# PETERSON'S® GRADUATE & PROFESSIONAL PROGRAMS

## AN OVERVIEW

# 2021



PETERSON'S®

**PETERSON'S®**

**About Peterson's®**

Peterson's® has been your trusted educational publisher for over 50 years. It's a milestone we're quite proud of, as we continue to offer the most accurate, dependable, high-quality educational content in the field, providing you with everything you need to succeed. No matter where you are on your academic or professional path, you can rely on Peterson's for its books, online information, expert test-prep tools, the most up-to-date education exploration data, and the highest quality career success resources—everything you need to achieve your education goals. For our complete line of products, visit **www.petersons.com**.

For more information about Peterson's range of educational products, contact Peterson's, 4380 S. Syracuse Street, Suite 200, Denver, CO 80237, or find us online at **www.petersons.com.**



ISSN 1093-8443
ISBN: 978-0-7689-4552-2

Printed in the United States of America

10 9 8 7 6 5 4 3 2 1    22 21 20

Fifty-fifth Edition

# CONTENTS


A Note from the Peterson's Editors v

THE GRADUATE ADVISER

The Admissions Process 3

Financial Support 5

Accreditation and Accrediting Agencies 9

How to Use This Guide 15

DIRECTORY OF GRADUATE AND PROFESSIONAL PROGRAMS BY FIELD

Directory of Graduate and Professional Programs by Field 19

DIRECTORY OF INSTITUTIONS AND THEIR OFFERINGS

Directory of Institutions and Their Offerings 141

PROFILES OF INSTITUTIONS OFFERING GRADUATE AND PROFESSIONAL WORK

Profiles 263

CLOSE-UPS OF INSTITUTIONS OFFERING GRADUATE AND PROFESSIONAL WORK

Close-Ups 629

APPENDIXES

Institutional Changes Since the 2020 Edition 639

Abbreviations Used in the Guides 641

INDEXES

Profiles, Displays, and Close-Ups 655

Directories and Subject Areas 669

# A Note from the Peterson's Editors

The six volumes of Peterson's *Graduate and Professional Programs*, the only annually updated reference work of its kind, provide wide-ranging information on the graduate and professional programs offered by accredited colleges and universities in the United States, U.S. territories, and Canada and by those institutions outside the United States that are accredited by U.S. accrediting bodies. More than 44,000 individual academic and professional programs at nearly 2,300 institutions are listed. Peterson's *Graduate and Professional Programs* have been used for more than fifty years by prospective graduate and professional students, placement counselors, faculty advisers, and all others interested in postbaccalaureate education.

***Graduate & Professional Programs: An Overview*** contains information on institutions as a whole, while the other books in the series are devoted to specific academic and professional fields:

- ***Graduate Programs in the Biological/Biomedical Sciences & Health-Related Medical Professions***
- ***Graduate Programs in Business, Education, Information Studies, Law & Social Work***
- ***Graduate Programs in Engineering & Applied Sciences***
- ***Graduate Programs in the Humanities, Arts & Social Sciences***
- ***Graduate Programs in the Physical Sciences, Mathematics, Agricultural Sciences, the Environment & Natural Resources***

The books may be used individually or as a set. For example, if you have chosen a field of study but do not know what institution you want to attend or if you have a college or university in mind but have not chosen an academic field of study, it is best to begin with the Overview guide.

***Graduate & Professional Programs: An Overview*** presents several directories to help you identify programs of study that might interest you; you can then research those programs further in the other books in the series by using the Directory of Graduate and Professional Programs by Field, which lists 500 fields and gives the names of those institutions that offer graduate degree programs in each.

For geographical or financial reasons, you may be interested in attending a particular institution and will want to know what it has to offer. You should turn to the Directory of Institutions and Their Offerings, which lists the degree programs available at each institution. As in the Directory of Graduate and Professional Programs by Field, the level of degrees offered is also indicated.

All books in the series include advice on graduate education, including topics such as admissions tests, financial aid, and accreditation. **The Graduate Adviser** includes two essays and information about accreditation. The first essay, "The Admissions Process," discusses general admission requirements, admission tests, factors to consider when selecting a graduate school or program, when and how to apply, and how admission decisions are made. Special information for international students and tips for minority students are also included. The second essay, "Financial Support," is an overview of the broad range of support available at the graduate level. Fellowships, scholarships, and grants; assistantships and internships; federal and private loan programs, as well as Federal Work-Study; and the GI bill are detailed. This essay concludes with advice on applying for need-based financial aid. "Accreditation and Accrediting Agencies" gives information on accreditation and its purpose and lists institutional accrediting agencies first and then specialized accrediting agencies relevant to each volume's specific fields of study.

With information on more than 40,000 graduate programs in more than 500 disciplines, Peterson's *Graduate and Professional Programs* give you all the information you need about the programs that are of interest to you in three formats: **Profiles** (capsule summaries of basic information), **Displays** (information that an institution or program wants to emphasize), and **Close-Ups** (written by administrators, with more expansive information than the **Profiles**, emphasizing different aspects of the programs). By using these various formats of program information, coupled with **Appendixes** and **Indexes** covering directories and subject areas for all six books, you will find that these guides provide the most comprehensive, accurate, and up-to-date graduate study information available.

Peterson's publishes a full line of resources with information you need to guide you through the graduate admissions process. Peterson's publications can be found at college libraries and career centers and your local bookstore or library—or visit us on the Web at www.petersons.com.

Colleges and universities will be pleased to know that Peterson's helped you in your selection. Admissions staff members are more than happy to answer questions, address specific problems, and help in any way they can. The editors at Peterson's wish you great success in your graduate program search!

# THE GRADUATE ADVISER

# The Admissions Process

Generalizations about graduate admissions practices are not always helpful because each institution has its own set of guidelines and procedures. Nevertheless, some broad statements can be made about the admissions process that may help you plan your strategy.

## Factors Involved in Selecting a Graduate School or Program

Selecting a graduate school and a specific program of study is a complex matter. Quality of the faculty; program and course offerings; the nature, size, and location of the institution; admission requirements; cost; and the availability of financial assistance are among the many factors that affect one's choice of institution. Other considerations are job placement and achievements of the program's graduates and the institution's resources, such as libraries, laboratories, and computer facilities. If you are to make the best possible choice, you need to learn as much as you can about the schools and programs you are considering before you apply.

The following steps may help you narrow your choices.

- Talk to alumni of the programs or institutions you are considering to get their impressions of how well they were prepared for work in their fields of study.
- Remember that graduate school requirements change, so be sure to get the most up-to-date information possible.
- Talk to department faculty members and the graduate adviser at your undergraduate institution. They often have information about programs of study at other institutions.
- Visit the websites of the graduate schools in which you are interested to request a graduate catalog. Contact the department chair in your chosen field of study for additional information about the department and the field.
- Visit as many campuses as possible. Call ahead for an appointment with the graduate adviser in your field of interest and be sure to check out the facilities and talk to students.

## General Requirements

Graduate schools and departments have requirements that applicants for admission must meet. Typically, these requirements include undergraduate transcripts (which provide information about undergraduate grade point average and course work applied toward a major), admission test scores, and letters of recommendation. Most graduate programs also ask for an essay or personal statement that describes your personal reasons for seeking graduate study. In some fields, such as art and music, portfolios or auditions may be required in addition to other evidence of talent. Some institutions require that the applicant have an undergraduate degree in the same subject as the intended graduate major.

Most institutions evaluate each applicant on the basis of the applicant's total record, and the weight accorded any given factor varies widely from institution to institution and from program to program.

## The Application Process

You should begin the application process at least one year before you expect to begin your graduate study. Find out the application deadline for each institution (many are provided in the **Profile** section of this guide). Go to the institution's website and find out if you can apply online. If not, request a paper application form. Fill out this form thoroughly and neatly. Assume that the school needs all the information it is requesting and that the admissions officer will be sensitive to the neatness and overall quality of what you submit. Do not supply more information than the school requires.

The institution may ask at least one question that will require a three- or four-paragraph answer. Compose your response on the assumption that the admissions officer is interested in both what you think and how you express yourself. Keep your statement brief and to the point, but, at the same time, include all pertinent information about your past experiences and your educational goals. Individual statements vary greatly in style and content, which helps admissions officers differentiate among applicants. Many graduate departments give considerable weight to the statement in making their admissions decisions, so be sure to take the time to prepare a thoughtful and concise statement.

If recommendations are a part of the admissions requirements, carefully choose the individuals you ask to write them. It is generally best to ask current or former professors to write the recommendations, provided they are able to attest to your intellectual ability and motivation for doing the work required of a graduate student. It is advisable to provide stamped, preaddressed envelopes to people being asked to submit recommendations on your behalf.

Completed applications, including references, transcripts, and admission test scores, should be received at the institution by the specified date.

Be advised that institutions do not usually make admissions decisions until all materials have been received. Enclose a self-addressed postcard with your application, requesting confirmation of receipt. Allow at least ten days for the return of the postcard before making further inquiries.

If you plan to apply for financial support, it is imperative that you file your application early.

### ADMISSION TESTS

The major testing program used in graduate admissions is the Graduate Record Examinations (GRE®) testing program, sponsored by the GRE Board and administered by Educational Testing Service, Princeton, New Jersey.

The Graduate Record Examinations testing program consists of a General Test and six Subject Tests. The General Test measures critical thinking, verbal reasoning, quantitative reasoning, and analytical writing skills. It is offered as an Internet-based test (iBT) in the United States, Canada, and many other countries.

The GRE® revised General Test's questions were designed to reflect the kind of thinking that students need to do in graduate or business school and demonstrate that students are indeed ready for graduate-level work.

- **Verbal Reasoning**—Measures ability to analyze and evaluate written material and synthesize information obtained from it, analyze relationships among component parts of sentences, and recognize relationships among words and concepts.
- **Quantitative Reasoning**—Measures problem-solving ability, focusing on basic concepts of arithmetic, algebra, geometry, and data analysis.
- **Analytical Writing**—Measures critical thinking and analytical writing skills, specifically the ability to articulate and support complex ideas clearly and effectively.

The computer-delivered GRE® revised General Test is offered year-round at Prometric™ test centers and on specific dates at testing locations outside of the Prometric test center network. Appointments are scheduled on a first-come, first-served basis. The GRE® revised General Test is also offered as a paper-based test three times a year in areas where computer-based testing is not available.

You can take the computer-delivered GRE® revised General Test once every twenty-one days, up to five times within any continuous rolling twelve-month period (365 days)—even if you canceled your scores on a previously taken test. You may take the paper-based GRE® revised General Test as often as it is offered.

Three scores are reported on the revised General Test:

1. A **Verbal Reasoning score** is reported on a 130–170 score scale, in 1-point increments.
2. A **Quantitative Reasoning score** is reported on a 130–170 score scale, in 1-point increments.
3. An **Analytical Writing score** is reported on a 0–6 score level, in half-point increments.

The GRE® Subject Tests measure achievement and assume undergraduate majors or extensive background in the following six disciplines:

- Biology
- Chemistry
- Literature in English
- Mathematics
- Physics
- Psychology

The Subject Tests are available three times per year as paper-based administrations around the world. Testing time is approximately 2 hours and 50 minutes. You can obtain more information about the GRE® by visiting the ETS website at **www.ets.org** or consulting the *GRE® Information Bulletin.* The *Bulletin* can be obtained at many undergraduate colleges. You can also download it from the ETS website or obtain it by contacting Graduate Record Examinations, Educational Testing Service, P.O. Box 6000, Princeton, NJ 08541-6000; phone: 609-771-7670 or 866-473-4373.

If you expect to apply for admission to a program that requires any of the GRE® tests, you should select a test date well in advance of the application deadline. Scores on the computer-based General Test are reported within ten to fifteen days; scores on the paper-based Subject Tests are reported within six weeks.

Another testing program, the Miller Analogies Test® (MAT®), is administered at more than 500 Controlled Testing Centers in the United States, Canada, and other countries. The MAT® computer-based test is now available. Testing time is 60 minutes. The test consists of 120 partial analogies. You can obtain the *Candidate Information Booklet,* which contains a list of test centers and instructions for taking the test, from **www.milleranalogies.com** or by calling 800-328-5999 (toll-free).

Check the specific requirements of the programs to which you are applying.

## How Admission Decisions Are Made

The program you apply to is directly involved in the admissions process. Although the final decision is usually made by the graduate dean (or an associate) or the faculty admissions committee, recommendations from faculty members in your intended field are important. At some institutions, an interview is incorporated into the decision process.

## A Special Note for International Students

In addition to the steps already described, there are some special considerations for international students who intend to apply for graduate study in the United States. All graduate schools require an indication of competence in English. The purpose of the Test of English as a Foreign Language (TOEFL®) is to evaluate the English proficiency of people who are nonnative speakers of English and want to study at colleges and universities where English is the language of instruction. The TOEFL® is administered by Educational Testing Service (ETS) under the general direction of a policy board established by the College Board and the Graduate Record Examinations Board.

The TOEFL iBT® assesses four basic language skills: listening, reading, writing, and speaking. The Internet-based test is administered at secure, official test centers. The testing time is approximately 4 hours.

The TOEFL® is also offered in a paper-based format in areas of the world where internet-based testing is not available. In 2017, ETS launched a revised TOEFL® paper-based Test, that more closely aligned to the TOEFL iBT® test. This revised paper-based test consists of three sections—listening, reading, and writing. The testing time is approximately 3 hours.

You can obtain more information for both versions of the TOEFL® by visiting the ETS website at **www.ets.org/toefl**. Information can also be obtained by contacting TOEFL® Services, Educational Testing Service, P.O. Box 6151, Princeton, NJ 08541-6151. Phone: 609-771-7100 or 877-863-3546 (toll free).

International students should apply especially early because of the number of steps required to complete the admissions process. Furthermore, many United States graduate schools have a limited number of spaces for international students, and many more students apply than the schools can accommodate.

International students may find financial assistance from institutions very limited. The U.S. government requires international applicants to submit a certification of support, which is a statement attesting to the applicant's financial resources. In addition, international students *must* have health insurance coverage.

## Tips for Minority Students

Indicators of a university's values in terms of diversity are found both in its recruitment programs and its resources directed to student success. Important questions: Does the institution vigorously recruit minorities for its graduate programs? Is there funding available to help with the costs associated with visiting the school? Are minorities represented in the institution's brochures or website or on their faculty rolls? What campus-based resources or services (including assistance in locating housing or career counseling and placement) are available? Is funding available to members of underrepresented groups?

At the program level, it is particularly important for minority students to investigate the "climate" of a program under consideration. How many minority students are enrolled and how many have graduated? What opportunities are there to work with diverse faculty and mentors whose research interests match yours? How are conflicts resolved or concerns addressed? How interested are faculty in building strong and supportive relations with students? "Climate" concerns should be addressed by posing questions to various individuals, including faculty members, current students, and alumni.

Information is also available through various organizations, such as the Hispanic Association of Colleges & Universities (HACU), and publications such as *Diverse Issues in Higher Education* and *Hispanic Outlook* magazine. There are also books devoted to this topic, such as *The Multicultural Student's Guide to Colleges* by Robert Mitchell.

# Financial Support

The range of financial support at the graduate level is very broad. The following descriptions will give you a general idea of what you might expect and what will be expected of you as a financial support recipient.

## Fellowships, Scholarships, and Grants

These are usually outright awards of a few hundred to many thousands of dollars with no service to the institution required in return. Fellowships and scholarships are usually awarded on the basis of merit and are highly competitive. Grants are made on the basis of financial need or special talent in a field of study. Many fellowships, scholarships, and grants not only cover tuition, fees, and supplies but also include stipends for living expenses with allowances for dependents. However, the terms of each should be examined because some do not permit recipients to supplement their income with outside work. Fellowships, scholarships, and grants may vary in the number of years for which they are awarded.

In addition to the availability of these funds at the university or program level, many excellent fellowship programs are available at the national level and may be applied for before and during enrollment in a graduate program. A listing of many of these programs can be found at the Council of Graduate Schools' website, **https://cgsnet.org/**. There is a wealth of information in the "Programs" and "Awards" sections.

## Assistantships and Internships

Many graduate students receive financial support through assistantships, particularly involving teaching or research duties. It is important to recognize that such appointments should not be viewed simply as employment relationships but rather should constitute an integral and important part of a student's graduate education. As such, the appointments should be accompanied by strong faculty mentoring and increasingly responsible apprenticeship experiences. The specific nature of these appointments in a given program should be considered in selecting that graduate program.

### TEACHING ASSISTANTSHIPS

These usually provide a salary and full or partial tuition remission and may also provide health benefits. Unlike fellowships, scholarships, and grants, which require no service to the institution, teaching assistantships require recipients to provide the institution with a specific amount of undergraduate teaching, ideally related to the student's field of study. Some teaching assistants are limited to grading papers, compiling bibliographies, taking notes, or monitoring laboratories. At some graduate schools, teaching assistants must carry lighter course loads than regular full-time students.

### RESEARCH ASSISTANTSHIPS

These are very similar to teaching assistantships in the manner in which financial assistance is provided. The difference is that recipients are given basic research assignments in their disciplines rather than teaching responsibilities. The work required is normally related to the student's field of study; in most instances, the assistantship supports the student's thesis or dissertation research.

### ADMINISTRATIVE INTERNSHIPS

These are similar to assistantships in application of financial assistance funds, but the student is given an assignment on a part-time basis, usually as a special assistant with one of the university's administrative offices. The assignment may not necessarily be directly related to the recipient's discipline.

### RESIDENCE HALL AND COUNSELING ASSISTANTSHIPS

These assistantships are frequently assigned to graduate students in psychology, counseling, and social work, but they may be offered to students in other disciplines, especially if the student has worked in this capacity during his or her undergraduate years. Duties can vary from being available in a dean's office for a specific number of hours for consultation with undergraduates to living in campus residences and being responsible for both counseling and administrative tasks or advising student activity groups. Residence hall assistantships often include a room and board allowance and, in some cases, tuition assistance and stipends. Contact the Housing and Student Life Office for more information.

## Health Insurance

The availability and affordability of health insurance is an important issue and one that should be considered in an applicant's choice of institution and program. While often included with assistantships and fellowships, this is not always the case and, even if provided, the benefits may be limited. It is important to note that the U.S. government requires international students to have health insurance.

## The GI Bill

This provides financial assistance for students who are veterans of the United States armed forces. If you are a veteran, contact your local Veterans Administration office to determine your eligibility and to get full details about benefits. There are a number of programs that offer educational benefits to current military enlistees. Some states have tuition assistance programs for members of the National Guard. Contact the VA office at the college for more information.

## Federal Work-Study Program (FWS)

Employment is another way some students finance their graduate studies. The federally funded Federal Work-Study Program provides eligible students with employment opportunities, usually in public and private nonprofit organizations. Federal funds pay up to 75 percent of the wages, with the remainder paid by the employing agency. FWS is available to graduate students who demonstrate financial need. Not all schools have these funds, and some only award them to undergraduates. Each school sets its application deadline and workstudy earnings limits. Wages vary and are related to the type of work done. You must file the Free Application for Federal Student Aid (FAFSA) to be eligible for this program.

## Loans

Many graduate students borrow to finance their graduate programs when other sources of assistance (which do not have to be repaid) prove insufficient. You should always read and understand the terms of any loan program before submitting your application.

### FEDERAL DIRECT LOANS

**Federal Direct Loans.** The Federal Direct Loan Program offers a variable-fixed interest rate loan to graduate students with the Department of Education acting as the lender. Students receive a new rate with each new loan, but that rate is fixed for the life of the loan. Beginning with loans made on or after July 1, 2013, the interest rate for loans made each July 1st to June 30th period are determined based on the last 10-year Treasury note auction prior to June 1st of that year, plus an added percentage. The interest rate can be no higher than 9.5%.

Beginning July 1, 2012, the Federal Direct Loan for graduate students is an unsubsidized loan. Under the *unsubsidized* program, the grad borrower pays the interest on the loan from the day proceeds are issued and is responsible for paying interest during all periods. If the borrower chooses not to pay the interest while in school, or during the grace periods, deferment, or forbearance, the interest accrues and will be capitalized.

Graduate students may borrow up to $20,500 per year through the Direct Loan Program, up to a cumulative maximum of $138,500, including undergraduate borrowing. No more than $65,500 of the $138,500 can be from subsidized loans, including loans the grad borrower may have received for periods of enrollment that began before July 1, 2012, or for prior undergraduate borrowing. You may borrow up to the cost of attendance at the school in which you are enrolled or will attend, minus estimated financial assistance from other federal, state, and private sources, up to a maximum of $20,500. Grad borrowers who reach the aggregate loan limit over the course of their education cannot receive additional loans; however, if they repay some of their loans to bring the outstanding balance below the aggregate limit, they could be eligible to borrow again, up to that limit.

Under the *subsidized* Federal Direct Loan Program, repayment begins six months after your last date of enrollment on at least a half-time basis. Under the *unsubsidized* program, repayment of interest begins within thirty days from disbursement of the loan proceeds, and repayment of the principal begins six months after your last enrollment on at least a half-time basis. Some borrowers may choose to defer interest payments while they are in school. The accrued interest is added to the loan balance when the borrower begins repayment. There are several repayment options.

**Federal Perkins Loans.** The Federal Perkins Loan is available to students demonstrating financial need and is administered directly by the school. Not all schools have these funds, and some may award them to undergraduates only. Eligibility is determined from the information you provide on the FAFSA. The school will notify you of your eligibility.

Eligible graduate students may borrow up to $8,000 per year, up to a maximum of $60,000, including undergraduate borrowing (even if your previous Perkins Loans have been repaid). The interest rate for Federal Perkins Loans is 5 percent, and no interest accrues while you remain in school at least half-time. Students who are attending less than half-time need to check with their school to determine the length of their grace period. There are no guarantee, loan, or disbursement fees. Repayment begins nine months after your last date of enrollment on at least a half-time basis and may extend over a maximum of ten years with no prepayment penalty.

**Federal Direct Graduate PLUS Loans.** Effective July 1, 2006, graduate and professional students are eligible for Graduate PLUS loans. This program allows students to borrow up to the cost of attendance, less any other aid received. These loans have a fixed interest rate (5.30% for loans first disbursed on or after July 1, 2020, and before July 1, 2021) and interest begins to accrue at the time of disbursement. Beginning with loans made on or after July 1, 2013, the interest rate for loans made each July 1st to June 30th period are determined based on the last 10-year Treasury note auction prior to June 1st of that year. The interest rate can be no higher than 10.5%. The PLUS loans do involve a credit check; a PLUS borrower may obtain a loan with a cosigner if his or her credit is not good enough. Grad PLUS loans may be deferred while a student is in school and for the six months following a drop below half-time enrollment. For more information, you should contact a representative in your college's financial aid office.

**Deferring Your Federal Loan Repayments.** If you borrowed under the Federal Direct Loan Program, Federal Direct PLUS Loan Program, or the Federal Perkins Loan Program for previous undergraduate or graduate study, your payments may be deferred when you return to graduate school, depending on when you borrowed and under which program.

There are other deferment options available if you are temporarily unable to repay your loan. Information about these deferments is provided at your entrance and exit interviews. If you believe you are eligible for a deferment of your loan payments, you must contact your lender or loan servicer to request a deferment. The deferment must be filed prior to the time your payment is due, and it must be re-filed when it expires if you remain eligible for deferment at that time.

### SUPPLEMENTAL (PRIVATE) LOANS

Many lending institutions offer supplemental loan programs and other financing plans, such as the ones described here, to students seeking additional assistance in meeting their education expenses. Some loan programs target all types of graduate students; others are designed specifically for business, law, or medical students. In addition, you can use private loans not specifically designed for education to help finance your graduate degree.

If you are considering borrowing through a supplemental or private loan program, you should carefully consider the terms and be sure to read the fine print. Check with the program sponsor for the most current terms that will be applicable to the amounts you intend to borrow for graduate study. Most supplemental loan programs for graduate study offer unsubsidized, credit-based loans. In general, a credit-ready borrower is one who has a satisfactory credit history or no credit history at all. A creditworthy borrower generally must pass a credit test to be eligible to borrow or act as a cosigner for the loan funds.

Many supplemental loan programs have minimum and maximum annual loan limits. Some offer amounts equal to the cost of attendance minus any other aid you will receive for graduate study. If you are planning to borrow for several years of graduate study, consider whether there is a cumulative or aggregate limit on the amount you may borrow. Often this cumulative or aggregate limit will include any amounts you borrowed and have not repaid for undergraduate or previous graduate study.

The combination of the annual interest rate, loan fees, and the repayment terms you choose will determine how much you will repay over time. Compare these features in combination before you decide which loan program to use. Some loans offer interest rates that are adjusted monthly, quarterly, or annually. Some offer interest rates that are lower during the in-school, grace, and deferment periods and then increase when you begin repayment. Some programs include a loan origination fee, which is usually deducted from the principal amount you receive when the loan is disbursed and must be repaid along with the interest and other principal when you graduate, withdraw from school, or drop below half-time study. Sometimes the loan fees are reduced if you borrow with a qualified cosigner. Some programs allow you to defer interest and/or principal payments while you are enrolled in graduate school. Many programs allow you to capitalize your interest payments; the interest due on your loan is added to the outstanding balance of your loan, so you don't have to repay immediately, but this increases the amount you owe. Other programs allow you to pay the interest as you go, which reduces the amount you later have to repay. The private loan market is very competitive, and your financial aid office can help you evaluate these programs.

## Applying for Need-Based Financial Aid

Schools that award federal and institutional financial assistance based on need will require you to complete the FAFSA and, in some cases, an institutional financial aid application.

If you are applying for federal student assistance, you **must** complete the FAFSA. A service of the U.S. Department of Education, the FAFSA is free to all applicants. Most applicants apply online at **www.fafsa.ed.gov**. Paper applications are available at the financial aid office of your local college.

After your FAFSA information has been processed, you will receive a Student Aid Report (SAR). If you provided an e-mail address on the FAFSA, this will be sent to you electronically; otherwise, it will be mailed to your home address.

Follow the instructions on the SAR if you need to correct information reported on your original application. If your situation changes after you file your FAFSA, contact your financial aid officer to discuss amending your information. You can also appeal your financial aid award if you have extenuating circumstances.

If you would like more information on federal student financial aid, visit the FAFSA website or download the most recent version of *Do You Need Money for College* at www.studentaid.ed.gov/sites/default/files/do-you-need-money.pdf. This guide is also available in Spanish.

The U.S. Department of Education also has a toll-free number for questions concerning federal student aid programs. The number is 1-800-4-FED AID (1-800-433-3243). If you are hearing impaired, call toll-free, 1-800-730-8913.

# Summary

Remember that these are generalized statements about financial assistance at the graduate level. Because each institution allots its aid differently, you should communicate directly with the school and the specific department of interest to you. It is not unusual, for example, to find that an endowment vested within a specific department supports one or more fellowships. You may fit its requirements and specifications precisely.

# Accreditation and Accrediting Agencies

Colleges and universities in the United States, and their individual academic and professional programs, are accredited by nongovernmental agencies concerned with monitoring the quality of education in this country. Agencies with both regional and national jurisdictions grant accreditation to institutions as a whole, while specialized bodies acting on a nationwide basis—often national professional associations—grant accreditation to departments and programs in specific fields.

Institutional and specialized accrediting agencies share the same basic concerns: the purpose an academic unit—whether university or program—has set for itself and how well it fulfills that purpose, the adequacy of its financial and other resources, the quality of its academic offerings, and the level of services it provides. Agencies that grant institutional accreditation take a broader view, of course, and examine university-wide or college-wide services with which a specialized agency may not concern itself.

Both types of agencies follow the same general procedures when considering an application for accreditation. The academic unit prepares a self-evaluation, focusing on the concerns mentioned above and usually including an assessment of both its strengths and weaknesses; a team of representatives of the accrediting body reviews this evaluation, visits the campus, and makes its own report; and finally, the accrediting body makes a decision on the application. Often, even when accreditation is granted, the agency makes a recommendation regarding how the institution or program can improve. All institutions and programs are also reviewed every few years to determine whether they continue to meet established standards; if they do not, they may lose their accreditation.

Accrediting agencies themselves are reviewed and evaluated periodically by the U.S. Department of Education and the Council for Higher Education Accreditation (CHEA). Recognized agencies adhere to certain standards and practices, and their authority in matters of accreditation is widely accepted in the educational community.

This does not mean, however, that accreditation is a simple matter, either for schools wishing to become accredited or for students deciding where to apply. Indeed, in certain fields the very meaning and methods of accreditation are the subject of a good deal of debate. For their part, those applying to graduate school should be aware of the safeguards provided by regional accreditation, especially in terms of degree acceptance and institutional longevity. Beyond this, applicants should understand the role that specialized accreditation plays in their field, as this varies considerably from one discipline to another. In certain professional fields, it is necessary to have graduated from a program that is accredited in order to be eligible for a license to practice, and in some fields the federal government also makes this a hiring requirement. In other disciplines, however, accreditation is not as essential, and there can be excellent programs that are not accredited. In fact, some programs choose not to seek accreditation, although most do.

Institutions and programs that present themselves for accreditation are sometimes granted the status of candidate for accreditation, or what is known as "preaccreditation." This may happen, for example, when an academic unit is too new to have met all the requirements for accreditation. Such status signifies initial recognition and indicates that the school or program in question is working to fulfill all requirements; it does not, however, guarantee that accreditation will be granted.

## Institutional Accrediting Agencies—Regional

*MIDDLE STATES COMMISSION ON HIGHER EDUCATION*

Accredits institutions in Delaware, District of Columbia, Maryland, New Jersey, New York, Pennsylvania, Puerto Rico, and the Virgin Islands.

Dr. Elizabeth Sibolski, President
Middle States Commission on Higher Education
3624 Market Street, Second Floor West
Philadelphia, Pennsylvania 19104
Phone: 267-284-5000
Fax: 215-662-5501
E-mail: info@msche.org
Website: www.msche.org

*NEW ENGLAND ASSOCIATION OF SCHOOLS AND COLLEGES*

Accredits institutions in Connecticut, Maine, Massachusetts, New Hampshire, Rhode Island, and Vermont.

Dr. Barbara E. Brittingham, President/Director
Commission on Institutions of Higher Education
3 Burlington Woods Drive, Suite 100
Burlington, Massachusetts 01803-4531
Phone: 855-886-3272 or 781-425-7714
Fax: 781-425-1001
E-mail: cihe@neasc.org
Website: https://cihe.neasc.org

*THE HIGHER LEARNING COMMISSION*

Accredits institutions in Arizona, Arkansas, Colorado, Illinois, Indiana, Iowa, Kansas, Michigan, Minnesota, Missouri, Nebraska, New Mexico, North Dakota, Ohio, Oklahoma, South Dakota, West Virginia, Wisconsin, and Wyoming.

Dr. Barbara Gellman-Danley, President
The Higher Learning Commission
230 South LaSalle Street, Suite 7-500
Chicago, Illinois 60604-1413
Phone: 800-621-7440 or 312-263-0456
Fax: 312-263-7462
E-mail: info@hlcommission.org
Website: www.hlcommission.org

*NORTHWEST COMMISSION ON COLLEGES AND UNIVERSITIES*

Accredits institutions in Alaska, Idaho, Montana, Nevada, Oregon, Utah, and Washington.

Dr. Sandra E. Elman, President
8060 165th Avenue, NE, Suite 100
Redmond, Washington 98052
Phone: 425-558-4224
Fax: 425-376-0596
E-mail: selman@nwccu.org
Website: www.nwccu.org

*SOUTHERN ASSOCIATION OF COLLEGES AND SCHOOLS*

Accredits institutions in Alabama, Florida, Georgia, Kentucky, Louisiana, Mississippi, North Carolina, South Carolina, Tennessee, Texas, and Virginia.

Dr. Belle S. Wheelan, President
Commission on Colleges
1866 Southern Lane
Decatur, Georgia 30033-4097
Phone: 404-679-4500 Ext. 4504
Fax: 404-679-4558
E-mail: questions@sacscoc.org
Website: www.sacscoc.org

*WESTERN ASSOCIATION OF SCHOOLS AND COLLEGES*

Accredits institutions in California, Guam, and Hawaii.

Jamienne S. Studley, President
WASC Senior College and University Commission
985 Atlantic Avenue, Suite 100
Alameda, California 94501
Phone: 510-748-9001
Fax: 510-748-9797
E-mail: wasc@wscuc.org
Website: https://www.wscuc.org/

## Institutional Accrediting Agencies—Other

*ACCREDITING COUNCIL FOR INDEPENDENT COLLEGES AND SCHOOLS*
Michelle Edwards, President
750 First Street NE, Suite 980
Washington, DC 20002-4223
Phone: 202-336-6780
Fax: 202-842-2593
E-mail: info@acics.org
Website: www.acics.org

*DISTANCE EDUCATION ACCREDITING COMMISSION (DEAC)*
Leah Matthews, Executive Director
1101 17th Street NW, Suite 808
Washington, DC 20036-4704
Phone: 202-234-5100
Fax: 202-332-1386
E-mail: info@deac.org
Website: www.deac.org

## Specialized Accrediting Agencies

*ACUPUNCTURE AND ORIENTAL MEDICINE*
Mark S. McKenzie, LAc MsOM DiplOM, Executive Director
Accreditation Commission for Acupuncture and Oriental Medicine
8941 Aztec Drive, Suite 2
Eden Prairie, Minnesota 55347
Phone: 952-212-2434
Fax: 301-313-0912
E-mail: info@acaom.org
Website: www.acaom.org

*ALLIED HEALTH*
Kathleen Megivern, Executive Director
Commission on Accreditation of Allied Health Education Programs (CAAHEP)
25400 US Hwy 19 North, Suite 158
Clearwater, Florida 33763
Phone: 727-210-2350
Fax: 727-210-2354
E-mail: mail@caahep.org
Website: www.caahep.org

*ART AND DESIGN*
Karen P. Moynahan, Executive Director
National Association of Schools of Art and Design (NASAD)
Commission on Accreditation
11250 Roger Bacon Drive, Suite 21
Reston, Virginia 20190-5248
Phone: 703-437-0700
Fax: 703-437-6312
E-mail: info@arts-accredit.org
Website: http://nasad.arts-accredit.org

*ATHLETIC TRAINING EDUCATION*
Pamela Hansen, CAATE Director of Accreditation
Commission on Accreditation of Athletic Training Education (CAATE)
6850 Austin Center Blvd., Suite 100
Austin, Texas 78731-3184
Phone: 512-733-9700
E-mail: pamela@caate.net
Website: www.caate.net

*AUDIOLOGY EDUCATION*
Meggan Olek, Director
Accreditation Commission for Audiology Education (ACAE)
11480 Commerce Park Drive, Suite 220
Reston, Virginia 20191
Phone: 202-986-9500
Fax: 202-986-9550
E-mail: info@acaeaccred.org
Website: https://acaeaccred.org/

*AVIATION*
Dr. Gary J. Northam, President
Aviation Accreditation Board International (AABI)
3410 Skyway Drive
Auburn, Alabama 36830
Phone: 334-844-2431
Fax: 334-844-2432
E-mail: gary.northam@auburn.edu
Website: www.aabi.aero

*BUSINESS*
Stephanie Bryant, Executive Vice President and Chief Accreditation Officer
AACSB International—The Association to Advance Collegiate Schools of Business
777 South Harbour Island Boulevard, Suite 750
Tampa, Florida 33602
Phone: 813-769-6500
Fax: 813-769-6559
E-mail: stephanie.bryant@aacsb.edu
Website: www.aacsb.edu

*BUSINESS EDUCATION*
Dr. Phyllis Okrepkie, President
International Assembly for Collegiate Business Education (IACBE)
11374 Strang Line Road
Lenexa, Kansas 66215
Phone: 913-631-3009
Fax: 913-631-9154
E-mail: iacbe@iacbe.org
Website: www.iacbe.org

*CHIROPRACTIC*
Dr. Craig S. Little, President
Council on Chiropractic Education (CCE)
Commission on Accreditation
8049 North 85th Way
Scottsdale, Arizona 85258-4321
Phone: 480-443-8877 or 888-443-3506
Fax: 480-483-7333
E-mail: cce@cce-usa.org
Website: www.cce-usa.org

*CLINICAL LABORATORY SCIENCES*
Dianne M. Cearlock, Ph.D., Chief Executive Officer
National Accrediting Agency for Clinical Laboratory Sciences
5600 North River Road, Suite 720
Rosemont, Illinois 60018-5119
Phone: 773-714-8880 or 847-939-3597
Fax: 773-714-8886
E-mail: info@naacls.org
Website: www.naacls.org

*CLINICAL PASTORAL EDUCATION*
Trace Haythorn, Ph.D., Executive Director/CEO
Association for Clinical Pastoral Education, Inc.
One West Court Square, Suite 325
Decatur, Georgia 30030-2576
Phone: 678-363-6226
Fax: 404-320-0849
E-mail: acpe@acpe.edu
Website: www.acpe.edu

*DANCE*
Karen P. Moynahan, Executive Director
National Association of Schools of Dance (NASD)
Commission on Accreditation
11250 Roger Bacon Drive, Suite 21
Reston, Virginia 20190-5248
Phone: 703-437-0700
Fax: 703-437-6312
E-mail: info@arts-accredit.org
Website: http://nasd.arts-accredit.org

*DENTISTRY*
Dr. Kathleen T. O'Loughlin, Executive Director
Commission on Dental Accreditation
American Dental Association
211 East Chicago Avenue
Chicago, Illinois 60611
Phone: 312-440-2500
E-mail: accreditation@ada.org
Website: www.ada.org

*DIETETICS AND NUTRITION*
Mary B. Gregoire, Ph.D., Executive Director; RD, FADA, FAND
Academy of Nutrition and Dietetics
Accreditation Council for Education in Nutrition and Dietetics (ACEND)
120 South Riverside Plaza
Chicago, Illinois 60606-6995
Phone: 800-877-1600 or 312-899-0040
E-mail: acend@eatright.org
Website: www.eatright.org/cade

*EDUCATION PREPARATION*
Christopher Koch, President
Council for the Accreditation of Educator Preparation (CAEP)
1140 19th Street NW, Suite 400
Washington, DC 20036
Phone: 202-223-0077
Fax: 202-296-6620
E-mail: caep@caepnet.org
Website: www.caepnet.org

*ENGINEERING*
Michael Milligan, Ph.D., PE, Executive Director
Accreditation Board for Engineering and Technology, Inc. (ABET)
415 North Charles Street
Baltimore, Maryland 21201
Phone: 410-347-7700
E-mail: accreditation@abet.org
Website: www.abet.org

*FORENSIC SCIENCES*
Nancy J. Jackson, Director of Development and Accreditation
American Academy of Forensic Sciences (AAFS)
Forensic Science Education Program Accreditation Commission (FEPAC)
410 North 21st Street
Colorado Springs, Colorado 80904
Phone: 719-636-1100
Fax: 719-636-1993
E-mail: njackson@aafs.org
Website: www.fepac-edu.org

*FORESTRY*
Carol L. Redelsheimer
Director of Science and Education
Society of American Foresters
10100 Laureate Way
Bethesda, Maryland 20814-2198
Phone: 301-897-8720 or 866-897-8720
Fax: 301-897-3690
E-mail: membership@safnet.org
Website: www.eforester.com

*HEALTHCARE MANAGEMENT*
Commission on Accreditation of Healthcare Management Education (CAHME)
Anthony Stanowski, President and CEO
6110 Executive Boulevard, Suite 614
Rockville, Maryland 20852
Phone: 301-298-1820
E-mail: info@cahme.org
Website: www.cahme.org

*HEALTH INFORMATICS AND HEALTH MANAGEMENT*
Angela Kennedy, EdD, MBA, RHIA, Chief Executive Officer
Commission on Accreditation for Health Informatics and Information Management Education (CAHIIM)
233 North Michigan Avenue, 21st Floor
Chicago, Illinois 60601-5800
Phone: 312-233-1134
Fax: 312-233-1948
E-mail: info@cahiim.org
Website: www.cahiim.org

*HUMAN SERVICE EDUCATION*
Dr. Elaine Green, President
Council for Standards in Human Service Education (CSHSE)
3337 Duke Street
Alexandria, Virginia 22314
Phone: 571-257-3959
E-mail: info@cshse.org
Website: www.cshse.org

*INTERIOR DESIGN*
Holly Mattson, Executive Director
Council for Interior Design Accreditation
206 Grandview Avenue, Suite 350
Grand Rapids, Michigan 49503-4014
Phone: 616-458-0400
Fax: 616-458-0460
E-mail: info@accredit-id.org
Website: www.accredit-id.org

*JOURNALISM AND MASS COMMUNICATIONS*
Patricia Thompson, Executive Director
Accrediting Council on Education in Journalism and Mass Communications (ACEJMC)
201 Bishop Hall
P.O. Box 1848
University, MS 38677-1848
Phone: 662-915-5504
E-mail: pthomps1@olemiss.edu
Website: www.acejmc.org

*LANDSCAPE ARCHITECTURE*
Nancy Somerville, Executive Vice President, CEO
American Society of Landscape Architects (ASLA)
636 Eye Street, NW
Washington, DC 20001-3736
Phone: 202-898-2444
Fax: 202-898-1185
E-mail: info@asla.org
Website: www.asla.org

*LAW*
Barry Currier, Managing Director of Accreditation & Legal Education
American Bar Association
321 North Clark Street, 21st Floor
Chicago, Illinois 60654
Phone: 312-988-6738
Fax: 312-988-5681
E-mail: legaled@americanbar.org
Website: https://www.americanbar.org/groups/legal_education/accreditation.html

*LIBRARY*
Karen O'Brien, Director
Office for Accreditation
American Library Association
50 East Huron Street
Chicago, Illinois 60611-2795
Phone: 800-545-2433, ext. 2432 or 312-280-2432
Fax: 312-280-2433
E-mail: accred@ala.org
Website: http://www.ala.org/aboutala/offices/accreditation/

*MARRIAGE AND FAMILY THERAPY*
Tanya A. Tamarkin, Director of Educational Affairs
Commission on Accreditation for Marriage and Family Therapy Education (COAMFTE)
American Association for Marriage and Family Therapy
112 South Alfred Street
Alexandria, Virginia 22314-3061
Phone: 703-838-9808
Fax: 703-838-9805
E-mail: coa@aamft.org
Website: www.aamft.org

*MEDICAL ILLUSTRATION*
Kathleen Megivern, Executive Director
Commission on Accreditation of Allied Health Education Programs (CAAHEP)
25400 US Highway 19 North, Suite 158
Clearwater, Florida 33756
Phone: 727-210-2350
Fax: 727-210-2354
E-mail: mail@caahep.org
Website: www.caahep.org

*MEDICINE*
Liaison Committee on Medical Education (LCME)
Robert B. Hash, M.D., LCME Secretary
American Medical Association
Council on Medical Education
330 North Wabash Avenue, Suite 39300
Chicago, Illinois 60611-5885
Phone: 312-464-4933
E-mail: lcme@aamc.org
Website: www.ama-assn.org

Liaison Committee on Medical Education (LCME)
Heather Lent, M.A., Director
Accreditation Services
Association of American Medical Colleges
655 K Street, NW
Washington, DC 20001-2399
Phone: 202-828-0596
E-mail: lcme@aamc.org
Website: www.lcme.org

*MUSIC*
Karen P. Moynahan, Executive Director
National Association of Schools of Music (NASM)
Commission on Accreditation
11250 Roger Bacon Drive, Suite 21
Reston, Virginia 20190-5248
Phone: 703-437-0700
Fax: 703-437-6312
E-mail: info@arts-accredit.org
Website: http://nasm.arts-accredit.org/

*NATUROPATHIC MEDICINE*
Daniel Seitz, J.D., Ed.D., Executive Director
Council on Naturopathic Medical Education
P.O. Box 178
Great Barrington, Massachusetts 01230
Phone: 413-528-8877
E-mail: https://cnme.org/contact-us/
Website: www.cnme.org

*NURSE ANESTHESIA*
Francis R.Gerbasi, Ph.D., CRNA, COA Executive Director
Council on Accreditation of Nurse Anesthesia Educational Programs (CoA-NAEP)
American Association of Nurse Anesthetists
222 South Prospect Avenue
Park Ridge, Illinois 60068-4001
Phone: 847-655-1160
Fax: 847-692-7137
E-mail: accreditation@coa.us.com
Website: http://www.coacrna.org

*NURSE EDUCATION*
Jennifer L. Butlin, Executive Director
Commission on Collegiate Nursing Education (CCNE)
One Dupont Circle, NW, Suite 530
Washington, DC 20036-1120
Phone: 202-887-6791
Fax: 202-887-8476
E-mail: jbutlin@aacn.nche.edu
Website: www.aacn.nche.edu/accreditation

Marsal P. Stoll, Chief Executive Officer
Accreditation Commission for Education in Nursing (ACEN)
3343 Peachtree Road, NE, Suite 850
Atlanta, Georgia 30326
Phone: 404-975-5000
Fax: 404-975-5020
E-mail: mstoll@acenursing.org
Website: www.acenursing.org

*NURSE MIDWIFERY*
Heather L. Maurer, M.A., Executive Director
Accreditation Commission for Midwifery Education (ACME)
American College of Nurse-Midwives
8403 Colesville Road, Suite 1550
Silver Spring, Maryland 20910
Phone: 240-485-1800
Fax: 240-485-1818
E-mail: info@acnm.org
Website: www.midwife.org/Program-Accreditation

*NURSE PRACTITIONER*
Gay Johnson, CEO
National Association of Nurse Practitioners in Women's Health
Council on Accreditation
505 C Street, NE
Washington, DC 20002
Phone: 202-543-9693 Ext. 1
Fax: 202-543-9858
E-mail: info@npwh.org
Website: www.npwh.org

*NURSING*
Marsal P. Stoll, Chief Executive Director
Accreditation Commission for Education in Nursing (ACEN)
3343 Peachtree Road, NE, Suite 850
Atlanta, Georgia 30326
Phone: 404-975-5000
Fax: 404-975-5020
E-mail: info@acenursing.org
Website: www.acenursing.org

*OCCUPATIONAL THERAPY*
Heather Stagliano, DHSc, OTR/L, Executive Director
The American Occupational Therapy Association, Inc.
4720 Montgomery Lane, Suite 200
Bethesda, Maryland 20814-3449
Phone: 301-652-6611 Ext. 2682
TDD: 800-377-8555
Fax: 240-762-5150
E-mail: accred@aota.org
Website: www.aoteonline.org

*OPTOMETRY*
Joyce L. Urbeck, Administrative Director
Accreditation Council on Optometric Education (ACOE)
American Optometric Association
243 North Lindbergh Boulevard
St. Louis, Missouri 63141-7881
Phone: 314-991-4100, Ext. 4246
Fax: 314-991-4101
E-mail: accredit@aoa.org
Website: www.theacoe.org

*OSTEOPATHIC MEDICINE*
Director, Department of Accreditation
Commission on Osteopathic College Accreditation (COCA)
American Osteopathic Association
142 East Ontario Street
Chicago, Illinois 60611
Phone: 312-202-8048
Fax: 312-202-8202
E-mail: predoc@osteopathic.org
Website: www.aoacoca.org

*PHARMACY*
Peter H. Vlasses, PharmD, Executive Director
Accreditation Council for Pharmacy Education
135 South LaSalle Street, Suite 4100
Chicago, Illinois 60603-4810
Phone: 312-664-3575
Fax: 312-664-4652
E-mail: csinfo@acpe-accredit.org
Website: www.acpe-accredit.org

*PHYSICAL THERAPY*
Sandra Wise, Senior Director
Commission on Accreditation in Physical Therapy Education (CAPTE)
American Physical Therapy Association (APTA)
1111 North Fairfax Street
Alexandria, Virginia 22314-1488
Phone: 703-706-3245
Fax: 703-706-3387
E-mail: accreditation@apta.org
Website: www.capteonline.org

*PHYSICIAN ASSISTANT STUDIES*
Sharon L. Luke, Executive Director
Accredittion Review Commission on Education for the Physician Assistant, Inc. (ARC-PA)
12000 Findley Road, Suite 275
Johns Creek, Georgia 30097
Phone: 770-476-1224
Fax: 770-476-1738
E-mail: arc-pa@arc-pa.org
Website: www.arc-pa.org

*PLANNING*
Jesmarie Soto Johnson, Executive Director
American Institute of Certified Planners/Association of Collegiate Schools of Planning/American Planning Association
Planning Accreditation Board (PAB)
2334 West Lawrence Avenue, Suite 209
Chicago, Illinois 60625
Phone: 773-334-7200
E-mail: smerits@planningaccreditationboard.org
Website: www.planningaccreditationboard.org

*PODIATRIC MEDICINE*
Heather Stagliano, OTR/L, DHSc, Executive Director
Council on Podiatric Medical Education (CPME)
American Podiatric Medical Association (APMA)
9312 Old Georgetown Road
Bethesda, Maryland 20814-1621
Phone: 301-581-9200
Fax: 301-571-4903
Website: www.cpme.org

*PSYCHOLOGY AND COUNSELING*
Jacqueline Remondet, Associate Executive Director, CEO of the Accrediting Unit,
Office of Program Consultation and Accreditation
American Psychological Association
750 First Street, NE
Washington, DC 20002-4202
Phone: 202-336-5979 or 800-374-2721
TDD/TTY: 202-336-6123
Fax: 202-336-5978
E-mail: apaaccred@apa.org
Website: www.apa.org/ed/accreditation

Kelly Coker, Executive Director
Council for Accreditation of Counseling and Related Educational Programs (CACREP)
1001 North Fairfax Street, Suite 510
Alexandria, Virginia 22314
Phone: 703-535-5990
Fax: 703-739-6209
E-mail: cacrep@cacrep.org
Website: www.cacrep.org

Richard M. McFall, Executive Director
Psychological Clinical Science Accreditation System (PCSAS)
1101 East Tenth Street
IU Psychology Building
Bloomington, Indiana 47405-7007
Phone: 812-856-2570
Fax: 812-322-5545
E-mail: rmmcfall@pcsas.org
Website: www.pcsas.org

*PUBLIC HEALTH*
Laura Rasar King, M.P.H., MCHES, Executive Director
Council on Education for Public Health
1010 Wayne Avenue, Suite 220
Silver Spring, Maryland 20910
Phone: 202-789-1050
Fax: 202-789-1895
E-mail: Lking@ceph.org
Website: www.ceph.org

*PUBLIC POLICY, AFFAIRS AND ADMINISTRATION*
Crystal Calarusse, Chief Accreditation Officer
Commission on Peer Review and Accreditation
Network of Schools of Public Policy, Affairs, and Administration (NASPAA-COPRA)
1029 Vermont Avenue, NW, Suite 1100
Washington, DC 20005
Phone: 202-628-8965
Fax: 202-626-4978
E-mail: copra@naspaa.org
Website: accreditation.naspaa.org

*RADIOLOGIC TECHNOLOGY*
Leslie Winter, Chief Executive Officer Joint Review Committee on Education in Radiologic Technology (JRCERT)
20 North Wacker Drive, Suite 2850
Chicago, Illinois 60606-3182
Phone: 312-704-5300
Fax: 312-704-5304
E-mail: mail@jrcert.org
Website: www.jrcert.org

*REHABILITATION EDUCATION*
Frank Lane, Ph.D., Executive Director
Council for Accreditation of Counseling and Related Educational Programs (CACREP)
1001 North Fairfax Street, Suite 510
Alexandria, Virginia 22314
Phone: 703-535-5990
Fax: 703-739-6209
E-mail: cacrep@cacrep.org
Website: www.cacrep.org

*RESPIRATORY CARE*
Thomas Smalling, Executive Director
Commission on Accreditation for Respiratory Care (CoARC)
1248 Harwood Road
Bedford, Texas 76021-4244
Phone: 817-283-2835
Fax: 817-354-8519
E-mail: tom@coarc.com
Website: www.coarc.com

*SOCIAL WORK*
Dr. Stacey Borasky, Director of Accreditation
Office of Social Work Accreditation
Council on Social Work Education
1701 Duke Street, Suite 200
Alexandria, Virginia 22314
Phone: 703-683-8080
Fax: 703-519-2078
E-mail: info@cswe.org
Website: www.cswe.org

*SPEECH-LANGUAGE PATHOLOGY AND AUDIOLOGY*
Kimberlee Moore, Accreditation Executive Director
American Speech-Language-Hearing Association
Council on Academic Accreditation in Audiology and Speech-Language Pathology
2200 Research Boulevard #310
Rockville, Maryland 20850-3289
Phone: 301-296-5700
Fax: 301-296-8750
E-mail: accreditation@asha.org
Website: http://caa.asha.org

*TEACHER EDUCATION*
Christopher A. Koch, President
National Council for Accreditation of Teacher Education (NCATE)
Teacher Education Accreditation Council (TEAC)
1140 19th Street, Suite 400
Washington, DC 20036
Phone: 202-223-0077
Fax: 202-296-6620
E-mail: caep@caepnet.org
Website: www.ncate.org

*TECHNOLOGY*
Michale S. McComis, Ed.D., Executive Director
Accrediting Commission of Career Schools and Colleges
2101 Wilson Boulevard, Suite 302
Arlington, Virginia 22201
Phone: 703-247-4212
Fax: 703-247-4533
E-mail: mccomis@accsc.org
Website: www.accsc.org

*TECHNOLOGY, MANAGEMENT, AND APPLIED ENGINEERING*
Kelly Schild, Director of Accreditation
The Association of Technology, Management, and Applied Engineering (ATMAE)
275 N. York Street, Suite 401
Elmhurst, Illinois 60126
Phone: 630-433-4514
Fax: 630-563-9181
E-mail: Kelly@atmae.org
Website: www.atmae.org

*THEATER*
Karen P. Moynahan, Executive Director
National Association of Schools of Theatre Commission on Accreditation
11250 Roger Bacon Drive, Suite 21
Reston, Virginia 20190
Phone: 703-437-0700
Fax: 703-437-6312
E-mail: info@arts-accredit.org
Website: http://nast.arts-accredit.org/

*THEOLOGY*
Dr. Bernard Fryshman, Executive VP
Emeritus and Interim Executive Director
Association of Advanced Rabbinical and Talmudic Schools (AARTS)
Accreditation Commission
11 Broadway, Suite 405
New York, New York 10004
Phone: 212-363-1991
Fax: 212-533-5335
E-mail: k.sharfman.aarts@gmail.com

Frank Yamada, Executive Director
Association of Theological Schools in the United States and Canada (ATS)
Commission on Accrediting
10 Summit Park Drive
Pittsburgh, Pennsylvania 15275
Phone: 412-788-6505
Fax: 412-788-6510
E-mail: ats@ats.edu
Website: www.ats.edu

Dr. Timothy Eaton, President
Transnational Association of Christian Colleges and Schools (TRACS)
Accreditation Commission
15935 Forest Road
Forest, Virginia 24551
Phone: 434-525-9539
Fax: 434-525-9538
E-mail: info@tracs.org
Website: www.tracs.org

*VETERINARY MEDICINE*
Dr. Karen Brandt, Director of Education and Research
American Veterinary Medical Association (AVMA)
Council on Education
1931 North Meacham Road, Suite 100
Schaumburg, Illinois 60173-4360
Phone: 847-925-8070 Ext. 6674
Fax: 847-285-5732
E-mail: info@avma.org
Website: www.avma.org

# How to Use These Guides

As you identify the particular programs and institutions that interest you, you can use both the ***Graduate & Professional Programs: An Overview*** volume and the specialized volumes in the series to obtain detailed information.

- ***Graduate Programs in the Biological/Biomedical Sciences & Health-Related Professions***
- ***Graduate Programs in Business, Education, Information Studies, Law & Social Work***
- ***Graduate Programs in Engineering & Applied Sciences***
- ***Graduate Programs the Humanities, Arts & Social Sciences***
- ***Graduate Programs in the Physical Sciences, Mathematics, Agricultural Sciences, the Environment & Natural Resources***

Each of the specialized volumes in the series is divided into sections that contain one or more directories devoted to programs in a particular field. If you do not find a directory devoted to your field of interest in a specific volume, consult "Directories and Subject Areas" (located at the end of each volume). After you have identified the correct volume, consult the "Directories and Subject Areas in This Book" index, which shows (as does the more general directory) what directories cover subjects not specifically named in a directory or section title.

Each of the specialized volumes in the series has a number of general directories. These directories have entries for the largest unit at an institution granting graduate degrees in that field. For example, the general Engineering and Applied Sciences directory in the ***Graduate Programs in Engineering & Applied Sciences*** volume consists of **Profiles** for colleges, schools, and departments of engineering and applied sciences.

General directories are followed by other directories, or sections, that give more detailed information about programs in particular areas of the general field that has been covered. The general Engineering and Applied Sciences directory, in the previous example, is followed by nineteen sections with directories in specific areas of engineering, such as Chemical Engineering, Industrial/Management Engineering, and Mechanical Engineering.

Because of the broad nature of many fields, any system of organization is bound to involve a certain amount of overlap. Environmental studies, for example, is a field whose various aspects are studied in several types of departments and schools. Readers interested in such studies will find information on relevant programs in the ***Graduate Programs in the Biological/Biomedical Sciences & Health-Related Professions*** volume under Ecology and Environmental Biology and Environmental and Occupational Health; in the ***Graduate Programs in the Physical Sciences, Mathematics, Agricultural Sciences, the Environment & Natural Resources*** volume under Environmental Management and Policy and Natural Resources; and in the ***Graduate Programs in Engineering & Applied Sciences*** volume under Energy Management and Policy and Environmental Engineering. To help you find all of the programs of interest to you, the introduction to each section within the specialized volumes includes, if applicable, a paragraph suggesting other sections and directories with information on related areas of study.

## Directory of Institutions and Their Offerings

This directory lists institutions in alphabetical order and includes beneath each name the academic fields in which each institution offers graduate programs. The degree level in each field is also indicated, provided that the institution has supplied that information in response to Peterson's Annual Survey of Graduate and Professional Institutions.

An M indicates that a master's degree program is offered; a D indicates that a doctoral degree program is offered; an O signifies that other advanced degrees (e.g., certificates or specialist degrees) are offered; and an * (asterisk) indicates that a **Close-Up** and/or **Display** is located in this volume. See the index, "Close-Ups and Displays," for the specific page number.

## Profiles of Academic and Professional Programs in the Specialized Volumes

Each section of **Profiles** has a table of contents that lists the Program Directories, **Displays**, and **Close-Ups.** Program Directories consist of the **Profiles** of programs in the relevant fields, with **Displays** following if programs have chosen to include them. **Close-Ups,** which are more individualized statements, are also listed for those graduate schools or programs that have chosen to submit them.

The **Profiles** found in the 500 directories in the specialized volumes provide basic data about the graduate units in capsule form for quick reference. To make these directories as useful as possible, **Profiles** are generally listed for an institution's smallest academic unit within a subject area. In other words, if an institution has a College of Liberal Arts that administers many related programs, the **Profile** for the individual program (e.g., Program in History), not the entire College, appears in the directory.

There are some programs that do not fit into any current directory and are not given individual **Profiles**. The directory structure is reviewed annually in order to keep this number to a minimum and to accommodate major trends in graduate education.

Some institutions maintain a "Premium Profile" at Peterson's where prospective students can find more in-depth school program descriptions and information. You can learn more about those schools by visiting **www.petersons.com.**

The following outline describes the **Profile** information found in the guides and explains how best to use that information. Any item that does not apply to or was not provided by a graduate unit is omitted from its listing. The format of the **Profiles** is constant, making it easy to compare one institution with another and one program with another.

**Identifying Information**. The institution's name, in boldface type, is followed by a complete listing of the administrative structure for that field of study. (For example, University of Akron, Buchtel College of Arts and Sciences, Department of Theoretical and Applied Mathematics, Program in Mathematics.) The last unit listed is the one to which all information in the **Profile** pertains. The institution's city, state, and ZIP code follow.

**Offerings**. Each field of study offered by the unit is listed with all postbaccalaureate degrees awarded. Degrees that are not preceded by a specific concentration are awarded in the general field listed in the unit name. Frequently, fields of study are broken down into subspecializations, and those appear following the degrees awarded; for example, "Offerings in secondary education (M.Ed.), including English education, mathematics education, science education." Students enrolled in the M.Ed. program would be able to specialize in any of the three fields mentioned.

**Professional Accreditation**. Some **Profiles** indicate whether a program is professionally accredited. Because it is possible for a program to receive or lose professional accreditation at any time, students entering fields in which accreditation is important to a career should verify the status of programs by contacting either the chairperson or the appropriate accrediting association.

**Jointly Offered Degrees**. Explanatory statements concerning programs that are offered in cooperation with other institutions are included in the list of degrees offered. This occurs most commonly on a regional basis (for example, two state universities offering a cooperative Ph.D. in special education) or where the specialized nature of the institutions encourages joint efforts (a J.D./M.B.A. offered by a law school at an institution with no formal business programs and an institution with a business school but lacking a law school). Only programs that are truly cooperative are listed; those involving only limited course work at another institution are not. Interested students should contact the heads of such units for further information.

**Program Availability**. This may include the following: part-time, evening/weekend, online only, 100% online, blended/hybrid learning, and/or minimal on-campus study. When information regarding the availability of part-time or evening/weekend study appears in the **Profile**, it means that students are able to earn a degree exclusively through such study. Blended/hybrid learning describes those courses in which some traditional in-class time has been replaced by online learning activities. Hybrid courses take advantage of the best features of both face-to-face and online learning.

**Faculty**. Figures on the number of faculty members actively involved with graduate students through teaching or research are separated into full- and part-time as well as men and women whenever the information has been supplied.

**Students**. Figures for the number of students enrolled in graduate and professional programs pertain to the semester of highest enrollment from the 2019-20 academic year. These figures are broken down into full-and part-time and men and women whenever the data have been supplied. Information on the number of matriculated students enrolled in the unit who are members of a minority group or are international students appears here. The average age of the matriculated students is followed by the number of applicants, the percentage accepted, and the number enrolled for fall 2019.

**Degrees Awarded.** The number of degrees awarded in the calendar year is listed. Many doctoral programs offer a terminal master's degree if students leave the program after completing only part of the requirements for a doctoral degree; that is indicated here. All degrees are classified into one of four types: master's, doctoral, first professional, and other advanced degrees. A unit may award one or several degrees at a given level; however, the data are only collected by type and may therefore represent several different degree programs.

**Degree Requirements**. The information in this section is also broken down by type of degree, and all information for a degree level pertains to all degrees of that type unless otherwise specified. Degree requirements are collected in a simplified form to provide some very basic information on the nature of the program and on foreign language, thesis or dissertation, comprehensive exam, and registration requirements. Many units also provide a short list of additional requirements, such as fieldwork or an internship. For complete information on graduation requirements, contact the graduate school or program directly.

**Entrance Requirements**. Entrance requirements are broken down into the four degree levels of master's, doctoral, first professional, and other advanced degrees. Within each level, information may be provided in two basic categories: entrance exams and other requirements. The entrance exams are identified by the standard acronyms used by the testing agencies, unless they are not well known. Other entrance requirements are quite varied, but they often contain an undergraduate or graduate grade point average (GPA). Unless otherwise stated, the GPA is calculated on a 4.0 scale and is listed as a minimum required for admission. Additional exam requirements/recommendations for international students may be listed here. Application deadlines for domestic and international students, the application fee, and whether electronic applications are accepted may be listed here. Note that the deadline should be used for reference only; these dates are subject to change, and students interested in applying should always contact the graduate unit directly about application procedures and deadlines.

**Expenses.** The typical cost of study for the 2019-20 academic year (2018-19 if 2019-20 figures were not available) is given in two basic categories: tuition and fees. Cost of study may be quite complex at a graduate institution. There are often sliding scales for part-time study, a different cost for first-year students, and other variables that make it impossible to completely cover the cost of study for each graduate program. To provide the most usable information, figures are given for full-time study for a full year where available and for part-time study in terms of a per-unit rate (per credit, per semester hour, etc.). Occasionally, variances may be noted in tuition and fees for reasons such as the type of program, whether courses are taken during the day or evening, whether courses are at the master's or doctoral level, or other institution-specific reasons. Respondents were also given the opportunity to provide more specific and detailed tuition and fees information at the unit level. When provided, this information will appear in place of any typical costs entered elsewhere on the university-level survey. Expenses are usually subject to change; for exact costs at any given time, contact your chosen schools and programs directly. Keep in mind that the tuition of Canadian institutions is usually given in Canadian dollars.

**Financial Support**. This section contains data on the number of awards administered by the institution and given to graduate students during the 2017–18 academic year. The first figure given represents the total number of students receiving financial support enrolled in that unit. If the unit has provided information on graduate appointments, these are broken down into three major categories: fellowships give money to graduate students to cover the cost of study and living expenses and are not based on a work obligation or research commitment, research assistantships provide stipends to graduate students for assistance in a formal research project with a faculty member, and teaching assistantships provide stipends to graduate students for teaching or for assisting faculty members in teaching undergraduate classes. Within each category, figures are given for the total number of awards, the average yearly amount per award, and whether full or partial tuition reimbursements are awarded. In addition to graduate appointments, the availability of several other financial aid sources is covered in this section. Tuition waivers are routinely part of a graduate appointment, but units sometimes waive part or all of a student's tuition even if a graduate appointment is not available. Federal Work Study is made available to students who demonstrate need and meet the federal guidelines; this form of aid normally includes 10 or more hours of work per week in an office of the institution. Institutionally sponsored loans are low-interest loans available to graduate students to cover both educational and living expenses. Career-related internships or fieldwork offer money to students who are participating in a formal off-campus research project or practicum. Grants, scholarships, traineeships, unspecified assistantships, and other awards may also be noted. The availability of financial support to part-time students is also indicated here.

Some programs list the financial aid application deadline and the forms that need to be completed for students to be eligible for financial awards. There are two forms: FAFSA, the Free Application for Federal Student Aid, which is required for federal aid, and the CSS PROFILE®.

**Faculty Research**. Each unit has the opportunity to list several keyword phrases describing the current research involving faculty members and graduate students. Space limitations prevent the unit from listing complete information on all research programs. The total expenditure for funded research from the previous academic year may also be included.

**Unit Head and Application Contact**. The head of the graduate program for each unit may be listed with academic title, phone and fax numbers, and e-mail address. In addition to the unit head's contact information, many graduate programs also list a separate contact for application and admission information, followed by the graduate school, program, or department's website. If no unit head or application contact is given, you should contact the overall institution for information on graduate admissions.

# Displays and Close-Ups

Any **Displays** and **Close-Ups** are supplementary insertions submitted by deans, chairs, and other administrators who wish to offer an additional, more individualized statement to readers. A number of graduate school and program administrators have attached a **Display** ad near the **Profile** listing. Here you will find information that an institution or program wants to emphasize. The **Close-Ups** are by their very nature more expansive and flexible than the **Profiles**, and the administrators who have written them may emphasize different aspects of their programs. All of the **Close-Ups** are organized in the same way (with the exception of a few that describe research and training opportunities instead of degree programs), and in each one you will find information on the same basic topics, such as programs of study, research facilities, tuition and fees, financial aid, and application procedures. If an institution or program has submitted a **Close-Up**, a boldface cross-reference appears below its **Profile**. As with the **Displays**, all of the **Close-Ups** in the guides have been submitted by choice; the absence of a **Display** or **Close-Up** does not reflect any type of editorial judgment on the part of Peterson's, and their presence in the guides should not be taken as an indication of status, quality, or approval. Statements regarding a university's objectives and accomplishments are a reflection of its own beliefs and are not the opinions of the Peterson's editors.

## Appendixes

This section contains two appendixes. The first, "Institutional Changes Since the 2020 Edition," lists institutions that have closed, merged, or changed their name or status since the last edition of the guides. The second, "Abbreviations Used in the Guides," gives abbreviations of degree names, along with what those abbreviations stand for. These appendixes are identical in all six volumes of ***Peterson's Graduate and Professional Programs***.

## Indexes

There are three indexes presented here. The first index, "Close-Ups and Displays," gives page references for all programs that have chosen to place **Close-Ups** and **Displays** in this volume. It is arranged alphabetically by institution; within institutions, the arrangement is alphabetical by subject area. It is not an index to all programs in the book's directories of **Profiles**; readers must refer to the directories themselves for **Profile** information on programs that have not submitted the additional, more individualized statements. The second index, "Directories and Subject Areas in Other Books in This Series", gives book references for the directories in the specialized volumes and also includes cross-references for subject area names not used in the directory structure, for example, "Computing Technology (see Computer Science)." The third index, "Directories and Subject Areas in This Book," gives page references for the directories in this volume and cross-references for subject area names not used in this volume's directory structure.

## Data Collection Procedures

The information published in the directories and Profiles of all the books is collected through Peterson's Annual Survey of Graduate and Professional Institutions. The survey is sent each spring to nearly 2,300 institutions offering postbaccalaureate degree programs, including accredited institutions in the United States, U.S. territories, and Canada and those institutions outside the United States that are accredited by U.S. accrediting bodies. Deans and other administrators complete these surveys, providing information on programs in the 500 academic and professional fields covered in the guides as well as overall institutional information. While every effort has been made to ensure the accuracy and completeness of the data, information is sometimes unavailable or changes occur after publication deadlines. All usable information received in time for publication has been included. The omission of any particular item from a directory or Profile signifies either that the item is not applicable to the institution or program or that information was not available. Profiles of programs scheduled to begin during the 2019-20 academic year cannot, obviously, include statistics on enrollment or, in many cases, the number of faculty members. If no usable data were submitted by an institution, its name, address, and program name appear in order to indicate the availability of graduate work.

## Criteria for Inclusion in This Guide

To be included in this guide, an institution must have full accreditation or be a candidate for accreditation (preaccreditation) status by an institutional or specialized accrediting body recognized by the U.S. Department of Education or the Council for Higher Education Accreditation (CHEA). Institutional accrediting bodies, which review each institution as a whole, include the six regional associations of schools and colleges (Middle States, New England, North Central, Northwest, Southern, and Western), each of which is responsible for a specified portion of the United States and its territories. Other institutional accrediting bodies are national in scope and accredit specific kinds of institutions (e.g., Bible colleges, independent colleges, and rabbinical and Talmudic schools). Program registration by the New York State Board of Regents is considered to be the equivalent of institutional accreditation, since the board requires that all programs offered by an institution meet its standards before recognition is granted. A Canadian institution must be chartered and authorized to grant degrees by the provincial government, affiliated with a chartered institution, or accredited by a recognized U.S. accrediting body. This guide also includes institutions outside the United States that are accredited by these U.S. accrediting bodies. There are recognized specialized or professional accrediting bodies in more than fifty different fields, each of which is authorized to accredit institutions or specific programs in its particular field. For specialized institutions that offer programs in one field only, we designate this to be the equivalent of institutional accreditation. A full explanation of the accrediting process and complete information on recognized institutional (regional and national) and specialized accrediting bodies can be found online at **www.chea.org** or at **www.ed.gov/admins/finaid/accred/index.html.**

# DIRECTORY OF GRADUATE AND PROFESSIONAL PROGRAMS BY FIELD

## ACCOUNTING

| | |
|---|---|
| Adelphi University | M |
| Adrian College | M |
| Alabama State University | M |
| Albany State University | M |
| Albertus Magnus College | M |
| Alfred University | M |
| American Business & Technology University | M |
| American InterContinental University Online | M |
| American International College | M,D,O |
| American Public University System | M,D |
| American University | M,O |
| American University of Sharjah | M,D |
| Anderson University (IN) | M,D |
| Andrews University | M |
| Angelo State University | M |
| Appalachian State University | M |
| Argosy University, Atlanta | M,D |
| Argosy University, Chicago | M,D |
| Argosy University, Hawaii | M,D,O |
| Argosy University, Los Angeles | M,D |
| Argosy University, Northern Virginia | M,D,O |
| Argosy University, Orange County | M,D,O |
| Argosy University, Phoenix | M,D |
| Argosy University, Seattle | M,D |
| Argosy University, Tampa | M,D |
| Argosy University, Twin Cities | M,D |
| Arizona State University at Tempe | M,D |
| Arkansas State University | M |
| Ashland University | M |
| Assumption University | M,O |
| Auburn University | M |
| Auburn University at Montgomery | M |
| Augustana University | M |
| Aurora University | M |
| Averett University | M |
| Azusa Pacific University | M |
| Babson College | M,O |
| Baker College Center for Graduate Studies–Online | M,D |
| Ball State University | M |
| Barry University | M |
| Baruch College of the City University of New York | M,D |
| Bayamón Central University | M |
| Baylor University | M |
| Bay Path University | M |
| Belmont University | M |
| Benedictine University | M |
| Bentley University | M,D |
| Binghamton University, State University of New York | M |
| Bloomfield College | M |
| Bloomsburg University of Pennsylvania | M |
| Bluffton University | M |
| Bob Jones University | M,D,O |
| Boise State University | M |
| Boston College | M |
| Bowling Green State University | M |
| Bradley University | M |
| Brandman University | M |
| Brenau University | M |
| Bridgewater State University | M |
| Brock University | M |
| Brooklyn College of the City University of New York | M |
| Bryant University | M |
| Bushnell University | M |
| Cabrini University | M,D |
| Cairn University | M,O |
| California Baptist University | M |
| California Polytechnic State University, San Luis Obispo | M |
| California State Polytechnic University, Pomona | M |
| California State University, East Bay | M |
| California State University, Fullerton | M |
| California State University, Los Angeles | M |
| California State University, Sacramento | M |
| California State University, San Bernardino | M |
| California Western School of Law | M,D |
| Calvin College | M |
| Canisius College | M |
| Capella University | M,D |
| Carnegie Mellon University | D |
| Case Western Reserve University | M,D |
| The Catholic University of America | M |
| Centenary University | M |
| Central Connecticut State University | M |
| Central Michigan University | M,O |
| Chaminade University of Honolulu | M |
| Chapman University | M |
| Charleston Southern University | M |
| Chatham University | M |
| Christian Brothers University | M,O |
| City University of Seattle | M,O |
| Clarion University of Pennsylvania | M |
| Clark Atlanta University | M |
| Clark University | M |
| Clayton State University | M |
| Clemson University | M |
| Cleveland State University | M |
| Coastal Carolina University | M,O |
| College of Charleston | M |
| The College of Saint Rose | M |
| College of Staten Island of the City University of New York | M |
| Colorado State University | M |
| Colorado State University–Global Campus | M |
| Colorado Technical University Aurora | M |
| Colorado Technical University Colorado Springs | M,D |
| Columbia College (MO) | M |
| Columbia University | M,D |
| Cornell University | M,D |
| Creighton University | M,D |
| Culver-Stockton College | M |
| Daemen College | M |
| Dallas Baptist University | M |
| Davenport University | M |
| Delaware Valley University | M |
| Delta State University | M |
| DePaul University | M,D |
| DeSales University | M |
| DeVry University–Folsom Campus | M |
| Dominican College | M |
| Dominican University | M |
| Drake University | M |
| Drexel University | M,D,O |
| Duke University | D |
| Duquesne University | M |
| East Carolina University | M |
| East Central University | M |
| Eastern Connecticut State University | M |
| Eastern Illinois University | M |
| Eastern Michigan University | M |
| Eastern Washington University | M |
| East Tennessee State University | M |
| Elms College | M,O |
| Emory University | M,D |
| Emporia State University | M |
| Everglades University | M |
| Fairfield University | M,O |
| Fairleigh Dickinson University, Florham Campus | M |
| Fairleigh Dickinson University, Metropolitan Campus | M,O |
| Fitchburg State University | M |
| Florida Agricultural and Mechanical University | M |
| Florida Atlantic University | M |
| Florida Gulf Coast University | M |
| Florida International University | M |
| Florida National University | M |
| Florida Southern College | M |
| Florida State University | M,D |
| Fontbonne University | M |
| Fordham University | M,D |
| Franklin University | M |
| Freed-Hardeman University | M |
| Friends University | M |
| George Fox University | M,D |
| George Mason University | M |
| The George Washington University | M |
| Georgia College & State University | M |
| Georgia Southern University | M |
| Georgia State University | M |
| Golden Gate University | M,D,O |
| Gonzaga University | M |
| Governors State University | M |
| The Graduate Center, City University of New York | D |
| Grand Canyon University | M |
| Grand Valley State University | M |
| Harvard University | D* |
| HEC Montreal | M,D,O |
| Hendrix College | M |
| Herzing University Online | M |
| Hodges University | M |
| Hofstra University | M,O |
| Holy Family University | M |
| Hood College | M,O |
| Howard University | M |
| Hunter College of the City University of New York | M |
| IGlobal University | M |
| Illinois State University | M |
| Indiana Tech | M |
| Indiana University Kokomo | M,O |
| Indiana University Northwest | M,O |
| Indiana University-Purdue University Indianapolis | M |
| Indiana University South Bend | M,O |
| Indiana Wesleyan University | M,O |
| Instituto Tecnologico de Santo Domingo | M,O |
| Inter American University of Puerto Rico, Aguadilla Campus | M |
| Inter American University of Puerto Rico, Arecibo Campus | M |
| Inter American University of Puerto Rico, Barranquitas Campus | M |
| Inter American University of Puerto Rico, Metropolitan Campus | M |
| Inter American University of Puerto Rico, Ponce Campus | M |
| Inter American University of Puerto Rico, San Germán Campus | M,D |
| Iona College | M,O |
| Iowa State University of Science and Technology | M |
| Ithaca College | M |
| Jackson State University | M |
| Jacksonville University | M |
| James Madison University | M |
| John Carroll University | M |
| Johnson & Wales University | M |
| Juniata College | M |
| Kansas State University | M |
| Kean University | M |
| Keiser University | M |
| Kennesaw State University | M |
| Kent State University | M,D |
| Keystone College | M |
| King University | M |
| Lamar University | M |
| La Roche University | M |
| La Salle University | M,O |
| La Sierra University | M,O |
| Lehigh University | M |
| Lehman College of the City University of New York | M |
| Lenoir-Rhyne University | M |
| Lewis University | M |
| Liberty University | M,D |
| Lipscomb University | M,O |
| Long Island University - Brooklyn | M,O |
| Long Island University - Post | M |
| Louisiana State University and Agricultural & Mechanical College | M,D |
| Louisiana Tech University | M,D |
| Loyola Marymount University | M |
| Loyola University Chicago | M |
| Maharishi International University | M,D |
| Manhattanville College | M,O |
| Marist College | M |
| Marquette University | M |
| Marshall University | M |
| Maryville University of Saint Louis | M,O |
| McGill University | M,D,O |
| Mercer University | M |
| Mercy College | M |
| Mercyhurst University | M,O |
| Merrimack College | M |
| Metropolitan State University of Denver | M |
| Miami University | M |
| Michigan State University | M,D |
| Middle Tennessee State University | M |
| Millennia Atlantic University | M |
| Millsaps College | M |
| Minnesota State University Mankato | M |
| Misericordia University | M |
| Mississippi College | M,O |
| Mississippi State University | M |
| Missouri State University | M |
| Missouri Western State University | M |
| Molloy College | M,O |
| Monmouth University | M,O |
| Monroe College | M |
| Montana State University | M |
| Montclair State University | M,O |
| Moravian College | M |
| Morgan State University | M,D |
| Mount Aloysius College | M |
| Murray State University | M |
| National American University (TX) | M,D |
| National University | M,O |
| Neumann University | M |
| New England College | M |
| New Jersey City University | M,O |
| New Mexico State University | M |
| New York University | M,D |
| Niagara University | M |
| North Carolina Agricultural and Technical State University | M |
| North Carolina State University | M |
| North Dakota State University | M |
| Northeastern Illinois University | M |
| Northeastern State University | M |
| Northeastern University | M |
| Northern Illinois University | M |
| Northern Kentucky University | M,O |
| Nova Southeastern University | M |
| Oakland University | M,O |
| Ohio Christian University | M |
| Ohio Dominican University | M |
| Ohio Northern University | M |
| The Ohio State University | M |
| Oklahoma Christian University | M |
| Oklahoma State University | M,D |
| Old Dominion University | M |
| Oral Roberts University | M |
| Oregon State University | M,D |
| Our Lady of the Lake University | M |
| Pace University | M,O |
| Pacific Lutheran University | M |
| Pacific States University | M,O |
| Penn State Erie, The Behrend College | M |
| Penn State Harrisburg | M,O |
| Penn State University Park | M,D* |
| Pepperdine University | M |
| Pittsburg State University | M |
| Plymouth State University | M |
| Polytechnic University of Puerto Rico, Miami Campus | M |
| Polytechnic University of Puerto Rico, Orlando Campus | M |
| Pontifical Catholic University of Puerto Rico | M,O |
| Post University | M |
| Prairie View A&M University | M |
| Providence College | M |
| Purdue University Northwest | M |
| Queens College of the City University of New York | M |
| Quinnipiac University | M |
| Ramapo College of New Jersey | M |
| Regent University | M,D,O |
| Regis University | M,O |
| Rhode Island College | M,O |
| Rhodes College | M |
| Rider University | M,O |
| Robert Morris University Illinois | M |
| Rochester Institute of Technology | M |
| Rockhurst University | M,O |
| Rocky Mountain College | M |
| Roosevelt University | M |
| Rutgers University - Newark | M,D |
| Sacred Heart University | M,O |
| St. Ambrose University | M |
| St. Bonaventure University | M |
| St. Edward's University | M |
| St. Francis College | M |
| St. John's University (NY) | M |
| St. Joseph's College, Long Island Campus | M |
| St. Joseph's College, New York | M |
| Saint Joseph's College of Maine | M |
| Saint Joseph's University | M,O |
| Saint Leo University | M,D |
| Saint Louis University | M |
| Saint Mary's College of California | M |
| Saint Mary's University of Minnesota | M |
| Saint Peter's University | M |
| St. Thomas University - Florida | M,O |
| Samford University | M |
| Sam Houston State University | M |
| San Diego State University | M |
| San Francisco State University | M |
| Seattle University | M |
| Seton Hall University | M,O |
| Seton Hill University | M |
| Shorter University | M |
| Siena College | M |
| Southeast Missouri State University | M |
| Southern Adventist University | M |
| Southern Illinois University Carbondale | M,D |
| Southern Illinois University Edwardsville | M |
| Southern Methodist University | M |
| Southern New Hampshire University | M,D,O |
| Southern Oregon University | M,O |
| Southern Utah University | M |
| Southwestern Adventist University | M |
| State University of New York at New Paltz | M |
| State University of New York College at Geneseo | M |
| State University of New York College at Old Westbury | M |
| State University of New York Polytechnic Institute | M |
| Stephen F. Austin State University | M |
| Stetson University | M |
| Stony Brook University, State University of New York | M,O |
| Stratford University (VA) | M,D |
| Strayer University | M |
| Suffolk University | M,O |
| SUNY Brockport | M,O |
| Syracuse University | M |
| Tabor College | M |
| Tarleton State University | M |
| Temple University | M,D* |
| Tennessee Technological University | M |
| Tennessee Wesleyan University | M |
| Texas A&M International University | M |
| Texas A&M University | M |
| Texas A&M University–Central Texas | M,O |
| Texas A&M University–Commerce | M |
| Texas A&M University–Corpus Christi | M |
| Texas A&M University–San Antonio | M |
| Texas A&M University–Texarkana | M |
| Texas Christian University | M |
| Texas Lutheran University | M |
| Texas State University | M |
| Texas Tech University | M,D |
| Texas Woman's University | M |
| Thomas Edison State University | M |
| Towson University | M |
| Trinity University | M |
| Troy University | M |
| Truman State University | M |
| Tulane University | M,D |
| Union University | M |
| Universidad del Este | M |
| Universidad del Turabo | M |
| Universidad Metropolitana | M |
| Université de Sherbrooke | M |
| Université du Québec à Montréal | M,O |
| Université du Québec à Trois-Rivières | M |
| Université du Québec en Outaouais | M,O |
| University at Albany, State University of New York | M |
| University at Buffalo, the State University of New York | M,D |
| The University of Akron | M |
| The University of Alabama | M,D |
| The University of Alabama at Birmingham | M |
| The University of Alabama in Huntsville | M,O |
| University of Alberta | D |
| The University of Arizona | M |
| University of Arkansas | M |
| University of Baltimore | M,O |
| University of Bridgeport | M |
| The University of British Columbia | D |
| University of California, Berkeley | D,O |
| University of California, Davis | M |
| University of California, Irvine | M |
| University of California, Los Angeles | M,D |
| University of California, Riverside | M,D |
| University of Central Arkansas | M |
| University of Central Florida | M |
| University of Central Missouri | M,D,O |
| University of Charleston | M |
| University of Chicago | M,O |
| University of Cincinnati | M,D |
| University of Colorado Denver | M |
| University of Connecticut | M,D |
| University of Dallas | M,D |
| University of Dayton | M |
| University of Delaware | M |
| University of Denver | M |
| University of Detroit Mercy | M,O |
| The University of Findlay | M,D |
| University of Florida | M,D |
| University of Georgia | M |
| University of Hartford | M,O |
| University of Hawaii at Manoa | M,D |
| University of Houston | M,D |

| | |
|---|---|
| University of Houston–Clear Lake | M |
| University of Houston - Downtown | M |
| University of Houston–Victoria | M |
| University of Idaho | M |
| University of Illinois at Chicago | M |
| University of Illinois at Springfield | M |
| University of Illinois at Urbana-Champaign | M,D |
| The University of Iowa | M,D |
| The University of Kansas | M |
| University of Kentucky | M |
| University of La Verne | M |
| University of Lethbridge | M,D |
| University of Louisiana at Lafayette | M |
| University of Louisville | M |
| The University of Manchester | M |
| University of Mary Hardin-Baylor | M |
| University of Maryland Global Campus | M,O |
| University of Massachusetts Amherst | M,D |
| University of Massachusetts Boston | M |
| University of Massachusetts Dartmouth | M,O |
| University of Memphis | M,D |
| University of Miami | M,D |
| University of Michigan | M,D |
| University of Michigan–Dearborn | M |
| University of Michigan–Flint | M,O |
| University of Minnesota, Twin Cities Campus | M,D |
| University of Mississippi | M,D |
| University of Missouri | M,D,O |
| University of Missouri–Kansas City | M,D |
| University of Missouri–St. Louis | M,D,O |
| University of Montana | M |
| University of Nebraska at Kearney | M |
| University of Nebraska at Omaha | M |
| University of Nebraska–Lincoln | M,D |
| University of Nevada, Las Vegas | M,O |
| University of Nevada, Reno | M |
| University of New Hampshire | M |
| University of New Haven | M,O |
| University of New Mexico | M |
| University of New Orleans | M |
| University of North Alabama | M |
| The University of North Carolina at Chapel Hill | M,D |
| The University of North Carolina at Charlotte | M |
| The University of North Carolina at Greensboro | M,O |
| The University of North Carolina Wilmington | M |
| University of Northern Colorado | M |
| University of Northern Iowa | M |
| University of North Florida | M |
| University of North Texas | M,D,O |
| University of North Texas at Dallas | M |
| University of Notre Dame | M |
| University of Oklahoma | M |
| University of Oregon | M,D |
| University of Pennsylvania | M,D |
| University of Phoenix - Bay Area Campus | M,D |
| University of Phoenix - Central Valley Campus | M |
| University of Phoenix - Dallas Campus | M |
| University of Phoenix - Hawaii Campus | M |
| University of Phoenix - Houston Campus | M |
| University of Phoenix - Las Vegas Campus | M |
| University of Phoenix–Online Campus | M,O |
| University of Phoenix - Phoenix Campus | M,O |
| University of Phoenix - Sacramento Valley Campus | M |
| University of Phoenix - San Antonio Campus | M |
| University of Phoenix - San Diego Campus | M |
| University of Pittsburgh | M,D* |
| University of Puerto Rico at Rio Piedras | M,D |
| University of Rhode Island | M |
| University of Rochester | M,D |
| University of St. Francis (IL) | M,O |
| University of St. Thomas (TX) | M |
| University of St. Thomas (MN) | M |
| University of San Diego | M |
| University of Saskatchewan | M |
| The University of Scranton | M |
| University of South Africa | M,D |
| University of South Alabama | M |
| University of South Carolina | M |
| University of South Dakota | M |
| University of Southern California | M |
| University of Southern Indiana | M |
| University of Southern Maine | M |
| University of Southern Mississippi | M |
| University of South Florida | M,D |
| The University of Tampa | M,O |
| The University of Tennessee | M,D |
| The University of Tennessee at Chattanooga | M |
| The University of Texas at Arlington | M,D |
| The University of Texas at Austin | M,D |
| The University of Texas at Dallas | M |
| The University of Texas at El Paso | M |
| The University of Texas at San Antonio | M,D |
| The University of Texas at Tyler | M |
| The University of Texas of the Permian Basin | M |
| The University of Texas Rio Grande Valley | M |
| University of the Cumberlands | M |
| University of the Incarnate Word | M |
| University of the Sacred Heart | M,O |
| The University of Toledo | M |
| The University of Tulsa | M |
| University of Utah | M,D |
| University of Vermont | M |
| University of Virginia | M |
| University of Washington | M,D |
| University of Washington, Tacoma | M |
| University of Waterloo | M,D |
| University of West Florida | M |
| University of Wisconsin–Madison | M,D |
| University of Wisconsin–Whitewater | M |
| University of Wyoming | M |
| Université Laval | M,O |
| Upper Iowa University | M |
| Utah State University | M |
| Utah Valley University | M |
| Utica College | M |
| Valdosta State University | M |
| Vanderbilt University | M* |
| Villanova University | M |
| Virginia Commonwealth University | M |
| Virginia International University | M,O |
| Virginia Polytechnic Institute and State University | M,D |
| Wagner College | M |
| Wake Forest University | M |
| Walden University | M,D,O |
| Walsh College of Accountancy and Business Administration | M |
| Warner University | M |
| Washburn University | M |
| Washington & Jefferson College | M,O |
| Washington State University | M |
| Washington University in St. Louis | M |
| Wayland Baptist University | M,D |
| Wayne State University | M,D,O |
| Webber International University | M |
| Weber State University | M |
| Webster University | M |
| Western Carolina University | M |
| Western Connecticut State University | M |
| Western Governors University | M |
| Western Illinois University | M |
| Western Michigan University | M |
| Western New England University | M |
| Westfield State University | M |
| West Liberty University | M |
| Westminster College (UT) | M,O |
| West Texas A&M University | M |
| West Virginia University | M,D,O |
| Wheeling Jesuit University | M |
| Wichita State University | M |
| Wilfrid Laurier University | M,D |
| William & Mary | M* |
| Wilmington University | M,D |
| Wilson College | M |
| Wingate University | M |
| Worcester State University | M |
| Wright State University | M |
| Xavier University | M* |
| Yale University | D |
| Yeshiva University | M |
| York University | M,D |
| Youngstown State University | M |

## ACOUSTICS

| | |
|---|---|
| Naval Postgraduate School | M,D |
| Penn State University Park | M,D* |
| Rensselaer Polytechnic Institute | D |
| The University of Kansas | M,D,O |

## ACTUARIAL SCIENCE

| | |
|---|---|
| Ball State University | M |
| Boston University | M |
| California State University, East Bay | M |
| Central Connecticut State University | M,O |
| Columbia University | M |
| Florida State University | M,D |
| Georgia State University | M |
| Governors State University | M |
| Lock Haven University of Pennsylvania | M |
| Maryville University of Saint Louis | M |
| Middle Tennessee State University | M |
| The Ohio State University | M,D |
| Oregon State University | M,D |
| Roosevelt University | M |
| St. John's University (NY) | M |
| Simon Fraser University | M,D |
| Temple University | M* |
| Université du Québec à Montréal | O |
| University of Illinois at Urbana-Champaign | M,D |
| The University of Iowa | M,D |
| The University of Manchester | M,D |
| University of Nebraska–Lincoln | M |
| The University of Texas at Austin | M,D |
| The University of Texas at Dallas | M,D |
| University of Waterloo | M,D |
| University of Wisconsin–Madison | D |
| University of Wisconsin–Milwaukee | M,D* |
| Youngstown State University | M |

## ACUPUNCTURE AND ORIENTAL MEDICINE

| | |
|---|---|
| Academy for Five Element Acupuncture | M |
| Academy of Chinese Culture and Health Sciences | M |
| Acupuncture & Integrative Medicine College, Berkeley | M |
| Acupuncture and Massage College | M |
| American Academy of Acupuncture and Oriental Medicine | M,D |
| American College of Acupuncture and Oriental Medicine | M |
| American Institute of Alternative Medicine | M |
| AOMA Graduate School of Integrative Medicine | M,D |
| Arizona School of Acupuncture and Oriental Medicine | M |
| Atlantic Institute of Oriental Medicine | M,D |
| Bastyr University | M,D |
| Canadian Memorial Chiropractic College | O |
| Colorado School of Traditional Chinese Medicine | M |
| Daoist Traditions College of Chinese Medical Arts | M,D |
| Dongguk University Los Angeles | M |
| Dragon Rises College of Oriental Medicine | M |
| Eastern School of Acupuncture and Traditional Medicine | M |
| East West College of Natural Medicine | M |
| Emperor's College of Traditional Oriental Medicine | M,D |
| Five Branches University | M,D |
| Florida College of Integrative Medicine | M |
| Institute of Clinical Acupuncture and Oriental Medicine | M |
| Institute of Taoist Education and Acupuncture | M |
| Maryland University of Integrative Health | M,D,O |
| MCPHS University | M |
| Midwest College of Oriental Medicine | M,O |
| National University of Health Sciences | M,D |
| National University of Natural Medicine | M,D |
| New York Chiropractic College | M |
| New York College of Health Professions | M |
| New York College of Traditional Chinese Medicine | M |
| Northwestern Health Sciences University | M |
| Oregon College of Oriental Medicine | M,D |
| Pacific College of Oriental Medicine | M,D |
| Pacific College of Oriental Medicine–Chicago | M |
| Pacific College of Oriental Medicine-New York | M |
| Phoenix Institute of Herbal Medicine & Acupuncture | M |
| Seattle Institute of East Asian Medicine | M |
| South Baylo University | M |
| Southern California University of Health Sciences | M,D |
| Southwest Acupuncture College | M |
| Swedish Institute, College of Health Sciences | M |
| Texas Health and Science University | M,D |
| University of Bridgeport | M |
| University of East-West Medicine | M,D |
| Virginia University of Integrative Medicine | M,D,O |
| Wongu University of Oriental Medicine | M |
| Won Institute of Graduate Studies | M,O |
| Yo San University of Traditional Chinese Medicine | M |

## ACUTE CARE/CRITICAL CARE NURSING

| | |
|---|---|
| Augusta University | D |
| Barry University | M,O |
| Case Western Reserve University | M |
| The College of New Rochelle | M,O |
| Columbia University | M,O |
| Drexel University | M |
| Duke University | M,D,O |
| Elms College | M,D |
| Georgetown University | M,D |
| Goldfarb School of Nursing at Barnes-Jewish College | M |
| Grand Canyon University | M,D,O |
| Indiana University-Purdue University Indianapolis | M |
| Inter American University of Puerto Rico, Arecibo Campus | M |
| Inter American University of Puerto Rico, Barranquitas Campus | M |
| Marquette University | M,D,O |
| Maryville University of Saint Louis | M,D |
| Moravian College | M |
| Mount Carmel College of Nursing | M,D |
| New York University | M,D,O |
| Northeastern University | M,D,O |
| Point Loma Nazarene University | M |
| Purdue University Northwest | M |
| San Francisco State University | M,O |
| Southern Adventist University | M,D |
| Tennessee Technological University | D |
| Texas Tech University Health Sciences Center | M,D,O |
| Texas Woman's University | M,D |
| Universidad de Iberoamerica | M,D |
| The University of Alabama in Huntsville | M,D,O |
| University of Cincinnati | M,D |
| University of Guelph | M,D,O |
| University of Illinois at Chicago | M,O |
| University of Miami | M,D |
| The University of North Carolina at Charlotte | M,D,O |
| University of Northern Colorado | M,D |
| University of Pennsylvania | M |
| University of Puerto Rico - Medical Sciences Campus | M |
| University of Rhode Island | M,D,O |
| University of Rochester | M,D |
| University of South Africa | M,D |
| University of South Carolina | M,O |
| University of South Florida | M,D,O |
| The University of Texas Health Science Center at San Antonio | M,D,O |
| University of Virginia | M,D |
| Wayne State University | M,D |
| Winona State University | M,D,O |
| Wright State University | M |

## ADDICTIONS/SUBSTANCE ABUSE COUNSELING

| | |
|---|---|
| Alliant International University - Los Angeles | M |
| Antioch University New England | M,D,O |
| Argosy University, Hawaii | O |
| Arkansas State University | M,O |
| Assumption University | O |
| Bay Path University | M |
| Cambridge College | M,O |
| Capella University | M,D |
| The College of New Jersey | M,O |
| College of St. Joseph | M |
| Coppin State University | M |
| East Carolina University | M,D,O |
| Fairfield University | M,O |
| The George Washington University | M |
| Governors State University | M |
| Hazelden Betty Ford Graduate School of Addiction Studies | M,O |
| Indiana University Northwest | M,O |
| Indiana University South Bend | M,O |
| Indiana Wesleyan University | M |
| Johnson & Wales University | M |
| Kean University | M |
| Lenoir-Rhyne University | M |
| Lewis & Clark College | M |
| Liberty University | M,D,O |
| Loma Linda University | M,D,O |
| Long Island University - Hudson | M,O |
| Maryville University of Saint Louis | M |
| Metropolitan State University | M |
| Monmouth University | M,O |
| Montclair State University | O |
| Northern Vermont University–Johnson | M |
| Northwest Nazarene University | M |
| Nova Southeastern University | M,D,O |
| Oral Roberts University | M,D |
| Pace University | M,D |
| Palm Beach Atlantic University | M |
| Plymouth State University | M |
| Post University | M |
| Regent University | M,D,O |
| Salve Regina University | M,O |
| Stephens College | M,O |
| Stony Brook University, State University of New York | M,O |
| Syracuse University | M,O |
| Texas Tech University Health Sciences Center | M |
| United States International University–Africa | M |
| Universidad Central del Caribe | M |
| University of California, Berkeley | O |
| University of Central Oklahoma | M |
| University of Cincinnati | M,D,O |
| University of Detroit Mercy | M,D,O |
| University of Illinois at Springfield | M,O |
| University of Indianapolis | M,D |
| University of Lethbridge | M,D |
| University of Louisville | M,D,O |
| University of Nevada, Las Vegas | M,D,O |
| University of New Hampshire | M,O |
| The University of North Carolina at Charlotte | M,D,O |
| University of South Dakota | M |
| University of Southern Maine | M,O |
| University of South Florida | M,D |
| The University of Tennessee at Martin | M |
| Viterbo University | M |
| Walden University | M,D |
| Washburn University | M |
| Waynesburg University | M,D |
| Winona State University | M,O |

## ADULT EDUCATION

| | |
|---|---|
| Alverno College | M |
| Antioch University Seattle | M |
| Argosy University, Chicago | M,D,O |
| Argosy University, Hawaii | M,D |
| Argosy University, Phoenix | M,D,O |
| Argosy University, Seattle | M,D |
| Athabasca University | M,O |
| Auburn University | M,D,O |
| Aurora University | M,D |

*M—masters degree; D—doctorate; O—other advanced degree; *—Close-Up and/or Display*

| | |
|---|---|
| Ball State University | M,D |
| Buffalo State College, State University of New York | M,O |
| California Baptist University | M |
| Capella University | M,D |
| Carroll University | M |
| Chicago State University | M |
| Cleveland State University | M,D,O |
| Colorado State University | M,D |
| Concordia University (Canada) | M,O |
| Coppin State University | M |
| Cornell University | M,D |
| Dallas Theological Seminary | M,D,O |
| Delaware State University | M |
| DePaul University | M |
| East Carolina University | M,O |
| Eastern Washington University | M |
| Florida Agricultural and Mechanical University | M,D |
| Florida Atlantic University | M,D,O |
| The George Washington University | O |
| Indiana University of Pennsylvania | M |
| Instituto Tecnologico de Santo Domingo | M,O |
| Kansas State University | M,D,O |
| Lesley University | M,D,O |
| Marshall University | M |
| Memorial University of Newfoundland | M,D,O |
| Michigan State University | M,D,O |
| Montana State University | M,D,O |
| Morehead State University | M,O |
| Mount Saint Vincent University | M |
| National Louis University | M,D,O |
| North Carolina Agricultural and Technical State University | M,D |
| North Carolina State University | M,D |
| Northern Illinois University | M,D |
| Northwestern Oklahoma State University | M |
| Northwestern State University of Louisiana | M |
| Oregon State University | M,D |
| Penn State Harrisburg | M,D,O |
| Penn State University Park | M,D,O* |
| Plymouth State University | D |
| Point Park University | M,D |
| Regent University | M,D,O |
| St. Francis Xavier University | M |
| Saint Joseph's College of Maine | M |
| San Francisco State University | M |
| Seattle University | M,O |
| Southern Arkansas University–Magnolia | M |
| State University of New York Empire State College | M |
| Teachers College, Columbia University | M,D |
| Texas A&M University–Kingsville | M |
| Texas A&M University–Texarkana | M |
| Texas State University | M,D |
| Trident University International | M |
| Troy University | M |
| Universidad del Este | M |
| Universidad Metropolitana | M |
| University of Alberta | M,D,O |
| University of Arkansas | M,D |
| University of Arkansas at Little Rock | M |
| The University of British Columbia | M,D |
| University of Calgary | M,D |
| University of Central Arkansas | M,O |
| University of Central Oklahoma | M |
| University of Colorado Denver | M |
| University of Connecticut | M,O |
| University of Georgia | D,O |
| University of Houston–Victoria | M,O |
| University of Manitoba | M |
| University of Memphis | M,D,O |
| University of Minnesota, Twin Cities Campus | M,D,O |
| University of Missouri | M,D,O |
| University of Missouri–St. Louis | M,O |
| University of Nebraska–Lincoln | M,D,O |
| The University of North Carolina at Greensboro | M,D,O |
| University of North Florida | M |
| University of Oklahoma | M,D |
| University of Phoenix - Bay Area Campus | M,D,O |
| University of Phoenix–Online Campus | M,O |
| University of Phoenix - Phoenix Campus | M |
| University of Phoenix - Sacramento Valley Campus | M,O |
| University of Regina | M |
| University of South Africa | M,D |
| University of South Dakota | M,D,O |
| University of Southern Maine | M,O |
| University of South Florida | M,D,O |
| The University of Tennessee | M,D |
| University of the District of Columbia | O |
| The University of West Alabama | M |
| University of Wisconsin–Milwaukee | M,D,O* |
| University of Wisconsin–Platteville | M |
| Virginia Commonwealth University | M |
| Walden University | M,D,O |
| Western Kentucky University | M,D,O |
| Western Washington University | M |
| Widener University | M,D |

## ADULT NURSING

| | |
|---|---|
| Adelphi University | M |
| Allen College | M,D |
| Azusa Pacific University | M,D |
| Bloomsburg University of Pennsylvania | M,D |
| Boston College | M,D |
| California Baptist University | M |
| Clarkson College | M,O |
| College of Staten Island of the City University of New York | M,O |
| Columbia University | M,O |
| Creighton University | M,D,O |
| Daemen College | M,D,O |
| Duke University | M,D,O |
| Eastern Michigan University | M,O |
| Emory University | M |
| Felician University | M,O |
| Florida International University | M,D |
| Florida Southern College | M |
| George Mason University | M,D,O |
| The George Washington University | M,D,O |
| Georgia State University | M,D,O |
| Gwynedd Mercy University | M,D |
| Hunter College of the City University of New York | M |
| Jacksonville University | M,D,O |
| Kent State University | M,D |
| La Salle University | M,D,O |
| Lehman College of the City University of New York | M |
| Lewis University | M,D |
| Loma Linda University | M |
| Long Island University - Brooklyn | M,O |
| Loyola University Chicago | M,D,O |
| Madonna University | M |
| Marian University (WI) | M |
| Marquette University | M,D,O |
| Maryville University of Saint Louis | M,D |
| Medical University of South Carolina | M,D |
| Monmouth University | M,D,O |
| Mount Carmel College of Nursing | M,D |
| Mount Saint Mary College | M,O |
| Neumann University | M,O |
| New York University | M,D,O |
| North Park University | M |
| Nova Southeastern University | M,D |
| Old Dominion University | M,D |
| Purdue University Fort Wayne | M,O |
| Purdue University Northwest | M |
| Quinnipiac University | D |
| Rutgers University - Newark | M,D,O |
| St. Catherine University | M,D |
| St. Joseph's College, Long Island Campus | M |
| St. Joseph's College, New York | M |
| Saint Mary's College | D |
| Saint Peter's University | M,D,O |
| Seattle Pacific University | M,O |
| Seton Hall University | M,D |
| Shenandoah University | M,D,O |
| Southern Adventist University | M,D |
| South University - Tampa | M |
| Spalding University | M,D,O |
| Stony Brook University, State University of New York | M,D,O |
| Temple University | D* |
| Texas Christian University | M,O |
| Texas Woman's University | M,D |
| Troy University | M,D |
| Universidad del Turabo | M,O |
| University at Buffalo, the State University of New York | M,D,O |
| The University of Alabama at Birmingham | M,D |
| University of Central Arkansas | M,O |
| University of Cincinnati | M,D |
| University of Colorado Colorado Springs | M,D |
| University of Colorado Denver | M,D |
| University of Delaware | M,O |
| University of Hawaii at Manoa | M,D,O |
| University of Illinois at Chicago | M,O |
| The University of Kansas | M,D,O |
| University of Massachusetts Amherst | M,D |
| University of Massachusetts Medical School | M,D,O |
| University of Miami | M,D |
| University of Missouri | M,D,O |
| University of Missouri–Kansas City | M,D |
| University of Missouri–St. Louis | D,O |
| The University of North Carolina at Chapel Hill | M,D,O |
| The University of North Carolina at Greensboro | M,D,O |
| University of Pennsylvania | M |
| University of Puerto Rico - Medical Sciences Campus | M |
| University of Rhode Island | M,D,O |
| University of Rochester | M,D |
| University of San Diego | M,D |
| University of South Carolina | M |
| University of Southern Maine | M,D,O |
| University of South Florida | M,D,O |
| The University of Tampa | M |
| The University of Texas at Austin | M,D |
| University of Wisconsin–Eau Claire | M,D |
| University of Wisconsin–Madison | D |
| University of Wisconsin–Oshkosh | M |
| Ursuline College | M,D |
| Villanova University | M,D,O |
| Virginia Commonwealth University | M,D,O |
| Walden University | M,D,O |
| Walsh University | M,D |
| Wayne State University | M,D |
| Western Connecticut State University | M,D |
| Wilmington University | M,D |
| Winona State University | M,D,O |
| Wright State University | M |

## ADVERTISING AND PUBLIC RELATIONS

| | |
|---|---|
| Academy of Art University | M |
| Ball State University | M |
| Boston University | M |
| Central Connecticut State University | M,O |
| Colorado State University | M,D |
| DePaul University | M |
| Georgetown University | M |
| Hofstra University | M |
| Iona College | M,O |
| Kansas State University | M |
| Kent State University | M |
| La Salle University | M,O |
| Lasell College | M,O |
| La Sierra University | M |
| Liberty University | M,D |
| Lindenwood University | M |
| Marquette University | M,O |
| Marshall University | M,O |
| Michigan State University | M |
| Mississippi College | M |
| Monmouth University | M,O |
| Montana State University Billings | M |
| Montclair State University | M |
| Mount Saint Vincent University | M |
| Murray State University | M |
| New York University | M |
| Northern Kentucky University | M,O |
| Quinnipiac University | M |
| Rowan University | M |
| San Diego State University | M |
| Savannah College of Art and Design | M |
| Seton Hall University | M |
| Southeastern Louisiana University | M |
| Southern Illinois University Edwardsville | M |
| Southern Methodist University | M |
| Southern New Hampshire University | M,D,O |
| Suffolk University | M |
| Syracuse University | M |
| Universidad Autonoma de Guadalajara | M,D |
| The University of Alabama | M |
| University of Colorado Boulder | M,D |
| University of Florida | M,D |
| University of Houston | M |
| University of Illinois at Urbana-Champaign | M |
| University of Maryland, College Park | M,D |
| University of Miami | M,D |
| University of Nebraska–Lincoln | M,D |
| University of North Texas | M,D,O |
| University of Saint Mary | M |
| University of Southern California | M,D |
| University of Southern Mississippi | M,D |
| The University of Tennessee | M,D |
| The University of Texas at Austin | M,D |
| University of the Sacred Heart | M |
| University of Wisconsin–Stevens Point | M |
| Université Laval | O |
| Virginia Commonwealth University | M |
| Virginia International University | M,O |
| Wayne State University | M,D,O |
| Webster University | M |
| Western New England University | M |
| William Woods University | M,D,O |

## AEROSPACE/AERONAUTICAL ENGINEERING

| | |
|---|---|
| Air Force Institute of Technology | M,D |
| Arizona State University at Tempe | M,D |
| Auburn University | M,D |
| California Institute of Technology | M,D,O |
| California Polytechnic State University, San Luis Obispo | M |
| California State Polytechnic University, Pomona | M |
| Carleton University | M,D |
| Case Western Reserve University | M,D |
| The Citadel, The Military College of South Carolina | M,O |
| Concordia University (Canada) | M |
| Cornell University | M,D |
| Embry-Riddle Aeronautical University–Daytona | M,D |
| Embry-Riddle Aeronautical University–Worldwide | M |
| Florida Institute of Technology | M,D |
| The George Washington University | M,D,O |
| Georgia Institute of Technology | M,D |
| Illinois Institute of Technology | M,D |
| Inter American University of Puerto Rico, Bayamón Campus | M |
| Iowa State University of Science and Technology | M,D |
| Johns Hopkins University | M |
| Kent State University | M |
| Massachusetts Institute of Technology | M,D,O |
| McGill University | M,D |
| Middle Tennessee State University | M |
| Mississippi State University | M,D |
| Missouri University of Science and Technology | M,D |
| Naval Postgraduate School | M,D,O |
| North Carolina State University | M,D |
| The Ohio State University | M,D |
| Old Dominion University | M,D |
| Penn State University Park | M,D* |
| Polytechnique Montréal | M,D,O |
| Princeton University | M,D |
| Purdue University | M,D |
| Rensselaer Polytechnic Institute | M,D |
| Rutgers University - New Brunswick | M,D |
| San Diego State University | M,D |
| San Jose State University | M |
| Stevens Institute of Technology | M,O |
| Syracuse University | M,D |
| Texas A&M University | M,D |
| University at Buffalo, the State University of New York | M,D |
| The University of Alabama | M,D |
| The University of Alabama in Huntsville | M,D |
| The University of Arizona | M,D |
| University of California, Davis | M,D,O |
| University of California, Irvine | M,D |
| University of California, Los Angeles | M,D |
| University of California, San Diego | M,D |
| University of Central Florida | M |
| University of Central Missouri | M,D,O |
| University of Cincinnati | M,D |
| University of Colorado Boulder | M,D |
| University of Colorado Colorado Springs | M,D |
| University of Dayton | M,D |
| University of Florida | M,D |
| University of Illinois at Urbana-Champaign | M,D |
| The University of Kansas | M,D |
| The University of Manchester | M,D |
| University of Maryland, College Park | M,D |
| University of Miami | M,D |
| University of Michigan | M,D |
| University of Minnesota, Twin Cities Campus | M,D |
| University of Missouri | M,D |
| University of Nevada, Las Vegas | M,D,O |
| University of Notre Dame | M,D |
| University of Oklahoma | M,D |
| University of Ottawa | M,D |
| University of Puerto Rico at Mayagüez | M,D |
| University of Southern California | M,D,O |
| The University of Tennessee | M,D |
| The University of Texas at Arlington | M,D |
| The University of Texas at Austin | M,D |
| University of Toronto | M,D |
| University of Virginia | M,D |
| University of Washington | M,D |
| Université Laval | M |
| Utah State University | M,D |
| Virginia Polytechnic Institute and State University | M,D,O |
| Washington University in St. Louis | M,D |
| Webster University | M,D,O |
| Western Michigan University | M,D |
| West Virginia University | M,D |
| Wichita State University | M,D |
| Worcester Polytechnic Institute | M,D |
| Wright State University | M |

## AFRICAN-AMERICAN STUDIES

| | |
|---|---|
| Boston University | M |
| Capital University | M |
| Carnegie Mellon University | D |
| Clark Atlanta University | M,D |
| Columbia University | M,D |
| Cornell University | M,D |
| Eastern Michigan University | O |
| Georgia State University | M |
| Harvard University | D* |
| Indiana University Bloomington | M,D |
| Michigan State University | M,D |
| Morgan State University | M,D |
| North Carolina Agricultural and Technical State University | M |
| Northwestern University | D |
| Oblate School of Theology | M,D,O |
| The Ohio State University | M,D |
| Rutgers University - New Brunswick | D |
| Syracuse University | M |
| Temple University | M,D* |
| University at Albany, State University of New York | M |
| University of California, Berkeley | D |
| University of California, Los Angeles | M |
| University of California, Santa Barbara | D |
| The University of Kansas | M,O |
| University of Louisville | M |
| University of Massachusetts Amherst | M,D |
| University of Memphis | M,D,O |
| University of Wisconsin–Madison | M |
| Wayne State University | M,D,O |
| Yale University | D |

## AFRICAN STUDIES

| | |
|---|---|
| Arizona State University at Tempe | M,D,O |
| California State University, Long Beach | M |
| Carnegie Mellon University | D |
| Claremont Graduate University | M,D,O |
| College of Staten Island of the City University of New York | M |
| Columbia University | M,D |
| Cornell University | M,D |
| Florida International University | M |
| Harvard University | D* |
| Howard University | M,D |
| Indiana University Bloomington | M |
| Michigan State University | M,D |
| New York University | M,D,O |
| Northwestern University | O |
| The Ohio State University | M,D |
| Ohio University | M |
| Rice University | D |
| Rutgers University - New Brunswick | D |
| Stony Brook University, State University of New York | M,O |
| Syracuse University | M |
| University at Albany, State University of New York | M |
| The University of Arizona | M,D,O |
| University of California, Los Angeles | M |

University of Illinois at Urbana-Champaign M
The University of Kansas M,O
University of Louisville M
University of Michigan M
The University of North Carolina at Charlotte O
University of Pennsylvania M,D
University of Pittsburgh O*
University of South Florida O
The University of Texas at Austin M,D
University of Wisconsin–Madison M,D
University of Wisconsin–Milwaukee D*
Yale University M

### AGRICULTURAL ECONOMICS AND AGRIBUSINESS

Alcorn State University M
Arizona State University at Tempe D
Auburn University M
Colorado State University M,D
Cornell University M,D
Delaware Valley University M
Illinois State University M
Instituto Centroamericano de Administracion de Empresas M
Iowa State University of Science and Technology M,D
Kansas State University M,D
Louisiana State University and Agricultural & Mechanical College M,D
McGill University M
Michigan State University M,D
Mississippi State University M
New Mexico State University M,D
North Carolina Agricultural and Technical State University M
North Carolina State University M,D
North Dakota State University M
Northwest Missouri State University M
The Ohio State University M,D
Oklahoma State University M,D
Penn State University Park M,D,O*
Purdue University M,D
Rutgers University - New Brunswick M
South Carolina State University M
Southern Illinois University Carbondale M
Texas A&M University M,D
Texas A&M University–Kingsville M,D
Texas Tech University M,D
Tropical Agriculture Research and Higher Education Center M,D
Tuskegee University M
Universidad del Este M
University of Alberta M,D
The University of Arizona M
University of Arkansas M
The University of British Columbia M
University of California, Berkeley D
University of California, Davis M,D
University of California, Santa Barbara M,D
University of Connecticut M,D
University of Delaware M
University of Florida M,D
University of Georgia M,D
University of Guelph M,D
University of Idaho M
University of Illinois at Urbana-Champaign M,D
University of Kentucky M,D
University of Maine M
University of Manitoba M,D
University of Maryland, College Park M,D
University of Massachusetts Amherst M,D
University of Missouri M,D
University of Nebraska–Lincoln M,D
University of Puerto Rico at Mayagüez M
University of Saskatchewan M,D,O
The University of Tennessee at Martin M
University of Vermont M
University of Wisconsin–Madison M,D
University of Wyoming M
Université Laval M
Utah State University M,D
Virginia Polytechnic Institute and State University M,D
Washington State University M,D,O
West Texas A&M University M

### AGRICULTURAL EDUCATION

Alcorn State University M,O
Arkansas State University M,O
California Polytechnic State University, San Luis Obispo M
California State University, Chico M
Clemson University M,D
Colorado State University M
Cornell University M,D
Eastern Kentucky University M
Iowa State University of Science and Technology M,D
Ithaca College M
Kansas State University M
Louisiana State University and Agricultural & Mechanical College M,D
Mississippi State University M,D
Montana State University M
Murray State University M,O
New Mexico State University M
North Carolina Agricultural and Technical State University M
North Dakota State University M
Northwest Missouri State University M
The Ohio State University M
Oklahoma State University M,D
Oregon State University M,D
Penn State University Park M,D,O*
Purdue University M,D,O
Saint Leo University M,D
South Dakota State University M
State University of New York at Oswego M
Tennessee State University M,D
Texas A&M University M,D
Texas State University M
Texas Tech University M,D
The University of Arizona M,O
University of Arkansas M
University of Connecticut M,D
University of Delaware M
University of Florida M,D
University of Illinois at Urbana-Champaign M
University of Missouri M,D,O
University of Nebraska–Lincoln M
University of Puerto Rico at Mayagüez M
The University of Tennessee M
University of Wisconsin–River Falls M
Utah State University M
West Virginia University M,D

### AGRICULTURAL ENGINEERING

Cornell University M,D
Illinois Institute of Technology M
Instituto Tecnológico y de Estudios Superiores de Monterrey, Campus Monterrey M,D
Iowa State University of Science and Technology M,D
Kansas State University M,D
Louisiana State University and Agricultural & Mechanical College M,D
McGill University M,D
North Carolina State University M,D,O
North Dakota State University M,D
The Ohio State University M,D
Oklahoma State University M,D
Oregon State University M,D
Penn State University Park M,D*
Purdue University M,D
South Dakota State University M,D
Texas A&M University M,D
The University of Arizona M,D
University of Arkansas M,D
University of Florida M,D,O
University of Illinois at Urbana-Champaign M,D
University of Kentucky M,D
University of Nebraska–Lincoln M,D
The University of Tennessee M
University of Wisconsin–Madison M,D
Université Laval M
Virginia Polytechnic Institute and State University M,D
Washington State University M,D

### AGRICULTURAL SCIENCES—GENERAL

Alabama Agricultural and Mechanical University M,D
Alcorn State University M
Angelo State University M
Arkansas State University M,O
Auburn University M,D
Brigham Young University M,D
California Polytechnic State University, San Luis Obispo M
California State Polytechnic University, Pomona M
California State University, Chico M
Clemson University M,D
Colorado State University M,D
Dalhousie University M
Illinois State University M
Instituto Tecnológico y de Estudios Superiores de Monterrey, Campus Monterrey M,D
Iowa State University of Science and Technology M,D
Kansas State University M,D,O
Louisiana State University and Agricultural & Mechanical College M,D
Louisiana Tech University M,D,O
McGill University M,D,O
McNeese State University M
Michigan State University M,D
Mississippi State University M,D
Missouri State University M
Montana State University M,D
Murray State University M,O
New Mexico State University M,D
North Carolina Agricultural and Technical State University M
North Carolina State University M,D,O
North Dakota State University M,D
Northwest Missouri State University M
The Ohio State University M,D
Oklahoma State University M,D
Penn State University Park M,D,O*
Prairie View A&M University M,D
Purdue University M,D
Sam Houston State University M
South Dakota State University M,D
Southern Arkansas University–Magnolia M
Southern Illinois University Carbondale M
Southern University and Agricultural and Mechanical College M
Stephen F. Austin State University M
Tarleton State University M
Tennessee State University M,D
Tennessee Technological University D
Texas A&M University M,D
Texas A&M University–Commerce M
Texas A&M University–Kingsville M,D
Texas Tech University M,D
Tropical Agriculture Research and Higher Education Center M,D
Universidad Nacional Pedro Henriquez Urena M
University of Alberta M,D
The University of Arizona M,D,O
University of Arkansas M,D
The University of British Columbia M,D
University of California, Davis M
University of Connecticut M,D
University of Delaware M,D
University of Florida M,D,O
University of Georgia M,D
University of Guelph M,D,O
University of Hawaii at Manoa M,D
University of Illinois at Urbana-Champaign M
The University of Iowa M,D,O
University of Kentucky M,D
University of Lethbridge M,D
University of Maine M,D,O
University of Manitoba M,D
University of Maryland, College Park M,D
University of Maryland Eastern Shore M
University of Minnesota, Twin Cities Campus M,D
University of Missouri M,D
University of Nebraska–Lincoln M,D
University of Nevada, Reno M,D
University of New Hampshire M,D
University of Puerto Rico at Mayagüez M
University of Saskatchewan M,D,O
University of South Africa M,D
The University of Tennessee M,D
The University of Tennessee at Martin M
The University of Texas Rio Grande Valley M
University of Vermont M,D,O
University of Wisconsin–Madison M,D
University of Wisconsin–River Falls M
University of Wyoming M,D
Université Laval M,D,O
Utah State University M,D
Virginia Polytechnic Institute and State University M,D,O
Western Kentucky University M
West Texas A&M University M,D
West Virginia University M,D

### AGRONOMY AND SOIL SCIENCES

Alabama Agricultural and Mechanical University M,D
Alcorn State University M
Auburn University M,D
Colorado State University M,D
Cornell University M,D
Dalhousie University M
Iowa State University of Science and Technology M,D
Kansas State University M,D,O
Louisiana State University and Agricultural & Mechanical College M,D
McGill University M,D
Michigan State University M,D
Mississippi State University M,D
North Carolina Agricultural and Technical State University M
North Carolina State University M,D
North Dakota State University M,D
The Ohio State University M,D
Oklahoma State University M,D
Oregon State University M,D
Penn State University Park M,D*
Purdue University M,D
Southern Illinois University Carbondale M
Tennessee State University M,D
Texas A&M University M,D
Texas A&M University–Kingsville M
Texas Tech University M,D
Tuskegee University M
University of Alberta M,D
The University of Arizona M,D,O
University of Arkansas M,D
The University of British Columbia M,D
University of California, Davis M,D
University of California, Riverside M,D
University of Connecticut M,D
University of Delaware M,D
University of Florida M,D
University of Georgia M,D
University of Guelph M,D
University of Idaho M,D
University of Illinois at Urbana-Champaign M,D
University of Kentucky M,D
University of Manitoba M,D
University of Minnesota, Twin Cities Campus M,D
University of Missouri M,D,O
University of Nebraska–Lincoln M,D
University of Puerto Rico at Mayagüez M
University of Saskatchewan M,D
University of Vermont M,D,O
University of Wisconsin–Madison M,D
University of Wyoming M,D
Université Laval M,D
Utah State University M,D
Virginia Polytechnic Institute and State University M,D
Washington State University M,D,O
West Virginia University M,D

### ALLIED HEALTH—GENERAL

Alabama State University M,D
American College of Healthcare Sciences M,O
Andrews University M
Athabasca University M,O
A.T. Still University M,D,O
Augusta University D
Belmont University M,D
Bennington College O
Boston University M,D
Brock University M,D
Canisius College M,O
Cleveland State University M
Concordia University, St. Paul M,D
Creighton University M,D
Dominican College M,D
Drexel University M,D,O
Duquesne University M,D,O
East Carolina University M,D,O
Eastern Kentucky University M
East Tennessee State University M
Emory University M,D
Ferris State University M
Florida Agricultural and Mechanical University M,D
Florida Gulf Coast University M,D
Georgia Southern University M,D,O
Georgia State University M
Grand Valley State University M,D
Hampton University M
Harding University M,D
Howard University M,D
Idaho State University M,D,O
Ithaca College M,D
Jacksonville University M,D
Loma Linda University M,D
Long Island University - Post M,O
Marymount University M,D,O
Maryville University of Saint Louis M,D,O
Medical University of South Carolina M,D
Mercy College M,D
Midwestern University, Glendale Campus M,D
Minnesota State University Mankato M,D,O
Misericordia University M,D
New Jersey City University M
Northeastern University M,D,O
Northern Arizona University M,D,O
Northern Kentucky University M
Nova Southeastern University M,D
Oakland University M,D,O
The Ohio State University M
Old Dominion University M,D
Oregon State University M,D
Purdue University M,D
Quinnipiac University M
Regis University M,D,O
Rosalind Franklin University of Medicine and Science M,D,O
Rutgers University - Newark M,D,O
Saint Louis University M,D,O
Sam Houston State University M
Seton Hall University D
Shenandoah University M,D,O
South Carolina State University M
Temple University M,D*
Tennessee State University M,D,O
Texas Christian University M,D,O
Texas State University M,D
Texas Woman's University M,D
Towson University M
University at Buffalo, the State University of New York M,D,O
The University of Alabama at Birmingham M,D,O
University of Detroit Mercy M,D,O
University of Florida M,D,O
University of Illinois at Chicago M,D,O
The University of Kansas M,D,O
University of Kentucky M,D
University of Maryland, Baltimore M
University of Massachusetts Lowell M,D
University of Memphis M,O
University of Mississippi Medical Center M
University of Nebraska Medical Center M,D,O
University of Nevada, Las Vegas M,D,O
University of New Mexico M,D,O
University of Northern Iowa M,D
University of North Florida M,D,O
University of Oklahoma Health Sciences Center M,D,O
University of Phoenix - Las Vegas Campus M
University of Puerto Rico - Medical Sciences Campus M,D,O
University of South Alabama M,D

*M—masters degree; D—doctorate; O—other advanced degree; *—Close-Up and/or Display*

| | |
|---|---|
| University of South Dakota | M,D,O |
| The University of Tennessee Health Science Center | M,D |
| The University of Texas at El Paso | D |
| The University of Texas Medical Branch | M,D |
| University of Vermont | M,D,O |
| University of Wisconsin–Milwaukee | M,D,O* |
| Virginia Commonwealth University | D |
| Western University of Health Sciences | M,D |
| Wichita State University | M,D |

**ALLOPATHIC MEDICINE**

| | |
|---|---|
| Albany Medical College | D |
| Albert Einstein College of Medicine | D |
| Augusta University | D |
| Baylor College of Medicine | D |
| Boston University | D |
| Brown University | D |
| California Northstate University | D |
| Case Western Reserve University | D |
| Central Michigan University | D |
| Charles R. Drew University of Medicine and Science | D |
| Columbia University | M,D |
| Creighton University | D |
| Dalhousie University | M,D |
| Dartmouth College | D |
| Drexel University | D |
| Duke University | D |
| East Carolina University | D |
| Eastern Virginia Medical School | D |
| East Tennessee State University | D |
| Emory University | D |
| Florida Atlantic University | M,D |
| Florida International University | M,D |
| Florida State University | D |
| Geisinger Commonwealth School of Medicine | D |
| Georgetown University | D |
| The George Washington University | D |
| Harvard University | D* |
| Hofstra University | D |
| Howard University | D |
| Icahn School of Medicine at Mount Sinai | D |
| Indiana University-Purdue University Indianapolis | M,D |
| Instituto Tecnologico de Santo Domingo | M,D |
| Johns Hopkins University | D |
| Loma Linda University | M,D |
| Louisiana State University Health Sciences Center | M,D |
| Louisiana State University Health Sciences Center at Shreveport | D |
| Marshall University | D |
| Mayo Clinic Alix School of Medicine | D |
| McGill University | M,D |
| Medical College of Wisconsin | D |
| Medical University of South Carolina | D |
| Meharry Medical College | D |
| Mercer University | M,D |
| Michigan State University | D |
| Morehouse School of Medicine | D |
| New York Medical College | D |
| New York University | M,D |
| Northeast Ohio Medical University | D |
| Northwestern University | |
| Nova Southeastern University | D |
| The Ohio State University | D |
| Oregon Health & Science University | D |
| Penn State Hershey Medical Center | M,D |
| Pontificia Universidad Catolica Madre y Maestra | D |
| Queen's University at Kingston | D |
| Quinnipiac University | D |
| Rosalind Franklin University of Medicine and Science | D |
| Rowan University | D |
| Rush University | D |
| Rutgers University - Newark | D |
| Rutgers University - New Brunswick | D |
| Saint Louis University | D |
| San Juan Bautista School of Medicine | M,D |
| Seton Hall University | D |
| Stanford University | D |
| State University of New York Downstate Medical Center | M,D |
| State University of New York Upstate Medical University | D |
| Stony Brook University, State University of New York | D |
| Temple University | D* |
| Texas A&M University | M,D |
| Texas Tech University Health Sciences Center | D |
| Texas Tech University Health Sciences Center El Paso | D |
| Thomas Jefferson University | D |
| Tufts University | D |
| Tulane University | D |
| Uniformed Services University of the Health Sciences | M,D |
| Universidad Autonoma de Guadalajara | D |
| Universidad Central del Caribe | M,D |
| Universidad Central del Este | D |
| Universidad de Ciencias Medicas | M,D,O |
| Universidad de Iberoamerica | M,D |
| Universidad Iberoamericana | D |
| Universidad Nacional Pedro Henriquez Urena | D |
| Université de Montréal | D |
| Université de Sherbrooke | D |
| University at Buffalo, the State University of New York | D |
| The University of Alabama at Birmingham | D |
| University of Alberta | D |
| The University of Arizona | M,D |
| University of Arkansas for Medical Sciences | D |
| The University of British Columbia | M,D |
| University of Calgary | D |
| University of California, Berkeley | |
| University of California, Davis | D |
| University of California, Irvine | D |
| University of California, Los Angeles | D |
| University of California, Riverside | D |
| University of California, San Diego | D |
| University of California, San Francisco | D |
| University of Central Florida | M,D |
| University of Chicago | D |
| University of Cincinnati | D |
| University of Colorado Denver | D |
| University of Connecticut Health Center | D |
| University of Florida | D |
| University of Hawaii at Manoa | D |
| University of Illinois at Chicago | D |
| The University of Iowa | D |
| The University of Kansas | D |
| University of Kentucky | D |
| University of Louisville | D |
| University of Lynchburg | D |
| University of Manitoba | M |
| University of Maryland, Baltimore | D |
| University of Massachusetts Medical School | D |
| University of Miami | D |
| University of Michigan | D |
| University of Minnesota, Duluth | D |
| University of Minnesota, Twin Cities Campus | M,D |
| University of Mississippi Medical Center | D |
| University of Missouri | D |
| University of Missouri–Kansas City | M,D |
| University of Nebraska Medical Center | D,O |
| University of Nevada, Reno | D |
| University of New Mexico | D |
| The University of North Carolina at Chapel Hill | D |
| University of Oklahoma Health Sciences Center | D |
| University of Ottawa | M,D |
| University of Pennsylvania | D |
| University of Pittsburgh | D* |
| University of Puerto Rico - Medical Sciences Campus | D |
| University of Rochester | D |
| University of Saskatchewan | D |
| University of South Alabama | D |
| University of South Carolina | D |
| University of South Dakota | D,O |
| University of Southern California | D |
| University of South Florida | M,D |
| The University of Tennessee Health Science Center | D |
| The University of Texas at Austin | D |
| The University of Texas Health Science Center at Houston | D |
| The University of Texas Health Science Center at San Antonio | M,D |
| The University of Texas Medical Branch | D |
| The University of Texas Rio Grande Valley | D |
| The University of Texas Southwestern Medical Center | D |
| The University of Toledo | M,D,O |
| University of Toronto | M,D |
| University of Utah | D |
| University of Vermont | M,D,O |
| University of Virginia | M,D |
| University of Washington | D |
| The University of Western Ontario | M,D |
| University of Wisconsin–Madison | D |
| Université Laval | D,O |
| Vanderbilt University | M,D* |
| Virginia Commonwealth University | D |
| Virginia Polytechnic Institute and State University | D |
| Wake Forest University | D |
| Washington State University | M,D |
| Washington University in St. Louis | D |
| Western Michigan University Homer Stryker MD School of Medicine | D |
| West Virginia University | M,D |
| Wright State University | D |
| Yale University | D |

**AMERICAN INDIAN/NATIVE AMERICAN STUDIES**

| | |
|---|---|
| Central Michigan University | M |
| Montana State University | M |
| Navajo Technical University | M |
| Northeastern State University | M |
| Northern Arizona University | O |
| Trent University | M,D |
| The University of Arizona | M,D |
| University of California, Davis | M,D |
| University of California, Los Angeles | M |
| The University of Kansas | M,O |
| University of Lethbridge | M,D |
| University of Manitoba | M |
| University of New Mexico | M,D |
| University of Oklahoma | M |
| University of South Dakota | M,D,O |
| The University of Tulsa | M,D,O |

**AMERICAN STUDIES**

| | |
|---|---|
| American Public University System | M,D |
| American University | M,D,O |
| Appalachian State University | M |
| Baylor University | M |
| Boston University | D |
| Bowling Green State University | M,D |
| Brown University | M,D |
| California State University, Fullerton | M |
| The Catholic University of America | M,D |
| Central Michigan University | M,O |
| Claremont Graduate University | M,D,O |
| Clark University | D |
| College of Staten Island of the City University of New York | M |
| The Colorado College | M |
| Columbia University | M,D |
| Cornell University | M,D |
| Drew University | M,D,O |
| East Carolina University | M |
| Emory & Henry College | M,D |
| Fairfield University | M |
| Florida State University | M,D |
| Georgetown University | M,D |
| The George Washington University | M,D |
| Harvard University | D* |
| Indiana University-Purdue University Indianapolis | M,D |
| Inter American University of Puerto Rico, Metropolitan Campus | M,D |
| James Madison University | M |
| Kennesaw State University | M |
| Lake Forest College | M |
| Lehigh University | M,D |
| Michigan State University | M,D |
| Monmouth University | M |
| New Mexico Highlands University | M |
| New York University | M,D |
| Northwestern Oklahoma State University | M |
| Northwestern University | M |
| Penn State Harrisburg | M,D,O |
| Pepperdine University | M |
| Portland State University | M |
| Providence College | M |
| Purdue University | M,D |
| Regent University | M |
| Rice University | D |
| Rutgers University - Newark | M,D |
| Saint Louis University | M,D |
| Salisbury University | M |
| Stockton University | M,O |
| SUNY Brockport | M |
| Texas Christian University | M,D |
| Trinity College (United States) | M |
| Universidad de las Américas Puebla | M |
| University at Buffalo, the State University of New York | M,D |
| The University of Alabama | M |
| University of Colorado Denver | M |
| University of Delaware | M |
| University of Hawaii at Manoa | M,D,O |
| The University of Iowa | M,D |
| The University of Kansas | M,D |
| University of Louisiana at Lafayette | M |
| University of Maryland, College Park | M,D |
| University of Massachusetts Amherst | M,D |
| University of Massachusetts Boston | M |
| University of Michigan | M,D |
| University of Michigan–Flint | M |
| University of Minnesota, Twin Cities Campus | D |
| University of Missouri–St. Louis | M,D |
| University of New Mexico | M,D |
| University of Southern California | D |
| University of South Florida | M,D |
| The University of Texas at Austin | M,D |
| University of Utah | M,D |
| University of West Florida | M |
| University of Wisconsin–Madison | M,D |
| University of Wyoming | M |
| Utah State University | M |
| Washington State University | M,D |
| Wilfrid Laurier University | M,D |
| Yale University | D |
| Youngstown State University | M |

**ANALYTICAL CHEMISTRY**

| | |
|---|---|
| Auburn University | M,D |
| Binghamton University, State University of New York | M,D |
| Brigham Young University | M,D |
| California State University, Los Angeles | M |
| Cornell University | D |
| Eastern New Mexico University | M |
| Florida State University | M,D |
| Georgetown University | D |
| The George Washington University | M,D |
| Georgia State University | M,D |
| Governors State University | M |
| Howard University | M,D |
| Illinois Institute of Technology | M,D |
| Indiana University Bloomington | M,D |
| Iowa State University of Science and Technology | M,D |
| Laurentian University | M |
| Marquette University | M,D |
| McMaster University | M,D |
| Old Dominion University | M,D |
| Oregon State University | M,D |
| Purdue University | M,D |
| Rutgers University - Newark | M,D |
| Seton Hall University | M,D |
| Southern University and Agricultural and Mechanical College | M |
| University of Calgary | M,D |
| University of Cincinnati | M,D |
| University of Georgia | M,D |
| University of Louisville | M,D |
| The University of Manchester | M,D |
| University of Maryland, College Park | M,D |
| University of Massachusetts Lowell | M,D |
| University of Memphis | M,D |
| University of Michigan | M,D |
| University of Missouri | D |
| University of Missouri–Kansas City | M,D |
| University of Montana | M,D |
| University of Nebraska–Lincoln | M,D |
| University of Oklahoma | M,D |
| University of Regina | M,D |
| The University of Tennessee | M,D |
| The University of Texas at Austin | D |
| The University of Toledo | M,D |
| Virginia Commonwealth University | M,D |
| Wake Forest University | M,D |
| Wayne State University | M,D |
| Youngstown State University | M |

**ANATOMY**

| | |
|---|---|
| Albert Einstein College of Medicine | D |
| Augusta University | D |
| Barry University | M |
| Boston University | M,D |
| Case Western Reserve University | M |
| Columbia University | M,D |
| Creighton University | M |
| Dalhousie University | M,D |
| Des Moines University | M |
| Duke University | D |
| D'Youville College | M |
| East Carolina University | M,D |
| East Tennessee State University | D |
| Howard University | M,D |
| Indiana University-Purdue University Indianapolis | M,D |
| Johns Hopkins University | D |
| Liberty University | M,D |
| Loma Linda University | D |
| Louisiana State University Health Sciences Center | D |
| Louisiana State University Health Sciences Center at Shreveport | M,D |
| McGill University | M,D |
| New York Academy of Art | M |
| New York Chiropractic College | M |
| The Ohio State University | M,D |
| Palmer College of Chiropractic | M |
| Penn State Hershey Medical Center | M,D |
| Purdue University | M,D |
| Rosalind Franklin University of Medicine and Science | D |
| Rush University | M,D |
| Saint Louis University | M,D |
| State University of New York Upstate Medical University | M,D |
| Stony Brook University, State University of New York | D |
| Universidad Central del Caribe | M,D |
| Universidad de Ciencias Medicas | M,D,O |
| University at Buffalo, the State University of New York | M,D |
| University of California, Irvine | M,D |
| University of California, Los Angeles | M,D |
| University of Chicago | D |
| University of Colorado Denver | M,D |
| University of Connecticut Health Center | D |
| University of Guelph | M,D |
| University of Illinois at Chicago | M |
| The University of Iowa | D |
| The University of Kansas | M,D |
| University of Kentucky | D |
| University of Louisville | M,D |
| University of Manitoba | M,D |
| University of Mississippi Medical Center | M,D |
| University of Missouri | M,D |
| University of Nebraska Medical Center | M,D |
| University of North Texas Health Science Center at Fort Worth | M,D |
| University of Prince Edward Island | M,D |
| University of Puerto Rico - Medical Sciences Campus | M,D |
| University of Rochester | D |
| University of Saskatchewan | M,D |
| The University of Tennessee | M,D |
| University of Utah | D |
| The University of Western Ontario | M,D |
| Université Laval | O |
| Virginia Commonwealth University | M |
| Wake Forest University | D |
| Wright State University | M |
| Youngstown State University | M |

**ANESTHESIOLOGIST ASSISTANT STUDIES**

| | |
|---|---|
| Case Western Reserve University | M |
| Emory University | M |
| Medical College of Wisconsin | M |
| Nova Southeastern University | M,D |
| Quinnipiac University | M |
| South University - Savannah | M |
| University of Colorado Denver | M |
| University of Guelph | M,D,O |
| Université Laval | O |

**ANIMAL BEHAVIOR**

| | |
|---|---|
| Arizona State University at Tempe | M,D |
| Bucknell University | M |
| Cornell University | D |
| Emory University | D |
| Hunter College of the City University of New York | M,O |
| Illinois State University | M,D |
| University of California, Davis | D |
| University of Massachusetts Amherst | M,D |

| | |
|---|---|
| University of Minnesota, Twin Cities Campus | M,D |
| University of Montana | M,D,O |
| The University of Tennessee | M,D |
| The University of Texas at Austin | D |
| University of Washington | M,D |

**ANIMAL SCIENCES**

| | |
|---|---|
| Alcorn State University | M |
| Auburn University | M,D |
| Bergin University of Canine Studies | M |
| Boise State University | M,D |
| Brigham Young University | M,D |
| California State University, Fresno | M |
| Clemson University | M,D |
| Colorado State University | M,D |
| Cornell University | M,D |
| Dalhousie University | M |
| Fort Valley State University | M |
| Iowa State University of Science and Technology | M,D |
| Kansas State University | M,D |
| Louisiana State University and Agricultural & Mechanical College | M,D |
| McGill University | M,D |
| Michigan State University | M,D |
| Mississippi State University | M,D |
| Missouri Western State University | M |
| Montana State University | M,D |
| North Carolina Agricultural and Technical State University | M |
| North Carolina State University | M,D |
| North Dakota State University | M,D |
| The Ohio State University | M,D |
| Oklahoma State University | M,D |
| Oregon State University | M |
| Penn State University Park | M,D* |
| Purdue University | M,D |
| Rutgers University - New Brunswick | M,D |
| South Dakota State University | M,D |
| Southern Illinois University Carbondale | M |
| Sul Ross State University | M |
| Texas A&M University | M,D |
| Texas A&M University–Kingsville | M |
| Texas Tech University | M,D |
| Tufts University | M |
| Tuskegee University | M |
| Universidad Nacional Pedro Henriquez Urena | M |
| The University of Arizona | M,D |
| University of Arkansas | M,D |
| The University of British Columbia | M,D |
| University of California, Davis | M,D |
| University of Connecticut | M,D |
| University of Delaware | M,D |
| University of Florida | M,D |
| University of Georgia | M,D |
| University of Guelph | M,D |
| University of Hawaii at Manoa | M |
| University of Idaho | M,D |
| University of Illinois at Urbana-Champaign | M,D |
| University of Kentucky | M,D |
| University of Manitoba | M,D |
| University of Maryland, College Park | M,D |
| University of Massachusetts Amherst | M,D |
| University of Minnesota, Twin Cities Campus | M,D |
| University of Missouri | M,D |
| University of Nebraska–Lincoln | M,D |
| University of Nevada, Reno | M |
| University of New Hampshire | M,D |
| University of Puerto Rico at Mayagüez | M |
| University of Rhode Island | M,D |
| University of Saskatchewan | M,D |
| The University of Tennessee | M,D |
| University of Vermont | M,D |
| University of Wisconsin–Madison | M,D |
| University of Wyoming | M,D |
| Université Laval | M,D |
| Utah State University | M,D |
| Virginia Polytechnic Institute and State University | M,D |
| Washington State University | M,D |
| West Texas A&M University | M |
| West Virginia University | M,D |

**ANTHROPOLOGY**

| | |
|---|---|
| American University | M,D,O |
| Arizona State University at Tempe | M,D,O |
| Ball State University | M,O |
| Binghamton University, State University of New York | M,D |
| Biola University | M,D,O |
| Boise State University | M |
| Boston University | M,D |
| Brandeis University | M,D |
| Brigham Young University | M |
| Brown University | M,D |
| California State University, Chico | M |
| California State University, East Bay | M |
| California State University, Fullerton | M |
| California State University, Long Beach | M |
| California State University, Los Angeles | M |
| California State University, Northridge | M |
| California State University, Sacramento | M |
| Carleton University | M |
| Case Western Reserve University | M,D |
| The Catholic University of America | M |
| Central European University | M,D |
| Central Washington University | M |
| Clemson University | M |
| Colorado State University | M,D |
| Columbia University | M,D |
| Concordia University (Canada) | M,D |
| Cornell University | D |
| Dalhousie University | M,D |
| East Carolina University | M |
| Eastern New Mexico University | M |
| Emory University | D |
| Florida Atlantic University | M |
| Florida State University | M,D |
| George Mason University | M,D |
| The George Washington University | M,D |
| Georgia State University | M |
| The Graduate Center, City University of New York | D |
| Harvard University | M,D* |
| Humboldt State University | M |
| Hunter College of the City University of New York | M |
| Idaho State University | M |
| Indiana University Bloomington | M,D |
| Iowa State University of Science and Technology | M |
| Johns Hopkins University | D |
| Kent State University | M |
| Louisiana State University and Agricultural & Mechanical College | M,D |
| McGill University | M,D |
| McMaster University | M,D |
| Memorial University of Newfoundland | M,D |
| Mercyhurst University | M |
| Michigan State University | M,D |
| Minnesota State University Mankato | M |
| Mississippi State University | M |
| Monmouth University | M |
| New Mexico Highlands University | M |
| New Mexico State University | M,O |
| The New School | M,D |
| New York University | M,D |
| North Carolina State University | M |
| North Dakota State University | M |
| Northern Arizona University | M |
| Northern Illinois University | M |
| Northwestern University | D |
| The Ohio State University | M,D |
| Oregon State University | M |
| Penn State University Park | M,D* |
| Portland State University | M,D,O |
| Princeton University | D |
| Purdue University | M,D |
| Rice University | M,D |
| Rutgers University - New Brunswick | M,D |
| San Diego State University | M |
| San Francisco State University | M |
| San Jose State University | M |
| Simon Fraser University | M,D |
| Sonoma State University | M |
| Southern Illinois University Carbondale | M,D |
| Southern Methodist University | M,D |
| Stanford University | M,D |
| Stony Brook University, State University of New York | M,D |
| Syracuse University | M,D |
| Teachers College, Columbia University | M,D |
| Temple University | D* |
| Texas A&M University | M,D |
| Texas State University | M |
| Texas Tech University | M |
| Trent University | M |
| Tulane University | D |
| UNB Fredericton | M |
| Universidad de las Américas Puebla | M |
| Université de Montréal | M,D |
| University at Albany, State University of New York | M,D |
| University at Buffalo, the State University of New York | M,D |
| The University of Alabama | M,D |
| The University of Alabama at Birmingham | M |
| University of Alaska Anchorage | M |
| University of Alaska Fairbanks | M,D |
| University of Alberta | M,D |
| The University of Arizona | M,D,O |
| University of Arkansas | M,D |
| The University of British Columbia | M,D |
| University of California, Berkeley | D |
| University of California, Davis | M,D |
| University of California, Irvine | M,D |
| University of California, Los Angeles | M,D |
| University of California, Riverside | M,D |
| University of California, San Diego | D |
| University of California, San Francisco | D |
| University of California, Santa Barbara | M,D |
| University of California, Santa Cruz | D |
| University of Central Florida | M |
| University of Chicago | D |
| University of Cincinnati | M |
| University of Colorado Boulder | M,D |
| University of Colorado Denver | M |
| University of Connecticut | M,D |
| University of Denver | M |
| University of Florida | M,D |
| University of Georgia | M,D |
| University of Guelph | M,D |
| University of Hawaii at Manoa | M,D |
| University of Houston | M |
| University of Idaho | M |
| University of Illinois at Chicago | M,D |
| University of Illinois at Urbana-Champaign | M,D |
| University of Indianapolis | M,D |
| The University of Iowa | M,D |
| The University of Kansas | M,D |
| University of Kentucky | M,D |
| University of Lethbridge | M,D |
| University of Louisville | M |
| University of Maine | D |
| The University of Manchester | M,D |
| University of Manitoba | M,D |
| University of Maryland, College Park | M |
| University of Massachusetts Amherst | M,D |
| University of Memphis | M |
| University of Michigan | D |
| University of Minnesota, Duluth | M |
| University of Minnesota, Twin Cities Campus | M,D |
| University of Mississippi | M,D |
| University of Missouri | M,D |
| University of Montana | M,D |
| University of Nebraska–Lincoln | M |
| University of Nevada, Las Vegas | M,D |
| University of Nevada, Reno | M,D |
| University of New Mexico | M,D |
| The University of North Carolina at Chapel Hill | M,D |
| The University of North Carolina at Charlotte | M |
| University of North Georgia | M |
| University of North Texas | M,D,O |
| University of Oklahoma | M,D |
| University of Oregon | M,D |
| University of Ottawa | M |
| University of Pennsylvania | M,D |
| University of Pittsburgh | M,D* |
| University of Regina | M |
| University of Rhode Island | M |
| University of Saskatchewan | M |
| University of South Africa | M,D |
| University of South Carolina | M,D |
| University of South Florida | M,D,O |
| The University of Tennessee | M,D |
| The University of Texas at Arlington | M |
| The University of Texas at Austin | M,D |
| The University of Texas at El Paso | M,O |
| The University of Texas at San Antonio | M,D |
| University of Toronto | M,D |
| The University of Tulsa | M,D |
| University of Utah | M,D |
| University of Victoria | M |
| University of Virginia | M,D |
| University of Washington | M,D |
| University of Waterloo | M |
| The University of Western Ontario | M,D |
| University of West Florida | M |
| University of Wisconsin–Madison | D |
| University of Wisconsin–Milwaukee | M,D,O* |
| University of Wyoming | M,D |
| Université Laval | M,D |
| Utah State University | M,D |
| Vanderbilt University | M,D* |
| Washington State University | M,D |
| Washington University in St. Louis | D |
| Wayne State University | M,D |
| Western Kentucky University | M |
| Western Michigan University | M |
| Western Washington University | M |
| Wichita State University | M |
| Yale University | M,D |
| York University | M,D |

**APPLIED ARTS AND DESIGN—GENERAL**

| | |
|---|---|
| Academy of Art University | M |
| Alfred University | M |
| Arizona State University at Tempe | M,D |
| The Art Institute of Dallas, a branch of Miami International University of Art & Design | M |
| Bowling Green State University | M |
| California College of the Arts | M |
| California Institute of the Arts | M,O |
| California State University, Fresno | M |
| California State University, Fullerton | M |
| California State University, Los Angeles | M |
| Carnegie Mellon University | M,D |
| College for Creative Studies | M |
| Concordia University (Canada) | M,O |
| Drexel University | M,D |
| Emily Carr University of Art + Design | M |
| Fashion Institute of Technology | M |
| Ferris State University | M |
| Florida Atlantic University | M |
| Howard University | M |
| Illinois Institute of Technology | M,D |
| Indiana University Bloomington | M |
| Iowa State University of Science and Technology | M,D |
| Louisiana State University and Agricultural & Mechanical College | M |
| Maryland Institute College of Art | M |
| Massachusetts College of Art and Design | M,O |
| Miami International University of Art & Design | M |
| Millersville University of Pennsylvania | M |
| Minneapolis College of Art and Design | M |
| The New School | M |
| New York Institute of Technology | M |
| New York University | M |
| North Carolina State University | M |
| Northeastern University | M |
| NSCAD University | M |
| Oklahoma State University | M,D |
| Pacific Northwest College of Art | M |
| Pratt Institute | M,O |
| Purdue University | M,D |
| Rhode Island School of Design | M |
| Rutgers University - New Brunswick | M |
| San Diego State University | M |
| San Francisco State University | M |
| Savannah College of Art and Design | M |
| School of Visual Arts (NY) | M |
| Southern Illinois University Carbondale | M |
| Stanford University | M,D,O |
| Stephen F. Austin State University | M |
| Suffolk University | M |
| Syracuse University | M |
| Texas State University | M |
| University of Alberta | M |
| University of Baltimore | M |
| University of Bridgeport | M |
| University of California, Berkeley | O |
| University of California, Los Angeles | M |
| University of Central Oklahoma | M |
| University of Cincinnati | M |
| University of Connecticut | M |
| University of Delaware | M |
| University of Illinois at Chicago | M |
| University of Illinois at Urbana-Champaign | M,D |
| The University of Kansas | M |
| University of Kentucky | M |
| University of Louisville | M,D |
| University of Michigan | M,D |
| University of Minnesota, Twin Cities Campus | M,D,O |
| University of North Texas | M,D,O |
| University of Notre Dame | M |
| University of Oklahoma | M,D |
| University of Oregon | M |
| The University of Texas at Austin | M |
| University of Washington | M |
| University of Wisconsin–Madison | M,D |
| University of Wisconsin–Milwaukee | M* |
| Western Carolina University | M |
| Western Michigan University | M |
| Yale University | M |
| York University | M |

**APPLIED BEHAVIOR ANALYSIS**

| | |
|---|---|
| Antioch University New England | M,D,O |
| Arcadia University | M |
| Arizona State University at Tempe | M,D |
| Assumption University | M,O |
| Aurora University | M,D |
| Ball State University | M |
| Bay Path University | M |
| Cairn University | M,O |
| Caldwell University | M,D,O |
| California State University, Fresno | M,O |
| California State University, Sacramento | M |
| California State University, Stanislaus | M |
| Capella University | M |
| The Chicago School of Professional Psychology | M,D |
| The Chicago School of Professional Psychology at Downtown Los Angeles | M,D |
| The Chicago School of Professional Psychology at San Diego | M,D |
| College of Saint Elizabeth | M,O |
| Drake University | M,D,O |
| Drexel University | M,D |
| Elms College | M,O |
| Endicott College | M,D,O |
| Fairfield University | M,O |
| Florida Institute of Technology | M |
| Florida International University | M,D |
| Florida State University | M |
| Georgian Court University | M,O |
| Hofstra University | M,D,O |
| James Madison University | M |
| Lindenwood University | M,D,O |
| Lipscomb University | M,D,O |
| Long Island University - Brooklyn | M,O |
| Long Island University - Post | M,O |
| Long Island University - Riverhead | M,O |
| Mary Baldwin University | M |
| McNeese State University | M,O |
| Mercyhurst University | M |
| Missouri State University | M,O |
| Monmouth University | M,D,O |
| Montana State University Billings | M |
| National University | M,O |
| Niagara University | M,D,O |
| Northeastern University | M,D,O |
| Northern Michigan University | M |
| Northern Vermont University–Johnson | M |
| Oakland University | M,O |
| Oklahoma City University | M |
| Penn State Harrisburg | M,D,O |
| Philadelphia College of Osteopathic Medicine | M,D,O |
| Queens College of the City University of New York | M |
| Regis College (MA) | M,D,O |

*M—masters degree; D—doctorate; O—other advanced degree; *—Close-Up and/or Display*

| | |
|---|---|
| Rollins College | M |
| Rowan University | M,O |
| Sage Graduate School | M,O |
| St. Cloud State University | M |
| Saint Louis University | M,D |
| Saint Peter's University | M,D,O |
| Salve Regina University | M,O |
| Shenandoah University | M |
| Simmons University | M,D,O |
| Teachers College, Columbia University | M,D,O |
| Temple University | M,D,O* |
| Tennessee Technological University | D |
| University of California, Riverside | M,D,O |
| The University of Kansas | M,D,O |
| University of Louisville | M,D,O |
| University of Massachusetts Dartmouth | M,O |
| University of Memphis | M,D,O |
| University of Michigan–Dearborn | M |
| University of Nebraska at Omaha | M,D,O |
| University of Nebraska Medical Center | M,D |
| University of Nevada, Reno | M,D |
| The University of North Carolina Wilmington | M,D |
| University of North Florida | M |
| University of North Texas | M,D,O |
| University of Oklahoma | M,D |
| University of Southern Maine | M,O |
| University of South Florida | M,D |
| The University of Texas at San Antonio | M,O |
| University of Utah | M,D |
| University of West Florida | M |
| Wayne State University | M,D,O |
| Western New England University | M,D |
| Westfield State University | M |
| Wright State University | M |

## APPLIED ECONOMICS

| | |
|---|---|
| Auburn University | M,D |
| Auburn University at Montgomery | M |
| Brandeis University | M |
| Buffalo State College, State University of New York | M |
| Clemson University | M,D |
| Cornell University | M,D |
| DePaul University | M,D |
| East Carolina University | M |
| Florida State University | M,D |
| Georgia Southern University | M,O |
| HEC Montreal | M,D |
| Johns Hopkins University | M |
| Mills College | M |
| New York University | M,D,O |
| Ohio University | M |
| Oregon State University | M,D |
| St. Cloud State University | M |
| San Jose State University | M |
| Southern Methodist University | M,D |
| Southern New Hampshire University | M,D,O |
| Texas Tech University | M,D |
| Thomas Jefferson University | M,D,O |
| UNB Fredericton | M |
| The University of Arizona | M |
| University of California, Los Angeles | M |
| University of California, Santa Cruz | M |
| University of Cincinnati | M |
| University of Georgia | M,D |
| University of Houston | M,D |
| University of Illinois at Urbana-Champaign | M,D |
| University of Massachusetts Boston | M |
| University of Michigan | M |
| University of Minnesota, Twin Cities Campus | M,D |
| University of Nevada, Las Vegas | M,O |
| The University of North Carolina at Charlotte | M,O |
| The University of North Carolina at Greensboro | M |
| University of North Dakota | M |
| University of Oklahoma | M,D |
| University of Pennsylvania | D |
| University of Vermont | M |
| University of Wisconsin–Madison | M,D |
| University of Wyoming | M |
| Utah State University | M,D |
| Virginia Polytechnic Institute and State University | M,D |
| Washington & Jefferson College | M,O |
| Western Kentucky University | M |
| Western Michigan University | M,D |
| Wright State University | M |

## APPLIED MATHEMATICS

| | |
|---|---|
| Air Force Institute of Technology | M,D |
| Arizona State University at Tempe | M,D,O |
| Auburn University | M,D |
| Bowie State University | M |
| Brown University | M,D |
| California Baptist University | M |
| California Institute of Technology | M,D |
| California State Polytechnic University, Pomona | M |
| California State University, Fullerton | M |
| California State University, Long Beach | M,D |
| California State University, Los Angeles | M |
| California State University, Northridge | M |
| Case Western Reserve University | M,D |
| Central European University | M,D |
| Claremont Graduate University | M,D |
| Colorado School of Mines | M,D |
| Columbia University | M,D |
| Cornell University | M,D |
| Dalhousie University | M,D |
| Delaware State University | M,D |
| DePaul University | M,D |
| Elizabeth City State University | M |
| Florida Atlantic University | M,D |
| Florida Institute of Technology | M,D |
| Florida State University | M,D |
| The George Washington University | M,D,O |
| Hampton University | M |
| Harvard University | M,D* |
| Howard University | M,D |
| Hunter College of the City University of New York | M |
| Illinois Institute of Technology | M,D |
| Indiana University Bloomington | M,D |
| Indiana University of Pennsylvania | M |
| Indiana University-Purdue University Indianapolis | M,D |
| Indiana University South Bend | M,O |
| Inter American University of Puerto Rico, San Germán Campus | M |
| Iowa State University of Science and Technology | M,D |
| Jackson State University | M |
| Johns Hopkins University | M,D,O |
| Kent State University | M,D |
| Lehigh University | M,D |
| Long Island University - Post | M,O |
| Manhattan College | M |
| McGill University | M,D |
| Michigan State University | M,D |
| Missouri University of Science and Technology | M,D |
| Montclair State University | M |
| Naval Postgraduate School | M,D |
| New Jersey Institute of Technology | M,D,O |
| New Mexico Institute of Mining and Technology | M,D |
| North Carolina Agricultural and Technical State University | M |
| North Dakota State University | M,D |
| Northeastern Illinois University | M |
| Northeastern University | M,D |
| Northwestern University | M,D |
| Oakland University | M,D |
| Oklahoma State University | M,D |
| Old Dominion University | M,D |
| Oregon State University | M,D |
| Polytechnique Montréal | M,D,O |
| Princeton University | D |
| Purdue University Fort Wayne | M,O |
| Queens College of the City University of New York | M |
| Rensselaer Polytechnic Institute | M,D |
| Rice University | M,D |
| Rochester Institute of Technology | M |
| Rutgers University - Camden | M |
| Rutgers University - New Brunswick | M,D |
| St. John's University (NY) | M |
| San Diego State University | M |
| Santa Clara University | M,D,O |
| Simon Fraser University | M,D |
| Southern Illinois University Edwardsville | M |
| Southern Methodist University | M,D |
| Stevens Institute of Technology | M |
| Stony Brook University, State University of New York | M,D,O |
| Temple University | M,D* |
| Texas Christian University | M |
| Towson University | M |
| The University of Akron | M |
| The University of Alabama | M,D |
| The University of Alabama at Birmingham | D |
| The University of Alabama in Huntsville | M,D |
| University of Alberta | M,D,O |
| The University of Arizona | M,D |
| University of Arkansas at Little Rock | M,O |
| University of California, Berkeley | M,D |
| University of California, Davis | M,D |
| University of California, Irvine | M,D |
| University of California, Merced | M,D |
| University of California, San Diego | M,D |
| University of California, Santa Barbara | M,D |
| University of California, Santa Cruz | M,D |
| University of Central Arkansas | M |
| University of Central Missouri | M,D,O |
| University of Central Oklahoma | M |
| University of Chicago | D |
| University of Cincinnati | M,D |
| University of Colorado Boulder | M,D |
| University of Colorado Denver | M,D |
| University of Connecticut | M |
| University of Dayton | M |
| University of Delaware | M,D |
| University of Georgia | M,D |
| University of Guelph | M,D |
| University of Houston | M,D |
| University of Illinois at Urbana-Champaign | M,D |
| The University of Iowa | D |
| The University of Kansas | M,D,O |
| University of Kentucky | M,D |
| University of Louisville | M,D |
| The University of Manchester | M,D |
| University of Maryland, Baltimore County | M,D |
| University of Maryland, College Park | M,D |
| University of Massachusetts Amherst | M,D |
| University of Memphis | M,D |
| University of Michigan–Dearborn | M |
| University of Minnesota, Duluth | M |
| University of Missouri | M,D |
| University of New Hampshire | M,D,O |
| The University of North Carolina at Charlotte | M,D |
| University of Northern Iowa | M |
| University of Notre Dame | M,D |
| University of Pennsylvania | D |
| University of Pittsburgh | M,D* |
| University of Puerto Rico at Mayagüez | M |
| University of Rhode Island | M,D |
| University of Southern California | M,D |
| University of South Florida | M,D |
| The University of Tennessee | M,D |
| The University of Tennessee at Chattanooga | M |
| The University of Texas at Arlington | M,D |
| The University of Texas at Austin | M,D |
| The University of Texas at Dallas | M,D |
| The University of Texas at San Antonio | M |
| The University of Toledo | M,D |
| University of Washington | M,D |
| University of Waterloo | M,D |
| The University of Western Ontario | M,D |
| University of Wisconsin–Milwaukee | M,D* |
| University of Wisconsin–Stout | M |
| Utah State University | M,D |
| Virginia Commonwealth University | M |
| Washington State University | M,D |
| Wayne State University | M,D |
| Western Michigan University | M,D |
| Wichita State University | M,D |
| Worcester Polytechnic Institute | M,D,O |
| Wright State University | M |
| Yale University | M,D |
| York University | M,D |
| Youngstown State University | M |

## APPLIED PHYSICS

| | |
|---|---|
| Air Force Institute of Technology | M,D |
| Binghamton University, State University of New York | M,D |
| California Institute of Technology | M,D |
| Carnegie Mellon University | M,D |
| Christopher Newport University | M |
| Colorado School of Mines | M,D |
| Columbia University | M,D |
| Cornell University | M,D |
| East Carolina University | M,D |
| Georgia Southern University | M |
| Harvard University | M,D* |
| Idaho State University | M,D |
| Illinois Institute of Technology | M,D |
| Iowa State University of Science and Technology | M,D |
| Johns Hopkins University | M,O |
| Laurentian University | M |
| Louisiana Tech University | M,D,O |
| Michigan Technological University | M,D |
| Naval Postgraduate School | M,D,O |
| New Jersey Institute of Technology | M,D,O |
| New York University | M |
| Northern Arizona University | M,D |
| Northwestern University | D |
| Rice University | M,D |
| Rutgers University - Newark | M,D |
| Southern Illinois University Carbondale | M,D |
| Stanford University | M,D |
| Texas A&M University | M,D |
| Towson University | M |
| University of Arkansas | M,D |
| University of California, San Diego | M,D |
| University of Massachusetts Boston | M |
| University of Michigan | D |
| University of Missouri–St. Louis | M,D |
| The University of North Carolina at Charlotte | M,D |
| The University of Texas at Austin | M,D |
| University of Washington | M,D |
| Virginia Commonwealth University | M |
| Yale University | M,D |

## APPLIED PSYCHOLOGY

| | |
|---|---|
| Antioch University New England | M,D,O |
| Arizona State University at Tempe | M,O |
| Athabasca University | M,O |
| California State University, Chico | M |
| The Catholic University of America | M,D |
| Central Michigan University | M,D |
| The Chicago School of Professional Psychology at San Diego | M,D |
| The Chicago School of Professional Psychology: Online | M,O |
| Clayton State University | M |
| Clemson University | M,D |
| DEREE - The American College of Greece | M |
| Eastern Washington University | M,O |
| Fairfield University | M,O |
| Fordham University | M,D |
| Francis Marion University | M,O |
| The George Washington University | D |
| Laurentian University | M |
| Liberty University | M,D,O |
| London Metropolitan University | M,D |
| Loras College | M |
| Lynn University | M |
| Mississippi State University | M,D |
| New York University | M,D,O |
| North Carolina State University | D |
| Old Dominion University | D |
| Penn State Erie, The Behrend College | M |
| Penn State Harrisburg | M,D,O |
| Rutgers University - New Brunswick | M,D |
| Sacred Heart University | M |
| Saint Mary's University (Canada) | M,D |
| Tarleton State University | M |
| Teachers College, Columbia University | M,D |
| University of Arkansas at Little Rock | M |
| University of Baltimore | M |
| University of Calgary | M,D |
| University of Guelph | M,D |
| University of Maryland, Baltimore County | D |
| University of Pennsylvania | M |
| University of Regina | M,D |
| University of South Carolina Aiken | M |
| The University of Tennessee | M,D |
| The University of Texas at El Paso | M,O |
| University of West Florida | M |
| University of Windsor | M,D |
| University of Wisconsin–Stout | M |
| Walden University | M,D,O |
| William James College | M,D,O |

## APPLIED SCIENCE AND TECHNOLOGY

| | |
|---|---|
| Colorado State University-Pueblo | M |
| Harvard University | M,O* |
| Kansas State University | M,O |
| Louisiana State University and Agricultural & Mechanical College | M |
| Missouri State University | M,O |
| Naval Postgraduate School | M,D |
| Saint Mary's University (Canada) | M |
| Southeastern Louisiana University | M |
| Thomas Edison State University | M,O |
| University of Arkansas at Little Rock | M,D |
| University of California, Berkeley | D |
| University of California, Davis | M,D |
| University of Colorado Denver | M |
| University of Mississippi | M,D |

## APPLIED SOCIAL RESEARCH

| | |
|---|---|
| American University | M,O |
| California State University, Dominguez Hills | M |
| Concordia University Irvine | M |
| Florida State University | M,D |
| Hunter College of the City University of New York | M |
| Laurentian University | M |
| Loma Linda University | M,D |
| The New School | M,D |
| New York University | M |
| Portland State University | M,D |
| Queens College of the City University of New York | M |

## APPLIED STATISTICS

| | |
|---|---|
| American University | M,O |
| Bay Path University | M |
| Bowling Green State University | M |
| Brigham Young University | M |
| California State University, East Bay | M |
| California State University, Long Beach | M |
| Clemson University | M,D |
| Cleveland State University | M |
| Colorado School of Mines | M,D |
| Cornell University | M,D |
| DePaul University | M,D |
| Florida State University | M,D |
| Fordham University | M,D |
| Indiana University Bloomington | M,D |
| Indiana University-Purdue University Indianapolis | M,D |
| Instituto Tecnológico y de Estudios Superiores de Monterrey, Campus Monterrey | M,D |
| Kennesaw State University | M |
| Louisiana State University and Agricultural & Mechanical College | M |
| Loyola University Chicago | M |
| McMaster University | M |
| Michigan State University | M,D |
| Minnesota State University Mankato | M |
| New Jersey Institute of Technology | M,D,O |
| New Mexico State University | M,D,O |
| New York University | M |
| Northern Arizona University | M,O |
| Oakland University | M |
| Penn State University Park | M,D* |
| Portland State University | M,D,O |
| Purdue University Fort Wayne | M,O |
| Rochester Institute of Technology | M,O |
| Rutgers University - New Brunswick | M,D |
| Southern Methodist University | M,D |
| Syracuse University | M |
| Teachers College, Columbia University | M,D |
| The University of Alabama | M,D |
| University of Arkansas at Little Rock | M,O |
| University of California, Santa Barbara | M,D |
| University of Chicago | M |
| University of Colorado Denver | M,D |
| University of Guelph | M,D |
| University of Illinois at Urbana-Champaign | M,D |
| The University of Kansas | M,D,O |
| University of Memphis | M,D |
| University of Michigan | M,D |
| The University of North Carolina Wilmington | M,O |
| University of Northern Colorado | M,D |
| University of Notre Dame | M,D |
| University of Pittsburgh | M,D* |
| University of South Carolina | M,D,O |
| The University of Tennessee at Chattanooga | M |
| The University of Texas at San Antonio | M,D |
| University of the Incarnate Word | M |
| University of Wyoming | M,D |
| Villanova University | M |

| | |
|---|---|
| Virginia Polytechnic Institute and State University | M,D |
| Western Illinois University | M |
| Worcester Polytechnic Institute | M,D,O |
| Wright State University | M |

## AQUACULTURE

| | |
|---|---|
| Auburn University | M,D |
| Dalhousie University | M |
| Memorial University of Newfoundland | M |
| Oregon State University | M,D |
| Purdue University | M,D |
| Texas A&M University–Corpus Christi | M |
| University of Arkansas at Pine Bluff | M,D |
| University of Florida | M,D |
| University of Guelph | M |
| University of Rhode Island | M,D |

## ARCHAEOLOGY

| | |
|---|---|
| Arizona State University at Tempe | M,D,O |
| Boston University | M,D |
| Brown University | D |
| Bryn Mawr College | M,D |
| California State University, Northridge | M |
| California State University, San Bernardino | M |
| Columbia University | M,D |
| Cornell University | M,D |
| Florida State University | M,D |
| Gordon-Conwell Theological Seminary | M,D |
| The Graduate Center, City University of New York | D |
| Harvard University | M,D* |
| Illinois State University | M |
| Indiana University Bloomington | M,D |
| Indiana University of Pennsylvania | M |
| Johns Hopkins University | D |
| Massachusetts Institute of Technology | M,D,O |
| Memorial University of Newfoundland | M,D |
| Mercyhurst University | M |
| New York University | M,D |
| Princeton University | D |
| Rice University | M,D |
| St. Cloud State University | M,O |
| San Francisco State University | M |
| Simon Fraser University | M,D |
| Southern Methodist University | M,D |
| Stanford University | M,D |
| Trinity International University | M,D,O |
| Universidad de las Américas Puebla | M |
| University of Alberta | M,D |
| The University of British Columbia | M |
| University of California, Berkeley | M,D |
| University of California, Los Angeles | M,D |
| University of Chicago | D |
| University of Colorado Denver | M |
| University of Denver | M |
| University of Lethbridge | M,D |
| The University of Manchester | D |
| University of Massachusetts Boston | M |
| University of Memphis | M,D,O |
| University of Michigan | M,D |
| University of Minnesota, Twin Cities Campus | M,D |
| University of Nebraska–Lincoln | M,D |
| University of New Mexico | M,D |
| The University of North Carolina at Chapel Hill | M,D |
| University of Oklahoma | M,D |
| University of Pennsylvania | M,D |
| University of Rhode Island | M |
| University of Saskatchewan | M |
| University of South Africa | M,D |
| University of South Florida | M,D,O |
| The University of Tennessee | M,D |
| The University of Texas at Austin | M,D |
| University of West Florida | M |
| University of Wisconsin–Madison | D |
| Université Laval | M,D |
| Washington State University | M,D |
| Washington University in St. Louis | M,D |
| Wheaton College | M,D |
| Yale University | M |

## ARCHITECTURAL ENGINEERING

| | |
|---|---|
| California Polytechnic State University, San Luis Obispo | M |
| California State University, Fullerton | M |
| Carnegie Mellon University | M,D |
| Drexel University | M,D |
| Illinois Institute of Technology | M,D |
| Kansas State University | M |
| Lawrence Technological University | M,D |
| Milwaukee School of Engineering | M |
| Penn State University Park | M,D* |
| University of California, San Diego | M |
| University of Colorado Boulder | M,D |
| University of Detroit Mercy | M |
| The University of Kansas | M |
| University of Louisiana at Lafayette | M |
| University of Massachusetts Amherst | M,D |
| University of Miami | M,D |
| University of Nebraska–Lincoln | M,D |
| The University of Texas at Austin | M |
| University of Wyoming | M,D |

## ARCHITECTURAL HISTORY

| | |
|---|---|
| Arizona State University at Tempe | D |
| Cornell University | M,D |
| The Graduate Center, City University of New York | D |
| Harvard University | D* |
| Massachusetts Institute of Technology | M,D |
| New York University | M |
| Roger Williams University | M,O |
| Savannah College of Art and Design | M |
| University of California, Berkeley | M,D |
| University of Colorado Denver | D |
| University of Pittsburgh | M,D* |
| The University of Texas at Austin | M,D |
| University of Virginia | M,D |

## ARCHITECTURE

| | |
|---|---|
| Academy of Art University | M |
| Andrews University | M |
| Arizona State University at Tempe | M,D |
| Athabasca University | M,O |
| Auburn University | M |
| Ball State University | M |
| Boston Architectural College | M |
| California Baptist University | M |
| California College of the Arts | M |
| California Polytechnic State University, San Luis Obispo | M |
| California State Polytechnic University, Pomona | M |
| Carleton University | M |
| Carnegie Mellon University | M,D |
| The Catholic University of America | M,O |
| City College of the City University of New York | M |
| Clemson University | M,D,O |
| Columbia University | M,D |
| Cooper Union for the Advancement of Science and Art | M |
| Cornell University | M,D |
| Cranbrook Academy of Art | M |
| Dalhousie University | M |
| Florida Agricultural and Mechanical University | M |
| Florida International University | M |
| Florida State University | M |
| Georgia Institute of Technology | M,D |
| Harvard University | M,D* |
| Illinois Institute of Technology | M,D |
| Indiana University Bloomington | M |
| Instituto Tecnológico y de Estudios Superiores de Monterrey, Campus Estado de México | M,D |
| Instituto Tecnológico y de Estudios Superiores de Monterrey, Campus Irapuato | M,D |
| Iowa State University of Science and Technology | M |
| Judson University | M |
| Kansas State University | M |
| Kent State University | M |
| Lawrence Technological University | M,O |
| London Metropolitan University | M,D |
| Louisiana State University and Agricultural & Mechanical College | M |
| Louisiana Tech University | M,D,O |
| Marywood University | M |
| Massachusetts College of Art and Design | M |
| Massachusetts Institute of Technology | M,D |
| McGill University | M,D,O |
| Miami University | M |
| Montana State University | M |
| Morgan State University | M |
| New Jersey Institute of Technology | M,D |
| The New School | M |
| NewSchool of Architecture and Design | M |
| New York Institute of Technology | M |
| North Carolina State University | M |
| North Dakota State University | M |
| Northeastern University | M |
| The Ohio State University | M,D |
| Penn State University Park | M,D* |
| Pontificia Universidad Catolica Madre y Maestra | M |
| Portland State University | M |
| Prairie View A&M University | M |
| Pratt Institute | M |
| Princeton University | M,D |
| Rensselaer Polytechnic Institute | M |
| Rhode Island School of Design | M |
| Rice University | M,D |
| Rochester Institute of Technology | M |
| Roger Williams University | M,O |
| Savannah College of Art and Design | M |
| School of Architecture at Taliesin | M |
| Southern California Institute of Architecture | M |
| Southern Illinois University Carbondale | M |
| Syracuse University | M |
| Temple University | M* |
| Texas A&M University | M,D |
| Texas Tech University | M,D |
| Thomas Jefferson University | M |
| Tulane University | M |
| Universidad Autonoma de Guadalajara | M,D |
| Universidad Nacional Pedro Henriquez Urena | M |
| University at Buffalo, the State University of New York | M |
| The University of Arizona | M |
| The University of British Columbia | M |
| University of Calgary | M,D |
| University of California, Berkeley | M,D |
| University of California, Los Angeles | M,D |
| University of Cincinnati | M |
| University of Colorado Denver | M |
| University of Florida | M,D |
| University of Hartford | M |
| University of Hawaii at Manoa | D |
| University of Houston | M |
| University of Idaho | M |
| University of Illinois at Chicago | M |
| University of Illinois at Urbana-Champaign | M,D |
| The University of Kansas | M,D,O |
| University of Kentucky | M |
| The University of Manchester | M,D |
| University of Manitoba | M |
| University of Maryland, College Park | M |
| University of Massachusetts Amherst | M |
| University of Memphis | M |
| University of Miami | M |
| University of Michigan | M |
| University of Minnesota, Twin Cities Campus | M |
| University of Missouri | M,D |
| University of Nebraska–Lincoln | M,D |
| University of Nevada, Las Vegas | M,O |
| University of New Mexico | M,D |
| The University of North Carolina at Charlotte | M |
| The University of North Carolina at Greensboro | M,O |
| University of Notre Dame | M |
| University of Oklahoma | M,D |
| University of Oregon | M,D |
| University of Pennsylvania | M,D,O |
| University of Puerto Rico at Rio Piedras | M |
| University of Southern California | M |
| University of South Florida | M |
| The University of Tennessee | M |
| The University of Texas at Arlington | M |
| The University of Texas at Austin | M |
| The University of Texas at San Antonio | M |
| University of the District of Columbia | M |
| University of Toronto | M |
| University of Utah | M |
| University of Virginia | M |
| University of Washington | M,D,O |
| University of Waterloo | M |
| University of Wisconsin–Milwaukee | M,D,O* |
| Université Laval | M |
| Washington State University | M |
| Washington University in St. Louis | M |
| Wentworth Institute of Technology | M |
| Woodbury University | M |
| Yale University | M,D |

## ARCHIVES/ARCHIVAL ADMINISTRATION

| | |
|---|---|
| Claremont Graduate University | M,D,O |
| Clayton State University | M |
| Columbia University | M |
| Drexel University | M |
| Middle Tennessee State University | M,D,O |
| Montclair State University | M |
| New York University | M,D,O |
| Queens College of the City University of New York | M,O |
| The University of British Columbia | M,D |
| University of California, Los Angeles | M,D,O |
| University of California, Riverside | M,D |
| University of Manitoba | M,D |
| University of Massachusetts Boston | M |
| University of Oklahoma | M,D,O |
| University of South Carolina | M,O |
| Wayne State University | M,O |

## ART/FINE ARTS

| | |
|---|---|
| Academy of Art University | M |
| Adelphi University | M |
| Alfred University | M,D |
| Anna Maria College | M,O |
| Arizona State University at Tempe | M,D |
| ArtCenter College of Design | M |
| Azusa Pacific University | M |
| Ball State University | M |
| Bard College | M |
| Barry University | M |
| Bob Jones University | M,D,O |
| Boise State University | M |
| Boston University | M |
| Bowling Green State University | M |
| Bradley University | M |
| Brandeis University | O |
| Brigham Young University | M |
| Brooklyn College of the City University of New York | M |
| Butler University | M |
| California College of the Arts | M |
| California Institute of the Arts | M,O |
| California State University, Chico | M |
| California State University, Fresno | M |
| California State University, Fullerton | M |
| California State University, Long Beach | M |
| California State University, Los Angeles | M |
| California State University, Northridge | M |
| California State University, Sacramento | M |
| California State University, San Bernardino | M |
| Carlow University | M |
| Carnegie Mellon University | M |
| Central Washington University | M |
| Chapman University | |
| Christie's Education | O |
| City College of the City University of New York | M |
| Claremont Graduate University | M |
| Clemson University | M |
| College for Creative Studies | M |
| Colorado State University | M |
| Columbia College Chicago | M |
| Columbia University | M,D |
| Columbus College of Art & Design | M |
| Concordia University (Canada) | M |
| Cornell University | M |
| Cranbrook Academy of Art | M |
| Drew University | M,D,O |
| Duke University | M,D |
| East Carolina University | M |
| Eastern Illinois University | M |
| Eastern Michigan University | M |
| East Tennessee State University | M |
| Edinboro University of Pennsylvania | M |
| Emily Carr University of Art + Design | M |
| Fairleigh Dickinson University, Metropolitan Campus | M |
| Ferris State University | M |
| Florida Atlantic University | M |
| Florida International University | M,O |
| Florida State University | M |
| Fontbonne University | M |
| Fort Hays State University | M |
| Full Sail University | M |
| George Mason University | M |
| The George Washington University | M,O |
| Georgia Southern University | M |
| Georgia State University | M |
| Governors State University | M |
| Hollins University | M |
| Hood College | M,O |
| Houston Baptist University | M |
| Howard University | M |
| Hunter College of the City University of New York | M |
| Idaho State University | M |
| Illinois State University | M |
| Indiana State University | M |
| Indiana University Bloomington | M |
| Indiana University of Pennsylvania | M |
| Indiana University-Purdue University Indianapolis | M |
| Institute for Doctoral Studies in the Visual Arts | D |
| Inter American University of Puerto Rico, San Germán Campus | M |
| Iowa State University of Science and Technology | M |
| Ithaca College | M |
| Jacksonville University | M |
| James Madison University | M |
| Kansas State University | M |
| Kent State University | M |
| Laguna College of Art & Design | M |
| Lake Forest College | M |
| Lee University | M,O |
| Lehman College of the City University of New York | M |
| Lesley University | M,D,O |
| Long Island University - Post | M |
| Louisiana State University and Agricultural & Mechanical College | M |
| Louisiana Tech University | M,D,O |
| Maine College of Art | M |
| Maryland Institute College of Art | M |
| Marywood University | M |
| Massachusetts College of Art and Design | M,O |
| Miami University | M |
| Michigan State University | M |
| Millersville University of Pennsylvania | M |
| Mills College | M |
| Minneapolis College of Art and Design | M |
| Minnesota State University Mankato | M |
| Mississippi College | M |
| Missouri State University | M |
| Montana State University | M |
| Montclair State University | M |
| Moore College of Art & Design | M |
| New Hampshire Institute of Art | M |
| New Jersey City University | M |
| New Mexico State University | M |
| The New School | M |
| New York Academy of Art | M |
| New York Institute of Technology | M |
| New York Studio School of Drawing, Painting and Sculpture | M,O* |
| New York University | M,D,O |
| Norfolk State University | M |
| Northern Illinois University | M |
| Northern Vermont University–Johnson | M |
| Northwestern State University of Louisiana | M |
| Northwestern University | M |
| Nova Southeastern University | M,D,O |
| NSCAD University | M |
| The Ohio State University | M |
| Ohio University | M |
| Otis College of Art and Design | M |
| Pacific Northwest College of Art | M |
| Paris College of Art | M |
| Penn State University Park | M,D,O* |
| Pennsylvania Academy of the Fine Arts | M,O |

*M—masters degree; D—doctorate; O—other advanced degree; *—Close-Up and/or Display*

| | |
|---|---|
| Pensacola Christian College | M,D,O |
| Pontifical Catholic University of Puerto Rico | M |
| Portland State University | M |
| Pratt Institute | M |
| Prescott College | M |
| Purchase College, State University of New York | M |
| Purdue University | M,D |
| Queens College of the City University of New York | M |
| Radford University | M |
| Rensselaer Polytechnic Institute | D |
| Rhode Island College | M |
| Rhode Island School of Design | M |
| Rochester Institute of Technology | M |
| Rutgers University - New Brunswick | M |
| San Diego State University | M |
| San Francisco Art Institute | M,O |
| San Francisco State University | M |
| Savannah College of Art and Design | M |
| School of Visual Arts (NY) | M |
| Sotheby's Institute of Art–London | M |
| Sotheby's Institute of Art–New York | M |
| Southern Illinois University Carbondale | M |
| Southern Illinois University Edwardsville | M |
| Southern Methodist University | M |
| Southwest University of Visual Arts | M |
| Spring Hill College | M,O |
| Stanford University | M,D |
| State University of New York at New Paltz | M |
| State University of New York at Oswego | M |
| Stephen F. Austin State University | M |
| Stony Brook University, State University of New York | M |
| Sul Ross State University | M |
| SUNY Brockport | M |
| Syracuse University | M |
| Temple University | M* |
| Texas A&M University | M |
| Texas A&M University–Commerce | M,D,O |
| Texas A&M University–Corpus Christi | M |
| Texas Christian University | M |
| Texas Southern University | M |
| Texas Tech University | M,D |
| Texas Woman's University | M |
| Thomas Jefferson University | M |
| Tiffin University | M |
| Towson University | M |
| Tufts University | M,O |
| Tulane University | M |
| United Theological Seminary of the Twin Cities | M,D,O |
| Universidad del Turabo | M |
| Université du Québec à Chicoutimi | M |
| Université du Québec à Montréal | M |
| University at Albany, State University of New York | M |
| University at Buffalo, the State University of New York | M |
| The University of Alabama | M |
| University of Alaska Fairbanks | M |
| University of Alberta | M |
| The University of Arizona | M |
| University of Arkansas | M |
| University of Arkansas at Little Rock | M |
| The University of British Columbia | M,D |
| University of California, Berkeley | M,O |
| University of California, Davis | M |
| University of California, Irvine | M,D |
| University of California, Los Angeles | M |
| University of California, Riverside | M |
| University of California, San Diego | M,D |
| University of California, Santa Barbara | M |
| University of California, Santa Cruz | M,D |
| University of Central Florida | M |
| University of Chicago | M |
| University of Cincinnati | M |
| University of Colorado Boulder | M |
| University of Colorado Denver | M,O |
| University of Dayton | M |
| University of Delaware | M |
| University of Denver | M |
| University of Florida | M,D |
| University of Georgia | M,D |
| University of Guam | M |
| University of Guelph | M |
| University of Hartford | M |
| University of Hawaii at Manoa | M |
| University of Houston | M |
| University of Idaho | M |
| University of Illinois at Chicago | M,D |
| University of Illinois at Urbana-Champaign | M |
| University of Indianapolis | M |
| The University of Iowa | M |
| The University of Kansas | M,D |
| University of Kentucky | M |
| University of Lethbridge | M,D |
| University of Maine | M |
| The University of Manchester | M,D |
| University of Maryland, College Park | M |
| University of Massachusetts Amherst | M |
| University of Massachusetts Dartmouth | M,O |
| University of Memphis | M,O |
| University of Miami | M |
| University of Michigan | M |
| University of Michigan–Flint | M |
| University of Minnesota, Duluth | M |
| University of Minnesota, Twin Cities Campus | M |
| University of Mississippi | M,D |
| University of Missouri | M |
| University of Missouri–Kansas City | M,D |
| University of Montana | M |
| University of Nebraska at Omaha | M |
| University of Nebraska–Lincoln | M |
| University of Nevada, Las Vegas | M |
| University of Nevada, Reno | M |
| University of New Mexico | M |
| University of New Orleans | M |
| The University of North Carolina at Chapel Hill | M |
| The University of North Carolina at Greensboro | M |
| University of North Dakota | M |
| University of Northern Colorado | M |
| University of Northern Iowa | M |
| University of North Texas | M,D,O |
| University of Notre Dame | M |
| University of Oklahoma | M,D |
| University of Oregon | M |
| University of Pennsylvania | M,O |
| University of Regina | M |
| University of Rochester | D |
| University of Saint Francis (IN) | M |
| University of Saskatchewan | M |
| The University of Scranton | M |
| University of South Alabama | M |
| University of South Carolina | M |
| University of South Dakota | M |
| University of Southern California | M,D,O |
| University of South Florida | M |
| The University of Tennessee | M |
| The University of Texas at Arlington | M |
| The University of Texas at Austin | M |
| The University of Texas at El Paso | M |
| The University of Texas at San Antonio | M |
| The University of Texas at Tyler | M |
| The University of Texas Rio Grande Valley | M |
| The University of the Arts | M |
| University of Utah | M |
| University of Victoria | M |
| University of Washington | M |
| University of Waterloo | M |
| University of Windsor | M |
| University of Wisconsin–Madison | M |
| University of Wisconsin–Milwaukee | M,O* |
| University of Wisconsin–River Falls | M |
| University of Wisconsin–Stout | M |
| University of Wisconsin–Superior | M |
| Université Laval | M |
| Utah State University | M |
| Vermont College of Fine Arts | M |
| Virginia Commonwealth University | M,D |
| Warren Wilson College | M |
| Washington State University | M |
| Washington University in St. Louis | M |
| Wayne State University | M |
| Webster University | M |
| Western Carolina University | M |
| Western Connecticut State University | M |
| West Texas A&M University | M |
| West Virginia University | M,D |
| Wichita State University | M |
| Wilson College | M |
| Winthrop University | M |
| Yale University | M |
| York University | M,D |

## ART EDUCATION

| | |
|---|---|
| Academy of Art University | M |
| Alabama Agricultural and Mechanical University | M |
| American University of Puerto Rico - Bayamon | M |
| Arcadia University | M,D,O |
| Arizona State University at Tempe | M,D |
| Art Academy of Cincinnati | M |
| Boston University | M |
| Bowling Green State University | M |
| Bridgewater State University | M |
| Brigham Young University | M |
| Brooklyn College of the City University of New York | M |
| Buffalo State College, State University of New York | M |
| California State University, Long Beach | M |
| California State University, Los Angeles | M |
| California State University, Northridge | M |
| Carthage College | M,O |
| Case Western Reserve University | M |
| Central Connecticut State University | M,O |
| Chatham University | M |
| Cleveland State University | M |
| The College of New Rochelle | M |
| The Colorado College | M |
| Colorado State University-Pueblo | M |
| Columbus State University | M |
| Concordia University (United States) | M,D |
| Concordia University (Canada) | M,D |
| Concordia University Wisconsin | M |
| Converse College | M |
| Delaware State University | M |
| East Carolina University | M |
| Eastern Illinois University | M |
| Eastern Kentucky University | M |
| Eastern Michigan University | M |
| Edinboro University of Pennsylvania | M |
| Fitchburg State University | M,O |
| Florida International University | M,D,O |
| Florida State University | M,D |
| Fontbonne University | M |
| Framingham State University | M |
| George Mason University | M |
| The George Washington University | M |
| Georgia State University | M |
| Harding University | M,O |
| Harvard University | M* |
| Hofstra University | M,D,O |
| Indiana University Bloomington | M,D,O |
| James Madison University | M |
| Kean University | M |
| Kennesaw State University | M |
| Kent State University | M |
| Kutztown University of Pennsylvania | M |
| Lake Forest College | M |
| Lehman College of the City University of New York | M |
| Lesley University | M,D,O |
| Long Island University - Post | M,D,O |
| Manhattanville College | M,O |
| Mansfield University of Pennsylvania | M |
| Maryland Institute College of Art | M |
| Marywood University | M |
| Massachusetts College of Art and Design | M,O |
| McNeese State University | O |
| Miami University | M |
| Millersville University of Pennsylvania | M |
| Minnesota State University Mankato | M |
| Mississippi College | M,D,O |
| Montclair State University | M |
| Moore College of Art & Design | M |
| Nazareth College of Rochester | M |
| New Hampshire Institute of Art | M |
| New Jersey City University | M |
| New York University | M,O |
| The Ohio State University | M,D |
| Penn State University Park | M,D,O* |
| Piedmont College | M,D,O |
| Plymouth State University | M |
| Pratt Institute | M,O |
| Purdue University | M,D,O |
| Queens College of the City University of New York | M,O |
| Rhode Island College | M |
| Rhode Island School of Design | M |
| Rochester Institute of Technology | M |
| Rocky Mountain College of Art + Design | M |
| Saint Michael's College | M,O |
| Salem College | M |
| Salem State University | M |
| School of Visual Arts (NY) | M |
| Simon Fraser University | M,D |
| Southern Connecticut State University | M |
| Southwestern Oklahoma State University | M |
| Spalding University | M |
| State University of New York at New Paltz | M |
| State University of New York at Oswego | M |
| Stephen F. Austin State University | M |
| Sul Ross State University | M |
| Syracuse University | M |
| Teachers College, Columbia University | M,D,O |
| Temple University | M* |
| Texas Tech University | M |
| Texas Woman's University | M |
| Towson University | M,O |
| Tufts University | M,D,O |
| The University of Akron | M |
| The University of Alabama at Birmingham | M |
| The University of Arizona | M,D |
| University of Arkansas at Little Rock | M |
| The University of British Columbia | M,D |
| University of Central Florida | M,O |
| University of Cincinnati | M |
| University of Denver | M,O |
| University of Florida | M,D |
| University of Illinois at Urbana-Champaign | M,D |
| University of Indianapolis | M |
| The University of Iowa | M,D |
| The University of Kansas | M |
| University of Kentucky | M |
| University of Louisville | M,D,O |
| University of Maryland, Baltimore County | M |
| University of Massachusetts Amherst | M |
| University of Massachusetts Dartmouth | M |
| University of Minnesota, Twin Cities Campus | M |
| University of Missouri | M,D,O |
| University of Montana | M |
| University of Nebraska at Kearney | M |
| University of New Mexico | M |
| The University of North Carolina at Charlotte | M,D,O |
| The University of North Carolina at Pembroke | M |
| University of Northern Colorado | M |
| University of Northern Iowa | M |
| University of North Texas | M,D,O |
| University of Rio Grande | M |
| University of St. Francis (IL) | M,D,O |
| University of South Alabama | M,D |
| University of South Carolina | M,D |
| University of South Dakota | M |
| The University of Tennessee | M,D,O |
| The University of Texas at Austin | M |
| The University of Texas at El Paso | M |
| The University of the Arts | M |
| The University of Toledo | M,D,O |
| University of Utah | M |
| University of Victoria | M,D |
| University of Wisconsin–Milwaukee | M,D,O* |
| University of Wisconsin–Superior | M |
| Vermont College of Fine Arts | M |
| Virginia Commonwealth University | M,D |
| Wayne State University | M,D,O |
| Western Kentucky University | M |
| Western Michigan University | M |
| West Virginia University | M,D |
| William Carey University | M,O |
| Winthrop University | M |

## ART HISTORY

| | |
|---|---|
| Academy of Art University | M |
| American University | M |
| Arizona State University at Tempe | M,D |
| Bard Graduate Center | M,D |
| Binghamton University, State University of New York | M,D |
| Boston University | M,D,O |
| Bowling Green State University | M |
| Brooklyn College of the City University of New York | M |
| Brown University | D |
| Bryn Mawr College | M,D |
| California State University, Chico | M |
| California State University, Fullerton | M |
| California State University, Los Angeles | M |
| California State University, Northridge | M |
| Caribbean University | M,D |
| Carleton University | M |
| Case Western Reserve University | M,D |
| Christie's Education | M |
| City College of the City University of New York | M |
| Cleveland State University | M |
| Colorado State University | M |
| Columbia College Chicago | M |
| Columbia University | M,D |
| Concordia University (Canada) | M,D |
| Cornell University | D |
| Duke University | M,D |
| Emory University | D |
| Fashion Institute of Technology | M |
| Florida State University | M,D |
| George Mason University | M |
| The George Washington University | M |
| Georgia State University | M |
| The Graduate Center, City University of New York | D |
| Graduate Theological Union | M,D,O |
| Harvard University | D* |
| Howard University | M |
| Hunter College of the City University of New York | M |
| Illinois State University | M |
| Indiana University Bloomington | M,D |
| James Madison University | M |
| John Cabot University | M |
| Johns Hopkins University | M,D |
| Kent State University | M |
| Lancaster Theological Seminary | M,D,O |
| Lindenwood University | M |
| Louisiana State University and Agricultural & Mechanical College | M |
| Massachusetts Institute of Technology | M,D |
| McGill University | M,D |
| Montana State University | M |
| New Mexico State University | M |
| New York University | M,D |
| Northwestern University | D |
| The Ohio State University | M,D |
| Ohio University | M |
| Oklahoma State University | M |
| Penn State University Park | M,D* |
| Purchase College, State University of New York | M |
| Queens College of the City University of New York | M |
| Rice University | D |
| Richmond, The American International University in London | M |
| Roger Williams University | M,O |
| Rutgers University - New Brunswick | M,D,O |
| San Francisco Art Institute | M |
| Savannah College of Art and Design | M |
| School of Visual Arts (NY) | M |
| Southern Methodist University | M,D |
| Stony Brook University, State University of New York | M,D |
| Sul Ross State University | M |
| Syracuse University | M |
| Temple University | M,D* |
| Texas Christian University | M |
| Texas Tech University | M |
| Texas Woman's University | M |
| Towson University | M |
| Tufts University | M |
| Tulane University | M |
| Université de Montréal | M,D |
| Université du Québec à Montréal | M,D |
| University at Buffalo, the State University of New York | M,D |
| The University of Alabama | M |
| The University of Alabama at Birmingham | M |

| | |
|---|---|
| University of Alberta | M |
| The University of Arizona | M,D |
| University of Arkansas at Little Rock | M |
| The University of British Columbia | M,D |
| University of California, Berkeley | D |
| University of California, Davis | M |
| University of California, Los Angeles | M,D |
| University of California, Riverside | M,D |
| University of California, San Diego | M,D |
| University of California, Santa Barbara | D |
| University of Chicago | M,D |
| University of Cincinnati | M |
| University of Colorado Boulder | M |
| University of Delaware | M,D |
| University of Denver | M |
| University of Florida | M,D |
| University of Georgia | M,D |
| University of Hawaii at Manoa | M |
| University of Houston | M |
| University of Illinois at Chicago | M,D |
| University of Illinois at Urbana-Champaign | M,D |
| The University of Iowa | M,D |
| The University of Kansas | M,D |
| University of Kentucky | M |
| University of Louisville | M,D |
| The University of Manchester | D |
| University of Maryland, College Park | M,D |
| University of Massachusetts Amherst | M |
| University of Massachusetts Dartmouth | M |
| University of Memphis | M,O |
| University of Miami | M |
| University of Michigan | M,D |
| University of Minnesota, Twin Cities Campus | M,D |
| University of Montana | M |
| University of Nebraska–Lincoln | M |
| University of New Mexico | M,D |
| The University of North Carolina at Chapel Hill | M,D |
| University of Northern Colorado | M |
| University of North Texas | M,D,O |
| University of Notre Dame | M |
| University of Oklahoma | M,D |
| University of Oregon | M,D |
| University of Pennsylvania | M,D |
| University of Pittsburgh | M,D* |
| University of Rochester | D |
| University of St. Thomas (MN) | M,O |
| University of South Africa | M,D |
| University of South Carolina | M |
| University of Southern California | M,D,O |
| University of South Florida | M |
| The University of Texas at Austin | M,D |
| The University of Texas at Dallas | M,D |
| The University of Texas at San Antonio | M |
| The University of Texas at Tyler | M |
| University of Toronto | M,D |
| University of Utah | M |
| University of Victoria | M,D |
| University of Virginia | M,D |
| University of Washington | M,D |
| University of Wisconsin–Madison | M,D |
| University of Wisconsin–Milwaukee | M* |
| University of Wisconsin–Superior | M |
| Université Laval | M,D |
| Virginia Commonwealth University | M,D |
| Washington University in St. Louis | M,D |
| Wayne State University | M |
| Webster University | M |
| West Virginia University | M,D |
| Williams College | M |
| Yale University | D |
| York University | M,D |

### ARTIFICIAL INTELLIGENCE/ROBOTICS

| | |
|---|---|
| The American University in Cairo | M,D,O |
| Brandeis University | M |
| California State University, Northridge | M |
| Carnegie Mellon University | M,D |
| College of Staten Island of the City University of New York | M |
| Cornell University | M,D |
| Illinois Institute of Technology | M,D |
| Indiana University Bloomington | D |
| Instituto Tecnológico y de Estudios Superiores de Monterrey, Campus Monterrey | M,D |
| Johns Hopkins University | M |
| Lawrence Technological University | M,O |
| New York University | M |
| Northwestern University | M |
| Oregon State University | M,D |
| Portland State University | M,D,O |
| Queen's University at Kingston | M |
| South Dakota School of Mines and Technology | M |
| Stevens Institute of Technology | M,D,O |
| Temple University | M,D* |
| Tufts University | M,D |
| University of California, Riverside | M,D |
| University of California, San Diego | M,D |
| University of Georgia | M |
| University of Michigan | M,D |
| University of Nebraska at Omaha | M,O |
| University of Pennsylvania | M |
| University of Pittsburgh | M,D* |
| University of Rochester | M,D |
| University of Southern California | M,D |
| Villanova University | M,O |
| Worcester Polytechnic Institute | M,D |

### ARTS ADMINISTRATION

| | |
|---|---|
| American University | M,O |
| The American University of Rome | M |
| Arizona State University at Tempe | M,D |
| Baruch College of the City University of New York | M |
| Boston University | M,O |
| Brooklyn College of the City University of New York | M |
| Carnegie Mellon University | M |
| Christie's Education | M,O |
| Claremont Graduate University | M |
| College of Charleston | O |
| Colorado State University | M |
| Drexel University | M |
| Eastern Michigan University | M |
| Fashion Institute of Technology | M |
| Florida State University | M,D |
| George Mason University | M |
| Goucher College | M |
| HEC Montreal | O |
| Indiana University Bloomington | M |
| Kutztown University of Pennsylvania | M |
| Le Moyne College | M |
| London Metropolitan University | M,D |
| Montclair State University | M |
| Moore College of Art & Design | M |
| New York University | M |
| Northeastern University | M |
| Northwestern University | M |
| The Ohio State University | M |
| Pratt Institute | M |
| Purchase College, State University of New York | M |
| Rhode Island College | M |
| Rider University | M |
| Rocky Mountain College of Art + Design | M |
| Roosevelt University | M,O |
| Rowan University | M |
| Ryerson University | M |
| St. Thomas University - Florida | M |
| Savannah College of Art and Design | M |
| Seattle University | M |
| Sotheby's Institute of Art–London | M |
| Sotheby's Institute of Art–New York | M |
| Southern Methodist University | M |
| Southern Utah University | M |
| SUNY Brockport | M,O |
| Teachers College, Columbia University | M,D,O |
| Temple University | M,D* |
| Universidad del Turabo | M |
| University at Buffalo, the State University of New York | M |
| The University of Akron | M |
| University of Cincinnati | M,D |
| University of Kentucky | M |
| The University of Manchester | D |
| University of Michigan–Flint | M |
| University of New Orleans | M |
| The University of North Carolina at Charlotte | M,O |
| University of Southern California | M |
| University of Wisconsin–Madison | M |
| Valparaiso University | M |
| Winthrop University | M |

### ARTS JOURNALISM

| | |
|---|---|
| Academy of Art University | M |
| Syracuse University | M |

### ART THERAPY

| | |
|---|---|
| Adler University | M,D |
| Albertus Magnus College | M |
| Athabasca University | M,O |
| California State University, Los Angeles | M |
| Cedar Crest College | M |
| The College of New Rochelle | M |
| Concordia University (Canada) | M |
| Drexel University | M,O |
| Eastern Virginia Medical School | M |
| Edinboro University of Pennsylvania | M,O |
| Emporia State University | M |
| Florida State University | M,D |
| The George Washington University | M,O |
| Georgia College & State University | M |
| Goddard College | M |
| Hofstra University | M,O |
| Indiana University-Purdue University Indianapolis | M |
| Lesley University | M,D,O |
| Long Island University - Post | M |
| Marywood University | M,O |
| Mount Mary University | M,D |
| Naropa University | M |
| Nazareth College of Rochester | M |
| New York University | M |
| Notre Dame de Namur University | M,D |
| Ottawa University | M |
| Phillips Graduate University | M |
| Pratt Institute | M |
| Prescott College | M |
| Saint Mary-of-the-Woods College | M,O |
| School of Visual Arts (NY) | M |
| Seton Hill University | M |
| Southern Illinois University Edwardsville | M |
| Southwestern College (NM) | M |
| Springfield College | M,O |
| University of Louisville | M,D |
| University of Maryland, College Park | M,D,O |
| University of Wisconsin–Superior | M |
| Ursuline College | M |

### ASIAN-AMERICAN STUDIES

| | |
|---|---|
| Binghamton University, State University of New York | M,O |
| California State University, Long Beach | M |
| San Francisco State University | M |
| Stony Brook University, State University of New York | M |
| University of California, Los Angeles | M |

### ASIAN LANGUAGES

| | |
|---|---|
| Cornell University | M,D |
| Harvard University | M,D* |
| Indiana University Bloomington | M,D |
| The Ohio State University | M,D |
| St. John's College (NM) | M |
| Stanford University | M,D |
| University of California, Berkeley | M,D |
| University of California, Irvine | M,D |
| University of California, Los Angeles | M,D |
| University of California, Santa Barbara | M,D |
| University of Chicago | D |
| University of Hawaii at Manoa | M,D |
| University of Illinois at Urbana-Champaign | M,D |
| The University of Iowa | M |
| The University of Kansas | M,O |
| University of Michigan | D |
| University of Minnesota, Twin Cities Campus | D |
| University of Oregon | M,D |
| University of Southern California | M,D |
| The University of Texas at Austin | M,D |
| University of Washington | M,D |
| University of Wisconsin–Madison | M,D |
| Washington University in St. Louis | M,D |
| Yale University | D |

### ASIAN STUDIES

| | |
|---|---|
| American University | O |
| Binghamton University, State University of New York | M,O |
| Brown University | D |
| California State University, Long Beach | M |
| College of Staten Island of the City University of New York | M |
| Columbia University | M,D,O |
| Cornell University | M,D |
| Dallas Baptist University | M |
| Duke University | M,O |
| Florida International University | M |
| Florida State University | M |
| Georgetown University | M |
| The George Washington University | M |
| Harvard University | M,D* |
| Indiana University Bloomington | M,D |
| Johns Hopkins University | M,D,O |
| Maharishi International University | M,D |
| McGill University | M,D |
| New York University | M,D |
| The Ohio State University | M |
| Ohio University | M |
| Princeton University | D |
| Rutgers University - New Brunswick | M,D |
| St. John's College (NM) | M |
| St. John's University (NY) | M |
| San Diego State University | M |
| Seton Hall University | M |
| Stanford University | M |
| Stony Brook University, State University of New York | M |
| United Theological Seminary of the Twin Cities | M,D,O |
| University of Alberta | M |
| The University of Arizona | M,D |
| University of Bridgeport | M |
| The University of British Columbia | M,D |
| University of California, Berkeley | M,D |
| University of California, Los Angeles | M,D |
| University of California, Riverside | M |
| University of California, Santa Barbara | M,D |
| University of Chicago | M,D |
| University of Colorado Boulder | M,D |
| University of Hawaii at Manoa | O |
| University of Illinois at Urbana-Champaign | M,D |
| The University of Iowa | M |
| The University of Kansas | M,O |
| The University of Manchester | D |
| University of Michigan | M,D,O |
| University of Minnesota, Twin Cities Campus | D |
| University of Oregon | M |
| University of Pennsylvania | M,D |
| University of Pittsburgh | M,O* |
| University of San Francisco | M |
| University of Southern California | M,D |
| The University of Texas at Austin | M,D |
| University of Toronto | M,D |
| University of Utah | M |
| University of Victoria | M |
| University of Virginia | M |
| University of Washington | M,D |
| University of Wisconsin–Madison | M,D |
| Washington University in St. Louis | M,D |
| Yale University | M |

### ASTRONOMY

| | |
|---|---|
| Boston University | M,D |
| Brigham Young University | M,D |
| California Institute of Technology | D |
| Case Western Reserve University | M,D |
| Columbia University | M,D |
| Cornell University | D |
| Dartmouth College | D |
| George Mason University | M,D |
| Georgia State University | D |
| Harvard University | D* |
| Hunter College of the City University of New York | M,D |
| Indiana University Bloomington | M,D |
| Johns Hopkins University | D |
| Louisiana State University and Agricultural & Mechanical College | M,D |
| Michigan State University | M,D |
| Minnesota State University Mankato | M |
| Northwestern University | D |
| The Ohio State University | M,D |
| Ohio University | M,D |
| Penn State University Park | M,D* |
| Princeton University | D |
| Queen's University at Kingston | M,D |
| Rensselaer Polytechnic Institute | M |
| Rice University | M,D |
| Rutgers University - New Brunswick | M,D |
| Saint Mary's University (Canada) | M,D |
| San Diego State University | M |
| San Francisco State University | M |
| Stony Brook University, State University of New York | D |
| Texas A&M University | M,D |
| Texas Tech University | M,D |
| Université de Moncton | M |
| The University of Alabama | M,D |
| The University of Alabama in Huntsville | M,D |
| The University of Arizona | D |
| The University of British Columbia | M,D |
| University of Calgary | M,D |
| University of California, Los Angeles | M,D |
| University of California, Santa Cruz | D |
| University of Chicago | D |
| University of Delaware | M,D |
| University of Florida | M,D |
| University of Hawaii at Manoa | M,D |
| University of Illinois at Urbana-Champaign | M,D |
| The University of Iowa | M |
| The University of Kansas | M,D |
| University of Kentucky | M,D |
| The University of Manchester | M,D |
| University of Maryland, College Park | M,D |
| University of Massachusetts Amherst | M,D |
| University of Michigan | D |
| University of Missouri | M,D |
| University of Nebraska–Lincoln | M,D |
| University of Nevada, Las Vegas | M,D |
| The University of North Carolina at Chapel Hill | M,D |
| University of Rochester | D |
| University of South Carolina | M,D |
| The University of Texas at Austin | M,D |
| University of Toronto | M,D |
| University of Victoria | M,D |
| University of Virginia | M,D |
| University of Washington | M,D |
| The University of Western Ontario | M,D |
| University of Wisconsin–Madison | D |
| Wesleyan University | M |
| Yale University | M,D |
| York University | M,D |

### ASTROPHYSICS

| | |
|---|---|
| Air Force Institute of Technology | M,D |
| Arizona State University at Tempe | M,D |
| Cornell University | D |
| Harvard University | D* |
| Indiana University Bloomington | M,D |
| Iowa State University of Science and Technology | M,D |
| Louisiana State University and Agricultural & Mechanical College | M,D |
| McMaster University | D |
| Michigan State University | M,D |
| New Mexico Institute of Mining and Technology | M,D |
| New Mexico State University | M,D |
| Penn State University Park | M,D* |
| Princeton University | D |
| Rochester Institute of Technology | M,D |
| Texas Christian University | M,D |
| Tufts University | M,D |
| University of Alaska Fairbanks | M,D |
| University of Alberta | M,D |
| University of California, Berkeley | D |
| University of California, Los Angeles | M,D |
| University of California, Santa Cruz | D |
| University of Chicago | D |
| University of Colorado Boulder | M,D |
| The University of Manchester | M,D |
| University of Michigan | D |
| University of Minnesota, Twin Cities Campus | M,D |
| University of Missouri–St. Louis | M,D |

*M—masters degree; D—doctorate; O—other advanced degree; *—Close-Up and/or Display*

| | |
|---|---|
| The University of North Carolina at Chapel Hill | M,D |
| University of North Dakota | M,D |
| The University of Toledo | M,D |
| University of Toronto | M,D |
| University of Victoria | M,D |
| Yale University | M,D |

### ATHLETIC TRAINING AND SPORTS MEDICINE

| | |
|---|---|
| Adrian College | M |
| A.T. Still University | M,D,O |
| Azusa Pacific University | M |
| Barry University | M |
| Baylor University | M,D |
| Bellarmine University | M,D |
| Bloomsburg University of Pennsylvania | M |
| Boston University | M,D |
| Bridgewater College | M |
| Brigham Young University | M,D |
| California Baptist University | M |
| California State University, Long Beach | M |
| California University of Pennsylvania | M |
| Campbell University | M,D |
| The College of St. Scholastica | M |
| Drake University | M,D |
| Eastern Michigan University | M,O |
| East Stroudsburg University of Pennsylvania | M |
| Florida International University | M |
| Franklin College | M |
| Gannon University | M |
| George Mason University | M,O |
| Georgia Southern University | M,O |
| Georgia State University | M |
| Grand View University | M,O |
| High Point University | M,D |
| Idaho State University | M |
| Indiana State University | M,D |
| Indiana University Bloomington | M,D |
| Indiana Wesleyan University | M,D |
| Inter American University of Puerto Rico, Metropolitan Campus | M |
| Kent State University | M,D |
| Lebanon Valley College | M |
| Lenoir-Rhyne University | M |
| Life University | M |
| Lock Haven University of Pennsylvania | M |
| London Metropolitan University | M,D |
| Long Island University - Brooklyn | M,D,O |
| Manchester University | M |
| Marshall University | M |
| Mercer University | M,D |
| Merrimack College | M |
| Missouri State University | M |
| Montana State University Billings | M |
| Moravian College | M,D |
| North Dakota State University | M,D |
| Northern Arizona University | M |
| Ohio University | M |
| Old Dominion University | M |
| Oregon State University | M |
| Pacific University | M,D |
| Plymouth State University | M |
| Saint Louis University | M,D |
| Salisbury University | M |
| Samford University | M,D |
| Seton Hall University | M |
| Shenandoah University | M,D,O |
| South Dakota State University | M,D |
| Spalding University | M |
| Springfield College | M |
| Stephen F. Austin State University | M |
| Tarleton State University | M |
| Temple University | M,D* |
| Texas A&M University | M,D |
| Texas State University | M |
| Texas Tech University Health Sciences Center | M |
| Thomas Jefferson University | M |
| Trinity International University | M |
| Universidad del Turabo | M |
| University of Arkansas | M |
| University of Central Florida | M |
| University of Central Oklahoma | M |
| University of Evansville | M |
| The University of Findlay | M,D |
| University of Florida | M,D |
| University of Idaho | M,D |
| The University of Iowa | M,D |
| University of Kentucky | M |
| University of Lynchburg | M |
| University of Miami | M,D |
| University of Nebraska at Omaha | M,D |
| The University of North Carolina at Chapel Hill | M |
| The University of North Carolina at Greensboro | M,D |
| University of Northern Iowa | M |
| University of North Georgia | M |
| University of Pittsburgh | M* |
| University of St. Augustine for Health Sciences | M |
| The University of Tennessee | M,D |
| The University of Tennessee at Chattanooga | M |
| The University of Texas at Arlington | M,D |
| The University of Toledo | M,D |
| University of Wisconsin–La Crosse | M |
| University of Wisconsin–Milwaukee | M,D* |
| University of Wisconsin–Stevens Point | M |
| Wayne State University | M,D |
| Weber State University | M |
| Western Michigan University | M |
| West Virginia University | M,D |
| West Virginia Wesleyan College | M |
| Xavier University | M* |
| Youngstown State University | M |

### ATMOSPHERIC SCIENCES

| | |
|---|---|
| Bard College | M,O |
| Carnegie Mellon University | D |
| City College of the City University of New York | M |
| Colorado State University | M,D |
| Columbia University | M,D |
| Cornell University | M,D |
| Florida State University | M,D |
| George Mason University | D |
| Georgia Institute of Technology | M,D |
| Hampton University | M,D |
| Howard University | M,D |
| Indiana University Bloomington | M,D |
| Jackson State University | M,D |
| Massachusetts Institute of Technology | M,D |
| McGill University | M,D |
| Mississippi State University | M,D |
| New Mexico Institute of Mining and Technology | M,D |
| North Carolina State University | M,D |
| Northern Arizona University | M,D,O |
| The Ohio State University | M,D |
| Oregon State University | M,D |
| Princeton University | D |
| Purdue University | M,D |
| Rutgers University - New Brunswick | M,D |
| South Dakota School of Mines and Technology | M,D |
| Stony Brook University, State University of New York | M,D |
| Texas Tech University | M,D |
| Université du Québec à Montréal | M,D,O |
| University at Albany, State University of New York | M,D |
| The University of Alabama in Huntsville | M,D |
| University of Alaska Fairbanks | M,D |
| The University of Arizona | M,D |
| The University of British Columbia | M,D |
| University of California, Davis | M,D |
| University of California, Los Angeles | M,D |
| University of Chicago | D |
| University of Colorado Boulder | M,D |
| University of Guelph | M,D |
| University of Houston | M,D |
| University of Illinois at Urbana-Champaign | M,D |
| The University of Kansas | M,D,O |
| The University of Manchester | M,D |
| University of Maryland, Baltimore County | M,D |
| University of Michigan | M,D |
| University of Nevada, Reno | M,D |
| University of North Dakota | M,D |
| University of Utah | M,D |
| University of Washington | M,D |
| University of Wisconsin–Madison | M,D |
| University of Wisconsin–Milwaukee | M,D* |
| University of Wyoming | M,D |
| Yale University | D |

### AUTOMOTIVE ENGINEERING

| | |
|---|---|
| Clemson University | M,D,O |
| College for Creative Studies | M |
| Lawrence Technological University | M,D |
| Minnesota State University Mankato | M |
| University of Michigan | M,D |
| University of Michigan–Dearborn | M |
| The University of Tennessee at Chattanooga | M |
| University of Wisconsin–Madison | M,D |
| Wayne State University | M,O |

### AVIATION

| | |
|---|---|
| Embry-Riddle Aeronautical University–Daytona | M |
| Embry-Riddle Aeronautical University–Prescott | M |
| Everglades University | M |
| Florida Institute of Technology | M,D |
| National Test Pilot School | M |
| Oklahoma State University | M,D,O |
| Southeastern Oklahoma State University | M |
| University of North Dakota | M |
| The University of Tennessee | M |

### AVIATION MANAGEMENT

| | |
|---|---|
| Arizona State University at Tempe | M |
| Delta State University | M |
| Embry-Riddle Aeronautical University–Worldwide | M |
| Florida Institute of Technology | M |
| Middle Tennessee State University | M |
| Midwest University | M,D |
| National American University (TX) | M,D |
| Purdue University | M |
| Southeastern Oklahoma State University | M |
| Vaughn College of Aeronautics and Technology | M |

### BACTERIOLOGY

| | |
|---|---|
| Illinois State University | M,D |
| The University of Iowa | M,D |
| University of Prince Edward Island | M,D |
| University of Wisconsin–Madison | M |

### BIOCHEMICAL ENGINEERING

| | |
|---|---|
| Brown University | M,D |
| Cornell University | M,D |
| Drexel University | M |
| Lehigh University | M,D |
| Rutgers University - New Brunswick | M,D |
| University of California, Irvine | M,D |
| University of Connecticut | M,D |
| University of Georgia | M |
| The University of Iowa | M,D |
| The University of Manchester | M,D |
| University of Maryland, Baltimore County | M,D,O |
| The University of Western Ontario | M,D |
| Villanova University | M,O |

### BIOCHEMISTRY

| | |
|---|---|
| Albert Einstein College of Medicine | D |
| Arizona State University at Tempe | M,D |
| Auburn University | M,D |
| Augusta University | D |
| Baylor College of Medicine | D |
| Baylor University | M,D |
| Boston College | M,D |
| Boston University | M,D |
| Bradley University | M |
| Brandeis University | M,D |
| Brigham Young University | M,D |
| Brown University | M,D |
| California Institute of Technology | M,D |
| California Polytechnic State University, San Luis Obispo | M |
| California State University, East Bay | M |
| California State University, Long Beach | M |
| California State University, Los Angeles | M |
| California State University, Northridge | M |
| California State University, Sacramento | M |
| Carnegie Mellon University | M,D |
| Case Western Reserve University | M,D |
| City College of the City University of New York | M,D |
| Clark University | D |
| Colorado State University | M,D |
| Colorado State University-Pueblo | M |
| Columbia University | M,D |
| Cornell University | M,D |
| Dalhousie University | M,D |
| Dartmouth College | M,D |
| Drexel University | M,D |
| Duke University | D |
| East Carolina University | M,D |
| Eastern New Mexico University | M |
| East Tennessee State University | D |
| Emory University | D |
| Florida Institute of Technology | M |
| Florida State University | M,D |
| George Mason University | M,D |
| Georgetown University | M,D |
| The George Washington University | D |
| Georgia State University | M,D |
| The Graduate Center, City University of New York | D |
| Harvard University | D* |
| Howard University | M,D |
| Hunter College of the City University of New York | M,D |
| Illinois Institute of Technology | M,D |
| Illinois State University | M,D |
| Indiana University Bloomington | M,D |
| Indiana University-Purdue University Indianapolis | M,D |
| Irell & Manella Graduate School of Biological Sciences | D |
| Johns Hopkins University | M,D |
| Kansas State University | M,D |
| Kennesaw State University | M |
| Laurentian University | M |
| Lehigh University | M,D |
| Loma Linda University | M,D |
| Louisiana State University and Agricultural & Mechanical College | M,D |
| Louisiana State University Health Sciences Center at Shreveport | M,D |
| Loyola University Chicago | M,D |
| Massachusetts Institute of Technology | D |
| Mayo Clinic Graduate School of Biomedical Sciences | M,D |
| McGill University | M,D |
| McMaster University | M,D |
| Medical College of Wisconsin | D |
| Medical University of South Carolina | M,D |
| Meharry Medical College | D |
| Memorial University of Newfoundland | M,D |
| Miami University | M,D |
| Michigan State University | M,D |
| Michigan Technological University | M,D,O |
| Mississippi College | M |
| Mississippi State University | M,D |
| Montana State University | M,D |
| Montclair State University | M |
| Mount Allison University | M |
| New York Medical College | M,D |
| North Carolina State University | D |
| North Dakota State University | M,D |
| Northern Illinois University | M,D |
| Northwestern University | D |
| The Ohio State University | M,D |
| Ohio University | M,D |
| Oklahoma State University | M,D |
| Old Dominion University | M,D |
| Oregon Health & Science University | M,D |
| Oregon State University | M,D |
| Pace University | M |
| Penn State Hershey Medical Center | M,D |
| Penn State University Park | M,D* |
| Purdue University | M,D |
| Rensselaer Polytechnic Institute | M,D |
| Rice University | M,D |
| Rosalind Franklin University of Medicine and Science | D |
| Rush University | M,D |
| Rutgers University - Newark | M,D |
| Rutgers University - New Brunswick | M,D |
| Saint Louis University | D |
| San Diego State University | M,D |
| San Francisco State University | M |
| Seton Hall University | M,D |
| Simon Fraser University | M,D,O |
| Sonoma State University | M |
| South Dakota State University | M,D |
| Southern Illinois University Carbondale | M,D |
| Southern University and Agricultural and Mechanical College | M |
| Stanford University | D |
| State University of New York College of Environmental Science and Forestry | M,D |
| State University of New York Upstate Medical University | M,D |
| Stevens Institute of Technology | M,D,O |
| Stony Brook University, State University of New York | M,D |
| Texas A&M University | M,D |
| Texas Christian University | M,D |
| Texas State University | M |
| Thomas Jefferson University | D |
| Tufts University | D |
| Tulane University | M |
| Universidad Central del Caribe | M,D |
| Université de Moncton | M |
| Université de Montréal | M,D,O |
| Université de Sherbrooke | M,D |
| University at Buffalo, the State University of New York | M,D |
| The University of Alabama at Birmingham | D |
| University of Alaska Fairbanks | M,D |
| University of Alberta | M,D |
| The University of Arizona | M,D |
| University of Arkansas for Medical Sciences | M,D,O |
| The University of British Columbia | M,D |
| University of Calgary | M,D |
| University of California, Berkeley | D |
| University of California, Davis | M,D |
| University of California, Irvine | M,D |
| University of California, Los Angeles | M,D |
| University of California, Merced | M,D |
| University of California, Riverside | M,D |
| University of California, San Diego | M,D |
| University of California, San Francisco | D |
| University of California, Santa Barbara | D |
| University of California, Santa Cruz | M,D |
| University of Cincinnati | M,D |
| University of Colorado Boulder | M,D |
| University of Colorado Denver | D |
| University of Connecticut Health Center | D |
| University of Dayton | M |
| University of Delaware | M,D |
| University of Florida | D |
| University of Georgia | M,D |
| University of Guelph | M,D |
| University of Houston | M,D |
| University of Idaho | M,D |
| University of Illinois at Chicago | D |
| University of Illinois at Urbana-Champaign | M,D |
| The University of Iowa | M,D |
| The University of Kansas | D |
| University of Kentucky | D |
| University of Lethbridge | M,D |
| University of Louisville | M,D |
| The University of Manchester | M,D |
| University of Manitoba | M,D |
| University of Maryland, Baltimore | M,D |
| University of Maryland, College Park | M,D |
| University of Massachusetts Amherst | M,D |
| University of Massachusetts Dartmouth | M,D |
| University of Massachusetts Lowell | M,D |
| University of Massachusetts Medical School | M,D |
| University of Miami | D |
| University of Michigan | M,D |
| University of Minnesota, Duluth | M,D |
| University of Minnesota, Twin Cities Campus | D |
| University of Mississippi Medical Center | D |
| University of Missouri | M,D |
| University of Missouri–Kansas City | D |
| University of Missouri–St. Louis | M,D |
| University of Montana | D |
| University of Nebraska–Lincoln | M,D |
| University of Nebraska Medical Center | M |
| University of Nevada, Las Vegas | M,D |
| University of Nevada, Reno | M,D |
| University of New Hampshire | M,D |
| University of New Mexico | M,D |
| The University of North Carolina at Chapel Hill | M,D |
| The University of North Carolina at Greensboro | M |
| University of North Texas | M,D,O |
| University of North Texas Health Science Center at Fort Worth | M,D |
| University of Notre Dame | M,D |
| University of Oklahoma | M,D |
| University of Oklahoma Health Sciences Center | M,D |
| University of Oregon | M,D |

| | |
|---|---|
| University of Ottawa | M,D |
| University of Pennsylvania | D |
| University of Puerto Rico - Medical Sciences Campus | M,D |
| University of Regina | M,D |
| University of Rhode Island | M,D |
| University of Rochester | D |
| University of Saint Joseph | M |
| University of Saskatchewan | M,D |
| The University of Scranton | M |
| University of South Carolina | M,D |
| University of Southern California | M |
| The University of Tennessee | M,D |
| The University of Texas at Austin | D |
| The University of Texas at Dallas | M,D |
| The University of Texas at El Paso | M,D |
| The University of Texas Health Science Center at Houston | M,D |
| The University of Texas Health Science Center at San Antonio | M,D |
| The University of Texas Medical Branch | D |
| The University of Texas Southwestern Medical Center | D |
| University of the Sciences | M,D |
| The University of Toledo | M,D |
| University of Toronto | M,D |
| University of Utah | M,D |
| University of Vermont | M,D |
| University of Victoria | M,D |
| University of Virginia | D |
| University of Washington | D |
| University of Waterloo | M,D |
| The University of Western Ontario | M,D |
| University of Windsor | M,D |
| University of Wisconsin–Madison | M,D |
| University of Wisconsin–Milwaukee | M,D* |
| Université Laval | M,D,O |
| Utah State University | M,D |
| Vanderbilt University | M,D* |
| Virginia Commonwealth University | M,D |
| Virginia Polytechnic Institute and State University | M,D |
| Wake Forest University | D |
| Washington State University | M,D |
| Washington University in St. Louis | D |
| Weill Cornell Medicine | M,D |
| Wesleyan University | D |
| West Virginia University | M,D |
| Worcester Polytechnic Institute | M,D |
| Wright State University | M |
| Yale University | D |
| Youngstown State University | M |

### BIOENGINEERING

| | |
|---|---|
| Alfred University | M,D |
| Baylor College of Medicine | D |
| California Institute of Technology | M,D |
| Carnegie Mellon University | M,D |
| Clemson University | M,D,O |
| Colorado School of Mines | M,D |
| Colorado State University | M,D |
| Cornell University | M,D |
| Dalhousie University | M,D |
| Florida Atlantic University | M,D |
| George Mason University | D |
| Harvard University | M,D* |
| Illinois Institute of Technology | M,D |
| Johns Hopkins University | M,D |
| Kansas State University | M,D |
| Lehigh University | M,D |
| Louisiana State University and Agricultural & Mechanical College | M,D |
| Massachusetts Institute of Technology | M,D |
| McGill University | M,D |
| Mississippi State University | M,D |
| North Carolina Agricultural and Technical State University | M |
| North Carolina State University | M,D,O |
| Northeastern University | M,D,O |
| Northern Arizona University | M,D |
| Northwestern University | D |
| The Ohio State University | M,D |
| Oklahoma State University | M,D |
| Oregon State University | M,D |
| Penn State University Park | M,D* |
| Princeton University | M,D |
| Rice University | M,D |
| Santa Clara University | M,D,O |
| South Dakota School of Mines and Technology | D |
| Stanford University | M,D |
| Syracuse University | M,D |
| Temple University | M,D* |
| Texas A&M University | M,D |
| Tufts University | M,D,O |
| University at Buffalo, the State University of New York | M,D,O |
| University of Arkansas | M |
| The University of British Columbia | M,D |
| University of California, Berkeley | M,D |
| University of California, Davis | M,D |
| University of California, Los Angeles | M,D |
| University of California, Merced | M,D |
| University of California, Riverside | M,D |
| University of California, San Diego | M,D |
| University of California, San Francisco | D |
| University of California, Santa Barbara | M,D |
| University of Chicago | D |
| University of Colorado Denver | M,D |
| University of Dayton | M |
| University of Denver | M,D |
| University of Florida | M,D,O |
| University of Guelph | M,D |
| University of Hawaii at Manoa | M |
| University of Idaho | M,D |
| University of Illinois at Chicago | M,D |
| University of Illinois at Urbana-Champaign | M,D |
| The University of Kansas | M,D |
| University of Louisville | M,D |
| University of Maryland, College Park | M,D |
| University of Michigan–Dearborn | M |
| University of Missouri | M,D |
| University of Nebraska–Lincoln | M,D |
| University of Notre Dame | M,D |
| University of Ottawa | M,D |
| University of Pennsylvania | M,D |
| University of Pittsburgh | M,D* |
| University of Puerto Rico at Mayagüez | M,D |
| University of Saskatchewan | M,D |
| The University of Texas at Arlington | M,D |
| The University of Toledo | M,D |
| University of Utah | M,D |
| University of Vermont | D |
| University of Washington | M,D |
| Utah State University | M,D |
| Virginia Polytechnic Institute and State University | M,D |
| Washington State University | M,D |

### BIOETHICS

| | |
|---|---|
| Albany Medical College | M,D,O |
| Case Western Reserve University | M |
| Clarkson University | M,O |
| Cleveland State University | M,O |
| Columbia University | M |
| Creighton University | M |
| Duke University | M |
| Duquesne University | M,D,O |
| Emory University | M |
| Hofstra University | M,D,O |
| Icahn School of Medicine at Mount Sinai | M |
| Indiana University-Purdue University Indianapolis | M,D,O |
| Instituto Tecnologico de Santo Domingo | M,O |
| Johns Hopkins University | M,D |
| Kansas City University of Medicine and Biosciences | M |
| Loma Linda University | M,O |
| Loyola Marymount University | M |
| Loyola University Chicago | M,D,O |
| McGill University | M,D,O |
| Medical College of Wisconsin | M,O |
| Northeast Ohio Medical University | M,D,O |
| Saint Louis University | D,O |
| Stony Brook University, State University of New York | M |
| Trinity International University | M,D |
| Université de Montréal | M,D,O |
| University of Louisville | M,D |
| University of Mary | M |
| University of Pennsylvania | M |
| University of Pittsburgh | M* |
| University of South Dakota | D,O |
| University of South Florida | O |
| The University of Tennessee | M,D |
| University of Toronto | M,D |
| University of Washington | M |
| Washington State University | M,D,O |
| Washington University in St. Louis | M |

### BIOINFORMATICS

| | |
|---|---|
| Arizona State University at Tempe | M,D |
| Boston University | M,D |
| Brandeis University | M |
| California State University, Dominguez Hills | M |
| Clemson University | M,D,O |
| Dalhousie University | M,D |
| Duke University | D,O |
| Emory University | M,D |
| George Mason University | M,D,O |
| Georgetown University | M,O |
| Georgia State University | M,D |
| Grand Valley State University | M |
| Hood College | M,O |
| Hunter College of the City University of New York | M |
| Indiana University Bloomington | M,D,O |
| Indiana University-Purdue University Indianapolis | M,D |
| Iowa State University of Science and Technology | M,D |
| Johns Hopkins University | M |
| Lawrence Technological University | M,O |
| Lewis University | M |
| Loyola University Chicago | M |
| Marquette University | M,D |
| Massachusetts Institute of Technology | M,D |
| McGill University | M,D |
| Morgan State University | M |
| New Mexico State University | M,D |
| New York University | M |
| North Dakota State University | M,D |
| Northeastern University | M,D |
| Nova Southeastern University | M,D,O |
| Oregon Health & Science University | M,D,O |
| Oregon State University | D |
| Penn State Hershey Medical Center | M,D |
| Rice University | M,D |
| Rochester Institute of Technology | M |
| Rowan University | M |
| Rutgers University - Newark | M,D |
| Saint Louis University | M |
| Simon Fraser University | M,D,O |
| State University of New York at Oswego | M |
| Stony Brook University, State University of New York | M,D,O |
| Tufts University | M,D |
| Université de Montréal | M,D |
| University at Buffalo, the State University of New York | M,D |
| The University of Alabama at Birmingham | D |
| University of Arkansas at Little Rock | M,D |
| University of Arkansas for Medical Sciences | M,D,O |
| The University of British Columbia | M,D |
| University of California, Los Angeles | M,D |
| University of California, Riverside | D |
| University of California, San Diego | D |
| University of California, San Francisco | D |
| University of California, Santa Cruz | M,D |
| University of Chicago | M |
| University of Cincinnati | D,O |
| University of Colorado Denver | D |
| University of Georgia | M,D |
| University of Idaho | M,D |
| University of Illinois at Chicago | M,D |
| University of Illinois at Urbana-Champaign | M,D,O |
| The University of Iowa | M,D,O |
| University of Louisville | M,D |
| University of Maine | M,D |
| The University of Manchester | M,D |
| University of Maryland, College Park | D |
| University of Massachusetts Medical School | M,D |
| University of Memphis | M,D |
| University of Michigan | M,D |
| University of Minnesota Rochester | M,D |
| University of Missouri | M |
| University of Missouri–Kansas City | M,D,O |
| University of Nebraska at Omaha | M,D |
| University of Nebraska–Lincoln | M,D |
| University of Nebraska Medical Center | M,D |
| The University of North Carolina at Chapel Hill | D |
| The University of North Carolina at Charlotte | D |
| University of Pittsburgh | M,D,O* |
| University of Rochester | M,D |
| University of Southern California | D |
| University of South Florida | M,D,O |
| The University of Tennessee at Chattanooga | M,O |
| The University of Texas at El Paso | M,D |
| The University of Texas Health Science Center at Houston | M,D,O |
| The University of Texas Medical Branch | D |
| University of the Sciences | M |
| The University of Toledo | M,O |
| University of Utah | M,D,O |
| University of Washington | M,D |
| University of Wisconsin–Madison | M,D |
| Vanderbilt University | M,D* |
| Virginia Polytechnic Institute and State University | M,D |
| Wayne State University | M,D |
| Wesleyan University | D |
| Worcester Polytechnic Institute | M,D |
| Yale University | D |

### BIOLOGICAL AND BIOMEDICAL SCIENCES—GENERAL

| | |
|---|---|
| Acadia University | M |
| Adelphi University | M |
| Alabama Agricultural and Mechanical University | M,D |
| Alabama State University | M,D |
| Albert Einstein College of Medicine | D |
| Alcorn State University | M |
| American Museum of Natural History–Richard Gilder Graduate School | D |
| American University | M |
| Andrews University | M |
| Angelo State University | M |
| Appalachian State University | M |
| Arizona State University at Tempe | M,D |
| Arkansas Colleges of Health Education | M |
| Arkansas State University | M,O |
| A.T. Still University | M,D |
| Auburn University | M,D |
| Austin Peay State University | M |
| Ball State University | M,D |
| Barry University | M |
| Baylor College of Medicine | M,D |
| Baylor University | M,D |
| Bemidji State University | M |
| Binghamton University, State University of New York | M,D |
| Bloomsburg University of Pennsylvania | M |
| Boise State University | M,D |
| Boston College | D |
| Boston University | M,D |
| Bowling Green State University | M,D |
| Bradley University | M |
| Brandeis University | M,D |
| Brigham Young University | M,D |
| Brock University | M,D |
| Brooklyn College of the City University of New York | M |
| Brown University | M,D |
| Bucknell University | M |
| Buffalo State College, State University of New York | M |
| Cabrini University | M,D |
| California Institute of Technology | D |
| California Polytechnic State University, San Luis Obispo | M |
| California State Polytechnic University, Pomona | M |
| California State University, Chico | M |
| California State University, Dominguez Hills | M |
| California State University, East Bay | M |
| California State University, Fresno | M |
| California State University, Fullerton | M |
| California State University, Long Beach | M |
| California State University, Los Angeles | M |
| California State University, Northridge | M |
| California State University, Sacramento | M |
| California State University, San Bernardino | M |
| California State University, San Marcos | M |
| Carleton University | M,D |
| Carnegie Mellon University | M,D |
| Case Western Reserve University | M,D |
| The Catholic University of America | M,D |
| Cedars-Sinai Medical Center | M,D |
| Central Connecticut State University | M,D |
| Central Michigan University | M |
| Central Washington University | M |
| Chatham University | M |
| Chicago State University | M |
| The Citadel, The Military College of South Carolina | M,O |
| City College of the City University of New York | M,D |
| Clark Atlanta University | M,D |
| Clarkson University | M |
| Clark University | M,D |
| Clayton State University | M |
| Clemson University | M,D |
| Cleveland State University | M,D |
| Cold Spring Harbor Laboratory | D |
| College of Staten Island of the City University of New York | M |
| Colorado State University | M,D |
| Colorado State University-Pueblo | M |
| Columbia University | M,D,O |
| Columbus State University | M |
| Concordia University (Canada) | M,D,O |
| Cornell University | D |
| Creighton University | M,D |
| Dalhousie University | M,D |
| Dartmouth College | D |
| Delaware State University | M |
| Delta State University | M |
| DePaul University | M,D |
| Des Moines University | M |
| Dominican University of California | M |
| Drew University | M,D,O |
| Drexel University | M,D,O |
| Duke University | D |
| Duquesne University | D |
| East Carolina University | M,D |
| Eastern Illinois University | M |
| Eastern Kentucky University | M |
| Eastern Mennonite University | M |
| Eastern Michigan University | M |
| Eastern New Mexico University | M |
| Eastern Virginia Medical School | M,D |
| Eastern Washington University | M |
| East Stroudsburg University of Pennsylvania | M |
| East Tennessee State University | M,D |
| Elizabeth City State University | M |
| Elms College | M |
| Emory University | D |
| Emporia State University | M |
| Fairleigh Dickinson University, Florham Campus | M |
| Fairleigh Dickinson University, Metropolitan Campus | M |
| Fisk University | M |
| Fitchburg State University | M |
| Florida Atlantic University | M,D |
| Florida Institute of Technology | M,D |
| Florida International University | M,D |
| Florida State University | M,D |
| Fordham University | M,D,O |
| Fort Hays State University | M |
| Frostburg State University | M |
| Geisinger Commonwealth School of Medicine | M |
| George Mason University | M,D,O |
| Georgetown University | D |
| The George Washington University | M,D |
| Georgia College & State University | M |
| Georgia Institute of Technology | M,D |
| Georgia Southern University | M |
| Georgia State University | M,D |
| Gerstner Sloan Kettering Graduate School of Biomedical Sciences | D |
| Goucher College | O |
| The Graduate Center, City University of New York | D |
| Grand Valley State University | M |
| Hampton University | M |
| Harvard University | M,D,O* |
| Hofstra University | M |

*M—masters degree; D—doctorate; O—other advanced degree; *—Close-Up and/or Display*

| | |
|---|---|
| Hood College | M |
| Howard University | M,D |
| Humboldt State University | M |
| Hunter College of the City University of New York | M,D |
| Icahn School of Medicine at Mount Sinai | M,D |
| Idaho State University | M,D |
| Illinois Institute of Technology | M,D |
| Illinois State University | M,D |
| Indiana State University | M,D |
| Indiana University Bloomington | M,D |
| Indiana University of Pennsylvania | M |
| Indiana University-Purdue University Indianapolis | M,D |
| Inter American University of Puerto Rico, Barranquitas Campus | M |
| Iowa State University of Science and Technology | M,D |
| Irell & Manella Graduate School of Biological Sciences | D |
| Jackson State University | M |
| Jacksonville State University | M |
| James Madison University | M |
| John Carroll University | M |
| Johns Hopkins University | M,D |
| Kansas City University of Medicine and Biosciences | M |
| Kansas State University | M,D |
| Kennesaw State University | M |
| Kent State University | M,D |
| Kutztown University of Pennsylvania | M,D |
| Lake Erie College of Osteopathic Medicine | M,D,O |
| Lakehead University | M |
| Lamar University | M |
| Laurentian University | M,D |
| Lee University | M,O |
| Lehigh University | M,D |
| Lehman College of the City University of New York | M |
| Liberty University | M,D |
| London Metropolitan University | M,D |
| Long Island University - Brooklyn | M,D,O |
| Long Island University - Post | M,O |
| Louisiana State University and Agricultural & Mechanical College | M,D |
| Louisiana State University Health Sciences Center | D |
| Louisiana State University Health Sciences Center at Shreveport | M |
| Louisiana State University in Shreveport | M |
| Louisiana Tech University | M,D,O |
| Loyola University Chicago | M,D |
| Loyola University Chicago | M,D |
| Manhattanville College | M,O |
| Marquette University | M,D |
| Marshall University | M,D |
| Massachusetts Institute of Technology | M,D |
| McGill University | M,D |
| McMaster University | M,D |
| Medical College of Wisconsin | M,D,O |
| Medical University of South Carolina | M,D |
| Meharry Medical College | D |
| Memorial University of Newfoundland | M,D,O |
| Miami University | M,D |
| Michigan State University | M,D |
| Michigan Technological University | M,D |
| Middle Tennessee State University | M |
| Midwestern State University | M |
| Midwestern University, Downers Grove Campus | M |
| Midwestern University, Glendale Campus | M |
| Mills College | O |
| Minnesota State University Mankato | M |
| Mississippi College | M |
| Mississippi State University | M,D |
| Missouri State University | M |
| Missouri University of Science and Technology | M |
| Missouri Western State University | M |
| Montana State University | M,D |
| Montclair State University | M |
| Morehead State University | M |
| Morehouse School of Medicine | M,D |
| Morgan State University | M,D |
| Mount Allison University | M |
| Murray State University | M |
| National University | M,O |
| New Jersey Institute of Technology | M,D,O |
| New Mexico Institute of Mining and Technology | M,D |
| New Mexico State University | M,D |
| New York Medical College | M,D |
| New York University | M,D |
| North Carolina Agricultural and Technical State University | M |
| North Carolina Central University | M |
| North Carolina State University | M,D,O |
| North Dakota State University | M,D |
| Northeastern Illinois University | M |
| Northeastern University | M,D |
| Northern Arizona University | M,D |
| Northern Illinois University | M,D |
| Northern Michigan University | M |
| Northwestern University | D |
| Northwest Missouri State University | M,O |
| Nova Southeastern University | M,D |
| Oakland University | M,D,O |
| Occidental College | M |
| The Ohio State University | M,D |
| Ohio University | M,D |
| Oklahoma State University | M,D |
| Oklahoma State University Center for Health Sciences | M,D |
| Old Dominion University | M,D |
| Oregon Health & Science University | M,D,O |
| Oregon State University | M,D |
| Pace University | M,O |
| Penn State Hershey Medical Center | M,D |
| Penn State University Park | M,D* |
| Philadelphia College of Osteopathic Medicine | M |
| Pittsburg State University | M |
| Point Loma Nazarene University | M |
| Ponce Health Sciences University | D |
| Pontifical Catholic University of Puerto Rico | M |
| Portland State University | M,D |
| Purdue University | M,D |
| Purdue University Fort Wayne | M |
| Purdue University Northwest | M |
| Queens College of the City University of New York | M,O |
| Queen's University at Kingston | M,D |
| Quinnipiac University | M |
| Regis University | M |
| Rensselaer Polytechnic Institute | M,D |
| Rhode Island College | M,O |
| Rochester Institute of Technology | M |
| The Rockefeller University | M,D* |
| Rocky Vista University | M |
| Rosalind Franklin University of Medicine and Science | M,D |
| Rowan University | M |
| Rutgers University - Camden | M |
| Rutgers University - Newark | M,D,O |
| Rutgers University - New Brunswick | M,D |
| St. Cloud State University | M |
| Saint Francis University | M |
| St. Francis Xavier University | M |
| St. John Fisher College | M |
| St. John's University (NY) | M,D |
| Saint Joseph's University | M |
| Saint Louis University | M,D |
| Salisbury University | M |
| Sam Houston State University | M |
| San Diego State University | M,D |
| Sanford Burnham Prebys Medical Discovery Institute | D |
| San Francisco State University | M |
| San Jose State University | M |
| The Scripps Research Institute | D |
| Seton Hall University | M,D |
| Shippensburg University of Pennsylvania | M |
| Simon Fraser University | M,D,O |
| Smith College | M |
| Sonoma State University | M |
| South Carolina State University | M |
| South Dakota State University | M,D |
| Southeastern Louisiana University | M |
| Southeast Missouri State University | M |
| Southern Connecticut State University | M |
| Southern Illinois University Carbondale | M,D |
| Southern Illinois University Edwardsville | M |
| Southern Methodist University | M,D |
| Southern University and Agricultural and Mechanical College | M |
| Stanford University | M,D |
| State University of New York at Fredonia | M,O |
| State University of New York College at Oneonta | M |
| State University of New York Downstate Medical Center | M,D |
| State University of New York Upstate Medical University | M,D |
| Stephen F. Austin State University | M |
| Stevenson University | M |
| Stony Brook University, State University of New York | M,D,O |
| Sul Ross State University | M |
| SUNY Brockport | M,O |
| Syracuse University | M,D |
| Tarleton State University | M |
| Teachers College, Columbia University | M,D |
| Temple University | M,D* |
| Tennessee State University | D |
| Tennessee Technological University | M,D |
| Texas A&M International University | M |
| Texas A&M University | M,D |
| Texas A&M University–Commerce | M,O |
| Texas A&M University–Corpus Christi | M,D |
| Texas A&M University–Kingsville | M |
| Texas Christian University | M,D |
| Texas Southern University | M |
| Texas State University | M |
| Texas Tech University | M,D |
| Texas Tech University Health Sciences Center | M,D |
| Texas Tech University Health Sciences Center El Paso | M |
| Texas Woman's University | M,D |
| Thomas Jefferson University | M,D,O |
| Towson University | M |
| Trent University | M,D |
| Troy University | M,O |
| Truett McConnell University | M |
| Tufts University | M,D,O |
| Tulane University | M,D |
| Tuskegee University | M,D |
| UNB Fredericton | M,D |
| Uniformed Services University of the Health Sciences | M,D |
| Universidad Central del Caribe | M,D |
| Universidad de Ciencias Medicas | M,D,O |
| Université de Moncton | M |
| Université de Montréal | M,D |
| Université de Sherbrooke | M,D,O |
| Université du Québec à Montréal | M,D |
| Université du Québec en Abitibi-Témiscamingue | M,D |
| Université du Québec, Institut National de la Recherche Scientifique | M,D |
| University at Albany, State University of New York | M,D |
| University at Buffalo, the State University of New York | M,D |
| The University of Akron | M,D |
| The University of Alabama | M,D |
| The University of Alabama at Birmingham | M,D |
| The University of Alabama in Huntsville | M,D |
| University of Alaska Anchorage | M |
| University of Alaska Fairbanks | M,D,O |
| University of Alberta | M,D |
| The University of Arizona | M,D |
| University of Arkansas | M,D |
| University of Arkansas at Little Rock | M |
| University of Arkansas for Medical Sciences | M,D,O |
| University of Calgary | M,D |
| University of California, Berkeley | D |
| University of California, Irvine | M,D |
| University of California, Los Angeles | M,D |
| University of California, Merced | M,D |
| University of California, Riverside | M,D |
| University of California, San Diego | M,D |
| University of California, San Francisco | D |
| University of Central Arkansas | M |
| University of Central Florida | M,D,O |
| University of Central Missouri | M,D,O |
| University of Central Oklahoma | M |
| University of Chicago | D |
| University of Cincinnati | M,D,O |
| University of Colorado Denver | M,D |
| University of Connecticut Health Center | D |
| University of Dayton | M,D |
| University of Delaware | M,D |
| University of Denver | M,D |
| University of Florida | M,D |
| University of Georgia | D |
| University of Guam | M |
| University of Guelph | M,D |
| University of Hawaii at Manoa | M,D |
| University of Holy Cross | M,D |
| University of Houston | M,D |
| University of Houston–Clear Lake | M |
| University of Houston–Victoria | M |
| University of Idaho | M,D |
| University of Illinois at Chicago | M,D |
| University of Illinois at Springfield | M |
| University of Illinois at Urbana-Champaign | M,D |
| University of Indianapolis | M |
| The University of Iowa | M,D |
| The University of Kansas | D |
| University of Kentucky | M,D |
| University of Lethbridge | M,D |
| University of Louisiana at Lafayette | M,D |
| University of Louisiana at Monroe | M |
| University of Louisville | M,D |
| University of Maine | M,D |
| The University of Manchester | M,D |
| University of Manitoba | M,D,O |
| University of Maryland, Baltimore | M,D,O |
| University of Maryland, Baltimore County | M,D |
| University of Maryland, College Park | M,D |
| University of Massachusetts Amherst | M,D |
| University of Massachusetts Boston | M,D |
| University of Massachusetts Dartmouth | M,D |
| University of Massachusetts Lowell | M |
| University of Massachusetts Medical School | M,D |
| University of Memphis | M,D |
| University of Miami | M,D |
| University of Michigan | M,D |
| University of Michigan–Flint | M |
| University of Minnesota, Duluth | M,D |
| University of Minnesota, Twin Cities Campus | M |
| University of Mississippi | M,D |
| University of Mississippi Medical Center | M,D |
| University of Missouri | M,D,O |
| University of Missouri–Kansas City | M,D |
| University of Missouri–St. Louis | M,D,O |
| University of Montana | M,D |
| University of Nebraska at Kearney | M |
| University of Nebraska at Omaha | M,O |
| University of Nebraska–Lincoln | M,D |
| University of Nebraska Medical Center | M,D |
| University of Nevada, Las Vegas | M,D |
| University of Nevada, Reno | M |
| University of New Brunswick Saint John | M,D |
| University of New England | M |
| University of New Hampshire | M,D |
| University of New Mexico | M,D |
| University of New Orleans | M |
| The University of North Carolina at Chapel Hill | M,D |
| The University of North Carolina at Charlotte | M,D |
| The University of North Carolina at Greensboro | M |
| The University of North Carolina Wilmington | M,D |
| University of North Dakota | M,D |
| University of Northern Colorado | M |
| University of Northern Iowa | M |
| University of North Florida | M |
| University of North Texas | M,D,O |
| University of North Texas Health Science Center at Fort Worth | M,D |
| University of Notre Dame | M,D |
| University of Oklahoma Health Sciences Center | M,D |
| University of Oregon | M,D |
| University of Ottawa | M,D |
| University of Pennsylvania | M,D |
| University of Pittsburgh | M,D* |
| University of Prince Edward Island | M,D |
| University of Puerto Rico at Mayagüez | M |
| University of Puerto Rico at Rio Piedras | M,D |
| University of Puerto Rico - Medical Sciences Campus | M,D |
| University of Regina | M,D |
| University of Rhode Island | M,D |
| University of Rochester | M,D |
| University of Saint Joseph | M |
| University of San Francisco | M |
| University of Saskatchewan | M,D |
| University of South Alabama | M,D |
| University of South Carolina | M,D,O |
| University of South Dakota | M,D |
| University of Southern California | M,D,O |
| University of Southern Maine | M |
| University of South Florida | M,D |
| The University of Tennessee | M,D |
| The University of Tennessee Health Science Center | M,D |
| The University of Tennessee–Oak Ridge National Laboratory | M,D |
| The University of Texas at Arlington | M,D |
| The University of Texas at Austin | M,D |
| The University of Texas at Dallas | M,D |
| The University of Texas at El Paso | M,D |
| The University of Texas at San Antonio | M,D |
| The University of Texas at Tyler | M |
| The University of Texas Health Science Center at Houston | M,D |
| The University of Texas Health Science Center at San Antonio | D |
| The University of Texas Medical Branch | M,D |
| The University of Texas of the Permian Basin | M |
| The University of Texas Rio Grande Valley | M |
| The University of Texas Southwestern Medical Center | M,D |
| University of the Incarnate Word | M |
| University of the Pacific | M |
| The University of Toledo | M,D,O |
| The University of Tulsa | M,D |
| University of Utah | M,D,O |
| University of Vermont | M,D |
| University of Victoria | M,D |
| University of Virginia | M,D |
| University of Washington | M,D |
| University of Waterloo | M,D |
| The University of Western Ontario | M,D |
| University of West Florida | M |
| University of Windsor | M,D |
| University of Wisconsin–La Crosse | M |
| University of Wisconsin–Madison | |
| University of Wisconsin–Milwaukee | M,D* |
| University of Wisconsin–Oshkosh | M |
| Université Laval | M,D,O |
| Utah State University | M,D |
| Vanderbilt University | M,D* |
| Villanova University | M |
| Virginia Commonwealth University | M,D,O |
| Virginia Polytechnic Institute and State University | M,D |
| Virginia State University | M |
| Wake Forest University | M,D |
| Walla Walla University | M |
| Washington State University | M,D |
| Washington University in St. Louis | D |
| Wayne State University | M,D |
| Weill Cornell Medicine | M,D |
| Wesleyan University | D |
| Western Carolina University | M |
| Western Illinois University | M,O |
| Western Kentucky University | M |
| Western Michigan University | M,D,O |
| Western University of Health Sciences | M |
| Western Washington University | M |
| West Liberty University | M |
| West Texas A&M University | M |
| West Virginia University | M,D |
| Wichita State University | M |
| Wilfrid Laurier University | M |
| Winthrop University | M |
| Worcester Polytechnic Institute | M,D |
| Wright State University | M,D |
| Yale University | D |
| York University | M,D |
| Youngstown State University | M |

**BIOLOGICAL ANTHROPOLOGY**

| | |
|---|---|
| Cornell University | D |
| Duke University | D |
| Harvard University | M,D* |
| Kent State University | M,D |
| Mercyhurst University | M |
| San Francisco State University | M |

University of Colorado Denver M
University of Michigan D
The University of Tennessee M,D
University of Wisconsin–Madison D

### BIOMATHEMATICS
Florida State University M,D
University of California, Los Angeles M,D

### BIOMEDICAL ENGINEERING
American University of Sharjah M,D
Arizona State University at Tempe M,D
Baylor College of Medicine D
Baylor University M,D
Binghamton University, State University of New York M,D
Boston University M,D
Brown University M,D
California Polytechnic State University, San Luis Obispo M
Carleton University M
Carnegie Mellon University M,D
Case Western Reserve University M,D
The Catholic University of America M,D
City College of the City University of New York M,D
Clemson University M,D,O
Cleveland State University D
Colorado State University M,D
Columbia University M,D
Cornell University M,D
Dalhousie University M,D
Dartmouth College M,D
Drexel University M,D
Duke University M,D
East Carolina University M
Florida Agricultural and Mechanical University M,D
Florida Institute of Technology M,D
Florida International University M,D
Florida State University M,D
The George Washington University M,D
Georgia Institute of Technology D
Harvard University D*
Illinois Institute of Technology M,D
Indiana University-Purdue University Indianapolis M,D
Johns Hopkins University M,D,O
Lawrence Technological University M,D
Louisiana Tech University M,D,O
Marquette University M,D
Massachusetts Institute of Technology M,D
Mayo Clinic Graduate School of Biomedical Sciences M,D
McGill University M,D
Mercer University M
Michigan Technological University M,D
Mississippi State University M,D
New Jersey Institute of Technology M,D
New York University M,D
Northwestern University M,D
The Ohio State University M,D
Ohio University M
Old Dominion University M,D
Oregon Health & Science University M,D
Polytechnique Montréal M,D,O
Purdue University M,D
Rensselaer Polytechnic Institute M,D
Rice University M,D
Rose-Hulman Institute of Technology M
Rutgers University - Newark O
Rutgers University - New Brunswick M,D
St. Cloud State University M,O
Saint Louis University M,D
South Dakota School of Mines and Technology M,D
Southern Illinois University Carbondale M
State University of New York Downstate Medical Center M,D
Stevens Institute of Technology M,D,O
Stony Brook University, State University of New York M,D,O
Tennessee State University M,D
Texas A&M University M,D
Tufts University M,D
Tulane University M,D
Université de Montréal M,D,O
University at Buffalo, the State University of New York M,D
The University of Akron M,D
The University of Alabama at Birmingham M,D
University of Alberta M,D
The University of Arizona M,D
University of Arkansas M
University of Bridgeport M
The University of British Columbia M,D
University of Calgary M,D
University of California, Davis M,D
University of California, Irvine M,D
University of California, Los Angeles M,D
University of Central Oklahoma M
University of Cincinnati M,D
University of Connecticut M,D
University of Florida M,D,O
University of Houston D
The University of Iowa M,D
University of Kentucky M,D
University of Maine M,D
University of Massachusetts Boston D
University of Massachusetts Dartmouth D
University of Memphis M,D
University of Miami M,D
University of Michigan M,D
University of Minnesota, Twin Cities Campus M,D
University of Nebraska–Lincoln M,D
University of Nevada, Las Vegas M,D,O
University of Nevada, Reno M,D
University of New Haven M
University of New Mexico M,D
University of North Texas M,D,O
University of Oklahoma M,D
University of Ottawa M
University of Portland M
University of Rhode Island M,D
University of Rochester M,D
University of Saskatchewan M,D,O
University of Southern California M,D
University of South Florida M,D,O
The University of Tennessee M,D
The University of Tennessee Health Science Center M,D
The University of Texas at Austin M,D
The University of Texas at Dallas M,D
The University of Texas at San Antonio M,D
The University of Texas Health Science Center at San Antonio M,D
The University of Texas Southwestern Medical Center M,D
The University of Toledo D
University of Toronto M,D
University of Vermont M
University of Virginia M,D
University of Wisconsin–Madison M,D
University of Wisconsin–Milwaukee M,D*
Vanderbilt University M,D*
Virginia Commonwealth University M,D
Virginia Polytechnic Institute and State University M,D
Wake Forest University M,D
Washington University in St. Louis M,D
Wayne State University M,D,O
Wichita State University M
Widener University M
Worcester Polytechnic Institute M,D,O
Wright State University M
Yale University M,D

### BIOMETRY
Cornell University M,D
San Diego State University M
University of Wisconsin–Madison M

### BIOPHYSICS
Albert Einstein College of Medicine D
Baylor College of Medicine D
Boston University M,D
Brandeis University M,D
California Institute of Technology D
Carnegie Mellon University M,D
Case Western Reserve University M,D
Columbia University M,D
Cornell University D
Dalhousie University M,D
East Carolina University M,D
Harvard University D*
Howard University D
Illinois State University M,D
Iowa State University of Science and Technology M,D
Johns Hopkins University D
Northwestern University D
The Ohio State University M,D
Oregon State University M,D
Purdue University D
Rensselaer Polytechnic Institute M,D
Rosalind Franklin University of Medicine and Science M,D
Stanford University D
Stony Brook University, State University of New York D
Texas Christian University M,D
Université de Sherbrooke M,D
Université du Québec à Trois-Rivières M,D
University at Buffalo, the State University of New York M,D
University of California, Berkeley D
University of California, Davis M,D
University of California, Irvine D
University of California, San Diego M,D
University of California, San Francisco D
University of California, Santa Barbara D
University of Chicago D
University of Cincinnati D
University of Colorado Denver M
University of Connecticut M,D
University of Guelph M,D
University of Illinois at Chicago M,D
University of Illinois at Urbana-Champaign M,D
The University of Iowa M,D
The University of Kansas D
The University of Manchester M,D
University of Maryland, College Park D
University of Miami D
University of Michigan D
University of Minnesota, Duluth M,D
University of Minnesota, Twin Cities Campus M,D
University of Mississippi Medical Center D
University of Missouri–Kansas City D
The University of North Carolina at Chapel Hill M,D
University of Regina M,D
University of Rochester D
University of Southern California M,D
The University of Texas Medical Branch D
University of Toronto M,D
University of Virginia M,D
University of Washington D
The University of Western Ontario M,D
University of Wisconsin–Madison D
Vanderbilt University M,D*
Washington State University M,D
Weill Cornell Medicine M,D
Yale University D

### BIOPSYCHOLOGY
American University M,D,O
Argosy University, Atlanta M,D,O
Argosy University, Twin Cities M,D,O
Binghamton University, State University of New York D
Boston University M
Carnegie Mellon University D
Cornell University D
Drexel University M,D
Duke University D
Florida State University M,D
The Graduate Center, City University of New York D
Harvard University D*
Howard University M,D
Liberty University M,D
Louisiana State University and Agricultural & Mechanical College M,D
Memorial University of Newfoundland M,D
Northwestern University D
Oregon Health & Science University D
Palo Alto University D
Penn State University Park M,D*
Philadelphia College of Osteopathic Medicine M,D,O
Rutgers University - Newark D
Rutgers University - New Brunswick D
The University of British Columbia M,D
University of Connecticut M,D
University of Michigan D
University of Minnesota, Twin Cities Campus D
University of Nebraska–Lincoln M,D
The University of North Carolina at Chapel Hill D
University of Oklahoma Health Sciences Center M,D
University of Oregon M,D
The University of Texas at Austin D
University of Windsor M,D
University of Wisconsin–Madison D

### BIOSTATISTICS
American University M,O
Boston University M,D
Brown University M,D
California State University, East Bay M
Case Western Reserve University M,D
Columbia University M,D
Dartmouth College M,D
Drexel University M,D,O
East Tennessee State University M,D,O
Emory University M,D
Florida International University M,D
Florida State University M,D
George Mason University M,D,O
Georgetown University M,O
The George Washington University M,D
Georgia Southern University M,D
Georgia State University M,D
Grand Valley State University M
Harvard University M,D*
Indiana University Bloomington M,D
Indiana University-Purdue University Indianapolis M,D,O
Iowa State University of Science and Technology M,D
Johns Hopkins University M,D
Kent State University M,D
Loma Linda University M,D
Louisiana State University Health Sciences Center M,D
McGill University M,D
Medical College of Wisconsin D
Medical University of South Carolina M,D
Middle Tennessee State University M
Monroe College M
New Jersey Institute of Technology M,D,O
New York Medical College M,D,O
Northwestern University D
The Ohio State University M,D
Old Dominion University M,D
Oregon State University M,D
Penn State Hershey Medical Center D
Rice University M,D
Rutgers University - New Brunswick M,D,O
San Diego State University M,D
Southern Methodist University M,D
Stanford University M,D
Texas A&M University M,D
Tufts University M,D,O
Tulane University M,D
University at Albany, State University of New York M,D
University at Buffalo, the State University of New York M,D
The University of Alabama at Birmingham M,D
University of Alberta M,D,O
The University of Arizona M,D
University of Arkansas for Medical Sciences M,D,O
University of California, Berkeley M,D
University of California, Davis M,D
University of California, Los Angeles M,D
University of California, San Diego D
University of Cincinnati M,D
University of Colorado Denver M,D
University of Florida M,D,O
University of Illinois at Chicago M,D
The University of Iowa M,D,O
The University of Kansas M,D,O
University of Kentucky D
University of Maryland, Baltimore M,D
University of Maryland, Baltimore County M,D
University of Maryland, College Park M,D
University of Massachusetts Amherst M,D
University of Memphis M,D
University of Miami M,D
University of Michigan M,D
University of Minnesota, Twin Cities Campus M,D
University of Nebraska Medical Center D
The University of North Carolina at Chapel Hill M,D
University of North Texas Health Science Center at Fort Worth M,D,O
University of Oklahoma Health Sciences Center M,D
University of Pennsylvania M,D
University of Pittsburgh M,D*
University of Puerto Rico - Medical Sciences Campus M
University of Rochester M
University of South Carolina M,D
University of Southern California M,D
University of Southern Mississippi M
University of South Florida O
The University of Texas Health Science Center at Houston M,D,O
The University of Toledo M,O
University of Toronto M,D
University of Utah M,D
University of Vermont M
University of Washington M,D
University of Waterloo M,D
The University of Western Ontario M,D
University of Wisconsin–Milwaukee M,D,O*
Virginia Commonwealth University M,D
Washington University in St. Louis M,D,O
Weill Cornell Medicine M
West Virginia University M,D
Yale University M,D

### BIOSYSTEMS ENGINEERING
Auburn University M,D
Clemson University M,D
Michigan State University M,D
North Dakota State University M,D
South Dakota State University M,D
The University of Arizona M,D
University of Manitoba M,D
University of Minnesota, Twin Cities Campus M,D
The University of Tennessee M,D

### BIOTECHNOLOGY
Adelphi University M
American University M
The American University in Cairo M,D,O
Arizona State University at Tempe M,D
Arkansas State University M,O
Azusa Pacific University M
Brandeis University M
Brigham Young University M,D
Brock University M,D
Brown University M,D
California State University, Fullerton M
California State University, San Marcos M
Carnegie Mellon University M
The Catholic University of America M,D
Claflin University M
Clarkson University M,D
College of Staten Island of the City University of New York M
Columbia University M,D
Concordia University (Canada) M,D,O
Cornell University M,D
Duquesne University M
East Carolina University M
Eastern Virginia Medical School M
Florida Institute of Technology M,D
The George Washington University M,D,O
Harvard University M,O*
Howard University M,D
Husson University M
Illinois State University M
Indiana University Bloomington M,D
Instituto Tecnológico y de Estudios Superiores de Monterrey, Campus Monterrey M,D
Inter American University of Puerto Rico, Barranquitas Campus M
Inter American University of Puerto Rico, Bayamón Campus M
Johns Hopkins University M
Kean University M
Marywood University M

*M—masters degree; D—doctorate; O—other advanced degree; *—Close-Up and/or Display*

| | |
|---|---|
| McGill University | M,D,O |
| Middle Tennessee State University | M |
| Mount St. Mary's University (MD) | M |
| New Mexico State University | M,D |
| New York University | M |
| Northeastern University | M,D |
| Northwestern University | M,D |
| Oregon State University | M,D |
| Penn State University Park | M,D* |
| Pontifical John Paul II Institute for Studies on Marriage and Family | M,D,O |
| Purdue University | D |
| Purdue University Northwest | M |
| Roosevelt University | M |
| St. John's University (NY) | M |
| San Francisco State University | M |
| Simon Fraser University | M,D,O |
| Southeastern Oklahoma State University | M |
| Stephen F. Austin State University | M |
| Temple University | M,D* |
| Tennessee State University | M,D |
| Texas Tech University | M,D |
| Texas Tech University Health Sciences Center | M |
| Thomas Jefferson University | M |
| Tufts University | M,D,O |
| Universidad de las Américas Puebla | M |
| University at Buffalo, the State University of New York | M |
| The University of Alabama at Birmingham | M |
| The University of Alabama in Huntsville | M,D |
| University of Alberta | M,D |
| University of Calgary | M |
| University of California, Irvine | M |
| University of Delaware | M,D |
| University of Guelph | M,D |
| University of Houston–Clear Lake | M |
| The University of Kansas | M |
| The University of Manchester | M,D |
| University of Maryland, Baltimore County | M,O |
| University of Maryland Global Campus | M,O |
| University of Massachusetts Amherst | M,D |
| University of Massachusetts Boston | M,D |
| University of Massachusetts Dartmouth | D |
| University of Minnesota, Twin Cities Campus | M |
| University of Missouri–St. Louis | M,D |
| University of Nevada, Reno | M |
| University of North Texas Health Science Center at Fort Worth | M,D |
| University of Pennsylvania | M |
| University of Rhode Island | M,D |
| University of San Francisco | M |
| University of Southern California | M |
| University of South Florida | O |
| The University of Texas at Dallas | M,D |
| The University of Texas at San Antonio | M,D |
| The University of Texas Health Science Center at Tyler | M |
| University of the Sciences | M |
| University of Toronto | M |
| University of Utah | M |
| University of Washington | D |
| University of Wyoming | D |
| Virginia Polytechnic Institute and State University | M,D |
| West Virginia State University | M |
| Worcester Polytechnic Institute | M,D |
| Worcester State University | M |
| Yeshiva University | M |

## BOTANY

| | |
|---|---|
| Auburn University | M,D |
| Central Washington University | M |
| Claremont Graduate University | M,D |
| Colorado State University | M,D |
| Dalhousie University | M |
| Emporia State University | M |
| Illinois State University | M,D |
| Kent State University | M,D |
| North Dakota State University | M,D |
| Oklahoma State University | M,D |
| Oregon State University | M,D |
| Purdue University | M,D |
| The University of British Columbia | M,D |
| University of California, Riverside | M,D |
| University of Connecticut | M,D |
| University of Florida | M,D |
| University of Guelph | M,D |
| University of Hawaii at Manoa | M,D |
| University of Maine | M,D |
| University of Manitoba | M,D |
| The University of North Carolina at Chapel Hill | M,D |
| University of Wisconsin–Madison | M,D |
| University of Wisconsin–Oshkosh | M |
| University of Wyoming | M,D |

## BROADCAST JOURNALISM

| | |
|---|---|
| American University | M |
| The American University in Cairo | M,O |
| Kent State University | M |
| Northwestern University | M |
| Quinnipiac University | M |
| Syracuse University | M |
| University of Maryland, College Park | M,D |
| University of Miami | M,D |
| University of the Sacred Heart | M,O |

## BUILDING SCIENCE

| | |
|---|---|
| Arizona State University at Tempe | M,D |
| Carnegie Mellon University | M,D |
| Georgia Institute of Technology | M,D |
| Pontificia Universidad Catolica Madre y Maestra | M |
| University of California, Berkeley | M,D |

## BUSINESS ADMINISTRATION AND MANAGEMENT—GENERAL

| | |
|---|---|
| Abilene Christian University | M |
| Adams State University | M |
| Adelphi University | M |
| Alabama Agricultural and Mechanical University | M |
| Alabama State University | M |
| Alaska Pacific University | M |
| Albany State University | M |
| Albertus Magnus College | M |
| Albizu University - Miami | M,D |
| Alcorn State University | M |
| Alfred University | M |
| Alliant International University - Los Angeles | D |
| Alliant International University - San Diego | M |
| Alvernia University | M |
| Alverno College | M |
| Amberton University | M |
| American Business & Technology University | M |
| American College Dublin | M |
| The American College of Financial Services | M |
| American College of Thessaloniki | M,O |
| American Graduate University | M,O |
| American InterContinental University Houston | M |
| American InterContinental University Online | M |
| American International College | M,D,O |
| American Jewish University | M |
| American National University - Roanoke Valley | M |
| American Public University System | M,D |
| American Sentinel University | M |
| American University | M,O |
| American University in Bulgaria | M |
| The American University in Cairo | M,O |
| The American University in Dubai | M |
| American University of Armenia | M |
| The American University of Paris | M |
| American University of Sharjah | M,D |
| Anaheim University | M,D,O |
| Anderson University (IN) | M,D |
| Anderson University (SC) | M |
| Angelo State University | M |
| Anna Maria College | M,O |
| Antioch University Los Angeles | M |
| Antioch University Santa Barbara | M |
| Apollos University | M,D |
| Appalachian State University | M |
| Aquinas College (MI) | M |
| Arcadia University | M |
| Argosy University, Atlanta | M,D |
| Argosy University, Chicago | M,D |
| Argosy University, Hawaii | M,D,O |
| Argosy University, Los Angeles | M,D |
| Argosy University, Northern Virginia | M,D,O |
| Argosy University, Orange County | M,D,O |
| Argosy University, Phoenix | M,D |
| Argosy University, Seattle | M,D |
| Argosy University, Tampa | M,D |
| Argosy University, Twin Cities | M,D |
| Arizona State University at Tempe | M,D |
| Arkansas State University | M |
| Arkansas Tech University | M |
| Ashland University | M |
| Ashworth College | M |
| Aspen University | M,O |
| Assumption University | M,O |
| Athabasca University | M,D,O |
| Atlantis University | M,D |
| Auburn University | M,D |
| Auburn University at Montgomery | M |
| Augsburg University | M |
| Augusta University | M |
| Aurora University | M |
| Austin Peay State University | M |
| Averett University | M |
| Avila University | M |
| Azusa Pacific University | M |
| Babson College | M,O |
| Baker College Center for Graduate Studies–Online | M,D |
| Baker University | M |
| Bakke Graduate University | M,D |
| Baldwin Wallace University | M |
| Ball State University | M,O |
| Barry University | M,O |
| Baruch College of the City University of New York | M,D,O |
| Bayamón Central University | M |
| Baylor University | M |
| Belhaven University (MS) | M |
| Bellarmine University | M |
| Bellevue University | M,D |
| Belmont University | M |
| Benedictine College | M |
| Benedictine University | M,D |
| Bentley University | M,D,O |
| Berkeley College–Woodland Park Campus | M |
| Berry College | M |
| Bethel University (IN) | M |
| Bethel University (MN) | M,D,O |
| Bethel University (TN) | M |
| Binghamton University, State University of New York | M,D |
| Biola University | M |
| Black Hills State University | M |
| Bloomsburg University of Pennsylvania | M,O |
| Bluffton University | M |
| Bob Jones University | M,D,O |
| Boise State University | M |
| Boston College | M |
| Boston University | M,D |
| Bowie State University | M |
| Bowling Green State University | M |
| Bradley University | M |
| Brandeis University | M |
| Brandman University | M |
| Brenau University | M |
| Brescia University | M |
| Bridgewater State University | M |
| Briercrest Seminary | M |
| Brigham Young University | M |
| Broadview University–West Jordan | M |
| Brock University | M |
| Brooklyn College of the City University of New York | M |
| Bryan College | M |
| Bryant University | M |
| Bryan University | M |
| Bushnell University | M |
| Butler University | M |
| Cairn University | M,O |
| Caldwell University | M |
| California Baptist University | M |
| California Coast University | M |
| California Institute of Advanced Management | M |
| California Intercontinental University | M,D |
| California International Business University | M,D |
| California Lutheran University | M,O |
| California Miramar University | M |
| California Polytechnic State University, San Luis Obispo | M |
| California State Polytechnic University, Pomona | M |
| California State University Channel Islands | M |
| California State University, Chico | M |
| California State University, Dominguez Hills | M |
| California State University, East Bay | M |
| California State University, Fresno | M |
| California State University, Fullerton | M |
| California State University, Long Beach | M |
| California State University, Los Angeles | M,O |
| California State University, Monterey Bay | M |
| California State University, Northridge | M |
| California State University, Sacramento | M |
| California State University, San Bernardino | M |
| California State University, Stanislaus | M |
| California University of Management and Sciences | M,D |
| California University of Pennsylvania | M |
| Cambridge College | M |
| Cameron University | M |
| Campbellsville University | M,D |
| Campbell University | M |
| Canisius College | M |
| Cape Breton University | M |
| Capella University | M,D |
| Capital University | M |
| Capitol Technology University | M |
| Cardinal Stritch University | M |
| Carleton University | M,D |
| Carlow University | M |
| Carnegie Mellon University | M,D |
| Carroll University | M |
| Case Western Reserve University | M,D |
| The Catholic University of America | M |
| Cedar Crest College | M |
| Cedarville University | M,D |
| Centenary College of Louisiana | M |
| Centenary University | M |
| Central Connecticut State University | M |
| Central European University | M,D |
| Central Michigan University | M,O |
| Chadron State College | M |
| Chaminade University of Honolulu | M |
| Champlain College | M |
| Chapman University | M |
| Charleston Southern University | M |
| Charter College | M |
| Chatham University | M |
| Christian Brothers University | M,O |
| The Citadel, The Military College of South Carolina | M |
| City College of the City University of New York | M |
| City University of Seattle | M,O |
| Claflin University | M |
| Claremont Graduate University | M,D,O |
| Clarion University of Pennsylvania | M |
| Clark Atlanta University | M |
| Clarke University | M |
| Clarkson University | M,O |
| Clark University | M |
| Clayton State University | M |
| Cleary University | M,O |
| Clemson University | M,D |
| Cleveland State University | M,D |
| Coastal Carolina University | M,O |
| Coker College | M |
| College of Charleston | M |
| College of Saint Elizabeth | M |
| College of St. Joseph | M |
| The College of Saint Rose | M |
| The College of St. Scholastica | M,O |
| College of Staten Island of the City University of New York | M |
| Colorado Christian University | M |
| Colorado Mesa University | M |
| Colorado State University | M |
| Colorado State University–Global Campus | M |
| Colorado State University-Pueblo | M |
| Colorado Technical University Aurora | M |
| Colorado Technical University Colorado Springs | M,D |
| Columbia College (MO) | M |
| Columbia College Chicago | M |
| Columbia Southern University | M,D |
| Columbia University | M,D |
| Columbus State University | M,O |
| Concordia University (United States) | M |
| Concordia University (Canada) | M,D,O |
| Concordia University Chicago | M,D |
| Concordia University Irvine | M |
| Concordia University, St. Paul | M |
| Concordia University Wisconsin | M |
| Copenhagen Business School | M,D |
| Corban University | M |
| Cornell University | M,D |
| Cornerstone University | M,O |
| Creighton University | M,D |
| Culver-Stockton College | M |
| Cumberland University | M |
| Curry College | M,O |
| Daemen College | M |
| Dakota State University | M,D,O |
| Dalhousie University | M,O |
| Dallas Baptist University | M,D |
| Dartmouth College | M |
| Davenport University | M |
| Defiance College | M |
| Delaware State University | M |
| Delaware Valley University | M |
| Delta State University | M |
| DePaul University | M,D |
| DeSales University | M |
| DeVry College of New York–Midtown Manhattan Campus | M |
| DeVry University–Alpharetta Campus | M |
| DeVry University–Arlington Campus | M |
| DeVry University–Charlotte Campus | M |
| DeVry University–Chesapeake Campus | M |
| DeVry University–Chicago Campus | M |
| DeVry University–Chicago Loop Campus | M |
| DeVry University–Cincinnati Campus | M |
| DeVry University–Columbus Campus | M |
| DeVry University–Decatur Campus | M |
| DeVry University–Folsom Campus | M |
| DeVry University–Fremont Campus | M |
| DeVry University–Ft. Washington Campus | M |
| DeVry University–Henderson Campus | M |
| DeVry University–Irving Campus | M |
| DeVry University–Jacksonville Campus | M |
| DeVry University–Long Beach Campus | M |
| DeVry University–Miramar Campus | M |
| DeVry University–Morrisville Campus | M |
| DeVry University–Nashville Campus | M |
| DeVry University–North Brunswick Campus | M |
| DeVry University Online | M |
| DeVry University–Orlando Campus | M |
| DeVry University–Phoenix Campus | M |
| DeVry University–Pomona Campus | M |
| DeVry University–San Diego Campus | M,O |
| DeVry University–Seven Hills Campus | M,O |
| DeVry University–Tinley Park Campus | M |
| Doane University | M |
| Dominican College | M |
| Dominican University | M |
| Dominican University of California | M |
| Drake University | M |
| Drexel University | M,D,O |
| Drury University | M |
| Duke University | D |
| Duquesne University | M |
| D'Youville College | M |
| East Carolina University | M,D,O |
| Eastern Illinois University | M |
| Eastern Kentucky University | M |
| Eastern Mennonite University | M |
| Eastern Michigan University | M,O |
| Eastern Nazarene College | M |
| Eastern New Mexico University | M |
| Eastern Oregon University | M |
| Eastern University | M |
| Eastern Washington University | M |
| East Tennessee State University | M,O |
| East Texas Baptist University | M |
| ECPI University | M |
| Elmhurst University | M |

| | |
|---|---|
| Elms College | M,O |
| Elon University | M |
| Embry-Riddle Aeronautical University–Daytona | M |
| Embry-Riddle Aeronautical University–Worldwide | M |
| Emmanuel College (United States) | M,O |
| Emory University | M,D |
| Emporia State University | M |
| Endicott College | M |
| ESSEC Business School | M,D |
| Everglades University | M |
| Fairfield University | M,O |
| Fairleigh Dickinson University, Florham Campus | M,O |
| Fairleigh Dickinson University, Metropolitan Campus | M,O |
| Fairmont State University | M |
| Fashion Institute of Technology | M |
| Faulkner University | M |
| Fayetteville State University | M |
| Felician University | M,D |
| Ferris State University | M |
| Fisher College | M |
| Fitchburg State University | M |
| Florida Agricultural and Mechanical University | M |
| Florida Atlantic University | M |
| Florida Gulf Coast University | M |
| Florida Institute of Technology | M |
| Florida Memorial University | M |
| Florida National University | M |
| Florida Southern College | M |
| Florida State University | M,D |
| Fontbonne University | M |
| Fordham University | M,D |
| Fort Hays State University | M |
| Framingham State University | M |
| Franciscan University of Steubenville | M |
| Francis Marion University | M |
| Franklin Pierce University | M,D,O |
| Franklin University | M |
| Freed-Hardeman University | M |
| Fresno Pacific University | M |
| Frostburg State University | M |
| Full Sail University | M |
| Gannon University | M |
| Gardner-Webb University | M |
| Geneva College | M |
| George Fox University | M,D |
| George Mason University | M |
| Georgetown University | M |
| The George Washington University | M,D,O |
| Georgia College & State University | M |
| Georgian Court University | M,O |
| Georgia Southern University | M,O |
| Georgia Southwestern State University | M |
| Georgia State University | M,D |
| Goddard College | M |
| Golden Gate University | M,D,O |
| Goldey-Beacom College | M |
| Gonzaga University | M |
| Governors State University | M |
| The Graduate Center, City University of New York | D |
| Grand Canyon University | M,D |
| Grand Valley State University | M |
| Grantham University | M,O |
| Hallmark University | M |
| Hamline University | M,D |
| Hampton University | M,D |
| Harding University | M |
| Hardin-Simmons University | M |
| Harvard University | M,D,O* |
| Hawaii Pacific University | M |
| HEC Montreal | M,D,O |
| Heidelberg University | M |
| Henderson State University | M |
| Herzing University Online | M |
| High Point University | M,D |
| Hodges University | M |
| Hofstra University | M,O |
| Holy Family College | M |
| Holy Family University | M |
| Holy Names University | M |
| Hood College | M,O |
| Houston Baptist University | M,D |
| Howard Payne University | M |
| Howard University | M |
| Hult International Business School (United States) | M |
| Humboldt State University | M |
| Huntington University | M,D |
| Husson University | M |
| Idaho State University | M,O |
| IGlobal University | M |
| Illinois Institute of Technology | M,D |
| Illinois State University | M |
| Independence University | M |
| Indiana State University | M |
| Indiana Tech | M |
| Indiana University Bloomington | M,D |
| Indiana University Kokomo | M,O |
| Indiana University Northwest | M,O |
| Indiana University of Pennsylvania | M |
| Indiana University-Purdue University Indianapolis | M |
| Indiana University South Bend | M,O |
| Indiana University Southeast | M |
| Indiana Wesleyan University | M,O |
| Instituto Centroamericano de Administracion de Empresas | M |
| Instituto Tecnologico de Santo Domingo | M,O |
| Instituto Tecnológico y de Estudios Superiores de Monterrey, Campus Central de Veracruz | M |
| Instituto Tecnológico y de Estudios Superiores de Monterrey, Campus Ciudad de México | M,D |
| Instituto Tecnológico y de Estudios Superiores de Monterrey, Campus Ciudad Juárez | M |
| Instituto Tecnológico y de Estudios Superiores de Monterrey, Campus Ciudad Obregón | M |
| Instituto Tecnológico y de Estudios Superiores de Monterrey, Campus Cuernavaca | M |
| Instituto Tecnológico y de Estudios Superiores de Monterrey, Campus Estado de México | M,D |
| Instituto Tecnológico y de Estudios Superiores de Monterrey, Campus Guadalajara | M |
| Instituto Tecnológico y de Estudios Superiores de Monterrey, Campus Irapuato | M,D |
| Instituto Tecnológico y de Estudios Superiores de Monterrey, Campus Laguna | M |
| Instituto Tecnológico y de Estudios Superiores de Monterrey, Campus León | M |
| Instituto Tecnológico y de Estudios Superiores de Monterrey, Campus Monterrey | M,D |
| Instituto Tecnológico y de Estudios Superiores de Monterrey, Campus Querétaro | M |
| Instituto Tecnológico y de Estudios Superiores de Monterrey, Campus Sonora Norte | M |
| Instituto Tecnológico y de Estudios Superiores de Monterrey, Campus Toluca | M |
| Inter American University of Puerto Rico, Aguadilla Campus | M |
| Inter American University of Puerto Rico, Arecibo Campus | M |
| Inter American University of Puerto Rico, Barranquitas Campus | M |
| Inter American University of Puerto Rico, Fajardo Campus | M |
| Inter American University of Puerto Rico, Guayama Campus | M |
| Inter American University of Puerto Rico, Metropolitan Campus | M |
| Inter American University of Puerto Rico, San Germán Campus | M,D |
| International Technological University | M,D |
| International University in Geneva | M,D |
| The International University of Monaco | M |
| Iona College | M,O |
| Iowa State University of Science and Technology | M |
| Jackson State University | M,D |
| Jacksonville State University | M |
| Jacksonville University | M,D |
| James Madison University | M |
| John Brown University | M |
| John Carroll University | M |
| John F. Kennedy University | M |
| Johns Hopkins University | M,O |
| Johnson & Wales University | M |
| Judson University | M |
| Juniata College | M |
| Kansas State University | M,O |
| Kansas Wesleyan University | M |
| Kean University | M |
| Keiser University | M,D |
| Kennesaw State University | M,D |
| Kent State University | M |
| Kent State University at Stark | M |
| Kettering University | M |
| Keuka College | M |
| Keystone College | M |
| King University | M |
| Kutztown University of Pennsylvania | M |
| Lake Erie College | M |
| Lake Forest Graduate School of Management | M |
| Lamar University | M |
| La Salle University | M,O |
| Lasell College | M,O |
| La Sierra University | M,O |
| Laurentian University | M |
| Lawrence Technological University | M,D,O |
| Lebanese American University | M |
| Lebanon Valley College | M |
| Lee University | M |
| Lehigh University | M |
| Lehman College of the City University of New York | M |
| Le Moyne College | M |
| Lenoir-Rhyne University | M |
| LeTourneau University | M |
| Lewis University | |
| Liberty University | M,D |
| LIM College | M |
| Limestone College | M |
| Lincoln Memorial University | M |
| Lincoln University (CA) | M,D |
| Lindenwood University | M,O |
| Lindenwood University–Belleville | M |
| Lipscomb University | M,O |
| Long Island University - Brooklyn | M,O |
| Long Island University - Post | M |
| Longwood University | M |
| Louisiana State University and Agricultural & Mechanical College | M,D |
| Louisiana State University in Shreveport | M |
| Louisiana Tech University | M,D,O |
| Lourdes University | M |
| Loyola Marymount University | M |
| Loyola University Chicago | M,O |
| Loyola University Maryland | M |
| Loyola University New Orleans | M |
| Lynn University | M |
| Maastricht School of Management | M,D |
| Madonna University | M |
| Maharishi International University | M,D |
| Malone University | M |
| Manhattan College | M |
| Marconi International University | M,D |
| Marian University (WI) | M |
| Marist College | M,O |
| Marlboro College | M |
| Marquette University | M,O |
| Marshall University | M,O |
| Maryland Institute College of Art | M |
| Marymount California University | M |
| Marymount University | M,O |
| Maryville University of Saint Louis | M,O |
| Marywood University | M |
| Massachusetts College of Liberal Arts | M,O |
| Massachusetts Institute of Technology | M,D |
| McGill University | M,D,O |
| McKendree University | M |
| McMaster University | M,D |
| McNeese State University | M |
| Medaille College | M |
| Melbourne Business School | M,D,O |
| Memorial University of Newfoundland | M |
| Mercer University | M |
| Mercer University | M |
| Mercy College | M |
| Meredith College | M |
| Merrimack College | M |
| Messiah University | M,O |
| Methodist University | M |
| Metropolitan College of New York | M |
| Metropolitan State University | M,D,O |
| Miami University | M |
| Michigan State University | M,D |
| Michigan Technological University | M |
| Mid-America Christian University | M |
| MidAmerica Nazarene University | M |
| Middle Tennessee State University | M |
| Midway University | M |
| Midwestern State University | M |
| Millennia Atlantic University | M |
| Milligan University | M,O |
| Millikin University | M |
| Millsaps College | M |
| Mills College | M |
| Milwaukee School of Engineering | M |
| Minnesota State University Mankato | M |
| Minnesota State University Moorhead | M |
| Minot State University | M |
| Misericordia University | M |
| Mississippi College | M,O |
| Mississippi State University | M,D |
| Missouri Baptist University | M,O |
| Missouri Southern State University | M |
| Missouri State University | M |
| Missouri University of Science and Technology | M |
| Missouri Western State University | M |
| Molloy College | M,O |
| Monmouth University | M,O |
| Monroe College | M |
| Montclair State University | M,O |
| Moravian College | M |
| Morehead State University | M |
| Morgan State University | M,D |
| Mount Aloysius College | M |
| Mount Marty University | M |
| Mount Mary University | M |
| Mount Mercy University | M |
| Mount St. Joseph University | M |
| Mount Saint Mary College | M |
| Mount Saint Mary's University (CA) | M,D,O |
| Mount St. Mary's University (MD) | M |
| Mount Vernon Nazarene University | M |
| Murray State University | M |
| National American University (TX) | M,D |
| National Louis University | M |
| National University | M,O |
| National University College | M |
| Naval Postgraduate School | M |
| Nazareth College of Rochester | M |
| Nebraska Christian College of Hope International University | M |
| Neumann University | M |
| New Charter University | M |
| New England College | M |
| New Jersey City University | M,O |
| New Jersey Institute of Technology | M,D,O |
| Newman University | M |
| New Mexico Highlands University | M |
| New Mexico State University | M,D |
| New York Institute of Technology | M |
| New York Medical College | M,D,O |
| New York University | M,D,O |
| Niagara University | M |
| Nicholls State University | M |
| Nichols College | M |
| North Carolina Agricultural and Technical State University | M |
| North Carolina Central University | M |
| North Carolina State University | M |
| North Central College | M |
| Northcentral University | M,D,O |
| North Dakota State University | M |
| Northeastern Illinois University | M |
| Northeastern State University | M |
| Northeastern University | M |
| Northern Arizona University | M,O |
| Northern Illinois University | M |
| Northern Kentucky University | M,O |
| Northern Michigan University | M |
| North Park University | M |
| Northwestern Polytechnic University | M,D |
| Northwestern University | M |
| Northwest Missouri State University | M |
| Northwest Nazarene University | M |
| Northwest University | M |
| Northwood University, Michigan Campus | M |
| Norwich University | M |
| Notre Dame de Namur University | M |
| Notre Dame of Maryland University | M |
| Nova Southeastern University | M |
| Nyack College | M |
| Oakland City University | M |
| Oakland University | M,O |
| Oglala Lakota College | M |
| Ohio Christian University | M |
| Ohio Dominican University | M |
| The Ohio State University | M,D |
| Ohio University | M |
| Oklahoma Baptist University | M |
| Oklahoma Christian University | M |
| Oklahoma City University | M |
| Oklahoma State University | M,D |
| Old Dominion University | M,D |
| Olivet Nazarene University | M |
| Open University | M |
| Oral Roberts University | M |
| Oregon State University | M,D |
| Ottawa University | M |
| Otterbein University | M |
| Our Lady of the Lake University | M |
| Pace University | M,D,O |
| Pacific Lutheran University | M |
| Pacific States University | M,O |
| Pacific University | M |
| Palm Beach Atlantic University | M |
| Park University | M,O |
| Penn State Erie, The Behrend College | M |
| Penn State Great Valley | M,O |
| Penn State Harrisburg | M,O |
| Penn State University Park | M,D* |
| Pensacola Christian College | M,D,O |
| Pfeiffer University | M |
| Phillips Theological Seminary | M,D |
| Piedmont College | M |
| Pittsburg State University | M |
| Plymouth State University | M |
| Point Loma Nazarene University | M |
| Point Park University | M |
| Point University | M |
| Polytechnic University of Puerto Rico | M |
| Polytechnic University of Puerto Rico, Miami Campus | M |
| Polytechnic University of Puerto Rico, Orlando Campus | M |
| Pontifical Catholic University of Puerto Rico | M,D,O |
| Pontificia Universidad Catolica Madre y Maestra | M |
| Portland State University | M,D,O |
| Post University | M |
| Prairie View A&M University | M |
| Presidio Graduate School (CA) | M,O |
| Providence College | M |
| Purdue University | M,D |
| Purdue University Fort Wayne | M |
| Purdue University Global | M |
| Purdue University Northwest | M |
| Queen's University at Kingston | M,D |
| Queens University of Charlotte | M |
| Quincy University | M |
| Quinnipiac University | M |
| Radford University | M |
| Ramapo College of New Jersey | M |
| Reformed University | M |
| Regent's University London | M |
| Regent University | M,D,O |
| Reinhardt University | M |
| Rensselaer at Hartford | M |
| Rensselaer Polytechnic Institute | M,D |
| Rice University | M |
| Rider University | M |
| Rivier University | M |
| Robert Morris University | M |
| Robert Morris University Illinois | M |
| Roberts Wesleyan College | M |
| Rochester Institute of Technology | M |
| Rockford University | M |
| Rockhurst University | M,O |
| Rogers State University | M |
| Roger Williams University | M |
| Rollins College | M |
| Roosevelt University | M |
| Roseman University of Health Sciences | M,O |
| Rosemont College | M |
| Rowan University | M,O |
| Royal Military College of Canada | M |
| Rutgers University - Camden | M |
| Rutgers University - Newark | M,D |
| Ryerson University | M |
| Sacred Heart University | M,O |
| Sage Graduate School | M |
| Saginaw Valley State University | M |
| St. Ambrose University | M,D |
| St. Bonaventure University | M |
| St. Catherine University | M |
| St. Cloud State University | M |
| Saint Francis University | M |
| St. John Fisher College | M |

*M—masters degree; D—doctorate; O—other advanced degree; *—Close-Up and/or Display*

| | |
|---|---|
| St. John's University (NY) | M |
| St. Joseph's College, Long Island Campus | M |
| St. Joseph's College, New York | M |
| Saint Joseph's College of Maine | M |
| Saint Joseph's University | M,O |
| Saint Leo University | M,D |
| Saint Louis University | M |
| Saint Martin's University | M |
| Saint Mary's College of California | M |
| Saint Mary's University (Canada) | M,D |
| St. Mary's University (United States) | M |
| Saint Mary's University of Minnesota | M,D |
| St. Norbert College | M |
| Saint Peter's University | M |
| St. Thomas Aquinas College | M |
| St. Thomas University - Florida | M,O |
| Saint Vincent College | M |
| Saint Xavier University | M,O |
| Salem International University | M |
| Salem State University | M |
| Salisbury University | M |
| Salve Regina University | M,O |
| Samford University | M |
| Sam Houston State University | M |
| San Diego State University | M |
| San Francisco State University | M |
| San Ignacio University | M |
| Santa Clara University | M |
| Savannah State University | M |
| Schiller International University - Heidelberg | M |
| Schiller International University - Madrid | M |
| Schiller International University - Paris | M |
| Schiller International University - Tampa | M |
| Schreiner University | M |
| Seattle Pacific University | M |
| Seattle University | M,O |
| Seton Hall University | M,O |
| Seton Hill University | M |
| Shenandoah University | M,O |
| Shippensburg University of Pennsylvania | M,D,O |
| Shorter University | M |
| Siena College | M |
| Simmons University | M |
| Simon Fraser University | M,D,O |
| SIT Graduate Institute | M |
| Sonoma State University | M |
| South Carolina State University | M |
| Southeastern Louisiana University | M |
| Southeastern Oklahoma State University | M |
| Southeastern University (FL) | M,D |
| Southeast Missouri State University | M |
| Southern Adventist University | M |
| Southern Arkansas University–Magnolia | M |
| Southern Connecticut State University | M |
| Southern Illinois University Carbondale | M,D |
| Southern Illinois University Edwardsville | M |
| Southern Methodist University | M |
| Southern Nazarene University | M |
| Southern New Hampshire University | M,D,O |
| Southern Oregon University | M,O |
| Southern States University | M |
| Southern University and Agricultural and Mechanical College | M |
| Southern Utah University | M |
| Southern Wesleyan University | M |
| South University - Austin | M |
| South University - Columbia | M |
| South University - Montgomery | M |
| South University - Richmond | M |
| South University - Savannah | M |
| South University - Tampa | M |
| South University - Virginia Beach | M |
| South University - West Palm Beach | M |
| Southwest Baptist University | M |
| Southwestern Adventist University | M |
| Southwestern College (KS) | M |
| Southwestern College (KS) | M |
| Southwestern Oklahoma State University | M |
| Southwest Minnesota State University | M |
| Southwest University | M |
| Spring Arbor University | M |
| Springfield College | M |
| Spring Hill College | M |
| Stanford University | M,D |
| State University of New York at New Paltz | M |
| State University of New York at Oswego | M |
| State University of New York College at Geneseo | M |
| State University of New York College at Old Westbury | M |
| State University of New York Empire State College | M |
| State University of New York Polytechnic Institute | M |
| Stephen F. Austin State University | M |
| Stetson University | M |
| Stevens Institute of Technology | M,O |
| Stockton University | M |
| Stony Brook University, State University of New York | M,O |
| Stratford University (VA) | M,D |
| Strayer University | M |
| Suffolk University | M |
| Sullivan University | M,D |
| Sul Ross State University | M |
| Syracuse University | M,D |
| Tabor College | M |
| Tarleton State University | M |
| Temple University | M,D* |
| Tennessee State University | M |
| Tennessee Technological University | M |
| Tennessee Wesleyan University | M |
| Texas A&M International University | M,D |
| Texas A&M University | M |
| Texas A&M University–Central Texas | M,O |
| Texas A&M University–Commerce | M |
| Texas A&M University–Corpus Christi | M |
| Texas A&M University–Kingsville | M |
| Texas A&M University–San Antonio | M |
| Texas A&M University–Texarkana | M |
| Texas Christian University | M |
| Texas Health and Science University | M,D |
| Texas Southern University | M |
| Texas State University | M |
| Texas Tech University | M,D |
| Texas Wesleyan University | M |
| Texas Woman's University | M |
| Thomas College | M |
| Thomas Edison State University | M |
| Thomas Jefferson University | M |
| Thomas More University | M |
| Thomas University | M |
| Thompson Rivers University | M |
| Tiffin University | M |
| Trevecca Nazarene University | M |
| Trident University International | M,D |
| Trine University | M |
| Trinity International University | M,D,O |
| Trinity University | M |
| Trinity Washington University | M |
| Trinity Western University | M |
| Troy University | M |
| Truett McConnell University | M |
| Tulane University | M,D |
| Tusculum University | M |
| UNB Fredericton | M |
| Union University | M |
| United States International University–Africa | M |
| Universidad Autonoma de Guadalajara | M,D |
| Universidad de las Americas, A.C. | M |
| Universidad de las Américas Puebla | M |
| Universidad del Este | M |
| Universidad del Turabo | M,D |
| Universidad Iberoamericana | M,D |
| Universidad Metropolitana | M |
| Université de Moncton | M |
| Université de Sherbrooke | M,D,O |
| Université du Québec à Chicoutimi | M |
| Université du Québec à Montréal | M,D,O |
| Université du Québec à Rimouski | M,O |
| Université du Québec à Trois-Rivières | M,D |
| Université du Québec en Abitibi-Témiscamingue | M |
| University at Albany, State University of New York | M |
| University at Buffalo, the State University of New York | M,D |
| The University of Akron | M |
| The University of Alabama | M,D |
| The University of Alabama at Birmingham | M |
| The University of Alabama in Huntsville | M,O |
| University of Alaska Anchorage | M |
| University of Alaska Fairbanks | M |
| University of Alberta | M,D |
| University of Antelope Valley | M |
| The University of Arizona | M,D,O |
| University of Arkansas | M,D |
| University of Arkansas at Little Rock | M,O |
| University of Baltimore | M,O |
| University of Bridgeport | M |
| The University of British Columbia | M,D |
| University of Calgary | M,D |
| University of California, Berkeley | M,D,O |
| University of California, Davis | M |
| University of California, Irvine | M,D |
| University of California, Los Angeles | M,D |
| University of California, Riverside | M,D |
| University of California, San Diego | M,D |
| University of Central Arkansas | M |
| University of Central Florida | M,D,O |
| University of Central Missouri | M,D,O |
| University of Charleston | M |
| University of Chicago | M,D,O |
| University of Cincinnati | M,D |
| University of Colorado Boulder | M,D |
| University of Colorado Colorado Springs | M |
| University of Colorado Denver | M |
| University of Connecticut | M,D |
| University of Dallas | M,D |
| University of Dayton | M |
| University of Delaware | M,D |
| University of Denver | M |
| University of Detroit Mercy | M,O |
| University of Dubuque | M |
| University of Fairfax | M,D |
| The University of Findlay | M,D |
| University of Florida | M,D |
| University of Georgia | M |
| University of Guam | M |
| University of Guelph | M,D |
| University of Hartford | M |
| University of Hawaii at Manoa | M |
| University of Holy Cross | M,D |
| University of Houston | M,D |
| University of Houston–Clear Lake | M |
| University of Houston - Downtown | M |
| University of Houston–Victoria | M |
| University of Idaho | M |
| University of Illinois at Chicago | M,D |
| University of Illinois at Springfield | M |
| University of Illinois at Urbana-Champaign | M,D |
| University of Indianapolis | M,O |
| The University of Iowa | M,D |
| The University of Kansas | M,D |
| University of Kentucky | M,D |
| University of La Verne | M,D,O |
| University of Lethbridge | M,D |
| University of Louisiana at Lafayette | M |
| University of Louisiana at Monroe | M,O |
| University of Louisville | M |
| University of Lynchburg | M |
| University of Maine | M,O |
| University of Management and Technology | M,D,O |
| The University of Manchester | M |
| University of Manitoba | M,D |
| University of Mary | M |
| University of Mary Hardin-Baylor | M |
| University of Maryland, College Park | M,D |
| University of Maryland Global Campus | M,O |
| University of Mary Washington | M |
| University of Massachusetts Amherst | M,D |
| University of Massachusetts Boston | M |
| University of Massachusetts Dartmouth | M,O |
| University of Massachusetts Lowell | M,D |
| University of Memphis | M,D |
| University of Miami | M,D |
| University of Michigan | M,D |
| University of Michigan–Dearborn | M |
| University of Michigan–Flint | M,O |
| University of Minnesota, Duluth | M |
| University of Minnesota Rochester | M,D |
| University of Minnesota, Twin Cities Campus | M,D |
| University of Mississippi | M,D |
| University of Missouri | M,D |
| University of Missouri–Kansas City | M,D |
| University of Missouri–St. Louis | M,D,O |
| University of Mobile | M |
| University of Montana | M |
| University of Montevallo | M |
| University of Mount Olive | M |
| University of Nebraska at Kearney | M |
| University of Nebraska at Omaha | M,O |
| University of Nebraska–Lincoln | M,D |
| University of Nevada, Las Vegas | M,O |
| University of Nevada, Reno | M |
| University of New Brunswick Saint John | M |
| University of New Hampshire | M,O |
| University of New Haven | M |
| University of New Mexico | M |
| University of New Orleans | M |
| University of North Alabama | M |
| The University of North Carolina at Chapel Hill | M,D |
| The University of North Carolina at Charlotte | M,D,O |
| The University of North Carolina at Greensboro | M,O |
| The University of North Carolina at Pembroke | M |
| The University of North Carolina Wilmington | M |
| University of North Dakota | M |
| University of Northern Colorado | M |
| University of Northern Iowa | M |
| University of North Florida | M |
| University of North Texas | M,D,O |
| University of North Texas at Dallas | M |
| University of Northwestern Ohio | M |
| University of Northwestern–St. Paul | M |
| University of Notre Dame | M |
| University of Oklahoma | M,D,O |
| University of Oregon | M,D |
| University of Ottawa | M |
| University of Pennsylvania | M,D |
| University of Phoenix - Bay Area Campus | M,D |
| University of Phoenix - Central Valley Campus | M |
| University of Phoenix - Dallas Campus | M |
| University of Phoenix - Hawaii Campus | M |
| University of Phoenix - Houston Campus | M |
| University of Phoenix - Las Vegas Campus | M |
| University of Phoenix–Online Campus | M,D,O |
| University of Phoenix - Phoenix Campus | M,O |
| University of Phoenix - Sacramento Valley Campus | M |
| University of Phoenix - San Antonio Campus | M |
| University of Phoenix - San Diego Campus | M |
| University of Pikeville | M |
| University of Pittsburgh | M,D* |
| University of Portland | M |
| University of Puerto Rico at Mayagüez | M |
| University of Puerto Rico at Rio Piedras | M,D |
| University of Redlands | M |
| University of Regina | M,O |
| University of Rhode Island | M,D |
| University of Richmond | M |
| University of Rochester | M,D |
| University of St. Francis (IL) | M,O |
| University of Saint Francis (IN) | M |
| University of Saint Joseph | M |
| University of Saint Mary | M |
| University of St. Thomas (TX) | M |
| University of St. Thomas (MN) | M |
| University of San Diego | M |
| University of San Francisco | M |
| University of Saskatchewan | M,D |
| The University of Scranton | M |
| University of Sioux Falls | M |
| University of South Africa | M,D |
| University of South Alabama | M,D |
| University of South Carolina | M,D |
| University of South Carolina Aiken | M |
| University of South Dakota | M,O |
| University of Southern California | M,D |
| University of Southern Indiana | M |
| University of Southern Maine | M,O |
| University of South Florida, St. Petersburg | M |
| University of South Florida Sarasota-Manatee | M |
| The University of Tampa | M,O |
| The University of Tennessee | M,D |
| The University of Tennessee at Chattanooga | M |
| The University of Tennessee at Martin | M |
| The University of Texas at Austin | M,D |
| The University of Texas at Dallas | M,D |
| The University of Texas at El Paso | M,D,O |
| The University of Texas at San Antonio | M,D,O |
| The University of Texas at Tyler | M |
| The University of Texas of the Permian Basin | M |
| The University of Texas Rio Grande Valley | M,D |
| University of the Cumberlands | M |
| University of the District of Columbia | M |
| University of the Incarnate Word | M,D |
| University of the Pacific | M |
| University of the People | M |
| University of the Potomac | M |
| University of the Sacred Heart | M,O |
| University of the Southwest | M |
| University of the Virgin Islands | M |
| University of the West | M |
| The University of Toledo | M |
| University of Toronto | M,D |
| The University of Tulsa | M |
| University of Utah | M,D,O |
| University of Vermont | M |
| University of Victoria | M |
| University of Virginia | M,D,O |
| University of Washington | M,D |
| University of Washington, Bothell | M |
| University of Washington, Tacoma | M |
| University of Waterloo | M |
| The University of West Alabama | M |
| The University of Western Ontario | M,D |
| University of West Florida | M |
| University of West Los Angeles | M |
| University of Windsor | M |
| University of Wisconsin–Eau Claire | M |
| University of Wisconsin–Green Bay | M |
| University of Wisconsin–Madison | M |
| University of Wisconsin–Milwaukee | M,D,O* |
| University of Wisconsin–Oshkosh | M |
| University of Wisconsin–Parkside | M |
| University of Wisconsin–River Falls | M |
| University of Wisconsin–Whitewater | M |
| University of Wyoming | M |
| Université Laval | M,D,O |
| Upper Iowa University | M |
| Urbana University–A Branch Campus of Franklin University | M |
| Utah State University | M |
| Utah Valley University | M |
| Valdosta State University | M |
| Valparaiso University | M,O |
| Vancouver Island University | M |
| Vanderbilt University | M* |
| Villanova University | M |
| Virginia Commonwealth University | M,D |
| Virginia International University | M,O |
| Virginia Polytechnic Institute and State University | M,D |
| Virginia Wesleyan University | M |
| Viterbo University | M |
| Wagner College | M |
| Wake Forest University | M |
| Walden University | M,D,O |
| Walsh College of Accountancy and Business Administration | M |
| Walsh University | M |

| | |
|---|---|
| Warner University | M |
| Washburn University | M |
| Washington Adventist University | M |
| Washington State University | M,D |
| Washington University in St. Louis | M,D |
| Wayland Baptist University | M,D |
| Waynesburg University | M,D |
| Wayne State College | M |
| Wayne State University | M,D,O |
| Webber International University | M |
| Weber State University | M,O |
| Webster University | M,D,O |
| Wesleyan College | M |
| Wesley College | M |
| Westcliff University | M,D |
| Western Carolina University | M |
| Western Connecticut State University | M |
| Western Governors University | M |
| Western Illinois University | M,O |
| Western Kentucky University | M |
| Western Michigan University | M |
| Western New England University | M |
| Western New Mexico University | M |
| Western Washington University | M |
| West Liberty University | M |
| Westminster College (UT) | M,O |
| West Texas A&M University | M |
| West Virginia University | M,D,O |
| West Virginia Wesleyan College | M |
| Wheeling Jesuit University | M |
| Whitworth University | M |
| WHU - Otto Beisheim School of Management | M |
| Wichita State University | M |
| Widener University | M |
| Wilfrid Laurier University | M,D |
| Willamette University | M |
| William & Mary | M* |
| William Carey University | M |
| William Woods University | M,D,O |
| Wilmington University | M,D |
| Wilson College | M |
| Wingate University | M |
| Winston-Salem State University | M |
| Winthrop University | M |
| Woodbury University | M |
| Worcester Polytechnic Institute | M,D,O |
| Worcester State University | M |
| Wright State University | M |
| Xavier University | M* |
| Yale University | M,D |
| Yeshiva University | M |
| York College of Pennsylvania | M |
| York University | M,D |
| Youngstown State University | M |

## BUSINESS ANALYTICS

| | |
|---|---|
| Abilene Christian University | M |
| American Public University System | M,D |
| Ashland University | M |
| Babson College | M,O |
| Baldwin Wallace University | M |
| Bentley University | M,O |
| Boston University | M,D |
| California Polytechnic State University, San Luis Obispo | M |
| California State University, East Bay | M |
| California State University, Fullerton | M |
| California University of Pennsylvania | M |
| Case Western Reserve University | M |
| Central European University | M,D |
| Clark University | M |
| Cleary University | M,O |
| Clemson University | M |
| The College of Saint Rose | M |
| Columbia University | M |
| Creighton University | M,D |
| Dakota State University | M,D,O |
| DePaul University | M,D |
| Fairfield University | M,O |
| The George Washington University | M,O |
| Golden Gate University | M,D,O |
| Grand Canyon University | M |
| HEC Montreal | M |
| Hult International Business School (United States) | M |
| Iowa State University of Science and Technology | M |
| Johns Hopkins University | M |
| Kent State University | M |
| La Salle University | M,O |
| Lenoir-Rhyne University | M |
| Lewis University | M |
| Loyola University Chicago | M,O |
| Marist College | M,O |
| Merrimack College | M |
| Metropolitan State University | M,D,O |
| Michigan State University | M |
| Montclair State University | M |
| National University | M,O |
| Northwest Missouri State University | M |
| Nova Southeastern University | M |
| Point Park University | M |
| Queen's University at Kingston | M,D |
| Regent University | M,D,O |
| Rensselaer Polytechnic Institute | M |
| Robert Morris University Illinois | M |
| Rockhurst University | M,O |
| St. John's University (NY) | M |
| Saint Joseph's University | M |
| Saint Mary's College of California | M |
| Santa Clara University | M |
| Seattle University | M,O |
| Shippensburg University of Pennsylvania | M,D,O |
| Southern Illinois University Edwardsville | M |
| Southern Methodist University | M |
| Southern New Hampshire University | M,D,O |
| Stevens Institute of Technology | M,O |
| Suffolk University | M |
| Syracuse University | M |
| Texas A&M University–Commerce | M |
| Texas Woman's University | M |
| Thomas Jefferson University | M |
| Tulane University | M,D |
| University at Albany, State University of New York | M |
| University at Buffalo, the State University of New York | M,D |
| The University of Alabama in Huntsville | M,O |
| The University of British Columbia | M |
| University of California, Davis | M |
| University of California, Irvine | M |
| University of California, Los Angeles | M,D |
| University of California, San Diego | M,D |
| University of Central Oklahoma | M |
| University of Cincinnati | M,D |
| University of Connecticut | M,D |
| University of Dallas | M,D |
| University of Denver | M |
| University of Georgia | M |
| The University of Iowa | M |
| The University of Manchester | M |
| University of Massachusetts Boston | M |
| University of Miami | M,D |
| University of Michigan–Dearborn | M |
| The University of North Carolina at Charlotte | M,D,O |
| University of Notre Dame | M |
| University of Oklahoma | M,O |
| University of Pittsburgh | D* |
| University of St. Francis (IL) | M,O |
| University of St. Thomas (MN) | M |
| University of South Dakota | M,O |
| The University of Tampa | M,O |
| The University of Tulsa | M |
| University of Utah | |
| University of Wisconsin–Milwaukee | M,O* |
| Villanova University | M |
| Virginia Polytechnic Institute and State University | M,D |
| Wake Forest University | M |
| Walsh College of Accountancy and Business Administration | M |
| West Virginia University | M,D,O |
| William & Mary | M* |
| York University | M,D |

## BUSINESS EDUCATION

| | |
|---|---|
| Alabama Agricultural and Mechanical University | M,O |
| Arkansas State University | O |
| Ball State University | M,O |
| Bloomsburg University of Pennsylvania | M |
| Bowling Green State University | M |
| Buffalo State College, State University of New York | M |
| Canisius College | M,O |
| Capella University | D |
| Chadron State College | M,O |
| Clemson University | M,D |
| Colorado Christian University | M |
| East Carolina University | M,O |
| Eastern Kentucky University | M |
| Florida Agricultural and Mechanical University | M |
| Hofstra University | M,D,O |
| Indiana University of Pennsylvania | M |
| Inter American University of Puerto Rico, Metropolitan Campus | M |
| Inter American University of Puerto Rico, San Germán Campus | M |
| Johnson & Wales University | M |
| Lock Haven University of Pennsylvania | M |
| Louisiana State University and Agricultural & Mechanical College | M,D |
| Manhattanville College | M,O |
| Maryville University of Saint Louis | M,O |
| Middle Tennessee State University | M |
| Milwaukee School of Engineering | M |
| Mississippi College | M,D,O |
| Morehead State University | M,O |
| New York University | M,O |
| North Carolina Agricultural and Technical State University | M |
| North Carolina State University | M |
| Nova Southeastern University | M |
| Old Dominion University | M,D |
| Pontifical Catholic University of Puerto Rico | M,D |
| Regis University | M,O |
| Salve Regina University | M,O |
| South Carolina State University | M |
| Spalding University | M |
| State University of New York at Oswego | M |
| Temple University | M* |
| Thomas College | M |
| University of Delaware | M,D |
| University of Georgia | M,D,O |
| University of Missouri | M,D,O |
| The University of North Carolina at Charlotte | D |
| University of South Carolina | M,D |
| University of the Cumberlands | M,D,O |
| The University of Toledo | M,D,O |
| University of Wisconsin–Whitewater | M |
| Utah State University | D |
| Washington State University | M,D |
| Wayne State College | M |

## CANADIAN STUDIES

| | |
|---|---|
| Carleton University | M,D |
| Queen's University at Kingston | M,D |
| Saint Mary's University (Canada) | M,O |
| Trent University | M,D |
| Université de Saint-Boniface | M |
| Université de Sherbrooke | M,D |
| Université du Québec à Chicoutimi | M |
| University at Buffalo, the State University of New York | M,D |
| University of Lethbridge | M,D |
| University of Manitoba | M |
| University of Ottawa | D |
| University of Saskatchewan | M,D |
| Wilfrid Laurier University | M,D |

## CANCER BIOLOGY/ONCOLOGY

| | |
|---|---|
| Augusta University | D |
| Baylor College of Medicine | D |
| Case Western Reserve University | D |
| Duke University | D |
| Emory University | D |
| Gerstner Sloan Kettering Graduate School of Biomedical Sciences | D |
| Grand Valley State University | M |
| Irell & Manella Graduate School of Biological Sciences | D |
| McMaster University | M,D |
| Medical University of South Carolina | D |
| Meharry Medical College | D |
| Memorial University of Newfoundland | M,D |
| New York University | M,D |
| Oregon Health & Science University | D |
| Purdue University | D |
| Rutgers University - New Brunswick | M,D |
| Saint Francis University | M |
| Thomas Jefferson University | D |
| Tufts University | D |
| University at Buffalo, the State University of New York | M |
| The University of Alabama at Birmingham | D |
| University of Alberta | M,D |
| The University of Arizona | D |
| University of Calgary | M,D |
| University of Chicago | D |
| University of Cincinnati | D |
| University of Colorado Denver | D |
| University of Delaware | M,D |
| The University of Kansas | M,D |
| The University of Manchester | M,D |
| University of Manitoba | M |
| University of Maryland, Baltimore | D |
| University of Massachusetts Medical School | M,D |
| University of Miami | D |
| University of Michigan | M,D |
| University of Minnesota, Twin Cities Campus | D |
| University of Nebraska Medical Center | D |
| University of North Texas Health Science Center at Fort Worth | M,D |
| University of Pennsylvania | D |
| University of Regina | M,D |
| University of Southern California | D |
| University of South Florida | M,D |
| The University of Texas Health Science Center at Houston | M,D |
| The University of Texas Southwestern Medical Center | D |
| University of the District of Columbia | M |
| The University of Toledo | M,D |
| University of Utah | M,D |
| University of Wisconsin–La Crosse | M |
| University of Wisconsin–Madison | D |
| Université Laval | O |
| Wake Forest University | D |
| West Virginia University | M,D |

## CARDIOVASCULAR SCIENCES

| | |
|---|---|
| Albany Medical College | M,D |
| Augusta University | D |
| Baylor College of Medicine | D |
| Johns Hopkins University | M,D |
| Marquette University | M |
| McMaster University | M,D |
| Medical University of South Carolina | D |
| Memorial University of Newfoundland | M,D |
| Midwestern University, Glendale Campus | M |
| Milwaukee School of Engineering | M |
| Quinnipiac University | M |
| University of Calgary | M,D |
| University of Guelph | M,D,O |
| University of Mary | M |
| University of South Dakota | M,D |
| University of South Florida | O |
| The University of Toledo | M,D |
| Université Laval | O |

## CELL BIOLOGY

| | |
|---|---|
| Albany College of Pharmacy and Health Sciences | M |
| Albany Medical College | M,D |
| Albert Einstein College of Medicine | D |
| Appalachian State University | M |
| Arizona State University at Tempe | M,D |
| Auburn University | M,D |
| Augusta University | D |
| Baylor College of Medicine | D |
| Boston University | M,D |
| Brandeis University | M,D |
| Brown University | M,D |
| California Institute of Technology | D |
| California State University, Sacramento | M |
| Carnegie Mellon University | M,D |
| Case Western Reserve University | D |
| The Catholic University of America | M,D |
| Columbia University | M,D |
| Cornell University | D |
| Dartmouth College | D |
| Drexel University | M,D |
| Duke University | D,O |
| East Carolina University | M,D |
| Emory University | D |
| Emporia State University | M |
| Florida Institute of Technology | M |
| Florida State University | M,D |
| Georgia State University | M,D |
| Grand Valley State University | M |
| Harvard University | D* |
| Illinois Institute of Technology | M,D |
| Illinois State University | M,D |
| Indiana State University | M,D |
| Indiana University Bloomington | M,D |
| Indiana University-Purdue University Indianapolis | M,D |
| Iowa State University of Science and Technology | M,D |
| Irell & Manella Graduate School of Biological Sciences | D |
| Johns Hopkins University | D |
| Kent State University | M,D |
| Lehigh University | M,D |
| Liberty University | M,D |
| Louisiana State University Health Sciences Center | D |
| Louisiana State University Health Sciences Center at Shreveport | M,D |
| Loyola University Chicago | M,D |
| Marquette University | M,D |
| Massachusetts Institute of Technology | D |
| McGill University | M,D |
| McMaster University | M,D |
| Medical University of South Carolina | D |
| Michigan State University | M,D |
| Missouri State University | M |
| New York Medical College | M,D |
| North Carolina State University | M,D |
| North Dakota State University | D |
| Northeastern Illinois University | M |
| Northwestern University | D |
| The Ohio State University | M,D |
| Ohio University | M,D |
| Oregon Health & Science University | D |
| Oregon State University | M,D |
| Penn State Hershey Medical Center | D |
| Penn State University Park | M,D* |
| Purdue University | M,D |
| Quinnipiac University | M |
| Rice University | M,D |
| Rosalind Franklin University of Medicine and Science | D |
| Rush University | M,D |
| Rutgers University - Newark | D |
| Rutgers University - New Brunswick | M,D |
| San Diego State University | M,D |
| San Francisco State University | M |
| Southern Methodist University | M,D |
| State University of New York Downstate Medical Center | D |
| State University of New York Upstate Medical University | M,D |
| Stony Brook University, State University of New York | M,D |
| Texas Tech University Health Sciences Center | M,D |
| Thomas Jefferson University | M,D |
| Tufts University | D |
| Tulane University | M,D |
| Uniformed Services University of the Health Sciences | M,D |
| Universidad Central del Caribe | M,D |
| Université de Montréal | M,D |
| Université de Sherbrooke | M,D |
| University at Buffalo, the State University of New York | M,D |
| The University of Alabama at Birmingham | D |
| University of Alberta | M,D |
| The University of Arizona | D |
| University of Arkansas | M,D |
| The University of British Columbia | M,D |
| University of California, Berkeley | D |
| University of California, Davis | M,D |
| University of California, Irvine | M,D |
| University of California, Los Angeles | M,D |
| University of California, Riverside | M,D |
| University of California, San Francisco | D |
| University of California, Santa Barbara | M,D |
| University of California, Santa Cruz | M,D |
| University of Chicago | D |
| University of Cincinnati | D |
| University of Colorado Boulder | M,D |
| University of Colorado Denver | M,D |

*M—masters degree; D—doctorate; O—other advanced degree; *—Close-Up and/or Display*

| | |
|---|---|
| University of Connecticut | M,D |
| University of Connecticut Health Center | D |
| University of Delaware | M,D |
| University of Denver | M,D |
| University of Florida | M,D |
| University of Georgia | M,D |
| University of Guelph | M,D |
| University of Illinois at Chicago | M,D |
| University of Illinois at Urbana-Champaign | D |
| The University of Iowa | M,D |
| The University of Kansas | M,D |
| The University of Manchester | M,D |
| University of Maryland, Baltimore | M,D |
| University of Maryland, Baltimore County | D |
| University of Maryland, College Park | M,D |
| University of Massachusetts Amherst | M,D |
| University of Miami | D |
| University of Michigan | M,D |
| University of Minnesota, Twin Cities Campus | M,D |
| University of Missouri–Kansas City | D |
| University of Montana | D |
| University of Nebraska Medical Center | M,D |
| University of Nevada, Reno | M,D |
| University of New Haven | M |
| University of New Mexico | M,D |
| The University of North Carolina at Chapel Hill | M,D |
| University of Notre Dame | M,D |
| University of Oklahoma Health Sciences Center | M,D |
| University of Ottawa | M,D |
| University of Pennsylvania | D |
| University of Pittsburgh | D* |
| University of Puerto Rico at Rio Piedras | M,D |
| University of Rhode Island | M,D |
| University of Saskatchewan | M,D |
| University of South Carolina | M,D |
| University of South Dakota | M,D |
| University of Southern California | M,D |
| University of South Florida | M,D |
| The University of Texas at Austin | D |
| The University of Texas at Dallas | M,D |
| The University of Texas at San Antonio | M,D |
| The University of Texas Health Science Center at Houston | M,D |
| The University of Texas Health Science Center at San Antonio | M,D |
| The University of Texas Medical Branch | M,D |
| The University of Texas Southwestern Medical Center | D |
| University of the Sciences | M |
| University of Toronto | M,D |
| University of Vermont | D |
| University of Virginia | D |
| University of Washington | D |
| The University of Western Ontario | M,D |
| University of Wisconsin–La Crosse | M |
| University of Wisconsin–Madison | D |
| University of Wisconsin–Milwaukee | M,D* |
| University of Wyoming | D |
| Université Laval | M,D |
| Vanderbilt University | M,D* |
| Washington University in St. Louis | D |
| Weill Cornell Medicine | M,D |
| Wesleyan University | D |
| Yale University | D |

## CELTIC LANGUAGES

| | |
|---|---|
| Harvard University | D* |

## CERAMIC SCIENCES AND ENGINEERING

| | |
|---|---|
| Alfred University | M,D |
| Missouri University of Science and Technology | M,D |

## CHEMICAL ENGINEERING

| | |
|---|---|
| American University of Sharjah | M,D |
| Arizona State University at Tempe | M,D |
| Auburn University | M,D |
| Brigham Young University | M,D |
| Brown University | M,D |
| Bucknell University | M |
| California Institute of Technology | M,D |
| Carnegie Mellon University | M,D |
| Case Western Reserve University | M,D |
| City College of the City University of New York | M,D |
| Clemson University | M,D |
| Cleveland State University | M,D |
| Colorado School of Mines | M,D |
| Colorado State University | M,D |
| Columbia University | M,D |
| Cooper Union for the Advancement of Science and Art | M |
| Cornell University | M,D |
| Dalhousie University | M,D |
| Dartmouth College | M,D |
| Drexel University | M,D |
| Fairleigh Dickinson University, Florham Campus | M,O |
| Florida Agricultural and Mechanical University | M,D |
| Florida Institute of Technology | M,D |
| Florida State University | M,D |
| Georgia Institute of Technology | M,D |
| Howard University | M |
| Illinois Institute of Technology | M,D |
| Instituto Tecnológico y de Estudios Superiores de Monterrey, Campus Monterrey | M,D |
| Iowa State University of Science and Technology | M,D |
| Johns Hopkins University | M,D |
| Kansas State University | M,D,O |
| Lamar University | M,D |
| Lehigh University | M,D |
| Louisiana State University and Agricultural & Mechanical College | M,D |
| Manhattan College | M |
| Massachusetts Institute of Technology | M,D |
| McGill University | M,D |
| McMaster University | M,D |
| McNeese State University | M |
| Miami University | M |
| Michigan State University | M,D |
| Michigan Technological University | M,D |
| Mississippi State University | M,D |
| Missouri University of Science and Technology | M,D |
| Montana State University | M,D |
| New Jersey Institute of Technology | M,D |
| New York University | M,D |
| North Carolina Agricultural and Technical State University | M |
| North Carolina State University | M,D |
| Northeastern University | M,D,O |
| Northwestern University | M,D |
| The Ohio State University | M,D |
| Ohio University | M,D |
| Oklahoma State University | M,D |
| Oregon State University | M,D |
| Penn State University Park | M,D* |
| Polytechnique Montréal | M,D,O |
| Princeton University | M,D |
| Purdue University | M,D |
| Queen's University at Kingston | M,D |
| Rensselaer Polytechnic Institute | M,D |
| Rice University | M,D |
| Rose-Hulman Institute of Technology | M |
| Rowan University | M |
| Royal Military College of Canada | M,D |
| Rutgers University - New Brunswick | M,D |
| San Jose State University | M |
| South Dakota School of Mines and Technology | M,D |
| Stanford University | M,D |
| Stevens Institute of Technology | M,D,O |
| Syracuse University | M,D |
| Tennessee Technological University | M |
| Texas A&M University | M,D |
| Texas A&M University–Kingsville | M |
| Tufts University | M,D |
| Tulane University | M,D |
| UNB Fredericton | M,D |
| Universidad de las Américas Puebla | M |
| Université de Sherbrooke | M,D |
| University at Buffalo, the State University of New York | M,D,O |
| The University of Akron | M,D |
| The University of Alabama | M,D |
| The University of Alabama in Huntsville | M,D |
| University of Alberta | M,D |
| The University of Arizona | M,D |
| University of Arkansas | M,D |
| The University of British Columbia | M,D |
| University of Calgary | M,D |
| University of California, Berkeley | M,D |
| University of California, Davis | M,D |
| University of California, Irvine | M,D |
| University of California, Los Angeles | M,D |
| University of California, Riverside | M,D |
| University of California, San Diego | M,D |
| University of California, Santa Barbara | M,D |
| University of Cincinnati | M,D |
| University of Colorado Boulder | M,D |
| University of Connecticut | M,D |
| University of Dayton | M |
| University of Delaware | M,D |
| University of Florida | M,D,O |
| University of Houston | M,D |
| University of Idaho | M,D |
| University of Illinois at Chicago | M,D |
| University of Illinois at Urbana-Champaign | M,D |
| The University of Iowa | M,D |
| The University of Kansas | M,D,O |
| University of Kentucky | M,D |
| University of Louisiana at Lafayette | M |
| University of Louisville | M,D |
| University of Maine | M,D |
| The University of Manchester | M,D |
| University of Maryland, Baltimore County | M,D |
| University of Maryland, College Park | M,D |
| University of Massachusetts Amherst | M,D |
| University of Massachusetts Lowell | M,D |
| University of Michigan | M,D,O |
| University of Minnesota, Twin Cities Campus | M,D |
| University of Mississippi | M,D |
| University of Missouri | M,D |
| University of Nebraska–Lincoln | M,D |
| University of Nevada, Reno | M,D |
| University of New Hampshire | M,D |
| University of New Mexico | M,D |
| University of North Dakota | M,D |
| University of Notre Dame | M,D |
| University of Oklahoma | M,D |
| University of Ottawa | M,D |
| University of Pennsylvania | M,D |
| University of Pittsburgh | M,D* |
| University of Puerto Rico at Mayagüez | M,D |
| University of Rhode Island | M,D,O |
| University of Rochester | M,D |
| University of Saskatchewan | M,D |
| University of South Africa | M |
| University of South Alabama | M |
| University of South Carolina | M,D |
| University of Southern California | M,D,O |
| University of South Florida | M,D,O |
| The University of Tennessee | M,D |
| The University of Tennessee at Chattanooga | M |
| The University of Texas at Austin | M,D |
| The University of Toledo | M,D |
| University of Toronto | M,D |
| The University of Tulsa | M,D |
| University of Utah | M,D |
| University of Virginia | M,D |
| University of Washington | M,D |
| University of Waterloo | M,D |
| The University of Western Ontario | M,D |
| University of Wisconsin–Madison | D |
| University of Wyoming | M,D |
| Université Laval | M,D |
| Vanderbilt University | M,D* |
| Villanova University | M,O |
| Virginia Polytechnic Institute and State University | M,D |
| Washington State University | M,D |
| Washington University in St. Louis | M,D |
| Wayne State University | M,D,O |
| Western Michigan University | M,D |
| West Virginia University | M,D |
| Widener University | M |
| Worcester Polytechnic Institute | M,D |
| Yale University | M,D |

## CHEMICAL PHYSICS

| | |
|---|---|
| Columbia University | M,D |
| Cornell University | D |
| Harvard University | D* |
| Kent State University | M,D |
| Marquette University | M,D |
| McMaster University | M,D |
| Michigan State University | M,D |
| The Ohio State University | M,D |
| Tufts University | M,D |
| University of Illinois at Urbana-Champaign | M,D |
| University of Louisville | M,D |
| University of Maryland, College Park | M,D |
| University of Minnesota, Twin Cities Campus | M,D |
| University of Nevada, Reno | D |
| The University of Tennessee | M,D |
| University of Utah | M,D |
| Virginia Commonwealth University | M,D |
| Wesleyan University | D |

## CHEMISTRY

| | |
|---|---|
| Acadia University | M |
| American University | M |
| The American University in Cairo | M,D,O |
| Arizona State University at Tempe | M,D |
| Arkansas State University | M,O |
| Auburn University | M,D |
| Ball State University | M,D |
| Baylor University | M,D |
| Binghamton University, State University of New York | M,D |
| Boise State University | M |
| Boston College | M,D |
| Boston University | M,D |
| Bowling Green State University | M,D |
| Bradley University | M |
| Brandeis University | M,D |
| Brigham Young University | M,D |
| Brock University | M,D |
| Brooklyn College of the City University of New York | M,D |
| Brown University | D |
| Bryn Mawr College | M,D |
| Bucknell University | M |
| Cabrini University | M,D |
| California Institute of Technology | M,D |
| California Polytechnic State University, San Luis Obispo | M |
| California State Polytechnic University, Pomona | M |
| California State University, East Bay | M |
| California State University, Fresno | M |
| California State University, Fullerton | M |
| California State University, Long Beach | M |
| California State University, Los Angeles | M |
| California State University, Northridge | M |
| California State University, Sacramento | M |
| Carleton University | M,D |
| Carnegie Mellon University | D |
| Case Western Reserve University | M,D |
| Central Michigan University | M |
| Central Washington University | M |
| City College of the City University of New York | M,D |
| Clark Atlanta University | M,D |
| Clarkson University | M,D |
| Clark University | D |
| Clemson University | M,D |
| Cleveland State University | M,D |
| Colorado School of Mines | M,D |
| Colorado State University | M,D |
| Colorado State University-Pueblo | M |
| Columbia University | M,D |
| Columbus State University | M,O |
| Concordia University (Canada) | M,D |
| Cornell University | D |
| Dalhousie University | M,D |
| Dartmouth College | M,D |
| Delaware State University | M,D |
| DePaul University | M,D |
| Drew University | M,D,O |
| Drexel University | M,D |
| Duke University | D |
| Duquesne University | D |
| East Carolina University | M |
| Eastern Illinois University | M |
| Eastern Kentucky University | M |
| Eastern Michigan University | M |
| Eastern New Mexico University | M |
| East Tennessee State University | M |
| Emory University | D |
| Fairleigh Dickinson University, Florham Campus | M |
| Fairleigh Dickinson University, Metropolitan Campus | M |
| Fisk University | M |
| Florida Agricultural and Mechanical University | M |
| Florida Atlantic University | M,D |
| Florida Institute of Technology | M,D |
| Florida International University | M,D |
| Florida State University | M,D |
| Furman University | M |
| George Mason University | M,D |
| Georgetown University | D |
| The George Washington University | M,D |
| Georgia Institute of Technology | M,D |
| Georgia State University | M,D |
| The Graduate Center, City University of New York | D |
| Hampton University | M |
| Harvard University | D* |
| Howard University | M,D |
| Hunter College of the City University of New York | D |
| Idaho State University | M |
| Illinois Institute of Technology | M,D |
| Indiana University Bloomington | M,D |
| Indiana University of Pennsylvania | M |
| Indiana University-Purdue University Indianapolis | M,D |
| Instituto Tecnológico y de Estudios Superiores de Monterrey, Campus Monterrey | M,D |
| Iowa State University of Science and Technology | M,D |
| Jackson State University | M,D |
| Johns Hopkins University | M,D |
| Kansas State University | M,D |
| Kennesaw State University | M |
| Kent State University | M,D |
| Lakehead University | M |
| Lamar University | M |
| Laurentian University | M |
| Lehigh University | M,D |
| Long Island University - Brooklyn | M,D,O |
| Louisiana State University and Agricultural & Mechanical College | M,D |
| Louisiana Tech University | M,D,O |
| Loyola University Chicago | M,D |
| Manhattanville College | M,O |
| Marquette University | M,D |
| Marshall University | M |
| Massachusetts Institute of Technology | D |
| McGill University | M,D |
| McMaster University | M,D |
| McNeese State University | M |
| MCPHS University | M,D |
| Memorial University of Newfoundland | M,D |
| Miami University | M,D |
| Michigan State University | M,D |
| Michigan Technological University | M,D |
| Middle Tennessee State University | M |
| Mississippi College | M |
| Mississippi State University | M,D |
| Missouri State University | M |
| Missouri University of Science and Technology | M,D |
| Missouri Western State University | M |
| Montana State University | M,D |
| Montclair State University | M |
| Morgan State University | M |
| Mount Allison University | M |
| Murray State University | M |
| New Jersey Institute of Technology | M,D,O |
| New Mexico Highlands University | M |
| New Mexico Institute of Mining and Technology | M,D |
| New York University | M,D |
| North Carolina Agricultural and Technical State University | M |
| North Carolina Central University | M |
| North Carolina State University | M,D |
| North Dakota State University | M,D |
| Northeastern Illinois University | M |
| Northeastern University | M,D |
| Northern Arizona University | M |
| Northern Illinois University | M,D |
| Northwestern University | D |
| Oakland University | M,D |
| The Ohio State University | M,D |
| Oklahoma State University | M,D |
| Old Dominion University | M,D |
| Oregon State University | M,D |
| Pace University | M,O |
| Penn State University Park | M,D* |
| Pittsburg State University | M |
| Pontifical Catholic University of Puerto Rico | M |
| Portland State University | M,D |
| Prairie View A&M University | M |
| Princeton University | M,D |
| Purdue University | M,D |
| Queens College of the City University of New York | M |
| Queen's University at Kingston | M,D |

| | |
|---|---|
| Rensselaer Polytechnic Institute | M,D |
| Rice University | M,D |
| Rochester Institute of Technology | M |
| Roosevelt University | M |
| Royal Military College of Canada | M,D |
| Rutgers University - Camden | M |
| Rutgers University - Newark | M,D |
| Rutgers University - New Brunswick | M,D |
| Sacred Heart University | M |
| St. Francis Xavier University | M |
| St. John Fisher College | M |
| St. John's University (NY) | M |
| Saint Louis University | M,D |
| Sam Houston State University | M |
| San Diego State University | M,D |
| San Francisco State University | M |
| San Jose State University | M |
| The Scripps Research Institute | D |
| Seton Hall University | M,D |
| Simon Fraser University | M,D |
| Smith College | M |
| South Dakota State University | M,D |
| Southeast Missouri State University | M |
| Southern Connecticut State University | M |
| Southern Illinois University Carbondale | M,D |
| Southern Illinois University Edwardsville | M |
| Southern Methodist University | M,D |
| Southern University and Agricultural and Mechanical College | M |
| Stanford University | D |
| State University of New York at New Paltz | M,O |
| State University of New York at Oswego | M |
| State University of New York College of Environmental Science and Forestry | M,D |
| Stephen F. Austin State University | M |
| Stevens Institute of Technology | M,D,O |
| Stevenson University | M |
| Stony Brook University, State University of New York | M,D |
| SUNY Brockport | M,O |
| Syracuse University | M,D |
| Teachers College, Columbia University | M,D |
| Temple University | M,D* |
| Tennessee State University | M |
| Tennessee Technological University | M,D |
| Texas A&M University | M,D |
| Texas A&M University–Commerce | M,O |
| Texas A&M University–Corpus Christi | M,D |
| Texas A&M University–Kingsville | M |
| Texas Christian University | M,D |
| Texas Southern University | M |
| Texas State University | M |
| Texas Tech University | M,D |
| Texas Woman's University | M |
| Trent University | M |
| Tufts University | M,D |
| Tulane University | M,D |
| Tuskegee University | M |
| UNB Fredericton | M,D |
| Universidad del Turabo | M,D |
| Université de Moncton | M |
| Université de Montréal | M,D |
| Université de Sherbrooke | M,D,O |
| Université du Québec à Montréal | M,D |
| Université du Québec à Trois-Rivières | M |
| University at Albany, State University of New York | M,D |
| University at Buffalo, the State University of New York | M,D |
| The University of Akron | M,D |
| The University of Alabama | M,D |
| The University of Alabama at Birmingham | M,D |
| The University of Alabama in Huntsville | M,D |
| University of Alaska Fairbanks | M,D |
| University of Alberta | M,D |
| The University of Arizona | M,D |
| University of Arkansas | M,D |
| University of Arkansas at Little Rock | M |
| The University of British Columbia | M,D |
| University of Calgary | M,D |
| University of California, Berkeley | D |
| University of California, Davis | M,D |
| University of California, Irvine | M,D |
| University of California, Los Angeles | M,D |
| University of California, Merced | M,D |
| University of California, Riverside | M,D |
| University of California, San Diego | M,D |
| University of California, San Francisco | D |
| University of California, Santa Barbara | M,D |
| University of California, Santa Cruz | M,D |
| University of Central Florida | M,D,O |
| University of Chicago | D |
| University of Cincinnati | M,D |
| University of Colorado Boulder | M,D |
| University of Colorado Denver | M |
| University of Connecticut | M,D |
| University of Dayton | M |
| University of Delaware | M,D |
| University of Denver | M,D |
| University of Detroit Mercy | M,D |
| University of Florida | M,D |
| University of Georgia | M,D |
| University of Guelph | M,D |
| University of Hawaii at Manoa | M,D |
| University of Houston | M,D |
| University of Houston–Clear Lake | M |
| University of Idaho | M,D |
| University of Illinois at Chicago | M,D |
| University of Illinois at Urbana-Champaign | M,D |
| The University of Iowa | D |
| The University of Kansas | M,D |
| University of Kentucky | M,D |
| University of Lethbridge | M,D |
| University of Louisville | M,D |
| University of Maine | M,D |
| The University of Manchester | M,D |
| University of Manitoba | M,D |
| University of Maryland, Baltimore County | M,D,O |
| University of Maryland, College Park | M,D |
| University of Maryland Eastern Shore | M,D |
| University of Massachusetts Amherst | M,D |
| University of Massachusetts Boston | M,D |
| University of Massachusetts Dartmouth | M,D |
| University of Massachusetts Lowell | M,D |
| University of Memphis | M,D |
| University of Miami | M,D |
| University of Michigan | M,D |
| University of Minnesota, Duluth | M |
| University of Minnesota, Twin Cities Campus | M,D |
| University of Mississippi | M,D |
| University of Missouri | D |
| University of Missouri–Kansas City | M,D |
| University of Missouri–St. Louis | M,D |
| University of Montana | M,D |
| University of Nebraska–Lincoln | M,D |
| University of Nevada, Las Vegas | M,D |
| University of Nevada, Reno | M,D |
| University of New Hampshire | M,D |
| University of New Mexico | M,D |
| University of New Orleans | M,D |
| The University of North Carolina at Chapel Hill | M,D |
| The University of North Carolina at Charlotte | M,D |
| The University of North Carolina at Greensboro | M |
| The University of North Carolina Wilmington | M |
| University of North Dakota | M,D |
| University of Northern Colorado | M,D |
| University of North Texas | M,D,O |
| University of Notre Dame | M,D |
| University of Oklahoma | M,D |
| University of Oregon | M,D |
| University of Ottawa | M,D |
| University of Pennsylvania | M,D |
| University of Pittsburgh | M,D* |
| University of Prince Edward Island | M,D |
| University of Puerto Rico at Mayagüez | M,D |
| University of Puerto Rico at Rio Piedras | M,D |
| University of Regina | M,D |
| University of Rhode Island | M,D |
| University of Rochester | D |
| University of Saint Joseph | M |
| University of San Francisco | M |
| University of Saskatchewan | M,D |
| The University of Scranton | M |
| University of South Alabama | M |
| University of South Carolina | M,D |
| University of South Dakota | M,D |
| University of Southern California | D |
| University of South Florida | M,D |
| The University of Tennessee | M,D |
| The University of Texas at Arlington | M,D |
| The University of Texas at Austin | D |
| The University of Texas at Dallas | M,D |
| The University of Texas at El Paso | M,D |
| The University of Texas at San Antonio | M,D |
| The University of Texas Rio Grande Valley | M |
| University of the Sciences | M,D |
| The University of Toledo | M,D |
| University of Toronto | M,D |
| University of Utah | M,D |
| University of Vermont | M,D |
| University of Victoria | M,D |
| University of Virginia | M,D |
| University of Washington | M,D |
| University of Waterloo | M,D |
| The University of Western Ontario | M,D |
| University of Windsor | M,D |
| University of Wisconsin–Madison | M,D |
| University of Wisconsin–Milwaukee | M,D* |
| University of Wyoming | M,D |
| Université Laval | M,D |
| Utah State University | M,D |
| Vanderbilt University | M,D* |
| Villanova University | M |
| Virginia Commonwealth University | M,D |
| Virginia Polytechnic Institute and State University | M,D |
| Wake Forest University | M,D |
| Washington State University | M,D |
| Washington University in St. Louis | D |
| Wayne State University | M,D |
| Wesleyan University | D |
| Western Carolina University | M |
| Western Illinois University | M |
| Western Kentucky University | M |
| Western Michigan University | M,D,O |
| Western Washington University | M |
| West Texas A&M University | M |
| West Virginia University | M,D |
| Wichita State University | M,D |
| Wilfrid Laurier University | M |
| Worcester Polytechnic Institute | M,D |
| Wright State University | M |
| Yale University | D |
| York University | M,D |
| Youngstown State University | M |

## CHILD AND FAMILY STUDIES

| | |
|---|---|
| Alabama Agricultural and Mechanical University | M |
| Amberton University | M |
| Arizona State University at Tempe | M,D |
| Asbury University | M |
| Assumption University | M,O |
| Auburn University | M,D |
| Bank Street College of Education | M |
| Brandeis University | M,D |
| Brigham Young University | M,D |
| Brock University | M |
| California State University, East Bay | M |
| California State University, Los Angeles | M |
| Capella University | M |
| Central Michigan University | M,O |
| Central Washington University | M |
| Colorado State University | M,D |
| Concordia University (Canada) | M |
| Concordia University, St. Paul | M |
| Concordia University Wisconsin | M |
| Cornell University | M,D |
| Dallas Theological Seminary | M,D,O |
| East Carolina University | M,D |
| Fairfield University | M,O |
| Florida State University | M,D |
| Iowa State University of Science and Technology | M,D |
| Kansas State University | M,D,O |
| Kent State University | M,D |
| Liberty University | M,D,O |
| Loma Linda University | M,D,O |
| London Metropolitan University | M,D |
| Miami University | M |
| Michigan State University | M,D |
| Mississippi State University | M,D |
| Missouri State University | M |
| Montclair State University | M,D,O |
| Mount Saint Vincent University | M |
| North Carolina Agricultural and Technical State University | M |
| North Dakota State University | M,D,O |
| Northern Illinois University | M |
| The Ohio State University | M,D |
| Ohio University | M |
| Oklahoma State University | M,D |
| Omega Graduate School | M,D |
| Oregon State University | M,D |
| Penn State University Park | M,D* |
| Purdue University | M,D |
| Purdue University Northwest | M |
| Queens College of the City University of New York | M,O |
| Roberts Wesleyan College | M |
| St. Cloud State University | M |
| San Diego State University | M |
| San Jose State University | M |
| South Carolina State University | M |
| Spring Arbor University | M |
| State University of New York at Oswego | M |
| Syracuse University | M,D |
| Texas State University | M |
| Texas Tech University | M,D |
| Texas Woman's University | M,D |
| Towson University | M,O |
| Tufts University | M,D |
| The University of Akron | M |
| The University of Alabama | M |
| The University of Arizona | M,D,O |
| University of Central Oklahoma | M |
| University of Colorado Denver | M,D |
| University of Connecticut | M,D |
| University of Delaware | M,D |
| University of Denver | M,D,O |
| University of Georgia | M |
| University of Guelph | M,D |
| University of Illinois at Springfield | M,O |
| University of Kentucky | M,D |
| University of La Verne | M |
| University of Maryland, College Park | M,D |
| University of Massachusetts Amherst | M,D,O |
| University of Minnesota, Twin Cities Campus | M,D |
| University of Missouri | M,D |
| University of Montana | M,D,O |
| University of Nebraska–Lincoln | M,D |
| University of Nevada, Reno | M |
| University of New Hampshire | M,O |
| University of New Mexico | M,D |
| University of North Alabama | M |
| The University of North Carolina at Charlotte | M,D,O |
| The University of North Carolina at Greensboro | M,D |
| University of North Texas | M,D,O |
| University of Rhode Island | M |
| University of Southern California | M,D |
| University of Southern Mississippi | M |
| University of South Florida | M,D,O |
| The University of Tennessee | M,D |
| The University of Tennessee at Martin | M |
| The University of Texas at Austin | M,D |
| The University of Texas at Dallas | M,D |
| University of Utah | M |
| University of Victoria | M,D |
| University of Wisconsin–Madison | M,D |
| Utah State University | M,D |
| Vanderbilt University | M* |
| Walden University | M,D |
| Washington University in St. Louis | M,D |

## CHILD DEVELOPMENT

| | |
|---|---|
| California State University, Los Angeles | M |
| California State University, Sacramento | M,D,O |
| California State University, San Bernardino | M |
| Chaminade University of Honolulu | M |
| East Carolina University | M,D |
| Erikson Institute | M |
| Fielding Graduate University | M,D,O |
| Kansas State University | M,D,O |
| Lee University | M |
| Michigan State University | M,D |
| Montclair State University | M,O |
| Mount Saint Mary College | M,O |
| North Carolina Agricultural and Technical State University | M |
| North Dakota State University | M |
| Ohio University | M |
| Purdue University | M,D |
| Purdue University Northwest | M |
| Rutgers University - Camden | M,D |
| San Diego State University | M |
| Sarah Lawrence College | M |
| Texas Woman's University | M,D |
| Tufts University | M,D |
| The University of Akron | M |
| University of California, Davis | M |
| University of Florida | M |
| University of La Verne | M |
| University of Minnesota, Twin Cities Campus | M,D |
| University of Nebraska–Lincoln | M,D |
| The University of North Carolina at Charlotte | M,D,O |
| The University of Tennessee at Martin | M |
| The University of Texas at Austin | M,D |
| The University of West Alabama | M,O |
| University of Wyoming | M |
| Whittier College | M |

## CHINESE

| | |
|---|---|
| Arizona State University at Tempe | M,D |
| Brandeis University | M |
| DePaul University | M |
| Harvard University | D* |
| Hunter College of the City University of New York | M |
| Indiana University Bloomington | M,D |
| Middlebury College | M |
| New York University | M,D,O |
| The Ohio State University | M,D |
| Saginaw Valley State University | M |
| San Francisco State University | M |
| Stanford University | M,D |
| University of Alberta | M |
| University of California, Berkeley | D |
| University of California, Irvine | M,D |
| University of Colorado Boulder | M,D |
| University of Delaware | M |
| University of Hawaii at Manoa | M,D,O |
| The University of Iowa | M |
| The University of Manchester | D |
| University of Massachusetts Amherst | M |
| University of Oregon | M,D |
| University of Pittsburgh | M* |
| University of Washington | M,D |
| University of Wisconsin–Madison | M,D |
| Washington University in St. Louis | M,D |

## CHIROPRACTIC

| | |
|---|---|
| Canadian Memorial Chiropractic College | D,O |
| Cleveland University–Kansas City | D |
| D'Youville College | D |
| Institut Franco-Européen de Chiropraxie | D |
| Life Chiropractic College West | D |
| Life University | D |
| Logan University | D |
| National University of Health Sciences | M,D |
| New York Chiropractic College | D |
| Northwestern Health Sciences University | D |
| Palmer College of Chiropractic | D |
| Parker University | D |
| Sherman College of Chiropractic | D |
| Southern California University of Health Sciences | D |
| Texas Chiropractic College | D |
| Université du Québec à Trois-Rivières | D |
| University of Bridgeport | D |
| University of Western States | D |

## CIVIL ENGINEERING

| | |
|---|---|
| American University of Sharjah | M,D |
| Arizona State University at Tempe | M,D |

*M—masters degree; D—doctorate; O—other advanced degree; *—Close-Up and/or Display*

| | |
|---|---|
| Auburn University | M,D |
| Boise State University | M |
| Bradley University | M |
| Brigham Young University | M,D |
| Bucknell University | M |
| California Institute of Technology | M,D,O |
| California Polytechnic State University, San Luis Obispo | M |
| California State Polytechnic University, Pomona | M |
| California State University, Fresno | M |
| California State University, Fullerton | M |
| California State University, Long Beach | M |
| California State University, Los Angeles | M |
| California State University, Northridge | M |
| California State University, Sacramento | M |
| Carleton University | M,D |
| Carnegie Mellon University | M,D |
| Case Western Reserve University | M,D |
| The Catholic University of America | M,D,O |
| The Citadel, The Military College of South Carolina | M,O |
| City College of the City University of New York | M,D |
| Clarkson University | M,D |
| Clemson University | M,D |
| Cleveland State University | M,D |
| Colorado School of Mines | M,D |
| Colorado State University | M,D |
| Columbia University | M,D |
| Concordia University (Canada) | M,D,O |
| Cooper Union for the Advancement of Science and Art | M |
| Cornell University | M,D |
| Dalhousie University | M,D |
| Drexel University | M,D |
| Duke University | M,D |
| Embry-Riddle Aeronautical University–Daytona | M |
| Florida Agricultural and Mechanical University | M,D |
| Florida Atlantic University | M |
| Florida Institute of Technology | M,D |
| Florida International University | M,D |
| Florida State University | M,D |
| George Mason University | M,D |
| The George Washington University | M,D,O |
| Georgia Institute of Technology | M,D |
| Georgia Southern University | M |
| Howard University | M |
| Idaho State University | M |
| Illinois Institute of Technology | M,D |
| Instituto Tecnológico y de Estudios Superiores de Monterrey, Campus Monterrey | M,D |
| Iowa State University of Science and Technology | M,D |
| Jackson State University | M,D |
| Johns Hopkins University | M,D,O |
| Kansas State University | M,D |
| Kennesaw State University | M |
| Lawrence Technological University | M,D |
| Lehigh University | M,D |
| Louisiana State University and Agricultural & Mechanical College | M,D |
| Loyola Marymount University | M |
| Manhattan College | M |
| Marquette University | M,D,O |
| Massachusetts Institute of Technology | M,D,O |
| McGill University | M,D |
| McMaster University | M,D |
| McNeese State University | M |
| Memorial University of Newfoundland | M,D |
| Merrimack College | M |
| Michigan State University | M,D |
| Michigan Technological University | M,D |
| Milwaukee School of Engineering | M |
| Mississippi State University | M,D |
| Missouri University of Science and Technology | M,D |
| Montana State University | M,D |
| Morgan State University | M,D,O |
| New York University | M,D |
| North Carolina Agricultural and Technical State University | M |
| North Carolina State University | M,D |
| North Dakota State University | M,D |
| Northeastern University | M,D,O |
| Northern Arizona University | M |
| Northwestern University | M,D |
| Norwich University | M |
| The Ohio State University | M,D |
| Ohio University | M,D |
| Oklahoma State University | M,D |
| Old Dominion University | M,D |
| Oregon State University | M,D |
| Penn State Harrisburg | M,O |
| Penn State University Park | M,D* |
| Polytechnic University of Puerto Rico | M |
| Polytechnique Montréal | M,D,O |
| Portland State University | M,D,O |
| Princeton University | M,D |
| Purdue University | M,D |
| Purdue University Fort Wayne | M |
| Queen's University at Kingston | M,D |
| Rensselaer Polytechnic Institute | M,D |
| Rice University | M,D |
| Rose-Hulman Institute of Technology | M |
| Rowan University | M |
| Royal Military College of Canada | M,D |
| Rutgers University - New Brunswick | M,D |
| Saint Martin's University | M |
| San Diego State University | M |
| San Jose State University | M |
| Santa Clara University | M,D,O |
| South Carolina State University | M |
| South Dakota School of Mines and Technology | M,D |
| South Dakota State University | M |
| Southern Illinois University Carbondale | M,D |
| Southern Illinois University Edwardsville | M |
| Southern Methodist University | M,D |
| Stevens Institute of Technology | M,D,O |
| Stony Brook University, State University of New York | M,D,O |
| Syracuse University | M,D |
| Temple University | M,O* |
| Tennessee State University | M,D |
| Tennessee Technological University | M |
| Texas A&M University | M,D |
| Texas A&M University–Kingsville | M |
| Texas State University | M |
| Tufts University | M,D |
| UNB Fredericton | M,D |
| United States Merchant Marine Academy | M |
| Université de Moncton | M |
| Université de Sherbrooke | M,D |
| University at Buffalo, the State University of New York | M,D |
| The University of Akron | M,D |
| The University of Alabama | M,D |
| The University of Alabama at Birmingham | M,D |
| The University of Alabama in Huntsville | M,D |
| University of Alaska Fairbanks | M,D,O |
| University of Alberta | M,D |
| University of Arkansas | M,D |
| The University of British Columbia | M,D |
| University of Calgary | M,D |
| University of California, Berkeley | M,D |
| University of California, Davis | M,D,O |
| University of California, Irvine | M,D |
| University of California, Los Angeles | M,D |
| University of Central Florida | M,D,O |
| University of Cincinnati | M,D |
| University of Colorado Boulder | M,D |
| University of Colorado Denver | M,D |
| University of Connecticut | M,D |
| University of Dayton | M |
| University of Delaware | M,D |
| University of Detroit Mercy | M,D |
| University of Florida | M,D |
| University of Hawaii at Manoa | M,D |
| University of Houston | M,D |
| University of Idaho | M,D |
| University of Illinois at Chicago | M,D |
| University of Illinois at Urbana-Champaign | M,D |
| The University of Iowa | M,D |
| The University of Kansas | M,D |
| University of Kentucky | M,D |
| University of Louisiana at Lafayette | M |
| University of Louisville | M,D |
| University of Maine | M,D |
| The University of Manchester | M,D |
| University of Manitoba | M,D |
| University of Maryland, College Park | M,D |
| University of Massachusetts Amherst | M,D |
| University of Massachusetts Dartmouth | M |
| University of Massachusetts Lowell | M,D |
| University of Memphis | M,D,O |
| University of Miami | M,D |
| University of Michigan | M,D,O |
| University of Minnesota, Twin Cities Campus | M,D,O |
| University of Mississippi | M,D |
| University of Missouri | M,D |
| University of Missouri–Kansas City | M,D,O |
| University of Nebraska–Lincoln | M,D |
| University of Nevada, Reno | M,D |
| University of New Hampshire | M,D |
| University of New Haven | M |
| University of New Mexico | M,D |
| University of New Orleans | M |
| University of North Dakota | M,D |
| University of North Florida | M |
| University of Notre Dame | M,D |
| University of Oklahoma | M,D |
| University of Ottawa | M,D |
| University of Pittsburgh | M,D* |
| University of Portland | M |
| University of Puerto Rico at Mayagüez | M,D |
| University of Rhode Island | M,D |
| University of Saskatchewan | M,D |
| University of South Alabama | M |
| University of South Carolina | M,D |
| University of Southern California | M,D,O |
| University of South Florida | M,D,O |
| The University of Tennessee | M,D |
| The University of Tennessee at Chattanooga | M |
| The University of Texas at Arlington | M,D |
| The University of Texas at Austin | M,D |
| The University of Texas at El Paso | M,D,O |
| The University of Texas at San Antonio | M,D |
| The University of Texas at Tyler | M |
| The University of Toledo | M,D |
| University of Toronto | M,D |
| University of Utah | M,D |
| University of Vermont | M,D |
| University of Virginia | M,D |
| University of Washington | M,D |
| University of Waterloo | M,D |
| The University of Western Ontario | M,D |
| University of Windsor | M,D |
| University of Wisconsin–Madison | M |
| University of Wisconsin–Milwaukee | M,D* |
| University of Wyoming | M,D |
| Université Laval | M,D,O |
| Utah State University | M,D,O |
| Vanderbilt University | M,D* |
| Villanova University | M |
| Virginia Polytechnic Institute and State University | M,D,O |
| Washington State University | M,D |
| Wayne State University | M,D |
| Wentworth Institute of Technology | M |
| Western Michigan University | M |
| Western New England University | M |
| West Virginia University | M,D |
| Widener University | M |
| Worcester Polytechnic Institute | M,D,O |
| Youngstown State University | M |

## CLASSICS

| | |
|---|---|
| Asbury University | M |
| Bethel Seminary | M,D,O |
| Boston College | M |
| Boston University | M,D |
| Brandeis University | M |
| Brigham Young University | M |
| Brock University | M |
| Brown University | M,D |
| Bryn Mawr College | M,D |
| The Catholic University of America | M,D,O |
| Columbia University | M,D |
| Cornell University | D |
| Dalhousie University | M,D |
| Duke University | D |
| Duquesne University | M |
| Florida State University | M,D |
| Fordham University | M,D |
| The Graduate Center, City University of New York | M,D |
| Harvard University | D* |
| Heritage Christian University | M |
| Hunter College of the City University of New York | M |
| Indiana University Bloomington | M,D |
| Johns Hopkins University | D |
| Knox Theological Seminary | M |
| McMaster University | M,D |
| Memorial University of Newfoundland | M |
| New York University | M,D,O |
| The Ohio State University | M,D |
| Princeton University | D |
| Queen's University at Kingston | M |
| Rutgers University - New Brunswick | M,D |
| San Francisco State University | M |
| Stanford University | M,D |
| Tufts University | M |
| Tulane University | M |
| UNB Fredericton | M |
| Université de Montréal | M |
| University at Buffalo, the State University of New York | M,D,O |
| University of Alberta | M,D |
| The University of Arizona | M |
| The University of British Columbia | M,D |
| University of Calgary | M,D |
| University of California, Berkeley | M,D |
| University of California, Irvine | M,D |
| University of California, Los Angeles | M,D |
| University of California, Riverside | D |
| University of California, Santa Barbara | M,D |
| University of Chicago | M,D |
| University of Cincinnati | M,D |
| University of Colorado Boulder | M,D |
| University of Florida | M,D |
| University of Georgia | M |
| University of Illinois at Urbana-Champaign | M,D |
| The University of Iowa | M,D |
| The University of Kansas | M |
| University of Kentucky | M |
| The University of Manchester | D |
| University of Manitoba | M |
| University of Maryland, College Park | M |
| University of Massachusetts Amherst | M |
| University of Massachusetts Boston | M |
| University of Michigan | M,D,O |
| University of Minnesota, Twin Cities Campus | M,D |
| University of Missouri | M,D |
| University of Nebraska–Lincoln | M |
| The University of North Carolina at Chapel Hill | M,D |
| The University of North Carolina at Greensboro | M |
| University of Oregon | M |
| University of Ottawa | M,D |
| University of Pennsylvania | M,D |
| University of South Africa | M,D |
| University of Southern California | M,D |
| The University of Texas at Austin | M,D |
| University of Toronto | M,D |
| University of Vermont | M,O |
| University of Victoria | M,D |
| University of Virginia | M,D |
| University of Washington | M,D |
| The University of Western Ontario | M |
| University of Wisconsin–Madison | M,D |
| University of Wisconsin–Milwaukee | M,O* |
| Villanova University | M |
| Washington University in St. Louis | M,D |
| Yale University | M,D |

## CLINICAL LABORATORY SCIENCES/ MEDICAL TECHNOLOGY

| | |
|---|---|
| Albany College of Pharmacy and Health Sciences | M |
| Austin Peay State University | M |
| Baylor College of Medicine | M,D |
| The Catholic University of America | M,D |
| Dominican University of California | M |
| Fairleigh Dickinson University, Metropolitan Campus | M |
| Inter American University of Puerto Rico, Metropolitan Campus | M |
| Lipscomb University | M |
| Mayo Clinic Graduate School of Biomedical Sciences | M,D |
| Medical College of Wisconsin | M |
| Michigan State University | M |
| Milwaukee School of Engineering | M |
| Northern Michigan University | M |
| Northwestern University | M |
| Pontifical Catholic University of Puerto Rico | O |
| Rush University | M |
| Rutgers University - Newark | M |
| Rutgers University - New Brunswick | M |
| State University of New York Upstate Medical University | M |
| Tarleton State University | M |
| Thomas Jefferson University | M |
| Tufts University | M,D,O |
| Universidad de las Américas Puebla | M |
| Université de Sherbrooke | M,D |
| University at Buffalo, the State University of New York | M |
| The University of Alabama at Birmingham | M,D |
| University of Alberta | M,D |
| University of California, San Diego | M,D |
| University of Colorado Denver | M,D |
| University of Florida | M,D |
| University of Maryland, Baltimore | M |
| University of Massachusetts Lowell | M |
| University of Minnesota, Twin Cities Campus | M |
| University of Nebraska Medical Center | M,O |
| University of New Mexico | M,O |
| University of North Dakota | M,D |
| University of Pennsylvania | M |
| University of Pittsburgh | D* |
| University of Puerto Rico - Medical Sciences Campus | M,O |
| University of Rhode Island | M,D |
| The University of Tennessee Health Science Center | M,D |
| The University of Texas at Austin | M,D |
| The University of Texas Health Science Center at San Antonio | D |
| The University of Texas Medical Branch | M,D |
| The University of Texas Rio Grande Valley | M |
| University of Utah | M |
| University of Vermont | M,D,O |
| University of Washington | M |
| Virginia Commonwealth University | M,D |
| Wake Forest University | M |

## CLINICAL PSYCHOLOGY

| | |
|---|---|
| Abilene Christian University | M,O |
| Acadia University | M |
| Adams State University | M,D |
| Adelphi University | D |
| Adler University | M,D |
| Alabama Agricultural and Mechanical University | M,O |
| Albizu University - Miami | M,D |
| Albizu University - San Juan | M,D |
| Alliant International University–Fresno | D |
| Alliant International University - Los Angeles | D |
| Alliant International University–Sacramento | D |
| Alliant International University - San Diego | M,D |
| Alliant International University–San Francisco | M,D,O |
| American International College | M,D,O |
| American University | M,D,O |
| Andrews University | M |
| Antioch University Los Angeles | M |
| Antioch University New England | M,D,O |
| Antioch University Santa Barbara | M,D |
| Antioch University Seattle | M,D |
| Appalachian State University | M |
| Argosy University, Atlanta | M,D,O |
| Argosy University, Chicago | M,D |
| Argosy University, Hawaii | M,D,O |
| Argosy University, Los Angeles | M,D |
| Argosy University, Northern Virginia | M,D |
| Argosy University, Orange County | M,D |
| Argosy University, Phoenix | M,D |
| Argosy University, Seattle | M,D,O |
| Argosy University, Tampa | M,D |
| Argosy University, Twin Cities | M,D,O |
| Arizona State University at Tempe | M,D |
| Arkansas State University | M,O |
| Ashland Theological Seminary | M,D |
| Auburn University at Montgomery | M,O |
| Augusta University | M,O |
| Austin Peay State University | M |
| Azusa Pacific University | D |
| Ball State University | M,D |
| Barry University | M,O |
| Baylor University | D |
| Bay Path University | M |
| Benedictine University | M |
| Bethel Seminary | M,D,O |

| | |
|---|---|
| Binghamton University, State University of New York | D |
| Biola University | D |
| Bowling Green State University | M,D |
| Bradley University | M |
| Brigham Young University | D |
| California Lutheran University | M,D |
| California State University, Dominguez Hills | M |
| California State University, Fullerton | M |
| California State University, Northridge | M |
| California State University, San Bernardino | M |
| California University of Pennsylvania | M |
| Capella University | M,D |
| Cardinal Stritch University | M |
| Case Western Reserve University | D |
| The Catholic University of America | M,D |
| Central Michigan University | D |
| Chestnut Hill College | M,D,O |
| The Chicago School of Professional Psychology | M,D |
| The Chicago School of Professional Psychology at Downtown Los Angeles | M,D |
| The Chicago School of Professional Psychology at Irvine | D |
| The Chicago School of Professional Psychology at San Diego | M,D |
| The Chicago School of Professional Psychology at Xavier University of Louisiana | D |
| The Chicago School of Professional Psychology: Online | M |
| Chicago State University | M |
| City College of the City University of New York | M,D |
| Clark University | D |
| Clayton State University | M |
| Clemson University | M,D,O |
| College of St. Joseph | M |
| College of Staten Island of the City University of New York | M |
| Columbus State University | M,D,O |
| Concordia University (Canada) | D,O |
| Dalhousie University | M,D |
| DePaul University | M,D |
| Divine Mercy University | M,D |
| Drexel University | D |
| Duke University | D |
| Duquesne University | M,D,O |
| East Carolina University | M,D,O |
| East Central University | M |
| Eastern Illinois University | M,O |
| Eastern Kentucky University | M,O |
| Eastern Michigan University | M,D |
| Eastern Virginia Medical School | D |
| Eastern Washington University | M,O |
| East Tennessee State University | M,D |
| Edinboro University of Pennsylvania | M,O |
| Emory University | D |
| Emporia State University | M |
| Evangel University | M |
| Fairfield University | M,O |
| Fairleigh Dickinson University, Florham Campus | M |
| Fairleigh Dickinson University, Metropolitan Campus | M,D |
| Fielding Graduate University | D,O |
| Fisk University | M |
| Florida Gulf Coast University | M |
| Florida Institute of Technology | D |
| Florida International University | M,D |
| Florida State University | D |
| Fordham University | D |
| Franciscan University of Steubenville | M |
| Francis Marion University | M,O |
| Fuller Theological Seminary | M,D,O |
| Gallaudet University | M,D,O |
| Gannon University | M |
| Geneva College | M |
| George Fox University | M,D,O |
| George Mason University | M,D,O |
| The George Washington University | M,D |
| Georgian Court University | M,O |
| Georgia Southern University | M,D |
| Georgia State University | D |
| Goddard College | M |
| Grace College | M |
| The Graduate Center, City University of New York | D |
| Hawaii Pacific University | M |
| Hodges University | M |
| Hofstra University | M,D |
| Hood College | M |
| Howard University | M,D |
| Husson University | M |
| Idaho State University | D |
| Illinois Institute of Technology | M,D |
| Illinois State University | M,D,O |
| Immaculata University | M,D,O |
| Indiana State University | M,D,O |
| Indiana University of Pennsylvania | M,D |
| Indiana University-Purdue University Indianapolis | M,D |
| Indiana University South Bend | M,O |
| Jackson State University | M,D |
| James Madison University | D |
| John Brown University | M,O |
| Johns Hopkins University | M,D |
| Johnson & Wales University | M |
| Johnson University | M,D,O |
| Judson University | M |
| Kean University | M,D |
| Kent State University | M,D |
| LaGrange College | M |
| Lakehead University | M,D |
| Lamar University | M |
| La Salle University | M,D |
| Lenoir-Rhyne University | M |
| Lesley University | M,D,O |
| Lewis University | M |
| Liberty University | M,D,O |
| Lipscomb University | M,O |
| Lock Haven University of Pennsylvania | M |
| Loma Linda University | D |
| London Metropolitan University | M,D |
| Long Island University - Brentwood Campus | M,O |
| Long Island University - Brooklyn | M,D,O |
| Long Island University - Post | M,D,O |
| Louisiana State University and Agricultural & Mechanical College | M,D |
| Louisiana Tech University | M,D,O |
| Loyola University Chicago | M,D,O |
| Loyola University Chicago | M,D,O |
| Loyola University Maryland | M,D,O |
| Loyola University New Orleans | M |
| Madonna University | M |
| Marquette University | M,D |
| Marshall University | M,D,O |
| Marymount University | M |
| Marywood University | M,D |
| McGill University | M,D |
| McKendree University | M |
| Medaille College | M,D |
| Memorial University of Newfoundland | M,D |
| Mercer University | M,D |
| Merrimack College | M,O |
| Messiah University | M,O |
| Michigan School of Psychology | M,D |
| MidAmerica Nazarene University | M |
| Middle Tennessee State University | M,O |
| Midwestern State University | M |
| Midwestern University, Downers Grove Campus | D |
| Midwestern University, Glendale Campus | D |
| Millersville University of Pennsylvania | M |
| Milligan University | M,O |
| Minnesota State University Mankato | M,D |
| Mississippi State University | M,D,O |
| Missouri State University | M,O |
| Molloy College | M |
| Montclair State University | M,O |
| Morehead State University | M |
| Mount Mary University | M,O |
| Murray State University | M,O |
| National University | M,O |
| Neumann University | M,D,O |
| New Mexico Highlands University | M |
| The New School | M,D |
| Nicholls State University | M,O |
| Norfolk State University | M |
| North Carolina Agricultural and Technical State University | M,D |
| North Carolina Central University | M |
| North Dakota State University | M,D |
| Northeastern Illinois University | M |
| Northern Kentucky University | M |
| Northern State University | M |
| Northwestern State University of Louisiana | M |
| Northwestern University | D |
| Northwest Nazarene University | M |
| Notre Dame de Namur University | M |
| Nova Southeastern University | M,D,O |
| The Ohio State University | D |
| Ohio University | D |
| Oklahoma State University | M,D |
| Old Dominion University | D |
| Oregon State University | M,D |
| Pace University | M,D |
| Pacifica Graduate Institute | M,D |
| Pacific University | M,D |
| Palo Alto University | M,D |
| Penn State Erie, The Behrend College | M |
| Penn State Harrisburg | M,D,O |
| Philadelphia College of Osteopathic Medicine | M,D,O |
| Pillar College | M |
| Pittsburg State University | M |
| Plymouth State University | O |
| Point Loma Nazarene University | M |
| Point Park University | M,D |
| Ponce Health Sciences University | D |
| Pontifical Catholic University of Puerto Rico | D |
| Pontificia Universidad Catolica Madre y Maestra | M |
| Post University | M |
| Prairie View A&M University | M,D |
| Purdue University | D |
| Queen's University at Kingston | M,D |
| Quincy University | M |
| Radford University | M |
| Regent University | M,D,O |
| Richmont Graduate University | M |
| Rider University | M,O |
| Rivier University | M |
| Roberts Wesleyan College | M,D |
| Roger Williams University | M |
| Roosevelt University | M |
| Rosalind Franklin University of Medicine and Science | M,D |
| Rowan University | M,O |
| Rutgers University - New Brunswick | M,D |
| St. John's University (NY) | M,D,O |
| Saint Louis University | M,D |
| Saint Michael's College | M |
| Sam Houston State University | M,D,O |
| San Diego State University | M,D |
| San Francisco State University | M,O |
| San Jose State University | M |
| Saybrook University | M |
| Seattle Pacific University | D |
| Shippensburg University of Pennsylvania | M,D |
| Siena Heights University | M,O |
| Slippery Rock University of Pennsylvania | M |
| Sofia University | M,D |
| Sonoma State University | M |
| Southeastern Oklahoma State University | M |
| Southern Illinois University Carbondale | M,D |
| Southern Illinois University Edwardsville | M |
| Southern Methodist University | D |
| Southern New Hampshire University | M |
| Spalding University | M,D |
| Springfield College | M,D,O |
| State University of New York at New Paltz | M,O |
| State University of New York at Plattsburgh | M,O |
| Stephens College | M,O |
| Stony Brook University, State University of New York | D |
| Suffolk University | M,D,O |
| Syracuse University | M,D |
| Teachers College, Columbia University | M,D |
| Texas A&M University–Central Texas | M,O |
| Texas A&M University–Corpus Christi | M |
| Texas A&M University–San Antonio | M |
| Texas State University | M |
| Texas Tech University | M,D |
| Texas Tech University Health Sciences Center | M |
| Trinity Washington University | M |
| Uniformed Services University of the Health Sciences | D |
| Union College (KY) | M |
| Union Institute & University | M |
| Universidad de Iberoamerica | M,D |
| University at Albany, State University of New York | M,D |
| The University of Akron | M |
| The University of Alabama | D |
| The University of Alabama at Birmingham | M,D |
| University of Alaska Anchorage | M,D |
| University of Bridgeport | M |
| The University of British Columbia | M,D |
| University of Calgary | M,D |
| University of California, San Diego | D |
| University of California, Santa Barbara | M,D,O |
| University of Central Florida | M,D |
| University of Cincinnati | D |
| University of Colorado Denver | M,D |
| University of Connecticut | M,D |
| University of Dayton | M,O |
| University of Delaware | D |
| University of Denver | M,D,O |
| University of Detroit Mercy | M,D,O |
| University of Florida | M,D |
| University of Guelph | M,D |
| University of Hartford | M,D |
| University of Hawaii at Manoa | M,D,O |
| University of Houston | M,D |
| University of Houston–Clear Lake | M |
| University of Indianapolis | M,D |
| The University of Kansas | M,D |
| University of La Verne | D |
| University of Louisiana at Monroe | M |
| University of Louisville | D |
| University of Lynchburg | M |
| The University of Manchester | M,D |
| University of Manitoba | M,D |
| University of Mary Hardin-Baylor | M |
| University of Maryland, Baltimore County | M,D |
| University of Maryland, College Park | M,D |
| University of Massachusetts Amherst | M,D |
| University of Massachusetts Boston | D |
| University of Massachusetts Dartmouth | M,O |
| University of Memphis | M,D,O |
| University of Miami | M,D |
| University of Michigan | D |
| University of Michigan–Dearborn | M |
| University of Minnesota, Twin Cities Campus | D |
| University of Missouri–St. Louis | M,D,O |
| University of Montana | M,D,O |
| University of Nebraska–Lincoln | M,D |
| University of Nevada, Las Vegas | M,D,O |
| University of Nevada, Reno | D |
| University of New Brunswick Saint John | M,D |
| University of New Mexico | D |
| University of North Alabama | M |
| The University of North Carolina at Chapel Hill | D |
| The University of North Carolina at Greensboro | M,D |
| The University of North Carolina Wilmington | M,D |
| University of North Dakota | M,D |
| University of Northern Colorado | M |
| University of North Texas | M,D,O |
| University of North Texas at Dallas | M |
| University of Oklahoma | M,O |
| University of Oregon | D |
| University of Phoenix - Phoenix Campus | M |
| University of Pittsburgh | M,D* |
| University of Puerto Rico at Rio Piedras | M,D |
| University of Regina | M,D |
| University of Rhode Island | M,D |
| University of Rochester | D |
| University of Saint Francis (IN) | M,O |
| University of Saint Joseph | M |
| University of San Francisco | D |
| The University of Scranton | M |
| University of South Africa | M,D |
| University of South Alabama | M,D,O |
| University of South Carolina | M,D |
| University of South Carolina Aiken | M |
| University of South Dakota | M,D |
| University of Southern California | M,D |
| University of South Florida | D |
| The University of Tennessee | M,D |
| The University of Texas at Austin | D |
| The University of Texas at El Paso | M,D |
| The University of Texas at Tyler | M |
| The University of Texas of the Permian Basin | M |
| The University of Texas Rio Grande Valley | M |
| The University of Texas Southwestern Medical Center | D |
| University of the Cumberlands | D |
| The University of Toledo | M,D |
| The University of Tulsa | M,D |
| University of Utah | M,D,O |
| University of Vermont | M,D |
| University of Victoria | M,D |
| University of Virginia | D |
| University of Washington | M,D |
| The University of West Alabama | M |
| University of Windsor | M,D |
| University of Wisconsin–Madison | D |
| University of Wisconsin–Parkside | M |
| University of Wisconsin–Stout | M |
| Université Laval | D |
| Utah State University | M,D |
| Valparaiso University | M |
| Vanguard University of Southern California | M |
| Virginia Commonwealth University | D |
| Virginia State University | M,D |
| Walden University | M,D,O |
| Washburn University | M |
| Washington State University | M,D |
| Waynesburg University | M,D |
| Wayne State University | M,D |
| Western Connecticut State University | M |
| Western Illinois University | M,O |
| Western Kentucky University | M,O |
| Western Michigan University | M,D |
| West Virginia University | M,D |
| Wheaton College | M,D |
| Wichita State University | D |
| Widener University | D |
| William James College | M,D,O |
| Wilmington University | M |
| Winona State University | M,O |
| Wisconsin School of Professional Psychology | M,D |
| The Wright Institute | D |
| Wright State University | D |
| Xavier University | M,D* |
| Yale University | D |
| Yeshiva University | D |

## CLINICAL RESEARCH

| | |
|---|---|
| Albert Einstein College of Medicine | D |
| American University of Health Sciences | M |
| Augusta University | M |
| Boston University | M |
| Case Western Reserve University | M,D |
| Clemson University | M,D,O |
| Duke University | M |
| Eastern Michigan University | M,O |
| Emory University | M |
| Fordham University | M |
| Icahn School of Medicine at Mount Sinai | M,D |
| Johns Hopkins University | M,D |
| Loyola University Chicago | M |
| Medical College of Wisconsin | |
| Medical University of South Carolina | M |
| Memorial University of Newfoundland | M |
| Morehouse School of Medicine | M |
| National University of Natural Medicine | M |
| New York University | M |
| Northwestern University | M,O |
| Oregon Health & Science University | M,O |
| Palmer College of Chiropractic | M |
| Stanford University | M,D |
| Thomas Jefferson University | M,O |
| Trident University International | M,D,O |
| University of California, Berkeley | O |
| University of California, Davis | M |
| University of California, Los Angeles | M |
| University of California, San Diego | M |
| University of Colorado Denver | M,D |

*M—masters degree; D—doctorate; O—other advanced degree; *—Close-Up and/or Display*

| | |
|---|---|
| University of Connecticut Health Center | M |
| University of Florida | M,D,O |
| The University of Iowa | M,D |
| The University of Kansas | M |
| University of Kentucky | M |
| University of Maryland, Baltimore | M,D,O |
| University of Massachusetts Medical School | M,D |
| University of Michigan | M |
| University of Minnesota, Twin Cities Campus | M |
| The University of North Carolina at Chapel Hill | M,D |
| The University of North Carolina Wilmington | M,D,O |
| University of Pittsburgh | M,O* |
| University of Puerto Rico - Medical Sciences Campus | M,O |
| University of Rochester | M |
| University of Southern California | M,D,O |
| University of South Florida | O |
| The University of Texas Health Science Center at San Antonio | M |
| University of Virginia | M |
| University of Washington | M,D |
| University of Wisconsin–Madison | M,D |
| Walden University | M,D,O |
| Washington University in St. Louis | M |

## CLOTHING AND TEXTILES

| | |
|---|---|
| Alabama Agricultural and Mechanical University | M |
| Auburn University | M,D |
| Central Michigan University | M,O |
| Cornell University | M,D |
| Drexel University | M |
| Eastern Michigan University | M |
| Fashion Institute of Technology | M |
| Georgia State University | M |
| Iowa State University of Science and Technology | M,D |
| Kansas State University | M,D |
| LIM College | M |
| Mississippi State University | M,D |
| New Mexico State University | M |
| The New School | M |
| North Carolina State University | M,D |
| Oklahoma State University | M,D |
| Rutgers University - Newark | M |
| Savannah College of Art and Design | M |
| Thomas Jefferson University | M |
| The University of Akron | M |
| The University of Alabama | M |
| University of Alberta | M,D |
| University of California, Davis | M |
| University of Delaware | M |
| University of Georgia | M,D |
| The University of Manchester | M,D |
| University of Minnesota, Twin Cities Campus | M,D,O |
| University of Missouri | M,D |
| University of Nebraska–Lincoln | M,D |
| University of Rhode Island | M,O |
| The University of Tennessee | M,D |
| University of the Incarnate Word | M |
| Washington State University | M |
| Wayne State University | M |

## COGNITIVE SCIENCES

| | |
|---|---|
| American University | M,D,O |
| Arizona State University at Tempe | M,D |
| Ball State University | M |
| Binghamton University, State University of New York | D |
| Brandeis University | M,D |
| Brigham Young University | D |
| Brown University | M,D |
| Carleton University | D |
| Carnegie Mellon University | D |
| Case Western Reserve University | M |
| Central European University | D |
| Claremont Graduate University | M,D,O |
| Cornell University | D |
| Dartmouth College | D |
| Duke University | D |
| Emory University | D |
| Florida International University | M,D |
| Florida State University | D |
| George Mason University | M,D,O |
| The George Washington University | D |
| Georgia State University | D |
| The Graduate Center, City University of New York | D |
| Grand Canyon University | D |
| Harvard University | M,D* |
| Illinois State University | M,D,O |
| Indiana University Bloomington | D |
| Iowa State University of Science and Technology | M,D |
| Johns Hopkins University | M,D |
| Louisiana State University and Agricultural & Mechanical College | M,D |
| Massachusetts Institute of Technology | D |
| Michigan Technological University | M,D,O |
| Mississippi State University | M,D |
| The New School | M,D |
| New York University | M,D,O |
| North Carolina State University | D |
| North Dakota State University | M,D |
| Northwestern University | D |
| The Ohio State University | D |
| Oregon State University | M,D |
| Purdue University | D |
| Queen's University at Kingston | M,D |
| Rensselaer Polytechnic Institute | D |
| Rice University | M,D |
| Rochester Institute of Technology | O |
| Rutgers University - Newark | D |
| Rutgers University - New Brunswick | D |
| Stony Brook University, State University of New York | D |
| Syracuse University | D |
| Texas Christian University | M,D |
| Tufts University | M,D |
| University at Albany, State University of New York | M,D |
| The University of British Columbia | M,D |
| University of California, Merced | M,D |
| University of California, San Diego | D |
| University of California, Santa Barbara | M,D |
| University of Central Florida | D |
| University of Connecticut | M,D |
| University of Delaware | M,D |
| University of Guelph | M,D |
| The University of Kansas | M,D |
| University of Louisville | D |
| University of Maryland, Baltimore County | D |
| University of Maryland, College Park | D |
| University of Massachusetts Amherst | M,D |
| University of Massachusetts Boston | M |
| University of Michigan | D |
| University of Minnesota, Twin Cities Campus | D |
| University of Nebraska–Lincoln | M,D,O |
| University of Nevada, Reno | M,D |
| University of New Mexico | D |
| The University of North Carolina at Chapel Hill | D |
| The University of North Carolina at Charlotte | M,D,O |
| The University of North Carolina at Greensboro | M,D |
| University of Notre Dame | D |
| University of Oregon | M,D |
| University of Rochester | D |
| University of Southern California | M,D |
| University of South Florida | D |
| The University of Texas at Dallas | M,D |
| University of Washington | M,D |
| University of Wisconsin–Madison | D |
| Wayne State University | M,D |
| Wilfrid Laurier University | M,D |
| Yale University | D |

## COMMUNICATION—GENERAL

| | |
|---|---|
| Abilene Christian University | M |
| American University | M,D |
| The American University in Cairo | M,D,O |
| The American University of Paris | M |
| Andrews University | M |
| Angelo State University | M |
| Arizona State University at Tempe | M,D |
| Arkansas State University | M,O |
| Ashland University | M |
| Auburn University | M,O |
| Austin Peay State University | M |
| Ball State University | M,O |
| Baylor University | M |
| Bay Path University | M |
| Bellarmine University | M |
| Boise State University | M |
| Boston University | M |
| Bowling Green State University | M,D |
| Brigham Young University | M |
| Bryant University | M,O |
| Cabrini University | M,O |
| California Baptist University | M |
| California State University, Chico | M |
| California State University, East Bay | M |
| California State University, Fresno | M |
| California State University, Fullerton | M |
| California State University, Long Beach | M |
| California State University, Los Angeles | M |
| California State University, Northridge | M |
| California State University, Sacramento | M |
| California State University, San Bernardino | M |
| Carleton University | M,D |
| Carnegie Mellon University | M,D |
| Central Connecticut State University | M,O |
| Central Michigan University | M |
| Chapman University | M |
| Chatham University | M |
| Clarks Summit University | M,D |
| Clark University | M |
| Clemson University | M |
| Cleveland State University | M,D,O |
| The College of New Rochelle | M,O |
| Columbia College Chicago | M |
| Columbia University | M,D |
| Concordia University (Canada) | M,D,O |
| Cornell University | M,D |
| Dallas Baptist University | M |
| DePaul University | M |
| DEREE - The American College of Greece | M |
| Drake University | M |
| Drexel University | M |
| Drury University | M |
| Duquesne University | M,D |
| Eastern Illinois University | M |
| Eastern Michigan University | M |
| Eastern New Mexico University | M |
| Eastern University | M,O |
| Eastern Washington University | M |
| East Stroudsburg University of Pennsylvania | M |
| East Tennessee State University | M,O |
| Edinboro University of Pennsylvania | M |
| Fairfield University | M |
| Fairleigh Dickinson University, Metropolitan Campus | M |
| Fitchburg State University | M,O |
| Florida Atlantic University | M,O |
| Florida Institute of Technology | M |
| Florida International University | M |
| Florida State University | M,D |
| Fordham University | M,D |
| Fordham University | M,D |
| Fort Hays State University | M |
| George Mason University | M,D,O |
| Georgetown University | M |
| The George Washington University | M |
| Georgia State University | M,D |
| Governors State University | M |
| Grand Valley State University | M |
| Harvard University | M,O* |
| Hawaii Pacific University | M |
| Howard University | M,D |
| Idaho State University | M |
| Illinois Institute of Technology | M,D |
| Illinois State University | M |
| Indiana State University | M |
| Indiana University of Pennsylvania | D |
| Indiana University-Purdue University Indianapolis | M,D |
| Indiana University South Bend | M,D |
| Instituto Tecnologico de Santo Domingo | M,O |
| Instituto Tecnológico y de Estudios Superiores de Monterrey, Campus Ciudad Obregón | M |
| Instituto Tecnológico y de Estudios Superiores de Monterrey, Campus Monterrey | M,D |
| International University in Geneva | M,D |
| James Madison University | M |
| Johns Hopkins University | M,O |
| Kansas State University | M,D,O |
| Kean University | M |
| Kennesaw State University | M |
| Kent State University | M |
| La Salle University | M,O |
| Lasell College | M,O |
| La Sierra University | M |
| Lawrence Technological University | M,O |
| Liberty University | M |
| Lindenwood University | M,O |
| Lindenwood University–Belleville | M |
| Louisiana State University and Agricultural & Mechanical College | M,D |
| Loyola University Chicago | M |
| Lynn University | M,O |
| Marist College | M |
| Marquette University | M,O |
| Marshall University | M |
| Marywood University | M |
| McGill University | M,D |
| Michigan State University | M,D |
| Minnesota State University Mankato | M,O |
| Mississippi College | M |
| Mississippi State University | M,D |
| Missouri State University | M,O |
| Monmouth University | M,O |
| Montana State University Billings | M |
| Moore College of Art & Design | M |
| Mount Saint Vincent University | M |
| New Mexico State University | M |
| New York Institute of Technology | M |
| New York University | M,D |
| Norfolk State University | M |
| North Carolina State University | M |
| North Dakota State University | M,D |
| Northeastern State University | M |
| Northern Arizona University | M,O |
| Northern Illinois University | M |
| Northern Kentucky University | M,O |
| Northwestern University | M,D |
| Notre Dame of Maryland University | M |
| The Ohio State University | M,D |
| Ohio University | M,D |
| Old Dominion University | M,O |
| Pace University | M |
| Penn State Harrisburg | M,D,O |
| Penn State University Park | M,D* |
| Pepperdine University | M |
| Pittsburg State University | M |
| Point Park University | M |
| Purdue University | M,D |
| Purdue University Fort Wayne | M |
| Purdue University Northwest | M |
| Queen's University at Kingston | M,D |
| Queens University of Charlotte | M |
| Quinnipiac University | M |
| Regent University | M,D |
| Rochester Institute of Technology | M |
| Roosevelt University | M |
| Rutgers University - New Brunswick | D |
| Sacred Heart University | M |
| Saginaw Valley State University | M |
| Saint Louis University | M |
| St. Mary's University (United States) | M |
| St. Thomas University - Florida | M,D,O |
| Sam Houston State University | M |
| San Diego State University | M |
| San Jose State University | M |
| Seton Hall University | M |
| Shippensburg University of Pennsylvania | M |
| Simon Fraser University | M,D |
| South Dakota State University | M |
| Southeastern Louisiana University | M |
| Southern Illinois University Carbondale | M,D |
| Southern Utah University | M |
| Spring Arbor University | M |
| Stanford University | M,D |
| State University of New York at Oswego | M |
| Stephen F. Austin State University | M |
| Stevens Institute of Technology | M,D,O |
| Stevenson University | M |
| Syracuse University | M,D |
| Tarleton State University | M |
| Teachers College, Columbia University | M,D |
| Temple University | M,D* |
| Texas A&M University | M,D |
| Texas A&M University–Corpus Christi | M |
| Texas Christian University | M |
| Texas Southern University | M |
| Texas State University | M |
| Texas Tech University | M |
| Tiffin University | M |
| Towson University | M |
| Trinity Washington University | M |
| Troy University | M |
| Université de Montréal | M,D |
| Université du Québec à Montréal | M,D |
| Université du Québec à Trois-Rivières | M,O |
| University at Albany, State University of New York | M,D |
| University at Buffalo, the State University of New York | M,D |
| The University of Akron | M |
| The University of Alabama | M,D |
| The University of Alabama at Birmingham | M |
| University of Alaska Fairbanks | M |
| University of Alberta | M |
| The University of Arizona | M,D |
| University of Arkansas | M |
| University of Bridgeport | M |
| University of California, Davis | M |
| University of California, San Diego | D |
| University of California, Santa Barbara | D |
| University of California, Santa Cruz | O |
| University of Central Missouri | M,D,O |
| University of Cincinnati | M |
| University of Colorado Boulder | M,D |
| University of Colorado Colorado Springs | M |
| University of Colorado Denver | M |
| University of Connecticut | M,D |
| University of Dayton | M |
| University of Delaware | M |
| University of Denver | M,O |
| University of Dubuque | M |
| University of Florida | M,D |
| University of Georgia | M,D |
| University of Hartford | M |
| University of Hawaii at Manoa | M,O |
| University of Houston | M |
| University of Illinois at Chicago | M,D |
| University of Illinois at Springfield | M |
| University of Illinois at Urbana-Champaign | M,D |
| The University of Iowa | M,D |
| The University of Kansas | M,D,O |
| University of Louisiana at Lafayette | M |
| University of Louisiana at Monroe | M |
| University of Louisville | M |
| University of Maine | M,D |
| University of Maryland, Baltimore County | M |
| University of Maryland, College Park | M,D |
| University of Massachusetts Amherst | M,D |
| University of Memphis | M,D |
| University of Miami | M,D |
| University of Michigan | D |
| University of Minnesota, Twin Cities Campus | M,D,O |
| University of Missouri | M,D |
| University of Missouri–St. Louis | M |
| University of Montana | M,O |
| University of Nebraska at Omaha | M,O |
| University of Nebraska–Lincoln | M,D |
| University of Nevada, Las Vegas | M |
| University of New Mexico | M,D |
| The University of North Carolina at Chapel Hill | M,D,O |
| The University of North Carolina at Charlotte | M |
| The University of North Carolina at Greensboro | M |
| University of North Dakota | D |
| University of Northern Colorado | M |
| University of Northern Iowa | M |
| University of North Texas | M,D,O |
| University of Oklahoma | M,D |
| University of Oregon | M,D |
| University of Ottawa | M |
| University of Pennsylvania | D |
| University of Pittsburgh | M,D* |
| University of Portland | M |
| University of Puerto Rico at Rio Piedras | M |
| University of Rhode Island | M |
| University of San Francisco | M |
| University of South Africa | M,D |
| University of South Alabama | M |
| University of South Dakota | M |
| University of Southern California | M,D |
| University of Southern Indiana | M |
| University of Southern Mississippi | M,D |
| University of South Florida | M,D |
| The University of Tennessee | M,D |
| The University of Tennessee at Martin | M |

| | |
|---|---|
| The University of Texas at Arlington | M |
| The University of Texas at Austin | M,D |
| The University of Texas at Dallas | M,D |
| The University of Texas at El Paso | M |
| The University of Texas at San Antonio | M |
| The University of Texas at Tyler | M |
| The University of Texas Rio Grande Valley | M |
| University of the Incarnate Word | M,D |
| University of the Pacific | M |
| University of the Sacred Heart | M,O |
| The University of Toledo | O |
| University of Utah | M,D |
| University of Washington | M,D |
| University of West Florida | M |
| University of Windsor | M |
| University of Wisconsin–Madison | M,D |
| University of Wisconsin–Milwaukee | M,D,O* |
| University of Wisconsin–Stevens Point | M |
| University of Wisconsin–Superior | M |
| University of Wisconsin–Whitewater | M |
| University of Wyoming | M |
| Utah State University | M |
| Valparaiso University | M,O |
| Villanova University | M |
| Virginia Commonwealth University | D |
| Virginia Polytechnic Institute and State University | M,D,O |
| Wake Forest University | M |
| Walden University | M,D,O |
| Walla Walla University | M |
| Washington State University | M,D |
| Wayne State College | M |
| Wayne State University | M,D,O |
| Weber State University | M |
| Webster University | M,O |
| Western Illinois University | M |
| Western Kentucky University | M,O |
| Western Michigan University | M |
| Western New England University | M |
| West Texas A&M University | M |
| West Virginia University | M,D |
| Wichita State University | M |
| Wilfrid Laurier University | M |
| York University | M,D |

## COMMUNICATION DISORDERS

| | |
|---|---|
| Abilene Christian University | M |
| Alabama Agricultural and Mechanical University | M |
| Albizu University - Miami | M,D |
| Albizu University - San Juan | M,D |
| Andrews University | M |
| Appalachian State University | M |
| Arizona State University at Tempe | M,D |
| Arkansas State University | M,O |
| A.T. Still University | M,D,O |
| Auburn University | M,D |
| Baldwin Wallace University | M |
| Ball State University | M,D |
| Barry University | M |
| Baylor University | M |
| Bloomsburg University of Pennsylvania | M,D |
| Boston University | M,D |
| Bowling Green State University | M,D |
| Bridgewater State University | M |
| Brigham Young University | M |
| Brooklyn College of the City University of New York | M,D |
| Buffalo State College, State University of New York | M |
| California Baptist University | M |
| California State University, Chico | M |
| California State University, East Bay | M |
| California State University, Fresno | M |
| California State University, Fullerton | M |
| California State University, Long Beach | M |
| California State University, Los Angeles | M |
| California State University, Northridge | M |
| California State University, Sacramento | M |
| California State University, San Marcos | M |
| California University of Pennsylvania | M |
| Calvin College | M |
| Canisius College | M,O |
| Case Western Reserve University | M,D |
| Central Michigan University | M,D |
| Chapman University | M |
| Clarion University of Pennsylvania | M |
| Cleveland State University | M |
| The College of Saint Rose | M |
| Dalhousie University | M,D |
| Duquesne University | M,D |
| East Carolina University | M,D |
| Eastern Illinois University | M |
| Eastern Kentucky University | M |
| Eastern Michigan University | M |
| Eastern New Mexico University | M |
| Eastern Washington University | M |
| East Stroudsburg University of Pennsylvania | M |
| East Tennessee State University | M,D |
| Edinboro University of Pennsylvania | M |
| Elmhurst University | M |
| Florida Atlantic University | M |
| Florida International University | M |
| Florida State University | M,D |
| Fontbonne University | M |
| Fort Hays State University | M |
| Francis Marion University | M |
| Gallaudet University | M,D,O |
| The George Washington University | M |
| Georgia Southern University | M |
| Georgia State University | M,D |
| Governors State University | M |
| The Graduate Center, City University of New York | D |
| Grand Valley State University | M |
| Hampton University | M |
| Harding University | M |
| Hofstra University | M,D,O |
| Howard University | M,D |
| Hunter College of the City University of New York | M |
| Idaho State University | M,D |
| Illinois State University | M |
| Indiana State University | M,D,O |
| Indiana University Bloomington | M,D |
| Indiana University of Pennsylvania | M |
| Iona College | M |
| Ithaca College | M |
| Jackson State University | M |
| Jacksonville University | M |
| James Madison University | M,D |
| Kansas State University | M,D,O |
| Kean University | M,D |
| Kent State University | M,D,O |
| Lamar University | M,D |
| La Salle University | M |
| Lebanon Valley College | M |
| Lehman College of the City University of New York | M |
| Lewis & Clark College | M |
| Lindenwood University | M,D,O |
| Loma Linda University | M,D |
| Long Island University - Brooklyn | M,D,O |
| Long Island University - Post | M,D,O |
| Longwood University | M |
| Louisiana State University and Agricultural & Mechanical College | M,D |
| Louisiana State University Health Sciences Center | M,D |
| Louisiana Tech University | M,D,O |
| Loyola University Maryland | M |
| Marquette University | M,[illegible]O |
| Marshall University | M |
| Maryville University of Saint Louis | M |
| Marywood University | M |
| Massachusetts Institute of Technology | M,D |
| McGill University | M,D |
| Mercy College | M |
| MGH Institute of Health Professions | M,O |
| Miami University | M |
| Michigan State University | M,D |
| Midwestern University, Downers Grove Campus | M |
| Midwestern University, Glendale Campus | M |
| Minnesota State University Mankato | M |
| Minot State University | M |
| Misericordia University | M |
| Mississippi University for Women | M,D,O |
| Missouri State University | M,D |
| Molloy College | M |
| Monmouth University | M,[illegible] |
| Montclair State University | M,D |
| Moravian College | M,D |
| Murray State University | M,O |
| Nazareth College of Rochester | M |
| New Mexico State University | M,D,O |
| New York Medical College | M,D,O |
| New York University | M,D |
| North Carolina Central University | M |
| Northeastern State University | M |
| Northeastern University | M,D,O |
| Northern Arizona University | M |
| Northern Illinois University | M,D |
| Northwestern University | M,D |
| Nova Southeastern University | M,D |
| The Ohio State University | M,D |
| Ohio University | M,D |
| Oklahoma State University | M |
| Old Dominion University | M |
| Our Lady of the Lake University | M |
| Pace University | M |
| Pacific University | M,D |
| Penn State University Park | M,D,O* |
| Portland State University | M |
| Purdue University | M,D |
| Queens College of the City University of New York | M,O |
| Radford University | M |
| Rockhurst University | M |
| Rocky Mountain University of Health Professions | D |
| Rush University | M,D |
| Sacred Heart University | M |
| St. Ambrose University | M |
| St. Cloud State University | M |
| St. John's University (NY) | M,D |
| Saint Joseph's University | M,D,O |
| Saint Louis University | M |
| Saint Mary's College | M |
| Saint Xavier University | M |
| Salus University | M,D,O |
| Samford University | M,D |
| San Diego State University | M,D |
| San Francisco State University | M |
| San Jose State University | M |
| Seton Hall University | M |
| South Carolina State University | M |
| Southeastern Louisiana University | M |
| Southeast Missouri State University | M |
| Southern Connecticut State University | M |
| Southern Illinois University Carbondale | M |
| Southern Illinois University Edwardsville | M |
| Southern University and Agricultural and Mechanical College | M |
| State University of New York at Fredonia | M,O |
| State University of New York at New Paltz | M |
| State University of New York at Plattsburgh | M |
| State University of New York College at Cortland | M |
| Stephen F. Austin State University | M |
| Stockton University | M |
| Syracuse University | M,D |
| Teachers College, Columbia University | M,D,O |
| Temple University | M,D* |
| Tennessee State University | M |
| Texas A&M University–Kingsville | M |
| Texas Christian University | M |
| Texas State University | M |
| Texas Tech University Health Sciences Center | M,D |
| Texas Woman's University | M |
| Towson University | M,D |
| Truman State University | M |
| Universidad del Turabo | M |
| Université de Montréal | M,O |
| University at Buffalo, the State University of New York | M,D |
| The University of Akron | M,D |
| The University of Alabama | M |
| University of Alberta | M |
| The University of Arizona | M,D,O |
| University of Arkansas | M |
| University of Arkansas for Medical Sciences | M,D |
| The University of British Columbia | M,D |
| University of California, San Diego | D |
| University of Central Arkansas | M,D |
| University of Central Florida | M,O |
| [illegible] of Central Missouri | M,D,O |
| Universi[illegible]f Central Oklahoma | M |
| University of Cincinnati | M,D |
| University of Colorado Boulder | M,D |
| University of Connecticut | M,D |
| University of Delaware | M |
| University of Florida | M,D |
| University of Georgia | M,D,O |
| University of Hawaii at Manoa | M |
| University of Houston | M |
| University of Illinois at Urbana-Champaign | M,D |
| The University of Iowa | M,D |
| The University of Kansas | M,D |
| University of Kentucky | M |
| University of Louisiana at Lafayette | M,D |
| University of Louisiana at Monroe | M |
| University of Louisville | M,D |
| University of Maine | M |
| The University of Manchester | M,D |
| [illegible] of Mary | M |
| [illegible] Maryland, College [illegible] | M,D |
| [illegible] Massachusetts [illegible] | M,D |
| [illegible] Memphis | M,D |
| [illegible]ersity of Minnesota, Duluth | M |
| University of Minnesota, Twin Cities Campus | M,D |
| University of Mississippi | M,D |
| University of Missouri | M,D |
| University of Montana | M,O |
| University of Montevallo | M |
| University of Nebraska at Kearney | M |
| University of Nebraska at Omaha | M |
| University of Nebraska–Lincoln | M,D |
| University of Nevada, Reno | M,D |
| University of New Hampshire | M |
| University of New Mexico | M |
| The University of North Carolina at Greensboro | M,D |
| University of North Dakota | M |
| University of Northern Colorado | M,D |
| University of Northern Iowa | M |
| University of North Florida | M |
| University of North Texas | M,D,O |
| University of Oklahoma Health Sciences Center | M,D,O |
| University of Oregon | M,D |
| University of Ottawa | M |
| University of Pittsburgh | M,D* |
| University of Puerto Rico - Medical Sciences Campus | M,D |
| University of Redlands | M |
| University of Rhode Island | M |
| University of South Alabama | M,D |
| University of South Carolina | M,D |
| University of South Dakota | M,D |
| University of Southern Mississippi | M,D |
| University of South Florida | M,D,O |
| The University of Tennessee | M,D,O |
| The University of Tennessee Health Science Center | M,D |
| The University of Texas at Austin | M,D |
| The University of Texas at Dallas | M,D |
| The University of Texas at El Paso | M |
| The University of Texas Health Science Center at San Antonio | M,D |
| The University of Texas Rio Grande Valley | M |
| University of the District of Columbia | M |
| University of the Pacific | M,D |
| The University of Toledo | M,D,O |
| University of Toronto | M,D |
| The University of Tulsa | M |
| University of Utah | M,D |
| University of Vermont | M |
| University of Virginia | M,D |
| University of Washington | M,D |
| The University of Western Ontario | M |
| University of Wisconsin–Eau Claire | M |
| University of Wisconsin–Madison | M,D |
| University of Wisconsin–Milwaukee | M* |
| University of Wisconsin–River Falls | M |
| University of Wisconsin–Stevens Point | M,D |
| University of Wisconsin–Whitewater | M |
| University of Wyoming | M |
| Université Laval | M |
| Utah State University | M,D,O |
| Valdosta State University | M,D,O |
| Vanderbilt University | M,D* |
| Washington State University | M |
| Washington University in St. Louis | M,D |
| Wayne State University | M,D |
| Webster University | M |
| Western Carolina University | M |
| Western Illinois University | M |
| Western Kentucky University | M |
| Western Michigan University | M,D |
| Western Washington University | M |
| West Texas A&M University | M |
| West Virginia University | M,D |
| Wichita State University | M,D |
| Worcester State University | M |
| Yeshiva University | M |

## COMMUNITY COLLEGE EDUCATION

| | |
|---|---|
| Argosy University, Chicago | M,D,O |
| Argosy University, Los Angeles | M,D |
| Argosy University, Northern Virginia | M,D,O |
| Argosy University, Orange County | M,D |
| Argosy University, Phoenix | M,D,O |
| Argosy University, Seattle | M,D |
| Argosy University, Tampa | M,D,O |
| Arkansas State University | M,D,O |
| California State University, San Bernardino | M |
| California State University, Stanislaus | D |
| Central Michigan University | M,D,O |
| Drew University | M,D,O |
| East Carolina University | M,D,O |
| Eastern Michigan University | M,D,O |
| Elizabeth City State University | M |
| Ferris State University | D |
| Lenoir-Rhyne University | M |
| Marymount University | M,O |
| Mississippi State University | M,D,O |
| Morgan State University | D |
| National American University (TX) | M,D |
| North Carolina State University | M,D |
| Northern Arizona University | M,D,O |
| Old Dominion University | M,D |
| University of Arkansas at Little Rock | M,D |
| University of Central Florida | M,O |
| University of Memphis | M,D,O |
| University of Northern Iowa | M |
| Wingate University | M,D,O |

## COMMUNITY HEALTH

| | |
|---|---|
| Adler University | M |
| Arizona State University at Tempe | M,D,O |
| Baylor University | M |
| Bloomsburg University of Pennsylvania | M,D |
| Brooklyn College of the City University of New York | M |
| Brown University | M,D |
| Canisius College | M,O |
| Clark University | M |
| Columbia University | M,D |
| Daemen College | M |
| Dalhousie University | M |
| Eastern Kentucky University | M |
| East Tennessee State University | M,D,O |
| George Mason University | M,O |
| The George Washington University | M,D |
| Georgia Southern University | M,D |
| Icahn School of Medicine at Mount Sinai | M,D |
| Idaho State University | O |
| Independence University | M |
| Indiana University Bloomington | M,D |
| Indiana University-Purdue University Indianapolis | M,D,O |
| Johns Hopkins University | M,D |
| Long Island University - Brooklyn | M,D,O |
| Louisiana State University Health Sciences Center | M,D |
| Medical College of Wisconsin | D |
| Memorial University of Newfoundland | M,D,O |
| Midwestern State University | M,O |
| Minnesota State University Mankato | M,O |
| Monroe College | M |
| New Jersey City University | M |
| New York University | M,D |
| North Dakota State University | M |
| Old Dominion University | M |
| Quinnipiac University | D |

*M—masters degree; D—doctorate; O—other advanced degree; *—Close-Up and/or Display*

| | |
|---|---|
| Saint Louis University | M |
| San Francisco State University | M |
| Southern Illinois University Carbondale | M |
| State University of New York College at Cortland | M |
| State University of New York College at Potsdam | M |
| State University of New York Downstate Medical Center | M |
| Stony Brook University, State University of New York | M,D,O |
| Suffolk University | M |
| SUNY Brockport | M |
| Teachers College, Columbia University | M,D,O |
| Tulane University | M,D |
| Universidad de Ciencias Medicas | M,D,O |
| Université de Montréal | M,D,O |
| University at Buffalo, the State University of New York | M,D,O |
| The University of Alabama | M |
| The University of Alabama at Birmingham | M |
| University of Alberta | M,D |
| University of Arkansas | M,D |
| University of Calgary | M,D |
| University of California, Los Angeles | M,D |
| University of Colorado Denver | M,D,O |
| University of Illinois at Chicago | M,D |
| University of Illinois at Springfield | M,O |
| University of Illinois at Urbana-Champaign | M,D |
| The University of Iowa | M,D |
| The University of Kansas | M,D,O |
| University of Louisville | M |
| University of Manitoba | M,D,O |
| University of Massachusetts Amherst | M,D |
| University of Miami | M,D |
| University of Minnesota, Twin Cities Campus | M |
| University of Montana | M |
| University of Nevada, Las Vegas | M,D,O |
| University of New Mexico | M |
| The University of North Carolina at Charlotte | M,D,O |
| The University of North Carolina at Greensboro | M,D |
| University of Northern British Columbia | M,D,O |
| University of Northern Colorado | M |
| University of Northern Iowa | M |
| University of North Florida | M,O |
| University of Ottawa | D,O |
| University of Phoenix - Central Valley Campus | M |
| University of Phoenix - Hawaii Campus | M |
| University of Pittsburgh | M,D,O* |
| University of Saskatchewan | M,D |
| University of South Florida | O |
| The University of Tennessee | M,D |
| The University of Texas Health Science Center at Houston | M,D,O |
| University of Toronto | M,D |
| University of Vermont | M |
| University of Virginia | M,D |
| University of Washington | M,D |
| University of Wisconsin–La Crosse | M |
| University of Wisconsin–Milwaukee | D* |
| University of Wyoming | M,D |
| Université Laval | M,D,O |
| Virginia Commonwealth University | M,D |
| Virginia State University | M,D |
| Walden University | M,D,O |
| Washington State University | M,D,O |
| William James College | M,D,O |

### COMMUNITY HEALTH NURSING

| | |
|---|---|
| Allen College | M,D |
| Binghamton University, State University of New York | M,D,O |
| Hampton University | M,D |
| Hunter College of the City University of New York | M |
| Husson University | M,O |
| Independence University | M |
| Johns Hopkins University | |
| Kean University | M |
| La Salle University | M,D,O |
| Louisiana State University Health Sciences Center | M,D,O |
| Oregon Health & Science University | M,O |
| San Francisco State University | M,O |
| University of Hartford | M |
| University of Hawaii at Manoa | M,D,O |
| University of Illinois at Chicago | M,O |
| The University of Kansas | M,D,O |
| University of Maryland, Baltimore | M,D,O |
| University of Massachusetts Amherst | M,D |
| University of Massachusetts Dartmouth | M,D |
| University of North Dakota | M,D,O |
| University of Puerto Rico - Medical Sciences Campus | M |
| University of South Carolina | M |
| The University of Texas at Austin | M,D |
| The University of Texas Health Science Center at San Antonio | M,D,O |
| The University of Toledo | M,O |
| University of Washington, Tacoma | M |
| Wayne State University | M,D |
| Worcester State University | M |

### COMPARATIVE AND INTERDISCIPLINARY ARTS

| | |
|---|---|
| Brigham Young University | M |
| Florida Atlantic University | D |
| Goddard College | M |
| Ohio University | D |
| Simon Fraser University | M |

### COMPARATIVE LITERATURE

| | |
|---|---|
| American University | M |
| The American University in Cairo | M,O |
| Arizona State University at Tempe | M,D,O |
| Binghamton University, State University of New York | M,D |
| Brigham Young University | M |
| Brock University | M |
| Brown University | D |
| California State University, Northridge | M |
| Carleton University | D |
| Carnegie Mellon University | M,D |
| Case Western Reserve University | M |
| Claremont Graduate University | M,D |
| Columbia University | M,D |
| Cornell University | D |
| Dartmouth College | M |
| Duke University | D |
| East Carolina University | M,D,O |
| Emory University | D,O |
| Fairleigh Dickinson University, Metropolitan Campus | M |
| Florida Atlantic University | M |
| Georgetown University | M,D |
| The Graduate Center, City University of New York | M,D |
| Harrison Middleton University | M,D |
| Harvard University | D* |
| Hunter College of the City University of New York | M |
| Indiana University Bloomington | M,D |
| Johns Hopkins University | D |
| Louisiana State University and Agricultural & Mechanical College | M,D |
| New York University | M,D |
| Northwestern University | M,D |
| Penn State University Park | M,D* |
| Princeton University | D |
| Purdue University | M,D |
| Rutgers University - New Brunswick | M,D |
| San Francisco State University | M |
| Stanford University | D |
| Stony Brook University, State University of New York | M,D,O |
| Université de Montréal | M,D |
| Université de Sherbrooke | M,D |
| Université du Québec à Chicoutimi | M[illegible] |
| Université du Québec à Montréal | M,D |
| Université du Québec à Rimouski | M,D |
| Université du Québec à Trois-Rivières | M |
| University at Buffalo, the State University of New York | M,D |
| University of Arkansas | M,D |
| University of California, Berkeley | D |
| University of California, Davis | D |
| University of California, Irvine | M,D |
| University of California, Los Angeles | M,D |
| University of California, Riverside | M,D |
| University of California, Santa Barbara | D |
| University of California, Santa Cruz | M,D |
| University of Chicago | [illegible] |
| University of Georgia | [illegible] |
| University of Guelph | [illegible] |
| University of Houston | [illegible] |
| University of Illinois at Urbana-Champaign | [illegible] |
| University of Maryland, College Park | M,D |
| University of Massachusetts Amherst | M,D |
| University of Memphis | M,D,O |
| University of Michigan | D |
| University of Minnesota, Twin Cities Campus | D |
| University of Nebraska–Lincoln | M,D |
| University of New Mexico | M,D |
| University of Notre Dame | D |
| University of Oregon | M,D |
| University of Pennsylvania | M,D |
| University of Puerto Rico at Rio Piedras | M |
| University of South Carolina | M,D |
| University of Southern California | D |
| University of South Florida | O |
| The University of Texas at Austin | M,D |
| The University of Texas at Dallas | M,D |
| University of Toronto | M,D |
| University of Utah | M,D |
| University of Washington | M,D |
| The University of Western Ontario | M,D |
| University of Wisconsin–Madison | M,D |
| University of Wisconsin–Milwaukee | M,O* |
| Université Laval | M,D |
| Washington University in St. Louis | M,D |
| Western Kentucky University | M |
| Yale University | D |

### COMPUTATIONAL BIOLOGY

| | |
|---|---|
| Albert Einstein College of Medicine | D |
| Baylor College of Medicine | D |
| Carnegie Mellon University | M,D |
| Claremont Graduate University | M,D |
| Cornell University | D |
| Duke University | D,O |
| George Mason University | M,D,O |
| Harvard University | M* |
| Iowa State University of Science and Technology | M,D |
| Lewis University | M |
| Massachusetts Institute of Technology | D |
| New York University | D |
| Oregon Health & Science University | M,D,O |
| Oregon State University | M,D |
| Princeton University | D |
| Rutgers University - Camden | M,D |
| Rutgers University - Newark | M |
| Rutgers University - New Brunswick | D |
| Saint Louis University | M |
| University of California, Irvine | D |
| University of Colorado Denver | M,D |
| University of Idaho | M,D |
| University of Illinois at Urbana-Champaign | M,D |
| The University of Iowa | M,D,O |
| The University of Kansas | D |
| University of Maryland, College Park | D |
| University of Massachusetts Medical School | M,D |
| University of Minnesota Rochester | M,D |
| The University of North Carolina at Chapel Hill | D |
| University of Pennsylvania | D |
| University of Rochester | M,D |
| University of Southern California | D |
| University of South Florida | M,D |
| The University of Texas Medical Branch | D |
| University of Wyoming | D |
| Washington University in St. Louis | D |
| Wayne State University | M,D |
| Weill Cornell Medicine | D |
| Worcester Polytechnic Institute | M,D |
| Yale University | D |

### COMPUTATIONAL SCIENCES

| | |
|---|---|
| California Institute of Technology | M,D |
| Chapman University | M,D |
| Claremont Graduate University | M,D |
| Cornell University | M,D |
| Duke University | M,D |
| Florida State University | M,D |
| George Mason University | M,D,O |
| Hampton University | M |
| Harvard University | M,D* |
| Marquette University | M,D |
| Massachusetts Institute of Technology | M |
| McGill University | M,D |
| Memorial University of Newfoundland | M |
| Michigan Technological University | M,D,O |
| Middle Tennessee State University | D |
| Morgan State University | M,D |
| North Carolina Agricultural and Technical State University | M |
| The Ohio State University | M,D |
| Oregon State University | M,D |
| Princeton University | D |
| Purdue University | D |
| Rice University | M,D |
| St. John's University (NY) | M |
| Sam Houston State University | M,D |
| San Diego State University | M,D |
| Simon Fraser University | M,D |
| South Dakota State University | M,D |
| Southern Illinois University Edwardsville | M |
| Southern Methodist University | M,D |
| Stanford University | M,D |
| Texas A&M University–Commerce | M,O |
| University at Buffalo, the State University of New York | D,O |
| The University of Alabama at Birmingham | D |
| University of Alaska Fairbanks | M,D |
| University of California, San Diego | M,D |
| University of California, Santa Barbara | M,D |
| University of Central Oklahoma | M |
| University of Chicago | M |
| University of Colorado Denver | M,D |
| The University of Iowa | D |
| University of Lethbridge | M,D |
| University of Manitoba | M |
| University of Massachusetts Boston | D |
| University of Memphis | M |
| University of Michigan–Dearborn | M |
| University of Minnesota, Duluth | M |
| University of Minnesota, Twin Cities Campus | M,D |
| University of Notre Dame | M,D |
| University of Pennsylvania | M,D |
| University of Pittsburgh | M,D,O* |
| University of Puerto Rico at Mayagüez | M |
| University of Southern Mississippi | M,D |
| The University of Tennessee at Chattanooga | D |
| The University of Texas at Austin | M,D |
| University of Utah | M |
| University of Washington | M,D |
| Valparaiso University | M |
| Western Michigan University | M,D |

### COMPUTER AND INFORMATION SYSTEMS SECURITY

| | |
|---|---|
| American InterContinental University Online | M |
| American Public University System | M,D |
| Augusta University | M |
| Austin Peay State University | M |
| Bay Path University | M |
| Benedictine University | M |
| Boston University | M,D,O |
| Brandeis University | M |
| California State University, San Bernardino | M |
| California State University, San Marcos | M |
| California University of Pennsylvania | M |
| Capella University | M,D |
| Capitol Technology University | M |
| Cardinal Stritch University | M |
| Carnegie Mellon University | M |
| Central Michigan University | O |
| Champlain College | M |
| City University of Seattle | M,O |
| Claremont Graduate University | M,D,O |
| College of Saint Elizabeth | M,O |
| College of Staten Island of the City University of New York | M |
| Colorado Christian University | M |
| Colorado Technical University Aurora | M |
| Colorado Technical University Colorado Springs | M,D |
| Columbus State University | M,O |
| Concordia University (Canada) | M,D,O |
| Concordia University, Nebraska | M |
| Concordia University of Edmonton | M |
| Concordia University, St. Paul | M |
| Davenport University | M |
| DePaul University | M,D |
| DeSales University | M,O |
| Drury University | O |
| East Carolina University | M,D,O |
| Eastern Illinois University | M |
| Eastern Michigan University | O |
| EC-Council University | M |
| ECPI University | M |
| Embry-Riddle Aeronautical University–Daytona | M |
| Embry-Riddle Aeronautical University–Worldwide | M |
| Endicott College | M,O |
| Fairfield University | M,O |
| Florida Institute of Technology | M |
| Florida International University | M,D |
| Florida State University | M,D |
| George Mason University | M |
| The George Washington University | M,D,O |
| Georgia Southern University | M,O |
| Hampton University | M |
| Harrisburg University of Science and Technology | M |
| Hofstra University | M |
| Hood College | M,O |
| Illinois Institute of Technology | M,D |
| Indiana University Bloomington | M,D |
| Indiana University-Purdue University Indianapolis | M,D,O |
| The Institute of World Politics | M,D,O |
| Inter American University of Puerto Rico, Guayama Campus | M |
| Iona College | M,O |
| James Madison University | M |
| Johns Hopkins University | M,O |
| Johnson & Wales University | M |
| Keiser University | M |
| Kennesaw State University | M,O |
| Kent State University | M |
| Lawrence Technological University | M,D,O |
| Lewis University | M |
| Liberty University | M,D |
| Lindenwood University | M,O |
| Lipscomb University | M,O |
| London Metropolitan University | M,D |
| Long Island University - Riverhead | M,O |
| Louisiana Tech University | M,D |
| Marymount University | M,D,O |
| Maryville University of Saint Louis | M,O |
| Marywood University | M |
| Mercy College | M |
| Mercyhurst University | M |
| Metropolitan State University | M,D,O |
| Middle Georgia State University | M |
| Mississippi College | M |
| Missouri Western State University | M |
| National University | M |
| Naval Postgraduate School | M,D |
| New Jersey City University | M,D,O |
| New Jersey Institute of Technology | M,D,O |
| New York Institute of Technology | M |
| New York University | M |
| Niagara University | M |
| Northcentral University | M,D,O |
| Northeastern University | M,D,O |
| Northern Kentucky University | M,O |
| Northwestern University | M |
| Norwich University | M |
| Nova Southeastern University | M,D |
| Our Lady of the Lake University | M |
| Pace University | M,D,O |
| Penn State Great Valley | M,O |
| Portland State University | M,D,O |
| Purdue University | M |
| Purdue University Global | M |
| Quinnipiac University | M |
| Regent University | M |
| Regis University | M,O |
| Robert Morris University | M,D |
| Robert Morris University Illinois | M |
| Rochester Institute of Technology | M,O |
| Roger Williams University | M |
| Rowan University | O |
| Sacred Heart University | M |
| Saginaw Valley State University | M |
| St. Cloud State University | M |
| Saint Leo University | M,D |
| St. Mary's University (United States) | M,O |
| Saint Mary's University of Minnesota | M |
| Salem International University | M |
| Salve Regina University | M,O |
| Sam Houston State University | M,D |
| The SANS Technology Institute | M |
| Seattle Pacific University | M |
| Southern Arkansas University–Magnolia | M |
| Southern New Hampshire University | M |

| | |
|---|---|
| Southern Utah University | M |
| State University of New York Polytechnic Institute | M |
| Stephen F. Austin State University | M |
| Stevens Institute of Technology | M,O |
| Stevenson University | M |
| Stratford University (VA) | M,D |
| Strayer University | M |
| Syracuse University | M,O |
| Temple University | M,D* |
| Thomas Edison State University | M,O |
| Trident University International | M,D |
| Tuskegee University | M |
| Universidad del Este | M |
| Université de Sherbrooke | M |
| University at Albany, State University of New York | M,D,O |
| University of Advancing Technology | M |
| The University of Alabama at Birmingham | M |
| The University of Alabama in Huntsville | M,D,O |
| University of Colorado Colorado Springs | M,D |
| University of Dallas | M,D |
| University of Dayton | M |
| University of Denver | M,D |
| University of Detroit Mercy | M,D,O |
| University of Fairfax | M,D |
| University of Houston | M |
| University of Louisville | M,D,O |
| University of Maryland, Baltimore County | M,O |
| University of Maryland Global Campus | M,O |
| University of Michigan–Dearborn | D |
| University of Minnesota, Twin Cities Campus | M |
| University of Missouri–St. Louis | M,D,O |
| University of Nebraska at Omaha | M,D,O |
| University of Nevada, Las Vegas | M,D,O |
| University of New Hampshire | M,O |
| University of New Haven | M |
| University of New Mexico | M |
| The University of North Carolina at Charlotte | M,O |
| University of Rhode Island | M,D,O |
| University of San Diego | M |
| University of Southern California | M,D |
| University of South Florida | M |
| The University of Tampa | M,O |
| The University of Texas at Austin | M,D |
| The University of Texas at El Paso | M,D,O |
| The University of Texas at San Antonio | M,D,O |
| The University of Texas at Tyler | M |
| The University of Tulsa | M,D |
| University of Utah | M,O |
| University of Washington | M,D |
| University of West Florida | M |
| University of Wisconsin–Madison | M |
| Utah Valley University | O |
| Utica College | M |
| Valparaiso University | M |
| Vanderbilt University | M* |
| Virginia International University | M,O |
| Virginia Polytechnic Institute and State University | M,O |
| Walden University | M,D,O |
| Walsh College of Accountancy and Business Administration | M |
| Webster University | M |
| Western Governors University | M |
| West Virginia University | M,D,O |
| Wilmington University | M |

## COMPUTER ART AND DESIGN

| | |
|---|---|
| Academy of Art University | M |
| Alfred University | M |
| ArtCenter College of Design | M |
| Bowling Green State University | M |
| California College of the Arts | M |
| Carnegie Mellon University | M |
| Chatham University | M |
| City College of the City University of New York | M |
| Claremont Graduate University | M |
| Concordia University (Canada) | M,O |
| Cornell University | M,D |
| DePaul University | M,D |
| DigiPen Institute of Technology | M |
| Drexel University | M,D |
| East Tennessee State University | M |
| Emily Carr University of Art + Design | M |
| Full Sail University | M |
| Georgia Institute of Technology | M,D |
| Georgian Court University | M,O |
| Goucher College | M |
| Indiana University-Purdue University Indianapolis | M |
| International Technological University | M |
| Lindenwood University–Belleville | M |
| Lynn University | M,O |
| New Mexico Highlands University | M |
| The New School | M |
| New York Institute of Technology | M |
| North Carolina State University | M,D |
| Northern Vermont University–Johnson | M |
| The Ohio State University | M |
| Old Dominion University | M |
| Purchase College, State University of New York | M |
| Purdue University | M,D |
| Rensselaer Polytechnic Institute | D |
| Rhode Island School of Design | M |
| Rochester Institute of Technology | M |
| Savannah College of Art and Design | M |
| School of Visual Arts (NY) | M |
| Syracuse University | M |
| Texas State University | M |
| Universidad Autonoma de Guadalajara | M,D |
| Universidad de las Américas Puebla | M |
| University of Alaska Fairbanks | M |
| University of California, Santa Cruz | M,D |
| University of Central Arkansas | M |
| University of Central Florida | M |
| University of Denver | M |
| University of Florida | M,D |
| University of Maryland, Baltimore County | M |
| University of Montana | M |
| University of Pennsylvania | M,D |
| University of Rhode Island | M |
| University of Southern California | M |
| University of South Florida, St. Petersburg | M |
| University of Victoria | M |
| University of Wisconsin–Milwaukee | M,O* |
| Virginia International University | M,O |

## COMPUTER EDUCATION

| | |
|---|---|
| Arcadia University | M,D,O |
| Ball State University | M,D,O |
| Eastern Washington University | M |
| Illinois Institute of Technology | M,D |
| Kent State University | M,D,O |
| Lesley University | M,D,O |
| Mississippi College | M,D,O |
| Ohio University | M,D |
| Stony Brook University, State University of New York | M |
| Teachers College, Columbia University | M,D |
| Thomas College | M |
| University of Bridgeport | M,D,O |
| University of Illinois at Chicago | D |
| University of Phoenix - Central Valley Campus | M |
| University of Phoenix–Online Campus | M,O |
| University of Phoenix - San Diego Campus | M |

## COMPUTER ENGINEERING

| | |
|---|---|
| Air Force Institute of Technology | M,D |
| American University of Sharjah | M,D |
| Arizona State University at Tempe | M,D |
| Atlantis University | M |
| Auburn University | M,D |
| Baylor University | M,D |
| Boise State University | M,D |
| Boston University | M,D,O |
| Brigham Young University | M,D |
| Brown University | M,D |
| Bucknell University | M |
| California State University, Chico | M |
| California State University, Fresno | M |
| California State University, Fullerton | M |
| California State University, Long Beach | M |
| Carnegie Mellon University | M,D |
| Case Western Reserve University | M,D |
| The Citadel, The Military College of South Carolina | M,O |
| Clemson University | M,D |
| Colorado Technical University Aurora | M |
| Colorado Technical University Colorado Springs | M |
| Columbia University | M,D |
| Concordia University (Canada) | M,D |
| Cornell University | M,D |
| Dalhousie University | M,D |
| Dartmouth College | M,D |
| Drexel University | M |
| Duke University | M,D |
| East Carolina University | M,D,O |
| Fairfield University | M,O |
| Fairleigh Dickinson University, Metropolitan Campus | M |
| Florida Atlantic University | M,D |
| Florida Institute of Technology | M,D |
| Florida International University | M,D |
| George Mason University | M,D,O |
| The George Washington University | M,D,O |
| Georgia Institute of Technology | M,D |
| Grand Valley State University | M |
| Illinois Institute of Technology | M,D |
| Indiana State University | M |
| Indiana University-Purdue University Indianapolis | M,D |
| Instituto Tecnológico y de Estudios Superiores de Monterrey, Campus Chihuahua | M,O |
| International Technological University | M |
| Iowa State University of Science and Technology | M,D |
| Johns Hopkins University | M,D,O |
| Kansas State University | M,D |
| Lakehead University | M |
| Lawrence Technological University | M,D |
| Lehigh University | M,D |
| Louisiana State University and Agricultural & Mechanical College | M,D |
| Manhattan College | M |
| Marquette University | M,D,O |
| Marshall University | M |
| Massachusetts Institute of Technology | M,D,O |
| McGill University | M,D |
| Memorial University of Newfoundland | M,D |
| Mercer University | M |
| Miami University | M |
| Michigan Technological University | M,D,O |
| Mississippi State University | M,D |
| Missouri University of Science and Technology | M,D |
| Montana State University | M,D |
| Naval Postgraduate School | M,D,O |
| New Jersey Institute of Technology | M,D |
| New York Institute of Technology | M |
| New York University | M |
| Norfolk State University | M |
| North Carolina Agricultural and Technical State University | M,D |
| North Carolina State University | M,D |
| North Dakota State University | M,D |
| Northeastern University | M,D,O |
| Northern Arizona University | M,D |
| Northwestern Polytechnic University | M,D |
| Northwestern University | M,D |
| Oakland University | M,D |
| The Ohio State University | M,D |
| Oklahoma Christian University | M |
| Oklahoma State University | M,D |
| Old Dominion University | M,D |
| Oregon Health & Science University | M,D |
| Oregon State University | M,D |
| Penn State University Park | M,D* |
| Polytechnic University of Puerto Rico | M |
| Polytechnique Montréal | M,D,O |
| Portland State University | M,D |
| Purdue University | M,D |
| Purdue University Fort Wayne | M |
| Purdue University Northwest | M |
| Queen's University at Kingston | M,D |
| Rensselaer at Hartford | M |
| Rensselaer Polytechnic Institute | M,D |
| Rice University | M,D |
| Rochester Institute of Technology | M |
| Rose-Hulman Institute of Technology | M |
| Royal Military College of Canada | M,D |
| Rutgers University - New Brunswick | M,D |
| St. Mary's University (United States) | M |
| San Jose State University | M |
| Santa Clara University | M,D,O |
| Southern Illinois University Carbondale | M,D |
| Southern Methodist University | M,D |
| Stevens Institute of Technology | M,D,O |
| Stony Brook University, State University of New York | M,D |
| Syracuse University | M,D |
| Tennessee State University | M,D |
| Texas A&M University | M,D |
| UNB Fredericton | M,D |
| Universidad del Turabo | M |
| The University of Akron | M,D |
| The University of Alabama | M,D |
| The University of Alabama at Birmingham | M,D |
| The University of Alabama in [illegible]ville | M,D |
| [illegible] Alberta | M,D |
| [illegible]ty of Arizona | M,D |
| [illegible] Arkansas | M,D |
| [illegible] Bridgeport | M,D |
| Th[illegible]sity of British Columbia | M,D |
| Un[illegible] of Calgary | M,D |
| University of California, Davis | M,D |
| University of California, Los Angeles | M,D |
| University of California, Riverside | M |
| University of California, San Diego | M,D |
| University of California, Santa Barbara | M,D |
| University of Central Florida | M,D |
| University of Cincinnati | M,D |
| University of Colorado Boulder | M,D |
| University of Connecticut | M,D |
| University of Dayton | M,D |
| University of Delaware | M,D |
| University of Denver | M,D |
| University of Detroit Mercy | M,D |
| University of Florida | M,D |
| University of Houston–Clear Lake | M |
| University of Illinois at Chicago | M,D |
| University of Illinois at Urbana-Champaign | M,D |
| The University of Iowa | M,D |
| The University of Kansas | M |
| University of Louisville | M,D,O |
| University of Maine | M,D |
| University of Manitoba | M,D |
| University of Maryland, Baltimore County | M,D |
| University of Maryland, College Park | M,D |
| University of Massachusetts Amherst | M,D |
| University of Massachusetts Dartmouth | M,D,O |
| University of Massachusetts Lowell | M,D |
| University of Memphis | M,D,O |
| University of Miami | M,D |
| University of Michigan | M,D |
| University of Michigan–Dearborn | M,D |
| University of Minnesota, Duluth | M |
| University of Minnesota, Twin Cities Campus | M,D |
| University of Missouri | M,D |
| University of Missouri–Kansas City | M,D,O |
| University of Nebraska–Lincoln | M,D |
| University of Nevada, Reno | M,D |
| University of New Haven | M |
| University of New Mexico | M,D |
| University of North Texas | M,D,O |
| University of Notre Dame | M,D |
| University of Oklahoma | M,D |
| University of Ottawa | M,D |
| University of Pittsburgh | M,D* |
| University of Puerto Rico at Mayagüez | M,D |
| University of Regina | M,D |
| University of Rhode Island | M,D |
| University of Rochester | M,D |
| University of San Diego | M |
| University of South Alabama | M |
| University of South Carolina | M,D |
| University of Southern California | M,D,O |
| University of South Florida | M,D |
| The University of Tennessee | M,D |
| The University of Texas at Arlington | M,D |
| The University of Texas at Austin | M,D |
| The University of Texas at Dallas | M,D |
| The University of Texas at El Paso | M,D,O |
| The University of Texas at San Antonio | M,D |
| University of Toronto | M,D |
| University of Utah | M,D |
| University of Victoria | M,D |
| University of Virginia | M,D |
| University of Washington | M,D |
| University of Washington, Bothell | M |
| University of Washington, Tacoma | M |
| University of Waterloo | M,D |
| The University of Western Ontario | M,D |
| University of Wisconsin–Milwaukee | M,D* |
| Villanova University | M,O |
| Virginia Polytechnic Institute and State University | M,D,O |
| Washington State University | M,D |
| Washington University in St. Louis | M,D |
| Wayne State University | M,D |
| Weber State University | M |
| Western Michigan University | M,D |
| West Virginia University | M,D |
| Wichita State University | M,D |
| Worcester Polytechnic Institute | M,D,O |
| Wright State University | M,D |
| Youngstown State University | M |

## COMPUTER SCIENCE

| | |
|---|---|
| Acadia University | M |
| Air Force Institute of Technology | M,D |
| Alabama Agricultural and Mechanical University | M |
| Alcorn State University | M |
| American Sentinel University | M |
| The American University in Cairo | M,D,O |
| American University of Armenia | M |
| Appalachian State University | M |
| Arizona State University at Tempe | M,D |
| Arkansas State University | M |
| Auburn University | M,D |
| Ball State University | M |
| Baylor University | M,D |
| Binghamton University, State University of New York | M,D |
| Boise State University | M,O |
| Boston University | M,D,O |
| Bowie State University | M,D |
| Bowling Green State University | M |
| Bradley University | M |
| Brandeis University | M,D |
| Bridgewater State University | M |
| Brigham Young University | M,D |
| Brock University | M |
| Brooklyn College of the City University of New York | M,O |
| Brown University | M,D |
| California Institute of Technology | M,D |
| California Polytechnic State University, San Luis Obispo | M |
| California State Polytechnic University, Pomona | M |
| California State University Channel Islands | M |
| California State University, Chico | M |
| California State University, Dominguez Hills | M |
| California State University, East Bay | M |
| California State University, Fresno | M |
| California State University, Fullerton | M |
| California State University, Long Beach | M |
| California State University, Los Angeles | M |
| California State University, Northridge | M |
| California State University, Sacramento | M |
| California State University, San Bernardino | M |
| California State University, San Marcos | M |
| Capitol Technology University | M |
| Carleton University | M,D |
| Carnegie Mellon University | M,D |
| Case Western Reserve University | M,D |
| The Catholic University of America | M,D |

*M—masters degree; D—doctorate; O—other advanced degree; *—Close-Up and/or Display*

| | |
|---|---|
| Central Connecticut State University | M,O |
| Central Michigan University | M |
| Chicago State University | M |
| Christopher Newport University | M |
| City College of the City University of New York | M,D |
| City University of Seattle | M,O |
| Clark Atlanta University | M |
| Clarkson University | M,D |
| Clemson University | M,D |
| Coastal Carolina University | M,D,O |
| College of Charleston | M |
| The College of Saint Rose | M,O |
| College of Staten Island of the City University of New York | M |
| Colorado School of Mines | M,D |
| Colorado State University | M,D |
| Colorado Technical University Aurora | M |
| Colorado Technical University Colorado Springs | M,D |
| Columbia University | M,D |
| Columbus State University | M,O |
| Concordia University (Canada) | M,D,O |
| Concordia University, Nebraska | M |
| Cornell University | M,D |
| Dakota State University | M,D,O |
| Dalhousie University | M,D |
| Dartmouth College | M,D |
| DePaul University | M,D |
| DigiPen Institute of Technology | M |
| Drexel University | M,D,O |
| Duke University | M,D |
| East Carolina University | M,D,O |
| Eastern Illinois University | M |
| Eastern Michigan University | M,O |
| Eastern Washington University | M |
| East Stroudsburg University of Pennsylvania | M |
| East Tennessee State University | M,O |
| Elizabeth City State University | M |
| Emory University | M,D |
| Fairleigh Dickinson University, Florham Campus | M |
| Fairleigh Dickinson University, Metropolitan Campus | M |
| Fitchburg State University | M |
| Florida Atlantic University | M,D |
| Florida Institute of Technology | M,D |
| Florida International University | M,D |
| Florida Polytechnic University | M |
| Fontbonne University | M |
| Fordham University | M |
| Franklin University | M |
| Frostburg State University | M |
| Gannon University | M |
| George Mason University | M,D,O |
| Georgetown University | M,D |
| The George Washington University | M,D,O |
| Georgia Southwestern State University | M,O |
| Georgia State University | M,D |
| Governors State University | M |
| The Graduate Center, City University of New York | D |
| Grand Valley State University | M |
| Hampton University | M |
| Harvard University | M,D* |
| Hood College | M,O |
| Howard University | M |
| Illinois Institute of Technology | M,D |
| Indiana State University | M |
| Indiana University Bloomington | M,D,O |
| Indiana University-Purdue University Indianapolis | M,D,O |
| Indiana University South Bend | M,O |
| Instituto Tecnológico y de Estudios Superiores de Monterrey, Campus Central de Veracruz | M |
| Instituto Tecnológico y de Estudios Superiores de Monterrey, Campus Ciudad de México | M,D |
| Instituto Tecnológico y de Estudios Superiores de Monterrey, Campus Cuernavaca | M,D |
| Instituto Tecnológico y de Estudios Superiores de Monterrey, Campus Estado de México | M,D |
| Instituto Tecnológico y de Estudios Superiores de Monterrey, Campus Irapuato | M,D |
| Instituto Tecnológico y de Estudios Superiores de Monterrey, Campus Monterrey | M,D |
| Inter American University of Puerto Rico, Fajardo Campus | M |
| Inter American University of Puerto Rico, Guayama Campus | M |
| Inter American University of Puerto Rico, Metropolitan Campus | M |
| Iona College | M |
| Iowa State University of Science and Technology | M,D |
| Jackson State University | M |
| Jacksonville State University | M |
| James Madison University | M |
| Johns Hopkins University | M,D,O |
| Kansas State University | M,D |
| Kennesaw State University | M |
| Kent State University | M,D |
| Kutztown University of Pennsylvania | M |
| Lakehead University | M |
| Lamar University | M |
| La Salle University | M,O |
| Lawrence Technological University | M,O |
| Lebanese American University | M |
| Lehigh University | M,D |
| Lehman College of the City University of New York | M |
| Lewis University | M |
| Long Island University - Brooklyn | M,O |
| Louisiana State University and Agricultural & Mechanical College | M,D |
| Louisiana State University in Shreveport | M |
| Louisiana Tech University | M,D,O |
| Loyola University Chicago | M |
| Maharishi International University | M |
| Marist College | M,O |
| Marquette University | M,D |
| Marshall University | M |
| Massachusetts Institute of Technology | M,D,O |
| McGill University | M,D |
| McMaster University | M,D |
| McNeese State University | M |
| Memorial University of Newfoundland | M,D |
| Merrimack College | M |
| Metropolitan State University | M |
| Michigan State University | M,D |
| Middle Tennessee State University | M |
| Midwestern State University | M |
| Mills College | M,O |
| Minnesota State University Mankato | M,O |
| Mississippi College | M |
| Mississippi State University | M,D |
| Missouri State University | M |
| Missouri University of Science and Technology | M,D |
| Monmouth University | M |
| Monroe College | M |
| Montana State University | M,D |
| Montclair State University | M,O |
| Morgan State University | M |
| Murray State University | M |
| National University | M |
| Naval Postgraduate School | M,D,O |
| New Jersey Institute of Technology | M,D,O |
| New Mexico Highlands University | M |
| New Mexico Institute of Mining and Technology | M,D |
| New York Institute of Technology | M |
| New York University | M,D |
| Norfolk State University | M |
| North Carolina Agricultural and Technical State University | M,D |
| North Carolina State University | M,D |
| North Central College | M |
| Northcentral University | M,D,O |
| North Dakota State University | M,D,O |
| Northeastern Illinois University | M |
| Northeastern University | M,D |
| Northern Arizona University | M,D |
| Northern Illinois University | M |
| Northern Kentucky University | M,O |
| Northwestern Polytechnic University | M,D |
| Northwestern University | M,D |
| Northwest Missouri State University | M |
| Notre Dame College (OH) | M,O |
| Nova Southeastern University | M,D |
| Oakland University | M,D |
| The Ohio State University | M,D |
| Ohio University | M,D |
| Oklahoma Christian University | M |
| Oklahoma City University | M |
| Oklahoma State University | M,D |
| Old Dominion University | M,D |
| Oregon Health & Science University | M,D |
| Oregon State University | M,D |
| Pace University | M,D,O |
| Pacific States University | [illegible] |
| Penn State Harrisburg | [illegible] |
| Penn State University Park | [illegible] |
| Polytechnic University of Puerto Rico | [illegible] |
| Polytechnique Montréal | [illegible]D |
| Portland State University | M,D,O |
| Prairie View A&M University | M,D |
| Princeton University | M,D |
| Purdue University | M,D |
| Purdue University Fort Wayne | M |
| Purdue University Northwest | M |
| Queens College of the City University of New York | M |
| Queen's University at Kingston | M,D |
| Regis University | M,O |
| Rensselaer at Hartford | M |
| Rensselaer Polytechnic Institute | M,D |
| Rice University | M,D |
| Rivier University | M |
| Rochester Institute of Technology | M,D |
| Roosevelt University | M |
| Rowan University | M |
| Royal Military College of Canada | M |
| Rutgers University - Camden | M |
| Rutgers University - New Brunswick | M,D |
| Sacred Heart University | M |
| Saginaw Valley State University | M |
| St. Cloud State University | M,O |
| St. Francis Xavier University | M |
| Saint Joseph's University | M,O |
| Saint Louis University | M |
| St. Mary's University (United States) | M |
| Saint Xavier University | M |
| Sam Houston State University | M,D |
| San Diego State University | M |
| San Francisco State University | M |
| Santa Clara University | M,D,O |
| Seattle University | M |
| Shippensburg University of Pennsylvania | M,O |
| Simon Fraser University | M,D |
| Sofia University | M,D |
| Southern Adventist University | M |
| Southern Arkansas University–Magnolia | M |
| Southern Connecticut State University | M |
| Southern Illinois University Carbondale | M,D |
| Southern Illinois University Edwardsville | M |
| Southern Methodist University | M,D |
| Southern Oregon University | M |
| Southern University and Agricultural and Mechanical College | M |
| Stanford University | M,D |
| State University of New York Polytechnic Institute | M |
| Stevens Institute of Technology | M,D,O |
| Stony Brook University, State University of New York | M,D,O |
| Stratford University (VA) | M,D |
| Syracuse University | M |
| Temple University | M,D* |
| Tennessee Technological University | M,D |
| Texas A&M University | M,D |
| Texas A&M University–Corpus Christi | M |
| Texas A&M University–Kingsville | M |
| Texas Southern University | M |
| Texas State University | M,D |
| Towson University | M |
| Toyota Technological Institute at Chicago | D |
| Trent University | M |
| Troy University | M |
| Tufts University | M,D,O |
| Universidad Autonoma de Guadalajara | M,D |
| Universidad de las Américas Puebla | M,D |
| Université de Moncton | M,O |
| Université de Montréal | M,D |
| Université du Québec à Trois-Rivières | M |
| Université du Québec en Outaouais | M,D,O |
| University at Albany, State University of New York | M,D |
| University at Buffalo, the State University of New York | M,D,O |
| University of Advancing Technology | M |
| The University of Akron | M |
| The University of Alabama | M,D |
| The University of Alabama at Birmingham | M,D |
| The University of Alabama in Huntsville | M,D,O |
| University of Alaska Fairbanks | M |
| University of Alberta | M,D |
| The University of Arizona | M,D |
| University of Arkansas | M,D |
| University of Arkansas at Little Rock | M,D |
| University of Bridgeport | M,D |
| The University of British Columbia | M,D |
| University of Calgary | M,D |
| University of California, Berkeley | M,D |
| University of California, Davis | M,D |
| University of California, Irvine | M,D |
| University of California, Los Angeles | M,D |
| University of California, Merced | M,D |
| University of California, Riverside | M,D |
| University of California, San Diego | M,D |
| University of California, Santa Barbara | M,D |
| University of California, Santa Cruz | M,D |
| University of Central Arkansas | M |
| University of Central Florida | M,D |
| University of Central Missouri | M,D,O |
| University of Central Oklahoma | M |
| University of Chicago | M,D |
| University of Cincinnati | M,D |
| University of Colorado Boulder | M,D |
| University of Colorado Denver | M,D |
| University of Connecticut | M,D |
| University of Dayton | M |
| University of Delaware | M,D |
| University of Denver | M,D |
| University of Detroit Mercy | M,D,O |
| University of Fairfax | M,D |
| University of Florida | M,D |
| University of Georgia | M,D |
| University of Guelph | M,D |
| University of Hawaii at Manoa | M,D,O |
| University of Houston | M,D |
| University of Houston–Clear Lake | M |
| University of Houston–Victoria | M |
| University of Idaho | M,D |
| University of Illinois at Chicago | M,D |
| University of Illinois at Springfield | M |
| University of Illinois at Urbana-Champaign | M,D |
| The University of Iowa | M,D |
| The University of Kansas | M,D |
| University of Kentucky | M,D |
| University of Lethbridge | M,D |
| University of Louisville | M,D,O |
| University of Maine | M,D,O |
| University of Management and Technology | M,O |
| The University of Manchester | M,D |
| University of Manitoba | M,D |
| University of Maryland, Baltimore County | M,D |
| University of Maryland, College Park | M,D |
| University of Maryland Eastern Shore | M |
| University of Massachusetts Amherst | M,D |
| University of Massachusetts Boston | M,D |
| University of Massachusetts Dartmouth | M,O |
| University of Massachusetts Lowell | M,D |
| University of Memphis | M,D |
| University of Miami | M,D |
| University of Michigan | M,D |
| University of Michigan–Dearborn | D |
| University of Michigan–Flint | M |
| University of Minnesota, Duluth | M |
| University of Minnesota, Twin Cities Campus | M,D |
| University of Mississippi | M,D |
| University of Missouri | M,D |
| University of Missouri–Kansas City | M,D,O |
| University of Missouri–St. Louis | M,D |
| University of Montana | M |
| University of Nebraska at Omaha | M,O |
| University of Nebraska–Lincoln | M,D |
| University of Nevada, Reno | M,D |
| University of New Hampshire | M,D |
| University of New Haven | M,O |
| University of New Mexico | M,D |
| University of New Orleans | M,D |
| The University of North Carolina at Chapel Hill | M,D |
| The University of North Carolina at Charlotte | D |
| The University of North Carolina at Greensboro | M |
| The University of North Carolina Wilmington | M |
| University of North Dakota | M |
| University of Northern British Columbia | M,D,O |
| University of North Florida | M |
| University of North Texas | M,D,O |
| University of Notre Dame | M,D |
| University of Oklahoma | M,D |
| University of Oregon | M,D |
| University of Ottawa | M,D |
| University of Pennsylvania | M,D |
| University of Pittsburgh | M,D* |
| University of Portland | M |
| University of Puerto Rico at Mayagüez | M,D |
| University of Regina | M,D |
| University of Rhode Island | M,D,O |
| University of Rochester | M,D |
| University of San Francisco | M |
| University of Saskatchewan | M,D |
| University of South Alabama | M,D |
| University of South Carolina | M,D |
| University of South Dakota | M |
| University of Southern California | M,D |
| University of Southern Maine | M,O |
| University of Southern Mississippi | M,D |
| University of South Florida | M,D |
| The University of Tennessee | M,D |
| The University of Tennessee at Chattanooga | M,O |
| The University of Texas at Arlington | M,D |
| The University of Texas at Austin | M,D |
| The University of Texas at Dallas | M,D |
| The University of Texas at El Paso | M,D,O |
| The University of Texas at San Antonio | M,D |
| The University of Texas at Tyler | M |
| The University of Texas of the Permian Basin | M |
| The University of Texas Rio Grande Valley | M |
| University of the District of Columbia | M |
| The University of Toledo | M,D |
| University of Toronto | M,D |
| The University of Tulsa | M,D |
| University of Utah | M,D |
| University of Vermont | M,D |
| University of Victoria | M,D |
| University of Virginia | M,D |
| University of Washington | M,D |
| University of Waterloo | M,D |
| The University of Western Ontario | M,D |
| University of West Florida | M |
| University of Windsor | M,D |
| University of Wisconsin–Madison | M,D |
| University of Wisconsin–Milwaukee | M,D* |
| University of Wisconsin–Parkside | M |
| University of Wisconsin–Platteville | M |
| University of Wyoming | M,D |
| Université Laval | M,D |
| Université TÉLUQ | M,D |
| Utah State University | M,D |
| Vanderbilt University | M,D* |
| Villanova University | M,O |
| Virginia Commonwealth University | M,D |
| Virginia International University | M,O |
| Virginia Polytechnic Institute and State University | M,D,O |
| Wake Forest University | M |
| Washington State University | M,D |
| Washington University in St. Louis | M,D |
| Wayne State University | M,D |
| Webster University | M |
| Wentworth Institute of Technology | M |
| Wesleyan University | M,D |
| Western Illinois University | M |
| Western Kentucky University | M |
| Western Michigan University | M,D |
| Western Washington University | M |
| West Virginia University | M,D |
| Wichita State University | M,D |
| Winston-Salem State University | M |
| Worcester Polytechnic Institute | M,D,O |
| Wright State University | M,D |
| Yale University | M,D |
| York University | M,D |
| Youngstown State University | M |

### CONDENSED MATTER PHYSICS

| | |
|---|---|
| Iowa State University of Science and Technology | M,D |
| Memorial University of Newfoundland | M,D |
| Rutgers University - New Brunswick | M,D |
| University of Alberta | M,D |
| The University of Manchester | M,D |
| University of Victoria | M,D |

### CONFLICT RESOLUTION AND MEDIATION/PEACE STUDIES

| | |
|---|---|
| American Public University System | M,D |
| American University | M,D,O |
| The American University of Paris | M |
| The American University of Rome | M |
| Anabaptist Mennonite Biblical Seminary | M,O |
| Arcadia University | M |
| Bethany Theological Seminary | M,O |
| Bethel University (TN) | M |
| Brandeis University | M,D |
| California State University, Dominguez Hills | M |
| California University of Pennsylvania | M |
| Cambridge College | M |
| Carleton University | M,O |
| Champlain College | M |
| Colgate Rochester Crozer Divinity School | M,D,O |
| Colorado Technical University Aurora | M |
| Colorado Technical University Colorado Springs | M,D |
| Columbia University | M |
| Cornell University | M,D |
| Creighton University | M,D,O |
| Dallas Baptist University | M |
| Drew University | M,D,O |
| Eastern Mennonite University | M,O |
| Fresno Pacific University | M,O |
| George Mason University | M,D,O |
| Georgetown University | M |
| Henley-Putnam School of Strategic Security | M |
| The Institute of World Politics | M,D,O |
| Kansas State University | M,D,O |
| Kennesaw State University | M,D |
| Kent State University | M,D |
| Lesley University | M,D,O |
| Lipscomb University | M,O |
| London Metropolitan University | M,D |
| Middlebury Institute of International Studies at Monterey | M |
| Montclair State University | M,O |
| Naval Postgraduate School | M,D |
| Norwich University | M |
| Nova Southeastern University | M,D,O |
| Old Dominion University | M,D |
| Portland State University | M |
| Regent University | M,D |
| Royal Roads University | M,O |
| Saint Mary's College of California | M |
| St. Mary's University (United States) | M,O |
| Saint Paul University | M |
| Salisbury University | M |
| Salve Regina University | M,D |
| SIT Graduate Institute | M |
| Southern Methodist University | M,O |
| Syracuse University | O |
| Trident University International | M,D |
| United States International University–Africa | M |
| United Theological Seminary of the Twin Cities | M,D,O |
| Universidad del Turabo | M |
| Université de Sherbrooke | M,D,O |
| University of Arkansas at Little Rock | O |
| University of Baltimore | M |
| University of Bridgeport | M |
| University of Denver | M,D,O |
| University of Hawaii at Manoa | M,O |
| The University of Manchester | D |
| University of Massachusetts Amherst | M,D |
| University of Massachusetts Boston | M,O |
| University of Massachusetts Lowell | M |
| University of Missouri | M,D |
| University of Missouri–St. Louis | M |
| University of New Haven | M,O |
| The University of North Carolina at Greensboro | M,O |
| The University of North Carolina Wilmington | M |
| University of Notre Dame | M,D |
| University of Phoenix–Online Campus | M,O |
| University of San Diego | M |
| University of the Sacred Heart | M |
| University of Victoria | M,D |
| University of Wisconsin–Milwaukee | M,D,O* |
| Walden University | M,D,O |
| Wayne State University | M,D,O |
| Wilfrid Laurier University | D |
| Willamette University | M,D |
| Yeshiva University | M,D |

### CONSERVATION BIOLOGY

| | |
|---|---|
| Antioch University New England | M,D |
| Arizona State University at Tempe | M,D |
| California State University, Sacramento | M |
| California State University, Stanislaus | M |
| Central Michigan University | M |
| Colorado State University | M,D |
| Columbia University | M,D |
| Cornell University | M,D |
| Florida Institute of Technology | M |
| Fordham University | M,D,O |
| Frostburg State University | M |
| Illinois State University | M,D |
| North Dakota State University | M,D |
| Oregon State University | M,D |
| State University of New York College of Environmental Science and Forestry | M,D |
| Texas State University | M |
| Tropical Agriculture Research and Higher Education Center | M,D |
| University of Alberta | M,D |
| University of Central Florida | M,D,O |
| University of Hawaii at Hilo | M |
| University of Illinois at Urbana-Champaign | M,D |
| University of Maryland, College Park | M |
| University of Minnesota, Twin Cities Campus | M,D |
| University of Missouri | M,D,O |
| University of Nevada, Reno | D |
| University of New Hampshire | M |
| The University of West Alabama | M |
| University of Wisconsin–Madison | M |
| University of Wisconsin–Stout | M |

### CONSTRUCTION ENGINEERING

| | |
|---|---|
| The American University in Cairo | M,D,O |
| Arizona State University at Tempe | M,D |
| Auburn University | M |
| Bradley University | M |
| Clemson University | M,D |
| Colorado School of Mines | M,D |
| Columbia University | M,D |
| Concordia University (Canada) | M,D,O |
| George Mason University | M,D |
| Illinois Institute of Technology | M,D |
| Iowa State University of Science and Technology | M,D |
| Lawrence Technological University | M,D |
| Marquette University | M,D,O |
| Massachusetts Institute of Technology | M,D,O |
| Montana State University | M,D |
| Ohio University | M,D |
| Oregon State University | M,D |
| Pittsburg State University | M |
| Stanford University | M,D,O |
| Stevens Institute of Technology | M,O |
| UNB Fredericton | M,D |
| The University of Alabama | M,D |
| The University of Alabama at Birmingham | M |
| University of Alberta | M,D |
| University of Michigan | M,D,O |
| University of Missouri–Kansas City | M,D,O |
| University of Puerto Rico at Mayagüez | M,D |
| University of Virginia | D |
| University of Washington | M,D |
| University of Wisconsin–Madison | M |
| Wentworth Institute of Technology | M |

### CONSTRUCTION MANAGEMENT

| | |
|---|---|
| The American University in Dubai | M |
| Arizona State University at Tempe | M,D |
| Brigham Young University | M |
| California Baptist University | M |
| California State University, Chico | M |
| California State University, East Bay | M |
| California State University, Northridge | M |
| Carnegie Mellon University | M,D |
| Central Connecticut State University | M,O |
| Clemson University | M,D |
| Colorado State University | M |
| Columbia University | M,D |
| Drexel University | M |
| East Carolina University | M,O |
| Eastern Michigan University | M,O |
| Farmingdale State College | M |
| Florida International University | M |
| Georgia Southern University | M |
| Illinois Institute of Technology | M,D |
| Instituto Tecnologico de Santo Domingo | M,O |
| Kennesaw State University | M |
| Louisiana State University and Agricultural & Mechanical College | M,D |
| Manhattan College | M |
| Marquette University | M,D,O |
| Michigan State University | M,D |
| Missouri State University | M |
| New England Institute of Technology | M |
| NewSchool of Architecture and Design | M |
| New York University | M |
| North Dakota State University | M,O |
| Norwich University | M |
| Pittsburg State University | M,O |
| Polytechnic University of Puerto Rico, Miami Campus | M |
| Polytechnic University of Puerto Rico, Orlando Campus | M |
| Purdue University | M |
| Purdue University Fort Wayne | M |
| South Dakota School of Mines and Technology | M |
| Stevens Institute of Technology | M,O |
| Texas A&M University | M |
| Thomas Jefferson University | M |
| Universidad de las Américas Puebla | M |
| The University of Alabama at Birmingham | M |
| University of Alaska Fairbanks | M,D,O |
| University of Arkansas at Little Rock | M |
| University of California, Berkeley | O |
| University of Denver | M |
| University of Florida | M,D |
| University of Houston | M |
| The University of Kansas | M |
| University of New Mexico | M,D |
| University of North Florida | M |
| University of Oklahoma | M,D |
| University of Southern California | M,D,O |
| The University of Tennessee at Chattanooga | M,O |
| The University of Texas at Arlington | M,D |
| The University of Texas at El Paso | M,D,O |
| University of Washington | M |
| University of Wisconsin–Stout | M |
| Wentworth Institute of Technology | M |
| Western Carolina University | M |

### CONSUMER ECONOMICS

| | |
|---|---|
| Colorado State University | M |
| Cornell University | M,D |
| Kansas State University | M,D,O |
| North Dakota State University | M,O |
| Ohio University | M |
| Oklahoma State University | M,D |
| Purdue University | M,D |
| South Dakota State University | M |
| State University of New York at Oswego | M |
| Texas Tech University | M,D |
| The University of Alabama | M |
| University of Guelph | M |
| University of Idaho | M |
| University of Illinois at Urbana-Champaign | M,D |
| University of Missouri | D |
| University of Nebraska–Lincoln | M,D |
| University of South Carolina | M |
| The University of Tennessee | M,D |
| University of Wisconsin–Madison | M,D |
| University of Wyoming | M |
| Université Laval | O |
| Utah State University | M |

### CORPORATE AND ORGANIZATIONAL COMMUNICATION

| | |
|---|---|
| American University | M |
| Ashland University | M |
| Austin Peay State University | M |
| Baruch College of the City University of New York | M |
| Bellevue University | M |
| Boston University | M |
| Bowie State University | M,O |
| Bryant University | M,O |
| California State University, San Bernardino | M |
| Carnegie Mellon University | M |
| City College of the City University of New York | M |
| Columbia University | M |
| Concordia University, St. Paul | M |
| Concordia University Wisconsin | M |
| Cornell University | M,D |
| DePaul University | M |
| Drexel University | M |
| East Carolina University | M,D,O |
| Eastern Michigan University | M,O |
| Fairleigh Dickinson University, Florham Campus | M |
| Florida State University | M,D |
| Franklin University | M |
| Georgia Southern University | M,O |
| HEC Montreal | O |
| High Point University | M,D |
| Howard University | M,D |
| Illinois Institute of Technology | M |
| Iowa State University of Science and Technology | M,D |
| La Salle University | M,O |
| Lasell College | M,O |
| Loyola University Chicago | M |
| Manhattanville College | M,O |
| Marist College | M |
| Minnesota State University Mankato | M,O |
| Mississippi College | M |
| Montclair State University | M |
| Murray State University | M |
| New Mexico State University | M,D |
| New York University | M |
| Northeastern University | M |
| Northwestern University | M,D |
| Ohio University | M,D |
| Radford University | M |
| Regent University | M,D |
| Regis College (MA) | M |
| Rider University | M |
| Roosevelt University | M |
| Rowan University | O |
| St. Bonaventure University | M |
| Seton Hall University | M |
| Southern Illinois University Edwardsville | M |
| Spalding University | M |
| State University of New York at Oswego | M |
| Suffolk University | M |
| Temple University | M,D* |
| Texas Christian University | M |
| Towson University | M |
| Troy University | M |
| Universidad Autonoma de Guadalajara | M,D |
| Universidad Iberoamericana | M,D |
| Université de Sherbrooke | M |
| University of Alaska Fairbanks | M |
| University of Colorado Denver | M |
| University of Illinois at Urbana-Champaign | M |
| University of Nebraska–Lincoln | M,D |
| University of Oklahoma | M,D |
| University of Portland | M |
| University of Southern California | M |
| University of South Florida | O |
| University of Wisconsin–Stevens Point | M |
| University of Wisconsin–Whitewater | M |
| Washington State University | M,D |
| Webster University | M |
| Western Kentucky University | M,O |
| West Virginia University | M,O |

### COUNSELING PSYCHOLOGY

| | |
|---|---|
| Abilene Christian University | M,O |
| Adelphi University | M |
| Alabama Agricultural and Mechanical University | M,O |
| Alaska Pacific University | M |
| Albizu University - Miami | M,D |
| Alfred University | M,D,O |
| Amberton University | M |
| American International College | M,D |
| Amridge University | M,D |
| Andrews University | M,D |
| Anna Maria College | M |
| Antioch University New England | M,D,O |
| Appalachian State University | M |
| Arcadia University | M |
| Argosy University, Chicago | D |
| Argosy University, Hawaii | D |
| Argosy University, Los Angeles | M,D |
| Argosy University, Northern Virginia | M,D |
| Argosy University, Orange County | M,D |
| Argosy University, Phoenix | M |
| Argosy University, Seattle | M,D |
| Argosy University, Tampa | M,D |
| Arizona State University at Tempe | D |
| Assumption University | M,O |
| Athabasca University | M,O |
| Austin Peay State University | M |
| Avila University | M |
| Ball State University | M,D |
| Baruch College of the City University of New York | M |
| Bastyr University | M,O |
| Becker College | M |
| Bethel University (MN) | M,D,O |
| Boston College | M,D |
| Boston Graduate School of Psychoanalysis | M |
| Boston University | M |
| Bowie State University | M |
| Bradley University | M |
| Brandman University | M |
| Brigham Young University | M,D,O |
| Brooklyn College of the City University of New York | M,D,O |
| Bushnell University | M |
| Caldwell University | M,O |
| California Baptist University | M |
| California State University, Fresno | M |
| California State University, San Bernardino | M |
| California State University, Stanislaus | M |
| California University of Pennsylvania | M |
| Cambridge College | M,O |
| Capella University | M |
| Carlow University | M,D,O |
| Centenary University | M |
| Central Michigan University | M,D,O |
| Central Washington University | M |
| Chatham University | M,D |
| Chestnut Hill College | M,O |
| City University of Seattle | M |
| Cleveland State University | M,D,O |
| The College of New Rochelle | M,O |
| College of Saint Elizabeth | M,D |
| College of St. Joseph | M |
| The College of Saint Rose | M,O |
| College of Staten Island of the City University of New York | M,O |
| Colorado Christian University | M |
| Concordia University Chicago | M |
| Dallas Baptist University | M |
| Delaware Valley University | M |
| DePaul University | M,D |
| Duquesne University | M,D,O |
| Eastern Nazarene College | M |
| Eastern Washington University | M,O |
| East Texas Baptist University | M |
| Edinboro University of Pennsylvania | M,O |
| Emporia State University | M |
| Evangel University | M |
| Fairfield University | M,O |
| Fairleigh Dickinson University, Florham Campus | M |
| Felician University | M,D |
| Fitchburg State University | M |
| Florida International University | M,D |
| Fordham University | M,D |
| Fort Valley State University | M |
| Framingham State University | M |

*M—masters degree; D—doctorate; O—other advanced degree; *—Close-Up and/or Display*

| | |
|---|---|
| Franciscan University of Steubenville | M |
| Francis Marion University | M,O |
| Frostburg State University | M |
| Gallaudet University | M,D,O |
| Gannon University | M |
| Gardner-Webb University | M |
| Geneva College | M |
| George Fox University | M,O |
| Georgian Court University | M,O |
| Georgia Southern University | M |
| Georgia State University | M,O |
| Governors State University | M |
| Hardin-Simmons University | M |
| Heidelberg University | M |
| Henderson State University | M,O |
| Hodges University | M |
| Hofstra University | M,O |
| Holy Family University | M |
| Holy Names University | M |
| Howard University | D |
| Humboldt State University | M |
| Husson University | M |
| Idaho State University | M,D,O |
| Illinois State University | M,D,O |
| Immaculata University | M,D,O |
| Indiana University Northwest | M,O |
| Indiana University South Bend | M,O |
| Indiana Wesleyan University | M |
| Instituto Tecnologico de Santo Domingo | M,O |
| Inter American University of Puerto Rico, Aguadilla Campus | M |
| Inter American University of Puerto Rico, Metropolitan Campus | M,D |
| Inter American University of Puerto Rico, San Germán Campus | M,D |
| Iona College | M,O |
| Iowa State University of Science and Technology | M,D |
| Jacksonville University | M |
| James Madison University | D |
| John Brown University | M,O |
| John Carroll University | M,O |
| John F. Kennedy University | M |
| Kean University | M |
| Kent State University | M |
| Kutztown University of Pennsylvania | M |
| Lamar University | M |
| Lancaster Bible College | M,D |
| La Salle University | M |
| Lee University | M |
| Lehigh University | M,D,O |
| Lenoir-Rhyne University | M |
| Lesley University | M,D,O |
| LeTourneau University | M |
| Lewis & Clark College | M |
| Lewis University | M |
| Liberty University | M,D,O |
| Lindenwood University | M,D,O |
| Lindsey Wilson College | M,D |
| Lipscomb University | M,O |
| Lock Haven University of Pennsylvania | M |
| London Metropolitan University | M,D |
| Long Island University - Brentwood Campus | M,O |
| Long Island University - Brooklyn | M,O |
| Long Island University - Hudson | M,O |
| Long Island University - Post | M,D,O |
| Louisiana Tech University | M,D,O |
| Loyola Marymount University | M |
| Loyola University Chicago | M,D,O |
| Loyola University Maryland | M,D,O |
| Lynn University | M |
| Manhattan College | M,O |
| Marian University (IN) | M |
| Marist College | M,O |
| Marquette University | M,D |
| Marymount University | M |
| Marywood University | M |
| McGill University | M,D,O |
| McKendree University | M |
| McNeese State University | M,O |
| Medaille College | M,D |
| Mercy College | M,O |
| Messiah University | M,O |
| Mid-America Christian University | M |
| Middle Tennessee State University | M |
| Midwestern State University | M |
| Minnesota State University Mankato | M,D |
| Mississippi College | M,O |
| Missouri State University | M |
| Monmouth University | M,O |
| Montana State University Billings | M |
| Moody Theological Seminary–Michigan | M,O |
| Morehead State University | M |
| Mount Mary University | M,O |
| Mount Saint Mary's University (CA) | M,D,O |
| Naropa University | M |
| National University | M,O |
| Nebraska Christian College of Hope International University | M |
| New England College | M |
| New Mexico Highlands University | M |
| New Mexico State University | M,D,O |
| New York University | M,D,O |
| Niagara University | M,D,O |
| North Dakota State University | M,D |
| Northeastern University | M,D,O |
| Northern Arizona University | M,D,O |
| Northern Kentucky University | M |
| Northern State University | M |
| Northwestern Oklahoma State University | M |
| Northwest University | M,D |
| Nova Southeastern University | M,D,O |
| Nyack College | M |
| Oakland University | M,D,O |
| Old Dominion University | M,D,O |
| Ottawa University | M |
| Our Lady of the Lake University | D |
| Pace University | M,D |
| Pacifica Graduate Institute | M,D |
| Palm Beach Atlantic University | M |
| Palo Alto University | M |
| Philadelphia College of Osteopathic Medicine | M,D,O |
| Phoenix Seminary | M,D,O |
| Prescott College | M |
| Providence University College & Theological Seminary | M,D,O |
| Purdue University Northwest | M |
| Queens College of the City University of New York | M,O |
| Radford University | D |
| Regent University | M,D,O |
| Regis College (MA) | M,D,O |
| Rhode Island College | M,O |
| Rivier University | M,D,O |
| Rosemont College | M |
| Rutgers University - New Brunswick | M |
| Sage Graduate School | M |
| St. Bonaventure University | M,O |
| St. Edward's University | M |
| St. John Fisher College | M |
| St. John's University (NY) | M,O |
| Saint Martin's University | M |
| St. Mary's University (United States) | M |
| Saint Mary's University of Minnesota | M,D,O |
| Saint Paul University | M |
| St. Thomas University - Florida | M |
| Salem State University | M,O |
| Salve Regina University | M,O |
| Santa Clara University | M,O |
| Saybrook University | M |
| The Seattle School of Theology and Psychology | M |
| Seton Hall University | M,D |
| Siena Heights University | M,O |
| Simpson University | M |
| Slippery Rock University of Pennsylvania | M |
| Sofia University | M,D |
| Sonoma State University | M |
| Southeastern Oklahoma State University | M |
| Southeastern University (FL) | M |
| Southeast Missouri State University | M,D,O |
| Southern Adventist University | M |
| Southern California Seminary | M,D |
| Southern Illinois University Carbondale | M,D |
| Southern Nazarene University | M |
| Southern Oregon University | M |
| South University - Austin | M |
| South University - Columbia | M |
| South University - Montgomery | M |
| South University - Richmond | M |
| South University - Savannah | M |
| South University - Virginia Beach | M |
| South University - West Palm Beach | M |
| Southwestern Assemblies of God University | M |
| Southwestern College (NM) | M,O |
| Spring Arbor University | M |
| Springfield College | M,D,O |
| State University of New York at New Paltz | M,O |
| State University of New York at Oswego | M |
| State University of New York at Plattsburgh | M,O |
| State University of New York College at Old Westbury | M |
| Suffolk University | M,D,O |
| SUNY Brockport | M,O |
| Tarleton State University | M |
| Teachers College, Columbia University | M,D |
| Temple University | M,D,O* |
| Tennessee State University | M |
| Texas A&M International University | M |
| Texas A&M University | M,D |
| Texas A&M University–Texarkana | M |
| Texas Tech University | M,D |
| Texas Woman's University | M,D,O |
| Towson University | M |
| Trinity Christian College | M |
| Trinity International University | M,D,O |
| Trinity International University Florida | M |
| Trinity Washington University | M |
| Trinity Western University | M |
| Truett McConnell University | M |
| Union College (KY) | M |
| United States International University–Africa | M |
| Universidad del Turabo | M,D,O |
| Universidad Metropolitana | M |
| University at Albany, State University of New York | M,D,O |
| University at Buffalo, the State University of New York | M,D,O |
| The University of Akron | M,D |
| University of Alberta | M,D |
| The University of Arizona | M |
| University of Baltimore | M |
| University of Bridgeport | M |
| The University of British Columbia | M,D,O |
| University of Calgary | M,D |
| University of California, Berkeley | O |
| University of California, Santa Barbara | M,D,O |
| University of Central Arkansas | M |
| University of Central Missouri | M,D,O |
| University of Central Oklahoma | M |
| University of Colorado Denver | M |
| University of Connecticut | M,D |
| University of Dayton | M,O |
| University of Denver | M,D,O |
| University of Florida | M,D |
| University of Hawaii at Hilo | M |
| University of Houston | M,D |
| University of Houston–Victoria | M |
| University of Indianapolis | M,D |
| The University of Iowa | M,D,O |
| The University of Kansas | M,D |
| University of Kentucky | M,D,O |
| University of Lethbridge | M,D |
| University of Louisiana at Monroe | M,D |
| University of Louisville | M,D |
| University of Lynchburg | M |
| The University of Manchester | M,D |
| University of Mary Hardin-Baylor | M |
| University of Maryland, College Park | M,D,O |
| University of Massachusetts Boston | M,D |
| University of Memphis | M,D |
| University of Miami | D |
| University of Minnesota, Twin Cities Campus | D |
| University of Missouri | M,D,O |
| University of Missouri–Kansas City | M,D,O |
| University of Montana | M,D,O |
| University of Nebraska at Kearney | M,O |
| University of Nebraska–Lincoln | M,D,O |
| University of Nevada, Las Vegas | M,D,O |
| The University of North Carolina at Greensboro | M,D,O |
| The University of North Carolina at Pembroke | M |
| University of North Dakota | M,D |
| University of Northern Colorado | D |
| University of Northern Iowa | M |
| University of North Florida | M |
| University of North Georgia | M |
| University of North Texas | M,D,O |
| University of Notre Dame | D |
| University of Oregon | M,D |
| University of Pennsylvania | M |
| University of Phoenix - Las Vegas Campus | M |
| University of Phoenix - Phoenix Campus | M |
| University of Providence | M |
| University of Puget Sound | M |
| University of Rhode Island | M |
| University of Saint Francis (IN) | M,O |
| University of Saint Joseph | M |
| University of Saint Mary | M |
| University of St. Thomas (MN) | M,D |
| University of San Diego | M |
| University of San Francisco | M |
| University of Saskatchewan | M,D |
| The University of Scranton | M |
| University of South Africa | M,D |
| University of South Alabama | M,D,O |
| University of South Dakota | M,D,O |
| University of Southern Maine | M,O |
| University of South Florida | M,D,O |
| The University of Tennessee | M,D |
| The University of Texas at Austin | M,D |
| The University of Texas at Tyler | M |
| University of the Cumberlands | M |
| University of the District of Columbia | M |
| University of the Southwest | M |
| University of Utah | M,D,O |
| University of Vermont | M |
| University of Victoria | M,D |
| The University of Western Ontario | M |
| University of West Florida | M |
| University of Wisconsin–Madison | D |
| University of Wisconsin–Milwaukee | M,D,O* |
| University of Wisconsin–Stout | M |
| Utah State University | M,D |
| Virginia Commonwealth University | M,D |
| Viterbo University | M |
| Walden University | M,D,O |
| Walsh University | M |
| Washington Adventist University | M |
| Washington State University | M,D |
| Wayland Baptist University | M |
| Waynesburg University | M,D |
| Wayne State University | M,D,O |
| Webster University | M |
| Western Kentucky University | M |
| Western Michigan University | M,D |
| Western Washington University | M |
| Westfield State University | M |
| Westminster College (UT) | M |
| West Virginia University | M,D |
| Wheaton College | M,D |
| William Carey University | M |
| William James College | M,D,O |
| Wilmington University | M |
| Winebrenner Theological Seminary | M,D |
| The Wright Institute | M |
| Xavier University | M* |
| Yeshiva University | M |

## COUNSELOR EDUCATION

| | |
|---|---|
| Acadia University | M |
| Adams State University | M,D |
| Adler University | D |
| Alabama Agricultural and Mechanical University | M,O |
| Alabama State University | M,D,O |
| Albany State University | M,O |
| Alcorn State University | M,O |
| Alfred University | M,D,O |
| Alliant International University–San Francisco | M |
| Amberton University | M |
| American International College | M,D,O |
| Amridge University | M,D |
| Angelo State University | M |
| Antioch University Seattle | M,D |
| Appalachian State University | M |
| Argosy University, Atlanta | M,D,O |
| Argosy University, Chicago | D |
| Argosy University, Northern Virginia | M,D |
| Argosy University, Tampa | M,D,O |
| Arizona State University at Tempe | M |
| Arkansas State University | M,O |
| Arkansas Tech University | M,D,O |
| Ashland Theological Seminary | M,D |
| Athabasca University | M,O |
| Auburn University at Montgomery | M,O |
| Augusta University | M,O |
| Austin Peay State University | M |
| Azusa Pacific University | M |
| Ball State University | M,D |
| Barry University | M,D,O |
| Bayamón Central University | M,O |
| Becker College | M |
| Bellevue University | M |
| Bloomsburg University of Pennsylvania | M |
| Bob Jones University | M,D,O |
| Boise State University | M,O |
| Bowie State University | M |
| Bowling Green State University | M |
| Bradley University | M |
| Brandman University | M,D |
| Brandon University | M,O |
| Bridgewater State University | M,O |
| Brooklyn College of the City University of New York | M |
| Buena Vista University | M |
| Bushnell University | M |
| California Baptist University | M |
| California Lutheran University | M,D |
| California State University, Dominguez Hills | M |
| California State University, East Bay | M |
| California State University, Fresno | M |
| California State University, Fullerton | M |
| California State University, Long Beach | M,D |
| California State University, Los Angeles | M,D |
| California State University, Northridge | M |
| California State University, Sacramento | M,D,O |
| California State University, San Bernardino | M |
| California State University, Stanislaus | M |
| California University of Pennsylvania | M |
| Cambridge College | M,O |
| Campbell University | M |
| Capella University | M,D |
| Carson-Newman University | M |
| Carthage College | M,O |
| Central Connecticut State University | M,O |
| Central Methodist University | M |
| Central Michigan University | M |
| Chadron State College | M,O |
| Chapman University | M,D,O |
| Chicago State University | M |
| The Citadel, The Military College of South Carolina | M,O |
| City University of Seattle | M,O |
| Clark Atlanta University | M |
| Clarks Summit University | M |
| Clemson University | M,D,O |
| Cleveland State University | M,D,O |
| The College of New Jersey | M |
| College of St. Joseph | M |
| The College of Saint Rose | M,O |
| Colorado State University | M,D |
| Columbia International University | M,D,O |
| Columbus State University | M,D,O |
| Concordia University Chicago | M |
| Concordia University Irvine | M |
| Concordia University Wisconsin | M |
| Creighton University | M |
| Dallas Baptist University | M |
| Delta State University | M,D,O |
| DePaul University | M,D |
| Doane University | M |
| Drake University | M,D,O |
| Duquesne University | M,D,O |
| East Carolina University | M,D,O |
| Eastern Illinois University | M |
| Eastern Kentucky University | M |
| Eastern Mennonite University | M |
| Eastern Michigan University | M,O |
| Eastern New Mexico University | M |
| Eastern Washington University | M,O |
| East Tennessee State University | M |
| Edinboro University of Pennsylvania | M,O |
| Emporia State University | M |
| Evangel University | M |
| Fairfield University | M,O |
| Faulkner University | M |
| Fitchburg State University | M,O |
| Florida Agricultural and Mechanical University | M,D |
| Florida Atlantic University | M,D |
| Fordham University | M,D |
| Fort Hays State University | M |
| Fort Valley State University | M,O |
| Freed-Hardeman University | M,O |
| Fresno Pacific University | M |
| Frostburg State University | M |
| Gallaudet University | M,D,O |
| Geneva College | M |
| George Fox University | M,O |
| George Mason University | M |
| The George Washington University | M,D,O |
| Georgian Court University | M,O |
| Georgia Southern University | M |

| | |
|---|---|
| Georgia State University | M,O |
| Grambling State University | M,D,O |
| Hampton University | M,D,O |
| Harding University | M,O |
| Hardin-Simmons University | M |
| Henderson State University | M,O |
| Heritage University | M |
| Hofstra University | M,O |
| Houston Baptist University | M,D |
| Howard University | M |
| Hunter College of the City University of New York | M |
| Husson University | M |
| Idaho State University | M,D,O |
| Indiana State University | M,D,O |
| Indiana University Bloomington | M,D,O |
| Indiana University of Pennsylvania | M |
| Indiana University-Purdue University Indianapolis | M,O |
| Indiana University South Bend | M,O |
| Indiana University Southeast | M |
| Indiana Wesleyan University | M |
| Inter American University of Puerto Rico, Arecibo Campus | M |
| Inter American University of Puerto Rico, Metropolitan Campus | M,D |
| Inter American University of Puerto Rico, San Germán Campus | M,D |
| Iowa State University of Science and Technology | M,D |
| Jackson State University | M |
| Jacksonville State University | M |
| John Brown University | M,O |
| John Carroll University | M,O |
| Johnson University | M,D,O |
| Kansas State University | M,D,O |
| Kean University | M |
| Kent State University | M,D,O |
| Kutztown University of Pennsylvania | M |
| Lakeland University | M |
| Lamar University | M |
| Lancaster Bible College | M,D |
| La Sierra University | M,O |
| Lehigh University | M,D,O |
| Lehman College of the City University of New York | M |
| Lenoir-Rhyne University | M |
| Lewis University | M |
| Liberty University | M,D,O |
| Lincoln Memorial University | M,D,O |
| Lincoln University (MO) | M |
| Lindenwood University–Belleville | M |
| Lindsey Wilson College | M,D |
| Loma Linda University | M,D,O |
| Long Island University - Brentwood Campus | M,O |
| Long Island University - Brooklyn | M,O |
| Long Island University - Hudson | M,O |
| Longwood University | M |
| Louisiana State University and Agricultural & Mechanical College | M,D,O |
| Louisiana State University in Shreveport | M |
| Loyola Marymount University | M |
| Loyola University Chicago | M,O |
| Loyola University Maryland | M,O |
| Malone University | M |
| Manhattan College | M,O |
| Marian University (IN) | M |
| Marquette University | M,D |
| Marshall University | M |
| Marymount University | M |
| Marywood University | M |
| McDaniel College | M |
| McNeese State University | M |
| Mercer University | M,D |
| Mercy College | M,O |
| Messiah University | M,O |
| Michigan State University | M,D,O |
| Middle Tennessee State University | M |
| Midwestern State University | M |
| Midwest University | M,D |
| Milligan University | M,O |
| Minnesota State University Mankato | M,D |
| Minnesota State University Moorhead | M,D,O |
| Mississippi College | M,O |
| Mississippi State University | M,D,O |
| Missouri Baptist University | M,O |
| Missouri State University | M |
| Montana State University Billings | M |
| Montana State University–Northern | M |
| Montclair State University | M,D |
| Morehead State University | M,O |
| Mount Mary University | M,O |
| Murray State University | M,D,O |
| Naropa University | M |
| National Louis University | M,D,O |
| National University | M,O |
| New Jersey City University | M |
| New Mexico Highlands University | M |
| New Mexico State University | M,D,O |
| New York University | M,D,O |
| Niagara University | M,O |
| Nicholls State University | M,O |
| North Carolina Agricultural and Technical State University | M,D |
| North Carolina Central University | M |
| North Carolina State University | M,D |
| North Dakota State University | M,D |
| Northeastern Illinois University | M |
| Northern Arizona University | M,D,O |
| Northern Illinois University | M,D |
| Northern Kentucky University | M |
| Northern State University | M |
| Northern Vermont University–Johnson | M |
| Northern Vermont University–Lyndon | M |
| Northwestern Oklahoma State University | M |
| Northwestern State University of Louisiana | M,O |
| Northwest Nazarene University | M |
| Nova Southeastern University | M,D,O |
| Nyack College | M |
| Ohio University | M,D |
| Oklahoma City University | M |
| Old Dominion University | M,D,O |
| Oregon State University | M,D |
| Ottawa University | M |
| Our Lady of the Lake University | M |
| Palm Beach Atlantic University | M |
| Penn State University Park | M,D,O* |
| Phillips Graduate University | M |
| Pittsburg State University | M |
| Plymouth State University | M |
| Point Loma Nazarene University | M |
| Pontifical Catholic University of Puerto Rico | M |
| Prairie View A&M University | M,D |
| Prescott College | M,D |
| Providence College | M |
| Purdue University Fort Wayne | M,O |
| Purdue University Northwest | M |
| Queens College of the City University of New York | M,O |
| Quincy University | M |
| Radford University | M |
| Regent University | M,D,O |
| Regis University | M,D,O |
| Rhode Island College | M,O |
| Richmont Graduate University | M |
| Rider University | M,O |
| Rivier University | M,D,O |
| Roberts Wesleyan College | M,D |
| Rollins College | M |
| Rosemont College | M |
| Rowan University | M |
| Rutgers University - New Brunswick | M |
| Sage Graduate School | M,O |
| St. Bonaventure University | M,O |
| St. Cloud State University | M |
| St. John's University (NY) | M,O |
| Saint Mary's College of California | M,O |
| St. Mary's University (United States) | D |
| Saint Peter's University | M,O |
| St. Thomas University - Florida | M,O |
| Saint Xavier University | M |
| Salem College | M |
| Salem State University | M |
| Sam Houston State University | M,D |
| San Diego State University | M |
| San Jose State University | M |
| Santa Clara University | M,O |
| Seattle Pacific University | M,D,O |
| Seattle University | M,D |
| Seton Hall University | M,D |
| Shippensburg University of Pennsylvania | M,D |
| Simon Fraser University | M |
| Slippery Rock University of Pennsylvania | M |
| South Carolina State University | M |
| South Dakota State University | M |
| Southeastern Louisiana University | M |
| Southeastern Oklahoma State University | M |
| Southeastern University (FL) | M |
| Southeast Missouri State University | M,D,O |
| Southern Adventist University | M |
| Southern Arkansas University–Magnolia | M |
| Southern Connecticut State University | M,O |
| Southern Methodist University | M,O |
| Southern University and Agricultural and Mechanical College | M |
| Southwestern Oklahoma State University | M |
| Spalding University | M |
| Springfield College | M,D,O |
| State University of New York at New Paltz | M,O |
| State University of New York at Plattsburgh | M,O |
| State University of New York College at Oneonta | M,O |
| Stephen F. Austin State University | M |
| Stephens College | M,O |
| Stetson University | M |
| Suffolk University | M,D,O |
| Sul Ross State University | M |
| SUNY Brockport | M,O |
| Syracuse University | M,D |
| Texas A&M International University | M |
| Texas A&M University–Central Texas | M,O |
| Texas A&M University–Commerce | M,D,O |
| Texas A&M University–Corpus Christi | M,D |
| Texas A&M University–Kingsville | M |
| Texas A&M University–San Antonio | M |
| Texas Christian University | M,D |
| Texas Southern University | M,D |
| Texas State University | M |
| Texas Tech University | M,D |
| Texas Woman's University | M,D |
| Trevecca Nazarene University | M,D |
| Trinity Washington University | M |
| Troy University | M,O |
| Universidad del Turabo | M |
| Université de Moncton | M |
| University at Buffalo, the State University of New York | M,D,O |
| The University of Akron | M,D |
| The University of Alabama | M,D,O |
| The University of Alabama at Birmingham | M |
| University of Alaska Fairbanks | M,O |
| University of Alberta | M,D |
| The University of Arizona | M |
| University of Arkansas | M,D |
| University of Arkansas at Little Rock | M |
| University of Central Arkansas | M |
| University of Central Florida | M,O |
| University of Central Missouri | M,D,O |
| University of Central Oklahoma | M |
| University of Cincinnati | M,D,O |
| University of Colorado Colorado Springs | M,D |
| University of Colorado Denver | M,D |
| University of Connecticut | M,D |
| University of Dayton | M,O |
| University of Florida | M,D,O |
| University of Georgia | M,D,O |
| University of Guam | M |
| University of Holy Cross | M,D |
| University of Houston–Clear Lake | M |
| University of Houston–Victoria | M,O |
| University of Idaho | M,O |
| University of Illinois at Urbana-Champaign | M,D,O |
| The University of Iowa | M,D |
| University of La Verne | M,D,O |
| University of Lethbridge | M,D |
| University of Louisiana at Lafayette | M |
| University of Louisiana at Monroe | M |
| University of Louisville | M,D |
| University of Lynchburg | M |
| University of Manitoba | M |
| University of Mary Hardin-Baylor | M |
| University of Maryland, College Park | M,D,O |
| University of Maryland Eastern Shore | M |
| University of Massachusetts Amherst | M,D,O |
| University of Massachusetts Boston | M |
| University of Memphis | M,D |
| University of Miami | M,O |
| University of Minnesota, Twin Cities Campus | M |
| University of Mississippi | M,D,O |
| University of Missouri–Kansas City | M,D,O |
| University of Montana | M,D,O |
| University of Montevallo | M |
| University of Nebraska at Kearney | M,O |
| University of Nebraska at Omaha | M |
| University of Nevada, Las Vegas | M,D,O |
| University of Nevada, Reno | M,D,O |
| University of New Mexico | M,D |
| University of New Orleans | M,D |
| University of North Alabama | M |
| The University of North Carolina at Chapel Hill | M |
| The University of North Carolina at Charlotte | M,D,O |
| The University of North Carolina at Greensboro | M,D,O |
| The University of North Carolina at Pembroke | M |
| University of Northern Colorado | M,D |
| University of Northern Iowa | M |
| University of North Florida | M,D |
| University of North Texas | M,D,O |
| University of North Texas at Dallas | M |
| University of Pennsylvania | M |
| University of Phoenix - Las Vegas Campus | M |
| University of Phoenix - Phoenix Campus | M |
| University of Puerto Rico at Rio Piedras | M,D |
| University of Puget Sound | M |
| University of Rochester | M,D |
| University of Saint Francis (IN) | M,O |
| University of Saint Joseph | M |
| University of St. Thomas (TX) | M,D |
| University of San Diego | M |
| University of San Francisco | M |
| The University of Scranton | M |
| University of South Africa | M,D |
| University of South Alabama | M,D,O |
| University of South Carolina | D,O |
| University of South Dakota | M,D,O |
| University of Southern California | M |
| University of Southern Maine | M,O |
| University of Southern Mississippi | M |
| University of South Florida | M,D,O |
| The University of Tennessee | M,D,O |
| The University of Tennessee at Chattanooga | M,D,O |
| The University of Tennessee at Martin | M |
| The University of Texas at Austin | M,D |
| The University of Texas at El Paso | M |
| The University of Texas at San Antonio | M,D |
| The University of Texas of the Permian Basin | M |
| The University of Texas Rio Grande Valley | M |
| University of the Cumberlands | M,D,O |
| University of the Southwest | M |
| The University of Toledo | M,D,O |
| University of Utah | M,D,O |
| University of Vermont | M |
| University of Victoria | M,D |
| University of Virginia | M,D,O |
| The University of West Alabama | M,O |
| University of Wisconsin–Madison | M |
| University of Wisconsin–Oshkosh | M |
| University of Wisconsin–River Falls | M,O |
| University of Wisconsin–Superior | M |
| University of Wyoming | M,D |
| Université Laval | M,D |
| Utah State University | M,D |
| Valdosta State University | M,O |
| Vanderbilt University | M* |
| Villanova University | M |
| Virginia Commonwealth University | M,D |
| Virginia Polytechnic Institute and State University | M,D,O |
| Virginia State University | M |
| Wake Forest University | M |
| Walden University | M,D |
| Walsh University | M |
| Waynesburg University | M,D |
| Wayne State College | M |
| Wayne State University | M,D,O |
| Western Connecticut State University | M |
| Western Illinois University | M |
| Western Kentucky University | M |
| Western Michigan University | M,D |
| Western Washington University | M |
| Westfield State University | M |
| West Texas A&M University | M |
| West Virginia University | M,D |
| Whitworth University | M |
| Wichita State University | M,D,O |
| Widener University | M,D |
| William & Mary | M,D* |
| Wilmington University | M,O |
| Winona State University | M,O |
| Winthrop University | M |
| Wright State University | M |
| Xavier University | M* |
| Xavier University of Louisiana | M |
| Youngstown State University | M,D,O |

## CRIMINAL JUSTICE AND CRIMINOLOGY

| | |
|---|---|
| Adler University | M |
| Adrian College | M |
| Albany State University | M |
| Albertus Magnus College | M |
| Alliant International University–San Francisco | M |
| American Public University System | M,D |
| American University | M,D |
| American University of Puerto Rico - Bayamon | M |
| Anderson University (SC) | M |
| Angelo State University | M |
| Anna Maria College | M |
| Arizona State University at Tempe | M,D,O |
| Arkansas State University | M,O |
| Ashworth College | M |
| Ball State University | M,O |
| Bellevue University | M |
| Boise State University | M |
| Boston University | M |
| Bowling Green State University | M |
| Bridgewater State University | M |
| Buffalo State College, State University of New York | M |
| Cabrini University | M,D |
| California Coast University | M |
| California State University, Fresno | M |
| California State University, Long Beach | M |
| California State University, Los Angeles | M |
| California State University, Sacramento | M |
| California State University, San Bernardino | M |
| California State University, Stanislaus | M |
| California University of Pennsylvania | M |
| Calumet College of Saint Joseph | M |
| Capella University | M,D |
| Cardinal Stritch University | M |
| Caribbean University | M,D |
| Carnegie Mellon University | M |
| The Catholic University of America | M |
| Central Connecticut State University | M |
| Chaminade University of Honolulu | M |
| Charleston Southern University | M |
| Chicago State University | M |
| Clark Atlanta University | M |
| Clayton State University | M |
| Clemson University | M |
| Coker College | M |
| College of Saint Elizabeth | M,O |
| Colorado State University–Global Campus | M |
| Colorado Technical University Aurora | M |
| Colorado Technical University Colorado Springs | M |
| Columbia College (MO) | M |
| Columbia College (SC) | M |
| Columbia Southern University | M |
| Columbus State University | M |
| Concordia University, St. Paul | M |
| Coppin State University | M |
| Curry College | M |
| Dallas Baptist University | M |
| Delaware Valley University | M |

*M—masters degree; D—doctorate; O—other advanced degree; *—Close-Up and/or Display*

| | |
|---|---|
| Delta State University | M |
| DeSales University | M,O |
| East Carolina University | M,O |
| East Central University | M |
| Eastern Kentucky University | M |
| Eastern Michigan University | M |
| East Tennessee State University | M,O |
| Fairleigh Dickinson University, Metropolitan Campus | M |
| Fairmont State University | M |
| Faulkner University | M |
| Fayetteville State University | M |
| Ferris State University | M |
| Florida Agricultural and Mechanical University | M |
| Florida Atlantic University | M |
| Florida Gulf Coast University | M |
| Florida International University | M,D |
| Florida State University | M,D |
| Franklin University | M |
| Gannon University | M |
| George Mason University | M,D |
| The George Washington University | M,O |
| Georgia College & State University | M |
| Georgian Court University | M,O |
| Georgia Southern University | M,O |
| Georgia State University | M,D,O |
| Governors State University | M |
| The Graduate Center, City University of New York | D |
| Grambling State University | M |
| Grand Valley State University | M |
| Guilford College | M |
| Hilbert College | M |
| Holy Family University | M |
| Howard Payne University | M |
| Husson University | M |
| Illinois State University | M |
| Indiana State University | M |
| Indiana University Bloomington | M,D |
| Indiana University Northwest | M,O |
| Indiana University of Pennsylvania | M,D |
| Indiana University-Purdue University Indianapolis | M,O |
| Inter American University of Puerto Rico, Aguadilla Campus | M |
| Inter American University of Puerto Rico, Barranquitas Campus | M |
| Inter American University of Puerto Rico, Metropolitan Campus | M |
| Inter American University of Puerto Rico, Ponce Campus | M |
| Iona College | M,O |
| Jackson State University | M |
| Jacksonville State University | M |
| John Jay College of Criminal Justice of the City University of New York | M,D |
| Johnson & Wales University | M |
| Kean University | M |
| Keiser University | M |
| Kennesaw State University | M |
| Kent State University | M,D |
| Lamar University | M |
| Lasell College | M,O |
| Lewis University | M |
| Liberty University | M,D,O |
| Lincoln University (MO) | M |
| Lindenwood University | M,O |
| Lindenwood University–Belleville | M |
| Loma Linda University | M,D |
| London Metropolitan University | M,D |
| Long Island University - Brentwood Campus | M,O |
| Long Island University - Post | M,O |
| Loyola University Chicago | M |
| Loyola University New Orleans | M |
| Lynn University | M |
| Madonna University | M |
| Marshall University | M |
| Marywood University | M |
| McNeese State University | M |
| Mercer University | M,D |
| Mercyhurst University | M,O |
| Methodist University | M |
| Metropolitan State University | M |
| Michigan State University | M,D |
| Middle Tennessee State University | M |
| Midwestern State University | M,O |
| Minnesota State University Mankato | M |
| Mississippi College | M,O |
| Mississippi Valley State University | M |
| Missouri Southern State University | M |
| Missouri State University | M,O |
| Molloy College | M |
| Monmouth University | M,O |
| Monroe College | M |
| Morehead State University | M |
| Mount Mercy University | M |
| National American University (TX) | M,D |
| National University | M |
| New Jersey City University | M,D,O |
| New Mexico State University | M |
| Niagara University | M |
| Norfolk State University | M |
| North Carolina Central University | M |
| North Dakota State University | M,D |
| Northeastern State University | M |
| Northeastern University | M,D |
| Northern Arizona University | M |
| Norwich University | M |
| Nova Southeastern University | M,D,O |
| Oklahoma City University | M |
| Old Dominion University | M,D |
| Penn State Harrisburg | M,D,O |
| Penn State University Park | M,D* |
| Point Park University | M |
| Pontifical Catholic University of Puerto Rico | M |
| Pontificia Universidad Catolica Madre y Maestra | M |
| Portland State University | M |
| Purdue University Global | M |
| Radford University | M,O |
| Regent University | M,D,O |
| Regis University | M,O |
| Robert Morris University Illinois | M |
| Rochester Institute of Technology | M |
| Roger Williams University | M |
| Rowan University | M |
| Rutgers University - Camden | M |
| Rutgers University - Newark | M,D |
| Sacred Heart University | M |
| St. Ambrose University | M |
| St. Cloud State University | M |
| St. John's University (NY) | M |
| Saint Joseph's University | M,O |
| Saint Leo University | M,D |
| Saint Louis University | M |
| Saint Mary's University (Canada) | M |
| St. Mary's University (United States) | M |
| Saint Peter's University | M |
| St. Thomas University - Florida | M,O |
| Salem State University | M |
| Salve Regina University | M,O |
| Sam Houston State University | M,D |
| San Diego State University | M |
| San Francisco State University | M |
| San Jose State University | M |
| Seattle University | M,O |
| Shippensburg University of Pennsylvania | M |
| Simon Fraser University | M,D |
| Simpson College | M |
| Slippery Rock University of Pennsylvania | M |
| Southeast Missouri State University | M |
| Southern Illinois University Carbondale | M,D |
| Southern New Hampshire University | M |
| Southern University and Agricultural and Mechanical College | M |
| Southern University at New Orleans | M |
| South University - Columbia | M |
| South University - Montgomery | M |
| South University - Savannah | M |
| South University - Tampa | M |
| South University - West Palm Beach | M |
| Southwestern College (KS) | M |
| Southwest University | M |
| Stockton University | M |
| Suffolk University | M |
| Sul Ross State University | M |
| Tarleton State University | M |
| Temple University | M,D* |
| Tennessee State University | M |
| Texas A&M International University | M |
| Texas A&M University–Central Texas | M,O |
| Texas A&M University–Commerce | M,D,O |
| Texas A&M University–Kingsville | M |
| Texas Christian University | M |
| Texas Southern University | M,D |
| Texas State University | M,D |
| Tiffin University | M |
| Trident University International | M,D |
| Trine University | M |
| Troy University | M |
| Universidad del Este | M |
| Universidad del Turabo | M |
| Université de Montréal | M,D |
| University at Albany, State University of New York | M,D |
| The University of Alabama | M |
| The University of Alabama at Birmingham | M |
| University of Alaska Fairbanks | M |
| University of Alberta | M,D |
| University of Antelope Valley | M |
| University of Arkansas at Little Rock | M,D |
| University of Baltimore | M |
| University of California, Irvine | M,D |
| University of Central Florida | M,D,O |
| University of Central Missouri | M,D,O |
| University of Central Oklahoma | M |
| University of Cincinnati | M,D |
| University of Colorado Colorado Springs | M |
| University of Colorado Denver | M,D |
| University of Delaware | M,D |
| University of Denver | M,O |
| University of Detroit Mercy | M,D,O |
| University of Florida | M,D |
| University of Guelph | M,D |
| University of Houston–Clear Lake | M |
| University of Houston - Downtown | M |
| University of Illinois at Chicago | M,D |
| University of Louisiana at Monroe | M |
| University of Louisville | M,D |
| University of Lynchburg | M |
| University of Management and Technology | M,O |
| The University of Manchester | M,D |
| University of Maryland, College Park | M,D |
| University of Maryland Eastern Shore | M |
| University of Massachusetts Lowell | M |
| University of Memphis | M |
| University of Michigan–Dearborn | M |
| University of Michigan–Flint | M |
| University of Minnesota, Duluth | M |
| University of Mississippi | M,D |
| University of Missouri–Kansas City | M |
| University of Missouri–St. Louis | M,D |
| University of Montana | M |
| University of Nebraska at Omaha | M,D,O |
| University of Nevada, Las Vegas | M,D |
| University of Nevada, Reno | M |
| University of New Haven | M,D,O |
| University of North Alabama | M |
| The University of North Carolina at Charlotte | M |
| The University of North Carolina at Greensboro | M |
| The University of North Carolina at Pembroke | M |
| The University of North Carolina Wilmington | M |
| University of North Dakota | D |
| University of Northern Colorado | M |
| University of North Florida | M |
| University of North Georgia | M |
| University of North Texas | M,D,O |
| University of North Texas at Dallas | M |
| University of Oklahoma | M,O |
| University of Ottawa | M,D |
| University of Pennsylvania | M,D |
| University of Phoenix - Bay Area Campus | M |
| University of Phoenix - Dallas Campus | M |
| University of Phoenix–Online Campus | M |
| University of Phoenix - Phoenix Campus | M |
| University of Phoenix - San Antonio Campus | M |
| University of Pittsburgh | M* |
| University of Providence | M |
| University of Regina | M |
| University of San Diego | M |
| University of South Africa | M,D |
| University of South Carolina | M,D |
| University of South Dakota | M |
| University of Southern Mississippi | M,D |
| University of South Florida | M,D,O |
| University of South Florida Sarasota-Manatee | M |
| The University of Tampa | M |
| The University of Tennessee | M,D |
| The University of Tennessee at Chattanooga | M |
| The University of Texas at Arlington | M |
| The University of Texas at Dallas | M,D |
| The University of Texas at San Antonio | M |
| The University of Texas at Tyler | M |
| The University of Texas of the Permian Basin | M |
| The University of Texas Rio Grande Valley | M |
| University of the Fraser Valley | M |
| The University of Toledo | M,O |
| University of Toronto | M,D |
| University of West Florida | M |
| University of Windsor | M,D |
| University of Wisconsin–Milwaukee | M,O* |
| University of Wisconsin–Platteville | M |
| Urbana University–A Branch Campus of Franklin University | M |
| Utica College | M |
| Virginia Commonwealth University | M,O |
| Virginia State University | M |
| Walden University | M,D,O |
| Waldorf University | M |
| Washburn University | M |
| Washington State University | M,D |
| Wayland Baptist University | M |
| Waynesburg University | M,D |
| Wayne State University | M |
| Webber International University | M |
| Webster University | M,D,O |
| Western Illinois University | M,O |
| Western Kentucky University | M |
| Western Oregon University | M |
| Westfield State University | M |
| West Texas A&M University | M |
| West Virginia State University | M |
| Wichita State University | M |
| Widener University | M |
| Wilfrid Laurier University | M |
| Wilmington University | M |
| Wright State University | M |
| Xavier University | M* |
| Youngstown State University | M |

## CULTURAL ANTHROPOLOGY

| | |
|---|---|
| Brandeis University | M,D |
| Concordia University (Canada) | M,D |
| Cornell University | D |
| Duke University | D |
| The Graduate Center, City University of New York | D |
| Memorial University of Newfoundland | M,D |
| Rice University | M,D |
| San Francisco State University | M |
| Southern Illinois University Edwardsville | M |
| Southern Methodist University | M,D |
| University of California, Santa Barbara | M,D |
| University of California, Santa Cruz | D |
| University of Denver | M |
| University of Michigan | D |
| The University of Tennessee | M,D |
| University of Wisconsin–Madison | D |
| Washington State University | M,D |

## CULTURAL STUDIES

| | |
|---|---|
| American University | M,D,O |
| The American University of Paris | M |
| Appalachian State University | M |
| Arizona State University at Tempe | M,D |
| Assemblies of God Theological Seminary | M,D |
| Athabasca University | M,O |
| Biola University | M,D,O |
| Boston University | M |
| Brock University | M |
| Carnegie Mellon University | D |
| Central Michigan University | M |
| Chapman University | M,D,O |
| Charlotte Christian College and Theological Seminary | M,D |
| Claremont Graduate University | M,D,O |
| Columbia International University | M,D,O |
| Concordia University Irvine | M |
| Cornell University | M,D |
| Drew University | M,D,O |
| Eastern Michigan University | O |
| Florida State University | M,D |
| Gardner-Webb University | M,D |
| George Fox University | M,D,O |
| George Mason University | D |
| Georgia State University | M,O |
| Goucher College | M |
| Grace Theological Seminary | M,D,O |
| Graduate Theological Union | M,D,O |
| Greensboro College | M |
| Johnson University | M,D,O |
| Lincoln Christian University | M |
| Maranatha Baptist University | M |
| McMaster University | M,D |
| Nazarene Theological Seminary | M,D,O |
| New Mexico State University | M,D,O |
| New York University | M,D,O |
| North Central College | M |
| Northern Kentucky University | M,O |
| Northwest University | M |
| Old Dominion University | M,D,O |
| Pacific Northwest College of Art | M |
| Plymouth State University | M |
| Regent University | M,D |
| St. Francis Xavier University | M |
| San Francisco State University | M |
| School of Visual Arts (NY) | M |
| Simmons University | M,D,O |
| Simon Fraser University | D |
| Southern Illinois University Carbondale | M |
| Stanford University | M,D |
| Stony Brook University, State University of New York | M,D,O |
| Taylor College and Seminary | M,O |
| Texas A&M University | M |
| Texas A&M University–Kingsville | M |
| Texas Tech University | M,D |
| Trent University | D |
| Trinity College (United States) | M |
| Union Institute & University | M,D |
| Union University | M |
| University of Alaska Fairbanks | M |
| University of Arkansas | M,D |
| University of California, Davis | M,D |
| University of California, Irvine | D |
| University of California, Riverside | D |
| University of California, Santa Barbara | M,D |
| University of Dayton | M |
| University of Denver | M,O |
| University of Hawaii at Hilo | M,D |
| University of Hawaii at Manoa | O |
| University of Houston | M |
| University of Houston–Clear Lake | M |
| The University of Kansas | M,D |
| University of Louisiana at Lafayette | M,D |
| University of Louisville | M,D |
| The University of Manchester | M,D |
| University of Massachusetts Boston | M |
| University of Minnesota, Twin Cities Campus | D |
| University of Missouri–St. Louis | O |
| University of Montana | M,D,O |
| University of New Mexico | M,D |
| The University of North Carolina at Charlotte | M,O |
| University of Oklahoma | M,D |
| University of Pittsburgh | O* |
| University of Saskatchewan | M |
| University of Southern California | D |
| University of Southern Indiana | M |
| University of Southern Maine | M,O |
| The University of Texas at Austin | M,D |
| The University of Texas at San Antonio | M,D |
| University of the Sacred Heart | M |
| University of Utah | M,D |
| University of Washington, Bothell | M |
| Washington State University | M,D |
| Wayne State University | M,D |
| Wilfrid Laurier University | M |
| Wilson College | M |

## CURRICULUM AND INSTRUCTION

| | |
|---|---|
| Acadia University | M |
| Adams State University | M |
| American College of Education | M |
| American InterContinental University Online | M |
| Andrews University | M,D,O |
| Angelo State University | M |
| Appalachian State University | M |
| Arcadia University | M,D,O |
| Arizona State University at Tempe | M |
| Arlington Baptist University | M |
| Auburn University | M,D,O |
| Augusta University | M,O |
| Aurora University | M,D |
| Azusa Pacific University | M |
| Ball State University | M,D |
| Barry University | D,O |
| Baylor University | M,D |

| | |
|---|---|
| Berry College | M,O |
| Biola University | M,O |
| Black Hills State University | M |
| Bloomsburg University of Pennsylvania | M,O |
| Bluffton University | M |
| Bob Jones University | M,D,O |
| Boise State University | M,D,O |
| Boston College | M,D,O |
| Bowling Green State University | M |
| Brandman University | M,D |
| Brandon University | M,O |
| Brescia University | M |
| Buena Vista University | M |
| Cabrini University | M,D |
| California Baptist University | M |
| California Coast University | M,D |
| California Polytechnic State University, San Luis Obispo | M |
| California State Polytechnic University, Pomona | M |
| California State University, Chico | M |
| California State University, Fresno | M |
| California State University, Los Angeles | M |
| California State University, Northridge | M |
| California State University, Sacramento | M,D,O |
| California State University, Stanislaus | M |
| Calvary University | M |
| Calvin College | M |
| Cambridge College | M,D,O |
| Capella University | M,D |
| Caribbean University | M,D |
| Carlow University | M |
| Carson-Newman University | M |
| Castleton University | M |
| Central Michigan University | M,D,O |
| Central Washington University | M |
| Chapman University | M,D,O |
| City University of Seattle | M,O |
| Clarion University of Pennsylvania | M |
| Clark Atlanta University | M |
| Clarks Summit University | M |
| Clemson University | M,D,O |
| Coker College | M |
| The College of Idaho | M |
| The College of Saint Rose | M,O |
| Colorado Christian University | M |
| Columbia International University | M,D,O |
| Columbus State University | M,D,O |
| Concordia University (United States) | M,D |
| Concordia University Ann Arbor | M |
| Concordia University Chicago | M |
| Concordia University Irvine | M |
| Concordia University, St. Paul | M,D,O |
| Coppin State University | M |
| Cornell University | M,D |
| Dakota Wesleyan University | M |
| Dallas Baptist University | M |
| Delaware State University | M |
| Delaware Valley University | M |
| DePaul University | M,D |
| DeVry University–Folsom Campus | M |
| Doane University | M,D,O |
| Drexel University | M,D |
| Drury University | M |
| Duquesne University | M,O |
| East Carolina University | M,O |
| Eastern Illinois University | M |
| Eastern Kentucky University | M |
| Eastern Mennonite University | M |
| Eastern Michigan University | M,O |
| Eastern New Mexico University | M |
| Eastern Washington University | M |
| East Tennessee State University | M,O |
| Emporia State University | M |
| Evangel University | M,D |
| Fairleigh Dickinson University, Metropolitan Campus | M,O |
| Faulkner University | M |
| Ferris State University | M |
| Fitchburg State University | M |
| Florida Atlantic University | M,D,O |
| Florida Gulf Coast University | M |
| Florida International University | M,D,O |
| Florida State University | M,D,O |
| Fontbonne University | M |
| Fordham University | M,O |
| Framingham State University | M |
| Franciscan University of Steubenville | M |
| Franklin Pierce University | M,D,O |
| Freed-Hardeman University | M,O |
| Fresno Pacific University | M |
| Frostburg State University | M,D |
| Furman University | M,O |
| Gannon University | M,O |
| Gardner-Webb University | M,D,O |
| George Mason University | M |
| The George Washington University | M,D,O |
| Georgia College & State University | M |
| Georgia Southern University | M,D |
| Georgia State University | M,D |
| Graceland University (IA) | M |
| Grambling State University | M,D,O |
| Grand Canyon University | M,D,O |
| Grand Valley State University | M |
| Harvard University | M* |
| Henderson State University | M,O |
| Hood College | M,O |
| Houston Baptist University | M,D |
| Illinois State University | M,D |
| Indiana State University | M,D |
| Indiana University Bloomington | M,D,O |
| Indiana University of Pennsylvania | D |
| Indiana University-Purdue University Indianapolis | M,O |
| Inter American University of Puerto Rico, Arecibo Campus | M |
| Inter American University of Puerto Rico, Barranquitas Campus | M |
| Inter American University of Puerto Rico, Metropolitan Campus | M,D |
| Inter American University of Puerto Rico, San Germán Campus | D |
| Iowa State University of Science and Technology | M,D |
| John Brown University | M |
| Kansas State University | M,D,O |
| Kean University | M |
| Kennesaw State University | O |
| Kent State University | M,D,O |
| Kent State University at Stark | M |
| Kutztown University of Pennsylvania | M,D |
| LaGrange College | M,O |
| Lasell College | M,O |
| La Sierra University | M,D,O |
| Lee University | M,O |
| Lehigh University | M,D,O |
| Lesley University | M,D,O |
| LeTourneau University | M |
| Lewis & Clark College | M |
| Lewis University | M |
| Lincoln Memorial University | M,D,O |
| Louisiana State University in Shreveport | M,D |
| Louisiana Tech University | M,D,O |
| Lourdes University | M |
| Loyola University Chicago | M,D |
| Loyola University Maryland | M |
| Marian University (WI) | M,D |
| Marquette University | M,D,O |
| Martin Luther College | M |
| Marygrove College | M,O |
| Marymount University | M |
| Massachusetts College of Liberal Arts | M,O |
| McDaniel College | M |
| McGill University | M,D,O |
| McKendree University | M,D,O |
| McNeese State University | M |
| Medaille College | M |
| Memorial University of Newfoundland | M,D,O |
| Mercer University | M,D,O |
| Mercer University | M,D,O |
| Messiah University | M |
| Metropolitan State University | M |
| Michigan State University | M,D,O |
| Middle Tennessee State University | M,O |
| Midwestern State University | M |
| Misericordia University | M |
| Mississippi College | M,D,O |
| Mississippi State University | M,D,O |
| Mississippi University for Women | M |
| Montana State University | M,D,O |
| Montana State University Billings | M |
| Montclair State University | M |
| Moravian College | M |
| Morehead State University | M,O |
| Mount Saint Vincent University | M |
| National Louis University | M,D,O |
| Newman University | M |
| New Mexico Highlands University | M |
| New Mexico State University | M,D,O |
| Nicholls State University | M |
| North Carolina State University | M,D |
| Northern Arizona University | M,D |
| Northern Illinois University | M,D |
| Northern Michigan University | M |
| Northern State University | M |
| Northern Vermont University–Johnson | M |
| Northern Vermont University–Lyndon | M |
| Northwestern Oklahoma State University | M |
| Northwestern State University of Louisiana | M |
| Northwest Nazarene University | M,D,O |
| Notre Dame de Namur University | M |
| Oakland City University | M,D |
| Ohio Dominican University | M |
| Ohio University | M,D |
| Ohio Valley University | M |
| Old Dominion University | M,D |
| Olivet Nazarene University | M |
| Oral Roberts University | M,D |
| Ottawa University | M |
| Our Lady of the Lake University | M |
| Pacific Lutheran University | M |
| Park University | M,O |
| Penn State Harrisburg | M,D,O |
| Penn State University Park | M,D,O* |
| Penn State York | M,O |
| Pensacola Christian College | M,D,O |
| Peru State College | M |
| Piedmont College | M,D,O |
| Piedmont International University | M,D |
| Plymouth State University | D |
| Point Park University | M,D |
| Pontifical Catholic University of Puerto Rico | M,D |
| Post University | M |
| Prairie View A&M University | M |
| Purdue University | M,D,O |
| Quincy University | M |
| Randolph College | M |
| Regent University | M,D,O |
| Regis University | M,O |
| Rivier University | M,D,O |
| St. Catherine University | M |
| St. Francis Xavier University | M |
| St. John's University (NY) | D |
| Saint Joseph's University | M,D,O |
| Saint Louis University | M,D |
| Saint Vincent College | M |
| Saint Xavier University | M |
| Salem International University | M |
| Salisbury University | M |
| Sam Houston State University | M,D |
| San Diego State University | M |
| San Jose State University | M,O |
| Shawnee State University | M |
| Shaw University | M |
| Shepherd University (WV) | M |
| Shippensburg University of Pennsylvania | M |
| Simon Fraser University | M,D |
| Simpson University | M |
| Sitting Bull College | M |
| Sonoma State University | M,O |
| South Dakota State University | M |
| Southeastern Louisiana University | M |
| Southeastern University (FL) | M,D |
| Southern Arkansas University–Magnolia | M |
| Southern Illinois University Carbondale | M,D |
| Southern Illinois University Edwardsville | M |
| Southern New Hampshire University | M,D,O |
| Southwestern Adventist University | M |
| Southwestern Assemblies of God University | M |
| Stanford University | M |
| State University of New York at Fredonia | M |
| State University of New York at Oswego | M |
| State University of New York at Plattsburgh | M |
| State University of New York College at Potsdam | M |
| SUNY Brockport | M,O |
| Syracuse University | M,D,O |
| Tarleton State University | M |
| Teachers College, Columbia University | M,D |
| Tennessee State University | M,D |
| Tennessee Technological University | M,O |
| Texas A&M International University | M |
| Texas A&M University | M,D |
| Texas A&M University–Central Texas | M,O |
| Texas A&M University–Commerce | M,D,O |
| Texas A&M University–Corpus Christi | M,D |
| Texas A&M University–Texarkana | M |
| Texas Christian University | M,D |
| Texas Southern University | M,D |
| Texas Tech University | M,D |
| Texas Woman's University | M,D |
| Trevecca Nazarene University | M,O |
| Trinity Baptist College | M |
| Trinity Washington University | M |
| Tusculum University | M |
| Universidad Adventista de las Antillas | M |
| Universidad del Turabo | M,D |
| Universidad Metropolitana | M |
| Université de Montréal | M,D,O |
| University at Albany, State University of New York | M,D,O |
| University at Buffalo, the State University of New York | M,D,O |
| The University of Akron | M |
| The University of Alabama at Birmingham | O |
| University of Arkansas | M,D,O |
| University of Arkansas at Little Rock | M |
| The University of British Columbia | M,D |
| University of Calgary | M,D |
| University of California, Davis | M,D |
| University of California, San Diego | M,D |
| University of Central Arkansas | M,O |
| University of Central Florida | M,O |
| University of Cincinnati | M,D |
| University of Colorado Boulder | M,D |
| University of Colorado Colorado Springs | M,D |
| University of Connecticut | M,D |
| University of Delaware | M,D,O |
| University of Denver | M,D,O |
| University of Detroit Mercy | M,D,O |
| University of Florida | M,D,O |
| University of Hawaii at Manoa | M,D |
| University of Houston | M,D |
| University of Houston–Clear Lake | M |
| University of Houston - Downtown | M |
| University of Houston–Victoria | M,O |
| University of Idaho | M,O |
| University of Illinois at Chicago | M,D |
| University of Illinois at Urbana-Champaign | M,D,O |
| University of Indianapolis | M |
| University of Jamestown | M |
| The University of Kansas | M,D |
| University of Kentucky | M,D |
| University of Louisiana at Lafayette | M |
| University of Louisiana at Monroe | M,D |
| University of Louisville | M,D,O |
| University of Lynchburg | M |
| University of Manitoba | M |
| University of Mary | M,D |
| University of Mary Hardin-Baylor | M,D |
| University of Maryland, College Park | M,D,O |
| University of Massachusetts Lowell | M |
| University of Memphis | M,D,O |
| University of Michigan–Dearborn | D,O |
| University of Michigan–Flint | M,D,O |
| University of Minnesota, Twin Cities Campus | M,D |
| University of Missouri | M,D,O |
| University of Missouri–Kansas City | M,D,O |
| University of Missouri–St. Louis | M |
| University of Montana | M,D |
| University of Nebraska at Kearney | M |
| University of Nebraska–Lincoln | M,D,O |
| University of Nevada, Las Vegas | M,D,O |
| University of Nevada, Reno | D |
| University of New England | M,D,O |
| University of New Hampshire | D,O |
| University of New Orleans | M |
| The University of North Carolina at Chapel Hill | M,D |
| The University of North Carolina at Charlotte | M,D,O |
| The University of North Carolina at Greensboro | M,D,O |
| The University of North Carolina Wilmington | M,D |
| University of Northern Colorado | M,D |
| University of Northern Iowa | D |
| University of North Georgia | M |
| University of North Texas | M,D,O |
| University of North Texas at Dallas | M |
| University of Oklahoma | M,D |
| University of Oregon | M,D |
| University of Phoenix - Central Valley Campus | M |
| University of Phoenix - Dallas Campus | M |
| University of Phoenix - Hawaii Campus | M |
| University of Phoenix - Houston Campus | M |
| University of Phoenix - Las Vegas Campus | M |
| University of Phoenix–Online Campus | M,D,O |
| University of Phoenix - Phoenix Campus | M |
| University of Phoenix - Sacramento Valley Campus | M,O |
| University of Phoenix - San Antonio Campus | M |
| University of Phoenix - San Diego Campus | M |
| University of Puerto Rico at Rio Piedras | M,D |
| University of Regina | M |
| University of Rochester | M,D |
| University of St. Francis (IL) | M,D,O |
| University of Saint Joseph | M |
| University of St. Thomas (TX) | M,D |
| University of San Diego | M |
| University of San Francisco | M,D |
| University of Saskatchewan | M,D,O |
| The University of Scranton | M |
| University of South Africa | M,D |
| University of South Carolina | D |
| University of South Dakota | M,D,O |
| University of South Florida Sarasota-Manatee | M |
| The University of Tampa | M |
| The University of Tennessee | M,D,O |
| The University of Tennessee at Martin | M |
| The University of Texas at Arlington | M |
| The University of Texas at Austin | M,D |
| The University of Texas at El Paso | M,D |
| The University of Texas at San Antonio | M,D |
| The University of Texas Rio Grande Valley | M,D |
| University of the Pacific | M,D,O |
| University of the Southwest | M |
| The University of Toledo | M,D,O |
| University of Vermont | M |
| University of Victoria | M,D |
| University of Virginia | M,D,O |
| University of Washington | M,D |
| The University of Western Ontario | M |
| University of West Florida | M,O |
| University of Wisconsin–Madison | M,D |
| University of Wisconsin–Milwaukee | M,D,O* |
| University of Wisconsin–Oshkosh | M |
| University of Wisconsin–Superior | M |
| University of Wyoming | M,D |
| Université Laval | M,D |
| Utah State University | D |
| Vanguard University of Southern California | M |
| Virginia Commonwealth University | D |
| Virginia Polytechnic Institute and State University | M,D,O |
| Virginia Union University | M |
| Walden University | M,D,O |
| Walla Walla University | M |
| Warner University | M |
| Washburn University | M |
| Washington State University | M,D |
| Waynesburg University | M,D |
| Wayne State College | M |
| Wayne State University | M,D,O |
| Weber State University | M |
| Western Connecticut State University | M |

*M—masters degree; D—doctorate; O—other advanced degree; *—Close-Up and/or Display*

Western Illinois University M
Western New England University M
West Texas A&M University M
West Virginia University M,D
Wichita State University M
William & Mary M*
William Woods University M,D,O
Wisconsin Lutheran College M
Worcester State University M,O
Wright State University O
Xavier University of Louisiana M
Youngstown State University M

## DANCE
Arizona State University at Tempe M
Bennington College M
California Institute of the Arts M,O
California State University, Long Beach M
Case Western Reserve University M
Eastern Michigan University M
Florida State University M
The George Washington University M,O
Hollins University M
Jacksonville University M
Mills College M
New York University M,D,O
Northern Illinois University M
The Ohio State University M,D
Saint Mary's College of California M
Sam Houston State University M
Sarah Lawrence College M
Smith College M
SUNY Brockport M
Temple University M,D*
Texas Woman's University M,D
Tulane University M
Université du Québec à Montréal M
University at Buffalo, the State University of New York M,D
The University of Arizona M
University of California, Irvine M
University of California, Los Angeles M,D
University of California, Riverside M
University of California, San Diego M,D
University of Colorado Boulder M,D
University of Hawaii at Manoa M,D
University of Illinois at Urbana-Champaign M
The University of Iowa M
University of Maryland, Baltimore County M
University of Maryland, College Park M
University of Michigan M
University of New Mexico M
The University of North Carolina at Greensboro M
University of Oklahoma M
University of Oregon M
The University of Texas at Austin M
The University of the Arts M
University of Utah M,O
University of Washington M
University of Wisconsin–Milwaukee M,O*
Washington University in St. Louis M
Wilson College M
York University M,D

## DATA SCIENCE/DATA ANALYTICS
American University M,O
Austin Peay State University M
Azusa Pacific University M
Boston University M,O
Brandman University M
Buffalo State College, State University of New York M
Central European University D
Claremont Graduate University M,D,O
College of Saint Elizabeth M
College of Staten Island of the City University of New York M,O
Colorado Technical University Aurora M
Colorado Technical University Colorado Springs M,D
Columbia University M
DePaul University M,D
DeSales University M,O
Elmhurst University M
Fairfield University M,O
Fitchburg State University M
Florida International University M,D
Fordham University M
George Mason University M,D,O
The Graduate Center, City University of New York M
Grand Canyon University D
HEC Montreal D
IGlobal University M
Illinois Institute of Technology M,D
Indiana University Bloomington M,O
Indiana University-Purdue University Indianapolis M,D,O
Johnson & Wales University M
Kansas State University M,O
Keck Graduate Institute M
Kennesaw State University M,D,O
Lawrence Technological University M,O
Lipscomb University M,O
London Metropolitan University M,D
Manhattan College M
Maryville University of Saint Louis M
Merrimack College M
Metropolitan State University M,D,O
Michigan Technological University M,D,O
Montclair State University O
National University M
New College of Florida M
New Jersey Institute of Technology M,D,O
The New School M
New York University M,D
Northcentral University M,D,O
Northeastern University M,D
Northwestern University M
Ohio Dominican University M
Oregon State University M
Penn State Great Valley M,O
Queens College of the City University of New York M
Radford University M
Regis University M,O
Robert Morris University M,D
Rochester Institute of Technology O
Rockhurst University M,O
St. John's University (NY) M
Saint Mary's University of Minnesota M
Saint Peter's University M
Seattle Pacific University M
Slippery Rock University of Pennsylvania M
Southern Arkansas University–Magnolia M
Southern Methodist University M,D
Southern New Hampshire University M,D,O
Stockton University M
Suffolk University M
Syracuse University M,O
Texas Tech University M,D
Tufts University M,D
University at Buffalo, the State University of New York M,D
The University of Arizona M
University of California, Berkeley M
University of California, San Diego M
University of Colorado Denver M
University of Denver M,D
University of Houston - Downtown M
University of Illinois at Springfield M
University of Louisville M,D,O
University of Maryland, Baltimore County M
University of Maryland Global Campus M,O
University of Massachusetts Dartmouth M
University of Michigan M,D,O
University of Michigan–Dearborn M,D
University of Minnesota, Twin Cities Campus M
University of Mississippi M,D
University of Nebraska at Omaha M,D,O
University of Nevada, Las Vegas M,O
The University of North Carolina Wilmington M
University of Pennsylvania M
University of Pittsburgh M,D,O*
University of Rochester M
University of St. Thomas (MN) M,O
University of San Francisco M
University of Southern Indiana M
University of South Florida O
The University of Tennessee D
The University of Texas at Dallas M,D
The University of Texas Health Science Center at Houston M,D,O
University of Vermont M,D
University of Virginia M
University of Washington M,D
University of West Florida M
University of Wisconsin–La Crosse M
University of Wisconsin–Stevens Point M
Virginia International University M,O
Walsh College of Accountancy and Business Administration M
Washington University in St. Louis M
Wayne State University M,D,O
Weill Cornell Medicine M
Western Governors University M
Worcester Polytechnic Institute M,D,O
Yeshiva University M

## DECORATIVE ARTS
Bard Graduate Center M,D
The George Washington University M
Sotheby's Institute of Art–London M
Sotheby's Institute of Art–New York M

## DEMOGRAPHY AND POPULATION STUDIES
Bowling Green State University M,D
Cornell University M,D
Florida State University M
Harvard University M,D*
Johns Hopkins University M,D
Miami University M,D
New York University M,D
Princeton University D,O
Université de Montréal M,D
Université du Québec, Institut National de la Recherche Scientifique M,D,O
University at Albany, State University of New York M,D,O
University of Alberta M,D
University of California, Berkeley M,D
University of California, Irvine M
University of Colorado Denver D
University of Guelph M,D
University of Hawaii at Manoa O
University of Pennsylvania M,D
University of Puerto Rico - Medical Sciences Campus M
The University of Texas at San Antonio D
The University of Texas Medical Branch D
University of Wisconsin–Madison M,D

## DENTAL HYGIENE
Eastern Washington University M
Idaho State University M
Missouri Southern State University M
The Ohio State University M,D
Old Dominion University M
Texas Woman's University M,D
Université de Montréal O
University of Alberta O
University of Bridgeport M
University of Michigan M
University of Missouri–Kansas City M,D,O
University of New Mexico M
The University of North Carolina at Chapel Hill M,D
West Virginia University M,D

## DENTISTRY
A.T. Still University M,D,O
Augusta University D
Case Western Reserve University D
Columbia University D
Creighton University D
East Carolina University D
Harvard University M,D,O*
Howard University D,O
Idaho State University O
Indiana University-Purdue University Indianapolis M,D,O
Jacksonville University M,O
Loma Linda University M,D,O
Louisiana State University Health Sciences Center D
Marquette University D
McGill University M,D,O
Medical University of South Carolina D
Meharry Medical College D
Midwestern University, Downers Grove Campus D
Midwestern University, Glendale Campus D
New York University D
Nova Southeastern University M,D
The Ohio State University M,D
Oregon Health & Science University D,O
Roseman University of Health Sciences M,D,O
Rutgers University - Newark M,D,O
Saint Louis University M
Southern Illinois University Edwardsville D
Stony Brook University, State University of New York D,O
Temple University D*
Texas A&M University M,D,O
Tufts University D
Universidad Central del Este D
Universidad Iberoamericana M,D
Universidad Nacional Pedro Henriquez Urena D
University at Buffalo, the State University of New York D
The University of Alabama at Birmingham D
University of Alberta D
The University of British Columbia D
University of California, Los Angeles D,O
University of California, San Francisco D
University of Colorado Denver D,O
University of Connecticut Health Center D,O
University of Detroit Mercy M,D,O
University of Florida D,O
University of Illinois at Chicago D
The University of Iowa M,D,O
University of Kentucky D
University of Louisville M,D
The University of Manchester M,D
University of Manitoba D
University of Maryland, Baltimore D,O
University of Michigan D
University of Minnesota, Twin Cities Campus D
University of Mississippi Medical Center M,D
University of Missouri–Kansas City M,D,O
University of Nebraska Medical Center M,D,O
University of Nevada, Las Vegas M,D,O
University of New England D
The University of North Carolina at Chapel Hill D
University of Oklahoma Health Sciences Center D,O
University of Pennsylvania D
University of Pittsburgh M,D,O*
University of Puerto Rico - Medical Sciences Campus D
University of Saskatchewan D
University of Southern California D
The University of Tennessee Health Science Center D
The University of Texas Health Science Center at Houston M,D
The University of Texas Health Science Center at San Antonio M,D,O
University of the Pacific M,D,O
University of Toronto D
University of Utah D
University of Washington M,D,O
The University of Western Ontario D
Université Laval D
Virginia Commonwealth University M,D
Western University of Health Sciences D
West Virginia University M,D

## DEVELOPMENTAL BIOLOGY
Albert Einstein College of Medicine D
Baylor College of Medicine D
Brigham Young University M,D
California Institute of Technology D
California State University, Sacramento M
Carnegie Mellon University M,D
Columbia University M,D
Cornell University D
Dalhousie University M,D
Duke University O
Emory University D
Illinois State University M,D
Iowa State University of Science and Technology M,D
Irell & Manella Graduate School of Biological Sciences D
Johns Hopkins University D
Louisiana State University Health Sciences Center D
Marquette University M,D
Massachusetts Institute of Technology D
Medical University of South Carolina D
New York University M,D
Northwestern University D
The Ohio State University M,D
Oregon Health & Science University D
Penn State Hershey Medical Center D
Purdue University M,D
Rutgers University - New Brunswick M,D
San Francisco State University M
Stanford University M,D
Stony Brook University, State University of New York M,D
Thomas Jefferson University M
Tufts University D
The University of Alabama at Birmingham D
The University of British Columbia M,D
University of California, Davis M,D
University of California, Irvine M,D
University of California, Los Angeles M,D
University of California, Riverside M,D
University of California, San Francisco D
University of California, Santa Barbara M,D
University of California, Santa Cruz M,D
University of Chicago D
University of Cincinnati D
University of Colorado Boulder M,D
University of Colorado Denver M,D
University of Connecticut M,D
University of Connecticut Health Center D
University of Delaware M,D
University of Hawaii at Manoa M,D
University of Illinois at Urbana-Champaign D
The University of Kansas D
The University of Manchester M,D
University of Massachusetts Amherst D
University of Miami D
University of Michigan M,D
University of Minnesota, Twin Cities Campus M,D
University of Montana D
The University of North Carolina at Chapel Hill M,D
University of Pennsylvania D
University of Pittsburgh D*
University of South Carolina M,D
University of Southern California D
The University of Texas Southwestern Medical Center D
Vanderbilt University M,D*
Washington University in St. Louis D
Wesleyan University D
West Virginia University M,D
Yale University D

## DEVELOPMENTAL EDUCATION
Ferris State University M
Grambling State University M,D,O
Instituto Tecnológico y de Estudios Superiores de Monterrey, Campus Ciudad Obregón M
National Louis University M,D,O
Penn State Harrisburg M,D,O
Rutgers University - New Brunswick M
Sam Houston State University M,D
Texas State University M,D
The University of Iowa M,D
Walden University M,D,O

## DEVELOPMENTAL PSYCHOLOGY
Andrews University M,D
Arizona State University at Tempe M,D
Azusa Pacific University M
Bay Path University M
Boston College M,D
Boston Graduate School of Psychoanalysis O
Bowling Green State University M,D
Brandeis University M,D
Capella University M
Carnegie Mellon University D
Chatham University M,D
Claremont Graduate University M,D,O
Clark University D
Clayton State University M
Cornell University M,D
Delaware Valley University M
Duke University D
Emory University D

| | |
|---|---|
| Erikson Institute | M,O |
| Fielding Graduate University | M,D,O |
| Florida International University | M,D |
| Florida State University | D |
| Fordham University | D |
| George Mason University | M,D,O |
| Georgia State University | D |
| The Graduate Center, City University of New York | D |
| Harvard University | D* |
| Howard University | M,D |
| Humboldt State University | M |
| Illinois State University | M,D,O |
| Indiana University Bloomington | D |
| La Salle University | M,D |
| Liberty University | M,D,O |
| Louisiana State University and Agricultural & Mechanical College | M,D |
| Loyola University Chicago | M,D |
| McGill University | M,D,O |
| New York University | M,D |
| North Carolina State University | D |
| North Dakota State University | D |
| The Ohio State University | D |
| Pace University | M,D |
| Pontificia Universidad Catolica Madre y Maestra | M |
| Queen's University at Kingston | M,D |
| Regis University | M,D,O |
| San Francisco State University | M,O |
| Teachers College, Columbia University | M,D |
| Texas Christian University | M,D |
| Université de Montréal | M,D |
| The University of Alabama at Birmingham | M,D |
| The University of British Columbia | M,D |
| University of Connecticut | M,D |
| University of Denver | D |
| University of Houston | M,D |
| University of Illinois at Chicago | M,D |
| The University of Kansas | M,D |
| University of Louisville | D |
| The University of Manchester | M,D |
| University of Maryland, Baltimore County | D |
| University of Maryland, College Park | M,D |
| University of Massachusetts Amherst | M,D |
| University of Miami | M,D |
| University of Michigan | D |
| University of Montana | M,D,O |
| University of Nebraska–Lincoln | M,D,O |
| University of New Mexico | D |
| The University of North Carolina at Chapel Hill | D |
| The University of North Carolina at Greensboro | M,D |
| University of Notre Dame | D |
| University of Oregon | M,D |
| University of Pittsburgh | D* |
| University of Rochester | D |
| University of Southern California | M,D |
| The University of Texas at Austin | D |
| University of Utah | D |
| University of Vermont | D |
| University of Victoria | M,D |
| University of Washington | M,D |
| University of Wisconsin–Madison | D |
| University of Wisconsin–Milwaukee | M,D,O* |
| Viterbo University | M |
| Washington University in St. Louis | D |
| Wilfrid Laurier University | M,D |
| Yale University | D |

**DISABILITY STUDIES**

| | |
|---|---|
| Brandeis University | D |
| Brock University | M,O |
| Chapman University | M,D,O |
| Montclair State University | M,O |
| Syracuse University | O |
| University of Hawaii at Manoa | O |
| University of Illinois at Chicago | M,D |
| University of Manitoba | M |
| University of Northern British Columbia | M,D,O |
| University of Pittsburgh | O* |
| Utah State University | M,D,O |
| York University | M,D |

**DISTANCE EDUCATION DEVELOPMENT**

| | |
|---|---|
| Athabasca University | M,D,O |
| Barry University | O |
| Boise State University | M,D,O |
| Brandeis University | M |
| California Baptist University | M |
| Capella University | M,D |
| Carlow University | M,O |
| Clemson University | M,D,O |
| Coastal Carolina University | M,O |
| College of Saint Elizabeth | M,O |
| Colorado Christian University | M |
| Dallas Baptist University | M |
| East Carolina University | M,O |
| Eastern Michigan University | M,O |
| Emporia State University | M,O |
| Endicott College | M |
| The George Washington University | O |
| Kansas State University | M,D,O |
| Keiser University | M |
| Lenoir-Rhyne University | M |
| Lesley University | M,D,O |
| Millersville University of Pennsylvania | M,D |
| National University | M,O |
| New Mexico State University | O |
| Nova Southeastern University | M,D,O |
| Post University | M |
| Regent University | M,D,O |
| Thomas Edison State University | M,O |
| University at Buffalo, the State University of New York | M,D,O |
| University of Colorado Denver | M |
| University of Maryland, Baltimore County | M,O |
| University of Maryland Global Campus | M |
| University of Nevada, Las Vegas | M,D,O |
| University of South Florida | O |
| Université TÉLUQ | M,D |
| Virginia Polytechnic Institute and State University | M,O |
| Walden University | M,D,O |
| Waynesburg University | M,D |
| Wayne State University | M,D,O |
| Western Illinois University | M,O |

**EARLY CHILDHOOD EDUCATION**

| | |
|---|---|
| Alabama Agricultural and Mechanical University | M,D,O |
| Alabama State University | M,O |
| Albany State University | M,O |
| Albright College | M |
| American International College | M,D,O |
| Anna Maria College | M,O |
| Antioch University New England | M,O |
| Arcadia University | M,D,O |
| Arkansas State University | M,D,O |
| Auburn University at Montgomery | M,O |
| Avila University | M,O |
| Bank Street College of Education | M |
| Barry University | M,D,O |
| Bayamón Central University | M,O |
| Binghamton University, State University of New York | M |
| Biola University | M,O |
| Bloomsburg University of Pennsylvania | M |
| Boise State University | M |
| Boston College | M,D,O |
| Brandman University | M,O |
| Brenau University | M,O |
| Bridgewater State University | M |
| Brooklyn College of the City University of New York | M,O |
| Buffalo State College, State University of New York | M |
| Cabrini University | M,D |
| California State University, Dominguez Hills | M |
| California State University, East Bay | M |
| California State University, Fresno | M |
| California State University, Northridge | M |
| California State University, Sacramento | M,D,O |
| California University of Pennsylvania | M |
| Cambridge College | M,D,O |
| Canisius College | M |
| Capella University | M |
| Caribbean University | M,D |
| Carlow University | M,O |
| Carroll University | M |
| The Catholic University of America | M,O |
| Central Connecticut State University | M,O |
| Central Michigan University | M,O |
| Chaminade University of Honolulu | M |
| Champlain College | M |
| Chatham University | M |
| Chestnut Hill College | M |
| Chicago State University | M |
| The Citadel, The Military College of South Carolina | M,O |
| City College of the City University of New York | M |
| Clarion University of Pennsylvania | M |
| Clemson University | M,D,O |
| Cleveland State University | M |
| College of Charleston | M |
| The College of New Jersey | M |
| The College of New Rochelle | M |
| College of Saint Elizabeth | M,O |
| The College of Saint Rose | M,O |
| College of Staten Island of the City University of New York | M |
| Colorado Christian University | M |
| Columbia International University | M,D,O |
| Columbus State University | M,O |
| Concordia University (United States) | M,D |
| Concordia University Chicago | M |
| Concordia University, Nebraska | M |
| Concordia University, St. Paul | M,D,O |
| Concordia University Wisconsin | M |
| Daemen College | M |
| Dallas Baptist University | M,D |
| DePaul University | M,D |
| Dickinson State University | M |
| Dominican University | M |
| Duquesne University | M |
| East Carolina University | M,D |
| Eastern Connecticut State University | M |
| Eastern Illinois University | M |
| Eastern Michigan University | M |
| Eastern Nazarene College | M,O |
| Eastern New Mexico University | M |
| Eastern University | M,O |
| Eastern Washington University | M |
| East Stroudsburg University of Pennsylvania | M |
| East Tennessee State University | M,D,O |
| Edinboro University of Pennsylvania | M,O |
| Elms College | M,O |
| Emporia State University | M |
| Endicott College | M |
| Erikson Institute | M,D |
| Fairleigh Dickinson University, Florham Campus | M,O |
| Fairleigh Dickinson University, Metropolitan Campus | M |
| Fielding Graduate University | M,D,O |
| Fitchburg State University | M |
| Five Towns College | M,D |
| Florida Atlantic University | M,D,O |
| Florida International University | M,D,O |
| Fontbonne University | M |
| Fordham University | M,O |
| Framingham State University | M |
| Furman University | M,O |
| Gallaudet University | M,D,O |
| Gateway Seminary | M,D,O |
| George Mason University | M |
| The George Washington University | M |
| Georgia College & State University | M |
| Georgia Southwestern State University | M,O |
| Georgia State University | M,D,O |
| Gordon College | M,O |
| Grand Canyon University | M,D,O |
| Harding University | M,O |
| Hebrew College | M,O |
| Henderson State University | M,O |
| Hofstra University | M,D,O |
| Holy Family University | M |
| Hunter College of the City University of New York | M,D,O |
| Indiana University-Purdue University Indianapolis | M,O |
| Inter American University of Puerto Rico, Guayama Campus | M |
| Iona College | M |
| Jackson State University | M,D,O |
| Jacksonville State University | M |
| James Madison University | M |
| Jose Maria Vargas University | M |
| Kansas State University | M,D,O |
| Kean University | M |
| Kennesaw State University | M |
| Kent State University | M,D,O |
| Keuka College | M |
| Keystone College | M |
| Lander University | M |
| La Salle University | M,O |
| Lee University | M,O |
| Lehigh University | M,D,O |
| Lehman College of the City University of New York | M |
| Le Moyne College | M,O |
| Lesley University | M,D,O |
| Lewis University | M |
| London Metropolitan University | M,D |
| Long Island University - Brentwood Campus | M,O |
| Long Island University - Brooklyn | M,O |
| Long Island University - Hudson | M,O |
| Long Island University - Post | M,D,O |
| Long Island University - Riverhead | M,O |
| Louisiana Tech University | M,D,O |
| Loyola University Maryland | M,O |
| Lynn University | M,D |
| Manhattan College | M,O |
| Manhattanville College | M,O |
| Martin Luther College | M |
| Marygrove College | M,O |
| Maryville University of Saint Louis | M,D |
| Marywood University | M |
| McNeese State University | O |
| Mercer University | M,D,O |
| Mercer University | M,D,O |
| Mercy College | M |
| Middle Tennessee State University | M,O |
| Millersville University of Pennsylvania | M |
| Milligan University | M,D,O |
| Mills College | M |
| Mississippi State University | M,D,O |
| Missouri Southern State University | M |
| Missouri State University | M |
| Missouri Western State University | M,O |
| Molloy College | M,O |
| Monmouth University | M,D,O |
| Mount St. Joseph University | M,O |
| Murray State University | M,O |
| National Louis University | M,D,O |
| Nazareth College of Rochester | M |
| New Jersey City University | M |
| New Mexico State University | M,D,O |
| New York University | M,D |
| Niagara University | M,O |
| Norfolk State University | M |
| North Carolina Agricultural and Technical State University | M |
| Northeastern Illinois University | M |
| Northeastern State University | M |
| Northern Arizona University | M,D,O |
| Northern Illinois University | M |
| Northwestern College | M,O |
| Northwestern State University of Louisiana | M |
| Northwest Missouri State University | M,D,O |
| Oakland University | M,D,O |
| Oklahoma City University | M |
| Old Dominion University | M,D |
| Ottawa University | M |
| Pace University | M,O |
| Pacific Oaks College | M |
| Pacific University | M |
| Piedmont College | M,D,O |
| Pontificia Universidad Catolica Madre y Maestra | M |
| Prescott College | M,D |
| Queens College of the City University of New York | M,O |
| Radford University | M |
| Regent University | M,D,O |
| Reinhardt University | M |
| Rhode Island College | M |
| Rider University | M |
| Rivier University | M,D,O |
| Roberts Wesleyan College | M |
| Rockford University | M |
| Roosevelt University | M |
| Rutgers University - New Brunswick | M,D |
| Saginaw Valley State University | M |
| St. Ambrose University | M |
| St. Bonaventure University | M |
| St. Catherine University | M |
| St. John's University (NY) | M,D,O |
| St. Joseph's College, Long Island Campus | M |
| Saint Joseph's University | M,D,O |
| Saint Mary's College of California | M |
| Saint Xavier University | M |
| Salem State University | M |
| San Francisco State University | M,D,O |
| San Ignacio University | M |
| Shenandoah University | M,D,O |
| Shippensburg University of Pennsylvania | M |
| Siena Heights University | M,O |
| Sonoma State University | M,O |
| South Carolina State University | M |
| Southern New Hampshire University | M,D,O |
| Southern Oregon University | M |
| Southwestern College (KS) | M,D |
| Southwestern Oklahoma State University | M |
| Southwest Minnesota State University | M |
| Springfield College | M,O |
| Spring Hill College | M |
| State University of New York at Fredonia | M |
| State University of New York at New Paltz | M |
| State University of New York at Oswego | M |
| State University of New York at Plattsburgh | O |
| State University of New York College at Cortland | M |
| State University of New York College at Potsdam | M |
| Stephen F. Austin State University | M |
| SUNY Brockport | M,O |
| Syracuse University | M |
| Teachers College, Columbia University | M,D |
| Teachers College of San Joaquin | M |
| Tennessee Technological University | M,O |
| Texas A&M University–Commerce | M,D,O |
| Texas A&M University–Corpus Christi | M,D |
| Texas A&M University–Kingsville | M |
| Texas A&M University–San Antonio | M |
| Texas State University | M |
| Texas Woman's University | M,D |
| Theological University of the Caribbean | M,D |
| Towson University | M,O |
| Trident University International | M |
| Trinity Washington University | M |
| Troy University | M,O |
| Universidad del Turabo | M |
| University at Buffalo, the State University of New York | M,D,O |
| The University of Alabama at Birmingham | M,D |
| University of Alaska Anchorage | M,O |
| University of Arkansas | M,D,O |
| University of Bridgeport | M,D,O |
| University of Central Missouri | M,D,O |
| University of Central Oklahoma | M |
| University of Colorado Denver | M,D |
| University of Dayton | M |
| University of Denver | M,D,O |
| University of Florida | M,D,O |
| University of Hartford | M |
| University of Hawaii at Manoa | M |
| University of Houston–Clear Lake | M |
| University of Illinois at Chicago | M,D |
| The University of Kansas | M,D,O |
| University of Kentucky | M,D |
| University of Louisiana at Lafayette | M |
| University of Louisville | M,D,O |
| University of Maine | M,D,O |
| University of Maine at Farmington | M |
| University of Maryland, Baltimore County | M |
| University of Massachusetts Amherst | M,D,O |
| University of Massachusetts Boston | D |
| University of Memphis | M,D,O |
| University of Miami | M,O |
| University of Michigan–Dearborn | M |
| University of Michigan–Flint | M,D,O |
| University of Minnesota, Twin Cities Campus | M,D,O |
| University of Mississippi | M,D,O |
| University of Missouri | M,D,O |
| University of Missouri–St. Louis | M |

*M—masters degree; D—doctorate; O—other advanced degree; *—Close-Up and/or Display*

| | |
|---|---|
| University of Montana | M,D |
| University of Nebraska at Kearney | M |
| University of Nebraska–Lincoln | M,D |
| University of Nevada, Las Vegas | M,D,O |
| University of New England | M,D,O |
| University of New Hampshire | M |
| University of New Mexico | D |
| The University of North Carolina at Chapel Hill | M,D |
| The University of North Carolina at Charlotte | M,D,O |
| The University of North Carolina at Greensboro | M,D,O |
| The University of North Carolina Wilmington | M |
| University of North Dakota | M |
| University of Northern Iowa | M |
| University of North Georgia | M |
| University of North Texas | M,D,O |
| University of Oklahoma | M,D |
| University of Phoenix - Bay Area Campus | M,D,O |
| University of Phoenix–Online Campus | M,O |
| University of Phoenix - Phoenix Campus | M |
| University of Puerto Rico at Rio Piedras | M |
| University of South Alabama | M,D |
| University of South Carolina | M,D |
| University of South Carolina Upstate | M |
| University of South Dakota | M,D,O |
| University of South Florida | M,D,O |
| The University of Tennessee | M,D,O |
| The University of Texas at Austin | M,D |
| The University of Texas at San Antonio | M,D |
| The University of Texas at Tyler | M |
| The University of Texas of the Permian Basin | M |
| The University of Texas Rio Grande Valley | M |
| University of the District of Columbia | M |
| University of the Sacred Heart | M,O |
| University of the Southwest | M |
| The University of Toledo | M,D,O |
| University of Utah | M,D |
| University of Vermont | M |
| University of Victoria | M,D |
| University of Virginia | M,D |
| The University of West Alabama | M,O |
| University of Wisconsin–Milwaukee | M* |
| University of Wisconsin–Oshkosh | M |
| Upper Iowa University | M |
| Virginia Commonwealth University | M |
| Viterbo University | M,O |
| Wagner College | M |
| Walden University | M,D,O |
| Wayne State College | M |
| Wayne State University | M,D,O |
| Webster University | M,O |
| Wesleyan College | M |
| Western Kentucky University | M,O |
| Western Oregon University | M |
| Westfield State University | M |
| West Virginia University | M,D |
| Wichita State University | M |
| Widener University | M,D |
| Worcester State University | M,O |
| Xavier University | M* |

## EAST EUROPEAN AND RUSSIAN STUDIES

| | |
|---|---|
| Boston College | M |
| Brown University | M,D |
| Carleton University | M,O |
| Columbia University | M,D |
| Cornell University | M,D |
| Florida State University | M |
| Georgetown University | M |
| The George Washington University | M |
| Harvard University | M* |
| Indiana University Bloomington | M,O |
| The Ohio State University | M,D |
| Stanford University | M |
| University of Alberta | M,D |
| The University of British Columbia | M,D |
| University of Colorado Boulder | M |
| University of Illinois at Chicago | M,D |
| University of Illinois at Urbana-Champaign | M |
| The University of Kansas | M,O |
| The University of Manchester | D |
| University of Michigan | M,O |
| The University of North Carolina at Chapel Hill | M |
| University of Pittsburgh | O* |
| The University of Texas at Austin | M |
| University of Toronto | M |
| University of Washington | M |
| Yale University | M,D |

## ECOLOGY

| | |
|---|---|
| Baylor University | D |
| Brown University | D |
| California State University, Stanislaus | M |
| Central Washington University | M |
| Columbia University | M,D |
| Cornell University | M,D |
| Dalhousie University | M |
| Dartmouth College | D |
| Duke University | D,O |
| Eastern Kentucky University | M |
| Emory University | D |
| Florida Institute of Technology | M,D |
| Florida State University | M,D |
| Frostburg State University | M |
| Illinois State University | M,D |
| Indiana State University | M,D |
| Indiana University Bloomington | M,D,O |
| Inter American University of Puerto Rico, Bayamón Campus | M |
| Iowa State University of Science and Technology | M,D |
| Kent State University | M,D |
| Laurentian University | M,D |
| Lesley University | M,D,O |
| Marquette University | M,D |
| Michigan State University | D |
| Montana State University | M,D |
| Montclair State University | M |
| Naropa University | M |
| Northeastern Illinois University | M |
| The Ohio State University | M,D |
| Ohio University | M,D |
| Oklahoma State University | M,D |
| Old Dominion University | D |
| Oregon State University | M,D |
| Penn State University Park | M,D* |
| Princeton University | D |
| Purdue University | M,D |
| Rice University | M,D |
| Rutgers University - New Brunswick | M,D |
| San Diego State University | M,D |
| San Francisco State University | M |
| San Jose State University | M |
| Stanford University | M,D |
| State University of New York College of Environmental Science and Forestry | M,D |
| Stony Brook University, State University of New York | M,D |
| Tulane University | M,D |
| Universidad Nacional Pedro Henriquez Urena | M |
| University at Buffalo, the State University of New York | M,D,O |
| University of Alberta | M,D |
| The University of Arizona | M,D |
| University of California, Davis | M,D |
| University of California, Irvine | M,D |
| University of California, Los Angeles | M,D |
| University of California, Santa Barbara | M,D |
| University of California, Santa Cruz | M,D |
| University of Chicago | D |
| University of Colorado Boulder | M,D |
| University of Colorado Denver | M |
| University of Connecticut | M,D |
| University of Delaware | M,D |
| University of Denver | M,D |
| University of Florida | M,D,O |
| University of Georgia | M,D |
| University of Guelph | M,D |
| University of Illinois at Urbana-Champaign | M,D |
| The University of Kansas | M,D |
| The University of Manchester | M,D |
| University of Manitoba | M,D |
| University of Maryland, College Park | M,D |
| University of Michigan | M,D |
| University of Minnesota, Twin Cities Campus | M,D |
| University of Missouri | M,D |
| University of Montana | M,D |
| University of Nevada, Reno | D |
| University of New Haven | M |
| The University of North Carolina at Chapel Hill | M,D |
| University of Notre Dame | M,D |
| University of Oklahoma | M,D |
| University of Oregon | M,D |
| University of Pittsburgh | D* |
| University of Puerto Rico at Rio Piedras | M,D |
| University of Rhode Island | M,D |
| University of Rochester | M,D |
| University of South Carolina | M,D |
| University of South Florida | M,D |
| The University of Tennessee | M,D |
| The University of Texas at Austin | D |
| The University of Texas at San Antonio | M |
| The University of Toledo | M,D |
| University of Toronto | M,D |
| University of Washington | M,D |
| University of Wisconsin–Madison | M |
| University of Wyoming | M,D |
| Utah State University | M,D |
| Washington University in St. Louis | D |
| Wesleyan University | D |
| Western Illinois University | D |
| Yale University | D |

## ECONOMIC DEVELOPMENT

| | |
|---|---|
| Albany State University | M |
| The American University in Cairo | M,O |
| Ball State University | M,O |
| Boston University | M |
| The Catholic University of America | M |
| Claremont Graduate University | M,D,O |
| Cleveland State University | M,O |
| Concordia University (Canada) | O |
| Cornell University | M,D |
| East Carolina University | M,O |
| East Tennessee State University | M,O |
| Fordham University | M,O |
| Georgetown University | D |
| Georgia Institute of Technology | M,D |
| Georgia State University | M,D,O |
| Indiana University Bloomington | M,D,O |
| Johnson & Wales University | M |
| Murray State University | M |
| New Mexico State University | M,D,O |
| Northeastern University | M |
| Southern New Hampshire University | M,D,O |
| State University of New York Empire State College | M |
| Thomas Edison State University | M |
| Troy University | M |
| Université de Sherbrooke | D |
| University at Buffalo, the State University of New York | M,D,O |
| University of Central Arkansas | M,O |
| University of Colorado Denver | M |
| University of Houston–Victoria | M |
| University of Massachusetts Lowell | M,O |
| University of New Hampshire | M |
| University of North Alabama | M |
| The University of North Carolina at Greensboro | M,D,O |
| University of Pennsylvania | M,O |
| University of Puerto Rico at Rio Piedras | M |
| University of Southern California | M,D |
| University of Southern Mississippi | M |
| Vanderbilt University | M,D* |
| Wayne State University | M,D,O |
| Western Illinois University | M |
| Williams College | M |
| Yale University | M |

## ECONOMICS

| | |
|---|---|
| Albany State University | M |
| American University | M,D,O |
| The American University in Cairo | M,O |
| American University of Armenia | M |
| Andrews University | M |
| Arizona State University at Tempe | D |
| Assumption University | M,O |
| Auburn University | M,D |
| Auburn University at Montgomery | M |
| Bard College | M |
| Baruch College of the City University of New York | M |
| Baylor University | M |
| Binghamton University, State University of New York | M,D |
| Boise State University | M |
| Boston College | D |
| Boston University | M |
| Bowling Green State University | M |
| Brandeis University | M,D |
| Brock University | M |
| Brooklyn College of the City University of New York | M |
| Brown University | D |
| Buffalo State College, State University of New York | M |
| California Polytechnic State University, San Luis Obispo | M |
| California State Polytechnic University, Pomona | M |
| California State University, East Bay | M |
| California State University, Fullerton | M |
| California State University, Long Beach | M |
| California State University, Los Angeles | M |
| California University of Management and Sciences | M,D |
| Campbellsville University | M,D |
| Carleton University | M,D |
| Carnegie Mellon University | D |
| Central European University | M,D |
| Central Michigan University | M |
| City College of the City University of New York | M |
| Claremont Graduate University | M,D,O |
| Clark Atlanta University | M |
| Clark University | D |
| Clemson University | M,D |
| Cleveland State University | M,O |
| Colorado State University | M,D |
| Columbia University | M,D |
| Concordia University (Canada) | M,D,O |
| Copenhagen Business School | M,D |
| Cornell University | M,D |
| Dalhousie University | M,D |
| DePaul University | M,D |
| Drexel University | M,D,O |
| Duke University | M,D |
| Eastern Illinois University | M |
| Eastern Michigan University | M,O |
| Emory University | D |
| Florida Atlantic University | M |
| Florida International University | M,D |
| Florida State University | M,D |
| Fordham University | M,D,O |
| George Mason University | M,D |
| Georgetown University | D |
| The George Washington University | M,D |
| Georgia Institute of Technology | M,D |
| Georgia State University | M,D |
| The Graduate Center, City University of New York | D |
| Harvard University | D* |
| Howard University | M,D |
| Hunter College of the City University of New York | M |
| Illinois State University | M |
| Indiana University Bloomington | M,D |
| Indiana University-Purdue University Indianapolis | M |
| Instituto Tecnologico de Santo Domingo | M,O |
| Instituto Tecnológico y de Estudios Superiores de Monterrey, Campus Ciudad de México | M,D |
| Iowa State University of Science and Technology | M,D |
| John Jay College of Criminal Justice of the City University of New York | M |
| Johns Hopkins University | D |
| Kansas State University | M,D |
| Kent State University | M |
| Lakehead University | M |
| Lee University | M,O |
| Lehigh University | M,D |
| Louisiana State University and Agricultural & Mechanical College | M,D |
| Loyola University Chicago | M |
| Marquette University | M,O |
| Massachusetts Institute of Technology | M,D |
| McGill University | M,D |
| McMaster University | M,D |
| Memorial University of Newfoundland | M |
| Miami University | M |
| Michigan State University | M,D |
| Middle Tennessee State University | M,D |
| Mississippi State University | M,D |
| Morgan State University | M |
| Murray State University | M |
| New Mexico State University | M,D,O |
| The New School | M,D |
| New York University | M,D,O |
| North Carolina State University | M,D |
| Northeastern University | M,D |
| Northern Illinois University | M,D |
| Northwestern University | D |
| Oakland University | M,O |
| The Ohio State University | M,D |
| Ohio University | M |
| Oklahoma State University | M,D |
| Old Dominion University | M |
| Pace University | O |
| Penn State University Park | M,D* |
| Pepperdine University | M |
| Peru State College | M |
| Portland State University | M,D,O |
| Princeton University | D,O |
| Purdue University | D |
| Queen's University at Kingston | M,D |
| Regent University | M,D,O |
| Regis University | M,O |
| Rice University | M,D |
| Roosevelt University | M |
| Rutgers University - Newark | M,D |
| Rutgers University - New Brunswick | M,D |
| St. Cloud State University | M |
| San Diego State University | M |
| San Francisco State University | M |
| San Jose State University | M |
| Simon Fraser University | M,D |
| South Dakota State University | M |
| Southern Illinois University Carbondale | M,D |
| Southern Illinois University Edwardsville | M |
| Southern Methodist University | M,D |
| Southern New Hampshire University | M,D,O |
| Stanford University | D |
| State University of New York College of Environmental Science and Forestry | M,D |
| Stony Brook University, State University of New York | M,D |
| Syracuse University | M,D |
| Teachers College, Columbia University | M,D |
| Temple University | M,D* |
| Texas A&M University | M,D |
| Texas Tech University | M,D |
| Troy University | M |
| Tufts University | M,D |
| Tulane University | M,D |
| UNB Fredericton | M |
| Universidad de las Américas Puebla | M |
| Université de Moncton | M |
| Université de Montréal | M,D,O |
| Université de Sherbrooke | M |
| Université du Québec à Montréal | M,D |
| University at Albany, State University of New York | M,D,O |
| University at Buffalo, the State University of New York | M,D,O |
| The University of Akron | M |
| The University of Alabama | M,D |
| University of Alberta | M,D |
| The University of Arizona | M,D |
| University of Arkansas | M,D |
| The University of British Columbia | M,D |
| University of California, Berkeley | D |
| University of California, Davis | M,D |
| University of California, Irvine | M,D |
| University of California, Los Angeles | D |
| University of California, Riverside | M,D |
| University of California, San Diego | D |
| University of California, Santa Barbara | M,D |
| University of California, Santa Cruz | D |
| University of Central Florida | M,D |
| University of Chicago | M,D,O |
| University of Cincinnati | D |
| University of Colorado Boulder | M,D |
| University of Colorado Denver | M |
| University of Connecticut | M,D |
| University of Delaware | M,D |
| University of Denver | M |
| University of Detroit Mercy | M,D,O |
| University of Florida | M,D |
| University of Georgia | M,D |
| University of Guelph | M,D |
| University of Hawaii at Manoa | M,D |
| University of Houston | M,D |
| University of Illinois at Chicago | M,D |
| University of Illinois at Urbana-Champaign | M,D |
| The University of Iowa | D |
| The University of Kansas | M,D |
| University of Kentucky | M,D |
| University of Lethbridge | M,D |
| University of Maine | M |
| University of Manitoba | M,D |

| | |
|---|---|
| University of Maryland, Baltimore County | M,D |
| University of Maryland, College Park | M,D |
| University of Massachusetts Amherst | M,D |
| University of Massachusetts Lowell | M,O |
| University of Memphis | M,D |
| University of Miami | M,D |
| University of Michigan | M,D |
| University of Minnesota, Twin Cities Campus | M,D |
| University of Mississippi | M,D |
| University of Missouri | M,D |
| University of Missouri–Kansas City | M,D |
| University of Missouri–St. Louis | M |
| University of Montana | M |
| University of Nebraska at Omaha | M |
| University of Nebraska–Lincoln | M,D |
| University of Nevada, Las Vegas | M |
| University of Nevada, Reno | M |
| University of New Hampshire | M,D |
| University of New Mexico | M,D |
| University of New Orleans | D |
| The University of North Carolina at Chapel Hill | M,D |
| The University of North Carolina at Charlotte | M,O |
| The University of North Carolina at Greensboro | D |
| University of North Florida | M |
| University of North Texas | M,D,O |
| University of Notre Dame | D |
| University of Oklahoma | M,D |
| University of Oregon | M,D |
| University of Ottawa | M,D |
| University of Pennsylvania | M,D |
| University of Pittsburgh | M,D* |
| University of Puerto Rico at Rio Piedras | M |
| University of Regina | M,D,O |
| University of Rhode Island | M,D |
| University of Rochester | D |
| University of Saskatchewan | M,O |
| University of South Africa | M,D |
| University of South Carolina | M,D |
| University of Southern California | M,D |
| University of South Florida | M,D |
| The University of Tennessee | M,D |
| The University of Texas at Arlington | M |
| The University of Texas at Austin | M,D |
| The University of Texas at Dallas | M,D |
| The University of Texas at El Paso | M |
| The University of Texas at San Antonio | M |
| The University of Toledo | M,D,O |
| University of Toronto | M,D |
| University of Utah | M,D |
| University of Vermont | M,D,O |
| University of Victoria | M,D |
| University of Virginia | M,D |
| University of Washington | D |
| University of Waterloo | M,D |
| The University of Western Ontario | M,D |
| University of Windsor | M |
| University of Wisconsin–Madison | D |
| University of Wisconsin–Milwaukee | M,D* |
| University of Wyoming | M,D |
| Université Laval | M,D |
| Utah State University | M |
| Vanderbilt University | M,D* |
| Virginia Commonwealth University | M |
| Virginia Polytechnic Institute and State University | M,D |
| Virginia State University | M |
| Washington State University | M,D,O |
| Washington University in St. Louis | D |
| Wayne State University | M,D |
| Western Illinois University | M |
| Western Michigan University | M,D |
| West Texas A&M University | M |
| West Virginia University | M,D,O |
| Wichita State University | M |
| Wilfrid Laurier University | M,D |
| Wright State University | M |
| Yale University | M,D |
| Yeshiva University | M |
| York University | M,D |
| Youngstown State University | M |

## EDUCATION—GENERAL

| | |
|---|---|
| Abilene Christian University | M,O |
| Acacia University | M |
| Acadia University | M,D |
| Adams State University | M |
| Adelphi University | M,D,O |
| Alabama Agricultural and Mechanical University | M,D,O |
| Alabama State University | M,D,O |
| Alaska Pacific University | M |
| Albany State University | M,O |
| Albertus Magnus College | M |
| Albright College | M |
| Alcorn State University | M,O |
| Alfred University | M |
| Alliant International University - Los Angeles | M,O |
| Alliant International University–Sacramento | M,O |
| Alliant International University - San Diego | M,O |
| Alliant International University–San Francisco | M,O |
| Alvernia University | M |
| Alverno College | M |
| American College of Education | M |
| American InterContinental University Online | M |
| American International College | M,D |
| American Jewish University | M |
| American University | M,O |
| The American University in Cairo | M |
| The American University in Dubai | M |
| American University of Puerto Rico - Bayamon | M |
| Anderson University (IN) | M |
| Anderson University (SC) | M |
| Andrews University | M,D,O |
| Anna Maria College | M,O |
| Antioch University Los Angeles | M |
| Antioch University New England | M,O |
| Antioch University Santa Barbara | M |
| Antioch University Seattle | M |
| Aquinas College (MI) | M |
| Aquinas College (TN) | M |
| Arcadia University | M,D,O |
| Argosy University, Atlanta | M,D,O |
| Argosy University, Chicago | M,D,O |
| Argosy University, Hawaii | M,D |
| Argosy University, Los Angeles | M,D |
| Argosy University, Northern Virginia | M,D,O |
| Argosy University, Orange County | M,D |
| Argosy University, Phoenix | M,D,O |
| Argosy University, Seattle | M,D |
| Argosy University, Tampa | M,D,O |
| Argosy University, Twin Cities | M,D,O |
| Arizona State University at Tempe | M,D,O |
| Arkansas State University | M,D,O |
| Arkansas Tech University | M,D,O |
| Arlington Baptist University | M |
| Ashland University | M,D |
| Athabasca University | M,D,O |
| Auburn University | M,D,O |
| Auburn University at Montgomery | M,O |
| Augsburg University | M |
| Augustana University | M |
| Augusta University | M,D,O |
| Aurora University | M,D |
| Austin College | M |
| Austin Peay State University | M,O |
| Averett University | M |
| Avila University | M,O |
| Azusa Pacific University | M,D |
| Baker University | M,D |
| Baldwin Wallace University | M |
| Ball State University | M,D,O |
| Bank Street College of Education | M |
| Bard College | M |
| Barry University | M,D,O |
| Bayamón Central University | M,O |
| Baylor University | M,D,O |
| Belhaven University (MS) | M,D,O |
| Bellarmine University | M,D,O |
| Bemidji State University | M |
| Benedictine College | M |
| Berry College | M,O |
| Bethany College | M |
| Bethel University (IN) | M |
| Bethel University (MN) | M,D,O |
| Binghamton University, State University of New York | M,D,O |
| Biola University | M,O |
| Bishop's University | M,O |
| Bloomsburg University of Pennsylvania | M,O |
| Bluefield College | M |
| Bluffton University | M |
| Boise State University | M,D,O |
| Boston College | M,D,O |
| Boston University | M,D,O |
| Bowie State University | M |
| Bradley University | M,D,O |
| Brandman University | M,D |
| Brandon University | M,O |
| Brenau University | M,O |
| Bridgewater State University | M,O |
| Brigham Young University | M,D,O |
| Brock University | M,D |
| Brooklyn College of the City University of New York | M,O |
| Brown University | M |
| Bucknell University | M |
| Buena Vista University | M |
| Buffalo State College, State University of New York | M,O |
| Bushnell University | M |
| Butler University | M,O |
| Cairn University | M,O |
| Caldwell University | M,D,O |
| California Baptist University | M |
| California Coast University | M,D |
| California Lutheran University | M,D |
| California Polytechnic State University, San Luis Obispo | M |
| California State University, Dominguez Hills | M |
| California State University, East Bay | M |
| California State University, Fresno | M,D |
| California State University, Long Beach | M,D |
| California State University, Los Angeles | M,D,O |
| California State University, Monterey Bay | M |
| California State University, Northridge | M,D |
| California State University, Sacramento | M,D,O |
| California State University, San Bernardino | M |
| California State University, San Marcos | M,D |
| California State University, Stanislaus | M,D |
| California University of Pennsylvania | M,D |
| Calvary University | M |
| Calvin College | M |
| Cambridge College | M,D,O |
| Cameron University | M |
| Campbellsville University | M |
| Campbell University | M |
| Canisius College | M,O |
| Capella University | M,D |
| Caribbean University | M,D |
| Carlow University | M,O |
| Carroll University | M |
| Carson-Newman University | M |
| Carthage College | M,O |
| Castleton University | M,O |
| The Catholic University of America | M,O |
| Cedar Crest College | M |
| Centenary College of Louisiana | M |
| Centenary University | M,D |
| Central Connecticut State University | M,D,O |
| Central Methodist University | M |
| Central Michigan University | M,D,O |
| Central Washington University | M |
| Chadron State College | M,O |
| Chaminade University of Honolulu | M |
| Chapman University | M,D,O |
| Charleston Southern University | M |
| Chatham University | M |
| Chestnut Hill College | M |
| Cheyney University of Pennsylvania | M,O |
| Chicago State University | M,D |
| Chowan University | M |
| Christian Brothers University | M |
| Christopher Newport University | M |
| The Citadel, The Military College of South Carolina | M,O |
| City College of the City University of New York | M,O |
| City University of Seattle | M,O |
| Claremont Graduate University | M,D,O |
| Clarion University of Pennsylvania | M |
| Clark Atlanta University | M,D,O |
| Clarke University | M |
| Clarkson University | M |
| Clark University | M,D |
| Clayton State University | M |
| Clemson University | M,D,O |
| Cleveland State University | M,D,O |
| Coastal Carolina University | M,O |
| College of Charleston | M,O |
| The College of Idaho | M |
| College of Mount Saint Vincent | M,O |
| The College of New Jersey | M,O |
| The College of New Rochelle | M,O |
| College of Saint Elizabeth | M,O |
| College of St. Joseph | M |
| College of Saint Mary | M |
| The College of Saint Rose | M,O |
| The College of St. Scholastica | M,O |
| College of Staten Island of the City University of New York | M,O |
| Colorado Christian University | M |
| The Colorado College | M |
| Colorado Mesa University | M,O |
| Colorado State University | M,D |
| Colorado State University–Global Campus | M |
| Colorado State University-Pueblo | M |
| Columbia College (MO) | M |
| Columbia College (SC) | M |
| Columbia International University | M,D,O |
| Columbus State University | M,D,O |
| Concordia College | M |
| Concordia University (United States) | M,D |
| Concordia University (Canada) | M,O |
| Concordia University Chicago | M |
| Concordia University Irvine | M |
| Concordia University, Nebraska | M |
| Concordia University, St. Paul | M,D,O |
| Concordia University Texas | M |
| Concordia University Wisconsin | M |
| Concord University | M |
| Coppin State University | M |
| Corban University | M |
| Cornell University | M,D |
| Cornerstone University | M,O |
| Covenant College | M |
| Crandall University | M |
| Creighton University | M |
| Cumberland University | M |
| Curry College | M,O |
| Daemen College | M |
| Dakota State University | M |
| Dakota Wesleyan University | M |
| Dallas Baptist University | M |
| Defiance College | M |
| Delaware State University | M,D |
| Delta State University | M,D,O |
| DePaul University | M,D |
| DeSales University | M,O |
| Dickinson State University | M |
| Doane University | M,D,O |
| Dominican College | M |
| Dominican University | M |
| Dominican University of California | M |
| Dordt University | M |
| Drake University | M,D,O |
| Drew University | M,D,O |
| Drexel University | M,D |
| Drury University | M |
| Duke University | M |
| Duquesne University | M,D,O |
| D'Youville College | M,D |
| Earlham College | M |
| East Carolina University | M,D,O |
| East Central University | M |
| Eastern Connecticut State University | M |
| Eastern Illinois University | M,O |
| Eastern Kentucky University | M |
| Eastern Mennonite University | M |
| Eastern Michigan University | M,D,O |
| Eastern Nazarene College | M,O |
| Eastern New Mexico University | M |
| Eastern Oregon University | M |
| Eastern Washington University | M |
| East Stroudsburg University of Pennsylvania | M,D |
| East Tennessee State University | M,D,O |
| East Texas Baptist University | M |
| Edgewood College | M,D,O |
| Elizabeth City State University | M |
| Elms College | M,O |
| Elon University | M |
| Embry-Riddle Aeronautical University–Worldwide | M |
| Emmanuel College (United States) | M,O |
| Emory & Henry College | M,D |
| Emory University | M,D |
| Emporia State University | M |
| Evangel University | M |
| The Evergreen State College | M |
| Fairfield University | M,O |
| Fairleigh Dickinson University, Florham Campus | M,O |
| Fairleigh Dickinson University, Metropolitan Campus | M,O |
| Fairmont State University | M |
| Faulkner University | M |
| Felician University | M,O |
| Ferris State University | M |
| Fielding Graduate University | M,D |
| Florida Agricultural and Mechanical University | M,D |
| Florida Atlantic University | M,D,O |
| Florida Gulf Coast University | M |
| Florida Memorial University | M |
| Florida Southern College | M,D |
| Florida State University | M,D,O |
| Fontbonne University | M |
| Fordham University | M,D,O |
| Fort Hays State University | M,O |
| Franciscan University of Steubenville | M |
| Francis Marion University | M |
| Freed-Hardeman University | M,O |
| Fresno Pacific University | M,O |
| Frostburg State University | M,D |
| Furman University | M,O |
| Gallaudet University | M,D,O |
| Gannon University | M,D,O |
| Gardner-Webb University | M,D,O |
| Geneva College | M |
| George Fox University | M,D,O |
| George Mason University | M,D,O |
| Georgetown College | M |
| The George Washington University | M,D,O |
| Georgia College & State University | M,O |
| Georgian Court University | M,O |
| Georgia Southern University | M,D,O |
| Georgia Southwestern State University | M,O |
| Georgia State University | M,D,O |
| Goddard College | M |
| Gonzaga University | M,D |
| Gordon College | M,O |
| Goucher College | M,O |
| Governors State University | M |
| Graceland University (IA) | M |
| Grambling State University | M,D,O |
| Grand Canyon University | M,D,O |
| Gratz College | M |
| Greensboro College | M |
| Greenville University | M |
| Hamline University | M,D |
| Hampton University | M,D,O |
| Hannibal-LaGrange University | M |
| Harding University | M,O |
| Hardin-Simmons University | M,D |
| Harrison Middleton University | M,D |
| Harvard University | M,D* |
| Hastings College | M |
| Hebrew College | M,O |
| Hebrew Union College–Jewish Institute of Religion (NY) | M |
| Henderson State University | M,O |
| Heritage University | M |
| Hofstra University | M,D,O |
| Hollins University | M |
| Holy Family College | M |
| Holy Family University | M,D |
| Holy Names University | M,O |
| Hood College | M,O |
| Hope International University | M |
| Houston Baptist University | M,D |
| Howard University | M,D,O |
| Humboldt State University | M |
| Hunter College of the City University of New York | M,D,O |
| Idaho State University | M,D,O |
| Illinois State University | M,D,O |
| Indiana State University | M,D,O |
| Indiana University Bloomington | M,D,O |
| Indiana University East | M |
| Indiana University Northwest | M,O |
| Indiana University of Pennsylvania | M,D,O |
| Indiana University-Purdue University Indianapolis | M,O |
| Indiana University South Bend | M,O |
| Indiana University Southeast | M |
| Institute for Christian Studies | M,D |
| Instituto Tecnologico de Santo Domingo | M,O |
| Instituto Tecnológico y de Estudios Superiores de Monterrey, Campus Central de Veracruz | M |

*M—masters degree; D—doctorate; O—other advanced degree; *—Close-Up and/or Display*

| | |
|---|---|
| Instituto Tecnológico y de Estudios Superiores de Monterrey, Campus Ciudad de México | M,D |
| Instituto Tecnológico y de Estudios Superiores de Monterrey, Campus Ciudad Juárez | M |
| Instituto Tecnológico y de Estudios Superiores de Monterrey, Campus Ciudad Obregón | M |
| Instituto Tecnológico y de Estudios Superiores de Monterrey, Campus Estado de México | M,D |
| Instituto Tecnológico y de Estudios Superiores de Monterrey, Campus Irapuato | M,D |
| Instituto Tecnológico y de Estudios Superiores de Monterrey, Campus Sonora Norte | M |
| Inter American University of Puerto Rico, Arecibo Campus | M |
| Inter American University of Puerto Rico, Barranquitas Campus | M |
| Inter American University of Puerto Rico, Metropolitan Campus | M,D |
| International Baptist College and Seminary | M |
| Iona College | M |
| Iowa State University of Science and Technology | M,D |
| Jackson State University | M,D,O |
| Jacksonville State University | M,O |
| John Brown University | M |
| Johns Hopkins University | M,D,O |
| Johnson & Wales University | M |
| Johnson University | M,D,O |
| Kansas State University | M,D,O |
| Kean University | M |
| Keiser University | M |
| Kennesaw State University | M,D,O |
| Kent State University | M,D,O |
| Kent State University at Stark | M |
| King's College | M |
| Kutztown University of Pennsylvania | M,D |
| LaGrange College | M,O |
| Lake Erie College | M |
| Lake Forest College | M |
| Lakehead University | M,D |
| Lakeland University | M |
| Lamar University | M,D,O |
| Lander University | M |
| Langston University | M |
| La Salle University | M,O |
| Lasell College | M,O |
| La Sierra University | M,D,O |
| Lee University | M,O |
| Lehigh University | M,D,O |
| Lehman College of the City University of New York | M |
| Le Moyne College | M,O |
| Lenoir-Rhyne University | M |
| Lesley University | M,D,O |
| Liberty University | M,D,O |
| Lincoln Memorial University | M,D,O |
| Lindenwood University | M,D,O |
| Lindenwood University–Belleville | M |
| Lipscomb University | M,D,O |
| Lock Haven University of Pennsylvania | M |
| London Metropolitan University | M,D |
| Long Island University - Brooklyn | M,O |
| Long Island University - Post | M,D,O |
| Longwood University | M |
| Louisiana College | M |
| Louisiana State University and Agricultural & Mechanical College | M,D,O |
| Louisiana State University in Shreveport | M,D |
| Louisiana Tech University | M,D,O |
| Loyola Marymount University | M,D |
| Loyola University Chicago | M,D,O |
| Loyola University Maryland | M,O |
| Loyola University New Orleans | M |
| Lynn University | M,D |
| Madonna University | M |
| Manhattan College | M,O |
| Manhattanville College | M,D,O |
| Mansfield University of Pennsylvania | M |
| Maranatha Baptist University | M |
| Marian University (IN) | M |
| Marian University (WI) | M,D |
| Marist College | M,O |
| Marquette University | M,D,O |
| Marshall University | M,D,O |
| Martin Luther College | M |
| Mary Baldwin University | M |
| Marymount University | M |
| Maryville University of Saint Louis | M,D |
| Marywood University | M |
| Massachusetts College of Liberal Arts | M,O |
| McGill University | M,D,O |
| McKendree University | M,D,O |
| McNeese State University | O |
| McPherson College | M |
| Medaille College | M |
| Memorial University of Newfoundland | M,D,O |
| Mercer University | M,D,O |
| Mercer University | M,D,O |
| Mercy College | M,O |
| Meredith College | M,O |
| Merrimack College | M,O |
| Metropolitan State University of Denver | M |
| Miami University | M,D,O |
| Michigan State University | M,D,O |
| MidAmerica Nazarene University | M |
| Middle Tennessee State University | M,D,O |
| Midway University | M |
| Midwestern State University | M |
| Midwest University | M,D |
| Millersville University of Pennsylvania | M,D,O |
| Milligan University | M,D,O |
| Mills College | M,D,O |
| Minnesota State University Mankato | M,D,O |
| Minnesota State University Moorhead | M,D,O |
| Misericordia University | M |
| Mississippi College | M,D,O |
| Mississippi State University | M,D,O |
| Mississippi University for Women | M |
| Mississippi Valley State University | M |
| Missouri Baptist University | M,O |
| Missouri Southern State University | M,O |
| Molloy College | M,O |
| Monmouth University | M,D,O |
| Montana State University | M,D,O |
| Montana State University Billings | M,O |
| Montana State University–Northern | M |
| Montclair State University | M,D,O |
| Moravian College | M |
| Morehead State University | M,O |
| Morgan State University | M,D |
| Morningside College | M |
| Mount Mary University | M |
| Mount Mercy University | M |
| Mount St. Joseph University | M,O |
| Mount Saint Mary College | M,O |
| Mount Saint Mary's University (CA) | M,D,O |
| Mount St. Mary's University (MD) | M |
| Mount Saint Vincent University | M |
| Mount Vernon Nazarene University | M |
| Multnomah University | M |
| Murray State University | M,D,O |
| Muskingum University | M |
| National Louis University | M,D,O |
| National University | M,O |
| Nazareth College of Rochester | M |
| Neumann University | M |
| New England College | M,D |
| New Jersey City University | M,D |
| Newman University | M |
| New Mexico Highlands University | M |
| New Mexico State University | M,D,O |
| New York University | M,D,O |
| Niagara University | M,D,O |
| Nicholls State University | M |
| Nipissing University | M,O |
| Norfolk State University | M |
| North Carolina Agricultural and Technical State University | M,D |
| North Carolina Central University | M |
| North Carolina State University | M,D,O |
| North Central College | M |
| Northcentral University | M,D,O |
| North Dakota State University | M,D,O |
| Northeastern Illinois University | M |
| Northeastern State University | M |
| Northern Arizona University | M,D,O |
| Northern Illinois University | M,D,O |
| Northern Kentucky University | M,D,O |
| Northern Michigan University | M |
| Northern State University | M |
| Northern Vermont University–Johnson | M |
| Northern Vermont University–Lyndon | M |
| North Greenville University | M,D |
| North Park University | M |
| Northwestern College | M,O |
| Northwestern Oklahoma State University | M |
| Northwestern State University of Louisiana | M,O |
| Northwestern University | M,D |
| Northwest Missouri State University | M,D,O |
| Northwest Nazarene University | M,D,O |
| Northwest University | M |
| Notre Dame de Namur University | M |
| Notre Dame of Maryland University | M |
| Nova Southeastern University | M,D,O |
| Oakland City University | M,D |
| Oakland University | M,D,O |
| Ohio Dominican University | M |
| The Ohio State University | M,D,O |
| The Ohio State University at Mansfield | M |
| The Ohio State University at Marion | M |
| The Ohio State University at Newark | M |
| Ohio University | M,D |
| Ohio Valley University | M |
| Oklahoma State University | M,D,O |
| Old Dominion University | M,D,O |
| Olivet Nazarene University | M |
| Open University | M |
| Oral Roberts University | M,D |
| Oregon State University | M,D |
| Oregon State University–Cascades | M |
| Ottawa University | M |
| Otterbein University | M |
| Pace University | M,O |
| Pacific Lutheran University | M |
| Pacific Oaks College | M |
| Pacific Union College | M |
| Pacific University | M |
| Palm Beach Atlantic University | M |
| Park University | M,O |
| Penn State Harrisburg | M,D,O |
| Penn State University Park | M,D,O* |
| Penn State York | M,O |
| Peru State College | M |
| Piedmont College | M,D,O |
| Pittsburg State University | M,O |
| Plymouth State University | O |
| Point Loma Nazarene University | M |
| Point Park University | M,D |
| Pontifical Catholic University of Puerto Rico | M,D |
| Portland State University | M,D |
| Post University | M |
| Prairie View A&M University | M,D |
| Prescott College | M,D |
| Purdue University | M,D,O |
| Purdue University Fort Wayne | M,O |
| Purdue University Global | M |
| Purdue University Northwest | M |
| Queens College of the City University of New York | M,O |
| Queen's University at Kingston | M,D |
| Queens University of Charlotte | M |
| Quincy University | M |
| Quinnipiac University | M,O |
| Randolph College | M |
| Regent University | M,D,O |
| Regis College (MA) | M,D |
| Regis University | M |
| Reinhardt University | M |
| Relay Graduate School of Education | M |
| Rhode Island College | D |
| Rice University | M |
| Rider University | M,O |
| Rivier University | M,D,O |
| Roberts Wesleyan College | M |
| Rockford University | M |
| Rockhurst University | M |
| Roger Williams University | M,O |
| Rollins College | M |
| Roosevelt University | M |
| Rosemont College | M |
| Rowan University | M,D,O |
| Rutgers University - New Brunswick | M,D |
| Sacred Heart University | M,O |
| Sage Graduate School | M,D,O |
| Saginaw Valley State University | M,O |
| St. Ambrose University | M |
| St. Bonaventure University | M,O |
| St. Catherine University | M,O |
| St. Cloud State University | M,D,O |
| St. Edward's University | M,O |
| Saint Francis University | M |
| St. Francis Xavier University | M |
| St. John Fisher College | M,D,O |
| St. John's University (NY) | M,D,O |
| St. Joseph's College, New York | M |
| Saint Joseph's College of Maine | M |
| Saint Joseph's University | M,D,O |
| Saint Leo University | M,D,O |
| Saint Louis University | M,D |
| Saint Martin's University | M |
| Saint Mary's College of California | M,D,O |
| St. Mary's College of Maryland | M |
| St. Mary's University (United States) | M |
| Saint Mary's University of Minnesota | M,O |
| Saint Michael's College | M,O |
| Saint Peter's University | M,D,O |
| St. Thomas Aquinas College | M,O |
| St. Thomas University - Florida | M,D,O |
| Saint Vincent College | M |
| Saint Xavier University | M |
| Salem College | M |
| Salem International University | M |
| Samford University | M,D,O |
| Sam Houston State University | M,D |
| San Diego Christian College | M |
| San Diego State University | M,D |
| San Francisco State University | M,D,O |
| San Ignacio University | M |
| Santa Clara University | M,O |
| Sarah Lawrence College | M |
| Schreiner University | M,O |
| Seattle Pacific University | D |
| Seattle University | M,D,O |
| Seton Hall University | M,D,O |
| Shawnee State University | M |
| Shenandoah University | M,D,O |
| Shippensburg University of Pennsylvania | M,D |
| Siena Heights University | M,O |
| Sierra Nevada College | M |
| Simon Fraser University | M,D,O |
| Simpson College | M |
| Simpson University | M |
| Sinte Gleska University | M |
| Slippery Rock University of Pennsylvania | M,D |
| Smith College | M |
| Sonoma State University | M,O |
| South Carolina State University | M |
| South Dakota State University | M,D |
| Southeastern Louisiana University | M,D |
| Southeastern Oklahoma State University | M |
| Southeastern University (FL) | M,D |
| Southern Adventist University | M |
| Southern Arkansas University–Magnolia | M |
| Southern Connecticut State University | M,D,O |
| Southern Illinois University Carbondale | M,D |
| Southern Illinois University Edwardsville | M,D,O |
| Southern Methodist University | M,D |
| Southern New Hampshire University | M,D,O |
| Southern Oregon University | M |
| Southern University and Agricultural and Mechanical College | M,D |
| Southern Utah University | M,O |
| Southern Wesleyan University | M |
| Southwest Baptist University | M,O |
| Southwestern Adventist University | M |
| Southwestern Assemblies of God University | M |
| Southwestern College (KS) | M,D |
| Southwestern Oklahoma State University | M,O |
| Southwest Minnesota State University | M |
| Spalding University | M,D |
| Spring Arbor University | M |
| Springfield College | M,O |
| Spring Hill College | M |
| Stanford University | M,D |
| State University of New York at Fredonia | M |
| State University of New York at New Paltz | M,O |
| State University of New York at Oswego | M,O |
| State University of New York College at Cortland | M,O |
| State University of New York College at Geneseo | M |
| State University of New York College at Old Westbury | M |
| State University of New York College at Oneonta | M,O |
| State University of New York Empire State College | M |
| Stephen F. Austin State University | M,D |
| Stetson University | M |
| Stevenson University | M |
| Stockton University | M |
| Strayer University | M |
| Sul Ross State University | M,O |
| SUNY Brockport | M,O |
| Sweet Briar College | M |
| Syracuse University | M,D,O |
| Taft University System | M |
| Tarleton State University | M,D,O |
| Teachers College, Columbia University | M,D |
| Teachers College of San Joaquin | M |
| Temple University | M,D,O* |
| Tennessee State University | M,D,O |
| Tennessee Technological University | M,D,O |
| Texas A&M International University | M |
| Texas A&M University | M,D |
| Texas A&M University–Commerce | M,D,O |
| Texas A&M University–Corpus Christi | M,D |
| Texas A&M University–Kingsville | M,D,O |
| Texas A&M University–San Antonio | M |
| Texas A&M University–Texarkana | M |
| Texas Christian University | M,D |
| Texas Southern University | M,D |
| Texas State University | M,D,O |
| Texas Tech University | M,D |
| Texas Wesleyan University | M,D |
| Texas Woman's University | M,D,O |
| Thomas More University | M |
| Thomas University | M |
| Thompson Rivers University | M |
| Tiffin University | M |
| Touro University California | M,D |
| Towson University | M |
| Trevecca Nazarene University | M,O |
| Trident University International | M,D |
| Trinity International University | M |
| Trinity University | M |
| Trinity Washington University | M |
| Troy University | M,O |
| Truman State University | M |
| Tufts University | M,D,O |
| Tusculum University | M |
| UNB Fredericton | M,D |
| Union College (KY) | M |
| Union Institute & University | D |
| Union University | M,D,O |
| Universidad Autonoma de Guadalajara | M,D |
| Universidad de las Americas, A.C. | M |
| Universidad de las Américas Puebla | M |
| Universidad del Turabo | M,D |
| Universidad Metropolitana | M |
| Université de Moncton | M |
| Université de Montréal | M,D,O |
| Université de Saint-Boniface | M |
| Université de Sherbrooke | M,O |
| Université du Québec à Chicoutimi | M,D |
| Université du Québec à Montréal | M,D,O |
| Université du Québec à Rimouski | M,D,O |
| Université du Québec à Trois-Rivières | M,D |
| Université du Québec en Abitibi-Témiscamingue | M,D,O |
| Université du Québec en Outaouais | M,D,O |
| Université Sainte-Anne | M |
| University at Albany, State University of New York | M,D,O |
| University at Buffalo, the State University of New York | M,D,O |
| The University of Akron | M |
| The University of Alabama at Birmingham | M,D,O |
| The University of Alabama in Huntsville | M,O |
| University of Alaska Anchorage | M,O |
| University of Alaska Fairbanks | M,O |
| University of Alaska Southeast | M |
| The University of Arizona | M,D,O |
| University of Arkansas | M,D,O |
| University of Arkansas at Little Rock | M,D,O |
| University of Arkansas at Monticello | M |

| | |
|---|---|
| University of Arkansas at Pine Bluff | M |
| University of Bridgeport | M,D,O |
| The University of British Columbia | M,D,O |
| University of California, Berkeley | M,D,O |
| University of California, Davis | M,D |
| University of California, Irvine | M,D |
| University of California, Los Angeles | M,D |
| University of California, Riverside | M,D,O |
| University of California, San Diego | M,D |
| University of California, Santa Barbara | M,D,O |
| University of California, Santa Cruz | M,D |
| University of Central Arkansas | M,O |
| University of Central Missouri | M,D,O |
| University of Central Oklahoma | M |
| University of Cincinnati | M,D,O |
| University of Colorado Boulder | M,D |
| University of Colorado Colorado Springs | M,D |
| University of Colorado Denver | M,D,O |
| University of Connecticut | M,D |
| University of Delaware | M,D,O |
| University of Denver | M,D,O |
| The University of Findlay | M,D |
| University of Florida | M,D,O |
| University of Georgia | M,D,O |
| University of Guam | M |
| University of Hartford | M,D,O |
| University of Hawaii at Hilo | M |
| University of Hawaii at Manoa | M,D,O |
| University of Holy Cross | M,D |
| University of Houston | M,D |
| University of Houston–Clear Lake | M,D |
| University of Houston–Victoria | M,O |
| University of Idaho | M,D,O |
| University of Illinois at Chicago | M,D |
| University of Illinois at Springfield | M,O |
| University of Illinois at Urbana-Champaign | M,D,O |
| University of Indianapolis | M |
| The University of Iowa | M,D,O |
| University of Jamestown | M |
| The University of Kansas | M,D,O |
| University of Kentucky | M,D,O |
| University of La Verne | M,O |
| University of Lethbridge | M,D |
| University of Louisiana at Lafayette | M,D |
| University of Louisiana at Monroe | M,D |
| University of Louisville | M,D,O |
| University of Maine | M,D,O |
| University of Maine at Farmington | M |
| The University of Manchester | M,D |
| University of Manitoba | M,D |
| University of Mary | M,D |
| University of Mary Hardin-Baylor | M,D |
| University of Maryland, Baltimore County | M,O |
| University of Maryland, College Park | M,D,O |
| University of Maryland Eastern Shore | M |
| University of Maryland Global Campus | M |
| University of Mary Washington | M |
| University of Massachusetts Amherst | M,D,O |
| University of Massachusetts Boston | M,D,O |
| University of Massachusetts Dartmouth | M,D,O |
| University of Massachusetts Lowell | M |
| University of Memphis | M,D,O |
| University of Miami | M,D,O |
| University of Michigan | M,D |
| University of Michigan–Dearborn | M |
| University of Michigan–Flint | M,D,O |
| University of Minnesota, Duluth | M,D |
| University of Minnesota, Twin Cities Campus | M,D,O |
| University of Mississippi | M,D,O |
| University of Missouri | M,D,O |
| University of Missouri–Kansas City | M,D,O |
| University of Missouri–St. Louis | M,D,O |
| University of Mobile | M |
| University of Montana | M,D,O |
| University of Montevallo | M,O |
| University of Nebraska at Kearney | M,O |
| University of Nebraska at Omaha | M,D,O |
| University of Nevada, Las Vegas | M,D,O |
| University of Nevada, Reno | M,D,O |
| University of New England | M,D,O |
| University of New Hampshire | M,D,O |
| University of New Mexico | M,D,O |
| University of North Alabama | M,O |
| The University of North Carolina at Chapel Hill | M,D |
| The University of North Carolina at Charlotte | M,D,O |
| The University of North Carolina at Greensboro | M,D,O |
| The University of North Carolina at Pembroke | M |
| The University of North Carolina Wilmington | M,D |
| University of North Dakota | M,D,O |
| University of Northern British Columbia | M,D,O |
| University of Northern Colorado | M,D,O |
| University of Northern Iowa | M,D,O |
| University of North Florida | M,D |
| University of North Georgia | M |
| University of North Texas | M,D,O |
| University of Northwestern–St. Paul | M |
| University of Notre Dame | M |
| University of Oklahoma | M,D,O |
| University of Oregon | M,D |
| University of Ottawa | M,D,O |
| University of Pennsylvania | M,D,O |
| University of Phoenix - Bay Area Campus | M,D,O |
| University of Phoenix - Central Valley Campus | M |
| University of Phoenix - Dallas Campus | M |
| University of Phoenix - Hawaii Campus | M |
| University of Phoenix - Houston Campus | M |
| University of Phoenix - Las Vegas Campus | M |
| University of Phoenix–Online Campus | M,O |
| University of Phoenix - Phoenix Campus | M |
| University of Phoenix - Sacramento Valley Campus | M,O |
| University of Phoenix - San Diego Campus | M |
| University of Pikeville | M |
| University of Pittsburgh | M,D* |
| University of Portland | M,D |
| University of Prince Edward Island | M,D |
| University of Puerto Rico at Rio Piedras | M,D |
| University of Puget Sound | M |
| University of Redlands | M,D,O |
| University of Regina | M,D,O |
| University of Rhode Island | M,D |
| University of Rio Grande | M |
| University of Rochester | M,D |
| University of St. Francis (IL) | M,D,O |
| University of Saint Francis (IN) | M |
| University of Saint Joseph | M |
| University of Saint Mary | M |
| University of St. Thomas (MN) | M,D,O |
| University of St. Thomas (TX) | M,D |
| University of San Diego | M,D,O |
| University of San Francisco | M,D |
| University of Saskatchewan | M,D,O |
| The University of Scranton | M |
| University of Sioux Falls | M,O |
| University of South Africa | M,D |
| University of South Alabama | M,D,O |
| University of South Carolina | M,D,O |
| University of South Carolina Upstate | M |
| University of South Dakota | M,D,O |
| University of Southern California | M,D |
| University of Southern Indiana | M,D |
| University of Southern Maine | M,D,O |
| University of Southern Mississippi | M,D,O |
| University of South Florida | M,D,O |
| University of South Florida, St. Petersburg | M |
| The University of Tampa | M |
| The University of Tennessee | M,D,O |
| The University of Tennessee at Chattanooga | M,D,O |
| The University of Tennessee at Martin | M |
| The University of Texas at Arlington | M,D |
| The University of Texas at Austin | M,D |
| The University of Texas at El Paso | M,D |
| The University of Texas of the Permian Basin | M |
| The University of Texas Rio Grande Valley | M,D |
| University of the Cumberlands | M,D,O |
| University of the Incarnate Word | M,D |
| University of the Pacific | M,D,O |
| University of the Sacred Heart | M,O |
| University of the Southwest | M |
| University of the Virgin Islands | M,D,O |
| The University of Toledo | M,D,O |
| University of Toronto | M,D |
| University of Utah | M,D,O |
| University of Vermont | M,D |
| University of Victoria | M,D |
| University of Virginia | M,D,O |
| University of Washington | M,D |
| University of Washington, Bothell | M |
| University of Washington, Tacoma | M |
| The University of West Alabama | M,O |
| The University of Western Ontario | M |
| University of Windsor | M,D |
| University of Wisconsin–Eau Claire | M |
| University of Wisconsin–Green Bay | M |
| University of Wisconsin–La Crosse | M,O |
| University of Wisconsin–Madison | M,D,O |
| University of Wisconsin–Milwaukee | M,D,O* |
| University of Wisconsin–Oshkosh | M |
| University of Wisconsin–Platteville | M |
| University of Wisconsin–River Falls | M |
| University of Wisconsin–Stevens Point | M,D |
| University of Wisconsin–Stout | M,D,O |
| University of Wisconsin–Superior | M |
| University of Wisconsin–Whitewater | M,O |
| Université Laval | M,D,O |
| Upper Iowa University | M |
| Urbana University–A Branch Campus of Franklin University | M |
| Utah State University | M,D,O |
| Utah Valley University | M |
| Utica College | M,O |
| Valley City State University | M |
| Valparaiso University | M,O |
| Vanderbilt University | M,D* |
| Vanguard University of Southern California | M |
| Villanova University | M |
| Virginia Commonwealth University | M,D,O |
| Virginia International University | M |
| Virginia Polytechnic Institute and State University | M,O |
| Virginia State University | M,D |
| Virginia Union University | M |
| Virginia Wesleyan University | M |
| Viterbo University | M,O |
| Wagner College | M |
| Wake Forest University | M |
| Walden University | M,D,O |
| Walla Walla University | M |
| Walsh University | M |
| Warner Pacific University | M |
| Warner University | M |
| Washburn University | M |
| Washington State University | M,D |
| Washington University in St. Louis | M,D |
| Wayland Baptist University | M |
| Wayne State College | M,O |
| Wayne State University | M,D,O |
| Weber State University | M |
| Webster University | M,O |
| Wesleyan College | M |
| Wesley College | M |
| Westcliff University | M |
| Western Carolina University | M |
| Western Colorado University | M |
| Western Connecticut State University | M,D |
| Western Governors University | M,O |
| Western Illinois University | M,D,O |
| Western Michigan University | M,D,O |
| Western New Mexico University | M |
| Western Oregon University | M |
| Western Washington University | M |
| Westfield State University | M |
| West Liberty University | M |
| Westminster College (UT) | M |
| West Texas A&M University | M |
| West Virginia University | M,D |
| Wheaton College | M |
| Whittier College | M |
| Whitworth University | M |
| Wichita State University | M,D,O |
| Widener University | M,D |
| William & Mary | M,D,O* |
| William Carey University | M,O |
| William Jessup University | M |
| William Jewell College | M |
| Williams Baptist University | M |
| Wilmington College | M |
| Wilmington University | M,D |
| Wilson College | M |
| Wingate University | M,D,O |
| Winona State University | O |
| Winston-Salem State University | M |
| Winthrop University | M |
| Wittenberg University | M |
| Worcester State University | M,O |
| Wright State University | M,O |
| Xavier University | M,D* |
| Xavier University of Louisiana | M |
| York College of Pennsylvania | M |
| York University | M,D |
| Youngstown State University | M,D,O |

## EDUCATIONAL LEADERSHIP AND ADMINISTRATION

| | |
|---|---|
| Abilene Christian University | D |
| Acacia University | M |
| Acadia University | M |
| Adams State University | M |
| Alabama State University | M,D,O |
| Albany State University | M,O |
| Alliant International University - San Diego | M,D,O |
| Alliant International University–San Francisco | M,D,O |
| Alverno College | M |
| American College of Education | M |
| American InterContinental University Online | M |
| American International College | M,D |
| American Public University System | M,D |
| American University | M,O |
| The American University in Cairo | M |
| Anderson University (SC) | M |
| Andrews University | M,D,O |
| Angelo State University | M |
| Antioch University New England | M,O |
| Appalachian State University | M,O |
| Arcadia University | M,D,O |
| Argosy University, Atlanta | M,D,O |
| Argosy University, Chicago | M,D,O |
| Argosy University, Hawaii | M,D |
| Argosy University, Los Angeles | M,D |
| Argosy University, Northern Virginia | M,D,O |
| Argosy University, Orange County | M,D |
| Argosy University, Phoenix | M,D,O |
| Argosy University, Seattle | M,D |
| Argosy University, Tampa | M,D,O |
| Argosy University, Twin Cities | M,D,O |
| Arizona State University at Tempe | M,D |
| Arkansas State University | M,D,O |
| Arkansas Tech University | M,D,O |
| Arlington Baptist University | M |
| Asbury University | M |
| Ashland University | M,D |
| Auburn University | M,D,O |
| Auburn University at Montgomery | M,O |
| Augusta University | M,O |
| Aurora University | M,D |
| Azusa Pacific University | M,D |
| Baldwin Wallace University | M |
| Ball State University | M,D,O |
| Bank Street College of Education | M |
| Barry University | M,D,O |
| Baruch College of the City University of New York | M,O |
| Bayamón Central University | M,O |
| Baylor University | M,O |
| Bay Path University | M |
| Belhaven University (MS) | M,D,O |
| Bellarmine University | M,D,O |
| Benedictine College | M |
| Berry College | O |
| Bethel University (MN) | M,D,O |
| Bethel University (TN) | M |
| Binghamton University, State University of New York | M,D,O |
| Bloomsburg University of Pennsylvania | M |
| Bluffton University | M |
| Bob Jones University | M,D,O |
| Boise State University | M,D,O |
| Bowie State University | M,D |
| Bowling Green State University | M,D,O |
| Bradley University | M |
| Brandeis University | M,O |
| Brandman University | M,D |
| Brandon University | M,O |
| Bridgewater State University | M,O |
| Brigham Young University | M,D |
| Brooklyn College of the City University of New York | M |
| Buffalo State College, State University of New York | O |
| Butler University | M,O |
| Cabrini University | M,D |
| Cairn University | M,O |
| Caldwell University | M,D,O |
| California Baptist University | M |
| California Coast University | M,D |
| California Lutheran University | M,D |
| California Polytechnic State University, San Luis Obispo | M |
| California State Polytechnic University, Pomona | D |
| California State University, East Bay | M,D |
| California State University, Fresno | M,D |
| California State University, Fullerton | M,D |
| California State University, Long Beach | M,D |
| California State University, Northridge | M,D |
| California State University, Sacramento | M,D,O |
| California State University, San Bernardino | M,D |
| California State University, San Marcos | M,D |
| California State University, Stanislaus | M,D |
| California University of Pennsylvania | M,D |
| Calumet College of Saint Joseph | M |
| Calvary University | M |
| Cambridge College | M,D,O |
| Cameron University | M |
| Campbellsville University | M |
| Campbell University | M |
| Canisius College | M,O |
| Capella University | M,D |
| Caribbean University | M,D |
| Carroll University | M |
| Carson-Newman University | M |
| Carthage College | M,O |
| Castleton University | M,O |
| The Catholic University of America | M,O |
| Centenary University | M,D |
| Central Connecticut State University | M,D,O |
| Central Michigan University | M,D,O |
| Central Washington University | M |
| Chadron State College | M,O |
| Chaminade University of Honolulu | M |
| Chapman University | M,D,O |
| Charleston Southern University | M |
| Chestnut Hill College | M |
| Cheyney University of Pennsylvania | M,O |
| Chicago State University | M,D |
| Christian Brothers University | M |
| The Citadel, The Military College of South Carolina | M,O |
| City College of the City University of New York | M,O |
| City University of Seattle | M,D,O |
| Claremont Graduate University | M,D,O |
| Clark Atlanta University | M,D,O |
| Clarke University | M |
| Clarks Summit University | M |
| Clemson University | M,D,O |
| Cleveland State University | M,D,O |
| Coastal Carolina University | M,O |
| The College of New Jersey | M,O |
| The College of New Rochelle | M,O |
| College of Saint Elizabeth | M,D,O |
| College of Saint Mary | M |
| The College of Saint Rose | M,O |
| College of Staten Island of the City University of New York | O |
| Colorado Mesa University | M,O |
| Colorado State University | M,D |

*M—masters degree; D—doctorate; O—other advanced degree; *—Close-Up and/or Display*

| | |
|---|---|
| Colorado State University–Global Campus | M |
| Columbia College (MO) | M |
| Columbia College (SC) | M |
| Columbia International University | M,D,O |
| Columbus State University | M,D,O |
| Concordia University (United States) | M,D |
| Concordia University Ann Arbor | M |
| Concordia University Chicago | M,D |
| Concordia University Irvine | M |
| Concordia University, Nebraska | M |
| Concordia University, St. Paul | M,D,O |
| Concordia University Wisconsin | M |
| Concord University | M |
| Converse College | M,O |
| Creighton University | M,D |
| Dakota Wesleyan University | M |
| Dallas Baptist University | M,D |
| Dallas Theological Seminary | M,D,O |
| Delaware State University | M,D |
| Delaware Valley University | M |
| Delta State University | M,D,O |
| DePaul University | M,D |
| DeVry University–Folsom Campus | M |
| Doane University | M,D,O |
| Drake University | M,D,O |
| Drexel University | M,D |
| Drury University | M |
| Duquesne University | M,D,O |
| D'Youville College | M,D |
| East Carolina University | M,D,O |
| Eastern Illinois University | M,O |
| Eastern Kentucky University | M |
| Eastern Michigan University | M,D,O |
| Eastern Nazarene College | M,O |
| Eastern New Mexico University | M |
| Eastern University | M,O |
| Eastern Washington University | M |
| East Tennessee State University | M,D,O |
| Edinboro University of Pennsylvania | M |
| Elizabeth City State University | M |
| Elmhurst University | M |
| Emporia State University | M |
| Endicott College | M,D |
| Evangel University | M,D |
| Fairleigh Dickinson University, Florham Campus | M |
| Fairleigh Dickinson University, Metropolitan Campus | M |
| Fayetteville State University | M,D |
| Felician University | M,O |
| Ferris State University | D |
| Fitchburg State University | M,O |
| Florida Agricultural and Mechanical University | M,D |
| Florida Atlantic University | M,D,O |
| Florida Gulf Coast University | M |
| Florida State University | M,D,O |
| Fordham University | M,D,O |
| Fort Hays State University | M,O |
| Fort Lewis College | M,O |
| Framingham State University | M |
| Franciscan University of Steubenville | M |
| Freed-Hardeman University | M,O |
| Fresno Pacific University | M |
| Frostburg State University | M,D |
| Furman University | M,O |
| Gannon University | D,O |
| Gardner-Webb University | M,D,O |
| Gateway Seminary | M,D,O |
| Geneva College | M |
| George Fox University | M,D,O |
| George Mason University | M,O |
| The George Washington University | M,D,O |
| Georgia College & State University | M,O |
| Georgian Court University | M,O |
| Georgia Southern University | M,D,O |
| Georgia State University | M,D,O |
| Gonzaga University | M,D |
| Gordon College | M,O |
| Goucher College | M,O |
| Governors State University | M,D |
| Graceland University (IA) | M |
| Grambling State University | M,D,O |
| Grand Canyon University | M,D,O |
| Grand Valley State University | M,O |
| Grand View University | M,O |
| Granite State College | M |
| Gratz College | M,D |
| Hampton University | M,D |
| Harding University | M,O |
| Hardin-Simmons University | D |
| Harvard University | M,D* |
| Hawaii Pacific University | M |
| Henderson State University | M,O |
| Heritage University | M |
| High Point University | M,D |
| High Tech High Graduate School of Education | M |
| Hofstra University | M,D,O |
| Holy Family College | M |
| Holy Family University | M,D |
| Hood College | M,O |
| Hope International University | M |
| Houston Baptist University | M,D |
| Howard Payne University | M |
| Howard University | M,D,O |
| Hunter College of the City University of New York | D,O |
| Husson University | M,O |
| Huston-Tillotson University | M |
| Idaho State University | M,D,O |
| Illinois State University | M,D |
| Immaculata University | M,D,O |
| Indiana State University | M,D,O |
| Indiana University Bloomington | M,D,O |
| Indiana University Northwest | M,O |
| Indiana University of Pennsylvania | D,O |
| Indiana University-Purdue University Indianapolis | M,O |
| Indiana University South Bend | M,O |
| Indiana Wesleyan University | M,O |
| Instituto Tecnologico de Santo Domingo | M,O |
| Instituto Tecnológico y de Estudios Superiores de Monterrey, Campus Central de Veracruz | M |
| Instituto Tecnológico y de Estudios Superiores de Monterrey, Campus Ciudad Juárez | M |
| Instituto Tecnológico y de Estudios Superiores de Monterrey, Campus Estado de México | M,D |
| Instituto Tecnológico y de Estudios Superiores de Monterrey, Campus Irapuato | M,D |
| Inter American University of Puerto Rico, Aguadilla Campus | M |
| Inter American University of Puerto Rico, Arecibo Campus | M |
| Inter American University of Puerto Rico, Barranquitas Campus | M |
| Inter American University of Puerto Rico, Fajardo Campus | M |
| Inter American University of Puerto Rico, Metropolitan Campus | M,D |
| Iona College | M |
| Iowa State University of Science and Technology | M,D |
| Jackson State University | M,D,O |
| Jacksonville State University | M,O |
| Jacksonville University | M |
| James Madison University | M |
| Johnson & Wales University | D |
| Kansas State University | M,D,O |
| Kean University | M,D |
| Keiser University | M,D,O |
| Kennesaw State University | M,D,O |
| Kent State University | M,D,O |
| Keystone College | M |
| Kutztown University of Pennsylvania | M |
| Lamar University | M,D |
| La Salle University | M,O |
| Lasell College | M,O |
| La Sierra University | M,D,O |
| Lee University | M,O |
| Lehigh University | M,D,O |
| Le Moyne College | M,O |
| Lenoir-Rhyne University | M |
| Lesley University | M,D,O |
| LeTourneau University | M |
| Lewis & Clark College | M,D,O |
| Lewis University | M,D |
| Lincoln Memorial University | M,D,O |
| Lindenwood University | M,D,O |
| Lindenwood University–Belleville | M |
| Lindsey Wilson College | M |
| Lipscomb University | M,D,O |
| Lock Haven University of Pennsylvania | M |
| Long Island University - Brentwood Campus | M,O |
| Long Island University - Brooklyn | M,O |
| Long Island University - Hudson | M,O |
| Long Island University - Post | M,D,O |
| Loras College | M |
| Louisiana College | M |
| Louisiana State University and Agricultural & Mechanical College | M,D,O |
| Louisiana State University in Shreveport | M,D |
| Louisiana Tech University | M,D,O |
| Lourdes University | M |
| Loyola Marymount University | M,D |
| Loyola University Chicago | M,D,O |
| Loyola University Maryland | M,O |
| Lynn University | M,D |
| Madonna University | M |
| Manhattan College | M,O |
| Manhattanville College | M,D,O |
| Marconi International University | M,D |
| Marian University (WI) | M,D |
| Marquette University | M,D,O |
| Marshall University | M |
| Martin Luther College | M |
| Mary Baldwin University | M |
| Marygrove College | M,O |
| Maryville University of Saint Louis | M,D |
| Marywood University | M,D |
| Massachusetts College of Liberal Arts | M,O |
| McDaniel College | M |
| McGill University | M,D,O |
| McKendree University | M,D,O |
| McNeese State University | M,O |
| Memorial University of Newfoundland | M,D,O |
| Mercer University | M,D,O |
| Mercer University | M,D,O |
| Mercy College | M,O |
| Mercyhurst University | M,O |
| Miami University | M,D |
| Michigan State University | M,D,O |
| Middle Tennessee State University | M,O |
| Midwestern State University | M |
| Millersville University of Pennsylvania | M,D |
| Milligan University | M,D,O |
| Mills College | |
| Minnesota State University Mankato | M |
| Minnesota State University Moorhead | M,D,O |
| Mississippi College | M,D,O |
| Mississippi State University | M,D,O |
| Mississippi University for Women | M |
| Missouri Baptist University | M,O |
| Missouri State University | M,O |
| Monmouth University | M,D,O |
| Montana State University | M,D,O |
| Montclair State University | M,D |
| Morehead State University | M,O |
| Morgan State University | M,D |
| Mount Holyoke College | M |
| Mount Mercy University | M |
| Murray State University | M,D,O |
| National American University (TX) | M,D |
| National Louis University | M,D,O |
| National University | M,O |
| Nebraska Christian College of Hope International University | M |
| Neumann University | M,D |
| New England College | M,D |
| New Jersey City University | M |
| Newman University | M |
| New Mexico Highlands University | M |
| New Mexico State University | M,D |
| New York University | M,D,O |
| Niagara University | M,D,O |
| Nicholls State University | M |
| Norfolk State University | M |
| North American University | M |
| North Carolina Agricultural and Technical State University | M,D |
| North Carolina Central University | M |
| North Carolina State University | M,D |
| North Central College | M |
| North Dakota State University | M,O |
| Northeastern Illinois University | M |
| Northeastern State University | M |
| Northeastern University | M |
| Northern Arizona University | M,D,O |
| Northern Illinois University | M,D,O |
| Northern Kentucky University | M,D,O |
| Northern Michigan University | M |
| Northern State University | M |
| Northwestern College | M,O |
| Northwestern Oklahoma State University | M |
| Northwestern State University of Louisiana | M,O |
| Northwestern University | M |
| Northwest Missouri State University | M,D,O |
| Northwest Nazarene University | M,D,O |
| Notre Dame de Namur University | M |
| Notre Dame of Maryland University | M,D |
| Oakland City University | M,D |
| Oakland University | M,D,O |
| Oglala Lakota College | M |
| Ohio Dominican University | M |
| The Ohio State University | M,D,O |
| Ohio University | M,D |
| Old Dominion University | M,D,O |
| Olivet Nazarene University | M |
| Oral Roberts University | M,D |
| Oregon State University | M,D |
| Ottawa University | M |
| Park University | M,O |
| Penn State University Park | M,D,O* |
| Pensacola Christian College | M,D,O |
| Piedmont International University | M,D |
| Pittsburg State University | M,O |
| Plymouth State University | M,D,O |
| Point Loma Nazarene University | M,O |
| Point Park University | M,D |
| Pontifical Catholic University of Puerto Rico | D |
| Post University | M |
| Prairie View A&M University | M,D |
| Prescott College | M,D |
| Providence College | M |
| Purdue University | M,D,O |
| Purdue University Fort Wayne | M,O |
| Purdue University Global | M |
| Purdue University Northwest | M |
| Queens College of the City University of New York | M,O |
| Queens University of Charlotte | M |
| Quincy University | M |
| Quinnipiac University | M,O |
| Radford University | M |
| Ramapo College of New Jersey | M |
| Regent University | M,D,O |
| Regis College (MA) | M,D |
| Regis University | M,O |
| Rhode Island College | M,O |
| Rivier University | M,D,O |
| Robert Morris University Illinois | M |
| Rocky Mountain College | M |
| Roosevelt University | M |
| Rowan University | M,D,O |
| Rutgers University - Camden | M |
| Rutgers University - New Brunswick | M,D |
| Sacred Heart University | O |
| Sage Graduate School | D |
| Saginaw Valley State University | M,O |
| St. Ambrose University | M |
| St. Bonaventure University | M,O |
| St. Cloud State University | M,D |
| Saint Francis University | M |
| St. Francis Xavier University | M |
| St. John Fisher College | M,D |
| St. John's University (NY) | M,D,O |
| St. Joseph's College, Long Island Campus | M |
| St. Joseph's College, New York | M |
| Saint Joseph's College of Maine | M |
| Saint Joseph's University | M,D,O |
| Saint Leo University | M,D,O |
| Saint Louis University | M,D,O |
| Saint Mary's College of California | M,D,O |
| St. Mary's University (United States) | M |
| Saint Mary's University of Minnesota | M,D,O |
| Saint Michael's College | M,O |
| Saint Peter's University | M,D |
| St. Thomas Aquinas College | M,O |
| St. Thomas University - Florida | M,D,O |
| Saint Vincent College | M |
| Saint Xavier University | M |
| Salem International University | M |
| Salem State University | M |
| Salisbury University | M |
| Samford University | M,D,O |
| Sam Houston State University | M,D |
| San Diego State University | M |
| San Francisco State University | M,D,O |
| San Ignacio University | M |
| San Jose State University | M,D |
| Santa Clara University | M,O |
| Schreiner University | M,O |
| Seattle Pacific University | M,D,O |
| Seattle University | M,D,O |
| Seton Hall University | M,D,O |
| Shasta Bible College | M |
| Shippensburg University of Pennsylvania | M,D |
| Siena Heights University | M,O |
| Sierra Nevada College | M |
| Simon Fraser University | M,D |
| Simpson University | M |
| SIT Graduate Institute | M |
| Slippery Rock University of Pennsylvania | M,D |
| Soka University of America | M |
| Sonoma State University | M,O |
| South Dakota State University | M |
| Southeastern Louisiana University | M,D |
| Southeastern Oklahoma State University | M |
| Southeastern University (FL) | M,D |
| Southeast Missouri State University | M,D,O |
| Southern Adventist University | M |
| Southern Arkansas University–Magnolia | M |
| Southern Connecticut State University | M,D,O |
| Southern Illinois University Carbondale | M,D |
| Southern Illinois University Edwardsville | M,D,O |
| Southern Methodist University | M,D |
| Southern New Hampshire University | M,D,O |
| Southern Oregon University | M |
| Southern University and Agricultural and Mechanical College | M |
| Southwest Baptist University | M,O |
| Southwestern Adventist University | M |
| Southwestern Assemblies of God University | M |
| Southwestern College (KS) | M,D |
| Southwestern Oklahoma State University | M |
| Southwest Minnesota State University | M |
| Spalding University | M,D |
| Springfield College | M,D,O |
| Stanford University | M |
| State University of New York at New Paltz | M,O |
| State University of New York at Oswego | O |
| State University of New York at Plattsburgh | O |
| State University of New York College at Cortland | O |
| Stephen F. Austin State University | M,D |
| Stetson University | M |
| Stevenson University | M |
| Stony Brook University, State University of New York | M,O |
| Suffolk University | M,O |
| Sul Ross State University | M |
| SUNY Brockport | M,O |
| Syracuse University | M,D,O |
| Tarleton State University | M,D,O |
| Teachers College, Columbia University | M,D |
| Teachers College of San Joaquin | M |
| Temple University | M,D* |
| Tennessee Technological University | M,O |
| Texas A&M International University | M |
| Texas A&M University | M,D |
| Texas A&M University–Central Texas | M,O |
| Texas A&M University–Commerce | M,D,O |
| Texas A&M University–Corpus Christi | M,D |
| Texas A&M University–Kingsville | M,D |
| Texas A&M University–San Antonio | M |
| Texas A&M University–Texarkana | M |
| Texas Christian University | M,D |
| Texas Southern University | M,D |
| Texas State University | M,D |
| Texas Tech University | M,D |
| Texas Woman's University | M,D |
| Thomas Edison State University | M,O |
| Thomas More University | M |
| Tiffin University | M |
| Towson University | M,O |
| Trevecca Nazarene University | M,D,O |
| Trident University International | M,D |
| Trinity Baptist College | M |
| Trinity University | M |
| Trinity Washington University | M |
| Trinity Western University | M |
| Troy University | M,O |
| Union College (KY) | M |
| Union University | M,D,O |
| Universidad Adventista de las Antillas | M |
| Universidad del Turabo | M,D |
| Universidad Iberoamericana | M,D |
| Universidad Metropolitana | M |
| Université de Moncton | M |
| Université de Montréal | M,D,O |
| Université de Sherbrooke | M |
| Université du Québec à Trois-Rivières | O |

| | |
|---|---|
| University at Albany, State University of New York | M,D,O |
| University at Buffalo, the State University of New York | M,D,O |
| The University of Akron | M,O |
| The University of Alabama | M,D,O |
| The University of Alabama at Birmingham | M,D,O |
| University of Alaska Anchorage | M,O |
| University of Alaska Southeast | M |
| University of Alberta | M,D,O |
| The University of Arizona | M,D,O |
| University of Arkansas | M,D,O |
| University of Arkansas at Little Rock | M,D,O |
| University of Arkansas at Monticello | M |
| University of Bridgeport | M,D,O |
| The University of British Columbia | M,D |
| University of Calgary | M,D |
| University of California, Berkeley | M,D |
| University of California, Irvine | M,D |
| University of California, Los Angeles | D |
| University of California, Riverside | M,D,O |
| University of California, San Diego | M,D |
| University of Central Arkansas | M,O |
| University of Central Florida | M,O |
| University of Central Missouri | M,D,O |
| University of Central Oklahoma | M |
| University of Cincinnati | M,D,O |
| University of Colorado Colorado Springs | M,D |
| University of Colorado Denver | M,D,O |
| University of Connecticut | M |
| University of Dayton | M,D,O |
| University of Delaware | M,D,O |
| University of Denver | M,D,O |
| University of Detroit Mercy | M,D,O |
| The University of Findlay | M,D |
| University of Florida | M,D,O |
| University of Georgia | D,O |
| University of Guam | M |
| University of Hartford | D |
| University of Hawaii at Manoa | M,D |
| University of Holy Cross | M,D |
| University of Houston | M,D |
| University of Houston–Clear Lake | M,D |
| University of Houston–Victoria | M,O |
| University of Idaho | M,O |
| University of Illinois at Chicago | M,D |
| University of Illinois at Springfield | M,O |
| University of Illinois at Urbana-Champaign | M,D,O |
| University of Indianapolis | M |
| The University of Iowa | M,D,O |
| The University of Kansas | M,D |
| University of Kentucky | M,D,O |
| University of La Verne | M,D,O |
| University of Lethbridge | M,D |
| University of Louisiana at Lafayette | M,D |
| University of Louisiana at Monroe | D |
| University of Louisville | M,D,O |
| University of Lynchburg | M,D |
| University of Maine | M,D,O |
| University of Maine at Farmington | M |
| University of Manitoba | M |
| University of Mary | M,D |
| University of Mary Hardin-Baylor | M,D |
| University of Maryland, College Park | M,D,O |
| University of Maryland Eastern Shore | D |
| University of Massachusetts Amherst | M,D,O |
| University of Massachusetts Boston | M,D,O |
| University of Massachusetts Dartmouth | D |
| University of Memphis | M,D,O |
| University of Michigan–Dearborn | M,D,O |
| University of Michigan–Flint | M,D,O |
| University of Minnesota, Twin Cities Campus | M,D |
| University of Mississippi | M,D,O |
| University of Missouri | M,D,O |
| University of Missouri–Kansas City | M,D,O |
| University of Mobile | M |
| University of Montana | M,D,O |
| University of Montevallo | M,O |
| University of Mount Union | M |
| University of Nebraska at Kearney | M,O |
| University of Nebraska at Omaha | M,D,O |
| University of Nebraska–Lincoln | M,D,O |
| University of Nevada, Las Vegas | M,D,O |
| University of Nevada, Reno | M,D,O |
| University of New England | M,D,O |
| University of New Hampshire | M,O |
| University of New Mexico | M,D,O |
| University of New Orleans | M,D |
| University of North Alabama | M,O |
| The University of North Carolina at Chapel Hill | M,D |
| The University of North Carolina at Charlotte | M,D,O |
| The University of North Carolina at Greensboro | M,D,O |
| The University of North Carolina at Pembroke | M |
| The University of North Carolina Wilmington | M,D |
| University of North Dakota | M,D,O |
| University of Northern Colorado | M,D,O |
| University of Northern Iowa | M,D |
| University of North Florida | M,D |
| University of North Georgia | D,O |
| University of North Texas | M,D,O |
| University of North Texas at Dallas | M |
| University of Oklahoma | M,D |
| University of Oregon | M,D |
| University of Pennsylvania | M,D |
| University of Phoenix - Bay Area Campus | M,D,O |
| University of Phoenix - Hawaii Campus | M |
| University of Phoenix - Las Vegas Campus | M |
| University of Phoenix–Online Campus | M,D,O |
| University of Phoenix - Phoenix Campus | M |
| University of Pikeville | M |
| University of Portland | M,D |
| University of Prince Edward Island | M,D |
| University of Puerto Rico at Rio Piedras | M,D |
| University of Regina | M |
| University of Rio Grande | M |
| University of Rochester | M,D |
| University of St. Francis (IL) | M,D,O |
| University of St. Thomas (MN) | M,D,O |
| University of St. Thomas (TX) | M,D |
| University of San Diego | M,D,O |
| University of San Francisco | M,D |
| University of Saskatchewan | M,D,O |
| The University of Scranton | M |
| University of Sioux Falls | M,O |
| University of South Africa | M,D |
| University of South Alabama | M,D |
| University of South Carolina | M,D,O |
| University of South Dakota | M,D,O |
| University of Southern California | D |
| University of Southern Indiana | M,O |
| University of Southern Maine | M,O |
| University of South Florida | M,D,O |
| University of South Florida, St. Petersburg | M |
| University of South Florida Sarasota-Manatee | M |
| The University of Tampa | M |
| The University of Tennessee | M,D,O |
| The University of Tennessee at Chattanooga | M,D,O |
| The University of Tennessee at Martin | M |
| The University of Texas at Arlington | M,D |
| The University of Texas at Austin | M,D |
| The University of Texas at El Paso | M,D |
| The University of Texas at San Antonio | M,D |
| The University of Texas of the Permian Basin | M |
| The University of Texas Rio Grande Valley | M,D |
| University of the Cumberlands | M,D,O |
| University of the Pacific | M,D,O |
| University of the Southwest | M |
| University of the Virgin Islands | M,D,O |
| The University of Toledo | M,D,O |
| University of Utah | M,D |
| University of Vermont | M,D |
| University of Victoria | M,D |
| University of Virginia | M,D,O |
| University of Washington | M,D |
| University of Washington, Bothell | M |
| University of Washington, Tacoma | M |
| The University of West Alabama | M,O |
| University of West Florida | M,D |
| University of Wisconsin–Madison | M,D,O |
| University of Wisconsin–Milwaukee | M,D,O* |
| University of Wisconsin–Oshkosh | M |
| University of Wisconsin–Stevens Point | M,D |
| University of Wisconsin–Superior | M,O |
| University of Wisconsin–Whitewater | M |
| University of Wyoming | M,D,O |
| Université Laval | M,D,O |
| Upper Iowa University | M |
| Ursuline College | M |
| Utah Valley University | M |
| Valdosta State University | M,D,O |
| Valparaiso University | M,O |
| Vanderbilt University | D* |
| Vanguard University of Southern California | M |
| Villanova University | M |
| Virginia Commonwealth University | M,D |
| Virginia Polytechnic Institute and State University | M,D,O |
| Virginia State University | M |
| Virginia Theological Seminary | M,D |
| Viterbo University | M,O |
| Walden University | M,D,O |
| Waldorf University | M |
| Walla Walla University | M |
| Washburn University | M |
| Washington State University | M,D |
| Wayland Baptist University | M |
| Waynesburg University | M,D |
| Wayne State College | M,O |
| Wayne State University | M,D,O |
| Western Colorado University | M |
| Western Connecticut State University | D |
| Western Governors University | M,O |
| Western Illinois University | M,D,O |
| Western Kentucky University | M,D,O |
| Western Michigan University | M,D,O |
| Western New Mexico University | M |
| Western Washington University | M |
| West Liberty University | M |
| West Texas A&M University | M |
| West Virginia University | M,D |
| Wheeling Jesuit University | M |
| Whittier College | M |
| Whitworth University | M |
| Wichita State University | M,D,O |
| Widener University | M,D |
| William & Mary | M,D* |
| William Woods University | M,D,O |
| Wilmington University | M,D |
| Wingate University | M,D,O |
| Winona State University | M,O |
| Winthrop University | M |
| Wisconsin Lutheran College | M |
| Worcester State University | M,O |
| Wright State University | O |
| Xavier University | M,D* |
| Xavier University of Louisiana | M |
| Yeshiva University | M,D,O |
| York College of Pennsylvania | M |
| Youngstown State University | M,D,O |

## EDUCATIONAL MEASUREMENT AND EVALUATION

| | |
|---|---|
| American InterContinental University Online | M |
| American University | M,O |
| Arizona State University at Tempe | D |
| Ball State University | M,D,O |
| Brandeis University | O |
| Brigham Young University | D |
| Cambridge College | M,D,O |
| Claremont Graduate University | M,D,O |
| Clemson University | M,D,O |
| College of Saint Mary | M |
| Duquesne University | M |
| Eastern Michigan University | M,O |
| Florida State University | M,D,O |
| Georgetown University | M |
| Georgia Southern University | M,D,O |
| Georgia State University | M,D |
| Houston Baptist University | M,D |
| Indiana University Bloomington | M,D,O |
| Iowa State University of Science and Technology | M,D |
| James Madison University | M,D |
| Kent State University | M,D |
| Louisiana State University and Agricultural & Mechanical College | M,D,O |
| Loyola University Chicago | M,D,O |
| McNeese State University | M,O |
| Michigan State University | M,D,O |
| Missouri State University | O |
| Missouri Western State University | M,O |
| Montclair State University | O |
| Mount Saint Vincent University | M |
| New Mexico State University | M,D,O |
| North Carolina State University | D |
| Ohio University | M,D |
| Old Dominion University | D |
| Rutgers University - New Brunswick | M |
| Seton Hall University | M,D,O |
| Southern Connecticut State University | M,D,O |
| Southwestern Oklahoma State University | M |
| Sul Ross State University | M,O |
| Syracuse University | M,D,O |
| Teachers College, Columbia University | M,D |
| Teachers College of San Joaquin | M |
| Tennessee Technological University | D |
| Texas A&M University–San Antonio | M |
| University of Arkansas | M,D |
| The University of British Columbia | M,D,O |
| University of Calgary | M,D |
| University of California, Riverside | M,D,O |
| University of Central Florida | O |
| University of Colorado Boulder | D |
| University of Colorado Denver | M,D |
| University of Denver | M,D,O |
| University of Florida | M,D,O |
| University of Illinois at Chicago | M,D |
| The University of Iowa | M,D,O |
| The University of Kansas | M,D |
| University of Kentucky | M,D |
| University of Louisville | M,D |
| University of Maryland, College Park | M,D |
| University of Massachusetts Amherst | M,D,O |
| University of Memphis | M,D |
| University of Miami | M,D |
| University of Michigan–Dearborn | M |
| University of Minnesota, Twin Cities Campus | M,D |
| University of Missouri–St. Louis | M,O |
| University of Nebraska–Lincoln | M,D,O |
| The University of North Carolina at Chapel Hill | M,D |
| The University of North Carolina at Greensboro | D |
| University of Northern Colorado | M,D |
| University of Northern Iowa | M |
| University of North Texas | M,D,O |
| University of Pennsylvania | M,D |
| University of Puerto Rico at Rio Piedras | M |
| University of St. Thomas (TX) | M,D |
| University of Saskatchewan | M,D |
| University of South Carolina | M,D |
| University of South Florida | O |
| The University of Tennessee | M,D,O |
| The University of Texas at El Paso | M |
| The University of Texas at San Antonio | M,O |
| The University of Toledo | M,D,O |
| University of Victoria | M,D |
| University of Virginia | M,D,O |
| University of Washington | M,D |
| University of Wisconsin–Milwaukee | M,D,O* |
| Université Laval | M,D,O |
| Utah State University | M,D |
| Virginia Commonwealth University | D |
| Virginia Polytechnic Institute and State University | M,D,O |
| Walden University | M,D,O |
| Washington University in St. Louis | D |
| Wayland Baptist University | M |
| Wayne State University | M,D,O |
| Western Michigan University | M,D,O |
| West Texas A&M University | M |

## EDUCATIONAL MEDIA/INSTRUCTIONAL TECHNOLOGY

| | |
|---|---|
| Alabama Agricultural and Mechanical University | M,O |
| Alabama State University | M,D,O |
| Alverno College | M |
| American College of Education | M |
| American InterContinental University Online | M |
| American University | M,O |
| Appalachian State University | M,O |
| Arcadia University | M,D,O |
| Argosy University, Atlanta | M,D,O |
| Argosy University, Orange County | M,D |
| Argosy University, Phoenix | M,D,O |
| Argosy University, Seattle | M,D |
| Argosy University, Twin Cities | M,D,O |
| Arizona State University at Tempe | M,O |
| Arkansas Tech University | M,D,O |
| Auburn University | M,D,O |
| Auburn University at Montgomery | M,O |
| Augustana University | M |
| Augusta University | D |
| Aurora University | M,D |
| Avila University | M |
| Azusa Pacific University | M |
| Baldwin Wallace University | M |
| Ball State University | M,D |
| Barry University | M,D,O |
| Bay Path University | M |
| Bellevue University | M |
| Bloomsburg University of Pennsylvania | M,O |
| Boise State University | M,D,O |
| Bowling Green State University | M |
| Brandman University | M,D |
| Bridgewater State University | M |
| Brigham Young University | M,D |
| Buffalo State College, State University of New York | M |
| California Baptist University | M |
| California State University, East Bay | M |
| California State University, Fullerton | M |
| California State University, Northridge | M |
| California State University, Sacramento | M,D,O |
| California State University, Stanislaus | M |
| Cambridge College | M,D,O |
| Canisius College | M,O |
| Capella University | M,D |
| Caribbean University | M,D |
| Central Michigan University | M,D,O |
| Chestnut Hill College | M,O |
| Clarion University of Pennsylvania | M |
| Cleveland State University | D |
| Coastal Carolina University | M,O |
| Coker College | M |
| College of Mount Saint Vincent | M,O |
| Colorado Christian University | M |
| Colorado State University-Pueblo | M |
| Concordia University (United States) | M,D |
| Concordia University (Canada) | M,O |
| Concordia University Chicago | M |
| Concordia University Irvine | M |
| Concordia University, St. Paul | M,D,O |
| Dakota State University | M |
| Dallas Baptist University | M |
| Delaware Valley University | M |
| DeSales University | M,O |
| DeVry University–Folsom Campus | M |
| Drexel University | M,D |
| Drury University | M |
| Duquesne University | M,D,O |
| East Carolina University | M,O |
| Eastern Connecticut State University | M |
| Eastern Michigan University | M,O |
| Eastern New Mexico University | M |
| East Stroudsburg University of Pennsylvania | M |
| East Tennessee State University | M,O |
| Emporia State University | M,O |
| Fairfield University | M,O |
| Fairleigh Dickinson University, Florham Campus | M,O |
| Fairleigh Dickinson University, Metropolitan Campus | M,O |
| Fairmont State University | M |
| Florida Atlantic University | M |
| Florida International University | M,D,O |
| Florida State University | M,D,O |
| Fontbonne University | M |
| Fort Hays State University | M |

*M—masters degree; D—doctorate; O—other advanced degree; *—Close-Up and/or Display*

| | |
|---|---|
| Framingham State University | M |
| Franklin University | M |
| Fresno Pacific University | M |
| Frostburg State University | M,D |
| Full Sail University | M |
| George Fox University | M,O |
| George Mason University | M |
| The George Washington University | M,O |
| Georgia College & State University | M |
| Georgian Court University | M,O |
| Georgia Southern University | M,O |
| Goucher College | M,O |
| Graceland University (IA) | M |
| Grambling State University | M,D,O |
| Grand Canyon University | M,D,O |
| Grand Valley State University | M |
| Harrisburg University of Science and Technology | M |
| Harvard University | M,O* |
| Hofstra University | M,D,O |
| Houston Baptist University | M,D |
| Idaho State University | M,D |
| Indiana State University | M,D |
| Indiana University Bloomington | M,D |
| Indiana University of Pennsylvania | M,D |
| Indiana University South Bend | M,O |
| Instituto Tecnológico y de Estudios Superiores de Monterrey, Campus Central de Veracruz | M |
| Instituto Tecnológico y de Estudios Superiores de Monterrey, Campus Ciudad de México | M,D |
| Instituto Tecnológico y de Estudios Superiores de Monterrey, Campus Ciudad Juárez | M,D |
| Instituto Tecnológico y de Estudios Superiores de Monterrey, Campus Estado de México | M,D |
| Instituto Tecnológico y de Estudios Superiores de Monterrey, Campus Irapuato | M,D |
| Inter American University of Puerto Rico, Metropolitan Campus | M |
| Iowa State University of Science and Technology | M,D |
| Jacksonville State University | M |
| James Madison University | M |
| Johnson University | M,D,O |
| Kansas State University | M,D,O |
| Keiser University | D,O |
| Kennesaw State University | M,D,O |
| Kent State University | M,D,O |
| Kutztown University of Pennsylvania | M |
| Lamar University | M,D |
| La Salle University | M,O |
| Lawrence Technological University | M,O |
| Lehigh University | M,D |
| Lenoir-Rhyne University | M |
| Lesley University | M,D,O |
| Lewis University | M |
| Lindenwood University | M,D,O |
| Lipscomb University | M,D,O |
| Long Island University - Post | M,D,O |
| Longwood University | M |
| Louisiana State University and Agricultural & Mechanical College | M,D,O |
| Loyola University Maryland | M |
| Manhattan College | M |
| Marconi International University | M,D |
| Marian University (WI) | M,D |
| Marlboro College | M,O |
| Martin Luther College | M |
| Marygrove College | M,O |
| Massachusetts College of Liberal Arts | M,O |
| McDaniel College | M |
| McNeese State University | M,O |
| Memorial University of Newfoundland | M,D,O |
| Michigan State University | M,D,O |
| MidAmerica Nazarene University | M |
| Middle Tennessee State University | M,O |
| Midwestern State University | M |
| Misericordia University | M |
| Mississippi State University | M,D,O |
| Missouri Southern State University | M |
| Missouri State University | M |
| Molloy College | M,O |
| Montana State University Billings | M |
| Morehead State University | M,O |
| Murray State University | M,D,O |
| National Louis University | M,D,O |
| National University | M,O |
| Nazareth College of Rochester | M |
| New Jersey City University | M,D |
| New York University | M,D,O |
| North Carolina Agricultural and Technical State University | M |
| North Carolina Central University | M |
| North Carolina State University | M,D |
| Northeastern State University | M |
| Northern Arizona University | M,O |
| Northern Illinois University | M,D |
| Northern State University | M |
| Northwestern State University of Louisiana | M,O |
| Northwestern University | M,D |
| Northwest Missouri State University | M |
| Nova Southeastern University | M,D,O |
| Ohio University | M,D |
| Old Dominion University | M,D,O |
| Ottawa University | M |
| Pace University | M,O |
| Penn State University Park | M,D,O* |
| Pittsburg State University | M |
| Post University | M |
| Purdue University | M,D,O |
| Purdue University Global | M |
| Purdue University Northwest | M |
| Quinnipiac University | M |
| Ramapo College of New Jersey | M |
| Regent University | M,D,O |

| | |
|---|---|
| Rockford University | M |
| Rowan University | M,O |
| Saginaw Valley State University | M |
| St. Cloud State University | M,O |
| St. John Fisher College | M |
| Saint Mary's University of Minnesota | M |
| St. Thomas University - Florida | M,D,O |
| Saint Vincent College | M |
| Saint Xavier University | M |
| Salem State University | M |
| Samford University | M,D,O |
| San Diego State University | M,D |
| San Francisco State University | M |
| Seattle Pacific University | M |
| Seton Hall University | M |
| Seton Hill University | M |
| Simon Fraser University | M,D |
| Slippery Rock University of Pennsylvania | M,D |
| Southern Illinois University Edwardsville | M,O |
| Southern New Hampshire University | M,D,O |
| Southern University and Agricultural and Mechanical College | M |
| Stanford University | M |
| State University of New York College at Potsdam | M |
| State University of New York Empire State College | M |
| Stockton University | M |
| Stony Brook University, State University of New York | M |
| Strayer University | M |
| Syracuse University | M,O |
| Tarleton State University | M |
| Teachers College, Columbia University | M,D |
| Tennessee Technological University | M,O |
| Texas A&M University | M,D |
| Texas A&M University–Commerce | M,D,O |
| Texas A&M University–Corpus Christi | M,D |
| Texas A&M University–Kingsville | M |
| Texas A&M University–Texarkana | M |
| Texas State University | M |
| Texas Tech University | M,D |
| Thomas Edison State University | M,O |
| Tiffin University | M |
| Touro College | M |
| Towson University | M |
| Trevecca Nazarene University | M |
| Trident University International | M,D |
| University at Albany, State University of New York | M,D,O |
| University at Buffalo, the State University of New York | M,D,O |
| University of Alaska Southeast | M |
| University of Alberta | M,D |
| University of Arkansas | M |
| University of Arkansas at Little Rock | M |
| University of Central Arkansas | M |
| University of Central Florida | M,O |
| University of Central Missouri | M,D,O |
| University of Central Oklahoma | M |
| University of Colorado Denver | M |
| University of Connecticut | M,D |
| University of Dayton | M |
| The University of Findlay | M,D |
| University of Georgia | M,D,O |
| University of Hawaii at Manoa | M,D |
| University of Houston–Clear Lake | M |
| University of Houston–Victoria | M,O |
| The University of Kansas | M,D |
| University of Kentucky | M,D |
| University of Louisiana at Lafayette | M |
| University of Maine | M,D,O |
| University of Maine at Farmington | M |
| University of Maryland, Baltimore County | M,O |
| University of Maryland, College Park | M,D,O |
| University of Maryland Global Campus | M |
| University of Massachusetts Amherst | M,D,O |
| University of Massachusetts Boston | M,O |
| University of Memphis | M,D,O |
| University of Michigan–Dearborn | M |
| University of Michigan–Flint | M,D,O |
| University of Minnesota, Twin Cities Campus | M,D,O |
| University of Missouri | D |
| University of Nebraska at Kearney | M |
| University of Nevada, Las Vegas | M,D,O |
| University of New Hampshire | M,O |
| University of New Mexico | M,D,O |
| The University of North Carolina at Charlotte | M,D,O |
| The University of North Carolina at Greensboro | M,D,O |
| The University of North Carolina Wilmington | M |
| University of North Dakota | M |
| University of Northern Iowa | M |
| University of North Florida | M,D |
| University of Oklahoma | M,D,O |
| University of Pennsylvania | M |
| University of Phoenix–Online Campus | D,O |
| University of Saint Joseph | M |
| University of San Francisco | M,D |
| University of Sioux Falls | M,O |
| University of South Africa | M,D |
| University of South Alabama | M,D,O |
| University of South Carolina | M |

| | |
|---|---|
| University of South Carolina Aiken | M |
| University of South Dakota | M |
| University of South Florida | O |
| The University of Tampa | M |
| The University of Tennessee | M,D,O |
| The University of Texas at Austin | M,D |
| The University of Texas at San Antonio | M,D |
| The University of Texas Rio Grande Valley | M,D |
| University of the Sacred Heart | M |
| The University of Toledo | M,D,O |
| University of Utah | M,D,O |
| University of Virginia | M,D,O |
| University of Washington | M,D |
| The University of West Alabama | M,O |
| University of West Florida | M,D |
| University of Wisconsin–Milwaukee | M* |
| University of Wyoming | M,D |
| Université Laval | M,D |
| Utah State University | M,D,O |
| Utah Valley University | M |
| Valley City State University | M |
| Virginia Commonwealth University | M |
| Virginia Polytechnic Institute and State University | M,O |
| Walden University | M,D,O |
| Warner University | M |
| Wayland Baptist University | M |
| Waynesburg University | M,D |
| Wayne State University | M,D,O |
| Webster University | M,O |
| Western Connecticut State University | M |
| Western Governors University | M,O |
| Western Illinois University | M,O |
| Western Kentucky University | M,O |
| Western Michigan University | M,D,O |
| Western Oregon University | M |
| West Texas A&M University | M |
| West Virginia University | M,D |
| Widener University | M,D |
| William Woods University | M,D,O |
| Wilmington University | M,D |
| Wilson College | M |
| Wisconsin Lutheran College | M |
| Worcester Polytechnic Institute | M,D |
| York College of Pennsylvania | M |

## EDUCATIONAL POLICY

| | |
|---|---|
| American University | M,O |
| Arizona State University at Tempe | D |
| Ball State University | D |
| Brigham Young University | M,D |
| California State University, Sacramento | M,D,O |
| Cleveland State University | D |
| Cornell University | M,D |
| Eastern Michigan University | M |
| Florida State University | M,D,O |
| The George Washington University | M,D,O |
| Georgia State University | M,D,O |
| Harvard University | M* |
| Howard University | M,D,O |
| Illinois State University | M,D |
| Indiana University Bloomington | M,D,O |
| Loyola University Chicago | M,D |
| Marquette University | M,D,O |
| Michigan State University | D |
| New York University | M,D |
| Niagara University | M,D,O |
| Northwest Missouri State University | M,D,O |
| The Ohio State University | M,D,O |
| Oregon State University | M,D |
| Penn State University Park | M,D,O* |
| Rutgers University - Camden | M |
| Rutgers University - New Brunswick | D |
| Stanford University | M |
| Teachers College, Columbia University | M,D |
| University at Albany, State University of New York | M,D,O |
| University of Alberta | M,D,O |
| University of Arkansas | D |
| The University of British Columbia | M,D |
| University of California, Riverside | M,D,O |
| University of Colorado Boulder | M,D |
| University of Colorado Denver | M,D,O |
| University of Denver | M,D,O |
| University of Florida | M,D,O |
| University of Georgia | D,O |
| University of Hawaii at Manoa | D |
| University of Illinois at Chicago | M,D |
| University of Illinois at Urbana-Champaign | M,D,O |
| The University of Iowa | M,D,O |
| The University of Kansas | M,D |
| University of Kentucky | M,D |
| University of Maryland, Baltimore County | M,D |
| University of Massachusetts Amherst | M,D,O |
| University of Massachusetts Boston | D |
| University of Massachusetts Dartmouth | M,D,O |
| University of Minnesota, Twin Cities Campus | M,D |
| University of Mobile | M |
| The University of North Carolina Wilmington | M |
| University of Northern Colorado | M,D,O |
| University of Pennsylvania | M,D |
| University of Rochester | M,D |
| University of Southern California | D |
| The University of Texas at Arlington | M,D |
| University of Utah | M,D |
| University of Vermont | D |
| University of Virginia | D |
| University of Washington | M,D |
| The University of Western Ontario | M |

| | |
|---|---|
| University of Wisconsin–Madison | M,D,O |
| University of Wisconsin–Milwaukee | M,O* |
| Virginia Polytechnic Institute and State University | M,D,O |
| Wayne State University | M,D,O |

## EDUCATIONAL PSYCHOLOGY

| | |
|---|---|
| Alliant International University–Irvine | M,D,O |
| Alliant International University - Los Angeles | M,D,O |
| Alliant International University - San Diego | M,D,O |
| Alliant International University–San Francisco | M,D,O |
| American International College | M,D,O |
| Andrews University | M,D |
| Ball State University | M,D |
| Baylor University | M,D,O |
| Boston College | M,D |
| Brigham Young University | M,D |
| California Coast University | M,D |
| California State University, Long Beach | M,D |
| California State University, Northridge | M |
| Capella University | M,D |
| Chapman University | M,D,O |
| Clark Atlanta University | M |
| The College of Saint Rose | M,O |
| Eastern Michigan University | M,O |
| Edinboro University of Pennsylvania | M,O |
| Florida State University | M,D,O |
| Fordham University | M,D |
| Fordham University | M,D |
| George Mason University | M,O |
| Georgia State University | M,D |
| The Graduate Center, City University of New York | D |
| Harvard University | M* |
| Holy Names University | M,O |
| Howard University | D |
| Immaculata University | M,D,O |
| Indiana University Bloomington | M,D,O |
| Indiana University of Pennsylvania | M,O |
| Instituto Tecnologico de Santo Domingo | M,O |
| John Carroll University | M,O |
| Kent State University | M |
| La Sierra University | M,O |
| McGill University | M,D,O |
| Memorial University of Newfoundland | M,D,O |
| Miami University | M,O |
| Michigan School of Psychology | M,D,O |
| Michigan State University | M,D,O |
| Mississippi State University | M,D,O |
| Mount Saint Vincent University | M |
| National Louis University | M,D,O |
| New York University | M,D |
| Northern Arizona University | M,D,O |
| Northern Illinois University | M,D,O |
| Old Dominion University | D |
| Penn State University Park | M,D,O* |
| Philadelphia College of Osteopathic Medicine | M,D,O |
| Pontifical Catholic University of Puerto Rico | M |
| Regent University | M,D,O |
| Rutgers University - New Brunswick | M,D |
| Simon Fraser University | M,D |
| Southern Illinois University Carbondale | M,D |
| State University of New York College at Oneonta | M,O |
| Teachers College, Columbia University | M,D,O |
| Temple University | M,D,O* |
| Tennessee Technological University | M,O |
| Texas A&M University | M,D |
| Texas A&M University–Central Texas | M,O |
| Texas A&M University–Commerce | M,D,O |
| Texas Tech University | M,D |
| Universidad de Iberoamerica | M,D |
| Université de Moncton | M |
| Université de Montréal | M,D,O |
| Université du Québec à Trois-Rivières | M,D |
| Université du Québec en Outaouais | M |
| University at Buffalo, the State University of New York | M,D,O |
| University of Alberta | M,D |
| The University of Arizona | M,D,O |
| University of California, Davis | M,D |
| University of California, Riverside | M,D,O |
| University of Colorado Boulder | M,D |
| University of Connecticut | M,D,O |
| University of Georgia | O |
| University of Hawaii at Manoa | M,D |
| University of Houston | M,D |
| University of Illinois at Chicago | M,D |
| University of Illinois at Urbana-Champaign | M,D,O |
| The University of Iowa | M,D,O |
| The University of Kansas | M,D |
| University of Kentucky | M,D,O |
| University of Louisville | M,D |
| The University of Manchester | M,D |
| University of Manitoba | M |
| University of Memphis | M,D |
| University of Minnesota, Twin Cities Campus | M,D,O |
| University of Missouri | M,D,O |
| University of Nebraska–Lincoln | M,D,O |
| University of Nevada, Reno | M,D,O |
| University of New Mexico | M,D |

| | |
|---|---|
| The University of North Carolina at Chapel Hill | M,D |
| University of Northern Colorado | M,D |
| University of Northern Iowa | M |
| University of North Texas | M,D,O |
| University of Oklahoma | M,D |
| University of Regina | M |
| University of Saskatchewan | M,D |
| University of South Africa | M,D |
| University of South Carolina | M,D |
| University of South Dakota | M,D,O |
| University of Southern California | D |
| University of Southern Maine | M,O |
| University of South Florida | M,D,O |
| The University of Tennessee | M,D,O |
| The University of Texas at Austin | M,D |
| The University of Texas at El Paso | M |
| The University of Texas at San Antonio | M,O |
| The University of Texas Rio Grande Valley | M |
| University of the Pacific | M,D,O |
| The University of Toledo | M,D,O |
| University of Utah | M,D,O |
| University of Victoria | M,D |
| University of Virginia | M,D,O |
| University of Washington | M,D |
| The University of Western Ontario | M |
| University of Wisconsin–Madison | M,D |
| University of Wisconsin–Milwaukee | M,D,O* |
| Université Laval | M,D |
| Virginia Commonwealth University | D |
| Walden University | M,D,O |
| Washington State University | M,D |
| Wayne State University | M,D,O |
| Webster University | M,O |
| West Virginia University | M,D |
| Wichita State University | M,D,O |
| Widener University | M,D |

## EDUCATION OF STUDENTS WITH SEVERE/MULTIPLE DISABILITIES

| | |
|---|---|
| California Baptist University | M |
| California State University, East Bay | M |
| California State University, Northridge | M |
| Chapman University | M,D,O |
| Cleveland State University | M |
| Georgia State University | M,D |
| Hofstra University | M,D,O |
| Hunter College of the City University of New York | M |
| Lesley University | M,D,O |
| Murray State University | M,O |
| Norfolk State University | M |
| Rhode Island College | M,O |
| Simmons University | M,D,O |
| Syracuse University | M |
| Teachers College, Columbia University | M,D,O |
| The University of Arizona | M,D,O |
| University of Central Oklahoma | M |
| University of Illinois at Urbana-Champaign | M,D,O |
| University of New Mexico | M,D,O |
| University of South Florida | O |
| University of Utah | M,D |
| University of Washington | M,D |
| Western Kentucky University | M,O |
| West Liberty University | M |

## EDUCATION OF THE GIFTED

| | |
|---|---|
| Albizu University - Miami | M,D |
| Arkansas State University | M,D,O |
| Ball State University | M,D,O |
| Barry University | M,D,O |
| Canisius College | M,O |
| Carthage College | M,O |
| The College of New Rochelle | O |
| Colorado Mesa University | M,O |
| Converse College | M |
| Eastern New Mexico University | M |
| Emporia State University | M |
| Florida Gulf Coast University | M |
| George Mason University | M |
| Grand Canyon University | M,D,O |
| Hardin-Simmons University | M |
| Hofstra University | M,D,O |
| James Madison University | M |
| Kent State University | M,D,O |
| Lindenwood University | M,D,O |
| Lynn University | M,D |
| Mary Baldwin University | M |
| McNeese State University | M |
| Meredith College | M,O |
| Midwest University | M,D |
| Millersville University of Pennsylvania | M |
| Mississippi University for Women | M |
| Morehead State University | M,O |
| Nebraska Christian College of Hope International University | M |
| Northeastern Illinois University | M |
| Pacific University | M |
| Regent University | M,D,O |
| St. Bonaventure University | M,O |
| St. John's University (NY) | D,O |
| St. Thomas University - Florida | M,D,O |
| Samford University | M,D,O |
| Southeastern University (FL) | M,D |
| Southern Arkansas University–Magnolia | M |
| Southern Methodist University | M,D |
| Teachers College, Columbia University | M,D |
| Tennessee Technological University | D |
| University at Buffalo, the State University of New York | M,D,O |
| The University of Alabama | M,D,O |
| University of Arkansas at Little Rock | M,O |
| University of Central Arkansas | M,O |
| University of Central Florida | M,O |
| University of Connecticut | O |
| University of Louisiana at Lafayette | M |
| University of Minnesota, Twin Cities Campus | M,D,O |
| University of Nebraska at Kearney | M |
| The University of North Carolina at Charlotte | M,D,O |
| University of Northern Colorado | M,D |
| University of North Texas | M,D,O |
| University of Southern Maine | M,O |
| The University of Toledo | M,D,O |
| University of Virginia | M,D,O |
| Viterbo University | M,O |
| Western Washington University | M |
| West Virginia University | M,D |
| Whitworth University | M |
| Wichita State University | M |
| William Carey University | M,O |
| Wilmington University | M,D |

## ELECTRICAL ENGINEERING

| | |
|---|---|
| Air Force Institute of Technology | M,D |
| Alfred University | M,D |
| The American University in Cairo | M,D,O |
| American University of Sharjah | M,D |
| Arizona State University at Tempe | M,D,O |
| Arkansas Tech University | M |
| Auburn University | M,D |
| Baylor University | M,D |
| Binghamton University, State University of New York | M,D |
| Boise State University | M,D |
| Boston University | M,D |
| Bradley University | M |
| Brigham Young University | M,D |
| Brown University | M,D |
| Bucknell University | M |
| California Institute of Technology | M,D,O |
| California Polytechnic State University, San Luis Obispo | M |
| California State Polytechnic University, Pomona | M |
| California State University, Chico | M |
| California State University, Fresno | M |
| California State University, Fullerton | M |
| California State University, Long Beach | M |
| California State University, Los Angeles | M |
| California State University, Northridge | M |
| California State University, Sacramento | M |
| Capitol Technology University | M |
| Carleton University | M,D |
| Carnegie Mellon University | M,D |
| Case Western Reserve University | M,D |
| The Catholic University of America | M,D |
| The Citadel, The Military College of South Carolina | M,O |
| City College of the City University of New York | M,D |
| Clarkson University | M |
| Clemson University | M,D |
| Cleveland State University | M,D |
| College of Staten Island of the City University of New York | M |
| Colorado School of Mines | M,D |
| Colorado State University | M,D |
| Colorado Technical University Aurora | M |
| Colorado Technical University Colorado Springs | M |
| Columbia University | M,D |
| Concordia University (Canada) | M,D |
| Cooper Union for the Advancement of Science and Art | M |
| Cornell University | M,D |
| Dalhousie University | M,D |
| Dartmouth College | M,D |
| Drexel University | M |
| Duke University | M,D |
| Embry-Riddle Aeronautical University–Daytona | M |
| Fairfield University | M,O |
| Fairleigh Dickinson University, Metropolitan Campus | M |
| Farmingdale State College | M |
| Florida Agricultural and Mechanical University | M,D |
| Florida Atlantic University | M,D |
| Florida Institute of Technology | M,D |
| Florida International University | M,D |
| Florida State University | M,D |
| Gannon University | M |
| George Mason University | M,D,O |
| The George Washington University | M,D,O |
| Georgia Institute of Technology | M,D |
| Georgia Southern University | M |
| Grand Valley State University | M |
| Harvard University | M,D* |
| Howard University | M,D |
| Illinois Institute of Technology | M,D |
| Indiana University-Purdue University Indianapolis | M,D |
| Instituto Tecnológico y de Estudios Superiores de Monterrey, Campus Chihuahua | M,O |
| Instituto Tecnológico y de Estudios Superiores de Monterrey, Campus Monterrey | M,D |
| Inter American University of Puerto Rico, Bayamón Campus | M |
| International Technological University | M,D |
| Iowa State University of Science and Technology | M,D |
| Johns Hopkins University | M,D,O |
| Kansas State University | M,D |
| Kennesaw State University | M |
| Kettering University | M |
| Lakehead University | M |
| Lamar University | M,D |
| Lawrence Technological University | M,D |
| Lehigh University | M,D |
| Louisiana State University and Agricultural & Mechanical College | M,D |
| Loyola Marymount University | M |
| Manhattan College | M |
| Marquette University | M,D,O |
| Marshall University | M |
| Massachusetts Institute of Technology | M,D,O |
| McGill University | M,D |
| McMaster University | M,D |
| McNeese State University | M |
| Memorial University of Newfoundland | M,D |
| Mercer University | M |
| Miami University | M |
| Michigan State University | M,D |
| Michigan Technological University | M,D,O |
| Mississippi State University | M,D |
| Missouri University of Science and Technology | M,D |
| Montana State University | M,D |
| Montana Technological University | M |
| Morgan State University | M,D,O |
| National University | M |
| Naval Postgraduate School | M,D,O |
| New Jersey Institute of Technology | M,D |
| New Mexico Institute of Mining and Technology | M |
| New York Institute of Technology | M |
| New York University | M,D |
| Norfolk State University | M |
| North Carolina Agricultural and Technical State University | M,D |
| North Carolina State University | M,D |
| North Dakota State University | M,D |
| Northeastern University | M,D,O |
| Northern Arizona University | M,D |
| Northern Illinois University | M |
| Northwestern Polytechnic University | M,D |
| Northwestern University | M,D |
| Oakland University | M,D |
| The Ohio State University | M,D |
| Ohio University | M,D |
| Oklahoma Christian University | M |
| Oklahoma State University | M,D |
| Old Dominion University | M,D |
| Oregon Health & Science University | M,D |
| Oregon State University | M,D |
| Penn State Harrisburg | M,O |
| Penn State University Park | M,D* |
| Pittsburg State University | M |
| Polytechnic University of Puerto Rico | M |
| Polytechnique Montréal | M,D,O |
| Portland State University | M,D |
| Prairie View A&M University | M,D |
| Princeton University | M,D |
| Purdue University | M,D |
| Purdue University Fort Wayne | M |
| Purdue University Northwest | M |
| Queen's University at Kingston | M,D |
| Rensselaer at Hartford | M |
| Rensselaer Polytechnic Institute | M,D |
| Rice University | M,D |
| Rochester Institute of Technology | M |
| Rose-Hulman Institute of Technology | M |
| Rowan University | M |
| Royal Military College of Canada | M,D |
| Rutgers University - New Brunswick | M,D |
| St. Cloud State University | M |
| St. Mary's University (United States) | M |
| San Diego State University | M |
| San Francisco State University | M |
| San Jose State University | M |
| Santa Clara University | M,D,O |
| South Dakota School of Mines and Technology | M |
| South Dakota State University | M,D |
| Southern Illinois University Carbondale | M,D |
| Southern Illinois University Edwardsville | M |
| Southern Methodist University | M,D |
| Stanford University | M,D |
| Stevens Institute of Technology | M,D,O |
| Stony Brook University, State University of New York | M,D |
| Syracuse University | M,D |
| Temple University | M,D* |
| Tennessee State University | M,D |
| Tennessee Technological University | M |
| Texas A&M University | M,D |
| Texas A&M University–Kingsville | M |
| Texas State University | M |
| Tufts University | M,D,O |
| Tuskegee University | M |
| UNB Fredericton | M,D |
| Universidad de las Américas Puebla | M |
| Universidad del Turabo | M |
| Université de Moncton | M |
| Université de Sherbrooke | M,D |
| Université du Québec à Trois-Rivières | M,D |
| University at Buffalo, the State University of New York | M,D |
| The University of Akron | M,D |
| The University of Alabama | M,D |
| The University of Alabama at Birmingham | M,D |
| The University of Alabama in Huntsville | M,D |
| University of Alaska Fairbanks | M |
| University of Alberta | M,D |
| The University of Arizona | M,D |
| University of Arkansas | M,D |
| University of Bridgeport | M |
| The University of British Columbia | M,D |
| University of Calgary | M,D |
| University of California, Berkeley | M,D |
| University of California, Davis | M,D |
| University of California, Irvine | M,D |
| University of California, Los Angeles | M,D |
| University of California, Merced | M,D |
| University of California, Riverside | M,D |
| University of California, San Diego | M,D |
| University of California, Santa Barbara | M,D |
| University of California, Santa Cruz | M,D |
| University of Central Florida | M,D |
| University of Central Oklahoma | M |
| University of Cincinnati | M,D |
| University of Colorado Boulder | M,D |
| University of Colorado Denver | M,D |
| University of Connecticut | M,D |
| University of Dayton | M,D |
| University of Delaware | M,D |
| University of Denver | M,D |
| University of Detroit Mercy | M,D |
| University of Florida | M,D |
| University of Hawaii at Manoa | M,D |
| University of Houston | M,D |
| University of Idaho | M,D |
| University of Illinois at Chicago | M,D |
| University of Illinois at Urbana-Champaign | M,D |
| The University of Iowa | M,D |
| The University of Kansas | M,D |
| University of Kentucky | M,D |
| University of Louisiana at Lafayette | M,D |
| University of Louisville | M,D |
| University of Maine | M,D |
| The University of Manchester | M,D |
| University of Manitoba | M,D |
| University of Maryland, Baltimore County | M,D |
| University of Maryland, College Park | M,D |
| University of Massachusetts Amherst | M,D |
| University of Massachusetts Dartmouth | M,D,O |
| University of Massachusetts Lowell | M,D |
| University of Memphis | M,D,O |
| University of Miami | M,D |
| University of Michigan | M,D |
| University of Michigan–Dearborn | M,D |
| University of Minnesota, Duluth | M |
| University of Minnesota, Twin Cities Campus | M,D |
| University of Mississippi | M,D |
| University of Missouri | M,D |
| University of Missouri–Kansas City | M,D,O |
| University of Nebraska–Lincoln | M,D |
| University of Nevada, Reno | M,D |
| University of New Hampshire | M,D,O |
| University of New Haven | M |
| University of New Mexico | M,D |
| University of New Orleans | M |
| University of North Dakota | M,D |
| University of North Florida | M |
| University of North Texas | M,D,O |
| University of Notre Dame | M,D |
| University of Oklahoma | M,D |
| University of Ottawa | M,D |
| University of Pennsylvania | M,D |
| University of Pittsburgh | M,D* |
| University of Portland | M |
| University of Puerto Rico at Mayagüez | M,D |
| University of Rhode Island | M,D |
| University of Rochester | M,D |
| University of St. Thomas (MN) | M,O |
| University of Saskatchewan | M,D,O |
| University of South Alabama | M |
| University of South Carolina | M,D |
| University of Southern California | M,D,O |
| University of South Florida | M,D |
| The University of Tennessee | M,D |
| The University of Tennessee at Chattanooga | M |
| The University of Texas at Arlington | M,D |
| The University of Texas at Austin | M,D |
| The University of Texas at Dallas | M,D |
| The University of Texas at El Paso | M,D,O |
| The University of Texas at San Antonio | M,D |
| The University of Texas at Tyler | M |
| The University of Texas Rio Grande Valley | M |
| University of the District of Columbia | M |
| The University of Toledo | M,D |
| University of Toronto | M,D |
| The University of Tulsa | M,D |
| University of Utah | M,D |

*M—masters degree; D—doctorate; O—other advanced degree; *—Close-Up and/or Display*

- University of Vermont M,D
- University of Victoria M,D
- University of Virginia M,D
- University of Washington M,D
- University of Waterloo M,D
- The University of Western Ontario M,D
- University of Windsor M,D
- University of Wisconsin–Madison M,D
- University of Wisconsin–Milwaukee M,D*
- University of Wyoming M,D
- Université Laval M,D
- Utah State University M,D
- Vanderbilt University M,D*
- Villanova University M,O
- Virginia Polytechnic Institute and State University M,D,O
- Washington State University M,D
- Wayne State University M,D
- Western Michigan University M,D
- Western New England University M
- West Virginia University M,D
- Wichita State University M,D
- Widener University M
- Worcester Polytechnic Institute M,D,O
- Wright State University M
- Yale University M,D
- Youngstown State University M

## ELECTRONIC COMMERCE

- California State University, Fullerton M
- Claremont Graduate University M,D,O
- Dalhousie University M,D
- DePaul University M,D
- Eastern Michigan University M,O
- Fairleigh Dickinson University, Metropolitan Campus M
- Fordham University M,D
- HEC Montreal M,O
- Instituto Tecnológico y de Estudios Superiores de Monterrey, Campus Central de Veracruz M
- Instituto Tecnológico y de Estudios Superiores de Monterrey, Campus Ciudad Juárez M
- Instituto Tecnológico y de Estudios Superiores de Monterrey, Campus Estado de México M,D
- Instituto Tecnológico y de Estudios Superiores de Monterrey, Campus Irapuato M,D
- Lewis University M
- Northwestern University M
- Pace University O
- Stevens Institute of Technology M,O
- Towson University M,O
- Universidad del Este M
- Université de Montréal M,D
- Université de Sherbrooke M
- University at Buffalo, the State University of New York M,D,O
- The University of Akron M
- University of New Brunswick Saint John M
- University of North Florida M
- University of Ottawa M,D,O
- University of Phoenix - Dallas Campus M
- University of Phoenix - Houston Campus M
- University of Phoenix - San Antonio Campus M
- Université Laval M,O

## ELECTRONIC MATERIALS

- Colorado School of Mines M,D
- Princeton University D
- University of Arkansas M,D
- University of Memphis M,O
- Wayne State University M

## ELEMENTARY EDUCATION

- Acacia University M
- Alabama Agricultural and Mechanical University M,D,O
- Alaska Pacific University M
- Albright College M
- Alcorn State University M,O
- American International College M,D,O
- American University of Puerto Rico - Bayamon M
- Anderson University (SC) M
- Andrews University M,D,O
- Anna Maria College M,O
- Antioch University New England M,O
- Appalachian State University M
- Aquinas College (TN) M
- Arcadia University M,D,O
- Argosy University, Atlanta M,D,O
- Argosy University, Chicago M,D,O
- Argosy University, Hawaii M,D
- Argosy University, Los Angeles M,D
- Argosy University, Northern Virginia M,D,O
- Argosy University, Orange County M,D
- Argosy University, Phoenix M,D,O
- Argosy University, Seattle M,D
- Argosy University, Tampa M,D,O
- Argosy University, Twin Cities M,D,O
- Arizona State University at Tempe M
- Arkansas State University M,D,O
- Arkansas Tech University M,D,O
- Auburn University at Montgomery M,O
- Augusta University M,O
- Avila University M,O
- Ball State University M,D,O
- Bank Street College of Education M
- Barry University M,D,O
- Barton College M
- Bayamón Central University M,O
- Bellarmine University M,D,O
- Bethel University (MN) M,D,O
- Blue Mountain College M
- Bob Jones University M,D,O
- Boston College M,D,O
- Bowie State University M
- Brandeis University M,O
- Brandman University M,D
- Bridgewater State University M
- Brooklyn College of the City University of New York M,O
- Brown University M
- Bushnell University M
- Cabrini University M,D
- California Lutheran University M,D
- California State University, Fullerton M
- California State University, Long Beach M
- California State University, Los Angeles M
- California State University, Northridge M
- California State University, Sacramento M,D,O
- California State University, Stanislaus M
- California University of Pennsylvania M
- Calvary University M
- Cambridge College M,D,O
- Campbell University M
- Canisius College M,O
- Capella University M,D
- Caribbean University M,D
- Carroll University M
- Carson-Newman University M
- Catawba College M
- Centenary College of Louisiana M
- Central Connecticut State University M,O
- Central Michigan University M,D,O
- Chadron State College M,O
- Chaminade University of Honolulu M
- Chapman University M,D,O
- Charleston Southern University M
- Chatham University M
- Chestnut Hill College M
- Cheyney University of Pennsylvania M
- Chicago State University M
- City University of Seattle M,O
- Clemson University M,D,O
- College of Charleston M
- The College of New Jersey M
- The College of New Rochelle M
- College of Saint Elizabeth M,O
- College of St. Joseph M
- College of Staten Island of the City University of New York M
- Colorado Christian University M
- The Colorado College M
- Columbia College (SC) M
- Columbia International University M,D,O
- Concordia University (United States) M,D
- Concordia University Chicago M
- Concordia University, Nebraska M
- Converse College M
- Creighton University M
- Curry College M,O
- Dallas Baptist University M
- Delta State University M,D,O
- DePaul University M,D
- Dominican College M
- Dominican University M
- Drew University M,D,O
- Drury University M
- Duquesne University M
- D'Youville College M,D
- East Carolina University M,O
- Eastern Connecticut State University M
- Eastern Illinois University M
- Eastern Kentucky University M
- Eastern Nazarene College M,O
- Eastern New Mexico University M
- Eastern Oregon University M
- Eastern University M,O
- Eastern Washington University M
- East Stroudsburg University of Pennsylvania M
- East Tennessee State University M,O
- Elizabeth City State University M
- Elms College M,O
- Elon University M
- Emporia State University M
- Endicott College M
- Fairfield University M,O
- Faulkner University M
- Fayetteville State University M
- Fitchburg State University M
- Florida Agricultural and Mechanical University M
- Florida Atlantic University M
- Florida Gulf Coast University M
- Florida International University M,D,O
- Florida Memorial University M
- Fontbonne University M
- Fordham University M,O
- Framingham State University M
- Franklin Pierce University M,D,O
- Frostburg State University M,D
- Gallaudet University M,D,O
- George Mason University M
- The George Washington University M
- Georgia Southern University M,O
- Georgia State University M,D,O
- Gonzaga University M,D
- Gordon College M,O
- Goucher College M,O
- Grand Canyon University M,D,O
- Greensboro College M
- Greenville University M
- Harding University M,O
- Hawaii Pacific University M
- High Point University M,D
- Hofstra University M,D,O
- Holy Family University M
- Hood College M,O
- Hope International University M
- Houston Baptist University M
- Howard University M
- Huntington University M,D
- Idaho State University M
- Indiana University Bloomington M,D,O
- Indiana University Northwest M,O
- Indiana University South Bend M,O
- Indiana University Southeast M
- Inter American University of Puerto Rico, Aguadilla Campus M
- Inter American University of Puerto Rico, Arecibo Campus M
- Inter American University of Puerto Rico, Barranquitas Campus M
- Inter American University of Puerto Rico, Guayama Campus M
- Inter American University of Puerto Rico, Metropolitan Campus M
- Inter American University of Puerto Rico, Ponce Campus M
- Inter American University of Puerto Rico, San Germán Campus M
- Iowa State University of Science and Technology M,D
- Ithaca College M
- Jackson State University M,D,O
- Jacksonville State University M
- James Madison University M
- Johnson & Wales University M
- Kansas State University M,D,O
- Keuka College M
- Kutztown University of Pennsylvania M
- Lake Forest College M
- Lancaster Bible College M,D
- Langston University M
- Lasell College M,O
- Lee University M,O
- Lehigh University M,D
- Lehman College of the City University of New York M
- Le Moyne College M,O
- Lesley University M,D,O
- Lewis & Clark College M
- Lewis University M
- Lincoln University (MO) M
- Lock Haven University of Pennsylvania M
- Long Island University - Brentwood Campus M,O
- Long Island University - Hudson M,O
- Long Island University - Riverhead M,O
- Longwood University M
- Louisiana State University and Agricultural & Mechanical College M,D,O
- Louisiana Tech University M,D,O
- Loyola Marymount University M
- Loyola University Chicago M
- Loyola University Maryland M,O
- Manhattan College M,O
- Manhattanville College M,O
- Mansfield University of Pennsylvania M
- Marquette University M,D,O
- Mars Hill University M
- Mary Baldwin University M
- Marygrove College M,O
- Marymount University M
- Maryville University of Saint Louis M,D
- Marywood University M
- McDaniel College M,O
- McNeese State University M,O
- Medaille College M
- Mercy College M
- Meredith College M,O
- Metropolitan College of New York M
- Metropolitan State University of Denver M
- Middle Tennessee State University M,O
- Milligan University M,D,O
- Minot State University M
- Mississippi College M,D,O
- Mississippi State University M,D,O
- Missouri State University M,O
- Monmouth University M,D,O
- Montana State University Billings M
- Morehead State University M,O
- Morgan State University M
- Mount Saint Vincent University M
- Murray State University M,O
- National Louis University M,D,O
- Nazareth College of Rochester M
- Nebraska Christian College of Hope International University M
- Neumann University M
- New Jersey City University M
- New York University M
- Niagara University M,O
- Nicholls State University M
- North Carolina Agricultural and Technical State University M
- North Carolina State University M
- Northeastern Illinois University M
- Northeastern University M
- Northern Arizona University M,D
- Northern Illinois University M
- Northwestern Oklahoma State University M
- Northwestern State University of Louisiana M,O
- Northwestern University M
- Northwest Missouri State University M,D,O
- Nyack College M
- Oakland City University M,D
- Oakland University M,O
- Oklahoma City University M
- Old Dominion University M,O
- Olivet Nazarene University M
- Oregon State University M
- Ottawa University M
- Pace University M,O
- Pacific Union College M
- Pacific University M
- Pfeiffer University M
- Point Park University M,D
- Prescott College M,D
- Providence College M
- Purdue University M,D,O
- Purdue University Fort Wayne M,O
- Queens College of the City University of New York M,O
- Queens University of Charlotte M
- Quinnipiac University M
- Regent University M,D,O
- Regis College (MA) M,D
- Regis University M,O
- Rhode Island College M
- Rider University M
- Rivier University M,D,O
- Rockford University M
- Rollins College M
- Roosevelt University M
- Rosemont College M
- Rutgers University - New Brunswick M,D
- Sage Graduate School M
- St. John Fisher College M,O
- St. John's University (NY) M
- Saint Joseph's University M,D,O
- Saint Mary's University of Minnesota M
- Saint Peter's University M,O
- St. Thomas Aquinas College M,O
- St. Thomas University - Florida M,D,O
- Saint Xavier University M
- Salem College M
- Salem State University M
- Samford University M,D,O
- San Diego State University M
- San Francisco State University M
- San Jose State University M,O
- Seton Hill University M
- Shippensburg University of Pennsylvania M
- Siena Heights University M,O
- Sierra Nevada College M
- Simmons University M,D,O
- Sinte Gleska University M
- Slippery Rock University of Pennsylvania M
- Smith College M
- South Carolina State University M
- Southeastern Louisiana University M
- Southeastern University (FL) M,D
- Southeast Missouri State University M,D,O
- Southern Connecticut State University M,O
- Southern New Hampshire University M,D,O
- Southern Oregon University M
- Southern University and Agricultural and Mechanical College M
- Southwestern College (KS) M,D
- Southwestern Oklahoma State University M
- Spalding University M
- Springfield College M,O
- Spring Hill College M
- State University of New York at New Paltz M
- State University of New York at Oswego M
- State University of New York at Plattsburgh M,O
- State University of New York College at Oneonta M
- State University of New York College at Potsdam M
- Stephen F. Austin State University M
- Sul Ross State University M
- Tarleton State University M
- Teachers College, Columbia University M,D
- Tennessee State University M,D
- Tennessee Technological University M,O
- Texas A&M University–Commerce M,D,O
- Texas A&M University–Corpus Christi M
- Texas State University M
- Texas Tech University M,D
- Towson University M
- Trevecca Nazarene University M,O
- Trinity Washington University M
- Troy University M,O
- Tufts University M,D
- Union College (KY) M
- Universidad del Este M
- Universidad Metropolitana M
- Université de Sherbrooke M,O
- University at Buffalo, the State University of New York M,D,O
- The University of Akron M
- The University of Alabama M,D,O
- The University of Alabama at Birmingham M
- University of Alaska Southeast M
- University of Alberta M,D
- The University of Arizona M,D
- University of Arkansas at Pine Bluff M
- University of Bridgeport M,D,O
- University of California, Irvine M,D
- University of Central Florida M
- University of Central Missouri M,D,O
- University of Central Oklahoma M
- University of Colorado Denver M
- University of Connecticut M,D
- University of Dayton M
- University of Florida M,D,O
- University of Hartford M
- University of Illinois at Chicago M,D
- University of Indianapolis M
- The University of Iowa M,D

University of Kentucky M,D
University of La Verne M,D,O
University of Louisiana at Monroe M
University of Louisville M,D,O
University of Mary Hardin-Baylor M,D
University of Maryland, Baltimore County M
University of Mary Washington M
University of Massachusetts Amherst M,D,O
University of Memphis M,D,O
University of Minnesota, Twin Cities Campus M
University of Mississippi M,D,O
University of Missouri M,D,O
University of Missouri–St. Louis M
University of Montevallo M
University of Nebraska at Kearney M
University of Nebraska at Omaha M
University of Nevada, Las Vegas M,D,O
University of Nevada, Reno M
University of New Hampshire M,O
University of New Mexico M
University of North Alabama M,O
The University of North Carolina at Charlotte M,O
The University of North Carolina at Greensboro D
The University of North Carolina at Pembroke M
The University of North Carolina Wilmington M
University of North Dakota M
University of Northern Colorado M
University of Northern Iowa M
University of North Florida M
University of Oklahoma M,D
University of Pennsylvania M
University of Phoenix - Bay Area Campus M,D,O
University of Phoenix - Central Valley Campus M
University of Phoenix - Hawaii Campus M
University of Phoenix - Las Vegas Campus M
University of Phoenix–Online Campus M,O
University of Phoenix - Phoenix Campus M
University of Phoenix - Sacramento Valley Campus M,O
University of Phoenix - San Diego Campus M
University of Puget Sound M
University of St. Francis (IL) M,D,O
University of Saint Joseph M
University of Saint Mary M
University of St. Thomas (TX) M,D
University of South Alabama M,D
University of South Carolina M,D
University of South Carolina Upstate M
University of South Dakota M
University of Southern Indiana M
University of South Florida, St. Petersburg M
University of South Florida Sarasota-Manatee M
The University of Tennessee M,D,O
The University of Tennessee at Chattanooga M,D,O
The University of Tennessee at Martin M
The University of Texas Rio Grande Valley M,D
University of the Cumberlands M,D,O
University of the District of Columbia M
The University of Toledo M,D,O
University of Utah M,D,O
University of Vermont M
University of Virginia M,D,O
University of Washington, Tacoma M
The University of West Alabama M,O
University of West Florida M
University of Wisconsin–Milwaukee M*
University of Wisconsin–River Falls M
University of Wisconsin–Stevens Point M
Utah State University M
Utah Valley University M
Valdosta State University M
Valley City State University M
Valparaiso University M,O
Vanderbilt University M*
Virginia Commonwealth University M
Wagner College M
Walden University M,D,O
Warner University M
Washington State University M,D
Washington University in St. Louis M
Wayland Baptist University M
Wayne State College M
Wayne State University M,D,O
Webster University M,O
Western Governors University M,O
Western Kentucky University M,O
Western New Mexico University M
Western Washington University M
Westfield State University M
West Virginia University M,D
Wheaton College M
Whittier College M
Whitworth University M
Widener University M,D
William Carey University M,O
Wilmington University M,D
Wilson College M
Wingate University M,D,O
Worcester State University M,O
Wright State University M
Xavier University M*

## EMERGENCY MANAGEMENT

Adelphi University O
Anna Maria College M,O
Arizona State University at Tempe M,D
Arkansas State University M,O
Arkansas Tech University M
Ball State University M,O
Benedictine University M
Boston University M
California State University, Long Beach M
California State University Maritime Academy M
Capella University M,D
Columbia Southern University M
Drexel University M
Endicott College M,O
Florida International University M
Fordham University M
Georgetown University M,D
The George Washington University M,D,O
Georgia State University M,D,O
Grand Canyon University M
Indiana University-Purdue University Indianapolis M,O
Jacksonville State University M,D
Lander University M
Lasell College M,O
Liberty University M,D,O
London Metropolitan University M,D
Massachusetts Maritime Academy M
Metropolitan College of New York M
Millersville University of Pennsylvania M
National University M
New York Medical College M,D,O
Norwich University M
Nova Southeastern University M,D,O
Oklahoma State University M,D
Pace University M
Park University M,O
Post University M
Regent University M
Royal Roads University M,O
Rutgers University - New Brunswick M,D,O
Saint Leo University M,D
Saint Louis University M
San Diego State University M,D
Sul Ross State University M
Syracuse University O
Thomas Jefferson University M
Trident University International M,D,O
Trine University M
Tulane University M,D
Université de Montréal O
University at Albany, State University of New York M,D,O
University of Alaska Fairbanks M
University of Central Florida M,O
University of Chicago M
University of Colorado Denver M,D
University of Delaware M,D
University of Denver M,O
University of Florida M
University of Hawaii at Manoa O
University of Illinois at Springfield M,O
University of Maryland, Baltimore County M,D,O
University of Nebraska Medical Center M
University of Nevada, Las Vegas M,D,O
University of New Haven M,O
The University of North Carolina at Charlotte M,O
The University of North Carolina at Pembroke M
University of North Texas M,D,O
University of South Florida O
The University of Texas Rio Grande Valley M
The University of Toledo M,O
Upper Iowa University M
Virginia Commonwealth University M,O
Walden University M,D,O
Waldorf University M
Wheaton College M
York University M

## EMERGENCY MEDICAL SERVICES

Creighton University M
Drexel University M
San Diego State University M,D
University of Guelph M,D,O
Université Laval O

## ENERGY AND POWER ENGINEERING

Appalachian State University M
Arizona State University at Tempe M,D
Carnegie Mellon University M,D
The Catholic University of America M,D
Clarkson University M
Cornell University M,D
Dartmouth College M,D
Florida State University M,D
Georgia Southern University M
Instituto Tecnologico de Santo Domingo M,D,O
Inter American University of Puerto Rico, Bayamón Campus M
Kansas State University M,D
Lawrence Technological University M,D
Lehigh University M
New Jersey Institute of Technology M,D
New York Institute of Technology O
North Carolina Agricultural and Technical State University M,D
Northeastern University M,D,O
Saginaw Valley State University M
San Francisco State University M
Santa Clara University M,D,O
Southern Illinois University Carbondale D
Stanford University M,D,O
Texas A&M University–Kingsville D
Texas Tech University M,D
Universidad Autonoma de Guadalajara M,D
University at Buffalo, the State University of New York M,D
University of Alberta M,D
The University of British Columbia M
University of Calgary M,D
University of Colorado Colorado Springs M,D
University of Illinois at Urbana-Champaign M,D
The University of Iowa M,D
University of Massachusetts Lowell M,D
University of Memphis M,D,O
University of Michigan M,D
University of Michigan–Dearborn M
The University of North Carolina at Charlotte M,O
University of North Texas M,D,O
University of Puerto Rico at Mayagüez M,D
The University of Tennessee D
The University of Tennessee at Chattanooga M,O
The University of Texas at El Paso M,D,O
Washington State University M,D
Wayne State University M,O
West Virginia University M,D
Worcester Polytechnic Institute M,D,O

## ENERGY MANAGEMENT AND POLICY

American College Dublin M
American University of Armenia M
Boston University M,D
Clarkson University M,O
Colorado School of Mines M,D
Colorado State University M
Eastern Illinois University M
Franklin Pierce University M,D,O
Indiana University Bloomington M,D,O
Instituto Tecnologico de Santo Domingo M,D,O
Johns Hopkins University M,O
Kansas State University M,D
New York Institute of Technology O
Norwich University M
Oklahoma Baptist University M
Oklahoma City University M
Portland State University M,D,O
Rice University M,D
Samford University M
SIT Graduate Institute M
Stony Brook University, State University of New York M
Tulane University M,D
Université du Québec, Institut National de la Recherche Scientifique M,D
University of Calgary M,D
University of California, Berkeley M,D
University of California, San Diego M
University of Colorado Denver M
University of Delaware M,D
University of Illinois at Urbana-Champaign M
University of Mary M
University of Phoenix - Bay Area Campus M,D
University of Phoenix–Online Campus M,O
University of Phoenix - Phoenix Campus M,O
University of Pittsburgh M*
University of San Francisco M
The University of Texas at Tyler M
The University of Tulsa M
Vermont Law School M
Waynesburg University M,D

## ENGINEERING AND APPLIED SCIENCES—GENERAL

Air Force Institute of Technology M,D
Alabama Agricultural and Mechanical University M,D
Alfred University M,D
The American University in Cairo M,D,O
Arizona State University at Tempe M,D,O
Arkansas State University M
Arkansas Tech University M
Atlantis University M
Auburn University M,D,O
Baylor University M,D
Binghamton University, State University of New York M,D
Boise State University M,D,O
Boston University M,D
Bradley University M
Brigham Young University M,D
Brown University M,D
Bucknell University M
California Institute of Technology M,D,O
California Polytechnic State University, San Luis Obispo M
California State University, Chico M
California State University, East Bay M
California State University, Fresno M
California State University, Fullerton M
California State University, Los Angeles M
California State University, Northridge M
California State University, Sacramento M
Carleton University M,D
Case Western Reserve University M,D
The Catholic University of America M,D,O
Central Connecticut State University M
Central Michigan University M
Christian Brothers University M
The Citadel, The Military College of South Carolina M,O
City College of the City University of New York M,D
Clarkson University M,D,O
Clemson University M,D,O
Cleveland State University M,D
Colorado School of Mines M,D,O
Colorado State University M,D
Colorado State University-Pueblo M
Columbia University M,D
Concordia University (Canada) M,D,O
Cooper Union for the Advancement of Science and Art M
Cornell University M,D
Dalhousie University M,D
Dartmouth College M,D
Drexel University M,D,O
Duke University M
Eastern Illinois University M,O
Eastern Michigan University M
Fairfield University M,O
Fairleigh Dickinson University, Metropolitan Campus M
Florida Agricultural and Mechanical University M,D
Florida Atlantic University M,D
Florida Institute of Technology M,D
Florida International University M,D
Florida Polytechnic University M
Florida State University M,D
George Mason University M,D,O
The George Washington University M,D,O
Georgia Institute of Technology M,D
Georgia Southern University M,O
Gonzaga University M,O
Grand Valley State University M
Grantham University M
Harvard University M,D*
Hofstra University M
Howard University M,D
Idaho State University M,D,O
Illinois Institute of Technology M,D
Indiana State University M
Instituto Tecnologico de Santo Domingo M,O
Instituto Tecnológico y de Estudios Superiores de Monterrey, Campus Ciudad Obregón M
Instituto Tecnológico y de Estudios Superiores de Monterrey, Campus Monterrey M,D
James Madison University M
Johns Hopkins University M,D,O
Kansas State University M,D,O
Kennesaw State University M
Lakehead University M
Lamar University M,D
Laurentian University M,D
Lawrence Technological University M,D
Lehigh University M,D,O
LeTourneau University M
Louisiana State University and Agricultural & Mechanical College M,D
Louisiana Tech University M,D,O
Manhattan College M
Marquette University M,D,O
Marshall University M,O
Massachusetts Institute of Technology M,D,O
McGill University M,D,O
McMaster University M,D
McNeese State University M
Memorial University of Newfoundland M,D
Mercer University M
Merrimack College M
Miami University M
Michigan State University M,D
Michigan Technological University M,D,O
Milwaukee School of Engineering M
Mississippi State University M,D
Missouri Western State University M
Montana State University M,D
Montana Technological University M
Morgan State University M,D,O
National University M
New Jersey Institute of Technology M,D
New Mexico State University M,D,O
New York Institute of Technology M,O
New York University M,D,O
North Carolina Agricultural and Technical State University M,D
North Carolina State University M,D
North Dakota State University M,D,O
Northeastern University M,D,O
Northern Arizona University M,D,O
Northern Illinois University M
Northwestern Polytechnic University M,D
Northwestern University M,D,O
Oakland University M,D,O
The Ohio State University M,D
Ohio University M,D

*M—masters degree; D—doctorate; O—other advanced degree; *—Close-Up and/or Display*

Oklahoma Christian University M
Oklahoma State University M,D
Old Dominion University M,D
Open University M
Oregon State University M,D
Penn State Great Valley M,O
Penn State Harrisburg M,O
Penn State University Park M,D*
Polytechnique Montréal M,D,O
Pontificia Universidad Catolica Madre y Maestra M
Portland State University M,D,O
Prairie View A&M University M,D
Princeton University M,D
Purdue University M,D,O
Purdue University Fort Wayne M,O
Purdue University Northwest M
Queen's University at Kingston M,D
Rensselaer at Hartford M
Rensselaer Polytechnic Institute M,D
Rice University M,D
Robert Morris University M
Rochester Institute of Technology M,D,O
Rose-Hulman Institute of Technology M
Rowan University M
Royal Military College of Canada M,D
Saginaw Valley State University M
St. Cloud State University M,O
San Diego State University M,D
San Francisco State University M
Santa Clara University M,D,O
Seattle University M
Simon Fraser University M,D
South Dakota School of Mines and Technology M,D
South Dakota State University M,D
Southern Illinois University Carbondale M,D
Southern Illinois University Edwardsville M
Southern Methodist University M,D
Southern University and Agricultural and Mechanical College M
Stanford University M,D,O
Stevens Institute of Technology M,D,O
Stony Brook University, State University of New York M,D,O
Syracuse University M,D,O
Tennessee State University M,D
Tennessee Technological University M,D
Texas A&M University–Kingsville M,D
Texas State University M
Texas Tech University M,D
Tufts University M,D
Tuskegee University M,D
UNB Fredericton M,D,O
Universidad de las Américas Puebla M,D
Universidad del Turabo M
Université de Moncton M
Université de Sherbrooke M,D,O
Université du Québec à Chicoutimi M,D
Université du Québec à Rimouski M
Université du Québec, École de technologie supérieure M,D,O
Université du Québec en Abitibi-Témiscamingue M,O
University at Albany, State University of New York M,D,O
University at Buffalo, the State University of New York M,D,O
The University of Akron M,D
The University of Alabama M,D
The University of Alabama at Birmingham D
The University of Alabama in Huntsville M,D
University of Alaska Fairbanks D
The University of Arizona M,D,O
University of Arkansas M,D
University of Bridgeport M,D
The University of British Columbia M,D
University of Calgary M,D
University of California, Berkeley M,D,O
University of California, Davis M,D,O
University of California, Irvine M,D
University of California, Los Angeles M,D
University of California, Merced M,D
University of California, Santa Barbara M,D
University of California, Santa Cruz M,D
University of Central Florida M,D,O
University of Central Oklahoma M
University of Cincinnati M,D
University of Colorado Boulder M,D
University of Colorado Colorado Springs M,D
University of Colorado Denver M,D
University of Connecticut M,D
University of Delaware M,D
University of Denver M,D
University of Detroit Mercy M,D
University of Florida M,D,O
University of Guelph M,D
University of Hartford M
University of Hawaii at Manoa M,D
University of Houston M,D
University of Idaho M,D
University of Illinois at Chicago M,D
University of Illinois at Urbana-Champaign M,D
The University of Iowa M,D
The University of Kansas M,D,O
University of Kentucky M,D
University of Louisville M,D,O
University of Maine M,D
University of Manitoba M,D
University of Maryland, Baltimore County M,D,O
University of Maryland, College Park M
University of Massachusetts Amherst M,D
University of Massachusetts Dartmouth D
University of Massachusetts Lowell M,D
University of Memphis M,D,O
University of Miami M,D
University of Michigan M,D,O
University of Michigan–Dearborn M,D
University of Minnesota, Twin Cities Campus M,D,O
University of Mississippi M,D
University of Missouri M,D,O
University of Missouri–Kansas City M,D,O
University of Nebraska–Lincoln M,D
University of Nevada, Las Vegas M,D,O
University of Nevada, Reno M,D
University of New Haven M,O
University of New Mexico M,O
University of New Orleans M,D
The University of North Carolina at Charlotte M,D,O
University of North Dakota D
University of North Texas M,D,O
University of Notre Dame M,D
University of Ottawa M,D,O
University of Pennsylvania M,D
University of Pittsburgh M,D*
University of Portland M
University of Puerto Rico at Mayagüez M,D
University of Regina M,D
University of Rhode Island M,D,O
University of Rochester M,O
University of St. Thomas (MN) M,O
University of Saskatchewan M,D,O
University of South Africa M,D
University of South Alabama M,D
University of South Carolina M,D
University of Southern California M,D,O
University of Southern Indiana M,D
University of South Florida M,D,O
The University of Tennessee M,D
The University of Texas at Arlington M,D
The University of Texas at Austin M,D
The University of Texas at Dallas M,D
The University of Texas at El Paso M,D,O
The University of Texas at San Antonio M,D
University of the District of Columbia M
University of the Pacific M
The University of Toledo M
University of Toronto M,D
The University of Tulsa M,D
University of Utah M,D
University of Vermont M,D
University of Victoria M,D
University of Virginia M,D
University of Washington M,D,O
University of Waterloo M,D
The University of Western Ontario M,D
University of Windsor M,D
University of Wisconsin–Madison M,D
University of Wisconsin–Milwaukee M,D*
University of Wisconsin–Platteville M
University of Wyoming M,D
Université Laval M,D,O
Utah State University M,D,O
Vanderbilt University M,D*
Villanova University M,D,O
Virginia Commonwealth University M,D
Virginia Polytechnic Institute and State University M,D
Washington State University M,D,O
Washington University in St. Louis M,D
Wayne State University M,D,O
Western Michigan University M,D
Western New England University M,D
West Texas A&M University M
West Virginia University M,D
Wichita State University M,D
Widener University M
Worcester Polytechnic Institute M,D,O
Wright State University M,D
Yale University M,D
Youngstown State University M,O

## ENGINEERING DESIGN

Harvard University M,D*
Northwestern University M
Ohio Dominican University M
Penn State University Park M*
Rochester Institute of Technology M
San Diego State University M,D
Stevens Institute of Technology M
The University of Alabama at Birmingham M
University of Michigan M,D
Worcester Polytechnic Institute M,D,O

## ENGINEERING MANAGEMENT

Air Force Institute of Technology M
American University of Sharjah M,D
Arkansas State University M
California State Polytechnic University, Pomona M
California State University, East Bay M
California State University, Long Beach M,D
California State University Maritime Academy M
California State University, Northridge M
Case Western Reserve University M
The Catholic University of America M,O
Central Michigan University M,O
The Citadel, The Military College of South Carolina M,O
Clarkson University M
Colorado School of Mines M,D
Cornell University M,D
Dartmouth College M
Drexel University M,O
Duke University M
Eastern Michigan University M
Embry-Riddle Aeronautical University–Worldwide M
Florida Institute of Technology M
Florida International University M
Gannon University M
The George Washington University M,D,O
Georgia Southern University M,O
Indiana Tech M
Instituto Tecnológico y de Estudios Superiores de Monterrey, Campus Chihuahua M,O
International Technological University M
Johns Hopkins University M
Kansas State University M,D
Kennesaw State University M
Kettering University M
Lawrence Technological University M,D
Lehigh University M,D,O
LeTourneau University M
Long Island University - Post M
Louisiana Tech University M,D,O
Loyola Marymount University
Marquette University M,D,O
Marshall University M
Massachusetts Institute of Technology M
McNeese State University M
Mercer University M
Merrimack College M
Middle Tennessee State University M
Milwaukee School of Engineering M
Missouri University of Science and Technology M,D
National University M
Naval Postgraduate School M,D,O
New England Institute of Technology M
New Jersey Institute of Technology M,D
New Mexico Institute of Mining and Technology M
Northeastern University M,D,O
Northwestern University M
Oakland University M
Oklahoma Christian University M
Old Dominion University M,D
Oregon State University M,D
Penn State Great Valley M,O
Penn State Harrisburg M,O
Point Park University M
Polytechnic University of Puerto Rico M
Polytechnic University of Puerto Rico, Orlando Campus M
Portland State University M,D,O
Robert Morris University M
Rochester Institute of Technology M
Rose-Hulman Institute of Technology M
Saint Martin's University M
St. Mary's University (United States) M
Santa Clara University M,D,O
South Dakota School of Mines and Technology M
Southern Illinois University Carbondale M
Southern Methodist University M,D
Southern New Hampshire University M,D,O
Stanford University M,D
Stevens Institute of Technology M,D,O
Syracuse University M
Tarleton State University M
Texas A&M University M,D
Texas Tech University M,D
Trine University M
Tufts University M
UNB Fredericton M
Université de Sherbrooke M,O
University at Buffalo, the State University of New York M,D,O
The University of Alabama at Birmingham M
University of Alberta M,D
The University of Arizona M,D,O
University of California, Berkeley M,D
University of California, Irvine M
University of Colorado Boulder M
University of Dayton M
University of Denver M,D
University of Detroit Mercy M,D
The University of Kansas M,O
University of Louisville M,D,O
University of Management and Technology M
The University of Manchester M,D
University of Maryland, Baltimore County M,O
University of Michigan–Dearborn M
University of Minnesota, Duluth M
University of Missouri–Kansas City M,D,O
University of Nebraska–Lincoln M,D
University of New Haven M,O
University of New Orleans M
University of Ottawa M,O
University of Puerto Rico at Mayagüez M,D
University of Regina M,O
University of St. Thomas (MN) M,O
University of Southern California M,D,O
University of Southern Indiana M
University of South Florida M,D
The University of Tennessee M,D
The University of Tennessee at Chattanooga M,O
The University of Texas at Arlington M
The University of Texas at Tyler M
The University of Texas Rio Grande Valley M
University of Vermont M
University of Waterloo M,D
Valparaiso University M,O
Virginia Polytechnic Institute and State University M,O
Washington State University M,O
Wayne State University M,D,O
Western Michigan University M,D
Western New England University M,D
Wichita State University M,D
Widener University M

## ENGINEERING PHYSICS

Air Force Institute of Technology M,D
Cornell University M,D
Embry-Riddle Aeronautical University–Daytona M,D
Louisiana Tech University M,D,O
McMaster University M,D
Polytechnique Montréal M,D,O
Queen's University at Kingston M,D
Rensselaer Polytechnic Institute M,D
Stanford University M,D
University of California, San Diego M,D
University of Central Oklahoma M
University of Oklahoma M,D
University of Saskatchewan M,D
University of Virginia M,D
University of Wisconsin–Madison M,D
Yale University M,D

## ENGLISH

Abilene Christian University M
Acadia University M
The American University in Cairo M,O
Andrews University M
Angelo State University M
Appalachian State University M
Arcadia University M
Arizona State University at Tempe M,D,O
Arkansas State University M,O
Arkansas Tech University M
Asbury University M
Auburn University M,D,O
Austin Peay State University M
Azusa Pacific University M
Ball State University M,D
Bard College M
Baylor University M,D
Bemidji State University M
Binghamton University, State University of New York M,D
Bob Jones University M,D,O
Boston College M,D
Boston University M,D
Bowie State University M
Bowling Green State University M,D
Bradley University M
Brandeis University M,D
Bridgewater State University M
Brigham Young University M
Brock University M
Brooklyn College of the City University of New York M
Brown University M,D
Bucknell University M
Buffalo State College, State University of New York M
Cabrini University M,D
California Baptist University M
California Polytechnic State University, San Luis Obispo M
California State Polytechnic University, Pomona M
California State University, Chico M
California State University, Dominguez Hills M,O
California State University, East Bay M
California State University, Fresno M
California State University, Fullerton M
California State University, Long Beach M
California State University, Los Angeles M,O
California State University, Northridge M
California State University, Sacramento M
California State University, San Bernardino M
California State University, San Marcos M
California State University, Stanislaus M,O
Carleton University M,D
Carnegie Mellon University M,D
Case Western Reserve University M,D
The Catholic University of America M,D,O
Central Connecticut State University M,O
Central Michigan University M
Central Washington University M
Chapman University M
Chicago State University M
The Citadel, The Military College of South Carolina M

| | |
|---|---|
| City College of the City University of New York | M |
| Claremont Graduate University | M,D |
| Clark Atlanta University | M |
| Clarks Summit University | M |
| Clark University | M |
| Cleveland State University | M |
| College of Charleston | M |
| The College of New Jersey | M |
| College of Staten Island of the City University of New York | M |
| Colorado State University | M |
| Columbia College Chicago | M |
| Columbia University | M,D |
| Concordia University (Canada) | M,D |
| Converse College | M |
| Cornell University | M,D |
| Creighton University | M |
| Dalhousie University | M,D |
| DePaul University | M |
| Drew University | M,D,O |
| Duke University | D |
| Duquesne University | M,D |
| East Carolina University | M,D,O |
| Eastern Illinois University | M |
| Eastern Kentucky University | M |
| Eastern Michigan University | M |
| Eastern New Mexico University | M |
| Eastern Washington University | M |
| East Tennessee State University | M,O |
| Emory University | D,O |
| Emporia State University | M |
| Fairleigh Dickinson University, Metropolitan Campus | M |
| Fitchburg State University | M,O |
| Florida Atlantic University | M |
| Florida Gulf Coast University | M |
| Florida International University | M |
| Florida State University | M,D |
| Fordham University | M,D |
| Fort Hays State University | M |
| Framingham State University | M |
| Gannon University | M |
| Gardner-Webb University | M |
| George Mason University | M,D,O |
| Georgetown University | M |
| The George Washington University | M,D |
| Georgia College & State University | M |
| Georgia Southern University | M |
| Georgia State University | M,D |
| Governors State University | M |
| The Graduate Center, City University of New York | D |
| Grambling State University | M,D,O |
| Grand Valley State University | M |
| Harvard University | M,D,O* |
| Heritage University | M |
| Hofstra University | M |
| Hollins University | M,O |
| Houston Baptist University | M,D |
| Howard University | M,D |
| Humboldt State University | M |
| Idaho State University | M,D,O |
| Illinois State University | M,D |
| Indiana State University | M |
| Indiana University Bloomington | M,D |
| Indiana University of Pennsylvania | M,D |
| Indiana University-Purdue University Indianapolis | M,O |
| Indiana University South Bend | M,O |
| Inter American University of Puerto Rico, Metropolitan Campus | M |
| Iona College | M |
| Iowa State University of Science and Technology | M,D |
| Jackson State University | M |
| Jacksonville State University | M |
| James Madison University | M |
| John Carroll University | M |
| Johns Hopkins University | D |
| Kansas State University | M,O |
| Kent State University | M,D |
| Kutztown University of Pennsylvania | M |
| Lakehead University | M |
| Lamar University | M |
| La Salle University | M,O |
| La Sierra University | M |
| Lee University | M,O |
| Lehigh University | M,D |
| Lehman College of the City University of New York | M |
| Liberty University | M |
| Lipscomb University | M,D,O |
| Long Island University - Brooklyn | M,D,O |
| Long Island University - Post | M,O |
| Louisiana State University and Agricultural & Mechanical College | M,D |
| Louisiana Tech University | M,D,O |
| Loyola Marymount University | M |
| Loyola University Chicago | M,D |
| Manhattan College | M,O |
| Manhattanville College | M,O |
| Marquette University | M,D |
| Marshall University | M,O |
| Mary Baldwin University | M |
| Marymount University | M,O |
| McGill University | M,D |
| McMaster University | M,D |
| McNeese State University | M |
| Memorial University of Newfoundland | M,D |
| Mercy College | M,D |
| Miami University | M,D |
| Michigan State University | M,D |
| Middlebury College | M |
| Middle Tennessee State University | M,D |
| Midwestern State University | M,D |
| Millersville University of Pennsylvania | M,O |
| Mills College | M,O |
| Minnesota State University Mankato | M,O |
| Mississippi College | M |
| Mississippi State University | M |
| Missouri State University | M,O |
| Monmouth University | M |
| Montana State University | M |
| Montclair State University | M |
| Morgan State University | M,D |
| Mount Mary University | M |
| Mount Saint Mary's University (CA) | M,D,O |
| Murray State University | M,D,O |
| National University | M,O |
| New Mexico Highlands University | M |
| New Mexico State University | M,D |
| New York University | M,D |
| North Carolina Agricultural and Technical State University | M |
| North Carolina Central University | M |
| North Carolina State University | M |
| North Dakota State University | M,D |
| Northeastern Illinois University | M |
| Northeastern State University | M |
| Northeastern University | M,D |
| Northern Arizona University | M,D,O |
| Northern Illinois University | M,D |
| Northern Kentucky University | M,O |
| Northern Michigan University | M,O |
| Northwestern State University of Louisiana | M |
| Northwestern University | M,D |
| Northwest Missouri State University | M,O |
| Oakland University | M |
| Ohio Dominican University | M |
| The Ohio State University | M,D |
| Ohio University | M,D |
| Oklahoma State University | M,D |
| Old Dominion University | M,D |
| Oregon State University | M |
| Our Lady of the Lake University | M |
| Pace University | M,O |
| Penn State University Park | M,D* |
| Pittsburg State University | M |
| Portland State University | M |
| Princeton University | D |
| Purdue University | M,D |
| Purdue University Fort Wayne | M,O |
| Purdue University Northwest | M |
| Queens College of the City University of New York | M |
| Queen's University at Kingston | M,D |
| Radford University | M |
| Rhode Island College | M,O |
| Rice University | M,D |
| Rivier University | M |
| Rutgers University - Camden | M |
| Rutgers University - Newark | M |
| Rutgers University - New Brunswick | D |
| St. Cloud State University | M |
| St. John's University (NY) | M,D |
| Saint Louis University | M,D |
| Saint Louis University–Madrid Campus | M |
| St. Mary's University (United States) | M |
| Salem State University | M |
| Salisbury University | M |
| Sam Houston State University | M |
| San Diego State University | M |
| San Francisco State University | M,O |
| Seton Hall University | M |
| Simmons University | M,D,O |
| Simon Fraser University | M,D |
| Slippery Rock University of Pennsylvania | M |
| Sonoma State University | M |
| South Carolina State University | M |
| South Dakota State University | M |
| Southeastern Louisiana University | M |
| Southeast Missouri State University | M |
| Southern Connecticut State University | M |
| Southern Illinois University Carbondale | M,D |
| Southern Illinois University Edwardsville | M,O |
| Southern Methodist University | M,D |
| Southern New Hampshire University | M |
| Spring Hill College | M,O |
| Stanford University | M,D |
| State University of New York at Fredonia | M,O |
| State University of New York at New Paltz | M |
| State University of New York College at Cortland | M |
| Stephen F. Austin State University | M |
| Stony Brook University, State University of New York | M,D,O |
| Sul Ross State University | M |
| SUNY Brockport | M,O |
| Syracuse University | M,D |
| Tarleton State University | M |
| Temple University | M,D* |
| Tennessee Technological University | M |
| Texas A&M International University | M |
| Texas A&M University | M,D |
| Texas A&M University–Commerce | M,D,O |
| Texas A&M University–Corpus Christi | M |
| Texas A&M University–Kingsville | M |
| Texas A&M University–San Antonio | M |
| Texas A&M University–Texarkana | M |
| Texas Christian University | M,D |
| Texas Southern University | M |
| Texas State University | M |
| Texas Tech University | M,D |
| Texas Woman's University | M,D |
| Tiffin University | M |
| Trinity College (United States) | M |
| Trinity Western University | M |
| Truman State University | M |
| Tufts University | M,D |
| Tulane University | M |
| UNB Fredericton | M,D |
| Universidad de las Américas Puebla | M |
| Université de Montréal | M,D |
| University at Albany, State University of New York | M,D |
| University at Buffalo, the State University of New York | M,D,O |
| The University of Akron | M |
| The University of Alabama | M,D |
| The University of Alabama at Birmingham | M |
| The University of Alabama in Huntsville | M,O |
| University of Alaska Anchorage | M |
| University of Alaska Fairbanks | M |
| University of Alberta | M,D |
| The University of Arizona | M,D |
| University of Arkansas | M,D |
| The University of British Columbia | M,D |
| University of California, Berkeley | D |
| University of California, Davis | M,D |
| University of California, Irvine | M,D |
| University of California, Los Angeles | M,D |
| University of California, Riverside | M,D |
| University of California, San Diego | M,D |
| University of California, Santa Barbara | D |
| University of California, Santa Cruz | M,D |
| University of Central Arkansas | M |
| University of Central Florida | M,D,O |
| University of Central Missouri | M,D,O |
| University of Central Oklahoma | M |
| University of Chicago | M,D |
| University of Cincinnati | M,D |
| University of Colorado Boulder | M,D |
| University of Colorado Denver | M |
| University of Connecticut | M,D |
| University of Dayton | M |
| University of Delaware | M,D |
| University of Denver | M,D |
| University of Florida | M,D |
| University of Georgia | M,D |
| University of Guam | M |
| University of Guelph | M |
| University of Hawaii at Manoa | M,D |
| University of Houston–Clear Lake | M |
| University of Houston - Downtown | M |
| University of Illinois at Chicago | M,D |
| University of Illinois at Springfield | M,O |
| University of Illinois at Urbana-Champaign | M,D |
| University of Indianapolis | M |
| The University of Iowa | M,D |
| The University of Kansas | M,D |
| University of Kentucky | M,D |
| University of La Verne | M,O |
| University of Lethbridge | M,D |
| University of Louisiana at Lafayette | M,D |
| University of Louisiana at Monroe | M |
| University of Louisville | M,D |
| University of Maine | M |
| The University of Manchester | D |
| University of Manitoba | M,D |
| University of Maryland, Baltimore County | M |
| University of Maryland, College Park | M,D |
| University of Massachusetts Amherst | M,D |
| University of Massachusetts Boston | M |
| University of Memphis | M,D,O |
| University of Miami | M,D |
| University of Michigan | M,D,O |
| University of Michigan–Flint | M |
| University of Minnesota, Duluth | M |
| University of Minnesota, Twin Cities Campus | M,D |
| University of Mississippi | M,D |
| University of Missouri | M,D |
| University of Missouri–Kansas City | M,D |
| University of Missouri–St. Louis | M |
| University of Montana | M |
| University of Montevallo | M |
| University of Nebraska at Kearney | M |
| University of Nebraska at Omaha | M,O |
| University of Nebraska–Lincoln | M,D |
| University of Nevada, Las Vegas | M,D |
| University of Nevada, Reno | M,D |
| University of New Hampshire | M,D |
| University of New Mexico | M,D |
| University of New Orleans | M |
| University of North Alabama | M |
| The University of North Carolina at Chapel Hill | M,D |
| The University of North Carolina at Charlotte | M,O |
| The University of North Carolina at Greensboro | M,D |
| The University of North Carolina Wilmington | M |
| University of North Dakota | M,D |
| University of Northern Colorado | M |
| University of Northern Iowa | M |
| University of North Florida | M |
| University of North Texas | M,D,O |
| University of Notre Dame | M,D |
| University of Oklahoma | M,D |
| University of Oregon | M,D |
| University of Ottawa | M,D |
| University of Pennsylvania | M,D |
| University of Pittsburgh | M,D* |
| University of Puerto Rico at Mayagüez | M |
| University of Puerto Rico at Rio Piedras | M,D |
| University of Regina | M,D |
| University of Rhode Island | M,D |
| University of Rochester | M,D |
| University of St. Thomas (MN) | M,O |
| University of Saskatchewan | M,D |
| University of South Africa | M,D |
| University of South Alabama | M |
| University of South Carolina | M,D |
| University of South Dakota | M,D |
| University of Southern California | M,D |
| University of Southern Indiana | M |
| University of South Florida | M,D,O |
| The University of Tennessee | M,D |
| The University of Tennessee at Chattanooga | M |
| The University of Texas at Arlington | M,D |
| The University of Texas at Austin | M,D |
| The University of Texas at El Paso | M,D,O |
| The University of Texas at San Antonio | M,D |
| The University of Texas at Tyler | M |
| The University of Texas of the Permian Basin | M |
| The University of Texas Rio Grande Valley | M |
| The University of the South | M |
| The University of Toledo | M,O |
| University of Toronto | M,D |
| The University of Tulsa | M,D |
| University of Utah | M,D |
| University of Vermont | M |
| University of Victoria | M,D |
| University of Virginia | M,D |
| University of Washington | M,D |
| University of Waterloo | M,D |
| The University of Western Ontario | M,D |
| University of West Florida | M |
| University of Windsor | M |
| University of Wisconsin–Eau Claire | M |
| University of Wisconsin–Madison | M,D |
| University of Wisconsin–Milwaukee | M,D* |
| University of Wisconsin–Oshkosh | M |
| University of Wyoming | M |
| Université Laval | M,D |
| Utah State University | M |
| Valdosta State University | M |
| Valparaiso University | M |
| Vanderbilt University | M,D* |
| Villanova University | M |
| Virginia Commonwealth University | M |
| Virginia Polytechnic Institute and State University | M,D,O |
| Wake Forest University | M |
| Washington State University | M,D |
| Washington University in St. Louis | M,D |
| Wayne State University | M,D |
| Weber State University | M |
| Western Carolina University | M,O |
| Western Connecticut State University | M |
| Western Illinois University | M,O |
| Western Kentucky University | M |
| Western Michigan University | M,D |
| Western Washington University | M |
| Westfield State University | M |
| West Texas A&M University | M |
| West Virginia University | M,D |
| Wichita State University | M |
| Wilfrid Laurier University | M,D |
| Wilson College | M |
| Winona State University | M |
| Winthrop University | M |
| Wright State University | M |
| Xavier University | M* |
| Yale University | M,D |
| York University | M,D |
| Youngstown State University | M |

## ENGLISH AS A SECOND LANGUAGE

| | |
|---|---|
| Acacia University | M |
| Albizu University - Miami | M,D |
| Albright College | M |
| Alliant International University - San Diego | M,D,O |
| Alliant International University–San Francisco | M,O |
| American College of Education | M |
| American University | M,O |
| The American University in Cairo | M,O |
| American University of Armenia | M |
| American University of Sharjah | M,D |
| Anaheim University | M,D,O |
| Andrews University | M,D,O |
| Angelo State University | M |
| Arizona State University at Tempe | M,D,O |
| Arkansas Tech University | M |
| Asbury University | M |
| Aurora University | M,D |
| Azusa Pacific University | M |
| Ball State University | M |
| Barry University | M,D,O |

*M—masters degree; D—doctorate; O—other advanced degree; *—Close-Up and/or Display*

| | |
|---|---|
| Binghamton University, State University of New York | M |
| Biola University | M,D,O |
| Bishop's University | M,O |
| Boise State University | M |
| Boricua College | M |
| Brigham Young University | M |
| Brock University | M |
| Brown University | M,D |
| Buena Vista University | M |
| Bushnell University | M |
| Cabrini University | M,D |
| California Baptist University | M |
| California State University, Dominguez Hills | M,O |
| California State University, East Bay | M |
| California State University, Fresno | M |
| California State University, Long Beach | M,O |
| California State University, Sacramento | M |
| California State University, Stanislaus | M,O |
| Cambridge College | M,D,O |
| Canisius College | M,O |
| Carson-Newman University | M |
| Central Michigan University | M |
| Central Washington University | M |
| City College of the City University of New York | M |
| Cleveland State University | M |
| Coastal Carolina University | M,O |
| College of Charleston | O |
| College of Mount Saint Vincent | M,O |
| The College of New Jersey | M,O |
| The College of New Rochelle | M,O |
| College of Saint Elizabeth | M,O |
| College of Saint Mary | M |
| College of Staten Island of the City University of New York | M,O |
| Colorado Mesa University | M,O |
| Columbia International University | M,D,O |
| Columbus State University | O |
| Concordia University (United States) | M,D |
| Concordia University (Canada) | M,D,O |
| Cornerstone University | M,O |
| Dallas Baptist University | M |
| DeSales University | M,O |
| Dominican University | M |
| Duquesne University | M |
| East Carolina University | M,D,O |
| Eastern Michigan University | M,O |
| Eastern Nazarene College | M,O |
| Eastern New Mexico University | M |
| Eastern University | M,O |
| Eastern Washington University | M |
| East Tennessee State University | M,O |
| Elms College | M,O |
| Emporia State University | M,O |
| Erikson Institute | M,O |
| Fairfield University | M,O |
| Florida Atlantic University | M,D,O |
| Florida Gulf Coast University | M |
| Florida International University | M,D,O |
| Florida State University | M,D,O |
| Fordham University | M,O |
| Framingham State University | M,O |
| Fresno Pacific University | M,O |
| Furman University | M,O |
| Gannon University | O |
| George Fox University | M,O |
| George Mason University | M |
| Gonzaga University | M |
| Gordon College | M,O |
| Grand Canyon University | M,D,O |
| Greensboro College | M |
| Hamline University | M,D |
| Harding University | M,O |
| Hawaii Pacific University | M |
| Henderson State University | M,O |
| Heritage University | M |
| Hofstra University | M,D,O |
| Holy Family University | M |
| Houston Baptist University | M,D |
| Humboldt State University | M |
| Hunter College of the City University of New York | M |
| Huntington University | M,D |
| Idaho State University | M,D,O |
| Immaculata University | M,O |
| Indiana State University | M,D,O |
| Indiana University Bloomington | M,D |
| Indiana University of Pennsylvania | M,D |
| Indiana University-Purdue University Indianapolis | M,O |
| Inter American University of Puerto Rico, Arecibo Campus | M |
| Inter American University of Puerto Rico, Barranquitas Campus | M |
| Inter American University of Puerto Rico, Metropolitan Campus | M |
| Inter American University of Puerto Rico, Ponce Campus | M |
| Inter American University of Puerto Rico, San Germán Campus | M |
| Iowa State University of Science and Technology | M |
| James Madison University | M |
| Kansas State University | M,D,O |
| Kean University | M |
| Kennesaw State University | M |
| Kent State University | M,D |
| Langston University | M |
| La Salle University | M,O |
| Lasell College | M,O |
| Lee University | M,O |
| Lehman College of the City University of New York | M |
| Le Moyne College | M,O |
| Lesley University | M,D,O |
| Lewis University | M |
| Lindenwood University | M,D,O |
| Long Island University - Brooklyn | M,O |
| Long Island University - Hudson | M,O |
| Long Island University - Post | M,D,O |
| Long Island University - Riverhead | M,O |
| Madonna University | M |
| Manhattanville College | M,O |
| Marlboro College | M |
| Mary Baldwin University | M |
| McDaniel College | M |
| Mercy College | M,O |
| Meredith College | M,O |
| Messiah University | M |
| Metropolitan State University | M |
| Michigan State University | M,D |
| MidAmerica Nazarene University | M |
| Middlebury Institute of International Studies at Monterey | M |
| Middle Tennessee State University | M,O |
| Midwest University | M,D |
| Millersville University of Pennsylvania | M |
| Minnesota State University Mankato | M,O |
| Mississippi College | M |
| Missouri State University | M,O |
| Missouri Western State University | M,O |
| Molloy College | M,O |
| Monmouth University | M,D,O |
| Montclair State University | M,O |
| Mount Saint Vincent University | M |
| Multnomah University | M |
| Murray State University | M,D,O |
| Nazareth College of Rochester | M |
| New Jersey City University | M |
| Newman University | M |
| New Mexico State University | M,D,O |
| New York University | M,D,O |
| Niagara University | M,O |
| Northeastern Illinois University | M |
| Northern Arizona University | M,D,O |
| Northern Michigan University | M,O |
| Northwest Missouri State University | M,D,O |
| Notre Dame of Maryland University | M |
| Nyack College | M |
| Oakland University | M,O |
| Ohio Dominican University | M |
| Oklahoma City University | M |
| Old Dominion University | M |
| Pacific University | M |
| Penn State Harrisburg | M,D,O |
| Penn State University Park | M,D* |
| Penn State York | M,O |
| Pittsburg State University | M,O |
| Pontifical Catholic University of Puerto Rico | M |
| Portland State University | M,O |
| Post University | M |
| Providence University College & Theological Seminary | M,D,O |
| Purdue University Fort Wayne | M,O |
| Queens College of the City University of New York | M,O |
| Quincy University | M |
| Regent University | M,D,O |
| Rhode Island College | M |
| Rider University | M |
| Rowan University | O |
| Rutgers University - New Brunswick | M,D |
| St. John's University (NY) | M,O |
| Saint Michael's College | M,O |
| St. Thomas University - Florida | M,D,O |
| Saint Xavier University | M |
| Salem College | M |
| Salem State University | M |
| San Diego State University | M,O |
| San Francisco State University | M |
| San Jose State University | M,O |
| Seattle University | M,O |
| Simon Fraser University | M |
| SIT Graduate Institute | M |
| Slippery Rock University of Pennsylvania | M |
| Southeastern University (FL) | M,D |
| Southeast Missouri State University | M |
| Southern Connecticut State University | M |
| Southern Illinois University Carbondale | M |
| Southern Illinois University Edwardsville | M,O |
| Southern Methodist University | M,D |
| Southern New Hampshire University | M,D,O |
| Southwest Minnesota State University | M |
| State University of New York at Fredonia | M |
| State University of New York at New Paltz | M,O |
| State University of New York College at Cortland | M |
| Stony Brook University, State University of New York | M |
| Syracuse University | M,O |
| Taylor College and Seminary | M,O |
| Teachers College, Columbia University | M,D,O |
| Temple University | M* |
| Tennessee Technological University | M |
| Texas A&M University–Commerce | M,D,O |
| Texas A&M University–Kingsville | M,D |
| Trevecca Nazarene University | M,O |
| Trinity Western University | M |
| Troy University | M |
| Universidad del Este | M |
| Universidad del Turabo | M |
| University at Buffalo, the State University of New York | M,D,O |
| The University of Alabama | M,D |
| The University of Alabama at Birmingham | M,O |
| The University of Alabama in Huntsville | M,O |
| University of Alberta | M,D |
| The University of Arizona | M,D |
| University of Arkansas at Little Rock | M |
| The University of British Columbia | M,D |
| University of California, Berkeley | O |
| University of California, Los Angeles | M,D,O |
| University of California, Riverside | M,D,O |
| University of Central Florida | M,O |
| University of Central Missouri | M,D,O |
| University of Central Oklahoma | M |
| University of Cincinnati | M,D |
| University of Colorado Colorado Springs | M,D |
| University of Dayton | M |
| University of Delaware | M,D,O |
| The University of Findlay | M,D |
| University of Florida | M,D,O |
| University of Guam | M |
| University of Hawaii at Manoa | M,D,O |
| University of Illinois at Chicago | M,D |
| University of Illinois at Urbana-Champaign | M,D |
| The University of Iowa | M,D |
| University of Louisiana at Lafayette | M,D |
| University of Manitoba | M |
| University of Maryland, Baltimore County | M,O |
| University of Maryland, College Park | M,D,O |
| University of Massachusetts Amherst | M,D,O |
| University of Massachusetts Dartmouth | M,D,O |
| University of Memphis | M,D,O |
| University of Minnesota, Twin Cities Campus | M,D,O |
| University of Missouri–St. Louis | M |
| University of Nebraska at Kearney | M |
| University of Nebraska at Omaha | M,O |
| University of Nevada, Las Vegas | M,D,O |
| University of Nevada, Reno | M |
| University of New Mexico | M,D |
| The University of North Carolina at Chapel Hill | M |
| The University of North Carolina at Charlotte | M,D,O |
| The University of North Carolina at Greensboro | M,D,O |
| The University of North Carolina Wilmington | M |
| University of Northern Colorado | M,D |
| University of Northern Iowa | M |
| University of North Florida | M |
| University of North Texas | M,D,O |
| University of Pennsylvania | M |
| University of Phoenix–Online Campus | M,O |
| University of Phoenix - San Diego Campus | M |
| University of Pittsburgh | D,O* |
| University of Portland | M,D |
| University of Puerto Rico at Rio Piedras | M |
| University of St. Francis (IL) | M,D,O |
| University of Saint Joseph | M |
| University of St. Thomas (TX) | M,D |
| University of San Diego | M |
| University of Saskatchewan | M |
| University of South Africa | M,D |
| University of South Carolina | M,D,O |
| University of South Dakota | M |
| University of Southern California | M |
| University of Southern Indiana | M |
| University of Southern Maine | M,O |
| University of South Florida | O |
| The University of Tennessee | M,D,O |
| The University of Texas at Arlington | M |
| The University of Texas at El Paso | M,O |
| The University of Texas at San Antonio | M,D,O |
| The University of Texas of the Permian Basin | M |
| The University of Texas Rio Grande Valley | M |
| University of the Southwest | M |
| The University of Toledo | M,D,O |
| University of Washington | M,D |
| University of Wisconsin–Madison | M,D |
| University of Wisconsin–Milwaukee | M,D,O* |
| University of Wisconsin–River Falls | M |
| Upper Iowa University | M |
| Utah Valley University | M |
| Valley City State University | M |
| Valparaiso University | M,O |
| Virginia International University | M |
| Walden University | M,D,O |
| Washington State University | M,D |
| Wayland Baptist University | M |
| Wayne State College | M |
| Wayne State University | M,D,O |
| Webster University | M,O |
| Westcliff University | M |
| Western Carolina University | M,O |
| Western Illinois University | M,O |
| Western Kentucky University | M |
| Western New Mexico University | M |
| Wilmington University | M,D |
| Winona State University | M |
| Worcester State University | M,O |

## ENGLISH EDUCATION

| | |
|---|---|
| Alabama Agricultural and Mechanical University | M,O |
| Alabama State University | M,O |
| Albany State University | M |
| Andrews University | M,D,O |
| Anna Maria College | M,O |
| Appalachian State University | M |
| Arcadia University | M,D,O |
| Arkansas State University | M,O |
| Arkansas Tech University | M |
| Binghamton University, State University of New York | M |
| Bloomsburg University of Pennsylvania | M |
| Bob Jones University | M,D,O |
| Boise State University | M |
| Boston College | M,D,O |
| Brooklyn College of the City University of New York | M |
| Brown University | M |
| Buffalo State College, State University of New York | M |
| California Baptist University | M |
| California State University, Northridge | M |
| Campbellsville University | M |
| Caribbean University | M,D |
| Carthage College | M,O |
| Central Connecticut State University | M,O |
| Chadron State College | M,O |
| Chatham University | M |
| The Citadel, The Military College of South Carolina | M,O |
| City College of the City University of New York | M,O |
| Clayton State University | M |
| College of St. Joseph | M |
| College of Staten Island of the City University of New York | M |
| The Colorado College | M |
| Columbus State University | M,O |
| Converse College | M |
| Delta State University | M |
| Duquesne University | M |
| East Carolina University | M,D,O |
| Eastern Kentucky University | M |
| Eastern Michigan University | M |
| Eastern University | M,O |
| Elms College | M,O |
| Fitchburg State University | M,O |
| Florida Agricultural and Mechanical University | M |
| Florida Gulf Coast University | M |
| Florida International University | M,D,O |
| Florida State University | M,D,O |
| Gardner-Webb University | M |
| George Mason University | M,D,O |
| Georgia Southwestern State University | M,O |
| Georgia State University | M,D |
| Hampton University | M |
| Harding University | M,O |
| Hofstra University | M,D,O |
| Hunter College of the City University of New York | M |
| Indiana University of Pennsylvania | D |
| Iona College | M |
| Ithaca College | M |
| Jackson State University | M |
| Kansas State University | M,D,O |
| Kennesaw State University | M |
| Kent State University | M,D |
| Kutztown University of Pennsylvania | M,D |
| Lake Forest College | M |
| Lehman College of the City University of New York | M |
| Le Moyne College | M,O |
| Lewis University | M |
| Lincoln Memorial University | M,D,O |
| Lipscomb University | M,D,O |
| London Metropolitan University | M,D |
| Manhattanville College | M,O |
| Marymount University | M,O |
| Metropolitan State University | M |
| Millersville University of Pennsylvania | M |
| Mississippi College | M,D,O |
| Missouri State University | M,O |
| Molloy College | M,O |
| Montclair State University | M,O |
| Morehead State University | M,O |
| Murray State University | M,D,O |
| National Louis University | M,D,O |
| New Mexico State University | M,D |
| New York University | M,D,O |
| North Carolina Agricultural and Technical State University | M |
| Northeastern Illinois University | M |
| Northwest Missouri State University | M,O |
| Oregon State University | M |
| Plymouth State University | M |
| Purdue University | M,D,O |
| Purdue University Fort Wayne | M,O |
| Queens College of the City University of New York | M,O |
| Quinnipiac University | M |
| Rhode Island College | M |
| Rowan University | O |
| Rutgers University - New Brunswick | M |
| St. John Fisher College | M |
| San Francisco State University | M,O |
| Simon Fraser University | M,D |
| Smith College | M |
| South Carolina State University | M |
| Southeastern Louisiana University | M |
| Southern Illinois University Edwardsville | M,O |
| State University of New York at Fredonia | M,O |
| State University of New York at New Paltz | M,O |
| State University of New York at Plattsburgh | M |

| | |
|---|---|
| State University of New York College at Cortland | M |
| State University of New York College at Geneseo | M |
| State University of New York College at Old Westbury | M |
| State University of New York College at Potsdam | M |
| SUNY Brockport | M,O |
| Syracuse University | M |
| Teachers College, Columbia University | M,D,O |
| Temple University | M* |
| Texas Woman's University | M,D |
| Trinity Washington University | M |
| University at Buffalo, the State University of New York | M,D,O |
| The University of Akron | M |
| The University of Alabama in Huntsville | M,O |
| The University of Arizona | M,D |
| University of Arkansas at Pine Bluff | M |
| University of Central Florida | M,O |
| University of Colorado Denver | M |
| University of Connecticut | M,D |
| University of Florida | M,D,O |
| University of Georgia | M,D |
| University of Indianapolis | M |
| The University of Iowa | M,D |
| University of Manitoba | M |
| University of Maryland, Baltimore County | M |
| University of Michigan | D |
| University of Minnesota, Twin Cities Campus | M |
| University of Missouri | M,D,O |
| University of Montana | M |
| University of New Mexico | M,D |
| The University of North Carolina at Chapel Hill | M |
| The University of North Carolina at Greensboro | M,D |
| The University of North Carolina at Pembroke | M |
| University of Northern Colorado | M,D |
| University of Northern Iowa | M |
| University of North Georgia | M |
| University of Oklahoma | M,D |
| University of Pennsylvania | M,D |
| University of Phoenix–Online Campus | M,O |
| University of Puerto Rico at Mayagüez | M |
| University of St. Francis (IL) | M,D,O |
| University of South Carolina | M,D |
| University of South Florida, St. Petersburg | M |
| University of South Florida Sarasota-Manatee | M |
| The University of Tennessee | M,D,O |
| The University of Texas at El Paso | M,D,O |
| University of the District of Columbia | M |
| University of the Sacred Heart | M,O |
| The University of Toledo | M,D,O |
| University of Victoria | M,D |
| University of Virginia | M,D,O |
| University of Washington | M,D |
| The University of West Alabama | M |
| University of Wisconsin–La Crosse | M,O |
| University of Wisconsin–Milwaukee | M,D* |
| University of Wisconsin–Stevens Point | M |
| Valdosta State University | M |
| Valley City State University | M |
| Vanderbilt University | M* |
| Wagner College | M |
| Wayland Baptist University | M |
| Wayne State College | M |
| Wayne State University | M,D,O |
| Western Governors University | M,O |
| Western Kentucky University | M |
| Western Michigan University | M,D |
| Western New England University | M |
| West Virginia University | M,D |
| Widener University | M,D |
| William Carey University | M,O |
| William Jessup University | M |
| Worcester State University | M |

## ENTERTAINMENT MANAGEMENT

| | |
|---|---|
| Berklee College of Music | M |
| California Intercontinental University | M |
| California State University, Northridge | M,O |
| Carnegie Mellon University | M |
| Columbia College Chicago | M |
| Full Sail University | M |
| Hofstra University | M,O |
| Manhattanville College | M,O |
| Point Park University | M |
| Southern New Hampshire University | M,D,O |
| Syracuse University | M |
| Universidad Autonoma de Guadalajara | M,D |
| University of Colorado Denver | M |
| University of Dallas | M,D |
| University of Massachusetts Amherst | |
| University of South Carolina | M |
| Valparaiso University | M |

## ENTOMOLOGY

| | |
|---|---|
| Auburn University | M,D |
| Clemson University | M,D |
| Colorado State University | M,D |
| Cornell University | M,D |
| Illinois State University | M,D |
| Iowa State University of Science and Technology | M,D |
| Kansas State University | M,D |
| Louisiana State University and Agricultural & Mechanical College | M,D |
| McGill University | M,D |
| Michigan State University | M,D |
| New Mexico State University | M |
| North Carolina State University | M,D |
| North Dakota State University | M,D |
| The Ohio State University | M,D |
| Oklahoma State University | M,D |
| Penn State University Park | M,D* |
| Purdue University | M,D |
| Rutgers University - New Brunswick | M,D |
| Simon Fraser University | M,D,O |
| State University of New York College of Environmental Science and Forestry | M,D |
| Texas A&M University | M,D |
| The University of Arizona | M,D |
| University of Arkansas | M,D |
| University of California, Davis | M,D |
| University of California, Riverside | M,D |
| University of Delaware | M,D |
| University of Georgia | M,D |
| University of Guelph | M,D |
| University of Hawaii at Manoa | M,D |
| University of Idaho | M,D |
| University of Illinois at Urbana-Champaign | M,D |
| University of Kentucky | M,D |
| University of Maine | M,D |
| University of Manitoba | M,D |
| University of Maryland, College Park | M,D |
| University of Minnesota, Twin Cities Campus | M,D |
| University of Missouri | M,D |
| University of Nebraska–Lincoln | M,D |
| The University of Tennessee | M,D |
| University of Vermont | M,D,O |
| University of Wisconsin–Madison | M,D |
| University of Wyoming | M,D |
| Virginia Polytechnic Institute and State University | M,D |
| Washington State University | M,D |
| West Virginia University | M,D |

## ENTREPRENEURSHIP

| | |
|---|---|
| Albizu University - Miami | M,D |
| American College of Thessaloniki | M,O |
| American University | M,D,O |
| Anaheim University | M,D,O |
| Arizona State University at Tempe | M,D |
| Ashland University | M |
| Azusa Pacific University | M |
| Babson College | M,O |
| Bakke Graduate University | M,D |
| Baruch College of the City University of New York | M,D |
| Baylor University | D |
| Bay Path University | M |
| Benedictine University | M |
| Brandeis University | M |
| Brandman University | M |
| Brigham Young University | M |
| Cairn University | M,O |
| California Institute of Advanced Management | M |
| California Intercontinental University | M,D |
| California Lutheran University | M,O |
| California State University, San Bernardino | M |
| California University of Pennsylvania | M |
| Cambridge College | M |
| Cameron University | M |
| Capella University | M,D |
| Carnegie Mellon University | D |
| City Vision University | M |
| Clarion University of Pennsylvania | M |
| Clemson University | M,D |
| Cogswell Polytechnical College | M |
| Columbia University | M |
| Dallas Baptist University | M |
| Dartmouth College | D |
| Delaware Valley University | M |
| DePaul University | M,D |
| Dickinson State University | M |
| Drexel University | M |
| Eastern Michigan University | M,O |
| East Tennessee State University | M,O |
| Elms College | M,O |
| Embry-Riddle Aeronautical University–Worldwide | M |
| Emory University | M |
| Everglades University | M |
| Fairleigh Dickinson University, Florham Campus | M,O |
| Fairleigh Dickinson University, Metropolitan Campus | M,O |
| Felician University | M,D |
| Florida Atlantic University | M |
| Fordham University | M,D |
| Georgia State University | M,D |
| Golden Gate University | M,D,O |
| Grand Canyon University | M |
| Harrisburg University of Science and Technology | M |
| HEC Montreal | M,O |
| Hult International Business School (United States) | M |
| IGlobal University | M |
| Illinois Institute of Technology | M |
| Indiana University-Purdue University Indianapolis | M |
| International University in Geneva | M,D |
| The International University of Monaco | M |
| James Madison University | M |
| Kansas State University | M,O |
| Lehigh University | M |
| Lenoir-Rhyne University | M |
| Lindenwood University | M |
| Loyola University Chicago | M |
| Manhattanville College | M |
| Marlboro College | M |
| Marquette University | M,O |
| McGill University | M,D,O |
| Mercer University | M |
| Mercyhurst University | M,O |
| Midwest University | M,D |
| Monroe College | M |
| Nebraska Christian College of Hope International University | M |
| New York University | M |
| North Carolina State University | M |
| Northeastern University | M |
| Nova Southeastern University | M |
| Oakland University | M,O |
| Oklahoma State University | M,D |
| Old Dominion University | M,O |
| Oral Roberts University | M |
| Pace University | M |
| Penn State Great Valley | M,O |
| Penn State University Park | M* |
| Peru State College | M |
| Point Loma Nazarene University | M |
| Pontificia Universidad Catolica Madre y Maestra | M |
| Purchase College, State University of New York | M |
| Purdue University Global | M |
| Queen's University at Kingston | M |
| Regent University | M,D,O |
| Rochester Institute of Technology | M |
| Rockhurst University | M,O |
| Rollins College | M |
| Salve Regina University | M |
| Samford University | M |
| San Diego State University | M |
| San Francisco State University | M |
| Seton Hall University | M,O |
| Seton Hill University | M |
| SIT Graduate Institute | M |
| South Carolina State University | M |
| Southeastern University (FL) | M,D |
| Southeast Missouri State University | M |
| Southern Methodist University | M |
| Southern New Hampshire University | M,D,O |
| South University - Savannah | M |
| Stevens Institute of Technology | M,O |
| Stony Brook University, State University of New York | M,O |
| Suffolk University | M |
| Syracuse University | M |
| Temple University | M,D* |
| Texas A&M University | M |
| Tufts University | M |
| Tulane University | M,D |
| UNB Fredericton | M |
| United States International University–Africa | M |
| University at Albany, State University of New York | M |
| The University of Alabama in Huntsville | M,O |
| University of Arkansas at Little Rock | O |
| University of Baltimore | M |
| University of Bridgeport | M |
| University of California, Davis | M |
| University of California, Merced | M,D |
| University of Central Florida | M,O |
| University of Chicago | M,O |
| University of Colorado Denver | M |
| University of Delaware | M,D |
| University of Florida | M,D,O |
| University of Hawaii at Manoa | M,O |
| University of Houston–Victoria | M |
| University of Louisiana at Lafayette | M |
| University of Louisville | M,D |
| The University of Manchester | M |
| University of Massachusetts Amherst | M,D |
| University of Massachusetts Lowell | M,D |
| University of Minnesota, Twin Cities Campus | D |
| University of New Mexico | M |
| University of Notre Dame | M |
| University of Oklahoma | M,D,O |
| University of Pennsylvania | M |
| University of Pikeville | M |
| University of Portland | M |
| University of Rhode Island | M,D,O |
| University of Rochester | M |
| University of San Francisco | M |
| University of Sioux Falls | M |
| University of Southern California | M |
| University of South Florida | M,O |
| The University of Tampa | M,O |
| The University of Texas at Austin | M,D |
| The University of Texas at Dallas | M,D |
| University of Washington | M,D |
| University of Waterloo | M |
| The University of Western Ontario | M,D |
| University of West Los Angeles | M |
| University of Wisconsin–Milwaukee | M,D,O* |
| Université Laval | M,O |
| Virginia International University | M,O |
| Walden University | M,D,O |
| Washington University in St. Louis | M |
| Wayne State University | M,D,O |
| Western Carolina University | M |
| Wichita State University | M |
| Wingate University | M |

## ENVIRONMENTAL AND OCCUPATIONAL HEALTH

| | |
|---|---|
| Augusta University | M |
| Boise State University | M,O |
| California State University, Fullerton | M |
| California State University, Northridge | M |
| Capella University | M,D |
| Clemson University | M,D |
| Colorado State University | M,D |
| Columbia Southern University | M |
| Columbia University | M,D |
| Duke University | O |
| East Carolina University | M,D,O |
| Eastern Kentucky University | M |
| East Tennessee State University | M,D,O |
| Embry-Riddle Aeronautical University–Worldwide | M |
| Emory University | M,D |
| Florida International University | M,D |
| Fort Valley State University | M |
| Gannon University | M |
| The George Washington University | D |
| Georgia Southern University | M,D,O |
| Harvard University | M,D* |
| Indiana State University | M |
| Indiana University Bloomington | M,D |
| Indiana University of Pennsylvania | M,D |
| Indiana University-Purdue University Indianapolis | M,D,O |
| Johns Hopkins University | M,D |
| Kent State University | M,D |
| Lehigh University | M,O |
| Lewis University | M |
| Loma Linda University | M |
| Louisiana State University Health Sciences Center | M,D |
| McGill University | M,D |
| Meharry Medical College | M |
| Mercer University | M,D |
| Mississippi Valley State University | M |
| Murray State University | M |
| New York Medical College | M,D,O |
| Oakland University | M |
| Old Dominion University | M |
| Oregon State University | M,D |
| Purdue University | M,D |
| Rochester Institute of Technology | M |
| Rutgers University - New Brunswick | M,D,O |
| San Diego State University | M,D |
| Southeastern Oklahoma State University | M |
| Syracuse University | O |
| Temple University | M,D* |
| Texas A&M University | M,D |
| Towson University | D |
| Trident University International | M,D,O |
| Tufts University | M,D |
| Tulane University | M,D |
| Uniformed Services University of the Health Sciences | M,D |
| Universidad Autonoma de Guadalajara | M,D |
| Universidad de Ciencias Medicas | M,D,O |
| Université de Montréal | M |
| Université du Québec à Montréal | O |
| University at Albany, State University of New York | M,D |
| The University of Alabama at Birmingham | M,D |
| University of Alberta | M,D |
| University of Arkansas for Medical Sciences | M,D,O |
| University of California, Berkeley | M,D |
| University of California, Irvine | M,D |
| University of California, Los Angeles | M,D |
| University of Central Missouri | M,D,O |
| University of Cincinnati | M,D |
| University of Colorado Denver | M |
| University of Connecticut | O |
| University of Florida | M,D,O |
| University of Georgia | M,D |
| University of Illinois at Chicago | M,D |
| University of Illinois at Springfield | M,O |
| The University of Iowa | M,D,O |
| University of Louisville | M,D |
| University of Maryland, College Park | M |
| University of Massachusetts Amherst | M,D |
| University of Memphis | M,D |
| University of Miami | M |
| University of Michigan | M,D |
| University of Minnesota, Twin Cities Campus | M,D,O |
| University of Nebraska Medical Center | D |
| University of Nevada, Reno | M,D |
| University of New Haven | M |
| The University of North Carolina at Chapel Hill | M,D |
| University of Oklahoma Health Sciences Center | M,D |
| University of Pennsylvania | M |
| University of Pittsburgh | M,D* |
| University of Puerto Rico - Medical Sciences Campus | M,D |
| University of Saint Francis (IN) | M |
| University of South Alabama | M |

*M—masters degree; D—doctorate; O—other advanced degree; *—Close-Up and/or Display*

- University of South Carolina M,D
- University of Southern California M
- University of South Florida O
- The University of Texas at Tyler M
- The University of Texas Health Science Center at Houston M,D,O
- University of the Sacred Heart M
- The University of Toledo M,D,O
- University of Toronto M,D
- University of Vermont M,O
- University of Washington M,D
- University of Wisconsin–Milwaukee M,D,O*
- University of Wisconsin–Whitewater M
- Université Laval O
- West Virginia University M,D
- Yale University M,D

## ENVIRONMENTAL BIOLOGY

- Chatham University M
- Dalhousie University M
- Dartmouth College D
- Emporia State University M
- Georgia State University M,D
- Governors State University M
- Hampton University M
- Hood College M,O
- Massachusetts Institute of Technology M,D,O
- Missouri University of Science and Technology M
- Morgan State University D
- Nicholls State University M
- Ohio University M,D
- Oregon State University M,D
- Regis University M
- Rutgers University - New Brunswick M,D
- State University of New York College of Environmental Science and Forestry M,D
- Universidad del Turabo M,D
- University of Alberta M,D
- University of California, Santa Cruz M,D
- University of Guelph M,D
- University of Louisiana at Lafayette M,D
- University of Louisville M,D
- The University of Manchester M,D
- University of Massachusetts Amherst M,D
- University of Southern California M,D
- University of South Florida M,D
- University of Wisconsin–Madison M,D
- Washington University in St. Louis D
- Youngstown State University M

## ENVIRONMENTAL DESIGN

- Arizona State University at Tempe D
- ArtCenter College of Design M
- Columbia University M
- Cornell University M
- Kansas State University D
- Kent State University M
- Michigan State University M,D
- North Carolina Agricultural and Technical State University M
- Texas Tech University M,D
- Université de Montréal M,D,O
- University of Calgary M,D
- University of California, Berkeley M,D
- University of California, Irvine D
- University of Georgia M
- The University of Manchester M,D
- Virginia Polytechnic Institute and State University M,D
- Yale University M,D

## ENVIRONMENTAL EDUCATION

- Alaska Pacific University M
- Antioch University New England M,D
- Arcadia University M,D,O
- Ball State University M,O
- Brooklyn College of the City University of New York M
- Chatham University M
- Concordia University (United States) M,D
- Concordia University Wisconsin M
- Florida Atlantic University M
- Goshen College M
- Hamline University M,D
- Instituto Tecnologico de Santo Domingo M,D,O
- Mary Baldwin University M
- Montclair State University M
- New York University M
- Oregon State University M,D
- Prescott College M,D
- Royal Roads University M,O
- Slippery Rock University of Pennsylvania M
- Southern Connecticut State University M,O
- Southern Oregon University M
- State University of New York College at Cortland M
- Université du Québec à Montréal M,D,O
- University of Florida M,D,O
- University of South Africa M,D
- University of Victoria M,D
- Western Washington University M

## ENVIRONMENTAL ENGINEERING

- Air Force Institute of Technology M
- The American University in Cairo M,D,O
- Arizona State University at Tempe M,D
- California Institute of Technology M,D
- California Polytechnic State University, San Luis Obispo M
- California State University, Fullerton M
- Carleton University M,D
- Carnegie Mellon University M,D
- The Catholic University of America M,D
- Clarkson University M,D
- Clemson University M,D
- Cleveland State University M,D
- Colorado School of Mines M,D
- Columbia University M,D
- Concordia University (Canada) M,D,O
- Cornell University M,D
- Dalhousie University M,D
- Drexel University M,D
- Duke University M,D
- Florida Atlantic University M
- Florida International University M,D
- Florida State University M,D
- Gannon University M
- The George Washington University M,D,O
- Georgia Institute of Technology M,D
- Harvard University M,D*
- Idaho State University M
- Illinois Institute of Technology M,D
- Instituto Tecnologico de Santo Domingo M,O
- Instituto Tecnológico y de Estudios Superiores de Monterrey, Campus Ciudad de México M,D
- Instituto Tecnológico y de Estudios Superiores de Monterrey, Campus Monterrey M,D
- Iowa State University of Science and Technology M,D
- Jackson State University M,D
- Johns Hopkins University M,D,O
- Kansas State University M,D
- Kennesaw State University M
- Lakehead University M
- Lehigh University M,D
- Louisiana State University and Agricultural & Mechanical College M,D
- Manhattan College M
- Marquette University M,D,O
- Marshall University M
- Massachusetts Institute of Technology M,D,O
- McGill University M,D
- Memorial University of Newfoundland M
- Mercer University M
- Michigan State University M,D
- Michigan Technological University M,D
- Missouri University of Science and Technology M,D
- Montana State University M,D
- Montana Technological University M
- New Jersey Institute of Technology M,D
- New Mexico Institute of Mining and Technology M
- New Mexico State University M,D
- New York Institute of Technology M
- New York University M
- North Dakota State University M,D
- Northeastern University M,D,O
- Northwestern University M,D
- Norwich University M
- Ohio University M,D
- Oklahoma State University M,D
- Old Dominion University M,D
- Oregon Health & Science University M,D
- Oregon State University M,D
- Penn State Harrisburg M,O
- Penn State University Park M,D*
- Polytechnic University of Puerto Rico, Miami Campus M
- Polytechnic University of Puerto Rico, Orlando Campus M
- Polytechnique Montréal M,D,O
- Portland State University M,D
- Princeton University M,D
- Purdue University M,D
- Rensselaer Polytechnic Institute M,D
- Rice University M,D
- Rose-Hulman Institute of Technology M
- Rutgers University - New Brunswick M,D
- Southern Illinois University Carbondale D
- Southern Illinois University Edwardsville M
- Southern Methodist University M,D
- State University of New York College of Environmental Science and Forestry M,D
- Stevens Institute of Technology M,D,O
- Syracuse University M
- Temple University M,O*
- Tennessee State University M,D
- Texas A&M University–Kingsville M,D
- Tufts University M,D
- UNB Fredericton M,D
- Universidad Central del Este M
- Universidad Nacional Pedro Henriquez Urena M
- Université de Sherbrooke M
- University at Buffalo, the State University of New York M,D
- The University of Alabama M,D
- The University of Alabama in Huntsville M,D
- University of Alaska Fairbanks M,D,O
- University of Alberta M,D
- The University of Arizona M,D
- University of Arkansas M,D
- University of Calgary M,D
- University of California, Berkeley M,D
- University of California, Davis M,D,O
- University of California, Irvine M,D
- University of California, Los Angeles M,D
- University of California, Merced M,D
- University of California, Riverside M,D
- University of Central Florida M,D
- University of Cincinnati M,D
- University of Colorado Boulder M,D
- University of Colorado Denver M,D
- University of Connecticut M,D
- University of Dayton M
- University of Delaware M,D
- University of Detroit Mercy M,D
- University of Florida M,D,O
- University of Georgia M
- University of Guelph M,D
- University of Hawaii at Manoa M,D
- University of Illinois at Urbana-Champaign M,D
- The University of Iowa M,D
- The University of Kansas M,D
- The University of Manchester M,D
- University of Maryland, Baltimore County M,D
- University of Maryland, College Park M,D
- University of Massachusetts Amherst M,D
- University of Massachusetts Lowell M,D
- University of Memphis M,D,O
- University of Michigan M,D,O
- University of Mississippi M,D
- University of Missouri M,D
- University of Nebraska–Lincoln M,D
- University of New Hampshire M,D
- University of New Haven M
- The University of North Carolina at Chapel Hill M,D
- The University of North Carolina at Charlotte M,D
- University of North Dakota M,D
- University of Notre Dame M,D
- University of Oklahoma M,D
- University of Pittsburgh M,D*
- University of Puerto Rico at Mayagüez M,D
- University of Regina M,D
- University of Rhode Island M,D
- University of South Alabama M
- University of Southern California M,D,O
- University of South Florida M,D
- The University of Tennessee M
- The University of Texas at Austin M,D
- The University of Texas at El Paso M,D,O
- The University of Texas at San Antonio M,D
- The University of Texas at Tyler M
- University of Utah M,D
- University of Vermont M,D
- University of Washington M,D
- University of Waterloo M,D
- The University of Western Ontario M,D
- University of Windsor M,D
- University of Wisconsin–Madison M
- University of Wyoming M
- Université Laval M,D
- Utah State University M,D,O
- Vanderbilt University M,D*
- Villanova University M,O
- Virginia Polytechnic Institute and State University M,O
- Washington State University M,D
- Washington University in St. Louis M,D
- Worcester Polytechnic Institute M,D,O
- Yale University M,D
- Youngstown State University M

## ENVIRONMENTAL LAW

- Chapman University M,D
- Florida State University M,D
- Georgetown University M,D
- Golden Gate University M,D
- Lehigh University M,O
- Lewis & Clark College M,D
- Montclair State University O
- Pace University M,D
- St. Mary's University (United States) M
- University at Buffalo, the State University of New York M,D
- University of Calgary M,O
- University of Colorado Denver M,D
- University of Florida M,D
- University of Houston M,D
- University of Pittsburgh M*
- The University of Tulsa M,D,O
- Vermont Law School M
- Western Michigan University Cooley Law School M,D

## ENVIRONMENTAL MANAGEMENT AND POLICY

- Adelphi University M
- Air Force Institute of Technology M
- American Public University System M,D
- American University M,D,O
- Antioch University New England M,D
- Arizona State University at Tempe M
- Ball State University M,O
- Bard College M,O
- Baylor University M,D
- Bemidji State University M
- Binghamton University, State University of New York M,D
- California State University, Fullerton M
- Central European University M,D
- Central Washington University M
- The Citadel, The Military College of South Carolina M,O
- Clarkson University M
- Clark University M
- Clemson University M,D
- Cleveland State University M,O
- College of the Atlantic M
- Colorado State University M,D
- Columbia University M
- Columbus State University M
- Concordia University (Canada) M,D,O
- Cornell University M,D
- Dalhousie University M
- Drexel University M
- Duke University D
- Duquesne University M,O
- The Evergreen State College M
- Florida Gulf Coast University M
- Florida Institute of Technology M
- Florida International University M,D
- George Mason University M,D
- The George Washington University M
- Georgia Institute of Technology M,D
- Georgia State University M,D,O
- Harvard University M,O*
- Humboldt State University M
- Idaho State University M
- Illinois Institute of Technology M
- Indiana University Bloomington M,D,O
- Indiana University Northwest M,O
- Indiana University of Pennsylvania M
- Instituto Tecnologico de Santo Domingo M,D,O
- Instituto Tecnológico y de Estudios Superiores de Monterrey, Campus Estado de México M,D
- Instituto Tecnológico y de Estudios Superiores de Monterrey, Campus Irapuato M,D
- Inter American University of Puerto Rico, Metropolitan Campus M
- James Madison University M
- Johns Hopkins University M,O
- Lake Forest College M
- Lehigh University M,O
- Long Island University - Post M,O
- Louisiana State University and Agricultural & Mechanical College M,D
- McGill University M,D
- Middlebury Institute of International Studies at Monterey M
- Millersville University of Pennsylvania M
- Missouri State University M,O
- Montclair State University M,D
- Morehead State University M
- New Jersey Institute of Technology M,D,O
- The New School M
- New York Institute of Technology O
- Northeastern Illinois University M,O
- Northeastern University M,D
- Northern Arizona University M,D,O
- The Ohio State University M,D
- Ohio University M,O
- Oregon State University M,O
- Pace University M
- Penn State University Park M*
- Point Park University M
- Polytechnic University of Puerto Rico M
- Polytechnic University of Puerto Rico, Miami Campus M
- Polytechnic University of Puerto Rico, Orlando Campus M
- Portland State University M,D,O
- Prescott College M
- Purdue University M,D
- Rice University M
- Royal Roads University M,O
- St. Edward's University M
- Samford University M
- San Francisco State University M
- San Jose State University M
- Shippensburg University of Pennsylvania M
- Simon Fraser University M,D,O
- SIT Graduate Institute M
- Slippery Rock University of Pennsylvania M
- Southeast Missouri State University M
- Southern Illinois University Carbondale M,D
- Southern Illinois University Edwardsville M
- Southern New Hampshire University M,D,O
- State University of New York College of Environmental Science and Forestry M,D
- Stony Brook University, State University of New York M,O
- Tennessee Technological University M
- Texas Southern University M,D
- Texas Tech University M,D
- Thomas Edison State University M
- Towson University M
- Trent University M,D
- Tropical Agriculture Research and Higher Education Center M,D
- Troy University M
- Tufts University M,D,O
- UNB Fredericton M,D
- Universidad Autonoma de Guadalajara M,D
- Universidad del Turabo M,D
- Universidad Metropolitana M
- Université de Montréal O
- Université du Québec à Chicoutimi M
- University of Alaska Fairbanks M
- University of Alberta M
- The University of Arizona M,D
- The University of British Columbia M,D
- University of Calgary M,D,O
- University of California, Berkeley M,D,O
- University of California, San Diego M
- University of California, Santa Barbara M,D
- University of California, Santa Cruz D
- University of Central Missouri M,D,O
- University of Chicago M
- University of Colorado Boulder M,D
- University of Colorado Denver M,D,O

| | |
|---|---|
| University of Dayton | M,D |
| University of Delaware | M,D |
| University of Denver | M,O |
| The University of Findlay | M,D |
| University of Guelph | M,D |
| University of Hawaii at Manoa | M,D,O |
| University of Houston–Clear Lake | M |
| University of Illinois at Springfield | M |
| University of Maine | D |
| The University of Manchester | M,D |
| University of Maryland, Baltimore County | M,D |
| University of Maryland Eastern Shore | M,D |
| University of Maryland Global Campus | M |
| University of Massachusetts Amherst | M,D |
| University of Massachusetts Dartmouth | M,O |
| University of Michigan | M,D |
| University of Minnesota, Twin Cities Campus | M,D |
| University of Montana | M |
| University of Nevada, Reno | M |
| University of New Hampshire | M |
| University of New Haven | M |
| University of New Mexico | M |
| The University of North Carolina Wilmington | M |
| University of Northern British Columbia | M,D,O |
| University of Oregon | M,D |
| University of Pennsylvania | M |
| University of Puerto Rico at Rio Piedras | M |
| University of Rhode Island | M,D |
| University of South Africa | M,D |
| University of South Alabama | M,D |
| University of South Carolina | M |
| University of South Florida | O |
| University of South Florida, St. Petersburg | M |
| The University of Tennessee | M,D |
| The University of Texas at Austin | M |
| University of Washington | M,D |
| University of Waterloo | M,D |
| University of Wisconsin–Green Bay | M |
| Université Laval | M,D,O |
| Utah State University | M,D |
| Vanderbilt University | M,D* |
| Vermont Law School | M |
| Virginia Commonwealth University | M |
| Virginia Polytechnic Institute and State University | M,D,O |
| Webster University | M |
| Wesley College | M |
| Western Colorado University | M |
| Wilfrid Laurier University | M,D |
| Wilmington University | M,D |
| Yale University | M,D |
| York University | M,D |
| Youngstown State University | M,O |

## ENVIRONMENTAL SCIENCES

| | |
|---|---|
| Adelphi University | M |
| Alaska Pacific University | M |
| American University | M,O |
| Antioch University New England | M,D |
| Arizona State University at Tempe | M,D,O |
| Arkansas State University | M,D |
| Ball State University | D |
| Baylor University | D |
| Boston University | M,D |
| Brigham Young University | M,D |
| California Institute of Technology | M,D |
| California State Polytechnic University, Pomona | M |
| California State University, Chico | M |
| California State University, East Bay | M |
| California State University, Northridge | M |
| California State University, San Bernardino | M |
| Carnegie Mellon University | D |
| Christopher Newport University | M |
| Clarkson University | M,D |
| Clark University | M |
| Clemson University | M,D |
| Cleveland State University | M,D |
| College of Charleston | M |
| College of Staten Island of the City University of New York | M |
| Colorado School of Mines | M,D |
| Columbia University | M,D |
| Columbus State University | M,O |
| Cornell University | M,D |
| Dalhousie University | M |
| DePaul University | M,D |
| Drexel University | M,D |
| Duke University | M,D |
| Duquesne University | M,O |
| Florida Agricultural and Mechanical University | M,D |
| Florida Gulf Coast University | M |
| Florida Institute of Technology | M,D |
| Florida State University | M,D |
| Gannon University | M |
| George Mason University | M,D |
| The Graduate Center, City University of New York | D |
| Harvard University | M,D* |
| Howard University | M,D |
| Humboldt State University | M |
| Idaho State University | M,O |
| Indiana University Bloomington | M,D,O |
| Instituto Tecnologico de Santo Domingo | M,D,O |
| Instituto Tecnológico y de Estudios Superiores de Monterrey, Campus Ciudad de México | M,D |
| Inter American University of Puerto Rico, San Germán Campus | M |
| Iowa State University of Science and Technology | M,D |
| Jackson State University | M |
| Johns Hopkins University | M,O |
| Kansas State University | M,D,O |
| Laurentian University | M |
| Lehigh University | M,D |
| Lincoln University (MO) | M |
| Louisiana State University and Agricultural & Mechanical College | M,D |
| Loyola Marymount University | M |
| Marshall University | M |
| Massachusetts Institute of Technology | M,D,O |
| McNeese State University | M |
| Memorial University of Newfoundland | M,D |
| Mercer University | M |
| Michigan State University | M,D |
| Minnesota State University Mankato | M |
| Montana State University | M,D |
| Montclair State University | M |
| Murray State University | M,O |
| New Jersey Institute of Technology | M,D,O |
| New York University | M |
| North Carolina Agricultural and Technical State University | M |
| North Carolina Central University | M |
| North Dakota State University | M,D |
| Northeastern University | M,D |
| Northern Arizona University | M,D,O |
| Oakland University | M,D |
| The Ohio State University | M,D |
| Oklahoma State University | M,D,O |
| Old Dominion University | M,D |
| Oregon Health & Science University | M,D |
| Oregon State University | M,D |
| Pace University | M |
| Penn State Harrisburg | M,O |
| Penn State University Park | M* |
| Pontifical Catholic University of Puerto Rico | M |
| Portland State University | M,D,O |
| Queens College of the City University of New York | M |
| Rice University | M,D |
| Rochester Institute of Technology | M |
| Rutgers University - Newark | M,D |
| Rutgers University - New Brunswick | M,D |
| Sitting Bull College | M |
| South Dakota School of Mines and Technology | D |
| Southern Connecticut State University | M,O |
| Southern Illinois University Carbondale | D |
| Southern Illinois University Edwardsville | M |
| Southern University and Agricultural and Mechanical College | M |
| Stanford University | M,D,O |
| State University of New York College of Environmental Science and Forestry | M,D |
| Stephen F. Austin State University | M |
| Stockton University | M |
| SUNY Brockport | M |
| Tarleton State University | M |
| Tennessee Technological University | M,D |
| Texas A&M University–Commerce | M,O |
| Texas A&M University–Corpus Christi | M |
| Texas Tech University | M,D |
| Thompson Rivers University | M |
| Towson University | M,O |
| Tuskegee University | M |
| Universidad del Turabo | M,D |
| Universidad Nacional Pedro Henriquez Urena | M |
| Université de Sherbrooke | M,O |
| Université du Québec à Montréal | M,D,O |
| Université du Québec à Trois-Rivières | M,D |
| Université du Québec en Abitibi-Témiscamingue | M,D |
| University at Buffalo, the State University of New York | M,D |
| University of Alberta | M,D |
| The University of Arizona | M,D,O |
| University of California, Berkeley | M,D |
| University of California, Davis | M,D |
| University of California, Los Angeles | M,D |
| University of California, Riverside | M |
| University of California, Santa Barbara | M,D |
| University of Chicago | M |
| University of Cincinnati | M,D |
| University of Colorado Denver | M |
| University of Guam | M |
| University of Guelph | M,D |
| University of Hawaii at Hilo | M |
| University of Houston–Clear Lake | M |
| University of Idaho | M,D |
| University of Illinois at Springfield | M |
| University of Illinois at Urbana-Champaign | M,D |
| The University of Kansas | M,D |
| University of Lethbridge | M,D |
| University of Louisiana at Lafayette | M |
| The University of Manchester | M,D |
| University of Manitoba | M,D |
| University of Maryland, Baltimore | M,D |
| University of Maryland, Baltimore County | M,D |
| University of Maryland, College Park | M,D |
| University of Maryland Eastern Shore | M,D |
| University of Massachusetts Boston | M,D |
| University of Massachusetts Lowell | M,D |
| University of Michigan | M,D |
| University of Michigan–Dearborn | M |
| University of Missouri | M,D,O |
| University of Montana | M |
| University of Nevada, Las Vegas | M,D,O |
| University of Nevada, Reno | M |
| University of New Haven | M |
| University of New Orleans | M,D |
| The University of North Carolina at Chapel Hill | M,D |
| The University of North Carolina Wilmington | M |
| University of North Texas | M,D,O |
| University of Oklahoma | M,D |
| University of Pennsylvania | M,D |
| University of Pittsburgh | M,D* |
| University of Prince Edward Island | M,D |
| University of Puerto Rico at Mayagüez | M,D |
| University of Puerto Rico at Rio Piedras | M,D |
| University of Rhode Island | M,D |
| University of San Diego | M |
| University of Saskatchewan | M,D |
| University of South Africa | M,D |
| University of South Florida, St. Petersburg | M |
| The University of Tennessee at Chattanooga | M |
| The University of Texas at Arlington | M,D |
| The University of Texas at El Paso | M,D |
| The University of Texas at San Antonio | M,D |
| The University of Texas Rio Grande Valley | M |
| University of the Virgin Islands | M |
| The University of Toledo | M,D |
| University of Toronto | M,D |
| University of Utah | M |
| University of Vermont | M |
| University of Virginia | M,D |
| University of Waterloo | M,D |
| The University of Western Ontario | M,D |
| University of West Florida | M |
| University of Windsor | M,D |
| University of Wisconsin–Green Bay | M |
| University of Wisconsin–Madison | M |
| University of Wisconsin–Milwaukee | M,D* |
| Université Laval | M,D |
| Vanderbilt University | M* |
| Virginia Polytechnic Institute and State University | M,O |
| Washington State University | M,D |
| Wesleyan University | M |
| Western Illinois University | D |
| Western Washington University | M |
| West Texas A&M University | M |
| Wichita State University | M |
| Wilfrid Laurier University | M,D |
| Wright State University | D |
| Yale University | M,D |

## EPIDEMIOLOGY

| | |
|---|---|
| Brown University | M,D |
| California State University, Northridge | M |
| Capella University | D |
| Case Western Reserve University | D |
| Colorado State University | M,D |
| Columbia University | M,D |
| Daemen College | M |
| Dalhousie University | M |
| Dartmouth College | M,D |
| Drexel University | M,D,O |
| East Tennessee State University | M,D,O |
| Emory University | M,D |
| Florida International University | M,D |
| George Mason University | M,O |
| Georgetown University | M,O |
| The George Washington University | M |
| Georgia Southern University | M,D |
| Harvard University | M,D* |
| Indiana University Bloomington | M,D |
| Indiana University-Purdue University Indianapolis | M,D,O |
| Johns Hopkins University | M,D |
| Kent State University | M,D |
| Liberty University | M,D |
| Loma Linda University | M,D |
| Louisiana State University Health Sciences Center | M,D |
| McGill University | M,D |
| Medical University of South Carolina | M,D |
| Memorial University of Newfoundland | M,D,O |
| Michigan State University | M,D |
| Monroe College | M |
| New York Medical College | M,D,O |
| North Carolina State University | M,D |
| Northwestern University | D |
| Oregon State University | M,D |
| Ponce Health Sciences University | M,D |
| Purdue University | M,D |
| Queen's University at Kingston | M,D |
| Rutgers University - Newark | M,O |
| Rutgers University - New Brunswick | M,D,O |
| San Diego State University | M,D |
| Stanford University | M,D |
| Temple University | M,D* |
| Texas A&M University | M,D |
| Tufts University | M,D,O |
| Tulane University | M,D |
| University at Albany, State University of New York | M,D |
| University at Buffalo, the State University of New York | M,D |
| The University of Alabama at Birmingham | M,D |
| University of Alberta | M,D |
| The University of Arizona | M,D |
| University of Arkansas for Medical Sciences | M,D,O |
| University of California, Berkeley | M,D |
| University of California, Davis | M,D |
| University of California, Irvine | M,D |
| University of California, Los Angeles | M,D |
| University of California, San Diego | D |
| University of Cincinnati | M,D |
| University of Colorado Denver | M,D |
| University of Florida | M,D,O |
| University of Guelph | M,D |
| University of Hawaii at Manoa | D |
| University of Illinois at Chicago | M,D |
| University of Illinois at Springfield | M,O |
| The University of Iowa | M,D |
| The University of Kansas | M |
| University of Kentucky | D |
| University of Louisville | M,D |
| University of Maryland, Baltimore | M,D,O |
| University of Maryland, Baltimore County | M,D,O |
| University of Maryland, College Park | M,D |
| University of Massachusetts Amherst | M,D |
| University of Memphis | M,D |
| University of Miami | M,D |
| University of Michigan | M,D |
| University of Minnesota, Twin Cities Campus | M,D |
| University of Nebraska Medical Center | D |
| University of New Mexico | M |
| The University of North Carolina at Chapel Hill | M,D |
| University of North Texas Health Science Center at Fort Worth | M,D,O |
| University of Oklahoma Health Sciences Center | M,D |
| University of Ottawa | M |
| University of Pennsylvania | M |
| University of Pittsburgh | M,D* |
| University of Prince Edward Island | M,D |
| University of Puerto Rico - Medical Sciences Campus | M |
| University of Rochester | D |
| University of Saskatchewan | M,D |
| University of South Carolina | M,D |
| University of Southern California | M,D |
| University of Southern Mississippi | M |
| University of South Florida | O |
| The University of Tennessee Health Science Center | M,D |
| The University of Texas Health Science Center at Houston | M,D,O |
| The University of Toledo | M,O |
| University of Toronto | M,D |
| University of Vermont | M,O |
| University of Washington | M,D |
| The University of Western Ontario | M,D |
| University of Wisconsin–Madison | M,D |
| University of Wisconsin–Milwaukee | M,D,O* |
| Université Laval | M,D |
| Virginia Commonwealth University | M,D |
| Walden University | M,D,O |
| Washington University in St. Louis | M,D |
| Weill Cornell Medicine | M |
| West Virginia University | M,D |
| Yale University | M,D |

## ERGONOMICS AND HUMAN FACTORS

| | |
|---|---|
| Arizona State University at Tempe | M |
| Bentley University | M |
| California State University, Long Beach | M |
| The Catholic University of America | M,D |
| Clemson University | M,D |
| Cornell University | M |
| Embry-Riddle Aeronautical University–Daytona | M,D |
| Florida Institute of Technology | M |
| Harvard University | M,D* |
| Indiana University Bloomington | M,D |
| Michigan Technological University | M,D,O |
| Mississippi State University | M,D |
| North Carolina State University | D |
| Old Dominion University | D |
| Purdue University | M,D |
| Queen's University at Kingston | M,D |
| Tufts University | M,D |
| Université de Montréal | O |
| Université du Québec à Montréal | O |
| The University of Alabama | M |
| University of Cincinnati | M,D |
| The University of Iowa | M,D,O |

*M—masters degree; D—doctorate; O—other advanced degree; *—Close-Up and/or Display*

| | |
|---|---|
| University of Miami | M |
| University of Wisconsin–Madison | M,D |
| University of Wisconsin–Milwaukee | M* |
| Wright State University | M,D |

### ETHICS

| | |
|---|---|
| American University | M,D,O |
| Anabaptist Mennonite Biblical Seminary | M,O |
| Arizona State University at Tempe | M,D |
| Azusa Pacific University | M |
| Chicago Theological Seminary | M,D |
| Claremont Graduate University | M,D |
| Claremont Lincoln University | M |
| Claremont School of Theology | M,D |
| Columbia University | M |
| Emory University | M,D |
| Epic Bible College | M,D |
| Fordham University | M,O |
| Freed-Hardeman University | M |
| George Mason University | M |
| Georgetown University | M,D |
| Graduate Theological Union | M,D,O |
| Greensboro College | M |
| John Brown University | M |
| Lancaster Theological Seminary | M,D,O |
| Lebanon Valley College | M |
| Lee University | M |
| Loyola University Chicago | M |
| Lutheran Theological Seminary Saskatoon | M,D |
| Marquette University | M,D |
| New England College of Business and Finance | M |
| Northwestern University | M |
| Oregon State University | M |
| Phillips Theological Seminary | M,D |
| Pontifical John Paul II Institute for Studies on Marriage and Family | M,D,O |
| Santa Clara University | M,D,O |
| Schreiner University | M |
| Southeastern Baptist Theological Seminary | M,D |
| Spring Hill College | M,O |
| Stevens Institute of Technology | M,O |
| Suffolk University | M,O |
| Texas State University | M |
| Université de Sherbrooke | M,D,O |
| Université du Québec à Chicoutimi | O |
| Université du Québec à Rimouski | M,O |
| University of Chicago | D |
| University of Detroit Mercy | M,O |
| University of Maryland, Baltimore | O |
| The University of North Carolina at Charlotte | M,O |
| University of North Florida | M,O |
| University of Pennsylvania | M,D |
| University of St. Thomas (MN) | M,D |
| University of South Africa | M,D |
| The University of Tennessee at Chattanooga | M,O |
| Université Laval | O |
| Valparaiso University | M,O |
| Viterbo University | M,O |
| Xavier University | M* |

### ETHNIC STUDIES

| | |
|---|---|
| Colorado State University | M |
| Cornell University | M,D |
| DePaul University | M |
| Minnesota State University Mankato | M |
| Northern Arizona University | O |
| San Francisco State University | M |
| United Theological Seminary of the Twin Cities | M,D,O |
| The University of British Columbia | M |
| University of California, Berkeley | D |
| University of California, Riverside | D |
| University of California, San Diego | D |
| University of Colorado Boulder | D |
| University of Colorado Denver | M,O |
| University of New Mexico | M,D |
| Université Laval | M,D |

### EVOLUTIONARY BIOLOGY

| | |
|---|---|
| Arizona State University at Tempe | M,D |
| Brown University | D |
| Columbia University | M,D |
| Cornell University | D |
| Dartmouth College | D |
| Emory University | D |
| Florida State University | M,D |
| Harvard University | D* |
| Illinois State University | M,D |
| Indiana State University | M,D |
| Indiana University Bloomington | M,D |
| Iowa State University of Science and Technology | M,D |
| Johns Hopkins University | D |
| Michigan State University | D |
| Montclair State University | M |
| The Ohio State University | M,D |
| Ohio University | M,D |
| Oklahoma State University | M,D |
| Princeton University | D |
| Purdue University | D |
| Rice University | M,D |
| Rutgers University - New Brunswick | M,D |
| Stony Brook University, State University of New York | M,D |
| Tulane University | M,D |
| University at Buffalo, the State University of New York | M,D,O |
| University of Alberta | M,D |
| The University of Arizona | M,D |
| University of California, Davis | D |
| University of California, Irvine | M,D |
| University of California, Los Angeles | M,D |
| University of California, Riverside | M,D |
| University of California, Santa Barbara | M,D |
| University of California, Santa Cruz | M,D |
| University of Chicago | D |
| University of Colorado Boulder | M,D |
| University of Delaware | M,D |
| University of Denver | M,D |
| University of Guelph | M,D |
| University of Illinois at Urbana-Champaign | M,D |
| The University of Iowa | M,D |
| The University of Kansas | M,D |
| University of Louisiana at Lafayette | M,D |
| The University of Manchester | M,D |
| University of Maryland, College Park | M,D |
| University of Massachusetts Amherst | M,D |
| University of Miami | M,D |
| University of Michigan | M,D |
| University of Minnesota, Twin Cities Campus | M,D |
| University of Missouri | M,D |
| University of Nevada, Reno | D |
| University of New Hampshire | D |
| The University of North Carolina at Chapel Hill | M,D |
| University of Notre Dame | M,D |
| University of Oklahoma | M,D |
| University of Oregon | M,D |
| University of Pittsburgh | D* |
| University of Puerto Rico at Rio Piedras | M,D |
| University of Rhode Island | M,D |
| University of South Carolina | M,D |
| University of Southern California | D |
| University of South Florida | M,D |
| The University of Tennessee | M,D |
| The University of Texas at Austin | D |
| University of Toronto | M,D |
| Washington University in St. Louis | D |
| Wesleyan University | D |
| Yale University | D |

### EXERCISE AND SPORTS SCIENCE

| | |
|---|---|
| Adams State University | M |
| American International College | M,D,O |
| Appalachian State University | M |
| Arizona State University at Tempe | M,D |
| Arkansas State University | M,O |
| Ashland University | M |
| Auburn University | M,D,O |
| Auburn University at Montgomery | M,O |
| Austin Peay State University | M |
| Ball State University | M,D |
| Barry University | M |
| Baylor University | M,D |
| Benedictine University | M |
| Bloomsburg University of Pennsylvania | M |
| Brigham Young University | M,D |
| Brooklyn College of the City University of New York | M |
| California Baptist University | M |
| California State University, Fresno | M |
| California State University, Long Beach | M |
| California State University, Sacramento | M |
| California University of Pennsylvania | M |
| Carroll University | M |
| Central Connecticut State University | M,O |
| Central Michigan University | M,D |
| The Citadel, The Military College of South Carolina | M,O |
| The College of St. Scholastica | M |
| Colorado State University | M,D |
| Columbus State University | M |
| Concordia University (Canada) | M |
| Concordia University Chicago | M |
| Concordia University, St. Paul | M,D |
| Delaware State University | M |
| Delta State University | M |
| East Carolina University | M,D,O |
| Eastern Illinois University | M |
| Eastern Kentucky University | M |
| Eastern Michigan University | M |
| Eastern New Mexico University | M |
| Eastern Washington University | M |
| East Tennessee State University | M,D |
| Fairmont State University | M |
| Florida Atlantic University | M |
| Florida State University | M,D |
| Gannon University | M |
| Gardner-Webb University | M |
| George Mason University | M,O |
| The George Washington University | M |
| Georgia College & State University | M |
| Georgia State University | M |
| Hofstra University | M,O |
| Howard University | M |
| Indiana University Bloomington | M,D |
| Indiana University of Pennsylvania | M |
| Inter American University of Puerto Rico, Metropolitan Campus | M |
| Iowa State University of Science and Technology | M |
| Ithaca College | M |
| James Madison University | M |
| Kean University | M |
| Kennesaw State University | M |
| Kent State University | M,D |
| Lakehead University | M |
| Liberty University | M,D |
| Life University | M |
| Lipscomb University | M |
| Logan University | M,D |
| Long Island University - Brooklyn | M,D,O |
| Manhattanville College | M,O |
| Marshall University | M |
| Marywood University | M |
| McNeese State University | M |
| Memorial University of Newfoundland | M |
| Merrimack College | M |
| Miami University | M |
| Middle Tennessee State University | M,D |
| Midwestern State University | M |
| Mississippi State University | M,D |
| Montclair State University | M,O |
| New Mexico Highlands University | M |
| North Dakota State University | M,D |
| Northeastern Illinois University | M |
| Northeastern University | M,D,O |
| Northern Michigan University | M |
| Northwest Missouri State University | M |
| Oakland University | M,O |
| Ohio University | M,D |
| Old Dominion University | M |
| Pittsburg State University | M |
| Point Loma Nazarene University | M |
| Purdue University | M,D |
| Queens College of the City University of New York | M,O |
| Queen's University at Kingston | M,D |
| Rowan University | M |
| Sacred Heart University | M |
| St. Ambrose University | M |
| Saint Mary's College of California | M |
| San Diego State University | M |
| Smith College | M |
| Sonoma State University | M |
| South Dakota State University | M,D |
| Southeast Missouri State University | M |
| Southern Connecticut State University | M |
| Southern Illinois University Edwardsville | M |
| Southern Utah University | M |
| Springfield College | M,D,O |
| Syracuse University | M |
| Tennessee State University | M |
| Texas A&M University–Commerce | M,D,O |
| Texas Tech University | M |
| Texas Woman's University | M,D |
| UNB Fredericton | M |
| United States Sports Academy | M |
| University at Buffalo, the State University of New York | M,D,O |
| The University of Akron | M |
| The University of Alabama | M,D |
| University of Alberta | M,D |
| University of Arkansas at Little Rock | M |
| University of California, Davis | M |
| University of Central Florida | M,O |
| University of Central Oklahoma | M |
| University of Connecticut | M,D |
| University of Dayton | M |
| University of Florida | M,D |
| University of Houston | M,D |
| University of Houston–Clear Lake | M |
| University of Idaho | M,D |
| The University of Iowa | M,D |
| The University of Kansas | M,D |
| University of Kentucky | M,D |
| University of Lethbridge | M,D |
| University of Louisiana at Monroe | M |
| University of Louisville | M,D,O |
| University of Maine | M,D,O |
| University of Mary | M |
| University of Mary Hardin-Baylor | M |
| University of Massachusetts Boston | M,D |
| University of Memphis | M,O |
| University of Miami | M,D |
| University of Minnesota, Twin Cities Campus | M,D |
| University of Mississippi | M,D |
| University of Montana | M |
| University of Nebraska at Kearney | M |
| University of Nebraska at Omaha | M,D |
| University of Nebraska–Lincoln | M,D |
| University of Nevada, Las Vegas | M,D |
| University of New Mexico | D |
| University of North Alabama | M |
| The University of North Carolina at Chapel Hill | M |
| The University of North Carolina at Pembroke | M |
| University of Northern Colorado | M,D |
| University of North Florida | M,D |
| University of Oklahoma | M,D |
| University of Puerto Rico at Mayagüez | M |
| University of Puerto Rico at Rio Piedras | M |
| University of Rhode Island | M |
| University of South Alabama | M |
| University of South Carolina | M,D |
| University of South Dakota | M |
| The University of Tampa | M |
| The University of Tennessee | M,D,O |
| The University of Texas at Arlington | M,D |
| The University of Texas at Austin | M,D |
| The University of Texas Rio Grande Valley | M |
| University of the Pacific | M |
| The University of Toledo | M,D |
| University of West Florida | M |
| University of Wisconsin–La Crosse | M |
| University of Wisconsin–Milwaukee | M,D* |
| University of Wyoming | M |
| Valdosta State University | M |
| Virginia Commonwealth University | M |
| Virginia Polytechnic Institute and State University | M,D |
| Wake Forest University | M |
| Washington State University | M |
| Wayne State College | M |
| Wayne State University | M,D |
| Western Michigan University | M |
| Western Washington University | M |
| West Texas A&M University | M |
| West Virginia University | M,D |
| Wichita State University | M |

### EXPERIMENTAL PSYCHOLOGY

| | |
|---|---|
| Azusa Pacific University | M |
| Bowling Green State University | M,D |
| Brooklyn College of the City University of New York | M,D |
| California State University, Fresno | M,O |
| California State University, Northridge | M |
| Case Western Reserve University | D |
| The Catholic University of America | M,D |
| Central Michigan University | M,D |
| Central Washington University | M |
| Cornell University | D |
| Duke University | D |
| Eastern Washington University | M,O |
| East Tennessee State University | D |
| Fairleigh Dickinson University, Metropolitan Campus | M,O |
| The Graduate Center, City University of New York | D |
| Harvard University | D* |
| Howard University | M,D |
| Idaho State University | D |
| Iona College | M,O |
| James Madison University | M |
| Kent State University | M,D |
| Lakehead University | M,D |
| Laurentian University | M |
| McGill University | M,D |
| McNeese State University | M,O |
| Memorial University of Newfoundland | M,D |
| Middle Tennessee State University | M,O |
| Missouri State University | M,O |
| Morehead State University | M |
| Murray State University | M,O |
| Nova Southeastern University | M,D,O |
| Ohio University | D |
| Radford University | M |
| Rivier University | M |
| Rochester Institute of Technology | M |
| Saint Louis University | M,D |
| San Jose State University | M |
| Seton Hall University | M |
| Southern Illinois University Carbondale | M,D |
| Texas A&M University–Central Texas | M,O |
| Texas Christian University | M,D |
| Texas Tech University | M,D |
| Towson University | M |
| The University of Alabama | D |
| University of Central Oklahoma | M |
| University of Cincinnati | D |
| University of Connecticut | M,D |
| University of Idaho | M,D |
| University of Louisville | D |
| University of Maryland, College Park | M,D |
| University of Massachusetts Dartmouth | M,O |
| University of Memphis | M,D,O |
| University of Mississippi | M,D |
| University of Montana | M,D,O |
| University of New Brunswick Saint John | M,D |
| University of Regina | M,D |
| University of South Carolina | M,D |
| The University of Tennessee | M,D |
| The University of Tennessee at Chattanooga | M |
| The University of Texas at Arlington | M,D |
| The University of Texas at El Paso | M,D |
| The University of Texas of the Permian Basin | M |
| The University of Texas Rio Grande Valley | M |
| The University of Toledo | M,D |
| University of Vermont | D |
| University of Victoria | M,D |
| The University of West Alabama | M |
| University of West Florida | M |
| University of Wisconsin–Oshkosh | M |
| Washington State University | M,D |
| Western Illinois University | M,O |
| Western Kentucky University | M,O |
| Western Washington University | M |

### FACILITIES MANAGEMENT

| | |
|---|---|
| Cornell University | M |
| Liberty University | M,D |
| Maastricht School of Management | M,D |
| Massachusetts Maritime Academy | M |
| Pratt Institute | M |
| Purdue University Fort Wayne | M |
| University of California, Berkeley | O |
| University of New Haven | M,O |
| The University of North Carolina at Charlotte | M,O |
| Université Laval | M,O |
| Wentworth Institute of Technology | M |

### FAMILY AND CONSUMER SCIENCES-GENERAL

| | |
|---|---|
| Alabama Agricultural and Mechanical University | M |
| Ball State University | M |

| | |
|---|---|
| California State University, Northridge | M |
| Central Michigan University | M,O |
| Central Washington University | M |
| Clemson University | D,O |
| Florida State University | M,D |
| Fontbonne University | M |
| Hofstra University | M,D,O |
| Illinois State University | M |
| Iowa State University of Science and Technology | M |
| Kansas State University | M,D,O |
| Lamar University | M |
| Louisiana State University and Agricultural & Mechanical College | M,D |
| New Mexico State University | M |
| North Carolina Agricultural and Technical State University | M |
| North Dakota State University | M |
| The Ohio State University | M,D |
| Oklahoma State University | M,D |
| Queens College of the City University of New York | M,O |
| Saint Peter's University | M |
| Sam Houston State University | M |
| San Francisco State University | M |
| South Carolina State University | M |
| South Dakota State University | M |
| Stephen F. Austin State University | M |
| Tennessee State University | M,D |
| Texas A&M University–Kingsville | M |
| Texas Southern University | M |
| Texas State University | M |
| Tufts University | M,D |
| The University of Alabama | M,D |
| University of Alberta | M,D |
| The University of Arizona | D |
| University of Arkansas | M |
| University of Central Arkansas | M |
| University of Central Oklahoma | M |
| University of Colorado Denver | M,D |
| University of Florida | M |
| University of Georgia | M,D |
| University of Houston | M |
| University of Maryland, College Park | M,D |
| University of Missouri | M,D,O |
| University of Nebraska–Lincoln | M,D |
| University of Puerto Rico at Rio Piedras | M |
| University of South Africa | M,D |
| The University of Tennessee | D |
| The University of Tennessee at Martin | M |
| The University of Texas at Austin | M,D |
| University of Wisconsin–Madison | M,D |
| University of Wisconsin–Stevens Point | O |
| Utah State University | M,D |
| Western Michigan University | M |

## FAMILY NURSE PRACTITIONER STUDIES

| | |
|---|---|
| Albany State University | M |
| Allen College | M,D |
| Alvernia University | M,D,O |
| Alverno College | M,D |
| American International College | M,D,O |
| Anderson University (SC) | M,D |
| Angelo State University | M |
| Arizona State University at Tempe | M,D,O |
| Ashland University | D |
| Auburn University at Montgomery | M |
| Augsburg University | M,D |
| Augusta University | D |
| Austin Peay State University | M |
| Azusa Pacific University | M,D |
| Ball State University | M,D,O |
| Barry University | M,O |
| Bellarmine University | M,D |
| Bellin College | M |
| Binghamton University, State University of New York | M,D,O |
| Bloomsburg University of Pennsylvania | M,D |
| Bowie State University | M |
| Bradley University | M,D,O |
| Brenau University | M |
| Brigham Young University | M |
| California Baptist University | M |
| California State University, San Marcos | M |
| Carlow University | M,O |
| Case Western Reserve University | M |
| Cedarville University | M,D |
| Clarion University of Pennsylvania | M |
| Clarke University | D |
| Clarkson College | M,O |
| Clayton State University | M |
| Clemson University | M,D,O |
| College of Mount Saint Vincent | M,O |
| The College of New Rochelle | M,O |
| Colorado Mesa University | M,D,O |
| Columbia University | M,O |
| Columbus State University | M |
| Concordia University Wisconsin | M,D |
| Coppin State University | M,O |
| Cox College | M |
| Creighton University | M,D,O |
| Delta State University | M,D |
| DePaul University | M,D |
| DeSales University | M,D,O |
| Dominican College | M,D |
| Drexel University | M |
| Duke University | M,D,O |
| Duquesne University | M,O |
| D'Youville College | M,D,O |
| Eastern Kentucky University | M |
| East Tennessee State University | M,D,O |
| Edinboro University of Pennsylvania | M,D |
| Elms College | M,D |
| Emory University | M |
| Endicott College | M,O |
| Fairfield University | M,D |
| Felician University | M,O |
| Florida National University | M |
| Florida Southern College | M |
| Florida State University | D,O |
| Franciscan Missionaries of Our Lady University | M |
| Francis Marion University | M |
| Fresno Pacific University | M |
| Gannon University | M,O |
| Gardner-Webb University | M,D |
| George Mason University | M,D,O |
| Georgetown University | M,D |
| The George Washington University | M,D,O |
| Georgia Southern University | M |
| Georgia Southwestern State University | M,O |
| Georgia State University | M,D,O |
| Goshen College | M |
| Graceland University (IA) | M,D,O |
| Grambling State University | M,O |
| Grand Canyon University | M,D,O |
| Gwynedd Mercy University | M,D |
| Hampton University | M,D |
| Hardin-Simmons University | M |
| Hofstra University | M |
| Holy Names University | M,O |
| Houston Baptist University | M |
| Howard University | M |
| Hunter College of the City University of New York | D |
| Husson University | M,O |
| Illinois State University | M,D,O |
| Indiana State University | M,D |
| Indiana University Kokomo | M |
| Indiana University-Purdue University Indianapolis | M |
| Indiana University South Bend | M |
| Jacksonville University | M |
| James Madison University | M,D |
| Johns Hopkins University | D |
| Keiser University | M |
| Kent State University | M,D |
| King University | M,D,O |
| La Salle University | M,D,O |
| Le Moyne College | M,O |
| Lewis University | M,D |
| Liberty University | M,D |
| Lincoln Memorial University | M |
| Long Island University - Brentwood Campus | M,O |
| Long Island University - Brooklyn | M,O |
| Long Island University - Post | M,O |
| Louisiana State University Health Sciences Center | M,D,O |
| Loyola University Chicago | M,D,O |
| Loyola University New Orleans | M,D |
| Malone University | M |
| Marian University (IN) | M,D |
| Marquette University | M,D,O |
| Marymount University | M,D,O |
| Maryville University of Saint Louis | M,D |
| McGill University | M,D,O |
| McMurry University | M |
| McNeese State University | M |
| Medical University of South Carolina | M,D |
| Mercer University | M,D,O |
| Middle Tennessee State University | M,O |
| Midwestern State University | M |
| Millersville University of Pennsylvania | M,D,O |
| Minnesota State University Mankato | M,D |
| Missouri State University | M,D |
| Molloy College | M,D,O |
| Montana State University | M,D,O |
| Morningside College | M |
| Mount Carmel College of Nursing | M,D |
| Murray State University | D |
| National University | M,O |
| New Mexico State University | M,D,O |
| New York University | M,D,O |
| Nicholls State University | M |
| Northeastern University | M,D,O |
| Northern Arizona University | M,D,O |
| Nova Southeastern University | M,D |
| Oakland University | M,O |
| Ohio University | M,D |
| Old Dominion University | M,D |
| Olivet Nazarene University | M |
| Oregon Health & Science University | M |
| Otterbein University | M,D,O |
| Pace University | M,D,O |
| Pacific Lutheran University | D |
| Palm Beach Atlantic University | M,D |
| Point Loma Nazarene University | M |
| Purdue University | M,D,O |
| Purdue University Fort Wayne | M,O |
| Purdue University Northwest | M |
| Queen's University at Kingston | M,D,O |
| Quinnipiac University | D |
| Ramapo College of New Jersey | M |
| Regis College (MA) | M,D,O |
| Rivier University | M,D |
| Rocky Mountain University of Health Professions | D |
| Rutgers University - Camden | D |
| Rutgers University - Newark | M,D,O |
| Sacred Heart University | M,D,O |
| Sage Graduate School | M |
| Saginaw Valley State University | M,D |
| Saint Francis Medical Center College of Nursing | M,D,O |
| Saint Joseph's College of Maine | M,O |
| Saint Mary's College | D |
| Salisbury University | D |
| Samford University | M,D |
| Samuel Merritt University | M,D,O |
| San Francisco State University | M,O |
| Seattle Pacific University | M,O |
| Shenandoah University | M,D,O |
| Simmons University | M,D |
| Sonoma State University | M |
| Southern Adventist University | M,D |
| Southern Connecticut State University | M,D |
| Southern Illinois University Edwardsville | M,D,O |
| Southern University and Agricultural and Mechanical College | M,D,O |
| South University - Tampa | M |
| South University - Virginia Beach | M |
| South University - West Palm Beach | M |
| Spalding University | M,D,O |
| State University of New York Downstate Medical Center | M,O |
| State University of New York Polytechnic Institute | M,O |
| State University of New York Upstate Medical University | M,O |
| Stephen F. Austin State University | M |
| Stony Brook University, State University of New York | M,D,O |
| Temple University | D* |
| Tennessee State University | M,O |
| Tennessee Technological University | M,D |
| Texas A&M International University | M |
| Texas A&M University | M |
| Texas A&M University–Corpus Christi | M,D |
| Texas Christian University | D |
| Texas State University | M |
| Texas Tech University Health Sciences Center | M,D,O |
| Texas Woman's University | M,D |
| Troy University | M,D |
| Tusculum University | M |
| Uniformed Services University of the Health Sciences | M,D |
| Union University | M,D,O |
| United States University | M |
| Universidad del Turabo | M,O |
| University at Buffalo, the State University of New York | M,D,O |
| The University of Alabama at Birmingham | M,D |
| The University of Alabama in Huntsville | M,D,O |
| The University of Arizona | M,D,O |
| University of Central Arkansas | M,O |
| University of Colorado Denver | M,D |
| University of Connecticut | M |
| University of Delaware | M,O |
| University of Detroit Mercy | M,D,O |
| University of Hawaii at Manoa | M,D,O |
| University of Houston | M |
| University of Illinois at Chicago | M,O |
| University of Indianapolis | M,D |
| University of Louisiana at Lafayette | M,D |
| University of Louisville | M,D |
| University of Maine | M,O |
| University of Mary | M,D |
| University of Mary Hardin-Baylor | M,D,O |
| University of Maryland, Baltimore | M,D,O |
| University of Massachusetts Amherst | M,D |
| University of Massachusetts Lowell | M |
| University of Massachusetts Medical School | M,D,O |
| University of Memphis | M,O |
| University of Miami | M,D |
| University of Michigan–Flint | M,D,O |
| University of Minnesota, Twin Cities Campus | M,D |
| University of Missouri | M,D,O |
| University of Missouri–Kansas City | M,D |
| University of Missouri–St. Louis | D,O |
| University of Nevada, Las Vegas | M,D,O |
| University of New Hampshire | M,D,O |
| The University of North Carolina at Chapel Hill | M,D,O |
| The University of North Carolina at Charlotte | M,D,O |
| The University of North Carolina Wilmington | M,D,O |
| University of North Dakota | M,D,O |
| University of Northern Colorado | M,D |
| University of North Florida | M,D,O |
| University of North Georgia | M,O |
| University of Pennsylvania | M,O |
| University of Phoenix - Hawaii Campus | M |
| University of Phoenix–Online Campus | M,O |
| University of Phoenix - Phoenix Campus | M,O |
| University of Phoenix - Sacramento Valley Campus | M |
| University of Pittsburgh | M,D* |
| University of Portland | M,D |
| University of Puerto Rico - Medical Sciences Campus | M |
| University of Rhode Island | M,D,O |
| University of Rochester | M,D |
| University of St. Francis (IL) | M,D,O |
| University of Saint Francis (IN) | M,D,O |
| University of Saint Joseph | M,D |
| University of San Diego | M,D |
| The University of Scranton | M,D,O |
| University of South Carolina | M |
| University of Southern Indiana | M,D,O |
| University of Southern Maine | M,D,O |
| University of South Florida | M,D,O |
| The University of Tampa | M |
| The University of Tennessee at Chattanooga | M,D,O |
| The University of Tennessee Health Science Center | D,O |
| The University of Texas at Arlington | M,D |
| The University of Texas at Austin | M,D |
| The University of Texas at El Paso | M,D,O |
| The University of Texas at Tyler | M,D |
| The University of Texas Health Science Center at San Antonio | M,D,O |
| The University of Toledo | M,O |
| The University of Tulsa | D |
| University of Victoria | M,D |
| University of Wisconsin–Eau Claire | M,D |
| University of Wisconsin–Milwaukee | M,D,O* |
| University of Wisconsin–Oshkosh | M |
| Ursuline College | M,D |
| Valdosta State University | M |
| Villanova University | M,D,O |
| Virginia Commonwealth University | M |
| Wagner College | M,D,O |
| Walden University | M,D,O |
| Washington State University | M,D,O |
| West Coast University | M,D |
| Westminster College (UT) | M |
| West Texas A&M University | M |
| West Virginia Wesleyan College | M,D,O |
| Wilmington University | M,D |
| Winona State University | M,D,O |
| Winston-Salem State University | M,D |
| Wright State University | M |

## FILM, TELEVISION, AND VIDEO PRODUCTION

| | |
|---|---|
| Academy of Art University | M |
| American Film Institute Conservatory | M |
| American University | M |
| Arizona State University at Tempe | M |
| ArtCenter College of Design | M |
| Azusa Pacific University | M |
| Bard College | M |
| Bob Jones University | M,D,O |
| Boston University | M |
| Bowling Green State University | M,D |
| Brigham Young University | M |
| Brooklyn College of the City University of New York | M |
| California College of the Arts | M |
| California Institute of the Arts | M,O |
| California State University, Fullerton | M |
| California State University, Northridge | M |
| Carleton University | M |
| Carnegie Mellon University | M |
| Central Michigan University | M |
| Chapman University | M |
| Chatham University | M |
| Columbia College Chicago | M |
| Columbia University | M |
| Concordia University (Canada) | M,D |
| DePaul University | M,D |
| Drexel University | M |
| Florida Atlantic University | M,O |
| Florida State University | M |
| Georgia State University | M,D |
| Governors State University | M |
| Hollins University | M |
| Howard University | M |
| Johns Hopkins University | M |
| Lake Forest College | M |
| Lindenwood University | M |
| Lipscomb University | M |
| Loyola Marymount University | M |
| Maryland Institute College of Art | M |
| Massachusetts College of Art and Design | M,O |
| Miami International University of Art & Design | M |
| Minneapolis College of Art and Design | M |
| Missouri State University | M,O |
| Montana State University | M |
| Mount Saint Mary's University (CA) | M,D,O |
| National University | M |
| New York Film Academy | M |
| New York University | M |
| Northwestern University | M,D |
| Ohio University | M |
| Quinnipiac University | M |
| Regent University | M,D |
| Rochester Institute of Technology | M |
| Sacred Heart University | M |
| St. Thomas University - Florida | M |
| San Diego State University | M |
| San Francisco State University | M |
| San Jose State University | M |
| Savannah College of Art and Design | M |
| School of Visual Arts (NY) | M |
| Stephen F. Austin State University | M |
| Stevens Institute of Technology | M |
| Stony Brook University, State University of New York | M |
| Syracuse University | M |
| Temple University | M* |
| Universidad Autonoma de Guadalajara | M,D |
| The University of British Columbia | M |
| University of California, Los Angeles | M,D |

*M—masters degree; D—doctorate; O—other advanced degree; *—Close-Up and/or Display*

| | |
|---|---|
| University of California, Santa Barbara | D |
| University of Central Arkansas | M |
| University of Central Florida | M |
| University of Colorado Boulder | M |
| The University of Iowa | M |
| University of Memphis | M,D |
| University of Miami | M,D |
| University of Mississippi | M,D |
| University of Montana | M |
| University of Nevada, Las Vegas | M,O |
| University of New Orleans | M |
| The University of North Carolina at Greensboro | M |
| University of North Carolina School of the Arts | M |
| University of North Texas | M,D,O |
| University of Regina | M |
| University of Rhode Island | M,D |
| University of Southern California | M |
| The University of Texas at Arlington | M |
| The University of Texas at Austin | M,D |
| University of the Sacred Heart | M,O |
| University of Utah | M |
| University of Victoria | M |
| University of Wisconsin–Milwaukee | M,O* |
| Vermont College of Fine Arts | M |
| Virginia Commonwealth University | M,D |
| Watkins College of Art, Design, & Film | M |
| Western Colorado University | M |
| York University | M,D |

## FILM, TELEVISION, AND VIDEO THEORY AND CRITICISM

| | |
|---|---|
| Brooklyn College of the City University of New York | M |
| California College of the Arts | M |
| Central Michigan University | M |
| Claremont Graduate University | M,D |
| College of Staten Island of the City University of New York | M |
| Columbia University | M |
| Concordia University (Canada) | M,D |
| DePaul University | M |
| Emory University | M,D,O |
| Hollins University | M |
| National University | M,O |
| New York University | M,D |
| Ohio University | M |
| San Francisco State University | M |
| Savannah College of Art and Design | M |
| Texas A&M University–Commerce | M,D,O |
| Tiffin University | M |
| Université de Montréal | M,D |
| University at Buffalo, the State University of New York | M,D,O |
| The University of Arizona | M |
| The University of British Columbia | M |
| University of California, Berkeley | D |
| University of California, Santa Cruz | D |
| University of Chicago | D |
| The University of Iowa | M,D |
| The University of Kansas | M,D |
| University of Miami | M,D |
| University of Michigan | D,O |
| University of Oklahoma | M,D |
| University of Pittsburgh | M,D,O* |
| University of Southern California | M,D |
| University of South Florida | M |
| University of Toronto | M,D |
| University of Wisconsin–Madison | M,D |
| University of Wisconsin–Milwaukee | M,D* |
| Université Laval | M,D |
| Walla Walla University | M |
| Wayne State University | M,D |
| Wilfrid Laurier University | M,D |
| Yale University | D |

## FINANCE AND BANKING

| | |
|---|---|
| Adelphi University | M |
| American Business & Technology University | M |
| The American College of Financial Services | M |
| American College of Thessaloniki | M,O |
| American InterContinental University Online | M |
| American University | M,O |
| The American University in Cairo | M,O |
| The American University in Dubai | M |
| Andrews University | M |
| Argosy University, Atlanta | M,D |
| Argosy University, Chicago | M,D |
| Argosy University, Hawaii | M,D,O |
| Argosy University, Los Angeles | M,D |
| Argosy University, Northern Virginia | M,D,O |
| Argosy University, Orange County | M,D,O |
| Argosy University, Phoenix | M,D |
| Argosy University, Seattle | M,D |
| Argosy University, Tampa | M,D |
| Argosy University, Twin Cities | M,D |
| Arizona State University at Tempe | M,D |
| Ashland University | M |
| Aspen University | M,O |
| Assumption University | M,O |
| Auburn University | M |
| Azusa Pacific University | M |
| Babson College | M,O |
| Baker College Center for Graduate Studies–Online | M,D |
| Barry University | O |
| Baruch College of the City University of New York | M,D |
| Bayamón Central University | M,D |
| Bellevue University | M,D |
| Benedictine University | M |
| Bentley University | M |
| Binghamton University, State University of New York | D |
| Bluffton University | M |
| Boston College | M,D |
| Boston University | M |
| Brandeis University | M,D |
| Brandman University | M |
| Bridgewater State University | M |
| Brigham Young University | M |
| Brooklyn College of the City University of New York | M |
| California College of the Arts | M |
| California Intercontinental University | M,D |
| California Lutheran University | M,O |
| California State University, East Bay | M |
| California State University, Fullerton | M |
| California State University, Los Angeles | M |
| California State University, San Bernardino | M |
| Capella University | M,D |
| Carnegie Mellon University | D |
| Case Western Reserve University | M |
| Central European University | M,D |
| Central Michigan University | M |
| Charleston Southern University | M |
| City University of Seattle | M,O |
| Clarion University of Pennsylvania | M |
| Clark University | M |
| Cleary University | M,O |
| College for Financial Planning | M |
| The College of Saint Rose | O |
| Colorado State University | M |
| Colorado State University–Global Campus | M |
| Colorado Technical University Aurora | M |
| Colorado Technical University Colorado Springs | M,D |
| Columbia Southern University | M |
| Columbia University | M,D |
| Concordia University (Canada) | M,D,O |
| Concordia University Wisconsin | M |
| Cornell University | D |
| Creighton University | M,D |
| Culver-Stockton College | M |
| Curry College | M,O |
| Dalhousie University | M |
| Dallas Baptist University | M |
| Davenport University | M |
| Delaware Valley University | M |
| DePaul University | M,D |
| DeSales University | M |
| DeVry University–Folsom Campus | M |
| Drew University | M,D,O |
| Drexel University | M,D,O |
| Duke University | D |
| Duquesne University | M |
| Eastern Michigan University | M,O |
| Elms College | M,O |
| Embry-Riddle Aeronautical University–Daytona | M |
| Embry-Riddle Aeronautical University–Worldwide | M |
| Emory University | M,D |
| Fairfield University | M,O |
| Fairleigh Dickinson University, Florham Campus | M,O |
| Fairleigh Dickinson University, Metropolitan Campus | M,O |
| Florida Agricultural and Mechanical University | M |
| Florida International University | M |
| Florida National University | M |
| Florida State University | M,D |
| Fordham University | M,D |
| Gannon University | M |
| Geneva College | M |
| George Fox University | M,D |
| Georgetown University | M,D |
| The George Washington University | M,D |
| Georgia State University | M,D,O |
| Golden Gate University | M,D,O |
| Goldey-Beacom College | M |
| Gordon College | M |
| The Graduate Center, City University of New York | D |
| Grand Canyon University | M |
| Hawaii Pacific University | M |
| HEC Montreal | M,D,O |
| Hofstra University | M,O |
| Holy Family University | M |
| Holy Names University | M |
| Howard University | M |
| Hult International Business School (United States) | M |
| IGlobal University | M |
| Illinois Institute of Technology | M,D |
| Indiana University Bloomington | M,D,O |
| Indiana University-Purdue University Indianapolis | M |
| Indiana University South Bend | M,O |
| Indiana University Southeast | M |
| Instituto Centroamericano de Administracion de Empresas | M |
| Instituto Tecnologico de Santo Domingo | M,O |
| Instituto Tecnológico y de Estudios Superiores de Monterrey, Campus Central de Veracruz | M |
| Instituto Tecnológico y de Estudios Superiores de Monterrey, Campus Ciudad de México | M,D |
| Instituto Tecnológico y de Estudios Superiores de Monterrey, Campus Ciudad Obregón | M |
| Instituto Tecnológico y de Estudios Superiores de Monterrey, Campus Cuernavaca | M |
| Instituto Tecnológico y de Estudios Superiores de Monterrey, Campus Estado de México | M,D |
| Instituto Tecnológico y de Estudios Superiores de Monterrey, Campus Guadalajara | M |
| Instituto Tecnológico y de Estudios Superiores de Monterrey, Campus Irapuato | M,D |
| Instituto Tecnológico y de Estudios Superiores de Monterrey, Campus Monterrey | M |
| Inter American University of Puerto Rico, Aguadilla Campus | M |
| Inter American University of Puerto Rico, Arecibo Campus | M |
| Inter American University of Puerto Rico, Metropolitan Campus | M |
| Inter American University of Puerto Rico, Ponce Campus | M |
| Inter American University of Puerto Rico, San Germán Campus | M,D |
| The International University of Monaco | M |
| Iona College | M,O |
| Iowa State University of Science and Technology | M |
| Jacksonville University | M |
| John F. Kennedy University | M |
| Johns Hopkins University | M,D,O |
| Johnson & Wales University | M |
| Kansas State University | M,D,O |
| Kent State University | D |
| King University | M |
| Lake Forest Graduate School of Management | M |
| La Salle University | M,O |
| La Sierra University | M,O |
| Lawrence Technological University | M,D,O |
| Lehigh University | M |
| Lewis University | M |
| Liberty University | M,D |
| Lincoln University (CA) | M,D |
| Lipscomb University | M,O |
| Long Island University - Post | M |
| Louisiana State University and Agricultural & Mechanical College | M,D |
| Louisiana Tech University | M,D |
| Loyola University Chicago | M |
| Loyola University Maryland | M |
| Manhattanville College | M,O |
| Marquette University | M,O |
| Maryville University of Saint Louis | M,O |
| Marywood University | M |
| McGill University | M,D,O |
| Metropolitan College of New York | M |
| Michigan State University | M,D |
| Mississippi College | M,O |
| Mississippi State University | M,D |
| Molloy College | M,O |
| Monmouth University | M,O |
| Monroe College | M |
| Montclair State University | M |
| Murray State University | M |
| Naval Postgraduate School | M |
| New Charter University | M |
| New England College of Business and Finance | M |
| New Jersey City University | M,O |
| Newman University | M |
| New Mexico State University | M,O |
| The New School | M,D |
| New York Institute of Technology | M |
| New York University | M,D |
| Niagara University | M |
| North Central College | M |
| Northeastern State University | M |
| Northeastern University | M |
| Northern State University | M |
| North Greenville University | M,D |
| Norwich University | M |
| Notre Dame de Namur University | M |
| Nova Southeastern University | M |
| Oakland University | M,O |
| Ohio Christian University | M |
| Ohio Dominican University | M |
| The Ohio State University | M |
| Ohio University | M |
| Oklahoma Christian University | M |
| Oklahoma State University | M,D |
| Old Dominion University | D |
| Oral Roberts University | M |
| Oregon State University | M,D |
| Ottawa University | M |
| Our Lady of the Lake University | M |
| Pace University | M,D,O |
| Pacific Lutheran University | M |
| Pacific States University | M,O |
| Pacific University | M |
| Park University | M,O |
| Penn State Great Valley | M,O |
| Penn State Harrisburg | M,D,O |
| Polytechnic University of Puerto Rico, Miami Campus | M |
| Polytechnic University of Puerto Rico, Orlando Campus | M |
| Pontifical Catholic University of Puerto Rico | M |
| Pontificia Universidad Catolica Madre y Maestra | M |
| Portland State University | M |
| Post University | M |
| Princeton University | M |
| Providence College | M |
| Purdue University | M |
| Purdue University Global | M |
| Queens College of the City University of New York | M |
| Queen's University at Kingston | M,D |
| Quinnipiac University | M |
| Regent's University London | M |
| Regent University | M,D,O |
| Regis University | M,O |
| Rhode Island College | M,O |
| Rider University | M |
| Robert Morris University Illinois | M |
| Rochester Institute of Technology | M |
| Rockhurst University | M,O |
| Rollins College | M |
| Rutgers University - Newark | M,D |
| Sacred Heart University | M,D,O |
| St. John's University (NY) | M |
| Saint Joseph's University | M,O |
| Saint Louis University | M |
| Saint Mary's College of California | M |
| Saint Peter's University | M |
| St. Thomas Aquinas College | M |
| Saint Xavier University | M,O |
| Samford University | M |
| Sam Houston State University | M |
| San Diego State University | M |
| San Francisco State University | M |
| Santa Clara University | M |
| Schiller International University - Tampa | M |
| Seattle University | M,O |
| Seton Hall University | M,O |
| Shippensburg University of Pennsylvania | M,D,O |
| Simon Fraser University | M,D,O |
| Southeast Missouri State University | M |
| Southern Adventist University | M |
| Southern Illinois University Edwardsville | M |
| Southern Methodist University | M |
| Southern New Hampshire University | M,D,O |
| Southwestern Adventist University | M |
| State University of New York Polytechnic Institute | M |
| Stevens Institute of Technology | M,O |
| Stony Brook University, State University of New York | M,O |
| Strayer University | M |
| Suffolk University | M |
| Syracuse University | M,D |
| Temple University | M,D* |
| Tennessee Technological University | M |
| Texas A&M International University | M |
| Texas A&M University | M |
| Texas A&M University–Commerce | M |
| Texas A&M University–Corpus Christi | M |
| Texas Tech University | M,D |
| Thomas Edison State University | M |
| Tiffin University | M |
| Trident University International | M,D |
| Troy University | M |
| Tulane University | M,D |
| United States International University–Africa | M |
| Universidad Central del Este | M |
| Universidad de las Americas, A.C. | M |
| Universidad de las Américas Puebla | M |
| Universidad Metropolitana | M |
| Université de Sherbrooke | M |
| Université du Québec à Montréal | O |
| Université du Québec à Trois-Rivières | O |
| Université du Québec en Outaouais | M,O |
| University at Albany, State University of New York | M,D,O |
| University at Buffalo, the State University of New York | M,D |
| The University of Akron | M |
| The University of Alabama | M,D |
| The University of Alabama at Birmingham | M |
| The University of Alabama in Huntsville | M,O |
| University of Alaska Fairbanks | M |
| University of Alberta | M,D |
| The University of Arizona | M |
| University of Baltimore | M |
| University of Bridgeport | M |
| The University of British Columbia | D |
| University of California, Berkeley | D,O |
| University of California, Davis | M |
| University of California, Los Angeles | M,D |
| University of California, Riverside | M,D |
| University of California, San Diego | M,D |
| University of California, Santa Barbara | M,D |
| University of California, Santa Cruz | M |
| University of Central Missouri | M,D,O |
| University of Chicago | M,O |
| University of Cincinnati | M,D |
| University of Colorado Denver | M |
| University of Connecticut | M,D,O |
| University of Dallas | M,D |
| University of Dayton | M |
| University of Delaware | M |
| University of Denver | M |
| University of Detroit Mercy | M,D,O |
| University of Florida | M,D,O |
| University of Hawaii at Manoa | M,D |
| University of Houston | M |
| University of Houston–Clear Lake | M |
| University of Houston - Downtown | M |
| University of Houston–Victoria | M |
| University of Illinois at Chicago | M |
| University of Illinois at Urbana-Champaign | M,D |
| The University of Iowa | M,D |
| The University of Kansas | M,D |

| | |
|---|---|
| University of La Verne | M |
| University of Lethbridge | M,D |
| University of Louisiana at Lafayette | M |
| University of Maine | M |
| The University of Manchester | M |
| University of Maryland Global Campus | M |
| University of Massachusetts Amherst | M,D |
| University of Massachusetts Boston | M |
| University of Massachusetts Dartmouth | M,O |
| University of Memphis | M,D |
| University of Miami | M,D |
| University of Michigan–Dearborn | M |
| University of Michigan–Flint | M,O |
| University of Minnesota, Twin Cities Campus | M,D |
| University of Mississippi | M,D |
| University of Missouri | M,D |
| University of Missouri–Kansas City | M,D |
| University of Nebraska–Lincoln | M,D |
| University of Nevada, Las Vegas | O |
| University of Nevada, Reno | M |
| University of New Haven | M,O |
| University of New Mexico | M |
| University of New Orleans | M |
| University of North Alabama | M |
| The University of North Carolina at Chapel Hill | D |
| The University of North Carolina at Charlotte | M,O |
| The University of North Carolina at Greensboro | M,O |
| The University of North Carolina Wilmington | M |
| University of North Florida | M |
| University of North Texas | M,D,O |
| University of Notre Dame | M |
| University of Oregon | D |
| University of Ottawa | D,O |
| University of Pennsylvania | M,D |
| University of Pittsburgh | M,D* |
| University of Portland | M |
| University of Puerto Rico at Mayagüez | M |
| University of Puerto Rico at Rio Piedras | M,D |
| University of Rhode Island | M,D |
| University of Rochester | M,D |
| University of St. Francis (IL) | M,O |
| University of Saint Mary | M |
| University of St. Thomas (TX) | M |
| University of San Diego | M |
| University of San Francisco | M |
| University of Saskatchewan | M |
| The University of Scranton | M |
| University of Southern Maine | M |
| University of South Florida | M,D |
| The University of Tampa | M,O |
| The University of Tennessee | M,D |
| The University of Tennessee at Martin | M |
| The University of Texas at Arlington | M,D |
| The University of Texas at Austin | M,D |
| The University of Texas at Dallas | M |
| The University of Texas at San Antonio | M,D |
| The University of Texas Rio Grande Valley | M,D |
| University of the West | M |
| The University of Toledo | M |
| University of Toronto | M |
| University of Utah | M,D |
| University of Virginia | M |
| University of Washington, Tacoma | M |
| University of Waterloo | M,D |
| The University of West Alabama | M |
| The University of Western Ontario | M,D |
| University of Wisconsin–Madison | M,D |
| University of Wisconsin–Whitewater | M |
| University of Wyoming | M |
| Université Laval | M,O |
| Université TÉLUQ | M,D |
| Upper Iowa University | M |
| Utah State University | M |
| Valparaiso University | M,O |
| Vancouver Island University | M |
| Vanderbilt University | M* |
| Villanova University | M |
| Virginia Commonwealth University | M |
| Virginia International University | M,O |
| Virginia Polytechnic Institute and State University | M,D |
| Wagner College | M |
| Walden University | M,D,O |
| Walsh College of Accountancy and Business Administration | M |
| Washington University in St. Louis | M,D |
| Waynesburg University | M,D |
| Wayne State University | M,D,O |
| Webster University | M |
| Western Michigan University Cooley Law School | M,D |
| West Texas A&M University | M |
| West Virginia University | M,D,O |
| Wilfrid Laurier University | M,D |
| Wilmington University | M,D |
| Wingate University | M |
| Xavier University | M* |
| Yale University | D |
| York College of Pennsylvania | M |
| York University | M,D |
| Youngstown State University | M |

## FINANCIAL ENGINEERING

| | |
|---|---|
| Baruch College of the City University of New York | M |
| Claremont Graduate University | M |
| Columbia University | M,D |
| HEC Montreal | M,D |
| The International University of Monaco | M |
| New York University | M |
| North Carolina State University | M |
| Princeton University | M,D |
| Rensselaer Polytechnic Institute | M |
| Stevens Institute of Technology | M,D,O |
| Temple University | M* |
| University of California, Berkeley | M |
| University of California, Los Angeles | M,D |
| University of Illinois at Urbana-Champaign | M |

## FIRE PROTECTION ENGINEERING

| | |
|---|---|
| Oklahoma State University | M,D |
| University of Maryland, College Park | M |
| University of New Haven | M,O |
| The University of North Carolina at Charlotte | M,O |
| Worcester Polytechnic Institute | M,D,O |

## FISH, GAME, AND WILDLIFE MANAGEMENT

| | |
|---|---|
| Arkansas Tech University | M |
| Auburn University | M,D |
| Brigham Young University | M,D |
| Central Washington University | M |
| Clemson University | M,D |
| Colorado State University | M,D |
| Cornell University | M,D |
| Frostburg State University | M |
| Humboldt State University | M |
| Iowa State University of Science and Technology | M,D |
| Louisiana State University and Agricultural & Mechanical College | M,D |
| McGill University | M,D |
| Memorial University of Newfoundland | M,O |
| Michigan State University | M,D |
| Mississippi State University | M,D |
| Montana State University | M,D |
| The Ohio State University | M,D |
| Oregon State University | M,D |
| Penn State University Park | M,D* |
| Purdue University | M,D |
| Simon Fraser University | M,D,O |
| South Dakota State University | M,D |
| State University of New York College of Environmental Science and Forestry | M,D |
| Sul Ross State University | M |
| Tarleton State University | M |
| Tennessee Technological University | M |
| Texas A&M University | M,D |
| Texas A&M University–Kingsville | M,D |
| Texas State University | M |
| Texas Tech University | M,D |
| Université du Québec à Rimouski | M,D,O |
| University of Alaska Fairbanks | M,D,O |
| University of Arkansas at Pine Bluff | M,D |
| University of Delaware | M,D |
| University of Florida | M,D,O |
| University of Maine | M,D |
| University of Maryland Eastern Shore | M,D |
| University of Massachusetts Amherst | M,D |
| University of Miami | M,D |
| University of Missouri | M,D,O |
| University of Montana | M,D |
| University of New Hampshire | M |
| University of North Dakota | M,D |
| University of Rhode Island | M,D |
| The University of Tennessee | M |
| University of Washington | M,D |
| University of Wisconsin–Madison | M,D |
| Utah State University | M,D |
| Virginia Polytechnic Institute and State University | M,D |
| West Virginia University | M,D |

## FOLKLORE

| | |
|---|---|
| The George Washington University | M,D |
| Indiana University Bloomington | M,D |
| Memorial University of Newfoundland | M,D |
| Penn State Harrisburg | M,D,O |
| University of Alberta | M,D |
| University of California, Berkeley | M |
| University of Louisiana at Lafayette | M,D |
| The University of North Carolina at Chapel Hill | M |
| University of Oregon | M |
| The University of Texas at Austin | M,D |
| University of Wisconsin–Madison | M,D |
| Utah State University | M |

## FOOD SCIENCE AND TECHNOLOGY

| | |
|---|---|
| Alabama Agricultural and Mechanical University | M,D |
| The American University of Rome | M |
| Auburn University | M,D,O |
| Boston University | M |
| Brigham Young University | M |
| California Polytechnic State University, San Luis Obispo | M |
| Chapman University | M |
| Clemson University | M,D |
| Colorado State University | M,D |
| Cornell University | M,D |
| Dalhousie University | M,D |
| Drexel University | M |
| Florida State University | M,D |
| Illinois Institute of Technology | M |
| Iowa State University of Science and Technology | M,D |
| Kansas State University | M,D |
| London Metropolitan University | M,D |
| Louisiana State University and Agricultural & Mechanical College | M,D |
| McGill University | M,D |
| Memorial University of Newfoundland | M,D |
| Michigan State University | M,D |
| Mississippi State University | M,D |
| New Mexico State University | M |
| New York University | M,D |
| North Carolina Agricultural and Technical State University | M |
| North Carolina State University | M,D |
| North Dakota State University | M,D |
| The Ohio State University | M,D |
| Oklahoma State University | M,D |
| Oregon State University | M,D |
| Penn State University Park | M,D* |
| Portland State University | M,D,O |
| Purdue University | M,D |
| Rutgers University - New Brunswick | M,D |
| South Dakota State University | M,D |
| Texas A&M University | M,D |
| Texas Tech University | M,D |
| Texas Woman's University | M,D |
| Tuskegee University | M |
| Universidad de las Américas Puebla | M |
| Université de Moncton | M |
| University at Buffalo, the State University of New York | M,D,O |
| University of Arkansas | M,D |
| The University of British Columbia | M,D |
| University of California, Davis | M,D |
| University of Delaware | M,D |
| University of Florida | M,D |
| University of Georgia | M,D |
| University of Guelph | M,D |
| University of Hawaii at Manoa | M |
| University of Idaho | M,D |
| University of Illinois at Urbana-Champaign | M,D |
| University of Kentucky | M,D |
| University of Manitoba | M,D |
| University of Maryland, College Park | M,D |
| University of Maryland Eastern Shore | M,D |
| University of Massachusetts Amherst | M,D |
| University of Minnesota, Twin Cities Campus | M,D |
| University of Mississippi | M,D |
| University of Missouri | M,D |
| University of Nebraska–Lincoln | M,D |
| University of Puerto Rico at Mayagüez | M |
| University of Rhode Island | M,D |
| University of Saskatchewan | M,D |
| University of Southern California | M,D,O |
| The University of Tennessee | M,D |
| The University of Tennessee at Martin | M |
| University of Vermont | M,D |
| University of Wisconsin–Madison | M,D |
| University of Wisconsin–Stout | M |
| University of Wyoming | M |
| Université Laval | M,D |
| Utah State University | M,D |
| Washington State University | M,D |
| Wayne State University | M,D,O |
| West Virginia University | M,D |

## FOREIGN LANGUAGES EDUCATION

| | |
|---|---|
| Andrews University | M,D,O |
| Appalachian State University | M |
| Arizona State University at Tempe | M,D |
| Augusta University | M,O |
| Binghamton University, State University of New York | M |
| Boston College | M,D,O |
| Brandeis University | M |
| Brigham Young University | M |
| Brooklyn College of the City University of New York | M |
| California State University, Sacramento | M |
| Caribbean University | M,D |
| Central Connecticut State University | M,O |
| Cleveland State University | M |
| College of Charleston | M |
| The Colorado College | M |
| Colorado State University-Pueblo | M |
| Columbia University | M,D |
| Concordia College | M |
| Cornell University | M,D |
| Delaware State University | M |
| DePaul University | M,D |
| Duquesne University | M |
| Eastern Michigan University | M,O |
| Eastern University | M,O |
| Elms College | M,O |
| Florida International University | M,D,O |
| George Mason University | M |
| The George Washington University | M |
| Georgia Southern University | M,O |
| Georgia State University | M,O |
| Harding University | M,O |
| Hofstra University | M,D,O |
| Hunter College of the City University of New York | M |
| Indiana State University | M,D,O |
| Indiana University Bloomington | M,D |
| Indiana University-Purdue University Indianapolis | M,O |
| Inter American University of Puerto Rico, Arecibo Campus | M |
| Inter American University of Puerto Rico, Barranquitas Campus | M |
| Inter American University of Puerto Rico, Metropolitan Campus | M |
| Iona College | M |
| James Madison University | M |
| Kean University | M |
| Lamar University | M |
| Le Moyne College | M,O |
| Lewis University | M |
| London Metropolitan University | M,D |
| Manhattanville College | M,O |
| Marquette University | M |
| McGill University | M,D,O |
| Michigan State University | D |
| Middlebury Institute of International Studies at Monterey | M |
| Middle Tennessee State University | M |
| Minnesota State University Mankato | M |
| Mississippi State University | M |
| Molloy College | M,O |
| Morehead State University | M |
| New York University | M,D,O |
| Northern Arizona University | M |
| Pace University | M,O |
| Portland State University | M |
| Purdue University | M,D,O |
| Queens College of the City University of New York | M,O |
| Quinnipiac University | M |
| Rhode Island College | M |
| Rider University | M |
| Rivier University | M |
| Rutgers University - New Brunswick | M,D |
| Saginaw Valley State University | M |
| St. John Fisher College | M |
| Saint Xavier University | M |
| Shippensburg University of Pennsylvania | M |
| Southern Connecticut State University | M |
| Southern Oregon University | M |
| Spalding University | M |
| State University of New York at Plattsburgh | M |
| State University of New York College at Old Westbury | M |
| Stony Brook University, State University of New York | M,O |
| Texas A&M International University | M |
| Texas A&M University–Kingsville | M |
| Universidad del Este | M |
| Université du Québec en Outaouais | O |
| University at Buffalo, the State University of New York | M,D,O |
| University of Arkansas at Little Rock | M |
| University of California, Irvine | M,D |
| University of Central Florida | M,O |
| University of Connecticut | M,D |
| University of Dayton | M |
| University of Delaware | M |
| University of Florida | M,D |
| University of Hawaii at Hilo | M,D |
| University of Hawaii at Manoa | M,D,O |
| University of Illinois at Chicago | M,D |
| University of Illinois at Urbana-Champaign | M,D |
| University of Indianapolis | M |
| The University of Iowa | M,D |
| University of Kentucky | M |
| University of Maine | M |
| University of Maryland, Baltimore County | M |
| University of Maryland, College Park | D |
| University of Massachusetts Amherst | M |
| University of Michigan | M,D |
| University of Minnesota, Twin Cities Campus | M |
| University of Mississippi | M,D |
| University of Missouri | M,D,O |
| University of Nebraska at Kearney | M |
| University of Nebraska at Omaha | M |
| The University of North Carolina at Chapel Hill | M |
| The University of North Carolina at Charlotte | M,D,O |
| The University of North Carolina at Greensboro | M,D,O |
| University of Northern Colorado | M,D |
| University of Northern Iowa | M |
| University of Oklahoma | M,D |
| University of Puerto Rico at Rio Piedras | M,D |
| University of South Carolina | M,D |
| University of South Florida | O |
| The University of Tennessee | M,D,O |
| University of the Sacred Heart | M,O |
| The University of Toledo | M,D,O |
| University of Vermont | M,O |
| University of Victoria | M |
| University of Virginia | M,D,O |
| University of Wisconsin–Milwaukee | M,O* |
| Vanderbilt University | M,D* |
| Wagner College | M |
| Washington State University | M |

*M—masters degree; D—doctorate; O—other advanced degree; *—Close-Up and/or Display*

| | |
|---|---|
| Wayne State University | M,D,O |
| Western Kentucky University | M |
| Worcester State University | M |

## FORENSIC NURSING

| | |
|---|---|
| Aspen University | M |
| Duquesne University | M,O |
| Fitchburg State University | M,O |
| Monmouth University | M,D,O |
| Texas A&M University | M |

## FORENSIC PSYCHOLOGY

| | |
|---|---|
| Adler University | M |
| Alliant International University–Fresno | D |
| Alliant International University–Irvine | D |
| Alliant International University - Los Angeles | D |
| Alliant International University–Sacramento | D |
| Alliant International University–San Francisco | M,D |
| American International College | M,D,O |
| Argosy University, Atlanta | M,D,O |
| Argosy University, Chicago | D |
| Argosy University, Hawaii | M |
| Argosy University, Los Angeles | M,D |
| Argosy University, Northern Virginia | M,D |
| Argosy University, Orange County | M |
| Argosy University, Phoenix | M |
| Argosy University, Twin Cities | M,D,O |
| California Baptist University | M |
| Castleton University | M |
| The Chicago School of Professional Psychology | M,D |
| The Chicago School of Professional Psychology at Downtown Los Angeles | D |
| The Chicago School of Professional Psychology at Irvine | D |
| The Chicago School of Professional Psychology: Online | M,O |
| Drexel University | D |
| Fairleigh Dickinson University, Metropolitan Campus | M |
| The George Washington University | M,D,O |
| Holy Names University | M |
| Immaculata University | M,D,O |
| John Jay College of Criminal Justice of the City University of New York | M,D |
| Kean University | M |
| Liberty University | M |
| London Metropolitan University | M,D |
| Marymount University | M |
| Montclair State University | O |
| Nova Southeastern University | M,D,O |
| Pontificia Universidad Catolica Madre y Maestra | M |
| Post University | M |
| Prairie View A&M University | M,D |
| Roger Williams University | M |
| Sage Graduate School | M,O |
| Tiffin University | M |
| Universidad de Iberoamerica | M,D |
| Universidad del Turabo | M,D,O |
| University of Central Oklahoma | M |
| University of Denver | M,D,O |
| University of Houston–Victoria | M |
| University of Louisiana at Monroe | M |
| University of New Haven | M,O |
| University of North Dakota | M,D |
| Walden University | M,D,O |
| Westfield State University | M |
| William James College | M,D,O |

## FORENSIC SCIENCES

| | |
|---|---|
| Alabama State University | M |
| Alliant International University–Irvine | D |
| Arcadia University | M |
| Bay Path University | M |
| Boston University | M |
| Buffalo State College, State University of New York | M |
| Carlow University | M |
| Cedar Crest College | M |
| Champlain College | M |
| DeSales University | M,O |
| Duquesne University | M |
| Emporia State University | M,O |
| Florida Gulf Coast University | M |
| Florida International University | M,D |
| George Mason University | M |
| The George Washington University | M,O |
| Georgia State University | M,O |
| Golden Gate University | M,O |
| Indiana University-Purdue University Indianapolis | M |
| Iona College | M,O |
| James Madison University | M |
| John Jay College of Criminal Justice of the City University of New York | M,D |
| La Salle University | M,O |
| Long Island University - Brooklyn | M,D,O |
| Marshall University | M,O |
| McGill University | M,D,O |
| Mercyhurst University | M |
| Michigan State University | M,D |
| Middle Georgia State University | M |
| Missouri Western State University | M,O |
| National University | M,O |
| Niagara University | M |
| Oklahoma State University Center for Health Sciences | M |
| Pace University | M |
| Penn State University Park | M* |
| Philadelphia College of Osteopathic Medicine | M |
| St. Joseph's College, Long Island Campus | M |
| St. Joseph's College, New York | M |
| Saint Leo University | M,D |
| Salve Regina University | M,O |
| Sam Houston State University | M,D |
| Seattle University | M,O |
| Stevenson University | M |
| Stratford University (VA) | M,D |
| Syracuse University | M,O |
| Towson University | M |
| Universidad del Turabo | M |
| University at Albany, State University of New York | M |
| The University of Alabama at Birmingham | M |
| University of California, Davis | M |
| University of Central Oklahoma | M |
| University of Charleston | M |
| University of Colorado Denver | M |
| University of Detroit Mercy | M,O |
| University of Florida | M,O |
| University of Houston–Victoria | M |
| University of Illinois at Chicago | M |
| University of Maryland, Baltimore | M |
| University of New Haven | M,O |
| University of North Texas Health Science Center at Fort Worth | M,D |
| University of Rhode Island | M,D,O |
| University of St. Francis (IL) | M,D |
| University of Southern Mississippi | M,D |
| University of South Florida | M,D,O |
| Virginia Commonwealth University | M |
| Webster University | M |
| West Virginia University | M,D |

## FORESTRY

| | |
|---|---|
| Auburn University | M,D |
| California Polytechnic State University, San Luis Obispo | M |
| Clemson University | M,D |
| Cornell University | M,D |
| Harvard University | M* |
| Humboldt State University | M |
| Iowa State University of Science and Technology | M,D |
| Lakehead University | M,D |
| Louisiana State University and Agricultural & Mechanical College | M,D |
| McGill University | M,D |
| Michigan State University | M,D |
| Michigan Technological University | M,D |
| Mississippi State University | M,D |
| North Carolina State University | M,D |
| Northern Arizona University | M,D |
| The Ohio State University | M,D |
| Oklahoma State University | M,D |
| Oregon State University | M,D |
| Penn State University Park | M,D* |
| Purdue University | M,D |
| Southern Illinois University Carbondale | M |
| Southern University and Agricultural and Mechanical College | M |
| State University of New York College of Environmental Science and Forestry | M,D |
| Stephen F. Austin State University | M,D |
| Texas A&M University | M,D |
| Tropical Agriculture Research and Higher Education Center | M,D |
| UNB Fredericton | M,D |
| Université du Québec en Abitibi-Témiscamingue | M,D |
| University of Alberta | M,D |
| The University of Arizona | M,D |
| University of Arkansas at Monticello | M |
| The University of British Columbia | M,D |
| University of California, Berkeley | M,D |
| University of Florida | M,D |
| University of Georgia | M,D |
| University of Kentucky | M |
| University of Maine | M,D |
| University of Massachusetts Amherst | M,D |
| University of Minnesota, Twin Cities Campus | M,D |
| University of Missouri | M,D,O |
| University of Montana | M,D |
| University of New Hampshire | M |
| The University of Tennessee | M |
| University of Toronto | M,D |
| University of Vermont | M,D,O |
| University of Washington | M,D |
| University of Wisconsin–Madison | M,D |
| Université Laval | M,D |
| Utah State University | M,D |
| Virginia Polytechnic Institute and State University | M,D |
| West Virginia University | M,D |
| Yale University | M,D |

## FOUNDATIONS AND PHILOSOPHY OF EDUCATION

| | |
|---|---|
| Antioch University New England | M,O |
| Arkansas State University | M,D,O |
| Ball State University | D |
| Bank Street College of Education | M |
| Binghamton University, State University of New York | D |
| Brigham Young University | M,D |
| Chicago State University | M |
| Columbia University | M,O |
| Curry College | M,O |
| DePaul University | M,D |
| Duquesne University | M |
| Eastern Michigan University | M |
| Eastern Washington University | M |
| Fairfield University | M,O |
| Fairleigh Dickinson University, Metropolitan Campus | M |
| Florida State University | M,D,O |
| Georgia State University | M,D |
| Harvard University | M,O* |
| Indiana University Bloomington | M,D,O |
| Iowa State University of Science and Technology | M,D |
| Kent State University | M,D |
| Marquette University | M,D,O |
| McGill University | M,D,O |
| Mount Saint Vincent University | M |
| New York University | M,D |
| Northern Arizona University | M,D,O |
| Northern Illinois University | M,D,O |
| Northern Vermont University–Johnson | M |
| Penn State University Park | M,D,O* |
| Purdue University | M,D,O |
| Rutgers University - New Brunswick | M,D |
| Saint Louis University | M,D |
| Simon Fraser University | M,D |
| Southern Illinois University Edwardsville | M |
| Spring Hill College | M |
| Syracuse University | M,D,O |
| Teachers College, Columbia University | M,D,O |
| University at Buffalo, the State University of New York | M,D,O |
| The University of British Columbia | M,D |
| University of California, Riverside | M,D,O |
| University of Central Oklahoma | M |
| University of Cincinnati | M,D |
| University of Hawaii at Manoa | M,D |
| University of Houston | M,D |
| University of Houston–Clear Lake | M |
| The University of Iowa | M,D,O |
| University of Manitoba | M |
| University of Maryland, College Park | M,D,O |
| University of Minnesota, Twin Cities Campus | M,D |
| University of New Mexico | M,D |
| University of Pennsylvania | M,D |
| University of Rochester | D |
| University of Saskatchewan | M,D,O |
| University of South Africa | M,D |
| University of South Carolina | D |
| The University of Tennessee | M,D,O |
| The University of Texas of the Permian Basin | M |
| The University of Toledo | M,D,O |
| University of Utah | M,D |
| University of Victoria | M,D |
| University of Washington | M,D |
| University of Wisconsin–Milwaukee | M,D,O* |
| Wayne State University | M,D,O |
| Western Illinois University | M,O |
| Widener University | M,D |

## FRENCH

| | |
|---|---|
| American University | M,O |
| Arizona State University at Tempe | M |
| Asbury University | M |
| Binghamton University, State University of New York | M |
| Boston College | M |
| Bowling Green State University | M |
| Brooklyn College of the City University of New York | M |
| Brown University | D |
| California State University, Long Beach | M |
| California State University, Los Angeles | M |
| Carleton University | M |
| Case Western Reserve University | M |
| Central Connecticut State University | M,O |
| Colorado State University | M |
| Columbia University | M,D |
| Concordia University (Canada) | M,O |
| Cornell University | D |
| Dalhousie University | M,D |
| DePaul University | M |
| Drew University | M,D,O |
| Duke University | D |
| Emory University | D |
| Florida Atlantic University | M |
| Florida State University | M,D |
| George Mason University | M |
| Georgia State University | M,O |
| The Graduate Center, City University of New York | D |
| Harvard University | M,D* |
| Howard University | M |
| Hunter College of the City University of New York | M |
| Illinois State University | M |
| Indiana University Bloomington | M,D |
| Johns Hopkins University | M,D |
| Kansas State University | M |
| Kent State University | M,D |
| Lake Forest College | M |
| Louisiana State University and Agricultural & Mechanical College | M,D |
| McGill University | M,D |
| McMaster University | M |
| Memorial University of Newfoundland | M |
| Miami University | M |
| Michigan State University | M,D |
| Middlebury College | M,D |
| Middle Tennessee State University | M |
| Millersville University of Pennsylvania | M |
| Minnesota State University Mankato | M |
| Montclair State University | M |
| New York University | M,D,O |
| North Carolina State University | M |
| Northern Illinois University | M |
| Northwestern University | D,O |
| The Ohio State University | M,D |
| Ohio University | M |
| Penn State University Park | M,D* |
| Portland State University | M |
| Princeton University | D |
| Purdue University | M |
| Queens College of the City University of New York | M |
| Queen's University at Kingston | M,D |
| Rutgers University - New Brunswick | M,D |
| St. John Fisher College | M |
| Saint Louis University | M |
| San Francisco State University | M |
| Simon Fraser University | M |
| Southern Oregon University | M |
| Stanford University | M,D |
| State University of New York at New Paltz | M,O |
| State University of New York College at Geneseo | M |
| Stony Brook University, State University of New York | M |
| Syracuse University | M |
| Tufts University | M |
| Tulane University | M,D |
| Université de Moncton | M,D |
| Université de Montréal | M,D |
| Université de Sherbrooke | M,D |
| Université du Québec à Chicoutimi | O |
| University at Buffalo, the State University of New York | M,D,O |
| The University of Alabama | M,D |
| University of Alberta | M,D |
| The University of Arizona | M |
| University of Arkansas | M |
| The University of British Columbia | M,D |
| University of California, Berkeley | D |
| University of California, Davis | D |
| University of California, Irvine | M,D |
| University of California, Los Angeles | M,D |
| University of California, Santa Barbara | D |
| University of Chicago | D |
| University of Cincinnati | M,D |
| University of Colorado Boulder | M,D |
| University of Delaware | M |
| University of Florida | M,D |
| University of Georgia | M,D |
| University of Guelph | M |
| University of Hawaii at Manoa | M |
| University of Illinois at Chicago | M |
| University of Illinois at Urbana-Champaign | M,D |
| The University of Iowa | M,D |
| The University of Kansas | M,D |
| University of Lethbridge | M,D |
| University of Louisiana at Lafayette | M,D |
| University of Louisville | M,O |
| University of Maine | M |
| The University of Manchester | D |
| University of Manitoba | M,D |
| University of Maryland, College Park | M,D |
| University of Massachusetts Amherst | M |
| University of Memphis | M |
| University of Miami | D |
| University of Michigan | D |
| University of Minnesota, Twin Cities Campus | M,D |
| University of Missouri | M,D |
| University of Missouri–Kansas City | M |
| University of Montana | M |
| University of Nebraska–Lincoln | M,D |
| University of New Mexico | M,D |
| The University of North Carolina at Chapel Hill | M,D |
| The University of North Carolina at Greensboro | M |
| University of North Texas | M,D,O |
| University of Notre Dame | M |
| University of Oklahoma | M,D |
| University of Oregon | M |
| University of Ottawa | M,D |
| University of Pennsylvania | M,D |
| University of Pittsburgh | M,D* |
| University of Regina | M |
| University of Saskatchewan | M |
| University of South Africa | M,D |
| University of South Carolina | M,D |
| The University of Tennessee | M,D |
| The University of Texas at Arlington | M |
| The University of Texas at Austin | M,D |
| The University of Toledo | M |
| University of Toronto | M,D |
| University of Utah | M,D |
| University of Victoria | M |
| University of Virginia | M,D |
| University of Washington | M,D |
| University of Waterloo | M,D |
| The University of Western Ontario | M,D |
| University of Wisconsin–Madison | M,D,O |
| University of Wisconsin–Milwaukee | M,O* |
| University of Wyoming | M |
| Vanderbilt University | M,D* |
| Washington University in St. Louis | D |
| Wayne State University | M,D |
| Western Kentucky University | M |
| Yale University | M,D |
| York University | M,D |

## GAME DESIGN AND DEVELOPMENT

| | |
|---|---|
| Academy of Art University | M |
| Concordia University (Canada) | M,D,O |
| DePaul University | M,D |
| Full Sail University | M |
| Iona College | M |

| | |
|---|---|
| Long Island University - Post | M |
| Michigan State University | M |
| New York University | M |
| Rochester Institute of Technology | M |
| Sacred Heart University | M |
| Savannah College of Art and Design | M |
| University of Advancing Technology | M |
| University of California, Santa Cruz | M,D |
| The University of North Carolina at Charlotte | M,O |
| University of Pennsylvania | M,D |
| University of Southern California | M,D |
| University of Utah | M |
| Virginia International University | M,O |
| Worcester Polytechnic Institute | M |

### GENDER STUDIES

| | |
|---|---|
| American University | M,D,O |
| The American University in Cairo | M,O |
| Arizona State University at Tempe | M,D,O |
| Brandeis University | M,D |
| Carnegie Mellon University | D |
| Central European University | M,D |
| Central Michigan University | M |
| The College of New Jersey | O |
| Cornell University | M,D |
| Delta State University | M |
| DePaul University | M |
| Eastern Michigan University | M,O |
| George Mason University | M |
| The George Washington University | O |
| Georgia State University | M,O |
| Indiana University Bloomington | D |
| Indiana University Northwest | M,O |
| Instituto Tecnologico de Santo Domingo | M,O |
| Kansas State University | O |
| Loyola University Chicago | M |
| Memorial University of Newfoundland | M,D |
| Middle Tennessee State University | O |
| Minnesota State University Mankato | M |
| Murray State University | M,D,O |
| Northern Arizona University | O |
| Northwestern University | O |
| The Ohio State University | M,D |
| Old Dominion University | M,O |
| Oregon State University | M,D |
| Queen's University at Kingston | M,D |
| Rutgers University - New Brunswick | M,D |
| Saint Mary's University (Canada) | M |
| San Diego State University | O |
| Simmons University | M,D,O |
| Simon Fraser University | M,D |
| Stony Brook University, State University of New York | O |
| Texas Woman's University | M,D |
| University at Albany, State University of New York | M |
| University at Buffalo, the State University of New York | M,D |
| The University of Arizona | M,D,O |
| The University of British Columbia | M,D |
| University of California, Los Angeles | M,D |
| University of Chicago | M |
| University of Colorado Denver | M,O |
| University of Florida | M,O |
| University of Lethbridge | M,D |
| University of Maryland, Baltimore County | O |
| University of Memphis | O |
| University of Michigan–Flint | M |
| University of Missouri–St. Louis | O |
| The University of North Carolina at Charlotte | M,D,O |
| The University of North Carolina at Greensboro | M,O |
| University of Northern British Columbia | M,D,O |
| University of Northern Iowa | M |
| University of Oklahoma | O |
| University of Rhode Island | M,D,O |
| University of South Florida | M,O |
| The University of Toledo | O |
| University of Toronto | M,D |
| University of Wisconsin–Milwaukee | M,O* |
| Wayne State University | M,D,O |
| Wilfrid Laurier University | M |
| York University | M,D |

### GENETIC COUNSELING

| | |
|---|---|
| Augustana University | M |
| Baylor College of Medicine | M |
| Bay Path University | M |
| Boston University | M |
| Brandeis University | M |
| California State University, Stanislaus | M |
| Case Western Reserve University | M,D |
| Emory University | M |
| Icahn School of Medicine at Mount Sinai | M,D |
| Johns Hopkins University | M,D |
| Long Island University - Post | M,O |
| McGill University | M,D |
| Northwestern University | M |
| Sarah Lawrence College | M |
| Thomas Jefferson University | M |
| Université de Montréal | O |
| The University of Alabama at Birmingham | M |
| University of Arkansas for Medical Sciences | M,D |
| The University of British Columbia | M |
| University of California, Irvine | M |
| University of Cincinnati | M |
| University of Colorado Denver | M |
| University of Manitoba | M,D |
| University of Maryland, Baltimore | M |
| University of Michigan | M,D |
| University of Minnesota, Twin Cities Campus | M,D |
| The University of North Carolina at Greensboro | M |
| University of Oklahoma Health Sciences Center | M |
| University of Pittsburgh | M,D,O* |
| University of South Carolina | M |
| The University of Texas Health Science Center at Houston | M,D |
| University of Toronto | M,D |
| University of Wisconsin–Madison | M,D |

### GENETICS

| | |
|---|---|
| Albert Einstein College of Medicine | D |
| Baylor College of Medicine | D |
| Boston University | D |
| Brandeis University | M,D |
| California Institute of Technology | D |
| Carnegie Mellon University | M,D |
| Clemson University | M,D,O |
| Columbia University | M,D |
| Cornell University | D |
| Drexel University | M,D |
| Duke University | D |
| Emory University | D |
| Harvard University | M,D* |
| Illinois State University | M,D |
| Indiana University Bloomington | M,D |
| Iowa State University of Science and Technology | M,D |
| Irell & Manella Graduate School of Biological Sciences | D |
| Johns Hopkins University | M,D |
| Kansas State University | M,D |
| Kent State University | M,D |
| Marquette University | M,D |
| Massachusetts Institute of Technology | D |
| Mayo Clinic Graduate School of Biomedical Sciences | D |
| McMaster University | M,D |
| Medical University of South Carolina | D |
| Michigan State University | M,D |
| Mississippi State University | M,D |
| New York University | M,D |
| The Ohio State University | M,D |
| Oregon Health & Science University | D |
| Oregon State University | M,D |
| Purdue University | M,D |
| Rutgers University - New Brunswick | M,D |
| Stanford University | D |
| Stony Brook University, State University of New York | D |
| Thomas Jefferson University | D |
| Tufts University | D |
| Université de Montréal | O |
| Université du Québec à Chicoutimi | M |
| University at Buffalo, the State University of New York | M,D |
| The University of Alabama at Birmingham | D |
| University of Alberta | M,D |
| The University of Arizona | M,D |
| The University of British Columbia | M,D |
| University of Calgary | M,D |
| University of California, Davis | M,D |
| University of California, Irvine | D |
| University of California, Riverside | D |
| University of California, San Francisco | D |
| University of Chicago | D |
| University of Colorado Denver | D |
| University of Connecticut | M,D |
| University of Connecticut Health Center | D |
| University of Delaware | M,D |
| University of Florida | D |
| University of Georgia | M,D |
| University of Hawaii at Manoa | M,D |
| University of Illinois at Chicago | D |
| The University of Iowa | M,D |
| The University of Manchester | M,D |
| University of Massachusetts Amherst | M,D |
| University of Miami | M,D |
| University of Minnesota, Twin Cities Campus | M,D |
| University of Nebraska Medical Center | M,D |
| University of New Hampshire | M,D |
| University of New Mexico | M,D |
| The University of North Carolina at Chapel Hill | M,D |
| University of North Dakota | M,D |
| University of North Texas Health Science Center at Fort Worth | M,D |
| University of Notre Dame | M,D |
| University of Oregon | M,D |
| University of Pennsylvania | D |
| University of Puerto Rico at Rio Piedras | M,D |
| University of Rochester | M,D |
| The University of Tennessee | M,D |
| The University of Texas Health Science Center at Houston | M,D |
| The University of Texas MD Anderson Cancer Center | M |
| The University of Texas Southwestern Medical Center | D |
| University of Washington | M,D,O |
| University of Wisconsin–Madison | M,D |
| University of Wyoming | D |
| Van Andel Institute Graduate School | D |
| Virginia Polytechnic Institute and State University | M,D |
| Washington State University | M,D |
| Washington University in St. Louis | M,D |
| Wesleyan University | D |
| West Virginia University | M,D |
| Yale University | D |

### GENOMIC SCIENCES

| | |
|---|---|
| Albert Einstein College of Medicine | D |
| Augusta University | D |
| Black Hills State University | M |
| Boston University | D |
| Case Western Reserve University | M,D |
| Concordia University (Canada) | M,D,O |
| Cornell University | D |
| Duke University | D |
| Manchester University | M |
| Massachusetts Institute of Technology | M,D |
| North Carolina State University | M,D |
| North Dakota State University | M,D |
| Oregon State University | M,D |
| Penn State Hershey Medical Center | M,D |
| Purdue University | D |
| Thomas Jefferson University | D |
| University at Buffalo, the State University of New York | M,D |
| The University of Alabama at Birmingham | D |
| University of California, Riverside | D |
| University of California, San Francisco | D |
| University of Chicago | D |
| University of Cincinnati | M,D |
| University of Colorado Denver | D |
| University of Connecticut | M,D |
| University of Georgia | M,D |
| University of Maryland, Baltimore | M,D |
| University of Maryland, College Park | D |
| University of Pennsylvania | D |
| University of Rochester | D |
| University of Southern California | D |
| The University of Tennessee | M,D |
| The University of Tennessee–Oak Ridge National Laboratory | M,D |
| The University of Texas Health Science Center at Houston | M,D,O |
| The University of Toledo | M,O |
| University of Washington | D |
| Wake Forest University | D |
| Washington University in St. Louis | M |
| Wesleyan University | D |
| Yale University | D |

### GEOCHEMISTRY

| | |
|---|---|
| California Institute of Technology | M,D |
| Colorado School of Mines | M,D |
| Cornell University | M,D |
| Georgia State University | M,D |
| Indiana University Bloomington | M,D |
| Massachusetts Institute of Technology | M,D |
| McMaster University | M,D |
| Missouri University of Science and Technology | M,D |
| Montana Technological University | M |
| New Mexico Institute of Mining and Technology | M,D |
| Ohio University | M |
| Oregon State University | M,D |
| University of California, Los Angeles | M,D |
| University of Hawaii at Manoa | M,D |
| The University of Manchester | M,D |
| University of Nevada, Reno | M,D |
| Yale University | D |

### GEODETIC SCIENCES

| | |
|---|---|
| The Ohio State University | M,D |
| UNB Fredericton | M,D |
| Université Laval | M,D |

### GEOGRAPHIC INFORMATION SYSTEMS

| | |
|---|---|
| Acadia University | M |
| Appalachian State University | M |
| Arizona State University at Tempe | M,D,O |
| Auburn University at Montgomery | M |
| Ball State University | M,O |
| Boston University | M,D |
| Central Michigan University | M |
| Chicago State University | M |
| Claremont Graduate University | M,D,O |
| Clark University | M |
| Cleveland State University | M,O |
| East Carolina University | M,O |
| Eastern Illinois University | M |
| Eastern Michigan University | M,O |
| East Tennessee State University | M,O |
| Elizabeth City State University | M |
| Elmhurst University | M |
| Florida State University | M,D |
| George Mason University | M,D,O |
| Georgia Institute of Technology | M,D |
| Georgia State University | O |
| The Graduate Center, City University of New York | M |
| Hood College | M,O |
| Hunter College of the City University of New York | M,O |
| Idaho State University | M,O |
| Indiana University of Pennsylvania | M,O |
| Indiana University-Purdue University Indianapolis | M,O |
| Johns Hopkins University | M,O |
| Kansas State University | M,D,O |
| Kent State University | M,D |
| Millersville University of Pennsylvania | M |
| Montclair State University | O |
| Naval Postgraduate School | M,D,O |
| North Carolina Central University | M |
| North Carolina State University | M,D |
| Northeastern Illinois University | M,O |
| Northeastern University | M |
| Northern Arizona University | M,O |
| Northern Kentucky University | M,O |
| Northwest Missouri State University | M,O |
| Oregon State University | M |
| Saint Mary's University of Minnesota | M,O |
| Salisbury University | M |
| Sam Houston State University | M,O |
| San Francisco State University | M |
| State University of New York College of Environmental Science and Forestry | M,D |
| Stony Brook University, State University of New York | O |
| Temple University | M,D,O* |
| Texas A&M University–Corpus Christi | M,D |
| Texas State University | M,D |
| Université du Québec à Montréal | O |
| University at Albany, State University of New York | M,O |
| University at Buffalo, the State University of New York | M,D |
| The University of Alabama | M,D |
| University of Alaska Fairbanks | M |
| The University of Arizona | M,D,O |
| University of Central Arkansas | M,O |
| University of Colorado Denver | M,D |
| University of Denver | M,D,O |
| University of Florida | M,D |
| The University of Iowa | M,D,O |
| The University of Kansas | M,D,O |
| University of Lethbridge | M,D |
| University of Maryland, Baltimore County | M,O |
| University of Memphis | M,D,O |
| University of Minnesota, Twin Cities Campus | M,D |
| University of Missouri | M,D,O |
| University of Nebraska at Omaha | M,O |
| University of New Hampshire | O |
| University of New Haven | M |
| University of North Alabama | M |
| The University of North Carolina at Charlotte | M,D |
| The University of North Carolina at Greensboro | M,D,O |
| The University of North Carolina Wilmington | M,O |
| University of North Dakota | M |
| University of North Texas Health Science Center at Fort Worth | M,D,O |
| University of Pennsylvania | M,D,O |
| University of Pittsburgh | M,D* |
| University of Redlands | M |
| University of Southern California | M,O |
| University of South Florida | O |
| The University of Texas at Dallas | M,D |
| The University of Toledo | M,D,O |
| University of Utah | M,D |
| University of West Florida | M |
| University of Wisconsin–Madison | M,D,O |
| University of Wisconsin–Milwaukee | M,D,O* |
| Université Laval | M,O |
| Virginia Commonwealth University | O |
| Western Illinois University | M,O |
| Western Michigan University | M,O |

### GEOGRAPHY

| | |
|---|---|
| Appalachian State University | M |
| Arizona State University at Tempe | M,D,O |
| Auburn University | M |
| Ball State University | M,O |
| Binghamton University, State University of New York | M |
| Brock University | M |
| California State University, East Bay | M |
| California State University, Fullerton | M |
| California State University, Long Beach | M |
| California State University, Los Angeles | M |
| California State University, Northridge | M |
| Carleton University | M,D |
| Central Connecticut State University | M |
| Central Washington University | M |
| Clark University | D |
| Concordia University (Canada) | M,D,O |
| East Carolina University | M,O |
| East Stroudsburg University of Pennsylvania | M |
| Florida State University | M,D |
| Fort Hays State University | M |
| George Mason University | M,D,O |
| The George Washington University | M,O |
| Georgia State University | M,D |
| Hunter College of the City University of New York | M,O |
| Indiana University Bloomington | D |
| Indiana University of Pennsylvania | M,O |
| Kansas State University | M,D,O |
| Kent State University | M,D |

*M—masters degree; D—doctorate; O—other advanced degree; *—Close-Up and/or Display*

| | |
|---|---|
| Louisiana State University and Agricultural & Mechanical College | M,D |
| Marshall University | M,O |
| McGill University | M,D |
| McMaster University | M,D |
| Memorial University of Newfoundland | M,D |
| Miami University | M |
| Michigan State University | M,D |
| Minnesota State University Mankato | M |
| Mississippi State University | M,D |
| Missouri State University | M,O |
| New Mexico State University | M |
| Northeastern Illinois University | M,O |
| Northern Arizona University | M,O |
| Northern Illinois University | M,D |
| The Ohio State University | M,D |
| Ohio University | M |
| Oklahoma State University | M,D |
| Oregon State University | M,D |
| Penn State University Park | M,D* |
| Portland State University | M,D |
| Queen's University at Kingston | M,D |
| Rutgers University - New Brunswick | M,D |
| St. Cloud State University | M,O |
| Salem State University | M |
| San Diego State University | M,D |
| San Francisco State University | M |
| Shippensburg University of Pennsylvania | M |
| Simon Fraser University | M,D |
| South Dakota State University | M |
| Southern Illinois University Carbondale | M,D |
| Southern Illinois University Edwardsville | M |
| Syracuse University | M,D |
| Temple University | M,D,O* |
| Texas A&M University | M,D |
| Texas State University | M,D |
| Texas Tech University | M,D |
| Thomas Jefferson University | M |
| Towson University | M |
| Trent University | M,D |
| Université de Montréal | M,D,O |
| Université de Sherbrooke | M,D |
| Université du Québec à Montréal | M |
| University at Albany, State University of New York | M,O |
| University at Buffalo, the State University of New York | M,D |
| The University of Alabama | M,D |
| The University of Arizona | M,D,O |
| University of Arkansas | M |
| The University of British Columbia | M,D |
| University of Calgary | M,D |
| University of California, Berkeley | D |
| University of California, Davis | M,D |
| University of California, Los Angeles | M,D |
| University of California, Santa Barbara | M,D |
| University of Central Arkansas | M,O |
| University of Cincinnati | M,D |
| University of Colorado Boulder | M,D |
| University of Colorado Colorado Springs | M |
| University of Connecticut | M,D |
| University of Delaware | M,D |
| University of Denver | M,D |
| University of Florida | M,D |
| University of Georgia | M,D |
| University of Guelph | M,D |
| University of Hawaii at Manoa | M,D,O |
| University of Idaho | M,D |
| University of Illinois at Chicago | M |
| University of Illinois at Urbana-Champaign | M,D |
| The University of Iowa | M,D,O |
| The University of Kansas | M,D,O |
| University of Kentucky | M,D |
| University of Lethbridge | M,D |
| University of Louisville | M |
| The University of Manchester | M,D |
| University of Manitoba | M,D |
| University of Maryland, Baltimore County | M,D |
| University of Maryland, College Park | M,D |
| University of Massachusetts Amherst | M |
| University of Memphis | M,D,O |
| University of Miami | M |
| University of Minnesota, Twin Cities Campus | M,D |
| University of Missouri | M,O |
| University of Montana | M |
| University of Nebraska at Omaha | M,O |
| University of Nebraska–Lincoln | M,D |
| University of Nevada, Reno | M,D |
| University of New Mexico | M |
| The University of North Carolina at Chapel Hill | M,D |
| The University of North Carolina at Charlotte | M,D |
| The University of North Carolina at Greensboro | M,D,O |
| University of North Dakota | M |
| University of Northern Iowa | M |
| University of North Texas | M,D,O |
| University of Oklahoma | M,D |
| University of Oregon | M,D |
| University of Ottawa | M,D |
| University of Prince Edward Island | M |
| University of Regina | M,D |
| University of Saskatchewan | M,D |
| University of South Africa | M,D |
| University of South Carolina | M,D |
| University of Southern California | M,O |
| University of South Florida | O |
| The University of Tennessee | M,D |
| The University of Texas at Austin | M,D |
| The University of Texas at Dallas | M,D |
| The University of Toledo | M,D,O |
| University of Toronto | M,D |
| University of Utah | M,D |
| University of Victoria | M,D |
| University of Washington | M,D |
| University of Waterloo | M,D |
| The University of Western Ontario | M,D |
| University of Wisconsin–Madison | M,D,O |
| University of Wisconsin–Milwaukee | M,D* |
| University of Wyoming | M |
| Université Laval | M,D |
| Utah State University | M,D |
| Virginia Polytechnic Institute and State University | M,D |
| Western Illinois University | M,O |
| Western Michigan University | M,D,O |
| Western Washington University | M |
| West Virginia University | M,D |
| Wilfrid Laurier University | M,D |
| York University | M,D |

**GEOLOGICAL ENGINEERING**

| | |
|---|---|
| Arizona State University at Tempe | M,D |
| Colorado School of Mines | M,D |
| Missouri University of Science and Technology | M,D |
| Montana Technological University | M |
| New Mexico Institute of Mining and Technology | M |
| South Dakota School of Mines and Technology | M,D |
| The University of Akron | M |
| University of Alaska Fairbanks | M |
| The University of Arizona | M,D,O |
| The University of British Columbia | M,D |
| University of Hawaii at Manoa | M,D |
| University of Idaho | M,D |
| University of Minnesota, Twin Cities Campus | M,D,O |
| University of Mississippi | M,D |
| University of Nevada, Reno | M,D |
| University of North Dakota | M,D |
| University of Oklahoma | M,D,O |
| University of Saskatchewan | M,D |
| University of Utah | M,D |
| University of Wisconsin–Madison | M,D |

**GEOLOGY**

| | |
|---|---|
| Acadia University | M |
| Arizona State University at Tempe | M,D |
| Auburn University | M |
| Ball State University | M,D |
| Binghamton University, State University of New York | M,D |
| Boston College | M |
| Bowling Green State University | M |
| Brigham Young University | M |
| Brooklyn College of the City University of New York | M,D |
| California Institute of Technology | M,D |
| California State Polytechnic University, Pomona | M |
| California State University, Chico | M |
| California State University, East Bay | M |
| California State University, Fresno | M |
| California State University, Fullerton | M |
| California State University, Long Beach | M |
| California State University, Los Angeles | M |
| California State University, Northridge | M |
| Case Western Reserve University | M,D |
| Central Washington University | M |
| City College of the City University of New York | M |
| Colorado School of Mines | M,D |
| Cornell University | M,D |
| Duke University | M,D |
| East Carolina University | M,O |
| Eastern Kentucky University | M,D |
| Florida Atlantic University | M,D |
| Florida State University | M,D |
| Fort Hays State University | M |
| Georgia State University | M |
| Humboldt State University | M |
| Idaho State University | M,O |
| Indiana University-Purdue University Indianapolis | M,D |
| Iowa State University of Science and Technology | M,D |
| Kansas State University | M |
| Kent State University | M,D |
| Lakehead University | M |
| Laurentian University | M,D |
| Lehigh University | M,D |
| Louisiana State University and Agricultural & Mechanical College | M,D |
| Massachusetts Institute of Technology | M,D |
| McMaster University | M,D |
| Memorial University of Newfoundland | M,D |
| Miami University | M,D |
| Mississippi State University | M,D |
| Missouri State University | M,O |
| Missouri University of Science and Technology | M,D |
| Montana Technological University | M |
| New Mexico Institute of Mining and Technology | M,D |
| Northern Arizona University | M,D,O |
| Northern Illinois University | M,D |
| Northwestern University | D |
| The Ohio State University | M,D |
| Ohio University | M |
| Oklahoma State University | M,D |
| Oregon State University | M,D |
| Portland State University | M,D,O |
| Queens College of the City University of New York | M |
| Queen's University at Kingston | M,D |
| Rensselaer Polytechnic Institute | M,D |
| Rutgers University - Newark | M |
| Rutgers University - New Brunswick | M,D |
| St. Francis Xavier University | M |
| San Diego State University | M |
| San Jose State University | M |
| South Dakota School of Mines and Technology | M,D |
| Southern Illinois University Carbondale | M,D |
| Southern Methodist University | M,D |
| Stephen F. Austin State University | M |
| Sul Ross State University | M |
| Syracuse University | M,D |
| Temple University | M,D* |
| Texas A&M University | M,D |
| UNB Fredericton | M,D |
| Université du Québec à Montréal | M,D,O |
| University at Buffalo, the State University of New York | M,D |
| The University of Akron | M |
| The University of Alabama | M,D |
| University of Arkansas | M |
| The University of British Columbia | M,D |
| University of Calgary | M,D |
| University of California, Berkeley | M,D |
| University of California, Davis | M,D |
| University of California, Los Angeles | M,D |
| University of California, Riverside | M,D |
| University of Cincinnati | M,D |
| University of Colorado Boulder | M,D |
| University of Connecticut | M,D |
| University of Delaware | M,D |
| University of Florida | M,D |
| University of Georgia | M,D |
| University of Hawaii at Manoa | M,D |
| University of Houston | M,D |
| University of Idaho | M,D |
| University of Illinois at Chicago | M,D |
| University of Illinois at Urbana-Champaign | M,D |
| The University of Kansas | M,D |
| University of Kentucky | M,D |
| University of Maine | M,O |
| University of Manitoba | M,D |
| University of Maryland, College Park | M,D |
| University of Memphis | M,D,O |
| University of Minnesota, Duluth | M,D |
| University of Minnesota, Twin Cities Campus | M,D |
| University of Mississippi | M,D |
| University of Missouri | M,D |
| University of Montana | M,D |
| University of Nevada, Reno | M,D |
| University of New Hampshire | M |
| The University of North Carolina at Chapel Hill | M,D |
| University of North Dakota | M,D |
| University of Oklahoma | M,D |
| University of Oregon | M,D |
| University of Pittsburgh | M,D* |
| University of Puerto Rico at Mayagüez | M |
| University of Regina | M,D |
| University of Rochester | M,D |
| University of Saskatchewan | M,D,O |
| University of South Carolina | M,D |
| University of South Florida | O |
| The University of Tennessee | M,D |
| The University of Texas at Arlington | M,D |
| The University of Texas at Austin | M,D |
| The University of Texas at El Paso | M,D |
| The University of Texas at San Antonio | M |
| The University of Texas of the Permian Basin | M |
| The University of Toledo | M,D |
| University of Toronto | M,D |
| University of Utah | M,D |
| University of Vermont | M |
| University of Washington | M,D |
| The University of Western Ontario | M,D |
| University of Wisconsin–Madison | M,D |
| University of Wisconsin–Milwaukee | M,D* |
| University of Wyoming | M,D |
| Université Laval | M,D |
| Utah State University | M |
| Vanderbilt University | M* |
| Washington State University | M,D |
| Wayne State University | M |
| Western Kentucky University | M |
| Western Washington University | M |
| West Virginia University | M,D |
| Wichita State University | M |
| Wright State University | O |
| Yale University | D |

**GEOPHYSICS**

| | |
|---|---|
| Boise State University | M,D |
| Boston College | M |
| Bowling Green State University | M |
| California Institute of Technology | M,D |
| Colorado School of Mines | M,D |
| Cornell University | M,D |
| Idaho State University | M,O |
| Indiana University Bloomington | M,D |
| Louisiana State University and Agricultural & Mechanical College | M,D |
| Massachusetts Institute of Technology | M,D |
| Memorial University of Newfoundland | M,D |
| Michigan Technological University | M,D |
| Missouri University of Science and Technology | M,D |
| New Mexico Institute of Mining and Technology | M,D |
| Oregon State University | M,D |
| Rice University | M |
| Saint Louis University | M,D |
| Southern Methodist University | M,D |
| Stanford University | M,D |
| Texas A&M University | M,D |
| University of Alaska Fairbanks | M |
| University of Alberta | M,D |
| The University of British Columbia | M,D |
| University of Calgary | M,D |
| University of California, Berkeley | M,D |
| University of California, Los Angeles | M,D |
| University of California, San Diego | M,D |
| University of Chicago | D |
| University of Colorado Boulder | M,D |
| University of Hawaii at Manoa | M,D |
| University of Houston | M,D |
| University of Manitoba | M,D |
| University of Memphis | M,D,O |
| University of Miami | M,D |
| University of Minnesota, Twin Cities Campus | M,D |
| University of Nevada, Reno | M,D |
| University of Oklahoma | M,D |
| University of Rhode Island | M,D |
| The University of Texas at El Paso | M,D |
| The University of Tulsa | M,D |
| University of Utah | M,D |
| University of Washington | M,D |
| The University of Western Ontario | M,D |
| University of Wisconsin–Madison | M,D |
| University of Wyoming | M,D |
| Wright State University | M |
| Yale University | D |

**GEOSCIENCES**

| | |
|---|---|
| Arizona State University at Tempe | M,D |
| Ball State University | M |
| Baylor University | M,D |
| Boise State University | M,D |
| Boston University | M,D |
| Brock University | M |
| Brooklyn College of the City University of New York | M |
| Brown University | D |
| California State University, Chico | M |
| California State University, San Bernardino | M |
| Carleton University | M,D |
| Case Western Reserve University | M,D |
| City College of the City University of New York | M |
| Colorado State University | M,D |
| Columbia University | M,D |
| Cornell University | M,D |
| Dalhousie University | M,D |
| Dartmouth College | M,D |
| Duke University | M,D |
| Eastern Michigan University | M |
| East Tennessee State University | M,O |
| Emporia State University | M,O |
| Florida Atlantic University | M,D |
| Florida Institute of Technology | M |
| Florida International University | M,D |
| Florida State University | M,D |
| Fort Hays State University | M |
| George Mason University | M,D,O |
| Georgia Institute of Technology | M,D |
| Georgia State University | M,D,O |
| The Graduate Center, City University of New York | D |
| Harvard University | M,D* |
| Hunter College of the City University of New York | M |
| Idaho State University | M,O |
| Indiana University Bloomington | M,D |
| Indiana University-Purdue University Indianapolis | M,D |
| Iowa State University of Science and Technology | M,D |
| Jackson State University | M,D |
| Johns Hopkins University | M,D |
| Lehigh University | M,D |
| Long Island University - Post | M,O |
| Manhattanville College | M,O |
| Massachusetts Institute of Technology | M,D |
| McGill University | M,D |
| McMaster University | M,D |
| Memorial University of Newfoundland | M,D |
| Michigan State University | M,D |
| Middle Tennessee State University | O |
| Mississippi State University | M,D |
| Missouri State University | M,O |
| Montana State University | M,D |
| Montana Technological University | M |
| Montclair State University | M |
| Murray State University | M,O |
| New Mexico Institute of Mining and Technology | M,D |
| North Carolina Central University | M |
| North Carolina State University | M,D |
| Northwestern University | D |
| The Ohio State University | M,D |
| Pace University | M,O |
| Penn State University Park | M,D* |
| Princeton University | D |
| Purdue University | M,D |
| Queens College of the City University of New York | M |
| Rice University | M,D |
| St. Francis Xavier University | M |
| Saint Louis University | M,D |

| | |
|---|---|
| St. Thomas University - Florida | M,D,O |
| San Francisco State University | M |
| Simon Fraser University | M,D |
| South Dakota State University | D |
| Southern Illinois University Carbondale | M,D |
| Stanford University | M,D,O |
| State University of New York at New Paltz | M,O |
| Stony Brook University, State University of New York | M,D |
| Teachers College, Columbia University | M,D |
| Temple University | M,D* |
| Tennessee Technological University | D |
| Texas Tech University | M,D |
| Université du Québec à Chicoutimi | M |
| Université du Québec à Montréal | M,D,O |
| Université du Québec, Institut National de la Recherche Scientifique | M,D |
| University at Buffalo, the State University of New York | M,D |
| The University of Akron | M |
| The University of Alabama | M,D |
| The University of Alabama in Huntsville | M,D |
| University of Alberta | M,D |
| The University of Arizona | M,D |
| University of Arkansas at Little Rock | O |
| University of Calgary | M,D |
| University of California, Irvine | M,D |
| University of California, Los Angeles | M,D |
| University of California, San Diego | M,D |
| University of California, Santa Barbara | M,D |
| University of California, Santa Cruz | M,D |
| University of Chicago | D |
| University of Florida | M,D |
| University of Illinois at Chicago | M,D |
| University of Illinois at Urbana-Champaign | M,D |
| The University of Iowa | M,D |
| University of Louisiana at Lafayette | M |
| University of Lynchburg | M |
| University of Maine | M,D |
| The University of Manchester | M,D |
| University of Massachusetts Amherst | M,D |
| University of Michigan | M,D |
| University of Missouri–Kansas City | M,D |
| University of Montana | M,D |
| University of Nebraska–Lincoln | M,D |
| University of Nevada, Las Vegas | M,D |
| University of New Hampshire | M |
| University of New Haven | M |
| University of New Mexico | M,D |
| University of New Orleans | M,D |
| The University of North Carolina at Charlotte | M,D |
| The University of North Carolina Wilmington | M,O |
| University of North Dakota | M,D |
| University of Northern Colorado | M |
| University of Northern Iowa | M |
| University of Notre Dame | M,D |
| University of Ottawa | M,D |
| University of Pennsylvania | M,D |
| University of Rhode Island | M,D,O |
| University of Rochester | M,D |
| University of South Carolina | M,D |
| University of Southern California | M,D |
| University of South Florida | M,D |
| The University of Texas at Austin | M,D |
| The University of Texas at Dallas | M,D |
| The University of Texas Rio Grande Valley | M |
| The University of Tulsa | M,D |
| University of Victoria | M,D |
| University of Waterloo | M,D |
| The University of Western Ontario | M,D |
| University of Windsor | M,D |
| Université Laval | M,D |
| Virginia Polytechnic Institute and State University | M,D |
| Washington University in St. Louis | D |
| Wesleyan University | M |
| Western Connecticut State University | M |
| Western Kentucky University | M |
| Western Michigan University | M,D,O |
| Yale University | D |
| York University | M,D |

## GEOTECHNICAL ENGINEERING

| | |
|---|---|
| The Citadel, The Military College of South Carolina | M,O |
| Clemson University | M,D |
| Cornell University | M,D |
| Drexel University | M,D |
| Illinois Institute of Technology | M,D |
| Iowa State University of Science and Technology | M,D |
| Kansas State University | M,D |
| Kennesaw State University | M |
| Louisiana State University and Agricultural & Mechanical College | M,D |
| Massachusetts Institute of Technology | M,D,O |
| McGill University | M,D |
| Missouri University of Science and Technology | M |
| Northwestern University | M,D |
| Norwich University | M |
| Ohio University | M,D |
| Old Dominion University | M |
| Oregon State University | M,D |
| Penn State University Park | M,D* |
| Polytechnique Montréal | M,D,O |
| Southern Illinois University Edwardsville | M |
| Southern Methodist University | M,D |
| Tufts University | M,D |
| UNB Fredericton | M,D |
| University of Alberta | M,D |
| University of Calgary | M,D |
| University of California, Berkeley | M,D |
| University of Colorado Denver | M,D |
| University of Dayton | M |
| University of Delaware | M,D |
| University of Massachusetts Amherst | M,D |
| University of Memphis | M,D,O |
| University of Puerto Rico at Mayagüez | M,D |
| University of Rhode Island | M,D |
| University of Southern California | M,D,O |
| University of South Florida | M,D |
| The University of Texas at Austin | M,D |
| University of Washington | M,D |
| University of Wisconsin–Madison | M |

## GERMAN

| | |
|---|---|
| Arizona State University at Tempe | M |
| Bowling Green State University | M |
| Brown University | D |
| California State University, Long Beach | M |
| Central Connecticut State University | M,O |
| Columbia University | M,D |
| Cornell University | M,D |
| Dalhousie University | M |
| DePaul University | M |
| Duke University | D |
| Florida State University | M |
| Georgetown University | M,D |
| Georgia State University | O |
| Harvard University | D* |
| Illinois State University | M |
| Indiana University Bloomington | M,D |
| Johns Hopkins University | M,D |
| Kansas State University | M |
| Kent State University | M,D |
| McGill University | M,D |
| Memorial University of Newfoundland | M |
| Michigan State University | M,D |
| Middlebury College | M,D |
| Middle Tennessee State University | M |
| Millersville University of Pennsylvania | M |
| New York University | M,D |
| Northwestern University | D |
| The Ohio State University | M,D |
| Penn State University Park | M,D* |
| Portland State University | M |
| Princeton University | D |
| Purdue University | M |
| Rutgers University - New Brunswick | M,D |
| San Francisco State University | M |
| Stanford University | M,D |
| Tufts University | M |
| Université de Montréal | M |
| University at Buffalo, the State University of New York | M,D,O |
| The University of Alabama | M,D |
| University of Alberta | M,D |
| The University of Arizona | M,D |
| University of Arkansas | M |
| The University of British Columbia | M,D |
| University of Calgary | M,D |
| University of California, Berkeley | D |
| University of California, Davis | M,D |
| University of California, Irvine | M,D |
| University of California, Los Angeles | M,D |
| University of Chicago | M,D |
| University of Cincinnati | M,D |
| University of Colorado Boulder | M |
| University of Delaware | M |
| University of Florida | M,D |
| University of Georgia | M |
| University of Illinois at Chicago | M,D |
| University of Illinois at Urbana-Champaign | M,D |
| University of Kentucky | M |
| University of Lethbridge | M,D |
| The University of Manchester | D |
| University of Manitoba | M |
| University of Maryland, College Park | M,D |
| University of Massachusetts Amherst | M,D |
| University of Michigan | M,D,O |
| University of Minnesota, Twin Cities Campus | M,D |
| University of Missouri | M |
| University of Montana | M |
| University of Nebraska–Lincoln | M,D |
| University of New Mexico | M,D |
| The University of North Carolina at Chapel Hill | D |
| University of Oklahoma | M,D |
| University of Oregon | M,D |
| University of Pennsylvania | M,D |
| University of South Africa | M,D |
| University of South Carolina | M,D |
| The University of Tennessee | M,D |
| The University of Texas at Austin | M,D |
| The University of Toledo | M |
| University of Toronto | M,D |
| University of Vermont | M |
| University of Victoria | M |
| University of Virginia | M |
| University of Washington | M,D |
| University of Waterloo | M,D |
| University of Wisconsin–Madison | M,D |
| University of Wisconsin–Milwaukee | M,O* |
| University of Wyoming | M |
| Vanderbilt University | M,D* |
| Washington University in St. Louis | D |
| Wayne State University | M,D |
| Western Kentucky University | M |
| Yale University | D |

## GERONTOLOGICAL NURSING

| | |
|---|---|
| Allen College | M,D |
| Alvernia University | M,D,O |
| Arizona State University at Tempe | M,D,O |
| Augusta University | D |
| Azusa Pacific University | M,D |
| Ball State University | M,D,O |
| Binghamton University, State University of New York | M,D,O |
| Boise State University | M,D,O |
| Boston College | M,D |
| California State University, Stanislaus | M |
| Capella University | M |
| Caribbean University | M,D |
| Case Western Reserve University | M |
| Clemson University | M,D,O |
| College of Staten Island of the City University of New York | M,O |
| Columbia University | M,O |
| Creighton University | M,D,O |
| Duke University | M,D,O |
| East Tennessee State University | M,D,O |
| Elms College | M,D |
| Fairleigh Dickinson University, Florham Campus | M |
| Felician University | M,O |
| Florida Southern College | M |
| George Mason University | M,D,O |
| Goldfarb School of Nursing at Barnes-Jewish College | M |
| Graceland University (IA) | M,D,O |
| Gwynedd Mercy University | M,D |
| Hofstra University | M |
| Hunter College of the City University of New York | M,D |
| Independence University | M |
| Indiana University-Purdue University Indianapolis | M |
| Jacksonville University | M,D,O |
| James Madison University | M,D |
| Johns Hopkins University | D |
| Kent State University | M,D |
| Keuka College | M |
| La Salle University | M,D,O |
| Lehman College of the City University of New York | M |
| Loma Linda University | M |
| Louisiana State University Health Sciences Center | M,D,O |
| Marquette University | M,D,O |
| Maryville University of Saint Louis | M,D |
| Medical University of South Carolina | M,D |
| Mercer University | M,D,O |
| MGH Institute of Health Professions | M,D,O |
| Middle Georgia State University | M |
| Molloy College | M,D,O |
| Monmouth University | M,D,O |
| Morningside College | M |
| Mount Carmel College of Nursing | M,D |
| Neumann University | M,O |
| New York University | M,D,O |
| Northeastern University | M,D,O |
| Nova Southeastern University | M,D |
| Oakland University | M,O |
| Old Dominion University | M,D |
| Oregon Health & Science University | M |
| Point Loma Nazarene University | M |
| Purdue University | M,D,O |
| Purdue University Fort Wayne | M,O |
| Rutgers University - Camden | D |
| Sage Graduate School | M,O |
| St. Catherine University | M,D |
| Saint Francis Medical Center College of Nursing | M,D,O |
| St. Joseph's College, Long Island Campus | M |
| St. Joseph's College, New York | M |
| Saint Mary's College | D |
| Salem State University | M |
| San Jose State University | M,O |
| Seattle Pacific University | M,O |
| Seton Hall University | M,D |
| Shenandoah University | M,D,O |
| Southern Adventist University | M,D |
| Southern University and Agricultural and Mechanical College | M,D,O |
| Stony Brook University, State University of New York | M,D,O |
| Tennessee Technological University | D |
| Texas Christian University | M,O |
| Texas Tech University Health Sciences Center | M,D,O |
| Texas Woman's University | M,D |
| Uniformed Services University of the Health Sciences | M,D |
| University at Buffalo, the State University of New York | M,D,O |
| The University of Alabama at Birmingham | M,D |
| The University of Alabama in Huntsville | M,D,O |
| University of Cincinnati | M,D |
| University of Colorado Colorado Springs | M,D |
| University of Connecticut | M,O |
| University of Delaware | M,O |
| University of Illinois at Chicago | M,O |
| The University of Kansas | M,D,O |
| University of Louisville | M,D |
| University of Maryland, Baltimore | M,D,O |
| University of Massachusetts Amherst | M,D |
| University of Massachusetts Lowell | M |
| University of Massachusetts Medical School | M,D,O |
| University of Minnesota, Twin Cities Campus | M,D |
| University of Missouri | M,D,O |
| University of Missouri–Kansas City | M,D |
| University of Missouri–St. Louis | D,O |
| The University of North Carolina at Chapel Hill | M,D,O |
| The University of North Carolina at Charlotte | M,D,O |
| The University of North Carolina at Greensboro | M,D,O |
| University of North Dakota | M,D,O |
| University of Pennsylvania | M |
| University of Phoenix - Bay Area Campus | M,D |
| University of Phoenix - Phoenix Campus | M,O |
| University of Pittsburgh | D* |
| University of Puerto Rico - Medical Sciences Campus | M |
| University of Rhode Island | M,D,O |
| University of Rochester | M,D |
| University of San Diego | M,D |
| University of Southern Maine | M,D,O |
| University of South Florida | M,D,O |
| The University of Tennessee at Chattanooga | M,D,O |
| The University of Tennessee Health Science Center | D,O |
| The University of Texas at Austin | M,D |
| The University of Texas Health Science Center at San Antonio | M,D,O |
| The University of Tulsa | D |
| University of Utah | M,O |
| University of Wisconsin–Eau Claire | M,D |
| University of Wisconsin–Madison | D |
| Ursuline College | M,D |
| Valdosta State University | M |
| Villanova University | M,D,O |
| Walden University | M,D,O |
| Wayne State University | M,D |
| Western Connecticut State University | M,D |
| Wilmington University | M,D |
| Winona State University | M,D,O |
| Wright State University | M |
| York College of Pennsylvania | M |

## GERONTOLOGY

| | |
|---|---|
| Alliant International University - Los Angeles | M |
| Arizona State University at Tempe | M,D,O |
| Arkansas State University | M,D,O |
| California State University, Fullerton | M |
| California State University, Long Beach | M |
| Capella University | M |
| Central Michigan University | M,O |
| Concordia University Chicago | M |
| DeSales University | M,D,O |
| Duke University | M,D,O |
| East Carolina University | M,O |
| Eastern Illinois University | M |
| Eastern Michigan University | O |
| East Tennessee State University | M,D,O |
| Georgia State University | M,O |
| Kansas State University | M,O |
| Kent State University | M,D |
| Lakehead University | M,D |
| La Salle University | M,D,O |
| Loma Linda University | M,D |
| Long Island University - Brooklyn | M,O |
| Long Island University - Post | M,O |
| Marywood University | M |
| McDaniel College | M,O |
| Mercer University | M,D |
| Miami University | M,D |
| Middle Tennessee State University | O |
| Minnesota State University Mankato | M |
| Morehead State University | M |
| Mount Saint Vincent University | M |
| North Dakota State University | D,O |
| Northeastern Illinois University | M |
| Oregon Health & Science University | M,O |
| Sage Graduate School | M |
| St. Cloud State University | M,O |
| San Diego State University | M |
| San Francisco State University | M |
| Simon Fraser University | M,D |
| SUNY Brockport | M,O |
| Temple University | D* |
| Texas Christian University | D |
| Texas State University | M |
| Texas Tech University | M,D |
| Université de Sherbrooke | M |
| The University of Akron | D |
| University of Arkansas at Little Rock | O |
| University of Central Missouri | M,D,O |
| University of Central Oklahoma | M |

*M—masters degree; D—doctorate; O—other advanced degree; *—Close-Up and/or Display*

University of Georgia O
University of Illinois at Springfield M,O
University of Indianapolis M,D,O
The University of Kansas D
University of Kentucky D,O
University of La Verne M,O
University of Louisiana at Monroe M,O
University of Louisville M,D,O
University of Maryland, Baltimore M,D
University of Maryland, Baltimore County M,D
University of Massachusetts Boston M,D,O
University of Michigan–Flint M,D,O
University of Nebraska at Omaha M,D,O
University of Nebraska–Lincoln M,D
The University of North Carolina at Charlotte M,D,O
The University of North Carolina at Greensboro M,O
The University of North Carolina Wilmington M
University of Northern Colorado M,D
University of North Texas M,D,O
University of Phoenix - Central Valley Campus M
University of Phoenix - Hawaii Campus M
University of Puerto Rico - Medical Sciences Campus M,O
University of Regina M
University of South Carolina O
University of Southern California M,D,O
University of Southern Indiana M,D,O
University of South Florida M,D,O
The University of Tennessee M
The University of Toledo M,O
University of Utah M,O
University of Wisconsin–Milwaukee M,D,O*
Université Laval O
Virginia Commonwealth University M,D
Walden University M,D
Washington University in St. Louis M,D
Wayne State University M,D,O
Webster University M
Wichita State University M
Youngstown State University M

## GRAPHIC DESIGN

Academy of Art University M
ArtCenter College of Design M
Atlantic University College M
Bob Jones University M,D,O
Bowling Green State University M
Bradley University M
California College of the Arts M
California Institute of the Arts M,O
California State University, Fullerton M
California State University, Los Angeles M
Central Connecticut State University M
Central Washington University M
City College of the City University of New York M
East Carolina University M
Florida Atlantic University M
Full Sail University M
George Mason University M
Georgia Southern University M
Georgia State University M
Illinois State University M
Indiana State University M
Indiana University-Purdue University Indianapolis M
Inter American University of Puerto Rico, San Germán Campus M
Iowa State University of Science and Technology M
Kent State University M
Louisiana State University and Agricultural & Mechanical College M
Louisiana Tech University M,D,O
Lynn University M,O
Maryland Institute College of Art M
Marywood University M
Minneapolis College of Art and Design M
New York Institute of Technology M
North Carolina State University M
Ohio University M
Oklahoma State University M
Otis College of Art and Design M
Pensacola Christian College M,D,O
Pittsburg State University M,O
Pratt Institute M
Rhode Island School of Design M
Rochester Institute of Technology M
San Diego State University M
Savannah College of Art and Design M
School of Visual Arts (NY) M
State University of New York at Oswego M
Suffolk University M
Temple University M*
Texas State University M
Texas Woman's University M
University of Baltimore D
University of Cincinnati M
University of Guam M
University of Illinois at Chicago M
University of Illinois at Urbana-Champaign M
University of Memphis M,O
University of Miami M
University of Minnesota, Duluth M
University of Notre Dame M
University of Pennsylvania M,O
University of South Dakota M
The University of Tennessee M
University of Utah M
Université Laval M
Vermont College of Fine Arts M
Wayne State University M
West Virginia University M,D
Yale University M

## HAZARDOUS MATERIALS MANAGEMENT

Humboldt State University M
Indiana University Bloomington M,D,O
Jackson State University M,D
Marquette University M,D,O
New Mexico Institute of Mining and Technology M
Rutgers University - New Brunswick M,D
University of Colorado Denver M
The University of Manchester M,D
University of New Haven M
University of South Carolina M,D
University of Southern California M,D,O

## HEALTH COMMUNICATION

Arkansas State University M,O
Boston University M
Chatham University M
The College of New Jersey M
Cornell University M,D
DePaul University M
East Carolina University M,O
Fontbonne University M
Gannon University M
The George Washington University M,D
Indiana University-Purdue University Indianapolis M,D
Johns Hopkins University M,D
Kansas State University M
Lasell College M,O
Marquette University M,O
Michigan State University M
Ohio University M,D
Rider University M
Southeastern Louisiana University M
Southern Illinois University Edwardsville M
State University of New York at Oswego M
Stony Brook University, State University of New York M,O
Tufts University M,D,O
University of Florida M,D,O
University of Houston M
University of Missouri M,D
The University of North Carolina at Chapel Hill M,D,O
University of Oklahoma M,D
University of St. Thomas (MN) M
University of Southern California M,D
Wayne State University M,D,O

## HEALTH EDUCATION

Alabama State University M
Albany State University M,O
Alcorn State University M,O
Allen College M,D
Arcadia University M
Arizona State University at Tempe D
Arkansas State University M,D,O
Auburn University M,D,O
Austin Peay State University M
Baldwin Wallace University M
Baylor University M,D
Benedictine University M
Boston University M
Brandeis University D
California Baptist University M
California State University, Long Beach M
California State University, Northridge M,O
Cambridge College M,D,O
Central Washington University M
Clark University M
Cleveland State University M
Cleveland University–Kansas City M
College of Saint Mary D
Colorado State University-Pueblo M
Columbus State University M
Concordia University (United States) M,D
Concordia University Wisconsin M,D
Daemen College M
Dalhousie University M
Delta State University M
Drew University M,D,O
East Carolina University M
Eastern Kentucky University M
Eastern Michigan University M,O
Eastern University M,O
East Stroudsburg University of Pennsylvania M
Emory University M,D
Fairfield University M,D
Florida State University M,D
Fort Hays State University M
Georgia College & State University M
Georgia Southern University M,D
Georgia State University M
Harding University M,O
Hofstra University M,D,O
Howard University M
Idaho State University M
Illinois State University M
Indiana State University M,D
Indiana University Bloomington M,D
Indiana University of Pennsylvania M
Indiana University-Purdue University Indianapolis M,D
Inter American University of Puerto Rico, Metropolitan Campus M
Inter American University of Puerto Rico, San Germán Campus M
Jackson State University M
James Madison University M
John F. Kennedy University M
Johns Hopkins University M,D
Kansas State University M,D
Keiser University M
Kent State University M,D
Lake Erie College of Osteopathic Medicine M,D,O
Lehman College of the City University of New York M
Lock Haven University of Pennsylvania M
Logan University M,D
Loma Linda University M,D
Longwood University M
Marshall University M
Marymount University M
Marywood University D
Massachusetts College of Liberal Arts M,O
McNeese State University O
Meredith College M,O
Merrimack College M
Middle Tennessee State University M
Minnesota State University Mankato M,O
Mississippi University for Women M,D,O
Montana State University M
Montclair State University M
Morehead State University M
New Jersey City University M
New Mexico Highlands University M
New York Medical College M,D,O
Nicholls State University M
Northeastern State University M
Northwestern State University of Louisiana M
Northwest Missouri State University M
Nova Southeastern University M,D,O
Old Dominion University M,D
Penn State Harrisburg M,D,O
Pennsylvania College of Health Sciences M
Pittsburg State University M
Plymouth State University M
Prairie View A&M University M
Purdue University M,D
Rhode Island College M,O
Rosalind Franklin University of Medicine and Science M
Rutgers University - Newark M,D
Rutgers University - New Brunswick M,D,O
Sage Graduate School M
Saint Francis University M
Saint Joseph's College of Maine M
San Francisco State University M
Southeastern Louisiana University M
Southern Connecticut State University M
Southern Illinois University Carbondale M,D
Southern Illinois University Edwardsville M,D,O
Southwestern Oklahoma State University M
State University of New York College at Cortland M
Stony Brook University, State University of New York M,O
SUNY Brockport M
Teachers College, Columbia University M,D,O
Tennessee Technological University M
Texas A&M University M,D
Texas A&M University–Kingsville M
Texas Southern University M
Texas State University M
Texas Woman's University M,D
Thomas Jefferson University M,D,O
Trident University International M,D,O
Union College (KY) M
The University of Alabama M,D
The University of Alabama at Birmingham D
University of Arkansas M,D
University of Arkansas at Little Rock M,D
University of Arkansas for Medical Sciences M,D,O
University of Central Arkansas M
University of Cincinnati M,D
University of Colorado Denver M,D
University of Florida M,D,O
University of Georgia M,D
University of Houston M,D
University of Illinois at Chicago M
University of Illinois at Springfield M,O
The University of Kansas M,D,O
University of Louisville M,D,O
University of Maryland, College Park M,D
University of Massachusetts Amherst M,D
University of Michigan M,D
University of Michigan–Flint M
University of Missouri M,D,O
University of Missouri–Kansas City M,D
University of Montana M
University of Nebraska at Omaha M,D
University of New Mexico M
The University of North Carolina at Pembroke M
University of Northern Colorado M
University of Northern Iowa M
University of Oklahoma Health Sciences Center D
University of Phoenix–Online Campus M,O
University of Pittsburgh M,D*
University of Puerto Rico - Medical Sciences Campus M
University of Rhode Island M
University of St. Augustine for Health Sciences M,D
University of South Africa M,D
University of South Alabama M
University of South Carolina M,D,O
University of Southern California M
University of South Florida M,D
The University of Tennessee M
The University of Texas at Austin M,D
The University of Texas at San Antonio M
The University of Texas at Tyler M
The University of Toledo M,D,O
University of Waterloo M,D
University of Wisconsin–La Crosse M
University of Wyoming M
Utah State University M,D
Virginia State University M,D
Walden University M,D,O
Washburn University M
Wayne State University M,D
Western Illinois University M
Western Michigan University D,O
Western Oregon University M
Western University of Health Sciences M
Widener University M,D
Worcester State University M,O
Wright State University M

## HEALTH INFORMATICS

Adelphi University M,O
American Public University System M,D
American Sentinel University M
Arkansas Tech University M
Augusta University M
Barry University O
Bay Path University M
Belmont University D
Benedictine University M
Boston University M,O
Brandeis University M
Brooklyn College of the City University of New York M,O
Canisius College M,O
Capella University M
Chatham University M
Claremont Graduate University M,D,O
Clarkson University M
The College of St. Scholastica M,O
Colorado Mesa University M,D,O
Dakota State University M,D,O
Dartmouth College M,D
DePaul University M,D
DeSales University M,O
Duke University M
East Carolina University M,O
Emory University M,D
George Mason University M,D,O
Georgia Southwestern State University M,O
Georgia State University M,D,O
Grand Canyon University M,D,O
Hofstra University M,O
Indiana University Bloomington M,D
Indiana University-Purdue University Indianapolis M,D
Jacksonville University M
Johns Hopkins University M,D,O
Kennesaw State University M,O
Kent State University M
Liberty University M,D
Lipscomb University M,D
Logan University M,D
Louisiana Tech University M,D,O
Marshall University M,O
Marymount University M,O
Mercer University M,D
Middle Georgia State University M
Midwestern State University M,O
Millennia Atlantic University M
Montana Technological University O
National University M,O
Northeastern University M,D
Northern Kentucky University M,O
Northwestern University M,D
Nova Southeastern University M,D,O
Oregon Health & Science University M,D,O
Regis University M,O
Roberts Wesleyan College M
Rochester Institute of Technology M
Rutgers University - New Brunswick M
Sacred Heart University M
St. Catherine University M
St. Joseph's College, Long Island Campus M
St. Joseph's College, New York M
Saint Joseph's University M
Samford University M
Slippery Rock University of Pennsylvania M
Southern Illinois University Edwardsville M
Southern New Hampshire University M,D,O
State University of New York at Oswego M
Stephens College M,O
Stony Brook University, State University of New York M,D,O
Temple University M,D*
Texas State University M
Trident University International M,D,O
The University of Alabama at Birmingham M
University of Central Florida M,O
University of Cincinnati M
University of Colorado Denver M
The University of Findlay M,D
University of Illinois at Chicago M,O
University of Illinois at Urbana-Champaign M,D,O
The University of Iowa M,D,O

The University of Kansas M,O
University of Lynchburg O
University of Maryland, Baltimore County M
University of Maryland Global Campus M
University of Michigan M,D
University of Michigan–Dearborn M
University of Michigan–Flint M
University of Minnesota, Twin Cities Campus M,D
University of Missouri M,O
University of New England M,D,O
University of Phoenix–Online Campus M,O
University of Pittsburgh M*
University of Puerto Rico - Medical Sciences Campus M
University of St. Augustine for Health Sciences M
University of San Diego M,D
University of San Francisco M
University of South Carolina Upstate M
University of South Florida O
The University of Tennessee Health Science Center M,D
The University of Texas Health Science Center at Houston M,D,O
University of Toronto M
University of Victoria M
University of Virginia M
University of Washington M,D
University of Waterloo M,D
University of Wisconsin–Milwaukee M,D*
Virginia International University M,O
Walden University M,D,O
Weill Cornell Medicine M

**HEALTH LAW**

Case Western Reserve University M,D
DePaul University M,D
Drexel University M,D
Florida State University M,D
Georgetown University M,D
Hofstra University M,D,O
Indiana University-Purdue University Indianapolis M,D,O
Loyola University Chicago M,D,O
Nova Southeastern University M,D
St. Mary's University (United States) M
Seattle University M,D
Seton Hall University M,D
Southern Illinois University Carbondale M
Suffolk University M,D
Université de Sherbrooke M,D,O
University of California, San Francisco M
University of Houston M,D
The University of Manchester M,D
University of Pittsburgh M*
The University of Tulsa M,D,O
Widener University M,D

**HEALTH PHYSICS/RADIOLOGICAL HEALTH**

East Carolina University M,D
Georgetown University M
Georgia Institute of Technology M,D
Idaho State University M,D
Illinois Institute of Technology M,D
John Patrick University of Health and Applied Sciences M
McMaster University M,D
Midwestern State University M
Northwestern State University of Louisiana M
Oregon State University M,D
Purdue University M,D
Quinnipiac University M
Rutgers University - Newark M
San Diego State University M
Thomas Jefferson University M
University of Alberta M,D
University of Arkansas for Medical Sciences M,D
University of Cincinnati M
University of Kentucky M
University of Massachusetts Lowell M
University of Michigan M,D,O
University of Missouri M
University of Nevada, Las Vegas M,D,O
University of Oklahoma Health Sciences Center M,D
University of Toronto M,D
Université Laval O
Virginia Commonwealth University D
Weber State University M

**HEALTH PROMOTION**

American College of Healthcare Sciences M,O
American University M,O
Arizona State University at Tempe M,D
Ball State University M
Boise State University M,O
Bridgewater State University M
Brigham Young University M,D
California Baptist University M
California State University, Fresno M
California State University, Fullerton M
Claremont Graduate University M,D
Cleveland University–Kansas City M
Concord University M
Creighton University M
East Carolina University M
Eastern Kentucky University M
Eastern Michigan University M,O
Emory University M
Fairmont State University M
Florida Atlantic University M
Florida International University M,D
George Mason University M,O
Georgetown University M,D
Georgia College & State University M
Goddard College M
Harvard University M,D*
Immaculata University M
Independence University M
Indiana University Bloomington M,D
Instituto Tecnologico de Santo Domingo M,O
Kent State University M,D
Lehman College of the City University of New York M
Liberty University M,D,O
Lindenwood University M
Lock Haven University of Pennsylvania M
Manhattanville College M,O
Maryland University of Integrative Health M,O
Marymount University M
McNeese State University M
Merrimack College M
Morehead State University M
Mount St. Joseph University M,O
National University M,O
Nebraska Methodist College M
New York University M,D,O
Old Dominion University M
Oregon State University M,D
Plymouth State University M,O
Portland State University M,D
Queen's University at Kingston M,D
Rosalind Franklin University of Medicine and Science M
Rowan University M
San Diego State University M,D
Simmons University M,D,O
Sonoma State University M
Southern Methodist University M,D
Springfield College M,D,O
Stony Brook University, State University of New York M,O
Tennessee Technological University M
Tulane University M
Union Institute & University M
Universidad del Turabo M
The University of Alabama M,D
The University of Alabama at Birmingham D
University of Alberta M,O
University of Arkansas M,D
University of Arkansas for Medical Sciences M,D,O
University of Central Oklahoma M
University of Chicago M,D
University of Cincinnati M,D
University of Delaware M
University of Georgia M,D
The University of Kansas M,D,O
University of Kentucky M,D
University of Louisville D
University of Lynchburg M
University of Massachusetts Lowell D
University of Memphis M,O
University of Michigan M,D
University of Mississippi M,D
University of Missouri M,O
University of Nebraska–Lincoln M,D
University of Nebraska Medical Center D
University of North Alabama M
The University of North Carolina at Chapel Hill M
University of Northern Iowa M
University of Oklahoma M,D
University of Oklahoma Health Sciences Center M,D
University of Puerto Rico - Medical Sciences Campus O
University of South Carolina M,D,O
University of Southern California M
The University of Tennessee M
The University of Texas Health Science Center at Houston M,D,O
The University of Toledo M,D,O
University of Toronto M,D
University of Vermont M
University of West Florida M
University of Wisconsin–Milwaukee M,D,O*
University of Wisconsin–Parkside M
University of Wisconsin–Stevens Point M
University of Wyoming M
Utah State University M,D
Walden University M,D,O
Wilfrid Laurier University M
Wright State University M

**HEALTH PSYCHOLOGY**

Adler University M
Alliant International University - Los Angeles D
Appalachian State University M
Argosy University, Atlanta M,D,O
Argosy University, Chicago D
Argosy University, Northern Virginia M,D
Argosy University, Twin Cities M,D,O
Bastyr University M,O
California State University, Dominguez Hills M
Central Michigan University M,D
Chatham University M,D
Claremont Graduate University M,D,O
Drexel University D
Duke University D
East Carolina University M,D,O
Georgian Court University M,O
John F. Kennedy University M
La Salle University M,D
Lesley University M,D,O
North Dakota State University M,D
Northern Kentucky University M,O
Oregon State University M,D
Penn State Harrisburg M,D,O
Prescott College M
Rhode Island College M,O
Rutgers University - New Brunswick D
San Diego State University M,D
Saybrook University M,D
Southwestern College (NM) O
Stony Brook University, State University of New York D
United States International University–Africa M
The University of Alabama at Birmingham M,D
The University of British Columbia M,D
University of Colorado Denver D
University of Florida M,D
University of Michigan–Dearborn M
University of New Mexico D
The University of North Carolina at Chapel Hill M,D
The University of North Carolina at Charlotte M,D,O
University of Pittsburgh D*
The University of Texas at Arlington M,D
University of the Sciences M
Virginia Commonwealth University D
Virginia State University M,D
Viterbo University M
Walden University M,D,O
Yeshiva University D

**HEALTH SERVICES MANAGEMENT AND HOSPITAL ADMINISTRATION**

Abilene Christian University M
Adelphi University M
AdventHealth University M
Alaska Pacific University M
Albany State University M
Albertus Magnus College M
American InterContinental University Online M
American Sentinel University M
American University M,O
Anderson University (SC) M
Antioch University Midwest M
Aquinas Institute of Theology M,D,O
Argosy University, Atlanta M,D
Argosy University, Chicago M,D
Argosy University, Hawaii M,D,O
Argosy University, Los Angeles M,D
Argosy University, Northern Virginia M,D,O
Argosy University, Orange County M,D,O
Argosy University, Phoenix M,D
Argosy University, Seattle M,D
Argosy University, Tampa M,D
Argosy University, Twin Cities M,D
Arizona State University at Tempe M,D
Arkansas State University M,D,O
Ashland University M
Ashworth College M
Assumption University M,O
Atlantis University M
A.T. Still University M,D,O
Baker College Center for Graduate Studies–Online M,D
Baldwin Wallace University M
Barry University M,O
Baruch College of the City University of New York M
Baylor University M
Bay Path University M
Belhaven University (MS) M
Bellevue University M
Belmont University M
Benedictine University M
Binghamton University, State University of New York M,D
Bluffton University M
Boston University M
Bradley University M,D,O
Brandeis University M
Brandman University M
Brenau University M
Brigham Young University M
Broadview University–West Jordan M
Brooklyn College of the City University of New York M
Bryan College M
California Baptist University M
California Coast University M
California Intercontinental University M,D
California State University, Chico M
California State University, East Bay M
California State University, Fresno M
California State University, Long Beach M
California State University, Los Angeles M,O
California State University, Northridge M
California State University, San Bernardino M
California University of Pennsylvania M
Cambridge College M
Capella University M,D
Cardinal Stritch University M
Carlow University M
Carnegie Mellon University M
Case Western Reserve University M
The Catholic University of America M
Cedarville University M,D
Central Michigan University M,D,O
Champlain College M
The Chicago School of Professional Psychology: Online M
Clarion University of Pennsylvania M
Clarkson University M,O
Cleary University M,O
Cleveland State University M
College of Saint Elizabeth M
College of Staten Island of the City University of New York M
Colorado State University–Global Campus M
Columbia Southern University M
Columbia University M
Columbus State University M
Concordia University Irvine M
Concordia University, St. Paul M
Concordia University Wisconsin M
Copenhagen Business School M,D
Cornell University M,D
Creighton University M,D
Daemen College M
Dalhousie University M,D
Dallas Baptist University M
Dartmouth College M,D
Davenport University M
Delta State University M,D
DeSales University M
Des Moines University M
Dominican College M
Drew University M,D,O
Duquesne University M,D
D'Youville College M,D,O
East Carolina University M,O
Eastern Kentucky University M
Eastern Mennonite University M
Eastern Michigan University M,O
Eastern University M
East Tennessee State University M,D,O
Elmhurst University M
Elms College M,O
Emory University M,D
Fairleigh Dickinson University, Florham Campus M
Fairleigh Dickinson University, Metropolitan Campus M
Felician University M
Ferris State University M
Florida Atlantic University M
Florida Institute of Technology M
Florida International University M,D
Florida National University M
Fordham University M,D
Framingham State University M
Franciscan Missionaries of Our Lady University M,D
Francis Marion University M
Franklin Pierce University M,D,O
Friends University M
George Mason University M,D,O
Georgetown University M,D
The George Washington University M,D,O
Georgia Institute of Technology M,D
Georgia Southern University M,D
Georgia State University M,D,O
Goldey-Beacom College M
Governors State University M
Grambling State University M
Grand Canyon University M,D,O
Grand Valley State University M
Grantham University M
Harvard University M,D*
Herzing University Online M
Hilbert College M
Hodges University M
Hofstra University M,O
Holy Family University M
Husson University M
IGlobal University M
Independence University M
Indiana Tech M
Indiana University Bloomington M,D
Indiana University Kokomo M,O
Indiana University Northwest M,O
Indiana University of Pennsylvania M
Indiana University-Purdue University Indianapolis M,D,O
Indiana University South Bend M,O
Indiana Wesleyan University M,O
Institute of Public Administration M,O
Iona College M,O
John F. Kennedy University M
Johns Hopkins University M,D
Kean University M
Keiser University M
Kennesaw State University M
Kent State University M,D
King's College M
King University M
Lake Erie College M
Lake Forest Graduate School of Management M
Lasell College M,O
Lawrence Technological University M,D,O
Lebanon Valley College M
Lehigh University M,O

*M—masters degree; D—doctorate; O—other advanced degree; *—Close-Up and/or Display*

| | |
|---|---|
| Lenoir-Rhyne University | M |
| LeTourneau University | M |
| Lewis University | M |
| Lindenwood University | M,O |
| Lindenwood University–Belleville | M |
| Lipscomb University | M,O |
| Lock Haven University of Pennsylvania | M |
| Loma Linda University | M |
| London Metropolitan University | M,D |
| Long Island University - Brentwood Campus | M,O |
| Long Island University - Brooklyn | M,O |
| Long Island University - Hudson | M,O |
| Long Island University - Post | M,O |
| Louisiana State University Health Sciences Center | M,D |
| Louisiana State University in Shreveport | M |
| Loyola University Chicago | M |
| Madonna University | M |
| Marshall University | M |
| Marymount University | M |
| Maryville University of Saint Louis | M,O |
| Marywood University | M,O |
| MCPHS University | M |
| Medical University of South Carolina | M,D |
| Meharry Medical College | M |
| Mercy College | M |
| Mercy College of Ohio | M |
| Midwestern State University | M,O |
| Milligan University | M,O |
| Milwaukee School of Engineering | M |
| Minnesota State University Moorhead | M,O |
| Misericordia University | M |
| Mississippi College | M |
| Molloy College | M,D,O |
| Monroe College | M |
| Montana State University Billings | M |
| Moravian College | M |
| Mount Aloysius College | M |
| Mount St. Joseph University | D |
| Mount Saint Mary's University (CA) | M,D,O |
| Mount St. Mary's University (MD) | M |
| National American University (TX) | M,D |
| National University | M,O |
| Nebraska Methodist College | M |
| New Charter University | M |
| New England College | M |
| New Jersey City University | M |
| New Jersey Institute of Technology | M,D |
| New York Medical College | M,D,O |
| New York University | M,D,O |
| Niagara University | M |
| Northeast Ohio Medical University | M,D,O |
| Northern Arizona University | D |
| Northwestern University | M,D |
| Ohio Christian University | M |
| Ohio Dominican University | M |
| The Ohio State University | M,D |
| Ohio University | M |
| Oklahoma Christian University | M |
| Oklahoma State University Center for Health Sciences | M |
| Oregon Health & Science University | M,O |
| Oregon State University | M,D |
| Our Lady of the Lake University | M |
| Pace University | M |
| Pacific University | M |
| Park University | M,O |
| Penn State Great Valley | M,O |
| Penn State Harrisburg | M,D,O |
| Penn State University Park | M,D* |
| Pennsylvania College of Health Sciences | M |
| Pfeiffer University | M |
| Philadelphia College of Osteopathic Medicine | M,D,O |
| Point Loma Nazarene University | M |
| Point Park University | M |
| Portland State University | M,D,O |
| Post University | M |
| Purdue University Global | M,O |
| Quinnipiac University | M |
| Regent University | M,D,O |
| Regis College (MA) | M,D,O |
| Regis University | M,D,O |
| Rhode Island College | M |
| Rice University | M |
| Robert Morris University Illinois | M |
| Roberts Wesleyan College | M |
| Rochester Institute of Technology | M,O |
| Rockhurst University | M,O |
| Roger Williams University | M |
| Rosalind Franklin University of Medicine and Science | M,O |
| Rush University | M,D |
| Rutgers University - Camden | M,O |
| Rutgers University - Newark | M,D,O |
| Rutgers University - New Brunswick | M,D,O |
| Sage Graduate School | M |
| Saginaw Valley State University | M |
| St. Ambrose University | M,D |
| St. Catherine University | M |
| St. Joseph's College, Long Island Campus | M |
| St. Joseph's College, New York | M |
| Saint Joseph's College of Maine | M |
| Saint Joseph's University | M,O |
| Saint Leo University | M,D |
| Saint Louis University | M,D |
| Saint Mary-of-the-Woods College | M |
| Saint Mary's University of Minnesota | M |
| St. Norbert College | M |
| Saint Peter's University | M |
| St. Thomas University - Florida | M,O |
| Saint Xavier University | M,O |
| Salve Regina University | M,O |
| Samford University | M |
| San Diego State University | M,D |
| San Francisco State University | M |
| Seton Hall University | M,D |
| Seton Hill University | M |
| Shenandoah University | M,D,O |
| Shippensburg University of Pennsylvania | M,D,O |
| Siena Heights University | M,O |
| Simmons University | M |
| South Carolina State University | M |
| Southeastern University (FL) | M,D |
| Southern Adventist University | M |
| Southern Illinois University Carbondale | M |
| Southern Nazarene University | M |
| Southern New Hampshire University | M,D,O |
| South University - Columbia | M |
| South University - Montgomery | M |
| South University - Savannah | M |
| South University - Tampa | M |
| South University - West Palm Beach | M |
| Southwest Baptist University | M |
| Stevenson University | M |
| Stony Brook University, State University of New York | M,D,O |
| Stratford University (VA) | M,D |
| Strayer University | M |
| Suffolk University | M |
| SUNY Brockport | M,O |
| Syracuse University | O |
| Temple University | M* |
| Texas A&M University | M,D |
| Texas A&M University–Corpus Christi | M,D |
| Texas Health and Science University | M,D |
| Texas Southern University | M |
| Texas State University | M |
| Texas Tech University | M,D |
| Texas Tech University Health Sciences Center | M |
| Texas Woman's University | M |
| Thomas Jefferson University | M,D,O |
| Tiffin University | M |
| Towson University | M,O |
| Trevecca Nazarene University | M |
| Trident University International | M,D,O |
| Trinity University | M |
| Trinity Western University | M,O |
| Troy University | M |
| Tufts University | M,D,O |
| Tulane University | M,D |
| Uniformed Services University of the Health Sciences | M,D |
| Union Institute & University | M |
| Universidad de Ciencias Medicas | M,D,O |
| Universidad de Iberoamerica | M,D |
| Université de Montréal | M,O |
| University at Albany, State University of New York | M,D,O |
| University at Buffalo, the State University of New York | M,D |
| The University of Alabama at Birmingham | M,D |
| The University of Alabama in Huntsville | M,D,O |
| University of Alberta | M,D |
| University of Arkansas for Medical Sciences | M,D,O |
| University of Arkansas-Fort Smith | M |
| University of Baltimore | M |
| The University of British Columbia | M,D |
| University of California, Berkeley | D |
| University of California, Irvine | M |
| University of California, Los Angeles | M,D |
| University of California, San Diego | M |
| University of Central Florida | M,O |
| University of Chicago | M,O |
| University of Colorado Denver | M,D |
| University of Connecticut | M,D |
| University of Dallas | M,D |
| University of Denver | M,O |
| University of Detroit Mercy | M,D,O |
| University of Evansville | M |
| The University of Findlay | M,D |
| University of Florida | M,D |
| University of Holy Cross | M,D |
| University of Houston–Clear Lake | M |
| University of Illinois at Chicago | M,D |
| University of Illinois at Urbana-Champaign | M,D |
| The University of Iowa | M,D |
| University of Kentucky | M,D |
| University of La Verne | M,D,O |
| University of Louisville | M |
| University of Management and Technology | M |
| University of Mary | M |
| University of Maryland, Baltimore County | M,D,O |
| University of Maryland, College Park | M,D |
| University of Maryland Global Campus | M |
| University of Massachusetts Amherst | M,D |
| University of Massachusetts Dartmouth | M |
| University of Memphis | M,D |
| University of Miami | M,D |
| University of Michigan | M,D |
| University of Michigan–Flint | M,O |
| University of Minnesota, Twin Cities Campus | M,D |
| University of Missouri | M,O |
| University of Nebraska Medical Center | M,D |
| University of Nevada, Las Vegas | M |
| University of New England | M,D,O |
| University of New Mexico | M |
| University of New Orleans | M |
| University of North Alabama | M |
| The University of North Carolina at Chapel Hill | M,D |
| The University of North Carolina at Charlotte | M,D,O |
| The University of North Carolina at Pembroke | M |
| University of Northern Colorado | M |
| University of North Florida | M |
| University of North Texas | M,D,O |
| University of North Texas Health Science Center at Fort Worth | M,D,O |
| University of Oklahoma | M,O |
| University of Oklahoma Health Sciences Center | M,D |
| University of Ottawa | M |
| University of Pennsylvania | M,D |
| University of Phoenix - Bay Area Campus | M,D |
| University of Phoenix - Central Valley Campus | M |
| University of Phoenix - Hawaii Campus | M |
| University of Phoenix - Houston Campus | M |
| University of Phoenix–Online Campus | M,D,O |
| University of Phoenix - Phoenix Campus | M,O |
| University of Phoenix - Sacramento Valley Campus | M |
| University of Phoenix - San Antonio Campus | M |
| University of Pikeville | M |
| University of Pittsburgh | M,D,O* |
| University of Portland | M |
| University of Puerto Rico - Medical Sciences Campus | M |
| University of Regina | M,D,O |
| University of Rhode Island | M,D,O |
| University of Rochester | M,D |
| University of St. Augustine for Health Sciences | M |
| University of St. Francis (IL) | M,O |
| University of Saint Francis (IN) | M |
| University of Saint Mary | M |
| University of St. Thomas (MN) | M |
| University of San Francisco | M |
| The University of Scranton | M |
| University of Sioux Falls | M |
| University of South Africa | M,D |
| University of South Carolina | M,D |
| University of South Dakota | M,O |
| University of Southern California | M,O |
| University of Southern Indiana | M |
| University of Southern Maine | M |
| University of Southern Mississippi | M |
| University of South Florida | O |
| The University of Tennessee | M |
| The University of Texas at Arlington | M |
| The University of Texas at Dallas | M,D |
| The University of Texas at El Paso | M,D,O |
| The University of Texas at Tyler | M |
| The University of Texas Health Science Center at Houston | M,D,O |
| The University of Texas Health Science Center at Tyler | M |
| The University of Texas Rio Grande Valley | M |
| University of the Incarnate Word | M,D |
| University of the Sciences | M,D |
| The University of Toledo | M,O |
| University of Toronto | M |
| University of Utah | M,D |
| University of Vermont | M,O |
| University of Virginia | M |
| University of Washington | M |
| The University of Western Ontario | M,D |
| University of West Florida | M |
| University of Wisconsin–Milwaukee | M,D* |
| University of Wisconsin–Oshkosh | M |
| University of Wyoming | M,D |
| Utica College | M |
| Valdosta State University | M |
| Valparaiso University | M |
| Vanderbilt University | M* |
| Villanova University | M |
| Virginia Commonwealth University | M,D |
| Virginia International University | M,O |
| Viterbo University | M |
| Walden University | M,D,O |
| Walsh University | M |
| Washington Adventist University | M |
| Washington State University | M |
| Wayland Baptist University | M,D |
| Waynesburg University | M,D |
| Wayne State University | M,D |
| Weber State University | M |
| Webster University | M,D,O |
| Weill Cornell Medicine | M |
| West Coast University | M,D |
| Western Carolina University | M |
| Western Connecticut State University | M |
| Western Governors University | M |
| Western Kentucky University | M |
| Western Michigan University | M,D,O |
| Widener University | M |
| William Woods University | M,D,O |
| Wilmington University | M,D |
| Wilson College | M |
| Wingate University | M |
| Winston-Salem State University | M |
| Worcester State University | M |
| Xavier University | M* |
| Yale University | M,D |
| York College of Pennsylvania | M |
| Youngstown State University | M |

## HEALTH SERVICES RESEARCH

| | |
|---|---|
| Albany College of Pharmacy and Health Sciences | M,D |
| Brown University | D |
| Clarkson University | M |
| Dartmouth College | M,D |
| Emory University | M,D |
| Florida Agricultural and Mechanical University | M,D |
| George Mason University | M,D,O |
| The George Washington University | M,D,O |
| Lakehead University | M |
| McMaster University | M,D |
| Northwestern University | D |
| Old Dominion University | D |
| Penn State Hershey Medical Center | M |
| Stanford University | M,D |
| Texas A&M University | M,D |
| Thomas Jefferson University | M,D,O |
| UNB Fredericton | M |
| The University of Alabama at Birmingham | M,D |
| University of Alberta | M,D |
| University of Arkansas for Medical Sciences | M,D,O |
| University of Cincinnati | M |
| University of Colorado Denver | M,D |
| University of Florida | M,D |
| University of Illinois at Chicago | M,D |
| University of La Verne | M |
| University of Maryland, Baltimore | M,D |
| University of Massachusetts Medical School | M,D |
| University of Minnesota, Twin Cities Campus | M,D |
| University of Nebraska Medical Center | M,D |
| The University of North Carolina at Charlotte | D |
| University of North Texas Health Science Center at Fort Worth | M,D,O |
| University of Ottawa | D,O |
| University of Pennsylvania | M |
| University of Pittsburgh | M* |
| University of Puerto Rico - Medical Sciences Campus | M |
| University of Rochester | D |
| University of Southern California | D |
| The University of Tennessee Health Science Center | M,D |
| University of Utah | M,D |
| University of Virginia | M |
| University of Washington | M,D |
| Virginia Commonwealth University | D |
| Washington University in St. Louis | M,O |
| Wayne State University | M,D |
| Weill Cornell Medicine | M |

## HIGHER EDUCATION

| | |
|---|---|
| Alliant International University - San Diego | M,D,O |
| Alliant International University–San Francisco | M,D,O |
| Andrews University | M,D,O |
| Angelo State University | M |
| Appalachian State University | M,O |
| Argosy University, Atlanta | M,D,O |
| Argosy University, Chicago | M,D,O |
| Argosy University, Hawaii | M,D |
| Argosy University, Los Angeles | M,D |
| Argosy University, Northern Virginia | M,D,O |
| Argosy University, Orange County | M,D |
| Argosy University, Phoenix | M,D,O |
| Argosy University, Seattle | M,D |
| Argosy University, Tampa | M,D,O |
| Argosy University, Twin Cities | M,D,O |
| Arizona State University at Tempe | M |
| Auburn University | M,D,O |
| Azusa Pacific University | M,D |
| Ball State University | M,D |
| Barry University | M,D |
| Baruch College of the City University of New York | M |
| Bay Path University | M |
| Bellarmine University | M,D,O |
| Bowling Green State University | D |
| California Baptist University | M |
| California Lutheran University | M,D |
| California State University, Long Beach | M,D |
| California State University, Sacramento | M,D,O |
| Capella University | M,D,O |
| Central Michigan University | M,D,O |
| Central Washington University | M |
| Chicago State University | M,D |
| Claremont Graduate University | M,D,O |
| Clemson University | M,D,O |
| Cleveland State University | D |
| College of Saint Elizabeth | M,D,O |
| The College of Saint Rose | M,O |
| Colorado State University | M,D |
| Columbia College (SC) | M |
| Columbus State University | M,D,O |
| Concordia University (United States) | M,D |
| Dallas Baptist University | M,D |
| Delta State University | D |
| DePaul University | M,D |
| DeVry University–Folsom Campus | M |
| Drexel University | M,D |
| East Carolina University | M,O |
| Eastern Kentucky University | M |
| Eastern Michigan University | M,D,O |
| Fitchburg State University | M,O |
| Florida Atlantic University | M,D,O |
| Florida State University | M,D,O |
| Geneva College | M |
| George Mason University | M,D,O |
| The George Washington University | M,D,O |
| Georgia Southern University | M,D |

| | |
|---|---|
| Grambling State University | M,D,O |
| Grand Valley State University | M |
| Hardin-Simmons University | D |
| Hofstra University | M,D,O |
| Houston Baptist University | M,D |
| Illinois State University | M,D |
| Indiana State University | M,D,O |
| Indiana University Bloomington | M,D,O |
| Indiana University of Pennsylvania | M |
| Indiana Wesleyan University | M |
| Inter American University of Puerto Rico, Metropolitan Campus | M |
| Iowa State University of Science and Technology | M,D |
| Jackson State University | M,D,O |
| James Madison University | M |
| Johnson University | M,D,O |
| Kent State University | M,D,O |
| Lee University | M,O |
| Lewis University | M |
| Lincoln Memorial University | M,D,O |
| Lincoln University (MO) | M |
| London Metropolitan University | M,D |
| Louisiana State University and Agricultural & Mechanical College | M,D,O |
| Louisiana Tech University | M,D,O |
| Loyola Marymount University | M |
| Loyola University Chicago | M,D |
| Mary Baldwin University | M |
| Maryville University of Saint Louis | M,D |
| Marywood University | M,D |
| McKendree University | M,D,O |
| Mercer University | M,D,O |
| Mercer University | M,D,O |
| Mercyhurst University | M,O |
| Messiah University | M |
| Michigan State University | M,D,O |
| Minnesota State University Mankato | M,D |
| Mississippi College | M,D,O |
| Mississippi State University | M,D,O |
| Missouri State University | M |
| Montana State University | M,D,O |
| Morehead State University | M,O |
| Morgan State University | M,D |
| National American University (TX) | M,D |
| National University | M,D |
| New England College | M,D |
| New Mexico State University | M,D |
| New York University | M,D |
| North Dakota State University | O |
| Northeastern University | M |
| Northern Arizona University | M,D,O |
| Northern Illinois University | M,D |
| Northwest Missouri State University | M,D,O |
| Oakland University | M,D,O |
| Ohio University | M,D |
| Old Dominion University | M,D,O |
| Oral Roberts University | M,D |
| Oregon State University | M,D |
| Penn State University Park | M,D,O* |
| Phillips Theological Seminary | M,D |
| Plymouth State University | D,O |
| Purdue University | M,D,O |
| Purdue University Global | M |
| Regent University | M,D,O |
| Regis College (MA) | M,D |
| Robert Morris University Illinois | M |
| Rowan University | M |
| St. Cloud State University | D |
| Saint Louis University | M,D,O |
| Saint Peter's University | M,D |
| Salem State University | M |
| Sam Houston State University | M,D |
| San Diego State University | M |
| San Jose State University | M,D |
| Seton Hall University | M,D,O |
| Siena Heights University | M,O |
| Southeast Missouri State University | M,D,O |
| Southern Arkansas University–Magnolia | M |
| Southern Illinois University Carbondale | M |
| Southern Illinois University Edwardsville | M |
| Southern Methodist University | M,D |
| Southern New Hampshire University | M,D,O |
| Southwestern College (KS) | M,D |
| Springfield College | M,D,O |
| Stony Brook University, State University of New York | M,O |
| Syracuse University | M,D |
| Taylor University | M |
| Teachers College, Columbia University | M,D |
| Texas A&M University–Commerce | M,D,O |
| Texas Southern University | M,D |
| Texas State University | M |
| Texas Tech University | M,D |
| Tiffin University | M |
| Trident University International | M,D |
| Union University | M,D,O |
| Universidad Central del Este | M |
| Université de Sherbrooke | M,O |
| University at Albany, State University of New York | M,D,O |
| University at Buffalo, the State University of New York | M,D,O |
| The University of Alabama | M,D,O |
| The University of Arizona | M,D |
| University of Arkansas | M,D,O |
| University of Arkansas at Little Rock | M,D |
| The University of British Columbia | M,D |
| University of California, Riverside | M,D,O |
| University of Central Florida | M,O |
| University of Connecticut | M |
| University of Delaware | M,D,O |
| University of Denver | M,D,O |
| University of Florida | M,D,O |
| University of Georgia | M,D,O |
| University of Houston | M,D |
| University of Houston–Victoria | M,O |
| The University of Iowa | M,D |
| The University of Kansas | M,D |
| University of Kentucky | M,D |
| University of Louisville | M,D,O |
| University of Lynchburg | M |
| University of Maine | M,D,O |
| University of Manitoba | M |
| University of Mary Hardin-Baylor | M,D |
| University of Massachusetts Amherst | M,D,O |
| University of Massachusetts Boston | D |
| University of Memphis | M,D,O |
| University of Miami | M,D,O |
| University of Minnesota, Twin Cities Campus | M,D |
| University of Mississippi | M,D,O |
| University of Missouri | M,D,O |
| University of Missouri–Kansas City | M,D,O |
| University of Missouri–St. Louis | M,O |
| University of Nevada, Las Vegas | M,D,O |
| University of New Hampshire | O |
| University of New Mexico | O |
| University of New Orleans | M,D |
| University of North Alabama | M |
| The University of North Carolina at Greensboro | D |
| The University of North Carolina Wilmington | M,D |
| University of Northern Colorado | M,D |
| University of Northern Iowa | M |
| University of North Georgia | D |
| University of North Texas | M,D,O |
| University of Oklahoma | M,D |
| University of Pennsylvania | M,D |
| University of Phoenix - Bay Area Campus | M,D,O |
| University of Phoenix–Online Campus | D,O |
| University of Puerto Rico at Mayagüez | M |
| University of Rochester | M,D |
| University of San Diego | M,D,O |
| University of South Carolina | M |
| University of South Dakota | M,D,O |
| University of Southern California | D |
| University of Southern Maine | M,O |
| University of South Florida | M,D,O |
| The University of Texas at Arlington | M,D |
| The University of Texas at San Antonio | M,D |
| The University of Toledo | M,D,O |
| University of Utah | M,D |
| University of Vermont | M,D |
| University of Virginia | M,D,O |
| University of Washington | M,D |
| The University of West Alabama | M |
| University of Wisconsin–La Crosse | M,D |
| University of Wisconsin–Madison | M,D,O |
| University of Wisconsin–Milwaukee | M,O* |
| Upper Iowa University | M |
| Wagner College | M |
| Walden University | M,D,O |
| Walsh University | M |
| Wayland Baptist University | M |
| Western Illinois University | M |
| Western Kentucky University | M |
| Western Michigan University | M,D |
| Western Washington University | M |
| West Virginia University | M,D |
| Wilmington University | M,D |

**HISPANIC AND LATIN AMERICAN LANGUAGES**

| | |
|---|---|
| Boston University | M,D |
| Brigham Young University | M |
| California State University, San Marcos | M |
| Cornell University | D |
| The Graduate Center, City University of New York | D |
| Indiana University Bloomington | M,D |
| Michigan State University | M,D |
| Queens College of the City University of New York | M |
| Stony Brook University, State University of New York | M,D |
| Université de Montréal | M,D |
| University of California, Berkeley | D |
| University of California, Los Angeles | D |
| University of California, Santa Barbara | M,D |
| University of Colorado Boulder | M,D |
| University of Illinois at Chicago | M,D |
| University of Massachusetts Amherst | M,D |
| University of Minnesota, Twin Cities Campus | M,D |
| The University of North Carolina at Greensboro | M,O |
| The University of Texas at Austin | M,D |
| University of Washington | M |

**HISPANIC STUDIES**

| | |
|---|---|
| Brown University | D |
| California State University, Los Angeles | M |
| California State University, Northridge | M |
| California State University, San Marcos | M |
| The Catholic University of America | M,D |
| The Citadel, The Military College of South Carolina | O |
| Columbia University | M,D |
| La Salle University | M,O |
| Louisiana State University and Agricultural & Mechanical College | M |
| McGill University | M,D |
| Michigan State University | M,D |
| Oregon State University | M |
| Pontifical Catholic University of Puerto Rico | M,O |
| St. Thomas University - Florida | M,O |
| Stephen F. Austin State University | M |
| Texas A&M University–Kingsville | D |
| University of Alberta | M,D |
| The University of British Columbia | M,D |
| University of California, Riverside | M,D |
| University of California, Santa Barbara | M,D |
| University of Houston | M,D |
| University of Illinois at Chicago | M,D |
| University of Kentucky | M,D |
| University of Nevada, Las Vegas | M,O |
| The University of North Carolina at Greensboro | M,O |
| The University of North Carolina Wilmington | M,O |
| University of Puerto Rico at Mayagüez | M |
| University of Puerto Rico at Rio Piedras | M,D |
| The University of Texas at Austin | M |
| University of Victoria | M |
| Villanova University | M |

**HISTORIC PRESERVATION**

| | |
|---|---|
| The American University of Rome | M |
| Arkansas State University | M,D |
| Ball State University | M |
| Boston Architectural College | M |
| Boston University | M |
| Buffalo State College, State University of New York | M,O |
| Clemson University | M,O |
| Cleveland State University | M,O |
| College of Charleston | M |
| Columbia University | M,D,O |
| Cornell University | M,D |
| Delaware State University | M |
| Eastern Michigan University | M,O |
| The George Washington University | M,D |
| Georgia State University | M |
| Goucher College | M |
| Morgan State University | M,D |
| New York University | M |
| Penn State Harrisburg | M,D,O |
| Plymouth State University | M,O |
| Pratt Institute | M |
| Roger Williams University | M,O |
| Rutgers University - New Brunswick | M,D,O |
| St. Cloud State University | M,O |
| Savannah College of Art and Design | M |
| Universidad Nacional Pedro Henriquez Urena | M |
| University at Buffalo, the State University of New York | M,D,O |
| University of California, Los Angeles | M |
| University of Colorado Denver | M |
| University of Delaware | M,D |
| University of Florida | M,D |
| University of Georgia | M |
| University of Hawaii at Manoa | O |
| The University of Kansas | M,D,O |
| University of Kentucky | M |
| University of Maryland, College Park | M,O |
| University of Massachusetts Amherst | M |
| University of New Mexico | O |
| University of North Alabama | M |
| The University of North Carolina at Greensboro | M,O |
| University of Oregon | M |
| University of Pennsylvania | M,O |
| University of South Carolina | M,O |
| University of Southern California | M |
| The University of Texas at Austin | M |
| University of Vermont | M |
| University of Washington | O |
| Ursuline College | M |

**HISTORY**

| | |
|---|---|
| Adams State University | M |
| Alabama State University | M |
| American Public University System | M,D |
| American University | M,D |
| Appalachian State University | M |
| Arizona State University at Tempe | M,D,O |
| Arkansas State University | M,O |
| Arkansas Tech University | M |
| Ashland University | M |
| Auburn University | M,D,O |
| Ball State University | M |
| Bard College | M |
| Baylor University | M,D |
| Binghamton University, State University of New York | M,D |
| Bob Jones University | M,D,O |
| Boise State University | M |
| Boston College | M,D |
| Boston University | M,D |
| Bowling Green State University | M,D |
| Brandeis University | M,D |
| Brock University | M |
| Brooklyn College of the City University of New York | M |
| Brown University | M,D |
| Buffalo State College, State University of New York | M |
| Cabrini University | M,D |
| California Polytechnic State University, San Luis Obispo | M |
| California State Polytechnic University, Pomona | M |
| California State University, Chico | M |
| California State University, East Bay | M |
| California State University, Fresno | M |
| California State University, Fullerton | M |
| California State University, Long Beach | M |
| California State University, Los Angeles | M |
| California State University, Northridge | M |
| California State University, San Marcos | M |
| California State University, Stanislaus | M |
| Carleton University | M,D |
| Carnegie Mellon University | D |
| Case Western Reserve University | M,D |
| The Catholic University of America | M,D |
| Central Connecticut State University | M,O |
| Central European University | M,D |
| Central Michigan University | M,O |
| Central Washington University | M |
| Centro de Estudios Avanzados de Puerto Rico y el Caribe | M,D |
| Chicago State University | M |
| The Citadel, The Military College of South Carolina | M,O |
| City College of the City University of New York | M |
| Claremont Graduate University | M,D,O |
| Clark University | D |
| Clayton State University | M |
| Clemson University | M |
| Cleveland State University | M |
| College of Charleston | M |
| College of Staten Island of the City University of New York | M |
| Colorado State University | M |
| Columbia University | M,D |
| Columbus State University | M,O |
| Concordia University (Canada) | M,D |
| Converse College | M |
| Cornell University | M,D |
| Dalhousie University | M,D |
| DePaul University | M |
| Drew University | M,D,O |
| Duke University | M,D |
| Duquesne University | M |
| East Carolina University | M |
| Eastern Illinois University | M |
| Eastern Kentucky University | M |
| Eastern Michigan University | M |
| Eastern Washington University | M |
| East Stroudsburg University of Pennsylvania | M |
| East Tennessee State University | M,O |
| Emory & Henry College | M,D |
| Emory University | D |
| Emporia State University | M |
| Fairleigh Dickinson University, Metropolitan Campus | M |
| Fitchburg State University | M |
| Florida Agricultural and Mechanical University | M |
| Florida Atlantic University | M |
| Florida Gulf Coast University | M |
| Florida International University | M,D |
| Florida State University | M,D |
| Fordham University | M,D |
| Fort Hays State University | M |
| George Mason University | M,D,O |
| Georgetown University | M,D |
| The George Washington University | M,D |
| Georgia Southern University | M,O |
| Georgia State University | M,D |
| The Graduate Center, City University of New York | D |
| Harvard University | D* |
| Howard University | M,D |
| Hunter College of the City University of New York | M |
| Idaho State University | M |
| Illinois State University | M |
| Indiana State University | M |
| Indiana University Bloomington | M,D |
| Indiana University of Pennsylvania | M |
| Indiana University-Purdue University Indianapolis | M |
| Inter American University of Puerto Rico, Barranquitas Campus | M |
| Inter American University of Puerto Rico, Metropolitan Campus | M,D |
| Iona College | M |
| Iowa State University of Science and Technology | M,D |
| Jackson State University | M |
| Jacksonville State University | M |
| James Madison University | M |
| Johns Hopkins University | D |
| Kansas State University | M,D |
| Kent State University | M,D |
| Lake Forest College | M |
| Lakehead University | M |
| Lamar University | M |
| Laurentian University | M |
| Lee University | M,O |

*M—masters degree; D—doctorate; O—other advanced degree; *—Close-Up and/or Display*

| | |
|---|---|
| Lehigh University | M,D |
| Lehman College of the City University of New York | M |
| Liberty University | M |
| Lincoln University (MO) | M |
| Long Island University - Post | M,O |
| Louisiana State University and Agricultural & Mechanical College | M,D |
| Louisiana Tech University | M,D,O |
| Loyola University Chicago | M,D |
| Marquette University | M,D |
| Marshall University | M,O |
| McGill University | M,D |
| McMaster University | M,D |
| Memorial University of Newfoundland | M,D |
| Miami University | M |
| Michigan State University | M,D |
| Middle Tennessee State University | M |
| Midwestern State University | M |
| Millersville University of Pennsylvania | M |
| Minnesota State University Mankato | M |
| Mississippi College | M,O |
| Mississippi State University | M,D |
| Missouri State University | M,O |
| Monmouth University | M |
| Montana State University | M,D |
| Morgan State University | M,D |
| Murray State University | M |
| New Jersey Institute of Technology | M,D,O |
| New Mexico Highlands University | M |
| New Mexico State University | M |
| The New School | M,D |
| New York University | M,D,O |
| North Carolina Central University | M |
| North Carolina State University | M |
| North Dakota State University | M,D |
| Northeastern Illinois University | M |
| Northeastern University | M,D |
| Northern Arizona University | M |
| Northern Illinois University | M,D |
| Northwestern University | M,D |
| Norwich University | M |
| Oakland University | M |
| The Ohio State University | M,D |
| Ohio University | M,D |
| Oklahoma State University | M,D |
| Old Dominion University | M |
| Open University | M |
| Penn State University Park | M,D* |
| Pittsburg State University | M |
| Pontifical Catholic University of Puerto Rico | M |
| Portland State University | M |
| Princeton University | D |
| Providence College | M |
| Purdue University | M,D |
| Purdue University Northwest | M |
| Queens College of the City University of New York | M |
| Rhode Island College | M |
| Rice University | M,D |
| Roosevelt University | M |
| Rowan University | M,O |
| Rutgers University - Camden | M |
| Rutgers University - Newark | M |
| Rutgers University - New Brunswick | D |
| St. Cloud State University | M |
| St. John's University (NY) | M,D |
| Saint Louis University | M,D |
| Saint Mary's University (Canada) | M |
| Salem State University | M |
| Salisbury University | M |
| Sam Houston State University | M |
| San Diego State University | M |
| San Francisco State University | M |
| San Jose State University | M |
| Sarah Lawrence College | M |
| Seton Hall University | M |
| Shippensburg University of Pennsylvania | M |
| Simmons University | M,D,O |
| Simon Fraser University | M,D |
| Slippery Rock University of Pennsylvania | M |
| Smith College | M |
| Sonoma State University | M |
| Southeastern Louisiana University | M |
| Southeast Missouri State University | M,O |
| Southern Connecticut State University | M |
| Southern Illinois University Carbondale | M,D |
| Southern Illinois University Edwardsville | M |
| Southern Methodist University | M,D |
| Southern New Hampshire University | M |
| Southern University and Agricultural and Mechanical College | M |
| Southwestern Assemblies of God University | M |
| Stanford University | M,D |
| State University of New York College at Cortland | M |
| Stephen F. Austin State University | M |
| Stony Brook University, State University of New York | M,D |
| Sul Ross State University | M |
| SUNY Brockport | M |
| Syracuse University | M,D |
| Tarleton State University | M |
| Temple University | M,D* |
| Texas A&M International University | M |
| Texas A&M University | M,D |
| Texas A&M University–Central Texas | M,O |
| Texas A&M University–Commerce | M,D,O |
| Texas A&M University–Corpus Christi | M |
| Texas Christian University | M,D |
| Texas Southern University | M |
| Texas State University | M |
| Texas Tech University | M,D |
| Texas Woman's University | M |
| Trinity Western University | M |
| Troy University | M |
| Tufts University | M,D |
| Tulane University | M,D |
| UNB Fredericton | M,D |
| Union Institute & University | M |
| Université de Moncton | M |
| Université de Montréal | M,D |
| Université de Sherbrooke | M |
| Université du Québec à Montréal | M,D |
| University at Albany, State University of New York | M,D,O |
| University at Buffalo, the State University of New York | M,D,O |
| The University of Akron | M,D |
| The University of Alabama | M,D |
| The University of Alabama at Birmingham | M |
| The University of Alabama in Huntsville | M |
| University of Alaska Fairbanks | M |
| University of Alberta | M,D |
| The University of Arizona | M,D,O |
| University of Arkansas | M,D |
| The University of British Columbia | M,D |
| University of Calgary | M,D |
| University of California, Berkeley | M,D |
| University of California, Davis | M,D |
| University of California, Irvine | M,D |
| University of California, Los Angeles | M,D |
| University of California, Riverside | M,D |
| University of California, San Diego | M,D |
| University of California, Santa Barbara | D |
| University of California, Santa Cruz | M,D |
| University of Central Arkansas | M |
| University of Central Florida | M |
| University of Central Missouri | M,D,O |
| University of Central Oklahoma | M |
| University of Chicago | D |
| University of Cincinnati | M,D |
| University of Colorado Boulder | M,D |
| University of Colorado Colorado Springs | M |
| University of Colorado Denver | M |
| University of Connecticut | M,D |
| University of Delaware | M,D |
| University of Denver | M,O |
| University of Florida | M,D |
| University of Georgia | M,D |
| University of Guelph | M,D |
| University of Hawaii at Manoa | M,D |
| University of Houston | M,D |
| University of Houston–Clear Lake | M |
| University of Idaho | M,D |
| University of Illinois at Chicago | M,D |
| University of Illinois at Springfield | M |
| University of Illinois at Urbana-Champaign | M,D |
| University of Indianapolis | M |
| The University of Iowa | M,D |
| The University of Kansas | M,D |
| University of Kentucky | M,D |
| University of Louisiana at Lafayette | M,D |
| University of Louisiana at Monroe | M |
| University of Louisville | M,O |
| University of Maine | M,D |
| The University of Manchester | D |
| University of Manitoba | M,D |
| University of Maryland, Baltimore County | M |
| University of Maryland, College Park | M,D |
| University of Massachusetts Amherst | M,D |
| University of Massachusetts Boston | M |
| University of Memphis | M,D |
| University of Miami | M,D |
| University of Michigan | D,O |
| University of Minnesota, Twin Cities Campus | M,D |
| University of Mississippi | M,D |
| University of Missouri | M,D |
| University of Missouri–Kansas City | M,D |
| University of Missouri–St. Louis | M,O |
| University of Montana | M,D |
| University of Nebraska at Kearney | M |
| University of Nebraska at Omaha | M |
| University of Nebraska–Lincoln | M,D |
| University of Nevada, Las Vegas | M,D |
| University of Nevada, Reno | M,D |
| University of New Hampshire | M,D |
| University of New Mexico | M,D |
| University of New Orleans | M |
| University of North Alabama | M |
| The University of North Carolina at Chapel Hill | M,D |
| The University of North Carolina at Charlotte | M |
| The University of North Carolina at Greensboro | M,D,O |
| The University of North Carolina Wilmington | M |
| University of North Dakota | M,D |
| University of Northern British Columbia | M,D,O |
| University of Northern Colorado | M |
| University of Northern Iowa | M |
| University of North Florida | M |
| University of North Georgia | M |
| University of North Texas | M,D,O |
| University of Notre Dame | M,D |
| University of Oklahoma | M,D |
| University of Oregon | M,D |
| University of Ottawa | M,D |
| University of Pennsylvania | M,D |
| University of Pittsburgh | M,D* |
| University of Puerto Rico at Rio Piedras | M,D |
| University of Regina | M |
| University of Rhode Island | M |
| University of Rochester | M,D |
| University of Saskatchewan | M,D |
| University of South Africa | M,D |
| University of South Alabama | M |
| University of South Carolina | M,D,O |
| University of South Dakota | M |
| University of Southern California | D |
| University of South Florida | M,D |
| The University of Tennessee | M,D |
| The University of Texas at Arlington | M,D |
| The University of Texas at Austin | M,D |
| The University of Texas at Dallas | M,D |
| The University of Texas at El Paso | M,D |
| The University of Texas at San Antonio | M |
| The University of Texas at Tyler | M |
| The University of Texas of the Permian Basin | M |
| The University of Texas Rio Grande Valley | M |
| The University of Toledo | M,D |
| University of Toronto | M,D |
| University of Utah | M,D |
| University of Vermont | M |
| University of Victoria | M,D |
| University of Virginia | M,D |
| University of Washington | M,D |
| University of Waterloo | M,D |
| The University of West Alabama | M |
| The University of Western Ontario | M,D |
| University of West Florida | M |
| University of Windsor | M |
| The University of Winnipeg | M |
| University of Wisconsin–Eau Claire | M |
| University of Wisconsin–Madison | M,D |
| University of Wisconsin–Milwaukee | M,D* |
| University of Wyoming | M |
| Université Laval | M,D |
| Utah State University | M |
| Vanderbilt University | M,D* |
| Villanova University | M |
| Virginia Commonwealth University | M |
| Washington State University | M,D |
| Washington University in St. Louis | D |
| Wayland Baptist University | M |
| Wayne State University | M,D,O |
| Western Carolina University | M |
| Western Connecticut State University | M |
| Western Illinois University | M |
| Western Kentucky University | M |
| Western Michigan University | M,D |
| Western Washington University | M |
| West Texas A&M University | M |
| West Virginia University | M,D |
| Wichita State University | M |
| Wilfrid Laurier University | M,D |
| Winthrop University | M |
| Worcester State University | M |
| Wright State University | M |
| Yale University | M,D |
| York University | M,D |
| Youngstown State University | M |

## HISTORY OF MEDICINE

| | |
|---|---|
| Indiana University Bloomington | M,D |
| McGill University | M,D |
| Rutgers University - New Brunswick | D |
| SUNY Brockport | M,O |
| The University of Manchester | M,D |
| University of Minnesota, Twin Cities Campus | M,D |
| University of Wisconsin–Madison | M,D |
| Yale University | M,D |

## HISTORY OF SCIENCE AND TECHNOLOGY

| | |
|---|---|
| Arizona State University at Tempe | M,D |
| Brown University | D |
| Carnegie Mellon University | D |
| Cornell University | M,D |
| Drexel University | M |
| Georgia Institute of Technology | M,D |
| Harvard University | M,D* |
| Indiana University Bloomington | M,D |
| Johns Hopkins University | M,D |
| Massachusetts Institute of Technology | D |
| Oregon State University | M,D |
| Princeton University | D |
| Rensselaer Polytechnic Institute | M,D |
| Rutgers University - New Brunswick | D |
| University of California, Berkeley | D |
| University of California, San Diego | D |
| University of California, San Francisco | M,D |
| University of Delaware | M,D |
| The University of Manchester | M,D |
| University of Minnesota, Twin Cities Campus | M,D |
| University of Notre Dame | M,D |
| University of Oklahoma | M,D |
| University of Pennsylvania | M,D |
| University of Pittsburgh | D* |
| University of Toronto | M,D |
| University of Wisconsin–Madison | M,D |
| Yale University | M,D |

## HIV/AIDS NURSING

| | |
|---|---|
| University of Delaware | M,O |

## HOLOCAUST AND GENOCIDE STUDIES

| | |
|---|---|
| Chapman University | M |
| Clark University | D |
| College of Saint Elizabeth | M,O |
| Gratz College | M,D |
| Kean University | M |
| Stockton University | M |
| Texas A&M University–Commerce | M,D,O |
| University of South Florida | O |

## HOME ECONOMICS EDUCATION

| | |
|---|---|
| Alabama Agricultural and Mechanical University | M,O |
| Central Washington University | M |
| Eastern Kentucky University | M |
| Louisiana State University and Agricultural & Mechanical College | M,D |
| Montana State University | M |
| Purdue University | M,D,O |
| South Carolina State University | M |
| Texas Tech University | M,D |
| The University of British Columbia | M,D |
| University of Nebraska–Lincoln | M,D |
| Utah State University | M |
| Wayne State College | M |

## HOMELAND SECURITY

| | |
|---|---|
| Angelo State University | M |
| Arizona State University at Tempe | M,D |
| Aurora University | M |
| Ball State University | M,O |
| Capella University | M |
| The Citadel, The Military College of South Carolina | M,O |
| Columbus State University | M |
| Drexel University | M |
| Endicott College | M,O |
| Fairleigh Dickinson University, Metropolitan Campus | M |
| Georgian Court University | M,O |
| Henley-Putnam School of Strategic Security | M |
| Indiana University-Purdue University Indianapolis | M,O |
| The Institute of World Politics | M,D,O |
| Johns Hopkins University | M,O |
| Keiser University | M |
| Lasell College | M,O |
| Liberty University | M |
| London Metropolitan University | M,D |
| Long Island University - Riverhead | M,O |
| Missouri State University | M,O |
| Monmouth University | M,O |
| National Defense University | M |
| National University | M |
| Naval Postgraduate School | M,D |
| Nichols College | M |
| Northeastern University | M,D |
| Northwestern State University of Louisiana | M |
| Notre Dame College (OH) | M,O |
| Pace University | M |
| Penn State Harrisburg | M,D,O |
| Post University | M |
| Regent University | M |
| Rider University | M |
| St. John's University (NY) | M |
| St. Mary's University (United States) | M,O |
| Salve Regina University | M,O |
| Sam Houston State University | M |
| Southern Illinois University Carbondale | M |
| Texas A&M University–Commerce | M,D,O |
| Thomas Edison State University | M |
| Tiffin University | M |
| Towson University | M,O |
| Tulane University | M |
| University at Albany, State University of New York | M,D,O |
| University of Alaska Fairbanks | M |
| University of Central Florida | M,O |
| University of Colorado Denver | M,D |
| University of Denver | M,D,O |
| University of Illinois at Springfield | M,O |
| University of Management and Technology | M |
| University of Oklahoma Health Sciences Center | M |
| University of Phoenix–Online Campus | M |
| University of Phoenix - Phoenix Campus | M |
| University of Southern California | M,O |
| University of the District of Columbia | M |
| Upper Iowa University | M |
| Virginia Commonwealth University | M,O |
| Walden University | M,D,O |
| Wayland Baptist University | M |
| Western Kentucky University | M |
| Western Michigan University Cooley Law School | M,D |
| Wilmington University | M,D |

## HORTICULTURE

| | |
|---|---|
| Auburn University | M,D |
| Colorado State University | M,D |
| Cornell University | M,D |
| Dalhousie University | M |
| Iowa State University of Science and Technology | M,D |
| Kansas State University | M,D |
| Louisiana State University and Agricultural & Mechanical College | M,D |
| Michigan State University | M,D |
| Mississippi State University | M,D |

North Carolina State University M,D,O
North Dakota State University M,D
The Ohio State University M,D
Oklahoma State University M,D
Oregon State University M,D
Penn State University Park M,D*
Purdue University M,D
Rutgers University - New Brunswick M,D
Texas A&M University M,D
Texas A&M University–Kingsville M,D
Texas Tech University M,D
Universidad Nacional Pedro Henriquez Urena M
University of Arkansas M
University of California, Davis M
University of Delaware M
University of Florida M,D
University of Georgia M,D
University of Guelph M,D
University of Hawaii at Manoa M,D
University of Maine M,D,O
University of Manitoba M,D
University of Maryland, College Park M,D
University of Missouri M,D
University of Nebraska–Lincoln M,D
University of Puerto Rico at Mayagüez M
University of South Africa M,D
University of Vermont M,D,O
University of Washington M,D
University of Wisconsin–Madison M,D
Utah State University M,D
Virginia Polytechnic Institute and State University M,D
Washington State University M,D
West Virginia University M,D

## HOSPICE NURSING

Central Connecticut State University M
Madonna University M

## HOSPITALITY MANAGEMENT

Alabama Agricultural and Mechanical University M
American International College M,D,O
Boston University M
California State Polytechnic University, Pomona M
California State University, Northridge M,O
Cornell University M,D
DePaul University M,D
Drexel University M
East Carolina University M,O
Eastern Michigan University O
Ecole Hôtelière de Lausanne M
ESSEC Business School M,D
Fairleigh Dickinson University, Florham Campus M
Fairleigh Dickinson University, Metropolitan Campus M
Florida International University M
Georgetown University M,D
The George Washington University M,O
Glion Institute of Higher Education M
Husson University M
IGlobal University M
Johnson & Wales University M
Kansas State University M,D
Kent State University M
Lasell College M,O
Les Roches International School of Hotel Management M
Michigan State University M
Monroe College M
Morgan State University M
New York University M,D
North Carolina Agricultural and Technical State University M
Oklahoma State University M,D
Penn State University Park M,D*
Pontificia Universidad Catolica Madre y Maestra M
Purdue University M,D
Rochester Institute of Technology M
Roosevelt University M
San Diego State University M
San Francisco State University M
San Ignacio University M
Schiller International University - Tampa M
South University - Savannah M
Stratford University (MD) M
Strayer University M
Syracuse University M,O
Temple University M,D*
Texas Tech University M,D
Thomas Edison State University M
The University of Alabama M
University of Central Florida M,D,O
University of Delaware M
The University of Findlay M,D
University of Guelph M
University of Houston M
University of Kentucky M
University of Louisiana at Lafayette M
University of Massachusetts Amherst M,D
University of Memphis M,O
University of Mississippi M,D
University of Missouri M,D
University of Nevada, Las Vegas M,D
University of New Orleans M
University of North Texas M,D,O
University of South Carolina M
University of South Florida Sarasota-Manatee M
The University of Tennessee M
University of the Pacific M
Virginia International University M,O

## HUMAN-COMPUTER INTERACTION

Brandeis University M
Carnegie Mellon University M,D
Cornell University M,D
Dalhousie University M,D
DePaul University M,D
Florida Institute of Technology M
Harrisburg University of Science and Technology M
Indiana University Bloomington M,D
Indiana University-Purdue University Indianapolis M,D
Iowa State University of Science and Technology M,D
Rochester Institute of Technology M
State University of New York at Oswego M
Tufts University O
University of Baltimore M
University of Illinois at Urbana-Champaign M,D,O
University of Rochester M,D
University of Washington M,D,O

## HUMAN DEVELOPMENT

Alabama Agricultural and Mechanical University M
Argosy University, Chicago D
Arizona State University at Tempe M,D
Auburn University M,D
Ball State University M,D,O
Bradley University M
Brigham Young University M,D
Brock University M,D
California State University, Fresno M,D
Central Michigan University M,O
Claremont Graduate University M,D,O
Colorado State University M,D
Cornell University M,D
Duke University D
Eastern Illinois University M
Erikson Institute M,O
Fielding Graduate University M,D,O
Florida State University M,D
Georgetown University M,D
The George Washington University M
Georgia State University M,D,O
Harvard University M*
Iowa State University of Science and Technology M,D
Kansas State University M,D,O
Kent State University M,D
Laurentian University M
Lindsey Wilson College M,D
Marywood University D
Michigan State University M,D
Mississippi State University M,D
Montana State University M
Murray State University M,D,O
National Louis University M,D,O
New York University M,D,O
Northern Arizona University O
Northwestern University D
The Ohio State University M,D
Oregon State University M,D
Pacific Oaks College M
Penn State University Park M,D*
Purdue University M,D
Saint Mary's University of Minnesota M
Syracuse University M,D
Texas A&M University–Corpus Christi M,D
Texas Tech University M,D
Tufts University M,D
The University of Alabama M
The University of Arizona M,D,O
The University of British Columbia M,D,O
University of California, Berkeley M,D
University of California, Davis D
University of Central Oklahoma M
University of Chicago D
University of Colorado Denver M,D
University of Connecticut M,D
University of Dayton M,O
University of Delaware M,D
University of Guelph M,D
University of Illinois at Chicago M,D
University of Illinois at Springfield M
University of Illinois at Urbana-Champaign M,D
University of Maine M,D,O
University of Maryland, College Park M,D
University of Missouri M,D
University of Nebraska–Lincoln M,D,O
University of Nevada, Reno M
University of New Mexico M,D
The University of North Carolina at Greensboro M,D
University of North Texas M,D,O
University of Pennsylvania M,D
University of Rhode Island M
University of Rochester M,D
University of St. Thomas (MN) D
University of South Africa M,D
University of South Dakota M,D,O
The University of Texas at Austin M,D
University of Utah M
University of Victoria M,D
University of Washington M,D
University of Wisconsin–Madison M,D
Utah State University M,D
Vanderbilt University M*
Washington State University D
Wright Graduate University for the Realization of Human Potential M,D,O

## HUMAN GENETICS

Baylor College of Medicine D
Case Western Reserve University M,D
Emory University M
Louisiana State University Health Sciences Center D
McGill University M,D
Memorial University of Newfoundland M,D
Sarah Lawrence College M
Thomas Jefferson University M
Tulane University M
University of California, Los Angeles M,D
University of Chicago D
University of Manitoba M,D
University of Maryland, Baltimore M,D
University of Michigan M,D
University of Pennsylvania M
University of Pittsburgh M,D,O*
University of Utah M,D
Vanderbilt University D*
Virginia Commonwealth University M,D
Washington University in St. Louis D

## HUMANITIES

Adams State University M
The American University in Cairo M,O
Brigham Young University M
California State University, Dominguez Hills M
Central Michigan University M
Claremont Graduate University M,D,O
The Colorado College M
Colorado School of Mines O
Concordia University (Canada) D
Duke University M
Faulkner University M,D
Georgetown University M,D
The Graduate Center, City University of New York M
Harrison Middleton University M,D
Hollins University M
Hood College M
Illinois Institute of Technology M,D
Instituto Tecnologico de Santo Domingo M,O
Instituto Tecnológico y de Estudios Superiores de Monterrey, Campus Central de Veracruz M
Instituto Tecnológico y de Estudios Superiores de Monterrey, Campus Ciudad de México M,D
Instituto Tecnológico y de Estudios Superiores de Monterrey, Campus Ciudad Juárez M
Instituto Tecnológico y de Estudios Superiores de Monterrey, Campus Estado de México M,D
Instituto Tecnológico y de Estudios Superiores de Monterrey, Campus Irapuato M,D
Laurentian University M
Loyola University Chicago M
Marshall University M,O
Memorial University of Newfoundland M
Mount Saint Mary's University (CA) M,D,O
New York University M,O
Northeast Ohio Medical University M,D,O
Nova Southeastern University M,D,O
Old Dominion University M,O
Penn State Harrisburg M,D,O
Pepperdine University M
Prescott College M
Roosevelt University M
St. Edward's University M,O
Salve Regina University M,D
Sam Houston State University M,D,O
San Francisco State University M
Simon Fraser University M
Tiffin University M
Towson University M
Trinity Western University M
Union Institute & University D
United Theological Seminary of the Twin Cities M,D,O
University at Buffalo, the State University of New York M
University of California, Merced M,D
University of California, Santa Cruz D
University of Chicago M
University of Colorado Denver M,O
University of Houston–Clear Lake M
University of Louisville M,D
University of South Florida M
The University of Texas at Dallas M,D
The University of Texas Medical Branch M,D
University of Utah M
Virginia Polytechnic Institute and State University M,D,O
Wayland Baptist University M
Wilson College M
Wright State University M
York University M,D

## HUMAN RESOURCES DEVELOPMENT

Amberton University M
Antioch University Los Angeles M
Barry University M,D
Bowie State University M
California State University, Sacramento M
Claremont Graduate University M,D,O
Clemson University M,D,O
The College of New Rochelle M,O
Drexel University M,D
The George Washington University M,D,O
Grantham University M,O
HEC Montreal O
Illinois Institute of Technology M,D
Indiana State University M
Indiana Tech M
Indiana University of Pennsylvania M
Inter American University of Puerto Rico, Metropolitan Campus M
Inter American University of Puerto Rico, San Germán Campus M,D
Iowa State University of Science and Technology M,D
La Salle University M,O
Lawrence Technological University M,O
Lincoln Memorial University M,D,O
Louisiana State University and Agricultural & Mechanical College M,D
Marquette University M
McDaniel College M
Midwestern State University M
Mississippi State University M,D,O
National Louis University M
New York University M
North Carolina State University M
Northeastern Illinois University M
Ottawa University M
Penn State Great Valley M,O
Penn State University Park M*
Pittsburg State University M
Regent University M,D,O
Rochester Institute of Technology M
Rockhurst University M,O
Rollins College M
Roosevelt University M
South Dakota State University M
Texas A&M University M,D
Towson University M
Tusculum University M
Universidad Central del Este M
Universidad Iberoamericana M,D
University of Arkansas M,D,O
University of Bridgeport M
University of Houston M
University of Louisville M,D,O
University of Minnesota, Twin Cities Campus M,D,O
University of Nebraska at Omaha M,D,O
University of Regina M
The University of Scranton M
University of South Africa M,D
University of South Florida O
The University of Tennessee M
The University of Texas at Tyler M,D
University of Wisconsin–Stout M
Villanova University M
Virginia Commonwealth University M
Waldorf University M
Webster University M,D,O
Western Seminary - Portland M
William Woods University M,D,O
Xavier University M,D*

## HUMAN RESOURCES MANAGEMENT

Adelphi University M,O
Albany State University M
Albertus Magnus College M
Amberton University M
American InterContinental University Online M
American University M,O
Anderson University (SC) M
Ashland University M
Ashworth College M
Assumption University M,O
Averett University M
Avila University M
Baker College Center for Graduate Studies–Online M,D
Baldwin Wallace University M
Barry University O
Baruch College of the City University of New York M,D
Belhaven University (MS) M
Bellevue University M,D
Benedictine University M
Brandman University M
Brigham Young University M
Bryan College M
Buffalo State College, State University of New York M,O
California Coast University M
California Intercontinental University M,D
California State University, East Bay M
California State University, Sacramento M
Capella University M,D
Caribbean University M,D
Carlow University M
The Catholic University of America M
Central Michigan University M,O
Charleston Southern University M
City University of Seattle M,O
Claremont Graduate University M
Clarkson University M,O
Clayton State University M
Cleveland State University M
College of Saint Elizabeth M
Colorado State University–Global Campus M

*M—masters degree; D—doctorate; O—other advanced degree; *—Close-Up and/or Display*

| | |
|---|---|
| Colorado Technical University Aurora | M |
| Colorado Technical University Colorado Springs | M,D |
| Columbia College (MO) | M |
| Columbia Southern University | M |
| Columbia University | M |
| Columbus State University | M,O |
| Concordia University, St. Paul | M |
| Concordia University Wisconsin | M |
| Cornell University | M,D |
| Dallas Baptist University | M |
| Davenport University | M |
| Delaware Valley University | M |
| DePaul University | M,D |
| DeSales University | M |
| DeVry University–Folsom Campus | M |
| East Central University | M |
| Eastern Michigan University | M,O |
| Embry-Riddle Aeronautical University–Daytona | M |
| Embry-Riddle Aeronautical University–Worldwide | M |
| Emmanuel College (United States) | M,O |
| Everglades University | M |
| Fairleigh Dickinson University, Florham Campus | M |
| Fairleigh Dickinson University, Metropolitan Campus | M,O |
| Fitchburg State University | M |
| Florida Institute of Technology | M |
| Florida International University | M,D |
| Florida State University | M,D |
| Framingham State University | M |
| Franklin Pierce University | M,D,O |
| Gannon University | M |
| George Fox University | M,D |
| George Mason University | M |
| Georgetown University | M,D |
| The George Washington University | M,O |
| Georgia State University | M,D |
| Golden Gate University | M,D,O |
| Goldey-Beacom College | M |
| Grambling State University | M |
| Grand Canyon University | M |
| Grantham University | M,O |
| Hawaii Pacific University | M |
| HEC Montreal | M,D,O |
| Herzing University Online | M |
| Hofstra University | M,O |
| Holy Family University | M |
| Houston Baptist University | M |
| Howard University | M |
| Idaho State University | M,D |
| IGlobal University | M |
| Indiana Tech | M |
| Indiana University South Bend | M,O |
| Indiana Wesleyan University | M,O |
| Instituto Tecnologico de Santo Domingo | M,O |
| Instituto Tecnológico y de Estudios Superiores de Monterrey, Campus Cuernavaca | M |
| Inter American University of Puerto Rico, Aguadilla Campus | M |
| Inter American University of Puerto Rico, Arecibo Campus | M |
| Inter American University of Puerto Rico, Barranquitas Campus | M |
| Inter American University of Puerto Rico, Bayamón Campus | M |
| Inter American University of Puerto Rico, Fajardo Campus | M |
| Inter American University of Puerto Rico, Metropolitan Campus | M |
| Inter American University of Puerto Rico, Ponce Campus | M |
| Inter American University of Puerto Rico, San Germán Campus | M,D |
| Iona College | M,O |
| James Madison University | M |
| John F. Kennedy University | M |
| Johnson & Wales University | M |
| King University | M |
| La Roche University | M,O |
| La Salle University | M,O |
| Lasell College | M,O |
| La Sierra University | M,O |
| Lebanon Valley College | M |
| Lewis University | M |
| Lincoln University (CA) | M,D |
| Lindenwood University | M,O |
| Lindenwood University–Belleville | M |
| London Metropolitan University | M,D |
| Long Island University - Brooklyn | M,O |
| Loyola University Chicago | M |
| Manhattanville College | M,O |
| Marquette University | M,O |
| Marshall University | M |
| Marygrove College | M,O |
| Marymount University | O |
| Maryville University of Saint Louis | M,O |
| McKendree University | M |
| McMaster University | M,D |
| Mercy College | M |
| Mercyhurst University | M,O |
| Michigan State University | M,D |
| Middle Tennessee State University | M |
| Millennia Atlantic University | M |
| Misericordia University | M |
| Monroe College | M |
| Montclair State University | M |
| Moravian College | M |
| Mount Mercy University | M |
| Murray State University | M |
| National American University (TX) | M,D |
| National Louis University | M |
| National University | M,O |
| Nazareth College of Rochester | M |
| New Mexico Highlands University | M |
| New York Institute of Technology | M,O |
| New York University | M |
| Niagara University | M |
| North Carolina Agricultural and Technical State University | M |
| North Central College | M |
| North Greenville University | M,D |
| Northwest Missouri State University | M |
| Norwich University | M |
| Nova Southeastern University | M |
| Oakland University | M,O |
| Ohio Christian University | M |
| The Ohio State University | M,D |
| Oklahoma Christian University | M |
| Ottawa University | M |
| Pace University | M |
| Penn State Great Valley | M,O |
| Penn State Harrisburg | M,D,O |
| Penn State University Park | M* |
| Polytechnic University of Puerto Rico, Miami Campus | M |
| Polytechnic University of Puerto Rico, Orlando Campus | M |
| Pontifical Catholic University of Puerto Rico | M,O |
| Pontificia Universidad Catolica Madre y Maestra | M |
| Portland State University | M,D,O |
| Purdue University | M,D |
| Purdue University Global | M |
| Regent's University London | M |
| Regent University | M,D,O |
| Regis University | M,O |
| Robert Morris University | M |
| Robert Morris University Illinois | M |
| Rollins College | M |
| Roosevelt University | M |
| Rutgers University - Newark | M,D |
| Rutgers University - New Brunswick | M,D |
| Sacred Heart University | M,O |
| St. Ambrose University | M,D |
| Saint Francis University | M |
| St. Joseph's College, Long Island Campus | M |
| St. Joseph's College, New York | M |
| Saint Joseph's University | M |
| Saint Leo University | M,D |
| Saint Mary's University of Minnesota | M |
| Saint Peter's University | M |
| St. Thomas University - Florida | M,O |
| Salve Regina University | M,O |
| San Diego State University | M |
| San Ignacio University | M |
| Savannah State University | M |
| Seattle Pacific University | M |
| Southern New Hampshire University | M,D,O |
| State University of New York Polytechnic Institute | M |
| Stevens Institute of Technology | M |
| Stony Brook University, State University of New York | M,O |
| Strayer University | M |
| Tarleton State University | M |
| Temple University | M* |
| Tennessee State University | M,D |
| Tennessee Technological University | M |
| Texas A&M University | M |
| Texas A&M University–Central Texas | M,O |
| Texas State University | M |
| Texas Woman's University | M |
| Thomas College | M |
| Thomas Edison State University | M |
| Tiffin University | M |
| Towson University | M |
| Trident University International | M,D |
| Trinity International University | M,D |
| Trinity Washington University | M |
| Troy University | M |
| United States International University–Africa | M |
| Universidad del Este | M |
| Universidad del Turabo | M |
| Universidad Metropolitana | M |
| University at Albany, State University of New York | M,D,O |
| University at Buffalo, the State University of New York | M,D,O |
| The University of Alabama in Huntsville | M,O |
| University of Bridgeport | M |
| University of California, Berkeley | O |
| University of Cincinnati | M |
| University of Colorado Denver | M |
| University of Connecticut | M,D |
| University of Dallas | M,O |
| University of Denver | M,O |
| University of Florida | M,D |
| University of Hawaii at Manoa | M |
| University of Houston–Clear Lake | M |
| University of Houston - Downtown | M |
| University of Illinois at Urbana-Champaign | M,D,O |
| The University of Kansas | M,O |
| University of La Verne | M,O |
| University of Lethbridge | M,D |
| University of Louisiana at Lafayette | M |
| University of Louisville | M,D,O |
| The University of Manchester | M |
| University of Mary | M |
| University of Memphis | M,O |
| University of Minnesota, Twin Cities Campus | M |
| University of Missouri–St. Louis | M,D,O |
| University of Nebraska at Kearney | M |
| University of New Haven | M,O |
| University of New Mexico | M |
| University of Northern Colorado | M |
| University of North Florida | M |
| University of North Texas | M,D,O |
| University of North Texas at Dallas | M |
| University of Oklahoma | M,D,O |
| University of Phoenix - Bay Area Campus | M,D |
| University of Phoenix - Central Valley Campus | M |
| University of Phoenix - Dallas Campus | M |
| University of Phoenix - Hawaii Campus | M |
| University of Phoenix - Houston Campus | M |
| University of Phoenix - Las Vegas Campus | M |
| University of Phoenix–Online Campus | M,O |
| University of Phoenix - Phoenix Campus | M,O |
| University of Phoenix - Sacramento Valley Campus | M |
| University of Phoenix - San Antonio Campus | M |
| University of Phoenix - San Diego Campus | M |
| University of Pittsburgh | M,D* |
| University of Puerto Rico at Mayagüez | M |
| University of Puerto Rico at Rio Piedras | M,D |
| University of Regina | M,O |
| University of Rhode Island | M,O |
| University of St. Francis (IL) | M,O |
| University of Saint Mary | M |
| University of South Carolina | M |
| University of South Dakota | M |
| University of Southern Indiana | M |
| The University of Texas at Arlington | M |
| University of the Sacred Heart | M |
| University of Toronto | M,D |
| University of Wisconsin–Madison | M,D |
| University of Wisconsin–Milwaukee | M,O* |
| Upper Iowa University | M |
| Utah State University | M |
| Virginia Commonwealth University | M |
| Virginia International University | M,O |
| Walden University | M,D,O |
| Walsh College of Accountancy and Business Administration | M |
| Warner University | M |
| Wayland Baptist University | M,D |
| Waynesburg University | M,D |
| Wayne State University | M,D |
| Webster University | M,D,O |
| Wilfrid Laurier University | M,D |
| Wilmington University | M,D |
| York University | M,D |

## HUMAN SERVICES

| | |
|---|---|
| Abilene Christian University | M,O |
| Albertus Magnus College | M |
| Albizu University - Miami | M,D |
| Amridge University | M,D |
| Bellevue University | M |
| Boricua College | M |
| Brandeis University | M |
| California State University, Sacramento | M |
| Capella University | M,D |
| Chestnut Hill College | M,O |
| Concordia University Chicago | M |
| Concordia University, St. Paul | M |
| Coppin State University | M |
| Eastern Illinois University | M |
| Eastern Michigan University | O |
| East Tennessee State University | M |
| Ferris State University | M |
| Georgia State University | M,O |
| Governors State University | M,D |
| Judson University | M |
| Kansas State University | M,D,O |
| Kent State University | M,D,O |
| Lehigh University | M,D,O |
| Lenoir-Rhyne University | M |
| Liberty University | M,D,O |
| Lock Haven University of Pennsylvania | M |
| Louisiana Tech University | M,D,O |
| McDaniel College | M |
| Mercer University | M,D |
| Minnesota State University Mankato | M |
| Murray State University | M,D,O |
| National Louis University | M,D,O |
| National University | M,O |
| New England College | M |
| Northeastern University | M |
| Pontifical Catholic University of Puerto Rico | M,D |
| Post University | M |
| Purdue University Northwest | M |
| Regent University | M,D,O |
| Roberts Wesleyan College | M |
| Rosemont College | M |
| St. Cloud State University | M |
| St. Joseph's College, Long Island Campus | M |
| St. Joseph's College, New York | M |
| Saint Leo University | M |
| South Carolina State University | M |
| Southeastern University (FL) | M |
| Springfield College | M |
| Texas Southern University | M |
| Thomas University | M |
| Universidad del Turabo | M |
| Université de Montréal | D |
| University of Baltimore | M |
| University of Bridgeport | M |
| University of Central Missouri | M,D,O |
| University of Colorado Colorado Springs | M,D |
| University of Idaho | M,O |
| University of Illinois at Springfield | M,O |
| University of Illinois at Urbana-Champaign | M,D |
| University of Maryland, Baltimore County | M,D |
| University of Massachusetts Boston | M |
| University of Nebraska at Kearney | M |
| University of Northern Iowa | M |
| University of North Georgia | M |
| University of Northwestern–St. Paul | M |
| University of Oklahoma | M,O |
| University of Providence | M |
| Upper Iowa University | M |
| Walden University | M,D |
| Warner Pacific University | M |
| Washburn University | M |
| Webster University | M |
| Western Michigan University | D,O |
| West Virginia University | M,D |
| Wichita State University | M |
| Wilmington University | M |
| Winona State University | M,O |
| Youngstown State University | M |

## HYDRAULICS

| | |
|---|---|
| Drexel University | M,D |
| McGill University | M,D |
| Old Dominion University | M |
| Polytechnique Montréal | M,D,O |
| Stevens Institute of Technology | M,D,O |
| University of Colorado Denver | M,D |
| The University of Iowa | M,D |

## HYDROGEOLOGY

| | |
|---|---|
| Clemson University | M,D |
| East Carolina University | M,O |
| Indiana University Bloomington | M,D |
| Montana Technological University | M |
| Oregon State University | M,D |
| University of Hawaii at Manoa | M,D |
| University of Nevada, Reno | M,D |
| University of South Florida | O |

## HYDROLOGY

| | |
|---|---|
| Boise State University | M,D |
| Colorado School of Mines | M,D |
| Cornell University | M,D |
| Drexel University | M,D |
| Idaho State University | M,O |
| Massachusetts Institute of Technology | M,D,O |
| New Mexico Institute of Mining and Technology | M,D |
| New Mexico State University | M,D |
| Oregon State University | M,D |
| Portland State University | M,D,O |
| Stanford University | M,D,O |
| Stevens Institute of Technology | M,D,O |
| Temple University | M,O* |
| UNB Fredericton | M,D |
| The University of Arizona | D,O |
| University of Calgary | M,D |
| University of California, Davis | M,D |
| University of Colorado Denver | M,D |
| University of Florida | M,D |
| University of Minnesota, Twin Cities Campus | M,D |
| University of Mississippi | M,D |
| University of Nevada, Reno | M,D |
| University of New Hampshire | M,D |
| University of Rhode Island | M,D,O |
| University of Washington | M,D |

## ILLUSTRATION

| | |
|---|---|
| Academy of Art University | M |
| Bob Jones University | M,D,O |
| California College of the Arts | M |
| California State University, Fullerton | M |
| East Carolina University | M |
| Fashion Institute of Technology | M |
| Hollins University | M,O |
| Kent State University | M |
| Maryland Institute College of Art | M |
| Marywood University | M |
| Mills College | M,O |
| Minneapolis College of Art and Design | M |
| Savannah College of Art and Design | M |
| School of Visual Arts (NY) | M |
| Syracuse University | M |
| Western Connecticut State University | M |

## IMMUNOLOGY

| | |
|---|---|
| Albany Medical College | M,D |
| Albert Einstein College of Medicine | D |
| Baylor College of Medicine | D |
| Boston University | D |
| California Institute of Technology | D |
| Colorado State University | M,D |
| Creighton University | M,D |
| Dalhousie University | M,D |
| Drexel University | M,D |
| Duke University | D |
| East Carolina University | M,D |
| Emory University | D |
| Georgetown University | M,D |
| The George Washington University | D |
| Illinois State University | M,D |
| Indiana University-Purdue University Indianapolis | M,D |
| Iowa State University of Science and Technology | M,D |
| Irell & Manella Graduate School of Biological Sciences | D |
| Johns Hopkins University | M,D |
| London Metropolitan University | M,D |
| Louisiana State University Health Sciences Center | D |

| | |
|---|---|
| Louisiana State University Health Sciences Center at Shreveport | M,D |
| Loyola University Chicago | M,D |
| Massachusetts Institute of Technology | D |
| Mayo Clinic Graduate School of Biomedical Sciences | D |
| McGill University | M,D |
| McMaster University | M,D |
| Medical University of South Carolina | M,D |
| Meharry Medical College | D |
| Memorial University of Newfoundland | M,D |
| Montana State University | M,D |
| New York Medical College | M,D |
| New York University | M,D |
| Old Dominion University | M |
| Oregon Health & Science University | D |
| Oregon State University | M,D |
| Penn State Hershey Medical Center | M,D |
| Purdue University | M,D |
| Rosalind Franklin University of Medicine and Science | D |
| Rush University | M,D |
| Rutgers University - Newark | D |
| Rutgers University - New Brunswick | M,D |
| Saint Louis University | D |
| Stanford University | D |
| State University of New York Upstate Medical University | M,D |
| Stony Brook University, State University of New York | M,D |
| Thomas Jefferson University | D |
| Tufts University | D |
| Tulane University | M |
| Uniformed Services University of the Health Sciences | D |
| Universidad Central del Caribe | M,D |
| Université de Montréal | M,D |
| Université de Sherbrooke | M,D |
| Université du Québec, Institut National de la Recherche Scientifique | M,D |
| University at Buffalo, the State University of New York | M,D |
| The University of Alabama at Birmingham | D |
| University of Alberta | M,D |
| The University of Arizona | D |
| University of Arkansas for Medical Sciences | M,D,O |
| The University of British Columbia | M,D |
| University of Calgary | M,D |
| University of California, Berkeley | D |
| University of California, Davis | M,D |
| University of California, Los Angeles | M,D |
| University of Chicago | D |
| University of Cincinnati | M,D |
| University of Colorado Denver | D |
| University of Connecticut Health Center | D |
| University of Florida | D |
| University of Guelph | M,D,O |
| University of Illinois at Chicago | D |
| The University of Iowa | M,D |
| University of Kentucky | D |
| University of Louisville | M,D |
| The University of Manchester | M,D |
| University of Manitoba | M,D |
| University of Maryland, Baltimore | D |
| University of Massachusetts Medical School | M,D |
| University of Miami | D |
| University of Michigan | M,D |
| University of Minnesota, Duluth | M,D |
| University of Minnesota, Twin Cities Campus | D |
| University of Missouri | D |
| University of Montana | D |
| University of Nebraska Medical Center | M,D |
| The University of North Carolina at Chapel Hill | M,D |
| University of North Texas Health Science Center at Fort Worth | M,D |
| University of Oklahoma Health Sciences Center | M,D |
| University of Ottawa | M,D |
| University of Pennsylvania | D |
| University of Pittsburgh | D* |
| University of Prince Edward Island | M,D |
| University of Rochester | M,D |
| University of Saskatchewan | M,D |
| University of South Dakota | M,D |
| University of Southern California | M |
| The University of Texas Health Science Center at Houston | M,D |
| The University of Texas Health Science Center at San Antonio | M,D |
| The University of Texas Medical Branch | M,D |
| The University of Texas Southwestern Medical Center | D |
| The University of Toledo | M,D |
| University of Toronto | M,D |
| University of Washington | D |
| The University of Western Ontario | M,D |
| Université Laval | M,D |
| Vanderbilt University | M,D* |
| Virginia Commonwealth University | M,D |
| Wake Forest University | D |
| Washington State University | M,D |
| Washington University in St. Louis | D |
| Weill Cornell Medicine | M,D |
| West Virginia University | M,D |
| Wright State University | M |
| Yale University | D |

### INDUSTRIAL/MANAGEMENT ENGINEERING

| | |
|---|---|
| American University of Armenia | M |
| Arizona State University at Tempe | M,D |
| Auburn University | M,D,O |
| Binghamton University, State University of New York | M,D |
| Bradley University | M |
| Buffalo State College, State University of New York | M |
| California Polytechnic State University, San Luis Obispo | M |
| California State University, Fresno | M |
| California State University, Northridge | M |
| Clemson University | M,D |
| Colorado State University-Pueblo | M |
| Columbia University | M,D |
| Concordia University (Canada) | M,D,O |
| Cornell University | M,D |
| Dalhousie University | M,D |
| Eastern Kentucky University | M |
| Florida Agricultural and Mechanical University | M,D |
| Florida State University | M,D |
| Georgia Institute of Technology | M,D |
| Illinois State University | M |
| Instituto Tecnologico de Santo Domingo | M,O |
| Instituto Tecnológico y de Estudios Superiores de Monterrey, Campus Chihuahua | M,O |
| Instituto Tecnológico y de Estudios Superiores de Monterrey, Campus Ciudad de México | M,D |
| Instituto Tecnológico y de Estudios Superiores de Monterrey, Campus Laguna | M |
| Instituto Tecnológico y de Estudios Superiores de Monterrey, Campus Monterrey | M,D |
| Iowa State University of Science and Technology | M,D |
| Kansas State University | M,D |
| Lawrence Technological University | M,D |
| Lehigh University | M,D,O |
| Mississippi State University | M,D |
| Montana State University | M,D |
| Montana Technological University | M |
| Morgan State University | M,D,O |
| New Jersey Institute of Technology | M,D |
| New York University | M |
| North Carolina Agricultural and Technical State University | M,D |
| North Carolina State University | M,D |
| North Dakota State University | M,D |
| Northeastern University | M,D,O |
| Northern Illinois University | M |
| Northwestern University | M,D |
| The Ohio State University | M,D |
| Ohio University | M,D |
| Oklahoma State University | M,D |
| Oregon State University | M,D |
| Penn State University Park | M,D* |
| Polytechnique Montréal | M,D,O |
| Purdue University | M,D |
| Purdue University Fort Wayne | M |
| Rensselaer Polytechnic Institute | M,D |
| Rochester Institute of Technology | M |
| Rutgers University - New Brunswick | M,D |
| St. Mary's University (United States) | M |
| San Jose State University | M |
| Southern Illinois University Edwardsville | M |
| Stanford University | M,D |
| Texas A&M University | M,D |
| Texas A&M University–Kingsville | M |
| Texas Southern University | M |
| Texas State University | M |
| Universidad de las Américas Puebla | M |
| Université de Moncton | M |
| Université du Québec à Trois-Rivières | M,O |
| University at Buffalo, the State University of New York | M,D,O |
| The University of Alabama in Huntsville | M,D |
| The University of Arizona | M,D,O |
| University of Arkansas | M,D |
| University of California, Berkeley | M,D |
| University of Central Florida | M,D,O |
| University of Cincinnati | M,D |
| University of Florida | M,D,O |
| University of Houston | M,D |
| University of Illinois at Chicago | M,D |
| University of Illinois at Urbana-Champaign | M,D |
| The University of Iowa | M,D |
| University of Louisville | M,D,O |
| University of Manitoba | M,D |
| University of Massachusetts Amherst | M,D |
| University of Massachusetts Dartmouth | M,O |
| University of Massachusetts Lowell | D |
| University of Miami | M,D |
| University of Michigan | M,D |
| University of Michigan–Dearborn | M,D |
| University of Minnesota, Twin Cities Campus | M,D |
| University of Missouri | M,D |
| University of Nebraska–Lincoln | M,D |
| University of New Haven | M,O |
| University of Oklahoma | M,D |
| University of Pittsburgh | M,D* |
| University of Puerto Rico at Mayagüez | M |
| University of Regina | M,D |
| University of Rhode Island | M,D |
| University of Southern California | M,D,O |
| University of South Florida | M,D,O |
| The University of Tennessee | M,D |
| The University of Texas at Arlington | M,D |
| The University of Texas at Austin | M,D |
| The University of Texas at El Paso | M |
| The University of Toledo | M,D |
| University of Toronto | M,D |
| University of Washington | M,D |
| University of Windsor | M,D |
| University of Wisconsin–Madison | M,D |
| University of Wisconsin–Milwaukee | M,D* |
| University of Wisconsin–Stout | M |
| Université Laval | O |
| Virginia Polytechnic Institute and State University | M,O |
| Wayne State University | M,D,O |
| Western Carolina University | M |
| Western Michigan University | M,D |
| Western New England University | M |
| West Virginia University | M,D |
| Wichita State University | M,D |
| Wright State University | M |
| Youngstown State University | M |

### INDUSTRIAL AND LABOR RELATIONS

| | |
|---|---|
| Baruch College of the City University of New York | M |
| Carnegie Mellon University | D |
| Cleveland State University | M |
| Cornell University | M,D |
| Georgetown University | D |
| Georgia State University | M,D |
| Indiana University of Pennsylvania | M |
| Inter American University of Puerto Rico, Metropolitan Campus | M,D |
| McMaster University | M |
| Memorial University of Newfoundland | M |
| Michigan State University | M,D |
| New York Institute of Technology | M,O |
| The Ohio State University | M,D |
| Penn State University Park | M* |
| Queen's University at Kingston | M |
| Rutgers University - New Brunswick | M,D |
| State University of New York Empire State College | M |
| Temple University | M,O* |
| Université de Montréal | M,D,O |
| Université du Québec à Trois-Rivières | O |
| Université du Québec en Outaouais | M,D,O |
| University of Alberta | D |
| University of California, Berkeley | D |
| University of Cincinnati | M |
| University of Illinois at Urbana-Champaign | M,D |
| The University of Manchester | M |
| University of Massachusetts Amherst | M |
| University of Minnesota, Twin Cities Campus | M |
| University of Rhode Island | M,O |
| University of Toronto | M,D |
| University of Wisconsin–Milwaukee | M,O* |
| Université Laval | M,D |
| Wayne State University | M,D |
| West Virginia University | M,D,O |

### INDUSTRIAL AND MANUFACTURING MANAGEMENT

| | |
|---|---|
| American InterContinental University Online | M |
| Baruch College of the City University of New York | M,D |
| Bluffton University | M |
| California State University, East Bay | M |
| Carnegie Mellon University | M,D |
| Case Western Reserve University | M,D |
| Cedarville University | M,D |
| Central Connecticut State University | M,O |
| Central Michigan University | M |
| Colorado Technical University Aurora | M |
| Colorado Technical University Colorado Springs | M,D |
| Duke University | D |
| East Carolina University | M,D,O |
| Emory University | M |
| Everglades University | M |
| Georgetown University | D |
| Harvard University | D* |
| HEC Montreal | M |
| Illinois Institute of Technology | M |
| Instituto Tecnologico de Santo Domingo | M,O |
| Instituto Tecnológico y de Estudios Superiores de Monterrey, Campus Estado de México | M,D |
| Instituto Tecnológico y de Estudios Superiores de Monterrey, Campus Irapuato | M,D |
| Inter American University of Puerto Rico, Metropolitan Campus | M |
| Inter American University of Puerto Rico, San Germán Campus | M,D |
| Lawrence Technological University | M,D |
| Marquette University | M,O |
| McGill University | M,D,O |
| Milligan University | M,O |
| Milwaukee School of Engineering | M |
| Mississippi State University | M,D |
| Northern Illinois University | M |
| Oakland University | M,O |
| Penn State Erie, The Behrend College | M |
| Polytechnic University of Puerto Rico | M |
| Polytechnic University of Puerto Rico, Miami Campus | M |
| Polytechnic University of Puerto Rico, Orlando Campus | M |
| Regis University | M,O |
| Rochester Institute of Technology | M |
| San Francisco State University | M |
| Southern New Hampshire University | M,D,O |
| Stevens Institute of Technology | M |
| Texas A&M University–Kingsville | M |
| Universidad de las Américas Puebla | M |
| The University of Alabama | M,D |
| University of Arkansas | M |
| University of Bridgeport | M |
| University of Central Missouri | M,D,O |
| University of Chicago | M,O |
| University of Cincinnati | D |
| The University of Manchester | M,D |
| University of Michigan–Flint | M,O |
| University of New Haven | M,O |
| The University of North Carolina at Charlotte | M,D,O |
| University of North Texas | M,D,O |
| University of Pittsburgh | M* |
| University of Portland | M |
| University of Puerto Rico at Mayagüez | M |
| University of Puerto Rico at Rio Piedras | M,D |
| University of Rochester | D |
| University of Southern Indiana | M |
| The University of Tennessee | M,D |
| The University of Texas at Austin | M,D |
| The University of Texas at Dallas | M,D |
| The University of Texas at Tyler | M |
| University of Utah | M,D,O |
| Wayne State University | M,D |

### INDUSTRIAL AND ORGANIZATIONAL PSYCHOLOGY

| | |
|---|---|
| Adler University | M |
| Albizu University - Miami | M,D |
| Albizu University - San Juan | M,D |
| Alliant International University–Fresno | M,D |
| Alliant International University - Los Angeles | M,D |
| Alliant International University - San Diego | M,D |
| Alliant International University–San Francisco | M,D |
| American InterContinental University Online | M |
| Angelo State University | M |
| Anna Maria College | M |
| Argosy University, Atlanta | M,D,O |
| Argosy University, Chicago | M,D |
| Argosy University, Phoenix | M |
| Argosy University, Tampa | M,D |
| Argosy University, Twin Cities | M,D,O |
| Austin Peay State University | M |
| Azusa Pacific University | M |
| Baruch College of the City University of New York | M,D |
| Bayamón Central University | M |
| Bowling Green State University | M,D |
| Brooklyn College of the City University of New York | M,D |
| California State University, Long Beach | M |
| California State University, Sacramento | M |
| California State University, San Bernardino | M |
| Capella University | M,D |
| Central Michigan University | M,D |
| Chatham University | M,D |
| The Chicago School of Professional Psychology | M,D |
| The Chicago School of Professional Psychology at Downtown Los Angeles | M |
| The Chicago School of Professional Psychology at San Diego | M,D |
| The Chicago School of Professional Psychology: Online | M,D,O |
| Claremont Graduate University | M,D,O |
| Clemson University | M,D |
| East Carolina University | M,D,O |
| Eastern Kentucky University | M,O |
| Elmhurst University | M |
| Emporia State University | M |
| Fairleigh Dickinson University, Florham Campus | M |
| Florida Institute of Technology | M,D |
| Florida International University | M,D |
| George Mason University | M,D,O |
| The Graduate Center, City University of New York | D |
| Grand Canyon University | D |
| Hofstra University | M,D |
| Illinois Institute of Technology | M,D |
| Illinois State University | M,D,O |
| Indiana University-Purdue University Indianapolis | M,D |
| Inter American University of Puerto Rico, Metropolitan Campus | M,D |
| Iona College | M,O |
| Kean University | M |

*M—masters degree; D—doctorate; O—other advanced degree; *—Close-Up and/or Display*

Keiser University M,D
La Salle University M
Liberty University M,D,O
London Metropolitan University M,D
Louisiana Tech University M,D,O
Meredith College M
Middle Tennessee State University M,O
Minnesota State University Mankato M,D
Missouri State University M,O
Missouri University of Science and Technology M
Montclair State University M
New York University M,D,O
North Carolina State University D
Northern Kentucky University M,O
Ohio University D
Old Dominion University D
Philadelphia College of Osteopathic Medicine M,D,O
Pontifical Catholic University of Puerto Rico D
Purdue University D
Radford University M
Rice University M,D
Roosevelt University M,D
Sacred Heart University M
St. Cloud State University M
Saint Louis University M,D
Saint Mary's University (Canada) M,D
St. Mary's University (United States) M
San Diego State University M,D
San Francisco State University M,O
San Jose State University M
Seattle Pacific University M,D
South Dakota State University M
Southeastern Louisiana University M
Southern Illinois University Edwardsville M
Springfield College M,D,O
Teachers College, Columbia University M,D
Thomas Edison State University M,O
University at Albany, State University of New York M,D
The University of Akron M,D
The University of Alabama in Huntsville M
University of Central Florida M,D
University of Connecticut M,D
University of Detroit Mercy M,D,O
University of Guelph M,D
University of Houston M,D
The University of Manchester M
University of Maryland, Baltimore County M
University of Maryland, College Park M,D
University of Minnesota, Twin Cities Campus D
University of Nebraska at Omaha M,D,O
University of New Haven M,O
The University of North Carolina at Charlotte M,D,O
University of Phoenix–Online Campus M,D,O
University of Puerto Rico at Rio Piedras M,D
University of South Africa M,D
University of South Florida D
The University of Tennessee D
The University of Tennessee at Chattanooga M
The University of Texas at Arlington M,D
University of the Incarnate Word M,D
The University of Tulsa M,D
University of West Florida M
University of Wisconsin–Oshkosh M
Valdosta State University M,O
Vanguard University of Southern California M
Walden University M,D,O
Wayne State University M,D
Western Kentucky University M,O
Western Michigan University M,D
William James College M,D,O
Wright State University M,D
Xavier University M,D*

## INDUSTRIAL DESIGN

Academy of Art University M
ArtCenter College of Design M
Auburn University M
California College of the Arts M
Carleton University M
Georgia Institute of Technology M
Iowa State University of Science and Technology M
The New School M
North Carolina State University M
The Ohio State University M
Pratt Institute M
Purdue University M,D
Rhode Island School of Design M
Rochester Institute of Technology M
Savannah College of Art and Design M
Thomas Jefferson University M
University of Cincinnati M
University of Detroit Mercy M,D
University of Illinois at Urbana-Champaign M
University of Notre Dame M
The University of the Arts M
University of Washington M
Wayne State University M

## INDUSTRIAL HYGIENE

California State University, Northridge M
Eastern Kentucky University M
Montana Technological University M
New York Medical College M,D,O
Old Dominion University M
The University of Alabama at Birmingham M,D
University of Central Missouri M,D,O
University of Cincinnati M,D
The University of Iowa M,D,O
University of Michigan M,D
University of Minnesota, Twin Cities Campus M,D
University of Puerto Rico - Medical Sciences Campus M
University of South Carolina M,D
The University of Toledo M,D,O
University of Wisconsin–Stout M
West Virginia University M,D

## INFECTIOUS DISEASES

Georgetown University M,D
The George Washington University M,D,O
Johns Hopkins University M,D
Loyola University Chicago M,D,O
Montana State University M,D
North Carolina State University M,D
North Dakota State University M
Thomas Jefferson University O
Tufts University M,D
Uniformed Services University of the Health Sciences D
The University of British Columbia M,D
University of Calgary M,D
University of California, Berkeley M,D
University of Georgia D
University of Guelph M,D,O
University of Manitoba M,D
University of Minnesota, Twin Cities Campus M,D
University of Nebraska Medical Center M,D
University of Pittsburgh M,D*
The University of Texas Health Science Center at Houston M,D
University of Washington D
Université Laval O
Washington State University M,D
Yale University D

## INFORMATION SCIENCE

Alcorn State University M
American InterContinental University Atlanta M
American InterContinental University Online M
American University of Armenia M
Arizona State University at Tempe M
Arkansas Tech University M
Aspen University M,O
Ball State University M,O
Barry University M
Bellevue University M
Bentley University M
Bradley University M
Brigham Young University M
Brooklyn College of the City University of New York M,O
California State University, Fullerton M
Capitol Technology University M
Carleton University M,D
Carnegie Mellon University M,D
Case Western Reserve University M,D
The Citadel, The Military College of South Carolina M
Claremont Graduate University M,D,O
Clark Atlanta University M
Clark University M
The College of Saint Rose M,O
Cornell University D
Dakota State University M,D,O
DePaul University M,D
Drexel University M,D,O
East Tennessee State University M,O
Florida Institute of Technology M
Florida International University M,D
Gannon University M
George Mason University M,D,O
Georgia State University M,D,O
Grand Valley State University M
Hardin-Simmons University M
Harvard University M,D,O*
Hood College M,O
Indiana University Bloomington M,D,O
Indiana University-Purdue University Indianapolis M
Instituto Tecnologico de Santo Domingo M,O
Instituto Tecnológico y de Estudios Superiores de Monterrey, Campus Cuernavaca M,D
Instituto Tecnológico y de Estudios Superiores de Monterrey, Campus Estado de México M,D
Instituto Tecnológico y de Estudios Superiores de Monterrey, Campus Irapuato M,D
Instituto Tecnológico y de Estudios Superiores de Monterrey, Campus Monterrey M,D
Instituto Tecnológico y de Estudios Superiores de Monterrey, Campus Sonora Norte M
Iowa State University of Science and Technology M
Kennesaw State University M,O
Kent State University M
Lawrence Technological University M,D,O
Lehigh University M
Loyola University Chicago M
Marshall University M
Maryville University of Saint Louis M,O
Massachusetts Institute of Technology M,D,O
Minnesota State University Mankato M,O
Missouri University of Science and Technology M
Monroe College M
Naval Postgraduate School M,D,O
New Jersey Institute of Technology M,D,O
Northern Kentucky University M,O
Northwestern University M
Nova Southeastern University M,D
Oklahoma State University M,D
Old Dominion University D
Pace University M,D,O
Penn State Great Valley M,O
Penn State University Park M,D*
Purdue University Fort Wayne M
Regis University M,O
Rensselaer at Hartford M
Rensselaer Polytechnic Institute M
Robert Morris University M,D
Rochester Institute of Technology M,D
Rutgers University - New Brunswick M
Sacred Heart University M
St. John's University (NY)
St. Mary's University (United States) M
Sam Houston State University M,D
Shippensburg University of Pennsylvania M,O
Southern Methodist University M,D
Southern States University M
State University of New York Polytechnic Institute M
Stevens Institute of Technology M,O
Strayer University M
Syracuse University M,D
Temple University M,D*
Texas Woman's University M
Thomas Edison State University M,O
Towson University M,D,O
Trevecca Nazarene University M,O
Université de Sherbrooke M,D
University at Albany, State University of New York M,D
The University of Alabama at Birmingham M,D
University of Arkansas at Little Rock M,D,O
University of California, Irvine M,D
University of California, Merced M,D
University of Central Missouri M,D,O
University of Cincinnati M,O
University of Colorado Boulder D
University of Colorado Denver M,D
University of Delaware M,D
University of Denver M,O
University of Fairfax M,D
University of Florida M,D
University of Hawaii at Manoa M,D
University of Houston M,D
University of Houston–Clear Lake M
University of Illinois at Urbana-Champaign M,D,O
The University of Iowa M,D,O
University of Kentucky M,D
University of Maine M,D,O
University of Maryland, Baltimore County M,D
University of Maryland Global Campus M
University of Michigan M,D
University of Michigan–Dearborn M,D
University of Michigan–Flint M
University of Nebraska at Omaha M,D,O
University of Nebraska–Lincoln M,D
University of North Alabama M
The University of North Carolina at Charlotte M,O
University of North Texas M,D,O
University of Oregon M,D
University of Ottawa M,O
University of Pennsylvania M,D
University of Pittsburgh M,D,O*
University of Puerto Rico at Mayagüez M,D
University of Puerto Rico at Rio Piedras M,O
University of St. Thomas (MN) M,O
University of South Africa M,D
University of South Carolina Upstate M
University of Southern Mississippi M,O
University of South Florida M
The University of Tennessee M,D
The University of Texas at El Paso M,D,O
The University of Texas at San Antonio M,D,O
University of the Sacred Heart O
University of Washington M,D
University of Waterloo M,D
University of Wisconsin–Parkside M
University of Wisconsin–Stout M
Western Governors University M
Youngstown State University M

## INFORMATION STUDIES

The Catholic University of America M,O
Central Connecticut State University M
Columbia University M
Cornell University D
Dalhousie University M
Dominican University M,D,O
Florida State University M,D,O
Lock Haven University of Pennsylvania M
Louisiana State University and Agricultural & Mechanical College M
Mansfield University of Pennsylvania M
McGill University M,D,O
Metropolitan State University M,D,O
Monmouth University M
North Carolina Central University M
Pratt Institute M,O
Queens College of the City University of New York M,O
Queen's University at Kingston M,D
Rutgers University - New Brunswick M,D
St. Catherine University M
St. John's University (NY) M,O
Southern Connecticut State University M,O
Syracuse University M
Universidad del Turabo M
Université de Montréal M,D
University at Buffalo, the State University of New York M,O
The University of Alabama M,D
The University of Alberta M
The University of Arizona M,D
The University of British Columbia M,D
University of California, Berkeley M,D
University of California, Los Angeles M,D,O
University of Hawaii at Manoa M,O
University of Illinois at Urbana-Champaign M,D,O
The University of Iowa M,D
University of Maryland, College Park M,D
University of Michigan M,D
University of Missouri D
The University of North Carolina at Chapel Hill M,D,O
The University of North Carolina at Greensboro M
University of Oklahoma M,D,O
University of Puerto Rico at Rio Piedras M,O
University of Rhode Island M
University of South Carolina M,D,O
University of South Florida M,O
The University of Texas at Austin M,D
University of Toronto M,D
The University of Western Ontario M,D
University of Wisconsin–Madison M,D
University of Wisconsin–Milwaukee M,D,O*
Valdosta State University M
Wayne State University M,O

## INORGANIC CHEMISTRY

Auburn University M,D
Binghamton University, State University of New York M,D
Boston College M,D
Brandeis University M,D
Cornell University D
Florida State University M,D
Georgetown University D
The George Washington University M,D
Harvard University D*
Howard University M,D
Illinois Institute of Technology M,D
Indiana University Bloomington M,D
Iowa State University of Science and Technology M,D
Marquette University M,D
Massachusetts Institute of Technology D
McMaster University M,D
Old Dominion University M,D
Purdue University M,D
Rice University M,D
Rutgers University - Newark M,D
Rutgers University - New Brunswick M,D
Seton Hall University M,D
Southern University and Agricultural and Mechanical College M
University of Calgary M,D
University of Cincinnati M,D
University of Louisville M,D
The University of Manchester M,D
University of Maryland, College Park M,D
University of Massachusetts Lowell M,D
University of Memphis M,D
University of Miami M,D
University of Michigan M,D
University of Missouri–Kansas City M,D
University of Montana M,D
University of Nebraska–Lincoln M,D
University of Notre Dame M,D
University of Oklahoma M,D
University of Regina M,D
University of Rochester D
The University of Tennessee M,D
The University of Texas at Austin D
The University of Toledo M,D
Virginia Commonwealth University M,D
Wake Forest University M,D
Wesleyan University D
Yale University D
Youngstown State University M

## INSURANCE

California State University, Fullerton M
Florida State University M,D
Georgia State University M,D,O
Olivet College M
Pontificia Universidad Catolica Madre y Maestra M
St. John's University (NY) M
Temple University D*
University of Colorado Denver M
University of Florida M,D,O
University of Pennsylvania M,D
University of Wisconsin–Madison M,D

| | |
|---|---|
| Western Michigan University Cooley Law School | M,D |

## INTELLECTUAL PROPERTY LAW

| | |
|---|---|
| Case Western Reserve University | M,D |
| DePaul University | M,D |
| Drexel University | M,D |
| Fordham University | M,D |
| Golden Gate University | M,D |
| Hofstra University | M,D,O |
| Indiana University-Purdue University Indianapolis | M,D,O |
| Michigan State University College of Law | M,D |
| Montclair State University | M,O |
| Santa Clara University | M,D,O |
| Suffolk University | M,D |
| Texas A&M University | M,D |
| University of Baltimore | M,D |
| University of Houston | M,D |
| University of New Hampshire | M,D,O |
| University of Pittsburgh | M* |
| University of San Francisco | M |
| University of Washington | M,D |
| Western Michigan University Cooley Law School | M,D |
| Yeshiva University | M,D |

## INTERDISCIPLINARY STUDIES

| | |
|---|---|
| Alaska Pacific University | M |
| Amberton University | M |
| Antioch University New England | M,D |
| Arizona State University at Tempe | M |
| Athabasca University | M,O |
| Baylor University | D |
| Boise State University | M |
| Bowling Green State University | M,D |
| Buffalo State College, State University of New York | M |
| California State University, East Bay | M |
| California State University, San Bernardino | M |
| California State University, Stanislaus | M |
| Cambridge College | M,D,O |
| Campbell University | M |
| Central Washington University | M |
| The Citadel, The Military College of South Carolina | M,O |
| Clarkson University | M,D |
| Colorado State University | M,D |
| Concordia University (Canada) | M,D |
| Dalhousie University | D |
| Dallas Baptist University | M |
| DePaul University | M |
| Eastern Washington University | M |
| Emory University | D |
| Fitchburg State University | O |
| Florida Gulf Coast University | M |
| Florida Institute of Technology | M |
| Fresno Pacific University | M |
| Frostburg State University | M,D |
| George Mason University | M |
| Georgetown University | M,D |
| Goddard College | M* |
| Grand Rapids Theological Seminary of Cornerstone University | M |
| Harrison Middleton University | M,D |
| Hiram College | M |
| Hollins University | M |
| Indiana University Southeast | M,O |
| Iowa State University of Science and Technology | M |
| Kansas State University | M,O |
| Lehigh University | M,D |
| Lesley University | M,D,O |
| Long Island University - Post | M,D,O |
| Marquette University | D |
| Marywood University | D |
| Massachusetts College of Art and Design | M,O |
| Michigan Technological University | M,D,O |
| Mills College | M,O |
| Minnesota State University Mankato | M |
| Montana State University Billings | M |
| Montana Technological University | M |
| Murray State University | M,O |
| New Mexico State University | M,D |
| New York University | M |
| Niagara University | M |
| Northeastern University | M,D,O |
| Nova Southeastern University | M,D,O |
| The Ohio State University | M,D |
| Oregon State University | M |
| Regent University | M,D,O |
| Rensselaer Polytechnic Institute | M,D |
| Rochester Institute of Technology | M |
| Rosalind Franklin University of Medicine and Science | D |
| Rutgers University - New Brunswick | D |
| San Diego State University | M |
| Sonoma State University | M |
| Southern Illinois University Edwardsville | M |
| Southern Oregon University | M |
| Southern Utah University | M |
| State University of New York at Fredonia | M,O |
| Stephen F. Austin State University | M |
| Teachers College, Columbia University | M,D |
| Texas A&M University–Texarkana | M |
| Texas State University | M |
| Texas Tech University | M,D |
| Trinity Western University | M |
| Tufts University | D |
| Tulane University | D |
| UNB Fredericton | M,D |
| Union Institute & University | D |
| University at Buffalo, the State University of New York | M |
| University of Alaska Fairbanks | M,D |
| The University of Arizona | M,D |
| University of Arkansas at Little Rock | M |
| University of California, Santa Barbara | D |
| University of California, Santa Cruz | M,D |
| University of Central Florida | M,O |
| University of Central Oklahoma | M |
| University of Cincinnati | D |
| University of Colorado Colorado Springs | M |
| University of Dayton | M |
| University of Florida | M,D |
| University of Houston–Victoria | M |
| University of Idaho | M |
| University of Illinois at Chicago | D |
| University of Illinois at Springfield | M |
| University of Illinois at Urbana-Champaign | D |
| The University of Kansas | D |
| University of Louisville | M,D |
| University of Maine | M,D |
| University of Manitoba | M,D |
| University of Massachusetts Medical School | M,D |
| University of Memphis | M,D,O |
| University of Minnesota, Twin Cities Campus | D |
| University of Missouri–Kansas City | D |
| University of Missouri–St. Louis | O |
| University of Montana | M,D |
| University of North Alabama | M |
| The University of North Carolina at Charlotte | M,D,O |
| University of Northern British Columbia | M,D,O |
| University of North Texas | M,D,O |
| University of Oregon | M |
| University of Ottawa | D,O |
| University of Pittsburgh | D* |
| University of Regina | M |
| University of South Dakota | M |
| University of South Florida | M,D |
| The University of Tennessee at Martin | M |
| The University of Texas at Dallas | M |
| The University of Texas at El Paso | M |
| The University of Texas at San Antonio | M,D |
| The University of Texas at Tyler | M |
| The University of Texas Health Science Center at San Antonio | D |
| The University of Texas Rio Grande Valley | M |
| University of Vermont | M |
| University of Virginia | M,D |
| University of Washington, Tacoma | M |
| The University of Western Ontario | M,D |
| Virginia Commonwealth University | M |
| Virginia Polytechnic Institute and State University | M,D |
| Virginia State University | M |
| Walden University | M,D,O |
| Washington State University | D |
| Western Kentucky University | M,O |
| Western New Mexico University | M |
| West Texas A&M University | M |
| Worcester Polytechnic Institute | M,D,O |
| York University | M |

## INTERIOR DESIGN

| | |
|---|---|
| Academy of Art University | M |
| Ball State University | M |
| Boston Architectural College | M |
| Brenau University | M |
| California State Polytechnic University, Pomona | M |
| Chatham University | M |
| Cornell University | M |
| Drexel University | M |
| Eastern Michigan University | M |
| Endicott College | M |
| Florida International University | M,O |
| Florida State University | M |
| The George Washington University | M |
| Georgia State University | M |
| Interior Designers Institute | M |
| Iowa State University of Science and Technology | M |
| Kansas State University | M |
| Lawrence Technological University | M,O |
| Marymount University | M |
| Marywood University | M |
| Miami University | M |
| Michigan State University | M,D |
| Moore College of Art & Design | M |
| The New School | M |
| New York School of Interior Design | M |
| The Ohio State University | M |
| Paris College of Art | M |
| Pontificia Universidad Catolica Madre y Maestra | M |
| Pratt Institute | M |
| Purdue University | M,D |
| Queens University of Charlotte | M |
| Rhode Island School of Design | M |
| San Diego State University | M |
| Savannah College of Art and Design | M |
| Suffolk University | M |
| Texas Tech University | M,D |
| Thomas Jefferson University | M |
| University of California, Berkeley | O |
| University of Cincinnati | M |
| University of Florida | M,D |
| University of Georgia | M,D |
| University of Kentucky | M |
| University of Manitoba | M |
| University of Massachusetts Amherst | M |
| University of Minnesota, Twin Cities Campus | M,D,O |
| University of Nebraska–Lincoln | M,D |
| The University of North Carolina at Greensboro | M,O |
| University of North Texas | M,D,O |
| University of Oklahoma | M,O |
| University of Oregon | M |
| The University of Texas at Austin | M |
| Virginia Commonwealth University | M,D |
| Washington State University | M |
| Wayne State University | M |

## INTERNATIONAL AFFAIRS

| | |
|---|---|
| American Graduate School in Paris | M,D |
| American Public University System | M,D |
| American University | M,D,O |
| The American University in Cairo | M,O |
| American University of Armenia | M |
| The American University of Paris | M |
| Anabaptist Mennonite Biblical Seminary | M,O |
| Baruch College of the City University of New York | M |
| Baylor University | M |
| Boston University | M |
| Brigham Young University | M |
| Brock University | M |
| Brooklyn College of the City University of New York | M |
| Carleton University | M,D |
| The Catholic University of America | M,D |
| Central Connecticut State University | M |
| Central European University | M,D |
| Central Michigan University | M,O |
| Chapman University | M |
| City College of the City University of New York | M |
| Claremont Graduate University | M,D |
| Cleveland State University | M |
| Columbia University | M,D |
| Concordia University Irvine | M |
| Cornell University | D |
| Dallas Baptist University | M |
| DePaul University | M |
| East Carolina University | M,O |
| Embry-Riddle Aeronautical University–Worldwide | M |
| Fairleigh Dickinson University, Metropolitan Campus | M |
| Florida International University | M,D |
| Florida State University | M |
| Fordham University | M,O |
| George Mason University | M |
| Georgetown University | M,D |
| The George Washington University | M,D |
| Georgia Institute of Technology | M |
| Harvard University | D* |
| Indiana University Bloomington | M |
| Indiana University South Bend | M,O |
| The Institute of World Politics | M,D,O |
| Instituto Tecnologico de Santo Domingo | M,O |
| Instituto Tecnológico y de Estudios Superiores de Monterrey, Campus Ciudad Obregón | M |
| International University in Geneva | M,D |
| Johns Hopkins University | M,D,O |
| Kennesaw State University | M |
| Lebanese American University | M |
| Lesley University | M,D,O |
| Liberty University | M,D |
| Lipscomb University | M,O |
| London Metropolitan University | M,D |
| Marquette University | M,D |
| McMaster University | M,D |
| Middlebury Institute of International Studies at Monterey | M |
| Middle Tennessee State University | M |
| Missouri State University | M |
| Morgan State University | M |
| New England College | M |
| The New School | M |
| New York University | M,D |
| North Carolina State University | M |
| Northeastern University | M,D |
| Northwestern University | M,D,O |
| Norwich University | M |
| Ohio University | M |
| Oklahoma State University | M,D,O |
| Old Dominion University | M,D |
| Penn State University Park | M* |
| Pepperdine University | M |
| Pontificia Universidad Catolica Madre y Maestra | M |
| Portland State University | M |
| Princeton University | M,D |
| Queen's University at Kingston | M,D |
| Regent's University London | M |
| Regent University | M |
| Richmond, The American International University in London | M |
| Rutgers University - Camden | M |
| Rutgers University - Newark | M,D |
| Rutgers University - New Brunswick | M,D |
| St. Mary's University (United States) | M,O |
| Salve Regina University | M,D,O |
| San Francisco State University | M |
| Schiller International University - Paris | M |
| Seton Hall University | M,O |
| Simon Fraser University | M |
| SIT Graduate Institute | M |
| Syracuse University | M |
| Teachers College, Columbia University | M,D,O |
| Texas A&M University | M,O |
| Texas State University | M |
| Troy University | M |
| Tufts University | M,D |
| United States International University–Africa | M |
| Universidad de las Americas, A.C. | M |
| Universidad Nacional Pedro Henriquez Urena | M |
| Université de Montréal | M,O |
| University of Bridgeport | M |
| The University of British Columbia | M |
| University of California, Berkeley | M |
| University of California, San Diego | M,D |
| University of California, Santa Barbara | M,D |
| University of California, Santa Cruz | D |
| University of Chicago | M |
| University of Colorado Denver | M,O |
| University of Connecticut | M |
| University of Delaware | M,D |
| University of Denver | M,D,O |
| University of Florida | M |
| University of Georgia | M,D |
| University of Hawaii at Manoa | O |
| University of Indianapolis | M |
| The University of Kansas | M |
| University of Kentucky | M |
| University of Maine | M |
| The University of Manchester | D |
| University of Massachusetts Boston | M |
| University of Miami | M,D |
| University of Michigan–Flint | M |
| The University of North Carolina at Chapel Hill | M |
| University of Northern British Columbia | M,D,O |
| University of North Georgia | M |
| University of North Texas | M,D,O |
| University of Notre Dame | M |
| University of Oklahoma | M |
| University of Oregon | M |
| University of Pennsylvania | M |
| University of Pittsburgh | M,D,O* |
| University of San Diego | M |
| University of San Francisco | M |
| University of South Carolina | M,D |
| University of Southern California | M,D |
| University of South Florida | O |
| University of the Pacific | M,D |
| University of Toronto | M |
| University of Utah | M,D |
| University of Virginia | M,D |
| University of Washington | M,D |
| University of Waterloo | M,D |
| University of Wyoming | M |
| Université Laval | M,D |
| Virginia International University | M |
| Virginia Polytechnic Institute and State University | M,D |
| Walden University | M,D,O |
| Webster University | M |
| Western Michigan University | M,D |
| Wilfrid Laurier University | M,D |
| Yale University | M |
| York University | M |

## INTERNATIONAL AND COMPARATIVE EDUCATION

| | |
|---|---|
| American University | M,O |
| The American University in Cairo | M |
| Andrews University | M |
| Bowling Green State University | M |
| California Baptist University | M |
| California State University, Dominguez Hills | M |
| The College of New Jersey | M,O |
| Drexel University | M,D |
| East Carolina University | M,O |
| Florida State University | M,D,O |
| Gallaudet University | M,D,O |
| The George Washington University | M,D,O |
| Harvard University | M* |
| Indiana University Bloomington | M,D,O |
| Louisiana State University and Agricultural & Mechanical College | M,D |
| Loyola University Chicago | M,D |
| Middlebury Institute of International Studies at Monterey | M |
| New York University | M,D,O |
| St. John's University (NY) | D |
| SIT Graduate Institute | M |
| Stanford University | M,D |
| Teachers College, Columbia University | M,D |
| University at Albany, State University of New York | M,D,O |
| University of Bridgeport | M,D,O |
| University of Massachusetts Amherst | M,D,O |
| University of Minnesota, Twin Cities Campus | M,D |
| University of Pennsylvania | M |
| University of San Francisco | M,D |
| University of South Africa | M,D |
| University of Wisconsin–Madison | M,D,O |
| Walden University | M,D,O |

## INTERNATIONAL BUSINESS

| | |
|---|---|
| Abilene Christian University | M |
| Amberton University | M |
| American Business & Technology University | M |

*M—masters degree; D—doctorate; O—other advanced degree; *—Close-Up and/or Display*

American College Dublin M
American InterContinental University Atlanta M
American InterContinental University Online M
The American University in Dubai M
The American University of Paris M
Anaheim University M,D,O
Argosy University, Atlanta M,D
Argosy University, Chicago M,D
Argosy University, Hawaii M,D,O
Argosy University, Los Angeles M,D
Argosy University, Northern Virginia M,D,O
Argosy University, Orange County M,D,O
Argosy University, Phoenix M,D
Argosy University, Seattle M,D
Argosy University, Tampa M,D
Argosy University, Twin Cities M,D
Arizona State University at Tempe M,D
Ashland University M
Ashworth College M
Assumption University M,O
Azusa Pacific University M
Barry University O
Baruch College of the City University of New York M,D
Benedictine University M
Boston University M
Brandeis University M,D
Brandman University M
Brooklyn College of the City University of New York M
California Intercontinental University M,D
California Lutheran University M,O
California State University, Fullerton M
California State University, Los Angeles M
California State University, San Bernardino M
California University of Management and Sciences M,D
Canisius College M
Central European University M,D
Central Michigan University M,O
Christian Brothers University M,O
City University of Seattle M,O
Clarkson University M,O
Clayton State University M
Colorado State University–Global Campus M
Columbia University M
Concordia University Wisconsin M
Copenhagen Business School M,D
Daemen College M
Dallas Baptist University M
Delaware Valley University M
DePaul University M,D
D'Youville College M
Eastern Michigan University M,O
Embry-Riddle Aeronautical University–Worldwide M
Emory University M
ESSEC Business School M,D
Fairleigh Dickinson University, Florham Campus M,O
Fairleigh Dickinson University, Metropolitan Campus M
Florida Atlantic University M
Florida Institute of Technology M
Florida International University M,D
George Mason University M,O
Georgetown University M,D
The George Washington University M,D
Georgia State University M,D
Golden Gate University M,D,O
Goldey-Beacom College M
Hallmark University M
Harding University M
Hawaii Pacific University M
HEC Montreal M,D
Hofstra University M,O
Hope International University M
Houston Baptist University M
Howard University M
Hult International Business School (United States) M
IGlobal University M
Indiana Tech D
Instituto Tecnologico de Santo Domingo M,O
Instituto Tecnológico y de Estudios Superiores de Monterrey, Campus Central de Veracruz M
Instituto Tecnológico y de Estudios Superiores de Monterrey, Campus Chihuahua M,O
Instituto Tecnológico y de Estudios Superiores de Monterrey, Campus Ciudad de México M,D
Instituto Tecnológico y de Estudios Superiores de Monterrey, Campus Cuernavaca M
Instituto Tecnológico y de Estudios Superiores de Monterrey, Campus Irapuato M,D
Instituto Tecnológico y de Estudios Superiores de Monterrey, Campus Monterrey M
Inter American University of Puerto Rico, Metropolitan Campus M,D
Inter American University of Puerto Rico, San Germán Campus M,D
International University in Geneva M,D
The International University of Monaco M
Iona College M,O
John Brown University M
Kean University M
Keiser University M,D
Lake Forest Graduate School of Management M
La Salle University M,O
Lenoir-Rhyne University M
Lewis University M
Liberty University M,D
Lincoln University (CA) M,D
Long Island University - Post M
Loyola University Chicago M
Madonna University M
Maine Maritime Academy M
Marconi International University M,D
Marquette University M,O
McGill University M,D,O
McKendree University M
Midwest University M,D
Milwaukee School of Engineering M
National American University (TX) M,D
National University M,O
Nebraska Christian College of Hope International University M
Newman University M
New Mexico Highlands University M
New York University M,D
Niagara University M
Northeastern University M
Northern Arizona University M
Northwest University M
Norwich University M
Nova Southeastern University M
Oakland University M,O
Oklahoma Christian University M
Oklahoma State University M,D
Old Dominion University M
Oral Roberts University M
Pace University M,O
Pacific States University M,O
Park University M,O
Pittsburg State University M
Point Park University M
Polytechnic University of Puerto Rico M
Polytechnic University of Puerto Rico, Miami Campus M
Polytechnic University of Puerto Rico, Orlando Campus M
Pontifical Catholic University of Puerto Rico M
Pontificia Universidad Catolica Madre y Maestra M
Providence College M
Purdue University M
Purdue University Global M
Queen's University at Kingston M
Regent's University London M
Rochester Institute of Technology M
Rockhurst University M,O
Rollins College M
Rutgers University - Newark D
St. John's University (NY) M
Saint Joseph's University M,O
Saint Louis University M,D
Saint Peter's University M
St. Thomas University - Florida M,O
Salem International University M
San Francisco State University M
San Ignacio University M
Schiller International University - Heidelberg M
Schiller International University - Madrid M
Schiller International University - Paris M
Schiller International University - Tampa M
Seton Hall University M,O
SIT Graduate Institute M
Southeastern University (FL) M,D
Southern New Hampshire University M,D,O
Southern Oregon University M,O
State University of New York Empire State College M
Stevens Institute of Technology M
Suffolk University M
Temple University M,D*
Tennessee Technological University M
Texas A&M International University M,D
Texas A&M University–Corpus Christi M
Thomas Edison State University M
Tiffin University M
Trident University International M,D
Trinity Western University M
Tufts University M,D
Tulane University M,D
United States International University–Africa M
Universidad Autonoma de Guadalajara M,D
Universidad Metropolitana M
Université de Sherbrooke M
Université du Québec, École nationale d'administration publique M,O
University at Buffalo, the State University of New York M,D
University of Alberta M
University of Baltimore M
University of Bridgeport M
University of California, Berkeley O
University of California, San Diego M
University of Chicago M,O
University of Colorado Denver M
University of Dallas M,D
University of Florida M,D
University of Hawaii at Manoa M,D
University of Houston - Downtown M
University of Houston–Victoria M
University of Kentucky M
University of La Verne M
University of Lethbridge M,D
University of Louisiana at Lafayette M
University of Louisville M
The University of Manchester M
University of Mary Hardin-Baylor M
University of Massachusetts Boston M
University of Miami M,D
University of Michigan–Flint M,O
University of New Brunswick Saint John M
University of New Haven M
University of New Mexico M
University of North Alabama M
The University of North Carolina Wilmington M
University of North Florida M
University of Pennsylvania M
University of Phoenix - Bay Area Campus M,D
University of Phoenix - Central Valley Campus M
University of Phoenix - Dallas Campus M
University of Phoenix - Hawaii Campus M
University of Phoenix - Houston Campus M
University of Phoenix - Las Vegas Campus M
University of Phoenix–Online Campus M,O
University of Phoenix - Phoenix Campus M,O
University of Phoenix - Sacramento Valley Campus M
University of Phoenix - San Antonio Campus M
University of Phoenix - San Diego Campus M
University of Pittsburgh O*
University of Puerto Rico at Rio Piedras M,D
University of Regina M,O
University of St. Thomas (TX) M
University of San Diego M
University of San Francisco M
The University of Scranton M
University of South Carolina M
The University of Tampa M,O
The University of Texas at Dallas M,D
The University of Texas at El Paso M,D,O
University of the West M
The University of Toledo M
University of Virginia M,O
University of Washington M,D,O
The University of Western Ontario M,D
University of Wisconsin–Oshkosh M
Université Laval M,O
Vancouver Island University M
Villanova University M
Virginia International University M,O
Viterbo University M
Walden University M,D,O
Walsh College of Accountancy and Business Administration M
Warner University M
Wayland Baptist University M,D
Webber International University M
Webster University M
Xavier University M*
York University M,D

## INTERNATIONAL DEVELOPMENT

American University M,D,O
Andrews University M
Athabasca University M,O
Clark University M
Dalhousie University M
Duke University M
Fordham University M,O
Georgetown University M
The George Washington University M,D
Harvard University M*
Hope International University M
Indiana University Bloomington M,D,O
Johns Hopkins University M,D,O
Marymount California University M
McGill University M,D,O
Middlebury Institute of International Studies at Monterey M
Norwich University M
Ohio University M
Old Dominion University M,D
Rutgers University - Camden M
Saint Mary's University (Canada) M,O
St. Mary's University (United States) M,O
Tufts University M
University of California, San Diego M
University of Denver M,D,O
University of Florida M,D,O
University of Guelph M,D
University of Hawaii at Manoa M,D,O
The University of Manchester M,D
University of Massachusetts Boston M,D
University of Minnesota, Twin Cities Campus M
University of New Mexico M,D
University of Ottawa M
University of Pittsburgh M,D*
University of San Francisco M
Walden University M,D,O

## INTERNATIONAL ECONOMICS

American University M,D,O
Baruch College of the City University of New York M
Claremont Graduate University M,D,O
Cleveland State University M
Fordham University M,D,O
Fordham University M,D,O
The Institute of World Politics M,D,O
Johns Hopkins University M,D,O
The New School M,D
Pace University O
University of California, San Diego M
University of New Mexico M,D
Valparaiso University M
Wayne State University M,D
Wichita State University M
Wilfrid Laurier University M
Yale University M

## INTERNATIONAL HEALTH

Arizona State University at Tempe M,D,O
A.T. Still University M,D,O
Brandeis University M,D
Cedarville University M,D
Central Michigan University M,D,O
Clark University M
Clemson University M,D,O
The College of New Jersey M
Duke University M
East Tennessee State University M,D,O
Emory University M
Endicott College M,O
George Mason University M,O
Georgetown University M,D
The George Washington University M,D
Harvard University M,D*
Indiana University-Purdue University Indianapolis M,D,O
Johns Hopkins University M,D
Liberty University M,D
Loma Linda University M
Medical University of South Carolina M
National University of Natural Medicine M
New York Institute of Technology O
New York Medical College M,D,O
New York University M,D
Northwestern University M
Oregon State University M,D
Park University M,O
St. Catherine University M
San Diego State University M,D
Seton Hall University M,O
Simon Fraser University M,D,O
Syracuse University M
Trident University International M,D,O
Tulane University M,D
Uniformed Services University of the Health Sciences M,D
University of Alberta M,D
University of California, Riverside M,D
University of California, San Diego D
University of Colorado Denver M
University of Denver M,D,O
University of Florida M,D
University of Maryland, Baltimore M,D,O
University of Michigan M,D
University of Minnesota, Twin Cities Campus M,D
University of Missouri M,O
University of Northern Colorado M
University of North Texas Health Science Center at Fort Worth M,D,O
University of Pennsylvania M
University of Pittsburgh M,D,O*
University of Southern California M,O
University of South Florida O
The University of Toledo M,O
University of Vermont M,O
University of Washington M,D
Walden University M,D,O
Washington University in St. Louis M,D
William James College M,D,O
Yale University M,D

## INTERNATIONAL TRADE POLICY

Baruch College of the City University of New York M
The George Washington University M
Middlebury Institute of International Studies at Monterey M
University at Buffalo, the State University of New York M,D
Valparaiso University M

## INTERNET AND INTERACTIVE MULTIMEDIA

Academy of Art University M
Agnes Scott College M
Alfred University M
Ball State University M
Boston University M,O
Brandeis University M
Brooklyn College of the City University of New York M
California State University, East Bay M
Champlain College M
College of Saint Elizabeth M
Concordia University (Canada) M,D,O
DePaul University M,D
Elon University M
Fairfield University M,O
Full Sail University M
Georgetown University M
Georgia Institute of Technology M,D
Ithaca College M
Kutztown University of Pennsylvania M
Liberty University M
Lindenwood University M
Lindenwood University–Belleville M
Lindsey Wilson College M
London Metropolitan University M,D
Long Island University - Post M
Louisiana State University and Agricultural & Mechanical College M
Lynn University M,O
Minneapolis College of Art and Design M

Montclair State University M
Mount Mary University M
National University M
New Mexico Highlands University M
The New School M
New York University M
Northeastern University M
Northwestern University M
The Ohio State University M
Ohio University M
Pace University M
Pratt Institute M
Quinnipiac University M
Rochester Institute of Technology O
Rocky Mountain College of Art + Design M
Sam Houston State University M
San Diego State University M
Savannah College of Art and Design M
School of Visual Arts (NY) M
Southern New Hampshire University M,D,O
State University of New York at Oswego M
Stonehill College M
Texas Woman's University M
Thomas Jefferson University M
Touro College M
Towson University M,O
Universidad Autonoma de Guadalajara M,D
University of Advancing Technology M
The University of British Columbia M
University of California, Santa Cruz M,D
University of Chicago M
University of Colorado Boulder D
University of Miami M
University of Montana M
University of North Texas M,D,O
University of Pennsylvania M,O
University of Southern California M,D,O
University of South Florida O
The University of Tennessee M,D
The University of Texas at Dallas M,O
University of the Sacred Heart M,O
University of Utah M,D
Virginia Polytechnic Institute and State University M,D
Walla Walla University M
Webster University M
Wilmington University M
Worcester Polytechnic Institute M

## INTERNET ENGINEERING

Dalhousie University M,D
New Jersey Institute of Technology M,D
Wilmington University M

## INVESTMENT MANAGEMENT

Alaska Pacific University M,O
Creighton University M,D
Fordham University M,D
The George Washington University M,D
Hofstra University M,O
Johns Hopkins University M,O
Lincoln University (CA) M,D
Loyola University Maryland M
Manhattanville College M,O
Marywood University M,D
Midwest University M,D
New York University M
Pace University M,O
Regent University M,D,O
Sacred Heart University M,D,O
Saint Mary's College of California M
Southern New Hampshire University M,D,O
Temple University M,O*
University of Houston - Downtown M
The University of North Carolina Wilmington M
University of Notre Dame M
University of Wisconsin–Madison D
University of Wisconsin–Milwaukee M,O*
Walsh College of Accountancy and Business Administration M

## ITALIAN

Binghamton University, State University of New York M
Boston College M
Brown University D
Central Connecticut State University M,O
Columbia University M,D
Cornell University D
DePaul University M
Drew University M,D,O
Duke University D
Florida State University M
The Graduate Center, City University of New York M,D
Harvard University M,D*
Hunter College of the City University of New York M
Indiana University Bloomington M,D
Johns Hopkins University M,D
McGill University M,D
Middlebury College M,D
New York University M,D,O
Northwestern University D,O
The Ohio State University M,D
Queens College of the City University of New York M
Rutgers University - New Brunswick M,D
San Francisco State University M
Stanford University M,D
Stony Brook University, State University of New York M
University of Alberta M,D
University of California, Berkeley D
University of California, Los Angeles M,D
University of Chicago D
University of Georgia M,D
University of Illinois at Urbana-Champaign M,D
University of Massachusetts Amherst M
University of Michigan D
The University of North Carolina at Chapel Hill M,D
University of Notre Dame M
University of Oregon M
University of Pennsylvania M,D
University of Pittsburgh M,D*
University of South Africa M,D
The University of Tennessee D
The University of Texas at Austin M,D
University of Toronto M,D
University of Victoria M
University of Washington M,D
University of Wisconsin–Madison M,D
Wayne State University M,D
Yale University D

## JAPANESE

Arizona State University at Tempe M
Columbia University M,D
DePaul University M
Harvard University D*
Indiana University Bloomington M,D
Kent State University M,D
New York University M,D,O
The Ohio State University M,D
Portland State University M
Purdue University M
San Francisco State University M
Stanford University M,D
University of Alberta M
University of California, Berkeley D
University of California, Irvine M,D
University of Colorado Boulder M,D
University of Hawaii at Manoa M,D,O
The University of Manchester D
University of Massachusetts Amherst M
University of Oregon M,D
University of Pittsburgh M*
University of Washington M,D
University of Wisconsin–Madison M,D
Washington University in St. Louis M,D

## JEWISH STUDIES

Academy for Jewish Religion California M
American Jewish University M
Biola University M,D,O
Brandeis University M,D
Brooklyn College of the City University of New York M
Central Yeshiva Tomchei Tmimim-Lubavitch M
Columbia University M,D
Concordia University (Canada) M
Cornell University M,D
Criswell College M
Dallas Theological Seminary M,D,O
Graduate Theological Union M,D,O
Gratz College M,O
Harvard University M,D*
Hebrew College M,O
Hebrew Union College–Jewish Institute of Religion (NY) M
Indiana University Bloomington M
The Jewish Theological Seminary M,D
McGill University M
New York University M,D
Reconstructionist Rabbinical College M,D,O
Rice University D
Rutgers University - New Brunswick M,O
Seton Hall University M,O
Southern Evangelical Seminary M,D,O
Spertus Institute for Jewish Learning and Leadership M,D
Telshe Yeshiva - Chicago O
Towson University M,O
University of California, San Diego M,D
University of Connecticut M,D
University of Florida M,D
University of Maryland, College Park M
University of Michigan M,D,O
University of St. Michael's College M,D,O
University of Wisconsin–Madison M,D
Washington University in St. Louis M
Yeshiva University M,D

## JOURNALISM

American University M
The American University in Cairo M,O
Arizona State University at Tempe M,D
Arkansas State University M
Arkansas Tech University M
Ball State University M
Baylor University M
Boston University M
California State University, Northridge M
Carleton University M,D
Columbia University M,D
Concordia University (Canada) M,O
CUNY Craig Newmark Graduate School of Journalism M
DePaul University M
Florida Agricultural and Mechanical University M
Florida International University M
Full Sail University M
Georgetown University M,D
Harvard University M,O*
Hofstra University M
Iowa State University of Science and Technology M
Kansas State University M
Kent State University M
Lindenwood University M
Marquette University M,O
Marshall University M,O
Michigan State University M
Morgan State University M
Murray State University M
National University M
New York University M,D,O
Northeastern University M
Northwestern University M
Ohio University M,D
Point Park University M
Quinnipiac University M
Regent University M,D
Sacred Heart University M
South Dakota State University M
Southeastern Louisiana University M
Stony Brook University, State University of New York M,O
Syracuse University M
Temple University M*
The University of Alabama M
The University of Arizona M
University of Arkansas M
The University of British Columbia M
University of California, Berkeley M
University of Colorado Boulder M,D
University of Florida M,D
University of Georgia M,D
University of Illinois at Springfield M
University of Illinois at Urbana-Champaign M
The University of Iowa M,D
The University of Kansas M,D
University of King's College M
University of Maryland, College Park M,D
University of Memphis M,O
University of Miami M,D
University of Mississippi M
University of Missouri M,D
University of Montana M
University of Nebraska–Lincoln M
University of Nevada, Las Vegas M
University of Nevada, Reno M
The University of North Carolina at Chapel Hill M,D,O
University of North Texas M,D,O
University of Oregon M,D
University of Puerto Rico at Rio Piedras M
University of Regina M
University of South Carolina M,D
University of Southern California M
University of South Florida O
University of South Florida, St. Petersburg M
The University of Tennessee M,D
The University of Texas at Austin M,D
The University of Western Ontario M
University of Wisconsin–Madison M,D
Université Laval O
Virginia Commonwealth University M
Wayne State University M,D,O
West Virginia University M,O

## KINESIOLOGY AND MOVEMENT STUDIES

Alabama Agricultural and Mechanical University M
A.T. Still University M,D,O
Azusa Pacific University M
Ball State University M,D,O
Barry University M
Baylor University M,D
Boise State University M
Bowling Green State University M
Brooklyn College of the City University of New York M
California Polytechnic State University, San Luis Obispo M
California State Polytechnic University, Pomona M
California State University, Chico M
California State University, Fresno M
California State University, Long Beach M
California State University, Los Angeles M,O
California State University, Northridge M
Canisius College M
Columbia University M,D
Dalhousie University M
Dallas Baptist University M
East Carolina University M,D,O
Eastern Illinois University M
Eastern Michigan University M
East Tennessee State University M,D
East Texas Baptist University M
Fresno Pacific University M
Georgia College & State University M
Georgia Southern University M
Georgia State University D
Hardin-Simmons University M
Houston Baptist University M
Humboldt State University M
Indiana University Bloomington M,D
Indiana University-Purdue University Indianapolis M,O
Inter American University of Puerto Rico, San Germán Campus M
Iowa State University of Science and Technology M,D
Jacksonville University M
James Madison University M
Kansas State University M,D
Lakehead University M
Lamar University M
Louisiana State University and Agricultural & Mechanical College M,D
Louisiana Tech University M,D,O
McDaniel College M
McGill University M,D,O
McMaster University M,D
Memorial University of Newfoundland M
Michigan State University M,D
Michigan Technological University M,D
Mississippi College M
Mississippi State University M,D
Missouri State University M
New Mexico State University D
New York University M,D,O
Northeastern State University M
Northwestern University D
The Ohio State University M,D
Old Dominion University M,D
Oregon State University M,D
Penn State University Park M,D,O*
Point Loma Nazarene University M
Prairie View A&M University M
Purdue University M,D
Saint Mary's College of California M
Sam Houston State University M
San Diego State University M
San Francisco State University M
San Jose State University M
Sarah Lawrence College M
Simon Fraser University M,D
Sonoma State University M
Southeastern Louisiana University M
Southeastern University (FL) M,D
Southern Arkansas University–Magnolia M
Southern Illinois University Carbondale M
Southern Illinois University Edwardsville M
Southwestern Oklahoma State University M
Stephen F. Austin State University M
Syracuse University M,D,O
Tarleton State University M
Teachers College, Columbia University M,D
Temple University M,D*
Tennessee Technological University M
Texas A&M University M,D
Texas A&M University–Commerce M,D,O
Texas A&M University–Corpus Christi M,D
Texas A&M University–Kingsville M
Texas A&M University–San Antonio M
Texas Christian University M
Texas Tech University M
Université de Montréal M,D,O
Université de Sherbrooke M,O
Université du Québec à Montréal M
The University of Alabama M,D
University of Alberta M,D
University of Arkansas M,D
The University of British Columbia M,D
University of Calgary M,D
University of Central Arkansas M
University of Central Florida M
University of Central Missouri M,D,O
University of Colorado Boulder M,D
University of Delaware M,D
University of Florida M,D
University of Georgia M,D
University of Hawaii at Manoa M,D
University of Houston M,D
University of Idaho M,D
University of Illinois at Chicago M,D
University of Illinois at Urbana-Champaign M,D
University of Kentucky M,D
University of Lethbridge M,D
University of Maine M,D,O
University of Manitoba M
University of Mary M
University of Maryland, College Park M,D
University of Massachusetts Amherst M,D
University of Michigan M,D
University of Minnesota, Twin Cities Campus M,D
University of Mississippi M,D
University of Nebraska at Omaha M,D
University of Nevada, Las Vegas M,D
University of New Hampshire M,O
University of North Alabama M
The University of North Carolina at Charlotte M
The University of North Carolina at Greensboro M,D
University of North Dakota M
University of Northern Iowa M
University of North Georgia M
University of North Texas M,D,O

*M—masters degree; D—doctorate; O—other advanced degree; *—Close-Up and/or Display*

| | |
|---|---|
| University of Ottawa | M |
| University of Puerto Rico at Mayagüez | M |
| University of Regina | M,D |
| University of Saskatchewan | M,D |
| University of South Alabama | M |
| University of South Dakota | M |
| University of Southern California | M,D |
| The University of Tennessee | M,D |
| The University of Texas at Arlington | M,D |
| The University of Texas at Austin | M,D |
| The University of Texas at El Paso | M |
| The University of Texas at San Antonio | M |
| The University of Texas at Tyler | M |
| The University of Texas of the Permian Basin | M |
| The University of Texas Rio Grande Valley | M |
| University of the Incarnate Word | M,D |
| University of Toronto | M,D |
| The University of Tulsa | M |
| University of Utah | M,D |
| University of Victoria | M |
| University of Virginia | M,D |
| University of Waterloo | M,D |
| The University of Western Ontario | M,D |
| University of Windsor | M |
| University of Wisconsin–Madison | M,D |
| University of Wisconsin–Milwaukee | M,D* |
| University of Wyoming | M |
| Université Laval | M,D |
| Utah State University | M,D |
| Washington University in St. Louis | D |
| Wayne State University | M,D |
| Western Illinois University | M |
| Wilfrid Laurier University | M |
| York University | M,D |

## LANDSCAPE ARCHITECTURE

| | |
|---|---|
| Academy of Art University | M |
| Arizona State University at Tempe | M,D |
| Auburn University | M |
| Ball State University | M |
| Boston Architectural College | M |
| California State Polytechnic University, Pomona | M |
| City College of the City University of New York | M |
| Clemson University | M,D |
| Colorado State University | M,D |
| Columbia University | M |
| The Conway School | M |
| Cornell University | M |
| Florida Agricultural and Mechanical University | M |
| Florida International University | M |
| Harvard University | M,D* |
| Illinois Institute of Technology | M,D |
| Iowa State University of Science and Technology | M |
| Kansas State University | M |
| Kent State University | M |
| Louisiana State University and Agricultural & Mechanical College | M |
| Mississippi State University | M |
| Morgan State University | M |
| North Carolina State University | M |
| North Dakota State University | M |
| The Ohio State University | M,D |
| Oklahoma State University | M,D |
| Penn State University Park | M,D* |
| Polytechnic University of Puerto Rico | M |
| Pontificia Universidad Catolica Madre y Maestra | M |
| Rhode Island School of Design | M |
| Rutgers University - New Brunswick | M |
| State University of New York College of Environmental Science and Forestry | M |
| Texas A&M University | M,D |
| Texas Tech University | M |
| The University of Arizona | M |
| The University of British Columbia | M |
| University of Calgary | M,D |
| University of California, Berkeley | M,D,O |
| University of Colorado Denver | M |
| University of Connecticut | M,D |
| University of Florida | M,D |
| University of Georgia | M |
| University of Guelph | M |
| University of Idaho | M |
| University of Illinois at Urbana-Champaign | M,D |
| The University of Manchester | M,D |
| University of Manitoba | M |
| University of Maryland, College Park | M |
| University of Massachusetts Amherst | M |
| University of Michigan | M |
| University of Minnesota, Twin Cities Campus | M |
| University of New Mexico | M |
| University of Oklahoma | M |
| University of Oregon | M,D |
| University of Pennsylvania | M,O |
| University of Southern California | M |
| The University of Tennessee | M |
| The University of Texas at Arlington | M |
| The University of Texas at Austin | M |
| University of Toronto | M |
| University of Virginia | M |
| University of Washington | M |
| University of Wisconsin–Madison | M,D |
| Utah State University | M |
| Virginia Polytechnic Institute and State University | M,D |
| Washington State University | M |
| Washington University in St. Louis | M |
| West Virginia University | M,D |

## LATIN AMERICAN STUDIES

| | |
|---|---|
| American University | M,O |
| Brown University | M,D |
| California State University, Los Angeles | M |
| Centro de Estudios Avanzados de Puerto Rico y el Caribe | M,D |
| College of Staten Island of the City University of New York | M |
| Columbia University | M,D |
| Cornell University | M,D |
| Duke University | M,D |
| Georgetown University | M |
| The George Washington University | M |
| Georgia State University | M,O |
| Indiana University Bloomington | M |
| La Salle University | M,O |
| Michigan State University | D |
| New York University | M |
| Northeastern Illinois University | M |
| The Ohio State University | M |
| Ohio University | M |
| San Diego State University | M |
| Simon Fraser University | M,O |
| Texas Christian University | M,D |
| Tulane University | M,D |
| University at Albany, State University of New York | M,D,O |
| The University of Arizona | M |
| University of California, Los Angeles | M |
| University of California, San Diego | M |
| University of California, Santa Barbara | M |
| University of Chicago | M |
| University of Connecticut | M |
| University of Florida | M,O |
| University of Illinois at Chicago | M |
| University of Illinois at Urbana-Champaign | M |
| The University of Kansas | M,O |
| University of Louisiana at Lafayette | M |
| The University of Manchester | D |
| University of Massachusetts Dartmouth | M,D |
| University of Miami | M |
| University of New Mexico | M,D |
| The University of North Carolina at Chapel Hill | M,D,O |
| The University of North Carolina at Charlotte | M,D,O |
| University of Notre Dame | M |
| University of Pittsburgh | O* |
| University of Southern California | D |
| University of South Florida | O |
| The University of Texas at Austin | M,D |
| The University of Texas at Dallas | M,D |
| University of Utah | M |
| University of Wisconsin–Madison | M,D |
| University of Wisconsin–Milwaukee | M,O* |
| Vanderbilt University | M* |
| Yale University | D |

## LAW

| | |
|---|---|
| Abraham Lincoln University | D |
| Albany Law School | M,D |
| Alliant International University–San Francisco | D |
| American University | M,D |
| The American University in Cairo | M,O |
| American University of Armenia | M |
| The American University of Paris | M |
| Appalachian School of Law | D |
| Arizona State University at Tempe | M,D |
| Atlanta's John Marshall Law School | M,D |
| Ave Maria School of Law | D |
| Barry University | D |
| Baylor University | D |
| Belmont University | D |
| Boston College | D |
| Boston University | M,D |
| Brigham Young University | M,D |
| Brooklyn Law School | M,D |
| California Western School of Law | M,D |
| Campbell University | D |
| Capital University | M,D |
| Case Western Reserve University | M,D |
| The Catholic University of America | M,D |
| Central European University | M,D |
| Champlain College | M |
| Chapman University | M,D |
| Charleston School of Law | D |
| City University of New York School of Law | D |
| Cleveland State University | M,D,O |
| Columbia University | M,D |
| Concordia University (United States) | D |
| Concord Law School | D |
| Cornell University | M,D |
| Creighton University | M,D,O |
| Dalhousie University | M,D |
| DePaul University | M,D |
| Drake University | M,D |
| Drexel University | M,D |
| Duke University | M,D |
| Dunlap-Stone University | M |
| Duquesne University | M,D |
| Elon University | D |
| Emory University | M,D,O |
| Empire College | M,D |
| Faulkner University | D |
| Florida Agricultural and Mechanical University | D |
| Florida Coastal School of Law | D |
| Florida International University | M,D |
| Florida State University | M,D |
| Fordham University | M,D |
| Friends University | M |
| George Mason University | M,D |
| Georgetown University | M,D |
| The George Washington University | M,D |
| Georgia State University | D |
| Golden Gate University | M,D |
| Gonzaga University | D |
| Harvard University | M,D* |
| Hofstra University | M,D,O |
| Howard University | M,D |
| Humphreys University | D |
| Illinois Institute of Technology | M,D |
| Indiana University Bloomington | M,D,O |
| Indiana University-Purdue University Indianapolis | M,D,O |
| Instituto Tecnológico y de Estudios Superiores de Monterrey, Campus Ciudad de México | O |
| Inter American University of Puerto Rico School of Law | D |
| John F. Kennedy University | D |
| The Judge Advocate General's School, U.S. Army | M |
| Lewis & Clark College | M,D |
| Liberty University | M |
| Lincoln Memorial University | D |
| London Metropolitan University | M,D |
| Louisiana State University and Agricultural & Mechanical College | M,D |
| Loyola Marymount University | M,D |
| Loyola University Chicago | M,D,O |
| Loyola University New Orleans | M,D |
| Marquette University | D |
| Massachusetts School of Law at Andover | D |
| McGill University | M,D,O |
| Mercer University | D |
| Michigan State University College of Law | M,D |
| Mississippi College | D,O |
| Mitchell Hamline School of Law | M,D |
| Montclair State University | M,O |
| New England Law - Boston | M,D |
| New York Law School | M,D |
| New York University | M,D,O |
| North Carolina Central University | D |
| Northeastern University | M,D |
| Northern Illinois University | D |
| Northern Kentucky University | D |
| Northwestern University | M,D |
| Nova Southeastern University | M,D |
| Ohio Northern University | M,D |
| The Ohio State University | M,D |
| Oklahoma City University | M,D |
| Pace University | M,D |
| Penn State University–Dickinson Law | M,D |
| Penn State University Park | M,D* |
| Pontifical Catholic University of Puerto Rico | D |
| Pontificia Universidad Catolica Madre y Maestra | M |
| Purdue University Global | M |
| Queen's University at Kingston | M,D |
| Quinnipiac University | M,D |
| Regent University | M,D |
| Roger Williams University | M,D |
| Rutgers University - Camden | D |
| Rutgers University - Newark | D |
| St. John's University (NY) | D |
| Saint Joseph's University | M,O |
| Saint Louis University | M,D |
| St. Mary's University (United States) | M,D |
| St. Thomas University - Florida | M,D |
| Samford University | M,D |
| San Joaquin College of Law | D |
| The Santa Barbara and Ventura Colleges of Law–Santa Barbara | M,D |
| The Santa Barbara and Ventura Colleges of Law–Ventura | M,D |
| Santa Clara University | M,D,O |
| Seattle University | M,D |
| Seton Hall University | M,D |
| Southern Illinois University Carbondale | M,D |
| Southern Methodist University | M,D |
| Southern University and Agricultural and Mechanical College | D |
| South Texas College of Law Houston | D |
| Southwestern Law School | M,D |
| Stanford University | M,D |
| Stetson University | M,D |
| Suffolk University | M,D |
| Syracuse University | M,D |
| Taft University System | M,D |
| Temple University | M,D,O* |
| Texas A&M University | M,D |
| Texas Southern University | D |
| Texas Tech University | M,D |
| Thomas Jefferson School of Law | D |
| Touro College | M,D |
| Trinity International University | M,D |
| Tufts University | M,D |
| UNB Fredericton | O |
| Universidad Autonoma de Guadalajara | M,D |
| Universidad Central del Este | D |
| Universidad Iberoamericana | M,D |
| Université de Montréal | M,D,O |
| Université de Sherbrooke | M,D,O |
| Université du Québec à Montréal | O |
| University at Albany, State University of New York | M |
| University at Buffalo, the State University of New York | M,D |
| The University of Akron | M,D |
| The University of Alabama | M,D |
| University of Alberta | M,D |
| The University of Arizona | M,D |
| University of Arkansas | M,D |
| University of Arkansas at Little Rock | D |
| University of Baltimore | M,D |
| The University of British Columbia | M,D |
| University of Calgary | M,D,O |
| University of California, Berkeley | M,D |
| University of California, Davis | M,D |
| University of California, Hastings College of the Law | M,D |
| University of California, Irvine | D |
| University of California, Los Angeles | M,D |
| University of Chicago | M,D |
| University of Cincinnati | M,D |
| University of Colorado Boulder | D |
| University of Connecticut | D |
| University of Dayton | M,D |
| University of Denver | M,D,O |
| University of Detroit Mercy | D |
| University of Florida | M,D |
| University of Georgia | M,D |
| University of Hawaii at Manoa | M,D,O |
| University of Houston | M,D |
| University of Idaho | M,D |
| University of Illinois at Chicago | M,D |
| University of Illinois at Urbana-Champaign | M,D |
| The University of Iowa | M,D |
| The University of Kansas | D |
| University of Kentucky | D |
| University of La Verne | D |
| University of Louisville | D |
| University of Maine | D |
| The University of Manchester | M,D |
| University of Manitoba | M |
| University of Maryland, Baltimore | M,D |
| University of Maryland, College Park | |
| University of Massachusetts Dartmouth | D |
| University of Memphis | D |
| University of Miami | M,D |
| University of Michigan | M,D |
| University of Minnesota, Twin Cities Campus | M,D |
| University of Mississippi | M,D |
| University of Missouri | M,D |
| University of Missouri–Kansas City | M,D |
| University of Montana | D |
| University of Nebraska–Lincoln | M,D |
| University of Nevada, Las Vegas | M,D |
| University of New Hampshire | M,D,O |
| University of New Mexico | D |
| University of North Alabama | M |
| The University of North Carolina at Chapel Hill | M,D |
| University of North Dakota | D |
| University of North Texas at Dallas | D |
| University of Notre Dame | M,D |
| University of Oklahoma | M,D |
| University of Oregon | M,D |
| University of Ottawa | M,D |
| University of Pennsylvania | M,D |
| University of Pittsburgh | M* |
| University of Puerto Rico at Rio Piedras | M,D |
| University of Richmond | D |
| University of St. Thomas (MN) | M,D |
| University of San Diego | M,D,O |
| University of San Francisco | D |
| University of Saskatchewan | M,D |
| University of South Africa | M,D |
| University of South Carolina | D |
| University of South Dakota | D |
| University of Southern California | M,D |
| The University of Tennessee | D |
| The University of Texas at Austin | M,D |
| The University of Texas at Dallas | M,D |
| University of the District of Columbia | M,D |
| University of the Pacific | M,D |
| The University of Toledo | M,D,O |
| University of Toronto | M,D |
| The University of Tulsa | M,D,O |
| University of Utah | M,D |
| University of Victoria | M,D |
| University of Virginia | M,D |
| University of Washington | M,D |
| The University of Western Ontario | M,D,O |
| University of West Los Angeles | D |
| University of Wisconsin–Madison | M,D |
| University of Wyoming | D |
| Université Laval | M,D,O |
| Vanderbilt University | M,D* |
| Vermont Law School | D |
| Villanova University | D |
| Wake Forest University | M,D |
| Walden University | M,D,O |
| Washburn University | M,D |
| Washington and Lee University | D |
| Washington University in St. Louis | M,D |
| Wayne State University | M,D |
| Western Michigan University Cooley Law School | M,D |
| Western New England University | M,D |
| Western State College of Law at Westcliff University | D |
| West Virginia University | M,D |
| Widener University | M,D |
| Willamette University | M,D |
| William & Mary | M,D* |
| Yale University | M,D |
| Yeshiva University | M,D |
| York University | M,D |

## LEGAL AND JUSTICE STUDIES

| | |
|---|---|
| Arizona State University at Tempe | M,D,O |
| Binghamton University, State University of New York | M,D |

Brock University M
California University of Pennsylvania M
Campbellsville University M
Capital University M
Carleton University M,O
Case Western Reserve University M,D
The Catholic University of America M,D,O
Central European University M,D
Columbia University M,D
The George Washington University M,D,O
Georgian Court University M,O
Golden Gate University M,D
Governors State University M
Harrison Middleton University M,D
Harvard University D*
Hodges University M
Hofstra University M,D,O
Illinois Institute of Technology M,D
Indiana University South Bend M,O
John Jay College of Criminal Justice of the City University of New York M,D
Liberty University M
Loyola University Chicago M,O
Marlboro College M
Marygrove College M,O
Michigan State University College of Law M,D
Mississippi College M,O
Montclair State University O
National Paralegal College M
National University M
New York University M,D
Northeastern University M,D
Nova Southeastern University M,D
Pace University M,D
Prairie View A&M University M,D
Prescott College M
Purdue University Global M,O
Queen's University at Kingston M,D
Regent University M,D
Rhode Island College M
Royal Roads University M,O
Rutgers University - New Brunswick M,D
St. John's University (NY) M
Saint Leo University M,D
St. Mary's University (United States) M
San Francisco State University M
The Santa Barbara and Ventura Colleges of Law–Santa Barbara M,D
The Santa Barbara and Ventura Colleges of Law–Ventura M,D
Simon Fraser University M,D
Southern Illinois University Carbondale M
Southern New Hampshire University M,D,O
Taft University System M,D
Temple University M,D*
Texas State University M
Texas Tech University M,D
Touro College M,D
Trident University International M,D,O
Universidad Autonoma de Guadalajara M,D
University at Buffalo, the State University of New York M,D
University of Baltimore M
University of Calgary M,O
University of California, Berkeley D
University of Charleston M
University of Denver M,O
University of Illinois at Springfield M
University of Massachusetts Lowell M
University of Montana M
University of Nebraska–Lincoln M
University of Nevada, Reno M,D
University of New Hampshire M,D,O
University of Pennsylvania M,D
University of Pittsburgh M*
University of San Diego M,D,O
University of South Florida O
University of the District of Columbia M,D
University of the Sacred Heart M
University of Washington M,D
University of Windsor M
Université Laval O
Vermont Law School M
Washburn University M,D
Weber State University M
Webster University M,O
Western Michigan University Cooley Law School M,D
West Virginia University M,D
Wilfrid Laurier University D

## LEISURE STUDIES

Bowling Green State University M
California State University, Long Beach M
Dalhousie University M
East Carolina University M,O
Howard University M
Indiana University Bloomington M,D
Penn State University Park M,D*
Prescott College M
San Francisco State University M
Southeast Missouri State University M
Southern Connecticut State University M
Texas State University M
Universidad Metropolitana M
Université du Québec à Trois-Rivières M,O
University of Illinois at Urbana-Champaign M,D
The University of Iowa M,D
University of Nebraska at Kearney M
The University of Tennessee M,D
The University of Toledo M,D
University of Utah M,D
University of Victoria M
University of Waterloo M,D
University of West Florida M

## LIBERAL STUDIES

Abilene Christian University M
Alaska Pacific University M
Albertus Magnus College M
Alvernia University M
Arizona State University at Tempe M
Arkansas Tech University M
Baker University M
Barry University M
Binghamton University, State University of New York M
Brooklyn College of the City University of New York M
Cardinal Stritch University M
Clayton State University M
Coastal Carolina University M
College of Staten Island of the City University of New York M
The Colorado College M
Colorado State University M
Converse College M
Dallas Baptist University M
Dartmouth College M
Delta State University M
DePaul University M
Dominican University of California M
Drew University M,D,O
Duke University M
Eastern Washington University M
Fort Hays State University M
Georgetown University M,D
The Graduate Center, City University of New York M
Hampton University M,D,O
Harvard University M,O*
Hawaii Pacific University M
Henderson State University M
Hollins University M
Houston Baptist University M
Indiana University Northwest M,O
Indiana University-Purdue University Indianapolis M,D,O
Indiana University South Bend M,O
Jacksonville State University M
Johns Hopkins University M,O
Kean University M
Lake Forest College M
Louisiana State University and Agricultural & Mechanical College M
Louisiana State University in Shreveport M
Madonna University M
McDaniel College M,O
Metropolitan State University M
Mississippi College M
The New School M
North Central College M
Northern Arizona University M
Northern Kentucky University M
Northwestern University M
Notre Dame of Maryland University M
Oakland University M
Queens College of the City University of New York M
Reed College M
Rice University M
Rollins College M
Rutgers University - Camden M
St. Edward's University M,O
St. John's College (MD) M
St. John's College (NM) M
St. John's University (NY) M
St. Norbert College M
San Diego State University M
San Francisco State University M
Simon Fraser University M
Southern Methodist University M,D
Spring Hill College M,O
State University of New York College at Old Westbury M
State University of New York Empire State College M
Stony Brook University, State University of New York M,O
SUNY Brockport M
Texas A&M University–Central Texas M,O
Texas Christian University M
Thomas Edison State University M,O
Towson University M
Tulane University M
University of Central Oklahoma M
University of Chicago M
University of Delaware M
University of Detroit Mercy M,D,O
University of Memphis M,O
University of Miami M
University of Michigan–Flint M
University of Minnesota, Duluth M
University of New Hampshire M
University of North Carolina Asheville M,O
The University of North Carolina at Charlotte M,D,O
The University of North Carolina at Greensboro M
The University of North Carolina Wilmington M
University of Pennsylvania M
University of St. Thomas (TX) M
University of Southern Indiana M
University of South Florida M,D
University of South Florida, St. Petersburg M
University of South Florida Sarasota-Manatee M
The University of Texas at El Paso M
University of the Virgin Islands M
The University of Toledo M
University of Wisconsin–Milwaukee M*
Vanderbilt University M*
Villanova University M
Virginia Polytechnic Institute and State University M,O
Wake Forest University M
Washburn University M
Wesleyan University M,O
Western Illinois University M
Wichita State University M
Winthrop University M

## LIBRARY SCIENCE

Appalachian State University M,O
The Catholic University of America M,O
Chicago State University M
Clarion University of Pennsylvania M
Dalhousie University M
Drexel University M,D,O
East Carolina University M,O
Eastern Kentucky University M
East Tennessee State University M,O
Emporia State University M,D,O
Florida State University M,D,O
Indiana University Bloomington M,D,O
Indiana University-Purdue University Indianapolis M,O
Instituto Tecnológico y de Estudios Superiores de Monterrey, Campus Irapuato M,D
Inter American University of Puerto Rico, Barranquitas Campus M
Inter American University of Puerto Rico, San Germán Campus M
Kent State University M
Kutztown University of Pennsylvania M
Long Island University - Brentwood Campus M,O
Long Island University - Post M,D,O
Louisiana State University and Agricultural & Mechanical College M
Mansfield University of Pennsylvania M
McDaniel College M
McGill University M,D,O
McNeese State University O
North Carolina Central University M
Old Dominion University M,O
Olivet Nazarene University M
Pratt Institute M,O
Queens College of the City University of New York M,O
Rowan University M,D,O
Rutgers University - New Brunswick D
St. Catherine University M
St. John's University (NY) M,O
Sam Houston State University M
Southern Arkansas University–Magnolia M
Southern Connecticut State University M,O
Syracuse University M
Tennessee Technological University M,O
Texas A&M University–Commerce M,D,O
Texas Woman's University M
Trevecca Nazarene University M,O
Universidad del Turabo M
Université de Montréal M,D
University at Buffalo, the State University of New York M,O
The University of Alabama M,D
University of Alberta M
The University of Arizona M,D
The University of British Columbia M,D
University of California, Los Angeles M,D,O
University of Central Arkansas M
University of Central Missouri M,D,O
University of Central Oklahoma M
University of Denver M,D,O
University of Hawaii at Manoa M,O
University of Houston–Clear Lake M
University of Illinois at Urbana-Champaign M,D,O
The University of Iowa M,D
University of Kentucky M
University of Maryland, College Park M
University of Missouri D
University of Nebraska at Kearney M
The University of North Carolina at Chapel Hill M,D,O
The University of North Carolina at Greensboro M
University of Oklahoma M,D,O
University of Pittsburgh M,D*
University of Puerto Rico at Rio Piedras M,O
University of Rhode Island M
University of South Carolina M,D,O
University of Southern Mississippi M,O
University of South Florida M
University of Washington M,D
The University of Western Ontario M,D
University of Wisconsin–Eau Claire M
University of Wisconsin–Madison M,D
University of Wisconsin–Milwaukee M,D,O*
Valdosta State University M
Valley City State University M
Wayne State University M,O

## LIGHTING DESIGN

The New School M
New York School of Interior Design M
Rensselaer Polytechnic Institute M,D
University of Washington M,D,O

## LIMNOLOGY

Cornell University D
Oregon State University M,D
University of Alaska Fairbanks M,D
University of Florida M,D

## LINGUISTICS

Arizona State University at Tempe M,D,O
Ball State University M
Biola University M,D,O
Boston College M
Boston University M,D
Brigham Young University M
Brown University M,D
California State University, Fresno M
California State University, Fullerton M
California State University, Long Beach M,O
California State University, Northridge M
Carleton University M
Carnegie Mellon University M,D
Case Western Reserve University M
Concordia University (Canada) M,O
Cornell University M,D
Dallas International University M,O
East Carolina University M,D,O
Eastern Michigan University M
Florida Atlantic University M
Florida International University M
Gallaudet University M,D,O
George Mason University M,D,O
Georgetown University M,D
Georgia State University M,D
The Graduate Center, City University of New York M,D
Grand Valley State University M
Harvard University D*
Hofstra University M
Indiana State University M,D,O
Indiana University Bloomington M,D
Instituto Tecnologico de Santo Domingo M,O
Iowa State University of Science and Technology M,D
Kent State University M,D
Massachusetts Institute of Technology D
McGill University M,D
Memorial University of Newfoundland M,D
Michigan State University M,D
Montclair State University M,O
New York University M,D
Northeastern Illinois University M
Northern Arizona University M,D,O
Northwestern University D
Oakland University M,O
The Ohio State University M,D
Ohio University M
Old Dominion University M
Penn State University Park M,D*
Purdue University M,D
Queens College of the City University of New York M,O
Rice University M,D
Rutgers University - New Brunswick D
San Diego State University M,O
San Francisco State University M
San Jose State University M,O
Simon Fraser University M,D
Southern Illinois University Carbondale M
Stanford University M,D
Stony Brook University, State University of New York M,D
Syracuse University M
Teachers College, Columbia University M,D,O
Texas A&M University–Commerce M,D,O
Trinity Western University M
Universidad de las Américas Puebla M
Université de Montréal M,D,O
Université de Sherbrooke M,D
Université du Québec à Chicoutimi M
Université du Québec à Montréal M,D
University at Buffalo, the State University of New York M,D
University of Alaska Fairbanks M
University of Alberta M,D
The University of Arizona M,D
The University of British Columbia M,D
University of Calgary M,D
University of California, Berkeley D
University of California, Davis M,D
University of California, Los Angeles M,D
University of California, San Diego D
University of California, Santa Barbara M,D
University of California, Santa Cruz M,D
University of Chicago M,D

*M—masters degree; D—doctorate; O—other advanced degree; *—Close-Up and/or Display*

| | |
|---|---|
| University of Colorado Boulder | M,D |
| University of Colorado Denver | M |
| University of Connecticut | M,D |
| University of Delaware | M,D |
| The University of Findlay | M,D |
| University of Florida | M,D,O |
| University of Georgia | M,D |
| University of Hawaii at Manoa | M,D |
| University of Houston | M,D |
| University of Illinois at Chicago | M |
| University of Illinois at Urbana-Champaign | M,D |
| The University of Iowa | M,D |
| The University of Kansas | M,D |
| University of Louisville | M,D |
| The University of Manchester | D |
| University of Manitoba | M,D |
| University of Maryland, Baltimore County | M |
| University of Maryland, College Park | M,D |
| University of Massachusetts Amherst | M,D |
| University of Massachusetts Boston | M,D |
| University of Memphis | M,D,O |
| University of Michigan | D |
| University of Minnesota, Twin Cities Campus | M,D |
| University of Montana | M,D |
| University of New Hampshire | M,D |
| University of New Mexico | M,D |
| The University of North Carolina at Chapel Hill | M |
| The University of North Carolina at Charlotte | M,O |
| University of North Dakota | M |
| University of North Texas | M,D,O |
| University of Oregon | M,D |
| University of Ottawa | M,D |
| University of Pennsylvania | M,D |
| University of Pittsburgh | M,D* |
| University of Puerto Rico at Rio Piedras | M,D |
| University of Rochester | M |
| University of Saskatchewan | M |
| University of South Africa | M,D |
| University of South Carolina | M,D,O |
| University of Southern California | M,D |
| The University of Tennessee | D |
| The University of Texas at Arlington | M,D |
| The University of Texas at Austin | M,D |
| The University of Texas at El Paso | M,O |
| University of Toronto | M,D |
| University of Utah | M,D |
| University of Victoria | M,D |
| University of Virginia | M |
| University of Washington | M,D |
| University of Wisconsin–Madison | M,D |
| University of Wisconsin–Milwaukee | M,D,O* |
| Université Laval | M,D |
| Virginia International University | M |
| Wayne State University | M |
| Wesley Biblical Seminary | M |
| Yale University | D |
| York University | M,D |

**LOGISTICS**

| | |
|---|---|
| Air Force Institute of Technology | M,D |
| Albany State University | M |
| American Public University System | M,D |
| Athens State University | M |
| Benedictine University | M |
| Case Western Reserve University | M,D |
| Central Connecticut State University | M,O |
| Central Michigan University | M,O |
| Colorado Technical University Colorado Springs | M,D |
| Copenhagen Business School | M,D |
| East Carolina University | M,D,O |
| Embry-Riddle Aeronautical University–Worldwide | M |
| Florida Institute of Technology | M |
| Friends University | M |
| George Mason University | M |
| Georgia College & State University | M |
| Georgia Institute of Technology | M,D |
| Georgia Southern University | D |
| HEC Montreal | M |
| Maryville University of Saint Louis | M,O |
| Massachusetts Institute of Technology | M |
| Michigan State University | M,D |
| Naval Postgraduate School | M |
| North Dakota State University | M,D |
| Norwich University | M |
| The Ohio State University | M |
| Polytechnic University of Puerto Rico, Miami Campus | M |
| Pontifical Catholic University of Puerto Rico | O |
| Pontificia Universidad Catolica Madre y Maestra | M |
| Purdue University Global | M |
| Rutgers University - Newark | M |
| Shippensburg University of Pennsylvania | M,D,O |
| Trident University International | M,D |
| Universidad del Turabo | M |
| University at Buffalo, the State University of New York | M,D |
| The University of Alabama in Huntsville | M,O |
| University of Alaska Anchorage | M |
| University of Dallas | M,D |
| University of Houston | M |
| The University of Kansas | M,D |
| University of Louisville | M,D,O |
| University of Missouri–St. Louis | M,D,O |
| The University of North Carolina at Charlotte | M,O |
| University of North Florida | M |
| University of North Texas | M,D,O |
| University of St. Francis (IL) | M,O |
| University of South Africa | M,D |
| The University of Tennessee | M,D |
| The University of Tennessee at Chattanooga | M,O |
| The University of Texas at Arlington | M |
| University of Washington | O |
| Virginia International University | M,O |
| Wright State University | M |

**MANAGEMENT INFORMATION SYSTEMS**

| | |
|---|---|
| Adelphi University | M |
| Air Force Institute of Technology | M |
| American Business & Technology University | M |
| American InterContinental University Atlanta | M |
| American Sentinel University | M |
| American University | M,D,O |
| American University of Armenia | M |
| Argosy University, Atlanta | M,D |
| Argosy University, Chicago | M,D |
| Argosy University, Hawaii | M,D,O |
| Argosy University, Los Angeles | M,D |
| Argosy University, Northern Virginia | M,D,O |
| Argosy University, Orange County | M,D,O |
| Argosy University, Phoenix | M,D |
| Argosy University, Seattle | M,D |
| Argosy University, Tampa | M,D |
| Argosy University, Twin Cities | M,D |
| Arizona State University at Tempe | M,D |
| Arkansas State University | O |
| Ashland University | M |
| Aspen University | M,O |
| Auburn University at Montgomery | M |
| Baker College Center for Graduate Studies–Online | M,D |
| Ball State University | M,O |
| Barry University | O |
| Baruch College of the City University of New York | M,D |
| Baylor University | M,D |
| Bay Path University | M |
| Bellevue University | M |
| Benedictine University | M |
| Binghamton University, State University of New York | D |
| Boston University | M,O |
| Bowie State University | M,O |
| Brandeis University | M |
| Broadview University–West Jordan | M |
| California Intercontinental University | M,D |
| California Lutheran University | M,O |
| California State Polytechnic University, Pomona | M |
| California State University, Fullerton | M |
| California State University, Los Angeles | M |
| California State University, Monterey Bay | M |
| California State University, San Bernardino | M |
| California University of Management and Sciences | M,D |
| Capella University | M,D |
| Capitol Technology University | M |
| Carnegie Mellon University | M,D |
| The Catholic University of America | M,O |
| Central Michigan University | M,O |
| Central Penn College | M |
| Charleston Southern University | M |
| City College of the City University of New York | M,D |
| City University of Seattle | M,O |
| Claremont Graduate University | M,D,O |
| Clark University | M |
| Clemson University | M,D |
| Cleveland State University | D |
| Coastal Carolina University | M,D,O |
| College of Charleston | M |
| The College of St. Scholastica | M,O |
| Colorado State University | M |
| Colorado State University–Global Campus | M |
| Concordia University Wisconsin | M |
| Copenhagen Business School | M,D |
| Daemen College | M |
| Dakota State University | M,D,O |
| Dalhousie University | M |
| Dallas Baptist University | M |
| DePaul University | M,D |
| DeSales University | M,O |
| DeVry University–Folsom Campus | M |
| Dominican University | M,D,O |
| Drexel University | M,D,O |
| Duquesne University | M |
| East Carolina University | M,D,O |
| Eastern Michigan University | M,O |
| ECPI University | M |
| Elmhurst University | M |
| Embry-Riddle Aeronautical University–Worldwide | M |
| Emory University | M,D |
| Endicott College | M |
| Fairfield University | M,O |
| Fairleigh Dickinson University, Metropolitan Campus | M,O |
| Ferris State University | M |
| Florida Agricultural and Mechanical University | M |
| Florida Atlantic University | M |
| Florida Gulf Coast University | M |
| Florida Institute of Technology | M |
| Florida International University | M,D |
| Florida State University | M,D,O |
| Fordham University | M,D |
| Franklin Pierce University | M,D,O |
| Friends University | M |
| George Mason University | M |
| The George Washington University | M,D |
| Georgia College & State University | M |
| Georgia Southern University | M,O |
| Georgia Southwestern State University | M,O |
| Georgia State University | M,D,O |
| Golden Gate University | M,D,O |
| Goldey-Beacom College | M |
| Governors State University | M |
| The Graduate Center, City University of New York | D |
| Grantham University | M,O |
| Harrisburg University of Science and Technology | M |
| Hawaii Pacific University | M |
| HEC Montreal | M,O |
| Hodges University | M |
| Hofstra University | M,O |
| Holy Family University | M |
| Hood College | M,O |
| Howard University | M |
| Idaho State University | M,O |
| IGlobal University | M |
| Illinois Institute of Technology | M,D |
| Illinois State University | M |
| Indiana University Bloomington | M,D,O |
| Indiana University Northwest | M,O |
| Instituto Tecnológico y de Estudios Superiores de Monterrey, Campus Central de Veracruz | M |
| Instituto Tecnológico y de Estudios Superiores de Monterrey, Campus Ciudad de México | M,D |
| Instituto Tecnológico y de Estudios Superiores de Monterrey, Campus Ciudad Juárez | M |
| Instituto Tecnológico y de Estudios Superiores de Monterrey, Campus Ciudad Obregón | M |
| Instituto Tecnológico y de Estudios Superiores de Monterrey, Campus Estado de México | M,D |
| Instituto Tecnológico y de Estudios Superiores de Monterrey, Campus Irapuato | M,D |
| Instituto Tecnológico y de Estudios Superiores de Monterrey, Campus Laguna | M |
| Inter American University of Puerto Rico, Aguadilla Campus | M |
| Inter American University of Puerto Rico, Fajardo Campus | M |
| Inter American University of Puerto Rico, Metropolitan Campus | M |
| Inter American University of Puerto Rico, San Germán Campus | M,D |
| Iona College | M,O |
| Iowa State University of Science and Technology | M,D |
| James Madison University | M |
| Johns Hopkins University | M,O |
| Johnson & Wales University | M |
| Kean University | M |
| Keiser University | M |
| Kent State University | D |
| Lake Erie College | M |
| Le Moyne College | M |
| Lenoir-Rhyne University | M |
| Lewis University | M |
| Lincoln University (CA) | M,D |
| Lindenwood University | M,O |
| Lipscomb University | M,O |
| London Metropolitan University | M,D |
| Long Island University - Post | M |
| Louisiana State University and Agricultural & Mechanical College | M,D |
| Louisiana Tech University | M,D |
| Loyola University Chicago | M,O |
| Loyola University Maryland | M |
| Marist College | M,O |
| Marquette University | M,O |
| Marymount University | M,O |
| Marywood University | M |
| McGill University | M,D,O |
| McMaster University | D |
| Metropolitan State University | M,D,O |
| Michigan State University | M,D |
| Middle Georgia State University | M |
| Middle Tennessee State University | M |
| Minot State University | M |
| Mississippi State University | M,D |
| Montclair State University | M |
| Morehead State University | M |
| Morgan State University | D |
| Murray State University | M |
| National American University (TX) | M,D |
| National University | M,O |
| Naval Postgraduate School | M,D,O |
| New England Institute of Technology | M |
| New Jersey Institute of Technology | M,D,O |
| Newman University | M |
| New Mexico State University | M |
| New York University | M,D |
| Northeastern University | M,D,O |
| Northern Illinois University | M |
| Northwestern University | M |
| Northwest Missouri State University | M |
| Nova Southeastern University | M,D |
| Oakland University | M,D,O |
| The Ohio State University | M,D |
| Oklahoma State University | M,D |
| Old Dominion University | M,D |
| Our Lady of the Lake University | M |
| Pace University | M,D,O |
| Pacific States University | M,O |
| Park University | M,O |
| Penn State Harrisburg | M,O |
| Penn State University Park | M,D* |
| Point Park University | M |
| Polytechnic University of Puerto Rico | M |
| Pontifical Catholic University of Puerto Rico | M,O |
| Prairie View A&M University | M,D |
| Purdue University | M |
| Purdue University Global | M |
| Queen's University at Kingston | M,D |
| Radford University | M |
| Regent's University London | M |
| Regis University | M,O |
| Rivier University | M |
| Robert Morris University | M,D |
| Robert Morris University Illinois | M |
| Rochester Institute of Technology | O |
| Rose-Hulman Institute of Technology | M |
| Rutgers University - Newark | M,D |
| St. John's University (NY) | M |
| Saint Peter's University | M |
| San Diego State University | M |
| San Francisco State University | M |
| Santa Clara University | M |
| Schiller International University - Heidelberg | M |
| Schiller International University - Tampa | M |
| Seattle Pacific University | M |
| Shippensburg University of Pennsylvania | M,D,O |
| Southeastern Oklahoma State University | M |
| Southern Illinois University Edwardsville | M |
| Southern Methodist University | M |
| Southern New Hampshire University | M,D,O |
| Southern University at New Orleans | M |
| South University - Austin | M |
| South University - Montgomery | M |
| South University - Tampa | M |
| South University - Virginia Beach | M |
| South University - West Palm Beach | M |
| Stevens Institute of Technology | M,D,O |
| Stratford University (VA) | M,D |
| Strayer University | M |
| Suffolk University | M |
| Syracuse University | M,D,O |
| Tarleton State University | M |
| Temple University | M,D* |
| Tennessee Technological University | M |
| Texas A&M International University | M,D |
| Texas A&M University | M |
| Texas A&M University–Central Texas | M,O |
| Texas Southern University | M |
| Texas State University | M |
| Texas Tech University | M,D |
| Touro College | M |
| Trident University International | M,D,O |
| Trine University | M |
| Troy University | M |
| Tulane University | M |
| Tuskegee University | M |
| United States International University–Africa | M |
| Universidad del Este | M |
| Universidad del Turabo | D |
| Universidad Metropolitana | M |
| Université de Sherbrooke | M,O |
| Université du Québec à Montréal | M |
| University at Albany, State University of New York | M,D,O |
| University at Buffalo, the State University of New York | M,D,O |
| The University of Akron | M |
| The University of Alabama at Birmingham | M |
| The University of Alabama in Huntsville | M,O |
| The University of Arizona | M,O |
| University of Arkansas | M |
| University of Arkansas at Little Rock | M,O |
| University of Baltimore | M,O |
| University of Bridgeport | M |
| The University of British Columbia | D |
| University of California, Berkeley | M,D,O |
| University of Central Missouri | M,D,O |
| University of Cincinnati | M,D |
| University of Colorado Denver | M,D |
| University of Connecticut | M,D |
| University of Dallas | M,D |
| University of Delaware | M,D |
| University of Detroit Mercy | M,D,O |
| University of Florida | M,D,O |
| University of Hawaii at Manoa | M,D,O |
| University of Houston–Clear Lake | M |
| University of Houston–Victoria | M |
| University of Illinois at Chicago | M,D |
| University of Illinois at Springfield | M |
| University of Illinois at Urbana-Champaign | M,D,O |
| The University of Kansas | M |
| University of La Verne | M |
| University of Lethbridge | M,D |
| University of Management and Technology | M,O |
| University of Mary Hardin-Baylor | M |
| University of Maryland Global Campus | M,O |
| University of Massachusetts Boston | M |
| University of Memphis | M,D,O |
| University of Michigan–Dearborn | M |
| University of Michigan–Flint | M,O |

| | |
|---|---|
| University of Minnesota, Twin Cities Campus | M,D |
| University of Mississippi | M,D |
| University of Missouri–St. Louis | M,D,O |
| University of Nebraska at Kearney | M |
| University of Nebraska at Omaha | M,D,O |
| University of Nebraska–Lincoln | M |
| University of Nevada, Las Vegas | M,O |
| University of Nevada, Reno | M |
| University of New Hampshire | M,O |
| University of New Mexico | M |
| University of North Alabama | M |
| The University of North Carolina at Chapel Hill | D |
| The University of North Carolina at Charlotte | M,D,O |
| The University of North Carolina at Greensboro | M,D,O |
| The University of North Carolina Wilmington | M |
| University of North Florida | M |
| University of North Texas | M,D,O |
| University of Oklahoma | M,O |
| University of Oregon | M |
| University of Pennsylvania | M,D |
| University of Phoenix - Bay Area Campus | M,D |
| University of Phoenix - Central Valley Campus | M |
| University of Phoenix - Dallas Campus | M |
| University of Phoenix - Hawaii Campus | M |
| University of Phoenix - Houston Campus | M |
| University of Phoenix - Las Vegas Campus | M |
| University of Phoenix–Online Campus | M |
| University of Phoenix - Sacramento Valley Campus | M |
| University of Phoenix - San Antonio Campus | M |
| University of Phoenix - San Diego Campus | M |
| University of Pittsburgh | M,D* |
| University of Redlands | M |
| University of Rochester | M,D |
| University of San Francisco | M |
| The University of Scranton | M |
| University of South Africa | M |
| University of South Alabama | M,D |
| University of South Florida | M,D,O |
| The University of Tampa | M,O |
| The University of Texas at Arlington | M,D |
| The University of Texas at Austin | M,D |
| The University of Texas at Dallas | M |
| The University of Texas Rio Grande Valley | M |
| University of the Sacred Heart | M |
| University of the West | M |
| University of Utah | M,D,O |
| University of Washington | M,D |
| University of Wisconsin–Madison | D |
| Université Laval | M,O |
| Utah State University | M |
| Valparaiso University | M |
| Virginia Commonwealth University | M |
| Virginia International University | M,O |
| Virginia Polytechnic Institute and State University | M,D,O |
| Walden University | M,D,O |
| Walsh College of Accountancy and Business Administration | M |
| Wayland Baptist University | M,D |
| Wayne State University | M,D,O |
| Webster University | M,D,O |
| Western Governors University | M |
| Wichita State University | M |
| Wilmington University | M,D |
| Winston-Salem State University | M |
| Worcester Polytechnic Institute | M,D,O |
| Wright State University | M |

## MANAGEMENT OF TECHNOLOGY

| | |
|---|---|
| Air Force Institute of Technology | M,D |
| Arizona State University at Tempe | M |
| Athabasca University | M,D,O |
| Atlantis University | M |
| Boston University | M |
| California Lutheran University | M,O |
| California State University, Los Angeles | M |
| Cambridge College | M |
| Campbellsville University | M,D |
| Capella University | M,D |
| Carleton University | M |
| The Catholic University of America | M,O |
| Central Connecticut State University | M,O |
| Central European University | M,D |
| Champlain College | M |
| City University of Seattle | M,O |
| Colorado School of Mines | M,D |
| Colorado Technical University Aurora | M |
| Colorado Technical University Colorado Springs | M,D |
| Columbia University | M |
| East Carolina University | M,D,O |
| Eastern Michigan University | D |
| Embry-Riddle Aeronautical University–Worldwide | M |
| Fairfield University | M,O |
| Fairleigh Dickinson University, Florham Campus | M,O |
| Farmingdale State College | M |
| George Mason University | M |
| Georgetown University | M,D |
| The George Washington University | M,D |
| Golden Gate University | M,D,O |
| Grand Canyon University | M |
| Harrisburg University of Science and Technology | M |
| Harvard University | D* |
| Herzing University Online | M |
| Illinois State University | M |
| Indiana State University | M,D |
| Indiana University-Purdue University Indianapolis | M |
| Instituto Centroamericano de Administracion de Empresas | M |
| Instituto Tecnológico y de Estudios Superiores de Monterrey, Campus Cuernavaca | M,D |
| Instituto Tecnológico y de Estudios Superiores de Monterrey, Campus Irapuato | M,D |
| Iona College | M,O |
| John F. Kennedy University | M |
| Johns Hopkins University | M,O |
| Kansas State University | M |
| Keiser University | M |
| Kennesaw State University | M |
| La Salle University | M,O |
| Lewis University | M |
| Lipscomb University | M,O |
| London Metropolitan University | M,D |
| Louisiana Tech University | M,D,O |
| Marquette University | M,D |
| Marshall University | M,O |
| Mercer University | M |
| Montclair State University | M |
| National University | M |
| New Jersey Institute of Technology | M,D,O |
| New York University | M,D |
| North Carolina State University | M,D |
| Northern Kentucky University | M |
| Pacific States University | M,O |
| Pittsburg State University | M,O |
| Polytechnic University of Puerto Rico | M |
| Polytechnic University of Puerto Rico, Orlando Campus | M |
| Polytechnique Montréal | M,D,O |
| Portland State University | M,D |
| Purdue University | M,D |
| Rutgers University - Newark | D |
| Ryerson University | M |
| St. Ambrose University | M |
| Seton Hall University | M,O |
| Simon Fraser University | M,D,O |
| South Dakota School of Mines and Technology | M |
| Southeast Missouri State University | M |
| State University of New York Polytechnic Institute | M |
| Stevens Institute of Technology | M,D,O |
| Stevenson University | M |
| Stony Brook University, State University of New York | M |
| Stratford University (VA) | M,D |
| Texas A&M University–Commerce | M,O |
| Texas State University | M |
| Towson University | M,O |
| University of Advancing Technology | M |
| The University of Alabama in Huntsville | M,O |
| University of Bridgeport | M,D |
| University of California, Los Angeles | M,D |
| University of California, Santa Barbara | M |
| University of Central Missouri | M,D,O |
| University of Colorado Denver | M |
| University of Dallas | M,D |
| University of Delaware | M |
| University of Illinois at Urbana-Champaign | M,D |
| University of Maryland, Baltimore County | M |
| University of Massachusetts Dartmouth | M |
| University of Miami | M,D |
| University of Minnesota, Twin Cities Campus | M |
| University of New Mexico | M |
| University of Phoenix - Bay Area Campus | M,D |
| University of Phoenix - Central Valley Campus | M |
| University of Phoenix - Dallas Campus | M |
| University of Phoenix - Hawaii Campus | M |
| University of Phoenix - Houston Campus | M |
| University of Phoenix - Las Vegas Campus | M |
| University of Phoenix–Online Campus | M,O |
| University of Phoenix - Phoenix Campus | M,O |
| University of Phoenix - Sacramento Valley Campus | M |
| University of Phoenix - San Antonio Campus | M |
| University of Phoenix - San Diego Campus | M |
| University of Portland | M |
| University of St. Thomas (MN) | M,O |
| University of South Florida | O |
| The University of Texas at Dallas | M |
| The University of Texas at San Antonio | M,D,O |
| University of Toronto | M |
| University of Virginia | M |
| University of Washington | M,D |
| University of Waterloo | M,D |
| University of Wisconsin–Madison | M |
| University of Wisconsin–Milwaukee | M,O* |
| Walsh College of Accountancy and Business Administration | M |
| Washington State University | M,O |
| Webster University | M,D,O |
| Wentworth Institute of Technology | M |
| Western Kentucky University | M |
| Wilfrid Laurier University | M,D |

## MANAGEMENT STRATEGY AND POLICY

| | |
|---|---|
| Amberton University | M |
| Antioch University Santa Barbara | M |
| Arizona State University at Tempe | M,D |
| Bay Path University | M |
| Black Hills State University | M |
| Boston University | M,O |
| Brandeis University | M |
| California Miramar University | M |
| California State University, East Bay | M |
| Capella University | M,D |
| Claremont Graduate University | M,D,O |
| Cleary University | M,O |
| College of Staten Island of the City University of New York | M |
| Davenport University | M |
| Defiance College | M |
| DePaul University | M,D |
| Drexel University | M,D,O |
| Duke University | D |
| Fisher College | M |
| Florida State University | M,D |
| Freed-Hardeman University | M |
| Friends University | M |
| The George Washington University | M,D,O |
| Georgia State University | M,D |
| Grantham University | M,O |
| Harrisburg University of Science and Technology | M |
| Harvard University | D* |
| HEC Montreal | M |
| Hofstra University | M,O |
| James Madison University | D |
| John F. Kennedy University | M |
| Lawrence Technological University | M,D,O |
| Lenoir-Rhyne University | M |
| LeTourneau University | M |
| Lipscomb University | M,O |
| Manhattanville College | M,O |
| McGill University | M,D,O |
| Mercyhurst University | M,O |
| Messiah University | M,O |
| Michigan State University | M,D |
| Middle Tennessee State University | M |
| Mount Mercy University | M |
| Neumann University | M |
| New England College | M |
| The New School | M,O |
| New York University | M,D |
| Niagara University | M |
| North Central College | M |
| Northwestern University | M |
| Norwich University | M |
| Nova Southeastern University | M |
| Oakland City University | M |
| Ohio Dominican University | M |
| Oklahoma Wesleyan University | M |
| Pace University | M |
| Pontificia Universidad Catolica Madre y Maestra | M |
| Queen's University at Kingston | M,D |
| Regent University | M,D,O |
| Regis University | M,O |
| Roberts Wesleyan College | M |
| Rockhurst University | M,O |
| St. John's University (NY) | M |
| Saint Mary-of-the-Woods College | M |
| Salve Regina University | M,O |
| Southeastern University (FL) | M,D |
| Southern Methodist University | M,D |
| Stevens Institute of Technology | M |
| Stockton University | M |
| Suffolk University | M |
| Temple University | D* |
| Tennessee State University | M,D |
| Tennessee Technological University | M |
| Thomas Jefferson University | M,D |
| Tufts University | O |
| Tulane University | M,D |
| United States International University–Africa | M |
| Universidad del Este | M |
| The University of Arizona | M,D |
| The University of British Columbia | D |
| University of Calgary | M,D |
| University of California, Davis | M |
| University of California, Los Angeles | M,D |
| University of Charleston | M |
| University of Chicago | M,O |
| University of Colorado Denver | M |
| University of Dallas | M,D |
| University of Detroit Mercy | M,O |
| University of Illinois at Urbana-Champaign | M,D,O |
| The University of Kansas | M,D |
| University of Lethbridge | M,D |
| The University of Manchester | M |
| University of Massachusetts Amherst | M,D |
| University of Memphis | M,O |
| University of Minnesota, Twin Cities Campus | D |
| University of New Haven | M |
| University of New Mexico | M |
| The University of North Carolina at Chapel Hill | D |
| University of North Texas | M,D,O |
| University of North Texas at Dallas | M |
| University of Pittsburgh | M,D* |
| University of Rhode Island | M,D,O |
| University of Rochester | M |
| University of South Florida | O |
| The University of Texas at Dallas | M |
| University of Utah | M,D,O |
| University of Virginia | M,O |
| The University of Western Ontario | M,D |
| University of Wisconsin–Madison | M,D |
| University of Wisconsin–Milwaukee | M,D,O* |
| Valparaiso University | M,O |
| Vanderbilt University | M* |
| Villanova University | M |
| Walsh College of Accountancy and Business Administration | M |
| Wayne State University | M,D,O |
| Western Governors University | M |
| Xavier University | M* |

## MANUFACTURING ENGINEERING

| | |
|---|---|
| American University of Armenia | M |
| Arizona State University at Tempe | M |
| Boston University | M,D |
| Bradley University | M |
| Brigham Young University | M |
| Buffalo State College, State University of New York | M |
| California State University, Northridge | M |
| The Citadel, The Military College of South Carolina | M,O |
| Cornell University | M,D |
| Eastern Kentucky University | M |
| East Tennessee State University | M |
| Florida State University | M,D |
| Georgia Southern University | M,O |
| Grand Valley State University | M |
| Illinois Institute of Technology | M,D |
| Instituto Tecnológico y de Estudios Superiores de Monterrey, Campus Monterrey | M,D |
| Kansas State University | M,D |
| Kettering University | M |
| Lawrence Technological University | M,D |
| Massachusetts Institute of Technology | M,D,O |
| Michigan State University | M,D |
| Minnesota State University Mankato | M |
| Missouri University of Science and Technology | M,D |
| New Jersey Institute of Technology | M,D |
| New York University | M |
| North Carolina State University | M |
| North Dakota State University | M,D |
| Oregon Institute of Technology | M |
| Oregon State University | M,D |
| Pittsburg State University | M |
| Polytechnic University of Puerto Rico | M |
| Rochester Institute of Technology | M |
| Southern Methodist University | M,D |
| Stevens Institute of Technology | M |
| Tennessee State University | M,D |
| Texas A&M University | M |
| Texas State University | M |
| Tufts University | O |
| Universidad Autonoma de Guadalajara | M,D |
| Universidad de las Américas Puebla | M |
| University at Buffalo, the State University of New York | M,D,O |
| University of Calgary | M,D |
| University of California, Irvine | M,D |
| University of California, Los Angeles | M |
| The University of Iowa | M,D |
| University of Kentucky | M |
| University of Manitoba | M,D |
| University of Maryland, College Park | M,D |
| University of Michigan | M,D |
| University of Michigan–Dearborn | M |
| University of Missouri | M,D |
| University of Nebraska–Lincoln | M,D |
| University of New Mexico | M |
| University of Puerto Rico at Mayagüez | M,D |
| University of St. Thomas (MN) | M,O |
| University of Southern California | M,D,O |
| The University of Texas at El Paso | M |
| The University of Texas at San Antonio | M,D |
| The University of Texas Rio Grande Valley | M |
| University of Toronto | M |
| University of Windsor | M,D |
| University of Wisconsin–Madison | M |
| University of Wisconsin–Milwaukee | M,D* |
| University of Wisconsin–Stout | M |
| Villanova University | M,O |
| Wayne State University | M,D,O |
| Western Illinois University | M |
| Western Michigan University | M |
| Western New England University | M |
| Wichita State University | M,D |
| Worcester Polytechnic Institute | M,D |

*M—masters degree; D—doctorate; O—other advanced degree; *—Close-Up and/or Display*

### MARINE AFFAIRS

| | |
|---|---|
| Dalhousie University | M |
| Louisiana State University and Agricultural & Mechanical College | M,D |
| Memorial University of Newfoundland | M,D,O |
| Oregon State University | M |
| Stony Brook University, State University of New York | M |
| Université du Québec à Rimouski | M,O |
| University of Delaware | M,D |
| University of Massachusetts Dartmouth | M,D |
| University of Miami | M,D |
| University of Rhode Island | M,D |
| University of Washington | M,O |

### MARINE BIOLOGY

| | |
|---|---|
| College of Charleston | M |
| Florida Institute of Technology | M,D |
| Montclair State University | M |
| Nicholls State University | M |
| Northeastern University | M,D |
| Nova Southeastern University | M,D |
| Princeton University | D |
| Rutgers University - New Brunswick | M,D |
| San Francisco State University | M |
| Texas A&M University | M,D |
| Texas A&M University–Corpus Christi | M,D |
| Texas State University | M,D |
| University of Alaska Fairbanks | M,D |
| University of California, Santa Barbara | M,D |
| University of Guam | M |
| University of Hawaii at Hilo | M |
| University of Hawaii at Manoa | M,D |
| University of Massachusetts Dartmouth | M,D |
| University of Miami | M,D |
| University of New Hampshire | M,D |
| The University of North Carolina Wilmington | M,D |
| University of Oregon | M,D |
| University of Rhode Island | M,D |
| University of Southern California | M,D |
| Western Illinois University | M,O |
| Woods Hole Oceanographic Institution | D |

### MARINE GEOLOGY

| | |
|---|---|
| Cornell University | M,D |
| Massachusetts Institute of Technology | M,D |
| University of Delaware | M,D |
| University of Hawaii at Manoa | M,D |
| University of Miami | M,D |
| University of Rhode Island | M,D |
| University of Washington | M,D |
| Woods Hole Oceanographic Institution | D |

### MARINE SCIENCES

| | |
|---|---|
| California State University, East Bay | M |
| California State University, Fresno | M |
| California State University, Monterey Bay | M |
| Coastal Carolina University | M,D,O |
| College of Charleston | M |
| Cornell University | M,D |
| Duke University | M,D |
| Florida Institute of Technology | M,D |
| Florida State University | M,D |
| Hawaii Pacific University | M |
| Instituto Tecnologico de Santo Domingo | M,D,O |
| Jacksonville University | M |
| Medical University of South Carolina | D |
| Memorial University of Newfoundland | M,O |
| North Carolina State University | M,D |
| Oregon State University | M |
| San Francisco State University | M |
| San Jose State University | M |
| Savannah State University | M |
| Southern Connecticut State University | M,O |
| Stony Brook University, State University of New York | M,D |
| Texas A&M University | M |
| Texas A&M University–Corpus Christi | M,D |
| University of Alaska Fairbanks | M,D |
| The University of British Columbia | M,D |
| University of California, San Diego | M |
| University of California, Santa Barbara | M,D |
| University of California, Santa Cruz | M,D |
| University of Delaware | M,D |
| University of Florida | M,D |
| University of Georgia | M,D |
| University of Hawaii at Manoa | O |
| University of Maine | M,D |
| University of Maryland, Baltimore | M,D |
| University of Maryland, Baltimore County | M,D |
| University of Maryland, College Park | M,D |
| University of Maryland Eastern Shore | M,D |
| University of Massachusetts Amherst | M,D |
| University of Massachusetts Boston | M,D |
| University of Massachusetts Dartmouth | M,D |
| University of Miami | M,D |
| University of New England | M |
| The University of North Carolina at Chapel Hill | M,D |
| The University of North Carolina Wilmington | M,D,O |
| University of Puerto Rico at Mayagüez | M,D |
| University of Rhode Island | M,D |
| University of South Alabama | M,D |
| University of South Carolina | M,D |
| University of Southern California | M,D |
| University of South Florida | M,D |
| The University of Texas at Austin | M,D |
| University of the Virgin Islands | M |
| University of Wisconsin–La Crosse | M |
| University of Wisconsin–Madison | M,D |
| Western Washington University | M |
| William & Mary | M,D* |

### MARKETING

| | |
|---|---|
| Abilene Christian University | M |
| Adelphi University | M |
| American Business & Technology University | M |
| American College of Thessaloniki | M,O |
| American InterContinental University Online | M |
| American University | M |
| The American University in Dubai | M |
| Anderson University (SC) | M |
| Argosy University, Atlanta | M,D |
| Argosy University, Chicago | M,D |
| Argosy University, Hawaii | M,D,O |
| Argosy University, Los Angeles | M,D |
| Argosy University, Northern Virginia | M,D,O |
| Argosy University, Orange County | M,D,O |
| Argosy University, Phoenix | M,D |
| Argosy University, Seattle | M,D |
| Argosy University, Tampa | M,D |
| Argosy University, Twin Cities | M,D |
| Arizona State University at Tempe | M,D |
| Ashworth College | M |
| Assumption University | M,O |
| Averett University | M |
| Azusa Pacific University | M |
| Baker College Center for Graduate Studies–Online | M,D |
| Barry University | O |
| Baruch College of the City University of New York | M,D |
| Bayamón Central University | M |
| Benedictine University | M |
| Bentley University | M |
| Binghamton University, State University of New York | D |
| Brandeis University | M |
| Brandman University | M |
| Brigham Young University | M |
| Bryan College | M |
| California Coast University | M |
| California Intercontinental University | M,D |
| California Lutheran University | M,O |
| California State University, East Bay | M |
| California State University, Los Angeles | M |
| California State University, San Bernardino | M |
| Capella University | M,D |
| Cardinal Stritch University | M |
| Carnegie Mellon University | D |
| Central Michigan University | M,O |
| City College of the City University of New York | M |
| City University of Seattle | M,O |
| Clark University | M |
| Clemson University | M |
| Cleveland State University | D |
| Colorado Technical University Aurora | M |
| Colorado Technical University Colorado Springs | M,D |
| Columbia Southern University | M |
| Columbia University | M,D |
| Concordia University (Canada) | M,D,O |
| Concordia University Wisconsin | M |
| Cornell University | D |
| Daemen College | M |
| DePaul University | M,D |
| DEREE - The American College of Greece | M |
| DeSales University | M |
| Drexel University | M,D,O |
| Duke University | D |
| Duquesne University | M |
| Eastern Michigan University | M,O |
| East Tennessee State University | M,O |
| Emory University | M,D |
| Fairfield University | M,O |
| Fairleigh Dickinson University, Florham Campus | M,O |
| Fairleigh Dickinson University, Metropolitan Campus | M,O |
| Fashion Institute of Technology | M |
| Florida Agricultural and Mechanical University | M |
| Florida International University | M |
| Florida National University | M |
| Florida State University | M,D |
| Fordham University | M,D |
| Franklin University | M |
| Full Sail University | M |
| Gannon University | M |
| Geneva College | M |
| George Fox University | M,D |
| The George Washington University | M,D |
| Georgia State University | M,D |
| Golden Gate University | M,D,O |
| Goldey-Beacom College | M |
| Grand Canyon University | M,D |
| Harvard University | D* |
| Hawaii Pacific University | M |
| HEC Montreal | M,D |
| Herzing University Online | M |
| Hofstra University | M,O |
| Holy Names University | M |
| Hope International University | M |
| Howard University | M |
| Hult International Business School (United States) | M |
| Illinois Institute of Technology | M |
| Indiana Tech | M |
| Indiana University-Purdue University Indianapolis | M |
| Indiana University South Bend | M,O |
| Instituto Tecnologico de Santo Domingo | M,O |
| Instituto Tecnológico y de Estudios Superiores de Monterrey, Campus Central de Veracruz | M |
| Instituto Tecnológico y de Estudios Superiores de Monterrey, Campus Ciudad Obregón | M |
| Instituto Tecnológico y de Estudios Superiores de Monterrey, Campus Cuernavaca | M |
| Instituto Tecnológico y de Estudios Superiores de Monterrey, Campus Estado de México | M,D |
| Instituto Tecnológico y de Estudios Superiores de Monterrey, Campus Monterrey | M |
| Inter American University of Puerto Rico, Aguadilla Campus | M |
| Inter American University of Puerto Rico, Fajardo Campus | M |
| Inter American University of Puerto Rico, Guayama Campus | M |
| Inter American University of Puerto Rico, Metropolitan Campus | M |
| Inter American University of Puerto Rico, Ponce Campus | M |
| Inter American University of Puerto Rico, San Germán Campus | M,D |
| International University in Geneva | M,D |
| The International University of Monaco | M |
| Iona College | M,O |
| Jacksonville University | M |
| Johns Hopkins University | M |
| Kansas State University | M,O |
| Keiser University | M,D |
| Kent State University | D |
| King University | M |
| Lake Forest Graduate School of Management | M |
| La Salle University | M,O |
| Lasell College | M,O |
| La Sierra University | M,O |
| Lawrence Technological University | M,D,O |
| Lewis University | M |
| Liberty University | M,D |
| LIM College | M |
| Lindenwood University | M,O |
| Long Island University - Post | M |
| Louisiana Tech University | M,D |
| Loyola University Chicago | M |
| Loyola University Maryland | M |
| Manhattanville College | M,O |
| Marist College | M |
| Marquette University | M,O |
| Maryville University of Saint Louis | M,O |
| McGill University | M,D,O |
| Melbourne Business School | M,D,O |
| Michigan State University | M,D |
| Milwaukee School of Engineering | M |
| Mississippi State University | D |
| Molloy College | M,O |
| Monmouth University | M,O |
| Monroe College | M |
| Montclair State University | M |
| Morgan State University | D |
| Murray State University | M |
| National American University (TX) | M,D |
| National University | M,O |
| National University College | M |
| Nebraska Christian College of Hope International University | M |
| New England College | M |
| New Jersey City University | M |
| New Mexico State University | D |
| New York Institute of Technology | M |
| New York University | M,D |
| Niagara University | M |
| Northwestern University | M |
| Northwest Missouri State University | M |
| Nova Southeastern University | M |
| Oakland University | M,O |
| Ohio Christian University | M |
| Oklahoma Christian University | M |
| Oklahoma State University | M,D |
| Old Dominion University | M,D |
| Oral Roberts University | M |
| Ottawa University | M |
| Pace University | M,D,O |
| Polytechnic University of Puerto Rico, Miami Campus | M |
| Pontifical Catholic University of Puerto Rico | M |
| Pontificia Universidad Catolica Madre y Maestra | M |
| Post University | M |
| Providence College | M |
| Purdue University Global | M |
| Queen's University at Kingston | M,D |
| Regent's University London | M |
| Regent University | M,D,O |
| Regis University | M,O |
| Roberts Wesleyan College | M |
| Roosevelt University | M |
| Rowan University | O |
| Rutgers University - Newark | D |
| Sacred Heart University | M,O |
| St. Bonaventure University | M |
| St. Catherine University | M |
| St. John's University (NY) | M |
| Saint Joseph's University | M,O |
| Saint Leo University | M,D |
| Saint Peter's University | M |
| St. Thomas Aquinas College | M |
| Saint Xavier University | M,O |
| Samford University | M |
| San Diego State University | M |
| San Francisco State University | M |
| San Ignacio University | M |
| Seton Hall University | M,O |
| Southeastern Louisiana University | M |
| Southern Adventist University | M |
| Southern Methodist University | M |
| Southern New Hampshire University | M,D,O |
| Southwest Minnesota State University | M |
| State University of New York Polytechnic Institute | M |
| Stephen F. Austin State University | M |
| Stevens Institute of Technology | M,O |
| Stony Brook University, State University of New York | M,O |
| Strayer University | M |
| Suffolk University | M |
| Syracuse University | M |
| Tarleton State University | M |
| Temple University | M,D* |
| Texas A&M University | M |
| Texas A&M University–Commerce | M |
| Texas Tech University | M,D |
| Thomas Jefferson University | M |
| Tiffin University | M |
| Trident University International | M,D |
| UNB Fredericton | M,D |
| United States International University–Africa | M |
| Universidad del Turabo | M |
| Universidad Iberoamericana | M,D |
| Universidad Metropolitana | M |
| Université de Sherbrooke | M |
| University at Albany, State University of New York | M |
| University at Buffalo, the State University of New York | M,D |
| The University of Akron | M |
| The University of Alabama | M,D |
| The University of Alabama at Birmingham | M |
| The University of Alabama in Huntsville | M,O |
| University of Alberta | D |
| The University of Arizona | M,D |
| University of Baltimore | M |
| University of Bridgeport | M |
| The University of British Columbia | D |
| University of California, Berkeley | D,O |
| University of California, Davis | M |
| University of California, Los Angeles | M,D |
| University of Central Missouri | M,D,O |
| University of Chicago | M,O |
| University of Cincinnati | M,D |
| University of Colorado Denver | M |
| University of Connecticut | M,D |
| University of Dallas | M,D |
| University of Dayton | M |
| University of Denver | M |
| University of Florida | M,D |
| University of Hawaii at Manoa | M,D |
| University of Houston | D |
| University of Houston–Victoria | M |
| The University of Iowa | M,D |
| The University of Kansas | M,D |
| University of La Verne | M |
| University of Lethbridge | M,D |
| The University of Manchester | M |
| University of Massachusetts Amherst | M,D |
| University of Memphis | M,D |
| University of Michigan–Flint | M,O |
| University of Minnesota, Twin Cities Campus | M,D |
| University of Mississippi | M,D |
| University of Missouri–St. Louis | M,D,O |
| University of Nebraska at Kearney | M |
| University of Nebraska–Lincoln | M,D |
| University of New Haven | M |
| University of New Mexico | M |
| The University of North Carolina at Chapel Hill | D |
| The University of North Carolina at Greensboro | M,D |
| University of North Texas | M,D,O |
| University of Notre Dame | M |
| University of Oregon | D |
| University of Pennsylvania | M,D |
| University of Phoenix - Bay Area Campus | M,D |
| University of Phoenix - Central Valley Campus | M |
| University of Phoenix - Dallas Campus | M |
| University of Phoenix - Hawaii Campus | M |
| University of Phoenix - Houston Campus | M |
| University of Phoenix - Las Vegas Campus | M |
| University of Phoenix–Online Campus | M,O |
| University of Phoenix - Phoenix Campus | M,O |
| University of Phoenix - Sacramento Valley Campus | M |
| University of Phoenix - San Antonio Campus | M |
| University of Phoenix - San Diego Campus | M |

| | |
|---|---|
| University of Pittsburgh | M,D* |
| University of Portland | M |
| University of Puerto Rico at Rio Piedras | M,D |
| University of Rhode Island | M,D |
| University of Rochester | M,D |
| University of Saint Mary | M |
| University of San Francisco | M |
| University of Saskatchewan | M |
| The University of Scranton | M |
| University of Sioux Falls | M |
| University of South Africa | M,D |
| University of South Alabama | M,D |
| University of South Dakota | M,O |
| University of South Florida | M,D |
| The University of Tampa | M,O |
| The University of Tennessee | M,D |
| The University of Texas at Arlington | M |
| The University of Texas at Austin | M,D |
| The University of Texas at Dallas | M |
| The University of Texas at San Antonio | M,D |
| The University of Texas at Tyler | M |
| The University of Texas Rio Grande Valley | M,D |
| University of the Cumberlands | M,D,O |
| University of the Sacred Heart | M |
| The University of Toledo | M |
| University of Utah | M,D |
| University of Virginia | M |
| The University of Western Ontario | M,D |
| University of Wisconsin–Madison | D |
| University of Wisconsin–Whitewater | M |
| Université Laval | M,O |
| Vancouver Island University | M |
| Vanderbilt University | M* |
| Villanova University | M |
| Virginia International University | M,O |
| Virginia Polytechnic Institute and State University | M,D |
| Wagner College | M |
| Walden University | M,D,O |
| Walsh College of Accountancy and Business Administration | M |
| Walsh University | M |
| Webster University | M,D,O |
| West Virginia University | M,D,O |
| Wilfrid Laurier University | M,D |
| William Woods University | M,D,O |
| Wilmington University | M,D |
| Wingate University | M |
| Worcester Polytechnic Institute | M,D,O |
| Worcester State University | M |
| Xavier University | M* |
| Yale University | D |
| Yeshiva University | M |

## MARKETING RESEARCH

| | |
|---|---|
| Hofstra University | M,O |
| Instituto Tecnológico y de Estudios Superiores de Monterrey, Campus Irapuato | M,D |
| Marquette University | M |
| Michigan State University | M,D |
| Pacific Lutheran University | M |
| Saint Leo University | M,D |
| Southern Illinois University Edwardsville | M |
| Towson University | M,O |
| Universidad Autonoma de Guadalajara | M,D |
| Universidad de las Americas, A.C. | M |
| University of Missouri–St. Louis | M,D,O |
| University of Rochester | M |
| The University of Texas at Arlington | M |
| University of Wisconsin–Madison | M |

## MARRIAGE AND FAMILY THERAPY

| | |
|---|---|
| Abilene Christian University | M |
| Adler University | M,D |
| Albizu University - Miami | M,D |
| Alliant International University–Irvine | M,D |
| Alliant International University - Los Angeles | M,D |
| Alliant International University–Sacramento | M,D |
| Alliant International University - San Diego | M,D |
| Amberton University | M |
| Amridge University | M,D |
| Antioch University New England | M,D,O |
| Antioch University Seattle | M,D |
| Appalachian State University | M |
| Arcadia University | M |
| Argosy University, Atlanta | M,D,O |
| Argosy University, Chicago | D |
| Argosy University, Hawaii | M |
| Argosy University, Los Angeles | M,D |
| Argosy University, Northern Virginia | M,D |
| Argosy University, Orange County | M,D |
| Argosy University, Tampa | M,D |
| Argosy University, Twin Cities | M,D,O |
| Arizona State University at Tempe | M,D |
| Azusa Pacific University | D |
| Barry University | M,O |
| Bayamón Central University | M,O |
| Bethel Seminary | M,D,O |
| Brandman University | M |
| Briercrest Seminary | M |
| Brigham Young University | M,D |
| California Lutheran University | M,D |
| California State University, Chico | M |
| California State University, Dominguez Hills | M |
| California State University, East Bay | M |
| California State University, Fresno | M |
| California State University, Long Beach | M,D |
| California State University, Northridge | M |
| Cambridge College | M,O |
| Campbellsville University | M |
| Capella University | M |
| Central Connecticut State University | M,O |
| Chapman University | M |
| Chatham University | M,D |
| Chestnut Hill College | M,D,O |
| The Chicago School of Professional Psychology at Downtown Los Angeles | M,D |
| The Chicago School of Professional Psychology at Irvine | M,D |
| Christian Theological Seminary | M,D |
| The College of New Jersey | M,O |
| The College of New Rochelle | M |
| Colorado State University | M,D |
| Converse College | M |
| Denver Seminary | M,D,O |
| Drexel University | M,D |
| Duquesne University | M,D,O |
| East Carolina University | M,D |
| Eastern Nazarene College | M |
| East Tennessee State University | M |
| Evangelical Seminary | M |
| Fairfield University | M,O |
| Florida State University | M,D |
| Fresno Pacific University | M |
| Friends University | M |
| Fuller Theological Seminary | M,D,O |
| Geneva College | M |
| George Fox University | M,O |
| Gonzaga University | M,D |
| Hampton University | M |
| Hardin-Simmons University | M |
| Hofstra University | M,O |
| Hope International University | M |
| Idaho State University | M,D,O |
| Indiana University South Bend | M,O |
| Indiana Wesleyan University | M |
| Instituto Tecnologico de Santo Domingo | M,O |
| Iona College | M |
| Jacksonville University | M |
| John Brown University | M,O |
| Kansas State University | M,D,O |
| Kean University | M |
| Lancaster Bible College | M,D |
| La Salle University | M |
| LeTourneau University | M |
| Lewis & Clark College | M |
| Liberty University | M,D,O |
| Lipscomb University | M,O |
| Loma Linda University | M,D,O |
| Long Island University - Brooklyn | M,O |
| Long Island University - Hudson | M,O |
| Loyola Marymount University | M |
| Loyola University New Orleans | M |
| Manhattan College | M |
| Maryville University of Saint Louis | M |
| Medaille College | M,D |
| Mercy College | M,O |
| Messiah University | M,O |
| Mid-America Christian University | M |
| MidAmerica Nazarene University | M |
| Midwest University | M,D |
| Mississippi College | M,O |
| Mount Mercy University | M |
| National University | M,O |
| Northcentral University | M,D,O |
| Northeastern Illinois University | M |
| Northern Kentucky University | M,O |
| Northwestern University | M |
| Northwest Nazarene University | M |
| Notre Dame de Namur University | M |
| Nova Southeastern University | M,D,O |
| Nyack College | M |
| Oklahoma Baptist University | M |
| Oral Roberts University | M,D |
| Ottawa University | M |
| Our Lady of the Lake University | M |
| Pacific Lutheran University | M |
| Pacific Oaks College | M |
| Palm Beach Atlantic University | M |
| Palo Alto University | M |
| Phillips Graduate University | M |
| Pillar College | M |
| Plymouth State University | M |
| Point Loma Nazarene University | M |
| Pontifical John Paul II Institute for Studies on Marriage and Family | M,D,O |
| Purdue University | M,D |
| Purdue University Fort Wayne | M,O |
| Purdue University Northwest | M |
| Reformed Theological Seminary–Jackson Campus | M,D,O |
| Regent University | M,D,O |
| Regis University | M,D,O |
| Richmont Graduate University | M |
| St. Cloud State University | M |
| Saint Mary's College of California | M,O |
| Saint Mary's University of Minnesota | M |
| Saint Paul University | M |
| St. Thomas University - Florida | M,O |
| San Francisco State University | M |
| Saybrook University | M,D |
| Seattle Pacific University | M,O |
| Seattle University | M |
| Sioux Falls Seminary | M |
| Southeastern University (FL) | M |
| Southern California Seminary | M,D |
| Southern Nazarene University | M |
| Syracuse University | M,D |
| Texas A&M University–Central Texas | M,O |
| Texas A&M University–San Antonio | M |
| Texas State University | M |
| Texas Tech University | M,D |
| Texas Woman's University | M,D |
| Thomas Jefferson University | M,D |
| Trevecca Nazarene University | M,D |
| Universidad de las Americas, A.C. | M |
| The University of Akron | M |
| The University of Alabama | M |
| University of Central Florida | M,O |
| University of Central Oklahoma | M |
| University of Colorado Denver | M |
| University of Denver | M,D,O |
| University of Florida | M,D,O |
| University of Guelph | M,D |
| University of Holy Cross | M,D |
| University of Houston–Clear Lake | M |
| The University of Iowa | M,D |
| University of La Verne | M |
| University of Louisiana at Monroe | M,D |
| University of Louisville | M,D,O |
| University of Mary Hardin-Baylor | M |
| University of Maryland, College Park | M,D |
| University of Massachusetts Boston | M,O |
| University of Miami | M,O |
| University of Minnesota, Twin Cities Campus | M,D |
| University of Mobile | M |
| University of Nebraska–Lincoln | M,D |
| University of New Hampshire | M,O |
| The University of North Carolina at Greensboro | M,D,O |
| University of Oregon | M,D |
| University of Phoenix - Bay Area Campus | M |
| University of Phoenix - Central Valley Campus | M |
| University of Phoenix - Las Vegas Campus | M |
| University of Phoenix - Phoenix Campus | M |
| University of Rhode Island | M |
| University of Rochester | M |
| University of Saint Joseph | M |
| University of San Diego | M |
| University of San Francisco | M |
| University of Southern California | M |
| University of Southern Mississippi | M |
| University of South Florida | M,D,O |
| The University of Texas at Tyler | M |
| The University of West Alabama | M |
| The University of Winnipeg | M,O |
| University of Wisconsin–Stout | M |
| Utah State University | M,D |
| Valdosta State University | M,O |
| Walden University | M,D |
| Western Kentucky University | M |
| Western Seminary–Sacramento Campus | M |
| Western Seminary - San Jose Campus | M,O |
| Wheaton College | M,D |
| William & Mary | M,D* |

## MASS COMMUNICATION

| | |
|---|---|
| American University | M,D,O |
| The American University in Cairo | M,O |
| Arizona State University at Tempe | M,D |
| Arkansas State University | M |
| Boston University | M |
| Brigham Young University | M |
| California State University, Fullerton | M |
| California State University, Northridge | M |
| Drexel University | M |
| Florida International University | M |
| Fordham University | M |
| The George Washington University | M,O |
| Georgia State University | M,D |
| Grambling State University | M |
| Howard University | M,D |
| Iona College | M,O |
| Iowa State University of Science and Technology | M |
| Kansas State University | M |
| Kent State University | M |
| Lindenwood University | M |
| Louisiana State University and Agricultural & Mechanical College | M,D |
| Lynn University | M,O |
| Marquette University | M,O |
| Middle Tennessee State University | M |
| Murray State University | M |
| North Dakota State University | M,D |
| Oklahoma State University | M |
| Penn State University Park | M,D* |
| Point Park University | M |
| St. Cloud State University | M |
| St. John's University (NY) | M |
| San Jose State University | M |
| Southern Illinois University Carbondale | M,D |
| Southern Illinois University Edwardsville | M |
| Southern University and Agricultural and Mechanical College | M |
| Stephen F. Austin State University | M |
| Syracuse University | M,D |
| Texas Christian University | M |
| Texas State University | M |
| Texas Tech University | M,D |
| The University of Alabama | D |
| University of Arkansas at Little Rock | M |
| University of Colorado Boulder | M,D |
| University of Denver | M |
| University of Florida | M,D |
| University of Georgia | M,D |
| University of Houston | M |
| The University of Iowa | M,D |
| University of Minnesota, Twin Cities Campus | M,D |
| University of Nebraska–Lincoln | M |
| University of Oklahoma | M,D |
| University of Puerto Rico at Rio Piedras | M |
| University of South Florida | M,O |
| University of Wisconsin–Madison | M,D |
| University of Wisconsin–Superior | M |
| University of Wisconsin–Whitewater | M |
| Université Laval | M,D |
| Virginia Commonwealth University | M |

## MATERIALS ENGINEERING

| | |
|---|---|
| Alabama Agricultural and Mechanical University | M |
| Arizona State University at Tempe | M,D |
| Auburn University | M,D |
| Binghamton University, State University of New York | M,D |
| Boise State University | M,D |
| Boston University | M,D |
| California State University, Northridge | M |
| Carleton University | M,D |
| Carnegie Mellon University | M,D |
| Case Western Reserve University | M,D |
| The Catholic University of America | M |
| Clarkson University | D |
| Clemson University | M,D |
| Colorado School of Mines | M,D |
| Columbia University | M,D |
| Cornell University | M,D |
| Dartmouth College | M,D |
| Drexel University | M,D |
| Duke University | M |
| Florida International University | M,D |
| Florida State University | M,D |
| Georgia Institute of Technology | M,D |
| Illinois Institute of Technology | M,D |
| Instituto Tecnológico y de Estudios Superiores de Monterrey, Campus Estado de México | M,D |
| Iowa State University of Science and Technology | M,D |
| Johns Hopkins University | M,D |
| Lehigh University | M,D |
| Massachusetts Institute of Technology | M,D,O |
| McGill University | M,D,O |
| McMaster University | M,D |
| Michigan State University | M,D |
| Michigan Technological University | M,D |
| Missouri University of Science and Technology | M,D |
| New Jersey Institute of Technology | M,D,O |
| New Mexico Institute of Mining and Technology | M,D |
| North Carolina State University | M,D |
| Northwestern University | M,D,O |
| The Ohio State University | M,D |
| Oklahoma State University | M,D |
| Penn State University Park | M,D* |
| Portland State University | M,D |
| Purdue University | M,D |
| Queen's University at Kingston | M,D |
| Rensselaer Polytechnic Institute | M,D |
| Rochester Institute of Technology | M |
| Rutgers University - New Brunswick | M,D |
| San Jose State University | M |
| South Dakota School of Mines and Technology | M,D |
| Stanford University | M,D,O |
| Stevens Institute of Technology | M,D |
| Stony Brook University, State University of New York | M,D |
| Texas A&M University | M,D |
| Texas State University | D |
| Tuskegee University | D |
| The University of Alabama | M,D |
| The University of Alabama at Birmingham | M,D |
| University of Alberta | M,D |
| The University of Arizona | M,D |
| The University of British Columbia | M,D |
| University of California, Berkeley | M,D |
| University of California, Davis | M,D |
| University of California, Irvine | M,D |
| University of California, Los Angeles | M,D |
| University of California, Riverside | M |
| University of California, Santa Barbara | M,D |
| University of Central Florida | M,D |
| University of Cincinnati | M,D |
| University of Colorado Boulder | M,D |
| University of Connecticut | M |
| University of Dayton | M,D |
| University of Delaware | M,D |
| University of Denver | M,D |
| University of Florida | M,D |
| University of Illinois at Chicago | M,D |
| University of Illinois at Urbana-Champaign | M,D |
| The University of Iowa | M,D |

*M—masters degree; D—doctorate; O—other advanced degree; *—Close-Up and/or Display*

University of Kentucky M,D
University of Maryland, College Park M,D
University of Michigan M,D
University of Minnesota, Twin Cities Campus M,D
University of Nebraska–Lincoln M,D
University of Nevada, Las Vegas M,D,O
University of Nevada, Reno M,D
University of New Hampshire M,D
University of Pennsylvania M,D
University of Puerto Rico at Mayagüez M,D
University of Southern California M,D,O
University of South Florida M,D,O
The University of Tennessee M,D
The University of Texas at Arlington M,D
The University of Texas at Austin M,D
The University of Texas at Dallas M,D
The University of Texas at El Paso M,D
The University of Texas at San Antonio M,D
University of Toronto M,D
University of Utah M,D
University of Washington M,D
The University of Western Ontario M,D
University of Windsor M,D
University of Wisconsin–Madison M,D
University of Wisconsin–Milwaukee M,D*
Washington State University M,D
West Virginia University M,D
Worcester Polytechnic Institute M,D
Wright State University M

## MATERIALS SCIENCES

Air Force Institute of Technology M,D
Alabama Agricultural and Mechanical University M,D
Alfred University M,D
Arizona State University at Tempe M,D
Binghamton University, State University of New York M,D
Boston University M,D
Brown University M,D
California Institute of Technology M,D
Carnegie Mellon University M,D
Case Western Reserve University M,D
The Catholic University of America M
Central Michigan University D
Clarkson University D
Clemson University M,D
Colorado School of Mines M,D
Colorado State University M,D
Columbia University M,D
Cornell University M,D
Dartmouth College M,D
Duke University M,D
Florida International University M,D
Florida State University M,D
Georgetown University D
The George Washington University M,D
Harvard University M,D*
Illinois Institute of Technology M,D
Indiana University Bloomington M,D
Instituto Tecnológico y de Estudios Superiores de Monterrey, Campus Estado de México M,D
Iowa State University of Science and Technology M,D
Jackson State University M,D
Johns Hopkins University M,D
Lehigh University M,D
Louisiana Tech University M,D,O
Massachusetts Institute of Technology M,D,O
McMaster University M,D
Michigan State University M,D
Missouri State University M
Missouri University of Science and Technology M,D
Montana Technological University D
New Jersey Institute of Technology M,D,O
Norfolk State University M
North Carolina State University M,D
North Dakota State University M,D
Northwestern University M,D,O
The Ohio State University M,D
Oklahoma State University M,D
Oregon State University M,D
Penn State University Park M,D*
Princeton University D
Rice University M,D
Rochester Institute of Technology M
Rutgers University - New Brunswick M,D
South Dakota School of Mines and Technology M,D
Stanford University M,D,O
State University of New York College of Environmental Science and Forestry M,D,O
Stevens Institute of Technology M,D
Stony Brook University, State University of New York M,D
Texas A&M University M,D
Texas State University D
Trent University M
UNB Fredericton M,D
Université du Québec, Institut National de la Recherche Scientifique M,D
University at Buffalo, the State University of New York M,D
The University of Alabama in Huntsville M,D
The University of Arizona M,D
University of Calgary M,D
University of California, Berkeley M,D
University of California, Davis M,D
University of California, Irvine M,D
University of California, Los Angeles M,D
University of California, Riverside M
University of California, San Diego M,D
University of California, Santa Barbara M,D
University of Central Florida M,D
University of Cincinnati M,D
University of Colorado Boulder M,D
University of Connecticut M,D
University of Delaware M,D
University of Denver M,D
University of Florida M,D
University of Idaho M,D
University of Illinois at Urbana-Champaign M,D
University of Kentucky M,D
The University of Manchester M,D
University of Maryland, College Park M,D
University of Michigan M,D
University of Minnesota, Twin Cities Campus M,D
University of Mississippi Medical Center M,D
University of Nebraska–Lincoln M,D
University of New Hampshire M,D
University of Pennsylvania M,D
University of Pittsburgh M,D*
University of Puerto Rico at Mayagüez M,D
University of Rochester M,D
University of Southern California M,D,O
University of South Florida O
The University of Tennessee M,D
The University of Texas at Arlington M,D
The University of Texas at Austin M,D
The University of Texas at Dallas M,D
The University of Texas at El Paso M,D
The University of Toledo M,D
University of Toronto M,D
University of Utah M,D
University of Vermont M,D
University of Virginia M,D
University of Washington M,D
Vanderbilt University M,D*
Washington State University M,D
Washington University in St. Louis M,D
Wayne State University M,D,O
West Virginia University M,D
Worcester Polytechnic Institute M,D
Wright State University M

## MATERNAL AND CHILD/NEONATAL NURSING

Boston College M,D
Case Western Reserve University M
Creighton University M,D,O
Duke University M,D,O
Hardin-Simmons University M
Lehman College of the City University of New York M
Louisiana State University Health Sciences Center M,D,O
Medical University of South Carolina M,D
Northeastern University M,D,O
Old Dominion University M,D
Regis University M,D,O
Saint Francis Medical Center College of Nursing M,D,O
Stony Brook University, State University of New York M,D,O
University of Alberta D
University of Cincinnati M,D
University of Connecticut M,O
University of Delaware M,O
University of Illinois at Chicago M,O
University of Indianapolis M,D
University of Louisville M,D
University of Maryland, Baltimore M,D,O
University of Missouri–Kansas City M,D
University of Pennsylvania M
University of Puerto Rico - Medical Sciences Campus M
University of Rochester M,D
University of South Africa M,D
The University of Texas at Austin M,D
Wayne State University M,D
Wright State University M

## MATERNAL AND CHILD HEALTH

Bank Street College of Education M
Bastyr University M,O
Columbia University M,D
East Carolina University M,D,O
Instituto Tecnologico de Santo Domingo M,O
Troy University M,D
The University of Alabama at Birmingham M,D
University of California, Davis M
University of Manitoba M
University of Maryland, College Park M,D
University of Minnesota, Twin Cities Campus M
The University of North Carolina at Chapel Hill M,D
University of Puerto Rico - Medical Sciences Campus M
University of South Florida O
The University of Texas Health Science Center at Houston M,D,O
University of Washington M,D

## MATHEMATICAL AND COMPUTATIONAL FINANCE

Austin Peay State University M
Boston University M,D
Carnegie Mellon University M,D
DePaul University M,D
Florida State University M,D
The George Washington University M,D,O
Illinois Institute of Technology M,D
Johns Hopkins University M,D,O
New Jersey Institute of Technology M,D,O
New York University M,D
North Carolina State University M
Oregon State University M,D
Rice University M,D
Rochester Institute of Technology M
Université de Montréal M,D,O
University of Alberta M,D,O
University of California, Santa Barbara M,D
University of Chicago M
University of Connecticut M
University of Dayton M
The University of Manchester M,D
University of Miami M,D
University of Notre Dame M,D
University of Southern California M,D
University of Toronto M

## MATHEMATICAL PHYSICS

Indiana University Bloomington M,D
New Mexico Institute of Mining and Technology M,D
University of Alberta M,D,O
University of Colorado Boulder M,D

## MATHEMATICS

Acadia University M
Alabama State University M
American University M,O
American University of Sharjah M,D
Appalachian State University M
Arizona State University at Tempe M,D,O
Arkansas State University M
Auburn University M,D
Augustana University M
Aurora University M
Ball State University M
Baylor University M,D
Bemidji State University M
Binghamton University, State University of New York M,D
Boise State University M
Boston College D
Boston University M,D
Bowling Green State University M,D
Brandeis University M,D
Brigham Young University M,D
Brock University M
Brooklyn College of the City University of New York M
Brown University D
Bryn Mawr College M,D
Bucknell University M
Cabrini University M,D
California Institute of Technology D
California Polytechnic State University, San Luis Obispo M
California State Polytechnic University, Pomona M
California State University Channel Islands M
California State University, East Bay M
California State University, Fresno M
California State University, Fullerton M
California State University, Long Beach M
California State University, Los Angeles M
California State University, Northridge M
California State University, Sacramento M
California State University, San Bernardino M
California State University, San Marcos M
Carleton University M,D
Carlow University M
Carnegie Mellon University M,D
Case Western Reserve University M,D
Central Connecticut State University M,O
Central European University M,D
Central Michigan University M,D
Chicago State University M
City College of the City University of New York M
Claremont Graduate University M,D
Clark Atlanta University M
Clarkson University M,D
Clemson University M,D
Cleveland State University M
College of Charleston M
Colorado State University M,D
Columbia University M,D
Columbus State University M,O
Concordia University (Canada) M,D
Cornell University D
Dalhousie University M,D
Dartmouth College M,D
Delaware State University M
DePaul University M,D
Drew University M,D,O
Drexel University M,D
Duke University D
Duquesne University M
East Carolina University M
Eastern Illinois University M
Eastern Kentucky University M
Eastern Michigan University M
East Tennessee State University M,O
Elizabeth City State University M
Emory University M,D
Emporia State University M
Fairfield University M
Fairleigh Dickinson University, Metropolitan Campus M
Florida Atlantic University M,D
Florida Gulf Coast University M
Florida International University M
George Mason University M,D
Georgetown University M
The George Washington University M,D,O
Georgia Institute of Technology M,D
Georgia Southern University M
Georgia State University M,D
Governors State University M
The Graduate Center, City University of New York D
Harvard University D*
Hofstra University M,D,O
Houston Baptist University M,D
Howard University M,D
Hunter College of the City University of New York M
Idaho State University M,D
Illinois State University M,D
Indiana State University M
Indiana University Bloomington M,D
Indiana University of Pennsylvania M
Indiana University-Purdue University Indianapolis M,D
Instituto Tecnologico de Santo Domingo M,D,O
Iowa State University of Science and Technology M,D
Jackson State University M
Jacksonville State University M
Johns Hopkins University D
Kansas State University M,D,O
Kent State University M,D,O
Kutztown University of Pennsylvania M
Lakehead University M
Lamar University M
Lee University M,O
Lehigh University M,D
Lehman College of the City University of New York M
Louisiana State University and Agricultural & Mechanical College M,D
Louisiana Tech University M,D,O
Loyola University Chicago M
Manhattan College M,O
Manhattanville College M,O
Marquette University M,D
Marshall University M
Marygrove College M,O
Massachusetts Institute of Technology D
McGill University M,D
McMaster University M,D
McNeese State University M
Memorial University of Newfoundland M,D
Mercer University M,D,O
Miami University M
Michigan State University M,D
Michigan Technological University M,D
Middle Tennessee State University M
Minnesota State University Mankato M
Mississippi College M
Mississippi State University M,D
Missouri State University M
Missouri University of Science and Technology M,D
Montana State University M,D
Montclair State University M
Morgan State University M,D
Murray State University M
New Jersey Institute of Technology M,D,O
New Mexico Institute of Mining and Technology M,D
New York University M,D
North Carolina Agricultural and Technical State University M
North Carolina Central University M
North Carolina State University M,D
North Dakota State University M,D
Northeastern Illinois University M
Northeastern University M,D
Northern Arizona University M,O
Northern Illinois University M,D
Northwestern University D
Northwest Missouri State University M,O
Oakland University M
The Ohio State University M,D
Ohio University M,D
Oklahoma State University M,D
Old Dominion University M,D
Oregon State University M,D
Pace University M,O
Penn State University Park M,D*
Pittsburg State University M
Portland State University M,D,O
Princeton University D
Purdue University M,D
Purdue University Fort Wayne M,O
Purdue University Northwest M
Queens College of the City University of New York M
Queen's University at Kingston M,D
Regent University M,D,O
Rensselaer Polytechnic Institute M,D
Rhode Island College M,O
Rice University D
Rivier University M
Rochester Institute of Technology M,D,O
Roosevelt University M
Rowan University M
Royal Military College of Canada M
Rutgers University - Camden M
Rutgers University - Newark D
Rutgers University - New Brunswick M,D
St. John's University (NY) M
Saint Joseph's University M,O
Saint Louis University M,D

Salem State University M
Sam Houston State University M
San Diego State University M,D
San Francisco State University M
Simon Fraser University M,D
Smith College O
South Carolina State University M
South Dakota State University M,D
Southeast Missouri State University M
Southern Connecticut State University M
Southern Illinois University Carbondale M,D
Southern Illinois University Edwardsville M
Southern Methodist University M,D
Southern University and Agricultural and Mechanical College M
Stanford University M,D
State University of New York College at Cortland M
State University of New York College at Potsdam M
Stephen F. Austin State University M
Stevens Institute of Technology M,D
Stony Brook University, State University of New York M,D
SUNY Brockport M
Syracuse University M,D
Tarleton State University M
Temple University M,D*
Tennessee State University M,D
Tennessee Technological University M
Texas A&M International University M
Texas A&M University M,D
Texas A&M University–Central Texas M,O
Texas A&M University–Commerce M,O
Texas A&M University–Corpus Christi M
Texas A&M University–Kingsville M
Texas Christian University M,D
Texas Southern University M
Texas State University M
Texas Tech University M,D
Texas Woman's University M
Tufts University M,D
Tulane University M,D
UNB Fredericton M,D
Université de Moncton M
Université de Montréal M,D,O
Université de Sherbrooke M,D
Université du Québec à Montréal M,D
Université du Québec à Trois-Rivières M
University at Albany, State University of New York M,D
University at Buffalo, the State University of New York M,D
The University of Akron M
The University of Alabama M,D
The University of Alabama at Birmingham M
The University of Alabama in Huntsville M,D
University of Alaska Fairbanks M,D,O
University of Alberta M,D,O
The University of Arizona M,D
University of Arkansas M,D
University of Arkansas at Little Rock M,O
The University of British Columbia M,D
University of Calgary M,D
University of California, Berkeley M,D
University of California, Davis M,D
University of California, Irvine M,D
University of California, Los Angeles M,D
University of California, Riverside M,D
University of California, San Diego M,D
University of California, Santa Barbara M,D
University of California, Santa Cruz M,D
University of Central Arkansas M
University of Central Florida M,D,O
University of Central Missouri M,D,O
University of Central Oklahoma M
University of Chicago D
University of Cincinnati M,D
University of Colorado Boulder M,D
University of Colorado Colorado Springs D
University of Colorado Denver M,D
University of Delaware M,D
University of Denver M,D
The University of Findlay M,D
University of Florida M,D
University of Georgia M,D
University of Guelph M,D
University of Hawaii at Manoa M,D
University of Houston M,D
University of Houston–Clear Lake M
University of Idaho M,D
University of Illinois at Chicago M,D
University of Illinois at Urbana-Champaign M,D
The University of Iowa M,D
The University of Kansas M,D,O
University of Kentucky M,D
University of Lethbridge M,D
University of Louisiana at Lafayette M,D
University of Louisville M,D
University of Lynchburg M
University of Maine M
The University of Manchester M,D
University of Manitoba M,D
University of Maryland, College Park M,D
University of Massachusetts Amherst M,D
University of Massachusetts Lowell D
University of Memphis M,D,O
University of Miami M,D
University of Michigan M,D
University of Minnesota, Twin Cities Campus M,D,O
University of Mississippi M,D
University of Missouri M,D
University of Missouri–Kansas City M,D
University of Missouri–St. Louis M,D
University of Montana M,D
University of Nebraska at Omaha M
University of Nebraska–Lincoln M,D
University of Nevada, Las Vegas M,D
University of Nevada, Reno M
University of New Hampshire M,D,O
University of New Mexico M,D
University of New Orleans M
The University of North Carolina at Chapel Hill M,D
The University of North Carolina at Charlotte M,D,O
The University of North Carolina at Greensboro M,D
The University of North Carolina Wilmington M,O
University of North Dakota M
University of Northern British Columbia M,D,O
University of Northern Colorado M,D
University of Northern Iowa M
University of North Florida M
University of North Texas M,D,O
University of Notre Dame M,D
University of Oklahoma M,D
University of Oregon M,D
University of Ottawa M,D
University of Pennsylvania M,D
University of Pittsburgh M,D*
University of Puerto Rico at Mayagüez M
University of Puerto Rico at Rio Piedras M,D
University of Regina M,D
University of Rhode Island M,D
University of Rochester D
University of San Diego M
University of Saskatchewan M,D
University of South Alabama M
University of South Carolina M,D
University of South Dakota M
University of Southern California M,D
University of South Florida M,D,O
The University of Tennessee M,D
The University of Tennessee at Chattanooga M
The University of Texas at Arlington M,D
The University of Texas at Austin M,D
The University of Texas at Dallas M,D
The University of Texas at El Paso M
The University of Texas at San Antonio M
The University of Texas at Tyler M
The University of Texas Rio Grande Valley M
University of the Incarnate Word M
University of the Virgin Islands M
The University of Toledo M,D
University of Toronto M,D
The University of Tulsa M,D
University of Utah M,D
University of Vermont M,D
University of Victoria M,D
University of Virginia M,D
University of Washington M,D
University of Waterloo M,D
The University of Western Ontario M,D
University of West Florida M
University of Windsor M,D
University of Wisconsin–Madison D
University of Wisconsin–Milwaukee M,D*
University of Wyoming M,D
Université Laval M,D
Utah State University M,D
Vanderbilt University M,D*
Villanova University M
Virginia Commonwealth University M
Virginia Polytechnic Institute and State University M,D
Virginia State University M
Wake Forest University M
Washington State University M,D
Washington University in St. Louis M,D
Wayne State University M,D,O
Wesleyan University M,D
Western Connecticut State University M
Western Illinois University M
Western Kentucky University M
Western Michigan University M,D
Western Washington University M
West Texas A&M University M
West Virginia University M,D
Wichita State University M,D
Wilfrid Laurier University M
Worcester Polytechnic Institute M,D,O
Wright State University M
Yale University M,D
Yeshiva University M
York University M,D
Youngstown State University M

## MATHEMATICS EDUCATION

Adams State University M
Alabama Agricultural and Mechanical University M,O
Alabama State University M,O
Appalachian State University M
Arcadia University M,D,O
Arizona State University at Tempe M,D,O
Arkansas State University M
Asbury University M
Aurora University M
Austin Peay State University M
Ball State University M
Bank Street College of Education M
Bard College M
Bemidji State University M
Binghamton University, State University of New York M
Bloomsburg University of Pennsylvania M
Bob Jones University M,D,O
Boise State University M
Boston College M,D,O
Bowling Green State University M,D
Bridgewater State University M
Brigham Young University M
Brooklyn College of the City University of New York M
Buffalo State College, State University of New York M
California State University, Chico M
California State University, East Bay M
California State University, Fresno M
California State University, Fullerton M
California State University, Long Beach M
California State University, Northridge M
California State University, San Bernardino M
California University of Pennsylvania M
Cambridge College M,D,O
Caribbean University M,D
Central Michigan University M,D
Chatham University M
The Citadel, The Military College of South Carolina M,O
City College of the City University of New York M,O
Clarion University of Pennsylvania M
Clark Atlanta University M
Clayton State University M
Clemson University M,D,O
Cleveland State University M
College of Charleston M
College of Staten Island of the City University of New York M
The Colorado College M
Columbus State University M,O
Concordia University (United States) M,D
Concordia University (Canada) M,D
Converse College M
Cornell University M,D
Delaware State University M
DePaul University M,D
Duquesne University M
East Carolina University M,O
Eastern Illinois University M
Eastern Kentucky University M
Eastern University M,O
Elizabeth City State University M
Fitchburg State University M
Florida Agricultural and Mechanical University M
Florida Gulf Coast University M
Florida International University M,D,O
Framingham State University M
Fresno Pacific University M
George Mason University M
The George Washington University M
Georgia Southwestern State University M,O
Georgia State University M,D,O
Gordon College M,O
Grambling State University M,D,O
Hampton University M
Harding University M,O
Harvard University M,O*
High Point University M,D
Hofstra University M,D,O
Hood College M,O
Hunter College of the City University of New York M
Idaho State University M,D
Illinois Institute of Technology M,D
Illinois State University M,D
Indiana University Bloomington M,D,O
Indiana University of Pennsylvania M
Indiana University-Purdue University Indianapolis M,D
Instituto Tecnológico y de Estudios Superiores de Monterrey, Campus Ciudad Obregón M
Inter American University of Puerto Rico, Arecibo Campus M
Inter American University of Puerto Rico, Metropolitan Campus M
Inter American University of Puerto Rico, Ponce Campus M
Inter American University of Puerto Rico, San Germán Campus M
Iona College M
Iowa State University of Science and Technology M,D
Jackson State University M
James Madison University M
Kennesaw State University M
Kent State University M,D
Lake Forest College M
Lebanon Valley College M,O
Lee University M,O
Lehman College of the City University of New York M
Lesley University M,D,O
Longwood University M
Loyola Marymount University M
Manhattanville College M,O
Marquette University M,D
McDaniel College M,O
McNeese State University O
Metropolitan State University M
Miami University M
Michigan State University M,D
Middle Tennessee State University M,D
Millersville University of Pennsylvania M,D
Minnesota State University Mankato M
Minot State University M
Mississippi College M,D,O
Missouri State University M
Missouri University of Science and Technology M,D
Molloy College M,O
Montana State University M,D
Montclair State University M,D,O
Morehead State University M
Morgan State University M,D
Mount Holyoke College M
Murray State University M
National Louis University M,D,O
National University M,O
New Jersey City University M
New York University M
North Carolina Agricultural and Technical State University M
North Carolina State University M,D
North Dakota State University D
Northeastern Illinois University M
Northeastern State University M
Northern Arizona University M,O
Northwest Missouri State University M,D,O
The Ohio State University M,D
Oregon State University M,D
Plymouth State University M
Portland State University M,D,O
Providence College M
Purdue University M,D,O
Purdue University Fort Wayne M,O
Purdue University Global M
Purdue University Northwest M
Queens College of the City University of New York M,O
Quinnipiac University M
Radford University M
Rhode Island College M
Rowan University M,O
Rutgers University - Camden M
Rutgers University - New Brunswick M,D
St. John Fisher College M
St. John's University (NY) D
St. Joseph's College, Long Island Campus M
Saint Peter's University M,D,O
Salem State University M
Salisbury University M
San Diego State University M,D
San Francisco State University M,O
Seattle Pacific University M
Shippensburg University of Pennsylvania M
Simon Fraser University M,D
Slippery Rock University of Pennsylvania M
Smith College M
South Carolina State University M
Southeastern Oklahoma State University M
Southern Illinois University Edwardsville M
Southern University and Agricultural and Mechanical College D
Southwestern Oklahoma State University M
Southwest Minnesota State University M
State University of New York at Fredonia M,O
State University of New York at Plattsburgh M
State University of New York College at Cortland M
State University of New York College at Old Westbury M
State University of New York College at Potsdam M
Stephen F. Austin State University M
Stevenson University M
Stony Brook University, State University of New York M,O
SUNY Brockport M,O
Syracuse University M,D
Teachers College, Columbia University M,D
Teachers College of San Joaquin M
Temple University M*
Tennessee Technological University M,O
Texas Christian University M
Texas State University D
Texas Woman's University M
Towson University M
Tufts University M,D

*M—masters degree; D—doctorate; O—other advanced degree; *—Close-Up and/or Display*

| | |
|---|---|
| Universidad Autonoma de Guadalajara | M,D |
| University at Buffalo, the State University of New York | M,D,O |
| The University of Akron | M |
| The University of Alabama in Huntsville | M,D,O |
| University of Alaska Southeast | M |
| The University of Arizona | M |
| University of Arkansas | M |
| University of Arkansas at Pine Bluff | M |
| The University of British Columbia | M,D |
| University of California, Berkeley | M,D |
| University of California, San Diego | D |
| University of Central Arkansas | M |
| University of Central Florida | M,O |
| University of Cincinnati | M,D |
| University of Colorado Denver | M,D |
| University of Connecticut | M,D |
| University of Dayton | M |
| University of Detroit Mercy | M,D |
| University of Florida | M,D,O |
| University of Georgia | M,D,O |
| University of Illinois at Chicago | M,D |
| University of Illinois at Urbana-Champaign | M,D |
| University of Indianapolis | M |
| The University of Iowa | M,D |
| University of Louisiana at Lafayette | M |
| University of Maryland, Baltimore County | M |
| University of Massachusetts Dartmouth | M,D,O |
| University of Memphis | M,D |
| University of Miami | D |
| University of Minnesota, Twin Cities Campus | M,D,O |
| University of Mississippi | M,D,O |
| University of Missouri | M,D,O |
| University of Montana | M,D |
| University of Nebraska at Kearney | M |
| University of Nevada, Reno | M |
| University of New Hampshire | M,D,O |
| The University of North Carolina at Chapel Hill | M |
| The University of North Carolina at Greensboro | M,D,O |
| The University of North Carolina at Pembroke | M |
| University of Northern Colorado | M,D |
| University of Northern Iowa | M |
| University of North Georgia | M |
| University of Oklahoma | M,D |
| University of Phoenix–Online Campus | M,O |
| University of Puerto Rico at Mayagüez | M |
| University of Puerto Rico at Rio Piedras | M,D |
| University of St. Francis (IL) | M,D,O |
| University of South Africa | M,D |
| University of South Carolina | M,D |
| University of South Dakota | M |
| University of Southern Indiana | M |
| University of Southern Mississippi | M,D |
| University of South Florida, St. Petersburg | M |
| The University of Tennessee | M,D,O |
| The University of Tennessee at Chattanooga | M |
| The University of Texas at Arlington | M,D |
| The University of Texas at Dallas | M |
| The University of Texas at San Antonio | M |
| University of the District of Columbia | M |
| University of the Incarnate Word | M |
| University of the Sacred Heart | M,O |
| University of the Virgin Islands | M |
| The University of Toledo | M,D,O |
| University of Utah | M,D |
| University of Victoria | M,D |
| University of Virginia | M,D,O |
| University of Washington | M,D |
| University of Washington, Tacoma | M |
| The University of West Alabama | M |
| University of Wisconsin–Milwaukee | M,D,O* |
| University of Wisconsin–Oshkosh | M |
| University of Wisconsin–River Falls | M |
| University of Wyoming | M,D |
| Utah Valley University | M |
| Wagner College | M |
| Walden University | M,D,O |
| Washington State University | M,D |
| Wayne State College | M |
| Wayne State University | M,D,O |
| Webster University | M,O |
| Western Governors University | M,O |
| Western Michigan University | M,D |
| Western New England University | M |
| Western Oregon University | M |
| Westfield State University | M |
| Widener University | M,D |
| William Jessup University | M |
| Wright State University | D |
| Youngstown State University | M |

## MECHANICAL ENGINEERING

| | |
|---|---|
| Alfred University | M,D |
| The American University in Cairo | M,D,O |
| American University of Sharjah | M,D |
| Arizona State University at Tempe | M,D |
| Arkansas Tech University | M |
| Auburn University | M,D |
| Baylor University | M,D |
| Binghamton University, State University of New York | M,D |
| Boise State University | M |
| Boston University | M,D |
| Bradley University | M |
| Brigham Young University | M,D |
| Brown University | M,D |
| Bucknell University | M |
| Buffalo State College, State University of New York | M |
| California Institute of Technology | M,D,O |
| California Polytechnic State University, San Luis Obispo | M |
| California State Polytechnic University, Pomona | M |
| California State University, Fresno | M |
| California State University, Fullerton | M |
| California State University, Long Beach | M,D |
| California State University, Los Angeles | M |
| California State University, Northridge | M |
| California State University, Sacramento | M |
| Carleton University | M,D |
| Carnegie Mellon University | M,D |
| Case Western Reserve University | M,D |
| The Catholic University of America | M,D |
| The Citadel, The Military College of South Carolina | M,O |
| City College of the City University of New York | M,D |
| Clemson University | M,D |
| Cleveland State University | M,D |
| Colorado School of Mines | M,D |
| Colorado State University | M,D |
| Columbia University | M,D |
| Concordia University (Canada) | M,D,O |
| Cooper Union for the Advancement of Science and Art | M |
| Cornell University | M,D |
| Dalhousie University | M,D |
| Dartmouth College | M,D |
| Drexel University | M,D |
| Duke University | M,D |
| Embry-Riddle Aeronautical University–Daytona | M,D |
| Fairfield University | M,O |
| Farmingdale State College | M |
| Florida Agricultural and Mechanical University | M,D |
| Florida Atlantic University | M,D |
| Florida Institute of Technology | M,D |
| Florida International University | M,D |
| Florida State University | M,D |
| Gannon University | M |
| The George Washington University | M,D,O |
| Georgia Institute of Technology | M,D |
| Georgia Southern University | M |
| Grand Valley State University | M |
| Harvard University | M,D* |
| Howard University | M,D |
| Idaho State University | M |
| Illinois Institute of Technology | M,D |
| Indiana University-Purdue University Indianapolis | M,D |
| Instituto Tecnológico y de Estudios Superiores de Monterrey, Campus Chihuahua | M,O |
| Instituto Tecnológico y de Estudios Superiores de Monterrey, Campus Monterrey | M,D |
| Inter American University of Puerto Rico, Bayamón Campus | M |
| Iowa State University of Science and Technology | M,D |
| Johns Hopkins University | M,D,O |
| Kansas State University | M,D |
| Kennesaw State University | M |
| Kettering University | M |
| Lamar University | M,D |
| Lawrence Technological University | M,D |
| Lehigh University | M,D |
| Louisiana State University and Agricultural & Mechanical College | M,D |
| Loyola Marymount University | M |
| Manhattan College | M |
| Marquette University | M,D,O |
| Marshall University | M |
| Massachusetts Institute of Technology | M,D,O |
| McGill University | M,D |
| McMaster University | M,D |
| McNeese State University | M |
| Memorial University of Newfoundland | M,D |
| Mercer University | M |
| Merrimack College | M |
| Miami University | M |
| Michigan State University | M,D |
| Michigan Technological University | M,D,O |
| Mississippi State University | M,D |
| Missouri University of Science and Technology | M,D |
| Montana State University | M,D |
| Naval Postgraduate School | M,D,O |
| New Jersey Institute of Technology | M,D |
| New Mexico Institute of Mining and Technology | M |
| New York Institute of Technology | M |
| New York University | M,D |
| North Carolina Agricultural and Technical State University | M,D |
| North Carolina State University | M,D |
| North Dakota State University | M,D |
| Northeastern University | M,D,O |
| Northern Arizona University | M,D |
| Northern Illinois University | M |
| Northwestern University | M,D |
| Oakland University | M,D |
| The Ohio State University | M,D |
| Ohio University | M |
| Oklahoma Christian University | M |
| Oklahoma State University | M,D |
| Old Dominion University | M,D |
| Oregon State University | M,D |
| Penn State Harrisburg | M,O |
| Penn State University Park | M,D* |
| Pittsburg State University | M |
| Polytechnic University of Puerto Rico | M |
| Polytechnique Montréal | M,D,O |
| Portland State University | M,D,O |
| Princeton University | M,D |
| Purdue University | M,D,O |
| Purdue University Fort Wayne | M |
| Purdue University Northwest | M |
| Queen's University at Kingston | M,D |
| Rensselaer at Hartford | M |
| Rensselaer Polytechnic Institute | M,D |
| Rice University | M,D |
| Rochester Institute of Technology | M |
| Rose-Hulman Institute of Technology | M |
| Rowan University | M,D |
| Royal Military College of Canada | M,D |
| Rutgers University - New Brunswick | M,D |
| Saint Martin's University | M |
| San Diego State University | M,D |
| San Jose State University | M |
| Santa Clara University | M,D,O |
| Simon Fraser University | M,D |
| South Carolina State University | M |
| South Dakota School of Mines and Technology | M,D |
| South Dakota State University | M,D |
| Southern Illinois University Carbondale | M,D |
| Southern Illinois University Edwardsville | M |
| Southern Methodist University | M,D |
| Stanford University | M,D,O |
| Stevens Institute of Technology | M,D,O |
| Stony Brook University, State University of New York | M,D |
| Syracuse University | M,D |
| Temple University | M* |
| Tennessee State University | M,D |
| Tennessee Technological University | M |
| Texas A&M University | M,D |
| Texas A&M University–Kingsville | M |
| Texas State University | M |
| Tufts University | M,D |
| Tuskegee University | M |
| UNB Fredericton | M,D |
| Universidad del Turabo | M |
| Université de Moncton | M |
| Université de Sherbrooke | M,D |
| University at Buffalo, the State University of New York | M,D |
| The University of Akron | M,D |
| The University of Alabama | M,D |
| The University of Alabama at Birmingham | M |
| The University of Alabama in Huntsville | M,D |
| University of Alaska Fairbanks | M |
| University of Alberta | M,D |
| The University of Arizona | M,D |
| University of Arkansas | M,D |
| University of Bridgeport | M |
| The University of British Columbia | M,D |
| University of Calgary | M,D |
| University of California, Berkeley | M,D |
| University of California, Davis | M,D,O |
| University of California, Irvine | M,D |
| University of California, Los Angeles | M,D |
| University of California, Merced | M,D |
| University of California, Riverside | M,D |
| University of California, San Diego | M,D |
| University of California, Santa Barbara | M,D |
| University of Central Florida | M,D |
| University of Central Oklahoma | M |
| University of Cincinnati | M,D |
| University of Colorado Boulder | M,D |
| University of Colorado Denver | M |
| University of Connecticut | M,D |
| University of Dayton | M,D |
| University of Delaware | M,D |
| University of Denver | M,D |
| University of Detroit Mercy | M,D |
| University of Florida | M,D |
| University of Hawaii at Manoa | M,D |
| University of Houston | M,D |
| University of Idaho | M,D |
| University of Illinois at Chicago | M,D |
| University of Illinois at Urbana-Champaign | M,D |
| The University of Iowa | M,D |
| The University of Kansas | M,D |
| University of Kentucky | M,D |
| University of Louisiana at Lafayette | M |
| University of Louisville | M,D |
| University of Maine | M,D |
| The University of Manchester | M,D |
| University of Manitoba | M,D |
| University of Maryland, Baltimore County | M,D |
| University of Maryland, College Park | M,D |
| University of Massachusetts Amherst | M,D |
| University of Massachusetts Dartmouth | M,O |
| University of Massachusetts Lowell | M,D |
| University of Memphis | M,D,O |
| University of Miami | M,D |
| University of Michigan | M,D |
| University of Michigan–Dearborn | M,D |
| University of Michigan–Flint | M |
| University of Minnesota, Twin Cities Campus | M,D |
| University of Mississippi | M,D |
| University of Missouri | M,D |
| University of Missouri–Kansas City | M,D,O |
| University of Nebraska–Lincoln | M,D |
| University of Nevada, Reno | M,D |
| University of New Hampshire | M,D |
| University of New Haven | M |
| University of New Mexico | M,D |
| University of New Orleans | M |
| University of North Dakota | M,D |
| University of North Florida | M |
| University of North Texas | M,D,O |
| University of Notre Dame | M,D |
| University of Oklahoma | M,D |
| University of Ottawa | M,D |
| University of Pennsylvania | M,D |
| University of Pittsburgh | M,D* |
| University of Portland | M |
| University of Puerto Rico at Mayagüez | M,D |
| University of Rochester | M,D |
| University of St. Thomas (MN) | M,O |
| University of Saskatchewan | M,D |
| University of South Alabama | M |
| University of South Carolina | M,D |
| University of Southern California | M,D,O |
| University of South Florida | M,D |
| The University of Tennessee | M,D |
| The University of Tennessee at Chattanooga | M |
| The University of Texas at Arlington | M,D |
| The University of Texas at Austin | M,D |
| The University of Texas at Dallas | M,D |
| The University of Texas at El Paso | M,D |
| The University of Texas at San Antonio | M,D |
| The University of Texas at Tyler | M |
| The University of Texas Rio Grande Valley | M |
| The University of Toledo | M,D |
| University of Toronto | M,D |
| The University of Tulsa | M,D |
| University of Utah | M,D |
| University of Vermont | M,D |
| University of Victoria | M,D |
| University of Virginia | M,D |
| University of Washington | M,D |
| University of Waterloo | M,D |
| The University of Western Ontario | M,D |
| University of Windsor | M,D |
| University of Wisconsin–Madison | M,D |
| University of Wisconsin–Milwaukee | M,D* |
| University of Wyoming | M,D |
| Université Laval | M,D |
| Utah State University | M,D |
| Vanderbilt University | M,D* |
| Villanova University | M,O |
| Virginia Commonwealth University | M,D |
| Washington State University | M,D |
| Washington University in St. Louis | M,D |
| Wayne State University | M,D |
| Western Michigan University | M,D |
| Western New England University | M |
| West Virginia University | M,D |
| Wichita State University | M,D |
| Widener University | M |
| Worcester Polytechnic Institute | M,D,O |
| Wright State University | M |
| Yale University | M,D |
| Youngstown State University | M |

## MECHANICS

| | |
|---|---|
| Brown University | M,D |
| California Institute of Technology | M,D |
| Carnegie Mellon University | M,D |
| Columbia University | M,D |
| Cornell University | M,D |
| Drexel University | M,D |
| Georgia Institute of Technology | M,D |
| Iowa State University of Science and Technology | M,D |
| Johns Hopkins University | M |
| Lehigh University | M,D |
| Louisiana State University and Agricultural & Mechanical College | M,D |
| McGill University | M,D |
| Michigan State University | M,D |
| Michigan Technological University | M,D,O |
| Montana State University | M,D |
| New Mexico Institute of Mining and Technology | M |
| Northwestern University | M,D |
| Ohio University | M,D |
| Penn State University Park | M,D* |
| Polytechnique Montréal | M,D,O |
| Rutgers University - New Brunswick | M,D |
| San Diego State University | M,D |
| Southern Illinois University Carbondale | M |
| Stanford University | M,D,O |
| UNB Fredericton | M,D |
| The University of Alabama | M,D |
| University of Calgary | M,D |
| University of California, Berkeley | M,D |
| University of California, Merced | M,D |
| University of California, San Diego | M,D |
| University of Cincinnati | M,D |
| University of Colorado Denver | M |
| University of Dayton | M |
| University of Illinois at Urbana-Champaign | M,D |
| University of Maryland, Baltimore County | O |
| University of Maryland, College Park | M,D |

University of Massachusetts Amherst M,D
University of Minnesota, Twin Cities Campus M,D
University of Nebraska–Lincoln M,D
University of Pennsylvania M,D
University of Southern California M,D,O
The University of Texas at Austin M,D
University of Washington M,D
University of Wisconsin–Madison M,D
University of Wisconsin–Milwaukee M,D*

### MEDIA STUDIES
American University M,D
Angelo State University M
Arizona State University at Tempe M,D
Arkansas State University M
Austin Peay State University M
Boston University M,D
Bowling Green State University M,D
Brooklyn College of the City University of New York M
Carnegie Mellon University M
Central Michigan University M
Champlain College M
City College of the City University of New York M
Claremont Graduate University M,D,O
College of Staten Island of the City University of New York M
Colorado State University M,D
Columbia University M
Concordia University (Canada) M,D,O
Cornell University M,D
Dallas Theological Seminary M,D,O
DePaul University M
Drexel University M
Duke University M
Fairleigh Dickinson University, Metropolitan Campus M
Fielding Graduate University M,D,O
Florida Atlantic University M,O
Florida State University M,D
Fordham University M,D
Fordham University M,D
Full Sail University M
Georgetown University M,D
Georgia State University M,D
Howard University M,D
Hunter College of the City University of New York M
Indiana State University M
Indiana University Bloomington M,D
Indiana University of Pennsylvania D
International University in Geneva M,D
Johns Hopkins University M
Kent State University M
La Salle University M,O
Lindenwood University M,O
Lindenwood University–Belleville M
Long Island University - Brooklyn M,D,O
Louisiana State University and Agricultural & Mechanical College M,D
Loyola University Maryland M
Lynn University M,O
Massachusetts College of Art and Design M,O
Massachusetts Institute of Technology M,D
Metropolitan College of New York M
Michigan State University M,D
Monmouth University M,O
New Mexico Highlands University M
The New School M,O
New York University M,D
Norfolk State University M
Northeastern University M
Northern Kentucky University M,O
Northwestern University M,D
Ohio University M,D
Old Dominion University M,O
Pace University M
Paris College of Art M
Penn State University Park M,D*
Pepperdine University M
Point Park University M
Pratt Institute M
Queens College of the City University of New York M
Rhode Island School of Design M
Rochester Institute of Technology M
Rowan University O
Saginaw Valley State University M
San Diego State University M
San Francisco State University M
Savannah College of Art and Design M
Southern Illinois University Carbondale M,D
Southern Illinois University Edwardsville O
Stevens Institute of Technology M
Syracuse University M
Temple University M*
Texas Tech University M,D
Trinity College (United States) M
University at Buffalo, the State University of New York M,D,O
University of Bridgeport M
University of California, Los Angeles M,D
University of California, Santa Barbara M,D
University of Chicago M,D
University of Colorado Boulder M,D
University of Colorado Denver M
University of Denver M
University of Illinois at Urbana-Champaign M,D
The University of Iowa M,D
The University of Kansas M,D
University of Lethbridge M,D
University of Maryland, College Park M,D
University of Massachusetts Dartmouth M
University of Michigan M
University of Nevada, Las Vegas M
The University of North Carolina at Chapel Hill M,D,O
The University of North Carolina at Greensboro M
University of Oregon M,D
University of South Carolina M
University of Southern California M,D
University of South Florida, St. Petersburg M
The University of Texas at Austin M,D
The University of Western Ontario M,D
University of Wisconsin–Madison M,D
University of Wisconsin–Milwaukee M,D*
University of Wisconsin–Stevens Point M
Valparaiso University M,O
Virginia Commonwealth University M,D
Virginia State University M
Wagner College M
Wayne State University M,D,O
Webster University M
West Virginia State University M
West Virginia University M,O
Wilfrid Laurier University M

### MEDICAL/SURGICAL NURSING
Case Western Reserve University M
Daemen College M,D,O
Eastern Virginia Medical School M
Inter American University of Puerto Rico, Arecibo Campus M
Inter American University of Puerto Rico, Barranquitas Campus M
Pontifical Catholic University of Puerto Rico M
Saint Francis Medical Center College of Nursing M,D,O
State University of New York Downstate Medical Center M,O
Universidad Adventista de las Antillas M
University of South Africa M,D
University of South Carolina M
Ursuline College M,D

### MEDICAL ILLUSTRATION
Augusta University M
Johns Hopkins University M
Rochester Institute of Technology M
University of Illinois at Chicago M

### MEDICAL IMAGING
Boston University M
Cedars-Sinai Medical Center M,D
Illinois Institute of Technology M,D
Medical University of South Carolina D
National University of Health Sciences M,D
Oregon State University M,D
Rutgers University - Newark M
Thomas Jefferson University M
University of California, San Francisco M
University of Cincinnati M,D
University of Guelph M,D,O
University of Southern California M,D
University of Wisconsin–Milwaukee D*
Wayne State University M,D,O

### MEDICAL INFORMATICS
Arizona State University at Tempe M,D
Brandeis University M
Columbia University M,D,O
Dalhousie University M,D
Grand Valley State University M
Johns Hopkins University M,D,O
Middle Tennessee State University M
Northwestern University M,D
Nova Southeastern University M,D,O
Oregon Health & Science University M,D,O
Regis University M,O
Rutgers University - Newark M,D,O
Stanford University M,D
University at Buffalo, the State University of New York M,D
The University of Arizona M,D,O
University of California, Davis M
University of Colorado Denver M,D
University of Illinois at Urbana-Champaign M,D,O
The University of Kansas M,D,O
University of Phoenix - Phoenix Campus M,O
University of Washington M,D
University of Wisconsin–Milwaukee M*

### MEDICAL MICROBIOLOGY
The Citadel, The Military College of South Carolina M,O
Creighton University M,D
HEC Montreal D
Idaho State University M,D
Rutgers University - New Brunswick M,D
Université du Québec, Institut National de la Recherche Scientifique M,D
University of Alberta M,D
University of Hawaii at Manoa M,D
University of Manitoba M,D
University of Minnesota, Duluth M,D
University of Southern California D
University of Wisconsin–La Crosse M
University of Wisconsin–Madison D

### MEDICAL PHYSICS
Columbia University M,D
Duke University M,D
East Carolina University M,D
Hampton University M,D
Harvard University D*
Hofstra University M
Indiana University Bloomington M,D
John Patrick University of Health and Applied Sciences M
Louisiana State University and Agricultural & Mechanical College M,D
Massachusetts Institute of Technology M,D
McGill University M,D
McMaster University M,D
Oakland University M,D
Oregon State University M,D
Purdue University M,D
Rush University M,D
Southern Illinois University Carbondale M
Stony Brook University, State University of New York M,D
Thomas Jefferson University M
University at Buffalo, the State University of New York M,D
University of Alberta M,D
The University of Arizona M
University of California, Los Angeles M,D
University of Chicago D
University of Cincinnati M
University of Florida M,D,O
University of Kentucky M
University of Minnesota, Twin Cities Campus M,D
University of Oklahoma Health Sciences Center M,D
University of Pennsylvania M,D
University of Rhode Island M,D
The University of Texas Health Science Center at Houston M,D
The University of Texas Health Science Center at San Antonio D
The University of Toledo M,D
University of Utah M,D
University of Victoria M,D
University of Wisconsin–Madison M,D
Virginia Commonwealth University M,D

### MEDICINAL AND PHARMACEUTICAL CHEMISTRY
Duquesne University M,D
Florida Agricultural and Mechanical University M,D
Idaho State University M,D
Medical University of South Carolina D
New Jersey Institute of Technology M,D,O
Purdue University D
Rutgers University - New Brunswick M,D
Temple University M,D*
University at Buffalo, the State University of New York M,D
University of California, Irvine D
University of California, San Francisco D
University of Connecticut M,D
University of Florida M,D
University of Illinois at Chicago M,D
The University of Iowa M,D
The University of Kansas M,D
University of Michigan D
University of Minnesota, Twin Cities Campus M,D
University of Mississippi M,D
University of Montana M,D
University of Rhode Island M,D
The University of Texas at Austin M,D
University of the Sciences M,D
The University of Toledo M,D
University of Utah M,D
University of Washington D
Virginia Commonwealth University M,D
Wayne State University M,D

### MEDIEVAL AND RENAISSANCE STUDIES
Arizona State University at Tempe M,D,O
The Catholic University of America M,D,O
Central European University M,D
Columbia University M,D
Cornell University M,D
Fordham University M,O
Georgetown University M
Harvard University D*
Indiana University Bloomington M,D
Loyola University Chicago M,D
Rutgers University - New Brunswick D
Southern Methodist University M
University of California, Santa Barbara M,D
University of Chicago D
University of Connecticut M,D
University of Guelph D
University of Minnesota, Twin Cities Campus M,D
University of Notre Dame M,D
University of Pittsburgh O*
University of Toronto M,D
Yale University M,D

### METALLURGICAL ENGINEERING AND METALLURGY
Colorado School of Mines M,D
Michigan Technological University M,D
Missouri University of Science and Technology M,D
Montana Technological University M
The Ohio State University M,D
The University of Alabama M,D
The University of Manchester M,D
University of Nebraska–Lincoln M,D
University of Nevada, Reno M,D
The University of Texas at El Paso M,D
Université Laval M,D

### METEOROLOGY
Ball State University M,O
Florida Institute of Technology M
Florida State University M,D
Iowa State University of Science and Technology M,D
McGill University M,D
Millersville University of Pennsylvania M
Mississippi State University M,D
Naval Postgraduate School M,D
North Carolina State University M,D
Northern Arizona University M,D,O
Penn State University Park M,D*
Saint Louis University M,D
San Jose State University M
SIT Graduate Institute M
Texas A&M University M,D
Université du Québec à Montréal M,D,O
University of California, San Diego M
University of Hawaii at Manoa M,D
University of Maryland, College Park M,D
University of Miami M,D
University of Oklahoma M,D
Utah State University M,D
Yale University D

### MICROBIOLOGY
Alabama State University M,D
Albany Medical College M,D
Albert Einstein College of Medicine D
Arizona State University at Tempe M,D
Baylor College of Medicine D
Boston University D
Brandeis University M,D
Brigham Young University M,D
California State University, Long Beach M
Case Western Reserve University D
The Catholic University of America M,D
Central Washington University M
Clemson University M,D
Colorado State University M,D
Columbia University M,D
Cornell University D
Dalhousie University M,D
Dartmouth College D
Drexel University M,D
Duke University D
East Carolina University M,D
East Tennessee State University M,D
Emory University D
Emporia State University M
Georgetown University M,D
The George Washington University M,D,O
Georgia State University M,D
Harvard University D*
Howard University D
Idaho State University M,D
Illinois Institute of Technology M,D
Illinois State University M,D
Indiana University Bloomington M,D
Indiana University-Purdue University Indianapolis M,D
Inter American University of Puerto Rico, Metropolitan Campus M
Iowa State University of Science and Technology M,D
Johns Hopkins University M,D
Loma Linda University M,D
Louisiana State University Health Sciences Center D
Louisiana State University Health Sciences Center at Shreveport M,D
Loyola University Chicago M,D
Marquette University M,D
Massachusetts Institute of Technology D
McGill University M,D
Medical University of South Carolina M,D
Meharry Medical College D
Miami University M,D
Michigan State University M,D
Montana State University M,D
New York Medical College M,D
New York University M,D
North Carolina State University M,D
North Dakota State University M,D
The Ohio State University M,D
Ohio University M,D
Oklahoma State University M,D
Old Dominion University M
Oregon Health & Science University D
Oregon State University M,D
Purdue University M,D
Rosalind Franklin University of Medicine and Science D
Rush University M,D
Rutgers University - Newark D

*M—masters degree; D—doctorate; O—other advanced degree; *—Close-Up and/or Display*

Rutgers University - New Brunswick M,D
Saint Louis University D
San Diego State University M
San Francisco State University M
San Jose State University M
Seton Hall University M,D
South Dakota State University M,D
Southern Illinois University Carbondale M,D
Southwestern Oklahoma State University M
Stanford University D
State University of New York Upstate Medical University M,D
Stony Brook University, State University of New York D
Texas A&M University M,D
Texas Tech University M,D
Thomas Jefferson University M,D
Tufts University D
Tulane University M
Universidad Central del Caribe M,D
Université de Montréal M,D
Université de Sherbrooke M,D
Université du Québec, Institut National de la Recherche Scientifique M,D
University at Buffalo, the State University of New York M,D
The University of Alabama at Birmingham D
University of Alberta M,D
The University of Arizona D
University of Arkansas for Medical Sciences M,D,O
The University of British Columbia M,D
University of Calgary M,D
University of California, Berkeley D
University of California, Davis M,D
University of California, Irvine M,D
University of California, Los Angeles M,D
University of California, Riverside M,D
University of California, Santa Cruz M,D
University of Chicago D
University of Cincinnati M,D
University of Colorado Denver D
University of Connecticut M,D
University of Delaware M,D
University of Florida M,D
University of Georgia M,D
University of Guelph M,D
University of Hawaii at Manoa M,D
University of Idaho M,D
University of Illinois at Chicago D
University of Illinois at Urbana-Champaign M,D
The University of Iowa M,D
The University of Kansas M,D
University of Kentucky D
University of Louisville M,D
University of Maine M,D
The University of Manchester M,D
University of Manitoba M,D
University of Maryland, Baltimore D
University of Massachusetts Amherst M,D
University of Massachusetts Medical School M,D
University of Miami D
University of Michigan M,D
University of Minnesota, Twin Cities Campus D
University of Mississippi Medical Center D
University of Missouri D
University of Montana D
University of New Hampshire M,D
University of New Mexico M,D
The University of North Carolina at Chapel Hill M,D
University of North Texas Health Science Center at Fort Worth M,D
University of Oklahoma M,D
University of Oklahoma Health Sciences Center M,D
University of Ottawa M,D
University of Pennsylvania D
University of Pittsburgh M,D*
University of Puerto Rico - Medical Sciences Campus M,D
University of Rhode Island M,D
University of Rochester M,D
University of Saskatchewan M,D
University of South Dakota M,D
University of Southern California M
University of South Florida M,D
The University of Tennessee M,D
The University of Texas at Austin D
The University of Texas Health Science Center at Houston M,D
The University of Texas Health Science Center at San Antonio M,D
The University of Texas Medical Branch M,D
The University of Texas Southwestern Medical Center D
University of Victoria M,D
University of Virginia D
University of Washington D
The University of Western Ontario M,D
University of Wisconsin–La Crosse M
University of Wisconsin–Madison D
University of Wisconsin–Milwaukee M,D*
University of Wisconsin–Oshkosh M
University of Wyoming D
Université Laval M,D
Vanderbilt University M,D*
Virginia Commonwealth University M,D
Wagner College M
Wake Forest University D
Washington University in St. Louis D
Wright State University M
Yale University D
Youngstown State University M

## MIDDLE SCHOOL EDUCATION

Alaska Pacific University M
Albany State University M,O
American International College M,D,O
Appalachian State University M
Arkansas State University M,D,O
Augusta University M,O
Avila University M,O
Ball State University M,O
Bellarmine University M,D,O
Berry College M,O
Bloomsburg University of Pennsylvania M
Brenau University M,O
Brooklyn College of the City University of New York M,O
Cabrini University M,D
California Lutheran University M,D
Campbell University M
Canisius College M
Capella University M,D
Chestnut Hill College M
Chicago State University M
The Citadel, The Military College of South Carolina M,O
City College of the City University of New York M,O
Clemson University M,D,O
College of Mount Saint Vincent M,O
College of Saint Elizabeth M,O
The College of Saint Rose M,O
College of Staten Island of the City University of New York M
Columbus State University M,O
Converse College M
Daemen College M
DePaul University M,D
Dickinson State University M
Drury University M
Duquesne University M
East Carolina University M
Eastern Illinois University M
Eastern Michigan University M
Eastern Nazarene College M,O
Eastern University M,O
East Tennessee State University M,O
Edinboro University of Pennsylvania M
Emory University M,D
Fayetteville State University M
Fitchburg State University M
Florida Gulf Coast University M
Fontbonne University M
Georgia College & State University M
Georgia Southern University M,O
Georgia Southwestern State University M,O
Georgia State University M,D
Gordon College M,O
Goucher College M,O
Hampton University M
Hebrew College M,O
Henderson State University M,O
Hofstra University M,D,O
Hood College M,O
Houston Baptist University M
Huntington University M,D
James Madison University M
Kansas State University M,D,O
Kennesaw State University D,O
Kent State University M,D,O
Kutztown University of Pennsylvania M,D
LaGrange College M,O
La Salle University M,O
Lee University M,O
Lehman College of the City University of New York M
Le Moyne College M,O
Lesley University M,D,O
Lewis University M
Lincoln University (MO) M
Long Island University - Hudson M,O
Long Island University - Post M,D,O
Longwood University M
Louisiana Tech University M,D,O
Lynn University M,D
Manhattanville College M,O
Mary Baldwin University M
Marygrove College M,O
Maryville University of Saint Louis M,D
McNeese State University O
Mercer University M,D,O
Mercy College M,O
Middle Tennessee State University M,O
Milligan University M,D,O
Minot State University M
Mississippi State University M,D,O
Morehead State University M,O
Mount St. Joseph University M,O
Mount Saint Mary College M,O
Mount Saint Vincent University M
Murray State University M,D,O
National Louis University M,D,O
Nazareth College of Rochester M
Niagara University M,O
Nicholls State University M
North Carolina State University M
Northeastern Illinois University M
Northwestern State University of Louisiana M
Northwest Missouri State University M,D,O
Ohio University M,D
Old Dominion University M,O
Pacific University M
Piedmont College M,D,O
Point Park University M,D
Portland State University M,D,O
Queens College of the City University of New York M,O
Roberts Wesleyan College M
Roger Williams University M,O
Rowan University O
St. Bonaventure University M
St. John Fisher College M
Saint Joseph's University M,D,O
Saint Peter's University M,O
St. Thomas Aquinas College M,O
Salem College M
Salem State University M
Salisbury University M
Seton Hill University M
Shippensburg University of Pennsylvania M
Smith College M
Spalding University M
State University of New York at Fredonia M,O
State University of New York at Oswego M
State University of New York College at Potsdam M
SUNY Brockport M,O
Temple University M*
Tennessee Technological University M
Theological University of the Caribbean M,D
Tufts University M,D
Union College (KY) M
University of Arkansas M,D,O
University of Arkansas at Little Rock M
University of Bridgeport M,D,O
University of Central Florida M,O
University of Dayton M
University of Kentucky M,D
University of Louisville M,D,O
University of Massachusetts Dartmouth M,D,O
University of Missouri–St. Louis M
The University of North Carolina at Charlotte M,D,O
The University of North Carolina at Greensboro M,D,O
The University of North Carolina Wilmington M
University of Northern Iowa M
University of North Georgia M
University of Phoenix–Online Campus M,O
University of South Florida, St. Petersburg M
University of the Cumberlands M,D,O
University of the District of Columbia M
The University of Toledo M,D,O
University of Vermont M
University of Washington, Bothell M
University of West Florida M
University of Wisconsin–Milwaukee M*
Wagner College M
Webster University M,O
Western Kentucky University M,O
Wichita State University M
Widener University M,D
Winston-Salem State University M
Worcester State University M,O

## MILITARY AND DEFENSE STUDIES

American Public University System M,D
Austin Peay State University M
Bellevue University M
The Citadel, The Military College of South Carolina M,O
East Carolina University M
Embry-Riddle Aeronautical University–Prescott M
George Mason University M
The George Washington University M
Hawaii Pacific University M
Henley-Putnam School of Strategic Security M
The Institute of World Politics M,D,O
The Judge Advocate General's School, U.S. Army M
Liberty University M,D
London Metropolitan University M,D
Missouri State University M,O
National Defense University M
National Intelligence University M
Naval Postgraduate School M,D
Norwich University M
Royal Military College of Canada M,D
School of Advanced Air and Space Studies M
United States Army Command and General Staff College M
University of Calgary M,D
University of Colorado Denver M,D
University of Pittsburgh M*

## MINERAL/MINING ENGINEERING

Colorado School of Mines M,D
Dalhousie University M,D
Laurentian University M,D
McGill University M,D,O
Missouri University of Science and Technology M,D
Montana Technological University M
New Mexico Institute of Mining and Technology M
Penn State University Park M,D*
Queen's University at Kingston M,D
South Dakota School of Mines and Technology M
Southern Illinois University Carbondale M,D
Université du Québec en Abitibi-Témiscamingue M,O
University of Alaska Fairbanks M,D
University of Alberta M,D
The University of Arizona M,D,O
The University of British Columbia M,D
University of Kentucky M,D
University of Nevada, Reno M,D
The University of Texas at Austin M
University of Utah M,D
Université Laval M,D
West Virginia University M,D

## MINERAL ECONOMICS

Colorado School of Mines M,D
Michigan Technological University M
The University of Texas at Austin M

## MINERALOGY

Cornell University M,D
Indiana University Bloomington M,D
Université du Québec à Chicoutimi D
Université du Québec à Montréal M,D,O
The University of Texas at Dallas M,D

## MISSIONS AND MISSIOLOGY

Abilene Christian University M,D
Acadia University M,D
Anderson University (IN) M,D
Asbury Theological Seminary M,D,O
Assemblies of God Theological Seminary M,D
Bethel Seminary M,D,O
Biola University M,D,O
Briercrest Seminary M
Calvin Theological Seminary M,D
Capital University M
Catholic Theological Union M,D,O
Cedarville University M,D
Central Baptist Theological Seminary M,O
Clarks Summit University M,D
Columbia International University M,D,O
Dallas Baptist University M
Dallas Theological Seminary M,D,O
Ecclesia College M
Evangelical Seminary M
Fresno Pacific University M
Fuller Theological Seminary M,D,O
Gardner-Webb University M,D
Global University M,D
Gordon-Conwell Theological Seminary M,D
Grace Mission University M,D
Grace Theological Seminary M,D,O
Hope International University M
Liberty University M,D
Luther Seminary M,D
Mid-America Baptist Theological Seminary M,D
Midwest University M,D
Milligan University M,D,O
Missio Seminary M,D,O
Nebraska Christian College of Hope International University M
Northern Seminary M,D
Northwest Nazarene University M
Northwest University M
Nyack College M,D
Oral Roberts University M,D
Phillips Theological Seminary M,D
Providence University College & Theological Seminary M,D,O
Reformed Theological Seminary–Jackson Campus M,D,O
Regent University M,D
Rochester University M
Saint Paul University M
Simpson University M
Southeastern Baptist Theological Seminary M,D
Southern Adventist University M
The Southern Baptist Theological Seminary M,D
Southern Evangelical Seminary M,D,O
Southwestern Assemblies of God University M
Southwestern Baptist Theological Seminary M,D
Southwestern Christian University M
Taylor College and Seminary M,O
Theological University of the Caribbean M,D
Trinity Bible College and Graduate School M
Trinity International University M,D,O
Trinity School for Ministry M,D,O
Tyndale University College & Seminary M,O
University of South Africa M,D
Villanova University M
Wesley Biblical Seminary M
Westminster Theological Seminary M,D,O
Wheaton College M
Whitworth University M

## MODELING AND SIMULATION

Arizona State University at Tempe M,D
Carnegie Mellon University M,D
Columbus State University M,O
Naval Postgraduate School M,D
Old Dominion University M,D
Portland State University M,D,O
Rochester Institute of Technology D
Stevens Institute of Technology M,D,O
Trent University M,D
University at Buffalo, the State University of New York M,D
The University of Alabama in Huntsville M,D,O

University of California, San Diego M,D
University of Central Florida M,D,O
The University of Manchester M,D
University of Southern California M,D
Université Laval M,O
Worcester Polytechnic Institute M,D,O

## MOLECULAR BIOLOGY

Albany College of Pharmacy and Health Sciences M
Albany Medical College M,D
Albert Einstein College of Medicine D
Appalachian State University M
Arizona State University at Tempe M,D
Arkansas State University M,D
Auburn University M,D
Baylor College of Medicine D
Boise State University M,D
Boston University M,D
Brandeis University M,D
Brigham Young University M,D
Brown University M,D
California Institute of Technology D
California State University, Sacramento M
Carnegie Mellon University M,D
Case Western Reserve University D
Central Connecticut State University M,O
Clemson University D
Columbia University D
Cornell University M,D
Dartmouth College D
Drexel University M,D
Duke University D,O
East Carolina University M,D
Emory University D
Florida Institute of Technology M
Florida State University M,D
Georgetown University M,D
Georgia State University M,D
Grand Valley State University M
Harvard University D*
Howard University M,D
Illinois Institute of Technology M,D
Illinois State University M,D
Indiana State University M,D
Indiana University Bloomington M,D
Indiana University-Purdue University Indianapolis M,D
Inter American University of Puerto Rico, Metropolitan Campus M
Iowa State University of Science and Technology M,D
Irell & Manella Graduate School of Biological Sciences D
Johns Hopkins University M,D
Kent State University M,D
Lehigh University M,D
Lipscomb University M
Louisiana State University Health Sciences Center at Shreveport M,D
Louisiana Tech University M,D,O
Loyola University Chicago M,D
Marquette University M,D
Massachusetts Institute of Technology M,D,O
Mayo Clinic Graduate School of Biomedical Sciences M,D
McMaster University M,D
Medical University of South Carolina M,D
Michigan State University M,D
Michigan Technological University M,D,O
Middle Tennessee State University D
Mississippi State University M,D
Missouri State University M
Montclair State University M,O
New Mexico State University M,D
New York Medical College M,D
New York University M,D
North Dakota State University D
Northeastern Illinois University M
Northwestern University D
The Ohio State University M,D
Ohio University D
Oklahoma State University M,D
Oregon Health & Science University M,D
Oregon State University M,D
Pace University M
Penn State University Park M,D*
Princeton University D
Purdue University D
Quinnipiac University M
Rosalind Franklin University of Medicine and Science D
Rutgers University - Newark M,D
Rutgers University - New Brunswick M,D
Sacred Heart University M
Saint Louis University D
San Diego State University M,D
San Francisco State University M
San Jose State University M
Seton Hall University M,D
Simon Fraser University M,D,O
Southern Illinois University Carbondale M,D
Southern Methodist University M,D
State University of New York Downstate Medical Center D
State University of New York Upstate Medical University M,D
Stony Brook University, State University of New York M,D
Texas Woman's University M,D
Tufts University D
Tulane University M,D
Uniformed Services University of the Health Sciences M,D
Universidad Central del Caribe M,D
Université de Montréal M,D
University at Buffalo, the State University of New York M,D
The University of Alabama at Birmingham D
University of Alberta M,D
The University of Arizona D
University of Arkansas M,D
University of Arkansas for Medical Sciences M,D,O
The University of British Columbia M,D
University of Calgary M,D
University of California, Berkeley D
University of California, Davis M,D
University of California, Irvine M,D
University of California, Los Angeles M,D
University of California, Riverside M,D
University of California, San Francisco D
University of California, Santa Barbara M,D
University of California, Santa Cruz M,D
University of Chicago D
University of Cincinnati M,D
University of Colorado Boulder M,D
University of Colorado Denver D
University of Connecticut M,D
University of Connecticut Health Center D
University of Delaware M,D
University of Denver M,D
University of Florida M,D
University of Georgia M,D
University of Guelph M,D
University of Hawaii at Manoa M,D
University of Illinois at Chicago D
The University of Iowa D
The University of Kansas D
University of Lethbridge M,D
University of Maine M,D
The University of Manchester M,D
University of Maryland, Baltimore M,D
University of Maryland, Baltimore County M,D
University of Maryland, College Park D
University of Miami D
University of Michigan M,D
University of Minnesota, Duluth M,D
University of Minnesota, Twin Cities Campus M,D
University of Missouri–Kansas City D
University of Montana D
University of Nebraska Medical Center M
University of Nevada, Reno M,D
University of New Haven M
University of New Mexico M,D
The University of North Carolina at Chapel Hill M,D
University of North Texas M,D,O
University of Notre Dame M,D
University of Oklahoma Health Sciences Center M,D
University of Oregon M,D
University of Ottawa M,D
University of Pennsylvania D
University of Pittsburgh D*
University of Puerto Rico at Rio Piedras M,D
University of Rhode Island M,D
University of Rochester M,D
University of South Carolina M,D
University of South Dakota M,D
University of Southern California D
University of South Florida M,D
The University of Texas at Austin D
The University of Texas at Dallas M,D
The University of Texas at San Antonio M,D
University of Utah D
University of Vermont D
University of Washington D
University of Wisconsin–La Crosse M
University of Wisconsin–Madison D
University of Wisconsin–Milwaukee M,D*
University of Wisconsin–Parkside M
University of Wyoming M,D
Université Laval M,D
Vanderbilt University M,D*
Virginia Commonwealth University M,D
Washington University in St. Louis D
Weill Cornell Medicine M,D
Wesleyan University D
West Virginia University M,D
Wright State University M
Yale University D
Youngstown State University M

## MOLECULAR BIOPHYSICS

Baylor College of Medicine D
California Institute of Technology M,D
Carnegie Mellon University D
Duke University O
Florida State University D
Illinois Institute of Technology M,D
Johns Hopkins University M,D
Rutgers University - New Brunswick D
University at Buffalo, the State University of New York M,D
University of Arkansas for Medical Sciences M,D,O
University of Chicago D
University of Massachusetts Amherst D
University of Pennsylvania D
University of Pittsburgh D*
The University of Texas Medical Branch D
The University of Texas Southwestern Medical Center D
Washington University in St. Louis D
Wesleyan University D
Yale University D

## MOLECULAR GENETICS

Albert Einstein College of Medicine D
Duke University D
Emory University D
Georgia State University M,D
Harvard University D*
Illinois State University M,D
Indiana University-Purdue University Indianapolis M,D
Iowa State University of Science and Technology M,D
Michigan State University M,D
New York University M,D
Northern Michigan University M
The Ohio State University M,D
Oklahoma State University M,D
Penn State Hershey Medical Center M,D
Rutgers University - Newark D
Rutgers University - New Brunswick M,D
Stony Brook University, State University of New York D
University of Calgary M,D
University of California, Irvine M,D
University of California, Los Angeles M,D
University of Cincinnati M,D
University of Colorado Denver D
University of Florida M
University of Guelph M,D
University of Illinois at Chicago D
University of Louisville M,D
The University of Manchester M,D
University of Maryland, College Park M,D
University of Nebraska Medical Center M,D
University of Rhode Island M,D
University of Toronto M,D
University of Virginia D
Van Andel Institute Graduate School D
Virginia Commonwealth University M,D
Wake Forest University D
Washington University in St. Louis D

## MOLECULAR MEDICINE

Augusta University D
Baylor College of Medicine D
Boston University D
Case Western Reserve University D
Cleveland State University M,D
Dartmouth College D
Drexel University M
Elmezzi Graduate School of Molecular Medicine D
The George Washington University D
Hofstra University D
Johns Hopkins University D
Liberty University M,D
Oregon Health & Science University M,D
Penn State Hershey Medical Center D
Queen's University at Kingston M,D
Rutgers University - Newark D
Tufts University D
The University of Alabama at Birmingham D
The University of Arizona M,D
University of Cincinnati D
University of Maryland, Baltimore D
University of Nebraska Medical Center D
University of Southern California M
The University of Texas Health Science Center at San Antonio M,D
University of Washington D
Wake Forest University M,D
Yale University D

## MOLECULAR PATHOGENESIS

Dartmouth College D
Emory University D
North Dakota State University M,D
Washington University in St. Louis D

## MOLECULAR PATHOLOGY

Rutgers University - Newark D
Texas Tech University Health Sciences Center M
University of California, Los Angeles D
University of Michigan D
University of Wisconsin–Madison D

## MOLECULAR PHARMACOLOGY

Albert Einstein College of Medicine D
Brown University M,D
Harvard University D*
Loyola University Chicago M,D
Mayo Clinic Graduate School of Biomedical Sciences M,D
Medical University of South Carolina M,D
Purdue University D
Rosalind Franklin University of Medicine and Science M,D
Rutgers University - New Brunswick M,D
Thomas Jefferson University D
University at Buffalo, the State University of New York M,D
University of Maryland, Baltimore D
University of Massachusetts Medical School M,D
University of Nevada, Reno D
University of Southern California M,D

## MOLECULAR PHYSIOLOGY

Baylor College of Medicine D
Loyola University Chicago M,D
Rutgers University - New Brunswick M,D
Stony Brook University, State University of New York D
University of California, Los Angeles D
University of Illinois at Urbana-Champaign M,D
The University of North Carolina at Chapel Hill D
University of Virginia M,D
Vanderbilt University M,D*
Yale University D

## MOLECULAR TOXICOLOGY

Massachusetts Institute of Technology D
Oregon State University M,D
Penn State Hershey Medical Center D
University of California, Berkeley D
University of California, Los Angeles D
University of Cincinnati M,D
University of Maryland, Baltimore D

## MULTILINGUAL AND MULTICULTURAL EDUCATION

Alliant International University–San Francisco M,O
American College of Education M
Bank Street College of Education M
Boise State University M
Brooklyn College of the City University of New York M
Brown University M,D
Buffalo State College, State University of New York O
California State University, Fullerton M
California State University, Northridge M
California State University, Sacramento M,D,O
California State University, Stanislaus M
Chicago State University M
City College of the City University of New York M
College of Mount Saint Vincent M,O
The College of New Rochelle M,O
College of Staten Island of the City University of New York O
Columbia International University M,D,O
Dallas Baptist University M
Dallas International University M,O
DePaul University M,D
Eastern New Mexico University M
Eastern University M,O
Fairfield University M,O
Fairleigh Dickinson University, Metropolitan Campus M
Florida Atlantic University M,D,O
Gallaudet University M,D,O
The George Washington University M,D,O
Georgia Southern University D
Heritage University M
Hofstra University M,D,O
Houston Baptist University M,D
Howard University M,D
Hunter College of the City University of New York M
Immaculata University M
Indiana State University M,D,O
Indiana University Bloomington M,D
James Madison University M
Kean University M
Langston University M
La Salle University M,O
Lehman College of the City University of New York M
Long Island University - Brooklyn M,O
Long Island University - Hudson M,O
Loyola Marymount University M
Manhattan College M,O
Manhattanville College M,O
Mercy College M
Molloy College M,O
Mount St. Joseph University M,O
New Jersey City University M
New Mexico State University M,D,O
New York University M,D,O
Northern Arizona University M,O
Queens College of the City University of New York M,O
Quincy University M
Rider University M
Rutgers University - New Brunswick M,D
St. John's University (NY) M,O
San Diego State University M,D
Southern Connecticut State University M
Southern Methodist University M,D
State University of New York at New Paltz M,O
Sul Ross State University M
SUNY Brockport M,O
Teachers College, Columbia University M,D,O
Texas A&M University M,D

*M—masters degree; D—doctorate; O—other advanced degree; *—Close-Up and/or Display*

Texas A&M University–Kingsville M,D
Texas A&M University–San Antonio M
Texas Southern University M,D
Texas State University M
Texas Tech University M,D
University at Buffalo, the State University of New York M,D,O
University of Alaska Fairbanks M
University of Alberta M
University of Calgary M,D
University of California, Riverside M,D,O
University of California, San Diego M,D
University of Colorado Boulder M,D
University of Colorado Denver M
University of Connecticut M,D
University of Delaware M,D,O
University of Houston–Clear Lake M
University of Maryland, Baltimore County M,D
University of Massachusetts Amherst M,D,O
University of Miami D
University of Minnesota, Twin Cities Campus M,D,O
University of New Mexico M,D
The University of North Carolina at Greensboro M,D,O
University of Northern Colorado M,D
University of Pennsylvania M
University of St. Thomas (TX) M,D
University of San Francisco M,D
University of Southern California D
The University of Tennessee M,D,O
The University of Texas at Austin M,D
The University of Texas at El Paso M,D,O
The University of Texas at San Antonio M,D
The University of Texas Rio Grande Valley M
University of the Southwest M
University of Washington M,D
University of Wisconsin–Milwaukee M,D,O*
Utah State University M
Vanderbilt University D*
Walden University M,D,O
Wayne State University M,D,O
Western New Mexico University M
Western Oregon University M
Winona State University O
Xavier University M*

## MUSEUM EDUCATION

Bank Street College of Education M
City College of the City University of New York M
Eastern Michigan University O
The George Washington University M
Tufts University M,D
University of Nebraska at Kearney M
The University of the Arts M

## MUSEUM STUDIES

American Museum of Natural History–Richard Gilder Graduate School D
Arizona State University at Tempe M,D,O
Bard College M
Baylor University M
Boston University M,D,O
Buffalo State College, State University of New York M
California College of the Arts M
California State University, Chico M
California State University, Fullerton M
Caribbean University M,D
Case Western Reserve University M
Christie's Education M
City College of the City University of New York M
Claremont Graduate University M,D,O
Cleveland State University M
Columbia University M,D
Eastern Michigan University M,O
Fashion Institute of Technology M
Florida International University M,O
Florida State University M,D
The George Washington University M,D,O
Harvard University M,O*
Indiana University-Purdue University Indianapolis M,O
John F. Kennedy University O
Johns Hopkins University M,O
Long Island University - Post M
Marist College M
Maryland Institute College of Art M
Morgan State University M,D
New Mexico State University M,O
The New School M
New York University M,O
Penn State Harrisburg M,D,O
St. John's University (NY) M
San Francisco Art Institute M
San Francisco State University M
Seton Hall University M
Southern Illinois University Edwardsville O
Southern University at New Orleans M
State University of New York College at Oneonta M
Syracuse University M
Texas Tech University M,D
Trinity College (United States) M
Tufts University M,D,O
Université de Montréal M
Université du Québec à Montréal M
University at Buffalo, the State University of New York M,D
The University of British Columbia M,D
University of Central Oklahoma M
University of Colorado Boulder M
University of Denver M
University of Florida M,D
University of Hawaii at Manoa O
University of Illinois at Chicago M,D
The University of Kansas M,O
University of Louisville M,D
The University of Manchester D
University of Memphis M,O
University of Michigan–Flint M
University of Missouri–St. Louis M,O
University of New Hampshire M,D
The University of North Carolina at Greensboro M,D,O
University of Oklahoma M,O
University of St. Thomas (MN) M,O
University of San Francisco M
University of South Carolina M,O
University of South Florida O
The University of the Arts M
University of Toronto M
The University of Tulsa M
University of Washington M
University of Wisconsin–Milwaukee M,D,O*
Université Laval O
Virginia Commonwealth University M,D
Wayne State University M,D,O
Western Illinois University M,O

## MUSIC

Academy of Art University M
American University M,O
Andrews University M
Appalachian State University M
Aquinas Institute of Theology M,D,O
Arizona State University at Tempe M,D
Arkansas State University M,O
Austin Peay State University M
Azusa Pacific University M
Ball State University M,D,O
The Baptist College of Florida M
Bard College M,O
Baylor University M,D
Bennington College M
Berklee College of Music M,O
Bethesda University M
Binghamton University, State University of New York M
Bob Jones University M,D,O
Boise State University M
Boston University M,D,O
Bowling Green State University M,D
Brandeis University M,D
Brandon University M
Brigham Young University M
Brooklyn College of the City University of New York M
Brown University D
Butler University M
California Baptist University M
California Institute of the Arts M,O
California State University, East Bay M
California State University, Fresno M
California State University, Fullerton M
California State University, Long Beach M
California State University, Los Angeles M
California State University, Northridge M
California State University, Sacramento M
Campbellsville University M
Capital University M
Carleton University M
Carnegie Mellon University M
Case Western Reserve University M,D
The Catholic University of America M,D,O
Central Michigan University M
Central Washington University M
Claremont Graduate University M,D
Cleveland Institute of Music M,D,O
Cleveland State University M
The Colburn School Conservatory of Music M,O
Colorado State University M
Columbia College Chicago M
Columbia University M,D
Columbus State University M,O
Concordia University (Canada) O
Concordia University Chicago M
Concordia University Wisconsin M
Conservatorio de Musica de Puerto Rico O
Converse College M
Cornell University M,D
Curtis Institute of Music M
Dalhousie University M
Dartmouth College M
DePaul University M,O
Duke University D
Duquesne University M,O
East Carolina University M,O
Eastern Illinois University M
Eastern Kentucky University M
Eastern Michigan University M
Eastern University M,O
Eastern Washington University M
Emory University M
Emporia State University M
Five Towns College M,D
Florida Atlantic University M
Florida International University M
Florida State University M,D
Fuller Theological Seminary M,D,O
Garrett-Evangelical Theological Seminary M,D
George Mason University M,D
Georgia Institute of Technology M,D
Georgia Southern University M
The Graduate Center, City University of New York D
Hardin-Simmons University M
Harvard University M,D*
Hebrew College M,O
Hebrew Union College–Jewish Institute of Religion (NY) M
Hollins University M
Holy Family College M
Holy Names University M,O
Hope International University M
Houghton College M
Houston Baptist University M,D
Howard University M
Hunter College of the City University of New York M
Illinois State University M
Indiana State University M
Indiana University Bloomington M,D,O
Indiana University of Pennsylvania M
Indiana University-Purdue University Indianapolis M,D
Indiana University South Bend M,D
Inter American University of Puerto Rico, San Germán Campus M
Ithaca College M
Jacksonville State University M
James Madison University M,D
The Jewish Theological Seminary M
Johns Hopkins University M,D,O
The Juilliard School M,D,O
Kansas State University M
Kent State University M,D
Lamar University M
Lee University M
Liberty University M,D
Long Island University - Post M
Louisiana State University and Agricultural & Mechanical College M,D
Loyola University New Orleans M
Lynn University M,O
Manhattan School of Music M,D,O
Mansfield University of Pennsylvania M
Marshall University M
McGill University M,D
Memorial University of Newfoundland M,D
Mercer University M
Messiah University M
Miami University M
Michigan State University M,D
Middle Tennessee State University M
Midwestern Baptist Theological Seminary M,D,O
Midwest University M,D
Mills College M
Minnesota State University Mankato M
Mississippi College M
Missouri State University M
Montclair State University M,O
Morgan State University M
Murray State University M
Nazareth College of Rochester M
New England Conservatory of Music M,D,O
New Jersey City University M
New Mexico State University M
New Orleans Baptist Theological Seminary M,D
The New School M,O
New York University M,D,O
Norfolk State University M
North Carolina Central University M
North Dakota State University M,D
Northeastern Illinois University M
Northern Arizona University M,O
Northern Illinois University M,O
North Park University M
Northwestern State University of Louisiana M
Northwestern University M,D
Oakland University M,D
Oberlin College M,O
The Ohio State University M,D
Ohio University M,O
Oklahoma City University M
Oklahoma State University M
Old Dominion University M
Open University M
Park University M,O
Penn State University Park M,D,O*
Pensacola Christian College M,D,O
Phillips Theological Seminary M,D
Pittsburg State University M
Point Park University M
Portland State University M
Pratt Institute M
Princeton University D
Purchase College, State University of New York M
Queens College of the City University of New York M,O
Radford University M
Rice University M,D
Rider University M
Roosevelt University M,O
Rowan University M
Rutgers University - Newark M
Rutgers University - New Brunswick M,D,O
Saint John's University (MN) M
Salem College M
Samford University M
Sam Houston State University M
San Diego State University M
San Francisco Conservatory of Music M,O
San Francisco State University M
Savannah College of Art and Design M
Shenandoah University M,D,O
Southeastern Baptist Theological Seminary M,D
Southeastern Louisiana University M
Southern Illinois University Carbondale M
Southern Illinois University Edwardsville M
Southern Methodist University M,D
Southern Oregon University M
Southern Utah University M
Southwestern Baptist Theological Seminary M,D
Southwestern Oklahoma State University M
Stanford University M,D
State University of New York at Fredonia M
State University of New York at New Paltz M
State University of New York College at Potsdam M
Stephen F. Austin State University M
Stony Brook University, State University of New York M,D
Syracuse University M
Temple University M,D*
Texas A&M University M
Texas A&M University–Commerce M,D,O
Texas A&M University–Kingsville M
Texas Christian University M,D
Texas Southern University M
Texas State University M
Texas Tech University M,D
Texas Woman's University M
Towson University M
Trinity College (Canada) M,D,O
Truman State University M
Tufts University M
Tulane University M
Université de Montréal M,D,O
University at Buffalo, the State University of New York M,D,O
The University of Akron M
The University of Alabama M,D
University of Alberta M,D
The University of Arizona M,D
University of Arkansas M
The University of British Columbia M,D
University of Calgary M,D
University of California, Berkeley D
University of California, Davis M,D
University of California, Irvine M
University of California, Los Angeles M,D
University of California, Riverside M,D
University of California, San Diego M,D
University of California, Santa Barbara M,D
University of California, Santa Cruz M,D
University of Central Arkansas M,O
University of Central Florida M
University of Central Missouri M,D,O
University of Central Oklahoma M
University of Chicago M,D
University of Cincinnati M,D,O
University of Colorado Boulder M,D
University of Colorado Denver M
University of Connecticut M,D
University of Delaware M
University of Denver M,O
University of Florida M,D
University of Georgia M,D
University of Hartford M,D,O
University of Hawaii at Manoa M,D
University of Houston M,D
University of Idaho M
University of Illinois at Urbana-Champaign M,D
The University of Iowa M,D
The University of Kansas M,D
University of Kentucky M,D
University of Lethbridge M,D
University of Louisiana at Lafayette M
University of Louisville M
University of Maine M
The University of Manchester D
University of Manitoba M
University of Maryland, Baltimore County O
University of Maryland, College Park M,D
University of Massachusetts Amherst M,D
University of Massachusetts Lowell M
University of Memphis M,D
University of Miami M,D,O
University of Michigan M,D,O
University of Michigan–Flint M
University of Minnesota, Duluth M
University of Minnesota, Twin Cities Campus M,D
University of Mississippi M,D
University of Missouri M,O
University of Missouri–Kansas City M,D
University of Mobile M,D
University of Montana M
University of Nebraska at Omaha M
University of Nebraska–Lincoln M,D
University of Nevada, Las Vegas M,D,O
University of Nevada, Reno M
University of New Hampshire M
University of New Mexico M
University of New Orleans M
The University of North Carolina at Chapel Hill M,D
The University of North Carolina at Charlotte O
The University of North Carolina at Greensboro M,D

| | |
|---|---|
| University of North Carolina School of the Arts | M,O |
| University of North Dakota | M,D |
| University of Northern Colorado | M,D |
| University of Northern Iowa | M |
| University of North Texas | M,D,O |
| University of Oklahoma | M,D,O |
| University of Oregon | M,D |
| University of Ottawa | M,O |
| University of Pennsylvania | M,D |
| University of Pittsburgh | M,D* |
| University of Redlands | M |
| University of Regina | M |
| University of Rhode Island | M |
| University of Rochester | M,D |
| University of St. Thomas (MN) | M,D |
| University of St. Thomas (TX) | M |
| University of Saskatchewan | M |
| University of South Africa | M,D |
| University of South Alabama | M |
| University of South Carolina | M,D,O |
| University of South Dakota | M |
| University of Southern California | M,D,O |
| University of Southern Maine | M |
| University of Southern Mississippi | M,D |
| University of South Florida | M,D |
| The University of Tennessee | M |
| The University of Texas at Arlington | M |
| The University of Texas at Austin | M,D |
| The University of Texas at El Paso | M |
| The University of Texas at San Antonio | M |
| The University of Texas Rio Grande Valley | M |
| The University of the Arts | M |
| University of the Pacific | M |
| The University of Toledo | M,O |
| University of Toronto | M,D |
| University of Utah | M,D |
| University of Valley Forge | M |
| University of Victoria | M,D |
| University of Virginia | M,D |
| University of Washington | M,D |
| The University of Western Ontario | M,D |
| University of Wisconsin–Madison | M,D |
| University of Wisconsin–Milwaukee | M,O* |
| University of Wyoming | M |
| Université Laval | M,D |
| Utah State University | M |
| Vermont College of Fine Arts | M |
| Virginia Commonwealth University | M |
| Washington State University | M |
| Washington University in St. Louis | M,D |
| Wayne State University | M,O |
| Webster University | M |
| Wesleyan University | M,D |
| Western Illinois University | M,O |
| Western Michigan University | M,O |
| Western Oregon University | M |
| Western Washington University | M |
| West Texas A&M University | M |
| West Virginia University | M,D |
| Wichita State University | M |
| Winthrop University | M |
| World Mission University | M,D |
| Yale University | M,D,O |
| York University | M,D |
| Youngstown State University | M |

## MUSIC EDUCATION

| | |
|---|---|
| Acadia University | M |
| Adams State University | M |
| Alabama Agricultural and Mechanical University | M |
| Alabama State University | M,O |
| Anderson University (SC) | M |
| Arcadia University | M,D,O |
| Arizona State University at Tempe | M,D |
| Arkansas State University | M,O |
| Augusta University | M,O |
| Austin Peay State University | M |
| Azusa Pacific University | M |
| Ball State University | M,D,O |
| Bob Jones University | M,D,O |
| Boise State University | M |
| Boston University | M,D |
| Bowling Green State University | M,D |
| Brandon University | M |
| Brigham Young University | M |
| Brooklyn College of the City University of New York | M |
| Butler University | M |
| California Baptist University | M |
| California State University, Fresno | M |
| California State University, Fullerton | M |
| California State University, Los Angeles | M |
| California State University, Northridge | M |
| Campbellsville University | M |
| Capital University | M |
| Carnegie Mellon University | M |
| Case Western Reserve University | M,D |
| The Catholic University of America | M,D,O |
| Central Connecticut State University | M,O |
| Central Methodist University | M |
| Central Michigan University | M |
| Central Washington University | M |
| Cleveland State University | M |
| College of Charleston | M |
| The Colorado College | M |
| Colorado State University-Pueblo | M |
| Columbus State University | M,O |
| Conservatorio de Musica de Puerto Rico | M |
| Converse College | M |
| DePaul University | M,O |
| Duquesne University | M,O |
| East Carolina University | M,O |
| Eastern Illinois University | M |
| Eastern Kentucky University | M |
| Eastern Washington University | M |
| Five Towns College | M,D |
| Florida International University | M |
| George Mason University | M |
| Georgia College & State University | M |
| Georgia Southern University | M |
| Georgia State University | M,D |
| Gordon College | M |
| Hardin-Simmons University | M |
| Hebrew College | M,O |
| Heidelberg University | M |
| Hofstra University | M,D,O |
| Holy Names University | M,O |
| Howard University | M |
| Hunter College of the City University of New York | M |
| Idaho State University | M |
| Indiana State University | M |
| Indiana University of Pennsylvania | M |
| Inter American University of Puerto Rico, Metropolitan Campus | M |
| Inter American University of Puerto Rico, San Germán Campus | M |
| Ithaca College | M |
| Jackson State University | M |
| James Madison University | M |
| Kent State University | M,D |
| Kutztown University of Pennsylvania | M |
| Lake Forest College | M |
| Lebanon Valley College | M |
| Lee University | M |
| Lehman College of the City University of New York | M |
| Liberty University | M,D |
| Long Island University - Post | M,D,O |
| Louisiana State University and Agricultural & Mechanical College | M,D |
| Loyola University Maryland | M |
| Manhattanville College | M,O |
| Marywood University | M |
| McGill University | M,D |
| McKendree University | M,D,O |
| McNeese State University | O |
| Miami University | M |
| Michigan State University | M,D |
| Minnesota State University Mankato | M |
| Mississippi College | M |
| Mississippi State University | M |
| Montclair State University | M |
| Murray State University | M |
| Nazareth College of Rochester | M |
| Nebraska Christian College of Hope International University | M |
| New Jersey City University | M |
| New Mexico State University | M |
| New York University | M,D,O |
| Norfolk State University | M |
| North Dakota State University | M,D |
| Northeastern Illinois University | M |
| Northern State University | M |
| Northwestern University | M,D |
| Oakland University | M,D |
| Ohio University | M,O |
| Oklahoma State University | M |
| Old Dominion University | M |
| Oregon State University | M |
| Penn State University Park | M,D,O* |
| Piedmont College | M,D,O |
| Pittsburg State University | M |
| Plymouth State University | M |
| Queens College of the City University of New York | M,O |
| Queens College of the City University of New York | M,O |
| Rhode Island College | M |
| Rider University | M |
| Rutgers University - New Brunswick | M,D,O |
| Saint Xavier University | M |
| Samford University | M |
| San Diego State University | M |
| San Francisco Conservatory of Music | M,O |
| San Francisco State University | M |
| Southern Illinois University Edwardsville | M,O |
| Southern Methodist University | M |
| Southwestern Oklahoma State University | M |
| State University of New York at Fredonia | M |
| State University of New York College at Potsdam | M |
| Syracuse University | M |
| Tarleton State University | M |
| Teachers College, Columbia University | M,D,O |
| Temple University | M,D* |
| Tennessee Technological University | M |
| Texas A&M University–Commerce | M,D,O |
| Texas A&M University–Kingsville | M |
| Texas Christian University | M,D |
| Texas State University | M |
| Texas Tech University | M,D |
| Texas Woman's University | M |
| Towson University | M |
| Union College (KY) | M |
| University at Buffalo, the State University of New York | M,D,O |
| The University of Akron | M |
| The University of Alabama | M,D |
| The University of Arizona | M,D |
| University of Bridgeport | M,D,O |
| The University of British Columbia | M,D |
| University of Central Arkansas | M,O |
| University of Central Oklahoma | M |
| University of Cincinnati | M,D |
| University of Colorado Boulder | M,D |
| University of Connecticut | M,D |
| University of Dayton | M |
| University of Delaware | M |
| University of Denver | M,O |
| University of Florida | M,D |
| University of Georgia | M,D |
| University of Hartford | M,D,O |
| University of Houston | M,D |
| University of Illinois at Urbana-Champaign | M,D |
| The University of Iowa | M,D |
| The University of Kansas | M,D |
| University of Kentucky | M,D |
| University of Louisiana at Lafayette | M |
| University of Louisville | M,D,O |
| University of Maryland, Baltimore County | M |
| University of Maryland, College Park | M,D |
| University of Massachusetts Amherst | M,D |
| University of Massachusetts Lowell | M |
| University of Memphis | M,D |
| University of Miami | M,D,O |
| University of Michigan | M,D,O |
| University of Minnesota, Duluth | M |
| University of Missouri | M,D,O |
| University of Missouri–Kansas City | M,D |
| University of Missouri–St. Louis | M |
| University of Nebraska at Kearney | M |
| University of Nebraska–Lincoln | M,D |
| University of New Mexico | M |
| The University of North Carolina at Chapel Hill | M |
| The University of North Carolina at Greensboro | M,D |
| University of North Dakota | M,D |
| University of Northern Colorado | M,D |
| University of Northern Iowa | M |
| University of North Texas | M,D,O |
| University of Oklahoma | M,D,O |
| University of Oregon | M,D |
| University of Ottawa | M,O |
| University of Rhode Island | M |
| University of Rochester | M,D |
| University of St. Thomas (MN) | M,D |
| University of South Alabama | M |
| University of South Carolina | M,D,O |
| University of South Dakota | M |
| University of Southern California | M,D,O |
| University of Southern Maine | M |
| University of Southern Mississippi | M,D |
| The University of Tennessee | M |
| The University of Texas at Arlington | M |
| The University of Texas at Austin | M,D |
| The University of Texas at El Paso | M |
| The University of the Arts | M |
| University of the Pacific | M |
| The University of Toledo | M,O |
| University of Toronto | M,D |
| University of Utah | M,D |
| University of Victoria | M,D |
| University of Washington | M,D |
| University of Wisconsin–Madison | M,D |
| University of Wisconsin–Milwaukee | M,O* |
| University of Wisconsin–Stevens Point | M |
| University of Wyoming | M |
| Université Laval | M,D |
| Utah State University | M |
| VanderCook College of Music | M |
| Virginia Commonwealth University | M |
| Wayne State College | M |
| Wayne State University | M,O |
| Webster University | M |
| Western Connecticut State University | M |
| Western Kentucky University | M |
| Western Michigan University | M,O |
| West Virginia University | M,D |
| Wichita State University | M |
| Winthrop University | M |
| Wright State University | M |
| Youngstown State University | M |

## NANOTECHNOLOGY

| | |
|---|---|
| The American University in Cairo | M,D,O |
| Arizona State University at Tempe | M,D |
| Carnegie Mellon University | D |
| Cornell University | M,D |
| Indiana University of Pennsylvania | M |
| Johns Hopkins University | M |
| Louisiana Tech University | M,D,O |
| North Dakota State University | M,D |
| South Dakota School of Mines and Technology | D |
| State University of New York Polytechnic Institute | M,D |
| University at Buffalo, the State University of New York | M,D,O |
| University of Alberta | M,D |
| University of California, Riverside | M |
| University of California, San Diego | M,D |
| University of New Mexico | M,D |
| University of Pennsylvania | M |
| University of South Florida | M,D |
| University of Washington | M,D |
| Virginia Commonwealth University | M,D |

## NATIONAL SECURITY

| | |
|---|---|
| American Public University System | M,D |
| American University | M,D,O |
| Angelo State University | M |
| Bellevue University | M |
| California State University, San Bernardino | M |
| The Citadel, The Military College of South Carolina | M,O |
| Daniel Morgan Graduate School of National Security | M |
| George Mason University | M,D,O |
| The George Washington University | M,D |
| Henley-Putnam School of Strategic Security | D |
| The Institute of World Politics | M,D,O |
| Kansas State University | M,D |
| National Defense University | M |
| Naval Postgraduate School | M,D |
| Naval War College | M |
| New Jersey City University | M,D,O |
| Regent University | M,D |
| Trinity Washington University | M |
| University of Nebraska at Omaha | M,O |
| University of New Haven | M,O |
| Virginia Polytechnic Institute and State University | M,O |
| Western Michigan University Cooley Law School | M,D |

## NATURAL RESOURCES

| | |
|---|---|
| American University | M,D,O |
| Auburn University | M,D |
| Ball State University | M,O |
| Boise State University | M,D,O |
| California Polytechnic State University, San Luis Obispo | M |
| Central Washington University | M |
| Colorado State University | M,D |
| Cornell University | M,D |
| Dalhousie University | M |
| Delaware State University | M |
| Duke University | M,D |
| Florida International University | M,D |
| Humboldt State University | M |
| Indiana University-Purdue University Indianapolis | M,D,O |
| Instituto Tecnologico de Santo Domingo | M,D,O |
| Iowa State University of Science and Technology | M,D |
| Kansas State University | M,D |
| Laurentian University | M,D |
| Louisiana State University and Agricultural & Mechanical College | M,D |
| McGill University | M,D |
| Michigan State University | M,D |
| Montana State University | M |
| New Mexico Highlands University | M |
| North Carolina Agricultural and Technical State University | M |
| North Carolina State University | M,D |
| North Dakota State University | M,D |
| Northeastern State University | M |
| The Ohio State University | M,D |
| Oklahoma State University | M,D |
| Oregon State University | M |
| Purdue University | M,D |
| State University of New York College of Environmental Science and Forestry | M,D |
| Sul Ross State University | M |
| Tarleton State University | M |
| Texas A&M University | M,D |
| Texas Tech University | M,D |
| Unity College | M |
| Universidad Metropolitana | M |
| Universidad Nacional Pedro Henriquez Urena | M |
| Université du Québec à Montréal | M,D,O |
| Université du Québec en Abitibi-Témiscamingue | M,D |
| University of Alaska Fairbanks | M,D |
| University of Alberta | M,D |
| The University of Arizona | M,D |
| University of Arkansas at Monticello | M |
| The University of British Columbia | M,D |
| University of California, Berkeley | M,D |
| University of Connecticut | M,D |
| University of Delaware | M |
| University of Florida | M,D |
| University of Georgia | M,D |
| University of Guelph | M,D |
| University of Hawaii at Manoa | M,D |
| University of Idaho | M,D |
| University of Illinois at Urbana-Champaign | M,D |
| University of Louisiana at Lafayette | M |
| The University of Manchester | M,D |
| University of Manitoba | M,D |
| University of Maryland, College Park | M,D |
| University of Michigan | M,D |
| University of Minnesota, Twin Cities Campus | M,D |
| University of Missouri | M |
| University of Montana | M,D |
| University of Nebraska–Lincoln | M,D |
| University of New Brunswick Saint John | M |
| University of New Hampshire | M,D |
| University of New Mexico | M,D |
| University of Northern British Columbia | M,D,O |
| University of Rhode Island | M,D |

*M—masters degree; D—doctorate; O—other advanced degree; *—Close-Up and/or Display*

| | |
|---|---|
| University of San Francisco | M |
| University of South Africa | M,D |
| The University of Texas at Austin | M |
| University of Vermont | M,D,O |
| University of Washington | M,D |
| University of Wisconsin–Madison | M,D |
| University of Wisconsin–Stevens Point | M |
| University of Wyoming | M,D |
| Utah State University | M |
| Virginia Polytechnic Institute and State University | M,D,O |
| Washington State University | M,D |
| West Virginia University | M,D |

### NATUROPATHIC MEDICINE

| | |
|---|---|
| Bastyr University | D,O |
| Canadian College of Naturopathic Medicine | D |
| Maryland University of Integrative Health | D |
| National University of Health Sciences | M,D |
| National University of Natural Medicine | M,D |
| Southwest College of Naturopathic Medicine and Health Sciences | D |
| Universidad del Turabo | D |
| University of Bridgeport | D |

### NEAR AND MIDDLE EASTERN LANGUAGES

| | |
|---|---|
| The American University in Cairo | M,O |
| Bethel Seminary | M,D,O |
| Brandeis University | M,D |
| California University of Pennsylvania | M |
| The Catholic University of America | M,D |
| DePaul University | M |
| Georgetown University | M,O |
| Harvard University | M,D* |
| Hebrew Union College–Jewish Institute of Religion (NY) | D |
| Houston Baptist University | M |
| Indiana University Bloomington | M,D |
| Johns Hopkins University | D |
| Kent State University | M,D |
| London Metropolitan University | M,D |
| Middlebury College | M |
| The Ohio State University | M,D |
| Oral Roberts University | M,D |
| University of California, Los Angeles | M,D |
| University of Chicago | D |
| University of Michigan | M,D |
| University of South Africa | M,D |
| The University of Texas at Austin | M,D |
| University of Utah | M,D |
| University of Wisconsin–Madison | M,D |
| Wayne State University | M,D |
| Yale University | M,D |

### NEAR AND MIDDLE EASTERN STUDIES

| | |
|---|---|
| The American University in Cairo | M,O |
| The American University of Paris | M |
| Brandeis University | M,D |
| Brown University | D |
| California State University, Long Beach | M |
| The Catholic University of America | M,D,O |
| College of Staten Island of the City University of New York | M |
| Columbia University | M,D |
| Cornell University | M,D |
| George Mason University | M,O |
| Georgetown University | M,O |
| The George Washington University | M |
| Harvard University | M,D* |
| Johns Hopkins University | D |
| McGill University | M,D,O |
| New York University | M,D |
| Princeton University | M,D |
| Rice University | D |
| Southern Evangelical Seminary | M,D,O |
| Southwestern Baptist Theological Seminary | M,D |
| The University of Arizona | M,D,O |
| University of California, Berkeley | M,D |
| University of California, Los Angeles | M,D |
| University of Chicago | M,D |
| University of Illinois at Urbana-Champaign | M |
| The University of Kansas | M,O |
| The University of Manchester | D |
| University of Memphis | M,D |
| University of Michigan | M,D |
| University of Pennsylvania | M,D |
| University of South Africa | M,D |
| The University of Texas at Austin | M,D |
| University of Toronto | M,D |
| University of Utah | M,D |
| University of Virginia | M |
| University of Washington | M,D |
| University of Waterloo | M |
| University of Wisconsin–Madison | M,D |
| Washington University in St. Louis | M |
| Wayne State University | M,D |
| Yale University | M,D |

### NEUROBIOLOGY

| | |
|---|---|
| Boston University | M,D |
| Brandeis University | M,D |
| California Institute of Technology | D |
| Carnegie Mellon University | M,D |
| Columbia University | D |
| Cornell University | D |
| Duke University | D |
| Georgia State University | M,D |
| Harvard University | D* |
| Illinois State University | M,D |
| Indiana University-Purdue University Indianapolis | D |
| Louisiana State University Health Sciences Center | D |
| Massachusetts Institute of Technology | D |
| New York University | M,D |
| Northwestern University | M,D |
| Penn State Hershey Medical Center | D |
| Purdue University | M,D |
| University of Arkansas for Medical Sciences | M,D,O |
| University of California, Irvine | M,D |
| University of California, Los Angeles | M,D |
| University of Chicago | D |
| University of Connecticut | M,D |
| The University of Iowa | M,D |
| University of Kentucky | D |
| University of Louisville | M,D |
| The University of Manchester | M,D |
| University of Maryland, Baltimore | D |
| University of Minnesota, Twin Cities Campus | M,D |
| The University of North Carolina at Chapel Hill | D |
| University of Oklahoma | M,D |
| University of Rochester | D |
| University of Southern California | D |
| The University of Texas at Austin | D |
| The University of Texas at San Antonio | M,D |
| University of Utah | D |
| University of Washington | D |
| Université Laval | M,D |
| Virginia Commonwealth University | M |
| Wake Forest University | D |
| Wesleyan University | D |
| Yale University | D |

### NEUROSCIENCE

| | |
|---|---|
| Albany Medical College | M,D |
| Albert Einstein College of Medicine | D |
| Alliant International University - San Diego | M,D,O |
| American University | M,D,O |
| Argosy University, Chicago | D |
| Argosy University, Phoenix | M,D |
| Argosy University, Tampa | M,D |
| Arizona State University at Tempe | M,D |
| Augusta University | D |
| Ball State University | M,D,O |
| Baylor College of Medicine | D |
| Boston University | D |
| Brandeis University | M,D |
| Brigham Young University | M,D |
| Brock University | M,D |
| Brown University | D |
| California Institute of Technology | M,D |
| Carleton University | M,D |
| Carnegie Mellon University | D |
| Case Western Reserve University | D |
| Central Michigan University | M,D |
| College of Staten Island of the City University of New York | M |
| Dalhousie University | M,D |
| Dartmouth College | D |
| Delaware State University | M,D |
| Drexel University | M,D |
| Duke University | D,O |
| Emory University | D |
| Fielding Graduate University | O |
| Florida Atlantic University | D |
| Florida International University | M,D |
| Florida State University | M,D |
| Gallaudet University | M,D,O |
| George Mason University | M,D,O |
| Georgetown University | D |
| Georgia State University | D |
| The Graduate Center, City University of New York | M,D |
| Harvard University | D* |
| Icahn School of Medicine at Mount Sinai | M,D |
| Illinois State University | M,D |
| Immaculata University | M,D,O |
| Indiana University Bloomington | D |
| Iowa State University of Science and Technology | M,D |
| Irell & Manella Graduate School of Biological Sciences | D |
| Johns Hopkins University | D |
| Kent State University | M,D |
| Louisiana State University Health Sciences Center | D |
| Loyola University Chicago | M,D |
| Marquette University | M,D |
| Massachusetts Institute of Technology | D |
| Mayo Clinic Graduate School of Biomedical Sciences | M,D |
| McGill University | M,D |
| McMaster University | M,D |
| Medical College of Wisconsin | D |
| Medical University of South Carolina | M,D |
| Meharry Medical College | D |
| Memorial University of Newfoundland | M,D |
| Michigan State University | M,D |
| Montana State University | M,D |
| New York University | D |
| Northwestern University | D |
| The Ohio State University | D |
| Ohio University | M,D |
| Oregon Health & Science University | D |
| Penn State Hershey Medical Center | M,D |
| Princeton University | D |
| Purdue University | D |
| Queens College of the City University of New York | M |
| Rosalind Franklin University of Medicine and Science | D |
| Rush University | M,D |
| Rutgers University - Newark | D |
| Rutgers University - New Brunswick | M,D |
| Seton Hall University | M,D |
| State University of New York Downstate Medical Center | D |
| State University of New York Upstate Medical University | D |
| Stony Brook University, State University of New York | M,D |
| Syracuse University | M,D |
| Teachers College, Columbia University | M,D |
| Texas Christian University | M,D |
| Thomas Jefferson University | D |
| Tufts University | M,D |
| Tulane University | M,D |
| Uniformed Services University of the Health Sciences | D |
| Universidad de Iberoamerica | M,D |
| Université de Montréal | M,D |
| University at Albany, State University of New York | M,D |
| University at Buffalo, the State University of New York | M,D |
| The University of Alabama at Birmingham | M,D |
| University of Alaska Fairbanks | M,D |
| University of Alberta | M,D |
| The University of Arizona | D |
| The University of British Columbia | M,D |
| University of Calgary | M,D |
| University of California, Berkeley | D |
| University of California, Davis | D |
| University of California, Irvine | D |
| University of California, Los Angeles | D |
| University of California, Riverside | D |
| University of California, San Diego | M,D |
| University of California, San Francisco | D |
| University of California, Santa Barbara | D |
| University of Chicago | D |
| University of Cincinnati | D |
| University of Colorado Denver | D |
| University of Connecticut | M,D |
| University of Connecticut Health Center | D |
| University of Delaware | D |
| University of Florida | D |
| University of Georgia | D |
| University of Guelph | M,D,O |
| University of Hartford | M |
| University of Illinois at Chicago | M,D |
| University of Illinois at Urbana-Champaign | D |
| The University of Iowa | D |
| The University of Kansas | M,D |
| University of Lethbridge | M,D |
| The University of Manchester | M,D |
| University of Maryland, Baltimore | D |
| University of Maryland, Baltimore County | D |
| University of Maryland, College Park | M,D |
| University of Massachusetts Amherst | M,D |
| University of Massachusetts Medical School | M,D |
| University of Miami | M,D |
| University of Michigan | D |
| University of Michigan–Flint | D,O |
| University of Minnesota, Twin Cities Campus | M,D |
| University of Mississippi Medical Center | D |
| University of Missouri | M,D,O |
| University of Missouri–St. Louis | M,D,O |
| University of Montana | M,D |
| University of Nebraska Medical Center | D |
| University of New Mexico | M,D |
| The University of North Carolina at Chapel Hill | D |
| University of North Texas Health Science Center at Fort Worth | M,D |
| University of Oklahoma Health Sciences Center | M,D |
| University of Oregon | M,D |
| University of Pennsylvania | D |
| University of Pittsburgh | D* |
| University of Puerto Rico at Rio Piedras | M,D |
| University of Rochester | D |
| University of South Dakota | M,D |
| University of Southern California | M,D |
| University of South Florida | D,O |
| The University of Texas at Austin | D |
| The University of Texas at Dallas | M,D |
| The University of Texas Health Science Center at Houston | M,D |
| The University of Texas Health Science Center at San Antonio | D |
| The University of Texas Medical Branch | D |
| The University of Texas Southwestern Medical Center | D |
| The University of Toledo | M,D |
| University of Utah | D |
| University of Vermont | D |
| University of Virginia | D |
| University of Washington | M,D |
| The University of Western Ontario | M,D |
| University of Wisconsin–Madison | D |
| Virginia Commonwealth University | M,D,O |
| Wake Forest University | D |
| Washington State University | M,D |
| Washington University in St. Louis | D |
| Wayne State University | M,D |
| Weill Cornell Medicine | M,D |
| Wilfrid Laurier University | M,D |
| Wright State University | M |
| Yale University | D |

### NONPROFIT MANAGEMENT

| | |
|---|---|
| Abilene Christian University | M |
| Albizu University - Miami | M,D |
| American Jewish University | M |
| American University | M,D,O |
| Antioch University Santa Barbara | M |
| Arizona State University at Tempe | M,D,O |
| Assumption University | M,O |
| Avila University | M |
| Baruch College of the City University of New York | M |
| Bay Path University | M |
| Bradley University | M |
| Brandeis University | M |
| Brigham Young University | M |
| Cairn University | M,O |
| California State University, Northridge | O |
| Capella University | D |
| Case Western Reserve University | M,D,O |
| Central Michigan University | M,O |
| Chaminade University of Honolulu | M |
| Cleveland State University | M,O |
| Columbia University | M |
| Corban University | M |
| Daemen College | M |
| Dallas Baptist University | M |
| DePaul University | M |
| Drury University | M |
| Eastern Mennonite University | M |
| Eastern Michigan University | M,O |
| East Tennessee State University | M,O |
| Fairleigh Dickinson University, Metropolitan Campus | M,O |
| Florida Atlantic University | M,D |
| Fordham University | M,D |
| Geneva College | M |
| The George Washington University | M,O |
| Georgian Court University | M,O |
| Georgia Southern University | M,O |
| Georgia State University | M,D,O |
| Grand Valley State University | M |
| Gratz College | M |
| Hamline University | M,D |
| Hebrew Union College–Jewish Institute of Religion (NY) | M |
| Hope International University | M |
| Indiana University Bloomington | M,D,O |
| Indiana University Northwest | M,O |
| Indiana University of Pennsylvania | D |
| Indiana University-Purdue University Indianapolis | M,O |
| Indiana University South Bend | M,O |
| James Madison University | M,D |
| John Carroll University | M |
| Johns Hopkins University | M,O |
| Johnson & Wales University | M |
| Johnson University | M,D,O |
| Kean University | M |
| La Salle University | M |
| Lawrence Technological University | M,D,O |
| Liberty University | M |
| Lipscomb University | M,O |
| Long Island University - Brooklyn | M,O |
| Long Island University - Post | M,O |
| Louisiana State University in Shreveport | M |
| Marymount University | M,O |
| Mercer University | M,D |
| Metropolitan State University | M |
| Minnesota State University Mankato | M,O |
| Mount Aloysius College | M |
| Murray State University | M,O |
| Nebraska Christian College of Hope International University | M |
| New England College | M |
| New York University | M,D,O |
| North Carolina State University | M,D,O |
| Northeastern University | M |
| Northern Kentucky University | M,O |
| North Park University | M |
| Norwich University | M |
| Notre Dame of Maryland University | M |
| Oakland University | M,O |
| Oklahoma Christian University | M |
| Oklahoma State University | M,D,O |
| Oral Roberts University | M |
| Our Lady of the Lake University | M |
| Pace University | M |
| Park University | M,O |
| Penn State Harrisburg | M,D,O |
| Portland State University | M,D,O |
| Post University | M |
| Regent University | M,D,O |
| Regis University | M,O |
| Rockhurst University | M,O |
| Saint Mary-of-the-Woods College | M |
| Salve Regina University | M,O |
| San Francisco State University | M |
| Seton Hall University | M,O |
| Southern New Hampshire University | M,D,O |
| Suffolk University | M |
| SUNY Brockport | M,O |
| Thomas Edison State University | M |
| Tiffin University | M |
| Trinity Washington University | M |
| Trinity Western University | M,O |
| Tufts University | O |
| University at Albany, State University of New York | M,D,O |
| University of Arkansas at Little Rock | O |
| University of California, San Diego | M |
| University of Central Florida | M,O |
| University of Central Oklahoma | M |
| University of Colorado Denver | M,D |
| University of Connecticut | M,O |
| University of Florida | M |

| | |
|---|---|
| University of Georgia | M,D,O |
| University of Houston - Downtown | M |
| University of La Verne | M,O |
| University of Louisville | M,D |
| University of Lynchburg | M |
| University of Maryland, Baltimore County | M,O |
| University of Memphis | M,O |
| University of Michigan–Flint | M |
| University of Missouri | M,D,O |
| University of Nevada, Las Vegas | M,D,O |
| University of New Haven | M,O |
| The University of North Carolina at Charlotte | M,O |
| The University of North Carolina at Greensboro | M,O |
| University of Northern Iowa | M |
| University of North Florida | M,O |
| University of North Texas | M,D,O |
| University of Notre Dame | M |
| University of Oklahoma | M,D,O |
| University of Oregon | M,O |
| University of Pennsylvania | M,O |
| University of Pittsburgh | M* |
| University of Portland | M |
| University of San Diego | M,D,O |
| University of San Francisco | M |
| University of Southern California | M,O |
| University of Southern Indiana | M |
| University of South Florida | O |
| The University of Tampa | M,O |
| The University of Tennessee at Chattanooga | M,O |
| The University of Texas at Dallas | M,D |
| University of the Sacred Heart | M |
| University of the West | M |
| The University of Toledo | M,O |
| University of Wisconsin–Milwaukee | M,D,O* |
| Upper Iowa University | M |
| Villanova University | M,O |
| Virginia Commonwealth University | O |
| Virginia Polytechnic Institute and State University | M,O |
| Walden University | M,D,O |
| Warner Pacific University | M |
| Wayne State University | M,D |
| Webster University | M,D,O |
| Western Michigan University | M,D,O |
| Westfield State University | M |
| Worcester State University | M |

## NORTHERN STUDIES

| | |
|---|---|
| University of Alaska Fairbanks | M |
| University of Manitoba | M |

## NUCLEAR ENGINEERING

| | |
|---|---|
| Air Force Institute of Technology | M,D |
| Arizona State University at Tempe | M,D,O |
| Colorado School of Mines | M,D |
| Georgia Institute of Technology | M,D |
| Idaho State University | M,D |
| Kansas State University | M,D |
| Massachusetts Institute of Technology | M,D,O |
| McMaster University | M,D |
| Missouri University of Science and Technology | M,D |
| North Carolina State University | M,D |
| The Ohio State University | M,D |
| Oregon State University | M,D |
| Penn State University Park | M,D* |
| Polytechnique Montréal | M,D,O |
| Purdue University | M,D |
| Rensselaer Polytechnic Institute | M,D |
| Texas A&M University | M,D |
| University of California, Berkeley | M,D |
| University of Cincinnati | M,D |
| University of Florida | M,D |
| University of Idaho | M,D |
| University of Illinois at Urbana-Champaign | M,D |
| The University of Manchester | M,D |
| University of Maryland, College Park | M,D |
| University of Massachusetts Lowell | M,D |
| University of Michigan | M,D,O |
| University of Nevada, Las Vegas | M,D,O |
| University of New Mexico | M,D |
| University of South Carolina | M,D |
| The University of Tennessee | M,D |
| University of Utah | M,D |
| University of Wisconsin–Madison | M,D |
| Virginia Commonwealth University | M,D |
| Worcester Polytechnic Institute | M,D,O |

## NURSE ANESTHESIA

| | |
|---|---|
| AdventHealth University | M |
| Albany Medical College | M |
| Arkansas State University | M,D,O |
| Augusta University | D |
| Barry University | M |
| Baylor College of Medicine | D |
| Bloomsburg University of Pennsylvania | M,D |
| Boston College | M,D |
| Bryan College of Health Sciences | M |
| California State University, Fullerton | M,D |
| Case Western Reserve University | M |
| Columbia University | M,O |
| DeSales University | M,D,O |
| Drexel University | M |
| Duke University | M,D,O |
| Fairfield University | M,D |
| Florida Gulf Coast University | M |
| Florida International University | M,D |
| Franciscan Missionaries of Our Lady University | D |
| Gannon University | M,O |
| Georgetown University | M,D |
| Goldfarb School of Nursing at Barnes-Jewish College | M |
| Inter American University of Puerto Rico, Arecibo Campus | M |
| Keiser University | M,D |
| La Roche University | M,D |
| La Salle University | M,D,O |
| Lincoln Memorial University | M |
| Louisiana State University Health Sciences Center | M,D,O |
| Lourdes University | M |
| Marian University (IN) | M,D |
| Marshall University | D |
| Mayo Clinic School of Health Sciences | D |
| Medical University of South Carolina | M |
| Midwestern University, Glendale Campus | M |
| Missouri State University | D |
| Mount Marty University | M |
| Murray State University | D |
| National University | M,O |
| Newman University | M |
| Northeastern University | M,D,O |
| Oakland University | M,O |
| Old Dominion University | D |
| Oregon Health & Science University | M |
| Otterbein University | M,D,O |
| Quinnipiac University | D |
| Rosalind Franklin University of Medicine and Science | D |
| Rutgers University - Newark | M,D,O |
| Saint Mary's University of Minnesota | M |
| Saint Vincent College | M,D |
| Samford University | M,D |
| Samuel Merritt University | M,D,O |
| Southern Illinois University Edwardsville | D |
| State University of New York Downstate Medical Center | M |
| Texas Christian University | D |
| Texas Wesleyan University | M,D |
| Uniformed Services University of the Health Sciences | M,D |
| Union University | M,D,O |
| University at Buffalo, the State University of New York | M,D,O |
| The University of Alabama at Birmingham | M,D |
| University of Cincinnati | M,D |
| University of Detroit Mercy | M,D,O |
| The University of Kansas | D |
| University of Maryland, Baltimore | M,D,O |
| University of Miami | M,D |
| University of Michigan–Flint | D |
| University of Minnesota, Twin Cities Campus | M,D |
| University of New England | M,D |
| The University of North Carolina at Charlotte | M,D,O |
| The University of North Carolina at Greensboro | M,D,O |
| University of North Dakota | M,D,O |
| University of North Florida | M,D,O |
| University of Pennsylvania | M |
| University of Pittsburgh | D* |
| University of Saint Francis (IN) | M,D,O |
| The University of Scranton | M,D,O |
| University of South Carolina | M |
| University of Southern California | D |
| University of South Florida | M,D,O |
| The University of Tennessee at Chattanooga | M,D,O |
| University of Wisconsin–La Crosse | M |
| Villanova University | M,D,O |
| Virginia Commonwealth University | M,D |
| Wake Forest University | M |
| Wayne State University | M,D,O |
| Webster University | D |
| Westminster College (UT) | M |
| York College of Pennsylvania | M |

## NURSE MIDWIFERY

| | |
|---|---|
| Bastyr University | M,O |
| Bethel University (MN) | M,D,O |
| Case Western Reserve University | M |
| Columbia University | M |
| DeSales University | M,D,O |
| Emory University | M |
| Georgetown University | M,D |
| James Madison University | M,D |
| Marquette University | M,D,O |
| Midwives College of Utah | M |
| National College of Midwifery | M,D |
| New York University | M,D,O |
| Oregon Health & Science University | M |
| Shenandoah University | M,D,O |
| State University of New York Downstate Medical Center | M,O |
| Stony Brook University, State University of New York | M,D,O |
| Thomas Jefferson University | M |
| University of Cincinnati | M,D |
| University of Colorado Denver | M,D |
| University of Illinois at Chicago | M,O |
| University of Indianapolis | M,O |
| The University of Kansas | M,D,O |
| The University of Manchester | M,D |
| University of Miami | M,D |
| University of Minnesota, Twin Cities Campus | M,D |
| University of Pennsylvania | M |
| University of Pittsburgh | D* |
| University of Puerto Rico - Medical Sciences Campus | M,O |
| University of South Africa | M,D |
| Wayne State University | M,D |
| West Virginia Wesleyan College | M,D,O |

## NURSING—GENERAL

| | |
|---|---|
| Abilene Christian University | D |
| Adelphi University | D |
| Albany State University | M |
| Alcorn State University | M |
| Allen College | M,D |
| Alvernia University | M,D,O |
| Alverno College | M,D |
| American Public University System | M,D |
| American Sentinel University | M |
| Anderson University (SC) | M,D |
| Andrews University | M,D |
| Angelo State University | M |
| Arizona State University at Tempe | M,D,O |
| Arkansas State University | M,D,O |
| Arkansas Tech University | M |
| Ashland University | D |
| Aspen University | M |
| Athabasca University | M,O |
| Auburn University | M |
| Auburn University at Montgomery | M |
| Augsburg University | M,D |
| Augusta University | D |
| Austin Peay State University | M |
| Azusa Pacific University | M,D |
| Ball State University | M,D,O |
| Barry University | M,D,O |
| Baylor University | M,D |
| Bellarmine University | M,D |
| Bellin College | M |
| Belmont University | M,D |
| Benedictine University | M |
| Bethel University (IN) | M |
| Binghamton University, State University of New York | M,D,O |
| Blessing-Rieman College of Nursing & Health Sciences | M |
| Bloomsburg University of Pennsylvania | M,D |
| Boise State University | M,D,O |
| Boston College | M,D |
| Bowie State University | M |
| Bradley University | M,D,O |
| Brandman University | D |
| Briar Cliff University | M,D,O |
| Brigham Young University | M |
| Brookline College - Phoenix Campus | M |
| California Baptist University | M,D |
| California State University, Chico | M |
| California State University, Dominguez Hills | M |
| California State University, Fresno | M,D |
| California State University, Fullerton | M,D |
| California State University, Long Beach | M,D,O |
| California State University, Los Angeles | M,O |
| California State University, Sacramento | M |
| California State University, San Bernardino | M |
| California State University, San Marcos | M |
| California State University, Stanislaus | M |
| California University of Pennsylvania | M |
| Capella University | M,D |
| Capital University | M |
| Cardinal Stritch University | M |
| Carlow University | D |
| Case Western Reserve University | M,D |
| The Catholic University of America | M,D,O |
| Cedar Crest College | M |
| Central Connecticut State University | M |
| Central Methodist University | M |
| Chatham University | M,D |
| Chicago State University | M |
| Clarion University of Pennsylvania | M |
| Clarke University | D |
| Clarkson College | M,O |
| Clayton State University | M |
| Clemson University | M,D,O |
| Cleveland State University | M,D |
| College of Mount Saint Vincent | M,O |
| The College of New Jersey | M,O |
| The College of New Rochelle | M,O |
| College of Saint Elizabeth | M |
| College of Saint Mary | M |
| The College of St. Scholastica | M,O |
| Colorado Mesa University | M,D,O |
| Colorado State University-Pueblo | M |
| Columbia College of Nursing | M |
| Columbia University | M,D,O |
| Columbus State University | M |
| Concordia University Irvine | M |
| Concordia University Wisconsin | M,D |
| Coppin State University | M,O |
| Cox College | M |
| Creighton University | M,D,O |
| Curry College | M |
| Daemen College | M,D,O |
| Dalhousie University | M,D |
| Delaware State University | M |
| Delta State University | M,D |
| DePaul University | M,D |
| DeSales University | M,D,O |
| Drexel University | M,D |
| Duke University | D |
| Duquesne University | M,D,O |
| D'Youville College | M,D,O |
| East Carolina University | M,D |
| Eastern Kentucky University | M |
| Eastern Mennonite University | M,D |
| Eastern New Mexico University | M |
| East Tennessee State University | M,D,O |
| Edgewood College | M,D |
| Edinboro University of Pennsylvania | M,D |
| EDP University of Puerto Rico–San Sebastian | M |
| Elmhurst University | M |
| Elms College | M,D |
| Emmanuel College (United States) | M,O |
| Emory University | M,D |
| Endicott College | M,O |
| Fairfield University | M,D |
| Fairleigh Dickinson University, Florham Campus | M |
| Fairleigh Dickinson University, Metropolitan Campus | M,D,O |
| Felician University | M,D,O |
| Ferris State University | M |
| Florida Agricultural and Mechanical University | M,D |
| Florida Atlantic University | M,D,O |
| Florida International University | M,D |
| Florida National University | M |
| Florida Southern College | M |
| Florida State University | D,O |
| Fort Hays State University | M |
| Framingham State University | M |
| Franciscan Missionaries of Our Lady University | M,D |
| Franciscan University of Steubenville | M |
| Francis Marion University | M |
| Fresno Pacific University | M |
| Frostburg State University | M |
| Gannon University | D |
| Gardner-Webb University | M,D |
| George Mason University | M,D,O |
| Georgetown University | M,D |
| The George Washington University | M,D,O |
| Georgia College & State University | M,D,O |
| Georgia Southern University | D |
| Georgia Southwestern State University | M,O |
| Georgia State University | M,D,O |
| Goldfarb School of Nursing at Barnes-Jewish College | M |
| Gonzaga University | M,D |
| Goshen College | M |
| Governors State University | M |
| Graceland University (IA) | M,D,O |
| The Graduate Center, City University of New York | D |
| Grambling State University | M,O |
| Grand Canyon University | M,D,O |
| Grand Valley State University | M,D |
| Grantham University | M |
| Gwynedd Mercy University | M,D |
| Hampton University | M,D |
| Hardin-Simmons University | M |
| Hawaii Pacific University | M,D |
| Herzing University Online | M |
| Hofstra University | M |
| Holy Family University | M |
| Holy Names University | M,O |
| Houston Baptist University | M |
| Howard University | M |
| Hunter College of the City University of New York | M,D,O |
| Husson University | M,O |
| Idaho State University | M,D |
| Illinois State University | M,D,O |
| Immaculata University | M |
| Independence University | M |
| Indiana State University | M,D |
| Indiana University East | M |
| Indiana University Kokomo | M |
| Indiana University of Pennsylvania | D |
| Indiana University-Purdue University Indianapolis | M,D |
| Indiana University South Bend | M |
| Indiana Wesleyan University | M |
| Inter American University of Puerto Rico, Arecibo Campus | M |
| Inter American University of Puerto Rico, Barranquitas Campus | M |
| Jacksonville State University | M |
| Jacksonville University | M,D |
| James Madison University | M,D |
| Jefferson College of Health Sciences | M |
| Johns Hopkins University | M,D,O |
| Kean University | M |
| Keiser University | M |
| Kennesaw State University | M |
| Kent State University | M,D |
| Keuka College | M |
| King University | M,D,O |
| Lamar University | M |
| Lander University | M |
| La Roche University | M |
| La Salle University | M,D,O |
| Laurentian University | M |
| Lehman College of the City University of New York | M |
| Le Moyne College | M,O |
| Lenoir-Rhyne University | M |
| Lewis University | M,D |
| Liberty University | M,D |
| Lincoln Memorial University | M |
| Lindenwood University | M |
| Loma Linda University | D |
| Long Island University - Brooklyn | M,O |
| Louisiana College | M |
| Louisiana State University Health Sciences Center | M,D,O |
| Loyola University Chicago | M,D,O |
| Loyola University New Orleans | M,D |
| Madonna University | M |
| Malone University | M |
| Mansfield University of Pennsylvania | M |
| Marian University (IN) | M,D |
| Marian University (WI) | M |

*M—masters degree; D—doctorate; O—other advanced degree; *—Close-Up and/or Display*

| | |
|---|---|
| Marquette University | M,D,O |
| Marshall University | M,O |
| Mary Baldwin University | M |
| Marymount University | M,D,O |
| Maryville University of Saint Louis | M,D |
| McGill University | M,D,O |
| McKendree University | M |
| McMaster University | M,D |
| McMurry University | M |
| McNeese State University | M,O |
| MCPHS University | M |
| Medical University of South Carolina | D |
| Memorial University of Newfoundland | M,D |
| Mercer University | M,D,O |
| Mercy College | M |
| Mercy College of Ohio | M,O |
| Metropolitan State University | M,D |
| MGH Institute of Health Professions | M,D,O |
| Miami Regional University | M |
| Michigan State University | M,D |
| MidAmerica Nazarene University | M |
| Middle Tennessee State University | M,O |
| Midwestern State University | M |
| Millersville University of Pennsylvania | M,D,O |
| Millikin University | M,D |
| Minnesota State University Mankato | M,D |
| Minnesota State University Moorhead | M,O |
| Misericordia University | M,D |
| Mississippi University for Women | M,D,O |
| Missouri Southern State University | M |
| Missouri State University | M,D |
| Missouri Western State University | M,O |
| Molloy College | M,D,O |
| Monmouth University | M,D,O |
| Montana State University | M,D,O |
| Moravian College | M |
| Morgan State University | M,D |
| Morningside College | M |
| Mount Carmel College of Nursing | M,D |
| Mount Marty University | M |
| Mount Mercy University | M |
| Mount St. Joseph University | M,D |
| Mount Saint Mary College | M,O |
| Mount Saint Mary's University (CA) | M,D,O |
| Murray State University | D |
| Nebraska Methodist College | M |
| Nebraska Wesleyan University | M |
| Neumann University | M,O |
| New Mexico State University | M,D,O |
| New York University | M,D,O |
| Nicholls State University | M |
| North Dakota State University | D |
| Northeastern University | M,D,O |
| Northern Arizona University | M,D,O |
| Northern Illinois University | M,D |
| Northern Kentucky University | M,D,O |
| Northern Michigan University | D |
| North Park University | M |
| Northwestern State University of Louisiana | M |
| Norwich University | M |
| Nova Southeastern University | M,D |
| Oakland University | M,D,O |
| The Ohio State University | M,D |
| Ohio University | M,D |
| Oklahoma Baptist University | M |
| Oklahoma City University | M,D |
| Old Dominion University | D |
| Olivet Nazarene University | M |
| Oregon Health & Science University | M,D,O |
| Otterbein University | M,D,O |
| Pace University | M,D,O |
| Pacific Lutheran University | M,D |
| Palm Beach Atlantic University | M,D |
| Penn State University Park | M,D* |
| Pensacola Christian College | M,D,O |
| Pittsburg State University | M,D |
| Point Loma Nazarene University | M,D,O |
| Pontifical Catholic University of Puerto Rico | M |
| Prairie View A&M University | M,D |
| Purdue University | M,D,O |
| Purdue University Fort Wayne | M,O |
| Purdue University Global | M |
| Purdue University Northwest | M |
| Queen's University at Kingston | M,D,O |
| Queens University of Charlotte | M |
| Quinnipiac University | D |
| Radford University | D |
| Ramapo College of New Jersey | M |
| Regis College (MA) | M,D,O |
| Resurrection University | M |
| Rhode Island College | M,D |
| Rivier University | M,D |
| Robert Morris University | M,D |
| Roberts Wesleyan College | M |
| Rowan University | M |
| Rutgers University - Camden | D |
| Rutgers University - Newark | M,D,O |
| Sacred Heart University | M,D,O |
| Sage Graduate School | M,D,O |
| Saginaw Valley State University | M |
| Saint Anthony College of Nursing | M |
| St. Catherine University | M,D |
| Saint Francis Medical Center College of Nursing | M,D,O |
| Saint Francis University | M |
| St. John Fisher College | M,D,O |
| St. Joseph's College, Long Island Campus | M |
| St. Joseph's College, New York | M |
| Saint Joseph's College of Maine | M,O |
| Saint Louis University | M,D,O |
| Saint Mary-of-the-Woods College | M |
| Saint Mary's College | D |
| Saint Peter's University | M,D,O |
| Saint Xavier University | M,O |
| Salem State University | M |
| Salisbury University | M,D |
| Salve Regina University | D |
| Samford University | M,D |
| Samuel Merritt University | M,D,O |
| San Diego State University | M |
| San Francisco State University | M,O |
| San Jose State University | M,O |
| Seattle Pacific University | M,O |
| Seattle University | D |
| Seton Hall University | M,D |
| Shenandoah University | M,D,O |
| Simmons University | M,D |
| Sonoma State University | M |
| South Dakota State University | M,D |
| Southeastern Louisiana University | M,D |
| Southeast Missouri State University | M |
| Southern Adventist University | M,D |
| Southern Connecticut State University | M,D |
| Southern Illinois University Edwardsville | M,D,O |
| Southern Nazarene University | M |
| Southern New Hampshire University | M,O |
| Southern University and Agricultural and Mechanical College | M,D,O |
| South University - Columbia | M |
| South University - Montgomery | M |
| South University - Richmond | M |
| South University - Savannah | M |
| South University - Tampa | M |
| South University - Virginia Beach | M |
| South University - West Palm Beach | M |
| Spalding University | M,D,O |
| Spring Arbor University | M |
| Spring Hill College | M,O |
| Stanbridge University | M |
| State University of New York College of Technology at Delhi | M |
| State University of New York Downstate Medical Center | M,O |
| State University of New York Upstate Medical University | M,O |
| Stephen F. Austin State University | M |
| Stevenson University | M |
| Stockton University | M |
| Stony Brook University, State University of New York | M,D,O |
| Tarleton State University | M |
| Temple University | D* |
| Tennessee State University | M,O |
| Tennessee Technological University | M,D |
| Texas A&M International University | M |
| Texas A&M University | M |
| Texas A&M University–Corpus Christi | M,D |
| Texas Christian University | M,D,O |
| Texas Tech University Health Sciences Center | M,D,O |
| Texas Tech University Health Sciences Center El Paso | M |
| Texas Woman's University | M,D |
| Thomas Edison State University | M,D |
| Thomas Jefferson University | M,D |
| Thomas University | M |
| Trinity Washington University | M |
| Trinity Western University | M |
| Troy University | M,D |
| Tusculum University | M |
| UNB Fredericton | M |
| Uniformed Services University of the Health Sciences | M,D |
| Union University | M,D,O |
| Universidad Metropolitana | M,O |
| Université de Montréal | M,D,O |
| Université du Québec à Rimouski | M,O |
| Université du Québec à Trois-Rivières | M,O |
| Université du Québec en Outaouais | M,O |
| University at Buffalo, the State University of New York | M,D,O |
| The University of Akron | M,D |
| The University of Alabama | M,D |
| The University of Alabama at Birmingham | M,D |
| The University of Alabama in Huntsville | M,D,O |
| University of Alaska Anchorage | M,D,O |
| University of Alberta | M,D |
| The University of Arizona | M,D,O |
| University of Arkansas | M |
| University of Arkansas for Medical Sciences | D |
| The University of British Columbia | M,D |
| University of Calgary | M,D,O |
| University of California, Irvine | M |
| University of California, Los Angeles | M,D |
| University of California, San Francisco | M,D |
| University of Central Arkansas | M,O |
| University of Central Florida | M,D,O |
| University of Central Missouri | M,D,O |
| University of Central Oklahoma | M |
| University of Cincinnati | M,D |
| University of Colorado Colorado Springs | M,D |
| University of Colorado Denver | M,D |
| University of Connecticut | M,D,O |
| University of Delaware | M,O |
| University of Detroit Mercy | M,D,O |
| University of Florida | M,D |
| University of Hartford | M |
| University of Hawaii at Hilo | D |
| University of Hawaii at Manoa | M,D,O |
| University of Houston | M |
| University of Illinois at Chicago | M,D,O |
| University of Indianapolis | M,D |
| The University of Iowa | M,D |
| The University of Kansas | M,D,O |
| University of Kentucky | M |
| University of Lethbridge | M,D |
| University of Louisiana at Lafayette | M,D |
| University of Louisville | M,D |
| University of Maine | M,O |
| The University of Manchester | M,D |
| University of Manitoba | M |
| University of Mary | M,D |
| University of Mary Hardin-Baylor | M,D,O |
| University of Maryland, Baltimore | M,D,O |
| University of Massachusetts Amherst | M,D |
| University of Massachusetts Boston | M,D |
| University of Massachusetts Dartmouth | M,D |
| University of Massachusetts Lowell | M,D |
| University of Massachusetts Medical School | M,D,O |
| University of Memphis | M,O |
| University of Miami | M,D |
| University of Michigan | M,D,O |
| University of Michigan–Flint | M,D,O |
| University of Minnesota, Twin Cities Campus | M,D |
| University of Mississippi Medical Center | M,D |
| University of Missouri | M,D,O |
| University of Missouri–Kansas City | M,D |
| University of Missouri–St. Louis | D,O |
| University of Mobile | M,D |
| University of Mount Olive | M |
| University of Nebraska Medical Center | D |
| University of Nevada, Las Vegas | M,D,O |
| University of Nevada, Reno | M,D |
| University of New Hampshire | M,D,O |
| University of New Mexico | M,D |
| University of North Alabama | M |
| The University of North Carolina at Chapel Hill | M,D,O |
| The University of North Carolina at Charlotte | M,D,O |
| The University of North Carolina at Greensboro | M,D,O |
| The University of North Carolina at Pembroke | M |
| The University of North Carolina Wilmington | M,D,O |
| University of North Dakota | M,D,O |
| University of Northern Colorado | M,D |
| University of North Florida | M,D,O |
| University of Oklahoma Health Sciences Center | M |
| University of Ottawa | M,D,O |
| University of Pennsylvania | M,D,O |
| University of Phoenix - Bay Area Campus | M,D |
| University of Phoenix - Central Valley Campus | M |
| University of Phoenix - Hawaii Campus | M |
| University of Phoenix - Houston Campus | M |
| University of Phoenix–Online Campus | M,D,O |
| University of Phoenix - Phoenix Campus | M,O |
| University of Phoenix - Sacramento Valley Campus | M |
| University of Phoenix - San Antonio Campus | M |
| University of Phoenix - San Diego Campus | M |
| University of Pittsburgh | D* |
| University of Portland | M,D |
| University of Puerto Rico - Medical Sciences Campus | M |
| University of Regina | M,D |
| University of Rhode Island | M,D,O |
| University of Rochester | M,D |
| University of St. Augustine for Health Sciences | M,D |
| University of St. Francis (IL) | M,D,O |
| University of Saint Francis (IN) | M,D,O |
| University of Saint Joseph | M,D |
| University of Saint Mary | M |
| University of San Diego | M,D |
| University of San Francisco | D |
| University of Saskatchewan | M,D |
| The University of Scranton | M,D,O |
| University of South Alabama | M,D,O |
| University of South Carolina | M,O |
| University of Southern Indiana | M,D,O |
| University of Southern Maine | M,D,O |
| University of Southern Mississippi | M,D,O |
| University of South Florida | M,D,O |
| The University of Tampa | M |
| The University of Tennessee | M,D |
| The University of Tennessee at Chattanooga | M,D,O |
| The University of Tennessee Health Science Center | M,D,O |
| The University of Texas at Arlington | M,D |
| The University of Texas at Austin | M,D |
| The University of Texas at El Paso | M,D,O |
| The University of Texas at Tyler | M,D |
| The University of Texas Health Science Center at Houston | M,D |
| The University of Texas Health Science Center at San Antonio | M,D,O |
| The University of Texas Medical Branch | M,D |
| University of the Incarnate Word | M,D |
| The University of Toledo | M,D,O |
| University of Toronto | M,D |
| The University of Tulsa | D |
| University of Utah | M,D |
| University of Vermont | M,D,O |
| University of Victoria | M,D |
| University of Virginia | M,D |
| University of Washington | M,D,O |
| University of Washington, Bothell | M |
| University of Washington, Tacoma | M |
| The University of Western Ontario | M,D |
| University of West Florida | M |
| University of Windsor | M |
| University of Wisconsin–Eau Claire | M,D |
| University of Wisconsin–Madison | D |
| University of Wisconsin–Milwaukee | M,D,O* |
| University of Wisconsin–Oshkosh | M |
| University of Wyoming | M |
| Université Laval | M,D,O |
| Urbana University–A Branch Campus of Franklin University | M |
| Ursuline College | M,D |
| Utah Valley University | M |
| Valdosta State University | M |
| Valparaiso University | M,D,O |
| Vanderbilt University | M,D,O* |
| Vanguard University of Southern California | M |
| Villanova University | M,D,O |
| Virginia Commonwealth University | M,D,O |
| Viterbo University | D |
| Wagner College | M,D,O |
| Walden University | M,D,O |
| Walsh University | M,D |
| Washburn University | M,D,O |
| Washington Adventist University | M |
| Washington State University | M,D,O |
| Waynesburg University | M,D |
| Wayne State University | M,D |
| Weber State University | M |
| Webster University | M |
| Wesley College | M |
| West Coast University | M,D |
| Western Carolina University | M,D,O |
| Western Connecticut State University | M,D |
| Western Kentucky University | M |
| Western Michigan University | M |
| Western University of Health Sciences | M,D |
| Westminster College (UT) | M |
| West Texas A&M University | M |
| West Virginia University | M,D,O |
| West Virginia Wesleyan College | M,D,O |
| Wheeling Jesuit University | M |
| Wichita State University | M,D |
| Widener University | M,D,O |
| William Carey University | M |
| Wilmington University | M,D |
| Wilson College | M |
| Winona State University | M,D,O |
| Winston-Salem State University | M,D |
| Wright State University | M |
| Xavier University | M,D,O* |
| Yale University | M,D,O |
| York College of Pennsylvania | M |
| York University | M |
| Youngstown State University | M |

## NURSING AND HEALTHCARE ADMINISTRATION

| | |
|---|---|
| Abilene Christian University | D |
| Adelphi University | M,O |
| Allen College | M,D |
| Alvernia University | M,D,O |
| American International College | M,D,O |
| Anderson University (SC) | M,D |
| Arizona State University at Tempe | M,D,O |
| Aspen University | M |
| Athabasca University | M,O |
| Augusta University | M,D |
| Austin Peay State University | M |
| Azusa Pacific University | M,D |
| Barry University | M,D,O |
| Bellarmine University | M,D |
| Blessing-Rieman College of Nursing & Health Sciences | M |
| Bloomsburg University of Pennsylvania | M,D |
| Bowie State University | M |
| Bradley University | M,D,O |
| Brenau University | M |
| Brookline College - Phoenix Campus | M |
| California Baptist University | M |
| California State University, Fullerton | M,D |
| California State University, San Marcos | M |
| California University of Pennsylvania | M |
| Capella University | M |
| Capital University | M |
| Carlow University | M |
| Cedar Crest College | M |
| Central Methodist University | M |
| Chatham University | M,D |
| Clarke University | D |
| Clarkson College | M,O |
| Clarkson University | M,O |
| College of Mount Saint Vincent | M,O |
| The College of New Rochelle | M,O |
| Columbus State University | M |
| Cox College | M |
| Creighton University | M,D,O |
| Daemen College | M,D,O |
| DeSales University | M,D,O |
| Drexel University | M |
| Duke University | M,D,O |
| Eastern Mennonite University | M,D |
| Eastern Michigan University | M,O |
| East Tennessee State University | M,D,O |
| Elms College | M,D |
| Emmanuel College (United States) | M,O |
| Emory University | M |
| Endicott College | M,O |

| | |
|---|---|
| Fairfield University | M,D |
| Felician University | M,D,O |
| Ferris State University | M |
| Florida Agricultural and Mechanical University | M,D |
| Florida Atlantic University | M,D,O |
| Florida National University | M |
| Florida Southern College | M |
| Framingham State University | M |
| Franklin Pierce University | M,D,O |
| Frostburg State University | M |
| Gannon University | M |
| George Mason University | M,D,O |
| The George Washington University | M,D,O |
| Georgia Southwestern State University | M,O |
| Georgia State University | M,D,O |
| Goldfarb School of Nursing at Barnes-Jewish College | M |
| Grand Valley State University | M,D |
| Grand View University | M,O |
| Grantham University | M |
| Hampton University | M,D |
| Herzing University Online | M |
| Hofstra University | M,D,O |
| Holy Family University | M |
| Holy Names University | M,O |
| Immaculata University | M |
| Independence University | M |
| Indiana State University | M,D |
| Indiana University Kokomo | M |
| Indiana University of Pennsylvania | M |
| Indiana University-Purdue University Indianapolis | M,D |
| Indiana Wesleyan University | M |
| Jacksonville University | M |
| James Madison University | M,D |
| Jefferson College of Health Sciences | M |
| Johns Hopkins University | M,D |
| Kean University | M |
| Kennesaw State University | M |
| Kent State University | M,D |
| King University | M,D,O |
| Lamar University | M |
| La Roche University | M |
| La Salle University | M,D,O |
| Le Moyne College | M,O |
| Lenoir-Rhyne University | M |
| Lewis University | M,D |
| Liberty University | M,D |
| Loma Linda University | M |
| Louisiana College | M |
| Louisiana State University Health Sciences Center | M,D,O |
| Lourdes University | M |
| Loyola University Chicago | M,D,O |
| Madonna University | M |
| Marquette University | M,D,O |
| McKendree University | M |
| Medical University of South Carolina | M |
| Mercer University | M,D |
| Mercy College | M |
| Metropolitan State University | M,D |
| Miami Regional University | M |
| MidAmerica Nazarene University | M |
| Middle Tennessee State University | M |
| Milwaukee School of Engineering | M |
| Missouri Western State University | M,O |
| Montana State University | M,D,O |
| Moravian College | M |
| Mount Carmel College of Nursing | M,D |
| Mount Mary University | M |
| Mount Mercy University | M |
| Mount St. Joseph University | M |
| Mount Saint Mary College | M,O |
| National American University (TX) | M,D |
| National University | M,O |
| Nebraska Methodist College | M |
| New Mexico State University | M,D,O |
| New York University | M,O |
| Nicholls State University | M |
| Northeastern State University | M |
| Northeastern University | M,D,O |
| North Park University | M |
| Northwest Nazarene University | M |
| Norwich University | M |
| Ohio University | M,D |
| Oklahoma Wesleyan University | M |
| Old Dominion University | M,D |
| Oregon Health & Science University | M |
| Otterbein University | M,D,O |
| Pace University | M,D,O |
| Palm Beach Atlantic University | M,D |
| Pennsylvania College of Health Sciences | M |
| Purdue University Fort Wayne | M,O |
| Purdue University Global | M |
| Purdue University Northwest | M |
| Queens University of Charlotte | M |
| Quinnipiac University | D |
| Ramapo College of New Jersey | M |
| Regis University | M,D,O |
| Rivier University | M,D |
| Roberts Wesleyan College | M |
| Sacred Heart University | M,D,O |
| Saint Francis Medical Center College of Nursing | M,D,O |
| Saint Francis University | M |
| Saint Joseph's College of Maine | M,O |
| Saint Peter's University | M,D,O |
| Salem State University | M |
| Salisbury University | M,D |
| Samford University | M,D |
| Samuel Merritt University | M,D,O |
| San Francisco State University | M,O |
| San Jose State University | M,O |
| Seattle Pacific University | M,O |
| Seton Hall University | M,D |
| Shenandoah University | M,D,O |
| Southern Illinois University Edwardsville | M,O |
| Southern Nazarene University | M |
| Southern New Hampshire University | M,O |
| Southern University and Agricultural and Mechanical College | M,D,O |
| Spalding University | M,D,O |
| Spring Hill College | M,O |
| State University of New York College of Technology at Delhi | M |
| Stevenson University | M |
| Stony Brook University, State University of New York | M,D,O |
| Tarleton State University | M |
| Teachers College, Columbia University | M,D |
| Tennessee Technological University | M,D |
| Texas A&M University–Corpus Christi | M,D |
| Texas Christian University | M,D,O |
| Texas Tech University Health Sciences Center | M,D,O |
| Texas Woman's University | M,D |
| Thomas Edison State University | M |
| Union University | M,D,O |
| Universidad Metropolitana | M,O |
| University at Buffalo, the State University of New York | M,D,O |
| The University of Alabama at Birmingham | M,D |
| University of Central Arkansas | M,O |
| University of Cincinnati | M,D |
| University of Colorado Denver | M,D |
| University of Delaware | M,O |
| University of Hawaii at Manoa | M,D,O |
| University of Houston | M |
| University of Illinois at Chicago | M,O |
| University of Indianapolis | M,D |
| University of Louisiana at Lafayette | M |
| University of Louisville | M,D |
| University of Mary | M,D |
| University of Maryland, Baltimore | M,D,O |
| University of Massachusetts Amherst | M,D |
| University of Massachusetts Medical School | M,D,O |
| University of Memphis | M,O |
| University of Minnesota, Twin Cities Campus | M,D |
| University of Missouri | M,D,O |
| University of Missouri–Kansas City | M,D |
| University of Mobile | M,D |
| The University of North Carolina at Chapel Hill | M,D,O |
| The University of North Carolina at Charlotte | M,D,O |
| The University of North Carolina at Greensboro | M,D,O |
| The University of North Carolina at Pembroke | M |
| University of Pennsylvania | M,D |
| University of Phoenix - Bay Area Campus | M,D |
| University of Pittsburgh | M,D* |
| University of Rochester | M,D |
| University of St. Augustine for Health Sciences | M |
| University of St. Francis (IL) | M,D,O |
| University of Saint Mary | M |
| University of San Diego | M,D |
| The University of Scranton | M,D,O |
| University of South Alabama | M,D,O |
| University of South Carolina | M |
| University of Southern Indiana | M,D,O |
| University of Southern Maine | M,D,O |
| The University of Texas at Arlington | M,D |
| The University of Texas at Austin | M,D |
| The University of Texas at El Paso | M,D,O |
| The University of Texas at Tyler | M,D |
| The University of Texas Health Science Center at San Antonio | M,D,O |
| The University of Toledo | M,D,O |
| University of Victoria | M,D |
| University of Virginia | M,D |
| University of Washington, Tacoma | M |
| University of Wisconsin–Eau Claire | M,D |
| University of Wisconsin–Green Bay | M |
| Virginia Commonwealth University | M,D,O |
| Walden University | M,D,O |
| Walsh University | M,D |
| Washburn University | M,D,O |
| Washington Adventist University | M |
| Waynesburg University | M,D |
| Weber State University | M |
| Western Governors University | M |
| Western University of Health Sciences | M |
| West Virginia Wesleyan College | M,D,O |
| Wilmington University | M,D |
| Wilson College | M |
| Winona State University | M,D,O |
| Wright State University | M |

## NURSING EDUCATION

| | |
|---|---|
| Abilene Christian University | D |
| Adelphi University | M,O |
| Albany State University | M |
| Allen College | M,D |
| Alvernia University | M,D,O |
| American International College | M,D,O |
| Anderson University (SC) | M,D |
| Angelo State University | M |
| Arizona State University at Tempe | M,D,O |
| Aspen University | M |
| Auburn University | M |
| Auburn University at Montgomery | M |
| Austin Peay State University | M |
| Azusa Pacific University | M,D |
| Ball State University | M,D,O |
| Barry University | M,O |
| Bellarmine University | M,D |
| Bellin College | M |
| Bethel University (MN) | M,D,O |
| Blessing-Rieman College of Nursing & Health Sciences | M |
| Bowie State University | M |
| Bradley University | M,D,O |
| Brenau University | M |
| California Baptist University | M |
| California State University, Fullerton | M,D |
| California State University, San Marcos | M |
| California State University, Stanislaus | M |
| California University of Pennsylvania | M |
| Capella University | M,D |
| Carlow University | M |
| Case Western Reserve University | M |
| Cedar Crest College | M |
| Cedarville University | M,D |
| Central Methodist University | M |
| Chatham University | M,D |
| Clarkson College | M,O |
| Cleveland State University | D |
| College of Mount Saint Vincent | M,O |
| The College of New Rochelle | M,O |
| Colorado Mesa University | M,D,O |
| Columbus State University | M |
| Cox College | M |
| Daemen College | M,D,O |
| Delta State University | M,D |
| DeSales University | M,D,O |
| Drexel University | M |
| Duke University | M,D,O |
| Duquesne University | M,O |
| Eastern Michigan University | M,O |
| East Tennessee State University | M,D,O |
| Edinboro University of Pennsylvania | M,D |
| Elms College | M,D |
| Emmanuel College (United States) | M,O |
| Endicott College | M,O |
| Felician University | M,O |
| Ferris State University | M |
| Florida Gulf Coast University | M |
| Florida National University | M |
| Florida Southern College | M |
| Framingham State University | M |
| Francis Marion University | M |
| Franklin Pierce University | M,D,O |
| Frostburg State University | M |
| George Mason University | M,D,O |
| Georgetown University | M,D |
| Georgia Southern University | O |
| Georgia Southwestern State University | M,O |
| Graceland University (IA) | M,D,O |
| Grand Canyon University | M,D,O |
| Grand View University | M,O |
| Grantham University | M |
| Gwynedd Mercy University | M,D |
| Hampton University | M,D |
| Hardin-Simmons University | M |
| Herzing University Online | M |
| Holy Family University | M |
| Howard University | M |
| Immaculata University | M |
| Indiana State University | M,D |
| Indiana University Kokomo | M |
| Indiana University of Pennsylvania | M |
| Indiana University-Purdue University Indianapolis | M |
| Indiana Wesleyan University | M |
| Jacksonville University | M |
| Jefferson College of Health Sciences | M |
| Johns Hopkins University | O |
| Kennesaw State University | M |
| Kent State University | M,D |
| Keuka College | M |
| King University | M,D,O |
| Lamar University | M |
| La Roche University | M |
| La Salle University | M,D,O |
| Le Moyne College | M,O |
| Lenoir-Rhyne University | M |
| Lewis University | M,D |
| Liberty University | M,D |
| Loma Linda University | M |
| Long Island University - Brooklyn | M,O |
| Long Island University - Post | M,O |
| Louisiana State University Health Sciences Center | M,D,O |
| Lourdes University | M |
| Marian University (IN) | M,D |
| Marian University (WI) | M |
| McKendree University | M |
| McMurry University | M |
| McNeese State University | M |
| Medical University of South Carolina | M |
| Mercy College | M |
| Messiah University | M |
| Metropolitan State University | M,D |
| MGH Institute of Health Professions | M,D,O |
| Miami Regional University | M |
| MidAmerica Nazarene University | M |
| Middle Tennessee State University | M |
| Midwestern State University | M |
| Millersville University of Pennsylvania | M,D,O |
| Minnesota State University Mankato | M,D |
| Missouri State University | M,D |
| Missouri Western State University | M,O |
| Molloy College | M,D,O |
| Montana State University | M,D,O |
| Moravian College | M |
| Mount Carmel College of Nursing | M,D |
| Mount Mercy University | M |
| Mount St. Joseph University | M |
| Mount Saint Mary College | M,O |
| National American University (TX) | M,D |
| Nebraska Methodist College | M |
| New York University | M,O |
| Nicholls State University | M |
| Northeastern State University | M |
| Norwich University | M |
| Nova Southeastern University | M,D |
| Ohio University | M,D |
| Oklahoma Baptist University | M |
| Oklahoma City University | M,D |
| Oklahoma Wesleyan University | M |
| Old Dominion University | M,D |
| Oregon Health & Science University | M,O |
| Otterbein University | M,D,O |
| Pennsylvania College of Health Sciences | M |
| Pittsburg State University | M,D |
| Purdue University Fort Wayne | M,O |
| Purdue University Global | M |
| Queens University of Charlotte | M |
| Ramapo College of New Jersey | M |
| Regis College (MA) | M,D,O |
| Regis University | M,D,O |
| Rivier University | M,D |
| Roberts Wesleyan College | M |
| Sacred Heart University | M,D,O |
| Sage Graduate School | D |
| St. Catherine University | M,D |
| Saint Francis Medical Center College of Nursing | M,D,O |
| Saint Francis University | M |
| St. Joseph's College, Long Island Campus | M |
| St. Joseph's College, New York | M |
| Saint Joseph's College of Maine | M,O |
| Salem State University | M |
| Salisbury University | M |
| San Jose State University | M,O |
| Seattle Pacific University | M,O |
| Seton Hall University | M,D |
| Shenandoah University | M,D,O |
| Southern Adventist University | M,D |
| Southern Connecticut State University | M,D |
| Southern Illinois University Edwardsville | M,O |
| Southern Nazarene University | M |
| Southern New Hampshire University | M,O |
| Southern University and Agricultural and Mechanical College | M,D,O |
| South University - Savannah | M |
| South University - Tampa | M |
| Spalding University | M,D,O |
| State University of New York College of Technology at Delhi | M |
| State University of New York Empire State College | M |
| State University of New York Polytechnic Institute | M,O |
| Stevenson University | M |
| Stony Brook University, State University of New York | M,O |
| Tarleton State University | M |
| Teachers College, Columbia University | M,D,O |
| Tennessee Technological University | M |
| Texas A&M University | M |
| Texas A&M University–Corpus Christi | M,D |
| Texas Christian University | M,O |
| Texas Tech University Health Sciences Center | M,D,O |
| Texas Woman's University | M,D |
| Thomas Edison State University | M |
| UNB Fredericton | M |
| Union University | M,D,O |
| The University of Alabama in Huntsville | M,D,O |
| University of Central Arkansas | M,O |
| University of Detroit Mercy | M,D,O |
| University of Hartford | M |
| University of Houston | M |
| University of Indianapolis | M,D |
| University of Louisiana at Lafayette | M,D |
| University of Louisville | M,D |
| University of Maine | M,O |
| University of Mary | M,D |
| University of Mary Hardin-Baylor | M,D,O |
| University of Maryland, Baltimore | M,D,O |
| University of Massachusetts Medical School | M,D,O |
| University of Memphis | M,O |
| University of Missouri–Kansas City | M,D |
| University of Mobile | M,D |
| University of Nevada, Las Vegas | M,D,O |
| The University of North Carolina at Chapel Hill | M,D,O |
| The University of North Carolina at Charlotte | M,D,O |
| The University of North Carolina at Greensboro | M,D,O |
| The University of North Carolina at Pembroke | M |
| The University of North Carolina Wilmington | M,D,O |
| University of North Dakota | M,D,O |
| University of Northern Colorado | M,D |
| University of North Georgia | M |

*M—masters degree; D—doctorate; O—other advanced degree; *—Close-Up and/or Display*

University of Phoenix - Bay Area Campus M,D
University of Phoenix - Hawaii Campus M
University of Phoenix–Online Campus M,O
University of Phoenix - Phoenix Campus M,O
University of Phoenix - Sacramento Valley Campus M
University of Phoenix - San Diego Campus M
University of Portland M,D
University of Rhode Island M,D,O
University of Rochester M,D
University of St. Augustine for Health Sciences M
University of St. Francis (IL) M,D,O
University of Saint Joseph M,D
University of Saint Mary M
University of South Alabama M,D,O
University of Southern Indiana M,D,O
University of Southern Maine M,D,O
University of South Florida M,D,O
The University of Tennessee at Chattanooga M,D,O
The University of Texas at Arlington M,D
The University of Texas at Austin M,D
The University of Texas at El Paso M,D,O
The University of Texas at Tyler M,D
The University of Texas Health Science Center at San Antonio M,D,O
The University of Toledo M,O
University of Victoria M,D
University of Washington, Tacoma M
University of Wisconsin–Eau Claire M,D
Ursuline College M,D
Valparaiso University M,D,O
Villanova University M,D,O
Virginia Commonwealth University M,D,O
Wagner College M,D,O
Walden University M,D,O
Walsh University M,D
Washington Adventist University M
Waynesburg University M,D
Weber State University M
Webster University M
Western Connecticut State University D
Western Governors University M
Wilson College M
Winona State University M,D,O
Winston-Salem State University M,D
Worcester State University M

## NURSING INFORMATICS

Allen College M,D
Aspen University M
Austin Peay State University M
Columbus State University M
Duke University M,D,O
Ferris State University M
Georgia Southwestern State University M,O
Georgia State University M,D,O
Grantham University M
Holy Names University M,O
Jacksonville University M
Le Moyne College M,O
Liberty University M,D
National American University (TX) M,D
National University M,O
New York University M,O
Nova Southeastern University M,D
Roberts Wesleyan College M
Rutgers University - Newark M
Samford University M,D
Seattle Pacific University M,O
Thomas Edison State University M
Troy University M,D
The University of Alabama at Birmingham M,D
University of Maryland, Baltimore M,D,O
University of Minnesota, Twin Cities Campus M,D
The University of North Carolina at Chapel Hill M,D,O
University of Phoenix - Bay Area Campus M,D
University of Phoenix - Phoenix Campus M,O
University of St. Augustine for Health Sciences M
Walden University M,D,O
Waynesburg University M,D
Western Governors University M

## NUTRITION

Abilene Christian University M,O
Adelphi University M,D,O
Alabama Agricultural and Mechanical University M
American College of Healthcare Sciences M,O
American University M,O
Andrews University M,O
Appalachian State University M
Arizona State University at Tempe M,D
Auburn University M,D,O
Ball State University M
Bastyr University M,O
Baylor University M,D
Benedictine University M
Boston University M,D
Bradley University M
Brigham Young University M
Brooklyn College of the City University of New York M
Buffalo State College, State University of New York M
California Polytechnic State University, San Luis Obispo M
California State University, Chico M
California State University, Long Beach M
California State University, Los Angeles M,O
California University of Pennsylvania M
Canisius College M,O
Case Western Reserve University M,D
Cedar Crest College O
Central Michigan University M,D,O
Central Washington University M
Chapman University M
Clemson University M,D
College of Saint Elizabeth M,O
Colorado State University M,D
Columbia University M,D
Cornell University M,D
D'Youville College M
East Carolina University M
Eastern Illinois University M
Eastern Kentucky University M
Eastern Michigan University M
East Tennessee State University M
Emory University M,D
Florida International University M,D
Florida State University M,D
Framingham State University M
Franciscan Missionaries of Our Lady University M,D
George Mason University M,O
Georgia Southern University O
Georgia State University M
Grand Valley State University M
Harvard University D*
Howard University M,D
Hunter College of the City University of New York M
Huntington University of Health Sciences M,D
Immaculata University M
Indiana University Bloomington M,D
Indiana University of Pennsylvania M
Indiana University-Purdue University Indianapolis M,D
Instituto Tecnologico de Santo Domingo M,O
Iowa State University of Science and Technology M,D
James Madison University M
Johns Hopkins University M,D
Kansas State University M,D
Kent State University M
Lehman College of the City University of New York M
Liberty University M,D
Life University M
Lipscomb University M
Logan University M,D
Loma Linda University M,D
London Metropolitan University M,D
Long Island University - Post M,O
Louisiana State University and Agricultural & Mechanical College M,D
Louisiana Tech University M,D,O
Loyola University Chicago M,D,O
Loyola University Chicago M,D,O
Marshall University M,O
Maryland University of Integrative Health M,D,O
Marywood University M,O
McGill University M,D,O
McMaster University M,D
McNeese State University M
Meredith College M,O
Michigan State University M,D
Mississippi State University M,D
Missouri State University M,D,O
Montclair State University M,O
Mount Mary University M
Mount Saint Vincent University M
Murray State University M,O
National University of Natural Medicine M
New York Chiropractic College M
New York Institute of Technology M
New York University M,D
North Carolina Agricultural and Technical State University M
North Carolina State University M,D
North Dakota State University M,D
Northeastern University M
Northern Illinois University M
Northwestern Health Sciences University M
Nova Southeastern University M,D,O
The Ohio State University M,D
Ohio University M
Oklahoma State University M,D
Oregon Health & Science University M,O
Oregon State University M,D
Penn State University Park M,D*
Purdue University M,D
Queens College of the City University of New York M,O
Rosalind Franklin University of Medicine and Science M
Rush University M
Rutgers University - Newark M,D,O
Rutgers University - New Brunswick M,D
Sacred Heart University M
Sage Graduate School M,O
Saint Louis University M
Samford University M
Sam Houston State University M
San Diego State University M
San Jose State University M
Saybrook University M,D,O
Simmons University M,D,O
South Carolina State University M
South Dakota State University M,D
Southern Illinois University Carbondale M
State University of New York College at Oneonta M
Stony Brook University, State University of New York M,O
Syracuse University M,D
Teachers College, Columbia University M,D,O
Texas A&M University M,D
Texas State University M
Texas Tech University M,D
Texas Woman's University M,D
Tufts University M,D,O
Tuskegee University M
Université de Moncton M
Université de Montréal M,D,O
University at Buffalo, the State University of New York M,D,O
The University of Alabama M
The University of Alabama at Birmingham M,D
The University of Arizona M,D
University of Arkansas for Medical Sciences M,D,O
University of Bridgeport M
The University of British Columbia M,D
University of California, Berkeley M,D
University of California, Davis M,D
University of Central Arkansas M
University of Central Oklahoma M
University of Chicago D
University of Cincinnati M
University of Connecticut M,D
University of Delaware M
University of Florida M,D
University of Georgia M,D
University of Guelph M,D
University of Hawaii at Manoa M,D
University of Houston M,D
University of Illinois at Chicago M,D
University of Illinois at Urbana-Champaign M,D
The University of Kansas M,D,O
University of Kentucky M,D
University of Manitoba M,D
University of Maryland, College Park M,D
University of Massachusetts Amherst M,D
University of Memphis M,O
University of Miami M
University of Michigan M,D
University of Minnesota, Twin Cities Campus M,D
University of Mississippi M,D
University of Missouri M,D
University of Nebraska–Lincoln M,D
University of Nebraska Medical Center O
University of Nevada, Las Vegas M,D
University of Nevada, Reno M
University of New England M,D,O
University of New Hampshire M,D
University of New Mexico M
The University of North Carolina at Chapel Hill M,D
The University of North Carolina at Greensboro M,D
University of North Florida M
University of Oklahoma Health Sciences Center M
University of Pittsburgh M*
University of Puerto Rico at Rio Piedras M
University of Puerto Rico - Medical Sciences Campus M,D,O
University of Rhode Island M
University of Saint Joseph M
University of Saskatchewan M,D
University of South Florida O
The University of Tampa M
The University of Tennessee M
The University of Tennessee at Martin M
The University of Texas at Austin M,D
The University of Texas Rio Grande Valley M
The University of Texas Southwestern Medical Center M
University of the District of Columbia M
University of the Incarnate Word M
The University of Toledo M,O
University of Toronto M,D
University of Utah M,D
University of Vermont M
University of Washington M,D
University of Wisconsin–Madison M,D
University of Wisconsin–Milwaukee M,D*
University of Wisconsin–Stevens Point M
University of Wisconsin–Stout M
University of Wyoming M
Université Laval M,D
Utah State University M,D
Virginia Polytechnic Institute and State University M,D
Virginia University of Integrative Medicine M,D,O
Washington State University M
Wayne State University M,D,O
West Virginia University M,D
Winthrop University M,O

## OCCUPATIONAL HEALTH NURSING

Rutgers University - Newark M,D,O
University of Cincinnati M,D
University of Illinois at Chicago M,O
University of Minnesota, Twin Cities Campus M,D
The University of North Carolina at Chapel Hill M
University of South Florida M,D,O
University of the Sacred Heart M

## OCCUPATIONAL THERAPY

Abilene Christian University M
AdventHealth University M
Alabama State University M
Allen College M,D
Alvernia University M
American International College M,D,O
Arkansas State University D
A.T. Still University M,D,O
Augusta University M
Baker College Center for Graduate Studies–Online M,D
Barry University M
Bay Path University M,D
Belmont University M,D
Boston University D
Brenau University M
Cabarrus College of Health Sciences M
California State University, Dominguez Hills M
Carroll University M
Chatham University M,D
Chicago State University M
Clarkson University M
Cleveland State University M
College of Saint Mary M
The College of St. Scholastica M
Colorado State University M,D
Columbia University M,D
Concordia University Wisconsin M
Cox College M
Creighton University D
Dalhousie University M
Davenport University M
Dominican College M
Dominican University of California M
Duquesne University M,D
D'Youville College M
East Carolina University M,D,O
Eastern Kentucky University M
Eastern Michigan University M
Eastern Washington University M
Elizabethtown College M
Elmhurst University M
Emory & Henry College M,D
Florida Agricultural and Mechanical University M
Florida Gulf Coast University M
Florida International University M
Gannon University M,D
Georgia State University M
Governors State University M
Grand Valley State University M
Hofstra University M,O
Howard University M,D
Huntington University M,D
Idaho State University M
Indiana State University M,D
Indiana University-Purdue University Indianapolis M,D
Indiana Wesleyan University M,D
Ithaca College M
Jacksonville University D
James Madison University M
Jefferson College of Health Sciences M
Johnson & Wales University D
Kean University M
Keiser University M
Kettering College D
Keuka College M
Le Moyne College M
Lenoir-Rhyne University M
Loma Linda University M,D
Long Island University - Brooklyn M,D,O
Louisiana State University Health Sciences Center M
Mary Baldwin University D
Maryville University of Saint Louis M
McMaster University M
Medical University of South Carolina M
Mercy College M
MGH Institute of Health Professions D
Midwestern University, Downers Grove Campus M
Midwestern University, Glendale Campus M
Milligan University M
Misericordia University M,D
Missouri State University M
Mount Mary University M,D
Nebraska Methodist College M
New England Institute of Technology M,D
New York Institute of Technology M
New York University M,D
Northeastern State University M
Northern Arizona University D
Nova Southeastern University M,D
The Ohio State University M
Pacific University D
Queen's University at Kingston M,D
Radford University M
Regis College (MA) M,D,O
Regis University M,D,O
Rockhurst University M
Rocky Mountain College D
Rocky Mountain University of Health Professions D
Rush University D
Sacred Heart University M
Sage Graduate School M
Saginaw Valley State University M
St. Ambrose University D
St. Catherine University M,D
Saint Francis University M
Saint Louis University M

Salem State University M
Salus University M,O
Samuel Merritt University D
San Jose State University M
Seton Hall University M
Shawnee State University M
Shenandoah University M
Sonoma State University M
South University - West Palm Beach D
Spalding University M
Springfield College M
Stanbridge University M
State University of New York Downstate Medical Center M
Stockton University M
Stony Brook University, State University of New York M,D,O
Temple University M,D*
Tennessee State University M
Texas Tech University Health Sciences Center M
Texas Woman's University M,D
Thomas Jefferson University M
Towson University M
Trinity Washington University M
Tufts University M,D,O
Tuskegee University M
Université de Montréal O
University at Buffalo, the State University of New York M
The University of Alabama at Birmingham M,O
University of Alberta M,D
The University of British Columbia M
University of Central Arkansas M
The University of Findlay M,D
University of Florida M
University of Illinois at Chicago M,D
University of Indianapolis M,D
The University of Kansas M,D
University of Louisiana at Monroe M
University of Manitoba M,D
University of Mary M
University of Minnesota Rochester M,D
University of Minnesota, Twin Cities Campus M
University of Mississippi Medical Center M
University of New England M,D
University of New Hampshire M,O
University of New Mexico M
University of North Dakota M
University of Oklahoma Health Sciences Center M
University of Pittsburgh M,D*
University of Puerto Rico - Medical Sciences Campus M
University of Puget Sound M,D
University of St. Augustine for Health Sciences M,D
The University of Scranton M
University of South Alabama M
University of South Dakota M,D
University of Southern California M,D
University of Southern Indiana M
University of Southern Maine M
The University of Tennessee at Chattanooga D
The University of Tennessee Health Science Center M,D
The University of Texas at El Paso M
The University of Texas Health Science Center at San Antonio M,D
The University of Texas Medical Branch M
The University of Texas Rio Grande Valley M
University of the Sciences M,D
The University of Toledo M,D
University of Toronto M
University of Utah M,D
University of Washington M,D
The University of Western Ontario M
University of Wisconsin–La Crosse M
University of Wisconsin–Madison M,D
University of Wisconsin–Milwaukee M*
Utica College M
Virginia Commonwealth University M,D
Washington University in St. Louis M,D
Wayne State University M,D,O
Wesley College M
West Coast University M,D
Western Michigan University M
Western New England University D
Western New Mexico University M
West Virginia University M,D
Winston-Salem State University M
Worcester State University M
Xavier University M*

## OCEAN ENGINEERING

Florida Atlantic University M,D
Florida Institute of Technology M,D
Massachusetts Institute of Technology M,D,O
Memorial University of Newfoundland M,D
Oregon State University M,D
Princeton University D
Stevens Institute of Technology M,D
University of California, San Diego M,D
University of Delaware M,D
University of Florida M,D
University of Hawaii at Manoa M,D
University of Michigan M,D,O
University of New Hampshire M,D,O
University of Rhode Island M,D
Virginia Polytechnic Institute and State University M,O
Woods Hole Oceanographic Institution D

## OCEANOGRAPHY

Cornell University D
Dalhousie University M,D
Florida Institute of Technology M,D
Florida State University M,D
Louisiana State University and Agricultural & Mechanical College M,D
Massachusetts Institute of Technology M,D,O
McGill University M,D
Memorial University of Newfoundland M,D
Naval Postgraduate School M,D
North Carolina State University M,D
Nova Southeastern University M,D
Old Dominion University M,D
Oregon State University M,D
Princeton University D
Rutgers University - New Brunswick M,D
Texas A&M University M,D
Université du Québec à Rimouski M,D
University of Alaska Fairbanks M,D
The University of British Columbia M,D
University of California, Los Angeles M,D
University of California, San Diego M,D
University of Colorado Boulder M,D
University of Delaware M,D
University of Hawaii at Manoa M,D
University of Maryland, College Park M,D
University of Miami M,D
University of New Hampshire M,D,O
University of Rhode Island M,D
University of San Diego M
University of Southern California M,D
University of South Florida M,D
The University of Texas Rio Grande Valley M
University of Victoria M,D
University of Washington M,D
University of Wisconsin–Madison M,D
Université Laval D
Woods Hole Oceanographic Institution D
Yale University D

## ONCOLOGY NURSING

Gwynedd Mercy University M,D
Universidad Metropolitana M,O
University of Delaware M,O
University of South Florida M,D,O

## OPERATIONS RESEARCH

Air Force Institute of Technology M,D
Bowling Green State University M
Capella University M
Carnegie Mellon University D
Case Western Reserve University M,D
Claremont Graduate University M,D
Colorado School of Mines M,D
Columbia University M,D
Cornell University M,D
Florida Institute of Technology M,D
George Mason University M,D,O
Georgia Institute of Technology M,D
Georgia State University M,D
HEC Montreal O
Idaho State University M
Iowa State University of Science and Technology M,D
Johns Hopkins University M,D
Kansas State University M,D
Massachusetts Institute of Technology M,D
Mississippi State University M,D
Naval Postgraduate School M,D
New Mexico Institute of Mining and Technology M,D
North Carolina State University M,D
Northeastern University M,D,O
The Ohio State University M
Polytechnique Montréal M,D,O
Princeton University M,D
Purdue University Fort Wayne M,O
Rutgers University - New Brunswick D
Simon Fraser University M,D
South Dakota State University M
Southern Illinois University Edwardsville M
Southern Methodist University M,D
The University of Alabama in Huntsville M,D
University of California, Berkeley M,D
University of Colorado Denver M,D
University of Delaware M
University of Illinois at Chicago M,D
The University of Iowa M,D
University of Massachusetts Amherst M,D
University of Michigan M,D
The University of North Carolina at Chapel Hill M,D
University of Southern California M,D,O
The University of Texas at Austin M,D
University of Waterloo M,D

## OPTICAL SCIENCES

Air Force Institute of Technology M,D
Alabama Agricultural and Mechanical University M,D
Delaware State University M,D
Duke University M
Norfolk State University M
North Carolina Agricultural and Technical State University M,D
The Ohio State University M,D
Polytechnique Montréal M,D,O
Rochester Institute of Technology M,D
Rose-Hulman Institute of Technology M
The University of Alabama in Huntsville M,D
The University of Arizona M,D,O
University of Central Florida M,D
University of Dayton M,D
University of New Mexico M,D
The University of North Carolina at Charlotte M,D
University of Rochester M,D

## OPTOMETRY

Ferris State University D
Illinois College of Optometry D
Indiana University Bloomington M,D
Inter American University of Puerto Rico School of Optometry D
Marshall B. Ketchum University M,D
MCPHS University D
Midwestern University, Downers Grove Campus D
Midwestern University, Glendale Campus D
New England College of Optometry M,D
Northeastern State University D
Nova Southeastern University M,D
The Ohio State University M,D
Pacific University M,D
Salus University D
Southern College of Optometry D
State University of New York College of Optometry D
Université de Montréal D
The University of Alabama at Birmingham D
University of California, Berkeley D,O
University of Houston D
The University of Manchester M,D
University of Pikeville D
University of the Incarnate Word D
University of Waterloo M,D
Western University of Health Sciences D

## ORAL AND DENTAL SCIENCES

A.T. Still University M,D,O
Augusta University M,D
Boston University M,D
Case Western Reserve University M,O
Columbia University M,D,O
Dalhousie University M,D
Harvard University M,D,O*
Howard University D,O
Idaho State University O
Jacksonville University M,O
Loma Linda University M,O
Marquette University M,O
McGill University M,D,O
Metropolitan State University M,D
New York University M,D,O
The Ohio State University M,D
Oregon Health & Science University M,D,O
Rutgers University - Newark M,D,O
Saint Louis University M
Seton Hill University M,O
Stony Brook University, State University of New York M,D,O
Temple University M,O*
Texas A&M University M,D,O
Tufts University M,O
Université de Montréal M,O
University at Buffalo, the State University of New York M,D,O
The University of Alabama at Birmingham M
University of Alberta M,D
The University of British Columbia M,D
University of California, Los Angeles M,D
University of California, San Francisco M,D
University of Colorado Denver D,O
University of Connecticut Health Center M
University of Detroit Mercy M,D,O
University of Florida M,D,O
University of Illinois at Chicago M,D
The University of Iowa M,D,O
University of Kentucky M
University of Louisville M,D
The University of Manchester M,D
University of Manitoba M,D
University of Maryland, Baltimore M,D,O
University of Michigan M,D
University of Minnesota, Twin Cities Campus M,D,O
University of Mississippi Medical Center M,D
University of Missouri–Kansas City M,D,O
University of Nebraska Medical Center M,D
University of Nevada, Las Vegas M,D,O
The University of North Carolina at Chapel Hill M,D
University of Oklahoma Health Sciences Center M
University of Pittsburgh M,D,O*
University of Puerto Rico - Medical Sciences Campus O
University of Rochester M
University of Southern California M,D,O
The University of Tennessee Health Science Center M,D
The University of Toledo M
University of Toronto M,D
University of Washington M,D,O
The University of Western Ontario M
Université Laval M,O
West Virginia University M,D

## ORGANIC CHEMISTRY

Auburn University M,D
Boston College M,D
Brandeis University M,D
Cleveland State University M,D
Cornell University D
Eastern New Mexico University M
Florida State University M,D
Georgetown University D
The George Washington University M,D
Georgia State University M,D
Harvard University D*
Howard University M,D
Indiana University Bloomington M,D
Instituto Tecnológico y de Estudios Superiores de Monterrey, Campus Monterrey M,D
Iowa State University of Science and Technology M,D
Laurentian University M
Marquette University M,D
Massachusetts Institute of Technology M,D,O
McMaster University M,D
Old Dominion University M,D
Purdue University M,D
Rice University M,D
Rutgers University - Newark M,D
Rutgers University - New Brunswick M,D
Seton Hall University M,D
Southern University and Agricultural and Mechanical College M
State University of New York College of Environmental Science and Forestry M,D
University of Calgary M,D
University of Cincinnati M,D
University of Louisville M,D
The University of Manchester M,D
University of Maryland, College Park M,D
University of Massachusetts Lowell M,D
University of Memphis M,D
University of Miami M,D
University of Michigan M,D
University of Missouri–Kansas City M,D
University of Montana M,D
University of Nebraska–Lincoln M,D
University of Notre Dame M,D
University of Oklahoma M,D
University of Regina M,D
University of Rochester D
The University of Tennessee M,D
The University of Texas at Austin D
The University of Toledo M,D
Virginia Commonwealth University M,D
Wake Forest University M,D
Wesleyan University D
Yale University D
Youngstown State University M

## ORGANIZATIONAL BEHAVIOR

Argosy University, Chicago D
Arizona State University at Tempe M,D
A.T. Still University M,D,O
Baruch College of the City University of New York M,D
Benedictine University M,D
Boston College D
Brooklyn College of the City University of New York M,D
California State University, East Bay M
Carnegie Mellon University D
Case Western Reserve University M,D
Clemson University M,D
Cornell University M,D
Drexel University M,D,O
Fairleigh Dickinson University, Florham Campus M,O
Florida Institute of Technology M
Florida State University M,D
The Graduate Center, City University of New York D
Hampton University M
Harvard University D*
International Institute for Restorative Practices M,O
John Jay College of Criminal Justice of the City University of New York M,D
Lake Forest Graduate School of Management M
New York University M,D
Northwestern University M
Phillips Graduate University D
Purdue University D
Queen's University at Kingston M,D
Saybrook University M,D
Suffolk University M
Universidad de las Americas, A.C. M
Université de Sherbrooke M
University at Albany, State University of New York M,D,O
The University of British Columbia D
University of California, Berkeley D
University of California, Davis M
University of Chicago M,O
University of Hartford M
University of Hawaii at Manoa M
The University of Kansas M,D
University of New Mexico M

*M—masters degree; D—doctorate; O—other advanced degree; *—Close-Up and/or Display*

The University of North Carolina at Chapel Hill D
University of North Texas at Dallas M
University of Oklahoma M,D,O
University of Pittsburgh M,D*
The University of Texas at Austin M
University of Utah M,D
Wayne State University M,D
Wilfrid Laurier University M,D

## ORGANIZATIONAL MANAGEMENT

Albertus Magnus College M
Albizu University - Miami M,D
Alvernia University D
The American College of Financial Services M
American University M,D,O
Anderson University (SC) M
Antioch University Los Angeles M
Apollos University M,D
Aquinas College (MI) M
Argosy University, Chicago D
Argosy University, Hawaii D
Argosy University, Los Angeles M,D
Argosy University, Northern Virginia M,D,O
Argosy University, Orange County D
Argosy University, Seattle M,D
Argosy University, Tampa M,D
Argosy University, Twin Cities M,D
Athabasca University M,O
Atlantic University M,O
Augsburg University M
Austin Peay State University M
Avila University M
Azusa Pacific University M
Baker University M
Bellevue University M
Benedictine University M,D
Bethel University (MN) M,D,O
Binghamton University, State University of New York D
Boise State University M,O
Boston College D
Boston University M
Bowling Green State University M
Brandman University M
Brenau University M
Briercrest Seminary M
Buffalo State College, State University of New York M
Cabrini University M,D
Cairn University M,O
California Baptist University M
California Coast University M,D
California College of the Arts M
California Intercontinental University M,D
California State University, Fullerton M
Calvary University M
Capella University M,D
Central Penn College M
Charleston Southern University M
Charter Oak State College M
The Chicago School of Professional Psychology M,D
City University of Seattle M,O
Clarks Summit University M,D
College of Saint Elizabeth M
College of Saint Mary M
The College of Saint Rose O
Colorado State University–Global Campus M
Columbia College (SC) M
Columbia Southern University M
Columbus State University M,O
Concordia College–New York M
Concordia University (Canada) M,O
Concordia University Ann Arbor M
Concordia University, St. Paul M
Concordia University Wisconsin M
Crandall University M
Creighton University M
Dallas Baptist University M,D
Duke University D
Duquesne University M
Eastern Connecticut State University M
Eastern Mennonite University M
Eastern Michigan University M,O
Eastern University M
Emory & Henry College M,D
Emory University M,D
Endicott College M
Evangel University M
Fairleigh Dickinson University, Florham Campus M,O
Fielding Graduate University O
Florida Institute of Technology M
Gannon University D
Gardner-Webb University M,D,O
Geneva College M
George Fox University M,D
George Mason University M
The George Washington University M,O
Georgia State University M,D
Gonzaga University M,D
Graceland University (IA) M,D,O
Grand Canyon University M,D
Grand View University M,O
Granite State College M
Harding University M
Hawaii Pacific University M
HEC Montreal M
Hood College M,D,O
Huntington University M,D
Husson University M
Immaculata University M
Indiana Tech M
Indiana University Bloomington M,D,O
Indiana University-Purdue University Indianapolis M,O
Indiana Wesleyan University M,D,O
Instituto Tecnologico de Santo Domingo M,O
Jacksonville University M
James Madison University D
Johnson & Wales University M
Judson University M
Juniata College M
Keiser University M
LaGrange College M
Lenoir-Rhyne University M
Lewis University M
Lincoln Christian University M
Lipscomb University M,O
Lourdes University M
Loyola University New Orleans M
Malone University M
Manhattan College M
Manhattanville College M,O
Mansfield University of Pennsylvania M
Maranatha Baptist University M
Marian University (WI) M
Marlboro College M
Medaille College M
Mercer University M,D
Mercy College M
Mercyhurst University M,O
Messiah University M,O
Mid-America Christian University M
Midway University M
Midwest University M,D
Misericordia University M
Mount St. Joseph University M
National University M,O
Neumann University M
New Jersey City University M
Newman University M
New York University M,D
Nichols College M
Northern Kentucky University M
Northwestern University M
Northwest University M
Norwich University M
Nyack College M
Oakland City University M,D
Oakland University M,D,O
Ohio Christian University M
Oklahoma Christian University M
Olivet Nazarene University M
Omega Graduate School M,D
Our Lady of the Lake University M,D
Palm Beach Atlantic University M
Peirce College M
Penn State University Park M,D*
Peru State College M
Pfeiffer University M
Point Loma Nazarene University M
Point Park University M
Purdue University Fort Wayne M,O
Purdue University Global M
Queens University of Charlotte M
Quinnipiac University M
Regent University M,D,O
Regis University M,O
Rider University M
Robert Morris University M,D
Rochester Institute of Technology O
Roosevelt University M
Rutgers University - Newark D
Sage Graduate School M
St. Ambrose University M
St. Catherine University M
St. Edward's University M
St. Joseph's College, Long Island Campus M
St. Joseph's College, New York M
Saint Mary-of-the-Woods College M
Saint Mary's College of California M
Saint Mary's University of Minnesota M
Salve Regina University M,O
San Diego Christian College M
Saybrook University M,D
Seattle University M,O
Shippensburg University of Pennsylvania M
Siena Heights University M,O
Simpson University M
SIT Graduate Institute M
Southeastern University (FL) M,D
Southern Arkansas University–Magnolia M
Southern New Hampshire University M,D,O
South University - Columbia M
South University - Savannah M
South University - Virginia Beach M
Southwest University M
Springfield College M
Stockton University D
Syracuse University O
Thomas Edison State University M
Trevecca Nazarene University M,D
Trine University M
Trinity Washington University M
Trinity Western University M,O
Tufts University M
Union Institute & University M
United States International University–Africa M
University of Alberta D
The University of Arizona M,D
University of Central Arkansas D
University of Charleston D
University of Cincinnati M
University of Colorado Boulder
University of Dallas M,D
University of Denver M,O
University of Guelph M
University of Hawaii at Manoa M,D
The University of Kansas M,D,O
University of La Verne M,D,O
University of Maryland Eastern Shore D
University of Massachusetts Amherst M,D
University of Michigan–Flint M,O
University of Missouri M,D,O
University of Nebraska at Omaha M
University of New Haven M,O
University of New Mexico M
University of Northwestern–St. Paul M
University of Oklahoma M,O
University of Pennsylvania M,O
University of Phoenix - Bay Area Campus M,D
University of Phoenix–Online Campus D,O
University of Portland M,D
University of Regina M,O
University of Saint Francis (IN) M
University of St. Thomas (MN) D
University of San Francisco M
University of South Dakota M
University of Southern California M
The University of Texas at San Antonio D
The University of Texas at Tyler M
University of the Incarnate Word M,D
University of West Los Angeles M
University of Wisconsin–Platteville M
Université Laval M,O
Upper Iowa University M
Vanderbilt University M*
Viterbo University M,O
Walden University M,D,O
Waldorf University M
Warner Pacific University M
Washington University in St. Louis M
Wayland Baptist University M,D
Waynesburg University M,D
Wayne State College M
Wayne State University M,D
Western New England University M
West Liberty University M
Wheeling Jesuit University M
Wilfrid Laurier University M,D
William Penn University M
Williamson College M
Wilmington University M,D
Winona State University M,D,O
Woodbury University M
Worcester Polytechnic Institute M,D,O
Worcester State University M
Yale University D

## OSTEOPATHIC MEDICINE

Alabama College of Osteopathic Medicine D
Arkansas Colleges of Health Education D
A.T. Still University M,D
Burrell College of Osteopathic Medicine D
Campbell University D
Des Moines University D
Edward Via College of Osteopathic Medicine–Carolinas Campus D
Edward Via College of Osteopathic Medicine–Virginia Campus D
Georgia Campus–Philadelphia College of Osteopathic Medicine D
Kansas City University of Medicine and Biosciences D
Lake Erie College of Osteopathic Medicine M,D,O
Liberty University D
Lincoln Memorial University D
Marian University (IN) M,D
Michigan State University D
Midwestern University, Downers Grove Campus D
Midwestern University, Glendale Campus D
New York Institute of Technology O
Nova Southeastern University M,D,O
Ohio University D
Oklahoma State University Center for Health Sciences D
Pacific Northwest University of Health Sciences D
Philadelphia College of Osteopathic Medicine D
Rocky Vista University D
Rowan University D
Touro University California M,D
University of New England D
University of North Texas Health Science Center at Fort Worth D
University of Pikeville D
University of the Incarnate Word M,D
Western University of Health Sciences D
West Virginia School of Osteopathic Medicine D
William Carey University D

## PACIFIC AREA/PACIFIC RIM STUDIES

Naval Postgraduate School M,D
University of Bridgeport M
The University of British Columbia M
University of Guam M
University of Hawaii at Manoa M,O
University of San Francisco M
University of Victoria M

## PALEONTOLOGY

Cornell University M,D
Duke University D
East Tennessee State University M,O
South Dakota School of Mines and Technology M,D
University of Chicago D
The University of Manchester M,D
Yale University D

## PAPER AND PULP ENGINEERING

State University of New York College of Environmental Science and Forestry M,D,O
The University of Manchester M,D
University of Minnesota, Twin Cities Campus M,D
Western Michigan University M,D

## PARASITOLOGY

Illinois State University M,D
Louisiana State University Health Sciences Center D
McGill University M,D,O
Oregon State University M,D
Tulane University M,D,O
University of Notre Dame M,D
University of Prince Edward Island M,D

## PASTORAL MINISTRY AND COUNSELING

Abilene Christian University M,D
Acadia University M,D
Ambrose University M,O
American Baptist Seminary of the West M
Amridge University M,D
Anabaptist Mennonite Biblical Seminary M,O
Anderson University (SC) M,D
Andrews University M,D,O
Appalachian Bible College M
Aquinas Institute of Theology M,D,O
Asbury Theological Seminary M,D,O
Ashland Theological Seminary M,D
Assemblies of God Theological Seminary M,D
Atlantic School of Theology M,O
Atlantic University O
Austin Presbyterian Theological Seminary M,D
Ave Maria University M,D
Azusa Pacific University M
Bakke Graduate University M,D
Baptist Bible College M
The Baptist College of Florida M
Barry University M,D
Bethany Theological Seminary M,O
Bethel Seminary M,D,O
Bethel University (IN) M
Biola University M,D,O
Bob Jones University M,D,O
Boston College M,D,O
Briercrest Seminary M,O
Brite Divinity School M,D,O
Bryan College M
Cairn University M
California Baptist University M
Calvary University M
Calvin Theological Seminary M,D
Campbell University M,D
Canadian Southern Baptist Seminary M
Capital University M
Carolina Christian College M
Catholic Theological Union M,D,O
The Catholic University of America M,D,O
Cedarville University M,D
Charlotte Christian College and Theological Seminary M,D
Chicago Theological Seminary M,D
Christian Theological Seminary M,D
Christ the King Seminary M
Cincinnati Christian University M
City Vision University M
Claremont Lincoln University M
Claremont School of Theology M,D
Clarks Summit University M,D
College of Saint Elizabeth M,O
Columbia International University M,D,O
Concordia University, Nebraska M
Corban University M,D,O
Covenant Theological Seminary M,D,O
Criswell College M
Dallas Baptist University M,D
Dallas Theological Seminary M,D,O
Denver Seminary M,D,O
Earlham School of Religion M
Eastern Mennonite University M,O
Ecumenical Theological Seminary D
Emory University M,D
Epic Bible College M,D
Evangelical Seminary M
Fairfield University M,O
Faith Baptist Bible College and Theological Seminary M
Faulkner University M,D
Fordham University M,D,O
Freed-Hardeman University M
Fresno Pacific University M
Fuller Theological Seminary M,D,O
Gannon University M,O
Gardner-Webb University M,D
Garrett-Evangelical Theological Seminary M,D
Gateway Seminary M,D,O
The General Theological Seminary M,D,O
Geneva College M
George Fox University M,D,O
Global University M,D
Gordon-Conwell Theological Seminary M,D
Grace Theological Seminary M,D,O
Grand Canyon University D
Grand Rapids Theological Seminary of Cornerstone University M
Greenville University M
Hampton University M,D,O
Harding School of Theology M,D
Harding University M
Hardin-Simmons University M,D
Hartford Seminary M,D,O
Heritage Christian University M
Holmes Institute M
Holy Names University M

Houston Graduate School of Theology M,D
Howard Payne University M
Huntington University M,D
Huntsville Bible College M
Iliff School of Theology M,D
Indiana Wesleyan University M
Inter American University of Puerto Rico, Metropolitan Campus D
Interdenominational Theological Center M,D
International Baptist College and Seminary M,D
Johnson University M,D,O
Johnson University Florida M
Judson University M
The King's University M,D,O
Kingswood University M
Knox Theological Seminary D
Lancaster Bible College M,D,O
La Sierra University M
Lee University M
Liberty University M,D,O
Lincoln Christian Seminary M,D
Lincoln Christian University M
Lipscomb University M,D
Loras College M
Loyola Marymount University M
Loyola University Chicago M,O
Lutheran School of Theology at Chicago M,D
Lutheran Theological Seminary Saskatoon M,D
Luther Rice College & Seminary M,D
Luther Seminary M,D
Madonna University M
Maple Springs Baptist Bible College and Seminary M,D,O
Maranatha Baptist University M,D
Martin University M
Marymount University M
The Master's University M,D
McCormick Theological Seminary M,D,O
McMaster University M,D,O
Meadville Lombard Theological School M,D
Mercer University M,D
Mid-America Baptist Theological Seminary M,D
Mid-America Christian University M
Midwestern Baptist Theological Seminary M,D,O
Midwest University M,D
Milligan University M,D,O
Missio Seminary M,D,O
Missouri Baptist University M,O
Moody Bible Institute M,O
Mount Marty University M
Mount St. Joseph University M,O
Nashotah House Theological Seminary M,D,O
Nebraska Christian College of Hope International University M
Neumann University M,D,O
New Brunswick Theological Seminary M,D
New Orleans Baptist Theological Seminary M,D
Northern Seminary M,D
North Greenville University M,D
North Park Theological Seminary M,O
Northwest Nazarene University M
Northwest University M
Nyack College M,D
Oakland City University M,D
Oakwood University M
Oblate School of Theology M,D,O
Ohio Christian University M
Olivet Nazarene University M
Oral Roberts University M,D
Ottawa University M
Pacific Rim Christian University M
Pentecostal Theological Seminary M,D
Pepperdine University M
Phillips Theological Seminary D
Phoenix Seminary M,D,O
Piedmont International University M,D
Pittsburgh Theological Seminary M,D
Point Loma Nazarene University M
Point University M
Providence University College & Theological Seminary M,D,O
Randall University M
Reformed Theological Seminary–Charlotte Campus M,D
Reformed Theological Seminary–Jackson Campus M,D,O
Reformed Theological Seminary–Orlando Campus M,D,O
Regent University M,D,O
Regis College (Canada) M,D,O
Richmont Graduate University M,O
Sacred Heart Major Seminary M
St. Ambrose University M
St. Augustine's Seminary of Toronto M,O
St. Bernard's School of Theology and Ministry M,O
St. Catherine University M,O
St. John's Seminary (CA) M
Saint John's University (MN) M
Saint Joseph's College of Maine M
St. Joseph's Seminary M
Saint Paul University M,D,O
Saints Cyril and Methodius Seminary M
St. Stephen's College M,D
St. Thomas University - Florida M,D,O
Santa Clara University M
Seattle University M
Selma University M
Seton Hall University M,O
Shasta Bible College M
Shepherds Theological Seminary M
Shiloh University M,D
Simpson University M
Sioux Falls Seminary M
Southeastern University (FL) M,D
The Southern Baptist Theological Seminary M,D
Southern Evangelical Seminary M,D,O
Southern Methodist University M,D
Southern Wesleyan University M
South University - Savannah D
Southwestern Assemblies of God University M
Southwestern Baptist Theological Seminary M,D,O
Southwestern Christian University M
Spring Arbor University M
SUM Bible College & Theological Seminary M
Theological University of the Caribbean M,D
Trevecca Nazarene University M
Trinity Bible College and Graduate School M
Trinity College (Canada) M,D,O
Trinity International University M,D,O
Trinity School for Ministry M,D,O
Trinity Western University M,D
Tyndale University College & Seminary M,O
Union University M,D
United Lutheran Seminary M,D
United Lutheran Seminary M,D,O
United Theological Seminary M,D
United Theological Seminary of the Twin Cities M,D,O
University of Chicago M
University of Dallas M
University of Dayton M,D
University of Fort Lauderdale M
University of Northwestern–St. Paul M
University of Saint Mary of the Lake–Mundelein Seminary M,D
University of St. Michael's College M,D,O
University of St. Thomas (MN) M
University of St. Thomas (TX) M
University of South Africa M,D
University of the Incarnate Word M
Ursuline College M
Virginia Beach Theological Seminary M
Virginia University of Lynchburg M,D
Viterbo University M,O
Walla Walla University M
Walsh University M
Wayland Baptist University M
Welch College M
Wesley Biblical Seminary M
Western Seminary - Portland M,D,O
Western Seminary–Sacramento Campus M,O
Western Seminary - San Jose Campus M,O
Western Theological Seminary M,D,O
Westminster Theological Seminary M,D,O
Whitworth University M
Wilfrid Laurier University M,D,O
World Mission University M,D
Xavier University M*
Xavier University of Louisiana M

## PATHOBIOLOGY
Brown University M,D
Columbia University M,D
Drexel University M,D
Johns Hopkins University D
Kansas State University M,D
Medical University of South Carolina D
Michigan State University M,D
Penn State University Park M,D*
Purdue University M,D
The University of Alabama at Birmingham D
University of Cincinnati D
University of Connecticut M,D
University of Illinois at Urbana-Champaign M,D
University of Missouri M,D
University of Toronto M,D
University of Washington D
University of Wyoming M

## PATHOLOGY
Albert Einstein College of Medicine D
Boston University M,D
Case Western Reserve University M,D
Colorado State University M,D
Columbia University M,D
Dalhousie University M,D
Duke University M,D
Harvard University D*
Indiana University-Purdue University Indianapolis M,D
Iowa State University of Science and Technology M,D
Johns Hopkins University D
Loma Linda University D
McGill University M,D
Medical University of South Carolina M,D
Michigan State University M,D
New York Medical College M,D
North Carolina State University M,D
North Dakota State University M,D
Purdue University M,D
Queen's University at Kingston M,D
Quinnipiac University M
Rosalind Franklin University of Medicine and Science M
Rutgers University - Newark D
Saint Louis University D
Stony Brook University, State University of New York M,D
Tufts University M,D
Université de Montréal M,D
University at Buffalo, the State University of New York M,D
University of Alberta M,D
The University of British Columbia M,D
University of Calgary M,D
University of California, Davis M,D
University of California, Irvine D
University of California, Los Angeles M,D
University of Cincinnati D
University of Georgia M,D
University of Guelph M,D,O
The University of Iowa M
The University of Kansas M,D
University of Manitoba M
University of Maryland, Baltimore M
University of Michigan D
University of Mississippi Medical Center D
University of Missouri M,D
University of Nebraska Medical Center M,D
University of New Mexico M,D
The University of North Carolina at Chapel Hill D
University of Oklahoma Health Sciences Center D
University of Prince Edward Island M,D
University of Rochester D
University of Saskatchewan M,D
University of Southern California M
The University of Tennessee Health Science Center M,D
The University of Texas Medical Branch D
The University of Toledo M,O
University of Utah M,D
University of Vermont M
University of Virginia D
University of Washington D
The University of Western Ontario M,D
University of Wisconsin–Madison D
Université Laval O
Vanderbilt University D*
West Virginia University M,D
Yale University M,D

## PEDIATRIC NURSING
Augusta University D
Azusa Pacific University M,D
Boston College M,D
Caribbean University M,D
Case Western Reserve University M
Columbia University M,O
Creighton University M,D,O
Drexel University M
Duke University M,D,O
East Tennessee State University M,D,O
Emory University M
Florida International University M,D
Georgia State University M,D,O
Gwynedd Mercy University M,D
Houston Baptist University M
Indiana University-Purdue University Indianapolis M
Johns Hopkins University D,O
Kent State University M,D
King University M,D,O
Lehman College of the City University of New York M
Loma Linda University M
Marquette University M,D,O
Maryville University of Saint Louis M,D
MGH Institute of Health Professions M,D,O
Molloy College M,D,O
New York University M,D,O
Northeastern University M,D,O
Old Dominion University M,D
Oregon Health & Science University M
Point Loma Nazarene University M
Purdue University M,D,O
Queen's University at Kingston M,D,O
St. Catherine University M,D
San Francisco State University M,O
Seton Hall University M,D
Spalding University M,D,O
Stony Brook University, State University of New York M,D,O
Texas Christian University M,D,O
Texas Tech University Health Sciences Center M,D,O
Texas Woman's University M,D
The University of Alabama at Birmingham M,D
University of Cincinnati M,D
University of Colorado Denver M,D
University of Delaware M,O
University of Illinois at Chicago M,O
University of Maryland, Baltimore M,D,O
University of Michigan M,D,O
University of Minnesota, Twin Cities Campus M,D
University of Missouri M,D,O
University of Missouri–Kansas City M,D
University of Missouri–St. Louis D,O
The University of North Carolina at Chapel Hill M,D,O
University of Pennsylvania M
University of Puerto Rico - Medical Sciences Campus M
University of Rochester M,D
University of San Diego M,D
University of South Carolina M
University of South Florida M,D,O
The University of Tennessee Health Science Center D,O
The University of Texas at Austin M,D
The University of Texas Health Science Center at San Antonio M,D,O
The University of Toledo M,O
University of Wisconsin–Madison D
Villanova University M,D,O
Virginia Commonwealth University M,D,O
Wayne State University M,D,O
Wright State University M

## PERFUSION
Long Island University - Post M,O
Milwaukee School of Engineering M
Quinnipiac University M
Rush University M
The University of Arizona M,D
University of Nebraska Medical Center M

## PETROLEUM ENGINEERING
Colorado School of Mines M,D
Louisiana State University and Agricultural & Mechanical College M,D
Missouri University of Science and Technology M,D
Montana Technological University M
New Mexico Institute of Mining and Technology M,D
Texas A&M University M,D
Texas A&M University–Kingsville M
University of Alaska Fairbanks M
University of Alberta M,D
University of Calgary M,D
University of Houston M,D
The University of Kansas M,D,O
University of Louisiana at Lafayette M
University of Oklahoma M,D,O
University of Pittsburgh M,D*
University of Regina M,D
University of Southern California M,D,O
The University of Texas at Austin M,D
The University of Tulsa M,D
University of Utah M,D
University of Wyoming M,D
West Virginia University M,D

## PHARMACEUTICAL ADMINISTRATION
Belmont University D
Columbia University M
Duquesne University M
Fairleigh Dickinson University, Metropolitan Campus M,O
Florida Agricultural and Mechanical University M,D
Idaho State University M,D
New Jersey Institute of Technology M,D
Northeast Ohio Medical University M,D,O
The Ohio State University M,D
Purdue University M,D,O
Rutgers University - Newark M
St. John's University (NY) M
San Diego State University M
Southwestern Oklahoma State University D
Temple University M*
University of Florida M,D
University of Georgia D
University of Houston M,D
University of Illinois at Chicago M,D
University of Maryland, Baltimore M,D
University of Michigan D
University of Minnesota, Twin Cities Campus M,D
University of Mississippi M,D
The University of North Carolina at Chapel Hill M,D
University of Pittsburgh M*
University of Southern California M
University of the Sciences M
The University of Toledo M
University of Utah M,D
University of Wisconsin–Madison M,D
Virginia Commonwealth University M,D

## PHARMACEUTICAL ENGINEERING
New Jersey Institute of Technology M,D
University of Michigan M,D

## PHARMACEUTICAL SCIENCES
Albany College of Pharmacy and Health Sciences M,D
Auburn University M,D
Boston University D
Butler University M,D
Campbell University M,D
Chapman University M,D
Creighton University M,D
Drexel University M
Duquesne University M,D
East Tennessee State University D
Florida Agricultural and Mechanical University M,D
Idaho State University M,D
Irell & Manella Graduate School of Biological Sciences D

*M—masters degree; D—doctorate; O—other advanced degree; *—Close-Up and/or Display*

| | |
|---|---|
| Johns Hopkins University | M |
| Long Island University - Brooklyn | M,D |
| Long Island University - Hudson | M,O |
| MCPHS University | M,D |
| Memorial University of Newfoundland | M,D |
| Mercer University | D |
| Northeastern University | M,D,O |
| Northeast Ohio Medical University | M,D,O |
| Oregon State University | M,D |
| Purdue University | M,D,O |
| Rowan University | M |
| Rush University | M,D |
| Rutgers University - New Brunswick | M,D |
| St. John's University (NY) | M,D |
| South Dakota State University | M,D |
| Stevens Institute of Technology | M,O |
| Temple University | M,D* |
| Texas Southern University | M,D |
| Texas Tech University Health Sciences Center | M,D |
| Université de Montréal | M,D,O |
| University at Buffalo, the State University of New York | M,D |
| University of Alberta | M,D |
| The University of Arizona | M,D |
| The University of British Columbia | M,D |
| University of California, Irvine | D |
| University of California, San Francisco | D |
| University of Cincinnati | M,D |
| University of Colorado Denver | D |
| University of Connecticut | M,D |
| University of Florida | M,D |
| University of Georgia | M,D |
| University of Hawaii at Hilo | D |
| University of Houston | M,D |
| University of Illinois at Chicago | M,D |
| The University of Iowa | M,D |
| University of Kentucky | M,D |
| The University of Manchester | M,D |
| University of Manitoba | M,D |
| University of Maryland, Baltimore | D |
| University of Maryland Eastern Shore | M,D |
| University of Michigan | D |
| University of Minnesota, Twin Cities Campus | M,D |
| University of Mississippi | M,D |
| University of Montana | M,D |
| University of Nebraska Medical Center | M,D |
| University of New Mexico | M,D |
| The University of North Carolina at Chapel Hill | M,D |
| University of North Texas Health Science Center at Fort Worth | M,D |
| University of Oklahoma Health Sciences Center | M,D |
| University of Pittsburgh | M,D* |
| University of Puerto Rico - Medical Sciences Campus | M,D |
| University of Rhode Island | M,D |
| University of South Carolina | M,D |
| University of Southern California | M,D,O |
| University of South Florida | M,D |
| The University of Tennessee Health Science Center | M,D |
| The University of Texas at Austin | M,D |
| University of the Pacific | M,D |
| University of the Sciences | M,D |
| The University of Toledo | M |
| University of Toronto | M,D |
| University of Utah | M,D |
| University of Washington | M,D |
| University of Wisconsin–Madison | M,D |
| Université Laval | M,D,O |
| Virginia Commonwealth University | M,D |
| Wayne State University | M,D |
| Western University of Health Sciences | M |
| West Virginia University | D |
| York College of the City University of New York | M |

**PHARMACOLOGY**

| | |
|---|---|
| Albany College of Pharmacy and Health Sciences | M,D |
| Albany Medical College | M,D |
| Alliant International University–San Francisco | M |
| Argosy University, Hawaii | M,O |
| Augusta University | D |
| Baylor College of Medicine | D |
| Boston University | M,D |
| Case Western Reserve University | D |
| The Chicago School of Professional Psychology: Online | M |
| Columbia University | M,D |
| Creighton University | M,D |
| Dalhousie University | M,D |
| Drexel University | M,D |
| Duke University | D |
| Duquesne University | M,D |
| East Carolina University | M,D |
| East Tennessee State University | D |
| Emory University | D |
| Fairleigh Dickinson University, Florham Campus | M,O |
| Florida Agricultural and Mechanical University | M,D |
| Georgetown University | M,D |
| Howard University | M,D |
| Husson University | M,D |
| Idaho State University | M,D |
| Indiana University-Purdue University Indianapolis | M,D |
| Johns Hopkins University | D |
| Kent State University | M,D |
| Loma Linda University | D |
| London Metropolitan University | M,D |
| Long Island University - Brooklyn | M,D |
| Louisiana State University Health Sciences Center | D |
| Louisiana State University Health Sciences Center at Shreveport | M,D |
| McGill University | M,D |
| McMaster University | M,D |
| MCPHS University | M,D |
| Medical College of Wisconsin | D |
| Meharry Medical College | D |
| Michigan State University | M,D |
| Montclair State University | M |
| New Jersey Institute of Technology | M,D |
| New York Medical College | M,D |
| North Carolina State University | M,D |
| Northeastern University | M,D,O |
| The Ohio State University | M,D |
| Oregon Health & Science University | D |
| Purdue University | M,D |
| Rush University | M,D |
| Rutgers University - Newark | D |
| Saint Louis University | D |
| Southern Illinois University Carbondale | M,D |
| State University of New York Upstate Medical University | D |
| Stony Brook University, State University of New York | M,D |
| Thomas Jefferson University | M |
| Tulane University | M |
| Universidad Central del Caribe | M,D |
| Université de Montréal | M,D |
| Université de Sherbrooke | M,D |
| University at Buffalo, the State University of New York | M,D |
| The University of Alabama at Birmingham | D |
| University of Alberta | M,D |
| The University of Arizona | M,D |
| University of Arkansas for Medical Sciences | M,D,O |
| The University of British Columbia | M,D |
| University of California, Davis | M,D |
| University of California, Los Angeles | M,D |
| University of California, San Francisco | D |
| University of Cincinnati | D |
| University of Colorado Denver | D |
| University of Connecticut | M,D |
| University of Florida | M,D |
| University of Georgia | M,D |
| University of Guelph | M,D |
| University of Hawaii at Hilo | M |
| University of Houston | M,D |
| University of Illinois at Chicago | D |
| The University of Iowa | M,D |
| The University of Kansas | M,D |
| University of Kentucky | D |
| University of Louisville | M,D |
| The University of Manchester | M,D |
| University of Manitoba | M,D |
| University of Maryland, Baltimore | M |
| University of Miami | D |
| University of Michigan | M,D |
| University of Minnesota, Duluth | M,D |
| University of Minnesota, Twin Cities Campus | M,D |
| University of Mississippi | M,D |
| University of Mississippi Medical Center | D |
| University of Missouri | M,D |
| University of Nebraska Medical Center | D |
| The University of North Carolina at Chapel Hill | D |
| University of North Texas Health Science Center at Fort Worth | M,D |
| University of Pennsylvania | D |
| University of Prince Edward Island | M,D |
| University of Puerto Rico - Medical Sciences Campus | M,D |
| University of Rhode Island | M,D |
| University of Rochester | M,D |
| University of Saskatchewan | M,D |
| University of South Dakota | M,D |
| The University of Tennessee Health Science Center | M,D |
| The University of Texas at Austin | M,D |
| The University of Texas Health Science Center at Houston | M,D |
| The University of Texas Health Science Center at San Antonio | D |
| The University of Texas Medical Branch | M,D |
| University of the Sciences | M,D |
| The University of Toledo | M,D |
| University of Toronto | M,D |
| University of Utah | D |
| University of Vermont | M,D |
| University of Virginia | D |
| University of Washington | D |
| University of Wisconsin–Madison | D |
| Vanderbilt University | D* |
| Virginia Commonwealth University | M,D,O |
| Wake Forest University | D |
| Wayne State University | M,D |
| Weill Cornell Medicine | M,D |
| Wright State University | M |
| Yale University | D |

**PHARMACY**

| | |
|---|---|
| Albany College of Pharmacy and Health Sciences | M,D |
| Appalachian College of Pharmacy | D |
| Auburn University | D |
| Belmont University | D |
| Binghamton University, State University of New York | D |
| Butler University | M,D |
| California Health Sciences University | D |
| California Northstate University | D |
| Campbell University | M,D |
| Cedarville University | M,D |
| Chapman University | M,D |
| Chicago State University | D |
| Concordia University Wisconsin | M,D |
| Creighton University | D |
| Drake University | M,D |
| Duquesne University | D |
| D'Youville College | D |
| East Tennessee State University | D |
| Fairleigh Dickinson University, Florham Campus | D |
| Ferris State University | D |
| Florida Agricultural and Mechanical University | D |
| Georgia Campus–Philadelphia College of Osteopathic Medicine | D |
| Harding University | D |
| High Point University | M,D |
| Howard University | D |
| Husson University | M,D |
| Idaho State University | M,D |
| Lake Erie College of Osteopathic Medicine | M,D,O |
| Lebanese American University | D |
| Lipscomb University | M,D |
| Loma Linda University | D |
| Long Island University - Brooklyn | M,D |
| Long Island University - Hudson | M,O |
| Manchester University | D |
| Marshall B. Ketchum University | M,D |
| Marshall University | D |
| MCPHS University | D |
| Medical College of Wisconsin | D |
| Medical University of South Carolina | D |
| Mercer University | D |
| Midwestern University, Downers Grove Campus | D |
| Midwestern University, Glendale Campus | D |
| North Dakota State University | M,D |
| Northeastern University | M,D,O |
| Northeast Ohio Medical University | D |
| Notre Dame of Maryland University | D |
| Nova Southeastern University | M,D |
| Ohio Northern University | D |
| The Ohio State University | M,D |
| Oregon State University | D |
| Pacific University | D |
| Palm Beach Atlantic University | D |
| Presbyterian College | D |
| Purdue University | D |
| Regis University | M,D,O |
| Roosevelt University | D |
| Rosalind Franklin University of Medicine and Science | D |
| Roseman University of Health Sciences | D |
| Rutgers University - New Brunswick | M,D |
| St. John Fisher College | D |
| St. John's University (NY) | M,D |
| St. Louis College of Pharmacy | D |
| Samford University | D |
| Shenandoah University | D |
| South College | D |
| South Dakota State University | D |
| Southern Illinois University Edwardsville | D |
| South University - Columbia | D |
| South University - Savannah | D |
| Southwestern Oklahoma State University | D |
| Sullivan University | D |
| Temple University | M,D* |
| Texas A&M University | D |
| Texas Southern University | D |
| Texas Tech University Health Sciences Center | D |
| Thomas Jefferson University | D |
| Touro University California | M,D |
| Union University | D |
| Universidad de Ciencias Medicas | M,D,O |
| University at Buffalo, the State University of New York | D |
| University of Alberta | M,D |
| The University of Arizona | D |
| University of Arkansas for Medical Sciences | M,D |
| The University of British Columbia | M,D |
| University of California, San Diego | D |
| University of California, San Francisco | D |
| University of Charleston | D |
| University of Cincinnati | D |
| University of Colorado Denver | D |
| University of Connecticut | D |
| The University of Findlay | M,D |
| University of Florida | M,D |
| University of Georgia | M,D,O |
| University of Hawaii at Hilo | D |
| University of Houston | M,D |
| University of Illinois at Chicago | D |
| The University of Iowa | M,D |
| The University of Kansas | M,D |
| University of Kentucky | D |
| University of Louisiana at Monroe | D |
| The University of Manchester | M,D |
| University of Maryland, Baltimore | M,D |
| University of Maryland Eastern Shore | M,D |
| University of Michigan | D |
| University of Minnesota, Duluth | M,D |
| University of Minnesota, Twin Cities Campus | D |
| University of Mississippi | M,D |
| University of Missouri–Kansas City | D |
| University of Montana | M,D |
| University of Nebraska Medical Center | D |
| University of New England | D |
| University of New Mexico | D |
| The University of North Carolina at Chapel Hill | M,D |
| University of Oklahoma Health Sciences Center | D |
| University of Pittsburgh | D* |
| University of Puerto Rico - Medical Sciences Campus | M,D |
| University of Rhode Island | D |
| University of Saint Joseph | D |
| University of Saskatchewan | M,D |
| University of South Carolina | D |
| University of Southern California | D |
| University of South Florida | M,D,O |
| The University of Tennessee Health Science Center | M,D |
| The University of Texas at Austin | D |
| The University of Texas at Tyler | D |
| University of the Incarnate Word | D |
| University of the Pacific | D |
| University of the Sciences | D |
| The University of Toledo | M,D |
| University of Utah | M,D |
| University of Washington | M,D |
| University of Wisconsin–Madison | D |
| University of Wyoming | M,D |
| Virginia Commonwealth University | D |
| Washington State University | M,D |
| Wayne State University | D |
| West Coast University | M,D |
| Western New England University | D |
| Western University of Health Sciences | D |
| West Virginia University | D |
| William Carey University | D |
| Wingate University | D |
| Xavier University of Louisiana | D |

**PHILANTHROPIC STUDIES**

| | |
|---|---|
| Central Michigan University | M,O |
| Indiana University-Purdue University Indianapolis | M,D |
| Saint Mary's University of Minnesota | M |
| University of Denver | M,O |
| University of Memphis | M,O |

**PHILOSOPHY**

| | |
|---|---|
| Acadia University | M |
| American University | M |
| The American University in Cairo | M,O |
| Arizona State University at Tempe | M,D,O |
| Baylor University | M,D |
| Binghamton University, State University of New York | M,D |
| Boston College | M,D |
| Boston University | M,D |
| Bowling Green State University | M,D |
| Brandeis University | M |
| Brock University | M |
| Brown University | D |
| California State University, Long Beach | M |
| California State University, Los Angeles | M,O |
| Carleton University | M |
| Carnegie Mellon University | M,D |
| The Catholic University of America | M,D,O |
| Central European University | M,D |
| Claremont Graduate University | M,D |
| Cleveland State University | M,O |
| Collège Dominicain de Philosophie et de Théologie | M,D |
| Colorado State University | M |
| Columbia University | M,D |
| Concordia University (Canada) | M |
| Cornell University | D |
| Dalhousie University | M,D |
| Dallas Theological Seminary | M,D,O |
| Delta State University | M |
| Dominican School of Philosophy and Theology | M,O |
| Duke University | D |
| Duquesne University | M,D |
| Eastern Michigan University | M |
| Emory University | D,O |
| Florida State University | M,D |
| Fordham University | M,D |
| Franciscan University of Steubenville | M |
| George Mason University | M |
| Georgetown University | M,D |
| The George Washington University | M |
| Georgia State University | M |
| Gonzaga University | M |
| The Graduate Center, City University of New York | M,D |
| Harrison Middleton University | M,D |
| Harvard University | M,D* |
| Houston Baptist University | M |
| Howard University | M |
| Indiana University Bloomington | M,D |
| Indiana University-Purdue University Indianapolis | M,O |
| Institute for Christian Studies | M,D |
| Institute for Doctoral Studies in the Visual Arts | D |
| Johns Hopkins University | M,D |
| Kent State University | M |
| Lake Forest College | M |
| Lincoln Christian University | M |
| Louisiana State University and Agricultural & Mechanical College | M |
| Loyola Marymount University | M |
| Loyola University Chicago | M,D |
| Marquette University | M,D |
| Massachusetts Institute of Technology | D |
| McGill University | M,D |
| McMaster University | M,D |
| Memorial University of Newfoundland | M,D |
| Miami University | M |
| Michigan State University | M,D |
| Midwestern State University | M,D |

Mount St. Mary's University (MD) M
The New School M,D
New York University M,D
Northern Illinois University M
Northwestern University D
The Ohio State University M,D
Ohio University M
Oklahoma State University M
Old Dominion University M,O
Open University M
Penn State University Park M,D*
Princeton University D
Purdue University M,D
Queen's University at Kingston M,D
Regis College (Canada) M,D,O
Rice University M,D
Roosevelt University M
Rutgers University - New Brunswick D
Saint Charles Borromeo Seminary, Overbrook M
Saint Louis University M,D
Saint Mary's University (Canada) M
San Diego State University M
San Francisco State University M
San Jose State University M
Simon Fraser University M,D
Southeastern Baptist Theological Seminary M,D
The Southern Baptist Theological Seminary M,D
Southern Evangelical Seminary M,D,O
Southern Illinois University Carbondale M,D
Stanford University M,D
Stony Brook University, State University of New York M,D,O
Syracuse University M,D
Teachers College, Columbia University M,D,O
Temple University M,D*
Texas A&M University M,D
Texas State University M
Texas Tech University M
Trinity Western University M
Tufts University M
Tulane University M,D
Universidad Autonoma de Guadalajara M,D
Université de Montréal M,D
Université de Sherbrooke M,D,O
Université du Québec à Montréal M,D
Université du Québec à Trois-Rivières M,D
University at Albany, State University of New York M,D
University at Buffalo, the State University of New York M,D
University of Alberta M,D
The University of Arizona M,D
University of Arkansas M,D
The University of British Columbia M,D
University of Calgary M,D
University of California, Berkeley D
University of California, Davis M,D
University of California, Irvine M,D
University of California, Los Angeles M,D
University of California, Riverside M,D
University of California, San Diego D
University of California, Santa Barbara D
University of California, Santa Cruz M,D
University of Chicago M,D
University of Cincinnati M,D
University of Colorado Boulder M,D
University of Connecticut M,D
University of Florida M,D
University of Georgia M,D
University of Guelph M,D
University of Hawaii at Manoa M,D
University of Houston M
University of Idaho M,D
University of Illinois at Chicago M,D
University of Illinois at Urbana-Champaign M,D
The University of Iowa D
The University of Kansas M,D
University of Kentucky M,D
University of Lethbridge M,D
University of Louisville M,D
The University of Manchester M,D
University of Manitoba M
University of Maryland, College Park M,D
University of Massachusetts Amherst M,D
University of Memphis M,D
University of Miami M,D
University of Michigan M,D
University of Minnesota, Twin Cities Campus M,D
University of Mississippi M,D
University of Missouri M,D
University of Missouri–St. Louis M
University of Montana M
University of Nebraska–Lincoln M,D
University of Nevada, Reno M
University of New Mexico M,D
The University of North Carolina at Chapel Hill M,D
The University of North Carolina at Charlotte M,O
University of North Florida M,O
University of North Georgia M
University of North Texas M,D,O
University of Notre Dame D
University of Oklahoma M,D
University of Oregon M,D
University of Ottawa M,D
University of Pennsylvania M,D
University of Pittsburgh D*
University of Puerto Rico at Rio Piedras M
University of Regina M
University of Rochester D
University of St. Thomas (TX) M,D
University of Saskatchewan M
University of South Africa M,D
University of South Carolina M,D
University of Southern California M,D
University of South Florida M,D
The University of Tennessee M,D
The University of Texas at Austin D
The University of Texas at El Paso M
The University of Texas at San Antonio M
The University of Toledo M
University of Toronto M,D
University of Utah M,D
University of Victoria M
University of Virginia M,D
University of Washington M,D
University of Waterloo M,D
The University of Western Ontario M,D
University of Windsor M
University of Wisconsin–Madison M,D
University of Wisconsin–Milwaukee M*
University of Wyoming M
Université Laval M,D
Vanderbilt University M,D*
Villanova University D
Washington University in St. Louis D
Wayne State University M,D
Western Michigan University M
Wilfrid Laurier University M
Yale University D
York University M,D

## PHOTOGRAPHY

Academy of Art University M
Ball State University M
Bard College M
Barry University M
Bradley University M
Brooklyn College of the City University of New York M
California Institute of the Arts M,O
California State University, Fullerton M
California State University, Los Angeles M
Central Washington University M
Claremont Graduate University M
Columbia College Chicago M
Cornell University M,D
Cranbrook Academy of Art M
East Carolina University M
Ferris State University M
The George Washington University M,O
Georgia State University M,D
Governors State University M
Howard University M
Illinois State University M
Indiana State University M
Indiana University-Purdue University Indianapolis M
Inter American University of Puerto Rico, San Germán Campus M
Ithaca College M
James Madison University M
Kent State University M
Lesley University M
Louisiana State University and Agricultural & Mechanical College M
Louisiana Tech University M,D,O
Maryland Institute College of Art M
Marywood University M
Massachusetts College of Art and Design M,O
Mills College M
Minneapolis College of Art and Design M
New Hampshire Institute of Art M
The New School M
New York Film Academy M
Northern Vermont University–Johnson M
Ohio University M
Oklahoma City University M
Otis College of Art and Design M
Paris College of Art M
Rhode Island School of Design M
Rochester Institute of Technology M
San Diego State University M
Savannah College of Art and Design M
School of Visual Arts (NY) M
Southwest University of Visual Arts M
Syracuse University M
Temple University M*
Texas Woman's University M
The University of Alabama M
University of Alaska Fairbanks M
University of Colorado Boulder M
University of Illinois at Urbana-Champaign M
University of Memphis M,O
University of Miami M
University of Montana M
University of New Mexico M,D
University of Notre Dame M
University of Oklahoma M,D
University of South Dakota M
University of Southern California M
The University of Tennessee M
University of Utah M
University of Victoria M
University of Washington M
Virginia Commonwealth University M,D
Wayne State University M
West Virginia University M,D
Wichita State University M
Yale University M

## PHOTONICS

Duke University M
Johns Hopkins University M,O
Lehigh University M,D
Oklahoma State University M,D
Princeton University D
Queens College of the City University of New York M
Stevens Institute of Technology M,D,O
The University of Alabama in Huntsville M,D
University of Arkansas M,D
University of California, San Diego M,D
University of California, Santa Barbara M,D
University of Central Florida M,D
University of Dayton M,D
University of New Mexico M,D

## PHYSICAL CHEMISTRY

Auburn University M,D
Binghamton University, State University of New York M,D
Boston College M,D
Brandeis University M,D
Cleveland State University M,D
Cornell University D
Dartmouth College M,D
Eastern New Mexico University M
Florida State University M,D
The George Washington University M,D
Georgia State University M,D
Harvard University D*
Howard University M,D
Indiana University Bloomington M,D
Iowa State University of Science and Technology M,D
Laurentian University M
Marquette University M,D
Massachusetts Institute of Technology D
McMaster University M,D
Old Dominion University M,D
Purdue University M,D
Rice University M,D
Rutgers University - Newark M,D
Rutgers University - New Brunswick M,D
Seton Hall University M,D
Southern University and Agricultural and Mechanical College M
University of Calgary M,D
University of Cincinnati M,D
University of Louisville M,D
The University of Manchester M,D
University of Maryland, College Park M,D
University of Memphis M,D
University of Miami M,D
University of Michigan M,D
University of Missouri–Kansas City M,D
University of Montana M,D
University of Nebraska–Lincoln M,D
University of Notre Dame M,D
University of Oklahoma M,D
University of Puerto Rico at Mayagüez M,D
University of Rochester D
University of Southern California D
The University of Tennessee M,D
The University of Texas at Austin D
The University of Toledo M,D
Virginia Commonwealth University M,D
Wake Forest University M,D
Yale University D
Youngstown State University M

## PHYSICAL EDUCATION

Adams State University M
Alabama Agricultural and Mechanical University M
Alabama State University M
Albany State University M,O
Alcorn State University M,O
American University of Puerto Rico - Bayamon M
Arizona State University at Tempe M
Arkansas State University M,O
Auburn University M,D,O
Auburn University at Montgomery M,O
Avila University M,O
Ball State University M
Baylor University M,D
Bridgewater State University M
Brooklyn College of the City University of New York M
California Baptist University M
California State University, East Bay M
California State University, Fullerton M
California State University, Long Beach M
California State University, Los Angeles M,O
California State University, Sacramento M
California State University, Stanislaus M
Campbell University M
Canisius College M
Caribbean University M,D
Central Connecticut State University M,O
Central Washington University M
Chicago State University M
The Citadel, The Military College of South Carolina M,O
Cleveland State University M
Colorado State University-Pueblo M
Columbus State University M
Concordia University (United States) M,D
Concordia University Irvine M
Delta State University M
DePaul University M,D
East Carolina University M,D,O
Eastern Kentucky University M
Eastern Michigan University M
Eastern New Mexico University M
Eastern University M,O
Eastern Washington University M
East Stroudsburg University of Pennsylvania M
Emporia State University M
Florida Agricultural and Mechanical University M
Florida International University M,D,O
Fort Hays State University M
Gardner-Webb University M
George Mason University M
Georgia College & State University M
Georgia State University M
Goucher College M,O
Henderson State University M
Hofstra University M,D,O
Howard University M
Idaho State University M
Illinois State University M
Indiana State University M,D
Indiana University Bloomington M,D
Indiana University of Pennsylvania M
Indiana University-Purdue University Indianapolis M,O
Inter American University of Puerto Rico, Metropolitan Campus M
Inter American University of Puerto Rico, San Germán Campus M
Jackson State University M
Jacksonville State University M,O
James Madison University M
Longwood University M
Massachusetts College of Liberal Arts M,O
McGill University M,D,O
McNeese State University O
Memorial University of Newfoundland M
Meredith College M,O
Middle Tennessee State University M
Millersville University of Pennsylvania M,O
Minnesota State University Mankato M
Mississippi State University M,D
Missouri State University M
Montclair State University M
Morehead State University M
North Carolina Central University M
Northern Illinois University M
Northwest Missouri State University M
The Ohio State University M,D
Ohio University M
Old Dominion University M,D
Pittsburg State University M
Purdue University M,D
Queens College of the City University of New York M,O
Rhode Island College M,O
Salem State University M
Slippery Rock University of Pennsylvania M
Southern Connecticut State University M
Southern Illinois University Carbondale M
Southern Illinois University Edwardsville M
Southwestern Oklahoma State University M
Springfield College M,D,O
State University of New York College at Cortland M
Stony Brook University, State University of New York M,O
Sul Ross State University M
SUNY Brockport M,O
Teachers College, Columbia University M,D
Temple University M,D*
Tennessee State University M
Tennessee Technological University M
Texas Southern University M
UNB Fredericton M
Union College (KY) M
United States Sports Academy M
Universidad del Turabo M
Universidad Metropolitana M
Université de Montréal M,D,O
Université de Sherbrooke M
Université du Québec à Trois-Rivières M
The University of Akron M
The University of Alabama M,D
University of Alberta M,D
University of Arkansas M
The University of British Columbia M,D
University of Dayton M

*M—masters degree; D—doctorate; O—other advanced degree; *—Close-Up and/or Display*

| | |
|---|---|
| University of Florida | M,D |
| University of Georgia | M,D |
| University of Houston | M,D |
| University of Idaho | M,D |
| University of Indianapolis | M |
| The University of Kansas | M,D |
| University of Kentucky | M,D |
| University of Louisville | M,D,O |
| University of Maine | M,D,O |
| University of Manitoba | M |
| University of Mary | M |
| University of Memphis | M,O |
| University of Montana | M |
| University of Nebraska at Kearney | M |
| University of New Hampshire | M,O |
| University of New Mexico | D |
| University of North Alabama | M |
| The University of North Carolina at Chapel Hill | M |
| The University of North Carolina at Pembroke | M |
| University of Northern Colorado | M,D |
| University of Northern Iowa | M |
| University of North Georgia | M |
| University of Rhode Island | M |
| University of Rio Grande | M |
| University of South Alabama | M |
| University of South Carolina | M,D |
| The University of Tennessee at Chattanooga | M |
| The University of Tennessee at Martin | M |
| The University of Texas at Austin | M,D |
| The University of Toledo | M |
| University of Toronto | M,D |
| University of Victoria | M |
| University of Virginia | M,D |
| University of Washington | M,D |
| The University of West Alabama | M |
| University of West Florida | M,D |
| University of Wisconsin–La Crosse | M |
| University of Wyoming | M |
| Utah State University | M,D |
| Wayne State College | M |
| Wayne State University | M,D |
| Western Kentucky University | M |
| Western Michigan University | M |
| Western Washington University | M |
| Westfield State University | M |
| West Liberty University | M |
| West Virginia University | M,D |
| Wilfrid Laurier University | M |
| William Woods University | M,D,O |
| Winthrop University | M |

## PHYSICAL THERAPY

| | |
|---|---|
| AdventHealth University | D |
| Alabama State University | D |
| American International College | M,D,O |
| Andrews University | D |
| Angelo State University | D |
| Arcadia University | D |
| Arkansas State University | D |
| A.T. Still University | M,D,O |
| Augusta University | D |
| Azusa Pacific University | D |
| Bellarmine University | M,D |
| Belmont University | M,D |
| Boston University | M,D |
| Bradley University | D |
| California State University, Fresno | D |
| California State University, Long Beach | D |
| California State University, Northridge | M |
| California State University, Sacramento | D |
| Campbell University | M,D |
| Carroll University | D |
| Central Michigan University | M,D |
| Chapman University | D |
| Chatham University | D |
| Clarke University | D |
| Clarkson University | D |
| Cleveland State University | D |
| The College of St. Scholastica | D |
| College of Staten Island of the City University of New York | D |
| Columbia University | D |
| Concordia University, St. Paul | M,D |
| Concordia University Wisconsin | D |
| Creighton University | D |
| Daemen College | D,O |
| Dalhousie University | M |
| Des Moines University | D |
| Dominican College | M,D |
| Drexel University | M,D,O |
| Duke University | D |
| Duquesne University | M,D |
| D'Youville College | D,O |
| East Carolina University | D |
| Eastern Washington University | D |
| East Tennessee State University | D |
| Elon University | D |
| Emory & Henry College | M,D |
| Emory University | D |
| Florida Agricultural and Mechanical University | D |
| Florida Gulf Coast University | D |
| Florida International University | D |
| Franciscan Missionaries of Our Lady University | M,D |
| Franklin Pierce University | M,D,O |
| Gannon University | D |
| George Fox University | D |
| The George Washington University | D |
| Georgia Campus–Philadelphia College of Osteopathic Medicine | D |
| Georgia Southern University | D |
| Georgia State University | D |
| Governors State University | D |
| Grand Valley State University | D |
| Hampton University | D |
| Harding University | D |
| Hardin-Simmons University | D |
| High Point University | M,D |
| Howard University | M,D |
| Hunter College of the City University of New York | D |
| Husson University | D |
| Idaho State University | D |
| Indiana State University | M,D |
| Indiana University-Purdue University Indianapolis | M,D |
| Ithaca College | D |
| Kean University | D |
| Langston University | D |
| Lebanon Valley College | D |
| Loma Linda University | M,D |
| Long Island University - Brooklyn | M,D,O |
| Louisiana State University Health Sciences Center | D |
| Marist College | D |
| Marquette University | D |
| Marshall University | D |
| Mary Baldwin University | D |
| Marymount University | D |
| Maryville University of Saint Louis | D |
| Mayo Clinic School of Health Sciences | D |
| McMaster University | M |
| MCPHS University | D |
| Medical University of South Carolina | D |
| Mercer University | M,D |
| Mercy College | D |
| MGH Institute of Health Professions | M,D,O |
| Midwestern University, Downers Grove Campus | D |
| Midwestern University, Glendale Campus | D |
| Misericordia University | D |
| Missouri State University | D |
| Mount St. Joseph University | D |
| Mount Saint Mary's University (CA) | M,D,O |
| Nazareth College of Rochester | D |
| Neumann University | D |
| New York Institute of Technology | D |
| New York Medical College | M,D,O |
| New York University | M,D,O |
| Northern Arizona University | D |
| Northern Illinois University | M,D |
| Northwestern University | D |
| Nova Southeastern University | M,D |
| The Ohio State University | D |
| Ohio University | D |
| Old Dominion University | D |
| Pacific University | M,D |
| Queen's University at Kingston | M,D |
| Radford University | D |
| Regis University | M,D,O |
| Rockhurst University | D |
| Rocky Mountain University of Health Professions | D |
| Rosalind Franklin University of Medicine and Science | M,D |
| Rush University | M |
| Rutgers University - Camden | D |
| Rutgers University - Newark | D |
| Sacred Heart University | D |
| Sage Graduate School | D |
| St. Ambrose University | D |
| St. Catherine University | D |
| Saint Francis University | D |
| Saint Louis University | M,D |
| Samford University | M,D |
| Samuel Merritt University | D |
| San Diego State University | D |
| San Francisco State University | D |
| Seton Hall University | D |
| Shenandoah University | D |
| Simmons University | M,D,O |
| Slippery Rock University of Pennsylvania | D |
| Sonoma State University | M |
| Southwest Baptist University | D |
| Springfield College | D |
| State University of New York Upstate Medical University | D |
| Stockton University | D |
| Stony Brook University, State University of New York | M,D,O |
| Tennessee State University | D |
| Texas State University | D |
| Texas Tech University Health Sciences Center | D |
| Texas Woman's University | D |
| Thomas Jefferson University | D |
| Trine University | D |
| University at Buffalo, the State University of New York | D |
| The University of Alabama at Birmingham | D |
| University of Alberta | M,D |
| The University of British Columbia | M |
| University of California, San Francisco | D |
| University of Central Arkansas | D |
| University of Central Florida | D |
| University of Cincinnati | D |
| University of Colorado Denver | D |
| University of Connecticut | D |
| University of Dayton | D |
| University of Delaware | D |
| University of Evansville | D |
| The University of Findlay | M,D |
| University of Florida | D |
| University of Hartford | M,D |
| University of Illinois at Chicago | M,D |
| University of Indianapolis | M,D |
| The University of Iowa | M,D |
| University of Jamestown | D |
| The University of Kansas | D |
| University of Kentucky | D |
| University of Lynchburg | D |
| University of Manitoba | M,D |
| University of Mary | D |
| University of Mary Hardin-Baylor | D |
| University of Maryland, Baltimore | D |
| University of Maryland Eastern Shore | D |
| University of Massachusetts Lowell | D |
| University of Miami | D |
| University of Michigan–Flint | D,O |
| University of Minnesota, Twin Cities Campus | M,D |
| University of Mississippi Medical Center | M |
| University of Montana | D |
| University of Mount Union | D |
| University of Nebraska Medical Center | D |
| University of Nevada, Las Vegas | D |
| University of New England | M,D |
| University of New Mexico | D |
| University of North Dakota | D |
| University of North Florida | M,D |
| University of North Georgia | D |
| University of North Texas Health Science Center at Fort Worth | M,D |
| University of Oklahoma Health Sciences Center | M |
| University of Pittsburgh | M,D* |
| University of Puerto Rico - Medical Sciences Campus | M |
| University of Puget Sound | D |
| University of Rhode Island | D |
| University of St. Augustine for Health Sciences | D |
| University of Saint Mary | D |
| The University of Scranton | D |
| University of South Alabama | D |
| University of South Dakota | D |
| University of Southern California | M,D |
| University of South Florida | D |
| The University of Tennessee at Chattanooga | D |
| The University of Tennessee Health Science Center | M,D |
| The University of Texas at El Paso | D |
| The University of Texas Health Science Center at San Antonio | M,D |
| The University of Texas Medical Branch | M,D |
| The University of Texas Southwestern Medical Center | D |
| University of the Incarnate Word | D |
| University of the Pacific | M,D |
| University of the Sciences | D |
| The University of Toledo | M,D |
| University of Toronto | M |
| University of Utah | D |
| University of Vermont | D |
| University of Washington | M,D |
| The University of Western Ontario | M,O |
| University of Wisconsin–La Crosse | D |
| University of Wisconsin–Madison | D |
| University of Wisconsin–Milwaukee | M,D* |
| Utica College | D |
| Virginia Commonwealth University | M,D |
| Walsh University | D |
| Washington University in St. Louis | D |
| Wayne State University | M,D,O |
| West Coast University | M,D |
| Western Carolina University | D |
| Western Kentucky University | D |
| Western University of Health Sciences | D |
| West Virginia University | M,D |
| Wheeling Jesuit University | D |
| Wichita State University | D |
| Widener University | M,D |
| Wingate University | D |
| Winston-Salem State University | D |
| Youngstown State University | D |

## PHYSICIAN ASSISTANT STUDIES

| | |
|---|---|
| AdventHealth University | M |
| Albany Medical College | M |
| Alderson Broaddus University | M |
| Arcadia University | M |
| A.T. Still University | M,D,O |
| Augsburg University | M |
| Augusta University | M |
| Baldwin Wallace University | M |
| Barry University | M |
| Baylor College of Medicine | M |
| Bay Path University | M |
| Bethel University (MN) | M,D,O |
| Bethel University (TN) | M |
| Boston University | M |
| Bryant University | M |
| Butler University | M,D |
| California Baptist University | M |
| Campbell University | M,D |
| Carroll University | M |
| Case Western Reserve University | M |
| Central Michigan University | M,D |
| Chapman University | M |
| Chatham University | M |
| Christian Brothers University | M |
| Clarkson University | M |
| Cleveland State University | M |
| Daemen College | M |
| Des Moines University | M |
| Drexel University | M |
| Duke University | M |
| Duquesne University | M,D |
| D'Youville College | M |
| East Carolina University | M |
| Eastern Michigan University | M |
| Eastern Virginia Medical School | M |
| Elon University | M |
| Emory & Henry College | M,D |
| Emory University | M |
| Florida Gulf Coast University | M |
| Florida International University | M,D |
| Franciscan Missionaries of Our Lady University | M,D |
| Francis Marion University | M |
| Franklin Pierce University | M,D,O |
| Gannon University | M |
| Gardner-Webb University | M |
| The George Washington University | M |
| Grand Valley State University | M |
| Harding University | M |
| Hardin-Simmons University | M,D |
| High Point University | M,D |
| Hofstra University | M |
| Howard University | M,D |
| Idaho State University | M |
| Indiana State University | M,D |
| James Madison University | M |
| Jefferson College of Health Sciences | M |
| Johnson & Wales University | M |
| Keiser University | M |
| Kettering College | M |
| King's College | M |
| Le Moyne College | M |
| Lenoir-Rhyne University | M |
| Lock Haven University of Pennsylvania | M |
| Loma Linda University | M |
| Long Island University - Brooklyn | M,D,O |
| Louisiana State University Health Sciences Center | M |
| Marietta College | M |
| Marquette University | M |
| Mary Baldwin University | M |
| Marywood University | M |
| MCPHS University | M |
| Medical University of South Carolina | M |
| Mercer University | M,D |
| Mercy College | M |
| Mercyhurst University | M |
| Methodist University | M |
| MGH Institute of Health Professions | M |
| Midwestern University, Downers Grove Campus | M |
| Midwestern University, Glendale Campus | M |
| Milligan University | M |
| Missouri State University | M |
| New York Institute of Technology | M |
| Northern Arizona University | M |
| Nova Southeastern University | M,D |
| Ohio Dominican University | M |
| Oregon Health & Science University | M |
| Pace University | M |
| Pacific University | M |
| Philadelphia College of Osteopathic Medicine | M |
| Quinnipiac University | M |
| Rocky Mountain College | M |
| Rocky Mountain University of Health Professions | M |
| Rocky Vista University | M |
| Rosalind Franklin University of Medicine and Science | M |
| Rush University | M |
| Rutgers University - Newark | M |
| Sacred Heart University | M |
| St. Ambrose University | M |
| St. Catherine University | M |
| Saint Francis University | M |
| Saint Louis University | M |
| Salus University | M |
| Samuel Merritt University | M |
| Seton Hall University | M |
| Seton Hill University | M |
| Shenandoah University | M,D,O |
| Slippery Rock University of Pennsylvania | M |
| South College | M |
| Southern Illinois University Carbondale | M |
| South University - Savannah | M |
| South University - Tampa | M |
| Springfield College | M |
| Stephens College | M,O |
| Stony Brook University, State University of New York | M,D,O |
| Texas Tech University Health Sciences Center | M |
| Thomas Jefferson University | M |
| Towson University | M |
| Trevecca Nazarene University | M |
| Trine University | M |
| Tufts University | M,D,O |
| Union College (NE) | M |
| The University of Alabama at Birmingham | M |
| University of Alaska Anchorage | M |
| University of Arkansas for Medical Sciences | M,D |
| University of Bridgeport | M |
| University of Charleston | M |
| University of Colorado Denver | M |
| University of Dayton | M |
| University of Detroit Mercy | M,D,O |
| The University of Findlay | M,D |
| University of Florida | M |
| The University of Iowa | M |
| University of Kentucky | M |
| University of Lynchburg | M |
| University of Mount Union | M |
| University of Nebraska Medical Center | M |
| University of New England | M,D |
| University of New Mexico | M |
| University of North Dakota | M |
| University of North Texas Health Science Center at Fort Worth | M,D |

| | |
|---|---|
| University of Oklahoma Health Sciences Center | M |
| University of Pittsburgh | M,D* |
| University of St. Francis (IL) | M,O |
| University of Saint Francis (IN) | M |
| University of South Alabama | M |
| University of South Dakota | M |
| University of Southern California | M |
| The University of Tennessee Health Science Center | M,D |
| The University of Texas Health Science Center at San Antonio | M,D |
| The University of Texas Medical Branch | M |
| The University of Texas Rio Grande Valley | M |
| The University of Texas Southwestern Medical Center | M |
| University of the Cumberlands | M |
| The University of Toledo | M |
| University of Utah | M |
| University of Wisconsin–La Crosse | M |
| University of Wisconsin–Madison | M |
| Valparaiso University | M,D,O |
| Wayne State University | M,D,O |
| Weill Cornell Medicine | M |
| Western Michigan University | M |
| Western University of Health Sciences | M |
| Westfield State University | M |
| West Liberty University | M |
| Wichita State University | M |
| Wingate University | M |
| Yale University | M |
| York College of the City University of New York | M |

## PHYSICS

| | |
|---|---|
| Alabama Agricultural and Mechanical University | M,D |
| The American University in Cairo | M,D,O |
| Arizona State University at Tempe | M,D |
| Auburn University | M,D |
| Ball State University | M |
| Baylor University | M,D |
| Binghamton University, State University of New York | M,D |
| Boston College | M,D |
| Boston University | D |
| Bowling Green State University | M |
| Brandeis University | M,D |
| Brigham Young University | M,D |
| Brock University | M |
| Brooklyn College of the City University of New York | M |
| Brown University | M,D |
| Bryn Mawr College | M,D |
| California Institute of Technology | D |
| California State University, Fresno | M |
| California State University, Fullerton | M |
| California State University, Long Beach | M |
| California State University, Los Angeles | M |
| California State University, Northridge | M |
| Carleton University | M,D |
| Carnegie Mellon University | M,D |
| Case Western Reserve University | M,D |
| The Catholic University of America | M,D |
| Central Michigan University | M,D |
| Christopher Newport University | M |
| City College of the City University of New York | M,D |
| Clark Atlanta University | M |
| Clark University | D |
| Clemson University | M,D |
| Cleveland State University | M |
| Colorado School of Mines | M,D |
| Colorado State University | M,D |
| Columbia University | M,D |
| Concordia University (Canada) | M,D |
| Cornell University | M,D |
| Creighton University | M |
| Dalhousie University | M,D |
| Dartmouth College | D |
| Delaware State University | M,D |
| DePaul University | M,D |
| Drexel University | M,D |
| Duke University | D |
| East Carolina University | M,D |
| Eastern Michigan University | M |
| Emory University | D |
| Fisk University | M |
| Florida Agricultural and Mechanical University | M,D |
| Florida Atlantic University | M,D |
| Florida Institute of Technology | M,D |
| Florida International University | M,D |
| Florida State University | M,D |
| George Mason University | M,D |
| The George Washington University | M,D |
| Georgia Institute of Technology | M,D |
| Georgia State University | M,D |
| The Graduate Center, City University of New York | D |
| Hampton University | M,D |
| Harvard University | D* |
| Howard University | M,D |
| Hunter College of the City University of New York | M,D |
| Idaho State University | M,D |
| Illinois Institute of Technology | M,D |
| Indiana University Bloomington | M,D |
| Indiana University of Pennsylvania | M |
| Indiana University-Purdue University Indianapolis | M,D |
| Iowa State University of Science and Technology | M,D |
| Jackson State University | M,D |
| Johns Hopkins University | D |
| Kansas State University | M,D |
| Kent State University | M,D |
| Lakehead University | M |
| Lehigh University | M,D |
| Louisiana State University and Agricultural & Mechanical College | M,D |
| Manhattanville College | M,O |
| Marshall University | M |
| Massachusetts Institute of Technology | M,D |
| McGill University | M,D |
| McMaster University | D |
| Memorial University of Newfoundland | M,D |
| Miami University | M |
| Michigan State University | M,D |
| Michigan Technological University | M,D |
| Minnesota State University Mankato | M |
| Mississippi State University | M,D |
| Missouri State University | M |
| Missouri University of Science and Technology | M,D |
| Montana State University | M,D |
| Morgan State University | M |
| Naval Postgraduate School | M,D |
| New Mexico Institute of Mining and Technology | M,D |
| New York University | M,D |
| North Carolina Agricultural and Technical State University | M |
| North Carolina Central University | M |
| North Carolina State University | M,D |
| North Dakota State University | M,D |
| Northeastern University | M,D |
| Northern Arizona University | M,D |
| Northern Illinois University | M,D |
| Northwestern University | D |
| Oakland University | M,D |
| The Ohio State University | M,D |
| Ohio University | M,D |
| Oklahoma State University | M,D |
| Old Dominion University | M,D |
| Oregon State University | M,D |
| Pace University | M,O |
| Penn State University Park | M,D* |
| Pittsburg State University | M |
| Portland State University | M,D |
| Princeton University | D |
| Purdue University | M,D |
| Queens College of the City University of New York | M |
| Queen's University at Kingston | M,D |
| Rensselaer Polytechnic Institute | M,D |
| Rice University | M,D |
| Royal Military College of Canada | M |
| Rutgers University - New Brunswick | M,D |
| St. John Fisher College | M |
| San Diego State University | M |
| San Francisco State University | M |
| San Jose State University | M |
| Simon Fraser University | M,D |
| South Dakota School of Mines and Technology | M,D |
| South Dakota State University | M |
| Southern Illinois University Carbondale | M,D |
| Southern Methodist University | M,D |
| Southern University and Agricultural and Mechanical College | M |
| Stanford University | D |
| State University of New York College at Cortland | M |
| Stephen F. Austin State University | M,D |
| Stony Brook University, State University of New York | M,D |
| Syracuse University | M,D |
| Teachers College, Columbia University | M,D |
| Temple University | M,D* |
| Texas A&M University | M,D |
| Texas A&M University–Commerce | M,O |
| Texas Christian University | M,D |
| Texas State University | M |
| Texas Tech University | M,D |
| Trent University | M |
| Tufts University | M,D |
| Tulane University | M,D |
| UNB Fredericton | M,D |
| Université de Moncton | M |
| Université de Montréal | M,D |
| Université de Sherbrooke | M,D |
| Université du Québec à Trois-Rivières | M,D |
| University at Albany, State University of New York | M,D |
| University at Buffalo, the State University of New York | M,D |
| The University of Alabama | M,D |
| The University of Alabama at Birmingham | M,D |
| The University of Alabama in Huntsville | M,D |
| University of Alaska Fairbanks | M,D |
| University of Alberta | M,D |
| The University of Arizona | M,D |
| University of Arkansas | M,D |
| The University of British Columbia | M,D |
| University of Calgary | M,D |
| University of California, Berkeley | D |
| University of California, Davis | M,D |
| University of California, Irvine | M,D |
| University of California, Los Angeles | M,D |
| University of California, Merced | M,D |
| University of California, Riverside | M,D |
| University of California, San Diego | M,D |
| University of California, Santa Barbara | D |
| University of California, Santa Cruz | M,D |
| University of Central Florida | M,D |
| University of Central Oklahoma | M |
| University of Chicago | M,D |
| University of Cincinnati | M,D |
| University of Colorado Boulder | M,D |
| University of Connecticut | M,D |
| University of Delaware | M,D |
| University of Denver | M,D |
| University of Florida | M,D |
| University of Georgia | M,D |
| University of Guelph | M,D |
| University of Hawaii at Manoa | M,D |
| University of Houston | M,D |
| University of Houston–Clear Lake | M |
| University of Idaho | M,D |
| University of Illinois at Chicago | M,D |
| University of Illinois at Urbana-Champaign | M,D |
| The University of Iowa | M,D |
| The University of Kansas | M,D |
| University of Kentucky | M,D |
| University of Lethbridge | M,D |
| University of Louisiana at Lafayette | M |
| University of Louisville | M,D |
| University of Maine | M,D |
| The University of Manchester | M,D |
| University of Manitoba | M,D |
| University of Maryland, Baltimore County | M,D |
| University of Maryland, College Park | M,D |
| University of Massachusetts Amherst | M,D |
| University of Massachusetts Dartmouth | M |
| University of Massachusetts Lowell | M,D |
| University of Memphis | M |
| University of Miami | M,D |
| University of Michigan | D |
| University of Minnesota, Duluth | M |
| University of Minnesota, Twin Cities Campus | M,D |
| University of Mississippi | M,D |
| University of Missouri | M,D |
| University of Missouri–Kansas City | M,D |
| University of Missouri–St. Louis | M,D |
| University of Nebraska–Lincoln | M,D |
| University of Nevada, Las Vegas | M,D |
| University of Nevada, Reno | M,D |
| University of New Hampshire | M,D |
| University of New Mexico | M,D |
| University of New Orleans | M,D |
| The University of North Carolina at Chapel Hill | M,D |
| University of North Dakota | M,D |
| University of Northern Iowa | M |
| University of Notre Dame | M,D |
| University of Oklahoma | M,D |
| University of Oregon | M,D |
| University of Ottawa | M,D |
| University of Pennsylvania | M,D |
| University of Pittsburgh | M,D* |
| University of Puerto Rico at Mayagüez | M |
| University of Puerto Rico at Rio Piedras | M,D |
| University of Regina | M,D |
| University of Rhode Island | M,D |
| University of Rochester | D |
| University of Saskatchewan | M,D |
| University of South Carolina | M,D |
| University of South Dakota | M,D |
| University of Southern California | M,D |
| University of South Florida | M,D |
| The University of Tennessee | M,D |
| The University of Texas at Arlington | M,D |
| The University of Texas at Austin | M,D |
| The University of Texas at Dallas | M,D |
| The University of Texas at El Paso | M |
| The University of Texas at San Antonio | M,D |
| The University of Texas Rio Grande Valley | M |
| The University of Toledo | M,D |
| University of Toronto | M,D |
| University of Utah | M,D |
| University of Vermont | M |
| University of Victoria | M,D |
| University of Virginia | M,D |
| University of Washington | M,D |
| University of Waterloo | M,D |
| The University of Western Ontario | M,D |
| University of Windsor | M,D |
| University of Wisconsin–Madison | M,D |
| University of Wisconsin–Milwaukee | M,D* |
| Université Laval | M,D |
| Utah State University | M,D |
| Vanderbilt University | M,D* |
| Virginia Commonwealth University | M |
| Virginia Polytechnic Institute and State University | M,D |
| Wake Forest University | M,D |
| Washington State University | M,D |
| Washington University in St. Louis | D |
| Wayne State University | M,D |
| Wesleyan University | D |
| Western Illinois University | M |
| Western Kentucky University | M |
| Western Michigan University | M,D,O |
| West Virginia University | M,D |
| Wichita State University | M,D |
| Worcester Polytechnic Institute | M,D |
| Wright State University | M |
| Yale University | D |
| York University | M,D |

## PHYSIOLOGY

| | |
|---|---|
| Albert Einstein College of Medicine | D |
| American College of Healthcare Sciences | M,O |
| Augusta University | D |
| Ball State University | M |
| Baylor University | M,D |
| Boston University | M,D |
| Brigham Young University | M,D |
| Brown University | M,D |
| Case Western Reserve University | M,D |
| Central Washington University | M |
| Columbia University | M,D |
| Cornell University | M,D |
| Dalhousie University | M,D |
| East Carolina University | M,D |
| Eastern Michigan University | M |
| East Tennessee State University | D |
| Georgetown University | M,D |
| Georgia Institute of Technology | M,D |
| Georgia State University | M,D |
| Gonzaga University | M,D |
| Howard University | D |
| Illinois State University | M,D |
| Indiana State University | M,D |
| James Madison University | M |
| Johns Hopkins University | D |
| Kansas State University | M,D |
| Kent State University | M,D |
| Loma Linda University | D |
| Louisiana State University Health Sciences Center | D |
| Louisiana State University Health Sciences Center at Shreveport | M,D |
| Loyola University Chicago | M,D |
| Maharishi International University | D |
| Marquette University | M,D |
| Mayo Clinic Graduate School of Biomedical Sciences | M,D |
| McGill University | M,D |
| McMaster University | M,D |
| Medical College of Wisconsin | D |
| Michigan State University | M,D |
| Montclair State University | M |
| New York Medical College | M,D |
| Northwestern University | M |
| Ohio University | M,D |
| Oregon Health & Science University | D |
| Oregon State University | M,D |
| Penn State University Park | M,D* |
| Purdue University | M,D |
| Rocky Mountain University of Health Professions | D |
| Rosalind Franklin University of Medicine and Science | M,D |
| Rush University | D |
| Rutgers University - Newark | D |
| Rutgers University - New Brunswick | M,D |
| Saint Louis University | D |
| Salisbury University | M |
| San Francisco State University | M |
| San Jose State University | M |
| Southern Illinois University Carbondale | M,D |
| Southern Methodist University | M,D |
| Stanford University | D |
| State University of New York Upstate Medical University | M,D |
| Stony Brook University, State University of New York | D |
| Teachers College, Columbia University | M,D |
| Tulane University | M |
| Universidad Central del Caribe | M,D |
| Université de Montréal | M,D |
| Université de Sherbrooke | M,D |
| University at Buffalo, the State University of New York | M,D |
| University of Alberta | M,D |
| The University of Arizona | M,D |
| University of Arkansas for Medical Sciences | M,D,O |
| University of Calgary | M,D |
| University of California, Berkeley | M,D |
| University of California, Davis | M,D |
| University of California, Irvine | D |
| University of California, Los Angeles | M,D |
| University of Central Florida | M,O |
| University of Colorado Boulder | M,D |
| University of Connecticut | M,D |
| University of Delaware | M,D |
| University of Florida | M,D |
| University of Georgia | M,D |
| University of Guelph | M,D |
| University of Hawaii at Manoa | M,D |
| University of Illinois at Chicago | M,D |
| University of Illinois at Urbana-Champaign | M,D |
| The University of Iowa | M,D |
| The University of Kansas | D |
| University of Kentucky | D |
| University of Louisville | M,D |
| The University of Manchester | M,D |
| University of Manitoba | M,D |
| University of Massachusetts Amherst | M,D |
| University of Miami | D |
| University of Michigan | M,D |

*M—masters degree; D—doctorate; O—other advanced degree; *—Close-Up and/or Display*

| | |
|---|---|
| University of Minnesota, Duluth | M,D |
| University of Minnesota, Twin Cities Campus | D |
| University of Mississippi Medical Center | D |
| University of Missouri | M,D |
| University of Nebraska Medical Center | D |
| University of Nevada, Reno | D |
| University of New Mexico | M,D |
| University of North Texas Health Science Center at Fort Worth | M,D |
| University of Notre Dame | M,D |
| University of Oklahoma Health Sciences Center | M,D |
| University of Oregon | M,D |
| University of Pennsylvania | D |
| University of Prince Edward Island | M,D |
| University of Puerto Rico - Medical Sciences Campus | M,D |
| University of Rochester | M,D |
| University of Saskatchewan | M,D |
| University of South Dakota | M,D |
| University of Southern California | M |
| University of South Florida | M,D |
| The University of Tennessee | M,D |
| The University of Texas Medical Branch | M,D |
| University of Toronto | M,D |
| University of Utah | M,D |
| University of Virginia | D |
| University of Washington | D |
| The University of Western Ontario | M,D |
| University of Wisconsin–La Crosse | M |
| University of Wisconsin–Madison | M,D |
| University of Wyoming | M,D |
| Université Laval | M,D |
| Virginia Commonwealth University | M,D |
| Wake Forest University | D |
| Weill Cornell Medicine | M,D |
| Western Michigan University | M |
| Wright State University | M |
| Yale University | D |
| Youngstown State University | M |

## PLANETARY AND SPACE SCIENCES

| | |
|---|---|
| Air Force Institute of Technology | M,D |
| Alabama Agricultural and Mechanical University | M,D |
| Arizona State University at Tempe | M,D |
| California Institute of Technology | M,D |
| Cornell University | D |
| Florida Institute of Technology | M,D |
| Hampton University | M,D |
| Harvard University | M,D* |
| Johns Hopkins University | M,D |
| Massachusetts Institute of Technology | M,D |
| McGill University | M,D |
| St. Thomas University - Florida | M,D,O |
| The University of Arizona | M,D |
| University of Arkansas | M,D |
| University of California, Los Angeles | M,D |
| University of California, Santa Cruz | M,D |
| University of Chicago | D |
| University of Hawaii at Manoa | M,D |
| University of Houston | M,D |
| University of Michigan | M,D |
| University of New Mexico | M,D |
| University of North Dakota | M |
| Washington University in St. Louis | D |
| Western Connecticut State University | M |
| Yale University | M,D |
| York University | M,D |

## PLANT BIOLOGY

| | |
|---|---|
| Arizona State University at Tempe | M,D |
| Clemson University | M,D |
| Cornell University | M,D |
| Illinois State University | M,D |
| Indiana University Bloomington | M,D |
| Iowa State University of Science and Technology | M,D |
| Michigan State University | M,D |
| New York University | M,D |
| North Carolina State University | M,D |
| Northwestern University | M,D |
| Ohio University | M,D |
| Oklahoma State University | M,D |
| Penn State University Park | M,D* |
| Rutgers University - New Brunswick | M,D |
| Southern Illinois University Carbondale | M,D |
| University of Alberta | M,D |
| University of California, Berkeley | D |
| University of California, Davis | M,D |
| University of California, Riverside | M,D |
| University of Florida | M,D |
| University of Georgia | M,D |
| University of Illinois at Urbana-Champaign | M,D |
| University of Maryland, College Park | M,D |
| University of Massachusetts Amherst | M,D |
| University of Minnesota, Twin Cities Campus | M,D |
| University of Missouri | M,D |
| University of Oklahoma | M,D |
| The University of Texas at Austin | M,D |
| University of Vermont | M,D |
| Université Laval | M,D |
| Washington University in St. Louis | D |
| Yale University | D |

## PLANT MOLECULAR BIOLOGY

| | |
|---|---|
| Cornell University | M,D |
| Illinois State University | M,D |
| Oregon State University | D |
| Rutgers University - New Brunswick | M,D |
| University of California, Riverside | M,D |
| University of Florida | M,D |
| University of Massachusetts Amherst | M,D |

## PLANT PATHOLOGY

| | |
|---|---|
| Auburn University | M,D |
| Colorado State University | M,D |
| Cornell University | M,D |
| Dalhousie University | M |
| Iowa State University of Science and Technology | M,D |
| Kansas State University | M,D |
| Louisiana State University and Agricultural & Mechanical College | M,D |
| Michigan State University | M,D |
| Montana State University | M,D |
| New Mexico State University | M |
| North Dakota State University | M,D |
| The Ohio State University | M,D |
| Oklahoma State University | M,D |
| Oregon State University | M,D |
| Penn State University Park | M,D* |
| Purdue University | M,D |
| Rutgers University - New Brunswick | M,D |
| State University of New York College of Environmental Science and Forestry | M,D |
| Texas A&M University | M,D |
| The University of Arizona | M,D |
| University of Arkansas | M |
| University of California, Davis | M,D |
| University of California, Riverside | M,D |
| University of Florida | M,D |
| University of Georgia | M,D |
| University of Guelph | M,D |
| University of Hawaii at Manoa | M,D |
| University of Idaho | M,D |
| University of Kentucky | M,D |
| University of Maine | M,D |
| University of Minnesota, Twin Cities Campus | M,D |
| The University of Tennessee | M,D |
| University of Vermont | M,D,O |
| University of Wisconsin–Madison | M,D |
| Virginia Polytechnic Institute and State University | M,D |
| Washington State University | M,D |
| West Virginia University | M,D |

## PLANT PHYSIOLOGY

| | |
|---|---|
| Cornell University | M,D |
| Dalhousie University | M |
| Oregon State University | M,D |
| University of Manitoba | M,D |
| University of Massachusetts Amherst | M,D |
| The University of Tennessee | M,D |
| Virginia Polytechnic Institute and State University | M,D |

## PLANT SCIENCES

| | |
|---|---|
| Alabama Agricultural and Mechanical University | M,D |
| Brigham Young University | M,D |
| California State University, Fresno | M |
| Colorado State University | M,D |
| Cornell University | M,D |
| Delaware State University | M |
| Illinois State University | M,D |
| Iowa State University of Science and Technology | M,D |
| Kansas State University | M,D,O |
| McGill University | M,D,O |
| Michigan State University | M,D |
| Mississippi State University | M,D |
| Missouri State University | M |
| Montana State University | M,D |
| North Carolina Agricultural and Technical State University | M |
| North Dakota State University | M,D |
| The Ohio State University | D |
| Oklahoma State University | M,D |
| Penn State University Park | M,D* |
| Purdue University | D |
| South Dakota State University | M,D |
| Southern Illinois University Carbondale | M |
| State University of New York College of Environmental Science and Forestry | M,D |
| Tennessee State University | M,D |
| Texas A&M University–Kingsville | M |
| Texas Tech University | M,D |
| Tuskegee University | M |
| The University of Arizona | M,D |
| University of Arkansas | D |
| The University of British Columbia | M,D |
| University of California, Riverside | M,D |
| University of Connecticut | M,D |
| University of Delaware | M,D |
| University of Florida | D |
| University of Georgia | M,D |
| University of Hawaii at Manoa | M,D |
| University of Idaho | M,D |
| University of Kentucky | M,D |
| The University of Manchester | M,D |
| University of Manitoba | M,D |
| University of Massachusetts Amherst | M,D |
| University of Minnesota, Twin Cities Campus | M,D |
| University of Missouri | M,D |
| University of Saskatchewan | M,D |
| The University of Tennessee | M |
| University of Vermont | M,D,O |
| University of Wisconsin–Madison | M,D |
| Utah State University | M,D |
| West Texas A&M University | M |
| West Virginia University | M,D |

## PLASMA PHYSICS

| | |
|---|---|
| Princeton University | D |
| University of Colorado Boulder | M,D |

## PODIATRIC MEDICINE

| | |
|---|---|
| Barry University | D |
| Des Moines University | D |
| Kent State University | D |
| Midwestern University, Glendale Campus | D |
| New York College of Podiatric Medicine | D |
| Rosalind Franklin University of Medicine and Science | D |
| Samuel Merritt University | D |
| Temple University | D* |
| Western University of Health Sciences | D |

## POLITICAL SCIENCE

| | |
|---|---|
| Acadia University | M |
| American Public University System | M,D |
| American University | M,D,O |
| American University of Armenia | M |
| Appalachian State University | M |
| Arizona State University at Tempe | M,D |
| Arkansas State University | M,O |
| Ashland University | M |
| Auburn University | M,D,O |
| Auburn University at Montgomery | M,D |
| Ball State University | M |
| Baylor University | M,D |
| Binghamton University, State University of New York | M,D |
| Boise State University | M |
| Boston College | M,D |
| Boston University | D |
| Brandeis University | M,D |
| Brigham Young University | M |
| Brock University | M |
| Brooklyn College of the City University of New York | M |
| Brown University | D |
| California Polytechnic State University, San Luis Obispo | M |
| California State University, Chico | M |
| California State University, Fullerton | M |
| California State University, Long Beach | M |
| California State University, Los Angeles | M |
| California State University, Northridge | M |
| California State University, Sacramento | M |
| Carleton University | M,D |
| Case Western Reserve University | M,D |
| The Catholic University of America | M,D |
| Central European University | M,D |
| Central Michigan University | M,O |
| The Citadel, The Military College of South Carolina | M |
| Claremont Graduate University | M,D |
| Clark Atlanta University | M,D |
| Colorado State University | M,D |
| Columbia University | M,D |
| Columbus State University | M |
| Concordia University (Canada) | M,D |
| Converse College | M |
| Cornell University | D |
| Dalhousie University | M,D |
| Duke University | M,D |
| East Carolina University | M,O |
| Eastern Illinois University | M |
| Eastern Kentucky University | M |
| East Stroudsburg University of Pennsylvania | M |
| Emory University | D |
| Fairleigh Dickinson University, Metropolitan Campus | M |
| Florida Agricultural and Mechanical University | M |
| Florida Atlantic University | M |
| Florida International University | M,D |
| Florida State University | M,D |
| Fordham University | M |
| George Mason University | M,D |
| Georgetown University | M,D |
| The George Washington University | M,D |
| Georgia State University | M,D |
| Governors State University | M |
| The Graduate Center, City University of New York | M,D |
| Grambling State University | M |
| Harvard University | M,D* |
| Hillsdale College | M,D |
| Howard University | M,D |
| Idaho State University | M,D |
| Illinois State University | M |
| Indiana University Bloomington | M,D |
| Indiana University-Purdue University Indianapolis | M |
| Institute for Christian Studies | M,D |
| The Institute of World Politics | M,D,O |
| Iowa State University of Science and Technology | M |
| Jackson State University | M |
| James Madison University | M |
| Johns Hopkins University | M,D,O |
| Kansas State University | M,D |
| Kent State University | M,D |
| Lamar University | M |
| Lehigh University | M |
| Liberty University | M |
| Long Island University - Brooklyn | M,D,O |
| Long Island University - Post | M,O |
| Louisiana State University and Agricultural & Mechanical College | M,D |
| Loyola University Chicago | M,D |
| Marquette University | M |
| Marshall University | M |
| Massachusetts Institute of Technology | M,D |
| McGill University | M,D |
| McMaster University | M,D |
| Memorial University of Newfoundland | M |
| Miami University | M |
| Michigan State University | M,D |
| Middle Tennessee State University | M |
| Midwestern State University | M |
| Mississippi College | M,O |
| Mississippi State University | M,D |
| Missouri State University | M,O |
| Montclair State University | M,O |
| Murray State University | M |
| New Mexico Highlands University | M |
| New Mexico State University | M |
| The New School | M,D |
| New York University | M,D |
| Northeastern Illinois University | M |
| Northeastern University | M,D |
| Northern Arizona University | M,D,O |
| Northern Illinois University | M,D |
| Northwestern University | D |
| The Ohio State University | D |
| Ohio University | M |
| Oklahoma State University | M,D |
| Penn State University Park | M,D* |
| Pepperdine University | M |
| Portland State University | M |
| Princeton University | D |
| Purdue University | M,D |
| Purdue University Global | M,O |
| Queen's University at Kingston | M,D |
| Regent University | M |
| Rice University | D |
| Rutgers University - Newark | M |
| Rutgers University - New Brunswick | M,D |
| St. John's University (NY) | M,O |
| Saint Louis University | M |
| Sam Houston State University | M |
| San Diego State University | M |
| San Francisco State University | M |
| Simon Fraser University | M,D |
| Sonoma State University | M |
| Southern Connecticut State University | M |
| Southern Illinois University Carbondale | M,D |
| Southern New Hampshire University | M |
| Southern University and Agricultural and Mechanical College | M |
| Stanford University | M,D |
| Stony Brook University, State University of New York | M,D |
| Suffolk University | M,O |
| Sul Ross State University | M |
| Syracuse University | M,D,O |
| Tarleton State University | M |
| Teachers College, Columbia University | M,D |
| Temple University | M,D* |
| Texas A&M International University | M |
| Texas A&M University | M,D |
| Texas A&M University–Central Texas | M,O |
| Texas A&M University–Commerce | M,D,O |
| Texas State University | M |
| Texas Tech University | M,D |
| Texas Woman's University | M |
| Tulane University | D |
| UNB Fredericton | M,D |
| Universidad Nacional Pedro Henriquez Urena | M |
| Université de Montréal | M,D |
| Université du Québec à Montréal | M,D |
| University at Albany, State University of New York | M,D |
| University at Buffalo, the State University of New York | M,D |
| The University of Akron | M |
| The University of Alabama | M,D |
| University of Alberta | M,D |
| The University of Arizona | M,D |
| University of Arkansas | M |
| The University of British Columbia | M,D |
| University of Calgary | M,D |
| University of California, Berkeley | D |
| University of California, Davis | M,D |
| University of California, Irvine | D |
| University of California, Los Angeles | M,D |
| University of California, Riverside | M,D |
| University of California, San Diego | M,D |
| University of California, Santa Barbara | M,D |
| University of California, Santa Cruz | D |
| University of Central Oklahoma | M |
| University of Chicago | D |
| University of Cincinnati | M,D |
| University of Colorado Boulder | M,D |
| University of Colorado Denver | M,D |
| University of Connecticut | M,D |
| University of Delaware | M,D |
| University of Florida | M,D,O |
| University of Georgia | M,D |
| University of Guelph | M |
| University of Hawaii at Manoa | M,D |
| University of Houston | M,D |
| University of Idaho | M,D |
| University of Illinois at Chicago | M,D |
| University of Illinois at Springfield | M |
| University of Illinois at Urbana-Champaign | M,D |
| The University of Iowa | D |
| The University of Kansas | M,D |

| | |
|---|---|
| University of Kentucky | M,D |
| University of Lethbridge | M,D |
| University of Louisville | M |
| The University of Manchester | M,D |
| University of Manitoba | M |
| University of Maryland, College Park | D |
| University of Massachusetts Amherst | M,D |
| University of Memphis | M |
| University of Miami | M |
| University of Michigan | D |
| University of Michigan–Flint | M |
| University of Minnesota, Twin Cities Campus | D |
| University of Mississippi | M,D |
| University of Missouri | M,D,O |
| University of Missouri–Kansas City | M |
| University of Missouri–St. Louis | M,D |
| University of Montana | M |
| University of Nebraska at Omaha | M,O |
| University of Nebraska–Lincoln | M,D,O |
| University of Nevada, Las Vegas | M,D |
| University of Nevada, Reno | M,D |
| University of New Hampshire | M,O |
| University of New Mexico | M,D |
| University of New Orleans | M,D |
| University of North Alabama | M |
| The University of North Carolina at Chapel Hill | M,D,O |
| The University of North Carolina at Greensboro | M,O |
| University of Northern British Columbia | M,D,O |
| University of North Texas | M,D,O |
| University of Notre Dame | D |
| University of Oklahoma | M,D |
| University of Oregon | M,D |
| University of Ottawa | M,D |
| University of Pennsylvania | M,D,O |
| University of Pittsburgh | M,D* |
| University of Rhode Island | M |
| University of Rochester | D |
| University of Saskatchewan | M |
| University of South Africa | M,D |
| University of South Carolina | M,D |
| University of Southern California | M,D |
| University of South Florida | O |
| The University of Tennessee | M,D |
| The University of Texas at Arlington | M |
| The University of Texas at Austin | M,D |
| The University of Texas at Dallas | M,D |
| The University of Texas at El Paso | M |
| The University of Texas at San Antonio | M |
| The University of Texas of the Permian Basin | M |
| The University of Toledo | M,O |
| University of Toronto | M,D |
| University of Utah | M,D |
| University of Victoria | M,D |
| University of Virginia | M,D |
| University of Washington | M,D |
| University of Waterloo | M,D |
| The University of Western Ontario | M,D |
| University of West Florida | M |
| University of Windsor | M |
| University of Wisconsin–Madison | D |
| University of Wisconsin–Milwaukee | M,D* |
| University of Wyoming | M |
| Université Laval | M,D |
| Utah State University | M |
| Vanderbilt University | M,D* |
| Villanova University | M |
| Virginia Commonwealth University | M,D,O |
| Virginia Polytechnic Institute and State University | M,O |
| Walden University | M,D,O |
| Washington State University | M,D,O |
| Washington University in St. Louis | D |
| Wayne State University | M,D |
| Western Illinois University | M |
| Western Kentucky University | M |
| Western Michigan University | M,D |
| Western Washington University | M |
| West Virginia University | M,D |
| Wilfrid Laurier University | M,D |
| Yale University | D |
| York University | M,D |

## POLYMER SCIENCE AND ENGINEERING

| | |
|---|---|
| California Polytechnic State University, San Luis Obispo | M |
| Carnegie Mellon University | M |
| Case Western Reserve University | M,D |
| Cornell University | M,D |
| DePaul University | M,D |
| Eastern Michigan University | M,O |
| Lehigh University | M,D |
| North Carolina State University | M,D |
| North Dakota State University | M,D |
| Pittsburg State University | M |
| The University of Akron | M,D |
| University of Connecticut | M,D |
| The University of Manchester | M,D |
| University of Massachusetts Amherst | M,D |
| University of Massachusetts Lowell | M,D |
| University of Missouri–Kansas City | M,D |
| University of Southern Mississippi | M,D |
| Wayne State University | M,D,O |

## PORTUGUESE

| | |
|---|---|
| Brigham Young University | M |
| Emory University | D,O |
| Harvard University | M,D* |
| Indiana University Bloomington | M,D |
| New York University | M,D |
| Northwestern University | D |
| The Ohio State University | M,D |
| Princeton University | D |
| Tulane University | M,D |
| University of California, Los Angeles | M |
| University of California, Santa Barbara | M,D |
| University of Georgia | M,D |
| University of Illinois at Urbana-Champaign | M,D |
| The University of Manchester | D |
| University of Maryland, College Park | M,D |
| University of Massachusetts Amherst | M,D |
| University of Massachusetts Dartmouth | M,D |
| University of Minnesota, Twin Cities Campus | M,D |
| University of New Mexico | M,D |
| The University of North Carolina at Chapel Hill | M,D |
| University of South Africa | M,D |
| The University of Tennessee | D |
| The University of Texas at Austin | M,D |
| University of Toronto | M,D |
| University of Washington | M |
| University of Wisconsin–Madison | M,D |
| University of Wisconsin–Milwaukee | M* |
| Vanderbilt University | M,D* |
| Yale University | D |

## PROJECT MANAGEMENT

| | |
|---|---|
| Albertus Magnus College | M |
| Amberton University | M |
| American Business & Technology University | M |
| American InterContinental University Online | M |
| American University | M,O |
| Ashland University | M |
| Aspen University | M,O |
| Athabasca University | M,D,O |
| Avila University | M |
| Bellevue University | M |
| Boston University | M,O |
| Brandeis University | M |
| Brenau University | M |
| California Intercontinental University | M,D |
| Capella University | M,D |
| Carlow University | M |
| The Catholic University of America | M,O |
| Christian Brothers University | M,O |
| The Citadel, The Military College of South Carolina | M,O |
| City University of Seattle | M,O |
| Colorado Christian University | M |
| Colorado State University–Global Campus | M |
| Colorado Technical University Aurora | M |
| Colorado Technical University Colorado Springs | M,D |
| DeSales University | M,O |
| DeVry University–Folsom Campus | M |
| Drexel University | M |
| Elmhurst University | M |
| Embry-Riddle Aeronautical University–Worldwide | M |
| Everglades University | M |
| Ferris State University | M |
| Geneva College | M |
| George Mason University | M,D |
| The George Washington University | M,D,O |
| Golden Gate University | M,D,O |
| Grand Canyon University | M |
| Granite State College | M |
| Grantham University | M,O |
| Harrisburg University of Science and Technology | M |
| Herzing University Online | M |
| Hult International Business School (United States) | M |
| IGlobal University | M |
| Iona College | M,O |
| King University | M |
| Lasell College | M,O |
| Lawrence Technological University | M,D,O |
| Lebanon Valley College | M |
| Lehigh University | M |
| Lewis University | M |
| Liberty University | M,D |
| Lindenwood University | M,O |
| Marlboro College | M |
| Marymount University | M,O |
| Maryville University of Saint Louis | M,O |
| Metropolitan State University | M,D,O |
| Mississippi State University | M,D |
| Missouri State University | M |
| Montana Technological University | M |
| Montclair State University | M |
| Morgan State University | M |
| Mount Aloysius College | M |
| National American University (TX) | M,D |
| New England College | M |
| New York University | M |
| Northeastern University | M |
| Northwestern University | M |
| Northwest University | M |
| Norwich University | M |
| Oklahoma Christian University | M |
| Pacific States University | M,O |
| Point Loma Nazarene University | M |
| Polytechnic University of Puerto Rico, Miami Campus | M |
| Post University | M |
| Purdue University Global | M |
| Queen's University at Kingston | M |
| Regis University | M,O |
| Robert Morris University | M,D |
| Rochester Institute of Technology | O |
| Saint Mary's University of Minnesota | M,O |
| Saint Xavier University | M,O |
| Sam Houston State University | M |
| Southern Illinois University Edwardsville | M |
| Southern New Hampshire University | M,D,O |
| Stevens Institute of Technology | M,O |
| Stevenson University | M |
| Thomas Edison State University | M |
| Trident University International | M,D |
| Universidad del Turabo | M |
| Universidad Nacional Pedro Henriquez Urena | M |
| Université du Québec à Chicoutimi | M |
| Université du Québec à Montréal | M,O |
| Université du Québec à Rimouski | M,O |
| Université du Québec en Abitibi-Témiscamingue | M,O |
| Université du Québec en Outaouais | M,O |
| The University of Alabama in Huntsville | M,O |
| University of Calgary | M,D |
| University of California, Berkeley | O |
| University of Connecticut | M,D |
| University of Dallas | M,D |
| University of Denver | M,O |
| University of Fairfax | M,D |
| University of Houston | M |
| University of Houston - Downtown | M |
| The University of Kansas | M |
| University of Louisiana at Lafayette | M |
| University of Management and Technology | M,D,O |
| The University of Manchester | M |
| University of Mary | M |
| University of Michigan–Dearborn | M |
| University of Nebraska at Omaha | M,D,O |
| University of North Alabama | M |
| University of Oklahoma | M,D,O |
| University of Ottawa | M,O |
| University of Phoenix - Bay Area Campus | M,D |
| University of Phoenix–Online Campus | M,O |
| University of Phoenix - Phoenix Campus | M,O |
| University of Regina | M,O |
| The University of Tennessee at Chattanooga | M,O |
| The University of Texas at Dallas | M,D |
| University of Wisconsin–Platteville | M |
| University of Wisconsin–Stout | M |
| Virginia International University | M,O |
| Viterbo University | M |
| Walden University | M,D,O |
| Walsh College of Accountancy and Business Administration | M |
| Wayland Baptist University | M,D |
| Western Carolina University | M,O |
| Wilmington University | M |
| Wingate University | M |

## PSYCHIATRIC NURSING

| | |
|---|---|
| Allen College | M,D |
| Alverno College | M,D |
| Anderson University (SC) | M,D |
| Arizona State University at Tempe | M,D,O |
| Augusta University | D |
| Azusa Pacific University | M,D |
| Binghamton University, State University of New York | M,D,O |
| Boston College | M,D |
| California State University, San Marcos | M |
| Case Western Reserve University | M |
| Clarke University | D |
| Columbia University | M,O |
| Creighton University | M,D,O |
| Drexel University | M |
| East Tennessee State University | M,D,O |
| Fairfield University | M,D |
| Fairleigh Dickinson University, Florham Campus | M |
| Florida International University | M,D |
| Florida State University | D,O |
| George Mason University | M,D,O |
| Georgia Southern University | M |
| Georgia State University | M,D,O |
| Hofstra University | M |
| Hunter College of the City University of New York | M,D,O |
| Husson University | M,O |
| Jacksonville University | M |
| James Madison University | M,D |
| Johns Hopkins University | O |
| Kent State University | M,D |
| Lincoln Memorial University | M |
| McNeese State University | M,O |
| MGH Institute of Health Professions | M,D,O |
| Midwestern State University | M |
| Molloy College | M,D,O |
| Montana State University | M,D,O |
| National University | M,O |
| New Mexico State University | M,D,O |
| New York University | M,D,O |
| Nicholls State University | M |
| Northeastern University | M,D,O |
| Nova Southeastern University | M,D |
| Oregon Health & Science University | M |
| Pontifical Catholic University of Puerto Rico | M |
| Rivier University | M,D |
| Sage Graduate School | M,O |
| Saint Francis Medical Center College of Nursing | M,D,O |
| Shenandoah University | M,D,O |
| Southern Adventist University | M,D |
| Southern Arkansas University–Magnolia | M |
| Stony Brook University, State University of New York | M,D,O |
| Tennessee Technological University | D |
| Uniformed Services University of the Health Sciences | M,D |
| University at Buffalo, the State University of New York | M,D,O |
| The University of Alabama at Birmingham | M,D |
| University of Colorado Denver | M,D |
| University of Delaware | M,O |
| The University of Kansas | M,D,O |
| University of Louisville | M,D |
| University of Maryland, Baltimore | M,D,O |
| University of Michigan–Flint | M,D,O |
| University of Minnesota, Twin Cities Campus | M,D |
| University of Missouri | M,D,O |
| University of Missouri–St. Louis | D,O |
| University of New Hampshire | M,D,O |
| The University of North Carolina at Chapel Hill | M,D,O |
| University of North Dakota | M,D,O |
| University of Pennsylvania | M |
| University of Puerto Rico - Medical Sciences Campus | M |
| University of Rochester | M,D |
| University of St. Francis (IL) | M,D,O |
| University of Saint Joseph | M,D |
| University of San Diego | M,D |
| University of South Carolina | M,O |
| University of Southern Indiana | M,D,O |
| University of Southern Maine | M,D,O |
| The University of Tennessee Health Science Center | D,O |
| The University of Texas at Austin | M,D |
| The University of Texas Health Science Center at San Antonio | M,D,O |
| University of Virginia | M,D |
| University of Wisconsin–Madison | D |
| Valdosta State University | M |
| Virginia Commonwealth University | M,D,O |
| Washington State University | M,D,O |
| Wayne State University | M,D,O |
| West Virginia Wesleyan College | M,D,O |
| Wright State University | M |

## PSYCHOANALYSIS AND PSYCHOTHERAPY

| | |
|---|---|
| Argosy University, Chicago | D |
| Atlantic University | O |
| Boston Graduate School of Psychoanalysis | M,D,O |
| Immaculata University | M,D,O |
| Naropa University | M |
| The New School | M,D |
| New York University | M,D,O |
| Prescott College | M |
| University of Manitoba | M |

## PSYCHOLOGY—GENERAL

| | |
|---|---|
| Abilene Christian University | M,O |
| Acadia University | M |
| Adelphi University | M |
| Alabama Agricultural and Mechanical University | M,O |
| Albizu University - Miami | M,D |
| Albizu University - San Juan | M,D |
| Alliant International University–Fresno | M,D |
| Alliant International University - Los Angeles | M,D |
| Alliant International University–Sacramento | M,D |
| Alliant International University - San Diego | M,D |
| Alliant International University–San Francisco | M,D,O |
| American International College | M,D,O |
| American University | M,D,O |
| The American University in Cairo | M,O |
| Andrews University | M,D,O |
| Angelo State University | M |
| Antioch University Los Angeles | M |
| Appalachian State University | M |
| Arcadia University | M,D,O |
| Argosy University, Atlanta | M,D,O |
| Argosy University, Chicago | M,D |
| Argosy University, Hawaii | M,D,O |
| Argosy University, Los Angeles | M,D |
| Argosy University, Northern Virginia | M,D |
| Argosy University, Orange County | M,D |
| Argosy University, Phoenix | M,D |
| Argosy University, Seattle | M,D,O |
| Argosy University, Tampa | M,D |
| Argosy University, Twin Cities | M,D,O |
| Arizona State University at Tempe | M,D |
| Arkansas Tech University | M |
| Auburn University | M,D |

*M—masters degree; D—doctorate; O—other advanced degree; *—Close-Up and/or Display*

| | |
|---|---|
| Auburn University at Montgomery | M |
| Augusta University | M |
| Austin Peay State University | M |
| Avila University | M |
| Azusa Pacific University | M |
| Ball State University | M |
| Barry University | M,O |
| Baylor University | M,D |
| Binghamton University, State University of New York | D |
| Biola University | D |
| Boston College | D |
| Boston Graduate School of Psychoanalysis | M |
| Boston University | M,D |
| Bowling Green State University | M,D |
| Brandeis University | M,D |
| Brandman University | M |
| Brenau University | M |
| Bridgewater State University | M |
| Brigham Young University | D |
| Brock University | M,D |
| Brooklyn College of the City University of New York | M,D |
| Brown University | M,D |
| Bucknell University | M |
| California Coast University | M |
| California Lutheran University | M,D |
| California Polytechnic State University, San Luis Obispo | M |
| California State Polytechnic University, Pomona | M |
| California State University, Chico | M |
| California State University, Dominguez Hills | M |
| California State University, Fresno | M,O |
| California State University, Fullerton | M |
| California State University, Long Beach | M |
| California State University, Los Angeles | M |
| California State University, Northridge | M |
| California State University, Sacramento | M |
| California State University, San Bernardino | M |
| California State University, San Marcos | M |
| California State University, Stanislaus | M |
| Cambridge College | M,O |
| Cameron University | M |
| Capella University | M,D |
| Cardinal Stritch University | M |
| Carleton University | M,D |
| Carnegie Mellon University | D |
| Case Western Reserve University | M,D |
| Castleton University | M |
| The Catholic University of America | M,D |
| Central Connecticut State University | M |
| Central Michigan University | M,D,O |
| Central Washington University | M,O |
| Chapman University | M,D |
| Chestnut Hill College | M,D,O |
| The Chicago School of Professional Psychology | M,D |
| The Chicago School of Professional Psychology at Irvine | D |
| The Chicago School of Professional Psychology: Online | M,D |
| The Citadel, The Military College of South Carolina | M,O |
| City College of the City University of New York | M,D |
| Claremont Graduate University | M,D,O |
| Clayton State University | M |
| Cleveland State University | M,D,O |
| College of Saint Elizabeth | M,D |
| College of St. Joseph | M |
| Colorado State University | M,D |
| Columbia University | M,D |
| Concordia University (Canada) | M |
| Cornell University | D |
| Dalhousie University | M,D |
| Dartmouth College | D |
| DePaul University | M,D |
| Divine Mercy University | M |
| Drexel University | M,D |
| Duke University | D |
| Duquesne University | D |
| East Central University | M |
| Eastern Illinois University | M,O |
| Eastern Kentucky University | M,O |
| Eastern Michigan University | M,D |
| Eastern Washington University | M,O |
| East Tennessee State University | D |
| Elizabeth City State University | M |
| Emory University | D |
| Emporia State University | M |
| Fairleigh Dickinson University, Florham Campus | M,O |
| Fairleigh Dickinson University, Metropolitan Campus | M,D,O |
| Fayetteville State University | M |
| Fielding Graduate University | M,D,O |
| Fisk University | M |
| Fitchburg State University | O |
| Florida Agricultural and Mechanical University | M |
| Florida Atlantic University | M |
| Florida Institute of Technology | M,D |
| Florida International University | M,D |
| Florida State University | M,D |
| Fordham University | M,D |
| Fort Hays State University | M,O |
| Francis Marion University | M,O |
| Frostburg State University | M |
| Gardner-Webb University | M |
| Geneva College | M |
| George Mason University | M,D,O |
| Georgetown University | D |
| The George Washington University | M,D,O |
| Georgia Institute of Technology | M,D |
| Georgia Southern University | M,D |
| Georgia State University | D |
| Goddard College | M |
| Golden Gate University | M,D,O |
| Governors State University | M |
| The Graduate Center, City University of New York | D |
| Grand Canyon University | D |
| Hampton University | M |
| Hardin-Simmons University | M |
| Harvard University | D* |
| Hofstra University | M,D |
| Howard University | M,D |
| Humboldt State University | M |
| Hunter College of the City University of New York | M,O |
| Idaho State University | D |
| Illinois Institute of Technology | M,D |
| Illinois State University | M,D,O |
| Immaculata University | M,D,O |
| Indiana State University | M,D |
| Indiana Tech | M |
| Indiana University Bloomington | D |
| Indiana University of Pennsylvania | M,D |
| Indiana University-Purdue University Indianapolis | M,D |
| Inter American University of Puerto Rico, Metropolitan Campus | M,D |
| Inter American University of Puerto Rico, San Germán Campus | M,D |
| Iona College | M,O |
| Iowa State University of Science and Technology | M,D |
| Jackson State University | D |
| Jacksonville State University | M |
| James Madison University | M |
| John F. Kennedy University | M,D,O |
| Johns Hopkins University | D |
| Kansas State University | M,D |
| Kean University | M |
| Keiser University | M,D |
| Kent State University | M,D |
| Lakehead University | M,D |
| Lamar University | M |
| La Salle University | M,D |
| Laurentian University | M |
| Lehigh University | M,D |
| Lesley University | M,D,O |
| LeTourneau University | M |
| Liberty University | M,D,O |
| Lipscomb University | M,O |
| Loma Linda University | D |
| Long Island University - Brooklyn | M,D,O |
| Long Island University - Post | M,O |
| Louisiana State University and Agricultural & Mechanical College | M,D |
| Loyola University Maryland | M,D,O |
| Lynn University | M |
| Madonna University | M |
| Mansfield University of Pennsylvania | M |
| Marietta College | M |
| Marist College | M,O |
| Marquette University | D |
| Marshall University | M,D,O |
| Martin University | M |
| Marywood University | M |
| McGill University | M,D |
| McMaster University | M,D |
| McNeese State University | M,O |
| Medaille College | M,D |
| Memorial University of Newfoundland | M,D |
| Mercy College | M |
| Meredith College | M |
| Miami University | M,D |
| Michigan School of Psychology | M,D |
| Michigan State University | M,D |
| Middle Tennessee State University | M,O |
| Millersville University of Pennsylvania | M |
| Minnesota State University Mankato | M,D |
| Mississippi State University | M,D |
| Missouri State University | M,O |
| Monmouth University | M,O |
| Montana State University | M |
| Montana State University Billings | M |
| Montclair State University | M |
| Morehead State University | M |
| Morgan State University | M,D |
| Murray State University | M,O |
| Naropa University | M |
| National Louis University | M,D,O |
| New Mexico Highlands University | M |
| New Mexico State University | M,D |
| The New School | M,D |
| New York Medical College | M,D,O |
| New York University | M,D,O |
| Norfolk State University | M,D |
| North Carolina Central University | M |
| North Carolina State University | D |
| Northcentral University | M,D,O |
| North Dakota State University | M,D |
| Northeastern State University | M |
| Northeastern University | M,D |
| Northern Arizona University | M |
| Northern Illinois University | M,D |
| Northern Michigan University | M |
| Northwestern State University of Louisiana | M |
| Northwestern University | D |
| Northwest University | M,D |
| Nova Southeastern University | M,D,O |
| The Ohio State University | D |
| Ohio University | D |
| Oklahoma State University | M,D |
| Old Dominion University | M,D |
| Oregon State University | M,D |
| Our Lady of the Lake University | M |
| Pace University | M |
| Pacifica Graduate Institute | M,D |
| Pacific University | M,D |
| Palo Alto University | M,D |
| Penn State Harrisburg | M,D,O |
| Penn State University Park | M,D* |
| Philadelphia College of Osteopathic Medicine | M,D,O |
| Phillips Graduate University | M |
| Pittsburg State University | M |
| Pontifical Catholic University of Puerto Rico | M,D |
| Pontificia Universidad Catolica Madre y Maestra | M |
| Portland State University | M,D,O |
| Princeton University | D |
| Purdue University | D |
| Queens College of the City University of New York | M |
| Queen's University at Kingston | M,D |
| Radford University | M |
| Rhode Island College | M,O |
| Rice University | M,D |
| Rivier University | M |
| Roberts Wesleyan College | M,D |
| Rochester Institute of Technology | M,O |
| Roosevelt University | M,D |
| Rosalind Franklin University of Medicine and Science | M,D |
| Rowan University | M,O |
| Rutgers University - Camden | M |
| Rutgers University - Newark | D |
| Rutgers University - New Brunswick | D |
| Sage Graduate School | M,O |
| St. John's University (NY) | M |
| Saint Joseph's University | M,O |
| Saint Leo University | M |
| Saint Louis University | M,D |
| Saint Mary's University (Canada) | M,D |
| Salem State University | M,O |
| Sam Houston State University | M,D,O |
| San Diego State University | M,D |
| San Francisco State University | M,O |
| San Jose State University | M |
| Saybrook University | M,D |
| The Seattle School of Theology and Psychology | M |
| Seattle University | M |
| Seton Hall University | M |
| Shippensburg University of Pennsylvania | M |
| Simon Fraser University | M,D |
| Sofia University | M,D |
| Southeastern Baptist Theological Seminary | M,D |
| Southeastern Louisiana University | M |
| Southern Adventist University | M |
| Southern California Seminary | M,D |
| Southern Connecticut State University | M |
| Southern Illinois University Carbondale | M,D |
| Southern Illinois University Edwardsville | M,O |
| Southern Methodist University | D |
| Southern Nazarene University | M |
| Southern New Hampshire University | M |
| Southern Oregon University | M |
| Southern University and Agricultural and Mechanical College | M |
| Southwestern College (NM) | O |
| Spalding University | M,D |
| Stanford University | D |
| State University of New York at New Paltz | M,O |
| State University of New York at Plattsburgh | M,O |
| Stephen F. Austin State University | M |
| Stony Brook University, State University of New York | M,D |
| Suffolk University | M,D,O |
| Sul Ross State University | M |
| SUNY Brockport | M |
| Syracuse University | D |
| Teachers College, Columbia University | M,D |
| Temple University | M,D* |
| Tennessee State University | M |
| Texas A&M International University | M |
| Texas A&M University | M,D |
| Texas A&M University–Commerce | M,D,O |
| Texas A&M University–Corpus Christi | M |
| Texas A&M University–Kingsville | M |
| Texas A&M University–Texarkana | M |
| Texas Christian University | M,D |
| Texas Southern University | M |
| Texas State University | M |
| Texas Tech University | M,D |
| Texas Woman's University | M,D,O |
| Tiffin University | M |
| Towson University | M |
| Tufts University | M,D |
| Tulane University | M,D |
| UNB Fredericton | M,D |
| Uniformed Services University of the Health Sciences | D |
| Union College (KY) | M |
| Universidad de las Americas, A.C. | M |
| Universidad de las Américas Puebla | M |
| Université de Montréal | M,D |
| Université de Sherbrooke | M |
| Université du Québec à Montréal | D |
| Université du Québec à Trois-Rivières | D,O |
| University at Albany, State University of New York | M,D |
| University at Buffalo, the State University of New York | M,D |
| The University of Akron | M,D |
| The University of Alabama | D |
| The University of Alabama at Birmingham | M,D |
| The University of Alabama in Huntsville | M |
| University of Alaska Anchorage | M,D |
| University of Alberta | M,D |
| The University of Arizona | M,D |
| University of Arkansas | M,D |
| University of Arkansas at Little Rock | M |
| The University of British Columbia | M,D |
| University of Calgary | M,D |
| University of California, Berkeley | D |
| University of California, Davis | D |
| University of California, Irvine | D |
| University of California, Los Angeles | M,D |
| University of California, Merced | M,D |
| University of California, Riverside | D |
| University of California, San Diego | D |
| University of California, Santa Barbara | D |
| University of California, Santa Cruz | D |
| University of Central Arkansas | M,D,O |
| University of Central Florida | M,D |
| University of Central Missouri | M,D,O |
| University of Central Oklahoma | M |
| University of Chicago | D |
| University of Cincinnati | D |
| University of Colorado Boulder | M,D |
| University of Colorado Colorado Springs | M,D |
| University of Connecticut | M,D |
| University of Dayton | M |
| University of Delaware | D |
| University of Denver | M,D,O |
| University of Florida | M,D |
| University of Georgia | D |
| University of Guelph | M,D |
| University of Hawaii at Manoa | M,D,O |
| University of Houston | M,D |
| University of Houston–Clear Lake | M |
| University of Houston–Victoria | M |
| University of Idaho | M,D |
| University of Illinois at Chicago | M,D |
| University of Illinois at Urbana-Champaign | M,D |
| University of Indianapolis | M,D |
| The University of Iowa | M,D,O |
| The University of Kansas | M,D,O |
| University of Kentucky | M,D |
| University of La Verne | M,D |
| University of Lethbridge | M,D |
| University of Louisiana at Lafayette | M |
| University of Louisiana at Monroe | M |
| University of Louisville | D |
| University of Maine | M,D |
| The University of Manchester | M,D |
| University of Manitoba | M,D |
| University of Maryland, Baltimore County | M,D |
| University of Maryland, College Park | M,D |
| University of Massachusetts Amherst | M,D |
| University of Massachusetts Dartmouth | M,O |
| University of Massachusetts Lowell | M |
| University of Memphis | M,D,O |
| University of Miami | M,D |
| University of Michigan | D,O |
| University of Minnesota, Twin Cities Campus | D |
| University of Missouri | M,D,O |
| University of Missouri–Kansas City | M,D |
| University of Missouri–St. Louis | M,D,O |
| University of Montana | M,D,O |
| University of Nebraska at Omaha | M,D,O |
| University of Nebraska–Lincoln | M,D |
| University of Nevada, Las Vegas | M,D,O |
| University of Nevada, Reno | M,D |
| University of New Brunswick Saint John | M,D |
| University of New Hampshire | D |
| University of New Mexico | D |
| University of New Orleans | M,D |
| The University of North Carolina at Chapel Hill | D |
| The University of North Carolina at Charlotte | M,D,O |
| The University of North Carolina at Greensboro | M,D |
| The University of North Carolina Wilmington | M,D |
| University of North Dakota | M,D |
| University of Northern British Columbia | M,D,O |
| University of Northern Iowa | M |
| University of North Florida | M |
| University of North Texas | M,D,O |
| University of Notre Dame | D |
| University of Oklahoma | M,D,O |
| University of Oregon | M,D |
| University of Ottawa | D |
| University of Pennsylvania | D |
| University of Philosophical Research | M |
| University of Phoenix–Online Campus | M,O |
| University of Phoenix - Phoenix Campus | M |
| University of Pittsburgh | D* |

| | |
|---|---|
| University of Puerto Rico at Rio Piedras | M,D |
| University of Regina | M,D |
| University of Rhode Island | M,D |
| University of Rochester | D |
| University of Saint Mary | M |
| University of Saskatchewan | M,D |
| University of South Africa | M,D |
| University of South Alabama | M |
| University of South Carolina | M,D |
| University of South Dakota | M,D |
| University of Southern California | M,D |
| University of Southern Mississippi | M,D |
| University of South Florida | D |
| University of South Florida, St. Petersburg | M |
| The University of Tennessee | M,D |
| The University of Tennessee at Chattanooga | M |
| The University of Texas at Arlington | M,D |
| The University of Texas at Austin | D |
| The University of Texas at Dallas | M,D |
| The University of Texas at El Paso | M,D |
| The University of Texas at San Antonio | M,D |
| The University of Texas at Tyler | M |
| The University of Texas of the Permian Basin | M |
| The University of Texas Rio Grande Valley | M |
| University of the Pacific | M |
| University of the West | M |
| The University of Toledo | M,D |
| University of Toronto | M,D |
| The University of Tulsa | M,D |
| University of Utah | D |
| University of Vermont | D |
| University of Victoria | M,D |
| University of Virginia | M,D |
| University of Washington | M,D |
| University of Waterloo | M,D |
| The University of Western Ontario | M,D |
| University of West Florida | M |
| University of Windsor | M,D |
| University of Wisconsin–Eau Claire | M,O |
| University of Wisconsin–La Crosse | M,O |
| University of Wisconsin–Madison | D |
| University of Wisconsin–Milwaukee | M,D* |
| University of Wisconsin–Oshkosh | M |
| University of Wisconsin–Whitewater | M,O |
| University of Wyoming | M,D |
| Université Laval | D |
| Utah State University | M,D |
| Valdosta State University | M,O |
| Vanderbilt University | D* |
| Villanova University | M |
| Virginia Polytechnic Institute and State University | M,D |
| Virginia State University | M,D |
| Wake Forest University | M |
| Walden University | M,D,O |
| Washburn University | M |
| Washington State University | M,D |
| Washington University in St. Louis | D |
| Wayne State University | M,D |
| Webster University | M |
| Western Carolina University | M |
| Western Illinois University | M,O |
| Western Kentucky University | M,O |
| Western Michigan University | M,D |
| Western Washington University | M |
| Westfield State University | M |
| West Texas A&M University | M |
| West Virginia University | M,D |
| Wheaton College | M,D |
| Wichita State University | D |
| Widener University | |
| Wilfrid Laurier University | M,D |
| William Carey University | M |
| William James College | M,D,O |
| Winthrop University | M,O |
| Wisconsin School of Professional Psychology | M,D |
| The Wright Institute | D |
| Wright State University | M,D |
| Xavier University | M,D* |
| Yale University | D |
| Yeshiva University | M,D |
| York University | M,D |

## PUBLIC ADMINISTRATION

| | |
|---|---|
| Adams State University | M |
| Adler University | M |
| Albany State University | M |
| Alfred University | M |
| American University | M,D,O |
| The American University in Cairo | M,O |
| Anabaptist Mennonite Biblical Seminary | M,O |
| Anna Maria College | M |
| Appalachian State University | M |
| Argosy University, Chicago | M,D |
| Argosy University, Los Angeles | M,D |
| Argosy University, Northern Virginia | M,D,O |
| Argosy University, Orange County | M,D,O |
| Argosy University, Phoenix | M,D |
| Argosy University, Seattle | M,D |
| Argosy University, Tampa | M,D |
| Argosy University, Twin Cities | M,D |
| Arizona State University at Tempe | M,D |
| Arkansas State University | M,O |
| Auburn University | M,D,O |
| Auburn University at Montgomery | M,D |
| Ball State University | M,O |
| Barry University | M |
| Baruch College of the City University of New York | M |
| Bellevue University | M |
| Binghamton University, State University of New York | M |
| Boise State University | M,D,O |
| Bowie State University | M |
| Bowling Green State University | M |
| Brandman University | M |
| Bridgewater State University | M |
| Brigham Young University | M |
| California Baptist University | M |
| California State Polytechnic University, Pomona | M |
| California State University, Chico | M |
| California State University, Dominguez Hills | M |
| California State University, East Bay | M |
| California State University, Fresno | M |
| California State University, Fullerton | M |
| California State University, Long Beach | M,O |
| California State University, Los Angeles | M |
| California State University, Northridge | M,O |
| California State University, Sacramento | M |
| California State University, San Bernardino | M |
| California State University, Stanislaus | M |
| Capella University | M,D |
| Carleton University | M,D |
| Carnegie Mellon University | M |
| Central European University | M,D |
| Central Michigan University | M,O |
| Cheyney University of Pennsylvania | M |
| City College of the City University of New York | M,D |
| Clark Atlanta University | M |
| Clark University | M,O |
| Clemson University | M,D,O |
| Cleveland State University | M,D,O |
| College of Charleston | M |
| The College of New Rochelle | M |
| College of Saint Elizabeth | M,O |
| Columbia University | M |
| Columbus State University | M |
| Concordia University (Canada) | M,D |
| Concordia University Wisconsin | M |
| Copenhagen Business School | M,D |
| Cumberland University | M |
| Dalhousie University | M,O |
| DePaul University | M |
| DeVry University–Folsom Campus | M |
| Drake University | M |
| East Carolina University | M,O |
| Eastern Kentucky University | M |
| Eastern Michigan University | M,O |
| Eastern Washington University | M |
| East Stroudsburg University of Pennsylvania | M |
| East Tennessee State University | M,O |
| The Evergreen State College | M |
| Fairfield University | M |
| Fairleigh Dickinson University, Florham Campus | M |
| Fairleigh Dickinson University, Metropolitan Campus | M,O |
| Florida Agricultural and Mechanical University | M |
| Florida Atlantic University | M,D |
| Florida Gulf Coast University | M |
| Florida Institute of Technology | M |
| Florida International University | M,D |
| Florida National University | M |
| Florida State University | M,D,O |
| Framingham State University | M |
| Gallaudet University | M,D,O |
| Gannon University | M |
| George Mason University | M |
| The George Washington University | M,D |
| Georgia College & State University | M |
| Georgia Southern University | M,O |
| Georgia State University | M,D,O |
| Golden Gate University | M,D,O |
| Governors State University | M |
| Grambling State University | M |
| Grand Valley State University | M |
| Hamline University | M,D |
| Harvard University | M* |
| Hawaii Pacific University | M |
| Hilbert College | M |
| Howard University | M |
| Idaho State University | M |
| IGlobal University | M |
| Illinois Institute of Technology | M |
| Indiana State University | M |
| Indiana University Bloomington | M,D,O |
| Indiana University Kokomo | M,O |
| Indiana University Northwest | M,O |
| Indiana University-Purdue University Indianapolis | M,O |
| Indiana University South Bend | M,O |
| Institute of Public Administration | M,O |
| Instituto Tecnológico y de Estudios Superiores de Monterrey, Campus Ciudad Juárez | M |
| International University in Geneva | M,D |
| Iowa State University of Science and Technology | M |
| Jackson State University | M,D |
| Jacksonville State University | M |
| James Madison University | M |
| John Jay College of Criminal Justice of the City University of New York | M |
| Johns Hopkins University | M,O |
| Kansas State University | M |
| Kean University | M |
| Kennesaw State University | M |
| Kent State University | M,D |
| Kutztown University of Pennsylvania | M |
| Liberty University | M |
| Lipscomb University | M |
| London Metropolitan University | M,D |
| Long Island University - Brooklyn | M,O |
| Long Island University - Hudson | M,O |
| Long Island University - Post | M,O |
| Louisiana State University and Agricultural & Mechanical College | M,D |
| Marist College | M |
| Marshall University | M |
| Marywood University | M |
| McMaster University | M,D |
| Metropolitan College of New York | M |
| Metropolitan State University | M |
| Mid-America Christian University | M |
| Middlebury Institute of International Studies at Monterey | M |
| Midwest University | M,D |
| Minnesota State University Mankato | M |
| Mississippi State University | M,D |
| Missouri State University | M,O |
| Montana State University | M |
| National University | M |
| New Mexico State University | M |
| New York University | M,D,O |
| North Carolina Central University | M |
| North Carolina State University | M,D |
| Northeastern University | M,D |
| Northern Arizona University | M,D,O |
| Northern Illinois University | M |
| Northern Kentucky University | M,O |
| Northwestern University | M |
| Norwich University | M |
| Notre Dame de Namur University | M |
| Nova Southeastern University | M |
| Oakland University | M,O |
| The Ohio State University | M,D |
| Ohio University | M,O |
| Old Dominion University | M,D |
| Pace University | M |
| Park University | M,O |
| Penn State Harrisburg | M,D,O |
| Pontifical Catholic University of Puerto Rico | M |
| Portland State University | M,D,O |
| Post University | M |
| Queen's University at Kingston | M |
| Regent University | M |
| Reinhardt University | M |
| Roger Williams University | M |
| Roosevelt University | M |
| Rutgers University - Camden | M |
| Rutgers University - Newark | M,D |
| Sacred Heart University | M |
| Saginaw Valley State University | M |
| St. John's University (NY) | M,O |
| St. Mary's University (United States) | M,O |
| Saint Mary's University of Minnesota | M |
| Saint Peter's University | M |
| St. Thomas University - Florida | M,O |
| Sam Houston State University | M |
| San Diego State University | M |
| San Francisco State University | M |
| San Jose State University | M |
| Savannah State University | M |
| Seattle University | M |
| Seton Hall University | M,O |
| Shippensburg University of Pennsylvania | M |
| Sonoma State University | M |
| Southeast Missouri State University | M |
| Southern Arkansas University–Magnolia | M |
| Southern Illinois University Carbondale | M |
| Southern Illinois University Edwardsville | M |
| Southern New Hampshire University | M,D,O |
| Southern University and Agricultural and Mechanical College | M |
| Southern Utah University | M |
| South University - Montgomery | M |
| South University - Savannah | M |
| South University - West Palm Beach | M |
| Stephen F. Austin State University | M |
| Strayer University | M |
| Suffolk University | M |
| SUNY Brockport | M,O |
| Syracuse University | M,D |
| Tennessee State University | M,D |
| Texas A&M International University | M |
| Texas A&M University–Corpus Christi | M |
| Texas Southern University | M |
| Texas State University | M |
| Texas Tech University | M,D |
| Thomas Edison State University | M |
| Trident University International | M,D |
| Troy University | M |
| Tufts University | O |
| UNB Fredericton | M |
| Université de Moncton | M |
| Université de Sherbrooke | M |
| Université du Québec à Montréal | M |
| Université du Québec, École nationale d'administration publique | D,O |
| University at Albany, State University of New York | M,D,O |
| The University of Akron | M |
| The University of Alabama | M,D |
| The University of Alabama at Birmingham | M |
| University of Alaska Anchorage | M |
| University of Alaska Southeast | M |
| The University of Arizona | M,D,O |
| University of Arkansas | M |
| University of Arkansas at Little Rock | M |
| University of Baltimore | M,D |
| University of Central Florida | M,O |
| University of Central Oklahoma | M |
| University of Colorado Colorado Springs | M |
| University of Colorado Denver | M,D |
| University of Connecticut | M |
| University of Dayton | M |
| University of Delaware | M |
| University of Evansville | M |
| The University of Findlay | M,D |
| University of Georgia | M,D |
| University of Guam | M |
| University of Guelph | M |
| University of Hawaii at Manoa | M,O |
| University of Houston | M,D |
| University of Idaho | M,D |
| University of Illinois at Chicago | M,D |
| University of Illinois at Springfield | M,D,O |
| University of Kentucky | M,D,O |
| University of La Verne | M,D |
| University of Louisiana at Monroe | M |
| University of Louisville | M,D |
| University of Management and Technology | M,O |
| University of Manitoba | M |
| University of Maryland, College Park | M |
| University of Massachusetts Amherst | M |
| University of Massachusetts Boston | M |
| University of Massachusetts Dartmouth | M,O |
| University of Memphis | M,O |
| University of Michigan–Dearborn | M |
| University of Michigan–Flint | M |
| University of Missouri | M,D,O |
| University of Missouri–Kansas City | M,D |
| University of Missouri–St. Louis | M,D |
| University of Montana | M |
| University of Nebraska at Omaha | M,D,O |
| University of Nevada, Las Vegas | M,D,O |
| University of Nevada, Reno | M |
| University of New Hampshire | M,O |
| University of New Haven | M,O |
| University of New Mexico | M |
| University of New Orleans | M |
| The University of North Carolina at Chapel Hill | M |
| The University of North Carolina at Charlotte | M,O |
| The University of North Carolina at Pembroke | M |
| The University of North Carolina Wilmington | M |
| University of North Dakota | M |
| University of North Florida | M,O |
| University of North Georgia | M |
| University of North Texas | M,D,O |
| University of North Texas at Dallas | M |
| University of Oklahoma | M,D |
| University of Oregon | M |
| University of Ottawa | D,O |
| University of Pennsylvania | M,O |
| University of Phoenix - Bay Area Campus | M,D |
| University of Phoenix - Central Valley Campus | M |
| University of Phoenix - Dallas Campus | M |
| University of Phoenix - Hawaii Campus | M |
| University of Phoenix - Houston Campus | M |
| University of Phoenix - Las Vegas Campus | M |
| University of Phoenix–Online Campus | M,O |
| University of Phoenix - Phoenix Campus | M |
| University of Phoenix - Sacramento Valley Campus | M |
| University of Phoenix - San Antonio Campus | M |
| University of Phoenix - San Diego Campus | M |
| University of Pittsburgh | M,D* |
| University of Puerto Rico at Rio Piedras | M |
| University of Regina | M,D,O |
| University of Rhode Island | M |
| University of St. Thomas (TX) | M |
| University of San Francisco | M |
| University of South Africa | M,D |
| University of South Alabama | M |
| University of South Carolina | M |
| University of Southern California | M,O |
| University of Southern Indiana | M |
| University of South Florida | O |
| The University of Tennessee | M |
| The University of Tennessee at Chattanooga | M,O |
| The University of Texas at Arlington | M |

*M—masters degree; D—doctorate; O—other advanced degree; *—Close-Up and/or Display*

| | |
|---|---|
| The University of Texas at Austin | M,D |
| The University of Texas at Dallas | M,D |
| The University of Texas at San Antonio | M |
| The University of Texas at Tyler | M |
| The University of Texas Rio Grande Valley | M |
| University of the District of Columbia | M |
| The University of Toledo | M,O |
| University of Utah | M,D |
| University of Vermont | M |
| University of Victoria | M,D |
| University of Washington | M,D |
| University of West Florida | M |
| The University of Winnipeg | M |
| University of Wisconsin–Milwaukee | M* |
| University of Wisconsin–Oshkosh | M |
| University of Wyoming | M |
| Upper Iowa University | M |
| Valdosta State University | M,D |
| Villanova University | M,O |
| Virginia Commonwealth University | M |
| Virginia International University | M |
| Virginia Polytechnic Institute and State University | M,D |
| Walden University | M,D,O |
| Waldorf University | M |
| Washington Adventist University | M |
| Wayne State University | M,D |
| Webster University | M,D,O |
| Western Kentucky University | M |
| Western Michigan University | M,D,O |
| Westfield State University | M |
| West Virginia University | M,D |
| Wichita State University | M |
| Widener University | M |
| Wilmington University | M,D |
| Wright State University | M |
| York University | M |

**PUBLIC AFFAIRS**

| | |
|---|---|
| Arizona State University at Tempe | M,D |
| Binghamton University, State University of New York | D |
| Cleveland State University | D |
| Concordia University (Canada) | O |
| Cornell University | M |
| Drake University | M |
| Florida International University | M,D |
| George Mason University | M |
| The George Washington University | M,O |
| Indiana University Bloomington | M,D,O |
| Indiana University Northwest | M,O |
| Indiana University of Pennsylvania | M |
| Indiana University-Purdue University Indianapolis | M,O |
| Indiana University South Bend | M,O |
| The Institute of World Politics | M,D,O |
| Jackson State University | M,D |
| McMaster University | M,D |
| Merrimack College | M,O |
| Metropolitan College of New York | M |
| Metropolitan State University | M |
| New Mexico Highlands University | M |
| The Ohio State University | M,D |
| Park University | M,O |
| Penn State Harrisburg | M,D,O |
| Portland State University | M,D,O |
| Princeton University | M,D,O |
| Syracuse University | |
| Texas A&M University | M,O |
| The University of Alabama in Huntsville | M |
| University of Arkansas at Little Rock | M,O |
| University of Baltimore | M,D |
| University of California, Berkeley | M |
| University of California, Los Angeles | M,D |
| University of Central Florida | D |
| University of Colorado Colorado Springs | M |
| University of Colorado Denver | M,D |
| University of Florida | M,D,O |
| University of Louisville | M,D |
| University of Minnesota, Twin Cities Campus | M,D |
| University of Missouri | M,D,O |
| University of Missouri–Kansas City | M,D |
| University of Nevada, Las Vegas | M,D,O |
| The University of North Carolina at Greensboro | M,O |
| University of South Florida | O |
| The University of Texas at Austin | M,D |
| The University of Texas Rio Grande Valley | M |
| University of Washington | M,D |
| University of Waterloo | M |
| University of Wisconsin–Madison | M |
| Virginia Commonwealth University | M,D,O |
| Virginia Polytechnic Institute and State University | M,D |
| Washington State University | M,D,O |
| Western Carolina University | M |
| Western Michigan University | M,D,O |
| York University | M |

**PUBLIC HEALTH—GENERAL**

| | |
|---|---|
| Adelphi University | M |
| Allen College | M,D |
| American University of Armenia | M |
| Andrews University | M,O |
| Arcadia University | M |
| Argosy University, Atlanta | M |
| Argosy University, Chicago | M |
| Argosy University, Hawaii | M |
| Argosy University, Los Angeles | M |
| Argosy University, Northern Virginia | M |
| Argosy University, Orange County | M |
| Argosy University, Phoenix | M |
| Argosy University, Seattle | M |
| Argosy University, Tampa | M |
| Argosy University, Twin Cities | M |
| Arizona State University at Tempe | M,D,O |
| A.T. Still University | M,D,O |
| Augusta University | M |
| Austin Peay State University | M |
| Azusa Pacific University | M |
| Baldwin Wallace University | M |
| Barry University | |
| Baylor University | M |
| Belmont University | D |
| Benedictine University | M |
| Boise State University | M,D,O |
| Boston University | M,D |
| Bowling Green State University | M |
| Brigham Young University | M |
| Brooklyn College of the City University of New York | M |
| Brown University | M |
| California Baptist University | M |
| California State University, Fresno | M |
| California State University, Fullerton | M |
| California State University, Long Beach | M |
| California State University, Northridge | M |
| California State University, San Bernardino | M |
| California State University, San Marcos | M |
| Campbell University | M,D |
| Case Western Reserve University | M |
| Charles R. Drew University of Medicine and Science | M |
| Chicago State University | M |
| Claremont Graduate University | M,D |
| Clemson University | M,D,O |
| Cleveland State University | M |
| The College of New Jersey | M |
| College of Saint Elizabeth | M |
| Columbia University | M,D |
| Creighton University | M |
| Daemen College | M |
| Dartmouth College | M |
| Davenport University | M |
| DePaul University | M |
| Des Moines University | M |
| Drexel University | M,D,O |
| East Carolina University | M,D,O |
| Eastern Virginia Medical School | M |
| Eastern Washington University | M |
| East Stroudsburg University of Pennsylvania | M |
| East Tennessee State University | M,D,O |
| Elmhurst University | M |
| Emory University | M,D |
| Everglades University | M |
| Ferris State University | M |
| Florida Agricultural and Mechanical University | M,D |
| Florida International University | M,D |
| Florida State University | M |
| Fort Valley State University | M |
| George Mason University | M,O |
| Georgetown University | M,D |
| The George Washington University | M,D |
| Georgia Southern University | M,D |
| Georgia State University | M,D,O |
| Grand Canyon University | M,D,O |
| Grand Valley State University | M |
| Harvard University | M,D* |
| Hawaii Pacific University | M |
| Hofstra University | M,O |
| Howard University | M |
| Hunter College of the City University of New York | M |
| Icahn School of Medicine at Mount Sinai | M,D |
| Idaho State University | M |
| Independence University | M |
| Indiana University Bloomington | M,D |
| Indiana University-Purdue University Indianapolis | M,D,O |
| Indiana Wesleyan University | M,D |
| Jackson State University | M,D |
| Johns Hopkins University | M,D |
| Kansas State University | M,D,O |
| Kent State University | M,D |
| La Salle University | M |
| Laurentian University | D |
| Lenoir-Rhyne University | M |
| Liberty University | M,D |
| Loma Linda University | M,D |
| London Metropolitan University | M,D |
| Long Island University - Brooklyn | M,D,O |
| Louisiana State University Health Sciences Center | M,D |
| Louisiana State University in Shreveport | M |
| Loyola University Chicago | M,O |
| Marshall University | M |
| McGill University | M,D |
| MCPHS University | M |
| Medical College of Wisconsin | M,D,O |
| Meharry Medical College | M |
| Mercer University | M,D |
| Michigan State University | M |
| MidAmerica Nazarene University | M |
| Mississippi University for Women | M,D,O |
| Missouri State University | M |
| Monroe College | M |
| Montclair State University | M |
| Morehouse School of Medicine | M |
| Morgan State University | M,D |
| National University | M,O |
| New England Institute of Technology | M |
| New Mexico State University | M,O |
| New York Medical College | M,D,O |
| New York University | M,D |
| North Dakota State University | M |
| Northeastern University | M,D,O |
| Northeast Ohio Medical University | M,D,O |
| Northern Illinois University | M |
| Northwestern University | M |
| Nova Southeastern University | M,D,O |
| Oakland University | M |
| The Ohio State University | M,D |
| Ohio University | M |
| Old Dominion University | M |
| Oregon State University | M,D |
| Penn State Hershey Medical Center | M,D |
| Philadelphia College of Osteopathic Medicine | M,D,O |
| Ponce Health Sciences University | M,D |
| Portland State University | M,D |
| Purdue University | M,D |
| Queen's University at Kingston | M,D |
| Rivier University | M,D |
| Rollins College | M |
| Rutgers University - Camden | M,O |
| Rutgers University - Newark | M,O |
| Rutgers University - New Brunswick | M,D |
| Sacred Heart University | M |
| St. Ambrose University | M |
| St. Catherine University | M |
| St. John's University (NY) | M |
| Saint Louis University | M,D |
| Salus University | M |
| Samford University | M |
| San Diego State University | M,D |
| San Francisco State University | M |
| San Juan Bautista School of Medicine | M,D |
| Sarah Lawrence College | M |
| Shenandoah University | M,D,O |
| Simmons University | M,D,O |
| Simon Fraser University | M,D,O |
| Slippery Rock University of Pennsylvania | M |
| Southern Connecticut State University | M |
| State University of New York Downstate Medical Center | M |
| State University of New York Upstate Medical University | M |
| Stony Brook University, State University of New York | M,O |
| SUNY Brockport | M |
| Tarleton State University | M |
| Temple University | M,D* |
| Tennessee State University | M |
| Texas A&M University | M,D |
| Thomas Edison State University | M |
| Thomas Jefferson University | M,O |
| Touro University California | M,D |
| Trinity Washington University | M |
| Tufts University | M,D,O |
| Tulane University | M,D |
| Uniformed Services University of the Health Sciences | M,D |
| Université de Montréal | M,D,O |
| University at Albany, State University of New York | M,D |
| University at Buffalo, the State University of New York | M,D |
| The University of Alabama at Birmingham | M,D |
| University of Alaska Anchorage | M |
| University of Alberta | M,D |
| The University of Arizona | M,D |
| University of Arkansas for Medical Sciences | M,D,O |
| The University of British Columbia | M,D |
| University of California, Berkeley | M,D |
| University of California, Irvine | M,D |
| University of California, Los Angeles | M,D |
| University of California, San Diego | D |
| University of Cincinnati | M,D |
| University of Colorado Denver | M,D |
| University of Connecticut Health Center | M |
| University of Florida | M,D,O |
| University of Georgia | D |
| University of Hawaii at Manoa | M,D,O |
| University of Illinois at Chicago | M,D |
| University of Illinois at Springfield | M,O |
| University of Illinois at Urbana-Champaign | M,D |
| University of Indianapolis | M |
| The University of Iowa | M,D,O |
| The University of Kansas | M,D |
| University of Kentucky | M,D |
| University of La Verne | M |
| University of Louisville | M,D |
| University of Lynchburg | M |
| The University of Manchester | M,D |
| University of Maryland, College Park | M,D |
| University of Massachusetts Amherst | M,D |
| University of Memphis | M,D |
| University of Miami | M,D |
| University of Michigan | M,D |
| University of Michigan–Flint | M |
| University of Minnesota, Twin Cities Campus | M,D,O |
| University of Missouri | M,O |
| University of Montana | M,O |
| University of Nebraska Medical Center | M |
| University of Nevada, Las Vegas | M,D,O |
| University of Nevada, Reno | M,D |
| University of New England | M,D,O |
| University of New Hampshire | M,O |
| University of New Mexico | M |
| The University of North Carolina at Chapel Hill | M,D |
| The University of North Carolina at Charlotte | M,D,O |
| University of North Dakota | M |
| University of Northern Colorado | M |
| University of North Florida | M,O |
| University of North Texas Health Science Center at Fort Worth | M,D,O |
| University of Oklahoma Health Sciences Center | M,D |
| University of Ottawa | D |
| University of Pennsylvania | M |
| University of Pittsburgh | M,D,O* |
| University of Rochester | M |
| University of Saint Joseph | M |
| University of San Francisco | M |
| University of South Africa | M,D |
| University of South Carolina | M |
| University of South Dakota | M |
| University of Southern California | M |
| University of Southern Maine | M,O |
| University of Southern Mississippi | M |
| University of South Florida | M,D,O |
| The University of Tennessee | M |
| The University of Texas at El Paso | M,O |
| The University of Texas Health Science Center at Houston | M,D,O |
| The University of Texas Health Science Center at Tyler | M |
| The University of Texas Medical Branch | M |
| University of the Sciences | M |
| The University of Toledo | M,D,O |
| University of Toronto | M,D |
| University of Utah | M,D |
| University of Vermont | M,O |
| University of Virginia | M,D |
| University of Washington | M,D |
| University of Waterloo | M,D |
| University of West Florida | M |
| University of Wisconsin–La Crosse | M |
| University of Wisconsin–Madison | M |
| University of Wisconsin–Milwaukee | M,D,O* |
| Utah State University | M,D |
| Valparaiso University | M,D,O |
| Vanderbilt University | M* |
| Virginia Commonwealth University | M,D |
| Virginia Polytechnic Institute and State University | M,D |
| Walden University | M,D,O |
| Washington University in St. Louis | M,D |
| Western Illinois University | M |
| Western Kentucky University | M |
| Westminster College (UT) | M |
| West Virginia University | M,D |
| Wright State University | M |
| Yale University | M,D |
| Youngstown State University | M |

**PUBLIC HISTORY**

| | |
|---|---|
| Arizona State University at Tempe | M,D,O |
| California State University, East Bay | M |
| California State University, Sacramento | M,D |
| Colorado State University | M |
| Drew University | M,D,O |
| Duquesne University | M |
| East Carolina University | M |
| Florida State University | M,D |
| Georgia Southern University | M,O |
| Georgia State University | M,D |
| Indiana University of Pennsylvania | M |
| Indiana University-Purdue University Indianapolis | M |
| James Madison University | M |
| Lehigh University | M,D |
| Loyola University Chicago | M,D |
| Middle Tennessee State University | D |
| New York University | M,D,O |
| North Carolina State University | M |
| Northern Kentucky University | M |
| Rutgers University - Camden | M |
| St. John's University (NY) | M,D |
| Shippensburg University of Pennsylvania | M |
| Sonoma State University | M |
| SUNY Brockport | M |
| Texas A&M University–Commerce | M,D,O |
| University at Albany, State University of New York | M,D,O |
| University at Buffalo, the State University of New York | M,D,O |
| University of Arkansas at Little Rock | M |
| University of California, Santa Barbara | D |
| University of Colorado Denver | M |
| University of Illinois at Springfield | M |
| University of Louisiana at Lafayette | M |
| University of Louisville | M,O |
| University of Maryland, Baltimore County | M,D |
| University of North Alabama | M |
| University of Northern Iowa | M |
| University of South Carolina | M,D |
| The University of Texas at Austin | M,D |
| University of West Florida | M |
| Wayne State University | M,D,O |

**PUBLIC POLICY**

| | |
|---|---|
| Adler University | M |
| Albany State University | M |
| American Public University System | M |
| American University | M,D,O |
| The American University in Cairo | M,O |
| The American University of Paris | M |
| Arizona State University at Tempe | M,D |
| Auburn University at Montgomery | M,D |
| Aurora University | M |
| Baruch College of the City University of New York | M |

Boise State University M,D,O
Brandeis University M
Brock University M
Brooklyn College of the City University of New York M
Brown University M
California Lutheran University M,O
California State University, East Bay M
California State University, Long Beach M,O
California State University, Sacramento M
Carleton University M,D
Carnegie Mellon University M,D
The Catholic University of America M
Central European University M,D
Claremont Graduate University M,D,O
Clemson University D,O
Columbia University M
Concordia University (Canada) M,D
Cornell University M,D
DePaul University M
Duke University M,D
Eastern Michigan University M,O
Florida State University M,D,O
Frederick S. Pardee RAND Graduate School D
George Mason University M,D
Georgetown University M,D
The George Washington University M,D
Georgia Institute of Technology M,D
Georgia State University M,D,O
Harvard University M,D*
Indiana University Bloomington M,D,O
Indiana University Kokomo M,O
The Institute of World Politics M,D,O
Jackson State University M,D
Jacksonville University M
John Jay College of Criminal Justice of the City University of New York M,D
Johns Hopkins University M,D
Liberty University M
Lipscomb University M
London Metropolitan University M,D
Loyola University Chicago M
McMaster University M,D
Midwest University M,D
Mills College M
Mississippi State University M,D
National Louis University M,D,O
New England College M
The New School M,D
New York University M
Northeastern University M,D,O
Northwestern University M,D
Norwich University M
The Ohio State University M,D
Old Dominion University D
Oregon State University M,D
Pepperdine University M
Portland State University M,D,O
Princeton University M,D
Purdue University Fort Wayne M,O
Regent University M
Rochester Institute of Technology M
Rutgers University - Camden M
Rutgers University - Newark M,D,O
Rutgers University - New Brunswick M,D
San Francisco State University M
Seton Hall University M,O
Simmons University M,D,O
Simon Fraser University M
Southern University and Agricultural and Mechanical College D
State University of New York Empire State College M
Stony Brook University, State University of New York M
Suffolk University M,O
Trinity College (United States) M
Tufts University M,D
Union Institute & University M,D
Universidad Autonoma de Guadalajara M,D
Universidad del Este M
Université de Montréal O
University at Albany, State University of New York M,D,O
The University of Arizona M,D,O
University of Arkansas D
The University of British Columbia M
University of Calgary M
University of California, Berkeley M,D
University of California, Los Angeles M
University of California, Riverside M,D
University of California, San Diego M
University of Chicago M,D
University of Delaware M,D
University of Denver M
University of Georgia M,D
University of Guelph M
University of Hawaii at Manoa O
University of Houston M
University of Kentucky M,D,O
University of Louisville M,D
University of Maryland, Baltimore County M,D,O
University of Maryland, College Park M,D
University of Massachusetts Amherst M
University of Massachusetts Boston M,D
University of Massachusetts Dartmouth M,O
University of Memphis M,O
University of Michigan M,D
University of Minnesota, Twin Cities Campus M,D
University of Missouri M,D,O
University of Missouri–St. Louis M,D
University of Nebraska–Lincoln M,D,O
University of Nevada, Las Vegas M,D,O
University of New Hampshire M
The University of North Carolina at Chapel Hill D
The University of North Carolina at Charlotte M,D,O
University of Northern Iowa M
University of Oklahoma M,D
University of Pennsylvania M,D
University of Pittsburgh M,D*
University of Puerto Rico at Rio Piedras M
University of Regina M,D,O
University of Rhode Island M
University of St. Thomas (TX) M
University of Saskatchewan M,D
University of Southern California M,D,O
University of Southern Maine M
The University of Texas at Arlington M,D
The University of Texas at Austin M,D
The University of Texas at Dallas M,D
The University of Texas Rio Grande Valley M
University of the Pacific M,D
University of Virginia M
University of Washington M,D
University of Washington, Bothell M
Vanderbilt University D*
Virginia Commonwealth University D
Virginia Polytechnic Institute and State University M,D
Walden University M,D,O
Wayne State University M,D,O
Wilfrid Laurier University M
York University M

## PUBLISHING

Arizona State University at Tempe M,D,O
Brown University M,D
Carnegie Mellon University M
DePaul University M
The George Washington University M
The Graduate Center, City University of New York M
New York University M
Northwestern University M
Pace University M,O
Rosemont College M
Rowan University O
Sam Houston State University M
Simon Fraser University M
Stephen F. Austin State University M
University of Baltimore M
University of Houston–Victoria M
Vermont College of Fine Arts M

## QUALITY MANAGEMENT

California Intercontinental University M,D
California State University, Dominguez Hills M
Calumet College of Saint Joseph M
Eastern Michigan University M,O
Hofstra University M,O
Instituto Tecnologico de Santo Domingo M,O
Instituto Tecnológico y de Estudios Superiores de Monterrey, Campus Ciudad de México M,D
Instituto Tecnológico y de Estudios Superiores de Monterrey, Campus Ciudad Juárez M
Instituto Tecnológico y de Estudios Superiores de Monterrey, Campus Estado de México M,D
Instituto Tecnológico y de Estudios Superiores de Monterrey, Campus Irapuato M,D
Madonna University M
Mount Mercy University M
New England College of Business and Finance M
Northwestern University M
Penn State Erie, The Behrend College M
Rutgers University - New Brunswick M,D
San Jose State University M
Southern New Hampshire University M,D,O
Stevens Institute of Technology M,O
Stevenson University M
Trident University International M,D,O
Universidad de las Americas, A.C. M
Universidad del Turabo M
The University of Alabama M
University of Massachusetts Boston M,O
The University of Tennessee at Chattanooga M,O
The University of Texas at Tyler M
University of Wisconsin–Stout M

## QUANTITATIVE ANALYSIS

Baruch College of the City University of New York M
Columbia University M,D
Drexel University M,D,O
Duke University D
Fordham University M,D
The Graduate Center, City University of New York M
Harvard University M,D*
Hofstra University M,O
Instituto Tecnologico de Santo Domingo M,O
Lehigh University M
Rutgers University - Newark M,O
San Francisco State University M
Southern New Hampshire University M,D,O
Stockton University M
University at Buffalo, the State University of New York M,D
The University of Alabama at Birmingham M,D
The University of British Columbia M,D
University of California, Santa Barbara M,D
University of Connecticut M,O
University of Florida M,D,O
The University of Iowa M,D,O
University of Maryland, College Park M,D
University of Michigan M,D
University of Minnesota, Twin Cities Campus M,D,O
University of New Mexico D
University of North Texas M,D,O
University of Oregon M
University of Puerto Rico at Rio Piedras M,D
University of South Africa M,D
University of Southern California M,D
The University of Texas at Arlington M,D
The University of Texas at Austin M,D
The University of Texas Health Science Center at Houston M,D
Vanderbilt University M*
Virginia Polytechnic Institute and State University M,O

## RADIATION BIOLOGY

Georgetown University M
Université de Sherbrooke M,D
The University of Iowa M
University of Oklahoma Health Sciences Center M,D

## RANGE SCIENCE

Kansas State University M,D,O
Montana State University M,D
Oregon State University M,D
Sul Ross State University M
Texas A&M University–Kingsville M
The University of Arizona M,D
University of California, Berkeley M
University of Nevada, Reno M
University of Wyoming M,D
Utah State University M,D

## READING EDUCATION

Abilene Christian University M
Alabama Agricultural and Mechanical University M,D,O
Alabama State University M,O
Alfred University M
Alverno College M
American International College M,D,O
Appalachian State University M
Arcadia University M,D,O
Arkansas State University M,D,O
Asbury University M
Augustana University M
Aurora University M,D
Baldwin Wallace University M
Ball State University M,D,O
Bank Street College of Education M
Barry University M,D,O
Belhaven University (MS) M,D,O
Bellarmine University M,D,O
Berry College M,O
Binghamton University, State University of New York M
Bloomsburg University of Pennsylvania M
Blue Mountain College M
Bluffton University M
Boise State University M
Boston College M,D,O
Bowie State University M
Bowling Green State University M,O
Bridgewater State University M,O
Buffalo State College, State University of New York M
Cabrini University M,D
California Baptist University M
California State University, East Bay M
California State University, Fresno M
California State University, Fullerton M
California State University, Northridge M
California State University, Sacramento M,D,O
California State University, San Marcos M,D
California State University, Stanislaus M
California University of Pennsylvania M
Canisius College M,O
Capella University M,D
Cardinal Stritch University M,O
Carthage College M,O
Castleton University M,O
Centenary University M,D
Central Connecticut State University M,O
Central Michigan University M,D,O
Central Washington University M
Chestnut Hill College M
Chicago State University M
The Citadel, The Military College of South Carolina M,O
City College of the City University of New York M
City University of Seattle M,O
Clarion University of Pennsylvania M
Clemson University M,D,O
Coastal Carolina University M,O
Coker College M
The College of New Jersey M,O
The College of New Rochelle M
College of St. Joseph M
The College of Saint Rose M,O
Concordia University (United States) M,D
Concordia University Chicago M
Concordia University, Nebraska M
Concordia University, St. Paul M,D,O
Concordia University Wisconsin M
Concord University M
Converse College O
Crandall University M
Curry College M,O
Dallas Baptist University M
Delaware State University M
DePaul University M,D
Dickinson State University M
Dominican University M
Drake University M,D,O
Drury University M
Duquesne University M
East Carolina University M
Eastern Mennonite University M
Eastern Michigan University M,O
Eastern Nazarene College M,O
Eastern New Mexico University M
Eastern University M,O
Eastern Washington University M
East Stroudsburg University of Pennsylvania M
East Tennessee State University M,O
Edinboro University of Pennsylvania M,O
Elms College M,O
Emory & Henry College M,D
Emporia State University M
Endicott College M
Evangel University M
Fairleigh Dickinson University, Florham Campus M,O
Fairleigh Dickinson University, Metropolitan Campus M,O
Fairmont State University M
Fitchburg State University O
Florida Atlantic University M
Florida Gulf Coast University M
Florida International University M,D,O
Florida Memorial University M
Florida State University M,D,O
Fontbonne University M
Framingham State University M
Fresno Pacific University M,O
Frostburg State University M,D
Furman University M,O
Gannon University M,O
George Fox University M,O
George Mason University M
Georgetown College M
Georgia Southern University M,O
Georgia State University M,D
Gordon College M,O
Goucher College M,O
Governors State University M
Graceland University (IA) M
Grambling State University M,D,O
Grand Canyon University M,D,O
Grand Valley State University M
Hamline University M,D
Hannibal-LaGrange University M
Harding University M,O
Hardin-Simmons University M
Harvard University M*
Heritage University M
Hofstra University M,D,O
Holy Family University M
Hood College M,O
Houston Baptist University M,D
Idaho State University M
Illinois State University M
Indiana University Bloomington M,D,O
Indiana University of Pennsylvania M,O
Indiana University-Purdue University Indianapolis M,O
Jackson State University M,D,O
Jacksonville State University M
James Madison University M
Judson University M,D
Kansas State University M,D,O
Kennesaw State University M
Kent State University M
Kutztown University of Pennsylvania M
La Salle University M,O
Lehman College of the City University of New York M
Le Moyne College M,O
Lesley University M,D,O
Lewis University M
Liberty University M,D,O
Lipscomb University M,D,O
Long Island University - Brentwood Campus M,O
Long Island University - Hudson M,O
Long Island University - Post M,D,O
Long Island University - Riverhead M,O
Longwood University M
Lourdes University M
Loyola Marymount University M
Loyola University Maryland M
Madonna University M
Manhattanville College M,O

*M—masters degree; D—doctorate; O—other advanced degree; *—Close-Up and/or Display*

| | |
|---|---|
| Marquette University | M,D,O |
| Marshall University | M |
| Mary Baldwin University | M |
| Marygrove College | M,O |
| Maryville University of Saint Louis | M,D |
| Marywood University | M |
| Massachusetts College of Liberal Arts | M,O |
| McDaniel College | M |
| McKendree University | M,D,O |
| McNeese State University | M |
| Medaille College | M |
| Mercy College | M,O |
| Meredith College | M,O |
| MGH Institute of Health Professions | M,O |
| Michigan State University | M |
| MidAmerica Nazarene University | M |
| Middle Tennessee State University | M,D |
| Midwestern State University | M |
| Millersville University of Pennsylvania | M |
| Misericordia University | M |
| Mississippi State University | M,D,O |
| Mississippi University for Women | M |
| Missouri State University | M,O |
| Monmouth University | M,D,O |
| Montana State University Billings | M |
| Montclair State University | M |
| Morehead State University | M,O |
| Mount Mercy University | M |
| Mount St. Joseph University | M,O |
| Mount Saint Mary College | M,O |
| Mount Saint Vincent University | M |
| National Louis University | M,D,O |
| Nazareth College of Rochester | M |
| Newman University | M |
| New Mexico State University | M,D,O |
| New York University | M |
| Niagara University | M |
| North Carolina Agricultural and Technical State University | M |
| Northeastern Illinois University | M |
| Northeastern State University | M |
| Northern Michigan University | M |
| Northern Vermont University–Lyndon | M |
| Northwestern Oklahoma State University | M |
| Northwestern State University of Louisiana | M,O |
| Northwest Missouri State University | M,D,O |
| Notre Dame College (OH) | M,O |
| Oakland University | M,D,O |
| Ohio University | M,D |
| Old Dominion University | M,D |
| Olivet Nazarene University | M |
| Pace University | M,O |
| Park University | M,O |
| Penn State Harrisburg | M,D,O |
| Providence College | M |
| Purdue University | M,D,O |
| Purdue University Global | M |
| Queens College of the City University of New York | M,O |
| Queens University of Charlotte | M |
| Quincy University | M |
| Radford University | M |
| Regent University | M,D,O |
| Regis University | M,O |
| Rhode Island College | M |
| Rivier University | M,D,O |
| Roberts Wesleyan College | M |
| Rockford University | M |
| Roger Williams University | M,O |
| Roosevelt University | M |
| Rowan University | M,O |
| Rutgers University - New Brunswick | M,D |
| Sacred Heart University | O |
| Sage Graduate School | M |
| Saginaw Valley State University | M |
| St. Bonaventure University | M |
| Saint Francis University | M |
| St. John Fisher College | M |
| St. John's University (NY) | M,D,O |
| St. Joseph's College, Long Island Campus | M |
| St. Joseph's College, New York | M |
| Saint Joseph's University | M,D,O |
| Saint Michael's College | M,O |
| Saint Peter's University | M,O |
| St. Thomas Aquinas College | M,O |
| St. Thomas University - Florida | M,D,O |
| Saint Xavier University | M |
| Salem College | M |
| Salem State University | M |
| Salisbury University | M,D |
| Sam Houston State University | M,D |
| San Diego State University | M |
| San Francisco State University | M,O |
| San Jose State University | M,O |
| Seattle Pacific University | M |
| Shippensburg University of Pennsylvania | M |
| Siena Heights University | M,O |
| Simon Fraser University | D |
| Slippery Rock University of Pennsylvania | M |
| Sonoma State University | M,O |
| Southeastern Louisiana University | M |
| Southeastern Oklahoma State University | M |
| Southeastern University (FL) | M,D |
| Southern Adventist University | M |
| Southern Connecticut State University | M,O |
| Southern Illinois University Edwardsville | M,O |
| Southern Methodist University | M,D |
| Southern New Hampshire University | M,D,O |
| Southern Oregon University | M |
| Southwestern Adventist University | M |
| Southwest Minnesota State University | M |
| Spring Arbor University | M |
| State University of New York at Fredonia | M |
| State University of New York at New Paltz | M |
| State University of New York at Oswego | M |
| State University of New York at Plattsburgh | M |
| State University of New York College at Cortland | M |
| State University of New York College at Geneseo | M |
| State University of New York College at Oneonta | M |
| State University of New York College at Potsdam | M |
| Sul Ross State University | M,O |
| SUNY Brockport | M,O |
| Syracuse University | M,D |
| Teachers College, Columbia University | M,D,O |
| Tennessee Technological University | M,D,O |
| Texas A&M University–Commerce | M,D,O |
| Texas A&M University–Corpus Christi | M,D |
| Texas A&M University–Kingsville | M |
| Texas A&M University–San Antonio | M |
| Texas Christian University | M |
| Texas State University | M |
| Texas Tech University | M,D |
| Texas Woman's University | M,D,O |
| Towson University | M,O |
| Trident University International | M |
| Trinity Washington University | M |
| Union College (KY) | M |
| University at Albany, State University of New York | M,D,O |
| University at Buffalo, the State University of New York | M,D,O |
| The University of Akron | M |
| The University of Alabama at Birmingham | M |
| The University of Alabama in Huntsville | M,O |
| University of Alaska Southeast | M |
| The University of Arizona | M,D,O |
| University of Arkansas at Little Rock | M,D,O |
| University of Bridgeport | M,D,O |
| The University of British Columbia | M,D |
| University of Central Arkansas | M |
| University of Central Florida | M,O |
| University of Central Missouri | M,D,O |
| University of Central Oklahoma | M |
| University of Cincinnati | M,D |
| University of Colorado Denver | M |
| University of Connecticut | M,D |
| University of Dayton | M |
| The University of Findlay | M,D |
| University of Florida | M,D,O |
| University of Georgia | M,D |
| University of Guam | M |
| University of Houston–Clear Lake | M |
| University of Houston–Victoria | M,O |
| University of Kentucky | M,D |
| University of Lynchburg | M |
| University of Maine | M,D,O |
| University of Mary | M,D |
| University of Maryland, College Park | M,D,O |
| University of Massachusetts Amherst | M,D,O |
| University of Memphis | M,D,O |
| University of Miami | D |
| University of Michigan–Flint | M,D,O |
| University of Minnesota, Twin Cities Campus | M,D,O |
| University of Mississippi | M,D,O |
| University of Missouri | M,D,O |
| University of Missouri–Kansas City | M,D,O |
| University of Missouri–St. Louis | M |
| University of Nebraska at Kearney | M |
| University of Nevada, Reno | M,D |
| University of New England | M,D,O |
| University of New Mexico | M,D |
| The University of North Carolina at Chapel Hill | M,D |
| The University of North Carolina at Charlotte | M,O |
| The University of North Carolina at Greensboro | M,D,O |
| The University of North Carolina at Pembroke | M |
| The University of North Carolina Wilmington | M |
| University of North Dakota | M |
| University of Northern Colorado | M |
| University of Northern Iowa | M |
| University of North Florida | M |
| University of Oklahoma | M,D |
| University of Oklahoma Health Sciences Center | M,D,O |
| University of Pennsylvania | M |
| University of Phoenix–Online Campus | M,O |
| University of Phoenix - Phoenix Campus | M |
| University of Portland | M,D |
| University of Rhode Island | M,D |
| University of St. Francis (IL) | M,D,O |
| University of Saint Joseph | M |
| University of St. Thomas (TX) | M,D |
| University of San Diego | M |
| University of San Francisco | M,D |
| The University of Scranton | M |
| University of Sioux Falls | M,O |
| University of South Alabama | M,D |
| University of South Carolina | M,D |
| University of South Dakota | M |
| University of Southern Maine | M,O |
| University of South Florida | M,D,O |
| University of South Florida, St. Petersburg | M |
| The University of Tennessee | M,D,O |
| The University of Texas at Arlington | M |
| The University of Texas at Austin | M,D |
| The University of Texas at El Paso | M,D |
| The University of Texas at San Antonio | M,D |
| The University of Texas at Tyler | M |
| The University of Texas of the Permian Basin | M |
| The University of Texas Rio Grande Valley | M |
| University of the Cumberlands | M,D,O |
| University of Utah | M,D,O |
| University of Victoria | M,D |
| University of Virginia | M,D |
| University of Washington | M,D |
| University of West Florida | M |
| University of Wisconsin–Eau Claire | M |
| University of Wisconsin–La Crosse | M,O |
| University of Wisconsin–Milwaukee | M* |
| University of Wisconsin–Oshkosh | M |
| University of Wisconsin–River Falls | M |
| University of Wisconsin–Stevens Point | M |
| University of Wisconsin–Superior | M |
| Upper Iowa University | M |
| Utah Valley University | M |
| Vanderbilt University | M* |
| Virginia Commonwealth University | M,O |
| Viterbo University | M,O |
| Walden University | M,D,O |
| Walla Walla University | M |
| Walsh University | M |
| Washburn University | M |
| Washington State University | M,D |
| Wayne State University | M,D,O |
| Webster University | M,O |
| Western Colorado University | M |
| Western Connecticut State University | M,D |
| Western Illinois University | M |
| Western Kentucky University | M,O |
| Western Michigan University | M,D |
| Western New Mexico University | M |
| Westfield State University | M |
| West Liberty University | M |
| West Texas A&M University | M |
| West Virginia University | M,D |
| Widener University | M,D |
| Wilmington College | M |
| Wilmington University | M,D |
| Worcester State University | M,O |
| Xavier University | M* |
| York College of Pennsylvania | M |
| Youngstown State University | M |

## REAL ESTATE

| | |
|---|---|
| American University | M,O |
| Arizona State University at Tempe | M,D |
| Auburn University | M |
| Baruch College of the City University of New York | M |
| Brandeis University | M |
| California State University, Sacramento | M |
| Clemson University | M |
| Cleveland State University | M,O |
| Columbia University | M |
| Cornell University | M |
| DePaul University | M,D |
| Drexel University | M |
| Emory University | M |
| Florida International University | M |
| Georgetown University | M,D |
| The George Washington University | O |
| Georgia State University | M,D,O |
| Instituto Centroamericano de Administracion de Empresas | M |
| Johns Hopkins University | M |
| Longwood University | M |
| Marquette University | M |
| Massachusetts Institute of Technology | M |
| Midwest University | M,D |
| Monmouth University | M,O |
| New York University | M |
| Pacific States University | M,O |
| Pontificia Universidad Catolica Madre y Maestra | M |
| Portland State University | M,D,O |
| Pratt Institute | M |
| Roosevelt University | M |
| Rutgers University - Newark | M |
| Southern Methodist University | M |
| Syracuse University | M |
| Thomas Jefferson University | M |
| Universidad Iberoamericana | M,D |
| University at Buffalo, the State University of New York | M,D,O |
| University of California, Berkeley | D |
| University of Central Florida | M |
| University of Denver | M |
| University of Florida | M,D,O |
| University of Hawaii at Manoa | M |
| University of Illinois at Chicago | M |
| University of Maryland, College Park | M |
| University of Memphis | M,D |
| University of Miami | M,D |
| The University of North Carolina at Charlotte | M,O |
| University of Pennsylvania | M,D |
| University of San Diego | M |
| University of South Africa | M,D |
| University of Southern California | M |
| University of South Florida | M,D |
| The University of Texas at Arlington | M,D |
| The University of Texas at Dallas | M |
| University of Utah | M |
| University of Wisconsin–Madison | M,D |
| Villanova University | M |
| Virginia Commonwealth University | O |

## RECREATION AND PARK MANAGEMENT

| | |
|---|---|
| Acadia University | M |
| Bowling Green State University | M |
| California State University, Chico | M |
| California State University, East Bay | M |
| California State University, Long Beach | M |
| California State University, Northridge | M,O |
| California State University, Sacramento | M |
| Central Michigan University | M,O |
| Clemson University | M,D,O |
| Colorado State University | M,D |
| Delta State University | M |
| East Carolina University | M,O |
| Eastern Kentucky University | M |
| Eastern Washington University | M |
| Frostburg State University | M |
| Hardin-Simmons University | M |
| Indiana State University | M,D |
| Indiana University Bloomington | M,D |
| Iona College | M,O |
| Kent State University | M |
| Lasell College | M,O |
| Lehman College of the City University of New York | M |
| Loyola Marymount University | M |
| Michigan State University | M,D |
| Middle Tennessee State University | M |
| Naropa University | M |
| New England College | M |
| North Carolina Central University | M |
| North Carolina State University | M,D |
| Northern Arizona University | M,O |
| Northwest Missouri State University | M |
| Ohio University | M |
| Old Dominion University | M |
| Penn State University Park | M,D* |
| Purdue University | M,D |
| San Francisco State University | M |
| Slippery Rock University of Pennsylvania | M |
| South Dakota State University | M,D |
| Southern Connecticut State University | M |
| Southern Illinois University Carbondale | M |
| Southern University and Agricultural and Mechanical College | M |
| Southwestern Oklahoma State University | M |
| Springfield College | M |
| State University of New York College at Cortland | M |
| Temple University | M,D* |
| Texas A&M University | M,D |
| Texas State University | M |
| UNB Fredericton | M |
| United States Sports Academy | M |
| Universidad Metropolitana | M |
| University of Alberta | M,D |
| University of Arkansas | M,D |
| University of Florida | M,D |
| The University of Iowa | M,D |
| University of Louisiana at Monroe | M |
| University of Manitoba | M |
| University of Mississippi | M,D |
| University of Montana | M,D |
| University of Nebraska at Kearney | M |
| University of New Hampshire | M |
| The University of North Carolina at Greensboro | M |
| University of Rhode Island | M |
| The University of Tennessee | M,D |
| The University of Toledo | M,D |
| University of Utah | M,D |
| University of Waterloo | M,D |
| University of Wisconsin–La Crosse | M |
| University of Wisconsin–Milwaukee | M* |
| Utah State University | M,D |
| Virginia Commonwealth University | M |
| Western Illinois University | M |
| Western Kentucky University | M |
| West Virginia University | M,D |

## REHABILITATION COUNSELING

| | |
|---|---|
| Adler University | M |
| Alabama Agricultural and Mechanical University | M,O |
| Alabama State University | M |
| Arkansas State University | M,O |
| Assumption University | M,O |
| Ball State University | M,D |
| Barry University | M,O |
| Bayamón Central University | M,O |
| California State University, Fresno | M |
| California State University, Los Angeles | M,D |
| California State University, San Bernardino | M |

| | |
|---|---|
| Cambridge College | M,O |
| Central Connecticut State University | M,O |
| Coppin State University | M |
| East Carolina University | M,D,O |
| East Central University | M |
| Edinboro University of Pennsylvania | M,O |
| Emporia State University | M |
| Fort Valley State University | M |
| The George Washington University | M |
| Georgia State University | M |
| Hofstra University | M,O |
| Hunter College of the City University of New York | M |
| Illinois Institute of Technology | M,D |
| Kent State University | M |
| Langston University | M |
| Louisiana State University Health Sciences Center | M |
| Maryville University of Saint Louis | M |
| Mercer University | M,D |
| Michigan State University | M,D,O |
| Minnesota State University Mankato | M |
| Mississippi State University | M,D,O |
| Montana State University Billings | M |
| Mount Mary University | M,O |
| North Carolina Agricultural and Technical State University | M,D |
| Northeastern Illinois University | M |
| Ohio University | M,D |
| Pontifical Catholic University of Puerto Rico | M |
| Rutgers University - Newark | M,D |
| St. Bonaventure University | M,O |
| Salve Regina University | M,O |
| San Diego State University | M |
| South Carolina State University | M |
| Southern University and Agricultural and Mechanical College | M |
| Springfield College | M |
| Texas Tech University Health Sciences Center | M |
| Thomas University | M |
| University at Buffalo, the State University of New York | M,D,O |
| The University of Arizona | M,D |
| University of Arkansas | M,D |
| University of Arkansas at Little Rock | M,O |
| University of Idaho | M,O |
| The University of Iowa | M,D |
| University of Kentucky | M,D |
| University of Maryland, College Park | M,D,O |
| University of Maryland Eastern Shore | M |
| University of Massachusetts Boston | M |
| University of Memphis | M,D |
| University of Northern Colorado | M,D |
| University of North Texas | M,D,O |
| University of Pittsburgh | M,D* |
| University of Puerto Rico at Rio Piedras | M |
| The University of Scranton | M |
| University of South Carolina | M,O |
| University of Southern Maine | M,O |
| University of South Florida | M,D,O |
| The University of Tennessee | M,D |
| The University of Texas at Austin | M,D |
| The University of Texas at El Paso | M |
| The University of Texas Rio Grande Valley | M,D |
| The University of Texas Southwestern Medical Center | M |
| University of the District of Columbia | M |
| University of Wisconsin–Madison | M,D |
| University of Wisconsin–Stout | M |
| Utah State University | M |
| Virginia Commonwealth University | M |
| Wayne State University | M,D,O |
| Western Oregon University | M |
| Western Washington University | M |
| West Virginia University | M,D |
| Wilberforce University | M |
| Winston-Salem State University | M |
| Wright State University | M |

## REHABILITATION SCIENCES

| | |
|---|---|
| Alabama State University | M |
| Augusta University | D |
| Boston University | M,D |
| Central Michigan University | M,D |
| Concordia University Wisconsin | M |
| Duquesne University | M,D |
| East Carolina University | M,D,O |
| East Stroudsburg University of Pennsylvania | M |
| George Mason University | D,O |
| Indiana University-Purdue University Indianapolis | M,D |
| Jackson State University | M |
| Lasell College | M |
| Logan University | M,D |
| Loma Linda University | M,D |
| Marquette University | M,D |
| McGill University | M,D,O |
| McMaster University | M,D |
| Medical University of South Carolina | D |
| New York University | M,D |
| Northwestern University | D |
| The Ohio State University | D |
| Old Dominion University | D |
| Queen's University at Kingston | M,D |
| Salus University | M,O |
| Stony Brook University, State University of New York | M,D,O |
| Temple University | M,D* |
| Texas Tech University Health Sciences Center | D |
| Université de Montréal | O |
| University at Buffalo, the State University of New York | O |
| The University of Alabama at Birmingham | D |
| University of Alberta | M,D |
| The University of British Columbia | M,D |
| University of Colorado Denver | D |
| University of Florida | D |
| University of Illinois at Urbana-Champaign | M,D |
| The University of Iowa | M,D |
| The University of Kansas | M,D |
| University of Kentucky | D |
| University of Manitoba | M,D |
| University of Maryland, Baltimore | D |
| University of Maryland Eastern Shore | M |
| University of Northern Colorado | M,D |
| University of North Texas Health Science Center at Fort Worth | M,D |
| University of Oklahoma Health Sciences Center | M |
| University of Ottawa | M |
| University of Pittsburgh | M,D* |
| University of South Carolina | M,O |
| University of South Florida | D |
| The University of Texas Medical Branch | D |
| University of Toronto | M,D |
| The University of Tulsa | M |
| University of Utah | D |
| University of Vermont | D |
| University of Washington | M,D |
| University of Wisconsin–La Crosse | M |
| University of Wisconsin–Milwaukee | D* |
| Virginia Commonwealth University | D |
| Washington University in St. Louis | D |
| Western Michigan University | M |

## RELIABILITY ENGINEERING

| | |
|---|---|
| Arizona State University at Tempe | M |
| Rutgers University - New Brunswick | M,D |
| University of Maryland, College Park | M,D |
| The University of Tennessee | M,D |

## RELIGION

| | |
|---|---|
| Abilene Christian University | M,D |
| Ambrose University | M,O |
| The American University of Rome | M |
| Amridge University | M,D |
| Arizona State University at Tempe | M,D,O |
| Athens State University | M |
| Baylor University | M,D |
| Bethany Theological Seminary | M,O |
| Bethel Seminary | M,D,O |
| Bethesda University | M |
| Beulah Heights University | M |
| Biola University | M,D,O |
| Bob Jones University | M,D,O |
| Boston University | M,D |
| Briercrest Seminary | M |
| Brown University | D |
| Bryn Athyn College of the New Church | M |
| Cairn University | M |
| California State University, Long Beach | M |
| Calvin Theological Seminary | M,D |
| Canadian Southern Baptist Seminary | M |
| The Catholic University of America | M,D,O |
| Charlotte Christian College and Theological Seminary | M,D |
| Chicago Theological Seminary | M,D |
| Christian Brothers University | M |
| Christian Theological Seminary | M,D |
| Cincinnati Christian University | M |
| Claremont Graduate University | M,D |
| Claremont Lincoln University | M |
| Claremont School of Theology | M,D |
| Clarks Summit University | M,D |
| Columbia University | M,D |
| Concordia University (Canada) | M,D |
| Concordia University Chicago | M |
| Concordia University Irvine | M |
| Concordia University of Edmonton | M |
| Cornell University | M,D |
| Dallas Baptist University | M |
| Dallas Theological Seminary | M,D,O |
| Delta State University | M |
| Denver Seminary | M,D,O |
| Drew University | M,D,O |
| Duke University | M,D |
| Earlham School of Religion | M |
| Eastern Mennonite University | M,O |
| East Texas Baptist University | M |
| Elms College | M |
| Emory University | D |
| Faith Baptist Bible College and Theological Seminary | M |
| Florida International University | M |
| Florida State University | M,D |
| Fordham University | M,D,O |
| The General Theological Seminary | M,D,O |
| George Mason University | M |
| Georgetown University | M,D |
| The George Washington University | M |
| Georgia State University | M |
| Gordon-Conwell Theological Seminary | M,D |
| Grace College of Divinity | M |
| Graceland University (IA) | M |
| Graduate Theological Union | M,D,O |
| Grand Rapids Theological Seminary of Cornerstone University | M |
| Hardin-Simmons University | M |
| Harrison Middleton University | M,D |
| Hartford Seminary | M,D,O |
| Harvard University | D* |
| Heritage Christian University | M |
| Hope International University | M |
| Iliff School of Theology | M,D |
| Indiana University Bloomington | M,D |
| The Jewish Theological Seminary | M,D |
| John Carroll University | M |
| Kentucky Christian University | M |
| Knox Theological Seminary | M |
| Lancaster Theological Seminary | M,D,O |
| La Sierra University | M |
| Lee University | M |
| Liberty University | M,D |
| Lincoln Christian University | M |
| Loma Linda University | M |
| Louisville Presbyterian Theological Seminary | M,D |
| Lutheran Theological Seminary Saskatoon | M,D |
| Luther Rice College & Seminary | M,D |
| Maranatha Baptist University | M |
| McGill University | M,D |
| McMaster University | M,D |
| Memorial University of Newfoundland | M |
| Milligan University | M,D,O |
| Missouri State University | M,O |
| Moody Theological Seminary–Michigan | M,O |
| Mount St. Joseph University | M,O |
| Mount Saint Mary's University (CA) | M,D,O |
| Naropa University | M |
| Nashotah House Theological Seminary | M,D,O |
| New Saint Andrews College | M,O |
| New York University | M,O |
| Northern Seminary | M,D |
| Northwestern University | M,D |
| Northwest Nazarene University | M,D |
| Nyack College | M |
| Oblate School of Theology | M,D,O |
| Olivet Nazarene University | M |
| Omega Graduate School | M,D |
| Pacific School of Religion | M,D,O |
| Pepperdine University | M |
| Princeton Theological Seminary | M,D |
| Princeton University | D |
| Queen's University at Kingston | M |
| Reformed Theological Seminary–Charlotte Campus | M,D |
| Reformed Theological Seminary–Houston Campus | M |
| Reformed Theological Seminary–Jackson Campus | M,D,O |
| Reformed Theological Seminary–Washington D.C. | M |
| Regent University | M,D |
| Rice University | D |
| The Robert E. Webber Institute for Worship Studies | M,D |
| Rutgers University - New Brunswick | M,O |
| Saint John's Seminary (MA) | M |
| St. Joseph's Seminary | M |
| Saint Mary's University (Canada) | M |
| Salve Regina University | M,D |
| Santa Clara University | M,D,O |
| Seattle Pacific University | M,O |
| The Seattle School of Theology and Psychology | M |
| Selma University | M |
| Seton Hall University | M,O |
| Sioux Falls Seminary | M |
| Southern Adventist University | M |
| The Southern Baptist Theological Seminary | M,D |
| Southern California Seminary | M,D |
| Southern Evangelical Seminary | M,D,O |
| Southern Methodist University | M,D |
| Southwestern Assemblies of God University | M |
| Stanford University | D |
| SUM Bible College & Theological Seminary | M |
| Syracuse University | M,D |
| Temple University | M,D* |
| Trevecca Nazarene University | M |
| Trinity Baptist College | M |
| Trinity International University Florida | M,O |
| Trinity School for Ministry | M,D,O |
| Union University | M,D |
| United Lutheran Seminary | M,D |
| United Lutheran Seminary | M,D,O |
| United Theological Seminary of the Twin Cities | M,D,O |
| Université de Montréal | M,D,O |
| Université de Sherbrooke | M,D,O |
| Université du Québec à Montréal | M,D |
| The University of British Columbia | M,D |
| University of Calgary | M,D |
| University of California, Berkeley | D |
| University of California, Riverside | M,D |
| University of California, Santa Barbara | M,D |
| University of Chicago | M,D |
| University of Colorado Boulder | M |
| University of Denver | M,D,O |
| University of Florida | M,D |
| University of Georgia | M |
| University of Hawaii at Manoa | M |
| University of Illinois at Urbana-Champaign | M |
| The University of Iowa | M,D |
| The University of Kansas | M,O |
| University of Lethbridge | M,D |
| The University of Manchester | D |
| University of Manitoba | M,D |
| University of Michigan | M,D |
| University of Minnesota, Twin Cities Campus | M,D |
| The University of North Carolina at Chapel Hill | M,D |
| The University of North Carolina at Charlotte | M |
| University of Notre Dame | M |
| University of Ottawa | M,D |
| University of Pennsylvania | D |
| University of Regina | M |
| University of St. Thomas (MN) | M |
| University of St. Thomas (TX) | M |
| University of Saskatchewan | M |
| University of South Africa | M,D |
| University of South Carolina | M |
| University of South Florida | M,D |
| The University of Tennessee | M,D |
| University of the Cumberlands | M |
| University of the West | M,D |
| University of Toronto | M,D |
| University of Valley Forge | M |
| University of Virginia | M,D |
| University of Washington | M,D |
| University of Waterloo | D |
| The University of Winnipeg | M |
| Université Laval | M,D |
| Vancouver School of Theology | M,O |
| Vanderbilt University | M,D* |
| Vanguard University of Southern California | M |
| Virginia University of Lynchburg | M,D |
| Wake Forest University | M |
| Walla Walla University | M |
| Washington Adventist University | M |
| Washington University in St. Louis | M |
| Wayland Baptist University | M |
| Wesley Biblical Seminary | M |
| Western Michigan University | M,O |
| Western Seminary - Portland | M,O |
| Westminster Seminary California | M |
| Westminster Theological Seminary | M,D,O |
| Wilfrid Laurier University | M,D |
| Won Institute of Graduate Studies | M |
| Wycliffe College | M,D,O |
| Yale University | D |
| Yeshiva Derech Chaim | D |

## RELIGIOUS EDUCATION

| | |
|---|---|
| Andrews University | M,D,O |
| Asbury Theological Seminary | M,D,O |
| Biola University | M,D,O |
| Boston College | M,D,O |
| Brandeis University | M,O |
| Calvary University | M |
| Calvin Theological Seminary | M,D |
| Capital University | M |
| Carolina Christian College | M |
| Claremont School of Theology | M,D |
| Clarks Summit University | M,D |
| Columbia International University | M,D,O |
| Concordia University Chicago | M |
| Concordia University, Nebraska | M |
| Dallas Baptist University | M |
| Dallas Theological Seminary | M,D,O |
| Felician University | M,O |
| Fordham University | M,D,O |
| Gardner-Webb University | M,D |
| Garrett-Evangelical Theological Seminary | M,D |
| Global University | M,D |
| Gratz College | M,D |
| Hebrew College | M,O |
| Hebrew Union College–Jewish Institute of Religion (NY) | M |
| Houston Baptist University | M,D |
| Inter American University of Puerto Rico, Metropolitan Campus | D |
| Interdenominational Theological Center | M,D |
| The Jewish Theological Seminary | M,D |
| Lancaster Theological Seminary | M,D,O |
| La Sierra University | M |
| Liberty University | M,D |
| Lincoln Christian Seminary | M,D |
| Loyola University Chicago | M,O |
| Maple Springs Baptist Bible College and Seminary | M,D,O |
| Midwestern Baptist Theological Seminary | M,D,O |
| Milligan University | M,D,O |
| Moody Theological Seminary–Michigan | M,O |
| Newman Theological College | M,O |
| New Orleans Baptist Theological Seminary | M,D |
| Oral Roberts University | M,D |
| Palm Beach Atlantic University | M |
| Pfeiffer University | M |
| Phillips Theological Seminary | M,D |
| Pontifical Catholic University of Puerto Rico | M |
| Providence University College & Theological Seminary | M,D,O |
| Reformed Theological Seminary–Jackson Campus | M,D,O |
| Regent University | M,D,O |
| Rochester University | M |
| St. Augustine's Seminary of Toronto | M,O |
| Saint Mary's University of Minnesota | M |
| Saints Cyril and Methodius Seminary | M |

*M—masters degree; D—doctorate; O—other advanced degree; *—Close-Up and/or Display*

| | |
|---|---|
| Selma University | M |
| Shasta Bible College | M |
| Southeastern Baptist Theological Seminary | M,D |
| Southern Adventist University | M |
| Southern Evangelical Seminary | M,D,O |
| Southwestern Assemblies of God University | M |
| Southwestern Baptist Theological Seminary | M,D |
| Trinity International University | M,D,O |
| Unification Theological Seminary | M,D |
| Union Presbyterian Seminary | M,D |
| University of Detroit Mercy | M,D,O |
| University of St. Michael's College | M,D,O |
| University of St. Thomas (TX) | M,D |
| University of St. Thomas (MN) | M |
| University of San Francisco | M,D |
| Vancouver School of Theology | M,O |
| Vanguard University of Southern California | M |
| Walsh University | M |
| Wesley Biblical Seminary | M |
| Wheaton College | M |
| Xavier University | M* |
| Yeshiva University | M,D,O |

## REPRODUCTIVE BIOLOGY

| | |
|---|---|
| Eastern Virginia Medical School | M |
| Rutgers University - New Brunswick | M,D |
| Tufts University | M,D |
| The University of British Columbia | M,D |
| University of Hawaii at Manoa | M,D |
| University of Saskatchewan | M,D |
| University of Wyoming | M,D |

## RHETORIC

| | |
|---|---|
| Abilene Christian University | M |
| Arizona State University at Tempe | M,D,O |
| Ball State University | M,D |
| Bob Jones University | M,D,O |
| Boise State University | M |
| Bowling Green State University | M,D |
| Brigham Young University | M |
| California State University, Dominguez Hills | M,O |
| California State University, Fresno | M |
| California State University, Northridge | M |
| California State University, Stanislaus | M,O |
| Carnegie Mellon University | M,D |
| The Catholic University of America | M,D,O |
| Clemson University | M,D |
| Colorado State University | M |
| DePaul University | M |
| Duquesne University | M,D |
| East Carolina University | M,D,O |
| Eastern Washington University | M |
| Florida State University | M,D |
| George Mason University | M,D,O |
| Georgia State University | M,D |
| Indiana University Bloomington | M,D |
| Iowa State University of Science and Technology | M,D |
| James Madison University | M |
| Kent State University | M,D |
| Michigan State University | M,D |
| Monmouth University | M |
| New Mexico Highlands University | M |
| New Mexico State University | M,D |
| North Carolina State University | M,D |
| North Dakota State University | M,D |
| Northern Arizona University | M,D,O |
| Northern Kentucky University | M,O |
| Northwestern University | M,D |
| Ohio University | M,D |
| Old Dominion University | M |
| Oregon State University | M |
| Rensselaer Polytechnic Institute | M,D |
| Rowan University | O |
| St. Cloud State University | M |
| San Diego State University | M |
| Southern Illinois University Carbondale | M,D |
| Syracuse University | M,D |
| Texas Christian University | M,D |
| Texas State University | M |
| Texas Tech University | M,D |
| Texas Woman's University | M,D |
| The University of Alabama | M,D |
| The University of Alabama at Birmingham | M |
| The University of Arizona | M,D |
| University of Arkansas at Little Rock | M |
| University of California, Berkeley | D |
| University of Central Oklahoma | M |
| University of Dayton | M |
| The University of Findlay | M,D |
| University of Houston - Downtown | M |
| The University of Iowa | M,D |
| University of Louisiana at Lafayette | M,D |
| University of Louisville | M,D |
| University of Massachusetts Amherst | M,D |
| University of Michigan–Flint | M |
| University of Nebraska–Lincoln | M,D |
| University of North Alabama | M |
| The University of North Carolina at Greensboro | M,D |
| University of Oklahoma | M,D |
| University of Southern California | D |
| The University of Tennessee at Chattanooga | M |
| The University of Texas at El Paso | M,D,O |
| University of Utah | M,D |
| University of Wisconsin–Madison | M,D |
| University of Wisconsin–Milwaukee | M,D,O* |
| Wayne State University | M,D |
| Western Carolina University | M,O |

## RISK MANAGEMENT

| | |
|---|---|
| Boston University | M |
| Brandeis University | M |
| California State University, Fullerton | M |
| Concordia University Wisconsin | M |
| DePaul University | M,D |
| Florida State University | M,D |
| Georgia State University | M,D,O |
| Husson University | M |
| Iona College | M,O |
| Johns Hopkins University | M |
| Loyola University Chicago | M |
| Metropolitan College of New York | M |
| New York University | M |
| Ohio Dominican University | M |
| Pace University | M |
| Queens College of the City University of New York | M |
| St. John's University (NY) | M |
| Saint Peter's University | M |
| Temple University | D* |
| University of Colorado Denver | M |
| University of Connecticut | M,D |
| University of Michigan | M,D |
| University of Pennsylvania | M,D |
| University of Saint Mary | M |
| The University of Texas at Austin | M,D |
| University of Wisconsin–Madison | M,D |
| Yeshiva University | M |

## ROMANCE LANGUAGES

| | |
|---|---|
| Boston University | M,D |
| Columbia University | M,D |
| Cornell University | M,D |
| Hunter College of the City University of New York | M |
| Johns Hopkins University | M,D |
| Michigan State University | M,D |
| New York University | M,D |
| Northern Illinois University | M |
| Queens College of the City University of New York | M |
| San Diego State University | M |
| Stony Brook University, State University of New York | M |
| Texas Tech University | M,D |
| University at Buffalo, the State University of New York | M,D |
| The University of Alabama | M,D |
| University of California, Berkeley | D |
| University of Chicago | M,D |
| University of Cincinnati | M,D |
| University of Illinois at Urbana-Champaign | D |
| University of Miami | D |
| University of Missouri | M,D |
| University of Missouri–Kansas City | M |
| University of New Orleans | M |
| The University of North Carolina at Chapel Hill | M,D |
| University of Notre Dame | M |
| University of Oregon | M,D |
| University of Pennsylvania | M,D |
| University of South Africa | M,D |
| The University of Texas at Austin | M,D |
| Washington University in St. Louis | D |
| Wayne State University | M,D |

## RURAL PLANNING AND STUDIES

| | |
|---|---|
| Brandon University | M,O |
| Dalhousie University | M |
| East Carolina University | M,O |
| Iowa State University of Science and Technology | D |
| University of Alaska Fairbanks | M |
| University of Guelph | M,D |
| University of Montana | M |
| University of Wyoming | M |
| Université Laval | O |

## RURAL SOCIOLOGY

| | |
|---|---|
| Auburn University | M |
| Cornell University | M,D |
| Iowa State University of Science and Technology | M,D |
| The Ohio State University | M,D |
| Penn State University Park | M,D,O* |
| University of Alberta | M,D |
| University of Missouri | M,D |
| University of Montana | M |
| University of Puerto Rico at Mayagüez | M |
| University of Wisconsin–Madison | M,D |

## RUSSIAN

| | |
|---|---|
| American University | M,O |
| Boston College | M |
| Brown University | M,D |
| Columbia University | M,D |
| Harvard University | D* |
| Kent State University | M,D |
| McGill University | M,D |
| Middlebury College | M,D |
| New York University | M |
| Penn State University Park | M,D* |
| Princeton University | D |
| The University of Arizona | M |
| University of California, Berkeley | D |
| University of Missouri | M |
| University of Oregon | M |
| University of South Africa | M,D |
| The University of Tennessee | D |
| University of Washington | M,D |
| University of Waterloo | M,D |
| Yale University | D |

## SAFETY ENGINEERING

| | |
|---|---|
| Embry-Riddle Aeronautical University–Prescott | M |
| Florida Institute of Technology | M |
| Indiana University Bloomington | M,D |
| Murray State University | M |
| New Jersey Institute of Technology | M,D |
| Rochester Institute of Technology | M |
| The University of Alabama at Birmingham | M |
| University of Minnesota, Duluth | M |
| University of Southern California | M,D,O |
| West Virginia University | M,D |

## SCANDINAVIAN LANGUAGES

| | |
|---|---|
| Cornell University | M,D |
| Harvard University | D* |
| University of California, Berkeley | D |
| University of California, Los Angeles | M |
| University of Massachusetts Amherst | M,D |
| University of Minnesota, Twin Cities Campus | M,D |
| University of Washington | M,D |
| University of Wisconsin–Madison | M,D |

## SCHOOL NURSING

| | |
|---|---|
| California State University, Fullerton | M,D |
| Cambridge College | M,D,O |
| Eastern Mennonite University | M,D |
| La Salle University | M,D,O |
| Lewis University | M,D |
| Rowan University | M,D,O |
| Seton Hall University | M,D |
| University of Illinois at Chicago | M,O |
| Wright State University | M |

## SCHOOL PSYCHOLOGY

| | |
|---|---|
| Abilene Christian University | M,O |
| Adelphi University | M |
| Adler University | M |
| Alabama Agricultural and Mechanical University | M,O |
| Alfred University | M,D,O |
| Alliant International University–Irvine | M,D,O |
| Alliant International University - Los Angeles | M,D,O |
| Alliant International University - San Diego | M,D,O |
| Alliant International University–San Francisco | M,D,O |
| Andrews University | M,O |
| Appalachian State University | M |
| Argosy University, Hawaii | M |
| Argosy University, Phoenix | M,D |
| Arkansas State University | M,O |
| Assumption University | M,O |
| Auburn University at Montgomery | M,O |
| Augusta University | M,O |
| Azusa Pacific University | M,D |
| Ball State University | M,D,O |
| Barry University | M,O |
| Baylor University | M,D,O |
| Brigham Young University | M,D,O |
| Brooklyn College of the City University of New York | M,O |
| California Baptist University | M |
| California State University, Chico | M |
| California State University, Dominguez Hills | M |
| California State University, Fresno | M,O |
| California State University, Los Angeles | M,D |
| California State University, Northridge | M |
| California State University, Sacramento | M,D,O |
| California University of Pennsylvania | M |
| Cambridge College | M,O |
| Campbellsville University | M |
| Capella University | M,D |
| Central Connecticut State University | M,O |
| Central Michigan University | D,O |
| Central Washington University | O |
| Chapman University | M,D,O |
| The Chicago School of Professional Psychology | D,O |
| The Chicago School of Professional Psychology at Washington DC | O |
| The Citadel, The Military College of South Carolina | M,O |
| The College of New Rochelle | M |
| College of Saint Elizabeth | M,D |
| College of St. Joseph | M |
| The College of Saint Rose | M,O |
| Creighton University | M |
| DePaul University | M,D |
| Doane University | M,D,O |
| Duquesne University | M,D |
| Eastern Illinois University | M,O |
| Eastern Kentucky University | M,O |
| Eastern University | M,O |
| Eastern Washington University | M,O |
| East Tennessee State University | M |
| Edinboro University of Pennsylvania | M,O |
| Emporia State University | M,O |
| Evangel University | M |
| Fairfield University | M,O |
| Fairleigh Dickinson University, Metropolitan Campus | M,D |
| Florida Gulf Coast University | M |
| Fordham University | M,D |
| Fort Hays State University | O |
| Francis Marion University | M,O |
| Fresno Pacific University | M |
| Gallaudet University | M,D,O |
| Gardner-Webb University | M |
| George Fox University | M,O |
| Georgian Court University | M,O |
| Georgia Southern University | M,O |
| Georgia State University | M,D,O |
| Grand Valley State University | M,O |
| Hofstra University | M,D |
| Hood College | M |
| Howard University | M,D |
| Humboldt State University | M |
| Husson University | M |
| Idaho State University | M,D,O |
| Illinois State University | M,D,O |
| Immaculata University | M,D,O |
| Indiana State University | M,D,O |
| Indiana University Bloomington | M,D,O |
| Indiana University of Pennsylvania | D,O |
| Indiana University South Bend | M,O |
| Inter American University of Puerto Rico, Metropolitan Campus | M,D |
| Inter American University of Puerto Rico, San Germán Campus | M,D |
| Iona College | M,O |
| Jackson State University | M |
| James Madison University | M,D,O |
| Kean University | D,O |
| Kent State University | M,D,O |
| La Sierra University | M,O |
| Lehigh University | D,O |
| Lesley University | M,D,O |
| Lewis & Clark College | M,O |
| Liberty University | M,D,O |
| Lindenwood University | M,D,O |
| Lipscomb University | M,D,O |
| Long Island University - Hudson | M,O |
| Long Island University - Post | M,D,O |
| Louisiana State University and Agricultural & Mechanical College | M,D |
| Louisiana State University in Shreveport | O |
| Loyola Marymount University | M |
| Loyola University Chicago | D,O |
| Marist College | M,O |
| Marshall University | O |
| McGill University | M,D,O |
| McNeese State University | M,O |
| Mercer University | M,D |
| Mercy College | M |
| Michigan State University | M,D,O |
| MidAmerica Nazarene University | M |
| Middle Tennessee State University | M,O |
| Millersville University of Pennsylvania | M |
| Minnesota State University Mankato | M,D |
| Minnesota State University Moorhead | M,O |
| Minot State University | O |
| Mississippi State University | M,D,O |
| Monmouth University | M,D,O |
| Montana State University | M,D,O |
| Mount Saint Vincent University | M |
| Murray State University | M,D,O |
| National Louis University | M,D,O |
| National University | M,O |
| New Mexico State University | M,D,O |
| Niagara University | M |
| Nicholls State University | M,O |
| North Carolina State University | D |
| North Dakota State University | M,D |
| Northeastern University | M,D,O |
| Northern Arizona University | M,D,O |
| Northern Vermont University–Johnson | M |
| Northwest Nazarene University | M |
| Nova Southeastern University | M,D,O |
| Old Dominion University | M,D,O |
| Oregon State University | M,D |
| Oregon State University–Cascades | M |
| Ottawa University | M |
| Our Lady of the Lake University | M |
| Pace University | M,D |
| Penn State University Park | M,D,O* |
| Philadelphia College of Osteopathic Medicine | M,D,O |
| Phillips Graduate University | M |
| Pittsburg State University | O |
| Plymouth State University | O |
| Purdue University Northwest | M |
| Queens College of the City University of New York | M,O |
| Quincy University | M |
| Radford University | O |
| Rhode Island College | M,O |
| Rider University | O |
| Roberts Wesleyan College | M,D |
| Rochester Institute of Technology | M,O |
| Roosevelt University | M |
| Rowan University | M,O |
| Rutgers University - New Brunswick | M,D |
| St. John's University (NY) | M,D |
| Saint Mary's College of California | M,O |
| Sam Houston State University | M,D,O |
| San Diego State University | M |
| San Francisco State University | M,O |
| Seattle University | M,O |
| Seton Hall University | M |
| Sonoma State University | M |
| Southern Connecticut State University | M,O |
| Southern Illinois University Edwardsville | O |
| Southwestern Oklahoma State University | O |
| State University of New York at Plattsburgh | M,O |
| Stephen F. Austin State University | M |
| Syracuse University | M,D,O |
| Teachers College, Columbia University | M,D,O |
| Temple University | M,D,O* |
| Texas A&M University | M,D |
| Texas A&M University–Central Texas | M,O |
| Texas State University | O |
| Texas Woman's University | M,D,O |
| Towson University | M |

Trinity University M
Tufts University M,O
Union College (KY) M
University of Alberta M,D
The University of Arizona D,O
The University of British Columbia M,D,O
University of Calgary M,D
University of California, Riverside M,D,O
University of California, Santa Barbara M,D,O
University of Central Arkansas M,D,O
University of Central Florida O
University of Central Oklahoma M
University of Cincinnati D,O
University of Colorado Denver M,D
University of Dayton M,O
University of Delaware M,D,O
University of Denver M,D,O
University of Detroit Mercy M,D,O
University of Florida M,D,O
University of Hartford M
University of Houston–Clear Lake M
University of Houston–Victoria M
The University of Iowa M,D,O
The University of Kansas D,O
University of Kentucky M,D,O
University of La Verne M,O
University of Louisville M,D
University of Lynchburg M
University of Manitoba M,D
University of Maryland, College Park M,D,O
University of Massachusetts Amherst M,D,O
University of Massachusetts Boston M,D
University of Memphis M,D,O
University of Minnesota, Twin Cities Campus M,D,O
University of Missouri M,D,O
University of Missouri–St. Louis M,O
University of Montana M,D,O
University of Nebraska at Kearney M,O
University of Nebraska at Omaha M,D,O
University of Nebraska–Lincoln M,D,O
The University of North Carolina at Chapel Hill M,D
The University of North Carolina at Greensboro M,D,O
University of Northern Colorado O
University of Northern Iowa M,O
University of Oregon M,D
University of Phoenix - Las Vegas Campus M
University of Rhode Island M,D
University of San Diego M
University of Saskatchewan M,D
University of South Carolina D
University of South Dakota M,D,O
University of Southern Maine M,D
The University of Tennessee M,D,O
The University of Tennessee at Chattanooga M,D,O
The University of Texas at Austin M,D
The University of Texas at San Antonio M,O
The University of Texas at Tyler M
The University of Texas Rio Grande Valley M
University of the Pacific M,D,O
University of the Virgin Islands M,D,O
The University of Toledo M,D,O
University of Utah M,D,O
University of Vermont M
University of Virginia M,D
University of Washington M,D
University of Wisconsin–Eau Claire M,O
University of Wisconsin–La Crosse M,O
University of Wisconsin–Milwaukee M,D,O*
University of Wisconsin–River Falls M,O
University of Wisconsin–Stout M,O
University of Wisconsin–Superior M
University of Wisconsin–Whitewater M,O
Utah State University M,D
Valparaiso University M,O
Wayne State University M,D,O
Western Illinois University M,O
Western Kentucky University M,O
Wichita State University M,D,O
William & Mary M,O*
William James College M,D,O
Worcester State University M,O
Yeshiva University D
Youngstown State University M,D,O

## SCIENCE EDUCATION

Adams State University M
Alabama Agricultural and Mechanical University M,O
Alabama State University M,O
Alverno College M
American University of Puerto Rico - Bayamon M
Andrews University M,D,O
Antioch University New England M,D
Appalachian State University M
Arcadia University M,D,O
Arkansas State University M,O
Asbury University M
Athabasca University M,O
Augustana University M
Aurora University M
Austin Peay State University M
Bard College M
Binghamton University, State University of New York M
Bloomsburg University of Pennsylvania M
Blue Mountain College M
Boston College M,D,O
Bowling Green State University M
Bridgewater State University M
Brigham Young University M,D
Brooklyn College of the City University of New York M
Brown University M
Buffalo State College, State University of New York M
California Baptist University M
California State University, Long Beach M
California State University, Northridge M
California University of Pennsylvania M
Cambridge College M,D,O
Campbellsville University M
Caribbean University M,D
Carlow University M
Carthage College M,O
Catawba College M
Central Connecticut State University M,O
Central Michigan University M
Chatham University M
The Citadel, The Military College of South Carolina M,O
City College of the City University of New York M
Clarion University of Pennsylvania M
Clark Atlanta University M
Clemson University D,O
Cleveland State University M
College of Charleston M
The Colorado College M
Columbia University M,D,O
Columbus State University M,O
Concordia University (United States) M,D
Converse College M
Delaware State University M,D
DePaul University M,D
Duquesne University M
East Carolina University M,O
Eastern Kentucky University M
Eastern Michigan University M
Eastern University M,O
Elizabeth City State University M
Elms College M,O
Fairleigh Dickinson University, Metropolitan Campus M
Fitchburg State University M
Florida Agricultural and Mechanical University M
Florida Atlantic University M,D
Florida Gulf Coast University M
Florida International University M,D,O
Florida State University M,D
Fresno Pacific University M
George Mason University M
The George Washington University M
Georgia State University M,D
Grambling State University M,D,O
Grand Canyon University M,D,O
Hamline University M,D
Harrison Middleton University M,D
Heritage University M
Hofstra University M,D,O
Hood College M,O
Houston Baptist University M,D
Hunter College of the City University of New York M
Illinois Institute of Technology M,D
Indiana State University M,D
Indiana University Bloomington M,D,O
Instituto Tecnológico y de Estudios Superiores de Monterrey, Campus Monterrey M,D
Inter American University of Puerto Rico, Arecibo Campus M
Inter American University of Puerto Rico, Metropolitan Campus M
Inter American University of Puerto Rico, Ponce Campus M
Inter American University of Puerto Rico, San Germán Campus M
Iona College M
Iowa State University of Science and Technology M
Jackson State University M,D
Kennesaw State University M
Lake Forest College M
Laurentian University O
Lawrence Technological University M,O
Lebanon Valley College M,O
Lehman College of the City University of New York M
Lesley University M,D,O
Lewis University M
Manhattanville College M,O
McDaniel College M,O
McNeese State University O
Mercer University M,D,O
Metropolitan State University M
Michigan Technological University M,D,O
Middle Tennessee State University M,D
Millersville University of Pennsylvania M,D
Minnesota State University Mankato M
Minot State University M
Mississippi College M,D,O
Missouri State University M,O
Molloy College M,O
Montclair State University M
Morehead State University M
Morgan State University M,D
National Louis University M,D,O
New Mexico Institute of Mining and Technology M
New York University M,D,O
North Carolina Agricultural and Technical State University M
North Carolina State University M,D
North Dakota State University D
Northeastern Illinois University M
Northeastern State University M
Northern Arizona University M
Northern Michigan University M
Northern Vermont University–Lyndon M
Northwest Missouri State University M,O
Oregon State University M,D
Our Lady of the Lake University M
Pacific University M
Portland State University M,D,O
Purdue University M,D,O
Purdue University Global M
Purdue University Northwest M
Queens College of the City University of New York M,O
Quinnipiac University M
Regent University M,D,O
Rice University M,D
Rowan University M,O
Rutgers University - New Brunswick M,D
St. John's University (NY) D
Saint Xavier University M
Salem State University M
San Diego State University M,D
Seattle Pacific University M
Shippensburg University of Pennsylvania M
Slippery Rock University of Pennsylvania M
Smith College M
South Carolina State University M
Southern Connecticut State University M,O
Southern University and Agricultural and Mechanical College D
Southwestern Oklahoma State University M
State University of New York at New Paltz M,O
State University of New York at Plattsburgh M
State University of New York College at Cortland M
State University of New York College at Old Westbury M
State University of New York College at Potsdam M
Stevenson University M
Stony Brook University, State University of New York M,D
SUNY Brockport M,O
Syracuse University M,D
Teachers College, Columbia University M,D
Teachers College of San Joaquin M
Temple University M*
Tennessee Technological University M,O
Texas A&M University–Kingsville M
Texas Christian University M,D
Texas Tech University M,D
Tufts University M,D
Universidad Nacional Pedro Henriquez Urena M
University at Buffalo, the State University of New York M,D,O
The University of Akron M
The University of Alabama in Huntsville M,D,O
University of Arkansas at Pine Bluff M
The University of British Columbia M,D
University of California, Berkeley M,D
University of California, San Diego D
University of Central Florida M,O
University of Chicago D
University of Colorado Denver M,D
University of Connecticut M,D
The University of Findlay M,D
University of Florida M,D,O
University of Georgia M,D,O
University of Illinois at Chicago D
University of Illinois at Urbana-Champaign M,D
University of Indianapolis M
The University of Iowa M,D
University of Lynchburg M
University of Maryland, Baltimore County M
University of Massachusetts Amherst M,D,O
University of Massachusetts Dartmouth M,D,O
University of Memphis M,D,O
University of Miami D
University of Minnesota, Twin Cities Campus M
University of Missouri M,D,O
University of Nebraska at Kearney M
University of Nebraska at Omaha M,O
University of New Hampshire M,D
University of New Mexico O
The University of North Carolina at Chapel Hill M
The University of North Carolina at Greensboro M,D,O
The University of North Carolina at Pembroke M
University of Northern Colorado M,D
University of Northern Iowa M
University of North Georgia M
University of Oklahoma M,D
University of Pennsylvania M,O
University of Phoenix–Online Campus M,O
University of Puerto Rico at Rio Piedras M,D
University of St. Francis (IL) M,D,O
University of San Diego M
University of South Africa M,D
University of South Alabama M,D
University of South Carolina M,D
University of South Dakota M
University of Southern Mississippi M,D
University of South Florida, St. Petersburg M
The University of Tennessee M,D,O
The University of Texas at Arlington M
The University of Texas at Dallas M
The University of Toledo M,D,O
University of Utah M,D
University of Vermont M,D
University of Victoria M,D
University of Virginia M,D,O
University of Washington M,D
University of Washington, Tacoma M
The University of West Alabama M
University of Wisconsin–Milwaukee M*
University of Wisconsin–River Falls M
University of Wisconsin–Stevens Point M
University of Wyoming M
Wagner College M
Walden University M,D,O
Warner University M
Wayland Baptist University M
Wayne State College M
Wayne State University M,D,O
Western Governors University M,O
Western Michigan University M,D,O
Western Oregon University M
Western Washington University M
Westfield State University M
Widener University M,D
Wisconsin Lutheran College M
Wright State University M,D
Youngstown State University M

## SECONDARY EDUCATION

Acacia University M
Alabama Agricultural and Mechanical University M,O
Alabama State University M,O
Alcorn State University M,O
American International College M,D,O
American Public University System M,D
Andrews University M,D,O
Aquinas College (TN) M
Arcadia University M,D,O
Argosy University, Atlanta M,D,O
Argosy University, Chicago M,D,O
Argosy University, Hawaii M,D
Argosy University, Los Angeles M,D
Argosy University, Northern Virginia M,D,O
Argosy University, Orange County M,D
Argosy University, Phoenix M,D,O
Argosy University, Seattle M,D
Argosy University, Tampa M,D,O
Argosy University, Twin Cities M,D,O
Arizona State University at Tempe M
Auburn University at Montgomery M,O
Augusta University M,O
Avila University M,O
Ball State University M
Bard College M
Bellarmine University M,D,O
Berry College M,O
Bethel University (MN) M,D,O
Binghamton University, State University of New York M
Blue Mountain College M
Bob Jones University M,D,O
Boston College M,D,O
Bowie State University M
Brandeis University M,O
Brandman University M,D
Brenau University M,O
Bridgewater State University M
Brooklyn College of the City University of New York M
Brown University M
Bushnell University M
Cabrini University M,D
California State University, Fullerton M
California State University, Long Beach M
California State University, Northridge M
California State University, Stanislaus M
California University of Pennsylvania M
Campbell University M
Canisius College M,O
Carroll University M
Carson-Newman University M
The Catholic University of America M,O
Centenary College of Louisiana M
Central Connecticut State University M,O

*M—masters degree; D—doctorate; O—other advanced degree; *—Close-Up and/or Display*

| | |
|---|---|
| Central Michigan University | M,D,O |
| Chadron State College | M,O |
| Chaminade University of Honolulu | M |
| Chapman University | M,D,O |
| Chatham University | M |
| Chestnut Hill College | M |
| Chicago State University | M |
| The Citadel, The Military College of South Carolina | M,O |
| City College of the City University of New York | M,O |
| Clemson University | M,D,O |
| Colgate University | M |
| The College of New Jersey | M |
| College of St. Joseph | M |
| The College of Saint Rose | M,O |
| College of Staten Island of the City University of New York | M |
| The Colorado College | M |
| Columbus State University | M,O |
| Concordia University (United States) | M,D |
| Concordia University Chicago | M |
| Concordia University, Nebraska | M |
| Converse College | M |
| Cornell University | M,D |
| Creighton University | M |
| Dakota Wesleyan University | M |
| Dallas Baptist University | M |
| Delta State University | M,D,O |
| DePaul University | M,D |
| DeSales University | M,O |
| Dominican University | M |
| Drew University | M,D,O |
| Drury University | M |
| Duquesne University | M |
| D'Youville College | M,D |
| Eastern Connecticut State University | M |
| Eastern Illinois University | M |
| Eastern Kentucky University | M |
| Eastern Michigan University | M |
| Eastern Nazarene College | M,O |
| Eastern New Mexico University | M |
| Eastern Oregon University | M |
| Eastern University | M,O |
| East Stroudsburg University of Pennsylvania | M,D |
| East Tennessee State University | M,O |
| Edinboro University of Pennsylvania | M |
| Elms College | M,O |
| Emory University | M,D |
| Endicott College | M |
| Evangel University | M |
| Fairfield University | M,O |
| Fayetteville State University | M |
| Florida Agricultural and Mechanical University | M |
| Florida Atlantic University | M |
| Fontbonne University | M |
| Frostburg State University | M,D |
| Gallaudet University | M,D,O |
| George Mason University | M |
| The George Washington University | M |
| Georgia College & State University | M |
| Georgia Southern University | M,O |
| Georgia State University | M,D |
| Gonzaga University | M,D |
| Gordon College | M,O |
| Goucher College | M,O |
| Grand Canyon University | M,D,O |
| Greenville University | M |
| Harding University | M,O |
| Hawaii Pacific University | M |
| High Point University | M,D |
| Hofstra University | M,D,O |
| Hood College | M,O |
| Hope International University | M |
| Howard University | M |
| Hunter College of the City University of New York | M |
| Idaho State University | M |
| Immaculata University | M,D,O |
| Indiana University Bloomington | M,D,O |
| Indiana University Northwest | M,O |
| Indiana University South Bend | M,O |
| Indiana University Southeast | M |
| Instituto Tecnologico de Santo Domingo | M,O |
| Ithaca College | M |
| Jacksonville State University | M |
| James Madison University | M |
| John Brown University | M |
| Johnson & Wales University | M |
| Kennesaw State University | M,D,O |
| Kent State University | M,D |
| Keuka College | M |
| Kutztown University of Pennsylvania | M,D |
| LaGrange College | M,O |
| Lake Forest College | M |
| Lancaster Bible College | M,D |
| La Salle University | M,O |
| Lee University | M,O |
| Lehman College of the City University of New York | M |
| Le Moyne College | M,O |
| Lenoir-Rhyne University | M |
| Lesley University | M,D,O |
| Lewis & Clark College | M |
| Lewis University | M |
| Lincoln University (MO) | M |
| Long Island University - Post | M,D,O |
| Louisiana State University and Agricultural & Mechanical College | M,D,O |
| Louisiana Tech University | M,D,O |
| Loyola Marymount University | M |
| Loyola University Chicago | M |
| Loyola University Maryland | M |
| Loyola University New Orleans | M |
| Manhattanville College | M,O |
| Mansfield University of Pennsylvania | M |
| Marquette University | M,D,O |
| Marymount University | M |
| Maryville University of Saint Louis | M,D |
| Marywood University | M |
| McDaniel College | M,O |
| McNeese State University | M,O |
| Medaille College | M |
| Mercer University | M,D,O |
| Mercer University | M,D,O |
| Mercy College | M,O |
| Mercyhurst University | M |
| Metropolitan State University | M |
| Middle Tennessee State University | M,O |
| Milligan University | M,D,O |
| Mississippi College | M,D,O |
| Mississippi State University | M,D,O |
| Missouri State University | M,O |
| Monmouth University | M,D,O |
| Montana State University Billings | M |
| Morehead State University | M |
| Mount St. Joseph University | M,O |
| Murray State University | M,D,O |
| National Louis University | M,D,O |
| Nebraska Christian College of Hope International University | M |
| Neumann University | M |
| New Jersey City University | M |
| New York University | M,D,O |
| Niagara University | M,O |
| Nicholls State University | M |
| Norfolk State University | M |
| North Carolina Agricultural and Technical State University | M |
| Northeastern Illinois University | M |
| Northern Arizona University | M,D,O |
| Northwestern Oklahoma State University | M |
| Northwestern State University of Louisiana | M,O |
| Northwestern University | M |
| Oakland City University | M,D |
| Oakland University | M,O |
| Ohio University | M,D |
| Old Dominion University | M |
| Olivet Nazarene University | M |
| Pacific Union College | M |
| Pacific University | M |
| Piedmont College | M,D,O |
| Pittsburg State University | M,O |
| Point Park University | M,D |
| Prescott College | M,D |
| Providence College | M |
| Purdue University Fort Wayne | M,O |
| Purdue University Global | M |
| Queens College of the City University of New York | M,O |
| Quinnipiac University | M |
| Regis University | M,O |
| Rhode Island College | M |
| Rider University | M |
| Roberts Wesleyan College | M |
| Rochester Institute of Technology | M |
| Rockford University | M |
| Roosevelt University | M |
| St. Bonaventure University | M |
| St. John's University (NY) | M |
| Saint Joseph's University | M,D,O |
| Saint Mary's University of Minnesota | M |
| Saint Peter's University | M,O |
| St. Thomas Aquinas College | M,O |
| Saint Xavier University | M |
| Salem College | M |
| Salem State University | M |
| Salisbury University | M |
| Samford University | M,D,O |
| San Diego State University | M |
| San Francisco State University | M,O |
| Seattle Pacific University | M |
| Siena Heights University | M,O |
| Sierra Nevada College | M |
| Simpson College | M |
| Slippery Rock University of Pennsylvania | M |
| Smith College | M |
| South Carolina State University | M |
| Southeast Missouri State University | M,D,O |
| Southern Oregon University | M |
| Southern University and Agricultural and Mechanical College | M |
| Southwestern Assemblies of God University | M |
| Spalding University | M |
| Springfield College | M,O |
| Spring Hill College | M |
| Stanford University | M |
| State University of New York at Fredonia | M |
| State University of New York at New Paltz | M |
| State University of New York at Oswego | M |
| State University of New York at Plattsburgh | M |
| State University of New York College at Cortland | M |
| State University of New York College at Geneseo | M |
| State University of New York College at Potsdam | M |
| Stephen F. Austin State University | M,D |
| Sul Ross State University | M |
| Tarleton State University | M |
| Teachers College, Columbia University | M,D |
| Temple University | M* |
| Tennessee Technological University | M,O |
| Texas A&M University–Commerce | M,D,O |
| Texas A&M University–Corpus Christi | M |
| Texas Southern University | M,D |
| Texas State University | M |
| Texas Tech University | M,D |
| Towson University | M |
| Trevecca Nazarene University | M,O |
| Trinity Washington University | M |
| Troy University | M |
| Tufts University | M,D |
| Union College (KY) | M |
| Universidad Metropolitana | M |
| The University of Akron | M |
| The University of Alabama | M,D,O |
| The University of Alabama at Birmingham | M |
| The University of Alabama in Huntsville | M,O |
| University of Alaska Southeast | M |
| University of Alberta | M,D |
| The University of Arizona | M,D |
| University of Arkansas | M,O |
| University of Arkansas at Little Rock | M |
| University of Arkansas at Pine Bluff | M |
| University of Bridgeport | M,D,O |
| University of California, Irvine | M,D |
| University of Central Oklahoma | M |
| University of Colorado Denver | M |
| University of Connecticut | M,D |
| University of Dayton | M |
| University of Guam | M |
| University of Illinois at Chicago | M,D |
| University of Indianapolis | M |
| The University of Iowa | M,D |
| University of Kentucky | M,D |
| University of La Verne | M,D,O |
| University of Louisiana at Monroe | M |
| University of Louisville | M,D,O |
| University of Mary Hardin-Baylor | M,D |
| University of Maryland, College Park | M,D,O |
| University of Massachusetts Amherst | M,D,O |
| University of Massachusetts Dartmouth | M,D,O |
| University of Memphis | M,D,O |
| University of Michigan–Flint | M,D,O |
| University of Mississippi | M,D,O |
| University of Missouri–St. Louis | M |
| University of Montevallo | M |
| University of Nebraska at Kearney | M |
| University of Nebraska at Omaha | M,O |
| University of Nevada, Las Vegas | M,D,O |
| University of Nevada, Reno | M,O |
| University of New Hampshire | M,O |
| University of New Mexico | M |
| University of North Alabama | M |
| The University of North Carolina at Chapel Hill | M |
| The University of North Carolina at Charlotte | M,D,O |
| The University of North Carolina Wilmington | M |
| University of Northern Iowa | M |
| University of North Florida | M |
| University of North Georgia | M |
| University of Pennsylvania | M |
| University of Phoenix - Bay Area Campus | M,D,O |
| University of Phoenix - Central Valley Campus | M |
| University of Phoenix - Hawaii Campus | M |
| University of Phoenix–Online Campus | M,O |
| University of Phoenix - Phoenix Campus | M |
| University of Phoenix - Sacramento Valley Campus | M,O |
| University of Phoenix - San Diego Campus | M |
| University of Puget Sound | M |
| University of St. Francis (IL) | M,D,O |
| University of Saint Francis (IN) | M |
| University of Saint Joseph | M |
| University of St. Thomas (TX) | M,D |
| The University of Scranton | M |
| University of South Alabama | M,D |
| University of South Carolina | M,D |
| University of South Dakota | M |
| University of Southern Indiana | M |
| University of South Florida | O |
| The University of Tennessee | M,D,O |
| The University of Tennessee at Chattanooga | M,D,O |
| The University of Tennessee at Martin | M |
| The University of Texas Rio Grande Valley | M,D |
| University of the Cumberlands | M,D,O |
| University of the District of Columbia | M |
| University of the Virgin Islands | M |
| The University of Toledo | M,D,O |
| University of Utah | M,D |
| University of Vermont | M |
| University of Washington, Bothell | M |
| The University of West Alabama | M |
| University of West Florida | M |
| University of Wisconsin–Eau Claire | M |
| University of Wisconsin–Milwaukee | M,D* |
| University of Wisconsin–Stevens Point | M |
| Utah State University | M |
| Valparaiso University | M,O |
| Vanderbilt University | M* |
| Virginia Wesleyan University | M |
| Wagner College | M |
| Wake Forest University | M |
| Washington State University | M,D |
| Washington University in St. Louis | M |
| Wayland Baptist University | M |
| Wayne State University | M,D,O |
| Webster University | M,O |
| Western Kentucky University | M,O |
| Western New Mexico University | M |
| Western Oregon University | M |
| Western Washington University | M |
| Westfield State University | M |
| West Virginia University | M,D |
| Wheaton College | M |
| Whittier College | M |
| Whitworth University | M |
| Wichita State University | M |
| William Carey University | M,O |
| Wilmington University | M,D |
| Wilson College | M |
| Winthrop University | M |
| Worcester State University | M,O |
| Wright State University | M |
| Xavier University | M* |

## SLAVIC LANGUAGES

| | |
|---|---|
| Brown University | M,D |
| Columbia University | M,D |
| Cornell University | M,D |
| Duke University | M,O |
| Florida State University | M |
| Harvard University | D* |
| Indiana University Bloomington | M,D |
| New York University | M |
| Northwestern University | D |
| The Ohio State University | M,D |
| Princeton University | D |
| Stanford University | D |
| University of Alberta | M,D |
| University of California, Berkeley | D |
| University of California, Los Angeles | M,D |
| University of Chicago | M |
| University of Illinois at Chicago | M,D |
| University of Illinois at Urbana-Champaign | M,D |
| The University of Kansas | M,D |
| University of Manitoba | M |
| University of Michigan | M,D |
| The University of North Carolina at Chapel Hill | D |
| University of Pittsburgh | M,D* |
| University of Southern California | M,D |
| The University of Texas at Austin | M,D |
| University of Toronto | M,D |
| University of Virginia | M,D |
| University of Washington | M,D |
| University of Wisconsin–Madison | M,D |
| Yale University | D |

## SOCIAL PSYCHOLOGY

| | |
|---|---|
| Adler University | M |
| Alliant International University - Los Angeles | D |
| Alvernia University | M |
| Alverno College | M |
| Andrews University | M |
| Argosy University, Atlanta | M,D,O |
| Argosy University, Chicago | M,D |
| Argosy University, Northern Virginia | M,D |
| Arizona State University at Tempe | M,D |
| Ball State University | M |
| Becker College | M |
| Bowling Green State University | M,D |
| Brandeis University | M,D |
| Brock University | M,D |
| Brooklyn College of the City University of New York | M,D |
| California State University, East Bay | M |
| California State University, Fullerton | M |
| Carnegie Mellon University | D |
| Claremont Graduate University | M,D,O |
| Clark University | D |
| College of St. Joseph | M |
| Concordia University (United States) | M |
| Cornell University | M,D |
| Delaware Valley University | M |
| Florida Agricultural and Mechanical University | M |
| Florida State University | D |
| Future Generations University | M |
| The George Washington University | D |
| Georgia State University | D |
| The Graduate Center, City University of New York | D |
| Harvard University | D* |
| Hofstra University | M,D |
| Howard University | M,D |
| Humboldt State University | M |
| Husson University | M |
| Indiana University Bloomington | D |
| Indiana University of Pennsylvania | M |
| Indiana University-Purdue University Indianapolis | M,D |
| Indiana Wesleyan University | M |
| Iowa State University of Science and Technology | M,D |
| Lesley University | M,D,O |
| Loyola University Chicago | M,O |
| Marquette University | M,D |
| Martin University | M |
| Marymount California University | M |
| Missouri Valley College | M |
| Mount Aloysius College | M |
| The New School | M,D |
| New York University | M,D,O |
| Norfolk State University | M,D |
| North Carolina State University | M,D |
| North Dakota State University | M,D |
| Northwestern University | D |
| The Ohio State University | D |
| Oregon State University–Cascades | M |
| Penn State Harrisburg | M,D,O |

| | |
|---|---|
| Queen's University at Kingston | M,D |
| Rutgers University - Newark | D |
| Rutgers University - New Brunswick | D |
| Sacred Heart University | M |
| Sage Graduate School | M |
| St. Bonaventure University | M,O |
| Saint Martin's University | M |
| San Francisco State University | M,O |
| Southwestern College (NM) | O |
| Stony Brook University, State University of New York | D |
| Syracuse University | D |
| Teachers College, Columbia University | M,D |
| Temple University | M,D,O* |
| Texas Christian University | M,D |
| Thomas Jefferson University | M |
| Thomas University | M |
| Université du Québec à Rimouski | M |
| University at Albany, State University of New York | M,D |
| University of Alaska Anchorage | M,D |
| University of Alaska Fairbanks | M,O |
| University of Bridgeport | M |
| The University of British Columbia | M,D |
| University of Central Arkansas | M |
| University of Connecticut | M,D |
| University of Delaware | D |
| University of Denver | D |
| University of Guelph | M,D |
| University of Hawaii at Manoa | M,D,O |
| University of Houston | M,D |
| The University of Kansas | M,D |
| University of Maryland, Baltimore County | M,D |
| University of Maryland, College Park | M,D |
| University of Massachusetts Amherst | M,D |
| University of Massachusetts Lowell | M |
| University of Michigan | D |
| University of Minnesota, Twin Cities Campus | D |
| University of Missouri–Kansas City | M,D |
| University of Nebraska–Lincoln | M,D |
| University of Nevada, Reno | D |
| University of New Haven | M,O |
| The University of North Carolina at Chapel Hill | D |
| The University of North Carolina at Greensboro | M,D |
| University of Oregon | M,D |
| University of Phoenix - Phoenix Campus | M |
| University of Pittsburgh | D* |
| University of Puerto Rico at Rio Piedras | M,D |
| University of Rochester | M,D |
| University of South Carolina | M,D |
| University of Southern California | M,D |
| The University of Tennessee at Chattanooga | M,D,O |
| The University of Tennessee at Martin | M |
| University of Utah | D |
| University of Vermont | D |
| University of Victoria | M,D |
| University of Washington | M,D |
| University of Windsor | M,D |
| University of Wisconsin–Madison | D |
| University of Wisconsin–Superior | M |
| Université Laval | D |
| Walden University | M,D,O |
| Wayne State University | M,D,O |
| Western Illinois University | M |
| Wichita State University | D |
| Wilfrid Laurier University | M,D |
| Yale University | D |

## SOCIAL SCIENCES

| | |
|---|---|
| Assumption University | O |
| Augusta University | M |
| California Institute of Technology | M,D |
| California State University, Chico | M |
| California State University, San Bernardino | M |
| Campbellsville University | M |
| Carnegie Mellon University | D |
| The Citadel, The Military College of South Carolina | M |
| Colorado School of Mines | O |
| Columbia University | M,D |
| East Carolina University | M,D,O |
| Eastern Michigan University | M |
| Elms College | M,O |
| Evangel University | M |
| Florida Agricultural and Mechanical University | M |
| The Graduate Center, City University of New York | M |
| Graduate Theological Union | M,D,O |
| Harrison Middleton University | M,D |
| Hollins University | M |
| Humboldt State University | M |
| Indiana University Bloomington | M,D,O |
| Indiana University-Purdue University Indianapolis | M,D,O |
| Massachusetts Institute of Technology | D |
| Mississippi College | M,O |
| Montclair State University | M |
| The New School | M,D |
| New York University | M,D |
| Nova Southeastern University | M,D,O |
| The Ohio State University | M,D |
| Ohio University | M |
| Oregon State University | M,D |
| Southern University and Agricultural and Mechanical College | M |
| Syracuse University | M,D |
| Texas A&M International University | M |
| Towson University | M |
| Troy University | M |
| University at Buffalo, the State University of New York | M |
| University of California, Merced | M,D |
| University of California, Santa Barbara | D |
| University of California, Santa Cruz | D |
| University of Chicago | M,D |
| University of Florida | M,D,O |
| University of Illinois at Springfield | M,O |
| The University of Manchester | M,D |
| University of Maryland, Baltimore County | D |
| University of Memphis | M,D |
| University of Michigan | D |
| University of Michigan–Flint | M |
| University of Northern Iowa | M |
| University of Regina | M |
| University of South Florida Sarasota-Manatee | M |
| The University of Texas at Tyler | M |
| University of the Virgin Islands | M |
| University of Toronto | M,D |
| University of Washington | M,D |
| Wilfrid Laurier University | M,D |
| Worcester Polytechnic Institute | M,D,O |
| Yale University | M,D |

## SOCIAL SCIENCES EDUCATION

| | |
|---|---|
| Alabama Agricultural and Mechanical University | M,O |
| Alabama State University | M,O |
| Andrews University | M,D,O |
| Appalachian State University | M |
| Arkansas State University | M,D,O |
| Asbury University | M |
| Binghamton University, State University of New York | M |
| Bloomsburg University of Pennsylvania | M |
| Bob Jones University | M,D,O |
| Boston College | M,D,O |
| Bridgewater State University | M |
| Brooklyn College of the City University of New York | M |
| Brown University | M |
| Buffalo State College, State University of New York | M |
| California State University, East Bay | M |
| California State University, Fresno | M |
| Caribbean University | M,D |
| Carthage College | M,O |
| Chadron State College | M,O |
| Chatham University | M |
| The Citadel, The Military College of South Carolina | M,O |
| City College of the City University of New York | M,O |
| College of St. Joseph | M |
| The Colorado College | M |
| Columbus State University | M,O |
| Concordia University (United States) | M,D |
| Converse College | M |
| Delta State University | M |
| Duquesne University | M |
| East Carolina University | M |
| Eastern Kentucky University | M |
| Eastern University | M,O |
| Fayetteville State University | M |
| Fitchburg State University | M |
| Florida Agricultural and Mechanical University | M |
| Florida Gulf Coast University | M |
| Florida International University | M,D,O |
| George Mason University | M |
| Georgia State University | M,D |
| Grambling State University | M |
| Harding University | M,O |
| Hofstra University | M,D,O |
| Hunter College of the City University of New York | M |
| Indiana University Bloomington | M,D,O |
| Instituto Tecnologico de Santo Domingo | M,O |
| Inter American University of Puerto Rico, Arecibo Campus | M |
| Inter American University of Puerto Rico, Metropolitan Campus | M |
| Inter American University of Puerto Rico, Ponce Campus | M |
| Iona College | M |
| Kent State University | M,D |
| Kutztown University of Pennsylvania | M,D |
| Lake Forest College | M |
| La Salle University | M,O |
| Lebanon Valley College | M,O |
| Lee University | M,O |
| Lehman College of the City University of New York | M |
| Le Moyne College | M,O |
| Lewis University | M |
| Long Island University - Brooklyn | M,D,O |
| Manhattanville College | M,O |
| Metropolitan State University | M |
| Michigan State University | M,D |
| Minnesota State University Mankato | M |
| Mississippi College | M,D,O |
| Missouri State University | M,O |
| Molloy College | M,O |
| Morehead State University | M,O |
| New York University | M,D,O |
| Northeastern Illinois University | M |
| Northwest Missouri State University | M,O |
| Oregon State University | M,D |
| Pace University | M,O |
| Plymouth State University | M |
| Portland State University | M |
| Purdue University | M,D,O |
| Queens College of the City University of New York | M,O |
| Quinnipiac University | M |
| Rhode Island College | M |
| Rivier University | M |
| Rutgers University - New Brunswick | M,D |
| St. John Fisher College | M |
| Smith College | M |
| South Carolina State University | M |
| Southwestern Oklahoma State University | M |
| State University of New York at New Paltz | M,O |
| State University of New York at Plattsburgh | M |
| State University of New York College at Geneseo | M |
| State University of New York College at Old Westbury | M |
| State University of New York College at Potsdam | M |
| Stony Brook University, State University of New York | M,O |
| SUNY Brockport | M,O |
| Syracuse University | M |
| Teachers College, Columbia University | M,D,O |
| Temple University | M* |
| Texas Tech University | M,D |
| Trinity Washington University | M |
| University at Buffalo, the State University of New York | M,D,O |
| The University of Akron | M |
| The University of Alabama in Huntsville | M,O |
| University of Arkansas at Pine Bluff | M |
| The University of British Columbia | M,D |
| University of California, Santa Cruz | M |
| University of Central Florida | M,O |
| University of Connecticut | M,D |
| University of Florida | M,D,O |
| University of Illinois at Chicago | D |
| University of Indianapolis | M |
| The University of Iowa | M,D |
| University of Maine | M,D,O |
| University of Maryland, Baltimore County | M |
| University of Minnesota, Twin Cities Campus | M |
| University of Missouri | M,D,O |
| University of Missouri–St. Louis | M,O |
| The University of North Carolina at Chapel Hill | M |
| The University of North Carolina at Greensboro | M,D,O |
| The University of North Carolina at Pembroke | M |
| University of North Georgia | M |
| University of Oklahoma | M,D |
| University of Puerto Rico at Rio Piedras | M,D |
| University of St. Francis (IL) | M,D,O |
| University of South Carolina | M,D |
| University of South Florida | M,D,O |
| The University of Tennessee | M,D,O |
| University of the District of Columbia | M |
| The University of Toledo | M,D,O |
| University of Victoria | M,D |
| University of Virginia | M,D,O |
| University of Washington | M,D |
| The University of West Alabama | M |
| University of Wisconsin–Milwaukee | M* |
| University of Wisconsin–River Falls | M |
| University of Wisconsin–Stevens Point | M |
| Virginia Polytechnic Institute and State University | M,D,O |
| Wagner College | M |
| Wayland Baptist University | M |
| Wayne State College | M |
| Wayne State University | M,D,O |
| Western Oregon University | M |
| Westfield State University | M |
| Widener University | M,D |
| William Carey University | M,O |
| Worcester State University | M |

## SOCIAL WORK

| | |
|---|---|
| Abilene Christian University | M |
| Adelphi University | M,D |
| Alabama Agricultural and Mechanical University | M,O |
| Alabama State University | M |
| Albany State University | M |
| American Jewish University | M |
| Andrews University | M |
| Anna Maria College | M |
| Appalachian State University | M |
| Arizona State University at Tempe | M,D,O |
| Arkansas State University | M,O |
| Asbury University | M |
| Auburn University | M |
| Augsburg University | M |
| Aurora University | M,D |
| Austin Peay State University | M |
| Azusa Pacific University | M |
| Barry University | M,D |
| Baylor University | M,D |
| Binghamton University, State University of New York | M |
| Boise State University | M |
| Boston College | M,D |
| Boston University | M,D |
| Bowling Green State University | M |
| Brandman University | M |
| Brescia University | M |
| Bridgewater State University | M |
| Brigham Young University | M |
| Bryn Mawr College | M,D |
| California Baptist University | M |
| California State University, Chico | M |
| California State University, Dominguez Hills | M |
| California State University, East Bay | M |
| California State University, Fresno | M |
| California State University, Fullerton | M |
| California State University, Long Beach | M |
| California State University, Los Angeles | M |
| California State University, Monterey Bay | M |
| California State University, Northridge | M,O |
| California State University, Sacramento | M |
| California State University, San Bernardino | M |
| California State University, Stanislaus | M |
| California University of Pennsylvania | M |
| Campbellsville University | M |
| Capella University | D |
| Carleton University | M |
| Carlow University | M |
| Case Western Reserve University | M,D |
| The Catholic University of America | M,D |
| Chicago State University | M |
| Clark Atlanta University | M,D |
| Clarke University | M |
| Cleveland State University | M |
| The College of Saint Rose | M |
| The College of St. Scholastica | M |
| College of Staten Island of the City University of New York | M |
| Colorado State University | M,D |
| Columbia University | M,D |
| Concordia University Wisconsin | M |
| Concord University | M |
| Cornell University | M,D |
| Daemen College | M |
| Dalhousie University | M |
| Delaware State University | M |
| DePaul University | M |
| Dominican University | M |
| East Carolina University | M,O |
| Eastern Michigan University | M |
| Eastern Washington University | M |
| East Tennessee State University | M |
| Edinboro University of Pennsylvania | M |
| Erikson Institute | M |
| Fayetteville State University | M |
| Ferris State University | M |
| Florida Agricultural and Mechanical University | M |
| Florida Atlantic University | M,D |
| Florida Gulf Coast University | M |
| Florida International University | M,D |
| Florida State University | M,D |
| Fordham University | M,D |
| Gallaudet University | M,D,O |
| George Fox University | M |
| George Mason University | M |
| Georgia State University | M,O |
| Governors State University | M |
| The Graduate Center, City University of New York | D |
| Grambling State University | M |
| Grand Valley State University | M |
| Gratz College | M,O |
| Hawaii Pacific University | M |
| Howard University | M,D |
| Humboldt State University | M |
| Hunter College of the City University of New York | M |
| Illinois State University | M |
| Indiana State University | M |
| Indiana University East | M |
| Indiana University Northwest | M |
| Indiana University-Purdue University Indianapolis | M,D,O |
| Indiana University South Bend | M |
| Institute for Clinical Social Work | D |
| Inter American University of Puerto Rico, Metropolitan Campus | M |
| Jackson State University | M,D |
| Jacksonville State University | M |
| Johnson C. Smith University | M |
| Kean University | M |
| Kennesaw State University | M |
| Keuka College | M |
| Kutztown University of Pennsylvania | M,D |
| Lakehead University | M |
| Laurentian University | M |
| Lehman College of the City University of New York | M |
| Lewis University | M |
| Loma Linda University | M,D |
| London Metropolitan University | M,D |

*M—masters degree; D—doctorate; O—other advanced degree; *—Close-Up and/or Display*

| | |
|---|---|
| Long Island University - Brentwood Campus | M,O |
| Long Island University - Brooklyn | M,D,O |
| Long Island University - Post | M,O |
| Louisiana College | M |
| Louisiana State University and Agricultural & Mechanical College | M,D |
| Loyola University Chicago | M,D,O |
| Madonna University | M |
| Marshall University | M |
| Marywood University | M,D |
| McGill University | M,D,O |
| McMaster University | M |
| Memorial University of Newfoundland | M,D |
| Metropolitan State University of Denver | M |
| Michigan State University | M,D |
| Middle Tennessee State University | M |
| Millersville University of Pennsylvania | M,D |
| Minnesota State University Mankato | M |
| Missouri State University | M |
| Monmouth University | M,O |
| Morgan State University | M |
| Nazareth College of Rochester | M |
| Newman University | M |
| New Mexico Highlands University | M |
| New Mexico State University | M |
| New York University | M,D |
| Norfolk State University | M,D |
| North Carolina Agricultural and Technical State University | M |
| North Carolina Central University | M |
| North Carolina State University | M |
| Northeastern Illinois University | M |
| Northern Kentucky University | M |
| Northwest Nazarene University | M |
| Nyack College | M |
| The Ohio State University | M,D |
| The Ohio State University at Lima | M |
| The Ohio State University at Mansfield | M |
| The Ohio State University at Newark | M |
| Ohio University | M |
| Our Lady of the Lake University | M,D |
| Pacific University | M |
| Park University | M,O |
| Phillips Theological Seminary | M,D |
| Pontifical Catholic University of Puerto Rico | M |
| Portland State University | M,D |
| Quinnipiac University | M |
| Radford University | M |
| Ramapo College of New Jersey | M |
| Rhode Island College | M |
| Roberts Wesleyan College | M |
| Rutgers University - New Brunswick | M,D |
| Sacred Heart University | M |
| Saginaw Valley State University | M |
| St. Ambrose University | M |
| St. Catherine University | M,D |
| St. Cloud State University | M |
| Saint Leo University | M |
| Saint Louis University | M,D |
| Salem State University | M |
| Salisbury University | M |
| Samford University | M |
| San Diego State University | M |
| San Francisco State University | M |
| Savannah State University | M |
| Seattle University | M |
| Seton Hall University | M |
| Shippensburg University of Pennsylvania | M |
| Simmons University | M,D |
| Smith College | M,D |
| Southeastern University (FL) | M |
| Southern Adventist University | M |
| Southern Connecticut State University | M |
| Southern Illinois University Carbondale | M |
| Southern Illinois University Edwardsville | M |
| Southern University at New Orleans | M |
| Spalding University | M |
| Spring Arbor University | M |
| Springfield College | M,O |
| Stephen F. Austin State University | M |
| Stockton University | M |
| Stony Brook University, State University of New York | M,D |
| SUNY Brockport | M,O |
| Syracuse University | M |
| Tarleton State University | M |
| Temple University | M* |
| Tennessee State University | M,D |
| Texas A&M University–Commerce | M,D,O |
| Texas A&M University–Kingsville | M |
| Texas Christian University | M |
| Texas State University | M |
| Texas Tech University | M |
| Thompson Rivers University | M |
| Troy University | M |
| Tulane University | M,D |
| Union University | M |
| Universidad del Este | M |
| Université de Moncton | M |
| Université de Montréal | O |
| Université de Sherbrooke | M |
| Université du Québec à Montréal | M |
| Université du Québec en Abitibi-Témiscamingue | M |
| Université du Québec en Outaouais | M |
| University at Albany, State University of New York | M,D |
| University at Buffalo, the State University of New York | M,D |
| The University of Akron | M |
| The University of Alabama | M,D |
| The University of Alabama at Birmingham | M |
| University of Alaska Anchorage | M,O |
| University of Arkansas | M |
| University of Arkansas at Little Rock | M |
| The University of British Columbia | M,D |
| University of Calgary | M,D,O |
| University of California, Berkeley | M,D |
| University of California, Los Angeles | M,D |
| University of Central Florida | M,O |
| University of Chicago | M,D |
| University of Cincinnati | M |
| University of Connecticut | M,D |
| University of Denver | M,D,O |
| University of Georgia | M,D,O |
| University of Guam | M |
| University of Hawaii at Manoa | M,D |
| University of Houston | M,D |
| University of Houston - Downtown | M |
| University of Illinois at Chicago | M,D,O |
| University of Illinois at Urbana-Champaign | M,D |
| University of Indianapolis | M,D |
| The University of Iowa | M,D |
| The University of Kansas | M,D |
| University of Kentucky | M,D |
| University of Louisville | M,D,O |
| University of Maine | M,O |
| The University of Manchester | M,D |
| University of Manitoba | M,D |
| University of Maryland, Baltimore | M,D |
| University of Maryland, College Park | |
| University of Memphis | M |
| University of Michigan | M |
| University of Minnesota, Duluth | M |
| University of Minnesota, Twin Cities Campus | M,D |
| University of Mississippi | M,D |
| University of Missouri | M,D,O |
| University of Missouri–Kansas City | M |
| University of Missouri–St. Louis | M |
| University of Montana | M |
| University of Nebraska at Omaha | M |
| University of Nevada, Las Vegas | M |
| University of Nevada, Reno | M |
| University of New England | M,D,O |
| University of New Hampshire | M,O |
| The University of North Carolina at Chapel Hill | M,D |
| The University of North Carolina at Charlotte | M |
| The University of North Carolina at Greensboro | M |
| The University of North Carolina at Pembroke | M |
| The University of North Carolina Wilmington | M |
| University of North Dakota | M |
| University of Northern British Columbia | M,D,O |
| University of Northern Iowa | M |
| University of North Florida | M |
| University of Oklahoma | M |
| University of Ottawa | M |
| University of Pennsylvania | M,D |
| University of Pittsburgh | M,D,O* |
| University of Puerto Rico at Rio Piedras | M,D |
| University of Regina | M,D |
| University of St. Francis (IL) | M,O |
| University of Saint Joseph | M |
| University of St. Thomas (MN) | M |
| University of South Africa | M,D |
| University of South Carolina | M,D |
| University of South Dakota | M |
| University of Southern California | M,D |
| University of Southern Indiana | M |
| University of Southern Maine | M |
| University of Southern Mississippi | M |
| University of South Florida | M,D,O |
| University of South Florida Sarasota-Manatee | M |
| The University of Tennessee | M,D |
| The University of Tennessee at Chattanooga | M |
| The University of Texas at Arlington | M,D |
| The University of Texas at Austin | M,D |
| The University of Texas at El Paso | M |
| The University of Texas at San Antonio | M |
| The University of Texas Rio Grande Valley | M |
| University of the Fraser Valley | M |
| The University of Toledo | M,O |
| University of Toronto | M,D |
| University of Utah | M,D |
| University of Vermont | M |
| University of Victoria | M |
| University of Washington | M,D |
| University of Washington, Tacoma | M |
| University of West Florida | M |
| University of Windsor | M |
| University of Wisconsin–Green Bay | M |
| University of Wisconsin–Madison | M,D |
| University of Wisconsin–Milwaukee | M,D,O* |
| University of Wisconsin–Oshkosh | M |
| University of Wyoming | M |
| Université Laval | M,D |
| Utah State University | M,D |
| Utah Valley University | M |
| Valdosta State University | M |
| Virginia Commonwealth University | M,D |
| Walden University | M,D |
| Walla Walla University | M |
| Washburn University | M |
| Washington University in St. Louis | M,D |
| Wayne State University | M,D,O |
| Western Carolina University | M |
| Western Illinois University | M |
| Western Kentucky University | M |
| Western Michigan University | M |
| Western New Mexico University | M |
| Westfield State University | M |
| West Texas A&M University | M |
| West Virginia University | M |
| Wichita State University | M |
| Widener University | M,D |
| Wilfrid Laurier University | M,D |
| Winthrop University | M |
| Yeshiva University | M,D |
| York University | M,D |
| Youngstown State University | M |

## SOCIOLOGY

| | |
|---|---|
| Acadia University | M |
| American University | M,O |
| Angelo State University | M |
| Arizona State University at Tempe | M,D |
| Arkansas State University | M,O |
| Arkansas Tech University | M |
| Auburn University | M |
| Ball State University | M |
| Baylor University | M,D |
| Binghamton University, State University of New York | M,D |
| Boston College | M,D |
| Boston University | M,D |
| Bowling Green State University | M,D |
| Brandeis University | M,D |
| Brigham Young University | M |
| Brock University | M |
| Brooklyn College of the City University of New York | M,D |
| Brown University | M,D |
| California State University, Dominguez Hills | M |
| California State University, Fullerton | M |
| California State University, Los Angeles | M |
| California State University, Northridge | M |
| California State University, Sacramento | M |
| California State University, San Marcos | M |
| Carleton University | M,D |
| Case Western Reserve University | M,D |
| The Catholic University of America | M |
| Central European University | M,D |
| City College of the City University of New York | M |
| Clark Atlanta University | M |
| Clemson University | M |
| Colorado State University | M,D |
| Columbia University | M,D |
| Concordia University (Canada) | M,D |
| Cornell University | M,D |
| Dalhousie University | M,D |
| DePaul University | M |
| Duke University | M,D |
| East Carolina University | M |
| Eastern Michigan University | M |
| East Tennessee State University | M |
| Emory University | D |
| Fayetteville State University | M |
| Florida Atlantic University | M |
| Florida International University | M,D |
| Florida State University | M,D |
| George Mason University | M,D |
| The George Washington University | M |
| Georgia Southern University | M |
| Georgia State University | M,D |
| The Graduate Center, City University of New York | D |
| Harvard University | D* |
| Howard University | M,D |
| Humboldt State University | M |
| Hunter College of the City University of New York | M |
| Idaho State University | M |
| Illinois State University | M |
| Indiana University Bloomington | M,D |
| Indiana University of Pennsylvania | M |
| Indiana University-Purdue University Indianapolis | M |
| Iowa State University of Science and Technology | M,D |
| Jackson State University | M |
| Johns Hopkins University | D |
| Kansas State University | M,D |
| Kent State University | M,D |
| Lakehead University | M |
| Laurentian University | M |
| Lincoln University (MO) | M |
| Louisiana State University and Agricultural & Mechanical College | M,D |
| Loyola University Chicago | M,D |
| Marshall University | M |
| McGill University | M,D,O |
| McMaster University | M,D |
| Memorial University of Newfoundland | M,D |
| Michigan State University | M,D |
| Middle Tennessee State University | M |
| Minnesota State University Mankato | M |
| Mississippi State University | M,D |
| Morehead State University | M |
| Morgan State University | M |
| Murray State University | M |
| New Mexico Highlands University | M |
| New Mexico State University | M |
| The New School | M,D |
| New York University | M,D |
| North Carolina State University | D |
| North Dakota State University | M |
| Northeastern University | M,D |
| Northern Arizona University | M |
| Northern Illinois University | M |
| Northwestern University | D |
| The Ohio State University | D |
| Ohio University | M |
| Oklahoma City University | M |
| Oklahoma State University | M,D |
| Old Dominion University | M |
| Omega Graduate School | M,D |
| Our Lady of the Lake University | M |
| Penn State University Park | M,D* |
| Portland State University | M,D,O |
| Prairie View A&M University | M |
| Princeton University | D,O |
| Purdue University | M,D |
| Queens College of the City University of New York | M |
| Queen's University at Kingston | M,D |
| Rice University | D |
| Roosevelt University | M |
| Rutgers University - New Brunswick | M,D |
| St. John's University (NY) | M |
| Sam Houston State University | M |
| San Diego State University | M |
| Shippensburg University of Pennsylvania | M |
| Simon Fraser University | M,D |
| South Dakota State University | M,D |
| Southeastern Louisiana University | M |
| Southern Connecticut State University | M |
| Southern Illinois University Carbondale | M,D |
| Southern Illinois University Edwardsville | M |
| Stanford University | D |
| Stony Brook University, State University of New York | M,D |
| Syracuse University | M,D |
| Teachers College, Columbia University | M,D |
| Temple University | M,D* |
| Texas A&M International University | M |
| Texas A&M University | M,D |
| Texas A&M University–Commerce | M,D,O |
| Texas A&M University–Kingsville | M |
| Texas Southern University | M |
| Texas State University | M |
| Texas Tech University | M |
| Texas Woman's University | M,D |
| Tulane University | M |
| UNB Fredericton | M,D |
| Université de Montréal | M,D |
| Université du Québec à Montréal | M,D |
| University at Albany, State University of New York | M,D,O |
| University at Buffalo, the State University of New York | M,D |
| The University of Alabama at Birmingham | D |
| University of Alberta | M,D |
| The University of Arizona | M,D |
| University of Arkansas | M |
| The University of British Columbia | M,D |
| University of Calgary | M,D |
| University of California, Berkeley | D |
| University of California, Davis | M,D |
| University of California, Irvine | D |
| University of California, Los Angeles | M,D |
| University of California, Merced | M,D |
| University of California, Riverside | M,D |
| University of California, San Diego | D |
| University of California, San Francisco | D |
| University of California, Santa Barbara | D |
| University of California, Santa Cruz | D |
| University of Central Florida | M,D |
| University of Central Missouri | M,D,O |
| University of Central Oklahoma | M |
| University of Chicago | D |
| University of Cincinnati | M,D |
| University of Colorado Boulder | D |
| University of Colorado Colorado Springs | M |
| University of Colorado Denver | M,O |
| University of Connecticut | M,D |
| University of Delaware | M,D |
| University of Florida | M,D |
| University of Georgia | M,D |
| University of Guelph | M,D |
| University of Hawaii at Manoa | M,D |
| University of Houston | M |
| University of Houston–Clear Lake | M |
| University of Illinois at Chicago | M,D |
| University of Illinois at Urbana-Champaign | M,D |
| University of Indianapolis | M |
| The University of Iowa | M,D |
| The University of Kansas | D |
| University of Kentucky | M,D |
| University of Lethbridge | M,D |
| University of Louisiana at Lafayette | M,D |
| University of Louisville | M,D |
| The University of Manchester | M,D |
| University of Manitoba | M,D |
| University of Maryland, Baltimore County | M |
| University of Maryland, College Park | M,D |
| University of Massachusetts Amherst | M,D |
| University of Massachusetts Boston | M,D |

| | |
|---|---|
| University of Massachusetts Lowell | M,O |
| University of Memphis | M |
| University of Miami | M,D |
| University of Michigan | D |
| University of Minnesota, Duluth | M |
| University of Minnesota, Twin Cities Campus | M,D |
| University of Missouri | M,D |
| University of Missouri–Kansas City | M |
| University of Missouri–St. Louis | M |
| University of Montana | M |
| University of Nebraska at Omaha | M |
| University of Nebraska–Lincoln | M,D |
| University of Nevada, Las Vegas | M,D |
| University of Nevada, Reno | M |
| University of New Hampshire | M,D |
| University of New Mexico | M,D |
| University of New Orleans | M |
| The University of North Carolina at Chapel Hill | M,D |
| The University of North Carolina at Charlotte | M |
| The University of North Carolina at Greensboro | M |
| The University of North Carolina Wilmington | M |
| University of North Dakota | M |
| University of Northern Colorado | M |
| University of North Texas | M,D,O |
| University of Notre Dame | D |
| University of Oklahoma | M,D |
| University of Oregon | M,D |
| University of Ottawa | M |
| University of Pennsylvania | M,D |
| University of Pittsburgh | M,D* |
| University of Puerto Rico at Rio Piedras | M |
| University of Regina | M |
| University of Saskatchewan | M,D |
| University of South Africa | M,D |
| University of South Alabama | M |
| University of South Carolina | M,D |
| University of Southern California | D |
| University of South Florida | M,D |
| The University of Tennessee | M,D |
| The University of Texas at Arlington | M |
| The University of Texas at Austin | M,D |
| The University of Texas at El Paso | M,O |
| The University of Texas at San Antonio | M |
| The University of Texas at Tyler | M |
| The University of Texas Rio Grande Valley | M |
| The University of Toledo | M |
| University of Toronto | M,D |
| University of Utah | M,D |
| University of Victoria | M,D |
| University of Virginia | M,D |
| University of Washington | M,D |
| University of Waterloo | M,D |
| The University of Western Ontario | M,D |
| University of Windsor | M,D |
| University of Wisconsin–Madison | M,D |
| University of Wisconsin–Milwaukee | M,D* |
| University of Wyoming | M,D |
| Université Laval | M,D |
| Utah State University | M,D |
| Vanderbilt University | M,D* |
| Virginia Commonwealth University | M |
| Washington State University | M,D |
| Wayne State University | M,D |
| Western Illinois University | M |
| Western Kentucky University | M |
| Western Michigan University | M,D |
| West Virginia University | M,D |
| Wichita State University | M |
| Wilfrid Laurier University | M |
| Yale University | D |
| York University | M,D |

## SOFTWARE ENGINEERING

| | |
|---|---|
| Arizona State University at Tempe | M,D |
| Auburn University | M,D |
| Boston University | M,O |
| Bowling Green State University | M |
| Brandeis University | M |
| California State University, Fullerton | M |
| California State University, Northridge | M |
| California State University, Sacramento | M |
| Carnegie Mellon University | M,D |
| Carroll University | M |
| Cleveland State University | M,D |
| College of Staten Island of the City University of New York | M |
| Colorado Technical University Aurora | M |
| Colorado Technical University Colorado Springs | M,D |
| Concordia University (Canada) | M,D,O |
| DePaul University | M,D |
| Drexel University | M,D,O |
| East Carolina University | M |
| Embry-Riddle Aeronautical University–Daytona | M |
| Fairfield University | M,O |
| Florida Agricultural and Mechanical University | M |
| Florida Institute of Technology | M |
| Gannon University | M |
| Harrisburg University of Science and Technology | M |
| Illinois Institute of Technology | M,D |
| Indiana University-Purdue University Indianapolis | M,D,O |
| Instituto Tecnologico de Santo Domingo | M,O |
| International Technological University | M |
| Jacksonville State University | M |
| Kennesaw State University | M,O |
| Lewis University | M |
| Lipscomb University | M,O |
| Loyola University Chicago | M |
| Marist College | M,O |
| Marymount University | M,O |
| McMaster University | M,D |
| Mercer University | M |
| Monmouth University | M,O |
| Naval Postgraduate School | M,D |
| New Jersey Institute of Technology | M,D,O |
| New York University | O |
| North Dakota State University | M,D,O |
| Northern Kentucky University | M,O |
| Northwestern University | M |
| Oakland University | M,D |
| Oklahoma Christian University | M |
| Pace University | M,D,O |
| Penn State Great Valley | M,O |
| Regis University | M,O |
| Rochester Institute of Technology | M |
| Royal Military College of Canada | M,D |
| Saint Louis University | M |
| St. Mary's University (United States) | M,O |
| San Jose State University | M |
| Santa Clara University | M,D,O |
| Shippensburg University of Pennsylvania | M,O |
| Southern Methodist University | M,D |
| Stevens Institute of Technology | M,O |
| Stratford University (VA) | M,D |
| Strayer University | M |
| Texas State University | M |
| Texas Tech University | M,D |
| The University of Alabama in Huntsville | M,D,O |
| University of Calgary | M,D |
| University of Colorado Colorado Springs | M,D |
| University of Connecticut | M,D |
| University of Detroit Mercy | M,D |
| University of Houston–Clear Lake | M |
| University of Management and Technology | M,O |
| University of Massachusetts Dartmouth | M,O |
| University of Michigan–Dearborn | M,D |
| University of Minnesota, Twin Cities Campus | M |
| University of Missouri–Kansas City | M,D,O |
| University of Nebraska at Omaha | M,O |
| University of New Haven | M,O |
| University of North Florida | M |
| University of Regina | M,D |
| University of St. Thomas (MN) | M,O |
| The University of Scranton | M |
| University of South Carolina | M,D |
| University of Southern California | M,D |
| University of Southern Maine | M,O |
| The University of Texas at Arlington | M,D |
| The University of Texas at Dallas | M,D |
| The University of Texas at El Paso | M,D,O |
| University of Utah | M,D,O |
| University of Washington, Bothell | M |
| University of Washington, Tacoma | M |
| University of Waterloo | M,D |
| University of West Florida | M |
| University of Wisconsin–La Crosse | M |
| Université Laval | O |
| Vermont Technical College | M |
| Virginia International University | M,O |
| Virginia Polytechnic Institute and State University | M,O |
| West Virginia University | M,D |

## SPANISH

| | |
|---|---|
| American University | M,O |
| Arizona State University at Tempe | M,D |
| Asbury University | M |
| Auburn University | M |
| Bard College | M |
| Baylor University | M |
| Binghamton University, State University of New York | M |
| Boston College | M |
| Bowling Green State University | M |
| Brigham Young University | M |
| Brooklyn College of the City University of New York | M |
| California State University, Fresno | M |
| California State University, Fullerton | M |
| California State University, Long Beach | M |
| California State University, Los Angeles | M |
| California State University, Northridge | M |
| California State University, San Bernardino | M |
| California State University, San Marcos | M |
| The Catholic University of America | M,D |
| Central Connecticut State University | M,O |
| Central Michigan University | M |
| City College of the City University of New York | M |
| Cleveland State University | M |
| Columbia University | M,D |
| Cornell University | D |
| DePaul University | M |
| Duke University | D |
| Eastern University | M,O |
| Emory University | D,O |
| Florida Atlantic University | M |
| Florida International University | M,D |
| Florida State University | M,D |
| George Mason University | M |
| Georgetown University | M,D |
| Georgia Southern University | M |
| Georgia State University | M,O |
| Harvard University | M,D* |
| Houston Baptist University | M |
| Howard University | M |
| Hunter College of the City University of New York | M |
| Illinois State University | M |
| Indiana State University | M,D,O |
| Indiana University Bloomington | M,D |
| Inter American University of Puerto Rico, Metropolitan Campus | M |
| Inter American University of Puerto Rico, Ponce Campus | M |
| Iona College | M |
| Johns Hopkins University | M,D |
| Kansas State University | M |
| Kent State University | M,D |
| Lake Forest College | M |
| Lamar University | M |
| Lee University | M,O |
| Lehman College of the City University of New York | M |
| Loyola University Chicago | M |
| Manhattanville College | M,O |
| Marquette University | M |
| Miami University | M |
| Michigan State University | M,D |
| Middlebury College | M,D |
| Middle Tennessee State University | M |
| Millersville University of Pennsylvania | M |
| Minnesota State University Mankato | M |
| Montclair State University | M |
| New Mexico State University | M |
| New York University | M,D,O |
| North Carolina State University | M |
| Northern Arizona University | M |
| Northern Illinois University | M |
| Northwestern University | D |
| The Ohio State University | M,D |
| Ohio University | M |
| Penn State University Park | M,D* |
| Pontifical Catholic University of Puerto Rico | M,O |
| Portland State University | M |
| Princeton University | D |
| Purdue University | M |
| Queens College of the City University of New York | M |
| Rutgers University - New Brunswick | M,D |
| St. John's University (NY) | M |
| Saint Louis University | M |
| Saint Louis University–Madrid Campus | M |
| Saint Xavier University | M |
| Salem State University | M |
| Sam Houston State University | M |
| San Diego State University | M |
| San Francisco State University | M |
| Southern Oregon University | M |
| Stanford University | M,D |
| State University of New York at New Paltz | M,O |
| State University of New York College at Geneseo | M |
| Syracuse University | M |
| Temple University | M,D* |
| Texas A&M University | M,D |
| Texas A&M University–Commerce | M,D,O |
| Texas A&M University–Kingsville | M |
| Texas State University | M |
| Texas Tech University | M,D |
| Tulane University | M,D |
| Universidad Autonoma de Guadalajara | M,D |
| Université de Montréal | M |
| University at Albany, State University of New York | M,D |
| University at Buffalo, the State University of New York | M,D,O |
| The University of Alabama | M,D |
| The University of Arizona | M,D |
| University of Arkansas | M |
| University of California, Berkeley | D |
| University of California, Davis | M,D |
| University of California, Irvine | M,D |
| University of California, Los Angeles | M |
| University of California, Riverside | M,D |
| University of California, Santa Barbara | M,D |
| University of Central Arkansas | M |
| University of Central Florida | M |
| University of Chicago | D |
| University of Cincinnati | M,D |
| University of Colorado Boulder | M,D |
| University of Colorado Denver | M |
| University of Delaware | M |
| University of Florida | M,D |
| University of Georgia | M,D |
| University of Hawaii at Manoa | M |
| University of Houston | M,D |
| University of Illinois at Chicago | M,D |
| University of Illinois at Urbana-Champaign | M,D |
| The University of Iowa | M,D |
| The University of Kansas | M,D |
| University of Lethbridge | M,D |
| University of Louisville | M,O |
| The University of Manchester | D |
| University of Maryland, College Park | M,D |
| University of Massachusetts Amherst | M,D |
| University of Memphis | M |
| University of Miami | M,D |
| University of Michigan | D |
| University of Minnesota, Twin Cities Campus | M,D |
| University of Missouri–Kansas City | M |
| University of Montana | M |
| University of Nebraska–Lincoln | M,D |
| University of Nevada, Reno | M |
| University of New Hampshire | M,O |
| University of New Mexico | M,D |
| The University of North Carolina at Chapel Hill | M,D |
| The University of North Carolina at Charlotte | M,O |
| The University of North Carolina at Greensboro | M,O |
| The University of North Carolina Wilmington | M,O |
| University of Northern Iowa | M |
| University of North Texas | M,D,O |
| University of Notre Dame | M |
| University of Oklahoma | M,D |
| University of Oregon | M |
| University of Ottawa | M,D |
| University of Pennsylvania | M,D |
| University of Pittsburgh | D* |
| University of Rhode Island | M |
| University of South Africa | M,D |
| University of South Carolina | M,D |
| University of Southern California | D |
| The University of Tennessee | M,D |
| The University of Texas at Arlington | M |
| The University of Texas at Austin | M,D |
| The University of Texas at El Paso | M,O |
| The University of Texas at San Antonio | M |
| The University of Texas of the Permian Basin | M |
| The University of Texas Rio Grande Valley | M |
| The University of Toledo | M |
| University of Toronto | M,D |
| University of Utah | M,D |
| University of Virginia | M,D |
| University of Washington | M |
| The University of Western Ontario | M,D |
| University of Wisconsin–Madison | M,D |
| University of Wisconsin–Milwaukee | M,O* |
| University of Wyoming | M,D |
| Université Laval | M,D |
| Vanderbilt University | M,D* |
| Washington University in St. Louis | D |
| Wayne State University | M,D |
| Western Kentucky University | M |
| Western Michigan University | M,D |
| Wichita State University | M |
| Worcester State University | M |
| Yale University | D |

## SPECIAL EDUCATION

| | |
|---|---|
| Acacia University | M |
| Acadia University | M |
| Alabama Agricultural and Mechanical University | M,D,O |
| Albany State University | M,O |
| Albizu University - Miami | M,D |
| Albright College | M |
| Alcorn State University | M,O |
| Alliant International University–San Francisco | M,O |
| Alverno College | M |
| American International College | M,D,O |
| American University | M,O |
| American University of Puerto Rico - Bayamon | M |
| Andrews University | M |
| Antioch University New England | M,D,O |
| Appalachian State University | M |
| Arcadia University | M,D,O |
| Arizona State University at Tempe | M,O |
| Arkansas State University | M,D,O |
| Arkansas Tech University | M,D,O |
| Asbury University | M |
| Assumption University | M,O |
| Auburn University | M,D,O |
| Auburn University at Montgomery | M,O |
| Augustana University | M |
| Augusta University | M,O |
| Aurora University | M,D |
| Averett University | M |
| Azusa Pacific University | M |
| Baldwin Wallace University | M |
| Ball State University | M,D,O |
| Bank Street College of Education | M |
| Barry University | M,D,O |
| Bayamón Central University | M,O |
| Baylor University | M,D,O |
| Bay Path University | M |
| Bemidji State University | M |
| Bethel University (MN) | M,D,O |
| Binghamton University, State University of New York | M |
| Biola University | M,O |

*M—masters degree; D—doctorate; O—other advanced degree; *—Close-Up and/or Display*

| | |
|---|---|
| Bloomsburg University of Pennsylvania | M,O |
| Bluffton University | M |
| Bob Jones University | M,D,O |
| Boise State University | M |
| Boston College | M,D,O |
| Bowie State University | M |
| Bowling Green State University | M |
| Brandman University | M,D |
| Brandon University | M,O |
| Brenau University | M,O |
| Bridgewater State University | M |
| Brigham Young University | M,D,O |
| Brooklyn College of the City University of New York | M,O |
| Buffalo State College, State University of New York | M |
| Bushnell University | M |
| Cabrini University | M,D |
| Caldwell University | M,D,O |
| California Baptist University | M |
| California Lutheran University | M,D |
| California Polytechnic State University, San Luis Obispo | M |
| California State University, Chico | M |
| California State University, Dominguez Hills | M |
| California State University, East Bay | M |
| California State University, Fresno | M |
| California State University, Fullerton | M |
| California State University, Long Beach | M,D |
| California State University, Los Angeles | M,D |
| California State University, Northridge | M |
| California State University, Sacramento | M,D,O |
| California State University, San Marcos | M,D |
| California State University, Stanislaus | M |
| California University of Pennsylvania | M |
| Cambridge College | M,D,O |
| Campbellsville University | M |
| Canisius College | M,O |
| Capella University | M,D |
| Caribbean University | M,D |
| Carlow University | M,O |
| Castleton University | M,O |
| The Catholic University of America | M,O |
| Centenary University | M,D |
| Central Connecticut State University | M,O |
| Central Michigan University | M,O |
| Chaminade University of Honolulu | M |
| Chapman University | M,D,O |
| Chatham University | M |
| Chestnut Hill College | M,O |
| Cheyney University of Pennsylvania | M |
| Chicago State University | M |
| City College of the City University of New York | M,O |
| City University of Seattle | M,O |
| Claremont Graduate University | M,D,O |
| Clarion University of Pennsylvania | M |
| Clark Atlanta University | M |
| Clemson University | M,D,O |
| Cleveland State University | M |
| Coastal Carolina University | M,O |
| College of Charleston | M |
| The College of New Jersey | M,O |
| The College of New Rochelle | M |
| College of Saint Elizabeth | M,O |
| College of St. Joseph | M |
| The College of Saint Rose | M,O |
| College of Staten Island of the City University of New York | M,O |
| Colorado Christian University | M |
| Colorado Mesa University | M,O |
| Colorado State University-Pueblo | M |
| Columbus State University | M,O |
| Concordia College–New York | M |
| Concordia University, St. Paul | M,D,O |
| Concordia University Wisconsin | M |
| Concord University | M |
| Converse College | M |
| Coppin State University | M |
| Curry College | M,O |
| Daemen College | M |
| Dallas Baptist University | M |
| Delaware State University | M |
| Delta State University | M |
| DePaul University | M,D |
| DeSales University | M,O |
| Dominican College | M |
| Dominican University | M |
| Dominican University of California | M |
| Drew University | M,D,O |
| Drexel University | M,D |
| Drury University | M |
| Duquesne University | M,D |
| D'Youville College | M,D |
| East Carolina University | M,O |
| Eastern Illinois University | M |
| Eastern Kentucky University | M |
| Eastern Mennonite University | M |
| Eastern Michigan University | M,O |
| Eastern Nazarene College | M,O |
| Eastern New Mexico University | M |
| Eastern University | M,O |
| East Stroudsburg University of Pennsylvania | M |
| East Tennessee State University | M,O |
| Edinboro University of Pennsylvania | M,O |
| Elmhurst University | M |
| Elms College | M,O |
| Emmanuel College (United States) | M,O |
| Emporia State University | M |
| Endicott College | M,D,O |
| Fairfield University | M,O |
| Fairleigh Dickinson University, Metropolitan Campus | M |
| Fairmont State University | M |
| Ferris State University | M |
| Fitchburg State University | M |
| Flagler College | M |
| Florida Atlantic University | M,D |
| Florida Gulf Coast University | M |
| Florida International University | M,D,O |
| Florida Memorial University | M |
| Fontbonne University | M |
| Fordham University | M,O |
| Fort Hays State University | M |
| Framingham State University | M |
| Francis Marion University | M |
| Franklin Pierce University | M,D,O |
| Freed-Hardeman University | M,O |
| Fresno Pacific University | M |
| Frostburg State University | M |
| Furman University | M,O |
| Gallaudet University | M,D,O |
| George Fox University | M,O |
| George Mason University | M,O |
| Georgetown College | M |
| The George Washington University | M,D,O |
| Georgia College & State University | M,O |
| Georgian Court University | M,O |
| Georgia Southern University | M,O |
| Georgia Southwestern State University | M,O |
| Georgia State University | D |
| Gonzaga University | M,D |
| Gordon College | M,O |
| Goucher College | M,O |
| Governors State University | M |
| Graceland University (IA) | M |
| Grambling State University | M |
| Grand Canyon University | M,D,O |
| Grand Valley State University | M |
| Greensboro College | M |
| Harding University | M,O |
| Hebrew College | M,O |
| Henderson State University | M,O |
| Heritage University | M |
| High Point University | M,D |
| Hofstra University | M,D,O |
| Holy Family University | M |
| Holy Names University | M,O |
| Hood College | M,O |
| Houston Baptist University | M,D |
| Howard University | M |
| Hunter College of the City University of New York | M |
| Idaho State University | M |
| Illinois State University | M,D,O |
| Immaculata University | M,D,O |
| Indiana University Bloomington | M,D,O |
| Indiana University of Pennsylvania | M |
| Indiana University-Purdue University Indianapolis | M,O |
| Indiana University South Bend | M,O |
| Inter American University of Puerto Rico, Barranquitas Campus | M |
| Inter American University of Puerto Rico, Fajardo Campus | M |
| Inter American University of Puerto Rico, Metropolitan Campus | M |
| Inter American University of Puerto Rico, San Germán Campus | M |
| Iona College | M |
| Iowa State University of Science and Technology | M,D |
| Jackson State University | M,O |
| Jacksonville State University | M |
| James Madison University | M |
| Johnson & Wales University | M |
| Kansas State University | M,D,O |
| Kean University | M |
| Kennesaw State University | M,D,O |
| Kent State University | M,D,O |
| Lamar University | M,D |
| Lancaster Bible College | M,D |
| La Salle University | M,O |
| Lasell College | M,O |
| Lee University | M,O |
| Lehigh University | M,D |
| Lehman College of the City University of New York | M |
| Le Moyne College | M,O |
| Lesley University | M,D,O |
| Lewis & Clark College | M,O |
| Lewis University | M |
| Lipscomb University | M,D,O |
| London Metropolitan University | M,D |
| Long Island University - Brentwood Campus | M,O |
| Long Island University - Brooklyn | M,O |
| Long Island University - Hudson | M,O |
| Long Island University - Post | M,D,O |
| Long Island University - Riverhead | M,O |
| Longwood University | M |
| Loras College | M |
| Louisiana Tech University | M,D,O |
| Loyola Marymount University | M |
| Loyola University Chicago | M |
| Lynn University | M,D |
| Madonna University | M |
| Manhattan College | M,O |
| Manhattanville College | M,O |
| Mansfield University of Pennsylvania | M |
| Marian University (WI) | M,D |
| Marshall University | M |
| Martin Luther College | M |
| Mary Baldwin University | M |
| Marygrove College | M,O |
| Marymount University | M |
| Marywood University | M |
| Massachusetts College of Liberal Arts | M,O |
| McDaniel College | M |
| McKendree University | M,D,O |
| McNeese State University | M,O |
| Medaille College | M |
| Mercyhurst University | M |
| Meredith College | M,O |
| Messiah University | M |
| Metropolitan College of New York | M |
| Metropolitan State University | M |
| Metropolitan State University of Denver | M |
| Michigan State University | M,D,O |
| Middle Tennessee State University | M |
| Midwestern State University | M |
| Millersville University of Pennsylvania | M |
| Milligan University | M,D,O |
| Minnesota State University Mankato | M,O |
| Minot State University | M |
| Misericordia University | M |
| Mississippi College | M,D,O |
| Mississippi State University | M,D,O |
| Missouri State University | M |
| Missouri Western State University | M,O |
| Molloy College | M,O |
| Monmouth University | M,D,O |
| Montana State University Billings | M |
| Montclair State University | M |
| Morehead State University | M,O |
| Morningside College | M |
| Mount Mercy University | M |
| Mount St. Joseph University | M,O |
| Mount Saint Mary College | M,O |
| Mount Saint Vincent University | M |
| Murray State University | M,O |
| National Louis University | M,D,O |
| National University | M,O |
| National University College | M |
| Neumann University | M |
| New England College | M,D |
| New Jersey City University | M |
| New Mexico Highlands University | M |
| New Mexico State University | M,D,O |
| New York University | M |
| Niagara University | M,O |
| Norfolk State University | M |
| North Carolina Central University | M |
| North Carolina State University | M |
| Northeastern Illinois University | M |
| Northeastern State University | M |
| Northeastern University | M |
| Northern Arizona University | M,O |
| Northern Illinois University | M |
| Northern Kentucky University | M,O |
| Northern Michigan University | M |
| Northern Vermont University–Johnson | M |
| Northern Vermont University–Lyndon | M |
| Northwestern State University of Louisiana | M,O |
| Northwest Missouri State University | M,D,O |
| Northwest Nazarene University | M,D,O |
| Notre Dame College (OH) | M,O |
| Notre Dame de Namur University | M |
| Nyack College | M |
| Oakland University | M,O |
| The Ohio State University | D |
| Ohio University | M,D |
| Old Dominion University | M,D |
| Ottawa University | M |
| Pace University | M,O |
| Pacific Oaks College | M |
| Pacific University | M |
| Penn State University Park | M,D,O* |
| Piedmont College | M,D,O |
| Pittsburg State University | M,O |
| Point Loma Nazarene University | M |
| Point Park University | M,D |
| Prescott College | M,D |
| Providence College | M |
| Purdue University Fort Wayne | M,O |
| Purdue University Global | M |
| Purdue University Northwest | M |
| Queens College of the City University of New York | M,O |
| Radford University | M,O |
| Ramapo College of New Jersey | M |
| Randolph College | M |
| Regent University | M,D,O |
| Regis College (MA) | M,D |
| Regis University | M,O |
| Rhode Island College | M,O |
| Rider University | M,O |
| Rivier University | M,D,O |
| Roberts Wesleyan College | M |
| Rochester Institute of Technology | M |
| Rockford University | M |
| Roosevelt University | M |
| Rowan University | M,O |
| Rutgers University - New Brunswick | M,D |
| Sage Graduate School | M |
| Saginaw Valley State University | M |
| St. Bonaventure University | M,O |
| St. Cloud State University | M,O |
| St. John Fisher College | M,O |
| St. John's University (NY) | M,O |
| St. Joseph's College, Long Island Campus | M |
| St. Joseph's College, New York | M |
| Saint Joseph's University | M,D,O |
| Saint Louis University | M,D |
| Saint Mary's College of California | M |
| Saint Mary's University of Minnesota | M,O |
| Saint Michael's College | M,O |
| Saint Peter's University | M,O |
| St. Thomas Aquinas College | M,O |
| St. Thomas University - Florida | M,D,O |
| Saint Vincent College | M |
| Saint Xavier University | M |
| Salem College | M |
| Salem State University | M |
| Salus University | M,O |
| Samford University | M,D,O |
| Sam Houston State University | M,D |
| San Diego State University | M |
| San Francisco State University | M,D,O |
| San Ignacio University | M |
| San Jose State University | M |
| Seattle University | M,O |
| Seton Hall University | M |
| Seton Hill University | M |
| Shippensburg University of Pennsylvania | M,D |
| Siena Heights University | M,O |
| Simmons University | M,D,O |
| Slippery Rock University of Pennsylvania | M,D |
| Sonoma State University | M,O |
| South Carolina State University | M |
| Southeastern Louisiana University | M |
| Southeast Missouri State University | M |
| Southern Connecticut State University | M |
| Southern Illinois University Carbondale | M,D |
| Southern Illinois University Edwardsville | M,O |
| Southern Methodist University | M,D |
| Southern New Hampshire University | M,D,O |
| Southern Oregon University | M |
| Southwestern Oklahoma State University | M |
| Southwest Minnesota State University | M |
| Spalding University | M |
| Spring Arbor University | M |
| Springfield College | M,O |
| State University of New York at New Paltz | M |
| State University of New York at Oswego | M |
| State University of New York at Plattsburgh | M |
| State University of New York College at Cortland | M |
| State University of New York College at Oneonta | M,O |
| State University of New York College at Potsdam | M |
| Stephen F. Austin State University | M |
| Stonehill College | M |
| Syracuse University | M,D |
| Tarleton State University | M |
| Teachers College, Columbia University | M,D,O |
| Teachers College of San Joaquin | M |
| Tennessee State University | M,D |
| Tennessee Technological University | M,O |
| Texas A&M International University | M |
| Texas A&M University | M,D |
| Texas A&M University–Commerce | M,D,O |
| Texas A&M University–Corpus Christi | M |
| Texas A&M University–Kingsville | M |
| Texas A&M University–San Antonio | M |
| Texas A&M University–Texarkana | M |
| Texas Christian University | M |
| Texas State University | M |
| Texas Tech University | M,D |
| Texas Woman's University | M,D |
| Towson University | M,O |
| Trevecca Nazarene University | M,O |
| Trinity Baptist College | M |
| Trinity Christian College | M |
| Trinity Washington University | M |
| Tusculum University | M |
| Union College (KY) | M |
| Universidad del Este | M |
| Universidad del Turabo | M |
| Universidad Iberoamericana | M,D |
| Universidad Metropolitana | M |
| Université de Sherbrooke | M,O |
| University at Buffalo, the State University of New York | M,D,O |
| The University of Alabama | M,D,O |
| The University of Alabama at Birmingham | M |
| The University of Alabama in Huntsville | M,O |
| University of Alaska Anchorage | M,O |
| University of Alaska Fairbanks | M |
| University of Alaska Southeast | M |
| University of Alberta | M,D |
| The University of Arizona | M,D |
| University of Arkansas | M |
| University of Arkansas at Little Rock | M,O |
| The University of British Columbia | M,D,O |
| University of California, Berkeley | M,D |
| University of California, Los Angeles | D |
| University of California, Riverside | M,D,O |
| University of Central Arkansas | M,O |
| University of Central Florida | M,O |
| University of Central Missouri | M,D,O |
| University of Central Oklahoma | M |
| University of Cincinnati | M,D |
| University of Colorado Colorado Springs | M,D |
| University of Colorado Denver | M,D |
| University of Denver | M,D,O |
| University of Detroit Mercy | M,D,O |
| University of Florida | M,D,O |
| University of Georgia | M,D,O |
| University of Guam | M |
| University of Hawaii at Manoa | M,D |
| University of Houston | M,D |
| University of Houston–Victoria | M,O |

| | |
|---|---|
| University of Idaho | M,O |
| University of Illinois at Chicago | M,D |
| University of Illinois at Urbana-Champaign | M,D,O |
| The University of Iowa | M,D |
| The University of Kansas | M,D,O |
| University of Kentucky | M,D |
| University of La Verne | M,D,O |
| University of Louisiana at Lafayette | M |
| University of Louisville | M,D,O |
| University of Lynchburg | M |
| University of Maine | M,D,O |
| University of Manitoba | M |
| University of Mary | M,D |
| University of Maryland Eastern Shore | M |
| University of Massachusetts Amherst | M,D,O |
| University of Massachusetts Boston | M |
| University of Massachusetts Dartmouth | M,O |
| University of Memphis | M,D,O |
| University of Miami | M,D,O |
| University of Minnesota, Twin Cities Campus | M,D |
| University of Mississippi | M,D,O |
| University of Missouri | D |
| University of Missouri–Kansas City | M,D,O |
| University of Missouri–St. Louis | M |
| University of Nebraska at Kearney | M,O |
| University of Nebraska at Omaha | M |
| University of Nebraska–Lincoln | M,D,O |
| University of Nevada, Las Vegas | M,D,O |
| University of Nevada, Reno | M,D |
| University of New Hampshire | M,O |
| University of New Mexico | M,D,O |
| University of New Orleans | M |
| University of North Alabama | M |
| The University of North Carolina at Charlotte | M,D,O |
| The University of North Carolina at Greensboro | M,D,O |
| The University of North Carolina Wilmington | M |
| University of North Dakota | M |
| University of Northern Colorado | M,D |
| University of Northern Iowa | M |
| University of North Florida | M |
| University of North Texas | M,D,O |
| University of Oklahoma | M,D |
| University of Oklahoma Health Sciences Center | M,D,O |
| University of Oregon | M,D |
| University of Phoenix - Bay Area Campus | M,D,O |
| University of Phoenix - Hawaii Campus | M |
| University of Phoenix–Online Campus | M,O |
| University of Phoenix - Phoenix Campus | M |
| University of Portland | M,D |
| University of Puerto Rico at Rio Piedras | M |
| University of Puerto Rico - Medical Sciences Campus | O |
| University of Rhode Island | M,D |
| University of Rio Grande | M |
| University of St. Francis (IL) | M,D,O |
| University of Saint Francis (IN) | M |
| University of Saint Joseph | M,O |
| University of Saint Mary | M |
| University of St. Thomas (MN) | M,O |
| University of St. Thomas (TX) | M,D |
| University of San Diego | M |
| University of San Francisco | M,D |
| University of Saskatchewan | M,D |
| The University of Scranton | M |
| University of South Alabama | M,D |
| University of South Carolina | M,D |
| University of South Carolina Upstate | M |
| University of South Dakota | M,D,O |
| University of Southern Maine | M,O |
| University of South Florida | O |
| The University of Tennessee | M,D,O |
| The University of Tennessee at Chattanooga | M,D,O |
| The University of Tennessee at Martin | M |
| The University of Texas at Austin | M,D |
| The University of Texas at El Paso | M |
| The University of Texas at San Antonio | M,D |
| The University of Texas at Tyler | M |
| The University of Texas Health Science Center at San Antonio | M,D |
| The University of Texas of the Permian Basin | M |
| The University of Texas Rio Grande Valley | M |
| University of the Cumberlands | M,D,O |
| University of the Pacific | M,D,O |
| University of the Southwest | M |
| The University of Toledo | M,D,O |
| University of Utah | M,D |
| University of Vermont | M |
| University of Victoria | M,D |
| University of Virginia | M,D,O |
| University of Washington | M,D |
| University of Washington, Tacoma | M |
| The University of West Alabama | M,O |
| The University of Western Ontario | M |
| University of West Florida | M |
| University of Wisconsin–Eau Claire | M |
| University of Wisconsin–La Crosse | M,O |
| University of Wisconsin–Madison | M,D |
| University of Wisconsin–Milwaukee | M,D,O* |
| University of Wisconsin–Oshkosh | M |
| University of Wisconsin–Stevens Point | M |
| University of Wisconsin–Superior | M |
| University of Wisconsin–Whitewater | M,O |
| University of Wyoming | M,D,O |
| Utah State University | M,D,O |
| Valdosta State University | M,D,O |
| Vanderbilt University | M,D* |
| Virginia Commonwealth University | M,D |
| Viterbo University | M,O |
| Wagner College | M |
| Walden University | M,D,O |
| Walla Walla University | M |
| Washburn University | M |
| Washington State University | M,D |
| Washington University in St. Louis | M,D |
| Wayland Baptist University | M |
| Waynesburg University | M,D |
| Wayne State College | M |
| Wayne State University | M,D,O |
| Webster University | M,O |
| Western Connecticut State University | M |
| Western Governors University | M,O |
| Western Illinois University | M |
| Western Kentucky University | M,O |
| Western Michigan University | M,D |
| Western New Mexico University | M |
| Western Oregon University | M |
| Westfield State University | M |
| West Liberty University | M |
| West Virginia University | M,D |
| Whitworth University | M |
| Wichita State University | M |
| Widener University | M,D |
| William Carey University | M,O |
| Wilmington College | M |
| Wilmington University | M,D |
| Wilson College | M |
| Winona State University | M |
| Winston-Salem State University | M |
| Winthrop University | M |
| Worcester State University | M,O |
| Wright State University | M |
| Xavier University | M* |
| Youngstown State University | M |

## SPEECH AND INTERPERSONAL COMMUNICATION

| | |
|---|---|
| Ball State University | M |
| Bob Jones University | M,D,O |
| Brooklyn College of the City University of New York | M,D |
| California State University, Fullerton | M |
| California State University, Northridge | M |
| Colorado State University | M,D |
| Georgia State University | M,D |
| Marquette University | M,O |
| New York University | M,D |
| North Dakota State University | M,D |
| Northeastern Illinois University | M |
| Northwestern University | M,D |
| Ohio University | M,D |
| Old Dominion University | M |
| Portland State University | M,O |
| Rensselaer Polytechnic Institute | M,D |
| San Francisco State University | M |
| San Jose State University | M |
| Seton Hall University | M |
| Southern Illinois University Carbondale | M,D |
| Southern Illinois University Edwardsville | M |
| Texas Christian University | M |
| The University of Alabama | M |
| University of Arkansas at Little Rock | M |
| University of California, Santa Barbara | D |
| University of Hawaii at Manoa | M |
| University of Houston | M |
| The University of Iowa | M,D |
| University of Maryland, College Park | M,D |
| University of Nebraska–Lincoln | M,D |
| University of Nevada, Reno | M |
| University of South Carolina | M,D |
| University of Wisconsin–Madison | M,D |
| University of Wisconsin–Stevens Point | M |
| University of Wisconsin–Superior | M |
| Wake Forest University | M |
| Washington University in St. Louis | M,D |

## SPORT PSYCHOLOGY

| | |
|---|---|
| Adams State University | M |
| Adler University | M |
| Argosy University, Atlanta | M,D,O |
| Argosy University, Orange County | M |
| Argosy University, Phoenix | M,D |
| A.T. Still University | M,D,O |
| Ball State University | M |
| Barry University | M |
| California State University, Fresno | M |
| California State University, Long Beach | M |
| California University of Pennsylvania | M |
| Capella University | M |
| Chatham University | M,D |
| John F. Kennedy University | M,O |
| Lock Haven University of Pennsylvania | M |
| Purdue University | M,D |
| Queen's University at Kingston | M,D |
| Southern Illinois University Edwardsville | M |
| Springfield College | M,D,O |
| University of Denver | M,D,O |
| University of Rhode Island | M |
| The University of Texas at Austin | M,D |
| West Virginia University | M,D |

## SPORTS AND ENTERTAINMENT LAW

| | |
|---|---|
| Arizona State University at Tempe | M,D |
| Chapman University | M,D |
| Drexel University | M,D |
| London Metropolitan University | M,D |
| New York University | M |
| University of New Hampshire | M,D,O |

## SPORTS MANAGEMENT

| | |
|---|---|
| Adams State University | M |
| Adelphi University | M |
| Alcorn State University | M,O |
| American Public University System | M,D |
| American University | M,O |
| Angelo State University | M |
| Arkansas State University | M,O |
| Ashland University | M |
| Auburn University at Montgomery | M,O |
| Augustana University | M |
| Austin Peay State University | M |
| Azusa Pacific University | M |
| Ball State University | M |
| Barry University | M |
| Belhaven University (MS) | M |
| Boise State University | M |
| Bowling Green State University | M |
| Brooklyn College of the City University of New York | M |
| Bryan College | M |
| California Baptist University | M |
| California State University, Fresno | M |
| California State University, Long Beach | M |
| California University of Management and Sciences | M,D |
| California University of Pennsylvania | M |
| Campbellsville University | M |
| Canisius College | M |
| Cardinal Stritch University | M |
| Central Michigan University | M,O |
| Central Washington University | M |
| The Citadel, The Military College of South Carolina | M,O |
| Clayton State University | M |
| Clemson University | M,D,O |
| Coastal Carolina University | M,D,O |
| Coker College | M |
| Columbia University | M |
| Concordia University Irvine | M |
| Concordia University, St. Paul | M,D |
| Dallas Baptist University | M |
| Drexel University | M |
| Duquesne University | M |
| East Carolina University | M,D,O |
| Eastern Kentucky University | M |
| Eastern Michigan University | M |
| Eastern New Mexico University | M |
| Eastern Washington University | M |
| East Stroudsburg University of Pennsylvania | M |
| East Tennessee State University | M,D |
| Endicott College | M |
| Fairleigh Dickinson University, Florham Campus | M |
| Fairleigh Dickinson University, Metropolitan Campus | M |
| Florida Agricultural and Mechanical University | M |
| Florida Atlantic University | M |
| Florida State University | M,D |
| Franklin Pierce University | M,D,O |
| George Mason University | M,O |
| Georgetown University | M,D |
| The George Washington University | M,O |
| Georgia Southern University | M |
| Georgia State University | M |
| Gonzaga University | M,D |
| Grambling State University | M |
| Grand Canyon University | M |
| Grand View University | M,O |
| Hampton University | M |
| Hardin-Simmons University | M |
| Henderson State University | M |
| Hofstra University | M,O |
| Houston Baptist University | M |
| Howard Payne University | M |
| Howard University | M |
| Husson University | M |
| Idaho State University | M |
| Indiana State University | M,D |
| Indiana University Bloomington | M,D |
| Indiana University of Pennsylvania | M |
| Iona College | M,O |
| Jackson State University | M |
| Jacksonville University | M |
| Johnson & Wales University | M |
| Kansas Wesleyan University | M |
| Kennesaw State University | M |
| Kent State University | M |
| Lasell College | M,O |
| Lewis University | M |
| Lock Haven University of Pennsylvania | M |
| Manhattanville College | M,O |
| Marquette University | M,O |
| Marshall University | M |
| Maryville University of Saint Louis | M,O |
| Mercyhurst University | M,O |
| Messiah University | M |
| Midwestern State University | M |
| Millersville University of Pennsylvania | M,O |
| Misericordia University | M |
| Mississippi State University | M,D |
| Missouri State University | M,O |
| Missouri Western State University | M |
| Montclair State University | M |
| Mount St. Mary's University (MD) | M |
| Neumann University | M |
| New England College | M |
| New Mexico Highlands University | M |
| North Carolina State University | M,D |
| Northeastern University | M |
| Northern State University | M |
| Northwestern University | M |
| Ohio Dominican University | M |
| Ohio University | M |
| Old Dominion University | M |
| Pittsburg State University | M |
| Point Loma Nazarene University | M |
| Point Park University | M |
| Purdue University | M,D |
| Robert Morris University Illinois | M |
| St. John's University (NY) | M |
| Saint Mary's College of California | M |
| St. Thomas University - Florida | M,O |
| Sam Houston State University | M |
| San Diego State University | M |
| Seattle University | M |
| Seton Hall University | M,O |
| Sonoma State University | M |
| Southeastern University (FL) | M,D |
| Southeast Missouri State University | M |
| Southern Methodist University | M,D |
| Southern Nazarene University | M |
| Southern New Hampshire University | M,D,O |
| Southwestern Oklahoma State University | M |
| Springfield College | M,D,O |
| State University of New York College at Cortland | M |
| SUNY Brockport | M,O |
| Syracuse University | M |
| Temple University | M,D* |
| Tennessee State University | M |
| Tennessee Technological University | M |
| Texas A&M University | M,D |
| Texas Tech University | M,D |
| Tiffin University | M |
| Troy University | M,D |
| UNB Fredericton | M |
| United States Sports Academy | M,D |
| The University of Alabama | M |
| University of Alberta | M |
| University of Arkansas | M,D |
| University of Arkansas at Little Rock | M |
| University of Central Florida | M |
| University of Cincinnati | M |
| University of Colorado Denver | M |
| University of Connecticut | M |
| University of Dallas | M,D |
| University of Florida | M,D |
| University of Idaho | M,D |
| University of Indianapolis | M |
| The University of Iowa | M,D |
| The University of Kansas | M,D |
| University of Louisiana at Monroe | M |
| University of Louisville | M,D,O |
| University of Mary | M |
| University of Mary Hardin-Baylor | M |
| University of Massachusetts Amherst | M,D |
| University of Miami | M |
| University of Michigan | M,D |
| University of Minnesota, Twin Cities Campus | M,D |
| University of Nebraska at Kearney | M |
| University of New Haven | M,O |
| University of New Mexico | D |
| The University of North Carolina at Chapel Hill | M |
| The University of North Carolina at Pembroke | M |
| University of Northern Colorado | M,D |
| University of Northern Iowa | M |
| University of North Florida | M,D |
| University of Oregon | M |
| University of San Francisco | M |
| University of South Alabama | M |
| University of South Carolina | M |
| University of Southern Indiana | M |
| University of Southern Mississippi | M |
| University of South Florida | M,D |
| The University of Tennessee | M,D |
| University of the Incarnate Word | M,D |
| University of the Southwest | M |
| University of Wisconsin–Parkside | M |
| Upper Iowa University | M |
| Valparaiso University | M |
| Waldorf University | M |
| Washington State University | M,D |
| Wayland Baptist University | M |
| Wayne State College | M |
| Wayne State University | M,D |

*M—masters degree; D—doctorate; O—other advanced degree; *—Close-Up and/or Display*

Webber International University M
Western Illinois University M
Western Kentucky University M
Western Michigan University M
Western New England University M
West Liberty University M
West Texas A&M University M
West Virginia University M,D
Wichita State University M
Wingate University M
Winona State University M,O
Xavier University M*

## STATISTICS
Acadia University M
American University M,O
Arizona State University at Tempe M,D,O
Auburn University M,D
Ball State University M
Baruch College of the City University of New York M
Baylor University M,D
Binghamton University, State University of New York M,D
Bowling Green State University M,D
Brigham Young University M
Brock University M
California State University, East Bay M
Carnegie Mellon University M,D
Central Connecticut State University M,O
Claremont Graduate University M,D
Clemson University M,D
Colorado State University M,D
Columbia University M,D
Concordia University (Canada) M,D
Cornell University M,D
Dalhousie University M,D
Duke University M,D
East Carolina University M
Florida Atlantic University M,D
Florida International University M
George Mason University M,D,O
Georgetown University M
The George Washington University M,D,O
Georgia State University M,D
Hampton University M
Harvard University M,D*
Hunter College of the City University of New York M
Indiana University Bloomington M,D
Indiana University-Purdue University Indianapolis M,D
Iowa State University of Science and Technology M,D
Jackson State University M
Johns Hopkins University M,D
Kansas State University M,D,O
Lehigh University M,D
Louisiana State University and Agricultural & Mechanical College M
Loyola University Chicago M
McGill University M,D,O
McMaster University M
McNeese State University M
Memorial University of Newfoundland M,D
Miami University M
Michigan State University M,D
Minnesota State University Mankato M
Mississippi State University M,D
Missouri University of Science and Technology M,D
Montana State University M,D
Montclair State University M
Murray State University M
New Jersey Institute of Technology M,D,O
New Mexico Institute of Mining and Technology M,D
New York University M,D
North Carolina State University M,D
North Dakota State University M,D
Northern Arizona University M,O
Northern Illinois University M,D
Northwestern University M,D
Oakland University O
The Ohio State University M,D
Oklahoma State University M,D
Old Dominion University M,D
Oregon State University M,D
Penn State University Park M,D*
Portland State University M,D,O
Purdue University M,D
Queen's University at Kingston M,D
Rice University M,D
Rochester Institute of Technology O
Rutgers University - New Brunswick M,D
St. John's University (NY) M
Sam Houston State University M
San Diego State University M
Simon Fraser University M,D
South Dakota State University M,D
Southern Illinois University Edwardsville M
Southern Methodist University M,D
Stanford University M,D
Stephen F. Austin State University M
Stevens Institute of Technology M,O
Stony Brook University, State University of New York M,D,O
Temple University M,D*
Texas A&M University M,D
Texas A&M University–Kingsville M
Texas Tech University M,D
UNB Fredericton M,D
Université de Montréal M,D,O
The University of Akron M
University of Alaska Fairbanks M,D,O
University of Alberta M,D,O
The University of Arizona M,D
University of Arkansas M
The University of British Columbia M,D
University of Calgary M,D
University of California, Berkeley M,D
University of California, Davis M,D
University of California, Irvine M,D
University of California, Los Angeles M,D
University of California, Riverside M
University of California, San Diego M,D
University of California, Santa Barbara M,D
University of California, Santa Cruz M,D
University of Central Oklahoma M
University of Chicago M,D,O
University of Cincinnati M,D
University of Colorado Denver M,D
University of Connecticut M,D
University of Delaware M
University of Florida M,D
University of Georgia M,D
University of Guelph M,D
University of Houston–Clear Lake M
University of Idaho M
University of Illinois at Chicago M,D
University of Illinois at Urbana-Champaign M,D
The University of Iowa M,D,O
The University of Kansas M,D,O
University of Kentucky M,D
The University of Manchester M,D
University of Manitoba M,D
University of Maryland, Baltimore County M,D
University of Maryland, College Park M,D
University of Massachusetts Amherst M,D
University of Memphis M,D
University of Michigan M,D,O
University of Minnesota, Twin Cities Campus M,D
University of Missouri M,D
University of Missouri–Kansas City M,D
University of Nebraska–Lincoln M,D
University of New Mexico M,D
The University of North Carolina at Chapel Hill M,D
The University of North Carolina Wilmington M,O
University of North Florida M
University of Notre Dame M,D
University of Ottawa M,D
University of Pennsylvania M,D
University of Pittsburgh M,D*
University of Regina M,D
University of Rhode Island M,D,O
University of Rochester M,D
University of Saskatchewan M,D
University of South Africa M,D
University of South Carolina M,D,O
University of Southern California M,D
University of Southern Maine M,O
University of South Florida M,D
The University of Tennessee M,D
The University of Texas at Austin M,D
The University of Texas at Dallas M,D
The University of Texas at El Paso M
The University of Texas at San Antonio M,D
The University of Toledo M,D
University of Toronto M,D
University of Utah M,D,O
University of Vermont M
University of Victoria M,D
University of Virginia M,D
University of Washington M,D
University of Waterloo M,D
The University of Western Ontario M,D
University of Windsor M,D
University of Wisconsin–Madison M,D
University of Wisconsin–Milwaukee M,D*
Université Laval M
Utah State University M,D
Virginia Polytechnic Institute and State University M,D
Washington University in St. Louis M,D
Wayne State University M,D
Western Michigan University M,D,O
West Virginia University M,D
Yale University M,D
York University M,D
Youngstown State University M

## STRUCTURAL BIOLOGY
Albert Einstein College of Medicine D
Baylor College of Medicine D
Carnegie Mellon University M,D
Columbia University D
Duke University O
Florida State University D
Illinois State University M,D
Iowa State University of Science and Technology M,D
Massachusetts Institute of Technology D
Michigan State University D
Northwestern University D
Stanford University D
Stony Brook University, State University of New York D
Tufts University D
Tulane University M,D
University at Buffalo, the State University of New York M,D
The University of Alabama at Birmingham D
University of Connecticut M,D
The University of Manchester M,D
University of Minnesota, Twin Cities Campus D
University of Oklahoma M,D
University of Pittsburgh D*
University of Rochester D
The University of Texas Health Science Center at San Antonio M,D
The University of Texas Medical Branch D
University of Washington D
Weill Cornell Medicine M,D

## STRUCTURAL ENGINEERING
California State University, Northridge M
The Citadel, The Military College of South Carolina M,O
Clemson University M,D
Cornell University M,D
Drexel University M,D
Illinois Institute of Technology M,D
Instituto Tecnologico de Santo Domingo M,O
Iowa State University of Science and Technology M,D
Kansas State University M,D
Kennesaw State University M
Louisiana State University and Agricultural & Mechanical College M,D
Marquette University M,D,O
Massachusetts Institute of Technology M,D,O
McGill University M,D
Northwestern University M,D
Norwich University M
Ohio University M,D
Old Dominion University M
Oregon State University M,D
Penn State Harrisburg M,O
Polytechnique Montréal M,D,O
Pontificia Universidad Catolica Madre y Maestra M
Southern Illinois University Edwardsville M
Southern Methodist University M,D
Stanford University M,D,O
Stevens Institute of Technology M,D,O
Tufts University M,D
UNB Fredericton M,D
University at Buffalo, the State University of New York M,D
The University of Alabama at Birmingham M
University of Alberta M,D
University of Calgary M,D
University of California, Berkeley M,D
University of California, San Diego M,D
University of Central Florida M,D,O
University of Colorado Denver M,D
University of Dayton M
University of Delaware M,D
The University of Manchester M,D
University of Massachusetts Amherst M,D
University of Memphis M,D,O
University of Michigan M,D,O
University of Puerto Rico at Mayagüez M,D
University of South Florida M,D
The University of Texas at Tyler M
University of Washington M,D
University of Wisconsin–Madison M

## STUDENT AFFAIRS
Alfred University M
Alliant International University - Los Angeles M,D,O
Alliant International University - San Diego M,D,O
Appalachian State University M
Arkansas State University M,O
Arkansas Tech University M,D,O
Binghamton University, State University of New York M
Bloomsburg University of Pennsylvania M
Bob Jones University M,D,O
Bowling Green State University M
Bucknell University M
California State University, Fresno M
California State University, Long Beach M,D
Canisius College M,O
Carlow University M
Central Michigan University M,D,O
The Citadel, The Military College of South Carolina M,O
Claremont Graduate University M,D,O
Clemson University M,D,O
The College of Saint Rose M
Colorado State University M,D
Dallas Baptist University M
DePaul University M
Eastern Illinois University M
Eastern Michigan University M,D,O
Fresno Pacific University M,O
The George Washington University M,D,O
Grambling State University M,D,O
Hampton University M,D,O
Illinois State University M,D
Indiana State University M,D,O
Indiana University Bloomington M,D,O
Indiana University of Pennsylvania M
Iowa State University of Science and Technology M,D
Kansas State University M,D,O
Kent State University M
Lewis & Clark College M,D,O
Lewis University M
Manhattan College M,O
Marquette University M,D,O
Messiah University M
Miami University M
Minnesota State University Mankato M,D
Mississippi State University M,D,O
Missouri State University M
Monmouth University M,D,O
Morgan State University M,D
New York University M,D
Northern Arizona University M,D,O
Northwestern State University of Louisiana M
Nova Southeastern University M,D,O
Ohio University M,D
Oregon State University M
Providence University College & Theological Seminary M,D,O
Purdue University Global M
Quincy University M
Regent University M,D,O
Rutgers University - New Brunswick M
St. Cloud State University M
St. Edward's University M
Saint Louis University M,D,O
San Jose State University M
Seton Hall University M,D,O
Shippensburg University of Pennsylvania M,D
Southern Arkansas University–Magnolia M
Southern Illinois University Edwardsville M
Springfield College M,D,O
State University of New York at Plattsburgh M,O
Syracuse University M
Texas State University M
University of Arkansas at Little Rock M,D
University of Bridgeport M
University of Central Arkansas M
University of Central Florida M,O
University of Central Missouri M,D,O
University of Central Oklahoma M
University of Dayton M,O
University of Florida M,D,O
University of Georgia M,D,O
The University of Iowa M,D
University of Louisville M,D
University of Maryland, College Park M,D,O
University of Minnesota, Twin Cities Campus M
University of Nebraska at Kearney M,O
University of Northern Colorado M,D
University of Northern Iowa M
University of Rhode Island M
University of Rochester M
University of St. Thomas (MN) M,D,O
University of South Carolina M
University of Southern California M
The University of Tennessee M
The University of Tennessee at Martin M
University of the Cumberlands M,D,O
University of Utah M,D
University of Virginia M,D,O
The University of West Alabama M
University of West Florida M
University of Wisconsin–La Crosse M,D
University of Wyoming M,D
Virginia Commonwealth University M
Walsh University M
Western Illinois University M
Western Kentucky University M
William James College M,D,O

## SUPPLY CHAIN MANAGEMENT
Abilene Christian University M
Adelphi University M
Albany State University M
American Graduate University M,O
Anderson University (SC) M
Arizona State University at Tempe M,D
Ashland University M
Athens State University M
Binghamton University, State University of New York D
Boston University M
Brigham Young University M
California Polytechnic State University, San Luis Obispo M
California State University, East Bay M
California State University, San Bernardino M
Capella University M,D
Case Western Reserve University M,D
Central Connecticut State University M,O
Clarkson University M,O
Clayton State University M
Clemson University M,D
Concordia University (Canada) M,D,O
Delaware Valley University M
DePaul University M,D
DeSales University M
Duquesne University M
Eastern Michigan University M,O
Elmhurst University M
Embry-Riddle Aeronautical University–Worldwide M
Fairleigh Dickinson University, Florham Campus M
Ferris State University M
Fontbonne University M
Friends University M
Georgia Southern University D
Golden Gate University M,D,O
HEC Montreal M,O
Howard University M

| | |
|---|---|
| Indiana University-Purdue University Indianapolis | M |
| Johnson & Wales University | M |
| Loyola University Chicago | M,O |
| Maine Maritime Academy | M |
| Marquette University | M,O |
| Maryville University of Saint Louis | M,O |
| McGill University | M,D,O |
| Metropolitan State University | M,D,O |
| Michigan State University | M,D |
| Moravian College | M |
| Naval Postgraduate School | M |
| New York Institute of Technology | M |
| Niagara University | M |
| North Carolina Agricultural and Technical State University | M |
| North Carolina State University | M |
| Norwich University | M |
| Nova Southeastern University | M |
| Old Dominion University | M |
| Penn State Harrisburg | M,O |
| Polytechnic University of Puerto Rico, Miami Campus | M |
| Portland State University | M |
| Purdue University Global | M |
| Quinnipiac University | M |
| Rensselaer Polytechnic Institute | M |
| Rutgers University - Newark | D |
| St. Norbert College | M |
| Santa Clara University | M |
| Seton Hall University | M,O |
| Shippensburg University of Pennsylvania | M,D,O |
| Southern Arkansas University–Magnolia | M |
| Southern New Hampshire University | M,D,O |
| Strayer University | M |
| Suffolk University | M |
| Syracuse University | M |
| Towson University | M,O |
| University at Buffalo, the State University of New York | M,D |
| The University of Akron | M |
| The University of Alabama in Huntsville | M,O |
| University of Dallas | M,D |
| University of Florida | M,D,O |
| University of Houston | M |
| University of Houston - Downtown | M |
| The University of Kansas | M,D |
| University of La Verne | M |
| University of Louisville | M,D,O |
| The University of Manchester | M |
| University of Memphis | M,D |
| University of Michigan | M,D |
| University of Michigan–Dearborn | M |
| University of Minnesota, Twin Cities Campus | M,D |
| University of Missouri–St. Louis | M,D,O |
| The University of North Carolina at Charlotte | M,O |
| The University of North Carolina at Greensboro | M,D,O |
| University of North Texas | M,D,O |
| University of Pittsburgh | M* |
| University of Rhode Island | M,D |
| University of St. Francis (IL) | M,O |
| University of San Diego | M,O |
| University of South Dakota | M,O |
| University of Southern California | M,D,O |
| The University of Tennessee at Chattanooga | M,O |
| The University of Texas at Austin | M,D |
| The University of Texas at Dallas | M |
| University of Washington | M,D |
| University of Wisconsin–Madison | M |
| University of Wisconsin–Platteville | M |
| University of Wisconsin–Stout | M |
| Walden University | M,D,O |
| Washington University in St. Louis | M |
| Western Illinois University | M,O |
| Wichita State University | M |
| Wilfrid Laurier University | M,D |
| Worcester Polytechnic Institute | M,D,O |
| Wright State University | M |
| Youngstown State University | O |

### SURVEYING SCIENCE AND ENGINEERING

| | |
|---|---|
| UNB Fredericton | M,D |

### SURVEY METHODOLOGY

| | |
|---|---|
| University of Maryland, College Park | M,D |
| University of Michigan | M,D,O |
| University of Nebraska–Lincoln | M,D |

### SUSTAINABILITY MANAGEMENT

| | |
|---|---|
| Adler University | M |
| American University | M |
| Anaheim University | M,D,O |
| Argosy University, Chicago | M,D |
| Argosy University, Hawaii | M,D,O |
| Argosy University, Los Angeles | M,D |
| Argosy University, Northern Virginia | M,D,O |
| Argosy University, Orange County | M,D,O |
| Argosy University, Phoenix | M,D |
| Argosy University, Seattle | M,D |
| Argosy University, Tampa | M,D |
| Argosy University, Twin Cities | M,D |
| Bard College | M,O |
| Baruch College of the City University of New York | M,D |
| Bluffton University | M |
| Case Western Reserve University | D |
| Chatham University | M |
| City University of Seattle | M,O |
| Clark University | M |
| Colorado State University | M |
| Columbia University | M |
| DePaul University | M,D |
| Duquesne University | M |
| Edgewood College | M |
| Fairleigh Dickinson University, Florham Campus | O |
| Franklin Pierce University | M,D,O |
| Goddard College | M |
| Illinois Institute of Technology | M |
| Indiana University Bloomington | M,D,O |
| James Madison University | M |
| Maastricht School of Management | M,D |
| Maharishi International University | M,D |
| Michigan Technological University | M,D,O |
| Naropa University | M |
| National University | M |
| The New School | M |
| Oklahoma State University | M,D,O |
| Oregon State University | M,D |
| Penn State Great Valley | M,O |
| Presidio Graduate School (CA) | M,O |
| Rochester Institute of Technology | M,D |
| Royal Roads University | M,O |
| San Francisco State University | M |
| Seattle Pacific University | M |
| SIT Graduate Institute | M |
| Southeastern Louisiana University | M |
| Southern New Hampshire University | M,D,O |
| South University - Savannah | M |
| State University of New York College of Environmental Science and Forestry | M,D,O |
| Syracuse University | O |
| Tufts University | M,D |
| The University of British Columbia | M,D |
| University of California, Berkeley | O |
| University of California, Merced | M,D |
| University of Colorado Denver | M |
| University of Louisville | M,D |
| University of New Hampshire | M,O |
| University of Portland | M |
| University of Saint Francis (IN) | M |
| University of Saskatchewan | M,D |
| University of Southern Maine | M |
| University of South Florida | M,O |
| University of Vermont | M |
| University of Wisconsin–Green Bay | M |
| University of Wisconsin–Parkside | M |
| University of Wisconsin–Stout | M |
| University of Wisconsin–Superior | M |

### SUSTAINABLE DEVELOPMENT

| | |
|---|---|
| American University | M,D,O |
| The American University in Cairo | M,D,O |
| Antioch University Los Angeles | M |
| Antioch University New England | M,D |
| Arizona State University at Tempe | M,D,O |
| Baruch College of the City University of New York | M |
| Binghamton University, State University of New York | M |
| Boston Architectural College | M |
| Brandeis University | M |
| California State University, Stanislaus | M |
| Carnegie Mellon University | M,D |
| The Catholic University of America | M,O |
| City College of the City University of New York | M |
| Clarkson University | M,D |
| Clark University | M |
| Cleveland State University | M,O |
| Colorado State University | M,O |
| Columbia University | M,D |
| Cornell University | M,D |
| Dartmouth College | D |
| DePaul University | M |
| Eastern Illinois University | M |
| Eastern Michigan University | M,O |
| Emory University | M |
| Future Generations University | M |
| Hawaii Pacific University | M |
| HEC Montreal | O |
| Hofstra University | M |
| Hunter College of the City University of New York | M,O |
| Instituto Centroamericano de Administracion de Empresas | M |
| Instituto Tecnologico de Santo Domingo | M,O |
| Iowa State University of Science and Technology | M,D |
| Johnson & Wales University | M |
| Judson University | M |
| Lehigh University | M,O |
| Lenoir-Rhyne University | M |
| Lesley University | M,D,O |
| Lipscomb University | M,O |
| Long Island University - Post | M,O |
| Manhattanville College | M,O |
| Michigan State University | M,D |
| Minneapolis College of Art and Design | M |
| Mississippi State University | M,D |
| Montclair State University | M |
| New Jersey Institute of Technology | M,D,O |
| New York School of Interior Design | M |
| New York University | M |
| Northern Arizona University | M |
| Penn State University Park | M* |
| Pratt Institute | M |
| Rochester Institute of Technology | M,D |
| St. Edward's University | M |
| Savannah College of Art and Design | M |
| Saybrook University | M,D |
| SIT Graduate Institute | M |
| Southern Illinois University Edwardsville | M |
| Southern Methodist University | M,D |
| Stanford University | M,D,O |
| State University of New York College of Environmental Science and Forestry | M,D,O |
| Texas A&M University–Kingsville | D |
| Texas State University | M |
| Texas Tech University | M,D |
| Thomas Jefferson University | M |
| Unity College | M |
| University at Buffalo, the State University of New York | M,D |
| The University of Alabama at Birmingham | M |
| University of Alaska Fairbanks | M,D |
| The University of British Columbia | M |
| University of Calgary | M,D |
| University of California, Berkeley | M,O |
| University of California, Santa Barbara | M,D |
| University of Colorado Denver | M,D |
| University of Florida | M,O |
| University of Georgia | M,D |
| University of Hawaii at Manoa | M,D,O |
| University of Houston | M |
| The University of Iowa | M,D |
| University of Maryland, College Park | M |
| University of Massachusetts Amherst | M |
| University of Michigan | M,D |
| University of Notre Dame | M |
| University of Oklahoma | M,D |
| University of South Dakota | M,D |
| University of Southern California | M,D,O |
| University of South Florida | M,O |
| The University of Texas at Austin | M |
| The University of Texas Rio Grande Valley | M |
| University of Vermont | M |
| University of Washington | M,D |
| The University of Western Ontario | M,D |
| University of Wisconsin–Madison | M |
| University of Wisconsin–Stevens Point | D |
| Walden University | M,D,O |
| Xavier University | M* |

### SYSTEMS BIOLOGY

| | |
|---|---|
| Albert Einstein College of Medicine | D |
| George Mason University | M,D,O |
| The George Washington University | D |
| Harvard University | D* |
| Massachusetts Institute of Technology | D |
| Michigan State University | D |
| Northwestern University | D |
| Oregon State University | M,D |
| Purdue University | D |
| Rutgers University - New Brunswick | D |
| Stanford University | D |
| University of California, Irvine | D |
| University of California, Merced | M,D |
| University of California, San Diego | D |
| University of Chicago | D |
| University of Cincinnati | D |
| University of Colorado Denver | M,D |
| University of Pittsburgh | D* |
| University of Toronto | M,D |
| Virginia Commonwealth University | D |
| Washington University in St. Louis | D |
| Weill Cornell Medicine | M,D |

### SYSTEMS ENGINEERING

| | |
|---|---|
| Air Force Institute of Technology | M,D |
| Arizona State University at Tempe | M |
| Auburn University | M,D,O |
| Boston University | M,D |
| California Institute of Technology | M,D |
| California State Polytechnic University, Pomona | M |
| California State University, Fullerton | M |
| California State University, Northridge | M |
| Carleton University | M,D |
| Carnegie Mellon University | M |
| Case Western Reserve University | M,D |
| The Catholic University of America | M,O |
| The Citadel, The Military College of South Carolina | M,O |
| Colorado State University | M,D |
| Colorado State University-Pueblo | M |
| Colorado Technical University Aurora | M |
| Colorado Technical University Colorado Springs | M |
| Concordia University (Canada) | M,D,O |
| Cornell University | M,D |
| Dartmouth College | M,D |
| Embry-Riddle Aeronautical University–Daytona | M |
| Embry-Riddle Aeronautical University–Worldwide | M |
| Florida Institute of Technology | M,D |
| George Mason University | M,D,O |
| Georgetown University | M,D |
| The George Washington University | M,D,O |
| Georgia Southern University | M |
| Harrisburg University of Science and Technology | M |
| Indiana University Bloomington | D |
| Instituto Tecnológico y de Estudios Superiores de Monterrey, Campus Chihuahua | M,O |
| Instituto Tecnológico y de Estudios Superiores de Monterrey, Campus Monterrey | M,D |
| Iowa State University of Science and Technology | M |
| Johns Hopkins University | M,O |
| Kennesaw State University | M |
| Lehigh University | M,D,O |
| Loyola Marymount University | M |
| Massachusetts Institute of Technology | M,D |
| Mississippi State University | M,D |
| Missouri University of Science and Technology | M,D |
| Naval Postgraduate School | M,D,O |
| New Mexico Institute of Mining and Technology | M |
| New Mexico State University | M,D,O |
| North Carolina Agricultural and Technical State University | M,D |
| Northeastern University | M,D,O |
| Oakland University | M,D |
| The Ohio State University | M,D |
| Ohio University | M |
| Old Dominion University | M,D |
| Oregon State University | M,D |
| Penn State Great Valley | M,O |
| Purdue University Fort Wayne | M |
| Regis University | M,O |
| Rensselaer Polytechnic Institute | M,D |
| Rochester Institute of Technology | M,D |
| Rose-Hulman Institute of Technology | M |
| Rutgers University - New Brunswick | M,D |
| San Jose State University | M |
| Simon Fraser University | M,D |
| Southern Methodist University | M,D |
| Stevens Institute of Technology | M,D,O |
| Stony Brook University, State University of New York | M |
| Tennessee State University | M,D |
| Texas A&M University–Kingsville | D |
| The University of Alabama in Huntsville | M,D |
| University of Alberta | M,D |
| The University of Arizona | M,D,O |
| University of Arkansas at Little Rock | M,D,O |
| University of California, Merced | M,D |
| University of Colorado Colorado Springs | M,D |
| University of Florida | M,D,O |
| University of Houston–Clear Lake | M |
| University of Illinois at Urbana-Champaign | M,D |
| University of Louisiana at Lafayette | M,D |
| University of Maryland, Baltimore County | M,O |
| University of Maryland, College Park | M |
| University of Massachusetts Dartmouth | M,O |
| University of Michigan | M,D |
| University of Michigan–Dearborn | M,D |
| University of Nebraska at Omaha | M,O |
| University of New Mexico | M,D |
| The University of North Carolina at Charlotte | M,D |
| University of Pennsylvania | M,D |
| University of Regina | M,D |
| University of Rhode Island | M,D |
| University of St. Thomas (MN) | M,O |
| University of South Alabama | D |
| University of Southern California | M,D,O |
| University of South Florida | O |
| The University of Texas at Arlington | M |
| The University of Texas at Dallas | M,D |
| The University of Texas at El Paso | M |
| The University of Texas Rio Grande Valley | M |
| University of Utah | M,O |
| University of Virginia | M,D |
| University of Washington | M,D |
| University of Waterloo | M,D |
| University of Wisconsin–Madison | M,D |
| Virginia Polytechnic Institute and State University | M,O |
| Wayne State University | M,D,O |
| Worcester Polytechnic Institute | M,D,O |
| Youngstown State University | M |

### SYSTEMS SCIENCE

| | |
|---|---|
| Arizona State University at Tempe | M,D |
| Binghamton University, State University of New York | M,D |
| Carleton University | M,D |
| Claremont Graduate University | M,D,O |
| Eastern Illinois University | M,O |
| Fairleigh Dickinson University, Metropolitan Campus | M |
| Harrisburg University of Science and Technology | M |
| Hood College | M |
| Louisiana State University and Agricultural & Mechanical College | M,D |
| Louisiana State University in Shreveport | M |
| Miami University | M |
| Oakland University | M,D |
| Portland State University | M,D,O |
| Rensselaer at Hartford | M |

*M—masters degree; D—doctorate; O—other advanced degree; *—Close-Up and/or Display*

| | |
|---|---|
| Stevens Institute of Technology | M,D |
| Strayer University | M |
| Universidad Autonoma de Guadalajara | M,D |
| University of Michigan | M,D |
| University of Ottawa | M,D,O |
| Worcester Polytechnic Institute | M,D,O |

## TAXATION

| | |
|---|---|
| American International College | M,D,O |
| American University | M,O |
| Appalachian State University | M |
| Baruch College of the City University of New York | M |
| Bentley University | M |
| Boise State University | M |
| Bryant University | M |
| California Miramar University | M |
| California Polytechnic State University, San Luis Obispo | M |
| California State University, Fullerton | M |
| California State University, Northridge | M,O |
| Capital University | M |
| Chapman University | M,D |
| DePaul University | M,D |
| Fairfield University | M,O |
| Fairleigh Dickinson University, Florham Campus | M,O |
| Fairleigh Dickinson University, Metropolitan Campus | M |
| Florida Gulf Coast University | M |
| Florida State University | M,D |
| Fordham University | M,D |
| Georgetown University | M,D |
| Georgia State University | M |
| Golden Gate University | M,D,O |
| Goldey-Beacom College | M |
| Gonzaga University | M |
| Grand Valley State University | M |
| HEC Montreal | M,O |
| Hofstra University | M,O |
| Illinois Institute of Technology | M,D |
| Instituto Tecnologico de Santo Domingo | M,O |
| James Madison University | M |
| Liberty University | M,D |
| Lipscomb University | M,O |
| Long Island University - Brooklyn | M,O |
| Long Island University - Post | M |
| Loyola University Chicago | M,D,O |
| Metropolitan State University of Denver | M |
| Michigan State University | M,D |
| Mississippi State University | M |
| National Paralegal College | M |
| New York University | M,D,O |
| Northeastern University | M |
| Northern Illinois University | M |
| Northern Kentucky University | M,O |
| Northwestern University | M,D |
| Pace University | M |
| Robert Morris University | M |
| St. John's University (NY) | M |
| St. Thomas University - Florida | M,D |
| Seton Hall University | O |
| Southern Illinois University Edwardsville | M |
| Southern Methodist University | M,D |
| Southern New Hampshire University | M,D,O |
| State University of New York College at Old Westbury | M |
| Strayer University | M |
| Suffolk University | M,O |
| Taft University System | M,D |
| Temple University | M,D* |
| Texas Christian University | M |
| Texas Tech University | M,D |
| Thomas Jefferson University | M |
| Université de Montréal | M,D,O |
| Université de Sherbrooke | M,O |
| University at Albany, State University of New York | M |
| The University of Akron | M |
| The University of Alabama | M,D |
| The University of Alabama in Huntsville | M |
| University of Baltimore | M,D |
| The University of British Columbia | M,D |
| University of Cincinnati | M |
| University of Colorado Denver | M |
| University of Denver | M |
| University of Florida | M,D |
| University of Hartford | M,O |
| University of Hawaii at Manoa | M |
| University of Houston | M,D |
| University of Miami | M,D |
| University of Michigan | M,D |
| University of Minnesota, Twin Cities Campus | M |
| University of Mississippi | M,D |
| University of Missouri | M,D,O |
| University of New Haven | M,O |
| University of New Mexico | M |
| University of New Orleans | M |
| University of Notre Dame | M |
| University of San Diego | M,D,O |
| University of Southern California | M |
| University of South Florida | M,D |
| The University of Texas at Arlington | M,D |
| University of the Sacred Heart | M |
| University of Washington | M,D |
| University of Waterloo | M,D |
| University of Wisconsin–Madison | M |
| University of Wisconsin–Milwaukee | M,O* |
| Villanova University | M |
| Wake Forest University | M |
| Walsh College of Accountancy and Business Administration | M |
| Wayne State University | M,D,O |
| Weber State University | M |
| Western Michigan University Cooley Law School | M,D |
| Wichita State University | M |
| Widener University | M |
| Yeshiva University | M |

## TECHNICAL COMMUNICATION

| | |
|---|---|
| Auburn University | M,D,O |
| Boise State University | M |
| Bowling Green State University | M,D |
| Drexel University | M |
| East Carolina University | M,D,O |
| Eastern Michigan University | M,O |
| Eastern Washington University | M |
| Harvard University | M* |
| Indiana University-Purdue University Indianapolis | M |
| Lawrence Technological University | M,O |
| Minnesota State University Mankato | M,O |
| Missouri University of Science and Technology | M |
| New Jersey Institute of Technology | M,D,O |
| Northeastern University | M |
| Texas State University | M |
| University of Houston - Downtown | M |
| University of Nebraska at Omaha | M,O |
| University of South Florida | O |
| University of Wisconsin–Stout | M |

## TECHNICAL WRITING

| | |
|---|---|
| Carnegie Mellon University | M |
| Drexel University | M |
| Illinois Institute of Technology | M,D |
| James Madison University | M |
| Johns Hopkins University | M,O |
| Laurentian University | O |
| Louisiana Tech University | M,D,O |
| Massachusetts Institute of Technology | M |
| Metropolitan State University | M |
| Texas Tech University | M,D |
| The University of Alabama in Huntsville | M,O |
| University of Arkansas at Little Rock | M |
| University of North Alabama | M |
| The University of North Carolina at Charlotte | M,O |
| The University of North Carolina at Greensboro | M,D,O |
| University of the Sciences | M,O |
| University of Waterloo | M,D |
| Western Carolina University | M,O |

## TECHNOLOGY AND PUBLIC POLICY

| | |
|---|---|
| Arizona State University at Tempe | M |
| Carnegie Mellon University | M,D |
| Eastern Michigan University | M |
| The George Washington University | M,O |
| Massachusetts Institute of Technology | M,D |
| Rensselaer Polytechnic Institute | M,D |
| Rochester Institute of Technology | M |
| University of Minnesota, Twin Cities Campus | M |
| University of South Africa | M,D |
| The University of Texas at Austin | M |

## TELECOMMUNICATIONS

| | |
|---|---|
| Ball State University | M |
| Boston University | M,O |
| California Miramar University | M |
| Claremont Graduate University | M,D,O |
| Drexel University | M |
| Fairfield University | M,O |
| Florida International University | M,D |
| Franklin Pierce University | M,D,O |
| The George Washington University | M,D,O |
| Illinois Institute of Technology | M,D |
| Instituto Tecnologico de Santo Domingo | M,O |
| New Jersey Institute of Technology | M,D |
| Northeastern University | M,D,O |
| Ohio University | M |
| Pace University | M,D,O |
| Rochester Institute of Technology | M |
| Southern Methodist University | M,D |
| Stevens Institute of Technology | M,D,O |
| Stony Brook University, State University of New York | M,D,O |
| Stratford University (VA) | M,D |
| Universidad del Turabo | M |
| Université du Québec, Institut National de la Recherche Scientifique | M,D |
| University of Alberta | M,D |
| University of Arkansas | M,D |
| University of California, San Diego | M,D |
| University of Colorado Boulder | M |
| University of Florida | M,D |
| University of Hawaii at Manoa | O |
| University of Houston | M |
| University of Maryland, College Park | M |
| University of Massachusetts Dartmouth | M,D,O |
| University of Mississippi | M,D |
| University of Missouri–Kansas City | M,D,O |
| The University of North Carolina at Chapel Hill | M,D,O |
| University of Oklahoma | M,D |
| University of Southern California | M,D,O |
| The University of Texas at Dallas | M,D |

## TELECOMMUNICATIONS MANAGEMENT

| | |
|---|---|
| Alaska Pacific University | M |
| Boston University | M,O |
| California Miramar University | M |
| Capitol Technology University | M |
| Carnegie Mellon University | M |
| Concordia University (Canada) | M,D,O |
| East Carolina University | M,D,O |
| Instituto Tecnológico y de Estudios Superiores de Monterrey, Campus Ciudad de México | M |
| Instituto Tecnológico y de Estudios Superiores de Monterrey, Campus Ciudad Obregón | M |
| Instituto Tecnológico y de Estudios Superiores de Monterrey, Campus Estado de México | M,D |
| Instituto Tecnológico y de Estudios Superiores de Monterrey, Campus Irapuato | M,D |
| Murray State University | M |
| Oklahoma State University | M,D,O |
| San Diego State University | M |
| Stevens Institute of Technology | M,D,O |
| Strayer University | M |
| University of Colorado Boulder | M |
| University of South Africa | M,D |
| University of Wisconsin–Stout | M |

## TEXTILE DESIGN

| | |
|---|---|
| Academy of Art University | M |
| Arizona State University at Tempe | M,D |
| California State University, Los Angeles | M |
| Concordia University (Canada) | M |
| Cornell University | M,D |
| Cranbrook Academy of Art | M |
| Drexel University | M |
| East Carolina University | M |
| Illinois State University | M |
| Kent State University | M |
| Massachusetts College of Art and Design | M,O |
| The New School | M |
| Paris College of Art | M |
| Rhode Island School of Design | M |
| Savannah College of Art and Design | M |
| Temple University | M* |
| Thomas Jefferson University | M |
| University of California, Davis | M |
| University of Cincinnati | M |
| The University of Kansas | M |
| The University of Manchester | M,D |
| University of Minnesota, Twin Cities Campus | M,D,O |
| The University of North Carolina at Greensboro | M,D |
| University of North Texas | M,D,O |
| Wayne State University | M |

## TEXTILE SCIENCES AND ENGINEERING

| | |
|---|---|
| Cornell University | M,D |
| North Carolina State University | M,D |
| Thomas Jefferson University | M,D |
| The University of Texas at Austin | M |

## THANATOLOGY

| | |
|---|---|
| Brooklyn College of the City University of New York | M |
| The College of New Rochelle | M,O |
| Marian University (WI) | M |
| Southwestern College (NM) | M,O |
| University of Maryland, Baltimore | O |
| Washington & Jefferson College | M,O |

## THEATER

| | |
|---|---|
| Academy of Art University | M |
| American Conservatory Theater | M,O |
| Arcadia University | M,D,O |
| Arizona State University at Tempe | M,D |
| Baylor University | M |
| Berklee College of Music | M,O |
| Binghamton University, State University of New York | M |
| Bob Jones University | M,D,O |
| Boston University | M,O |
| Bowling Green State University | M,D |
| Brigham Young University | M |
| Brooklyn College of the City University of New York | M |
| Brown University | M,D |
| California Institute of the Arts | M,O |
| California State University, Fullerton | M |
| California State University, Long Beach | M |
| California State University, Los Angeles | M |
| California State University, Northridge | M |
| Carnegie Mellon University | M |
| Case Western Reserve University | M |
| The Catholic University of America | M,O |
| Central Washington University | M |
| Columbia University | M,D |
| Columbus State University | M |
| Cornell University | D |
| Dell'Arte International School of Physical Theatre | M |
| DePaul University | M |
| Eastern Michigan University | M |
| Florida Atlantic University | M |
| Florida State University | M,D |
| Fontbonne University | M |
| Fordham University | M |
| The George Washington University | M,O |
| The Graduate Center, City University of New York | D |
| Hollins University | M,O |
| Hunter College of the City University of New York | M |
| Idaho State University | M |
| Illinois State University | M |
| Indiana University Bloomington | M,D |
| The Juilliard School | M,D,O |
| Kansas State University | M |
| Kent State University | M |
| Long Island University - Post | M |
| Louisiana State University and Agricultural & Mechanical College | M,D |
| Mary Baldwin University | M |
| Miami University | M |
| Michigan State University | M |
| Minnesota State University Mankato | M |
| Montclair State University | M |
| Naropa University | M |
| The New School | M |
| New York University | M,D,O |
| Northern Illinois University | M |
| Northern Michigan University | M,O |
| Northwestern University | M,D |
| The Ohio State University | M,D |
| Ohio University | M |
| Pace University | M |
| Penn State University Park | M* |
| Pensacola Christian College | M,D,O |
| Point Park University | M |
| Portland State University | M |
| Regent University | M,D |
| Roosevelt University | M |
| Rowan University | M |
| Rutgers University - New Brunswick | M |
| San Diego State University | M |
| San Francisco State University | M |
| San Jose State University | M |
| Sarah Lawrence College | M |
| Savannah College of Art and Design | M |
| Smith College | M |
| Southern Illinois University Carbondale | M,D |
| Southern Methodist University | M |
| Southern Oregon University | M |
| Stanford University | D |
| Stony Brook University, State University of New York | M |
| Temple University | M* |
| Texas A&M University–Commerce | M,D,O |
| Texas State University | M |
| Texas Tech University | M |
| Texas Woman's University | M |
| Towson University | M |
| Tufts University | M,D |
| Tulane University | M |
| Université de Sherbrooke | M,D |
| University at Buffalo, the State University of New York | M,D |
| The University of Akron | M |
| The University of Alabama | M |
| University of Alberta | M |
| The University of Arizona | M |
| University of Arkansas | M |
| The University of British Columbia | M,D |
| University of California, Berkeley | D |
| University of California, Davis | M,D |
| University of California, Irvine | M,D |
| University of California, Los Angeles | M,D |
| University of California, San Diego | M,D |
| University of California, Santa Barbara | M,D |
| University of California, Santa Cruz | O |
| University of Central Florida | M |
| University of Central Missouri | M,D,O |
| University of Chicago | M |
| University of Cincinnati | M,D |
| University of Colorado Boulder | M,D |
| University of Connecticut | M |
| University of Delaware | M |
| University of Florida | M |
| University of Georgia | M,D |
| University of Guelph | M |
| University of Hawaii at Manoa | M,D |
| University of Houston | M |
| University of Idaho | M |
| University of Illinois at Urbana-Champaign | M,D |
| The University of Iowa | M |
| The University of Kansas | M,D |
| University of Lethbridge | M,D |
| University of Louisville | M |
| The University of Manchester | D |
| University of Maryland, Baltimore County | M |
| University of Maryland, College Park | M,D |
| University of Massachusetts Amherst | M |
| University of Memphis | M |
| University of Minnesota, Twin Cities Campus | M,D |
| University of Missouri | M,D |
| University of Missouri–Kansas City | M |
| University of Montana | M |
| University of Nebraska–Lincoln | M |
| University of Nevada, Las Vegas | M |
| University of New Mexico | M |
| University of New Orleans | M |
| The University of North Carolina at Chapel Hill | M |
| The University of North Carolina at Charlotte | M,D,O |
| The University of North Carolina at Greensboro | M |
| University of North Carolina School of the Arts | M |
| University of Oklahoma | M |
| University of Oregon | M,D |
| University of Ottawa | M |
| University of Pittsburgh | M,D* |
| University of San Diego | M |
| University of Saskatchewan | M |
| University of South Carolina | M,D |
| University of South Dakota | M |
| University of Southern California | M |
| The University of Tennessee | M |
| The University of Texas at Austin | M,D |
| The University of the Arts | M,O |
| University of the Cumberlands | M,D,O |
| University of Toronto | M,D |
| University of Victoria | M |
| University of Virginia | M |

| | |
|---|---|
| University of Washington | M,D |
| University of Wisconsin–Madison | M,D |
| University of Wisconsin–Superior | M |
| Université Laval | M,D |
| Utah State University | M |
| Villanova University | M |
| Virginia Commonwealth University | M |
| Washington University in St. Louis | M |
| Wayne State University | M |
| Western Illinois University | M |
| West Virginia University | M,D |
| Yale University | M,D,O |
| York University | M,D |

## THEOLOGY

| | |
|---|---|
| Abilene Christian University | M,D |
| Acadia University | M,D |
| Ambrose University | M,O |
| American Baptist Seminary of the West | M |
| American Jewish University | M |
| Amridge University | M,D |
| Anabaptist Mennonite Biblical Seminary | M,O |
| Anderson University (IN) | M,D |
| Andrews University | M,D,O |
| Apex School of Theology | M,D |
| Aquinas Institute of Theology | M,D,O |
| Arlington Baptist University | M |
| Asbury Theological Seminary | M,D,O |
| Ashland Theological Seminary | M,D |
| Assemblies of God Theological Seminary | M,D |
| The Athenaeum of Ohio | M,O |
| Atlantic School of Theology | M,O |
| Austin Presbyterian Theological Seminary | M,D |
| Ave Maria University | M,D |
| Azusa Pacific University | M,D |
| Bakke Graduate University | M,D |
| Baptist Bible College | M |
| The Baptist College of Florida | M |
| Baptist Missionary Association Theological Seminary | M |
| Barclay College | M |
| Barry University | M,D |
| Baylor University | M,D |
| Bethany Theological Seminary | M,O |
| Bethel Seminary | M,D,O |
| Bethel University (IN) | M |
| Bethesda University | M |
| Beth HaMedrash Shaarei Yosher Institute | |
| Beth Hatalmud Rabbinical College | |
| Bethlehem College & Seminary | M |
| Beth Medrash Govoha | |
| Bethune-Cookman University | M |
| Bexley Seabury Seminary | M,D,O |
| Biola University | M,D,O |
| Bob Jones University | M,D,O |
| Boston College | M,D,O |
| Briercrest Seminary | M |
| Brite Divinity School | M,D,O |
| Bryn Athyn College of the New Church | M |
| Byzantine Catholic Seminary of Saints Cyril and Methodius | M |
| Cairn University | M |
| California Lutheran University | M,D,O |
| Calvary University | M |
| Calvin Theological Seminary | M,D |
| Campbellsville University | M |
| Campbell University | M,D |
| Canadian Southern Baptist Seminary | M |
| Capital University | M |
| Carey Theological College | M,D |
| Carson-Newman University | M |
| Catholic Distance University | M |
| Catholic Theological Union | M,D,O |
| The Catholic University of America | M,D,O |
| Central Baptist Theological Seminary | M,O |
| Central Yeshiva Tomchei Tmimim-Lubavitch | M |
| Charlotte Christian College and Theological Seminary | M,D |
| Chicago Theological Seminary | M,D |
| Christendom College | M |
| Christian Theological Seminary | M,D |
| Christ the King Seminary | M |
| Church Divinity School of the Pacific | M,D,O |
| Cincinnati Christian University | M |
| Claremont Graduate University | M,D |
| Claremont School of Theology | M,D |
| Clarks Summit University | M,D |
| Colgate Rochester Crozer Divinity School | M,D,O |
| Collège Dominicain de Philosophie et de Théologie | M,D,O |
| College of Emmanuel and St. Chad | M,D,O |
| College of Saint Elizabeth | M,O |
| Columbia International University | M,D,O |
| Columbia Theological Seminary | M,D |
| Concordia Lutheran Seminary | M,O |
| Concordia Seminary | M,D,O |
| Concordia Theological Seminary | M,D |
| Concordia University (Canada) | M |
| Concordia University Irvine | M |
| Concordia University of Edmonton | M |
| Corban University | M,D,O |
| Covenant Theological Seminary | M,D,O |
| Criswell College | M |
| Crown College | M |
| Dallas Baptist University | M |
| Dallas Theological Seminary | M,D,O |
| Denver Seminary | M,D,O |
| Dominican House of Studies, Pontifical Faculty of the Immaculate Conception | M,D,O |
| Dominican School of Philosophy and Theology | M,O |
| Drew University | M,D,O |
| Duke University | M,D |
| Duquesne University | M,D |
| Earlham School of Religion | M |
| Eastern Mennonite University | M,O |
| Eastern University | M |
| Ecumenical Theological Seminary | M |
| Eden Theological Seminary | M,D |
| Emory University | M,D |
| Erskine Theological Seminary | M,D |
| Evangelical Seminary | M |
| Evangelical Seminary of Puerto Rico | M,D |
| Faith Baptist Bible College and Theological Seminary | M |
| Faith International University | M,D |
| Faith Theological Seminary | M,D |
| Faulkner University | M,D |
| Fordham University | M,D |
| Franciscan School of Theology | M |
| Franciscan University of Steubenville | M |
| Freed-Hardeman University | M |
| Fresno Pacific University | M |
| Fuller Theological Seminary | M,D,O |
| Gannon University | M,O |
| Gardner-Webb University | M,D |
| Garrett-Evangelical Theological Seminary | M,D |
| Gateway Seminary | M,D,O |
| The General Theological Seminary | M,D,O |
| George Fox University | M,D,O |
| Georgetown University | D |
| Georgian Court University | M,O |
| Global University | M,D |
| Gonzaga University | M |
| Gordon-Conwell Theological Seminary | M,D |
| Graceland University (IA) | M |
| Grace School of Theology | M |
| Grace Theological Seminary | M,D,O |
| Graduate Theological Union | M,D,O |
| Grand Rapids Theological Seminary of Cornerstone University | M |
| Greensboro College | M |
| Harding School of Theology | M,D |
| Hardin-Simmons University | M |
| Hartford Seminary | M,D,O |
| Harvard University | M* |
| Hebrew College | M |
| Hebrew Union College–Jewish Institute of Religion (NY) | M,D |
| Heritage College and Seminary | M,O |
| Holy Apostles College and Seminary | M,O |
| Holy Cross Greek Orthodox School of Theology | M |
| Hood Theological Seminary | M,D |
| Houston Baptist University | M |
| Houston Graduate School of Theology | M,D |
| Howard Payne University | M |
| Howard University | M,D |
| Iliff School of Theology | M,D |
| Indiana Wesleyan University | M |
| Institute for Christian Studies | M,D |
| Inter American University of Puerto Rico, Metropolitan Campus | D |
| Interdenominational Theological Center | M,D |
| International Baptist College and Seminary | M |
| The Jewish Theological Seminary | M,D,O |
| John Carroll University | M |
| John Paul the Great Catholic University | M |
| Johnson University | M,D,O |
| Kehilath Yakov Rabbinical Seminary | |
| Kenrick-Glennon Seminary | M |
| Kentucky Christian University | M |
| The King's University | M,D,O |
| Kingswood University | M |
| Knox College | M,D |
| Knox Theological Seminary | M |
| Lakeland University | M |
| Lancaster Bible College | M,D,O |
| Lancaster Theological Seminary | M,D,O |
| Lee University | M |
| Lenoir-Rhyne University | M |
| Lexington Theological Seminary | M,D |
| Liberty University | M,D,O |
| Lincoln Christian Seminary | M,D |
| Lincoln Christian University | M |
| Lipscomb University | M,D |
| Logos Evangelical Seminary | M,D,O |
| Loras College | M |
| Louisville Presbyterian Theological Seminary | M,D |
| Lourdes University | M |
| Loyola Marymount University | M |
| Loyola University Chicago | M,D,O |
| Loyola University Maryland | M |
| Loyola University New Orleans | M,O |
| Lubbock Christian University | M |
| Lutheran School of Theology at Chicago | M,D |
| Lutheran Theological Seminary Saskatoon | M,D |
| Luther Rice College & Seminary | M,D |
| Luther Seminary | M,D |
| Machzikei Hadath Rabbinical College | O |
| Madonna University | M |
| Maple Springs Baptist Bible College and Seminary | M,D,O |
| Maranatha Baptist University | M |
| Marquette University | M,D |
| The Master's University | M,D |
| McCormick Theological Seminary | M,D,O |
| McGill University | M,D |
| McMaster University | M,D,O |
| Meadville Lombard Theological School | M,D |
| Memphis Theological Seminary | M,D |
| Mercer University | M,D |
| Merrimack College | M,O |
| Mesivta of Eastern Parkway–Yeshiva Zichron Meilech | |
| Mesivtha Tifereth Jerusalem of America | |
| Methodist Theological School in Ohio | M,D |
| Mid-America Baptist Theological Seminary | M,D |
| Mid-America Baptist Theological Seminary Northeast Branch | M |
| Mid-America Reformed Seminary | M |
| Midwestern Baptist Theological Seminary | M,D,O |
| Midwest University | M,D |
| Milligan University | M,D,O |
| Mirrer Yeshiva Central Institute | |
| Missio Seminary | M,D,O |
| Moody Bible Institute | M,O |
| Moody Theological Seminary–Michigan | M,O |
| Moravian Theological Seminary | M,O |
| Mount Angel Seminary | M |
| Mount St. Joseph University | M,O |
| Mount St. Mary's University (MD) | M |
| Mount Vernon Nazarene University | M |
| Multnomah University | M,D |
| Naropa University | M |
| Nashotah House Theological Seminary | M,D,O |
| Nazarene Theological Seminary | M,D,O |
| Nebraska Christian College of Hope International University | M |
| Ner Israel Rabbinical College | M,D,O |
| Ner Israel Yeshiva College of Toronto | |
| New Brunswick Theological Seminary | M,D |
| Newman Theological College | M |
| Newman University | M |
| New Orleans Baptist Theological Seminary | M,D |
| New Saint Andrews College | M,O |
| New York Theological Seminary | M,D |
| Northeastern Seminary at Roberts Wesleyan College | M,D |
| Northern Seminary | M,D |
| North Park Theological Seminary | M,D |
| Northwest Nazarene University | M |
| Northwest University | M |
| Notre Dame Seminary | M |
| Nyack College | M,D |
| Oakland City University | M,D |
| Oblate School of Theology | M,D,O |
| Ohio Christian University | M |
| Ohio Dominican University | M |
| Ohr Hameir Theological Seminary | |
| Oklahoma Christian University | M |
| Oklahoma Wesleyan University | M |
| Olivet Nazarene University | M |
| Oral Roberts University | M,D |
| Pacific School of Religion | M,D,O |
| Palm Beach Atlantic University | M |
| Payne Theological Seminary | M |
| Pentecostal Theological Seminary | M,D |
| Pfeiffer University | M |
| Phillips Theological Seminary | M,D |
| Phoenix Seminary | M,D,O |
| Piedmont International University | M,D |
| Pittsburgh Theological Seminary | M,D |
| Point Loma Nazarene University | M |
| Pontifical Catholic University of Puerto Rico | M |
| Pontifical College Josephinum | M |
| Pontifical John Paul II Institute for Studies on Marriage and Family | M,D,O |
| Pope St. John XXIII National Seminary | M |
| Princeton Theological Seminary | M,D |
| Providence College | M |
| Providence University College & Theological Seminary | M,D,O |
| Rabbinical Academy Mesivta Rabbi Chaim Berlin | O |
| Rabbinical College Beth Shraga | |
| Rabbinical College Bobover Yeshiva B'nei Zion | O |
| Rabbinical College of Long Island | |
| Rabbinical Seminary of America | |
| Reconstructionist Rabbinical College | M,D,O |
| Reformed Episcopal Seminary | M |
| Reformed Presbyterian Theological Seminary | M,D |
| Reformed Theological Seminary–Atlanta Campus | M,D,O |
| Reformed Theological Seminary–Charlotte Campus | M,D |
| Reformed Theological Seminary–Dallas Campus | M |
| Reformed Theological Seminary–Jackson Campus | M,D,O |
| Reformed Theological Seminary–Orlando Campus | M,D,O |
| Reformed Theological Seminary–Washington D.C. | M |
| Reformed University | M |
| Regent College | M,O |
| Regent University | M,D |
| Regis College (Canada) | M,D,O |
| Sacred Heart Major Seminary | M |
| Sacred Heart Seminary and School of Theology | M,O |
| St. Andrew's College | M,D,O |
| St. Andrew's College in Winnipeg | M |
| St. Augustine's Seminary of Toronto | M,O |
| St. Bernard's School of Theology and Ministry | M,O |
| St. Catherine University | M,O |
| Saint Charles Borromeo Seminary, Overbrook | M |
| St. John's Seminary (CA) | M |
| Saint John's Seminary (MA) | M |
| Saint John's University (MN) | M |
| St. John's University (NY) | M |
| St. Joseph's Seminary | M |
| Saint Leo University | M,O |
| Saint Louis University | M,D |
| Saint Mary Seminary and Graduate School of Theology | M,D |
| St. Mary's Seminary and University | M,D,O |
| Saint Mary's University (Canada) | M |
| St. Mary's University (United States) | M |
| Saint Meinrad School of Theology | M |
| St. Norbert College | M |
| St. Patrick's Seminary & University | M,O |
| Saint Paul School of Theology | M,D |
| Saint Paul University | M,D,O |
| St. Peter's Seminary | M |
| Saints Cyril and Methodius Seminary | M |
| St. Stephen's College | M,D |
| St. Thomas University - Florida | M,D,O |
| St. Tikhon's Orthodox Theological Seminary | M |
| St. Vincent de Paul Regional Seminary | M |
| Saint Vincent Seminary | M |
| St. Vladimir's Orthodox Theological Seminary | M,D |
| Samford University | M,D |
| San Francisco Theological Seminary | M,D |
| Santa Clara University | M,D,O |
| Seattle Pacific University | M,O |
| The Seattle School of Theology and Psychology | M |
| Seattle University | M,D,O |
| Seton Hall University | M,O |
| Shaw University | M |
| Shepherds Theological Seminary | M |
| Shiloh University | M,D |
| Sh'or Yoshuv Rabbinical College | |
| Sioux Falls Seminary | M,D,O |
| Southeastern Baptist Theological Seminary | M,D |
| Southeastern University (FL) | M,D |
| Southern Adventist University | M |
| The Southern Baptist Theological Seminary | M,D |
| Southern California Seminary | M,D |
| Southern Evangelical Seminary | M,D,O |
| Southern Methodist University | M,D |
| South Florida Bible College and Theological Seminary | M |
| Southwestern Assemblies of God University | M |
| Southwestern Baptist Theological Seminary | M,D |
| Spring Arbor University | M |
| Spring Hill College | M,O |
| Starr King School for the Ministry | M |
| SUM Bible College & Theological Seminary | M |
| Talmudic University | M |
| Taylor College and Seminary | M,O |
| Toronto School of Theology | M,D |
| Trinity Bible College and Graduate School | M |
| Trinity College (Canada) | M,D,O |
| Trinity International University | M,D,O |
| Trinity School for Ministry | M,D,O |
| Trinity Western University | M,D |
| Tri-State Bible College | M |
| Truett McConnell University | M |
| Tyndale University College & Seminary | M,O |
| Unification Theological Seminary | M,D |
| Union Theological Seminary in the City of New York | M,D |
| United Lutheran Seminary | M,D |
| United Lutheran Seminary | M,D,O |
| United Talmudical Seminary | |
| United Theological Seminary | M,D |
| United Theological Seminary of the Twin Cities | M,D,O |
| Université de Montréal | M,D,O |
| Université de Sherbrooke | M,D,O |
| Université du Québec à Chicoutimi | M,D |
| University of Chicago | D |
| University of Dayton | M,D |
| University of Denver | D,O |
| University of Dubuque | M,D |
| University of Holy Cross | M,D |
| The University of Manchester | D |
| University of Mobile | M |
| University of Northwestern–St. Paul | M |
| University of Notre Dame | M,D |
| University of Philosophical Research | M |
| University of Saint Mary of the Lake–Mundelein Seminary | M,D |
| University of St. Michael's College | M,D,O |
| University of St. Thomas (MN) | M |
| University of St. Thomas (TX) | M |

*M—masters degree; D—doctorate; O—other advanced degree; *—Close-Up and/or Display*

| | |
|---|---|
| The University of Scranton | M |
| University of South Africa | M,D |
| The University of the South | M,D |
| University of the West | M |
| University of Valley Forge | M |
| The University of Winnipeg | M,O |
| Université Laval | M,D |
| Urshan Graduate School of Theology | M |
| Ursuline College | M |
| Vancouver School of Theology | M,O |
| Vanderbilt University | M* |
| Vanguard University of Southern California | M |
| Victoria University | M,D,O |
| Villanova University | M,D |
| Virginia Baptist College | M |
| Virginia Beach Theological Seminary | M |
| Virginia Theological Seminary | M,D |
| Virginia Union University | M,D |
| Walsh University | M |
| Wartburg Theological Seminary | M |
| Wayland Baptist University | M |
| Welch College | M |
| Wesley Biblical Seminary | M |
| Wesley Theological Seminary | M,D |
| Western Seminary - Portland | M,O |
| Western Seminary–Sacramento Campus | M,O |
| Western Seminary - San Jose Campus | M,O |
| Western Theological Seminary | M,D,O |
| Westminster Seminary California | M |
| Westminster Theological Seminary | M,D,O |
| Wheaton College | M,D |
| Whitworth University | M |
| Wilfrid Laurier University | M,D,O |
| Winebrenner Theological Seminary | M,D |
| World Mission University | M,D |
| Wycliffe College | M,D,O |
| Xavier University | M* |
| Xavier University of Louisiana | M |
| Yale University | M |
| Yeshiva Beth Moshe | O |
| Yeshiva Karlin Stolin | O |
| Yeshiva of Nitra Rabbinical College | O |
| Yeshiva Shaar Hatorah Talmudic Research Institute | |
| Yeshivath Zichron Moshe | O |

## THEORETICAL CHEMISTRY

| | |
|---|---|
| Carnegie Mellon University | D |
| Cornell University | D |
| Georgetown University | D |
| Laurentian University | M |
| University of Calgary | M,D |
| The University of Manchester | M,D |
| University of Regina | M,D |
| The University of Tennessee | M,D |
| Wesleyan University | D |
| Yale University | D |

## THEORETICAL PHYSICS

| | |
|---|---|
| Cornell University | M,D |
| Delaware State University | D |
| Harvard University | D* |
| Rutgers University - New Brunswick | M,D |
| The University of Manchester | M,D |
| University of Victoria | M,D |

## THERAPIES—DANCE, DRAMA, AND MUSIC

| | |
|---|---|
| Antioch University New England | M,D,O |
| Antioch University Seattle | M |
| Appalachian State University | M |
| Arizona State University at Tempe | M,D |
| Concordia University (Canada) | M |
| Drexel University | M,O |
| East Carolina University | M,O |
| Florida State University | M,D |
| Georgia College & State University | M |
| Immaculata University | M |
| Indiana University-Purdue University Indianapolis | M,D |
| Lesley University | M,D,O |
| Loyola University New Orleans | M |
| Maryville University of Saint Louis | M |
| Michigan State University | M,D |
| Molloy College | M |
| Montclair State University | M,O |
| Naropa University | M |
| Nazareth College of Rochester | M |
| New York University | M |
| Ohio University | M,O |
| Pratt Institute | M |
| Saint Mary-of-the-Woods College | M |
| Slippery Rock University of Pennsylvania | M |
| Southwestern Oklahoma State University | M |
| State University of New York at New Paltz | M |
| Temple University | M,D* |
| Texas Woman's University | M |
| The University of Kansas | M,D |
| University of Kentucky | M,D |
| University of Miami | M,D,O |
| University of Missouri–Kansas City | M,D |
| University of the Pacific | M |
| Western Michigan University | M,O |
| Wilfrid Laurier University | M |

## TOXICOLOGY

| | |
|---|---|
| Clemson University | M,D |
| Columbia University | M,D |
| Cornell University | M,D |
| Duke University | O |
| East Carolina University | M,D |
| Florida Agricultural and Mechanical University | M,D |
| The George Washington University | M,O |
| Indiana University Bloomington | M,D,O |
| Indiana University-Purdue University Indianapolis | M,D |
| Iowa State University of Science and Technology | M,D |
| Long Island University - Brooklyn | M,D |
| Louisiana State University and Agricultural & Mechanical College | M,D |
| Massachusetts Institute of Technology | M,D |
| Medical College of Wisconsin | D |
| Medical University of South Carolina | D |
| Michigan State University | M,D |
| Oklahoma State University Center for Health Sciences | M |
| Oregon State University | M,D |
| Purdue University | M,D |
| Rutgers University - New Brunswick | M,D |
| St. John's University (NY) | M |
| San Diego State University | M,D |
| Simon Fraser University | M,D,O |
| Texas Southern University | M,D |
| Texas Tech University | M,D |
| Thomas Jefferson University | M |
| Université de Montréal | O |
| University at Albany, State University of New York | M,D |
| University at Buffalo, the State University of New York | M,D |
| The University of Alabama at Birmingham | M,D |
| University of Arkansas for Medical Sciences | M,D,O |
| University of California, Davis | M,D |
| University of California, Irvine | M,D |
| University of California, Riverside | M,D |
| University of California, Santa Cruz | M,D |
| University of Colorado Denver | D |
| University of Connecticut | M,D |
| University of Florida | M,D,O |
| University of Guelph | M,D |
| University of Illinois at Chicago | M,D |
| The University of Iowa | M,D |
| The University of Kansas | M,D |
| University of Kentucky | M,D |
| University of Louisiana at Monroe | D |
| University of Louisville | M,D |
| The University of Manchester | M,D |
| University of Maryland, Baltimore | M,D |
| University of Maryland Eastern Shore | M,D |
| University of Michigan | M,D |
| University of Minnesota, Duluth | M,D |
| University of Minnesota, Twin Cities Campus | M,D |
| University of Mississippi | M,D |
| University of Mississippi Medical Center | D |
| University of Montana | M,D |
| University of Nebraska–Lincoln | M,D |
| University of Nebraska Medical Center | D |
| University of New Mexico | M,D |
| The University of North Carolina at Chapel Hill | M,D |
| University of Prince Edward Island | M,D |
| University of Puerto Rico - Medical Sciences Campus | M,D |
| University of Rhode Island | M,D |
| University of Rochester | D |
| University of Saskatchewan | M,D,O |
| University of South Alabama | M |
| University of Southern California | M,D |
| University of South Florida | O |
| The University of Texas at Austin | M,D |
| The University of Texas Health Science Center at San Antonio | M |
| The University of Texas Medical Branch | M,D |
| University of the Sciences | M,D |
| University of Utah | D |
| University of Washington | M,D |
| University of Wisconsin–Madison | M,D |
| Utah State University | M,D |
| Virginia Commonwealth University | M,D,O |
| Wayne State University | M,D |
| Wright State University | M |

## TRANSCULTURAL NURSING

| | |
|---|---|
| Augsburg University | M,D |
| Rutgers University - Newark | M,D,O |

## TRANSLATIONAL BIOLOGY

| | |
|---|---|
| Baylor College of Medicine | D |
| Boston University | D |
| Cedars-Sinai Medical Center | M,D |
| Rutgers University - New Brunswick | M |
| University of California, Irvine | M |
| The University of Iowa | M,D |
| University of Massachusetts Medical School | M,D |
| The University of Texas at San Antonio | D |
| The University of Texas Medical Branch | M,D |
| Virginia Polytechnic Institute and State University | M,D |
| Wake Forest University | M,D |

## TRANSLATION AND INTERPRETATION

| | |
|---|---|
| American University of Sharjah | M,D |
| Arizona State University at Tempe | M,D,O |
| Babel University Professional School of Translation | M |
| Binghamton University, State University of New York | D,O |
| Columbia University | M,D |
| Concordia University (Canada) | M,O |
| East Tennessee State University | M,O |
| Gallaudet University | M,D,O |
| Georgia State University | O |
| Kent State University | M,D |
| La Salle University | M,O |
| London Metropolitan University | M,D |
| Middlebury Institute of International Studies at Monterey | M |
| Mills College | M,O |
| Montclair State University | O |
| New York University | M |
| Rochester Institute of Technology | M |
| Rutgers University - New Brunswick | M,D |
| Texas A&M International University | M |
| Universidad Autonoma de Guadalajara | M,D |
| Université de Montréal | M,D,O |
| University of California, Santa Barbara | M,D |
| University of Delaware | M |
| University of Denver | M,O |
| University of Illinois at Urbana-Champaign | M |
| The University of Manchester | D |
| University of Nevada, Las Vegas | M,O |
| University of Northern Colorado | M |
| University of North Florida | M |
| University of Ottawa | M,D |
| University of Puerto Rico at Rio Piedras | M,O |
| University of Rochester | M,O |
| The University of Texas Rio Grande Valley | M |
| University of Wisconsin–Milwaukee | M,O* |
| Université Laval | M,O |
| Vermont College of Fine Arts | M |
| Wesley Biblical Seminary | M |
| York University | M |

## TRANSPERSONAL AND HUMANISTIC PSYCHOLOGY

| | |
|---|---|
| Atlantic University | M |
| John F. Kennedy University | M |
| Michigan School of Psychology | M,D |
| Naropa University | M |
| Saybrook University | M,D |
| Seattle University | M |
| Sofia University | M,D |

## TRANSPORTATION AND HIGHWAY ENGINEERING

| | |
|---|---|
| Arizona State University at Tempe | M,D,O |
| ArtCenter College of Design | M |
| The Catholic University of America | M,D,O |
| The Citadel, The Military College of South Carolina | M,O |
| Clemson University | M,D |
| College for Creative Studies | M |
| Cornell University | M,D |
| George Mason University | M,D |
| Illinois Institute of Technology | M,D |
| Iowa State University of Science and Technology | M,D |
| Kansas State University | M,D |
| Kennesaw State University | M |
| Louisiana State University and Agricultural & Mechanical College | M,D |
| Marquette University | M,D,O |
| Marshall University | M |
| Massachusetts Institute of Technology | M,D,O |
| Morgan State University | M,D,O |
| New Jersey Institute of Technology | M,D |
| New York University | M,D |
| North Dakota State University | D |
| Northwestern University | M,D |
| Ohio University | M,D |
| Old Dominion University | M |
| Oregon State University | M,D |
| Polytechnique Montréal | M,D,O |
| Rensselaer Polytechnic Institute | M,D |
| South Carolina State University | M |
| Southern Illinois University Edwardsville | M |
| Southern Methodist University | M,D |
| Stevens Institute of Technology | M,D,O |
| Texas Southern University | M |
| UNB Fredericton | M,D |
| University of Arkansas | M,D |
| University of Calgary | M,D |
| University of California, Berkeley | M,D |
| University of California, Davis | M,D |
| University of California, Irvine | M,D |
| University of Central Florida | M,D,O |
| University of Colorado Denver | M,D |
| University of Dayton | M |
| University of Delaware | M,D |
| The University of Iowa | M,D |
| University of Massachusetts Amherst | M,D |
| University of Memphis | M,D,O |
| University of Nevada, Las Vegas | M,D |
| University of Puerto Rico at Mayagüez | M,D |
| University of Southern California | M,D,O |
| University of South Florida | M,D,O |
| The University of Texas at Tyler | M |
| University of Washington | M,D |
| University of Wisconsin–Madison | M |
| Virginia Polytechnic Institute and State University | M,O |
| Wentworth Institute of Technology | M |

## TRANSPORTATION MANAGEMENT

| | |
|---|---|
| American Public University System | M,D |
| California State University Maritime Academy | M |
| George Mason University | M |
| Instituto Tecnologico de Santo Domingo | M,O |
| Iowa State University of Science and Technology | M |
| Maine Maritime Academy | M |
| McGill University | M,D |
| Naval Postgraduate School | M |
| New Jersey Institute of Technology | M,D |
| New York University | M |
| North Dakota State University | M,D |
| Pontifical Catholic University of Puerto Rico | O |
| State University of New York Maritime College | M |
| Texas A&M University | M |
| Texas Southern University | M |
| University at Buffalo, the State University of New York | M |
| The University of British Columbia | D |
| University of California, Davis | M,D |
| University of California, Santa Barbara | M,D |
| University of Hawaii at Manoa | M,D,O |
| University of New Orleans | M |
| The University of Tennessee | M,D |
| University of Washington | O |

## TRAVEL AND TOURISM

| | |
|---|---|
| Arizona State University at Tempe | M,D,O |
| Boston University | M |
| California State University, Chico | M |
| California State University, East Bay | M |
| California State University, Fullerton | M |
| California State University, Northridge | M |
| Clemson University | M,D,O |
| Colorado State University | M,D |
| The George Washington University | M,O |
| IGlobal University | M |
| Indiana University Bloomington | M,D |
| Johnson & Wales University | M |
| Kent State University | M |
| Lasell College | M,O |
| New Mexico State University | M |
| New York University | M |
| North Carolina State University | M,D |
| Old Dominion University | M |
| Penn State University Park | M,D* |
| Pontificia Universidad Catolica Madre y Maestra | M |
| Purdue University | M,D |
| Rochester Institute of Technology | M |
| Royal Roads University | M,O |
| San Diego State University | M |
| San Francisco State University | M |
| San Ignacio University | M |
| Savannah College of Art and Design | M |
| Schiller International University - Tampa | M |
| Strayer University | M |
| Syracuse University | M |
| Temple University | M,D* |
| Tropical Agriculture Research and Higher Education Center | M,D |
| Université du Québec à Trois-Rivières | M,O |
| University of Central Florida | M,D,O |
| University of Florida | M,D |
| University of Hawaii at Manoa | M |
| University of Idaho | M,D |
| University of Massachusetts Amherst | M,D |
| University of Minnesota, Twin Cities Campus | M,D |
| University of New Orleans | M |
| University of North Texas | M,D,O |
| University of South Africa | M,D |
| University of South Carolina | M |
| University of South Florida | M,O |
| The University of Tennessee | M |
| Western Illinois University | M |
| West Virginia University | M,D |

## URBAN AND REGIONAL PLANNING

| | |
|---|---|
| Alabama Agricultural and Mechanical University | M |
| American University of Sharjah | M,D |
| Andrews University | M |
| Arizona State University at Tempe | M,D,O |
| Auburn University | M |
| Ball State University | M,O |
| Boston University | M |
| California Polytechnic State University, San Luis Obispo | M |
| California State Polytechnic University, Pomona | M |
| The Catholic University of America | M,O |
| Clark University | M |
| Cleveland State University | M,O |
| College of Charleston | O |
| Columbia University | M,D |
| Concordia University (Canada) | O |
| Cornell University | M,D |
| Dalhousie University | M |
| Delta State University | M |
| East Carolina University | M,O |
| Eastern Kentucky University | M |
| Eastern Michigan University | M,O |
| East Tennessee State University | M,O |
| Florida Atlantic University | M |
| Florida State University | M,D |
| Future Generations University | M |
| Georgetown University | M,D |
| Georgia Institute of Technology | M,D |
| Georgia State University | M,D,O |
| Harvard University | M,D* |
| Hunter College of the City University of New York | M |
| Indiana University of Pennsylvania | M |
| Iowa State University of Science and Technology | M |
| Jackson State University | M,D |
| Kansas State University | M |
| Lesley University | M,D,O |
| Massachusetts Institute of Technology | M,D |
| McGill University | M,D |
| Michigan State University | M,D |
| Minnesota State University Mankato | M,O |
| Missouri State University | M,O |
| Morgan State University | M |

| | |
|---|---|
| New York University | M |
| North Dakota State University | M |
| Northern Arizona University | M,O |
| Northwest University | M,D |
| The Ohio State University | M,D |
| Pratt Institute | M |
| Queen's University at Kingston | M |
| Roger Williams University | M,O |
| Rutgers University - New Brunswick | M,D |
| St. Francis Xavier University | M |
| Saint Louis University | M |
| San Diego State University | M |
| Savannah State University | M |
| Southeastern University (FL) | M |
| Southern California Institute of Architecture | M |
| State University of New York College of Environmental Science and Forestry | M,D |
| Syracuse University | O |
| Texas A&M University | M,D |
| Texas Southern University | M,D |
| Thomas Edison State University | M |
| Thomas Jefferson University | M |
| Tufts University | M |
| Université de Montréal | M,D,O |
| Université du Québec à Rimouski | M,D,O |
| Université du Québec en Outaouais | M |
| University at Albany, State University of New York | M,O |
| University at Buffalo, the State University of New York | M,D,O |
| The University of Arizona | M |
| The University of British Columbia | M,D |
| University of California, Berkeley | M,D |
| University of California, Davis | M |
| University of California, Irvine | M,D |
| University of California, Los Angeles | M,D |
| University of Central Arkansas | M,O |
| University of Central Florida | M,O |
| University of Central Oklahoma | M |
| University of Cincinnati | M |
| University of Colorado Denver | M,D |
| University of Detroit Mercy | M |
| University of Florida | M,D |
| University of Hawaii at Manoa | M,D,O |
| University of Idaho | M |
| University of Illinois at Chicago | M,D |
| University of Illinois at Urbana-Champaign | M,D |
| The University of Iowa | M |
| The University of Kansas | M |
| University of Louisville | M,D |
| University of Manitoba | M |
| University of Maryland, College Park | M,D |
| University of Massachusetts Amherst | M,D |
| University of Massachusetts Boston | M |
| University of Massachusetts Lowell | M,O |
| University of Memphis | M |
| University of Michigan | M,D |
| University of Minnesota, Twin Cities Campus | M,D |
| University of Nebraska–Lincoln | M,D |
| University of New Mexico | M |
| University of New Orleans | M |
| The University of North Carolina at Chapel Hill | M,D |
| The University of North Carolina at Charlotte | M,O |
| University of Oklahoma | M,D |
| University of Oregon | M |
| University of Pennsylvania | M,D,O |
| University of Pittsburgh | M* |
| University of Puerto Rico at Rio Piedras | M |
| University of Southern California | M,D,O |
| University of Southern Maine | M,O |
| University of South Florida | O |
| The University of Texas at Arlington | D |
| The University of Texas at Austin | M,D |
| The University of Texas at San Antonio | M |
| The University of Toledo | M,D,O |
| University of Toronto | M,D |
| University of Utah | M,D |
| University of Virginia | M |
| University of Washington | M,D |
| University of Waterloo | M,D |
| University of Wisconsin–Madison | M,D |
| University of Wisconsin–Milwaukee | M* |
| Université Laval | M,D |
| Utah State University | M,D |
| Vanderbilt University | M* |
| Virginia Commonwealth University | M |
| Virginia Polytechnic Institute and State University | M,D |
| Wayne State University | M,O |

## URBAN DESIGN

| | |
|---|---|
| Arizona State University at Tempe | M,D |
| Ball State University | M |
| Carnegie Mellon University | M,D |
| City College of the City University of New York | M |
| Cornell University | M,D |
| DePaul University | M |
| Drexel University | M |
| Georgia Institute of Technology | M,D |
| Harvard University | M* |
| Hofstra University | M |
| Judson University | M |
| Kent State University | M |
| Lawrence Technological University | M,O |
| London Metropolitan University | M,D |
| The New School | M |
| New York Institute of Technology | M |
| Pratt Institute | M |
| Rice University | M,D |
| Savannah College of Art and Design | M |
| Southern California Institute of Architecture | M |
| State University of New York College of Environmental Science and Forestry | M |
| University at Buffalo, the State University of New York | M,D,O |
| The University of British Columbia | M |
| University of California, Berkeley | M,D |
| University of California, Los Angeles | M,D |
| University of Colorado Denver | M,D |
| University of Houston | M |
| The University of Kansas | M,D,O |
| University of Miami | M |
| University of Michigan | M |
| The University of North Carolina at Charlotte | M |
| University of Pennsylvania | M,D,O |
| The University of Texas at Austin | M |
| University of Toronto | M,D |
| University of Utah | M,D |
| University of Washington | M,D,O |
| Washington University in St. Louis | M |

## URBAN EDUCATION

| | |
|---|---|
| Alvernia University | M |
| Bakke Graduate University | M,D |
| Brown University | M |
| Buffalo State College, State University of New York | M |
| Cheyney University of Pennsylvania | M |
| Claremont Graduate University | M,D,O |
| Cleveland State University | D |
| College of Mount Saint Vincent | M,O |
| Eastern Michigan University | M,O |
| Emmanuel College (United States) | M,O |
| Georgia State University | M,D,O |
| The Graduate Center, City University of New York | D |
| Grand View University | M,O |
| Holy Names University | M,O |
| Langston University | M |
| Long Island University - Brooklyn | M,O |
| Loyola Marymount University | M |
| Manhattanville College | M,O |
| Metropolitan State University | M |
| Morgan State University | D |
| New Jersey City University | M |
| Norfolk State University | M |
| Northeastern Illinois University | M |
| Providence College | M |
| Teachers College, Columbia University | M,D |
| Temple University | M* |
| University of Chicago | M |
| University of Houston - Downtown | M |
| University of Illinois at Chicago | M,D |
| University of Massachusetts Boston | D |
| University of Memphis | M,D,O |
| University of Michigan–Dearborn | M,D |
| University of Nebraska at Omaha | M,O |
| University of Pennsylvania | M |
| University of San Francisco | M |
| University of Southern California | D |
| University of Wisconsin–Milwaukee | M,D,O* |
| Virginia Commonwealth University | D |

## URBAN STUDIES

| | |
|---|---|
| Arizona State University at Tempe | M,D,O |
| Azusa Pacific University | M |
| Boston University | M |
| Brooklyn College of the City University of New York | M |
| Cleveland State University | M,D,O |
| Columbus State University | M |
| Concordia University (Canada) | M,D,O |
| Fordham University | M |
| Fresno Pacific University | M |
| Hunter College of the City University of New York | M |
| Indiana University Northwest | M,O |
| Le Moyne College | M,O |
| Long Island University - Brooklyn | M,D,O |
| Loyola University Chicago | M |
| Massachusetts Institute of Technology | M,D |
| Minnesota State University Mankato | M,O |
| Moody Bible Institute | M,O |
| New Jersey City University | M |
| New York University | M |
| Norfolk State University | M |
| North Dakota State University | M,D |
| Northeastern University | M,D |
| Queens College of the City University of New York | M |
| Rutgers University - Newark | M,D |
| Savannah State University | M |
| Simon Fraser University | M,O |
| Temple University | M,D,O* |
| Tufts University | M |
| Université du Québec à Montréal | M,D |
| Université du Québec, École nationale d'administration publique | M |
| Université du Québec, Institut National de la Recherche Scientifique | M,D,O |
| University at Albany, State University of New York | M,D,O |
| University of California, Irvine | M,D |
| University of Delaware | M,D |
| University of Lethbridge | M,D |
| University of Louisville | M,D |
| University of Maryland, Baltimore County | M,D |
| University of New Orleans | M,D |
| University of San Francisco | M |
| University of Wisconsin–Milwaukee | M,D* |
| Virginia Polytechnic Institute and State University | M,D |
| Wayne State University | M,D,O |

## VETERINARY MEDICINE

| | |
|---|---|
| Auburn University | D |
| Colorado State University | D |
| Cornell University | D |
| Iowa State University of Science and Technology | M |
| Kansas State University | D |
| Lincoln Memorial University | D |
| Louisiana State University and Agricultural & Mechanical College | D |
| Michigan State University | D |
| Midwestern University, Glendale Campus | D |
| Mississippi State University | D |
| Oklahoma State University | D |
| Oregon State University | D |
| Purdue University | D |
| Texas A&M University | M,D |
| Tufts University | M,D |
| Tuskegee University | M,D |
| Université de Montréal | D |
| University of California, Davis | D |
| University of Florida | D |
| University of Georgia | M,D |
| University of Guelph | M,D,O |
| University of Illinois at Urbana-Champaign | D |
| University of Maryland, College Park | D |
| University of Minnesota, Twin Cities Campus | D |
| University of Missouri | M,D |
| University of Pennsylvania | D |
| University of Prince Edward Island | D |
| University of Saskatchewan | M,D |
| The University of Tennessee | D |
| University of Wisconsin–Madison | M,D |
| Virginia Polytechnic Institute and State University | M,D |
| Washington State University | D |
| Western University of Health Sciences | D |

## VETERINARY SCIENCES

| | |
|---|---|
| Clemson University | M,D |
| Colorado State University | M,D |
| Drexel University | M |
| Iowa State University of Science and Technology | M,D |
| Kansas State University | M,O |
| Louisiana State University and Agricultural & Mechanical College | M,D |
| Michigan State University | M,D |
| Mississippi State University | M,D |
| North Carolina State University | M,D |
| The Ohio State University | M,D |
| Oklahoma State University | M,D |
| Penn State Hershey Medical Center | M |
| Purdue University | M,D |
| South Dakota State University | M,D |
| Texas A&M University | M,D |
| Tuskegee University | M,D |
| Université de Montréal | M,D |
| University of California, Davis | M,O |
| University of Florida | M,D,O |
| University of Guelph | M,D,O |
| University of Idaho | M,D |
| University of Illinois at Urbana-Champaign | M,D |
| University of Kentucky | M,D |
| University of Maryland, College Park | M,D |
| University of Minnesota, Twin Cities Campus | M,D |
| University of Missouri | M |
| University of Nebraska–Lincoln | M,D |
| University of Prince Edward Island | M,D |
| University of Saskatchewan | M,D |
| University of Vermont | M,D |
| University of Washington | M |
| University of Wisconsin–Madison | M,D |
| Utah State University | M,D |
| Virginia Polytechnic Institute and State University | M,D |
| Washington State University | M,D |

## VIROLOGY

| | |
|---|---|
| Baylor College of Medicine | D |
| Case Western Reserve University | D |
| Mayo Clinic Graduate School of Biomedical Sciences | D |
| McMaster University | M,D |
| Oregon State University | M,D |
| Penn State Hershey Medical Center | M,D |
| Purdue University | M,D |
| Rush University | M,D |
| Rutgers University - New Brunswick | M,D |
| Université de Montréal | D |
| Université du Québec, Institut National de la Recherche Scientifique | M,D |
| The University of Iowa | M,D |
| University of Minnesota, Twin Cities Campus | D |
| University of Pennsylvania | D |
| University of Prince Edward Island | M,D |
| Yale University | D |

## VISION SCIENCES

| | |
|---|---|
| Eastern Virginia Medical School | O |
| Marshall B. Ketchum University | M,D |
| New England College of Optometry | M,D |
| Pacific University | M,D |
| Salus University | M,O |
| State University of New York College of Optometry | D |
| Université de Montréal | M,O |
| The University of Alabama at Birmingham | M,D |
| University of Alberta | M,D |
| University of California, Berkeley | M,D |
| University of Guelph | M,D,O |
| University of Houston | M,D |
| The University of Manchester | M,D |
| University of Massachusetts Boston | M |
| University of Waterloo | M,D |
| Western Michigan University | M |

## VITICULTURE AND ENOLOGY

| | |
|---|---|
| California State University, Fresno | M |
| Cornell University | M,D |
| Oregon State University | M,D |
| University of California, Davis | M,D |

## VOCATIONAL AND TECHNICAL EDUCATION

| | |
|---|---|
| Alcorn State University | M,O |
| Appalachian State University | M |
| Athens State University | M |
| Bowling Green State University | M |
| Buffalo State College, State University of New York | M |
| California Baptist University | M |
| California University of Pennsylvania | M |
| Capella University | D |
| Central Connecticut State University | M |
| Central Washington University | M |
| Chicago State University | M |
| Clarion University of Pennsylvania | M |
| Concordia University (United States) | M,D |
| East Carolina University | M,O |
| Eastern Kentucky University | M |
| Eastern New Mexico University | M |
| Fitchburg State University | M |
| Florida Agricultural and Mechanical University | M |
| The George Washington University | O |
| Indiana State University | M |
| Indiana University of Pennsylvania | M |
| Inter American University of Puerto Rico, Metropolitan Campus | M |
| Iowa State University of Science and Technology | M,D |
| Jackson State University | M,D |
| James Madison University | M |
| Kent State University | M |
| Louisiana State University and Agricultural & Mechanical College | M,D |
| Middle Tennessee State University | M |
| Millersville University of Pennsylvania | M |
| Mississippi State University | M,D,O |
| Montana State University | M,D,O |
| Morehead State University | M |
| Murray State University | M,O |
| North Carolina State University | M,D,O |
| Northern Arizona University | M,O |
| Old Dominion University | M,D |
| Penn State University Park | M,D,O* |
| Pittsburg State University | M,O |
| Purdue University | M,D,O |
| Rochester Institute of Technology | O |
| South Carolina State University | M |
| Southern Illinois University Carbondale | M,D |
| State University of New York at Oswego | M |
| Temple University | M* |
| Texas State University | M |
| University of Arkansas | M,D,O |
| The University of British Columbia | M,D |
| University of Central Florida | M,O |
| University of Central Missouri | M,D,O |
| University of Georgia | M,D,O |
| University of Idaho | M,O |
| University of Maryland Eastern Shore | M |
| University of Minnesota, Twin Cities Campus | M,D,O |
| University of Missouri | M,D,O |
| University of Nebraska–Lincoln | M,D,O |
| University of New England | M,D,O |
| University of Northern Iowa | M,D |
| University of North Texas | M,D,O |
| University of Phoenix - Phoenix Campus | M |
| University of South Africa | M,D |
| University of South Florida | M,D,O |
| The University of Toledo | M,D,O |
| University of Victoria | M,D |
| University of Wisconsin–Stout | M,D,O |
| Utah State University | D |
| Valley City State University | M |
| Virginia Polytechnic Institute and State University | M,D,O |
| Washington State University | M,D |
| Wayne State College | M |
| Western Michigan University | M |
| Westfield State University | M |
| Wilmington University | M,D |

*M—masters degree; D—doctorate; O—other advanced degree; *—Close-Up and/or Display*

### WATER RESOURCES

| | |
|---|---|
| Albany State University | M |
| California State University, Monterey Bay | M |
| Colorado State University | M,D |
| Cornell University | M,D |
| Dalhousie University | M |
| Humboldt State University | M |
| Marquette University | M,D,O |
| Missouri University of Science and Technology | M,D |
| Montclair State University | O |
| New Mexico State University | M,D |
| Old Dominion University | M |
| Oregon State University | M,D |
| Rutgers University - New Brunswick | M,D |
| State University of New York College of Environmental Science and Forestry | M,D |
| Tropical Agriculture Research and Higher Education Center | M,D |
| Tufts University | M,D |
| UNB Fredericton | M,D |
| The University of Arizona | M,D,O |
| The University of British Columbia | M,D |
| University of Calgary | M,D |
| University of California, Riverside | M,D |
| University of Colorado Denver | M |
| University of Florida | M,D |
| University of Idaho | M,D |
| The University of Iowa | M,D |
| University of Maine | M,D |
| University of Massachusetts Amherst | M,D |
| University of Minnesota, Twin Cities Campus | M,D |
| University of Missouri | M,D,O |
| University of Nevada, Las Vegas | M |
| University of New Hampshire | M |
| University of New Mexico | M |
| University of Southern California | M,D,O |
| University of the District of Columbia | M |
| University of the Pacific | M,D |
| University of Wisconsin–Madison | M |
| University of Wisconsin–Milwaukee | M,D* |
| University of Wyoming | M,D |
| Utah State University | M,D |

### WATER RESOURCES ENGINEERING

| | |
|---|---|
| Carnegie Mellon University | M,D |
| Clemson University | M,D |
| Cornell University | M,D |
| Indiana University Bloomington | M,D,O |
| Kansas State University | M,D |
| Kennesaw State University | M |
| Lawrence Technological University | M,D |
| Louisiana State University and Agricultural & Mechanical College | M,D |
| Marquette University | M,D,O |
| McGill University | M,D |
| New Mexico Institute of Mining and Technology | M |
| Ohio University | M,D |
| Oregon State University | M,D |
| State University of New York College of Environmental Science and Forestry | M,D |
| Stevens Institute of Technology | M,D,O |
| Tufts University | M,D |
| University at Buffalo, the State University of New York | M,D |
| University of Alberta | M,D |
| University of California, Berkeley | M,D |
| University of Dayton | M |
| University of Delaware | M,D |
| University of Guelph | M,D |
| University of Idaho | M,D |
| The University of Iowa | M,D |
| University of Massachusetts Amherst | M,D |
| University of Memphis | M,D,O |
| University of New Haven | M |
| University of South Florida | M,D,O |
| The University of Texas at Austin | M,D |
| The University of Texas at Tyler | M |
| University of Wisconsin–Madison | M |
| Villanova University | M,O |

### WESTERN EUROPEAN STUDIES

| | |
|---|---|
| American University | M,D,O |
| Boston College | M,D |
| Brown University | M,D |
| Carleton University | M,O |
| The Catholic University of America | M,D |
| Central Michigan University | M,O |
| Claremont Graduate University | M,D,O |
| College of Staten Island of the City University of New York | M |
| Columbia University | M,D |
| Cornell University | M,D |
| Dallas Baptist University | M |
| Drew University | M,D,O |
| East Carolina University | M |
| Georgetown University | M |
| The George Washington University | M |
| Indiana University Bloomington | M |
| Indiana University-Purdue University Indianapolis | M |
| Monmouth University | M |
| New York University | M |
| San Diego State University | M |
| University of Colorado Denver | M |
| University of Guelph | M |
| University of Illinois at Urbana-Champaign | M |
| University of Louisiana at Lafayette | M |
| University of Nevada, Reno | D |
| University of Pittsburgh | O* |
| University of Virginia | M |

### WOMEN&APOSS HEALTH NURSING

| | |
|---|---|
| Boston College | M,D |
| California State University, Fullerton | M,D |
| Carlow University | M,O |
| Case Western Reserve University | M |
| Drexel University | M |
| Duke University | M,D,O |
| East Tennessee State University | M,D,O |
| Emory University | M |
| Georgia State University | M,D,O |
| Loyola University Chicago | M,D,O |
| MGH Institute of Health Professions | M,D,O |
| Queen's University at Kingston | M,D,O |
| Rutgers University - Newark | M,D,O |
| San Francisco State University | M,O |
| Stony Brook University, State University of New York | M,D,O |
| Tennessee Technological University | D |
| Texas Woman's University | M,D |
| Uniformed Services University of the Health Sciences | M,D |
| The University of Alabama at Birmingham | M,D |
| University of Cincinnati | M,D |
| University of Colorado Denver | M,D |
| University of Delaware | M,O |
| University of Illinois at Chicago | M,O |
| University of Indianapolis | M,D |
| University of Louisville | M,D |
| University of Minnesota, Twin Cities Campus | M,D |
| University of Missouri–Kansas City | M,D |
| University of Missouri–St. Louis | D,O |
| University of Pennsylvania | M |
| University of South Carolina | M |
| Virginia Commonwealth University | M,D,O |
| Wayne State University | M,D |

### WOMEN&APOSS STUDIES

| | |
|---|---|
| American University | O |
| The American University in Cairo | M,O |
| Brandeis University | M,D |
| Carnegie Mellon University | D |
| Chatham University | M |
| Claremont Graduate University | M,D |
| Cornell University | M,D |
| DePaul University | M |
| Eastern Michigan University | M,O |
| Emory University | D,O |
| Florida Atlantic University | M |
| George Mason University | M |
| The George Washington University | M,O |
| Georgia State University | M,O |
| Grace Theological Seminary | M,D,O |
| Inter American University of Puerto Rico, Metropolitan Campus | M |
| The Jewish Theological Seminary | M,D |
| Kansas State University | O |
| Lakehead University | M,D |
| Lesley University | M,D,O |
| London Metropolitan University | M,D |
| Loyola University Chicago | M |
| Middle Tennessee State University | O |
| Minnesota State University Mankato | M |
| Mount Saint Vincent University | M |
| Northern Arizona University | O |
| The Ohio State University | M,D |
| Old Dominion University | M |
| Oregon State University | M,D |
| Queen's University at Kingston | M,D |
| Reconstructionist Rabbinical College | M,D,O |
| Rutgers University - New Brunswick | M,D |
| Saint Mary's University (Canada) | M |
| San Diego State University | M |
| San Francisco State University | M |
| Sarah Lawrence College | M |
| Simon Fraser University | M,D |
| Smith College | O |
| Southeastern Baptist Theological Seminary | M,D |
| Southern Connecticut State University | M |
| Stony Brook University, State University of New York | O |
| Texas Woman's University | M,D |
| Towson University | M,O |
| United Theological Seminary of the Twin Cities | M,D,O |
| University at Albany, State University of New York | M |
| The University of Alabama | M |
| The University of Arizona | M,D,O |
| University of California, Santa Barbara | M,D |
| University of Cincinnati | M,O |
| University of Colorado Denver | M,O |
| University of Florida | M,O |
| University of Georgia | O |
| University of Hawaii at Manoa | O |
| The University of Iowa | O |
| University of Lethbridge | M,D |
| University of Louisville | M,O |
| University of Maryland, Baltimore County | O |
| University of Maryland, College Park | M,D |
| University of Michigan | D,O |
| University of Minnesota, Twin Cities Campus | D |
| University of New Hampshire | O |
| The University of North Carolina at Charlotte | M,D,O |
| The University of North Carolina at Greensboro | M,D,O |
| University of Northern Iowa | M |
| University of Oklahoma | O |
| University of Ottawa | M |
| University of Pittsburgh | O* |
| University of Regina | M |
| University of Rhode Island | O |
| University of South Carolina | O |
| University of South Florida | M |
| The University of Toledo | O |
| University of Toronto | M,D |
| University of Washington | D |
| University of Wisconsin–Madison | M,D |
| University of Wisconsin–Milwaukee | M,O* |
| Université Laval | O |
| Wayne State University | M,D,O |
| Western Seminary - Portland | M |
| Western Seminary–Sacramento Campus | O |
| Western Seminary - San Jose Campus | M,O |
| Wilson College | M |
| York University | M,D |

### WRITING

| | |
|---|---|
| Abilene Christian University | M |
| Academy of Art University | M |
| Adelphi University | M |
| Agnes Scott College | M |
| Albertus Magnus College | M |
| American College Dublin | M |
| American University | M |
| Antioch University Santa Barbara | M |
| Arcadia University | M |
| Arizona State University at Tempe | M,D |
| Asbury University | M |
| Ashland University | M |
| Auburn University at Montgomery | M |
| Ball State University | M,D |
| Bard College | M |
| Bay Path University | M |
| Bennington College | M |
| Binghamton University, State University of New York | M,D |
| Boston University | M |
| Bowling Green State University | M,D |
| Brigham Young University | M |
| Brooklyn College of the City University of New York | M |
| Brown University | M,D |
| California College of the Arts | M |
| California Institute of the Arts | M,O |
| California State University, Fresno | M |
| California State University, Long Beach | M |
| California State University, Northridge | M |
| California State University, Sacramento | M |
| California State University, San Bernardino | M |
| California State University, San Marcos | M |
| California State University, Stanislaus | M,O |
| Carlow University | M |
| Carnegie Mellon University | M |
| Cedar Crest College | M |
| Central Michigan University | M |
| Central Washington University | M |
| Chapman University | M |
| Chatham University | M |
| Chicago State University | M |
| City College of the City University of New York | M |
| Claremont Graduate University | M,D |
| Clemson University | M,D |
| Cleveland State University | M |
| Coastal Carolina University | M |
| College of Charleston | M |
| Colorado State University | M |
| Columbia College Chicago | M |
| Columbia University | M |
| Concordia University (Canada) | M |
| Concordia University, St. Paul | M |
| Converse College | M |
| Cornell University | M,D |
| Creighton University | M |
| DePaul University | M |
| Drew University | M,D,O |
| East Carolina University | M,D,O |
| Eastern Kentucky University | M |
| Eastern Michigan University | M,O |
| Fairfield University | M |
| Fairleigh Dickinson University, Florham Campus | M |
| Fitchburg State University | M |
| Florida International University | M |
| Florida State University | M,D |
| Full Sail University | M |
| George Mason University | M |
| Georgia College & State University | M |
| Georgia Southern University | M,O |
| Georgia State University | M,D |
| Goddard College | M |
| Goucher College | M |
| Hamline University | M |
| Hofstra University | M |
| Hollins University | M,O |
| Holy Names University | M |
| Hunter College of the City University of New York | M |
| Illinois State University | M,D |
| Indiana State University | M |
| Indiana University Bloomington | M,D |
| Indiana University-Purdue University Indianapolis | M,O |
| Indiana University South Bend | M,O |
| Institute of American Indian Arts | M |
| Iowa State University of Science and Technology | M,D |
| Ithaca College | M |
| James Madison University | M |
| Johns Hopkins University | M,O |
| Kean University | M |
| Kennesaw State University | M |
| Kent State University | M,D |
| Lake Forest College | M |
| La Sierra University | M |
| Lenoir-Rhyne University | M |
| Lesley University | M,D,O |
| Lindenwood University | M,O |
| Lipscomb University | M |
| London Metropolitan University | M,D |
| Long Island University - Brooklyn | M,D,O |
| Louisiana State University and Agricultural & Mechanical College | M,D |
| Loyola Marymount University | M |
| Maharishi International University | M |
| Manhattanville College | M |
| Massachusetts Institute of Technology | M |
| McDaniel College | M,O |
| McNeese State University | M |
| Michigan State University | M,D |
| Millersville University of Pennsylvania | M,O |
| Mills College | M,O |
| Minnesota State University Mankato | M,O |
| Missouri State University | M,O |
| Monmouth University | M |
| Montclair State University | O |
| Mount Mary University | M |
| Mount Saint Mary's University (CA) | M,D,O |
| Murray State University | M,D,O |
| Naropa University | M |
| National Louis University | M,D,O |
| National University | M,O |
| New England College | M |
| New Hampshire Institute of Art | M |
| New Mexico Highlands University | M |
| New Mexico State University | M,D |
| New Saint Andrews College | M,O |
| The New School | M |
| New York University | M |
| North Carolina State University | M |
| North Dakota State University | M,D |
| Northern Arizona University | M,D,O |
| Northern Kentucky University | M,O |
| Northern Michigan University | M,O |
| Northwestern University | M,O |
| Oklahoma City University | M |
| Oklahoma State University | M,D |
| Old Dominion University | M |
| Oregon State University | M |
| Otis College of Art and Design | M |
| Our Lady of the Lake University | M |
| Pacific Lutheran University | M |
| Pacific University | M |
| Park University | M,O |
| Pepperdine University | M |
| Pittsburg State University | M |
| Portland State University | M |
| Pratt Institute | M |
| Purdue University | M,D |
| Queens College of the City University of New York | M |
| Queens University of Charlotte | M |
| Randolph College | M |
| Regent University | M,D |
| Regis University | M,O |
| Reinhardt University | M |
| Rhode Island College | M,O |
| Rivier University | M |
| Roosevelt University | M |
| Rosemont College | M |
| Rowan University | M,O |
| Rutgers University - Camden | M |
| Rutgers University - Newark | M |
| Rutgers University - New Brunswick | M |
| St. Cloud State University | M |
| St. Joseph's College, New York | M |
| Saint Joseph's University | M |
| Saint Leo University | M |
| Saint Mary's College of California | M |
| Salve Regina University | M |
| Sam Houston State University | M |
| San Diego State University | M |
| San Francisco State University | M |
| Sarah Lawrence College | M |
| Savannah College of Art and Design | M |
| School of the Art Institute of Chicago | M,O |
| School of Visual Arts (NY) | M |
| Seattle Pacific University | M |
| Seton Hill University | M |
| Shenandoah University | M,D,O |
| Simmons University | M,D,O |
| Sonoma State University | M |
| Southeastern Louisiana University | M |
| Southern Illinois University Carbondale | M |
| Southern Illinois University Edwardsville | M |
| Southern New Hampshire University | M |
| Spalding University | M |
| State University of New York at Fredonia | M,O |
| Stephens College | M,O |
| Stetson University | M |
| Stony Brook University, State University of New York | M,O |
| SUNY Brockport | M,O |
| Syracuse University | M,D |
| Temple University | M,D* |
| Texas A&M University–Commerce | M,D,O |
| Texas State University | M |
| Tiffin University | M |
| Towson University | M |
| Trinity College (United States) | M |
| Union Institute & University | M |
| The University of Akron | M |
| The University of Alabama | M,D |
| The University of Alabama at Birmingham | M |

| | |
|---|---|
| University of Alaska Anchorage | M |
| University of Alaska Fairbanks | M |
| The University of Arizona | M |
| University of Arkansas | M |
| University of Arkansas at Little Rock | M |
| University of Baltimore | M |
| The University of British Columbia | M,D |
| University of California, Berkeley | O |
| University of California, Davis | M,D |
| University of California, Irvine | M |
| University of California, Riverside | M |
| University of California, San Diego | M,D |
| University of California, Santa Barbara | D |
| University of California, Santa Cruz | M |
| University of Central Arkansas | M |
| University of Central Oklahoma | M |
| University of Chicago | M |
| University of Colorado Boulder | M,D |
| University of Colorado Denver | M |
| University of Dayton | M |
| University of Denver | M,D,O |
| The University of Findlay | M,D |
| University of Florida | M,D |
| University of Houston | M,D |
| University of Houston–Victoria | M |
| University of Idaho | M |
| University of Illinois at Urbana-Champaign | M,D |
| The University of Iowa | M,D |
| The University of Kansas | M,D |
| University of King's College | M |
| University of Louisiana at Lafayette | M,D |
| University of Louisville | M,D |
| The University of Manchester | D |
| University of Maryland, College Park | M,D |
| University of Massachusetts Amherst | M,D |
| University of Massachusetts Boston | M |
| University of Massachusetts Dartmouth | M,O |
| University of Memphis | M,D,O |
| University of Miami | M,D |
| University of Michigan | M |
| University of Michigan–Flint | M |
| University of Mississippi | M,D |
| University of Missouri–St. Louis | M |
| University of Montana | M |
| University of Nebraska at Kearney | M |
| University of Nebraska at Omaha | M,O |
| University of Nebraska–Lincoln | M,D |
| University of Nevada, Las Vegas | M,D,O |
| University of New Hampshire | M,D |
| University of New Mexico | M |
| University of New Orleans | M |
| University of North Alabama | M |
| The University of North Carolina at Charlotte | M,O |
| The University of North Carolina at Greensboro | M |
| The University of North Carolina Wilmington | M |
| University of Northern Iowa | M |
| University of North Florida | M |
| University of North Texas | M,D,O |
| University of Notre Dame | M |
| University of Oklahoma | M,D |
| University of Oregon | M |
| University of Pittsburgh | M,D* |
| University of Regina | M,D |
| University of Rhode Island | M,D |
| University of San Francisco | M |
| University of South Alabama | M |
| University of South Carolina | M,D |
| University of Southern California | M,D |
| University of Southern Maine | M |
| University of South Florida | O |
| The University of Tampa | M |
| The University of Tennessee at Chattanooga | M |
| The University of Texas at Austin | M,D |
| The University of Texas at El Paso | M,D,O |
| The University of Texas Rio Grande Valley | M |
| University of the Sacred Heart | M,O |
| The University of the South | M |
| The University of Toledo | M,O |
| University of Toronto | M,D |
| University of Utah | M,D |
| University of Victoria | M |
| University of Virginia | M |
| University of Washington | M |
| University of Washington, Bothell | M |
| University of West Florida | M |
| University of Windsor | M |
| University of Wisconsin–Eau Claire | M |
| University of Wisconsin–Madison | M,D |
| University of Wisconsin–Milwaukee | M,D* |
| University of Wyoming | M |
| Utah State University | M |
| Vanderbilt University | M* |
| Vermont College of Fine Arts | M |
| Virginia Commonwealth University | M |
| Virginia Polytechnic Institute and State University | M,D,O |
| Warren Wilson College | M |
| Washington & Jefferson College | M,O |
| Washington University in St. Louis | M |
| Wayne State University | M,D |
| Wesleyan University | M,O |
| Western Carolina University | M,O |
| Western Colorado University | M |
| Western Connecticut State University | M |
| Western Kentucky University | M |
| Western Michigan University | M,D |
| Western New England University | M |
| West Virginia University | M,D |
| West Virginia Wesleyan College | M |
| Wichita State University | M |
| Yale University | M,D,O |

## ZOOLOGY

| | |
|---|---|
| Auburn University | M,D |
| Colorado State University | M,D |
| Emporia State University | M |
| Illinois State University | M,D |
| Indiana University Bloomington | M,D |
| Michigan State University | M,D |
| North Dakota State University | M,D |
| Southern Illinois University Carbondale | M,D |
| Texas Tech University | M,D |
| Uniformed Services University of the Health Sciences | M,D |
| The University of British Columbia | M,D |
| University of California, Davis | M |
| University of Florida | M,D |
| University of Guelph | M,D |
| University of Hawaii at Manoa | M,D |
| University of Illinois at Urbana-Champaign | M,D |
| University of Maine | M,D |
| University of Manitoba | M,D |
| University of Montana | M,D |
| University of North Dakota | M,D |
| University of Wisconsin–Madison | M,D |
| University of Wisconsin–Oshkosh | M |
| University of Wyoming | M,D |
| Western Illinois University | M,O |
| West Liberty University | M |

*M—masters degree; D—doctorate; O—other advanced degree; *—Close-Up and/or Display*

# DIRECTORY OF INSTITUTIONS AND THEIR OFFERINGS

### ABILENE CHRISTIAN UNIVERSITY
Business Administration and Management—General M
Business Analytics M
Clinical Psychology M,O
Communication Disorders M
Communication—General M
Counseling Psychology M,O
Education—General M,O
Educational Leadership and Administration D
English M
Health Services Management and Hospital Administration M
Human Services M,O
International Business M
Liberal Studies M
Marketing M
Marriage and Family Therapy M
Missions and Missiology M,D
Nonprofit Management M
Nursing and Healthcare Administration D
Nursing Education D
Nursing—General D
Nutrition M,O
Occupational Therapy M
Pastoral Ministry and Counseling M,D
Psychology—General M,O
Reading Education M
Religion M,D
Rhetoric M
School Psychology M,O
Social Work M
Supply Chain Management M
Theology M,D
Writing M

### ABRAHAM LINCOLN UNIVERSITY
Law D

### ACACIA UNIVERSITY
Education—General M
Educational Leadership and Administration M
Elementary Education M
English as a Second Language M
Secondary Education M
Special Education M

### ACADEMY FOR FIVE ELEMENT ACUPUNCTURE
Acupuncture and Oriental Medicine M

### ACADEMY FOR JEWISH RELIGION CALIFORNIA
Jewish Studies M

### ACADEMY OF ART UNIVERSITY
Advertising and Public Relations M
Applied Arts and Design—General M
Architecture M
Art Education M
Art History M
Art/Fine Arts M
Arts Journalism M
Computer Art and Design M
Film, Television, and Video Production M
Game Design and Development M
Graphic Design M
Illustration M
Industrial Design M
Interior Design M
Internet and Interactive Multimedia M
Landscape Architecture M
Music M
Photography M
Textile Design M
Theater M
Writing M

### ACADEMY OF CHINESE CULTURE AND HEALTH SCIENCES
Acupuncture and Oriental Medicine M

### ACADIA UNIVERSITY
Biological and Biomedical Sciences—General M
Chemistry M
Clinical Psychology M
Computer Science M
Counselor Education M
Curriculum and Instruction M
Education—General M,D
Educational Leadership and Administration M
English M
Geographic Information Systems M
Geology M
Mathematics M
Missions and Missiology M,D
Music Education M
Pastoral Ministry and Counseling M,D
Philosophy M
Political Science M
Psychology—General M
Recreation and Park Management M
Sociology M
Special Education M
Statistics M
Theology M,D

### ACUPUNCTURE & INTEGRATIVE MEDICINE COLLEGE, BERKELEY
Acupuncture and Oriental Medicine M

### ACUPUNCTURE AND MASSAGE COLLEGE
Acupuncture and Oriental Medicine M

### ADAMS STATE UNIVERSITY
Business Administration and Management—General M
Clinical Psychology M,D
Counselor Education M,D
Curriculum and Instruction M
Education—General M
Educational Leadership and Administration M
Exercise and Sports Science M
History M
Humanities M
Mathematics Education M
Music Education M
Physical Education M
Public Administration M
Science Education M
Sport Psychology M
Sports Management M

### ADELPHI UNIVERSITY
Accounting M
Adult Nursing M
Art/Fine Arts M
Biological and Biomedical Sciences—General M
Biotechnology M
Business Administration and Management—General M
Clinical Psychology D
Counseling Psychology M
Education—General M,D,O
Emergency Management O
Environmental Management and Policy M
Environmental Sciences M
Finance and Banking M
Health Informatics M,O
Health Services Management and Hospital Administration M
Human Resources Management M,O
Management Information Systems M
Marketing M
Nursing and Healthcare Administration M,O
Nursing Education M,O
Nursing—General D
Nutrition M,D,O
Psychology—General M
Public Health—General M
School Psychology M
Social Work M,D
Sports Management M
Supply Chain Management M
Writing M

### ADLER UNIVERSITY
Art Therapy M,D
Clinical Psychology M,D
Community Health M
Counselor Education D
Criminal Justice and Criminology M
Forensic Psychology M
Health Psychology M
Industrial and Organizational Psychology M
Marriage and Family Therapy M,D
Public Administration M
Public Policy M
Rehabilitation Counseling M
School Psychology M
Social Psychology M
Sport Psychology M
Sustainability Management M

### ADRIAN COLLEGE
Accounting M
Athletic Training and Sports Medicine M
Criminal Justice and Criminology M

### ADVENTHEALTH UNIVERSITY
Health Services Management and Hospital Administration M
Nurse Anesthesia M
Occupational Therapy M
Physical Therapy D
Physician Assistant Studies M

### AGNES SCOTT COLLEGE
Internet and Interactive Multimedia M
Writing M

### AIR FORCE INSTITUTE OF TECHNOLOGY
Aerospace/Aeronautical Engineering M,D
Applied Mathematics M,D
Applied Physics M,D
Astrophysics M,D
Computer Engineering M,D
Computer Science M,D
Electrical Engineering M,D
Engineering and Applied Sciences—General M,D
Engineering Management M
Engineering Physics M,D
Environmental Engineering M
Environmental Management and Policy M
Logistics M,D
Management Information Systems M
Management of Technology M,D
Materials Sciences M,D
Nuclear Engineering M,D
Operations Research M,D
Optical Sciences M,D
Planetary and Space Sciences M,D
Systems Engineering M,D

### ALABAMA AGRICULTURAL AND MECHANICAL UNIVERSITY
Agricultural Sciences—General M,D
Agronomy and Soil Sciences M,D
Art Education M
Biological and Biomedical Sciences—General M,D
Business Administration and Management—General M
Business Education M,O
Child and Family Studies M
Clinical Psychology M,O
Clothing and Textiles M
Communication Disorders M
Computer Science M
Counseling Psychology M,O
Counselor Education M,O
Early Childhood Education M,D,O
Education—General M,D,O
Educational Media/Instructional Technology M,O
Elementary Education M,D,O
Engineering and Applied Sciences—General M,D
English Education M,O
Family and Consumer Sciences-General M
Food Science and Technology M,D
Home Economics Education M,O
Hospitality Management M
Human Development M
Kinesiology and Movement Studies M
Materials Engineering M
Materials Sciences M,D
Mathematics Education M,O
Music Education M
Nutrition M
Optical Sciences M,D
Physical Education M
Physics M,D
Planetary and Space Sciences M,D
Plant Sciences M,D
Psychology—General M,O
Reading Education M,D,O
Rehabilitation Counseling M,O
School Psychology M,O
Science Education M,O
Secondary Education M,O
Social Sciences Education M,O
Social Work M,O
Special Education M,D,O
Urban and Regional Planning M

### ALABAMA COLLEGE OF OSTEOPATHIC MEDICINE
Osteopathic Medicine D

### ALABAMA STATE UNIVERSITY
Accounting M
Allied Health—General M,D
Biological and Biomedical Sciences—General M,D
Business Administration and Management—General M
Counselor Education M,D,O
Early Childhood Education M,O
Education—General M,D,O
Educational Leadership and Administration M,D,O
Educational Media/Instructional Technology M,D,O
English Education M,O
Forensic Sciences M
Health Education M
History M
Mathematics Education M,O
Mathematics M
Microbiology M,D
Music Education M,O
Occupational Therapy M
Physical Education M
Physical Therapy D
Reading Education M,O
Rehabilitation Counseling M
Rehabilitation Sciences M
Science Education M,O
Secondary Education M,O
Social Sciences Education M,O
Social Work M

### ALASKA PACIFIC UNIVERSITY
Business Administration and Management—General M
Counseling Psychology M
Education—General M
Elementary Education M
Environmental Education M
Environmental Sciences M
Health Services Management and Hospital Administration M
Interdisciplinary Studies M
Investment Management M,O
Liberal Studies M
Middle School Education M
Telecommunications Management M

### ALBANY COLLEGE OF PHARMACY AND HEALTH SCIENCES
Cell Biology M
Clinical Laboratory Sciences/Medical Technology M
Health Services Research M,D
Molecular Biology M
Pharmaceutical Sciences M,D
Pharmacology M,D
Pharmacy M,D

### ALBANY LAW SCHOOL
Law M,D

### ALBANY MEDICAL COLLEGE
Allopathic Medicine D
Bioethics M,D,O
Cardiovascular Sciences M,D
Cell Biology M,D
Immunology M,D
Microbiology M,D
Molecular Biology M,D
Neuroscience M,D
Nurse Anesthesia M
Pharmacology M,D
Physician Assistant Studies M

### ALBANY STATE UNIVERSITY
Accounting M
Business Administration and Management—General M
Counselor Education M,O
Criminal Justice and Criminology M
Early Childhood Education M,O
Economic Development M
Economics M
Education—General M,O
Educational Leadership and Administration M,O
English Education M
Family Nurse Practitioner Studies M
Health Education M,O
Health Services Management and Hospital Administration M
Human Resources Management M
Logistics M
Middle School Education M,O
Nursing Education M
Nursing—General M
Physical Education M,O
Public Administration M
Public Policy M
Social Work M
Special Education M,O
Supply Chain Management M
Water Resources M

### ALBERT EINSTEIN COLLEGE OF MEDICINE
Allopathic Medicine D
Anatomy D
Biochemistry D
Biological and Biomedical Sciences—General D
Biophysics D
Cell Biology D
Clinical Research D
Computational Biology D
Developmental Biology D
Genetics D
Genomic Sciences D
Immunology D
Microbiology D
Molecular Biology D
Molecular Genetics D
Molecular Pharmacology D
Neuroscience D
Pathology D
Physiology D
Structural Biology D
Systems Biology D

### ALBERTUS MAGNUS COLLEGE
Accounting M
Art Therapy M
Business Administration and Management—General M
Criminal Justice and Criminology M
Education—General M
Health Services Management and Hospital Administration M
Human Resources Management M
Human Services M
Liberal Studies M
Organizational Management M
Project Management M
Writing M

### ALBIZU UNIVERSITY - MIAMI
Business Administration and Management—General M,D
Clinical Psychology M,D
Communication Disorders M,D
Counseling Psychology M,D
Education of the Gifted M,D
English as a Second Language M,D
Entrepreneurship M,D
Human Services M,D
Industrial and Organizational Psychology M,D
Marriage and Family Therapy M,D
Nonprofit Management M,D
Organizational Management M,D
Psychology—General M,D
Special Education M,D

### ALBIZU UNIVERSITY - SAN JUAN
Clinical Psychology M,D
Communication Disorders M,D
Industrial and Organizational Psychology M,D
Psychology—General M,D

### ALBRIGHT COLLEGE
Early Childhood Education M
Education—General M
Elementary Education M
English as a Second Language M
Special Education M

### ALCORN STATE UNIVERSITY
Agricultural Economics and Agribusiness M
Agricultural Education M,O
Agricultural Sciences—General M
Agronomy and Soil Sciences M
Animal Sciences M
Biological and Biomedical Sciences—General M
Business Administration and Management—General M
Computer Science M
Counselor Education M,O
Education—General M,O
Elementary Education M,O
Health Education M,O
Information Science M

Nursing—General M
Physical Education M,O
Secondary Education M,O
Special Education M,O
Sports Management M,O
Vocational and Technical Education M,O

**ALDERSON BROADDUS UNIVERSITY**
Physician Assistant Studies M

**ALFRED UNIVERSITY**
Accounting M
Applied Arts and Design—General M
Art/Fine Arts M,D
Bioengineering M,D
Business Administration and Management—General M
Ceramic Sciences and Engineering M,D
Computer Art and Design M
Counseling Psychology M,D,O
Counselor Education M,D,O
Education—General M
Electrical Engineering M,D
Engineering and Applied Sciences—General M,D
Internet and Interactive Multimedia M
Materials Sciences M,D
Mechanical Engineering M,D
Public Administration M
Reading Education M
School Psychology M,D,O
Student Affairs M

**ALLEN COLLEGE**
Adult Nursing M,D
Community Health Nursing M,D
Family Nurse Practitioner Studies M,D
Gerontological Nursing M,D
Health Education M,D
Nursing and Healthcare Administration M,D
Nursing Education M,D
Nursing Informatics M,D
Nursing—General M,D
Occupational Therapy M,D
Psychiatric Nursing M,D
Public Health—General M,D

**ALLIANT INTERNATIONAL UNIVERSITY–FRESNO**
Clinical Psychology D
Forensic Psychology D
Industrial and Organizational Psychology M,D
Psychology—General M,D

**ALLIANT INTERNATIONAL UNIVERSITY–IRVINE**
Educational Psychology M,D,O
Forensic Psychology D
Forensic Sciences D
Marriage and Family Therapy M,D
School Psychology M,D,O

**ALLIANT INTERNATIONAL UNIVERSITY - LOS ANGELES**
Addictions/Substance Abuse Counseling M
Business Administration and Management—General D
Clinical Psychology D
Education—General M,O
Educational Psychology M,D,O
Forensic Psychology D
Gerontology M
Health Psychology D
Industrial and Organizational Psychology M,D
Marriage and Family Therapy M,D
Psychology—General M,D
School Psychology M,D,O
Social Psychology D
Student Affairs M,D,O

**ALLIANT INTERNATIONAL UNIVERSITY–SACRAMENTO**
Clinical Psychology D
Education—General M,O
Forensic Psychology D
Marriage and Family Therapy M,D
Psychology—General M,D

**ALLIANT INTERNATIONAL UNIVERSITY - SAN DIEGO**
Business Administration and Management—General M
Clinical Psychology M,D
Education—General M,O
Educational Leadership and Administration M,D,O
Educational Psychology M,D,O
English as a Second Language M,D,O
Higher Education M,D,O
Industrial and Organizational Psychology M,D
Marriage and Family Therapy M,D
Neuroscience M,D,O
Psychology—General M,D
School Psychology M,D,O
Student Affairs M,D,O

**ALLIANT INTERNATIONAL UNIVERSITY–SAN FRANCISCO**
Clinical Psychology M,D,O
Counselor Education M
Criminal Justice and Criminology M
Education—General M,O
Educational Leadership and Administration M,D,O
Educational Psychology M,D,O
English as a Second Language M,O
Forensic Psychology M,D
Higher Education M,D,O
Industrial and Organizational Psychology M,D
Law D
Multilingual and Multicultural Education M,O
Pharmacology M,D,O
Psychology—General M,D,O
School Psychology M,D,O
Special Education M,O

**ALVERNIA UNIVERSITY**
Business Administration and Management—General M
Education—General M
Family Nurse Practitioner Studies M,D,O
Gerontological Nursing M,D,O
Liberal Studies M
Nursing and Healthcare Administration M,D,O
Nursing Education M,D,O
Nursing—General M,D,O
Occupational Therapy M
Organizational Management D
Social Psychology M
Urban Education M

**ALVERNO COLLEGE**
Adult Education M
Business Administration and Management—General M
Education—General M
Educational Leadership and Administration M
Educational Media/Instructional Technology M
Family Nurse Practitioner Studies M,D
Nursing—General M,D
Psychiatric Nursing M,D
Reading Education M
Science Education M
Social Psychology M
Special Education M

**AMBERTON UNIVERSITY**
Business Administration and Management—General M
Child and Family Studies M
Counseling Psychology M
Counselor Education M
Human Resources Development M
Human Resources Management M
Interdisciplinary Studies M
International Business M
Management Strategy and Policy M
Marriage and Family Therapy M
Project Management M

**AMBROSE UNIVERSITY**
Pastoral Ministry and Counseling M,O
Religion M,O
Theology M,O

**AMERICAN ACADEMY OF ACUPUNCTURE AND ORIENTAL MEDICINE**
Acupuncture and Oriental Medicine M,D

**AMERICAN BAPTIST SEMINARY OF THE WEST**
Pastoral Ministry and Counseling M
Theology M

**AMERICAN BUSINESS & TECHNOLOGY UNIVERSITY**
Accounting M
Business Administration and Management—General M
Finance and Banking M
International Business M
Management Information Systems M
Marketing M
Project Management M

**AMERICAN COLLEGE DUBLIN**
Business Administration and Management—General M
Energy Management and Policy M
International Business M
Writing M

**AMERICAN COLLEGE OF ACUPUNCTURE AND ORIENTAL MEDICINE**
Acupuncture and Oriental Medicine M

**AMERICAN COLLEGE OF EDUCATION**
Curriculum and Instruction M
Education—General M
Educational Leadership and Administration M
Educational Media/Instructional Technology M
English as a Second Language M
Multilingual and Multicultural Education M

**THE AMERICAN COLLEGE OF FINANCIAL SERVICES**
Business Administration and Management—General M
Finance and Banking M
Organizational Management M

**AMERICAN COLLEGE OF HEALTHCARE SCIENCES**
Allied Health—General M,O
Health Promotion M,O
Nutrition M,O
Physiology M,O

**AMERICAN COLLEGE OF THESSALONIKI**
Business Administration and Management—General M,O
Entrepreneurship M,O
Finance and Banking M,O
Marketing M,O

**AMERICAN CONSERVATORY THEATER**
Theater M,O

**AMERICAN FILM INSTITUTE CONSERVATORY**
Film, Television, and Video Production M

**AMERICAN GRADUATE SCHOOL IN PARIS**
International Affairs M,D

**AMERICAN GRADUATE UNIVERSITY**
Business Administration and Management—General M,O
Supply Chain Management M,O

**AMERICAN INSTITUTE OF ALTERNATIVE MEDICINE**
Acupuncture and Oriental Medicine M

**AMERICAN INTERCONTINENTAL UNIVERSITY ATLANTA**
Information Science M
International Business M
Management Information Systems M

**AMERICAN INTERCONTINENTAL UNIVERSITY HOUSTON**
Business Administration and Management—General M

**AMERICAN INTERCONTINENTAL UNIVERSITY ONLINE**
Accounting M
Business Administration and Management—General M
Computer and Information Systems Security M
Curriculum and Instruction M
Education—General M
Educational Leadership and Administration M
Educational Measurement and Evaluation M
Educational Media/Instructional Technology M
Finance and Banking M
Health Services Management and Hospital Administration M
Human Resources Management M
Industrial and Manufacturing Management M
Industrial and Organizational Psychology M
Information Science M
International Business M
Marketing M
Project Management M

**AMERICAN INTERNATIONAL COLLEGE**
Accounting M,D,O
Business Administration and Management—General M,D,O
Clinical Psychology M,D,O
Counseling Psychology M,D
Counselor Education M,D,O
Early Childhood Education M,D,O
Education—General M,D
Educational Leadership and Administration M,D
Educational Psychology M,D,O
Elementary Education M,D,O
Exercise and Sports Science M,D,O
Family Nurse Practitioner Studies M,D,O
Forensic Psychology M,D,O
Hospitality Management M,D,O
Middle School Education M,D,O
Nursing and Healthcare Administration M,D,O
Nursing Education M,D,O
Occupational Therapy M,D,O
Physical Therapy M,D,O
Psychology—General M,D,O
Reading Education M,D,O
Secondary Education M,D,O
Special Education M,D,O
Taxation M,D,O

**AMERICAN JEWISH UNIVERSITY**
Business Administration and Management—General M
Education—General M
Jewish Studies M
Nonprofit Management M
Social Work M
Theology M

**AMERICAN MUSEUM OF NATURAL HISTORY–RICHARD GILDER GRADUATE SCHOOL**
Biological and Biomedical Sciences—General D
Museum Studies D

**AMERICAN NATIONAL UNIVERSITY - ROANOKE VALLEY**
Business Administration and Management—General M

**AMERICAN PUBLIC UNIVERSITY SYSTEM**
Accounting M,D
American Studies M,D
Business Administration and Management—General M,D
Business Analytics M,D
Computer and Information Systems Security M,D
Conflict Resolution and Mediation/Peace Studies M,D
Criminal Justice and Criminology M,D
Educational Leadership and Administration M,D
Environmental Management and Policy M,D
Health Informatics M,D
History M,D
International Affairs M,D
Logistics M,D
Military and Defense Studies M,D
National Security M,D
Nursing—General M,D
Political Science M,D
Public Policy M,D
Secondary Education M,D
Sports Management M,D
Transportation Management M,D

**AMERICAN SENTINEL UNIVERSITY**
Business Administration and Management—General M
Computer Science M
Health Informatics M
Health Services Management and Hospital Administration M
Management Information Systems M
Nursing—General M

**AMERICAN UNIVERSITY**
Accounting M,O
American Studies M,D,O
Anthropology M,D,O
Applied Social Research M,O
Applied Statistics M,O
Art History M
Arts Administration M,O
Asian Studies O
Biological and Biomedical Sciences—General M
Biopsychology M,D,O
Biostatistics M,O
Biotechnology M
Broadcast Journalism M
Business Administration and Management—General M,O
Chemistry M
Clinical Psychology M,D,O
Cognitive Sciences M,D,O
Communication—General M,D
Comparative Literature M
Conflict Resolution and Mediation/Peace Studies M,D,O
Corporate and Organizational Communication M
Criminal Justice and Criminology M,D
Cultural Studies M,D,O
Data Science/Data Analytics M,O
Economics M,D,O
Education—General M,O
Educational Leadership and Administration M,O
Educational Measurement and Evaluation M,O
Educational Media/Instructional Technology M,O
Educational Policy M,O
English as a Second Language M,O
Entrepreneurship M,D,O
Environmental Management and Policy M,D,O
Environmental Sciences M,O
Ethics M,D,O
Film, Television, and Video Production M
Finance and Banking M,O
French M,O
Gender Studies M,D,O
Health Promotion M,O
Health Services Management and Hospital Administration M,O
History M,D
Human Resources Management M,O
International Affairs M,D,O
International and Comparative Education M,O
International Development M,D,O
International Economics M,D,O
Journalism M
Latin American Studies M,O
Law M,D
Management Information Systems M,D,O
Marketing M
Mass Communication M,D,O
Mathematics M,O
Media Studies M,O
Music M,O
National Security M,D,O
Natural Resources M,D,O
Neuroscience M,D,O
Nonprofit Management M,D,O
Nutrition M,O
Organizational Management M,D,O
Philosophy M
Political Science M,D,O
Project Management M,D,O
Psychology—General M,D,O
Public Administration M,D,O
Public Policy M,D,O
Real Estate M,O
Russian M,O
Sociology M,O
Spanish M,O
Special Education M,O
Sports Management M,O
Statistics M,O
Sustainability Management M

*M—masters degree; D—doctorate; O—other advanced degree; *—Close-Up and/or Display*

Sustainable Development M,D,O
Taxation M,O
Western European Studies M,D,O
Women's Studies O
Writing M

**AMERICAN UNIVERSITY IN BULGARIA**
Business Administration and Management—General M

**THE AMERICAN UNIVERSITY IN CAIRO**
Artificial Intelligence/Robotics M,D,O
Biotechnology M,D,O
Broadcast Journalism M,O
Business Administration and Management—General M,O
Chemistry M,D,O
Communication—General M,D,O
Comparative Literature M,O
Computer Science M,D,O
Construction Engineering M,D,O
Economic Development M,O
Economics M,O
Education—General M
Educational Leadership and Administration M
Electrical Engineering M,D,O
Engineering and Applied Sciences—General M,D,O
English as a Second Language M,O
English M,O
Environmental Engineering M,D,O
Finance and Banking M,O
Gender Studies M,O
Humanities M,O
International Affairs M,O
International and Comparative Education M
Journalism M,O
Law M,O
Mass Communication M,O
Mechanical Engineering M,D,O
Nanotechnology M,D,O
Near and Middle Eastern Languages M,O
Near and Middle Eastern Studies M,O
Philosophy M,O
Physics M,D,O
Psychology—General M,O
Public Administration M,O
Public Policy M,O
Sustainable Development M,D,O
Women's Studies M,O

**THE AMERICAN UNIVERSITY IN DUBAI**
Business Administration and Management—General M
Construction Management M
Education—General M
Finance and Banking M
International Business M
Marketing M

**AMERICAN UNIVERSITY OF ARMENIA**
Business Administration and Management—General M
Computer Science M
Economics M
Energy Management and Policy M
English as a Second Language M
Industrial/Management Engineering M
Information Science M
International Affairs M
Law M
Management Information Systems M
Manufacturing Engineering M
Political Science M
Public Health—General M

**AMERICAN UNIVERSITY OF HEALTH SCIENCES**
Clinical Research M

**THE AMERICAN UNIVERSITY OF PARIS**
Business Administration and Management—General M
Communication—General M
Conflict Resolution and Mediation/Peace Studies M
Cultural Studies M
International Affairs M
International Business M
Law M
Near and Middle Eastern Studies M
Public Policy M

**AMERICAN UNIVERSITY OF PUERTO RICO - BAYAMON**
Art Education M
Criminal Justice and Criminology M
Education—General M
Elementary Education M
Physical Education M
Science Education M
Special Education M

**THE AMERICAN UNIVERSITY OF ROME**
Arts Administration M
Conflict Resolution and Mediation/Peace Studies M
Food Science and Technology M
Historic Preservation M
Religion M

**AMERICAN UNIVERSITY OF SHARJAH**
Accounting M,D
Biomedical Engineering M,D
Business Administration and Management—General M,D
Chemical Engineering M,D
Civil Engineering M,D
Computer Engineering M,D
Electrical Engineering M,D
Engineering Management M,D
English as a Second Language M,D
Mathematics M,D
Mechanical Engineering M,D
Translation and Interpretation M,D
Urban and Regional Planning M,D

**AMRIDGE UNIVERSITY**
Counseling Psychology M,D
Counselor Education M,D
Human Services M,D
Marriage and Family Therapy M,D
Pastoral Ministry and Counseling M,D
Religion M,D
Theology M,D

**ANABAPTIST MENNONITE BIBLICAL SEMINARY**
Conflict Resolution and Mediation/Peace Studies M,O
Ethics M,O
International Affairs M,O
Pastoral Ministry and Counseling M,O
Public Administration M,O
Theology M,O

**ANAHEIM UNIVERSITY**
Business Administration and Management—General M,D,O
English as a Second Language M,D,O
Entrepreneurship M,D,O
International Business M,D,O
Sustainability Management M,D,O

**ANDERSON UNIVERSITY (IN)**
Accounting M,D
Business Administration and Management—General M,D
Education—General M
Missions and Missiology M,D
Theology M,D

**ANDERSON UNIVERSITY (SC)**
Business Administration and Management—General M
Criminal Justice and Criminology M
Education—General M
Educational Leadership and Administration M
Elementary Education M
Family Nurse Practitioner Studies M,D
Health Services Management and Hospital Administration M
Human Resources Management M
Marketing M
Music Education M
Nursing and Healthcare Administration M,D
Nursing Education M,D
Nursing—General M,D
Organizational Management M
Pastoral Ministry and Counseling M,D
Psychiatric Nursing M,D
Supply Chain Management M

**ANDREWS UNIVERSITY**
Accounting M
Allied Health—General M
Architecture M
Biological and Biomedical Sciences—General M
Clinical Psychology M
Communication Disorders M
Communication—General M
Counseling Psychology M,D
Curriculum and Instruction M,D,O
Developmental Psychology M,D
Economics M
Education—General M,D,O
Educational Leadership and Administration M,D,O
Educational Psychology M,D
Elementary Education M,D,O
English as a Second Language M,D,O
English Education M,D,O
English M
Finance and Banking M
Foreign Languages Education M,D,O
Higher Education M,D,O
International and Comparative Education M
International Development M
Music M
Nursing—General M,D
Nutrition M,O
Pastoral Ministry and Counseling M,D,O
Physical Therapy D
Psychology—General M,D,O
Public Health—General M,O
Religious Education M,D,O
School Psychology M,O
Science Education M,D,O
Secondary Education M,D,O
Social Psychology M
Social Sciences Education M,D,O
Social Work M
Special Education M
Theology M,D,O
Urban and Regional Planning M

**ANGELO STATE UNIVERSITY**
Accounting M
Agricultural Sciences—General M
Biological and Biomedical Sciences—General M
Business Administration and Management—General M
Communication—General M
Counselor Education M
Criminal Justice and Criminology M
Curriculum and Instruction M
Educational Leadership and Administration M
English as a Second Language M
English M
Family Nurse Practitioner Studies M
Higher Education M
Homeland Security M
Industrial and Organizational Psychology M
Media Studies M
National Security M
Nursing Education M
Nursing—General M
Physical Therapy D
Psychology—General M
Sociology M
Sports Management M

**ANNA MARIA COLLEGE**
Art/Fine Arts M,O
Business Administration and Management—General M,O
Counseling Psychology M
Criminal Justice and Criminology M
Early Childhood Education M,O
Education—General M,O
Elementary Education M,O
Emergency Management M,O
English Education M,O
Industrial and Organizational Psychology M
Public Administration M
Social Work M

**ANTIOCH UNIVERSITY LOS ANGELES**
Business Administration and Management—General M
Clinical Psychology M
Education—General M
Human Resources Development M
Organizational Management M
Psychology—General M
Sustainable Development M

**ANTIOCH UNIVERSITY MIDWEST**
Health Services Management and Hospital Administration M

**ANTIOCH UNIVERSITY NEW ENGLAND**
Addictions/Substance Abuse Counseling M,D,O
Applied Behavior Analysis M,D,O
Applied Psychology M,D,O
Clinical Psychology M,D,O
Conservation Biology M,D
Counseling Psychology M,D,O
Early Childhood Education M,O
Education—General M,O
Educational Leadership and Administration M,O
Elementary Education M,O
Environmental Education M,D
Environmental Management and Policy M,D
Environmental Sciences M,D
Foundations and Philosophy of Education M,O
Interdisciplinary Studies M,D
Marriage and Family Therapy M,D,O
Science Education M,D
Special Education M,D,O
Sustainable Development M,D
Therapies—Dance, Drama, and Music M,D,O

**ANTIOCH UNIVERSITY SANTA BARBARA**
Business Administration and Management—General M
Clinical Psychology M,D
Education—General M
Management Strategy and Policy M
Nonprofit Management M
Writing M

**ANTIOCH UNIVERSITY SEATTLE**
Adult Education M
Clinical Psychology M,D
Counselor Education M,D
Education—General M
Marriage and Family Therapy M,D
Therapies—Dance, Drama, and Music M

**AOMA GRADUATE SCHOOL OF INTEGRATIVE MEDICINE**
Acupuncture and Oriental Medicine M,D

**APEX SCHOOL OF THEOLOGY**
Theology M,D

**APOLLOS UNIVERSITY**
Business Administration and Management—General M,D
Organizational Management M,D

**APPALACHIAN BIBLE COLLEGE**
Pastoral Ministry and Counseling M

**APPALACHIAN COLLEGE OF PHARMACY**
Pharmacy D

**APPALACHIAN SCHOOL OF LAW**
Law D

**APPALACHIAN STATE UNIVERSITY**
Accounting M
American Studies M
Biological and Biomedical Sciences—General M
Business Administration and Management—General M
Cell Biology M
Clinical Psychology M
Communication Disorders M
Computer Science M
Counseling Psychology M
Counselor Education M
Cultural Studies M
Curriculum and Instruction M
Educational Leadership and Administration M,O
Educational Media/Instructional Technology M,O
Elementary Education M
Energy and Power Engineering M
English Education M
English M
Exercise and Sports Science M
Foreign Languages Education M
Geographic Information Systems M
Geography M
Health Psychology M
Higher Education M,O
History M
Library Science M,O
Marriage and Family Therapy M
Mathematics Education M
Mathematics M
Middle School Education M
Molecular Biology M
Music M
Nutrition M
Political Science M
Psychology—General M
Public Administration M
Reading Education M
School Psychology M
Science Education M
Social Sciences Education M
Social Work M
Special Education M
Student Affairs M
Taxation M
Therapies—Dance, Drama, and Music M
Vocational and Technical Education M

**AQUINAS COLLEGE (MI)**
Business Administration and Management—General M
Education—General M
Organizational Management M

**AQUINAS COLLEGE (TN)**
Education—General M
Elementary Education M
Secondary Education M

**AQUINAS INSTITUTE OF THEOLOGY**
Health Services Management and Hospital Administration M,D,O
Music M,D,O
Pastoral Ministry and Counseling M,D,O
Theology M,D,O

**ARCADIA UNIVERSITY**
Applied Behavior Analysis M
Art Education M,D,O
Business Administration and Management—General M
Computer Education M,D,O
Conflict Resolution and Mediation/Peace Studies M
Counseling Psychology M
Curriculum and Instruction M,D,O
Early Childhood Education M,D,O
Education—General M,D,O
Educational Leadership and Administration M,D,O
Educational Media/Instructional Technology M,D,O
Elementary Education M,D,O
English Education M,D,O
English M
Environmental Education M,D,O
Forensic Sciences M
Health Education M
Marriage and Family Therapy M
Mathematics Education M,D,O
Music Education M,D,O
Physical Therapy D
Physician Assistant Studies M
Psychology—General M,D,O
Public Health—General M
Reading Education M,D,O
Science Education M,D,O
Secondary Education M,D,O
Special Education M,D,O
Theater M,D,O
Writing M

**ARGOSY UNIVERSITY, ATLANTA**
Accounting M,D
Biopsychology M,D,O
Business Administration and Management—General M,D
Clinical Psychology M,D,O
Counselor Education M,D,O
Education—General M,D,O
Educational Leadership and Administration M,D,O
Educational Media/Instructional Technology M,D,O
Elementary Education M,D,O
Finance and Banking M,D
Forensic Psychology M,D,O
Health Psychology M,D,O
Health Services Management and Hospital Administration M,D
Higher Education M,D,O
Industrial and Organizational Psychology M,D,O
International Business M,D
Management Information Systems M,D
Marketing M,D
Marriage and Family Therapy M,D,O
Psychology—General M,D,O
Public Health—General M
Secondary Education M,D,O
Social Psychology M,D,O
Sport Psychology M,D,O

**ARGOSY UNIVERSITY, CHICAGO**
Accounting M,D
Adult Education M,D,O

| | |
|---|---|
| Business Administration and Management—General | M,D |
| Clinical Psychology | M,D |
| Community College Education | M,D,O |
| Counseling Psychology | D |
| Counselor Education | D |
| Education—General | M,D,O |
| Educational Leadership and Administration | M,D,O |
| Elementary Education | M,D,O |
| Finance and Banking | M,D |
| Forensic Psychology | D |
| Health Psychology | D |
| Health Services Management and Hospital Administration | M,D |
| Higher Education | M,D,O |
| Human Development | D |
| Industrial and Organizational Psychology | M,D |
| International Business | M,D |
| Management Information Systems | M,D |
| Marketing | M,D |
| Marriage and Family Therapy | D |
| Neuroscience | D |
| Organizational Behavior | D |
| Organizational Management | D |
| Psychoanalysis and Psychotherapy | D |
| Psychology—General | M,D |
| Public Administration | M,D |
| Public Health—General | M |
| Secondary Education | M,D,O |
| Social Psychology | M,D |
| Sustainability Management | M,D |

**ARGOSY UNIVERSITY, HAWAII**

| | |
|---|---|
| Accounting | M,D,O |
| Addictions/Substance Abuse Counseling | O |
| Adult Education | M,D |
| Business Administration and Management—General | M,D,O |
| Clinical Psychology | M,D,O |
| Counseling Psychology | D |
| Education—General | M,D |
| Educational Leadership and Administration | M,D |
| Elementary Education | M,D |
| Finance and Banking | M,D,O |
| Forensic Psychology | M |
| Health Services Management and Hospital Administration | M,D,O |
| Higher Education | M,D |
| International Business | M,D,O |
| Management Information Systems | M,D,O |
| Marketing | M,D,O |
| Marriage and Family Therapy | M |
| Organizational Management | D |
| Pharmacology | M,O |
| Psychology—General | M,D,O |
| Public Health—General | M |
| School Psychology | M |
| Secondary Education | M,D |
| Sustainability Management | M,D,O |

**ARGOSY UNIVERSITY, LOS ANGELES**

| | |
|---|---|
| Accounting | M,D |
| Business Administration and Management—General | M,D |
| Clinical Psychology | M,D |
| Community College Education | M,D |
| Counseling Psychology | M,D |
| Education—General | M,D |
| Educational Leadership and Administration | M,D |
| Elementary Education | M,D |
| Finance and Banking | M,D |
| Forensic Psychology | M,D |
| Health Services Management and Hospital Administration | M,D |
| Higher Education | M,D |
| International Business | M,D |
| Management Information Systems | M,D |
| Marketing | M,D |
| Marriage and Family Therapy | M,D |
| Organizational Management | M,D |
| Psychology—General | M,D |
| Public Administration | M,D |
| Public Health—General | M |
| Secondary Education | M,D |
| Sustainability Management | M,D |

**ARGOSY UNIVERSITY, NORTHERN VIRGINIA**

| | |
|---|---|
| Accounting | M,D,O |
| Business Administration and Management—General | M,D,O |
| Clinical Psychology | M,D |
| Community College Education | M,D,O |
| Counseling Psychology | M,D |
| Counselor Education | M,D |
| Education—General | M,D,O |
| Educational Leadership and Administration | M,D,O |
| Elementary Education | M,D,O |
| Finance and Banking | M,D,O |
| Forensic Psychology | M,D |
| Health Psychology | M,D |
| Health Services Management and Hospital Administration | M,D,O |
| Higher Education | M,D,O |
| International Business | M,D,O |
| Management Information Systems | M,D,O |
| Marketing | M,D,O |
| Marriage and Family Therapy | M,D |
| Organizational Management | M,D,O |
| Psychology—General | M,D |
| Public Administration | M,D,O |
| Public Health—General | M |
| Secondary Education | M,D,O |
| Social Psychology | M,D |
| Sustainability Management | M,D,O |

**ARGOSY UNIVERSITY, ORANGE COUNTY**

| | |
|---|---|
| Accounting | M,D,O |
| Business Administration and Management—General | M,D,O |
| Clinical Psychology | M,D |
| Community College Education | M,D |
| Counseling Psychology | M,D |
| Education—General | M,D |
| Educational Leadership and Administration | M,D |
| Educational Media/Instructional Technology | M,D |
| Elementary Education | M,D |
| Finance and Banking | M,D,O |
| Forensic Psychology | M |
| Health Services Management and Hospital Administration | M,D,O |
| Higher Education | M,D |
| International Business | M,D,O |
| Management Information Systems | M,D,O |
| Marketing | M,D,O |
| Marriage and Family Therapy | M,D |
| Organizational Management | D |
| Psychology—General | M,D |
| Public Administration | M,D,O |
| Public Health—General | M |
| Secondary Education | M,D |
| Sport Psychology | M |
| Sustainability Management | M,D,O |

**ARGOSY UNIVERSITY, PHOENIX**

| | |
|---|---|
| Accounting | M,D |
| Adult Education | M,D,O |
| Business Administration and Management—General | M,D |
| Clinical Psychology | M,D |
| Community College Education | M,D,O |
| Counseling Psychology | M |
| Education—General | M,D,O |
| Educational Leadership and Administration | M,D,O |
| Educational Media/Instructional Technology | M,D,O |
| Elementary Education | M,D,O |
| Finance and Banking | M,D |
| Forensic Psychology | M |
| Health Services Management and Hospital Administration | M,D |
| Higher Education | M,D,O |
| Industrial and Organizational Psychology | M |
| International Business | M,D |
| Management Information Systems | M,D |
| Marketing | M,D |
| Neuroscience | M,D |
| Psychology—General | M,D |
| Public Administration | M,D |
| Public Health—General | M |
| School Psychology | M,D |
| Secondary Education | M,D,O |
| Sport Psychology | M,D |
| Sustainability Management | M,D |

**ARGOSY UNIVERSITY, SEATTLE**

| | |
|---|---|
| Accounting | M,D |
| Adult Education | M,D |
| Business Administration and Management—General | M,D |
| Clinical Psychology | M,D,O |
| Community College Education | M,D |
| Counseling Psychology | M,D |
| Education—General | M,D |
| Educational Leadership and Administration | M,D |
| Educational Media/Instructional Technology | M,D |
| Elementary Education | M,D |
| Finance and Banking | M,D |
| Health Services Management and Hospital Administration | M,D |
| Higher Education | M,D |
| International Business | M,D |
| Management Information Systems | M,D |
| Marketing | M,D |
| Organizational Management | M,D |
| Psychology—General | M,D,O |
| Public Administration | M,D |
| Public Health—General | M |
| Secondary Education | M,D |
| Sustainability Management | M,D |

**ARGOSY UNIVERSITY, TAMPA**

| | |
|---|---|
| Accounting | M,D |
| Business Administration and Management—General | M,D |
| Clinical Psychology | M,D |
| Community College Education | M,D,O |
| Counseling Psychology | M,D |
| Counselor Education | M,D,O |
| Education—General | M,D,O |
| Educational Leadership and Administration | M,D,O |
| Elementary Education | M,D,O |
| Finance and Banking | M,D |
| Health Services Management and Hospital Administration | M,D |
| Higher Education | M,D,O |
| Industrial and Organizational Psychology | M,D |
| International Business | M,D |
| Management Information Systems | M,D |
| Marketing | M,D |
| Marriage and Family Therapy | M,D |
| Neuroscience | M,D |
| Organizational Management | M,D |
| Psychology—General | M,D |
| Public Administration | M,D |
| Public Health—General | M |
| Secondary Education | M,D,O |
| Sustainability Management | M,D |

**ARGOSY UNIVERSITY, TWIN CITIES**

| | |
|---|---|
| Accounting | M,D |
| Biopsychology | M,D,O |
| Business Administration and Management—General | M,D |
| Clinical Psychology | M,D,O |
| Education—General | M,D,O |
| Educational Leadership and Administration | M,D,O |
| Educational Media/Instructional Technology | M,D,O |
| Elementary Education | M,D,O |
| Finance and Banking | M,D |
| Forensic Psychology | M,D,O |
| Health Psychology | M,D,O |
| Health Services Management and Hospital Administration | M,D |
| Higher Education | M,D,O |
| Industrial and Organizational Psychology | M,D,O |
| International Business | M,D |
| Management Information Systems | M,D |
| Marketing | M,D |
| Marriage and Family Therapy | M,D,O |
| Organizational Management | M,D |
| Psychology—General | M,D,O |
| Public Administration | M,D |
| Public Health—General | M |
| Secondary Education | M,D,O |
| Sustainability Management | M,D |

**ARIZONA SCHOOL OF ACUPUNCTURE AND ORIENTAL MEDICINE**

| | |
|---|---|
| Acupuncture and Oriental Medicine | M |

**ARIZONA STATE UNIVERSITY AT TEMPE**

| | |
|---|---|
| Accounting | M,D |
| Aerospace/Aeronautical Engineering | M,D |
| African Studies | M,D,O |
| Agricultural Economics and Agribusiness | D |
| Animal Behavior | M,D |
| Anthropology | M,D,O |
| Applied Arts and Design—General | M,D |
| Applied Behavior Analysis | M,D |
| Applied Mathematics | M,D,O |
| Applied Psychology | M |
| Archaeology | M,D,O |
| Architectural History | D |
| Architecture | M,D |
| Art Education | M,D |
| Art History | M,D |
| Art/Fine Arts | M,D |
| Arts Administration | M,D |
| Astrophysics | M,D |
| Aviation Management | M |
| Biochemistry | M,D |
| Bioinformatics | M,D |
| Biological and Biomedical Sciences—General | M,D |
| Biomedical Engineering | M,D |
| Biotechnology | M,D |
| Building Science | M,D |
| Business Administration and Management—General | M,D |
| Cell Biology | M,D |
| Chemical Engineering | M,D |
| Chemistry | M,D |
| Child and Family Studies | M,D |
| Chinese | M,D |
| Civil Engineering | M,D |
| Clinical Psychology | M,D |
| Cognitive Sciences | M,D |
| Communication Disorders | M,D |
| Communication—General | M,D |
| Community Health | M,D,O |
| Comparative Literature | M,D,O |
| Computer Engineering | M,D |
| Computer Science | M,D |
| Conservation Biology | M,D |
| Construction Engineering | M,D |
| Construction Management | M,D |
| Counseling Psychology | D |
| Counselor Education | M |
| Criminal Justice and Criminology | M,D,O |
| Cultural Studies | M,D |
| Curriculum and Instruction | M |
| Dance | M |
| Developmental Psychology | M,D |
| Economics | D |
| Education—General | M,D,O |
| Educational Leadership and Administration | M,D |
| Educational Measurement and Evaluation | D |
| Educational Media/Instructional Technology | M,O |
| Educational Policy | D |
| Electrical Engineering | M,D,O |
| Elementary Education | M |
| Emergency Management | M,D |
| Energy and Power Engineering | M,D |
| Engineering and Applied Sciences—General | M,D,O |
| English as a Second Language | M,D,O |
| English | M,D,O |
| Entrepreneurship | M,D |
| Environmental Design | D |
| Environmental Engineering | M,D |
| Environmental Management and Policy | M |
| Environmental Sciences | M,D,O |
| Ergonomics and Human Factors | M |
| Ethics | M,D |
| Evolutionary Biology | M,D |
| Exercise and Sports Science | M,D |
| Family Nurse Practitioner Studies | M,D,O |
| Film, Television, and Video Production | M |
| Finance and Banking | M,D |
| Foreign Languages Education | M,D |
| French | M |
| Gender Studies | M,D,O |
| Geographic Information Systems | M,D,O |
| Geography | M,D,O |
| Geological Engineering | M,D |
| Geology | M,D |
| Geosciences | M,D |
| German | M |
| Gerontological Nursing | M,D,O |
| Gerontology | M,D,O |
| Health Education | D |
| Health Promotion | M,D |
| Health Services Management and Hospital Administration | M,D |
| Higher Education | M |
| History of Science and Technology | M,D |
| History | M,D,O |
| Homeland Security | M,D |
| Human Development | M,D |
| Industrial/Management Engineering | M,D |
| Information Science | M |
| Interdisciplinary Studies | M |
| International Business | M,D |
| International Health | M,D,O |
| Japanese | M |
| Journalism | M,D |
| Landscape Architecture | M,D |
| Law | M,D |
| Legal and Justice Studies | M,D,O |
| Liberal Studies | M |
| Linguistics | M,D,O |
| Management Information Systems | M,D |
| Management of Technology | M |
| Management Strategy and Policy | M,D |
| Manufacturing Engineering | M |
| Marketing | M,D |
| Marriage and Family Therapy | M,D |
| Mass Communication | M,D |
| Materials Engineering | M,D |
| Materials Sciences | M,D |
| Mathematics Education | M,D,O |
| Mathematics | M,D,O |
| Mechanical Engineering | M,D |
| Media Studies | M,D |
| Medical Informatics | M,D |
| Medieval and Renaissance Studies | M,D,O |
| Microbiology | M,D |
| Modeling and Simulation | M,D |
| Molecular Biology | M,D |
| Museum Studies | M,D,O |
| Music Education | M,D |
| Music | M,D |
| Nanotechnology | M,D |
| Neuroscience | M,D |
| Nonprofit Management | M,D,O |
| Nuclear Engineering | M,D,O |
| Nursing and Healthcare Administration | M,D,O |
| Nursing Education | M,D,O |
| Nursing—General | M,D,O |
| Nutrition | M,D |
| Organizational Behavior | M,D |
| Philosophy | M,D,O |
| Physical Education | M |
| Physics | M,D |
| Planetary and Space Sciences | M,D |
| Plant Biology | M,D |
| Political Science | M,D |
| Psychiatric Nursing | M,D,O |
| Psychology—General | M,D |
| Public Administration | M,D |
| Public Affairs | M,D |
| Public Health—General | M,D,O |
| Public History | M,D,O |
| Public Policy | M,D |
| Publishing | M,D,O |
| Real Estate | M,D |
| Reliability Engineering | M |
| Religion | M,D,O |
| Rhetoric | M,D,O |
| Secondary Education | M |
| Social Psychology | M,D |
| Social Work | M,D,O |
| Sociology | M,D |
| Software Engineering | M,D |
| Spanish | M,D |
| Special Education | M,O |
| Sports and Entertainment Law | M,D |
| Statistics | M,D,O |
| Supply Chain Management | M,D,O |
| Sustainable Development | M,D,O |
| Systems Engineering | M |
| Systems Science | M,D |
| Technology and Public Policy | M |
| Textile Design | M,D |
| Theater | M,D |
| Therapies—Dance, Drama, and Music | M,D |
| Translation and Interpretation | M,D,O |
| Transportation and Highway Engineering | M,D,O |
| Travel and Tourism | M,D,O |
| Urban and Regional Planning | M,D,O |
| Urban Design | M,D |
| Urban Studies | M,D,O |
| Writing | M,D |

**ARKANSAS COLLEGES OF HEALTH EDUCATION**

| | |
|---|---|
| Biological and Biomedical Sciences—General | M |
| Osteopathic Medicine | D |

*M—masters degree; D—doctorate; O—other advanced degree; *—Close-Up and/or Display*

### ARKANSAS STATE UNIVERSITY
Accounting M
Addictions/Substance Abuse Counseling M,O
Agricultural Education M,O
Agricultural Sciences—General M,O
Biological and Biomedical Sciences—General M,O
Biotechnology M,O
Business Administration and Management—General M
Business Education O
Chemistry M,O
Clinical Psychology M,O
Communication Disorders M,O
Communication—General M,O
Community College Education M,D,O
Computer Science M
Counselor Education M,O
Criminal Justice and Criminology M,O
Early Childhood Education M,D,O
Education of the Gifted M,D,O
Education—General M,D,O
Educational Leadership and Administration M,D,O
Elementary Education M,D,O
Emergency Management M,O
Engineering and Applied Sciences—General M
Engineering Management M
English Education M,O
English M,O
Environmental Sciences M,D
Exercise and Sports Science M,O
Foundations and Philosophy of Education M,D,O
Gerontology M,D,O
Health Communication M,O
Health Education M,D,O
Health Services Management and Hospital Administration M,D,O
Historic Preservation M,D
History M,O
Journalism M
Management Information Systems O
Mass Communication M
Mathematics Education M
Mathematics M
Media Studies M
Middle School Education M,D,O
Molecular Biology M,D
Music Education M,O
Music M,O
Nurse Anesthesia M,D,O
Nursing—General M,D,O
Occupational Therapy D
Physical Education M,O
Physical Therapy D
Political Science M,O
Public Administration M,O
Reading Education M,D,O
Rehabilitation Counseling M,O
School Psychology M,O
Science Education M,O
Social Sciences Education M,D,O
Social Work M,O
Sociology M,O
Special Education M,D,O
Sports Management M,O
Student Affairs M,O

### ARKANSAS TECH UNIVERSITY
Business Administration and Management—General M
Counselor Education M,D,O
Education—General M,D,O
Educational Leadership and Administration M,D,O
Educational Media/Instructional Technology M,D,O
Electrical Engineering M
Elementary Education M,D,O
Emergency Management M
Engineering and Applied Sciences—General M
English as a Second Language M
English Education M
English M
Fish, Game, and Wildlife Management M
Health Informatics M
History M
Information Science M
Journalism M
Liberal Studies M
Mechanical Engineering M
Nursing—General M
Psychology—General M
Sociology M
Special Education M,D,O
Student Affairs M,D,O

### ARLINGTON BAPTIST UNIVERSITY
Curriculum and Instruction M
Education—General M
Educational Leadership and Administration M
Theology M

### ART ACADEMY OF CINCINNATI
Art Education M

### ARTCENTER COLLEGE OF DESIGN
Art/Fine Arts M
Computer Art and Design M
Environmental Design M
Film, Television, and Video Production M
Graphic Design M
Industrial Design M
Transportation and Highway Engineering M

### THE ART INSTITUTE OF DALLAS, A BRANCH OF MIAMI INTERNATIONAL UNIVERSITY OF ART & DESIGN
Applied Arts and Design—General M

### ASBURY THEOLOGICAL SEMINARY
Missions and Missiology M,D,O
Pastoral Ministry and Counseling M,D,O
Religious Education M,D,O
Theology M,D,O

### ASBURY UNIVERSITY
Child and Family Studies M
Classics M
Educational Leadership and Administration M
English as a Second Language M
English M
French M
Mathematics Education M
Reading Education M
Science Education M
Social Sciences Education M
Social Work M
Spanish M
Special Education M
Writing M

### ASHLAND THEOLOGICAL SEMINARY
Clinical Psychology M,D
Counselor Education M,D
Pastoral Ministry and Counseling M,D
Theology M,D

### ASHLAND UNIVERSITY
Accounting M
Business Administration and Management—General M
Business Analytics M
Communication—General M
Corporate and Organizational Communication M
Education—General M,D
Educational Leadership and Administration M,D
Entrepreneurship M
Exercise and Sports Science M
Family Nurse Practitioner Studies D
Finance and Banking M
Health Services Management and Hospital Administration M
History M
Human Resources Management M
International Business M
Management Information Systems M
Nursing—General D
Political Science M
Project Management M
Sports Management M
Supply Chain Management M
Writing M

### ASHWORTH COLLEGE
Business Administration and Management—General M
Criminal Justice and Criminology M
Health Services Management and Hospital Administration M
Human Resources Management M
International Business M
Marketing M

### ASPEN UNIVERSITY
Business Administration and Management—General M,O
Finance and Banking M,O
Forensic Nursing M
Information Science M,O
Management Information Systems M,O
Nursing and Healthcare Administration M
Nursing Education M
Nursing Informatics M
Nursing—General M
Project Management M,O

### ASSEMBLIES OF GOD THEOLOGICAL SEMINARY
Cultural Studies M,D
Missions and Missiology M,D
Pastoral Ministry and Counseling M,D
Theology M,D

### ASSUMPTION UNIVERSITY
Accounting M,O
Addictions/Substance Abuse Counseling O
Applied Behavior Analysis M,O
Business Administration and Management—General M,O
Child and Family Studies M,O
Counseling Psychology M,O
Economics M,O
Finance and Banking M,O
Health Services Management and Hospital Administration M,O
Human Resources Management M,O
International Business M,O
Marketing M,O
Nonprofit Management M,O
Rehabilitation Counseling M,O
School Psychology M,O
Social Sciences O
Special Education M,O

### ATHABASCA UNIVERSITY
Adult Education M,O
Allied Health—General M,O
Applied Psychology M,O
Architecture M,O
Art Therapy M,O
Business Administration and Management—General M,D,O
Counseling Psychology M,O
Counselor Education M,O
Cultural Studies M,O
Distance Education Development M,D,O
Education—General M,D,O
Interdisciplinary Studies M,O
International Development M,O
Management of Technology M,D,O
Nursing and Healthcare Administration M,O
Nursing—General M,O
Organizational Management M,O
Project Management M,D,O
Science Education M,O

### THE ATHENAEUM OF OHIO
Theology M,O

### ATHENS STATE UNIVERSITY
Logistics M
Religion M
Supply Chain Management M
Vocational and Technical Education M

### ATLANTA'S JOHN MARSHALL LAW SCHOOL
Law M,D

### ATLANTIC INSTITUTE OF ORIENTAL MEDICINE
Acupuncture and Oriental Medicine M,D

### ATLANTIC SCHOOL OF THEOLOGY
Pastoral Ministry and Counseling M,O
Theology M,O

### ATLANTIC UNIVERSITY
Organizational Management M,O
Pastoral Ministry and Counseling O
Psychoanalysis and Psychotherapy O
Transpersonal and Humanistic Psychology M

### ATLANTIC UNIVERSITY COLLEGE
Graphic Design M

### ATLANTIS UNIVERSITY
Business Administration and Management—General M,D
Computer Engineering M
Engineering and Applied Sciences—General M
Health Services Management and Hospital Administration M
Management of Technology M

### A.T. STILL UNIVERSITY
Allied Health—General M,D,O
Athletic Training and Sports Medicine M,D,O
Biological and Biomedical Sciences—General M,D
Communication Disorders M,D,O
Dentistry M,D,O
Health Services Management and Hospital Administration M,D,O
International Health M,D,O
Kinesiology and Movement Studies M,D,O
Occupational Therapy M,D,O
Oral and Dental Sciences M,D,O
Organizational Behavior M,D,O
Osteopathic Medicine M,D
Physical Therapy M,D,O
Physician Assistant Studies M,D,O
Public Health—General M,D,O
Sport Psychology M,D,O

### AUBURN UNIVERSITY
Accounting M
Adult Education M,D,O
Aerospace/Aeronautical Engineering M,D
Agricultural Economics and Agribusiness M
Agricultural Sciences—General M,D
Agronomy and Soil Sciences M,D
Analytical Chemistry M,D
Animal Sciences M,D
Applied Economics M,D
Applied Mathematics M,D
Aquaculture M,D
Architecture M
Biochemistry M,D
Biological and Biomedical Sciences—General M,D
Biosystems Engineering M,D
Botany M,D
Business Administration and Management—General M,D
Cell Biology M,D
Chemical Engineering M,D
Chemistry M,D
Child and Family Studies M,D
Civil Engineering M,D
Clothing and Textiles M,D
Communication Disorders M,D
Communication—General M,D
Computer Engineering M,D
Computer Science M,D
Construction Engineering M
Curriculum and Instruction M,D,O
Economics M,D
Education—General M,D,O
Educational Leadership and Administration M,D,O
Educational Media/Instructional Technology M,D,O
Electrical Engineering M,D
Engineering and Applied Sciences—General M,D,O
English M,D,O
Entomology M,D
Exercise and Sports Science M,D,O
Finance and Banking M
Fish, Game, and Wildlife Management M,D
Food Science and Technology M,D,O
Forestry M,D
Geography M
Geology M
Health Education M,D,O
Higher Education M,D,O
History M,D,O
Horticulture M,D
Human Development M,D
Industrial Design M
Industrial/Management Engineering M,D,O
Inorganic Chemistry M,D
Landscape Architecture M
Materials Engineering M,D
Mathematics M,D
Mechanical Engineering M,D
Molecular Biology M,D
Natural Resources M,D
Nursing Education M
Nursing—General M
Nutrition M,D,O
Organic Chemistry M,D
Pharmaceutical Sciences M,D
Pharmacy D
Physical Chemistry M,D
Physical Education M,D,O
Physics M,D
Plant Pathology M,D
Political Science M,D,O
Psychology—General M,D
Public Administration M,D,O
Real Estate M
Rural Sociology M
Social Work M
Sociology M
Software Engineering M,D
Spanish M
Special Education M,D
Statistics M,D
Systems Engineering M,D,O
Technical Communication M,D,O
Urban and Regional Planning M
Veterinary Medicine D
Zoology M,D

### AUBURN UNIVERSITY AT MONTGOMERY
Accounting M
Applied Economics M
Business Administration and Management—General M
Clinical Psychology M,O
Counselor Education M,O
Early Childhood Education M,O
Economics M
Education—General M,O
Educational Leadership and Administration M,O
Educational Media/Instructional Technology M,O
Elementary Education M,O
Exercise and Sports Science M,O
Family Nurse Practitioner Studies M
Geographic Information Systems M
Management Information Systems M
Nursing Education M
Nursing—General M
Physical Education M,O
Political Science M,D
Psychology—General M
Public Administration M,D
Public Policy M,D
School Psychology M,O
Secondary Education M,O
Special Education M,O
Sports Management M,O
Writing M

### AUGSBURG UNIVERSITY
Business Administration and Management—General M
Education—General M
Family Nurse Practitioner Studies M,D
Nursing—General M,D
Organizational Management M
Physician Assistant Studies M
Social Work M
Transcultural Nursing M,D

### AUGUSTANA UNIVERSITY
Accounting M
Education—General M
Educational Media/Instructional Technology M
Genetic Counseling M
Mathematics M
Reading Education M
Science Education M
Special Education M
Sports Management M

### AUGUSTA UNIVERSITY
Acute Care/Critical Care Nursing D
Allied Health—General D
Allopathic Medicine D
Anatomy D
Biochemistry D
Business Administration and Management—General M
Cancer Biology/Oncology D
Cardiovascular Sciences D
Cell Biology D
Clinical Psychology M,O
Clinical Research M
Computer and Information Systems Security M
Counselor Education M,O
Curriculum and Instruction M,O
Dentistry D
Education—General M,D,O
Educational Leadership and Administration M,O
Educational Media/Instructional Technology D
Elementary Education M,O

Environmental and Occupational Health M
Family Nurse Practitioner Studies D
Foreign Languages Education M,O
Genomic Sciences D
Gerontological Nursing D
Health Informatics M
Medical Illustration M
Middle School Education M,O
Molecular Medicine D
Music Education M,O
Neuroscience D
Nurse Anesthesia D
Nursing and Healthcare Administration M,D
Nursing—General D
Occupational Therapy M
Oral and Dental Sciences M,D
Pediatric Nursing D
Pharmacology D
Physical Therapy D
Physician Assistant Studies M
Physiology D
Psychiatric Nursing D
Psychology—General M
Public Health—General M
Rehabilitation Sciences D
School Psychology M,O
Secondary Education M,O
Social Sciences M
Special Education M,O

### AURORA UNIVERSITY
Accounting M
Adult Education M,D
Applied Behavior Analysis M,D
Business Administration and Management—General M
Curriculum and Instruction M,D
Education—General M,D
Educational Leadership and Administration M,D
Educational Media/Instructional Technology M,D
English as a Second Language M,D
Homeland Security M
Mathematics Education M
Mathematics M
Public Policy M
Reading Education M,D
Science Education M
Social Work M,D
Special Education M,D

### AUSTIN COLLEGE
Education—General M

### AUSTIN PEAY STATE UNIVERSITY
Biological and Biomedical Sciences—General M
Business Administration and Management—General M
Clinical Laboratory Sciences/Medical Technology M
Clinical Psychology M
Communication—General M
Computer and Information Systems Security M
Corporate and Organizational Communication M
Counseling Psychology M
Counselor Education M
Data Science/Data Analytics M
Education—General M,O
English M
Exercise and Sports Science M
Family Nurse Practitioner Studies M
Health Education M
Industrial and Organizational Psychology M
Mathematical and Computational Finance M
Mathematics Education M
Media Studies M
Military and Defense Studies M
Music Education M
Music M
Nursing and Healthcare Administration M
Nursing Education M
Nursing Informatics M
Nursing—General M
Organizational Management M
Psychology—General M
Public Health—General M
Science Education M
Social Work M
Sports Management M

### AUSTIN PRESBYTERIAN THEOLOGICAL SEMINARY
Pastoral Ministry and Counseling M,D
Theology M,D

### AVE MARIA SCHOOL OF LAW
Law D

### AVE MARIA UNIVERSITY
Pastoral Ministry and Counseling M,D
Theology M,D

### AVERETT UNIVERSITY
Accounting M
Business Administration and Management—General M
Education—General M
Human Resources Management M
Marketing M
Special Education M

### AVILA UNIVERSITY
Business Administration and Management—General M
Counseling Psychology M
Early Childhood Education M,O
Education—General M,O
Educational Media/Instructional Technology M
Elementary Education M,O
Human Resources Management M
Middle School Education M,O
Nonprofit Management M
Organizational Management M
Physical Education M,O
Project Management M
Psychology—General M
Secondary Education M,O

### AZUSA PACIFIC UNIVERSITY
Accounting M
Adult Nursing M,D
Art/Fine Arts M
Athletic Training and Sports Medicine M
Biotechnology M
Business Administration and Management—General M
Clinical Psychology D
Counselor Education M
Curriculum and Instruction M
Data Science/Data Analytics M
Developmental Psychology M
Education—General M,D
Educational Leadership and Administration M,D
Educational Media/Instructional Technology M
English as a Second Language M
English M
Entrepreneurship M
Ethics M
Experimental Psychology M
Family Nurse Practitioner Studies M,D
Film, Television, and Video Production M
Finance and Banking M
Gerontological Nursing M,D
Higher Education M,D
Industrial and Organizational Psychology M
International Business M
Kinesiology and Movement Studies M
Marketing M
Marriage and Family Therapy D
Music Education M
Music M
Nursing and Healthcare Administration M,D
Nursing Education M,D
Nursing—General M,D
Organizational Management M
Pastoral Ministry and Counseling M
Pediatric Nursing M,D
Physical Therapy D
Psychiatric Nursing M,D
Psychology—General M
Public Health—General M
School Psychology M,D
Social Work M
Special Education M
Sports Management M
Theology M,D
Urban Studies M

### BABEL UNIVERSITY PROFESSIONAL SCHOOL OF TRANSLATION
Translation and Interpretation M

### BABSON COLLEGE
Accounting M,O
Business Administration and Management—General M,O
Business Analytics M,O
Entrepreneurship M,O
Finance and Banking M,O

### BAKER COLLEGE CENTER FOR GRADUATE STUDIES–ONLINE
Accounting M,D
Business Administration and Management—General M,D
Finance and Banking M,D
Health Services Management and Hospital Administration M,D
Human Resources Management M,D
Management Information Systems M,D
Marketing M,D
Occupational Therapy M,D

### BAKER UNIVERSITY
Business Administration and Management—General M
Education—General M,D
Liberal Studies M
Organizational Management M

### BAKKE GRADUATE UNIVERSITY
Business Administration and Management—General M,D
Entrepreneurship M,D
Pastoral Ministry and Counseling M,D
Theology M,D
Urban Education M,D

### BALDWIN WALLACE UNIVERSITY
Business Administration and Management—General M
Business Analytics M
Communication Disorders M
Education—General M
Educational Leadership and Administration M
Educational Media/Instructional Technology M
Health Education M
Health Services Management and Hospital Administration M
Human Resources Management M
Physician Assistant Studies M
Public Health—General M
Reading Education M
Special Education M

### BALL STATE UNIVERSITY
Accounting M
Actuarial Science M
Adult Education M,D
Advertising and Public Relations M
Anthropology M,O
Applied Behavior Analysis M
Architecture M
Art/Fine Arts M
Biological and Biomedical Sciences—General M,D
Business Administration and Management—General M,O
Business Education M,O
Chemistry M,D
Clinical Psychology M,D
Cognitive Sciences M
Communication Disorders M,D
Communication—General M,O
Computer Education M,D,O
Computer Science M
Counseling Psychology M,D
Counselor Education M,D
Criminal Justice and Criminology M,O
Curriculum and Instruction M,D
Economic Development M,O
Education of the Gifted M,D,O
Education—General M,D,O
Educational Leadership and Administration M,D,O
Educational Measurement and Evaluation M,D,O
Educational Media/Instructional Technology M,D
Educational Policy D
Educational Psychology M,D
Elementary Education M,D,O
Emergency Management M,O
English as a Second Language M
English M,D
Environmental Education M,O
Environmental Management and Policy M,O
Environmental Sciences D
Exercise and Sports Science M,D
Family and Consumer Sciences-General M
Family Nurse Practitioner Studies M,D,O
Foundations and Philosophy of Education D
Geographic Information Systems M,O
Geography M,O
Geology M,D
Geosciences M
Gerontological Nursing M,D,O
Health Promotion M
Higher Education M,D
Historic Preservation M
History M
Homeland Security M,O
Human Development M,D,O
Information Science M,O
Interior Design M
Internet and Interactive Multimedia M
Journalism M
Kinesiology and Movement Studies M,D,O
Landscape Architecture M
Linguistics M
Management Information Systems M,O
Mathematics Education M
Mathematics M
Meteorology M,O
Middle School Education M,O
Music Education M,D,O
Music M,D,O
Natural Resources M,O
Neuroscience M,D,O
Nursing Education M,D,O
Nursing—General M,D,O
Nutrition M
Photography M
Physical Education M
Physics M
Physiology M
Political Science M
Psychology—General M
Public Administration M,O
Reading Education M,D,O
Rehabilitation Counseling M,D
Rhetoric M,D
School Psychology M,D,O
Secondary Education M
Social Psychology M
Sociology M
Special Education M,D,O
Speech and Interpersonal Communication M
Sport Psychology M
Sports Management M
Statistics M
Telecommunications M
Urban and Regional Planning M,O
Urban Design M
Writing M,D

### BANK STREET COLLEGE OF EDUCATION
Child and Family Studies M
Early Childhood Education M
Education—General M
Educational Leadership and Administration M
Elementary Education M
Foundations and Philosophy of Education M
Maternal and Child Health M
Mathematics Education M
Multilingual and Multicultural Education M
Museum Illustration M
Reading Education M
Special Education M

### BAPTIST BIBLE COLLEGE
Pastoral Ministry and Counseling M
Theology M

### THE BAPTIST COLLEGE OF FLORIDA
Music M
Pastoral Ministry and Counseling M
Theology M

### BAPTIST MISSIONARY ASSOCIATION THEOLOGICAL SEMINARY
Theology M

### BARCLAY COLLEGE
Theology M

### BARD COLLEGE
Art/Fine Arts M
Atmospheric Sciences M,O
Economics M
Education—General M
English M
Environmental Management and Policy M,O
Film, Television, and Video Production M
History M
Mathematics Education M
Museum Studies M
Music M,O
Photography M
Science Education M
Secondary Education M
Spanish M
Sustainability Management M,O
Writing M

### BARD GRADUATE CENTER
Art History M,D
Decorative Arts M,D

### BARRY UNIVERSITY
Accounting M
Acute Care/Critical Care Nursing M,O
Anatomy M
Art/Fine Arts M
Athletic Training and Sports Medicine M
Biological and Biomedical Sciences—General M
Business Administration and Management—General M,O
Clinical Psychology M,O
Communication Disorders M
Counselor Education M,D,O
Curriculum and Instruction D,O
Distance Education Development O
Early Childhood Education M,D,O
Education of the Gifted M,D,O
Education—General M,D,O
Educational Leadership and Administration M,D,O
Educational Media/Instructional Technology M,D,O
Elementary Education M,D,O
English as a Second Language M,D,O
Exercise and Sports Science M
Family Nurse Practitioner Studies M,O
Finance and Banking O
Health Informatics O
Health Services Management and Hospital Administration M,O
Higher Education M,D
Human Resources Development M,D
Human Resources Management O
Information Science O
International Business O
Kinesiology and Movement Studies M
Law D
Liberal Studies M
Management Information Systems O
Marketing O
Marriage and Family Therapy M,O
Nurse Anesthesia M
Nursing and Healthcare Administration M,D,O
Nursing Education M,O
Nursing—General M,D,O
Occupational Therapy M
Pastoral Ministry and Counseling M,D
Photography M
Physician Assistant Studies M
Podiatric Medicine D
Psychology—General M,O
Public Administration M
Public Health—General
Reading Education M,D,O
Rehabilitation Counseling M,O
School Psychology M,O
Social Work M,D
Special Education M,D,O
Sport Psychology M
Sports Management M
Theology M,D

### BARTON COLLEGE
Elementary Education M

### BARUCH COLLEGE OF THE CITY UNIVERSITY OF NEW YORK
Accounting M,D
Arts Administration M

*M—masters degree; D—doctorate; O—other advanced degree; *—Close-Up and/or Display*

Business Administration and Management—General M,D,O
Corporate and Organizational Communication M
Counseling Psychology M
Economics M
Educational Leadership and Administration M,O
Entrepreneurship M,D
Finance and Banking M,D
Financial Engineering M
Health Services Management and Hospital Administration M
Higher Education M
Human Resources Management M,D
Industrial and Labor Relations M
Industrial and Manufacturing Management M,D
Industrial and Organizational Psychology M,D
International Affairs M
International Business M,D
International Economics M
International Trade Policy M
Management Information Systems M,D
Marketing M,D
Nonprofit Management M
Organizational Behavior M,D
Public Administration M
Public Policy M
Quantitative Analysis M
Real Estate M
Statistics M
Sustainability Management M,D
Sustainable Development M
Taxation M

### BASTYR UNIVERSITY
Acupuncture and Oriental Medicine M,D
Counseling Psychology M,O
Health Psychology M,O
Maternal and Child Health M,O
Naturopathic Medicine D,O
Nurse Midwifery M,O
Nutrition M,O

### BAYAMÓN CENTRAL UNIVERSITY
Accounting M
Business Administration and Management—General M
Counselor Education M,O
Early Childhood Education M,O
Education—General M,O
Educational Leadership and Administration M,O
Elementary Education M,O
Finance and Banking M
Industrial and Organizational Psychology M
Marketing M
Marriage and Family Therapy M,O
Rehabilitation Counseling M,O
Special Education M,O

### BAYLOR COLLEGE OF MEDICINE
Allopathic Medicine D
Biochemistry D
Bioengineering D
Biological and Biomedical Sciences—General M,D
Biomedical Engineering D
Biophysics D
Cancer Biology/Oncology D
Cardiovascular Sciences D
Cell Biology D
Clinical Laboratory Sciences/Medical Technology M,D
Computational Biology D
Developmental Biology D
Genetic Counseling M
Genetics D
Human Genetics D
Immunology D
Microbiology D
Molecular Biology D
Molecular Biophysics D
Molecular Medicine D
Molecular Physiology D
Neuroscience D
Nurse Anesthesia D
Pharmacology D
Physician Assistant Studies M
Structural Biology D
Translational Biology D
Virology D

### BAYLOR UNIVERSITY
Accounting M
American Studies M
Athletic Training and Sports Medicine M,D
Biochemistry M,D
Biological and Biomedical Sciences—General M,D
Biomedical Engineering M,D
Business Administration and Management—General M
Chemistry M,D
Clinical Psychology D
Communication Disorders M
Communication—General M
Community Health M
Computer Engineering M,D
Computer Science M,D
Curriculum and Instruction M,D
Ecology D
Economics M
Education—General M,D,O
Educational Leadership and Administration M,O
Educational Psychology M,D,O
Electrical Engineering M,D
Engineering and Applied Sciences—General M,D
English M,D
Entrepreneurship D
Environmental Management and Policy M,D
Environmental Sciences D
Exercise and Sports Science M,D
Geosciences M,D
Health Education M,D
Health Services Management and Hospital Administration M
History M,D
Interdisciplinary Studies D
International Affairs M
Journalism M
Kinesiology and Movement Studies M,D
Law D
Management Information Systems M,D
Mathematics M,D
Mechanical Engineering M,D
Museum Studies M
Music M,D
Nursing—General M,D
Nutrition M,D
Philosophy M,D
Physical Education M,D
Physics M,D
Physiology M,D
Political Science M,D
Psychology—General M,D
Public Health—General M
Religion M,D
School Psychology M,D,O
Social Work M,D
Sociology M,D
Spanish M
Special Education M,D,O
Statistics M,D
Theater M
Theology M,D

### BAY PATH UNIVERSITY
Accounting M
Addictions/Substance Abuse Counseling M
Applied Behavior Analysis M
Applied Statistics M
Clinical Psychology M
Communication—General M
Computer and Information Systems Security M
Developmental Psychology M
Educational Leadership and Administration M
Educational Media/Instructional Technology M
Entrepreneurship M
Forensic Sciences M
Genetic Counseling M
Health Informatics M
Health Services Management and Hospital Administration M
Higher Education M
Management Information Systems M
Management Strategy and Policy M
Nonprofit Management M
Occupational Therapy M,D
Physician Assistant Studies M
Special Education M
Writing M

### BECKER COLLEGE
Counseling Psychology M
Counselor Education M
Social Psychology M

### BELHAVEN UNIVERSITY (MS)
Business Administration and Management—General M
Education—General M,D,O
Educational Leadership and Administration M,D,O
Health Services Management and Hospital Administration M
Human Resources Management M
Reading Education M,D,O
Sports Management M

### BELLARMINE UNIVERSITY
Athletic Training and Sports Medicine M,D
Business Administration and Management—General M
Communication—General M
Education—General M,D,O
Educational Leadership and Administration M,D,O
Elementary Education M,D,O
Family Nurse Practitioner Studies M,D
Higher Education M,D,O
Middle School Education M,D,O
Nursing and Healthcare Administration M,D
Nursing Education M,D
Nursing—General M,D
Physical Therapy M,D
Reading Education M,D,O
Secondary Education M,D,O

### BELLEVUE UNIVERSITY
Business Administration and Management—General M,D
Corporate and Organizational Communication M
Counselor Education M
Criminal Justice and Criminology M
Educational Media/Instructional Technology M
Finance and Banking M,D
Health Services Management and Hospital Administration M
Human Resources Management M,D
Human Services M
Information Science M
Management Information Systems M
Military and Defense Studies M
National Security M
Organizational Management M
Project Management M
Public Administration M

### BELLIN COLLEGE
Family Nurse Practitioner Studies M
Nursing Education M
Nursing—General M

### BELMONT UNIVERSITY
Accounting M
Allied Health—General M,D
Business Administration and Management—General M
Health Informatics D
Health Services Management and Hospital Administration M
Law D
Nursing—General M,D
Occupational Therapy M,D
Pharmaceutical Administration D
Pharmacy D
Physical Therapy M,D
Public Health—General D

### BEMIDJI STATE UNIVERSITY
Biological and Biomedical Sciences—General M
Education—General M
English M
Environmental Management and Policy M
Mathematics Education M
Mathematics M
Special Education M

### BENEDICTINE COLLEGE
Business Administration and Management—General M
Education—General M
Educational Leadership and Administration M

### BENEDICTINE UNIVERSITY
Accounting M
Business Administration and Management—General M,D
Clinical Psychology M
Computer and Information Systems Security M
Emergency Management M
Entrepreneurship M
Exercise and Sports Science M
Finance and Banking M
Health Education M
Health Informatics M
Health Services Management and Hospital Administration M
Human Resources Management M
International Business M
Logistics M
Management Information Systems M
Marketing M
Nursing—General M
Nutrition M
Organizational Behavior M,D
Organizational Management M,D
Public Health—General M

### BENNINGTON COLLEGE
Allied Health—General O
Dance M
Music M
Writing M

### BENTLEY UNIVERSITY
Accounting M,D
Business Administration and Management—General M,D,O
Business Analytics M,O
Ergonomics and Human Factors M
Finance and Banking M
Information Science M
Marketing M
Taxation M

### BERGIN UNIVERSITY OF CANINE STUDIES
Animal Sciences M

### BERKELEY COLLEGE–WOODLAND PARK CAMPUS
Business Administration and Management—General M

### BERKLEE COLLEGE OF MUSIC
Entertainment Management M
Music M,O
Theater M,O

### BERRY COLLEGE
Business Administration and Management—General M
Curriculum and Instruction M,O
Education—General M,O
Educational Leadership and Administration O
Middle School Education M,O
Reading Education M,O
Secondary Education M,O

### BETHANY COLLEGE
Education—General M

### BETHANY THEOLOGICAL SEMINARY
Conflict Resolution and Mediation/Peace Studies M,O
Pastoral Ministry and Counseling M,O
Religion M,O
Theology M,O

### BETHEL SEMINARY
Classics M,D,O
Clinical Psychology M,D,O
Marriage and Family Therapy M,D,O
Missions and Missiology M,D,O
Near and Middle Eastern Languages M,D,O
Pastoral Ministry and Counseling M,D,O
Religion M,D,O
Theology M,D,O

### BETHEL UNIVERSITY (IN)
Business Administration and Management—General M
Education—General M
Nursing—General M
Pastoral Ministry and Counseling M
Theology M

### BETHEL UNIVERSITY (MN)
Business Administration and Management—General M,D,O
Counseling Psychology M,D,O
Education—General M,D,O
Educational Leadership and Administration M,D,O
Elementary Education M,D,O
Nurse Midwifery M,D,O
Nursing Education M,D,O
Organizational Management M,D,O
Physician Assistant Studies M,D,O
Secondary Education M,D,O
Special Education M,D,O

### BETHEL UNIVERSITY (TN)
Business Administration and Management—General M
Conflict Resolution and Mediation/Peace Studies M
Educational Leadership and Administration M
Physician Assistant Studies M

### BETHESDA UNIVERSITY
Music M
Religion M
Theology M

### BETH HAMEDRASH SHAAREI YOSHER INSTITUTE
Theology

### BETH HATALMUD RABBINICAL COLLEGE
Theology

### BETHLEHEM COLLEGE & SEMINARY
Theology M

### BETH MEDRASH GOVOHA
Theology

### BETHUNE-COOKMAN UNIVERSITY
Theology M

### BEULAH HEIGHTS UNIVERSITY
Religion M

### BEXLEY SEABURY SEMINARY
Theology M,D,O

### BINGHAMTON UNIVERSITY, STATE UNIVERSITY OF NEW YORK
Accounting M
Analytical Chemistry M,D
Anthropology M,D
Applied Physics M,D
Art History M,D
Asian Studies M,O
Asian-American Studies M,O
Biological and Biomedical Sciences—General M,D
Biomedical Engineering M,D
Biopsychology D
Business Administration and Management—General M,D
Chemistry M,D
Clinical Psychology D
Cognitive Sciences D
Community Health Nursing M,D,O
Comparative Literature M,D
Computer Science M,D
Early Childhood Education M
Economics M,D
Education—General M,D,O
Educational Leadership and Administration M,D,O
Electrical Engineering M,D
Engineering and Applied Sciences—General M,D
English as a Second Language M
English Education M
English M,D
Environmental Management and Policy M,D
Family Nurse Practitioner Studies M,D,O
Finance and Banking D
Foreign Languages Education M
Foundations and Philosophy of Education D
French M
Geography M
Geology M,D
Gerontological Nursing M,D,O
Health Services Management and Hospital Administration M,D
History M,D
Industrial/Management Engineering M,D
Inorganic Chemistry M,D
Italian M
Legal and Justice Studies M,D
Liberal Studies M
Management Information Systems D
Marketing D
Materials Engineering M,D
Materials Sciences M,D
Mathematics Education M
Mathematics M,D
Mechanical Engineering M,D
Music M
Nursing—General M,D,O
Organizational Management D
Pharmacy D
Philosophy M,D
Physical Chemistry M,D
Physics M,D

| | |
|---|---|
| Political Science | M,D |
| Psychiatric Nursing | M,D,O |
| Psychology—General | D |
| Public Administration | M |
| Public Affairs | D |
| Reading Education | M |
| Science Education | M |
| Secondary Education | M |
| Social Sciences Education | M |
| Social Work | M |
| Sociology | M,D |
| Spanish | M |
| Special Education | M |
| Statistics | M,D |
| Student Affairs | M |
| Supply Chain Management | D |
| Sustainable Development | M |
| Systems Science | M,D |
| Theater | M |
| Translation and Interpretation | D,O |
| Writing | M,D |

### BIOLA UNIVERSITY

| | |
|---|---|
| Anthropology | M,D,O |
| Business Administration and Management—General | M |
| Clinical Psychology | D |
| Cultural Studies | M,D,O |
| Curriculum and Instruction | M,O |
| Early Childhood Education | M,O |
| Education—General | M,O |
| English as a Second Language | M,D,O |
| Jewish Studies | M,D,O |
| Linguistics | M,D,O |
| Missions and Missiology | M,D,O |
| Pastoral Ministry and Counseling | M,D,O |
| Psychology—General | D |
| Religion | M,D,O |
| Religious Education | M,D,O |
| Special Education | M,O |
| Theology | M,D,O |

### BISHOP'S UNIVERSITY

| | |
|---|---|
| Education—General | M,O |
| English as a Second Language | M,O |

### BLACK HILLS STATE UNIVERSITY

| | |
|---|---|
| Business Administration and Management—General | M |
| Curriculum and Instruction | M |
| Genomic Sciences | M |
| Management Strategy and Policy | M |

### BLESSING-RIEMAN COLLEGE OF NURSING & HEALTH SCIENCES

| | |
|---|---|
| Nursing and Healthcare Administration | M |
| Nursing Education | M |
| Nursing—General | M |

### BLOOMFIELD COLLEGE

| | |
|---|---|
| Accounting | M |

### BLOOMSBURG UNIVERSITY OF PENNSYLVANIA

| | |
|---|---|
| Accounting | M |
| Adult Nursing | M,D |
| Athletic Training and Sports Medicine | M |
| Biological and Biomedical Sciences—General | M |
| Business Administration and Management—General | M,O |
| Business Education | M |
| Communication Disorders | M,D |
| Community Health | M,D |
| Counselor Education | M |
| Curriculum and Instruction | M,O |
| Early Childhood Education | M |
| Education—General | M,O |
| Educational Leadership and Administration | M |
| Educational Media/Instructional Technology | M,O |
| English Education | M |
| Exercise and Sports Science | M |
| Family Nurse Practitioner Studies | M,D |
| Mathematics Education | M |
| Middle School Education | M |
| Nurse Anesthesia | M,D |
| Nursing and Healthcare Administration | M,D |
| Nursing—General | M,D |
| Reading Education | M |
| Science Education | M |
| Social Sciences Education | M |
| Special Education | M,O |
| Student Affairs | M |

### BLUEFIELD COLLEGE

| | |
|---|---|
| Education—General | M |

### BLUE MOUNTAIN COLLEGE

| | |
|---|---|
| Elementary Education | M |
| Reading Education | M |
| Science Education | M |
| Secondary Education | M |

### BLUFFTON UNIVERSITY

| | |
|---|---|
| Accounting | M |
| Business Administration and Management—General | M |
| Curriculum and Instruction | M |
| Education—General | M |
| Educational Leadership and Administration | M |
| Finance and Banking | M |
| Health Services Management and Hospital Administration | M |
| Industrial and Manufacturing Management | M |
| Reading Education | M |
| Special Education | M |
| Sustainability Management | M |

### BOB JONES UNIVERSITY

| | |
|---|---|
| Accounting | M,D,O |
| Art/Fine Arts | M,D,O |
| Business Administration and Management—General | M,D,O |
| Counselor Education | M,D,O |
| Curriculum and Instruction | M,D,O |
| Educational Leadership and Administration | M,D,O |
| Elementary Education | M,D,O |
| English Education | M,D,O |
| English | M,D,O |
| Film, Television, and Video Production | M,D,O |
| Graphic Design | M,D,O |
| History | M,D,O |
| Illustration | M,D,O |
| Mathematics Education | M,D,O |
| Music Education | M,D,O |
| Music | M,D,O |
| Pastoral Ministry and Counseling | M,D,O |
| Religion | M,D,O |
| Rhetoric | M,D,O |
| Secondary Education | M,D,O |
| Social Sciences Education | M,D,O |
| Special Education | M,D,O |
| Speech and Interpersonal Communication | M,D,O |
| Student Affairs | M,D,O |
| Theater | M,D,O |
| Theology | M,D,O |

### BOISE STATE UNIVERSITY

| | |
|---|---|
| Accounting | M |
| Animal Sciences | M,D |
| Anthropology | M |
| Art/Fine Arts | M |
| Biological and Biomedical Sciences—General | M,D |
| Business Administration and Management—General | M |
| Chemistry | M |
| Civil Engineering | M |
| Communication—General | M |
| Computer Engineering | M,D |
| Computer Science | M,D |
| Counselor Education | M,O |
| Criminal Justice and Criminology | M |
| Curriculum and Instruction | M,D,O |
| Distance Education Development | M,D,O |
| Early Childhood Education | M |
| Economics | M |
| Education—General | M,D,O |
| Educational Leadership and Administration | M,D,O |
| Educational Media/Instructional Technology | M,D,O |
| Electrical Engineering | M,D |
| Engineering and Applied Sciences—General | M,D,O |
| English as a Second Language | M |
| English Education | M |
| Environmental and Occupational Health | M,O |
| Geophysics | M,D |
| Geosciences | M,D |
| Gerontological Nursing | M,D,O |
| Health Promotion | M,O |
| History | M |
| Hydrology | M,D |
| Interdisciplinary Studies | M |
| Kinesiology and Movement Studies | M |
| Materials Engineering | M,D |
| Mathematics Education | M |
| Mathematics | M |
| Mechanical Engineering | M |
| Molecular Biology | M,D |
| Multilingual and Multicultural Education | M |
| Music Education | M |
| Music | M |
| Natural Resources | M,D,O |
| Nursing—General | M,D,O |
| Organizational Management | M,O |
| Political Science | M |
| Public Administration | M,D,O |
| Public Health—General | M,D,O |
| Public Policy | M,D,O |
| Reading Education | M |
| Rhetoric | M |
| Social Work | M |
| Special Education | M |
| Sports Management | M |
| Taxation | M |
| Technical Communication | M |

### BORICUA COLLEGE

| | |
|---|---|
| English as a Second Language | M |
| Human Services | M |

### BOSTON ARCHITECTURAL COLLEGE

| | |
|---|---|
| Architecture | M |
| Historic Preservation | M |
| Interior Design | M |
| Landscape Architecture | M |
| Sustainable Development | M |

### BOSTON COLLEGE

| | |
|---|---|
| Accounting | M |
| Adult Nursing | M,D |
| Biochemistry | M,D |
| Biological and Biomedical Sciences—General | D |
| Business Administration and Management—General | M |
| Chemistry | M,D |
| Classics | M |
| Counseling Psychology | M,D |
| Curriculum and Instruction | M,D,O |
| Developmental Psychology | M,D |
| Early Childhood Education | M,D,O |
| East European and Russian Studies | M |
| Economics | D |
| Education—General | M,D,O |
| Educational Psychology | M,D |
| Elementary Education | M,D,O |
| English Education | M,D,O |
| English | M,D |
| Finance and Banking | M,D |
| Foreign Languages Education | M,D,O |
| French | M |
| Geology | M |
| Geophysics | M |
| Gerontological Nursing | M,D |
| History | M,D |
| Inorganic Chemistry | M,D |
| Italian | M |
| Law | D |
| Linguistics | M |
| Maternal and Child/Neonatal Nursing | M,D |
| Mathematics Education | M,D,O |
| Mathematics | D |
| Nurse Anesthesia | M,D |
| Nursing—General | M,D |
| Organic Chemistry | M,D |
| Organizational Behavior | D |
| Organizational Management | D |
| Pastoral Ministry and Counseling | M,D,O |
| Pediatric Nursing | M,D |
| Philosophy | M,D |
| Physical Chemistry | M,D |
| Physics | M,D |
| Political Science | M,D |
| Psychiatric Nursing | M,D |
| Psychology—General | D |
| Reading Education | M,D,O |
| Religious Education | M,D,O |
| Russian | M |
| Science Education | M,D,O |
| Secondary Education | M,D,O |
| Social Sciences Education | M,D,O |
| Social Work | M,D |
| Sociology | M,D |
| Spanish | M |
| Special Education | M,D,O |
| Theology | M,D,O |
| Western European Studies | M,D |
| Women's Health Nursing | M,D |

### BOSTON GRADUATE SCHOOL OF PSYCHOANALYSIS

| | |
|---|---|
| Counseling Psychology | M |
| Developmental Psychology | O |
| Psychoanalysis and Psychotherapy | M,D,O |
| Psychology—General | M |

### BOSTON UNIVERSITY

| | |
|---|---|
| Actuarial Science | M |
| Advertising and Public Relations | M |
| African-American Studies | M |
| Allied Health—General | M,D |
| Allopathic Medicine | D |
| American Studies | D |
| Anatomy | M,D |
| Anthropology | M,D |
| Archaeology | M,D |
| Art Education | M |
| Art History | M,D,O |
| Art/Fine Arts | M |
| Arts Administration | M,O |
| Astronomy | M,D |
| Athletic Training and Sports Medicine | M,D |
| Biochemistry | M,D |
| Bioinformatics | M,D |
| Biological and Biomedical Sciences—General | M,D |
| Biomedical Engineering | M,D |
| Biophysics | M,D |
| Biopsychology | M |
| Biostatistics | M,D |
| Business Administration and Management—General | M,D |
| Business Analytics | M,D |
| Cell Biology | M,D |
| Chemistry | M,D |
| Classics | M,D |
| Clinical Research | M |
| Communication Disorders | M,D |
| Communication—General | M |
| Computer and Information Systems Security | M,D,O |
| Computer Engineering | M,D,O |
| Computer Science | M,D,O |
| Corporate and Organizational Communication | M |
| Counseling Psychology | M |
| Criminal Justice and Criminology | M |
| Cultural Studies | M |
| Data Science/Data Analytics | M,O |
| Economic Development | M |
| Economics | M |
| Education—General | M,D,O |
| Electrical Engineering | M,D |
| Emergency Management | M |
| Energy Management and Policy | M,D |
| Engineering and Applied Sciences—General | M,D |
| English | M,D |
| Environmental Sciences | M,D |
| Film, Television, and Video Production | M |
| Finance and Banking | M |
| Food Science and Technology | M |
| Forensic Sciences | M |
| Genetic Counseling | M |
| Genetics | D |
| Genomic Sciences | D |
| Geographic Information Systems | M,D |
| Geosciences | M,D |
| Health Communication | M |
| Health Education | M |
| Health Informatics | M,O |
| Health Services Management and Hospital Administration | M |
| Hispanic and Latin American Languages | M,D |
| Historic Preservation | M |
| History | M,D |
| Hospitality Management | M |
| Immunology | D |
| International Affairs | M |
| International Business | M |
| Internet and Interactive Multimedia | M,O |
| Journalism | M |
| Law | M,D |
| Linguistics | M,D |
| Management Information Systems | M,O |
| Management of Technology | M |
| Management Strategy and Policy | M,O |
| Manufacturing Engineering | M,D |
| Mass Communication | M |
| Materials Engineering | M,D |
| Materials Sciences | M,D |
| Mathematical and Computational Finance | M,D |
| Mathematics | M,D |
| Mechanical Engineering | M,D |
| Media Studies | M,D |
| Medical Imaging | M |
| Microbiology | D |
| Molecular Biology | M,D |
| Molecular Medicine | D |
| Museum Studies | M,D,O |
| Music Education | M,D |
| Music | M,D,O |
| Neurobiology | M,D |
| Neuroscience | D |
| Nutrition | M,D |
| Occupational Therapy | D |
| Oral and Dental Sciences | M,D |
| Organizational Management | M |
| Pathology | M,D |
| Pharmaceutical Sciences | D |
| Pharmacology | M,D |
| Philosophy | M,D |
| Physical Therapy | M,D |
| Physician Assistant Studies | M |
| Physics | D |
| Physiology | M,D |
| Political Science | D |
| Project Management | M,O |
| Psychology—General | M,D |
| Public Health—General | M,D |
| Rehabilitation Sciences | M,D |
| Religion | M,D |
| Risk Management | M |
| Romance Languages | M,D |
| Social Work | M,D |
| Sociology | M,D |
| Software Engineering | M,O |
| Supply Chain Management | M |
| Systems Engineering | M,D |
| Telecommunications Management | M,O |
| Telecommunications | M,O |
| Theater | M,O |
| Translational Biology | D |
| Travel and Tourism | M |
| Urban and Regional Planning | M |
| Urban Studies | M |
| Writing | M |

### BOWIE STATE UNIVERSITY

| | |
|---|---|
| Applied Mathematics | M |
| Business Administration and Management—General | M |
| Computer Science | M,D |
| Corporate and Organizational Communication | M,O |
| Counseling Psychology | M |
| Counselor Education | M |
| Education—General | M |
| Educational Leadership and Administration | M,D |
| Elementary Education | M |
| English | M |
| Family Nurse Practitioner Studies | M |
| Human Resources Development | M |
| Management Information Systems | M,O |
| Nursing and Healthcare Administration | M |
| Nursing Education | M |
| Nursing—General | M |
| Public Administration | M |
| Reading Education | M |
| Secondary Education | M |
| Special Education | M |

### BOWLING GREEN STATE UNIVERSITY

| | |
|---|---|
| Accounting | M |
| American Studies | M,D |
| Applied Arts and Design—General | M |
| Applied Statistics | M |
| Art Education | M |
| Art History | M |
| Art/Fine Arts | M |
| Biological and Biomedical Sciences—General | M,D |
| Business Administration and Management—General | M |
| Business Education | M |
| Chemistry | M,D |
| Clinical Psychology | M,D |
| Communication Disorders | M,D |
| Communication—General | M,D |
| Computer Art and Design | M |
| Computer Science | M |
| Counselor Education | M |

*M—masters degree; D—doctorate; O—other advanced degree; *—Close-Up and/or Display*

- Criminal Justice and Criminology M
- Curriculum and Instruction M
- Demography and Population Studies M,D
- Developmental Psychology M,D
- Economics M
- Educational Leadership and Administration M,D,O
- Educational Media/Instructional Technology M
- English M,D
- Experimental Psychology M,D
- Film, Television, and Video Production M,D
- French M
- Geology M
- Geophysics M
- German M
- Graphic Design M
- Higher Education D
- History M,D
- Industrial and Organizational Psychology M,D
- Interdisciplinary Studies M,D
- International and Comparative Education M
- Kinesiology and Movement Studies M
- Leisure Studies M
- Mathematics Education M,D
- Mathematics M,D
- Media Studies M,D
- Music Education M,D
- Music M,D
- Operations Research M
- Organizational Management M
- Philosophy M,D
- Physics M
- Psychology—General M,D
- Public Administration M
- Public Health—General M
- Reading Education M,O
- Recreation and Park Management M
- Rhetoric M,D
- Science Education M
- Social Psychology M,D
- Social Work M
- Sociology M,D
- Software Engineering M
- Spanish M
- Special Education M
- Sports Management M
- Statistics M,D
- Student Affairs M
- Technical Communication M,D
- Theater M,D
- Vocational and Technical Education M
- Writing M,D

### BRADLEY UNIVERSITY
- Accounting M
- Art/Fine Arts M
- Biochemistry M
- Biological and Biomedical Sciences—General M
- Business Administration and Management—General M
- Chemistry M
- Civil Engineering M
- Clinical Psychology M
- Computer Science M
- Construction Engineering M
- Counseling Psychology M
- Counselor Education M
- Education—General M,D,O
- Educational Leadership and Administration M
- Electrical Engineering M
- Engineering and Applied Sciences—General M
- English M
- Family Nurse Practitioner Studies M,D,O
- Graphic Design M
- Health Services Management and Hospital Administration M,D,O
- Human Development M
- Industrial/Management Engineering M
- Information Science M
- Manufacturing Engineering M
- Mechanical Engineering M
- Nonprofit Management M
- Nursing and Healthcare Administration M,D,O
- Nursing Education M,D,O
- Nursing—General M,D,O
- Nutrition M
- Photography M
- Physical Therapy D

### BRANDEIS UNIVERSITY
- Anthropology M,D
- Applied Economics M
- Art/Fine Arts O
- Artificial Intelligence/Robotics M
- Biochemistry M,D
- Bioinformatics M
- Biological and Biomedical Sciences—General M,D
- Biophysics M,D
- Biotechnology M
- Business Administration and Management—General M
- Cell Biology M,D
- Chemistry M,D
- Child and Family Studies M,D
- Chinese M
- Classics M
- Cognitive Sciences M,D
- Computer and Information Systems Security M
- Computer Science M,D
- Conflict Resolution and Mediation/Peace Studies M,D
- Cultural Anthropology M,D
- Developmental Psychology M,D
- Disability Studies D
- Distance Education Development M
- Economics M,D
- Educational Leadership and Administration M,O
- Educational Measurement and Evaluation O
- Elementary Education M,O
- English M,D
- Entrepreneurship M
- Finance and Banking M,D
- Foreign Languages Education M
- Gender Studies M,D
- Genetic Counseling M
- Genetics M,D
- Health Education D
- Health Informatics M
- Health Services Management and Hospital Administration M
- History M,D
- Human Services M
- Human-Computer Interaction M
- Inorganic Chemistry M,D
- International Business M,D
- International Health M,D
- Internet and Interactive Multimedia M
- Jewish Studies M,D
- Management Information Systems M
- Management Strategy and Policy M
- Marketing M
- Mathematics M,D
- Medical Informatics M
- Microbiology M,D
- Molecular Biology M,D
- Music M,D
- Near and Middle Eastern Languages M,D
- Near and Middle Eastern Studies M,D
- Neurobiology M,D
- Neuroscience M,D
- Nonprofit Management M
- Organic Chemistry M,D
- Philosophy M
- Physical Chemistry M,D
- Physics M,D
- Political Science M,D
- Project Management M
- Psychology—General M,D
- Public Policy M,D
- Real Estate M
- Religious Education M,O
- Risk Management M
- Secondary Education M,O
- Social Psychology M,D
- Sociology M,D
- Software Engineering M
- Sustainable Development M
- Women's Studies M,D

### BRANDMAN UNIVERSITY
- Accounting M
- Business Administration and Management—General M
- Counseling Psychology M
- Counselor Education M,D
- Curriculum and Instruction M,D
- Data Science/Data Analytics M
- Early Childhood Education M,D
- Education—General M,D
- Educational Leadership and Administration M,D
- Educational Media/Instructional Technology M,D
- Elementary Education M,D
- Entrepreneurship M
- Finance and Banking M
- Health Services Management and Hospital Administration M
- Human Resources Management M
- International Business M
- Marketing M
- Marriage and Family Therapy M
- Nursing—General D
- Organizational Management M
- Psychology—General M
- Public Administration M
- Secondary Education M,D
- Social Work M
- Special Education M,D

### BRANDON UNIVERSITY
- Counselor Education M,O
- Curriculum and Instruction M,O
- Education—General M,O
- Educational Leadership and Administration M,O
- Music Education M
- Music M
- Rural Planning and Studies M,O
- Special Education M,O

### BRENAU UNIVERSITY
- Accounting M
- Business Administration and Management—General M
- Early Childhood Education M,O
- Education—General M,O
- Family Nurse Practitioner Studies M
- Health Services Management and Hospital Administration M
- Interior Design M
- Middle School Education M,O
- Nursing and Healthcare Administration M
- Nursing Education M
- Occupational Therapy M
- Organizational Management M
- Project Management M
- Psychology—General M
- Secondary Education M,O
- Special Education M,O

### BRESCIA UNIVERSITY
- Business Administration and Management—General M
- Curriculum and Instruction M
- Social Work M

### BRIAR CLIFF UNIVERSITY
- Nursing—General M,D,O

### BRIDGEWATER COLLEGE
- Athletic Training and Sports Medicine M

### BRIDGEWATER STATE UNIVERSITY
- Accounting M
- Art Education M
- Business Administration and Management—General M
- Communication Disorders M
- Computer Science M
- Counselor Education M,O
- Criminal Justice and Criminology M
- Early Childhood Education M
- Education—General M,O
- Educational Leadership and Administration M,O
- Educational Media/Instructional Technology M
- Elementary Education M
- English M
- Finance and Banking M
- Health Promotion M
- Mathematics Education M
- Physical Education M
- Psychology—General M
- Public Administration M
- Reading Education M,O
- Science Education M
- Secondary Education M
- Social Sciences Education M
- Social Work M
- Special Education M

### BRIERCREST SEMINARY
- Business Administration and Management—General M
- Marriage and Family Therapy M
- Missions and Missiology M
- Organizational Management M
- Pastoral Ministry and Counseling M
- Religion M
- Theology M

### BRIGHAM YOUNG UNIVERSITY
- Agricultural Sciences—General M,D
- Analytical Chemistry M,D
- Animal Sciences M,D
- Anthropology M
- Applied Statistics M
- Art Education M
- Art/Fine Arts M
- Astronomy M,D
- Athletic Training and Sports Medicine M,D
- Biochemistry M,D
- Biological and Biomedical Sciences—General M,D
- Biotechnology M,D
- Business Administration and Management—General M
- Chemical Engineering M,D
- Chemistry M,D
- Child and Family Studies M,D
- Civil Engineering M,D
- Classics M
- Clinical Psychology D
- Cognitive Sciences D
- Communication Disorders M
- Communication—General M
- Comparative and Interdisciplinary Arts M
- Comparative Literature M
- Computer Engineering M,D
- Computer Science M,D
- Construction Management M
- Counseling Psychology M,D,O
- Developmental Biology M,D
- Education—General M,D,O
- Educational Leadership and Administration M,D
- Educational Measurement and Evaluation D
- Educational Media/Instructional Technology M,D
- Educational Policy M,D
- Educational Psychology M,D
- Electrical Engineering M,D
- Engineering and Applied Sciences—General M,D
- English as a Second Language M
- English M
- Entrepreneurship M
- Environmental Sciences M,D
- Exercise and Sports Science M,D
- Family Nurse Practitioner Studies M
- Film, Television, and Video Production M
- Finance and Banking M
- Fish, Game, and Wildlife Management M,D
- Food Science and Technology M
- Foreign Languages Education M
- Foundations and Philosophy of Education M,D
- Geology M
- Health Promotion M,D
- Health Services Management and Hospital Administration M
- Hispanic and Latin American Languages M
- Human Development M,D
- Human Resources Management M
- Humanities M
- Information Science M
- International Affairs M
- Law M,D
- Linguistics M
- Manufacturing Engineering M
- Marketing M
- Marriage and Family Therapy M,D
- Mass Communication M
- Mathematics Education M
- Mathematics M,D
- Mechanical Engineering M,D
- Microbiology M,D
- Molecular Biology M,D
- Music Education M
- Music M
- Neuroscience M,D
- Nonprofit Management M
- Nursing—General M
- Nutrition M
- Physics M,D
- Physiology M,D
- Plant Sciences M,D
- Political Science M
- Portuguese M
- Psychology—General D
- Public Administration M
- Public Health—General M
- Rhetoric M
- School Psychology M,D,O
- Science Education M,D
- Social Work M
- Sociology M
- Spanish M
- Special Education M,D,O
- Statistics M
- Supply Chain Management M
- Theater M
- Writing M

### BRITE DIVINITY SCHOOL
- Pastoral Ministry and Counseling M,D,O
- Theology M,D,O

### BROADVIEW UNIVERSITY–WEST JORDAN
- Business Administration and Management—General M
- Health Services Management and Hospital Administration M
- Management Information Systems M

### BROCK UNIVERSITY
- Accounting M
- Allied Health—General M,D
- Biological and Biomedical Sciences—General M,D
- Biotechnology M,D
- Business Administration and Management—General M
- Chemistry M,D
- Child and Family Studies M
- Classics M
- Comparative Literature M
- Computer Science M
- Cultural Studies M
- Disability Studies M,O
- Economics M
- Education—General M,D
- English as a Second Language M
- English M
- Geography M
- Geosciences M
- History M
- Human Development M,D
- International Affairs M
- Legal and Justice Studies M
- Mathematics M
- Neuroscience M,D
- Philosophy M
- Physics M
- Political Science M
- Psychology—General M,D
- Public Policy M
- Social Psychology M,D
- Sociology M
- Statistics M

### BROOKLINE COLLEGE - PHOENIX CAMPUS
- Nursing and Healthcare Administration M
- Nursing—General M

### BROOKLYN COLLEGE OF THE CITY UNIVERSITY OF NEW YORK
- Accounting M
- Art Education M
- Art History M
- Art/Fine Arts M
- Arts Administration M
- Biological and Biomedical Sciences—General M
- Business Administration and Management—General M
- Chemistry M,D
- Communication Disorders M,D
- Community Health M
- Computer Science M,O
- Counseling Psychology M,D,O
- Counselor Education M
- Early Childhood Education M,O
- Economics M
- Education—General M,O
- Educational Leadership and Administration M
- Elementary Education M,O
- English Education M
- English M
- Environmental Education M
- Exercise and Sports Science M
- Experimental Psychology M,D
- Film, Television, and Video Production M
- Film, Television, and Video Theory and Criticism M
- Finance and Banking M
- Foreign Languages Education M
- French M
- Geology M,D
- Geosciences M

Health Informatics M,O
Health Services Management and Hospital Administration M
History M
Industrial and Organizational Psychology M,D
Information Science M,O
International Affairs M
International Business M
Internet and Interactive Multimedia M
Jewish Studies M
Kinesiology and Movement Studies M
Liberal Studies M
Mathematics Education M
Mathematics M
Media Studies M
Middle School Education M,O
Multilingual and Multicultural Education M
Music Education M
Music M
Nutrition M
Organizational Behavior M,D
Photography M
Physical Education M
Physics M
Political Science M
Psychology—General M,D
Public Health—General M
Public Policy M
School Psychology M,O
Science Education M
Secondary Education M
Social Psychology M,D
Social Sciences Education M
Sociology M,D
Spanish M
Special Education M,O
Speech and Interpersonal Communication M,D
Sports Management M
Thanatology M
Theater M
Urban Studies M
Writing M

**BROOKLYN LAW SCHOOL**
Law M,D

**BROWN UNIVERSITY**
Allopathic Medicine D
American Studies M,D
Anthropology M,D
Applied Mathematics M,D
Archaeology D
Art History D
Asian Studies D
Biochemical Engineering M,D
Biochemistry M,D
Biological and Biomedical Sciences—General M,D
Biomedical Engineering M,D
Biostatistics M,D
Biotechnology M,D
Cell Biology M,D
Chemical Engineering M,D
Chemistry D
Classics M,D
Cognitive Sciences M,D
Community Health M,D
Comparative Literature D
Computer Engineering M,D
Computer Science M,D
East European and Russian Studies M,D
Ecology D
Economics D
Education—General M
Electrical Engineering M,D
Elementary Education M
Engineering and Applied Sciences—General M,D
English as a Second Language M,D
English Education M
English M,D
Epidemiology M,D
Evolutionary Biology D
French D
Geosciences D
German D
Health Services Research D
Hispanic Studies D
History of Science and Technology D
History M,D
Italian D
Latin American Studies M,D
Linguistics M,D
Materials Sciences M,D
Mathematics D
Mechanical Engineering M,D
Mechanics M,D
Molecular Biology M,D
Molecular Pharmacology M,D
Multilingual and Multicultural Education M,D
Music D
Near and Middle Eastern Studies D
Neuroscience D
Pathobiology M,D
Philosophy D
Physics M,D
Physiology M,D
Political Science D
Psychology—General M,D
Public Health—General M
Public Policy M
Publishing M,D
Religion D
Russian M,D
Science Education M
Secondary Education M

Slavic Languages M,D
Social Sciences Education M
Sociology M,D
Theater M,D
Urban Education M
Western European Studies M,D
Writing M,D

**BRYAN COLLEGE**
Business Administration and Management—General M
Health Services Management and Hospital Administration M
Human Resources Management M
Marketing M
Pastoral Ministry and Counseling M
Sports Management M

**BRYAN COLLEGE OF HEALTH SCIENCES**
Nurse Anesthesia M

**BRYANT UNIVERSITY**
Accounting M
Business Administration and Management—General M
Communication—General M,O
Corporate and Organizational Communication M,O
Physician Assistant Studies M
Taxation M

**BRYAN UNIVERSITY**
Business Administration and Management—General M

**BRYN ATHYN COLLEGE OF THE NEW CHURCH**
Religion M
Theology M

**BRYN MAWR COLLEGE**
Archaeology M,D
Art History M,D
Chemistry M,D
Classics M,D
Mathematics M,D
Physics M,D
Social Work M,D

**BUCKNELL UNIVERSITY**
Animal Behavior M
Biological and Biomedical Sciences—General M
Chemical Engineering M
Chemistry M
Civil Engineering M
Computer Engineering M
Education—General M
Electrical Engineering M
Engineering and Applied Sciences—General M
English M
Mathematics M
Mechanical Engineering M
Psychology—General M
Student Affairs M

**BUENA VISTA UNIVERSITY**
Counselor Education M
Curriculum and Instruction M
Education—General M
English as a Second Language M

**BUFFALO STATE COLLEGE, STATE UNIVERSITY OF NEW YORK**
Adult Education M,O
Applied Economics M
Art Education M
Biological and Biomedical Sciences—General M
Business Education M
Communication Disorders M
Criminal Justice and Criminology M
Data Science/Data Analytics M
Early Childhood Education M
Economics M
Education—General M,O
Educational Leadership and Administration O
Educational Media/Instructional Technology M
English Education M
English M
Forensic Sciences M
Historic Preservation M,O
History M
Human Resources Management M,O
Industrial/Management Engineering M
Interdisciplinary Studies M
Manufacturing Engineering M
Mathematics Education M
Mechanical Engineering M
Multilingual and Multicultural Education O
Museum Studies M
Nutrition M
Organizational Management M
Reading Education M
Science Education M
Social Sciences Education M
Special Education M
Urban Education M
Vocational and Technical Education M

**BURRELL COLLEGE OF OSTEOPATHIC MEDICINE**
Osteopathic Medicine D

**BUSHNELL UNIVERSITY**
Accounting M
Business Administration and Management—General M

Counseling Psychology M
Counselor Education M
Education—General M
Elementary Education M
English as a Second Language M
Secondary Education M
Special Education M

**BUTLER UNIVERSITY**
Art/Fine Arts M
Business Administration and Management—General M
Education—General M,O
Educational Leadership and Administration M,O
Music Education M
Music M
Pharmaceutical Sciences M,D
Pharmacy M,D
Physician Assistant Studies M,D

**BYZANTINE CATHOLIC SEMINARY OF SAINTS CYRIL AND METHODIUS**
Theology M

**CABARRUS COLLEGE OF HEALTH SCIENCES**
Occupational Therapy M

**CABRINI UNIVERSITY**
Accounting M,D
Biological and Biomedical Sciences—General M,D
Chemistry M,D
Communication—General M,D
Criminal Justice and Criminology M,D
Curriculum and Instruction M,D
Early Childhood Education M,D
Educational Leadership and Administration M,D
Elementary Education M,D
English as a Second Language M,D
English M,D
History M,D
Mathematics M,D
Middle School Education M,D
Organizational Management M,D
Reading Education M,D
Secondary Education M,D
Special Education M,D

**CAIRN UNIVERSITY**
Accounting M,O
Applied Behavior Analysis M,O
Business Administration and Management—General M,O
Education—General M,O
Educational Leadership and Administration M,O
Entrepreneurship M,O
Nonprofit Management M,O
Organizational Management M,O
Pastoral Ministry and Counseling M
Religion M
Theology M

**CALDWELL UNIVERSITY**
Applied Behavior Analysis M,D,O
Business Administration and Management—General M
Counseling Psychology M,O
Education—General M,D,O
Educational Leadership and Administration M,D,O
Special Education M,D,O

**CALIFORNIA BAPTIST UNIVERSITY**
Accounting M
Adult Education M
Adult Nursing M
Applied Mathematics M
Architecture M
Athletic Training and Sports Medicine M
Business Administration and Management—General M
Communication Disorders M
Communication—General M
Construction Management M
Counseling Psychology M
Counselor Education M
Curriculum and Instruction M
Distance Education Development M
Education of Students with Severe/Multiple Disabilities M
Education—General M
Educational Leadership and Administration M
Educational Media/Instructional Technology M
English as a Second Language M
English Education M
English M
Exercise and Sports Science M
Family Nurse Practitioner Studies M
Forensic Psychology M
Health Education M
Health Promotion M
Health Services Management and Hospital Administration M
Higher Education M
International and Comparative Education M
Music Education M
Music M
Nursing and Healthcare Administration M
Nursing Education M
Nursing—General M,D
Organizational Management M
Pastoral Ministry and Counseling M
Physical Education M
Physician Assistant Studies M

Public Administration M
Public Health—General M
Reading Education M
School Psychology M
Science Education M
Social Work M
Special Education M
Sports Management M
Vocational and Technical Education M

**CALIFORNIA COAST UNIVERSITY**
Business Administration and Management—General M
Criminal Justice and Criminology M
Curriculum and Instruction M,D
Education—General M,D
Educational Leadership and Administration M,D
Educational Psychology M,D
Health Services Management and Hospital Administration M
Human Resources Management M
Marketing M
Organizational Management M,D
Psychology—General M

**CALIFORNIA COLLEGE OF THE ARTS**
Applied Arts and Design—General M
Architecture M
Art/Fine Arts M
Computer Art and Design M
Film, Television, and Video Production M
Film, Television, and Video Theory and Criticism M
Finance and Banking M
Graphic Design M
Illustration M
Industrial Design M
Museum Studies M
Organizational Management M
Writing M

**CALIFORNIA HEALTH SCIENCES UNIVERSITY**
Pharmacy D

**CALIFORNIA INSTITUTE OF ADVANCED MANAGEMENT**
Business Administration and Management—General M
Entrepreneurship M

**CALIFORNIA INSTITUTE OF TECHNOLOGY**
Aerospace/Aeronautical Engineering M,D,O
Applied Mathematics M,D
Applied Physics M,D
Astronomy D
Biochemistry M,D
Bioengineering M,D
Biological and Biomedical Sciences—General D
Biophysics D
Cell Biology D
Chemical Engineering M,D
Chemistry M,D
Civil Engineering M,D,O
Computational Sciences M,D
Computer Science M,D
Developmental Biology D
Electrical Engineering M,D,O
Engineering and Applied Sciences—General M,D,O
Environmental Engineering M,D
Environmental Sciences M,D
Genetics D
Geochemistry M,D
Geology M,D
Geophysics M,D
Immunology D
Materials Sciences M,D
Mathematics D
Mechanical Engineering M,D,O
Mechanics M,D
Molecular Biology D
Molecular Biophysics M,D
Neurobiology D
Neuroscience M,D
Physics D
Planetary and Space Sciences M,D
Social Sciences M,D
Systems Engineering M,D

**CALIFORNIA INSTITUTE OF THE ARTS**
Applied Arts and Design—General M,O
Art/Fine Arts M,O
Dance M,O
Film, Television, and Video Production M,O
Graphic Design M,O
Music M,O
Photography M,O
Theater M,O
Writing M,O

**CALIFORNIA INTERCONTINENTAL UNIVERSITY**
Business Administration and Management—General M,D
Entertainment Management M
Entrepreneurship M,D
Finance and Banking M,D
Health Services Management and Hospital Administration M,D
Human Resources Management M,D
International Business M,D
Management Information Systems M,D
Marketing M,D

*M—masters degree; D—doctorate; O—other advanced degree; *—Close-Up and/or Display*

| | |
|---|---|
| Organizational Management | M,D |
| Project Management | M,D |
| Quality Management | M,D |

**CALIFORNIA INTERNATIONAL BUSINESS UNIVERSITY**

| | |
|---|---|
| Business Administration and Management—General | M,D |

**CALIFORNIA LUTHERAN UNIVERSITY**

| | |
|---|---|
| Business Administration and Management—General | M,O |
| Clinical Psychology | M,D |
| Counselor Education | M,D |
| Education—General | M,D |
| Educational Leadership and Administration | M,D |
| Elementary Education | M,D |
| Entrepreneurship | M,O |
| Finance and Banking | M,O |
| Higher Education | M,D |
| International Business | M,O |
| Management Information Systems | M,O |
| Management of Technology | M,O |
| Marketing | M,O |
| Marriage and Family Therapy | M,D |
| Middle School Education | M,D |
| Psychology—General | M,D |
| Public Policy | M,O |
| Special Education | M,D |
| Theology | M,D,O |

**CALIFORNIA MIRAMAR UNIVERSITY**

| | |
|---|---|
| Business Administration and Management—General | M |
| Management Strategy and Policy | M |
| Taxation | M |
| Telecommunications Management | M |
| Telecommunications | M |

**CALIFORNIA NORTHSTATE UNIVERSITY**

| | |
|---|---|
| Allopathic Medicine | D |
| Pharmacy | D |

**CALIFORNIA POLYTECHNIC STATE UNIVERSITY, SAN LUIS OBISPO**

| | |
|---|---|
| Accounting | M |
| Aerospace/Aeronautical Engineering | M |
| Agricultural Education | M |
| Agricultural Sciences—General | M |
| Architectural Engineering | M |
| Architecture | M |
| Biochemistry | M |
| Biological and Biomedical Sciences—General | M |
| Biomedical Engineering | M |
| Business Administration and Management—General | M |
| Business Analytics | M |
| Chemistry | M |
| Civil Engineering | M |
| Computer Science | M |
| Curriculum and Instruction | M |
| Economics | M |
| Education—General | M |
| Educational Leadership and Administration | M |
| Electrical Engineering | M |
| Engineering and Applied Sciences—General | M |
| English | M |
| Environmental Engineering | M |
| Food Science and Technology | M |
| Forestry | M |
| History | M |
| Industrial/Management Engineering | M |
| Kinesiology and Movement Studies | M |
| Mathematics | M |
| Mechanical Engineering | M |
| Natural Resources | M |
| Nutrition | M |
| Political Science | M |
| Polymer Science and Engineering | M |
| Psychology—General | M |
| Special Education | M |
| Supply Chain Management | M |
| Taxation | M |
| Urban and Regional Planning | M |

**CALIFORNIA STATE POLYTECHNIC UNIVERSITY, POMONA**

| | |
|---|---|
| Accounting | M |
| Aerospace/Aeronautical Engineering | M |
| Agricultural Sciences—General | M |
| Applied Mathematics | M |
| Architecture | M |
| Biological and Biomedical Sciences—General | M |
| Business Administration and Management—General | M |
| Chemistry | M |
| Civil Engineering | M |
| Computer Science | M |
| Curriculum and Instruction | M |
| Economics | M |
| Educational Leadership and Administration | D |
| Electrical Engineering | M |
| Engineering Management | M |
| English | M |
| Environmental Sciences | M |
| Geology | M |
| History | M |
| Hospitality Management | M |
| Interior Design | M |
| Kinesiology and Movement Studies | M |
| Landscape Architecture | M |
| Management Information Systems | M |
| Mathematics | M |
| Mechanical Engineering | M |
| Psychology—General | M |
| Public Administration | M |
| Systems Engineering | M |
| Urban and Regional Planning | M |

**CALIFORNIA STATE UNIVERSITY CHANNEL ISLANDS**

| | |
|---|---|
| Business Administration and Management—General | M |
| Computer Science | M |
| Mathematics | M |

**CALIFORNIA STATE UNIVERSITY, CHICO**

| | |
|---|---|
| Agricultural Education | M |
| Agricultural Sciences—General | M |
| Anthropology | M |
| Applied Psychology | M |
| Art History | M |
| Art/Fine Arts | M |
| Biological and Biomedical Sciences—General | M |
| Business Administration and Management—General | M |
| Communication Disorders | M |
| Communication—General | M |
| Computer Engineering | M |
| Computer Science | M |
| Construction Management | M |
| Curriculum and Instruction | M |
| Electrical Engineering | M |
| Engineering and Applied Sciences—General | M |
| English | M |
| Environmental Sciences | M |
| Geology | M |
| Geosciences | M |
| Health Services Management and Hospital Administration | M |
| History | M |
| Kinesiology and Movement Studies | M |
| Marriage and Family Therapy | M |
| Mathematics Education | M |
| Museum Studies | M |
| Nursing—General | M |
| Nutrition | M |
| Political Science | M |
| Psychology—General | M |
| Public Administration | M |
| Recreation and Park Management | M |
| School Psychology | M |
| Social Sciences | M |
| Social Work | M |
| Special Education | M |
| Travel and Tourism | M |

**CALIFORNIA STATE UNIVERSITY, DOMINGUEZ HILLS**

| | |
|---|---|
| Applied Social Research | M |
| Bioinformatics | M |
| Biological and Biomedical Sciences—General | M |
| Business Administration and Management—General | M |
| Clinical Psychology | M |
| Computer Science | M |
| Conflict Resolution and Mediation/Peace Studies | M |
| Counselor Education | M |
| Early Childhood Education | M |
| Education—General | M |
| English as a Second Language | M,O |
| English | M,O |
| Health Psychology | M |
| Humanities | M |
| International and Comparative Education | M |
| Marriage and Family Therapy | M |
| Nursing—General | M |
| Occupational Therapy | M |
| Psychology—General | M |
| Public Administration | M |
| Quality Management | M |
| Rhetoric | M,O |
| School Psychology | M |
| Social Work | M |
| Sociology | M |
| Special Education | M |

**CALIFORNIA STATE UNIVERSITY, EAST BAY**

| | |
|---|---|
| Accounting | M |
| Actuarial Science | M |
| Anthropology | M |
| Applied Statistics | M |
| Biochemistry | M |
| Biological and Biomedical Sciences—General | M |
| Biostatistics | M |
| Business Administration and Management—General | M |
| Business Analytics | M |
| Chemistry | M |
| Child and Family Studies | M |
| Communication Disorders | M |
| Communication—General | M |
| Computer Science | M |
| Construction Management | M |
| Counselor Education | M |
| Early Childhood Education | M |
| Economics | M |
| Education of Students with Severe/Multiple Disabilities | M |
| Education—General | M |
| Educational Leadership and Administration | M,D |
| Educational Media/Instructional Technology | M |
| Engineering and Applied Sciences—General | M |
| Engineering Management | M |
| English as a Second Language | M |
| English | M |
| Environmental Sciences | M |
| Finance and Banking | M |
| Geography | M |
| Geology | M |
| Health Services Management and Hospital Administration | M |
| History | M |
| Human Resources Management | M |
| Industrial and Manufacturing Management | M |
| Interdisciplinary Studies | M |
| Internet and Interactive Multimedia | M |
| Management Strategy and Policy | M |
| Marine Sciences | M |
| Marketing | M |
| Marriage and Family Therapy | M |
| Mathematics Education | M |
| Mathematics | M |
| Music | M |
| Organizational Behavior | M |
| Physical Education | M |
| Public Administration | M |
| Public History | M |
| Public Policy | M |
| Reading Education | M |
| Recreation and Park Management | M |
| Social Psychology | M |
| Social Sciences Education | M |
| Social Work | M |
| Special Education | M |
| Statistics | M |
| Supply Chain Management | M |
| Travel and Tourism | M |

**CALIFORNIA STATE UNIVERSITY, FRESNO**

| | |
|---|---|
| Animal Sciences | M |
| Applied Arts and Design—General | M |
| Applied Behavior Analysis | M,O |
| Art/Fine Arts | M |
| Biological and Biomedical Sciences—General | M |
| Business Administration and Management—General | M |
| Chemistry | M |
| Civil Engineering | M |
| Communication Disorders | M |
| Communication—General | M |
| Computer Engineering | M |
| Computer Science | M |
| Counseling Psychology | M |
| Counselor Education | M |
| Criminal Justice and Criminology | M |
| Curriculum and Instruction | M |
| Early Childhood Education | M |
| Education—General | M,D |
| Educational Leadership and Administration | M,D |
| Electrical Engineering | M |
| Engineering and Applied Sciences—General | M |
| English as a Second Language | M |
| English | M |
| Exercise and Sports Science | M |
| Experimental Psychology | M,O |
| Geology | M |
| Health Promotion | M |
| Health Services Management and Hospital Administration | M |
| History | M |
| Human Development | M,D |
| Industrial/Management Engineering | M |
| Kinesiology and Movement Studies | M |
| Linguistics | M |
| Marine Sciences | M |
| Marriage and Family Therapy | M |
| Mathematics Education | M |
| Mathematics | M |
| Mechanical Engineering | M |
| Music Education | M |
| Music | M |
| Nursing—General | M,D |
| Physical Therapy | D |
| Physics | M |
| Plant Sciences | M |
| Psychology—General | M,O |
| Public Administration | M |
| Public Health—General | M |
| Reading Education | M |
| Rehabilitation Counseling | M |
| Rhetoric | M |
| School Psychology | M,O |
| Social Sciences Education | M |
| Social Work | M |
| Spanish | M |
| Special Education | M |
| Sport Psychology | M |
| Sports Management | M |
| Student Affairs | M |
| Viticulture and Enology | M |
| Writing | M |

**CALIFORNIA STATE UNIVERSITY, FULLERTON**

| | |
|---|---|
| Accounting | M |
| American Studies | M |
| Anthropology | M |
| Applied Arts and Design—General | M |
| Applied Mathematics | M |
| Architectural Engineering | M |
| Art History | M |
| Art/Fine Arts | M |
| Biological and Biomedical Sciences—General | M |
| Biotechnology | M |
| Business Administration and Management—General | M |
| Business Analytics | M |
| Chemistry | M |
| Civil Engineering | M |
| Clinical Psychology | M |
| Communication Disorders | M |
| Communication—General | M |
| Computer Engineering | M |
| Computer Science | M |
| Counselor Education | M |
| Economics | M |
| Educational Leadership and Administration | M,D |
| Educational Media/Instructional Technology | M |
| Electrical Engineering | M |
| Electronic Commerce | M |
| Elementary Education | M |
| Engineering and Applied Sciences—General | M |
| English | M |
| Environmental and Occupational Health | M |
| Environmental Engineering | M |
| Environmental Management and Policy | M |
| Film, Television, and Video Production | M |
| Finance and Banking | M |
| Geography | M |
| Geology | M |
| Gerontology | M |
| Graphic Design | M |
| Health Promotion | M |
| History | M |
| Illustration | M |
| Information Science | M |
| Insurance | M |
| International Business | M |
| Linguistics | M |
| Management Information Systems | M |
| Mass Communication | M |
| Mathematics Education | M |
| Mathematics | M |
| Mechanical Engineering | M |
| Multilingual and Multicultural Education | M |
| Museum Studies | M |
| Music Education | M |
| Music | M |
| Nurse Anesthesia | M,D |
| Nursing and Healthcare Administration | M,D |
| Nursing Education | M,D |
| Nursing—General | M,D |
| Organizational Management | M |
| Photography | M |
| Physical Education | M |
| Physics | M |
| Political Science | M |
| Psychology—General | M |
| Public Administration | M |
| Public Health—General | M |
| Reading Education | M |
| Risk Management | M |
| School Nursing | M,D |
| Secondary Education | M |
| Social Psychology | M |
| Social Work | M |
| Sociology | M |
| Software Engineering | M |
| Spanish | M |
| Special Education | M |
| Speech and Interpersonal Communication | M |
| Systems Engineering | M |
| Taxation | M |
| Theater | M |
| Travel and Tourism | M |
| Women's Health Nursing | M,D |

**CALIFORNIA STATE UNIVERSITY, LONG BEACH**

| | |
|---|---|
| African Studies | M |
| Anthropology | M |
| Applied Mathematics | M,D |
| Applied Statistics | M |
| Art Education | M |
| Art/Fine Arts | M |
| Asian Studies | M |
| Asian-American Studies | M |
| Athletic Training and Sports Medicine | M |
| Biochemistry | M |
| Biological and Biomedical Sciences—General | M |
| Business Administration and Management—General | M |
| Chemistry | M |
| Civil Engineering | M |
| Communication Disorders | M |
| Communication—General | M |
| Computer Engineering | M |
| Computer Science | M |
| Counselor Education | M,D |
| Criminal Justice and Criminology | M |
| Dance | M |
| Economics | M |
| Education—General | M,D |
| Educational Leadership and Administration | M,D |
| Educational Psychology | M,D |
| Electrical Engineering | M |
| Elementary Education | M |
| Emergency Management | M |
| Engineering Management | M,D |
| English as a Second Language | M,O |
| English | M |
| Ergonomics and Human Factors | M |
| Exercise and Sports Science | M |
| French | M |
| Geography | M |
| Geology | M |
| German | M |
| Gerontology | M |
| Health Education | M |

| | |
|---|---|
| Health Services Management and Hospital Administration | M |
| Higher Education | M,D |
| History | M |
| Industrial and Organizational Psychology | M |
| Kinesiology and Movement Studies | M |
| Leisure Studies | M |
| Linguistics | M,O |
| Marriage and Family Therapy | M,D |
| Mathematics Education | M |
| Mathematics | M |
| Mechanical Engineering | M,D |
| Microbiology | M |
| Music | M |
| Near and Middle Eastern Studies | M |
| Nursing—General | M,D,O |
| Nutrition | M |
| Philosophy | M |
| Physical Education | M |
| Physical Therapy | D |
| Physics | M |
| Political Science | M |
| Psychology—General | M |
| Public Administration | M,O |
| Public Health—General | M |
| Public Policy | M,O |
| Recreation and Park Management | M |
| Religion | M |
| Science Education | M |
| Secondary Education | M |
| Social Work | M |
| Spanish | M |
| Special Education | M,D |
| Sport Psychology | M |
| Sports Management | M |
| Student Affairs | M,D |
| Theater | M |
| Writing | M |

**CALIFORNIA STATE UNIVERSITY, LOS ANGELES**

| | |
|---|---|
| Accounting | M |
| Analytical Chemistry | M |
| Anthropology | M |
| Applied Arts and Design—General | M |
| Applied Mathematics | M |
| Art Education | M |
| Art History | M |
| Art Therapy | M |
| Art/Fine Arts | M |
| Biochemistry | M |
| Biological and Biomedical Sciences—General | M |
| Business Administration and Management—General | M,O |
| Chemistry | M |
| Child and Family Studies | M |
| Child Development | M |
| Civil Engineering | M |
| Communication Disorders | M |
| Communication—General | M |
| Computer Science | M |
| Counselor Education | M,D |
| Criminal Justice and Criminology | M |
| Curriculum and Instruction | M |
| Economics | M |
| Education—General | M,D,O |
| Electrical Engineering | M |
| Elementary Education | M |
| Engineering and Applied Sciences—General | M |
| English | M,O |
| Finance and Banking | M |
| French | M |
| Geography | M |
| Geology | M |
| Graphic Design | M |
| Health Services Management and Hospital Administration | M,O |
| Hispanic Studies | M |
| History | M |
| International Business | M |
| Kinesiology and Movement Studies | M,O |
| Latin American Studies | M |
| Management Information Systems | M |
| Management of Technology | M |
| Marketing | M |
| Mathematics | M |
| Mechanical Engineering | M |
| Music Education | M |
| Music | M |
| Nursing—General | M,O |
| Nutrition | M,O |
| Philosophy | M,O |
| Photography | M |
| Physical Education | M,O |
| Physics | M |
| Political Science | M |
| Psychology—General | M |
| Public Administration | M |
| Rehabilitation Counseling | M,D |
| School Psychology | M,D |
| Social Work | M |
| Sociology | M |
| Spanish | M |
| Special Education | M,D |
| Textile Design | M |
| Theater | M |

**CALIFORNIA STATE UNIVERSITY MARITIME ACADEMY**

| | |
|---|---|
| Emergency Management | M |
| Engineering Management | M |
| Transportation Management | M |

**CALIFORNIA STATE UNIVERSITY, MONTEREY BAY**

| | |
|---|---|
| Business Administration and Management—General | M |
| Education—General | M |
| Management Information Systems | M |
| Marine Sciences | M |
| Social Work | M |
| Water Resources | M |

**CALIFORNIA STATE UNIVERSITY, NORTHRIDGE**

| | |
|---|---|
| Anthropology | M |
| Applied Mathematics | M |
| Archaeology | M |
| Art Education | M |
| Art History | M |
| Art/Fine Arts | M |
| Artificial Intelligence/Robotics | M |
| Biochemistry | M |
| Biological and Biomedical Sciences—General | M |
| Business Administration and Management—General | M |
| Chemistry | M |
| Civil Engineering | M |
| Clinical Psychology | M |
| Communication Disorders | M |
| Communication—General | M |
| Comparative Literature | M |
| Computer Science | M |
| Construction Management | M |
| Counselor Education | M |
| Curriculum and Instruction | M |
| Early Childhood Education | M |
| Education of Students with Severe/Multiple Disabilities | M |
| Education—General | M,D |
| Educational Leadership and Administration | M,D |
| Educational Media/Instructional Technology | M |
| Educational Psychology | M |
| Electrical Engineering | M |
| Elementary Education | M |
| Engineering and Applied Sciences—General | M |
| Engineering Management | M |
| English Education | M |
| English | M |
| Entertainment Management | M,O |
| Environmental and Occupational Health | M |
| Environmental Sciences | M |
| Epidemiology | M |
| Experimental Psychology | M |
| Family and Consumer Sciences-General | M |
| Film, Television, and Video Production | M |
| Geography | M |
| Geology | M |
| Health Education | M,O |
| Health Services Management and Hospital Administration | M |
| Hispanic Studies | M |
| History | M |
| Hospitality Management | M,O |
| Industrial Hygiene | M |
| Industrial/Management Engineering | M |
| Journalism | M |
| Kinesiology and Movement Studies | M |
| Linguistics | M |
| Manufacturing Engineering | M |
| Marriage and Family Therapy | M |
| Mass Communication | M |
| Materials Engineering | M |
| Mathematics Education | M |
| Mathematics | M |
| Mechanical Engineering | M |
| Multilingual and Multicultural Education | M |
| Music Education | M |
| Music | M |
| Nonprofit Management | O |
| Physical Therapy | M |
| Physics | M |
| Political Science | M |
| Psychology—General | M |
| Public Administration | M,O |
| Public Health—General | M |
| Reading Education | M |
| Recreation and Park Management | M,O |
| Rhetoric | M |
| School Psychology | M |
| Science Education | M |
| Secondary Education | M |
| Social Work | M,O |
| Sociology | M |
| Software Engineering | M |
| Spanish | M |
| Special Education | M |
| Speech and Interpersonal Communication | M |
| Structural Engineering | M |
| Systems Engineering | M |
| Taxation | M,O |
| Theater | M |
| Travel and Tourism | M |
| Writing | M |

**CALIFORNIA STATE UNIVERSITY, SACRAMENTO**

| | |
|---|---|
| Accounting | M |
| Anthropology | M |
| Applied Behavior Analysis | M |
| Art/Fine Arts | M |
| Biochemistry | M |
| Biological and Biomedical Sciences—General | M |
| Business Administration and Management—General | M |
| Cell Biology | M |
| Chemistry | M |
| Child Development | M,D,O |
| Civil Engineering | M |
| Communication Disorders | M |
| Communication—General | M |
| Computer Science | M |
| Conservation Biology | M |
| Counselor Education | M,D,O |
| Criminal Justice and Criminology | M |
| Curriculum and Instruction | M,D,O |
| Developmental Biology | M |
| Early Childhood Education | M,D,O |
| Education—General | M,D,O |
| Educational Leadership and Administration | M,D,O |
| Educational Media/Instructional Technology | M,D,O |
| Educational Policy | M,D,O |
| Electrical Engineering | M |
| Elementary Education | M,D,O |
| Engineering and Applied Sciences—General | M |
| English as a Second Language | M |
| English | M |
| Exercise and Sports Science | M |
| Foreign Languages Education | M |
| Higher Education | M,D,O |
| Human Resources Development | M |
| Human Resources Management | M |
| Human Services | M |
| Industrial and Organizational Psychology | M |
| Mathematics | M |
| Mechanical Engineering | M |
| Molecular Biology | M |
| Multilingual and Multicultural Education | M,D,O |
| Music | M |
| Nursing—General | M |
| Physical Education | M |
| Physical Therapy | D |
| Political Science | M |
| Psychology—General | M |
| Public Administration | M |
| Public History | M,D |
| Public Policy | M |
| Reading Education | M,D,O |
| Real Estate | M |
| Recreation and Park Management | M |
| School Psychology | M,D,O |
| Social Work | M |
| Sociology | M |
| Software Engineering | M |
| Special Education | M,D,O |
| Writing | M |

**CALIFORNIA STATE UNIVERSITY, SAN BERNARDINO**

| | |
|---|---|
| Accounting | M |
| Archaeology | M |
| Art/Fine Arts | M |
| Biological and Biomedical Sciences—General | M |
| Business Administration and Management—General | M |
| Child Development | M |
| Clinical Psychology | M |
| Communication—General | M |
| Community College Education | M |
| Computer and Information Systems Security | M |
| Computer Science | M |
| Corporate and Organizational Communication | M |
| Counseling Psychology | M |
| Counselor Education | M |
| Criminal Justice and Criminology | M |
| Education—General | M |
| Educational Leadership and Administration | M,D |
| English | M |
| Entrepreneurship | M |
| Environmental Sciences | M |
| Finance and Banking | M |
| Geosciences | M |
| Health Services Management and Hospital Administration | M |
| Industrial and Organizational Psychology | M |
| Interdisciplinary Studies | M |
| International Business | M |
| Management Information Systems | M |
| Marketing | M |
| Mathematics Education | M |
| Mathematics | M |
| National Security | M |
| Nursing—General | M |
| Psychology—General | M |
| Public Administration | M |
| Public Health—General | M |
| Rehabilitation Counseling | M |
| Social Sciences | M |
| Social Work | M |
| Spanish | M |
| Supply Chain Management | M |
| Writing | M |

**CALIFORNIA STATE UNIVERSITY, SAN MARCOS**

| | |
|---|---|
| Biological and Biomedical Sciences—General | M |
| Biotechnology | M |
| Communication Disorders | M |
| Computer and Information Systems Security | M |
| Computer Science | M |
| Education—General | M,D |
| Educational Leadership and Administration | M,D |
| English | M |
| Family Nurse Practitioner Studies | M |
| Hispanic and Latin American Languages | M |
| Hispanic Studies | M |
| History | M |
| Mathematics | M |
| Nursing and Healthcare Administration | M |
| Nursing Education | M |
| Nursing—General | M |
| Psychiatric Nursing | M |
| Psychology—General | M |
| Public Health—General | M |
| Reading Education | M,D |
| Sociology | M |
| Spanish | M |
| Special Education | M,D |
| Writing | M |

**CALIFORNIA STATE UNIVERSITY, STANISLAUS**

| | |
|---|---|
| Applied Behavior Analysis | M |
| Business Administration and Management—General | M |
| Community College Education | D |
| Conservation Biology | M |
| Counseling Psychology | M |
| Counselor Education | M |
| Criminal Justice and Criminology | M |
| Curriculum and Instruction | M |
| Ecology | M |
| Education—General | M,D |
| Educational Leadership and Administration | M,D |
| Educational Media/Instructional Technology | M |
| Elementary Education | M |
| English as a Second Language | M,O |
| English | M,O |
| Genetic Counseling | M |
| Gerontological Nursing | M |
| History | M |
| Interdisciplinary Studies | M |
| Multilingual and Multicultural Education | M |
| Nursing Education | M |
| Nursing—General | M |
| Physical Education | M |
| Psychology—General | M |
| Public Administration | M |
| Reading Education | M |
| Rhetoric | M,O |
| Secondary Education | M |
| Social Work | M |
| Special Education | M |
| Sustainable Development | M |
| Writing | M,O |

**CALIFORNIA UNIVERSITY OF MANAGEMENT AND SCIENCES**

| | |
|---|---|
| Business Administration and Management—General | M,D |
| Economics | M,D |
| International Business | M,D |
| Management Information Systems | M,D |
| Sports Management | M,D |

**CALIFORNIA UNIVERSITY OF PENNSYLVANIA**

| | |
|---|---|
| Athletic Training and Sports Medicine | M |
| Business Administration and Management—General | M |
| Business Analytics | M |
| Clinical Psychology | M |
| Communication Disorders | M |
| Computer and Information Systems Security | M |
| Conflict Resolution and Mediation/Peace Studies | M |
| Counseling Psychology | M |
| Counselor Education | M |
| Criminal Justice and Criminology | M |
| Early Childhood Education | M |
| Education—General | M,D |
| Educational Leadership and Administration | M,D |
| Elementary Education | M |
| Entrepreneurship | M |
| Exercise and Sports Science | M |
| Health Services Management and Hospital Administration | M |
| Legal and Justice Studies | M |
| Mathematics Education | M |
| Near and Middle Eastern Languages | M |
| Nursing and Healthcare Administration | M |
| Nursing Education | M |
| Nursing—General | M |
| Nutrition | M |
| Reading Education | M |
| School Psychology | M |
| Science Education | M |
| Secondary Education | M |
| Social Work | M |
| Special Education | M |
| Sport Psychology | M |
| Sports Management | M |
| Vocational and Technical Education | M |

**CALIFORNIA WESTERN SCHOOL OF LAW**

| | |
|---|---|
| Accounting | M,D |
| Law | M,D |

**CALUMET COLLEGE OF SAINT JOSEPH**

| | |
|---|---|
| Criminal Justice and Criminology | M |
| Educational Leadership and Administration | M |
| Quality Management | M |

**CALVARY UNIVERSITY**

| | |
|---|---|
| Curriculum and Instruction | M |

*M—masters degree; D—doctorate; O—other advanced degree; *—Close-Up and/or Display*

| | |
|---|---|
| Education—General | M |
| Educational Leadership and Administration | M |
| Elementary Education | M |
| Organizational Management | M |
| Pastoral Ministry and Counseling | M |
| Religious Education | M |
| Theology | M |

### CALVIN COLLEGE

| | |
|---|---|
| Accounting | M |
| Communication Disorders | M |
| Curriculum and Instruction | M |
| Education—General | M |

### CALVIN THEOLOGICAL SEMINARY

| | |
|---|---|
| Missions and Missiology | M,D |
| Pastoral Ministry and Counseling | M,D |
| Religion | M,D |
| Religious Education | M,D |
| Theology | M,D |

### CAMBRIDGE COLLEGE

| | |
|---|---|
| Addictions/Substance Abuse Counseling | M,O |
| Business Administration and Management—General | M |
| Conflict Resolution and Mediation/Peace Studies | M |
| Counseling Psychology | M,O |
| Counselor Education | M,O |
| Curriculum and Instruction | M,D,O |
| Early Childhood Education | M,D,O |
| Education—General | M,D,O |
| Educational Leadership and Administration | M,D,O |
| Educational Measurement and Evaluation | M,D,O |
| Educational Media/Instructional Technology | M,D,O |
| Elementary Education | M,D,O |
| English as a Second Language | M,D,O |
| Entrepreneurship | M |
| Health Education | M,D,O |
| Health Services Management and Hospital Administration | M |
| Interdisciplinary Studies | M,D,O |
| Management of Technology | M,O |
| Marriage and Family Therapy | M,O |
| Mathematics Education | M,D,O |
| Psychology—General | M,O |
| Rehabilitation Counseling | M,O |
| School Nursing | M,D,O |
| School Psychology | M,O |
| Science Education | M,D,O |
| Special Education | M,D,O |

### CAMERON UNIVERSITY

| | |
|---|---|
| Business Administration and Management—General | M |
| Education—General | M |
| Educational Leadership and Administration | M |
| Entrepreneurship | M |
| Psychology—General | M |

### CAMPBELLSVILLE UNIVERSITY

| | |
|---|---|
| Business Administration and Management—General | M,D |
| Economics | M,D |
| Education—General | M |
| Educational Leadership and Administration | M |
| English Education | M |
| Legal and Justice Studies | M |
| Management of Technology | M,D |
| Marriage and Family Therapy | M |
| Music Education | M |
| Music | M |
| School Psychology | M |
| Science Education | M |
| Social Sciences | M |
| Social Work | M |
| Special Education | M |
| Sports Management | M |
| Theology | M |

### CAMPBELL UNIVERSITY

| | |
|---|---|
| Athletic Training and Sports Medicine | M,D |
| Business Administration and Management—General | M |
| Counselor Education | M |
| Education—General | M |
| Educational Leadership and Administration | M |
| Elementary Education | M |
| Interdisciplinary Studies | M |
| Law | D |
| Middle School Education | M |
| Osteopathic Medicine | D |
| Pastoral Ministry and Counseling | M,D |
| Pharmaceutical Sciences | M,D |
| Pharmacy | M,D |
| Physical Education | M |
| Physical Therapy | M,D |
| Physician Assistant Studies | M,D |
| Public Health—General | M,D |
| Secondary Education | M |
| Theology | M,D |

### CANADIAN COLLEGE OF NATUROPATHIC MEDICINE

| | |
|---|---|
| Naturopathic Medicine | D |

### CANADIAN MEMORIAL CHIROPRACTIC COLLEGE

| | |
|---|---|
| Acupuncture and Oriental Medicine | O |
| Chiropractic | D,O |

### CANADIAN SOUTHERN BAPTIST SEMINARY

| | |
|---|---|
| Pastoral Ministry and Counseling | M |
| Religion | M |
| Theology | M |

### CANISIUS COLLEGE

| | |
|---|---|
| Accounting | M |
| Allied Health—General | M,O |
| Business Administration and Management—General | M |
| Business Education | M,O |
| Communication Disorders | M,O |
| Community Health | M,O |
| Early Childhood Education | M,O |
| Education of the Gifted | M,O |
| Education—General | M,O |
| Educational Leadership and Administration | M,O |
| Educational Media/Instructional Technology | M,O |
| Elementary Education | M,O |
| English as a Second Language | M,O |
| Health Informatics | M,O |
| International Business | M |
| Kinesiology and Movement Studies | M |
| Middle School Education | M |
| Nutrition | M,O |
| Physical Education | M |
| Reading Education | M,O |
| Secondary Education | M,O |
| Special Education | M,O |
| Sports Management | M |
| Student Affairs | M,O |

### CAPE BRETON UNIVERSITY

| | |
|---|---|
| Business Administration and Management—General | M |

### CAPELLA UNIVERSITY

| | |
|---|---|
| Accounting | M,D |
| Addictions/Substance Abuse Counseling | M,D |
| Adult Education | M,D |
| Applied Behavior Analysis | M |
| Business Administration and Management—General | M,D |
| Business Education | D |
| Child and Family Studies | M |
| Clinical Psychology | M,D |
| Computer and Information Systems Security | M,D |
| Counseling Psychology | M |
| Counselor Education | M,D |
| Criminal Justice and Criminology | M,D |
| Curriculum and Instruction | M,D |
| Developmental Psychology | M |
| Distance Education Development | M,D |
| Early Childhood Education | M |
| Education—General | M,D |
| Educational Leadership and Administration | M,D |
| Educational Media/Instructional Technology | M,D |
| Educational Psychology | M,D |
| Elementary Education | M,D |
| Emergency Management | M,D |
| Entrepreneurship | M,D |
| Environmental and Occupational Health | M,D |
| Epidemiology | D |
| Finance and Banking | M,D |
| Gerontological Nursing | M |
| Gerontology | M |
| Health Informatics | M |
| Health Services Management and Hospital Administration | M,D |
| Higher Education | M,D |
| Homeland Security | M |
| Human Resources Management | M,D |
| Human Services | M,D |
| Industrial and Organizational Psychology | M,D |
| Management Information Systems | M,D |
| Management of Technology | M,D |
| Management Strategy and Policy | M,D |
| Marketing | M,D |
| Marriage and Family Therapy | M |
| Middle School Education | M,D |
| Nonprofit Management | D |
| Nursing and Healthcare Administration | M |
| Nursing Education | M,D |
| Nursing—General | M,D |
| Operations Research | M |
| Organizational Management | M,D |
| Project Management | M,D |
| Psychology—General | M,D |
| Public Administration | M,D |
| Reading Education | M,D |
| School Psychology | M,D |
| Social Work | D |
| Special Education | M,D |
| Sport Psychology | M |
| Supply Chain Management | M,D |
| Vocational and Technical Education | D |

### CAPITAL UNIVERSITY

| | |
|---|---|
| African-American Studies | M |
| Business Administration and Management—General | M |
| Law | M,D |
| Legal and Justice Studies | M |
| Missions and Missiology | M |
| Music Education | M |
| Music | M |
| Nursing and Healthcare Administration | M |
| Nursing—General | M |
| Pastoral Ministry and Counseling | M |
| Religious Education | M |
| Taxation | M |
| Theology | M |

### CAPITOL TECHNOLOGY UNIVERSITY

| | |
|---|---|
| Business Administration and Management—General | M |
| Computer and Information Systems Security | M |
| Computer Science | M |
| Electrical Engineering | M |
| Information Science | M |
| Management Information Systems | M |
| Telecommunications Management | M |

### CARDINAL STRITCH UNIVERSITY

| | |
|---|---|
| Business Administration and Management—General | M |
| Clinical Psychology | M |
| Computer and Information Systems Security | M |
| Criminal Justice and Criminology | M |
| Health Services Management and Hospital Administration | M |
| Liberal Studies | M |
| Marketing | M |
| Nursing—General | M |
| Psychology—General | M |
| Reading Education | M,D |
| Sports Management | M |

### CAREY THEOLOGICAL COLLEGE

| | |
|---|---|
| Theology | M,D |

### CARIBBEAN UNIVERSITY

| | |
|---|---|
| Art History | M,D |
| Criminal Justice and Criminology | M,D |
| Curriculum and Instruction | M,D |
| Early Childhood Education | M,D |
| Education—General | M,D |
| Educational Leadership and Administration | M,D |
| Educational Media/Instructional Technology | M,D |
| Elementary Education | M,D |
| English Education | M,D |
| Foreign Languages Education | M,D |
| Gerontological Nursing | M,D |
| Human Resources Management | M,D |
| Mathematics Education | M,D |
| Museum Studies | M,D |
| Pediatric Nursing | M,D |
| Physical Education | M,D |
| Science Education | M,D |
| Social Sciences Education | M,D |
| Special Education | M,D |

### CARLETON UNIVERSITY

| | |
|---|---|
| Aerospace/Aeronautical Engineering | M,D |
| Anthropology | M |
| Architecture | M |
| Art History | M |
| Biological and Biomedical Sciences—General | M,D |
| Biomedical Engineering | M |
| Business Administration and Management—General | M,D |
| Canadian Studies | M,D |
| Chemistry | M,D |
| Civil Engineering | M,D |
| Cognitive Sciences | D |
| Communication—General | M,D |
| Comparative Literature | D |
| Computer Science | M,D |
| Conflict Resolution and Mediation/Peace Studies | M,O |
| East European and Russian Studies | M,O |
| Economics | M,D |
| Electrical Engineering | M,D |
| Engineering and Applied Sciences—General | M,D |
| English | M,D |
| Environmental Engineering | M,D |
| Film, Television, and Video Production | M |
| French | M |
| Geography | M,D |
| Geosciences | M,D |
| History | M,D |
| Industrial Design | M |
| Information Science | M,D |
| International Affairs | M,D |
| Journalism | M,D |
| Legal and Justice Studies | M,O |
| Linguistics | M |
| Management of Technology | M |
| Materials Engineering | M,D |
| Mathematics | M,D |
| Mechanical Engineering | M,D |
| Music | M |
| Neuroscience | M,D |
| Philosophy | M |
| Physics | M,D |
| Political Science | M,D |
| Psychology—General | M,D |
| Public Administration | M,D |
| Public Policy | M,D |
| Social Work | M |
| Sociology | M,D |
| Systems Engineering | M,D |
| Systems Science | M,D |
| Western European Studies | M,O |

### CARLOW UNIVERSITY

| | |
|---|---|
| Art/Fine Arts | M |
| Business Administration and Management—General | M |
| Counseling Psychology | M,D,O |
| Curriculum and Instruction | M |
| Distance Education Development | M,O |
| Early Childhood Education | M,O |
| Education—General | M,O |
| Family Nurse Practitioner Studies | M,O |
| Forensic Sciences | M |
| Health Services Management and Hospital Administration | M |
| Human Resources Management | M |
| Mathematics | M |
| Nursing and Healthcare Administration | M |
| Nursing Education | M |
| Nursing—General | D |
| Project Management | M |
| Science Education | M |
| Social Work | M |
| Special Education | M,O |
| Student Affairs | M |
| Women's Health Nursing | M,O |
| Writing | M |

### CARNEGIE MELLON UNIVERSITY

| | |
|---|---|
| Accounting | D |
| African Studies | D |
| African-American Studies | D |
| Applied Arts and Design—General | M,D |
| Applied Physics | M,D |
| Architectural Engineering | M,D |
| Architecture | M,D |
| Art/Fine Arts | M |
| Artificial Intelligence/Robotics | M,D |
| Arts Administration | M |
| Atmospheric Sciences | D |
| Biochemistry | M,D |
| Bioengineering | M,D |
| Biological and Biomedical Sciences—General | M,D |
| Biomedical Engineering | M,D |
| Biophysics | M,D |
| Biopsychology | D |
| Biotechnology | M |
| Building Science | M,D |
| Business Administration and Management—General | M,D |
| Cell Biology | M,D |
| Chemical Engineering | M,D |
| Chemistry | D |
| Civil Engineering | M,D |
| Cognitive Sciences | D |
| Communication—General | M,D |
| Comparative Literature | M,D |
| Computational Biology | M,D |
| Computer and Information Systems Security | M |
| Computer Art and Design | M |
| Computer Engineering | M,D |
| Computer Science | M,D |
| Construction Management | M,D |
| Corporate and Organizational Communication | M |
| Criminal Justice and Criminology | M |
| Cultural Studies | D |
| Developmental Biology | M,D |
| Developmental Psychology | D |
| Economics | D |
| Electrical Engineering | M,D |
| Energy and Power Engineering | M,D |
| English | M,D |
| Entertainment Management | M |
| Entrepreneurship | D |
| Environmental Engineering | M,D |
| Environmental Sciences | D |
| Film, Television, and Video Production | M |
| Finance and Banking | D |
| Gender Studies | D |
| Genetics | M,D |
| Health Services Management and Hospital Administration | M |
| History of Science and Technology | D |
| History | D |
| Human-Computer Interaction | M,D |
| Industrial and Labor Relations | D |
| Industrial and Manufacturing Management | M,D |
| Information Science | M,D |
| Linguistics | M,D |
| Management Information Systems | M,D |
| Marketing | D |
| Materials Engineering | M,D |
| Materials Sciences | M,D |
| Mathematical and Computational Finance | M,D |
| Mathematics | M,D |
| Mechanical Engineering | M,D |
| Mechanics | M,D |
| Media Studies | M |
| Modeling and Simulation | M,D |
| Molecular Biology | M,D |
| Molecular Biophysics | D |
| Music Education | M |
| Music | M |
| Nanotechnology | D |
| Neurobiology | M,D |
| Neuroscience | D |
| Operations Research | D |
| Organizational Behavior | D |
| Philosophy | M,D |
| Physics | M,D |
| Polymer Science and Engineering | M |
| Psychology—General | D |
| Public Administration | M |
| Public Policy | M,D |
| Publishing | M |
| Rhetoric | M,D |
| Social Psychology | D |
| Social Sciences | D |
| Software Engineering | M,D |
| Statistics | M,D |
| Structural Biology | M,D |
| Sustainable Development | M,D |
| Systems Engineering | M |
| Technical Writing | M |
| Technology and Public Policy | M,D |
| Telecommunications Management | M |
| Theater | M |
| Theoretical Chemistry | D |
| Urban Design | M,D |
| Water Resources Engineering | M,D |
| Women's Studies | D |
| Writing | M |

### CAROLINA CHRISTIAN COLLEGE

| | |
|---|---|
| Pastoral Ministry and Counseling | M |
| Religious Education | M |

### CARROLL UNIVERSITY
Adult Education M
Business Administration and Management—General M
Early Childhood Education M
Education—General M
Educational Leadership and Administration M
Elementary Education M
Exercise and Sports Science M
Occupational Therapy M
Physical Therapy D
Physician Assistant Studies M
Secondary Education M
Software Engineering M

### CARSON-NEWMAN UNIVERSITY
Counselor Education M
Curriculum and Instruction M
Education—General M
Educational Leadership and Administration M
Elementary Education M
English as a Second Language M
Secondary Education M
Theology M

### CARTHAGE COLLEGE
Art Education M,O
Counselor Education M,O
Education of the Gifted M,O
Education—General M,O
Educational Leadership and Administration M,O
English Education M,O
Reading Education M,O
Science Education M,O
Social Sciences Education M,O

### CASE WESTERN RESERVE UNIVERSITY
Accounting M,D
Acute Care/Critical Care Nursing M
Aerospace/Aeronautical Engineering M,D
Allopathic Medicine D
Anatomy M
Anesthesiologist Assistant Studies M
Anthropology M,D
Applied Mathematics M,D
Art Education M
Art History M,D
Astronomy M,D
Biochemistry M,D
Bioethics M
Biological and Biomedical Sciences—General M,D
Biomedical Engineering M,D
Biophysics M,D
Biostatistics M,D
Business Administration and Management—General M,D
Business Analytics M
Cancer Biology/Oncology D
Cell Biology D
Chemical Engineering M,D
Chemistry M,D
Civil Engineering M,D
Clinical Psychology D
Clinical Research M,D
Cognitive Sciences M
Communication Disorders M,D
Comparative Literature M
Computer Engineering M,D
Computer Science M,D
Dance M
Dentistry D
Electrical Engineering M,D
Engineering and Applied Sciences—General M,D
Engineering Management M
English M,D
Epidemiology D
Experimental Psychology D
Family Nurse Practitioner Studies M
Finance and Banking M
French M
Genetic Counseling M,D
Genomic Sciences M,D
Geology M,D
Geosciences M,D
Gerontological Nursing M
Health Law M,D
Health Services Management and Hospital Administration M
History M,D
Human Genetics M,D
Industrial and Manufacturing Management M,D
Information Science M,D
Intellectual Property Law M,D
Law M,D
Legal and Justice Studies M,D
Linguistics M
Logistics M,D
Materials Engineering M,D
Materials Sciences M,D
Maternal and Child/Neonatal Nursing M
Mathematics M,D
Mechanical Engineering M,D
Medical/Surgical Nursing M
Microbiology D
Molecular Biology D
Molecular Medicine D
Museum Studies M
Music Education M,D
Music M,D
Neuroscience D
Nonprofit Management M,D,O
Nurse Anesthesia M
Nurse Midwifery M
Nursing Education M
Nursing—General M,D
Nutrition M,D
Operations Research M,D
Oral and Dental Sciences M,O
Organizational Behavior M,D
Pathology M,D
Pediatric Nursing M
Pharmacology D
Physician Assistant Studies M
Physics M,D
Physiology M,D
Political Science M,D
Polymer Science and Engineering M,D
Psychiatric Nursing M
Psychology—General M,D
Public Health—General M
Social Work M,D
Sociology M,D
Supply Chain Management M,D
Sustainability Management D
Systems Engineering M,D
Theater M
Virology D
Women's Health Nursing M

### CASTLETON UNIVERSITY
Curriculum and Instruction M
Education—General M,O
Educational Leadership and Administration M,O
Forensic Psychology M
Psychology—General M
Reading Education M,O
Special Education M,O

### CATAWBA COLLEGE
Elementary Education M
Science Education M

### CATHOLIC DISTANCE UNIVERSITY
Theology M

### CATHOLIC THEOLOGICAL UNION
Missions and Missiology M,D,O
Pastoral Ministry and Counseling M,D,O
Theology M,D,O

### THE CATHOLIC UNIVERSITY OF AMERICA
Accounting M
American Studies M,D
Anthropology M
Applied Psychology M,D
Architecture M,O
Biological and Biomedical Sciences—General M,D
Biomedical Engineering M,D
Biotechnology M,D
Business Administration and Management—General M
Cell Biology M,D
Civil Engineering M,D,O
Classics M,D,O
Clinical Laboratory Sciences/Medical Technology M,D
Clinical Psychology M,D
Computer Science M,D
Criminal Justice and Criminology M
Early Childhood Education M,O
Economic Development M
Education—General M,O
Educational Leadership and Administration M,O
Electrical Engineering M,D
Energy and Power Engineering M,D
Engineering and Applied Sciences—General M,D,O
Engineering Management M,O
English M,D,O
Environmental Engineering M,D
Ergonomics and Human Factors M,D
Experimental Psychology M,D
Health Services Management and Hospital Administration M
Hispanic Studies M,D
History M,D
Human Resources Management M
Information Studies M,O
International Affairs M,D
Law M,D
Legal and Justice Studies M,D,O
Library Science M,O
Management Information Systems M,O
Management of Technology M,O
Materials Engineering M,D
Materials Sciences M
Mechanical Engineering M,D
Medieval and Renaissance Studies M,D,O
Microbiology M,D
Music Education M,D,O
Music M,D,O
Near and Middle Eastern Languages M,D
Near and Middle Eastern Studies M,D,O
Nursing—General M,D,O
Pastoral Ministry and Counseling M,D,O
Philosophy M,D,O
Physics M,D
Political Science M,D
Project Management M,O
Psychology—General M,D
Public Policy M
Religion M,D,O
Rhetoric M,D,O
Secondary Education M,O
Social Work M,D
Sociology M
Spanish M,D
Special Education M,O
Sustainable Development M,O

Systems Engineering M,O
Theater M,O
Theology M,D,O
Transportation and Highway Engineering M,D,O
Urban and Regional Planning M,O
Western European Studies M,D

### CEDAR CREST COLLEGE
Art Therapy M
Business Administration and Management—General M
Education—General M
Forensic Sciences M
Nursing and Healthcare Administration M
Nursing Education M
Nursing—General M
Nutrition O
Writing M

### CEDARS-SINAI MEDICAL CENTER
Biological and Biomedical Sciences—General M,D
Medical Imaging M,D
Translational Biology M,D

### CEDARVILLE UNIVERSITY
Business Administration and Management—General M,D
Family Nurse Practitioner Studies M,D
Health Services Management and Hospital Administration M,D
Industrial and Manufacturing Management M,D
International Health M,D
Missions and Missiology M,D
Nursing Education M,D
Pastoral Ministry and Counseling M,D
Pharmacy M,D

### CENTENARY COLLEGE OF LOUISIANA
Business Administration and Management—General M
Education—General M
Elementary Education M
Secondary Education M

### CENTENARY UNIVERSITY
Accounting M
Business Administration and Management—General M
Counseling Psychology M
Education—General M,D
Educational Leadership and Administration M,D
Reading Education M,D
Special Education M,D

### CENTRAL BAPTIST THEOLOGICAL SEMINARY
Missions and Missiology M,O
Theology M,O

### CENTRAL CONNECTICUT STATE UNIVERSITY
Accounting M
Actuarial Science M,O
Advertising and Public Relations M,O
Art Education M,O
Biological and Biomedical Sciences—General M,D
Business Administration and Management—General M
Communication—General M,O
Computer Science M,O
Construction Management M,O
Counselor Education M,O
Criminal Justice and Criminology M
Early Childhood Education M,O
Education—General M,D,O
Educational Leadership and Administration M,D,O
Elementary Education M,O
Engineering and Applied Sciences—General M
English Education M,O
English M,O
Exercise and Sports Science M,O
Foreign Languages Education M,O
French M,O
Geography M
German M,O
Graphic Design M
History M,O
Hospice Nursing M
Industrial and Manufacturing Management M,O
Information Studies M
International Affairs M
Italian M,O
Logistics M,O
Management of Technology M,O
Marriage and Family Therapy M,O
Mathematics M,O
Molecular Biology M,O
Music Education M,O
Nursing—General M
Physical Education M,O
Psychology—General M
Reading Education M,O
Rehabilitation Counseling M,O
School Psychology M,O
Science Education M,O
Secondary Education M,O
Spanish M,O
Special Education M,O
Statistics M,O
Supply Chain Management M,O
Vocational and Technical Education M

### CENTRAL EUROPEAN UNIVERSITY
Anthropology M,D
Applied Mathematics M,D
Business Administration and Management—General M,D
Business Analytics M,D
Cognitive Sciences D
Data Science/Data Analytics D
Economics M,D
Environmental Management and Policy M,D
Finance and Banking M,D
Gender Studies M,D
History M,D
International Affairs M,D
International Business M,D
Law M,D
Legal and Justice Studies M,D
Management of Technology M,D
Mathematics M,D
Medieval and Renaissance Studies M,D
Philosophy M,D
Political Science M,D
Public Administration M,D
Public Policy M,D
Sociology M,D

### CENTRAL METHODIST UNIVERSITY
Counselor Education M
Education—General M
Music Education M
Nursing and Healthcare Administration M
Nursing Education M
Nursing—General M

### CENTRAL MICHIGAN UNIVERSITY
Accounting M,O
Allopathic Medicine D
American Indian/Native American Studies M
American Studies M,O
Applied Psychology M,D
Biological and Biomedical Sciences—General M
Business Administration and Management—General M,O
Chemistry M
Child and Family Studies M,O
Clinical Psychology D
Clothing and Textiles M,O
Communication Disorders M,D
Communication—General M
Community College Education M,D,O
Computer and Information Systems Security O
Computer Science M
Conservation Biology M
Counseling Psychology M,D,O
Counselor Education M
Cultural Studies M
Curriculum and Instruction M,D,O
Early Childhood Education M,O
Economics M
Education—General M,D,O
Educational Leadership and Administration M,D,O
Educational Media/Instructional Technology M,D,O
Elementary Education M,D,O
Engineering and Applied Sciences—General M
Engineering Management M,O
English as a Second Language M
English M
Exercise and Sports Science M,D
Experimental Psychology M,D
Family and Consumer Sciences-General M,O
Film, Television, and Video Production M
Film, Television, and Video Theory and Criticism M
Finance and Banking M
Gender Studies M
Geographic Information Systems M
Gerontology M,O
Health Psychology M,D
Health Services Management and Hospital Administration M,D,O
Higher Education M,D,O
History M,O
Human Development M,O
Human Resources Management M,O
Humanities M
Industrial and Manufacturing Management M
Industrial and Organizational Psychology M,D
International Affairs M,O
International Business M,O
International Health M,D,O
Logistics M,O
Management Information Systems M,O
Marketing M,O
Materials Sciences D
Mathematics Education M,D
Mathematics M,D
Media Studies M
Music Education M
Music M
Neuroscience M,D
Nonprofit Management M,O
Nutrition M,D,O
Philanthropic Studies M,O
Physical Therapy M,D
Physician Assistant Studies M,D
Physics M,D
Political Science M,D
Psychology—General M,D,O
Public Administration M,O
Reading Education M,D,O
Recreation and Park Management M,O

M—masters degree; D—doctorate; O—other advanced degree; *—Close-Up and/or Display

| | |
|---|---|
| Rehabilitation Sciences | M,D |
| School Psychology | D,O |
| Science Education | M |
| Secondary Education | M,D,O |
| Spanish | M |
| Special Education | M,O |
| Sports Management | M,O |
| Student Affairs | M,D,O |
| Western European Studies | M,O |
| Writing | M |

**CENTRAL PENN COLLEGE**

| | |
|---|---|
| Management Information Systems | M |
| Organizational Management | M |

**CENTRAL WASHINGTON UNIVERSITY**

| | |
|---|---|
| Anthropology | M |
| Art/Fine Arts | M |
| Biological and Biomedical Sciences—General | M |
| Botany | M |
| Chemistry | M |
| Child and Family Studies | M |
| Counseling Psychology | M |
| Curriculum and Instruction | M |
| Ecology | M |
| Education—General | M |
| Educational Leadership and Administration | M |
| English as a Second Language | M |
| English | M |
| Environmental Management and Policy | M |
| Experimental Psychology | M |
| Family and Consumer Sciences-General | M |
| Fish, Game, and Wildlife Management | M |
| Geography | M |
| Geology | M |
| Graphic Design | M |
| Health Education | M |
| Higher Education | M |
| History | M |
| Home Economics Education | M |
| Interdisciplinary Studies | M |
| Microbiology | M |
| Music Education | M |
| Music | M |
| Natural Resources | M |
| Nutrition | M |
| Photography | M |
| Physical Education | M |
| Physiology | M |
| Psychology—General | M,O |
| Reading Education | M |
| School Psychology | O |
| Sports Management | M |
| Theater | M |
| Vocational and Technical Education | M |
| Writing | M |

**CENTRAL YESHIVA TOMCHEI TMIMIM-LUBAVITCH**

| | |
|---|---|
| Jewish Studies | M |
| Theology | M |

**CENTRO DE ESTUDIOS AVANZADOS DE PUERTO RICO Y EL CARIBE**

| | |
|---|---|
| History | M,D |
| Latin American Studies | M,D |

**CHADRON STATE COLLEGE**

| | |
|---|---|
| Business Administration and Management—General | M |
| Business Education | M,O |
| Counselor Education | M,O |
| Education—General | M,O |
| Educational Leadership and Administration | M,O |
| Elementary Education | M,O |
| English Education | M,O |
| Secondary Education | M,O |
| Social Sciences Education | M,O |

**CHAMINADE UNIVERSITY OF HONOLULU**

| | |
|---|---|
| Accounting | M |
| Business Administration and Management—General | M |
| Child Development | M |
| Criminal Justice and Criminology | M |
| Early Childhood Education | M |
| Education—General | M |
| Educational Leadership and Administration | M |
| Elementary Education | M |
| Nonprofit Management | M |
| Secondary Education | M |
| Special Education | M |

**CHAMPLAIN COLLEGE**

| | |
|---|---|
| Business Administration and Management—General | M |
| Computer and Information Systems Security | M |
| Conflict Resolution and Mediation/Peace Studies | M |
| Early Childhood Education | M |
| Forensic Sciences | M |
| Health Services Management and Hospital Administration | M |
| Internet and Interactive Multimedia | M |
| Law | M |
| Management of Technology | M |
| Media Studies | M |

**CHAPMAN UNIVERSITY**

| | |
|---|---|
| Accounting | M |
| Art/Fine Arts | |
| Business Administration and Management—General | M |
| Communication Disorders | M |
| Communication—General | M |
| Computational Sciences | M,D |
| Counselor Education | M,D,O |
| Cultural Studies | M,D,O |
| Curriculum and Instruction | M,D,O |
| Disability Studies | M,D,O |
| Education of Students with Severe/Multiple Disabilities | M,D,O |
| Education—General | M,D,O |
| Educational Leadership and Administration | M,D,O |
| Educational Psychology | M,D,O |
| Elementary Education | M,D,O |
| English | M |
| Environmental Law | M,D |
| Film, Television, and Video Production | M |
| Food Science and Technology | M |
| Holocaust and Genocide Studies | M |
| International Affairs | M |
| Law | M,D |
| Marriage and Family Therapy | M |
| Nutrition | M |
| Pharmaceutical Sciences | M,D |
| Pharmacy | M,D |
| Physical Therapy | D |
| Physician Assistant Studies | M |
| Psychology—General | M,D |
| School Psychology | M,D,O |
| Secondary Education | M,D,O |
| Special Education | M,D,O |
| Sports and Entertainment Law | M,D |
| Taxation | M,D |
| Writing | M |

**CHARLES R. DREW UNIVERSITY OF MEDICINE AND SCIENCE**

| | |
|---|---|
| Allopathic Medicine | D |
| Public Health—General | M |

**CHARLESTON SCHOOL OF LAW**

| | |
|---|---|
| Law | D |

**CHARLESTON SOUTHERN UNIVERSITY**

| | |
|---|---|
| Accounting | M |
| Business Administration and Management—General | M |
| Criminal Justice and Criminology | M |
| Education—General | M |
| Educational Leadership and Administration | M |
| Elementary Education | M |
| Finance and Banking | M |
| Human Resources Management | M |
| Management Information Systems | M |
| Organizational Management | M |

**CHARLOTTE CHRISTIAN COLLEGE AND THEOLOGICAL SEMINARY**

| | |
|---|---|
| Cultural Studies | M,D |
| Pastoral Ministry and Counseling | M,D |
| Religion | M,D |
| Theology | M,D |

**CHARTER COLLEGE**

| | |
|---|---|
| Business Administration and Management—General | M |

**CHARTER OAK STATE COLLEGE**

| | |
|---|---|
| Organizational Management | M |

**CHATHAM UNIVERSITY**

| | |
|---|---|
| Accounting | M |
| Art Education | M |
| Biological and Biomedical Sciences—General | M |
| Business Administration and Management—General | M |
| Communication—General | M |
| Computer Art and Design | M |
| Counseling Psychology | M,D |
| Developmental Psychology | M,D |
| Early Childhood Education | M |
| Education—General | M |
| Elementary Education | M |
| English Education | M |
| Environmental Biology | M |
| Environmental Education | M |
| Film, Television, and Video Production | M |
| Health Communication | M |
| Health Informatics | M |
| Health Psychology | M,D |
| Industrial and Organizational Psychology | M,D |
| Interior Design | M |
| Marriage and Family Therapy | M,D |
| Mathematics Education | M |
| Nursing and Healthcare Administration | M,D |
| Nursing Education | M,D |
| Nursing—General | M,D |
| Occupational Therapy | M,D |
| Physical Therapy | D |
| Physician Assistant Studies | M |
| Science Education | M |
| Secondary Education | M |
| Social Sciences Education | M |
| Special Education | M |
| Sport Psychology | M,D |
| Sustainability Management | M |
| Women's Studies | M |
| Writing | M |

**CHESTNUT HILL COLLEGE**

| | |
|---|---|
| Clinical Psychology | M,D,O |
| Counseling Psychology | M,O |
| Early Childhood Education | M |
| Education—General | M |
| Educational Leadership and Administration | M |
| Educational Media/Instructional Technology | M,O |
| Elementary Education | M |
| Human Services | M,O |
| Marriage and Family Therapy | M,D,O |
| Middle School Education | M |
| Psychology—General | M,D,O |
| Reading Education | M |
| Secondary Education | M |
| Special Education | M,O |

**CHEYNEY UNIVERSITY OF PENNSYLVANIA**

| | |
|---|---|
| Education—General | M,O |
| Educational Leadership and Administration | M,O |
| Elementary Education | M |
| Public Administration | M |
| Special Education | M |
| Urban Education | M |

**THE CHICAGO SCHOOL OF PROFESSIONAL PSYCHOLOGY**

| | |
|---|---|
| Applied Behavior Analysis | M,D |
| Clinical Psychology | M,D |
| Forensic Psychology | M,D |
| Industrial and Organizational Psychology | M,D |
| Organizational Management | M,D |
| Psychology—General | M,D |
| School Psychology | D,O |

**THE CHICAGO SCHOOL OF PROFESSIONAL PSYCHOLOGY AT DOWNTOWN LOS ANGELES**

| | |
|---|---|
| Applied Behavior Analysis | M,D |
| Clinical Psychology | M,D |
| Forensic Psychology | D |
| Industrial and Organizational Psychology | M |
| Marriage and Family Therapy | M,D |

**THE CHICAGO SCHOOL OF PROFESSIONAL PSYCHOLOGY AT IRVINE**

| | |
|---|---|
| Clinical Psychology | D |
| Forensic Psychology | D |
| Marriage and Family Therapy | M,D |
| Psychology—General | D |

**THE CHICAGO SCHOOL OF PROFESSIONAL PSYCHOLOGY AT SAN DIEGO**

| | |
|---|---|
| Applied Behavior Analysis | M,D |
| Applied Psychology | M,D |
| Clinical Psychology | M,D |
| Industrial and Organizational Psychology | M,D |

**THE CHICAGO SCHOOL OF PROFESSIONAL PSYCHOLOGY AT WASHINGTON DC**

| | |
|---|---|
| School Psychology | O |

**THE CHICAGO SCHOOL OF PROFESSIONAL PSYCHOLOGY AT XAVIER UNIVERSITY OF LOUISIANA**

| | |
|---|---|
| Clinical Psychology | D |

**THE CHICAGO SCHOOL OF PROFESSIONAL PSYCHOLOGY: ONLINE**

| | |
|---|---|
| Applied Psychology | M,O |
| Clinical Psychology | M |
| Forensic Psychology | M,O |
| Health Services Management and Hospital Administration | M |
| Industrial and Organizational Psychology | M,D,O |
| Pharmacology | M |
| Psychology—General | M,D |

**CHICAGO STATE UNIVERSITY**

| | |
|---|---|
| Adult Education | M |
| Biological and Biomedical Sciences—General | M |
| Clinical Psychology | M |
| Computer Science | M |
| Counselor Education | M |
| Criminal Justice and Criminology | M |
| Early Childhood Education | M |
| Education—General | M,D |
| Educational Leadership and Administration | M,D |
| Elementary Education | M |
| English | M |
| Foundations and Philosophy of Education | M |
| Geographic Information Systems | M |
| Higher Education | M,D |
| History | M |
| Library Science | M |
| Mathematics | M |
| Middle School Education | M |
| Multilingual and Multicultural Education | M |
| Nursing—General | M |
| Occupational Therapy | M |
| Pharmacy | D |
| Physical Education | M |
| Public Health—General | M |
| Reading Education | M |
| Secondary Education | M |
| Social Work | M |
| Special Education | M |
| Vocational and Technical Education | M |
| Writing | M |

**CHICAGO THEOLOGICAL SEMINARY**

| | |
|---|---|
| Ethics | M,D |
| Pastoral Ministry and Counseling | M,D |
| Religion | M,D |
| Theology | M,D |

**CHOWAN UNIVERSITY**

| | |
|---|---|
| Education—General | M |

**CHRISTENDOM COLLEGE**

| | |
|---|---|
| Theology | M |

**CHRISTIAN BROTHERS UNIVERSITY**

| | |
|---|---|
| Accounting | M,O |
| Business Administration and Management—General | M,O |
| Education—General | M |
| Educational Leadership and Administration | M |
| Engineering and Applied Sciences—General | M |
| International Business | M,O |
| Physician Assistant Studies | M |
| Project Management | M,O |
| Religion | M |

**CHRISTIAN THEOLOGICAL SEMINARY**

| | |
|---|---|
| Marriage and Family Therapy | M,D |
| Pastoral Ministry and Counseling | M,D |
| Religion | M,D |
| Theology | M,D |

**CHRISTIE'S EDUCATION**

| | |
|---|---|
| Art History | M |
| Art/Fine Arts | O |
| Arts Administration | M,O |
| Museum Studies | M |

**CHRISTOPHER NEWPORT UNIVERSITY**

| | |
|---|---|
| Applied Physics | M |
| Computer Science | M |
| Education—General | M |
| Environmental Sciences | M |
| Physics | M |

**CHRIST THE KING SEMINARY**

| | |
|---|---|
| Pastoral Ministry and Counseling | M |
| Theology | M |

**CHURCH DIVINITY SCHOOL OF THE PACIFIC**

| | |
|---|---|
| Theology | M,D,O |

**CINCINNATI CHRISTIAN UNIVERSITY**

| | |
|---|---|
| Pastoral Ministry and Counseling | M |
| Religion | M |
| Theology | M |

**THE CITADEL, THE MILITARY COLLEGE OF SOUTH CAROLINA**

| | |
|---|---|
| Aerospace/Aeronautical Engineering | M,O |
| Biological and Biomedical Sciences—General | M,O |
| Business Administration and Management—General | M |
| Civil Engineering | M,O |
| Computer Engineering | M,O |
| Counselor Education | M,O |
| Early Childhood Education | M,O |
| Education—General | M,O |
| Educational Leadership and Administration | M,O |
| Electrical Engineering | M,O |
| Engineering and Applied Sciences—General | M,O |
| Engineering Management | M,O |
| English Education | M,O |
| English | M |
| Environmental Management and Policy | M,O |
| Exercise and Sports Science | M,O |
| Geotechnical Engineering | M,O |
| Hispanic Studies | O |
| History | M,O |
| Homeland Security | M,O |
| Information Science | M |
| Interdisciplinary Studies | M,O |
| Manufacturing Engineering | M,O |
| Mathematics Education | M,O |
| Mechanical Engineering | M,O |
| Medical Microbiology | M,O |
| Middle School Education | M,O |
| Military and Defense Studies | M,O |
| National Security | M,O |
| Physical Education | M,O |
| Political Science | M |
| Project Management | M,O |
| Psychology—General | M,O |
| Reading Education | M,O |
| School Psychology | M,O |
| Science Education | M,O |
| Secondary Education | M,O |
| Social Sciences Education | M,O |
| Social Sciences | M |
| Sports Management | M,O |
| Structural Engineering | M,O |
| Student Affairs | M,O |
| Systems Engineering | M,O |
| Transportation and Highway Engineering | M,O |

**CITY COLLEGE OF THE CITY UNIVERSITY OF NEW YORK**

| | |
|---|---|
| Architecture | M |
| Art History | M |
| Art/Fine Arts | M |
| Atmospheric Sciences | M |
| Biochemistry | M,D |
| Biological and Biomedical Sciences—General | M,D |
| Biomedical Engineering | M,D |
| Business Administration and Management—General | M |
| Chemical Engineering | M,D |
| Chemistry | M,D |
| Civil Engineering | M,D |
| Clinical Psychology | M,D |
| Computer Art and Design | M |
| Computer Science | M,D |
| Corporate and Organizational Communication | M |
| Early Childhood Education | M |
| Economics | M |
| Education—General | M,O |
| Educational Leadership and Administration | M,O |
| Electrical Engineering | M,D |
| Engineering and Applied Sciences—General | M,D |
| English as a Second Language | M |
| English Education | M,O |
| English | M |
| Geology | M |

| | |
|---|---|
| Geosciences | M |
| Graphic Design | M |
| History | M |
| International Affairs | M |
| Landscape Architecture | M |
| Management Information Systems | M,D |
| Marketing | M |
| Mathematics Education | M,O |
| Mathematics | M |
| Mechanical Engineering | M,D |
| Media Studies | M |
| Middle School Education | M,O |
| Multilingual and Multicultural Education | M |
| Museum Education | M |
| Museum Studies | M |
| Physics | M,D |
| Psychology—General | M,D |
| Public Administration | M,D |
| Reading Education | M |
| Science Education | M |
| Secondary Education | M,O |
| Social Sciences Education | M,O |
| Sociology | M |
| Spanish | M |
| Special Education | M,O |
| Sustainable Development | M |
| Urban Design | M |
| Writing | M |

### CITY UNIVERSITY OF NEW YORK SCHOOL OF LAW

| | |
|---|---|
| Law | D |

### CITY UNIVERSITY OF SEATTLE

| | |
|---|---|
| Accounting | M,O |
| Business Administration and Management—General | M,O |
| Computer and Information Systems Security | M,O |
| Computer Science | M,O |
| Counseling Psychology | M |
| Counselor Education | M,O |
| Curriculum and Instruction | M,O |
| Education—General | M,O |
| Educational Leadership and Administration | M,D,O |
| Elementary Education | M,O |
| Finance and Banking | M,O |
| Human Resources Management | M,O |
| International Business | M,O |
| Management Information Systems | M,O |
| Management of Technology | M,O |
| Marketing | M,O |
| Organizational Management | M,O |
| Project Management | M,O |
| Reading Education | M,O |
| Special Education | M,O |
| Sustainability Management | M,O |

### CITY VISION UNIVERSITY

| | |
|---|---|
| Entrepreneurship | M |
| Pastoral Ministry and Counseling | M |

### CLAFLIN UNIVERSITY

| | |
|---|---|
| Biotechnology | M |
| Business Administration and Management—General | M |

### CLAREMONT GRADUATE UNIVERSITY

| | |
|---|---|
| African Studies | M,D,O |
| American Studies | M,D,O |
| Applied Mathematics | M,D |
| Archives/Archival Administration | M,D,O |
| Art/Fine Arts | M |
| Arts Administration | M |
| Botany | M,D |
| Business Administration and Management—General | M,D,O |
| Cognitive Sciences | M,D,O |
| Comparative Literature | M,D |
| Computational Biology | M,D |
| Computational Sciences | M,D |
| Computer and Information Systems Security | M,D,O |
| Computer Art and Design | M |
| Cultural Studies | M,D,O |
| Data Science/Data Analytics | M,D,O |
| Developmental Psychology | M,D,O |
| Economic Development | M,D,O |
| Economics | M,D,O |
| Education—General | M,D,O |
| Educational Leadership and Administration | M,D,O |
| Educational Measurement and Evaluation | M,D,O |
| Electronic Commerce | M,D,O |
| English | M,D |
| Ethics | M,D |
| Film, Television, and Video Theory and Criticism | M,D |
| Financial Engineering | M |
| Geographic Information Systems | M,D,O |
| Health Informatics | M,D,O |
| Health Promotion | M,D |
| Health Psychology | M,D,O |
| Higher Education | M,D,O |
| History | M,D,O |
| Human Development | M,D,O |
| Human Resources Development | M,D,O |
| Human Resources Management | M |
| Humanities | M,D,O |
| Industrial and Organizational Psychology | M,D,O |
| Information Science | M,D,O |
| International Affairs | M,D |
| International Economics | M,D,O |
| Management Information Systems | M,D,O |
| Management Strategy and Policy | M,D,O |
| Mathematics | M,D |
| Media Studies | M,D,O |
| Museum Studies | M,D,O |
| Music | M,D |
| Operations Research | M,D |
| Philosophy | M,D |
| Photography | M |
| Political Science | M,D |
| Psychology—General | M,D,O |
| Public Health—General | M,D |
| Public Policy | M,D,O |
| Religion | M,D |
| Social Psychology | M,D,O |
| Special Education | M,D,O |
| Statistics | M,D |
| Student Affairs | M,D,O |
| Systems Science | M,D,O |
| Telecommunications | M,D,O |
| Theology | M,D |
| Urban Education | M,D,O |
| Western European Studies | M,D,O |
| Women's Studies | M,D |
| Writing | M,D |

### CLAREMONT LINCOLN UNIVERSITY

| | |
|---|---|
| Ethics | M |
| Pastoral Ministry and Counseling | M |
| Religion | M |

### CLAREMONT SCHOOL OF THEOLOGY

| | |
|---|---|
| Ethics | M,D |
| Pastoral Ministry and Counseling | M,D |
| Religion | M,D |
| Religious Education | M,D |
| Theology | M,D |

### CLARION UNIVERSITY OF PENNSYLVANIA

| | |
|---|---|
| Accounting | M |
| Business Administration and Management—General | M |
| Communication Disorders | M |
| Curriculum and Instruction | M |
| Early Childhood Education | M |
| Education—General | M |
| Educational Media/Instructional Technology | M |
| Entrepreneurship | M |
| Family Nurse Practitioner Studies | M |
| Finance and Banking | M |
| Health Services Management and Hospital Administration | M |
| Library Science | M |
| Mathematics Education | M |
| Nursing—General | M |
| Reading Education | M |
| Science Education | M |
| Special Education | M |
| Vocational and Technical Education | M |

### CLARK ATLANTA UNIVERSITY

| | |
|---|---|
| Accounting | M |
| African-American Studies | M,D |
| Biological and Biomedical Sciences—General | M,D |
| Business Administration and Management—General | M |
| Chemistry | M,D |
| Computer Science | M |
| Counselor Education | M |
| Criminal Justice and Criminology | M |
| Curriculum and Instruction | M |
| Economics | M |
| Education—General | M,D,O |
| Educational Leadership and Administration | M,D,O |
| Educational Psychology | M |
| English | M,D |
| Information Science | M |
| Mathematics Education | M |
| Mathematics | M |
| Physics | M |
| Political Science | M,D |
| Public Administration | M |
| Science Education | M |
| Social Work | M,D |
| Sociology | M |
| Special Education | M |

### CLARKE UNIVERSITY

| | |
|---|---|
| Business Administration and Management—General | M |
| Education—General | M |
| Educational Leadership and Administration | M |
| Family Nurse Practitioner Studies | D |
| Nursing and Healthcare Administration | D |
| Nursing—General | D |
| Physical Therapy | D |
| Psychiatric Nursing | D |
| Social Work | M |

### CLARKSON COLLEGE

| | |
|---|---|
| Adult Nursing | M,O |
| Family Nurse Practitioner Studies | M,O |
| Nursing and Healthcare Administration | M,O |
| Nursing Education | M,O |
| Nursing—General | M,O |

### CLARKSON UNIVERSITY

| | |
|---|---|
| Bioethics | M,O |
| Biological and Biomedical Sciences—General | M |
| Biotechnology | M,D |
| Business Administration and Management—General | M,O |
| Chemistry | M,D |
| Civil Engineering | M,D |
| Computer Science | M,D |
| Education—General | M |
| Electrical Engineering | M |
| Energy and Power Engineering | M |
| Energy Management and Policy | M,O |
| Engineering and Applied Sciences—General | M,D,O |
| Engineering Management | M |
| Environmental Engineering | M,D |
| Environmental Management and Policy | M |
| Environmental Sciences | M,D |
| Health Informatics | M |
| Health Services Management and Hospital Administration | M,O |
| Health Services Research | M |
| Human Resources Management | M,O |
| Interdisciplinary Studies | M,D |
| International Business | M,O |
| Materials Engineering | D |
| Materials Sciences | D |
| Mathematics | M,D |
| Nursing and Healthcare Administration | M,O |
| Occupational Therapy | M |
| Physical Therapy | D |
| Physician Assistant Studies | M |
| Supply Chain Management | M,O |
| Sustainable Development | M,D |

### CLARKS SUMMIT UNIVERSITY

| | |
|---|---|
| Communication—General | M,D |
| Counselor Education | M |
| Curriculum and Instruction | M |
| Educational Leadership and Administration | M |
| English | M |
| Missions and Missiology | M,D |
| Organizational Management | M,D |
| Pastoral Ministry and Counseling | M,D |
| Religion | M,D |
| Religious Education | M,D |
| Theology | M,D |

### CLARK UNIVERSITY

| | |
|---|---|
| Accounting | M |
| American Studies | D |
| Biochemistry | D |
| Biological and Biomedical Sciences—General | M,D |
| Business Administration and Management—General | M |
| Business Analytics | M |
| Chemistry | D |
| Clinical Psychology | D |
| Communication—General | M |
| Community Health | M |
| Developmental Psychology | D |
| Economics | D |
| Education—General | M,D |
| English | M |
| Environmental Management and Policy | M |
| Environmental Sciences | M |
| Finance and Banking | M |
| Geographic Information Systems | M |
| Geography | D |
| Health Education | M |
| History | D |
| Holocaust and Genocide Studies | D |
| Information Science | M |
| International Development | M |
| International Health | M |
| Management Information Systems | M |
| Marketing | M |
| Physics | D |
| Public Administration | M,O |
| Social Psychology | D |
| Sustainability Management | M |
| Sustainable Development | M |
| Urban and Regional Planning | M |

### CLAYTON STATE UNIVERSITY

| | |
|---|---|
| Accounting | M |
| Applied Psychology | M |
| Archives/Archival Administration | M |
| Biological and Biomedical Sciences—General | M |
| Business Administration and Management—General | M |
| Clinical Psychology | M |
| Criminal Justice and Criminology | M |
| Developmental Psychology | M |
| Education—General | M |
| English Education | M |
| Family Nurse Practitioner Studies | M |
| History | M |
| Human Resources Management | M |
| International Business | M |
| Liberal Studies | M |
| Mathematics Education | M |
| Nursing—General | M |
| Psychology—General | M |
| Sports Management | M |
| Supply Chain Management | M |

### CLEARY UNIVERSITY

| | |
|---|---|
| Business Administration and Management—General | M,O |
| Business Analytics | M,O |
| Finance and Banking | M,O |
| Health Services Management and Hospital Administration | M,O |
| Management Strategy and Policy | M,O |

### CLEMSON UNIVERSITY

| | |
|---|---|
| Accounting | M |
| Agricultural Education | M,D |
| Agricultural Sciences—General | M,D |
| Animal Sciences | M,D |
| Anthropology | M |
| Applied Economics | M,D |
| Applied Psychology | M,D |
| Applied Statistics | M,D |
| Architecture | M,D,O |
| Art/Fine Arts | M |
| Automotive Engineering | M,D,O |
| Bioengineering | M,D,O |
| Bioinformatics | M,D,O |
| Biological and Biomedical Sciences—General | M,D |
| Biomedical Engineering | M,D,O |
| Biosystems Engineering | M,D |
| Business Administration and Management—General | M,D |
| Business Analytics | M |
| Business Education | M,D |
| Chemical Engineering | M,D |
| Chemistry | M,D |
| Civil Engineering | M,D |
| Clinical Psychology | M,D,O |
| Clinical Research | M,D,O |
| Communication—General | M |
| Computer Engineering | M,D |
| Computer Science | M,D |
| Construction Engineering | M,D |
| Construction Management | M,D |
| Counselor Education | M,D,O |
| Criminal Justice and Criminology | M |
| Curriculum and Instruction | M,D,O |
| Distance Education Development | M,D,O |
| Early Childhood Education | M,D,O |
| Economics | M,D |
| Education—General | M,D,O |
| Educational Leadership and Administration | M,D,O |
| Educational Measurement and Evaluation | M,D,O |
| Electrical Engineering | M,D |
| Elementary Education | M,D,O |
| Engineering and Applied Sciences—General | M,D,O |
| Entomology | M,D |
| Entrepreneurship | M,D |
| Environmental and Occupational Health | M,D |
| Environmental Engineering | M,D |
| Environmental Management and Policy | M,D |
| Environmental Sciences | M,D |
| Ergonomics and Human Factors | M,D |
| Family and Consumer Sciences-General | D,O |
| Family Nurse Practitioner Studies | M,D,O |
| Fish, Game, and Wildlife Management | M,D |
| Food Science and Technology | M,D |
| Forestry | M,D |
| Genetics | M,D,O |
| Geotechnical Engineering | M,D |
| Gerontological Nursing | M,D,O |
| Higher Education | M,D,O |
| Historic Preservation | M,O |
| History | M |
| Human Resources Development | M,D,O |
| Hydrogeology | M,D |
| Industrial and Organizational Psychology | M,D |
| Industrial/Management Engineering | M,D |
| International Health | M,D,O |
| Landscape Architecture | M |
| Management Information Systems | M,D |
| Marketing | M |
| Materials Engineering | M,D |
| Materials Sciences | M,D |
| Mathematics Education | M,D,O |
| Mathematics | M,D |
| Mechanical Engineering | M,D |
| Microbiology | M,D |
| Middle School Education | M,D,O |
| Molecular Biology | D |
| Nursing—General | M,D,O |
| Nutrition | M,D |
| Organizational Behavior | M,D |
| Physics | M,D |
| Plant Biology | M,D |
| Public Administration | M,D,O |
| Public Health—General | M,D,O |
| Public Policy | D,O |
| Reading Education | M,D,O |
| Real Estate | M |
| Recreation and Park Management | M,D,O |
| Rhetoric | M,D |
| Science Education | D,O |
| Secondary Education | M,D,O |
| Sociology | M |
| Special Education | M,D,O |
| Sports Management | M,D,O |
| Statistics | M,D |
| Structural Engineering | M,D |
| Student Affairs | M,D,O |
| Supply Chain Management | M,D |
| Toxicology | M,D |
| Transportation and Highway Engineering | M,D |
| Travel and Tourism | M,D,O |
| Veterinary Sciences | M,D |
| Water Resources Engineering | M,D |
| Writing | M,D |

### CLEVELAND INSTITUTE OF MUSIC

| | |
|---|---|
| Music | M,D,O |

### CLEVELAND STATE UNIVERSITY

| | |
|---|---|
| Accounting | M |
| Adult Education | M,D,O |
| Allied Health—General | M |
| Applied Statistics | M |
| Art Education | M |
| Art History | M |
| Bioethics | M,O |

*M—masters degree; D—doctorate; O—other advanced degree; *—Close-Up and/or Display*

- Biological and Biomedical Sciences—General M,D
- Biomedical Engineering D
- Business Administration and Management—General M,D
- Chemical Engineering M,D
- Chemistry M,D
- Civil Engineering M,D
- Communication Disorders M
- Communication—General M,D,O
- Counseling Psychology M,D,O
- Counselor Education M,D,O
- Early Childhood Education M
- Economic Development M,O
- Economics M,O
- Education of Students with Severe/Multiple Disabilities M
- Education—General M,D,O
- Educational Leadership and Administration M,D,O
- Educational Media/Instructional Technology D
- Educational Policy D
- Electrical Engineering M,D
- Engineering and Applied Sciences—General M,D
- English as a Second Language M
- English M
- Environmental Engineering M,D
- Environmental Management and Policy M,O
- Environmental Sciences M,D
- Foreign Languages Education M
- Geographic Information Systems M,O
- Health Education M
- Health Services Management and Hospital Administration M
- Higher Education D
- Historic Preservation M,O
- History M
- Human Resources Management M
- Industrial and Labor Relations M
- International Affairs M
- International Economics M
- Law M,D,O
- Management Information Systems D
- Marketing D
- Mathematics Education M
- Mathematics M
- Mechanical Engineering M,D
- Molecular Medicine M,D
- Museum Studies M
- Music Education M
- Music M
- Nonprofit Management M,O
- Nursing Education D
- Nursing—General M,D
- Occupational Therapy M
- Organic Chemistry M,D
- Philosophy M,O
- Physical Chemistry M,D
- Physical Education M
- Physical Therapy D
- Physician Assistant Studies M
- Physics M
- Psychology—General M,D,O
- Public Administration M,D,O
- Public Affairs D
- Public Health—General M
- Real Estate M,O
- Science Education M
- Social Work M
- Software Engineering M,D
- Spanish M
- Special Education M
- Sustainable Development M,O
- Urban and Regional Planning M,O
- Urban Education D
- Urban Studies M,D,O
- Writing M

### CLEVELAND UNIVERSITY–KANSAS CITY
- Chiropractic D
- Health Education M
- Health Promotion M

### COASTAL CAROLINA UNIVERSITY
- Accounting M,O
- Business Administration and Management—General M,O
- Computer Science M,D,O
- Distance Education Development M,O
- Education—General M,O
- Educational Leadership and Administration M,O
- Educational Media/Instructional Technology M,O
- English as a Second Language M,O
- Liberal Studies M
- Management Information Systems M,D,O
- Marine Sciences M,D,O
- Reading Education M,O
- Special Education M,O
- Sports Management M,D,O
- Writing M

### COGSWELL POLYTECHNICAL COLLEGE
- Entrepreneurship M

### COKER COLLEGE
- Business Administration and Management—General M
- Criminal Justice and Criminology M
- Curriculum and Instruction M
- Educational Media/Instructional Technology M
- Reading Education M
- Sports Management M

### THE COLBURN SCHOOL CONSERVATORY OF MUSIC
- Music M,O

### COLD SPRING HARBOR LABORATORY
- Biological and Biomedical Sciences—General D

### COLGATE ROCHESTER CROZER DIVINITY SCHOOL
- Conflict Resolution and Mediation/Peace Studies M,D,O
- Theology M,D,O

### COLGATE UNIVERSITY
- Secondary Education M

### COLLÊGE DOMINICAIN DE PHILOSOPHIE ET DE THÊOLOGIE
- Philosophy M,D
- Theology M,D,O

### COLLEGE FOR CREATIVE STUDIES
- Applied Arts and Design—General M
- Art/Fine Arts M
- Automotive Engineering M
- Transportation and Highway Engineering M

### COLLEGE FOR FINANCIAL PLANNING
- Finance and Banking M

### COLLEGE OF CHARLESTON
- Accounting M
- Arts Administration O
- Business Administration and Management—General M
- Computer Science M
- Early Childhood Education M
- Education—General M,O
- Elementary Education M
- English as a Second Language O
- English M
- Environmental Sciences M
- Foreign Languages Education M
- Historic Preservation M
- History M
- Management Information Systems M
- Marine Biology M
- Marine Sciences M
- Mathematics Education M
- Mathematics M
- Music Education M
- Public Administration M
- Science Education M
- Special Education M
- Urban and Regional Planning O
- Writing M

### COLLEGE OF EMMANUEL AND ST. CHAD
- Theology M,D,O

### THE COLLEGE OF IDAHO
- Curriculum and Instruction M
- Education—General M

### COLLEGE OF MOUNT SAINT VINCENT
- Education—General M,O
- Educational Media/Instructional Technology M,O
- English as a Second Language M,O
- Family Nurse Practitioner Studies M,O
- Middle School Education M,O
- Multilingual and Multicultural Education M,O
- Nursing and Healthcare Administration M,O
- Nursing Education M,O
- Nursing—General M,O
- Urban Education M,O

### THE COLLEGE OF NEW JERSEY
- Addictions/Substance Abuse Counseling M,O
- Counselor Education M
- Early Childhood Education M
- Education—General M,O
- Educational Leadership and Administration M,O
- Elementary Education M
- English as a Second Language M,O
- English M
- Gender Studies O
- Health Communication M
- International and Comparative Education M,O
- International Health M
- Marriage and Family Therapy M,O
- Nursing—General M,O
- Public Health—General M
- Reading Education M,O
- Secondary Education M
- Special Education M,O

### THE COLLEGE OF NEW ROCHELLE
- Acute Care/Critical Care Nursing M,O
- Art Education M
- Art Therapy M
- Communication—General M,O
- Counseling Psychology M,O
- Early Childhood Education M
- Education of the Gifted O
- Education—General M,O
- Educational Leadership and Administration M,O
- Elementary Education M
- English as a Second Language M,O
- Family Nurse Practitioner Studies M,O
- Human Resources Development M,O
- Marriage and Family Therapy M
- Multilingual and Multicultural Education M,O
- Nursing and Healthcare Administration M,O
- Nursing Education M,O
- Nursing—General M,O
- Public Administration M
- Reading Education M
- School Psychology M
- Special Education M
- Thanatology M,O

### COLLEGE OF SAINT ELIZABETH
- Applied Behavior Analysis M,O
- Business Administration and Management—General M
- Computer and Information Systems Security M,O
- Counseling Psychology M,D
- Criminal Justice and Criminology M,O
- Data Science/Data Analytics M
- Distance Education Development M,O
- Early Childhood Education M,O
- Education—General M,O
- Educational Leadership and Administration M,D,O
- Elementary Education M,O
- English as a Second Language M,O
- Health Services Management and Hospital Administration M
- Higher Education M,D,O
- Holocaust and Genocide Studies M,O
- Human Resources Management M
- Internet and Interactive Multimedia M
- Middle School Education M,O
- Nursing—General M
- Nutrition M,O
- Organizational Management M
- Pastoral Ministry and Counseling M,O
- Psychology—General M,D
- Public Administration M,O
- Public Health—General M
- School Psychology M,D
- Special Education M,O
- Theology M,O

### COLLEGE OF ST. JOSEPH
- Addictions/Substance Abuse Counseling M
- Business Administration and Management—General M
- Clinical Psychology M
- Counseling Psychology M
- Counselor Education M
- Education—General M
- Elementary Education M
- English Education M
- Psychology—General M
- Reading Education M
- School Psychology M
- Secondary Education M
- Social Psychology M
- Social Sciences Education M
- Special Education M

### COLLEGE OF SAINT MARY
- Education—General M
- Educational Leadership and Administration M
- Educational Measurement and Evaluation M
- English as a Second Language M
- Health Education D
- Nursing—General M
- Occupational Therapy M
- Organizational Management M

### THE COLLEGE OF SAINT ROSE
- Accounting M
- Business Administration and Management—General M
- Business Analytics M
- Communication Disorders M
- Computer Science M,O
- Counseling Psychology M,O
- Counselor Education M,O
- Curriculum and Instruction M,O
- Early Childhood Education M,O
- Education—General M,O
- Educational Leadership and Administration M,O
- Educational Psychology M,O
- Finance and Banking O
- Higher Education M,O
- Information Science M,O
- Middle School Education M,O
- Organizational Management O
- Reading Education M,O
- School Psychology M,O
- Secondary Education M,O
- Social Work M
- Special Education M,O
- Student Affairs M

### THE COLLEGE OF ST. SCHOLASTICA
- Athletic Training and Sports Medicine M
- Business Administration and Management—General M,O
- Education—General M,O
- Exercise and Sports Science M
- Health Informatics M,O
- Management Information Systems M,O
- Nursing—General M,O
- Occupational Therapy M
- Physical Therapy D
- Social Work M

### COLLEGE OF STATEN ISLAND OF THE CITY UNIVERSITY OF NEW YORK
- Accounting M
- Adult Nursing M,O
- African Studies M
- American Studies M
- Artificial Intelligence/Robotics M
- Asian Studies M
- Biological and Biomedical Sciences—General M
- Biotechnology M
- Business Administration and Management—General M
- Clinical Psychology M
- Computer and Information Systems Security M
- Computer Science M
- Counseling Psychology M,O
- Data Science/Data Analytics M,O
- Early Childhood Education M
- Education—General M,O
- Educational Leadership and Administration O
- Electrical Engineering M
- Elementary Education M
- English as a Second Language M,O
- English Education M
- English M
- Environmental Sciences M
- Film, Television, and Video Theory and Criticism M
- Gerontological Nursing M,O
- Health Services Management and Hospital Administration M
- History M
- Latin American Studies M
- Liberal Studies M
- Management Strategy and Policy M
- Mathematics Education M
- Media Studies M
- Middle School Education M
- Multilingual and Multicultural Education O
- Near and Middle Eastern Studies M
- Neuroscience M
- Physical Therapy D
- Secondary Education M
- Social Work M
- Software Engineering M
- Special Education M,O
- Western European Studies M

### COLLEGE OF THE ATLANTIC
- Environmental Management and Policy M

### COLORADO CHRISTIAN UNIVERSITY
- Business Administration and Management—General M
- Business Education M
- Computer and Information Systems Security M
- Counseling Psychology M
- Curriculum and Instruction M
- Distance Education Development M
- Early Childhood Education M
- Education—General M
- Educational Media/Instructional Technology M
- Elementary Education M
- Project Management M
- Special Education M

### THE COLORADO COLLEGE
- American Studies M
- Art Education M
- Education—General M
- Elementary Education M
- English Education M
- Foreign Languages Education M
- Humanities M
- Liberal Studies M
- Mathematics Education M
- Music Education M
- Science Education M
- Secondary Education M
- Social Sciences Education M

### COLORADO MESA UNIVERSITY
- Business Administration and Management—General M
- Education of the Gifted M,O
- Education—General M,O
- Educational Leadership and Administration M,O
- English as a Second Language M,O
- Family Nurse Practitioner Studies M,D,O
- Health Informatics M,D,O
- Nursing Education M,D,O
- Nursing—General M,D,O
- Special Education M,O

### COLORADO SCHOOL OF MINES
- Applied Mathematics M,D
- Applied Physics M,D
- Applied Statistics M,D
- Bioengineering M,D
- Chemical Engineering M,D
- Chemistry M,D
- Civil Engineering M,D
- Computer Science M,D
- Construction Engineering M,D
- Electrical Engineering M,D
- Electronic Materials M,D
- Energy Management and Policy M,D
- Engineering and Applied Sciences—General M,D,O
- Engineering Management M,D
- Environmental Engineering M,D
- Environmental Sciences M,D
- Geochemistry M,D
- Geological Engineering M,D
- Geology M,D
- Geophysics M,D
- Humanities O
- Hydrology M,D
- Management of Technology M,D
- Materials Engineering M,D
- Materials Sciences M,D
- Mechanical Engineering M,D
- Metallurgical Engineering and Metallurgy M,D
- Mineral Economics M,D
- Mineral/Mining Engineering M,D
- Nuclear Engineering M,D
- Operations Research M,D
- Petroleum Engineering M,D
- Physics M,D
- Social Sciences O

### COLORADO SCHOOL OF TRADITIONAL CHINESE MEDICINE

| | |
|---|---|
| Acupuncture and Oriental Medicine | M |

### COLORADO STATE UNIVERSITY

| | |
|---|---|
| Accounting | M |
| Adult Education | M,D |
| Advertising and Public Relations | M,D |
| Agricultural Economics and Agribusiness | M,D |
| Agricultural Education | M |
| Agricultural Sciences—General | M,D |
| Agronomy and Soil Sciences | M,D |
| Animal Sciences | M,D |
| Anthropology | M,D |
| Art History | M |
| Art/Fine Arts | M |
| Arts Administration | M |
| Atmospheric Sciences | M,D |
| Biochemistry | M,D |
| Bioengineering | M,D |
| Biological and Biomedical Sciences—General | M,D |
| Biomedical Engineering | M,D |
| Botany | M,D |
| Business Administration and Management—General | M |
| Chemical Engineering | M,D |
| Chemistry | M,D |
| Child and Family Studies | M,D |
| Civil Engineering | M,D |
| Computer Science | M,D |
| Conservation Biology | M,D |
| Construction Management | M |
| Consumer Economics | M |
| Counselor Education | M,D |
| Economics | M,D |
| Education—General | M,D |
| Educational Leadership and Administration | M,D |
| Electrical Engineering | M,D |
| Energy Management and Policy | M |
| Engineering and Applied Sciences—General | M,D |
| English | M |
| Entomology | M,D |
| Environmental and Occupational Health | M,D |
| Environmental Management and Policy | M,D |
| Epidemiology | M,D |
| Ethnic Studies | M |
| Exercise and Sports Science | M,D |
| Finance and Banking | M |
| Fish, Game, and Wildlife Management | M,D |
| Food Science and Technology | M,D |
| French | M |
| Geosciences | M,D |
| Higher Education | M,D |
| History | M |
| Horticulture | M,D |
| Human Development | M,D |
| Immunology | M,D |
| Interdisciplinary Studies | M,D |
| Landscape Architecture | M,D |
| Liberal Studies | M |
| Management Information Systems | M,D |
| Marriage and Family Therapy | M,D |
| Materials Sciences | M,D |
| Mathematics | M,D |
| Mechanical Engineering | M,D |
| Media Studies | M,D |
| Microbiology | M,D |
| Music | M |
| Natural Resources | M,D |
| Nutrition | M,D |
| Occupational Therapy | M,D |
| Pathology | M,D |
| Philosophy | M |
| Physics | M,D |
| Plant Pathology | M,D |
| Plant Sciences | M,D |
| Political Science | M,D |
| Psychology—General | M,D |
| Public History | M |
| Recreation and Park Management | M,D |
| Rhetoric | M |
| Social Work | M,D |
| Sociology | M,D |
| Speech and Interpersonal Communication | M,D |
| Statistics | M,D |
| Student Affairs | M,D |
| Sustainability Management | M |
| Sustainable Development | M,O |
| Systems Engineering | M,D |
| Travel and Tourism | M,D |
| Veterinary Medicine | D |
| Veterinary Sciences | M,D |
| Water Resources | M,D |
| Writing | M |
| Zoology | M,D |

### COLORADO STATE UNIVERSITY–GLOBAL CAMPUS

| | |
|---|---|
| Accounting | M |
| Business Administration and Management—General | M |
| Criminal Justice and Criminology | M |
| Education—General | M |
| Educational Leadership and Administration | M |
| Finance and Banking | M |
| Health Services Management and Hospital Administration | M |
| Human Resources Management | M |
| International Business | M |
| Management Information Systems | M |
| Organizational Management | M |
| Project Management | M |

### COLORADO STATE UNIVERSITY-PUEBLO

| | |
|---|---|
| Applied Science and Technology | M |
| Art Education | M |
| Biochemistry | M |
| Biological and Biomedical Sciences—General | M |
| Business Administration and Management—General | M |
| Chemistry | M |
| Education—General | M |
| Educational Media/Instructional Technology | M |
| Engineering and Applied Sciences—General | M |
| Foreign Languages Education | M |
| Health Education | M |
| Industrial/Management Engineering | M |
| Music Education | M |
| Nursing—General | M |
| Physical Education | M |
| Special Education | M |
| Systems Engineering | M |

### COLORADO TECHNICAL UNIVERSITY AURORA

| | |
|---|---|
| Accounting | M |
| Business Administration and Management—General | M |
| Computer and Information Systems Security | M |
| Computer Engineering | M |
| Computer Science | M |
| Conflict Resolution and Mediation/Peace Studies | M |
| Criminal Justice and Criminology | M |
| Data Science/Data Analytics | M |
| Electrical Engineering | M |
| Finance and Banking | M |
| Human Resources Management | M |
| Industrial and Manufacturing Management | M |
| Management of Technology | M |
| Marketing | M |
| Project Management | M |
| Software Engineering | M |
| Systems Engineering | M |

### COLORADO TECHNICAL UNIVERSITY COLORADO SPRINGS

| | |
|---|---|
| Accounting | M,D |
| Business Administration and Management—General | M,D |
| Computer and Information Systems Security | M,D |
| Computer Engineering | M |
| Computer Science | M,D |
| Conflict Resolution and Mediation/Peace Studies | M,D |
| Criminal Justice and Criminology | M |
| Data Science/Data Analytics | M,D |
| Electrical Engineering | M |
| Finance and Banking | M,D |
| Human Resources Management | M,D |
| Industrial and Manufacturing Management | M,D |
| Logistics | M,D |
| Management of Technology | M,D |
| Marketing | M,D |
| Project Management | M,D |
| Software Engineering | M,D |
| Systems Engineering | M |

### COLUMBIA COLLEGE (MO)

| | |
|---|---|
| Accounting | M |
| Business Administration and Management—General | M |
| Criminal Justice and Criminology | M |
| Education—General | M |
| Educational Leadership and Administration | M |
| Human Resources Management | M |

### COLUMBIA COLLEGE (SC)

| | |
|---|---|
| Criminal Justice and Criminology | M |
| Education—General | M |
| Educational Leadership and Administration | M |
| Elementary Education | M |
| Higher Education | M |
| Organizational Management | M |

### COLUMBIA COLLEGE CHICAGO

| | |
|---|---|
| Art History | M |
| Art/Fine Arts | M |
| Business Administration and Management—General | M |
| Communication—General | M |
| English | M |
| Entertainment Management | M |
| Film, Television, and Video Production | M |
| Music | M |
| Photography | M |
| Writing | M |

### COLUMBIA COLLEGE OF NURSING

| | |
|---|---|
| Nursing—General | M |

### COLUMBIA INTERNATIONAL UNIVERSITY

| | |
|---|---|
| Counselor Education | M,D,O |
| Cultural Studies | M,D,O |
| Curriculum and Instruction | M,D,O |
| Early Childhood Education | M,D,O |
| Education—General | M,D,O |
| Educational Leadership and Administration | M,D,O |
| Elementary Education | M,D,O |
| English as a Second Language | M,D,O |
| Missions and Missiology | M,D,O |
| Multilingual and Multicultural Education | M,D,O |
| Pastoral Ministry and Counseling | M,D,O |
| Religious Education | M,D,O |
| Theology | M,D,O |

### COLUMBIA SOUTHERN UNIVERSITY

| | |
|---|---|
| Business Administration and Management—General | M,D |
| Criminal Justice and Criminology | M |
| Emergency Management | M |
| Environmental and Occupational Health | M |
| Finance and Banking | M |
| Health Services Management and Hospital Administration | M |
| Human Resources Management | M |
| Marketing | M |
| Organizational Management | M |

### COLUMBIA THEOLOGICAL SEMINARY

| | |
|---|---|
| Theology | M,D |

### COLUMBIA UNIVERSITY

| | |
|---|---|
| Accounting | M,D |
| Actuarial Science | M |
| Acute Care/Critical Care Nursing | M,O |
| Adult Nursing | M,O |
| African Studies | M,D |
| African-American Studies | M,D |
| Allopathic Medicine | M,D |
| American Studies | M,D |
| Anatomy | M,D |
| Anthropology | M,D |
| Applied Mathematics | M,D |
| Applied Physics | M,D |
| Archaeology | M,D |
| Architecture | M,D |
| Archives/Archival Administration | M |
| Art History | M,D |
| Art/Fine Arts | M,D |
| Asian Studies | M,D,O |
| Astronomy | M,D |
| Atmospheric Sciences | M,D |
| Biochemistry | M,D |
| Bioethics | M |
| Biological and Biomedical Sciences—General | M,D,O |
| Biomedical Engineering | M,D |
| Biophysics | M,D |
| Biostatistics | M,D |
| Biotechnology | M,D |
| Business Administration and Management—General | M,D |
| Business Analytics | M |
| Cell Biology | M,D |
| Chemical Engineering | M,D |
| Chemical Physics | M,D |
| Chemistry | M,D |
| Civil Engineering | M,D |
| Classics | M,D |
| Communication—General | M,D |
| Community Health | M,D |
| Comparative Literature | M,D |
| Computer Engineering | M,D |
| Computer Science | M,D |
| Conflict Resolution and Mediation/Peace Studies | M |
| Conservation Biology | M,D |
| Construction Engineering | M,D |
| Construction Management | M,D |
| Corporate and Organizational Communication | M |
| Data Science/Data Analytics | M |
| Dentistry | D |
| Developmental Biology | M,D |
| East European and Russian Studies | M,D |
| Ecology | M,D |
| Economics | M,D |
| Electrical Engineering | M,D |
| Engineering and Applied Sciences—General | M,D |
| English | M,D |
| Entrepreneurship | M |
| Environmental and Occupational Health | M,D |
| Environmental Design | M |
| Environmental Engineering | M,D |
| Environmental Management and Policy | M |
| Environmental Sciences | M,D |
| Epidemiology | M,D |
| Ethics | M |
| Evolutionary Biology | M,D |
| Family Nurse Practitioner Studies | M,O |
| Film, Television, and Video Production | M |
| Film, Television, and Video Theory and Criticism | M |
| Finance and Banking | M,D |
| Financial Engineering | M,D |
| Foreign Languages Education | M,D |
| Foundations and Philosophy of Education | M,D |
| French | M,D |
| Genetics | M,D |
| Geosciences | M,D |
| German | M,D |
| Gerontological Nursing | M,O |
| Health Services Management and Hospital Administration | M |
| Hispanic Studies | M,D |
| Historic Preservation | M,D,O |
| History | M,D |
| Human Resources Management | M |
| Industrial/Management Engineering | M,D |
| Information Studies | M |
| International Affairs | M,D |
| International Business | M |
| Italian | M,D |
| Japanese | M,D |
| Jewish Studies | M,D |
| Journalism | M,D |
| Kinesiology and Movement Studies | M,D |
| Landscape Architecture | M |
| Latin American Studies | M,D |
| Law | M,D |
| Legal and Justice Studies | M,D |
| Management of Technology | M |
| Marketing | M,D |
| Materials Engineering | M,D |
| Materials Sciences | M,D |
| Maternal and Child Health | M,D |
| Mathematics | M,D |
| Mechanical Engineering | M,D |
| Mechanics | M,D |
| Media Studies | M |
| Medical Informatics | M,D,O |
| Medical Physics | M,D |
| Medieval and Renaissance Studies | M,D |
| Microbiology | M,D |
| Molecular Biology | D |
| Museum Studies | M,D |
| Music | M,D |
| Near and Middle Eastern Studies | M,D |
| Neurobiology | D |
| Nonprofit Management | M |
| Nurse Anesthesia | M,O |
| Nurse Midwifery | M |
| Nursing—General | M,D,O |
| Nutrition | M,D |
| Occupational Therapy | M,D |
| Operations Research | M,D |
| Oral and Dental Sciences | M,D,O |
| Pathobiology | M,D |
| Pathology | M,D |
| Pediatric Nursing | M,O |
| Pharmaceutical Administration | M |
| Pharmacology | M,D |
| Philosophy | M,D |
| Physical Therapy | D |
| Physics | M,D |
| Physiology | M,D |
| Political Science | M,D |
| Psychiatric Nursing | M,O |
| Psychology—General | M,D |
| Public Administration | M |
| Public Health—General | M,D |
| Public Policy | M |
| Quantitative Analysis | M,D |
| Real Estate | M |
| Religion | M,D |
| Romance Languages | M,D |
| Russian | M,D |
| Science Education | M,D,O |
| Slavic Languages | M,D |
| Social Sciences | M,D |
| Social Work | M,D |
| Sociology | M,D |
| Spanish | M,D |
| Sports Management | M |
| Statistics | M,D |
| Structural Biology | D |
| Sustainability Management | M |
| Sustainable Development | M,D |
| Theater | M,D |
| Toxicology | M,D |
| Translation and Interpretation | M,D |
| Urban and Regional Planning | M,D |
| Western European Studies | M,D |
| Writing | M |

### COLUMBUS COLLEGE OF ART & DESIGN

| | |
|---|---|
| Art/Fine Arts | M |

### COLUMBUS STATE UNIVERSITY

| | |
|---|---|
| Art Education | M |
| Biological and Biomedical Sciences—General | M |
| Business Administration and Management—General | M,O |
| Chemistry | M,O |
| Clinical Psychology | M,D,O |
| Computer and Information Systems Security | M,O |
| Computer Science | M,O |
| Counselor Education | M,D,O |
| Criminal Justice and Criminology | M |
| Curriculum and Instruction | M,D,O |
| Early Childhood Education | M,O |
| Education—General | M,D,O |
| Educational Leadership and Administration | M,D,O |
| English as a Second Language | O |
| English Education | M,O |
| Environmental Management and Policy | M |
| Environmental Sciences | M,O |
| Exercise and Sports Science | M |
| Family Nurse Practitioner Studies | M |
| Health Education | M |
| Health Services Management and Hospital Administration | M |
| Higher Education | M,D,O |
| History | M,O |
| Homeland Security | M |
| Human Resources Management | M,O |
| Mathematics Education | M,O |
| Mathematics | M,O |
| Middle School Education | M,O |
| Modeling and Simulation | M,O |
| Music Education | M,O |
| Music | M,O |
| Nursing and Healthcare Administration | M |
| Nursing Education | M |

*M—masters degree; D—doctorate; O—other advanced degree; *—Close-Up and/or Display*

Nursing Informatics M
Nursing—General M
Organizational Management M,O
Physical Education M
Political Science M
Public Administration M
Science Education M,O
Secondary Education M,O
Social Sciences Education M,O
Special Education M,O
Theater M
Urban Studies M

## CONCORDIA COLLEGE
Education—General M
Foreign Languages Education M

## CONCORDIA COLLEGE–NEW YORK
Organizational Management M
Special Education M

## CONCORDIA LUTHERAN SEMINARY
Theology M,O

## CONCORDIA SEMINARY
Theology M,D,O

## CONCORDIA THEOLOGICAL SEMINARY
Theology M,D

## CONCORDIA UNIVERSITY (CANADA)
Adult Education M,O
Aerospace/Aeronautical Engineering M
Anthropology M,D
Applied Arts and Design—General M,O
Art Education M,D
Art History M,D
Art Therapy M
Art/Fine Arts M
Biological and Biomedical Sciences—General M,D,O
Biotechnology M,D,O
Business Administration and Management—General M,D,O
Chemistry M,D
Child and Family Studies M
Civil Engineering M,D,O
Clinical Psychology D,O
Communication—General M,D,O
Computer and Information Systems Security M,D,O
Computer Art and Design M,O
Computer Engineering M,D
Computer Science M,D,O
Construction Engineering M,D,O
Cultural Anthropology M,D
Economic Development O
Economics M,D,O
Education—General M,O
Educational Media/Instructional Technology M,O
Electrical Engineering M,D
Engineering and Applied Sciences—General M,D,O
English as a Second Language M,O
English M,D
Environmental Engineering M,D,O
Environmental Management and Policy M,D,O
Exercise and Sports Science M
Film, Television, and Video Production M,D
Film, Television, and Video Theory and Criticism M,D
Finance and Banking M,D,O
French M,O
Game Design and Development M,D,O
Genomic Sciences M,D,O
Geography M,D,O
History M,D
Humanities D
Industrial/Management Engineering M,D,O
Interdisciplinary Studies M,D
Internet and Interactive Multimedia M,D,O
Jewish Studies M
Journalism M,O
Linguistics M,O
Marketing M,D,O
Mathematics Education M,D
Mathematics M,D
Mechanical Engineering M,D,O
Media Studies M,D,O
Music O
Organizational Management M,O
Philosophy M
Physics M,D
Political Science M,D
Psychology—General M
Public Administration M,D
Public Affairs O
Public Policy M,D
Religion M,D
Sociology M,D
Software Engineering M,D,O
Statistics M,D
Supply Chain Management M,D,O
Systems Engineering M,D,O
Telecommunications Management M,D,O
Textile Design M
Theology M
Therapies—Dance, Drama, and Music M
Translation and Interpretation M,O
Urban and Regional Planning O
Urban Studies M,D,O
Writing M

## CONCORDIA UNIVERSITY (UNITED STATES)
Art Education M,D
Business Administration and Management—General M
Curriculum and Instruction M,D
Early Childhood Education M,D
Education—General M,D
Educational Leadership and Administration M,D
Educational Media/Instructional Technology M,D
Elementary Education M,D
English as a Second Language M,D
Environmental Education M,D
Health Education M,D
Higher Education M,D
Law D
Mathematics Education M,D
Physical Education M,D
Reading Education M,D
Science Education M,D
Secondary Education M,D
Social Psychology M
Social Sciences Education M,D
Vocational and Technical Education M,D

## CONCORDIA UNIVERSITY ANN ARBOR
Curriculum and Instruction M
Educational Leadership and Administration M
Organizational Management M

## CONCORDIA UNIVERSITY CHICAGO
Business Administration and Management—General M,D
Counseling Psychology M
Counselor Education M
Curriculum and Instruction M
Early Childhood Education M
Education—General M
Educational Leadership and Administration M,D
Educational Media/Instructional Technology M
Elementary Education M
Exercise and Sports Science M
Gerontology M
Human Services M
Music M
Reading Education M
Religion M
Religious Education M
Secondary Education M

## CONCORDIA UNIVERSITY IRVINE
Applied Social Research M
Business Administration and Management—General M
Counselor Education M
Cultural Studies M
Curriculum and Instruction M
Education—General M
Educational Leadership and Administration M
Educational Media/Instructional Technology M
Health Services Management and Hospital Administration M
International Affairs M
Nursing—General M
Physical Education M
Religion M
Sports Management M
Theology M

## CONCORDIA UNIVERSITY, NEBRASKA
Computer and Information Systems Security M
Computer Science M
Early Childhood Education M
Education—General M
Educational Leadership and Administration M
Elementary Education M
Pastoral Ministry and Counseling M
Reading Education M
Religious Education M
Secondary Education M

## CONCORDIA UNIVERSITY OF EDMONTON
Computer and Information Systems Security M
Religion M
Theology M

## CONCORDIA UNIVERSITY, ST. PAUL
Allied Health—General M,D
Business Administration and Management—General M
Child and Family Studies M
Computer and Information Systems Security M
Corporate and Organizational Communication M
Criminal Justice and Criminology M
Curriculum and Instruction M,D,O
Early Childhood Education M,D,O
Education—General M,D,O
Educational Leadership and Administration M,D,O
Educational Media/Instructional Technology M,D,O
Exercise and Sports Science M,D
Health Services Management and Hospital Administration M
Human Resources Management M
Human Services M
Organizational Management M
Physical Therapy M,D
Reading Education M,D,O
Special Education M,D,O
Sports Management M,D
Writing M

## CONCORDIA UNIVERSITY TEXAS
Education—General M

## CONCORDIA UNIVERSITY WISCONSIN
Art Education M
Business Administration and Management—General M
Child and Family Studies M
Corporate and Organizational Communication M
Counselor Education M
Early Childhood Education M
Education—General M
Educational Leadership and Administration M
Environmental Education M
Family Nurse Practitioner Studies M,D
Finance and Banking M
Health Education M,D
Health Services Management and Hospital Administration M
Human Resources Management M
International Business M
Management Information Systems M
Marketing M
Music M
Nursing—General M,D
Occupational Therapy M
Organizational Management M
Pharmacy M,D
Physical Therapy D
Public Administration M
Reading Education M
Rehabilitation Sciences M
Risk Management M
Social Work M
Special Education M

## CONCORD LAW SCHOOL
Law D

## CONCORD UNIVERSITY
Education—General M
Educational Leadership and Administration M
Health Promotion M
Reading Education M
Social Work M
Special Education M

## CONSERVATORIO DE MUSICA DE PUERTO RICO
Music Education M
Music O

## CONVERSE COLLEGE
Art Education M
Education of the Gifted M
Educational Leadership and Administration M,O
Elementary Education M
English Education M
English M
History M
Liberal Studies M
Marriage and Family Therapy M
Mathematics Education M
Middle School Education M
Music Education M
Music M
Political Science M
Reading Education O
Science Education M
Secondary Education M
Social Sciences Education M
Special Education M
Writing M

## THE CONWAY SCHOOL
Landscape Architecture M

## COOPER UNION FOR THE ADVANCEMENT OF SCIENCE AND ART
Architecture M
Chemical Engineering M
Civil Engineering M
Electrical Engineering M
Engineering and Applied Sciences—General M
Mechanical Engineering M

## COPENHAGEN BUSINESS SCHOOL
Business Administration and Management—General M,D
Economics M,D
Health Services Management and Hospital Administration M,D
International Business M,D
Logistics M,D
Management Information Systems M,D
Public Administration M,D

## COPPIN STATE UNIVERSITY
Addictions/Substance Abuse Counseling M
Adult Education M
Criminal Justice and Criminology M
Curriculum and Instruction M
Education—General M
Family Nurse Practitioner Studies M,O
Human Services M
Nursing—General M,O
Rehabilitation Counseling M
Special Education M

## CORBAN UNIVERSITY
Business Administration and Management—General M
Education—General M
Nonprofit Management M
Pastoral Ministry and Counseling M,D,O
Theology M,D,O

## CORNELL UNIVERSITY
Accounting M,D
Adult Education M,D
Aerospace/Aeronautical Engineering M,D
African Studies M,D
African-American Studies M,D
Agricultural Economics and Agribusiness M,D
Agricultural Education M,D
Agricultural Engineering M,D
Agronomy and Soil Sciences M,D
American Studies M,D
Analytical Chemistry D
Animal Behavior D
Animal Sciences M,D
Anthropology D
Applied Economics M,D
Applied Mathematics M,D
Applied Physics M,D
Applied Statistics M,D
Archaeology M,D
Architectural History M,D
Architecture M,D
Art History D
Art/Fine Arts M
Artificial Intelligence/Robotics M,D
Asian Languages M,D
Asian Studies M,D
Astronomy D
Astrophysics D
Atmospheric Sciences M,D
Biochemical Engineering M,D
Biochemistry M,D
Bioengineering M,D
Biological and Biomedical Sciences—General D
Biological Anthropology D
Biomedical Engineering M,D
Biometry M,D
Biophysics D
Biopsychology D
Biotechnology M,D
Business Administration and Management—General M,D
Cell Biology D
Chemical Engineering M,D
Chemical Physics D
Chemistry D
Child and Family Studies M,D
Civil Engineering M,D
Classics D
Clothing and Textiles M,D
Cognitive Sciences D
Communication—General M,D
Comparative Literature D
Computational Biology D
Computational Sciences M,D
Computer Art and Design M,D
Computer Engineering M,D
Computer Science M,D
Conflict Resolution and Mediation/Peace Studies M,D
Conservation Biology M,D
Consumer Economics M,D
Corporate and Organizational Communication M,D
Cultural Anthropology D
Cultural Studies M,D
Curriculum and Instruction M,D
Demography and Population Studies M,D
Developmental Biology D
Developmental Psychology M,D
East European and Russian Studies M,D
Ecology M,D
Economic Development M,D
Economics M,D
Education—General M,D
Educational Policy M,D
Electrical Engineering M,D
Energy and Power Engineering M,D
Engineering and Applied Sciences—General M,D
Engineering Management M,D
Engineering Physics M,D
English M,D
Entomology M,D
Environmental Design M
Environmental Engineering M,D
Environmental Management and Policy M,D
Environmental Sciences M,D
Ergonomics and Human Factors M
Ethnic Studies M,D
Evolutionary Biology D
Experimental Psychology D
Facilities Management M
Finance and Banking D
Fish, Game, and Wildlife Management M,D
Food Science and Technology M,D
Foreign Languages Education M,D
Forestry M,D
French D
Gender Studies M,D
Genetics D
Genomic Sciences D
Geochemistry M,D
Geology M,D
Geophysics M,D
Geosciences M,D
Geotechnical Engineering M,D
German M,D
Health Communication M,D
Health Services Management and Hospital Administration M,D
Hispanic and Latin American Languages D
Historic Preservation M,D
History of Science and Technology M,D
History M,D
Horticulture M,D
Hospitality Management M,D
Human Development M,D
Human Resources Management M,D
Human-Computer Interaction M,D
Hydrology M,D
Industrial and Labor Relations M,D

Industrial/Management Engineering M,D
Information Science D
Information Studies D
Inorganic Chemistry D
Interior Design M
International Affairs D
Italian D
Jewish Studies M,D
Landscape Architecture M
Latin American Studies M,D
Law M,D
Limnology D
Linguistics M,D
Manufacturing Engineering M,D
Marine Geology M,D
Marine Sciences M,D
Marketing D
Materials Engineering M,D
Materials Sciences M,D
Mathematics Education M,D
Mathematics D
Mechanical Engineering M,D
Mechanics M,D
Media Studies M,D
Medieval and Renaissance Studies M,D
Microbiology D
Mineralogy M,D
Molecular Biology M,D
Music M,D
Nanotechnology M,D
Natural Resources M,D
Near and Middle Eastern Studies M,D
Neurobiology D
Nutrition M,D
Oceanography D
Operations Research M,D
Organic Chemistry D
Organizational Behavior M,D
Paleontology M,D
Philosophy D
Photography M,D
Physical Chemistry D
Physics M,D
Physiology M,D
Planetary and Space Sciences D
Plant Biology M,D
Plant Molecular Biology M,D
Plant Pathology M,D
Plant Physiology M,D
Plant Sciences M,D
Political Science D
Polymer Science and Engineering M,D
Psychology—General D
Public Affairs M
Public Policy M,D
Real Estate M
Religion M,D
Romance Languages M,D
Rural Sociology M,D
Scandinavian Languages M,D
Secondary Education M,D
Slavic Languages M,D
Social Psychology M,D
Social Work M,D
Sociology M,D
Spanish D
Statistics M,D
Structural Engineering M,D
Sustainable Development M,D
Systems Engineering M,D
Textile Design M,D
Textile Sciences and Engineering M,D
Theater D
Theoretical Chemistry D
Theoretical Physics M,D
Toxicology M,D
Transportation and Highway Engineering M,D
Urban and Regional Planning M,D
Urban Design M,D
Veterinary Medicine D
Viticulture and Enology M,D
Water Resources Engineering M,D
Water Resources M,D
Western European Studies M,D
Women's Studies M,D
Writing M,D

### CORNERSTONE UNIVERSITY
Business Administration and Management—General M,O
Education—General M,O
English as a Second Language M,O

### COVENANT COLLEGE
Education—General M

### COVENANT THEOLOGICAL SEMINARY
Pastoral Ministry and Counseling M,D,O
Theology M,D,O

### COX COLLEGE
Family Nurse Practitioner Studies M
Nursing and Healthcare Administration M
Nursing Education M
Nursing—General M
Occupational Therapy M

### CRANBROOK ACADEMY OF ART
Architecture M
Art/Fine Arts M
Photography M
Textile Design M

### CRANDALL UNIVERSITY
Education—General M
Organizational Management M
Reading Education M

### CREIGHTON UNIVERSITY
Accounting M,D
Adult Nursing M,D,O
Allied Health—General M,D
Allopathic Medicine D
Anatomy M
Bioethics M
Biological and Biomedical Sciences—General M,D
Business Administration and Management—General M,D
Business Analytics M,D
Conflict Resolution and Mediation/Peace Studies M,D,O
Counselor Education M
Dentistry D
Education—General M
Educational Leadership and Administration M,D
Elementary Education M
Emergency Medical Services M
English M
Family Nurse Practitioner Studies M,D,O
Finance and Banking M,D
Gerontological Nursing M,D,O
Health Promotion M
Health Services Management and Hospital Administration M,D
Immunology M,D
Investment Management M,D
Law M,D,O
Maternal and Child/Neonatal Nursing M,D,O
Medical Microbiology M,D
Nursing and Healthcare Administration M,D,O
Nursing—General M,D,O
Occupational Therapy D
Organizational Management M
Pediatric Nursing M,D,O
Pharmaceutical Sciences M,D
Pharmacology M,D
Pharmacy D
Physical Therapy D
Physics M
Psychiatric Nursing M,D,O
Public Health—General M
School Psychology M
Secondary Education M
Writing M

### CRISWELL COLLEGE
Jewish Studies M
Pastoral Ministry and Counseling M
Theology M

### CROWN COLLEGE
Theology M

### CULVER-STOCKTON COLLEGE
Accounting M
Business Administration and Management—General M
Finance and Banking M

### CUMBERLAND UNIVERSITY
Business Administration and Management—General M
Education—General M
Public Administration M

### CUNY CRAIG NEWMARK GRADUATE SCHOOL OF JOURNALISM
Journalism M

### CURRY COLLEGE
Business Administration and Management—General M,O
Criminal Justice and Criminology M
Education—General M,O
Elementary Education M,O
Finance and Banking M,O
Foundations and Philosophy of Education M,O
Nursing—General M
Reading Education M,O
Special Education M,O

### CURTIS INSTITUTE OF MUSIC
Music M

### DAEMEN COLLEGE
Accounting M
Adult Nursing M,D,O
Business Administration and Management—General M
Community Health M
Early Childhood Education M
Education—General M
Epidemiology M
Health Education M
Health Services Management and Hospital Administration M
International Business M
Management Information Systems M
Marketing M
Medical/Surgical Nursing M,D,O
Middle School Education M
Nonprofit Management M
Nursing and Healthcare Administration M,D,O
Nursing Education M,D,O
Nursing—General M,D,O
Physical Therapy D,O
Physician Assistant Studies M
Public Health—General M
Social Work M
Special Education M

### DAKOTA STATE UNIVERSITY
Business Administration and Management—General M,D,O
Business Analytics M,D,O
Computer Science M,D,O
Education—General M
Educational Media/Instructional Technology M
Health Informatics M,D,O
Information Science M,D,O
Management Information Systems M,D,O

### DAKOTA WESLEYAN UNIVERSITY
Curriculum and Instruction M
Education—General M
Educational Leadership and Administration M
Secondary Education M

### DALHOUSIE UNIVERSITY
Agricultural Sciences—General M
Agronomy and Soil Sciences M
Allopathic Medicine M,D
Anatomy M,D
Animal Sciences M
Anthropology M,D
Applied Mathematics M,D
Aquaculture M
Architecture M
Biochemistry M,D
Bioengineering M,D
Bioinformatics M,D
Biological and Biomedical Sciences—General M,D
Biomedical Engineering M,D
Biophysics M,D
Botany M
Business Administration and Management—General M,O
Chemical Engineering M,D
Chemistry M,D
Civil Engineering M,D
Classics M,D
Clinical Psychology M,D
Communication Disorders M,D
Community Health M
Computer Engineering M,D
Computer Science M,D
Developmental Biology M,D
Ecology M
Economics M,D
Electrical Engineering M,D
Electronic Commerce M,D
Engineering and Applied Sciences—General M,D
English M,D
Environmental Biology M
Environmental Engineering M,D
Environmental Management and Policy M
Environmental Sciences M
Epidemiology M
Finance and Banking M
Food Science and Technology M,D
French M,D
Geosciences M,D
German M
Health Education M
Health Services Management and Hospital Administration M,D
History M,D
Horticulture M
Human-Computer Interaction M,D
Immunology M,D
Industrial/Management Engineering M,D
Information Studies M
Interdisciplinary Studies D
International Development M
Internet Engineering M,D
Kinesiology and Movement Studies M
Law M,D
Leisure Studies M
Library Science M
Management Information Systems M
Marine Affairs M
Mathematics M,D
Mechanical Engineering M,D
Medical Informatics M,D
Microbiology M,D
Mineral/Mining Engineering M,D
Music M
Natural Resources M
Neuroscience M,D
Nursing—General M,D
Occupational Therapy M
Oceanography M,D
Oral and Dental Sciences M
Pathology M,D
Pharmacology M,D
Philosophy M,D
Physical Therapy M
Physics M,D
Physiology M,D
Plant Pathology M
Plant Physiology M
Political Science M,D
Psychology—General M,D
Public Administration M,O
Rural Planning and Studies M
Social Work M
Sociology M,D
Statistics M,D
Urban and Regional Planning M
Water Resources M

### DALLAS BAPTIST UNIVERSITY
Accounting M
Asian Studies M
Business Administration and Management—General M,D
Communication—General M
Conflict Resolution and Mediation/Peace Studies M
Counseling Psychology M
Counselor Education M
Criminal Justice and Criminology M
Curriculum and Instruction M
Distance Education Development M
Early Childhood Education M,D
Education—General M
Educational Leadership and Administration M,D
Educational Media/Instructional Technology M
Elementary Education M
English as a Second Language M
Entrepreneurship M
Finance and Banking M
Health Services Management and Hospital Administration M
Higher Education M,D
Human Resources Management M
Interdisciplinary Studies M
International Affairs M
International Business M
Kinesiology and Movement Studies M
Liberal Studies M
Management Information Systems M
Missions and Missiology M
Multilingual and Multicultural Education M
Nonprofit Management M
Organizational Management M,D
Pastoral Ministry and Counseling M,D
Reading Education M
Religion M
Religious Education M
Secondary Education M
Special Education M
Sports Management M
Student Affairs M
Theology M
Western European Studies M

### DALLAS INTERNATIONAL UNIVERSITY
Linguistics M,O
Multilingual and Multicultural Education M,O

### DALLAS THEOLOGICAL SEMINARY
Adult Education M,D,O
Child and Family Studies M,D,O
Educational Leadership and Administration M,D,O
Jewish Studies M,D,O
Media Studies M,D,O
Missions and Missiology M,D,O
Pastoral Ministry and Counseling M,D,O
Philosophy M,D,O
Religion M,D,O
Religious Education M,D,O
Theology M,D,O

### DANIEL MORGAN GRADUATE SCHOOL OF NATIONAL SECURITY
National Security M

### DAOIST TRADITIONS COLLEGE OF CHINESE MEDICAL ARTS
Acupuncture and Oriental Medicine M,D

### DARTMOUTH COLLEGE
Allopathic Medicine D
Astronomy D
Biochemistry M,D
Biological and Biomedical Sciences—General D
Biomedical Engineering M,D
Biostatistics M,D
Business Administration and Management—General M
Cell Biology D
Chemical Engineering M,D
Chemistry M,D
Cognitive Sciences D
Comparative Literature M
Computer Engineering M,D
Computer Science M,D
Ecology D
Electrical Engineering M,D
Energy and Power Engineering M,D
Engineering and Applied Sciences—General M,D
Engineering Management M
Entrepreneurship D
Environmental Biology D
Epidemiology M,D
Evolutionary Biology D
Geosciences M,D
Health Informatics M,D
Health Services Management and Hospital Administration M,D
Health Services Research M,D
Liberal Studies M
Materials Engineering M,D
Materials Sciences M,D
Mathematics M,D
Mechanical Engineering M,D
Microbiology D
Molecular Biology D
Molecular Medicine D
Molecular Pathogenesis D
Music M
Neuroscience D
Physical Chemistry M,D
Physics D
Psychology—General D
Public Health—General M
Sustainable Development D
Systems Engineering M,D

### DAVENPORT UNIVERSITY
Accounting M
Business Administration and Management—General M

*M—masters degree; D—doctorate; O—other advanced degree; *—Close-Up and/or Display*

Computer and Information Systems Security M
Finance and Banking M
Health Services Management and Hospital Administration M
Human Resources Management M
Management Strategy and Policy M
Occupational Therapy M
Public Health—General M

### DEFIANCE COLLEGE
Business Administration and Management—General M
Education—General M
Management Strategy and Policy M

### DELAWARE STATE UNIVERSITY
Adult Education M
Applied Mathematics M,D
Art Education M
Biological and Biomedical Sciences—General M
Business Administration and Management—General M
Chemistry M,D
Curriculum and Instruction M
Education—General M,D
Educational Leadership and Administration M,D
Exercise and Sports Science M
Foreign Languages Education M
Historic Preservation M
Mathematics Education M
Mathematics M
Natural Resources M
Neuroscience M,D
Nursing—General M
Optical Sciences M,D
Physics M,D
Plant Sciences M
Reading Education M
Science Education M,D
Social Work M
Special Education M
Theoretical Physics D

### DELAWARE VALLEY UNIVERSITY
Accounting M
Agricultural Economics and Agribusiness M
Business Administration and Management—General M
Counseling Psychology M
Criminal Justice and Criminology M
Curriculum and Instruction M
Developmental Psychology M
Educational Leadership and Administration M
Educational Media/Instructional Technology M
Entrepreneurship M
Finance and Banking M
Human Resources Management M
International Business M
Social Psychology M
Supply Chain Management M

### DELL'ARTE INTERNATIONAL SCHOOL OF PHYSICAL THEATRE
Theater M

### DELTA STATE UNIVERSITY
Accounting M
Aviation Management M
Biological and Biomedical Sciences—General M
Business Administration and Management—General M
Counselor Education M,D,O
Criminal Justice and Criminology M
Education—General M,D,O
Educational Leadership and Administration M,D,O
Elementary Education M,D,O
English Education M
Exercise and Sports Science M
Family Nurse Practitioner Studies M,D
Gender Studies M
Health Education M
Health Services Management and Hospital Administration M,D
Higher Education D
Liberal Studies M
Nursing Education M,D
Nursing—General M,D
Philosophy M
Physical Education M
Recreation and Park Management M
Religion M
Secondary Education M,D,O
Social Sciences Education M
Special Education M
Urban and Regional Planning M

### DENVER SEMINARY
Marriage and Family Therapy M,D,O
Pastoral Ministry and Counseling M,D,O
Religion M,D,O
Theology M,D,O

### DEPAUL UNIVERSITY
Accounting M,D
Adult Education M
Advertising and Public Relations M
Applied Economics M,D
Applied Mathematics M,D
Applied Statistics M,D
Biological and Biomedical Sciences—General M,D
Business Administration and Management—General M,D
Business Analytics M,D
Chemistry M,D
Chinese M
Clinical Psychology M,D
Communication—General M
Computer and Information Systems Security M,D
Computer Art and Design M,D
Computer Science M,D
Corporate and Organizational Communication M
Counseling Psychology M,D
Counselor Education M,D
Curriculum and Instruction M,D
Data Science/Data Analytics M,D
Early Childhood Education M,D
Economics M,D
Education—General M,D
Educational Leadership and Administration M,D
Electronic Commerce M,D
Elementary Education M,D
English M
Entrepreneurship M,D
Environmental Sciences M,D
Ethnic Studies M
Family Nurse Practitioner Studies M,D
Film, Television, and Video Production M,D
Film, Television, and Video Theory and Criticism M
Finance and Banking M,D
Foreign Languages Education M,D
Foundations and Philosophy of Education M,D
French M
Game Design and Development M,D
Gender Studies M
German M
Health Communication M
Health Informatics M,D
Health Law M,D
Higher Education M,D
History M
Hospitality Management M,D
Human Resources Management M,D
Human-Computer Interaction M,D
Information Science M,D
Intellectual Property Law M,D
Interdisciplinary Studies M
International Affairs M
International Business M,D
Internet and Interactive Multimedia M,D
Italian M
Japanese M
Journalism M
Law M,D
Liberal Studies M
Management Information Systems M,D
Management Strategy and Policy M,D
Marketing M,D
Mathematical and Computational Finance M,D
Mathematics Education M,D
Mathematics M,D
Media Studies M
Middle School Education M,D
Multilingual and Multicultural Education M,D
Music Education M,O
Music M,O
Near and Middle Eastern Languages M
Nonprofit Management M
Nursing—General M,D
Physical Education M,D
Physics M,D
Polymer Science and Engineering M,D
Psychology—General M,D
Public Administration M
Public Health—General M
Public Policy M
Publishing M
Reading Education M,D
Real Estate M,D
Rhetoric M
Risk Management M,D
School Psychology M,D
Science Education M,D
Secondary Education M,D
Social Work M
Sociology M
Software Engineering M,D
Spanish M
Special Education M,D
Student Affairs M,D
Supply Chain Management M,D
Sustainability Management M,D
Sustainable Development M
Taxation M,D
Theater M
Urban Design M
Women's Studies M
Writing M

### DEREE - THE AMERICAN COLLEGE OF GREECE
Applied Psychology M
Communication—General M
Marketing M

### DESALES UNIVERSITY
Accounting M
Business Administration and Management—General M
Computer and Information Systems Security M,O
Criminal Justice and Criminology M,O
Data Science/Data Analytics M,O
Education—General M,O
Educational Media/Instructional Technology M,O
English as a Second Language M,O
Family Nurse Practitioner Studies M,D,O
Finance and Banking M
Forensic Sciences M,O
Gerontology M,D,O
Health Informatics M,O
Health Services Management and Hospital Administration M
Human Resources Management M
Management Information Systems M,O
Marketing M
Nurse Anesthesia M,D,O
Nurse Midwifery M,D,O
Nursing and Healthcare Administration M,D,O
Nursing Education M,D,O
Nursing—General M,D,O
Project Management M,O
Secondary Education M,O
Special Education M,O
Supply Chain Management M

### DES MOINES UNIVERSITY
Anatomy M
Biological and Biomedical Sciences—General M
Health Services Management and Hospital Administration M
Osteopathic Medicine D
Physical Therapy D
Physician Assistant Studies M
Podiatric Medicine D
Public Health—General M

### DEVRY COLLEGE OF NEW YORK–MIDTOWN MANHATTAN CAMPUS
Business Administration and Management—General M

### DEVRY UNIVERSITY–ALPHARETTA CAMPUS
Business Administration and Management—General M

### DEVRY UNIVERSITY–ARLINGTON CAMPUS
Business Administration and Management—General M

### DEVRY UNIVERSITY–CHARLOTTE CAMPUS
Business Administration and Management—General M

### DEVRY UNIVERSITY–CHESAPEAKE CAMPUS
Business Administration and Management—General M

### DEVRY UNIVERSITY–CHICAGO CAMPUS
Business Administration and Management—General M

### DEVRY UNIVERSITY–CHICAGO LOOP CAMPUS
Business Administration and Management—General M

### DEVRY UNIVERSITY–CINCINNATI CAMPUS
Business Administration and Management—General M

### DEVRY UNIVERSITY–COLUMBUS CAMPUS
Business Administration and Management—General M

### DEVRY UNIVERSITY–DECATUR CAMPUS
Business Administration and Management—General M

### DEVRY UNIVERSITY–FOLSOM CAMPUS
Accounting M
Business Administration and Management—General M
Curriculum and Instruction M
Educational Leadership and Administration M
Educational Media/Instructional Technology M
Finance and Banking M
Higher Education M
Human Resources Management M
Management Information Systems M
Project Management M
Public Administration M

### DEVRY UNIVERSITY–FREMONT CAMPUS
Business Administration and Management—General M

### DEVRY UNIVERSITY–FT. WASHINGTON CAMPUS
Business Administration and Management—General M

### DEVRY UNIVERSITY–HENDERSON CAMPUS
Business Administration and Management—General M

### DEVRY UNIVERSITY–IRVING CAMPUS
Business Administration and Management—General M

### DEVRY UNIVERSITY–JACKSONVILLE CAMPUS
Business Administration and Management—General M

### DEVRY UNIVERSITY–LONG BEACH CAMPUS
Business Administration and Management—General M

### DEVRY UNIVERSITY–MIRAMAR CAMPUS
Business Administration and Management—General M

### DEVRY UNIVERSITY–MORRISVILLE CAMPUS
Business Administration and Management—General M

### DEVRY UNIVERSITY–NASHVILLE CAMPUS
Business Administration and Management—General M

### DEVRY UNIVERSITY–NORTH BRUNSWICK CAMPUS
Business Administration and Management—General M

### DEVRY UNIVERSITY ONLINE
Business Administration and Management—General M

### DEVRY UNIVERSITY–ORLANDO CAMPUS
Business Administration and Management—General M

### DEVRY UNIVERSITY–PHOENIX CAMPUS
Business Administration and Management—General M

### DEVRY UNIVERSITY–POMONA CAMPUS
Business Administration and Management—General M

### DEVRY UNIVERSITY–SAN DIEGO CAMPUS
Business Administration and Management—General M,O

### DEVRY UNIVERSITY–SEVEN HILLS CAMPUS
Business Administration and Management—General M,O

### DEVRY UNIVERSITY–TINLEY PARK CAMPUS
Business Administration and Management—General M

### DICKINSON STATE UNIVERSITY
Early Childhood Education M
Education—General M
Entrepreneurship M
Middle School Education M
Reading Education M

### DIGIPEN INSTITUTE OF TECHNOLOGY
Computer Art and Design M
Computer Science M

### DIVINE MERCY UNIVERSITY
Clinical Psychology M,D
Psychology—General M

### DOANE UNIVERSITY
Business Administration and Management—General M
Counselor Education M
Curriculum and Instruction M,D,O
Education—General M,D,O
Educational Leadership and Administration M,D,O
School Psychology M,D,O

### DOMINICAN COLLEGE
Accounting M
Allied Health—General M,D
Business Administration and Management—General M
Education—General M
Elementary Education M
Family Nurse Practitioner Studies M,D
Health Services Management and Hospital Administration M
Occupational Therapy M
Physical Therapy M,D
Special Education M

### DOMINICAN HOUSE OF STUDIES, PONTIFICAL FACULTY OF THE IMMACULATE CONCEPTION
Theology M,D,O

### DOMINICAN SCHOOL OF PHILOSOPHY AND THEOLOGY
Philosophy M,O
Theology M,O

### DOMINICAN UNIVERSITY
Accounting M
Business Administration and Management—General M
Early Childhood Education M
Education—General M
Elementary Education M
English as a Second Language M
Information Studies M,D,O
Management Information Systems M,D,O
Reading Education M
Secondary Education M
Social Work M
Special Education M

### DOMINICAN UNIVERSITY OF CALIFORNIA
Biological and Biomedical Sciences—General M
Business Administration and Management—General M
Clinical Laboratory Sciences/Medical Technology M
Education—General M
Liberal Studies M
Occupational Therapy M
Special Education M

### DONGGUK UNIVERSITY LOS ANGELES
Acupuncture and Oriental Medicine M

### DORDT UNIVERSITY
Education—General M

### DRAGON RISES COLLEGE OF ORIENTAL MEDICINE
Acupuncture and Oriental Medicine M

### DRAKE UNIVERSITY
Accounting M
Applied Behavior Analysis M,D,O
Athletic Training and Sports Medicine M,D
Business Administration and Management—General M
Communication—General M
Counselor Education M,D,O
Education—General M,D,O
Educational Leadership and Administration M,D,O
Law M,D
Pharmacy M,D
Public Administration M
Public Affairs M
Reading Education M,D,O

### DREW UNIVERSITY
American Studies M,D,O
Art/Fine Arts M,D,O
Biological and Biomedical Sciences—General M,D,O
Chemistry M,D,O
Community College Education M,D,O
Conflict Resolution and Mediation/Peace Studies M,D,O
Cultural Studies M,D,O
Education—General M,D,O
Elementary Education M,D,O
English M,D,O
Finance and Banking M,D,O
French M,D,O
Health Education M,D,O
Health Services Management and Hospital Administration M,D,O
History M,D,O
Italian M,D,O
Liberal Studies M,D,O
Mathematics M,D,O
Public History M,D,O
Religion M,D,O
Secondary Education M,D,O
Special Education M,D,O
Theology M,D,O
Western European Studies M,D,O
Writing M,D,O

### DREXEL UNIVERSITY
Accounting M,D,O
Acute Care/Critical Care Nursing M
Allied Health—General M,D,O
Allopathic Medicine D
Applied Arts and Design—General M,D
Applied Behavior Analysis M,D
Architectural Engineering M,D
Archives/Archival Administration M
Art Therapy M,O
Arts Administration M
Biochemical Engineering M
Biochemistry M,D
Biological and Biomedical Sciences—General M,D,O
Biomedical Engineering M,D
Biopsychology M,D
Biostatistics M,D,O
Business Administration and Management—General M,D,O
Cell Biology M,D
Chemical Engineering M,D
Chemistry M,D
Civil Engineering M,D
Clinical Psychology D
Clothing and Textiles M
Communication—General M
Computer Art and Design M,D
Computer Engineering M
Computer Science M,D,O
Construction Management M
Corporate and Organizational Communication M
Curriculum and Instruction M,D
Economics M,D,O
Education—General M,D
Educational Leadership and Administration M,D
Educational Media/Instructional Technology M,D
Electrical Engineering M
Emergency Management M
Emergency Medical Services M
Engineering and Applied Sciences—General M,D,O
Engineering Management M,O
Entrepreneurship M
Environmental Engineering M,D
Environmental Management and Policy M
Environmental Sciences M,D
Epidemiology M,D,O
Family Nurse Practitioner Studies M
Film, Television, and Video Production M
Finance and Banking M,D,O
Food Science and Technology M
Forensic Psychology D
Genetics M,D
Geotechnical Engineering M,D
Health Law M,D
Health Psychology D
Higher Education M,D
History of Science and Technology M
Homeland Security M
Hospitality Management M
Human Resources Development M,D
Hydraulics M,D
Hydrology M,D
Immunology M,D
Information Science M,D,O
Intellectual Property Law M,D
Interior Design M
International and Comparative Education M,D
Law M,D
Library Science M,D,O
Management Information Systems M,D,O
Management Strategy and Policy M,D,O
Marketing M,D,O
Marriage and Family Therapy M,D
Mass Communication M
Materials Engineering M,D
Mathematics M,D
Mechanical Engineering M,D
Mechanics M,D
Media Studies M
Microbiology M,D
Molecular Biology M,D
Molecular Medicine M
Neuroscience M,D
Nurse Anesthesia M
Nursing and Healthcare Administration M
Nursing Education M
Nursing—General M,D
Organizational Behavior M,D,O
Pathobiology M,D
Pediatric Nursing M
Pharmaceutical Sciences M
Pharmacology M,D
Physical Therapy M,D,O
Physician Assistant Studies M
Physics M,D
Project Management M
Psychiatric Nursing M
Psychology—General M,D
Public Health—General M,D,O
Quantitative Analysis M,D,O
Real Estate M
Software Engineering M,D,O
Special Education M,D
Sports and Entertainment Law M,D
Sports Management M
Structural Engineering M,D
Technical Communication M
Technical Writing M
Telecommunications M
Textile Design M
Therapies—Dance, Drama, and Music M,O
Urban Design M
Veterinary Sciences M
Women's Health Nursing M

### DRURY UNIVERSITY
Business Administration and Management—General M
Communication—General M
Computer and Information Systems Security O
Curriculum and Instruction M
Education—General M
Educational Leadership and Administration M
Educational Media/Instructional Technology M
Elementary Education M
Middle School Education M
Nonprofit Management M
Reading Education M
Secondary Education M
Special Education M

### DUKE UNIVERSITY
Accounting D
Acute Care/Critical Care Nursing M,D,O
Adult Nursing M,D,O
Allopathic Medicine D
Anatomy D
Art History M,D
Art/Fine Arts M,D
Asian Studies M,O
Biochemistry D
Bioethics M
Bioinformatics D,O
Biological and Biomedical Sciences—General D
Biological Anthropology D
Biomedical Engineering M,D
Biopsychology D
Business Administration and Management—General D
Cancer Biology/Oncology D
Cell Biology D,O
Chemistry D
Civil Engineering M,D
Classics D
Clinical Psychology D
Clinical Research M
Cognitive Sciences D
Comparative Literature D
Computational Biology D,O
Computational Sciences M,D
Computer Engineering M,D
Computer Science M,D
Cultural Anthropology D
Developmental Biology O
Developmental Psychology D
Ecology D,O
Economics M,D
Education—General M
Electrical Engineering M,D
Engineering and Applied Sciences—General M
Engineering Management M
English D
Environmental and Occupational Health O
Environmental Engineering M,D
Environmental Management and Policy D
Environmental Sciences M,D
Experimental Psychology D
Family Nurse Practitioner Studies M,D,O
Finance and Banking D
French D
Genetics D
Genomic Sciences D
Geology M,D
Geosciences M,D
German D
Gerontological Nursing M,D,O
Gerontology M,D,O
Health Informatics M
Health Psychology D
History M,D
Human Development D
Humanities M
Immunology D
Industrial and Manufacturing Management D
International Development M
International Health M
Italian D
Latin American Studies M,D
Law M,D
Liberal Studies M
Management Strategy and Policy D
Marine Sciences M,D
Marketing D
Materials Engineering M
Materials Sciences M,D
Maternal and Child/Neonatal Nursing M,D,O
Mathematics D
Mechanical Engineering M,D
Media Studies M
Medical Physics M,D
Microbiology D
Molecular Biology D,O
Molecular Biophysics O
Molecular Genetics D
Music D
Natural Resources M,D
Neurobiology D
Neuroscience D,O
Nurse Anesthesia M,D,O
Nursing and Healthcare Administration M,D,O
Nursing Education M,D,O
Nursing Informatics M,D,O
Nursing—General D
Optical Sciences M
Organizational Management D
Paleontology D
Pathology M,D
Pediatric Nursing M,D,O
Pharmacology D
Philosophy D
Photonics M
Physical Therapy D
Physician Assistant Studies M
Physics D
Political Science M,D
Psychology—General D
Public Policy M,D
Quantitative Analysis D
Religion M,D
Slavic Languages M,O
Sociology M,D
Spanish D
Statistics M,D
Structural Biology O
Theology M,D
Toxicology O
Women's Health Nursing M,D,O

### DUNLAP-STONE UNIVERSITY
Law M

### DUQUESNE UNIVERSITY
Accounting M
Allied Health—General M,D,O
Bioethics M,D,O
Biological and Biomedical Sciences—General D
Biotechnology M
Business Administration and Management—General M
Chemistry D
Classics M
Clinical Psychology M,D,O
Communication Disorders M,D
Communication—General M,D
Counseling Psychology M,D,O
Counselor Education M,D,O
Curriculum and Instruction M,O
Early Childhood Education M
Education—General M,D,O
Educational Leadership and Administration M,D,O
Educational Measurement and Evaluation M
Educational Media/Instructional Technology M,D,O
Elementary Education M
English as a Second Language M
English Education M
English M,D
Environmental Management and Policy M,O
Environmental Sciences M,O
Family Nurse Practitioner Studies M,O
Finance and Banking M
Foreign Languages Education M
Forensic Nursing M,O
Forensic Sciences M
Foundations and Philosophy of Education M
Health Services Management and Hospital Administration M,D
History M
Law M,D
Management Information Systems M
Marketing M
Marriage and Family Therapy M,D,O
Mathematics Education M
Mathematics M
Medicinal and Pharmaceutical Chemistry M,D
Middle School Education M
Music Education M,O
Music M,O
Nursing Education M,O
Nursing—General M,D,O
Occupational Therapy M,D
Organizational Management M
Pharmaceutical Administration M
Pharmaceutical Sciences M,D
Pharmacology M,D
Pharmacy D
Philosophy M,D
Physical Therapy M,D
Physician Assistant Studies M,D
Psychology—General D
Public History M
Reading Education M
Rehabilitation Sciences M,D
Rhetoric M,D
School Psychology M,D
Science Education M
Secondary Education M
Social Sciences Education M
Special Education M,D
Sports Management M
Supply Chain Management M
Sustainability Management M
Theology M,D

### D'YOUVILLE COLLEGE
Anatomy M
Business Administration and Management—General M
Chiropractic D
Education—General M,D
Educational Leadership and Administration M,D
Elementary Education M,D
Family Nurse Practitioner Studies M,D,O
Health Services Management and Hospital Administration M,D,O
International Business M
Nursing—General M,D,O
Nutrition M
Occupational Therapy M
Pharmacy D
Physical Therapy D,O
Physician Assistant Studies M
Secondary Education M,D
Special Education M,D

### EARLHAM COLLEGE
Education—General M

### EARLHAM SCHOOL OF RELIGION
Pastoral Ministry and Counseling M
Religion M
Theology M

### EAST CAROLINA UNIVERSITY
Accounting M
Addictions/Substance Abuse Counseling M,D,O
Adult Education M,O
Allied Health—General M,D,O
Allopathic Medicine D
American Studies M
Anatomy M,D
Anthropology M
Applied Economics M
Applied Physics M,D
Art Education M
Art/Fine Arts M
Biochemistry M,D
Biological and Biomedical Sciences—General M,D
Biomedical Engineering M
Biophysics M,D
Biotechnology M
Business Administration and Management—General M,D,O
Business Education M,O
Cell Biology M,D
Chemistry M
Child and Family Studies M,D
Child Development M,D
Clinical Psychology M,D,O
Communication Disorders M,D
Community College Education M,D,O
Comparative Literature M,D,O
Computer and Information Systems Security M,D,O
Computer Engineering M,D,O
Computer Science M,D,O
Construction Management M,O
Corporate and Organizational Communication M,D,O
Counselor Education M,D,O
Criminal Justice and Criminology M,O
Curriculum and Instruction M,O
Dentistry D
Distance Education Development M,O
Early Childhood Education M,D
Economic Development M,O
Education—General M,D,O
Educational Leadership and Administration M,D,O
Educational Media/Instructional Technology M,O
Elementary Education M,O
English as a Second Language M,D,O

*M—masters degree; D—doctorate; O—other advanced degree; *—Close-Up and/or Display*

| | |
|---|---|
| English Education | M,D,O |
| English | M,D,O |
| Environmental and Occupational Health | M,D,O |
| Exercise and Sports Science | M,D,O |
| Geographic Information Systems | M,O |
| Geography | M,O |
| Geology | M,O |
| Gerontology | M,O |
| Graphic Design | M |
| Health Communication | M,O |
| Health Education | M |
| Health Informatics | M,O |
| Health Physics/Radiological Health | M,D |
| Health Promotion | M |
| Health Psychology | M,D,O |
| Health Services Management and Hospital Administration | M,O |
| Higher Education | M,O |
| History | M |
| Hospitality Management | M,O |
| Hydrogeology | M,O |
| Illustration | M |
| Immunology | M,D |
| Industrial and Manufacturing Management | M,D,O |
| Industrial and Organizational Psychology | M,D,O |
| International Affairs | M,O |
| International and Comparative Education | M,O |
| Kinesiology and Movement Studies | M,D,O |
| Leisure Studies | M,O |
| Library Science | M,O |
| Linguistics | M,D,O |
| Logistics | M,D,O |
| Management Information Systems | M,D,O |
| Management of Technology | M,D,O |
| Marriage and Family Therapy | M,D |
| Maternal and Child Health | M,D,O |
| Mathematics Education | M,O |
| Mathematics | M |
| Medical Physics | M,D |
| Microbiology | M,D |
| Middle School Education | M |
| Military and Defense Studies | M |
| Molecular Biology | M,D |
| Music Education | M,O |
| Music | M,O |
| Nursing—General | M,D |
| Nutrition | M |
| Occupational Therapy | M,D,O |
| Pharmacology | M,D |
| Photography | M |
| Physical Education | M,D,O |
| Physical Therapy | D |
| Physician Assistant Studies | M |
| Physics | M,D |
| Physiology | M,D |
| Political Science | M,O |
| Public Administration | M,O |
| Public Health—General | M,D,O |
| Public History | M |
| Reading Education | M |
| Recreation and Park Management | M,O |
| Rehabilitation Counseling | M,D,O |
| Rehabilitation Sciences | M,D,O |
| Rhetoric | M,D,O |
| Rural Planning and Studies | M,O |
| Science Education | M,O |
| Social Sciences Education | M |
| Social Sciences | M,D,O |
| Social Work | M,O |
| Sociology | M |
| Software Engineering | M,O |
| Special Education | M,O |
| Sports Management | M,D,O |
| Statistics | M |
| Technical Communication | M,D,O |
| Telecommunications Management | M,D,O |
| Textile Design | M |
| Therapies—Dance, Drama, and Music | M,O |
| Toxicology | M,D |
| Urban and Regional Planning | M,O |
| Vocational and Technical Education | M,O |
| Western European Studies | M |
| Writing | M,D,O |

## EAST CENTRAL UNIVERSITY

| | |
|---|---|
| Accounting | M |
| Clinical Psychology | M |
| Criminal Justice and Criminology | M |
| Education—General | M |
| Human Resources Management | M |
| Psychology—General | M |
| Rehabilitation Counseling | M |

## EASTERN CONNECTICUT STATE UNIVERSITY

| | |
|---|---|
| Accounting | M |
| Early Childhood Education | M |
| Education—General | M |
| Educational Media/Instructional Technology | M |
| Elementary Education | M |
| Organizational Management | M |
| Secondary Education | M |

## EASTERN ILLINOIS UNIVERSITY

| | |
|---|---|
| Accounting | M |
| Art Education | M |
| Art/Fine Arts | M |
| Biological and Biomedical Sciences—General | M |
| Business Administration and Management—General | M |
| Chemistry | M |
| Clinical Psychology | M,O |
| Communication Disorders | M |
| Communication—General | M |
| Computer and Information Systems Security | M |
| Computer Science | M |
| Counselor Education | M |
| Curriculum and Instruction | M |
| Early Childhood Education | M |
| Economics | M |
| Education—General | M,O |
| Educational Leadership and Administration | M,O |
| Elementary Education | M |
| Energy Management and Policy | M |
| Engineering and Applied Sciences—General | M,O |
| English | M |
| Exercise and Sports Science | M |
| Geographic Information Systems | M |
| Gerontology | M |
| History | M |
| Human Development | M |
| Human Services | M |
| Kinesiology and Movement Studies | M |
| Mathematics Education | M |
| Mathematics | M |
| Middle School Education | M |
| Music Education | M |
| Music | M |
| Nutrition | M |
| Political Science | M |
| Psychology—General | M,O |
| School Psychology | M,O |
| Secondary Education | M |
| Special Education | M |
| Student Affairs | M |
| Sustainable Development | M |
| Systems Science | M,O |

## EASTERN KENTUCKY UNIVERSITY

| | |
|---|---|
| Agricultural Education | M |
| Allied Health—General | M |
| Art Education | M |
| Biological and Biomedical Sciences—General | M |
| Business Administration and Management—General | M |
| Business Education | M |
| Chemistry | M |
| Clinical Psychology | M,O |
| Communication Disorders | M |
| Community Health | M |
| Counselor Education | M |
| Criminal Justice and Criminology | M |
| Curriculum and Instruction | M |
| Ecology | M |
| Education—General | M |
| Educational Leadership and Administration | M |
| Elementary Education | M |
| English Education | M |
| English | M |
| Environmental and Occupational Health | M |
| Exercise and Sports Science | M |
| Family Nurse Practitioner Studies | M |
| Geology | M,D |
| Health Education | M |
| Health Promotion | M |
| Health Services Management and Hospital Administration | M |
| Higher Education | M |
| History | M |
| Home Economics Education | M |
| Industrial and Organizational Psychology | M,O |
| Industrial Hygiene | M |
| Industrial/Management Engineering | M |
| Library Science | M |
| Manufacturing Engineering | M |
| Mathematics Education | M |
| Mathematics | M |
| Music Education | M |
| Music | M |
| Nursing—General | M |
| Nutrition | M |
| Occupational Therapy | M |
| Physical Education | M |
| Political Science | M |
| Psychology—General | M,O |
| Public Administration | M |
| Recreation and Park Management | M |
| School Psychology | M,O |
| Science Education | M |
| Secondary Education | M |
| Social Sciences Education | M |
| Special Education | M |
| Sports Management | M |
| Urban and Regional Planning | M |
| Vocational and Technical Education | M |
| Writing | M |

## EASTERN MENNONITE UNIVERSITY

| | |
|---|---|
| Biological and Biomedical Sciences—General | M |
| Business Administration and Management—General | M |
| Conflict Resolution and Mediation/Peace Studies | M,O |
| Counselor Education | M |
| Curriculum and Instruction | M |
| Education—General | M |
| Health Services Management and Hospital Administration | M |
| Nonprofit Management | M |
| Nursing and Healthcare Administration | M,D |
| Nursing—General | M,D |
| Organizational Management | M |
| Pastoral Ministry and Counseling | M,O |
| Reading Education | M |
| Religion | M,O |
| School Nursing | M,D |
| Special Education | M |
| Theology | M,O |

## EASTERN MICHIGAN UNIVERSITY

| | |
|---|---|
| Accounting | M |
| Adult Nursing | M,O |
| African-American Studies | O |
| Art Education | M |
| Art/Fine Arts | M |
| Arts Administration | M |
| Athletic Training and Sports Medicine | M,O |
| Biological and Biomedical Sciences—General | M |
| Business Administration and Management—General | M,O |
| Chemistry | M |
| Clinical Psychology | M,D |
| Clinical Research | M,O |
| Clothing and Textiles | M |
| Communication Disorders | M |
| Communication—General | M |
| Community College Education | M,D,O |
| Computer and Information Systems Security | O |
| Computer Science | M,O |
| Construction Management | M,O |
| Corporate and Organizational Communication | M,O |
| Counselor Education | M,O |
| Criminal Justice and Criminology | M |
| Cultural Studies | O |
| Curriculum and Instruction | M,O |
| Dance | M |
| Distance Education Development | M,O |
| Early Childhood Education | M |
| Economics | M,O |
| Education—General | M,D,O |
| Educational Leadership and Administration | M,D,O |
| Educational Measurement and Evaluation | M,O |
| Educational Media/Instructional Technology | M,O |
| Educational Policy | M |
| Educational Psychology | M,O |
| Electronic Commerce | M,O |
| Engineering and Applied Sciences—General | M |
| Engineering Management | M |
| English as a Second Language | M,O |
| English Education | M |
| English | M |
| Entrepreneurship | M,O |
| Exercise and Sports Science | M |
| Finance and Banking | M,O |
| Foreign Languages Education | M,O |
| Foundations and Philosophy of Education | M |
| Gender Studies | M,O |
| Geographic Information Systems | M,O |
| Geosciences | M |
| Gerontology | O |
| Health Education | M,O |
| Health Promotion | M,O |
| Health Services Management and Hospital Administration | M,O |
| Higher Education | M,D,O |
| Historic Preservation | M,O |
| History | M |
| Hospitality Management | O |
| Human Resources Management | M,O |
| Human Services | O |
| Interior Design | M |
| International Business | M,O |
| Kinesiology and Movement Studies | M |
| Linguistics | M |
| Management Information Systems | M,O |
| Management of Technology | D |
| Marketing | M,O |
| Mathematics | M |
| Middle School Education | M |
| Museum Education | O |
| Museum Studies | M,O |
| Music | M |
| Nonprofit Management | M,O |
| Nursing and Healthcare Administration | M,O |
| Nursing Education | M,O |
| Nutrition | M |
| Occupational Therapy | M |
| Organizational Management | M,O |
| Philosophy | M |
| Physical Education | M |
| Physician Assistant Studies | M |
| Physics | M |
| Physiology | M |
| Polymer Science and Engineering | M,O |
| Psychology—General | M,D |
| Public Administration | M,O |
| Public Policy | M,O |
| Quality Management | M,O |
| Reading Education | M,O |
| Science Education | M |
| Secondary Education | M |
| Social Sciences | M |
| Social Work | M |
| Sociology | M |
| Special Education | M,O |
| Sports Management | M |
| Student Affairs | M,D,O |
| Supply Chain Management | M,O |
| Sustainable Development | M,O |
| Technical Communication | M,O |
| Technology and Public Policy | M |
| Theater | M |
| Urban and Regional Planning | M,O |
| Urban Education | M,O |
| Women's Studies | M,O |
| Writing | M,O |

## EASTERN NAZARENE COLLEGE

| | |
|---|---|
| Business Administration and Management—General | M |
| Counseling Psychology | M |
| Early Childhood Education | M,O |
| Education—General | M,O |
| Educational Leadership and Administration | M,O |
| Elementary Education | M,O |
| English as a Second Language | M,O |
| Marriage and Family Therapy | M |
| Middle School Education | M,O |
| Reading Education | M,O |
| Secondary Education | M,O |
| Special Education | M,O |

## EASTERN NEW MEXICO UNIVERSITY

| | |
|---|---|
| Analytical Chemistry | M |
| Anthropology | M |
| Biochemistry | M |
| Biological and Biomedical Sciences—General | M |
| Business Administration and Management—General | M |
| Chemistry | M |
| Communication Disorders | M |
| Communication—General | M |
| Counselor Education | M |
| Curriculum and Instruction | M |
| Early Childhood Education | M |
| Education of the Gifted | M |
| Education—General | M |
| Educational Leadership and Administration | M |
| Educational Media/Instructional Technology | M |
| Elementary Education | M |
| English as a Second Language | M |
| English | M |
| Exercise and Sports Science | M |
| Multilingual and Multicultural Education | M |
| Nursing—General | M |
| Organic Chemistry | M |
| Physical Chemistry | M |
| Physical Education | M |
| Reading Education | M |
| Secondary Education | M |
| Special Education | M |
| Sports Management | M |
| Vocational and Technical Education | M |

## EASTERN OREGON UNIVERSITY

| | |
|---|---|
| Business Administration and Management—General | M |
| Education—General | M |
| Elementary Education | M |
| Secondary Education | M |

## EASTERN SCHOOL OF ACUPUNCTURE AND TRADITIONAL MEDICINE

| | |
|---|---|
| Acupuncture and Oriental Medicine | M |

## EASTERN UNIVERSITY

| | |
|---|---|
| Business Administration and Management—General | M |
| Communication—General | M,O |
| Early Childhood Education | M,O |
| Educational Leadership and Administration | M,O |
| Elementary Education | M,O |
| English as a Second Language | M,O |
| English Education | M,O |
| Foreign Languages Education | M,O |
| Health Education | M,O |
| Health Services Management and Hospital Administration | M |
| Mathematics Education | M,O |
| Middle School Education | M,O |
| Multilingual and Multicultural Education | M,O |
| Music | M,O |
| Organizational Management | M |
| Physical Education | M,O |
| Reading Education | M,O |
| School Psychology | M,O |
| Science Education | M,O |
| Secondary Education | M,O |
| Social Sciences Education | M,O |
| Spanish | M,O |
| Special Education | M,O |
| Theology | M |

## EASTERN VIRGINIA MEDICAL SCHOOL

| | |
|---|---|
| Allopathic Medicine | D |
| Art Therapy | M |
| Biological and Biomedical Sciences—General | M,D |
| Biotechnology | M |
| Clinical Psychology | D |
| Medical/Surgical Nursing | M |
| Physician Assistant Studies | M |
| Public Health—General | M |
| Reproductive Biology | M |
| Vision Sciences | O |

## EASTERN WASHINGTON UNIVERSITY

| | |
|---|---|
| Accounting | M |
| Adult Education | M |
| Applied Psychology | M,O |
| Biological and Biomedical Sciences—General | M |
| Business Administration and Management—General | M |
| Clinical Psychology | M,O |
| Communication Disorders | M |
| Communication—General | M |
| Computer Education | M |
| Computer Science | M |
| Counseling Psychology | M,O |
| Counselor Education | M,O |
| Curriculum and Instruction | M |
| Dental Hygiene | M |
| Early Childhood Education | M |
| Education—General | M |
| Educational Leadership and Administration | M |
| Elementary Education | M |
| English as a Second Language | M |
| English | M |
| Exercise and Sports Science | M |
| Experimental Psychology | M,O |

- Foundations and Philosophy of Education M
- History M
- Interdisciplinary Studies M
- Liberal Studies M
- Music Education M
- Music M
- Occupational Therapy M
- Physical Education M
- Physical Therapy D
- Psychology—General M,O
- Public Administration M
- Public Health—General M
- Reading Education M
- Recreation and Park Management M
- Rhetoric M
- School Psychology M,O
- Social Work M
- Sports Management M
- Technical Communication M

**EAST STROUDSBURG UNIVERSITY OF PENNSYLVANIA**

- Athletic Training and Sports Medicine M
- Biological and Biomedical Sciences—General M
- Communication Disorders M
- Communication—General M
- Computer Science M
- Early Childhood Education M
- Education—General M,D
- Educational Media/Instructional Technology M
- Elementary Education M
- Geography M
- Health Education M
- History M
- Physical Education M
- Political Science M
- Public Administration M
- Public Health—General M
- Reading Education M
- Rehabilitation Sciences M
- Secondary Education M,D
- Special Education M
- Sports Management M

**EAST TENNESSEE STATE UNIVERSITY**

- Accounting M
- Allied Health—General M
- Allopathic Medicine D
- Anatomy D
- Art/Fine Arts M
- Biochemistry D
- Biological and Biomedical Sciences—General M,D
- Biostatistics M,D,O
- Business Administration and Management—General M,O
- Chemistry M
- Clinical Psychology M,D
- Communication Disorders M,D
- Communication—General M,O
- Community Health M,D,O
- Computer Art and Design M
- Computer Science M,O
- Counselor Education M
- Criminal Justice and Criminology M,O
- Curriculum and Instruction M,O
- Early Childhood Education M,D,O
- Economic Development M,O
- Education—General M,D,O
- Educational Leadership and Administration M,D,O
- Educational Media/Instructional Technology M,O
- Elementary Education M,O
- English as a Second Language M,O
- English M,O
- Entrepreneurship M,O
- Environmental and Occupational Health M,D,O
- Epidemiology M,D,O
- Exercise and Sports Science M,D
- Experimental Psychology D
- Family Nurse Practitioner Studies M,D,O
- Geographic Information Systems M,O
- Geosciences M,O
- Gerontological Nursing M,D,O
- Gerontology M,D,O
- Health Services Management and Hospital Administration M,D,O
- History M,O
- Human Services M
- Information Science M,O
- International Health M,D,O
- Kinesiology and Movement Studies M,D
- Library Science M,O
- Manufacturing Engineering M
- Marketing M,O
- Marriage and Family Therapy M
- Mathematics M,O
- Microbiology M,D
- Middle School Education M,O
- Nonprofit Management M,O
- Nursing and Healthcare Administration M,D,O
- Nursing Education M,D,O
- Nursing—General M,D,O
- Nutrition M
- Paleontology M,O
- Pediatric Nursing M,D,O
- Pharmaceutical Sciences D
- Pharmacology D
- Pharmacy D
- Physical Therapy D
- Physiology D
- Psychiatric Nursing M,D,O
- Psychology—General D
- Public Administration M,O
- Public Health—General M,D,O
- Reading Education M,O
- School Psychology M
- Secondary Education M,O
- Social Work M
- Sociology M
- Special Education M,O
- Sports Management M,D
- Translation and Interpretation M,O
- Urban and Regional Planning M,O
- Women's Health Nursing M,D,O

**EAST TEXAS BAPTIST UNIVERSITY**

- Business Administration and Management—General M
- Counseling Psychology M
- Education—General M
- Kinesiology and Movement Studies M
- Religion M

**EAST WEST COLLEGE OF NATURAL MEDICINE**

- Acupuncture and Oriental Medicine M

**ECCLESIA COLLEGE**

- Missions and Missiology M

**EC-COUNCIL UNIVERSITY**

- Computer and Information Systems Security M

**ECOLE HÔTELIÈRE DE LAUSANNE**

- Hospitality Management M

**ECPI UNIVERSITY**

- Business Administration and Management—General M
- Computer and Information Systems Security M
- Management Information Systems M

**ECUMENICAL THEOLOGICAL SEMINARY**

- Pastoral Ministry and Counseling D
- Theology M

**EDEN THEOLOGICAL SEMINARY**

- Theology M,D

**EDGEWOOD COLLEGE**

- Education—General M,D,O
- Nursing—General M,D
- Sustainability Management M

**EDINBORO UNIVERSITY OF PENNSYLVANIA**

- Art Education M
- Art Therapy M,O
- Art/Fine Arts M
- Clinical Psychology M,O
- Communication Disorders M
- Communication—General M
- Counseling Psychology M,O
- Counselor Education M,O
- Early Childhood Education M,O
- Educational Leadership and Administration M
- Educational Psychology M,O
- Family Nurse Practitioner Studies M,D
- Middle School Education M,O
- Nursing Education M,D
- Nursing—General M,D
- Reading Education M,O
- Rehabilitation Counseling M,O
- School Psychology M,O
- Secondary Education M
- Social Work M
- Special Education M,O

**EDP UNIVERSITY OF PUERTO RICO–SAN SEBASTIAN**

- Nursing—General M

**EDWARD VIA COLLEGE OF OSTEOPATHIC MEDICINE–CAROLINAS CAMPUS**

- Osteopathic Medicine D

**EDWARD VIA COLLEGE OF OSTEOPATHIC MEDICINE–VIRGINIA CAMPUS**

- Osteopathic Medicine D

**ELIZABETH CITY STATE UNIVERSITY**

- Applied Mathematics M
- Biological and Biomedical Sciences—General M
- Community College Education M
- Computer Science M
- Education—General M
- Educational Leadership and Administration M
- Elementary Education M
- Geographic Information Systems M
- Mathematics Education M
- Mathematics M
- Psychology—General M
- Science Education M

**ELIZABETHTOWN COLLEGE**

- Occupational Therapy M

**ELMEZZI GRADUATE SCHOOL OF MOLECULAR MEDICINE**

- Molecular Medicine D

**ELMHURST UNIVERSITY**

- Business Administration and Management—General M
- Communication Disorders M
- Data Science/Data Analytics M
- Educational Leadership and Administration M
- Geographic Information Systems M
- Health Services Management and Hospital Administration M
- Industrial and Organizational Psychology M
- Management Information Systems M
- Nursing—General M
- Occupational Therapy M
- Project Management M
- Public Health—General M
- Special Education M
- Supply Chain Management M

**ELMS COLLEGE**

- Accounting M,O
- Acute Care/Critical Care Nursing M,D
- Applied Behavior Analysis M,O
- Biological and Biomedical Sciences—General M
- Business Administration and Management—General M,O
- Early Childhood Education M,O
- Education—General M,O
- Elementary Education M,O
- English as a Second Language M,O
- English Education M,O
- Entrepreneurship M,O
- Family Nurse Practitioner Studies M,D
- Finance and Banking M,O
- Foreign Languages Education M,O
- Gerontological Nursing M,D
- Health Services Management and Hospital Administration M,O
- Nursing and Healthcare Administration M,D
- Nursing Education M,D
- Nursing—General M,D
- Reading Education M,O
- Religion M
- Science Education M,O
- Secondary Education M,O
- Social Sciences M,O
- Special Education M,O

**ELON UNIVERSITY**

- Business Administration and Management—General M
- Education—General M
- Elementary Education M
- Internet and Interactive Multimedia M
- Law D
- Physical Therapy D
- Physician Assistant Studies M

**EMBRY-RIDDLE AERONAUTICAL UNIVERSITY–DAYTONA**

- Aerospace/Aeronautical Engineering M,D
- Aviation M
- Business Administration and Management—General M
- Civil Engineering M
- Computer and Information Systems Security M
- Electrical Engineering M
- Engineering Physics M,D
- Ergonomics and Human Factors M,D
- Finance and Banking M
- Human Resources Management M
- Mechanical Engineering M,D
- Software Engineering M
- Systems Engineering M

**EMBRY-RIDDLE AERONAUTICAL UNIVERSITY–PRESCOTT**

- Aviation M
- Military and Defense Studies M
- Safety Engineering M

**EMBRY-RIDDLE AERONAUTICAL UNIVERSITY–WORLDWIDE**

- Aerospace/Aeronautical Engineering M
- Aviation Management M
- Business Administration and Management—General M
- Computer and Information Systems Security M
- Education—General M
- Engineering Management M
- Entrepreneurship M
- Environmental and Occupational Health M
- Finance and Banking M
- Human Resources Management M
- International Affairs M
- International Business M
- Logistics M
- Management Information Systems M
- Management of Technology M
- Project Management M
- Supply Chain Management M
- Systems Engineering M

**EMILY CARR UNIVERSITY OF ART + DESIGN**

- Applied Arts and Design—General M
- Art/Fine Arts M
- Computer Art and Design M

**EMMANUEL COLLEGE (UNITED STATES)**

- Business Administration and Management—General M,O
- Education—General M,O
- Human Resources Management M,O
- Nursing and Healthcare Administration M,O
- Nursing Education M,O
- Nursing—General M,O
- Special Education M,O
- Urban Education M,O

**EMORY & HENRY COLLEGE**

- American Studies M,D
- Education—General M,D
- History M,D
- Occupational Therapy M,D
- Organizational Management M,D
- Physical Therapy M,D
- Physician Assistant Studies M,D
- Reading Education M,D

**EMORY UNIVERSITY**

- Accounting M,D
- Adult Nursing M
- Allied Health—General M,D
- Allopathic Medicine D
- Anesthesiologist Assistant Studies M
- Animal Behavior D
- Anthropology D
- Art History D
- Biochemistry D
- Bioethics M
- Bioinformatics M,D
- Biological and Biomedical Sciences—General D
- Biostatistics M,D
- Business Administration and Management—General M,D
- Cancer Biology/Oncology D
- Cell Biology D
- Chemistry D
- Clinical Psychology D
- Clinical Research M
- Cognitive Sciences D
- Comparative Literature D,O
- Computer Science M,D
- Developmental Biology D
- Developmental Psychology D
- Ecology D
- Economics D
- Education—General M,D
- English D,O
- Entrepreneurship M
- Environmental and Occupational Health M,D
- Epidemiology M,D
- Ethics M,D
- Evolutionary Biology D
- Family Nurse Practitioner Studies M
- Film, Television, and Video Theory and Criticism M,D,O
- Finance and Banking M,D
- French D
- Genetic Counseling M
- Genetics D
- Health Education M,D
- Health Informatics M,D
- Health Promotion M
- Health Services Management and Hospital Administration M,D
- Health Services Research M,D
- History D
- Human Genetics M
- Immunology D
- Industrial and Manufacturing Management M
- Interdisciplinary Studies D
- International Business M
- International Health M
- Law M,D,O
- Management Information Systems M,D
- Marketing M,D
- Mathematics M,D
- Microbiology D
- Middle School Education M,D
- Molecular Biology D
- Molecular Genetics D
- Molecular Pathogenesis D
- Music M
- Neuroscience D
- Nurse Midwifery M
- Nursing and Healthcare Administration M
- Nursing—General M,D
- Nutrition M,D
- Organizational Management M,D
- Pastoral Ministry and Counseling M,D
- Pediatric Nursing M
- Pharmacology D
- Philosophy D,O
- Physical Therapy D
- Physician Assistant Studies M
- Physics D
- Political Science D
- Portuguese D,O
- Psychology—General D
- Public Health—General M,D
- Real Estate M
- Religion D
- Secondary Education M,D
- Sociology D
- Spanish D,O
- Sustainable Development M
- Theology M,D
- Women's Health Nursing M
- Women's Studies D,O

**EMPEROR'S COLLEGE OF TRADITIONAL ORIENTAL MEDICINE**

- Acupuncture and Oriental Medicine M,D

**EMPIRE COLLEGE**

- Law M,D

**EMPORIA STATE UNIVERSITY**

- Accounting M
- Art Therapy M
- Biological and Biomedical Sciences—General M
- Botany M
- Business Administration and Management—General M
- Cell Biology M

*M—masters degree; D—doctorate; O—other advanced degree; *—Close-Up and/or Display*

Clinical Psychology M
Counseling Psychology M
Counselor Education M
Curriculum and Instruction M
Distance Education Development M,O
Early Childhood Education M
Education of the Gifted M
Education—General M
Educational Leadership and Administration M
Educational Media/Instructional Technology M,O
Elementary Education M
English as a Second Language M,O
English M
Environmental Biology M
Forensic Sciences M,O
Geosciences M,O
History M
Industrial and Organizational Psychology M
Library Science M,D,O
Mathematics M
Microbiology M
Music M
Physical Education M
Psychology—General M
Reading Education M
Rehabilitation Counseling M
School Psychology M,O
Special Education M
Zoology M

### ENDICOTT COLLEGE
Applied Behavior Analysis M,D,O
Business Administration and Management—General M
Computer and Information Systems Security M,O
Distance Education Development M
Early Childhood Education M
Educational Leadership and Administration M,D
Elementary Education M
Emergency Management M,O
Family Nurse Practitioner Studies M,O
Homeland Security M,O
Interior Design M
International Health M,O
Management Information Systems M
Nursing and Healthcare Administration M,O
Nursing Education M,O
Nursing—General M,O
Organizational Management M
Reading Education M
Secondary Education M
Special Education M,D,O
Sports Management M

### EPIC BIBLE COLLEGE
Ethics M,D
Pastoral Ministry and Counseling M,D

### ERIKSON INSTITUTE
Child Development M
Developmental Psychology M,O
Early Childhood Education M,D
English as a Second Language M,O
Human Development M,O
Social Work M

### ERSKINE THEOLOGICAL SEMINARY
Theology M,D

### ESSEC BUSINESS SCHOOL
Business Administration and Management—General M,D
Hospitality Management M,D
International Business M,D

### EVANGELICAL SEMINARY
Marriage and Family Therapy M
Missions and Missiology M
Pastoral Ministry and Counseling M
Theology M

### EVANGELICAL SEMINARY OF PUERTO RICO
Theology M,D

### EVANGEL UNIVERSITY
Clinical Psychology M
Counseling Psychology M
Counselor Education M
Curriculum and Instruction M,D
Education—General M
Educational Leadership and Administration M,D
Organizational Management M
Reading Education M
School Psychology M
Secondary Education M
Social Sciences M

### EVERGLADES UNIVERSITY
Accounting M
Aviation M
Business Administration and Management—General M
Entrepreneurship M
Human Resources Management M
Industrial and Manufacturing Management M
Project Management M
Public Health—General M

### THE EVERGREEN STATE COLLEGE
Education—General M
Environmental Management and Policy M
Public Administration M

### FAIRFIELD UNIVERSITY
Accounting M,O
Addictions/Substance Abuse Counseling M,O
American Studies M
Applied Behavior Analysis M,O
Applied Psychology M,O
Business Administration and Management—General M,O
Business Analytics M,O
Child and Family Studies M,O
Clinical Psychology M,O
Communication—General M
Computer and Information Systems Security M,O
Computer Engineering M,O
Counseling Psychology M,O
Counselor Education M,O
Data Science/Data Analytics M,O
Education—General M,O
Educational Media/Instructional Technology M,O
Electrical Engineering M,O
Elementary Education M,O
Engineering and Applied Sciences—General M,O
English as a Second Language M,O
Family Nurse Practitioner Studies M,D
Finance and Banking M,O
Foundations and Philosophy of Education M,O
Health Education M,D
Internet and Interactive Multimedia M,O
Management Information Systems M,O
Management of Technology M,O
Marketing M,O
Marriage and Family Therapy M,O
Mathematics M
Mechanical Engineering M,O
Multilingual and Multicultural Education M,O
Nurse Anesthesia M,D
Nursing and Healthcare Administration M,D
Nursing—General M,D
Pastoral Ministry and Counseling M,O
Psychiatric Nursing M,D
Public Administration M
School Psychology M,O
Secondary Education M,O
Software Engineering M,O
Special Education M,O
Taxation M,O
Telecommunications M,O
Writing M

### FAIRLEIGH DICKINSON UNIVERSITY, FLORHAM CAMPUS
Accounting M
Biological and Biomedical Sciences—General M
Business Administration and Management—General M,O
Chemical Engineering M,O
Chemistry M
Clinical Psychology M
Computer Science M
Corporate and Organizational Communication M
Counseling Psychology M
Early Childhood Education M,O
Education—General M,O
Educational Leadership and Administration M
Educational Media/Instructional Technology M,O
Entrepreneurship M,O
Finance and Banking M,O
Gerontological Nursing M
Health Services Management and Hospital Administration M
Hospitality Management M
Human Resources Management M
Industrial and Organizational Psychology M
International Business M,O
Management of Technology M,O
Marketing M,O
Nursing—General M
Organizational Behavior M,O
Organizational Management M,O
Pharmacology M,O
Pharmacy D
Psychiatric Nursing M
Psychology—General M,O
Public Administration M
Reading Education M,O
Sports Management M
Supply Chain Management M
Sustainability Management O
Taxation M,O
Writing M

### FAIRLEIGH DICKINSON UNIVERSITY, METROPOLITAN CAMPUS
Accounting M,O
Art/Fine Arts M
Biological and Biomedical Sciences—General M
Business Administration and Management—General M,O
Chemistry M
Clinical Laboratory Sciences/Medical Technology M
Clinical Psychology M,D
Communication—General M
Comparative Literature M
Computer Engineering M
Computer Science M
Criminal Justice and Criminology M
Curriculum and Instruction M,O
Early Childhood Education M
Education—General M,O
Educational Leadership and Administration M
Educational Media/Instructional Technology M,O
Electrical Engineering M
Electronic Commerce M
Engineering and Applied Sciences—General M
English M
Entrepreneurship M,O
Experimental Psychology M,O
Finance and Banking M,O
Forensic Psychology M
Foundations and Philosophy of Education M
Health Services Management and Hospital Administration M
History M
Homeland Security M
Hospitality Management M
Human Resources Management M,O
International Affairs M
International Business M
Management Information Systems M,O
Marketing M,O
Mathematics M
Media Studies M
Multilingual and Multicultural Education M
Nonprofit Management M,O
Nursing—General M,D,O
Pharmaceutical Administration M,O
Political Science M
Psychology—General M,D,O
Public Administration M,O
Reading Education M,O
School Psychology M,D
Science Education M
Special Education M
Sports Management M
Systems Science M
Taxation M

### FAIRMONT STATE UNIVERSITY
Business Administration and Management—General M
Criminal Justice and Criminology M
Education—General M
Educational Media/Instructional Technology M
Exercise and Sports Science M
Health Promotion M
Reading Education M
Special Education M

### FAITH BAPTIST BIBLE COLLEGE AND THEOLOGICAL SEMINARY
Pastoral Ministry and Counseling M
Religion M
Theology M

### FAITH INTERNATIONAL UNIVERSITY
Theology M,D

### FAITH THEOLOGICAL SEMINARY
Theology M,D

### FARMINGDALE STATE COLLEGE
Construction Management M
Electrical Engineering M
Management of Technology M
Mechanical Engineering M

### FASHION INSTITUTE OF TECHNOLOGY
Applied Arts and Design—General M
Art History M
Arts Administration M
Business Administration and Management—General M
Clothing and Textiles M
Illustration M
Marketing M
Museum Studies M

### FAULKNER UNIVERSITY
Business Administration and Management—General M
Counselor Education M
Criminal Justice and Criminology M
Curriculum and Instruction M
Education—General M
Elementary Education M
Humanities M,D
Law D
Pastoral Ministry and Counseling M,D
Theology M,D

### FAYETTEVILLE STATE UNIVERSITY
Business Administration and Management—General M
Criminal Justice and Criminology M
Educational Leadership and Administration M,D
Elementary Education M
Middle School Education M
Psychology—General M
Secondary Education M
Social Sciences Education M
Social Work M
Sociology M

### FELICIAN UNIVERSITY
Adult Nursing M,O
Business Administration and Management—General M,D
Counseling Psychology M,D
Education—General M,O
Educational Leadership and Administration M,O
Entrepreneurship M,D
Family Nurse Practitioner Studies M,O
Gerontological Nursing M,O
Health Services Management and Hospital Administration M
Nursing and Healthcare Administration M,D,O
Nursing Education M,O
Nursing—General M,D,O
Religious Education M,O

### FERRIS STATE UNIVERSITY
Allied Health—General M
Applied Arts and Design—General M
Art/Fine Arts M
Business Administration and Management—General M
Community College Education D
Criminal Justice and Criminology M
Curriculum and Instruction M
Developmental Education M
Education—General M
Educational Leadership and Administration D
Health Services Management and Hospital Administration M
Human Services M
Management Information Systems M
Nursing and Healthcare Administration M
Nursing Education M
Nursing Informatics M
Nursing—General M
Optometry D
Pharmacy D
Photography M
Project Management M
Public Health—General M
Social Work M
Special Education M
Supply Chain Management M

### FIELDING GRADUATE UNIVERSITY
Child Development M,D,O
Clinical Psychology D,O
Developmental Psychology M,D,O
Early Childhood Education M,D,O
Education—General M,D
Human Development M,D,O
Media Studies M,D,O
Neuroscience O
Organizational Management O
Psychology—General M,D,O

### FISHER COLLEGE
Business Administration and Management—General M
Management Strategy and Policy M

### FISK UNIVERSITY
Biological and Biomedical Sciences—General M
Chemistry M
Clinical Psychology M
Physics M
Psychology—General M

### FITCHBURG STATE UNIVERSITY
Accounting M
Art Education M,O
Biological and Biomedical Sciences—General M
Business Administration and Management—General M
Communication—General M,O
Computer Science M
Counseling Psychology M
Counselor Education M,O
Curriculum and Instruction M
Data Science/Data Analytics M
Early Childhood Education M
Educational Leadership and Administration M,O
Elementary Education M
English Education M,O
English M,O
Forensic Nursing M,O
Higher Education M,O
History M
Human Resources Management M
Interdisciplinary Studies O
Mathematics Education M
Middle School Education M
Psychology—General O
Reading Education O
Science Education M
Social Sciences Education M
Special Education M
Vocational and Technical Education M
Writing M

### FIVE BRANCHES UNIVERSITY
Acupuncture and Oriental Medicine M,D

### FIVE TOWNS COLLEGE
Early Childhood Education M,D
Music Education M,D
Music M,D

### FLAGLER COLLEGE
Special Education M

### FLORIDA AGRICULTURAL AND MECHANICAL UNIVERSITY
Accounting M
Adult Education M,D
Allied Health—General M,D
Architecture M
Biomedical Engineering M,D
Business Administration and Management—General M
Business Education M
Chemical Engineering M,D
Chemistry M
Civil Engineering M,D
Counselor Education M,D
Criminal Justice and Criminology M
Education—General M,D
Educational Leadership and Administration M,D
Electrical Engineering M,D
Elementary Education M
Engineering and Applied Sciences—General M,D
English Education M
Environmental Sciences M,D
Finance and Banking M

Health Services Research M,D
History M
Industrial/Management Engineering M,D
Journalism M
Landscape Architecture M
Law D
Management Information Systems M
Marketing M
Mathematics Education M
Mechanical Engineering M,D
Medicinal and Pharmaceutical Chemistry M,D
Nursing and Healthcare Administration M,D
Nursing—General M,D
Occupational Therapy M
Pharmaceutical Administration M,D
Pharmaceutical Sciences M,D
Pharmacology M,D
Pharmacy D
Physical Education M
Physical Therapy D
Physics M,D
Political Science M
Psychology—General M
Public Administration M
Public Health—General M,D
Science Education M
Secondary Education M
Social Psychology M
Social Sciences Education M
Social Sciences M
Social Work M
Software Engineering M
Sports Management M
Toxicology M,D
Vocational and Technical Education M

**FLORIDA ATLANTIC UNIVERSITY**

Accounting M
Adult Education M,D,O
Allopathic Medicine M,D
Anthropology M
Applied Arts and Design—General M
Applied Mathematics M,D
Art/Fine Arts M
Bioengineering M,D
Biological and Biomedical Sciences—General M,D
Business Administration and Management—General M
Chemistry M,D
Civil Engineering M
Communication Disorders M
Communication—General M,O
Comparative and Interdisciplinary Arts D
Comparative Literature M
Computer Engineering M,D
Computer Science M,D
Counselor Education M,D
Criminal Justice and Criminology M
Curriculum and Instruction M,D,O
Early Childhood Education M,D,O
Economics M
Education—General M,D,O
Educational Leadership and Administration M,D,O
Educational Media/Instructional Technology M
Electrical Engineering M,D
Elementary Education M
Engineering and Applied Sciences—General M,D
English as a Second Language M,D,O
English M
Entrepreneurship M
Environmental Education M
Environmental Engineering M
Exercise and Sports Science M
Film, Television, and Video Production M,O
French M
Geology M,D
Geosciences M,D
Graphic Design M
Health Promotion M
Health Services Management and Hospital Administration M
Higher Education M,D,O
History M
International Business M
Linguistics M
Management Information Systems M
Mathematics M,D
Mechanical Engineering M,D
Media Studies M,O
Multilingual and Multicultural Education M,D,O
Music M
Neuroscience D
Nonprofit Management M,D
Nursing and Healthcare Administration M,D,O
Nursing—General M,D,O
Ocean Engineering M,D
Physics M,D
Political Science M
Psychology—General M
Public Administration M,D
Reading Education M
Science Education M,D
Secondary Education M
Social Work M,D
Sociology M
Spanish M
Special Education M,D
Sports Management M
Statistics M,D

Theater M
Urban and Regional Planning M
Women's Studies M

**FLORIDA COASTAL SCHOOL OF LAW**

Law D

**FLORIDA COLLEGE OF INTEGRATIVE MEDICINE**

Acupuncture and Oriental Medicine M

**FLORIDA GULF COAST UNIVERSITY**

Accounting M
Allied Health—General M,D
Business Administration and Management—General M
Clinical Psychology M
Criminal Justice and Criminology M
Curriculum and Instruction M
Education of the Gifted M
Education—General M
Educational Leadership and Administration M
Elementary Education M
English as a Second Language M
English Education M
English M
Environmental Management and Policy M
Environmental Sciences M
Forensic Sciences M
History M
Interdisciplinary Studies M
Management Information Systems M
Mathematics Education M
Mathematics M
Middle School Education M
Nurse Anesthesia M
Nursing Education M
Occupational Therapy M
Physical Therapy D
Physician Assistant Studies M
Public Administration M
Reading Education M
School Psychology M
Science Education M
Social Sciences Education M
Social Work M
Special Education M
Taxation M

**FLORIDA INSTITUTE OF TECHNOLOGY**

Aerospace/Aeronautical Engineering M,D
Applied Behavior Analysis M
Applied Mathematics M,D
Aviation Management M
Aviation M,D
Biochemistry M
Biological and Biomedical Sciences—General M,D
Biomedical Engineering M,D
Biotechnology M,D
Business Administration and Management—General M
Cell Biology M
Chemical Engineering M,D
Chemistry M,D
Civil Engineering M,D
Clinical Psychology D
Communication—General M
Computer and Information Systems Security M
Computer Engineering M,D
Computer Science M,D
Conservation Biology M
Ecology M,D
Electrical Engineering M,D
Engineering and Applied Sciences—General M,D
Engineering Management M
Environmental Management and Policy M
Environmental Sciences M,D
Ergonomics and Human Factors M
Geosciences M
Health Services Management and Hospital Administration M
Human Resources Management M
Human-Computer Interaction M
Industrial and Organizational Psychology M,D
Information Science M
Interdisciplinary Studies M
International Business M
Logistics M
Management Information Systems M
Marine Biology M,D
Marine Sciences M,D
Mechanical Engineering M,D
Meteorology M
Molecular Biology M
Ocean Engineering M,D
Oceanography M,D
Operations Research M,D
Organizational Behavior M
Organizational Management M
Physics M,D
Planetary and Space Sciences M,D
Psychology—General M,D
Public Administration M
Safety Engineering M
Software Engineering M
Systems Engineering M,D

**FLORIDA INTERNATIONAL UNIVERSITY**

Accounting M
Adult Nursing M,D
African Studies M
Allopathic Medicine M,D
Applied Behavior Analysis M,D
Architecture M
Art Education M,D,O
Art/Fine Arts M,O
Asian Studies M
Athletic Training and Sports Medicine M
Biological and Biomedical Sciences—General M,D
Biomedical Engineering M,D
Biostatistics M,D
Chemistry M,D
Civil Engineering M,D
Clinical Psychology M,D
Cognitive Sciences M,D
Communication Disorders M
Communication—General M
Computer and Information Systems Security M,D
Computer Engineering M,D
Computer Science M,D
Construction Management M
Counseling Psychology M,D
Criminal Justice and Criminology M,D
Curriculum and Instruction M,D,O
Data Science/Data Analytics M,D
Developmental Psychology M,D
Early Childhood Education M,D,O
Economics M,D
Educational Media/Instructional Technology M,D,O
Electrical Engineering M,D
Elementary Education M,D,O
Emergency Management M
Engineering and Applied Sciences—General M,D
Engineering Management M
English as a Second Language M,D,O
English Education M,D,O
English M
Environmental and Occupational Health M,D
Environmental Engineering M,D
Environmental Management and Policy M,D
Epidemiology M,D
Finance and Banking M
Foreign Languages Education M,D,O
Forensic Sciences M,D
Geosciences M,D
Health Promotion M,D
Health Services Management and Hospital Administration M,D
History M,D
Hospitality Management M
Human Resources Management M,D
Industrial and Organizational Psychology M,D
Information Science M,D
Interior Design M,O
International Affairs M,D
International Business M,D
Journalism M
Landscape Architecture M
Law M,D
Linguistics M
Management Information Systems M,D
Marketing M
Mass Communication M
Materials Engineering M,D
Materials Sciences M,D
Mathematics Education M,D,O
Mathematics M
Mechanical Engineering M,D
Museum Studies M,O
Music Education M
Music M
Natural Resources M,D
Neuroscience M,D
Nurse Anesthesia M,D
Nursing—General M,D
Nutrition M,D
Occupational Therapy M
Pediatric Nursing M,D
Physical Education M,D,O
Physical Therapy D
Physician Assistant Studies M,D
Physics M,D
Political Science M,D
Psychiatric Nursing M,D
Psychology—General M,D
Public Administration M,D
Public Affairs M,D
Public Health—General M,D
Reading Education M,D,O
Real Estate M
Religion M
Science Education M,D,O
Social Sciences Education M,D,O
Social Work M,D
Sociology M,D
Spanish M,D
Special Education M,D,O
Statistics M
Telecommunications M,D
Writing M

**FLORIDA MEMORIAL UNIVERSITY**

Business Administration and Management—General M
Education—General M
Elementary Education M
Reading Education M
Special Education M

**FLORIDA NATIONAL UNIVERSITY**

Accounting M
Business Administration and Management—General M
Family Nurse Practitioner Studies M
Finance and Banking M
Health Services Management and Hospital Administration M
Marketing M
Nursing and Healthcare Administration M
Nursing Education M
Nursing—General M
Public Administration M

**FLORIDA POLYTECHNIC UNIVERSITY**

Computer Science M
Engineering and Applied Sciences—General M

**FLORIDA SOUTHERN COLLEGE**

Accounting M
Adult Nursing M
Business Administration and Management—General M
Education—General M,D
Family Nurse Practitioner Studies M
Gerontological Nursing M
Nursing and Healthcare Administration M
Nursing Education M
Nursing—General M

**FLORIDA STATE UNIVERSITY**

Accounting M,D
Actuarial Science M,D
Allopathic Medicine D
American Studies M,D
Analytical Chemistry M,D
Anthropology M,D
Applied Behavior Analysis M
Applied Economics M,D
Applied Mathematics M,D
Applied Social Research M,D
Applied Statistics M,D
Archaeology M,D
Architecture M
Art Education M,D
Art History M,D
Art Therapy M,D
Art/Fine Arts M
Arts Administration M,D
Asian Studies M
Atmospheric Sciences M,D
Biochemistry M,D
Biological and Biomedical Sciences—General M,D
Biomathematics M,D
Biomedical Engineering M,D
Biopsychology M,D
Biostatistics M,D
Business Administration and Management—General M,D
Cell Biology M,D
Chemical Engineering M,D
Chemistry M,D
Child and Family Studies M,D
Civil Engineering M,D
Classics M,D
Clinical Psychology D
Cognitive Sciences D
Communication Disorders M,D
Communication—General M,D
Computational Sciences M,D
Computer and Information Systems Security M,D
Corporate and Organizational Communication M,D
Criminal Justice and Criminology M,D
Cultural Studies M,D
Curriculum and Instruction M,D,O
Dance M
Demography and Population Studies M
Developmental Psychology D
East European and Russian Studies M
Ecology M,D
Economics M,D
Education—General M,D,O
Educational Leadership and Administration M,D,O
Educational Measurement and Evaluation M,D,O
Educational Media/Instructional Technology M,D,O
Educational Policy M,D,O
Educational Psychology M,D,O
Electrical Engineering M,D
Energy and Power Engineering M,D
Engineering and Applied Sciences—General M,D
English as a Second Language M,D,O
English Education M,D,O
English M,D
Environmental Engineering M,D
Environmental Law M,D
Environmental Sciences M,D
Evolutionary Biology M,D
Exercise and Sports Science M,D
Family and Consumer Sciences-General M,D
Family Nurse Practitioner Studies D,O
Film, Television, and Video Production M
Finance and Banking M,D
Food Science and Technology M,D
Foundations and Philosophy of Education M,D,O
French M,D
Geographic Information Systems M,D
Geography M,D
Geology M,D
Geosciences M,D
German M
Health Education M,D
Health Law M,D
Higher Education M,D,O

*M—masters degree; D—doctorate; O—other advanced degree; *—Close-Up and/or Display*

History M,D
Human Development M,D
Human Resources Management M,D
Industrial/Management Engineering M,D
Information Studies M,D,O
Inorganic Chemistry M,D
Insurance M,D
Interior Design M
International Affairs M
International and Comparative Education M,D,O
Italian M
Law M,D
Library Science M,D,O
Management Information Systems M,D,O
Management Strategy and Policy M,D
Manufacturing Engineering M,D
Marine Sciences M,D
Marketing M,D
Marriage and Family Therapy M,D
Materials Engineering M,D
Materials Sciences M,D
Mathematical and Computational Finance M,D
Mechanical Engineering M,D
Media Studies M,D
Meteorology M,D
Molecular Biology M,D
Molecular Biophysics D
Museum Studies M,D
Music M,D
Neuroscience M,D
Nursing—General D,O
Nutrition M,D
Oceanography M,D
Organic Chemistry M,D
Organizational Behavior M,D
Philosophy M,D
Physical Chemistry M,D
Physics M,D
Political Science M,D
Psychiatric Nursing D,O
Psychology—General M,D
Public Administration M,D,O
Public Health—General M
Public History M,D
Public Policy M,D,O
Reading Education M,D,O
Religion M,D
Rhetoric M,D
Risk Management M,D
Science Education M,D
Slavic Languages M
Social Psychology D
Social Work M,D
Sociology M,D
Spanish M,D
Sports Management M,D
Structural Biology D
Taxation M,D
Theater M,D
Therapies—Dance, Drama, and Music M,D
Urban and Regional Planning M,D
Writing M,D

## FONTBONNE UNIVERSITY
Accounting M
Art Education M
Art/Fine Arts M
Business Administration and Management—General M
Communication Disorders M
Computer Science M
Curriculum and Instruction M
Early Childhood Education M
Education—General M
Educational Media/Instructional Technology M
Elementary Education M
Family and Consumer Sciences-General M
Health Communication M
Middle School Education M
Reading Education M
Secondary Education M
Special Education M
Supply Chain Management M
Theater M

## FORDHAM UNIVERSITY
Accounting M,D
Applied Psychology M,D
Applied Statistics M,D
Biological and Biomedical Sciences—General M,D,O
Business Administration and Management—General M,D
Classics M,D
Clinical Psychology D
Clinical Research M
Communication—General M,D
Computer Science M
Conservation Biology M,D,O
Counseling Psychology M,D
Counselor Education M,D
Curriculum and Instruction M,O
Data Science/Data Analytics M
Developmental Psychology D
Early Childhood Education M,O
Economic Development M,O
Economics M,D,O
Education—General M,D,O
Educational Leadership and Administration M,D,O
Educational Psychology M,D
Electronic Commerce M,D
Elementary Education M,O
Emergency Management M
English as a Second Language M,O
English M,D
Entrepreneurship M,D
Ethics M,O
Finance and Banking M,D
Health Services Management and Hospital Administration M,D
History M,D
Intellectual Property Law M,D
International Affairs M,O
International Development M,O
International Economics M,D,O
Investment Management M,D
Law M,D
Management Information Systems M,D
Marketing M,D
Mass Communication M
Media Studies M,D
Medieval and Renaissance Studies M,O
Nonprofit Management M,D
Pastoral Ministry and Counseling M,D,O
Philosophy M,D
Political Science M
Psychology—General M,D
Quantitative Analysis M,D
Religion M,D,O
Religious Education M,D,O
School Psychology M,D
Social Work M,D
Special Education M,O
Taxation M,D
Theater M
Theology M,D
Urban Studies M

## FORT HAYS STATE UNIVERSITY
Art/Fine Arts M
Biological and Biomedical Sciences—General M
Business Administration and Management—General M
Communication Disorders M
Communication—General M
Counselor Education M
Education—General M,O
Educational Leadership and Administration M,O
Educational Media/Instructional Technology M
English M
Geography M
Geology M
Geosciences M
Health Education M
History M
Liberal Studies M
Nursing—General M
Physical Education M
Psychology—General M,O
School Psychology O
Special Education M

## FORT LEWIS COLLEGE
Educational Leadership and Administration M,O

## FORT VALLEY STATE UNIVERSITY
Animal Sciences M
Counseling Psychology M
Counselor Education M,O
Environmental and Occupational Health M
Public Health—General M
Rehabilitation Counseling M

## FRAMINGHAM STATE UNIVERSITY
Art Education M
Business Administration and Management—General M
Counseling Psychology M
Curriculum and Instruction M
Early Childhood Education M
Educational Leadership and Administration M
Educational Media/Instructional Technology M
Elementary Education M
English as a Second Language M,O
English M
Health Services Management and Hospital Administration M
Human Resources Management M
Mathematics Education M
Nursing and Healthcare Administration M
Nursing Education M
Nursing—General M
Nutrition M
Public Administration M
Reading Education M
Special Education M

## FRANCISCAN MISSIONARIES OF OUR LADY UNIVERSITY
Family Nurse Practitioner Studies M
Health Services Management and Hospital Administration M,D
Nurse Anesthesia D
Nursing—General M,D
Nutrition M,D
Physical Therapy M,D
Physician Assistant Studies M,D

## FRANCISCAN SCHOOL OF THEOLOGY
Theology M

## FRANCISCAN UNIVERSITY OF STEUBENVILLE
Business Administration and Management—General M
Clinical Psychology M
Counseling Psychology M
Curriculum and Instruction M
Education—General M
Educational Leadership and Administration M
Nursing—General M
Philosophy M
Theology M

## FRANCIS MARION UNIVERSITY
Applied Psychology M,O
Business Administration and Management—General M
Clinical Psychology M,O
Communication Disorders M
Counseling Psychology M,O
Education—General M
Family Nurse Practitioner Studies M
Health Services Management and Hospital Administration M
Nursing Education M
Nursing—General M
Physician Assistant Studies M
Psychology—General M,O
School Psychology M,O
Special Education M

## FRANKLIN COLLEGE
Athletic Training and Sports Medicine M

## FRANKLIN PIERCE UNIVERSITY
Business Administration and Management—General M,D,O
Curriculum and Instruction M,D,O
Elementary Education M,D,O
Energy Management and Policy M,D,O
Health Services Management and Hospital Administration M,D,O
Human Resources Management M,D,O
Management Information Systems M,D,O
Nursing and Healthcare Administration M,D,O
Nursing Education M,D,O
Physical Therapy M,D,O
Physician Assistant Studies M,D,O
Special Education M,D,O
Sports Management M,D,O
Sustainability Management M,D,O
Telecommunications M,D,O

## FRANKLIN UNIVERSITY
Accounting M
Business Administration and Management—General M
Computer Science M
Corporate and Organizational Communication M
Criminal Justice and Criminology M
Educational Media/Instructional Technology M
Marketing M

## FREDERICK S. PARDEE RAND GRADUATE SCHOOL
Public Policy D

## FREED-HARDEMAN UNIVERSITY
Accounting M
Business Administration and Management—General M
Counselor Education M,O
Curriculum and Instruction M,O
Education—General M,O
Educational Leadership and Administration M,O
Ethics M
Management Strategy and Policy M
Pastoral Ministry and Counseling M
Special Education M,O
Theology M

## FRESNO PACIFIC UNIVERSITY
Business Administration and Management—General M
Conflict Resolution and Mediation/Peace Studies M,O
Counselor Education M
Curriculum and Instruction M
Education—General M,O
Educational Leadership and Administration M
Educational Media/Instructional Technology M
English as a Second Language M,O
Family Nurse Practitioner Studies M
Interdisciplinary Studies M
Kinesiology and Movement Studies M
Marriage and Family Therapy M
Mathematics Education M
Missions and Missiology M
Nursing—General M
Pastoral Ministry and Counseling M
Reading Education M,O
School Psychology M
Science Education M
Special Education M
Student Affairs M,O
Theology M
Urban Studies M

## FRIENDS UNIVERSITY
Accounting M
Health Services Management and Hospital Administration M
Law M
Logistics M
Management Information Systems M
Management Strategy and Policy M
Marriage and Family Therapy M
Supply Chain Management M

## FROSTBURG STATE UNIVERSITY
Biological and Biomedical Sciences—General M
Business Administration and Management—General M
Computer Science M
Conservation Biology M
Counseling Psychology M
Counselor Education M
Curriculum and Instruction M,D
Ecology M
Education—General M,D
Educational Leadership and Administration M,D
Educational Media/Instructional Technology M,D
Elementary Education M,D
Fish, Game, and Wildlife Management M
Interdisciplinary Studies M,D
Nursing and Healthcare Administration M
Nursing Education M
Nursing—General M
Psychology—General M
Reading Education M,D
Recreation and Park Management M
Secondary Education M,D
Special Education M

## FULLER THEOLOGICAL SEMINARY
Clinical Psychology M,D,O
Marriage and Family Therapy M,D,O
Missions and Missiology M,D,O
Music M,D,O
Pastoral Ministry and Counseling M,D,O
Theology M,D,O

## FULL SAIL UNIVERSITY
Art/Fine Arts M
Business Administration and Management—General M
Computer Art and Design M
Educational Media/Instructional Technology M
Entertainment Management M
Game Design and Development M
Graphic Design M
Internet and Interactive Multimedia M
Journalism M
Marketing M
Media Studies M
Writing M

## FURMAN UNIVERSITY
Chemistry M
Curriculum and Instruction M,O
Early Childhood Education M,O
Education—General M,O
Educational Leadership and Administration M,O
English as a Second Language M,O
Reading Education M,O
Special Education M,O

## FUTURE GENERATIONS UNIVERSITY
Social Psychology M
Sustainable Development M
Urban and Regional Planning M

## GALLAUDET UNIVERSITY
Clinical Psychology M,D,O
Communication Disorders M,D,O
Counseling Psychology M,D,O
Counselor Education M,D,O
Early Childhood Education M,D,O
Education—General M,D,O
Elementary Education M,D,O
International and Comparative Education M,D,O
Linguistics M,D,O
Multilingual and Multicultural Education M,D,O
Neuroscience M,D,O
Public Administration M,D,O
School Psychology M,D,O
Secondary Education M,D,O
Social Work M,D,O
Special Education M,D,O
Translation and Interpretation M,D,O

## GANNON UNIVERSITY
Athletic Training and Sports Medicine M
Business Administration and Management—General M
Clinical Psychology M
Computer Science M
Counseling Psychology M
Criminal Justice and Criminology M
Curriculum and Instruction M,O
Education—General M,O
Educational Leadership and Administration D,O
Electrical Engineering M
Engineering Management M
English as a Second Language O
English M
Environmental and Occupational Health M
Environmental Engineering M
Environmental Sciences M
Exercise and Sports Science M
Family Nurse Practitioner Studies M,O
Finance and Banking M
Health Communication M
Human Resources Management M
Information Science M
Marketing M
Mechanical Engineering M
Nurse Anesthesia M,O
Nursing and Healthcare Administration M
Nursing—General D
Occupational Therapy M,D
Organizational Management D
Pastoral Ministry and Counseling M,O
Physical Therapy D
Physician Assistant Studies M
Public Administration M
Reading Education M,O
Software Engineering M
Theology M,O

## GARDNER-WEBB UNIVERSITY
Business Administration and Management—General M
Counseling Psychology M

| | |
|---|---|
| Cultural Studies | M,D |
| Curriculum and Instruction | M,D,O |
| Education—General | M,D,O |
| Educational Leadership and Administration | M,D,O |
| English Education | M |
| English | M |
| Exercise and Sports Science | M |
| Family Nurse Practitioner Studies | M,D |
| Missions and Missiology | M,D |
| Nursing—General | M,D |
| Organizational Management | M,D,O |
| Pastoral Ministry and Counseling | M,D |
| Physical Education | M |
| Physician Assistant Studies | M |
| Psychology—General | M |
| Religious Education | M,D |
| School Psychology | M |
| Theology | M,D |

### GARRETT-EVANGELICAL THEOLOGICAL SEMINARY

| | |
|---|---|
| Music | M,D |
| Pastoral Ministry and Counseling | M,D |
| Religious Education | M,D |
| Theology | M,D |

### GATEWAY SEMINARY

| | |
|---|---|
| Early Childhood Education | M,D,O |
| Educational Leadership and Administration | M,D,O |
| Pastoral Ministry and Counseling | M,D,O |
| Theology | M,D,O |

### GEISINGER COMMONWEALTH SCHOOL OF MEDICINE

| | |
|---|---|
| Allopathic Medicine | D |
| Biological and Biomedical Sciences—General | M |

### THE GENERAL THEOLOGICAL SEMINARY

| | |
|---|---|
| Pastoral Ministry and Counseling | M,D,O |
| Religion | M,D,O |
| Theology | M,D,O |

### GENEVA COLLEGE

| | |
|---|---|
| Business Administration and Management—General | M |
| Clinical Psychology | M |
| Counseling Psychology | M |
| Counselor Education | M |
| Education—General | M |
| Educational Leadership and Administration | M |
| Finance and Banking | M |
| Higher Education | M |
| Marketing | M |
| Marriage and Family Therapy | M |
| Nonprofit Management | M |
| Organizational Management | M |
| Pastoral Ministry and Counseling | M |
| Project Management | M |
| Psychology—General | M |

### GEORGE FOX UNIVERSITY

| | |
|---|---|
| Accounting | M,D |
| Business Administration and Management—General | M,D |
| Clinical Psychology | M,D,O |
| Counseling Psychology | M,O |
| Counselor Education | M,O |
| Cultural Studies | M,D,O |
| Education—General | M,D,O |
| Educational Leadership and Administration | M,D,O |
| Educational Media/Instructional Technology | M,O |
| English as a Second Language | M,O |
| Finance and Banking | M,D |
| Human Resources Management | M,D |
| Marketing | M,D |
| Marriage and Family Therapy | M,O |
| Organizational Management | M,D |
| Pastoral Ministry and Counseling | M,D,O |
| Physical Therapy | D |
| Reading Education | M,O |
| School Psychology | M,O |
| Social Work | M |
| Special Education | M,O |
| Theology | M,D,O |

### GEORGE MASON UNIVERSITY

| | |
|---|---|
| Accounting | M |
| Adult Nursing | M,D,O |
| Anthropology | M,D |
| Art Education | M |
| Art History | M |
| Art/Fine Arts | M |
| Arts Administration | M |
| Astronomy | M,D |
| Athletic Training and Sports Medicine | M,O |
| Atmospheric Sciences | D |
| Biochemistry | M,D |
| Bioengineering | D |
| Bioinformatics | M,D,O |
| Biological and Biomedical Sciences—General | M,D,O |
| Biostatistics | M,D,O |
| Business Administration and Management—General | M |
| Chemistry | M,D |
| Civil Engineering | M,D |
| Clinical Psychology | M,D,O |
| Cognitive Sciences | M,D,O |
| Communication—General | M,D,O |
| Community Health | M,O |
| Computational Biology | M,D,O |
| Computational Sciences | M,D,O |
| Computer and Information Systems Security | M |
| Computer Engineering | M,D,O |
| Computer Science | M,D,O |
| Conflict Resolution and Mediation/Peace Studies | M,D,O |
| Construction Engineering | M,D |
| Counselor Education | M |
| Criminal Justice and Criminology | M,D |
| Cultural Studies | D |
| Curriculum and Instruction | M |
| Data Science/Data Analytics | M,D,O |
| Developmental Psychology | M,D,O |
| Early Childhood Education | M |
| Economics | M,D |
| Education of the Gifted | M |
| Education—General | M,D,O |
| Educational Leadership and Administration | M,O |
| Educational Media/Instructional Technology | M |
| Educational Psychology | M,O |
| Electrical Engineering | M,D,O |
| Elementary Education | M |
| Engineering and Applied Sciences—General | M,D,O |
| English as a Second Language | M |
| English Education | M,D,O |
| English | M,D,O |
| Environmental Management and Policy | M,D |
| Environmental Sciences | M,D |
| Epidemiology | M,O |
| Ethics | M |
| Exercise and Sports Science | M,O |
| Family Nurse Practitioner Studies | M,D,O |
| Foreign Languages Education | M |
| Forensic Sciences | M |
| French | M |
| Gender Studies | M |
| Geographic Information Systems | M,D,O |
| Geography | M,D,O |
| Geosciences | M,D,O |
| Gerontological Nursing | M,D,O |
| Graphic Design | M |
| Health Informatics | M,D,O |
| Health Promotion | M,O |
| Health Services Management and Hospital Administration | M,D,O |
| Health Services Research | M,D,O |
| Higher Education | M,D,O |
| History | M,D,O |
| Human Resources Management | M |
| Industrial and Organizational Psychology | M,D,O |
| Information Science | M,D,O |
| Interdisciplinary Studies | M |
| International Affairs | M |
| International Business | M,O |
| International Health | M,O |
| Law | M,D |
| Linguistics | M,D,O |
| Logistics | M |
| Management Information Systems | M |
| Management of Technology | M |
| Mathematics Education | M |
| Mathematics | M,D |
| Military and Defense Studies | M |
| Music Education | M |
| Music | M,D |
| National Security | M,D,O |
| Near and Middle Eastern Studies | M,O |
| Neuroscience | M,D,O |
| Nursing and Healthcare Administration | M,D,O |
| Nursing Education | M,D,O |
| Nursing—General | M,D,O |
| Nutrition | M,O |
| Operations Research | M,D,O |
| Organizational Management | M |
| Philosophy | M |
| Physical Education | M |
| Physics | M,D |
| Political Science | M,D |
| Project Management | M,D |
| Psychiatric Nursing | M,D,O |
| Psychology—General | M,D,O |
| Public Administration | M |
| Public Affairs | M |
| Public Health—General | M,O |
| Public Policy | M,D |
| Reading Education | M |
| Rehabilitation Sciences | D,O |
| Religion | M |
| Rhetoric | M,D,O |
| Science Education | M |
| Secondary Education | M |
| Social Sciences Education | M |
| Social Work | M |
| Sociology | M,D |
| Spanish | M |
| Special Education | M,O |
| Sports Management | M,O |
| Statistics | M,D,O |
| Systems Biology | M,D,O |
| Systems Engineering | M,D,O |
| Transportation and Highway Engineering | M,D |
| Transportation Management | M |
| Women's Studies | M |
| Writing | M |

### GEORGETOWN COLLEGE

| | |
|---|---|
| Education—General | M |
| Reading Education | M |
| Special Education | M |

### GEORGETOWN UNIVERSITY

| | |
|---|---|
| Acute Care/Critical Care Nursing | M,D |
| Advertising and Public Relations | M |
| Allopathic Medicine | D |
| American Studies | M,D |
| Analytical Chemistry | D |
| Asian Studies | M |
| Biochemistry | M,D |
| Bioinformatics | M,O |
| Biological and Biomedical Sciences—General | D |
| Biostatistics | M,O |
| Business Administration and Management—General | M |
| Chemistry | D |
| Communication—General | M |
| Comparative Literature | M,D |
| Computer Science | M,D |
| Conflict Resolution and Mediation/Peace Studies | M |
| East European and Russian Studies | M |
| Economic Development | D |
| Economics | D |
| Educational Measurement and Evaluation | M |
| Emergency Management | M,D |
| English | M |
| Environmental Law | M,D |
| Epidemiology | M,O |
| Ethics | M,D |
| Family Nurse Practitioner Studies | M,D |
| Finance and Banking | M,D |
| German | M,D |
| Health Law | M,D |
| Health Physics/Radiological Health | M |
| Health Promotion | M,D |
| Health Services Management and Hospital Administration | M,D |
| History | M,D |
| Hospitality Management | M,D |
| Human Development | M,D |
| Human Resources Management | M,D |
| Humanities | M,D |
| Immunology | M,D |
| Industrial and Labor Relations | D |
| Industrial and Manufacturing Management | D |
| Infectious Diseases | M,D |
| Inorganic Chemistry | D |
| Interdisciplinary Studies | M,D |
| International Affairs | M,D |
| International Business | M,D |
| International Development | M |
| International Health | M,D |
| Internet and Interactive Multimedia | M |
| Journalism | M,D |
| Latin American Studies | M |
| Law | M,D |
| Liberal Studies | M,D |
| Linguistics | M,D |
| Management of Technology | M,D |
| Materials Sciences | D |
| Mathematics | M |
| Media Studies | M,D |
| Medieval and Renaissance Studies | M,D |
| Microbiology | M,D |
| Molecular Biology | M,D |
| Near and Middle Eastern Languages | M,O |
| Near and Middle Eastern Studies | M,O |
| Neuroscience | D |
| Nurse Anesthesia | M,D |
| Nurse Midwifery | M,D |
| Nursing Education | M,D |
| Nursing—General | M,D |
| Organic Chemistry | D |
| Pharmacology | M,D |
| Philosophy | M,D |
| Physiology | M,D |
| Political Science | M,D |
| Psychology—General | D |
| Public Health—General | M,D |
| Public Policy | M,D |
| Radiation Biology | M |
| Real Estate | M,D |
| Religion | M,D |
| Spanish | M,D |
| Sports Management | M,D |
| Statistics | M |
| Systems Engineering | M,D |
| Taxation | M,D |
| Theology | D |
| Theoretical Chemistry | D |
| Urban and Regional Planning | M,D |
| Western European Studies | M |

### THE GEORGE WASHINGTON UNIVERSITY

| | |
|---|---|
| Accounting | M |
| Addictions/Substance Abuse Counseling | M |
| Adult Education | O |
| Adult Nursing | M,D,O |
| Aerospace/Aeronautical Engineering | M,D,O |
| Allopathic Medicine | D |
| American Studies | M,D |
| Analytical Chemistry | M,D |
| Anthropology | M,D |
| Applied Mathematics | M,D,O |
| Applied Psychology | D |
| Art Education | M |
| Art History | M |
| Art Therapy | M,O |
| Art/Fine Arts | M,O |
| Asian Studies | M |
| Biochemistry | D |
| Biological and Biomedical Sciences—General | M,D |
| Biomedical Engineering | M,D |
| Biostatistics | M,D |
| Biotechnology | M,D,O |
| Business Administration and Management—General | M,D,O |
| Business Analytics | M,O |
| Chemistry | M,D |
| Civil Engineering | M,D,O |
| Clinical Psychology | M,D |
| Cognitive Sciences | D |
| Communication Disorders | M |
| Communication—General | M |
| Community Health | M,D |
| Computer and Information Systems Security | M,D,O |
| Computer Engineering | M,D,O |
| Computer Science | M,D,O |
| Counselor Education | M,D,O |
| Criminal Justice and Criminology | M,O |
| Curriculum and Instruction | M,D,O |
| Dance | M,O |
| Decorative Arts | M |
| Distance Education Development | O |
| Early Childhood Education | M |
| East European and Russian Studies | M |
| Economics | M,D |
| Education—General | M,D,O |
| Educational Leadership and Administration | M,D,O |
| Educational Media/Instructional Technology | M,O |
| Educational Policy | M,D,O |
| Electrical Engineering | M,D,O |
| Elementary Education | M |
| Emergency Management | M,D,O |
| Engineering and Applied Sciences—General | M,D,O |
| Engineering Management | M,D,O |
| English | M,D |
| Environmental and Occupational Health | D |
| Environmental Engineering | M,D,O |
| Environmental Management and Policy | M |
| Epidemiology | M |
| Exercise and Sports Science | M |
| Family Nurse Practitioner Studies | M,D,O |
| Finance and Banking | M,D |
| Folklore | M,D |
| Foreign Languages Education | M |
| Forensic Psychology | M,D,O |
| Forensic Sciences | M,O |
| Gender Studies | O |
| Geography | M,O |
| Health Communication | M,D |
| Health Services Management and Hospital Administration | M,D,O |
| Health Services Research | M,D,O |
| Higher Education | M,D,O |
| Historic Preservation | M,D |
| History | M,D |
| Hospitality Management | M,O |
| Human Development | M |
| Human Resources Development | M,D,O |
| Human Resources Management | M,O |
| Immunology | D |
| Infectious Diseases | M,D,O |
| Inorganic Chemistry | M,D |
| Interior Design | M |
| International Affairs | M,D |
| International and Comparative Education | M,D,O |
| International Business | M,D |
| International Development | M,D |
| International Health | M,D |
| International Trade Policy | M |
| Investment Management | M,D |
| Latin American Studies | M |
| Law | M,D |
| Legal and Justice Studies | M,D,O |
| Management Information Systems | M,D |
| Management of Technology | M,D |
| Management Strategy and Policy | M,D,O |
| Marketing | M,D |
| Mass Communication | M,O |
| Materials Sciences | M,D |
| Mathematical and Computational Finance | M,D,O |
| Mathematics Education | M |
| Mathematics | M,D,O |
| Mechanical Engineering | M,D,O |
| Microbiology | M,D,O |
| Military and Defense Studies | M |
| Molecular Medicine | D |
| Multilingual and Multicultural Education | M,D,O |
| Museum Education | M |
| Museum Studies | M,D,O |
| National Security | M,D |
| Near and Middle Eastern Studies | M |
| Nonprofit Management | M,O |
| Nursing and Healthcare Administration | M,D,O |
| Nursing—General | M,D,O |
| Organic Chemistry | M,D |
| Organizational Management | M,D |
| Philosophy | M |
| Photography | M,O |
| Physical Chemistry | M,D |
| Physical Therapy | D |
| Physician Assistant Studies | M |
| Physics | M,D |
| Political Science | M,D |
| Project Management | M,D,O |
| Psychology—General | M,D,O |
| Public Administration | M,D |
| Public Affairs | M,O |
| Public Health—General | M,D |
| Public Policy | M,D |
| Publishing | M |
| Real Estate | O |
| Rehabilitation Counseling | M |
| Religion | M |
| Science Education | M |
| Secondary Education | M |
| Social Psychology | D |
| Sociology | M |
| Special Education | M,D,O |
| Sports Management | M,O |
| Statistics | M,D,O |

*M—masters degree; D—doctorate; O—other advanced degree; *—Close-Up and/or Display*

| | |
|---|---|
| Student Affairs | M,D,O |
| Systems Biology | D |
| Systems Engineering | M,D,O |
| Technology and Public Policy | M,O |
| Telecommunications | M,D,O |
| Theater | M,O |
| Toxicology | M,O |
| Travel and Tourism | M,O |
| Vocational and Technical Education | O |
| Western European Studies | M |
| Women's Studies | M,O |

**GEORGIA CAMPUS–PHILADELPHIA COLLEGE OF OSTEOPATHIC MEDICINE**

| | |
|---|---|
| Osteopathic Medicine | D |
| Pharmacy | D |
| Physical Therapy | D |

**GEORGIA COLLEGE & STATE UNIVERSITY**

| | |
|---|---|
| Accounting | M |
| Art Therapy | M |
| Biological and Biomedical Sciences—General | M |
| Business Administration and Management—General | M |
| Criminal Justice and Criminology | M |
| Curriculum and Instruction | M |
| Early Childhood Education | M |
| Education—General | M,O |
| Educational Leadership and Administration | M,O |
| Educational Media/Instructional Technology | M |
| English | M |
| Exercise and Sports Science | M |
| Health Education | M |
| Health Promotion | M |
| Kinesiology and Movement Studies | M |
| Logistics | M |
| Management Information Systems | M |
| Middle School Education | M |
| Music Education | M |
| Nursing—General | M,D,O |
| Physical Education | M |
| Public Administration | M |
| Secondary Education | M |
| Special Education | M,O |
| Therapies—Dance, Drama, and Music | M |
| Writing | M |

**GEORGIA INSTITUTE OF TECHNOLOGY**

| | |
|---|---|
| Aerospace/Aeronautical Engineering | M,D |
| Architecture | M,D |
| Atmospheric Sciences | M,D |
| Biological and Biomedical Sciences—General | M,D |
| Biomedical Engineering | D |
| Building Science | M,D |
| Chemical Engineering | M,D |
| Chemistry | M,D |
| Civil Engineering | M,D |
| Computer Art and Design | M,D |
| Computer Engineering | M,D |
| Economic Development | M,D |
| Economics | M,D |
| Electrical Engineering | M,D |
| Engineering and Applied Sciences—General | M,D |
| Environmental Engineering | M,D |
| Environmental Management and Policy | M,D |
| Geographic Information Systems | M,D |
| Geosciences | M,D |
| Health Physics/Radiological Health | M,D |
| Health Services Management and Hospital Administration | M,D |
| History of Science and Technology | M,D |
| Industrial Design | M |
| Industrial/Management Engineering | M,D |
| International Affairs | M |
| Internet and Interactive Multimedia | M,D |
| Logistics | M,D |
| Materials Engineering | M,D |
| Mathematics | M,D |
| Mechanical Engineering | M,D |
| Mechanics | M,D |
| Music | M,D |
| Nuclear Engineering | M,D |
| Operations Research | M,D |
| Physics | M,D |
| Physiology | M,D |
| Psychology—General | M,D |
| Public Policy | M,D |
| Urban and Regional Planning | M,D |
| Urban Design | M,D |

**GEORGIAN COURT UNIVERSITY**

| | |
|---|---|
| Applied Behavior Analysis | M,O |
| Business Administration and Management—General | M,O |
| Clinical Psychology | M,O |
| Computer Art and Design | M,O |
| Counseling Psychology | M,O |
| Counselor Education | M,O |
| Criminal Justice and Criminology | M,O |
| Education—General | M,O |
| Educational Leadership and Administration | M,O |
| Educational Media/Instructional Technology | M,O |
| Health Psychology | M,O |
| Homeland Security | M,O |
| Legal and Justice Studies | M,O |
| Nonprofit Management | M,O |
| School Psychology | M,O |
| Special Education | M,O |
| Theology | M,O |

**GEORGIA SOUTHERN UNIVERSITY**

| | |
|---|---|
| Accounting | M |
| Allied Health—General | M,D,O |
| Applied Economics | M,O |
| Applied Physics | M |
| Art/Fine Arts | M |
| Athletic Training and Sports Medicine | M,O |
| Biological and Biomedical Sciences—General | M |
| Biostatistics | M,D |
| Business Administration and Management—General | M,O |
| Civil Engineering | M |
| Clinical Psychology | M,D |
| Communication Disorders | M |
| Community Health | M,D |
| Computer and Information Systems Security | M,O |
| Construction Management | M |
| Corporate and Organizational Communication | M,O |
| Counseling Psychology | M |
| Counselor Education | M |
| Criminal Justice and Criminology | M,O |
| Curriculum and Instruction | M,D |
| Education—General | M,D,O |
| Educational Leadership and Administration | M,D,O |
| Educational Measurement and Evaluation | M,D,O |
| Educational Media/Instructional Technology | M,O |
| Electrical Engineering | M |
| Elementary Education | M,O |
| Energy and Power Engineering | M |
| Engineering and Applied Sciences—General | M,O |
| Engineering Management | M,O |
| English | M |
| Environmental and Occupational Health | M,D,O |
| Epidemiology | M,D |
| Family Nurse Practitioner Studies | M |
| Foreign Languages Education | M,O |
| Graphic Design | M |
| Health Education | M,D |
| Health Services Management and Hospital Administration | M,D |
| Higher Education | M,D |
| History | M,O |
| Kinesiology and Movement Studies | M |
| Logistics | D |
| Management Information Systems | M,O |
| Manufacturing Engineering | M,O |
| Mathematics | M |
| Mechanical Engineering | M |
| Middle School Education | M,O |
| Multilingual and Multicultural Education | D |
| Music Education | M |
| Music | M |
| Nonprofit Management | M,O |
| Nursing Education | O |
| Nursing—General | D |
| Nutrition | O |
| Physical Therapy | D |
| Psychiatric Nursing | O |
| Psychology—General | M,D |
| Public Administration | M,D |
| Public Health—General | M,D |
| Public History | M,O |
| Reading Education | M,O |
| School Psychology | M,O |
| Secondary Education | M,O |
| Sociology | M |
| Spanish | M |
| Special Education | M,O |
| Sports Management | M |
| Supply Chain Management | D |
| Systems Engineering | M |
| Writing | M,O |

**GEORGIA SOUTHWESTERN STATE UNIVERSITY**

| | |
|---|---|
| Business Administration and Management—General | M |
| Computer Science | M,O |
| Early Childhood Education | M,O |
| Education—General | M,O |
| English Education | M,O |
| Family Nurse Practitioner Studies | M,O |
| Health Informatics | M,O |
| Management Information Systems | M,O |
| Mathematics Education | M,O |
| Middle School Education | M,O |
| Nursing and Healthcare Administration | M,O |
| Nursing Education | M,O |
| Nursing Informatics | M,O |
| Nursing—General | M,O |
| Special Education | M,O |

**GEORGIA STATE UNIVERSITY**

| | |
|---|---|
| Accounting | M |
| Actuarial Science | M |
| Adult Nursing | M,D,O |
| African-American Studies | M |
| Allied Health—General | M |
| Analytical Chemistry | M,D |
| Anthropology | M |
| Art Education | M |
| Art History | M |
| Art/Fine Arts | M |
| Astronomy | D |
| Athletic Training and Sports Medicine | M |
| Biochemistry | M,D |
| Bioinformatics | M,D |
| Biological and Biomedical Sciences—General | M,D |
| Biostatistics | M,D |
| Business Administration and Management—General | M,D |
| Cell Biology | M,D |
| Chemistry | M,D |
| Clinical Psychology | D |
| Clothing and Textiles | M |
| Cognitive Sciences | D |
| Communication Disorders | M,D |
| Communication—General | M,D |
| Computer Science | M,D |
| Counseling Psychology | M,O |
| Counselor Education | M,O |
| Criminal Justice and Criminology | M,D,O |
| Cultural Studies | M,O |
| Curriculum and Instruction | M,D |
| Developmental Psychology | D |
| Early Childhood Education | M,D,O |
| Economic Development | M,D,O |
| Economics | M,D |
| Education of Students with Severe/Multiple Disabilities | M,D |
| Education—General | M,D,O |
| Educational Leadership and Administration | M,D,O |
| Educational Measurement and Evaluation | M,D |
| Educational Policy | M,D,O |
| Educational Psychology | M,D |
| Elementary Education | M,D,O |
| Emergency Management | M,D,O |
| English Education | M,D |
| English | M,D |
| Entrepreneurship | M,D |
| Environmental Biology | M,D |
| Environmental Management and Policy | M,D,O |
| Exercise and Sports Science | M |
| Family Nurse Practitioner Studies | M,D,O |
| Film, Television, and Video Production | M,D |
| Finance and Banking | M,D,O |
| Foreign Languages Education | M,O |
| Forensic Sciences | M,O |
| Foundations and Philosophy of Education | M,D |
| French | M,O |
| Gender Studies | M,O |
| Geochemistry | M,D |
| Geographic Information Systems | O |
| Geography | M,D |
| Geology | M |
| Geosciences | M,D,O |
| German | O |
| Gerontology | M,O |
| Graphic Design | M |
| Health Education | M |
| Health Informatics | M,D,O |
| Health Services Management and Hospital Administration | M,D,O |
| Historic Preservation | M |
| History | M,D |
| Human Development | M,D,O |
| Human Resources Management | M,D |
| Human Services | M,O |
| Industrial and Labor Relations | M,D |
| Information Science | M,D,O |
| Insurance | M,D,O |
| Interior Design | M |
| International Business | M |
| Kinesiology and Movement Studies | D |
| Latin American Studies | M,O |
| Law | D |
| Linguistics | M,D |
| Management Information Systems | M,D,O |
| Management Strategy and Policy | M,D |
| Marketing | M,D |
| Mass Communication | M,D |
| Mathematics Education | M,D,O |
| Mathematics | M,D |
| Media Studies | M,D |
| Microbiology | M,D |
| Middle School Education | M,D |
| Molecular Biology | M,D |
| Molecular Genetics | M,D |
| Music Education | M,D |
| Neurobiology | M,D |
| Neuroscience | D |
| Nonprofit Management | M,D,O |
| Nursing and Healthcare Administration | M,D,O |
| Nursing Informatics | M,D,O |
| Nursing—General | M,D,O |
| Nutrition | M |
| Occupational Therapy | M |
| Operations Research | M,D |
| Organic Chemistry | M,D |
| Organizational Management | M,D |
| Pediatric Nursing | M,D,O |
| Philosophy | M |
| Photography | M,D |
| Physical Chemistry | M,D |
| Physical Education | M |
| Physical Therapy | D |
| Physics | M,D |
| Physiology | M,D |
| Political Science | M,D |
| Psychiatric Nursing | M,D,O |
| Psychology—General | D |
| Public Administration | M,D,O |
| Public Health—General | M,D,O |
| Public History | M,D |
| Public Policy | M,D,O |
| Reading Education | M,D |
| Real Estate | M,D,O |
| Rehabilitation Counseling | M |
| Religion | M |
| Rhetoric | M,D |
| Risk Management | M,D,O |
| School Psychology | M,D,O |
| Science Education | M,D |
| Secondary Education | M,D |
| Social Psychology | D |
| Social Sciences Education | M,D |
| Social Work | M,O |
| Sociology | M,D |
| Spanish | M,O |
| Special Education | D |
| Speech and Interpersonal Communication | M,D |
| Sports Management | M |
| Statistics | M,D |
| Taxation | M |
| Translation and Interpretation | O |
| Urban and Regional Planning | M,D,O |
| Urban Education | M,D,O |
| Women's Health Nursing | M,D,O |
| Women's Studies | M,O |
| Writing | M,D |

**GERSTNER SLOAN KETTERING GRADUATE SCHOOL OF BIOMEDICAL SCIENCES**

| | |
|---|---|
| Biological and Biomedical Sciences—General | D |
| Cancer Biology/Oncology | D |

**GLION INSTITUTE OF HIGHER EDUCATION**

| | |
|---|---|
| Hospitality Management | M |

**GLOBAL UNIVERSITY**

| | |
|---|---|
| Missions and Missiology | M,D |
| Pastoral Ministry and Counseling | M,D |
| Religious Education | M,D |
| Theology | M,D |

**GODDARD COLLEGE**

| | |
|---|---|
| Art Therapy | M |
| Business Administration and Management—General | M |
| Clinical Psychology | M |
| Comparative and Interdisciplinary Arts | M |
| Education—General | M |
| Health Promotion | M |
| Interdisciplinary Studies | M |
| Psychology—General | M |
| Sustainability Management | M |
| Writing | M |

**GOLDEN GATE UNIVERSITY**

| | |
|---|---|
| Accounting | M,D,O |
| Business Administration and Management—General | M,D,O |
| Business Analytics | M,D,O |
| Entrepreneurship | M,D,O |
| Environmental Law | M,D |
| Finance and Banking | M,D,O |
| Forensic Sciences | M,O |
| Human Resources Management | M,D,O |
| Intellectual Property Law | M,D |
| International Business | M,D,O |
| Law | M,D |
| Legal and Justice Studies | M,D |
| Management Information Systems | M,D,O |
| Management of Technology | M,D,O |
| Marketing | M,D,O |
| Project Management | M,D,O |
| Psychology—General | M,D,O |
| Public Administration | M,D,O |
| Supply Chain Management | M,D,O |
| Taxation | M,D,O |

**GOLDEY-BEACOM COLLEGE**

| | |
|---|---|
| Business Administration and Management—General | M |
| Finance and Banking | M |
| Health Services Management and Hospital Administration | M |
| Human Resources Management | M |
| International Business | M |
| Management Information Systems | M |
| Marketing | M |
| Taxation | M |

**GOLDFARB SCHOOL OF NURSING AT BARNES-JEWISH COLLEGE**

| | |
|---|---|
| Acute Care/Critical Care Nursing | M |
| Gerontological Nursing | M |
| Nurse Anesthesia | M |
| Nursing and Healthcare Administration | M |
| Nursing—General | M |

**GONZAGA UNIVERSITY**

| | |
|---|---|
| Accounting | M |
| Business Administration and Management—General | M |
| Education—General | M,D |
| Educational Leadership and Administration | M,D |
| Elementary Education | M,D |
| Engineering and Applied Sciences—General | M,O |
| English as a Second Language | M |
| Law | D |
| Marriage and Family Therapy | M,D |
| Nursing—General | M,D |
| Organizational Management | M,D |
| Philosophy | M |
| Physiology | M,D |
| Secondary Education | M,D |
| Special Education | M,D |
| Sports Management | M,D |
| Taxation | M |
| Theology | M |

**GORDON COLLEGE**

| | |
|---|---|
| Early Childhood Education | M,O |
| Education—General | M,O |
| Educational Leadership and Administration | M,O |
| Elementary Education | M,O |
| English as a Second Language | M,O |
| Finance and Banking | M |
| Mathematics Education | M,O |
| Middle School Education | M,O |
| Music Education | M |
| Reading Education | M,O |
| Secondary Education | M,O |
| Special Education | M,O |

**GORDON-CONWELL THEOLOGICAL SEMINARY**

| | |
|---|---|
| Archaeology | M,D |
| Missions and Missiology | M,D |

Pastoral Ministry and Counseling M,D
Religion M,D
Theology M,D

**GOSHEN COLLEGE**
Environmental Education M
Family Nurse Practitioner Studies M
Nursing—General M

**GOUCHER COLLEGE**
Arts Administration M
Biological and Biomedical Sciences—General O
Computer Art and Design M
Cultural Studies M
Education—General M,O
Educational Leadership and Administration M,O
Educational Media/Instructional Technology M,O
Elementary Education M,O
Historic Preservation M
Middle School Education M,O
Physical Education M,O
Reading Education M,O
Secondary Education M,O
Special Education M,O
Writing M

**GOVERNORS STATE UNIVERSITY**
Accounting M
Actuarial Science M
Addictions/Substance Abuse Counseling M
Analytical Chemistry M
Art/Fine Arts M
Business Administration and Management—General M
Communication Disorders M
Communication—General M
Computer Science M
Counseling Psychology M
Criminal Justice and Criminology M
Education—General M
Educational Leadership and Administration M,D
English M
Environmental Biology M
Film, Television, and Video Production M
Health Services Management and Hospital Administration M
Human Services M,D
Legal and Justice Studies M
Management Information Systems M
Mathematics M
Nursing—General M
Occupational Therapy M
Photography M
Physical Therapy D
Political Science M
Psychology—General M
Public Administration M
Reading Education M
Social Work M
Special Education M

**GRACE COLLEGE**
Clinical Psychology M

**GRACE COLLEGE OF DIVINITY**
Religion M

**GRACELAND UNIVERSITY (IA)**
Curriculum and Instruction M
Education—General M
Educational Leadership and Administration M
Educational Media/Instructional Technology M
Family Nurse Practitioner Studies M,D,O
Gerontological Nursing M,D,O
Nursing Education M,D,O
Nursing—General M,D,O
Organizational Management M,D,O
Reading Education M
Religion M
Special Education M
Theology M

**GRACE MISSION UNIVERSITY**
Missions and Missiology M,D

**GRACE SCHOOL OF THEOLOGY**
Theology M

**GRACE THEOLOGICAL SEMINARY**
Cultural Studies M,D,O
Missions and Missiology M,D,O
Pastoral Ministry and Counseling M,D,O
Theology M,D,O
Women's Studies M,D,O

**THE GRADUATE CENTER, CITY UNIVERSITY OF NEW YORK**
Accounting D
Anthropology D
Archaeology D
Architectural History D
Art History D
Biochemistry D
Biological and Biomedical Sciences—General D
Biopsychology D
Business Administration and Management—General D
Chemistry D
Classics M,D
Clinical Psychology D
Cognitive Sciences D
Communication Disorders D
Comparative Literature M,D
Computer Science D
Criminal Justice and Criminology D
Cultural Anthropology D
Data Science/Data Analytics M
Developmental Psychology D
Economics D
Educational Psychology D
English D
Environmental Sciences D
Experimental Psychology D
Finance and Banking D
French D
Geographic Information Systems M
Geosciences D
Hispanic and Latin American Languages D
History D
Humanities M
Industrial and Organizational Psychology D
Italian M,D
Liberal Studies M
Linguistics M,D
Management Information Systems D
Mathematics D
Music D
Neuroscience M,D
Nursing—General D
Organizational Behavior D
Philosophy M,D
Physics D
Political Science M,D
Psychology—General D
Publishing M
Quantitative Analysis M
Social Psychology D
Social Sciences M
Social Work D
Sociology D
Theater D
Urban Education D

**GRADUATE THEOLOGICAL UNION**
Art History M,D,O
Cultural Studies M,D,O
Ethics M,D,O
Jewish Studies M,D,O
Religion M,D,O
Social Sciences M,D,O
Theology M,D,O

**GRAMBLING STATE UNIVERSITY**
Counselor Education M,D,O
Criminal Justice and Criminology M
Curriculum and Instruction M,D,O
Developmental Education M,D,O
Education—General M,D,O
Educational Leadership and Administration M,D,O
Educational Media/Instructional Technology M,D,O
English M,D,O
Family Nurse Practitioner Studies M,O
Health Services Management and Hospital Administration M
Higher Education M,D,O
Human Resources Management M
Mass Communication M
Mathematics Education M,D,O
Nursing—General M,O
Political Science M
Public Administration M
Reading Education M,D,O
Science Education M,D,O
Social Sciences Education M
Social Work M
Special Education M
Sports Management M
Student Affairs M,D,O

**GRAND CANYON UNIVERSITY**
Accounting M
Acute Care/Critical Care Nursing M,D,O
Business Administration and Management—General M,D
Business Analytics M
Cognitive Sciences D
Curriculum and Instruction M,D,O
Data Science/Data Analytics D
Early Childhood Education M,D,O
Education of the Gifted M,D,O
Education—General M,D,O
Educational Leadership and Administration M,D,O
Educational Media/Instructional Technology M,D,O
Elementary Education M,D,O
Emergency Management M
English as a Second Language M,D,O
Entrepreneurship M
Family Nurse Practitioner Studies M,D,O
Finance and Banking M
Health Informatics M,D,O
Health Services Management and Hospital Administration M,D,O
Human Resources Management M
Industrial and Organizational Psychology D
Management of Technology M
Marketing M,D
Nursing Education M,D,O
Nursing—General M,D,O
Organizational Management M,D
Pastoral Ministry and Counseling D
Project Management M
Psychology—General D
Public Health—General M,D,O
Reading Education M,D,O
Science Education M,D,O
Secondary Education M,D,O
Special Education M,D,O
Sports Management M

**GRAND RAPIDS THEOLOGICAL SEMINARY OF CORNERSTONE UNIVERSITY**
Interdisciplinary Studies M
Pastoral Ministry and Counseling M
Religion M
Theology M

**GRAND VALLEY STATE UNIVERSITY**
Accounting M
Allied Health—General M,D
Bioinformatics M
Biological and Biomedical Sciences—General M
Biostatistics M
Business Administration and Management—General M
Cancer Biology/Oncology M
Cell Biology M
Communication Disorders M
Communication—General M
Computer Engineering M
Computer Science M
Criminal Justice and Criminology M
Curriculum and Instruction M
Educational Leadership and Administration M,O
Educational Media/Instructional Technology M
Electrical Engineering M
Engineering and Applied Sciences—General M
English M
Health Services Management and Hospital Administration M
Higher Education M
Information Science M
Linguistics M
Manufacturing Engineering M
Mechanical Engineering M
Medical Informatics M
Molecular Biology M
Nonprofit Management M
Nursing and Healthcare Administration M,D
Nursing—General M,D
Nutrition M
Occupational Therapy M
Physical Therapy D
Physician Assistant Studies M
Public Administration M
Public Health—General M
Reading Education M
School Psychology M,O
Social Work M
Special Education M
Taxation M

**GRAND VIEW UNIVERSITY**
Athletic Training and Sports Medicine M,O
Educational Leadership and Administration M,O
Nursing and Healthcare Administration M,O
Nursing Education M,O
Organizational Management M,O
Sports Management M,O
Urban Education M,O

**GRANITE STATE COLLEGE**
Educational Leadership and Administration M
Organizational Management M
Project Management M

**GRANTHAM UNIVERSITY**
Business Administration and Management—General M,O
Engineering and Applied Sciences—General M
Health Services Management and Hospital Administration M
Human Resources Development M,O
Human Resources Management M,O
Management Information Systems M,O
Management Strategy and Policy M,O
Nursing and Healthcare Administration M
Nursing Education M
Nursing Informatics M
Nursing—General M
Project Management M,O

**GRATZ COLLEGE**
Education—General M
Educational Leadership and Administration M,D
Holocaust and Genocide Studies M,D
Jewish Studies M,O
Nonprofit Management M
Religious Education M,D
Social Work M,O

**GREENSBORO COLLEGE**
Cultural Studies M
Education—General M
Elementary Education M
English as a Second Language M
Ethics M
Special Education M
Theology M

**GREENVILLE UNIVERSITY**
Education—General M
Elementary Education M
Pastoral Ministry and Counseling M
Secondary Education M

**GUILFORD COLLEGE**
Criminal Justice and Criminology M

**GWYNEDD MERCY UNIVERSITY**
Adult Nursing M,D
Family Nurse Practitioner Studies M,D
Gerontological Nursing M,D
Nursing Education M,D
Nursing—General M,D
Oncology Nursing M,D
Pediatric Nursing M,D

**HALLMARK UNIVERSITY**
Business Administration and Management—General M
International Business M

**HAMLINE UNIVERSITY**
Business Administration and Management—General M,D
Education—General M,D
English as a Second Language M,D
Environmental Education M,D
Nonprofit Management M,D
Public Administration M,D
Reading Education M,D
Science Education M,D
Writing M

**HAMPTON UNIVERSITY**
Allied Health—General M
Applied Mathematics M
Atmospheric Sciences M,D
Biological and Biomedical Sciences—General M
Business Administration and Management—General M,D
Chemistry M
Communication Disorders M
Community Health Nursing M,D
Computational Sciences M
Computer and Information Systems Security M
Computer Science M
Counselor Education M,D,O
Education—General M,D,O
Educational Leadership and Administration M,D
English Education M
Environmental Biology M
Family Nurse Practitioner Studies M,D
Liberal Studies M,D,O
Marriage and Family Therapy M
Mathematics Education M
Medical Physics M,D
Middle School Education M
Nursing and Healthcare Administration M,D
Nursing Education M,D
Nursing—General M,D
Organizational Behavior M
Pastoral Ministry and Counseling M,D,O
Physical Therapy D
Physics M,D
Planetary and Space Sciences M,D
Psychology—General M
Sports Management M
Statistics M
Student Affairs M,D,O

**HANNIBAL-LAGRANGE UNIVERSITY**
Education—General M
Reading Education M

**HARDING SCHOOL OF THEOLOGY**
Pastoral Ministry and Counseling M,D
Theology M,D

**HARDING UNIVERSITY**
Allied Health—General M,D
Art Education M,O
Business Administration and Management—General M
Communication Disorders M
Counselor Education M,O
Early Childhood Education M,O
Education—General M,O
Educational Leadership and Administration M,O
Elementary Education M,O
English as a Second Language M,O
English Education M,O
Foreign Languages Education M,O
Health Education M,O
International Business M
Mathematics Education M,O
Organizational Management M
Pastoral Ministry and Counseling M
Pharmacy D
Physical Therapy D
Physician Assistant Studies M
Reading Education M,O
Secondary Education M,O
Social Sciences Education M,O
Special Education M,O

**HARDIN-SIMMONS UNIVERSITY**
Business Administration and Management—General M
Counseling Psychology M
Counselor Education M
Education of the Gifted M
Education—General M,D
Educational Leadership and Administration D
Family Nurse Practitioner Studies M
Higher Education D
Information Science M
Kinesiology and Movement Studies M
Marriage and Family Therapy M
Maternal and Child/Neonatal Nursing M
Music Education M
Music M
Nursing Education M
Nursing—General M
Pastoral Ministry and Counseling M,D

*M—masters degree; D—doctorate; O—other advanced degree; *—Close-Up and/or Display*

| | |
|---|---|
| Physical Therapy | D |
| Physician Assistant Studies | M,D |
| Psychology—General | M |
| Reading Education | M |
| Recreation and Park Management | M |
| Religion | M |
| Sports Management | M |
| Theology | M |

### HARRISBURG UNIVERSITY OF SCIENCE AND TECHNOLOGY

| | |
|---|---|
| Computer and Information Systems Security | M |
| Educational Media/Instructional Technology | M |
| Entrepreneurship | M |
| Human-Computer Interaction | M |
| Management Information Systems | M |
| Management of Technology | M |
| Management Strategy and Policy | M |
| Project Management | M |
| Software Engineering | M |
| Systems Engineering | M |
| Systems Science | M |

### HARRISON MIDDLETON UNIVERSITY

| | |
|---|---|
| Comparative Literature | M,D |
| Education—General | M,D |
| Humanities | M,D |
| Interdisciplinary Studies | M,D |
| Legal and Justice Studies | M,D |
| Philosophy | M,D |
| Religion | M,D |
| Science Education | M,D |
| Social Sciences | M,D |

### HARTFORD SEMINARY

| | |
|---|---|
| Pastoral Ministry and Counseling | M,D,O |
| Religion | M,D,O |
| Theology | M,D,O |

### HARVARD UNIVERSITY

| | |
|---|---|
| Accounting | D |
| African Studies | D |
| African-American Studies | D |
| Allopathic Medicine | D |
| American Studies | D |
| Anthropology | M,D |
| Applied Mathematics | M,D |
| Applied Physics | M,D |
| Applied Science and Technology | M,O |
| Archaeology | M,D |
| Architectural History | D |
| Architecture | M,D |
| Art Education | M |
| Art History | D |
| Asian Languages | M,D |
| Asian Studies | M,D |
| Astronomy | D |
| Astrophysics | D |
| Biochemistry | D |
| Bioengineering | M,D |
| Biological and Biomedical Sciences—General | M,D,O |
| Biological Anthropology | M,D |
| Biomedical Engineering | D |
| Biophysics | D |
| Biopsychology | D |
| Biostatistics | M,D |
| Biotechnology | M,O |
| Business Administration and Management—General | M,D,O |
| Cell Biology | D |
| Celtic Languages | D |
| Chemical Physics | D |
| Chemistry | D |
| Chinese | D |
| Classics | D |
| Cognitive Sciences | M,D |
| Communication—General | M,O |
| Comparative Literature | D |
| Computational Biology | M |
| Computational Sciences | M,D |
| Computer Science | M,D |
| Curriculum and Instruction | M |
| Demography and Population Studies | M,D |
| Dentistry | M,D,O |
| Developmental Psychology | D |
| East European and Russian Studies | M |
| Economics | D |
| Education—General | M,D |
| Educational Leadership and Administration | M,D |
| Educational Media/Instructional Technology | M,O |
| Educational Policy | M,O |
| Educational Psychology | M |
| Electrical Engineering | M,D |
| Engineering and Applied Sciences—General | M,D |
| Engineering Design | M,D |
| English | M,D,O |
| Environmental and Occupational Health | M,D |
| Environmental Engineering | M,D |
| Environmental Management and Policy | M,O |
| Environmental Sciences | M,D |
| Epidemiology | M,D |
| Ergonomics and Human Factors | M,D |
| Evolutionary Biology | D |
| Experimental Psychology | D |
| Forestry | M |
| Foundations and Philosophy of Education | M,O |
| French | M,D |
| Genetics | M,D |
| Geosciences | M,D |
| German | D |
| Health Promotion | M,D |
| Health Services Management and Hospital Administration | M,D |
| History of Science and Technology | M,D |
| History | D |
| Human Development | M |
| Industrial and Manufacturing Management | D |
| Information Science | M,D,O |
| Inorganic Chemistry | D |
| International Affairs | D |
| International and Comparative Education | M |
| International Development | M |
| International Health | M,D |
| Italian | M,D |
| Japanese | D |
| Jewish Studies | M,D |
| Journalism | M,O |
| Landscape Architecture | M,D |
| Law | M,D |
| Legal and Justice Studies | D |
| Liberal Studies | M,O |
| Linguistics | D |
| Management of Technology | D |
| Management Strategy and Policy | D |
| Marketing | D |
| Materials Sciences | M,D |
| Mathematics Education | M,O |
| Mathematics | D |
| Mechanical Engineering | M,D |
| Medical Physics | D |
| Medieval and Renaissance Studies | D |
| Microbiology | D |
| Molecular Biology | D |
| Molecular Genetics | D |
| Molecular Pharmacology | D |
| Museum Studies | M,O |
| Music | M,D |
| Near and Middle Eastern Languages | M,D |
| Near and Middle Eastern Studies | M,D |
| Neurobiology | D |
| Neuroscience | D |
| Nutrition | D |
| Oral and Dental Sciences | M,D,O |
| Organic Chemistry | D |
| Organizational Behavior | D |
| Pathology | D |
| Philosophy | M,D |
| Physical Chemistry | D |
| Physics | D |
| Planetary and Space Sciences | M,D |
| Political Science | M,D |
| Portuguese | M,D |
| Psychology—General | D |
| Public Administration | M |
| Public Health—General | M,D* |
| Public Policy | M,D |
| Quantitative Analysis | M,D |
| Reading Education | M |
| Religion | D |
| Russian | D |
| Scandinavian Languages | D |
| Slavic Languages | D |
| Social Psychology | D |
| Sociology | D |
| Spanish | M,D |
| Statistics | M,D |
| Systems Biology | D |
| Technical Communication | M |
| Theology | M |
| Theoretical Physics | D |
| Urban and Regional Planning | M,D |
| Urban Design | M |

### HASTINGS COLLEGE

| | |
|---|---|
| Education—General | M |

### HAWAII PACIFIC UNIVERSITY

| | |
|---|---|
| Business Administration and Management—General | M |
| Clinical Psychology | M |
| Communication—General | M |
| Educational Leadership and Administration | M |
| Elementary Education | M |
| English as a Second Language | M |
| Finance and Banking | M |
| Human Resources Management | M |
| International Business | M |
| Liberal Studies | M |
| Management Information Systems | M |
| Marine Sciences | M |
| Marketing | M |
| Military and Defense Studies | M |
| Nursing—General | M,D |
| Organizational Management | M |
| Public Administration | M |
| Public Health—General | M |
| Secondary Education | M |
| Social Work | M |
| Sustainable Development | M |

### HAZELDEN BETTY FORD GRADUATE SCHOOL OF ADDICTION STUDIES

| | |
|---|---|
| Addictions/Substance Abuse Counseling | M,O |

### HEBREW COLLEGE

| | |
|---|---|
| Early Childhood Education | M,O |
| Education—General | M,O |
| Jewish Studies | M,O |
| Middle School Education | M,O |
| Music Education | M,O |
| Music | M,O |
| Religious Education | M,O |
| Special Education | M,O |
| Theology | M |

### HEBREW UNION COLLEGE–JEWISH INSTITUTE OF RELIGION (NY)

| | |
|---|---|
| Education—General | M |
| Jewish Studies | M |
| Music | M |
| Near and Middle Eastern Languages | D |
| Nonprofit Management | M |
| Religious Education | M |
| Theology | M,D |

### HEC MONTREAL

| | |
|---|---|
| Accounting | M,D,O |
| Applied Economics | M,D |
| Arts Administration | O |
| Business Administration and Management—General | M,D,O |
| Business Analytics | M |
| Corporate and Organizational Communication | O |
| Data Science/Data Analytics | D |
| Electronic Commerce | M,O |
| Entrepreneurship | M,O |
| Finance and Banking | M,D,O |
| Financial Engineering | M,D |
| Human Resources Development | O |
| Human Resources Management | M,D,O |
| Industrial and Manufacturing Management | M |
| International Business | M,D |
| Logistics | M |
| Management Information Systems | M,O |
| Management Strategy and Policy | M,O |
| Marketing | M,D |
| Medical Microbiology | D |
| Operations Research | O |
| Organizational Management | M |
| Supply Chain Management | M,O |
| Sustainable Development | O |
| Taxation | M,O |

### HEIDELBERG UNIVERSITY

| | |
|---|---|
| Business Administration and Management—General | M |
| Counseling Psychology | M |
| Music Education | M |

### HENDERSON STATE UNIVERSITY

| | |
|---|---|
| Business Administration and Management—General | M |
| Counseling Psychology | M,O |
| Counselor Education | M,O |
| Curriculum and Instruction | M,O |
| Early Childhood Education | M,O |
| Education—General | M,O |
| Educational Leadership and Administration | M,O |
| English as a Second Language | M,O |
| Liberal Studies | M |
| Middle School Education | M,O |
| Physical Education | M |
| Special Education | M,O |
| Sports Management | M |

### HENDRIX COLLEGE

| | |
|---|---|
| Accounting | M |

### HENLEY-PUTNAM SCHOOL OF STRATEGIC SECURITY

| | |
|---|---|
| Conflict Resolution and Mediation/Peace Studies | M |
| Homeland Security | M |
| Military and Defense Studies | M |
| National Security | D |

### HERITAGE CHRISTIAN UNIVERSITY

| | |
|---|---|
| Classics | M |
| Pastoral Ministry and Counseling | M |
| Religion | M |

### HERITAGE COLLEGE AND SEMINARY

| | |
|---|---|
| Theology | M,O |

### HERITAGE UNIVERSITY

| | |
|---|---|
| Counselor Education | M |
| Education—General | M |
| Educational Leadership and Administration | M |
| English as a Second Language | M |
| English | M |
| Multilingual and Multicultural Education | M |
| Reading Education | M |
| Science Education | M |
| Special Education | M |

### HERZING UNIVERSITY ONLINE

| | |
|---|---|
| Accounting | M |
| Business Administration and Management—General | M |
| Health Services Management and Hospital Administration | M |
| Human Resources Management | M |
| Management of Technology | M |
| Marketing | M |
| Nursing and Healthcare Administration | M |
| Nursing Education | M |
| Nursing—General | M |
| Project Management | M |

### HIGH POINT UNIVERSITY

| | |
|---|---|
| Athletic Training and Sports Medicine | M,D |
| Business Administration and Management—General | M,D |
| Corporate and Organizational Communication | M,D |
| Educational Leadership and Administration | M,D |
| Elementary Education | M,D |
| Mathematics Education | M,D |
| Pharmacy | M,D |
| Physical Therapy | M,D |
| Physician Assistant Studies | M,D |
| Secondary Education | M,D |
| Special Education | M,D |

### HIGH TECH HIGH GRADUATE SCHOOL OF EDUCATION

| | |
|---|---|
| Educational Leadership and Administration | M |

### HILBERT COLLEGE

| | |
|---|---|
| Criminal Justice and Criminology | M |
| Health Services Management and Hospital Administration | M |
| Public Administration | M |

### HILLSDALE COLLEGE

| | |
|---|---|
| Political Science | M,D |

### HIRAM COLLEGE

| | |
|---|---|
| Interdisciplinary Studies | M |

### HODGES UNIVERSITY

| | |
|---|---|
| Accounting | M |
| Business Administration and Management—General | M |
| Clinical Psychology | M |
| Counseling Psychology | M |
| Health Services Management and Hospital Administration | M |
| Legal and Justice Studies | M |
| Management Information Systems | M |

### HOFSTRA UNIVERSITY

| | |
|---|---|
| Accounting | M,O |
| Advertising and Public Relations | M |
| Allopathic Medicine | D |
| Applied Behavior Analysis | M,D,O |
| Art Education | M,D,O |
| Art Therapy | M,O |
| Bioethics | M,D,O |
| Biological and Biomedical Sciences—General | M |
| Business Administration and Management—General | M,O |
| Business Education | M,D,O |
| Clinical Psychology | M,D |
| Communication Disorders | M,D,O |
| Computer and Information Systems Security | M |
| Counseling Psychology | M,O |
| Counselor Education | M,O |
| Early Childhood Education | M,D,O |
| Education of Students with Severe/Multiple Disabilities | M,D,O |
| Education of the Gifted | M,D,O |
| Education—General | M,D,O |
| Educational Leadership and Administration | M,D,O |
| Educational Media/Instructional Technology | M,D,O |
| Elementary Education | M,D,O |
| Engineering and Applied Sciences—General | M |
| English as a Second Language | M,D,O |
| English Education | M,D,O |
| English | M |
| Entertainment Management | M,O |
| Exercise and Sports Science | M,O |
| Family and Consumer Sciences-General | M,D,O |
| Family Nurse Practitioner Studies | M |
| Finance and Banking | M,O |
| Foreign Languages Education | M,D,O |
| Gerontological Nursing | M |
| Health Education | M,D,O |
| Health Informatics | M,O |
| Health Law | M,D,O |
| Health Services Management and Hospital Administration | M,O |
| Higher Education | M,D,O |
| Human Resources Management | M,O |
| Industrial and Organizational Psychology | M,D |
| Intellectual Property Law | M,D,O |
| International Business | M,O |
| Investment Management | M,O |
| Journalism | M |
| Law | M,D,O |
| Legal and Justice Studies | M,D,O |
| Linguistics | M |
| Management Information Systems | M,O |
| Management Strategy and Policy | M,O |
| Marketing Research | M,O |
| Marketing | M,O |
| Marriage and Family Therapy | M,O |
| Mathematics Education | M,D,O |
| Mathematics | M,D,O |
| Medical Physics | M |
| Middle School Education | M,D,O |
| Molecular Medicine | D |
| Multilingual and Multicultural Education | M,D,O |
| Music Education | M,D,O |
| Nursing and Healthcare Administration | M,D,O |
| Nursing—General | M |
| Occupational Therapy | M,O |
| Physical Education | M,D,O |
| Physician Assistant Studies | M |
| Psychiatric Nursing | M,O |
| Psychology—General | M,D |
| Public Health—General | M,O |
| Quality Management | M,O |
| Quantitative Analysis | M,O |
| Reading Education | M,D,O |
| Rehabilitation Counseling | M,O |
| School Psychology | M,D |
| Science Education | M,D,O |
| Secondary Education | M,D,O |
| Social Psychology | M,D |
| Social Sciences Education | M,D,O |
| Special Education | M,D,O |
| Sports Management | M,O |
| Sustainable Development | M |
| Taxation | M,O |
| Urban Design | M |
| Writing | M |

### HOLLINS UNIVERSITY

| | |
|---|---|
| Art/Fine Arts | M |
| Dance | M |
| Education—General | M |
| English | M,O |
| Film, Television, and Video Production | M |
| Film, Television, and Video Theory and Criticism | M |
| Humanities | M |
| Illustration | M,O |
| Interdisciplinary Studies | M |

Liberal Studies M
Music M
Social Sciences M
Theater M,O
Writing M,O

### HOLMES INSTITUTE
Pastoral Ministry and Counseling M

### HOLY APOSTLES COLLEGE AND SEMINARY
Theology M,O

### HOLY CROSS GREEK ORTHODOX SCHOOL OF THEOLOGY
Theology M

### HOLY FAMILY COLLEGE
Business Administration and Management—General M
Education—General M
Educational Leadership and Administration M
Music M

### HOLY FAMILY UNIVERSITY
Accounting M
Business Administration and Management—General M
Counseling Psychology M
Criminal Justice and Criminology M
Early Childhood Education M
Education—General M,D
Educational Leadership and Administration M,D
Elementary Education M
English as a Second Language M
Finance and Banking M
Health Services Management and Hospital Administration M
Human Resources Management M
Management Information Systems M
Nursing and Healthcare Administration M
Nursing Education M
Nursing—General M
Reading Education M
Special Education M

### HOLY NAMES UNIVERSITY
Business Administration and Management—General M
Counseling Psychology M
Education—General M,O
Educational Psychology M,O
Family Nurse Practitioner Studies M,O
Finance and Banking M
Forensic Psychology M
Marketing M
Music Education M,O
Music M,O
Nursing and Healthcare Administration M,O
Nursing Informatics M,O
Nursing—General M,O
Pastoral Ministry and Counseling M
Special Education M,O
Urban Education M,O
Writing M

### HOOD COLLEGE
Accounting M,O
Art/Fine Arts M,O
Bioinformatics M,O
Biological and Biomedical Sciences—General M
Business Administration and Management—General M,O
Clinical Psychology M
Computer and Information Systems Security M,O
Computer Science M,O
Curriculum and Instruction M,O
Education—General M,O
Educational Leadership and Administration M,O
Elementary Education M,O
Environmental Biology M,O
Geographic Information Systems M,O
Humanities M
Information Science M,O
Management Information Systems M,O
Mathematics Education M,O
Middle School Education M,O
Organizational Management M,D,O
Reading Education M,O
School Psychology M
Science Education M,O
Secondary Education M,O
Special Education M,O
Systems Science M

### HOOD THEOLOGICAL SEMINARY
Theology M,D

### HOPE INTERNATIONAL UNIVERSITY
Education—General M
Educational Leadership and Administration M
Elementary Education M
International Business M
International Development M
Marketing M
Marriage and Family Therapy M
Missions and Missiology M
Music M
Nonprofit Management M
Religion M
Secondary Education M

### HOUGHTON COLLEGE
Music M

### HOUSTON BAPTIST UNIVERSITY
Art/Fine Arts M
Business Administration and Management—General M,D
Counselor Education M,D
Curriculum and Instruction M,D
Education—General M,D
Educational Leadership and Administration M,D
Educational Measurement and Evaluation M,D
Educational Media/Instructional Technology M,D
Elementary Education M
English as a Second Language M,D
English M,D
Family Nurse Practitioner Studies M
Higher Education M,D
Human Resources Management M
International Business M
Kinesiology and Movement Studies M
Liberal Studies M
Mathematics M,D
Middle School Education M
Multilingual and Multicultural Education M,D
Music M,D
Near and Middle Eastern Languages M
Nursing—General M
Pediatric Nursing M
Philosophy M
Reading Education M,D
Religious Education M,D
Science Education M,D
Spanish M
Special Education M,D
Sports Management M
Theology M

### HOUSTON GRADUATE SCHOOL OF THEOLOGY
Pastoral Ministry and Counseling M,D
Theology M,D

### HOWARD PAYNE UNIVERSITY
Business Administration and Management—General M
Criminal Justice and Criminology M
Educational Leadership and Administration M
Pastoral Ministry and Counseling M
Sports Management M
Theology M

### HOWARD UNIVERSITY
Accounting M
African Studies M,D
Allied Health—General M,D
Allopathic Medicine D
Analytical Chemistry M,D
Anatomy M,D
Applied Arts and Design—General M
Applied Mathematics M,D
Art History M
Art/Fine Arts M
Atmospheric Sciences M,D
Biochemistry M,D
Biological and Biomedical Sciences—General M,D
Biophysics D
Biopsychology M,D
Biotechnology M,D
Business Administration and Management—General M
Chemical Engineering M
Chemistry M,D
Civil Engineering M
Clinical Psychology M,D
Communication Disorders M,D
Communication—General M,D
Computer Science M
Corporate and Organizational Communication M,D
Counseling Psychology D
Counselor Education M
Dentistry D,O
Developmental Psychology M,D
Economics M,D
Education—General M,D,O
Educational Leadership and Administration M,D,O
Educational Policy M,D,O
Educational Psychology D
Electrical Engineering M,D
Elementary Education M
Engineering and Applied Sciences—General M,D
English M,D
Environmental Sciences M,D
Exercise and Sports Science M
Experimental Psychology M,D
Family Nurse Practitioner Studies M
Film, Television, and Video Production M
Finance and Banking M
French M
Health Education M
History M,D
Human Resources Management M
Inorganic Chemistry M,D
International Business M
Law M,D
Leisure Studies M
Management Information Systems M
Marketing M
Mass Communication M,D
Mathematics M,D
Mechanical Engineering M,D
Media Studies M,D
Microbiology D
Molecular Biology M,D
Multilingual and Multicultural Education M,D
Music Education M
Music M
Nursing Education M
Nursing—General M
Nutrition M,D
Occupational Therapy M,D
Oral and Dental Sciences D,O
Organic Chemistry M,D
Pharmacology M,D
Pharmacy D
Philosophy M
Photography M
Physical Chemistry M,D
Physical Education M
Physical Therapy M,D
Physician Assistant Studies M,D
Physics M,D
Physiology D
Political Science M,D
Psychology—General M,D
Public Administration M
Public Health—General M
School Psychology M,D
Secondary Education M
Social Psychology M,D
Social Work M,D
Sociology M,D
Spanish M
Special Education M
Sports Management M
Supply Chain Management M
Theology M,D

### HULT INTERNATIONAL BUSINESS SCHOOL (UNITED STATES)
Business Administration and Management—General M
Business Analytics M
Entrepreneurship M
Finance and Banking M
International Business M
Marketing M
Project Management M

### HUMBOLDT STATE UNIVERSITY
Anthropology M
Biological and Biomedical Sciences—General M
Business Administration and Management—General M
Counseling Psychology M
Developmental Psychology M
Education—General M
English as a Second Language M
English M
Environmental Management and Policy M
Environmental Sciences M
Fish, Game, and Wildlife Management M
Forestry M
Geology M
Hazardous Materials Management M
Kinesiology and Movement Studies M
Natural Resources M
Psychology—General M
School Psychology M
Social Psychology M
Social Sciences M
Social Work M
Sociology M
Water Resources M

### HUMPHREYS UNIVERSITY
Law D

### HUNTER COLLEGE OF THE CITY UNIVERSITY OF NEW YORK
Accounting M
Adult Nursing M
Animal Behavior M,O
Anthropology M
Applied Mathematics M
Applied Social Research M
Art History M
Art/Fine Arts M
Astronomy M,D
Biochemistry M,D
Bioinformatics M
Biological and Biomedical Sciences—General M,D
Chemistry D
Chinese M
Classics M
Communication Disorders M
Community Health Nursing M
Comparative Literature M
Counselor Education M
Early Childhood Education M,D,O
Economics M
Education of Students with Severe/Multiple Disabilities M
Education—General M,D,O
Educational Leadership and Administration D,O
English as a Second Language M
English Education M
Family Nurse Practitioner Studies D
Foreign Languages Education M
French M
Geographic Information Systems M,O
Geography M,O
Geosciences M
Gerontological Nursing M,D
History M
Italian M
Mathematics Education M
Mathematics M
Media Studies M
Multilingual and Multicultural Education M
Music Education M
Music M
Nursing—General M,D,O
Nutrition M
Physical Therapy D
Physics M,D
Psychiatric Nursing M,D,O
Psychology—General M,O
Public Health—General M
Rehabilitation Counseling M
Romance Languages M
Science Education M
Secondary Education M
Social Sciences Education M
Social Work M
Sociology M
Spanish M
Special Education M
Statistics M
Sustainable Development M,O
Theater M
Urban and Regional Planning M
Urban Studies M
Writing M

### HUNTINGTON UNIVERSITY
Business Administration and Management—General M,D
Elementary Education M,D
English as a Second Language M,D
Middle School Education M,D
Occupational Therapy M,D
Organizational Management M,D
Pastoral Ministry and Counseling M,D

### HUNTINGTON UNIVERSITY OF HEALTH SCIENCES
Nutrition M,D

### HUNTSVILLE BIBLE COLLEGE
Pastoral Ministry and Counseling M

### HUSSON UNIVERSITY
Biotechnology M
Business Administration and Management—General M
Clinical Psychology M
Community Health Nursing M,O
Counseling Psychology M
Counselor Education M
Criminal Justice and Criminology M
Educational Leadership and Administration M,O
Family Nurse Practitioner Studies M,O
Health Services Management and Hospital Administration M
Hospitality Management M
Nursing—General M,O
Organizational Management M
Pharmacology M,D
Pharmacy M,D
Physical Therapy D
Psychiatric Nursing M,O
Risk Management M
School Psychology M
Social Psychology M
Sports Management M

### HUSTON-TILLOTSON UNIVERSITY
Educational Leadership and Administration M

### ICAHN SCHOOL OF MEDICINE AT MOUNT SINAI
Allopathic Medicine D
Bioethics M
Biological and Biomedical Sciences—General M,D
Clinical Research M,D
Community Health M,D
Genetic Counseling M,D
Neuroscience M,D
Public Health—General M,D

### IDAHO STATE UNIVERSITY
Allied Health—General M,D,O
Anthropology M
Applied Physics M,D
Art/Fine Arts M
Athletic Training and Sports Medicine M
Biological and Biomedical Sciences—General M,D
Business Administration and Management—General M,O
Chemistry M
Civil Engineering M
Clinical Psychology D
Communication Disorders M,D
Communication—General M
Community Health O
Counseling Psychology M,D,O
Counselor Education M,D,O
Dental Hygiene M
Dentistry O
Education—General M,D,O
Educational Leadership and Administration M,D,O
Educational Media/Instructional Technology M,D
Elementary Education M
Engineering and Applied Sciences—General M,D,O
English as a Second Language M,D,O
English M,D,O
Environmental Engineering M
Environmental Management and Policy M
Environmental Sciences M,O
Experimental Psychology D
Geographic Information Systems M,O

*M—masters degree; D—doctorate; O—other advanced degree; *—Close-Up and/or Display*

| | |
|---|---|
| Geology | M,O |
| Geophysics | M,O |
| Geosciences | M,O |
| Health Education | M |
| Health Physics/Radiological Health | M,D |
| History | M |
| Human Resources Management | M,D |
| Hydrology | M,O |
| Management Information Systems | M,O |
| Marriage and Family Therapy | M,D,O |
| Mathematics Education | M,D |
| Mathematics | M,D |
| Mechanical Engineering | M |
| Medical Microbiology | M,D |
| Medicinal and Pharmaceutical Chemistry | M,D |
| Microbiology | M,D |
| Music Education | M |
| Nuclear Engineering | M,D |
| Nursing—General | M,D |
| Occupational Therapy | M |
| Operations Research | M |
| Oral and Dental Sciences | O |
| Pharmaceutical Administration | M,D |
| Pharmaceutical Sciences | M,D |
| Pharmacology | M,D |
| Pharmacy | M,D |
| Physical Education | M |
| Physical Therapy | D |
| Physician Assistant Studies | M |
| Physics | M,D |
| Political Science | M,D |
| Psychology—General | D |
| Public Administration | M |
| Public Health—General | M |
| Reading Education | M |
| School Psychology | M,D,O |
| Secondary Education | M |
| Sociology | M |
| Special Education | M |
| Sports Management | M |
| Theater | M |

### IGLOBAL UNIVERSITY

| | |
|---|---|
| Accounting | M |
| Business Administration and Management—General | M |
| Data Science/Data Analytics | M |
| Entrepreneurship | M |
| Finance and Banking | M |
| Health Services Management and Hospital Administration | M |
| Hospitality Management | M |
| Human Resources Management | M |
| International Business | M |
| Management Information Systems | M |
| Project Management | M |
| Public Administration | M |
| Travel and Tourism | M |

### ILIFF SCHOOL OF THEOLOGY

| | |
|---|---|
| Pastoral Ministry and Counseling | M,D |
| Religion | M,D |
| Theology | M,D |

### ILLINOIS COLLEGE OF OPTOMETRY

| | |
|---|---|
| Optometry | D |

### ILLINOIS INSTITUTE OF TECHNOLOGY

| | |
|---|---|
| Aerospace/Aeronautical Engineering | M,D |
| Agricultural Engineering | M |
| Analytical Chemistry | M,D |
| Applied Arts and Design—General | M,D |
| Applied Mathematics | M,D |
| Applied Physics | M,D |
| Architectural Engineering | M,D |
| Architecture | M,D |
| Artificial Intelligence/Robotics | M,D |
| Biochemistry | M,D |
| Bioengineering | M,D |
| Biological and Biomedical Sciences—General | M,D |
| Biomedical Engineering | M,D |
| Business Administration and Management—General | M,D |
| Cell Biology | M,D |
| Chemical Engineering | M,D |
| Chemistry | M,D |
| Civil Engineering | M,D |
| Clinical Psychology | M,D |
| Communication—General | M,D |
| Computer and Information Systems Security | M,D |
| Computer Education | M,D |
| Computer Engineering | M,D |
| Computer Science | M,D |
| Construction Engineering | M,D |
| Construction Management | M,D |
| Corporate and Organizational Communication | M |
| Data Science/Data Analytics | M,D |
| Electrical Engineering | M,D |
| Engineering and Applied Sciences—General | M,D |
| Entrepreneurship | M |
| Environmental Engineering | M,D |
| Environmental Management and Policy | M |
| Finance and Banking | M,D |
| Food Science and Technology | M |
| Geotechnical Engineering | M,D |
| Health Physics/Radiological Health | M,D |
| Human Resources Development | M,D |
| Humanities | M,D |
| Industrial and Manufacturing Management | M |
| Industrial and Organizational Psychology | M,D |
| Inorganic Chemistry | M,D |
| Landscape Architecture | M,D |
| Law | M,D |
| Legal and Justice Studies | M,D |
| Management Information Systems | M,D |
| Manufacturing Engineering | M,D |
| Marketing | M |
| Materials Engineering | M,D |
| Materials Sciences | M,D |
| Mathematical and Computational Finance | M,D |
| Mathematics Education | M,D |
| Mechanical Engineering | M,D |
| Medical Imaging | M,D |
| Microbiology | M,D |
| Molecular Biology | M,D |
| Molecular Biophysics | M,D |
| Physics | M,D |
| Psychology—General | M,D |
| Public Administration | M |
| Rehabilitation Counseling | M,D |
| Science Education | M,D |
| Software Engineering | M,D |
| Structural Engineering | M,D |
| Sustainability Management | M |
| Taxation | M,D |
| Technical Writing | M,D |
| Telecommunications | M,D |
| Transportation and Highway Engineering | M,D |

### ILLINOIS STATE UNIVERSITY

| | |
|---|---|
| Accounting | M |
| Agricultural Economics and Agribusiness | M |
| Agricultural Sciences—General | M |
| Animal Behavior | M,D |
| Archaeology | M |
| Art History | M |
| Art/Fine Arts | M |
| Bacteriology | M,D |
| Biochemistry | M,D |
| Biological and Biomedical Sciences—General | M,D |
| Biophysics | M,D |
| Biotechnology | M |
| Botany | M,D |
| Business Administration and Management—General | M |
| Cell Biology | M,D |
| Clinical Psychology | M,D,O |
| Cognitive Sciences | M,D,O |
| Communication Disorders | M |
| Communication—General | M |
| Conservation Biology | M,D |
| Counseling Psychology | M,D,O |
| Criminal Justice and Criminology | M |
| Curriculum and Instruction | M,D |
| Developmental Biology | M,D |
| Developmental Psychology | M,D,O |
| Ecology | M,D |
| Economics | M |
| Education—General | M,D,O |
| Educational Leadership and Administration | M,D |
| Educational Policy | M,D |
| English | M,D |
| Entomology | M,D |
| Evolutionary Biology | M,D |
| Family and Consumer Sciences-General | M |
| Family Nurse Practitioner Studies | M,D,O |
| French | M |
| Genetics | M,D |
| German | M |
| Graphic Design | M |
| Health Education | M |
| Higher Education | M,D |
| History | M |
| Immunology | M,D |
| Industrial and Organizational Psychology | M,D,O |
| Industrial/Management Engineering | M |
| Management Information Systems | M |
| Management of Technology | M |
| Mathematics Education | M,D |
| Mathematics | M |
| Microbiology | M,D |
| Molecular Biology | M,D |
| Molecular Genetics | M,D |
| Music | M |
| Neurobiology | M,D |
| Neuroscience | M,D |
| Nursing—General | M,D,O |
| Parasitology | M,D |
| Photography | M |
| Physical Education | M |
| Physiology | M,D |
| Plant Biology | M,D |
| Plant Molecular Biology | M,D |
| Plant Sciences | M,D |
| Political Science | M |
| Psychology—General | M,D,O |
| Reading Education | M |
| School Psychology | M,D,O |
| Social Work | M |
| Sociology | M |
| Spanish | M |
| Special Education | M,D,O |
| Structural Biology | M,D |
| Student Affairs | M |
| Textile Design | M |
| Theater | M |
| Writing | M,D |
| Zoology | M,D |

### IMMACULATA UNIVERSITY

| | |
|---|---|
| Clinical Psychology | M,D,O |
| Counseling Psychology | M,D,O |
| Educational Leadership and Administration | M,D,O |
| Educational Psychology | M,D,O |
| English as a Second Language | M |
| Forensic Psychology | M,D,O |
| Health Promotion | M |
| Multilingual and Multicultural Education | M |
| Neuroscience | M,D,O |
| Nursing and Healthcare Administration | M |
| Nursing Education | M |
| Nursing—General | M |
| Nutrition | M |
| Organizational Management | M |
| Psychoanalysis and Psychotherapy | M,D,O |
| Psychology—General | M,D,O |
| School Psychology | M,D,O |
| Secondary Education | M,D,O |
| Special Education | M,D,O |
| Therapies—Dance, Drama, and Music | M |

### INDEPENDENCE UNIVERSITY

| | |
|---|---|
| Business Administration and Management—General | M |
| Community Health Nursing | M |
| Community Health | M |
| Gerontological Nursing | M |
| Health Promotion | M |
| Health Services Management and Hospital Administration | M |
| Nursing and Healthcare Administration | M |
| Nursing—General | M |
| Public Health—General | M |

### INDIANA STATE UNIVERSITY

| | |
|---|---|
| Art/Fine Arts | M |
| Athletic Training and Sports Medicine | M,D |
| Biological and Biomedical Sciences—General | M,D |
| Business Administration and Management—General | M |
| Cell Biology | M,D |
| Clinical Psychology | M,D,O |
| Communication Disorders | M,D,O |
| Communication—General | M |
| Computer Engineering | M |
| Computer Science | M |
| Counselor Education | M,D,O |
| Criminal Justice and Criminology | M |
| Curriculum and Instruction | M,D |
| Ecology | M,D |
| Education—General | M,D,O |
| Educational Leadership and Administration | M,D,O |
| Educational Media/Instructional Technology | M,D |
| Engineering and Applied Sciences—General | M |
| English as a Second Language | M,D,O |
| English | M |
| Environmental and Occupational Health | M |
| Evolutionary Biology | M,D |
| Family Nurse Practitioner Studies | M,D |
| Foreign Languages Education | M,D,O |
| Graphic Design | M |
| Health Education | M,D |
| Higher Education | M,D,O |
| History | M |
| Human Resources Development | M |
| Linguistics | M,D,O |
| Management of Technology | M,D |
| Mathematics | M |
| Media Studies | M |
| Molecular Biology | M,D |
| Multilingual and Multicultural Education | M,D,O |
| Music Education | M |
| Music | M |
| Nursing and Healthcare Administration | M,D |
| Nursing Education | M,D |
| Nursing—General | M,D |
| Occupational Therapy | M,D |
| Photography | M |
| Physical Education | M,D |
| Physical Therapy | M,D |
| Physician Assistant Studies | M,D |
| Physiology | M,D |
| Psychology—General | M,D |
| Public Administration | M |
| Recreation and Park Management | M,D |
| School Psychology | M,D,O |
| Science Education | M,D |
| Social Work | M |
| Spanish | M,D,O |
| Sports Management | M,D |
| Student Affairs | M,D,O |
| Vocational and Technical Education | M |
| Writing | M |

### INDIANA TECH

| | |
|---|---|
| Accounting | M |
| Business Administration and Management—General | M |
| Engineering Management | M |
| Health Services Management and Hospital Administration | M |
| Human Resources Development | M |
| Human Resources Management | M |
| International Business | D |
| Marketing | M |
| Organizational Management | M |
| Psychology—General | M |

### INDIANA UNIVERSITY BLOOMINGTON

| | |
|---|---|
| African Studies | M |
| African-American Studies | M,D |
| Analytical Chemistry | M,D |
| Anthropology | M,D |
| Applied Arts and Design—General | M |
| Applied Mathematics | M,D |
| Applied Statistics | M,D |
| Archaeology | M,D |
| Architecture | M |
| Art Education | M,D,O |
| Art History | M,D |
| Art/Fine Arts | M |
| Artificial Intelligence/Robotics | D |
| Arts Administration | M |
| Asian Languages | M,D |
| Asian Studies | M,D |
| Astronomy | M,D |
| Astrophysics | M,D |
| Athletic Training and Sports Medicine | M,D |
| Atmospheric Sciences | M,D |
| Biochemistry | M,D |
| Bioinformatics | M,D,O |
| Biological and Biomedical Sciences—General | M,D |
| Biostatistics | M,D |
| Biotechnology | M,D |
| Business Administration and Management—General | M,D |
| Cell Biology | M,D |
| Chemistry | M,D |
| Chinese | M,D |
| Classics | M,D |
| Cognitive Sciences | D |
| Communication Disorders | M,D |
| Community Health | M,D |
| Comparative Literature | M,D |
| Computer and Information Systems Security | M,D |
| Computer Science | M,D,O |
| Counselor Education | M,D,O |
| Criminal Justice and Criminology | M,D |
| Curriculum and Instruction | M,D,O |
| Data Science/Data Analytics | M,O |
| Developmental Psychology | D |
| East European and Russian Studies | M,O |
| Ecology | M,D,O |
| Economic Development | M,D,O |
| Economics | M,D |
| Education—General | M,D,O |
| Educational Leadership and Administration | M,D,O |
| Educational Measurement and Evaluation | M,D,O |
| Educational Media/Instructional Technology | M,D |
| Educational Policy | M,D,O |
| Educational Psychology | M,D,O |
| Elementary Education | M,D,O |
| Energy Management and Policy | M,D,O |
| English as a Second Language | M,D |
| English | M,D |
| Environmental and Occupational Health | M,D |
| Environmental Management and Policy | M,D,O |
| Environmental Sciences | M,D,O |
| Epidemiology | M,D |
| Ergonomics and Human Factors | M,D |
| Evolutionary Biology | M,D |
| Exercise and Sports Science | M,D |
| Finance and Banking | M,D,O |
| Folklore | M,D |
| Foreign Languages Education | M,D |
| Foundations and Philosophy of Education | M,D,O |
| French | M,D |
| Gender Studies | D |
| Genetics | M,D |
| Geochemistry | M,D |
| Geography | D |
| Geophysics | M,D |
| Geosciences | M,D |
| German | M,D |
| Hazardous Materials Management | M,D,O |
| Health Education | M,D |
| Health Informatics | M,D |
| Health Promotion | M,D |
| Health Services Management and Hospital Administration | M,D |
| Higher Education | M,D,O |
| Hispanic and Latin American Languages | M,D |
| History of Medicine | M,D |
| History of Science and Technology | M,D |
| History | M,D |
| Human-Computer Interaction | M,D |
| Hydrogeology | M,D |
| Information Science | M,D,O |
| Inorganic Chemistry | M,D |
| International Affairs | M |
| International and Comparative Education | M,D,O |
| International Development | M,D,O |
| Italian | M,D |
| Japanese | M,D |
| Jewish Studies | M |
| Kinesiology and Movement Studies | M,D |
| Latin American Studies | M |
| Law | M,D,O |
| Leisure Studies | M,D |
| Library Science | M,D,O |
| Linguistics | M,D |
| Management Information Systems | M,D,O |
| Materials Sciences | M,D |
| Mathematical Physics | M,D |
| Mathematics Education | M,D,O |
| Mathematics | M,D |
| Media Studies | M,D |
| Medical Physics | M,D |
| Medieval and Renaissance Studies | M,D |
| Microbiology | M,D |
| Mineralogy | M,D |
| Molecular Biology | M,D |
| Multilingual and Multicultural Education | M,D |
| Music | M,D,O |
| Near and Middle Eastern Languages | M,D |
| Neuroscience | D |
| Nonprofit Management | M,D,O |
| Nutrition | M,D |
| Optometry | M,D |
| Organic Chemistry | M,D |

| | |
|---|---|
| Organizational Management | M,D,O |
| Philosophy | M,D |
| Physical Chemistry | M,D |
| Physical Education | M,D |
| Physics | M,D |
| Plant Biology | M,D |
| Political Science | M,D |
| Portuguese | M,D |
| Psychology—General | D |
| Public Administration | M,D,O |
| Public Affairs | M,D,O |
| Public Health—General | M,D |
| Public Policy | M,D,O |
| Reading Education | M,D,O |
| Recreation and Park Management | M,D |
| Religion | M,D |
| Rhetoric | M,D |
| Safety Engineering | M,D |
| School Psychology | M,D,O |
| Science Education | M,D,O |
| Secondary Education | M,D,O |
| Slavic Languages | M,D |
| Social Psychology | D |
| Social Sciences Education | M,D,O |
| Social Sciences | M,D,O |
| Sociology | M,D |
| Spanish | M,D |
| Special Education | M,D,O |
| Sports Management | M,D |
| Statistics | M,D |
| Student Affairs | M,D,O |
| Sustainability Management | M,D,O |
| Systems Engineering | D |
| Theater | M,D |
| Toxicology | M,D,O |
| Travel and Tourism | M,D |
| Water Resources Engineering | M,D,O |
| Western European Studies | M |
| Writing | M,D |
| Zoology | M,D |

**INDIANA UNIVERSITY EAST**

| | |
|---|---|
| Education—General | M |
| Nursing—General | M |
| Social Work | M |

**INDIANA UNIVERSITY KOKOMO**

| | |
|---|---|
| Accounting | M,O |
| Business Administration and Management—General | M,O |
| Family Nurse Practitioner Studies | M |
| Health Services Management and Hospital Administration | M,O |
| Nursing and Healthcare Administration | M |
| Nursing Education | M |
| Nursing—General | M |
| Public Administration | M,O |
| Public Policy | M,O |

**INDIANA UNIVERSITY NORTHWEST**

| | |
|---|---|
| Accounting | M,O |
| Addictions/Substance Abuse Counseling | M,O |
| Business Administration and Management—General | M,O |
| Counseling Psychology | M,O |
| Criminal Justice and Criminology | M,O |
| Education—General | M,O |
| Educational Leadership and Administration | M,O |
| Elementary Education | M,O |
| Environmental Management and Policy | M,O |
| Gender Studies | M,O |
| Health Services Management and Hospital Administration | M,O |
| Liberal Studies | M,O |
| Management Information Systems | M,O |
| Nonprofit Management | M,O |
| Public Administration | M,O |
| Public Affairs | M,O |
| Secondary Education | M,O |
| Social Work | M |
| Urban Studies | M,O |

**INDIANA UNIVERSITY OF PENNSYLVANIA**

| | |
|---|---|
| Adult Education | M |
| Applied Mathematics | M |
| Archaeology | M |
| Art/Fine Arts | M |
| Biological and Biomedical Sciences—General | M |
| Business Administration and Management—General | M |
| Business Education | M |
| Chemistry | M |
| Clinical Psychology | M,D |
| Communication Disorders | M |
| Communication—General | D |
| Counselor Education | M |
| Criminal Justice and Criminology | M,D |
| Curriculum and Instruction | D |
| Education—General | M,D,O |
| Educational Leadership and Administration | D,O |
| Educational Media/Instructional Technology | M,D |
| Educational Psychology | M,O |
| English as a Second Language | M,D |
| English Education | D |
| English | M,D |
| Environmental and Occupational Health | M,D |
| Environmental Management and Policy | M |
| Exercise and Sports Science | M |
| Geographic Information Systems | M,O |
| Geography | M,O |
| Health Education | M |
| Health Services Management and Hospital Administration | M |
| Higher Education | M |
| History | M |
| Human Resources Development | M |
| Industrial and Labor Relations | M |
| Mathematics Education | M |
| Mathematics | M |
| Media Studies | D |
| Music Education | M |
| Music | M |
| Nanotechnology | M |
| Nonprofit Management | D |
| Nursing and Healthcare Administration | M |
| Nursing Education | M |
| Nursing—General | D |
| Nutrition | M |
| Physical Education | M |
| Physics | M |
| Psychology—General | M,D |
| Public Affairs | M |
| Public History | M |
| Reading Education | M,O |
| School Psychology | D,O |
| Social Psychology | M |
| Sociology | M |
| Special Education | M |
| Sports Management | M |
| Student Affairs | M |
| Urban and Regional Planning | M |
| Vocational and Technical Education | M |

**INDIANA UNIVERSITY-PURDUE UNIVERSITY INDIANAPOLIS**

| | |
|---|---|
| Accounting | M |
| Acute Care/Critical Care Nursing | M |
| Allopathic Medicine | M,D |
| American Studies | M,D |
| Anatomy | M,D |
| Applied Mathematics | M,D |
| Applied Statistics | M,D |
| Art Therapy | M |
| Art/Fine Arts | M |
| Biochemistry | M,D |
| Bioethics | M,D,O |
| Bioinformatics | M,D |
| Biological and Biomedical Sciences—General | M,D |
| Biomedical Engineering | M,D |
| Biostatistics | M,D,O |
| Business Administration and Management—General | M |
| Cell Biology | M,D |
| Chemistry | M,D |
| Clinical Psychology | M,D |
| Communication—General | M,D |
| Community Health | M,D,O |
| Computer and Information Systems Security | M,D,O |
| Computer Art and Design | M |
| Computer Engineering | M,D |
| Computer Science | M,D,O |
| Counselor Education | M,O |
| Criminal Justice and Criminology | M,O |
| Curriculum and Instruction | M,O |
| Data Science/Data Analytics | M,D,O |
| Dentistry | M,D,O |
| Early Childhood Education | M,O |
| Economics | M |
| Education—General | M,O |
| Educational Leadership and Administration | M,O |
| Electrical Engineering | M,D |
| Emergency Management | M,O |
| English as a Second Language | M,O |
| English | M,O |
| Entrepreneurship | M |
| Environmental and Occupational Health | M,D,O |
| Epidemiology | M,D,O |
| Family Nurse Practitioner Studies | M |
| Finance and Banking | M |
| Foreign Languages Education | M,O |
| Forensic Sciences | M |
| Geographic Information Systems | M,O |
| Geology | M,D |
| Geosciences | M,D |
| Gerontological Nursing | M |
| Graphic Design | M |
| Health Communication | M,D |
| Health Education | M,D |
| Health Informatics | M,D |
| Health Law | M,D,O |
| Health Services Management and Hospital Administration | M,D,O |
| History | M |
| Homeland Security | M,O |
| Human-Computer Interaction | M,D |
| Immunology | M,D |
| Industrial and Organizational Psychology | M,D |
| Information Science | M |
| Intellectual Property Law | M,D,O |
| International Health | M,D,O |
| Kinesiology and Movement Studies | M,O |
| Law | M,D,O |
| Liberal Studies | M,D,O |
| Library Science | M,O |
| Management of Technology | M |
| Marketing | M |
| Mathematics Education | M,D |
| Mathematics | M,D |
| Mechanical Engineering | M,D |
| Microbiology | M,D |
| Molecular Biology | M,D |
| Molecular Genetics | M,D |
| Museum Studies | M,O |
| Music | M,D |
| Natural Resources | M,D,O |
| Neurobiology | D |
| Nonprofit Management | M,O |
| Nursing and Healthcare Administration | M,D |
| Nursing Education | M |
| Nursing—General | M,D |
| Nutrition | M,D |
| Occupational Therapy | M,D |
| Organizational Management | M,O |
| Pathology | M,D |
| Pediatric Nursing | M |
| Pharmacology | M,D |
| Philanthropic Studies | M,D |
| Philosophy | M,O |
| Photography | M |
| Physical Education | M,O |
| Physical Therapy | M,D |
| Physics | M,D |
| Political Science | M |
| Psychology—General | M,D |
| Public Administration | M,O |
| Public Affairs | M,O |
| Public Health—General | M,D,O |
| Public History | M |
| Reading Education | M,O |
| Rehabilitation Sciences | M,D |
| Social Psychology | M,D |
| Social Sciences | M,D,O |
| Social Work | M,D,O |
| Sociology | M |
| Software Engineering | M,D,O |
| Special Education | M,O |
| Statistics | M,D |
| Supply Chain Management | M |
| Technical Communication | M |
| Therapies—Dance, Drama, and Music | M,D |
| Toxicology | M,D |
| Western European Studies | M |
| Writing | M,O |

**INDIANA UNIVERSITY SOUTH BEND**

| | |
|---|---|
| Accounting | M,O |
| Addictions/Substance Abuse Counseling | M,O |
| Applied Mathematics | M,O |
| Business Administration and Management—General | M,O |
| Clinical Psychology | M,O |
| Communication—General | M,D |
| Computer Science | M,O |
| Counseling Psychology | M,O |
| Counselor Education | M,O |
| Education—General | M,O |
| Educational Leadership and Administration | M,O |
| Educational Media/Instructional Technology | M,O |
| Elementary Education | M,O |
| English | M,O |
| Family Nurse Practitioner Studies | M |
| Finance and Banking | M,O |
| Health Services Management and Hospital Administration | M,O |
| Human Resources Management | M,O |
| International Affairs | M,O |
| Legal and Justice Studies | M,O |
| Liberal Studies | M,O |
| Marketing | M,O |
| Marriage and Family Therapy | M,O |
| Music | M,D |
| Nonprofit Management | M,O |
| Nursing—General | M |
| Public Administration | M,O |
| Public Affairs | M,O |
| School Psychology | M,O |
| Secondary Education | M,O |
| Social Work | M |
| Special Education | M,O |
| Writing | M,O |

**INDIANA UNIVERSITY SOUTHEAST**

| | |
|---|---|
| Business Administration and Management—General | M |
| Counselor Education | M |
| Education—General | M |
| Elementary Education | M |
| Finance and Banking | M |
| Interdisciplinary Studies | M,O |
| Secondary Education | M |

**INDIANA WESLEYAN UNIVERSITY**

| | |
|---|---|
| Accounting | M,O |
| Addictions/Substance Abuse Counseling | M |
| Athletic Training and Sports Medicine | M,D |
| Business Administration and Management—General | M,O |
| Counseling Psychology | M,O |
| Counselor Education | M |
| Educational Leadership and Administration | M,O |
| Health Services Management and Hospital Administration | M,O |
| Higher Education | M |
| Human Resources Management | M,O |
| Marriage and Family Therapy | M |
| Nursing and Healthcare Administration | M |
| Nursing Education | M |
| Nursing—General | M |
| Occupational Therapy | M,D |
| Organizational Management | M,D,O |
| Pastoral Ministry and Counseling | M |
| Public Health—General | M,D |
| Social Psychology | M |
| Theology | M |

**INSTITUTE FOR CHRISTIAN STUDIES**

| | |
|---|---|
| Education—General | M,D |
| Philosophy | M,D |
| Political Science | M,D |
| Theology | M,D |

**INSTITUTE FOR CLINICAL SOCIAL WORK**

| | |
|---|---|
| Social Work | D |

**INSTITUTE FOR DOCTORAL STUDIES IN THE VISUAL ARTS**

| | |
|---|---|
| Art/Fine Arts | D |
| Philosophy | D |

**INSTITUTE OF AMERICAN INDIAN ARTS**

| | |
|---|---|
| Writing | M |

**INSTITUTE OF CLINICAL ACUPUNCTURE AND ORIENTAL MEDICINE**

| | |
|---|---|
| Acupuncture and Oriental Medicine | M |

**INSTITUTE OF PUBLIC ADMINISTRATION**

| | |
|---|---|
| Health Services Management and Hospital Administration | M,O |
| Public Administration | M,O |

**INSTITUTE OF TAOIST EDUCATION AND ACUPUNCTURE**

| | |
|---|---|
| Acupuncture and Oriental Medicine | M |

**THE INSTITUTE OF WORLD POLITICS**

| | |
|---|---|
| Computer and Information Systems Security | M,D,O |
| Conflict Resolution and Mediation/Peace Studies | M,D,O |
| Homeland Security | M,D,O |
| International Affairs | M,D,O |
| International Economics | M,D,O |
| Military and Defense Studies | M,D,O |
| National Security | M,D,O |
| Political Science | M,D,O |
| Public Affairs | M,D,O |
| Public Policy | M,D,O |

**INSTITUT FRANCO-EUROPÉEN DE CHIROPRAXIE**

| | |
|---|---|
| Chiropractic | D |

**INSTITUTO CENTROAMERICANO DE ADMINISTRACION DE EMPRESAS**

| | |
|---|---|
| Agricultural Economics and Agribusiness | M |
| Business Administration and Management—General | M |
| Finance and Banking | M |
| Management of Technology | M |
| Real Estate | M |
| Sustainable Development | M |

**INSTITUTO TECNOLOGICO DE SANTO DOMINGO**

| | |
|---|---|
| Accounting | M,O |
| Adult Education | M,O |
| Allopathic Medicine | M,D |
| Bioethics | M,O |
| Business Administration and Management—General | M,O |
| Communication—General | M,O |
| Construction Management | M,O |
| Counseling Psychology | M,O |
| Economics | M,O |
| Education—General | M,O |
| Educational Leadership and Administration | M,O |
| Educational Psychology | M,O |
| Energy and Power Engineering | M,D,O |
| Energy Management and Policy | M,D,O |
| Engineering and Applied Sciences—General | M,O |
| Environmental Education | M,D,O |
| Environmental Engineering | M,O |
| Environmental Management and Policy | M,D,O |
| Environmental Sciences | M,D,O |
| Finance and Banking | M,O |
| Gender Studies | M,O |
| Health Promotion | M,O |
| Human Resources Management | M,O |
| Humanities | M,O |
| Industrial and Manufacturing Management | M,O |
| Industrial/Management Engineering | M,O |
| Information Science | M,O |
| International Affairs | M,O |
| International Business | M,O |
| Linguistics | M,O |
| Marine Sciences | M,D,O |
| Marketing | M,O |
| Marriage and Family Therapy | M,O |
| Maternal and Child Health | M,O |
| Mathematics | M,D,O |
| Natural Resources | M,D,O |
| Nutrition | M,O |
| Organizational Management | M,O |
| Quality Management | M,O |
| Quantitative Analysis | M,O |
| Secondary Education | M,O |
| Social Sciences Education | M,O |
| Software Engineering | M,O |
| Structural Engineering | M,O |
| Sustainable Development | M,O |
| Taxation | M,O |
| Telecommunications | M,O |
| Transportation Management | M,O |

**INSTITUTO TECNOLÓGICO Y DE ESTUDIOS SUPERIORES DE MONTERREY, CAMPUS CENTRAL DE VERACRUZ**

| | |
|---|---|
| Business Administration and Management—General | M |
| Computer Science | M |

*M—masters degree; D—doctorate; O—other advanced degree; *—Close-Up and/or Display*

Education—General M
Educational Leadership and Administration M
Educational Media/Instructional Technology M
Electronic Commerce M
Finance and Banking M
Humanities M
International Business M
Management Information Systems M
Marketing M

**INSTITUTO TECNOLÓGICO Y DE ESTUDIOS SUPERIORES DE MONTERREY, CAMPUS CHIHUAHUA**
Computer Engineering M,O
Electrical Engineering M,O
Engineering Management M,O
Industrial/Management Engineering M,O
International Business M,O
Mechanical Engineering M,O
Systems Engineering M,O

**INSTITUTO TECNOLÓGICO Y DE ESTUDIOS SUPERIORES DE MONTERREY, CAMPUS CIUDAD DE MÉXICO**
Business Administration and Management—General M,D
Computer Science M,D
Economics M,D
Education—General M,D
Educational Media/Instructional Technology M,D
Environmental Engineering M,D
Environmental Sciences M,D
Finance and Banking M,D
Humanities M,D
Industrial/Management Engineering M,D
International Business M,D
Law O
Management Information Systems M,D
Quality Management M,D
Telecommunications Management M

**INSTITUTO TECNOLÓGICO Y DE ESTUDIOS SUPERIORES DE MONTERREY, CAMPUS CIUDAD JUÁREZ**
Business Administration and Management—General M
Education—General M
Educational Leadership and Administration M
Educational Media/Instructional Technology M,D
Electronic Commerce M
Humanities M
Management Information Systems M
Public Administration M
Quality Management M

**INSTITUTO TECNOLÓGICO Y DE ESTUDIOS SUPERIORES DE MONTERREY, CAMPUS CIUDAD OBREGÓN**
Business Administration and Management—General M
Communication—General M
Developmental Education M
Education—General M
Engineering and Applied Sciences—General M
Finance and Banking M
International Affairs M
Management Information Systems M
Marketing M
Mathematics Education M
Telecommunications Management M

**INSTITUTO TECNOLÓGICO Y DE ESTUDIOS SUPERIORES DE MONTERREY, CAMPUS CUERNAVACA**
Business Administration and Management—General M
Computer Science M,D
Finance and Banking M
Human Resources Management M
Information Science M,D
International Business M
Management of Technology M,D
Marketing M

**INSTITUTO TECNOLÓGICO Y DE ESTUDIOS SUPERIORES DE MONTERREY, CAMPUS ESTADO DE MÉXICO**
Architecture M,D
Business Administration and Management—General M,D
Computer Science M,D
Education—General M,D
Educational Leadership and Administration M,D
Educational Media/Instructional Technology M,D
Electronic Commerce M,D
Environmental Management and Policy M,D
Finance and Banking M,D
Humanities M,D
Industrial and Manufacturing Management M,D
Information Science M,D
Management Information Systems M,D
Marketing M,D
Materials Engineering M,D
Materials Sciences M,D
Quality Management M,D
Telecommunications Management M,D

**INSTITUTO TECNOLÓGICO Y DE ESTUDIOS SUPERIORES DE MONTERREY, CAMPUS GUADALAJARA**
Business Administration and Management—General M
Finance and Banking M

**INSTITUTO TECNOLÓGICO Y DE ESTUDIOS SUPERIORES DE MONTERREY, CAMPUS IRAPUATO**
Architecture M,D
Business Administration and Management—General M,D
Computer Science M,D
Education—General M,D
Educational Leadership and Administration M,D
Educational Media/Instructional Technology M,D
Electronic Commerce M,D
Environmental Management and Policy M,D
Finance and Banking M,D
Humanities M,D
Industrial and Manufacturing Management M,D
Information Science M,D
International Business M,D
Library Science M,D
Management Information Systems M,D
Management of Technology M,D
Marketing Research M,D
Quality Management M,D
Telecommunications Management M,D

**INSTITUTO TECNOLÓGICO Y DE ESTUDIOS SUPERIORES DE MONTERREY, CAMPUS LAGUNA**
Business Administration and Management—General M
Industrial/Management Engineering M
Management Information Systems M

**INSTITUTO TECNOLÓGICO Y DE ESTUDIOS SUPERIORES DE MONTERREY, CAMPUS LEÓN**
Business Administration and Management—General M

**INSTITUTO TECNOLÓGICO Y DE ESTUDIOS SUPERIORES DE MONTERREY, CAMPUS MONTERREY**
Agricultural Engineering M,D
Agricultural Sciences—General M,D
Applied Statistics M,D
Artificial Intelligence/Robotics M,D
Biotechnology M,D
Business Administration and Management—General M,D
Chemical Engineering M,D
Chemistry M,D
Civil Engineering M,D
Communication—General M,D
Computer Science M,D
Electrical Engineering M,D
Engineering and Applied Sciences—General M,D
Environmental Engineering M,D
Finance and Banking M
Industrial/Management Engineering M,D
Information Science M,D
International Business M,D
Manufacturing Engineering M,D
Marketing M
Mechanical Engineering M,D
Organic Chemistry M,D
Science Education M,D
Systems Engineering M,D

**INSTITUTO TECNOLÓGICO Y DE ESTUDIOS SUPERIORES DE MONTERREY, CAMPUS QUERÉTARO**
Business Administration and Management—General M

**INSTITUTO TECNOLÓGICO Y DE ESTUDIOS SUPERIORES DE MONTERREY, CAMPUS SONORA NORTE**
Business Administration and Management—General M
Education—General M
Information Science M

**INSTITUTO TECNOLÓGICO Y DE ESTUDIOS SUPERIORES DE MONTERREY, CAMPUS TOLUCA**
Business Administration and Management—General M

**INTER AMERICAN UNIVERSITY OF PUERTO RICO, AGUADILLA CAMPUS**
Accounting M
Business Administration and Management—General M
Counseling Psychology M
Criminal Justice and Criminology M
Educational Leadership and Administration M
Elementary Education M
Finance and Banking M
Human Resources Management M
Management Information Systems M
Marketing M

**INTER AMERICAN UNIVERSITY OF PUERTO RICO, ARECIBO CAMPUS**
Accounting M
Acute Care/Critical Care Nursing M
Business Administration and Management—General M
Counselor Education M
Curriculum and Instruction M
Education—General M
Educational Leadership and Administration M
Elementary Education M
English as a Second Language M
Finance and Banking M
Foreign Languages Education M
Human Resources Management M
Mathematics Education M
Medical/Surgical Nursing M
Nurse Anesthesia M
Nursing—General M
Science Education M
Social Sciences Education M

**INTER AMERICAN UNIVERSITY OF PUERTO RICO, BARRANQUITAS CAMPUS**
Accounting M
Acute Care/Critical Care Nursing M
Biological and Biomedical Sciences—General M
Biotechnology M
Business Administration and Management—General M
Criminal Justice and Criminology M
Curriculum and Instruction M
Education—General M
Educational Leadership and Administration M
Elementary Education M
English as a Second Language M
Foreign Languages Education M
History M
Human Resources Management M
Library Science M
Medical/Surgical Nursing M
Nursing—General M
Special Education M

**INTER AMERICAN UNIVERSITY OF PUERTO RICO, BAYAMÓN CAMPUS**
Aerospace/Aeronautical Engineering M
Biotechnology M
Ecology M
Electrical Engineering M
Energy and Power Engineering M
Human Resources Management M
Mechanical Engineering M

**INTER AMERICAN UNIVERSITY OF PUERTO RICO, FAJARDO CAMPUS**
Business Administration and Management—General M
Computer Science M
Educational Leadership and Administration M
Human Resources Management M
Management Information Systems M
Marketing M
Special Education M

**INTER AMERICAN UNIVERSITY OF PUERTO RICO, GUAYAMA CAMPUS**
Business Administration and Management—General M
Computer and Information Systems Security M
Computer Science M
Early Childhood Education M
Elementary Education M
Marketing M

**INTER AMERICAN UNIVERSITY OF PUERTO RICO, METROPOLITAN CAMPUS**
Accounting M
American Studies M,D
Athletic Training and Sports Medicine M
Business Administration and Management—General M
Business Education M
Clinical Laboratory Sciences/Medical Technology M
Computer Science M
Counseling Psychology M,D
Counselor Education M,D
Criminal Justice and Criminology M
Curriculum and Instruction M,D
Education—General M,D
Educational Leadership and Administration M,D
Educational Media/Instructional Technology M
Elementary Education M
English as a Second Language M
English M
Environmental Management and Policy M
Exercise and Sports Science M
Finance and Banking M
Foreign Languages Education M
Health Education M
Higher Education M
History M,D
Human Resources Development M
Human Resources Management M
Industrial and Labor Relations M,D
Industrial and Manufacturing Management M
Industrial and Organizational Psychology M,D
International Business M,D
Management Information Systems M
Marketing M
Mathematics Education M
Microbiology M
Molecular Biology M
Music Education M
Pastoral Ministry and Counseling D
Physical Education M
Psychology—General M,D
Religious Education D
School Psychology M,D
Science Education M
Social Sciences Education M
Social Work M
Spanish M
Special Education M
Theology D
Vocational and Technical Education M
Women's Studies M

**INTER AMERICAN UNIVERSITY OF PUERTO RICO, PONCE CAMPUS**
Accounting M
Criminal Justice and Criminology M
Elementary Education M
English as a Second Language M
Finance and Banking M
Human Resources Management M
Marketing M
Mathematics Education M
Science Education M
Social Sciences Education M
Spanish M

**INTER AMERICAN UNIVERSITY OF PUERTO RICO, SAN GERMÁN CAMPUS**
Accounting M,D
Applied Mathematics M
Art/Fine Arts M
Business Administration and Management—General M,D
Business Education M
Counseling Psychology M,D
Counselor Education M,D
Curriculum and Instruction D
Elementary Education M
English as a Second Language M
Environmental Sciences M
Finance and Banking M,D
Graphic Design M
Health Education M
Human Resources Development M,D
Human Resources Management M,D
Industrial and Manufacturing Management M,D
International Business M,D
Kinesiology and Movement Studies M
Library Science M
Management Information Systems M,D
Marketing M,D
Mathematics Education M
Music Education M
Music M
Photography M
Physical Education M
Psychology—General M,D
School Psychology M,D
Science Education M
Special Education M

**INTER AMERICAN UNIVERSITY OF PUERTO RICO SCHOOL OF LAW**
Law D

**INTER AMERICAN UNIVERSITY OF PUERTO RICO SCHOOL OF OPTOMETRY**
Optometry D

**INTERDENOMINATIONAL THEOLOGICAL CENTER**
Pastoral Ministry and Counseling M,D
Religious Education M,D
Theology M,D

**INTERIOR DESIGNERS INSTITUTE**
Interior Design M

**INTERNATIONAL BAPTIST COLLEGE AND SEMINARY**
Education—General M
Pastoral Ministry and Counseling M,D
Theology M

**INTERNATIONAL INSTITUTE FOR RESTORATIVE PRACTICES**
Organizational Behavior M,O

**INTERNATIONAL TECHNOLOGICAL UNIVERSITY**
Business Administration and Management—General M,D
Computer Art and Design M
Computer Engineering M
Electrical Engineering M,D
Engineering Management M
Software Engineering M

**INTERNATIONAL UNIVERSITY IN GENEVA**
Business Administration and Management—General M,D
Communication—General M,D
Entrepreneurship M,D
International Affairs M,D
International Business M,D
Marketing M,D
Media Studies M,D
Public Administration M,D

**THE INTERNATIONAL UNIVERSITY OF MONACO**
Business Administration and Management—General M
Entrepreneurship M
Finance and Banking M
Financial Engineering M
International Business M
Marketing M

**IONA COLLEGE**
Accounting M,O
Advertising and Public Relations M,O

| | |
|---|---|
| Business Administration and Management—General | M,O |
| Communication Disorders | M |
| Computer and Information Systems Security | M,O |
| Computer Science | M |
| Counseling Psychology | M,O |
| Criminal Justice and Criminology | M,O |
| Early Childhood Education | M |
| Education—General | M |
| Educational Leadership and Administration | M |
| English Education | M |
| English | M |
| Experimental Psychology | M,O |
| Finance and Banking | M,O |
| Foreign Languages Education | M |
| Forensic Sciences | M,O |
| Game Design and Development | M |
| Health Services Management and Hospital Administration | M,O |
| History | M |
| Human Resources Management | M,O |
| Industrial and Organizational Psychology | M,O |
| International Business | M,O |
| Management Information Systems | M,O |
| Management of Technology | M,O |
| Marketing | M,O |
| Marriage and Family Therapy | M |
| Mass Communication | M,O |
| Mathematics Education | M |
| Project Management | M,O |
| Psychology—General | M,O |
| Recreation and Park Management | M,O |
| Risk Management | M,O |
| School Psychology | M,O |
| Science Education | M |
| Social Sciences Education | M |
| Spanish | M |
| Special Education | M |
| Sports Management | M,O |

## IOWA STATE UNIVERSITY OF SCIENCE AND TECHNOLOGY

| | |
|---|---|
| Accounting | M |
| Aerospace/Aeronautical Engineering | M,D |
| Agricultural Economics and Agribusiness | M,D |
| Agricultural Education | M,D |
| Agricultural Engineering | M,D |
| Agricultural Sciences—General | M,D |
| Agronomy and Soil Sciences | M,D |
| Analytical Chemistry | M,D |
| Animal Sciences | M,D |
| Anthropology | M |
| Applied Arts and Design—General | M,D |
| Applied Mathematics | M,D |
| Applied Physics | M,D |
| Architecture | M |
| Art/Fine Arts | M |
| Astrophysics | M,D |
| Bioinformatics | M,D |
| Biological and Biomedical Sciences—General | M,D |
| Biophysics | M,D |
| Biostatistics | M,D |
| Business Administration and Management—General | M |
| Business Analytics | M |
| Cell Biology | M,D |
| Chemical Engineering | M,D |
| Chemistry | M,D |
| Child and Family Studies | M,D |
| Civil Engineering | M,D |
| Clothing and Textiles | M,D |
| Cognitive Sciences | M,D |
| Computational Biology | M,D |
| Computer Engineering | M,D |
| Computer Science | M,D |
| Condensed Matter Physics | M,D |
| Construction Engineering | M,D |
| Corporate and Organizational Communication | M,D |
| Counseling Psychology | M,D |
| Counselor Education | M,D |
| Curriculum and Instruction | M,D |
| Developmental Biology | M,D |
| Ecology | M,D |
| Economics | M,D |
| Education—General | M,D |
| Educational Leadership and Administration | M,D |
| Educational Measurement and Evaluation | M,D |
| Educational Media/Instructional Technology | M,D |
| Electrical Engineering | M,D |
| Elementary Education | M,D |
| English as a Second Language | M |
| English | M,D |
| Entomology | M,D |
| Environmental Engineering | M,D |
| Environmental Sciences | M,D |
| Evolutionary Biology | M,D |
| Exercise and Sports Science | M |
| Family and Consumer Sciences-General | M |
| Finance and Banking | M |
| Fish, Game, and Wildlife Management | M,D |
| Food Science and Technology | M,D |
| Forestry | M,D |
| Foundations and Philosophy of Education | M,D |
| Genetics | M,D |
| Geology | M,D |
| Geosciences | M,D |
| Geotechnical Engineering | M,D |
| Graphic Design | M |
| Higher Education | M,D |
| History | M,D |
| Horticulture | M,D |
| Human Development | M,D |
| Human Resources Development | M,D |
| Human-Computer Interaction | M,D |
| Immunology | M,D |
| Industrial Design | M |
| Industrial/Management Engineering | M,D |
| Information Science | M |
| Inorganic Chemistry | M,D |
| Interdisciplinary Studies | M |
| Interior Design | M |
| Journalism | M |
| Kinesiology and Movement Studies | M,D |
| Landscape Architecture | M |
| Linguistics | M,D |
| Management Information Systems | M,D |
| Mass Communication | M |
| Materials Engineering | M,D |
| Materials Sciences | M,D |
| Mathematics Education | M,D |
| Mathematics | M,D |
| Mechanical Engineering | M,D |
| Mechanics | M,D |
| Meteorology | M,D |
| Microbiology | M,D |
| Molecular Biology | M,D |
| Molecular Genetics | M,D |
| Natural Resources | M,D |
| Neuroscience | M,D |
| Nutrition | M,D |
| Operations Research | M,D |
| Organic Chemistry | M,D |
| Pathology | M,D |
| Physical Chemistry | M,D |
| Physics | M,D |
| Plant Biology | M,D |
| Plant Pathology | M,D |
| Plant Sciences | M,D |
| Political Science | M |
| Psychology—General | M,D |
| Public Administration | M |
| Rhetoric | M,D |
| Rural Planning and Studies | D |
| Rural Sociology | M,D |
| Science Education | M |
| Social Psychology | M,D |
| Sociology | M,D |
| Special Education | M,D |
| Statistics | M,D |
| Structural Biology | M,D |
| Structural Engineering | M,D |
| Student Affairs | M,D |
| Sustainable Development | M,D |
| Systems Engineering | M |
| Toxicology | M,D |
| Transportation and Highway Engineering | M,D |
| Transportation Management | M |
| Urban and Regional Planning | M |
| Veterinary Medicine | M |
| Veterinary Sciences | M,D |
| Vocational and Technical Education | M,D |
| Writing | M,D |

## IRELL & MANELLA GRADUATE SCHOOL OF BIOLOGICAL SCIENCES

| | |
|---|---|
| Biochemistry | D |
| Biological and Biomedical Sciences—General | D |
| Cancer Biology/Oncology | D |
| Cell Biology | D |
| Developmental Biology | D |
| Genetics | D |
| Immunology | D |
| Molecular Biology | D |
| Neuroscience | D |
| Pharmaceutical Sciences | D |

## ITHACA COLLEGE

| | |
|---|---|
| Accounting | M |
| Agricultural Education | M |
| Allied Health—General | M,D |
| Art/Fine Arts | M |
| Communication Disorders | M |
| Elementary Education | M |
| English Education | M |
| Exercise and Sports Science | M |
| Internet and Interactive Multimedia | M |
| Music Education | M |
| Music | M |
| Occupational Therapy | M |
| Photography | M |
| Physical Therapy | D |
| Secondary Education | M |
| Writing | M |

## JACKSON STATE UNIVERSITY

| | |
|---|---|
| Accounting | M |
| Applied Mathematics | M |
| Atmospheric Sciences | M,D |
| Biological and Biomedical Sciences—General | M |
| Business Administration and Management—General | M,D |
| Chemistry | M,D |
| Civil Engineering | M,D |
| Clinical Psychology | M,D |
| Communication Disorders | M |
| Computer Science | M |
| Counselor Education | M |
| Criminal Justice and Criminology | M |
| Early Childhood Education | M,D,O |
| Education—General | M,D,O |
| Educational Leadership and Administration | M,D,O |
| Elementary Education | M,D,O |
| English Education | M |
| English | M |
| Environmental Engineering | M,D |
| Environmental Sciences | M |
| Geosciences | M,D |
| Hazardous Materials Management | M,D |
| Health Education | M |
| Higher Education | M,D,O |
| History | M |
| Materials Sciences | M,D |
| Mathematics Education | M |
| Mathematics | M |
| Music Education | M |
| Physical Education | M |
| Physics | M,D |
| Political Science | M |
| Psychology—General | D |
| Public Administration | M,D |
| Public Affairs | M,D |
| Public Health—General | M,D |
| Public Policy | M,D |
| Reading Education | M,D,O |
| Rehabilitation Sciences | M |
| School Psychology | M |
| Science Education | M,D |
| Social Work | M,D |
| Sociology | M |
| Special Education | M,O |
| Sports Management | M |
| Statistics | M |
| Urban and Regional Planning | M,D |
| Vocational and Technical Education | M,D |

## JACKSONVILLE STATE UNIVERSITY

| | |
|---|---|
| Biological and Biomedical Sciences—General | M |
| Business Administration and Management—General | M |
| Computer Science | M |
| Counselor Education | M |
| Criminal Justice and Criminology | M |
| Early Childhood Education | M |
| Education—General | M,O |
| Educational Leadership and Administration | M,O |
| Educational Media/Instructional Technology | M |
| Elementary Education | M |
| Emergency Management | M,D |
| English | M |
| History | M |
| Liberal Studies | M |
| Mathematics | M |
| Music | M |
| Nursing—General | M |
| Physical Education | M,O |
| Psychology—General | M |
| Public Administration | M |
| Reading Education | M |
| Secondary Education | M |
| Social Work | M |
| Software Engineering | M |
| Special Education | M |

## JACKSONVILLE UNIVERSITY

| | |
|---|---|
| Accounting | M |
| Adult Nursing | M,D,O |
| Allied Health—General | M,D |
| Art/Fine Arts | M |
| Business Administration and Management—General | M,D |
| Communication Disorders | M |
| Counseling Psychology | M |
| Dance | M |
| Dentistry | M,O |
| Educational Leadership and Administration | M |
| Family Nurse Practitioner Studies | M |
| Finance and Banking | M |
| Gerontological Nursing | M,D,O |
| Health Informatics | M |
| Kinesiology and Movement Studies | M |
| Marine Sciences | M |
| Marketing | M |
| Marriage and Family Therapy | M |
| Nursing and Healthcare Administration | M |
| Nursing Education | M |
| Nursing Informatics | M |
| Nursing—General | M,D |
| Occupational Therapy | D |
| Oral and Dental Sciences | M,O |
| Organizational Management | M |
| Psychiatric Nursing | M |
| Public Policy | M |
| Sports Management | M |

## JAMES MADISON UNIVERSITY

| | |
|---|---|
| Accounting | M |
| American Studies | M |
| Applied Behavior Analysis | M |
| Art Education | M |
| Art History | M |
| Art/Fine Arts | M |
| Biological and Biomedical Sciences—General | M |
| Business Administration and Management—General | M |
| Clinical Psychology | D |
| Communication Disorders | M,D |
| Communication—General | M |
| Computer and Information Systems Security | M |
| Computer Science | M |
| Counseling Psychology | D |
| Early Childhood Education | M |
| Education of the Gifted | M |
| Educational Leadership and Administration | M |
| Educational Measurement and Evaluation | M,D |
| Educational Media/Instructional Technology | M |
| Elementary Education | M |
| Engineering and Applied Sciences—General | M |
| English as a Second Language | M |
| English | M |
| Entrepreneurship | M |
| Environmental Management and Policy | M |
| Exercise and Sports Science | M |
| Experimental Psychology | M |
| Family Nurse Practitioner Studies | M,D |
| Foreign Languages Education | M |
| Forensic Sciences | M |
| Gerontological Nursing | M,D |
| Health Education | M |
| Higher Education | M |
| History | M |
| Human Resources Management | M |
| Kinesiology and Movement Studies | M |
| Management Information Systems | M |
| Management Strategy and Policy | D |
| Mathematics Education | M |
| Middle School Education | M |
| Multilingual and Multicultural Education | M |
| Music Education | M |
| Music | M,D |
| Nonprofit Management | M,D |
| Nurse Midwifery | M,D |
| Nursing and Healthcare Administration | M,D |
| Nursing—General | M,D |
| Nutrition | M |
| Occupational Therapy | M |
| Organizational Management | D |
| Photography | M |
| Physical Education | M |
| Physician Assistant Studies | M |
| Physiology | M |
| Political Science | M |
| Psychiatric Nursing | M,D |
| Psychology—General | M |
| Public Administration | M |
| Public History | M |
| Reading Education | M |
| Rhetoric | M |
| School Psychology | M,D,O |
| Secondary Education | M |
| Special Education | M |
| Sustainability Management | M |
| Taxation | M |
| Technical Writing | M |
| Vocational and Technical Education | M |
| Writing | M |

## JEFFERSON COLLEGE OF HEALTH SCIENCES

| | |
|---|---|
| Nursing and Healthcare Administration | M |
| Nursing Education | M |
| Nursing—General | M |
| Occupational Therapy | M |
| Physician Assistant Studies | M |

## THE JEWISH THEOLOGICAL SEMINARY

| | |
|---|---|
| Jewish Studies | M,D |
| Music | M |
| Religion | M,D |
| Religious Education | M,D |
| Theology | M,D,O |
| Women's Studies | M,D |

## JOHN BROWN UNIVERSITY

| | |
|---|---|
| Business Administration and Management—General | M |
| Clinical Psychology | M,O |
| Counseling Psychology | M,O |
| Counselor Education | M,O |
| Curriculum and Instruction | M |
| Education—General | M |
| Ethics | M |
| International Business | M |
| Marriage and Family Therapy | M,O |
| Secondary Education | M |

## JOHN CABOT UNIVERSITY

| | |
|---|---|
| Art History | M |

## JOHN CARROLL UNIVERSITY

| | |
|---|---|
| Accounting | M |
| Biological and Biomedical Sciences—General | M |
| Business Administration and Management—General | M |
| Counseling Psychology | M,O |
| Counselor Education | M,O |
| Educational Psychology | M,O |
| English | M |
| Nonprofit Management | M |
| Religion | M |
| Theology | M |

## JOHN F. KENNEDY UNIVERSITY

| | |
|---|---|
| Business Administration and Management—General | M |
| Counseling Psychology | M |
| Finance and Banking | M |
| Health Education | M |
| Health Psychology | M |
| Health Services Management and Hospital Administration | M |
| Human Resources Management | M |
| Law | D |
| Management of Technology | M |
| Management Strategy and Policy | M |
| Museum Studies | O |
| Psychology—General | M,D,O |

*M—masters degree; D—doctorate; O—other advanced degree; *—Close-Up and/or Display*

Sport Psychology M,O
Transpersonal and Humanistic Psychology M

### JOHN JAY COLLEGE OF CRIMINAL JUSTICE OF THE CITY UNIVERSITY OF NEW YORK
Criminal Justice and Criminology M,D
Economics M
Forensic Psychology M,D
Forensic Sciences M,D
Legal and Justice Studies M,D
Organizational Behavior M,D
Public Administration M
Public Policy M,D

### JOHN PATRICK UNIVERSITY OF HEALTH AND APPLIED SCIENCES
Health Physics/Radiological Health M
Medical Physics M

### JOHN PAUL THE GREAT CATHOLIC UNIVERSITY
Theology M

### JOHNS HOPKINS UNIVERSITY
Aerospace/Aeronautical Engineering M
Allopathic Medicine D
Anatomy D
Anthropology D
Applied Economics M
Applied Mathematics M,D,O
Applied Physics M,O
Archaeology D
Art History M,D
Artificial Intelligence/Robotics M
Asian Studies M,D,O
Astronomy D
Biochemistry M,D
Bioengineering M,D
Bioethics M,D
Bioinformatics M
Biological and Biomedical Sciences—General M,D
Biomedical Engineering M,D,O
Biophysics D
Biostatistics M,D
Biotechnology M
Business Administration and Management—General M,O
Business Analytics M
Cardiovascular Sciences M,D
Cell Biology D
Chemical Engineering M,D
Chemistry M,D
Civil Engineering M,D,O
Classics D
Clinical Psychology M,D
Clinical Research M,D
Cognitive Sciences M,D
Communication—General M,O
Community Health Nursing
Community Health M,D
Comparative Literature D
Computer and Information Systems Security M,O
Computer Engineering M,D,O
Computer Science M,D,O
Demography and Population Studies M,D
Developmental Biology D
Economics D
Education—General M,D,O
Electrical Engineering M,D,O
Energy Management and Policy M,O
Engineering and Applied Sciences—General M,D,O
Engineering Management M
English D
Environmental and Occupational Health M,D
Environmental Engineering M,D,O
Environmental Management and Policy M,O
Environmental Sciences M,O
Epidemiology M,D
Evolutionary Biology D
Family Nurse Practitioner Studies D
Film, Television, and Video Production M
Finance and Banking M,D,O
French M,D
Genetic Counseling M,D
Genetics M,D
Geographic Information Systems M,O
Geosciences M,D
German M,D
Gerontological Nursing D
Health Communication M,D
Health Education M,D
Health Informatics M,D,O
Health Services Management and Hospital Administration M,D
History of Science and Technology M,D
History D
Homeland Security M,O
Immunology M,D
Infectious Diseases M,D
International Affairs M,D,O
International Development M,D,O
International Economics M,D,O
International Health M,D
Investment Management M,O
Italian M,D
Liberal Studies M,O
Management Information Systems M,O
Management of Technology M,O
Marketing M
Materials Engineering M,D
Materials Sciences M,D
Mathematical and Computational Finance M,D,O
Mathematics D
Mechanical Engineering M,D,O
Mechanics M
Media Studies M
Medical Illustration M
Medical Informatics M,D,O
Microbiology M,D
Molecular Biology M,D
Molecular Biophysics M,D
Molecular Medicine D
Museum Studies M,O
Music M,D,O
Nanotechnology M
Near and Middle Eastern Languages D
Near and Middle Eastern Studies D
Neuroscience D
Nonprofit Management M,O
Nursing and Healthcare Administration M,D
Nursing Education O
Nursing—General M,D,O
Nutrition M,D
Operations Research M,D
Pathobiology D
Pathology D
Pediatric Nursing D,O
Pharmaceutical Sciences M
Pharmacology D
Philosophy M,D
Photonics M,O
Physics D
Physiology D
Planetary and Space Sciences M,D
Political Science M,D,O
Psychiatric Nursing O
Psychology—General D
Public Administration M,O
Public Health—General M,D
Public Policy M,D
Real Estate M
Risk Management M
Romance Languages M,D
Sociology D
Spanish M,D
Statistics M,D
Systems Engineering M,O
Technical Writing M,O
Writing M,O

### JOHNSON & WALES UNIVERSITY
Accounting M
Addictions/Substance Abuse Counseling M
Business Administration and Management—General M
Business Education M
Clinical Psychology M
Computer and Information Systems Security M
Criminal Justice and Criminology M
Data Science/Data Analytics M
Economic Development M
Education—General M
Educational Leadership and Administration D
Elementary Education M
Finance and Banking M
Hospitality Management M
Human Resources Management M
Management Information Systems M
Nonprofit Management M
Occupational Therapy D
Organizational Management M
Physician Assistant Studies M
Secondary Education M
Special Education M
Sports Management M
Supply Chain Management M
Sustainable Development M
Travel and Tourism M

### JOHNSON C. SMITH UNIVERSITY
Social Work M

### JOHNSON UNIVERSITY
Clinical Psychology M,D,O
Counselor Education M,D,O
Cultural Studies M,D,O
Education—General M,D,O
Educational Media/Instructional Technology M,D,O
Higher Education M,D,O
Nonprofit Management M,D,O
Pastoral Ministry and Counseling M,D,O
Theology M,D,O

### JOHNSON UNIVERSITY FLORIDA
Pastoral Ministry and Counseling M

### JOSE MARIA VARGAS UNIVERSITY
Early Childhood Education M

### THE JUDGE ADVOCATE GENERAL'S SCHOOL, U.S. ARMY
Law M
Military and Defense Studies M

### JUDSON UNIVERSITY
Architecture M
Business Administration and Management—General M
Clinical Psychology M
Human Services M
Organizational Management M
Pastoral Ministry and Counseling M
Reading Education M,D
Sustainable Development M
Urban Design M

### THE JUILLIARD SCHOOL
Music M,D,O
Theater M,D,O

### JUNIATA COLLEGE
Accounting M
Business Administration and Management—General M
Organizational Management M

### KANSAS CITY UNIVERSITY OF MEDICINE AND BIOSCIENCES
Bioethics M
Biological and Biomedical Sciences—General M
Osteopathic Medicine D

### KANSAS STATE UNIVERSITY
Accounting M
Adult Education M,D,O
Advertising and Public Relations M
Agricultural Economics and Agribusiness M,D
Agricultural Education M
Agricultural Engineering M,D
Agricultural Sciences—General M,D,O
Agronomy and Soil Sciences M,D,O
Animal Sciences M,D
Applied Science and Technology M,O
Architectural Engineering M
Architecture M
Art/Fine Arts M
Biochemistry M,D
Bioengineering M,D
Biological and Biomedical Sciences—General M,D
Business Administration and Management—General M,O
Chemical Engineering M,D,O
Chemistry M,D
Child and Family Studies M,D,O
Child Development M,D,O
Civil Engineering M,D
Clothing and Textiles M,D
Communication Disorders M,D,O
Communication—General M,D,O
Computer Engineering M,D
Computer Science M,D
Conflict Resolution and Mediation/Peace Studies M,D,O
Consumer Economics M,D,O
Counselor Education M,D,O
Curriculum and Instruction M,D,O
Data Science/Data Analytics M,O
Distance Education Development M,D,O
Early Childhood Education M,D,O
Economics M,D
Education—General M,D,O
Educational Leadership and Administration M,D,O
Educational Media/Instructional Technology M,D,O
Electrical Engineering M,D
Elementary Education M,D,O
Energy and Power Engineering M,D
Energy Management and Policy M,D
Engineering and Applied Sciences—General M,D,O
Engineering Management M,D
English as a Second Language M,D,O
English Education M,D,O
English M,O
Entomology M,D
Entrepreneurship M,O
Environmental Design D
Environmental Engineering M,D
Environmental Sciences M,D,O
Family and Consumer Sciences-General M,D,O
Finance and Banking M,D,O
Food Science and Technology M,D
French M
Gender Studies O
Genetics M,D
Geographic Information Systems M,D,O
Geography M,D,O
Geology M
Geotechnical Engineering M,D
German M
Gerontology M,O
Health Communication M
Health Education M,D
History M,D
Horticulture M,D
Hospitality Management M,D
Human Development M,D,O
Human Services M,D,O
Industrial/Management Engineering M,D
Interdisciplinary Studies M,O
Interior Design M
Journalism M
Kinesiology and Movement Studies M,D
Landscape Architecture M
Management of Technology M
Manufacturing Engineering M,D
Marketing M,O
Marriage and Family Therapy M,D,O
Mass Communication M
Mathematics M,D,O
Mechanical Engineering M,D
Middle School Education M,D,O
Music M
National Security M,D
Natural Resources M,D
Nuclear Engineering M,D
Nutrition M,D
Operations Research M,D
Pathobiology M,D
Physics M,D
Physiology M,D
Plant Pathology M,D
Plant Sciences M,D,O
Political Science M
Psychology—General M,D
Public Administration M
Public Health—General M,D,O
Range Science M,D,O
Reading Education M,D,O
Sociology M,D
Spanish M
Special Education M,D,O
Statistics M,D,O
Structural Engineering M,D
Student Affairs M,D,O
Theater M
Transportation and Highway Engineering M,D
Urban and Regional Planning M
Veterinary Medicine D
Veterinary Sciences M,O
Water Resources Engineering M,D
Women's Studies O

### KANSAS WESLEYAN UNIVERSITY
Business Administration and Management—General M
Sports Management M

### KEAN UNIVERSITY
Accounting M
Addictions/Substance Abuse Counseling M
Art Education M
Biotechnology M
Business Administration and Management—General M
Clinical Psychology M,D
Communication Disorders M,D
Communication—General M
Community Health Nursing M
Counseling Psychology M
Counselor Education M
Criminal Justice and Criminology M
Curriculum and Instruction M
Early Childhood Education M
Education—General M
Educational Leadership and Administration M,D
English as a Second Language M
Exercise and Sports Science M
Foreign Languages Education M
Forensic Psychology M
Health Services Management and Hospital Administration M
Holocaust and Genocide Studies M
Industrial and Organizational Psychology M
International Business M
Liberal Studies M
Management Information Systems M
Marriage and Family Therapy M
Multilingual and Multicultural Education M
Nonprofit Management M
Nursing and Healthcare Administration M
Nursing—General M
Occupational Therapy M
Physical Therapy D
Psychology—General M
Public Administration M
School Psychology D,O
Social Work M
Special Education M
Writing M

### KECK GRADUATE INSTITUTE
Data Science/Data Analytics M

### KEHILATH YAKOV RABBINICAL SEMINARY
Theology

### KEISER UNIVERSITY
Accounting M
Business Administration and Management—General M,D
Computer and Information Systems Security M
Criminal Justice and Criminology M
Distance Education Development M
Education—General M
Educational Leadership and Administration M,D,O
Educational Media/Instructional Technology D,O
Family Nurse Practitioner Studies M
Health Education M
Health Services Management and Hospital Administration M
Homeland Security M
Industrial and Organizational Psychology M,D
International Business M,D
Management Information Systems M
Management of Technology M
Marketing M,D
Nurse Anesthesia M,D
Nursing—General M
Occupational Therapy M
Organizational Management M
Physician Assistant Studies M
Psychology—General M,D

### KENNESAW STATE UNIVERSITY
Accounting M
American Studies M
Applied Statistics M
Art Education M
Biochemistry M
Biological and Biomedical Sciences—General M
Business Administration and Management—General M,D
Chemistry M
Civil Engineering M
Communication—General M
Computer and Information Systems Security M,O
Computer Science M
Conflict Resolution and Mediation/Peace Studies M,D
Construction Management M
Criminal Justice and Criminology M

| | |
|---|---|
| Curriculum and Instruction | O |
| Data Science/Data Analytics | M,D,O |
| Early Childhood Education | M |
| Education—General | M,D,O |
| Educational Leadership and Administration | M,D,O |
| Educational Media/Instructional Technology | M,D,O |
| Electrical Engineering | M |
| Engineering and Applied Sciences—General | M |
| Engineering Management | M |
| English as a Second Language | M |
| English Education | M |
| Environmental Engineering | M |
| Exercise and Sports Science | M |
| Geotechnical Engineering | M |
| Health Informatics | M,O |
| Health Services Management and Hospital Administration | M |
| Information Science | M,O |
| International Affairs | M |
| Management of Technology | M |
| Mathematics Education | M |
| Mechanical Engineering | M |
| Middle School Education | D,O |
| Nursing and Healthcare Administration | M |
| Nursing Education | M |
| Nursing—General | M |
| Public Administration | M |
| Reading Education | M |
| Science Education | M |
| Secondary Education | M,D,O |
| Social Work | M |
| Software Engineering | M,O |
| Special Education | M,D,O |
| Sports Management | M |
| Structural Engineering | M |
| Systems Engineering | M |
| Transportation and Highway Engineering | M |
| Water Resources Engineering | M |
| Writing | M |

**KENRICK-GLENNON SEMINARY**

| | |
|---|---|
| Theology | M |

**KENT STATE UNIVERSITY**

| | |
|---|---|
| Accounting | M,D |
| Adult Nursing | M,D |
| Advertising and Public Relations | M |
| Aerospace/Aeronautical Engineering | M |
| Anthropology | M |
| Applied Mathematics | M,D |
| Architecture | M |
| Art Education | M |
| Art History | M |
| Art/Fine Arts | M |
| Athletic Training and Sports Medicine | M,D |
| Biological and Biomedical Sciences—General | M,D |
| Biological Anthropology | M,D |
| Biostatistics | M,D |
| Botany | M,D |
| Broadcast Journalism | M |
| Business Administration and Management—General | M |
| Business Analytics | M |
| Cell Biology | M,D |
| Chemical Physics | M,D |
| Chemistry | M,D |
| Child and Family Studies | M |
| Clinical Psychology | M,D |
| Communication Disorders | M,D,O |
| Communication—General | M |
| Computer and Information Systems Security | M |
| Computer Education | M,D,O |
| Computer Science | M,D |
| Conflict Resolution and Mediation/Peace Studies | M,D |
| Counseling Psychology | M |
| Counselor Education | M,D,O |
| Criminal Justice and Criminology | M,D |
| Curriculum and Instruction | M,D,O |
| Early Childhood Education | M,D,O |
| Ecology | M,D |
| Economics | M |
| Education of the Gifted | M,D,O |
| Education—General | M,D,O |
| Educational Leadership and Administration | M,D,O |
| Educational Measurement and Evaluation | M,D |
| Educational Media/Instructional Technology | M,D,O |
| Educational Psychology | M |
| English as a Second Language | M,D |
| English Education | M,D |
| English | M,D |
| Environmental and Occupational Health | M,D |
| Environmental Design | M |
| Epidemiology | M,D |
| Exercise and Sports Science | M,D |
| Experimental Psychology | M,D |
| Family Nurse Practitioner Studies | M,D |
| Finance and Banking | D |
| Foundations and Philosophy of Education | M,D |
| French | M,D |
| Genetics | M,D |
| Geographic Information Systems | M,D |
| Geography | M,D |
| Geology | M,D |
| German | M,D |
| Gerontological Nursing | M,D |
| Gerontology | M,D |
| Graphic Design | M |
| Health Education | M,D |
| Health Informatics | M |
| Health Promotion | M,D |
| Health Services Management and Hospital Administration | M,D |
| Higher Education | M,D,O |
| History | M,D |
| Hospitality Management | M |
| Human Development | M,D |
| Human Services | M,D,O |
| Illustration | M |
| Information Science | M |
| Japanese | M,D |
| Journalism | M |
| Landscape Architecture | M |
| Library Science | M |
| Linguistics | M,D |
| Management Information Systems | D |
| Marketing | D |
| Mass Communication | M |
| Mathematics Education | M,D |
| Mathematics | M,D,O |
| Media Studies | M |
| Middle School Education | M,D,O |
| Molecular Biology | M,D |
| Music Education | M,D |
| Music | M,D |
| Near and Middle Eastern Languages | M,D |
| Neuroscience | M,D |
| Nursing and Healthcare Administration | M,D |
| Nursing Education | M,D |
| Nursing—General | M,D |
| Nutrition | M |
| Pediatric Nursing | M,D |
| Pharmacology | M,D |
| Philosophy | M |
| Photography | M |
| Physics | M,D |
| Physiology | M,D |
| Podiatric Medicine | D |
| Political Science | M,D |
| Psychiatric Nursing | M,D |
| Psychology—General | M,D |
| Public Administration | M,D |
| Public Health—General | M,D |
| Reading Education | M |
| Recreation and Park Management | M |
| Rehabilitation Counseling | M |
| Rhetoric | M,D |
| Russian | M,D |
| School Psychology | M,D,O |
| Secondary Education | M,D |
| Social Sciences Education | M,D |
| Sociology | M,D |
| Spanish | M,D |
| Special Education | M,D,O |
| Sports Management | M |
| Student Affairs | M |
| Textile Design | M |
| Theater | M |
| Translation and Interpretation | M,D |
| Travel and Tourism | M |
| Urban Design | M |
| Vocational and Technical Education | M |
| Writing | M,D |

**KENT STATE UNIVERSITY AT STARK**

| | |
|---|---|
| Business Administration and Management—General | M |
| Curriculum and Instruction | M |
| Education—General | M |

**KENTUCKY CHRISTIAN UNIVERSITY**

| | |
|---|---|
| Religion | M |
| Theology | M |

**KETTERING COLLEGE**

| | |
|---|---|
| Occupational Therapy | D |
| Physician Assistant Studies | M |

**KETTERING UNIVERSITY**

| | |
|---|---|
| Business Administration and Management—General | M |
| Electrical Engineering | M |
| Engineering Management | M |
| Manufacturing Engineering | M |
| Mechanical Engineering | M |

**KEUKA COLLEGE**

| | |
|---|---|
| Business Administration and Management—General | M |
| Early Childhood Education | M |
| Elementary Education | M |
| Gerontological Nursing | M |
| Nursing Education | M |
| Nursing—General | M |
| Occupational Therapy | M |
| Secondary Education | M |
| Social Work | M |

**KEYSTONE COLLEGE**

| | |
|---|---|
| Accounting | M |
| Business Administration and Management—General | M |
| Early Childhood Education | M |
| Educational Leadership and Administration | M |

**KING'S COLLEGE**

| | |
|---|---|
| Education—General | M |
| Health Services Management and Hospital Administration | M |
| Physician Assistant Studies | M |

**THE KING'S UNIVERSITY**

| | |
|---|---|
| Pastoral Ministry and Counseling | M,D,O |
| Theology | M,D,O |

**KINGSWOOD UNIVERSITY**

| | |
|---|---|
| Pastoral Ministry and Counseling | M |
| Theology | M |

**KING UNIVERSITY**

| | |
|---|---|
| Accounting | M |
| Business Administration and Management—General | M |
| Family Nurse Practitioner Studies | M,D,O |
| Finance and Banking | M |
| Health Services Management and Hospital Administration | M |
| Human Resources Management | M |
| Marketing | M |
| Nursing and Healthcare Administration | M,D,O |
| Nursing Education | M,D,O |
| Nursing—General | M,D,O |
| Pediatric Nursing | M,D,O |
| Project Management | M |

**KNOX COLLEGE**

| | |
|---|---|
| Theology | M,D |

**KNOX THEOLOGICAL SEMINARY**

| | |
|---|---|
| Classics | M |
| Pastoral Ministry and Counseling | D |
| Religion | M |
| Theology | M |

**KUTZTOWN UNIVERSITY OF PENNSYLVANIA**

| | |
|---|---|
| Art Education | M |
| Arts Administration | M |
| Biological and Biomedical Sciences—General | M,D |
| Business Administration and Management—General | M |
| Computer Science | M |
| Counseling Psychology | M |
| Counselor Education | M |
| Curriculum and Instruction | M,D |
| Education—General | M,D |
| Educational Leadership and Administration | M |
| Educational Media/Instructional Technology | M |
| Elementary Education | M |
| English Education | M,D |
| English | M |
| Internet and Interactive Multimedia | M |
| Library Science | M |
| Mathematics | M,D |
| Middle School Education | M,D |
| Music Education | M |
| Public Administration | M |
| Reading Education | M |
| Secondary Education | M,D |
| Social Sciences Education | M,D |
| Social Work | M,D |

**LAGRANGE COLLEGE**

| | |
|---|---|
| Clinical Psychology | M |
| Curriculum and Instruction | M,O |
| Education—General | M,O |
| Middle School Education | M,O |
| Organizational Management | M |
| Secondary Education | M,O |

**LAGUNA COLLEGE OF ART & DESIGN**

| | |
|---|---|
| Art/Fine Arts | M |

**LAKE ERIE COLLEGE**

| | |
|---|---|
| Business Administration and Management—General | M |
| Education—General | M |
| Health Services Management and Hospital Administration | M |
| Management Information Systems | M |

**LAKE ERIE COLLEGE OF OSTEOPATHIC MEDICINE**

| | |
|---|---|
| Biological and Biomedical Sciences—General | M,D,O |
| Health Education | M,D,O |
| Osteopathic Medicine | M,D,O |
| Pharmacy | M,D,O |

**LAKE FOREST COLLEGE**

| | |
|---|---|
| American Studies | M |
| Art Education | M |
| Art/Fine Arts | M |
| Education—General | M |
| Elementary Education | M |
| English Education | M |
| Environmental Management and Policy | M |
| Film, Television, and Video Production | M |
| French | M |
| History | M |
| Liberal Studies | M |
| Mathematics Education | M |
| Music Education | M |
| Philosophy | M |
| Science Education | M |
| Secondary Education | M |
| Social Sciences Education | M |
| Spanish | M |
| Writing | M |

**LAKE FOREST GRADUATE SCHOOL OF MANAGEMENT**

| | |
|---|---|
| Business Administration and Management—General | M |
| Finance and Banking | M |
| Health Services Management and Hospital Administration | M |
| International Business | M |
| Marketing | M |
| Organizational Behavior | M |

**LAKEHEAD UNIVERSITY**

| | |
|---|---|
| Biological and Biomedical Sciences—General | M |
| Chemistry | M |
| Clinical Psychology | M,D |
| Computer Engineering | M |
| Computer Science | M |
| Economics | M |
| Education—General | M,D |
| Electrical Engineering | M |
| Engineering and Applied Sciences—General | M |
| English | M |
| Environmental Engineering | M |
| Exercise and Sports Science | M |
| Experimental Psychology | M,D |
| Forestry | M,D |
| Geology | M |
| Gerontology | M,D |
| Health Services Research | M |
| History | M |
| Kinesiology and Movement Studies | M |
| Mathematics | M |
| Physics | M |
| Psychology—General | M,D |
| Social Work | M |
| Sociology | M |
| Women's Studies | M,D |

**LAKELAND UNIVERSITY**

| | |
|---|---|
| Counselor Education | M |
| Education—General | M |
| Theology | M |

**LAMAR UNIVERSITY**

| | |
|---|---|
| Accounting | M |
| Biological and Biomedical Sciences—General | M |
| Business Administration and Management—General | M |
| Chemical Engineering | M,D |
| Chemistry | M |
| Clinical Psychology | M |
| Communication Disorders | M,D |
| Computer Science | M |
| Counseling Psychology | M |
| Counselor Education | M |
| Criminal Justice and Criminology | M |
| Education—General | M,D,O |
| Educational Leadership and Administration | M,D |
| Educational Media/Instructional Technology | M,D |
| Electrical Engineering | M,D |
| Engineering and Applied Sciences—General | M,D |
| English | M |
| Family and Consumer Sciences-General | M |
| Foreign Languages Education | M |
| History | M |
| Kinesiology and Movement Studies | M |
| Mathematics | M |
| Mechanical Engineering | M,D |
| Music | M |
| Nursing and Healthcare Administration | M |
| Nursing Education | M |
| Nursing—General | M |
| Political Science | M |
| Psychology—General | M |
| Spanish | M |
| Special Education | M,D |

**LANCASTER BIBLE COLLEGE**

| | |
|---|---|
| Counseling Psychology | M,D |
| Counselor Education | M,D |
| Elementary Education | M,D |
| Marriage and Family Therapy | M,D |
| Pastoral Ministry and Counseling | M,D,O |
| Secondary Education | M,D |
| Special Education | M,D |
| Theology | M,D,O |

**LANCASTER THEOLOGICAL SEMINARY**

| | |
|---|---|
| Art History | M,D,O |
| Ethics | M,D,O |
| Religion | M,D,O |
| Religious Education | M,D,O |
| Theology | M,D,O |

**LANDER UNIVERSITY**

| | |
|---|---|
| Early Childhood Education | M |
| Education—General | M |
| Emergency Management | M |
| Nursing—General | M |

**LANGSTON UNIVERSITY**

| | |
|---|---|
| Education—General | M |
| Elementary Education | M |
| English as a Second Language | M |
| Multilingual and Multicultural Education | M |
| Physical Therapy | D |
| Rehabilitation Counseling | M |
| Urban Education | M |

**LA ROCHE UNIVERSITY**

| | |
|---|---|
| Accounting | M |
| Human Resources Management | M,O |
| Nurse Anesthesia | M,D |
| Nursing and Healthcare Administration | M |
| Nursing Education | M |
| Nursing—General | M |

**LA SALLE UNIVERSITY**

| | |
|---|---|
| Accounting | M,O |
| Adult Nursing | M,D,O |
| Advertising and Public Relations | M,O |
| Business Administration and Management—General | M,O |
| Business Analytics | M,O |
| Clinical Psychology | M,D |
| Communication Disorders | M |
| Communication—General | M,O |
| Community Health Nursing | M,D,O |
| Computer Science | M,O |

*M—masters degree; D—doctorate; O—other advanced degree; *—Close-Up and/or Display*

| | |
|---|---|
| Corporate and Organizational Communication | M,O |
| Counseling Psychology | M |
| Developmental Psychology | M,D |
| Early Childhood Education | M,O |
| Education—General | M,O |
| Educational Leadership and Administration | M,O |
| Educational Media/Instructional Technology | M,O |
| English as a Second Language | M,O |
| English | M,O |
| Family Nurse Practitioner Studies | M,D,O |
| Finance and Banking | M,O |
| Forensic Sciences | M,O |
| Gerontological Nursing | M,D,O |
| Gerontology | M,D,O |
| Health Psychology | M,D |
| Hispanic Studies | M,O |
| Human Resources Development | M,O |
| Human Resources Management | M,O |
| Industrial and Organizational Psychology | M |
| International Business | M,O |
| Latin American Studies | M,O |
| Management of Technology | M,O |
| Marketing | M,O |
| Marriage and Family Therapy | M |
| Media Studies | M,O |
| Middle School Education | M,O |
| Multilingual and Multicultural Education | M,O |
| Nonprofit Management | M |
| Nurse Anesthesia | M,D,O |
| Nursing and Healthcare Administration | M,D,O |
| Nursing Education | M,D,O |
| Nursing—General | M,D,O |
| Psychology—General | M,D |
| Public Health—General | M |
| Reading Education | M,O |
| School Nursing | M,D,O |
| Secondary Education | M,O |
| Social Sciences Education | M,O |
| Special Education | M,O |
| Translation and Interpretation | M,O |

### LASELL COLLEGE

| | |
|---|---|
| Advertising and Public Relations | M,O |
| Business Administration and Management—General | M,O |
| Communication—General | M,O |
| Corporate and Organizational Communication | M,O |
| Criminal Justice and Criminology | M,O |
| Curriculum and Instruction | M,O |
| Education—General | M,O |
| Educational Leadership and Administration | M,O |
| Elementary Education | M,O |
| Emergency Management | M,O |
| English as a Second Language | M,O |
| Health Communication | M,O |
| Health Services Management and Hospital Administration | M,O |
| Homeland Security | M,O |
| Hospitality Management | M,O |
| Human Resources Management | M,O |
| Marketing | M,O |
| Project Management | M,O |
| Recreation and Park Management | M,O |
| Rehabilitation Sciences | M |
| Special Education | M,O |
| Sports Management | M,O |
| Travel and Tourism | M,O |

### LA SIERRA UNIVERSITY

| | |
|---|---|
| Accounting | M,O |
| Advertising and Public Relations | M |
| Business Administration and Management—General | M,O |
| Communication—General | M |
| Counselor Education | M,O |
| Curriculum and Instruction | M,D,O |
| Education—General | M,D,O |
| Educational Leadership and Administration | M,D,O |
| Educational Psychology | M,O |
| English | M |
| Finance and Banking | M,O |
| Human Resources Management | M,O |
| Marketing | M,O |
| Pastoral Ministry and Counseling | M |
| Religion | M |
| Religious Education | M |
| School Psychology | M,O |
| Writing | M |

### LAURENTIAN UNIVERSITY

| | |
|---|---|
| Analytical Chemistry | M |
| Applied Physics | M |
| Applied Psychology | M |
| Applied Social Research | M |
| Biochemistry | M |
| Biological and Biomedical Sciences—General | M,D |
| Business Administration and Management—General | M |
| Chemistry | M |
| Ecology | M,D |
| Engineering and Applied Sciences—General | M,D |
| Environmental Sciences | M |
| Experimental Psychology | M |
| Geology | M,D |
| History | M |
| Human Development | M |
| Humanities | M |
| Mineral/Mining Engineering | M,D |
| Natural Resources | M,D |
| Nursing—General | M |
| Organic Chemistry | M |
| Physical Chemistry | M |
| Psychology—General | M |
| Public Health—General | D |
| Science Education | O |
| Social Work | M |
| Sociology | M |
| Technical Writing | O |
| Theoretical Chemistry | M |

### LAWRENCE TECHNOLOGICAL UNIVERSITY

| | |
|---|---|
| Architectural Engineering | M,D |
| Architecture | M,O |
| Artificial Intelligence/Robotics | M,O |
| Automotive Engineering | M,D |
| Bioinformatics | M,O |
| Biomedical Engineering | M,D |
| Business Administration and Management—General | M,D,O |
| Civil Engineering | M,D |
| Communication—General | M,O |
| Computer and Information Systems Security | M,D,O |
| Computer Engineering | M,D |
| Computer Science | M,O |
| Construction Engineering | M,D |
| Data Science/Data Analytics | M,O |
| Educational Media/Instructional Technology | M,O |
| Electrical Engineering | M,D |
| Energy and Power Engineering | M,D |
| Engineering and Applied Sciences—General | M,D |
| Engineering Management | M,D |
| Finance and Banking | M,D,O |
| Health Services Management and Hospital Administration | M,D,O |
| Human Resources Development | M,O |
| Industrial and Manufacturing Management | M,D |
| Industrial/Management Engineering | M,D |
| Information Science | M,D,O |
| Interior Design | M,O |
| Management Strategy and Policy | M,D,O |
| Manufacturing Engineering | M,D |
| Marketing | M,D,O |
| Mechanical Engineering | M,D |
| Nonprofit Management | M,D,O |
| Project Management | M,D,O |
| Science Education | M,O |
| Technical Communication | M,O |
| Urban Design | M,O |
| Water Resources Engineering | M,D |

### LEBANESE AMERICAN UNIVERSITY

| | |
|---|---|
| Business Administration and Management—General | M |
| Computer Science | M |
| International Affairs | M |
| Pharmacy | D |

### LEBANON VALLEY COLLEGE

| | |
|---|---|
| Athletic Training and Sports Medicine | M |
| Business Administration and Management—General | M |
| Communication Disorders | M |
| Ethics | M |
| Health Services Management and Hospital Administration | M |
| Human Resources Management | M |
| Mathematics Education | M,O |
| Music Education | M |
| Physical Therapy | D |
| Project Management | M |
| Science Education | M,O |
| Social Sciences Education | M,O |

### LEE UNIVERSITY

| | |
|---|---|
| Art/Fine Arts | M,O |
| Biological and Biomedical Sciences—General | M,O |
| Business Administration and Management—General | M |
| Child Development | M |
| Counseling Psychology | M |
| Curriculum and Instruction | M,O |
| Early Childhood Education | M,O |
| Economics | M,O |
| Education—General | M,O |
| Educational Leadership and Administration | M,O |
| Elementary Education | M,O |
| English as a Second Language | M,O |
| English | M,O |
| Ethics | M |
| Higher Education | M,O |
| History | M,O |
| Mathematics Education | M,O |
| Mathematics | M,O |
| Middle School Education | M,O |
| Music Education | M |
| Music | M |
| Pastoral Ministry and Counseling | M |
| Religion | M |
| Secondary Education | M,O |
| Social Sciences Education | M,O |
| Spanish | M,O |
| Special Education | M,O |
| Theology | M |

### LEHIGH UNIVERSITY

| | |
|---|---|
| Accounting | M |
| American Studies | M,D |
| Applied Mathematics | M,D |
| Biochemical Engineering | M,D |
| Biochemistry | M,D |
| Bioengineering | M,D |
| Biological and Biomedical Sciences—General | M,D |
| Business Administration and Management—General | M |
| Cell Biology | M,D |
| Chemical Engineering | M,D |
| Chemistry | M,D |
| Civil Engineering | M,D |
| Computer Engineering | M,D |
| Computer Science | M,D |
| Counseling Psychology | M,D,O |
| Counselor Education | M,D,O |
| Curriculum and Instruction | M,D,O |
| Early Childhood Education | M,D,O |
| Economics | M,D |
| Education—General | M,D,O |
| Educational Leadership and Administration | M,D,O |
| Educational Media/Instructional Technology | M,D |
| Electrical Engineering | M,D |
| Elementary Education | M,D |
| Energy and Power Engineering | M |
| Engineering and Applied Sciences—General | M,D,O |
| Engineering Management | M,D,O |
| English | M,D |
| Entrepreneurship | M |
| Environmental and Occupational Health | M,O |
| Environmental Engineering | M,D |
| Environmental Law | M,O |
| Environmental Management and Policy | M,O |
| Environmental Sciences | M,D |
| Finance and Banking | M |
| Geology | M,D |
| Geosciences | M,D |
| Health Services Management and Hospital Administration | M,O |
| History | M,D |
| Human Services | M,D,O |
| Industrial/Management Engineering | M,D,O |
| Information Science | M |
| Interdisciplinary Studies | M,D |
| Materials Engineering | M,D |
| Materials Sciences | M,D |
| Mathematics | M,D |
| Mechanical Engineering | M,D |
| Mechanics | M,D |
| Molecular Biology | M,D |
| Photonics | M,D |
| Physics | M,D |
| Political Science | M |
| Polymer Science and Engineering | M,D |
| Project Management | M |
| Psychology—General | M,D |
| Public History | M,D |
| Quantitative Analysis | M |
| School Psychology | D,O |
| Special Education | M,D |
| Statistics | M,D |
| Sustainable Development | M,O |
| Systems Engineering | M,D,O |

### LEHMAN COLLEGE OF THE CITY UNIVERSITY OF NEW YORK

| | |
|---|---|
| Accounting | M |
| Adult Nursing | M |
| Art Education | M |
| Art/Fine Arts | M |
| Biological and Biomedical Sciences—General | M |
| Business Administration and Management—General | M |
| Communication Disorders | M |
| Computer Science | M |
| Counselor Education | M |
| Early Childhood Education | M |
| Education—General | M |
| Elementary Education | M |
| English as a Second Language | M |
| English Education | M |
| English | M |
| Gerontological Nursing | M |
| Health Education | M |
| Health Promotion | M |
| History | M |
| Maternal and Child/Neonatal Nursing | M |
| Mathematics Education | M |
| Mathematics | M |
| Middle School Education | M |
| Multilingual and Multicultural Education | M |
| Music Education | M |
| Nursing—General | M |
| Nutrition | M |
| Pediatric Nursing | M |
| Reading Education | M |
| Recreation and Park Management | M |
| Science Education | M |
| Secondary Education | M |
| Social Sciences Education | M |
| Social Work | M |
| Spanish | M |
| Special Education | M |

### LE MOYNE COLLEGE

| | |
|---|---|
| Arts Administration | M |
| Business Administration and Management—General | M |
| Early Childhood Education | M,O |
| Education—General | M,O |
| Educational Leadership and Administration | M,O |
| Elementary Education | M,O |
| English as a Second Language | M,O |
| English Education | M,O |
| Family Nurse Practitioner Studies | M,O |
| Foreign Languages Education | M,O |
| Management Information Systems | M,O |
| Middle School Education | M,O |
| Nursing and Healthcare Administration | M,O |
| Nursing Education | M,O |
| Nursing Informatics | M,O |
| Nursing—General | M,O |
| Occupational Therapy | M |
| Physician Assistant Studies | M |
| Reading Education | M,O |
| Secondary Education | M,O |
| Social Sciences Education | M,O |
| Special Education | M,O |
| Urban Studies | M,O |

### LENOIR-RHYNE UNIVERSITY

| | |
|---|---|
| Accounting | M |
| Addictions/Substance Abuse Counseling | M |
| Athletic Training and Sports Medicine | M |
| Business Administration and Management—General | M |
| Business Analytics | M |
| Clinical Psychology | M |
| Community College Education | M |
| Counseling Psychology | M |
| Counselor Education | M |
| Distance Education Development | M |
| Education—General | M |
| Educational Leadership and Administration | M |
| Educational Media/Instructional Technology | M |
| Entrepreneurship | M |
| Health Services Management and Hospital Administration | M |
| Human Services | M |
| International Business | M |
| Management Information Systems | M |
| Management Strategy and Policy | M |
| Nursing and Healthcare Administration | M |
| Nursing Education | M |
| Nursing—General | M |
| Occupational Therapy | M |
| Organizational Management | M |
| Physician Assistant Studies | M |
| Public Health—General | M |
| Secondary Education | M |
| Sustainable Development | M |
| Theology | M |
| Writing | M |

### LESLEY UNIVERSITY

| | |
|---|---|
| Adult Education | M,D,O |
| Art Education | M,D,O |
| Art Therapy | M,D,O |
| Art/Fine Arts | M,D,O |
| Clinical Psychology | M,D,O |
| Computer Education | M,D,O |
| Conflict Resolution and Mediation/Peace Studies | M,D,O |
| Counseling Psychology | M,D,O |
| Curriculum and Instruction | M,D,O |
| Distance Education Development | M,D,O |
| Early Childhood Education | M,D,O |
| Ecology | M,D,O |
| Education of Students with Severe/Multiple Disabilities | M,D,O |
| Education—General | M,D,O |
| Educational Leadership and Administration | M,D,O |
| Educational Media/Instructional Technology | M,D,O |
| Elementary Education | M,D,O |
| English as a Second Language | M,D,O |
| Health Psychology | M,D,O |
| Interdisciplinary Studies | M,D,O |
| International Affairs | M,D,O |
| Mathematics Education | M,D,O |
| Middle School Education | M,D,O |
| Photography | M |
| Psychology—General | M,D,O |
| Reading Education | M,D,O |
| School Psychology | M,D,O |
| Science Education | M,D,O |
| Secondary Education | M,D,O |
| Social Psychology | M,D,O |
| Special Education | M,D,O |
| Sustainable Development | M,D,O |
| Therapies—Dance, Drama, and Music | M,D,O |
| Urban and Regional Planning | M,D,O |
| Women's Studies | M,D,O |
| Writing | M,D,O |

### LES ROCHES INTERNATIONAL SCHOOL OF HOTEL MANAGEMENT

| | |
|---|---|
| Hospitality Management | M |

### LETOURNEAU UNIVERSITY

| | |
|---|---|
| Business Administration and Management—General | M |
| Counseling Psychology | M |
| Curriculum and Instruction | M |
| Educational Leadership and Administration | M |
| Engineering and Applied Sciences—General | M |
| Engineering Management | M |
| Health Services Management and Hospital Administration | M |
| Management Strategy and Policy | M |
| Marriage and Family Therapy | M |
| Psychology—General | M |

### LEWIS & CLARK COLLEGE

| | |
|---|---|
| Addictions/Substance Abuse Counseling | M |
| Communication Disorders | M |
| Counseling Psychology | M |
| Curriculum and Instruction | M |
| Educational Leadership and Administration | M,D,O |
| Elementary Education | M |
| Environmental Law | M |
| Law | M,D |
| Marriage and Family Therapy | M |
| School Psychology | M,O |
| Secondary Education | M |
| Special Education | M |
| Student Affairs | M,D,O |

### LEWIS UNIVERSITY

| | |
|---|---|
| Accounting | M |

Adult Nursing M,D
Bioinformatics M
Business Administration and Management—General
Business Analytics M
Clinical Psychology M
Computational Biology M
Computer and Information Systems Security M
Computer Science M
Counseling Psychology M
Counselor Education M
Criminal Justice and Criminology M
Curriculum and Instruction M
Early Childhood Education M
Educational Leadership and Administration M,D
Educational Media/Instructional Technology M
Electronic Commerce M
Elementary Education M
English as a Second Language M
English Education M
Environmental and Occupational Health M
Family Nurse Practitioner Studies M,D
Finance and Banking M
Foreign Languages Education M
Health Services Management and Hospital Administration M
Higher Education M
Human Resources Management M
International Business M
Management Information Systems M
Management of Technology M
Marketing M
Middle School Education M
Nursing and Healthcare Administration M,D
Nursing Education M,D
Nursing—General M,D
Organizational Management M
Project Management M
Reading Education M
School Nursing M,D
Science Education M
Secondary Education M
Social Sciences Education M
Social Work M
Software Engineering M
Special Education M
Sports Management M
Student Affairs M

### LEXINGTON THEOLOGICAL SEMINARY
Theology M,D

### LIBERTY UNIVERSITY
Accounting M,D
Addictions/Substance Abuse Counseling M,D,O
Advertising and Public Relations M,D
Anatomy M,D
Applied Psychology M,D,O
Biological and Biomedical Sciences—General M,D
Biopsychology M,D
Business Administration and Management—General M,D
Cell Biology M,D
Child and Family Studies M,D,O
Clinical Psychology M,D,O
Communication—General M
Computer and Information Systems Security M,D
Counseling Psychology M,D,O
Counselor Education M,D,O
Criminal Justice and Criminology M,D,O
Developmental Psychology M,D,O
Education—General M,D,O
Emergency Management M,D,O
English M
Epidemiology M,D
Exercise and Sports Science M,D
Facilities Management M,D
Family Nurse Practitioner Studies M,D
Finance and Banking M,D
Forensic Psychology M
Health Informatics M,D
Health Promotion M,D,O
History M
Homeland Security M
Human Services M,D,O
Industrial and Organizational Psychology M,D,O
International Affairs M,D
International Business M,D
International Health M,D
Internet and Interactive Multimedia M
Law M
Legal and Justice Studies M
Marketing M,D
Marriage and Family Therapy M,D,O
Military and Defense Studies M,D
Missions and Missiology M,D
Molecular Medicine M,D
Music Education M,D
Music M,D
Nonprofit Management M
Nursing and Healthcare Administration M,D
Nursing Education M,D
Nursing Informatics M,D
Nursing—General M,D
Nutrition M,D
Osteopathic Medicine D
Pastoral Ministry and Counseling M,D,O
Political Science M
Project Management M,D
Psychology—General M,D,O
Public Administration M
Public Health—General M,D
Public Policy M
Reading Education M,D,O
Religion M,D
Religious Education M,D
School Psychology M,D,O
Taxation M,D
Theology M,D,O

### LIFE CHIROPRACTIC COLLEGE WEST
Chiropractic D

### LIFE UNIVERSITY
Athletic Training and Sports Medicine M
Chiropractic D
Exercise and Sports Science M
Nutrition M

### LIM COLLEGE
Business Administration and Management—General M
Clothing and Textiles M
Marketing M

### LIMESTONE COLLEGE
Business Administration and Management—General M

### LINCOLN CHRISTIAN SEMINARY
Pastoral Ministry and Counseling M,D
Religious Education M,D
Theology M,D

### LINCOLN CHRISTIAN UNIVERSITY
Cultural Studies M
Organizational Management M
Pastoral Ministry and Counseling M
Philosophy M
Religion M
Theology M

### LINCOLN MEMORIAL UNIVERSITY
Business Administration and Management—General M
Counselor Education M,D,O
Curriculum and Instruction M,D,O
Education—General M,D,O
Educational Leadership and Administration M,D,O
English Education M,D,O
Family Nurse Practitioner Studies M
Higher Education M,D,O
Human Resources Development M,D,O
Law D
Nurse Anesthesia M
Nursing—General M
Osteopathic Medicine D
Psychiatric Nursing M
Veterinary Medicine D

### LINCOLN UNIVERSITY (CA)
Business Administration and Management—General M,D
Finance and Banking M,D
Human Resources Management M,D
International Business M,D
Investment Management M,D
Management Information Systems M,D

### LINCOLN UNIVERSITY (MO)
Counselor Education M
Criminal Justice and Criminology M
Elementary Education M
Environmental Sciences M
Higher Education M
History M
Middle School Education M
Secondary Education M
Sociology M

### LINDENWOOD UNIVERSITY
Advertising and Public Relations M
Applied Behavior Analysis M,D,O
Art History M
Business Administration and Management—General M,O
Communication Disorders M,D,O
Communication—General M,O
Computer and Information Systems Security M,O
Counseling Psychology M,D,O
Criminal Justice and Criminology M,O
Education of the Gifted M,D,O
Education—General M,D,O
Educational Leadership and Administration M,D,O
Educational Media/Instructional Technology M,D,O
English as a Second Language M,D,O
Entrepreneurship M
Film, Television, and Video Production M
Health Promotion M
Health Services Management and Hospital Administration M,O
Human Resources Management M,O
Internet and Interactive Multimedia M
Journalism M
Management Information Systems M,O
Marketing M,O
Mass Communication M
Media Studies M,O
Nursing—General M
Project Management M,O
School Psychology M,D,O
Writing M,O

### LINDENWOOD UNIVERSITY–BELLEVILLE
Business Administration and Management—General M
Communication—General M
Computer Art and Design M
Counselor Education M
Criminal Justice and Criminology M
Education—General M
Educational Leadership and Administration M
Health Services Management and Hospital Administration M
Human Resources Management M
Internet and Interactive Multimedia M
Media Studies M

### LINDSEY WILSON COLLEGE
Counseling Psychology M,D
Counselor Education M,D
Educational Leadership and Administration M
Human Development M,D
Internet and Interactive Multimedia M

### LIPSCOMB UNIVERSITY
Accounting M,O
Applied Behavior Analysis M,D,O
Business Administration and Management—General M,O
Clinical Laboratory Sciences/Medical Technology M
Clinical Psychology M,O
Computer and Information Systems Security M,O
Conflict Resolution and Mediation/Peace Studies M,O
Counseling Psychology M,O
Data Science/Data Analytics M,O
Education—General M,D,O
Educational Leadership and Administration M,D,O
Educational Media/Instructional Technology M,D,O
English Education M,D,O
English M,D,O
Exercise and Sports Science M
Film, Television, and Video Production M
Finance and Banking M,O
Health Informatics M,D
Health Services Management and Hospital Administration M,O
International Affairs M,O
Management Information Systems M,O
Management of Technology M,O
Management Strategy and Policy M,O
Marriage and Family Therapy M,O
Molecular Biology M
Nonprofit Management M,O
Nutrition M
Organizational Management M,O
Pastoral Ministry and Counseling M,D
Pharmacy M,D
Psychology—General M,O
Public Administration M
Public Policy M
Reading Education M,D,O
School Psychology M,D,O
Software Engineering M,O
Special Education M,D,O
Sustainable Development M,O
Taxation M,O
Theology M,D
Writing M

### LOCK HAVEN UNIVERSITY OF PENNSYLVANIA
Actuarial Science M
Athletic Training and Sports Medicine M
Business Education M
Clinical Psychology M
Counseling Psychology M
Education—General M
Educational Leadership and Administration M
Elementary Education M
Health Education M
Health Promotion M
Health Services Management and Hospital Administration M
Human Services M
Information Studies M
Physician Assistant Studies M
Sport Psychology M
Sports Management M

### LOGAN UNIVERSITY
Chiropractic D
Exercise and Sports Science M,D
Health Education M,D
Health Informatics M,D
Nutrition M,D
Rehabilitation Sciences M,D

### LOGOS EVANGELICAL SEMINARY
Theology M,D,O

### LOMA LINDA UNIVERSITY
Addictions/Substance Abuse Counseling M,D,O
Adult Nursing M
Allied Health—General M,D
Allopathic Medicine M,D
Anatomy D
Applied Social Research M,D
Biochemistry M,D
Bioethics M,O
Biostatistics M,D
Child and Family Studies M,D,O
Clinical Psychology D
Communication Disorders M,D
Counselor Education M,D,O
Criminal Justice and Criminology M,D
Dentistry M,D,O
Environmental and Occupational Health M
Epidemiology M,D
Gerontological Nursing M
Gerontology M,D
Health Education M,D
Health Services Management and Hospital Administration M
International Health M
Marriage and Family Therapy M,D,O
Microbiology M,D
Nursing and Healthcare Administration M
Nursing Education M
Nursing—General D
Nutrition M,D
Occupational Therapy M,D
Oral and Dental Sciences M,O
Pathology D
Pediatric Nursing M
Pharmacology D
Pharmacy D
Physical Therapy M,D
Physician Assistant Studies M
Physiology D
Psychology—General D
Public Health—General M,D
Rehabilitation Sciences M,D
Religion M
Social Work M,D

### LONDON METROPOLITAN UNIVERSITY
Applied Psychology M,D
Architecture M,D
Arts Administration M,D
Athletic Training and Sports Medicine M,D
Biological and Biomedical Sciences—General M,D
Child and Family Studies M,D
Clinical Psychology M,D
Computer and Information Systems Security M,D
Conflict Resolution and Mediation/Peace Studies M,D
Counseling Psychology M,D
Criminal Justice and Criminology M,D
Data Science/Data Analytics M,D
Early Childhood Education M,D
Education—General M,D
Emergency Management M,D
English Education M,D
Food Science and Technology M,D
Foreign Languages Education M,D
Forensic Psychology M,D
Health Services Management and Hospital Administration M,D
Higher Education M,D
Homeland Security M,D
Human Resources Management M,D
Immunology M,D
Industrial and Organizational Psychology M,D
International Affairs M,D
Internet and Interactive Multimedia M,D
Law M,D
Management Information Systems M,D
Management of Technology M,D
Military and Defense Studies M,D
Near and Middle Eastern Languages M,D
Nutrition M,D
Pharmacology M,D
Public Administration M,D
Public Health—General M,D
Public Policy M,D
Social Work M,D
Special Education M,D
Sports and Entertainment Law M,D
Translation and Interpretation M,D
Urban Design M,D
Women's Studies M,D
Writing M,D

### LONG ISLAND UNIVERSITY - BRENTWOOD CAMPUS
Clinical Psychology M,O
Counseling Psychology M,O
Counselor Education M,O
Criminal Justice and Criminology M,O
Early Childhood Education M,O
Educational Leadership and Administration M,O
Elementary Education M,O
Family Nurse Practitioner Studies M,O
Health Services Management and Hospital Administration M,O
Library Science M,O
Reading Education M,O
Social Work M,O
Special Education M,O

### LONG ISLAND UNIVERSITY - BROOKLYN
Accounting M,O
Adult Nursing M,O
Applied Behavior Analysis M,O
Athletic Training and Sports Medicine M,D,O
Biological and Biomedical Sciences—General M,D,O
Business Administration and Management—General M,O
Chemistry M,D,O
Clinical Psychology M,D,O
Communication Disorders M,D,O
Community Health M,D,O
Computer Science M,O
Counseling Psychology M,O
Counselor Education M,O
Early Childhood Education M,O

*M—masters degree; D—doctorate; O—other advanced degree; *—Close-Up and/or Display*

Education—General M,O
Educational Leadership and Administration M,O
English as a Second Language M,O
English M,D,O
Exercise and Sports Science M,D,O
Family Nurse Practitioner Studies M,O
Forensic Sciences M,D,O
Gerontology M,O
Health Services Management and Hospital Administration M,O
Human Resources Management M,O
Marriage and Family Therapy M,O
Media Studies M,D,O
Multilingual and Multicultural Education M,O
Nonprofit Management M,O
Nursing Education M,O
Nursing—General M,O
Occupational Therapy M,D,O
Pharmaceutical Sciences M,D
Pharmacology M,D
Pharmacy M,D
Physical Therapy M,D,O
Physician Assistant Studies M,D,O
Political Science M,D,O
Psychology—General M,D,O
Public Administration M,O
Public Health—General M,D,O
Social Sciences Education M,D,O
Social Work M,D,O
Special Education M,O
Taxation M,O
Toxicology M,D
Urban Education M,O
Urban Studies M,D,O
Writing M,D,O

### LONG ISLAND UNIVERSITY - HUDSON

Addictions/Substance Abuse Counseling M,O
Counseling Psychology M,O
Counselor Education M,O
Early Childhood Education M,O
Educational Leadership and Administration M,O
Elementary Education M,O
English as a Second Language M,O
Health Services Management and Hospital Administration M,O
Marriage and Family Therapy M,O
Middle School Education M,O
Multilingual and Multicultural Education M,O
Pharmaceutical Sciences M,O
Pharmacy M,O
Public Administration M,O
Reading Education M,O
School Psychology M,O
Special Education M,O

### LONG ISLAND UNIVERSITY - POST

Accounting M
Allied Health—General M,O
Applied Behavior Analysis M,O
Applied Mathematics M,O
Art Education M,D,O
Art Therapy M
Art/Fine Arts M
Biological and Biomedical Sciences—General M,O
Business Administration and Management—General M
Clinical Psychology M,D,O
Communication Disorders M,D,O
Counseling Psychology M,D,O
Criminal Justice and Criminology M,O
Early Childhood Education M,D,O
Education—General M,D,O
Educational Leadership and Administration M,D,O
Educational Media/Instructional Technology M,D,O
Engineering Management M
English as a Second Language M,D,O
English M,O
Environmental Management and Policy M,O
Family Nurse Practitioner Studies M,O
Finance and Banking M
Game Design and Development M
Genetic Counseling M,O
Geosciences M,O
Gerontology M,O
Health Services Management and Hospital Administration M,O
History M,O
Interdisciplinary Studies M,D,O
International Business M
Internet and Interactive Multimedia M
Library Science M,D,O
Management Information Systems M
Marketing M
Middle School Education M,D,O
Museum Studies M
Music Education M,D,O
Music M
Nonprofit Management M,O
Nursing Education M,O
Nutrition M,O
Perfusion M,O
Political Science M,O
Psychology—General M,O
Public Administration M,O
Reading Education M,D,O
School Psychology M,D,O
Secondary Education M,D,O
Social Work M,O
Special Education M,D,O
Sustainable Development M,O
Taxation M
Theater M

### LONG ISLAND UNIVERSITY - RIVERHEAD

Applied Behavior Analysis M,O
Computer and Information Systems Security M,O
Early Childhood Education M,O
Elementary Education M,O
English as a Second Language M,O
Homeland Security M,O
Reading Education M,O
Special Education M,O

### LONGWOOD UNIVERSITY

Business Administration and Management—General M
Communication Disorders M
Counselor Education M
Education—General M
Educational Media/Instructional Technology M
Elementary Education M
Health Education M
Mathematics Education M
Middle School Education M
Physical Education M
Reading Education M
Real Estate M
Special Education M

### LORAS COLLEGE

Applied Psychology M
Educational Leadership and Administration M
Pastoral Ministry and Counseling M
Special Education M
Theology M

### LOUISIANA COLLEGE

Education—General M
Educational Leadership and Administration M
Nursing and Healthcare Administration M
Nursing—General M
Social Work M

### LOUISIANA STATE UNIVERSITY AND AGRICULTURAL & MECHANICAL COLLEGE

Accounting M,D
Agricultural Economics and Agribusiness M,D
Agricultural Education M,D
Agricultural Engineering M,D
Agricultural Sciences—General M,D
Agronomy and Soil Sciences M,D
Animal Sciences M,D
Anthropology M,D
Applied Arts and Design—General M
Applied Science and Technology M
Applied Statistics M
Architecture M
Art History M
Art/Fine Arts M
Astronomy M,D
Astrophysics M,D
Biochemistry M,D
Bioengineering M,D
Biological and Biomedical Sciences—General M,D
Biopsychology M,D
Business Administration and Management—General M,D
Business Education M,D
Chemical Engineering M,D
Chemistry M,D
Civil Engineering M,D
Clinical Psychology M,D
Cognitive Sciences M,D
Communication Disorders M,D
Communication—General M,D
Comparative Literature M,D
Computer Engineering M,D
Computer Science M,D
Construction Management M,D
Counselor Education M,D,O
Developmental Psychology M,D
Economics M,D
Education—General M,D,O
Educational Leadership and Administration M,D,O
Educational Measurement and Evaluation M,D,O
Educational Media/Instructional Technology M,D,O
Electrical Engineering M,D
Elementary Education M,D,O
Engineering and Applied Sciences—General M,D
English M,D
Entomology M,D
Environmental Engineering M,D
Environmental Management and Policy M,D
Environmental Sciences M,D
Family and Consumer Sciences-General M,D
Finance and Banking M,D
Fish, Game, and Wildlife Management M,D
Food Science and Technology M,D
Forestry M,D
French M,D
Geography M,D
Geology M,D
Geophysics M,D
Geotechnical Engineering M,D
Graphic Design M
Higher Education M,D,O
Hispanic Studies M
History M,D
Home Economics Education M,D
Horticulture M,D
Human Resources Development M,D
Information Studies M
International and Comparative Education M,D
Internet and Interactive Multimedia M
Kinesiology and Movement Studies M,D
Landscape Architecture M
Law M,D
Liberal Studies M
Library Science M
Management Information Systems M,D
Marine Affairs M,D
Mass Communication M,D
Mathematics M,D
Mechanical Engineering M,D
Mechanics M,D
Media Studies M,D
Medical Physics M,D
Music Education M,D
Music M,D
Natural Resources M,D
Nutrition M,D
Oceanography M,D
Petroleum Engineering M,D
Philosophy M
Photography M
Physics M,D
Plant Pathology M,D
Political Science M,D
Psychology—General M,D
Public Administration M,D
School Psychology M,D
Secondary Education M,D,O
Social Work M,D
Sociology M,D
Statistics M
Structural Engineering M,D
Systems Science M,D
Theater M,D
Toxicology M,D
Transportation and Highway Engineering M,D
Veterinary Medicine D
Veterinary Sciences M,D
Vocational and Technical Education M,D
Water Resources Engineering M,D
Writing M,D

### LOUISIANA STATE UNIVERSITY HEALTH SCIENCES CENTER

Allopathic Medicine M,D
Anatomy D
Biological and Biomedical Sciences—General D
Biostatistics M,D
Cell Biology D
Communication Disorders M,D
Community Health Nursing M,D,O
Community Health M,D
Dentistry D
Developmental Biology D
Environmental and Occupational Health M,D
Epidemiology M,D
Family Nurse Practitioner Studies M,D,O
Gerontological Nursing M,D,O
Health Services Management and Hospital Administration M,D
Human Genetics D
Immunology D
Maternal and Child/Neonatal Nursing M,D,O
Microbiology D
Neurobiology D
Neuroscience D
Nurse Anesthesia M,D,O
Nursing and Healthcare Administration M,D,O
Nursing Education M,D,O
Nursing—General M,D,O
Occupational Therapy M
Parasitology D
Pharmacology D
Physical Therapy D
Physician Assistant Studies M
Physiology D
Public Health—General M,D
Rehabilitation Counseling M

### LOUISIANA STATE UNIVERSITY HEALTH SCIENCES CENTER AT SHREVEPORT

Allopathic Medicine D
Anatomy M,D
Biochemistry M,D
Biological and Biomedical Sciences—General M
Cell Biology M,D
Immunology M,D
Microbiology M,D
Molecular Biology M,D
Pharmacology M,D
Physiology M,D

### LOUISIANA STATE UNIVERSITY IN SHREVEPORT

Biological and Biomedical Sciences—General M
Business Administration and Management—General M
Computer Science M
Counselor Education M
Curriculum and Instruction M,D
Education—General M,D
Educational Leadership and Administration M,D
Health Services Management and Hospital Administration M
Liberal Studies M
Nonprofit Management M
Public Health—General M
School Psychology O
Systems Science M

### LOUISIANA TECH UNIVERSITY

Accounting M,D
Agricultural Sciences—General M,D,O
Applied Physics M,D,O
Architecture M,D,O
Art/Fine Arts M,D,O
Biological and Biomedical Sciences—General M,D,O
Biomedical Engineering M,D,O
Business Administration and Management—General M,D,O
Chemistry M,D,O
Clinical Psychology M,D,O
Communication Disorders M,D,O
Computer and Information Systems Security M,D
Computer Science M,D,O
Counseling Psychology M,D,O
Curriculum and Instruction M,D,O
Early Childhood Education M,D,O
Education—General M,D,O
Educational Leadership and Administration M,D,O
Elementary Education M,D,O
Engineering and Applied Sciences—General M,D,O
Engineering Management M,D,O
Engineering Physics M,D,O
English M,D,O
Finance and Banking M,D
Graphic Design M,D,O
Health Informatics M,D,O
Higher Education M,D,O
History M,D,O
Human Services M,D,O
Industrial and Organizational Psychology M,D,O
Kinesiology and Movement Studies M,D,O
Management Information Systems M,D
Management of Technology M,D,O
Marketing M,D
Materials Sciences M,D,O
Mathematics M,D,O
Middle School Education M,D,O
Molecular Biology M,D,O
Nanotechnology M,D,O
Nutrition M,D,O
Photography M,D,O
Secondary Education M,D,O
Special Education M,D,O
Technical Writing M,D,O

### LOUISVILLE PRESBYTERIAN THEOLOGICAL SEMINARY

Religion M,D
Theology M,D

### LOURDES UNIVERSITY

Business Administration and Management—General M
Curriculum and Instruction M
Educational Leadership and Administration M
Nurse Anesthesia M
Nursing and Healthcare Administration M
Nursing Education M
Organizational Management M
Reading Education M
Theology M

### LOYOLA MARYMOUNT UNIVERSITY

Accounting M
Bioethics M
Business Administration and Management—General M
Civil Engineering M
Counseling Psychology M
Counselor Education M
Education—General M,D
Educational Leadership and Administration M,D
Electrical Engineering M
Elementary Education M
Engineering Management
English M
Environmental Sciences M
Film, Television, and Video Production M
Higher Education M
Law M,D
Marriage and Family Therapy M
Mathematics Education M
Mechanical Engineering M
Multilingual and Multicultural Education M
Pastoral Ministry and Counseling M
Philosophy M
Reading Education M
Recreation and Park Management M
School Psychology M
Secondary Education M
Special Education M
Systems Engineering M
Theology M
Urban Education M
Writing M

### LOYOLA UNIVERSITY CHICAGO

Accounting M
Adult Nursing M,D,O
Applied Statistics M
Biochemistry M,D
Bioethics M,D,O
Bioinformatics M
Biological and Biomedical Sciences—General M,D
Business Administration and Management—General M,O
Business Analytics M,O
Cell Biology M,D
Chemistry M,D
Clinical Psychology M,D,O

| | |
|---|---|
| Clinical Research | M |
| Communication—General | M |
| Computer Science | M |
| Corporate and Organizational Communication | M |
| Counseling Psychology | M,D,O |
| Counselor Education | M,O |
| Criminal Justice and Criminology | M |
| Curriculum and Instruction | M,D |
| Developmental Psychology | M,D |
| Economics | M |
| Education—General | M,D,O |
| Educational Leadership and Administration | M,D,O |
| Educational Measurement and Evaluation | M,D,O |
| Educational Policy | M,D |
| Elementary Education | M |
| English | M,D |
| Entrepreneurship | M |
| Ethics | M |
| Family Nurse Practitioner Studies | M,D,O |
| Finance and Banking | M |
| Gender Studies | M |
| Health Law | M,D,O |
| Health Services Management and Hospital Administration | M |
| Higher Education | M,D |
| History | M,D |
| Human Resources Management | M |
| Humanities | M |
| Immunology | M,D |
| Infectious Diseases | M,D,O |
| Information Science | M |
| International and Comparative Education | M,D |
| International Business | M |
| Law | M,D,O |
| Legal and Justice Studies | M,O |
| Management Information Systems | M,O |
| Marketing | M |
| Mathematics | M |
| Medieval and Renaissance Studies | M,D |
| Microbiology | M,D |
| Molecular Biology | M,D |
| Molecular Pharmacology | M,D |
| Molecular Physiology | M,D |
| Neuroscience | M,D |
| Nursing and Healthcare Administration | M,D,O |
| Nursing—General | M,D,O |
| Nutrition | M,D,O |
| Pastoral Ministry and Counseling | M,O |
| Philosophy | M,D |
| Physiology | M,D |
| Political Science | M,D |
| Public Health—General | M,O |
| Public History | M,D |
| Public Policy | M |
| Religious Education | M,O |
| Risk Management | M |
| School Psychology | D,O |
| Secondary Education | M |
| Social Psychology | M,O |
| Social Work | M,D,O |
| Sociology | M,D |
| Software Engineering | M |
| Spanish | M |
| Special Education | M |
| Statistics | M |
| Supply Chain Management | M,O |
| Taxation | M,D,O |
| Theology | M,D,O |
| Urban Studies | M |
| Women's Health Nursing | M,D,O |
| Women's Studies | M |

## LOYOLA UNIVERSITY MARYLAND

| | |
|---|---|
| Business Administration and Management—General | M |
| Clinical Psychology | M,D,O |
| Communication Disorders | M |
| Counseling Psychology | M,D,O |
| Counselor Education | M,O |
| Curriculum and Instruction | M |
| Early Childhood Education | M,O |
| Education—General | M,O |
| Educational Leadership and Administration | M,O |
| Educational Media/Instructional Technology | M |
| Elementary Education | M,O |
| Finance and Banking | M |
| Investment Management | M |
| Management Information Systems | M |
| Marketing | M |
| Media Studies | M |
| Music Education | M |
| Psychology—General | M,D,O |
| Reading Education | M |
| Secondary Education | M |
| Theology | M |

## LOYOLA UNIVERSITY NEW ORLEANS

| | |
|---|---|
| Business Administration and Management—General | M |
| Clinical Psychology | M |
| Criminal Justice and Criminology | M |
| Education—General | M |
| Family Nurse Practitioner Studies | M,D |
| Law | M,D |
| Marriage and Family Therapy | M |
| Music | M |
| Nursing—General | M,D |
| Organizational Management | M |
| Secondary Education | M |
| Theology | M,O |
| Therapies—Dance, Drama, and Music | M |

## LUBBOCK CHRISTIAN UNIVERSITY

| | |
|---|---|
| Theology | M |

## LUTHERAN SCHOOL OF THEOLOGY AT CHICAGO

| | |
|---|---|
| Pastoral Ministry and Counseling | M,D |
| Theology | M,D |

## LUTHERAN THEOLOGICAL SEMINARY SASKATOON

| | |
|---|---|
| Ethics | M,D |
| Pastoral Ministry and Counseling | M,D |
| Religion | M,D |
| Theology | M,D |

## LUTHER RICE COLLEGE & SEMINARY

| | |
|---|---|
| Pastoral Ministry and Counseling | M,D |
| Religion | M,D |
| Theology | M,D |

## LUTHER SEMINARY

| | |
|---|---|
| Missions and Missiology | M,D |
| Pastoral Ministry and Counseling | M,D |
| Theology | M,D |

## LYNN UNIVERSITY

| | |
|---|---|
| Applied Psychology | M |
| Business Administration and Management—General | M |
| Communication—General | M,O |
| Computer Art and Design | M,O |
| Counseling Psychology | M |
| Criminal Justice and Criminology | M |
| Early Childhood Education | M,D |
| Education of the Gifted | M,D |
| Education—General | M,D |
| Educational Leadership and Administration | M,D |
| Graphic Design | M,O |
| Internet and Interactive Multimedia | M,O |
| Mass Communication | M,O |
| Media Studies | M,O |
| Middle School Education | M,D |
| Music | M,O |
| Psychology—General | M |
| Special Education | M,D |

## MAASTRICHT SCHOOL OF MANAGEMENT

| | |
|---|---|
| Business Administration and Management—General | M,D |
| Facilities Management | M,D |
| Sustainability Management | M,D |

## MACHZIKEI HADATH RABBINICAL COLLEGE

| | |
|---|---|
| Theology | O |

## MADONNA UNIVERSITY

| | |
|---|---|
| Adult Nursing | M |
| Business Administration and Management—General | M |
| Clinical Psychology | M |
| Criminal Justice and Criminology | M |
| Education—General | M |
| Educational Leadership and Administration | M |
| English as a Second Language | M |
| Health Services Management and Hospital Administration | M |
| Hospice Nursing | M |
| International Business | M |
| Liberal Studies | M |
| Nursing and Healthcare Administration | M |
| Nursing—General | M |
| Pastoral Ministry and Counseling | M |
| Psychology—General | M |
| Quality Management | M |
| Reading Education | M |
| Social Work | M |
| Special Education | M |
| Theology | M |

## MAHARISHI INTERNATIONAL UNIVERSITY

| | |
|---|---|
| Accounting | M,D |
| Asian Studies | M,D |
| Business Administration and Management—General | M,D |
| Computer Science | M |
| Physiology | D |
| Sustainability Management | M,D |
| Writing | M |

## MAINE COLLEGE OF ART

| | |
|---|---|
| Art/Fine Arts | M |

## MAINE MARITIME ACADEMY

| | |
|---|---|
| International Business | M |
| Supply Chain Management | M |
| Transportation Management | M |

## MALONE UNIVERSITY

| | |
|---|---|
| Business Administration and Management—General | M |
| Counselor Education | M |
| Family Nurse Practitioner Studies | M |
| Nursing—General | M |
| Organizational Management | M |

## MANCHESTER UNIVERSITY

| | |
|---|---|
| Athletic Training and Sports Medicine | M |
| Genomic Sciences | M |
| Pharmacy | D |

## MANHATTAN COLLEGE

| | |
|---|---|
| Applied Mathematics | M |
| Business Administration and Management—General | M |
| Chemical Engineering | M |
| Civil Engineering | M |
| Computer Engineering | M |
| Construction Management | M |
| Counseling Psychology | M,O |
| Counselor Education | M,O |
| Data Science/Data Analytics | M |
| Early Childhood Education | M,O |
| Education—General | M,O |
| Educational Leadership and Administration | M,O |
| Educational Media/Instructional Technology | M |
| Electrical Engineering | M |
| Elementary Education | M,O |
| Engineering and Applied Sciences—General | M |
| English | M,O |
| Environmental Engineering | M |
| Marriage and Family Therapy | M |
| Mathematics | M,O |
| Mechanical Engineering | M |
| Multilingual and Multicultural Education | M,O |
| Organizational Management | M |
| Special Education | M,O |
| Student Affairs | M,O |

## MANHATTAN SCHOOL OF MUSIC

| | |
|---|---|
| Music | M,D,O |

## MANHATTANVILLE COLLEGE

| | |
|---|---|
| Accounting | M,O |
| Art Education | M,O |
| Biological and Biomedical Sciences—General | M,O |
| Business Education | M,O |
| Chemistry | M,O |
| Corporate and Organizational Communication | M,O |
| Early Childhood Education | M,O |
| Education—General | M,D,O |
| Educational Leadership and Administration | M,D,O |
| Elementary Education | M,O |
| English as a Second Language | M,O |
| English Education | M,O |
| English | M,O |
| Entertainment Management | M,O |
| Entrepreneurship | M |
| Exercise and Sports Science | M,O |
| Finance and Banking | M,O |
| Foreign Languages Education | M,O |
| Geosciences | M,O |
| Health Promotion | M,O |
| Human Resources Management | M,O |
| Investment Management | M,O |
| Management Strategy and Policy | M,O |
| Marketing | M,O |
| Mathematics Education | M,O |
| Mathematics | M,O |
| Middle School Education | M,O |
| Multilingual and Multicultural Education | M,O |
| Music Education | M,O |
| Organizational Management | M,O |
| Physics | M,O |
| Reading Education | M,O |
| Science Education | M,O |
| Secondary Education | M,O |
| Social Sciences Education | M,O |
| Spanish | M,O |
| Special Education | M,O |
| Sports Management | M,O |
| Sustainable Development | M,O |
| Urban Education | M,O |
| Writing | M |

## MANSFIELD UNIVERSITY OF PENNSYLVANIA

| | |
|---|---|
| Art Education | M |
| Education—General | M |
| Elementary Education | M |
| Information Studies | M |
| Library Science | M |
| Music | M |
| Nursing—General | M |
| Organizational Management | M |
| Psychology—General | M |
| Secondary Education | M |
| Special Education | M |

## MAPLE SPRINGS BAPTIST BIBLE COLLEGE AND SEMINARY

| | |
|---|---|
| Pastoral Ministry and Counseling | M,D,O |
| Religious Education | M,D,O |
| Theology | M,D,O |

## MARANATHA BAPTIST UNIVERSITY

| | |
|---|---|
| Cultural Studies | M |
| Education—General | M |
| Organizational Management | M |
| Pastoral Ministry and Counseling | M,D |
| Religion | M |
| Theology | M |

## MARCONI INTERNATIONAL UNIVERSITY

| | |
|---|---|
| Business Administration and Management—General | M,D |
| Educational Leadership and Administration | M,D |
| Educational Media/Instructional Technology | M,D |
| International Business | M,D |

## MARIAN UNIVERSITY (IN)

| | |
|---|---|
| Counseling Psychology | M |
| Counselor Education | M |
| Education—General | M |
| Family Nurse Practitioner Studies | M,D |
| Nurse Anesthesia | M,D |
| Nursing Education | M,D |
| Nursing—General | M,D |
| Osteopathic Medicine | M,D |

## MARIAN UNIVERSITY (WI)

| | |
|---|---|
| Adult Nursing | M |
| Business Administration and Management—General | M |
| Curriculum and Instruction | M,D |
| Education—General | M,D |
| Educational Leadership and Administration | M,D |
| Educational Media/Instructional Technology | M,D |
| Nursing Education | M |
| Nursing—General | M |
| Organizational Management | M |
| Special Education | M,D |
| Thanatology | M |

## MARIETTA COLLEGE

| | |
|---|---|
| Physician Assistant Studies | M |
| Psychology—General | M |

## MARIST COLLEGE

| | |
|---|---|
| Accounting | M |
| Business Administration and Management—General | M,O |
| Business Analytics | M,O |
| Communication—General | M |
| Computer Science | M,O |
| Corporate and Organizational Communication | M |
| Counseling Psychology | M,O |
| Education—General | M,O |
| Management Information Systems | M,O |
| Marketing | M |
| Museum Studies | M |
| Physical Therapy | D |
| Psychology—General | M,O |
| Public Administration | M |
| School Psychology | M,O |
| Software Engineering | M,O |

## MARLBORO COLLEGE

| | |
|---|---|
| Business Administration and Management—General | M |
| Educational Media/Instructional Technology | M,O |
| English as a Second Language | M |
| Entrepreneurship | M |
| Legal and Justice Studies | M |
| Organizational Management | M |
| Project Management | M |

## MARQUETTE UNIVERSITY

| | |
|---|---|
| Accounting | M |
| Acute Care/Critical Care Nursing | M,D,O |
| Adult Nursing | M,D,O |
| Advertising and Public Relations | M,O |
| Analytical Chemistry | M,D |
| Bioinformatics | M,D |
| Biological and Biomedical Sciences—General | M,D |
| Biomedical Engineering | M,D |
| Business Administration and Management—General | M,O |
| Cardiovascular Sciences | M |
| Cell Biology | M,D |
| Chemical Physics | M,D |
| Chemistry | M,D |
| Civil Engineering | M,D,O |
| Clinical Psychology | M,D |
| Communication Disorders | M,O |
| Communication—General | M,D |
| Computational Sciences | M,D |
| Computer Engineering | M,D,O |
| Computer Science | M,D |
| Construction Engineering | M,D,O |
| Construction Management | M,D,O |
| Counseling Psychology | M,D |
| Counselor Education | M,D |
| Curriculum and Instruction | M,D,O |
| Dentistry | D |
| Developmental Biology | M,D |
| Ecology | M,D |
| Economics | M,O |
| Education—General | M,D,O |
| Educational Leadership and Administration | M,D,O |
| Educational Policy | M,D,O |
| Electrical Engineering | M,D,O |
| Elementary Education | M,D,O |
| Engineering and Applied Sciences—General | M,D,O |
| Engineering Management | M,D,O |
| English | M,D |
| Entrepreneurship | M,O |
| Environmental Engineering | M,D,O |
| Ethics | M,D |
| Family Nurse Practitioner Studies | M,D,O |
| Finance and Banking | M,O |
| Foreign Languages Education | M |
| Foundations and Philosophy of Education | M,D,O |
| Genetics | M,D |
| Gerontological Nursing | M,D,O |
| Hazardous Materials Management | M,D,O |
| Health Communication | M,O |
| History | M,D |
| Human Resources Development | M |
| Human Resources Management | M,O |
| Industrial and Manufacturing Management | M,O |
| Inorganic Chemistry | M,D |
| Interdisciplinary Studies | D |
| International Affairs | M,D |
| International Business | M,O |
| Journalism | M,O |
| Law | D |
| Management Information Systems | M,O |
| Management of Technology | M,D |
| Marketing Research | M |
| Marketing | M,O |
| Mass Communication | M,O |
| Mathematics Education | M,D |
| Mathematics | M,D |
| Mechanical Engineering | M,D,O |
| Microbiology | M,D |

*M—masters degree; D—doctorate; O—other advanced degree; *—Close-Up and/or Display*

| | |
|---|---|
| Molecular Biology | M,D |
| Neuroscience | M,D |
| Nurse Midwifery | M,D,O |
| Nursing and Healthcare Administration | M,D,O |
| Nursing—General | M,D,O |
| Oral and Dental Sciences | M,O |
| Organic Chemistry | M,D |
| Pediatric Nursing | M,D,O |
| Philosophy | M,D |
| Physical Chemistry | M,D |
| Physical Therapy | D |
| Physician Assistant Studies | M |
| Physiology | M,D |
| Political Science | M |
| Psychology—General | D |
| Reading Education | M,D,O |
| Real Estate | M |
| Rehabilitation Sciences | M,D |
| Secondary Education | M,D,O |
| Social Psychology | M,D |
| Spanish | M |
| Speech and Interpersonal Communication | M,O |
| Sports Management | M,O |
| Structural Engineering | M,D,O |
| Student Affairs | M,D,O |
| Supply Chain Management | M,O |
| Theology | M,D |
| Transportation and Highway Engineering | M,D,O |
| Water Resources Engineering | M,D,O |
| Water Resources | M,D,O |

### MARSHALL B. KETCHUM UNIVERSITY

| | |
|---|---|
| Optometry | M,D |
| Pharmacy | M,D |
| Vision Sciences | M,D |

### MARSHALL UNIVERSITY

| | |
|---|---|
| Accounting | M |
| Adult Education | M |
| Advertising and Public Relations | M,O |
| Allopathic Medicine | D |
| Athletic Training and Sports Medicine | M |
| Biological and Biomedical Sciences—General | M,D |
| Business Administration and Management—General | M,O |
| Chemistry | M |
| Clinical Psychology | M,D,O |
| Communication Disorders | M |
| Communication—General | M |
| Computer Engineering | M |
| Computer Science | M |
| Counselor Education | M |
| Criminal Justice and Criminology | M |
| Education—General | M,D,O |
| Educational Leadership and Administration | M |
| Electrical Engineering | M |
| Engineering and Applied Sciences—General | M,O |
| Engineering Management | M |
| English | M,O |
| Environmental Engineering | M |
| Environmental Sciences | M |
| Exercise and Sports Science | M |
| Forensic Sciences | M,O |
| Geography | M,O |
| Health Education | M |
| Health Informatics | M |
| Health Services Management and Hospital Administration | M |
| History | M,O |
| Human Resources Management | M |
| Humanities | M,O |
| Information Science | M |
| Journalism | M,O |
| Management of Technology | M,O |
| Mathematics | M |
| Mechanical Engineering | M |
| Music | M |
| Nurse Anesthesia | D |
| Nursing—General | M,O |
| Nutrition | M,O |
| Pharmacy | D |
| Physical Therapy | D |
| Physics | M |
| Political Science | M |
| Psychology—General | M,D,O |
| Public Administration | M |
| Public Health—General | M |
| Reading Education | M |
| School Psychology | O |
| Social Work | M |
| Sociology | M |
| Special Education | M |
| Sports Management | M |
| Transportation and Highway Engineering | M |

### MARS HILL UNIVERSITY

| | |
|---|---|
| Elementary Education | M |

### MARTIN LUTHER COLLEGE

| | |
|---|---|
| Curriculum and Instruction | M |
| Early Childhood Education | M |
| Education—General | M |
| Educational Leadership and Administration | M |
| Educational Media/Instructional Technology | M |
| Special Education | M |

### MARTIN UNIVERSITY

| | |
|---|---|
| Pastoral Ministry and Counseling | M |
| Psychology—General | M |
| Social Psychology | M |

### MARY BALDWIN UNIVERSITY

| | |
|---|---|
| Applied Behavior Analysis | M |
| Education of the Gifted | M |
| Education—General | M |
| Educational Leadership and Administration | M |
| Elementary Education | M |
| English as a Second Language | M |
| English | M |
| Environmental Education | M |
| Higher Education | M |
| Middle School Education | M |
| Nursing—General | M |
| Occupational Therapy | D |
| Physical Therapy | D |
| Physician Assistant Studies | M |
| Reading Education | M |
| Special Education | M |
| Theater | M |

### MARYGROVE COLLEGE

| | |
|---|---|
| Curriculum and Instruction | M,O |
| Early Childhood Education | M,O |
| Educational Leadership and Administration | M,O |
| Educational Media/Instructional Technology | M,O |
| Elementary Education | M,O |
| Human Resources Management | M,O |
| Legal and Justice Studies | M,O |
| Mathematics | M,O |
| Middle School Education | M,O |
| Reading Education | M,O |
| Special Education | M,O |

### MARYLAND INSTITUTE COLLEGE OF ART

| | |
|---|---|
| Applied Arts and Design—General | M |
| Art Education | M |
| Art/Fine Arts | M |
| Business Administration and Management—General | M |
| Film, Television, and Video Production | M |
| Graphic Design | M |
| Illustration | M |
| Museum Studies | M |
| Photography | M |

### MARYLAND UNIVERSITY OF INTEGRATIVE HEALTH

| | |
|---|---|
| Acupuncture and Oriental Medicine | M,D,O |
| Health Promotion | M,O |
| Naturopathic Medicine | D |
| Nutrition | M,D,O |

### MARYMOUNT CALIFORNIA UNIVERSITY

| | |
|---|---|
| Business Administration and Management—General | M |
| International Development | M |
| Social Psychology | M |

### MARYMOUNT UNIVERSITY

| | |
|---|---|
| Allied Health—General | M,D,O |
| Business Administration and Management—General | M,O |
| Clinical Psychology | M |
| Community College Education | M,O |
| Computer and Information Systems Security | M,D,O |
| Counseling Psychology | M |
| Counselor Education | M |
| Curriculum and Instruction | M |
| Education—General | M |
| Elementary Education | M |
| English Education | M,O |
| English | M,O |
| Family Nurse Practitioner Studies | M,D,O |
| Forensic Psychology | M |
| Health Education | M |
| Health Informatics | M,O |
| Health Promotion | M |
| Health Services Management and Hospital Administration | M |
| Human Resources Management | O |
| Interior Design | M |
| Management Information Systems | M,O |
| Nonprofit Management | M,O |
| Nursing—General | M,D,O |
| Pastoral Ministry and Counseling | M |
| Physical Therapy | D |
| Project Management | M,O |
| Secondary Education | M |
| Software Engineering | M,O |
| Special Education | M |

### MARYVILLE UNIVERSITY OF SAINT LOUIS

| | |
|---|---|
| Accounting | M,O |
| Actuarial Science | M |
| Acute Care/Critical Care Nursing | M,D |
| Addictions/Substance Abuse Counseling | M |
| Adult Nursing | M,D |
| Allied Health—General | M,D,O |
| Business Administration and Management—General | M,O |
| Business Education | M,O |
| Communication Disorders | M |
| Computer and Information Systems Security | M,O |
| Data Science/Data Analytics | M |
| Early Childhood Education | M,D |
| Education—General | M,D |
| Educational Leadership and Administration | M,D |
| Elementary Education | M,D |
| Family Nurse Practitioner Studies | M,D |
| Finance and Banking | M,O |
| Gerontological Nursing | M,D |
| Health Services Management and Hospital Administration | M,O |
| Higher Education | M,O |
| Human Resources Management | M,O |
| Information Science | M,O |
| Logistics | M,O |
| Marketing | M,O |
| Marriage and Family Therapy | M |
| Middle School Education | M,D |
| Nursing—General | M,D |
| Occupational Therapy | M |
| Pediatric Nursing | M,D |
| Physical Therapy | D |
| Project Management | M,O |
| Reading Education | M,D |
| Rehabilitation Counseling | M |
| Secondary Education | M,D |
| Sports Management | M,O |
| Supply Chain Management | M,O |
| Therapies—Dance, Drama, and Music | M |

### MARYWOOD UNIVERSITY

| | |
|---|---|
| Architecture | M |
| Art Education | M |
| Art Therapy | M,O |
| Art/Fine Arts | M |
| Biotechnology | M |
| Business Administration and Management—General | M |
| Clinical Psychology | M,D |
| Communication Disorders | M |
| Communication—General | M |
| Computer and Information Systems Security | M |
| Counseling Psychology | M |
| Counselor Education | M |
| Criminal Justice and Criminology | M |
| Early Childhood Education | M |
| Education—General | M |
| Educational Leadership and Administration | M,D |
| Elementary Education | M |
| Exercise and Sports Science | M |
| Finance and Banking | M |
| Gerontology | M |
| Graphic Design | M |
| Health Education | D |
| Health Services Management and Hospital Administration | M |
| Higher Education | M,D |
| Human Development | D |
| Illustration | M |
| Interdisciplinary Studies | D |
| Interior Design | M |
| Investment Management | M |
| Management Information Systems | M |
| Music Education | M |
| Nutrition | M,O |
| Photography | M |
| Physician Assistant Studies | M |
| Psychology—General | M |
| Public Administration | M |
| Reading Education | M |
| Secondary Education | M |
| Social Work | M,D |
| Special Education | M |

### MASSACHUSETTS COLLEGE OF ART AND DESIGN

| | |
|---|---|
| Applied Arts and Design—General | M,O |
| Architecture | M |
| Art Education | M,O |
| Art/Fine Arts | M,O |
| Film, Television, and Video Production | M,O |
| Interdisciplinary Studies | M,O |
| Media Studies | M,O |
| Photography | M,O |
| Textile Design | M,O |

### MASSACHUSETTS COLLEGE OF LIBERAL ARTS

| | |
|---|---|
| Business Administration and Management—General | M,O |
| Curriculum and Instruction | M,O |
| Education—General | M,O |
| Educational Leadership and Administration | M,O |
| Educational Media/Instructional Technology | M,O |
| Health Education | M,O |
| Physical Education | M,O |
| Reading Education | M,O |
| Special Education | M,O |

### MASSACHUSETTS INSTITUTE OF TECHNOLOGY

| | |
|---|---|
| Aerospace/Aeronautical Engineering | M,D,O |
| Archaeology | M,D,O |
| Architectural History | M,D |
| Architecture | M,D |
| Art History | M,D |
| Atmospheric Sciences | M,D |
| Biochemistry | D |
| Bioengineering | M,D |
| Bioinformatics | M,D |
| Biological and Biomedical Sciences—General | M,D |
| Biomedical Engineering | M,D |
| Business Administration and Management—General | M,D |
| Cell Biology | D |
| Chemical Engineering | M,D |
| Chemistry | D |
| Civil Engineering | M,D,O |
| Cognitive Sciences | D |
| Communication Disorders | M,D |
| Computational Biology | D |
| Computational Sciences | M |
| Computer Engineering | M,D,O |
| Computer Science | M,D,O |
| Construction Engineering | M,D,O |
| Developmental Biology | D |
| Economics | M,D |
| Electrical Engineering | M,D,O |
| Engineering and Applied Sciences—General | M,D,O |
| Engineering Management | M |
| Environmental Biology | M,D,O |
| Environmental Engineering | M,D,O |
| Environmental Sciences | M,D,O |
| Genetics | D |
| Genomic Sciences | M,D |
| Geochemistry | M,D |
| Geology | M,D |
| Geophysics | M,D |
| Geosciences | M,D |
| Geotechnical Engineering | M,D,O |
| History of Science and Technology | D |
| Hydrology | M,D,O |
| Immunology | D |
| Information Science | M,D,O |
| Inorganic Chemistry | D |
| Linguistics | D |
| Logistics | M |
| Manufacturing Engineering | M,D,O |
| Marine Geology | M,D |
| Materials Engineering | M,D,O |
| Materials Sciences | M,D,O |
| Mathematics | D |
| Mechanical Engineering | M,D,O |
| Media Studies | M,D |
| Medical Physics | M,D |
| Microbiology | D |
| Molecular Biology | M,D,O |
| Molecular Toxicology | D |
| Neurobiology | D |
| Neuroscience | D |
| Nuclear Engineering | M,D,O |
| Ocean Engineering | M,D,O |
| Oceanography | M,D,O |
| Operations Research | M,D |
| Organic Chemistry | M,D,O |
| Philosophy | D |
| Physical Chemistry | D |
| Physics | M,D |
| Planetary and Space Sciences | M,D |
| Political Science | M,D |
| Real Estate | M |
| Social Sciences | D |
| Structural Biology | D |
| Structural Engineering | M,D,O |
| Systems Biology | D |
| Systems Engineering | M,D |
| Technical Writing | M |
| Technology and Public Policy | M,D |
| Toxicology | M,D |
| Transportation and Highway Engineering | M,D,O |
| Urban and Regional Planning | M,D |
| Urban Studies | M,D |
| Writing | M |

### MASSACHUSETTS MARITIME ACADEMY

| | |
|---|---|
| Emergency Management | M |
| Facilities Management | M |

### MASSACHUSETTS SCHOOL OF LAW AT ANDOVER

| | |
|---|---|
| Law | D |

### THE MASTER'S UNIVERSITY

| | |
|---|---|
| Pastoral Ministry and Counseling | M,D |
| Theology | M,D |

### MAYO CLINIC ALIX SCHOOL OF MEDICINE

| | |
|---|---|
| Allopathic Medicine | D |

### MAYO CLINIC GRADUATE SCHOOL OF BIOMEDICAL SCIENCES

| | |
|---|---|
| Biochemistry | M,D |
| Biomedical Engineering | M,D |
| Clinical Laboratory Sciences/Medical Technology | M,D |
| Genetics | D |
| Immunology | D |
| Molecular Biology | M,D |
| Molecular Pharmacology | M,D |
| Neuroscience | M,D |
| Physiology | M,D |
| Virology | D |

### MAYO CLINIC SCHOOL OF HEALTH SCIENCES

| | |
|---|---|
| Nurse Anesthesia | D |
| Physical Therapy | D |

### MCCORMICK THEOLOGICAL SEMINARY

| | |
|---|---|
| Pastoral Ministry and Counseling | M,D,O |
| Theology | M,D,O |

### MCDANIEL COLLEGE

| | |
|---|---|
| Counselor Education | M |
| Curriculum and Instruction | M |
| Educational Leadership and Administration | M |
| Educational Media/Instructional Technology | M |
| Elementary Education | M,O |
| English as a Second Language | M |
| Gerontology | M,O |
| Human Resources Development | M |
| Human Services | M |
| Kinesiology and Movement Studies | M |
| Liberal Studies | M,O |
| Library Science | M |
| Mathematics Education | M,O |
| Reading Education | M |
| Science Education | M,O |
| Secondary Education | M,O |
| Special Education | M |
| Writing | M,O |

### MCGILL UNIVERSITY

| | |
|---|---|
| Accounting | M,D,O |
| Aerospace/Aeronautical Engineering | M,D |
| Agricultural Economics and Agribusiness | M |
| Agricultural Engineering | M,D |
| Agricultural Sciences—General | M,D,O |
| Agronomy and Soil Sciences | M,D |
| Allopathic Medicine | M,D |
| Anatomy | M,D |
| Animal Sciences | M,D |

| | |
|---|---|
| Anthropology | M,D |
| Applied Mathematics | M,D |
| Architecture | M,D,O |
| Art History | M,D |
| Asian Studies | M,D |
| Atmospheric Sciences | M,D |
| Biochemistry | M,D |
| Bioengineering | M,D |
| Bioethics | M,D,O |
| Bioinformatics | M,D |
| Biological and Biomedical Sciences—General | M,D |
| Biomedical Engineering | M,D |
| Biostatistics | M,D |
| Biotechnology | M,D,O |
| Business Administration and Management—General | M,D,O |
| Cell Biology | M,D |
| Chemical Engineering | M,D |
| Chemistry | M,D |
| Civil Engineering | M,D |
| Clinical Psychology | M,D |
| Communication Disorders | M,D |
| Communication—General | M,D |
| Computational Sciences | M,D |
| Computer Engineering | M,D |
| Computer Science | M,D |
| Counseling Psychology | M,D,O |
| Curriculum and Instruction | M,D,O |
| Dentistry | M,D,O |
| Developmental Psychology | M,D,O |
| Economics | M,D |
| Education—General | M,D,O |
| Educational Leadership and Administration | M,D,O |
| Educational Psychology | M,D,O |
| Electrical Engineering | M,D |
| Engineering and Applied Sciences—General | M,D,O |
| English | M,D |
| Entomology | M,D |
| Entrepreneurship | M,D,O |
| Environmental and Occupational Health | M,D |
| Environmental Engineering | M,D |
| Environmental Management and Policy | M,D |
| Epidemiology | M,D |
| Experimental Psychology | M,D |
| Family Nurse Practitioner Studies | M,D,O |
| Finance and Banking | M,D,O |
| Fish, Game, and Wildlife Management | M,D |
| Food Science and Technology | M,D |
| Foreign Languages Education | M,D,O |
| Forensic Sciences | M,D,O |
| Forestry | M,D |
| Foundations and Philosophy of Education | M,D,O |
| French | M,D |
| Genetic Counseling | M,D |
| Geography | M,D |
| Geosciences | M,D |
| Geotechnical Engineering | M,D |
| German | M,D |
| Hispanic Studies | M,D |
| History of Medicine | M,D |
| History | M,D |
| Human Genetics | M,D |
| Hydraulics | M,D |
| Immunology | M,D |
| Industrial and Manufacturing Management | M,D,O |
| Information Studies | M,D,O |
| International Business | M,D,O |
| International Development | M,D,O |
| Italian | M,D |
| Jewish Studies | M |
| Kinesiology and Movement Studies | M,D,O |
| Law | M,D,O |
| Library Science | M,D,O |
| Linguistics | M,D |
| Management Information Systems | M,D,O |
| Management Strategy and Policy | M,D,O |
| Marketing | M,D,O |
| Materials Engineering | M,D,O |
| Mathematics | M,D |
| Mechanical Engineering | M,D |
| Mechanics | M,D |
| Medical Physics | M,D |
| Meteorology | M,D |
| Microbiology | M,D |
| Mineral/Mining Engineering | M,D,O |
| Music Education | M,D |
| Music | M,D |
| Natural Resources | M,D |
| Near and Middle Eastern Studies | M,D,O |
| Neuroscience | M,D |
| Nursing—General | M,D,O |
| Nutrition | M,D,O |
| Oceanography | M,D |
| Oral and Dental Sciences | M,D,O |
| Parasitology | M,D,O |
| Pathology | M,D |
| Pharmacology | M,D |
| Philosophy | M,D |
| Physical Education | M,D,O |
| Physics | M,D |
| Physiology | M,D |
| Planetary and Space Sciences | M,D |
| Plant Sciences | M,D,O |
| Political Science | M,D |
| Psychology—General | M,D |
| Public Health—General | M,D |
| Rehabilitation Sciences | M,D,O |
| Religion | M,D |
| Russian | M,D |
| School Psychology | M,D,O |
| Social Work | M,D,O |
| Sociology | M,D,O |
| Statistics | M,D,O |
| Structural Engineering | M,D |
| Supply Chain Management | M,D,O |
| Theology | M,D |
| Transportation Management | M,D |
| Urban and Regional Planning | M,D |
| Water Resources Engineering | M,D |

**MCKENDREE UNIVERSITY**

| | |
|---|---|
| Business Administration and Management—General | M |
| Clinical Psychology | M |
| Counseling Psychology | M |
| Curriculum and Instruction | M,D,O |
| Education—General | M,D,O |
| Educational Leadership and Administration | M,D,O |
| Higher Education | M,D,O |
| Human Resources Management | M |
| International Business | M |
| Music Education | M,D,O |
| Nursing and Healthcare Administration | M |
| Nursing Education | M |
| Nursing—General | M |
| Reading Education | M,D,O |
| Special Education | M,D,O |

**MCMASTER UNIVERSITY**

| | |
|---|---|
| Analytical Chemistry | M,D |
| Anthropology | M,D |
| Applied Statistics | M |
| Astrophysics | D |
| Biochemistry | M,D |
| Biological and Biomedical Sciences—General | M,D |
| Business Administration and Management—General | M,D |
| Cancer Biology/Oncology | M,D |
| Cardiovascular Sciences | M,D |
| Cell Biology | M,D |
| Chemical Engineering | M,D |
| Chemical Physics | M,D |
| Chemistry | M,D |
| Civil Engineering | M,D |
| Classics | M,D |
| Computer Science | M,D |
| Cultural Studies | M,D |
| Economics | M,D |
| Electrical Engineering | M,D |
| Engineering and Applied Sciences—General | M,D |
| Engineering Physics | M,D |
| English | M,D |
| French | M |
| Genetics | M,D |
| Geochemistry | M,D |
| Geography | M,D |
| Geology | M,D |
| Geosciences | M,D |
| Health Physics/Radiological Health | M,D |
| Health Services Research | M,D |
| History | M,D |
| Human Resources Management | M,D |
| Immunology | M,D |
| Industrial and Labor Relations | M |
| Inorganic Chemistry | M,D |
| International Affairs | M,D |
| Kinesiology and Movement Studies | M,D |
| Management Information Systems | D |
| Materials Engineering | M,D |
| Materials Sciences | M,D |
| Mathematics | M,D |
| Mechanical Engineering | M,D |
| Medical Physics | M,D |
| Molecular Biology | M,D |
| Neuroscience | M,D |
| Nuclear Engineering | M,D |
| Nursing—General | M,D |
| Nutrition | M,D |
| Occupational Therapy | M |
| Organic Chemistry | M,D |
| Pastoral Ministry and Counseling | M,D,O |
| Pharmacology | M,D |
| Philosophy | M,D |
| Physical Chemistry | M,D |
| Physical Therapy | M |
| Physics | D |
| Physiology | M,D |
| Political Science | M,D |
| Psychology—General | M,D |
| Public Administration | M,D |
| Public Affairs | M,D |
| Public Policy | M,D |
| Rehabilitation Sciences | M,D |
| Religion | M,D |
| Social Work | M |
| Sociology | M,D |
| Software Engineering | M,D |
| Statistics | M |
| Theology | M,D,O |
| Virology | M,D |

**MCMURRY UNIVERSITY**

| | |
|---|---|
| Family Nurse Practitioner Studies | M |
| Nursing Education | M |
| Nursing—General | M |

**MCNEESE STATE UNIVERSITY**

| | |
|---|---|
| Agricultural Sciences—General | M |
| Applied Behavior Analysis | M,O |
| Art Education | O |
| Business Administration and Management—General | M |
| Chemical Engineering | M |
| Chemistry | M |
| Civil Engineering | M |
| Computer Science | M |
| Counseling Psychology | M,O |
| Counselor Education | M |
| Criminal Justice and Criminology | M |
| Curriculum and Instruction | M |
| Early Childhood Education | O |
| Education of the Gifted | M |
| Education—General | O |
| Educational Leadership and Administration | M,O |
| Educational Measurement and Evaluation | M,O |
| Educational Media/Instructional Technology | M,O |
| Electrical Engineering | M |
| Elementary Education | M,O |
| Engineering and Applied Sciences—General | M |
| Engineering Management | M |
| English | M |
| Environmental Sciences | M |
| Exercise and Sports Science | M |
| Experimental Psychology | M,O |
| Family Nurse Practitioner Studies | M |
| Health Education | O |
| Health Promotion | M |
| Library Science | O |
| Mathematics Education | O |
| Mathematics | M |
| Mechanical Engineering | M |
| Middle School Education | O |
| Music Education | O |
| Nursing Education | M |
| Nursing—General | M,O |
| Nutrition | M |
| Physical Education | O |
| Psychiatric Nursing | M,O |
| Psychology—General | M,O |
| Reading Education | M |
| School Psychology | M,O |
| Science Education | O |
| Secondary Education | M,O |
| Special Education | M,O |
| Statistics | M |
| Writing | M |

**MCPHERSON COLLEGE**

| | |
|---|---|
| Education—General | M |

**MCPHS UNIVERSITY**

| | |
|---|---|
| Acupuncture and Oriental Medicine | M |
| Chemistry | M,D |
| Health Services Management and Hospital Administration | M |
| Nursing—General | M |
| Optometry | D |
| Pharmaceutical Sciences | M,D |
| Pharmacology | M,D |
| Pharmacy | D |
| Physical Therapy | D |
| Physician Assistant Studies | M |
| Public Health—General | M |

**MEADVILLE LOMBARD THEOLOGICAL SCHOOL**

| | |
|---|---|
| Pastoral Ministry and Counseling | M,D |
| Theology | M,D |

**MEDAILLE COLLEGE**

| | |
|---|---|
| Business Administration and Management—General | M |
| Clinical Psychology | M,D |
| Counseling Psychology | M,D |
| Curriculum and Instruction | M |
| Education—General | M |
| Elementary Education | M |
| Marriage and Family Therapy | M,D |
| Organizational Management | M |
| Psychology—General | M,D |
| Reading Education | M |
| Secondary Education | M |
| Special Education | M |

**MEDICAL COLLEGE OF WISCONSIN**

| | |
|---|---|
| Allopathic Medicine | D |
| Anesthesiologist Assistant Studies | M |
| Biochemistry | D |
| Bioethics | M,O |
| Biological and Biomedical Sciences—General | M,D,O |
| Biostatistics | D |
| Clinical Laboratory Sciences/Medical Technology | M |
| Clinical Research | |
| Community Health | D |
| Neuroscience | D |
| Pharmacology | D |
| Pharmacy | D |
| Physiology | D |
| Public Health—General | M,D,O |
| Toxicology | D |

**MEDICAL UNIVERSITY OF SOUTH CAROLINA**

| | |
|---|---|
| Adult Nursing | M,D |
| Allied Health—General | M,D |
| Allopathic Medicine | D |
| Biochemistry | M,D |
| Biological and Biomedical Sciences—General | M,D |
| Biostatistics | M,D |
| Cancer Biology/Oncology | D |
| Cardiovascular Sciences | D |
| Cell Biology | D |
| Clinical Research | M |
| Dentistry | D |
| Developmental Biology | D |
| Epidemiology | M,D |
| Family Nurse Practitioner Studies | M,D |
| Genetics | D |
| Gerontological Nursing | M,D |
| Health Services Management and Hospital Administration | M,D |
| Immunology | M,D |
| International Health | M |
| Marine Sciences | D |
| Maternal and Child/Neonatal Nursing | M,D |
| Medical Imaging | D |
| Medicinal and Pharmaceutical Chemistry | D |
| Microbiology | M,D |
| Molecular Biology | M,D |
| Molecular Pharmacology | M,D |
| Neuroscience | M,D |
| Nurse Anesthesia | M |
| Nursing and Healthcare Administration | M |
| Nursing Education | M |
| Nursing—General | D |
| Occupational Therapy | M |
| Pathobiology | D |
| Pathology | M,D |
| Pharmacy | D |
| Physical Therapy | D |
| Physician Assistant Studies | M |
| Rehabilitation Sciences | D |
| Toxicology | D |

**MEHARRY MEDICAL COLLEGE**

| | |
|---|---|
| Allopathic Medicine | D |
| Biochemistry | D |
| Biological and Biomedical Sciences—General | D |
| Cancer Biology/Oncology | D |
| Dentistry | D |
| Environmental and Occupational Health | M |
| Health Services Management and Hospital Administration | M |
| Immunology | D |
| Microbiology | D |
| Neuroscience | D |
| Pharmacology | D |
| Public Health—General | M |

**MELBOURNE BUSINESS SCHOOL**

| | |
|---|---|
| Business Administration and Management—General | M,D,O |
| Marketing | M,D,O |

**MEMORIAL UNIVERSITY OF NEWFOUNDLAND**

| | |
|---|---|
| Adult Education | M,D,O |
| Anthropology | M,D |
| Aquaculture | M |
| Archaeology | M,D |
| Biochemistry | M,D |
| Biological and Biomedical Sciences—General | M,D,O |
| Biopsychology | M,D |
| Business Administration and Management—General | M |
| Cancer Biology/Oncology | M,D |
| Cardiovascular Sciences | M,D |
| Chemistry | M,D |
| Civil Engineering | M,D |
| Classics | M |
| Clinical Psychology | M,D |
| Clinical Research | M |
| Community Health | M,D,O |
| Computational Sciences | M |
| Computer Engineering | M,D |
| Computer Science | M,D |
| Condensed Matter Physics | M,D |
| Cultural Anthropology | M,D |
| Curriculum and Instruction | M,D,O |
| Economics | M |
| Education—General | M,D,O |
| Educational Leadership and Administration | M,D,O |
| Educational Media/Instructional Technology | M,D,O |
| Educational Psychology | M,D,O |
| Electrical Engineering | M,D |
| Engineering and Applied Sciences—General | M,D |
| English | M,D |
| Environmental Engineering | M |
| Environmental Sciences | M,D |
| Epidemiology | M,D,O |
| Exercise and Sports Science | M |
| Experimental Psychology | M,D |
| Fish, Game, and Wildlife Management | M,O |
| Folklore | M,D |
| Food Science and Technology | M,D |
| French | M |
| Gender Studies | M,D |
| Geography | M,D |
| Geology | M,D |
| Geophysics | M,D |
| Geosciences | M,D |
| German | M |
| History | M,D |
| Human Genetics | M,D |
| Humanities | M |
| Immunology | M,D |
| Industrial and Labor Relations | M |
| Kinesiology and Movement Studies | M |
| Linguistics | M,D |
| Marine Affairs | M,D,O |
| Marine Sciences | M,O |
| Mathematics | M,D |
| Mechanical Engineering | M,D |
| Music | M,D |
| Neuroscience | M,D |
| Nursing—General | M,D |
| Ocean Engineering | M,D |
| Oceanography | M,D |
| Pharmaceutical Sciences | M,D |
| Philosophy | M,D |
| Physical Education | M |
| Physics | M,D |
| Political Science | M |
| Psychology—General | M,D |
| Religion | M |

*M—masters degree; D—doctorate; O—other advanced degree; *—Close-Up and/or Display*

| | |
|---|---|
| Social Work | M,D |
| Sociology | M,D |
| Statistics | M,D |

## MEMPHIS THEOLOGICAL SEMINARY

| | |
|---|---|
| Theology | M,D |

## MERCER UNIVERSITY

| | |
|---|---|
| Accounting | M |
| Allopathic Medicine | M,D |
| Athletic Training and Sports Medicine | M,D |
| Biomedical Engineering | M |
| Business Administration and Management—General | M |
| Clinical Psychology | M,D |
| Computer Engineering | M |
| Counselor Education | M,D |
| Criminal Justice and Criminology | M,D |
| Curriculum and Instruction | M,D,O |
| Early Childhood Education | M,D,O |
| Education—General | M,D,O |
| Educational Leadership and Administration | M,D,O |
| Electrical Engineering | M |
| Engineering and Applied Sciences—General | M |
| Engineering Management | M |
| Entrepreneurship | M |
| Environmental and Occupational Health | M,D |
| Environmental Engineering | M |
| Environmental Sciences | M |
| Family Nurse Practitioner Studies | M,D,O |
| Gerontological Nursing | M,D,O |
| Gerontology | M,D |
| Health Informatics | M,D |
| Higher Education | M,D,O |
| Human Services | M,D |
| Law | D |
| Management of Technology | M |
| Mathematics | M,D,O |
| Mechanical Engineering | M |
| Middle School Education | M,D,O |
| Music | M |
| Nonprofit Management | M,D |
| Nursing and Healthcare Administration | M,D |
| Nursing—General | M,D,O |
| Organizational Management | M,D |
| Pastoral Ministry and Counseling | M,D |
| Pharmaceutical Sciences | D |
| Pharmacy | D |
| Physical Therapy | M,D |
| Physician Assistant Studies | M,D |
| Public Health—General | M,D |
| Rehabilitation Counseling | M,D |
| School Psychology | M,D |
| Science Education | M,D,O |
| Secondary Education | M,D,O |
| Software Engineering | M |
| Theology | M,D |

## MERCY COLLEGE

| | |
|---|---|
| Accounting | M |
| Allied Health—General | M,D |
| Business Administration and Management—General | M |
| Communication Disorders | M |
| Computer and Information Systems Security | M |
| Counseling Psychology | M,O |
| Counselor Education | M,O |
| Early Childhood Education | M |
| Education—General | M,O |
| Educational Leadership and Administration | M,O |
| Elementary Education | M |
| English as a Second Language | M,O |
| English | M |
| Health Services Management and Hospital Administration | M |
| Human Resources Management | M |
| Marriage and Family Therapy | M,O |
| Middle School Education | M,O |
| Multilingual and Multicultural Education | M |
| Nursing and Healthcare Administration | M |
| Nursing Education | M |
| Nursing—General | M |
| Occupational Therapy | M |
| Organizational Management | M |
| Physical Therapy | D |
| Physician Assistant Studies | M |
| Psychology—General | M |
| Reading Education | M,O |
| School Psychology | M,O |
| Secondary Education | M,O |

## MERCY COLLEGE OF OHIO

| | |
|---|---|
| Health Services Management and Hospital Administration | M |
| Nursing—General | M,O |

## MERCYHURST UNIVERSITY

| | |
|---|---|
| Accounting | M,O |
| Anthropology | M |
| Applied Behavior Analysis | M |
| Archaeology | M |
| Biological Anthropology | M |
| Computer and Information Systems Security | M |
| Criminal Justice and Criminology | M,O |
| Educational Leadership and Administration | M,O |
| Entrepreneurship | M,O |
| Forensic Sciences | M |
| Higher Education | M,O |
| Human Resources Management | M,O |
| Management Strategy and Policy | M,O |
| Organizational Management | M,O |
| Physician Assistant Studies | M |
| Secondary Education | M |
| Special Education | M |
| Sports Management | M,O |

## MEREDITH COLLEGE

| | |
|---|---|
| Business Administration and Management—General | M |
| Education of the Gifted | M,O |
| Education—General | M,O |
| Elementary Education | M,O |
| English as a Second Language | M,O |
| Health Education | M,O |
| Industrial and Organizational Psychology | M |
| Nutrition | M,O |
| Physical Education | M,O |
| Psychology—General | M |
| Reading Education | M,O |
| Special Education | M,O |

## MERRIMACK COLLEGE

| | |
|---|---|
| Accounting | M |
| Athletic Training and Sports Medicine | M |
| Business Administration and Management—General | M |
| Business Analytics | M |
| Civil Engineering | M |
| Clinical Psychology | M,O |
| Computer Science | M |
| Data Science/Data Analytics | M |
| Education—General | M,O |
| Engineering and Applied Sciences—General | M |
| Engineering Management | M |
| Exercise and Sports Science | M |
| Health Education | M |
| Health Promotion | M |
| Mechanical Engineering | M |
| Public Affairs | M,O |
| Theology | M,O |

## MESIVTA OF EASTERN PARKWAY–YESHIVA ZICHRON MEILECH

| | |
|---|---|
| Theology | |

## MESIVTHA TIFERETH JERUSALEM OF AMERICA

| | |
|---|---|
| Theology | |

## MESSIAH UNIVERSITY

| | |
|---|---|
| Business Administration and Management—General | M,O |
| Clinical Psychology | M,O |
| Counseling Psychology | M,O |
| Counselor Education | M,O |
| Curriculum and Instruction | M,O |
| English as a Second Language | M |
| Higher Education | M |
| Management Strategy and Policy | M,O |
| Marriage and Family Therapy | M,O |
| Music | M |
| Nursing Education | M |
| Organizational Management | M,O |
| Special Education | M |
| Sports Management | M |
| Student Affairs | M |

## METHODIST THEOLOGICAL SCHOOL IN OHIO

| | |
|---|---|
| Theology | M,D |

## METHODIST UNIVERSITY

| | |
|---|---|
| Business Administration and Management—General | M |
| Criminal Justice and Criminology | M |
| Physician Assistant Studies | M |

## METROPOLITAN COLLEGE OF NEW YORK

| | |
|---|---|
| Business Administration and Management—General | M |
| Elementary Education | M |
| Emergency Management | M |
| Finance and Banking | M |
| Media Studies | M |
| Public Administration | M |
| Public Affairs | M |
| Risk Management | M |
| Special Education | M |

## METROPOLITAN STATE UNIVERSITY

| | |
|---|---|
| Addictions/Substance Abuse Counseling | M |
| Business Administration and Management—General | M,D,O |
| Business Analytics | M,D,O |
| Computer and Information Systems Security | M,D,O |
| Computer Science | M |
| Criminal Justice and Criminology | M |
| Curriculum and Instruction | M |
| Data Science/Data Analytics | M,D,O |
| English as a Second Language | M |
| English Education | M |
| Information Studies | M,D,O |
| Liberal Studies | M |
| Management Information Systems | M,D,O |
| Mathematics Education | M |
| Nonprofit Management | M |
| Nursing and Healthcare Administration | M,D |
| Nursing Education | M,D |
| Nursing—General | M,D |
| Oral and Dental Sciences | M,D |
| Project Management | M,D,O |
| Public Administration | M |
| Public Affairs | M |
| Science Education | M |
| Secondary Education | M |
| Social Sciences Education | M |
| Special Education | M |
| Supply Chain Management | M,D,O |
| Technical Writing | M |
| Urban Education | M |

## METROPOLITAN STATE UNIVERSITY OF DENVER

| | |
|---|---|
| Accounting | M |
| Education—General | M |
| Elementary Education | M |
| Social Work | M |
| Special Education | M |
| Taxation | M |

## MGH INSTITUTE OF HEALTH PROFESSIONS

| | |
|---|---|
| Communication Disorders | M,O |
| Gerontological Nursing | M,D,O |
| Nursing Education | M,D,O |
| Nursing—General | M,D,O |
| Occupational Therapy | D |
| Pediatric Nursing | M,D,O |
| Physical Therapy | M,D,O |
| Physician Assistant Studies | M |
| Psychiatric Nursing | M,D,O |
| Reading Education | M,O |
| Women's Health Nursing | M,D,O |

## MIAMI INTERNATIONAL UNIVERSITY OF ART & DESIGN

| | |
|---|---|
| Applied Arts and Design—General | M |
| Film, Television, and Video Production | M |

## MIAMI REGIONAL UNIVERSITY

| | |
|---|---|
| Nursing and Healthcare Administration | M |
| Nursing Education | M |
| Nursing—General | M |

## MIAMI UNIVERSITY

| | |
|---|---|
| Accounting | M |
| Architecture | M |
| Art Education | M |
| Art/Fine Arts | M |
| Biochemistry | M,D |
| Biological and Biomedical Sciences—General | M,D |
| Business Administration and Management—General | M |
| Chemical Engineering | M |
| Chemistry | M,D |
| Child and Family Studies | M |
| Communication Disorders | M |
| Computer Engineering | M |
| Demography and Population Studies | M,D |
| Economics | M |
| Education—General | M,D,O |
| Educational Leadership and Administration | M,D |
| Educational Psychology | M,O |
| Electrical Engineering | M |
| Engineering and Applied Sciences—General | M |
| English | M,D |
| Exercise and Sports Science | M |
| French | M |
| Geography | M |
| Geology | M,D |
| Gerontology | M,D |
| History | M |
| Interior Design | M |
| Mathematics Education | M |
| Mathematics | M |
| Mechanical Engineering | M |
| Microbiology | M,D |
| Music Education | M |
| Music | M |
| Philosophy | M |
| Physics | M |
| Political Science | M |
| Psychology—General | M,D |
| Spanish | M |
| Statistics | M |
| Student Affairs | M,D |
| Systems Science | M |
| Theater | M |

## MICHIGAN SCHOOL OF PSYCHOLOGY

| | |
|---|---|
| Clinical Psychology | M,D |
| Educational Psychology | M,D |
| Psychology—General | M,D |
| Transpersonal and Humanistic Psychology | M,D |

## MICHIGAN STATE UNIVERSITY

| | |
|---|---|
| Accounting | M,D |
| Adult Education | M,D,O |
| Advertising and Public Relations | M |
| African Studies | M,D |
| African-American Studies | M,D |
| Agricultural Economics and Agribusiness | M,D |
| Agricultural Sciences—General | M,D |
| Agronomy and Soil Sciences | M,D |
| Allopathic Medicine | D |
| American Studies | M,D |
| Animal Sciences | M,D |
| Anthropology | M,D |
| Applied Mathematics | M,D |
| Applied Statistics | M,D |
| Art/Fine Arts | M |
| Astronomy | M,D |
| Astrophysics | M,D |
| Biochemistry | M,D |
| Biological and Biomedical Sciences—General | M,D |
| Biosystems Engineering | M,D |
| Business Administration and Management—General | M,D |
| Business Analytics | M |
| Cell Biology | M,D |
| Chemical Engineering | M,D |
| Chemical Physics | M,D |
| Chemistry | M,D |
| Child and Family Studies | M,D |
| Child Development | M,D |
| Civil Engineering | M,D |
| Clinical Laboratory Sciences/Medical Technology | M |
| Communication Disorders | M,D |
| Communication—General | M,D |
| Computer Science | M,D |
| Construction Management | M,D |
| Counselor Education | M,D,O |
| Criminal Justice and Criminology | M,D |
| Curriculum and Instruction | M,D,O |
| Ecology | D |
| Economics | M,D |
| Education—General | M,D,O |
| Educational Leadership and Administration | M,D,O |
| Educational Measurement and Evaluation | M,D,O |
| Educational Media/Instructional Technology | M,D,O |
| Educational Policy | D |
| Educational Psychology | M,D,O |
| Electrical Engineering | M,D |
| Engineering and Applied Sciences—General | M,D |
| English as a Second Language | M,D |
| English | M,D |
| Entomology | M,D |
| Environmental Design | M,D |
| Environmental Engineering | M,D |
| Environmental Sciences | M,D |
| Epidemiology | M,D |
| Evolutionary Biology | D |
| Finance and Banking | M,D |
| Fish, Game, and Wildlife Management | M,D |
| Food Science and Technology | M,D |
| Foreign Languages Education | D |
| Forensic Sciences | M,D |
| Forestry | M,D |
| French | M,D |
| Game Design and Development | M |
| Genetics | M,D |
| Geography | M,D |
| Geosciences | M,D |
| German | M,D |
| Health Communication | M |
| Higher Education | M,D,O |
| Hispanic and Latin American Languages | M,D |
| Hispanic Studies | M,D |
| History | M,D |
| Horticulture | M,D |
| Hospitality Management | M |
| Human Development | M,D |
| Human Resources Management | M,D |
| Industrial and Labor Relations | M,D |
| Interior Design | M,D |
| Journalism | M |
| Kinesiology and Movement Studies | M,D |
| Latin American Studies | D |
| Linguistics | M,D |
| Logistics | M,D |
| Management Information Systems | M,D |
| Management Strategy and Policy | M,D |
| Manufacturing Engineering | M,D |
| Marketing Research | M,D |
| Marketing | M,D |
| Materials Engineering | M,D |
| Materials Sciences | M,D |
| Mathematics Education | M,D |
| Mathematics | M,D |
| Mechanical Engineering | M,D |
| Mechanics | M,D |
| Media Studies | M,D |
| Microbiology | M,D |
| Molecular Biology | M,D |
| Molecular Genetics | M,D |
| Music Education | M,D |
| Music | M,D |
| Natural Resources | M,D |
| Neuroscience | M,D |
| Nursing—General | M,D |
| Nutrition | M,D |
| Osteopathic Medicine | D |
| Pathobiology | M,D |
| Pathology | M,D |
| Pharmacology | M,D |
| Philosophy | M,D |
| Physics | M,D |
| Physiology | M,D |
| Plant Biology | M,D |
| Plant Pathology | M,D |
| Plant Sciences | M,D |
| Political Science | M,D |
| Psychology—General | M,D |
| Public Health—General | M |
| Reading Education | M |
| Recreation and Park Management | M,D |
| Rehabilitation Counseling | M,D,O |
| Rhetoric | M,D |
| Romance Languages | M,D |
| School Psychology | M,D,O |
| Social Sciences Education | M,D |
| Social Work | M,D |
| Sociology | M,D |
| Spanish | M,D |
| Special Education | M,D,O |
| Statistics | M,D |
| Structural Biology | D |
| Supply Chain Management | M,D |
| Sustainable Development | M,D |
| Systems Biology | D |
| Taxation | M,D |
| Theater | M |
| Therapies—Dance, Drama, and Music | M,D |
| Toxicology | M,D |
| Urban and Regional Planning | M,D |
| Veterinary Medicine | D |
| Veterinary Sciences | M,D |
| Writing | M,D |
| Zoology | M,D |

## MICHIGAN STATE UNIVERSITY COLLEGE OF LAW

| | |
|---|---|
| Intellectual Property Law | M,D |
| Law | M,D |
| Legal and Justice Studies | M,D |

**MICHIGAN TECHNOLOGICAL UNIVERSITY**
Applied Physics M,D
Biochemistry M,D,O
Biological and Biomedical Sciences—General M,D
Biomedical Engineering M,D
Business Administration and Management—General M
Chemical Engineering M,D
Chemistry M,D
Civil Engineering M,D
Cognitive Sciences M,D,O
Computational Sciences M,D,O
Computer Engineering M,D,O
Data Science/Data Analytics M,D,O
Electrical Engineering M,D,O
Engineering and Applied Sciences—General M,D,O
Environmental Engineering M,D
Ergonomics and Human Factors M,D,O
Forestry M,D
Geophysics M,D
Interdisciplinary Studies M,D,O
Kinesiology and Movement Studies M,D
Materials Engineering M,D
Mathematics M,D
Mechanical Engineering M,D,O
Mechanics M,D,O
Metallurgical Engineering and Metallurgy M,D
Mineral Economics M
Molecular Biology M,D,O
Physics M,D
Science Education M,D,O
Sustainability Management M,D,O

**MID-AMERICA BAPTIST THEOLOGICAL SEMINARY**
Missions and Missiology M,D
Pastoral Ministry and Counseling M,D
Theology M,D

**MID-AMERICA BAPTIST THEOLOGICAL SEMINARY NORTHEAST BRANCH**
Theology M

**MID-AMERICA CHRISTIAN UNIVERSITY**
Business Administration and Management—General M
Counseling Psychology M
Marriage and Family Therapy M
Organizational Management M
Pastoral Ministry and Counseling M
Public Administration M

**MIDAMERICA NAZARENE UNIVERSITY**
Business Administration and Management—General M
Clinical Psychology M
Education—General M
Educational Media/Instructional Technology M
English as a Second Language M
Marriage and Family Therapy M
Nursing and Healthcare Administration M
Nursing Education M
Nursing—General M
Public Health—General M
Reading Education M
School Psychology M

**MID-AMERICA REFORMED SEMINARY**
Theology M

**MIDDLEBURY COLLEGE**
Chinese M
English M
French M,D
German M,D
Italian M,D
Near and Middle Eastern Languages M
Russian M,D
Spanish M,D

**MIDDLEBURY INSTITUTE OF INTERNATIONAL STUDIES AT MONTEREY**
Conflict Resolution and Mediation/Peace Studies M
English as a Second Language M
Environmental Management and Policy M
Foreign Languages Education M
International Affairs M
International and Comparative Education M
International Development M
International Trade Policy M
Public Administration M
Translation and Interpretation M

**MIDDLE GEORGIA STATE UNIVERSITY**
Computer and Information Systems Security M
Forensic Sciences M
Gerontological Nursing M
Health Informatics M
Management Information Systems M

**MIDDLE TENNESSEE STATE UNIVERSITY**
Accounting M
Actuarial Science M
Aerospace/Aeronautical Engineering M
Archives/Archival Administration M,D,O
Aviation Management M
Biological and Biomedical Sciences—General M
Biostatistics M
Biotechnology M
Business Administration and Management—General M
Business Education M
Chemistry M
Clinical Psychology M,O
Computational Sciences D
Computer Science M
Counseling Psychology M
Counselor Education M
Criminal Justice and Criminology M
Curriculum and Instruction M,O
Early Childhood Education M,O
Economics M,D
Education—General M,D,O
Educational Leadership and Administration M,O
Educational Media/Instructional Technology M,O
Elementary Education M,O
Engineering Management M
English as a Second Language M,O
English M,D
Exercise and Sports Science M,D
Experimental Psychology M,O
Family Nurse Practitioner Studies M,O
Foreign Languages Education M
French M
Gender Studies O
Geosciences O
German M
Gerontology O
Health Education M
History M
Human Resources Management M
Industrial and Organizational Psychology M,O
International Affairs M
Management Information Systems M
Management Strategy and Policy M
Mass Communication M
Mathematics Education M,D
Mathematics M
Medical Informatics M
Middle School Education M,O
Molecular Biology D
Music M
Nursing and Healthcare Administration M
Nursing Education M
Nursing—General M,O
Physical Education M
Political Science M
Psychology—General M,O
Public History D
Reading Education M,D
Recreation and Park Management M
School Psychology M,O
Science Education M,D
Secondary Education M,O
Social Work M
Sociology M
Spanish M
Special Education M
Vocational and Technical Education M
Women's Studies O

**MIDWAY UNIVERSITY**
Business Administration and Management—General M
Education—General M
Organizational Management M

**MIDWEST COLLEGE OF ORIENTAL MEDICINE**
Acupuncture and Oriental Medicine M,O

**MIDWESTERN BAPTIST THEOLOGICAL SEMINARY**
Music M,D,O
Pastoral Ministry and Counseling M,D,O
Religious Education M,D,O
Theology M,D,O

**MIDWESTERN STATE UNIVERSITY**
Biological and Biomedical Sciences—General M
Business Administration and Management—General M
Clinical Psychology M
Community Health M,O
Computer Science M
Counseling Psychology M
Counselor Education M
Criminal Justice and Criminology M,O
Curriculum and Instruction M
Education—General M
Educational Leadership and Administration M
Educational Media/Instructional Technology M
English M,D
Exercise and Sports Science M
Family Nurse Practitioner Studies M
Health Informatics M,O
Health Physics/Radiological Health M
Health Services Management and Hospital Administration M,O
History M
Human Resources Development M
Nursing Education M
Nursing—General M
Philosophy M,D
Political Science M
Psychiatric Nursing M
Reading Education M
Special Education M
Sports Management M

**MIDWESTERN UNIVERSITY, DOWNERS GROVE CAMPUS**
Biological and Biomedical Sciences—General M
Clinical Psychology D
Communication Disorders M
Dentistry D
Occupational Therapy M
Optometry D
Osteopathic Medicine D
Pharmacy D
Physical Therapy D
Physician Assistant Studies M

**MIDWESTERN UNIVERSITY, GLENDALE CAMPUS**
Allied Health—General M,D
Biological and Biomedical Sciences—General M
Cardiovascular Sciences M
Clinical Psychology D
Communication Disorders M
Dentistry D
Nurse Anesthesia M
Occupational Therapy M
Optometry D
Osteopathic Medicine D
Pharmacy D
Physical Therapy D
Physician Assistant Studies M
Podiatric Medicine D
Veterinary Medicine D

**MIDWEST UNIVERSITY**
Aviation Management M,D
Counselor Education M,D
Education of the Gifted M,D
Education—General M,D
English as a Second Language M,D
Entrepreneurship M,D
International Business M,D
Investment Management M,D
Marriage and Family Therapy M,D
Missions and Missiology M,D
Music M,D
Organizational Management M,D
Pastoral Ministry and Counseling M,D
Public Administration M,D
Public Policy M,D
Real Estate M,D
Theology M,D

**MIDWIVES COLLEGE OF UTAH**
Nurse Midwifery M

**MILLENNIA ATLANTIC UNIVERSITY**
Accounting M
Business Administration and Management—General M
Health Informatics M
Human Resources Management M

**MILLERSVILLE UNIVERSITY OF PENNSYLVANIA**
Applied Arts and Design—General M
Art Education M
Art/Fine Arts M
Clinical Psychology M
Distance Education Development M,D
Early Childhood Education M
Education of the Gifted M
Education—General M,D,O
Educational Leadership and Administration M,D
Emergency Management M
English as a Second Language M
English Education M
English M,O
Environmental Management and Policy M
Family Nurse Practitioner Studies M,D,O
French M
Geographic Information Systems M
German M
History M
Mathematics Education M,D
Meteorology M
Nursing Education M,D,O
Nursing—General M,D,O
Physical Education M,O
Psychology—General M
Reading Education M
School Psychology M
Science Education M,D
Social Work M,D
Spanish M
Special Education M
Sports Management M,O
Vocational and Technical Education M
Writing M,O

**MILLIGAN UNIVERSITY**
Business Administration and Management—General M,O
Clinical Psychology M,O
Counselor Education M,O
Early Childhood Education M,D,O
Education—General M,D,O
Educational Leadership and Administration M,D,O
Elementary Education M,D,O
Health Services Management and Hospital Administration M,O
Industrial and Manufacturing Management M,O
Middle School Education M,D,O
Missions and Missiology M,D,O
Occupational Therapy M
Pastoral Ministry and Counseling M,D,O
Physician Assistant Studies M
Religion M,D,O
Religious Education M,D,O
Secondary Education M,D,O
Special Education M,D,O
Theology M,D,O

**MILLIKIN UNIVERSITY**
Business Administration and Management—General M
Nursing—General M,D

**MILLSAPS COLLEGE**
Accounting M
Business Administration and Management—General M

**MILLS COLLEGE**
Applied Economics M
Art/Fine Arts M
Biological and Biomedical Sciences—General O
Business Administration and Management—General M
Computer Science M,O
Dance M
Early Childhood Education M
Education—General M,D,O
Educational Leadership and Administration
English M,O
Illustration M,O
Interdisciplinary Studies M,O
Music M
Photography M
Public Policy M
Translation and Interpretation M,O
Writing M,O

**MILWAUKEE SCHOOL OF ENGINEERING**
Architectural Engineering M
Business Administration and Management—General M
Business Education M
Cardiovascular Sciences M
Civil Engineering M
Clinical Laboratory Sciences/Medical Technology M
Engineering and Applied Sciences—General M
Engineering Management M
Health Services Management and Hospital Administration M
Industrial and Manufacturing Management M
International Business M
Marketing M
Nursing and Healthcare Administration M
Perfusion M

**MINNEAPOLIS COLLEGE OF ART AND DESIGN**
Applied Arts and Design—General M
Art/Fine Arts M
Film, Television, and Video Production M
Graphic Design M
Illustration M
Internet and Interactive Multimedia M
Photography M
Sustainable Development M

**MINNESOTA STATE UNIVERSITY MANKATO**
Accounting M
Allied Health—General M,D,O
Anthropology M
Applied Statistics M
Art Education M
Art/Fine Arts M
Astronomy M
Automotive Engineering M
Biological and Biomedical Sciences—General M
Business Administration and Management—General M
Clinical Psychology M,D
Communication Disorders M
Communication—General M,O
Community Health M,O
Computer Science M,O
Corporate and Organizational Communication M,O
Counseling Psychology M,D
Counselor Education M,D
Criminal Justice and Criminology M
Education—General M,D,O
Educational Leadership and Administration M
English as a Second Language M,O
English M,O
Environmental Sciences M
Ethnic Studies M
Family Nurse Practitioner Studies M,D
Foreign Languages Education M
French M
Gender Studies M
Geography M
Gerontology M
Health Education M,O
Higher Education M
History M
Human Services M
Industrial and Organizational Psychology M,D
Information Science M,O
Interdisciplinary Studies M
Manufacturing Engineering M
Mathematics Education M
Mathematics M
Music Education M

*M—masters degree; D—doctorate; O—other advanced degree; *—Close-Up and/or Display*

| | |
|---|---|
| Music | M |
| Nonprofit Management | M,O |
| Nursing Education | M,D |
| Nursing—General | M,D |
| Physical Education | M |
| Physics | M |
| Psychology—General | M,D |
| Public Administration | M |
| Rehabilitation Counseling | M |
| School Psychology | M,D |
| Science Education | M |
| Social Sciences Education | M |
| Social Work | M |
| Sociology | M |
| Spanish | M |
| Special Education | M,O |
| Statistics | M |
| Student Affairs | M,D |
| Technical Communication | M,O |
| Theater | M |
| Urban and Regional Planning | M,O |
| Urban Studies | M,O |
| Women's Studies | M |
| Writing | M,O |

### MINNESOTA STATE UNIVERSITY MOORHEAD

| | |
|---|---|
| Business Administration and Management—General | M |
| Counselor Education | M,D,O |
| Education—General | M,D,O |
| Educational Leadership and Administration | M,D,O |
| Health Services Management and Hospital Administration | M,O |
| Nursing—General | M,O |
| School Psychology | M,O |

### MINOT STATE UNIVERSITY

| | |
|---|---|
| Business Administration and Management—General | M |
| Communication Disorders | M |
| Elementary Education | M |
| Management Information Systems | M |
| Mathematics Education | M |
| Middle School Education | M |
| School Psychology | O |
| Science Education | M |
| Special Education | M |

### MIRRER YESHIVA CENTRAL INSTITUTE

| | |
|---|---|
| Theology | |

### MISERICORDIA UNIVERSITY

| | |
|---|---|
| Accounting | M |
| Allied Health—General | M,D |
| Business Administration and Management—General | M |
| Communication Disorders | M |
| Curriculum and Instruction | M |
| Education—General | M |
| Educational Media/Instructional Technology | M |
| Health Services Management and Hospital Administration | M |
| Human Resources Management | M |
| Nursing—General | M,D |
| Occupational Therapy | M,D |
| Organizational Management | M |
| Physical Therapy | D |
| Reading Education | M |
| Special Education | M |
| Sports Management | M |

### MISSIO SEMINARY

| | |
|---|---|
| Missions and Missiology | M,D,O |
| Pastoral Ministry and Counseling | M,D,O |
| Theology | M,D,O |

### MISSISSIPPI COLLEGE

| | |
|---|---|
| Accounting | M,O |
| Advertising and Public Relations | M |
| Art Education | M,D,O |
| Art/Fine Arts | M |
| Biochemistry | M |
| Biological and Biomedical Sciences—General | M |
| Business Administration and Management—General | M,O |
| Business Education | M,D,O |
| Chemistry | M |
| Communication—General | M |
| Computer and Information Systems Security | M |
| Computer Education | M,D,O |
| Computer Science | M |
| Corporate and Organizational Communication | M |
| Counseling Psychology | M,O |
| Counselor Education | M,O |
| Criminal Justice and Criminology | M,O |
| Curriculum and Instruction | M,D,O |
| Education—General | M,D,O |
| Educational Leadership and Administration | M,D,O |
| Elementary Education | M,D,O |
| English as a Second Language | M |
| English Education | M,D,O |
| English | M |
| Finance and Banking | M,O |
| Health Services Management and Hospital Administration | M |
| Higher Education | M,D,O |
| History | M,O |
| Kinesiology and Movement Studies | M |
| Law | D,O |
| Legal and Justice Studies | M,O |
| Liberal Studies | M |
| Marriage and Family Therapy | M,O |
| Mathematics Education | M,D,O |
| Mathematics | M |
| Music Education | M |
| Music | M |
| Political Science | M,O |
| Science Education | M,D,O |
| Secondary Education | M,D,O |
| Social Sciences Education | M,D,O |
| Social Sciences | M,O |
| Special Education | M,D,O |

### MISSISSIPPI STATE UNIVERSITY

| | |
|---|---|
| Accounting | M |
| Aerospace/Aeronautical Engineering | M,D |
| Agricultural Economics and Agribusiness | M |
| Agricultural Education | M,D |
| Agricultural Sciences—General | M,D |
| Agronomy and Soil Sciences | M,D |
| Animal Sciences | M,D |
| Anthropology | M |
| Applied Psychology | M,D |
| Atmospheric Sciences | M,D |
| Biochemistry | M,D |
| Bioengineering | M,D |
| Biological and Biomedical Sciences—General | M,D |
| Biomedical Engineering | M,D |
| Business Administration and Management—General | M,D |
| Chemical Engineering | M,D |
| Chemistry | M,D |
| Child and Family Studies | M,D |
| Civil Engineering | M,D |
| Clinical Psychology | M,D,O |
| Clothing and Textiles | M,D |
| Cognitive Sciences | M,D |
| Communication—General | M,D |
| Community College Education | M,D,O |
| Computer Engineering | M,D |
| Computer Science | M,D |
| Counselor Education | M,D,O |
| Curriculum and Instruction | M,D,O |
| Early Childhood Education | M,D,O |
| Economics | M,D |
| Education—General | M,D,O |
| Educational Leadership and Administration | M,D,O |
| Educational Media/Instructional Technology | M,D,O |
| Educational Psychology | M,D,O |
| Electrical Engineering | M,D |
| Elementary Education | M,D,O |
| Engineering and Applied Sciences—General | M,D |
| English | M |
| Ergonomics and Human Factors | M,D |
| Exercise and Sports Science | M,D |
| Finance and Banking | M,D |
| Fish, Game, and Wildlife Management | M,D |
| Food Science and Technology | M,D |
| Foreign Languages Education | M |
| Forestry | M,D |
| Genetics | M,D |
| Geography | M,D |
| Geology | M,D |
| Geosciences | M,D |
| Higher Education | M,D,O |
| History | M,D |
| Horticulture | M,D |
| Human Development | M,D |
| Human Resources Development | M,D,O |
| Industrial and Manufacturing Management | M,D |
| Industrial/Management Engineering | M,D |
| Kinesiology and Movement Studies | M,D |
| Landscape Architecture | M |
| Management Information Systems | M,D |
| Marketing | D |
| Mathematics | M,D |
| Mechanical Engineering | M,D |
| Meteorology | M,D |
| Middle School Education | M,D,O |
| Molecular Biology | M,D |
| Music Education | M |
| Nutrition | M,D |
| Operations Research | M,D |
| Physical Education | M,D |
| Physics | M,D |
| Plant Sciences | M,D |
| Political Science | M,D |
| Project Management | M,D |
| Psychology—General | M,D |
| Public Administration | M,D |
| Public Policy | M,D |
| Reading Education | M,D,O |
| Rehabilitation Counseling | M,D,O |
| School Psychology | M,D,O |
| Secondary Education | M,D,O |
| Sociology | M,D |
| Special Education | M,D,O |
| Sports Management | M,D |
| Statistics | M,D |
| Student Affairs | M,D,O |
| Sustainable Development | M,D |
| Systems Engineering | M,D |
| Taxation | M |
| Veterinary Medicine | D |
| Veterinary Sciences | M,D |
| Vocational and Technical Education | M,D,O |

### MISSISSIPPI UNIVERSITY FOR WOMEN

| | |
|---|---|
| Communication Disorders | M,D,O |
| Curriculum and Instruction | M |
| Education of the Gifted | M |
| Education—General | M |
| Educational Leadership and Administration | M |
| Health Education | M,D,O |
| Nursing—General | M,D,O |
| Public Health—General | M,D,O |
| Reading Education | M |

### MISSISSIPPI VALLEY STATE UNIVERSITY

| | |
|---|---|
| Criminal Justice and Criminology | M |
| Education—General | M |
| Environmental and Occupational Health | M |

### MISSOURI BAPTIST UNIVERSITY

| | |
|---|---|
| Business Administration and Management—General | M,O |
| Counselor Education | M,O |
| Education—General | M,O |
| Educational Leadership and Administration | M,O |
| Pastoral Ministry and Counseling | M,O |

### MISSOURI SOUTHERN STATE UNIVERSITY

| | |
|---|---|
| Business Administration and Management—General | M |
| Criminal Justice and Criminology | M |
| Dental Hygiene | M |
| Early Childhood Education | M |
| Education—General | M |
| Educational Media/Instructional Technology | M |
| Nursing—General | M |

### MISSOURI STATE UNIVERSITY

| | |
|---|---|
| Accounting | M |
| Agricultural Sciences—General | M |
| Applied Behavior Analysis | M,O |
| Applied Science and Technology | M,O |
| Art/Fine Arts | M |
| Athletic Training and Sports Medicine | M |
| Biological and Biomedical Sciences—General | M |
| Business Administration and Management—General | M |
| Cell Biology | M |
| Chemistry | M |
| Child and Family Studies | M |
| Clinical Psychology | M,O |
| Communication Disorders | M,D |
| Communication—General | M,O |
| Computer Science | M |
| Construction Management | M |
| Counseling Psychology | M |
| Counselor Education | M |
| Criminal Justice and Criminology | M,O |
| Early Childhood Education | M |
| Educational Leadership and Administration | M,O |
| Educational Measurement and Evaluation | O |
| Educational Media/Instructional Technology | M |
| Elementary Education | M,O |
| English as a Second Language | M,O |
| English Education | M,O |
| English | M,O |
| Environmental Management and Policy | M,O |
| Experimental Psychology | M,O |
| Family Nurse Practitioner Studies | M,D |
| Film, Television, and Video Production | M,O |
| Geography | M,O |
| Geology | M,O |
| Geosciences | M,O |
| Higher Education | M |
| History | M,O |
| Homeland Security | M,O |
| Industrial and Organizational Psychology | M,O |
| International Affairs | M |
| Kinesiology and Movement Studies | M |
| Materials Sciences | M |
| Mathematics Education | M |
| Mathematics | M |
| Military and Defense Studies | M,O |
| Molecular Biology | M |
| Music | M |
| Nurse Anesthesia | D |
| Nursing Education | M,D |
| Nursing—General | M,D |
| Nutrition | M,D,O |
| Occupational Therapy | M |
| Physical Education | M |
| Physical Therapy | D |
| Physician Assistant Studies | M |
| Physics | M |
| Plant Sciences | M |
| Political Science | M,O |
| Project Management | M |
| Psychology—General | M,O |
| Public Administration | M,O |
| Public Health—General | M |
| Reading Education | M,O |
| Religion | M,O |
| Science Education | M,O |
| Secondary Education | M,O |
| Social Sciences Education | M,O |
| Social Work | M |
| Special Education | M |
| Sports Management | M,O |
| Student Affairs | M |
| Urban and Regional Planning | M,O |
| Writing | M,O |

### MISSOURI UNIVERSITY OF SCIENCE AND TECHNOLOGY

| | |
|---|---|
| Aerospace/Aeronautical Engineering | M,D |
| Applied Mathematics | M,D |
| Biological and Biomedical Sciences—General | M |
| Business Administration and Management—General | M |
| Ceramic Sciences and Engineering | M,D |
| Chemical Engineering | M,D |
| Chemistry | M,D |
| Civil Engineering | M,D |
| Computer Engineering | M,D |
| Computer Science | M,D |
| Electrical Engineering | M,D |
| Engineering Management | M,D |
| Environmental Biology | M |
| Environmental Engineering | M,D |
| Geochemistry | M,D |
| Geological Engineering | M,D |
| Geology | M,D |
| Geophysics | M,D |
| Geotechnical Engineering | M |
| Industrial and Organizational Psychology | M |
| Information Science | M |
| Manufacturing Engineering | M,D |
| Materials Engineering | M,D |
| Materials Sciences | M,D |
| Mathematics Education | M,D |
| Mathematics | M,D |
| Mechanical Engineering | M,D |
| Metallurgical Engineering and Metallurgy | M,D |
| Mineral/Mining Engineering | M,D |
| Nuclear Engineering | M,D |
| Petroleum Engineering | M,D |
| Physics | M,D |
| Statistics | M,D |
| Systems Engineering | M,D |
| Technical Communication | M |
| Water Resources | M,D |

### MISSOURI VALLEY COLLEGE

| | |
|---|---|
| Social Psychology | M |

### MISSOURI WESTERN STATE UNIVERSITY

| | |
|---|---|
| Accounting | M |
| Animal Sciences | M |
| Biological and Biomedical Sciences—General | M |
| Business Administration and Management—General | M |
| Chemistry | M |
| Computer and Information Systems Security | M |
| Early Childhood Education | M,O |
| Educational Measurement and Evaluation | M,O |
| Engineering and Applied Sciences—General | M |
| English as a Second Language | M,O |
| Forensic Sciences | M,O |
| Nursing and Healthcare Administration | M,O |
| Nursing Education | M,O |
| Nursing—General | M,O |
| Special Education | M,O |
| Sports Management | M,O |

### MITCHELL HAMLINE SCHOOL OF LAW

| | |
|---|---|
| Law | M,D |

### MOLLOY COLLEGE

| | |
|---|---|
| Accounting | M,O |
| Business Administration and Management—General | M,O |
| Clinical Psychology | M |
| Communication Disorders | M |
| Criminal Justice and Criminology | M |
| Early Childhood Education | M,O |
| Education—General | M,O |
| Educational Media/Instructional Technology | M,O |
| English as a Second Language | M,O |
| English Education | M,O |
| Family Nurse Practitioner Studies | M,D,O |
| Finance and Banking | M,O |
| Foreign Languages Education | M,O |
| Gerontological Nursing | M,D,O |
| Health Services Management and Hospital Administration | M,D,O |
| Marketing | M,O |
| Mathematics Education | M,O |
| Multilingual and Multicultural Education | M,O |
| Nursing Education | M,D,O |
| Nursing—General | M,D,O |
| Pediatric Nursing | M,D,O |
| Psychiatric Nursing | M,D,O |
| Science Education | M,O |
| Social Sciences Education | M,O |
| Special Education | M,O |
| Therapies—Dance, Drama, and Music | M |

### MONMOUTH UNIVERSITY

| | |
|---|---|
| Accounting | M,O |
| Addictions/Substance Abuse Counseling | M,O |
| Adult Nursing | M,D,O |
| Advertising and Public Relations | M,O |
| American Studies | M |
| Anthropology | M |
| Applied Behavior Analysis | M,D,O |
| Business Administration and Management—General | M,O |
| Communication Disorders | M,D,O |
| Communication—General | M,O |
| Computer Science | M |
| Counseling Psychology | M,O |
| Criminal Justice and Criminology | M,O |
| Early Childhood Education | M,D,O |
| Education—General | M,D,O |
| Educational Leadership and Administration | M,D,O |
| Elementary Education | M,D,O |
| English as a Second Language | M,D,O |
| English | M |
| Finance and Banking | M,O |
| Forensic Nursing | M,D,O |
| Gerontological Nursing | M,D,O |
| History | M |
| Homeland Security | M,O |
| Information Studies | M |
| Marketing | M,O |
| Media Studies | M,O |
| Nursing—General | M,D,O |

Psychology—General M,O
Reading Education M,D,O
Real Estate M,O
Rhetoric M
School Psychology M,D,O
Secondary Education M,D,O
Social Work M,O
Software Engineering M,O
Special Education M,D,O
Student Affairs M,D,O
Western European Studies M
Writing M

**MONROE COLLEGE**
Accounting M
Biostatistics M
Business Administration and Management—General M
Community Health M
Computer Science M
Criminal Justice and Criminology M
Entrepreneurship M
Epidemiology M
Finance and Banking M
Health Services Management and Hospital Administration M
Hospitality Management M
Human Resources Management M
Information Science M
Marketing M
Public Health—General M

**MONTANA STATE UNIVERSITY**
Accounting M
Adult Education M,D,O
Agricultural Education M
Agricultural Sciences—General M,D
American Indian/Native American Studies M
Animal Sciences M,D
Architecture M
Art History M
Art/Fine Arts M
Biochemistry M,D
Biological and Biomedical Sciences—General M,D
Chemical Engineering M,D
Chemistry M,D
Civil Engineering M,D
Computer Engineering M,D
Computer Science M,D
Construction Engineering M,D
Curriculum and Instruction M,D,O
Ecology M,D
Education—General M,D,O
Educational Leadership and Administration M,D,O
Electrical Engineering M,D
Engineering and Applied Sciences—General M,D
English M
Environmental Engineering M,D
Environmental Sciences M,D
Family Nurse Practitioner Studies M,D,O
Film, Television, and Video Production M
Fish, Game, and Wildlife Management M,D
Geosciences M,D
Health Education M
Higher Education M,D,O
History M,D
Home Economics Education M
Human Development M
Immunology M,D
Industrial/Management Engineering M,D
Infectious Diseases M,D
Mathematics Education M,D
Mathematics M,D
Mechanical Engineering M,D
Mechanics M,D
Microbiology M,D
Natural Resources M
Neuroscience M,D
Nursing and Healthcare Administration M,D,O
Nursing Education M,D,O
Nursing—General M,D,O
Physics M,D
Plant Pathology M,D
Plant Sciences M,D
Psychiatric Nursing M,D,O
Psychology—General M
Public Administration M
Range Science M,D
School Psychology M,D,O
Statistics M,D
Vocational and Technical Education M,D,O

**MONTANA STATE UNIVERSITY BILLINGS**
Advertising and Public Relations M
Applied Behavior Analysis M
Athletic Training and Sports Medicine M
Communication—General M
Counseling Psychology M
Counselor Education M
Curriculum and Instruction M
Education—General M,O
Educational Media/Instructional Technology M
Elementary Education M
Health Services Management and Hospital Administration M
Interdisciplinary Studies M
Psychology—General M
Reading Education M
Rehabilitation Counseling M
Secondary Education M
Special Education M

**MONTANA STATE UNIVERSITY–NORTHERN**
Counselor Education M
Education—General M

**MONTANA TECHNOLOGICAL UNIVERSITY**
Electrical Engineering M
Engineering and Applied Sciences—General M
Environmental Engineering M
Geochemistry M
Geological Engineering M
Geology M
Geosciences M
Health Informatics O
Hydrogeology M
Industrial Hygiene M
Industrial/Management Engineering M
Interdisciplinary Studies M
Materials Sciences D
Metallurgical Engineering and Metallurgy M
Mineral/Mining Engineering M
Petroleum Engineering M
Project Management M

**MONTCLAIR STATE UNIVERSITY**
Accounting M,O
Addictions/Substance Abuse Counseling O
Advertising and Public Relations M
Applied Mathematics M
Archives/Archival Administration M
Art Education M
Art/Fine Arts M
Arts Administration M
Biochemistry M
Biological and Biomedical Sciences—General M
Business Administration and Management—General M,O
Business Analytics M
Chemistry M
Child and Family Studies M,D,O
Child Development M,O
Clinical Psychology M,O
Communication Disorders M,D
Computer Science M,O
Conflict Resolution and Mediation/Peace Studies M,O
Corporate and Organizational Communication M
Counselor Education M,D
Curriculum and Instruction M
Data Science/Data Analytics O
Disability Studies M,O
Ecology M
Education—General M,D,O
Educational Leadership and Administration M,D
Educational Measurement and Evaluation O
English as a Second Language M,O
English Education M,O
English M
Environmental Education M
Environmental Law O
Environmental Management and Policy M,D
Environmental Sciences M
Evolutionary Biology M
Exercise and Sports Science M,O
Finance and Banking M
Forensic Psychology O
French M
Geographic Information Systems O
Geosciences M
Health Education M
Human Resources Management M
Industrial and Organizational Psychology M
Intellectual Property Law M,O
Internet and Interactive Multimedia M
Law M,O
Legal and Justice Studies O
Linguistics M,O
Management Information Systems M
Management of Technology M
Marine Biology M
Marketing M
Mathematics Education M,D,O
Mathematics M
Molecular Biology M,O
Music Education M
Music M,O
Nutrition M,O
Pharmacology M
Physical Education M
Physiology M
Political Science M,O
Project Management M
Psychology—General M
Public Health—General M
Reading Education M
Science Education M
Social Sciences M
Spanish M
Special Education M
Sports Management M
Statistics M
Sustainable Development M
Theater M
Therapies—Dance, Drama, and Music M,O
Translation and Interpretation O
Water Resources O
Writing O

**MOODY BIBLE INSTITUTE**
Pastoral Ministry and Counseling M,O
Theology M,O
Urban Studies M,O

**MOODY THEOLOGICAL SEMINARY–MICHIGAN**
Counseling Psychology M,O
Religion M,O
Religious Education M,O
Theology M,O

**MOORE COLLEGE OF ART & DESIGN**
Art Education M
Art/Fine Arts M
Arts Administration M
Communication—General M
Interior Design M

**MORAVIAN COLLEGE**
Accounting M
Acute Care/Critical Care Nursing M
Athletic Training and Sports Medicine M,D
Business Administration and Management—General M
Communication Disorders M,D
Curriculum and Instruction M
Education—General M
Health Services Management and Hospital Administration M
Human Resources Management M
Nursing and Healthcare Administration M
Nursing Education M
Nursing—General M
Supply Chain Management M

**MORAVIAN THEOLOGICAL SEMINARY**
Theology M,O

**MOREHEAD STATE UNIVERSITY**
Adult Education M,O
Biological and Biomedical Sciences—General M
Business Administration and Management—General M
Business Education M,O
Clinical Psychology M
Counseling Psychology M
Counselor Education M,O
Criminal Justice and Criminology M
Curriculum and Instruction M,O
Education of the Gifted M,O
Education—General M,O
Educational Leadership and Administration M,O
Educational Media/Instructional Technology M,O
Elementary Education M,O
English Education M,O
Environmental Management and Policy M
Experimental Psychology M
Foreign Languages Education M
Gerontology M
Health Education M
Health Promotion M
Higher Education M,O
Management Information Systems M
Mathematics Education M
Middle School Education M,O
Physical Education M
Psychology—General M
Reading Education M,O
Science Education M
Secondary Education M
Social Sciences Education M,O
Sociology M
Special Education M,O
Vocational and Technical Education M

**MOREHOUSE SCHOOL OF MEDICINE**
Allopathic Medicine D
Biological and Biomedical Sciences—General M,D
Clinical Research M
Public Health—General M

**MORGAN STATE UNIVERSITY**
Accounting M,D
African-American Studies M,D
Architecture M
Bioinformatics M
Biological and Biomedical Sciences—General M,D
Business Administration and Management—General M,D
Chemistry M
Civil Engineering M,D,O
Community College Education D
Computational Sciences M,D
Computer Science M
Economics M
Education—General M,D
Educational Leadership and Administration M,D
Electrical Engineering M,D,O
Elementary Education M
Engineering and Applied Sciences—General M,D,O
English M,D
Environmental Biology D
Higher Education M,D
Historic Preservation M,D
History M,D
Hospitality Management M
Industrial/Management Engineering M,D,O
International Affairs M
Journalism M
Landscape Architecture M
Management Information Systems D
Marketing D
Mathematics Education M,D
Mathematics M,D
Museum Studies M,D
Music M
Nursing—General M,D
Physics M
Project Management M
Psychology—General M,D
Public Health—General M,D
Science Education M,D
Social Work M
Sociology M
Student Affairs M,D
Transportation and Highway Engineering M,D,O
Urban and Regional Planning M
Urban Education D

**MORNINGSIDE COLLEGE**
Education—General M
Family Nurse Practitioner Studies M
Gerontological Nursing M
Nursing—General M
Special Education M

**MOUNT ALLISON UNIVERSITY**
Biochemistry M
Biological and Biomedical Sciences—General M
Chemistry M

**MOUNT ALOYSIUS COLLEGE**
Accounting M
Business Administration and Management—General M
Health Services Management and Hospital Administration M
Nonprofit Management M
Project Management M
Social Psychology M

**MOUNT ANGEL SEMINARY**
Theology M

**MOUNT CARMEL COLLEGE OF NURSING**
Acute Care/Critical Care Nursing M,D
Adult Nursing M,D
Family Nurse Practitioner Studies M,D
Gerontological Nursing M,D
Nursing and Healthcare Administration M,D
Nursing Education M,D
Nursing—General M,D

**MOUNT HOLYOKE COLLEGE**
Educational Leadership and Administration M
Mathematics Education M

**MOUNT MARTY UNIVERSITY**
Business Administration and Management—General M
Nurse Anesthesia M
Nursing—General M
Pastoral Ministry and Counseling M

**MOUNT MARY UNIVERSITY**
Art Therapy M,D
Business Administration and Management—General M
Clinical Psychology M,O
Counseling Psychology M,O
Counselor Education M,O
Education—General M
English M
Internet and Interactive Multimedia M
Nursing and Healthcare Administration M
Nutrition M
Occupational Therapy M,D
Rehabilitation Counseling M,O
Writing M

**MOUNT MERCY UNIVERSITY**
Business Administration and Management—General M
Criminal Justice and Criminology M
Education—General M
Educational Leadership and Administration M
Human Resources Management M
Management Strategy and Policy M
Marriage and Family Therapy M
Nursing and Healthcare Administration M
Nursing Education M
Nursing—General M
Quality Management M
Reading Education M
Special Education M

**MOUNT ST. JOSEPH UNIVERSITY**
Business Administration and Management—General M
Early Childhood Education M,O
Education—General M,O
Health Promotion M,O
Health Services Management and Hospital Administration D
Middle School Education M,O
Multilingual and Multicultural Education M,O
Nursing and Healthcare Administration M
Nursing Education M
Nursing—General M,D
Organizational Management M
Pastoral Ministry and Counseling M,O
Physical Therapy D
Reading Education M,O
Religion M,O

*M—masters degree; D—doctorate; O—other advanced degree; *—Close-Up and/or Display*

Secondary Education M,O
Special Education M,O
Theology M,O

### MOUNT SAINT MARY COLLEGE
Adult Nursing M,O
Business Administration and Management—General M
Child Development M,O
Education—General M,O
Middle School Education M,O
Nursing and Healthcare Administration M,O
Nursing Education M,O
Nursing—General M,O
Reading Education M,O
Special Education M,O

### MOUNT SAINT MARY'S UNIVERSITY (CA)
Business Administration and Management—General M,D,O
Counseling Psychology M,D,O
Education—General M,D,O
English M,D,O
Film, Television, and Video Production M,D,O
Health Services Management and Hospital Administration M,D,O
Humanities M,D,O
Nursing—General M,D,O
Physical Therapy M,D,O
Religion M,D,O
Writing M,D,O

### MOUNT ST. MARY'S UNIVERSITY (MD)
Biotechnology M
Business Administration and Management—General M
Education—General M
Health Services Management and Hospital Administration M
Philosophy M
Sports Management M
Theology M

### MOUNT SAINT VINCENT UNIVERSITY
Adult Education M
Advertising and Public Relations M
Child and Family Studies M
Communication—General M
Curriculum and Instruction M
Education—General M
Educational Measurement and Evaluation M
Educational Psychology M
Elementary Education M
English as a Second Language M
Foundations and Philosophy of Education M
Gerontology M
Middle School Education M
Nutrition M
Reading Education M
School Psychology M
Special Education M
Women's Studies M

### MOUNT VERNON NAZARENE UNIVERSITY
Business Administration and Management—General M
Education—General M
Theology M

### MULTNOMAH UNIVERSITY
Education—General M
English as a Second Language M
Theology M,D

### MURRAY STATE UNIVERSITY
Accounting M
Advertising and Public Relations M
Agricultural Education M,O
Agricultural Sciences—General M,O
Biological and Biomedical Sciences—General M
Business Administration and Management—General M
Chemistry M
Clinical Psychology M,O
Communication Disorders M,O
Computer Science M
Corporate and Organizational Communication M
Counselor Education M,D,O
Early Childhood Education M,O
Economic Development M
Economics M
Education of Students with Severe/Multiple Disabilities M,O
Education—General M,D,O
Educational Leadership and Administration M,D,O
Educational Media/Instructional Technology M,D,O
Elementary Education M,O
English as a Second Language M,D,O
English Education M,D,O
English M,D,O
Environmental and Occupational Health M
Environmental Sciences M,O
Experimental Psychology M,O
Family Nurse Practitioner Studies D
Finance and Banking M
Gender Studies M,D,O
Geosciences M,O
History M,O
Human Development M,D,O
Human Resources Management M
Human Services M,D,O
Interdisciplinary Studies M,O
Journalism M
Management Information Systems M
Marketing M
Mass Communication M
Mathematics Education M
Mathematics M
Middle School Education M,D,O
Music Education M
Music M
Nonprofit Management M,O
Nurse Anesthesia D
Nursing—General D
Nutrition M,O
Political Science M
Psychology—General M,O
Safety Engineering M
School Psychology M,D,O
Secondary Education M,D,O
Sociology M
Special Education M,O
Statistics M
Telecommunications Management M
Vocational and Technical Education M,O
Writing M,D,O

### MUSKINGUM UNIVERSITY
Education—General M

### NAROPA UNIVERSITY
Art Therapy M
Counseling Psychology M
Counselor Education M
Ecology M
Psychoanalysis and Psychotherapy M
Psychology—General M
Recreation and Park Management M
Religion M
Sustainability Management M
Theater M
Theology M
Therapies—Dance, Drama, and Music M
Transpersonal and Humanistic Psychology M
Writing M

### NASHOTAH HOUSE THEOLOGICAL SEMINARY
Pastoral Ministry and Counseling M,D,O
Religion M,D,O
Theology M,D,O

### NATIONAL AMERICAN UNIVERSITY (TX)
Accounting M,D
Aviation Management M,D
Business Administration and Management—General M,D
Community College Education M,D
Criminal Justice and Criminology M,D
Educational Leadership and Administration M,D
Health Services Management and Hospital Administration M,D
Higher Education M,D
Human Resources Management M,D
International Business M,D
Management Information Systems M,D
Marketing M,D
Nursing and Healthcare Administration M,D
Nursing Education M,D
Nursing Informatics M,D
Project Management M,D

### NATIONAL COLLEGE OF MIDWIFERY
Nurse Midwifery M,D

### NATIONAL DEFENSE UNIVERSITY
Homeland Security M
Military and Defense Studies M
National Security M

### NATIONAL INTELLIGENCE UNIVERSITY
Military and Defense Studies M

### NATIONAL LOUIS UNIVERSITY
Adult Education M,D,O
Business Administration and Management—General M
Counselor Education M,D,O
Curriculum and Instruction M,D,O
Developmental Education M,D,O
Early Childhood Education M,D,O
Education—General M,D,O
Educational Leadership and Administration M,D,O
Educational Media/Instructional Technology M,D,O
Educational Psychology M,D,O
Elementary Education M,D,O
English Education M,D,O
Human Development M,D,O
Human Resources Development M
Human Resources Management M
Human Services M,D,O
Mathematics Education M,D,O
Middle School Education M,D,O
Psychology—General M,D,O
Public Policy M,D,O
Reading Education M,D,O
School Psychology M,D,O
Science Education M,D,O
Secondary Education M,D,O
Special Education M,D,O
Writing M,D,O

### NATIONAL PARALEGAL COLLEGE
Legal and Justice Studies M
Taxation M

### NATIONAL TEST PILOT SCHOOL
Aviation M

### NATIONAL UNIVERSITY
Accounting M,O
Applied Behavior Analysis M,O
Biological and Biomedical Sciences—General M,O
Business Administration and Management—General M,O
Business Analytics M,O
Clinical Psychology M,O
Computer and Information Systems Security M
Computer Science M
Counseling Psychology M,O
Counselor Education M,O
Criminal Justice and Criminology M
Data Science/Data Analytics M
Distance Education Development M,O
Education—General M,O
Educational Leadership and Administration M,O
Educational Media/Instructional Technology M,O
Electrical Engineering M
Emergency Management M
Engineering and Applied Sciences—General M
Engineering Management M
English M,O
Family Nurse Practitioner Studies M,O
Film, Television, and Video Production M
Film, Television, and Video Theory and Criticism M,O
Forensic Sciences M,O
Health Informatics M,O
Health Promotion M,O
Health Services Management and Hospital Administration M,O
Higher Education M,O
Homeland Security M,O
Human Resources Management M,O
Human Services M,O
International Business M,O
Internet and Interactive Multimedia M
Journalism M
Legal and Justice Studies M
Management Information Systems M,O
Management of Technology M
Marketing M,O
Marriage and Family Therapy M,O
Mathematics Education M,O
Nurse Anesthesia M,O
Nursing and Healthcare Administration M,O
Nursing Informatics M,O
Organizational Management M,O
Psychiatric Nursing M,O
Public Administration M
Public Health—General M,O
School Psychology M,O
Special Education M,O
Sustainability Management M
Writing M,O

### NATIONAL UNIVERSITY COLLEGE
Business Administration and Management—General M
Marketing M
Special Education M

### NATIONAL UNIVERSITY OF HEALTH SCIENCES
Acupuncture and Oriental Medicine M,D
Chiropractic M,D
Medical Imaging M,D
Naturopathic Medicine M,D

### NATIONAL UNIVERSITY OF NATURAL MEDICINE
Acupuncture and Oriental Medicine M,D
Clinical Research M
International Health M
Naturopathic Medicine M,D
Nutrition M

### NAVAJO TECHNICAL UNIVERSITY
American Indian/Native American Studies M

### NAVAL POSTGRADUATE SCHOOL
Acoustics M,D
Aerospace/Aeronautical Engineering M,D,O
Applied Mathematics M,D
Applied Physics M,D,O
Applied Science and Technology M,D
Business Administration and Management—General M
Computer and Information Systems Security M,D
Computer Engineering M,D,O
Computer Science M,D,O
Conflict Resolution and Mediation/Peace Studies M,D
Electrical Engineering M,D,O
Engineering Management M,D,O
Finance and Banking M
Geographic Information Systems M,D,O
Homeland Security M,D
Information Science M,D,O
Logistics M,D
Management Information Systems M,D,O
Mechanical Engineering M,D,O
Meteorology M,D
Military and Defense Studies M,D
Modeling and Simulation M,D
National Security M,D
Oceanography M,D
Operations Research M,D
Pacific Area/Pacific Rim Studies M,D
Physics M,D
Software Engineering M,D
Supply Chain Management M
Systems Engineering M,D,O
Transportation Management M

### NAVAL WAR COLLEGE
National Security M

### NAZARENE THEOLOGICAL SEMINARY
Cultural Studies M,D,O
Theology M,D,O

### NAZARETH COLLEGE OF ROCHESTER
Art Education M
Art Therapy M
Business Administration and Management—General M
Communication Disorders M
Early Childhood Education M
Education—General M
Educational Media/Instructional Technology M
Elementary Education M
English as a Second Language M
Human Resources Management M
Middle School Education M
Music Education M
Music M
Physical Therapy D
Reading Education M
Social Work M
Therapies—Dance, Drama, and Music M

### NEBRASKA CHRISTIAN COLLEGE OF HOPE INTERNATIONAL UNIVERSITY
Business Administration and Management—General M
Counseling Psychology M
Education of the Gifted M
Educational Leadership and Administration M
Elementary Education M
Entrepreneurship M
International Business M
Marketing M
Missions and Missiology M
Music Education M
Nonprofit Management M
Pastoral Ministry and Counseling M
Secondary Education M
Theology M

### NEBRASKA METHODIST COLLEGE
Health Promotion M
Health Services Management and Hospital Administration M
Nursing and Healthcare Administration M
Nursing Education M
Nursing—General M
Occupational Therapy M

### NEBRASKA WESLEYAN UNIVERSITY
Nursing—General M

### NER ISRAEL RABBINICAL COLLEGE
Theology M,D,O

### NER ISRAEL YESHIVA COLLEGE OF TORONTO
Theology

### NEUMANN UNIVERSITY
Accounting M
Adult Nursing M,O
Business Administration and Management—General M
Clinical Psychology M,D,O
Education—General M
Educational Leadership and Administration M,D
Elementary Education M
Gerontological Nursing M,O
Management Strategy and Policy M
Nursing—General M,O
Organizational Management M
Pastoral Ministry and Counseling M,D,O
Physical Therapy D
Secondary Education M
Special Education M
Sports Management M

### NEW BRUNSWICK THEOLOGICAL SEMINARY
Pastoral Ministry and Counseling M,D
Theology M,D

### NEW CHARTER UNIVERSITY
Business Administration and Management—General M
Finance and Banking M
Health Services Management and Hospital Administration M

### NEW COLLEGE OF FLORIDA
Data Science/Data Analytics M

### NEW ENGLAND COLLEGE
Accounting M
Business Administration and Management—General M
Counseling Psychology M
Education—General M,D
Educational Leadership and Administration M,D
Health Services Management and Hospital Administration M
Higher Education M,D
Human Services M
International Affairs M
Management Strategy and Policy M
Marketing M
Nonprofit Management M
Project Management M
Public Policy M
Recreation and Park Management M
Special Education M,D
Sports Management M
Writing M

### NEW ENGLAND COLLEGE OF BUSINESS AND FINANCE
Ethics M
Finance and Banking M
Quality Management M

### NEW ENGLAND COLLEGE OF OPTOMETRY
Optometry M,D
Vision Sciences M,D

### NEW ENGLAND CONSERVATORY OF MUSIC
Music M,D,O

### NEW ENGLAND INSTITUTE OF TECHNOLOGY
Construction Management M
Engineering Management M
Management Information Systems M
Occupational Therapy M,D
Public Health—General M

### NEW ENGLAND LAW - BOSTON
Law M,D

### NEW HAMPSHIRE INSTITUTE OF ART
Art Education M
Art/Fine Arts M
Photography M
Writing M

### NEW JERSEY CITY UNIVERSITY
Accounting M,O
Allied Health—General M
Art Education M
Art/Fine Arts M
Business Administration and Management—General M,O
Community Health M
Computer and Information Systems Security M,D,O
Counselor Education M
Criminal Justice and Criminology M,D,O
Early Childhood Education M
Education—General M,D
Educational Leadership and Administration M
Educational Media/Instructional Technology M,D
Elementary Education M
English as a Second Language M
Finance and Banking M,O
Health Education M
Health Services Management and Hospital Administration M
Marketing M
Mathematics Education M
Multilingual and Multicultural Education M
Music Education M
Music M
National Security M,D,O
Organizational Management M
Secondary Education M
Special Education M
Urban Education M
Urban Studies M

### NEW JERSEY INSTITUTE OF TECHNOLOGY
Applied Mathematics M,D,O
Applied Physics M,D,O
Applied Statistics M,D,O
Architecture M,D
Biological and Biomedical Sciences—General M,D,O
Biomedical Engineering M,D
Biostatistics M,D,O
Business Administration and Management—General M,D,O
Chemical Engineering M,D
Chemistry M,D,O
Computer and Information Systems Security M,D,O
Computer Engineering M,D
Computer Science M,D,O
Data Science/Data Analytics M,D,O
Electrical Engineering M,D
Energy and Power Engineering M,D
Engineering and Applied Sciences—General M,D
Engineering Management M,D
Environmental Engineering M,D
Environmental Management and Policy M,D,O
Environmental Sciences M,D,O
Health Services Management and Hospital Administration M,D
History M,D,O
Industrial/Management Engineering M,D
Information Science M,D,O
Internet Engineering M,D
Management Information Systems M,D,O
Management of Technology M,D,O
Manufacturing Engineering M,D
Materials Engineering M,D,O
Materials Sciences M,D,O
Mathematical and Computational Finance M,D,O
Mathematics M,D,O
Mechanical Engineering M,D
Medicinal and Pharmaceutical Chemistry M,D,O
Pharmaceutical Administration M,D
Pharmaceutical Engineering M,D
Pharmacology M,D
Safety Engineering M,D
Software Engineering M,D,O
Statistics M,D,O
Sustainable Development M,D,O
Technical Communication M,D,O
Telecommunications M,D
Transportation and Highway Engineering M,D
Transportation Management M,D

### NEWMAN THEOLOGICAL COLLEGE
Religious Education M,O
Theology M

### NEWMAN UNIVERSITY
Business Administration and Management—General M
Curriculum and Instruction M
Education—General M
Educational Leadership and Administration M
English as a Second Language M
Finance and Banking M
International Business M
Management Information Systems M
Nurse Anesthesia M
Organizational Management M
Reading Education M
Social Work M
Theology M

### NEW MEXICO HIGHLANDS UNIVERSITY
American Studies M
Anthropology M
Business Administration and Management—General M
Chemistry M
Clinical Psychology M
Computer Art and Design M
Computer Science M
Counseling Psychology M
Counselor Education M
Curriculum and Instruction M
Education—General M
Educational Leadership and Administration M
English M
Exercise and Sports Science M
Health Education M
History M
Human Resources Management M
International Business M
Internet and Interactive Multimedia M
Media Studies M
Natural Resources M
Political Science M
Psychology—General M
Public Affairs M
Rhetoric M
Social Work M
Sociology M
Special Education M
Sports Management M
Writing M

### NEW MEXICO INSTITUTE OF MINING AND TECHNOLOGY
Applied Mathematics M,D
Astrophysics M,D
Atmospheric Sciences M,D
Biological and Biomedical Sciences—General M,D
Chemistry M,D
Computer Science M,D
Electrical Engineering M
Engineering Management M
Environmental Engineering M
Geochemistry M,D
Geological Engineering M
Geology M,D
Geophysics M,D
Geosciences M,D
Hazardous Materials Management M
Hydrology M,D
Materials Engineering M,D
Mathematical Physics M,D
Mathematics M,D
Mechanical Engineering M
Mechanics M
Mineral/Mining Engineering M
Operations Research M,D
Petroleum Engineering M,D
Physics M,D
Science Education M
Statistics M,D
Systems Engineering M
Water Resources Engineering M

### NEW MEXICO STATE UNIVERSITY
Accounting M
Agricultural Economics and Agribusiness M,D
Agricultural Education M
Agricultural Sciences—General M,D
Anthropology M,O
Applied Statistics M,D,O
Art History M
Art/Fine Arts M
Astrophysics M,D
Bioinformatics M,D
Biological and Biomedical Sciences—General M,D
Biotechnology M,D
Business Administration and Management—General M,D
Clothing and Textiles M
Communication Disorders M,D,O
Communication—General M
Corporate and Organizational Communication M,D
Counseling Psychology M,D,O
Counselor Education M,D,O
Criminal Justice and Criminology M
Cultural Studies M,D,O
Curriculum and Instruction M,D,O
Distance Education Development O
Early Childhood Education M,D,O
Economic Development M,D,O
Economics M,D,O
Education—General M,D,O
Educational Leadership and Administration M,D
Educational Measurement and Evaluation M,D,O
Engineering and Applied Sciences—General M,D,O
English as a Second Language M,D,O
English Education M,D
English M,D
Entomology M
Environmental Engineering M,D
Family and Consumer Sciences-General M
Family Nurse Practitioner Studies M,D,O
Finance and Banking M,O
Food Science and Technology M
Geography M
Higher Education M,D
History M
Hydrology M,D
Interdisciplinary Studies M,D
Kinesiology and Movement Studies D
Management Information Systems M
Marketing D
Molecular Biology M,D
Multilingual and Multicultural Education M,D,O
Museum Studies M,O
Music Education M
Music M
Nursing and Healthcare Administration M,D,O
Nursing—General M,D,O
Plant Pathology M
Political Science M
Psychiatric Nursing M,D,O
Psychology—General M,D
Public Administration M
Public Health—General M,O
Reading Education M,D,O
Rhetoric M,D
School Psychology M,D,O
Social Work M
Sociology M
Spanish M
Special Education M,D,O
Systems Engineering M,D,O
Travel and Tourism M
Water Resources M,D
Writing M,D

### NEW ORLEANS BAPTIST THEOLOGICAL SEMINARY
Music M,D
Pastoral Ministry and Counseling M,D
Religious Education M,D
Theology M,D

### NEW SAINT ANDREWS COLLEGE
Religion M,O
Theology M,O
Writing M,O

### THE NEW SCHOOL
Anthropology M,D
Applied Arts and Design—General M
Applied Social Research M,D
Architecture M
Art/Fine Arts M
Clinical Psychology M,D
Clothing and Textiles M
Cognitive Sciences M,D
Computer Art and Design M
Data Science/Data Analytics M
Economics M,D
Environmental Management and Policy M
Finance and Banking M,D
History M,D
Industrial Design M
Interior Design M
International Affairs M
International Economics M,D
Internet and Interactive Multimedia M
Liberal Studies M
Lighting Design M
Management Strategy and Policy M,O
Media Studies M,O
Museum Studies M
Music M,O
Philosophy M,D
Photography M
Political Science M,D
Psychoanalysis and Psychotherapy M,D
Psychology—General M,D
Public Policy M,D
Social Psychology M,D
Social Sciences M,D
Sociology M,D
Sustainability Management M
Textile Design M
Theater M
Urban Design M
Writing M

### NEWSCHOOL OF ARCHITECTURE AND DESIGN
Architecture M
Construction Management M

### NEW YORK ACADEMY OF ART
Anatomy M
Art/Fine Arts M

### NEW YORK CHIROPRACTIC COLLEGE
Acupuncture and Oriental Medicine M
Anatomy M
Chiropractic D
Nutrition M

### NEW YORK COLLEGE OF HEALTH PROFESSIONS
Acupuncture and Oriental Medicine M

### NEW YORK COLLEGE OF PODIATRIC MEDICINE
Podiatric Medicine D

### NEW YORK COLLEGE OF TRADITIONAL CHINESE MEDICINE
Acupuncture and Oriental Medicine M

### NEW YORK FILM ACADEMY
Film, Television, and Video Production M
Photography M

### NEW YORK INSTITUTE OF TECHNOLOGY
Applied Arts and Design—General M
Architecture M
Art/Fine Arts M
Business Administration and Management—General M
Communication—General M
Computer and Information Systems Security M
Computer Art and Design M
Computer Engineering M
Computer Science M
Electrical Engineering M
Energy and Power Engineering O
Energy Management and Policy O
Engineering and Applied Sciences—General M,O
Environmental Engineering M
Environmental Management and Policy O
Finance and Banking M
Graphic Design M
Human Resources Management M,O
Industrial and Labor Relations M,O
International Health O
Marketing M
Mechanical Engineering M
Nutrition M
Occupational Therapy M
Osteopathic Medicine O
Physical Therapy D
Physician Assistant Studies M
Supply Chain Management M
Urban Design M

### NEW YORK LAW SCHOOL
Law M,D

### NEW YORK MEDICAL COLLEGE
Allopathic Medicine D
Biochemistry M,D
Biological and Biomedical Sciences—General M,D
Biostatistics M,D,O
Business Administration and Management—General M,D,O
Cell Biology M,D
Communication Disorders M,D,O
Emergency Management M,D,O
Environmental and Occupational Health M,D,O
Epidemiology M,D,O
Health Education M,D,O
Health Services Management and Hospital Administration M,D,O
Immunology M,D
Industrial Hygiene M,D,O
International Health M,D,O
Microbiology M,D
Molecular Biology M,D
Pathology M,D
Pharmacology M,D
Physical Therapy M,D,O
Physiology M,D
Psychology—General M,D,O
Public Health—General M,D,O

### NEW YORK SCHOOL OF INTERIOR DESIGN
Interior Design M
Lighting Design M
Sustainable Development M

### NEW YORK STUDIO SCHOOL OF DRAWING, PAINTING AND SCULPTURE
Art/Fine Arts M,O*

### NEW YORK THEOLOGICAL SEMINARY
Theology M,D

### NEW YORK UNIVERSITY
Accounting M,D
Acute Care/Critical Care Nursing M,D,O
Adult Nursing M,D,O
Advertising and Public Relations M
African Studies M,D,O
Allopathic Medicine M,D
American Studies M,D
Anthropology M,D
Applied Arts and Design—General M
Applied Economics M,D,O
Applied Physics M
Applied Psychology M,D,O
Applied Social Research M
Applied Statistics M
Archaeology M,D
Architectural History M
Archives/Archival Administration M,D,O
Art Education M,O
Art History M,D
Art Therapy M
Art/Fine Arts M,D,O

*M—masters degree; D—doctorate; O—other advanced degree; *—Close-Up and/or Display*

| | |
|---|---|
| Artificial Intelligence/Robotics | M |
| Arts Administration | M |
| Asian Studies | M,D |
| Bioinformatics | M |
| Biological and Biomedical Sciences—General | M,D |
| Biomedical Engineering | M,D |
| Biotechnology | M |
| Business Administration and Management—General | M,D,O |
| Business Education | M,O |
| Cancer Biology/Oncology | M,D |
| Chemical Engineering | M,D |
| Chemistry | M,D |
| Chinese | M,D,O |
| Civil Engineering | M,D |
| Classics | M,D,O |
| Clinical Research | M |
| Cognitive Sciences | M,D,O |
| Communication Disorders | M,D |
| Communication—General | M,D |
| Community Health | M,D |
| Comparative Literature | M,D |
| Computational Biology | D |
| Computer and Information Systems Security | M |
| Computer Engineering | M |
| Computer Science | M,D |
| Construction Management | M |
| Corporate and Organizational Communication | M |
| Counseling Psychology | M,D,O |
| Counselor Education | M,D,O |
| Cultural Studies | M,D,O |
| Dance | M,D,O |
| Data Science/Data Analytics | M |
| Demography and Population Studies | M,D |
| Dentistry | D |
| Developmental Biology | M,D |
| Developmental Psychology | M,D |
| Early Childhood Education | M |
| Economics | M,D,O |
| Education—General | M,D,O |
| Educational Leadership and Administration | M,D,O |
| Educational Media/Instructional Technology | M,D,O |
| Educational Policy | M,D |
| Educational Psychology | M,D |
| Electrical Engineering | M,D |
| Elementary Education | M |
| Engineering and Applied Sciences—General | M,D,O |
| English as a Second Language | M,D,O |
| English Education | M,D,O |
| English | M,D |
| Entrepreneurship | M |
| Environmental Education | M |
| Environmental Engineering | M |
| Environmental Sciences | M |
| Family Nurse Practitioner Studies | M,D,O |
| Film, Television, and Video Production | M |
| Film, Television, and Video Theory and Criticism | M,D |
| Finance and Banking | M,D |
| Financial Engineering | M |
| Food Science and Technology | M,D |
| Foreign Languages Education | M,D,O |
| Foundations and Philosophy of Education | M,D |
| French | M,D,O |
| Game Design and Development | M |
| Genetics | M,D |
| German | M,D |
| Gerontological Nursing | M,D,O |
| Health Promotion | M,D,O |
| Health Services Management and Hospital Administration | M,D,O |
| Higher Education | M,D |
| Historic Preservation | M |
| History | M,D,O |
| Hospitality Management | M,D |
| Human Development | M,D,O |
| Human Resources Development | M |
| Human Resources Management | M |
| Humanities | M,O |
| Immunology | M,D |
| Industrial and Organizational Psychology | M,D,O |
| Industrial/Management Engineering | M |
| Interdisciplinary Studies | M |
| International Affairs | M,D |
| International and Comparative Education | M,D,O |
| International Business | M,D |
| International Health | M,D |
| Internet and Interactive Multimedia | M |
| Investment Management | M |
| Italian | M,D,O |
| Japanese | M,D,O |
| Jewish Studies | M,D |
| Journalism | M,D,O |
| Kinesiology and Movement Studies | M,D,O |
| Latin American Studies | M |
| Law | M,D,O |
| Legal and Justice Studies | M,D |
| Linguistics | M,D |
| Management Information Systems | M,D |
| Management of Technology | M,D |
| Management Strategy and Policy | M,D |
| Manufacturing Engineering | M |
| Marketing | M,D |
| Mathematical and Computational Finance | M,D |
| Mathematics Education | M |
| Mathematics | M,D |
| Mechanical Engineering | M,D |
| Media Studies | M,D |
| Microbiology | M,D |
| Molecular Biology | M,D |
| Molecular Genetics | M,D |
| Multilingual and Multicultural Education | M,D,O |
| Museum Studies | M,O |
| Music Education | M,D,O |
| Music | M,D,O |
| Near and Middle Eastern Studies | M,D |
| Neurobiology | M,D |
| Neuroscience | D |
| Nonprofit Management | M,D,O |
| Nurse Midwifery | M,D,O |
| Nursing and Healthcare Administration | M,O |
| Nursing Education | M,O |
| Nursing Informatics | M,O |
| Nursing—General | M,D,O |
| Nutrition | M,D |
| Occupational Therapy | M,D |
| Oral and Dental Sciences | M,D,O |
| Organizational Behavior | M,D |
| Organizational Management | M,D |
| Pediatric Nursing | M,D,O |
| Philosophy | M,D |
| Physical Therapy | M,D,O |
| Physics | M,D |
| Plant Biology | M,D |
| Political Science | M,D |
| Portuguese | M,D |
| Project Management | M |
| Psychiatric Nursing | M,D,O |
| Psychoanalysis and Psychotherapy | M,D,O |
| Psychology—General | M,D,O |
| Public Administration | M,D,O |
| Public Health—General | M,D |
| Public History | M,D,O |
| Public Policy | M |
| Publishing | M |
| Reading Education | M |
| Real Estate | M |
| Rehabilitation Sciences | M,D |
| Religion | M,O |
| Risk Management | M |
| Romance Languages | M,D |
| Russian | M |
| Science Education | M,D,O |
| Secondary Education | M,D,O |
| Slavic Languages | M |
| Social Psychology | M,D,O |
| Social Sciences Education | M,D,O |
| Social Sciences | M,D |
| Social Work | M,D |
| Sociology | M,D |
| Software Engineering | O |
| Spanish | M,D,O |
| Special Education | M |
| Speech and Interpersonal Communication | M,D |
| Sports and Entertainment Law | M |
| Statistics | M,D |
| Student Affairs | M,D |
| Sustainable Development | M |
| Taxation | M,D,O |
| Theater | M,D,O |
| Therapies—Dance, Drama, and Music | M |
| Translation and Interpretation | M |
| Transportation and Highway Engineering | M,D |
| Transportation Management | M |
| Travel and Tourism | M |
| Urban and Regional Planning | M |
| Urban Studies | M |
| Western European Studies | M |
| Writing | M |

### NIAGARA UNIVERSITY

| | |
|---|---|
| Accounting | M |
| Applied Behavior Analysis | M,D,O |
| Business Administration and Management—General | M |
| Computer and Information Systems Security | M |
| Counseling Psychology | M,D,O |
| Counselor Education | M,O |
| Criminal Justice and Criminology | M |
| Early Childhood Education | M,O |
| Education—General | M,D,O |
| Educational Leadership and Administration | M,D,O |
| Educational Policy | M,D,O |
| Elementary Education | M,O |
| English as a Second Language | M,O |
| Finance and Banking | M |
| Forensic Sciences | M |
| Health Services Management and Hospital Administration | M |
| Human Resources Management | M |
| Interdisciplinary Studies | M |
| International Business | M |
| Management Strategy and Policy | M |
| Marketing | M |
| Middle School Education | M,O |
| Reading Education | M |
| School Psychology | M |
| Secondary Education | M,O |
| Special Education | M,O |
| Supply Chain Management | M |

### NICHOLLS STATE UNIVERSITY

| | |
|---|---|
| Business Administration and Management—General | M |
| Clinical Psychology | M,O |
| Counselor Education | M,O |
| Curriculum and Instruction | M |
| Education—General | M |
| Educational Leadership and Administration | M |
| Elementary Education | M |
| Environmental Biology | M |
| Family Nurse Practitioner Studies | M |
| Health Education | M |
| Marine Biology | M |
| Middle School Education | M |
| Nursing and Healthcare Administration | M |
| Nursing Education | M |
| Nursing—General | M |
| Psychiatric Nursing | M |
| School Psychology | M,O |
| Secondary Education | M |

### NICHOLS COLLEGE

| | |
|---|---|
| Business Administration and Management—General | M |
| Homeland Security | M |
| Organizational Management | M |

### NIPISSING UNIVERSITY

| | |
|---|---|
| Education—General | M,O |

### NORFOLK STATE UNIVERSITY

| | |
|---|---|
| Art/Fine Arts | M |
| Clinical Psychology | M |
| Communication—General | M |
| Computer Engineering | M |
| Computer Science | M |
| Criminal Justice and Criminology | M |
| Early Childhood Education | M |
| Education of Students with Severe/Multiple Disabilities | M |
| Education—General | M |
| Educational Leadership and Administration | M |
| Electrical Engineering | M |
| Materials Sciences | M |
| Media Studies | M |
| Music Education | M |
| Music | M |
| Optical Sciences | M |
| Psychology—General | M,D |
| Secondary Education | M |
| Social Psychology | M |
| Social Work | M,D |
| Special Education | M |
| Urban Education | M |
| Urban Studies | M |

### NORTH AMERICAN UNIVERSITY

| | |
|---|---|
| Educational Leadership and Administration | M |

### NORTH CAROLINA AGRICULTURAL AND TECHNICAL STATE UNIVERSITY

| | |
|---|---|
| Accounting | M |
| Adult Education | M,D |
| African-American Studies | M |
| Agricultural Economics and Agribusiness | M |
| Agricultural Education | M |
| Agricultural Sciences—General | M |
| Agronomy and Soil Sciences | M |
| Animal Sciences | M |
| Applied Mathematics | M |
| Bioengineering | M |
| Biological and Biomedical Sciences—General | M |
| Business Administration and Management—General | M |
| Business Education | M |
| Chemical Engineering | M |
| Chemistry | M |
| Child and Family Studies | M |
| Child Development | M |
| Civil Engineering | M |
| Clinical Psychology | M,D |
| Computational Sciences | M |
| Computer Engineering | M,D |
| Computer Science | M,D |
| Counselor Education | M,D |
| Early Childhood Education | M |
| Education—General | M,D |
| Educational Leadership and Administration | M,D |
| Educational Media/Instructional Technology | M |
| Electrical Engineering | M,D |
| Elementary Education | M |
| Energy and Power Engineering | M,D |
| Engineering and Applied Sciences—General | M,D |
| English Education | M |
| English | M |
| Environmental Design | M |
| Environmental Sciences | M |
| Family and Consumer Sciences-General | M |
| Food Science and Technology | M |
| Hospitality Management | M |
| Human Resources Management | M |
| Industrial/Management Engineering | M,D |
| Mathematics Education | M |
| Mathematics | M |
| Mechanical Engineering | M,D |
| Natural Resources | M |
| Nutrition | M |
| Optical Sciences | M,D |
| Physics | M |
| Plant Sciences | M |
| Reading Education | M |
| Rehabilitation Counseling | M,D |
| Science Education | M |
| Secondary Education | M |
| Social Work | M |
| Supply Chain Management | M |
| Systems Engineering | M,D |

### NORTH CAROLINA CENTRAL UNIVERSITY

| | |
|---|---|
| Biological and Biomedical Sciences—General | M |
| Business Administration and Management—General | M |
| Chemistry | M |
| Clinical Psychology | M |
| Communication Disorders | M |
| Counselor Education | M |
| Criminal Justice and Criminology | M |
| Education—General | M |
| Educational Leadership and Administration | M |
| Educational Media/Instructional Technology | M |
| English | M |
| Environmental Sciences | M |
| Geographic Information Systems | M |
| Geosciences | M |
| History | M |
| Information Studies | M |
| Law | D |
| Library Science | M |
| Mathematics | M |
| Music | M |
| Physical Education | M |
| Physics | M |
| Psychology—General | M |
| Public Administration | M |
| Recreation and Park Management | M |
| Social Work | M |
| Special Education | M |

### NORTH CAROLINA STATE UNIVERSITY

| | |
|---|---|
| Accounting | M |
| Adult Education | M,D |
| Aerospace/Aeronautical Engineering | M,D |
| Agricultural Economics and Agribusiness | M,D |
| Agricultural Engineering | M,D,O |
| Agricultural Sciences—General | M,D,O |
| Agronomy and Soil Sciences | M,D |
| Animal Sciences | M,D |
| Anthropology | M |
| Applied Arts and Design—General | M |
| Applied Psychology | D |
| Architecture | M |
| Atmospheric Sciences | M,D |
| Biochemistry | D |
| Bioengineering | M,D,O |
| Biological and Biomedical Sciences—General | M,D,O |
| Business Administration and Management—General | M |
| Business Education | M |
| Cell Biology | M,D |
| Chemical Engineering | M,D |
| Chemistry | M,D |
| Civil Engineering | M,D |
| Clothing and Textiles | M,D |
| Cognitive Sciences | D |
| Communication—General | M |
| Community College Education | M,D |
| Computer Art and Design | M,D |
| Computer Engineering | M,D |
| Computer Science | M,D |
| Counselor Education | M,D |
| Curriculum and Instruction | M,D |
| Developmental Psychology | D |
| Economics | M,D |
| Education—General | M,D,O |
| Educational Leadership and Administration | M,D |
| Educational Measurement and Evaluation | D |
| Educational Media/Instructional Technology | M,D |
| Electrical Engineering | M,D |
| Elementary Education | M |
| Engineering and Applied Sciences—General | M,D |
| English | M |
| Entomology | M,D |
| Entrepreneurship | M |
| Epidemiology | M,D |
| Ergonomics and Human Factors | D |
| Financial Engineering | M |
| Food Science and Technology | M,D |
| Forestry | M,D |
| French | M |
| Genomic Sciences | M,D |
| Geographic Information Systems | M,D |
| Geosciences | M,D |
| Graphic Design | M |
| History | M |
| Horticulture | M,D,O |
| Human Resources Development | M |
| Industrial and Organizational Psychology | D |
| Industrial Design | M |
| Industrial/Management Engineering | M,D |
| Infectious Diseases | M,D |
| International Affairs | M |
| Landscape Architecture | M |
| Management of Technology | M,D |
| Manufacturing Engineering | M |
| Marine Sciences | M,D |
| Materials Engineering | M,D |
| Materials Sciences | M,D |
| Mathematical and Computational Finance | M |
| Mathematics Education | M,D |
| Mathematics | M,D |
| Mechanical Engineering | M,D |
| Meteorology | M,D |
| Microbiology | M,D |
| Middle School Education | M |
| Natural Resources | M,D |
| Nonprofit Management | M,D,O |
| Nuclear Engineering | M,D |
| Nutrition | M,D |
| Oceanography | M,D |
| Operations Research | M,D |
| Pathology | M,D |
| Pharmacology | M,D |
| Physics | M,D |

| | |
|---|---|
| Plant Biology | M,D |
| Polymer Science and Engineering | M,D |
| Psychology—General | D |
| Public Administration | M,D |
| Public History | M |
| Recreation and Park Management | M,D |
| Rhetoric | M,D |
| School Psychology | D |
| Science Education | M,D |
| Social Psychology | M,D |
| Social Work | M |
| Sociology | D |
| Spanish | M |
| Special Education | M |
| Sports Management | M,D |
| Statistics | M,D |
| Supply Chain Management | M |
| Textile Sciences and Engineering | M,D |
| Travel and Tourism | M,D |
| Veterinary Sciences | M,D |
| Vocational and Technical Education | M,D,O |
| Writing | M |

## NORTH CENTRAL COLLEGE

| | |
|---|---|
| Business Administration and Management—General | M |
| Computer Science | M |
| Cultural Studies | M |
| Education—General | M |
| Educational Leadership and Administration | M |
| Finance and Banking | M |
| Human Resources Management | M |
| Liberal Studies | M |
| Management Strategy and Policy | M |

## NORTHCENTRAL UNIVERSITY

| | |
|---|---|
| Business Administration and Management—General | M,D,O |
| Computer and Information Systems Security | M,D,O |
| Computer Science | M,D,O |
| Data Science/Data Analytics | M,D,O |
| Education—General | M,D,O |
| Marriage and Family Therapy | M,D,O |
| Psychology—General | M,D,O |

## NORTH DAKOTA STATE UNIVERSITY

| | |
|---|---|
| Accounting | M |
| Agricultural Economics and Agribusiness | M |
| Agricultural Education | M |
| Agricultural Engineering | M,D |
| Agricultural Sciences—General | M,D |
| Agronomy and Soil Sciences | M,D |
| Animal Sciences | M,D |
| Anthropology | M |
| Applied Mathematics | M,D |
| Architecture | M |
| Athletic Training and Sports Medicine | M,D |
| Biochemistry | M,D |
| Bioinformatics | M,D |
| Biological and Biomedical Sciences—General | M,D |
| Biosystems Engineering | M,D |
| Botany | M,D |
| Business Administration and Management—General | M |
| Cell Biology | D |
| Chemistry | M,D |
| Child and Family Studies | M,D,O |
| Child Development | M |
| Civil Engineering | M,D |
| Clinical Psychology | M,D |
| Cognitive Sciences | M,D |
| Communication—General | M,D |
| Community Health | M |
| Computer Engineering | M,D |
| Computer Science | M,D,O |
| Conservation Biology | M,D |
| Construction Management | M,O |
| Consumer Economics | M,O |
| Counseling Psychology | M,D |
| Counselor Education | M,D |
| Criminal Justice and Criminology | M,D |
| Developmental Psychology | D |
| Education—General | M,D,O |
| Educational Leadership and Administration | M,O |
| Electrical Engineering | M,D |
| Engineering and Applied Sciences—General | M,D,O |
| English | M,D |
| Entomology | M,D |
| Environmental Engineering | M,D |
| Environmental Sciences | M,D |
| Exercise and Sports Science | M,D |
| Family and Consumer Sciences-General | M |
| Food Science and Technology | M,D |
| Genomic Sciences | M,D |
| Gerontology | D,O |
| Health Psychology | M,D |
| Higher Education | O |
| History | M,D |
| Horticulture | M,D |
| Industrial/Management Engineering | M,D |
| Infectious Diseases | M |
| Landscape Architecture | M |
| Logistics | M,D |
| Manufacturing Engineering | M,D |
| Mass Communication | M,D |
| Materials Sciences | M,D |
| Mathematics Education | D |
| Mathematics | M,D |
| Mechanical Engineering | M,D |
| Microbiology | M,D |
| Molecular Biology | D |
| Molecular Pathogenesis | M,D |
| Music Education | M,D |
| Music | M,D |
| Nanotechnology | M,D |
| Natural Resources | M,D |
| Nursing—General | D |
| Nutrition | M,D |
| Pathology | M,D |
| Pharmacy | M,D |
| Physics | M,D |
| Plant Pathology | M,D |
| Plant Sciences | M,D |
| Polymer Science and Engineering | M,D |
| Psychology—General | M,D |
| Public Health—General | M |
| Rhetoric | M,D |
| School Psychology | M,D |
| Science Education | D |
| Social Psychology | M,D |
| Sociology | M |
| Software Engineering | M,D,O |
| Speech and Interpersonal Communication | M,D |
| Statistics | M,D |
| Transportation and Highway Engineering | D |
| Transportation Management | M,D |
| Urban and Regional Planning | M |
| Urban Studies | M,D |
| Writing | M,D |
| Zoology | M,D |

## NORTHEASTERN ILLINOIS UNIVERSITY

| | |
|---|---|
| Accounting | M |
| Applied Mathematics | M |
| Biological and Biomedical Sciences—General | M |
| Business Administration and Management—General | M |
| Cell Biology | M |
| Chemistry | M |
| Clinical Psychology | M |
| Computer Science | M |
| Counselor Education | M |
| Early Childhood Education | M |
| Ecology | M |
| Education of the Gifted | M |
| Education—General | M |
| Educational Leadership and Administration | M |
| Elementary Education | M |
| English as a Second Language | M |
| English Education | M |
| English | M |
| Environmental Management and Policy | M,O |
| Exercise and Sports Science | M |
| Geographic Information Systems | M,O |
| Geography | M,O |
| Gerontology | M |
| History | M |
| Human Resources Development | M |
| Latin American Studies | M |
| Linguistics | M |
| Marriage and Family Therapy | M |
| Mathematics Education | M |
| Mathematics | M |
| Middle School Education | M |
| Molecular Biology | M |
| Music Education | M |
| Music | M |
| Political Science | M |
| Reading Education | M |
| Rehabilitation Counseling | M |
| Science Education | M |
| Secondary Education | M |
| Social Sciences Education | M |
| Social Work | M |
| Special Education | M |
| Speech and Interpersonal Communication | M |
| Urban Education | M |

## NORTHEASTERN SEMINARY AT ROBERTS WESLEYAN COLLEGE

| | |
|---|---|
| Theology | M,D |

## NORTHEASTERN STATE UNIVERSITY

| | |
|---|---|
| Accounting | M |
| American Indian/Native American Studies | M |
| Business Administration and Management—General | M |
| Communication Disorders | M |
| Communication—General | M |
| Criminal Justice and Criminology | M |
| Early Childhood Education | M |
| Education—General | M |
| Educational Leadership and Administration | M |
| Educational Media/Instructional Technology | M |
| English | M |
| Finance and Banking | M |
| Health Education | M |
| Kinesiology and Movement Studies | M |
| Mathematics Education | M |
| Natural Resources | M |
| Nursing and Healthcare Administration | M |
| Nursing Education | M |
| Occupational Therapy | M |
| Optometry | D |
| Psychology—General | M |
| Reading Education | M |
| Science Education | M |
| Special Education | M |

## NORTHEASTERN UNIVERSITY

| | |
|---|---|
| Accounting | M |
| Acute Care/Critical Care Nursing | M,D,O |
| Allied Health—General | M,D,O |
| Applied Arts and Design—General | M |
| Applied Behavior Analysis | M,D,O |
| Applied Mathematics | M,D |
| Architecture | M |
| Arts Administration | M |
| Bioengineering | M,D,O |
| Bioinformatics | M,D |
| Biological and Biomedical Sciences—General | M,D |
| Biotechnology | M,D |
| Business Administration and Management—General | M |
| Chemical Engineering | M,D,O |
| Chemistry | M,D |
| Civil Engineering | M,D,O |
| Communication Disorders | M,D,O |
| Computer and Information Systems Security | M,D,O |
| Computer Engineering | M,D,O |
| Computer Science | M,D |
| Corporate and Organizational Communication | M |
| Counseling Psychology | M,D,O |
| Criminal Justice and Criminology | M,D |
| Data Science/Data Analytics | M,D |
| Economic Development | M |
| Economics | M,D |
| Educational Leadership and Administration | M |
| Electrical Engineering | M,D,O |
| Elementary Education | M |
| Energy and Power Engineering | M,D,O |
| Engineering and Applied Sciences—General | M,D,O |
| Engineering Management | M,D,O |
| English | M,D |
| Entrepreneurship | M |
| Environmental Engineering | M,D,O |
| Environmental Management and Policy | M,D |
| Environmental Sciences | M,D |
| Exercise and Sports Science | M,D,O |
| Family Nurse Practitioner Studies | M,D,O |
| Finance and Banking | M |
| Geographic Information Systems | M |
| Gerontological Nursing | M,D,O |
| Health Informatics | M,D |
| Higher Education | M |
| History | M,D |
| Homeland Security | M,D |
| Human Services | M |
| Industrial/Management Engineering | M,D,O |
| Interdisciplinary Studies | M,D,O |
| International Affairs | M,D |
| International Business | M |
| Internet and Interactive Multimedia | M |
| Journalism | M |
| Law | M,D |
| Legal and Justice Studies | M,D |
| Management Information Systems | M,D,O |
| Marine Biology | M,D |
| Maternal and Child/Neonatal Nursing | M,D,O |
| Mathematics | M,D |
| Mechanical Engineering | M,D,O |
| Media Studies | M |
| Nonprofit Management | M |
| Nurse Anesthesia | M,D,O |
| Nursing and Healthcare Administration | M,D,O |
| Nursing—General | M,D,O |
| Nutrition | M |
| Operations Research | M,D,O |
| Pediatric Nursing | M,D,O |
| Pharmaceutical Sciences | M,D,O |
| Pharmacology | M,D,O |
| Pharmacy | M,D,O |
| Physics | M,D |
| Political Science | M,D |
| Project Management | M |
| Psychiatric Nursing | M,D,O |
| Psychology—General | M,D |
| Public Administration | M,D |
| Public Health—General | M,D,O |
| Public Policy | M,D,O |
| School Psychology | M,D,O |
| Sociology | M,D |
| Special Education | M |
| Sports Management | M |
| Systems Engineering | M,D,O |
| Taxation | M |
| Technical Communication | M |
| Telecommunications | M,D,O |
| Urban Studies | M,D |

## NORTHEAST OHIO MEDICAL UNIVERSITY

| | |
|---|---|
| Allopathic Medicine | D |
| Bioethics | M,D,O |
| Health Services Management and Hospital Administration | M,D,O |
| Humanities | M,D,O |
| Pharmaceutical Administration | M,D,O |
| Pharmaceutical Sciences | M,D,O |
| Pharmacy | D |
| Public Health—General | M,D,O |

## NORTHERN ARIZONA UNIVERSITY

| | |
|---|---|
| Allied Health—General | M,D,O |
| American Indian/Native American Studies | O |
| Anthropology | M |
| Applied Physics* | M,D |
| Applied Statistics | M,O |
| Athletic Training and Sports Medicine | M |
| Atmospheric Sciences | M,D,O |
| Bioengineering | M,D |
| Biological and Biomedical Sciences—General | M,D |
| Business Administration and Management—General | M,O |
| Chemistry | M |
| Civil Engineering | M |
| Communication Disorders | M |
| Communication—General | M,O |
| Community College Education | M,D,O |
| Computer Engineering | M,D |
| Computer Science | M,D |
| Counseling Psychology | M,D,O |
| Counselor Education | M,D,O |
| Criminal Justice and Criminology | M |
| Curriculum and Instruction | M,D |
| Early Childhood Education | M,D,O |
| Education—General | M,D,O |
| Educational Leadership and Administration | M,D,O |
| Educational Media/Instructional Technology | M,O |
| Educational Psychology | M,D,O |
| Electrical Engineering | M,D |
| Elementary Education | M,D |
| Engineering and Applied Sciences—General | M,D,O |
| English as a Second Language | M,D,O |
| English | M,D,O |
| Environmental Management and Policy | M,D,O |
| Environmental Sciences | M,D,O |
| Ethnic Studies | O |
| Family Nurse Practitioner Studies | M,D,O |
| Foreign Languages Education | M |
| Forestry | M,D |
| Foundations and Philosophy of Education | M,D,O |
| Gender Studies | O |
| Geographic Information Systems | M,O |
| Geography | M,O |
| Geology | M,D,O |
| Health Services Management and Hospital Administration | D |
| Higher Education | M,D,O |
| History | M |
| Human Development | O |
| International Business | M |
| Liberal Studies | M |
| Linguistics | M,D,O |
| Mathematics Education | M,O |
| Mathematics | M,O |
| Mechanical Engineering | M,D |
| Meteorology | M,D,O |
| Multilingual and Multicultural Education | M,O |
| Music | M,O |
| Nursing—General | M,D,O |
| Occupational Therapy | D |
| Physical Therapy | D |
| Physician Assistant Studies | M |
| Physics | M,D |
| Political Science | M,D,O |
| Psychology—General | M |
| Public Administration | M,D,O |
| Recreation and Park Management | M,O |
| Rhetoric | M,D,O |
| School Psychology | M,D,O |
| Science Education | M |
| Secondary Education | M,D,O |
| Sociology | M |
| Spanish | M |
| Special Education | M,O |
| Statistics | M,O |
| Student Affairs | M,D,O |
| Sustainable Development | M |
| Urban and Regional Planning | M,O |
| Vocational and Technical Education | M,O |
| Women's Studies | O |
| Writing | M,D,O |

## NORTHERN ILLINOIS UNIVERSITY

| | |
|---|---|
| Accounting | M |
| Adult Education | M,D |
| Anthropology | M |
| Art/Fine Arts | M |
| Biochemistry | M,D |
| Biological and Biomedical Sciences—General | M,D |
| Business Administration and Management—General | M |
| Chemistry | M,D |
| Child and Family Studies | M |
| Communication Disorders | M,D |
| Communication—General | M |
| Computer Science | M |
| Counselor Education | M,D |
| Curriculum and Instruction | M,D |
| Dance | M |
| Early Childhood Education | M |
| Economics | M,D |
| Education—General | M,D,O |
| Educational Leadership and Administration | M,D,O |
| Educational Media/Instructional Technology | M,D |
| Educational Psychology | M,D,O |
| Electrical Engineering | M |
| Elementary Education | M |
| Engineering and Applied Sciences—General | M |
| English | M,D |
| Foundations and Philosophy of Education | M,D,O |
| French | M |
| Geography | M,D |
| Geology | M,D |

*M—masters degree; D—doctorate; O—other advanced degree; *—Close-Up and/or Display*

| | |
|---|---|
| Higher Education | M,D |
| History | M,D |
| Industrial and Manufacturing Management | M |
| Industrial/Management Engineering | M |
| Law | D |
| Management Information Systems | M |
| Mathematics | M,D |
| Mechanical Engineering | M |
| Music | M,O |
| Nursing—General | M,O |
| Nutrition | M |
| Philosophy | M |
| Physical Education | M |
| Physical Therapy | M,D |
| Physics | M,D |
| Political Science | M,D |
| Psychology—General | M,D |
| Public Administration | M |
| Public Health—General | M |
| Romance Languages | M |
| Sociology | M |
| Spanish | M |
| Special Education | M |
| Statistics | M,D |
| Taxation | M |
| Theater | M |

**NORTHERN KENTUCKY UNIVERSITY**

| | |
|---|---|
| Accounting | M,O |
| Advertising and Public Relations | M,O |
| Allied Health—General | M |
| Business Administration and Management—General | M,O |
| Clinical Psychology | M |
| Communication—General | M,O |
| Computer and Information Systems Security | M,O |
| Computer Science | M,O |
| Counseling Psychology | M |
| Counselor Education | M |
| Cultural Studies | M,O |
| Education—General | M,D,O |
| Educational Leadership and Administration | M,D,O |
| English | M,O |
| Geographic Information Systems | M,O |
| Health Informatics | M,O |
| Health Psychology | M,O |
| Industrial and Organizational Psychology | M,O |
| Information Science | M,O |
| Law | D |
| Liberal Studies | M |
| Management of Technology | M |
| Marriage and Family Therapy | M,O |
| Media Studies | M,O |
| Nonprofit Management | M,O |
| Nursing—General | M,D,O |
| Organizational Management | M |
| Public Administration | M,O |
| Public History | M |
| Rhetoric | M,O |
| Social Work | M |
| Software Engineering | M,O |
| Special Education | M,O |
| Taxation | M,O |
| Writing | M,O |

**NORTHERN MICHIGAN UNIVERSITY**

| | |
|---|---|
| Applied Behavior Analysis | M |
| Biological and Biomedical Sciences—General | M |
| Business Administration and Management—General | M |
| Clinical Laboratory Sciences/Medical Technology | M |
| Curriculum and Instruction | M |
| Education—General | M |
| Educational Leadership and Administration | M |
| English as a Second Language | M,O |
| English | M,O |
| Exercise and Sports Science | M |
| Molecular Genetics | M |
| Nursing—General | D |
| Psychology—General | M |
| Reading Education | M |
| Science Education | M |
| Special Education | M |
| Theater | M,O |
| Writing | M,O |

**NORTHERN SEMINARY**

| | |
|---|---|
| Missions and Missiology | M,D |
| Pastoral Ministry and Counseling | M,D |
| Religion | M,D |
| Theology | M,D |

**NORTHERN STATE UNIVERSITY**

| | |
|---|---|
| Clinical Psychology | M |
| Counseling Psychology | M |
| Counselor Education | M |
| Curriculum and Instruction | M |
| Education—General | M |
| Educational Leadership and Administration | M |
| Educational Media/Instructional Technology | M |
| Finance and Banking | M |
| Music Education | M |
| Sports Management | M |

**NORTHERN VERMONT UNIVERSITY–JOHNSON**

| | |
|---|---|
| Addictions/Substance Abuse Counseling | M |
| Applied Behavior Analysis | M |
| Art/Fine Arts | M |
| Computer Art and Design | M |
| Counselor Education | M |
| Curriculum and Instruction | M |
| Education—General | M |
| Foundations and Philosophy of Education | M |
| Photography | M |
| School Psychology | M |
| Special Education | M |

**NORTHERN VERMONT UNIVERSITY–LYNDON**

| | |
|---|---|
| Counselor Education | M |
| Curriculum and Instruction | M |
| Education—General | M |
| Reading Education | M |
| Science Education | M |
| Special Education | M |

**NORTH GREENVILLE UNIVERSITY**

| | |
|---|---|
| Education—General | M,D |
| Finance and Banking | M,D |
| Human Resources Management | M,D |
| Pastoral Ministry and Counseling | M,D |

**NORTH PARK THEOLOGICAL SEMINARY**

| | |
|---|---|
| Pastoral Ministry and Counseling | M,O |
| Theology | M,D |

**NORTH PARK UNIVERSITY**

| | |
|---|---|
| Adult Nursing | M |
| Business Administration and Management—General | M |
| Education—General | M |
| Music | M |
| Nonprofit Management | M |
| Nursing and Healthcare Administration | M |
| Nursing—General | M |

**NORTHWESTERN COLLEGE**

| | |
|---|---|
| Early Childhood Education | M,O |
| Education—General | M,O |
| Educational Leadership and Administration | M,O |

**NORTHWESTERN HEALTH SCIENCES UNIVERSITY**

| | |
|---|---|
| Acupuncture and Oriental Medicine | M |
| Chiropractic | D |
| Nutrition | M |

**NORTHWESTERN OKLAHOMA STATE UNIVERSITY**

| | |
|---|---|
| Adult Education | M |
| American Studies | M |
| Counseling Psychology | M |
| Counselor Education | M |
| Curriculum and Instruction | M |
| Education—General | M |
| Educational Leadership and Administration | M |
| Elementary Education | M |
| Reading Education | M |
| Secondary Education | M |

**NORTHWESTERN POLYTECHNIC UNIVERSITY**

| | |
|---|---|
| Business Administration and Management—General | M,D |
| Computer Engineering | M,D |
| Computer Science | M,D |
| Electrical Engineering | M,D |
| Engineering and Applied Sciences—General | M,D |

**NORTHWESTERN STATE UNIVERSITY OF LOUISIANA**

| | |
|---|---|
| Adult Education | M |
| Art/Fine Arts | M |
| Clinical Psychology | M |
| Counselor Education | M,O |
| Curriculum and Instruction | M |
| Early Childhood Education | M |
| Education—General | M,O |
| Educational Leadership and Administration | M,O |
| Educational Media/Instructional Technology | M,O |
| Elementary Education | M,O |
| English | M |
| Health Education | M |
| Health Physics/Radiological Health | M |
| Homeland Security | M |
| Middle School Education | M |
| Music | M |
| Nursing—General | M |
| Psychology—General | M |
| Reading Education | M,O |
| Secondary Education | M,O |
| Special Education | M,O |
| Student Affairs | M |

**NORTHWESTERN UNIVERSITY**

| | |
|---|---|
| African Studies | O |
| African-American Studies | D |
| Allopathic Medicine | |
| American Studies | M |
| Anthropology | D |
| Applied Mathematics | M,D |
| Applied Physics | D |
| Art History | D |
| Art/Fine Arts | M |
| Artificial Intelligence/Robotics | M |
| Arts Administration | M |
| Astronomy | D |
| Biochemistry | D |
| Bioengineering | D |
| Biological and Biomedical Sciences—General | D |
| Biomedical Engineering | M,D |
| Biophysics | D |
| Biopsychology | D |
| Biostatistics | D |
| Biotechnology | M,D |
| Broadcast Journalism | M |
| Business Administration and Management—General | M |
| Cell Biology | D |
| Chemical Engineering | M,D |
| Chemistry | D |
| Civil Engineering | M,D |
| Clinical Laboratory Sciences/Medical Technology | M |
| Clinical Psychology | D |
| Clinical Research | M,O |
| Cognitive Sciences | D |
| Communication Disorders | M,D |
| Communication—General | M,D |
| Comparative Literature | M,D |
| Computer and Information Systems Security | M |
| Computer Engineering | M,D |
| Computer Science | M,D |
| Corporate and Organizational Communication | M,D |
| Data Science/Data Analytics | M |
| Developmental Biology | D |
| Economics | D |
| Education—General | M,D |
| Educational Leadership and Administration | M |
| Educational Media/Instructional Technology | M,D |
| Electrical Engineering | M,D |
| Electronic Commerce | M |
| Elementary Education | M |
| Engineering and Applied Sciences—General | M,D,O |
| Engineering Design | M |
| Engineering Management | M |
| English | M,D |
| Environmental Engineering | M,D |
| Epidemiology | D |
| Ethics | M |
| Film, Television, and Video Production | M,D |
| French | D,O |
| Gender Studies | O |
| Genetic Counseling | M |
| Geology | D |
| Geosciences | D |
| Geotechnical Engineering | M,D |
| German | D |
| Health Informatics | M,D |
| Health Services Management and Hospital Administration | M,D |
| Health Services Research | D |
| History | M,D |
| Human Development | D |
| Industrial/Management Engineering | M,D |
| Information Science | M |
| International Affairs | M,D,O |
| International Health | M |
| Internet and Interactive Multimedia | M |
| Italian | D,O |
| Journalism | M |
| Kinesiology and Movement Studies | D |
| Law | M,D |
| Liberal Studies | M |
| Linguistics | D |
| Management Information Systems | M |
| Management Strategy and Policy | M |
| Marketing | M |
| Marriage and Family Therapy | M |
| Materials Engineering | M,D,O |
| Materials Sciences | M,D,O |
| Mathematics | D |
| Mechanical Engineering | M,D |
| Mechanics | M,D |
| Media Studies | M,D |
| Medical Informatics | M,D |
| Molecular Biology | D |
| Music Education | M,D |
| Music | M,D |
| Neurobiology | M,D |
| Neuroscience | D |
| Organizational Behavior | M |
| Organizational Management | M |
| Philosophy | D |
| Physical Therapy | D |
| Physics | D |
| Physiology | M |
| Plant Biology | M,D |
| Political Science | D |
| Portuguese | D |
| Project Management | M |
| Psychology—General | D |
| Public Administration | M |
| Public Health—General | M |
| Public Policy | M,D |
| Publishing | M |
| Quality Management | M |
| Rehabilitation Sciences | D |
| Religion | M,D |
| Rhetoric | M,D |
| Secondary Education | M |
| Slavic Languages | D |
| Social Psychology | D |
| Sociology | D |
| Software Engineering | M |
| Spanish | D |
| Speech and Interpersonal Communication | M,D |
| Sports Management | M |
| Statistics | M,D |
| Structural Biology | D |
| Structural Engineering | M,D |
| Systems Biology | D |
| Taxation | M,D |
| Theater | M,D |
| Transportation and Highway Engineering | M,D |
| Writing | M |

**NORTHWEST MISSOURI STATE UNIVERSITY**

| | |
|---|---|
| Agricultural Economics and Agribusiness | M |
| Agricultural Education | M |
| Agricultural Sciences—General | M |
| Biological and Biomedical Sciences—General | M,O |
| Business Administration and Management—General | M |
| Business Analytics | M |
| Computer Science | M |
| Early Childhood Education | M,D,O |
| Education—General | M,D,O |
| Educational Leadership and Administration | M,D,O |
| Educational Media/Instructional Technology | M |
| Educational Policy | M,D,O |
| Elementary Education | M,D,O |
| English as a Second Language | M,D,O |
| English Education | M,O |
| English | M,O |
| Exercise and Sports Science | M |
| Geographic Information Systems | M,O |
| Health Education | M |
| Higher Education | M,D,O |
| Human Resources Management | M |
| Management Information Systems | M |
| Marketing | M |
| Mathematics Education | M,D,O |
| Mathematics | M,O |
| Middle School Education | M,D,O |
| Physical Education | M |
| Reading Education | M,D,O |
| Recreation and Park Management | M |
| Science Education | M,O |
| Social Sciences Education | M,O |
| Special Education | M,D,O |

**NORTHWEST NAZARENE UNIVERSITY**

| | |
|---|---|
| Addictions/Substance Abuse Counseling | M |
| Business Administration and Management—General | M |
| Clinical Psychology | M |
| Counselor Education | M |
| Curriculum and Instruction | M,D,O |
| Education—General | M,D,O |
| Educational Leadership and Administration | M,D,O |
| Marriage and Family Therapy | M |
| Missions and Missiology | M |
| Nursing and Healthcare Administration | M |
| Pastoral Ministry and Counseling | M |
| Religion | M |
| School Psychology | M |
| Social Work | M |
| Special Education | M,D,O |
| Theology | M |

**NORTHWEST UNIVERSITY**

| | |
|---|---|
| Business Administration and Management—General | M |
| Counseling Psychology | M,D |
| Cultural Studies | M |
| Education—General | M |
| International Business | M |
| Missions and Missiology | M |
| Organizational Management | M |
| Pastoral Ministry and Counseling | M |
| Project Management | M |
| Psychology—General | M,D |
| Theology | M |
| Urban and Regional Planning | M,D |

**NORTHWOOD UNIVERSITY, MICHIGAN CAMPUS**

| | |
|---|---|
| Business Administration and Management—General | M |

**NORWICH UNIVERSITY**

| | |
|---|---|
| Business Administration and Management—General | M |
| Civil Engineering | M |
| Computer and Information Systems Security | M |
| Conflict Resolution and Mediation/Peace Studies | M |
| Construction Management | M |
| Criminal Justice and Criminology | M |
| Emergency Management | M |
| Energy Management and Policy | M |
| Environmental Engineering | M |
| Finance and Banking | M |
| Geotechnical Engineering | M |
| History | M |
| Human Resources Management | M |
| International Affairs | M |
| International Business | M |
| International Development | M |
| Logistics | M |
| Management Strategy and Policy | M |
| Military and Defense Studies | M |
| Nonprofit Management | M |
| Nursing and Healthcare Administration | M |
| Nursing Education | M |
| Nursing—General | M |
| Organizational Management | M |
| Project Management | M |
| Public Administration | M |
| Public Policy | M |
| Structural Engineering | M |
| Supply Chain Management | M |

**NOTRE DAME COLLEGE (OH)**

| | |
|---|---|
| Computer Science | M,O |
| Homeland Security | M,O |
| Reading Education | M,O |
| Special Education | M,O |

**NOTRE DAME DE NAMUR UNIVERSITY**

| | |
|---|---|
| Art Therapy | M,D |
| Business Administration and Management—General | M |
| Clinical Psychology | M |
| Curriculum and Instruction | M |
| Education—General | M |
| Educational Leadership and Administration | M |
| Finance and Banking | M |

Marriage and Family Therapy M
Public Administration M
Special Education M

### NOTRE DAME OF MARYLAND UNIVERSITY

Business Administration and Management—General M
Communication—General M
Education—General M
Educational Leadership and Administration M,D
English as a Second Language M
Liberal Studies M
Nonprofit Management M
Pharmacy D

### NOTRE DAME SEMINARY

Theology M

### NOVA SOUTHEASTERN UNIVERSITY

Accounting M
Addictions/Substance Abuse Counseling M,D,O
Adult Nursing M,D
Allied Health—General M,D
Allopathic Medicine D
Anesthesiologist Assistant Studies M,D
Art/Fine Arts M,D,O
Bioinformatics M,D,O
Biological and Biomedical Sciences—General M,D
Business Administration and Management—General M
Business Analytics M
Business Education M
Clinical Psychology M,D,O
Communication Disorders M,D
Computer and Information Systems Security M,D
Computer Science M,D
Conflict Resolution and Mediation/Peace Studies M,D,O
Counseling Psychology M,D,O
Counselor Education M,D,O
Criminal Justice and Criminology M,D,O
Dentistry M,D
Distance Education Development M,D,O
Education—General M,D,O
Educational Media/Instructional Technology M,D,O
Emergency Management M,D,O
Entrepreneurship M
Experimental Psychology M,D,O
Family Nurse Practitioner Studies M,D
Finance and Banking M
Forensic Psychology M,D,O
Gerontological Nursing M,D
Health Education M,D,O
Health Informatics M,D,O
Health Law M,D
Human Resources Management M
Humanities M,D,O
Information Science M,D
Interdisciplinary Studies M,D,O
International Business M
Law M,D
Legal and Justice Studies M,D
Management Information Systems M,D
Management Strategy and Policy M
Marine Biology M,D
Marketing M
Marriage and Family Therapy M,D,O
Medical Informatics M,D,O
Nursing Education M,D
Nursing Informatics M,D
Nursing—General M,D
Nutrition M,D,O
Occupational Therapy M,D
Oceanography M,D
Optometry M,D
Osteopathic Medicine M,D,O
Pharmacy M,D
Physical Therapy M,D
Physician Assistant Studies M,D
Psychiatric Nursing M,D
Psychology—General M,D,O
Public Administration M
Public Health—General M,D,O
School Psychology M,D,O
Social Sciences M,D,O
Student Affairs M,D,O
Supply Chain Management M

### NSCAD UNIVERSITY

Applied Arts and Design—General M
Art/Fine Arts M

### NYACK COLLEGE

Business Administration and Management—General M
Counseling Psychology M
Counselor Education M
Elementary Education M
English as a Second Language M
Marriage and Family Therapy M
Missions and Missiology M,D
Organizational Management M
Pastoral Ministry and Counseling M,D
Religion M
Social Work M
Special Education M
Theology M,D

### OAKLAND CITY UNIVERSITY

Business Administration and Management—General M
Curriculum and Instruction M,D
Education—General M,D
Educational Leadership and Administration M,D
Elementary Education M,D
Management Strategy and Policy M
Organizational Management M,D
Pastoral Ministry and Counseling M,D
Secondary Education M,D
Theology M,D

### OAKLAND UNIVERSITY

Accounting M,O
Allied Health—General M,D,O
Applied Behavior Analysis M,O
Applied Mathematics M,D
Applied Statistics M
Biological and Biomedical Sciences—General M,D,O
Business Administration and Management—General M,O
Chemistry M,D
Computer Engineering M,D
Computer Science M,D
Counseling Psychology M,D,O
Early Childhood Education M,D,O
Economics M,O
Education—General M,D,O
Educational Leadership and Administration M,D,O
Electrical Engineering M,D
Elementary Education M,O
Engineering and Applied Sciences—General M,D,O
Engineering Management M
English as a Second Language M,O
English M
Entrepreneurship M,O
Environmental and Occupational Health M
Environmental Sciences M,D
Exercise and Sports Science M,O
Family Nurse Practitioner Studies M,O
Finance and Banking M,O
Gerontological Nursing M,O
Higher Education M,D,O
History M
Human Resources Management M,O
Industrial and Manufacturing Management M,O
International Business M,O
Liberal Studies M
Linguistics M,O
Management Information Systems M,D,O
Marketing M,O
Mathematics M
Mechanical Engineering M,D
Medical Physics M,D
Music Education M,D
Music M,D
Nonprofit Management M,O
Nurse Anesthesia M,O
Nursing—General M,D,O
Organizational Management M,D,O
Physics M,D
Public Administration M,O
Public Health—General M
Reading Education M,D,O
Secondary Education M,O
Software Engineering M,D
Special Education M,O
Statistics O
Systems Engineering M,D
Systems Science M,D

### OAKWOOD UNIVERSITY

Pastoral Ministry and Counseling M

### OBERLIN COLLEGE

Music M,O

### OBLATE SCHOOL OF THEOLOGY

African-American Studies M,D,O
Pastoral Ministry and Counseling M,D,O
Religion M,D,O
Theology M,D,O

### OCCIDENTAL COLLEGE

Biological and Biomedical Sciences—General M

### OGLALA LAKOTA COLLEGE

Business Administration and Management—General M
Educational Leadership and Administration M

### OHIO CHRISTIAN UNIVERSITY

Accounting M
Business Administration and Management—General M
Finance and Banking M
Health Services Management and Hospital Administration M
Human Resources Management M
Marketing M
Organizational Management M
Pastoral Ministry and Counseling M
Theology M

### OHIO DOMINICAN UNIVERSITY

Accounting M
Business Administration and Management—General M
Curriculum and Instruction M
Data Science/Data Analytics M
Education—General M
Educational Leadership and Administration M
Engineering Design M
English as a Second Language M
English M
Finance and Banking M
Health Services Management and Hospital Administration M
Management Strategy and Policy M
Physician Assistant Studies M
Risk Management M
Sports Management M

Theology M

### OHIO NORTHERN UNIVERSITY

Accounting M
Law M,D
Pharmacy D

### THE OHIO STATE UNIVERSITY

Accounting M
Actuarial Science M,D
Aerospace/Aeronautical Engineering M,D
African Studies M,D
African-American Studies M,D
Agricultural Economics and Agribusiness M,D
Agricultural Education M
Agricultural Engineering M,D
Agricultural Sciences—General M,D
Agronomy and Soil Sciences M,D
Allied Health—General M
Allopathic Medicine D
Anatomy M,D
Animal Sciences M,D
Anthropology M,D
Architecture M,D
Art Education M,D
Art History M,D
Art/Fine Arts M
Arts Administration M
Asian Languages M,D
Asian Studies M
Astronomy M,D
Atmospheric Sciences M,D
Biochemistry M,D
Bioengineering M,D
Biological and Biomedical Sciences—General M,D
Biomedical Engineering M,D
Biophysics M,D
Biostatistics M,D
Business Administration and Management—General M,D
Cell Biology M,D
Chemical Engineering M,D
Chemical Physics M,D
Chemistry M,D
Child and Family Studies M,D
Chinese M,D
Civil Engineering M,D
Classics M,D
Clinical Psychology D
Cognitive Sciences D
Communication Disorders M,D
Communication—General M,D
Computational Sciences M,D
Computer Art and Design M
Computer Engineering M,D
Computer Science M,D
Dance M,D
Dental Hygiene M,D
Dentistry M,D
Developmental Biology M,D
Developmental Psychology D
East European and Russian Studies M,D
Ecology M,D
Economics M,D
Education—General M,D,O
Educational Leadership and Administration M,D,O
Educational Policy M,D,O
Electrical Engineering M,D
Engineering and Applied Sciences—General M,D
English M,D
Entomology M,D
Environmental Management and Policy M,D
Environmental Sciences M,D
Evolutionary Biology M,D
Family and Consumer Sciences-General M,D
Finance and Banking M
Fish, Game, and Wildlife Management M,D
Food Science and Technology M,D
Forestry M,D
French M,D
Gender Studies M,D
Genetics M,D
Geodetic Sciences M,D
Geography M,D
Geology M,D
Geosciences M,D
German M,D
Health Services Management and Hospital Administration M,D
History M,D
Horticulture M,D
Human Development M,D
Human Resources Management M,D
Industrial and Labor Relations M,D
Industrial Design M
Industrial/Management Engineering M,D
Interdisciplinary Studies M,D
Interior Design M
Internet and Interactive Multimedia M
Italian M,D
Japanese M,D
Kinesiology and Movement Studies M,D
Landscape Architecture M,D
Latin American Studies M
Law M,D
Linguistics M,D
Logistics M
Management Information Systems M,D
Materials Engineering M,D
Materials Sciences M,D
Mathematics Education M,D
Mathematics M,D
Mechanical Engineering M,D
Metallurgical Engineering and Metallurgy M,D
Microbiology M,D
Molecular Biology M,D
Molecular Genetics M,D
Music M,D
Natural Resources M,D
Near and Middle Eastern Languages M,D
Neuroscience D
Nuclear Engineering M,D
Nursing—General M,D
Nutrition M,D
Occupational Therapy M
Operations Research M
Optical Sciences M,D
Optometry M,D
Oral and Dental Sciences M,D
Pharmaceutical Administration M,D
Pharmacology M,D
Pharmacy M,D
Philosophy M,D
Physical Education M,D
Physical Therapy D
Physics M,D
Plant Pathology M,D
Plant Sciences D
Political Science D
Portuguese M,D
Psychology—General D
Public Administration M,D
Public Affairs M,D
Public Health—General M,D
Public Policy M,D
Rehabilitation Sciences D
Rural Sociology M,D
Slavic Languages M,D
Social Psychology D
Social Sciences M,D
Social Work M,D
Sociology D
Spanish M,D
Special Education D
Statistics M,D
Systems Engineering M,D
Theater M,D
Urban and Regional Planning M,D
Veterinary Sciences M,D
Women's Studies M,D

### THE OHIO STATE UNIVERSITY AT LIMA

Social Work M

### THE OHIO STATE UNIVERSITY AT MANSFIELD

Education—General M
Social Work M

### THE OHIO STATE UNIVERSITY AT MARION

Education—General M

### THE OHIO STATE UNIVERSITY AT NEWARK

Education—General M
Social Work M

### OHIO UNIVERSITY

African Studies M
Applied Economics M
Art History M
Art/Fine Arts M
Asian Studies M
Astronomy M,D
Athletic Training and Sports Medicine M
Biochemistry M,D
Biological and Biomedical Sciences—General M,D
Biomedical Engineering M
Business Administration and Management—General M
Cell Biology M,D
Chemical Engineering M,D
Child and Family Studies M
Child Development M
Civil Engineering M,D
Clinical Psychology D
Communication Disorders M,D
Communication—General M,D
Comparative and Interdisciplinary Arts D
Computer Education M,D
Computer Science M,D
Construction Engineering M,D
Consumer Economics M
Corporate and Organizational Communication M,D
Counselor Education M,D
Curriculum and Instruction M,D
Ecology M,D
Economics M
Education—General M,D
Educational Leadership and Administration M,D
Educational Measurement and Evaluation M,D
Educational Media/Instructional Technology M,D
Electrical Engineering M,D
Engineering and Applied Sciences—General M,D
English M,D
Environmental Biology M,D
Environmental Engineering M,D
Environmental Management and Policy M,O
Evolutionary Biology M,D
Exercise and Sports Science M,D

*M—masters degree; D—doctorate; O—other advanced degree; *—Close-Up and/or Display*

| | |
|---|---|
| Experimental Psychology | D |
| Family Nurse Practitioner Studies | M,D |
| Film, Television, and Video Production | M |
| Film, Television, and Video Theory and Criticism | M |
| Finance and Banking | M |
| French | M |
| Geochemistry | M |
| Geography | M |
| Geology | M |
| Geotechnical Engineering | M,D |
| Graphic Design | M |
| Health Communication | M,D |
| Health Services Management and Hospital Administration | M |
| Higher Education | M,D |
| History | M,D |
| Industrial and Organizational Psychology | D |
| Industrial/Management Engineering | M,D |
| International Affairs | M |
| International Development | M |
| Internet and Interactive Multimedia | M |
| Journalism | M,D |
| Latin American Studies | M |
| Linguistics | M |
| Mathematics | M,D |
| Mechanical Engineering | M |
| Mechanics | M,D |
| Media Studies | M,D |
| Microbiology | M,D |
| Middle School Education | M,D |
| Molecular Biology | D |
| Music Education | M,O |
| Music | M,O |
| Neuroscience | M,D |
| Nursing and Healthcare Administration | M,D |
| Nursing Education | M,D |
| Nursing—General | M,D |
| Nutrition | M |
| Osteopathic Medicine | D |
| Philosophy | M |
| Photography | M |
| Physical Education | M |
| Physical Therapy | D |
| Physics | M,D |
| Physiology | M,D |
| Plant Biology | M,D |
| Political Science | M |
| Psychology—General | D |
| Public Administration | M,O |
| Public Health—General | M |
| Reading Education | M,D |
| Recreation and Park Management | M |
| Rehabilitation Counseling | M,D |
| Rhetoric | M,D |
| Secondary Education | M,D |
| Social Sciences | M |
| Social Work | M |
| Sociology | M |
| Spanish | M |
| Special Education | M,D |
| Speech and Interpersonal Communication | M,D |
| Sports Management | M |
| Structural Engineering | M,D |
| Student Affairs | M,D |
| Systems Engineering | M |
| Telecommunications | M |
| Theater | M |
| Therapies—Dance, Drama, and Music | M,O |
| Transportation and Highway Engineering | M,D |
| Water Resources Engineering | M,D |

**OHIO VALLEY UNIVERSITY**

| | |
|---|---|
| Curriculum and Instruction | M |
| Education—General | M |

**OHR HAMEIR THEOLOGICAL SEMINARY**

| | |
|---|---|
| Theology | |

**OKLAHOMA BAPTIST UNIVERSITY**

| | |
|---|---|
| Business Administration and Management—General | M |
| Energy Management and Policy | M |
| Marriage and Family Therapy | M |
| Nursing Education | M |
| Nursing—General | M |

**OKLAHOMA CHRISTIAN UNIVERSITY**

| | |
|---|---|
| Accounting | M |
| Business Administration and Management—General | M |
| Computer Engineering | M |
| Computer Science | M |
| Electrical Engineering | M |
| Engineering and Applied Sciences—General | M |
| Engineering Management | M |
| Finance and Banking | M |
| Health Services Management and Hospital Administration | M |
| Human Resources Management | M |
| International Business | M |
| Marketing | M |
| Mechanical Engineering | M |
| Nonprofit Management | M |
| Organizational Management | M |
| Project Management | M |
| Software Engineering | M |
| Theology | M |

**OKLAHOMA CITY UNIVERSITY**

| | |
|---|---|
| Applied Behavior Analysis | M |
| Business Administration and Management—General | M |
| Computer Science | M |
| Counselor Education | M |
| Criminal Justice and Criminology | M |
| Early Childhood Education | M |
| Elementary Education | M |
| Energy Management and Policy | M |
| English as a Second Language | M |
| Law | M,D |
| Music | M |
| Nursing Education | M,D |
| Nursing—General | M,D |
| Photography | M |
| Sociology | M |
| Writing | M |

**OKLAHOMA STATE UNIVERSITY**

| | |
|---|---|
| Accounting | M,D |
| Agricultural Economics and Agribusiness | M,D |
| Agricultural Education | M,D |
| Agricultural Engineering | M,D |
| Agricultural Sciences—General | M,D |
| Agronomy and Soil Sciences | M,D |
| Animal Sciences | M,D |
| Applied Arts and Design—General | M,D |
| Applied Mathematics | M,D |
| Art History | M |
| Aviation | M,D,O |
| Biochemistry | M,D |
| Bioengineering | M,D |
| Biological and Biomedical Sciences—General | M,D |
| Botany | M,D |
| Business Administration and Management—General | M,D |
| Chemical Engineering | M,D |
| Chemistry | M,D |
| Child and Family Studies | M,D |
| Civil Engineering | M,D |
| Clinical Psychology | M,D |
| Clothing and Textiles | M,D |
| Communication Disorders | M |
| Computer Engineering | M,D |
| Computer Science | M,D |
| Consumer Economics | M,D |
| Ecology | M,D |
| Economics | M,D |
| Education—General | M,D,O |
| Electrical Engineering | M,D |
| Emergency Management | M,D |
| Engineering and Applied Sciences—General | M,D |
| English | M,D |
| Entomology | M,D |
| Entrepreneurship | M,D |
| Environmental Engineering | M,D |
| Environmental Sciences | M,D,O |
| Evolutionary Biology | M,D |
| Family and Consumer Sciences-General | M,D |
| Finance and Banking | M,D |
| Fire Protection Engineering | M,D |
| Food Science and Technology | M,D |
| Forestry | M,D |
| Geography | M,D |
| Geology | M,D |
| Graphic Design | M |
| History | M,D |
| Horticulture | M,D |
| Hospitality Management | M,D |
| Industrial/Management Engineering | M,D |
| Information Science | M,D |
| International Affairs | M,D,O |
| International Business | M,D |
| Landscape Architecture | M,D |
| Management Information Systems | M,D |
| Marketing | M,D |
| Mass Communication | M |
| Materials Engineering | M,D |
| Materials Sciences | M,D |
| Mathematics | M,D |
| Mechanical Engineering | M,D |
| Microbiology | M,D |
| Molecular Biology | M,D |
| Molecular Genetics | M,D |
| Music Education | M |
| Music | M |
| Natural Resources | M,D |
| Nonprofit Management | M,D,O |
| Nutrition | M,D |
| Philosophy | M |
| Photonics | M,D |
| Physics | M,D |
| Plant Biology | M,D |
| Plant Pathology | M,D |
| Plant Sciences | M,D |
| Political Science | M,D |
| Psychology—General | M,D |
| Sociology | M,D |
| Statistics | M,D |
| Sustainability Management | M,D,O |
| Telecommunications Management | M,D,O |
| Veterinary Medicine | D |
| Veterinary Sciences | M,D |
| Writing | M,D |

**OKLAHOMA STATE UNIVERSITY CENTER FOR HEALTH SCIENCES**

| | |
|---|---|
| Biological and Biomedical Sciences—General | M,D |
| Forensic Sciences | M |
| Health Services Management and Hospital Administration | M |
| Osteopathic Medicine | D |
| Toxicology | M |

**OKLAHOMA WESLEYAN UNIVERSITY**

| | |
|---|---|
| Management Strategy and Policy | M |
| Nursing and Healthcare Administration | M |
| Nursing Education | M |
| Theology | M |

**OLD DOMINION UNIVERSITY**

| | |
|---|---|
| Accounting | M |
| Adult Nursing | M,D |
| Aerospace/Aeronautical Engineering | M,D |
| Allied Health—General | M,D |
| Analytical Chemistry | M,D |
| Applied Mathematics | M,D |
| Applied Psychology | D |
| Athletic Training and Sports Medicine | M |
| Biochemistry | M,D |
| Biological and Biomedical Sciences—General | M,D |
| Biomedical Engineering | M,D |
| Biostatistics | M,D |
| Business Administration and Management—General | M,D |
| Business Education | M,D |
| Chemistry | M,D |
| Civil Engineering | M,D |
| Clinical Psychology | D |
| Communication Disorders | M |
| Communication—General | M,O |
| Community College Education | M,D |
| Community Health | M |
| Computer Art and Design | M |
| Computer Engineering | M,D |
| Computer Science | M,D |
| Conflict Resolution and Mediation/Peace Studies | M,D |
| Counseling Psychology | M,D,O |
| Counselor Education | M,D,O |
| Criminal Justice and Criminology | M,D |
| Cultural Studies | M,D,O |
| Curriculum and Instruction | M,D |
| Dental Hygiene | M |
| Early Childhood Education | M,D |
| Ecology | D |
| Economics | M |
| Education—General | M,D,O |
| Educational Leadership and Administration | M,D,O |
| Educational Measurement and Evaluation | D |
| Educational Media/Instructional Technology | M,D,O |
| Educational Psychology | D |
| Electrical Engineering | M,D |
| Elementary Education | M,O |
| Engineering and Applied Sciences—General | M,D |
| Engineering Management | M,D |
| English as a Second Language | M |
| English | M,D |
| Entrepreneurship | M,O |
| Environmental and Occupational Health | M |
| Environmental Engineering | M,D |
| Environmental Sciences | M,D |
| Ergonomics and Human Factors | D |
| Exercise and Sports Science | M |
| Family Nurse Practitioner Studies | M |
| Finance and Banking | D |
| Gender Studies | M,O |
| Geotechnical Engineering | M |
| Gerontological Nursing | M,D |
| Health Education | M,D |
| Health Promotion | M,D |
| Health Services Research | D |
| Higher Education | M,D,O |
| History | M |
| Humanities | M,O |
| Hydraulics | M |
| Immunology | M |
| Industrial and Organizational Psychology | D |
| Industrial Hygiene | M |
| Information Science | D |
| Inorganic Chemistry | M,D |
| International Affairs | M,D |
| International Business | M |
| International Development | M,D |
| Kinesiology and Movement Studies | M,D |
| Library Science | M,O |
| Linguistics | M |
| Management Information Systems | M,D |
| Marketing | M,D |
| Maternal and Child/Neonatal Nursing | M,D |
| Mathematics | M,D |
| Mechanical Engineering | M,D |
| Media Studies | M,O |
| Microbiology | M |
| Middle School Education | M,O |
| Modeling and Simulation | M,D |
| Music Education | M |
| Music | M |
| Nurse Anesthesia | D |
| Nursing and Healthcare Administration | M,D |
| Nursing Education | M,D |
| Nursing—General | D |
| Oceanography | M,D |
| Organic Chemistry | M,D |
| Pediatric Nursing | M,D |
| Philosophy | M,O |
| Physical Chemistry | M,D |
| Physical Education | M,D |
| Physical Therapy | D |
| Physics | M,D |
| Psychology—General | M,D |
| Public Administration | M,D |
| Public Health—General | M |
| Public Policy | D |
| Reading Education | M,D |
| Recreation and Park Management | M |
| Rehabilitation Sciences | D |
| Rhetoric | M |
| School Psychology | M,D,O |
| Secondary Education | M |
| Sociology | M |
| Special Education | M,D |
| Speech and Interpersonal Communication | M |
| Sports Management | M |
| Statistics | M,D |
| Structural Engineering | M |
| Supply Chain Management | M |
| Systems Engineering | M,D |
| Transportation and Highway Engineering | M |
| Travel and Tourism | M |
| Vocational and Technical Education | M,D |
| Water Resources | M |
| Women's Studies | M |
| Writing | M |

**OLIVET COLLEGE**

| | |
|---|---|
| Insurance | M |

**OLIVET NAZARENE UNIVERSITY**

| | |
|---|---|
| Business Administration and Management—General | M |
| Curriculum and Instruction | M |
| Education—General | M |
| Educational Leadership and Administration | M |
| Elementary Education | M |
| Family Nurse Practitioner Studies | M |
| Library Science | M |
| Nursing—General | M |
| Organizational Management | M |
| Pastoral Ministry and Counseling | M |
| Reading Education | M |
| Religion | M |
| Secondary Education | M |
| Theology | M |

**OMEGA GRADUATE SCHOOL**

| | |
|---|---|
| Child and Family Studies | M,D |
| Organizational Management | M,D |
| Religion | M,D |
| Sociology | M,D |

**OPEN UNIVERSITY**

| | |
|---|---|
| Business Administration and Management—General | M |
| Education—General | M |
| Engineering and Applied Sciences—General | M |
| History | M |
| Music | M |
| Philosophy | M |

**ORAL ROBERTS UNIVERSITY**

| | |
|---|---|
| Accounting | M |
| Addictions/Substance Abuse Counseling | M,D |
| Business Administration and Management—General | M |
| Curriculum and Instruction | M,D |
| Education—General | M,D |
| Educational Leadership and Administration | M,D |
| Entrepreneurship | M |
| Finance and Banking | M |
| Higher Education | M,D |
| International Business | M |
| Marketing | M |
| Marriage and Family Therapy | M,D |
| Missions and Missiology | M,D |
| Near and Middle Eastern Languages | M,D |
| Nonprofit Management | M |
| Pastoral Ministry and Counseling | M,D |
| Religious Education | M,D |
| Theology | M,D |

**OREGON COLLEGE OF ORIENTAL MEDICINE**

| | |
|---|---|
| Acupuncture and Oriental Medicine | M,D |

**OREGON HEALTH & SCIENCE UNIVERSITY**

| | |
|---|---|
| Allopathic Medicine | D |
| Biochemistry | M,D |
| Bioinformatics | M,D,O |
| Biological and Biomedical Sciences—General | M,D,O |
| Biomedical Engineering | M,D |
| Biopsychology | D |
| Cancer Biology/Oncology | D |
| Cell Biology | D |
| Clinical Research | M,O |
| Community Health Nursing | M,O |
| Computational Biology | M,D,O |
| Computer Engineering | M,D |
| Computer Science | M,D |
| Dentistry | D,O |
| Developmental Biology | D |
| Electrical Engineering | M,D |
| Environmental Engineering | M,D |
| Environmental Sciences | M,D |
| Family Nurse Practitioner Studies | M |
| Genetics | D |
| Gerontological Nursing | M |
| Gerontology | M,O |
| Health Informatics | M,D,O |
| Health Services Management and Hospital Administration | M,O |
| Immunology | D |
| Medical Informatics | M,D,O |
| Microbiology | D |
| Molecular Biology | M,D |
| Molecular Medicine | M,D |
| Neuroscience | D |
| Nurse Anesthesia | M |
| Nurse Midwifery | M |
| Nursing and Healthcare Administration | M |
| Nursing Education | M,O |
| Nursing—General | M,D,O |
| Nutrition | M,O |
| Oral and Dental Sciences | M,D,O |
| Pediatric Nursing | M |
| Pharmacology | D |
| Physician Assistant Studies | M |
| Physiology | D |
| Psychiatric Nursing | M |

**OREGON INSTITUTE OF TECHNOLOGY**
- Manufacturing Engineering	M

**OREGON STATE UNIVERSITY**
- Accounting	M,D
- Actuarial Science	M,D
- Adult Education	M,D
- Agricultural Education	M,D
- Agricultural Engineering	M,D
- Agronomy and Soil Sciences	M,D
- Allied Health—General	M,D
- Analytical Chemistry	M,D
- Animal Sciences	M
- Anthropology	M
- Applied Economics	M,D
- Applied Mathematics	M,D
- Aquaculture	M,D
- Artificial Intelligence/Robotics	M,D
- Athletic Training and Sports Medicine	M
- Atmospheric Sciences	M,D
- Biochemistry	M,D
- Bioengineering	M,D
- Bioinformatics	D
- Biological and Biomedical Sciences—General	M,D
- Biophysics	M,D
- Biostatistics	M,D
- Biotechnology	M,D
- Botany	M,D
- Business Administration and Management—General	M,D
- Cell Biology	M,D
- Chemical Engineering	M,D
- Chemistry	M,D
- Child and Family Studies	M,D
- Civil Engineering	M,D
- Clinical Psychology	M,D
- Cognitive Sciences	M,D
- Computational Biology	M,D
- Computational Sciences	M,D
- Computer Engineering	M,D
- Computer Science	M,D
- Conservation Biology	M,D
- Construction Engineering	M,D
- Counselor Education	M,D
- Data Science/Data Analytics	M
- Ecology	M,D
- Education—General	M,D
- Educational Leadership and Administration	M,D
- Educational Policy	M,D
- Electrical Engineering	M,D
- Elementary Education	M
- Engineering and Applied Sciences—General	M,D
- Engineering Management	M,D
- English Education	M
- English	M
- Environmental and Occupational Health	M,D
- Environmental Biology	M,D
- Environmental Education	M,D
- Environmental Engineering	M,D
- Environmental Management and Policy	M,D
- Environmental Sciences	M,D
- Epidemiology	M,D
- Ethics	M
- Finance and Banking	M,D
- Fish, Game, and Wildlife Management	M,D
- Food Science and Technology	M,D
- Forestry	M,D
- Gender Studies	M,D
- Genetics	M,D
- Genomic Sciences	M,D
- Geochemistry	M,D
- Geographic Information Systems	M
- Geography	M,D
- Geology	M,D
- Geophysics	M,D
- Geotechnical Engineering	M,D
- Health Physics/Radiological Health	M,D
- Health Promotion	M,D
- Health Psychology	M,D
- Health Services Management and Hospital Administration	M,D
- Higher Education	M,D
- Hispanic Studies	M
- History of Science and Technology	M,D
- Horticulture	M,D
- Human Development	M,D
- Hydrogeology	M,D
- Hydrology	M,D
- Immunology	M,D
- Industrial/Management Engineering	M,D
- Interdisciplinary Studies	M
- International Health	M,D
- Kinesiology and Movement Studies	M,D
- Limnology	M,D
- Manufacturing Engineering	M,D
- Marine Affairs	M
- Marine Sciences	M
- Materials Sciences	M,D
- Mathematical and Computational Finance	M,D
- Mathematics Education	M,D
- Mathematics	M,D
- Mechanical Engineering	M,D
- Medical Imaging	M,D
- Medical Physics	M,D
- Microbiology	M,D
- Molecular Biology	M,D
- Molecular Toxicology	M,D
- Music Education	M
- Natural Resources	M
- Nuclear Engineering	M,D
- Nutrition	M,D
- Ocean Engineering	M,D
- Oceanography	M,D
- Parasitology	M,D
- Pharmaceutical Sciences	M,D
- Pharmacy	D
- Physics	M,D
- Physiology	M,D
- Plant Molecular Biology	D
- Plant Pathology	M,D
- Plant Physiology	M,D
- Psychology—General	M,D
- Public Health—General	M,D
- Public Policy	M,D
- Range Science	M,D
- Rhetoric	M
- School Psychology	M,D
- Science Education	M,D
- Social Sciences Education	M,D
- Social Sciences	M,D
- Statistics	M,D
- Structural Engineering	M,D
- Student Affairs	M
- Sustainability Management	M,D
- Systems Biology	M,D
- Systems Engineering	M,D
- Toxicology	M,D
- Transportation and Highway Engineering	M,D
- Veterinary Medicine	D
- Virology	M,D
- Viticulture and Enology	M,D
- Water Resources Engineering	M,D
- Water Resources	M,D
- Women's Studies	M,D
- Writing	M

**OREGON STATE UNIVERSITY–CASCADES**
- Education—General	M
- School Psychology	M
- Social Psychology	M

**OTIS COLLEGE OF ART AND DESIGN**
- Art/Fine Arts	M
- Graphic Design	M
- Photography	M
- Writing	M

**OTTAWA UNIVERSITY**
- Art Therapy	M
- Business Administration and Management—General	M
- Counseling Psychology	M
- Counselor Education	M
- Curriculum and Instruction	M
- Early Childhood Education	M
- Education—General	M
- Educational Leadership and Administration	M
- Educational Media/Instructional Technology	M
- Elementary Education	M
- Finance and Banking	M
- Human Resources Development	M
- Human Resources Management	M
- Marketing	M
- Marriage and Family Therapy	M
- Pastoral Ministry and Counseling	M
- School Psychology	M
- Special Education	M

**OTTERBEIN UNIVERSITY**
- Business Administration and Management—General	M
- Education—General	M
- Family Nurse Practitioner Studies	M,D,O
- Nurse Anesthesia	M,D,O
- Nursing and Healthcare Administration	M,D,O
- Nursing Education	M,D,O
- Nursing—General	M,D,O

**OUR LADY OF THE LAKE UNIVERSITY**
- Accounting	M
- Business Administration and Management—General	M
- Communication Disorders	M
- Computer and Information Systems Security	M
- Counseling Psychology	D
- Counselor Education	M
- Curriculum and Instruction	M
- English	M
- Finance and Banking	M
- Health Services Management and Hospital Administration	M
- Management Information Systems	M
- Marriage and Family Therapy	M
- Nonprofit Management	M
- Organizational Management	M,D
- Psychology—General	M
- School Psychology	M
- Science Education	M
- Social Work	M,D
- Sociology	M
- Writing	M

**PACE UNIVERSITY**
- Accounting	M,O
- Addictions/Substance Abuse Counseling	M,D
- Biochemistry	M
- Biological and Biomedical Sciences—General	M,O
- Business Administration and Management—General	M,D,O
- Chemistry	M,O
- Clinical Psychology	M,D
- Communication Disorders	M
- Communication—General	M
- Computer and Information Systems Security	M,D,O
- Computer Science	M,D,O
- Counseling Psychology	M,D
- Developmental Psychology	M,D
- Early Childhood Education	M,O
- Economics	O
- Education—General	M,O
- Educational Media/Instructional Technology	M,O
- Electronic Commerce	O
- Elementary Education	M,O
- Emergency Management	M
- English	M,O
- Entrepreneurship	M
- Environmental Law	M,D
- Environmental Management and Policy	M
- Environmental Sciences	M
- Family Nurse Practitioner Studies	M,D,O
- Finance and Banking	M,D,O
- Foreign Languages Education	M,O
- Forensic Sciences	M
- Geosciences	M,O
- Health Services Management and Hospital Administration	M
- Homeland Security	M
- Human Resources Management	M
- Information Science	M,D,O
- International Business	M,O
- International Economics	O
- Internet and Interactive Multimedia	M
- Investment Management	M,O
- Law	M,D
- Legal and Justice Studies	M,D
- Management Information Systems	M,D,O
- Management Strategy and Policy	M
- Marketing	M,D,O
- Mathematics	M,O
- Media Studies	M
- Molecular Biology	M
- Nonprofit Management	M
- Nursing and Healthcare Administration	M,D,O
- Nursing—General	M,D,O
- Physician Assistant Studies	M
- Physics	M,O
- Psychology—General	M
- Public Administration	M
- Publishing	M,O
- Reading Education	M,O
- Risk Management	M
- School Psychology	M,D
- Social Sciences Education	M,O
- Software Engineering	M,D,O
- Special Education	M,O
- Taxation	M
- Telecommunications	M,D,O
- Theater	M

**PACIFICA GRADUATE INSTITUTE**
- Clinical Psychology	M,D
- Counseling Psychology	M,D
- Psychology—General	M,D

**PACIFIC COLLEGE OF ORIENTAL MEDICINE**
- Acupuncture and Oriental Medicine	M,D

**PACIFIC COLLEGE OF ORIENTAL MEDICINE–CHICAGO**
- Acupuncture and Oriental Medicine	M

**PACIFIC COLLEGE OF ORIENTAL MEDICINE-NEW YORK**
- Acupuncture and Oriental Medicine	M

**PACIFIC LUTHERAN UNIVERSITY**
- Accounting	M
- Business Administration and Management—General	M
- Curriculum and Instruction	M
- Education—General	M
- Family Nurse Practitioner Studies	D
- Finance and Banking	M
- Marketing Research	M
- Marriage and Family Therapy	M
- Nursing—General	M,D
- Writing	M

**PACIFIC NORTHWEST COLLEGE OF ART**
- Applied Arts and Design—General	M
- Art/Fine Arts	M
- Cultural Studies	M

**PACIFIC NORTHWEST UNIVERSITY OF HEALTH SCIENCES**
- Osteopathic Medicine	D

**PACIFIC OAKS COLLEGE**
- Early Childhood Education	M
- Education—General	M
- Human Development	M
- Marriage and Family Therapy	M
- Special Education	M

**PACIFIC RIM CHRISTIAN UNIVERSITY**
- Pastoral Ministry and Counseling	M

**PACIFIC SCHOOL OF RELIGION**
- Religion	M,D,O
- Theology	M,D,O

**PACIFIC STATES UNIVERSITY**
- Accounting	M,O
- Business Administration and Management—General	M,O
- Computer Science	M
- Finance and Banking	M,O
- International Business	M,O
- Management Information Systems	M,O
- Management of Technology	M,O
- Project Management	M,O
- Real Estate	M,O

**PACIFIC UNION COLLEGE**
- Education—General	M
- Elementary Education	M
- Secondary Education	M

**PACIFIC UNIVERSITY**
- Athletic Training and Sports Medicine	M,D
- Business Administration and Management—General	M
- Clinical Psychology	M,D
- Communication Disorders	M,D
- Early Childhood Education	M
- Education of the Gifted	M
- Education—General	M
- Elementary Education	M
- English as a Second Language	M
- Finance and Banking	M
- Health Services Management and Hospital Administration	M
- Middle School Education	M
- Occupational Therapy	D
- Optometry	M,D
- Pharmacy	D
- Physical Therapy	M,D
- Physician Assistant Studies	M
- Psychology—General	M,D
- Science Education	M
- Secondary Education	M
- Social Work	M
- Special Education	M
- Vision Sciences	M,D
- Writing	M

**PALM BEACH ATLANTIC UNIVERSITY**
- Addictions/Substance Abuse Counseling	M
- Business Administration and Management—General	M
- Counseling Psychology	M
- Counselor Education	M
- Education—General	M
- Family Nurse Practitioner Studies	M,D
- Marriage and Family Therapy	M
- Nursing and Healthcare Administration	M,D
- Nursing—General	M,D
- Organizational Management	M
- Pharmacy	D
- Religious Education	M
- Theology	M

**PALMER COLLEGE OF CHIROPRACTIC**
- Anatomy	M
- Chiropractic	D
- Clinical Research	M

**PALO ALTO UNIVERSITY**
- Biopsychology	D
- Clinical Psychology	M,D
- Counseling Psychology	M
- Marriage and Family Therapy	M
- Psychology—General	M,D

**PARIS COLLEGE OF ART**
- Art/Fine Arts	M
- Interior Design	M
- Media Studies	M
- Photography	M
- Textile Design	M

**PARKER UNIVERSITY**
- Chiropractic	D

**PARK UNIVERSITY**
- Business Administration and Management—General	M,O
- Curriculum and Instruction	M,O
- Education—General	M,O
- Educational Leadership and Administration	M,O
- Emergency Management	M,O
- Finance and Banking	M,O
- Health Services Management and Hospital Administration	M,O
- International Business	M,O
- International Health	M,O
- Management Information Systems	M,O
- Music	M,O
- Nonprofit Management	M,O
- Public Administration	M,O
- Public Affairs	M,O
- Reading Education	M,O
- Social Work	M,O
- Writing	M,O

**PAYNE THEOLOGICAL SEMINARY**
- Theology	M

**PEIRCE COLLEGE**
- Organizational Management	M

**PENN STATE ERIE, THE BEHREND COLLEGE**
- Accounting	M
- Applied Psychology	M
- Business Administration and Management—General	M
- Clinical Psychology	M
- Industrial and Manufacturing Management	M
- Quality Management	M

**PENN STATE GREAT VALLEY**
- Business Administration and Management—General	M,O
- Computer and Information Systems Security	M,O
- Data Science/Data Analytics	M,O
- Engineering and Applied Sciences—General	M,O
- Engineering Management	M,O
- Entrepreneurship	M,O
- Finance and Banking	M,O

*M—masters degree; D—doctorate; O—other advanced degree; *—Close-Up and/or Display*

| | |
|---|---|
| Health Services Management and Hospital Administration | M,O |
| Human Resources Development | M,O |
| Human Resources Management | M,O |
| Information Science | M,O |
| Software Engineering | M,O |
| Sustainability Management | M,O |
| Systems Engineering | M,O |

### PENN STATE HARRISBURG

| | |
|---|---|
| Accounting | M,O |
| Adult Education | M,D,O |
| American Studies | M,D,O |
| Applied Behavior Analysis | M,D,O |
| Applied Psychology | M,D,O |
| Business Administration and Management—General | M,O |
| Civil Engineering | M,O |
| Clinical Psychology | M,D,O |
| Communication—General | M,D,O |
| Computer Science | M,O |
| Criminal Justice and Criminology | M,D,O |
| Curriculum and Instruction | M,D,O |
| Developmental Education | M,D,O |
| Education—General | M,D,O |
| Electrical Engineering | M,O |
| Engineering and Applied Sciences—General | M,O |
| Engineering Management | M,O |
| English as a Second Language | M,D,O |
| Environmental Engineering | M,O |
| Environmental Sciences | M,O |
| Finance and Banking | M,D,O |
| Folklore | M,D,O |
| Health Education | M,D,O |
| Health Psychology | M,D,O |
| Health Services Management and Hospital Administration | M,D,O |
| Historic Preservation | M,D,O |
| Homeland Security | M,D,O |
| Human Resources Management | M,D,O |
| Humanities | M,D,O |
| Management Information Systems | M,O |
| Mechanical Engineering | M,O |
| Museum Studies | M,D,O |
| Nonprofit Management | M,D,O |
| Psychology—General | M,D,O |
| Public Administration | M,D,O |
| Public Affairs | M,D,O |
| Reading Education | M,D,O |
| Social Psychology | M,D,O |
| Structural Engineering | M,O |
| Supply Chain Management | M,O |

### PENN STATE HERSHEY MEDICAL CENTER

| | |
|---|---|
| Allopathic Medicine | M,D |
| Anatomy | M,D |
| Biochemistry | M,D |
| Bioinformatics | M,D |
| Biological and Biomedical Sciences—General | M,D |
| Biostatistics | D |
| Cell Biology | D |
| Developmental Biology | D |
| Genomic Sciences | M,D |
| Health Services Research | M |
| Immunology | M,D |
| Molecular Genetics | M,D |
| Molecular Medicine | D |
| Molecular Toxicology | D |
| Neurobiology | D |
| Neuroscience | M,D |
| Public Health—General | M,D |
| Veterinary Sciences | M |
| Virology | M,D |

### PENN STATE UNIVERSITY–DICKINSON LAW

| | |
|---|---|
| Law | M,D |

### PENN STATE UNIVERSITY PARK

| | |
|---|---|
| Accounting | M,D |
| Acoustics | M,D |
| Adult Education | M,D,O |
| Aerospace/Aeronautical Engineering | M,D |
| Agricultural Economics and Agribusiness | M,D,O |
| Agricultural Education | M,D,O |
| Agricultural Engineering | M,D |
| Agricultural Sciences—General | M,D,O |
| Agronomy and Soil Sciences | M,D |
| Animal Sciences | M,D |
| Anthropology | M,D |
| Applied Statistics | M,D |
| Architectural Engineering | M,D |
| Architecture | M,D |
| Art Education | M,D,O |
| Art History | M,D |
| Art/Fine Arts | M,D,O |
| Astronomy | M,D |
| Astrophysics | M,D |
| Biochemistry | M,D |
| Bioengineering | M,D |
| Biological and Biomedical Sciences—General | M,D |
| Biopsychology | M,D |
| Biotechnology | M,D |
| Business Administration and Management—General | M,D |
| Cell Biology | M,D |
| Chemical Engineering | M,D |
| Chemistry | M,D |
| Child and Family Studies | M,D |
| Civil Engineering | M,D |
| Communication Disorders | M,D,O |
| Communication—General | M,D |
| Comparative Literature | M,D |
| Computer Engineering | M,D |
| Computer Science | M,D* |
| Counselor Education | M,D,O |
| Criminal Justice and Criminology | M,D |
| Curriculum and Instruction | M,D,O |
| Ecology | M,D |
| Economics | M,D |
| Education—General | M,D,O |
| Educational Leadership and Administration | M,D,O |
| Educational Media/Instructional Technology | M,D,O |
| Educational Policy | M,D,O |
| Educational Psychology | M,D,O |
| Electrical Engineering | M,D |
| Engineering and Applied Sciences—General | M,D |
| Engineering Design | M |
| English as a Second Language | M,D |
| English | M,D |
| Entomology | M,D |
| Entrepreneurship | M |
| Environmental Engineering | M,D |
| Environmental Management and Policy | M |
| Environmental Sciences | M |
| Fish, Game, and Wildlife Management | M,D |
| Food Science and Technology | M,D |
| Forensic Sciences | M |
| Forestry | M,D |
| Foundations and Philosophy of Education | M,D,O |
| French | M,D |
| Geography | M,D |
| Geosciences | M,D |
| Geotechnical Engineering | M,D |
| German | M,D |
| Health Services Management and Hospital Administration | M,D |
| Higher Education | M,D,O |
| History | M,D |
| Horticulture | M,D |
| Hospitality Management | M,D |
| Human Development | M,D |
| Human Resources Development | M |
| Human Resources Management | M |
| Industrial and Labor Relations | M |
| Industrial/Management Engineering | M,D |
| Information Science | M,D |
| International Affairs | M |
| Kinesiology and Movement Studies | M,D,O |
| Landscape Architecture | M,D |
| Law | M,D |
| Leisure Studies | M,D |
| Linguistics | M,D |
| Management Information Systems | M,D |
| Mass Communication | M,D |
| Materials Engineering | M,D |
| Materials Sciences | M,D |
| Mathematics | M,D |
| Mechanical Engineering | M,D |
| Mechanics | M,D |
| Media Studies | M,D |
| Meteorology | M,D |
| Mineral/Mining Engineering | M,D |
| Molecular Biology | M,D |
| Music Education | M,D,O |
| Music | M,D,O |
| Nuclear Engineering | M,D |
| Nursing—General | M,D |
| Nutrition | M,D |
| Organizational Management | M,D |
| Pathobiology | M,D |
| Philosophy | M,D |
| Physics | M,D |
| Physiology | M,D |
| Plant Biology | M,D |
| Plant Pathology | M,D |
| Plant Sciences | M,D |
| Political Science | M,D |
| Psychology—General | M,D |
| Recreation and Park Management | M,D |
| Rural Sociology | M,D,O |
| Russian | M,D |
| School Psychology | M,D,O |
| Sociology | M,D |
| Spanish | M,D |
| Special Education | M,D,O |
| Statistics | M,D |
| Sustainable Development | M |
| Theater | M |
| Travel and Tourism | M,D |
| Vocational and Technical Education | M,D,O |

### PENN STATE YORK

| | |
|---|---|
| Curriculum and Instruction | M,O |
| Education—General | M,O |
| English as a Second Language | M,O |

### PENNSYLVANIA ACADEMY OF THE FINE ARTS

| | |
|---|---|
| Art/Fine Arts | M,O |

### PENNSYLVANIA COLLEGE OF HEALTH SCIENCES

| | |
|---|---|
| Health Education | M |
| Health Services Management and Hospital Administration | M |
| Nursing and Healthcare Administration | M |
| Nursing Education | M |

### PENSACOLA CHRISTIAN COLLEGE

| | |
|---|---|
| Art/Fine Arts | M,D,O |
| Business Administration and Management—General | M,D,O |
| Curriculum and Instruction | M,D,O |
| Educational Leadership and Administration | M,D,O |
| Graphic Design | M,D,O |
| Music | M,D,O |
| Nursing—General | M,D,O |
| Theater | M,D,O |

### PENTECOSTAL THEOLOGICAL SEMINARY

| | |
|---|---|
| Pastoral Ministry and Counseling | M,D |
| Theology | M,D |

### PEPPERDINE UNIVERSITY

| | |
|---|---|
| Accounting | M |
| American Studies | M |
| Communication—General | M |
| Economics | M |
| Humanities | M |
| International Affairs | M |
| Media Studies | M |
| Pastoral Ministry and Counseling | M |
| Political Science | M |
| Public Policy | M |
| Religion | M |
| Writing | M |

### PERU STATE COLLEGE

| | |
|---|---|
| Curriculum and Instruction | M |
| Economics | M |
| Education—General | M |
| Entrepreneurship | M |
| Organizational Management | M |

### PFEIFFER UNIVERSITY

| | |
|---|---|
| Business Administration and Management—General | M |
| Elementary Education | M |
| Health Services Management and Hospital Administration | M |
| Organizational Management | M |
| Religious Education | M |
| Theology | M |

### PHILADELPHIA COLLEGE OF OSTEOPATHIC MEDICINE

| | |
|---|---|
| Applied Behavior Analysis | M,D,O |
| Biological and Biomedical Sciences—General | M |
| Biopsychology | M,D,O |
| Clinical Psychology | M,D,O |
| Counseling Psychology | M,D,O |
| Educational Psychology | M,D,O |
| Forensic Sciences | M |
| Health Services Management and Hospital Administration | M,D,O |
| Industrial and Organizational Psychology | M,D,O |
| Osteopathic Medicine | D |
| Physician Assistant Studies | M |
| Psychology—General | M,D,O |
| Public Health—General | M,D,O |
| School Psychology | M,D,O |

### PHILLIPS GRADUATE UNIVERSITY

| | |
|---|---|
| Art Therapy | M |
| Counselor Education | M |
| Marriage and Family Therapy | M |
| Organizational Behavior | D |
| Psychology—General | M |
| School Psychology | M |

### PHILLIPS THEOLOGICAL SEMINARY

| | |
|---|---|
| Business Administration and Management—General | M,D |
| Ethics | M,D |
| Higher Education | M,D |
| Missions and Missiology | M,D |
| Music | M,D |
| Pastoral Ministry and Counseling | D |
| Religious Education | M,D |
| Social Work | M,D |
| Theology | M,D |

### PHOENIX INSTITUTE OF HERBAL MEDICINE & ACUPUNCTURE

| | |
|---|---|
| Acupuncture and Oriental Medicine | M |

### PHOENIX SEMINARY

| | |
|---|---|
| Counseling Psychology | M,D,O |
| Pastoral Ministry and Counseling | M,D,O |
| Theology | M,D,O |

### PIEDMONT COLLEGE

| | |
|---|---|
| Art Education | M,D,O |
| Business Administration and Management—General | M |
| Curriculum and Instruction | M,D,O |
| Early Childhood Education | M,D,O |
| Education—General | M,D,O |
| Middle School Education | M,D,O |
| Music Education | M,D,O |
| Secondary Education | M,D,O |
| Special Education | M,D,O |

### PIEDMONT INTERNATIONAL UNIVERSITY

| | |
|---|---|
| Curriculum and Instruction | M,D |
| Educational Leadership and Administration | M,D |
| Pastoral Ministry and Counseling | M,D |
| Theology | M,D |

### PILLAR COLLEGE

| | |
|---|---|
| Clinical Psychology | M |
| Marriage and Family Therapy | M |

### PITTSBURGH THEOLOGICAL SEMINARY

| | |
|---|---|
| Pastoral Ministry and Counseling | M,D |
| Theology | M,D |

### PITTSBURG STATE UNIVERSITY

| | |
|---|---|
| Accounting | M |
| Biological and Biomedical Sciences—General | M |
| Business Administration and Management—General | M |
| Chemistry | M |
| Clinical Psychology | M |
| Communication—General | M |
| Construction Engineering | M |
| Construction Management | M,O |
| Counselor Education | M |
| Education—General | M,O |
| Educational Leadership and Administration | M,O |
| Educational Media/Instructional Technology | M |
| Electrical Engineering | M |
| English as a Second Language | M,O |
| English | M |
| Exercise and Sports Science | M |
| Graphic Design | M,O |
| Health Education | M |
| History | M |
| Human Resources Development | M |
| International Business | M |
| Management of Technology | M,O |
| Manufacturing Engineering | M |
| Mathematics | M |
| Mechanical Engineering | M |
| Music Education | M |
| Music | M |
| Nursing Education | M,D |
| Nursing—General | M,D |
| Physical Education | M |
| Physics | M |
| Polymer Science and Engineering | M |
| Psychology—General | M |
| School Psychology | O |
| Secondary Education | M,O |
| Special Education | M,O |
| Sports Management | M |
| Vocational and Technical Education | M,O |
| Writing | M |

### PLYMOUTH STATE UNIVERSITY

| | |
|---|---|
| Accounting | M |
| Addictions/Substance Abuse Counseling | M |
| Adult Education | D |
| Art Education | M |
| Athletic Training and Sports Medicine | M |
| Business Administration and Management—General | M |
| Clinical Psychology | O |
| Counselor Education | M |
| Cultural Studies | M |
| Curriculum and Instruction | D |
| Education—General | O |
| Educational Leadership and Administration | M,D,O |
| English Education | M |
| Health Education | M |
| Health Promotion | M,O |
| Higher Education | D,O |
| Historic Preservation | M,O |
| Marriage and Family Therapy | M |
| Mathematics Education | M |
| Music Education | M |
| School Psychology | O |
| Social Sciences Education | M |

### POINT LOMA NAZARENE UNIVERSITY

| | |
|---|---|
| Acute Care/Critical Care Nursing | M |
| Biological and Biomedical Sciences—General | M |
| Business Administration and Management—General | M |
| Clinical Psychology | M |
| Counselor Education | M |
| Education—General | M |
| Educational Leadership and Administration | M |
| Entrepreneurship | M |
| Exercise and Sports Science | M |
| Family Nurse Practitioner Studies | M |
| Gerontological Nursing | M |
| Health Services Management and Hospital Administration | M |
| Kinesiology and Movement Studies | M |
| Marriage and Family Therapy | M |
| Nursing—General | M,D,O |
| Organizational Management | M |
| Pastoral Ministry and Counseling | M |
| Pediatric Nursing | M |
| Project Management | M |
| Special Education | M |
| Sports Management | M |
| Theology | M |

### POINT PARK UNIVERSITY

| | |
|---|---|
| Adult Education | M,D |
| Business Administration and Management—General | M |
| Business Analytics | M |
| Clinical Psychology | M,D |
| Communication—General | M |
| Criminal Justice and Criminology | M |
| Curriculum and Instruction | M,D |
| Education—General | M,D |
| Educational Leadership and Administration | M,D |
| Elementary Education | M,D |
| Engineering Management | M |
| Entertainment Management | M |
| Environmental Management and Policy | M |
| Health Services Management and Hospital Administration | M |
| International Business | M |
| Journalism | M |
| Management Information Systems | M |
| Mass Communication | M |
| Media Studies | M |
| Middle School Education | M,D |
| Music | M |
| Organizational Management | M |
| Secondary Education | M,D |
| Special Education | M,D |
| Sports Management | M |
| Theater | M |

### POINT UNIVERSITY

| | |
|---|---|
| Business Administration and Management—General | M |
| Pastoral Ministry and Counseling | M |

### POLYTECHNIC UNIVERSITY OF PUERTO RICO

| | |
|---|---|
| Business Administration and Management—General | M |

| | |
|---|---|
| Civil Engineering | M |
| Computer Engineering | M |
| Computer Science | M |
| Electrical Engineering | M |
| Engineering Management | M |
| Environmental Management and Policy | M |
| Industrial and Manufacturing Management | M |
| International Business | M |
| Landscape Architecture | M |
| Management Information Systems | M |
| Management of Technology | M |
| Manufacturing Engineering | M |
| Mechanical Engineering | M |

### POLYTECHNIC UNIVERSITY OF PUERTO RICO, MIAMI CAMPUS

| | |
|---|---|
| Accounting | M |
| Business Administration and Management—General | M |
| Construction Management | M |
| Environmental Engineering | M |
| Environmental Management and Policy | M |
| Finance and Banking | M |
| Human Resources Management | M |
| Industrial and Manufacturing Management | M |
| International Business | M |
| Logistics | M |
| Marketing | M |
| Project Management | M |
| Supply Chain Management | M |

### POLYTECHNIC UNIVERSITY OF PUERTO RICO, ORLANDO CAMPUS

| | |
|---|---|
| Accounting | M |
| Business Administration and Management—General | M |
| Construction Management | M |
| Engineering Management | M |
| Environmental Engineering | M |
| Environmental Management and Policy | M |
| Finance and Banking | M |
| Human Resources Management | M |
| Industrial and Manufacturing Management | M |
| International Business | M |
| Management of Technology | M |

### POLYTECHNIQUE MONTRÉAL

| | |
|---|---|
| Aerospace/Aeronautical Engineering | M,D,O |
| Applied Mathematics | M,D,O |
| Biomedical Engineering | M,D,O |
| Chemical Engineering | M,D,O |
| Civil Engineering | M,D,O |
| Computer Engineering | M,D,O |
| Computer Science | M,D,O |
| Electrical Engineering | M,D,O |
| Engineering and Applied Sciences—General | M,D,O |
| Engineering Physics | M,D,O |
| Environmental Engineering | M,D,O |
| Geotechnical Engineering | M,D,O |
| Hydraulics | M,D,O |
| Industrial/Management Engineering | M,D,O |
| Management of Technology | M,D,O |
| Mechanical Engineering | M,D,O |
| Mechanics | M,D,O |
| Nuclear Engineering | M,D,O |
| Operations Research | M,D,O |
| Optical Sciences | M,D,O |
| Structural Engineering | M,D,O |
| Transportation and Highway Engineering | M,D,O |

### PONCE HEALTH SCIENCES UNIVERSITY

| | |
|---|---|
| Biological and Biomedical Sciences—General | D |
| Clinical Psychology | D |
| Epidemiology | M,D |
| Public Health—General | M,D |

### PONTIFICAL CATHOLIC UNIVERSITY OF PUERTO RICO

| | |
|---|---|
| Accounting | M,O |
| Art/Fine Arts | M |
| Biological and Biomedical Sciences—General | M |
| Business Administration and Management—General | M,D,O |
| Business Education | M,D |
| Chemistry | M |
| Clinical Laboratory Sciences/Medical Technology | O |
| Clinical Psychology | D |
| Counselor Education | M |
| Criminal Justice and Criminology | M |
| Curriculum and Instruction | M,D |
| Education—General | M,D |
| Educational Leadership and Administration | D |
| Educational Psychology | M |
| English as a Second Language | M |
| Environmental Sciences | M |
| Finance and Banking | M |
| Hispanic Studies | M,O |
| History | M |
| Human Resources Management | M,O |
| Human Services | M,D |
| Industrial and Organizational Psychology | D |
| International Business | M |
| Law | D |
| Logistics | O |
| Management Information Systems | M,O |
| Marketing | M |
| Medical/Surgical Nursing | M |
| Nursing—General | M |
| Psychiatric Nursing | M |
| Psychology—General | M,D |
| Public Administration | M |
| Rehabilitation Counseling | M |
| Religious Education | M |
| Social Work | M |
| Spanish | M,O |
| Theology | M |
| Transportation Management | O |

### PONTIFICAL COLLEGE JOSEPHINUM

| | |
|---|---|
| Theology | M |

### PONTIFICAL JOHN PAUL II INSTITUTE FOR STUDIES ON MARRIAGE AND FAMILY

| | |
|---|---|
| Biotechnology | M,D,O |
| Ethics | M,D,O |
| Marriage and Family Therapy | M,D,O |
| Theology | M,D,O |

### PONTIFICIA UNIVERSIDAD CATOLICA MADRE Y MAESTRA

| | |
|---|---|
| Allopathic Medicine | D |
| Architecture | M |
| Building Science | M |
| Business Administration and Management—General | M |
| Clinical Psychology | M |
| Criminal Justice and Criminology | M |
| Developmental Psychology | M |
| Early Childhood Education | M |
| Engineering and Applied Sciences—General | M |
| Entrepreneurship | M |
| Finance and Banking | M |
| Forensic Psychology | M |
| Hospitality Management | M |
| Human Resources Management | M |
| Insurance | M |
| Interior Design | M |
| International Affairs | M |
| International Business | M |
| Landscape Architecture | M |
| Law | M |
| Logistics | M |
| Management Strategy and Policy | M |
| Marketing | M |
| Psychology—General | M |
| Real Estate | M |
| Structural Engineering | M |
| Travel and Tourism | M |

### POPE ST. JOHN XXIII NATIONAL SEMINARY

| | |
|---|---|
| Theology | M |

### PORTLAND STATE UNIVERSITY

| | |
|---|---|
| American Studies | M |
| Anthropology | M,D,O |
| Applied Social Research | M,D |
| Applied Statistics | M,D,O |
| Architecture | M |
| Art/Fine Arts | M |
| Artificial Intelligence/Robotics | M,D,O |
| Biological and Biomedical Sciences—General | M,D |
| Business Administration and Management—General | M,D,O |
| Chemistry | M,D |
| Civil Engineering | M,D,O |
| Communication Disorders | M |
| Computer and Information Systems Security | M,D,O |
| Computer Engineering | M,D |
| Computer Science | M,D,O |
| Conflict Resolution and Mediation/Peace Studies | M |
| Criminal Justice and Criminology | M |
| Economics | M,D,O |
| Education—General | M,D |
| Electrical Engineering | M,D |
| Energy Management and Policy | M,D,O |
| Engineering and Applied Sciences—General | M,D,O |
| Engineering Management | M,D,O |
| English as a Second Language | M,O |
| English | M |
| Environmental Engineering | M,D |
| Environmental Management and Policy | M,D,O |
| Environmental Sciences | M,D,O |
| Finance and Banking | M |
| Food Science and Technology | M,D,O |
| Foreign Languages Education | M |
| French | M |
| Geography | M,D |
| Geology | M,D,O |
| German | M |
| Health Promotion | M,D |
| Health Services Management and Hospital Administration | M,D,O |
| History | M |
| Human Resources Management | M,D,O |
| Hydrology | M,D,O |
| International Affairs | M |
| Japanese | M |
| Management of Technology | M,D |
| Materials Engineering | M,D |
| Mathematics Education | M,D,O |
| Mathematics | M,D,O |
| Mechanical Engineering | M,D,O |
| Middle School Education | M,D,O |
| Modeling and Simulation | M,D,O |
| Music | M |
| Nonprofit Management | M,D,O |
| Physics | M,D |
| Political Science | M |
| Psychology—General | M,D,O |
| Public Administration | M,D,O |
| Public Affairs | M,D,O |
| Public Health—General | M,D |
| Public Policy | M,D,O |
| Real Estate | M,D,O |
| Science Education | M,D,O |
| Social Sciences Education | M |
| Social Work | M,D |
| Sociology | M,D,O |
| Spanish | M |
| Speech and Interpersonal Communication | M,O |
| Statistics | M,D,O |
| Supply Chain Management | M |
| Systems Science | M,D,O |
| Theater | M |
| Writing | M |

### POST UNIVERSITY

| | |
|---|---|
| Accounting | M |
| Addictions/Substance Abuse Counseling | M |
| Business Administration and Management—General | M |
| Clinical Psychology | M |
| Curriculum and Instruction | M |
| Distance Education Development | M |
| Education—General | M |
| Educational Leadership and Administration | M |
| Educational Media/Instructional Technology | M |
| Emergency Management | M |
| English as a Second Language | M |
| Finance and Banking | M |
| Forensic Psychology | M |
| Health Services Management and Hospital Administration | M |
| Homeland Security | M |
| Human Services | M |
| Marketing | M |
| Nonprofit Management | M |
| Project Management | M |
| Public Administration | M |

### PRAIRIE VIEW A&M UNIVERSITY

| | |
|---|---|
| Accounting | M |
| Agricultural Sciences—General | M |
| Architecture | M |
| Business Administration and Management—General | M |
| Chemistry | M |
| Clinical Psychology | M,D |
| Computer Science | M,D |
| Counselor Education | M,D |
| Curriculum and Instruction | M |
| Education—General | M,D |
| Educational Leadership and Administration | M,D |
| Electrical Engineering | M,D |
| Engineering and Applied Sciences—General | M,D |
| Forensic Psychology | M,D |
| Health Education | M |
| Kinesiology and Movement Studies | M |
| Legal and Justice Studies | M,D |
| Management Information Systems | M,D |
| Nursing—General | M,D |
| Sociology | M |

### PRATT INSTITUTE

| | |
|---|---|
| Applied Arts and Design—General | M,O |
| Architecture | M |
| Art Education | M,O |
| Art Therapy | M |
| Art/Fine Arts | M |
| Arts Administration | M |
| Facilities Management | M |
| Graphic Design | M |
| Historic Preservation | M |
| Industrial Design | M |
| Information Studies | M,O |
| Interior Design | M |
| Internet and Interactive Multimedia | M |
| Library Science | M,O |
| Media Studies | M |
| Music | M |
| Real Estate | M |
| Sustainable Development | M |
| Therapies—Dance, Drama, and Music | M |
| Urban and Regional Planning | M |
| Urban Design | M |
| Writing | M |

### PRESBYTERIAN COLLEGE

| | |
|---|---|
| Pharmacy | D |

### PRESCOTT COLLEGE

| | |
|---|---|
| Art Therapy | M |
| Art/Fine Arts | M |
| Counseling Psychology | M |
| Counselor Education | M,D |
| Early Childhood Education | M,D |
| Education—General | M,D |
| Educational Leadership and Administration | M,D |
| Elementary Education | M,D |
| Environmental Education | M,D |
| Environmental Management and Policy | M |
| Health Psychology | M |
| Humanities | M |
| Legal and Justice Studies | M |
| Leisure Studies | M |
| Psychoanalysis and Psychotherapy | M |
| Secondary Education | M,D |
| Special Education | M,D |

### PRESIDIO GRADUATE SCHOOL (CA)

| | |
|---|---|
| Business Administration and Management—General | M,O |
| Sustainability Management | M,O |

### PRINCETON THEOLOGICAL SEMINARY

| | |
|---|---|
| Religion | M,D |
| Theology | M,D |

### PRINCETON UNIVERSITY

| | |
|---|---|
| Aerospace/Aeronautical Engineering | M,D |
| Anthropology | D |
| Applied Mathematics | D |
| Archaeology | D |
| Architecture | M,D |
| Asian Studies | D |
| Astronomy | D |
| Astrophysics | D |
| Atmospheric Sciences | D |
| Bioengineering | M,D |
| Chemical Engineering | M,D |
| Chemistry | M,D |
| Civil Engineering | M,D |
| Classics | D |
| Comparative Literature | D |
| Computational Biology | D |
| Computational Sciences | D |
| Computer Science | M,D |
| Demography and Population Studies | D,O |
| Ecology | D |
| Economics | D,O |
| Electrical Engineering | M,D |
| Electronic Materials | D |
| Engineering and Applied Sciences—General | M,D |
| English | D |
| Environmental Engineering | M,D |
| Evolutionary Biology | D |
| Finance and Banking | M |
| Financial Engineering | M,D |
| French | D |
| Geosciences | D |
| German | D |
| History of Science and Technology | D |
| History | D |
| International Affairs | M,D |
| Marine Biology | D |
| Materials Sciences | D |
| Mathematics | D |
| Mechanical Engineering | M,D |
| Molecular Biology | D |
| Music | D |
| Near and Middle Eastern Studies | M,D |
| Neuroscience | D |
| Ocean Engineering | D |
| Oceanography | D |
| Operations Research | M,D |
| Philosophy | D |
| Photonics | D |
| Physics | D |
| Plasma Physics | D |
| Political Science | D |
| Portuguese | D |
| Psychology—General | D |
| Public Affairs | M,D,O |
| Public Policy | M,D |
| Religion | D |
| Russian | D |
| Slavic Languages | D |
| Sociology | D,O |
| Spanish | D |

### PROVIDENCE COLLEGE

| | |
|---|---|
| Accounting | M |
| American Studies | M |
| Business Administration and Management—General | M |
| Counselor Education | M |
| Educational Leadership and Administration | M |
| Elementary Education | M |
| Finance and Banking | M |
| History | M |
| International Business | M |
| Marketing | M |
| Mathematics Education | M |
| Reading Education | M |
| Secondary Education | M |
| Special Education | M |
| Theology | M |
| Urban Education | M |

### PROVIDENCE UNIVERSITY COLLEGE & THEOLOGICAL SEMINARY

| | |
|---|---|
| Counseling Psychology | M,D,O |
| English as a Second Language | M,D,O |
| Missions and Missiology | M,D,O |
| Pastoral Ministry and Counseling | M,D,O |
| Religious Education | M,D,O |
| Student Affairs | M,D,O |
| Theology | M,D,O |

### PURCHASE COLLEGE, STATE UNIVERSITY OF NEW YORK

| | |
|---|---|
| Art History | M |
| Art/Fine Arts | M |
| Arts Administration | M |
| Computer Art and Design | M |
| Entrepreneurship | M |
| Music | M |

### PURDUE UNIVERSITY

| | |
|---|---|
| Aerospace/Aeronautical Engineering | M,D |
| Agricultural Economics and Agribusiness | M,D |
| Agricultural Education | M,D,O |
| Agricultural Engineering | M,D |
| Agricultural Sciences—General | M,D |
| Agronomy and Soil Sciences | M,D |
| Allied Health—General | M,D |

*M—masters degree; D—doctorate; O—other advanced degree; *—Close-Up and/or Display*

| | |
|---|---|
| American Studies | M,D |
| Analytical Chemistry | M,D |
| Anatomy | M,D |
| Animal Sciences | M,D |
| Anthropology | M,D |
| Applied Arts and Design—General | M,D |
| Aquaculture | M,D |
| Art Education | M,D,O |
| Art/Fine Arts | M,D |
| Atmospheric Sciences | M,D |
| Aviation Management | M |
| Biochemistry | M,D |
| Biological and Biomedical Sciences—General | M,D |
| Biomedical Engineering | M,D |
| Biophysics | D |
| Biotechnology | D |
| Botany | M,D |
| Business Administration and Management—General | M,D |
| Cancer Biology/Oncology | D |
| Cell Biology | M,D |
| Chemical Engineering | M,D |
| Chemistry | M,D |
| Child and Family Studies | M,D |
| Child Development | M,D |
| Civil Engineering | M,D |
| Clinical Psychology | D |
| Cognitive Sciences | D |
| Communication Disorders | M,D |
| Communication—General | M,D |
| Comparative Literature | M,D |
| Computational Sciences | D |
| Computer and Information Systems Security | M |
| Computer Art and Design | M,D |
| Computer Engineering | M,D |
| Computer Science | M,D |
| Construction Management | M |
| Consumer Economics | M,D |
| Curriculum and Instruction | M,D,O |
| Developmental Biology | M,D |
| Ecology | M,D |
| Economics | D |
| Education—General | M,D,O |
| Educational Leadership and Administration | M,D,O |
| Educational Media/Instructional Technology | M,D,O |
| Electrical Engineering | M,D |
| Elementary Education | M,D,O |
| Engineering and Applied Sciences—General | M,D,O |
| English Education | M,D,O |
| English | M,D |
| Entomology | M,D |
| Environmental and Occupational Health | M,D |
| Environmental Engineering | M,D |
| Environmental Management and Policy | M,D |
| Epidemiology | M,D |
| Ergonomics and Human Factors | M,D |
| Evolutionary Biology | D |
| Exercise and Sports Science | M,D |
| Family Nurse Practitioner Studies | M,D,O |
| Finance and Banking | M |
| Fish, Game, and Wildlife Management | M,D |
| Food Science and Technology | M,D |
| Foreign Languages Education | M,D,O |
| Forestry | M,D |
| Foundations and Philosophy of Education | M,D,O |
| French | M |
| Genetics | M,D |
| Genomic Sciences | D |
| Geosciences | M,D |
| German | M |
| Gerontological Nursing | M,D,O |
| Health Education | M,D |
| Health Physics/Radiological Health | M,D |
| Higher Education | M,D,O |
| History | M,D |
| Home Economics Education | M,D,O |
| Horticulture | M,D |
| Hospitality Management | M,D |
| Human Development | M,D |
| Human Resources Management | M,D |
| Immunology | M,D |
| Industrial and Organizational Psychology | D |
| Industrial Design | M,D |
| Industrial/Management Engineering | M,D |
| Inorganic Chemistry | M,D |
| Interior Design | M,D |
| International Business | M |
| Japanese | M |
| Kinesiology and Movement Studies | M,D |
| Linguistics | M,D |
| Management Information Systems | M |
| Management of Technology | M,D |
| Marriage and Family Therapy | M,D |
| Materials Engineering | M,D |
| Mathematics Education | M,D,O |
| Mathematics | M,D |
| Mechanical Engineering | M,D,O |
| Medical Physics | M,D |
| Medicinal and Pharmaceutical Chemistry | D |
| Microbiology | M,D |
| Molecular Biology | D |
| Molecular Pharmacology | D |
| Natural Resources | M,D |
| Neurobiology | M,D |
| Neuroscience | D |
| Nuclear Engineering | M,D |
| Nursing—General | M,D,O |
| Nutrition | M,D |
| Organic Chemistry | M,D |
| Organizational Behavior | D |
| Pathobiology | M,D |
| Pathology | M,D |
| Pediatric Nursing | M,D,O |
| Pharmaceutical Administration | M,D,O |
| Pharmaceutical Sciences | M,D,O |
| Pharmacology | M,D |
| Pharmacy | D |
| Philosophy | M,D |
| Physical Chemistry | M,D |
| Physical Education | M,D |
| Physics | M,D |
| Physiology | M,D |
| Plant Pathology | M,D |
| Plant Sciences | D |
| Political Science | M,D |
| Psychology—General | D |
| Public Health—General | M,D |
| Reading Education | M,D,O |
| Recreation and Park Management | M,D |
| Science Education | M,D,O |
| Social Sciences Education | M,D,O |
| Sociology | M,D |
| Spanish | M |
| Sport Psychology | M,D |
| Sports Management | M,D |
| Statistics | M,D |
| Systems Biology | D |
| Toxicology | M,D |
| Travel and Tourism | M,D |
| Veterinary Medicine | D |
| Veterinary Sciences | M,D |
| Virology | M,D |
| Vocational and Technical Education | M,D,O |
| Writing | M,D |

### PURDUE UNIVERSITY FORT WAYNE

| | |
|---|---|
| Adult Nursing | M,O |
| Applied Mathematics | M,O |
| Applied Statistics | M,O |
| Biological and Biomedical Sciences—General | M |
| Business Administration and Management—General | M |
| Civil Engineering | M |
| Communication—General | M |
| Computer Engineering | M |
| Computer Science | M |
| Construction Management | M |
| Counselor Education | M,O |
| Education—General | M,O |
| Educational Leadership and Administration | M,O |
| Electrical Engineering | M,O |
| Elementary Education | M,O |
| Engineering and Applied Sciences—General | M,O |
| English as a Second Language | M,O |
| English Education | M,O |
| English | M,O |
| Facilities Management | M |
| Family Nurse Practitioner Studies | M,O |
| Gerontological Nursing | M,O |
| Industrial/Management Engineering | M |
| Information Science | M |
| Marriage and Family Therapy | M,O |
| Mathematics Education | M,O |
| Mathematics | M,O |
| Mechanical Engineering | M |
| Nursing and Healthcare Administration | M,O |
| Nursing Education | M,O |
| Nursing—General | M,O |
| Operations Research | M,O |
| Organizational Management | M,O |
| Public Policy | M,O |
| Secondary Education | M,O |
| Special Education | M,O |
| Systems Engineering | M |

### PURDUE UNIVERSITY GLOBAL

| | |
|---|---|
| Business Administration and Management—General | M |
| Computer and Information Systems Security | M |
| Criminal Justice and Criminology | M |
| Education—General | M |
| Educational Leadership and Administration | M |
| Educational Media/Instructional Technology | M |
| Entrepreneurship | M |
| Finance and Banking | M |
| Health Services Management and Hospital Administration | M,O |
| Higher Education | M |
| Human Resources Management | M |
| International Business | M |
| Law | M |
| Legal and Justice Studies | M,O |
| Logistics | M |
| Management Information Systems | M |
| Marketing | M |
| Mathematics Education | M |
| Nursing and Healthcare Administration | M |
| Nursing Education | M |
| Nursing—General | M |
| Organizational Management | M |
| Political Science | M,O |
| Project Management | M |
| Reading Education | M |
| Science Education | M |
| Secondary Education | M |
| Special Education | M |
| Student Affairs | M |
| Supply Chain Management | M |

### PURDUE UNIVERSITY NORTHWEST

| | |
|---|---|
| Accounting | M |
| Acute Care/Critical Care Nursing | M |
| Adult Nursing | M |
| Biological and Biomedical Sciences—General | M |
| Biotechnology | M |
| Business Administration and Management—General | M |
| Child and Family Studies | M |
| Child Development | M |
| Communication—General | M |
| Computer Engineering | M |
| Computer Science | M |
| Counseling Psychology | M |
| Counselor Education | M |
| Education—General | M |
| Educational Leadership and Administration | M |
| Educational Media/Instructional Technology | M |
| Electrical Engineering | M |
| Engineering and Applied Sciences—General | M |
| English | M |
| Family Nurse Practitioner Studies | M |
| History | M |
| Human Services | M |
| Marriage and Family Therapy | M |
| Mathematics Education | M |
| Mathematics | M |
| Mechanical Engineering | M |
| Nursing and Healthcare Administration | M |
| Nursing—General | M |
| School Psychology | M |
| Science Education | M |
| Special Education | M |

### QUEENS COLLEGE OF THE CITY UNIVERSITY OF NEW YORK

| | |
|---|---|
| Accounting | M |
| Applied Behavior Analysis | M |
| Applied Mathematics | M |
| Applied Social Research | M |
| Archives/Archival Administration | M,O |
| Art Education | M,O |
| Art History | M |
| Art/Fine Arts | M |
| Biological and Biomedical Sciences—General | M,O |
| Chemistry | M |
| Child and Family Studies | M,O |
| Communication Disorders | M,O |
| Computer Science | M |
| Counseling Psychology | M,O |
| Counselor Education | M,O |
| Data Science/Data Analytics | M |
| Early Childhood Education | M,O |
| Education—General | M,O |
| Educational Leadership and Administration | M,O |
| Elementary Education | M,O |
| English as a Second Language | M,O |
| English Education | M,O |
| English | M |
| Environmental Sciences | M |
| Exercise and Sports Science | M,O |
| Family and Consumer Sciences-General | M,O |
| Finance and Banking | M |
| Foreign Languages Education | M,O |
| French | M |
| Geology | M |
| Geosciences | M |
| Hispanic and Latin American Languages | M |
| History | M |
| Information Studies | M,O |
| Italian | M |
| Liberal Studies | M |
| Library Science | M,O |
| Linguistics | M,O |
| Mathematics Education | M,O |
| Mathematics | M |
| Media Studies | M |
| Middle School Education | M,O |
| Multilingual and Multicultural Education | M,O |
| Music Education | M,O |
| Music | M,O |
| Neuroscience | M |
| Nutrition | M,O |
| Photonics | M |
| Physical Education | M,O |
| Physics | M |
| Psychology—General | M |
| Reading Education | M,O |
| Risk Management | M |
| Romance Languages | M |
| School Psychology | M,O |
| Science Education | M,O |
| Secondary Education | M,O |
| Social Sciences Education | M,O |
| Sociology | M |
| Spanish | M |
| Special Education | M,O |
| Urban Studies | M |
| Writing | M |

### QUEEN'S UNIVERSITY AT KINGSTON

| | |
|---|---|
| Allopathic Medicine | D |
| Artificial Intelligence/Robotics | M |
| Astronomy | M,D |
| Biological and Biomedical Sciences—General | M,D |
| Business Administration and Management—General | M,D |
| Business Analytics | M,D |
| Canadian Studies | M,D |
| Chemical Engineering | M,D |
| Chemistry | M,D |
| Civil Engineering | M,D |
| Classics | M |
| Clinical Psychology | M,D |
| Cognitive Sciences | M,D |
| Communication—General | M,D |
| Computer Engineering | M,D |
| Computer Science | M,D |
| Developmental Psychology | M,D |
| Economics | M,D |
| Education—General | M,D |
| Electrical Engineering | M,D |
| Engineering and Applied Sciences—General | M,D |
| Engineering Physics | M,D |
| English | M,D |
| Entrepreneurship | M |
| Epidemiology | M,D |
| Ergonomics and Human Factors | M,D |
| Exercise and Sports Science | M,D |
| Family Nurse Practitioner Studies | M,D,O |
| Finance and Banking | M,D |
| French | M,D |
| Gender Studies | M,D |
| Geography | M,D |
| Geology | M,D |
| Health Promotion | M,D |
| Industrial and Labor Relations | M |
| Information Studies | M,D |
| International Affairs | M,D |
| International Business | M |
| Law | M,D |
| Legal and Justice Studies | M,D |
| Management Information Systems | M,D |
| Management Strategy and Policy | M,D |
| Marketing | M,D |
| Materials Engineering | M,D |
| Mathematics | M,D |
| Mechanical Engineering | M,D |
| Mineral/Mining Engineering | M,D |
| Molecular Medicine | M,D |
| Nursing—General | M,D,O |
| Occupational Therapy | M,D |
| Organizational Behavior | M,D |
| Pathology | M,D |
| Pediatric Nursing | M,D,O |
| Philosophy | M,D |
| Physical Therapy | M,D |
| Physics | M,D |
| Political Science | M,D |
| Project Management | M |
| Psychology—General | M,D |
| Public Administration | M |
| Public Health—General | M,D |
| Rehabilitation Sciences | M,D |
| Religion | M |
| Social Psychology | M,D |
| Sociology | M,D |
| Sport Psychology | M,D |
| Statistics | M,D |
| Urban and Regional Planning | M |
| Women's Health Nursing | M,D,O |
| Women's Studies | M,D |

### QUEENS UNIVERSITY OF CHARLOTTE

| | |
|---|---|
| Business Administration and Management—General | M |
| Communication—General | M |
| Education—General | M |
| Educational Leadership and Administration | M |
| Elementary Education | M |
| Interior Design | M |
| Nursing and Healthcare Administration | M |
| Nursing Education | M |
| Nursing—General | M |
| Organizational Management | M |
| Reading Education | M |
| Writing | M |

### QUINCY UNIVERSITY

| | |
|---|---|
| Business Administration and Management—General | M |
| Clinical Psychology | M |
| Counselor Education | M |
| Curriculum and Instruction | M |
| Education—General | M |
| Educational Leadership and Administration | M |
| English as a Second Language | M |
| Multilingual and Multicultural Education | M |
| Reading Education | M |
| School Psychology | M |
| Student Affairs | M |

### QUINNIPIAC UNIVERSITY

| | |
|---|---|
| Accounting | M |
| Adult Nursing | D |
| Advertising and Public Relations | M |
| Allied Health—General | M |
| Allopathic Medicine | D |
| Anesthesiologist Assistant Studies | M |
| Biological and Biomedical Sciences—General | M |
| Broadcast Journalism | M |
| Business Administration and Management—General | M |
| Cardiovascular Sciences | M |
| Cell Biology | M |
| Communication—General | M |
| Community Health | D |
| Computer and Information Systems Security | M |
| Education—General | M,O |
| Educational Leadership and Administration | M,O |
| Educational Media/Instructional Technology | M |
| Elementary Education | M |
| English Education | M |
| Family Nurse Practitioner Studies | D |
| Film, Television, and Video Production | M |
| Finance and Banking | M |
| Foreign Languages Education | M |
| Health Physics/Radiological Health | M |
| Health Services Management and Hospital Administration | M |
| Internet and Interactive Multimedia | M |
| Journalism | M |
| Law | M,D |

| | |
|---|---|
| Mathematics Education | M |
| Molecular Biology | M |
| Nurse Anesthesia | D |
| Nursing and Healthcare Administration | D |
| Nursing—General | D |
| Organizational Management | M |
| Pathology | M |
| Perfusion | M |
| Physician Assistant Studies | M |
| Science Education | M |
| Secondary Education | M |
| Social Sciences Education | M |
| Social Work | M |
| Supply Chain Management | M |

### RABBINICAL ACADEMY MESIVTA RABBI CHAIM BERLIN

| | |
|---|---|
| Theology | O |

### RABBINICAL COLLEGE BETH SHRAGA

| | |
|---|---|
| Theology | |

### RABBINICAL COLLEGE BOBOVER YESHIVA B'NEI ZION

| | |
|---|---|
| Theology | O |

### RABBINICAL COLLEGE OF LONG ISLAND

| | |
|---|---|
| Theology | |

### RABBINICAL SEMINARY OF AMERICA

| | |
|---|---|
| Theology | |

### RADFORD UNIVERSITY

| | |
|---|---|
| Art/Fine Arts | M |
| Business Administration and Management—General | M |
| Clinical Psychology | M |
| Communication Disorders | M |
| Corporate and Organizational Communication | M |
| Counseling Psychology | D |
| Counselor Education | M |
| Criminal Justice and Criminology | M,O |
| Data Science/Data Analytics | M |
| Early Childhood Education | M |
| Educational Leadership and Administration | M |
| English | M |
| Experimental Psychology | M |
| Industrial and Organizational Psychology | M |
| Management Information Systems | M |
| Mathematics Education | M |
| Music | M |
| Nursing—General | D |
| Occupational Therapy | M |
| Physical Therapy | D |
| Psychology—General | M |
| Reading Education | M |
| School Psychology | O |
| Social Work | M |
| Special Education | M,O |

### RAMAPO COLLEGE OF NEW JERSEY

| | |
|---|---|
| Accounting | M |
| Business Administration and Management—General | M |
| Educational Leadership and Administration | M |
| Educational Media/Instructional Technology | M |
| Family Nurse Practitioner Studies | M |
| Nursing and Healthcare Administration | M |
| Nursing Education | M |
| Nursing—General | M |
| Social Work | M |
| Special Education | M |

### RANDALL UNIVERSITY

| | |
|---|---|
| Pastoral Ministry and Counseling | M |

### RANDOLPH COLLEGE

| | |
|---|---|
| Curriculum and Instruction | M |
| Education—General | M |
| Special Education | M |
| Writing | M |

### RECONSTRUCTIONIST RABBINICAL COLLEGE

| | |
|---|---|
| Jewish Studies | M,D,O |
| Theology | M,D,O |
| Women's Studies | M,D,O |

### REED COLLEGE

| | |
|---|---|
| Liberal Studies | M |

### REFORMED EPISCOPAL SEMINARY

| | |
|---|---|
| Theology | M |

### REFORMED PRESBYTERIAN THEOLOGICAL SEMINARY

| | |
|---|---|
| Theology | M,D |

### REFORMED THEOLOGICAL SEMINARY–ATLANTA CAMPUS

| | |
|---|---|
| Theology | M,D,O |

### REFORMED THEOLOGICAL SEMINARY–CHARLOTTE CAMPUS

| | |
|---|---|
| Pastoral Ministry and Counseling | M,D |
| Religion | M,D |
| Theology | M,D |

### REFORMED THEOLOGICAL SEMINARY–DALLAS CAMPUS

| | |
|---|---|
| Theology | M |

### REFORMED THEOLOGICAL SEMINARY–HOUSTON CAMPUS

| | |
|---|---|
| Religion | M |

### REFORMED THEOLOGICAL SEMINARY–JACKSON CAMPUS

| | |
|---|---|
| Marriage and Family Therapy | M,D,O |
| Missions and Missiology | M,D,O |
| Pastoral Ministry and Counseling | M,D,O |
| Religion | M,D,O |
| Religious Education | M,D,O |
| Theology | M,D,O |

### REFORMED THEOLOGICAL SEMINARY–ORLANDO CAMPUS

| | |
|---|---|
| Pastoral Ministry and Counseling | M,D,O |
| Theology | M,D,O |

### REFORMED THEOLOGICAL SEMINARY–WASHINGTON D.C.

| | |
|---|---|
| Religion | M |
| Theology | M |

### REFORMED UNIVERSITY

| | |
|---|---|
| Business Administration and Management—General | M |
| Theology | M |

### REGENT COLLEGE

| | |
|---|---|
| Theology | M,O |

### REGENT'S UNIVERSITY LONDON

| | |
|---|---|
| Business Administration and Management—General | M |
| Finance and Banking | M |
| Human Resources Management | M |
| International Affairs | M |
| International Business | M |
| Management Information Systems | M |
| Marketing | M |

### REGENT UNIVERSITY

| | |
|---|---|
| Accounting | M,D,O |
| Addictions/Substance Abuse Counseling | M,D,O |
| Adult Education | M,D,O |
| American Studies | M |
| Business Administration and Management—General | M,D,O |
| Business Analytics | M,D,O |
| Clinical Psychology | M,D,O |
| Communication—General | M,D |
| Computer and Information Systems Security | M |
| Conflict Resolution and Mediation/Peace Studies | M,D |
| Corporate and Organizational Communication | M,D |
| Counseling Psychology | M,D,O |
| Counselor Education | M,D,O |
| Criminal Justice and Criminology | M,D,O |
| Cultural Studies | M,D |
| Curriculum and Instruction | M,D,O |
| Distance Education Development | M,D,O |
| Early Childhood Education | M,D,O |
| Economics | M,D,O |
| Education of the Gifted | M,D,O |
| Education—General | M,D,O |
| Educational Leadership and Administration | M,D,O |
| Educational Media/Instructional Technology | M,D,O |
| Educational Psychology | M,D,O |
| Elementary Education | M,D,O |
| Emergency Management | M |
| English as a Second Language | M,D,O |
| Entrepreneurship | M,D,O |
| Film, Television, and Video Production | M,D |
| Finance and Banking | M,D,O |
| Health Services Management and Hospital Administration | M,D,O |
| Higher Education | M,D,O |
| Homeland Security | M |
| Human Resources Development | M,D,O |
| Human Resources Management | M,D,O |
| Human Services | M,D,O |
| Interdisciplinary Studies | M,D,O |
| International Affairs | M |
| Investment Management | M,D,O |
| Journalism | M,D |
| Law | M,D |
| Legal and Justice Studies | M,D |
| Management Strategy and Policy | M,D,O |
| Marketing | M,D,O |
| Marriage and Family Therapy | M,D,O |
| Mathematics | M,D,O |
| Missions and Missiology | M,D |
| National Security | M,D |
| Nonprofit Management | M,D,O |
| Organizational Management | M,D,O |
| Pastoral Ministry and Counseling | M,D,O |
| Political Science | M |
| Public Administration | M |
| Public Policy | M |
| Reading Education | M,D,O |
| Religion | M,D |
| Religious Education | M,D,O |
| Science Education | M,D,O |
| Special Education | M,D,O |
| Student Affairs | M,D,O |
| Theater | M,D |
| Theology | M,D |
| Writing | M,D |

### REGIS COLLEGE (CANADA)

| | |
|---|---|
| Pastoral Ministry and Counseling | M,D,O |
| Philosophy | M,D,O |
| Theology | M,D,O |

### REGIS COLLEGE (MA)

| | |
|---|---|
| Applied Behavior Analysis | M,D,O |
| Corporate and Organizational Communication | M |
| Counseling Psychology | M,D,O |
| Education—General | M,D |
| Educational Leadership and Administration | M,D |
| Elementary Education | M,D |
| Family Nurse Practitioner Studies | M,D,O |
| Health Services Management and Hospital Administration | M,D,O |
| Higher Education | M,D |
| Nursing Education | M,D,O |
| Nursing—General | M,D,O |
| Occupational Therapy | M,D,O |
| Special Education | M,D |

### REGIS UNIVERSITY

| | |
|---|---|
| Accounting | M,O |
| Allied Health—General | M,D,O |
| Biological and Biomedical Sciences—General | M |
| Business Education | M,O |
| Computer and Information Systems Security | M,O |
| Computer Science | M,O |
| Counselor Education | M,D,O |
| Criminal Justice and Criminology | M,O |
| Curriculum and Instruction | M,O |
| Data Science/Data Analytics | M,O |
| Developmental Psychology | M,D,O |
| Economics | M,O |
| Education—General | M |
| Educational Leadership and Administration | M,O |
| Elementary Education | M,O |
| Environmental Biology | M |
| Finance and Banking | M,O |
| Health Informatics | M,O |
| Health Services Management and Hospital Administration | M,D,O |
| Human Resources Management | M,O |
| Industrial and Manufacturing Management | M,O |
| Information Science | M,O |
| Management Information Systems | M,O |
| Management Strategy and Policy | M,O |
| Marketing | M,O |
| Marriage and Family Therapy | M,D,O |
| Maternal and Child/Neonatal Nursing | M,D,O |
| Medical Informatics | M,O |
| Nonprofit Management | M,O |
| Nursing and Healthcare Administration | M,D,O |
| Nursing Education | M,D,O |
| Occupational Therapy | M,D,O |
| Organizational Management | M,D,O |
| Pharmacy | M,D,O |
| Physical Therapy | M,D,O |
| Project Management | M,O |
| Reading Education | M,O |
| Secondary Education | M,O |
| Software Engineering | M,O |
| Special Education | M,O |
| Systems Engineering | M,O |
| Writing | M,O |

### REINHARDT UNIVERSITY

| | |
|---|---|
| Business Administration and Management—General | M |
| Early Childhood Education | M |
| Education—General | M |
| Public Administration | M |
| Writing | M |

### RELAY GRADUATE SCHOOL OF EDUCATION

| | |
|---|---|
| Education—General | M |

### RENSSELAER AT HARTFORD

| | |
|---|---|
| Business Administration and Management—General | M |
| Computer Engineering | M |
| Computer Science | M |
| Electrical Engineering | M |
| Engineering and Applied Sciences—General | M |
| Information Science | M |
| Mechanical Engineering | M |
| Systems Science | M |

### RENSSELAER POLYTECHNIC INSTITUTE

| | |
|---|---|
| Acoustics | D |
| Aerospace/Aeronautical Engineering | M,D |
| Applied Mathematics | M |
| Architecture | M |
| Art/Fine Arts | D |
| Astronomy | M |
| Biochemistry | M,D |
| Biological and Biomedical Sciences—General | M,D |
| Biomedical Engineering | M,D |
| Biophysics | M,D |
| Business Administration and Management—General | M,D |
| Business Analytics | M |
| Chemical Engineering | M,D |
| Chemistry | M,D |
| Civil Engineering | M,D |
| Cognitive Sciences | D |
| Computer Art and Design | D |
| Computer Engineering | M,D |
| Computer Science | M,D |
| Electrical Engineering | M,D |
| Engineering and Applied Sciences—General | M,D |
| Engineering Physics | M,D |
| Environmental Engineering | M,D |
| Financial Engineering | M |
| Geology | M,D |
| History of Science and Technology | M,D |
| Industrial/Management Engineering | M,D |
| Information Science | M |
| Interdisciplinary Studies | M,D |
| Lighting Design | M,D |
| Materials Engineering | M,D |
| Mathematics | M,D |
| Mechanical Engineering | M,D |
| Nuclear Engineering | M,D |
| Physics | M,D |
| Rhetoric | M,D |
| Speech and Interpersonal Communication | M,D |
| Supply Chain Management | M |
| Systems Engineering | M,D |
| Technology and Public Policy | M,D |
| Transportation and Highway Engineering | M,D |

### RESURRECTION UNIVERSITY

| | |
|---|---|
| Nursing—General | M |

### RHODE ISLAND COLLEGE

| | |
|---|---|
| Accounting | M,O |
| Art Education | M |
| Art/Fine Arts | M |
| Arts Administration | M |
| Biological and Biomedical Sciences—General | M,O |
| Counseling Psychology | M,O |
| Counselor Education | M,O |
| Early Childhood Education | M |
| Education of Students with Severe/Multiple Disabilities | M,O |
| Education—General | D |
| Educational Leadership and Administration | M,O |
| Elementary Education | M |
| English as a Second Language | M |
| English Education | M |
| English | M,O |
| Finance and Banking | M,O |
| Foreign Languages Education | M |
| Health Education | M,O |
| Health Psychology | M,O |
| Health Services Management and Hospital Administration | M |
| History | M |
| Legal and Justice Studies | M |
| Mathematics Education | M |
| Mathematics | M,O |
| Music Education | M |
| Nursing—General | M,D |
| Physical Education | M,O |
| Psychology—General | M,O |
| Reading Education | M |
| School Psychology | M,O |
| Secondary Education | M |
| Social Sciences Education | M |
| Social Work | M |
| Special Education | M,O |
| Writing | M,O |

### RHODE ISLAND SCHOOL OF DESIGN

| | |
|---|---|
| Applied Arts and Design—General | M |
| Architecture | M |
| Art Education | M |
| Art/Fine Arts | M |
| Computer Art and Design | M |
| Graphic Design | M |
| Industrial Design | M |
| Interior Design | M |
| Landscape Architecture | M |
| Media Studies | M |
| Photography | M |
| Textile Design | M |

### RHODES COLLEGE

| | |
|---|---|
| Accounting | M |

### RICE UNIVERSITY

| | |
|---|---|
| African Studies | D |
| American Studies | D |
| Anthropology | M,D |
| Applied Mathematics | M,D |
| Applied Physics | M,D |
| Archaeology | M,D |
| Architecture | M,D |
| Art History | D |
| Astronomy | M,D |
| Biochemistry | M,D |
| Bioengineering | M,D |
| Bioinformatics | M,D |
| Biomedical Engineering | M,D |
| Biostatistics | M,D |
| Business Administration and Management—General | M |
| Cell Biology | M,D |
| Chemical Engineering | M,D |
| Chemistry | M,D |
| Civil Engineering | M,D |
| Cognitive Sciences | M,D |
| Computational Sciences | M,D |
| Computer Engineering | M,D |
| Computer Science | M,D |
| Cultural Anthropology | M,D |
| Ecology | M,D |
| Economics | M,D |
| Education—General | M |
| Electrical Engineering | M,D |
| Energy Management and Policy | M,D |
| Engineering and Applied Sciences—General | M,D |
| English | M,D |
| Environmental Engineering | M,D |
| Environmental Management and Policy | M |
| Environmental Sciences | M,D |
| Evolutionary Biology | M,D |
| Geophysics | M |
| Geosciences | M,D |
| Health Services Management and Hospital Administration | M |

*M—masters degree; D—doctorate; O—other advanced degree; *—Close-Up and/or Display*

| | |
|---|---|
| History | M,D |
| Industrial and Organizational Psychology | M,D |
| Inorganic Chemistry | M,D |
| Jewish Studies | D |
| Liberal Studies | M |
| Linguistics | M,D |
| Materials Sciences | M,D |
| Mathematical and Computational Finance | M,D |
| Mathematics | D |
| Mechanical Engineering | M,D |
| Music | M,D |
| Near and Middle Eastern Studies | D |
| Organic Chemistry | M,D |
| Philosophy | M,D |
| Physical Chemistry | M,D |
| Physics | M,D |
| Political Science | D |
| Psychology—General | M,D |
| Religion | D |
| Science Education | M,D |
| Sociology | D |
| Statistics | M,D |
| Urban Design | M,D |

### RICHMOND, THE AMERICAN INTERNATIONAL UNIVERSITY IN LONDON

| | |
|---|---|
| Art History | M |
| International Affairs | M |

### RICHMONT GRADUATE UNIVERSITY

| | |
|---|---|
| Clinical Psychology | M |
| Counselor Education | M |
| Marriage and Family Therapy | M |
| Pastoral Ministry and Counseling | M,O |

### RIDER UNIVERSITY

| | |
|---|---|
| Accounting | M,O |
| Arts Administration | M |
| Business Administration and Management—General | M |
| Clinical Psychology | M,O |
| Corporate and Organizational Communication | M |
| Counselor Education | M,O |
| Early Childhood Education | M |
| Education—General | M,O |
| Elementary Education | M |
| English as a Second Language | M |
| Finance and Banking | M |
| Foreign Languages Education | M |
| Health Communication | M |
| Homeland Security | M |
| Multilingual and Multicultural Education | M |
| Music Education | M |
| Music | M |
| Organizational Management | M |
| School Psychology | O |
| Secondary Education | M |
| Special Education | M,O |

### RIVIER UNIVERSITY

| | |
|---|---|
| Business Administration and Management—General | M |
| Clinical Psychology | M |
| Computer Science | M |
| Counseling Psychology | M,D,O |
| Counselor Education | M,D,O |
| Curriculum and Instruction | M,D,O |
| Early Childhood Education | M,D,O |
| Education—General | M,D,O |
| Educational Leadership and Administration | M,D,O |
| Elementary Education | M,D,O |
| English | M |
| Experimental Psychology | M |
| Family Nurse Practitioner Studies | M,D |
| Foreign Languages Education | M |
| Management Information Systems | M |
| Mathematics | M |
| Nursing and Healthcare Administration | M,D |
| Nursing Education | M,D |
| Nursing—General | M,D |
| Psychiatric Nursing | M,D |
| Psychology—General | M |
| Public Health—General | M,D |
| Reading Education | M,D,O |
| Social Sciences Education | M |
| Special Education | M,D,O |
| Writing | M |

### THE ROBERT E. WEBBER INSTITUTE FOR WORSHIP STUDIES

| | |
|---|---|
| Religion | M,D |

### ROBERT MORRIS UNIVERSITY

| | |
|---|---|
| Business Administration and Management—General | M |
| Computer and Information Systems Security | M,D |
| Data Science/Data Analytics | M,D |
| Engineering and Applied Sciences—General | M |
| Engineering Management | M |
| Human Resources Management | M |
| Information Science | M,D |
| Management Information Systems | M,D |
| Nursing—General | M,D |
| Organizational Management | M,D |
| Project Management | M,D |
| Taxation | M |

### ROBERT MORRIS UNIVERSITY ILLINOIS

| | |
|---|---|
| Accounting | M |
| Business Administration and Management—General | M |
| Business Analytics | M |
| Computer and Information Systems Security | M |
| Criminal Justice and Criminology | M |
| Educational Leadership and Administration | M |
| Finance and Banking | M |
| Health Services Management and Hospital Administration | M |
| Higher Education | M |
| Human Resources Management | M |
| Management Information Systems | M |
| Sports Management | M |

### ROBERTS WESLEYAN COLLEGE

| | |
|---|---|
| Business Administration and Management—General | M |
| Child and Family Studies | M |
| Clinical Psychology | M,D |
| Counselor Education | M,D |
| Early Childhood Education | M |
| Education—General | M |
| Health Informatics | M |
| Health Services Management and Hospital Administration | M |
| Human Services | M |
| Management Strategy and Policy | M |
| Marketing | M |
| Middle School Education | M |
| Nursing and Healthcare Administration | M |
| Nursing Education | M |
| Nursing Informatics | M |
| Nursing—General | M |
| Psychology—General | M,D |
| Reading Education | M |
| School Psychology | M,D |
| Secondary Education | M |
| Social Work | M |
| Special Education | M |

### ROCHESTER INSTITUTE OF TECHNOLOGY

| | |
|---|---|
| Accounting | M |
| Applied Mathematics | M |
| Applied Statistics | M,O |
| Architecture | M |
| Art Education | M |
| Art/Fine Arts | M |
| Astrophysics | M,D |
| Bioinformatics | M |
| Biological and Biomedical Sciences—General | M |
| Business Administration and Management—General | M |
| Chemistry | M |
| Cognitive Sciences | O |
| Communication—General | M |
| Computer and Information Systems Security | M,O |
| Computer Art and Design | M |
| Computer Engineering | M |
| Computer Science | M,D |
| Criminal Justice and Criminology | M |
| Data Science/Data Analytics | O |
| Electrical Engineering | M |
| Engineering and Applied Sciences—General | M,D,O |
| Engineering Design | M |
| Engineering Management | M |
| Entrepreneurship | M |
| Environmental and Occupational Health | M |
| Environmental Sciences | M |
| Experimental Psychology | M |
| Film, Television, and Video Production | M |
| Finance and Banking | M |
| Game Design and Development | M |
| Graphic Design | M |
| Health Informatics | M |
| Health Services Management and Hospital Administration | M,O |
| Hospitality Management | M |
| Human Resources Development | M |
| Human-Computer Interaction | M |
| Industrial and Manufacturing Management | M |
| Industrial Design | M |
| Industrial/Management Engineering | M |
| Information Science | M,D |
| Interdisciplinary Studies | M |
| International Business | M |
| Internet and Interactive Multimedia | O |
| Management Information Systems | O |
| Manufacturing Engineering | M |
| Materials Engineering | M |
| Materials Sciences | M |
| Mathematical and Computational Finance | M |
| Mathematics | M,D,O |
| Mechanical Engineering | M |
| Media Studies | M |
| Medical Illustration | M |
| Modeling and Simulation | D |
| Optical Sciences | M,D |
| Organizational Management | O |
| Photography | M |
| Project Management | O |
| Psychology—General | M,O |
| Public Policy | M |
| Safety Engineering | M |
| School Psychology | M,O |
| Secondary Education | M |
| Software Engineering | M |
| Special Education | M |
| Statistics | O |
| Sustainability Management | M,D |
| Sustainable Development | M,D |
| Systems Engineering | M,D |
| Technology and Public Policy | M |
| Telecommunications | M |
| Translation and Interpretation | M |
| Travel and Tourism | M |
| Vocational and Technical Education | O |

### ROCHESTER UNIVERSITY

| | |
|---|---|
| Missions and Missiology | M |
| Religious Education | M |

### THE ROCKEFELLER UNIVERSITY

| | |
|---|---|
| Biological and Biomedical Sciences—General | M,D* |

### ROCKFORD UNIVERSITY

| | |
|---|---|
| Business Administration and Management—General | M |
| Early Childhood Education | M |
| Education—General | M |
| Educational Media/Instructional Technology | M |
| Elementary Education | M |
| Reading Education | M |
| Secondary Education | M |
| Special Education | M |

### ROCKHURST UNIVERSITY

| | |
|---|---|
| Accounting | M,O |
| Business Administration and Management—General | M,O |
| Business Analytics | M,O |
| Communication Disorders | M |
| Data Science/Data Analytics | M,O |
| Education—General | M |
| Entrepreneurship | M,O |
| Finance and Banking | M,O |
| Health Services Management and Hospital Administration | M,O |
| Human Resources Development | M,O |
| International Business | M,O |
| Management Strategy and Policy | M,O |
| Nonprofit Management | M,O |
| Occupational Therapy | M |
| Physical Therapy | D |

### ROCKY MOUNTAIN COLLEGE

| | |
|---|---|
| Accounting | M |
| Educational Leadership and Administration | M |
| Occupational Therapy | D |
| Physician Assistant Studies | M |

### ROCKY MOUNTAIN COLLEGE OF ART + DESIGN

| | |
|---|---|
| Art Education | M |
| Arts Administration | M |
| Internet and Interactive Multimedia | M |

### ROCKY MOUNTAIN UNIVERSITY OF HEALTH PROFESSIONS

| | |
|---|---|
| Communication Disorders | D |
| Family Nurse Practitioner Studies | D |
| Occupational Therapy | D |
| Physical Therapy | D |
| Physician Assistant Studies | M |
| Physiology | D |

### ROCKY VISTA UNIVERSITY

| | |
|---|---|
| Biological and Biomedical Sciences—General | M |
| Osteopathic Medicine | D |
| Physician Assistant Studies | M |

### ROGERS STATE UNIVERSITY

| | |
|---|---|
| Business Administration and Management—General | M |

### ROGER WILLIAMS UNIVERSITY

| | |
|---|---|
| Architectural History | M,O |
| Architecture | M,O |
| Art History | M,O |
| Business Administration and Management—General | M |
| Clinical Psychology | M |
| Computer and Information Systems Security | M |
| Criminal Justice and Criminology | M |
| Education—General | M,O |
| Forensic Psychology | M |
| Health Services Management and Hospital Administration | M |
| Historic Preservation | M,O |
| Law | M,D |
| Middle School Education | M,O |
| Public Administration | M |
| Reading Education | M,O |
| Urban and Regional Planning | M,O |

### ROLLINS COLLEGE

| | |
|---|---|
| Applied Behavior Analysis | M |
| Business Administration and Management—General | M |
| Counselor Education | M |
| Education—General | M |
| Elementary Education | M |
| Entrepreneurship | M |
| Finance and Banking | M |
| Human Resources Development | M |
| Human Resources Management | M |
| International Business | M |
| Liberal Studies | M |
| Public Health—General | M |

### ROOSEVELT UNIVERSITY

| | |
|---|---|
| Accounting | M |
| Actuarial Science | M |
| Arts Administration | M,O |
| Biotechnology | M |
| Business Administration and Management—General | M |
| Chemistry | M |
| Clinical Psychology | M |
| Communication—General | M |
| Computer Science | M |
| Corporate and Organizational Communication | M |
| Early Childhood Education | M |
| Economics | M |
| Education—General | M |
| Educational Leadership and Administration | M |
| Elementary Education | M |
| History | M |
| Hospitality Management | M |
| Human Resources Development | M |
| Human Resources Management | M |
| Humanities | M |
| Industrial and Organizational Psychology | M,D |
| Marketing | M |
| Mathematics | M |
| Music | M,O |
| Organizational Management | M |
| Pharmacy | D |
| Philosophy | M |
| Psychology—General | M,D |
| Public Administration | M |
| Reading Education | M |
| Real Estate | M |
| School Psychology | M |
| Secondary Education | M |
| Sociology | M |
| Special Education | M |
| Theater | M |
| Writing | M |

### ROSALIND FRANKLIN UNIVERSITY OF MEDICINE AND SCIENCE

| | |
|---|---|
| Allied Health—General | M,D,O |
| Allopathic Medicine | D |
| Anatomy | D |
| Biochemistry | D |
| Biological and Biomedical Sciences—General | M,D |
| Biophysics | M,D |
| Cell Biology | D |
| Clinical Psychology | M,D |
| Health Education | M |
| Health Promotion | M |
| Health Services Management and Hospital Administration | M,O |
| Immunology | D |
| Interdisciplinary Studies | D |
| Microbiology | D |
| Molecular Biology | D |
| Molecular Pharmacology | M,D |
| Neuroscience | D |
| Nurse Anesthesia | D |
| Nutrition | M |
| Pathology | M |
| Pharmacy | D |
| Physical Therapy | M,D |
| Physician Assistant Studies | M |
| Physiology | M,D |
| Podiatric Medicine | D |
| Psychology—General | M,D |

### ROSE-HULMAN INSTITUTE OF TECHNOLOGY

| | |
|---|---|
| Biomedical Engineering | M |
| Chemical Engineering | M |
| Civil Engineering | M |
| Computer Engineering | M |
| Electrical Engineering | M |
| Engineering and Applied Sciences—General | M |
| Engineering Management | M |
| Environmental Engineering | M |
| Management Information Systems | M |
| Mechanical Engineering | M |
| Optical Sciences | M |
| Systems Engineering | M |

### ROSEMAN UNIVERSITY OF HEALTH SCIENCES

| | |
|---|---|
| Business Administration and Management—General | M,O |
| Dentistry | M,D,O |
| Pharmacy | D |

### ROSEMONT COLLEGE

| | |
|---|---|
| Business Administration and Management—General | M |
| Counseling Psychology | M |
| Counselor Education | M |
| Education—General | M |
| Elementary Education | M |
| Human Services | M |
| Publishing | M |
| Writing | M |

### ROWAN UNIVERSITY

| | |
|---|---|
| Advertising and Public Relations | M |
| Allopathic Medicine | D |
| Applied Behavior Analysis | M,O |
| Arts Administration | M |
| Bioinformatics | M |
| Biological and Biomedical Sciences—General | M |
| Business Administration and Management—General | M,O |
| Chemical Engineering | M |
| Civil Engineering | M |
| Clinical Psychology | M,O |
| Computer and Information Systems Security | O |
| Computer Science | M |
| Corporate and Organizational Communication | O |
| Counselor Education | M |
| Criminal Justice and Criminology | M |
| Education—General | M,D,O |
| Educational Leadership and Administration | M,D,O |
| Educational Media/Instructional Technology | M,O |
| Electrical Engineering | M |
| Engineering and Applied Sciences—General | M |
| English as a Second Language | O |
| English Education | O |
| Exercise and Sports Science | M |
| Health Promotion | M |
| Higher Education | M |
| History | M,O |
| Library Science | M,D,O |
| Marketing | O |
| Mathematics Education | M,O |
| Mathematics | M |
| Mechanical Engineering | M |

| | |
|---|---|
| Media Studies | O |
| Middle School Education | O |
| Music | M |
| Nursing—General | M |
| Osteopathic Medicine | D |
| Pharmaceutical Sciences | M |
| Psychology—General | M,O |
| Publishing | O |
| Reading Education | M,O |
| Rhetoric | O |
| School Nursing | M,D,O |
| School Psychology | M,O |
| Science Education | M,O |
| Special Education | M,O |
| Theater | M |
| Writing | M,O |

### ROYAL MILITARY COLLEGE OF CANADA

| | |
|---|---|
| Business Administration and Management—General | M |
| Chemical Engineering | M,D |
| Chemistry | M,D |
| Civil Engineering | M,D |
| Computer Engineering | M,D |
| Computer Science | M |
| Electrical Engineering | M,D |
| Engineering and Applied Sciences—General | M,D |
| Mathematics | M |
| Mechanical Engineering | M,D |
| Military and Defense Studies | M,D |
| Physics | M |
| Software Engineering | M,D |

### ROYAL ROADS UNIVERSITY

| | |
|---|---|
| Conflict Resolution and Mediation/Peace Studies | M,O |
| Emergency Management | M,O |
| Environmental Education | M,O |
| Environmental Management and Policy | M,O |
| Legal and Justice Studies | M,O |
| Sustainability Management | M,O |
| Travel and Tourism | M,O |

### RUSH UNIVERSITY

| | |
|---|---|
| Allopathic Medicine | D |
| Anatomy | M,D |
| Biochemistry | M,D |
| Cell Biology | M,D |
| Clinical Laboratory Sciences/Medical Technology | M |
| Communication Disorders | M,D |
| Health Services Management and Hospital Administration | M,D |
| Immunology | M,D |
| Medical Physics | M,D |
| Microbiology | M,D |
| Neuroscience | M,D |
| Nutrition | M |
| Occupational Therapy | D |
| Perfusion | M |
| Pharmaceutical Sciences | M,D |
| Pharmacology | M,D |
| Physical Therapy | M |
| Physician Assistant Studies | M |
| Physiology | D |
| Virology | M,D |

### RUTGERS UNIVERSITY - CAMDEN

| | |
|---|---|
| Applied Mathematics | M |
| Biological and Biomedical Sciences—General | M |
| Business Administration and Management—General | M |
| Chemistry | M |
| Child Development | M,D |
| Computational Biology | M,D |
| Computer Science | M |
| Criminal Justice and Criminology | M |
| Educational Leadership and Administration | M |
| Educational Policy | M |
| English | M |
| Family Nurse Practitioner Studies | D |
| Gerontological Nursing | D |
| Health Services Management and Hospital Administration | M,O |
| History | M |
| International Affairs | M |
| International Development | M |
| Law | D |
| Liberal Studies | M |
| Mathematics Education | M |
| Mathematics | M |
| Nursing—General | D |
| Physical Therapy | D |
| Psychology—General | M |
| Public Administration | M |
| Public Health—General | M,O |
| Public History | M |
| Public Policy | M |
| Writing | M |

### RUTGERS UNIVERSITY - NEWARK

| | |
|---|---|
| Accounting | M,D |
| Adult Nursing | M,D,O |
| Allied Health—General | M,D,O |
| Allopathic Medicine | D |
| American Studies | M,D |
| Analytical Chemistry | M,D |
| Applied Physics | M,D |
| Biochemistry | M,D |
| Bioinformatics | M,D |
| Biological and Biomedical Sciences—General | M,D,O |
| Biomedical Engineering | O |
| Biopsychology | D |
| Business Administration and Management—General | M,D |
| Cell Biology | D |
| Chemistry | M,D |
| Clinical Laboratory Sciences/Medical Technology | M |
| Clothing and Textiles | M |
| Cognitive Sciences | D |
| Computational Biology | M |
| Criminal Justice and Criminology | M,D |
| Dentistry | M,D,O |
| Economics | M,D |
| English | M |
| Environmental Sciences | M,D |
| Epidemiology | M,O |
| Family Nurse Practitioner Studies | M,D,O |
| Finance and Banking | M,D |
| Geology | M |
| Health Education | M,D |
| Health Physics/Radiological Health | M |
| Health Services Management and Hospital Administration | M,D,O |
| History | M |
| Human Resources Management | M,D |
| Immunology | D |
| Inorganic Chemistry | M,D |
| International Affairs | M,D |
| International Business | D |
| Law | D |
| Logistics | M |
| Management Information Systems | M,D |
| Management of Technology | D |
| Marketing | D |
| Mathematics | D |
| Medical Imaging | M |
| Medical Informatics | M,D,O |
| Microbiology | D |
| Molecular Biology | M,D |
| Molecular Genetics | D |
| Molecular Medicine | D |
| Molecular Pathology | D |
| Music | M |
| Neuroscience | D |
| Nurse Anesthesia | M,D,O |
| Nursing Informatics | M |
| Nursing—General | M,D,O |
| Nutrition | M,D,O |
| Occupational Health Nursing | M,D,O |
| Oral and Dental Sciences | M,D,O |
| Organic Chemistry | M,D |
| Organizational Management | D |
| Pathology | D |
| Pharmaceutical Administration | M |
| Pharmacology | D |
| Physical Chemistry | M,D |
| Physical Therapy | D |
| Physician Assistant Studies | M |
| Physiology | D |
| Political Science | M |
| Psychology—General | D |
| Public Administration | M,D |
| Public Health—General | M,O |
| Public Policy | M,D,O |
| Quantitative Analysis | M,O |
| Real Estate | M |
| Rehabilitation Counseling | M,D |
| Social Psychology | D |
| Supply Chain Management | D |
| Transcultural Nursing | M,D,O |
| Urban Studies | M,D |
| Women's Health Nursing | M,D,O |
| Writing | M |

### RUTGERS UNIVERSITY - NEW BRUNSWICK

| | |
|---|---|
| Aerospace/Aeronautical Engineering | M,D |
| African Studies | D |
| African-American Studies | D |
| Agricultural Economics and Agribusiness | M |
| Allopathic Medicine | D |
| Animal Sciences | M,D |
| Anthropology | M,D |
| Applied Arts and Design—General | M |
| Applied Mathematics | M,D |
| Applied Psychology | M,D |
| Applied Statistics | M,D |
| Art History | M,D,O |
| Art/Fine Arts | M |
| Asian Studies | M,D |
| Astronomy | M,D |
| Atmospheric Sciences | M,D |
| Biochemical Engineering | M,D |
| Biochemistry | M,D |
| Biological and Biomedical Sciences—General | M,D |
| Biomedical Engineering | M,D |
| Biopsychology | D |
| Biostatistics | M,D,O |
| Cancer Biology/Oncology | M,D |
| Cell Biology | M,D |
| Chemical Engineering | M,D |
| Chemistry | M,D |
| Civil Engineering | M,D |
| Classics | M,D |
| Clinical Laboratory Sciences/Medical Technology | M |
| Clinical Psychology | M,D |
| Cognitive Sciences | D |
| Communication—General | D |
| Comparative Literature | M,D |
| Computational Biology | D |
| Computer Engineering | M,D |
| Computer Science | M,D |
| Condensed Matter Physics | M,D |
| Counseling Psychology | M |
| Counselor Education | M |
| Developmental Biology | M,D |
| Developmental Education | M |
| Early Childhood Education | M,D |
| Ecology | M,D |
| Economics | M,D |
| Education—General | M,D |
| Educational Leadership and Administration | M,D |
| Educational Measurement and Evaluation | M |
| Educational Policy | D |
| Educational Psychology | M,D |
| Electrical Engineering | M,D |
| Elementary Education | M,D |
| Emergency Management | M,D,O |
| English as a Second Language | M,D |
| English Education | M |
| English | D |
| Entomology | M,D |
| Environmental and Occupational Health | M,D,O |
| Environmental Biology | M,D |
| Environmental Engineering | M,D |
| Environmental Sciences | M,D |
| Epidemiology | M,D,O |
| Evolutionary Biology | M,D |
| Food Science and Technology | M,D |
| Foreign Languages Education | M,D |
| Foundations and Philosophy of Education | M,D |
| French | M,D |
| Gender Studies | M,D |
| Genetics | M,D |
| Geography | M,D |
| Geology | M,D |
| German | M,D |
| Hazardous Materials Management | M,D |
| Health Education | M,D,O |
| Health Informatics | M |
| Health Psychology | D |
| Health Services Management and Hospital Administration | M,D,O |
| Historic Preservation | M,D,O |
| History of Medicine | D |
| History of Science and Technology | D |
| History | D |
| Horticulture | M,D |
| Human Resources Management | M,D |
| Immunology | M,D |
| Industrial and Labor Relations | M,D |
| Industrial/Management Engineering | M,D |
| Information Science | M |
| Information Studies | M,D |
| Inorganic Chemistry | M,D |
| Interdisciplinary Studies | D |
| International Affairs | M,D |
| Italian | M,D |
| Jewish Studies | M,O |
| Landscape Architecture | M |
| Legal and Justice Studies | M,D |
| Library Science | D |
| Linguistics | D |
| Marine Biology | M,D |
| Materials Engineering | M,D |
| Materials Sciences | M,D |
| Mathematics Education | M,D |
| Mathematics | M,D |
| Mechanical Engineering | M,D |
| Mechanics | M,D |
| Medical Microbiology | M,D |
| Medicinal and Pharmaceutical Chemistry | M,D |
| Medieval and Renaissance Studies | D |
| Microbiology | M,D |
| Molecular Biology | M,D |
| Molecular Biophysics | D |
| Molecular Genetics | M,D |
| Molecular Pharmacology | M,D |
| Molecular Physiology | M,D |
| Multilingual and Multicultural Education | M,D |
| Music Education | M,D,O |
| Music | M,D,O |
| Neuroscience | M,D |
| Nutrition | M,D |
| Oceanography | M,D |
| Operations Research | D |
| Organic Chemistry | M,D |
| Pharmaceutical Sciences | M,D |
| Pharmacy | M,D |
| Philosophy | D |
| Physical Chemistry | M,D |
| Physics | M,D |
| Physiology | M,D |
| Plant Biology | M,D |
| Plant Molecular Biology | M,D |
| Plant Pathology | M,D |
| Political Science | M,D |
| Psychology—General | D |
| Public Health—General | M,D |
| Public Policy | M,D |
| Quality Management | M,D |
| Reading Education | M,D |
| Reliability Engineering | M,D |
| Religion | M,O |
| Reproductive Biology | M,D |
| School Psychology | M,D |
| Science Education | M,D |
| Social Psychology | D |
| Social Sciences Education | M,D |
| Social Work | M,D |
| Sociology | M,D |
| Spanish | M,D |
| Special Education | M,D |
| Statistics | M,D |
| Student Affairs | M |
| Systems Biology | D |
| Systems Engineering | M,D |
| Theater | M |
| Theoretical Physics | M,D |
| Toxicology | M,D |
| Translation and Interpretation | M,D |
| Translational Biology | M |
| Urban and Regional Planning | M,D |
| Virology | M,D |
| Water Resources | M,D |
| Women's Studies | M,D |
| Writing | M |

### RYERSON UNIVERSITY

| | |
|---|---|
| Arts Administration | M |
| Business Administration and Management—General | M |
| Management of Technology | M |

### SACRED HEART MAJOR SEMINARY

| | |
|---|---|
| Pastoral Ministry and Counseling | M |
| Theology | M |

### SACRED HEART SEMINARY AND SCHOOL OF THEOLOGY

| | |
|---|---|
| Theology | M,O |

### SACRED HEART UNIVERSITY

| | |
|---|---|
| Accounting | M,O |
| Applied Psychology | M |
| Business Administration and Management—General | M,O |
| Chemistry | M |
| Communication Disorders | M |
| Communication—General | M |
| Computer and Information Systems Security | M |
| Computer Science | M |
| Criminal Justice and Criminology | M |
| Education—General | M,O |
| Educational Leadership and Administration | O |
| Exercise and Sports Science | M |
| Family Nurse Practitioner Studies | M,D,O |
| Film, Television, and Video Production | M |
| Finance and Banking | M,D,O |
| Game Design and Development | M |
| Health Informatics | M |
| Human Resources Management | M,O |
| Industrial and Organizational Psychology | M |
| Information Science | M |
| Investment Management | M,D,O |
| Journalism | M |
| Marketing | M,O |
| Molecular Biology | M |
| Nursing and Healthcare Administration | M,D,O |
| Nursing Education | M,D,O |
| Nursing—General | M,D,O |
| Nutrition | M |
| Occupational Therapy | M |
| Physical Therapy | D |
| Physician Assistant Studies | M |
| Public Administration | M |
| Public Health—General | M |
| Reading Education | O |
| Social Psychology | M |
| Social Work | M |

### SAGE GRADUATE SCHOOL

| | |
|---|---|
| Applied Behavior Analysis | M,O |
| Business Administration and Management—General | M |
| Counseling Psychology | M |
| Counselor Education | M,O |
| Education—General | M,D,O |
| Educational Leadership and Administration | D |
| Elementary Education | M |
| Family Nurse Practitioner Studies | M |
| Forensic Psychology | M,O |
| Gerontological Nursing | M,O |
| Gerontology | M |
| Health Education | M |
| Health Services Management and Hospital Administration | M |
| Nursing Education | D |
| Nursing—General | M,D,O |
| Nutrition | M,O |
| Occupational Therapy | M |
| Organizational Management | M |
| Physical Therapy | D |
| Psychiatric Nursing | M,O |
| Psychology—General | M,O |
| Reading Education | M |
| Social Psychology | M |
| Special Education | M |

### SAGINAW VALLEY STATE UNIVERSITY

| | |
|---|---|
| Business Administration and Management—General | M |
| Chinese | M |
| Communication—General | M |
| Computer and Information Systems Security | M |
| Computer Science | M |
| Early Childhood Education | M |
| Education—General | M,O |
| Educational Leadership and Administration | M,O |
| Educational Media/Instructional Technology | M |
| Energy and Power Engineering | M |
| Engineering and Applied Sciences—General | M |
| Family Nurse Practitioner Studies | M,D |
| Foreign Languages Education | M |
| Health Services Management and Hospital Administration | M |
| Media Studies | M |
| Nursing—General | M |
| Occupational Therapy | M |
| Public Administration | M |
| Reading Education | M |
| Social Work | M |
| Special Education | M |

*M—masters degree; D—doctorate; O—other advanced degree; *—Close-Up and/or Display*

### ST. AMBROSE UNIVERSITY

| | |
|---|---|
| Accounting | M |
| Business Administration and Management—General | M,D |
| Communication Disorders | M |
| Criminal Justice and Criminology | M |
| Early Childhood Education | M |
| Education—General | M |
| Educational Leadership and Administration | M |
| Exercise and Sports Science | M |
| Health Services Management and Hospital Administration | M,D |
| Human Resources Management | M,D |
| Management of Technology | M |
| Occupational Therapy | D |
| Organizational Management | M |
| Pastoral Ministry and Counseling | M |
| Physical Therapy | D |
| Physician Assistant Studies | M |
| Public Health—General | M |
| Social Work | M |

### ST. ANDREW'S COLLEGE

| | |
|---|---|
| Theology | M,D,O |

### ST. ANDREW'S COLLEGE IN WINNIPEG

| | |
|---|---|
| Theology | M |

### SAINT ANTHONY COLLEGE OF NURSING

| | |
|---|---|
| Nursing—General | M |

### ST. AUGUSTINE'S SEMINARY OF TORONTO

| | |
|---|---|
| Pastoral Ministry and Counseling | M,O |
| Religious Education | M,O |
| Theology | M,O |

### ST. BERNARD'S SCHOOL OF THEOLOGY AND MINISTRY

| | |
|---|---|
| Pastoral Ministry and Counseling | M,O |
| Theology | M,O |

### ST. BONAVENTURE UNIVERSITY

| | |
|---|---|
| Accounting | M |
| Business Administration and Management—General | M |
| Corporate and Organizational Communication | M |
| Counseling Psychology | M,O |
| Counselor Education | M,O |
| Early Childhood Education | M |
| Education of the Gifted | M,O |
| Education—General | M,O |
| Educational Leadership and Administration | M,O |
| Marketing | M |
| Middle School Education | M |
| Reading Education | M |
| Rehabilitation Counseling | M,O |
| Secondary Education | M |
| Social Psychology | M,O |
| Special Education | M,O |

### ST. CATHERINE UNIVERSITY

| | |
|---|---|
| Adult Nursing | M,D |
| Business Administration and Management—General | M |
| Curriculum and Instruction | M |
| Early Childhood Education | M |
| Education—General | M,O |
| Gerontological Nursing | M,D |
| Health Informatics | M |
| Health Services Management and Hospital Administration | M |
| Information Studies | M |
| International Health | M |
| Library Science | M |
| Marketing | M |
| Nursing Education | M,D |
| Nursing—General | M,D |
| Occupational Therapy | M,D |
| Organizational Management | M |
| Pastoral Ministry and Counseling | M,O |
| Pediatric Nursing | M,D |
| Physical Therapy | D |
| Physician Assistant Studies | M |
| Public Health—General | M |
| Social Work | M,D |
| Theology | M,O |

### SAINT CHARLES BORROMEO SEMINARY, OVERBROOK

| | |
|---|---|
| Philosophy | M |
| Theology | M |

### ST. CLOUD STATE UNIVERSITY

| | |
|---|---|
| Applied Behavior Analysis | M |
| Applied Economics | M |
| Archaeology | M,O |
| Biological and Biomedical Sciences—General | M |
| Biomedical Engineering | M,O |
| Business Administration and Management—General | M |
| Child and Family Studies | M |
| Communication Disorders | M |
| Computer and Information Systems Security | M |
| Computer Science | M,O |
| Counselor Education | M |
| Criminal Justice and Criminology | M |
| Economics | M |
| Education—General | M,D,O |
| Educational Leadership and Administration | M,D |
| Educational Media/Instructional Technology | M,O |
| Electrical Engineering | M |
| Engineering and Applied Sciences—General | M,O |
| English | M |
| Geography | M,O |
| Gerontology | M,O |
| Higher Education | D |
| Historic Preservation | M,O |
| History | M |
| Human Services | M |
| Industrial and Organizational Psychology | M |
| Marriage and Family Therapy | M |
| Mass Communication | M |
| Rhetoric | M |
| Social Work | M |
| Special Education | M,O |
| Student Affairs | M |
| Writing | M |

### ST. EDWARD'S UNIVERSITY

| | |
|---|---|
| Accounting | M |
| Counseling Psychology | M |
| Education—General | M,O |
| Environmental Management and Policy | M |
| Humanities | M,O |
| Liberal Studies | M,O |
| Organizational Management | M |
| Student Affairs | M |
| Sustainable Development | M |

### ST. FRANCIS COLLEGE

| | |
|---|---|
| Accounting | M |

### SAINT FRANCIS MEDICAL CENTER COLLEGE OF NURSING

| | |
|---|---|
| Family Nurse Practitioner Studies | M,D,O |
| Gerontological Nursing | M,D,O |
| Maternal and Child/Neonatal Nursing | M,D,O |
| Medical/Surgical Nursing | M,D,O |
| Nursing and Healthcare Administration | M,D,O |
| Nursing Education | M,D,O |
| Nursing—General | M,D,O |
| Psychiatric Nursing | M,D,O |

### SAINT FRANCIS UNIVERSITY

| | |
|---|---|
| Biological and Biomedical Sciences—General | M |
| Business Administration and Management—General | M |
| Cancer Biology/Oncology | M |
| Education—General | M |
| Educational Leadership and Administration | M |
| Health Education | M |
| Human Resources Management | M |
| Nursing and Healthcare Administration | M |
| Nursing Education | M |
| Nursing—General | M |
| Occupational Therapy | M |
| Physical Therapy | D |
| Physician Assistant Studies | M |
| Reading Education | M |

### ST. FRANCIS XAVIER UNIVERSITY

| | |
|---|---|
| Adult Education | M |
| Biological and Biomedical Sciences—General | M |
| Chemistry | M |
| Computer Science | M |
| Cultural Studies | M |
| Curriculum and Instruction | M |
| Education—General | M |
| Educational Leadership and Administration | M |
| Geology | M |
| Geosciences | M |
| Urban and Regional Planning | M |

### ST. JOHN FISHER COLLEGE

| | |
|---|---|
| Biological and Biomedical Sciences—General | M |
| Business Administration and Management—General | M |
| Chemistry | M |
| Counseling Psychology | M |
| Education—General | M,D,O |
| Educational Leadership and Administration | M,D |
| Educational Media/Instructional Technology | M |
| Elementary Education | M,O |
| English Education | M |
| Foreign Languages Education | M |
| French | M |
| Mathematics Education | M |
| Middle School Education | M |
| Nursing—General | M,D,O |
| Pharmacy | D |
| Physics | M |
| Reading Education | M |
| Social Sciences Education | M |
| Special Education | M,O |

### ST. JOHN'S COLLEGE (MD)

| | |
|---|---|
| Liberal Studies | M |

### ST. JOHN'S COLLEGE (NM)

| | |
|---|---|
| Asian Languages | M |
| Asian Studies | M |
| Liberal Studies | M |

### ST. JOHN'S SEMINARY (CA)

| | |
|---|---|
| Pastoral Ministry and Counseling | M |
| Theology | M |

### SAINT JOHN'S SEMINARY (MA)

| | |
|---|---|
| Religion | M |
| Theology | M |

### SAINT JOHN'S UNIVERSITY (MN)

| | |
|---|---|
| Music | M |
| Pastoral Ministry and Counseling | M |
| Theology | M |

### ST. JOHN'S UNIVERSITY (NY)

| | |
|---|---|
| Accounting | M |
| Actuarial Science | M |
| Applied Mathematics | M |
| Asian Studies | M |
| Biological and Biomedical Sciences—General | M,D |
| Biotechnology | M |
| Business Administration and Management—General | M |
| Business Analytics | M |
| Chemistry | M |
| Clinical Psychology | M,D,O |
| Communication Disorders | M,D |
| Computational Sciences | M |
| Counseling Psychology | M,O |
| Counselor Education | M,O |
| Criminal Justice and Criminology | M |
| Curriculum and Instruction | D |
| Data Science/Data Analytics | M |
| Early Childhood Education | M,D,O |
| Education of the Gifted | D,O |
| Education—General | M,D,O |
| Educational Leadership and Administration | M,D,O |
| Elementary Education | M |
| English as a Second Language | M,O |
| English | M,D |
| Finance and Banking | M |
| History | M,D |
| Homeland Security | M |
| Information Science | |
| Information Studies | M,O |
| Insurance | M |
| International and Comparative Education | D |
| International Business | M |
| Law | D |
| Legal and Justice Studies | M |
| Liberal Studies | M |
| Library Science | M,O |
| Management Information Systems | M |
| Management Strategy and Policy | M |
| Marketing | M |
| Mass Communication | M |
| Mathematics Education | D |
| Mathematics | M |
| Multilingual and Multicultural Education | M,O |
| Museum Studies | M |
| Pharmaceutical Administration | M |
| Pharmaceutical Sciences | M,D |
| Pharmacy | M,D |
| Political Science | M,O |
| Psychology—General | M |
| Public Administration | M,O |
| Public Health—General | M |
| Public History | M,D |
| Reading Education | M,D,O |
| Risk Management | M |
| School Psychology | M,D |
| Science Education | D |
| Secondary Education | M |
| Sociology | M |
| Spanish | M |
| Special Education | M,O |
| Sports Management | M |
| Statistics | M |
| Taxation | M |
| Theology | M |
| Toxicology | M |

### ST. JOSEPH'S COLLEGE, LONG ISLAND CAMPUS

| | |
|---|---|
| Accounting | M |
| Adult Nursing | M |
| Business Administration and Management—General | M |
| Early Childhood Education | M |
| Educational Leadership and Administration | M |
| Forensic Sciences | M |
| Gerontological Nursing | M |
| Health Informatics | M |
| Health Services Management and Hospital Administration | M |
| Human Resources Management | M |
| Human Services | M |
| Mathematics Education | M |
| Nursing Education | M |
| Nursing—General | M |
| Organizational Management | M |
| Reading Education | M |
| Special Education | M |

### ST. JOSEPH'S COLLEGE, NEW YORK

| | |
|---|---|
| Accounting | M |
| Adult Nursing | M |
| Business Administration and Management—General | M |
| Education—General | M |
| Educational Leadership and Administration | M |
| Forensic Sciences | M |
| Gerontological Nursing | M |
| Health Informatics | M |
| Health Services Management and Hospital Administration | M |
| Human Resources Management | M |
| Human Services | M |
| Nursing Education | M |
| Nursing—General | M |
| Organizational Management | M |
| Reading Education | M |
| Special Education | M |
| Writing | M |

### SAINT JOSEPH'S COLLEGE OF MAINE

| | |
|---|---|
| Accounting | M |
| Adult Education | M |
| Business Administration and Management—General | M |
| Education—General | M |
| Educational Leadership and Administration | M |
| Family Nurse Practitioner Studies | M,O |
| Health Education | M |
| Health Services Management and Hospital Administration | M |
| Nursing and Healthcare Administration | M,O |
| Nursing Education | M,O |
| Nursing—General | M,O |
| Pastoral Ministry and Counseling | M |

### ST. JOSEPH'S SEMINARY

| | |
|---|---|
| Pastoral Ministry and Counseling | M |
| Religion | M |
| Theology | M |

### SAINT JOSEPH'S UNIVERSITY

| | |
|---|---|
| Accounting | M,O |
| Biological and Biomedical Sciences—General | M |
| Business Administration and Management—General | M,O |
| Business Analytics | M |
| Communication Disorders | M,D,O |
| Computer Science | M,O |
| Criminal Justice and Criminology | M,O |
| Curriculum and Instruction | M,D,O |
| Early Childhood Education | M,D,O |
| Education—General | M,D,O |
| Educational Leadership and Administration | M,D,O |
| Elementary Education | M,D,O |
| Finance and Banking | M,O |
| Health Informatics | M |
| Health Services Management and Hospital Administration | M,O |
| Human Resources Management | M |
| International Business | M,O |
| Law | M,O |
| Marketing | M,O |
| Mathematics | M,O |
| Middle School Education | M,D,O |
| Psychology—General | M,O |
| Reading Education | M,D,O |
| Secondary Education | M,D,O |
| Special Education | M,D,O |
| Writing | M |

### SAINT LEO UNIVERSITY

| | |
|---|---|
| Accounting | M,D |
| Agricultural Education | M,D |
| Business Administration and Management—General | M,D |
| Computer and Information Systems Security | M,D |
| Criminal Justice and Criminology | M,D |
| Education—General | M,D,O |
| Educational Leadership and Administration | M,D,O |
| Emergency Management | M,D |
| Forensic Sciences | M,D |
| Health Services Management and Hospital Administration | M,D |
| Human Resources Management | M,D |
| Human Services | M |
| Legal and Justice Studies | M,D |
| Marketing Research | M,D |
| Marketing | M,D |
| Psychology—General | M |
| Social Work | M |
| Theology | M,O |
| Writing | M |

### ST. LOUIS COLLEGE OF PHARMACY

| | |
|---|---|
| Pharmacy | D |

### SAINT LOUIS UNIVERSITY

| | |
|---|---|
| Accounting | M |
| Allied Health—General | M,D,O |
| Allopathic Medicine | D |
| American Studies | M,D |
| Anatomy | M,D |
| Applied Behavior Analysis | M,D |
| Athletic Training and Sports Medicine | M,D |
| Biochemistry | D |
| Bioethics | D,O |
| Bioinformatics | M |
| Biological and Biomedical Sciences—General | M,D |
| Biomedical Engineering | M,D |
| Business Administration and Management—General | M |
| Chemistry | M,D |
| Clinical Psychology | M,D |
| Communication Disorders | M |
| Communication—General | M |
| Community Health | M |
| Computational Biology | M |
| Computer Science | M |
| Criminal Justice and Criminology | M |
| Curriculum and Instruction | M,D |
| Dentistry | M |
| Education—General | M,D |
| Educational Leadership and Administration | M,D,O |
| Emergency Management | M |
| English | M,D |
| Experimental Psychology | M,D |
| Finance and Banking | M |
| Foundations and Philosophy of Education | M,D |
| French | M |
| Geophysics | M,D |
| Geosciences | M,D |
| Health Services Management and Hospital Administration | M,D |
| Higher Education | M,D,O |
| History | M,D |
| Immunology | D |
| Industrial and Organizational Psychology | M,D |
| International Business | M,D |
| Law | M,D |
| Mathematics | M,D |
| Meteorology | M,D |
| Microbiology | D |
| Molecular Biology | D |
| Nursing—General | M,D,O |
| Nutrition | M |
| Occupational Therapy | M |
| Oral and Dental Sciences | M |
| Pathology | D |
| Pharmacology | D |

Philosophy M,D
Physical Therapy M,D
Physician Assistant Studies M
Physiology D
Political Science M
Psychology—General M,D
Public Health—General M,D
Social Work M,D
Software Engineering M
Spanish M
Special Education M,D
Student Affairs M,D,O
Theology M,D
Urban and Regional Planning M

### SAINT LOUIS UNIVERSITY–MADRID CAMPUS
English M
Spanish M

### SAINT MARTIN'S UNIVERSITY
Business Administration and Management—General M
Civil Engineering M
Counseling Psychology M
Education—General M
Engineering Management M
Mechanical Engineering M
Social Psychology M

### SAINT MARY-OF-THE-WOODS COLLEGE
Art Therapy M,O
Health Services Management and Hospital Administration M
Management Strategy and Policy M
Nonprofit Management M
Nursing—General M
Organizational Management M
Therapies—Dance, Drama, and Music M

### SAINT MARY'S COLLEGE
Adult Nursing D
Communication Disorders M
Family Nurse Practitioner Studies D
Gerontological Nursing D
Nursing—General D

### SAINT MARY'S COLLEGE OF CALIFORNIA
Accounting M
Business Administration and Management—General M
Business Analytics M
Conflict Resolution and Mediation/Peace Studies M
Counselor Education M,O
Dance M
Early Childhood Education M
Education—General M,D,O
Educational Leadership and Administration M,D,O
Exercise and Sports Science M
Finance and Banking M
Investment Management M
Kinesiology and Movement Studies M
Marriage and Family Therapy M,O
Organizational Management M
School Psychology M,O
Special Education M
Sports Management M
Writing M

### ST. MARY'S COLLEGE OF MARYLAND
Education—General M

### SAINT MARY SEMINARY AND GRADUATE SCHOOL OF THEOLOGY
Theology M,D

### ST. MARY'S SEMINARY AND UNIVERSITY
Theology M,D,O

### SAINT MARY'S UNIVERSITY (CANADA)
Applied Psychology M,D
Applied Science and Technology M
Astronomy M,D
Business Administration and Management—General M,D
Canadian Studies M,O
Criminal Justice and Criminology M
Gender Studies M
History M
Industrial and Organizational Psychology M,D
International Development M
Philosophy M
Psychology—General M,D
Religion M
Theology M
Women's Studies M

### ST. MARY'S UNIVERSITY (UNITED STATES)
Business Administration and Management—General M
Communication—General M
Computer and Information Systems Security M,O
Computer Engineering M
Computer Science M
Conflict Resolution and Mediation/Peace Studies M,O
Counseling Psychology M
Counselor Education D
Criminal Justice and Criminology M
Education—General M
Educational Leadership and Administration M
Electrical Engineering M
Engineering Management M
English M
Environmental Law M
Health Law M
Homeland Security M,O
Industrial and Organizational Psychology M
Industrial/Management Engineering M
Information Science M
International Affairs M,O
International Development M,O
Law M,D
Legal and Justice Studies M
Public Administration M,O
Software Engineering M,O
Theology M

### SAINT MARY'S UNIVERSITY OF MINNESOTA
Accounting M
Business Administration and Management—General M,D
Computer and Information Systems Security M
Counseling Psychology M,D,O
Data Science/Data Analytics M
Education—General M,O
Educational Leadership and Administration M,D,O
Educational Media/Instructional Technology M
Elementary Education M
Geographic Information Systems M,O
Health Services Management and Hospital Administration M
Human Development M
Human Resources Management M
Marriage and Family Therapy M
Nurse Anesthesia M
Organizational Management M
Philanthropic Studies M
Project Management M,O
Public Administration M
Religious Education M
Secondary Education M
Special Education M,O

### SAINT MEINRAD SCHOOL OF THEOLOGY
Theology M

### SAINT MICHAEL'S COLLEGE
Art Education M,O
Clinical Psychology M
Education—General M,O
Educational Leadership and Administration M,O
English as a Second Language M,O
Reading Education M,O
Special Education M,O

### ST. NORBERT COLLEGE
Business Administration and Management—General M
Health Services Management and Hospital Administration M
Liberal Studies M
Supply Chain Management M
Theology M

### ST. PATRICK'S SEMINARY & UNIVERSITY
Theology M,O

### SAINT PAUL SCHOOL OF THEOLOGY
Theology M,D

### SAINT PAUL UNIVERSITY
Conflict Resolution and Mediation/Peace Studies M
Counseling Psychology M
Marriage and Family Therapy M
Missions and Missiology M
Pastoral Ministry and Counseling M,D,O
Theology M,D,O

### ST. PETER'S SEMINARY
Theology M

### SAINT PETER'S UNIVERSITY
Accounting M
Adult Nursing M,D,O
Applied Behavior Analysis M,D,O
Business Administration and Management—General M
Counselor Education M,O
Criminal Justice and Criminology M
Data Science/Data Analytics M
Education—General M,D,O
Educational Leadership and Administration M,D
Elementary Education M,O
Family and Consumer Sciences-General M
Finance and Banking M
Health Services Management and Hospital Administration M
Higher Education M,D
Human Resources Management M
International Business M
Management Information Systems M
Marketing M
Mathematics Education M,D,O
Middle School Education M,O
Nursing and Healthcare Administration M,D,O
Nursing—General M,D,O
Public Administration M
Reading Education M,O
Risk Management M
Secondary Education M,O
Special Education M,O

### SAINTS CYRIL AND METHODIUS SEMINARY
Pastoral Ministry and Counseling M
Religious Education M
Theology M

### ST. STEPHEN'S COLLEGE
Pastoral Ministry and Counseling M,D
Theology M,D

### ST. THOMAS AQUINAS COLLEGE
Business Administration and Management—General M
Education—General M,O
Educational Leadership and Administration M,O
Elementary Education M,O
Finance and Banking M
Marketing M
Middle School Education M,O
Reading Education M,O
Secondary Education M,O
Special Education M,O

### ST. THOMAS UNIVERSITY - FLORIDA
Accounting M,O
Arts Administration M
Business Administration and Management—General M,O
Communication—General M,D,O
Counseling Psychology M
Counselor Education M,O
Criminal Justice and Criminology M,O
Education of the Gifted M,D,O
Education—General M,D,O
Educational Leadership and Administration M,D,O
Educational Media/Instructional Technology M,D,O
Elementary Education M,D,O
English as a Second Language M,D,O
Film, Television, and Video Production M
Geosciences M,D,O
Health Services Management and Hospital Administration M,O
Hispanic Studies M,O
Human Resources Management M,O
International Business M,O
Law M,D
Marriage and Family Therapy M,O
Pastoral Ministry and Counseling M,D,O
Planetary and Space Sciences M,D,O
Public Administration M,O
Reading Education M,D,O
Special Education M,D,O
Sports Management M,O
Taxation M,D
Theology M,D,O

### ST. TIKHON'S ORTHODOX THEOLOGICAL SEMINARY
Theology M

### SAINT VINCENT COLLEGE
Business Administration and Management—General M
Curriculum and Instruction M
Education—General M
Educational Leadership and Administration M
Educational Media/Instructional Technology M
Nurse Anesthesia M,D
Special Education M

### ST. VINCENT DE PAUL REGIONAL SEMINARY
Theology M

### SAINT VINCENT SEMINARY
Theology M

### ST. VLADIMIR'S ORTHODOX THEOLOGICAL SEMINARY
Theology M,D

### SAINT XAVIER UNIVERSITY
Business Administration and Management—General M,O
Communication Disorders M
Computer Science M
Counselor Education M
Curriculum and Instruction M
Early Childhood Education M
Education—General M
Educational Leadership and Administration M
Educational Media/Instructional Technology M
Elementary Education M
English as a Second Language M
Finance and Banking M,O
Foreign Languages Education M
Health Services Management and Hospital Administration M,O
Marketing M,O
Music Education M
Nursing—General M,O
Project Management M,O
Reading Education M
Science Education M
Secondary Education M
Spanish M
Special Education M

### SALEM COLLEGE
Art Education M
Counselor Education M
Education—General M
Elementary Education M
English as a Second Language M
Middle School Education M
Music M
Reading Education M
Secondary Education M
Special Education M

### SALEM INTERNATIONAL UNIVERSITY
Business Administration and Management—General M
Computer and Information Systems Security M
Curriculum and Instruction M
Education—General M
Educational Leadership and Administration M
International Business M

### SALEM STATE UNIVERSITY
Art Education M
Business Administration and Management—General M
Counseling Psychology M,O
Counselor Education M
Criminal Justice and Criminology M
Early Childhood Education M
Educational Leadership and Administration M
Educational Media/Instructional Technology M
Elementary Education M
English as a Second Language M
English M
Geography M
Gerontological Nursing M
Higher Education M
History M
Mathematics Education M
Mathematics M
Middle School Education M
Nursing and Healthcare Administration M
Nursing Education M
Nursing—General M
Occupational Therapy M
Physical Education M
Psychology—General M,O
Reading Education M
Science Education M
Secondary Education M
Social Work M
Spanish M
Special Education M

### SALISBURY UNIVERSITY
American Studies M
Athletic Training and Sports Medicine M
Biological and Biomedical Sciences—General M
Business Administration and Management—General M
Conflict Resolution and Mediation/Peace Studies M
Curriculum and Instruction M
Educational Leadership and Administration M
English M
Family Nurse Practitioner Studies D
Geographic Information Systems M
History M
Mathematics Education M
Middle School Education M
Nursing and Healthcare Administration M,D
Nursing Education M
Nursing—General M,D
Physiology M
Reading Education M,D
Secondary Education M
Social Work M

### SALUS UNIVERSITY
Communication Disorders M,D,O
Occupational Therapy M,O
Optometry D
Physician Assistant Studies M
Public Health—General M
Rehabilitation Sciences M,O
Special Education M,O
Vision Sciences M,O

### SALVE REGINA UNIVERSITY
Addictions/Substance Abuse Counseling M,O
Applied Behavior Analysis M,O
Business Administration and Management—General M,O
Business Education M,O
Computer and Information Systems Security M,O
Conflict Resolution and Mediation/Peace Studies M,D
Counseling Psychology M,O
Criminal Justice and Criminology M,O
Entrepreneurship M
Forensic Sciences M,O
Health Services Management and Hospital Administration M,O
Homeland Security M,O
Human Resources Management M,O
Humanities M,D
International Affairs M,D,O
Management Strategy and Policy M,O
Nonprofit Management M,O
Nursing—General D
Organizational Management M,O
Rehabilitation Counseling M,O
Religion M,D
Writing M

### SAMFORD UNIVERSITY
Accounting M
Athletic Training and Sports Medicine M,D

*M—masters degree; D—doctorate; O—other advanced degree; *—Close-Up and/or Display*

Business Administration and Management—General M
Communication Disorders M,D
Education of the Gifted M,D,O
Education—General M,D,O
Educational Leadership and Administration M,D,O
Educational Media/Instructional Technology M,D,O
Elementary Education M,D,O
Energy Management and Policy M
Entrepreneurship M
Environmental Management and Policy M
Family Nurse Practitioner Studies M,D
Finance and Banking M
Health Informatics M
Health Services Management and Hospital Administration M
Law M,D
Marketing M
Music Education M
Music M
Nurse Anesthesia M,D
Nursing and Healthcare Administration M,D
Nursing Informatics M,D
Nursing—General M,D
Nutrition M
Pharmacy D
Physical Therapy M,D
Public Health—General M
Secondary Education M,D,O
Social Work M
Special Education M,D,O
Theology M,D

### SAM HOUSTON STATE UNIVERSITY

Accounting M
Agricultural Sciences—General M
Allied Health—General M
Biological and Biomedical Sciences—General M
Business Administration and Management—General M
Chemistry M
Clinical Psychology M,D,O
Communication—General M
Computational Sciences M,D
Computer and Information Systems Security M,D
Computer Science M,D
Counselor Education M,D
Criminal Justice and Criminology M,D
Curriculum and Instruction M,D
Dance M
Developmental Education M,D
Education—General M,D
Educational Leadership and Administration M,D
English M
Family and Consumer Sciences-General M
Finance and Banking M
Forensic Sciences M,D
Geographic Information Systems M,O
Higher Education M,D
History M
Homeland Security M
Humanities M,D,O
Information Science M,D
Internet and Interactive Multimedia M
Kinesiology and Movement Studies M
Library Science M
Mathematics M
Music M
Nutrition M
Political Science M
Project Management M
Psychology—General M,D,O
Public Administration M
Publishing M
Reading Education M,D
School Psychology M,D,O
Sociology M
Spanish M
Special Education M,D
Sports Management M
Statistics M
Writing M

### SAMUEL MERRITT UNIVERSITY

Family Nurse Practitioner Studies M,D,O
Nurse Anesthesia M,D,O
Nursing and Healthcare Administration M,D,O
Nursing—General M,D,O
Occupational Therapy D
Physical Therapy D
Physician Assistant Studies M
Podiatric Medicine D

### SAN DIEGO CHRISTIAN COLLEGE

Education—General M
Organizational Management M

### SAN DIEGO STATE UNIVERSITY

Accounting M
Advertising and Public Relations M
Aerospace/Aeronautical Engineering M,D
Anthropology M
Applied Arts and Design—General M
Applied Mathematics M
Art/Fine Arts M
Asian Studies M
Astronomy M
Biochemistry M,D
Biological and Biomedical Sciences—General M,D
Biometry M
Biostatistics M,D
Business Administration and Management—General M
Cell Biology M,D
Chemistry M,D
Child and Family Studies M
Child Development M
Civil Engineering M
Clinical Psychology M,D
Communication Disorders M,D
Communication—General M
Computational Sciences M,D
Computer Science M
Counselor Education M
Criminal Justice and Criminology M
Curriculum and Instruction M
Ecology M,D
Economics M
Education—General M,D
Educational Leadership and Administration M
Educational Media/Instructional Technology M,D
Electrical Engineering M
Elementary Education M
Emergency Management M,D
Emergency Medical Services M,D
Engineering and Applied Sciences—General M,D
Engineering Design M,D
English as a Second Language M,O
English M
Entrepreneurship M
Environmental and Occupational Health M,D
Epidemiology M,D
Exercise and Sports Science M
Film, Television, and Video Production M
Finance and Banking M
Gender Studies O
Geography M,D
Geology M
Gerontology M
Graphic Design M
Health Physics/Radiological Health M
Health Promotion M,D
Health Psychology M,D
Health Services Management and Hospital Administration M,D
Higher Education M
History M
Hospitality Management M
Human Resources Management M
Industrial and Organizational Psychology M,D
Interdisciplinary Studies M
Interior Design M
International Health M,D
Internet and Interactive Multimedia M
Kinesiology and Movement Studies M
Latin American Studies M
Liberal Studies M
Linguistics M,O
Management Information Systems M
Marketing M
Mathematics Education M,D
Mathematics M,D
Mechanical Engineering M,D
Mechanics M,D
Media Studies M
Microbiology M
Molecular Biology M,D
Multilingual and Multicultural Education M,D
Music Education M
Music M
Nursing—General M
Nutrition M
Pharmaceutical Administration M
Philosophy M
Photography M
Physical Therapy D
Physics M
Political Science M
Psychology—General M,D
Public Administration M
Public Health—General M,D
Reading Education M
Rehabilitation Counseling M
Rhetoric M
Romance Languages M
School Psychology M
Science Education M,D
Secondary Education M
Social Work M
Sociology M
Spanish M
Special Education M
Sports Management M
Statistics M
Telecommunications Management M
Theater M
Toxicology M,D
Travel and Tourism M
Urban and Regional Planning M
Western European Studies M
Women's Studies M
Writing M

### SANFORD BURNHAM PREBYS MEDICAL DISCOVERY INSTITUTE

Biological and Biomedical Sciences—General D

### SAN FRANCISCO ART INSTITUTE

Art History M
Art/Fine Arts M,O
Museum Studies M

### SAN FRANCISCO CONSERVATORY OF MUSIC

Music Education M,O
Music M,O

### SAN FRANCISCO STATE UNIVERSITY

Accounting M
Acute Care/Critical Care Nursing M,O
Adult Education M
Anthropology M
Applied Arts and Design—General M
Archaeology M
Art/Fine Arts M
Asian-American Studies M
Astronomy M
Biochemistry M
Biological and Biomedical Sciences—General M
Biological Anthropology M
Biotechnology M
Business Administration and Management—General M
Cell Biology M
Chemistry M
Chinese M
Classics M
Clinical Psychology M,O
Communication Disorders M
Community Health Nursing M,O
Community Health M
Comparative Literature M
Computer Science M
Criminal Justice and Criminology M
Cultural Anthropology M
Cultural Studies M
Developmental Biology M
Developmental Psychology M,O
Early Childhood Education M,D,O
Ecology M
Economics M
Education—General M,D,O
Educational Leadership and Administration M,D,O
Educational Media/Instructional Technology M
Electrical Engineering M
Elementary Education M
Energy and Power Engineering M
Engineering and Applied Sciences—General M
English as a Second Language M
English Education M,O
English M,O
Entrepreneurship M
Environmental Management and Policy M
Ethnic Studies M
Family and Consumer Sciences-General M
Family Nurse Practitioner Studies M,O
Film, Television, and Video Production M
Film, Television, and Video Theory and Criticism M
Finance and Banking M
French M
Geographic Information Systems M
Geography M
Geosciences M
German M
Gerontology M
Health Education M
Health Services Management and Hospital Administration M
History M
Hospitality Management M
Humanities M
Industrial and Manufacturing Management M
Industrial and Organizational Psychology M,O
International Affairs M
International Business M
Italian M
Japanese M
Kinesiology and Movement Studies M
Legal and Justice Studies M
Leisure Studies M
Liberal Studies M
Linguistics M
Management Information Systems M
Marine Biology M
Marine Sciences M
Marketing M
Marriage and Family Therapy M
Mathematics Education M,O
Mathematics M
Media Studies M
Microbiology M
Molecular Biology M
Museum Studies M
Music Education M
Music M
Nonprofit Management M
Nursing and Healthcare Administration M,O
Nursing—General M,O
Pediatric Nursing M,O
Philosophy M
Physical Therapy D
Physics M
Physiology M
Political Science M
Psychology—General M,O
Public Administration M
Public Health—General M
Public Policy M
Quantitative Analysis M
Reading Education M,O
Recreation and Park Management M
School Psychology M,O
Secondary Education M,O
Social Psychology M,O
Social Work M
Spanish M
Special Education M,D,O
Speech and Interpersonal Communication M
Sustainability Management M
Theater M
Travel and Tourism M
Women's Health Nursing M,O
Women's Studies M
Writing M

### SAN FRANCISCO THEOLOGICAL SEMINARY

Theology M,D

### SAN IGNACIO UNIVERSITY

Business Administration and Management—General M
Early Childhood Education M
Education—General M
Educational Leadership and Administration M
Hospitality Management M
Human Resources Management M
International Business M
Marketing M
Special Education M
Travel and Tourism M

### SAN JOAQUIN COLLEGE OF LAW

Law D

### SAN JOSE STATE UNIVERSITY

Aerospace/Aeronautical Engineering M
Anthropology M
Applied Economics M
Biological and Biomedical Sciences—General M
Chemical Engineering M
Chemistry M
Child and Family Studies M
Civil Engineering M
Clinical Psychology M
Communication Disorders M
Communication—General M
Computer Engineering M
Counselor Education M
Criminal Justice and Criminology M
Curriculum and Instruction M,O
Ecology M
Economics M
Educational Leadership and Administration M,D
Electrical Engineering M
Elementary Education M,O
English as a Second Language M,O
Environmental Management and Policy M
Experimental Psychology M
Film, Television, and Video Production M
Geology M
Gerontological Nursing M,O
Higher Education M,D
History M
Industrial and Organizational Psychology M
Industrial/Management Engineering M
Kinesiology and Movement Studies M
Linguistics M,O
Marine Sciences M
Mass Communication M
Materials Engineering M
Mechanical Engineering M
Meteorology M
Microbiology M
Molecular Biology M
Nursing and Healthcare Administration M,O
Nursing Education M,O
Nursing—General M,O
Nutrition M
Occupational Therapy M
Philosophy M
Physics M
Physiology M
Psychology—General M
Public Administration M
Quality Management M
Reading Education M,O
Software Engineering M
Special Education M
Speech and Interpersonal Communication M
Student Affairs M
Systems Engineering M
Theater M

### SAN JUAN BAUTISTA SCHOOL OF MEDICINE

Allopathic Medicine M,D
Public Health—General M,D

### THE SANS TECHNOLOGY INSTITUTE

Computer and Information Systems Security M

### THE SANTA BARBARA AND VENTURA COLLEGES OF LAW–SANTA BARBARA

Law M,D
Legal and Justice Studies M,D

### THE SANTA BARBARA AND VENTURA COLLEGES OF LAW–VENTURA

Law M,D
Legal and Justice Studies M,D

### SANTA CLARA UNIVERSITY

Applied Mathematics M,D,O
Bioengineering M,D,O
Business Administration and Management—General M
Business Analytics M
Civil Engineering M,D,O
Computer Engineering M,D,O
Computer Science M,D,O

| | |
|---|---|
| Counseling Psychology | M,O |
| Counselor Education | M,O |
| Education—General | M,O |
| Educational Leadership and Administration | M,O |
| Electrical Engineering | M,D,O |
| Energy and Power Engineering | M,D,O |
| Engineering and Applied Sciences—General | M,D,O |
| Engineering Management | M,D,O |
| Ethics | M,D,O |
| Finance and Banking | M |
| Intellectual Property Law | M,D,O |
| Law | M,D,O |
| Management Information Systems | M |
| Mechanical Engineering | M,D,O |
| Pastoral Ministry and Counseling | M |
| Religion | M,D,O |
| Software Engineering | M,D,O |
| Supply Chain Management | M |
| Theology | M,D,O |

**SARAH LAWRENCE COLLEGE**

| | |
|---|---|
| Child Development | M |
| Dance | M |
| Education—General | M |
| Genetic Counseling | M |
| History | M |
| Human Genetics | M |
| Kinesiology and Movement Studies | M |
| Public Health—General | M |
| Theater | M |
| Women's Studies | M |
| Writing | M |

**SAVANNAH COLLEGE OF ART AND DESIGN**

| | |
|---|---|
| Advertising and Public Relations | M |
| Applied Arts and Design—General | M |
| Architectural History | M |
| Architecture | M |
| Art History | M |
| Art/Fine Arts | M |
| Arts Administration | M |
| Clothing and Textiles | M |
| Computer Art and Design | M |
| Film, Television, and Video Production | M |
| Film, Television, and Video Theory and Criticism | M |
| Game Design and Development | M |
| Graphic Design | M |
| Historic Preservation | M |
| Illustration | M |
| Industrial Design | M |
| Interior Design | M |
| Internet and Interactive Multimedia | M |
| Media Studies | M |
| Music | M |
| Photography | M |
| Sustainable Development | M |
| Textile Design | M |
| Theater | M |
| Travel and Tourism | M |
| Urban Design | M |
| Writing | M |

**SAVANNAH STATE UNIVERSITY**

| | |
|---|---|
| Business Administration and Management—General | M |
| Human Resources Management | M |
| Marine Sciences | M |
| Public Administration | M |
| Social Work | M |
| Urban and Regional Planning | M |
| Urban Studies | M |

**SAYBROOK UNIVERSITY**

| | |
|---|---|
| Clinical Psychology | M |
| Counseling Psychology | M |
| Health Psychology | M,D |
| Marriage and Family Therapy | M,D |
| Nutrition | M,D,O |
| Organizational Behavior | M,D |
| Organizational Management | M,D |
| Psychology—General | M,D |
| Sustainable Development | M,D |
| Transpersonal and Humanistic Psychology | M,D |

**SCHILLER INTERNATIONAL UNIVERSITY - HEIDELBERG**

| | |
|---|---|
| Business Administration and Management—General | M |
| International Business | M |
| Management Information Systems | M |

**SCHILLER INTERNATIONAL UNIVERSITY - MADRID**

| | |
|---|---|
| Business Administration and Management—General | M |
| International Business | M |

**SCHILLER INTERNATIONAL UNIVERSITY - PARIS**

| | |
|---|---|
| Business Administration and Management—General | M |
| International Affairs | M |
| International Business | M |

**SCHILLER INTERNATIONAL UNIVERSITY - TAMPA**

| | |
|---|---|
| Business Administration and Management—General | M |
| Finance and Banking | M |
| Hospitality Management | M |
| International Business | M |
| Management Information Systems | M |
| Travel and Tourism | M |

**SCHOOL OF ADVANCED AIR AND SPACE STUDIES**

| | |
|---|---|
| Military and Defense Studies | M |

**SCHOOL OF ARCHITECTURE AT TALIESIN**

| | |
|---|---|
| Architecture | M |

**SCHOOL OF THE ART INSTITUTE OF CHICAGO**

| | |
|---|---|
| Writing | M,O |

**SCHOOL OF VISUAL ARTS (NY)**

| | |
|---|---|
| Applied Arts and Design—General | M |
| Art Education | M |
| Art History | M |
| Art Therapy | M |
| Art/Fine Arts | M |
| Computer Art and Design | M |
| Cultural Studies | M |
| Film, Television, and Video Production | M |
| Graphic Design | M |
| Illustration | M |
| Internet and Interactive Multimedia | M |
| Photography | M |
| Writing | M |

**SCHREINER UNIVERSITY**

| | |
|---|---|
| Business Administration and Management—General | M |
| Education—General | M,O |
| Educational Leadership and Administration | M,O |
| Ethics | M |

**THE SCRIPPS RESEARCH INSTITUTE**

| | |
|---|---|
| Biological and Biomedical Sciences—General | D |
| Chemistry | D |

**SEATTLE INSTITUTE OF EAST ASIAN MEDICINE**

| | |
|---|---|
| Acupuncture and Oriental Medicine | M |

**SEATTLE PACIFIC UNIVERSITY**

| | |
|---|---|
| Adult Nursing | M,O |
| Business Administration and Management—General | M |
| Clinical Psychology | D |
| Computer and Information Systems Security | M |
| Counselor Education | M,D,O |
| Data Science/Data Analytics | M |
| Education—General | D |
| Educational Leadership and Administration | M,D,O |
| Educational Media/Instructional Technology | M |
| Family Nurse Practitioner Studies | M,O |
| Gerontological Nursing | M,O |
| Human Resources Management | M |
| Industrial and Organizational Psychology | M,D |
| Management Information Systems | M |
| Marriage and Family Therapy | M,O |
| Mathematics Education | M |
| Nursing and Healthcare Administration | M,O |
| Nursing Education | M,O |
| Nursing Informatics | M,O |
| Nursing—General | M,O |
| Reading Education | M |
| Religion | M,O |
| Science Education | M |
| Secondary Education | M |
| Sustainability Management | M |
| Theology | M,O |
| Writing | M |

**THE SEATTLE SCHOOL OF THEOLOGY AND PSYCHOLOGY**

| | |
|---|---|
| Counseling Psychology | M |
| Psychology—General | M |
| Religion | M |
| Theology | M |

**SEATTLE UNIVERSITY**

| | |
|---|---|
| Accounting | M |
| Adult Education | M,O |
| Arts Administration | M |
| Business Administration and Management—General | M,O |
| Business Analytics | M,O |
| Computer Science | M |
| Counselor Education | M,O |
| Criminal Justice and Criminology | M,O |
| Education—General | M,D,O |
| Educational Leadership and Administration | M,D,O |
| Engineering and Applied Sciences—General | M |
| English as a Second Language | M,O |
| Finance and Banking | M,O |
| Forensic Sciences | M,O |
| Health Law | M,D |
| Law | M,D |
| Marriage and Family Therapy | M |
| Nursing—General | D |
| Organizational Management | M,O |
| Pastoral Ministry and Counseling | M |
| Psychology—General | M |
| Public Administration | M |
| School Psychology | M,O |
| Social Work | M |
| Special Education | M,O |
| Sports Management | M |
| Theology | M,D,O |
| Transpersonal and Humanistic Psychology | M |

**SELMA UNIVERSITY**

| | |
|---|---|
| Pastoral Ministry and Counseling | M |
| Religion | M |
| Religious Education | M |

**SETON HALL UNIVERSITY**

| | |
|---|---|
| Accounting | M,O |
| Adult Nursing | M,D |
| Advertising and Public Relations | M |
| Allied Health—General | D |
| Allopathic Medicine | D |
| Analytical Chemistry | M,D |
| Asian Studies | M |
| Athletic Training and Sports Medicine | M |
| Biochemistry | M,D |
| Biological and Biomedical Sciences—General | M,D |
| Business Administration and Management—General | M,O |
| Chemistry | M,D |
| Communication Disorders | M |
| Communication—General | M |
| Corporate and Organizational Communication | M |
| Counseling Psychology | M,D |
| Counselor Education | M,D |
| Education—General | M,D,O |
| Educational Leadership and Administration | M,D,O |
| Educational Measurement and Evaluation | M,D,O |
| Educational Media/Instructional Technology | M |
| English | M |
| Entrepreneurship | M,O |
| Experimental Psychology | M |
| Finance and Banking | M,O |
| Gerontological Nursing | M,D |
| Health Law | M,D |
| Health Services Management and Hospital Administration | M,D |
| Higher Education | M,D,O |
| History | M |
| Inorganic Chemistry | M,D |
| International Affairs | M,O |
| International Business | M,O |
| International Health | M,O |
| Jewish Studies | M,O |
| Law | M,D |
| Management of Technology | M,O |
| Marketing | M,O |
| Microbiology | M,D |
| Molecular Biology | M,D |
| Museum Studies | M |
| Neuroscience | M,D |
| Nonprofit Management | M,O |
| Nursing and Healthcare Administration | M,D |
| Nursing Education | M,D |
| Nursing—General | M,D |
| Occupational Therapy | M |
| Organic Chemistry | M,D |
| Pastoral Ministry and Counseling | M,O |
| Pediatric Nursing | M,D |
| Physical Chemistry | M,D |
| Physical Therapy | D |
| Physician Assistant Studies | M |
| Psychology—General | M |
| Public Administration | M,O |
| Public Policy | M,O |
| Religion | M,O |
| School Nursing | M,D |
| School Psychology | M |
| Social Work | M |
| Special Education | M |
| Speech and Interpersonal Communication | M |
| Sports Management | M,O |
| Student Affairs | M,D,O |
| Supply Chain Management | M,O |
| Taxation | O |
| Theology | M,O |

**SETON HILL UNIVERSITY**

| | |
|---|---|
| Accounting | M |
| Art Therapy | M |
| Business Administration and Management—General | M |
| Educational Media/Instructional Technology | M |
| Elementary Education | M |
| Entrepreneurship | M |
| Health Services Management and Hospital Administration | M |
| Middle School Education | M |
| Oral and Dental Sciences | M,O |
| Physician Assistant Studies | M |
| Special Education | M |
| Writing | M |

**SHASTA BIBLE COLLEGE**

| | |
|---|---|
| Educational Leadership and Administration | M |
| Pastoral Ministry and Counseling | M |
| Religious Education | M |

**SHAWNEE STATE UNIVERSITY**

| | |
|---|---|
| Curriculum and Instruction | M |
| Education—General | M |
| Occupational Therapy | M |

**SHAW UNIVERSITY**

| | |
|---|---|
| Curriculum and Instruction | M |
| Theology | M |

**SHENANDOAH UNIVERSITY**

| | |
|---|---|
| Adult Nursing | M,D,O |
| Allied Health—General | M,D,O |
| Applied Behavior Analysis | M |
| Athletic Training and Sports Medicine | M,D,O |
| Business Administration and Management—General | M,O |
| Early Childhood Education | M,D,O |
| Education—General | M,D,O |
| Family Nurse Practitioner Studies | M,D,O |
| Gerontological Nursing | M,D,O |
| Health Services Management and Hospital Administration | M,D,O |
| Music | M,D,O |
| Nurse Midwifery | M,D,O |
| Nursing and Healthcare Administration | M,D,O |
| Nursing Education | M,D,O |
| Nursing—General | M,D,O |
| Occupational Therapy | M |
| Pharmacy | D |
| Physical Therapy | D |
| Physician Assistant Studies | M,D,O |
| Psychiatric Nursing | M,D,O |
| Public Health—General | M,D,O |
| Writing | M,D,O |

**SHEPHERDS THEOLOGICAL SEMINARY**

| | |
|---|---|
| Pastoral Ministry and Counseling | M |
| Theology | M |

**SHEPHERD UNIVERSITY (WV)**

| | |
|---|---|
| Curriculum and Instruction | M |

**SHERMAN COLLEGE OF CHIROPRACTIC**

| | |
|---|---|
| Chiropractic | D |

**SHILOH UNIVERSITY**

| | |
|---|---|
| Pastoral Ministry and Counseling | M,D |
| Theology | M,D |

**SHIPPENSBURG UNIVERSITY OF PENNSYLVANIA**

| | |
|---|---|
| Biological and Biomedical Sciences—General | M |
| Business Administration and Management—General | M,D,O |
| Business Analytics | M,D,O |
| Clinical Psychology | M,D |
| Communication—General | M |
| Computer Science | M,O |
| Counselor Education | M,D |
| Criminal Justice and Criminology | M |
| Curriculum and Instruction | M |
| Early Childhood Education | M |
| Education—General | M,D |
| Educational Leadership and Administration | M,D |
| Elementary Education | M |
| Environmental Management and Policy | M |
| Finance and Banking | M,D,O |
| Foreign Languages Education | M |
| Geography | M |
| Health Services Management and Hospital Administration | M,D,O |
| History | M |
| Information Science | M,O |
| Logistics | M,D,O |
| Management Information Systems | M,D,O |
| Mathematics Education | M |
| Middle School Education | M |
| Organizational Management | M |
| Psychology—General | M |
| Public Administration | M |
| Public History | M |
| Reading Education | M |
| Science Education | M |
| Social Work | M |
| Sociology | M |
| Software Engineering | M,O |
| Special Education | M,D |
| Student Affairs | M,D |
| Supply Chain Management | M,D,O |

**SHORTER UNIVERSITY**

| | |
|---|---|
| Accounting | M |
| Business Administration and Management—General | M |

**SH'OR YOSHUV RABBINICAL COLLEGE**

| | |
|---|---|
| Theology | |

**SIENA COLLEGE**

| | |
|---|---|
| Accounting | M |
| Business Administration and Management—General | M |

**SIENA HEIGHTS UNIVERSITY**

| | |
|---|---|
| Clinical Psychology | M,O |
| Counseling Psychology | M,O |
| Early Childhood Education | M,O |
| Education—General | M,O |
| Educational Leadership and Administration | M,O |
| Elementary Education | M,O |
| Health Services Management and Hospital Administration | M,O |
| Higher Education | M,O |
| Organizational Management | M,O |
| Reading Education | M,O |
| Secondary Education | M,O |
| Special Education | M,O |

**SIERRA NEVADA COLLEGE**

| | |
|---|---|
| Education—General | M |
| Educational Leadership and Administration | M |
| Elementary Education | M |
| Secondary Education | M |

**SIMMONS UNIVERSITY**

| | |
|---|---|
| Applied Behavior Analysis | M,D,O |
| Business Administration and Management—General | M |
| Cultural Studies | M,D,O |
| Education of Students with Severe/Multiple Disabilities | M,D,O |

*M—masters degree; D—doctorate; O—other advanced degree; *—Close-Up and/or Display*

Elementary Education M,D,O
English M,D,O
Family Nurse Practitioner Studies M,D
Gender Studies M,D,O
Health Promotion M,D,O
Health Services Management and Hospital Administration M
History M,D,O
Nursing—General M,D
Nutrition M,D,O
Physical Therapy M,D,O
Public Health—General M,D,O
Public Policy M,D,O
Social Work M,D
Special Education M,D,O
Writing M,D,O

**SIMON FRASER UNIVERSITY**
Actuarial Science M,D
Anthropology M,D
Applied Mathematics M,D
Archaeology M,D
Art Education M,D
Biochemistry M,D,O
Bioinformatics M,D,O
Biological and Biomedical Sciences—General M,D,O
Biotechnology M,D,O
Business Administration and Management—General M,D,O
Chemistry M,D
Communication—General M,D
Comparative and Interdisciplinary Arts M
Computational Sciences M,D
Computer Science M,D
Counselor Education M
Criminal Justice and Criminology M,D
Cultural Studies D
Curriculum and Instruction M,D
Economics M,D
Education—General M,D,O
Educational Leadership and Administration M,D
Educational Media/Instructional Technology M,D
Educational Psychology M,D
Engineering and Applied Sciences—General M,D
English as a Second Language M
English Education M,D
English M,D
Entomology M,D,O
Environmental Management and Policy M,D,O
Finance and Banking M,D,O
Fish, Game, and Wildlife Management M,D,O
Foundations and Philosophy of Education M,D
French M
Gender Studies M,D
Geography M,D
Geosciences M,D
Gerontology M,D
History M,D
Humanities M
International Affairs M
International Health M,D,O
Kinesiology and Movement Studies M,D
Latin American Studies M,O
Legal and Justice Studies M,D
Liberal Studies M
Linguistics M,D
Management of Technology M,D,O
Mathematics Education M,D
Mathematics M,D
Mechanical Engineering M,D
Molecular Biology M,D,O
Operations Research M,D
Philosophy M,D
Physics M,D
Political Science M,D
Psychology—General M,D
Public Health—General M,D,O
Public Policy M
Publishing M
Reading Education D
Sociology M,D
Statistics M,D
Systems Engineering M,D
Toxicology M,D,O
Urban Studies M,O
Women's Studies M,D

**SIMPSON COLLEGE**
Criminal Justice and Criminology M
Education—General M
Secondary Education M

**SIMPSON UNIVERSITY**
Counseling Psychology M
Curriculum and Instruction M
Education—General M
Educational Leadership and Administration M
Missions and Missiology M
Organizational Management M
Pastoral Ministry and Counseling M

**SINTE GLESKA UNIVERSITY**
Education—General M
Elementary Education M

**SIOUX FALLS SEMINARY**
Marriage and Family Therapy M
Pastoral Ministry and Counseling M
Religion M
Theology M,D,O

**SIT GRADUATE INSTITUTE**
Business Administration and Management—General M
Conflict Resolution and Mediation/Peace Studies M
Educational Leadership and Administration M
Energy Management and Policy M
English as a Second Language M
Entrepreneurship M
Environmental Management and Policy M
International Affairs M
International and Comparative Education M
International Business M
Meteorology M
Organizational Management M
Sustainability Management M
Sustainable Development M

**SITTING BULL COLLEGE**
Curriculum and Instruction M
Environmental Sciences M

**SLIPPERY ROCK UNIVERSITY OF PENNSYLVANIA**
Clinical Psychology M
Counseling Psychology M
Counselor Education M
Criminal Justice and Criminology M
Data Science/Data Analytics M
Education—General M,D
Educational Leadership and Administration M,D
Educational Media/Instructional Technology M,D
Elementary Education M
English as a Second Language M
English M
Environmental Education M
Environmental Management and Policy M
Health Informatics M
History M
Mathematics Education M
Physical Education M
Physical Therapy D
Physician Assistant Studies M
Public Health—General M
Reading Education M
Recreation and Park Management M
Science Education M
Secondary Education M
Special Education M,D
Therapies—Dance, Drama, and Music M

**SMITH COLLEGE**
Biological and Biomedical Sciences—General M
Chemistry M
Dance M
Education—General M
Elementary Education M
English Education M
Exercise and Sports Science M
History M
Mathematics Education M
Mathematics O
Middle School Education M
Science Education M
Secondary Education M
Social Sciences Education M
Social Work M,D
Theater M
Women's Studies O

**SOFIA UNIVERSITY**
Clinical Psychology M,D
Computer Science M,D
Counseling Psychology M,D
Psychology—General M,D
Transpersonal and Humanistic Psychology M,D

**SOKA UNIVERSITY OF AMERICA**
Educational Leadership and Administration M

**SONOMA STATE UNIVERSITY**
Anthropology M
Biochemistry M
Biological and Biomedical Sciences—General M
Business Administration and Management—General M
Clinical Psychology M
Counseling Psychology M
Curriculum and Instruction M,O
Early Childhood Education M,O
Education—General M,O
Educational Leadership and Administration M,O
English M
Exercise and Sports Science M
Family Nurse Practitioner Studies M
Health Promotion M
History M
Interdisciplinary Studies M
Kinesiology and Movement Studies M
Nursing—General M
Occupational Therapy M
Physical Therapy M
Political Science M
Public Administration M
Public History M
Reading Education M,O
School Psychology M
Special Education M,O
Sports Management M
Writing M

**SOTHEBY'S INSTITUTE OF ART–LONDON**
Art/Fine Arts M
Arts Administration M
Decorative Arts M

**SOTHEBY'S INSTITUTE OF ART–NEW YORK**
Art/Fine Arts M
Arts Administration M
Decorative Arts M

**SOUTH BAYLO UNIVERSITY**
Acupuncture and Oriental Medicine M

**SOUTH CAROLINA STATE UNIVERSITY**
Agricultural Economics and Agribusiness M
Allied Health—General M
Biological and Biomedical Sciences—General M
Business Administration and Management—General M
Business Education M
Child and Family Studies M
Civil Engineering M
Communication Disorders M
Counselor Education M
Early Childhood Education M
Education—General M
Elementary Education M
English Education M
English M
Entrepreneurship M
Family and Consumer Sciences-General M
Health Services Management and Hospital Administration M
Home Economics Education M
Human Services M
Mathematics Education M
Mathematics M
Mechanical Engineering M
Nutrition M
Rehabilitation Counseling M
Science Education M
Secondary Education M
Social Sciences Education M
Special Education M
Transportation and Highway Engineering M
Vocational and Technical Education M

**SOUTH COLLEGE**
Pharmacy D
Physician Assistant Studies M

**SOUTH DAKOTA SCHOOL OF MINES AND TECHNOLOGY**
Artificial Intelligence/Robotics M
Atmospheric Sciences M,D
Bioengineering D
Biomedical Engineering M,D
Chemical Engineering M,D
Civil Engineering M,D
Construction Management M
Electrical Engineering M
Engineering and Applied Sciences—General M,D
Engineering Management M
Environmental Sciences D
Geological Engineering M,D
Geology M,D
Management of Technology M
Materials Engineering M,D
Materials Sciences M,D
Mechanical Engineering M,D
Mineral/Mining Engineering M
Nanotechnology D
Paleontology M,D
Physics M,D

**SOUTH DAKOTA STATE UNIVERSITY**
Agricultural Education M
Agricultural Engineering M,D
Agricultural Sciences—General M,D
Animal Sciences M,D
Athletic Training and Sports Medicine M,D
Biochemistry M,D
Biological and Biomedical Sciences—General M,D
Biosystems Engineering M,D
Chemistry M,D
Civil Engineering M
Communication—General M
Computational Sciences M,D
Consumer Economics M
Counselor Education M
Curriculum and Instruction M
Economics M
Education—General M,D
Educational Leadership and Administration M
Electrical Engineering M,D
Engineering and Applied Sciences—General M,D
English M
Exercise and Sports Science M,D
Family and Consumer Sciences-General M
Fish, Game, and Wildlife Management M,D
Food Science and Technology M,D
Geography M
Geosciences D
Human Resources Development M
Industrial and Organizational Psychology M
Journalism M
Mathematics M,D
Mechanical Engineering M,D
Microbiology M,D
Nursing—General M,D
Nutrition M,D
Operations Research M
Pharmaceutical Sciences M,D
Pharmacy D
Physics M
Plant Sciences M,D
Recreation and Park Management M,D
Sociology M,D
Statistics M,D
Veterinary Sciences M,D

**SOUTHEASTERN BAPTIST THEOLOGICAL SEMINARY**
Ethics M,D
Missions and Missiology M,D
Music M,D
Philosophy M,D
Psychology—General M,D
Religious Education M,D
Theology M,D
Women's Studies M,D

**SOUTHEASTERN LOUISIANA UNIVERSITY**
Advertising and Public Relations M
Applied Science and Technology M
Biological and Biomedical Sciences—General M
Business Administration and Management—General M
Communication Disorders M
Communication—General M
Counselor Education M
Curriculum and Instruction M
Education—General M,D
Educational Leadership and Administration M,D
Elementary Education M
English Education M
English M
Health Communication M
Health Education M
History M
Industrial and Organizational Psychology M
Journalism M
Kinesiology and Movement Studies M
Marketing M
Music M
Nursing—General M,D
Psychology—General M
Reading Education M
Sociology M
Special Education M
Sustainability Management M
Writing M

**SOUTHEASTERN OKLAHOMA STATE UNIVERSITY**
Aviation Management M
Aviation M
Biotechnology M
Business Administration and Management—General M
Clinical Psychology M
Counseling Psychology M
Counselor Education M
Education—General M
Educational Leadership and Administration M
Environmental and Occupational Health M
Management Information Systems M
Mathematics Education M
Reading Education M

**SOUTHEASTERN UNIVERSITY (FL)**
Business Administration and Management—General M,D
Counseling Psychology M
Counselor Education M
Curriculum and Instruction M,D
Education of the Gifted M,D
Education—General M,D
Educational Leadership and Administration M,D
Elementary Education M,D
English as a Second Language M,D
Entrepreneurship M,D
Health Services Management and Hospital Administration M,D
Human Services M
International Business M,D
Kinesiology and Movement Studies M,D
Management Strategy and Policy M,D
Marriage and Family Therapy M
Organizational Management M,D
Pastoral Ministry and Counseling M,D
Reading Education M,D
Social Work M
Sports Management M,D
Theology M,D
Urban and Regional Planning M

**SOUTHEAST MISSOURI STATE UNIVERSITY**
Accounting M
Biological and Biomedical Sciences—General M
Business Administration and Management—General M
Chemistry M
Communication Disorders M
Counseling Psychology M,D,O
Counselor Education M,D,O
Criminal Justice and Criminology M
Educational Leadership and Administration M,D,O
Elementary Education M,D,O
English as a Second Language M
English M
Entrepreneurship M
Environmental Management and Policy M
Exercise and Sports Science M
Finance and Banking M
Higher Education M,D,O
History M,O
Leisure Studies M

Management of Technology M
Mathematics M
Nursing—General M
Public Administration M
Secondary Education M,D,O
Special Education M
Sports Management M

**SOUTHERN ADVENTIST UNIVERSITY**

Accounting M
Acute Care/Critical Care Nursing M,D
Adult Nursing M,D
Business Administration and Management—General M
Computer Science M
Counseling Psychology M
Counselor Education M
Education—General M
Educational Leadership and Administration M
Family Nurse Practitioner Studies M,D
Finance and Banking M
Gerontological Nursing M,D
Health Services Management and Hospital Administration M
Marketing M
Missions and Missiology M
Nursing Education M,D
Nursing—General M,D
Psychiatric Nursing M,D
Psychology—General M
Reading Education M
Religion M
Religious Education M
Social Work M
Theology M

**SOUTHERN ARKANSAS UNIVERSITY–MAGNOLIA**

Adult Education M
Agricultural Sciences—General M
Business Administration and Management—General M
Computer and Information Systems Security M
Computer Science M
Counselor Education M
Curriculum and Instruction M
Data Science/Data Analytics M
Education of the Gifted M
Education—General M
Educational Leadership and Administration M
Higher Education M
Kinesiology and Movement Studies M
Library Science M
Organizational Management M
Psychiatric Nursing M
Public Administration M
Student Affairs M
Supply Chain Management M

**THE SOUTHERN BAPTIST THEOLOGICAL SEMINARY**

Missions and Missiology M,D
Pastoral Ministry and Counseling M,D
Philosophy M,D
Religion M,D
Theology M,D

**SOUTHERN CALIFORNIA INSTITUTE OF ARCHITECTURE**

Architecture M
Urban and Regional Planning M
Urban Design M

**SOUTHERN CALIFORNIA SEMINARY**

Counseling Psychology M,D
Marriage and Family Therapy M,D
Psychology—General M,D
Religion M,D
Theology M,D

**SOUTHERN CALIFORNIA UNIVERSITY OF HEALTH SCIENCES**

Acupuncture and Oriental Medicine M,D
Chiropractic D

**SOUTHERN COLLEGE OF OPTOMETRY**

Optometry D

**SOUTHERN CONNECTICUT STATE UNIVERSITY**

Art Education M
Biological and Biomedical Sciences—General M
Business Administration and Management—General M
Chemistry M
Communication Disorders M
Computer Science M
Counselor Education M,O
Education—General M,D,O
Educational Leadership and Administration M,D,O
Educational Measurement and Evaluation M,D,O
Elementary Education M,O
English as a Second Language M
English M
Environmental Education M,O
Environmental Sciences M,O
Exercise and Sports Science M
Family Nurse Practitioner Studies M,D
Foreign Languages Education M
Health Education M
History M
Information Studies M,O
Leisure Studies M
Library Science M,O
Marine Sciences M,O
Mathematics M
Multilingual and Multicultural Education M
Nursing Education M,D
Nursing—General M,D
Physical Education M
Political Science M
Psychology—General M
Public Health—General M
Reading Education M,O
Recreation and Park Management M
School Psychology M,O
Science Education M,O
Social Work M
Sociology M
Special Education M
Women's Studies M

**SOUTHERN EVANGELICAL SEMINARY**

Jewish Studies M,D,O
Missions and Missiology M,D,O
Near and Middle Eastern Studies M,D,O
Pastoral Ministry and Counseling M,D,O
Philosophy M,D,O
Religion M,D,O
Religious Education M,D,O
Theology M,D,O

**SOUTHERN ILLINOIS UNIVERSITY CARBONDALE**

Accounting M,D
Agricultural Economics and Agribusiness M
Agricultural Sciences—General M
Agronomy and Soil Sciences M
Animal Sciences M
Anthropology M,D
Applied Arts and Design—General M
Applied Physics M,D
Architecture M
Art/Fine Arts M
Biochemistry M,D
Biological and Biomedical Sciences—General M,D
Biomedical Engineering M
Business Administration and Management—General M,D
Chemistry M,D
Civil Engineering M,D
Clinical Psychology M,D
Communication Disorders M
Communication—General M,D
Community Health M
Computer Engineering M,D
Computer Science M,D
Counseling Psychology M,D
Criminal Justice and Criminology M,D
Cultural Studies M
Curriculum and Instruction M,D
Economics M,D
Education—General M,D
Educational Leadership and Administration M,D
Educational Psychology M,D
Electrical Engineering M,D
Energy and Power Engineering D
Engineering and Applied Sciences—General M,D
Engineering Management M
English as a Second Language M
English M,D
Environmental Engineering D
Environmental Management and Policy M,D
Environmental Sciences D
Experimental Psychology M,D
Forestry M
Geography M,D
Geology M,D
Geosciences M,D
Health Education M,D
Health Law M
Health Services Management and Hospital Administration M
Higher Education M
History M,D
Homeland Security M
Kinesiology and Movement Studies M
Law M,D
Legal and Justice Studies M
Linguistics M
Mass Communication M,D
Mathematics M,D
Mechanical Engineering M,D
Mechanics M
Media Studies M,D
Medical Physics M
Microbiology M,D
Mineral/Mining Engineering M,D
Molecular Biology M,D
Music M
Nutrition M
Pharmacology M,D
Philosophy M,D
Physical Education M
Physician Assistant Studies M
Physics M,D
Physiology M,D
Plant Biology M,D
Plant Sciences M
Political Science M,D
Psychology—General M,D
Public Administration M
Recreation and Park Management M
Rhetoric M,D
Social Work M
Sociology M,D
Special Education M,D
Speech and Interpersonal Communication M,D
Theater M,D
Vocational and Technical Education M,D
Writing M
Zoology M,D

**SOUTHERN ILLINOIS UNIVERSITY EDWARDSVILLE**

Accounting M
Advertising and Public Relations M
Applied Mathematics M
Art Therapy M
Art/Fine Arts M
Biological and Biomedical Sciences—General M
Business Administration and Management—General M
Business Analytics M
Chemistry M
Civil Engineering M
Clinical Psychology M
Communication Disorders M
Computational Sciences M
Computer Science M
Corporate and Organizational Communication M
Cultural Anthropology M
Curriculum and Instruction M
Dentistry D
Economics M
Education—General M,D,O
Educational Leadership and Administration M,D,O
Educational Media/Instructional Technology M,O
Electrical Engineering M
Engineering and Applied Sciences—General M
English as a Second Language M,O
English Education M,O
English M,O
Environmental Engineering M
Environmental Management and Policy M
Environmental Sciences M
Exercise and Sports Science M
Family Nurse Practitioner Studies M,D,O
Finance and Banking M
Foundations and Philosophy of Education M
Geography M
Geotechnical Engineering M
Health Communication M
Health Education M,D,O
Health Informatics M
Higher Education M
History M
Industrial and Organizational Psychology M
Industrial/Management Engineering M
Interdisciplinary Studies M
Kinesiology and Movement Studies M
Management Information Systems M
Marketing Research M
Mass Communication M
Mathematics Education M
Mathematics M
Mechanical Engineering M
Media Studies O
Museum Studies O
Music Education M,O
Music M
Nurse Anesthesia D
Nursing and Healthcare Administration M,O
Nursing Education M,O
Nursing—General M,D,O
Operations Research M
Pharmacy D
Physical Education M
Project Management M
Psychology—General M,O
Public Administration M
Reading Education M,O
School Psychology O
Social Work M
Sociology M
Special Education M,O
Speech and Interpersonal Communication M
Sport Psychology M
Statistics M
Structural Engineering M
Student Affairs M
Sustainable Development M
Taxation M
Transportation and Highway Engineering M
Writing M

**SOUTHERN METHODIST UNIVERSITY**

Accounting M
Advertising and Public Relations M
Anthropology M,D
Applied Economics M,D
Applied Mathematics M,D
Applied Statistics M,D
Archaeology M,D
Art History M,D
Art/Fine Arts M
Arts Administration M
Biological and Biomedical Sciences—General M,D
Biostatistics M,D
Business Administration and Management—General M
Business Analytics M
Cell Biology M,D
Chemistry M,D
Civil Engineering M,D
Clinical Psychology D
Computational Sciences M,D
Computer Engineering M,D
Computer Science M,D
Conflict Resolution and Mediation/Peace Studies M,O
Counselor Education M,O
Cultural Anthropology M,D
Data Science/Data Analytics M,D
Economics M,D
Education of the Gifted M,D
Education—General M,D
Educational Leadership and Administration M,D
Electrical Engineering M,D
Engineering and Applied Sciences—General M,D
Engineering Management M,D
English as a Second Language M,D
English M,D
Entrepreneurship M
Environmental Engineering M,D
Finance and Banking M
Geology M,D
Geophysics M,D
Geotechnical Engineering M,D
Health Promotion M,D
Higher Education M,D
History M,D
Information Science M,D
Law M,D
Liberal Studies M,D
Management Information Systems M
Management Strategy and Policy M
Manufacturing Engineering M,D
Marketing M
Mathematics M,D
Mechanical Engineering M,D
Medieval and Renaissance Studies M
Molecular Biology M,D
Multilingual and Multicultural Education M,D
Music Education M
Music M,D
Operations Research M,D
Pastoral Ministry and Counseling M,D
Physics M,D
Physiology M,D
Psychology—General D
Reading Education M,D
Real Estate M
Religion M,D
Software Engineering M,D
Special Education M,D
Sports Management M,D
Statistics M,D
Structural Engineering M,D
Sustainable Development M,D
Systems Engineering M,D
Taxation M,D
Telecommunications M,D
Theater M
Theology M,D
Transportation and Highway Engineering M,D

**SOUTHERN NAZARENE UNIVERSITY**

Business Administration and Management—General M
Counseling Psychology M
Health Services Management and Hospital Administration M
Marriage and Family Therapy M
Nursing and Healthcare Administration M
Nursing Education M
Nursing—General M
Psychology—General M
Sports Management M

**SOUTHERN NEW HAMPSHIRE UNIVERSITY**

Accounting M,D,O
Advertising and Public Relations M,D,O
Applied Economics M,D,O
Business Administration and Management—General M,D,O
Business Analytics M,D,O
Clinical Psychology M
Computer and Information Systems Security M
Criminal Justice and Criminology M
Curriculum and Instruction M,D,O
Data Science/Data Analytics M,D,O
Early Childhood Education M,D,O
Economic Development M,D,O
Economics M,D,O
Education—General M,D,O
Educational Leadership and Administration M,D,O
Educational Media/Instructional Technology M,D,O
Elementary Education M,D,O
Engineering Management M,D,O
English as a Second Language M,D,O
English M
Entertainment Management M,D,O
Entrepreneurship M,D,O
Environmental Management and Policy M,D,O
Finance and Banking M,D,O
Health Informatics M,D,O
Health Services Management and Hospital Administration M,D,O
Higher Education M,D,O
History M
Human Resources Management M,D,O
Industrial and Manufacturing Management M,D,O
International Business M,D,O

*M—masters degree; D—doctorate; O—other advanced degree; *—Close-Up and/or Display*

Internet and Interactive Multimedia M,D,O
Investment Management M,D,O
Legal and Justice Studies M,D,O
Management Information Systems M,D,O
Marketing M,D,O
Nonprofit Management M,D,O
Nursing and Healthcare Administration M,O
Nursing Education M,O
Nursing—General M,O
Organizational Management M,D,O
Political Science M
Project Management M,D,O
Psychology—General M
Public Administration M,D,O
Quality Management M,D,O
Quantitative Analysis M,D,O
Reading Education M,D,O
Special Education M,D,O
Sports Management M,D,O
Supply Chain Management M,D,O
Sustainability Management M,D,O
Taxation M,D,O
Writing M

**SOUTHERN OREGON UNIVERSITY**
Accounting M,O
Business Administration and Management—General M,O
Computer Science M
Counseling Psychology M
Early Childhood Education M
Education—General M
Educational Leadership and Administration M
Elementary Education M
Environmental Education M
Foreign Languages Education M
French M
Interdisciplinary Studies M
International Business M,O
Music M
Psychology—General M
Reading Education M
Secondary Education M
Spanish M
Special Education M
Theater M

**SOUTHERN STATES UNIVERSITY**
Business Administration and Management—General M
Information Science M

**SOUTHERN UNIVERSITY AND AGRICULTURAL AND MECHANICAL COLLEGE**
Agricultural Sciences—General M
Analytical Chemistry M
Biochemistry M
Biological and Biomedical Sciences—General M
Business Administration and Management—General M
Chemistry M
Communication Disorders M
Computer Science M
Counselor Education M
Criminal Justice and Criminology M
Education—General M,D
Educational Leadership and Administration M
Educational Media/Instructional Technology M
Elementary Education M
Engineering and Applied Sciences—General M
Environmental Sciences M
Family Nurse Practitioner Studies M,D,O
Forestry M
Gerontological Nursing M,D,O
History M
Inorganic Chemistry M
Law D
Mass Communication M
Mathematics Education D
Mathematics M
Nursing and Healthcare Administration M,D,O
Nursing Education M,D,O
Nursing—General M,D,O
Organic Chemistry M
Physical Chemistry M
Physics M
Political Science M
Psychology—General M
Public Administration M
Public Policy D
Recreation and Park Management M
Rehabilitation Counseling M
Science Education D
Secondary Education M
Social Sciences M

**SOUTHERN UNIVERSITY AT NEW ORLEANS**
Criminal Justice and Criminology M
Management Information Systems M
Museum Studies M
Social Work M

**SOUTHERN UTAH UNIVERSITY**
Accounting M
Arts Administration M
Business Administration and Management—General M
Communication—General M
Computer and Information Systems Security M
Education—General M,O
Exercise and Sports Science M
Interdisciplinary Studies M
Music M

Public Administration M

**SOUTHERN WESLEYAN UNIVERSITY**
Business Administration and Management—General M
Education—General M
Pastoral Ministry and Counseling M

**SOUTH FLORIDA BIBLE COLLEGE AND THEOLOGICAL SEMINARY**
Theology M

**SOUTH TEXAS COLLEGE OF LAW HOUSTON**
Law D

**SOUTH UNIVERSITY - AUSTIN**
Business Administration and Management—General M
Counseling Psychology M
Management Information Systems M

**SOUTH UNIVERSITY - COLUMBIA**
Business Administration and Management—General M
Counseling Psychology M
Criminal Justice and Criminology M
Health Services Management and Hospital Administration M
Nursing—General M
Organizational Management M
Pharmacy D

**SOUTH UNIVERSITY - MONTGOMERY**
Business Administration and Management—General M
Counseling Psychology M
Criminal Justice and Criminology M
Health Services Management and Hospital Administration M
Management Information Systems M
Nursing—General M
Public Administration M

**SOUTH UNIVERSITY - RICHMOND**
Business Administration and Management—General M
Counseling Psychology M
Nursing—General M

**SOUTH UNIVERSITY - SAVANNAH**
Anesthesiologist Assistant Studies M
Business Administration and Management—General M
Counseling Psychology M
Criminal Justice and Criminology M
Entrepreneurship M
Health Services Management and Hospital Administration M
Hospitality Management M
Nursing Education M
Nursing—General M
Organizational Management M
Pastoral Ministry and Counseling D
Pharmacy
Physician Assistant Studies M
Public Administration M
Sustainability Management M

**SOUTH UNIVERSITY - TAMPA**
Adult Nursing M
Business Administration and Management—General M
Criminal Justice and Criminology M
Family Nurse Practitioner Studies M
Health Services Management and Hospital Administration M
Management Information Systems M
Nursing Education M
Nursing—General M
Physician Assistant Studies M

**SOUTH UNIVERSITY - VIRGINIA BEACH**
Business Administration and Management—General M
Counseling Psychology M
Family Nurse Practitioner Studies M
Management Information Systems M
Nursing—General M
Organizational Management M

**SOUTH UNIVERSITY - WEST PALM BEACH**
Business Administration and Management—General M
Counseling Psychology M
Criminal Justice and Criminology M
Family Nurse Practitioner Studies M
Health Services Management and Hospital Administration M
Management Information Systems M
Nursing—General M
Occupational Therapy D
Public Administration M

**SOUTHWEST ACUPUNCTURE COLLEGE**
Acupuncture and Oriental Medicine M

**SOUTHWEST BAPTIST UNIVERSITY**
Business Administration and Management—General M
Education—General M,O
Educational Leadership and Administration M,O
Health Services Management and Hospital Administration M
Physical Therapy D

**SOUTHWEST COLLEGE OF NATUROPATHIC MEDICINE AND HEALTH SCIENCES**
Naturopathic Medicine D

**SOUTHWESTERN ADVENTIST UNIVERSITY**
Accounting M
Business Administration and Management—General M
Curriculum and Instruction M

Education—General M
Educational Leadership and Administration M
Finance and Banking M
Reading Education M

**SOUTHWESTERN ASSEMBLIES OF GOD UNIVERSITY**
Counseling Psychology M
Curriculum and Instruction M
Education—General M
Educational Leadership and Administration M
History M
Missions and Missiology M
Pastoral Ministry and Counseling M
Religion M
Religious Education M
Secondary Education M
Theology M

**SOUTHWESTERN BAPTIST THEOLOGICAL SEMINARY**
Missions and Missiology M,D
Music M,D
Near and Middle Eastern Studies M,D
Pastoral Ministry and Counseling M,D,O
Religious Education M,D
Theology M,D

**SOUTHWESTERN CHRISTIAN UNIVERSITY**
Missions and Missiology M
Pastoral Ministry and Counseling M

**SOUTHWESTERN COLLEGE (KS)**
Business Administration and Management—General M
Criminal Justice and Criminology M
Early Childhood Education M,D
Education—General M,D
Educational Leadership and Administration M,D
Elementary Education M,D
Higher Education M,D

**SOUTHWESTERN COLLEGE (NM)**
Art Therapy M
Counseling Psychology M,O
Health Psychology O
Psychology—General O
Social Psychology O
Thanatology M,O

**SOUTHWESTERN LAW SCHOOL**
Law M,D

**SOUTHWESTERN OKLAHOMA STATE UNIVERSITY**
Art Education M
Business Administration and Management—General M
Counselor Education M
Early Childhood Education M
Education—General M,O
Educational Leadership and Administration M
Educational Measurement and Evaluation M
Elementary Education M
Health Education M
Kinesiology and Movement Studies M
Mathematics Education M
Microbiology M
Music Education M
Music M
Pharmaceutical Administration D
Pharmacy D
Physical Education M
Recreation and Park Management M
School Psychology O
Science Education M
Social Sciences Education M
Special Education M
Sports Management M
Therapies—Dance, Drama, and Music M

**SOUTHWEST MINNESOTA STATE UNIVERSITY**
Business Administration and Management—General M
Early Childhood Education M
Education—General M
Educational Leadership and Administration M
English as a Second Language M
Marketing M
Mathematics Education M
Reading Education M
Special Education M

**SOUTHWEST UNIVERSITY**
Business Administration and Management—General M
Criminal Justice and Criminology M
Organizational Management M

**SOUTHWEST UNIVERSITY OF VISUAL ARTS**
Art/Fine Arts M
Photography M

**SPALDING UNIVERSITY**
Adult Nursing M,D,O
Art Education M
Athletic Training and Sports Medicine M
Business Education M
Clinical Psychology M,D
Corporate and Organizational Communication M
Counselor Education M
Education—General M,D
Educational Leadership and Administration M,D
Elementary Education M

Family Nurse Practitioner Studies M,D,O
Foreign Languages Education M
Middle School Education M
Nursing and Healthcare Administration M,D,O
Nursing Education M,D,O
Nursing—General M,D,O
Occupational Therapy M
Pediatric Nursing M,D,O
Psychology—General M,D
Secondary Education M
Social Work M
Special Education M
Writing M

**SPERTUS INSTITUTE FOR JEWISH LEARNING AND LEADERSHIP**
Jewish Studies M,D

**SPRING ARBOR UNIVERSITY**
Business Administration and Management—General M
Child and Family Studies M
Communication—General M
Counseling Psychology M
Education—General M
Nursing—General M
Pastoral Ministry and Counseling M
Reading Education M
Social Work M
Special Education M
Theology M

**SPRINGFIELD COLLEGE**
Art Therapy M,O
Athletic Training and Sports Medicine M
Business Administration and Management—General M
Clinical Psychology M,D,O
Counseling Psychology M,D,O
Counselor Education M,D,O
Early Childhood Education M,O
Education—General M,O
Educational Leadership and Administration M,D,O
Elementary Education M,O
Exercise and Sports Science M,D,O
Health Promotion M,D,O
Higher Education M,D,O
Human Services M
Industrial and Organizational Psychology M,D,O
Occupational Therapy M
Organizational Management M
Physical Education M,D,O
Physical Therapy D
Physician Assistant Studies M
Recreation and Park Management M
Rehabilitation Counseling M
Secondary Education M,O
Social Work M,O
Special Education M,O
Sport Psychology M,D,O
Sports Management M,D,O
Student Affairs M,D,O

**SPRING HILL COLLEGE**
Art/Fine Arts M,O
Business Administration and Management—General M
Early Childhood Education M
Education—General M
Elementary Education M
English M,O
Ethics M,O
Foundations and Philosophy of Education M
Liberal Studies M,O
Nursing and Healthcare Administration M,O
Nursing—General M,O
Secondary Education M
Theology M,O

**STANBRIDGE UNIVERSITY**
Nursing—General M
Occupational Therapy M

**STANFORD UNIVERSITY**
Allopathic Medicine D
Anthropology M,D
Applied Arts and Design—General M,D,O
Applied Physics M,D
Archaeology M,D
Art/Fine Arts M,D
Asian Languages M,D
Asian Studies M
Biochemistry D
Bioengineering M,D
Biological and Biomedical Sciences—General M,D
Biophysics D
Biostatistics M,D
Business Administration and Management—General M,D
Chemical Engineering M,D
Chemistry D
Chinese M,D
Classics M,D
Clinical Research M,D
Communication—General M,D
Comparative Literature D
Computational Sciences M,D
Computer Science M,D
Construction Engineering M,D,O
Cultural Studies M,D
Curriculum and Instruction M
Developmental Biology M,D
East European and Russian Studies M
Ecology M,D
Economics D
Education—General M,D
Educational Leadership and Administration M

| | |
|---|---|
| Educational Media/Instructional Technology | M |
| Educational Policy | M |
| Electrical Engineering | M,D |
| Energy and Power Engineering | M,D,O |
| Engineering and Applied Sciences—General | M,D,O |
| Engineering Management | M,D |
| Engineering Physics | M,D |
| English | M,D |
| Environmental Sciences | M,D,O |
| Epidemiology | M,D |
| French | M,D |
| Genetics | D |
| Geophysics | M,D |
| Geosciences | M,D,O |
| German | M,D |
| Health Services Research | M,D |
| History | M,D |
| Hydrology | M,D,O |
| Immunology | D |
| Industrial/Management Engineering | M,D |
| International and Comparative Education | M,D |
| Italian | M,D |
| Japanese | M,D |
| Law | M,D |
| Linguistics | M,D |
| Materials Engineering | M,D,O |
| Materials Sciences | M,D,O |
| Mathematics | M,D |
| Mechanical Engineering | M,D,O |
| Mechanics | M,D,O |
| Medical Informatics | M,D |
| Microbiology | D |
| Music | M,D |
| Philosophy | M,D |
| Physics | D |
| Physiology | D |
| Political Science | M,D |
| Psychology—General | D |
| Religion | D |
| Secondary Education | M |
| Slavic Languages | D |
| Sociology | D |
| Spanish | M,D |
| Statistics | M,D |
| Structural Biology | D |
| Structural Engineering | M,D,O |
| Sustainable Development | M,D,O |
| Systems Biology | D |
| Theater | D |

**STARR KING SCHOOL FOR THE MINISTRY**

| | |
|---|---|
| Theology | M |

**STATE UNIVERSITY OF NEW YORK AT FREDONIA**

| | |
|---|---|
| Biological and Biomedical Sciences—General | M,O |
| Communication Disorders | M,O |
| Curriculum and Instruction | M |
| Early Childhood Education | M |
| Education—General | M |
| English as a Second Language | M |
| English Education | M,O |
| English | M,O |
| Interdisciplinary Studies | M,O |
| Mathematics Education | M,O |
| Middle School Education | M,O |
| Music Education | M |
| Music | M |
| Reading Education | M |
| Secondary Education | M |
| Writing | M,O |

**STATE UNIVERSITY OF NEW YORK AT NEW PALTZ**

| | |
|---|---|
| Accounting | M |
| Art Education | M |
| Art/Fine Arts | M |
| Business Administration and Management—General | M |
| Chemistry | M,O |
| Clinical Psychology | M,O |
| Communication Disorders | M |
| Counseling Psychology | M,O |
| Counselor Education | M,O |
| Early Childhood Education | M |
| Education—General | M,O |
| Educational Leadership and Administration | M,O |
| Elementary Education | M |
| English as a Second Language | M,O |
| English Education | M,O |
| English | M |
| French | M,O |
| Geosciences | M,O |
| Multilingual and Multicultural Education | M,O |
| Music | M |
| Psychology—General | M,O |
| Reading Education | M |
| Science Education | M,O |
| Secondary Education | M |
| Social Sciences Education | M,O |
| Spanish | M,O |
| Special Education | M |
| Therapies—Dance, Drama, and Music | M |

**STATE UNIVERSITY OF NEW YORK AT OSWEGO**

| | |
|---|---|
| Agricultural Education | M |
| Art Education | M |
| Art/Fine Arts | M |
| Bioinformatics | M |
| Business Administration and Management—General | M |
| Business Education | M |
| Chemistry | M |
| Child and Family Studies | M |
| Communication—General | M |
| Consumer Economics | M |
| Corporate and Organizational Communication | M |
| Counseling Psychology | M |
| Curriculum and Instruction | M |
| Early Childhood Education | M |
| Education—General | M,O |
| Educational Leadership and Administration | O |
| Elementary Education | M |
| Graphic Design | M |
| Health Communication | M |
| Health Informatics | M |
| Human-Computer Interaction | M |
| Internet and Interactive Multimedia | M |
| Middle School Education | M |
| Reading Education | M |
| Secondary Education | M |
| Special Education | M |
| Vocational and Technical Education | M |

**STATE UNIVERSITY OF NEW YORK AT PLATTSBURGH**

| | |
|---|---|
| Clinical Psychology | M,O |
| Communication Disorders | M |
| Counseling Psychology | M,O |
| Counselor Education | M,O |
| Curriculum and Instruction | M |
| Early Childhood Education | O |
| Educational Leadership and Administration | O |
| Elementary Education | M,O |
| English Education | M |
| Foreign Languages Education | M |
| Mathematics Education | M |
| Psychology—General | M,O |
| Reading Education | M |
| School Psychology | M,O |
| Science Education | M |
| Secondary Education | M |
| Social Sciences Education | M |
| Special Education | M |
| Student Affairs | M,O |

**STATE UNIVERSITY OF NEW YORK COLLEGE AT CORTLAND**

| | |
|---|---|
| Communication Disorders | M |
| Community Health | M |
| Early Childhood Education | M |
| Education—General | M,O |
| Educational Leadership and Administration | O |
| English as a Second Language | M |
| English Education | M |
| English | M |
| Environmental Education | M |
| Health Education | M |
| History | M |
| Mathematics Education | M |
| Mathematics | M |
| Physical Education | M |
| Physics | M |
| Reading Education | M |
| Recreation and Park Management | M |
| Science Education | M |
| Secondary Education | M |
| Special Education | M |
| Sports Management | M |

**STATE UNIVERSITY OF NEW YORK COLLEGE AT GENESEO**

| | |
|---|---|
| Accounting | M |
| Business Administration and Management—General | M |
| Education—General | M |
| English Education | M |
| French | M |
| Reading Education | M |
| Secondary Education | M |
| Social Sciences Education | M |
| Spanish | M |

**STATE UNIVERSITY OF NEW YORK COLLEGE AT OLD WESTBURY**

| | |
|---|---|
| Accounting | M |
| Business Administration and Management—General | M |
| Counseling Psychology | M |
| Education—General | M |
| English Education | M |
| Foreign Languages Education | M |
| Liberal Studies | M |
| Mathematics Education | M |
| Science Education | M |
| Social Sciences Education | M |
| Taxation | M |

**STATE UNIVERSITY OF NEW YORK COLLEGE AT ONEONTA**

| | |
|---|---|
| Biological and Biomedical Sciences—General | M |
| Counselor Education | M,O |
| Education—General | M,O |
| Educational Psychology | M,O |
| Elementary Education | M |
| Museum Studies | M |
| Nutrition | M |
| Reading Education | M |
| Special Education | M,O |

**STATE UNIVERSITY OF NEW YORK COLLEGE AT POTSDAM**

| | |
|---|---|
| Community Health | M |
| Curriculum and Instruction | M |
| Early Childhood Education | M |
| Educational Media/Instructional Technology | M |
| Elementary Education | M |
| English Education | M |
| Mathematics Education | M |
| Mathematics | M |
| Middle School Education | M |
| Music Education | M |
| Music | M |
| Reading Education | M |
| Science Education | M |
| Secondary Education | M |
| Social Sciences Education | M |
| Special Education | M |

**STATE UNIVERSITY OF NEW YORK COLLEGE OF ENVIRONMENTAL SCIENCE AND FORESTRY**

| | |
|---|---|
| Biochemistry | M,D |
| Chemistry | M,D |
| Conservation Biology | M,D |
| Ecology | M,D |
| Economics | M,D |
| Entomology | M,D |
| Environmental Biology | M,D |
| Environmental Engineering | M,D |
| Environmental Management and Policy | M,D |
| Environmental Sciences | M,D |
| Fish, Game, and Wildlife Management | M,D |
| Forestry | M,D |
| Geographic Information Systems | M,D |
| Landscape Architecture | M |
| Materials Sciences | M,D,O |
| Natural Resources | M,D |
| Organic Chemistry | M,D |
| Paper and Pulp Engineering | M,D,O |
| Plant Pathology | M,D |
| Plant Sciences | M,D |
| Sustainability Management | M,D,O |
| Sustainable Development | M,D,O |
| Urban and Regional Planning | M,D |
| Urban Design | M |
| Water Resources Engineering | M,D |
| Water Resources | M,D |

**STATE UNIVERSITY OF NEW YORK COLLEGE OF OPTOMETRY**

| | |
|---|---|
| Optometry | D |
| Vision Sciences | D |

**STATE UNIVERSITY OF NEW YORK COLLEGE OF TECHNOLOGY AT DELHI**

| | |
|---|---|
| Nursing and Healthcare Administration | M |
| Nursing Education | M |
| Nursing—General | M |

**STATE UNIVERSITY OF NEW YORK DOWNSTATE MEDICAL CENTER**

| | |
|---|---|
| Allopathic Medicine | M,D |
| Biological and Biomedical Sciences—General | M,D |
| Biomedical Engineering | M,D |
| Cell Biology | D |
| Community Health | M |
| Family Nurse Practitioner Studies | M,O |
| Medical/Surgical Nursing | M,O |
| Molecular Biology | D |
| Neuroscience | D |
| Nurse Anesthesia | M |
| Nurse Midwifery | M,O |
| Nursing—General | M,O |
| Occupational Therapy | M |
| Public Health—General | M |

**STATE UNIVERSITY OF NEW YORK EMPIRE STATE COLLEGE**

| | |
|---|---|
| Adult Education | M |
| Business Administration and Management—General | M |
| Economic Development | M |
| Education—General | M |
| Educational Media/Instructional Technology | M |
| Industrial and Labor Relations | M |
| International Business | M |
| Liberal Studies | M |
| Nursing Education | M |
| Public Policy | M |

**STATE UNIVERSITY OF NEW YORK MARITIME COLLEGE**

| | |
|---|---|
| Transportation Management | M |

**STATE UNIVERSITY OF NEW YORK POLYTECHNIC INSTITUTE**

| | |
|---|---|
| Accounting | M |
| Business Administration and Management—General | M |
| Computer and Information Systems Security | M |
| Computer Science | M |
| Family Nurse Practitioner Studies | M,O |
| Finance and Banking | M |
| Human Resources Management | M |
| Information Science | M |
| Management of Technology | M |
| Marketing | M |
| Nanotechnology | M,D |
| Nursing Education | M,O |

**STATE UNIVERSITY OF NEW YORK UPSTATE MEDICAL UNIVERSITY**

| | |
|---|---|
| Allopathic Medicine | D |
| Anatomy | M,D |
| Biochemistry | M,D |
| Biological and Biomedical Sciences—General | M,D |
| Cell Biology | M,D |
| Clinical Laboratory Sciences/Medical Technology | M |
| Family Nurse Practitioner Studies | M,O |
| Immunology | M,D |
| Microbiology | M,D |
| Molecular Biology | M,D |
| Neuroscience | D |
| Nursing—General | M,O |
| Pharmacology | D |
| Physical Therapy | D |
| Physiology | M,D |
| Public Health—General | M |

**STEPHEN F. AUSTIN STATE UNIVERSITY**

| | |
|---|---|
| Accounting | M |
| Agricultural Sciences—General | M |
| Applied Arts and Design—General | M |
| Art Education | M |
| Art/Fine Arts | M |
| Athletic Training and Sports Medicine | M |
| Biological and Biomedical Sciences—General | M |
| Biotechnology | M |
| Business Administration and Management—General | M |
| Chemistry | M |
| Communication Disorders | M |
| Communication—General | M |
| Computer and Information Systems Security | M |
| Counselor Education | M |
| Early Childhood Education | M |
| Education—General | M,D |
| Educational Leadership and Administration | M,D |
| Elementary Education | M |
| English | M |
| Environmental Sciences | M |
| Family and Consumer Sciences-General | M |
| Family Nurse Practitioner Studies | M |
| Film, Television, and Video Production | M |
| Forestry | M,D |
| Geology | M |
| Hispanic Studies | M |
| History | M |
| Interdisciplinary Studies | M |
| Kinesiology and Movement Studies | M |
| Marketing | M |
| Mass Communication | M |
| Mathematics Education | M |
| Mathematics | M |
| Music | M |
| Nursing—General | M |
| Physics | M,D |
| Psychology—General | M |
| Public Administration | M |
| Publishing | M |
| School Psychology | M |
| Secondary Education | M,D |
| Social Work | M |
| Special Education | M |
| Statistics | M |

**STEPHENS COLLEGE**

| | |
|---|---|
| Addictions/Substance Abuse Counseling | M,O |
| Clinical Psychology | M,O |
| Counselor Education | M,O |
| Health Informatics | M,O |
| Physician Assistant Studies | M,O |
| Writing | M,O |

**STETSON UNIVERSITY**

| | |
|---|---|
| Accounting | M |
| Business Administration and Management—General | M |
| Counselor Education | M |
| Education—General | M |
| Educational Leadership and Administration | M |
| Law | M,D |
| Writing | M |

**STEVENS INSTITUTE OF TECHNOLOGY**

| | |
|---|---|
| Aerospace/Aeronautical Engineering | M,O |
| Applied Mathematics | M |
| Artificial Intelligence/Robotics | M,D,O |
| Biochemistry | M,D,O |
| Biomedical Engineering | M,D,O |
| Business Administration and Management—General | M,O |
| Business Analytics | M,O |
| Chemical Engineering | M,D,O |
| Chemistry | M,D,O |
| Civil Engineering | M,D,O |
| Communication—General | M,D,O |
| Computer and Information Systems Security | M,O |
| Computer Engineering | M,D,O |
| Computer Science | M,D,O |
| Construction Engineering | M,O |
| Construction Management | M,O |
| Electrical Engineering | M,D,O |
| Electronic Commerce | M,O |
| Engineering and Applied Sciences—General | M,D,O |
| Engineering Design | M |
| Engineering Management | M,D,O |
| Entrepreneurship | M,O |
| Environmental Engineering | M,D,O |
| Ethics | M,O |
| Film, Television, and Video Production | M |
| Finance and Banking | M,O |
| Financial Engineering | M,D,O |
| Human Resources Management | M |
| Hydraulics | M,D,O |
| Hydrology | M,D,O |

*M—masters degree; D—doctorate; O—other advanced degree; *—Close-Up and/or Display*

| | |
|---|---|
| Industrial and Manufacturing Management | M |
| Information Science | M,O |
| International Business | M |
| Management Information Systems | M,D,O |
| Management of Technology | M,D,O |
| Management Strategy and Policy | M |
| Manufacturing Engineering | M |
| Marketing | M,O |
| Materials Engineering | M,D |
| Materials Sciences | M,D |
| Mathematics | M,D |
| Mechanical Engineering | M,D,O |
| Media Studies | M |
| Modeling and Simulation | M,D,O |
| Ocean Engineering | M,D |
| Pharmaceutical Sciences | M,O |
| Photonics | M,D,O |
| Project Management | M,O |
| Quality Management | M,O |
| Software Engineering | M,O |
| Statistics | M,O |
| Structural Engineering | M,D,O |
| Systems Engineering | M,D,O |
| Systems Science | M,D |
| Telecommunications Management | M,D,O |
| Telecommunications | M,D,O |
| Transportation and Highway Engineering | M,D,O |
| Water Resources Engineering | M,D,O |

## STEVENSON UNIVERSITY

| | |
|---|---|
| Biological and Biomedical Sciences—General | M |
| Chemistry | M |
| Communication—General | M |
| Computer and Information Systems Security | M |
| Education—General | M |
| Educational Leadership and Administration | M |
| Forensic Sciences | M |
| Health Services Management and Hospital Administration | M |
| Management of Technology | M |
| Mathematics Education | M |
| Nursing and Healthcare Administration | M |
| Nursing Education | M |
| Nursing—General | M |
| Project Management | M |
| Quality Management | M |
| Science Education | M |

## STOCKTON UNIVERSITY

| | |
|---|---|
| American Studies | M,O |
| Business Administration and Management—General | M |
| Communication Disorders | M |
| Criminal Justice and Criminology | M |
| Data Science/Data Analytics | M |
| Education—General | M |
| Educational Media/Instructional Technology | M |
| Environmental Sciences | M |
| Holocaust and Genocide Studies | M |
| Management Strategy and Policy | M |
| Nursing—General | M |
| Occupational Therapy | M |
| Organizational Management | D |
| Physical Therapy | D |
| Quantitative Analysis | M |
| Social Work | M |

## STONEHILL COLLEGE

| | |
|---|---|
| Internet and Interactive Multimedia | M |
| Special Education | M |

## STONY BROOK UNIVERSITY, STATE UNIVERSITY OF NEW YORK

| | |
|---|---|
| Accounting | M,O |
| Addictions/Substance Abuse Counseling | M,O |
| Adult Nursing | M,D,O |
| African Studies | M,O |
| Allopathic Medicine | D |
| Anatomy | D |
| Anthropology | M,D |
| Applied Mathematics | M,D,O |
| Art History | M,D |
| Art/Fine Arts | M |
| Asian Studies | M |
| Asian-American Studies | M |
| Astronomy | D |
| Atmospheric Sciences | M,D |
| Biochemistry | M,D |
| Bioethics | |
| Bioinformatics | M,D,O |
| Biological and Biomedical Sciences—General | M,D,O |
| Biomedical Engineering | M,D,O |
| Biophysics | D |
| Business Administration and Management—General | M,O |
| Cell Biology | M,D |
| Chemistry | M,D |
| Civil Engineering | M,D,O |
| Clinical Psychology | D |
| Cognitive Sciences | D |
| Community Health | M,D,O |
| Comparative Literature | M,D,O |
| Computer Education | M |
| Computer Engineering | M,D |
| Computer Science | M,D,O |
| Cultural Studies | M,D,O |
| Dentistry | D,O |
| Developmental Biology | M,D |
| Ecology | M,D |
| Economics | M,D |
| Educational Leadership and Administration | M,O |
| Educational Media/Instructional Technology | M |
| Electrical Engineering | M,D |
| Energy Management and Policy | M |
| Engineering and Applied Sciences—General | M,D,O |
| English as a Second Language | M |
| English | M,D,O |
| Entrepreneurship | M,O |
| Environmental Management and Policy | M,O |
| Evolutionary Biology | M,D |
| Family Nurse Practitioner Studies | M,D,O |
| Film, Television, and Video Production | M |
| Finance and Banking | M,O |
| Foreign Languages Education | M,O |
| French | M |
| Gender Studies | O |
| Genetics | D |
| Geographic Information Systems | O |
| Geosciences | M,D |
| Gerontological Nursing | M,D,O |
| Health Communication | M,O |
| Health Education | M,O |
| Health Informatics | M,D,O |
| Health Promotion | M,O |
| Health Psychology | D |
| Health Services Management and Hospital Administration | M,D,O |
| Higher Education | M,O |
| Hispanic and Latin American Languages | M,D |
| History | M,D |
| Human Resources Management | M,O |
| Immunology | M,D |
| Italian | M |
| Journalism | M,O |
| Liberal Studies | M,O |
| Linguistics | M,D |
| Management of Technology | M |
| Marine Affairs | M |
| Marine Sciences | M,D |
| Marketing | M,O |
| Materials Engineering | M,D |
| Materials Sciences | M,D |
| Maternal and Child/Neonatal Nursing | M,D,O |
| Mathematics Education | M,O |
| Mathematics | M,D |
| Mechanical Engineering | M,D |
| Medical Physics | M,D |
| Microbiology | D |
| Molecular Biology | M,D |
| Molecular Genetics | D |
| Molecular Physiology | D |
| Music | M,D |
| Neuroscience | M,D |
| Nurse Midwifery | M,D,O |
| Nursing and Healthcare Administration | M,D,O |
| Nursing Education | M,O |
| Nursing—General | M,D,O |
| Nutrition | M,O |
| Occupational Therapy | M,D,O |
| Oral and Dental Sciences | M,D,O |
| Pathology | M,D |
| Pediatric Nursing | M,D,O |
| Pharmacology | M,D |
| Philosophy | M,D,O |
| Physical Education | M,O |
| Physical Therapy | M,D,O |
| Physician Assistant Studies | M,D,O |
| Physics | M,D |
| Physiology | D |
| Political Science | M,D |
| Psychiatric Nursing | M,D,O |
| Psychology—General | M,D |
| Public Health—General | M,O |
| Public Policy | M |
| Rehabilitation Sciences | M,D,O |
| Romance Languages | M |
| Science Education | M,D |
| Social Psychology | D |
| Social Sciences Education | M,O |
| Social Work | M,D |
| Sociology | M,D |
| Statistics | M,D,O |
| Structural Biology | D |
| Systems Engineering | M |
| Telecommunications | M,D,O |
| Theater | M |
| Women's Health Nursing | M,D,O |
| Women's Studies | O |
| Writing | M,O |

## STRATFORD UNIVERSITY (MD)

| | |
|---|---|
| Hospitality Management | M |

## STRATFORD UNIVERSITY (VA)

| | |
|---|---|
| Accounting | M,D |
| Business Administration and Management—General | M,D |
| Computer and Information Systems Security | M,D |
| Computer Science | M,D |
| Forensic Sciences | M,D |
| Health Services Management and Hospital Administration | M,D |
| Management Information Systems | M,D |
| Management of Technology | M,D |
| Software Engineering | M,D |
| Telecommunications | M,D |

## STRAYER UNIVERSITY

| | |
|---|---|
| Accounting | M |
| Business Administration and Management—General | M |
| Computer and Information Systems Security | M |
| Education—General | M |
| Educational Media/Instructional Technology | M |
| Finance and Banking | M |
| Health Services Management and Hospital Administration | M |
| Hospitality Management | M |
| Human Resources Management | M |
| Information Science | M |
| Management Information Systems | M |
| Marketing | M |
| Public Administration | M |
| Software Engineering | M |
| Supply Chain Management | M |
| Systems Science | M |
| Taxation | M |
| Telecommunications Management | M |
| Travel and Tourism | M |

## SUFFOLK UNIVERSITY

| | |
|---|---|
| Accounting | M,O |
| Advertising and Public Relations | M |
| Applied Arts and Design—General | M |
| Business Administration and Management—General | M |
| Business Analytics | M |
| Clinical Psychology | M,D,O |
| Community Health | M |
| Corporate and Organizational Communication | M |
| Counseling Psychology | M,D,O |
| Counselor Education | M,D,O |
| Criminal Justice and Criminology | M |
| Data Science/Data Analytics | M |
| Educational Leadership and Administration | M,O |
| Entrepreneurship | M |
| Ethics | M,O |
| Finance and Banking | M |
| Graphic Design | M |
| Health Law | M,D |
| Health Services Management and Hospital Administration | M |
| Intellectual Property Law | M,D |
| Interior Design | M |
| International Business | M |
| Law | M,D |
| Management Information Systems | M |
| Management Strategy and Policy | M |
| Marketing | M |
| Nonprofit Management | M |
| Organizational Behavior | M |
| Political Science | M,O |
| Psychology—General | M,D,O |
| Public Administration | M |
| Public Policy | M,O |
| Supply Chain Management | M |
| Taxation | M,O |

## SULLIVAN UNIVERSITY

| | |
|---|---|
| Business Administration and Management—General | M,D |
| Pharmacy | D |

## SUL ROSS STATE UNIVERSITY

| | |
|---|---|
| Animal Sciences | M |
| Art Education | M |
| Art History | M |
| Art/Fine Arts | M |
| Biological and Biomedical Sciences—General | M |
| Business Administration and Management—General | M |
| Counselor Education | M |
| Criminal Justice and Criminology | M |
| Education—General | M,O |
| Educational Leadership and Administration | M |
| Educational Measurement and Evaluation | M,O |
| Elementary Education | M |
| Emergency Management | M |
| English | M |
| Fish, Game, and Wildlife Management | M |
| Geology | M |
| History | M |
| Multilingual and Multicultural Education | M |
| Natural Resources | M |
| Physical Education | M |
| Political Science | M |
| Psychology—General | M |
| Range Science | M |
| Reading Education | M,O |
| Secondary Education | M |

## SUM BIBLE COLLEGE & THEOLOGICAL SEMINARY

| | |
|---|---|
| Pastoral Ministry and Counseling | M |
| Religion | M |
| Theology | M |

## SUNY BROCKPORT

| | |
|---|---|
| Accounting | M,O |
| American Studies | M |
| Art/Fine Arts | M |
| Arts Administration | M,O |
| Biological and Biomedical Sciences—General | M,O |
| Chemistry | M,O |
| Community Health | M |
| Counseling Psychology | M,O |
| Counselor Education | M,O |
| Curriculum and Instruction | M,O |
| Dance | M |
| Early Childhood Education | M,O |
| Education—General | M,O |
| Educational Leadership and Administration | M,O |
| English Education | M,O |
| English | M,O |
| Environmental Sciences | M |
| Gerontology | M,O |
| Health Education | M |
| Health Services Management and Hospital Administration | M,O |
| History of Medicine | M,O |
| History | M |
| Liberal Studies | M |
| Mathematics Education | M,O |
| Mathematics | M |
| Middle School Education | M,O |
| Multilingual and Multicultural Education | M,O |
| Nonprofit Management | M,O |
| Physical Education | M,O |
| Psychology—General | M |
| Public Administration | M,O |
| Public Health—General | M |
| Public History | M |
| Reading Education | M,O |
| Science Education | M,O |
| Social Sciences Education | M,O |
| Social Work | M,O |
| Sports Management | M,O |
| Writing | M,O |

## SWEDISH INSTITUTE, COLLEGE OF HEALTH SCIENCES

| | |
|---|---|
| Acupuncture and Oriental Medicine | M |

## SWEET BRIAR COLLEGE

| | |
|---|---|
| Education—General | M |

## SYRACUSE UNIVERSITY

| | |
|---|---|
| Accounting | M |
| Addictions/Substance Abuse Counseling | M,O |
| Advertising and Public Relations | M |
| Aerospace/Aeronautical Engineering | M,D |
| African Studies | M |
| African-American Studies | M |
| Anthropology | M,D |
| Applied Arts and Design—General | M |
| Applied Statistics | M |
| Architecture | M |
| Art Education | M |
| Art History | M |
| Art/Fine Arts | M |
| Arts Journalism | M |
| Bioengineering | M,D |
| Biological and Biomedical Sciences—General | M,D |
| Broadcast Journalism | M |
| Business Administration and Management—General | M,D |
| Business Analytics | M |
| Chemical Engineering | M,D |
| Chemistry | M,D |
| Child and Family Studies | M,D |
| Civil Engineering | M,D |
| Clinical Psychology | M,D |
| Cognitive Sciences | D |
| Communication Disorders | M,D |
| Communication—General | M,D |
| Computer and Information Systems Security | M,O |
| Computer Art and Design | M |
| Computer Engineering | M,D |
| Computer Science | M |
| Conflict Resolution and Mediation/Peace Studies | O |
| Counselor Education | M,D |
| Curriculum and Instruction | M,D,O |
| Data Science/Data Analytics | M,O |
| Disability Studies | O |
| Early Childhood Education | M |
| Economics | M,D |
| Education of Students with Severe/Multiple Disabilities | M |
| Education—General | M,D,O |
| Educational Leadership and Administration | M,D,O |
| Educational Measurement and Evaluation | M,D,O |
| Educational Media/Instructional Technology | M,O |
| Electrical Engineering | M,D |
| Emergency Management | O |
| Engineering and Applied Sciences—General | M,D,O |
| Engineering Management | M |
| English as a Second Language | M,O |
| English Education | M |
| English | M,D |
| Entertainment Management | M |
| Entrepreneurship | M |
| Environmental and Occupational Health | O |
| Environmental Engineering | M |
| Exercise and Sports Science | M |
| Film, Television, and Video Production | M |
| Finance and Banking | M,D |
| Forensic Sciences | M,O |
| Foundations and Philosophy of Education | M,D,O |
| French | M |
| Geography | M,D |
| Geology | M,D |
| Health Services Management and Hospital Administration | O |
| Higher Education | M,D |
| History | M,D |
| Hospitality Management | M,O |
| Human Development | M,D |
| Illustration | M |
| Information Science | M,D |
| Information Studies | M |
| International Affairs | M |
| International Health | M |
| Journalism | M |
| Kinesiology and Movement Studies | M,D,O |
| Law | M,D |
| Library Science | M |
| Linguistics | M |
| Management Information Systems | M,D,O |
| Marketing | M |
| Marriage and Family Therapy | M,D |
| Mass Communication | M,D |
| Mathematics Education | M,D |
| Mathematics | M,D |

| | |
|---|---|
| Mechanical Engineering | M,D |
| Media Studies | M |
| Museum Studies | M |
| Music Education | M |
| Music | M |
| Neuroscience | M,D |
| Nutrition | M,D |
| Organizational Management | O |
| Philosophy | M,D |
| Photography | M |
| Physics | M,D |
| Political Science | M,D,O |
| Psychology—General | D |
| Public Administration | M,D |
| Public Affairs | |
| Reading Education | M,D |
| Real Estate | M |
| Religion | M,D |
| Rhetoric | M,D |
| School Psychology | M,D,O |
| Science Education | M,D |
| Social Psychology | D |
| Social Sciences Education | M |
| Social Sciences | M,D |
| Social Work | M |
| Sociology | M,D |
| Spanish | M |
| Special Education | M,D |
| Sports Management | M |
| Student Affairs | M |
| Supply Chain Management | M |
| Sustainability Management | O |
| Travel and Tourism | M |
| Urban and Regional Planning | O |
| Writing | M,D |

**TABOR COLLEGE**

| | |
|---|---|
| Accounting | M |
| Business Administration and Management—General | M |

**TAFT UNIVERSITY SYSTEM**

| | |
|---|---|
| Education—General | M |
| Law | M,D |
| Legal and Justice Studies | M,D |
| Taxation | M,D |

**TALMUDIC UNIVERSITY**

| | |
|---|---|
| Theology | M |

**TARLETON STATE UNIVERSITY**

| | |
|---|---|
| Accounting | M |
| Agricultural Sciences—General | M |
| Applied Psychology | M |
| Athletic Training and Sports Medicine | M |
| Biological and Biomedical Sciences—General | M |
| Business Administration and Management—General | M |
| Clinical Laboratory Sciences/Medical Technology | M |
| Communication—General | M |
| Counseling Psychology | M |
| Criminal Justice and Criminology | M |
| Curriculum and Instruction | M |
| Education—General | M,D,O |
| Educational Leadership and Administration | M,D,O |
| Educational Media/Instructional Technology | M |
| Elementary Education | M |
| Engineering Management | M |
| English | M |
| Environmental Sciences | M |
| Fish, Game, and Wildlife Management | M |
| History | M |
| Human Resources Management | M |
| Kinesiology and Movement Studies | M |
| Management Information Systems | M |
| Marketing | M |
| Mathematics | M |
| Music Education | M |
| Natural Resources | M |
| Nursing and Healthcare Administration | M |
| Nursing Education | M |
| Nursing—General | M |
| Political Science | M |
| Public Health—General | M |
| Secondary Education | M |
| Social Work | M |
| Special Education | M |

**TAYLOR COLLEGE AND SEMINARY**

| | |
|---|---|
| Cultural Studies | M,O |
| English as a Second Language | M,O |
| Missions and Missiology | M,O |
| Theology | M,O |

**TAYLOR UNIVERSITY**

| | |
|---|---|
| Higher Education | M |

**TEACHERS COLLEGE, COLUMBIA UNIVERSITY**

| | |
|---|---|
| Adult Education | M,D |
| Anthropology | M,D |
| Applied Behavior Analysis | M,D,O |
| Applied Psychology | M,D |
| Applied Statistics | M,D |
| Art Education | M,D,O |
| Arts Administration | M,D,O |
| Biological and Biomedical Sciences—General | M,D |
| Chemistry | M,D |
| Clinical Psychology | M,D |
| Communication Disorders | M,D,O |
| Communication—General | M,D |
| Community Health | M,D,O |
| Computer Education | M,D |
| Counseling Psychology | M,D |
| Curriculum and Instruction | M,D |
| Developmental Psychology | M,D |
| Early Childhood Education | M,D |
| Economics | M,D |
| Education of Students with Severe/Multiple Disabilities | M,D,O |
| Education of the Gifted | M,D |
| Education—General | M,D |
| Educational Leadership and Administration | M,D |
| Educational Measurement and Evaluation | M,D |
| Educational Media/Instructional Technology | M,D |
| Educational Policy | M,D |
| Educational Psychology | M,D,O |
| Elementary Education | M,D |
| English as a Second Language | M,D,O |
| English Education | M,D,O |
| Foundations and Philosophy of Education | M,D,O |
| Geosciences | M,D |
| Health Education | M,D,O |
| Higher Education | M,D |
| Industrial and Organizational Psychology | M,D |
| Interdisciplinary Studies | M,D |
| International Affairs | M,D,O |
| International and Comparative Education | M,D |
| Kinesiology and Movement Studies | M,D |
| Linguistics | M,D,O |
| Mathematics Education | M,D |
| Multilingual and Multicultural Education | M,D,O |
| Music Education | M,D,O |
| Neuroscience | M,D |
| Nursing and Healthcare Administration | M,D |
| Nursing Education | M,D,O |
| Nutrition | M,D,O |
| Philosophy | M,D,O |
| Physical Education | M,D |
| Physics | M,D |
| Physiology | M,D |
| Political Science | M,D |
| Psychology—General | M,D |
| Reading Education | M,D,O |
| School Psychology | M,D,O |
| Science Education | M,D |
| Secondary Education | M,D |
| Social Psychology | M,D |
| Social Sciences Education | M,D,O |
| Sociology | M,D |
| Special Education | M,D,O |
| Urban Education | M,D |

**TEACHERS COLLEGE OF SAN JOAQUIN**

| | |
|---|---|
| Early Childhood Education | M |
| Education—General | M |
| Educational Leadership and Administration | M |
| Educational Measurement and Evaluation | M |
| Mathematics Education | M |
| Science Education | M |
| Special Education | M |

**TELSHE YESHIVA - CHICAGO**

| | |
|---|---|
| Jewish Studies | O |

**TEMPLE UNIVERSITY**

| | |
|---|---|
| Accounting | M,D |
| Actuarial Science | M |
| Adult Nursing | D |
| African-American Studies | M,D |
| Allied Health—General | M,D |
| Allopathic Medicine | D |
| Anthropology | D |
| Applied Behavior Analysis | M,D,O |
| Applied Mathematics | M,D |
| Architecture | M |
| Art Education | M |
| Art History | M,D |
| Art/Fine Arts | M |
| Artificial Intelligence/Robotics | M,D |
| Arts Administration | M,D |
| Athletic Training and Sports Medicine | M,D |
| Bioengineering | M,D |
| Biological and Biomedical Sciences—General | M,D |
| Biotechnology | M,D |
| Business Administration and Management—General | M,D |
| Business Education | M |
| Chemistry | M,D |
| Civil Engineering | M,O |
| Communication Disorders | M,D |
| Communication—General | M,D |
| Computer and Information Systems Security | M,D |
| Computer Science | M,D |
| Corporate and Organizational Communication | M,D |
| Counseling Psychology | M,D,O |
| Criminal Justice and Criminology | M,D |
| Dance | M,D |
| Dentistry | D |
| Economics | M,D |
| Education—General | M,D,O |
| Educational Leadership and Administration | M,D |
| Educational Psychology | M,D,O |
| Electrical Engineering | M,D |
| English as a Second Language | M |
| English Education | M |
| English | M,D |
| Entrepreneurship | M,D |
| Environmental and Occupational Health | M,D |
| Environmental Engineering | M,O |
| Epidemiology | M,D |
| Family Nurse Practitioner Studies | D |
| Film, Television, and Video Production | M |
| Finance and Banking | M,D |
| Financial Engineering | M |
| Geographic Information Systems | M,D,O |
| Geography | M,D,O |
| Geology | M,D |
| Geosciences | M,D |
| Gerontology | D |
| Graphic Design | M |
| Health Informatics | M,D |
| Health Services Management and Hospital Administration | M |
| History | M,D |
| Hospitality Management | M,D |
| Human Resources Management | M |
| Hydrology | M,O |
| Industrial and Labor Relations | M,O |
| Information Science | M,D |
| Insurance | D |
| International Business | M,D |
| Investment Management | M,O |
| Journalism | M |
| Kinesiology and Movement Studies | M,D |
| Law | M,D,O |
| Legal and Justice Studies | M,D |
| Management Information Systems | M,D |
| Management Strategy and Policy | D |
| Marketing | M,D |
| Mathematics Education | M |
| Mathematics | M,D |
| Mechanical Engineering | M |
| Media Studies | M |
| Medicinal and Pharmaceutical Chemistry | M,D |
| Middle School Education | M |
| Music Education | M,D |
| Music | M,D |
| Nursing—General | D |
| Occupational Therapy | M,D |
| Oral and Dental Sciences | M,O |
| Pharmaceutical Administration | M |
| Pharmaceutical Sciences | M,D |
| Pharmacy | M,D |
| Philosophy | M,D |
| Photography | M |
| Physical Education | M,D |
| Physics | M,D |
| Podiatric Medicine | D |
| Political Science | M,D |
| Psychology—General | M,D |
| Public Health—General | M,D |
| Recreation and Park Management | M,D |
| Rehabilitation Sciences | M,D |
| Religion | M,D |
| Risk Management | D |
| School Psychology | M,D,O |
| Science Education | M |
| Secondary Education | M |
| Social Psychology | M,D,O |
| Social Sciences Education | M |
| Social Work | M |
| Sociology | M,D |
| Spanish | M,D |
| Sports Management | M,D |
| Statistics | M,D |
| Taxation | M,D |
| Textile Design | M |
| Theater | M |
| Therapies—Dance, Drama, and Music | M,D |
| Travel and Tourism | M,D |
| Urban Education | M |
| Urban Studies | M,D,O |
| Vocational and Technical Education | M |
| Writing | M,D |

**TENNESSEE STATE UNIVERSITY**

| | |
|---|---|
| Agricultural Education | M,D |
| Agricultural Sciences—General | M,D |
| Agronomy and Soil Sciences | M,D |
| Allied Health—General | M,D,O |
| Biological and Biomedical Sciences—General | D |
| Biomedical Engineering | M,D |
| Biotechnology | M,D |
| Business Administration and Management—General | M |
| Chemistry | M |
| Civil Engineering | M,D |
| Communication Disorders | M |
| Computer Engineering | M,D |
| Counseling Psychology | M |
| Criminal Justice and Criminology | M |
| Curriculum and Instruction | M,D |
| Education—General | M,D,O |
| Electrical Engineering | M,D |
| Elementary Education | M,D |
| Engineering and Applied Sciences—General | M,D |
| Environmental Engineering | M,D |
| Exercise and Sports Science | M |
| Family and Consumer Sciences-General | M,D |
| Family Nurse Practitioner Studies | M,O |
| Human Resources Management | M,D |
| Management Strategy and Policy | M,D |
| Manufacturing Engineering | M,D |
| Mathematics | M,D |
| Mechanical Engineering | M,D |
| Nursing—General | M,O |
| Occupational Therapy | M |
| Physical Education | M |
| Physical Therapy | D |
| Plant Sciences | M,D |
| Psychology—General | M |
| Public Administration | M,D |
| Public Health—General | M |
| Social Work | M,D |
| Special Education | M,D |
| Sports Management | M |
| Systems Engineering | M,D |

**TENNESSEE TECHNOLOGICAL UNIVERSITY**

| | |
|---|---|
| Accounting | M |
| Acute Care/Critical Care Nursing | D |
| Agricultural Sciences—General | D |
| Applied Behavior Analysis | D |
| Biological and Biomedical Sciences—General | M,D |
| Business Administration and Management—General | M |
| Chemical Engineering | M |
| Chemistry | M,D |
| Civil Engineering | M |
| Computer Science | M,D |
| Curriculum and Instruction | M,O |
| Early Childhood Education | M,O |
| Education of the Gifted | D |
| Education—General | M,D,O |
| Educational Leadership and Administration | M,O |
| Educational Measurement and Evaluation | D |
| Educational Media/Instructional Technology | M,O |
| Educational Psychology | M,O |
| Electrical Engineering | M |
| Elementary Education | M,O |
| Engineering and Applied Sciences—General | M,D |
| English as a Second Language | M |
| English | M |
| Environmental Management and Policy | M |
| Environmental Sciences | M,D |
| Family Nurse Practitioner Studies | M,D |
| Finance and Banking | M |
| Fish, Game, and Wildlife Management | M |
| Geosciences | D |
| Gerontological Nursing | D |
| Health Education | M |
| Health Promotion | M |
| Human Resources Management | M |
| International Business | M |
| Kinesiology and Movement Studies | M |
| Library Science | M,O |
| Management Information Systems | M |
| Management Strategy and Policy | M |
| Mathematics Education | M,O |
| Mathematics | M |
| Mechanical Engineering | M |
| Middle School Education | M |
| Music Education | M |
| Nursing and Healthcare Administration | M,D |
| Nursing Education | M |
| Nursing—General | M,D |
| Physical Education | M |
| Psychiatric Nursing | D |
| Reading Education | M,D,O |
| Science Education | M,O |
| Secondary Education | M,O |
| Special Education | M,O |
| Sports Management | M |
| Women's Health Nursing | D |

**TENNESSEE WESLEYAN UNIVERSITY**

| | |
|---|---|
| Accounting | M |
| Business Administration and Management—General | M |

**TEXAS A&M INTERNATIONAL UNIVERSITY**

| | |
|---|---|
| Accounting | M |
| Biological and Biomedical Sciences—General | M |
| Business Administration and Management—General | M,D |
| Counseling Psychology | M |
| Counselor Education | M |
| Criminal Justice and Criminology | M |
| Curriculum and Instruction | M |
| Education—General | M |
| Educational Leadership and Administration | M |
| English | M |
| Family Nurse Practitioner Studies | M |
| Finance and Banking | M |
| Foreign Languages Education | M |
| History | M |
| International Business | M,D |
| Management Information Systems | M,D |
| Mathematics | M |
| Nursing—General | M |
| Political Science | M |
| Psychology—General | M |
| Public Administration | M |
| Social Sciences | M |
| Sociology | M |
| Special Education | M |
| Translation and Interpretation | M |

**TEXAS A&M UNIVERSITY**

| | |
|---|---|
| Accounting | M |
| Aerospace/Aeronautical Engineering | M,D |
| Agricultural Economics and Agribusiness | M,D |
| Agricultural Education | M,D |
| Agricultural Engineering | M,D |
| Agricultural Sciences—General | M,D |
| Agronomy and Soil Sciences | M,D |
| Allopathic Medicine | M,D |
| Animal Sciences | M,D |
| Anthropology | M,D |

*M—masters degree; D—doctorate; O—other advanced degree; *—Close-Up and/or Display*

| | |
|---|---|
| Applied Physics | M,D |
| Architecture | M,D |
| Art/Fine Arts | M |
| Astronomy | M,D |
| Athletic Training and Sports Medicine | M,D |
| Biochemistry | M,D |
| Bioengineering | M,D |
| Biological and Biomedical Sciences—General | M,D |
| Biomedical Engineering | M,D |
| Biostatistics | M,D |
| Business Administration and Management—General | M |
| Chemical Engineering | M,D |
| Chemistry | M,D |
| Civil Engineering | M,D |
| Communication—General | M,D |
| Computer Engineering | M,D |
| Computer Science | M,D |
| Construction Management | M |
| Counseling Psychology | M,D |
| Cultural Studies | M |
| Curriculum and Instruction | M,D |
| Dentistry | M,D,O |
| Economics | M,D |
| Education—General | M,D |
| Educational Leadership and Administration | M,D |
| Educational Media/Instructional Technology | M,D |
| Educational Psychology | M,D |
| Electrical Engineering | M,D |
| Engineering Management | M,D |
| English | M,D |
| Entomology | M,D |
| Entrepreneurship | M |
| Environmental and Occupational Health | M,D |
| Epidemiology | M,D |
| Family Nurse Practitioner Studies | M |
| Finance and Banking | M |
| Fish, Game, and Wildlife Management | M,D |
| Food Science and Technology | M,D |
| Forensic Nursing | M |
| Forestry | M,D |
| Geography | M,D |
| Geology | M,D |
| Geophysics | M,D |
| Health Education | M,D |
| Health Services Management and Hospital Administration | M,D |
| Health Services Research | M,D |
| History | M,D |
| Horticulture | M,D |
| Human Resources Development | M,D |
| Human Resources Management | M |
| Industrial/Management Engineering | M,D |
| Intellectual Property Law | M,D |
| International Affairs | M,O |
| Kinesiology and Movement Studies | M,D |
| Landscape Architecture | M,D |
| Law | M,D |
| Management Information Systems | M |
| Manufacturing Engineering | M |
| Marine Biology | M,D |
| Marine Sciences | M |
| Marketing | M |
| Materials Engineering | M,D |
| Materials Sciences | M,D |
| Mathematics | M,D |
| Mechanical Engineering | M,D |
| Meteorology | M,D |
| Microbiology | M,D |
| Multilingual and Multicultural Education | M,D |
| Music | M |
| Natural Resources | M,D |
| Nuclear Engineering | M,D |
| Nursing Education | M |
| Nursing—General | M |
| Nutrition | M,D |
| Oceanography | M,D |
| Oral and Dental Sciences | M,D,O |
| Petroleum Engineering | M,D |
| Pharmacy | D |
| Philosophy | M,D |
| Physics | M,D |
| Plant Pathology | M,D |
| Political Science | M,D |
| Psychology—General | M,D |
| Public Affairs | M,O |
| Public Health—General | M,D |
| Recreation and Park Management | M,D |
| School Psychology | M,D |
| Sociology | M,D |
| Spanish | M,D |
| Special Education | M,D |
| Sports Management | M,D |
| Statistics | M,D |
| Transportation Management | M |
| Urban and Regional Planning | M,D |
| Veterinary Medicine | M,D |
| Veterinary Sciences | M,D |

## TEXAS A&M UNIVERSITY–CENTRAL TEXAS

| | |
|---|---|
| Accounting | M,O |
| Business Administration and Management—General | M,O |
| Clinical Psychology | M,O |
| Counselor Education | M,O |
| Criminal Justice and Criminology | M,O |
| Curriculum and Instruction | M,O |
| Educational Leadership and Administration | M,O |
| Educational Psychology | M,O |
| Experimental Psychology | M,O |
| History | M,O |
| Human Resources Management | M,O |
| Liberal Studies | M,O |
| Management Information Systems | M,O |
| Marriage and Family Therapy | M,O |
| Mathematics | M,O |
| Political Science | M,O |
| School Psychology | M,O |

## TEXAS A&M UNIVERSITY–COMMERCE

| | |
|---|---|
| Accounting | M |
| Agricultural Sciences—General | M |
| Art/Fine Arts | M,D,O |
| Biological and Biomedical Sciences—General | M,O |
| Business Administration and Management—General | M |
| Business Analytics | M |
| Chemistry | M,O |
| Computational Sciences | M,O |
| Counselor Education | M,D,O |
| Criminal Justice and Criminology | M,D,O |
| Curriculum and Instruction | M,D,O |
| Early Childhood Education | M,D,O |
| Education—General | M,D,O |
| Educational Leadership and Administration | M,D,O |
| Educational Media/Instructional Technology | M,D,O |
| Educational Psychology | M,D,O |
| Elementary Education | M,D,O |
| English as a Second Language | M,D,O |
| English | M,D,O |
| Environmental Sciences | M,O |
| Exercise and Sports Science | M,D,O |
| Film, Television, and Video Theory and Criticism | M,D,O |
| Finance and Banking | M |
| Higher Education | M,D,O |
| History | M,D,O |
| Holocaust and Genocide Studies | M,D,O |
| Homeland Security | M,D,O |
| Kinesiology and Movement Studies | M,D,O |
| Library Science | M,D,O |
| Linguistics | M,D,O |
| Management of Technology | M,O |
| Marketing | M |
| Mathematics | M,O |
| Music Education | M,D,O |
| Music | M,D,O |
| Physics | M,O |
| Political Science | M,D,O |
| Psychology—General | M,D,O |
| Public History | M,D,O |
| Reading Education | M,D,O |
| Secondary Education | M,D,O |
| Social Work | M,D,O |
| Sociology | M,D,O |
| Spanish | M,D,O |
| Special Education | M,D,O |
| Theater | M,D,O |
| Writing | M,D,O |

## TEXAS A&M UNIVERSITY–CORPUS CHRISTI

| | |
|---|---|
| Accounting | M |
| Aquaculture | M |
| Art/Fine Arts | M |
| Biological and Biomedical Sciences—General | M,D |
| Business Administration and Management—General | M |
| Chemistry | M,D |
| Clinical Psychology | M |
| Communication—General | M |
| Computer Science | M |
| Counselor Education | M,D |
| Curriculum and Instruction | M,D |
| Early Childhood Education | M,D |
| Education—General | M,D |
| Educational Leadership and Administration | M,D |
| Educational Media/Instructional Technology | M,D |
| Elementary Education | M |
| English | M |
| Environmental Sciences | M |
| Family Nurse Practitioner Studies | M,D |
| Finance and Banking | M |
| Geographic Information Systems | M,D |
| Health Services Management and Hospital Administration | M,D |
| History | M |
| Human Development | M,D |
| International Business | M |
| Kinesiology and Movement Studies | M,D |
| Marine Biology | M,D |
| Marine Sciences | M,D |
| Mathematics | M |
| Nursing and Healthcare Administration | M,D |
| Nursing Education | M,D |
| Nursing—General | M,D |
| Psychology—General | M |
| Public Administration | M |
| Reading Education | M,D |
| Secondary Education | M |
| Special Education | M |

## TEXAS A&M UNIVERSITY–KINGSVILLE

| | |
|---|---|
| Adult Education | M |
| Agricultural Economics and Agribusiness | M,D |
| Agricultural Sciences—General | M,D |
| Agronomy and Soil Sciences | M |
| Animal Sciences | M |
| Biological and Biomedical Sciences—General | M |
| Business Administration and Management—General | M |
| Chemical Engineering | M |
| Chemistry | M |
| Civil Engineering | M |
| Communication Disorders | M |
| Computer Science | M |
| Counselor Education | M |
| Criminal Justice and Criminology | M |
| Cultural Studies | M |
| Early Childhood Education | M |
| Education—General | M,D,O |
| Educational Leadership and Administration | M,D |
| Educational Media/Instructional Technology | M |
| Electrical Engineering | M |
| Energy and Power Engineering | D |
| Engineering and Applied Sciences—General | M,D |
| English as a Second Language | M,D |
| English | M |
| Environmental Engineering | M,D |
| Family and Consumer Sciences-General | M |
| Fish, Game, and Wildlife Management | M,D |
| Foreign Languages Education | M |
| Health Education | M |
| Hispanic Studies | D |
| Horticulture | M,D |
| Industrial and Manufacturing Management | M |
| Industrial/Management Engineering | M |
| Kinesiology and Movement Studies | M |
| Mathematics | M |
| Mechanical Engineering | M |
| Multilingual and Multicultural Education | M,D |
| Music Education | M |
| Music | M |
| Petroleum Engineering | M |
| Plant Sciences | M |
| Psychology—General | M |
| Range Science | M |
| Reading Education | M |
| Science Education | M |
| Social Work | M |
| Sociology | M |
| Spanish | M |
| Special Education | M |
| Statistics | M |
| Sustainable Development | D |
| Systems Engineering | D |

## TEXAS A&M UNIVERSITY–SAN ANTONIO

| | |
|---|---|
| Accounting | M |
| Business Administration and Management—General | M |
| Clinical Psychology | M |
| Counselor Education | M |
| Early Childhood Education | M |
| Education—General | M |
| Educational Leadership and Administration | M |
| Educational Measurement and Evaluation | M |
| English | M |
| Kinesiology and Movement Studies | M |
| Marriage and Family Therapy | M |
| Multilingual and Multicultural Education | M |
| Reading Education | M |
| Special Education | M |

## TEXAS A&M UNIVERSITY–TEXARKANA

| | |
|---|---|
| Accounting | M |
| Adult Education | M |
| Business Administration and Management—General | M |
| Counseling Psychology | M |
| Curriculum and Instruction | M |
| Education—General | M |
| Educational Leadership and Administration | M |
| Educational Media/Instructional Technology | M |
| English | M |
| Interdisciplinary Studies | M |
| Psychology—General | M |
| Special Education | M |

## TEXAS CHIROPRACTIC COLLEGE

| | |
|---|---|
| Chiropractic | D |

## TEXAS CHRISTIAN UNIVERSITY

| | |
|---|---|
| Accounting | M |
| Adult Nursing | M,O |
| Allied Health—General | M,D,O |
| American Studies | M,D |
| Applied Mathematics | M,D |
| Art History | M |
| Art/Fine Arts | M |
| Astrophysics | M,D |
| Biochemistry | M,D |
| Biological and Biomedical Sciences—General | M,D |
| Biophysics | M,D |
| Business Administration and Management—General | M |
| Chemistry | M,D |
| Cognitive Sciences | M,D |
| Communication Disorders | M |
| Communication—General | M |
| Corporate and Organizational Communication | M |
| Counselor Education | M,D |
| Criminal Justice and Criminology | M |
| Curriculum and Instruction | M,D |
| Developmental Psychology | M,D |
| Education—General | M,D |
| Educational Leadership and Administration | M,D |
| English | M,D |
| Experimental Psychology | M,D |
| Family Nurse Practitioner Studies | D |
| Gerontological Nursing | M,O |
| Gerontology | D |
| History | M,D |
| Kinesiology and Movement Studies | M |
| Latin American Studies | M,D |
| Liberal Studies | M |
| Mass Communication | M |
| Mathematics Education | M |
| Mathematics | M,D |
| Music Education | M,D |
| Music | M,D |
| Neuroscience | M,D |
| Nurse Anesthesia | D |
| Nursing and Healthcare Administration | M,D,O |
| Nursing Education | M,O |
| Nursing—General | M,D,O |
| Pediatric Nursing | M,D,O |
| Physics | M,D |
| Psychology—General | M,D |
| Reading Education | M |
| Rhetoric | M,D |
| Science Education | M,D |
| Social Psychology | M,D |
| Social Work | M |
| Special Education | M |
| Speech and Interpersonal Communication | M |
| Taxation | M |

## TEXAS HEALTH AND SCIENCE UNIVERSITY

| | |
|---|---|
| Acupuncture and Oriental Medicine | M,D |
| Business Administration and Management—General | M,D |
| Health Services Management and Hospital Administration | M,D |

## TEXAS LUTHERAN UNIVERSITY

| | |
|---|---|
| Accounting | M |

## TEXAS SOUTHERN UNIVERSITY

| | |
|---|---|
| Art/Fine Arts | M |
| Biological and Biomedical Sciences—General | M |
| Business Administration and Management—General | M |
| Chemistry | M |
| Communication—General | M |
| Computer Science | M |
| Counselor Education | M,D |
| Criminal Justice and Criminology | M,D |
| Curriculum and Instruction | M,D |
| Education—General | M,D |
| Educational Leadership and Administration | M,D |
| English | M |
| Environmental Management and Policy | M,D |
| Family and Consumer Sciences-General | M |
| Health Education | M |
| Health Services Management and Hospital Administration | M |
| Higher Education | M,D |
| History | M |
| Human Services | M |
| Industrial/Management Engineering | M |
| Law | D |
| Management Information Systems | M |
| Mathematics | M |
| Multilingual and Multicultural Education | M,D |
| Music | M |
| Pharmaceutical Sciences | M,D |
| Pharmacy | D |
| Physical Education | M |
| Psychology—General | M |
| Public Administration | M |
| Secondary Education | M,D |
| Sociology | M |
| Toxicology | M,D |
| Transportation and Highway Engineering | M |
| Transportation Management | M |
| Urban and Regional Planning | M,D |

## TEXAS STATE UNIVERSITY

| | |
|---|---|
| Accounting | M |
| Adult Education | M,D |
| Agricultural Education | M |
| Allied Health—General | M,D |
| Anthropology | M |
| Applied Arts and Design—General | M |
| Athletic Training and Sports Medicine | M |
| Biochemistry | M |
| Biological and Biomedical Sciences—General | M |
| Business Administration and Management—General | M |
| Chemistry | M |
| Child and Family Studies | M |
| Civil Engineering | M |
| Clinical Psychology | M |
| Communication Disorders | M |
| Communication—General | M |
| Computer Art and Design | M |
| Computer Science | M,D |
| Conservation Biology | M |
| Counselor Education | M |
| Criminal Justice and Criminology | M,D |
| Developmental Education | M,D |
| Early Childhood Education | M |
| Education—General | M,D,O |
| Educational Leadership and Administration | M,D |
| Educational Media/Instructional Technology | M |
| Electrical Engineering | M |
| Elementary Education | M |
| Engineering and Applied Sciences—General | M |
| English | M |
| Ethics | M |
| Family and Consumer Sciences-General | M |

| | |
|---|---|
| Family Nurse Practitioner Studies | M |
| Fish, Game, and Wildlife Management | M |
| Geographic Information Systems | M,D |
| Geography | M,D |
| Gerontology | M |
| Graphic Design | M |
| Health Education | M |
| Health Informatics | M |
| Health Services Management and Hospital Administration | M |
| Higher Education | M |
| History | M |
| Human Resources Management | M |
| Industrial/Management Engineering | M |
| Interdisciplinary Studies | M |
| International Affairs | M |
| Legal and Justice Studies | M |
| Leisure Studies | M |
| Management Information Systems | M |
| Management of Technology | M |
| Manufacturing Engineering | M |
| Marine Biology | M,D |
| Marriage and Family Therapy | M |
| Mass Communication | M |
| Materials Engineering | D |
| Materials Sciences | D |
| Mathematics Education | D |
| Mathematics | M |
| Mechanical Engineering | M |
| Multilingual and Multicultural Education | M |
| Music Education | M |
| Music | M |
| Nutrition | M |
| Philosophy | M |
| Physical Therapy | D |
| Physics | M |
| Political Science | M |
| Psychology—General | M |
| Public Administration | M |
| Reading Education | M |
| Recreation and Park Management | M |
| Rhetoric | M |
| School Psychology | O |
| Secondary Education | M |
| Social Work | M |
| Sociology | M |
| Software Engineering | M |
| Spanish | M |
| Special Education | M |
| Student Affairs | M |
| Sustainable Development | M |
| Technical Communication | M |
| Theater | M |
| Vocational and Technical Education | M |
| Writing | M |

## TEXAS TECH UNIVERSITY

| | |
|---|---|
| Accounting | M,D |
| Agricultural Economics and Agribusiness | M,D |
| Agricultural Education | M,D |
| Agricultural Sciences—General | M,D |
| Agronomy and Soil Sciences | M,D |
| Animal Sciences | M,D |
| Anthropology | M |
| Applied Economics | M,D |
| Architecture | M,D |
| Art Education | M |
| Art History | M |
| Art/Fine Arts | M,D |
| Astronomy | M,D |
| Atmospheric Sciences | M,D |
| Biological and Biomedical Sciences—General | M,D |
| Biotechnology | M,D |
| Business Administration and Management—General | M,D |
| Chemistry | M,D |
| Child and Family Studies | M,D |
| Clinical Psychology | M,D |
| Communication—General | M |
| Consumer Economics | M,D |
| Counseling Psychology | M,D |
| Counselor Education | M,D |
| Cultural Studies | M,D |
| Curriculum and Instruction | M,D |
| Data Science/Data Analytics | M,D |
| Economics | M,D |
| Education—General | M,D |
| Educational Leadership and Administration | M,D |
| Educational Media/Instructional Technology | M,D |
| Educational Psychology | M,D |
| Elementary Education | M,D |
| Energy and Power Engineering | M,D |
| Engineering and Applied Sciences—General | M,D |
| Engineering Management | M,D |
| English | M,D |
| Environmental Design | M,D |
| Environmental Management and Policy | M,D |
| Environmental Sciences | M,D |
| Exercise and Sports Science | M |
| Experimental Psychology | M,D |
| Finance and Banking | M,D |
| Fish, Game, and Wildlife Management | M,D |
| Food Science and Technology | M,D |
| Geography | M,D |
| Geosciences | M,D |
| Gerontology | M,D |
| Health Services Management and Hospital Administration | M,D |
| Higher Education | M,D |
| History | M,D |
| Home Economics Education | M,D |
| Horticulture | M,D |
| Hospitality Management | M,D |
| Human Development | M,D |
| Interdisciplinary Studies | M,D |
| Interior Design | M,D |
| Kinesiology and Movement Studies | M |
| Landscape Architecture | M |
| Law | M,D |
| Legal and Justice Studies | M,D |
| Management Information Systems | M,D |
| Marketing | M,D |
| Marriage and Family Therapy | M,D |
| Mass Communication | M,D |
| Mathematics | M,D |
| Media Studies | M,D |
| Microbiology | M,D |
| Multilingual and Multicultural Education | M,D |
| Museum Studies | M,D |
| Music Education | M,D |
| Music | M,D |
| Natural Resources | M,D |
| Nutrition | M,D |
| Philosophy | M |
| Physics | M,D |
| Plant Sciences | M,D |
| Political Science | M,D |
| Psychology—General | M,D |
| Public Administration | M,D |
| Reading Education | M,D |
| Rhetoric | M,D |
| Romance Languages | M,D |
| Science Education | M,D |
| Secondary Education | M,D |
| Social Sciences Education | M,D |
| Social Work | M |
| Sociology | M |
| Software Engineering | M,D |
| Spanish | M,D |
| Special Education | M,D |
| Sports Management | M |
| Statistics | M,D |
| Sustainable Development | M,D |
| Taxation | M,D |
| Technical Writing | M,D |
| Theater | M |
| Toxicology | M,D |
| Zoology | M,D |

## TEXAS TECH UNIVERSITY HEALTH SCIENCES CENTER

| | |
|---|---|
| Acute Care/Critical Care Nursing | M,D,O |
| Addictions/Substance Abuse Counseling | M |
| Allopathic Medicine | D |
| Athletic Training and Sports Medicine | M |
| Biological and Biomedical Sciences—General | M,D |
| Biotechnology | M |
| Cell Biology | M,D |
| Clinical Psychology | M |
| Communication Disorders | M,D |
| Family Nurse Practitioner Studies | M,D,O |
| Gerontological Nursing | M,D,O |
| Health Services Management and Hospital Administration | M |
| Molecular Pathology | M |
| Nursing and Healthcare Administration | M,D,O |
| Nursing Education | M,D,O |
| Nursing—General | M,D,O |
| Occupational Therapy | M |
| Pediatric Nursing | M,D,O |
| Pharmaceutical Sciences | M,D |
| Pharmacy | D |
| Physical Therapy | D |
| Physician Assistant Studies | M |
| Rehabilitation Counseling | M |
| Rehabilitation Sciences | D |

## TEXAS TECH UNIVERSITY HEALTH SCIENCES CENTER EL PASO

| | |
|---|---|
| Allopathic Medicine | D |
| Biological and Biomedical Sciences—General | M |
| Nursing—General | M |

## TEXAS WESLEYAN UNIVERSITY

| | |
|---|---|
| Business Administration and Management—General | M |
| Education—General | M,D |
| Nurse Anesthesia | M,D |

## TEXAS WOMAN'S UNIVERSITY

| | |
|---|---|
| Accounting | M |
| Acute Care/Critical Care Nursing | M,D |
| Adult Nursing | M,D |
| Allied Health—General | M,D |
| Art Education | M |
| Art History | M |
| Art/Fine Arts | M |
| Biological and Biomedical Sciences—General | M,D |
| Business Administration and Management—General | M |
| Business Analytics | M |
| Chemistry | M |
| Child and Family Studies | M,D |
| Child Development | M,D |
| Communication Disorders | M |
| Counseling Psychology | M,D,O |
| Counselor Education | M,D |
| Curriculum and Instruction | M,D |
| Dance | M,D |
| Dental Hygiene | M,D |
| Early Childhood Education | M,D |
| Education—General | M,D,O |
| Educational Leadership and Administration | M,D |
| English Education | M,D |
| English | M,D |
| Exercise and Sports Science | M,D |
| Family Nurse Practitioner Studies | M,D |
| Food Science and Technology | M,D |
| Gender Studies | M,D |
| Gerontological Nursing | M,D |
| Graphic Design | M |
| Health Education | M,D |
| Health Services Management and Hospital Administration | M |
| History | M |
| Human Resources Management | M |
| Information Science | M |
| Internet and Interactive Multimedia | M |
| Library Science | M |
| Marriage and Family Therapy | M,D |
| Mathematics Education | M |
| Mathematics | M |
| Molecular Biology | M,D |
| Music Education | M |
| Music | M |
| Nursing and Healthcare Administration | M,D |
| Nursing Education | M,D |
| Nursing—General | M,D |
| Nutrition | M,D |
| Occupational Therapy | M,D |
| Pediatric Nursing | M,D |
| Photography | M |
| Physical Therapy | D |
| Political Science | M |
| Psychology—General | M,D,O |
| Reading Education | M,D,O |
| Rhetoric | M,D |
| School Psychology | M,D,O |
| Sociology | M,D |
| Special Education | M,D |
| Theater | M |
| Therapies—Dance, Drama, and Music | M |
| Women's Health Nursing | M,D |
| Women's Studies | M,D |

## THEOLOGICAL UNIVERSITY OF THE CARIBBEAN

| | |
|---|---|
| Early Childhood Education | M,D |
| Middle School Education | M,D |
| Missions and Missiology | M,D |
| Pastoral Ministry and Counseling | M,D |

## THOMAS COLLEGE

| | |
|---|---|
| Business Administration and Management—General | M |
| Business Education | M |
| Computer Education | M |
| Human Resources Management | M |

## THOMAS EDISON STATE UNIVERSITY

| | |
|---|---|
| Accounting | M |
| Applied Science and Technology | M,O |
| Business Administration and Management—General | M |
| Computer and Information Systems Security | M,O |
| Distance Education Development | M,O |
| Economic Development | M |
| Educational Leadership and Administration | M,O |
| Educational Media/Instructional Technology | M,O |
| Environmental Management and Policy | M |
| Finance and Banking | M |
| Homeland Security | M |
| Hospitality Management | M |
| Human Resources Management | M |
| Industrial and Organizational Psychology | M,O |
| Information Science | M,O |
| International Business | M |
| Liberal Studies | M,O |
| Nonprofit Management | M |
| Nursing and Healthcare Administration | M |
| Nursing Education | M |
| Nursing Informatics | M |
| Nursing—General | M,D |
| Organizational Management | M |
| Project Management | M |
| Public Administration | M |
| Public Health—General | M |
| Urban and Regional Planning | M |

## THOMAS JEFFERSON SCHOOL OF LAW

| | |
|---|---|
| Law | D |

## THOMAS JEFFERSON UNIVERSITY

| | |
|---|---|
| Allopathic Medicine | D |
| Applied Economics | M,D,O |
| Architecture | M |
| Art/Fine Arts | M |
| Athletic Training and Sports Medicine | M |
| Biochemistry | D |
| Biological and Biomedical Sciences—General | M,D,O |
| Biotechnology | M |
| Business Administration and Management—General | M |
| Business Analytics | M |
| Cancer Biology/Oncology | D |
| Cell Biology | M,D |
| Clinical Laboratory Sciences/Medical Technology | M |
| Clinical Research | M,O |
| Clothing and Textiles | M |
| Construction Management | M |
| Developmental Biology | M |
| Emergency Management | M |
| Genetic Counseling | M |
| Genetics | D |
| Genomic Sciences | D |
| Geography | M |
| Health Education | M,D,O |
| Health Physics/Radiological Health | M |
| Health Services Management and Hospital Administration | M,D,O |
| Health Services Research | M,D,O |
| Human Genetics | M |
| Immunology | D |
| Industrial Design | M |
| Infectious Diseases | O |
| Interior Design | M |
| Internet and Interactive Multimedia | M |
| Management Strategy and Policy | M,D |
| Marketing | M |
| Marriage and Family Therapy | M |
| Medical Imaging | M |
| Medical Physics | M |
| Microbiology | M,D |
| Molecular Pharmacology | D |
| Neuroscience | D |
| Nurse Midwifery | M |
| Nursing—General | M,D |
| Occupational Therapy | M |
| Pharmacology | M |
| Pharmacy | D |
| Physical Therapy | D |
| Physician Assistant Studies | M |
| Public Health—General | M,O |
| Real Estate | M |
| Social Psychology | M |
| Sustainable Development | M |
| Taxation | M |
| Textile Design | M |
| Textile Sciences and Engineering | M,D |
| Toxicology | M |
| Urban and Regional Planning | M |

## THOMAS MORE UNIVERSITY

| | |
|---|---|
| Business Administration and Management—General | M |
| Education—General | M |
| Educational Leadership and Administration | M |

## THOMAS UNIVERSITY

| | |
|---|---|
| Business Administration and Management—General | M |
| Education—General | M |
| Human Services | M |
| Nursing—General | M |
| Rehabilitation Counseling | M |
| Social Psychology | M |

## THOMPSON RIVERS UNIVERSITY

| | |
|---|---|
| Business Administration and Management—General | M |
| Education—General | M |
| Environmental Sciences | M |
| Social Work | M |

## TIFFIN UNIVERSITY

| | |
|---|---|
| Art/Fine Arts | M |
| Business Administration and Management—General | M |
| Communication—General | M |
| Criminal Justice and Criminology | M |
| Education—General | M |
| Educational Leadership and Administration | M |
| Educational Media/Instructional Technology | M |
| English | M |
| Film, Television, and Video Theory and Criticism | M |
| Finance and Banking | M |
| Forensic Psychology | M |
| Health Services Management and Hospital Administration | M |
| Higher Education | M |
| Homeland Security | M |
| Human Resources Management | M |
| Humanities | M |
| International Business | M |
| Marketing | M |
| Nonprofit Management | M |
| Psychology—General | M |
| Sports Management | M |
| Writing | M |

## TORONTO SCHOOL OF THEOLOGY

| | |
|---|---|
| Theology | M,D |

## TOURO COLLEGE

| | |
|---|---|
| Educational Media/Instructional Technology | M |
| Internet and Interactive Multimedia | M |
| Law | M,D |
| Legal and Justice Studies | M,D |
| Management Information Systems | M |

## TOURO UNIVERSITY CALIFORNIA

| | |
|---|---|
| Education—General | M,D |
| Osteopathic Medicine | M,D |
| Pharmacy | M,D |
| Public Health—General | M,D |

## TOWSON UNIVERSITY

| | |
|---|---|
| Accounting | M |
| Allied Health—General | M |
| Applied Mathematics | M |
| Applied Physics | M |
| Art Education | M,O |
| Art History | M |
| Art/Fine Arts | M |

*M—masters degree; D—doctorate; O—other advanced degree; *—Close-Up and/or Display*

| | |
|---|---|
| Biological and Biomedical Sciences—General | M |
| Child and Family Studies | M,O |
| Communication Disorders | M,D |
| Communication—General | M |
| Computer Science | M |
| Corporate and Organizational Communication | M |
| Counseling Psychology | M |
| Early Childhood Education | M,O |
| Education—General | M |
| Educational Leadership and Administration | M,O |
| Educational Media/Instructional Technology | M |
| Electronic Commerce | M,O |
| Elementary Education | M |
| Environmental and Occupational Health | D |
| Environmental Management and Policy | M |
| Environmental Sciences | M,O |
| Experimental Psychology | M |
| Forensic Sciences | M |
| Geography | M |
| Health Services Management and Hospital Administration | M,O |
| Homeland Security | M,O |
| Human Resources Development | M |
| Human Resources Management | M |
| Humanities | M |
| Information Science | M,D,O |
| Internet and Interactive Multimedia | M,O |
| Jewish Studies | M,O |
| Liberal Studies | M |
| Management of Technology | M,O |
| Marketing Research | M,O |
| Mathematics Education | M |
| Music Education | M |
| Music | M |
| Occupational Therapy | M |
| Physician Assistant Studies | M |
| Psychology—General | M |
| Reading Education | M,O |
| School Psychology | M |
| Secondary Education | M |
| Social Sciences | M |
| Special Education | M,O |
| Supply Chain Management | M,O |
| Theater | M |
| Women's Studies | M,O |
| Writing | M |

### TOYOTA TECHNOLOGICAL INSTITUTE AT CHICAGO

| | |
|---|---|
| Computer Science | D |

### TRENT UNIVERSITY

| | |
|---|---|
| American Indian/Native American Studies | M,D |
| Anthropology | M |
| Biological and Biomedical Sciences—General | M,D |
| Canadian Studies | M,D |
| Chemistry | M |
| Computer Science | M |
| Cultural Studies | D |
| Environmental Management and Policy | M,D |
| Geography | M,D |
| Materials Sciences | M |
| Modeling and Simulation | M,D |
| Physics | M |

### TREVECCA NAZARENE UNIVERSITY

| | |
|---|---|
| Business Administration and Management—General | M |
| Counselor Education | M,D |
| Curriculum and Instruction | M,O |
| Education—General | M,O |
| Educational Leadership and Administration | M,D,O |
| Educational Media/Instructional Technology | M |
| Elementary Education | M,O |
| English as a Second Language | M,O |
| Health Services Management and Hospital Administration | M |
| Information Science | M,O |
| Library Science | M,O |
| Marriage and Family Therapy | M,D |
| Organizational Management | M,D |
| Pastoral Ministry and Counseling | M |
| Physician Assistant Studies | M |
| Religion | M |
| Secondary Education | M,O |
| Special Education | M,O |

### TRIDENT UNIVERSITY INTERNATIONAL

| | |
|---|---|
| Adult Education | M |
| Business Administration and Management—General | M,D |
| Clinical Research | M,D,O |
| Computer and Information Systems Security | M,D |
| Conflict Resolution and Mediation/Peace Studies | M,D |
| Criminal Justice and Criminology | M,D |
| Early Childhood Education | M |
| Education—General | M,D |
| Educational Leadership and Administration | M,D |
| Educational Media/Instructional Technology | M,D |
| Emergency Management | M,D,O |
| Environmental and Occupational Health | M,D,O |
| Finance and Banking | M,D |
| Health Education | M,D,O |
| Health Informatics | M,D,O |
| Health Services Management and Hospital Administration | M,D,O |
| Higher Education | M,D |
| Human Resources Management | M,D |
| International Business | M,D |
| International Health | M,D,O |
| Legal and Justice Studies | M,D,O |
| Logistics | M,D |
| Management Information Systems | M,D,O |
| Marketing | M,D |
| Project Management | M,D |
| Public Administration | M,D |
| Quality Management | M,D,O |
| Reading Education | M |

### TRINE UNIVERSITY

| | |
|---|---|
| Business Administration and Management—General | M |
| Criminal Justice and Criminology | M |
| Emergency Management | M |
| Engineering Management | M |
| Management Information Systems | M |
| Organizational Management | M |
| Physical Therapy | D |
| Physician Assistant Studies | M |

### TRINITY BAPTIST COLLEGE

| | |
|---|---|
| Curriculum and Instruction | M |
| Educational Leadership and Administration | M |
| Religion | M |
| Special Education | M |

### TRINITY BIBLE COLLEGE AND GRADUATE SCHOOL

| | |
|---|---|
| Missions and Missiology | M |
| Pastoral Ministry and Counseling | M |
| Theology | M |

### TRINITY CHRISTIAN COLLEGE

| | |
|---|---|
| Counseling Psychology | M |
| Special Education | M |

### TRINITY COLLEGE (CANADA)

| | |
|---|---|
| Music | M,D,O |
| Pastoral Ministry and Counseling | M,D,O |
| Theology | M,D,O |

### TRINITY COLLEGE (UNITED STATES)

| | |
|---|---|
| American Studies | M |
| Cultural Studies | M |
| English | M |
| Media Studies | M |
| Museum Studies | M |
| Public Policy | M |
| Writing | M |

### TRINITY INTERNATIONAL UNIVERSITY

| | |
|---|---|
| Archaeology | M,D,O |
| Athletic Training and Sports Medicine | M |
| Bioethics | M,D |
| Business Administration and Management—General | M,D,O |
| Counseling Psychology | M,D,O |
| Education—General | M |
| Human Resources Management | M,D |
| Law | M,D |
| Missions and Missiology | M,D,O |
| Pastoral Ministry and Counseling | M,D,O |
| Religious Education | M,D,O |
| Theology | M,D,O |

### TRINITY INTERNATIONAL UNIVERSITY FLORIDA

| | |
|---|---|
| Counseling Psychology | M |
| Religion | M,O |

### TRINITY SCHOOL FOR MINISTRY

| | |
|---|---|
| Missions and Missiology | M,D,O |
| Pastoral Ministry and Counseling | M,D,O |
| Religion | M,D,O |
| Theology | M,D,O |

### TRINITY UNIVERSITY

| | |
|---|---|
| Accounting | M |
| Business Administration and Management—General | M |
| Education—General | M |
| Educational Leadership and Administration | M |
| Health Services Management and Hospital Administration | M |
| School Psychology | M |

### TRINITY WASHINGTON UNIVERSITY

| | |
|---|---|
| Business Administration and Management—General | M |
| Clinical Psychology | M |
| Communication—General | M |
| Counseling Psychology | M |
| Counselor Education | M |
| Curriculum and Instruction | M |
| Early Childhood Education | M |
| Education—General | M |
| Educational Leadership and Administration | M |
| Elementary Education | M |
| English Education | M |
| Human Resources Management | M |
| National Security | M |
| Nonprofit Management | M |
| Nursing—General | M |
| Occupational Therapy | M |
| Organizational Management | M |
| Public Health—General | M |
| Reading Education | M |
| Secondary Education | M |
| Social Sciences Education | M |
| Special Education | M |

### TRINITY WESTERN UNIVERSITY

| | |
|---|---|
| Business Administration and Management—General | M |
| Counseling Psychology | M |
| Educational Leadership and Administration | M,O |
| English as a Second Language | M |
| English | M |
| Health Services Management and Hospital Administration | M,O |
| History | M |
| Humanities | M |
| Interdisciplinary Studies | M |
| International Business | M |
| Linguistics | M |
| Nonprofit Management | M,O |
| Nursing—General | M |
| Organizational Management | M,O |
| Pastoral Ministry and Counseling | M,D |
| Philosophy | M |
| Theology | M,D |

### TRI-STATE BIBLE COLLEGE

| | |
|---|---|
| Theology | M |

### TROPICAL AGRICULTURE RESEARCH AND HIGHER EDUCATION CENTER

| | |
|---|---|
| Agricultural Economics and Agribusiness | M,D |
| Agricultural Sciences—General | M,D |
| Conservation Biology | M,D |
| Environmental Management and Policy | M,D |
| Forestry | M,D |
| Travel and Tourism | M,D |
| Water Resources | M,D |

### TROY UNIVERSITY

| | |
|---|---|
| Accounting | M |
| Adult Education | M |
| Adult Nursing | M,D |
| Biological and Biomedical Sciences—General | M,O |
| Business Administration and Management—General | M |
| Communication—General | M |
| Computer Science | M |
| Corporate and Organizational Communication | M |
| Counselor Education | M,O |
| Criminal Justice and Criminology | M |
| Early Childhood Education | M,O |
| Economic Development | M |
| Economics | M |
| Education—General | M,O |
| Educational Leadership and Administration | M,O |
| Elementary Education | M,O |
| English as a Second Language | M |
| Environmental Management and Policy | M |
| Family Nurse Practitioner Studies | M,D |
| Finance and Banking | M |
| Health Services Management and Hospital Administration | M |
| History | M |
| Human Resources Management | M |
| International Affairs | M |
| Management Information Systems | M |
| Maternal and Child Health | M,D |
| Nursing Informatics | M,D |
| Nursing—General | M,D |
| Public Administration | M |
| Secondary Education | M |
| Social Sciences | M |
| Social Work | M |
| Sports Management | M,D |

### TRUETT MCCONNELL UNIVERSITY

| | |
|---|---|
| Biological and Biomedical Sciences—General | M |
| Business Administration and Management—General | M |
| Counseling Psychology | M |
| Theology | M |

### TRUMAN STATE UNIVERSITY

| | |
|---|---|
| Accounting | M |
| Communication Disorders | M |
| Education—General | M |
| English | M |
| Music | M |

### TUFTS UNIVERSITY

| | |
|---|---|
| Allopathic Medicine | D |
| Animal Sciences | M |
| Art Education | M,D,O |
| Art History | M |
| Art/Fine Arts | M,O |
| Artificial Intelligence/Robotics | M,D |
| Astrophysics | M,D |
| Biochemistry | D |
| Bioengineering | M,D,O |
| Bioinformatics | M,D |
| Biological and Biomedical Sciences—General | M,D,O |
| Biomedical Engineering | M,D |
| Biostatistics | M,D,O |
| Biotechnology | M,D,O |
| Cancer Biology/Oncology | D |
| Cell Biology | D |
| Chemical Engineering | M,D |
| Chemical Physics | M,D |
| Chemistry | M,D |
| Child and Family Studies | M,D |
| Child Development | M,D |
| Civil Engineering | M,D |
| Classics | M |
| Clinical Laboratory Sciences/Medical Technology | M,D,O |
| Cognitive Sciences | M,D |
| Computer Science | M,D,O |
| Data Science/Data Analytics | M,D |
| Dentistry | D |
| Developmental Biology | D |
| Economics | M,D |
| Education—General | M,D,O |
| Electrical Engineering | M,D,O |
| Elementary Education | M,D |
| Engineering and Applied Sciences—General | M,D |
| Engineering Management | M |
| English | M,D |
| Entrepreneurship | M |
| Environmental and Occupational Health | M,D |
| Environmental Engineering | M,D |
| Environmental Management and Policy | M,D,O |
| Epidemiology | M,D,O |
| Ergonomics and Human Factors | M,D |
| Family and Consumer Sciences-General | M,D |
| French | M |
| Genetics | D |
| Geotechnical Engineering | M,D |
| German | M |
| Health Communication | M,D,O |
| Health Services Management and Hospital Administration | M,D,O |
| History | M,D |
| Human Development | M,D |
| Human-Computer Interaction | O |
| Immunology | D |
| Infectious Diseases | M,D |
| Interdisciplinary Studies | D |
| International Affairs | M,D |
| International Business | M,D |
| International Development | M |
| Law | M,D |
| Management Strategy and Policy | O |
| Manufacturing Engineering | O |
| Mathematics Education | M,D |
| Mathematics | M,D |
| Mechanical Engineering | M,D |
| Microbiology | D |
| Middle School Education | M,D |
| Molecular Biology | D |
| Molecular Medicine | D |
| Museum Education | M,D |
| Museum Studies | M,D,O |
| Music | M |
| Neuroscience | M,D |
| Nonprofit Management | O |
| Nutrition | M,D,O |
| Occupational Therapy | M,D,O |
| Oral and Dental Sciences | M,O |
| Organizational Management | M |
| Pathology | M,D |
| Philosophy | M |
| Physician Assistant Studies | M,D,O |
| Physics | M,D |
| Psychology—General | M,D |
| Public Administration | O |
| Public Health—General | M,D,O |
| Public Policy | M,D |
| Reproductive Biology | M,D |
| School Psychology | M,O |
| Science Education | M,D |
| Secondary Education | M,D |
| Structural Biology | D |
| Structural Engineering | M,D |
| Sustainability Management | M,D |
| Theater | M,D |
| Urban and Regional Planning | M |
| Urban Studies | M |
| Veterinary Medicine | M,D |
| Water Resources Engineering | M,D |
| Water Resources | M,D |

### TULANE UNIVERSITY

| | |
|---|---|
| Accounting | M,D |
| Allopathic Medicine | D |
| Anthropology | D |
| Architecture | M |
| Art History | M |
| Art/Fine Arts | M |
| Biochemistry | M |
| Biological and Biomedical Sciences—General | M,D |
| Biomedical Engineering | M,D |
| Biostatistics | M,D |
| Business Administration and Management—General | M,D |
| Business Analytics | M,D |
| Cell Biology | M,D |
| Chemical Engineering | M,D |
| Chemistry | M,D |
| Classics | M,D |
| Community Health | M |
| Dance | M |
| Ecology | M,D |
| Economics | M,D |
| Emergency Management | M,D |
| Energy Management and Policy | M,D |
| English | M |
| Entrepreneurship | M,D |
| Environmental and Occupational Health | M,D |
| Epidemiology | M,D |
| Evolutionary Biology | M,D |
| Finance and Banking | M,D |
| French | M,D |
| Health Promotion | M |
| Health Services Management and Hospital Administration | M,D |
| History | M,D |
| Homeland Security | M |
| Human Genetics | M |
| Immunology | M |
| Interdisciplinary Studies | D |
| International Business | M,D |
| International Health | M,D |
| Latin American Studies | M,D |
| Liberal Studies | M |
| Management Information Systems | M |
| Management Strategy and Policy | M,D |
| Mathematics | M,D |
| Microbiology | M |
| Molecular Biology | M,D |
| Music | M |
| Neuroscience | M,D |
| Parasitology | M,D,O |
| Pharmacology | M,D |
| Philosophy | M |
| Physics | M,D |
| Physiology | M |
| Political Science | D |

Portuguese M,D
Psychology—General M,D
Public Health—General M,D
Social Work M,D
Sociology M
Spanish M,D
Structural Biology M,D
Theater M

**TUSCULUM UNIVERSITY**
Business Administration and Management—General M
Curriculum and Instruction M
Education—General M
Family Nurse Practitioner Studies M
Human Resources Development M
Nursing—General M
Special Education M

**TUSKEGEE UNIVERSITY**
Agricultural Economics and Agribusiness M
Agronomy and Soil Sciences M
Animal Sciences M
Biological and Biomedical Sciences—General M,D
Chemistry M
Computer and Information Systems Security M
Electrical Engineering M
Engineering and Applied Sciences—General M,D
Environmental Sciences M
Food Science and Technology M
Management Information Systems M
Materials Engineering D
Mechanical Engineering M
Nutrition M
Occupational Therapy M
Plant Sciences M
Veterinary Medicine M,D
Veterinary Sciences M,D

**TYNDALE UNIVERSITY COLLEGE & SEMINARY**
Missions and Missiology M,O
Pastoral Ministry and Counseling M,O
Theology M,O

**UNB FREDERICTON**
Anthropology M
Applied Economics M
Biological and Biomedical Sciences—General M,D
Business Administration and Management—General M
Chemical Engineering M,D
Chemistry M,D
Civil Engineering M,D
Classics M
Computer Engineering M,D
Construction Engineering M,D
Economics M
Education—General M,D
Electrical Engineering M,D
Engineering and Applied Sciences—General M,D,O
Engineering Management M
English M,D
Entrepreneurship M
Environmental Engineering M,D
Environmental Management and Policy M,D
Exercise and Sports Science M
Forestry M,D
Geodetic Sciences M,D
Geology M,D
Geotechnical Engineering M,D
Health Services Research M
History M,D
Hydrology M,D
Interdisciplinary Studies M,D
Law O
Marketing M,D
Materials Sciences M,D
Mathematics M,D
Mechanical Engineering M,D
Mechanics M,D
Nursing Education M
Nursing—General M
Physical Education M
Physics M,D
Political Science M
Psychology—General M,D
Public Administration M
Recreation and Park Management M
Sociology M,D
Sports Management M
Statistics M,D
Structural Engineering M,D
Surveying Science and Engineering M,D
Transportation and Highway Engineering M,D
Water Resources M,D

**UNIFICATION THEOLOGICAL SEMINARY**
Religious Education M,D
Theology M,D

**UNIFORMED SERVICES UNIVERSITY OF THE HEALTH SCIENCES**
Allopathic Medicine M,D
Biological and Biomedical Sciences—General M,D
Cell Biology M,D
Clinical Psychology D
Environmental and Occupational Health M,D
Family Nurse Practitioner Studies M,D
Gerontological Nursing M,D
Health Services Management and Hospital Administration M,D
Immunology D
Infectious Diseases D
International Health M,D
Molecular Biology M,D
Neuroscience D
Nurse Anesthesia M,D
Nursing—General M,D
Psychiatric Nursing M,D
Psychology—General D
Public Health—General M,D
Women's Health Nursing M,D
Zoology M,D

**UNION COLLEGE (KY)**
Clinical Psychology M
Counseling Psychology M
Education—General M
Educational Leadership and Administration M
Elementary Education M
Health Education M
Middle School Education M
Music Education M
Physical Education M
Psychology—General M
Reading Education M
School Psychology M
Secondary Education M
Special Education M

**UNION COLLEGE (NE)**
Physician Assistant Studies M

**UNION INSTITUTE & UNIVERSITY**
Clinical Psychology M
Cultural Studies M,D
Education—General D
Health Promotion M
Health Services Management and Hospital Administration M
History M
Humanities D
Interdisciplinary Studies D
Organizational Management M
Public Policy M,D
Writing M

**UNION PRESBYTERIAN SEMINARY**
Religious Education M,D

**UNION THEOLOGICAL SEMINARY IN THE CITY OF NEW YORK**
Theology M,D

**UNION UNIVERSITY**
Accounting M
Business Administration and Management—General M
Cultural Studies M
Education—General M,D,O
Educational Leadership and Administration M,D,O
Family Nurse Practitioner Studies M,D,O
Higher Education M,D,O
Nurse Anesthesia M,D,O
Nursing and Healthcare Administration M,D,O
Nursing Education M,D,O
Nursing—General M,D,O
Pastoral Ministry and Counseling M,D
Pharmacy D
Religion M,D
Social Work M

**UNITED LUTHERAN SEMINARY**
Pastoral Ministry and Counseling M,D
Religion M,D
Theology M,D

**UNITED LUTHERAN SEMINARY**
Pastoral Ministry and Counseling M,D,O
Religion M,D,O
Theology M,D,O

**UNITED STATES ARMY COMMAND AND GENERAL STAFF COLLEGE**
Military and Defense Studies M

**UNITED STATES INTERNATIONAL UNIVERSITY–AFRICA**
Addictions/Substance Abuse Counseling M
Business Administration and Management—General M
Conflict Resolution and Mediation/Peace Studies M
Counseling Psychology M
Entrepreneurship M
Finance and Banking M
Health Psychology M
Human Resources Management M
International Affairs M
International Business M
Management Information Systems M
Management Strategy and Policy M
Marketing M
Organizational Management M

**UNITED STATES MERCHANT MARINE ACADEMY**
Civil Engineering M

**UNITED STATES SPORTS ACADEMY**
Exercise and Sports Science M
Physical Education M
Recreation and Park Management M
Sports Management M,D

**UNITED STATES UNIVERSITY**
Family Nurse Practitioner Studies M

**UNITED TALMUDICAL SEMINARY**
Theology M

**UNITED THEOLOGICAL SEMINARY**
Pastoral Ministry and Counseling M,D
Theology M,D

**UNITED THEOLOGICAL SEMINARY OF THE TWIN CITIES**
Art/Fine Arts M,D,O
Asian Studies M,D,O
Conflict Resolution and Mediation/Peace Studies M,D,O
Ethnic Studies M,D,O
Humanities M,D,O
Pastoral Ministry and Counseling M,D,O
Religion M,D,O
Theology M,D,O
Women's Studies M,D,O

**UNITY COLLEGE**
Natural Resources M
Sustainable Development M

**UNIVERSIDAD ADVENTISTA DE LAS ANTILLAS**
Curriculum and Instruction M
Educational Leadership and Administration M
Medical/Surgical Nursing M

**UNIVERSIDAD AUTONOMA DE GUADALAJARA**
Advertising and Public Relations M,D
Allopathic Medicine D
Architecture M,D
Business Administration and Management—General M,D
Computer Art and Design M,D
Computer Science M,D
Corporate and Organizational Communication M,D
Education—General M,D
Energy and Power Engineering M,D
Entertainment Management M,D
Environmental and Occupational Health M,D
Environmental Management and Policy M,D
Film, Television, and Video Production M,D
International Business M,D
Internet and Interactive Multimedia M,D
Law M,D
Legal and Justice Studies M,D
Manufacturing Engineering M,D
Marketing Research M,D
Mathematics Education M,D
Philosophy M,D
Public Policy M,D
Spanish M,D
Systems Science M,D
Translation and Interpretation M,D

**UNIVERSIDAD CENTRAL DEL CARIBE**
Addictions/Substance Abuse Counseling M
Allopathic Medicine M,D
Anatomy M,D
Biochemistry M,D
Biological and Biomedical Sciences—General M,D
Cell Biology M,D
Immunology M,D
Microbiology M,D
Molecular Biology M,D
Pharmacology M,D
Physiology M,D

**UNIVERSIDAD CENTRAL DEL ESTE**
Allopathic Medicine D
Dentistry D
Environmental Engineering M
Finance and Banking M
Higher Education M
Human Resources Development M
Law D

**UNIVERSIDAD DE CIENCIAS MEDICAS**
Allopathic Medicine M,D,O
Anatomy M,D,O
Biological and Biomedical Sciences—General M,D,O
Community Health M,D,O
Environmental and Occupational Health M,D,O
Health Services Management and Hospital Administration M,D,O
Pharmacy M,D,O

**UNIVERSIDAD DE IBEROAMERICA**
Acute Care/Critical Care Nursing M,D
Allopathic Medicine M,D
Clinical Psychology M,D
Educational Psychology M,D
Forensic Psychology M,D
Health Services Management and Hospital Administration M,D
Neuroscience M,D

**UNIVERSIDAD DE LAS AMERICAS, A.C.**
Business Administration and Management—General M
Education—General M
Finance and Banking M
International Affairs M
Marketing Research M
Marriage and Family Therapy M
Organizational Behavior M
Psychology—General M
Quality Management M

**UNIVERSIDAD DE LAS AMÉRICAS PUEBLA**
American Studies M
Anthropology M
Archaeology M
Biotechnology M
Business Administration and Management—General M
Chemical Engineering M
Clinical Laboratory Sciences/Medical Technology M
Computer Art and Design M
Computer Science M,D
Construction Management M
Economics M
Education—General M
Electrical Engineering M
Engineering and Applied Sciences—General M,D
English M
Finance and Banking M
Food Science and Technology M
Industrial and Manufacturing Management M
Industrial/Management Engineering M
Linguistics M
Manufacturing Engineering M
Psychology—General M

**UNIVERSIDAD DEL ESTE**
Accounting M
Adult Education M
Agricultural Economics and Agribusiness M
Business Administration and Management—General M
Computer and Information Systems Security M
Criminal Justice and Criminology M
Electronic Commerce M
Elementary Education M
English as a Second Language M
Foreign Languages Education M
Human Resources Management M
Management Information Systems M
Management Strategy and Policy M
Public Policy M
Social Work M
Special Education M

**UNIVERSIDAD DEL TURABO**
Accounting M
Adult Nursing M,O
Art/Fine Arts M
Arts Administration M
Athletic Training and Sports Medicine M
Business Administration and Management—General M,D
Chemistry M,D
Communication Disorders M
Computer Engineering M
Conflict Resolution and Mediation/Peace Studies M
Counseling Psychology M,D,O
Counselor Education M
Criminal Justice and Criminology M
Curriculum and Instruction M,D
Early Childhood Education M
Education—General M,D
Educational Leadership and Administration M,D
Electrical Engineering M
Engineering and Applied Sciences—General M
English as a Second Language M
Environmental Biology M,D
Environmental Management and Policy M,D
Environmental Sciences M,D
Family Nurse Practitioner Studies M,O
Forensic Psychology M,D,O
Forensic Sciences M
Health Promotion M
Human Resources Management M
Human Services M
Information Studies M
Library Science M
Logistics M
Management Information Systems D
Marketing M
Mechanical Engineering M
Naturopathic Medicine D
Physical Education M
Project Management M
Quality Management M
Special Education M
Telecommunications M

**UNIVERSIDAD IBEROAMERICANA**
Allopathic Medicine D
Business Administration and Management—General M,D
Corporate and Organizational Communication M,D
Dentistry M,D
Educational Leadership and Administration M,D
Human Resources Development M,D
Law M,D
Marketing M,D
Real Estate M,D
Special Education M,D

**UNIVERSIDAD METROPOLITANA**
Accounting M
Adult Education M
Business Administration and Management—General M
Counseling Psychology M
Curriculum and Instruction M
Education—General M

*M—masters degree; D—doctorate; O—other advanced degree; *—Close-Up and/or Display*

| | |
|---|---|
| Educational Leadership and Administration | M |
| Elementary Education | M |
| Environmental Management and Policy | M |
| Finance and Banking | M |
| Human Resources Management | M |
| International Business | M |
| Leisure Studies | M |
| Management Information Systems | M |
| Marketing | M |
| Natural Resources | M |
| Nursing and Healthcare Administration | M,O |
| Nursing—General | M,O |
| Oncology Nursing | M,O |
| Physical Education | M |
| Recreation and Park Management | M |
| Secondary Education | M |
| Special Education | M |

**UNIVERSIDAD NACIONAL PEDRO HENRIQUEZ URENA**

| | |
|---|---|
| Agricultural Sciences—General | M |
| Allopathic Medicine | D |
| Animal Sciences | M |
| Architecture | M |
| Dentistry | D |
| Ecology | M |
| Environmental Engineering | M |
| Environmental Sciences | M |
| Historic Preservation | M |
| Horticulture | M |
| International Affairs | M |
| Natural Resources | M |
| Political Science | M |
| Project Management | M |
| Science Education | M |

**UNIVERSITÉ DE MONCTON**

| | |
|---|---|
| Astronomy | M |
| Biochemistry | M |
| Biological and Biomedical Sciences—General | M |
| Business Administration and Management—General | M |
| Chemistry | M |
| Civil Engineering | M |
| Computer Science | M,O |
| Counselor Education | M |
| Economics | M |
| Education—General | M |
| Educational Leadership and Administration | M |
| Educational Psychology | M |
| Electrical Engineering | M |
| Engineering and Applied Sciences—General | M |
| Food Science and Technology | M |
| French | M,D |
| History | M |
| Industrial/Management Engineering | M |
| Mathematics | M |
| Mechanical Engineering | M |
| Nutrition | M |
| Physics | M |
| Public Administration | M |
| Social Work | M |

**UNIVERSITÉ DE MONTRÉAL**

| | |
|---|---|
| Allopathic Medicine | D |
| Anthropology | M,D |
| Art History | M,D |
| Biochemistry | M,D,O |
| Bioethics | M,D,O |
| Bioinformatics | M,D |
| Biological and Biomedical Sciences—General | M,D |
| Biomedical Engineering | M,D,O |
| Cell Biology | M,D |
| Chemistry | M,D |
| Classics | M |
| Communication Disorders | M,O |
| Communication—General | M,D |
| Community Health | M,D,O |
| Comparative Literature | M,D |
| Computer Science | M,D |
| Criminal Justice and Criminology | M,D |
| Curriculum and Instruction | M,D,O |
| Demography and Population Studies | M,D |
| Dental Hygiene | O |
| Developmental Psychology | M,D |
| Economics | M,D,O |
| Education—General | M,D,O |
| Educational Leadership and Administration | M,D,O |
| Educational Psychology | M,D,O |
| Electronic Commerce | M,D |
| Emergency Management | O |
| English | M,D |
| Environmental and Occupational Health | M |
| Environmental Design | M,D,O |
| Environmental Management and Policy | O |
| Ergonomics and Human Factors | O |
| Film, Television, and Video Theory and Criticism | M,D |
| French | M,D |
| Genetic Counseling | O |
| Genetics | O |
| Geography | M,D,O |
| German | M |
| Health Services Management and Hospital Administration | M,O |
| Hispanic and Latin American Languages | M,D |
| History | M,D |
| Human Services | D |
| Immunology | M,D |
| Industrial and Labor Relations | M,D,O |
| Information Studies | M,D |
| International Affairs | M,O |
| Kinesiology and Movement Studies | M,D,O |
| Law | M,D,O |
| Library Science | M,D |
| Linguistics | M,D,O |
| Mathematical and Computational Finance | M,D,O |
| Mathematics | M,D,O |
| Microbiology | M,D |
| Molecular Biology | M,D |
| Museum Studies | M |
| Music | M,D,O |
| Neuroscience | M,D |
| Nursing—General | M,D,O |
| Nutrition | M,D,O |
| Occupational Therapy | O |
| Optometry | D |
| Oral and Dental Sciences | M,O |
| Pathology | M,D |
| Pharmaceutical Sciences | M,D,O |
| Pharmacology | M,D |
| Philosophy | M,D |
| Physical Education | M,D,O |
| Physics | M,D |
| Physiology | M,D |
| Political Science | M,D |
| Psychology—General | M,D |
| Public Health—General | M,D,O |
| Public Policy | O |
| Rehabilitation Sciences | O |
| Religion | M,D,O |
| Social Work | O |
| Sociology | M,D |
| Spanish | M |
| Statistics | M,D,O |
| Taxation | M,D,O |
| Theology | M,D,O |
| Toxicology | O |
| Translation and Interpretation | M,D,O |
| Urban and Regional Planning | M,D,O |
| Veterinary Medicine | D |
| Veterinary Sciences | M,D |
| Virology | D |
| Vision Sciences | M,O |

**UNIVERSITÉ DE SAINT-BONIFACE**

| | |
|---|---|
| Canadian Studies | M |
| Education—General | M |

**UNIVERSITÉ DE SHERBROOKE**

| | |
|---|---|
| Accounting | M |
| Allopathic Medicine | D |
| Biochemistry | M,D |
| Biological and Biomedical Sciences—General | M,D,O |
| Biophysics | M,D |
| Business Administration and Management—General | M,D,O |
| Canadian Studies | M,D |
| Cell Biology | M,D |
| Chemical Engineering | M,D |
| Chemistry | M,D,O |
| Civil Engineering | M,D |
| Clinical Laboratory Sciences/Medical Technology | M,D |
| Comparative Literature | M,D |
| Computer and Information Systems Security | M |
| Conflict Resolution and Mediation/Peace Studies | M,D,O |
| Corporate and Organizational Communication | M |
| Economic Development | D |
| Economics | M |
| Education—General | M,O |
| Educational Leadership and Administration | M |
| Electrical Engineering | M,D |
| Electronic Commerce | M |
| Elementary Education | M,O |
| Engineering and Applied Sciences—General | M,D,O |
| Engineering Management | M,O |
| Environmental Engineering | M |
| Environmental Sciences | M,O |
| Ethics | M,D,O |
| Finance and Banking | M |
| French | M,D |
| Geography | M,D |
| Gerontology | M |
| Health Law | M,D,O |
| Higher Education | M,O |
| History | M |
| Immunology | M,D |
| Information Science | M,D |
| International Business | M |
| Kinesiology and Movement Studies | M,O |
| Law | M,D,O |
| Linguistics | M,D |
| Management Information Systems | M,O |
| Marketing | M |
| Mathematics | M,D |
| Mechanical Engineering | M,D |
| Microbiology | M,D |
| Organizational Behavior | M |
| Pharmacology | M,D |
| Philosophy | M,D,O |
| Physical Education | M,D |
| Physics | M,D |
| Physiology | M,D |
| Psychology—General | M |
| Public Administration | M |
| Radiation Biology | M,D |
| Religion | M,D,O |
| Social Work | M |
| Special Education | M,O |
| Taxation | M,O |
| Theater | M,D |
| Theology | M,D,O |

**UNIVERSITÉ DU QUÉBEC À CHICOUTIMI**

| | |
|---|---|
| Art/Fine Arts | M |
| Business Administration and Management—General | M |
| Canadian Studies | M |
| Comparative Literature | M |
| Education—General | M,D |
| Engineering and Applied Sciences—General | M,D |
| Environmental Management and Policy | M |
| Ethics | O |
| French | O |
| Genetics | M |
| Geosciences | M |
| Linguistics | M |
| Mineralogy | D |
| Project Management | M |
| Theology | M,D |

**UNIVERSITÉ DU QUÉBEC À MONTRÉAL**

| | |
|---|---|
| Accounting | M,O |
| Actuarial Science | O |
| Art History | M,D |
| Art/Fine Arts | M |
| Atmospheric Sciences | M,D,O |
| Biological and Biomedical Sciences—General | M,D |
| Business Administration and Management—General | M,D,O |
| Chemistry | M,D |
| Communication—General | M,D |
| Comparative Literature | M,D |
| Dance | M |
| Economics | M,D |
| Education—General | M,D,O |
| Environmental and Occupational Health | O |
| Environmental Education | M,D,O |
| Environmental Sciences | M,D,O |
| Ergonomics and Human Factors | O |
| Finance and Banking | O |
| Geographic Information Systems | O |
| Geography | M |
| Geology | M,D,O |
| Geosciences | M,D,O |
| History | M,D |
| Kinesiology and Movement Studies | M |
| Law | O |
| Linguistics | M,D |
| Management Information Systems | M |
| Mathematics | M,D |
| Meteorology | M,D,O |
| Mineralogy | M,D,O |
| Museum Studies | M |
| Natural Resources | M,D,O |
| Philosophy | M,D |
| Political Science | M,D |
| Project Management | M,O |
| Psychology—General | D |
| Public Administration | M,O |
| Religion | M,D |
| Social Work | M |
| Sociology | M,D |
| Urban Studies | M,D |

**UNIVERSITÉ DU QUÉBEC À RIMOUSKI**

| | |
|---|---|
| Business Administration and Management—General | M,O |
| Comparative Literature | M,D |
| Education—General | M,D,O |
| Engineering and Applied Sciences—General | M |
| Ethics | M,O |
| Fish, Game, and Wildlife Management | M,D,O |
| Marine Affairs | M,O |
| Nursing—General | M,O |
| Oceanography | M,D |
| Project Management | M,O |
| Social Psychology | M |
| Urban and Regional Planning | M,D,O |

**UNIVERSITÉ DU QUÉBEC À TROIS-RIVIÈRES**

| | |
|---|---|
| Accounting | M |
| Biophysics | M,D |
| Business Administration and Management—General | M,D |
| Chemistry | M |
| Chiropractic | D |
| Communication—General | M,O |
| Comparative Literature | M |
| Computer Science | M |
| Education—General | M,D |
| Educational Leadership and Administration | O |
| Educational Psychology | M,D |
| Electrical Engineering | M,D |
| Environmental Sciences | M,D |
| Finance and Banking | O |
| Industrial and Labor Relations | O |
| Industrial/Management Engineering | M,O |
| Leisure Studies | M,O |
| Mathematics | M |
| Nursing—General | M,O |
| Philosophy | M,D |
| Physical Education | M |
| Physics | M,D |
| Psychology—General | D,O |
| Travel and Tourism | M,O |

**UNIVERSITÉ DU QUÉBEC, ÉCOLE DE TECHNOLOGIE SUPÉRIEURE**

| | |
|---|---|
| Engineering and Applied Sciences—General | M,D,O |

**UNIVERSITÉ DU QUÉBEC, ÉCOLE NATIONALE D'ADMINISTRATION PUBLIQUE**

| | |
|---|---|
| International Business | M,O |
| Public Administration | D,O |
| Urban Studies | M |

**UNIVERSITÉ DU QUÉBEC EN ABITIBI-TÉMISCAMINGUE**

| | |
|---|---|
| Biological and Biomedical Sciences—General | M,D |
| Business Administration and Management—General | M |
| Education—General | M,D,O |
| Engineering and Applied Sciences—General | M,O |
| Environmental Sciences | M,D |
| Forestry | M,D |
| Mineral/Mining Engineering | M,O |
| Natural Resources | M,D |
| Project Management | M,O |
| Social Work | M |

**UNIVERSITÉ DU QUÉBEC EN OUTAOUAIS**

| | |
|---|---|
| Accounting | M,O |
| Computer Science | M,D,O |
| Education—General | M,D,O |
| Educational Psychology | M |
| Finance and Banking | M,O |
| Foreign Languages Education | O |
| Industrial and Labor Relations | M,D,O |
| Nursing—General | M,O |
| Project Management | M,O |
| Social Work | M |
| Urban and Regional Planning | M |

**UNIVERSITÉ DU QUÉBEC, INSTITUT NATIONAL DE LA RECHERCHE SCIENTIFIQUE**

| | |
|---|---|
| Biological and Biomedical Sciences—General | M,D |
| Demography and Population Studies | M,D,O |
| Energy Management and Policy | M,D |
| Geosciences | M,D |
| Immunology | M,D |
| Materials Sciences | M,D |
| Medical Microbiology | M,D |
| Microbiology | M,D |
| Telecommunications | M,D |
| Urban Studies | M,D,O |
| Virology | M,D |

**UNIVERSITÉ SAINTE-ANNE**

| | |
|---|---|
| Education—General | M |

**UNIVERSITY AT ALBANY, STATE UNIVERSITY OF NEW YORK**

| | |
|---|---|
| Accounting | M |
| African Studies | M |
| African-American Studies | M |
| Anthropology | M,D |
| Art/Fine Arts | M |
| Atmospheric Sciences | M,D |
| Biological and Biomedical Sciences—General | M,D |
| Biostatistics | M,D |
| Business Administration and Management—General | M |
| Business Analytics | M |
| Chemistry | M,D |
| Clinical Psychology | M,D |
| Cognitive Sciences | M,D |
| Communication—General | M,D |
| Computer and Information Systems Security | M,D,O |
| Computer Science | M,D |
| Counseling Psychology | M,D,O |
| Criminal Justice and Criminology | M,D |
| Curriculum and Instruction | M,D,O |
| Demography and Population Studies | M,D,O |
| Economics | M,D,O |
| Education—General | M,D,O |
| Educational Leadership and Administration | M,D,O |
| Educational Media/Instructional Technology | M,D,O |
| Educational Policy | M,D,O |
| Emergency Management | M,D,O |
| Engineering and Applied Sciences—General | M,D,O |
| English | M,D |
| Entrepreneurship | M |
| Environmental and Occupational Health | M,D |
| Epidemiology | M,D |
| Finance and Banking | M,D,O |
| Forensic Sciences | M |
| Gender Studies | M |
| Geographic Information Systems | M,O |
| Geography | M,O |
| Health Services Management and Hospital Administration | M,D,O |
| Higher Education | M,D,O |
| History | M,D,O |
| Homeland Security | M,D,O |
| Human Resources Management | M,D,O |
| Industrial and Organizational Psychology | M,D |
| Information Science | M,D |
| International and Comparative Education | M,D,O |
| Latin American Studies | M,D,O |
| Law | M |
| Management Information Systems | M,D,O |
| Marketing | M |
| Mathematics | M,D |
| Neuroscience | M,D |
| Nonprofit Management | M,D,O |
| Organizational Behavior | M,D,O |
| Philosophy | M,D |
| Physics | M,D |
| Political Science | M,D |
| Psychology—General | M,D |
| Public Administration | M,D,O |
| Public Health—General | M,D |
| Public History | M,D,O |
| Public Policy | M,D,O |
| Reading Education | M,D,O |
| Social Psychology | M,D |
| Social Work | M,D |
| Sociology | M,D,O |
| Spanish | M,D |
| Taxation | M |
| Toxicology | M,D |

| | |
|---|---|
| Urban and Regional Planning | M,O |
| Urban Studies | M,D,O |
| Women's Studies | M |

### UNIVERSITY AT BUFFALO, THE STATE UNIVERSITY OF NEW YORK

| | |
|---|---|
| Accounting | M,D |
| Adult Nursing | M,D,O |
| Aerospace/Aeronautical Engineering | M,D |
| Allied Health—General | M,D,O |
| Allopathic Medicine | D |
| American Studies | M,D |
| Anatomy | M,D |
| Anthropology | M,D |
| Architecture | M |
| Art History | M,D |
| Art/Fine Arts | M |
| Arts Administration | M |
| Biochemistry | M,D |
| Bioengineering | M,D,O |
| Bioinformatics | M,D |
| Biological and Biomedical Sciences—General | M,D |
| Biomedical Engineering | M,D |
| Biophysics | M,D |
| Biostatistics | M,D |
| Biotechnology | M |
| Business Administration and Management—General | M,D |
| Business Analytics | M,D |
| Canadian Studies | M,D |
| Cancer Biology/Oncology | M |
| Cell Biology | M,D |
| Chemical Engineering | M,D,O |
| Chemistry | M,D |
| Civil Engineering | M,D |
| Classics | M,D,O |
| Clinical Laboratory Sciences/Medical Technology | M |
| Communication Disorders | M,D |
| Communication—General | M,D |
| Community Health | M,D,O |
| Comparative Literature | M,D |
| Computational Sciences | D,O |
| Computer Science | M,D,O |
| Counseling Psychology | M,D,O |
| Counselor Education | M,D,O |
| Curriculum and Instruction | M,D,O |
| Dance | M,D |
| Data Science/Data Analytics | M,D |
| Dentistry | D |
| Distance Education Development | M,D,O |
| Early Childhood Education | M,D,O |
| Ecology | M,D,O |
| Economic Development | M,D,O |
| Economics | M,D,O |
| Education of the Gifted | M,D,O |
| Education—General | M,D,O |
| Educational Leadership and Administration | M,D,O |
| Educational Media/Instructional Technology | M,D,O |
| Educational Psychology | M,D,O |
| Electrical Engineering | M,D |
| Electronic Commerce | M,D,O |
| Elementary Education | M,D,O |
| Energy and Power Engineering | M,D |
| Engineering and Applied Sciences—General | M,D,O |
| Engineering Management | M,D,O |
| English as a Second Language | M,D,O |
| English Education | M,D,O |
| English | M,D,O |
| Environmental Engineering | M,D |
| Environmental Law | M,D |
| Environmental Sciences | M,D |
| Epidemiology | M,D |
| Evolutionary Biology | M,D,O |
| Exercise and Sports Science | M,D,O |
| Family Nurse Practitioner Studies | M,D,O |
| Film, Television, and Video Theory and Criticism | M,D,O |
| Finance and Banking | M,D |
| Food Science and Technology | M,D,O |
| Foreign Languages Education | M,D,O |
| Foundations and Philosophy of Education | M,D,O |
| French | M,D,O |
| Gender Studies | M,D |
| Genetics | M,D |
| Genomic Sciences | M,D |
| Geographic Information Systems | M,D |
| Geography | M,D |
| Geology | M,D |
| Geosciences | M,D |
| German | M,D,O |
| Gerontological Nursing | M,D,O |
| Health Services Management and Hospital Administration | M,D |
| Higher Education | M,D,O |
| Historic Preservation | M,D,O |
| History | M,D,O |
| Human Resources Management | M,D,O |
| Humanities | M |
| Immunology | M,D |
| Industrial/Management Engineering | M,D,O |
| Information Studies | M,O |
| Interdisciplinary Studies | M |
| International Business | M,D |
| International Trade Policy | M,D |
| Law | M,D |
| Legal and Justice Studies | M,D |
| Library Science | M,O |
| Linguistics | M,D |
| Logistics | M,D |
| Management Information Systems | M,D,O |
| Manufacturing Engineering | M,D,O |
| Marketing | M,D |
| Materials Sciences | M,D |
| Mathematics Education | M,D,O |
| Mathematics | M,D |
| Mechanical Engineering | M,D |
| Media Studies | M,D,O |
| Medical Informatics | M,D |
| Medical Physics | M,D |
| Medicinal and Pharmaceutical Chemistry | M,D |
| Microbiology | M,D |
| Modeling and Simulation | M,D |
| Molecular Biology | M,D |
| Molecular Biophysics | M,D |
| Molecular Pharmacology | M,D |
| Multilingual and Multicultural Education | M,D,O |
| Museum Studies | M,D |
| Music Education | M,D,O |
| Music | M,D,O |
| Nanotechnology | M,D,O |
| Neuroscience | M,D |
| Nurse Anesthesia | M,D,O |
| Nursing and Healthcare Administration | M,D,O |
| Nursing—General | M,D,O |
| Nutrition | M,D,O |
| Occupational Therapy | M |
| Oral and Dental Sciences | M,D,O |
| Pathology | M,D |
| Pharmaceutical Sciences | M,D |
| Pharmacology | M,D |
| Pharmacy | D |
| Philosophy | M,D |
| Physical Therapy | D |
| Physics | M,D |
| Physiology | M,D |
| Political Science | M,D |
| Psychiatric Nursing | M,D,O |
| Psychology—General | M,D |
| Public Health—General | M,D |
| Public History | M,D,O |
| Quantitative Analysis | M,D |
| Reading Education | M,D,O |
| Real Estate | M,D,O |
| Rehabilitation Counseling | M,D,O |
| Rehabilitation Sciences | O |
| Romance Languages | M,D |
| Science Education | M,D,O |
| Social Sciences Education | M,D,O |
| Social Sciences | M |
| Social Work | M,D |
| Sociology | M,D |
| Spanish | M,D,O |
| Special Education | M,D,O |
| Structural Biology | M,D |
| Structural Engineering | M,D |
| Supply Chain Management | M,D |
| Sustainable Development | M,D |
| Theater | M,D |
| Toxicology | M,D |
| Transportation Management | M |
| Urban and Regional Planning | M,D,O |
| Urban Design | M,D,O |
| Water Resources Engineering | M,D |

### UNIVERSITY OF ADVANCING TECHNOLOGY

| | |
|---|---|
| Computer and Information Systems Security | M |
| Computer Science | M |
| Game Design and Development | M |
| Internet and Interactive Multimedia | M |
| Management of Technology | M |

### THE UNIVERSITY OF AKRON

| | |
|---|---|
| Accounting | M |
| Applied Mathematics | M |
| Art Education | M |
| Arts Administration | M |
| Biological and Biomedical Sciences—General | M,D |
| Biomedical Engineering | M,D |
| Business Administration and Management—General | M |
| Chemical Engineering | M,D |
| Chemistry | M,D |
| Child and Family Studies | M |
| Child Development | M |
| Civil Engineering | M,D |
| Clinical Psychology | M |
| Clothing and Textiles | M |
| Communication Disorders | M,D |
| Communication—General | M |
| Computer Engineering | M,D |
| Computer Science | M |
| Counseling Psychology | M,D |
| Counselor Education | M,D |
| Curriculum and Instruction | M |
| Economics | M |
| Education—General | M |
| Educational Leadership and Administration | M,O |
| Electrical Engineering | M,D |
| Electronic Commerce | M |
| Elementary Education | M |
| Engineering and Applied Sciences—General | M,D |
| English Education | M |
| English | M |
| Exercise and Sports Science | M |
| Finance and Banking | M |
| Geological Engineering | M |
| Geology | M |
| Geosciences | M |
| Gerontology | D |
| History | M,D |
| Industrial and Organizational Psychology | M,D |
| Law | M,D |
| Management Information Systems | M |
| Marketing | M |
| Marriage and Family Therapy | M |
| Mathematics Education | M |
| Mathematics | M |
| Mechanical Engineering | M,D |
| Music Education | M |
| Music | M |
| Nursing—General | M,D |
| Physical Education | M |
| Political Science | M |
| Polymer Science and Engineering | M,D |
| Psychology—General | M,D |
| Public Administration | M |
| Reading Education | M |
| Science Education | M |
| Secondary Education | M |
| Social Sciences Education | M |
| Social Work | M |
| Statistics | M |
| Supply Chain Management | M |
| Taxation | M |
| Theater | M |
| Writing | M |

### THE UNIVERSITY OF ALABAMA

| | |
|---|---|
| Accounting | M,D |
| Advertising and Public Relations | M |
| Aerospace/Aeronautical Engineering | M,D |
| American Studies | M |
| Anthropology | M,D |
| Applied Mathematics | M,D |
| Applied Statistics | M,D |
| Art History | M |
| Art/Fine Arts | M |
| Astronomy | M,D |
| Biological and Biomedical Sciences—General | M,D |
| Business Administration and Management—General | M,D |
| Chemical Engineering | M,D |
| Chemistry | M,D |
| Child and Family Studies | M |
| Civil Engineering | M,D |
| Clinical Psychology | D |
| Clothing and Textiles | M |
| Communication Disorders | M |
| Communication—General | M,D |
| Community Health | M |
| Computer Engineering | M,D |
| Computer Science | M,D |
| Construction Engineering | M,D |
| Consumer Economics | M |
| Counselor Education | M,D,O |
| Criminal Justice and Criminology | M |
| Economics | M,D |
| Education of the Gifted | M,D,O |
| Educational Leadership and Administration | M,D,O |
| Electrical Engineering | M,D |
| Elementary Education | M,D,O |
| Engineering and Applied Sciences—General | M,D |
| English as a Second Language | M,D |
| English | M,D |
| Environmental Engineering | M,D |
| Ergonomics and Human Factors | M |
| Exercise and Sports Science | M,D |
| Experimental Psychology | D |
| Family and Consumer Sciences-General | M,D |
| Finance and Banking | M,D |
| French | M,D |
| Geographic Information Systems | M,D |
| Geography | M,D |
| Geology | M,D |
| Geosciences | M,D |
| German | M,D |
| Health Education | M,D |
| Health Promotion | M,D |
| Higher Education | M,D,O |
| History | M,D |
| Hospitality Management | M |
| Human Development | M |
| Industrial and Manufacturing Management | M,D |
| Information Studies | M,D |
| Journalism | M |
| Kinesiology and Movement Studies | M,D |
| Law | M,D |
| Library Science | M,D |
| Marketing | M,D |
| Marriage and Family Therapy | M |
| Mass Communication | D |
| Materials Engineering | M,D |
| Mathematics | M,D |
| Mechanical Engineering | M,D |
| Mechanics | M,D |
| Metallurgical Engineering and Metallurgy | M,D |
| Music Education | M,D |
| Music | M,D |
| Nursing—General | M,D |
| Nutrition | M |
| Photography | M |
| Physical Education | M,D |
| Physics | M,D |
| Political Science | M,D |
| Psychology—General | D |
| Public Administration | M,D |
| Quality Management | M |
| Rhetoric | M,D |
| Romance Languages | M,D |
| Secondary Education | M,D,O |
| Social Work | M,D |
| Spanish | M,D |
| Special Education | M,D,O |
| Speech and Interpersonal Communication | M |
| Sports Management | M |
| Taxation | M,D |
| Theater | M |
| Women's Studies | M |
| Writing | M,D |

### THE UNIVERSITY OF ALABAMA AT BIRMINGHAM

| | |
|---|---|
| Accounting | M |
| Adult Nursing | M,D |
| Allied Health—General | M,D,O |
| Allopathic Medicine | D |
| Anthropology | M |
| Applied Mathematics | D |
| Art Education | M |
| Art History | M |
| Biochemistry | D |
| Bioinformatics | D |
| Biological and Biomedical Sciences—General | M,D |
| Biomedical Engineering | M,D |
| Biostatistics | M,D |
| Biotechnology | M |
| Business Administration and Management—General | M |
| Cancer Biology/Oncology | D |
| Cell Biology | D |
| Chemistry | M,D |
| Civil Engineering | M,D |
| Clinical Laboratory Sciences/Medical Technology | M,D |
| Clinical Psychology | M,D |
| Communication—General | M |
| Community Health | M |
| Computational Sciences | D |
| Computer and Information Systems Security | M |
| Computer Engineering | M,D |
| Computer Science | M,D |
| Construction Engineering | M |
| Construction Management | M |
| Counselor Education | M |
| Criminal Justice and Criminology | M |
| Curriculum and Instruction | O |
| Dentistry | D |
| Developmental Biology | D |
| Developmental Psychology | M,D |
| Early Childhood Education | M,D |
| Education—General | M,D,O |
| Educational Leadership and Administration | M,D,O |
| Electrical Engineering | M,D |
| Elementary Education | M |
| Engineering and Applied Sciences—General | D |
| Engineering Design | M |
| Engineering Management | M |
| English as a Second Language | M,O |
| English | M |
| Environmental and Occupational Health | M,D |
| Epidemiology | M,D |
| Family Nurse Practitioner Studies | M,D |
| Finance and Banking | M |
| Forensic Sciences | M |
| Genetic Counseling | M |
| Genetics | D |
| Genomic Sciences | D |
| Gerontological Nursing | M,D |
| Health Education | D |
| Health Informatics | M |
| Health Promotion | D |
| Health Psychology | M,D |
| Health Services Management and Hospital Administration | M,D |
| Health Services Research | M,D |
| History | M |
| Immunology | D |
| Industrial Hygiene | M,D |
| Information Science | M,D |
| Management Information Systems | M |
| Marketing | M |
| Materials Engineering | M,D |
| Maternal and Child Health | M,D |
| Mathematics | M |
| Mechanical Engineering | M |
| Microbiology | D |
| Molecular Biology | D |
| Molecular Medicine | D |
| Neuroscience | M,D |
| Nurse Anesthesia | M,D |
| Nursing and Healthcare Administration | M,D |
| Nursing Informatics | M,D |
| Nursing—General | M,D |
| Nutrition | M,D |
| Occupational Therapy | M,O |
| Optometry | D |
| Oral and Dental Sciences | M |
| Pathobiology | D |
| Pediatric Nursing | M,D |
| Pharmacology | D |
| Physical Therapy | D |
| Physician Assistant Studies | M |
| Physics | M,D |
| Psychiatric Nursing | M,D |
| Psychology—General | M,D |
| Public Administration | M |
| Public Health—General | M,D |
| Quantitative Analysis | M,D |
| Reading Education | M |
| Rehabilitation Sciences | D |
| Rhetoric | M |
| Safety Engineering | M |
| Secondary Education | M |
| Social Work | M |
| Sociology | D |
| Special Education | M |
| Structural Biology | D |

*M—masters degree; D—doctorate; O—other advanced degree; *—Close-Up and/or Display*

Structural Engineering M
Sustainable Development M
Toxicology M,D
Vision Sciences M,D
Women's Health Nursing M,D
Writing M

### THE UNIVERSITY OF ALABAMA IN HUNTSVILLE

Accounting M,O
Acute Care/Critical Care Nursing M,D,O
Aerospace/Aeronautical Engineering M,D
Applied Mathematics M,D
Astronomy M,D
Atmospheric Sciences M,D
Biological and Biomedical Sciences—General M,D
Biotechnology M,D
Business Administration and Management—General M,O
Business Analytics M,O
Chemical Engineering M,D
Chemistry M,D
Civil Engineering M,D
Computer and Information Systems Security M,D,O
Computer Engineering M,D
Computer Science M,D,O
Education—General M,O
Electrical Engineering M,D
Engineering and Applied Sciences—General M,D
English as a Second Language M,O
English Education M,O
English M,O
Entrepreneurship M,O
Environmental Engineering M,D
Family Nurse Practitioner Studies M,D,O
Finance and Banking M,O
Geosciences M,D
Gerontological Nursing M,D,O
Health Services Management and Hospital Administration M,D,O
History M
Human Resources Management M,O
Industrial and Organizational Psychology M
Industrial/Management Engineering M,D
Logistics M,O
Management Information Systems M,O
Management of Technology M,O
Marketing M,O
Materials Sciences M,D
Mathematics Education M,D,O
Mathematics M,D
Mechanical Engineering M,D
Modeling and Simulation M,D,O
Nursing Education M,D,O
Nursing—General M,D,O
Operations Research M,D
Optical Sciences M,D
Photonics M,D
Physics M,D
Project Management M,O
Psychology—General M
Public Affairs M
Reading Education M,O
Science Education M,D,O
Secondary Education M,O
Social Sciences Education M,O
Software Engineering M,D,O
Special Education M,O
Supply Chain Management M,O
Systems Engineering M,D
Taxation M
Technical Writing M,O

### UNIVERSITY OF ALASKA ANCHORAGE

Anthropology M
Biological and Biomedical Sciences—General M
Business Administration and Management—General M
Clinical Psychology M,D
Early Childhood Education M,O
Education—General M,O
Educational Leadership and Administration M,O
English M
Logistics M
Nursing—General M,D,O
Physician Assistant Studies M
Psychology—General M,D
Public Administration M
Public Health—General M
Social Psychology M,D
Social Work M,O
Special Education M,O
Writing M

### UNIVERSITY OF ALASKA FAIRBANKS

Anthropology M,D
Art/Fine Arts M
Astrophysics M,D
Atmospheric Sciences M,D
Biochemistry M,D
Biological and Biomedical Sciences—General M,D,O
Business Administration and Management—General M
Chemistry M,D
Civil Engineering M,D,O
Communication—General M
Computational Sciences M,D
Computer Art and Design M
Computer Science M
Construction Management M,D,O
Corporate and Organizational Communication M
Counselor Education M,O
Criminal Justice and Criminology M
Cultural Studies M
Education—General M,O
Electrical Engineering M
Emergency Management M
Engineering and Applied Sciences—General D
English M
Environmental Engineering M,D,O
Environmental Management and Policy M
Finance and Banking M
Fish, Game, and Wildlife Management M,D,O
Geographic Information Systems M
Geological Engineering M
Geophysics M
History M
Homeland Security M
Interdisciplinary Studies M,D
Limnology M,D
Linguistics M
Marine Biology M,D
Marine Sciences M,D
Mathematics M,D,O
Mechanical Engineering M
Mineral/Mining Engineering M
Multilingual and Multicultural Education M
Natural Resources M,D
Neuroscience M,D
Northern Studies M
Oceanography M,D
Petroleum Engineering M
Photography M
Physics M,D
Rural Planning and Studies M
Social Psychology M,O
Special Education M
Statistics M,D,O
Sustainable Development M,D
Writing M

### UNIVERSITY OF ALASKA SOUTHEAST

Education—General M
Educational Leadership and Administration M
Educational Media/Instructional Technology M
Elementary Education M
Mathematics Education M
Public Administration M
Reading Education M
Secondary Education M
Special Education M

### UNIVERSITY OF ALBERTA

Accounting D
Adult Education M,D,O
Agricultural Economics and Agribusiness M,D
Agricultural Sciences—General M,D
Agronomy and Soil Sciences M,D
Allopathic Medicine D
Anthropology M,D
Applied Arts and Design—General M
Applied Mathematics M,D,O
Archaeology M,D
Art History M
Art/Fine Arts M
Asian Studies M
Astrophysics M,D
Biochemistry M,D
Biological and Biomedical Sciences—General M,D
Biomedical Engineering M,D
Biostatistics M,D,O
Biotechnology M,D
Business Administration and Management—General M,D
Cancer Biology/Oncology M,D
Cell Biology M,D
Chemical Engineering M,D
Chemistry M,D
Chinese M
Civil Engineering M,D
Classics M,D
Clinical Laboratory Sciences/Medical Technology M,D
Clothing and Textiles M,D
Communication Disorders M
Communication—General M
Community Health M,D
Computer Engineering M,D
Computer Science M,D
Condensed Matter Physics M,D
Conservation Biology M,D
Construction Engineering M,D
Counseling Psychology M,D
Counselor Education M,D
Criminal Justice and Criminology M,D
Demography and Population Studies M,D
Dental Hygiene O
Dentistry D
East European and Russian Studies M,D
Ecology M,D
Economics M,D
Educational Leadership and Administration M,D,O
Educational Media/Instructional Technology M,D
Educational Policy M,D,O
Educational Psychology M,D
Electrical Engineering M,D
Elementary Education M,D
Energy and Power Engineering M,D
Engineering Management M,D
English as a Second Language M,D
English M,D
Environmental and Occupational Health M,D
Environmental Biology M,D
Environmental Engineering M,D
Environmental Management and Policy M,D
Environmental Sciences M,D
Epidemiology M,D
Evolutionary Biology M,D
Exercise and Sports Science M,D
Family and Consumer Sciences-General M,D
Finance and Banking M,D
Folklore M,D
Forestry M,D
French M,D
Genetics M,D
Geophysics M,D
Geosciences M,D
Geotechnical Engineering M,D
German M,D
Health Physics/Radiological Health M,D
Health Promotion M,O
Health Services Management and Hospital Administration M,D
Health Services Research M,D
Hispanic Studies M,D
History M,D
Immunology M,D
Industrial and Labor Relations D
Information Studies M
International Business M
International Health M,D
Italian M,D
Japanese M
Kinesiology and Movement Studies M,D
Law M,D
Library Science M
Linguistics M,D
Marketing D
Materials Engineering M,D
Maternal and Child/Neonatal Nursing D
Mathematical and Computational Finance M,D,O
Mathematical Physics M,D,O
Mathematics M,D,O
Mechanical Engineering M,D
Medical Microbiology M,D
Medical Physics M,D
Microbiology M,D
Mineral/Mining Engineering M,D
Molecular Biology M,D
Multilingual and Multicultural Education M
Music M,D
Nanotechnology M,D
Natural Resources M,D
Neuroscience M,D
Nursing—General M,D
Occupational Therapy M,D
Oral and Dental Sciences M,D
Organizational Management D
Pathology M,D
Petroleum Engineering M,D
Pharmaceutical Sciences M,D
Pharmacology M,D
Pharmacy M,D
Philosophy M,D
Physical Education M,D
Physical Therapy M,D
Physics M,D
Physiology M,D
Plant Biology M,D
Political Science M,D
Psychology—General M,D
Public Health—General M,D
Recreation and Park Management M,D
Rehabilitation Sciences M,D
Rural Sociology M,D
School Psychology M,D
Secondary Education M,D
Slavic Languages M,D
Sociology M,D
Special Education M,D
Sports Management M
Statistics M,D,O
Structural Engineering M,D
Systems Engineering M,D
Telecommunications M,D
Theater M
Vision Sciences M,D
Water Resources Engineering M,D

### UNIVERSITY OF ANTELOPE VALLEY

Business Administration and Management—General M
Criminal Justice and Criminology M

### THE UNIVERSITY OF ARIZONA

Accounting M
Aerospace/Aeronautical Engineering M,D
African Studies M,D,O
Agricultural Economics and Agribusiness M
Agricultural Education M,O
Agricultural Engineering M,D
Agricultural Sciences—General M,D,O
Agronomy and Soil Sciences M,D,O
Allopathic Medicine M,D
American Indian/Native American Studies M,D
Animal Sciences M,D
Anthropology M,D,O
Applied Economics M
Applied Mathematics M,D
Architecture M
Art Education M,D
Art History M,D
Art/Fine Arts M
Asian Studies M,D
Astronomy D
Atmospheric Sciences M,D
Biochemistry M,D
Biological and Biomedical Sciences—General M,D
Biomedical Engineering M,D
Biostatistics M,D
Biosystems Engineering M,D
Business Administration and Management—General M,D,O
Cancer Biology/Oncology D
Cell Biology D
Chemical Engineering M,D
Chemistry M,D
Child and Family Studies M,D,O
Classics M
Communication Disorders M,D,O
Communication—General M,D
Computer Engineering M,D
Computer Science M,D
Counseling Psychology M
Counselor Education M
Dance M
Data Science/Data Analytics M
Ecology M,D
Economics M,D
Education of Students with Severe/Multiple Disabilities M,D,O
Education—General M,D,O
Educational Leadership and Administration M,D,O
Educational Psychology M,D,O
Electrical Engineering M,D
Elementary Education M,D
Engineering and Applied Sciences—General M,D,O
Engineering Management M,D,O
English as a Second Language M,D
English Education M,D
English M,D
Entomology M,D
Environmental Engineering M,D
Environmental Management and Policy M,D
Environmental Sciences M,D,O
Epidemiology M,D
Evolutionary Biology M,D
Family and Consumer Sciences-General D
Family Nurse Practitioner Studies M,D,O
Film, Television, and Video Theory and Criticism M
Finance and Banking M
Forestry M,D
French M
Gender Studies M,D,O
Genetics M,D
Geographic Information Systems M,D,O
Geography M,D,O
Geological Engineering M,D,O
Geosciences M,D
German M,D
Higher Education M,D
History M,D,O
Human Development M,D,O
Hydrology D,O
Immunology D
Industrial/Management Engineering M,D,O
Information Studies M,D
Interdisciplinary Studies M,D
Journalism M
Landscape Architecture M
Latin American Studies M
Law M,D
Library Science M,D
Linguistics M,D
Management Information Systems M,O
Management Strategy and Policy M,D
Marketing M,D
Materials Engineering M,D
Materials Sciences M,D
Mathematics Education M
Mathematics M,D
Mechanical Engineering M,D
Medical Informatics M,D,O
Medical Physics M
Microbiology D
Mineral/Mining Engineering M,D,O
Molecular Biology D
Molecular Medicine M,D
Music Education M,D
Music M,D
Natural Resources M,D
Near and Middle Eastern Studies M,D,O
Neuroscience D
Nursing—General M,D,O
Nutrition M,D
Optical Sciences M,D,O
Organizational Management M,D
Perfusion M,D
Pharmaceutical Sciences M,D
Pharmacology M,D
Pharmacy D
Philosophy M,D
Physics M,D
Physiology M,D
Planetary and Space Sciences M,D
Plant Pathology M,D
Plant Sciences M,D
Political Science M,D
Psychology—General M,D
Public Administration M,D,O
Public Health—General M,D
Public Policy M,D,O
Range Science M,D
Reading Education M,D,O
Rehabilitation Counseling M,D
Rhetoric M,D
Russian M
School Psychology D,O
Secondary Education M,D
Sociology M,D
Spanish M,D
Special Education M,D
Statistics M,D
Systems Engineering M,D,O
Theater M
Urban and Regional Planning M
Water Resources M,D,O
Women's Studies M,D,O

| | |
|---|---|
| Writing | M |

### UNIVERSITY OF ARKANSAS

| | |
|---|---|
| Accounting | M |
| Adult Education | M,D |
| Agricultural Economics and Agribusiness | M |
| Agricultural Education | M |
| Agricultural Engineering | M,D |
| Agricultural Sciences—General | M,D |
| Agronomy and Soil Sciences | M,D |
| Animal Sciences | M,D |
| Anthropology | M,D |
| Applied Physics | M,D |
| Art/Fine Arts | M |
| Athletic Training and Sports Medicine | M |
| Bioengineering | M |
| Biological and Biomedical Sciences—General | M,D |
| Biomedical Engineering | M |
| Business Administration and Management—General | M,D |
| Cell Biology | M,D |
| Chemical Engineering | M,D |
| Chemistry | M,D |
| Civil Engineering | M,D |
| Communication Disorders | M |
| Communication—General | M |
| Community Health | M,D |
| Comparative Literature | M,D |
| Computer Engineering | M,D |
| Computer Science | M,D |
| Counselor Education | M,D |
| Cultural Studies | M,D |
| Curriculum and Instruction | M,D,O |
| Early Childhood Education | M,D,O |
| Economics | M,D |
| Education—General | M,D,O |
| Educational Leadership and Administration | M,D,O |
| Educational Measurement and Evaluation | M,D |
| Educational Media/Instructional Technology | M |
| Educational Policy | D |
| Electrical Engineering | M,D |
| Electronic Materials | M,D |
| Engineering and Applied Sciences—General | M,D |
| English | M,D |
| Entomology | M,D |
| Environmental Engineering | M,D |
| Family and Consumer Sciences-General | M |
| Food Science and Technology | M,D |
| French | M |
| Geography | M |
| Geology | M |
| German | M |
| Health Education | M,D |
| Health Promotion | M,D |
| Higher Education | M,D,O |
| History | M,D |
| Horticulture | M |
| Human Resources Development | M,D,O |
| Industrial and Manufacturing Management | M |
| Industrial/Management Engineering | M,D |
| Journalism | M |
| Kinesiology and Movement Studies | M,D |
| Law | M,D |
| Management Information Systems | M |
| Mathematics Education | M |
| Mathematics | M,D |
| Mechanical Engineering | M,D |
| Middle School Education | M,D,O |
| Molecular Biology | M,D |
| Music | M |
| Nursing—General | M |
| Philosophy | M,D |
| Photonics | M,D |
| Physical Education | M |
| Physics | M,D |
| Planetary and Space Sciences | M,D |
| Plant Pathology | M |
| Plant Sciences | D |
| Political Science | M |
| Psychology—General | M,D |
| Public Administration | M |
| Public Policy | D |
| Recreation and Park Management | M,D |
| Rehabilitation Counseling | M,D |
| Secondary Education | M,O |
| Social Work | M |
| Sociology | M |
| Spanish | M |
| Special Education | M |
| Sports Management | M,D |
| Statistics | M |
| Telecommunications | M,D |
| Theater | M |
| Transportation and Highway Engineering | M,D |
| Vocational and Technical Education | M,D,O |
| Writing | M |

### UNIVERSITY OF ARKANSAS AT LITTLE ROCK

| | |
|---|---|
| Adult Education | M |
| Applied Mathematics | M,O |
| Applied Psychology | M |
| Applied Science and Technology | M,D |
| Applied Statistics | M,O |
| Art Education | M |
| Art History | M |
| Art/Fine Arts | M |
| Bioinformatics | M,D |
| Biological and Biomedical Sciences—General | M |
| Business Administration and Management—General | M,O |
| Chemistry | M |
| Community College Education | M,D |
| Computer Science | M,D |
| Conflict Resolution and Mediation/Peace Studies | O |
| Construction Management | M |
| Counselor Education | M |
| Criminal Justice and Criminology | M,D |
| Curriculum and Instruction | M |
| Education of the Gifted | M,O |
| Education—General | M,D,O |
| Educational Leadership and Administration | M,D,O |
| Educational Media/Instructional Technology | M |
| English as a Second Language | M |
| Entrepreneurship | O |
| Exercise and Sports Science | M |
| Foreign Languages Education | M |
| Geosciences | O |
| Gerontology | O |
| Health Education | M,D |
| Higher Education | M,D |
| Information Science | M,D,O |
| Interdisciplinary Studies | M |
| Law | D |
| Management Information Systems | M,O |
| Mass Communication | M |
| Mathematics | M,O |
| Middle School Education | M |
| Nonprofit Management | O |
| Psychology—General | M |
| Public Administration | M |
| Public Affairs | M,O |
| Public History | M |
| Reading Education | M,D,O |
| Rehabilitation Counseling | M,O |
| Rhetoric | M |
| Secondary Education | M |
| Social Work | M |
| Special Education | M,O |
| Speech and Interpersonal Communication | M |
| Sports Management | M |
| Student Affairs | M,D |
| Systems Engineering | M,D,O |
| Technical Writing | M |
| Writing | M |

### UNIVERSITY OF ARKANSAS AT MONTICELLO

| | |
|---|---|
| Education—General | M |
| Educational Leadership and Administration | M |
| Forestry | M |
| Natural Resources | M |

### UNIVERSITY OF ARKANSAS AT PINE BLUFF

| | |
|---|---|
| Aquaculture | M,D |
| Education—General | M |
| Elementary Education | M |
| English Education | M |
| Fish, Game, and Wildlife Management | M,D |
| Mathematics Education | M |
| Science Education | M |
| Secondary Education | M |
| Social Sciences Education | M |

### UNIVERSITY OF ARKANSAS FOR MEDICAL SCIENCES

| | |
|---|---|
| Allopathic Medicine | D |
| Biochemistry | M,D,O |
| Bioinformatics | M,D,O |
| Biological and Biomedical Sciences—General | M,D,O |
| Biostatistics | M,D,O |
| Communication Disorders | M,D |
| Environmental and Occupational Health | M,D,O |
| Epidemiology | M,D,O |
| Genetic Counseling | M,D |
| Health Education | M,D,O |
| Health Physics/Radiological Health | M,D |
| Health Promotion | M,D,O |
| Health Services Management and Hospital Administration | M,D,O |
| Health Services Research | M,D,O |
| Immunology | M,D,O |
| Microbiology | M,D,O |
| Molecular Biology | M,D,O |
| Molecular Biophysics | M,D,O |
| Neurobiology | M,D,O |
| Nursing—General | D |
| Nutrition | M,D,O |
| Pharmacology | M,D,O |
| Pharmacy | M,D |
| Physician Assistant Studies | M,D |
| Physiology | M,D,O |
| Public Health—General | M,D,O |
| Toxicology | M,D,O |

### UNIVERSITY OF ARKANSAS-FORT SMITH

| | |
|---|---|
| Health Services Management and Hospital Administration | M |

### UNIVERSITY OF BALTIMORE

| | |
|---|---|
| Accounting | M,O |
| Applied Arts and Design—General | M |
| Applied Psychology | M |
| Business Administration and Management—General | M,O |
| Conflict Resolution and Mediation/Peace Studies | M |
| Counseling Psychology | M |
| Criminal Justice and Criminology | M |
| Entrepreneurship | M |
| Finance and Banking | M |
| Graphic Design | D |
| Health Services Management and Hospital Administration | M |
| Human Services | M |
| Human-Computer Interaction | M |
| Intellectual Property Law | M,D |
| International Business | M |
| Law | M,D |
| Legal and Justice Studies | M |
| Management Information Systems | M,O |
| Marketing | M |
| Public Administration | M,D |
| Public Affairs | M,D |
| Publishing | M |
| Taxation | M,D |
| Writing | M |

### UNIVERSITY OF BRIDGEPORT

| | |
|---|---|
| Accounting | M |
| Acupuncture and Oriental Medicine | M |
| Applied Arts and Design—General | M |
| Asian Studies | M |
| Biomedical Engineering | M |
| Business Administration and Management—General | M |
| Chiropractic | D |
| Clinical Psychology | M |
| Communication—General | M |
| Computer Education | M,D,O |
| Computer Engineering | M,D |
| Computer Science | M,D |
| Conflict Resolution and Mediation/Peace Studies | M |
| Counseling Psychology | M |
| Dental Hygiene | M |
| Early Childhood Education | M,D,O |
| Education—General | M,D,O |
| Educational Leadership and Administration | M,D,O |
| Electrical Engineering | M |
| Elementary Education | M,D,O |
| Engineering and Applied Sciences—General | M,D |
| Entrepreneurship | M |
| Finance and Banking | M |
| Human Resources Development | M |
| Human Resources Management | M |
| Human Services | M |
| Industrial and Manufacturing Management | M |
| International Affairs | M |
| International and Comparative Education | M,D,O |
| International Business | M |
| Management Information Systems | M |
| Management of Technology | M,D |
| Marketing | M |
| Mechanical Engineering | M |
| Media Studies | M |
| Middle School Education | M,D,O |
| Music Education | M,D,O |
| Naturopathic Medicine | D |
| Nutrition | M |
| Pacific Area/Pacific Rim Studies | M |
| Physician Assistant Studies | M |
| Reading Education | M,D,O |
| Secondary Education | M,D,O |
| Social Psychology | M |
| Student Affairs | M |

### THE UNIVERSITY OF BRITISH COLUMBIA

| | |
|---|---|
| Accounting | D |
| Adult Education | M,D |
| Agricultural Economics and Agribusiness | M |
| Agricultural Sciences—General | M,D |
| Agronomy and Soil Sciences | M,D |
| Allopathic Medicine | M,D |
| Animal Sciences | M,D |
| Anthropology | M,D |
| Archaeology | M |
| Architecture | M |
| Archives/Archival Administration | M,D |
| Art Education | M,D |
| Art History | M,D |
| Art/Fine Arts | M,D |
| Asian Studies | M,D |
| Astronomy | M,D |
| Atmospheric Sciences | M,D |
| Biochemistry | M,D |
| Bioengineering | M,D |
| Bioinformatics | M,D |
| Biomedical Engineering | M,D |
| Biopsychology | M,D |
| Botany | M,D |
| Business Administration and Management—General | M,D |
| Business Analytics | M |
| Cell Biology | M,D |
| Chemical Engineering | M,D |
| Chemistry | M,D |
| Civil Engineering | M,D |
| Classics | M,D |
| Clinical Psychology | M,D |
| Cognitive Sciences | M,D |
| Communication Disorders | M,D |
| Computer Engineering | M,D |
| Computer Science | M,D |
| Counseling Psychology | M,D,O |
| Curriculum and Instruction | M,D |
| Dentistry | D |
| Developmental Biology | M,D |
| Developmental Psychology | M,D |
| East European and Russian Studies | M,D |
| Economics | M,D |
| Education—General | M,D,O |
| Educational Leadership and Administration | M,D |
| Educational Measurement and Evaluation | M,D,O |
| Educational Policy | M,D |
| Electrical Engineering | M,D |
| Energy and Power Engineering | M |
| Engineering and Applied Sciences—General | M,D |
| English as a Second Language | M,D |
| English | M,D |
| Environmental Management and Policy | M,D |
| Ethnic Studies | M |
| Film, Television, and Video Production | M |
| Film, Television, and Video Theory and Criticism | M |
| Finance and Banking | D |
| Food Science and Technology | M,D |
| Forestry | M,D |
| Foundations and Philosophy of Education | M,D |
| French | M,D |
| Gender Studies | M,D |
| Genetic Counseling | M |
| Genetics | M,D |
| Geography | M,D |
| Geological Engineering | M,D |
| Geology | M,D |
| Geophysics | M,D |
| German | M,D |
| Health Psychology | M,D |
| Health Services Management and Hospital Administration | M,D |
| Higher Education | M,D |
| Hispanic Studies | M,D |
| History | M,D |
| Home Economics Education | M,D |
| Human Development | M,D,O |
| Immunology | M,D |
| Infectious Diseases | M,D |
| Information Studies | M,D |
| International Affairs | M |
| Internet and Interactive Multimedia | M |
| Journalism | M |
| Kinesiology and Movement Studies | M,D |
| Landscape Architecture | M |
| Law | M,D |
| Library Science | M,D |
| Linguistics | M,D |
| Management Information Systems | D |
| Management Strategy and Policy | D |
| Marine Sciences | M,D |
| Marketing | D |
| Materials Engineering | M,D |
| Mathematics Education | M,D |
| Mathematics | M,D |
| Mechanical Engineering | M,D |
| Microbiology | M,D |
| Mineral/Mining Engineering | M,D |
| Molecular Biology | M,D |
| Museum Studies | M,D |
| Music Education | M,D |
| Music | M,D |
| Natural Resources | M,D |
| Neuroscience | M,D |
| Nursing—General | M,D |
| Nutrition | M,D |
| Occupational Therapy | M |
| Oceanography | M,D |
| Oral and Dental Sciences | M,D |
| Organizational Behavior | D |
| Pacific Area/Pacific Rim Studies | M |
| Pathology | M,D |
| Pharmaceutical Sciences | M,D |
| Pharmacology | M,D |
| Pharmacy | M,D |
| Philosophy | M,D |
| Physical Education | M,D |
| Physical Therapy | M |
| Physics | M,D |
| Plant Sciences | M,D |
| Political Science | M,D |
| Psychology—General | M,D |
| Public Health—General | M,D |
| Public Policy | M |
| Quantitative Analysis | M,D |
| Reading Education | M,D |
| Rehabilitation Sciences | M,D |
| Religion | M,D |
| Reproductive Biology | M,D |
| School Psychology | M,D,O |
| Science Education | M,D |
| Social Psychology | M,D |
| Social Sciences Education | M,D |
| Social Work | M,D |
| Sociology | M,D |
| Special Education | M,D,O |
| Statistics | M,D |
| Sustainability Management | M,D |
| Sustainable Development | M |
| Taxation | M,D |
| Theater | M,D |
| Transportation Management | D |
| Urban and Regional Planning | M,D |
| Urban Design | M |
| Vocational and Technical Education | M,D |
| Water Resources | M |
| Writing | M,D |
| Zoology | M,D |

### UNIVERSITY OF CALGARY

| | |
|---|---|
| Adult Education | M,D |

*M—masters degree; D—doctorate; O—other advanced degree; *—Close-Up and/or Display*

| | |
|---|---|
| Allopathic Medicine | D |
| Analytical Chemistry | M,D |
| Applied Psychology | M,D |
| Architecture | M,D |
| Astronomy | M,D |
| Biochemistry | M,D |
| Biological and Biomedical Sciences—General | M,D |
| Biomedical Engineering | M,D |
| Biotechnology | M |
| Business Administration and Management—General | M,D |
| Cancer Biology/Oncology | M,D |
| Cardiovascular Sciences | M,D |
| Chemical Engineering | M,D |
| Chemistry | M,D |
| Civil Engineering | M,D |
| Classics | M,D |
| Clinical Psychology | M,D |
| Community Health | M,D |
| Computer Engineering | M,D |
| Computer Science | M,D |
| Counseling Psychology | M,D |
| Curriculum and Instruction | M,D |
| Educational Leadership and Administration | M,D |
| Educational Measurement and Evaluation | M,D |
| Electrical Engineering | M,D |
| Energy and Power Engineering | M,D |
| Energy Management and Policy | M,D |
| Engineering and Applied Sciences—General | M,D |
| Environmental Design | M,D |
| Environmental Engineering | M,D |
| Environmental Law | M,O |
| Environmental Management and Policy | M,D,O |
| Genetics | M,D |
| Geography | M,D |
| Geology | M,D |
| Geophysics | M,D |
| Geosciences | M,D |
| Geotechnical Engineering | M,D |
| German | M,D |
| History | M,D |
| Hydrology | M,D |
| Immunology | M,D |
| Infectious Diseases | M,D |
| Inorganic Chemistry | M,D |
| Kinesiology and Movement Studies | M,D |
| Landscape Architecture | M,D |
| Law | M,D,O |
| Legal and Justice Studies | M,O |
| Linguistics | M,D |
| Management Strategy and Policy | M,D |
| Manufacturing Engineering | M,D |
| Materials Sciences | M,D |
| Mathematics | M,D |
| Mechanical Engineering | M,D |
| Mechanics | M,D |
| Microbiology | M,D |
| Military and Defense Studies | M,D |
| Molecular Biology | M,D |
| Molecular Genetics | M,D |
| Multilingual and Multicultural Education | M,D |
| Music | M,D |
| Neuroscience | M,D |
| Nursing—General | M,D,O |
| Organic Chemistry | M,D |
| Pathology | M,D |
| Petroleum Engineering | M,D |
| Philosophy | M,D |
| Physical Chemistry | M,D |
| Physics | M,D |
| Physiology | M,D |
| Political Science | M,D |
| Project Management | M,D |
| Psychology—General | M,D |
| Public Policy | M |
| Religion | M,D |
| School Psychology | M,D |
| Social Work | M,D,O |
| Sociology | M,D |
| Software Engineering | M,D |
| Statistics | M,D |
| Structural Engineering | M,D |
| Sustainable Development | M,D |
| Theoretical Chemistry | M,D |
| Transportation and Highway Engineering | M,D |
| Water Resources | M,D |

**UNIVERSITY OF CALIFORNIA, BERKELEY**

| | |
|---|---|
| Accounting | D,O |
| Addictions/Substance Abuse Counseling | O |
| African-American Studies | D |
| Agricultural Economics and Agribusiness | D |
| Allopathic Medicine | |
| Anthropology | D |
| Applied Arts and Design—General | O |
| Applied Mathematics | M,D |
| Applied Science and Technology | D |
| Archaeology | M,D |
| Architectural History | M,D |
| Architecture | M,D |
| Art History | D |
| Art/Fine Arts | M,O |
| Asian Languages | M,D |
| Asian Studies | M,D |
| Astrophysics | D |
| Biochemistry | D |
| Bioengineering | M,D |
| Biological and Biomedical Sciences—General | D |
| Biophysics | D |
| Biostatistics | M,D |
| Building Science | M,D |
| Business Administration and Management—General | M,D,O |
| Cell Biology | D |
| Chemical Engineering | M,D |
| Chemistry | D |
| Chinese | D |
| Civil Engineering | M,D |
| Classics | M,D |
| Clinical Research | O |
| Comparative Literature | D |
| Computer Science | M,D |
| Construction Management | O |
| Counseling Psychology | M |
| Data Science/Data Analytics | M |
| Demography and Population Studies | M,D |
| Economics | D |
| Education—General | M,D,O |
| Educational Leadership and Administration | M,D |
| Electrical Engineering | M,D |
| Energy Management and Policy | M,D |
| Engineering and Applied Sciences—General | M,D,O |
| Engineering Management | M,D |
| English as a Second Language | O |
| English | D |
| Environmental and Occupational Health | M,D |
| Environmental Design | M,D |
| Environmental Engineering | M,D |
| Environmental Management and Policy | M,D,O |
| Environmental Sciences | M,D |
| Epidemiology | M,D |
| Ethnic Studies | D |
| Facilities Management | O |
| Film, Television, and Video Theory and Criticism | D |
| Finance and Banking | D,O |
| Financial Engineering | M |
| Folklore | M |
| Forestry | M,D |
| French | D |
| Geography | D |
| Geology | M,D |
| Geophysics | M,D |
| Geotechnical Engineering | M,D |
| German | D |
| Health Services Management and Hospital Administration | D |
| Hispanic and Latin American Languages | D |
| History of Science and Technology | D |
| History | M,D |
| Human Development | M,D |
| Human Resources Management | O |
| Immunology | D |
| Industrial and Labor Relations | D |
| Industrial/Management Engineering | M,D |
| Infectious Diseases | M,D |
| Information Studies | M,D |
| Interior Design | O |
| International Affairs | M |
| International Business | O |
| Italian | D |
| Japanese | D |
| Journalism | M |
| Landscape Architecture | M,D,O |
| Law | M,D |
| Legal and Justice Studies | D |
| Linguistics | D |
| Management Information Systems | M,D,O |
| Marketing | D,O |
| Materials Engineering | M,D |
| Materials Sciences | M,D |
| Mathematics Education | M,D |
| Mathematics | M,D |
| Mechanical Engineering | M,D |
| Mechanics | M,D |
| Microbiology | D |
| Molecular Biology | D |
| Molecular Toxicology | D |
| Music | D |
| Natural Resources | M,D |
| Near and Middle Eastern Studies | M,D |
| Neuroscience | D |
| Nuclear Engineering | M,D |
| Nutrition | M,D |
| Operations Research | M,D |
| Optometry | D,O |
| Organizational Behavior | D |
| Philosophy | D |
| Physics | D |
| Physiology | M,D |
| Plant Biology | D |
| Political Science | D |
| Project Management | O |
| Psychology—General | D |
| Public Affairs | M |
| Public Health—General | M,D |
| Public Policy | M,D |
| Range Science | M |
| Real Estate | D |
| Religion | D |
| Rhetoric | D |
| Romance Languages | D |
| Russian | D |
| Scandinavian Languages | D |
| Science Education | M,D |
| Slavic Languages | D |
| Social Work | M,D |
| Sociology | D |
| Spanish | D |
| Special Education | M,D |
| Statistics | M,D |
| Structural Engineering | M,D |
| Sustainability Management | O |
| Sustainable Development | M,O |
| Theater | D |
| Transportation and Highway Engineering | M,D |
| Urban and Regional Planning | M,D |
| Urban Design | M,D |
| Vision Sciences | M,D |
| Water Resources Engineering | M,D |
| Writing | O |

**UNIVERSITY OF CALIFORNIA, DAVIS**

| | |
|---|---|
| Accounting | M |
| Aerospace/Aeronautical Engineering | M,D,O |
| Agricultural Economics and Agribusiness | M,D |
| Agricultural Sciences—General | M |
| Agronomy and Soil Sciences | M,D |
| Allopathic Medicine | D |
| American Indian/Native American Studies | M,D |
| Animal Behavior | D |
| Animal Sciences | M,D |
| Anthropology | M,D |
| Applied Mathematics | M,D |
| Applied Science and Technology | M,D |
| Art History | M |
| Art/Fine Arts | M |
| Atmospheric Sciences | M,D |
| Biochemistry | M,D |
| Bioengineering | M,D |
| Biomedical Engineering | M,D |
| Biophysics | M,D |
| Biostatistics | M,D |
| Business Administration and Management—General | M |
| Business Analytics | M |
| Cell Biology | M,D |
| Chemical Engineering | M,D |
| Chemistry | M,D |
| Child Development | M |
| Civil Engineering | M,D,O |
| Clinical Research | M |
| Clothing and Textiles | M |
| Communication—General | M |
| Comparative Literature | D |
| Computer Engineering | M,D |
| Computer Science | M,D |
| Cultural Studies | M,D |
| Curriculum and Instruction | M,D |
| Developmental Biology | M,D |
| Ecology | M,D |
| Economics | M,D |
| Education—General | M,D |
| Educational Psychology | M,D |
| Electrical Engineering | M,D |
| Engineering and Applied Sciences—General | M,D,O |
| English | M,D |
| Entomology | M,D |
| Entrepreneurship | M |
| Environmental Engineering | M,D,O |
| Environmental Sciences | M,D |
| Epidemiology | M,D |
| Evolutionary Biology | D |
| Exercise and Sports Science | M |
| Finance and Banking | M |
| Food Science and Technology | M,D |
| Forensic Sciences | M |
| French | D |
| Genetics | M,D |
| Geography | M,D |
| Geology | M,D |
| German | M,D |
| History | M,D |
| Horticulture | M |
| Human Development | D |
| Hydrology | M,D |
| Immunology | M,D |
| Law | M,D |
| Linguistics | M,D |
| Management Strategy and Policy | M |
| Marketing | M |
| Materials Engineering | M,D |
| Materials Sciences | M,D |
| Maternal and Child Health | M |
| Mathematics | M,D |
| Mechanical Engineering | M,D,O |
| Medical Informatics | M |
| Microbiology | M,D |
| Molecular Biology | M,D |
| Music | M,D |
| Neuroscience | D |
| Nutrition | M,D |
| Organizational Behavior | M |
| Pathology | M,D |
| Pharmacology | M,D |
| Philosophy | M,D |
| Physics | M,D |
| Physiology | M,D |
| Plant Biology | M,D |
| Plant Pathology | M,D |
| Political Science | M,D |
| Psychology—General | D |
| Sociology | M,D |
| Spanish | M,D |
| Statistics | M,D |
| Textile Design | M |
| Theater | M,D |
| Toxicology | M,D |
| Transportation and Highway Engineering | M,D |
| Transportation Management | M |
| Urban and Regional Planning | M |
| Veterinary Medicine | D |
| Veterinary Sciences | M,O |
| Viticulture and Enology | M,D |
| Writing | M,D |
| Zoology | M |

**UNIVERSITY OF CALIFORNIA, HASTINGS COLLEGE OF THE LAW**

| | |
|---|---|
| Law | M,D |

**UNIVERSITY OF CALIFORNIA, IRVINE**

| | |
|---|---|
| Accounting | M |
| Aerospace/Aeronautical Engineering | M,D |
| Allopathic Medicine | D |
| Anatomy | M,D |
| Anthropology | M,D |
| Applied Mathematics | M,D |
| Art/Fine Arts | M,D |
| Asian Languages | M,D |
| Biochemical Engineering | M,D |
| Biochemistry | M,D |
| Biological and Biomedical Sciences—General | M,D |
| Biomedical Engineering | M,D |
| Biophysics | D |
| Biotechnology | M |
| Business Administration and Management—General | M,D |
| Business Analytics | M |
| Cell Biology | M,D |
| Chemical Engineering | M,D |
| Chemistry | M,D |
| Chinese | M,D |
| Civil Engineering | M,D |
| Classics | M,D |
| Comparative Literature | M,D |
| Computational Biology | D |
| Computer Science | M,D |
| Criminal Justice and Criminology | M,D |
| Cultural Studies | D |
| Dance | M |
| Demography and Population Studies | M |
| Developmental Biology | M,D |
| Ecology | M,D |
| Economics | M,D |
| Education—General | M,D |
| Educational Leadership and Administration | M,D |
| Electrical Engineering | M,D |
| Elementary Education | M,D |
| Engineering and Applied Sciences—General | M,D |
| Engineering Management | M |
| English | M,D |
| Environmental and Occupational Health | M,D |
| Environmental Design | D |
| Environmental Engineering | M,D |
| Epidemiology | M,D |
| Evolutionary Biology | M,D |
| Foreign Languages Education | M,D |
| French | M,D |
| Genetic Counseling | M |
| Genetics | D |
| Geosciences | M,D |
| German | M,D |
| Health Services Management and Hospital Administration | M |
| History | M,D |
| Information Science | M,D |
| Japanese | M,D |
| Law | D |
| Manufacturing Engineering | M,D |
| Materials Engineering | M,D |
| Materials Sciences | M,D |
| Mathematics | M,D |
| Mechanical Engineering | M,D |
| Medicinal and Pharmaceutical Chemistry | D |
| Microbiology | M,D |
| Molecular Biology | M,D |
| Molecular Genetics | M,D |
| Music | M |
| Neurobiology | M,D |
| Neuroscience | D |
| Nursing—General | M |
| Pathology | D |
| Pharmaceutical Sciences | D |
| Philosophy | M,D |
| Physics | M,D |
| Physiology | D |
| Political Science | D |
| Psychology—General | D |
| Public Health—General | M,D |
| Secondary Education | M,D |
| Sociology | D |
| Spanish | M,D |
| Statistics | M,D |
| Systems Biology | D |
| Theater | M,D |
| Toxicology | M,D |
| Translational Biology | M |
| Transportation and Highway Engineering | M,D |
| Urban and Regional Planning | M,D |
| Urban Studies | M,D |
| Writing | M |

**UNIVERSITY OF CALIFORNIA, LOS ANGELES**

| | |
|---|---|
| Accounting | M,D |
| Aerospace/Aeronautical Engineering | M,D |
| African Studies | M |
| African-American Studies | M |
| Allopathic Medicine | D |
| American Indian/Native American Studies | M |
| Anatomy | M,D |
| Anthropology | M,D |
| Applied Arts and Design—General | M |
| Applied Economics | M |
| Archaeology | M |
| Architecture | M |
| Archives/Archival Administration | M,D,O |
| Art History | M,D |
| Art/Fine Arts | M |
| Asian Languages | M,D |
| Asian Studies | M,D |
| Asian-American Studies | M |
| Astronomy | M,D |
| Astrophysics | M,D |

| | |
|---|---|
| Atmospheric Sciences | M,D |
| Biochemistry | M,D |
| Bioengineering | M,D |
| Bioinformatics | M,D |
| Biological and Biomedical Sciences—General | M,D |
| Biomathematics | M,D |
| Biomedical Engineering | M,D |
| Biostatistics | M,D |
| Business Administration and Management—General | M,D |
| Business Analytics | M,D |
| Cell Biology | M,D |
| Chemical Engineering | M,D |
| Chemistry | M,D |
| Civil Engineering | M,D |
| Classics | M,D |
| Clinical Research | M |
| Community Health | M,D |
| Comparative Literature | M,D |
| Computer Engineering | M,D |
| Computer Science | M,D |
| Dance | M,D |
| Dentistry | D,O |
| Developmental Biology | M,D |
| Ecology | M,D |
| Economics | D |
| Education—General | M,D |
| Educational Leadership and Administration | D |
| Electrical Engineering | M,D |
| Engineering and Applied Sciences—General | M,D |
| English as a Second Language | M,D,O |
| English | M,D |
| Environmental and Occupational Health | M,D |
| Environmental Engineering | M,D |
| Environmental Sciences | M,D |
| Epidemiology | M,D |
| Evolutionary Biology | M,D |
| Film, Television, and Video Production | M,D |
| Finance and Banking | M,D |
| Financial Engineering | M,D |
| French | M,D |
| Gender Studies | M,D |
| Geochemistry | M,D |
| Geography | M,D |
| Geology | M,D |
| Geophysics | M,D |
| Geosciences | M,D |
| German | M,D |
| Health Services Management and Hospital Administration | M,D |
| Hispanic and Latin American Languages | D |
| Historic Preservation | M |
| History | M,D |
| Human Genetics | M,D |
| Immunology | M,D |
| Information Studies | M,D,O |
| Italian | M,D |
| Latin American Studies | M |
| Law | M,D |
| Library Science | M,D,O |
| Linguistics | M,D |
| Management of Technology | M,D |
| Management Strategy and Policy | M,D |
| Manufacturing Engineering | M |
| Marketing | M,D |
| Materials Engineering | M,D |
| Materials Sciences | M,D |
| Mathematics | M,D |
| Mechanical Engineering | M,D |
| Media Studies | M,D |
| Medical Physics | M,D |
| Microbiology | M,D |
| Molecular Biology | M,D |
| Molecular Genetics | M,D |
| Molecular Pathology | D |
| Molecular Physiology | D |
| Molecular Toxicology | D |
| Music | M,D |
| Near and Middle Eastern Languages | M,D |
| Near and Middle Eastern Studies | M,D |
| Neurobiology | M,D |
| Neuroscience | D |
| Nursing—General | M,D |
| Oceanography | M,D |
| Oral and Dental Sciences | M,D |
| Pathology | M,D |
| Pharmacology | M,D |
| Philosophy | M,D |
| Physics | M,D |
| Physiology | M,D |
| Planetary and Space Sciences | M,D |
| Political Science | M,D |
| Portuguese | M |
| Psychology—General | M,D |
| Public Affairs | M,D |
| Public Health—General | M,D |
| Public Policy | M |
| Scandinavian Languages | M |
| Slavic Languages | M,D |
| Social Work | M,D |
| Sociology | M,D |
| Spanish | M |
| Special Education | D |
| Statistics | M,D |
| Theater | M,D |
| Urban and Regional Planning | M,D |
| Urban Design | M,D |

**UNIVERSITY OF CALIFORNIA, MERCED**

| | |
|---|---|
| Applied Mathematics | M,D |
| Biochemistry | M,D |
| Bioengineering | M,D |
| Biological and Biomedical Sciences—General | M,D |
| Chemistry | M,D |
| Cognitive Sciences | M,D |
| Computer Science | M,D |
| Electrical Engineering | M,D |
| Engineering and Applied Sciences—General | M,D |
| Entrepreneurship | M,D |
| Environmental Engineering | M,D |
| Humanities | M,D |
| Information Science | M,D |
| Mechanical Engineering | M,D |
| Mechanics | M,D |
| Physics | M,D |
| Psychology—General | M,D |
| Social Sciences | M,D |
| Sociology | M,D |
| Sustainability Management | M,D |
| Systems Biology | M,D |
| Systems Engineering | M,D |

**UNIVERSITY OF CALIFORNIA, RIVERSIDE**

| | |
|---|---|
| Accounting | M,D |
| Agronomy and Soil Sciences | M,D |
| Allopathic Medicine | D |
| Anthropology | M,D |
| Applied Behavior Analysis | M,D,O |
| Archives/Archival Administration | M,D |
| Art History | M,D |
| Art/Fine Arts | M |
| Artificial Intelligence/Robotics | M,D |
| Asian Studies | M |
| Biochemistry | M,D |
| Bioengineering | M,D |
| Bioinformatics | D |
| Biological and Biomedical Sciences—General | M,D |
| Botany | M,D |
| Business Administration and Management—General | M,D |
| Cell Biology | M,D |
| Chemical Engineering | M,D |
| Chemistry | M,D |
| Classics | D |
| Comparative Literature | M,D |
| Computer Engineering | M |
| Computer Science | M,D |
| Cultural Studies | D |
| Dance | M |
| Developmental Biology | M,D |
| Economics | M,D |
| Education—General | M,D,O |
| Educational Leadership and Administration | M,D,O |
| Educational Measurement and Evaluation | M,D,O |
| Educational Policy | M,D,O |
| Educational Psychology | M,D,O |
| Electrical Engineering | M,D |
| English as a Second Language | M,D,O |
| English | M,D |
| Entomology | M,D |
| Environmental Engineering | M,D |
| Environmental Sciences | M |
| Ethnic Studies | D |
| Evolutionary Biology | M,D |
| Finance and Banking | M,D |
| Foundations and Philosophy of Education | M,D,O |
| Genetics | D |
| Genomic Sciences | D |
| Geology | M,D |
| Higher Education | M,D,O |
| Hispanic Studies | M,D |
| History | M,D |
| International Health | M,D |
| Materials Engineering | M |
| Materials Sciences | M |
| Mathematics | M,D |
| Mechanical Engineering | M,D |
| Microbiology | M,D |
| Molecular Biology | M,D |
| Multilingual and Multicultural Education | M,D,O |
| Music | M,D |
| Nanotechnology | M |
| Neuroscience | D |
| Philosophy | M,D |
| Physics | M,D |
| Plant Biology | M,D |
| Plant Molecular Biology | M,D |
| Plant Pathology | M,D |
| Plant Sciences | M,D |
| Political Science | M,D |
| Psychology—General | D |
| Public Policy | M,D |
| Religion | M,D |
| School Psychology | M,D,O |
| Sociology | M,D |
| Spanish | M,D |
| Special Education | M,D,O |
| Statistics | M |
| Toxicology | M,D |
| Water Resources | M,D |
| Writing | M |

**UNIVERSITY OF CALIFORNIA, SAN DIEGO**

| | |
|---|---|
| Aerospace/Aeronautical Engineering | M,D |
| Allopathic Medicine | D |
| Anthropology | D |
| Applied Mathematics | M,D |
| Applied Physics | M,D |
| Architectural Engineering | M |
| Art History | M,D |
| Art/Fine Arts | M,D |
| Artificial Intelligence/Robotics | M,D |
| Biochemistry | M,D |
| Bioengineering | M,D |
| Bioinformatics | D |
| Biological and Biomedical Sciences—General | M,D |
| Biophysics | M,D |
| Biostatistics | D |
| Business Administration and Management—General | M,D |
| Business Analytics | M,D |
| Chemical Engineering | M,D |
| Chemistry | M,D |
| Clinical Laboratory Sciences/Medical Technology | M,D |
| Clinical Psychology | D |
| Clinical Research | M |
| Cognitive Sciences | D |
| Communication Disorders | D |
| Communication—General | D |
| Computational Sciences | M,D |
| Computer Engineering | M,D |
| Computer Science | M,D |
| Curriculum and Instruction | M,D |
| Dance | M,D |
| Data Science/Data Analytics | M |
| Economics | D |
| Education—General | M,D |
| Educational Leadership and Administration | M,D |
| Electrical Engineering | M,D |
| Energy Management and Policy | M |
| Engineering Physics | M,D |
| English | M,D |
| Environmental Management and Policy | M |
| Epidemiology | D |
| Ethnic Studies | D |
| Finance and Banking | M,D |
| Geophysics | M,D |
| Geosciences | M,D |
| Health Services Management and Hospital Administration | M |
| History of Science and Technology | D |
| History | M,D |
| International Affairs | M,D |
| International Business | M |
| International Development | M |
| International Economics | M |
| International Health | D |
| Jewish Studies | M,D |
| Latin American Studies | M |
| Linguistics | D |
| Marine Sciences | M |
| Materials Sciences | M,D |
| Mathematics Education | D |
| Mathematics | M,D |
| Mechanical Engineering | M,D |
| Mechanics | M,D |
| Meteorology | M |
| Modeling and Simulation | M,D |
| Multilingual and Multicultural Education | M,D |
| Music | M,D |
| Nanotechnology | M,D |
| Neuroscience | M,D |
| Nonprofit Management | M |
| Ocean Engineering | M,D |
| Oceanography | M,D |
| Pharmacy | D |
| Philosophy | D |
| Photonics | M,D |
| Physics | M,D |
| Political Science | M,D |
| Psychology—General | D |
| Public Health—General | D |
| Public Policy | M |
| Science Education | D |
| Sociology | D |
| Statistics | M,D |
| Structural Engineering | M,D |
| Systems Biology | D |
| Telecommunications | M,D |
| Theater | M,D |
| Writing | M,D |

**UNIVERSITY OF CALIFORNIA, SAN FRANCISCO**

| | |
|---|---|
| Allopathic Medicine | D |
| Anthropology | D |
| Biochemistry | D |
| Bioengineering | D |
| Bioinformatics | D |
| Biological and Biomedical Sciences—General | D |
| Biophysics | D |
| Cell Biology | D |
| Chemistry | D |
| Dentistry | D |
| Developmental Biology | D |
| Genetics | D |
| Genomic Sciences | D |
| Health Law | M |
| History of Science and Technology | M,D |
| Medical Imaging | M |
| Medicinal and Pharmaceutical Chemistry | D |
| Molecular Biology | D |
| Neuroscience | D |
| Nursing—General | M,D |
| Oral and Dental Sciences | M,D |
| Pharmaceutical Sciences | D |
| Pharmacology | D |
| Pharmacy | D |
| Physical Therapy | D |
| Sociology | D |

**UNIVERSITY OF CALIFORNIA, SANTA BARBARA**

| | |
|---|---|
| African-American Studies | D |
| Agricultural Economics and Agribusiness | M,D |
| Anthropology | M,D |
| Applied Mathematics | M,D |
| Applied Statistics | M,D |
| Art History | D |
| Art/Fine Arts | M |
| Asian Languages | M,D |
| Asian Studies | M,D |
| Biochemistry | D |
| Bioengineering | M,D |
| Biophysics | D |
| Cell Biology | M,D |
| Chemical Engineering | M,D |
| Chemistry | M,D |
| Classics | M,D |
| Clinical Psychology | M,D,O |
| Cognitive Sciences | M,D |
| Communication—General | D |
| Comparative Literature | D |
| Computational Sciences | M,D |
| Computer Engineering | M,D |
| Computer Science | M,D |
| Counseling Psychology | M,D,O |
| Cultural Anthropology | M,D |
| Cultural Studies | M,D |
| Developmental Biology | M,D |
| Ecology | M,D |
| Economics | M,D |
| Education—General | M,D,O |
| Electrical Engineering | M,D |
| Engineering and Applied Sciences—General | M,D |
| English | D |
| Environmental Management and Policy | M,D |
| Environmental Sciences | M,D |
| Evolutionary Biology | M,D |
| Film, Television, and Video Production | D |
| Finance and Banking | M,D |
| French | D |
| Geography | M,D |
| Geosciences | M,D |
| Hispanic and Latin American Languages | M,D |
| Hispanic Studies | M,D |
| History | D |
| Interdisciplinary Studies | D |
| International Affairs | M,D |
| Latin American Studies | M |
| Linguistics | M,D |
| Management of Technology | M |
| Marine Biology | M,D |
| Marine Sciences | M,D |
| Materials Engineering | M,D |
| Materials Sciences | M,D |
| Mathematical and Computational Finance | M,D |
| Mathematics | M,D |
| Mechanical Engineering | M,D |
| Media Studies | M,D |
| Medieval and Renaissance Studies | M,D |
| Molecular Biology | M,D |
| Music | M,D |
| Neuroscience | D |
| Philosophy | D |
| Photonics | M,D |
| Physics | D |
| Political Science | M,D |
| Portuguese | M,D |
| Psychology—General | D |
| Public History | D |
| Quantitative Analysis | M,D |
| Religion | M,D |
| School Psychology | M,D,O |
| Social Sciences | D |
| Sociology | D |
| Spanish | M,D |
| Speech and Interpersonal Communication | D |
| Statistics | M,D |
| Sustainable Development | M,D |
| Theater | M,D |
| Translation and Interpretation | M,D |
| Transportation Management | M,D |
| Women's Studies | M,D |
| Writing | D |

**UNIVERSITY OF CALIFORNIA, SANTA CRUZ**

| | |
|---|---|
| Anthropology | D |
| Applied Economics | M |
| Applied Mathematics | M,D |
| Art/Fine Arts | M,D |
| Astronomy | D |
| Astrophysics | D |
| Biochemistry | M,D |
| Bioinformatics | M,D |
| Cell Biology | M,D |
| Chemistry | M,D |
| Communication—General | O |
| Comparative Literature | M,D |
| Computer Art and Design | M,D |
| Computer Science | M,D |
| Cultural Anthropology | D |
| Developmental Biology | M,D |
| Ecology | M,D |
| Economics | D |
| Education—General | M,D |
| Electrical Engineering | M,D |
| Engineering and Applied Sciences—General | M,D |
| English | M,D |
| Environmental Biology | M,D |
| Environmental Management and Policy | D |
| Evolutionary Biology | M,D |
| Film, Television, and Video Theory and Criticism | D |
| Finance and Banking | M |
| Game Design and Development | M,D |
| Geosciences | M,D |
| History | M,D |

*M—masters degree; D—doctorate; O—other advanced degree; *—Close-Up and/or Display*

| | |
|---|---|
| Humanities | D |
| Interdisciplinary Studies | M,D |
| International Affairs | D |
| Internet and Interactive Multimedia | M,D |
| Linguistics | M,D |
| Marine Sciences | M,D |
| Mathematics | M,D |
| Microbiology | M,D |
| Molecular Biology | M,D |
| Music | M,D |
| Philosophy | M,D |
| Physics | M,D |
| Planetary and Space Sciences | M,D |
| Political Science | D |
| Psychology—General | D |
| Social Sciences Education | M |
| Social Sciences | D |
| Sociology | D |
| Statistics | M,D |
| Theater | O |
| Toxicology | M,D |
| Writing | M |

## UNIVERSITY OF CENTRAL ARKANSAS

| | |
|---|---|
| Accounting | M |
| Adult Education | M,O |
| Adult Nursing | M,O |
| Applied Mathematics | M |
| Biological and Biomedical Sciences—General | M |
| Business Administration and Management—General | M |
| Communication Disorders | M,D |
| Computer Art and Design | M |
| Computer Science | M |
| Counseling Psychology | M |
| Counselor Education | M |
| Curriculum and Instruction | M,O |
| Economic Development | M,O |
| Education of the Gifted | M,O |
| Education—General | M,O |
| Educational Leadership and Administration | M,O |
| Educational Media/Instructional Technology | M |
| English | M |
| Family and Consumer Sciences-General | M |
| Family Nurse Practitioner Studies | M,O |
| Film, Television, and Video Production | M |
| Geographic Information Systems | M,O |
| Geography | M,O |
| Health Education | M |
| History | M |
| Kinesiology and Movement Studies | M |
| Library Science | M |
| Mathematics Education | M |
| Mathematics | M |
| Music Education | M,O |
| Music | M,O |
| Nursing and Healthcare Administration | M,O |
| Nursing Education | M,O |
| Nursing—General | M,O |
| Nutrition | M |
| Occupational Therapy | M |
| Organizational Management | D |
| Physical Therapy | D |
| Psychology—General | M,D,O |
| Reading Education | M |
| School Psychology | M,D,O |
| Social Psychology | M |
| Spanish | M |
| Special Education | M,O |
| Student Affairs | M |
| Urban and Regional Planning | M,O |
| Writing | M |

## UNIVERSITY OF CENTRAL FLORIDA

| | |
|---|---|
| Accounting | M |
| Aerospace/Aeronautical Engineering | M |
| Allopathic Medicine | M,D |
| Anthropology | M |
| Art Education | M,O |
| Art/Fine Arts | M |
| Athletic Training and Sports Medicine | M |
| Biological and Biomedical Sciences—General | M,D,O |
| Business Administration and Management—General | M,D,O |
| Chemistry | M,D,O |
| Civil Engineering | M,D,O |
| Clinical Psychology | M,D |
| Cognitive Sciences | D |
| Communication Disorders | M,O |
| Community College Education | M,O |
| Computer Art and Design | M |
| Computer Engineering | M,D |
| Computer Science | M,D |
| Conservation Biology | M,D,O |
| Counselor Education | M,O |
| Criminal Justice and Criminology | M,D,O |
| Curriculum and Instruction | M,O |
| Economics | M,D |
| Education of the Gifted | M,O |
| Educational Leadership and Administration | M,O |
| Educational Measurement and Evaluation | O |
| Educational Media/Instructional Technology | M,O |
| Electrical Engineering | M,D |
| Elementary Education | M |
| Emergency Management | M,O |
| Engineering and Applied Sciences—General | M,D,O |
| English as a Second Language | M,O |
| English Education | M,O |
| English | M,D,O |
| Entrepreneurship | M,O |
| Environmental Engineering | M,D |
| Exercise and Sports Science | M,O |
| Film, Television, and Video Production | M |
| Foreign Languages Education | M,O |
| Health Informatics | M,O |
| Health Services Management and Hospital Administration | M,O |
| Higher Education | M,O |
| History | M |
| Homeland Security | M,O |
| Hospitality Management | M,D,O |
| Industrial and Organizational Psychology | M,D |
| Industrial/Management Engineering | M,D,O |
| Interdisciplinary Studies | M,O |
| Kinesiology and Movement Studies | M |
| Marriage and Family Therapy | M,O |
| Materials Engineering | M,D |
| Materials Sciences | M,D |
| Mathematics Education | M,O |
| Mathematics | M,D,O |
| Mechanical Engineering | M,D |
| Middle School Education | M,O |
| Modeling and Simulation | M,D,O |
| Music | M |
| Nonprofit Management | M,O |
| Nursing—General | M,D,O |
| Optical Sciences | M,D |
| Photonics | M,D |
| Physical Therapy | D |
| Physics | M,D |
| Physiology | M,O |
| Psychology—General | M,D |
| Public Administration | M,O |
| Public Affairs | D |
| Reading Education | M,O |
| Real Estate | M |
| School Psychology | O |
| Science Education | M,O |
| Social Sciences Education | M,O |
| Social Work | M,O |
| Sociology | M,D |
| Spanish | M |
| Special Education | M,O |
| Sports Management | M |
| Structural Engineering | M,D,O |
| Student Affairs | M,O |
| Theater | M |
| Transportation and Highway Engineering | M,D,O |
| Travel and Tourism | M,D,O |
| Urban and Regional Planning | M,O |
| Vocational and Technical Education | M,O |

## UNIVERSITY OF CENTRAL MISSOURI

| | |
|---|---|
| Accounting | M,D,O |
| Aerospace/Aeronautical Engineering | M,D,O |
| Applied Mathematics | M,D,O |
| Biological and Biomedical Sciences—General | M,D,O |
| Business Administration and Management—General | M,D,O |
| Communication Disorders | M,D,O |
| Communication—General | M,D,O |
| Computer Science | M,D,O |
| Counseling Psychology | M,D,O |
| Counselor Education | M,D,O |
| Criminal Justice and Criminology | M,D,O |
| Early Childhood Education | M,D,O |
| Education—General | M,D,O |
| Educational Leadership and Administration | M,D,O |
| Educational Media/Instructional Technology | M,D,O |
| Elementary Education | M,D,O |
| English as a Second Language | M,D,O |
| English | M,D,O |
| Environmental and Occupational Health | M,D,O |
| Environmental Management and Policy | M,D,O |
| Finance and Banking | M,D,O |
| Gerontology | M,D,O |
| History | M,D,O |
| Human Services | M,D,O |
| Industrial and Manufacturing Management | M,D,O |
| Industrial Hygiene | M,D,O |
| Information Science | M,D,O |
| Kinesiology and Movement Studies | M,D,O |
| Library Science | M,D,O |
| Management Information Systems | M,D,O |
| Management of Technology | M,D,O |
| Marketing | M,D,O |
| Mathematics | M,D,O |
| Music | M,D,O |
| Nursing—General | M,D,O |
| Psychology—General | M,D,O |
| Reading Education | M,D,O |
| Sociology | M,D,O |
| Special Education | M,D,O |
| Student Affairs | M,D,O |
| Theater | M,D,O |
| Vocational and Technical Education | M,D,O |

## UNIVERSITY OF CENTRAL OKLAHOMA

| | |
|---|---|
| Addictions/Substance Abuse Counseling | M |
| Adult Education | M |
| Applied Arts and Design—General | M |
| Applied Mathematics | M |
| Athletic Training and Sports Medicine | M |
| Biological and Biomedical Sciences—General | M |
| Biomedical Engineering | M |
| Business Analytics | M |
| Child and Family Studies | M |
| Communication Disorders | M |
| Computational Sciences | M |
| Computer Science | M |
| Counseling Psychology | M |
| Counselor Education | M |
| Criminal Justice and Criminology | M |
| Early Childhood Education | M |
| Education of Students with Severe/Multiple Disabilities | M |
| Education—General | M |
| Educational Leadership and Administration | M |
| Educational Media/Instructional Technology | M |
| Electrical Engineering | M |
| Elementary Education | M |
| Engineering and Applied Sciences—General | M |
| Engineering Physics | M |
| English as a Second Language | M |
| English | M |
| Exercise and Sports Science | M |
| Experimental Psychology | M |
| Family and Consumer Sciences-General | M |
| Forensic Psychology | M |
| Forensic Sciences | M |
| Foundations and Philosophy of Education | M |
| Gerontology | M |
| Health Promotion | M |
| History | M |
| Human Development | M |
| Interdisciplinary Studies | M |
| Liberal Studies | M |
| Library Science | M |
| Marriage and Family Therapy | M |
| Mathematics | M |
| Mechanical Engineering | M |
| Museum Studies | M |
| Music Education | M |
| Music | M |
| Nonprofit Management | M |
| Nursing—General | M |
| Nutrition | M |
| Physics | M |
| Political Science | M |
| Psychology—General | M |
| Public Administration | M |
| Reading Education | M |
| Rhetoric | M |
| School Psychology | M |
| Secondary Education | M |
| Sociology | M |
| Special Education | M |
| Statistics | M |
| Student Affairs | M |
| Urban and Regional Planning | M |
| Writing | M |

## UNIVERSITY OF CHARLESTON

| | |
|---|---|
| Accounting | M |
| Business Administration and Management—General | M |
| Forensic Sciences | M |
| Legal and Justice Studies | M |
| Management Strategy and Policy | M |
| Organizational Management | D |
| Pharmacy | D |
| Physician Assistant Studies | M |

## UNIVERSITY OF CHICAGO

| | |
|---|---|
| Accounting | M,O |
| Allopathic Medicine | D |
| Anatomy | D |
| Anthropology | D |
| Applied Mathematics | D |
| Applied Statistics | M |
| Archaeology | D |
| Art History | M,D |
| Art/Fine Arts | M |
| Asian Languages | D |
| Asian Studies | M,D |
| Astronomy | D |
| Astrophysics | D |
| Atmospheric Sciences | D |
| Bioengineering | D |
| Bioinformatics | M |
| Biological and Biomedical Sciences—General | D |
| Biophysics | D |
| Business Administration and Management—General | M,D,O |
| Cancer Biology/Oncology | D |
| Cell Biology | D |
| Chemistry | D |
| Classics | M,D |
| Comparative Literature | M,D |
| Computational Sciences | M |
| Computer Science | M,D |
| Developmental Biology | D |
| Ecology | D |
| Economics | M,D,O |
| Emergency Management | M |
| English | M,D |
| Entrepreneurship | M,O |
| Environmental Management and Policy | M |
| Environmental Sciences | M |
| Ethics | D |
| Evolutionary Biology | D |
| Film, Television, and Video Theory and Criticism | D |
| Finance and Banking | M,O |
| French | D |
| Gender Studies | M |
| Genetics | D |
| Genomic Sciences | D |
| Geophysics | D |
| Geosciences | D |
| German | M,D |
| Health Promotion | M,D |
| Health Services Management and Hospital Administration | M,O |
| History | D |
| Human Development | D |
| Human Genetics | D |
| Humanities | M |
| Immunology | D |
| Industrial and Manufacturing Management | M,O |
| International Affairs | M |
| International Business | M,O |
| Internet and Interactive Multimedia | M |
| Italian | D |
| Latin American Studies | M |
| Law | M,D |
| Liberal Studies | M |
| Linguistics | M,D |
| Management Strategy and Policy | M,O |
| Marketing | M,O |
| Mathematical and Computational Finance | M |
| Mathematics | D |
| Media Studies | M,D |
| Medical Physics | D |
| Medieval and Renaissance Studies | D |
| Microbiology | D |
| Molecular Biology | D |
| Molecular Biophysics | D |
| Music | M,D |
| Near and Middle Eastern Languages | D |
| Near and Middle Eastern Studies | M,D |
| Neurobiology | D |
| Neuroscience | D |
| Nutrition | D |
| Organizational Behavior | M,O |
| Paleontology | D |
| Pastoral Ministry and Counseling | M |
| Philosophy | M,D |
| Physics | M,D |
| Planetary and Space Sciences | D |
| Political Science | D |
| Psychology—General | D |
| Public Policy | M,D |
| Religion | M,D |
| Romance Languages | M,D |
| Science Education | D |
| Slavic Languages | M |
| Social Sciences | M,D |
| Social Work | M,D |
| Sociology | D |
| Spanish | D |
| Statistics | M,D,O |
| Systems Biology | D |
| Theater | M |
| Theology | D |
| Urban Education | M |
| Writing | M |

## UNIVERSITY OF CINCINNATI

| | |
|---|---|
| Accounting | M,D |
| Acute Care/Critical Care Nursing | M,D |
| Addictions/Substance Abuse Counseling | M,D,O |
| Adult Nursing | M,D |
| Aerospace/Aeronautical Engineering | M,D |
| Allopathic Medicine | D |
| Analytical Chemistry | M,D |
| Anthropology | M |
| Applied Arts and Design—General | M |
| Applied Economics | M |
| Applied Mathematics | M,D |
| Architecture | M |
| Art Education | M |
| Art History | M |
| Art/Fine Arts | M |
| Arts Administration | M,D |
| Biochemistry | M,D |
| Bioinformatics | D,O |
| Biological and Biomedical Sciences—General | M,D,O |
| Biomedical Engineering | M,D |
| Biophysics | D |
| Biostatistics | M,D |
| Business Administration and Management—General | M,D |
| Business Analytics | M,D |
| Cancer Biology/Oncology | D |
| Cell Biology | D |
| Chemical Engineering | M,D |
| Chemistry | M,D |
| Civil Engineering | M,D |
| Classics | M,D |
| Clinical Psychology | D |
| Communication Disorders | M,D |
| Communication—General | M |
| Computer Engineering | M,D |
| Computer Science | M,D |
| Counselor Education | M,D,O |
| Criminal Justice and Criminology | M,D |
| Curriculum and Instruction | M,D |
| Developmental Biology | D |
| Economics | D |
| Education—General | M,D,O |
| Educational Leadership and Administration | M,D,O |
| Electrical Engineering | M,D |
| Engineering and Applied Sciences—General | M,D |
| English as a Second Language | M,D |
| English | M,D |
| Environmental and Occupational Health | M,D |
| Environmental Engineering | M,D |
| Environmental Sciences | M,D |
| Epidemiology | M,D |
| Ergonomics and Human Factors | M,D |
| Experimental Psychology | D |
| Finance and Banking | M,D |
| Foundations and Philosophy of Education | M,D |
| French | M,D |
| Genetic Counseling | M |
| Genomic Sciences | M,D |
| Geography | M,D |
| Geology | M,D |

| | |
|---|---|
| German | M,D |
| Gerontological Nursing | M,D |
| Graphic Design | M |
| Health Education | M,D |
| Health Informatics | M |
| Health Physics/Radiological Health | M |
| Health Promotion | M,D |
| Health Services Research | M |
| History | M,D |
| Human Resources Management | M |
| Immunology | M,D |
| Industrial and Labor Relations | M |
| Industrial and Manufacturing Management | D |
| Industrial Design | M |
| Industrial Hygiene | M,D |
| Industrial/Management Engineering | M,D |
| Information Science | M,O |
| Inorganic Chemistry | M,D |
| Interdisciplinary Studies | D |
| Interior Design | M |
| Law | M,D |
| Management Information Systems | M,D |
| Marketing | M,D |
| Materials Engineering | M,D |
| Materials Sciences | M,D |
| Maternal and Child/Neonatal Nursing | M,D |
| Mathematics Education | M,D |
| Mathematics | M,D |
| Mechanical Engineering | M,D |
| Mechanics | M,D |
| Medical Imaging | M,D |
| Medical Physics | M |
| Microbiology | M,D |
| Molecular Biology | M,D |
| Molecular Genetics | M,D |
| Molecular Medicine | D |
| Molecular Toxicology | M,D |
| Music Education | M |
| Music | M,D,O |
| Neuroscience | D |
| Nuclear Engineering | M,D |
| Nurse Anesthesia | M,D |
| Nurse Midwifery | M,D |
| Nursing and Healthcare Administration | M,D |
| Nursing—General | M,D |
| Nutrition | M |
| Occupational Health Nursing | M,D |
| Organic Chemistry | M,D |
| Organizational Management | M |
| Pathobiology | D |
| Pathology | D |
| Pediatric Nursing | M,D |
| Pharmaceutical Sciences | M,D |
| Pharmacology | D |
| Pharmacy | D |
| Philosophy | M,D |
| Physical Chemistry | M,D |
| Physical Therapy | D |
| Physics | M,D |
| Political Science | M,D |
| Psychology—General | D |
| Public Health—General | M,D |
| Reading Education | M,D |
| Romance Languages | M,D |
| School Psychology | D,O |
| Social Work | M |
| Sociology | M,D |
| Spanish | M,D |
| Special Education | M,D |
| Sports Management | M |
| Statistics | M,D |
| Systems Biology | D |
| Taxation | M |
| Textile Design | M |
| Theater | M,D |
| Urban and Regional Planning | M |
| Women's Health Nursing | M,D |
| Women's Studies | M,O |

## UNIVERSITY OF COLORADO BOULDER

| | |
|---|---|
| Advertising and Public Relations | M,D |
| Aerospace/Aeronautical Engineering | M,D |
| Anthropology | M,D |
| Applied Mathematics | M,D |
| Architectural Engineering | M,D |
| Art History | M |
| Art/Fine Arts | M |
| Asian Studies | M,D |
| Astrophysics | M,D |
| Atmospheric Sciences | M,D |
| Biochemistry | M,D |
| Business Administration and Management—General | M,D |
| Cell Biology | M,D |
| Chemical Engineering | M,D |
| Chemistry | M,D |
| Chinese | M,D |
| Civil Engineering | M,D |
| Classics | M,D |
| Communication Disorders | M,D |
| Communication—General | M,D |
| Computer Engineering | M,D |
| Computer Science | M,D |
| Curriculum and Instruction | M,D |
| Dance | M,D |
| Developmental Biology | M,D |
| East European and Russian Studies | M |
| Ecology | M,D |
| Economics | M,D |
| Education—General | M,D |
| Educational Measurement and Evaluation | D |
| Educational Policy | M,D |
| Educational Psychology | M,D |
| Electrical Engineering | M,D |
| Engineering and Applied Sciences—General | M,D |
| Engineering Management | M |
| English | M,D |
| Environmental Engineering | M,D |
| Environmental Management and Policy | M,D |
| Ethnic Studies | D |
| Evolutionary Biology | M,D |
| Film, Television, and Video Production | M |
| French | M,D |
| Geography | M,D |
| Geology | M,D |
| Geophysics | M,D |
| German | M |
| Hispanic and Latin American Languages | M,D |
| History | M,D |
| Information Science | D |
| Internet and Interactive Multimedia | D |
| Japanese | M,D |
| Journalism | M,D |
| Kinesiology and Movement Studies | M,D |
| Law | D |
| Linguistics | M,D |
| Mass Communication | M,D |
| Materials Engineering | M,D |
| Materials Sciences | M,D |
| Mathematical Physics | M,D |
| Mathematics | M,D |
| Mechanical Engineering | M,D |
| Media Studies | M,D |
| Molecular Biology | M,D |
| Multilingual and Multicultural Education | M,D |
| Museum Studies | M |
| Music Education | M,D |
| Music | M,D |
| Oceanography | M,D |
| Organizational Management | |
| Philosophy | M,D |
| Photography | M |
| Physics | M,D |
| Physiology | M,D |
| Plasma Physics | M,D |
| Political Science | M,D |
| Psychology—General | M,D |
| Religion | M |
| Sociology | D |
| Spanish | M,D |
| Telecommunications Management | M |
| Telecommunications | M |
| Theater | M,D |
| Writing | M,D |

## UNIVERSITY OF COLORADO COLORADO SPRINGS

| | |
|---|---|
| Adult Nursing | M,D |
| Aerospace/Aeronautical Engineering | M,D |
| Business Administration and Management—General | M |
| Communication—General | M |
| Computer and Information Systems Security | M,D |
| Counselor Education | M,D |
| Criminal Justice and Criminology | M |
| Curriculum and Instruction | M,D |
| Education—General | M,D |
| Educational Leadership and Administration | M,D |
| Energy and Power Engineering | M,D |
| Engineering and Applied Sciences—General | M,D |
| English as a Second Language | M,D |
| Geography | M |
| Gerontological Nursing | M,D |
| History | M |
| Human Services | M,D |
| Interdisciplinary Studies | M |
| Mathematics | D |
| Nursing—General | M,D |
| Psychology—General | M,D |
| Public Administration | M |
| Public Affairs | M |
| Sociology | M |
| Software Engineering | M,D |
| Special Education | M,D |
| Systems Engineering | M,D |

## UNIVERSITY OF COLORADO DENVER

| | |
|---|---|
| Accounting | M |
| Adult Education | M |
| Adult Nursing | M,D |
| Allopathic Medicine | D |
| American Studies | M |
| Anatomy | M,D |
| Anesthesiologist Assistant Studies | M |
| Anthropology | M |
| Applied Mathematics | M,D |
| Applied Science and Technology | M |
| Applied Statistics | M,D |
| Archaeology | M |
| Architectural History | D |
| Architecture | M |
| Art/Fine Arts | M,O |
| Biochemistry | D |
| Bioengineering | M,D |
| Bioinformatics | D |
| Biological and Biomedical Sciences—General | M,D |
| Biological Anthropology | M |
| Biophysics | M |
| Biostatistics | M,D |
| Business Administration and Management—General | M |
| Cancer Biology/Oncology | D |
| Cell Biology | M,D |
| Chemistry | M |
| Child and Family Studies | M,D |
| Civil Engineering | M,D |
| Clinical Laboratory Sciences/Medical Technology | M,D |
| Clinical Psychology | M,D |
| Clinical Research | M,D |
| Communication—General | M |
| Community Health | M,D,O |
| Computational Biology | M,D |
| Computational Sciences | M,D |
| Computer Science | M,D |
| Corporate and Organizational Communication | M |
| Counseling Psychology | M |
| Counselor Education | M |
| Criminal Justice and Criminology | M,D |
| Data Science/Data Analytics | M |
| Demography and Population Studies | D |
| Dentistry | D,O |
| Developmental Biology | M,D |
| Distance Education Development | M |
| Early Childhood Education | M,D |
| Ecology | M |
| Economic Development | M |
| Economics | M |
| Education—General | M,D,O |
| Educational Leadership and Administration | M,D,O |
| Educational Measurement and Evaluation | M,D |
| Educational Media/Instructional Technology | M |
| Educational Policy | M,D,O |
| Electrical Engineering | M,D |
| Elementary Education | M |
| Emergency Management | M,D |
| Energy Management and Policy | M |
| Engineering and Applied Sciences—General | M,D |
| English Education | M |
| English | M |
| Entertainment Management | M |
| Entrepreneurship | M |
| Environmental and Occupational Health | M |
| Environmental Engineering | M,D |
| Environmental Law | M,D |
| Environmental Management and Policy | M,D,O |
| Environmental Sciences | M |
| Epidemiology | M,D |
| Ethnic Studies | M,O |
| Family and Consumer Sciences-General | M,D |
| Family Nurse Practitioner Studies | M,D |
| Finance and Banking | M |
| Forensic Sciences | M |
| Gender Studies | M,O |
| Genetic Counseling | M |
| Genetics | D |
| Genomic Sciences | D |
| Geographic Information Systems | M,D |
| Geotechnical Engineering | M,D |
| Hazardous Materials Management | M |
| Health Education | M,D |
| Health Informatics | M |
| Health Psychology | D |
| Health Services Management and Hospital Administration | M |
| Health Services Research | M,D |
| Historic Preservation | M |
| History | M |
| Homeland Security | M,D |
| Human Development | M,D |
| Human Resources Management | M |
| Humanities | M,O |
| Hydraulics | M,D |
| Hydrology | M,D |
| Immunology | D |
| Information Science | M,D |
| Insurance | M |
| International Affairs | M,O |
| International Business | M |
| International Health | M |
| Landscape Architecture | M |
| Linguistics | M |
| Management Information Systems | M,D |
| Management of Technology | M |
| Management Strategy and Policy | M |
| Marketing | M |
| Marriage and Family Therapy | M |
| Mathematics Education | M,D |
| Mathematics | M,D |
| Mechanical Engineering | M |
| Mechanics | M |
| Media Studies | M |
| Medical Informatics | M,D |
| Microbiology | D |
| Military and Defense Studies | M,D |
| Molecular Biology | D |
| Molecular Genetics | D |
| Multilingual and Multicultural Education | M |
| Music | M |
| Neuroscience | D |
| Nonprofit Management | M,D |
| Nurse Midwifery | M,D |
| Nursing and Healthcare Administration | M,D |
| Nursing—General | M,D |
| Operations Research | M,D |
| Oral and Dental Sciences | D,O |
| Pediatric Nursing | M,D |
| Pharmaceutical Sciences | D |
| Pharmacology | D |
| Pharmacy | D |
| Physical Therapy | D |
| Physician Assistant Studies | M |
| Political Science | M,D |
| Psychiatric Nursing | M,D |
| Public Administration | M,D |
| Public Affairs | M,D |
| Public Health—General | M,D |
| Public History | M |
| Reading Education | M |
| Rehabilitation Sciences | D |
| Risk Management | M |
| School Psychology | M,D |
| Science Education | M,D |
| Secondary Education | M |
| Sociology | M,O |
| Spanish | M |
| Special Education | M,D |
| Sports Management | M |
| Statistics | M,D |
| Structural Engineering | M,D |
| Sustainability Management | M |
| Sustainable Development | M,D |
| Systems Biology | M,D |
| Taxation | M |
| Toxicology | D |
| Transportation and Highway Engineering | M,D |
| Urban and Regional Planning | M,D |
| Urban Design | M,D |
| Water Resources | M |
| Western European Studies | M |
| Women's Health Nursing | M,D |
| Women's Studies | M,O |
| Writing | M |

## UNIVERSITY OF CONNECTICUT

| | |
|---|---|
| Accounting | M,D |
| Adult Education | M,O |
| Agricultural Economics and Agribusiness | M,D |
| Agricultural Education | M,D |
| Agricultural Sciences—General | M,D |
| Agronomy and Soil Sciences | M,D |
| Animal Sciences | M,D |
| Anthropology | M,D |
| Applied Arts and Design—General | M |
| Applied Mathematics | M |
| Biochemical Engineering | M,D |
| Biomedical Engineering | M,D |
| Biophysics | M,D |
| Biopsychology | M,D |
| Botany | M,D |
| Business Administration and Management—General | M,D |
| Business Analytics | M,D |
| Cell Biology | M,D |
| Chemical Engineering | M,D |
| Chemistry | M,D |
| Child and Family Studies | M,D |
| Civil Engineering | M,D |
| Clinical Psychology | M,D |
| Cognitive Sciences | M,D |
| Communication Disorders | M,D |
| Communication—General | M,D |
| Computer Engineering | M,D |
| Computer Science | M,D |
| Counseling Psychology | M,D |
| Counselor Education | M,D |
| Curriculum and Instruction | M,D |
| Developmental Biology | M,D |
| Developmental Psychology | M,D |
| Ecology | M,D |
| Economics | M,D |
| Education of the Gifted | O |
| Education—General | M,D |
| Educational Leadership and Administration | M |
| Educational Media/Instructional Technology | M,D |
| Educational Psychology | M,D,O |
| Electrical Engineering | M,D |
| Elementary Education | M,D |
| Engineering and Applied Sciences—General | M,D |
| English Education | M,D |
| English | M,D |
| Environmental and Occupational Health | O |
| Environmental Engineering | M,D |
| Exercise and Sports Science | M,D |
| Experimental Psychology | M,D |
| Family Nurse Practitioner Studies | M |
| Finance and Banking | M,D,O |
| Foreign Languages Education | M,D |
| Genetics | M,D |
| Genomic Sciences | M,D |
| Geography | M,D |
| Geology | M,D |
| Gerontological Nursing | M,O |
| Health Services Management and Hospital Administration | M,D |
| Higher Education | M |
| History | M,D |
| Human Development | M,D |
| Human Resources Management | M,D |
| Industrial and Organizational Psychology | M,D |
| International Affairs | M |
| Jewish Studies | M,D |
| Landscape Architecture | M,D |
| Latin American Studies | M |
| Law | D |
| Linguistics | M,D |
| Management Information Systems | M,D |
| Marketing | M,D |
| Materials Engineering | M |
| Materials Sciences | M,D |
| Maternal and Child/Neonatal Nursing | M,O |

*M—masters degree; D—doctorate; O—other advanced degree; *—Close-Up and/or Display*

Mathematical and Computational Finance M
Mathematics Education M,D
Mechanical Engineering M,D
Medicinal and Pharmaceutical Chemistry M,D
Medieval and Renaissance Studies M,D
Microbiology M,D
Molecular Biology M,D
Multilingual and Multicultural Education M,D
Music Education M,D
Music M,D
Natural Resources M,D
Neurobiology M,D
Neuroscience M,D
Nonprofit Management M,O
Nursing—General M,D,O
Nutrition M,D
Pathobiology M,D
Pharmaceutical Sciences M,D
Pharmacology M,D
Pharmacy D
Philosophy M,D
Physical Therapy D
Physics M,D
Physiology M,D
Plant Sciences M,D
Political Science M,D
Polymer Science and Engineering M,D
Project Management M,D
Psychology—General M,D
Public Administration M
Quantitative Analysis M,O
Reading Education M,D
Risk Management M,D
Science Education M,D
Secondary Education M,D
Social Psychology M,D
Social Sciences Education M,D
Social Work M,D
Sociology M,D
Software Engineering M,D
Sports Management M
Statistics M,D
Structural Biology M,D
Theater M
Toxicology M,D

## UNIVERSITY OF CONNECTICUT HEALTH CENTER

Allopathic Medicine D
Anatomy D
Biochemistry D
Biological and Biomedical Sciences—General D
Cell Biology D
Clinical Research M
Dentistry D,O
Developmental Biology D
Genetics D
Immunology D
Molecular Biology D
Neuroscience D
Oral and Dental Sciences M
Public Health—General M

## UNIVERSITY OF DALLAS

Accounting M,D
Business Administration and Management—General M,D
Business Analytics M,D
Computer and Information Systems Security M,D
Entertainment Management M,D
Finance and Banking M,D
Health Services Management and Hospital Administration M,D
Human Resources Management M,D
International Business M,D
Logistics M,D
Management Information Systems M,D
Management of Technology M,D
Management Strategy and Policy M,D
Marketing M,D
Organizational Management M,D
Pastoral Ministry and Counseling M
Project Management M,D
Sports Management M,D
Supply Chain Management M,D

## UNIVERSITY OF DAYTON

Accounting M
Aerospace/Aeronautical Engineering M,D
Applied Mathematics M
Art/Fine Arts M
Biochemistry M
Bioengineering M
Biological and Biomedical Sciences—General M,D
Business Administration and Management—General M
Chemical Engineering M
Chemistry M
Civil Engineering M
Clinical Psychology M,O
Communication—General M
Computer and Information Systems Security M
Computer Engineering M,D
Computer Science M
Counseling Psychology M,O
Counselor Education M,O
Cultural Studies M
Early Childhood Education M
Educational Leadership and Administration M,D,O
Educational Media/Instructional Technology M
Electrical Engineering M,D
Elementary Education M
Engineering Management M
English as a Second Language M
English M
Environmental Engineering M
Environmental Management and Policy M,D
Exercise and Sports Science M
Finance and Banking M
Foreign Languages Education M
Geotechnical Engineering M
Human Development M,O
Interdisciplinary Studies M
Law M,D
Marketing M
Materials Engineering M,D
Mathematical and Computational Finance M
Mathematics Education M
Mechanical Engineering M,D
Mechanics M
Middle School Education M
Music Education M
Optical Sciences M,D
Pastoral Ministry and Counseling M,D
Photonics M,D
Physical Education M
Physical Therapy D
Physician Assistant Studies M
Psychology—General M
Public Administration M
Reading Education M
Rhetoric M
School Psychology M,O
Secondary Education M
Structural Engineering M
Student Affairs M,O
Theology M,D
Transportation and Highway Engineering M
Water Resources Engineering M
Writing M

## UNIVERSITY OF DELAWARE

Accounting M
Adult Nursing M,O
Agricultural Economics and Agribusiness M
Agricultural Education M
Agricultural Sciences—General M,D
Agronomy and Soil Sciences M,D
American Studies M
Animal Sciences M,D
Applied Arts and Design—General M
Applied Mathematics M,D
Art History M,D
Art/Fine Arts M
Astronomy M,D
Biochemistry M,D
Biological and Biomedical Sciences—General M,D
Biotechnology M,D
Business Administration and Management—General M,D
Business Education M,D
Cancer Biology/Oncology M,D
Cell Biology M,D
Chemical Engineering M,D
Chemistry M,D
Child and Family Studies M,D
Chinese M
Civil Engineering M,D
Clinical Psychology D
Clothing and Textiles M
Cognitive Sciences M,D
Communication Disorders M
Communication—General M
Computer Engineering M,D
Computer Science M,D
Criminal Justice and Criminology M,D
Curriculum and Instruction M,D,O
Developmental Biology M,D
Ecology M,D
Economics M,D
Education—General M,D,O
Educational Leadership and Administration M,D,O
Electrical Engineering M,D
Emergency Management M,D
Energy Management and Policy M,D
Engineering and Applied Sciences—General M,D
English as a Second Language M,D,O
English M,D
Entomology M,D
Entrepreneurship M,D
Environmental Engineering M,D
Environmental Management and Policy M,D
Evolutionary Biology M,D
Family Nurse Practitioner Studies M,O
Finance and Banking M
Fish, Game, and Wildlife Management M,D
Food Science and Technology M,D
Foreign Languages Education M
French M
Genetics M,D
Geography M,D
Geology M,D
Geotechnical Engineering M,D
German M
Gerontological Nursing M,O
Health Promotion M
Higher Education M,D,O
Historic Preservation M,D
History of Science and Technology M,D
History M,D
HIV/AIDS Nursing M,O
Horticulture M
Hospitality Management M
Human Development M,D
Information Science M,D
International Affairs M,D
Kinesiology and Movement Studies M,D
Liberal Studies M
Linguistics M,D
Management Information Systems M,D
Management of Technology M
Marine Affairs M,D
Marine Geology M,D
Marine Sciences M,D
Materials Engineering M,D
Materials Sciences M,D
Maternal and Child/Neonatal Nursing M,O
Mathematics M,D
Mechanical Engineering M,D
Microbiology M,D
Molecular Biology M,D
Multilingual and Multicultural Education M,D,O
Music Education M
Music M
Natural Resources M
Neuroscience D
Nursing and Healthcare Administration M,O
Nursing—General M,O
Nutrition M
Ocean Engineering M,D
Oceanography M,D
Oncology Nursing M,O
Operations Research M
Pediatric Nursing M,O
Physical Therapy D
Physics M,D
Physiology M,D
Plant Sciences M,D
Political Science M,D
Psychiatric Nursing M,O
Psychology—General D
Public Administration M
Public Policy M,D
School Psychology M,D,O
Social Psychology D
Sociology M,D
Spanish M
Statistics M
Structural Engineering M,D
Theater M
Translation and Interpretation M
Transportation and Highway Engineering M,D
Urban Studies M,D
Water Resources Engineering M,D
Women's Health Nursing M,O

## UNIVERSITY OF DENVER

Accounting M
Anthropology M
Archaeology M
Art Education M,O
Art History M
Art/Fine Arts M
Bioengineering M,D
Biological and Biomedical Sciences—General M,D
Business Administration and Management—General M
Business Analytics M
Cell Biology M,D
Chemistry M,D
Child and Family Studies M,D,O
Clinical Psychology M,D,O
Communication—General M,O
Computer and Information Systems Security M,D
Computer Art and Design M
Computer Engineering M,D
Computer Science M,D
Conflict Resolution and Mediation/Peace Studies M,D,O
Construction Management M
Counseling Psychology M,D,O
Criminal Justice and Criminology M,O
Cultural Anthropology M
Cultural Studies M,O
Curriculum and Instruction M,D,O
Data Science/Data Analytics M,D
Developmental Psychology D
Early Childhood Education M,D,O
Ecology M,D
Economics M
Education—General M,D,O
Educational Leadership and Administration M,D,O
Educational Measurement and Evaluation M,D,O
Educational Policy M,D,O
Electrical Engineering M,D
Emergency Management M,O
Engineering and Applied Sciences—General M,D
Engineering Management M,D
English M,D
Environmental Management and Policy M,O
Evolutionary Biology M,D
Finance and Banking M
Forensic Psychology M,D,O
Geographic Information Systems M,D,O
Geography M,D
Health Services Management and Hospital Administration M,O
Higher Education M,D,O
History M,O
Homeland Security M,D,O
Human Resources Management M,O
Information Science M,O
International Affairs M,D,O
International Development M,D,O
International Health M,D,O
Law M,D,O
Legal and Justice Studies M,O
Library Science M,D,O
Marketing M
Marriage and Family Therapy M,D,O
Mass Communication M
Materials Engineering M,D
Materials Sciences M,D
Mathematics M,D
Mechanical Engineering M,D
Media Studies M
Molecular Biology M,D
Museum Studies M
Music Education M,O
Music M,O
Organizational Management M,O
Philanthropic Studies M,O
Physics M,D
Project Management M,O
Psychology—General M,D,O
Public Policy M
Real Estate M
Religion M,D,O
School Psychology M,D,O
Social Psychology D
Social Work M,D,O
Special Education M,D,O
Sport Psychology M,D,O
Taxation M
Theology D,O
Translation and Interpretation M,O
Writing M,D,O

## UNIVERSITY OF DETROIT MERCY

Accounting M,O
Addictions/Substance Abuse Counseling M,D,O
Allied Health—General M,D,O
Architectural Engineering M
Business Administration and Management—General M,O
Chemistry M,D
Civil Engineering M,D
Clinical Psychology M,D,O
Computer and Information Systems Security M,D,O
Computer Engineering M,D
Computer Science M,D,O
Criminal Justice and Criminology M,D,O
Curriculum and Instruction M,D,O
Dentistry M,D,O
Economics M,D,O
Educational Leadership and Administration M,D,O
Electrical Engineering M,D
Engineering and Applied Sciences—General M,D
Engineering Management M,D
Environmental Engineering M,D
Ethics M,O
Family Nurse Practitioner Studies M,D,O
Finance and Banking M,D,O
Forensic Sciences M,O
Health Services Management and Hospital Administration M,D,O
Industrial and Organizational Psychology M,D,O
Industrial Design M,D
Law D
Liberal Studies M,D,O
Management Information Systems M,D,O
Management Strategy and Policy M,O
Mathematics Education M,D
Mechanical Engineering M,D
Nurse Anesthesia M,D,O
Nursing Education M,D,O
Nursing—General M,D,O
Oral and Dental Sciences M,D,O
Physician Assistant Studies M,D,O
Religious Education M,D,O
School Psychology M,D,O
Software Engineering M,D
Special Education M,D,O
Urban and Regional Planning M

## UNIVERSITY OF DUBUQUE

Business Administration and Management—General M
Communication—General M
Theology M,D

## UNIVERSITY OF EAST-WEST MEDICINE

Acupuncture and Oriental Medicine M,D

## UNIVERSITY OF EVANSVILLE

Athletic Training and Sports Medicine M
Health Services Management and Hospital Administration M
Physical Therapy D
Public Administration M

## UNIVERSITY OF FAIRFAX

Business Administration and Management—General M,D
Computer and Information Systems Security M,D
Computer Science M,D
Information Science M,D
Project Management M,D

## THE UNIVERSITY OF FINDLAY

Accounting M,D
Athletic Training and Sports Medicine M,D
Business Administration and Management—General M,D
Education—General M,D
Educational Leadership and Administration M,D
Educational Media/Instructional Technology M,D
English as a Second Language M,D
Environmental Management and Policy M,D
Health Informatics M,D
Health Services Management and Hospital Administration M,D
Hospitality Management M,D
Linguistics M,D

| | |
|---|---|
| Mathematics | M,D |
| Occupational Therapy | M,D |
| Pharmacy | M,D |
| Physical Therapy | M,D |
| Physician Assistant Studies | M,D |
| Public Administration | M,D |
| Reading Education | M,D |
| Rhetoric | M,D |
| Science Education | M,D |
| Writing | M,D |

### UNIVERSITY OF FLORIDA

| | |
|---|---|
| Accounting | M,D |
| Advertising and Public Relations | M,D |
| Aerospace/Aeronautical Engineering | M,D |
| Agricultural Economics and Agribusiness | M,D |
| Agricultural Education | M,D |
| Agricultural Engineering | M,D,O |
| Agricultural Sciences—General | M,D,O |
| Agronomy and Soil Sciences | M,D |
| Allied Health—General | M,D,O |
| Allopathic Medicine | D |
| Animal Sciences | M,D |
| Anthropology | M,D |
| Aquaculture | M,D |
| Architecture | M,D |
| Art Education | M,D |
| Art History | M,D |
| Art/Fine Arts | M,D |
| Astronomy | M,D |
| Athletic Training and Sports Medicine | M,D |
| Biochemistry | D |
| Bioengineering | M,D,O |
| Biological and Biomedical Sciences—General | M,D |
| Biomedical Engineering | M,D,O |
| Biostatistics | M,D,O |
| Botany | M,D |
| Business Administration and Management—General | M,D |
| Cell Biology | M,D |
| Chemical Engineering | M,D,O |
| Chemistry | M,D |
| Child Development | M |
| Civil Engineering | M,D |
| Classics | M,D |
| Clinical Laboratory Sciences/Medical Technology | M,D |
| Clinical Psychology | M,D |
| Clinical Research | M,D,O |
| Communication Disorders | M,D |
| Communication—General | M,D |
| Computer Art and Design | M,D |
| Computer Engineering | M,D |
| Computer Science | M,D |
| Construction Management | M,D |
| Counseling Psychology | M,D |
| Counselor Education | M,D,O |
| Criminal Justice and Criminology | M,D |
| Curriculum and Instruction | M,D,O |
| Dentistry | D,O |
| Early Childhood Education | M,D,O |
| Ecology | M,D,O |
| Economics | M,D |
| Education—General | M,D,O |
| Educational Leadership and Administration | M,D,O |
| Educational Measurement and Evaluation | M,D,O |
| Educational Policy | M,D,O |
| Electrical Engineering | M,D |
| Elementary Education | M,D,O |
| Emergency Management | M |
| Engineering and Applied Sciences—General | M,D,O |
| English as a Second Language | M,D,O |
| English Education | M,D,O |
| English | M,D |
| Entrepreneurship | M,D,O |
| Environmental and Occupational Health | M,D,O |
| Environmental Education | M,D,O |
| Environmental Engineering | M,D,O |
| Environmental Law | M,D |
| Epidemiology | M,D,O |
| Exercise and Sports Science | M,D |
| Family and Consumer Sciences-General | M |
| Finance and Banking | M,D,O |
| Fish, Game, and Wildlife Management | M,D,O |
| Food Science and Technology | M,D |
| Foreign Languages Education | M,D |
| Forensic Sciences | M,O |
| Forestry | M,D |
| French | M,D |
| Gender Studies | M,O |
| Genetics | D |
| Geographic Information Systems | M,D |
| Geography | M,D |
| Geology | M,D |
| Geosciences | M,D |
| German | M,D |
| Health Communication | M,D,O |
| Health Education | M,D,O |
| Health Psychology | M,D |
| Health Services Management and Hospital Administration | M,D |
| Health Services Research | M,D |
| Higher Education | M,D,O |
| Historic Preservation | M,D |
| History | M,D |
| Horticulture | M,D |
| Human Resources Management | M,D |
| Hydrology | M,D |
| Immunology | D |
| Industrial/Management Engineering | M,D,O |
| Information Science | M,D |
| Insurance | M,D,O |
| Interdisciplinary Studies | M,D |
| Interior Design | M,D |
| International Affairs | M |
| International Business | M,D |
| International Development | M,D,O |
| International Health | M,D |
| Jewish Studies | M,D |
| Journalism | M,D |
| Kinesiology and Movement Studies | M,D |
| Landscape Architecture | M,D |
| Latin American Studies | M,O |
| Law | M,D |
| Limnology | M,D |
| Linguistics | M,D,O |
| Management Information Systems | M,D,O |
| Marine Sciences | M,D |
| Marketing | M,D |
| Marriage and Family Therapy | M,D,O |
| Mass Communication | M,D |
| Materials Engineering | M,D |
| Materials Sciences | M,D |
| Mathematics Education | M,D,O |
| Mathematics | M,D |
| Mechanical Engineering | M,D |
| Medical Physics | M,D,O |
| Medicinal and Pharmaceutical Chemistry | M,D |
| Microbiology | M,D |
| Molecular Biology | M,D |
| Molecular Genetics | M |
| Museum Studies | M,D |
| Music Education | M,D |
| Music | M,D |
| Natural Resources | M,D |
| Neuroscience | D |
| Nonprofit Management | M |
| Nuclear Engineering | M,D |
| Nursing—General | M,D |
| Nutrition | M,D |
| Occupational Therapy | M |
| Ocean Engineering | M,D |
| Oral and Dental Sciences | M,D,O |
| Pharmaceutical Administration | M,D |
| Pharmaceutical Sciences | M,D |
| Pharmacology | M,D |
| Pharmacy | M,D |
| Philosophy | M,D |
| Physical Education | M,D |
| Physical Therapy | D |
| Physician Assistant Studies | M |
| Physics | M,D |
| Physiology | M,D |
| Plant Biology | M,D |
| Plant Molecular Biology | M,D |
| Plant Pathology | M,D |
| Plant Sciences | D |
| Political Science | M,D,O |
| Psychology—General | M,D |
| Public Affairs | M,D,O |
| Public Health—General | M,D,O |
| Quantitative Analysis | M,D,O |
| Reading Education | M,D,O |
| Real Estate | M,D,O |
| Recreation and Park Management | M,D |
| Rehabilitation Sciences | D |
| Religion | M,D |
| School Psychology | M,D,O |
| Science Education | M,D,O |
| Social Sciences Education | M,D,O |
| Social Sciences | M,D,O |
| Sociology | M,D |
| Spanish | M,D |
| Special Education | M,D,O |
| Sports Management | M,D |
| Statistics | M,D |
| Student Affairs | M,D,O |
| Supply Chain Management | M,D,O |
| Sustainable Development | M,O |
| Systems Engineering | M,D,O |
| Taxation | M,D |
| Telecommunications | M,D |
| Theater | M |
| Toxicology | M,D,O |
| Travel and Tourism | M,D |
| Urban and Regional Planning | M,D |
| Veterinary Medicine | D |
| Veterinary Sciences | M,D,O |
| Water Resources | M,D |
| Women's Studies | M,O |
| Writing | M,D |
| Zoology | M,D |

### UNIVERSITY OF FORT LAUDERDALE

| | |
|---|---|
| Pastoral Ministry and Counseling | M |

### UNIVERSITY OF GEORGIA

| | |
|---|---|
| Accounting | M |
| Adult Education | D,O |
| Agricultural Economics and Agribusiness | M,D |
| Agricultural Sciences—General | M,D |
| Agronomy and Soil Sciences | M,D |
| Analytical Chemistry | M,D |
| Animal Sciences | M,D |
| Anthropology | M,D |
| Applied Economics | M,D |
| Applied Mathematics | M,D |
| Art History | M,D |
| Art/Fine Arts | M,D |
| Artificial Intelligence/Robotics | M |
| Biochemical Engineering | M |
| Biochemistry | M,D |
| Bioinformatics | M,D |
| Biological and Biomedical Sciences—General | D |
| Business Administration and Management—General | M |
| Business Analytics | M |
| Business Education | M,D,O |
| Cell Biology | M,D |
| Chemistry | M,D |
| Child and Family Studies | M |
| Classics | M |
| Clothing and Textiles | M,D |
| Communication Disorders | M,D,O |
| Communication—General | M,D |
| Comparative Literature | M,D |
| Computer Science | M,D |
| Counselor Education | M,D,O |
| Ecology | M,D |
| Economics | M,D |
| Education—General | M,D,O |
| Educational Leadership and Administration | D,O |
| Educational Media/Instructional Technology | M,D,O |
| Educational Policy | D,O |
| Educational Psychology | O |
| English Education | M,D |
| English | M,D |
| Entomology | M,D |
| Environmental and Occupational Health | M,D |
| Environmental Design | M |
| Environmental Engineering | M |
| Family and Consumer Sciences-General | M,D |
| Food Science and Technology | M,D |
| Forestry | M,D |
| French | M,D |
| Genetics | M,D |
| Genomic Sciences | M,D |
| Geography | M,D |
| Geology | M,D |
| German | M |
| Gerontology | O |
| Health Education | M,D |
| Health Promotion | M,D |
| Higher Education | M,D |
| Historic Preservation | M |
| History | M,D |
| Horticulture | M,D |
| Infectious Diseases | D |
| Interior Design | M,D |
| International Affairs | M,D |
| Italian | M,D |
| Journalism | M,D |
| Kinesiology and Movement Studies | M,D |
| Landscape Architecture | M |
| Law | M,D |
| Linguistics | M,D |
| Marine Sciences | M,D |
| Mass Communication | M,D |
| Mathematics Education | M,D,O |
| Mathematics | M,D |
| Microbiology | M,D |
| Molecular Biology | M,D |
| Music Education | M,D |
| Music | M,D |
| Natural Resources | M,D |
| Neuroscience | D |
| Nonprofit Management | M,D,O |
| Nutrition | M,D |
| Pathology | M,D |
| Pharmaceutical Administration | D |
| Pharmaceutical Sciences | M,D |
| Pharmacology | M,D |
| Pharmacy | M,D,O |
| Philosophy | M,D |
| Physical Education | M,D |
| Physics | M,D |
| Physiology | M,D |
| Plant Biology | M,D |
| Plant Pathology | M,D |
| Plant Sciences | M,D |
| Political Science | M,D |
| Portuguese | M,D |
| Psychology—General | D |
| Public Administration | M,D |
| Public Health—General | D |
| Public Policy | M,D |
| Reading Education | M,D |
| Religion | M |
| Science Education | M,D,O |
| Social Work | M,D,O |
| Sociology | M,D |
| Spanish | M,D |
| Special Education | M,D,O |
| Statistics | M,D |
| Student Affairs | M,D,O |
| Sustainable Development | M,D |
| Theater | M,D |
| Veterinary Medicine | M,D |
| Vocational and Technical Education | M,D,O |
| Women's Studies | O |

### UNIVERSITY OF GUAM

| | |
|---|---|
| Art/Fine Arts | M |
| Biological and Biomedical Sciences—General | M |
| Business Administration and Management—General | M |
| Counselor Education | M |
| Education—General | M |
| Educational Leadership and Administration | M |
| English as a Second Language | M |
| English | M |
| Environmental Sciences | M |
| Graphic Design | M |
| Marine Biology | M |
| Pacific Area/Pacific Rim Studies | M |
| Public Administration | M |
| Reading Education | M |
| Secondary Education | M |
| Social Work | M |
| Special Education | M |

### UNIVERSITY OF GUELPH

| | |
|---|---|
| Acute Care/Critical Care Nursing | M,D,O |
| Agricultural Economics and Agribusiness | M,D |
| Agricultural Sciences—General | M,D,O |
| Agronomy and Soil Sciences | M,D |
| Anatomy | M,D |
| Anesthesiologist Assistant Studies | M,D,O |
| Animal Sciences | M,D |
| Anthropology | M,D |
| Applied Mathematics | M,D |
| Applied Psychology | M,D |
| Applied Statistics | M,D |
| Aquaculture | M |
| Art/Fine Arts | M |
| Atmospheric Sciences | M,D |
| Biochemistry | M,D |
| Bioengineering | M,D |
| Biological and Biomedical Sciences—General | M,D |
| Biophysics | M,D |
| Biotechnology | M,D |
| Botany | M,D |
| Business Administration and Management—General | M,D |
| Cardiovascular Sciences | M,D,O |
| Cell Biology | M,D |
| Chemistry | M,D |
| Child and Family Studies | M,D |
| Clinical Psychology | M,D |
| Cognitive Sciences | M,D |
| Comparative Literature | D |
| Computer Science | M,D |
| Consumer Economics | M |
| Criminal Justice and Criminology | M,D |
| Demography and Population Studies | M,D |
| Ecology | M,D |
| Economics | M,D |
| Emergency Medical Services | M,D,O |
| Engineering and Applied Sciences—General | M,D |
| English | M |
| Entomology | M,D |
| Environmental Biology | M,D |
| Environmental Engineering | M,D |
| Environmental Management and Policy | M,D |
| Environmental Sciences | M,D |
| Epidemiology | M,D |
| Evolutionary Biology | M,D |
| Food Science and Technology | M,D |
| French | M |
| Geography | M,D |
| History | M,D |
| Horticulture | M,D |
| Hospitality Management | M |
| Human Development | M,D |
| Immunology | M,D,O |
| Industrial and Organizational Psychology | M,D |
| Infectious Diseases | M,D,O |
| International Development | M,D |
| Landscape Architecture | M |
| Marriage and Family Therapy | M,D |
| Mathematics | M,D |
| Medical Imaging | M,D,O |
| Medieval and Renaissance Studies | D |
| Microbiology | M,D |
| Molecular Biology | M,D |
| Molecular Genetics | M,D |
| Natural Resources | M,D |
| Neuroscience | M,D,O |
| Nutrition | M,D |
| Organizational Management | M |
| Pathology | M,D,O |
| Pharmacology | M,D |
| Philosophy | M,D |
| Physics | M,D |
| Physiology | M,D |
| Plant Pathology | M,D |
| Political Science | M |
| Psychology—General | M,D |
| Public Administration | M |
| Public Policy | M |
| Rural Planning and Studies | M,D |
| Social Psychology | M,D |
| Sociology | M,D |
| Statistics | M,D |
| Theater | M |
| Toxicology | M,D |
| Veterinary Medicine | M,D,O |
| Veterinary Sciences | M,D,O |
| Vision Sciences | M,D,O |
| Water Resources Engineering | M,D |
| Western European Studies | M |
| Zoology | M,D |

### UNIVERSITY OF HARTFORD

| | |
|---|---|
| Accounting | M,O |
| Architecture | M |
| Art/Fine Arts | M |
| Business Administration and Management—General | M |
| Clinical Psychology | M,D |
| Communication—General | M |
| Community Health Nursing | M |
| Early Childhood Education | M |
| Education—General | M,D,O |
| Educational Leadership and Administration | D |
| Elementary Education | M |
| Engineering and Applied Sciences—General | M |
| Music Education | M,D,O |
| Music | M,D,O |
| Neuroscience | M |

*M—masters degree; D—doctorate; O—other advanced degree; *—Close-Up and/or Display*

| | |
|---|---|
| Nursing Education | M |
| Nursing—General | M |
| Organizational Behavior | M |
| Physical Therapy | M,D |
| School Psychology | M |
| Taxation | M,O |

## UNIVERSITY OF HAWAII AT HILO

| | |
|---|---|
| Conservation Biology | M |
| Counseling Psychology | M |
| Cultural Studies | M,D |
| Education—General | M |
| Environmental Sciences | M |
| Foreign Languages Education | M,D |
| Marine Biology | M |
| Nursing—General | D |
| Pharmaceutical Sciences | D |
| Pharmacology | M |
| Pharmacy | D |

## UNIVERSITY OF HAWAII AT MANOA

| | |
|---|---|
| Accounting | M,D |
| Adult Nursing | M,D,O |
| Agricultural Sciences—General | M,D |
| Allopathic Medicine | D |
| American Studies | M,D,O |
| Animal Sciences | M |
| Anthropology | M,D |
| Architecture | D |
| Art History | M |
| Art/Fine Arts | M |
| Asian Languages | M,D |
| Asian Studies | O |
| Astronomy | M,D |
| Bioengineering | M |
| Biological and Biomedical Sciences—General | M,D |
| Botany | M,D |
| Business Administration and Management—General | M |
| Chemistry | M,D |
| Chinese | M,D,O |
| Civil Engineering | M,D |
| Clinical Psychology | M,D,O |
| Communication Disorders | M |
| Communication—General | M,O |
| Community Health Nursing | M,D,O |
| Computer Science | M,D,O |
| Conflict Resolution and Mediation/Peace Studies | M,O |
| Cultural Studies | O |
| Curriculum and Instruction | M,D |
| Dance | M,D |
| Demography and Population Studies | O |
| Developmental Biology | M,D |
| Disability Studies | O |
| Early Childhood Education | M |
| Economics | M,D |
| Education—General | M,D,O |
| Educational Leadership and Administration | M,D |
| Educational Media/Instructional Technology | M,D |
| Educational Policy | D |
| Educational Psychology | M,D |
| Electrical Engineering | M,D |
| Emergency Management | O |
| Engineering and Applied Sciences—General | M,D |
| English as a Second Language | M,D,O |
| English | M,D |
| Entomology | M,D |
| Entrepreneurship | M,O |
| Environmental Engineering | M,D |
| Environmental Management and Policy | M,D,O |
| Epidemiology | D |
| Family Nurse Practitioner Studies | M,D,O |
| Finance and Banking | M,D |
| Food Science and Technology | M |
| Foreign Languages Education | M,D,O |
| Foundations and Philosophy of Education | M,D |
| French | M |
| Genetics | M,D |
| Geochemistry | M,D |
| Geography | M,D,O |
| Geological Engineering | M,D |
| Geology | M,D |
| Geophysics | M,D |
| Historic Preservation | O |
| History | M,D |
| Horticulture | M,D |
| Human Resources Management | M |
| Hydrogeology | M,D |
| Information Science | M,D |
| Information Studies | M,O |
| International Affairs | O |
| International Business | M,D |
| International Development | M,D,O |
| Japanese | M,D,O |
| Kinesiology and Movement Studies | M,D |
| Law | M,D,O |
| Library Science | M,O |
| Linguistics | M,D |
| Management Information Systems | M,D,O |
| Marine Biology | M,D |
| Marine Geology | M,D |
| Marine Sciences | O |
| Marketing | M,D |
| Mathematics | M,D |
| Mechanical Engineering | M,D |
| Medical Microbiology | M,D |
| Meteorology | M,D |
| Microbiology | M,D |
| Molecular Biology | M,D |
| Museum Studies | O |
| Music | M,D |
| Natural Resources | M,D |
| Nursing and Healthcare Administration | M,D,O |
| Nursing—General | M,D,O |
| Nutrition | M,D |
| Ocean Engineering | M,D |
| Oceanography | M,D |
| Organizational Behavior | M |
| Organizational Management | M,D |
| Pacific Area/Pacific Rim Studies | M,O |
| Philosophy | M,D |
| Physics | M,D |
| Physiology | M,D |
| Planetary and Space Sciences | M,D |
| Plant Pathology | M,D |
| Plant Sciences | M,D |
| Political Science | M,D |
| Psychology—General | M,D,O |
| Public Administration | M,O |
| Public Health—General | M,D,O |
| Public Policy | O |
| Real Estate | M |
| Religion | M |
| Reproductive Biology | M,D |
| Social Psychology | M,D,O |
| Social Work | M,D |
| Sociology | M,D |
| Spanish | M |
| Special Education | M,D |
| Speech and Interpersonal Communication | M |
| Sustainable Development | M,D,O |
| Taxation | M |
| Telecommunications | O |
| Theater | M,D |
| Transportation Management | M,D,O |
| Travel and Tourism | M |
| Urban and Regional Planning | M,D,O |
| Women's Studies | O |
| Zoology | M,D |

## UNIVERSITY OF HOLY CROSS

| | |
|---|---|
| Biological and Biomedical Sciences—General | M,D |
| Business Administration and Management—General | M,D |
| Counselor Education | M,D |
| Education—General | M,D |
| Educational Leadership and Administration | M,D |
| Health Services Management and Hospital Administration | M,D |
| Marriage and Family Therapy | M,D |
| Theology | M,D |

## UNIVERSITY OF HOUSTON

| | |
|---|---|
| Accounting | M,D |
| Advertising and Public Relations | M |
| Anthropology | M |
| Applied Economics | M,D |
| Applied Mathematics | M,D |
| Architecture | M,D |
| Art History | M |
| Art/Fine Arts | M |
| Atmospheric Sciences | M,D |
| Biochemistry | M,D |
| Biological and Biomedical Sciences—General | M,D |
| Biomedical Engineering | D |
| Business Administration and Management—General | M,D |
| Chemical Engineering | M,D |
| Chemistry | M,D |
| Civil Engineering | M,D |
| Clinical Psychology | M,D |
| Communication Disorders | M |
| Communication—General | M |
| Comparative Literature | M |
| Computer and Information Systems Security | M |
| Computer Science | M,D |
| Construction Management | M |
| Counseling Psychology | M,D |
| Cultural Studies | M |
| Curriculum and Instruction | M,D |
| Developmental Psychology | M,D |
| Economics | M,D |
| Education—General | M,D |
| Educational Leadership and Administration | M,D |
| Educational Psychology | M,D |
| Electrical Engineering | M,D |
| Engineering and Applied Sciences—General | M,D |
| Environmental Law | M,D |
| Exercise and Sports Science | M,D |
| Family and Consumer Sciences-General | M |
| Family Nurse Practitioner Studies | M |
| Finance and Banking | M |
| Foundations and Philosophy of Education | M,D |
| Geology | M,D |
| Geophysics | M,D |
| Health Communication | M |
| Health Education | M,D |
| Health Law | M,D |
| Higher Education | M,D |
| Hispanic Studies | M,D |
| History | M,D |
| Hospitality Management | M |
| Human Resources Development | M |
| Industrial and Organizational Psychology | M,D |
| Industrial/Management Engineering | M,D |
| Information Science | M,D |
| Intellectual Property Law | M,D |
| Kinesiology and Movement Studies | M,D |
| Law | M,D |
| Linguistics | M,D |
| Logistics | M |
| Marketing | D |
| Mass Communication | M |
| Mathematics | M,D |
| Mechanical Engineering | M,D |
| Music Education | M,D |
| Music | M,D |
| Nursing and Healthcare Administration | M |
| Nursing Education | M |
| Nursing—General | M |
| Nutrition | M,D |
| Optometry | D |
| Petroleum Engineering | M,D |
| Pharmaceutical Administration | M,D |
| Pharmaceutical Sciences | M,D |
| Pharmacology | M,D |
| Pharmacy | M,D |
| Philosophy | M |
| Physical Education | M,D |
| Physics | M,D |
| Planetary and Space Sciences | M,D |
| Political Science | M,D |
| Project Management | M |
| Psychology—General | M,D |
| Public Administration | M,D |
| Public Policy | M |
| Social Psychology | M,D |
| Social Work | M,D |
| Sociology | M,D |
| Spanish | M,D |
| Special Education | M,D |
| Speech and Interpersonal Communication | M |
| Supply Chain Management | M |
| Sustainable Development | M |
| Taxation | M,D |
| Telecommunications | M |
| Theater | M |
| Urban Design | M |
| Vision Sciences | M,D |
| Writing | M,D |

## UNIVERSITY OF HOUSTON–CLEAR LAKE

| | |
|---|---|
| Accounting | M |
| Biological and Biomedical Sciences—General | M |
| Biotechnology | M |
| Business Administration and Management—General | M |
| Chemistry | M |
| Clinical Psychology | M |
| Computer Engineering | M |
| Computer Science | M |
| Counselor Education | M |
| Criminal Justice and Criminology | M |
| Cultural Studies | M |
| Curriculum and Instruction | M |
| Early Childhood Education | M |
| Education—General | M,D |
| Educational Leadership and Administration | M,D |
| Educational Media/Instructional Technology | M |
| English | M |
| Environmental Management and Policy | M |
| Environmental Sciences | M |
| Exercise and Sports Science | M |
| Finance and Banking | M |
| Foundations and Philosophy of Education | M |
| Health Services Management and Hospital Administration | M |
| History | M |
| Human Resources Management | M |
| Humanities | M |
| Information Science | M |
| Library Science | M |
| Management Information Systems | M |
| Marriage and Family Therapy | M |
| Mathematics | M |
| Multilingual and Multicultural Education | M |
| Physics | M |
| Psychology—General | M |
| Reading Education | M |
| School Psychology | M |
| Sociology | M |
| Software Engineering | M |
| Statistics | M |
| Systems Engineering | M |

## UNIVERSITY OF HOUSTON - DOWNTOWN

| | |
|---|---|
| Accounting | M |
| Business Administration and Management—General | M |
| Criminal Justice and Criminology | M |
| Curriculum and Instruction | M |
| Data Science/Data Analytics | M |
| English | M |
| Finance and Banking | M |
| Human Resources Management | M |
| International Business | M |
| Investment Management | M |
| Nonprofit Management | M |
| Project Management | M |
| Rhetoric | M |
| Social Work | M |
| Supply Chain Management | M |
| Technical Communication | M |
| Urban Education | M |

## UNIVERSITY OF HOUSTON–VICTORIA

| | |
|---|---|
| Accounting | M |
| Adult Education | M,O |
| Biological and Biomedical Sciences—General | M |
| Business Administration and Management—General | M |
| Computer Science | M |
| Counseling Psychology | M |
| Counselor Education | M,O |
| Curriculum and Instruction | M,O |
| Economic Development | M |
| Education—General | M,O |
| Educational Leadership and Administration | M,O |
| Educational Media/Instructional Technology | M,O |
| Entrepreneurship | M |
| Finance and Banking | M |
| Forensic Psychology | M |
| Forensic Sciences | M |
| Higher Education | M,O |
| Interdisciplinary Studies | M |
| International Business | M |
| Management Information Systems | M |
| Marketing | M |
| Psychology—General | M |
| Publishing | M |
| Reading Education | M,O |
| School Psychology | M |
| Special Education | M,O |
| Writing | M |

## UNIVERSITY OF IDAHO

| | |
|---|---|
| Accounting | M |
| Agricultural Economics and Agribusiness | M |
| Agronomy and Soil Sciences | M,D |
| Animal Sciences | M,D |
| Anthropology | M |
| Architecture | M |
| Art/Fine Arts | M |
| Athletic Training and Sports Medicine | M,D |
| Biochemistry | M,D |
| Bioengineering | M,D |
| Bioinformatics | M,D |
| Biological and Biomedical Sciences—General | M,D |
| Business Administration and Management—General | M |
| Chemical Engineering | M,D |
| Chemistry | M,D |
| Civil Engineering | M,D |
| Computational Biology | M,D |
| Computer Science | M,D |
| Consumer Economics | M |
| Counselor Education | M,O |
| Curriculum and Instruction | M,O |
| Education—General | M,D,O |
| Educational Leadership and Administration | M,O |
| Electrical Engineering | M,D |
| Engineering and Applied Sciences—General | M,D |
| Entomology | M,D |
| Environmental Sciences | M,D |
| Exercise and Sports Science | M,D |
| Experimental Psychology | M,D |
| Food Science and Technology | M,D |
| Geography | M,D |
| Geological Engineering | M,D |
| Geology | M,D |
| History | M,D |
| Human Services | M,O |
| Interdisciplinary Studies | M |
| Kinesiology and Movement Studies | M,D |
| Landscape Architecture | M |
| Law | M,D |
| Materials Sciences | M,D |
| Mathematics | M,D |
| Mechanical Engineering | M,D |
| Microbiology | M,D |
| Music | M |
| Natural Resources | M,D |
| Nuclear Engineering | M,D |
| Philosophy | M,D |
| Physical Education | M,D |
| Physics | M,D |
| Plant Pathology | M,D |
| Plant Sciences | M,D |
| Political Science | M,D |
| Psychology—General | M,D |
| Public Administration | M,D |
| Rehabilitation Counseling | M,O |
| Special Education | M,O |
| Sports Management | M,D |
| Statistics | M |
| Theater | M |
| Travel and Tourism | M,D |
| Urban and Regional Planning | M |
| Veterinary Sciences | M,D |
| Vocational and Technical Education | M,O |
| Water Resources Engineering | M,D |
| Water Resources | M,D |
| Writing | M |

## UNIVERSITY OF ILLINOIS AT CHICAGO

| | |
|---|---|
| Accounting | M |
| Acute Care/Critical Care Nursing | M,O |
| Adult Nursing | M,O |
| Allied Health—General | M,D,O |
| Allopathic Medicine | D |
| Anatomy | M |
| Anthropology | M,D |
| Applied Arts and Design—General | M |
| Architecture | M |
| Art History | M,D |
| Art/Fine Arts | M,D |
| Biochemistry | D |
| Bioengineering | M,D |
| Bioinformatics | M,D |
| Biological and Biomedical Sciences—General | M,D |
| Biophysics | M,D |
| Biostatistics | M,D |
| Business Administration and Management—General | M,D |
| Cell Biology | M,D |
| Chemical Engineering | M,D |
| Chemistry | M,D |
| Civil Engineering | M,D |
| Communication—General | M,D |
| Community Health Nursing | M,O |
| Community Health | M,D |
| Computer Education | D |
| Computer Engineering | M,D |
| Computer Science | M,D |

| | |
|---|---|
| Criminal Justice and Criminology | M,D |
| Curriculum and Instruction | M,D |
| Dentistry | D |
| Developmental Psychology | M,D |
| Disability Studies | M,D |
| Early Childhood Education | M,D |
| East European and Russian Studies | M,D |
| Economics | M,D |
| Education—General | M,D |
| Educational Leadership and Administration | M,D |
| Educational Measurement and Evaluation | M,D |
| Educational Policy | M,D |
| Educational Psychology | M,D |
| Electrical Engineering | M,D |
| Elementary Education | M,D |
| Engineering and Applied Sciences—General | M,D |
| English as a Second Language | M,D |
| English | M,D |
| Environmental and Occupational Health | M,D |
| Epidemiology | M,D |
| Family Nurse Practitioner Studies | M,O |
| Finance and Banking | M |
| Foreign Languages Education | M,D |
| Forensic Sciences | M |
| French | M |
| Genetics | D |
| Geography | M |
| Geology | M,D |
| Geosciences | M,D |
| German | M,D |
| Gerontological Nursing | M,O |
| Graphic Design | M |
| Health Education | M |
| Health Informatics | M,O |
| Health Services Management and Hospital Administration | M,D |
| Health Services Research | M,D |
| Hispanic and Latin American Languages | M,D |
| Hispanic Studies | M,D |
| History | M,D |
| Human Development | M,D |
| Immunology | D |
| Industrial/Management Engineering | M,D |
| Interdisciplinary Studies | D |
| Kinesiology and Movement Studies | M,D |
| Latin American Studies | M |
| Law | M,D |
| Linguistics | M |
| Management Information Systems | M,D |
| Materials Engineering | M,D |
| Maternal and Child/Neonatal Nursing | M,O |
| Mathematics Education | M,D |
| Mathematics | M,D |
| Mechanical Engineering | M,D |
| Medical Illustration | M |
| Medicinal and Pharmaceutical Chemistry | M,D |
| Microbiology | D |
| Molecular Biology | D |
| Molecular Genetics | D |
| Museum Studies | M,D |
| Neuroscience | M,D |
| Nurse Midwifery | M,O |
| Nursing and Healthcare Administration | M,O |
| Nursing—General | M,D,O |
| Nutrition | M,D |
| Occupational Health Nursing | M,O |
| Occupational Therapy | M,D |
| Operations Research | M,D |
| Oral and Dental Sciences | M,D |
| Pediatric Nursing | M,O |
| Pharmaceutical Administration | M,D |
| Pharmaceutical Sciences | M,D |
| Pharmacology | D |
| Pharmacy | D |
| Philosophy | M,D |
| Physical Therapy | M,D |
| Physics | M,D |
| Physiology | M,D |
| Political Science | M,D |
| Psychology—General | M,D |
| Public Administration | M,D |
| Public Health—General | M,D |
| Real Estate | M |
| School Nursing | M,O |
| Science Education | D |
| Secondary Education | M,D |
| Slavic Languages | M,D |
| Social Sciences Education | D |
| Social Work | M,D,O |
| Sociology | M,D |
| Spanish | M,D |
| Special Education | M,D |
| Statistics | M,D |
| Toxicology | M,D |
| Urban and Regional Planning | M,D |
| Urban Education | M,D |
| Women's Health Nursing | M,O |

**UNIVERSITY OF ILLINOIS AT SPRINGFIELD**

| | |
|---|---|
| Accounting | M |
| Addictions/Substance Abuse Counseling | M,O |
| Biological and Biomedical Sciences—General | M |
| Business Administration and Management—General | M |
| Child and Family Studies | M,O |
| Communication—General | M |
| Community Health | M,O |
| Computer Science | M |
| Data Science/Data Analytics | M |
| Education—General | M,O |
| Educational Leadership and Administration | M,O |
| Emergency Management | M,O |
| English | M,O |
| Environmental and Occupational Health | M,O |
| Environmental Management and Policy | M |
| Environmental Sciences | M |
| Epidemiology | M,O |
| Gerontology | M,O |
| Health Education | M,O |
| History | M |
| Homeland Security | M,O |
| Human Development | M |
| Human Services | M,O |
| Interdisciplinary Studies | M |
| Journalism | M |
| Legal and Justice Studies | M |
| Management Information Systems | M |
| Political Science | M |
| Public Administration | M,D,O |
| Public Health—General | M,O |
| Public History | M |
| Social Sciences | M,O |

**UNIVERSITY OF ILLINOIS AT URBANA-CHAMPAIGN**

| | |
|---|---|
| Accounting | M,D |
| Actuarial Science | M,D |
| Advertising and Public Relations | M |
| Aerospace/Aeronautical Engineering | M,D |
| African Studies | M |
| Agricultural Economics and Agribusiness | M,D |
| Agricultural Education | M |
| Agricultural Engineering | M,D |
| Agricultural Sciences—General | M |
| Agronomy and Soil Sciences | M,D |
| Animal Sciences | M,D |
| Anthropology | M,D |
| Applied Arts and Design—General | M,D |
| Applied Economics | M,D |
| Applied Mathematics | M,D |
| Applied Statistics | M,D |
| Architecture | M,D |
| Art Education | M,D |
| Art History | M,D |
| Art/Fine Arts | M |
| Asian Languages | M,D |
| Asian Studies | M,D |
| Astronomy | M,D |
| Atmospheric Sciences | M,D |
| Biochemistry | M,D |
| Bioengineering | M,D |
| Bioinformatics | M,D,O |
| Biological and Biomedical Sciences—General | M,D |
| Biophysics | M,D |
| Business Administration and Management—General | M,D |
| Cell Biology | D |
| Chemical Engineering | M,D |
| Chemical Physics | M,D |
| Chemistry | M,D |
| Civil Engineering | M,D |
| Classics | M,D |
| Communication Disorders | M,D |
| Communication—General | M,D |
| Community Health | M,D |
| Comparative Literature | M,D |
| Computational Biology | M,D |
| Computer Engineering | M,D |
| Computer Science | M,D |
| Conservation Biology | M,D |
| Consumer Economics | M,D |
| Corporate and Organizational Communication | M |
| Counselor Education | M,D,O |
| Curriculum and Instruction | M,D,O |
| Dance | M |
| Developmental Biology | D |
| East European and Russian Studies | M |
| Ecology | M,D |
| Economics | M,D |
| Education of Students with Severe/Multiple Disabilities | M,D,O |
| Education—General | M,D,O |
| Educational Leadership and Administration | M,D,O |
| Educational Policy | M,D,O |
| Educational Psychology | M,D,O |
| Electrical Engineering | M,D |
| Energy and Power Engineering | M,D |
| Energy Management and Policy | M |
| Engineering and Applied Sciences—General | M,D |
| English as a Second Language | M,D |
| English | M,D |
| Entomology | M,D |
| Environmental Engineering | M,D |
| Environmental Sciences | M,D |
| Evolutionary Biology | M,D |
| Finance and Banking | M,D |
| Financial Engineering | M |
| Food Science and Technology | M,D |
| Foreign Languages Education | M,D |
| French | M,D |
| Geography | M,D |
| Geology | M,D |
| Geosciences | M,D |
| German | M,D |
| Graphic Design | M |
| Health Informatics | M,D,O |
| Health Services Management and Hospital Administration | M,D |
| History | M,D |
| Human Development | M,D |
| Human Resources Management | M,D,O |
| Human Services | M,D |
| Human-Computer Interaction | M,D,O |
| Industrial and Labor Relations | M,D |
| Industrial Design | M |
| Industrial/Management Engineering | M,D |
| Information Science | M,D,O |
| Information Studies | M,D,O |
| Interdisciplinary Studies | D |
| Italian | M,D |
| Journalism | M |
| Kinesiology and Movement Studies | M,D |
| Landscape Architecture | M,D |
| Latin American Studies | M |
| Law | M,D |
| Leisure Studies | M,D |
| Library Science | M,D,O |
| Linguistics | M,D |
| Management Information Systems | M,D,O |
| Management of Technology | M,D |
| Management Strategy and Policy | M,D,O |
| Materials Engineering | M,D |
| Materials Sciences | M,D |
| Mathematics Education | M,D |
| Mathematics | M,D |
| Mechanical Engineering | M,D |
| Mechanics | M,D |
| Media Studies | M,D |
| Medical Informatics | M,D,O |
| Microbiology | M,D |
| Molecular Physiology | M,D |
| Music Education | M,D |
| Music | M,D |
| Natural Resources | M,D |
| Near and Middle Eastern Studies | M |
| Neuroscience | D |
| Nuclear Engineering | M,D |
| Nutrition | M,D |
| Pathobiology | M,D |
| Philosophy | M,D |
| Photography | M |
| Physics | M,D |
| Physiology | M,D |
| Plant Biology | M,D |
| Political Science | M,D |
| Portuguese | M,D |
| Psychology—General | M,D |
| Public Health—General | M,D |
| Rehabilitation Sciences | M,D |
| Religion | M |
| Romance Languages | D |
| Science Education | M,D |
| Slavic Languages | M,D |
| Social Work | M,D |
| Sociology | M,D |
| Spanish | M,D |
| Special Education | M,D,O |
| Statistics | M,D |
| Systems Engineering | M,D |
| Theater | M,D |
| Translation and Interpretation | M |
| Urban and Regional Planning | M,D |
| Veterinary Medicine | D |
| Veterinary Sciences | M,D |
| Western European Studies | M |
| Writing | M,D |
| Zoology | M,D |

**UNIVERSITY OF INDIANAPOLIS**

| | |
|---|---|
| Addictions/Substance Abuse Counseling | M,D |
| Anthropology | M |
| Art Education | M |
| Art/Fine Arts | M |
| Biological and Biomedical Sciences—General | M |
| Business Administration and Management—General | M,O |
| Clinical Psychology | M,D |
| Counseling Psychology | M,D |
| Curriculum and Instruction | M |
| Education—General | M |
| Educational Leadership and Administration | M |
| Elementary Education | M |
| English Education | M |
| English | M |
| Family Nurse Practitioner Studies | M,D |
| Foreign Languages Education | M |
| Gerontology | M,D,O |
| History | M |
| International Affairs | M |
| Maternal and Child/Neonatal Nursing | M,D |
| Mathematics Education | M |
| Nurse Midwifery | M,D |
| Nursing and Healthcare Administration | M,D |
| Nursing Education | M,D |
| Nursing—General | M,D |
| Occupational Therapy | M,D |
| Physical Education | M |
| Physical Therapy | M,D |
| Psychology—General | M,D |
| Public Health—General | M |
| Science Education | M |
| Secondary Education | M |
| Social Sciences Education | M |
| Social Work | M,D |
| Sociology | M |
| Sports Management | M |
| Women's Health Nursing | M,D |

**THE UNIVERSITY OF IOWA**

| | |
|---|---|
| Accounting | M,D |
| Actuarial Science | M,D |
| Agricultural Sciences—General | M,D,O |
| Allopathic Medicine | D |
| American Studies | M,D |
| Anatomy | D |
| Anthropology | M,D |
| Applied Mathematics | D |
| Art Education | M,D |
| Art History | M,D |
| Art/Fine Arts | M |
| Asian Languages | M |
| Asian Studies | M |
| Astronomy | M |
| Athletic Training and Sports Medicine | M,D |
| Bacteriology | M,D |
| Biochemical Engineering | M,D |
| Biochemistry | M,D |
| Bioinformatics | M,D,O |
| Biological and Biomedical Sciences—General | M,D |
| Biomedical Engineering | M,D |
| Biophysics | M,D |
| Biostatistics | M,D,O |
| Business Administration and Management—General | M,D |
| Business Analytics | M |
| Cell Biology | M,D |
| Chemical Engineering | M,D |
| Chemistry | D |
| Chinese | M |
| Civil Engineering | M,D |
| Classics | M,D |
| Clinical Research | M,D |
| Communication Disorders | M,D |
| Communication—General | M,D |
| Community Health | M,D |
| Computational Biology | M,D,O |
| Computational Sciences | D |
| Computer Engineering | M,D |
| Computer Science | M,D |
| Counseling Psychology | M,D,O |
| Counselor Education | M,D |
| Dance | M |
| Dentistry | M,D,O |
| Developmental Education | M,D |
| Economics | D |
| Education—General | M,D,O |
| Educational Leadership and Administration | M,D,O |
| Educational Measurement and Evaluation | M,D,O |
| Educational Policy | M,D,O |
| Educational Psychology | M,D,O |
| Electrical Engineering | M,D |
| Elementary Education | M,D |
| Energy and Power Engineering | M,D |
| Engineering and Applied Sciences—General | M,D |
| English as a Second Language | M,D |
| English Education | M,D |
| English | M,D |
| Environmental and Occupational Health | M,D,O |
| Environmental Engineering | M,D |
| Epidemiology | M,D |
| Ergonomics and Human Factors | M,D,O |
| Evolutionary Biology | M,D |
| Exercise and Sports Science | M,D |
| Film, Television, and Video Production | M |
| Film, Television, and Video Theory and Criticism | M,D |
| Finance and Banking | M,D |
| Foreign Languages Education | M,D |
| Foundations and Philosophy of Education | M,D,O |
| French | M,D |
| Genetics | M,D |
| Geographic Information Systems | M,D,O |
| Geography | M,D,O |
| Geosciences | M,D |
| Health Informatics | M,D,O |
| Health Services Management and Hospital Administration | M,D |
| Higher Education | M,D |
| History | M,D |
| Hydraulics | M,D |
| Immunology | M,D |
| Industrial Hygiene | M,D,O |
| Industrial/Management Engineering | M,D |
| Information Science | M,D,O |
| Information Studies | M,D |
| Journalism | M,D |
| Law | M,D |
| Leisure Studies | M,D |
| Library Science | M,D |
| Linguistics | M,D |
| Manufacturing Engineering | M,D |
| Marketing | M,D |
| Marriage and Family Therapy | M,D |
| Mass Communication | M,D |
| Materials Engineering | M,D |
| Mathematics Education | M,D |
| Mathematics | M,D |
| Mechanical Engineering | M,D |
| Media Studies | M,D |
| Medicinal and Pharmaceutical Chemistry | M,D |
| Microbiology | M,D |
| Molecular Biology | D |
| Music Education | M,D |
| Music | M,D |
| Neurobiology | M,D |
| Neuroscience | D |
| Nursing—General | M,D |
| Operations Research | M,D |
| Oral and Dental Sciences | M,D,O |

*M—masters degree; D—doctorate; O—other advanced degree; *—Close-Up and/or Display*

| | |
|---|---|
| Pathology | M |
| Pharmaceutical Sciences | M,D |
| Pharmacology | M,D |
| Pharmacy | M,D |
| Philosophy | D |
| Physical Therapy | M,D |
| Physician Assistant Studies | M |
| Physics | M,D |
| Physiology | M,D |
| Political Science | D |
| Psychology—General | M,D,O |
| Public Health—General | M,D,O |
| Quantitative Analysis | M,D,O |
| Radiation Biology | M |
| Recreation and Park Management | M,D |
| Rehabilitation Counseling | M,D |
| Rehabilitation Sciences | M,D |
| Religion | M,D |
| Rhetoric | M,D |
| School Psychology | M,D,O |
| Science Education | M,D |
| Secondary Education | M,D |
| Social Sciences Education | M,D |
| Social Work | M,D |
| Sociology | M,D |
| Spanish | M,D |
| Special Education | M,D |
| Speech and Interpersonal Communication | M,D |
| Sports Management | M,D |
| Statistics | M,D,O |
| Student Affairs | M,D |
| Sustainable Development | M,D |
| Theater | M |
| Toxicology | M,D |
| Translational Biology | M,D |
| Transportation and Highway Engineering | M,D |
| Urban and Regional Planning | M |
| Virology | M,D |
| Water Resources Engineering | M,D |
| Water Resources | M,D |
| Women's Studies | O |
| Writing | M,D |

**UNIVERSITY OF JAMESTOWN**

| | |
|---|---|
| Curriculum and Instruction | M |
| Education—General | M |
| Physical Therapy | D |

**THE UNIVERSITY OF KANSAS**

| | |
|---|---|
| Accounting | M |
| Acoustics | M,D,O |
| Adult Nursing | M,D,O |
| Aerospace/Aeronautical Engineering | M,D |
| African Studies | M,O |
| African-American Studies | M,O |
| Allied Health—General | M,D,O |
| Allopathic Medicine | D |
| American Indian/Native American Studies | M,O |
| American Studies | M,D |
| Anatomy | M,D |
| Anthropology | M,D |
| Applied Arts and Design—General | M |
| Applied Behavior Analysis | M,D,O |
| Applied Mathematics | M,D,O |
| Applied Statistics | M,D,O |
| Architectural Engineering | M |
| Architecture | M,D,O |
| Art Education | M |
| Art History | M,D |
| Art/Fine Arts | M,D |
| Asian Languages | M,O |
| Asian Studies | M,O |
| Astronomy | M,D |
| Atmospheric Sciences | M,D,O |
| Biochemistry | D |
| Bioengineering | M,D |
| Biological and Biomedical Sciences—General | D |
| Biophysics | D |
| Biostatistics | M,D,O |
| Biotechnology | M |
| Business Administration and Management—General | M,D |
| Cancer Biology/Oncology | M,D |
| Cell Biology | M,D |
| Chemical Engineering | M,D,O |
| Chemistry | M,D |
| Civil Engineering | M,D |
| Classics | M |
| Clinical Psychology | M,D |
| Clinical Research | M |
| Cognitive Sciences | M,D |
| Communication Disorders | M,D |
| Communication—General | M,D,O |
| Community Health Nursing | M,D,O |
| Community Health | M,D,O |
| Computational Biology | D |
| Computer Engineering | M |
| Computer Science | M,D |
| Construction Management | M |
| Counseling Psychology | M,D |
| Cultural Studies | M,D |
| Curriculum and Instruction | M,D |
| Developmental Biology | D |
| Developmental Psychology | M,D |
| Early Childhood Education | M,D,O |
| East European and Russian Studies | M,O |
| Ecology | M,D |
| Economics | M,D |
| Education—General | M,D,O |
| Educational Leadership and Administration | M,D |
| Educational Measurement and Evaluation | M,D |
| Educational Media/Instructional Technology | M,D |
| Educational Policy | M,D |
| Educational Psychology | M,D |
| Electrical Engineering | M,D |
| Engineering and Applied Sciences—General | M,D,O |
| Engineering Management | M,O |
| English | M,D |
| Environmental Engineering | M,D |
| Environmental Sciences | M,D |
| Epidemiology | M |
| Evolutionary Biology | M,D |
| Exercise and Sports Science | M,D |
| Film, Television, and Video Theory and Criticism | M,D |
| Finance and Banking | M,D |
| French | M,D |
| Geographic Information Systems | M,D,O |
| Geography | M,D,O |
| Geology | M,D |
| Gerontological Nursing | M,D,O |
| Gerontology | D |
| Health Education | M,D,O |
| Health Informatics | M,O |
| Health Promotion | M,D,O |
| Higher Education | M,D |
| Historic Preservation | M,D,O |
| History | M,D |
| Human Resources Management | M,D |
| Interdisciplinary Studies | D |
| International Affairs | M |
| Journalism | M,D |
| Latin American Studies | M,O |
| Law | D |
| Linguistics | M,D |
| Logistics | M,D |
| Management Information Systems | M |
| Management Strategy and Policy | M,D |
| Marketing | M,D |
| Mathematics | M,D,O |
| Mechanical Engineering | M,D |
| Media Studies | M,D |
| Medical Informatics | M,D,O |
| Medicinal and Pharmaceutical Chemistry | M,D |
| Microbiology | M,D |
| Molecular Biology | D |
| Museum Studies | M,O |
| Music Education | M,D |
| Music | M,D |
| Near and Middle Eastern Studies | M,O |
| Neuroscience | M,D |
| Nurse Anesthesia | D |
| Nurse Midwifery | M,D,O |
| Nursing—General | M,D,O |
| Nutrition | M,D,O |
| Occupational Therapy | M,D |
| Organizational Behavior | M,D |
| Organizational Management | M,D,O |
| Pathology | M,D |
| Petroleum Engineering | M,D,O |
| Pharmacology | M,D |
| Pharmacy | M,D |
| Philosophy | M,D |
| Physical Education | M,D |
| Physical Therapy | D |
| Physics | M,D |
| Physiology | D |
| Political Science | M,D |
| Project Management | M |
| Psychiatric Nursing | M,D,O |
| Psychology—General | M,D,O |
| Public Health—General | M |
| Rehabilitation Sciences | M,D |
| Religion | M,O |
| School Psychology | D,O |
| Slavic Languages | M,D |
| Social Psychology | M,D |
| Social Work | M,D |
| Sociology | D |
| Spanish | M,D |
| Special Education | M,D,O |
| Sports Management | M,D |
| Statistics | M,D,O |
| Supply Chain Management | M,D |
| Textile Design | M |
| Theater | M,D |
| Therapies—Dance, Drama, and Music | M,D |
| Toxicology | M,D |
| Urban and Regional Planning | M |
| Urban Design | M,D,O |
| Writing | M,D |

**UNIVERSITY OF KENTUCKY**

| | |
|---|---|
| Accounting | M |
| Agricultural Economics and Agribusiness | M,D |
| Agricultural Engineering | M,D |
| Agricultural Sciences—General | M,D |
| Agronomy and Soil Sciences | M,D |
| Allied Health—General | M,D |
| Allopathic Medicine | D |
| Anatomy | D |
| Animal Sciences | M,D |
| Anthropology | M,D |
| Applied Arts and Design—General | M |
| Applied Mathematics | M,D |
| Architecture | M |
| Art Education | M |
| Art History | M |
| Art/Fine Arts | M |
| Arts Administration | M |
| Astronomy | M,D |
| Athletic Training and Sports Medicine | M |
| Biochemistry | D |
| Biological and Biomedical Sciences—General | M,D |
| Biomedical Engineering | M,D |
| Biostatistics | D |
| Business Administration and Management—General | M,D |
| Chemical Engineering | M,D |
| Chemistry | M,D |
| Child and Family Studies | M,D |
| Civil Engineering | M,D |
| Classics | M |
| Clinical Research | M |
| Communication Disorders | M |
| Computer Science | M,D |
| Counseling Psychology | M,D,O |
| Curriculum and Instruction | M,D |
| Dentistry | D |
| Early Childhood Education | M,D |
| Economics | M,D |
| Education—General | M,D,O |
| Educational Leadership and Administration | M,D,O |
| Educational Measurement and Evaluation | M,D |
| Educational Media/Instructional Technology | M,D |
| Educational Policy | M,D |
| Educational Psychology | M,D,O |
| Electrical Engineering | M,D |
| Elementary Education | M,D |
| Engineering and Applied Sciences—General | M,D |
| English | M,D |
| Entomology | M,D |
| Epidemiology | D |
| Exercise and Sports Science | M,D |
| Food Science and Technology | M,D |
| Foreign Languages Education | M |
| Forestry | M |
| Geography | M,D |
| Geology | M,D |
| German | M |
| Gerontology | D,O |
| Health Physics/Radiological Health | M |
| Health Promotion | M,D |
| Health Services Management and Hospital Administration | M |
| Higher Education | M,D |
| Hispanic Studies | M,D |
| Historic Preservation | M |
| History | M,D |
| Hospitality Management | M |
| Immunology | D |
| Information Science | M,D |
| Interior Design | M |
| International Affairs | M |
| International Business | M |
| Kinesiology and Movement Studies | M,D |
| Law | D |
| Library Science | M |
| Manufacturing Engineering | M |
| Materials Engineering | M,D |
| Materials Sciences | M,D |
| Mathematics | M,D |
| Mechanical Engineering | M,D |
| Medical Physics | M |
| Microbiology | D |
| Middle School Education | M,D |
| Mineral/Mining Engineering | M,D |
| Music Education | M,D |
| Music | M,D |
| Neurobiology | D |
| Nursing—General | D |
| Nutrition | M,D |
| Oral and Dental Sciences | M |
| Pharmaceutical Sciences | M,D |
| Pharmacology | D |
| Pharmacy | D |
| Philosophy | M,D |
| Physical Education | M,D |
| Physical Therapy | D |
| Physician Assistant Studies | M |
| Physics | M,D |
| Physiology | D |
| Plant Pathology | M,D |
| Plant Sciences | M,D |
| Political Science | M,D |
| Psychology—General | M,D |
| Public Administration | M,D,O |
| Public Health—General | M,D |
| Public Policy | M,D,O |
| Reading Education | M,D |
| Rehabilitation Counseling | M,D |
| Rehabilitation Sciences | D |
| School Psychology | M,D,O |
| Secondary Education | M,D |
| Social Work | M,D |
| Sociology | M,D |
| Special Education | M,D |
| Statistics | M,D |
| Therapies—Dance, Drama, and Music | M,D |
| Toxicology | M,D |
| Veterinary Sciences | M,D |

**UNIVERSITY OF KING'S COLLEGE**

| | |
|---|---|
| Journalism | M |
| Writing | M |

**UNIVERSITY OF LA VERNE**

| | |
|---|---|
| Accounting | M |
| Business Administration and Management—General | M,D,O |
| Child and Family Studies | M |
| Child Development | M |
| Clinical Psychology | D |
| Counselor Education | M,D,O |
| Education—General | M,O |
| Educational Leadership and Administration | M,D,O |
| Elementary Education | M,D,O |
| English | M,O |
| Finance and Banking | M |
| Gerontology | M,O |
| Health Services Management and Hospital Administration | M,D,O |
| Health Services Research | M |
| Human Resources Management | M,O |
| International Business | M |
| Law | D |
| Management Information Systems | M |
| Marketing | M |
| Marriage and Family Therapy | M |
| Nonprofit Management | M,O |
| Organizational Management | M,D,O |
| Psychology—General | M,D |
| Public Administration | M,D |
| Public Health—General | M |
| School Psychology | M,O |
| Secondary Education | M,D,O |
| Special Education | M,D,O |
| Supply Chain Management | M |

**UNIVERSITY OF LETHBRIDGE**

| | |
|---|---|
| Accounting | M,D |
| Addictions/Substance Abuse Counseling | M,D |
| Agricultural Sciences—General | M,D |
| American Indian/Native American Studies | M,D |
| Anthropology | M,D |
| Archaeology | M,D |
| Art/Fine Arts | M,D |
| Biochemistry | M,D |
| Biological and Biomedical Sciences—General | M,D |
| Business Administration and Management—General | M,D |
| Canadian Studies | M,D |
| Chemistry | M,D |
| Computational Sciences | M,D |
| Computer Science | M,D |
| Counseling Psychology | M,D |
| Counselor Education | M,D |
| Economics | M,D |
| Education—General | M,D |
| Educational Leadership and Administration | M,D |
| English | M,D |
| Environmental Sciences | M,D |
| Exercise and Sports Science | M,D |
| Finance and Banking | M,D |
| French | M,D |
| Gender Studies | M,D |
| Geographic Information Systems | M,D |
| Geography | M,D |
| German | M,D |
| Human Resources Management | M,D |
| International Business | M,D |
| Kinesiology and Movement Studies | M,D |
| Management Information Systems | M,D |
| Management Strategy and Policy | M,D |
| Marketing | M,D |
| Mathematics | M,D |
| Media Studies | M,D |
| Molecular Biology | M,D |
| Music | M,D |
| Neuroscience | M,D |
| Nursing—General | M,D |
| Philosophy | M,D |
| Physics | M,D |
| Political Science | M,D |
| Psychology—General | M,D |
| Religion | M,D |
| Sociology | M,D |
| Spanish | M,D |
| Theater | M,D |
| Urban Studies | M,D |
| Women's Studies | M,D |

**UNIVERSITY OF LOUISIANA AT LAFAYETTE**

| | |
|---|---|
| Accounting | M |
| American Studies | M |
| Architectural Engineering | M |
| Biological and Biomedical Sciences—General | M,D |
| Business Administration and Management—General | M |
| Chemical Engineering | M |
| Civil Engineering | M |
| Communication Disorders | M,D |
| Communication—General | M |
| Counselor Education | M |
| Cultural Studies | M,D |
| Curriculum and Instruction | M |
| Early Childhood Education | M |
| Education of the Gifted | M |
| Education—General | M,D |
| Educational Leadership and Administration | M,D |
| Educational Media/Instructional Technology | M |
| Electrical Engineering | M,D |
| English as a Second Language | M,D |
| English | M,D |
| Entrepreneurship | M |
| Environmental Biology | M,D |
| Environmental Sciences | M |
| Evolutionary Biology | M,D |
| Family Nurse Practitioner Studies | M,D |
| Finance and Banking | M |
| Folklore | M,D |
| French | M,D |
| Geosciences | M |
| History | M,D |
| Hospitality Management | M |
| Human Resources Management | M |
| International Business | M |
| Latin American Studies | M |
| Mathematics Education | M |
| Mathematics | M,D |
| Mechanical Engineering | M |
| Music Education | M |
| Music | M |
| Natural Resources | M |
| Nursing and Healthcare Administration | M |
| Nursing Education | M,D |
| Nursing—General | M,D |
| Petroleum Engineering | M |
| Physics | M |
| Project Management | M |
| Psychology—General | M |
| Public History | M |
| Rhetoric | M,D |
| Sociology | M,D |

Special Education M
Systems Engineering M,D
Western European Studies M
Writing M,D

### UNIVERSITY OF LOUISIANA AT MONROE

Biological and Biomedical Sciences—General M
Business Administration and Management—General M,O
Clinical Psychology M
Communication Disorders M
Communication—General M
Counseling Psychology M
Counselor Education M
Criminal Justice and Criminology M
Curriculum and Instruction M,D
Education—General M,D
Educational Leadership and Administration D
Elementary Education M
English M
Exercise and Sports Science M
Forensic Psychology M
Gerontology M,O
History M
Marriage and Family Therapy M,D
Occupational Therapy M
Pharmacy D
Psychology—General M
Public Administration M
Recreation and Park Management M
Secondary Education M
Sports Management M
Toxicology D

### UNIVERSITY OF LOUISVILLE

Accounting M
Addictions/Substance Abuse Counseling M,D,O
African Studies M
African-American Studies M
Allopathic Medicine D
Analytical Chemistry M,D
Anatomy M,D
Anthropology M
Applied Arts and Design—General M,D
Applied Behavior Analysis M,D,O
Applied Mathematics M,D
Art Education M,D,O
Art History M,D
Art Therapy M,D
Biochemistry M,D
Bioengineering M,D
Bioethics M,D
Bioinformatics M,D
Biological and Biomedical Sciences—General M,D
Business Administration and Management—General M
Chemical Engineering M,D
Chemical Physics M,D
Chemistry M,D
Civil Engineering M,D
Clinical Psychology D
Cognitive Sciences D
Communication Disorders M,D
Communication—General M
Community Health M
Computer and Information Systems Security M,D,O
Computer Engineering M,D,O
Computer Science M,D,O
Counseling Psychology M,D
Counselor Education M,D
Criminal Justice and Criminology M,D
Cultural Studies M,D
Curriculum and Instruction M,D,O
Data Science/Data Analytics M,D,O
Dentistry M,D
Developmental Psychology D
Early Childhood Education M,D,O
Education—General M,D,O
Educational Leadership and Administration M,D,O
Educational Measurement and Evaluation M,D
Educational Psychology M,D
Electrical Engineering M,D
Elementary Education M,D,O
Engineering and Applied Sciences—General M,D,O
Engineering Management M,D,O
English M,D
Entrepreneurship M,D
Environmental and Occupational Health M,D
Environmental Biology M,D
Epidemiology M,D
Exercise and Sports Science M,D,O
Experimental Psychology D
Family Nurse Practitioner Studies M,D
French M,O
Geography M
Gerontological Nursing M,D
Gerontology M,D,O
Health Education M,D,O
Health Promotion D
Health Services Management and Hospital Administration M
Higher Education M,D,O
History M,O
Human Resources Development M,D,O
Human Resources Management M,D,O
Humanities M,D
Immunology M,D
Industrial/Management Engineering M,D,O
Inorganic Chemistry M,D
Interdisciplinary Studies M,D
International Business M
Law D
Linguistics M,D
Logistics M,D,O
Marriage and Family Therapy M,D,O
Maternal and Child/Neonatal Nursing M,D
Mathematics M,D
Mechanical Engineering M,D
Microbiology M,D
Middle School Education M,D,O
Molecular Genetics M,D
Museum Studies M,D
Music Education M,D,O
Music M
Neurobiology M,D
Nonprofit Management M,D
Nursing and Healthcare Administration M,D
Nursing Education M,D
Nursing—General M,D
Oral and Dental Sciences M,D
Organic Chemistry M,D
Pharmacology M,D
Philosophy M,D
Physical Chemistry M,D
Physical Education M,D,O
Physics M,D
Physiology M,D
Political Science M
Psychiatric Nursing M,D
Psychology—General D
Public Administration M,D
Public Affairs M,D
Public Health—General M,D
Public History M,O
Public Policy M,D
Rhetoric M,D
School Psychology M,D
Secondary Education M,D,O
Social Work M,D,O
Sociology M,D
Spanish M,O
Special Education M,D,O
Sports Management M,D,O
Student Affairs M,D
Supply Chain Management M,D,O
Sustainability Management M,D
Theater M
Toxicology M,D
Urban and Regional Planning M,D
Urban Studies M,D
Women's Health Nursing M,D
Women's Studies M,O
Writing M,D

### UNIVERSITY OF LYNCHBURG

Allopathic Medicine D
Athletic Training and Sports Medicine M
Business Administration and Management—General M
Clinical Psychology M
Counseling Psychology M
Counselor Education M
Criminal Justice and Criminology M
Curriculum and Instruction M
Educational Leadership and Administration M,D
Geosciences M
Health Informatics O
Health Promotion M
Higher Education M
Mathematics M
Nonprofit Management M
Physical Therapy D
Physician Assistant Studies M
Public Health—General M
Reading Education M
School Psychology M
Science Education M
Special Education M

### UNIVERSITY OF MAINE

Agricultural Economics and Agribusiness M
Agricultural Sciences—General M,D,O
Anthropology D
Art/Fine Arts M
Bioinformatics M,D
Biological and Biomedical Sciences—General M,D
Biomedical Engineering M,D
Botany M,D
Business Administration and Management—General M,O
Chemical Engineering M,D
Chemistry M,D
Civil Engineering M,D
Communication Disorders M
Communication—General M,D
Computer Engineering M,D
Computer Science M,D,O
Early Childhood Education M,D,O
Economics M
Education—General M,D,O
Educational Leadership and Administration M,D,O
Educational Media/Instructional Technology M,D,O
Electrical Engineering M,D
Engineering and Applied Sciences—General M,D
English M
Entomology M,D
Environmental Management and Policy D
Exercise and Sports Science M,D,O
Family Nurse Practitioner Studies M,O
Finance and Banking M
Fish, Game, and Wildlife Management M,D
Foreign Languages Education M
Forestry M,D
French M
Geology M,O
Geosciences M,D
Higher Education M,D,O
History M,D
Horticulture M,D,O
Human Development M,D,O
Information Science M,D,O
Interdisciplinary Studies M,D
International Affairs M
Kinesiology and Movement Studies M,D,O
Law D
Marine Sciences M,D
Mathematics M
Mechanical Engineering M,D
Microbiology M,D
Molecular Biology M,D
Music M
Nursing Education M,O
Nursing—General M,O
Physical Education M,D,O
Physics M,D
Plant Pathology M,D
Psychology—General M,D
Reading Education M,D,O
Social Sciences Education M,D,O
Social Work M,O
Special Education M,D,O
Water Resources M,D
Zoology M,D

### UNIVERSITY OF MAINE AT FARMINGTON

Early Childhood Education M
Education—General M
Educational Leadership and Administration M
Educational Media/Instructional Technology M

### UNIVERSITY OF MANAGEMENT AND TECHNOLOGY

Business Administration and Management—General M,D,O
Computer Science M,O
Criminal Justice and Criminology M,O
Engineering Management M
Health Services Management and Hospital Administration M
Homeland Security M
Management Information Systems M,O
Project Management M,D,O
Public Administration M,O
Software Engineering M,O

### THE UNIVERSITY OF MANCHESTER

Accounting M
Actuarial Science M,D
Aerospace/Aeronautical Engineering M,D
Analytical Chemistry M,D
Anthropology M,D
Applied Mathematics M,D
Archaeology D
Architecture M,D
Art History D
Art/Fine Arts M,D
Arts Administration D
Asian Studies D
Astronomy M,D
Astrophysics M,D
Atmospheric Sciences M,D
Biochemical Engineering M,D
Biochemistry M,D
Bioinformatics M,D
Biological and Biomedical Sciences—General M,D
Biophysics M,D
Biotechnology M,D
Business Administration and Management—General M
Business Analytics M
Cancer Biology/Oncology M,D
Cell Biology M,D
Chemical Engineering M,D
Chemistry M,D
Chinese D
Civil Engineering M,D
Classics D
Clinical Psychology M,D
Clothing and Textiles M,D
Communication Disorders M,D
Computer Science M,D
Condensed Matter Physics M,D
Conflict Resolution and Mediation/Peace Studies D
Counseling Psychology M,D
Criminal Justice and Criminology M,D
Cultural Studies M,D
Dentistry M,D
Developmental Biology M,D
Developmental Psychology M,D
East European and Russian Studies D
Ecology M,D
Education—General M,D
Educational Psychology M,D
Electrical Engineering M,D
Engineering Management M,D
English D
Entrepreneurship M
Environmental Biology M,D
Environmental Design M,D
Environmental Engineering M,D
Environmental Management and Policy M,D
Environmental Sciences M,D
Evolutionary Biology M,D
Finance and Banking M
French D
Genetics M,D
Geochemistry M,D
Geography M,D
Geosciences M,D
German D
Hazardous Materials Management M,D
Health Law M,D
History of Medicine M,D
History of Science and Technology M,D
History D
Human Resources Management M
Immunology M,D
Industrial and Labor Relations M
Industrial and Manufacturing Management M,D
Industrial and Organizational Psychology M
Inorganic Chemistry M,D
International Affairs D
International Business M
International Development M,D
Japanese D
Landscape Architecture M,D
Latin American Studies D
Law M,D
Linguistics D
Management Strategy and Policy M
Marketing M
Materials Sciences M,D
Mathematical and Computational Finance M,D
Mathematics M,D
Mechanical Engineering M,D
Metallurgical Engineering and Metallurgy M,D
Microbiology M,D
Modeling and Simulation M,D
Molecular Biology M,D
Molecular Genetics M,D
Museum Studies D
Music D
Natural Resources M,D
Near and Middle Eastern Studies D
Neurobiology M,D
Neuroscience M,D
Nuclear Engineering M,D
Nurse Midwifery M,D
Nursing—General M,D
Optometry M,D
Oral and Dental Sciences M,D
Organic Chemistry M,D
Paleontology M,D
Paper and Pulp Engineering M,D
Pharmaceutical Sciences M,D
Pharmacology M,D
Pharmacy M,D
Philosophy M,D
Physical Chemistry M,D
Physics M,D
Physiology M,D
Plant Sciences M,D
Political Science M,D
Polymer Science and Engineering M,D
Portuguese D
Project Management M
Psychology—General M,D
Public Health—General M,D
Religion D
Social Sciences M,D
Social Work M,D
Sociology M,D
Spanish D
Statistics M,D
Structural Biology M,D
Structural Engineering M,D
Supply Chain Management M
Textile Design M,D
Theater D
Theology D
Theoretical Chemistry M,D
Theoretical Physics M,D
Toxicology M,D
Translation and Interpretation D
Vision Sciences M,D
Writing D

### UNIVERSITY OF MANITOBA

Adult Education M
Agricultural Economics and Agribusiness M,D
Agricultural Sciences—General M,D
Agronomy and Soil Sciences M,D
Allopathic Medicine M
American Indian/Native American Studies M
Anatomy M,D
Animal Sciences M,D
Anthropology M,D
Architecture M
Archives/Archival Administration M,D
Biochemistry M,D
Biological and Biomedical Sciences—General M,D,O
Biosystems Engineering M,D
Botany M,D
Business Administration and Management—General M,D
Canadian Studies M
Cancer Biology/Oncology M
Chemistry M,D
Civil Engineering M,D
Classics M
Clinical Psychology M,D
Community Health M,D,O
Computational Sciences M
Computer Engineering M,D

*M—masters degree; D—doctorate; O—other advanced degree; *—Close-Up and/or Display*

| | |
|---|---|
| Computer Science | M,D |
| Counselor Education | M |
| Curriculum and Instruction | M |
| Dentistry | D |
| Disability Studies | M |
| Ecology | M,D |
| Economics | M,D |
| Education—General | M,D |
| Educational Leadership and Administration | M |
| Educational Psychology | M |
| Electrical Engineering | M,D |
| Engineering and Applied Sciences—General | M,D |
| English as a Second Language | M |
| English Education | M |
| English | M,D |
| Entomology | M,D |
| Environmental Sciences | M,D |
| Food Science and Technology | M,D |
| Foundations and Philosophy of Education | M |
| French | M,D |
| Genetic Counseling | M,D |
| Geography | M,D |
| Geology | M,D |
| Geophysics | M,D |
| German | M |
| Higher Education | M |
| History | M,D |
| Horticulture | M,D |
| Human Genetics | M,D |
| Immunology | M,D |
| Industrial/Management Engineering | M,D |
| Infectious Diseases | M,D |
| Interdisciplinary Studies | M,D |
| Interior Design | M |
| Kinesiology and Movement Studies | M |
| Landscape Architecture | M |
| Law | M |
| Linguistics | M,D |
| Manufacturing Engineering | M,D |
| Maternal and Child Health | M |
| Mathematics | M,D |
| Mechanical Engineering | M,D |
| Medical Microbiology | M,D |
| Microbiology | M,D |
| Music | M |
| Natural Resources | M,D |
| Northern Studies | M |
| Nursing—General | M |
| Nutrition | M,D |
| Occupational Therapy | M,D |
| Oral and Dental Sciences | M,D |
| Pathology | M |
| Pharmaceutical Sciences | M,D |
| Pharmacology | M,D |
| Philosophy | M |
| Physical Education | M |
| Physical Therapy | M,D |
| Physics | M,D |
| Physiology | M,D |
| Plant Physiology | M,D |
| Plant Sciences | M,D |
| Political Science | M |
| Psychoanalysis and Psychotherapy | M |
| Psychology—General | M,D |
| Public Administration | M |
| Recreation and Park Management | M |
| Rehabilitation Sciences | M,D |
| Religion | M,D |
| School Psychology | M,D |
| Slavic Languages | M |
| Social Work | M,D |
| Sociology | M,D |
| Special Education | M |
| Statistics | M,D |
| Urban and Regional Planning | M |
| Zoology | M,D |

**UNIVERSITY OF MARY**

| | |
|---|---|
| Bioethics | M |
| Business Administration and Management—General | M |
| Cardiovascular Sciences | M |
| Communication Disorders | M |
| Curriculum and Instruction | M,D |
| Education—General | M,D |
| Educational Leadership and Administration | M,D |
| Energy Management and Policy | M |
| Exercise and Sports Science | M |
| Family Nurse Practitioner Studies | M,D |
| Health Services Management and Hospital Administration | M |
| Human Resources Management | M |
| Kinesiology and Movement Studies | M |
| Nursing and Healthcare Administration | M,D |
| Nursing Education | M,D |
| Nursing—General | M,D |
| Occupational Therapy | M |
| Physical Education | M |
| Physical Therapy | D |
| Project Management | M |
| Reading Education | M,D |
| Special Education | M,D |
| Sports Management | M |

**UNIVERSITY OF MARY HARDIN-BAYLOR**

| | |
|---|---|
| Accounting | M |
| Business Administration and Management—General | M |
| Clinical Psychology | M |
| Counseling Psychology | M |
| Counselor Education | M |
| Curriculum and Instruction | M,D |
| Education—General | M,D |
| Educational Leadership and Administration | M,D |
| Elementary Education | M,D |
| Exercise and Sports Science | M |
| Family Nurse Practitioner Studies | M,D,O |
| Higher Education | M,D |
| International Business | M |
| Management Information Systems | M |
| Marriage and Family Therapy | M |
| Nursing Education | M,D,O |
| Nursing—General | M,D,O |
| Physical Therapy | D |
| Secondary Education | M,D |
| Sports Management | M |

**UNIVERSITY OF MARYLAND, BALTIMORE**

| | |
|---|---|
| Allied Health—General | M |
| Allopathic Medicine | D |
| Biochemistry | M,D |
| Biological and Biomedical Sciences—General | M,D,O |
| Biostatistics | M,D |
| Cancer Biology/Oncology | D |
| Cell Biology | M,D |
| Clinical Laboratory Sciences/Medical Technology | M |
| Clinical Research | M,D,O |
| Community Health Nursing | M,D,O |
| Dentistry | D,O |
| Environmental Sciences | M,D |
| Epidemiology | M,D,O |
| Ethics | O |
| Family Nurse Practitioner Studies | M,D,O |
| Forensic Sciences | M |
| Genetic Counseling | M |
| Genomic Sciences | M,D |
| Gerontological Nursing | M,D,O |
| Gerontology | M,D |
| Health Services Research | M,D |
| Human Genetics | M,D |
| Immunology | D |
| International Health | M,D,O |
| Law | M,D |
| Marine Sciences | M,D |
| Maternal and Child/Neonatal Nursing | M,D,O |
| Microbiology | D |
| Molecular Biology | M,D |
| Molecular Medicine | D |
| Molecular Pharmacology | D |
| Molecular Toxicology | D |
| Neurobiology | D |
| Neuroscience | D |
| Nurse Anesthesia | M,D,O |
| Nursing and Healthcare Administration | M,D,O |
| Nursing Education | M,D,O |
| Nursing Informatics | M,D,O |
| Nursing—General | M,D,O |
| Oral and Dental Sciences | M,D,O |
| Pathology | M |
| Pediatric Nursing | M,D,O |
| Pharmaceutical Administration | M,D |
| Pharmaceutical Sciences | D |
| Pharmacology | M |
| Pharmacy | M,D |
| Physical Therapy | D |
| Psychiatric Nursing | M,D,O |
| Rehabilitation Sciences | D |
| Social Work | M,D |
| Thanatology | O |
| Toxicology | M,D |

**UNIVERSITY OF MARYLAND, BALTIMORE COUNTY**

| | |
|---|---|
| Applied Mathematics | M,D |
| Applied Psychology | D |
| Art Education | M |
| Atmospheric Sciences | M,D |
| Biochemical Engineering | M,D,O |
| Biological and Biomedical Sciences—General | M,D |
| Biostatistics | M,D |
| Biotechnology | M,O |
| Cell Biology | D |
| Chemical Engineering | M,D |
| Chemistry | M,D,O |
| Clinical Psychology | M,D |
| Cognitive Sciences | D |
| Communication—General | M |
| Computer and Information Systems Security | M,O |
| Computer Art and Design | M |
| Computer Engineering | M,D |
| Computer Science | M,D |
| Dance | M |
| Data Science/Data Analytics | M |
| Developmental Psychology | D |
| Distance Education Development | M,O |
| Early Childhood Education | M |
| Economics | M,D |
| Education—General | M,O |
| Educational Media/Instructional Technology | M,O |
| Educational Policy | M,D |
| Electrical Engineering | M,D |
| Elementary Education | M |
| Emergency Management | M,D,O |
| Engineering and Applied Sciences—General | M,D,O |
| Engineering Management | M,O |
| English as a Second Language | M,O |
| English Education | M |
| English | M |
| Environmental Engineering | M,D |
| Environmental Management and Policy | M,D |
| Environmental Sciences | M,D |
| Epidemiology | M,D,O |
| Foreign Languages Education | M |
| Gender Studies | O |
| Geographic Information Systems | M,O |
| Geography | M,D |
| Gerontology | M,D |
| Health Informatics | M |
| Health Services Management and Hospital Administration | M,D,O |
| History | M |
| Human Services | M,D |
| Industrial and Organizational Psychology | M |
| Information Science | M,D |
| Linguistics | M |
| Management of Technology | M |
| Marine Sciences | M,D |
| Mathematics Education | M |
| Mechanical Engineering | M,D |
| Mechanics | O |
| Molecular Biology | M,D |
| Multilingual and Multicultural Education | M,D |
| Music Education | M |
| Music | O |
| Neuroscience | D |
| Nonprofit Management | M,O |
| Physics | M,D |
| Psychology—General | M,D |
| Public History | M,D |
| Public Policy | M,D,O |
| Science Education | M |
| Social Psychology | M,D |
| Social Sciences Education | M |
| Social Sciences | D |
| Sociology | M |
| Statistics | M,D |
| Systems Engineering | M,O |
| Theater | M |
| Urban Studies | M,D |
| Women's Studies | O |

**UNIVERSITY OF MARYLAND, COLLEGE PARK**

| | |
|---|---|
| Advertising and Public Relations | M,D |
| Aerospace/Aeronautical Engineering | M,D |
| Agricultural Economics and Agribusiness | M,D |
| Agricultural Sciences—General | M,D |
| American Studies | M,D |
| Analytical Chemistry | M,D |
| Animal Sciences | M,D |
| Anthropology | M |
| Applied Mathematics | M,D |
| Architecture | M |
| Art History | M,D |
| Art Therapy | M,D,O |
| Art/Fine Arts | M |
| Astronomy | M,D |
| Biochemistry | M,D |
| Bioengineering | M,D |
| Bioinformatics | D |
| Biological and Biomedical Sciences—General | M,D |
| Biophysics | D |
| Biostatistics | M,D |
| Broadcast Journalism | M,D |
| Business Administration and Management—General | M,D |
| Cell Biology | M,D |
| Chemical Engineering | M,D |
| Chemical Physics | M,D |
| Chemistry | M,D |
| Child and Family Studies | M,D |
| Civil Engineering | M,D |
| Classics | M |
| Clinical Psychology | M,D |
| Cognitive Sciences | D |
| Communication Disorders | M,D |
| Communication—General | M,D |
| Comparative Literature | M,D |
| Computational Biology | D |
| Computer Engineering | M,D |
| Computer Science | M,D |
| Conservation Biology | M |
| Counseling Psychology | M,D,O |
| Counselor Education | M,D,O |
| Criminal Justice and Criminology | M,D |
| Curriculum and Instruction | M,D,O |
| Dance | M |
| Developmental Psychology | M,D |
| Ecology | M,D |
| Economics | M,D |
| Education—General | M,D,O |
| Educational Leadership and Administration | M,D,O |
| Educational Measurement and Evaluation | M,D |
| Educational Media/Instructional Technology | M,D,O |
| Electrical Engineering | M,D |
| Engineering and Applied Sciences—General | M |
| English as a Second Language | M,D,O |
| English | M,D |
| Entomology | M,D |
| Environmental and Occupational Health | M |
| Environmental Engineering | M,D |
| Environmental Sciences | M,D |
| Epidemiology | M,D |
| Evolutionary Biology | M,D |
| Experimental Psychology | M,D |
| Family and Consumer Sciences-General | M,D |
| Fire Protection Engineering | M |
| Food Science and Technology | M,D |
| Foreign Languages Education | D |
| Foundations and Philosophy of Education | M,D,O |
| French | M,D |
| Genomic Sciences | D |
| Geography | M,D |
| Geology | M,D |
| German | M,D |
| Health Education | M,D |
| Health Services Management and Hospital Administration | M,D |
| Historic Preservation | M,O |
| History | M,D |
| Horticulture | M,D |
| Human Development | M,D |
| Industrial and Organizational Psychology | M,D |
| Information Studies | M,D |
| Inorganic Chemistry | M,D |
| Jewish Studies | M |
| Journalism | M,D |
| Kinesiology and Movement Studies | M,D |
| Landscape Architecture | M |
| Law | |
| Library Science | |
| Linguistics | M,D |
| Manufacturing Engineering | M,D |
| Marine Sciences | M,D |
| Marriage and Family Therapy | M,D |
| Materials Engineering | M,D |
| Materials Sciences | M,D |
| Maternal and Child Health | M,D |
| Mathematics | M,D |
| Mechanical Engineering | M,D |
| Mechanics | M,D |
| Media Studies | M,D |
| Meteorology | M,D |
| Molecular Biology | D |
| Molecular Genetics | M,D |
| Music Education | M,D |
| Music | M,D |
| Natural Resources | M,D |
| Neuroscience | M,D |
| Nuclear Engineering | M,D |
| Nutrition | M,D |
| Oceanography | M,D |
| Organic Chemistry | M,D |
| Philosophy | M,D |
| Physical Chemistry | M,D |
| Physics | M,D |
| Plant Biology | M,D |
| Political Science | D |
| Portuguese | M,D |
| Psychology—General | M,D |
| Public Administration | M |
| Public Health—General | M,D |
| Public Policy | M,D |
| Quantitative Analysis | M,D |
| Reading Education | M,D,O |
| Real Estate | M |
| Rehabilitation Counseling | M,D,O |
| Reliability Engineering | M,D |
| School Psychology | M,D,O |
| Secondary Education | M,D,O |
| Social Psychology | M,D |
| Social Work | |
| Sociology | M,D |
| Spanish | M,D |
| Speech and Interpersonal Communication | M,D |
| Statistics | M,D |
| Student Affairs | M,D,O |
| Survey Methodology | M,D |
| Sustainable Development | M |
| Systems Engineering | M |
| Telecommunications | M |
| Theater | M,D |
| Urban and Regional Planning | M,D |
| Veterinary Medicine | D |
| Veterinary Sciences | M,D |
| Women's Studies | M,D |
| Writing | M,D |

**UNIVERSITY OF MARYLAND EASTERN SHORE**

| | |
|---|---|
| Agricultural Sciences—General | M |
| Chemistry | M,D |
| Computer Science | M |
| Counselor Education | M |
| Criminal Justice and Criminology | M |
| Education—General | M |
| Educational Leadership and Administration | D |
| Environmental Management and Policy | M,D |
| Environmental Sciences | M,D |
| Fish, Game, and Wildlife Management | M,D |
| Food Science and Technology | M,D |
| Marine Sciences | M,D |
| Organizational Management | D |
| Pharmaceutical Sciences | M,D |
| Pharmacy | M,D |
| Physical Therapy | D |
| Rehabilitation Counseling | M |
| Rehabilitation Sciences | M |
| Special Education | M |
| Toxicology | M,D |
| Vocational and Technical Education | M |

**UNIVERSITY OF MARYLAND GLOBAL CAMPUS**

| | |
|---|---|
| Accounting | M,O |
| Biotechnology | M,O |
| Business Administration and Management—General | M,O |
| Computer and Information Systems Security | M,O |
| Data Science/Data Analytics | M,O |
| Distance Education Development | M |
| Education—General | M |
| Educational Media/Instructional Technology | M |
| Environmental Management and Policy | M |
| Finance and Banking | M |
| Health Informatics | M |
| Health Services Management and Hospital Administration | M |
| Information Science | M |
| Management Information Systems | M,O |

### UNIVERSITY OF MARY WASHINGTON

| | |
|---|---|
| Business Administration and Management—General | M |
| Education—General | M |
| Elementary Education | M |

### UNIVERSITY OF MASSACHUSETTS AMHERST

| | |
|---|---|
| Accounting | M,D |
| Adult Nursing | M,D |
| African-American Studies | M,D |
| Agricultural Economics and Agribusiness | M,D |
| American Studies | M,D |
| Animal Behavior | M,D |
| Animal Sciences | M,D |
| Anthropology | M,D |
| Applied Mathematics | M,D |
| Architectural Engineering | M,D |
| Architecture | M |
| Art Education | M |
| Art History | M |
| Art/Fine Arts | M |
| Astronomy | M,D |
| Biochemistry | M,D |
| Biological and Biomedical Sciences—General | M,D |
| Biostatistics | M,D |
| Biotechnology | M,D |
| Business Administration and Management—General | M,D |
| Cell Biology | M,D |
| Chemical Engineering | M,D |
| Chemistry | M,D |
| Child and Family Studies | M,D,O |
| Chinese | M |
| Civil Engineering | M,D |
| Classics | M |
| Clinical Psychology | M,D |
| Cognitive Sciences | M,D |
| Communication Disorders | M,D |
| Communication—General | M,D |
| Community Health Nursing | M,D |
| Community Health | M,D |
| Comparative Literature | M,D |
| Computer Engineering | M,D |
| Computer Science | M,D |
| Conflict Resolution and Mediation/Peace Studies | M,D |
| Counselor Education | M,D,O |
| Developmental Biology | D |
| Developmental Psychology | M,D |
| Early Childhood Education | M,D,O |
| Economics | M,D |
| Education—General | M,D,O |
| Educational Leadership and Administration | M,D,O |
| Educational Measurement and Evaluation | M,D,O |
| Educational Media/Instructional Technology | M,D,O |
| Educational Policy | M,D,O |
| Electrical Engineering | M,D |
| Elementary Education | M,D,O |
| Engineering and Applied Sciences—General | M,D |
| English as a Second Language | M,D,O |
| English | M,D |
| Entertainment Management | |
| Entrepreneurship | M,D |
| Environmental and Occupational Health | M,D |
| Environmental Biology | M,D |
| Environmental Engineering | M,D |
| Environmental Management and Policy | M,D |
| Epidemiology | M,D |
| Evolutionary Biology | M,D |
| Family Nurse Practitioner Studies | M,D |
| Finance and Banking | M,D |
| Fish, Game, and Wildlife Management | M,D |
| Food Science and Technology | M,D |
| Foreign Languages Education | M |
| Forestry | M,D |
| French | M |
| Genetics | M,D |
| Geography | M |
| Geosciences | M,D |
| Geotechnical Engineering | M,D |
| German | M,D |
| Gerontological Nursing | M,D |
| Health Education | M,D |
| Health Services Management and Hospital Administration | M,D |
| Higher Education | M,D,O |
| Hispanic and Latin American Languages | M,D |
| Historic Preservation | M |
| History | M,D |
| Hospitality Management | M,D |
| Industrial and Labor Relations | M |
| Industrial/Management Engineering | M,D |
| Interior Design | M |
| International and Comparative Education | M,D,O |
| Italian | M |
| Japanese | M |
| Kinesiology and Movement Studies | M,D |
| Landscape Architecture | M |
| Linguistics | M,D |
| Management Strategy and Policy | M,D |
| Marine Sciences | M,D |
| Marketing | M,D |
| Mathematics | M,D |
| Mechanical Engineering | M,D |
| Mechanics | M,D |
| Microbiology | M,D |
| Molecular Biophysics | D |
| Multilingual and Multicultural Education | M,D,O |
| Music Education | M,D |
| Music | M,D |
| Neuroscience | M,D |
| Nursing and Healthcare Administration | M,D |
| Nursing—General | M,D |
| Nutrition | M,D |
| Operations Research | M,D |
| Organizational Management | M,D |
| Philosophy | M,D |
| Physics | M,D |
| Physiology | M,D |
| Plant Biology | M,D |
| Plant Molecular Biology | M,D |
| Plant Physiology | M,D |
| Plant Sciences | M,D |
| Political Science | M,D |
| Polymer Science and Engineering | M,D |
| Portuguese | M,D |
| Psychology—General | M,D |
| Public Administration | M |
| Public Health—General | M,D |
| Public Policy | M |
| Reading Education | M,D,O |
| Rhetoric | M,D |
| Scandinavian Languages | M,D |
| School Psychology | M,D,O |
| Science Education | M,D,O |
| Secondary Education | M,D,O |
| Social Psychology | M,D |
| Sociology | M,D |
| Spanish | M,D |
| Special Education | M,D,O |
| Sports Management | M,D |
| Statistics | M,D |
| Structural Engineering | M,D |
| Sustainable Development | M |
| Theater | M |
| Transportation and Highway Engineering | M,D |
| Travel and Tourism | M,D |
| Urban and Regional Planning | M,D |
| Water Resources Engineering | M,D |
| Water Resources | M,D |
| Writing | M,D |

### UNIVERSITY OF MASSACHUSETTS BOSTON

| | |
|---|---|
| Accounting | M |
| American Studies | M |
| Applied Economics | M |
| Applied Physics | M |
| Archaeology | M |
| Archives/Archival Administration | M |
| Biological and Biomedical Sciences—General | M,D |
| Biomedical Engineering | D |
| Biotechnology | M,D |
| Business Administration and Management—General | M |
| Business Analytics | M |
| Chemistry | M,D |
| Classics | M |
| Clinical Psychology | D |
| Cognitive Sciences | M |
| Computational Sciences | D |
| Computer Science | M,D |
| Conflict Resolution and Mediation/Peace Studies | M,O |
| Counseling Psychology | M,D |
| Counselor Education | M |
| Cultural Studies | M |
| Early Childhood Education | D |
| Education—General | M,D,O |
| Educational Leadership and Administration | M,D,O |
| Educational Media/Instructional Technology | M,O |
| Educational Policy | D |
| English | M |
| Environmental Sciences | M,D |
| Exercise and Sports Science | M,D |
| Finance and Banking | M |
| Gerontology | M,D,O |
| Higher Education | D |
| History | M |
| Human Services | M |
| International Affairs | M |
| International Business | M |
| International Development | M,D |
| Linguistics | M,D |
| Management Information Systems | M |
| Marine Sciences | M,D |
| Marriage and Family Therapy | M |
| Nursing—General | M,D |
| Public Administration | M |
| Public Policy | M,D |
| Quality Management | M,O |
| Rehabilitation Counseling | M |
| School Psychology | M,D |
| Sociology | M,D |
| Special Education | M |
| Urban and Regional Planning | M |
| Urban Education | D |
| Vision Sciences | M |
| Writing | M |

### UNIVERSITY OF MASSACHUSETTS DARTMOUTH

| | |
|---|---|
| Accounting | M,O |
| Applied Behavior Analysis | M,O |
| Art Education | M |
| Art History | M |
| Art/Fine Arts | M,O |
| Biochemistry | M,D |
| Biological and Biomedical Sciences—General | M,D |
| Biomedical Engineering | D |
| Biotechnology | D |
| Business Administration and Management—General | M,O |
| Chemistry | M,D |
| Civil Engineering | M |
| Clinical Psychology | M,O |
| Community Health Nursing | M,D |
| Computer Engineering | M,D,O |
| Computer Science | M,O |
| Data Science/Data Analytics | M |
| Education—General | M,D,O |
| Educational Leadership and Administration | D |
| Educational Policy | M,D,O |
| Electrical Engineering | M,D,O |
| Engineering and Applied Sciences—General | D |
| English as a Second Language | M,D,O |
| Environmental Management and Policy | M,O |
| Experimental Psychology | M,O |
| Finance and Banking | M,O |
| Health Services Management and Hospital Administration | M |
| Industrial/Management Engineering | M,O |
| Latin American Studies | M,D |
| Law | D |
| Management of Technology | M |
| Marine Affairs | M,D |
| Marine Biology | M,D |
| Marine Sciences | M,D |
| Mathematics Education | M,D,O |
| Mechanical Engineering | M,O |
| Media Studies | M |
| Middle School Education | M,D,O |
| Nursing—General | M,D |
| Physics | M |
| Portuguese | M,D |
| Psychology—General | M,O |
| Public Administration | M,O |
| Public Policy | M,O |
| Science Education | M,D,O |
| Secondary Education | M,D,O |
| Software Engineering | M,O |
| Special Education | M,O |
| Systems Engineering | M,O |
| Telecommunications | M,D,O |
| Writing | M,O |

### UNIVERSITY OF MASSACHUSETTS LOWELL

| | |
|---|---|
| Allied Health—General | M,D |
| Analytical Chemistry | M,D |
| Biochemistry | M,D |
| Biological and Biomedical Sciences—General | M |
| Business Administration and Management—General | M,D |
| Chemical Engineering | M,D |
| Chemistry | M,D |
| Civil Engineering | M,D |
| Clinical Laboratory Sciences/Medical Technology | M |
| Computer Engineering | M,D |
| Computer Science | M,D |
| Conflict Resolution and Mediation/Peace Studies | M |
| Criminal Justice and Criminology | M |
| Curriculum and Instruction | M |
| Economic Development | M,O |
| Economics | M,O |
| Education—General | M |
| Electrical Engineering | M,D |
| Energy and Power Engineering | M,D |
| Engineering and Applied Sciences—General | M,D |
| Entrepreneurship | M,D |
| Environmental Engineering | M,D |
| Environmental Sciences | M,D |
| Family Nurse Practitioner Studies | M |
| Gerontological Nursing | M |
| Health Physics/Radiological Health | M |
| Health Promotion | D |
| Industrial/Management Engineering | D |
| Inorganic Chemistry | M,D |
| Legal and Justice Studies | M |
| Mathematics | D |
| Mechanical Engineering | M,D |
| Music Education | M |
| Music | M |
| Nuclear Engineering | M,D |
| Nursing—General | M,D |
| Organic Chemistry | M,D |
| Physical Therapy | D |
| Physics | M,D |
| Polymer Science and Engineering | M,D |
| Psychology—General | M |
| Social Psychology | M |
| Sociology | M,O |
| Urban and Regional Planning | M,O |

### UNIVERSITY OF MASSACHUSETTS MEDICAL SCHOOL

| | |
|---|---|
| Adult Nursing | M,D,O |
| Allopathic Medicine | D |
| Biochemistry | M,D |
| Bioinformatics | M,D |
| Biological and Biomedical Sciences—General | M,D |
| Cancer Biology/Oncology | M,D |
| Clinical Research | M,D |
| Computational Biology | M,D |
| Family Nurse Practitioner Studies | M,D,O |
| Gerontological Nursing | M,D,O |
| Health Services Research | M,D |
| Immunology | M,D |
| Interdisciplinary Studies | M,D |
| Microbiology | M,D |
| Molecular Pharmacology | M,D |
| Neuroscience | M,D |
| Nursing and Healthcare Administration | M,D,O |
| Nursing Education | M,D,O |
| Nursing—General | M,D,O |
| Translational Biology | M,D |

### UNIVERSITY OF MEMPHIS

| | |
|---|---|
| Accounting | M,D |
| Adult Education | M,D,O |
| African-American Studies | M,D,O |
| Allied Health—General | M,O |
| Analytical Chemistry | M,D |
| Anthropology | M |
| Applied Behavior Analysis | M,D,O |
| Applied Mathematics | M,D |
| Applied Statistics | M,D |
| Archaeology | M,D,O |
| Architecture | M |
| Art History | M,O |
| Art/Fine Arts | M,O |
| Bioinformatics | M,D |
| Biological and Biomedical Sciences—General | M,D |
| Biomedical Engineering | M,D |
| Biostatistics | M,D |
| Business Administration and Management—General | M,D |
| Chemistry | M,D |
| Civil Engineering | M,D,O |
| Clinical Psychology | M,D,O |
| Communication Disorders | M,D |
| Communication—General | M,D |
| Community College Education | M,D,O |
| Comparative Literature | M,D,O |
| Computational Sciences | M |
| Computer Engineering | M,D,O |
| Computer Science | M,D |
| Counseling Psychology | M,D |
| Counselor Education | M,D |
| Criminal Justice and Criminology | M |
| Curriculum and Instruction | M,D,O |
| Early Childhood Education | M,D,O |
| Economics | M,D |
| Education—General | M,D,O |
| Educational Leadership and Administration | M,D,O |
| Educational Measurement and Evaluation | M,D |
| Educational Media/Instructional Technology | M,D,O |
| Educational Psychology | M,D |
| Electrical Engineering | M,D,O |
| Electronic Materials | M,O |
| Elementary Education | M,D,O |
| Energy and Power Engineering | M,D,O |
| Engineering and Applied Sciences—General | M,D,O |
| English as a Second Language | M,D,O |
| English | M,D,O |
| Environmental and Occupational Health | M,D |
| Environmental Engineering | M,D,O |
| Epidemiology | M,D |
| Exercise and Sports Science | M,O |
| Experimental Psychology | M,D,O |
| Family Nurse Practitioner Studies | M,O |
| Film, Television, and Video Production | M,D |
| Finance and Banking | M,D |
| French | M |
| Gender Studies | O |
| Geographic Information Systems | M,D,O |
| Geography | M,D,O |
| Geology | M,D,O |
| Geophysics | M,D,O |
| Geotechnical Engineering | M,D,O |
| Graphic Design | M,O |
| Health Promotion | M,O |
| Health Services Management and Hospital Administration | M,D |
| Higher Education | M,D,O |
| History | M,D |
| Hospitality Management | M,O |
| Human Resources Management | M,O |
| Inorganic Chemistry | M,D |
| Interdisciplinary Studies | M,D,O |
| Journalism | M,O |
| Law | D |
| Liberal Studies | M,O |
| Linguistics | M,D,O |
| Management Information Systems | M,D,O |
| Management Strategy and Policy | M,O |
| Marketing | M,D |
| Mathematics Education | M,D |
| Mathematics | M,D,O |
| Mechanical Engineering | M,D,O |
| Museum Studies | M,O |
| Music Education | M,D |
| Music | M,D |
| Near and Middle Eastern Studies | M,D |
| Nonprofit Management | M,O |
| Nursing and Healthcare Administration | M,O |
| Nursing Education | M,O |
| Nursing—General | M,O |
| Nutrition | M,O |
| Organic Chemistry | M,D |
| Philanthropic Studies | M,O |
| Philosophy | M,D |
| Photography | M,O |
| Physical Chemistry | M,D |
| Physical Education | M,O |
| Physics | M |
| Political Science | M |
| Psychology—General | M,D,O |
| Public Administration | M,O |
| Public Health—General | M,D |

*M—masters degree; D—doctorate; O—other advanced degree; *—Close-Up and/or Display*

| | |
|---|---|
| Public Policy | M,O |
| Reading Education | M,D,O |
| Real Estate | M,D |
| Rehabilitation Counseling | M,D |
| School Psychology | M,D,O |
| Science Education | M,D,O |
| Secondary Education | M,D,O |
| Social Sciences | M,D |
| Social Work | M |
| Sociology | M |
| Spanish | M |
| Special Education | M,D,O |
| Statistics | M,D |
| Structural Engineering | M,D,O |
| Supply Chain Management | M,D |
| Theater | M |
| Transportation and Highway Engineering | M,D,O |
| Urban and Regional Planning | M |
| Urban Education | M,D,O |
| Water Resources Engineering | M,D,O |
| Writing | M,D,O |

**UNIVERSITY OF MIAMI**

| | |
|---|---|
| Accounting | M,D |
| Acute Care/Critical Care Nursing | M,D |
| Adult Nursing | M,D |
| Advertising and Public Relations | M,D |
| Aerospace/Aeronautical Engineering | M,D |
| Allopathic Medicine | D |
| Architectural Engineering | M,D |
| Architecture | M |
| Art History | M |
| Art/Fine Arts | M |
| Athletic Training and Sports Medicine | M,D |
| Biochemistry | D |
| Biological and Biomedical Sciences—General | M,D |
| Biomedical Engineering | M,D |
| Biophysics | D |
| Biostatistics | M,D |
| Broadcast Journalism | M,D |
| Business Administration and Management—General | M,D |
| Business Analytics | M,D |
| Cancer Biology/Oncology | D |
| Cell Biology | D |
| Chemistry | M,D |
| Civil Engineering | M,D |
| Clinical Psychology | M,D |
| Communication—General | M,D |
| Community Health | M,D |
| Computer Engineering | M,D |
| Computer Science | M,D |
| Counseling Psychology | D |
| Counselor Education | M,O |
| Developmental Biology | D |
| Developmental Psychology | M,D |
| Early Childhood Education | M,O |
| Economics | M,D |
| Education—General | M,D,O |
| Educational Measurement and Evaluation | M,D |
| Electrical Engineering | M,D |
| Engineering and Applied Sciences—General | M,D |
| English | M,D |
| Environmental and Occupational Health | M |
| Epidemiology | M,D |
| Ergonomics and Human Factors | M |
| Evolutionary Biology | M,D |
| Exercise and Sports Science | M,D |
| Family Nurse Practitioner Studies | M,D |
| Film, Television, and Video Production | M,D |
| Film, Television, and Video Theory and Criticism | M,D |
| Finance and Banking | M,D |
| Fish, Game, and Wildlife Management | M,D |
| French | D |
| Genetics | M,D |
| Geography | M |
| Geophysics | M,D |
| Graphic Design | M |
| Health Services Management and Hospital Administration | M,D |
| Higher Education | M,D,O |
| History | M,D |
| Immunology | D |
| Industrial/Management Engineering | M,D |
| Inorganic Chemistry | M,D |
| International Affairs | M,D |
| International Business | M,D |
| Internet and Interactive Multimedia | M |
| Journalism | M,D |
| Latin American Studies | M |
| Law | M,D |
| Liberal Studies | M |
| Management of Technology | M,D |
| Marine Affairs | M |
| Marine Biology | M,D |
| Marine Geology | M,D |
| Marine Sciences | M,D |
| Marriage and Family Therapy | M,O |
| Mathematical and Computational Finance | M,D |
| Mathematics Education | D |
| Mathematics | M,D |
| Mechanical Engineering | M,D |
| Meteorology | M,D |
| Microbiology | D |
| Molecular Biology | D |
| Multilingual and Multicultural Education | D |
| Music Education | M,D,O |
| Music | M,D,O |
| Neuroscience | M,D |
| Nurse Anesthesia | M,D |
| Nurse Midwifery | M,D |
| Nursing—General | M,D |
| Nutrition | M |
| Oceanography | M,D |
| Organic Chemistry | M,D |
| Pharmacology | D |
| Philosophy | M,D |
| Photography | M |
| Physical Chemistry | M,D |
| Physical Therapy | D |
| Physics | M,D |
| Physiology | D |
| Political Science | M |
| Psychology—General | M,D |
| Public Health—General | M,D |
| Reading Education | D |
| Real Estate | M,D |
| Romance Languages | D |
| Science Education | D |
| Sociology | M,D |
| Spanish | M,D |
| Special Education | M,D,O |
| Sports Management | M |
| Taxation | M,D |
| Therapies—Dance, Drama, and Music | M,D,O |
| Urban Design | M |
| Writing | M,D |

**UNIVERSITY OF MICHIGAN**

| | |
|---|---|
| Accounting | M,D |
| Aerospace/Aeronautical Engineering | M,D |
| African Studies | M |
| Allopathic Medicine | D |
| American Studies | M,D |
| Analytical Chemistry | M,D |
| Anthropology | D |
| Applied Arts and Design—General | M,D |
| Applied Economics | M |
| Applied Physics | D |
| Applied Statistics | M,D |
| Archaeology | M,D |
| Architecture | M |
| Art History | M,D |
| Art/Fine Arts | M |
| Artificial Intelligence/Robotics | M,D |
| Asian Languages | D |
| Asian Studies | M,D,O |
| Astronomy | D |
| Astrophysics | D |
| Atmospheric Sciences | M,D |
| Automotive Engineering | M,D |
| Biochemistry | M,D |
| Bioinformatics | M,D |
| Biological and Biomedical Sciences—General | M,D |
| Biological Anthropology | D |
| Biomedical Engineering | M,D |
| Biophysics | D |
| Biopsychology | D |
| Biostatistics | M,D |
| Business Administration and Management—General | M,D |
| Cancer Biology/Oncology | M,D |
| Cell Biology | M,D |
| Chemical Engineering | M,D,O |
| Chemistry | M,D |
| Civil Engineering | M,D,O |
| Classics | M,D,O |
| Clinical Psychology | D |
| Clinical Research | M |
| Cognitive Sciences | D |
| Communication—General | D |
| Comparative Literature | D |
| Computer Engineering | M,D |
| Computer Science | M,D |
| Construction Engineering | M,D,O |
| Cultural Anthropology | D |
| Dance | M |
| Data Science/Data Analytics | M,D,O |
| Dental Hygiene | M |
| Dentistry | D |
| Developmental Biology | M,D |
| Developmental Psychology | D |
| East European and Russian Studies | M,O |
| Ecology | M,D |
| Economics | M,D |
| Education—General | M,D |
| Electrical Engineering | M,D |
| Energy and Power Engineering | M,D |
| Engineering and Applied Sciences—General | M,D,O |
| Engineering Design | M,D |
| English Education | D |
| English | M,D,O |
| Environmental and Occupational Health | M,D |
| Environmental Engineering | M,D,O |
| Environmental Management and Policy | M,D |
| Environmental Sciences | M,D |
| Epidemiology | M,D |
| Evolutionary Biology | M,D |
| Film, Television, and Video Theory and Criticism | D,O |
| Foreign Languages Education | M,D |
| French | D |
| Genetic Counseling | M,D |
| Geosciences | M,D |
| German | M,D,O |
| Health Education | M,D |
| Health Informatics | M,D |
| Health Physics/Radiological Health | M,D,O |
| Health Promotion | M,D |
| Health Services Management and Hospital Administration | M,D |
| History | D,O |
| Human Genetics | M,D |
| Immunology | M,D |
| Industrial Hygiene | M,D |
| Industrial/Management Engineering | M,D |
| Information Science | M,D |
| Information Studies | M,D |
| Inorganic Chemistry | M,D |
| International Health | M,D |
| Italian | D |
| Jewish Studies | M,D,O |
| Kinesiology and Movement Studies | M,D |
| Landscape Architecture | M |
| Law | M,D |
| Linguistics | D |
| Manufacturing Engineering | M,D |
| Materials Engineering | M,D |
| Materials Sciences | M,D |
| Mathematics | M,D |
| Mechanical Engineering | M,D |
| Media Studies | M |
| Medicinal and Pharmaceutical Chemistry | D |
| Microbiology | M,D |
| Molecular Biology | M,D |
| Molecular Pathology | D |
| Music Education | M,D,O |
| Music | M,D,O |
| Natural Resources | M,D |
| Near and Middle Eastern Languages | M,D |
| Near and Middle Eastern Studies | M,D |
| Neuroscience | D |
| Nuclear Engineering | M,D,O |
| Nursing—General | M,D,O |
| Nutrition | M,D |
| Ocean Engineering | M,D,O |
| Operations Research | M,D |
| Oral and Dental Sciences | M,D |
| Organic Chemistry | M,D |
| Pathology | D |
| Pediatric Nursing | M,D,O |
| Pharmaceutical Administration | D |
| Pharmaceutical Engineering | M,D |
| Pharmaceutical Sciences | D |
| Pharmacology | M,D |
| Pharmacy | D |
| Philosophy | M,D |
| Physical Chemistry | M,D |
| Physics | D |
| Physiology | M,D |
| Planetary and Space Sciences | M,D |
| Political Science | D |
| Psychology—General | D,O |
| Public Health—General | M,D |
| Public Policy | M,D |
| Quantitative Analysis | M,D |
| Religion | M,D |
| Risk Management | M,D |
| Slavic Languages | M,D |
| Social Psychology | D |
| Social Sciences | D |
| Social Work | M |
| Sociology | D |
| Spanish | D |
| Sports Management | M,D |
| Statistics | M,D,O |
| Structural Engineering | M,D,O |
| Supply Chain Management | M,D |
| Survey Methodology | M,D,O |
| Sustainable Development | M,D |
| Systems Engineering | M,D |
| Systems Science | M,D |
| Taxation | M,D |
| Toxicology | M,D |
| Urban and Regional Planning | M,D |
| Urban Design | M |
| Women's Studies | D,O |
| Writing | M |

**UNIVERSITY OF MICHIGAN–DEARBORN**

| | |
|---|---|
| Accounting | M |
| Applied Behavior Analysis | M |
| Applied Mathematics | M |
| Automotive Engineering | M |
| Bioengineering | M |
| Business Administration and Management—General | M |
| Business Analytics | M |
| Clinical Psychology | M |
| Computational Sciences | M |
| Computer and Information Systems Security | D |
| Computer Engineering | M,D |
| Computer Science | D |
| Criminal Justice and Criminology | M |
| Curriculum and Instruction | D,O |
| Data Science/Data Analytics | M,D |
| Early Childhood Education | M |
| Education—General | M |
| Educational Leadership and Administration | M,D,O |
| Educational Measurement and Evaluation | M |
| Educational Media/Instructional Technology | M |
| Electrical Engineering | M,D |
| Energy and Power Engineering | M |
| Engineering and Applied Sciences—General | M,D |
| Engineering Management | M |
| Environmental Sciences | M |
| Finance and Banking | M |
| Health Informatics | M |
| Health Psychology | M |
| Industrial/Management Engineering | M,D |
| Information Science | M,D |
| Management Information Systems | M |
| Manufacturing Engineering | M |
| Mechanical Engineering | M,D |
| Project Management | M |
| Public Administration | M |
| Software Engineering | M,D |
| Supply Chain Management | M |
| Systems Engineering | M,D |
| Urban Education | M,D |

**UNIVERSITY OF MICHIGAN–FLINT**

| | |
|---|---|
| Accounting | M,O |
| American Studies | M |
| Art/Fine Arts | M |
| Arts Administration | M |
| Biological and Biomedical Sciences—General | M |
| Business Administration and Management—General | M,O |
| Computer Science | M |
| Criminal Justice and Criminology | M |
| Curriculum and Instruction | M,D,O |
| Early Childhood Education | M,D,O |
| Education—General | M,D,O |
| Educational Leadership and Administration | M,D,O |
| Educational Media/Instructional Technology | M,D,O |
| English | M |
| Family Nurse Practitioner Studies | M,D,O |
| Finance and Banking | M,O |
| Gender Studies | M |
| Gerontology | M,D,O |
| Health Education | M |
| Health Informatics | M |
| Health Services Management and Hospital Administration | M,O |
| Industrial and Manufacturing Management | M,O |
| Information Science | M |
| International Affairs | M |
| International Business | M,O |
| Liberal Studies | M |
| Management Information Systems | M,O |
| Marketing | M,O |
| Mechanical Engineering | M |
| Museum Studies | M |
| Music | M |
| Neuroscience | D,O |
| Nonprofit Management | M |
| Nurse Anesthesia | D |
| Nursing—General | M,D,O |
| Organizational Management | M,O |
| Physical Therapy | D,O |
| Political Science | M |
| Psychiatric Nursing | M,D,O |
| Public Administration | M |
| Public Health—General | M |
| Reading Education | M,D,O |
| Rhetoric | M |
| Secondary Education | M,D,O |
| Social Sciences | M |
| Writing | M |

**UNIVERSITY OF MINNESOTA, DULUTH**

| | |
|---|---|
| Allopathic Medicine | D |
| Anthropology | M |
| Applied Mathematics | M |
| Art/Fine Arts | M |
| Biochemistry | M,D |
| Biological and Biomedical Sciences—General | M,D |
| Biophysics | M,D |
| Business Administration and Management—General | M |
| Chemistry | M |
| Communication Disorders | M |
| Computational Sciences | M |
| Computer Engineering | M |
| Computer Science | M |
| Criminal Justice and Criminology | M |
| Education—General | M,D |
| Electrical Engineering | M |
| Engineering Management | M |
| English | M |
| Geology | M,D |
| Graphic Design | M |
| Immunology | M,D |
| Liberal Studies | M |
| Medical Microbiology | M,D |
| Molecular Biology | M,D |
| Music Education | M |
| Music | M |
| Pharmacology | M,D |
| Pharmacy | M,D |
| Physics | M |
| Physiology | M,D |
| Safety Engineering | M |
| Social Work | M |
| Sociology | M |
| Toxicology | M,D |

**UNIVERSITY OF MINNESOTA ROCHESTER**

| | |
|---|---|
| Bioinformatics | M,D |
| Business Administration and Management—General | M,D |
| Computational Biology | M,D |
| Occupational Therapy | M,D |

**UNIVERSITY OF MINNESOTA, TWIN CITIES CAMPUS**

| | |
|---|---|
| Accounting | M,D |
| Adult Education | M,D,O |
| Aerospace/Aeronautical Engineering | M,D |
| Agricultural Sciences—General | M,D |
| Agronomy and Soil Sciences | M,D |
| Allopathic Medicine | M,D |
| American Studies | D |
| Animal Behavior | M,D |
| Animal Sciences | M,D |
| Anthropology | M,D |
| Applied Arts and Design—General | M,D,O |
| Applied Economics | M,D |
| Archaeology | M,D |
| Architecture | M |
| Art Education | M |
| Art History | M,D |
| Art/Fine Arts | M |
| Asian Languages | D |

| | |
|---|---|
| Asian Studies | D |
| Astrophysics | M,D |
| Biochemistry | D |
| Biological and Biomedical Sciences—General | M |
| Biomedical Engineering | M,D |
| Biophysics | M,D |
| Biopsychology | D |
| Biostatistics | M,D |
| Biosystems Engineering | M,D |
| Biotechnology | M |
| Business Administration and Management—General | M,D |
| Cancer Biology/Oncology | D |
| Cell Biology | M,D |
| Chemical Engineering | M,D |
| Chemical Physics | M,D |
| Chemistry | M,D |
| Child and Family Studies | M,D |
| Child Development | M,D |
| Civil Engineering | M,D,O |
| Classics | M,D |
| Clinical Laboratory Sciences/Medical Technology | M |
| Clinical Psychology | D |
| Clinical Research | M |
| Clothing and Textiles | M,D,O |
| Cognitive Sciences | D |
| Communication Disorders | M,D |
| Communication—General | M,D,O |
| Community Health | M |
| Comparative Literature | D |
| Computational Sciences | M,D |
| Computer and Information Systems Security | M |
| Computer Engineering | M,D |
| Computer Science | M,D |
| Conservation Biology | M,D |
| Counseling Psychology | D |
| Counselor Education | M |
| Cultural Studies | D |
| Curriculum and Instruction | M,D |
| Data Science/Data Analytics | M |
| Dentistry | D |
| Developmental Biology | M,D |
| Early Childhood Education | M,D,O |
| Ecology | M,D |
| Economics | M,D |
| Education of the Gifted | M,D,O |
| Education—General | M,D,O |
| Educational Leadership and Administration | M,D |
| Educational Measurement and Evaluation | M,D |
| Educational Media/Instructional Technology | M,D,O |
| Educational Policy | M,D |
| Educational Psychology | M,D,O |
| Electrical Engineering | M,D |
| Elementary Education | M |
| Engineering and Applied Sciences—General | M,D,O |
| English as a Second Language | M,D,O |
| English Education | M |
| English | M,D |
| Entomology | M,D |
| Entrepreneurship | D |
| Environmental and Occupational Health | M,D,O |
| Environmental Management and Policy | M,D |
| Epidemiology | M,D |
| Evolutionary Biology | M,D |
| Exercise and Sports Science | M,D |
| Family Nurse Practitioner Studies | M,D |
| Finance and Banking | M,D |
| Food Science and Technology | M,D |
| Foreign Languages Education | M |
| Forestry | M,D |
| Foundations and Philosophy of Education | M,D |
| French | M,D |
| Genetic Counseling | M,D |
| Genetics | M,D |
| Geographic Information Systems | M,D |
| Geography | M,D |
| Geological Engineering | M,D,O |
| Geology | M,D |
| Geophysics | M,D |
| German | M,D |
| Gerontological Nursing | M,D |
| Health Informatics | M,D |
| Health Services Management and Hospital Administration | M,D |
| Health Services Research | M,D |
| Higher Education | M,D |
| Hispanic and Latin American Languages | M,D |
| History of Medicine | M,D |
| History of Science and Technology | M,D |
| History | M,D |
| Human Resources Development | M,D,O |
| Human Resources Management | M |
| Hydrology | M,D |
| Immunology | D |
| Industrial and Labor Relations | M |
| Industrial and Organizational Psychology | D |
| Industrial Hygiene | M,D |
| Industrial/Management Engineering | M,D |
| Infectious Diseases | M,D |
| Interdisciplinary Studies | D |
| Interior Design | M,D,O |
| International and Comparative Education | M,D |
| International Development | M |
| International Health | M,D |
| Kinesiology and Movement Studies | M,D |
| Landscape Architecture | M |
| Law | M,D |
| Linguistics | M,D |
| Management Information Systems | M,D |
| Management of Technology | M |
| Management Strategy and Policy | D |
| Marketing | M,D |
| Marriage and Family Therapy | M,D |
| Mass Communication | M,D |
| Materials Engineering | M,D |
| Materials Sciences | M,D |
| Maternal and Child Health | M |
| Mathematics Education | M,D,O |
| Mathematics | M,D,O |
| Mechanical Engineering | M,D |
| Mechanics | M,D |
| Medical Physics | M,D |
| Medicinal and Pharmaceutical Chemistry | M,D |
| Medieval and Renaissance Studies | M,D |
| Microbiology | D |
| Molecular Biology | M,D |
| Multilingual and Multicultural Education | M,D,O |
| Music | M,D |
| Natural Resources | M,D |
| Neurobiology | M,D |
| Neuroscience | M,D |
| Nurse Anesthesia | M,D |
| Nurse Midwifery | M,D |
| Nursing and Healthcare Administration | M,D |
| Nursing Informatics | M,D |
| Nursing—General | M,D |
| Nutrition | M,D |
| Occupational Health Nursing | M,D |
| Occupational Therapy | M |
| Oral and Dental Sciences | M,D,O |
| Paper and Pulp Engineering | M,D |
| Pediatric Nursing | M,D |
| Pharmaceutical Administration | M,D |
| Pharmaceutical Sciences | M,D |
| Pharmacology | M,D |
| Pharmacy | D |
| Philosophy | M,D |
| Physical Therapy | M,D |
| Physics | M,D |
| Physiology | D |
| Plant Biology | M,D |
| Plant Pathology | M,D |
| Plant Sciences | M,D |
| Political Science | D |
| Portuguese | M,D |
| Psychiatric Nursing | M,D |
| Psychology—General | D |
| Public Affairs | M,D |
| Public Health—General | M,D,O |
| Public Policy | M,D |
| Quantitative Analysis | M,D,O |
| Reading Education | M,D,O |
| Religion | M,D |
| Scandinavian Languages | M,D |
| School Psychology | M,D,O |
| Science Education | M |
| Social Psychology | D |
| Social Sciences Education | M |
| Social Work | M,D |
| Sociology | M,D |
| Software Engineering | M |
| Spanish | M,D |
| Special Education | M,D |
| Sports Management | M,D |
| Statistics | M,D |
| Structural Biology | D |
| Student Affairs | M |
| Supply Chain Management | M,D |
| Taxation | M |
| Technology and Public Policy | M |
| Textile Design | M,D,O |
| Theater | M,D |
| Toxicology | M,D |
| Travel and Tourism | M,D |
| Urban and Regional Planning | M,D |
| Veterinary Medicine | D |
| Veterinary Sciences | M,D |
| Virology | D |
| Vocational and Technical Education | M,D,O |
| Water Resources | M,D |
| Women's Health Nursing | M,D |
| Women's Studies | D |

### UNIVERSITY OF MISSISSIPPI

| | |
|---|---|
| Accounting | M,D |
| Anthropology | M,D |
| Applied Science and Technology | M,D |
| Art/Fine Arts | M,D |
| Biological and Biomedical Sciences—General | M,D |
| Business Administration and Management—General | M,D |
| Chemical Engineering | M,D |
| Chemistry | M,D |
| Civil Engineering | M,D |
| Communication Disorders | M,D |
| Computer Science | M,D |
| Counselor Education | M,D,O |
| Criminal Justice and Criminology | M,D |
| Data Science/Data Analytics | M,D |
| Early Childhood Education | M,D,O |
| Economics | M,D |
| Education—General | M,D,O |
| Educational Leadership and Administration | M,D,O |
| Electrical Engineering | M,D |
| Elementary Education | M,D,O |
| Engineering and Applied Sciences—General | M,D |
| English | M,D |
| Environmental Engineering | M,D |
| Exercise and Sports Science | M,D |
| Experimental Psychology | M,D |
| Film, Television, and Video Production | M,D |
| Finance and Banking | M,D |
| Food Science and Technology | M,D |
| Foreign Languages Education | M,D |
| Geological Engineering | M,D |
| Geology | M,D |
| Health Promotion | M,D |
| Higher Education | M,D,O |
| History | M,D |
| Hospitality Management | M,D |
| Hydrology | M,D |
| Journalism | M |
| Kinesiology and Movement Studies | M,D |
| Law | M,D |
| Management Information Systems | M,D |
| Marketing | M,D |
| Mathematics Education | M,D,O |
| Mathematics | M,D |
| Mechanical Engineering | M,D |
| Medicinal and Pharmaceutical Chemistry | M,D |
| Music | M,D |
| Nutrition | M,D |
| Pharmaceutical Administration | M,D |
| Pharmaceutical Sciences | M,D |
| Pharmacology | M,D |
| Pharmacy | M,D |
| Philosophy | M,D |
| Physics | M,D |
| Political Science | M,D |
| Reading Education | M,D,O |
| Recreation and Park Management | M,D |
| Secondary Education | M,D,O |
| Social Work | M,D |
| Special Education | M,D,O |
| Taxation | M,D |
| Telecommunications | M,D |
| Toxicology | M,D |
| Writing | M,D |

### UNIVERSITY OF MISSISSIPPI MEDICAL CENTER

| | |
|---|---|
| Allied Health—General | M |
| Allopathic Medicine | D |
| Anatomy | M,D |
| Biochemistry | D |
| Biological and Biomedical Sciences—General | M,D |
| Biophysics | D |
| Dentistry | M,D |
| Materials Sciences | M,D |
| Microbiology | D |
| Neuroscience | D |
| Nursing—General | M,D |
| Occupational Therapy | M,D |
| Oral and Dental Sciences | M,D |
| Pathology | D |
| Pharmacology | D |
| Physical Therapy | M |
| Physiology | D |
| Toxicology | D |

### UNIVERSITY OF MISSOURI

| | |
|---|---|
| Accounting | M,D,O |
| Adult Education | M,D,O |
| Adult Nursing | M,D,O |
| Aerospace/Aeronautical Engineering | M,D |
| Agricultural Economics and Agribusiness | M,D |
| Agricultural Education | M,D,O |
| Agricultural Sciences—General | M,D |
| Agronomy and Soil Sciences | M,D,O |
| Allopathic Medicine | D |
| Analytical Chemistry | D |
| Anatomy | M,D |
| Animal Sciences | M,D |
| Anthropology | M,D |
| Applied Mathematics | M,D |
| Architecture | M,D |
| Art Education | M,D,O |
| Art/Fine Arts | M |
| Astronomy | M,D |
| Biochemistry | M,D |
| Bioengineering | M,D |
| Bioinformatics | M |
| Biological and Biomedical Sciences—General | M,D,O |
| Business Administration and Management—General | M,D |
| Business Education | M,D,O |
| Chemical Engineering | M,D |
| Chemistry | D |
| Child and Family Studies | M,D |
| Civil Engineering | M,D |
| Classics | M,D |
| Clothing and Textiles | M,D |
| Communication Disorders | M,D |
| Communication—General | M,D |
| Computer Engineering | M,D |
| Computer Science | M,D |
| Conflict Resolution and Mediation/Peace Studies | M,D |
| Conservation Biology | M,D,O |
| Consumer Economics | D |
| Counseling Psychology | M,D,O |
| Curriculum and Instruction | M,D,O |
| Early Childhood Education | M,D,O |
| Ecology | M,D |
| Economics | M,D |
| Education—General | M,D,O |
| Educational Leadership and Administration | M,D,O |
| Educational Media/Instructional Technology | D |
| Educational Psychology | M,D,O |
| Electrical Engineering | M,D |
| Elementary Education | M,D,O |
| Engineering and Applied Sciences—General | M,D,O |
| English Education | M,D,O |
| English | M,D |
| Entomology | M,D |
| Environmental Engineering | M,D |
| Environmental Sciences | M,D,O |
| Evolutionary Biology | M,D |
| Family and Consumer Sciences-General | M,D,O |
| Family Nurse Practitioner Studies | M,D,O |
| Finance and Banking | M,D |
| Fish, Game, and Wildlife Management | M,D,O |
| Food Science and Technology | M,D |
| Foreign Languages Education | M,D,O |
| Forestry | M,D,O |
| French | M,D |
| Geographic Information Systems | M,D,O |
| Geography | M,O |
| Geology | M,D |
| German | M |
| Gerontological Nursing | M,D,O |
| Health Communication | M,D |
| Health Education | M,D,O |
| Health Informatics | M,O |
| Health Physics/Radiological Health | M |
| Health Promotion | M,O |
| Health Services Management and Hospital Administration | M,O |
| Higher Education | M,D,O |
| History | M,D |
| Horticulture | M,D |
| Hospitality Management | M,D |
| Human Development | M,D |
| Immunology | D |
| Industrial/Management Engineering | M,D |
| Information Studies | D |
| International Health | M,O |
| Journalism | M,D |
| Law | M,D |
| Library Science | D |
| Manufacturing Engineering | M,D |
| Mathematics Education | M,D,O |
| Mathematics | M,D |
| Mechanical Engineering | M,D |
| Microbiology | D |
| Music Education | M,D,O |
| Music | M,O |
| Natural Resources | M |
| Neuroscience | M,D,O |
| Nonprofit Management | M,D,O |
| Nursing and Healthcare Administration | M,D,O |
| Nursing—General | M,D,O |
| Nutrition | M,D |
| Organizational Management | M,D,O |
| Pathobiology | M,D |
| Pathology | M,D |
| Pediatric Nursing | M,D,O |
| Pharmacology | M,D |
| Philosophy | M,D |
| Physics | M,D |
| Physiology | M,D |
| Plant Biology | M,D |
| Plant Sciences | M,D |
| Political Science | M,D,O |
| Psychiatric Nursing | M,D,O |
| Psychology—General | M,D,O |
| Public Administration | M,D,O |
| Public Affairs | M,D,O |
| Public Health—General | M,O |
| Public Policy | M,D,O |
| Reading Education | M,D,O |
| Romance Languages | M,D |
| Rural Sociology | M,D |
| Russian | M |
| School Psychology | M,D,O |
| Science Education | M,D,O |
| Social Sciences Education | M,D,O |
| Social Work | M,D,O |
| Sociology | M,D |
| Special Education | D |
| Statistics | M,D |
| Taxation | M,D,O |
| Theater | M,D |
| Veterinary Medicine | M,D |
| Veterinary Sciences | M |
| Vocational and Technical Education | M,D,O |
| Water Resources | M,D,O |

### UNIVERSITY OF MISSOURI–KANSAS CITY

| | |
|---|---|
| Accounting | M,D |
| Adult Nursing | M,D |
| Allopathic Medicine | M,D |
| Analytical Chemistry | M,D |
| Art/Fine Arts | M,D |
| Biochemistry | D |
| Bioinformatics | M,D,O |
| Biological and Biomedical Sciences—General | M,D |
| Biophysics | D |
| Business Administration and Management—General | M,D |
| Cell Biology | D |
| Chemistry | M,D |
| Civil Engineering | M,D,O |
| Computer Engineering | M,D,O |
| Computer Science | M,D,O |
| Construction Engineering | M,D,O |
| Counseling Psychology | M,D,O |
| Counselor Education | M,D,O |
| Criminal Justice and Criminology | M |
| Curriculum and Instruction | M,D,O |
| Dental Hygiene | M,D,O |
| Dentistry | M,D,O |
| Economics | M,D |
| Education—General | M,D,O |

*M—masters degree; D—doctorate; O—other advanced degree; *—Close-Up and/or Display*

| | |
|---|---|
| Educational Leadership and Administration | M,D,O |
| Electrical Engineering | M,D,O |
| Engineering and Applied Sciences—General | M,D,O |
| Engineering Management | M,D,O |
| English | M,D |
| Family Nurse Practitioner Studies | M,D |
| Finance and Banking | M,D |
| French | M |
| Geosciences | M,D |
| Gerontological Nursing | M,D |
| Health Education | M,D |
| Higher Education | M,D,O |
| History | M,D |
| Inorganic Chemistry | M,D |
| Interdisciplinary Studies | D |
| Law | M,D |
| Maternal and Child/Neonatal Nursing | M,D |
| Mathematics | M,D |
| Mechanical Engineering | M,D,O |
| Molecular Biology | D |
| Music Education | M,D |
| Music | M,D |
| Nursing and Healthcare Administration | M,D |
| Nursing Education | M,D |
| Nursing—General | M,D |
| Oral and Dental Sciences | M,D,O |
| Organic Chemistry | M,D |
| Pediatric Nursing | M,D |
| Pharmacy | D |
| Physical Chemistry | M,D |
| Physics | M,D |
| Political Science | M |
| Polymer Science and Engineering | M,D |
| Psychology—General | M,D |
| Public Administration | M,D |
| Public Affairs | M,D |
| Reading Education | M,D,O |
| Romance Languages | M |
| Social Psychology | M,D |
| Social Work | M |
| Sociology | M |
| Software Engineering | M,D,O |
| Spanish | M |
| Special Education | M,D,O |
| Statistics | M,D |
| Telecommunications | M,D,O |
| Theater | M |
| Therapies—Dance, Drama, and Music | M,D |
| Women's Health Nursing | M,D |

## UNIVERSITY OF MISSOURI–ST. LOUIS

| | |
|---|---|
| Accounting | M,D,O |
| Adult Education | M,O |
| Adult Nursing | D,O |
| American Studies | M,D |
| Applied Physics | M,D |
| Astrophysics | M,D |
| Biochemistry | M,D |
| Biological and Biomedical Sciences—General | M,D,O |
| Biotechnology | M,D |
| Business Administration and Management—General | M,D,O |
| Chemistry | M,D |
| Clinical Psychology | M,D,O |
| Communication—General | M |
| Computer and Information Systems Security | M,D,O |
| Computer Science | M,D |
| Conflict Resolution and Mediation/Peace Studies | M |
| Criminal Justice and Criminology | M,D |
| Cultural Studies | O |
| Curriculum and Instruction | M |
| Early Childhood Education | M |
| Economics | M |
| Education—General | M,D,O |
| Educational Measurement and Evaluation | M,O |
| Elementary Education | M |
| English as a Second Language | M |
| English | M |
| Family Nurse Practitioner Studies | D,O |
| Gender Studies | O |
| Gerontological Nursing | D,O |
| Higher Education | M,O |
| History | M,O |
| Human Resources Management | M,D,O |
| Interdisciplinary Studies | O |
| Logistics | M,D,O |
| Management Information Systems | M,D,O |
| Marketing Research | M,D,O |
| Marketing | M,D,O |
| Mathematics | M,D |
| Middle School Education | M |
| Museum Studies | M,O |
| Music Education | M |
| Neuroscience | M,D,O |
| Nursing—General | D,O |
| Pediatric Nursing | D,O |
| Philosophy | M |
| Physics | M,D |
| Political Science | M,D |
| Psychiatric Nursing | D,O |
| Psychology—General | M,D,O |
| Public Administration | M,D |
| Public Policy | M,D |
| Reading Education | M |
| School Psychology | M,O |
| Secondary Education | M |
| Social Sciences Education | M,O |
| Social Work | M |
| Sociology | M |
| Special Education | M |
| Supply Chain Management | M,D,O |
| Women's Health Nursing | D,O |
| Writing | M |

## UNIVERSITY OF MOBILE

| | |
|---|---|
| Business Administration and Management—General | M |
| Education—General | M |
| Educational Leadership and Administration | M |
| Educational Policy | M |
| Marriage and Family Therapy | M |
| Music | M,D |
| Nursing and Healthcare Administration | M,D |
| Nursing Education | M,D |
| Nursing—General | M,D |
| Theology | M |

## UNIVERSITY OF MONTANA

| | |
|---|---|
| Accounting | M |
| Analytical Chemistry | M,D |
| Animal Behavior | M,D,O |
| Anthropology | M,D |
| Art Education | M |
| Art History | M |
| Art/Fine Arts | M |
| Biochemistry | D |
| Biological and Biomedical Sciences—General | M,D |
| Business Administration and Management—General | M |
| Cell Biology | D |
| Chemistry | M,D |
| Child and Family Studies | M,D,O |
| Clinical Psychology | M,D,O |
| Communication Disorders | M,O |
| Communication—General | M |
| Community Health | M |
| Computer Art and Design | M |
| Computer Science | M |
| Counseling Psychology | M,D,O |
| Counselor Education | M,D,O |
| Criminal Justice and Criminology | M |
| Cultural Studies | M,D,O |
| Curriculum and Instruction | M,D |
| Developmental Biology | D |
| Developmental Psychology | M,D,O |
| Early Childhood Education | M,D |
| Ecology | M,D |
| Economics | M |
| Education—General | M,D,O |
| Educational Leadership and Administration | M,D,O |
| English Education | M |
| English | M |
| Environmental Management and Policy | M |
| Environmental Sciences | M |
| Exercise and Sports Science | M |
| Experimental Psychology | M,D,O |
| Film, Television, and Video Production | M |
| Fish, Game, and Wildlife Management | M,D |
| Forestry | M,D |
| French | M |
| Geography | M |
| Geology | M,D |
| Geosciences | M,D |
| German | M |
| Health Education | M |
| History | M,D |
| Immunology | D |
| Inorganic Chemistry | M,D |
| Interdisciplinary Studies | M,D |
| Internet and Interactive Multimedia | M |
| Journalism | M |
| Law | D |
| Legal and Justice Studies | M |
| Linguistics | M,D |
| Mathematics Education | M,D |
| Mathematics | M,D |
| Medicinal and Pharmaceutical Chemistry | M,D |
| Microbiology | D |
| Molecular Biology | D |
| Music | M |
| Natural Resources | M,D |
| Neuroscience | M,D |
| Organic Chemistry | M,D |
| Pharmaceutical Sciences | M,D |
| Pharmacy | M,D |
| Philosophy | M |
| Photography | M |
| Physical Chemistry | M,D |
| Physical Education | M |
| Physical Therapy | D |
| Political Science | M |
| Psychology—General | M,D,O |
| Public Administration | M |
| Public Health—General | M,O |
| Recreation and Park Management | M,D |
| Rural Planning and Studies | M |
| Rural Sociology | M |
| School Psychology | M,D,O |
| Social Work | M |
| Sociology | M |
| Spanish | M |
| Theater | M |
| Toxicology | M,D |
| Writing | M |
| Zoology | M,D |

## UNIVERSITY OF MONTEVALLO

| | |
|---|---|
| Business Administration and Management—General | M |
| Communication Disorders | M |
| Counselor Education | M |
| Education—General | M,O |
| Educational Leadership and Administration | M,O |
| Elementary Education | M |
| English | M |
| Secondary Education | M |

## UNIVERSITY OF MOUNT OLIVE

| | |
|---|---|
| Business Administration and Management—General | M |
| Nursing—General | M |

## UNIVERSITY OF MOUNT UNION

| | |
|---|---|
| Educational Leadership and Administration | M |
| Physical Therapy | D |
| Physician Assistant Studies | M |

## UNIVERSITY OF NEBRASKA AT KEARNEY

| | |
|---|---|
| Accounting | M |
| Art Education | M |
| Biological and Biomedical Sciences—General | M |
| Business Administration and Management—General | M |
| Communication Disorders | M |
| Counseling Psychology | M,O |
| Counselor Education | M,O |
| Curriculum and Instruction | M |
| Early Childhood Education | M |
| Education of the Gifted | M |
| Education—General | M,O |
| Educational Leadership and Administration | M,O |
| Educational Media/Instructional Technology | M |
| Elementary Education | M |
| English as a Second Language | M |
| English | M |
| Exercise and Sports Science | M |
| Foreign Languages Education | M |
| History | M |
| Human Resources Management | M |
| Human Services | M |
| Leisure Studies | M |
| Library Science | M |
| Management Information Systems | M |
| Marketing | M |
| Mathematics Education | M |
| Museum Education | M |
| Music Education | M |
| Physical Education | M |
| Reading Education | M |
| Recreation and Park Management | M |
| School Psychology | M,O |
| Science Education | M |
| Secondary Education | M |
| Special Education | M,O |
| Sports Management | M |
| Student Affairs | M,O |
| Writing | M |

## UNIVERSITY OF NEBRASKA AT OMAHA

| | |
|---|---|
| Accounting | M |
| Applied Behavior Analysis | M,D,O |
| Art/Fine Arts | M |
| Artificial Intelligence/Robotics | M,O |
| Athletic Training and Sports Medicine | M,D |
| Bioinformatics | M,D |
| Biological and Biomedical Sciences—General | M,O |
| Business Administration and Management—General | M,O |
| Communication Disorders | M |
| Communication—General | M,O |
| Computer and Information Systems Security | M,D,O |
| Computer Science | M,O |
| Counselor Education | M |
| Criminal Justice and Criminology | M,D,O |
| Data Science/Data Analytics | M,D,O |
| Economics | M |
| Education—General | M,D,O |
| Educational Leadership and Administration | M,D,O |
| Elementary Education | M |
| English as a Second Language | M,O |
| English | M,O |
| Exercise and Sports Science | M,D |
| Foreign Languages Education | M |
| Geographic Information Systems | M,O |
| Geography | M,O |
| Gerontology | M,D,O |
| Health Education | M,D |
| History | M |
| Human Resources Development | M,D,O |
| Industrial and Organizational Psychology | M,D,O |
| Information Science | M,D,O |
| Kinesiology and Movement Studies | M,D |
| Management Information Systems | M,D,O |
| Mathematics | M |
| Music | M |
| National Security | M,O |
| Organizational Management | M |
| Political Science | M |
| Project Management | M,D,O |
| Psychology—General | M,D,O |
| Public Administration | M,D,O |
| School Psychology | M,D,O |
| Science Education | M,O |
| Secondary Education | M,O |
| Social Work | M |
| Sociology | M |
| Software Engineering | M,O |
| Special Education | M |
| Systems Engineering | M,O |
| Technical Communication | M,O |
| Urban Education | M,O |
| Writing | M,O |

## UNIVERSITY OF NEBRASKA–LINCOLN

| | |
|---|---|
| Accounting | M,D |
| Actuarial Science | M |
| Adult Education | M,D,O |
| Advertising and Public Relations | M,D |
| Agricultural Economics and Agribusiness | M,D |
| Agricultural Education | M |
| Agricultural Engineering | M,D |
| Agricultural Sciences—General | M,D |
| Agronomy and Soil Sciences | M,D |
| Analytical Chemistry | M,D |
| Animal Sciences | M,D |
| Anthropology | M |
| Archaeology | M,D |
| Architectural Engineering | M,D |
| Architecture | M,D |
| Art History | M |
| Art/Fine Arts | M |
| Astronomy | M,D |
| Biochemistry | M,D |
| Bioengineering | M,D |
| Bioinformatics | M,D |
| Biological and Biomedical Sciences—General | M,D |
| Biomedical Engineering | M,D |
| Biopsychology | M,D |
| Business Administration and Management—General | M,D |
| Chemical Engineering | M,D |
| Chemistry | M,D |
| Child and Family Studies | M,D |
| Child Development | M,D |
| Civil Engineering | M,D |
| Classics | M |
| Clinical Psychology | M,D |
| Clothing and Textiles | M,D |
| Cognitive Sciences | M,D,O |
| Communication Disorders | M,D |
| Communication—General | M,D |
| Comparative Literature | M,D |
| Computer Engineering | M,D |
| Computer Science | M,D |
| Consumer Economics | M,D |
| Corporate and Organizational Communication | M,D |
| Counseling Psychology | M,D,O |
| Curriculum and Instruction | M,D,O |
| Developmental Psychology | M,D,O |
| Early Childhood Education | M,D |
| Economics | M,D |
| Educational Leadership and Administration | M,D,O |
| Educational Measurement and Evaluation | M,D,O |
| Educational Psychology | M,D,O |
| Electrical Engineering | M,D |
| Engineering and Applied Sciences—General | M,D |
| Engineering Management | M,D |
| English | M,D |
| Entomology | M,D |
| Environmental Engineering | M,D |
| Exercise and Sports Science | M,D |
| Family and Consumer Sciences-General | M,D |
| Finance and Banking | M,D |
| Food Science and Technology | M,D |
| French | M,D |
| Geography | M,D |
| Geosciences | M,D |
| German | M,D |
| Gerontology | M,D |
| Health Promotion | M,D |
| History | M,D |
| Home Economics Education | M,D |
| Horticulture | M,D |
| Human Development | M,D,O |
| Industrial/Management Engineering | M,D |
| Information Science | M,D |
| Inorganic Chemistry | M,D |
| Interior Design | M,D |
| Journalism | M |
| Law | M,D |
| Legal and Justice Studies | M |
| Management Information Systems | M |
| Manufacturing Engineering | M,D |
| Marketing | M,D |
| Marriage and Family Therapy | M,D |
| Mass Communication | M |
| Materials Engineering | M,D |
| Materials Sciences | M,D |
| Mathematics | M,D |
| Mechanical Engineering | M,D |
| Mechanics | M,D |
| Metallurgical Engineering and Metallurgy | M,D |
| Music Education | M,D |
| Music | M,D |
| Natural Resources | M,D |
| Nutrition | M,D |
| Organic Chemistry | M,D |
| Philosophy | M,D |
| Physical Chemistry | M,D |
| Physics | M,D |
| Political Science | M,D,O |
| Psychology—General | M,D |
| Public Policy | M,D,O |
| Rhetoric | M,D |
| School Psychology | M,D,O |
| Social Psychology | M,D |
| Sociology | M,D |
| Spanish | M,D |
| Special Education | M,D,O |
| Speech and Interpersonal Communication | M,D |
| Statistics | M,D |
| Survey Methodology | M,D |
| Theater | M |
| Toxicology | M,D |
| Urban and Regional Planning | M,D |
| Veterinary Sciences | M,D |
| Vocational and Technical Education | M,D,O |
| Writing | M,D |

## UNIVERSITY OF NEBRASKA MEDICAL CENTER

| | |
|---|---|
| Allied Health—General | M,D,O |
| Allopathic Medicine | D,O |
| Anatomy | M,D |

| | |
|---|---|
| Applied Behavior Analysis | M,D |
| Biochemistry | M |
| Bioinformatics | M,D |
| Biological and Biomedical Sciences—General | M,D |
| Biostatistics | D |
| Cancer Biology/Oncology | D |
| Cell Biology | M,D |
| Clinical Laboratory Sciences/Medical Technology | M,O |
| Dentistry | M,D,O |
| Emergency Management | M |
| Environmental and Occupational Health | D |
| Epidemiology | D |
| Genetics | M,D |
| Health Promotion | D |
| Health Services Management and Hospital Administration | M,D |
| Health Services Research | M,D |
| Immunology | M,D |
| Infectious Diseases | M,D |
| Molecular Biology | M |
| Molecular Genetics | M,D |
| Molecular Medicine | D |
| Neuroscience | D |
| Nursing—General | D |
| Nutrition | O |
| Oral and Dental Sciences | M,D |
| Pathology | M,D |
| Perfusion | M |
| Pharmaceutical Sciences | M,D |
| Pharmacology | D |
| Pharmacy | D |
| Physical Therapy | D |
| Physician Assistant Studies | M |
| Physiology | D |
| Public Health—General | M |
| Toxicology | D |

### UNIVERSITY OF NEVADA, LAS VEGAS

| | |
|---|---|
| Accounting | M,O |
| Addictions/Substance Abuse Counseling | M,D,O |
| Aerospace/Aeronautical Engineering | M,D,O |
| Allied Health—General | M,D,O |
| Anthropology | M,D |
| Applied Economics | M,O |
| Architecture | M,O |
| Art/Fine Arts | M |
| Astronomy | M,D |
| Biochemistry | M,D |
| Biological and Biomedical Sciences—General | M,D |
| Biomedical Engineering | M,D,O |
| Business Administration and Management—General | M,O |
| Chemistry | M,D |
| Clinical Psychology | M,D,O |
| Communication—General | M |
| Community Health | M,D,O |
| Computer and Information Systems Security | M,D,O |
| Counseling Psychology | M,D,O |
| Counselor Education | M,D,O |
| Criminal Justice and Criminology | M,D |
| Curriculum and Instruction | M,D,O |
| Data Science/Data Analytics | M,O |
| Dentistry | M,D,O |
| Distance Education Development | M,D,O |
| Early Childhood Education | M,D,O |
| Economics | M |
| Education—General | M,D,O |
| Educational Leadership and Administration | M,D,O |
| Educational Media/Instructional Technology | M,D,O |
| Elementary Education | M,D,O |
| Emergency Management | M,D,O |
| Engineering and Applied Sciences—General | M,D,O |
| English as a Second Language | M,D,O |
| English | M,D |
| Environmental Sciences | M,D,O |
| Exercise and Sports Science | M,D |
| Family Nurse Practitioner Studies | M,D,O |
| Film, Television, and Video Production | M,O |
| Finance and Banking | O |
| Geosciences | M,D |
| Health Physics/Radiological Health | M,D,O |
| Health Services Management and Hospital Administration | M |
| Higher Education | M,D,O |
| Hispanic Studies | M,O |
| History | M,D |
| Hospitality Management | M,D |
| Journalism | M |
| Kinesiology and Movement Studies | M,D |
| Law | M,D |
| Management Information Systems | M,O |
| Materials Engineering | M,D,O |
| Mathematics | M,D |
| Media Studies | M |
| Music | M,D,O |
| Nonprofit Management | M,D,O |
| Nuclear Engineering | M,D,O |
| Nursing Education | M,D,O |
| Nursing—General | M,D,O |
| Nutrition | M,D |
| Oral and Dental Sciences | M,D,O |
| Physical Therapy | D |
| Physics | M,D |
| Political Science | M,D |
| Psychology—General | M,D,O |
| Public Administration | M,D,O |
| Public Affairs | M,D,O |
| Public Health—General | M,D,O |
| Public Policy | M,D,O |
| Secondary Education | M,D,O |
| Social Work | M |
| Sociology | M,D |
| Special Education | M,D,O |
| Theater | M |
| Translation and Interpretation | M,O |
| Transportation and Highway Engineering | M,D |
| Water Resources | M |
| Writing | M,D,O |

### UNIVERSITY OF NEVADA, RENO

| | |
|---|---|
| Accounting | M |
| Agricultural Sciences—General | M,D |
| Allopathic Medicine | D |
| Animal Sciences | M |
| Anthropology | M,D |
| Applied Behavior Analysis | M,D |
| Art/Fine Arts | M |
| Atmospheric Sciences | M,D |
| Biochemistry | M,D |
| Biological and Biomedical Sciences—General | M |
| Biomedical Engineering | M,D |
| Biotechnology | M |
| Business Administration and Management—General | M |
| Cell Biology | M,D |
| Chemical Engineering | M,D |
| Chemical Physics | D |
| Chemistry | M,D |
| Child and Family Studies | M |
| Civil Engineering | M,D |
| Clinical Psychology | D |
| Cognitive Sciences | M,D |
| Communication Disorders | M,D |
| Computer Engineering | M,D |
| Computer Science | M,D |
| Conservation Biology | D |
| Counselor Education | M,D,O |
| Criminal Justice and Criminology | M |
| Curriculum and Instruction | D |
| Ecology | D |
| Economics | M |
| Education—General | M,D,O |
| Educational Leadership and Administration | M,D,O |
| Educational Psychology | M,D,O |
| Electrical Engineering | M,D |
| Elementary Education | M |
| Engineering and Applied Sciences—General | M,D |
| English as a Second Language | M |
| English | M,D |
| Environmental and Occupational Health | M,D |
| Environmental Management and Policy | M |
| Environmental Sciences | M,D |
| Evolutionary Biology | D |
| Finance and Banking | M |
| Geochemistry | M,D |
| Geography | M,D |
| Geological Engineering | M,D |
| Geology | M,D |
| Geophysics | M,D |
| History | M,D |
| Human Development | M |
| Hydrogeology | M,D |
| Hydrology | M,D |
| Journalism | M |
| Legal and Justice Studies | M,D |
| Management Information Systems | M |
| Materials Engineering | M,D |
| Mathematics Education | M |
| Mathematics | M |
| Mechanical Engineering | M,D |
| Metallurgical Engineering and Metallurgy | M,D |
| Mineral/Mining Engineering | M,D |
| Molecular Biology | M,D |
| Molecular Pharmacology | D |
| Music | M |
| Nursing—General | M,D |
| Nutrition | M |
| Philosophy | M |
| Physics | M,D |
| Physiology | D |
| Political Science | M,D |
| Psychology—General | M,D |
| Public Administration | M |
| Public Health—General | M,D |
| Range Science | M |
| Reading Education | M,D |
| Secondary Education | M |
| Social Psychology | D |
| Social Work | M |
| Sociology | M |
| Spanish | M |
| Special Education | M,D |
| Speech and Interpersonal Communication | M |
| Western European Studies | D |

### UNIVERSITY OF NEW BRUNSWICK SAINT JOHN

| | |
|---|---|
| Biological and Biomedical Sciences—General | M,D |
| Business Administration and Management—General | M |
| Clinical Psychology | M,D |
| Electronic Commerce | M |
| Experimental Psychology | M,D |
| International Business | M |
| Natural Resources | M |
| Psychology—General | M,D |

### UNIVERSITY OF NEW ENGLAND

| | |
|---|---|
| Biological and Biomedical Sciences—General | M |
| Curriculum and Instruction | M,D,O |
| Dentistry | D |
| Early Childhood Education | M,D,O |
| Education—General | M,D,O |
| Educational Leadership and Administration | M,D,O |
| Health Informatics | M,D,O |
| Health Services Management and Hospital Administration | M,D,O |
| Marine Sciences | M |
| Nurse Anesthesia | M,D |
| Nutrition | M,D,O |
| Occupational Therapy | M,D |
| Osteopathic Medicine | D |
| Pharmacy | D |
| Physical Therapy | M,D |
| Physician Assistant Studies | M,D |
| Public Health—General | M,D,O |
| Reading Education | M,D,O |
| Social Work | M,D,O |
| Vocational and Technical Education | M,D,O |

### UNIVERSITY OF NEW HAMPSHIRE

| | |
|---|---|
| Accounting | M |
| Addictions/Substance Abuse Counseling | M,O |
| Agricultural Sciences—General | M,D |
| Animal Sciences | M,D |
| Applied Mathematics | M,D,O |
| Biochemistry | M,D |
| Biological and Biomedical Sciences—General | M,D |
| Business Administration and Management—General | M,O |
| Chemical Engineering | M,D |
| Chemistry | M,D |
| Child and Family Studies | M,O |
| Civil Engineering | M,D |
| Communication Disorders | M |
| Computer and Information Systems Security | M,O |
| Computer Science | M,D |
| Conservation Biology | M |
| Curriculum and Instruction | D,O |
| Early Childhood Education | M |
| Economic Development | M |
| Economics | M,D |
| Education—General | M,D,O |
| Educational Leadership and Administration | M,O |
| Educational Media/Instructional Technology | M,O |
| Electrical Engineering | M,D,O |
| Elementary Education | M,O |
| English | M,D |
| Environmental Engineering | M,D |
| Environmental Management and Policy | M |
| Evolutionary Biology | D |
| Family Nurse Practitioner Studies | M,D,O |
| Fish, Game, and Wildlife Management | M |
| Forestry | M |
| Genetics | M,D |
| Geographic Information Systems | O |
| Geology | M |
| Geosciences | M |
| Higher Education | O |
| History | M,D |
| Hydrology | M |
| Intellectual Property Law | M,D,O |
| Kinesiology and Movement Studies | M,O |
| Law | M,D,O |
| Legal and Justice Studies | M,D,O |
| Liberal Studies | M |
| Linguistics | M,D |
| Management Information Systems | M,O |
| Marine Biology | M,D |
| Marriage and Family Therapy | M,O |
| Materials Engineering | M,D |
| Materials Sciences | M,D |
| Mathematics Education | M,D,O |
| Mathematics | M,D,O |
| Mechanical Engineering | M,D |
| Microbiology | M,D |
| Museum Studies | M,D |
| Music | M |
| Natural Resources | M,D |
| Nursing—General | M,D,O |
| Nutrition | M,D |
| Occupational Therapy | M,O |
| Ocean Engineering | M,D,O |
| Oceanography | M,D,O |
| Physical Education | M,O |
| Physics | M,D |
| Political Science | M,O |
| Psychiatric Nursing | M,D,O |
| Psychology—General | D |
| Public Administration | M,O |
| Public Health—General | M,O |
| Public Policy | M |
| Recreation and Park Management | M |
| Science Education | M,D |
| Secondary Education | M,O |
| Social Work | M,O |
| Sociology | M,D |
| Spanish | M,O |
| Special Education | M,O |
| Sports and Entertainment Law | M,D,O |
| Sustainability Management | M,O |
| Water Resources | M |
| Women's Studies | O |
| Writing | M,D |

### UNIVERSITY OF NEW HAVEN

| | |
|---|---|
| Accounting | M,O |
| Biomedical Engineering | M |
| Business Administration and Management—General | M |
| Cell Biology | M |
| Civil Engineering | M |
| Computer and Information Systems Security | M |
| Computer Engineering | M |
| Computer Science | M,O |
| Conflict Resolution and Mediation/Peace Studies | M,O |
| Criminal Justice and Criminology | M,D,O |
| Ecology | M |
| Electrical Engineering | M |
| Emergency Management | M,O |
| Engineering and Applied Sciences—General | M,O |
| Engineering Management | M,O |
| Environmental and Occupational Health | M |
| Environmental Engineering | M |
| Environmental Management and Policy | M |
| Environmental Sciences | M |
| Facilities Management | M,O |
| Finance and Banking | M,O |
| Fire Protection Engineering | M,O |
| Forensic Psychology | M,O |
| Forensic Sciences | M,O |
| Geographic Information Systems | M |
| Geosciences | M |
| Hazardous Materials Management | M |
| Human Resources Management | M,O |
| Industrial and Manufacturing Management | M,O |
| Industrial and Organizational Psychology | M,O |
| Industrial/Management Engineering | M,O |
| International Business | M |
| Management Strategy and Policy | M |
| Marketing | M |
| Mechanical Engineering | M |
| Molecular Biology | M |
| National Security | M,O |
| Nonprofit Management | M,O |
| Organizational Management | M,O |
| Public Administration | M,O |
| Social Psychology | M,O |
| Software Engineering | M,O |
| Sports Management | M,O |
| Taxation | M,O |
| Water Resources Engineering | M |

### UNIVERSITY OF NEW MEXICO

| | |
|---|---|
| Accounting | M |
| Allied Health—General | M,D,O |
| Allopathic Medicine | D |
| American Indian/Native American Studies | M,D |
| American Studies | M,D |
| Anthropology | M,D |
| Archaeology | M,D |
| Architecture | M,D |
| Art Education | M |
| Art History | M,D |
| Art/Fine Arts | M |
| Biochemistry | M,D |
| Biological and Biomedical Sciences—General | M,D |
| Biomedical Engineering | M,D |
| Business Administration and Management—General | M |
| Cell Biology | M,D |
| Chemical Engineering | M,D |
| Chemistry | M,D |
| Child and Family Studies | M,D |
| Civil Engineering | M,D |
| Clinical Laboratory Sciences/Medical Technology | M,O |
| Clinical Psychology | D |
| Cognitive Sciences | D |
| Communication Disorders | M |
| Communication—General | M,D |
| Community Health | M |
| Comparative Literature | M,D |
| Computer and Information Systems Security | M |
| Computer Engineering | M,D |
| Computer Science | M,D |
| Construction Management | M,D |
| Counselor Education | M,D |
| Cultural Studies | M,D |
| Dance | M |
| Dental Hygiene | M |
| Developmental Psychology | D |
| Early Childhood Education | D |
| Economics | M,D |
| Education of Students with Severe/Multiple Disabilities | M,D,O |
| Education—General | M,D,O |
| Educational Leadership and Administration | M,D,O |
| Educational Media/Instructional Technology | M,D,O |
| Educational Psychology | M,D |
| Electrical Engineering | M,D |
| Elementary Education | M |
| Engineering and Applied Sciences—General | M,D |
| English as a Second Language | M,D |
| English Education | M,D |
| English | M,D |
| Entrepreneurship | M |
| Environmental Management and Policy | M |
| Epidemiology | M |
| Ethnic Studies | M,D |
| Exercise and Sports Science | D |
| Finance and Banking | M |
| Foundations and Philosophy of Education | M,D |
| French | M,D |
| Genetics | M,D |
| Geography | M |

*M—masters degree; D—doctorate; O—other advanced degree; *—Close-Up and/or Display*

| | |
|---|---|
| Geosciences | M,D |
| German | M,D |
| Health Education | M |
| Health Psychology | D |
| Health Services Management and Hospital Administration | M |
| Higher Education | O |
| Historic Preservation | O |
| History | M,D |
| Human Development | M,D |
| Human Resources Management | M |
| International Business | M |
| International Development | M,D |
| International Economics | M,D |
| Landscape Architecture | M |
| Latin American Studies | M,D |
| Law | D |
| Linguistics | M,D |
| Management Information Systems | M |
| Management of Technology | M |
| Management Strategy and Policy | M |
| Manufacturing Engineering | M |
| Marketing | M |
| Mathematics | M,D |
| Mechanical Engineering | M,D |
| Microbiology | M,D |
| Molecular Biology | M,D |
| Multilingual and Multicultural Education | M,D |
| Music Education | M |
| Music | M |
| Nanotechnology | M,D |
| Natural Resources | M,D |
| Neuroscience | M,D |
| Nuclear Engineering | M,D |
| Nursing—General | M,D |
| Nutrition | M |
| Occupational Therapy | M |
| Optical Sciences | M,D |
| Organizational Behavior | M |
| Organizational Management | M |
| Pathology | M,D |
| Pharmaceutical Sciences | M,D |
| Pharmacy | D |
| Philosophy | M,D |
| Photography | M,D |
| Photonics | M,D |
| Physical Education | D |
| Physical Therapy | D |
| Physician Assistant Studies | M |
| Physics | M,D |
| Physiology | M,D |
| Planetary and Space Sciences | M,D |
| Political Science | M,D |
| Portuguese | M,D |
| Psychology—General | D |
| Public Administration | M |
| Public Health—General | M |
| Quantitative Analysis | D |
| Reading Education | M,D |
| Science Education | O |
| Secondary Education | M |
| Sociology | M,D |
| Spanish | M,D |
| Special Education | M,D,O |
| Sports Management | D |
| Statistics | M,D |
| Systems Engineering | M,D |
| Taxation | M |
| Theater | M |
| Toxicology | M,D |
| Urban and Regional Planning | M |
| Water Resources | M |
| Writing | M |

**UNIVERSITY OF NEW ORLEANS**

| | |
|---|---|
| Accounting | M |
| Art/Fine Arts | M |
| Arts Administration | M |
| Biological and Biomedical Sciences—General | M |
| Business Administration and Management—General | M |
| Chemistry | M,D |
| Civil Engineering | M |
| Computer Science | M,D |
| Counselor Education | M,D |
| Curriculum and Instruction | M |
| Economics | D |
| Educational Leadership and Administration | M,D |
| Electrical Engineering | M |
| Engineering and Applied Sciences—General | M,D |
| Engineering Management | M |
| English | M |
| Environmental Sciences | M,D |
| Film, Television, and Video Production | M |
| Finance and Banking | M |
| Geosciences | M,D |
| Health Services Management and Hospital Administration | M |
| Higher Education | M,D |
| History | M |
| Hospitality Management | M |
| Mathematics | M |
| Mechanical Engineering | M |
| Music | M |
| Physics | M,D |
| Political Science | M,D |
| Psychology—General | M,D |
| Public Administration | M |
| Romance Languages | M |
| Sociology | M |
| Special Education | M |
| Taxation | M |
| Theater | M |
| Transportation Management | M |
| Travel and Tourism | M |
| Urban and Regional Planning | M |
| Urban Studies | M,D |
| Writing | M |

**UNIVERSITY OF NORTH ALABAMA**

| | |
|---|---|
| Accounting | M |
| Business Administration and Management—General | M |
| Child and Family Studies | M |
| Clinical Psychology | M |
| Counselor Education | M |
| Criminal Justice and Criminology | M |
| Economic Development | M |
| Education—General | M,O |
| Educational Leadership and Administration | M,O |
| Elementary Education | M,O |
| English | M |
| Exercise and Sports Science | M |
| Finance and Banking | M |
| Geographic Information Systems | M |
| Health Promotion | M |
| Health Services Management and Hospital Administration | M |
| Higher Education | M |
| Historic Preservation | M |
| History | M |
| Information Science | M |
| Interdisciplinary Studies | M |
| International Business | M |
| Kinesiology and Movement Studies | M |
| Law | M |
| Management Information Systems | M |
| Nursing—General | M |
| Physical Education | M |
| Political Science | M |
| Project Management | M |
| Public History | M |
| Rhetoric | M |
| Secondary Education | M |
| Special Education | M |
| Technical Writing | M |
| Writing | M |

**UNIVERSITY OF NORTH CAROLINA ASHEVILLE**

| | |
|---|---|
| Liberal Studies | M,O |

**THE UNIVERSITY OF NORTH CAROLINA AT CHAPEL HILL**

| | |
|---|---|
| Accounting | M,D |
| Adult Nursing | M,D,O |
| Allopathic Medicine | D |
| Anthropology | M,D |
| Archaeology | M,D |
| Art History | M,D |
| Art/Fine Arts | M |
| Astronomy | M,D |
| Astrophysics | M,D |
| Athletic Training and Sports Medicine | M |
| Biochemistry | M,D |
| Bioinformatics | D |
| Biological and Biomedical Sciences—General | M,D |
| Biophysics | M,D |
| Biopsychology | D |
| Biostatistics | M,D |
| Botany | M,D |
| Business Administration and Management—General | M,D |
| Cell Biology | M,D |
| Chemistry | M,D |
| Classics | M,D |
| Clinical Psychology | D |
| Clinical Research | M,D |
| Cognitive Sciences | D |
| Communication—General | M,D,O |
| Computational Biology | D |
| Computer Science | M,D |
| Counselor Education | M |
| Curriculum and Instruction | M,D |
| Dental Hygiene | M,D |
| Dentistry | D |
| Developmental Biology | M,D |
| Developmental Psychology | D |
| Early Childhood Education | M,D |
| East European and Russian Studies | M |
| Ecology | M,D |
| Economics | M,D |
| Education—General | M,D |
| Educational Leadership and Administration | M,D |
| Educational Measurement and Evaluation | M,D |
| Educational Psychology | M,D |
| English as a Second Language | M |
| English Education | M |
| English | M,D |
| Environmental and Occupational Health | M,D |
| Environmental Engineering | M,D |
| Environmental Sciences | M,D |
| Epidemiology | M,D |
| Evolutionary Biology | M,D |
| Exercise and Sports Science | M |
| Family Nurse Practitioner Studies | M,D,O |
| Finance and Banking | D |
| Folklore | M |
| Foreign Languages Education | M |
| French | M,D |
| Genetics | M,D |
| Geography | M,D |
| Geology | M,D |
| German | D |
| Gerontological Nursing | M,D,O |
| Health Communication | M,D,O |
| Health Promotion | M |
| Health Psychology | M,D |
| Health Services Management and Hospital Administration | M,D |
| History | M,D |
| Immunology | M,D |
| Information Studies | M,D,O |
| International Affairs | M |
| Italian | M,D |
| Journalism | M,D,O |
| Latin American Studies | M,D,O |
| Law | M,D |
| Library Science | M,D,O |
| Linguistics | M,D |
| Management Information Systems | D |
| Management Strategy and Policy | D |
| Marine Sciences | M,D |
| Marketing | D |
| Maternal and Child Health | M,D |
| Mathematics Education | M |
| Mathematics | M,D |
| Media Studies | M,D,O |
| Microbiology | M,D |
| Molecular Biology | M,D |
| Molecular Physiology | D |
| Music Education | M |
| Music | M,D |
| Neurobiology | D |
| Neuroscience | D |
| Nursing and Healthcare Administration | M,D,O |
| Nursing Education | M,D,O |
| Nursing Informatics | M,D,O |
| Nursing—General | M,D,O |
| Nutrition | M,D |
| Occupational Health Nursing | M |
| Operations Research | M,D |
| Oral and Dental Sciences | M,D |
| Organizational Behavior | D |
| Pathology | D |
| Pediatric Nursing | M,D,O |
| Pharmaceutical Administration | M,D |
| Pharmaceutical Sciences | M,D |
| Pharmacology | D |
| Pharmacy | M,D |
| Philosophy | M,D |
| Physical Education | M |
| Physics | M,D |
| Political Science | M,D,O |
| Portuguese | M,D |
| Psychiatric Nursing | M,D,O |
| Psychology—General | D |
| Public Administration | M |
| Public Health—General | M,D |
| Public Policy | D |
| Reading Education | M,D |
| Religion | M,D |
| Romance Languages | M,D |
| School Psychology | M,D |
| Science Education | M |
| Secondary Education | M |
| Slavic Languages | D |
| Social Psychology | D |
| Social Sciences Education | M |
| Social Work | M,D |
| Sociology | M,D |
| Spanish | M,D |
| Sports Management | M |
| Statistics | M,D |
| Telecommunications | M,D,O |
| Theater | M |
| Toxicology | M,D |
| Urban and Regional Planning | M,D |

**THE UNIVERSITY OF NORTH CAROLINA AT CHARLOTTE**

| | |
|---|---|
| Accounting | M |
| Acute Care/Critical Care Nursing | M,D,O |
| Addictions/Substance Abuse Counseling | M,D,O |
| African Studies | O |
| Anthropology | M |
| Applied Economics | M,O |
| Applied Mathematics | M,D |
| Applied Physics | M,D |
| Architecture | M |
| Art Education | M,D,O |
| Arts Administration | M,O |
| Bioinformatics | D |
| Biological and Biomedical Sciences—General | M,D |
| Business Administration and Management—General | M,D,O |
| Business Analytics | M,D,O |
| Business Education | D |
| Chemistry | M,D |
| Child and Family Studies | M,D,O |
| Child Development | M,D,O |
| Cognitive Sciences | M,D,O |
| Communication—General | M |
| Community Health | M,D,O |
| Computer and Information Systems Security | M,O |
| Computer Science | D |
| Counselor Education | M,D,O |
| Criminal Justice and Criminology | M |
| Cultural Studies | M,O |
| Curriculum and Instruction | M,D,O |
| Early Childhood Education | M,D,O |
| Economics | M,O |
| Education of the Gifted | M,D,O |
| Education—General | M,D,O |
| Educational Leadership and Administration | M,D,O |
| Educational Media/Instructional Technology | M,D,O |
| Elementary Education | M,O |
| Emergency Management | M,O |
| Energy and Power Engineering | M,O |
| Engineering and Applied Sciences—General | M,D,O |
| English as a Second Language | M,D,O |
| English | M,O |
| Environmental Engineering | M,D |
| Ethics | M,O |
| Facilities Management | M,O |
| Family Nurse Practitioner Studies | M,D,O |
| Finance and Banking | M,O |
| Fire Protection Engineering | M,O |
| Foreign Languages Education | M,D,O |
| Game Design and Development | M,O |
| Gender Studies | M,D,O |
| Geographic Information Systems | M,D |
| Geography | M,D |
| Geosciences | M,D |
| Gerontological Nursing | M,D,O |
| Gerontology | M,D,O |
| Health Psychology | M,D,O |
| Health Services Management and Hospital Administration | M,D,O |
| Health Services Research | D |
| History | M |
| Industrial and Manufacturing Management | M,D,O |
| Industrial and Organizational Psychology | M,D,O |
| Information Science | M,O |
| Interdisciplinary Studies | M,D,O |
| Kinesiology and Movement Studies | M |
| Latin American Studies | M,D,O |
| Liberal Studies | M,D,O |
| Linguistics | M,O |
| Logistics | M,O |
| Management Information Systems | M,D,O |
| Mathematics | M,D,O |
| Middle School Education | M,D,O |
| Music | O |
| Nonprofit Management | M,O |
| Nurse Anesthesia | M,D,O |
| Nursing and Healthcare Administration | M,D,O |
| Nursing Education | M,D,O |
| Nursing—General | M,D,O |
| Optical Sciences | M,D |
| Philosophy | M,O |
| Psychology—General | M,D,O |
| Public Administration | M,O |
| Public Health—General | M,D,O |
| Public Policy | M,D,O |
| Reading Education | M,O |
| Real Estate | M,O |
| Religion | M |
| Secondary Education | M,D,O |
| Social Work | M |
| Sociology | M,O |
| Spanish | M,O |
| Special Education | M,D,O |
| Supply Chain Management | M,O |
| Systems Engineering | M,D |
| Technical Writing | M,O |
| Theater | M,D,O |
| Urban and Regional Planning | M,O |
| Urban Design | M |
| Women's Studies | M,D,O |
| Writing | M,O |

**THE UNIVERSITY OF NORTH CAROLINA AT GREENSBORO**

| | |
|---|---|
| Accounting | M,O |
| Adult Education | M,D,O |
| Adult Nursing | M,D,O |
| Applied Economics | M |
| Architecture | M,O |
| Art/Fine Arts | M |
| Athletic Training and Sports Medicine | M,D |
| Biochemistry | M |
| Biological and Biomedical Sciences—General | M |
| Business Administration and Management—General | M,O |
| Chemistry | M |
| Child and Family Studies | M,D |
| Classics | M |
| Clinical Psychology | M,D |
| Cognitive Sciences | M,D |
| Communication Disorders | M,D |
| Communication—General | M |
| Community Health | M,D |
| Computer Science | M |
| Conflict Resolution and Mediation/Peace Studies | M,O |
| Counseling Psychology | M,D,O |
| Counselor Education | M,D,O |
| Criminal Justice and Criminology | M |
| Curriculum and Instruction | M,D,O |
| Dance | M |
| Developmental Psychology | M,D |
| Early Childhood Education | M,D,O |
| Economic Development | M,D,O |
| Economics | D |
| Education—General | M,D,O |
| Educational Leadership and Administration | M,D,O |
| Educational Measurement and Evaluation | D |
| Educational Media/Instructional Technology | M,D,O |
| Elementary Education | D |
| English as a Second Language | M,D,O |
| English Education | M,D |
| English | M,D |
| Film, Television, and Video Production | M |
| Finance and Banking | M,O |
| Foreign Languages Education | M,D,O |
| French | M |
| Gender Studies | M,O |
| Genetic Counseling | M |
| Geographic Information Systems | M,D,O |
| Geography | M,D,O |
| Gerontological Nursing | M,D,O |
| Gerontology | M,O |
| Higher Education | D |
| Hispanic and Latin American Languages | M,O |
| Hispanic Studies | M,O |
| Historic Preservation | M,O |
| History | M,D,O |
| Human Development | M,D |
| Information Studies | M |
| Interior Design | M,O |
| Kinesiology and Movement Studies | M,D |
| Liberal Studies | M |
| Library Science | M |
| Management Information Systems | M,D,O |
| Marketing | M,D |

Marriage and Family Therapy M,D,O
Mathematics Education M,D,O
Mathematics M,D
Media Studies M
Middle School Education M,D,O
Multilingual and Multicultural Education M,D,O
Museum Studies M,D,O
Music Education M,D
Music M,D
Nonprofit Management M,O
Nurse Anesthesia M,D,O
Nursing and Healthcare Administration M,D,O
Nursing Education M,D,O
Nursing—General M,D,O
Nutrition M,D
Political Science M,O
Psychology—General M,D
Public Affairs M,O
Reading Education M,D,O
Recreation and Park Management M
Rhetoric M,D
School Psychology M,D,O
Science Education M,D,O
Social Psychology M,D
Social Sciences Education M,D,O
Social Work M
Sociology M
Spanish M,O
Special Education M,D,O
Supply Chain Management M,D,O
Technical Writing M,D,O
Textile Design M,D
Theater M
Women's Studies M,D,O
Writing M

### THE UNIVERSITY OF NORTH CAROLINA AT PEMBROKE

Art Education M
Business Administration and Management—General M
Counseling Psychology M
Counselor Education M
Criminal Justice and Criminology M
Education—General M
Educational Leadership and Administration M
Elementary Education M
Emergency Management M
English Education M
Exercise and Sports Science M
Health Education M
Health Services Management and Hospital Administration M
Mathematics Education M
Nursing and Healthcare Administration M
Nursing Education M
Nursing—General M
Physical Education M
Public Administration M
Reading Education M
Science Education M
Social Sciences Education M
Social Work M
Sports Management M

### UNIVERSITY OF NORTH CAROLINA SCHOOL OF THE ARTS

Film, Television, and Video Production M
Music M,O
Theater M

### THE UNIVERSITY OF NORTH CAROLINA WILMINGTON

Accounting M
Applied Behavior Analysis M,D
Applied Statistics M,O
Biological and Biomedical Sciences—General M,D
Business Administration and Management—General M
Chemistry M
Clinical Psychology M,D
Clinical Research M,D,O
Computer Science M
Conflict Resolution and Mediation/Peace Studies M
Criminal Justice and Criminology M
Curriculum and Instruction M,D
Data Science/Data Analytics M
Early Childhood Education M
Education—General M,D
Educational Leadership and Administration M,D
Educational Media/Instructional Technology M
Educational Policy M
Elementary Education M
English as a Second Language M
English M
Environmental Management and Policy M
Environmental Sciences M
Family Nurse Practitioner Studies M,D,O
Finance and Banking M
Geographic Information Systems M,O
Geosciences M,O
Gerontology M
Higher Education M,D
Hispanic Studies M,O
History M
International Business M
Investment Management M
Liberal Studies M
Management Information Systems M
Marine Biology M,D
Marine Sciences M,D,O

Mathematics M,O
Middle School Education M
Nursing Education M,D,O
Nursing—General M,D,O
Psychology—General M,D
Public Administration M
Reading Education M
Secondary Education M
Social Work M
Sociology M
Spanish M,O
Special Education M
Statistics M,O
Writing M

### UNIVERSITY OF NORTH DAKOTA

Applied Economics M
Art/Fine Arts M
Astrophysics M,D
Atmospheric Sciences M,D
Aviation M
Biological and Biomedical Sciences—General M,D
Business Administration and Management—General M
Chemical Engineering M,D
Chemistry M,D
Civil Engineering M,D
Clinical Laboratory Sciences/Medical Technology M,D
Clinical Psychology M,D
Communication Disorders M
Communication—General D
Community Health Nursing M,D,O
Computer Science M
Counseling Psychology M,D
Criminal Justice and Criminology D
Early Childhood Education M
Education—General M,D,O
Educational Leadership and Administration M,D,O
Educational Media/Instructional Technology M
Electrical Engineering M,D
Elementary Education M
Engineering and Applied Sciences—General D
English M,D
Environmental Engineering M,D
Family Nurse Practitioner Studies M,D,O
Fish, Game, and Wildlife Management M,D
Forensic Psychology M,D
Genetics M,D
Geographic Information Systems M
Geography M
Geological Engineering M,D
Geology M,D
Geosciences M,D
Gerontological Nursing M,D,O
History M,D
Kinesiology and Movement Studies M
Law D
Linguistics M
Mathematics M
Mechanical Engineering M,D
Music Education M,D
Music M,D
Nurse Anesthesia M,D,O
Nursing Education M,D,O
Nursing—General M,D,O
Occupational Therapy M
Physical Therapy D
Physician Assistant Studies M
Physics M,D
Planetary and Space Sciences M
Psychiatric Nursing M,D,O
Psychology—General M,D
Public Administration M
Public Health—General M
Reading Education M
Social Work M
Sociology M
Special Education M
Zoology M,D

### UNIVERSITY OF NORTHERN BRITISH COLUMBIA

Community Health M,D,O
Computer Science M,D,O
Disability Studies M,D,O
Education—General M,D,O
Environmental Management and Policy M,D,O
Gender Studies M,D,O
History M,D,O
Interdisciplinary Studies M,D,O
International Affairs M,D,O
Mathematics M,D,O
Natural Resources M,D,O
Political Science M,D,O
Psychology—General M,D,O
Social Work M,D,O

### UNIVERSITY OF NORTHERN COLORADO

Accounting M
Acute Care/Critical Care Nursing M,D
Applied Statistics M,D
Art Education M
Art History M
Art/Fine Arts M
Biological and Biomedical Sciences—General M
Business Administration and Management—General M
Chemistry M,D
Clinical Psychology M
Communication Disorders M,D
Communication—General M
Community Health M

Counseling Psychology D
Counselor Education M,D
Criminal Justice and Criminology M
Curriculum and Instruction M,D
Education of the Gifted M,D
Education—General M,D,O
Educational Leadership and Administration M,D,O
Educational Measurement and Evaluation M,D
Educational Policy M,D,O
Educational Psychology M,D
Elementary Education M
English as a Second Language M,D
English Education M,D
English M
Exercise and Sports Science M,D
Family Nurse Practitioner Studies M,D
Foreign Languages Education M,D
Geosciences M
Gerontology M,D
Health Education M
Health Services Management and Hospital Administration M
Higher Education M,D
History M
Human Resources Management M
International Health M
Mathematics Education M,D
Mathematics M,D
Multilingual and Multicultural Education M,D
Music Education M,D
Music M,D
Nursing Education M,D
Nursing—General M,D
Physical Education M,D
Public Health—General M
Reading Education M
Rehabilitation Counseling M,D
Rehabilitation Sciences M,D
School Psychology O
Science Education M,D
Sociology M
Special Education M,D
Sports Management M,D
Student Affairs M,D
Translation and Interpretation M

### UNIVERSITY OF NORTHERN IOWA

Accounting M
Allied Health—General M,D
Applied Mathematics M
Art Education M
Art/Fine Arts M
Athletic Training and Sports Medicine M
Biological and Biomedical Sciences—General M
Business Administration and Management—General M
Communication Disorders M
Communication—General M
Community College Education M
Community Health M
Counseling Psychology M
Counselor Education M
Curriculum and Instruction D
Early Childhood Education M
Education—General M,D,O
Educational Leadership and Administration M,D
Educational Measurement and Evaluation M
Educational Media/Instructional Technology M
Educational Psychology M
Elementary Education M
English as a Second Language M
English Education M
English M
Foreign Languages Education M
Gender Studies M
Geography M
Geosciences M
Health Education M
Health Promotion M
Higher Education M
History M
Human Services M
Kinesiology and Movement Studies M
Mathematics Education M
Mathematics M
Middle School Education M
Music Education M
Music M
Nonprofit Management M
Physical Education M
Physics M
Psychology—General M
Public History M
Public Policy M
Reading Education M
School Psychology M,O
Science Education M
Secondary Education M
Social Sciences M
Social Work M
Spanish M
Special Education M
Sports Management M
Student Affairs M
Vocational and Technical Education M,D
Women's Studies M
Writing M

### UNIVERSITY OF NORTH FLORIDA

Accounting M
Adult Education M
Allied Health—General M,D,O
Applied Behavior Analysis M

Biological and Biomedical Sciences—General M
Business Administration and Management—General M
Civil Engineering M
Communication Disorders M
Community Health M,O
Computer Science M
Construction Management M
Counseling Psychology M
Counselor Education M,D
Criminal Justice and Criminology M
Economics M
Education—General M,D
Educational Leadership and Administration M,D
Educational Media/Instructional Technology M,D
Electrical Engineering M
Electronic Commerce M
Elementary Education M
English as a Second Language M
English M
Ethics M,O
Exercise and Sports Science M,D
Family Nurse Practitioner Studies M,D,O
Finance and Banking M
Health Services Management and Hospital Administration M
History M
Human Resources Management M
International Business M
Logistics M
Management Information Systems M
Mathematics M
Mechanical Engineering M
Nonprofit Management M,O
Nurse Anesthesia M,D,O
Nursing—General M,D,O
Nutrition M
Philosophy M,O
Physical Therapy M,D
Psychology—General M
Public Administration M,O
Public Health—General M,O
Reading Education M
Secondary Education M
Social Work M
Software Engineering M
Special Education M
Sports Management M,D
Statistics M
Translation and Interpretation M
Writing M

### UNIVERSITY OF NORTH GEORGIA

Anthropology M
Athletic Training and Sports Medicine M
Counseling Psychology M
Criminal Justice and Criminology M
Curriculum and Instruction M
Early Childhood Education M
Education—General M
Educational Leadership and Administration D,O
English Education M
Family Nurse Practitioner Studies M,O
Higher Education D
History M
Human Services M
International Affairs M
Kinesiology and Movement Studies M
Mathematics Education M
Middle School Education M
Nursing Education M
Philosophy M
Physical Education M
Physical Therapy D
Public Administration M
Science Education M
Secondary Education M
Social Sciences Education M

### UNIVERSITY OF NORTH TEXAS

Accounting M,D,O
Advertising and Public Relations M,D,O
Anthropology M,D,O
Applied Arts and Design—General M,D,O
Applied Behavior Analysis M,D,O
Art Education M,D,O
Art History M,D,O
Art/Fine Arts M,D,O
Biochemistry M,D,O
Biological and Biomedical Sciences—General M,D,O
Biomedical Engineering M,D,O
Business Administration and Management—General M,D,O
Chemistry M,D,O
Child and Family Studies M,D,O
Clinical Psychology M,D,O
Communication Disorders M,D,O
Communication—General M,D,O
Computer Engineering M,D,O
Computer Science M,D,O
Counseling Psychology M,D,O
Counselor Education M,D,O
Criminal Justice and Criminology M,D,O
Curriculum and Instruction M,D,O
Early Childhood Education M,D,O
Economics M,D,O
Education of the Gifted M,D,O
Education—General M,D,O
Educational Leadership and Administration M,D,O
Educational Measurement and Evaluation M,D,O
Educational Psychology M,D,O
Electrical Engineering M,D,O

*M—masters degree; D—doctorate; O—other advanced degree; *—Close-Up and/or Display*

Emergency Management M,D,O
Energy and Power Engineering M,D,O
Engineering and Applied Sciences—General M,D,O
English as a Second Language M,D,O
English M,D,O
Environmental Sciences M,D,O
Film, Television, and Video Production M,D,O
Finance and Banking M,D,O
French M,D,O
Geography M,D,O
Gerontology M,D,O
Health Services Management and Hospital Administration M,D,O
Higher Education M,D,O
History M,D,O
Hospitality Management M,D,O
Human Development M,D,O
Human Resources Management M,D,O
Industrial and Manufacturing Management M,D,O
Information Science M,D,O
Interdisciplinary Studies M,D,O
Interior Design M,D,O
International Affairs M,D,O
Internet and Interactive Multimedia M,D,O
Journalism M,D,O
Kinesiology and Movement Studies M,D,O
Linguistics M,D,O
Logistics M,D,O
Management Information Systems M,D,O
Management Strategy and Policy M,D,O
Marketing M,D,O
Mathematics M,D,O
Mechanical Engineering M,D,O
Molecular Biology M,D,O
Music Education M,D,O
Music M,D,O
Nonprofit Management M,D,O
Philosophy M,D,O
Political Science M,D,O
Psychology—General M,D,O
Public Administration M,D,O
Quantitative Analysis M,D,O
Rehabilitation Counseling M,D,O
Sociology M,D,O
Spanish M,D,O
Special Education M,D,O
Supply Chain Management M,D,O
Textile Design M,D,O
Travel and Tourism M,D,O
Vocational and Technical Education M,D,O
Writing M,D,O

## UNIVERSITY OF NORTH TEXAS AT DALLAS

Accounting M
Business Administration and Management—General M
Clinical Psychology M
Counselor Education M
Criminal Justice and Criminology M
Curriculum and Instruction M
Educational Leadership and Administration M
Human Resources Management M
Law D
Management Strategy and Policy M
Organizational Behavior M
Public Administration M

## UNIVERSITY OF NORTH TEXAS HEALTH SCIENCE CENTER AT FORT WORTH

Anatomy M,D
Biochemistry M,D
Biological and Biomedical Sciences—General M,D
Biostatistics M,D,O
Biotechnology M,D
Cancer Biology/Oncology M,D
Epidemiology M,D,O
Forensic Sciences M,D
Genetics M,D
Geographic Information Systems M,D,O
Health Services Management and Hospital Administration M,D,O
Health Services Research M,D,O
Immunology M,D
International Health M,D,O
Microbiology M,D
Neuroscience M,D
Osteopathic Medicine D
Pharmaceutical Sciences M,D
Pharmacology M,D
Physical Therapy M,D
Physician Assistant Studies M,D
Physiology M,D
Public Health—General M,D,O
Rehabilitation Sciences M,D

## UNIVERSITY OF NORTHWESTERN OHIO

Business Administration and Management—General M

## UNIVERSITY OF NORTHWESTERN–ST. PAUL

Business Administration and Management—General M
Education—General M
Human Services M
Organizational Management M
Pastoral Ministry and Counseling M
Theology M

## UNIVERSITY OF NOTRE DAME

Accounting M
Aerospace/Aeronautical Engineering M,D
Applied Arts and Design—General M
Applied Mathematics M,D
Applied Statistics M,D
Architecture M
Art History M
Art/Fine Arts M
Biochemistry M,D
Bioengineering M,D
Biological and Biomedical Sciences—General M,D
Business Administration and Management—General M
Business Analytics M
Cell Biology M,D
Chemical Engineering M,D
Chemistry M,D
Civil Engineering M,D
Cognitive Sciences D
Comparative Literature D
Computational Sciences M,D
Computer Engineering M,D
Computer Science M,D
Conflict Resolution and Mediation/Peace Studies M,D
Counseling Psychology D
Developmental Psychology D
Ecology M,D
Economics D
Education—General M
Electrical Engineering M,D
Engineering and Applied Sciences—General M,D
English M,D
Entrepreneurship M
Environmental Engineering M,D
Evolutionary Biology M,D
Finance and Banking M
French M
Genetics M,D
Geosciences M,D
Graphic Design M
History of Science and Technology M,D
History M,D
Industrial Design M
Inorganic Chemistry M,D
International Affairs M
Investment Management M
Italian M
Latin American Studies M
Law M,D
Marketing M
Mathematical and Computational Finance M,D
Mathematics M,D
Mechanical Engineering M,D
Medieval and Renaissance Studies M,D
Molecular Biology M,D
Nonprofit Management M
Organic Chemistry M,D
Parasitology M,D
Philosophy D
Photography M
Physical Chemistry M,D
Physics M,D
Physiology M,D
Political Science D
Psychology—General D
Religion M
Romance Languages M
Sociology D
Spanish M
Statistics M,D
Sustainable Development M
Taxation M
Theology M,D
Writing M

## UNIVERSITY OF OKLAHOMA

Accounting M
Adult Education M,D
Aerospace/Aeronautical Engineering M,D
American Indian/Native American Studies M
Analytical Chemistry M,D
Anthropology M,D
Applied Arts and Design—General M,D
Applied Behavior Analysis M,D
Applied Economics M,D
Archaeology M,D
Architecture M,D
Archives/Archival Administration M,D,O
Art History M,D
Art/Fine Arts M,D
Biochemistry M,D
Biomedical Engineering M,D
Business Administration and Management—General M,D,O
Business Analytics M,O
Chemical Engineering M,D
Chemistry M,D
Civil Engineering M,D
Clinical Psychology M,O
Communication—General M,D
Computer Engineering M,D
Computer Science M,D
Construction Management M,D
Corporate and Organizational Communication M,D
Criminal Justice and Criminology M,O
Cultural Studies M,D
Curriculum and Instruction M,D
Dance M
Early Childhood Education M,D
Ecology M,D
Economics M,D
Education—General M,D,O
Educational Leadership and Administration M,D
Educational Media/Instructional Technology M,D,O
Educational Psychology M,D
Electrical Engineering M,D
Elementary Education M,D
Engineering Physics M,D
English Education M,D
English M,D
Entrepreneurship M,D,O
Environmental Engineering M,D
Environmental Sciences M,D
Evolutionary Biology M,D
Exercise and Sports Science M,D
Film, Television, and Video Theory and Criticism M,D
Foreign Languages Education M,D
French M,D
Gender Studies O
Geography M,D
Geological Engineering M,D,O
Geology M,D
Geophysics M,D
German M,D
Health Communication M,D
Health Promotion M,D
Health Services Management and Hospital Administration M,O
Higher Education M,D
History of Science and Technology M,D
History M,D
Human Resources Management M,D,O
Human Services M,O
Industrial/Management Engineering M,D
Information Studies M,D,O
Inorganic Chemistry M,D
Interior Design M,O
International Affairs M
Landscape Architecture M
Law M,D
Library Science M,D,O
Management Information Systems M,O
Mass Communication M,D
Mathematics Education M,D
Mathematics M,D
Mechanical Engineering M,D
Meteorology M,D
Microbiology M,D
Museum Studies M,O
Music Education M,D,O
Music M,D,O
Neurobiology M,D
Nonprofit Management M,D,O
Organic Chemistry M,D
Organizational Behavior M,D,O
Organizational Management M,O
Petroleum Engineering M,D,O
Philosophy M,D
Photography M,D
Physical Chemistry M,D
Physics M,D
Plant Biology M,D
Political Science M,D
Project Management M,D,O
Psychology—General M,D,O
Public Administration M,D
Public Policy M,D
Reading Education M,D
Rhetoric M,D
Science Education M,D
Social Sciences Education M,D
Social Work M
Sociology M,D
Spanish M,D
Special Education M,D
Structural Biology M,D
Sustainable Development M,D
Telecommunications M,D
Theater M
Urban and Regional Planning M,D
Women's Studies O
Writing M,D

## UNIVERSITY OF OKLAHOMA HEALTH SCIENCES CENTER

Allied Health—General M,D,O
Allopathic Medicine D
Biochemistry M,D
Biological and Biomedical Sciences—General M,D
Biopsychology M,D
Biostatistics M,D
Cell Biology M,D
Communication Disorders M,D,O
Dentistry D,O
Environmental and Occupational Health M,D
Epidemiology M,D
Genetic Counseling M
Health Education D
Health Physics/Radiological Health M,D
Health Promotion M,D
Health Services Management and Hospital Administration M,D
Homeland Security M
Immunology M,D
Medical Physics M,D
Microbiology M,D
Molecular Biology M,D
Neuroscience M,D
Nursing—General M
Nutrition M
Occupational Therapy M
Oral and Dental Sciences M
Pathology D
Pharmaceutical Sciences M,D
Pharmacy D
Physical Therapy M
Physician Assistant Studies M
Physiology M,D
Public Health—General M,D
Radiation Biology M,D
Reading Education M,D,O
Rehabilitation Sciences M
Special Education M,D,O

## UNIVERSITY OF OREGON

Accounting M,D
Anthropology M,D
Applied Arts and Design—General M
Architecture M
Art History M,D
Art/Fine Arts M
Asian Languages M,D
Asian Studies M
Biochemistry M,D
Biological and Biomedical Sciences—General M,D
Biopsychology M,D
Business Administration and Management—General M,D
Chemistry M,D
Chinese M,D
Classics M
Clinical Psychology D
Cognitive Sciences M,D
Communication Disorders M,D
Communication—General M,D
Comparative Literature M,D
Computer Science M,D
Counseling Psychology M,D
Curriculum and Instruction M,D
Dance M
Developmental Psychology M,D
Ecology M,D
Economics M,D
Education—General M,D
Educational Leadership and Administration M,D
English M,D
Environmental Management and Policy M,D
Evolutionary Biology M,D
Finance and Banking D
Folklore M
French M
Genetics M,D
Geography M,D
Geology M,D
German M,D
Historic Preservation M
History M,D
Information Science M,D
Interdisciplinary Studies M
Interior Design M
International Affairs M
Italian M
Japanese M,D
Journalism M,D
Landscape Architecture M,D
Law M,D
Linguistics M,D
Management Information Systems M
Marine Biology M,D
Marketing D
Marriage and Family Therapy M,D
Mathematics M,D
Media Studies M,D
Molecular Biology M,D
Music Education M,D
Music M,D
Neuroscience M,D
Nonprofit Management M,O
Philosophy M,D
Physics M,D
Physiology M,D
Political Science M,D
Psychology—General M,D
Public Administration M
Quantitative Analysis M
Romance Languages M,D
Russian M
School Psychology M,D
Social Psychology M,D
Sociology M,D
Spanish M
Special Education M,D
Sports Management M
Theater M,D
Urban and Regional Planning M
Writing M

## UNIVERSITY OF OTTAWA

Aerospace/Aeronautical Engineering M,D
Allopathic Medicine M,D
Anthropology M
Biochemistry M,D
Bioengineering M,D
Biological and Biomedical Sciences—General M,D
Biomedical Engineering M
Business Administration and Management—General M
Canadian Studies D
Cell Biology M,D
Chemical Engineering M,D
Chemistry M,D
Civil Engineering M,D
Classics M,D
Communication Disorders M
Communication—General M
Community Health D,O
Computer Engineering M,D
Computer Science M,D
Criminal Justice and Criminology M,D
Economics M,D
Education—General M,D,O
Electrical Engineering M,D
Electronic Commerce M,D,O
Engineering and Applied Sciences—General M,D,O
Engineering Management M,O
English M,D
Epidemiology M
Finance and Banking D,O
French M,D
Geography M,D
Geosciences M,D
Health Services Management and Hospital Administration M
Health Services Research D,O
History M,D
Immunology M,D
Information Science M,O

| | |
|---|---|
| Interdisciplinary Studies | D,O |
| International Development | M |
| Kinesiology and Movement Studies | M |
| Law | M,D |
| Linguistics | M,D |
| Mathematics | M,D |
| Mechanical Engineering | M,D |
| Microbiology | M,D |
| Molecular Biology | M,D |
| Music Education | M,O |
| Music | M,O |
| Nursing—General | M,D,O |
| Philosophy | M,D |
| Physics | M,D |
| Political Science | M,D |
| Project Management | M,O |
| Psychology—General | D |
| Public Administration | D,O |
| Public Health—General | D |
| Rehabilitation Sciences | M |
| Religion | M,D |
| Social Work | M |
| Sociology | M |
| Spanish | M,D |
| Statistics | M,D |
| Systems Science | M,D,O |
| Theater | M |
| Translation and Interpretation | M,D |
| Women's Studies | M |

**UNIVERSITY OF PENNSYLVANIA**

| | |
|---|---|
| Accounting | M,D |
| Acute Care/Critical Care Nursing | M |
| Adult Nursing | M |
| African Studies | M,D |
| Allopathic Medicine | D |
| Anthropology | M,D |
| Applied Economics | D |
| Applied Mathematics | D |
| Applied Psychology | M |
| Archaeology | M,D |
| Architecture | M,D,O |
| Art History | M,D |
| Art/Fine Arts | M,O |
| Artificial Intelligence/Robotics | M |
| Asian Studies | M,D |
| Biochemistry | D |
| Bioengineering | M,D |
| Bioethics | M |
| Biological and Biomedical Sciences—General | M,D |
| Biostatistics | M,D |
| Biotechnology | M |
| Business Administration and Management—General | M,D |
| Cancer Biology/Oncology | D |
| Cell Biology | D |
| Chemical Engineering | M,D |
| Chemistry | M,D |
| Classics | M,D |
| Clinical Laboratory Sciences/Medical Technology | M |
| Communication—General | D |
| Comparative Literature | M,D |
| Computational Biology | D |
| Computational Sciences | M,D |
| Computer Art and Design | M,D |
| Computer Science | M,D |
| Counseling Psychology | M |
| Counselor Education | M |
| Criminal Justice and Criminology | M,D |
| Data Science/Data Analytics | M |
| Demography and Population Studies | M,D |
| Dentistry | D |
| Developmental Biology | D |
| Economic Development | M,O |
| Economics | M,D |
| Education—General | M,D,O |
| Educational Leadership and Administration | M,D |
| Educational Measurement and Evaluation | M,D |
| Educational Media/Instructional Technology | M |
| Educational Policy | M,D |
| Electrical Engineering | M,D |
| Elementary Education | M |
| Engineering and Applied Sciences—General | M,D |
| English as a Second Language | M |
| English Education | M,D |
| English | M,D |
| Entrepreneurship | M |
| Environmental and Occupational Health | M |
| Environmental Management and Policy | M |
| Environmental Sciences | M,D |
| Epidemiology | M |
| Ethics | M,D |
| Family Nurse Practitioner Studies | M,O |
| Finance and Banking | M,D |
| Foundations and Philosophy of Education | M,D |
| French | M,D |
| Game Design and Development | M,D |
| Genetics | D |
| Genomic Sciences | D |
| Geographic Information Systems | M,D,O |
| Geosciences | M,D |
| German | M,D |
| Gerontological Nursing | M |
| Graphic Design | M,O |
| Health Services Management and Hospital Administration | M,D |
| Health Services Research | M |
| Higher Education | M,D |
| Historic Preservation | M,O |
| History of Science and Technology | M,D |
| History | M,D |
| Human Development | M,D |
| Human Genetics | M |
| Immunology | D |
| Information Science | M,D |
| Insurance | M,D |
| International Affairs | M |
| International and Comparative Education | M |
| International Business | M |
| International Health | M |
| Internet and Interactive Multimedia | M,O |
| Italian | M,D |
| Landscape Architecture | M,O |
| Law | M,D |
| Legal and Justice Studies | M,D |
| Liberal Studies | M |
| Linguistics | M,D |
| Management Information Systems | M,D |
| Marketing | M,D |
| Materials Engineering | M,D |
| Materials Sciences | M,D |
| Maternal and Child/Neonatal Nursing | M |
| Mathematics | M,D |
| Mechanical Engineering | M,D |
| Mechanics | M,D |
| Medical Physics | M,D |
| Microbiology | D |
| Molecular Biology | D |
| Molecular Biophysics | D |
| Multilingual and Multicultural Education | M |
| Music | M,D |
| Nanotechnology | M |
| Near and Middle Eastern Studies | M,D |
| Neuroscience | D |
| Nonprofit Management | M,O |
| Nurse Anesthesia | M |
| Nurse Midwifery | M |
| Nursing and Healthcare Administration | M,D |
| Nursing—General | M,D,O |
| Organizational Management | M,O |
| Pediatric Nursing | M |
| Pharmacology | D |
| Philosophy | M,D |
| Physics | M,D |
| Physiology | D |
| Political Science | M,D,O |
| Psychiatric Nursing | M |
| Psychology—General | D |
| Public Administration | M,O |
| Public Health—General | M |
| Public Policy | M,D |
| Reading Education | M |
| Real Estate | M,D |
| Religion | D |
| Risk Management | M,D |
| Romance Languages | M,D |
| Science Education | M,O |
| Secondary Education | M |
| Social Work | M,D |
| Sociology | M,D |
| Spanish | M,D |
| Statistics | M,D |
| Systems Engineering | M,D |
| Urban and Regional Planning | M,D,O |
| Urban Design | M,D,O |
| Urban Education | M |
| Veterinary Medicine | D |
| Virology | D |
| Women's Health Nursing | M |

**UNIVERSITY OF PHILOSOPHICAL RESEARCH**

| | |
|---|---|
| Psychology—General | M |
| Theology | M |

**UNIVERSITY OF PHOENIX - BAY AREA CAMPUS**

| | |
|---|---|
| Accounting | M,D |
| Adult Education | M,D,O |
| Business Administration and Management—General | M,D |
| Criminal Justice and Criminology | M |
| Early Childhood Education | M,D,O |
| Education—General | M,D,O |
| Educational Leadership and Administration | M,D,O |
| Elementary Education | M,D,O |
| Energy Management and Policy | M,D |
| Gerontological Nursing | M,D |
| Health Services Management and Hospital Administration | M,D |
| Higher Education | M,D,O |
| Human Resources Management | M,D |
| International Business | M,D |
| Management Information Systems | M,D |
| Management of Technology | M,D |
| Marketing | M,D |
| Marriage and Family Therapy | M |
| Nursing and Healthcare Administration | M,D |
| Nursing Education | M,D |
| Nursing Informatics | M,D |
| Nursing—General | M,D |
| Organizational Management | M,D |
| Project Management | M,D |
| Public Administration | M,D |
| Secondary Education | M,D,O |
| Special Education | M,D,O |

**UNIVERSITY OF PHOENIX - CENTRAL VALLEY CAMPUS**

| | |
|---|---|
| Accounting | M |
| Business Administration and Management—General | M |
| Community Health | M |
| Computer Education | M |
| Curriculum and Instruction | M |
| Education—General | M |
| Elementary Education | M |
| Gerontology | M |
| Health Services Management and Hospital Administration | M |
| Human Resources Management | M |
| International Business | M |
| Management Information Systems | M |
| Management of Technology | M |
| Marketing | M |
| Marriage and Family Therapy | M |
| Nursing—General | M |
| Public Administration | M |
| Secondary Education | M |

**UNIVERSITY OF PHOENIX - DALLAS CAMPUS**

| | |
|---|---|
| Accounting | M |
| Business Administration and Management—General | M |
| Criminal Justice and Criminology | M |
| Curriculum and Instruction | M |
| Education—General | M |
| Electronic Commerce | M |
| Human Resources Management | M |
| International Business | M |
| Management Information Systems | M |
| Management of Technology | M |
| Marketing | M |
| Public Administration | M |

**UNIVERSITY OF PHOENIX - HAWAII CAMPUS**

| | |
|---|---|
| Accounting | M |
| Business Administration and Management—General | M |
| Community Health | M |
| Curriculum and Instruction | M |
| Education—General | M |
| Educational Leadership and Administration | M |
| Elementary Education | M |
| Family Nurse Practitioner Studies | M |
| Gerontology | M |
| Health Services Management and Hospital Administration | M |
| Human Resources Management | M |
| International Business | M |
| Management Information Systems | M |
| Management of Technology | M |
| Marketing | M |
| Nursing Education | M |
| Nursing—General | M |
| Public Administration | M |
| Secondary Education | M |
| Special Education | M |

**UNIVERSITY OF PHOENIX - HOUSTON CAMPUS**

| | |
|---|---|
| Accounting | M |
| Business Administration and Management—General | M |
| Curriculum and Instruction | M |
| Education—General | M |
| Electronic Commerce | M |
| Health Services Management and Hospital Administration | M |
| Human Resources Management | M |
| International Business | M |
| Management Information Systems | M |
| Management of Technology | M |
| Marketing | M |
| Nursing—General | M |
| Public Administration | M |

**UNIVERSITY OF PHOENIX - LAS VEGAS CAMPUS**

| | |
|---|---|
| Accounting | M |
| Allied Health—General | M |
| Business Administration and Management—General | M |
| Counseling Psychology | M |
| Counselor Education | M |
| Curriculum and Instruction | M |
| Education—General | M |
| Educational Leadership and Administration | M |
| Elementary Education | M |
| Human Resources Management | M |
| International Business | M |
| Management Information Systems | M |
| Management of Technology | M |
| Marketing | M |
| Marriage and Family Therapy | M |
| Public Administration | M |
| School Psychology | M |

**UNIVERSITY OF PHOENIX–ONLINE CAMPUS**

| | |
|---|---|
| Accounting | M,O |
| Adult Education | M,O |
| Business Administration and Management—General | M,D,O |
| Computer Education | M,O |
| Conflict Resolution and Mediation/Peace Studies | M,O |
| Criminal Justice and Criminology | M |
| Curriculum and Instruction | M,D,O |
| Early Childhood Education | M,O |
| Education—General | M,O |
| Educational Leadership and Administration | M,D,O |
| Educational Media/Instructional Technology | D,O |
| Elementary Education | M,O |
| Energy Management and Policy | M,O |
| English as a Second Language | M,O |
| English Education | M,O |
| Family Nurse Practitioner Studies | M,O |
| Health Education | M,O |
| Health Informatics | M,O |
| Health Services Management and Hospital Administration | M,D,O |
| Higher Education | D,O |
| Homeland Security | M |
| Human Resources Management | M,O |
| Industrial and Organizational Psychology | M,D,O |
| International Business | M,O |
| Management Information Systems | M |
| Management of Technology | M,O |
| Marketing | M,O |
| Mathematics Education | M,O |
| Middle School Education | M,O |
| Nursing Education | M,O |
| Nursing—General | M,D,O |
| Organizational Management | D,O |
| Project Management | M,O |
| Psychology—General | M,O |
| Public Administration | M,O |
| Reading Education | M,O |
| Science Education | M,O |
| Secondary Education | M,O |
| Special Education | M,O |

**UNIVERSITY OF PHOENIX - PHOENIX CAMPUS**

| | |
|---|---|
| Accounting | M,O |
| Adult Education | M |
| Business Administration and Management—General | M,O |
| Clinical Psychology | M |
| Counseling Psychology | M |
| Counselor Education | M |
| Criminal Justice and Criminology | M |
| Curriculum and Instruction | M |
| Early Childhood Education | M |
| Education—General | M |
| Educational Leadership and Administration | M |
| Elementary Education | M |
| Energy Management and Policy | M,O |
| Family Nurse Practitioner Studies | M,O |
| Gerontological Nursing | M,O |
| Health Services Management and Hospital Administration | M,O |
| Homeland Security | M |
| Human Resources Management | M,O |
| International Business | M,O |
| Management of Technology | M,O |
| Marketing | M,O |
| Marriage and Family Therapy | M |
| Medical Informatics | M,O |
| Nursing Education | M,O |
| Nursing Informatics | M,O |
| Nursing—General | M,O |
| Project Management | M,O |
| Psychology—General | M |
| Public Administration | M |
| Reading Education | M |
| Secondary Education | M |
| Social Psychology | M |
| Special Education | M |
| Vocational and Technical Education | M |

**UNIVERSITY OF PHOENIX - SACRAMENTO VALLEY CAMPUS**

| | |
|---|---|
| Accounting | M |
| Adult Education | M,O |
| Business Administration and Management—General | M |
| Curriculum and Instruction | M,O |
| Education—General | M,O |
| Elementary Education | M,O |
| Family Nurse Practitioner Studies | M |
| Health Services Management and Hospital Administration | M |
| Human Resources Management | M |
| International Business | M |
| Management Information Systems | M |
| Management of Technology | M |
| Marketing | M |
| Nursing Education | M |
| Nursing—General | M |
| Public Administration | M |
| Secondary Education | M,O |

**UNIVERSITY OF PHOENIX - SAN ANTONIO CAMPUS**

| | |
|---|---|
| Accounting | M |
| Business Administration and Management—General | M |
| Criminal Justice and Criminology | M |
| Curriculum and Instruction | M |
| Electronic Commerce | M |
| Health Services Management and Hospital Administration | M |
| Human Resources Management | M |
| International Business | M |
| Management Information Systems | M |
| Management of Technology | M |
| Marketing | M |
| Nursing—General | M |
| Public Administration | M |

**UNIVERSITY OF PHOENIX - SAN DIEGO CAMPUS**

| | |
|---|---|
| Accounting | M |
| Business Administration and Management—General | M |
| Computer Education | M |
| Curriculum and Instruction | M |
| Education—General | M |
| Elementary Education | M |
| English as a Second Language | M |
| Human Resources Management | M |
| International Business | M |
| Management Information Systems | M |
| Management of Technology | M |
| Marketing | M |
| Nursing Education | M |

*M—masters degree; D—doctorate; O—other advanced degree; *—Close-Up and/or Display*

Nursing—General M
Public Administration M
Secondary Education M

### UNIVERSITY OF PIKEVILLE
Business Administration and Management—General M
Education—General M
Educational Leadership and Administration M
Entrepreneurship M
Health Services Management and Hospital Administration M
Optometry D
Osteopathic Medicine D

### UNIVERSITY OF PITTSBURGH
Accounting M,D
African Studies O
Allopathic Medicine D
Anthropology M,D
Applied Mathematics M,D
Applied Statistics M,D
Architectural History M,D
Art History M,D
Artificial Intelligence/Robotics M,D
Asian Studies M,O
Athletic Training and Sports Medicine M
Bioengineering M,D
Bioethics M
Bioinformatics M,D,O
Biological and Biomedical Sciences—General M,D
Biostatistics M,D
Business Administration and Management—General M,D
Business Analytics D
Cell Biology D
Chemical Engineering M,D
Chemistry M,D
Chinese M
Civil Engineering M,D
Clinical Laboratory Sciences/Medical Technology D
Clinical Psychology M,D
Clinical Research M,O
Communication Disorders M,D
Communication—General M,D
Community Health M,D,O
Computational Sciences M,D,O
Computer Engineering M,D
Computer Science M,D
Criminal Justice and Criminology M
Cultural Studies O
Data Science/Data Analytics M,D,O
Dentistry M,D,O
Developmental Biology D
Developmental Psychology D
Disability Studies O
East European and Russian Studies O
Ecology D
Economics M,D
Education—General M,D
Electrical Engineering M,D
Energy Management and Policy M
Engineering and Applied Sciences—General M,D
English as a Second Language D,O
English M,D
Environmental and Occupational Health M,D
Environmental Engineering M,D
Environmental Law M
Environmental Sciences M,D
Epidemiology M,D
Evolutionary Biology D
Family Nurse Practitioner Studies M,D
Film, Television, and Video Theory and Criticism M,D,O
Finance and Banking M,D
French M,D
Genetic Counseling M,D,O
Geographic Information Systems M,D
Geology M,D
Gerontological Nursing D
Health Education M,D
Health Informatics M
Health Law M
Health Psychology D
Health Services Management and Hospital Administration M,D,O
Health Services Research M
History of Science and Technology D
History M,D
Human Genetics M,D,O
Human Resources Management M,D
Immunology D
Industrial and Manufacturing Management M
Industrial/Management Engineering M,D
Infectious Diseases M,D
Information Science M,D,O
Intellectual Property Law M
Interdisciplinary Studies D
International Affairs M,D,O
International Business O
International Development M,D
International Health M,D,O
Italian M,D
Japanese M
Latin American Studies O
Law M
Legal and Justice Studies M
Library Science M,D
Linguistics M,D
Management Information Systems M,D
Management Strategy and Policy M,D
Marketing M,D
Materials Sciences M,D
Mathematics M,D
Mechanical Engineering M,D
Medieval and Renaissance Studies O
Microbiology M,D
Military and Defense Studies M
Molecular Biology D
Molecular Biophysics D
Music M,D
Neuroscience D
Nonprofit Management M
Nurse Anesthesia D
Nurse Midwifery D
Nursing and Healthcare Administration M,D
Nursing—General D
Nutrition M
Occupational Therapy M,D
Oral and Dental Sciences M,D,O
Organizational Behavior M,D
Petroleum Engineering M,D
Pharmaceutical Administration M
Pharmaceutical Sciences M,D
Pharmacy D
Philosophy D
Physical Therapy M,D
Physician Assistant Studies M,D
Physics M,D*
Political Science M,D
Psychology—General D
Public Administration M,D
Public Health—General M,D,O
Public Policy M,D
Rehabilitation Counseling M,D
Rehabilitation Sciences M,D
Slavic Languages M,D
Social Psychology D
Social Work M,D,O
Sociology M,D
Spanish D
Statistics M,D
Structural Biology D
Supply Chain Management M
Systems Biology D
Theater M,D
Urban and Regional Planning M
Western European Studies O
Women's Studies O
Writing M,D

### UNIVERSITY OF PORTLAND
Biomedical Engineering M
Business Administration and Management—General M
Civil Engineering M
Communication—General M
Computer Science M
Corporate and Organizational Communication M
Education—General M,D
Educational Leadership and Administration M,D
Electrical Engineering M
Engineering and Applied Sciences—General M
English as a Second Language M,D
Entrepreneurship M
Family Nurse Practitioner Studies M,D
Finance and Banking M
Health Services Management and Hospital Administration M
Industrial and Manufacturing Management M
Management of Technology M
Marketing M
Mechanical Engineering M
Nonprofit Management M
Nursing Education M,D
Nursing—General M,D
Organizational Management M,D
Reading Education M,D
Special Education M,D
Sustainability Management M

### UNIVERSITY OF PRINCE EDWARD ISLAND
Anatomy M,D
Bacteriology M,D
Biological and Biomedical Sciences—General M,D
Chemistry M,D
Education—General M,D
Educational Leadership and Administration M,D
Environmental Sciences M,D
Epidemiology M,D
Geography M
Immunology M,D
Parasitology M,D
Pathology M,D
Pharmacology M,D
Physiology M,D
Toxicology M,D
Veterinary Medicine D
Veterinary Sciences M,D
Virology M,D

### UNIVERSITY OF PROVIDENCE
Counseling Psychology M
Criminal Justice and Criminology M
Human Services M

### UNIVERSITY OF PUERTO RICO AT MAYAGÜEZ
Aerospace/Aeronautical Engineering M,D
Agricultural Economics and Agribusiness M
Agricultural Education M
Agricultural Sciences—General M
Agronomy and Soil Sciences M
Animal Sciences M
Applied Mathematics M
Bioengineering M,D
Biological and Biomedical Sciences—General M
Business Administration and Management—General M
Chemical Engineering M,D
Chemistry M,D
Civil Engineering M,D
Computational Sciences M
Computer Engineering M,D
Computer Science M,D
Construction Engineering M,D
Electrical Engineering M,D
Energy and Power Engineering M,D
Engineering and Applied Sciences—General M,D
Engineering Management M,D
English Education M
English M
Environmental Engineering M,D
Environmental Sciences M,D
Exercise and Sports Science M
Finance and Banking M
Food Science and Technology M
Geology M
Geotechnical Engineering M,D
Higher Education M
Hispanic Studies M
Horticulture M
Human Resources Management M
Industrial and Manufacturing Management M
Industrial/Management Engineering M
Information Science M,D
Kinesiology and Movement Studies M
Manufacturing Engineering M,D
Marine Sciences M,D
Materials Engineering M,D
Materials Sciences M,D
Mathematics Education M
Mathematics M
Mechanical Engineering M,D
Physical Chemistry M,D
Physics M
Rural Sociology M
Structural Engineering M,D
Transportation and Highway Engineering M,D

### UNIVERSITY OF PUERTO RICO AT RIO PIEDRAS
Accounting M,D
Architecture M
Biological and Biomedical Sciences—General M,D
Business Administration and Management—General M,D
Cell Biology M,D
Chemistry M,D
Clinical Psychology M,D
Communication—General M
Comparative Literature M
Counselor Education M,D
Curriculum and Instruction M,D
Early Childhood Education M
Ecology M,D
Economic Development M
Economics M
Education—General M,D
Educational Leadership and Administration M,D
Educational Measurement and Evaluation M
English as a Second Language M
English M,D
Environmental Management and Policy M
Environmental Sciences M,D
Evolutionary Biology M,D
Exercise and Sports Science M
Family and Consumer Sciences-General M
Finance and Banking M,D
Foreign Languages Education M,D
Genetics M,D
Hispanic Studies M,D
History M,D
Human Resources Management M,D
Industrial and Manufacturing Management M,D
Industrial and Organizational Psychology M,D
Information Science M,O
Information Studies M,O
International Business M,D
Journalism M
Law M,D
Library Science M,O
Linguistics M,D
Marketing M,D
Mass Communication M
Mathematics Education M,D
Mathematics M,D
Molecular Biology M,D
Neuroscience M,D
Nutrition M
Philosophy M
Physics M,D
Psychology—General M,D
Public Administration M
Public Policy M
Quantitative Analysis M,D
Rehabilitation Counseling M
Science Education M,D
Social Psychology M,D
Social Sciences Education M,D
Social Work M,D
Sociology M
Special Education M
Translation and Interpretation M,O
Urban and Regional Planning M

### UNIVERSITY OF PUERTO RICO - MEDICAL SCIENCES CAMPUS
Acute Care/Critical Care Nursing M
Adult Nursing M
Allied Health—General M,D,O
Allopathic Medicine D
Anatomy M,D
Biochemistry M,D
Biological and Biomedical Sciences—General M,D
Biostatistics M
Clinical Laboratory Sciences/Medical Technology M,O
Clinical Research M,O
Communication Disorders M,D
Community Health Nursing M
Demography and Population Studies M
Dentistry D
Environmental and Occupational Health M,D
Epidemiology M
Family Nurse Practitioner Studies M
Gerontological Nursing M
Gerontology M,O
Health Education M
Health Informatics M
Health Promotion O
Health Services Management and Hospital Administration M
Health Services Research M
Industrial Hygiene M
Maternal and Child Health M
Maternal and Child/Neonatal Nursing M
Microbiology M,D
Nurse Midwifery M,O
Nursing—General M
Nutrition M,D,O
Occupational Therapy M
Oral and Dental Sciences O
Pediatric Nursing M
Pharmaceutical Sciences M,D
Pharmacology M,D
Pharmacy M,D
Physical Therapy M
Physiology M,D
Psychiatric Nursing M
Special Education O
Toxicology M,D

### UNIVERSITY OF PUGET SOUND
Counseling Psychology M
Counselor Education M
Education—General M
Elementary Education M
Occupational Therapy M,D
Physical Therapy D
Secondary Education M

### UNIVERSITY OF REDLANDS
Business Administration and Management—General M
Communication Disorders M
Education—General M,D,O
Geographic Information Systems M
Management Information Systems M
Music M

### UNIVERSITY OF REGINA
Adult Education M
Analytical Chemistry M,D
Anthropology M
Applied Psychology M,D
Art/Fine Arts M
Biochemistry M,D
Biological and Biomedical Sciences—General M,D
Biophysics M,D
Business Administration and Management—General M,O
Cancer Biology/Oncology M,D
Chemistry M,D
Clinical Psychology M,D
Computer Engineering M,D
Computer Science M,D
Criminal Justice and Criminology M
Curriculum and Instruction M
Economics M,D,O
Education—General M,D,O
Educational Leadership and Administration M
Educational Psychology M
Engineering and Applied Sciences—General M,D
Engineering Management M,O
English M,D
Environmental Engineering M,D
Experimental Psychology M,D
Film, Television, and Video Production M
French M
Geography M,D
Geology M,D
Gerontology M
Health Services Management and Hospital Administration M,D,O
History M
Human Resources Development M
Human Resources Management M,O
Industrial/Management Engineering M,D
Inorganic Chemistry M,D
Interdisciplinary Studies M
International Business M,O
Journalism M
Kinesiology and Movement Studies M,D
Mathematics M,D
Music M
Nursing—General M,D
Organic Chemistry M,D
Organizational Management M,O
Petroleum Engineering M,D
Philosophy M
Physics M,D
Project Management M,O
Psychology—General M,D
Public Administration M,D,O
Public Policy M,D,O
Religion M

| | |
|---|---|
| Social Sciences | M |
| Social Work | M,D |
| Sociology | M |
| Software Engineering | M,D |
| Statistics | M,D |
| Systems Engineering | M,D |
| Theoretical Chemistry | M,D |
| Women's Studies | M |
| Writing | M,D |

## UNIVERSITY OF RHODE ISLAND

| | |
|---|---|
| Accounting | M |
| Acute Care/Critical Care Nursing | M,D,O |
| Adult Nursing | M,D,O |
| Animal Sciences | M,D |
| Anthropology | M |
| Applied Mathematics | M,D |
| Aquaculture | M,D |
| Archaeology | M |
| Biochemistry | M,D |
| Biological and Biomedical Sciences—General | M,D |
| Biomedical Engineering | M,D |
| Biotechnology | M,D |
| Business Administration and Management—General | M,D |
| Cell Biology | M,D |
| Chemical Engineering | M,D,O |
| Chemistry | M,D |
| Child and Family Studies | M |
| Civil Engineering | M,D |
| Clinical Laboratory Sciences/Medical Technology | M,D |
| Clinical Psychology | M,D |
| Clothing and Textiles | M,O |
| Communication Disorders | M |
| Communication—General | M |
| Computer and Information Systems Security | M,D,O |
| Computer Art and Design | M |
| Computer Engineering | M,D |
| Computer Science | M,D,O |
| Counseling Psychology | M |
| Ecology | M,D |
| Economics | M,D |
| Education—General | M,D |
| Electrical Engineering | M,D |
| Engineering and Applied Sciences—General | M,D,O |
| English | M,D |
| Entrepreneurship | M,D,O |
| Environmental Engineering | M,D |
| Environmental Management and Policy | M,D |
| Environmental Sciences | M,D |
| Evolutionary Biology | M,D |
| Exercise and Sports Science | M |
| Family Nurse Practitioner Studies | M,D,O |
| Film, Television, and Video Production | M,D |
| Finance and Banking | M,D |
| Fish, Game, and Wildlife Management | M,D |
| Food Science and Technology | M,D |
| Forensic Sciences | M,D,O |
| Gender Studies | M,D,O |
| Geophysics | M,D |
| Geosciences | M,D,O |
| Geotechnical Engineering | M,D |
| Gerontological Nursing | M,D,O |
| Health Education | M |
| Health Services Management and Hospital Administration | M,D,O |
| History | M |
| Human Development | M |
| Human Resources Management | M,O |
| Hydrology | M,D,O |
| Industrial and Labor Relations | M,O |
| Industrial/Management Engineering | M,D |
| Information Studies | M |
| Library Science | M |
| Management Strategy and Policy | M,D,O |
| Marine Affairs | M,D |
| Marine Biology | M,D |
| Marine Geology | M,D |
| Marine Sciences | M,D |
| Marketing | M,D |
| Marriage and Family Therapy | M |
| Mathematics | M,D |
| Medical Physics | M,D |
| Medicinal and Pharmaceutical Chemistry | M,D |
| Microbiology | M,D |
| Molecular Biology | M,D |
| Molecular Genetics | M,D |
| Music Education | M |
| Music | M |
| Natural Resources | M,D |
| Nursing Education | M,D,O |
| Nursing—General | M,D,O |
| Nutrition | M |
| Ocean Engineering | M,D |
| Oceanography | M,D |
| Pharmaceutical Sciences | M,D |
| Pharmacology | M,D |
| Pharmacy | D |
| Physical Education | M |
| Physical Therapy | D |
| Physics | M,D |
| Political Science | M |
| Psychology—General | M,D |
| Public Administration | M |
| Public Policy | M |
| Reading Education | M,D |
| Recreation and Park Management | M |
| School Psychology | M,D |
| Spanish | M |
| Special Education | M,D |
| Sport Psychology | M |
| Statistics | M,D,O |
| Student Affairs | M |
| Supply Chain Management | M,D |
| Systems Engineering | M,D |
| Toxicology | M,D |
| Women's Studies | O |
| Writing | M,D |

## UNIVERSITY OF RICHMOND

| | |
|---|---|
| Business Administration and Management—General | M |
| Law | D |

## UNIVERSITY OF RIO GRANDE

| | |
|---|---|
| Art Education | M |
| Education—General | M |
| Educational Leadership and Administration | M |
| Physical Education | M |
| Special Education | M |

## UNIVERSITY OF ROCHESTER

| | |
|---|---|
| Accounting | M,D |
| Acute Care/Critical Care Nursing | M,D |
| Adult Nursing | M,D |
| Allopathic Medicine | D |
| Anatomy | D |
| Art History | D |
| Art/Fine Arts | D |
| Artificial Intelligence/Robotics | M,D |
| Astronomy | D |
| Biochemistry | D |
| Bioinformatics | M,D |
| Biological and Biomedical Sciences—General | M,D |
| Biomedical Engineering | M,D |
| Biophysics | D |
| Biostatistics | M |
| Business Administration and Management—General | M,D |
| Chemical Engineering | M,D |
| Chemistry | D |
| Clinical Psychology | D |
| Clinical Research | M |
| Cognitive Sciences | D |
| Computational Biology | M,D |
| Computer Engineering | M,D |
| Computer Science | M,D |
| Counselor Education | M,D |
| Curriculum and Instruction | M,D |
| Data Science/Data Analytics | M |
| Developmental Psychology | D |
| Ecology | M,D |
| Economics | D |
| Education—General | M,D |
| Educational Leadership and Administration | M,D |
| Educational Policy | M,D |
| Electrical Engineering | M,D |
| Engineering and Applied Sciences—General | M,D |
| English | M,D |
| Entrepreneurship | M |
| Epidemiology | D |
| Family Nurse Practitioner Studies | M,D |
| Finance and Banking | M,D |
| Foundations and Philosophy of Education | D |
| Genetics | M,D |
| Genomic Sciences | D |
| Geology | M,D |
| Geosciences | M,D |
| Gerontological Nursing | M,D |
| Health Services Management and Hospital Administration | M,D |
| Health Services Research | D |
| Higher Education | M,D |
| History | M,D |
| Human Development | M,D |
| Human-Computer Interaction | M,D |
| Immunology | M,D |
| Industrial and Manufacturing Management | D |
| Inorganic Chemistry | D |
| Linguistics | M |
| Management Information Systems | M,D |
| Management Strategy and Policy | M |
| Marketing Research | M |
| Marketing | M,D |
| Marriage and Family Therapy | M |
| Materials Sciences | M,D |
| Maternal and Child/Neonatal Nursing | M,D |
| Mathematics | D |
| Mechanical Engineering | M,D |
| Microbiology | M,D |
| Molecular Biology | M,D |
| Music Education | M,D |
| Music | M,D |
| Neurobiology | D |
| Neuroscience | D |
| Nursing and Healthcare Administration | M,D |
| Nursing Education | M,D |
| Nursing—General | M,D |
| Optical Sciences | M,D |
| Oral and Dental Sciences | M |
| Organic Chemistry | D |
| Pathology | D |
| Pediatric Nursing | M,D |
| Pharmacology | M,D |
| Philosophy | D |
| Physical Chemistry | D |
| Physics | D |
| Physiology | M,D |
| Political Science | D |
| Psychiatric Nursing | M,D |
| Psychology—General | D |
| Public Health—General | M |
| Social Psychology | M,D |
| Statistics | M,D |
| Structural Biology | D |
| Student Affairs | M |
| Toxicology | D |
| Translation and Interpretation | M,O |

## UNIVERSITY OF ST. AUGUSTINE FOR HEALTH SCIENCES

| | |
|---|---|
| Athletic Training and Sports Medicine | M |
| Health Education | M,D |
| Health Informatics | M |
| Health Services Management and Hospital Administration | M |
| Nursing and Healthcare Administration | M |
| Nursing Education | M |
| Nursing Informatics | M |
| Nursing—General | M,D |
| Occupational Therapy | M,D |
| Physical Therapy | D |

## UNIVERSITY OF ST. FRANCIS (IL)

| | |
|---|---|
| Accounting | M,O |
| Art Education | M,D,O |
| Business Administration and Management—General | M,O |
| Business Analytics | M,O |
| Curriculum and Instruction | M,D,O |
| Education—General | M,D,O |
| Educational Leadership and Administration | M,D,O |
| Elementary Education | M,D,O |
| English as a Second Language | M,D,O |
| English Education | M,D,O |
| Family Nurse Practitioner Studies | M,D,O |
| Finance and Banking | M,O |
| Forensic Sciences | M,O |
| Health Services Management and Hospital Administration | M,O |
| Human Resources Management | M,O |
| Logistics | M,O |
| Mathematics Education | M,D,O |
| Nursing and Healthcare Administration | M,D,O |
| Nursing Education | M,D,O |
| Nursing—General | M,D,O |
| Physician Assistant Studies | M,O |
| Psychiatric Nursing | M,D,O |
| Reading Education | M,D,O |
| Science Education | M,D,O |
| Secondary Education | M,D,O |
| Social Sciences Education | M,D,O |
| Social Work | M,O |
| Special Education | M,D,O |
| Supply Chain Management | M,O |

## UNIVERSITY OF SAINT FRANCIS (IN)

| | |
|---|---|
| Art/Fine Arts | M |
| Business Administration and Management—General | M |
| Clinical Psychology | M,O |
| Counseling Psychology | M,O |
| Counselor Education | M,O |
| Education—General | M |
| Environmental and Occupational Health | M |
| Family Nurse Practitioner Studies | M,D,O |
| Health Services Management and Hospital Administration | M |
| Nurse Anesthesia | M,D,O |
| Nursing—General | M,D,O |
| Organizational Management | M |
| Physician Assistant Studies | M |
| Secondary Education | M |
| Special Education | M |
| Sustainability Management | M |

## UNIVERSITY OF SAINT JOSEPH

| | |
|---|---|
| Biochemistry | M |
| Biological and Biomedical Sciences—General | M |
| Business Administration and Management—General | M |
| Chemistry | M |
| Clinical Psychology | M |
| Counseling Psychology | M |
| Counselor Education | M |
| Curriculum and Instruction | M |
| Education—General | M |
| Educational Media/Instructional Technology | M |
| Elementary Education | M |
| English as a Second Language | M |
| Family Nurse Practitioner Studies | M,D |
| Marriage and Family Therapy | M |
| Nursing Education | M,D |
| Nursing—General | M,D |
| Nutrition | M |
| Pharmacy | D |
| Psychiatric Nursing | M,D |
| Public Health—General | M |
| Reading Education | M |
| Secondary Education | M |
| Social Work | M |
| Special Education | M,O |

## UNIVERSITY OF SAINT MARY

| | |
|---|---|
| Advertising and Public Relations | M |
| Business Administration and Management—General | M |
| Counseling Psychology | M |
| Education—General | M |
| Elementary Education | M |
| Finance and Banking | M |
| Health Services Management and Hospital Administration | M |
| Human Resources Management | M |
| Marketing | M |
| Nursing and Healthcare Administration | M |
| Nursing Education | M |
| Nursing—General | M |
| Physical Therapy | D |
| Psychology—General | M |
| Risk Management | M |
| Special Education | M |

## UNIVERSITY OF SAINT MARY OF THE LAKE–MUNDELEIN SEMINARY

| | |
|---|---|
| Pastoral Ministry and Counseling | M,D |
| Theology | M,D |

## UNIVERSITY OF ST. MICHAEL'S COLLEGE

| | |
|---|---|
| Jewish Studies | M,D,O |
| Pastoral Ministry and Counseling | M,D,O |
| Religious Education | M,D,O |
| Theology | M,D,O |

## UNIVERSITY OF ST. THOMAS (MN)

| | |
|---|---|
| Accounting | M |
| Art History | M,O |
| Business Administration and Management—General | M |
| Business Analytics | M |
| Counseling Psychology | M,D |
| Data Science/Data Analytics | M,O |
| Education—General | M,D,O |
| Educational Leadership and Administration | M,D,O |
| Electrical Engineering | M,O |
| Engineering and Applied Sciences—General | M,O |
| Engineering Management | M,O |
| English | M,O |
| Ethics | M,D |
| Health Communication | M |
| Health Services Management and Hospital Administration | M |
| Human Development | D |
| Information Science | M,O |
| Law | M,D |
| Management of Technology | M,O |
| Manufacturing Engineering | M,O |
| Mechanical Engineering | M,O |
| Museum Studies | M,O |
| Music Education | M,D |
| Music | M,D |
| Organizational Management | D |
| Pastoral Ministry and Counseling | M |
| Religion | M |
| Religious Education | M |
| Social Work | M |
| Software Engineering | M,O |
| Special Education | M,O |
| Student Affairs | M,D,O |
| Systems Engineering | M,O |
| Theology | M |

## UNIVERSITY OF ST. THOMAS (TX)

| | |
|---|---|
| Accounting | M |
| Business Administration and Management—General | M |
| Counselor Education | M,D |
| Curriculum and Instruction | M,D |
| Education—General | M,D |
| Educational Leadership and Administration | M,D |
| Educational Measurement and Evaluation | M,D |
| Elementary Education | M,D |
| English as a Second Language | M,D |
| Finance and Banking | M |
| International Business | M |
| Liberal Studies | M |
| Multilingual and Multicultural Education | M,D |
| Music | M |
| Pastoral Ministry and Counseling | M |
| Philosophy | M,D |
| Public Administration | M |
| Public Policy | M |
| Reading Education | M,D |
| Religion | M |
| Religious Education | M,D |
| Secondary Education | M,D |
| Special Education | M,D |
| Theology | M |

## UNIVERSITY OF SAN DIEGO

| | |
|---|---|
| Accounting | M |
| Adult Nursing | M,D |
| Business Administration and Management—General | M |
| Computer and Information Systems Security | M |
| Computer Engineering | M |
| Conflict Resolution and Mediation/Peace Studies | M |
| Counseling Psychology | M |
| Counselor Education | M |
| Criminal Justice and Criminology | M |
| Curriculum and Instruction | M |
| Education—General | M,D,O |
| Educational Leadership and Administration | M,D,O |
| English as a Second Language | M |
| Environmental Sciences | M |
| Family Nurse Practitioner Studies | M,D |
| Finance and Banking | M |
| Gerontological Nursing | M,D |
| Health Informatics | M,D |
| Higher Education | M,D,O |
| International Affairs | M |
| International Business | M |
| Law | M,D,O |
| Legal and Justice Studies | M,D,O |
| Marriage and Family Therapy | M |
| Mathematics | M |
| Nonprofit Management | M,D,O |
| Nursing and Healthcare Administration | M,D |
| Nursing—General | M,D |
| Oceanography | M |
| Pediatric Nursing | M,D |

*M—masters degree; D—doctorate; O—other advanced degree; *—Close-Up and/or Display*

| | |
|---|---|
| Psychiatric Nursing | M,D |
| Reading Education | M |
| Real Estate | M |
| School Psychology | M |
| Science Education | M |
| Special Education | M |
| Supply Chain Management | M,O |
| Taxation | M,D,O |
| Theater | M |

**UNIVERSITY OF SAN FRANCISCO**

| | |
|---|---|
| Asian Studies | M |
| Biological and Biomedical Sciences—General | M |
| Biotechnology | M |
| Business Administration and Management—General | M |
| Chemistry | M |
| Clinical Psychology | D |
| Communication—General | M |
| Computer Science | M |
| Counseling Psychology | M |
| Counselor Education | M |
| Curriculum and Instruction | M,D |
| Data Science/Data Analytics | M |
| Education—General | M,D |
| Educational Leadership and Administration | M,D |
| Educational Media/Instructional Technology | M,D |
| Energy Management and Policy | M |
| Entrepreneurship | M |
| Finance and Banking | M |
| Health Informatics | M |
| Health Services Management and Hospital Administration | M |
| Intellectual Property Law | M |
| International Affairs | M |
| International and Comparative Education | M,D |
| International Business | M |
| International Development | M |
| Law | D |
| Management Information Systems | M |
| Marketing | M |
| Marriage and Family Therapy | M |
| Multilingual and Multicultural Education | M,D |
| Museum Studies | M |
| Natural Resources | M |
| Nonprofit Management | M |
| Nursing—General | D |
| Organizational Management | M |
| Pacific Area/Pacific Rim Studies | M |
| Public Administration | M |
| Public Health—General | M |
| Reading Education | M,D |
| Religious Education | M,D |
| Special Education | M,D |
| Sports Management | M |
| Urban Education | M |
| Urban Studies | M |
| Writing | M |

**UNIVERSITY OF SASKATCHEWAN**

| | |
|---|---|
| Accounting | M |
| Agricultural Economics and Agribusiness | M,D,O |
| Agricultural Sciences—General | M,D,O |
| Agronomy and Soil Sciences | M,D |
| Allopathic Medicine | D |
| Anatomy | M,D |
| Animal Sciences | M,D |
| Anthropology | M |
| Archaeology | M |
| Art/Fine Arts | M |
| Biochemistry | M,D |
| Bioengineering | M,D |
| Biological and Biomedical Sciences—General | M,D |
| Biomedical Engineering | M,D,O |
| Business Administration and Management—General | M,D |
| Canadian Studies | M,D |
| Cell Biology | M,D |
| Chemical Engineering | M,D |
| Chemistry | M,D |
| Civil Engineering | M,D |
| Community Health | M,D |
| Computer Science | M,D |
| Counseling Psychology | M,D |
| Cultural Studies | M |
| Curriculum and Instruction | M,D,O |
| Dentistry | D |
| Economics | M,O |
| Education—General | M,D,O |
| Educational Leadership and Administration | M,D,O |
| Educational Measurement and Evaluation | M,D |
| Educational Psychology | M,D |
| Electrical Engineering | M,D,O |
| Engineering and Applied Sciences—General | M,D,O |
| Engineering Physics | M,D |
| English as a Second Language | M |
| English | M,D |
| Environmental Sciences | M,D |
| Epidemiology | M,D |
| Finance and Banking | M |
| Food Science and Technology | M,D |
| Foundations and Philosophy of Education | M,D,O |
| French | M |
| Geography | M,D |
| Geological Engineering | M,D |
| Geology | M,D,O |
| History | M,D |
| Immunology | M,D |
| Kinesiology and Movement Studies | M,D |
| Law | M,D |
| Linguistics | M |
| Marketing | M |
| Mathematics | M,D |
| Mechanical Engineering | M,D |
| Microbiology | M,D |
| Music | M |
| Nursing—General | M,D |
| Nutrition | M,D |
| Pathology | M,D |
| Pharmacology | M,D |
| Pharmacy | M,D |
| Philosophy | M,D |
| Physics | M,D |
| Physiology | M,D |
| Plant Sciences | M,D |
| Political Science | M |
| Psychology—General | M,D |
| Public Policy | M,D |
| Religion | M |
| Reproductive Biology | M,D |
| School Psychology | M,D |
| Sociology | M,D |
| Special Education | M,D |
| Statistics | M,D |
| Sustainability Management | M,D |
| Theater | M |
| Toxicology | M,D,O |
| Veterinary Medicine | M,D |
| Veterinary Sciences | M,D |

**THE UNIVERSITY OF SCRANTON**

| | |
|---|---|
| Accounting | M |
| Art/Fine Arts | M |
| Biochemistry | M |
| Business Administration and Management—General | M |
| Chemistry | M |
| Clinical Psychology | M |
| Counseling Psychology | M |
| Counselor Education | M |
| Curriculum and Instruction | M |
| Education—General | M |
| Educational Leadership and Administration | M |
| Family Nurse Practitioner Studies | M,D,O |
| Finance and Banking | M |
| Health Services Management and Hospital Administration | M |
| Human Resources Development | M |
| International Business | M |
| Management Information Systems | M |
| Marketing | M |
| Nurse Anesthesia | M,D,O |
| Nursing and Healthcare Administration | M,D,O |
| Nursing—General | M,D,O |
| Occupational Therapy | M |
| Physical Therapy | D |
| Reading Education | M |
| Rehabilitation Counseling | M |
| Secondary Education | M |
| Software Engineering | M |
| Special Education | M |
| Theology | M |

**UNIVERSITY OF SIOUX FALLS**

| | |
|---|---|
| Business Administration and Management—General | M |
| Education—General | M,O |
| Educational Leadership and Administration | M,O |
| Educational Media/Instructional Technology | M,O |
| Entrepreneurship | M |
| Health Services Management and Hospital Administration | M |
| Marketing | M |
| Reading Education | M,O |

**UNIVERSITY OF SOUTH AFRICA**

| | |
|---|---|
| Accounting | M,D |
| Acute Care/Critical Care Nursing | M,D |
| Adult Education | M,D |
| Agricultural Sciences—General | M,D |
| Anthropology | M,D |
| Archaeology | M,D |
| Art History | M,D |
| Business Administration and Management—General | M,D |
| Chemical Engineering | M,D |
| Classics | M,D |
| Clinical Psychology | M,D |
| Communication—General | M,D |
| Counseling Psychology | M,D |
| Counselor Education | M,D |
| Criminal Justice and Criminology | M,D |
| Curriculum and Instruction | M,D |
| Economics | M,D |
| Education—General | M,D |
| Educational Leadership and Administration | M,D |
| Educational Media/Instructional Technology | M,D |
| Educational Psychology | M,D |
| Engineering and Applied Sciences—General | M |
| English as a Second Language | M,D |
| English | M,D |
| Environmental Education | M,D |
| Environmental Management and Policy | M,D |
| Environmental Sciences | M,D |
| Ethics | M,D |
| Family and Consumer Sciences-General | M,D |
| Foundations and Philosophy of Education | M,D |
| French | M,D |
| Geography | M,D |
| German | M,D |
| Health Education | M,D |
| Health Services Management and Hospital Administration | M,D |
| History | M,D |
| Horticulture | M,D |
| Human Development | M,D |
| Human Resources Development | M,D |
| Industrial and Organizational Psychology | M,D |
| Information Science | M,D |
| International and Comparative Education | M,D |
| Italian | M,D |
| Law | M,D |
| Linguistics | M,D |
| Logistics | M,D |
| Management Information Systems | M |
| Marketing | M,D |
| Maternal and Child/Neonatal Nursing | M,D |
| Mathematics Education | M,D |
| Medical/Surgical Nursing | M,D |
| Missions and Missiology | M,D |
| Music | M,D |
| Natural Resources | M,D |
| Near and Middle Eastern Languages | M,D |
| Near and Middle Eastern Studies | M,D |
| Nurse Midwifery | M,D |
| Pastoral Ministry and Counseling | M,D |
| Philosophy | M,D |
| Political Science | M,D |
| Portuguese | M,D |
| Psychology—General | M,D |
| Public Administration | M,D |
| Public Health—General | M,D |
| Quantitative Analysis | M,D |
| Real Estate | M,D |
| Religion | M,D |
| Romance Languages | M,D |
| Russian | M,D |
| Science Education | M,D |
| Social Work | M,D |
| Sociology | M,D |
| Spanish | M,D |
| Statistics | M,D |
| Technology and Public Policy | M,D |
| Telecommunications Management | M,D |
| Theology | M,D |
| Travel and Tourism | M,D |
| Vocational and Technical Education | M,D |

**UNIVERSITY OF SOUTH ALABAMA**

| | |
|---|---|
| Accounting | M |
| Allied Health—General | M,D |
| Allopathic Medicine | D |
| Art Education | M,D |
| Art/Fine Arts | M |
| Biological and Biomedical Sciences—General | M,D |
| Business Administration and Management—General | M,D |
| Chemical Engineering | M |
| Chemistry | M |
| Civil Engineering | M |
| Clinical Psychology | M,D,O |
| Communication Disorders | M,D |
| Communication—General | M |
| Computer Engineering | M |
| Computer Science | M,D |
| Counseling Psychology | M,D,O |
| Counselor Education | M,D,O |
| Early Childhood Education | M,D |
| Education—General | M,D,O |
| Educational Leadership and Administration | M,D |
| Educational Media/Instructional Technology | M,D,O |
| Electrical Engineering | M |
| Elementary Education | M,D |
| Engineering and Applied Sciences—General | M,D |
| English | M |
| Environmental and Occupational Health | M |
| Environmental Engineering | M |
| Environmental Management and Policy | M,D |
| Exercise and Sports Science | M |
| Health Education | M |
| History | M |
| Kinesiology and Movement Studies | M |
| Management Information Systems | M,D |
| Marine Sciences | M,D |
| Marketing | M,D |
| Mathematics | M |
| Mechanical Engineering | M |
| Music Education | M |
| Music | M |
| Nursing and Healthcare Administration | M,D,O |
| Nursing Education | M,D,O |
| Nursing—General | M,D,O |
| Occupational Therapy | M |
| Physical Education | M |
| Physical Therapy | D |
| Physician Assistant Studies | M |
| Psychology—General | M |
| Public Administration | M |
| Reading Education | M,D |
| Science Education | M,D |
| Secondary Education | M,D |
| Sociology | M |
| Special Education | M,D |
| Sports Management | M |
| Systems Engineering | D |
| Toxicology | M |
| Writing | M |

**UNIVERSITY OF SOUTH CAROLINA**

| | |
|---|---|
| Accounting | M |
| Acute Care/Critical Care Nursing | M,O |
| Adult Nursing | M |
| Allopathic Medicine | D |
| Anthropology | M,D |
| Applied Statistics | M,D,O |
| Archives/Archival Administration | M,O |
| Art Education | M,D |
| Art History | M |
| Art/Fine Arts | M |
| Astronomy | M,D |
| Biochemistry | M,D |
| Biological and Biomedical Sciences—General | M,D,O |
| Biostatistics | M,D |
| Business Administration and Management—General | M,D |
| Business Education | M,D |
| Cell Biology | M,D |
| Chemical Engineering | M,D |
| Chemistry | M,D |
| Civil Engineering | M,D |
| Clinical Psychology | M,D |
| Communication Disorders | M,D |
| Community Health Nursing | M |
| Comparative Literature | M,D |
| Computer Engineering | M,D |
| Computer Science | M,D |
| Consumer Economics | M |
| Counselor Education | D,O |
| Criminal Justice and Criminology | M,D |
| Curriculum and Instruction | D |
| Developmental Biology | M,D |
| Early Childhood Education | M,D |
| Ecology | M,D |
| Economics | M,D |
| Education—General | M,D,O |
| Educational Leadership and Administration | M,D,O |
| Educational Measurement and Evaluation | M,D |
| Educational Media/Instructional Technology | M |
| Educational Psychology | M,D |
| Electrical Engineering | M,D |
| Elementary Education | M,D |
| Engineering and Applied Sciences—General | M,D |
| English as a Second Language | M,D,O |
| English Education | M,D |
| English | M,D |
| Entertainment Management | M |
| Environmental and Occupational Health | M,D |
| Environmental Management and Policy | M |
| Epidemiology | M,D |
| Evolutionary Biology | M,D |
| Exercise and Sports Science | M,D |
| Experimental Psychology | M,D |
| Family Nurse Practitioner Studies | M |
| Foreign Languages Education | M,D |
| Foundations and Philosophy of Education | D |
| French | M,D |
| Genetic Counseling | M |
| Geography | M,D |
| Geology | M,D |
| Geosciences | M,D |
| German | M,D |
| Gerontology | O |
| Hazardous Materials Management | M,D |
| Health Education | M,D,O |
| Health Promotion | M,D,O |
| Health Services Management and Hospital Administration | M,D |
| Higher Education | M |
| Historic Preservation | M,O |
| History | M,D,O |
| Hospitality Management | M |
| Human Resources Management | M |
| Industrial Hygiene | M,D |
| Information Studies | M,D,O |
| International Affairs | M,D |
| International Business | M |
| Journalism | M,D |
| Law | D |
| Library Science | M,D,O |
| Linguistics | M,D,O |
| Marine Sciences | M,D |
| Mathematics Education | M,D |
| Mathematics | M,D |
| Mechanical Engineering | M,D |
| Media Studies | M |
| Medical/Surgical Nursing | M |
| Molecular Biology | M,D |
| Museum Studies | M,O |
| Music Education | M,D,O |
| Music | M,D,O |
| Nuclear Engineering | M,D |
| Nurse Anesthesia | M |
| Nursing and Healthcare Administration | M |
| Nursing—General | M,O |
| Pediatric Nursing | M |
| Pharmaceutical Sciences | M,D |
| Pharmacy | D |
| Philosophy | M,D |
| Physical Education | M,D |
| Physics | M,D |
| Political Science | M,D |
| Psychiatric Nursing | M,O |
| Psychology—General | M,D |
| Public Administration | M |
| Public Health—General | M |
| Public History | M,O |
| Reading Education | M,D |
| Rehabilitation Counseling | M,O |
| Rehabilitation Sciences | M,O |
| Religion | M |
| School Psychology | D |
| Science Education | M,D |
| Secondary Education | M,D |
| Social Psychology | M,D |
| Social Sciences Education | M,D |
| Social Work | M,D |
| Sociology | M,D |
| Software Engineering | M,D |
| Spanish | M,D |
| Special Education | M,D |
| Speech and Interpersonal Communication | M,D |
| Sports Management | M |

Statistics M,D,O
Student Affairs M
Theater M,D
Travel and Tourism M
Women's Health Nursing M
Women's Studies O
Writing M,D

### UNIVERSITY OF SOUTH CAROLINA AIKEN
Applied Psychology M
Business Administration and Management—General M
Clinical Psychology M
Educational Media/Instructional Technology M

### UNIVERSITY OF SOUTH CAROLINA UPSTATE
Early Childhood Education M
Education—General M
Elementary Education M
Health Informatics M
Information Science M
Special Education M

### UNIVERSITY OF SOUTH DAKOTA
Accounting M
Addictions/Substance Abuse Counseling M
Adult Education M,D,O
Allied Health—General M,D,O
Allopathic Medicine D,O
American Indian/Native American Studies M,D,O
Art Education M
Art/Fine Arts M
Bioethics D,O
Biological and Biomedical Sciences—General M,D
Business Administration and Management—General M,O
Business Analytics M,O
Cardiovascular Sciences M,D
Cell Biology M,D
Chemistry M,D
Clinical Psychology M,D
Communication Disorders M,D
Communication—General M
Computer Science M
Counseling Psychology M,D,O
Counselor Education M,D,O
Criminal Justice and Criminology M
Curriculum and Instruction M,D,O
Early Childhood Education M,D,O
Education—General M,D,O
Educational Leadership and Administration M,D,O
Educational Media/Instructional Technology M
Educational Psychology M,D,O
Elementary Education M
English as a Second Language M
English M,D
Exercise and Sports Science M
Graphic Design M
Health Services Management and Hospital Administration M,O
Higher Education M,D,O
History M
Human Development M,D,O
Human Resources Management M
Immunology M,D
Interdisciplinary Studies M
Kinesiology and Movement Studies M
Law D
Marketing M,O
Mathematics Education M
Mathematics M
Microbiology M,D
Molecular Biology M,D
Music Education M
Music M
Neuroscience M,D
Occupational Therapy M,D
Organizational Management M
Pharmacology M,D
Photography M
Physical Therapy D
Physician Assistant Studies M
Physics M,D
Physiology M,D
Psychology—General M,D
Public Health—General M
Reading Education M
School Psychology M,D,O
Science Education M
Secondary Education M
Social Work M
Special Education M,D,O
Supply Chain Management M,O
Sustainable Development M,D
Theater M

### UNIVERSITY OF SOUTHERN CALIFORNIA
Accounting M
Advertising and Public Relations M
Aerospace/Aeronautical Engineering M,D,O
Allopathic Medicine D
American Studies D
Applied Mathematics M,D
Architecture M
Art History M,D,O
Art/Fine Arts M,D,O
Artificial Intelligence/Robotics M,D
Arts Administration M
Asian Languages M,D
Asian Studies M,D
Biochemistry M
Bioinformatics D
Biological and Biomedical Sciences—General M,D,O
Biomedical Engineering M,D
Biophysics M,D
Biostatistics M,D
Biotechnology M
Business Administration and Management—General M,D
Cancer Biology/Oncology D
Cell Biology M,D
Chemical Engineering M,D,O
Chemistry D
Child and Family Studies M,D
Civil Engineering M,D,O
Classics M,D
Clinical Psychology M,D
Clinical Research M,D,O
Cognitive Sciences M,D
Communication—General M,D
Comparative Literature D
Computational Biology D
Computer and Information Systems Security M,D
Computer Art and Design M
Computer Engineering M,D,O
Computer Science M,D
Construction Management M,D,O
Corporate and Organizational Communication M
Counselor Education M
Cultural Studies D
Dentistry D
Developmental Biology D
Developmental Psychology M,D
Economic Development M,D
Economics M,D
Education—General M,D
Educational Leadership and Administration D
Educational Policy D
Educational Psychology D
Electrical Engineering M,D,O
Engineering and Applied Sciences—General M,D,O
Engineering Management M,D,O
English as a Second Language M
English M,D
Entrepreneurship M
Environmental and Occupational Health M
Environmental Biology M,D
Environmental Engineering M,D,O
Epidemiology M,D
Evolutionary Biology D
Film, Television, and Video Production M
Film, Television, and Video Theory and Criticism M,D
Food Science and Technology M,D,O
Game Design and Development M,D
Genomic Sciences D
Geographic Information Systems M,O
Geography M,O
Geosciences M,D
Geotechnical Engineering M,D,O
Gerontology M,D,O
Hazardous Materials Management M,D,O
Health Communication M,D
Health Education M
Health Promotion M
Health Services Management and Hospital Administration M,O
Health Services Research D
Higher Education D
Historic Preservation M
History D
Homeland Security M,O
Immunology M
Industrial/Management Engineering M,D,O
International Affairs M,D
International Health M,O
Internet and Interactive Multimedia M,D,O
Journalism M
Kinesiology and Movement Studies M,D
Landscape Architecture M
Latin American Studies D
Law M,D
Linguistics M,D
Manufacturing Engineering M,D,O
Marine Biology M,D
Marine Sciences M,D
Marriage and Family Therapy M
Materials Engineering M,D,O
Materials Sciences M,D,O
Mathematical and Computational Finance M,D
Mathematics M,D
Mechanical Engineering M,D,O
Mechanics M,D,O
Media Studies M,D
Medical Imaging M,D
Medical Microbiology D
Microbiology M
Modeling and Simulation M,D
Molecular Biology D
Molecular Medicine M
Molecular Pharmacology M,D
Multilingual and Multicultural Education D
Music Education M,D,O
Music M,D,O
Neurobiology D
Neuroscience M,D
Nonprofit Management M,O
Nurse Anesthesia D
Occupational Therapy M,D
Oceanography M,D
Operations Research M,D,O
Oral and Dental Sciences M,D,O
Organizational Management M
Pathology M
Petroleum Engineering M,D,O
Pharmaceutical Administration M
Pharmaceutical Sciences M,D,O
Pharmacy D
Philosophy M,D
Photography M
Physical Chemistry D
Physical Therapy M,D
Physician Assistant Studies M
Physics M,D
Physiology M
Political Science M,D
Psychology—General M,D
Public Administration M,O
Public Health—General M
Public Policy M,D,O
Quantitative Analysis M,D
Real Estate M
Rhetoric D
Safety Engineering M,D,O
Slavic Languages M,D
Social Psychology M,D
Social Work M,D
Sociology D
Software Engineering M,D
Spanish D
Statistics M,D
Student Affairs M
Supply Chain Management M,D,O
Sustainable Development M,D,O
Systems Engineering M,D,O
Taxation M
Telecommunications M,D,O
Theater M
Toxicology M,D
Transportation and Highway Engineering M,D,O
Urban and Regional Planning M,D,O
Urban Education D
Water Resources M,D,O
Writing M,D

### UNIVERSITY OF SOUTHERN INDIANA
Accounting M
Business Administration and Management—General M
Communication—General M
Cultural Studies M
Data Science/Data Analytics M
Education—General M,D
Educational Leadership and Administration M,D
Elementary Education M
Engineering and Applied Sciences—General M,D
Engineering Management M
English as a Second Language M
English M
Family Nurse Practitioner Studies M,D,O
Gerontology M,D,O
Health Services Management and Hospital Administration M
Human Resources Management M
Industrial and Manufacturing Management M
Liberal Studies M
Mathematics Education M
Nonprofit Management M
Nursing and Healthcare Administration M,D,O
Nursing Education M,D,O
Nursing—General M,D,O
Occupational Therapy M
Psychiatric Nursing M,D,O
Public Administration M
Secondary Education M
Social Work M
Sports Management M

### UNIVERSITY OF SOUTHERN MAINE
Accounting M
Addictions/Substance Abuse Counseling M,O
Adult Education M,O
Adult Nursing M,D,O
Applied Behavior Analysis M,O
Biological and Biomedical Sciences—General M
Business Administration and Management—General M,O
Computer Science M,O
Counseling Psychology M,O
Counselor Education M,O
Cultural Studies M,O
Education of the Gifted M,O
Education—General M,D,O
Educational Leadership and Administration M,O
Educational Psychology M,O
English as a Second Language M,O
Family Nurse Practitioner Studies M,D,O
Finance and Banking M
Gerontological Nursing M,D,O
Health Services Management and Hospital Administration M
Higher Education M,O
Music Education M
Music M
Nursing and Healthcare Administration M,D,O
Nursing Education M,D,O
Nursing—General M,D,O
Occupational Therapy M
Psychiatric Nursing M,D,O
Public Health—General M,O
Public Policy M
Reading Education M,O
Rehabilitation Counseling M,O
School Psychology M,D
Social Work M
Software Engineering M,O
Special Education M,O
Statistics M,O
Sustainability Management M
Urban and Regional Planning M,O
Writing M

### UNIVERSITY OF SOUTHERN MISSISSIPPI
Accounting M
Advertising and Public Relations M,D
Biostatistics M
Child and Family Studies M
Communication Disorders M,D
Communication—General M,D
Computational Sciences M,D
Computer Science M,D
Counselor Education M
Criminal Justice and Criminology M,D
Economic Development M
Education—General M,D,O
Epidemiology M
Forensic Sciences M,D
Health Services Management and Hospital Administration M
Information Science M,O
Library Science M,O
Marriage and Family Therapy M
Mathematics Education M,D
Music Education M,D
Music M,D
Nursing—General M,D,O
Polymer Science and Engineering M,D
Psychology—General M,D
Public Health—General M
Science Education M,D
Social Work M
Sports Management M

### UNIVERSITY OF SOUTH FLORIDA
Accounting M,D
Acute Care/Critical Care Nursing M,D,O
Addictions/Substance Abuse Counseling M,D
Adult Education M,D,O
Adult Nursing M,D,O
African Studies O
Allopathic Medicine M,D
American Studies M
Anthropology M,D,O
Applied Behavior Analysis M,D
Applied Mathematics M,D
Archaeology M,D,O
Architecture M
Art History M
Art/Fine Arts M
Bioethics O
Bioinformatics M,D,O
Biological and Biomedical Sciences—General M,D
Biomedical Engineering M,D,O
Biostatistics O
Biotechnology O
Cancer Biology/Oncology M,D
Cardiovascular Sciences O
Cell Biology M,D
Chemical Engineering M,D,O
Chemistry M,D
Child and Family Studies M,D,O
Civil Engineering M,D,O
Clinical Psychology D
Clinical Research O
Cognitive Sciences D
Communication Disorders M,D,O
Communication—General M,D
Community Health O
Comparative Literature O
Computational Biology M,D
Computer and Information Systems Security M
Computer Engineering M,D
Computer Science M,D
Corporate and Organizational Communication O
Counseling Psychology M,D,O
Counselor Education M,D,O
Criminal Justice and Criminology M,D,O
Data Science/Data Analytics O
Distance Education Development O
Early Childhood Education M,D,O
Ecology M,D
Economics M,D
Education of Students with Severe/Multiple Disabilities O
Education—General M,D,O
Educational Leadership and Administration M,D,O
Educational Measurement and Evaluation O
Educational Media/Instructional Technology O
Educational Psychology M,D,O
Electrical Engineering M,D
Emergency Management O
Engineering and Applied Sciences—General M,D,O
Engineering Management M,D
English as a Second Language O
English M,D,O
Entrepreneurship M,O
Environmental and Occupational Health O
Environmental Biology M,D
Environmental Engineering M,D
Environmental Management and Policy O

*M—masters degree; D—doctorate; O—other advanced degree; *—Close-Up and/or Display*

| | |
|---|---|
| Epidemiology | O |
| Evolutionary Biology | M,D |
| Family Nurse Practitioner Studies | M,D,O |
| Film, Television, and Video Theory and Criticism | M |
| Finance and Banking | M,D |
| Foreign Languages Education | O |
| Forensic Sciences | M,D,O |
| Gender Studies | M,O |
| Geographic Information Systems | O |
| Geography | O |
| Geology | O |
| Geosciences | M,D |
| Geotechnical Engineering | M,D |
| Gerontological Nursing | M,D,O |
| Gerontology | M,D,O |
| Health Education | M,D |
| Health Informatics | O |
| Health Services Management and Hospital Administration | O |
| Higher Education | M,D,O |
| History | M,D |
| Holocaust and Genocide Studies | O |
| Human Resources Development | O |
| Humanities | M |
| Hydrogeology | O |
| Industrial and Organizational Psychology | D |
| Industrial/Management Engineering | M,D,O |
| Information Science | M |
| Information Studies | M,O |
| Interdisciplinary Studies | M,D |
| International Affairs | O |
| International Health | O |
| Internet and Interactive Multimedia | O |
| Journalism | O |
| Latin American Studies | O |
| Legal and Justice Studies | O |
| Liberal Studies | M,D |
| Library Science | M |
| Management Information Systems | M,D,O |
| Management of Technology | O |
| Management Strategy and Policy | O |
| Marine Sciences | M,D |
| Marketing | M,D |
| Marriage and Family Therapy | M,D,O |
| Mass Communication | M,O |
| Materials Engineering | M,D,O |
| Materials Sciences | O |
| Maternal and Child Health | O |
| Mathematics | M,D,O |
| Mechanical Engineering | M,D |
| Microbiology | M,D |
| Molecular Biology | M,D |
| Museum Studies | O |
| Music | M,D |
| Nanotechnology | M,D |
| Neuroscience | D,O |
| Nonprofit Management | O |
| Nurse Anesthesia | M,D,O |
| Nursing Education | M,D,O |
| Nursing—General | M,D,O |
| Nutrition | O |
| Occupational Health Nursing | M,D,O |
| Oceanography | M,D |
| Oncology Nursing | M,D,O |
| Pediatric Nursing | M,D,O |
| Pharmaceutical Sciences | M,D |
| Pharmacy | M,D,O |
| Philosophy | M,D |
| Physical Therapy | D |
| Physics | M,D |
| Physiology | M,D |
| Political Science | O |
| Psychology—General | D |
| Public Administration | O |
| Public Affairs | O |
| Public Health—General | M,D,O |
| Reading Education | M,D,O |
| Real Estate | M,D |
| Rehabilitation Counseling | M,D,O |
| Rehabilitation Sciences | D |
| Religion | M,D |
| Secondary Education | O |
| Social Sciences Education | M,D,O |
| Social Work | M,D,O |
| Sociology | M,D |
| Special Education | O |
| Sports Management | M,D |
| Statistics | M,D |
| Structural Engineering | M,D |
| Sustainability Management | M,O |
| Sustainable Development | M,O |
| Systems Engineering | O |
| Taxation | M,D |
| Technical Communication | O |
| Toxicology | O |
| Transportation and Highway Engineering | M,D,O |
| Travel and Tourism | M,O |
| Urban and Regional Planning | O |
| Vocational and Technical Education | M,D,O |
| Water Resources Engineering | M,D,O |
| Women's Studies | M |
| Writing | O |

### UNIVERSITY OF SOUTH FLORIDA, ST. PETERSBURG

| | |
|---|---|
| Business Administration and Management—General | M |
| Computer Art and Design | M |
| Education—General | M |
| Educational Leadership and Administration | M |
| Elementary Education | M |
| English Education | M |
| Environmental Management and Policy | M |
| Environmental Sciences | M |
| Journalism | M |
| Liberal Studies | M |
| Mathematics Education | M |
| Media Studies | M |
| Middle School Education | M |
| Psychology—General | M |
| Reading Education | M |
| Science Education | M |

### UNIVERSITY OF SOUTH FLORIDA SARASOTA-MANATEE

| | |
|---|---|
| Business Administration and Management—General | M |
| Criminal Justice and Criminology | M |
| Curriculum and Instruction | M |
| Educational Leadership and Administration | M |
| Elementary Education | M |
| English Education | M |
| Hospitality Management | M |
| Liberal Studies | M |
| Social Sciences | M |
| Social Work | M |

### THE UNIVERSITY OF TAMPA

| | |
|---|---|
| Accounting | M,O |
| Adult Nursing | M |
| Business Administration and Management—General | M,O |
| Business Analytics | M,O |
| Computer and Information Systems Security | M,O |
| Criminal Justice and Criminology | M |
| Curriculum and Instruction | M |
| Education—General | M |
| Educational Leadership and Administration | M |
| Educational Media/Instructional Technology | M |
| Entrepreneurship | M,O |
| Exercise and Sports Science | M |
| Family Nurse Practitioner Studies | M |
| Finance and Banking | M,O |
| International Business | M,O |
| Management Information Systems | M,O |
| Marketing | M,O |
| Nonprofit Management | M,O |
| Nursing—General | M |
| Nutrition | M |
| Writing | M |

### THE UNIVERSITY OF TENNESSEE

| | |
|---|---|
| Accounting | M,D |
| Adult Education | M,D |
| Advertising and Public Relations | M,D |
| Aerospace/Aeronautical Engineering | M,D |
| Agricultural Education | M |
| Agricultural Engineering | M |
| Agricultural Sciences—General | M,D |
| Analytical Chemistry | M,D |
| Anatomy | M,D |
| Animal Behavior | M,D |
| Animal Sciences | M,D |
| Anthropology | M,D |
| Applied Mathematics | M,D |
| Applied Psychology | M,D |
| Archaeology | M,D |
| Architecture | M |
| Art Education | M,D,O |
| Art/Fine Arts | M |
| Athletic Training and Sports Medicine | M,D |
| Aviation | M |
| Biochemistry | M,D |
| Bioethics | M,D |
| Biological and Biomedical Sciences—General | M,D |
| Biological Anthropology | M,D |
| Biomedical Engineering | M,D |
| Biosystems Engineering | M,D |
| Business Administration and Management—General | M,D |
| Chemical Engineering | M,D |
| Chemical Physics | M,D |
| Chemistry | M,D |
| Child and Family Studies | M,D |
| Civil Engineering | M,D |
| Clinical Psychology | M,D |
| Clothing and Textiles | M,D |
| Communication Disorders | M,D,O |
| Communication—General | M,D |
| Community Health | M,D |
| Computer Engineering | M,D |
| Computer Science | M,D |
| Consumer Economics | M,D |
| Counseling Psychology | M,D |
| Counselor Education | M,D,O |
| Criminal Justice and Criminology | M,D |
| Cultural Anthropology | M,D |
| Curriculum and Instruction | M,D,O |
| Data Science/Data Analytics | D |
| Early Childhood Education | M,D,O |
| Ecology | M,D |
| Economics | M,D |
| Education—General | M,D,O |
| Educational Leadership and Administration | M,D,O |
| Educational Measurement and Evaluation | M,D,O |
| Educational Media/Instructional Technology | M,D,O |
| Educational Psychology | M,D,O |
| Electrical Engineering | M,D |
| Elementary Education | M,D,O |
| Energy and Power Engineering | D |
| Engineering and Applied Sciences—General | M,D |
| Engineering Management | M,D |
| English as a Second Language | M,D,O |
| English Education | M,D,O |
| English | M,D |
| Entomology | M,D |
| Environmental Engineering | M |
| Environmental Management and Policy | M,D |
| Evolutionary Biology | M,D |
| Exercise and Sports Science | M,D,O |
| Experimental Psychology | M,D |
| Family and Consumer Sciences-General | D |
| Finance and Banking | M,D |
| Fish, Game, and Wildlife Management | M |
| Food Science and Technology | M,D |
| Foreign Languages Education | M,D,O |
| Forestry | M |
| Foundations and Philosophy of Education | M,D,O |
| French | M,D |
| Genetics | M,D |
| Genomic Sciences | M,D |
| Geography | M,D |
| Geology | M,D |
| German | M,D |
| Gerontology | M |
| Graphic Design | M |
| Health Education | M |
| Health Promotion | M |
| Health Services Management and Hospital Administration | M |
| History | M,D |
| Hospitality Management | M |
| Human Resources Development | M |
| Industrial and Manufacturing Management | M,D |
| Industrial and Organizational Psychology | D |
| Industrial/Management Engineering | M,D |
| Information Science | M,D |
| Inorganic Chemistry | M,D |
| Internet and Interactive Multimedia | M,D |
| Italian | D |
| Journalism | M,D |
| Kinesiology and Movement Studies | M,D |
| Landscape Architecture | M |
| Law | D |
| Leisure Studies | M,D |
| Linguistics | D |
| Logistics | M,D |
| Marketing | M,D |
| Materials Engineering | M,D |
| Materials Sciences | M,D |
| Mathematics Education | M,D,O |
| Mathematics | M,D |
| Mechanical Engineering | M,D |
| Microbiology | M,D |
| Multilingual and Multicultural Education | M,D,O |
| Music Education | M |
| Music | M |
| Nuclear Engineering | M,D |
| Nursing—General | M,D |
| Nutrition | M |
| Organic Chemistry | M,D |
| Philosophy | M,D |
| Photography | M |
| Physical Chemistry | M,D |
| Physics | M,D |
| Physiology | M,D |
| Plant Pathology | M,D |
| Plant Physiology | M,D |
| Plant Sciences | M |
| Political Science | M,D |
| Portuguese | D |
| Psychology—General | M,D |
| Public Administration | M |
| Public Health—General | M |
| Reading Education | M,D,O |
| Recreation and Park Management | M,D |
| Rehabilitation Counseling | M,D |
| Reliability Engineering | M,D |
| Religion | M,D |
| Russian | D |
| School Psychology | M,D,O |
| Science Education | M,D,O |
| Secondary Education | M,D,O |
| Social Sciences Education | M,D,O |
| Social Work | M,D |
| Sociology | M,D |
| Spanish | M,D |
| Special Education | M,D,O |
| Sports Management | M,D |
| Statistics | M,D |
| Student Affairs | M |
| Theater | M |
| Theoretical Chemistry | M,D |
| Transportation Management | M,D |
| Travel and Tourism | M |
| Veterinary Medicine | D |

### THE UNIVERSITY OF TENNESSEE AT CHATTANOOGA

| | |
|---|---|
| Accounting | M |
| Applied Mathematics | M |
| Applied Statistics | M |
| Athletic Training and Sports Medicine | M |
| Automotive Engineering | M |
| Bioinformatics | M,O |
| Business Administration and Management—General | M |
| Chemical Engineering | M |
| Civil Engineering | M |
| Computational Sciences | D |
| Computer Science | M,O |
| Construction Management | M,O |
| Counselor Education | M,D,O |
| Criminal Justice and Criminology | M |
| Education—General | M,D,O |
| Educational Leadership and Administration | M,D,O |
| Electrical Engineering | M |
| Elementary Education | M,D,O |
| Energy and Power Engineering | M,O |
| Engineering Management | M,O |
| English | M |
| Environmental Sciences | M |
| Ethics | M,O |
| Experimental Psychology | M |
| Family Nurse Practitioner Studies | M,D,O |
| Gerontological Nursing | M,D,O |
| Industrial and Organizational Psychology | M |
| Logistics | M,O |
| Mathematics Education | M |
| Mathematics | M |
| Mechanical Engineering | M |
| Nonprofit Management | M,O |
| Nurse Anesthesia | M,D,O |
| Nursing Education | M,D,O |
| Nursing—General | M,D,O |
| Occupational Therapy | D |
| Physical Education | M |
| Physical Therapy | D |
| Project Management | M,O |
| Psychology—General | M |
| Public Administration | M,O |
| Quality Management | M,O |
| Rhetoric | M |
| School Psychology | M,D,O |
| Secondary Education | M,D,O |
| Social Psychology | M,D,O |
| Social Work | M |
| Special Education | M,D,O |
| Supply Chain Management | M,O |
| Writing | M |

### THE UNIVERSITY OF TENNESSEE AT MARTIN

| | |
|---|---|
| Addictions/Substance Abuse Counseling | M |
| Agricultural Economics and Agribusiness | M |
| Agricultural Sciences—General | M |
| Business Administration and Management—General | M |
| Child and Family Studies | M |
| Child Development | M |
| Communication—General | M |
| Counselor Education | M |
| Curriculum and Instruction | M |
| Education—General | M |
| Educational Leadership and Administration | M |
| Elementary Education | M |
| Family and Consumer Sciences-General | M |
| Finance and Banking | M |
| Food Science and Technology | M |
| Interdisciplinary Studies | M |
| Nutrition | M |
| Physical Education | M |
| Secondary Education | M |
| Social Psychology | M |
| Special Education | M |
| Student Affairs | M |

### THE UNIVERSITY OF TENNESSEE HEALTH SCIENCE CENTER

| | |
|---|---|
| Allied Health—General | M,D |
| Allopathic Medicine | D |
| Biological and Biomedical Sciences—General | M,D |
| Biomedical Engineering | M,D |
| Clinical Laboratory Sciences/Medical Technology | M,D |
| Communication Disorders | M,D |
| Dentistry | D |
| Epidemiology | M,D |
| Family Nurse Practitioner Studies | D,O |
| Gerontological Nursing | D,O |
| Health Informatics | M,D |
| Health Services Research | M,D |
| Nursing—General | M,D,O |
| Occupational Therapy | M,D |
| Oral and Dental Sciences | M,D |
| Pathology | M,D |
| Pediatric Nursing | D,O |
| Pharmaceutical Sciences | M,D |
| Pharmacology | M,D |
| Pharmacy | M,D |
| Physical Therapy | M,D |
| Physician Assistant Studies | M,D |
| Psychiatric Nursing | D,O |

### THE UNIVERSITY OF TENNESSEE–OAK RIDGE NATIONAL LABORATORY

| | |
|---|---|
| Biological and Biomedical Sciences—General | M,D |
| Genomic Sciences | M,D |

### THE UNIVERSITY OF TEXAS AT ARLINGTON

| | |
|---|---|
| Accounting | M,D |
| Aerospace/Aeronautical Engineering | M,D |
| Anthropology | M |
| Applied Mathematics | M,D |
| Architecture | M |
| Art/Fine Arts | M |
| Athletic Training and Sports Medicine | M,D |
| Bioengineering | M,D |
| Biological and Biomedical Sciences—General | M,D |
| Chemistry | M,D |
| Civil Engineering | M,D |
| Communication—General | M |
| Computer Engineering | M,D |
| Computer Science | M,D |
| Construction Management | M,D |
| Criminal Justice and Criminology | M |
| Curriculum and Instruction | M |
| Economics | M |
| Education—General | M,D |
| Educational Leadership and Administration | M,D |
| Educational Policy | M,D |

| | |
|---|---|
| Electrical Engineering | M,D |
| Engineering and Applied Sciences—General | M,D |
| Engineering Management | M |
| English as a Second Language | M |
| English | M,D |
| Environmental Sciences | M,D |
| Exercise and Sports Science | M,D |
| Experimental Psychology | M,D |
| Family Nurse Practitioner Studies | M,D |
| Film, Television, and Video Production | M |
| Finance and Banking | M,D |
| French | M |
| Geology | M,D |
| Health Psychology | M,D |
| Health Services Management and Hospital Administration | M |
| Higher Education | M,D |
| History | M,D |
| Human Resources Management | M |
| Industrial and Organizational Psychology | M,D |
| Industrial/Management Engineering | M,D |
| Kinesiology and Movement Studies | M,D |
| Landscape Architecture | M |
| Linguistics | M,D |
| Logistics | M |
| Management Information Systems | M,D |
| Marketing Research | M |
| Marketing | M |
| Materials Engineering | M,D |
| Materials Sciences | M,D |
| Mathematics Education | M,D |
| Mathematics | M,D |
| Mechanical Engineering | M,D |
| Music Education | M |
| Music | M |
| Nursing and Healthcare Administration | M,D |
| Nursing Education | M,D |
| Nursing—General | M,D |
| Physics | M,D |
| Political Science | M |
| Psychology—General | M,D |
| Public Administration | M |
| Public Policy | M,D |
| Quantitative Analysis | M,D |
| Reading Education | M |
| Real Estate | M,D |
| Science Education | M |
| Social Work | M,D |
| Sociology | M |
| Software Engineering | M,D |
| Spanish | M |
| Systems Engineering | M |
| Taxation | M,D |
| Urban and Regional Planning | D |

### THE UNIVERSITY OF TEXAS AT AUSTIN

| | |
|---|---|
| Accounting | M,D |
| Actuarial Science | M,D |
| Adult Nursing | M,D |
| Advertising and Public Relations | M,D |
| Aerospace/Aeronautical Engineering | M,D |
| African Studies | M,D |
| Allopathic Medicine | D |
| American Studies | M,D |
| Analytical Chemistry | D |
| Animal Behavior | D |
| Anthropology | M,D |
| Applied Arts and Design—General | M |
| Applied Mathematics | M,D |
| Applied Physics | M,D |
| Archaeology | M,D |
| Architectural Engineering | M |
| Architectural History | M,D |
| Architecture | M |
| Art Education | M |
| Art History | M,D |
| Art/Fine Arts | M |
| Asian Languages | M,D |
| Asian Studies | M,D |
| Astronomy | M,D |
| Biochemistry | D |
| Biological and Biomedical Sciences—General | M,D |
| Biomedical Engineering | M,D |
| Biopsychology | D |
| Business Administration and Management—General | M,D |
| Cell Biology | D |
| Chemical Engineering | M,D |
| Chemistry | D |
| Child and Family Studies | M,D |
| Child Development | M,D |
| Civil Engineering | M,D |
| Classics | M,D |
| Clinical Laboratory Sciences/Medical Technology | M,D |
| Clinical Psychology | D |
| Communication Disorders | M,D |
| Communication—General | M,D |
| Community Health Nursing | M,D |
| Comparative Literature | M,D |
| Computational Sciences | M,D |
| Computer and Information Systems Security | M,D |
| Computer Engineering | M,D |
| Computer Science | M,D |
| Counseling Psychology | M,D |
| Counselor Education | M,D |
| Cultural Studies | M,D |
| Curriculum and Instruction | M,D |
| Dance | M,D |
| Developmental Psychology | D |
| Early Childhood Education | M,D |
| East European and Russian Studies | M |
| Ecology | D |
| Economics | M,D |
| Education—General | M,D |
| Educational Leadership and Administration | M,D |
| Educational Media/Instructional Technology | M,D |
| Educational Psychology | M,D |
| Electrical Engineering | M,D |
| Engineering and Applied Sciences—General | M,D |
| English | M,D |
| Entrepreneurship | M |
| Environmental Engineering | M,D |
| Environmental Management and Policy | M |
| Evolutionary Biology | D |
| Exercise and Sports Science | M,D |
| Family and Consumer Sciences-General | M,D |
| Family Nurse Practitioner Studies | M,D |
| Film, Television, and Video Production | M,D |
| Finance and Banking | M,D |
| Folklore | M,D |
| French | M,D |
| Geography | M,D |
| Geology | M,D |
| Geosciences | M,D |
| Geotechnical Engineering | M,D |
| German | M,D |
| Gerontological Nursing | M,D |
| Health Education | M,D |
| Hispanic and Latin American Languages | M,D |
| Hispanic Studies | M |
| Historic Preservation | M |
| History | M,D |
| Human Development | M,D |
| Industrial and Manufacturing Management | M,D |
| Industrial/Management Engineering | M,D |
| Information Studies | M,D |
| Inorganic Chemistry | D |
| Interior Design | M |
| Italian | M,D |
| Journalism | M,D |
| Kinesiology and Movement Studies | M,D |
| Landscape Architecture | M |
| Latin American Studies | M |
| Law | M,D |
| Linguistics | M,D |
| Management Information Systems | M,D |
| Marine Sciences | M,D |
| Marketing | M,D |
| Materials Engineering | M,D |
| Materials Sciences | M,D |
| Maternal and Child/Neonatal Nursing | M,D |
| Mathematics | M,D |
| Mechanical Engineering | M,D |
| Mechanics | M,D |
| Media Studies | M,D |
| Medicinal and Pharmaceutical Chemistry | M,D |
| Microbiology | D |
| Mineral Economics | M |
| Mineral/Mining Engineering | M |
| Molecular Biology | D |
| Multilingual and Multicultural Education | M,D |
| Music Education | M,D |
| Music | M,D |
| Natural Resources | M |
| Near and Middle Eastern Languages | M,D |
| Near and Middle Eastern Studies | M,D |
| Neurobiology | D |
| Neuroscience | D |
| Nursing and Healthcare Administration | M,D |
| Nursing Education | M,D |
| Nursing—General | M,D |
| Nutrition | M,D |
| Operations Research | M,D |
| Organic Chemistry | D |
| Organizational Behavior | M |
| Pediatric Nursing | M,D |
| Petroleum Engineering | M,D |
| Pharmaceutical Sciences | M,D |
| Pharmacology | M,D |
| Pharmacy | D |
| Philosophy | D |
| Physical Chemistry | D |
| Physical Education | M,D |
| Physics | M,D |
| Plant Biology | M,D |
| Political Science | M,D |
| Portuguese | M,D |
| Psychiatric Nursing | M,D |
| Psychology—General | D |
| Public Administration | M,D |
| Public Affairs | M,D |
| Public History | M,D |
| Public Policy | M,D |
| Quantitative Analysis | M,D |
| Reading Education | M,D |
| Rehabilitation Counseling | M,D |
| Risk Management | M,D |
| Romance Languages | M,D |
| School Psychology | M,D |
| Slavic Languages | M,D |
| Social Work | M,D |
| Sociology | M,D |
| Spanish | M,D |
| Special Education | M,D |
| Sport Psychology | M,D |
| Statistics | M,D |
| Supply Chain Management | M,D |
| Sustainable Development | M |
| Technology and Public Policy | M |
| Textile Sciences and Engineering | M |
| Theater | M,D |
| Toxicology | M,D |
| Urban and Regional Planning | M,D |
| Urban Design | M |
| Water Resources Engineering | M,D |
| Writing | M,D |

### THE UNIVERSITY OF TEXAS AT DALLAS

| | |
|---|---|
| Accounting | M |
| Actuarial Science | M,D |
| Applied Mathematics | M,D |
| Art History | M,D |
| Biochemistry | M,D |
| Biological and Biomedical Sciences—General | M,D |
| Biomedical Engineering | M,D |
| Biotechnology | M,D |
| Business Administration and Management—General | M,D |
| Cell Biology | M,D |
| Chemistry | M,D |
| Child and Family Studies | M,D |
| Cognitive Sciences | M,D |
| Communication Disorders | M,D |
| Communication—General | M,D |
| Comparative Literature | M,D |
| Computer Engineering | M,D |
| Computer Science | M,D |
| Criminal Justice and Criminology | M,D |
| Data Science/Data Analytics | M,D |
| Economics | M,D |
| Electrical Engineering | M,D |
| Engineering and Applied Sciences—General | M,D |
| Entrepreneurship | M,D |
| Finance and Banking | M |
| Geographic Information Systems | M,D |
| Geography | M,D |
| Geosciences | M,D |
| Health Services Management and Hospital Administration | M,D |
| History | M,D |
| Humanities | M,D |
| Industrial and Manufacturing Management | M,D |
| Interdisciplinary Studies | M |
| International Business | M,D |
| Internet and Interactive Multimedia | M,D |
| Latin American Studies | M,D |
| Law | M,D |
| Management Information Systems | M |
| Management of Technology | M |
| Management Strategy and Policy | M |
| Marketing | M |
| Materials Engineering | M,D |
| Materials Sciences | M,D |
| Mathematics Education | M |
| Mathematics | M,D |
| Mechanical Engineering | M,D |
| Mineralogy | M,D |
| Molecular Biology | M,D |
| Neuroscience | M,D |
| Nonprofit Management | M,D |
| Physics | M,D |
| Political Science | M,D |
| Project Management | M,D |
| Psychology—General | M,D |
| Public Administration | M,D |
| Public Policy | M,D |
| Real Estate | M |
| Science Education | M |
| Software Engineering | M,D |
| Statistics | M,D |
| Supply Chain Management | M |
| Systems Engineering | M,D |
| Telecommunications | M,D |

### THE UNIVERSITY OF TEXAS AT EL PASO

| | |
|---|---|
| Accounting | M |
| Allied Health—General | D |
| Anthropology | M,O |
| Applied Psychology | M,O |
| Art Education | M |
| Art/Fine Arts | M |
| Biochemistry | M,D |
| Bioinformatics | M,D |
| Biological and Biomedical Sciences—General | M,D |
| Business Administration and Management—General | M,D,O |
| Chemistry | M,D |
| Civil Engineering | M,D,O |
| Clinical Psychology | M,D |
| Communication Disorders | M |
| Communication—General | M |
| Computer and Information Systems Security | M,D,O |
| Computer Engineering | M,D,O |
| Computer Science | M,D,O |
| Construction Management | M,D,O |
| Counselor Education | M |
| Curriculum and Instruction | M,D |
| Economics | M |
| Education—General | M,D |
| Educational Leadership and Administration | M,D |
| Educational Measurement and Evaluation | M |
| Educational Psychology | M |
| Electrical Engineering | M,D,O |
| Energy and Power Engineering | M,D,O |
| Engineering and Applied Sciences—General | M,D,O |
| English as a Second Language | M,O |
| English Education | M,D,O |
| English | M,D,O |
| Environmental Engineering | M,D,O |
| Environmental Sciences | M,D |
| Experimental Psychology | M,D |
| Family Nurse Practitioner Studies | M,D,O |
| Geology | M,D |
| Geophysics | M,D |
| Health Services Management and Hospital Administration | M,D,O |
| History | M,D |
| Industrial/Management Engineering | M |
| Information Science | M,D,O |
| Interdisciplinary Studies | M |
| International Business | M,D,O |
| Kinesiology and Movement Studies | M |
| Liberal Studies | M |
| Linguistics | M,O |
| Manufacturing Engineering | M |
| Materials Engineering | M,D |
| Materials Sciences | M,D |
| Mathematics | M |
| Mechanical Engineering | M,D |
| Metallurgical Engineering and Metallurgy | M,D |
| Multilingual and Multicultural Education | M,D,O |
| Music Education | M |
| Music | M |
| Nursing and Healthcare Administration | M,D,O |
| Nursing Education | M,D,O |
| Nursing—General | M,D,O |
| Occupational Therapy | M |
| Philosophy | M |
| Physical Therapy | D |
| Physics | M |
| Political Science | M |
| Psychology—General | M,D |
| Public Health—General | M,O |
| Reading Education | M,D |
| Rehabilitation Counseling | M |
| Rhetoric | M,D,O |
| Social Work | M |
| Sociology | M,O |
| Software Engineering | M,D,O |
| Spanish | M,O |
| Special Education | M |
| Statistics | M |
| Systems Engineering | M |
| Writing | M,D,O |

### THE UNIVERSITY OF TEXAS AT SAN ANTONIO

| | |
|---|---|
| Accounting | M,D |
| Anthropology | M,D |
| Applied Behavior Analysis | M,O |
| Applied Mathematics | M |
| Applied Statistics | M,D |
| Architecture | M |
| Art History | M |
| Art/Fine Arts | M |
| Biological and Biomedical Sciences—General | M,D |
| Biomedical Engineering | M,D |
| Biotechnology | M,D |
| Business Administration and Management—General | M,D,O |
| Cell Biology | M,D |
| Chemistry | M,D |
| Civil Engineering | M,D |
| Communication—General | M |
| Computer and Information Systems Security | M,D,O |
| Computer Engineering | M,D |
| Computer Science | M,D |
| Counselor Education | M,D |
| Criminal Justice and Criminology | M |
| Cultural Studies | M,D |
| Curriculum and Instruction | M,D |
| Demography and Population Studies | D |
| Early Childhood Education | M,D |
| Ecology | M |
| Economics | M |
| Educational Leadership and Administration | M,D |
| Educational Measurement and Evaluation | M,O |
| Educational Media/Instructional Technology | M,D |
| Educational Psychology | M,O |
| Electrical Engineering | M,D |
| Engineering and Applied Sciences—General | M,D |
| English as a Second Language | M,D,O |
| English | M,D |
| Environmental Engineering | M,D |
| Environmental Sciences | M,D |
| Finance and Banking | M,D |
| Geology | M |
| Health Education | M |
| Higher Education | M,D |
| History | M |
| Information Science | M,D,O |
| Interdisciplinary Studies | M,D |
| Kinesiology and Movement Studies | M |
| Management of Technology | M,D,O |
| Manufacturing Engineering | M,D |
| Marketing | M,D |
| Materials Engineering | M,D |
| Mathematics Education | M |
| Mathematics | M |
| Mechanical Engineering | M,D |
| Molecular Biology | M,D |
| Multilingual and Multicultural Education | M,D |
| Music | M |
| Neurobiology | M,D |
| Organizational Management | D |
| Philosophy | M |
| Physics | M,D |
| Political Science | M |

*M—masters degree; D—doctorate; O—other advanced degree; *—Close-Up and/or Display*

Psychology—General M,D
Public Administration M
Reading Education M,D
School Psychology M,O
Social Work M
Sociology M
Spanish M
Special Education M,D
Statistics M,D
Translational Biology D
Urban and Regional Planning M

### THE UNIVERSITY OF TEXAS AT TYLER
Accounting M
Art History M
Art/Fine Arts M
Biological and Biomedical Sciences—General M
Business Administration and Management—General M
Civil Engineering M
Clinical Psychology M
Communication—General M
Computer and Information Systems Security M
Computer Science M
Counseling Psychology M
Criminal Justice and Criminology M
Early Childhood Education M
Electrical Engineering M
Energy Management and Policy M
Engineering Management M
English M
Environmental and Occupational Health M
Environmental Engineering M
Family Nurse Practitioner Studies M,D
Health Education M
Health Services Management and Hospital Administration M
History M
Human Resources Development M,D
Industrial and Manufacturing Management M
Interdisciplinary Studies M
Kinesiology and Movement Studies M
Marketing M
Marriage and Family Therapy M
Mathematics M
Mechanical Engineering M
Nursing and Healthcare Administration M,D
Nursing Education M,D
Nursing—General M,D
Organizational Management M
Pharmacy D
Psychology—General M
Public Administration M
Quality Management M
Reading Education M
School Psychology M
Social Sciences M
Sociology M
Special Education M
Structural Engineering M
Transportation and Highway Engineering M
Water Resources Engineering M

### THE UNIVERSITY OF TEXAS HEALTH SCIENCE CENTER AT HOUSTON
Allopathic Medicine D
Biochemistry M,D
Bioinformatics M,D,O
Biological and Biomedical Sciences—General M,D
Biostatistics M,D,O
Cancer Biology/Oncology M,D
Cell Biology M,D
Community Health M,D,O
Data Science/Data Analytics M,D,O
Dentistry M,D
Environmental and Occupational Health M,D,O
Epidemiology M,D,O
Genetic Counseling M,D
Genetics M,D
Genomic Sciences M,D,O
Health Informatics M,D,O
Health Promotion M,D,O
Health Services Management and Hospital Administration M,D,O
Immunology M,D
Infectious Diseases M,D
Maternal and Child Health M,D,O
Medical Physics M,D
Microbiology M,D
Neuroscience M,D
Nursing—General M,D
Pharmacology M,D
Public Health—General M,D,O
Quantitative Analysis M,D

### THE UNIVERSITY OF TEXAS HEALTH SCIENCE CENTER AT SAN ANTONIO
Acute Care/Critical Care Nursing M,D,O
Allopathic Medicine M,D
Biochemistry M,D
Biological and Biomedical Sciences—General D
Biomedical Engineering M,D
Cell Biology M,D
Clinical Laboratory Sciences/Medical Technology D
Clinical Research M
Communication Disorders M,D
Community Health Nursing M,D,O
Dentistry M,D,O
Family Nurse Practitioner Studies M,D,O
Gerontological Nursing M,D,O
Immunology M,D
Interdisciplinary Studies D
Medical Physics D
Microbiology M,D
Molecular Medicine M,D
Neuroscience D
Nursing and Healthcare Administration M,D,O
Nursing Education M,D,O
Nursing—General M,D,O
Occupational Therapy M,D
Pediatric Nursing M,D,O
Pharmacology D
Physical Therapy M,D
Physician Assistant Studies M,D
Psychiatric Nursing M,D,O
Special Education M,D
Structural Biology M,D
Toxicology M

### THE UNIVERSITY OF TEXAS HEALTH SCIENCE CENTER AT TYLER
Biotechnology M
Health Services Management and Hospital Administration M
Public Health—General M

### THE UNIVERSITY OF TEXAS MD ANDERSON CANCER CENTER
Genetics M

### THE UNIVERSITY OF TEXAS MEDICAL BRANCH
Allied Health—General M,D
Allopathic Medicine D
Biochemistry D
Bioinformatics D
Biological and Biomedical Sciences—General M,D
Biophysics D
Cell Biology M,D
Clinical Laboratory Sciences/Medical Technology M,D
Computational Biology D
Demography and Population Studies D
Humanities M,D
Immunology M,D
Microbiology M,D
Molecular Biophysics D
Neuroscience D
Nursing—General M,D
Occupational Therapy M
Pathology D
Pharmacology M,D
Physical Therapy M,D
Physician Assistant Studies M
Physiology M,D
Public Health—General M
Rehabilitation Sciences D
Structural Biology D
Toxicology M,D
Translational Biology M,D

### THE UNIVERSITY OF TEXAS OF THE PERMIAN BASIN
Accounting M
Biological and Biomedical Sciences—General M
Business Administration and Management—General M
Clinical Psychology M
Computer Science M
Counselor Education M
Criminal Justice and Criminology M
Early Childhood Education M
Education—General M
Educational Leadership and Administration M
English as a Second Language M
English M
Experimental Psychology M
Foundations and Philosophy of Education M
Geology M
History M
Kinesiology and Movement Studies M
Political Science M
Psychology—General M
Reading Education M
Spanish M
Special Education M

### THE UNIVERSITY OF TEXAS RIO GRANDE VALLEY
Accounting M
Agricultural Sciences—General M
Allopathic Medicine D
Art/Fine Arts M
Biological and Biomedical Sciences—General M
Business Administration and Management—General M,D
Chemistry M
Clinical Laboratory Sciences/Medical Technology M
Clinical Psychology M
Communication Disorders M
Communication—General M
Computer Science M
Counselor Education M
Criminal Justice and Criminology M
Curriculum and Instruction M,D
Early Childhood Education M
Education—General M,D
Educational Leadership and Administration M,D
Educational Media/Instructional Technology M,D
Educational Psychology M
Electrical Engineering M
Elementary Education M,D
Emergency Management M
Engineering Management M
English as a Second Language M
English M
Environmental Sciences M
Exercise and Sports Science M
Experimental Psychology M
Finance and Banking M,D
Geosciences M
Health Services Management and Hospital Administration M
History M
Interdisciplinary Studies M
Kinesiology and Movement Studies M
Management Information Systems M
Manufacturing Engineering M
Marketing M,D
Mathematics M
Mechanical Engineering M
Multilingual and Multicultural Education M
Music M
Nutrition M
Occupational Therapy M
Oceanography M
Physician Assistant Studies M
Physics M
Psychology—General M
Public Administration M
Public Affairs M
Public Policy M
Reading Education M
Rehabilitation Counseling M,D
School Psychology M
Secondary Education M,D
Social Work M
Sociology M
Spanish M
Special Education M
Sustainable Development M
Systems Engineering M
Translation and Interpretation M
Writing M

### THE UNIVERSITY OF TEXAS SOUTHWESTERN MEDICAL CENTER
Allopathic Medicine D
Biochemistry D
Biological and Biomedical Sciences—General M,D
Biomedical Engineering M,D
Cancer Biology/Oncology D
Cell Biology D
Clinical Psychology D
Developmental Biology D
Genetics D
Immunology D
Microbiology D
Molecular Biophysics D
Neuroscience D
Nutrition M
Physical Therapy D
Physician Assistant Studies M
Rehabilitation Counseling M

### THE UNIVERSITY OF THE ARTS
Art Education M
Art/Fine Arts M
Dance M
Industrial Design M
Museum Education M
Museum Studies M
Music Education M
Music M
Theater M,O

### UNIVERSITY OF THE CUMBERLANDS
Accounting M
Business Administration and Management—General M
Business Education M,D,O
Clinical Psychology D
Counseling Psychology M
Counselor Education M,D,O
Education—General M,D,O
Educational Leadership and Administration M,D,O
Elementary Education M,D,O
Marketing M,D,O
Middle School Education M,D,O
Physician Assistant Studies M
Reading Education M,D,O
Religion M
Secondary Education M,D,O
Special Education M,D,O
Student Affairs M,D,O
Theater M,D,O

### UNIVERSITY OF THE DISTRICT OF COLUMBIA
Adult Education O
Architecture M
Business Administration and Management—General M
Cancer Biology/Oncology M
Communication Disorders M
Computer Science M
Counseling Psychology M
Early Childhood Education M
Electrical Engineering M
Elementary Education M
Engineering and Applied Sciences—General M
English Education M
Homeland Security M
Law M,D
Legal and Justice Studies M,D
Mathematics Education M
Middle School Education M
Nutrition M
Public Administration M
Rehabilitation Counseling M
Secondary Education M
Social Sciences Education M
Water Resources M

### UNIVERSITY OF THE FRASER VALLEY
Criminal Justice and Criminology M
Social Work M

### UNIVERSITY OF THE INCARNATE WORD
Accounting M
Applied Statistics M
Biological and Biomedical Sciences—General M
Business Administration and Management—General M,D
Clothing and Textiles M
Communication—General M,D
Education—General M,D
Health Services Management and Hospital Administration M,D
Industrial and Organizational Psychology M,D
Kinesiology and Movement Studies M,D
Mathematics Education M
Mathematics M
Nursing—General M,D
Nutrition M
Optometry D
Organizational Management M,D
Osteopathic Medicine M,D
Pastoral Ministry and Counseling M
Pharmacy D
Physical Therapy D
Sports Management M,D

### UNIVERSITY OF THE PACIFIC
Biological and Biomedical Sciences—General M
Business Administration and Management—General M
Communication Disorders M,D
Communication—General M
Curriculum and Instruction M,D,O
Dentistry M,D,O
Education—General M,D,O
Educational Leadership and Administration M,D,O
Educational Psychology M,D,O
Engineering and Applied Sciences—General M
Exercise and Sports Science M
Hospitality Management M
International Affairs M,D
Law M,D
Music Education M
Music M
Pharmaceutical Sciences M,D
Pharmacy D
Physical Therapy M,D
Psychology—General M
Public Policy M,D
School Psychology M,D,O
Special Education M,D,O
Therapies—Dance, Drama, and Music M
Water Resources M,D

### UNIVERSITY OF THE PEOPLE
Business Administration and Management—General M

### UNIVERSITY OF THE POTOMAC
Business Administration and Management—General M

### UNIVERSITY OF THE SACRED HEART
Accounting M,O
Advertising and Public Relations M
Broadcast Journalism M,O
Business Administration and Management—General M,O
Communication—General M,O
Conflict Resolution and Mediation/Peace Studies M
Cultural Studies M
Early Childhood Education M,O
Education—General M,O
Educational Media/Instructional Technology M
English Education M,O
Environmental and Occupational Health M
Film, Television, and Video Production M,O
Foreign Languages Education M,O
Human Resources Management M
Information Science O
Internet and Interactive Multimedia M,O
Legal and Justice Studies M
Management Information Systems M
Marketing M
Mathematics Education M,O
Nonprofit Management M
Occupational Health Nursing M
Taxation M
Writing M,O

### UNIVERSITY OF THE SCIENCES
Biochemistry M,D
Bioinformatics M
Biotechnology M
Cell Biology M
Chemistry M,D
Health Psychology M
Health Services Management and Hospital Administration M,D
Medicinal and Pharmaceutical Chemistry M,D
Occupational Therapy M,D
Pharmaceutical Administration M
Pharmaceutical Sciences M,D
Pharmacology M,D
Pharmacy D
Physical Therapy D
Public Health—General M
Technical Writing M,O
Toxicology M,D

### THE UNIVERSITY OF THE SOUTH
English M
Theology M,D
Writing M

### UNIVERSITY OF THE SOUTHWEST
Business Administration and Management—General M

| | |
|---|---|
| Counseling Psychology | M |
| Counselor Education | M |
| Curriculum and Instruction | M |
| Early Childhood Education | M |
| Education—General | M |
| Educational Leadership and Administration | M |
| English as a Second Language | M |
| Multilingual and Multicultural Education | M |
| Special Education | M |
| Sports Management | M |

### UNIVERSITY OF THE VIRGIN ISLANDS

| | |
|---|---|
| Business Administration and Management—General | M |
| Education—General | M,D,O |
| Educational Leadership and Administration | M,D,O |
| Environmental Sciences | M |
| Liberal Studies | M |
| Marine Sciences | M |
| Mathematics Education | M |
| Mathematics | M |
| School Psychology | M,D,O |
| Secondary Education | M |
| Social Sciences | M |

### UNIVERSITY OF THE WEST

| | |
|---|---|
| Business Administration and Management—General | M |
| Finance and Banking | M |
| International Business | M |
| Management Information Systems | M |
| Nonprofit Management | M |
| Psychology—General | M |
| Religion | M,D |
| Theology | M |

### THE UNIVERSITY OF TOLEDO

| | |
|---|---|
| Accounting | M |
| Allopathic Medicine | M,D,O |
| Analytical Chemistry | M,D |
| Applied Mathematics | M,D |
| Art Education | M,D,O |
| Astrophysics | M,D |
| Athletic Training and Sports Medicine | M,D |
| Biochemistry | M,D |
| Bioengineering | M,D |
| Bioinformatics | M,O |
| Biological and Biomedical Sciences—General | M,D,O |
| Biomedical Engineering | D |
| Biostatistics | M,O |
| Business Administration and Management—General | M |
| Business Education | M,D,O |
| Cancer Biology/Oncology | M,D |
| Cardiovascular Sciences | M,D |
| Chemical Engineering | M,D |
| Chemistry | M,D |
| Civil Engineering | M,D |
| Clinical Psychology | M,D |
| Communication Disorders | M,D,O |
| Communication—General | O |
| Community Health Nursing | M,O |
| Computer Science | M,D |
| Counselor Education | M,D,O |
| Criminal Justice and Criminology | M,O |
| Curriculum and Instruction | M,D,O |
| Early Childhood Education | M,D,O |
| Ecology | M,D |
| Economics | M,D,O |
| Education of the Gifted | M,D,O |
| Education—General | M,D,O |
| Educational Leadership and Administration | M,D,O |
| Educational Measurement and Evaluation | M,D,O |
| Educational Media/Instructional Technology | M,D,O |
| Educational Psychology | M,D,O |
| Electrical Engineering | M,D |
| Elementary Education | M,D,O |
| Emergency Management | M,O |
| Engineering and Applied Sciences—General | M |
| English as a Second Language | M,D,O |
| English Education | M,D,O |
| English | M,O |
| Environmental and Occupational Health | M,D,O |
| Environmental Sciences | M,D |
| Epidemiology | M,O |
| Exercise and Sports Science | M,D |
| Experimental Psychology | M,D |
| Family Nurse Practitioner Studies | M,O |
| Finance and Banking | M |
| Foreign Languages Education | M,D,O |
| Foundations and Philosophy of Education | M,D,O |
| French | M |
| Gender Studies | O |
| Genomic Sciences | M,O |
| Geographic Information Systems | M,D,O |
| Geography | M,D,O |
| Geology | M,D |
| German | M |
| Gerontology | M,O |
| Health Education | M,D,O |
| Health Promotion | M,D,O |
| Health Services Management and Hospital Administration | M,O |
| Higher Education | M,D,O |
| History | M,D |
| Immunology | M,D |
| Industrial Hygiene | M,D,O |
| Industrial/Management Engineering | M,D |
| Inorganic Chemistry | M,D |
| International Business | M |
| International Health | M,O |
| Law | M,D,O |
| Leisure Studies | M,D |
| Liberal Studies | M |
| Marketing | M |
| Materials Sciences | M,D |
| Mathematics Education | M,D,O |
| Mathematics | M,D |
| Mechanical Engineering | M,D |
| Medical Physics | M,D |
| Medicinal and Pharmaceutical Chemistry | M,D |
| Middle School Education | M,D,O |
| Music Education | M,O |
| Music | M,O |
| Neuroscience | M,D |
| Nonprofit Management | M,O |
| Nursing and Healthcare Administration | M,O |
| Nursing Education | M,O |
| Nursing—General | M,D,O |
| Nutrition | M,O |
| Occupational Therapy | M,D |
| Oral and Dental Sciences | M |
| Organic Chemistry | M,D |
| Pathology | M,O |
| Pediatric Nursing | M,O |
| Pharmaceutical Administration | M |
| Pharmaceutical Sciences | M |
| Pharmacology | M,D |
| Pharmacy | M,D |
| Philosophy | M |
| Physical Chemistry | M,D |
| Physical Education | M |
| Physical Therapy | M,D |
| Physician Assistant Studies | M |
| Physics | M,D |
| Political Science | M,O |
| Psychology—General | M,D |
| Public Administration | M,O |
| Public Health—General | M,D,O |
| Recreation and Park Management | M,D |
| School Psychology | M,D,O |
| Science Education | M,D,O |
| Secondary Education | M,D,O |
| Social Sciences Education | M,D,O |
| Social Work | M,O |
| Sociology | M |
| Spanish | M |
| Special Education | M,D,O |
| Statistics | M,D |
| Urban and Regional Planning | M,D,O |
| Vocational and Technical Education | M,D,O |
| Women's Studies | O |
| Writing | M,O |

### UNIVERSITY OF TORONTO

| | |
|---|---|
| Aerospace/Aeronautical Engineering | M,D |
| Allopathic Medicine | M,D |
| Anthropology | M,D |
| Architecture | M |
| Art History | M,D |
| Asian Studies | M,D |
| Astronomy | M,D |
| Astrophysics | M,D |
| Biochemistry | M,D |
| Bioethics | M,D |
| Biomedical Engineering | M,D |
| Biophysics | M,D |
| Biostatistics | M,D |
| Biotechnology | M |
| Business Administration and Management—General | M,D |
| Cell Biology | M,D |
| Chemical Engineering | M,D |
| Chemistry | M,D |
| Civil Engineering | M,D |
| Classics | M,D |
| Communication Disorders | M,D |
| Community Health | M,D |
| Comparative Literature | M,D |
| Computer Engineering | M,D |
| Computer Science | M,D |
| Criminal Justice and Criminology | M,D |
| Dentistry | D |
| East European and Russian Studies | M |
| Ecology | M,D |
| Economics | M,D |
| Education—General | M,D |
| Electrical Engineering | M,D |
| Engineering and Applied Sciences—General | M,D |
| English | M,D |
| Environmental and Occupational Health | M,D |
| Environmental Sciences | M,D |
| Epidemiology | M,D |
| Evolutionary Biology | M,D |
| Film, Television, and Video Theory and Criticism | M,D |
| Finance and Banking | M |
| Forestry | M,D |
| French | M,D |
| Gender Studies | M,D |
| Genetic Counseling | M,D |
| Geography | M,D |
| Geology | M,D |
| German | M,D |
| Health Informatics | M |
| Health Physics/Radiological Health | M,D |
| Health Promotion | M,D |
| Health Services Management and Hospital Administration | M |
| History of Science and Technology | M,D |
| History | M,D |
| Human Resources Management | M,D |
| Immunology | M,D |
| Industrial and Labor Relations | M,D |
| Industrial/Management Engineering | M,D |
| Information Studies | M,D |
| International Affairs | M |
| Italian | M,D |
| Kinesiology and Movement Studies | M,D |
| Landscape Architecture | M |
| Law | M,D |
| Linguistics | M,D |
| Management of Technology | M |
| Manufacturing Engineering | M |
| Materials Engineering | M,D |
| Materials Sciences | M,D |
| Mathematical and Computational Finance | M |
| Mathematics | M,D |
| Mechanical Engineering | M,D |
| Medieval and Renaissance Studies | M,D |
| Molecular Genetics | M,D |
| Museum Studies | M |
| Music Education | M,D |
| Music | M,D |
| Near and Middle Eastern Studies | M,D |
| Nursing—General | M,D |
| Nutrition | M,D |
| Occupational Therapy | M |
| Oral and Dental Sciences | M,D |
| Pathobiology | M,D |
| Pharmaceutical Sciences | M,D |
| Pharmacology | M,D |
| Philosophy | M,D |
| Physical Education | M,D |
| Physical Therapy | M |
| Physics | M,D |
| Physiology | M,D |
| Political Science | M,D |
| Portuguese | M,D |
| Psychology—General | M,D |
| Public Health—General | M,D |
| Rehabilitation Sciences | M,D |
| Religion | M,D |
| Slavic Languages | M,D |
| Social Sciences | M,D |
| Social Work | M,D |
| Sociology | M,D |
| Spanish | M,D |
| Statistics | M,D |
| Systems Biology | M,D |
| Theater | M,D |
| Urban and Regional Planning | M,D |
| Urban Design | M,D |
| Women's Studies | M,D |
| Writing | M,D |

### THE UNIVERSITY OF TULSA

| | |
|---|---|
| Accounting | M |
| American Indian/Native American Studies | M,D,O |
| Anthropology | M,D |
| Biological and Biomedical Sciences—General | M,D |
| Business Administration and Management—General | M |
| Business Analytics | M |
| Chemical Engineering | M,D |
| Clinical Psychology | M,D |
| Communication Disorders | M |
| Computer and Information Systems Security | M,D |
| Computer Science | M,D |
| Electrical Engineering | M,D |
| Energy Management and Policy | M |
| Engineering and Applied Sciences—General | M,D |
| English | M,D |
| Environmental Law | M,D,O |
| Family Nurse Practitioner Studies | D |
| Geophysics | M,D |
| Geosciences | M,D |
| Gerontological Nursing | D |
| Health Law | M,D,O |
| Industrial and Organizational Psychology | M,D |
| Kinesiology and Movement Studies | M |
| Law | M,D,O |
| Mathematics | M,D |
| Mechanical Engineering | M,D |
| Museum Studies | M |
| Nursing—General | D |
| Petroleum Engineering | M,D |
| Psychology—General | M,D |
| Rehabilitation Sciences | M |

### UNIVERSITY OF UTAH

| | |
|---|---|
| Accounting | M,D |
| Allopathic Medicine | D |
| American Studies | M,D |
| Anatomy | D |
| Anthropology | M,D |
| Applied Behavior Analysis | M,D |
| Architecture | M |
| Art Education | M |
| Art History | M |
| Art/Fine Arts | M |
| Asian Studies | M |
| Atmospheric Sciences | M,D |
| Biochemistry | M,D |
| Bioengineering | M,D |
| Bioinformatics | M,D,O |
| Biological and Biomedical Sciences—General | M,D,O |
| Biostatistics | M,D |
| Biotechnology | M |
| Business Administration and Management—General | M,D,O |
| Business Analytics | |
| Cancer Biology/Oncology | M,D |
| Chemical Engineering | M,D |
| Chemical Physics | M,D |
| Chemistry | M,D |
| Child and Family Studies | M |
| Civil Engineering | M,D |
| Clinical Laboratory Sciences/Medical Technology | M |
| Clinical Psychology | M,D,O |
| Communication Disorders | M,D |
| Communication—General | M,D |
| Comparative Literature | M,D |
| Computational Sciences | M |
| Computer and Information Systems Security | M,O |
| Computer Engineering | M,D |
| Computer Science | M,D |
| Counseling Psychology | M,D,O |
| Counselor Education | M,D,O |
| Cultural Studies | M,D |
| Dance | M,O |
| Dentistry | D |
| Developmental Psychology | D |
| Early Childhood Education | M,D |
| Economics | M,D |
| Education of Students with Severe/Multiple Disabilities | M,D |
| Education—General | M,D,O |
| Educational Leadership and Administration | M,D |
| Educational Media/Instructional Technology | M,D,O |
| Educational Policy | M,D |
| Educational Psychology | M,D,O |
| Electrical Engineering | M,D |
| Elementary Education | M,D,O |
| Engineering and Applied Sciences—General | M,D |
| English | M,D |
| Environmental Engineering | M,D |
| Environmental Sciences | M |
| Film, Television, and Video Production | M |
| Finance and Banking | M,D |
| Foundations and Philosophy of Education | M,D |
| French | M,D |
| Game Design and Development | M |
| Geographic Information Systems | M,D |
| Geography | M,D |
| Geological Engineering | M,D |
| Geology | M,D |
| Geophysics | M,D |
| Gerontological Nursing | M,O |
| Gerontology | M,O |
| Graphic Design | M |
| Health Services Management and Hospital Administration | M,D |
| Health Services Research | M,D |
| Higher Education | M,D |
| History | M,D |
| Human Development | M |
| Human Genetics | M,D |
| Humanities | M |
| Industrial and Manufacturing Management | M,D,O |
| International Affairs | M,D |
| Internet and Interactive Multimedia | M,D |
| Kinesiology and Movement Studies | M,D |
| Latin American Studies | M |
| Law | M,D |
| Leisure Studies | M,D |
| Linguistics | M,D |
| Management Information Systems | M,D,O |
| Management Strategy and Policy | M,D,O |
| Marketing | M,D |
| Materials Engineering | M,D |
| Materials Sciences | M,D |
| Mathematics Education | M,D |
| Mathematics | M,D |
| Mechanical Engineering | M,D |
| Medical Physics | M,D |
| Medicinal and Pharmaceutical Chemistry | M,D |
| Mineral/Mining Engineering | M,D |
| Molecular Biology | D |
| Music Education | M,D |
| Music | M,D |
| Near and Middle Eastern Languages | M,D |
| Near and Middle Eastern Studies | M,D |
| Neurobiology | D |
| Neuroscience | D |
| Nuclear Engineering | M,D |
| Nursing—General | M,D |
| Nutrition | M,D |
| Occupational Therapy | M,D |
| Organizational Behavior | M,D |
| Pathology | M,D |
| Petroleum Engineering | M,D |
| Pharmaceutical Administration | M,D |
| Pharmaceutical Sciences | M,D |
| Pharmacology | D |
| Pharmacy | M,D |
| Philosophy | M,D |
| Photography | M |
| Physical Therapy | D |
| Physician Assistant Studies | M |
| Physics | M,D |
| Physiology | M,D |
| Political Science | M,D |
| Psychology—General | D |
| Public Administration | M,D |
| Public Health—General | M,D |
| Reading Education | M,D,O |
| Real Estate | M |
| Recreation and Park Management | M,D |
| Rehabilitation Sciences | D |
| Rhetoric | M,D |
| School Psychology | M,D,O |
| Science Education | M,D |
| Secondary Education | M,D |
| Social Psychology | D |
| Social Work | M,D |
| Sociology | M,D |
| Software Engineering | M,D,O |

*M—masters degree; D—doctorate; O—other advanced degree; *—Close-Up and/or Display*

| | |
|---|---|
| Spanish | M,D |
| Special Education | M,D |
| Statistics | M,D,O |
| Student Affairs | M,D |
| Systems Engineering | M,O |
| Toxicology | D |
| Urban and Regional Planning | M,D |
| Urban Design | M,D |
| Writing | M,D |

## UNIVERSITY OF VALLEY FORGE

| | |
|---|---|
| Music | M |
| Religion | M |
| Theology | M |

## UNIVERSITY OF VERMONT

| | |
|---|---|
| Accounting | M |
| Agricultural Economics and Agribusiness | M |
| Agricultural Sciences—General | M,D,O |
| Agronomy and Soil Sciences | M,D,O |
| Allied Health—General | M,D,O |
| Allopathic Medicine | M,D,O |
| Animal Sciences | M,D |
| Applied Economics | M |
| Biochemistry | M,D |
| Bioengineering | D |
| Biological and Biomedical Sciences—General | M,D |
| Biomedical Engineering | M |
| Biostatistics | M |
| Business Administration and Management—General | M |
| Cell Biology | D |
| Chemistry | M,D |
| Civil Engineering | M,D |
| Classics | M,O |
| Clinical Laboratory Sciences/Medical Technology | M,D,O |
| Clinical Psychology | M,D |
| Communication Disorders | M |
| Community Health | M |
| Computer Science | M,D |
| Counseling Psychology | M |
| Counselor Education | M |
| Curriculum and Instruction | M |
| Data Science/Data Analytics | M,D |
| Developmental Psychology | D |
| Early Childhood Education | M |
| Economics | M,D,O |
| Education—General | M,D |
| Educational Leadership and Administration | M,D |
| Educational Policy | D |
| Electrical Engineering | M,D |
| Elementary Education | M |
| Engineering and Applied Sciences—General | M,D |
| Engineering Management | M |
| English | M |
| Entomology | M,D,O |
| Environmental and Occupational Health | M,O |
| Environmental Engineering | M,D |
| Environmental Sciences | M |
| Epidemiology | M,O |
| Experimental Psychology | D |
| Food Science and Technology | M,D |
| Foreign Languages Education | M,O |
| Forestry | M,D,O |
| Geology | M |
| German | M |
| Health Promotion | M |
| Health Services Management and Hospital Administration | M,O |
| Higher Education | M |
| Historic Preservation | M |
| History | M |
| Horticulture | M,D,O |
| Interdisciplinary Studies | M |
| International Health | M,O |
| Materials Sciences | M,D |
| Mathematics | M,D |
| Mechanical Engineering | M,D |
| Middle School Education | M |
| Molecular Biology | D |
| Natural Resources | M,D,O |
| Neuroscience | D |
| Nursing—General | M,D,O |
| Nutrition | M |
| Pathology | M |
| Pharmacology | M,D |
| Physical Therapy | D |
| Physics | M |
| Plant Biology | M,D |
| Plant Pathology | M,D,O |
| Plant Sciences | M,D,O |
| Psychology—General | D |
| Public Administration | M |
| Public Health—General | M,O |
| Rehabilitation Sciences | D |
| School Psychology | M |
| Science Education | M,D |
| Secondary Education | M |
| Social Psychology | D |
| Social Work | M |
| Special Education | M |
| Statistics | M |
| Sustainability Management | M |
| Sustainable Development | M |
| Veterinary Sciences | M,D |

## UNIVERSITY OF VICTORIA

| | |
|---|---|
| Anthropology | M |
| Art Education | M,D |
| Art History | M,D |
| Art/Fine Arts | M |
| Asian Studies | M |
| Astronomy | M,D |
| Astrophysics | M,D |
| Biochemistry | M,D |
| Biological and Biomedical Sciences—General | M,D |
| Business Administration and Management—General | M |
| Chemistry | M,D |
| Child and Family Studies | M,D |
| Classics | M,D |
| Clinical Psychology | M,D |
| Computer Art and Design | M |
| Computer Engineering | M,D |
| Computer Science | M,D |
| Condensed Matter Physics | M,D |
| Conflict Resolution and Mediation/Peace Studies | M,D |
| Counseling Psychology | M,D |
| Counselor Education | M,D |
| Curriculum and Instruction | M,D |
| Developmental Psychology | M,D |
| Early Childhood Education | M,D |
| Economics | M,D |
| Education—General | M,D |
| Educational Leadership and Administration | M,D |
| Educational Measurement and Evaluation | M,D |
| Educational Psychology | M,D |
| Electrical Engineering | M,D |
| Engineering and Applied Sciences—General | M,D |
| English Education | M,D |
| English | M,D |
| Environmental Education | M,D |
| Experimental Psychology | M,D |
| Family Nurse Practitioner Studies | M,D |
| Film, Television, and Video Production | M |
| Foreign Languages Education | M |
| Foundations and Philosophy of Education | M,D |
| French | M |
| Geography | M,D |
| Geosciences | M,D |
| German | M |
| Health Informatics | M |
| Hispanic Studies | M |
| History | M,D |
| Human Development | M,D |
| Italian | M |
| Kinesiology and Movement Studies | M,D |
| Law | M,D |
| Leisure Studies | M |
| Linguistics | M,D |
| Mathematics Education | M,D |
| Mathematics | M,D |
| Mechanical Engineering | M,D |
| Medical Physics | M,D |
| Microbiology | M,D |
| Music Education | M,D |
| Music | M,D |
| Nursing and Healthcare Administration | M,D |
| Nursing Education | M,D |
| Nursing—General | M,D |
| Oceanography | M,D |
| Pacific Area/Pacific Rim Studies | M |
| Philosophy | M |
| Photography | M |
| Physical Education | M |
| Physics | M,D |
| Political Science | M,D |
| Psychology—General | M,D |
| Public Administration | M,D |
| Reading Education | M,D |
| Science Education | M,D |
| Social Psychology | M,D |
| Social Sciences Education | M,D |
| Social Work | M |
| Sociology | M,D |
| Special Education | M,D |
| Statistics | M,D |
| Theater | M |
| Theoretical Physics | M,D |
| Vocational and Technical Education | M,D |
| Writing | M |

## UNIVERSITY OF VIRGINIA

| | |
|---|---|
| Accounting | M |
| Acute Care/Critical Care Nursing | M,D |
| Aerospace/Aeronautical Engineering | M,D |
| Allopathic Medicine | M,D |
| Anthropology | M,D |
| Architectural History | M,D |
| Architecture | M |
| Art History | M,D |
| Asian Studies | M |
| Astronomy | M,D |
| Biochemistry | D |
| Biological and Biomedical Sciences—General | M,D |
| Biomedical Engineering | M,D |
| Biophysics | M,D |
| Business Administration and Management—General | M,D,O |
| Cell Biology | D |
| Chemical Engineering | M,D |
| Chemistry | M,D |
| Civil Engineering | M,D |
| Classics | M,D |
| Clinical Psychology | D |
| Clinical Research | M |
| Communication Disorders | M,D |
| Community Health | M,D |
| Computer Engineering | M,D |
| Computer Science | M,D |
| Construction Engineering | D |
| Counselor Education | M,D,O |
| Curriculum and Instruction | M,D,O |
| Data Science/Data Analytics | M,D |
| Early Childhood Education | M,D |
| Economics | M,D |
| Education of the Gifted | M,D,O |
| Education—General | M,D,O |
| Educational Leadership and Administration | M,D,O |
| Educational Measurement and Evaluation | M,D,O |
| Educational Media/Instructional Technology | M,D,O |
| Educational Policy | D |
| Educational Psychology | M,D,O |
| Electrical Engineering | M,D |
| Elementary Education | M,D,O |
| Engineering and Applied Sciences—General | M,D |
| Engineering Physics | M,D |
| English Education | M,D,O |
| English | M,D |
| Environmental Sciences | M,D |
| Finance and Banking | M |
| Foreign Languages Education | M,D,O |
| French | M,D |
| German | M |
| Health Informatics | M |
| Health Services Management and Hospital Administration | M |
| Health Services Research | M |
| Higher Education | M,D,O |
| History | M,D |
| Interdisciplinary Studies | M,D |
| International Affairs | M,D |
| International Business | M,O |
| Kinesiology and Movement Studies | M,D |
| Landscape Architecture | M |
| Law | M,D |
| Linguistics | M |
| Management of Technology | M |
| Management Strategy and Policy | M,O |
| Marketing | M |
| Materials Sciences | M,D |
| Mathematics Education | M,D,O |
| Mathematics | M,D |
| Mechanical Engineering | M,D |
| Microbiology | D |
| Molecular Genetics | D |
| Molecular Physiology | M,D |
| Music | M,D |
| Near and Middle Eastern Studies | M |
| Neuroscience | D |
| Nursing and Healthcare Administration | M,D |
| Nursing—General | M,D |
| Pathology | D |
| Pharmacology | D |
| Philosophy | M,D |
| Physical Education | M,D |
| Physics | M,D |
| Physiology | D |
| Political Science | M,D |
| Psychiatric Nursing | M,D |
| Psychology—General | M,D |
| Public Health—General | M,D |
| Public Policy | M |
| Reading Education | M,D |
| Religion | M,D |
| School Psychology | M,D |
| Science Education | M,D,O |
| Slavic Languages | M,D |
| Social Sciences Education | M,D,O |
| Sociology | M,D |
| Spanish | M,D |
| Special Education | M,D,O |
| Statistics | M,D |
| Student Affairs | M,D,O |
| Systems Engineering | M,D |
| Theater | M |
| Urban and Regional Planning | M |
| Western European Studies | M |
| Writing | M |

## UNIVERSITY OF WASHINGTON

| | |
|---|---|
| Accounting | M,D |
| Aerospace/Aeronautical Engineering | M,D |
| Allopathic Medicine | D |
| Animal Behavior | M,D |
| Anthropology | M,D |
| Applied Arts and Design—General | M |
| Applied Mathematics | M,D |
| Applied Physics | M,D |
| Architecture | M,D,O |
| Art History | M,D |
| Art/Fine Arts | M |
| Asian Languages | M,D |
| Asian Studies | M,D |
| Astronomy | M,D |
| Atmospheric Sciences | M,D |
| Biochemistry | D |
| Bioengineering | M,D |
| Bioethics | M |
| Bioinformatics | M,D |
| Biological and Biomedical Sciences—General | M,D |
| Biophysics | D |
| Biostatistics | M,D |
| Biotechnology | D |
| Business Administration and Management—General | M,D |
| Cell Biology | D |
| Chemical Engineering | M,D |
| Chemistry | M,D |
| Chinese | M,D |
| Civil Engineering | M,D |
| Classics | M,D |
| Clinical Laboratory Sciences/Medical Technology | M |
| Clinical Psychology | M,D |
| Clinical Research | M,D |
| Cognitive Sciences | M,D |
| Communication Disorders | M,D |
| Communication—General | M,D |
| Community Health | M,D |
| Comparative Literature | M,D |
| Computational Sciences | M,D |
| Computer and Information Systems Security | M,D |
| Computer Engineering | M,D |
| Computer Science | M,D |
| Construction Engineering | M,D |
| Construction Management | M |
| Curriculum and Instruction | M,D |
| Dance | M |
| Data Science/Data Analytics | M,D |
| Dentistry | M,D,O |
| Developmental Psychology | M,D |
| East European and Russian Studies | M |
| Ecology | M,D |
| Economics | D |
| Education of Students with Severe/Multiple Disabilities | M,D |
| Education—General | M,D |
| Educational Leadership and Administration | M,D |
| Educational Measurement and Evaluation | M,D |
| Educational Media/Instructional Technology | M,D |
| Educational Policy | M,D |
| Educational Psychology | M,D |
| Electrical Engineering | M,D |
| Engineering and Applied Sciences—General | M,D,O |
| English as a Second Language | M,D |
| English Education | M,D |
| English | M,D |
| Entrepreneurship | M,D |
| Environmental and Occupational Health | M,D |
| Environmental Engineering | M,D |
| Environmental Management and Policy | M,D |
| Epidemiology | M,D |
| Fish, Game, and Wildlife Management | M,D |
| Forestry | M,D |
| Foundations and Philosophy of Education | M,D |
| French | M,D |
| Genetics | M,D,O |
| Genomic Sciences | D |
| Geography | M,D |
| Geology | M,D |
| Geophysics | M,D |
| Geotechnical Engineering | M,D |
| German | M,D |
| Health Informatics | M,D |
| Health Services Management and Hospital Administration | M |
| Health Services Research | M,D |
| Higher Education | M,D |
| Hispanic and Latin American Languages | M |
| Historic Preservation | O |
| History | M,D |
| Horticulture | M,D |
| Human Development | M,D |
| Human-Computer Interaction | M,D,O |
| Hydrology | M,D |
| Immunology | D |
| Industrial Design | M |
| Industrial/Management Engineering | M,D |
| Infectious Diseases | D |
| Information Science | M,D |
| Intellectual Property Law | M,D |
| International Affairs | M,D |
| International Business | M,D,O |
| International Health | M,D |
| Italian | M,D |
| Japanese | M,D |
| Landscape Architecture | M |
| Law | M,D |
| Legal and Justice Studies | M,D |
| Library Science | M,D |
| Lighting Design | M,D,O |
| Linguistics | M,D |
| Logistics | O |
| Management Information Systems | M,D |
| Management of Technology | M,D |
| Marine Affairs | M,O |
| Marine Geology | M,D |
| Materials Engineering | M,D |
| Materials Sciences | M,D |
| Maternal and Child Health | M,D |
| Mathematics Education | M,D |
| Mathematics | M,D |
| Mechanical Engineering | M,D |
| Mechanics | M,D |
| Medical Informatics | M,D |
| Medicinal and Pharmaceutical Chemistry | D |
| Microbiology | D |
| Molecular Biology | D |
| Molecular Medicine | D |
| Multilingual and Multicultural Education | M,D |
| Museum Studies | M |
| Music Education | M,D |
| Music | M,D |
| Nanotechnology | M,D |
| Natural Resources | M,D |
| Near and Middle Eastern Studies | M,D |
| Neurobiology | D |
| Neuroscience | D |
| Nursing—General | M,D,O |
| Nutrition | M,D |
| Occupational Therapy | M,D |
| Oceanography | M,D |
| Oral and Dental Sciences | M,D,O |
| Pathobiology | D |
| Pathology | D |
| Pharmaceutical Sciences | M,D |
| Pharmacology | D |
| Pharmacy | M,D |
| Philosophy | M,D |
| Photography | M |
| Physical Education | M,D |
| Physical Therapy | M,D |
| Physics | M,D |
| Physiology | D |
| Political Science | M,D |
| Portuguese | M |

Psychology—General M,D
Public Administration M,D
Public Affairs M,D
Public Health—General M
Public Policy M,D
Reading Education M,D
Rehabilitation Sciences M,D
Religion M,D
Russian M,D
Scandinavian Languages M,D
School Psychology M,D
Science Education M,D
Slavic Languages M,D
Social Psychology M,D
Social Sciences Education M,D
Social Sciences M,D
Social Work M,D
Sociology M,D
Spanish M
Special Education M,D
Statistics M,D
Structural Biology D
Structural Engineering M,D
Supply Chain Management M,D
Sustainable Development M,D
Systems Engineering M,D
Taxation M,D
Theater M,D
Toxicology M,D
Transportation and Highway Engineering M,D
Transportation Management O
Urban and Regional Planning M,D
Urban Design M,D,O
Veterinary Sciences M
Women's Studies D
Writing M

### UNIVERSITY OF WASHINGTON, BOTHELL
Business Administration and Management—General M
Computer Engineering M
Cultural Studies M
Education—General M
Educational Leadership and Administration M
Middle School Education M
Nursing—General M
Public Policy M
Secondary Education M
Software Engineering M
Writing M

### UNIVERSITY OF WASHINGTON, TACOMA
Accounting M
Business Administration and Management—General M
Community Health Nursing M
Computer Engineering M
Education—General M
Educational Leadership and Administration M
Elementary Education M
Finance and Banking M
Interdisciplinary Studies M
Mathematics Education M
Nursing and Healthcare Administration M
Nursing Education M
Nursing—General M
Science Education M
Social Work M
Software Engineering M
Special Education M

### UNIVERSITY OF WATERLOO
Accounting M,D
Actuarial Science M,D
Anthropology M
Applied Mathematics M,D
Architecture M
Art/Fine Arts M
Biochemistry M,D
Biological and Biomedical Sciences—General M,D
Biostatistics M,D
Business Administration and Management—General M
Chemical Engineering M,D
Chemistry M,D
Civil Engineering M,D
Computer Engineering M,D
Computer Science M,D
Economics M,D
Electrical Engineering M,D
Engineering and Applied Sciences—General M,D
Engineering Management M,D
English M,D
Entrepreneurship M
Environmental Engineering M,D
Environmental Management and Policy M,D
Environmental Sciences M,D
Finance and Banking M,D
French M,D
Geography M,D
Geosciences M,D
German M,D
Health Education M,D
Health Informatics M,D
History M,D
Information Science M,D
International Affairs M,D
Kinesiology and Movement Studies M,D
Leisure Studies M,D
Management of Technology M,D
Mathematics M,D
Mechanical Engineering M,D
Near and Middle Eastern Studies M
Operations Research M,D
Optometry M,D
Philosophy M,D
Physics M,D
Political Science M,D
Psychology—General M,D
Public Affairs M
Public Health—General M,D
Recreation and Park Management M,D
Religion D
Russian M,D
Sociology M,D
Software Engineering M,D
Statistics M,D
Systems Engineering M,D
Taxation M,D
Technical Writing M,D
Urban and Regional Planning M,D
Vision Sciences M,D

### THE UNIVERSITY OF WEST ALABAMA
Adult Education M
Business Administration and Management—General M
Child Development M,O
Clinical Psychology M
Conservation Biology M
Counselor Education M,O
Early Childhood Education M,O
Education—General M,O
Educational Leadership and Administration M,O
Educational Media/Instructional Technology M,O
Elementary Education M,O
English Education M
Experimental Psychology M
Finance and Banking M
Higher Education M
History M
Marriage and Family Therapy M
Mathematics Education M
Physical Education M
Science Education M
Secondary Education M
Social Sciences Education M
Special Education M,O
Student Affairs M

### THE UNIVERSITY OF WESTERN ONTARIO
Allopathic Medicine M,D
Anatomy M,D
Anthropology M,D
Applied Mathematics M,D
Astronomy M,D
Biochemical Engineering M,D
Biochemistry M,D
Biological and Biomedical Sciences—General M,D
Biophysics M,D
Biostatistics M,D
Business Administration and Management—General M,D
Cell Biology M,D
Chemical Engineering M,D
Chemistry M,D
Civil Engineering M,D
Classics M
Communication Disorders M
Comparative Literature M,D
Computer Engineering M,D
Computer Science M,D
Counseling Psychology M
Curriculum and Instruction M
Dentistry D
Economics M,D
Education—General M
Educational Policy M
Educational Psychology M
Electrical Engineering M,D
Engineering and Applied Sciences—General M,D
English M,D
Entrepreneurship M,D
Environmental Engineering M,D
Environmental Sciences M,D
Epidemiology M,D
Finance and Banking M,D
French M,D
Geography M,D
Geology M,D
Geophysics M,D
Geosciences M,D
Health Services Management and Hospital Administration M,D
History M,D
Immunology M,D
Information Studies M,D
Interdisciplinary Studies M,D
International Business M,D
Journalism M
Kinesiology and Movement Studies M,D
Law M,D,O
Library Science M,D
Management Strategy and Policy M,D
Marketing M,D
Materials Engineering M,D
Mathematics M,D
Mechanical Engineering M,D
Media Studies M,D
Microbiology M,D
Music M,D
Neuroscience M,D
Nursing—General M,D
Occupational Therapy M
Oral and Dental Sciences M
Pathology M,D
Philosophy M,D
Physical Therapy M,O
Physics M,D
Physiology M,D
Political Science M,D
Psychology—General M,D
Sociology M,D
Spanish M,D
Special Education M
Statistics M,D
Sustainable Development M,D

### UNIVERSITY OF WESTERN STATES
Chiropractic D

### UNIVERSITY OF WEST FLORIDA
Accounting M
American Studies M
Anthropology M
Applied Behavior Analysis M
Applied Psychology M
Archaeology M
Biological and Biomedical Sciences—General M
Business Administration and Management—General M
Communication—General M
Computer and Information Systems Security M
Computer Science M
Counseling Psychology M
Criminal Justice and Criminology M
Curriculum and Instruction M,O
Data Science/Data Analytics M
Educational Leadership and Administration M,D
Educational Media/Instructional Technology M,D
Elementary Education M
English M
Environmental Sciences M
Exercise and Sports Science M
Experimental Psychology M
Geographic Information Systems M
Health Promotion M
Health Services Management and Hospital Administration M
History M
Industrial and Organizational Psychology M
Leisure Studies M
Mathematics M
Middle School Education M
Nursing—General M
Physical Education M,D
Political Science M
Psychology—General M
Public Administration M
Public Health—General M
Public History M
Reading Education M
Secondary Education M
Social Work M
Software Engineering M
Special Education M
Student Affairs M
Writing M

### UNIVERSITY OF WEST LOS ANGELES
Business Administration and Management—General M
Entrepreneurship M
Law D
Organizational Management M

### UNIVERSITY OF WINDSOR
Applied Psychology M,D
Art/Fine Arts M
Biochemistry M,D
Biological and Biomedical Sciences—General M,D
Biopsychology M,D
Business Administration and Management—General M
Chemistry M,D
Civil Engineering M,D
Clinical Psychology M,D
Communication—General M
Computer Science M,D
Criminal Justice and Criminology M,D
Economics M
Education—General M,D
Electrical Engineering M,D
Engineering and Applied Sciences—General M,D
English M
Environmental Engineering M,D
Environmental Sciences M,D
Geosciences M,D
History M
Industrial/Management Engineering M,D
Kinesiology and Movement Studies M
Legal and Justice Studies M
Manufacturing Engineering M,D
Materials Engineering M,D
Mathematics M,D
Mechanical Engineering M,D
Nursing—General M
Philosophy M
Physics M,D
Political Science M
Psychology—General M,D
Social Psychology M,D
Social Work M
Sociology M,D
Statistics M,D
Writing M

### THE UNIVERSITY OF WINNIPEG
History M
Marriage and Family Therapy M,O
Public Administration M
Religion M
Theology M,O

### UNIVERSITY OF WISCONSIN–EAU CLAIRE
Adult Nursing M,D
Business Administration and Management—General M
Communication Disorders M
Education—General M
English M
Family Nurse Practitioner Studies M,D
Gerontological Nursing M,D
History M
Library Science M
Nursing and Healthcare Administration M,D
Nursing Education M,D
Nursing—General M,D
Psychology—General M,O
Reading Education M
School Psychology M,O
Secondary Education M
Special Education M
Writing M

### UNIVERSITY OF WISCONSIN–GREEN BAY
Business Administration and Management—General M
Education—General M
Environmental Management and Policy M
Environmental Sciences M
Nursing and Healthcare Administration M
Social Work M
Sustainability Management M

### UNIVERSITY OF WISCONSIN–LA CROSSE
Athletic Training and Sports Medicine M
Biological and Biomedical Sciences—General M
Cancer Biology/Oncology M
Cell Biology M
Community Health M
Data Science/Data Analytics M
Education—General M,O
English Education M,O
Exercise and Sports Science M
Health Education M
Higher Education M,D
Marine Sciences M
Medical Microbiology M
Microbiology M
Molecular Biology M
Nurse Anesthesia M
Occupational Therapy M
Physical Education M
Physical Therapy D
Physician Assistant Studies M
Physiology M
Psychology—General M,O
Public Health—General M
Reading Education M,O
Recreation and Park Management M
Rehabilitation Sciences M
School Psychology M,O
Software Engineering M
Special Education M,O
Student Affairs M

### UNIVERSITY OF WISCONSIN–MADISON
Accounting M,D
Actuarial Science D
Adult Nursing D
African Studies M,D
African-American Studies M
Agricultural Economics and Agribusiness M,D
Agricultural Engineering M,D
Agricultural Sciences—General M,D
Agronomy and Soil Sciences M,D
Allopathic Medicine D
American Studies M,D
Animal Sciences M,D
Anthropology D
Applied Arts and Design—General M,D
Applied Economics M,D
Archaeology D
Art History M,D
Art/Fine Arts M
Arts Administration M
Asian Languages M,D
Asian Studies M,D
Astronomy D
Atmospheric Sciences M,D
Automotive Engineering M,D
Bacteriology M
Biochemistry M,D
Bioinformatics M,D
Biological and Biomedical Sciences—General
Biological Anthropology D
Biomedical Engineering M,D
Biometry M
Biophysics D
Biopsychology D
Botany M,D
Business Administration and Management—General M
Cancer Biology/Oncology D
Cell Biology D
Chemical Engineering D
Chemistry M,D
Child and Family Studies M,D
Chinese M,D
Civil Engineering M
Classics M,D
Clinical Psychology D

*M—masters degree; D—doctorate; O—other advanced degree; *—Close-Up and/or Display*

| | |
|---|---|
| Clinical Research | M,D |
| Cognitive Sciences | D |
| Communication Disorders | M,D |
| Communication—General | M,D |
| Comparative Literature | M,D |
| Computer and Information Systems Security | M |
| Computer Science | M,D |
| Conservation Biology | M |
| Construction Engineering | M |
| Consumer Economics | M,D |
| Counseling Psychology | D |
| Counselor Education | M |
| Cultural Anthropology | D |
| Curriculum and Instruction | M,D |
| Demography and Population Studies | M,D |
| Developmental Psychology | D |
| Ecology | M |
| Economics | D |
| Education—General | M,D,O |
| Educational Leadership and Administration | M,D,O |
| Educational Policy | M,D,O |
| Educational Psychology | M,D |
| Electrical Engineering | M,D |
| Engineering and Applied Sciences—General | M,D |
| Engineering Physics | M,D |
| English as a Second Language | M,D |
| English | M,D |
| Entomology | M,D |
| Environmental Biology | M,D |
| Environmental Engineering | M |
| Environmental Sciences | M |
| Epidemiology | M,D |
| Ergonomics and Human Factors | M,D |
| Family and Consumer Sciences-General | M,D |
| Film, Television, and Video Theory and Criticism | M,D |
| Finance and Banking | M,D |
| Fish, Game, and Wildlife Management | M,D |
| Folklore | M,D |
| Food Science and Technology | M,D |
| Forestry | M,D |
| French | M,D,O |
| Genetic Counseling | M,D |
| Genetics | M,D |
| Geographic Information Systems | M,D,O |
| Geography | M,D,O |
| Geological Engineering | M,D |
| Geology | M,D |
| Geophysics | M,D |
| Geotechnical Engineering | M |
| German | M,D |
| Gerontological Nursing | D |
| Higher Education | M,D,O |
| History of Medicine | M,D |
| History of Science and Technology | M,D |
| History | M,D |
| Horticulture | M,D |
| Human Development | M,D |
| Human Resources Management | M,D |
| Industrial/Management Engineering | M,D |
| Information Studies | M,D |
| Insurance | M,D |
| International and Comparative Education | M,D,O |
| Investment Management | D |
| Italian | M,D |
| Japanese | M,D |
| Jewish Studies | M,D |
| Journalism | M,D |
| Kinesiology and Movement Studies | M,D |
| Landscape Architecture | M,D |
| Latin American Studies | M,D |
| Law | M,D |
| Library Science | M,D |
| Linguistics | M,D |
| Management Information Systems | D |
| Management of Technology | M |
| Management Strategy and Policy | M,D |
| Manufacturing Engineering | M |
| Marine Sciences | M,D |
| Marketing Research | M |
| Marketing | D |
| Mass Communication | M,D |
| Materials Engineering | M,D |
| Mathematics | D |
| Mechanical Engineering | M,D |
| Mechanics | M,D |
| Media Studies | M,D |
| Medical Microbiology | D |
| Medical Physics | M,D |
| Microbiology | D |
| Molecular Biology | D |
| Molecular Pathology | D |
| Music Education | M,D |
| Music | M,D |
| Natural Resources | M,D |
| Near and Middle Eastern Languages | M,D |
| Near and Middle Eastern Studies | M,D |
| Neuroscience | D |
| Nuclear Engineering | M,D |
| Nursing—General | D |
| Nutrition | M,D |
| Occupational Therapy | M,D |
| Oceanography | M,D |
| Pathology | D |
| Pediatric Nursing | D |
| Pharmaceutical Administration | M,D |
| Pharmaceutical Sciences | M,D |
| Pharmacology | D |
| Pharmacy | D |
| Philosophy | M,D |
| Physical Therapy | D |
| Physician Assistant Studies | M |
| Physics | M,D |
| Physiology | M,D |
| Plant Pathology | M,D |
| Plant Sciences | M,D |
| Political Science | D |
| Portuguese | M,D |
| Psychiatric Nursing | D |
| Psychology—General | D |
| Public Affairs | M |
| Public Health—General | M |
| Real Estate | M,D |
| Rehabilitation Counseling | M,D |
| Rhetoric | M,D |
| Risk Management | M,D |
| Rural Sociology | M,D |
| Scandinavian Languages | M,D |
| Slavic Languages | M,D |
| Social Psychology | D |
| Social Work | M,D |
| Sociology | M,D |
| Spanish | M,D |
| Special Education | M,D |
| Speech and Interpersonal Communication | M,D |
| Statistics | M,D |
| Structural Engineering | M |
| Supply Chain Management | M |
| Sustainable Development | M |
| Systems Engineering | M,D |
| Taxation | M |
| Theater | M,D |
| Toxicology | M,D |
| Transportation and Highway Engineering | M |
| Urban and Regional Planning | M,D |
| Veterinary Medicine | M,D |
| Veterinary Sciences | M,D |
| Water Resources Engineering | M |
| Water Resources | M |
| Women's Studies | M,D |
| Writing | M,D |
| Zoology | M,D |

## UNIVERSITY OF WISCONSIN–MILWAUKEE

| | |
|---|---|
| Actuarial Science | M,D |
| Adult Education | M,D,O |
| African Studies | D |
| Allied Health—General | M,D,O |
| Anthropology | M,D,O |
| Applied Arts and Design—General | M |
| Applied Mathematics | M,D |
| Architecture | M,D,O |
| Art Education | M,D,O |
| Art History | M |
| Art/Fine Arts | M,O |
| Athletic Training and Sports Medicine | M,D |
| Atmospheric Sciences | M,D |
| Biochemistry | M,D |
| Biological and Biomedical Sciences—General | M,D |
| Biomedical Engineering | M,D |
| Biostatistics | M,D,O |
| Business Administration and Management—General | M,D,O |
| Business Analytics | M,O |
| Cell Biology | M,D |
| Chemistry | M,D |
| Civil Engineering | M,D |
| Classics | M,O |
| Communication Disorders | M |
| Communication—General | M,D,O |
| Community Health | D |
| Comparative Literature | M,O |
| Computer Art and Design | M,O |
| Computer Engineering | M,D |
| Computer Science | M,D |
| Conflict Resolution and Mediation/Peace Studies | M,D,O |
| Counseling Psychology | M,D,O |
| Criminal Justice and Criminology | M,O |
| Curriculum and Instruction | M,D,O |
| Dance | M,O |
| Developmental Psychology | M,D,O |
| Early Childhood Education | M |
| Economics | M,D |
| Education—General | M,D,O |
| Educational Leadership and Administration | M,D,O |
| Educational Measurement and Evaluation | M,D,O |
| Educational Media/Instructional Technology | M |
| Educational Policy | M,O |
| Educational Psychology | M,D,O |
| Electrical Engineering | M,D |
| Elementary Education | M |
| Engineering and Applied Sciences—General | M,D |
| English as a Second Language | M,D,O |
| English Education | M,D |
| English | M,D |
| Entrepreneurship | M,D,O |
| Environmental and Occupational Health | M,D,O |
| Environmental Sciences | M,D |
| Epidemiology | M,D,O |
| Ergonomics and Human Factors | M |
| Exercise and Sports Science | M,D |
| Family Nurse Practitioner Studies | M,D,O |
| Film, Television, and Video Production | M,O |
| Film, Television, and Video Theory and Criticism | M,D |
| Foreign Languages Education | M,O |
| Foundations and Philosophy of Education | M,D,O |
| French | M,O |
| Gender Studies | M,O |
| Geographic Information Systems | M,D,O |
| Geography | M,D |
| Geology | M,D |
| German | M,O |
| Gerontology | M,D,O |
| Health Informatics | M,D |
| Health Promotion | M,D,O |
| Health Services Management and Hospital Administration | M,D |
| Higher Education | M,O |
| History | M,D |
| Human Resources Management | M,O |
| Industrial and Labor Relations | M,O |
| Industrial/Management Engineering | M,D |
| Information Studies | M,D,O |
| Investment Management | M,O |
| Kinesiology and Movement Studies | M,D |
| Latin American Studies | M,O |
| Liberal Studies | M |
| Library Science | M,D,O |
| Linguistics | M,D,O |
| Management of Technology | M,O |
| Management Strategy and Policy | M,D,O |
| Manufacturing Engineering | M,D |
| Materials Engineering | M,D |
| Mathematics Education | M,D,O |
| Mathematics | M,D |
| Mechanical Engineering | M,D |
| Mechanics | M,D |
| Media Studies | M,D |
| Medical Imaging | D |
| Medical Informatics | M |
| Microbiology | M,D |
| Middle School Education | M |
| Molecular Biology | M,D |
| Multilingual and Multicultural Education | M,D,O |
| Museum Studies | M,D,O |
| Music Education | M,O |
| Music | M,O |
| Nonprofit Management | M,D,O |
| Nursing—General | M,D,O* |
| Nutrition | M,D |
| Occupational Therapy | M |
| Philosophy | M |
| Physical Therapy | M,D |
| Physics | M,D |
| Political Science | M,D |
| Portuguese | M |
| Psychology—General | M,D |
| Public Administration | M |
| Public Health—General | M,D,O |
| Reading Education | M |
| Recreation and Park Management | M |
| Rehabilitation Sciences | D |
| Rhetoric | M,D,O |
| School Psychology | M,D,O |
| Science Education | M |
| Secondary Education | M,D |
| Social Sciences Education | M |
| Social Work | M,D,O |
| Sociology | M,D |
| Spanish | M,O |
| Special Education | M,D,O |
| Statistics | M,D |
| Taxation | M,O |
| Translation and Interpretation | M,O |
| Urban and Regional Planning | M |
| Urban Education | M,D,O |
| Urban Studies | M,D |
| Water Resources | M,D |
| Women's Studies | M,O |
| Writing | M,D |

## UNIVERSITY OF WISCONSIN–OSHKOSH

| | |
|---|---|
| Adult Nursing | M |
| Biological and Biomedical Sciences—General | M |
| Botany | M |
| Business Administration and Management—General | M |
| Counselor Education | M |
| Curriculum and Instruction | M |
| Early Childhood Education | M |
| Education—General | M |
| Educational Leadership and Administration | M |
| English | M |
| Experimental Psychology | M |
| Family Nurse Practitioner Studies | M |
| Health Services Management and Hospital Administration | M |
| Industrial and Organizational Psychology | M |
| International Business | M |
| Mathematics Education | M |
| Microbiology | M |
| Nursing—General | M |
| Psychology—General | M |
| Public Administration | M |
| Reading Education | M |
| Social Work | M |
| Special Education | M |
| Zoology | M |

## UNIVERSITY OF WISCONSIN–PARKSIDE

| | |
|---|---|
| Business Administration and Management—General | M |
| Clinical Psychology | M |
| Computer Science | M |
| Health Promotion | M |
| Information Science | M |
| Molecular Biology | M |
| Sports Management | M |
| Sustainability Management | M |

## UNIVERSITY OF WISCONSIN–PLATTEVILLE

| | |
|---|---|
| Adult Education | M |
| Computer Science | M |
| Criminal Justice and Criminology | M |
| Education—General | M |
| Engineering and Applied Sciences—General | M |
| Organizational Management | M |
| Project Management | M |
| Supply Chain Management | M |

## UNIVERSITY OF WISCONSIN–RIVER FALLS

| | |
|---|---|
| Agricultural Education | M |
| Agricultural Sciences—General | M |
| Art/Fine Arts | M |
| Business Administration and Management—General | M |
| Communication Disorders | M |
| Counselor Education | M,O |
| Education—General | M |
| Elementary Education | M |
| English as a Second Language | M |
| Mathematics Education | M |
| Reading Education | M |
| School Psychology | M,O |
| Science Education | M |
| Social Sciences Education | M |

## UNIVERSITY OF WISCONSIN–STEVENS POINT

| | |
|---|---|
| Advertising and Public Relations | M |
| Athletic Training and Sports Medicine | M |
| Communication Disorders | M,D |
| Communication—General | M |
| Corporate and Organizational Communication | M |
| Data Science/Data Analytics | M |
| Education—General | M,D |
| Educational Leadership and Administration | M,D |
| Elementary Education | M |
| English Education | M |
| Family and Consumer Sciences-General | O |
| Health Promotion | M |
| Media Studies | M |
| Music Education | M |
| Natural Resources | M |
| Nutrition | M |
| Reading Education | M |
| Science Education | M |
| Secondary Education | M |
| Social Sciences Education | M |
| Special Education | M |
| Speech and Interpersonal Communication | M |
| Sustainable Development | D |

## UNIVERSITY OF WISCONSIN–STOUT

| | |
|---|---|
| Applied Mathematics | M |
| Applied Psychology | M |
| Art/Fine Arts | M |
| Clinical Psychology | M |
| Conservation Biology | M |
| Construction Management | M |
| Counseling Psychology | M |
| Education—General | M,D,O |
| Food Science and Technology | M |
| Human Resources Development | M |
| Industrial Hygiene | M |
| Industrial/Management Engineering | M |
| Information Science | M |
| Manufacturing Engineering | M |
| Marriage and Family Therapy | M |
| Nutrition | M |
| Project Management | M |
| Quality Management | M |
| Rehabilitation Counseling | M |
| School Psychology | M,O |
| Supply Chain Management | M |
| Sustainability Management | M |
| Technical Communication | M |
| Telecommunications Management | M |
| Vocational and Technical Education | M,D,O |

## UNIVERSITY OF WISCONSIN–SUPERIOR

| | |
|---|---|
| Art Education | M |
| Art History | M |
| Art Therapy | M |
| Art/Fine Arts | M |
| Communication—General | M |
| Counselor Education | M |
| Curriculum and Instruction | M |
| Education—General | M |
| Educational Leadership and Administration | M,O |
| Mass Communication | M |
| Reading Education | M |
| School Psychology | M |
| Social Psychology | M |
| Special Education | M |
| Speech and Interpersonal Communication | M |
| Sustainability Management | M |
| Theater | M |

## UNIVERSITY OF WISCONSIN–WHITEWATER

| | |
|---|---|
| Accounting | M |
| Business Administration and Management—General | M |
| Business Education | M |
| Communication Disorders | M |
| Communication—General | M |
| Corporate and Organizational Communication | M |
| Education—General | M,O |
| Educational Leadership and Administration | M |
| Environmental and Occupational Health | M |
| Finance and Banking | M |
| Marketing | M |
| Mass Communication | M |
| Psychology—General | M,O |
| School Psychology | M,O |
| Special Education | M,O |

## UNIVERSITY OF WYOMING

| | |
|---|---|
| Accounting | M |

| | |
|---|---|
| Agricultural Economics and Agribusiness | M |
| Agricultural Sciences—General | M,D |
| Agronomy and Soil Sciences | M,D |
| American Studies | M |
| Animal Sciences | M,D |
| Anthropology | M,D |
| Applied Economics | M |
| Applied Statistics | M,D |
| Architectural Engineering | M,D |
| Atmospheric Sciences | M,D |
| Biotechnology | D |
| Botany | M,D |
| Business Administration and Management—General | M |
| Cell Biology | D |
| Chemical Engineering | M,D |
| Chemistry | M,D |
| Child Development | M |
| Civil Engineering | M,D |
| Communication Disorders | M |
| Communication—General | M |
| Community Health | M,D |
| Computational Biology | D |
| Computer Science | M,D |
| Consumer Economics | M |
| Counselor Education | M,D |
| Curriculum and Instruction | M,D |
| Ecology | M,D |
| Economics | M,D |
| Educational Leadership and Administration | M,D,O |
| Educational Media/Instructional Technology | M,D |
| Electrical Engineering | M,D |
| Engineering and Applied Sciences—General | M,D |
| English | M |
| Entomology | M,D |
| Environmental Engineering | M |
| Exercise and Sports Science | M |
| Finance and Banking | M |
| Food Science and Technology | M |
| French | M |
| Genetics | D |
| Geography | M |
| Geology | M,D |
| Geophysics | M,D |
| German | M |
| Health Education | M |
| Health Promotion | M |
| Health Services Management and Hospital Administration | M,D |
| History | M |
| International Affairs | M |
| Kinesiology and Movement Studies | M |
| Law | D |
| Mathematics Education | M,D |
| Mathematics | M,D |
| Mechanical Engineering | M,D |
| Microbiology | D |
| Molecular Biology | M,D |
| Music Education | M |
| Music | M |
| Natural Resources | M,D |
| Nursing—General | M |
| Nutrition | M |
| Pathobiology | M |
| Petroleum Engineering | M,D |
| Pharmacy | M,D |
| Philosophy | M |
| Physical Education | M |
| Physiology | M,D |
| Political Science | M |
| Psychology—General | M,D |
| Public Administration | M |
| Range Science | M,D |
| Reproductive Biology | M,D |
| Rural Planning and Studies | M |
| Science Education | M |
| Social Work | M |
| Sociology | M |
| Spanish | M |
| Special Education | M,D,O |
| Student Affairs | M,D |
| Water Resources | M,D |
| Writing | M |
| Zoology | M,D |

**UNIVERSITÉ LAVAL**

| | |
|---|---|
| Accounting | M,O |
| Advertising and Public Relations | O |
| Aerospace/Aeronautical Engineering | M |
| Agricultural Economics and Agribusiness | M |
| Agricultural Engineering | M |
| Agricultural Sciences—General | M,D,O |
| Agronomy and Soil Sciences | M,D |
| Allopathic Medicine | D,O |
| Anatomy | O |
| Anesthesiologist Assistant Studies | O |
| Animal Sciences | M,D |
| Anthropology | M,D |
| Archaeology | M,D |
| Architecture | M |
| Art History | M,D |
| Art/Fine Arts | M |
| Biochemistry | M,D,O |
| Biological and Biomedical Sciences—General | M,D,O |
| Business Administration and Management—General | M,D,O |
| Cancer Biology/Oncology | O |
| Cardiovascular Sciences | O |
| Cell Biology | M,D |
| Chemical Engineering | M,D |
| Chemistry | M,D |
| Civil Engineering | M,D,O |
| Clinical Psychology | D |
| Communication Disorders | M |
| Community Health | M,D,O |
| Comparative Literature | M,D |
| Computer Science | M,D |
| Consumer Economics | O |
| Counselor Education | M,D |
| Curriculum and Instruction | M,D |
| Dentistry | D |
| Economics | M,D |
| Education—General | M,D,O |
| Educational Leadership and Administration | M,D,O |
| Educational Measurement and Evaluation | M,D,O |
| Educational Media/Instructional Technology | M,D |
| Educational Psychology | M,D |
| Electrical Engineering | M,D |
| Electronic Commerce | M,O |
| Emergency Medical Services | O |
| Engineering and Applied Sciences—General | M,D,O |
| English | M,D |
| Entrepreneurship | M,O |
| Environmental and Occupational Health | O |
| Environmental Engineering | M,D |
| Environmental Management and Policy | M,D,O |
| Environmental Sciences | M,D |
| Epidemiology | M,D |
| Ethics | O |
| Ethnic Studies | M,D |
| Facilities Management | M,O |
| Film, Television, and Video Theory and Criticism | M,D |
| Finance and Banking | M,O |
| Food Science and Technology | M,D |
| Forestry | M,D |
| Geodetic Sciences | M,D |
| Geographic Information Systems | M,O |
| Geography | M,D |
| Geology | M,D |
| Geosciences | M,D |
| Gerontology | O |
| Graphic Design | M |
| Health Physics/Radiological Health | O |
| History | M,D |
| Immunology | M,D |
| Industrial and Labor Relations | M,D |
| Industrial/Management Engineering | O |
| Infectious Diseases | O |
| International Affairs | M,D |
| International Business | M,O |
| Journalism | O |
| Kinesiology and Movement Studies | M,D |
| Law | M,D,O |
| Legal and Justice Studies | O |
| Linguistics | M,D |
| Management Information Systems | M,O |
| Marketing | M,O |
| Mass Communication | M,D |
| Mathematics | M,D |
| Mechanical Engineering | M,D |
| Metallurgical Engineering and Metallurgy | M,D |
| Microbiology | M,D |
| Mineral/Mining Engineering | M,D |
| Modeling and Simulation | M,O |
| Molecular Biology | M,D |
| Museum Studies | O |
| Music Education | M,D |
| Music | M,D |
| Neurobiology | M,D |
| Nursing—General | M,D,O |
| Nutrition | M,D |
| Oceanography | D |
| Oral and Dental Sciences | M,O |
| Organizational Management | M,O |
| Pathology | O |
| Pharmaceutical Sciences | M,D,O |
| Philosophy | M,D |
| Physics | M,D |
| Physiology | M,D |
| Plant Biology | M,D |
| Political Science | M,D |
| Psychology—General | D |
| Religion | M,D |
| Rural Planning and Studies | O |
| Social Psychology | D |
| Social Work | M,D |
| Sociology | M,D |
| Software Engineering | O |
| Spanish | M,D |
| Statistics | M |
| Theater | M,D |
| Theology | M,D |
| Translation and Interpretation | M,O |
| Urban and Regional Planning | M,D |
| Women's Studies | O |

**UNIVERSITÉ TÉLUQ**

| | |
|---|---|
| Computer Science | M,D |
| Distance Education Development | M,D |
| Finance and Banking | M,D |

**UPPER IOWA UNIVERSITY**

| | |
|---|---|
| Accounting | M |
| Business Administration and Management—General | M |
| Early Childhood Education | M |
| Education—General | M |
| Educational Leadership and Administration | M |
| Emergency Management | M |
| English as a Second Language | M |
| Finance and Banking | M |
| Higher Education | M |
| Homeland Security | M |
| Human Resources Management | M |
| Human Services | M |
| Nonprofit Management | M |
| Organizational Management | M |
| Public Administration | M |
| Reading Education | M |
| Sports Management | M |

**URBANA UNIVERSITY–A BRANCH CAMPUS OF FRANKLIN UNIVERSITY**

| | |
|---|---|
| Business Administration and Management—General | M |
| Criminal Justice and Criminology | M |
| Education—General | M |
| Nursing—General | M |

**URSHAN GRADUATE SCHOOL OF THEOLOGY**

| | |
|---|---|
| Theology | M |

**URSULINE COLLEGE**

| | |
|---|---|
| Adult Nursing | M,D |
| Art Therapy | M |
| Educational Leadership and Administration | M |
| Family Nurse Practitioner Studies | M,D |
| Gerontological Nursing | M,D |
| Historic Preservation | M |
| Medical/Surgical Nursing | M,D |
| Nursing Education | M,D |
| Nursing—General | M,D |
| Pastoral Ministry and Counseling | M |
| Theology | M |

**UTAH STATE UNIVERSITY**

| | |
|---|---|
| Accounting | M |
| Aerospace/Aeronautical Engineering | M,D |
| Agricultural Economics and Agribusiness | M,D |
| Agricultural Education | M |
| Agricultural Sciences—General | M,D |
| Agronomy and Soil Sciences | M,D |
| American Studies | M |
| Animal Sciences | M,D |
| Anthropology | M,D |
| Applied Economics | M,D |
| Applied Mathematics | M,D |
| Art/Fine Arts | M |
| Biochemistry | M,D |
| Bioengineering | M,D |
| Biological and Biomedical Sciences—General | M,D |
| Business Administration and Management—General | M |
| Business Education | D |
| Chemistry | M,D |
| Child and Family Studies | M,D |
| Civil Engineering | M,D,O |
| Clinical Psychology | M,D |
| Communication Disorders | M,D,O |
| Communication—General | M |
| Computer Science | M,D |
| Consumer Economics | M |
| Counseling Psychology | M,D |
| Counselor Education | M,D |
| Curriculum and Instruction | D |
| Disability Studies | M,D,O |
| Ecology | M,D |
| Economics | M |
| Education—General | M,D,O |
| Educational Measurement and Evaluation | M,D |
| Educational Media/Instructional Technology | M,D,O |
| Electrical Engineering | M,D |
| Elementary Education | M |
| Engineering and Applied Sciences—General | M,D,O |
| English | M |
| Environmental Engineering | M,D,O |
| Environmental Management and Policy | M,D |
| Family and Consumer Sciences-General | M,D |
| Finance and Banking | M |
| Fish, Game, and Wildlife Management | M,D |
| Folklore | M |
| Food Science and Technology | M,D |
| Forestry | M,D |
| Geography | M,D |
| Geology | M |
| Health Education | M,D |
| Health Promotion | M,D |
| History | M |
| Home Economics Education | M |
| Horticulture | M,D |
| Human Development | M,D |
| Human Resources Management | M |
| Kinesiology and Movement Studies | M,D |
| Landscape Architecture | M |
| Management Information Systems | M |
| Marriage and Family Therapy | M,D |
| Mathematics | M,D |
| Mechanical Engineering | M,D |
| Meteorology | M,D |
| Multilingual and Multicultural Education | M |
| Music Education | M |
| Music | M |
| Natural Resources | M |
| Nutrition | M,D |
| Physical Education | M,D |
| Physics | M,D |
| Plant Sciences | M,D |
| Political Science | M |
| Psychology—General | M,D |
| Public Health—General | M,D |
| Range Science | M,D |
| Recreation and Park Management | M,D |
| Rehabilitation Counseling | M |
| School Psychology | M,D |
| Secondary Education | M |
| Social Work | M,D |
| Sociology | M,D |
| Special Education | M,D,O |
| Statistics | M,D |
| Theater | M |
| Toxicology | M,D |
| Urban and Regional Planning | M,D |
| Veterinary Sciences | M,D |
| Vocational and Technical Education | D |
| Water Resources | M,D |
| Writing | M |

**UTAH VALLEY UNIVERSITY**

| | |
|---|---|
| Accounting | M |
| Business Administration and Management—General | M |
| Computer and Information Systems Security | O |
| Education—General | M |
| Educational Leadership and Administration | M |
| Educational Media/Instructional Technology | M |
| Elementary Education | M |
| English as a Second Language | M |
| Mathematics Education | M |
| Nursing—General | M |
| Reading Education | M |
| Social Work | M |

**UTICA COLLEGE**

| | |
|---|---|
| Accounting | M |
| Computer and Information Systems Security | M |
| Criminal Justice and Criminology | M |
| Education—General | M,O |
| Health Services Management and Hospital Administration | M |
| Occupational Therapy | M |
| Physical Therapy | D |

**VALDOSTA STATE UNIVERSITY**

| | |
|---|---|
| Accounting | M |
| Business Administration and Management—General | M |
| Communication Disorders | M,D,O |
| Counselor Education | M,O |
| Educational Leadership and Administration | M,D,O |
| Elementary Education | M |
| English Education | M |
| English | M |
| Exercise and Sports Science | M |
| Family Nurse Practitioner Studies | M |
| Gerontological Nursing | M |
| Health Services Management and Hospital Administration | M |
| Industrial and Organizational Psychology | M,O |
| Information Studies | M |
| Library Science | M |
| Marriage and Family Therapy | M,O |
| Nursing—General | M |
| Psychiatric Nursing | M |
| Psychology—General | M,O |
| Public Administration | M,D |
| Social Work | M |
| Special Education | M,D,O |

**VALLEY CITY STATE UNIVERSITY**

| | |
|---|---|
| Education—General | M |
| Educational Media/Instructional Technology | M |
| Elementary Education | M |
| English as a Second Language | M |
| English Education | M |
| Library Science | M |
| Vocational and Technical Education | M |

**VALPARAISO UNIVERSITY**

| | |
|---|---|
| Arts Administration | M |
| Business Administration and Management—General | M,O |
| Clinical Psychology | M |
| Communication—General | M,O |
| Computational Sciences | M |
| Computer and Information Systems Security | M |
| Education—General | M,O |
| Educational Leadership and Administration | M,O |
| Elementary Education | M,O |
| Engineering Management | M,O |
| English as a Second Language | M,O |
| English | M |
| Entertainment Management | M |
| Ethics | M,O |
| Finance and Banking | M,O |
| Health Services Management and Hospital Administration | M |
| International Economics | M |
| International Trade Policy | M |
| Management Information Systems | M |
| Management Strategy and Policy | M,O |
| Media Studies | M,O |
| Nursing Education | M,D,O |
| Nursing—General | M,D,O |
| Physician Assistant Studies | M,D,O |
| Public Health—General | M,D,O |
| School Psychology | M,O |
| Secondary Education | M,O |
| Sports Management | M |

**VAN ANDEL INSTITUTE GRADUATE SCHOOL**

| | |
|---|---|
| Genetics | D |
| Molecular Genetics | D |

*M—masters degree; D—doctorate; O—other advanced degree; *—Close-Up and/or Display*

| **VANCOUVER ISLAND UNIVERSITY** | |
|---|---|
| Business Administration and Management—General | M |
| Finance and Banking | M |
| International Business | M |
| Marketing | M |

| **VANCOUVER SCHOOL OF THEOLOGY** | |
|---|---|
| Religion | M,O |
| Religious Education | M,O |
| Theology | M,O |

| **VANDERBILT UNIVERSITY** | |
|---|---|
| Accounting | M |
| Allopathic Medicine | M,D |
| Anthropology | M,D |
| Biochemistry | M,D |
| Bioinformatics | M,D |
| Biological and Biomedical Sciences—General | M,D |
| Biomedical Engineering | M,D |
| Biophysics | M,D |
| Business Administration and Management—General | M |
| Cell Biology | M,D |
| Chemical Engineering | M,D |
| Chemistry | M,D |
| Child and Family Studies | M |
| Civil Engineering | M,D |
| Communication Disorders | M,D |
| Computer and Information Systems Security | M |
| Computer Science | M,D |
| Counselor Education | M |
| Developmental Biology | M,D |
| Economic Development | M,D |
| Economics | M,D |
| Education—General | M,D* |
| Educational Leadership and Administration | D |
| Electrical Engineering | M,D |
| Elementary Education | M |
| Engineering and Applied Sciences—General | M,D |
| English Education | M |
| English | M,D |
| Environmental Engineering | M,D |
| Environmental Management and Policy | M,D |
| Environmental Sciences | M |
| Finance and Banking | M |
| Foreign Languages Education | M,D |
| French | M,D |
| Geology | M |
| German | M,D |
| Health Services Management and Hospital Administration | M |
| History | M,D |
| Human Development | M |
| Human Genetics | D |
| Immunology | M,D |
| Latin American Studies | M |
| Law | M,D |
| Liberal Studies | M |
| Management Strategy and Policy | M |
| Marketing | M |
| Materials Sciences | M,D |
| Mathematics | M,D |
| Mechanical Engineering | M,D |
| Microbiology | M,D |
| Molecular Biology | M,D |
| Molecular Physiology | M,D |
| Multilingual and Multicultural Education | D |
| Nursing—General | M,D,O |
| Organizational Management | M |
| Pathology | D |
| Pharmacology | D |
| Philosophy | M,D |
| Physics | M,D |
| Political Science | M,D |
| Portuguese | M,D |
| Psychology—General | D |
| Public Health—General | M |
| Public Policy | D |
| Quantitative Analysis | M |
| Reading Education | M |
| Religion | M,D |
| Secondary Education | M |
| Sociology | M,D |
| Spanish | M,D |
| Special Education | M,D |
| Theology | M |
| Urban and Regional Planning | M |
| Writing | M |

| **VANDERCOOK COLLEGE OF MUSIC** | |
|---|---|
| Music Education | M |

| **VANGUARD UNIVERSITY OF SOUTHERN CALIFORNIA** | |
|---|---|
| Clinical Psychology | M |
| Curriculum and Instruction | M |
| Education—General | M |
| Educational Leadership and Administration | M |
| Industrial and Organizational Psychology | M |
| Nursing—General | M |
| Religion | M |
| Religious Education | M |
| Theology | M |

| **VAUGHN COLLEGE OF AERONAUTICS AND TECHNOLOGY** | |
|---|---|
| Aviation Management | M |

| **VERMONT COLLEGE OF FINE ARTS** | |
|---|---|
| Art Education | M |
| Art/Fine Arts | M |
| Film, Television, and Video Production | M |
| Graphic Design | M |
| Music | M |
| Publishing | M |
| Translation and Interpretation | M |
| Writing | M |

| **VERMONT LAW SCHOOL** | |
|---|---|
| Energy Management and Policy | M |
| Environmental Law | M |
| Environmental Management and Policy | M |
| Law | D |
| Legal and Justice Studies | M |

| **VERMONT TECHNICAL COLLEGE** | |
|---|---|
| Software Engineering | M |

| **VICTORIA UNIVERSITY** | |
|---|---|
| Theology | M,D,O |

| **VILLANOVA UNIVERSITY** | |
|---|---|
| Accounting | M |
| Adult Nursing | M,D,O |
| Applied Statistics | M |
| Artificial Intelligence/Robotics | M,O |
| Biochemical Engineering | M,O |
| Biological and Biomedical Sciences—General | M |
| Business Administration and Management—General | M |
| Business Analytics | M |
| Chemical Engineering | M,O |
| Chemistry | M |
| Civil Engineering | M |
| Classics | M |
| Communication—General | M |
| Computer Engineering | M,O |
| Computer Science | M,O |
| Counselor Education | M |
| Education—General | M |
| Educational Leadership and Administration | M |
| Electrical Engineering | M,O |
| Engineering and Applied Sciences—General | M,D,O |
| English | M |
| Environmental Engineering | M,O |
| Family Nurse Practitioner Studies | M,D,O |
| Finance and Banking | M |
| Gerontological Nursing | M,D,O |
| Health Services Management and Hospital Administration | M |
| Hispanic Studies | M |
| History | M |
| Human Resources Development | M |
| International Business | M |
| Law | D |
| Liberal Studies | M |
| Management Strategy and Policy | M |
| Manufacturing Engineering | M,O |
| Marketing | M |
| Mathematics | M |
| Mechanical Engineering | M,O |
| Missions and Missiology | M |
| Nonprofit Management | M,O |
| Nurse Anesthesia | M,D,O |
| Nursing Education | M,D,O |
| Nursing—General | M,D,O |
| Pediatric Nursing | M,D,O |
| Philosophy | D |
| Political Science | M |
| Psychology—General | M |
| Public Administration | M,O |
| Real Estate | M |
| Taxation | M |
| Theater | M |
| Theology | M,D |
| Water Resources Engineering | M,O |

| **VIRGINIA BAPTIST COLLEGE** | |
|---|---|
| Theology | M |

| **VIRGINIA BEACH THEOLOGICAL SEMINARY** | |
|---|---|
| Pastoral Ministry and Counseling | M |
| Theology | M |

| **VIRGINIA COMMONWEALTH UNIVERSITY** | |
|---|---|
| Accounting | M |
| Adult Education | M |
| Adult Nursing | M,D,O |
| Advertising and Public Relations | M |
| Allied Health—General | D |
| Allopathic Medicine | D |
| Analytical Chemistry | M,D |
| Anatomy | M |
| Applied Mathematics | M |
| Applied Physics | M |
| Art Education | M,D |
| Art History | M,D |
| Art/Fine Arts | M,D |
| Biochemistry | M,D |
| Biological and Biomedical Sciences—General | M,D,O |
| Biomedical Engineering | M,D |
| Biostatistics | M,D |
| Business Administration and Management—General | M,D |
| Chemical Physics | M,D |
| Chemistry | M,D |
| Clinical Laboratory Sciences/Medical Technology | M,D |
| Clinical Psychology | D |
| Communication—General | D |
| Community Health | M,D |
| Computer Science | M,D |
| Counseling Psychology | M,D |
| Counselor Education | M,D |
| Criminal Justice and Criminology | M,O |
| Curriculum and Instruction | D |
| Dentistry | M,D |
| Early Childhood Education | M |
| Economics | M |
| Education—General | M,D,O |
| Educational Leadership and Administration | M,D |
| Educational Measurement and Evaluation | D |
| Educational Media/Instructional Technology | M |
| Educational Psychology | D |
| Elementary Education | M |
| Emergency Management | M,O |
| Engineering and Applied Sciences—General | M,D |
| English | M |
| Environmental Management and Policy | M |
| Epidemiology | M,D |
| Exercise and Sports Science | M |
| Family Nurse Practitioner Studies | M |
| Film, Television, and Video Production | M,D |
| Finance and Banking | M |
| Forensic Sciences | M |
| Geographic Information Systems | O |
| Gerontology | M,D |
| Health Physics/Radiological Health | D |
| Health Psychology | D |
| Health Services Management and Hospital Administration | M,D |
| Health Services Research | D |
| History | M |
| Homeland Security | M,O |
| Human Genetics | M,D |
| Human Resources Development | M |
| Human Resources Management | M |
| Immunology | M,D |
| Inorganic Chemistry | M,D |
| Interdisciplinary Studies | M |
| Interior Design | M,D |
| Journalism | M |
| Management Information Systems | M |
| Mass Communication | M |
| Mathematics | M |
| Mechanical Engineering | M,D |
| Media Studies | M,D |
| Medical Physics | M,D |
| Medicinal and Pharmaceutical Chemistry | M,D |
| Microbiology | M,D |
| Molecular Biology | M,D |
| Molecular Genetics | M,D |
| Museum Studies | M,D |
| Music Education | M |
| Music | M |
| Nanotechnology | M,D |
| Neurobiology | M |
| Neuroscience | M,D,O |
| Nonprofit Management | O |
| Nuclear Engineering | M,D |
| Nurse Anesthesia | M,D |
| Nursing and Healthcare Administration | M,D,O |
| Nursing Education | M,D,O |
| Nursing—General | M,D,O |
| Occupational Therapy | M,D |
| Organic Chemistry | M,D |
| Pediatric Nursing | M,D,O |
| Pharmaceutical Administration | M,D |
| Pharmaceutical Sciences | M,D |
| Pharmacology | M,D,O |
| Pharmacy | D |
| Photography | M,D |
| Physical Chemistry | M,D |
| Physical Therapy | M,D |
| Physics | M |
| Physiology | M,D |
| Political Science | M,D,O |
| Psychiatric Nursing | M,D,O |
| Public Administration | M |
| Public Affairs | M,D,O |
| Public Health—General | M,D |
| Public Policy | D |
| Reading Education | M,O |
| Real Estate | O |
| Recreation and Park Management | M |
| Rehabilitation Counseling | M |
| Rehabilitation Sciences | D |
| Social Work | M,D |
| Sociology | M |
| Special Education | M,D |
| Student Affairs | M |
| Systems Biology | D |
| Theater | M |
| Toxicology | M,D,O |
| Urban and Regional Planning | M |
| Urban Education | D |
| Women's Health Nursing | M,D,O |
| Writing | M |

| **VIRGINIA INTERNATIONAL UNIVERSITY** | |
|---|---|
| Accounting | M,O |
| Advertising and Public Relations | M,O |
| Business Administration and Management—General | M,O |
| Computer and Information Systems Security | M,O |
| Computer Art and Design | M,O |
| Computer Science | M,O |
| Data Science/Data Analytics | M,O |
| Education—General | M |
| English as a Second Language | M |
| Entrepreneurship | M,O |
| Finance and Banking | M,O |
| Game Design and Development | M,O |
| Health Informatics | M,O |
| Health Services Management and Hospital Administration | M,O |
| Hospitality Management | M,O |
| Human Resources Management | M,O |
| International Affairs | M |
| International Business | M,O |
| Linguistics | M |
| Logistics | M,O |
| Management Information Systems | M,O |
| Marketing | M,O |
| Project Management | M,O |
| Public Administration | M |
| Software Engineering | M,O |

| **VIRGINIA POLYTECHNIC INSTITUTE AND STATE UNIVERSITY** | |
|---|---|
| Accounting | M,D |
| Aerospace/Aeronautical Engineering | M,D,O |
| Agricultural Economics and Agribusiness | M,D |
| Agricultural Engineering | M,D |
| Agricultural Sciences—General | M,D,O |
| Agronomy and Soil Sciences | M,D |
| Allopathic Medicine | D |
| Animal Sciences | M,D |
| Applied Economics | M,D |
| Applied Statistics | M,D |
| Biochemistry | M,D |
| Bioengineering | M,D |
| Bioinformatics | M,D |
| Biological and Biomedical Sciences—General | M,D |
| Biomedical Engineering | M,D |
| Biotechnology | M,D |
| Business Administration and Management—General | M,D |
| Business Analytics | M,D |
| Chemical Engineering | M,D |
| Chemistry | M,D |
| Civil Engineering | M,D,O |
| Communication—General | M,D,O |
| Computer and Information Systems Security | M,O |
| Computer Engineering | M,D,O |
| Computer Science | M,D,O |
| Counselor Education | M,D,O |
| Curriculum and Instruction | M,D,O |
| Distance Education Development | M,O |
| Economics | M,D |
| Education—General | M,O |
| Educational Leadership and Administration | M,D,O |
| Educational Measurement and Evaluation | M,D,O |
| Educational Media/Instructional Technology | M,O |
| Educational Policy | M,D,O |
| Electrical Engineering | M,D,O |
| Engineering and Applied Sciences—General | M,D |
| Engineering Management | M,O |
| English | M,D,O |
| Entomology | M,D |
| Environmental Design | M,D |
| Environmental Engineering | M,O |
| Environmental Management and Policy | M,D,O |
| Environmental Sciences | M,O |
| Exercise and Sports Science | M,D |
| Finance and Banking | M,D |
| Fish, Game, and Wildlife Management | M,D |
| Forestry | M,D |
| Genetics | M,D |
| Geography | M,D |
| Geosciences | M,D |
| Horticulture | M,D |
| Humanities | M,D,O |
| Industrial/Management Engineering | M,O |
| Interdisciplinary Studies | M,D |
| International Affairs | M,D |
| Internet and Interactive Multimedia | M,D |
| Landscape Architecture | M,D |
| Liberal Studies | M,O |
| Management Information Systems | M,D,O |
| Marketing | M,D |
| Mathematics | M,D |
| National Security | M,O |
| Natural Resources | M,D,O |
| Nonprofit Management | M,O |
| Nutrition | M,D |
| Ocean Engineering | M,O |
| Physics | M,D |
| Plant Pathology | M,D |
| Plant Physiology | M,D |
| Political Science | M,O |
| Psychology—General | M,D |
| Public Administration | M,D |
| Public Affairs | M,D |
| Public Health—General | M,D |
| Public Policy | M,D |
| Quantitative Analysis | M,O |
| Social Sciences Education | M,D,O |
| Software Engineering | M,O |
| Statistics | M,D |
| Systems Engineering | M,O |
| Translational Biology | M,D |
| Transportation and Highway Engineering | M,O |
| Urban and Regional Planning | M,D |
| Urban Studies | M,D |
| Veterinary Medicine | M,D |
| Veterinary Sciences | M,D |
| Vocational and Technical Education | M,D,O |
| Writing | M,D,O |

| **VIRGINIA STATE UNIVERSITY** | |
|---|---|
| Biological and Biomedical Sciences—General | M |
| Clinical Psychology | M,D |
| Community Health | M,D |
| Counselor Education | M |
| Criminal Justice and Criminology | M |
| Economics | M |
| Education—General | M,D |
| Educational Leadership and Administration | M |
| Health Education | M,D |
| Health Psychology | M,D |
| Interdisciplinary Studies | M |
| Mathematics | M |
| Media Studies | M |
| Psychology—General | M,D |

**VIRGINIA THEOLOGICAL SEMINARY**

| | |
|---|---|
| Educational Leadership and Administration | M,D |
| Theology | M,D |

**VIRGINIA UNION UNIVERSITY**

| | |
|---|---|
| Curriculum and Instruction | M |
| Education—General | M |
| Theology | M,D |

**VIRGINIA UNIVERSITY OF INTEGRATIVE MEDICINE**

| | |
|---|---|
| Acupuncture and Oriental Medicine | M,D,O |
| Nutrition | M,D,O |

**VIRGINIA UNIVERSITY OF LYNCHBURG**

| | |
|---|---|
| Pastoral Ministry and Counseling | M,D |
| Religion | M,D |

**VIRGINIA WESLEYAN UNIVERSITY**

| | |
|---|---|
| Business Administration and Management—General | M |
| Education—General | M |
| Secondary Education | M |

**VITERBO UNIVERSITY**

| | |
|---|---|
| Addictions/Substance Abuse Counseling | M |
| Business Administration and Management—General | M |
| Counseling Psychology | M |
| Developmental Psychology | M |
| Early Childhood Education | M,O |
| Education of the Gifted | M,O |
| Education—General | M,O |
| Educational Leadership and Administration | M,O |
| Ethics | M,O |
| Health Psychology | M |
| Health Services Management and Hospital Administration | M |
| International Business | M |
| Nursing—General | D |
| Organizational Management | M,O |
| Pastoral Ministry and Counseling | M,O |
| Project Management | M |
| Reading Education | M,O |
| Special Education | M,O |

**WAGNER COLLEGE**

| | |
|---|---|
| Accounting | M |
| Business Administration and Management—General | M |
| Early Childhood Education | M |
| Education—General | M |
| Elementary Education | M |
| English Education | M |
| Family Nurse Practitioner Studies | M,D,O |
| Finance and Banking | M |
| Foreign Languages Education | M |
| Higher Education | M |
| Marketing | M |
| Mathematics Education | M |
| Media Studies | M |
| Microbiology | M |
| Middle School Education | M |
| Nursing Education | M,D,O |
| Nursing—General | M,D,O |
| Science Education | M |
| Secondary Education | M |
| Social Sciences Education | M |
| Special Education | M |

**WAKE FOREST UNIVERSITY**

| | |
|---|---|
| Accounting | M |
| Allopathic Medicine | D |
| Analytical Chemistry | M,D |
| Anatomy | D |
| Biochemistry | D |
| Biological and Biomedical Sciences—General | M,D |
| Biomedical Engineering | M,D |
| Business Administration and Management—General | M |
| Business Analytics | M |
| Cancer Biology/Oncology | D |
| Chemistry | M,D |
| Clinical Laboratory Sciences/Medical Technology | M |
| Communication—General | M |
| Computer Science | M |
| Counselor Education | M |
| Education—General | M |
| English | M |
| Exercise and Sports Science | M |
| Genomic Sciences | D |
| Immunology | D |
| Inorganic Chemistry | M,D |
| Law | M,D |
| Liberal Studies | M |
| Mathematics | M |
| Microbiology | D |
| Molecular Genetics | D |
| Molecular Medicine | M,D |
| Neurobiology | D |
| Neuroscience | D |
| Nurse Anesthesia | M |
| Organic Chemistry | M,D |
| Pharmacology | D |
| Physical Chemistry | M,D |
| Physics | M,D |
| Physiology | D |
| Psychology—General | M |
| Religion | M |
| Secondary Education | M |
| Speech and Interpersonal Communication | M |
| Taxation | M |
| Translational Biology | M,D |

**WALDEN UNIVERSITY**

| | |
|---|---|
| Accounting | M,D,O |
| Addictions/Substance Abuse Counseling | M,D |
| Adult Education | M,D,O |
| Adult Nursing | M,D,O |
| Applied Psychology | M,D,O |
| Business Administration and Management—General | M,D,O |
| Child and Family Studies | M,D |
| Clinical Psychology | M,D,O |
| Clinical Research | M,D,O |
| Communication—General | M,D,O |
| Community Health | M,D,O |
| Computer and Information Systems Security | M,D,O |
| Conflict Resolution and Mediation/Peace Studies | M,D,O |
| Counseling Psychology | M,D,O |
| Counselor Education | M,D |
| Criminal Justice and Criminology | M,D,O |
| Curriculum and Instruction | M,D,O |
| Developmental Education | M,D,O |
| Distance Education Development | M,D,O |
| Early Childhood Education | M,D,O |
| Education—General | M,D,O |
| Educational Leadership and Administration | M,D,O |
| Educational Measurement and Evaluation | M,D,O |
| Educational Media/Instructional Technology | M,D,O |
| Educational Psychology | M,D,O |
| Elementary Education | M,D,O |
| Emergency Management | M,D,O |
| English as a Second Language | M,D,O |
| Entrepreneurship | M,D,O |
| Epidemiology | M,D,O |
| Family Nurse Practitioner Studies | M,D,O |
| Finance and Banking | M,D,O |
| Forensic Psychology | M,D,O |
| Gerontological Nursing | M,D,O |
| Gerontology | M,D |
| Health Education | M,D,O |
| Health Informatics | M,D,O |
| Health Promotion | M,D,O |
| Health Psychology | M,D,O |
| Health Services Management and Hospital Administration | M,D,O |
| Higher Education | M,D,O |
| Homeland Security | M,D,O |
| Human Resources Management | M,D,O |
| Human Services | M,D |
| Industrial and Organizational Psychology | M,D,O |
| Interdisciplinary Studies | M,D,O |
| International Affairs | M,D,O |
| International and Comparative Education | M,D,O |
| International Business | M,D,O |
| International Development | M,D,O |
| International Health | M,D,O |
| Law | M,D,O |
| Management Information Systems | M,D,O |
| Marketing | M,D,O |
| Marriage and Family Therapy | M,D |
| Mathematics Education | M,D,O |
| Multilingual and Multicultural Education | M,D,O |
| Nonprofit Management | M,D,O |
| Nursing and Healthcare Administration | M,D,O |
| Nursing Education | M,D,O |
| Nursing Informatics | M,D,O |
| Nursing—General | M,D,O |
| Organizational Management | M,D,O |
| Political Science | M,D,O |
| Project Management | M,D,O |
| Psychology—General | M,D,O |
| Public Administration | M,D,O |
| Public Health—General | M,D,O |
| Public Policy | M,D,O |
| Reading Education | M,D,O |
| Science Education | M,D,O |
| Social Psychology | M,D,O |
| Social Work | M,D |
| Special Education | M,D,O |
| Supply Chain Management | M,D,O |
| Sustainable Development | M,D,O |

**WALDORF UNIVERSITY**

| | |
|---|---|
| Criminal Justice and Criminology | M |
| Educational Leadership and Administration | M |
| Emergency Management | M |
| Human Resources Development | M |
| Organizational Management | M |
| Public Administration | M |
| Sports Management | M |

**WALLA WALLA UNIVERSITY**

| | |
|---|---|
| Biological and Biomedical Sciences—General | M |
| Communication—General | M |
| Curriculum and Instruction | M |
| Education—General | M |
| Educational Leadership and Administration | M |
| Film, Television, and Video Theory and Criticism | M |
| Internet and Interactive Multimedia | M |
| Pastoral Ministry and Counseling | M |
| Reading Education | M |
| Religion | M |
| Social Work | M |
| Special Education | M |

**WALSH COLLEGE OF ACCOUNTANCY AND BUSINESS ADMINISTRATION**

| | |
|---|---|
| Accounting | M |
| Business Administration and Management—General | M |
| Business Analytics | M |
| Computer and Information Systems Security | M |
| Data Science/Data Analytics | M |
| Finance and Banking | M |
| Human Resources Management | M |
| International Business | M |
| Investment Management | M |
| Management Information Systems | M |
| Management of Technology | M |
| Management Strategy and Policy | M |
| Marketing | M |
| Project Management | M |
| Taxation | M |

**WALSH UNIVERSITY**

| | |
|---|---|
| Adult Nursing | M,D |
| Business Administration and Management—General | M |
| Counseling Psychology | M |
| Counselor Education | M |
| Education—General | M |
| Health Services Management and Hospital Administration | M |
| Higher Education | M |
| Marketing | M |
| Nursing and Healthcare Administration | M,D |
| Nursing Education | M,D |
| Nursing—General | M,D |
| Pastoral Ministry and Counseling | M |
| Physical Therapy | D |
| Reading Education | M |
| Religious Education | M |
| Student Affairs | M |
| Theology | M |

**WARNER PACIFIC UNIVERSITY**

| | |
|---|---|
| Education—General | M |
| Human Services | M |
| Nonprofit Management | M |
| Organizational Management | M |

**WARNER UNIVERSITY**

| | |
|---|---|
| Accounting | M |
| Business Administration and Management—General | M |
| Curriculum and Instruction | M |
| Education—General | M |
| Educational Media/Instructional Technology | M |
| Elementary Education | M |
| Human Resources Management | M |
| International Business | M |
| Science Education | M |

**WARREN WILSON COLLEGE**

| | |
|---|---|
| Art/Fine Arts | M |
| Writing | M |

**WARTBURG THEOLOGICAL SEMINARY**

| | |
|---|---|
| Theology | M |

**WASHBURN UNIVERSITY**

| | |
|---|---|
| Accounting | M |
| Addictions/Substance Abuse Counseling | M |
| Business Administration and Management—General | M |
| Clinical Psychology | M |
| Criminal Justice and Criminology | M |
| Curriculum and Instruction | M |
| Education—General | M |
| Educational Leadership and Administration | M |
| Health Education | M |
| Human Services | M |
| Law | M,D |
| Legal and Justice Studies | M,D |
| Liberal Studies | M |
| Nursing and Healthcare Administration | M,D,O |
| Nursing—General | M,D,O |
| Psychology—General | M |
| Reading Education | M |
| Social Work | M |
| Special Education | M |

**WASHINGTON ADVENTIST UNIVERSITY**

| | |
|---|---|
| Business Administration and Management—General | M |
| Counseling Psychology | M |
| Health Services Management and Hospital Administration | M |
| Nursing and Healthcare Administration | M |
| Nursing Education | M |
| Nursing—General | M |
| Public Administration | M |
| Religion | M |

**WASHINGTON & JEFFERSON COLLEGE**

| | |
|---|---|
| Accounting | M,O |
| Applied Economics | M,O |
| Thanatology | M,O |
| Writing | M,O |

**WASHINGTON AND LEE UNIVERSITY**

| | |
|---|---|
| Law | D |

**WASHINGTON STATE UNIVERSITY**

| | |
|---|---|
| Accounting | M |
| Agricultural Economics and Agribusiness | M,D,O |
| Agricultural Engineering | M,D |
| Agronomy and Soil Sciences | M,D,O |
| Allopathic Medicine | M,D |
| American Studies | M,D |
| Animal Sciences | M,D |
| Anthropology | M,D |
| Applied Mathematics | M,D |
| Archaeology | M,D |
| Architecture | M |
| Art/Fine Arts | M |
| Biochemistry | M,D |
| Bioengineering | M,D |
| Bioethics | M,D,O |
| Biological and Biomedical Sciences—General | M,D |
| Biophysics | M,D |
| Business Administration and Management—General | M,D |
| Business Education | M,D |
| Chemical Engineering | M,D |
| Chemistry | M,D |
| Civil Engineering | M,D |
| Clinical Psychology | M,D |
| Clothing and Textiles | M |
| Communication Disorders | M |
| Communication—General | M,D |
| Community Health | M,D,O |
| Computer Engineering | M,D |
| Computer Science | M,D |
| Corporate and Organizational Communication | M,D |
| Counseling Psychology | M,D |
| Criminal Justice and Criminology | M,D |
| Cultural Anthropology | M,D |
| Cultural Studies | M,D |
| Curriculum and Instruction | M,D |
| Economics | M,D,O |
| Education—General | M,D |
| Educational Leadership and Administration | M,D |
| Educational Psychology | M,D |
| Electrical Engineering | M,D |
| Elementary Education | M,D |
| Energy and Power Engineering | M,D |
| Engineering and Applied Sciences—General | M,D,O |
| Engineering Management | M,O |
| English as a Second Language | M,D |
| English | M,D |
| Entomology | M,D |
| Environmental Engineering | M,D |
| Environmental Sciences | M,D |
| Exercise and Sports Science | M |
| Experimental Psychology | M,D |
| Family Nurse Practitioner Studies | M,D,O |
| Food Science and Technology | M,D |
| Foreign Languages Education | M |
| Genetics | M,D |
| Geology | M,D |
| Health Services Management and Hospital Administration | M |
| History | M,D |
| Horticulture | M,D |
| Human Development | D |
| Immunology | M,D |
| Infectious Diseases | M,D |
| Interdisciplinary Studies | D |
| Interior Design | M |
| Landscape Architecture | M |
| Management of Technology | M,O |
| Materials Engineering | M,D |
| Materials Sciences | M,D |
| Mathematics Education | M,D |
| Mathematics | M,D |
| Mechanical Engineering | M,D |
| Music | M |
| Natural Resources | M,D |
| Neuroscience | M,D |
| Nursing—General | M,D,O |
| Nutrition | M |
| Pharmacy | M,D |
| Physics | M,D |
| Plant Pathology | M,D |
| Political Science | M,D,O |
| Psychiatric Nursing | M,D,O |
| Psychology—General | M,D |
| Public Affairs | M,D,O |
| Reading Education | M,D |
| Secondary Education | M,D |
| Sociology | M,D |
| Special Education | M,D |
| Sports Management | M,D |
| Veterinary Medicine | D |
| Veterinary Sciences | M,D |
| Vocational and Technical Education | M,D |

**WASHINGTON UNIVERSITY IN ST. LOUIS**

| | |
|---|---|
| Accounting | M |
| Aerospace/Aeronautical Engineering | M,D |
| Allopathic Medicine | D |
| Anthropology | D |
| Archaeology | M,D |
| Architecture | M |
| Art History | M,D |
| Art/Fine Arts | M |
| Asian Languages | M,D |
| Asian Studies | M,D |
| Biochemistry | D |
| Bioethics | M |
| Biological and Biomedical Sciences—General | D |
| Biomedical Engineering | M,D |
| Biostatistics | M,D,O |
| Business Administration and Management—General | M,D |
| Cell Biology | D |
| Chemical Engineering | M,D |
| Chemistry | D |
| Child and Family Studies | M,D |
| Chinese | M,D |
| Classics | M,D |
| Clinical Research | M |
| Communication Disorders | M,D |
| Comparative Literature | M,D |
| Computational Biology | D |
| Computer Engineering | M,D |
| Computer Science | M,D |
| Dance | M |

*M—masters degree; D—doctorate; O—other advanced degree; *—Close-Up and/or Display*

| | |
|---|---|
| Data Science/Data Analytics | M |
| Developmental Biology | D |
| Developmental Psychology | D |
| Ecology | D |
| Economics | D |
| Education—General | M,D |
| Educational Measurement and Evaluation | D |
| Elementary Education | M |
| Engineering and Applied Sciences—General | M,D |
| English | M,D |
| Entrepreneurship | M |
| Environmental Biology | D |
| Environmental Engineering | M,D |
| Epidemiology | M,D |
| Evolutionary Biology | D |
| Finance and Banking | M,D |
| French | M,D |
| Genetics | M,D |
| Genomic Sciences | D |
| Geosciences | D |
| German | D |
| Gerontology | M,D |
| Health Services Research | M,O |
| History | D |
| Human Genetics | D |
| Immunology | D |
| International Health | M,D |
| Japanese | M,D |
| Jewish Studies | M |
| Kinesiology and Movement Studies | D |
| Landscape Architecture | M |
| Law | M,D |
| Materials Sciences | M,D |
| Mathematics | M,D |
| Mechanical Engineering | M,D |
| Microbiology | D |
| Molecular Biology | D |
| Molecular Biophysics | D |
| Molecular Genetics | D |
| Molecular Pathogenesis | D |
| Music | M,D |
| Near and Middle Eastern Studies | M |
| Neuroscience | D |
| Occupational Therapy | M,D |
| Organizational Management | M |
| Philosophy | D |
| Physical Therapy | D |
| Physics | D |
| Planetary and Space Sciences | D |
| Plant Biology | D |
| Political Science | D |
| Psychology—General | D |
| Public Health—General | M,D |
| Rehabilitation Sciences | D |
| Religion | M |
| Romance Languages | D |
| Secondary Education | M |
| Social Work | M,D |
| Spanish | D |
| Special Education | M,D |
| Speech and Interpersonal Communication | M,D |
| Statistics | M,D |
| Supply Chain Management | M |
| Systems Biology | D |
| Theater | M |
| Urban Design | M |
| Writing | M |

## WATKINS COLLEGE OF ART, DESIGN, & FILM

| | |
|---|---|
| Film, Television, and Video Production | M |

## WAYLAND BAPTIST UNIVERSITY

| | |
|---|---|
| Accounting | M,D |
| Business Administration and Management—General | M,D |
| Counseling Psychology | M |
| Criminal Justice and Criminology | M |
| Education—General | M |
| Educational Leadership and Administration | M |
| Educational Measurement and Evaluation | M |
| Educational Media/Instructional Technology | M |
| Elementary Education | M |
| English as a Second Language | M |
| English Education | M |
| Health Services Management and Hospital Administration | M,D |
| Higher Education | M |
| History | M |
| Homeland Security | M |
| Human Resources Management | M,D |
| Humanities | M |
| International Business | M,D |
| Management Information Systems | M,D |
| Organizational Management | M,D |
| Pastoral Ministry and Counseling | M |
| Project Management | M,D |
| Religion | M |
| Science Education | M |
| Secondary Education | M |
| Social Sciences Education | M |
| Special Education | M |
| Sports Management | M |
| Theology | M |

## WAYNESBURG UNIVERSITY

| | |
|---|---|
| Addictions/Substance Abuse Counseling | M,D |
| Business Administration and Management—General | M,D |
| Clinical Psychology | M,D |
| Counseling Psychology | M,D |
| Counselor Education | M,D |
| Criminal Justice and Criminology | M,D |
| Curriculum and Instruction | M,D |
| Distance Education Development | M,D |
| Educational Leadership and Administration | M,D |
| Educational Media/Instructional Technology | M,D |
| Energy Management and Policy | M,D |
| Finance and Banking | M,D |
| Health Services Management and Hospital Administration | M,D |
| Human Resources Management | M,D |
| Nursing and Healthcare Administration | M,D |
| Nursing Education | M,D |
| Nursing Informatics | M,D |
| Nursing—General | M,D |
| Organizational Management | M,D |
| Special Education | M,D |

## WAYNE STATE COLLEGE

| | |
|---|---|
| Business Administration and Management—General | M |
| Business Education | M |
| Communication—General | M |
| Counselor Education | M |
| Curriculum and Instruction | M |
| Early Childhood Education | M |
| Education—General | M,O |
| Educational Leadership and Administration | M,O |
| Elementary Education | M |
| English as a Second Language | M |
| English Education | M |
| Exercise and Sports Science | M |
| Home Economics Education | M |
| Mathematics Education | M |
| Music Education | M |
| Organizational Management | M |
| Physical Education | M |
| Science Education | M |
| Social Sciences Education | M |
| Special Education | M |
| Sports Management | M |
| Vocational and Technical Education | M |

## WAYNE STATE UNIVERSITY

| | |
|---|---|
| Accounting | M,D,O |
| Acute Care/Critical Care Nursing | M,D |
| Adult Nursing | M,D |
| Advertising and Public Relations | M,D,O |
| African-American Studies | M,D,O |
| Analytical Chemistry | M,D |
| Anthropology | M,D |
| Applied Behavior Analysis | M,D,O |
| Applied Mathematics | M,D |
| Archives/Archival Administration | M,O |
| Art Education | M,D,O |
| Art History | M |
| Art/Fine Arts | M |
| Athletic Training and Sports Medicine | M,D |
| Automotive Engineering | M,O |
| Bioinformatics | M,D |
| Biological and Biomedical Sciences—General | M,D |
| Biomedical Engineering | M,D,O |
| Business Administration and Management—General | M,D,O |
| Chemical Engineering | M,D,O |
| Chemistry | M,D |
| Civil Engineering | M,D |
| Clinical Psychology | M,D |
| Clothing and Textiles | M |
| Cognitive Sciences | M,D |
| Communication Disorders | M,D |
| Communication—General | M,D,O |
| Community Health Nursing | M,D |
| Computational Biology | M,D |
| Computer Engineering | M,D |
| Computer Science | M,D |
| Conflict Resolution and Mediation/Peace Studies | M,D,O |
| Counseling Psychology | M,D,O |
| Counselor Education | M,D,O |
| Criminal Justice and Criminology | M |
| Cultural Studies | M,D |
| Curriculum and Instruction | M,D,O |
| Data Science/Data Analytics | M,D,O |
| Distance Education Development | M,D,O |
| Early Childhood Education | M,D,O |
| Economic Development | M,D,O |
| Economics | M,D |
| Education—General | M,D,O |
| Educational Leadership and Administration | M,D,O |
| Educational Measurement and Evaluation | M,D,O |
| Educational Media/Instructional Technology | M,D,O |
| Educational Policy | M,D,O |
| Educational Psychology | M,D,O |
| Electrical Engineering | M,D |
| Electronic Materials | M |
| Elementary Education | M,D,O |
| Energy and Power Engineering | M,O |
| Engineering and Applied Sciences—General | M,D,O |
| Engineering Management | M,D,O |
| English as a Second Language | M,D,O |
| English Education | M,D,O |
| English | M,D |
| Entrepreneurship | M,D,O |
| Exercise and Sports Science | M,D |
| Film, Television, and Video Theory and Criticism | M,D |
| Finance and Banking | M,D,O |
| Food Science and Technology | M,D,O |
| Foreign Languages Education | M,D,O |
| Foundations and Philosophy of Education | M,D,O |
| French | M,D |
| Gender Studies | M,D,O |
| Geology | M |
| German | M,D |
| Gerontological Nursing | M,D |
| Gerontology | M,D,O |
| Graphic Design | M |
| Health Communication | M,D,O |
| Health Education | M,D |
| Health Services Management and Hospital Administration | M,D |
| Health Services Research | M,D |
| History | M,D,O |
| Human Resources Management | M,D |
| Industrial and Labor Relations | M,D |
| Industrial and Manufacturing Management | M,D |
| Industrial and Organizational Psychology | M,D |
| Industrial Design | M |
| Industrial/Management Engineering | M,D,O |
| Information Studies | M,O |
| Interior Design | M |
| International Economics | M,D |
| Italian | M,D |
| Journalism | M,D,O |
| Kinesiology and Movement Studies | M,D |
| Law | M,D |
| Library Science | M,O |
| Linguistics | M |
| Management Information Systems | M,D,O |
| Management Strategy and Policy | M,D,O |
| Manufacturing Engineering | M,D,O |
| Materials Sciences | M,D,O |
| Maternal and Child/Neonatal Nursing | M,D |
| Mathematics Education | M,D,O |
| Mathematics | M,D,O |
| Mechanical Engineering | M,D |
| Media Studies | M,D,O |
| Medical Imaging | M,D,O |
| Medicinal and Pharmaceutical Chemistry | M,D |
| Multilingual and Multicultural Education | M,D,O |
| Museum Studies | M,D,O |
| Music Education | M,O |
| Music | M,O |
| Near and Middle Eastern Languages | M,D |
| Near and Middle Eastern Studies | M,D |
| Neuroscience | M,D |
| Nonprofit Management | M,D |
| Nurse Anesthesia | M,D,O |
| Nurse Midwifery | M,D |
| Nursing—General | M,D |
| Nutrition | M,D,O |
| Occupational Therapy | M,D,O |
| Organizational Behavior | M,D |
| Organizational Management | M,D |
| Pediatric Nursing | M,D,O |
| Pharmaceutical Sciences | M,D |
| Pharmacology | M,D |
| Pharmacy | D |
| Philosophy | M,D |
| Photography | M |
| Physical Education | M,D |
| Physical Therapy | M,D,O |
| Physician Assistant Studies | M,D,O |
| Physics | M,D |
| Political Science | M,D |
| Polymer Science and Engineering | M,D,O |
| Psychiatric Nursing | M,D |
| Psychology—General | M,D |
| Public Administration | M,D |
| Public History | M,D,O |
| Public Policy | M,D,O |
| Reading Education | M,D,O |
| Rehabilitation Counseling | M,D,O |
| Rhetoric | M,D |
| Romance Languages | M,D |
| School Psychology | M,D,O |
| Science Education | M,D,O |
| Secondary Education | M,D,O |
| Social Psychology | M,D,O |
| Social Sciences Education | M,D,O |
| Social Work | M,D,O |
| Sociology | M,D |
| Spanish | M,D |
| Special Education | M,D,O |
| Sports Management | M,D |
| Statistics | M,D |
| Systems Engineering | M,D,O |
| Taxation | M,D,O |
| Textile Design | M |
| Theater | M |
| Toxicology | M,D |
| Urban and Regional Planning | M,O |
| Urban Studies | M,D,O |
| Women's Health Nursing | M,D |
| Women's Studies | M,D,O |
| Writing | M,D |

## WEBBER INTERNATIONAL UNIVERSITY

| | |
|---|---|
| Accounting | M |
| Business Administration and Management—General | M |
| Criminal Justice and Criminology | M |
| International Business | M |
| Sports Management | M |

## WEBER STATE UNIVERSITY

| | |
|---|---|
| Accounting | M |
| Athletic Training and Sports Medicine | M |
| Business Administration and Management—General | M,O |
| Communication—General | M |
| Computer Engineering | M |
| Curriculum and Instruction | M |
| Education—General | M |
| English | M |
| Health Physics/Radiological Health | M |
| Health Services Management and Hospital Administration | M |
| Legal and Justice Studies | M |
| Nursing and Healthcare Administration | M |
| Nursing Education | M |
| Nursing—General | M |
| Taxation | M |

## WEBSTER UNIVERSITY

| | |
|---|---|
| Accounting | M |
| Advertising and Public Relations | M |
| Aerospace/Aeronautical Engineering | M,D,O |
| Art History | M |
| Art/Fine Arts | M |
| Business Administration and Management—General | M,D,O |
| Communication Disorders | M |
| Communication—General | M,O |
| Computer and Information Systems Security | M |
| Computer Science | M |
| Corporate and Organizational Communication | M |
| Counseling Psychology | M |
| Criminal Justice and Criminology | M,D,O |
| Early Childhood Education | M,O |
| Education—General | M,O |
| Educational Media/Instructional Technology | M,O |
| Educational Psychology | M,O |
| Elementary Education | M,O |
| English as a Second Language | M,O |
| Environmental Management and Policy | M |
| Finance and Banking | M |
| Forensic Sciences | M |
| Gerontology | M |
| Health Services Management and Hospital Administration | M,D,O |
| Human Resources Development | M,D,O |
| Human Resources Management | M,D,O |
| Human Services | M |
| International Affairs | M |
| International Business | M |
| Internet and Interactive Multimedia | M |
| Legal and Justice Studies | M,O |
| Management Information Systems | M,D,O |
| Management of Technology | M,D,O |
| Marketing | M,D,O |
| Mathematics Education | M,O |
| Media Studies | M |
| Middle School Education | M,O |
| Music Education | M |
| Music | M |
| Nonprofit Management | M,D,O |
| Nurse Anesthesia | D |
| Nursing Education | M |
| Nursing—General | M |
| Psychology—General | M |
| Public Administration | M,D,O |
| Reading Education | M,O |
| Secondary Education | M,O |
| Special Education | M,O |

## WEILL CORNELL MEDICINE

| | |
|---|---|
| Biochemistry | M,D |
| Biological and Biomedical Sciences—General | M,D |
| Biophysics | M,D |
| Biostatistics | M |
| Cell Biology | M,D |
| Computational Biology | D |
| Data Science/Data Analytics | M |
| Epidemiology | M |
| Health Informatics | M |
| Health Services Management and Hospital Administration | M |
| Health Services Research | M |
| Immunology | M,D |
| Molecular Biology | M,D |
| Neuroscience | M,D |
| Pharmacology | M,D |
| Physician Assistant Studies | M |
| Physiology | M,D |
| Structural Biology | M,D |
| Systems Biology | M,D |

## WELCH COLLEGE

| | |
|---|---|
| Pastoral Ministry and Counseling | M |
| Theology | M |

## WENTWORTH INSTITUTE OF TECHNOLOGY

| | |
|---|---|
| Architecture | M |
| Civil Engineering | M |
| Computer Science | M |
| Construction Engineering | M |
| Construction Management | M |
| Facilities Management | M |
| Management of Technology | M |
| Transportation and Highway Engineering | M |

## WESLEYAN COLLEGE

| | |
|---|---|
| Business Administration and Management—General | M |
| Early Childhood Education | M |
| Education—General | M |

## WESLEYAN UNIVERSITY

| | |
|---|---|
| Astronomy | M |
| Biochemistry | D |
| Bioinformatics | D |
| Biological and Biomedical Sciences—General | D |
| Cell Biology | D |
| Chemical Physics | D |
| Chemistry | D |
| Computer Science | M,D |
| Developmental Biology | D |
| Ecology | D |
| Environmental Sciences | M |
| Evolutionary Biology | D |
| Genetics | D |
| Genomic Sciences | D |
| Geosciences | M |
| Inorganic Chemistry | D |
| Liberal Studies | M,O |

| | |
|---|---|
| Mathematics | M,D |
| Molecular Biology | D |
| Molecular Biophysics | D |
| Music | M,D |
| Neurobiology | D |
| Organic Chemistry | D |
| Physics | D |
| Theoretical Chemistry | D |
| Writing | M,O |

**WESLEY BIBLICAL SEMINARY**

| | |
|---|---|
| Linguistics | M |
| Missions and Missiology | M |
| Pastoral Ministry and Counseling | M |
| Religion | M |
| Religious Education | M |
| Theology | M |
| Translation and Interpretation | M |

**WESLEY COLLEGE**

| | |
|---|---|
| Business Administration and Management—General | M |
| Education—General | M |
| Environmental Management and Policy | M |
| Nursing—General | M |
| Occupational Therapy | M |

**WESLEY THEOLOGICAL SEMINARY**

| | |
|---|---|
| Theology | M,D |

**WESTCLIFF UNIVERSITY**

| | |
|---|---|
| Business Administration and Management—General | M,D |
| Education—General | M |
| English as a Second Language | M |

**WEST COAST UNIVERSITY**

| | |
|---|---|
| Family Nurse Practitioner Studies | M,D |
| Health Services Management and Hospital Administration | M,D |
| Nursing—General | M,D |
| Occupational Therapy | M,D |
| Pharmacy | M,D |
| Physical Therapy | M,D |

**WESTERN CAROLINA UNIVERSITY**

| | |
|---|---|
| Accounting | M |
| Applied Arts and Design—General | M |
| Art/Fine Arts | M |
| Biological and Biomedical Sciences—General | M |
| Business Administration and Management—General | M |
| Chemistry | M |
| Communication Disorders | M |
| Construction Management | M |
| Education—General | M |
| English as a Second Language | M,O |
| English | M,O |
| Entrepreneurship | M |
| Health Services Management and Hospital Administration | M |
| History | M |
| Industrial/Management Engineering | M |
| Nursing—General | M,D,O |
| Physical Therapy | D |
| Project Management | M,O |
| Psychology—General | M |
| Public Affairs | M |
| Rhetoric | M,O |
| Social Work | M |
| Technical Writing | M,O |
| Writing | M,O |

**WESTERN COLORADO UNIVERSITY**

| | |
|---|---|
| Education—General | M |
| Educational Leadership and Administration | M |
| Environmental Management and Policy | M |
| Film, Television, and Video Production | M |
| Reading Education | M |
| Writing | M |

**WESTERN CONNECTICUT STATE UNIVERSITY**

| | |
|---|---|
| Accounting | M |
| Adult Nursing | M,D |
| Art/Fine Arts | M |
| Business Administration and Management—General | M |
| Clinical Psychology | M |
| Counselor Education | M |
| Curriculum and Instruction | M |
| Education—General | M,D |
| Educational Leadership and Administration | D |
| Educational Media/Instructional Technology | M |
| English | M |
| Geosciences | M |
| Gerontological Nursing | M,D |
| Health Services Management and Hospital Administration | M |
| History | M |
| Illustration | M |
| Mathematics | M |
| Music Education | M |
| Nursing Education | D |
| Nursing—General | M,D |
| Planetary and Space Sciences | M |
| Reading Education | M,D |
| Special Education | M,D |
| Writing | M |

**WESTERN GOVERNORS UNIVERSITY**

| | |
|---|---|
| Accounting | M |
| Business Administration and Management—General | M |
| Computer and Information Systems Security | M |
| Data Science/Data Analytics | M |
| Education—General | M,O |
| Educational Leadership and Administration | M,O |
| Educational Media/Instructional Technology | M,O |
| Elementary Education | M,O |
| English Education | M,O |
| Health Services Management and Hospital Administration | M |
| Information Science | M |
| Management Information Systems | M |
| Management Strategy and Policy | M |
| Mathematics Education | M,O |
| Nursing and Healthcare Administration | M |
| Nursing Education | M |
| Nursing Informatics | M |
| Science Education | M,O |
| Special Education | M,O |

**WESTERN ILLINOIS UNIVERSITY**

| | |
|---|---|
| Accounting | M |
| Applied Statistics | M |
| Biological and Biomedical Sciences—General | M,O |
| Business Administration and Management—General | M,O |
| Chemistry | M |
| Clinical Psychology | M,O |
| Communication Disorders | M |
| Communication—General | M |
| Computer Science | M |
| Counselor Education | M |
| Criminal Justice and Criminology | M,O |
| Curriculum and Instruction | M |
| Distance Education Development | M,O |
| Ecology | D |
| Economic Development | M |
| Economics | M |
| Education—General | M,D,O |
| Educational Leadership and Administration | M,D,O |
| Educational Media/Instructional Technology | M,O |
| English as a Second Language | M,O |
| English | M,O |
| Environmental Sciences | D |
| Experimental Psychology | M,O |
| Foundations and Philosophy of Education | M,O |
| Geographic Information Systems | M,O |
| Geography | M,O |
| Health Education | M |
| Higher Education | M |
| History | M |
| Kinesiology and Movement Studies | M |
| Liberal Studies | M |
| Manufacturing Engineering | M |
| Marine Biology | M,O |
| Mathematics | M |
| Museum Studies | M,O |
| Music | M |
| Physics | M |
| Political Science | M |
| Psychology—General | M,O |
| Public Health—General | M |
| Reading Education | M |
| Recreation and Park Management | M |
| School Psychology | M,O |
| Social Psychology | M,O |
| Social Work | M |
| Sociology | M |
| Special Education | M |
| Sports Management | M |
| Student Affairs | M |
| Supply Chain Management | M,O |
| Theater | M |
| Travel and Tourism | M |
| Zoology | M,O |

**WESTERN KENTUCKY UNIVERSITY**

| | |
|---|---|
| Adult Education | M,D,O |
| Agricultural Sciences—General | M |
| Anthropology | M |
| Applied Economics | M |
| Art Education | M |
| Biological and Biomedical Sciences—General | M |
| Business Administration and Management—General | M |
| Chemistry | M |
| Clinical Psychology | M,O |
| Communication Disorders | M |
| Communication—General | M,O |
| Comparative Literature | M |
| Computer Science | M |
| Corporate and Organizational Communication | M,O |
| Counseling Psychology | M |
| Counselor Education | M |
| Criminal Justice and Criminology | M |
| Early Childhood Education | M,O |
| Education of Students with Severe/Multiple Disabilities | M,O |
| Educational Leadership and Administration | M,D,O |
| Educational Media/Instructional Technology | M,O |
| Elementary Education | M,O |
| English as a Second Language | M |
| English Education | M |
| English | M |
| Experimental Psychology | M,O |
| Foreign Languages Education | M |
| French | M |
| Geology | M |
| Geosciences | M |
| German | M |
| Health Services Management and Hospital Administration | M |
| Higher Education | M |
| History | M |
| Homeland Security | M |
| Industrial and Organizational Psychology | M,O |
| Interdisciplinary Studies | M,O |
| Management of Technology | M |
| Marriage and Family Therapy | M |
| Mathematics | M |
| Middle School Education | M,O |
| Music Education | M |
| Nursing—General | M |
| Physical Education | M |
| Physical Therapy | D |
| Physics | M |
| Political Science | M |
| Psychology—General | M,O |
| Public Administration | M |
| Public Health—General | M |
| Reading Education | M,O |
| Recreation and Park Management | M |
| School Psychology | M,O |
| Secondary Education | M,O |
| Social Work | M |
| Sociology | M |
| Spanish | M |
| Special Education | M,O |
| Sports Management | M |
| Student Affairs | M |
| Writing | M |

**WESTERN MICHIGAN UNIVERSITY**

| | |
|---|---|
| Accounting | M |
| Aerospace/Aeronautical Engineering | M,D |
| Anthropology | M |
| Applied Arts and Design—General | M |
| Applied Economics | M,D |
| Applied Mathematics | M,D |
| Art Education | M |
| Athletic Training and Sports Medicine | M |
| Biological and Biomedical Sciences—General | M,D,O |
| Business Administration and Management—General | M |
| Chemical Engineering | M,D |
| Chemistry | M,D,O |
| Civil Engineering | M |
| Clinical Psychology | M,D |
| Communication Disorders | M,D |
| Communication—General | M |
| Computational Sciences | M |
| Computer Engineering | M,D |
| Computer Science | M,D |
| Counseling Psychology | M,D |
| Counselor Education | M,D |
| Economics | M,D |
| Education—General | M,D,O |
| Educational Leadership and Administration | M,D,O |
| Educational Measurement and Evaluation | M,D,O |
| Educational Media/Instructional Technology | M,D,O |
| Electrical Engineering | M,D |
| Engineering and Applied Sciences—General | M,D |
| Engineering Management | M,D |
| English Education | M,D |
| English | M,D |
| Exercise and Sports Science | M |
| Family and Consumer Sciences-General | M |
| Geographic Information Systems | M,O |
| Geography | M,D,O |
| Geosciences | M,D,O |
| Health Education | D,O |
| Health Services Management and Hospital Administration | M,D,O |
| Higher Education | M,D |
| History | M,D |
| Human Services | D,O |
| Industrial and Organizational Psychology | M,D |
| Industrial/Management Engineering | M,D |
| International Affairs | M,D |
| Manufacturing Engineering | M |
| Mathematics Education | M,D |
| Mathematics | M,D |
| Mechanical Engineering | M,D |
| Music Education | M,O |
| Music | M,O |
| Nonprofit Management | M,D,O |
| Nursing—General | M |
| Occupational Therapy | M |
| Paper and Pulp Engineering | M,D |
| Philosophy | M |
| Physical Education | M |
| Physician Assistant Studies | M |
| Physics | M,D,O |
| Physiology | M |
| Political Science | M,D |
| Psychology—General | M,D |
| Public Administration | M,D,O |
| Public Affairs | M,D,O |
| Reading Education | M,D |
| Rehabilitation Sciences | M |
| Religion | M,O |
| Science Education | M,D,O |
| Social Work | M |
| Sociology | M,D |
| Spanish | M,D |
| Special Education | M,D |
| Sports Management | M |
| Statistics | M,D,O |
| Therapies—Dance, Drama, and Music | M,O |
| Vision Sciences | M |
| Vocational and Technical Education | M |
| Writing | M,D |

**WESTERN MICHIGAN UNIVERSITY COOLEY LAW SCHOOL**

| | |
|---|---|
| Environmental Law | M,D |
| Finance and Banking | M,D |
| Homeland Security | M,D |
| Insurance | M,D |
| Intellectual Property Law | M,D |
| Law | M,D |
| Legal and Justice Studies | M,D |
| National Security | M,D |
| Taxation | M,D |

**WESTERN MICHIGAN UNIVERSITY HOMER STRYKER MD SCHOOL OF MEDICINE**

| | |
|---|---|
| Allopathic Medicine | D |

**WESTERN NEW ENGLAND UNIVERSITY**

| | |
|---|---|
| Accounting | M |
| Advertising and Public Relations | M |
| Applied Behavior Analysis | M,D |
| Business Administration and Management—General | M |
| Civil Engineering | M |
| Communication—General | M |
| Curriculum and Instruction | M |
| Electrical Engineering | M |
| Engineering and Applied Sciences—General | M,D |
| Engineering Management | M,D |
| English Education | M |
| Industrial/Management Engineering | M |
| Law | M,D |
| Manufacturing Engineering | M |
| Mathematics Education | M |
| Mechanical Engineering | M |
| Occupational Therapy | D |
| Organizational Management | M |
| Pharmacy | D |
| Sports Management | M |
| Writing | M |

**WESTERN NEW MEXICO UNIVERSITY**

| | |
|---|---|
| Business Administration and Management—General | M |
| Education—General | M |
| Educational Leadership and Administration | M |
| Elementary Education | M |
| English as a Second Language | M |
| Interdisciplinary Studies | M |
| Multilingual and Multicultural Education | M |
| Occupational Therapy | M |
| Reading Education | M |
| Secondary Education | M |
| Social Work | M |
| Special Education | M |

**WESTERN OREGON UNIVERSITY**

| | |
|---|---|
| Criminal Justice and Criminology | M |
| Early Childhood Education | M |
| Education—General | M |
| Educational Media/Instructional Technology | M |
| Health Education | M |
| Mathematics Education | M |
| Multilingual and Multicultural Education | M |
| Music | M |
| Rehabilitation Counseling | M |
| Science Education | M |
| Secondary Education | M |
| Social Sciences Education | M |
| Special Education | M |

**WESTERN SEMINARY - PORTLAND**

| | |
|---|---|
| Human Resources Development | M |
| Pastoral Ministry and Counseling | M,D,O |
| Religion | M,O |
| Theology | M,O |
| Women's Studies | M |

**WESTERN SEMINARY–SACRAMENTO CAMPUS**

| | |
|---|---|
| Marriage and Family Therapy | M |
| Pastoral Ministry and Counseling | M,O |
| Theology | M,O |
| Women's Studies | O |

**WESTERN SEMINARY - SAN JOSE CAMPUS**

| | |
|---|---|
| Marriage and Family Therapy | M,O |
| Pastoral Ministry and Counseling | M,O |
| Theology | M,O |
| Women's Studies | M,O |

**WESTERN STATE COLLEGE OF LAW AT WESTCLIFF UNIVERSITY**

| | |
|---|---|
| Law | D |

**WESTERN THEOLOGICAL SEMINARY**

| | |
|---|---|
| Pastoral Ministry and Counseling | M,D,O |
| Theology | M,D,O |

**WESTERN UNIVERSITY OF HEALTH SCIENCES**

| | |
|---|---|
| Allied Health—General | M,D |
| Biological and Biomedical Sciences—General | M |
| Dentistry | D |
| Health Education | M |
| Nursing and Healthcare Administration | M |
| Nursing—General | M,D |
| Optometry | D |
| Osteopathic Medicine | D |

*M—masters degree; D—doctorate; O—other advanced degree; *—Close-Up and/or Display*

| | |
|---|---|
| Pharmaceutical Sciences | M |
| Pharmacy | D |
| Physical Therapy | D |
| Physician Assistant Studies | M |
| Podiatric Medicine | D |
| Veterinary Medicine | D |

### WESTERN WASHINGTON UNIVERSITY

| | |
|---|---|
| Adult Education | M |
| Anthropology | M |
| Biological and Biomedical Sciences—General | M |
| Business Administration and Management—General | M |
| Chemistry | M |
| Communication Disorders | M |
| Computer Science | M |
| Counseling Psychology | M |
| Counselor Education | M |
| Education of the Gifted | M |
| Education—General | M |
| Educational Leadership and Administration | M |
| Elementary Education | M |
| English | M |
| Environmental Education | M |
| Environmental Sciences | M |
| Exercise and Sports Science | M |
| Experimental Psychology | M |
| Geography | M |
| Geology | M |
| Higher Education | M |
| History | M |
| Marine Sciences | M |
| Mathematics | M |
| Music | M |
| Physical Education | M |
| Political Science | M |
| Psychology—General | M |
| Rehabilitation Counseling | M |
| Science Education | M |
| Secondary Education | M |

### WESTFIELD STATE UNIVERSITY

| | |
|---|---|
| Accounting | M |
| Applied Behavior Analysis | M |
| Counseling Psychology | M |
| Counselor Education | M |
| Criminal Justice and Criminology | M |
| Early Childhood Education | M |
| Education—General | M |
| Elementary Education | M |
| English | M |
| Forensic Psychology | M |
| Mathematics Education | M |
| Nonprofit Management | M |
| Physical Education | M |
| Physician Assistant Studies | M |
| Psychology—General | M |
| Public Administration | M |
| Reading Education | M |
| Science Education | M |
| Secondary Education | M |
| Social Sciences Education | M |
| Social Work | M |
| Special Education | M |
| Vocational and Technical Education | M |

### WEST LIBERTY UNIVERSITY

| | |
|---|---|
| Accounting | M |
| Biological and Biomedical Sciences—General | M |
| Business Administration and Management—General | M |
| Education of Students with Severe/Multiple Disabilities | M |
| Education—General | M |
| Educational Leadership and Administration | M |
| Organizational Management | M |
| Physical Education | M |
| Physician Assistant Studies | M |
| Reading Education | M |
| Special Education | M |
| Sports Management | M |
| Zoology | M |

### WESTMINSTER COLLEGE (UT)

| | |
|---|---|
| Accounting | M,O |
| Business Administration and Management—General | M,O |
| Counseling Psychology | M |
| Education—General | M |
| Family Nurse Practitioner Studies | M |
| Nurse Anesthesia | M |
| Nursing—General | M |
| Public Health—General | M |

### WESTMINSTER SEMINARY CALIFORNIA

| | |
|---|---|
| Religion | M |
| Theology | M |

### WESTMINSTER THEOLOGICAL SEMINARY

| | |
|---|---|
| Missions and Missiology | M,D,O |
| Pastoral Ministry and Counseling | M,D,O |
| Religion | M,D,O |
| Theology | M,D,O |

### WEST TEXAS A&M UNIVERSITY

| | |
|---|---|
| Accounting | M |
| Agricultural Economics and Agribusiness | M |
| Agricultural Sciences—General | M,D |
| Animal Sciences | M |
| Art/Fine Arts | M |
| Biological and Biomedical Sciences—General | M |
| Business Administration and Management—General | M |
| Chemistry | M |
| Communication Disorders | M |
| Communication—General | M |
| Counselor Education | M |
| Criminal Justice and Criminology | M |
| Curriculum and Instruction | M |
| Economics | M |
| Education—General | M |
| Educational Leadership and Administration | M |
| Educational Measurement and Evaluation | M |
| Educational Media/Instructional Technology | M |
| Engineering and Applied Sciences—General | M |
| English | M |
| Environmental Sciences | M |
| Exercise and Sports Science | M |
| Family Nurse Practitioner Studies | M |
| Finance and Banking | M |
| History | M |
| Interdisciplinary Studies | M |
| Mathematics | M |
| Music | M |
| Nursing—General | M |
| Plant Sciences | M |
| Psychology—General | M |
| Reading Education | M |
| Social Work | M |
| Sports Management | M |

### WEST VIRGINIA SCHOOL OF OSTEOPATHIC MEDICINE

| | |
|---|---|
| Osteopathic Medicine | D |

### WEST VIRGINIA STATE UNIVERSITY

| | |
|---|---|
| Biotechnology | M |
| Criminal Justice and Criminology | M |
| Media Studies | M |

### WEST VIRGINIA UNIVERSITY

| | |
|---|---|
| Accounting | M,D,O |
| Aerospace/Aeronautical Engineering | M,D |
| Agricultural Education | M,D |
| Agricultural Sciences—General | M,D |
| Agronomy and Soil Sciences | M,D |
| Allopathic Medicine | M,D |
| Animal Sciences | M,D |
| Art Education | M,D |
| Art History | M,D |
| Art/Fine Arts | M,D |
| Athletic Training and Sports Medicine | M,D |
| Biochemistry | M,D |
| Biological and Biomedical Sciences—General | M,D |
| Biostatistics | M,D |
| Business Administration and Management—General | M,D,O |
| Business Analytics | M,D,O |
| Cancer Biology/Oncology | M,D |
| Chemical Engineering | M,D |
| Chemistry | M,D |
| Civil Engineering | M,D |
| Clinical Psychology | M,D |
| Communication Disorders | M,D |
| Communication—General | M,D |
| Computer and Information Systems Security | M,D,O |
| Computer Engineering | M,D |
| Computer Science | M,D |
| Corporate and Organizational Communication | M,O |
| Counseling Psychology | M,D |
| Counselor Education | M,D |
| Curriculum and Instruction | M,D |
| Dental Hygiene | M,D |
| Dentistry | M,D |
| Developmental Biology | M,D |
| Early Childhood Education | M,D |
| Economics | M,D,O |
| Education of the Gifted | M,D |
| Education—General | M,D |
| Educational Leadership and Administration | M,D |
| Educational Media/Instructional Technology | M,D |
| Educational Psychology | M,D |
| Electrical Engineering | M,D |
| Elementary Education | M,D |
| Energy and Power Engineering | M,D |
| Engineering and Applied Sciences—General | M,D |
| English Education | M,D |
| English | M,D |
| Entomology | M,D |
| Environmental and Occupational Health | M,D |
| Epidemiology | M,D |
| Exercise and Sports Science | M,D |
| Finance and Banking | M,D,O |
| Fish, Game, and Wildlife Management | M,D |
| Food Science and Technology | M,D |
| Forensic Sciences | M,D |
| Forestry | M,D |
| Genetics | M,D |
| Geography | M,D |
| Geology | M,D |
| Graphic Design | M,D |
| Higher Education | M,D |
| History | M,D |
| Horticulture | M,D |
| Human Services | M,D |
| Immunology | M,D |
| Industrial and Labor Relations | M,D,O |
| Industrial Hygiene | M,D |
| Industrial/Management Engineering | M,D |
| Journalism | M,O |
| Landscape Architecture | M,D |
| Law | M,D |
| Legal and Justice Studies | M,D |
| Marketing | M,D,O |
| Materials Engineering | M,D |
| Materials Sciences | M,D |
| Mathematics | M,D |
| Mechanical Engineering | M,D |
| Media Studies | M,O |
| Mineral/Mining Engineering | M,D |
| Molecular Biology | M,D |
| Music Education | M,D |
| Music | M,D |
| Natural Resources | M,D |
| Nursing—General | M,D,O |
| Nutrition | M,D |
| Occupational Therapy | M,D |
| Oral and Dental Sciences | M,D |
| Pathology | M,D |
| Petroleum Engineering | M,D |
| Pharmaceutical Sciences | D |
| Pharmacy | D |
| Photography | M,D |
| Physical Education | M,D |
| Physical Therapy | M,D |
| Physics | M,D |
| Plant Pathology | M,D |
| Plant Sciences | M,D |
| Political Science | M,D |
| Psychology—General | M,D |
| Public Administration | M,D |
| Public Health—General | M,D |
| Reading Education | M,D |
| Recreation and Park Management | M,D |
| Rehabilitation Counseling | M,D |
| Safety Engineering | M,D |
| Secondary Education | M,D |
| Social Work | M |
| Sociology | M,D |
| Software Engineering | M,D |
| Special Education | M,D |
| Sport Psychology | M,D |
| Sports Management | M,D |
| Statistics | M,D |
| Theater | M,D |
| Travel and Tourism | M,D |
| Writing | M,D |

### WEST VIRGINIA WESLEYAN COLLEGE

| | |
|---|---|
| Athletic Training and Sports Medicine | M |
| Business Administration and Management—General | M |
| Family Nurse Practitioner Studies | M,D,O |
| Nurse Midwifery | M,D,O |
| Nursing and Healthcare Administration | M,D,O |
| Nursing—General | M,D,O |
| Psychiatric Nursing | M,D,O |
| Writing | M |

### WHEATON COLLEGE

| | |
|---|---|
| Archaeology | M,D |
| Clinical Psychology | M,D |
| Counseling Psychology | M,D |
| Education—General | M |
| Elementary Education | M |
| Emergency Management | M |
| Marriage and Family Therapy | M,D |
| Missions and Missiology | M |
| Psychology—General | M,D |
| Religious Education | M |
| Secondary Education | M |
| Theology | M,D |

### WHEELING JESUIT UNIVERSITY

| | |
|---|---|
| Accounting | M |
| Business Administration and Management—General | M |
| Educational Leadership and Administration | M |
| Nursing—General | M |
| Organizational Management | M |
| Physical Therapy | D |

### WHITTIER COLLEGE

| | |
|---|---|
| Child Development | M |
| Education—General | M |
| Educational Leadership and Administration | M |
| Elementary Education | M |
| Secondary Education | M |

### WHITWORTH UNIVERSITY

| | |
|---|---|
| Business Administration and Management—General | M |
| Counselor Education | M |
| Education of the Gifted | M |
| Education—General | M |
| Educational Leadership and Administration | M |
| Elementary Education | M |
| Missions and Missiology | M |
| Pastoral Ministry and Counseling | M |
| Secondary Education | M |
| Special Education | M |
| Theology | M |

### WHU - OTTO BEISHEIM SCHOOL OF MANAGEMENT

| | |
|---|---|
| Business Administration and Management—General | M |

### WICHITA STATE UNIVERSITY

| | |
|---|---|
| Accounting | M |
| Aerospace/Aeronautical Engineering | M,D |
| Allied Health—General | M,D |
| Anthropology | M |
| Applied Mathematics | M,D |
| Art/Fine Arts | M |
| Biological and Biomedical Sciences—General | M |
| Biomedical Engineering | M |
| Business Administration and Management—General | M |
| Chemistry | M,D |
| Clinical Psychology | D |
| Communication Disorders | M,D |
| Communication—General | M |
| Computer Engineering | M,D |
| Computer Science | M,D |
| Counselor Education | M,D,O |
| Criminal Justice and Criminology | M |
| Curriculum and Instruction | M |
| Early Childhood Education | M |
| Economics | M |
| Education of the Gifted | M |
| Education—General | M,D,O |
| Educational Leadership and Administration | M,D,O |
| Educational Psychology | M,D,O |
| Electrical Engineering | M,D |
| Engineering and Applied Sciences—General | M,D |
| Engineering Management | M,D |
| English | M |
| Entrepreneurship | M |
| Environmental Sciences | M |
| Exercise and Sports Science | M |
| Geology | M |
| Gerontology | M |
| History | M |
| Human Services | M |
| Industrial/Management Engineering | M,D |
| International Economics | M |
| Liberal Studies | M |
| Management Information Systems | M |
| Manufacturing Engineering | M,D |
| Mathematics | M,D |
| Mechanical Engineering | M,D |
| Middle School Education | M |
| Music Education | M |
| Music | M |
| Nursing—General | M,D |
| Photography | M |
| Physical Therapy | D |
| Physician Assistant Studies | M |
| Physics | M,D |
| Psychology—General | D |
| Public Administration | M |
| School Psychology | M,D,O |
| Secondary Education | M |
| Social Psychology | D |
| Social Work | M |
| Sociology | M |
| Spanish | M |
| Special Education | M |
| Sports Management | M |
| Supply Chain Management | M |
| Taxation | M |
| Writing | M |

### WIDENER UNIVERSITY

| | |
|---|---|
| Adult Education | M,D |
| Biomedical Engineering | M |
| Business Administration and Management—General | M |
| Chemical Engineering | M |
| Civil Engineering | M |
| Clinical Psychology | D |
| Counselor Education | M,D |
| Criminal Justice and Criminology | M |
| Early Childhood Education | M,D |
| Education—General | M,D |
| Educational Leadership and Administration | M,D |
| Educational Media/Instructional Technology | M,D |
| Educational Psychology | M,D |
| Electrical Engineering | M |
| Elementary Education | M,D |
| Engineering and Applied Sciences—General | M |
| Engineering Management | M |
| English Education | M,D |
| Foundations and Philosophy of Education | M,D |
| Health Education | M,D |
| Health Law | M,D |
| Health Services Management and Hospital Administration | M |
| Law | M,D |
| Mathematics Education | M,D |
| Mechanical Engineering | M |
| Middle School Education | M,D |
| Nursing—General | M,D,O |
| Physical Therapy | M,D |
| Psychology—General | |
| Public Administration | M |
| Reading Education | M,D |
| Science Education | M,D |
| Social Sciences Education | M,D |
| Social Work | M,D |
| Special Education | M,D |
| Taxation | M |

### WILBERFORCE UNIVERSITY

| | |
|---|---|
| Rehabilitation Counseling | M |

### WILFRID LAURIER UNIVERSITY

| | |
|---|---|
| Accounting | M,D |
| American Studies | M,D |
| Biological and Biomedical Sciences—General | M |
| Business Administration and Management—General | M,D |
| Canadian Studies | M,D |
| Chemistry | M |
| Cognitive Sciences | M,D |
| Communication—General | M |
| Conflict Resolution and Mediation/Peace Studies | D |
| Criminal Justice and Criminology | M |
| Cultural Studies | M |
| Developmental Psychology | M,D |
| Economics | M,D |
| English | M,D |
| Environmental Management and Policy | M,D |
| Environmental Sciences | M,D |
| Film, Television, and Video Theory and Criticism | M,D |
| Finance and Banking | M,D |
| Gender Studies | M |

| | |
|---|---|
| Geography | M,D |
| Health Promotion | M |
| History | M,D |
| Human Resources Management | M,D |
| International Affairs | M,D |
| International Economics | M,D |
| Kinesiology and Movement Studies | M |
| Legal and Justice Studies | D |
| Management of Technology | M,D |
| Marketing | M,D |
| Mathematics | M |
| Media Studies | M |
| Neuroscience | M,D |
| Organizational Behavior | M,D |
| Organizational Management | M,D |
| Pastoral Ministry and Counseling | M,D,O |
| Philosophy | M |
| Physical Education | M |
| Political Science | M,D |
| Psychology—General | M,D |
| Public Policy | M |
| Religion | M,D |
| Social Psychology | M,D |
| Social Sciences | M |
| Social Work | M,D |
| Sociology | M |
| Supply Chain Management | M,D |
| Theology | M,D,O |
| Therapies—Dance, Drama, and Music | M |

### WILLAMETTE UNIVERSITY

| | |
|---|---|
| Business Administration and Management—General | M |
| Conflict Resolution and Mediation/Peace Studies | M,D |
| Law | M,D |

### WILLIAM & MARY

| | |
|---|---|
| Accounting | M |
| Business Administration and Management—General | M |
| Business Analytics | M |
| Counselor Education | M,D |
| Curriculum and Instruction | M |
| Education—General | M,D,O* |
| Educational Leadership and Administration | M,D |
| Law | M,D |
| Marine Sciences | M,D |
| Marriage and Family Therapy | M,D |
| School Psychology | M,O |

### WILLIAM CAREY UNIVERSITY

| | |
|---|---|
| Art Education | M,O |
| Business Administration and Management—General | M |
| Counseling Psychology | M |
| Education of the Gifted | M,O |
| Education—General | M,O |
| Elementary Education | M,O |
| English Education | M,O |
| Nursing—General | M |
| Osteopathic Medicine | D |
| Pharmacy | D |
| Psychology—General | M |
| Secondary Education | M,O |
| Social Sciences Education | M,O |
| Special Education | M,O |

### WILLIAM JAMES COLLEGE

| | |
|---|---|
| Applied Psychology | M,D,O |
| Clinical Psychology | M,D,O |
| Community Health | M,D,O |
| Counseling Psychology | M,D,O |
| Forensic Psychology | M,D,O |
| Industrial and Organizational Psychology | M,D,O |
| International Health | M,D,O |
| Psychology—General | M,D,O |
| School Psychology | M,D,O |
| Student Affairs | M,D,O |

### WILLIAM JESSUP UNIVERSITY

| | |
|---|---|
| Education—General | M |
| English Education | M |
| Mathematics Education | M |

### WILLIAM JEWELL COLLEGE

| | |
|---|---|
| Education—General | M |

### WILLIAM PENN UNIVERSITY

| | |
|---|---|
| Organizational Management | M |

### WILLIAMS BAPTIST UNIVERSITY

| | |
|---|---|
| Education—General | M |

### WILLIAMS COLLEGE

| | |
|---|---|
| Art History | M |
| Economic Development | M |

### WILLIAMSON COLLEGE

| | |
|---|---|
| Organizational Management | M |

### WILLIAM WOODS UNIVERSITY

| | |
|---|---|
| Advertising and Public Relations | M,D,O |
| Business Administration and Management—General | M,D,O |
| Curriculum and Instruction | M,D,O |
| Educational Leadership and Administration | M,D,O |
| Educational Media/Instructional Technology | M,D,O |
| Health Services Management and Hospital Administration | M,D,O |
| Human Resources Development | M,D,O |
| Marketing | M,D,O |
| Physical Education | M,D,O |

### WILMINGTON COLLEGE

| | |
|---|---|
| Education—General | M |
| Reading Education | M |
| Special Education | M |

### WILMINGTON UNIVERSITY

| | |
|---|---|
| Accounting | M,D |
| Adult Nursing | M,D |
| Business Administration and Management—General | M,D |
| Clinical Psychology | M |
| Computer and Information Systems Security | M |
| Counseling Psychology | M |
| Counselor Education | M,D |
| Criminal Justice and Criminology | M |
| Education of the Gifted | M,D |
| Education—General | M,D |
| Educational Leadership and Administration | M,D |
| Educational Media/Instructional Technology | M,D |
| Elementary Education | M,D |
| English as a Second Language | M,D |
| Environmental Management and Policy | M,D |
| Family Nurse Practitioner Studies | M,D |
| Finance and Banking | M,D |
| Gerontological Nursing | M,D |
| Health Services Management and Hospital Administration | M,D |
| Higher Education | M,D |
| Homeland Security | M,D |
| Human Resources Management | M,D |
| Human Services | M |
| Internet and Interactive Multimedia | M |
| Internet Engineering | M |
| Management Information Systems | M,D |
| Marketing | M,D |
| Nursing and Healthcare Administration | M,D |
| Nursing—General | M,D |
| Organizational Management | M,D |
| Project Management | M |
| Public Administration | M,D |
| Reading Education | M,D |
| Secondary Education | M,D |
| Special Education | M,D |
| Vocational and Technical Education | M,D |

### WILSON COLLEGE

| | |
|---|---|
| Accounting | M |
| Art/Fine Arts | M |
| Business Administration and Management—General | M |
| Cultural Studies | M |
| Dance | M |
| Education—General | M |
| Educational Media/Instructional Technology | M |
| Elementary Education | M |
| English | M |
| Health Services Management and Hospital Administration | M |
| Humanities | M |
| Nursing and Healthcare Administration | M |
| Nursing Education | M |
| Nursing—General | M |
| Secondary Education | M |
| Special Education | M |
| Women's Studies | M |

### WINEBRENNER THEOLOGICAL SEMINARY

| | |
|---|---|
| Counseling Psychology | M,D |
| Theology | M,D |

### WINGATE UNIVERSITY

| | |
|---|---|
| Accounting | M |
| Business Administration and Management—General | M |
| Community College Education | M,D,O |
| Education—General | M,D,O |
| Educational Leadership and Administration | M,D,O |
| Elementary Education | M,D,O |
| Entrepreneurship | M |
| Finance and Banking | M |
| Health Services Management and Hospital Administration | M |
| Marketing | M |
| Pharmacy | D |
| Physical Therapy | D |
| Physician Assistant Studies | M |
| Project Management | M |
| Sports Management | M |

### WINONA STATE UNIVERSITY

| | |
|---|---|
| Acute Care/Critical Care Nursing | M,D,O |
| Addictions/Substance Abuse Counseling | M,O |
| Adult Nursing | M,D,O |
| Clinical Psychology | M,O |
| Counselor Education | M,O |
| Education—General | O |
| Educational Leadership and Administration | M,O |
| English as a Second Language | M |
| English | M |
| Family Nurse Practitioner Studies | M,D,O |
| Gerontological Nursing | M,D,O |
| Human Services | M,O |
| Multilingual and Multicultural Education | O |
| Nursing and Healthcare Administration | M,D,O |
| Nursing Education | M,D,O |
| Nursing—General | M,D,O |
| Organizational Management | M,D,O |
| Special Education | M |
| Sports Management | M,O |

### WINSTON-SALEM STATE UNIVERSITY

| | |
|---|---|
| Business Administration and Management—General | M |
| Computer Science | M |
| Education—General | M |
| Family Nurse Practitioner Studies | M,D |
| Health Services Management and Hospital Administration | M |
| Management Information Systems | M |
| Middle School Education | M |
| Nursing Education | M,D |
| Nursing—General | M,D |
| Occupational Therapy | M |
| Physical Therapy | D |
| Rehabilitation Counseling | M |
| Special Education | M |

### WINTHROP UNIVERSITY

| | |
|---|---|
| Art Education | M |
| Art/Fine Arts | M |
| Arts Administration | M |
| Biological and Biomedical Sciences—General | M |
| Business Administration and Management—General | M |
| Counselor Education | M |
| Education—General | M |
| Educational Leadership and Administration | M |
| English | M |
| History | M |
| Liberal Studies | M |
| Music Education | M |
| Music | M |
| Nutrition | M,O |
| Physical Education | M |
| Psychology—General | M,O |
| Secondary Education | M |
| Social Work | M |
| Special Education | M |

### WISCONSIN LUTHERAN COLLEGE

| | |
|---|---|
| Curriculum and Instruction | M |
| Educational Leadership and Administration | M |
| Educational Media/Instructional Technology | M |
| Science Education | M |

### WISCONSIN SCHOOL OF PROFESSIONAL PSYCHOLOGY

| | |
|---|---|
| Clinical Psychology | M,D |
| Psychology—General | M,D |

### WITTENBERG UNIVERSITY

| | |
|---|---|
| Education—General | M |

### WONGU UNIVERSITY OF ORIENTAL MEDICINE

| | |
|---|---|
| Acupuncture and Oriental Medicine | M |

### WON INSTITUTE OF GRADUATE STUDIES

| | |
|---|---|
| Acupuncture and Oriental Medicine | M,O |
| Religion | M |

### WOODBURY UNIVERSITY

| | |
|---|---|
| Architecture | M |
| Business Administration and Management—General | M |
| Organizational Management | M |

### WOODS HOLE OCEANOGRAPHIC INSTITUTION

| | |
|---|---|
| Marine Biology | D |
| Marine Geology | D |
| Ocean Engineering | D |
| Oceanography | D |

### WORCESTER POLYTECHNIC INSTITUTE

| | |
|---|---|
| Aerospace/Aeronautical Engineering | M,D |
| Applied Mathematics | M,D,O |
| Applied Statistics | M,D,O |
| Artificial Intelligence/Robotics | M,D |
| Biochemistry | M,D |
| Bioinformatics | M,D |
| Biological and Biomedical Sciences—General | M,D |
| Biomedical Engineering | M,D,O |
| Biotechnology | M,D |
| Business Administration and Management—General | M,D,O |
| Chemical Engineering | M,D |
| Chemistry | M,D |
| Civil Engineering | M,D,O |
| Computational Biology | M,D |
| Computer Engineering | M,D,O |
| Computer Science | M,D,O |
| Data Science/Data Analytics | M,D,O |
| Educational Media/Instructional Technology | M,D |
| Electrical Engineering | M,D,O |
| Energy and Power Engineering | M,D,O |
| Engineering and Applied Sciences—General | M,D,O |
| Engineering Design | M,D,O |
| Environmental Engineering | M,D,O |
| Fire Protection Engineering | M,D,O |
| Game Design and Development | M |
| Interdisciplinary Studies | M,D,O |
| Internet and Interactive Multimedia | M |
| Management Information Systems | M,D,O |
| Manufacturing Engineering | M,D |
| Marketing | M,D,O |
| Materials Engineering | M,D |
| Materials Sciences | M,D |
| Mathematics | M,D,O |
| Mechanical Engineering | M,D,O |
| Modeling and Simulation | M,D,O |
| Nuclear Engineering | M,D,O |
| Organizational Management | M,D,O |
| Physics | M,D |
| Social Sciences | M,D,O |
| Supply Chain Management | M,D,O |
| Systems Engineering | M,D,O |
| Systems Science | M,D,O |

### WORCESTER STATE UNIVERSITY

| | |
|---|---|
| Accounting | M |
| Biotechnology | M |
| Business Administration and Management—General | M |
| Communication Disorders | M |
| Community Health Nursing | M |
| Curriculum and Instruction | M,O |
| Early Childhood Education | M,O |
| Education—General | M,O |
| Educational Leadership and Administration | M,O |
| Elementary Education | M,O |
| English as a Second Language | M,O |
| English Education | M |
| Foreign Languages Education | M |
| Health Education | M,O |
| Health Services Management and Hospital Administration | M |
| History | M |
| Marketing | M |
| Middle School Education | M,O |
| Nonprofit Management | M |
| Nursing Education | M |
| Occupational Therapy | M |
| Organizational Management | M |
| Reading Education | M,O |
| School Psychology | M,O |
| Secondary Education | M,O |
| Social Sciences Education | M |
| Spanish | M |
| Special Education | M,O |

### WORLD MISSION UNIVERSITY

| | |
|---|---|
| Music | M,D |
| Pastoral Ministry and Counseling | M,D |
| Theology | M,D |

### WRIGHT GRADUATE UNIVERSITY FOR THE REALIZATION OF HUMAN POTENTIAL

| | |
|---|---|
| Human Development | M,D,O |

### THE WRIGHT INSTITUTE

| | |
|---|---|
| Clinical Psychology | D |
| Counseling Psychology | M |
| Psychology—General | D |

### WRIGHT STATE UNIVERSITY

| | |
|---|---|
| Accounting | M |
| Acute Care/Critical Care Nursing | M |
| Adult Nursing | M |
| Aerospace/Aeronautical Engineering | M |
| Allopathic Medicine | D |
| Anatomy | M |
| Applied Behavior Analysis | M |
| Applied Economics | M |
| Applied Mathematics | M |
| Applied Statistics | M |
| Biochemistry | M |
| Biological and Biomedical Sciences—General | M,D |
| Biomedical Engineering | M |
| Business Administration and Management—General | M |
| Chemistry | M |
| Clinical Psychology | D |
| Computer Engineering | M,D |
| Computer Science | M,D |
| Counselor Education | M |
| Criminal Justice and Criminology | M |
| Curriculum and Instruction | O |
| Economics | M |
| Education—General | M,O |
| Educational Leadership and Administration | O |
| Electrical Engineering | M |
| Elementary Education | M |
| Engineering and Applied Sciences—General | M,D |
| English | M |
| Environmental Sciences | D |
| Ergonomics and Human Factors | M,D |
| Family Nurse Practitioner Studies | M |
| Geology | O |
| Geophysics | M |
| Gerontological Nursing | M |
| Health Education | M |
| Health Promotion | M |
| History | M |
| Humanities | M |
| Immunology | M |
| Industrial and Organizational Psychology | M,D |
| Industrial/Management Engineering | M |
| Logistics | M |
| Management Information Systems | M |
| Materials Engineering | M |
| Materials Sciences | M |
| Maternal and Child/Neonatal Nursing | M |
| Mathematics Education | D |
| Mathematics | M |
| Mechanical Engineering | M |
| Microbiology | M |
| Molecular Biology | M |
| Music Education | M |
| Neuroscience | M |
| Nursing and Healthcare Administration | M |
| Nursing—General | M |
| Pediatric Nursing | M |
| Pharmacology | M |
| Physics | M |
| Physiology | M |

*M—masters degree; D—doctorate; O—other advanced degree; *—Close-Up and/or Display*

Psychiatric Nursing M
Psychology—General M,D
Public Administration M
Public Health—General M
Rehabilitation Counseling M
School Nursing M
Science Education M,D
Secondary Education M
Special Education M
Supply Chain Management M
Toxicology M

**WYCLIFFE COLLEGE**

Religion M,D,O
Theology M,D,O

**XAVIER UNIVERSITY**

Accounting M
Athletic Training and Sports Medicine M
Business Administration and Management—General M
Clinical Psychology M,D
Counseling Psychology M
Counselor Education M
Criminal Justice and Criminology M
Early Childhood Education M
Education—General M,D
Educational Leadership and Administration M,D
Elementary Education M
English M
Ethics M
Finance and Banking M
Health Services Management and Hospital Administration M*
Human Resources Development M,D
Industrial and Organizational Psychology M,D
International Business M
Management Strategy and Policy M
Marketing M
Multilingual and Multicultural Education M
Nursing—General M,D,O
Occupational Therapy M
Pastoral Ministry and Counseling M
Psychology—General M,D
Reading Education M
Religious Education M
Secondary Education M
Special Education M
Sports Management M
Sustainable Development M
Theology M

**XAVIER UNIVERSITY OF LOUISIANA**

Counselor Education M
Curriculum and Instruction M
Education—General M
Educational Leadership and Administration M
Pastoral Ministry and Counseling M
Pharmacy D
Theology M

**YALE UNIVERSITY**

Accounting D
African Studies M
African-American Studies D
Allopathic Medicine D
American Studies D
Anthropology M,D
Applied Arts and Design—General M
Applied Mathematics M,D
Applied Physics M,D
Archaeology M
Architecture M,D
Art History D
Art/Fine Arts M
Asian Languages D
Asian Studies M
Astronomy M,D
Astrophysics M,D
Atmospheric Sciences D
Biochemistry D
Bioinformatics D
Biological and Biomedical Sciences—General D
Biomedical Engineering M,D
Biophysics D
Biostatistics M,D
Business Administration and Management—General M,D
Cell Biology D
Chemical Engineering M,D
Chemistry D
Classics M,D
Clinical Psychology D
Cognitive Sciences D
Comparative Literature D
Computational Biology D
Computer Science M,D
Developmental Biology D
Developmental Psychology D
East European and Russian Studies M,D
Ecology D
Economic Development M
Economics M,D
Electrical Engineering M,D
Engineering and Applied Sciences—General M,D
Engineering Physics M,D
English M,D
Environmental and Occupational Health M,D
Environmental Design M,D
Environmental Engineering M,D
Environmental Management and Policy M,D
Environmental Sciences M,D
Epidemiology M,D
Evolutionary Biology D
Film, Television, and Video Theory and Criticism D
Finance and Banking D
Forestry M,D
French M,D
Genetics D
Genomic Sciences D
Geochemistry D
Geology D
Geophysics D
Geosciences D
German D
Graphic Design M
Health Services Management and Hospital Administration M,D
History of Medicine M,D
History of Science and Technology M,D
History M,D
Immunology D
Infectious Diseases D
Inorganic Chemistry D
International Affairs M
International Economics M
International Health M,D
Italian D
Latin American Studies D
Law M,D
Linguistics D
Marketing D
Mathematics M,D
Mechanical Engineering M,D
Medieval and Renaissance Studies M,D
Meteorology D
Microbiology D
Molecular Biology D
Molecular Biophysics D
Molecular Medicine D
Molecular Physiology D
Music M,D,O
Near and Middle Eastern Languages M,D
Near and Middle Eastern Studies M,D
Neurobiology D
Neuroscience D
Nursing—General M,D,O
Oceanography D
Organic Chemistry D
Organizational Management D
Paleontology D
Pathology M,D
Pharmacology D
Philosophy D
Photography M
Physical Chemistry D
Physician Assistant Studies M
Physics D
Physiology D
Planetary and Space Sciences M,D
Plant Biology D
Political Science D
Portuguese D
Psychology—General D
Public Health—General M,D
Religion D
Russian D
Slavic Languages D
Social Psychology D
Social Sciences M,D
Sociology D
Spanish D
Statistics M,D
Theater M,D,O
Theology M
Theoretical Chemistry D
Virology D
Writing M,D,O

**YESHIVA BETH MOSHE**

Theology O

**YESHIVA DERECH CHAIM**

Religion D

**YESHIVA KARLIN STOLIN**

Theology O

**YESHIVA OF NITRA RABBINICAL COLLEGE**

Theology O

**YESHIVA SHAAR HATORAH TALMUDIC RESEARCH INSTITUTE**

Theology

**YESHIVATH ZICHRON MOSHE**

Theology O

**YESHIVA UNIVERSITY**

Accounting M
Biotechnology M
Business Administration and Management—General M
Clinical Psychology D
Communication Disorders M
Conflict Resolution and Mediation/Peace Studies M,D
Counseling Psychology M
Data Science/Data Analytics M
Economics M
Educational Leadership and Administration M,D,O
Health Psychology D
Intellectual Property Law M,D
Jewish Studies M,D
Law M,D
Marketing M
Mathematics M
Psychology—General M,D
Religious Education M,D,O
Risk Management M
School Psychology D
Social Work M,D
Taxation M

**YORK COLLEGE OF PENNSYLVANIA**

Business Administration and Management—General M
Education—General M
Educational Leadership and Administration M
Educational Media/Instructional Technology M
Finance and Banking M
Gerontological Nursing M
Health Services Management and Hospital Administration M
Nurse Anesthesia M
Nursing—General M
Reading Education M

**YORK COLLEGE OF THE CITY UNIVERSITY OF NEW YORK**

Pharmaceutical Sciences M
Physician Assistant Studies M

**YORK UNIVERSITY**

Accounting M,D
Anthropology M,D
Applied Arts and Design—General M
Applied Mathematics M,D
Art History M,D
Art/Fine Arts M,D
Astronomy M,D
Biological and Biomedical Sciences—General M,D
Business Administration and Management—General M,D
Business Analytics M,D
Chemistry M,D
Communication—General M,D
Computer Science M,D
Dance M,D
Disability Studies M,D
Economics M,D
Education—General M,D
Emergency Management M
English M,D
Environmental Management and Policy M,D
Film, Television, and Video Production M,D
Finance and Banking M,D
French M,D
Gender Studies M,D
Geography M,D
Geosciences M,D
History M,D
Human Resources Management M,D
Humanities M,D
Interdisciplinary Studies M
International Affairs M
International Business M,D
Kinesiology and Movement Studies M,D
Law M,D
Linguistics M,D
Mathematics M,D
Music M,D
Nursing—General M
Philosophy M,D
Physics M,D
Planetary and Space Sciences M,D
Political Science M,D
Psychology—General M,D
Public Administration M
Public Affairs M
Public Policy M
Social Work M,D
Sociology M,D
Statistics M,D
Theater M,D
Translation and Interpretation M
Women's Studies M,D

**YO SAN UNIVERSITY OF TRADITIONAL CHINESE MEDICINE**

Acupuncture and Oriental Medicine M

**YOUNGSTOWN STATE UNIVERSITY**

Accounting M
Actuarial Science M
American Studies M
Analytical Chemistry M
Anatomy M
Applied Mathematics M
Athletic Training and Sports Medicine M
Biochemistry M
Biological and Biomedical Sciences—General M
Business Administration and Management—General M
Chemistry M
Civil Engineering M
Computer Engineering M
Computer Science M
Counselor Education M,D,O
Criminal Justice and Criminology M
Curriculum and Instruction M
Economics M
Education—General M,D,O
Educational Leadership and Administration M,D,O
Electrical Engineering M
Engineering and Applied Sciences—General M,O
English M
Environmental Biology M
Environmental Engineering M
Environmental Management and Policy M,O
Finance and Banking M
Gerontology M
Health Services Management and Hospital Administration M
History M
Human Services M
Industrial/Management Engineering M
Information Science M
Inorganic Chemistry M
Mathematics Education M
Mathematics M
Mechanical Engineering M
Microbiology M
Molecular Biology M
Music Education M
Music M
Nursing—General M
Organic Chemistry M
Physical Chemistry M
Physical Therapy D
Physiology M
Public Health—General M
Reading Education M
School Psychology M,D,O
Science Education M
Social Work M
Special Education M
Statistics M
Supply Chain Management O
Systems Engineering M

# PROFILES OF INSTITUTIONS OFFERING GRADUATE AND PROFESSIONAL WORK

## ABILENE CHRISTIAN UNIVERSITY, Abilene, TX 79699

**General Information** Independent-religious, coed, university. CGS member. *Enrollment:* 5,292 graduate, professional, and undergraduate students; 1,150 full-time matriculated graduate/professional students (811 women), 638 part-time matriculated graduate/professional students (428 women). *Enrollment by degree level:* 1,068 master's, 686 doctoral, 34 other advanced degrees. *Graduate faculty:* 52 full-time (25 women), 160 part-time/adjunct (80 women). *Tuition:* Full-time $22,356; part-time $1242 per credit hour. Tuition and fees vary according to program. *Graduate housing:* On-campus housing not available. *Student services:* Campus employment opportunities, campus safety program, career counseling, exercise/wellness program, grant writing training, international student services, low-cost health insurance, multicultural affairs office, services for students with disabilities, teacher training, writing training. *Library facilities:* Brown Library. *Collection:* Books: 532,096 (physical), 489,972 (digital/electronic); Serial titles: 5,941 (physical), 58,956 (digital/electronic); Databases: 113. Weekly public service hours: 97; students can reserve study rooms. *Research affiliation:* Los Alamos National Laboratory (particle physics), Fermilab (peanut toxins).

**Computer facilities:** Computer purchase and lease plans are available. 500 computers available on campus for general student use. A campuswide network can be accessed from student residence rooms and from off campus. Online class registration is available.
Website: http://www.acu.edu/

**General Application Contact:** Graduate Admissions, 325-674-6911, E-mail: gradinfo@acu.edu.

**GRADUATE UNITS**

**College of Graduate and Professional Studies** Students: 719 full-time (508 women), 513 part-time (375 women); includes 653 minority (364 Black or African American, non-Hispanic/Latino; 6 American Indian or Alaska Native, non-Hispanic/Latino; 15 Asian, non-Hispanic/Latino; 223 Hispanic/Latino; 2 Native Hawaiian or other Pacific Islander, non-Hispanic/Latino; 43 Two or more races, non-Hispanic/Latino), 15 international. 335 applicants, 98% accepted, 248 enrolled. *Faculty:* 29 full-time (14 women), 80 part-time/adjunct (41 women). Expenses: Contact institution. *Financial support:* In 2019–20, 220 students received support. Scholarships/grants available. Support available to part-time students. Financial award application deadline: 7/1; financial award applicants required to submit FAFSA. In 2019, 199 master's, 25 doctorates, 33 other advanced degrees awarded. *Program availability:* Part-time, online only, 100% online, blended/hybrid learning. *Application deadline:* For fall admission, 10/7 for domestic students; for winter admission, 12/20 for domestic students; for spring admission, 2/24 for domestic students; for summer admission, 4/20 for domestic students. Applications are processed on a rolling basis. *Application fee:* $50. *Application Contact:* Graduate Advisor, 855-219-7300, E-mail: onlineadmissions@acu.edu. *Dean*, Dr. Joe Cope, 214-305-9508, E-mail: copej@acu.edu.

**Office of Graduate Programs** Students: 431 full-time (303 women), 125 part-time (53 women); includes 169 minority (63 Black or African American, non-Hispanic/Latino; 1 American Indian or Alaska Native, non-Hispanic/Latino; 8 Asian, non-Hispanic/Latino; 75 Hispanic/Latino; 22 Two or more races, non-Hispanic/Latino), 19 international. 1,568 applicants, 31% accepted, 250 enrolled. *Faculty:* 23 full-time (11 women), 80 part-time/adjunct (39 women). Expenses: Contact institution. *Financial support:* In 2019–20, 232 students received support, including 71 research assistantships with partial tuition reimbursements available, 8 teaching assistantships with partial tuition reimbursements available; career-related internships or fieldwork, Federal Work-Study, and scholarships/grants also available. Support available to part-time students. Financial award application deadline: 4/1; financial award applicants required to submit FAFSA. In 2019, 225 master's, 2 doctorates, 11 other advanced degrees awarded. *Program availability:* Part-time, evening/weekend, online learning. *Application deadline:* For fall admission, 4/1 priority date for domestic students; for spring admission, 11/1 priority date for domestic students. Applications are processed on a rolling basis. *Application fee:* $65. Electronic applications accepted. *Application Contact:* Graduate Admissions, 325-674-6911, E-mail: gradinfo@acu.edu. *Assistant Provost for Graduate Programs*, Dr. Donnie Snider, 325-674-2223, E-mail: gradinfo@acu.edu.

***COBA Accounting and Finance Department*** Students: 5 full-time (1 woman), 6 part-time (1 woman). 47 applicants, 28% accepted, 9 enrolled. *Faculty:* 6 part-time/adjunct (0 women). Expenses: Contact institution. *Financial support:* In 2019–20, 4 students received support. Federal Work-Study and scholarships/grants available. Support available to part-time students. Financial award application deadline: 4/1; financial award applicants required to submit FAFSA. In 2019, 44 master's awarded. *Program availability:* Part-time. *Application deadline:* For fall admission, 8/10 for domestic students; for spring admission, 11/1 for domestic students. Applications are processed on a rolling basis. *Application fee:* $65. Electronic applications accepted. *Application Contact:* Graduate Admissions, 325-674-6911, E-mail: gradinfo@acu.edu. *Graduate Director*, John Neill, 325-674-2053, Fax: 325-674-2507, E-mail: john.neill@acu.edu.

***College of Arts and Sciences*** Students: 36 full-time (28 women), 15 part-time (13 women); includes 15 minority (5 Black or African American, non-Hispanic/Latino; 7 Hispanic/Latino; 3 Two or more races, non-Hispanic/Latino), 4 international. 155 applicants, 25% accepted, 16 enrolled. *Faculty:* 26 part-time/adjunct (9 women). Expenses: Contact institution. *Financial support:* In 2019–20, 38 students received support, including 32 research assistantships with partial tuition reimbursements available, 8 teaching assistantships with partial tuition reimbursements available; career-related internships or fieldwork, Federal Work-Study, and scholarships/grants also available. Support available to part-time students. Financial award application deadline: 4/1; financial award applicants required to submit FAFSA. In 2019, 27 master's awarded. *Program availability:* Part-time. *Application deadline:* For fall admission, 4/10 priority date for domestic students; for spring admission, 11/1 for domestic students. Applications are processed on a rolling basis. *Application fee:* $65. Electronic applications accepted. *Application Contact:* Graduate Admissions, 325-674-6911, E-mail: gradinfo@acu.edu. *Dean*, Dr. Greg Straughn, 325-674-2209, Fax: 325-674-6800, E-mail: cas@acu.edu.

***College of Biblical Studies*** Students: 138 full-time (41 women), 87 part-time (24 women); includes 67 minority (37 Black or African American, non-Hispanic/Latino; 1 Asian, non-Hispanic/Latino; 24 Hispanic/Latino; 5 Two or more races, non-Hispanic/Latino), 12 international. 229 applicants, 51% accepted, 81 enrolled. *Faculty:* 17 full-time (6 women), 15 part-time/adjunct (5 women). Expenses: Contact institution. *Financial support:* In 2019–20, 61 students received support, including 18 research assistantships with partial tuition reimbursements available; career-related internships or fieldwork, Federal Work-Study, and scholarships/grants also available. Support available to part-time students. Financial award application deadline: 4/1; financial award applicants required to submit FAFSA. In 2019, 35 master's, 2 doctorates awarded. *Program availability:* Part-time, evening/weekend, blended/hybrid learning. *Application deadline:* For fall admission, 2/15 priority date for domestic students; for spring admission, 11/1 for domestic students. Applications are processed on a rolling basis. *Application fee:* $65. Electronic applications accepted. *Application Contact:* Graduate Admissions, 325-674-6911, E-mail: gradinfo@acu.edu. *Dean*, Dr. Ken Cukrowski, 325-674-3700, Fax: 325-674-3776, E-mail: cukrowski@bible.acu.edu.

***College of Education and Human Services*** Students: 252 full-time (233 women), 17 part-time (15 women); includes 87 minority (21 Black or African American, non-Hispanic/Latino; 1 American Indian or Alaska Native, non-Hispanic/Latino; 7 Asian, non-Hispanic/Latino; 44 Hispanic/Latino; 14 Two or more races, non-Hispanic/Latino), 3 international. 1,137 applicants, 28% accepted, 144 enrolled. *Faculty:* 6 full-time (5 women), 33 part-time/adjunct (25 women). Expenses: Contact institution. *Financial support:* In 2019–20, 129 students received support, including 21 research assistantships with partial tuition reimbursements available; career-related internships or fieldwork, Federal Work-Study, institutionally sponsored loans, and scholarships/grants also available. Support available to part-time students. Financial award application deadline: 4/1; financial award applicants required to submit FAFSA. In 2019, 119 master's, 11 other advanced degrees awarded. *Application deadline:* For fall admission, 8/15 priority date for domestic students; for winter admission, 10/1 priority date for domestic students; for spring admission, 12/15 priority date for domestic students; for summer admission, 4/15 for domestic students. Applications are processed on a rolling basis. *Application fee:* $65. Electronic applications accepted. *Application Contact:* Graduate Admission, 325-674-6911, E-mail: gradinfo@acu.edu. *Dean*, Dr. Jennifer Shewmaker, 325-674-2700, Fax: 325-674-3707, E-mail: cehs@acu.edu.

## ABRAHAM LINCOLN UNIVERSITY, Los Angeles, CA 90010

**General Information** Proprietary, coed, comprehensive institution.

**GRADUATE UNITS**

**School of Law**

## ACACIA UNIVERSITY, Tempe, AZ 85284

**General Information** Private, coed, graduate-only institution.

**GRADUATE UNITS**

**American Graduate School of Education**

## ACADEMY FOR FIVE ELEMENT ACUPUNCTURE, Gainesville, FL 32601

**General Information** Independent, coed, graduate-only institution.

**GRADUATE UNITS**

**Graduate Program**

## ACADEMY FOR JEWISH RELIGION CALIFORNIA, Los Angeles, CA 90024

**General Information** Independent-religious, coed, graduate-only institution. *Graduate housing:* On-campus housing not available.

**GRADUATE UNITS**

**Graduate Programs**

## ACADEMY OF ART UNIVERSITY, San Francisco, CA 94105-3410

**General Information** Proprietary, coed, comprehensive institution. *Enrollment:* 9,826 graduate, professional, and undergraduate students; 1,765 full-time matriculated graduate/professional students (1,139 women), 1,353 part-time matriculated graduate/professional students (919 women). *Enrollment by degree level:* 3,118 master's. *Graduate faculty:* 172 full-time (74 women), 514 part-time/adjunct (210 women). *Tuition:* Full-time $1083; part-time $1083 per credit hour. *Required fees:* $860; $860 per unit. $430 per term. One-time fee: $145. Tuition and fees vary according to program. *Graduate housing:* Room and/or apartments guaranteed to single students; on-campus housing not available to married students. *Student services:* Campus employment opportunities, campus safety program, career counseling, international student services, low-cost health insurance, services for students with disabilities, teacher training, writing training. *Library facilities:* Academy of Art University Library. *Collection:* Books: 30,674 (physical), 9,600 (digital/electronic); Serial titles: 792 (physical), 2 (digital/electronic); Databases: 20. Weekly public service hours: 83; students can reserve study rooms.

**Computer facilities:** 900 computers available on campus for general student use. A campuswide network can be accessed. Online class registration, support for students taking online courses are available.
Website: http://www.academyart.edu/

**GRADUATE UNITS**

**Graduate Programs** Students: 1,765 full-time (1,139 women), 1,353 part-time (919 women); includes 521 minority (162 Black or African American, non-Hispanic/Latino; 11 American Indian or Alaska Native, non-Hispanic/Latino; 126 Asian, non-Hispanic/Latino; 166 Hispanic/Latino; 7 Native Hawaiian or other Pacific Islander, non-Hispanic/Latino; 49 Two or more races, non-Hispanic/Latino), 1,518 international. Average age 32. 1,228 applicants, 100% accepted, 787 enrolled. *Faculty:* 172 full-time (74 women), 514 part-time/adjunct (210 women). Expenses: Contact institution. *Financial support:* Career-related internships or fieldwork, Federal Work-Study, and scholarships/grants available. Financial award application deadline: 8/10; financial award applicants required to submit FAFSA. In 2019, 1,270 master's awarded. *Program availability:* Part-time, 100% online. *Application deadline:* Applications are processed on a rolling basis. *Application fee:* $50. Electronic applications accepted. *Application Contact:* 800-544-ARTS, E-mail: info@academyart.edu.

***School of Acting*** Students: 25 full-time (13 women), 4 part-time (2 women); includes 8 minority (6 Black or African American, non-Hispanic/Latino; 2 Hispanic/Latino), 9 international. Average age 28. 36 applicants, 100% accepted, 6 enrolled. *Faculty:* 1 (woman) full-time, 8 part-time/adjunct (3 women). Expenses: Contact institution. *Financial support:* Career-related internships or fieldwork, Federal Work-Study, and scholarships/grants available. Financial award application deadline: 8/10; financial award applicants required to submit FAFSA. In 2019, 9 master's awarded. *Program availability:* Part-time. *Application deadline:* Applications are processed on a rolling basis. *Application fee:* $50. Electronic applications accepted.

***School of Advertising*** Students: 51 full-time (35 women), 23 part-time (13 women); includes 16 minority (5 Black or African American, non-Hispanic/Latino; 4 Asian, non-Hispanic/Latino; 6 Hispanic/Latino; 1 Two or more races, non-Hispanic/Latino), 41 international. Average age 29. 25 applicants, 100% accepted, 18 enrolled. *Faculty:* 4 full-time (1 woman), 15 part-time/adjunct (7 women). Expenses: Contact institution. *Financial support:* Career-related internships or fieldwork, Federal Work-Study, and scholarships/grants available. Financial award application deadline: 8/10; financial award applicants required to submit FAFSA. In 2019, 35 master's awarded. *Program* *availability:* Part-time, 100% online. *Application deadline:* Applications are processed on a rolling basis. *Application fee:* $50. Electronic applications accepted. *Application Contact:* 800-544-ARTS, E-mail: info@academyart.edu.

***School of Animation and Visual Effects*** Students: 215 full-time (113 women), 122 part-time (59 women); includes 59 minority (18 Black or African American, non-Hispanic/Latino; 12 Asian, non-Hispanic/Latino; 23 Hispanic/Latino; 1 Native Hawaiian or other Pacific Islander, non-Hispanic/Latino; 5 Two or more races, non-Hispanic/Latino), 193 international. Average age 29. 112 applicants, 100% accepted, 84 enrolled. *Faculty:* 16 full-time (3 women), 51 part-time/adjunct (12 women). Expenses: Contact institution. *Financial support:* Career-related internships or fieldwork, Federal Work-Study, and scholarships/grants available. Financial award application deadline: 8/10; financial award applicants required to submit FAFSA. In 2019, 135 master's awarded. *Program availability:* Part-time, 100% online. *Application deadline:* Applications are processed on a rolling basis. *Application fee:* $50. Electronic applications accepted.

***School of Architecture*** Students: 88 full-time (46 women), 78 part-time (36 women); includes 35 minority (9 Black or African American, non-Hispanic/Latino; 7 Asian, non-Hispanic/Latino; 19 Hispanic/Latino), 43 international. Average age 35. 68 applicants, 100% accepted, 37 enrolled. *Faculty:* 9 full-time (4 women), 29 part-time/adjunct (8 women). Expenses: Contact institution. *Financial support:* Career-related internships or fieldwork, Federal Work-Study, and scholarships/grants available. Financial award application deadline: 8/10; financial award applicants required to submit FAFSA. In 2019, 25 master's awarded. *Program availability:* Part-time, 100% online. *Application deadline:* Applications are processed on a rolling basis. *Application fee:* $50. Electronic applications accepted.

***School of Art Education*** Students: 15 full-time (13 women), 11 part-time (10 women); includes 4 minority (1 Black or African American, non-Hispanic/Latino; 1 American Indian or Alaska Native, non-Hispanic/Latino; 1 Asian, non-Hispanic/Latino; 1 Hispanic/Latino), 9 international. Average age 34. 16 applicants, 100% accepted, 1 enrolled. *Faculty:* 3 full-time (2 women), 2 part-time/adjunct (both women). Expenses: Contact institution. *Financial support:* Career-related internships or fieldwork, Federal Work-Study, and scholarships/grants available. Financial award application deadline: 8/10; financial award applicants required to submit FAFSA. In 2019, 7 master's awarded. *Program availability:* Part-time, 100% online. *Application deadline:* Applications are processed on a rolling basis. *Application fee:* $50. Electronic applications accepted.

***School of Art History*** Students: 2 full-time (both women), 27 part-time (24 women); includes 4 minority (1 Black or African American, non-Hispanic/Latino; 2 Hispanic/Latino; 1 Two or more races, non-Hispanic/Latino), 2 international. Average age 38. 9 applicants, 100% accepted, 5 enrolled. *Faculty:* 1 (woman) full-time, 3 part-time/adjunct (2 women). Expenses: Contact institution. *Financial support:* Career-related internships or fieldwork, Federal Work-Study, and scholarships/grants available. Financial award application deadline: 8/10; financial award applicants required to submit FAFSA. In 2019, 12 master's awarded. *Program availability:* Part-time, 100% online. *Application deadline:* Applications are processed on a rolling basis. *Application fee:* $50. Electronic applications accepted.

***School of Communications and Media Technologies*** Students: 25 full-time (15 women), 15 part-time (9 women); includes 5 minority (4 Black or African American, non-Hispanic/Latino; 1 Two or more races, non-Hispanic/Latino), 23 international. Average age 31. 14 applicants, 100% accepted, 9 enrolled. *Faculty:* 2 full-time (1 woman), 12 part-time/adjunct (6 women). Expenses: Contact institution. *Financial support:* Career-related internships or fieldwork, Federal Work-Study, and scholarships/grants available. Financial award application deadline: 8/10; financial award applicants required to submit FAFSA. In 2019, 17 master's awarded. *Program availability:* Part-time, 100% online. *Application deadline:* Applications are processed on a rolling basis. *Application fee:* $50. Electronic applications accepted.

***School of Fashion*** Students: 199 full-time (173 women), 136 part-time (126 women); includes 66 minority (30 Black or African American, non-Hispanic/Latino; 1 American Indian or Alaska Native, non-Hispanic/Latino; 17 Asian, non-Hispanic/Latino; 12 Hispanic/Latino; 6 Two or more races, non-Hispanic/Latino), 185 international. Average age 30. 154 applicants, 100% accepted, 89 enrolled. *Faculty:* 22 full-time (16 women), 54 part-time/adjunct (40 women). Expenses: Contact institution. *Financial support:* Career-related internships or fieldwork, Federal Work-Study, and scholarships/grants available. Financial award application deadline: 8/10; financial award applicants required to submit FAFSA. In 2019, 181 master's awarded. *Program availability:* Part-time, 100% online. *Application deadline:* Applications are processed on a rolling basis. *Application fee:* $50. Electronic applications accepted.

***School of Fine Art*** Students: 63 full-time (41 women), 104 part-time (79 women); includes 28 minority (3 Black or African American, non-Hispanic/Latino; 2 American Indian or Alaska Native, non-Hispanic/Latino; 9 Asian, non-Hispanic/Latino; 7 Hispanic/Latino; 3 Native Hawaiian or other Pacific Islander, non-Hispanic/Latino; 4 Two or more races, non-Hispanic/Latino), 45 international. Average age 42. 44 applicants, 100% accepted, 29 enrolled. *Faculty:* 12 full-time (6 women), 24 part-time/adjunct (13 women). Expenses: Contact institution. *Financial support:* Career-related internships or fieldwork, Federal Work-Study, and scholarships/grants available. Financial award application deadline: 8/10; financial award applicants required to submit FAFSA. In 2019, 71 master's awarded. *Program availability:* Part-time, 100% online. *Application deadline:* Applications are processed on a rolling basis. *Application fee:* $50. Electronic applications accepted.

***School of Game Development*** Students: 134 full-time (54 women), 67 part-time (22 women); includes 31 minority (4 Black or African American, non-Hispanic/Latino; 12 Asian, non-Hispanic/Latino; 8 Hispanic/Latino; 7 Two or more races, non-Hispanic/Latino), 100 international. Average age 29. 71 applicants, 100% accepted, 57 enrolled. *Faculty:* 10 full-time (0 women), 28 part-time/adjunct (8 women). Expenses: Contact institution. *Financial support:* Career-related internships or fieldwork, Federal Work-Study, and scholarships/grants available. Financial award application deadline: 8/10; financial award applicants required to submit FAFSA. In 2019, 41 master's awarded. *Program availability:* Part-time, 100% online. *Application deadline:* Applications are processed on a rolling basis. *Application fee:* $50. Electronic applications accepted.

***School of Graphic Design*** Students: 142 full-time (99 women), 119 part-time (82 women); includes 31 minority (9 Black or African American, non-Hispanic/Latino; 6 Asian, non-Hispanic/Latino; 13 Hispanic/Latino; 1 Native Hawaiian or other Pacific Islander, non-Hispanic/Latino; 2 Two or more races, non-Hispanic/Latino), 166 international. Average age 28. 125 applicants, 100% accepted, 80 enrolled. *Faculty:* 5 full-time (1 woman), 19 part-time/adjunct (9 women). Expenses: Contact institution. *Financial support:* Career-related internships or fieldwork, Federal Work-Study, and scholarships/grants available. Financial award application deadline: 8/10; financial award applicants required to submit FAFSA. In 2019, 105 master's awarded. *Program availability:* Part-time, 100% online. *Application deadline:* Applications are processed on a rolling basis. *Application fee:* $50. Electronic applications accepted.

***School of Illustration*** Students: 79 full-time (59 women), 83 part-time (66 women); includes 30 minority (11 Black or African American, non-Hispanic/Latino; 2 American Indian or Alaska Native, non-Hispanic/Latino; 8 Asian, non-Hispanic/Latino; 9 Hispanic/Latino), 67 international. Average age 32. 62 applicants, 100% accepted, 27 enrolled. *Faculty:* 10 full-time (2 women), 27 part-time/adjunct (12 women). Expenses: Contact institution. *Financial support:* Career-related internships or fieldwork, Federal Work-Study, and scholarships/grants available. Financial award application deadline: 8/10; financial award applicants required to submit FAFSA. In 2019, 68 master's awarded. *Program availability:* Part-time, 100% online. *Application deadline:* Applications are processed on a rolling basis. *Application fee:* $50. Electronic applications accepted.

***School of Industrial Design*** Students: 41 full-time (16 women), 48 part-time (19 women); includes 9 minority (2 Black or African American, non-Hispanic/Latino; 2 Asian, non-Hispanic/Latino; 3 Hispanic/Latino; 2 Two or more races, non-Hispanic/Latino), 63 international. Average age 28. 52 applicants, 100% accepted, 27 enrolled. *Faculty:* 4 full-time (0 women), 25 part-time/adjunct (3 women). Expenses: Contact institution. *Financial support:* Career-related internships or fieldwork, Federal Work-Study, and scholarships/grants available. Financial award application deadline: 8/10; financial award applicants required to submit FAFSA. In 2019, 37 master's awarded. *Program availability:* Part-time, 100% online. *Application deadline:* Applications are processed on a rolling basis. *Application fee:* $50. Electronic applications accepted. *Application Contact:* 800-544-ARTS, E-mail: info@academyart.edu.

***School of Interior Architecture and Design*** Students: 107 full-time (95 women), 157 part-time (143 women); includes 44 minority (11 Black or African American, non-Hispanic/Latino; 1 American Indian or Alaska Native, non-Hispanic/Latino; 10 Asian, non-Hispanic/Latino; 20 Hispanic/Latino; 2 Two or more races, non-Hispanic/Latino), 79 international. Average age 33. 110 applicants, 100% accepted, 82 enrolled. *Faculty:* 4 full-time (3 women), 28 part-time/adjunct (14 women). Expenses: Contact institution. *Financial support:* Career-related internships or fieldwork, Federal Work-Study, and scholarships/grants available. Financial award application deadline: 8/10; financial award applicants required to submit FAFSA. In 2019, 98 master's awarded. *Program availability:* Part-time, 100% online. *Application deadline:* Applications are processed on a rolling basis. *Application fee:* $50. Electronic applications accepted. *Application Contact:* 800-544-ARTS, E-mail: info@academyart.edu.

***School of Jewelry and Metal Arts*** Students: 16 full-time (14 women), 13 part-time (10 women); includes 2 minority (1 Asian, non-Hispanic/Latino; 1 Hispanic/Latino), 16 international. Average age 35. 14 applicants, 100% accepted, 10 enrolled. *Faculty:* 2 full-time (both women), 8 part-time/adjunct (6 women). Expenses: Contact institution. *Financial support:* Career-related internships or fieldwork, Federal Work-Study, and scholarships/grants available. Financial award application deadline: 8/10; financial award applicants required to submit FAFSA. In 2019, 11 master's awarded. *Program availability:* Part-time, 100% online. *Application deadline:* Applications are processed on a rolling basis. *Application fee:* $50. Electronic applications accepted.

***School of Landscape Architecture*** Students: 12 full-time (7 women), 11 part-time (6 women); includes 2 minority (both Hispanic/Latino), 15 international. Average age 35. 20 applicants, 100% accepted, 9 enrolled. *Faculty:* 2 full-time (1 woman), 10 part-time/adjunct (3 women). Expenses: Contact institution. *Financial support:* Career-related internships or fieldwork, Federal Work-Study, and scholarships/grants available. Financial award application deadline: 8/10; financial award applicants required to submit FAFSA. In 2019, 9 master's awarded. *Program availability:* Part-time, 100% online. *Application deadline:* Applications are processed on a rolling basis. *Application fee:* $50. Electronic applications accepted.

***School of Motion Pictures and Television*** Students: 88 full-time (40 women), 38 part-time (15 women); includes 22 minority (9 Black or African American, non-Hispanic/Latino; 1 American Indian or Alaska Native, non-Hispanic/Latino; 3 Asian, non-Hispanic/Latino; 8 Hispanic/Latino; 1 Two or more races, non-Hispanic/Latino), 71 international. Average age 32. 55 applicants, 100% accepted, 23 enrolled. *Faculty:* 8 full-time (3 women), 37 part-time/adjunct (13 women). Expenses: Contact institution. *Financial support:* Career-related internships or fieldwork, Federal Work-Study, and scholarships/grants available. Financial award application deadline: 8/10; financial award applicants required to submit FAFSA. In 2019, 73 master's awarded. *Program availability:* Part-time, 100% online. *Application deadline:* Applications are processed on a rolling basis. *Application fee:* $50. Electronic applications accepted. *Application Contact:* 800-544-ARTS, E-mail: info@academyart.edu.

***School of Music Production and Sound Design for Visual Media*** Students: 73 full-time (33 women), 23 part-time (7 women); includes 16 minority (7 Black or African American, non-Hispanic/Latino; 1 Asian, non-Hispanic/Latino; 4 Hispanic/Latino; 4 Two or more races, non-Hispanic/Latino), 54 international. Average age 30. 44 applicants, 100% accepted, 31 enrolled. *Faculty:* 1 full-time (0 women), 26 part-time/adjunct (4 women). Expenses: Contact institution. *Financial support:* Career-related internships or fieldwork, Federal Work-Study, and scholarships/grants available. Financial award application deadline: 8/10; financial award applicants required to submit FAFSA. In 2019, 34 master's awarded. *Program availability:* Part-time, 100% online. *Application deadline:* Applications are processed on a rolling basis. *Application fee:* $50. Electronic applications accepted.

***School of Photography*** Students: 100 full-time (50 women), 93 part-time (57 women); includes 40 minority (14 Black or African American, non-Hispanic/Latino; 2 American Indian or Alaska Native, non-Hispanic/Latino; 5 Asian, non-Hispanic/Latino; 12 Hispanic/Latino; 1 Native Hawaiian or other Pacific Islander, non-Hispanic/Latino; 6 Two or more races, non-Hispanic/Latino), 56 international. Average age 38. 50 applicants, 100% accepted, 43 enrolled. *Faculty:* 6 full-time (3 women), 26 part-time/adjunct (9 women). Expenses: Contact institution. *Financial support:* Career-related internships or fieldwork, Federal Work-Study, and scholarships/grants available. Financial award application deadline: 8/10; financial award applicants required to submit FAFSA. In 2019, 69 master's awarded. *Program availability:* Part-time, 100% online. *Application deadline:* Applications are processed on a rolling basis. *Application fee:* $50. Electronic applications accepted. *Application Contact:* 800-544-ARTS, E-mail: info@academyart.edu.

***School of Visual Development*** Students: 66 full-time (48 women), 41 part-time (30 women); includes 16 minority (4 Black or African American, non-Hispanic/Latino; 1 American Indian or Alaska Native, non-Hispanic/Latino; 4 Asian, non-Hispanic/Latino; 6 Hispanic/Latino; 1 Two or more races, non-Hispanic/Latino), 47 international. Average age 28. 34 applicants, 100% accepted, 33 enrolled. *Faculty:* 4 full-time (0 women), 8 part-time/adjunct (1 woman). Expenses: Contact institution. *Financial support:* Career-related internships or fieldwork, Federal Work-Study, and scholarships/grants available. Financial award application deadline: 8/10; financial award applicants required to submit FAFSA. In 2019, 53 master's awarded. *Program* *availability:* Part-time, 100% online. *Application deadline:* Applications are processed on a rolling basis. *Application fee:* $50. Electronic applications accepted.

***School of Web Design and New Media*** Students: 203 full-time (158 women), 113 part-time (82 women); includes 38 minority (4 Black or African American, non-Hispanic/Latino; 24 Asian, non-Hispanic/Latino; 5 Hispanic/Latino; 1 Native Hawaiian or other Pacific Islander, non-Hispanic/Latino; 4 Two or more races, non-Hispanic/Latino), 228 international. Average age 29. 87 applicants, 100% accepted, 71 enrolled. *Faculty:* 6 full-time (2 women), 23 part-time/adjunct (5 women). Expenses: Contact institution. *Financial support:* Career-related internships or fieldwork, Federal Work-Study, and scholarships/grants available. Financial award application deadline: 8/10; financial award applicants required to submit FAFSA. In 2019, 163 master's awarded. *Program availability:* Part-time, 100% online. *Application deadline:* Applications are processed on a rolling basis. *Application fee:* $50. Electronic applications accepted. *Application Contact:* 800-544-ARTS, E-mail: info@academyart.edu.

***School of Writing for Film, Television and Digital Media*** Students: 21 full-time (15 women), 27 part-time (18 women); includes 15 minority (10 Black or African American, non-Hispanic/Latino; 3 Hispanic/Latino; 2 Two or more races, non-Hispanic/Latino), 6 international. Average age 36. 13 applicants, 100% accepted, 12 enrolled. *Faculty:* 8 full-time (3 women), 37 part-time/adjunct (13 women). Expenses: Contact institution. *Financial support:* Career-related internships or fieldwork, Federal Work-Study, and scholarships/grants available. Financial award application deadline: 8/10; financial award applicants required to submit FAFSA. In 2019, 3 master's awarded. *Program availability:* Part-time, 100% online. *Application deadline:* Applications are processed on a rolling basis. *Application fee:* $50. Electronic applications accepted.

## ACADEMY OF CHINESE CULTURE AND HEALTH SCIENCES, Oakland, CA 94612

**General Information** Private, coed, graduate-only institution. *Graduate housing:* On-campus housing not available.

**GRADUATE UNITS**

**Program in Traditional Chinese Medicine** *Program availability:* Part-time, evening/weekend.

## ACADIA UNIVERSITY, Wolfville, NS B4P 2R6, Canada

**General Information** Province-supported, coed, comprehensive institution. *Graduate housing:* Room and/or apartments available on a first-come, first-served basis to single students; on-campus housing not available to married students. Housing application deadline: 5/31. *Research affiliation:* Atlantic Research Laboratory.

**GRADUATE UNITS**

**Divinity College** *Program availability:* Part-time.

**Faculty of Arts**

**Faculty of Professional Studies**

***School of Education***

***School of Recreation Management and Community Development***

**Faculty of Pure and Applied Science**

***Jodrey School of Computer Science***

## ACUPUNCTURE & INTEGRATIVE MEDICINE COLLEGE, BERKELEY, Berkeley, CA 94704

**General Information** Independent, coed, graduate-only institution. *Graduate housing:* On-campus housing not available.

**GRADUATE UNITS**

**Master of Science in Oriental Medicine Program** *Program availability:* Part-time. Electronic applications accepted.

## ACUPUNCTURE AND MASSAGE COLLEGE, Miami, FL 33176

**General Information** Proprietary, coed, graduate-only institution.

**GRADUATE UNITS**

**Program in Oriental Medicine**

## ADAMS STATE UNIVERSITY, Alamosa, CO 81101

**General Information** State-supported, coed, comprehensive institution. CGS member. *Enrollment:* 3,101 graduate, professional, and undergraduate students; 959 full-time matriculated graduate/professional students (673 women), 336 part-time matriculated graduate/professional students (196 women). *Enrollment by degree level:* 1,295 master's. *Graduate housing:* Rooms and/or apartments available on a first-come, first-served basis to single and married students. *Student services:* Campus employment opportunities, career counseling, child daycare facilities, exercise/wellness program, free psychological counseling, international student services, low-cost health insurance, multicultural affairs office, services for students with disabilities, writing training. *Library facilities:* Nielsen Library. *Collection:* Books: 252 (physical), 891 (digital/electronic); Serial titles: 102 (physical), 372 (digital/electronic); Databases: 60. Weekly public service hours: 84. *Research affiliation:* Sandia National Laboratories (science education).

**Computer facilities:** 322 computers available on campus for general student use. A campuswide network can be accessed from student residence rooms and from off campus. Online class registration is available.
Website: http://www.adams.edu/

**General Application Contact:** Information Contact, 719-587-8152, Fax: 719-587-8222, E-mail: graduatestudies@adams.edu.

**GRADUATE UNITS**

**Office of Graduate Studies** Expenses: Contact institution. *Financial support:* Fellowships with partial tuition reimbursements, career-related internships or fieldwork, Federal Work-Study, institutionally sponsored loans, and scholarships/grants available. Financial award application deadline: 3/1; financial award applicants required to submit FAFSA. *Program availability:* Part-time, 100% online, summer residency. *Application deadline:* For fall admission, 9/15 priority date for domestic students. Applications are processed on a rolling basis. *Application fee:* $30. Electronic applications accepted. *Application Contact:* Information Contact, 719-587-8152, Fax: 719-587-8222, E-mail: graduatestudies@adams.edu.

***School of Business*** Expenses: Contact institution. *Application Contact:* Information Contact, 719-587-8152, Fax: 719-587-8222, E-mail: graduatestudies@adams.edu. *Director of the MBA Program,* Dr. Liz Thomas-Hensley, 719-587-7477, E-mail: lthomas@adams.edu.

## ADELPHI UNIVERSITY, Garden City, NY 11530-0701

**General Information** Independent, coed, university. *Graduate housing:* Room and/or apartments available on a first-come, first-served basis to single students; on-campus housing not available to married students. Housing application deadline: 5/1. *Research affiliation:* The Hagedorn Foundation, North Shore Long Island Jewish Health System (medicine), National Science Foundation, The Research Corporation, Mount Sinai Medical Center, Albert Einstein College of Medicine.

**GRADUATE UNITS**

**College of Arts and Sciences** *Program availability:* Part-time. Electronic applications accepted.

**College of Education and Health Sciences** *Program availability:* Part-time, evening/weekend. Electronic applications accepted.

**College of Nursing and Public Health** *Program availability:* Part-time, evening/weekend. Electronic applications accepted.

**College of Professional and Continuing Studies**

**Gordon F. Derner School of Psychology** *Program availability:* Part-time. Electronic applications accepted.

**Robert B. Willumstad School of Business** *Program availability:* Part-time, evening/weekend. Electronic applications accepted.

**School of Social Work** *Program availability:* Part-time, evening/weekend. Electronic applications accepted.

## ADLER UNIVERSITY, Chicago, IL 60602

**General Information** Independent, coed, graduate-only institution. *Graduate faculty:* 90 full-time (58 women), 102 part-time/adjunct (59 women). *Graduate housing:* On-campus housing not available. *Student services:* Campus employment opportunities, campus safety program, career counseling, international student services, services for students with disabilities, writing training. *Library facilities:* Harold Mosak Library. *Research affiliation:* LGBTQ Mental Health and Inclusion Center, Adler Child Guidance Center, Adler Institute on Social Exclusion, Adler Institute on Public Safety and Social Justice.

**Computer facilities:** A campuswide network can be accessed.
Website: http://www.adler.edu/

**General Application Contact:** Michelle Brice, Associate Vice President of Admissions, 312-662-4100, E-mail: admissions@adler.edu.

**GRADUATE UNITS**

**Doctor of Philosophy (Ph.D.) in Counselor Education and Supervision** Expenses: Contact institution. In 2019, 1 doctorate awarded. *Application Contact:* Phyllis Horton, Director of Admissions, 312-662-4100, E-mail: admissions@adler.edu. *Director of Admissions,* Phyllis Horton, 312-662-4100, E-mail: admissions@adler.edu.

**Doctor of Philosophy (Ph.D.) in Couple and Family Therapy** Expenses: Contact institution. In 2019, 1 doctorate awarded. *Application Contact:* Phyllis Horton, Director of Admissions, 312-662-4100, E-mail: admissions@adler.edu. *Director of Admissions,* Phyllis Horton, 312-662-4100, E-mail: admissions@adler.edu.

**Doctor of Psychology (Psy.D.) in Clinical Psychology** Expenses: Contact institution. In 2019, 1 doctorate awarded. *Application Contact:* Michelle Brice, Director of Admissions, 312-662-4113, Fax: 312-662-4199, E-mail: admissions@adler.edu. *Director of Admissions,* Phyllis Horton, 312-662-4100, E-mail: admissions@adler.edu.

**Master of Arts (M.A.) in Counseling: Art Therapy/Ph.D. in Art Therapy** Expenses: Contact institution. In 2019, 1 doctorate awarded. *Program availability:* Part-time. *Application Contact:* Phyllis Horton, Director of Admissions, 312-662-4100, E-mail: admissions@adler.edu. *Director of Admissions,* Phyllis Horton, 312-662-4100, E-mail: admissions@adler.edu.

**Master of Arts (M.A.) in Counseling: Specialization in Clinical Mental Health Counseling** Expenses: Contact institution. In 2019, 2 master's awarded. *Program availability:* Part-time, evening/weekend, 100% online, blended/hybrid learning. *Application Contact:* Phyllis Horton, Director of Admissions, 312-662-4100, E-mail: admissions@adler.edu. *Director of Admissions,* Phyllis Horton, 312-662-4100, E-mail: admissions@adler.edu.

**Master of Arts (M.A.) in Counseling: Specialization in Rehabilitation Counseling** Expenses: Contact institution. In 2019, 1 master's awarded. *Program availability:* Part-time. *Application Contact:* Michelle Brice, 312-662-4113, Fax: 312-662-4199. *Director of Admissions,* Phyllis Horton, 312-662-4100, E-mail: admissions@adler.edu.

**Master of Arts (M.A.) in Couple and Family Therapy** Expenses: Contact institution. In 2019, 1 master's awarded. *Application Contact:* Phyllis Horton, Director of Admissions, 312-662-4100, E-mail: admissions@adler.edu. *Director of Admissions,* Phyllis Horton, 312-662-4100, E-mail: admissions@adler.edu.

**Master of Arts (M.A.) in Forensic Mental Health Leadership** Expenses: Contact institution. In 2019, 1 master's awarded. *Application Contact:* Phyllis Horton, Director of Admissions, 312-662-4100, E-mail: admissions@adler.edu. *Director of Admissions,* Phyllis Horton, 312-662-4100, E-mail: admissions@adler.edu.

**Master of Counselling Psychology: Art Therapy** Expenses: Contact institution. In 2019, 1 master's awarded. *Application Contact:* Michelle Brice, Associate Vice President of Admissions, 236-521-2409, E-mail: vanadmissions@adler.edu. *Associate Vice President of Admissions,* Michelle Brice, 236-521-2409, E-mail: vanadmissions@adler.edu.

**Master of Public Administration Program** Expenses: Contact institution. In 2019, 1 master's awarded. *Program availability:* Part-time, evening/weekend. *Application Contact:* Phyllis Horton, Director of Admissions, 312-662-4100, E-mail: admissions@adler.edu. *Director of Admissions,* Phyllis Horton, 312-662-4100, E-mail: admissions@adler.edu.

**Master of Public Policy and Administration Program: Social Change Leadership** Expenses: Contact institution. In 2019, 1 master's awarded. *Program availability:* Part-time, evening/weekend. *Application Contact:* Michelle Brice, Associate Vice President of Admissions, 236-521-2409, E-mail: vanadmissions@adler.edu. *Associate Vice President of Admissions,* Michelle Brice, 236-521-2409, E-mail: vanadmissions@adler.edu.

**Master of Public Policy Program** Expenses: Contact institution. In 2019, 1 master's awarded. *Program availability:* Part-time, evening/weekend. *Application Contact:* Phyllis Horton, Director of Admissions, 312-662-4100, E-mail: admissions@adler.edu. *Director of Admissions,* Phyllis Horton, 312-662-4100, E-mail: admissions@adler.edu.

**Master of Science (M.S.) in Sport and Human Performance** Expenses: Contact institution. In 2019, 1 master's awarded. *Application Contact:* Phyllis Horton, Director of Admissions, 312-662-4100, E-mail: admissions@adler.edu. *Director of Admissions,* Phyllis Horton, 312-662-4100, E-mail: admissions@adler.edu.

**Master's Degrees in Counselling Psychology** Expenses: Contact institution. In 2019, 2 master's awarded. *Application Contact:* Michelle Brice, Associate Vice President of Admissions, 236-521-2409, E-mail: vanadmissions@adler.edu. *Associate Vice*

*President of Admissions*, Michelle Brice, 236-521-2409, E-mail: vanadmissions@adler.edu.

**Master's Degrees in Counselling Psychology; School & Youth Concentration** Expenses: Contact institution. In 2019, 2 master's awarded. *Application Contact:* Michelle Brice, Associate Vice President of Admissions, 236-521-2409, E-mail: vanadmissions@adler.edu. *Associate Vice President of Admissions*, Michelle Brice, 236-521-2409, E-mail: vanadmissions@adler.edu.

**Master's Degrees in Industrial and Organizational Psychology** Expenses: Contact institution. In 2019, 2 master's awarded. *Program availability:* Part-time, evening/weekend. *Application Contact:* Michelle Brice, Associate Vice President of Admissions, 236-521-2409, E-mail: vanadmissions@adler.edu. *Associate Vice President of Admissions*, Michelle Brice, 236-521-2409, E-mail: vanadmissions@adler.edu.

## ADRIAN COLLEGE, Adrian, MI 49221-2575

**General Information** Independent-religious, coed, comprehensive institution. *Graduate housing:* On-campus housing not available.

**GRADUATE UNITS**

**Graduate Programs**

## ADVENTHEALTH UNIVERSITY, Orlando, FL 32803

**General Information** Independent, coed, comprehensive institution.

**GRADUATE UNITS**

**Program in Healthcare Administration**

**Program in Nurse Anesthesia**

**Program in Occupational Therapy**

**Program in Physical Therapy**

**Program in Physician Assistant Studies**

## AGNES SCOTT COLLEGE, Decatur, GA 30030-3797

**General Information** Independent-religious, women only, comprehensive institution. *Graduate housing:* On-campus housing not available.

**GRADUATE UNITS**

**Program in Writing and Digital Communication**

## AIR FORCE INSTITUTE OF TECHNOLOGY, Dayton, OH 45433-7765

**General Information** Federally supported, coed, primarily men, graduate-only institution. *Graduate housing:* On-campus housing not available. *Research affiliation:* U.S. Air Force Office of Scientific Research, U.S. Air Force Research Laboratory (AFRL), Dayton Area Graduate Studies Institute (aerospace), U.S. Department of Energy, National Security Agency.

**GRADUATE UNITS**

**Graduate School of Engineering and Management** *Program availability:* Part-time.

## ALABAMA AGRICULTURAL AND MECHANICAL UNIVERSITY, Huntsville, AL 35811

**General Information** State-supported, coed, university. CGS member. *Graduate housing:* Rooms and/or apartments available on a first-come, first-served basis to single and married students. Housing application deadline: 5/5. *Research affiliation:* NASA (utilization of space resources), Boeing Defense and Space Group (plant science), Lawrence Livermore National Laboratory (chemistry, physics), Alabama Supercomputer Network (computer services), Nichols Research Corporation (computer science), Hughes Aircraft Corporation (physics).

**GRADUATE UNITS**

**School of Graduate Studies** Electronic applications accepted.

***College of Agricultural, Life and Natural Sciences*** *Program availability:* Part-time, evening/weekend. Electronic applications accepted.

***College of Business and Public Affairs*** *Program availability:* Part-time, evening/weekend. Electronic applications accepted.

***College of Education, Humanities, and Behavioral Sciences*** *Program availability:* Part-time, evening/weekend. Electronic applications accepted.

***College of Engineering, Technology, and Physical Sciences*** *Program availability:* Part-time, evening/weekend. Electronic applications accepted.

## ALABAMA COLLEGE OF OSTEOPATHIC MEDICINE, Dothan, AL 36303

**General Information** Independent, coed, graduate-only institution.

**GRADUATE UNITS**

**Graduate Program**

## ALABAMA STATE UNIVERSITY, Montgomery, AL 36101-0271

**General Information** State-supported, coed, university. CGS member. *Graduate housing:* On-campus housing not available.

**GRADUATE UNITS**

**College of Business Administration** Students: 13 full-time (7 women), 3 part-time (2 women); includes 15 minority (all Black or African American, non-Hispanic/Latino), 1 international. Average age 32. 14 applicants, 36% accepted, 4 enrolled. *Faculty:* 4 full-time (1 woman), 1 part-time/adjunct (0 women). Expenses: Contact institution. *Financial support:* Fellowships, teaching assistantships, career-related internships or fieldwork, scholarships/grants, tuition waivers (partial), and unspecified assistantships available. Financial award application deadline: 6/30; financial award applicants required to submit FAFSA. In 2019, 15 master's awarded. *Program availability:* Part-time. *Application deadline:* For fall admission, 4/15 for domestic and international students; for spring admission, 11/15 for domestic students, 11/1 for international students; for summer admission, 3/15 for domestic and international students. *Application fee:* $25. Electronic applications accepted. *Application Contact:* Dr. Ed Brown, Dean of Graduate Studies, 334-229-4274, Fax: 334-229-4928, E-mail: ebrown@alasu.edu. *Director, Master of Accountancy*, Dr. Dave Thompson, 334-229-6809, E-mail: dthompson@alasu.edu.

**College of Education** Students: 65 full-time (46 women), 120 part-time (79 women); includes 171 minority (170 Black or African American, non-Hispanic/Latino; 1 Hispanic/Latino), 3 international. Average age 36. 174 applicants, 47% accepted, 38 enrolled. *Faculty:* 7 full-time (4 women), 7 part-time/adjunct (4 women). Expenses: Contact institution. *Financial support:* Fellowships, teaching assistantships, career-related internships or fieldwork, scholarships/grants, tuition waivers (partial), and unspecified assistantships available. Financial award application deadline: 6/30; financial award applicants required to submit FAFSA. In 2019, 53 master's, 3 doctorates, 6 other advanced degrees awarded. *Program availability:* Part-time. *Application deadline:* For fall admission, 4/15 for domestic and international students; for spring admission, 11/15 for domestic and international students; for summer admission, 3/15 for domestic and international students. Applications are processed on a rolling basis. *Application fee:* $25. Electronic applications accepted. *Application Contact:* Dr. Ed Brown, Dean of Graduate Studies, 334-229-4274, Fax: 334-229-4928, E-mail: ebrown@alasu.edu. *Dean*, Dr. Alethea Hampton, 334-229-4250, E-mail: ahampton@alasu.edu.

**College of Health Sciences** Students: 183 full-time (128 women), 1 part-time (0 women); includes 76 minority (64 Black or African American, non-Hispanic/Latino; 1 American Indian or Alaska Native, non-Hispanic/Latino; 6 Hispanic/Latino; 5 Two or more races, non-Hispanic/Latino). Average age 25. 146 applicants, 50% accepted, 71 enrolled. *Faculty:* 19 full-time (16 women), 19 part-time/adjunct (10 women). Expenses: Contact institution. *Financial support:* In 2019–20, 3 students received support. Research assistantships, Federal Work-Study, scholarships/grants, tuition waivers (partial), and unspecified assistantships available. Financial award application deadline: 6/30; financial award applicants required to submit FAFSA. In 2019, 33 master's, 23 doctorates awarded. *Program availability:* Part-time. *Application deadline:* For fall admission, 4/15 for domestic and international students; for spring admission, 11/15 for domestic and international students; for summer admission, 3/15 for domestic and international students. Applications are processed on a rolling basis. *Application fee:* $25. Electronic applications accepted. *Application Contact:* Dr. Ed Brown, Dean of Graduate Studies, 334-229-4274, Fax: 334-229-4928, E-mail: ebrown@alasu.edu. *Dean, College of Health Sciences*, Dr. Charlene Portee, 334-229-5053, E-mail: cportee@alasu.edu.

**College of Liberal Arts and Social Sciences** Students: 22 full-time (18 women), 4 part-time (all women); all minorities (25 Black or African American, non-Hispanic/Latino; 1 American Indian or Alaska Native, non-Hispanic/Latino). Average age 32. 25 applicants, 28% accepted, 7 enrolled. *Faculty:* 16 full-time (4 women). Expenses: Contact institution. *Financial support:* Fellowships, research assistantships, scholarships/grants, tuition waivers (partial), and unspecified assistantships available. Financial award application deadline: 6/30. In 2019, 11 master's awarded. *Program availability:* Part-time. *Application deadline:* For fall admission, 7/15 for domestic students; for spring admission, 12/15 for domestic students. Applications are processed on a rolling basis. *Application fee:* $25. Electronic applications accepted. *Application Contact:* Dr. Ed Brown, Dean of Graduate Studies, 334-229-4274, Fax: 334-229-4928, E-mail: ebrown@alasu.edu. *Associate Dean*, Dr. Kathaleen Amende, 334-229-5149, E-mail: kamende@alasu.edu.

**College of Science, Mathematics and Technology** Students: 15 full-time (10 women), 13 part-time (8 women); includes 21 minority (19 Black or African American, non-Hispanic/Latino; 1 Asian, non-Hispanic/Latino; 1 Hispanic/Latino), 5 international. Average age 28. 34 applicants, 21% accepted, 5 enrolled. *Faculty:* 11 full-time (4 women). Expenses: Contact institution. *Financial support:* In 2019–20, 22 students received support. Research assistantships, Federal Work-Study, scholarships/grants, tuition waivers (partial), and unspecified assistantships available. Financial award application deadline: 6/30; financial award applicants required to submit CSS PROFILE or FAFSA. In 2019, 8 master's, 1 doctorate awarded. *Application deadline:* For fall admission, 4/15 for domestic and international students; for spring admission, 11/15 for domestic and international students; for summer admission, 3/15 for domestic and international students. Applications are processed on a rolling basis. *Application fee:* $25. Electronic applications accepted. *Application Contact:* Dr. Ed Brown, Dean of Graduate Studies, 334-229-4274, Fax: 334-229-4928, E-mail: ebrown@alasu.edu. *Dean*, Dr. Kennedy Weskesa, 334-229-4316, Fax: 334-229-4916, E-mail: weskesa@alasu.edu.

## ALASKA PACIFIC UNIVERSITY, Anchorage, AK 99508-4672

**General Information** Independent, coed, comprehensive institution. *Graduate housing:* Room and/or apartments available on a first-come, first-served basis to single students; on-campus housing not available to married students. Housing application deadline: 8/15.

**GRADUATE UNITS**

**Graduate Programs** *Program availability:* Part-time, evening/weekend. Electronic applications accepted.

## ALBANY COLLEGE OF PHARMACY AND HEALTH SCIENCES, Albany, NY 12208

**General Information** Independent, coed, comprehensive institution. *Graduate housing:* Room and/or apartments available on a first-come, first-served basis to single students; on-campus housing not available to married students. Housing application deadline: 7/1.

**GRADUATE UNITS**

**School of Arts and Sciences** Electronic applications accepted.

**School of Pharmacy and Pharmaceutical Sciences** Electronic applications accepted.

## ALBANY LAW SCHOOL, Albany, NY 12208-3494

**General Information** Independent, coed, graduate-only institution. *Graduate housing:* On-campus housing not available.

**GRADUATE UNITS**

**Professional Program** *Program availability:* Part-time.

## ALBANY MEDICAL COLLEGE, Albany, NY 12208-3479

**General Information** Independent, coed, graduate-only institution. *Graduate housing:* On-campus housing not available. *Research affiliation:* X-Ray Optical Systems (diagnostic equipment), Integrated Tissue Dynamics INTIGYN (integrated tissue dynamics), Regenerative Research Foundation (biomedical research), Wadsworth Center for Laboratories and Research (biomedical research), ORDWAY Research Institute (biomedical research), General Electric Company (GE) (imaging).

**GRADUATE UNITS**

**Alden March Bioethics Institute** *Program availability:* Part-time, evening/weekend, online learning. Electronic applications accepted.

**Center for Cardiovascular Sciences** *Program availability:* Part-time.

**Center for Cell Biology and Cancer Research** *Program availability:* Part-time.

**Center for Immunology and Microbial Disease** *Program availability:* Part-time.

**Center for Neuropharmacology and Neuroscience**

**Center for Nurse Anesthesiology** Electronic applications accepted.

**Center for Physician Assistant Studies** Electronic applications accepted.

**Professional Program** Electronic applications accepted.

## ALBANY STATE UNIVERSITY, Albany, GA 31705-2717

**General Information** State-supported, coed, comprehensive institution. *Graduate housing:* Room and/or apartments available on a first-come, first-served basis to single students; on-campus housing not available to married students. Housing application deadline: 6/30.

**GRADUATE UNITS**

**College of Arts and Humanities** *Program availability:* Part-time. Electronic applications accepted.

**College of Business** *Program availability:* Part-time, evening/weekend. Electronic applications accepted.

**College of Education** *Program availability:* Part-time, evening/weekend, online learning. Electronic applications accepted.

**Darton College of Health Professions** *Program availability:* Part-time, evening/weekend, online learning. Electronic applications accepted.

## ALBERT EINSTEIN COLLEGE OF MEDICINE, Bronx, NY 10461

**General Information** Independent, coed, graduate-only institution. CGS member. *Graduate housing:* Room and/or apartments guaranteed to single students.

**GRADUATE UNITS**

**Graduate Programs in the Biomedical Sciences** Electronic applications accepted.

**Medical Scientist Training Program**

**Professional Program in Medicine**

## ALBERTUS MAGNUS COLLEGE, New Haven, CT 06511-1189

**General Information** Independent-religious, coed, comprehensive institution. *Enrollment:* 1,419 graduate, professional, and undergraduate students; 205 full-time matriculated graduate/professional students (148 women), 98 part-time matriculated graduate/professional students (77 women). *Enrollment by degree level:* 303 master's. *Library facilities:* Rosary Hall. *Collection:* Books: 38,339 (physical), 148,500 (digital/electronic); Databases: 88.

**Computer facilities:** 117 computers available on campus for general student use. A campuswide network can be accessed. Online class registration, online class sessions are available.
Website: http://www.albertus.edu/

**General Application Contact:** Annette Bosley-Boyce, Dean of the Division of Professional and Graduate Studies, 203-672-6685 Ext. 6685, E-mail: abosleyboyce@albertus.edu.

**GRADUATE UNITS**

**Master of Arts in Art Therapy and Counseling Program** Students: 10 full-time (9 women), 20 part-time (all women); includes 7 minority (2 Asian, non-Hispanic/Latino; 5 Hispanic/Latino). Average age 29. Expenses: Contact institution. *Application Contact:* Annette Bosley-Boyce, Dean of the Division of Professional and Graduate Studies, 203-672-6685, E-mail: abosleyboyce@albertus.edu. *Director of M.A.A.T.C Program,* Dr. Stephen Joy, 203-773-8555, E-mail: sjoy@albertus.edu.

**Master of Arts in Liberal Studies Program** Students: 5 full-time (4 women), 1 (woman) part-time; includes 3 minority (all Black or African American, non-Hispanic/Latino). Average age 40. *Faculty:* 1 full-time (0 women), 2 part-time/adjunct (0 women). Expenses: Contact institution. *Financial support:* Unspecified assistantships available. Financial award applicants required to submit FAFSA. *Program availability:* Part-time, evening/weekend, 100% online, blended/hybrid learning. *Application deadline:* For fall admission, 7/15 for international students; for spring admission, 11/15 for international students. Applications are processed on a rolling basis. *Application fee:* $50. Electronic applications accepted. *Application Contact:* Annette Bosley-Boyce, Dean of the Division of Professional and Graduate Studies, 203-672-6687, E-mail: abosleyboyce@albertus.edu.

**Master of Business Administration Program** Students: 57 full-time (40 women), 15 part-time (8 women); includes 32 minority (23 Black or African American, non-Hispanic/Latino; 1 Asian, non-Hispanic/Latino; 6 Hispanic/Latino; 2 Two or more races, non-Hispanic/Latino), 4 international. Average age 34. 30 applicants, 90% accepted, 23 enrolled. *Faculty:* 8 full-time (1 woman), 5 part-time/adjunct (2 women). Expenses: Contact institution. *Financial support:* In 2019–20, 5 students received support. Unspecified assistantships available. Financial award applicants required to submit FAFSA. In 2019, 50 master's awarded. *Program availability:* Part-time, evening/weekend, 100% online, blended/hybrid learning. *Application deadline:* For fall admission, 7/15 for international students; for spring admission, 11/15 for international students. Applications are processed on a rolling basis. *Application fee:* $50. Electronic applications accepted. *Application Contact:* Annette Bosley-Boyce, Dean of the Division of Professional and Graduate Studies, 203-672-6688, E-mail: abosleyboyce@albertus.edu. *Director of Master of Business Administration Programs,* Dr. Wayne Gineo, 203-672-6670, E-mail: wgineo@albertus.edu.

**Master of Fine Arts in Writing Program** Students: 3 full-time (2 women), 1 part-time (0 women); includes 2 minority (1 Black or African American, non-Hispanic/Latino; 1 Hispanic/Latino). Average age 35. 8 applicants, 50% accepted, 1 enrolled. *Faculty:* 2 full-time (1 woman), 1 part-time/adjunct (0 women). Expenses: Contact institution. *Financial support:* In 2019–20, 5 students received support. Unspecified assistantships available. Financial award applicants required to submit FAFSA. In 2019, 3 master's awarded. *Program availability:* Part-time, evening/weekend, 100% online, blended/hybrid learning. *Application deadline:* For fall admission, 7/15 for international students; for spring admission, 11/15 for international students. Applications are processed on a rolling basis. *Application fee:* $50. Electronic applications accepted. *Application Contact:* Prof. Sarah Wallman, Dean of the Division of Professional and Graduate Studies, 203-672-6689, E-mail: abosleyboyce@albertus.edu. *Co-Director MFA Program,* Charles Rafferty, 203-773-4473, E-mail: swallman@albertus.edu.

**Master of Science in Accounting Program** Students: 13 full-time (5 women), 6 part-time (1 woman); includes 8 minority (4 Black or African American, non-Hispanic/Latino; 1 Asian, non-Hispanic/Latino; 3 Hispanic/Latino), 1 international. Average age 35. 6 applicants, 100% accepted, 6 enrolled. *Faculty:* 8 full-time (1 woman), 5 part-time/adjunct (2 women). Expenses: Contact institution. *Financial support:* In 2019–20, 1 student received support. Unspecified assistantships available. Financial award applicants required to submit FAFSA. In 2019, 4 master's awarded. *Program availability:* Part-time, evening/weekend, 100% online, blended/hybrid learning. *Application deadline:* For fall admission, 7/15 for international students; for spring admission, 11/15 for international students. Applications are processed on a rolling basis. *Application fee:* $50. Electronic applications accepted. *Application Contact:* Dr. Nancy Fallon, Director, 203-773-8567, E-mail: nfallon@albertus.edu. *Director,* Dr. Nancy Fallon, 203-773-8567, E-mail: nfallon@albertus.edu.

**Master of Science in Clinical Counseling Program** Students: 19 full-time (15 women), 1 (woman) part-time; includes 9 minority (5 Black or African American, non-Hispanic/Latino; 4 Hispanic/Latino). Average age 33. 14 applicants, 71% accepted, 7 enrolled. *Faculty:* 11 full-time (10 women), 9 part-time/adjunct (6 women). Expenses: Contact institution. *Financial support:* In 2019–20, 3 students received support. Unspecified assistantships available. Financial award applicants required to submit FAFSA. *Program availability:* Part-time, evening/weekend. *Application deadline:* For fall admission, 7/15 for international students; for spring admission, 11/15 for international students. Applications are processed on a rolling basis. *Application fee:* $50. Electronic applications accepted. *Application Contact:* Annette Bosley-Boyce, Dean of the Division of Professional and Graduate Studies, 203-672-6691, E-mail: abosleyboyce@albertus.edu. *Director, Master of Science in Clinical Counseling Program,* Siobhan Evarts, 203-672-6675, E-mail: soevarts@albertus.edu.

**Master of Science in Criminal Justice Program** Students: 18 full-time (13 women), 3 part-time (2 women); includes 10 minority (4 Black or African American, non-Hispanic/Latino; 6 Hispanic/Latino). Average age 33. 10 applicants, 90% accepted, 7 enrolled. *Faculty:* 2 full-time (0 women), 1 part-time/adjunct (0 women). Expenses: Contact institution. *Financial support:* In 2019–20, 1 student received support. Unspecified assistantships available. Financial award applicants required to submit FAFSA. In 2019, 11 master's awarded. *Program availability:* Part-time, evening/weekend, 100% online, blended/hybrid learning. *Application deadline:* For fall admission, 7/15 for international students; for spring admission, 11/15 for international students. Applications are processed on a rolling basis. *Application fee:* $50. Electronic applications accepted. *Application Contact:* Dean of the Division of Professional and Graduate Studies, 203-672-6692, E-mail: abosleyboyce@albertus.edu. *Director of Graduate Leadership Programs,* John Lawrie, 203-773-4424, E-mail: hfero@albertus.edu.

**Master of Science in Education Program** Students: 5 full-time (3 women), 7 part-time (all women); includes 6 minority (3 Black or African American, non-Hispanic/Latino; 2 Hispanic/Latino; 1 Two or more races, non-Hispanic/Latino). Average age 40. 5 applicants, 100% accepted, 5 enrolled. *Faculty:* 2 full-time (1 woman), 3 part-time/adjunct (1 woman). Expenses: Contact institution. *Financial support:* Unspecified assistantships available. Financial award applicants required to submit FAFSA. In 2019, 7 master's awarded. *Program availability:* Part-time, evening/weekend. *Application deadline:* For fall admission, 7/15 for international students; for spring admission, 11/15 for international students. Applications are processed on a rolling basis. *Application fee:* $50. Electronic applications accepted. *Application Contact:* Anthony Reich, Dean of the Division of Professional and Graduate Studies, 203-672-6693, E-mail: abosleyboyce@albertus.edu. *Director, Education Programs,* Dr. Joan Venditto, 203-773-8087, Fax: 203-773-4422, E-mail: jvenditto@albertus.edu.

**Master of Science in Human Services Program** Students: 36 full-time (33 women), 2 part-time (both women); includes 27 minority (20 Black or African American, non-Hispanic/Latino; 1 American Indian or Alaska Native, non-Hispanic/Latino; 6 Hispanic/Latino), 2 international. Average age 41. 26 applicants, 54% accepted, 13 enrolled. *Faculty:* 4 full-time (all women), 4 part-time/adjunct (1 woman). Expenses: Contact institution. *Financial support:* In 2019–20, 2 students received support. Unspecified assistantships available. Financial award applicants required to submit FAFSA. In 2019, 25 master's awarded. *Program availability:* Part-time, evening/weekend. *Application deadline:* For fall admission, 7/15 for international students; for spring admission, 11/15 for international students. Applications are processed on a rolling basis. *Application fee:* $50. Electronic applications accepted. *Application Contact:* Anthony Reich, 203-672-6694, E-mail: abosleyboyce@albertus.edu. *Associate Director of Human Services,* Ragaa Mazen, 203-562-1590, E-mail: chuckaby@albertus.edu.

**Master of Science in Management and Organizational Leadership Program** Students: 17 full-time (12 women), 8 part-time (3 women); includes 14 minority (7 Black or African American, non-Hispanic/Latino; 6 Hispanic/Latino; 1 Two or more races, non-Hispanic/Latino). Average age 38. 14 applicants, 100% accepted, 11 enrolled. *Faculty:* 2 full-time (0 women), 4 part-time/adjunct (1 woman). Expenses: Contact institution. *Financial support:* In 2019–20, 3 students received support. Unspecified assistantships available. Financial award applicants required to submit FAFSA. In 2019, 7 master's awarded. *Program availability:* Part-time, evening/weekend, 100% online, blended/hybrid learning. *Application deadline:* For fall admission, 7/15 for international students; for spring admission, 11/15 for international students. Applications are processed on a rolling basis. *Application fee:* $50. Electronic applications accepted. *Application Contact:* Anthony Reich, Dean of the Division of Professional and Graduate Studies, 203-672-6695, E-mail: abosleyboyce@albertus.edu.

**Masters of Arts in Leadership**

**Masters of Public Administration Program** Students: 16 full-time (10 women), 5 part-time (3 women); includes 16 minority (12 Black or African American, non-Hispanic/Latino; 4 Hispanic/Latino). Average age 36. 4 applicants, 75% accepted, 1 enrolled. *Faculty:* 2 full-time (1 woman). Expenses: Contact institution. *Financial support:* Unspecified assistantships available. *Program availability:* Part-time, evening/weekend, 100% online, blended/hybrid learning. *Application deadline:* For fall admission, 7/15 for international students; for spring admission, 11/15 for international students. Applications are processed on a rolling basis. *Application fee:* $50. Electronic applications accepted. *Application Contact:* Annette Bosley-Boyce, Dean of the Division of Professional and Graduate Studies, 203-672-6696, E-mail: abosleyboyce@albertus.edu. *Director, Master of Public Administration Program,* Dr. Patricia Birungi, 203-672-5309, E-mail: pnbirungi@albertus.edu.

## ALBIZU UNIVERSITY - MIAMI, Miami, FL 33172-2209

**General Information** Independent, coed, comprehensive institution. *Enrollment:* 410 full-time matriculated graduate/professional students (351 women), 190 part-time matriculated graduate/professional students (163 women). *Enrollment by degree level:* 419 master's, 181 doctoral. *Graduate faculty:* 28 full-time (21 women), 27 part-time/adjunct (15 women). *Tuition:* Full-time $11,160; part-time $5580 per year. *Required fees:* $322 per term. Tuition and fees vary according to course load, degree level and program. *Graduate housing:* Room and/or apartments available to single students; on-campus housing not available to married students. *Student services:* Campus employment opportunities, campus safety program, career counseling, exercise/wellness program, international student services, services for students with disabilities, teacher training, writing training. *Library facilities:* Albizu Library. *Collection:* Books: 27,760 (physical), 22,900 (digital/electronic); Serial titles: 295 (physical), 17,034 (digital/electronic); Databases: 73. Weekly public service hours: 66.

**Computer facilities:** 268 computers available on campus for general student use. A campuswide network can be accessed from off campus. Online class registration, campus portal, virtual library, 24/7 support, Cloud computing, learning center are available.
Website: http://www.albizu.edu/

**General Application Contact:** Nancy Alvarez, Director of Enrollment Management, 305-593-1223 Ext. 3136, Fax: 305-593-1854, E-mail: nalvarez@albizu.edu.

GRADUATE UNITS

**Graduate Programs** Students: 410 full-time (351 women), 190 part-time (163 women); includes 519 minority (33 Black or African American, non-Hispanic/Latino; 3 Asian, non-Hispanic/Latino; 477 Hispanic/Latino; 6 Two or more races, non-Hispanic/Latino), 21 international. Average age 33. 286 applicants, 66% accepted, 127 enrolled. *Faculty:* 28 full-time (21 women), 27 part-time/adjunct (15 women). Expenses: Contact institution. *Financial support:* In 2019–20, 158 students received support. Federal Work-Study, scholarships/grants, unspecified assistantships, and tuition discounts available. Financial award application deadline: 6/1; financial award applicants required to submit FAFSA. In 2019, 96 master's, 54 doctorates awarded. *Program availability:* Part-time, 100% online, blended/hybrid learning. *Application deadline:* For fall admission, 4/1 priority date for domestic students, 5/1 priority date for international students; for spring admission, 11/1 priority date for domestic students, 9/1 priority date for international students. Applications are processed on a rolling basis. *Application fee:* $50. Electronic applications accepted. *Application Contact:* Nancy Alvarez, Director of Enrollment Management, 305-593-1223 Ext. 3136, Fax: 305-593-1854, E-mail: nalvarez@albizu.edu. *Chancellor*, Dr. Tilokie Depoo, PhD, 305-593-1223 Ext. 3138, Fax: 305-477-8983, E-mail: tdepoo@albizu.edu.

## ALBIZU UNIVERSITY - SAN JUAN, San Juan, PR 00901

**General Information** Independent, coed, university. *Graduate housing:* On-campus housing not available.

GRADUATE UNITS

**Graduate Programs** *Program availability:* Part-time, evening/weekend.

## ALBRIGHT COLLEGE, Reading, PA 19612-5234

**General Information** Independent-religious, coed, comprehensive institution. *Graduate housing:* On-campus housing not available.

GRADUATE UNITS

**Graduate Division** *Program availability:* Part-time, evening/weekend. Electronic applications accepted.

## ALCORN STATE UNIVERSITY, Lorman, MS 39096-7500

**General Information** State-supported, coed, comprehensive institution. CGS member. *Graduate housing:* Room and/or apartments available on a first-come, first-served basis to single students; on-campus housing not available to married students.

GRADUATE UNITS

**School of Graduate Studies** *Program availability:* Part-time. Electronic applications accepted.

***School of Agriculture and Applied Sciences***

***School of Arts and Sciences***

***School of Business***

***School of Education and Psychology***

***School of Nursing***

## ALDERSON BROADDUS UNIVERSITY, Philippi, WV 26416

**General Information** Independent-religious, coed, comprehensive institution. *Graduate housing:* Rooms and/or apartments available on a first-come, first-served basis to single and married students. Housing application deadline: 8/21.

GRADUATE UNITS

**Program in Physician Assistant Studies** Electronic applications accepted.

## ALFRED UNIVERSITY, Alfred, NY 14802-1205

**General Information** Independent, coed, university. *Graduate housing:* Room and/or apartments available on a first-come, first-served basis to single students; on-campus housing not available to married students. Housing application deadline: 5/1. *Student services:* Campus employment opportunities, campus safety program, career counseling, free psychological counseling, international student services, low-cost health insurance, multicultural affairs office, services for students with disabilities, teacher training, writing training. *Library facilities:* Herrick Memorial Library plus 1 other. *Collection:* Books: 189,737 (physical), 675,346 (digital/electronic); Serial titles: 4,013 (physical), 95,505 (digital/electronic); Databases: 211. Study areas open 24 hours, 5–7 days a week; students can reserve study rooms. *Research affiliation:* Whitewares Research Center (whitewares processing, traditional ceramics), National Science Foundation Industry-University Center for Biosurfaces (bioceramics), Center for High Temperature Characterization (materials science), New York State Center for Advanced Ceramic Technology (ceramic engineering and materials science), Center for Glass Research (glass engineering and science), National Science Foundation Industry-University Center for Glass Research.

**Computer facilities:** Computer purchase and lease plans are available. 1,231 computers available on campus for general student use. A campuswide network can be accessed. Online class registration, online bill pay are available.
Website: http://www.alfred.edu/

**General Application Contact:** Sara Love, Coordinator of Graduate Admissions, 607-871-2115, Fax: 607-871-2198, E-mail: gradinquiry@alfred.edu.

GRADUATE UNITS

**Graduate School** Students: 193 full-time (107 women), 276 part-time (202 women); includes 152 minority (82 Black or African American, non-Hispanic/Latino; 1 American Indian or Alaska Native, non-Hispanic/Latino; 10 Asian, non-Hispanic/Latino; 58 Hispanic/Latino; 1 Two or more races, non-Hispanic/Latino), 23 international. Average age 25. 543 applicants, 75% accepted, 355 enrolled. *Faculty:* 79 full-time (29 women), 33 part-time/adjunct (14 women). Expenses: Contact institution. *Financial support:* In 2019–20, 150 students received support, including 6 fellowships with full tuition reimbursements available (averaging $22,520 per year), 45 research assistantships with partial tuition reimbursements available (averaging $19,010 per year), 36 teaching assistantships with full tuition reimbursements available (averaging $27,270 per year); career-related internships or fieldwork and unspecified assistantships also available. Financial award application deadline: 8/1; financial award applicants required to submit FAFSA. In 2019, 264 master's, 10 doctorates, 111 other advanced degrees awarded. *Program availability:* Part-time. *Application deadline:* For fall admission, 8/1 for domestic students, 2/15 for international students; for spring admission, 12/1 for domestic students, 10/1 for international students. Applications are processed on a rolling basis. *Application fee:* $60. Electronic applications accepted. *Application Contact:* Lindsey Gertin, Assistant Director of Graduate Admissions, 607-871-2017, Fax: 607-871-2198, E-mail: gertin@alfred.edu. *Interim Provost and Vice President of Academic Affairs*, Dr. Beth Ann Dobie, 607-871-2967, Fax: 607-871-2198, E-mail: dobie@alfred.edu.

***College of Business*** Students: 37 full-time (19 women), 18 part-time (8 women); includes 15 minority (6 Black or African American, non-Hispanic/Latino; 1 Asian, non-Hispanic/Latino; 5 Hispanic/Latino; 3 Two or more races, non-Hispanic/Latino), 1 international. Average age 24. 52 applicants, 96% accepted, 46 enrolled. *Faculty:* 8 full-time (3 women), 1 part-time/adjunct (0 women). Expenses: Contact institution. *Financial support:* In 2019–20, 50 students received support. Research assistantships with partial tuition reimbursements available, tuition waivers (partial), and unspecified assistantships available. Financial award application deadline: 3/15; financial award applicants required to submit FAFSA. In 2019, 29 master's awarded. *Program availability:* Part-time, evening/weekend. *Application deadline:* For fall admission, 8/1 for domestic students, 3/15 for international students; for winter admission, 12/1 for domestic students; for spring admission, 10/1 for international students. Applications are processed on a rolling basis. *Application fee:* $60. Electronic applications accepted. *Application Contact:* Lindsey Getin, Assistant Director of Graduate Admissions, 607-871-2017, Fax: 607-871-2198, E-mail: gertin@alfred.edu. *Dean of the Colllege of Business*, Mark Lewis, 607-871-2124, Fax: 607-871-2114, E-mail: lewism@alfred.edu.

***College of Ceramics*** Students: 71 full-time (38 women), 10 part-time (5 women); includes 6 minority (3 Asian, non-Hispanic/Latino; 2 Hispanic/Latino; 1 Two or more races, non-Hispanic/Latino), 22 international. Average age 29. 194 applicants, 31% accepted, 38 enrolled. *Faculty:* 41 full-time (4 women), 21 part-time/adjunct (2 women). Expenses: Contact institution. *Financial support:* In 2019–20, 70 students received support. Fellowships with full tuition reimbursements available, research assistantships with full tuition reimbursements available, teaching assistantships with full tuition reimbursements available, and tuition waivers (full and partial) available. Financial award application deadline: 3/15; financial award applicants required to submit FAFSA. In 2019, 26 master's, 5 doctorates awarded. *Application deadline:* For fall admission, 3/1 priority date for domestic students, 3/15 for international students; for spring admission, 12/1 for domestic students, 10/1 for international students. Applications are processed on a rolling basis. *Application fee:* $60. Electronic applications accepted. *Application Contact:* Lindsey Gertin, Assistant Director of Graduate Admissions, 607-871-2017, Fax: 607-871-2198, E-mail: gradinquiry@alfred.edu. *Vice President*, Dr. Gabrielle Gaustad, 607-871-2953, E-mail: gaustad@alfred.edu.

***Division of Education*** Students: 7 full-time (4 women), 17 part-time (13 women); includes 6 minority (2 Black or African American, non-Hispanic/Latino; 3 Hispanic/Latino; 1 Two or more races, non-Hispanic/Latino). Average age 28. 9 applicants, 100% accepted, 9 enrolled. *Faculty:* 4 full-time (3 women), 2 part-time/adjunct (1 woman). Expenses: Contact institution. *Financial support:* In 2019–20, 15 students received support. Research assistantships with partial tuition reimbursements available, tuition waivers (partial), and unspecified assistantships available. Financial award application deadline: 3/15; financial award applicants required to submit FAFSA. In 2019, 13 master's awarded. *Program availability:* Evening/weekend. *Application deadline:* For fall admission, 3/15 for domestic and international students; for spring admission, 12/1 for domestic students, 10/1 for international students. Applications are processed on a rolling basis. *Application fee:* $60. Electronic applications accepted. *Application Contact:* Lindsey Gertin, Assistant Director of Graduate Admissions, 607-871-2017, Fax: 607-871-2198, E-mail: gertin@alfred.edu. *Division Chair*, Tim Nichols, 607-871-2399, E-mail: nichols@alfred.edu.

## ALLEN COLLEGE, Waterloo, IA 50703

**General Information** Independent, coed, primarily women, comprehensive institution. *Graduate housing:* On-campus housing not available.

GRADUATE UNITS

**Graduate Programs** Students: 193 full-time (175 women), 95 part-time (84 women); includes 22 minority (6 Black or African American, non-Hispanic/Latino; 1 American Indian or Alaska Native, non-Hispanic/Latino; 4 Asian, non-Hispanic/Latino; 5 Hispanic/Latino; 6 Two or more races, non-Hispanic/Latino). Average age 32. 376 applicants, 53% accepted, 122 enrolled. *Faculty:* 27 full-time (23 women), 9 part-time/adjunct (8 women). Expenses: Contact institution. *Financial support:* In 2019–20, 78 students received support. Federal Work-Study, institutionally sponsored loans, and scholarships/grants available. Support available to part-time students. Financial award application deadline: 8/1; financial award applicants required to submit FAFSA. *Application deadline:* For fall admission, 2/1 priority date for domestic students; for spring admission, 9/1 priority date for domestic students. Applications are processed on a rolling basis. *Application fee:* $50. Electronic applications accepted. *Application Contact:* Molly Quinn, Director of Admissions, 319-226-2001, Fax: 319-226-2010, E-mail: molly.quinn@allencollege.edu. *Provost*, Dr. Bob Loch, 319-226-2040, Fax: 319-226-2070, E-mail: bob.loch@allencollege.edu.

## ALLIANT INTERNATIONAL UNIVERSITY–FRESNO, Fresno, CA 93727

**General Information** Independent, coed, graduate-only institution. *Graduate housing:* On-campus housing not available.

GRADUATE UNITS

**California School of Forensic Studies** Electronic applications accepted.

**California School of Professional Psychology** Electronic applications accepted.

## ALLIANT INTERNATIONAL UNIVERSITY–IRVINE, Irvine, CA 92606

**General Information** Independent, coed, graduate-only institution. *Graduate housing:* On-campus housing not available.

GRADUATE UNITS

**California School of Forensic Studies** Electronic applications accepted.

**California School of Professional Psychology** *Program availability:* Part-time. Electronic applications accepted.

**Shirley M. Hufstedler School of Education** *Program availability:* Part-time, evening/weekend, online learning. Electronic applications accepted.

## ALLIANT INTERNATIONAL UNIVERSITY - LOS ANGELES, Alhambra, CA 91803

**General Information** Independent, coed, graduate-only institution. *Graduate housing:* Room and/or apartments available to single students; on-campus housing not available to married students.

GRADUATE UNITS

**California School of Forensic Studies**

**California School of Professional Psychology** Electronic applications accepted.

***Organizational Psychology Division*** *Program availability:* Part-time. Electronic applications accepted.

**Marshall Goldsmith School of Management**

***Business Division***

**Shirley M. Hufstedler School of Education** *Program availability:* Part-time, evening/weekend, online learning. Electronic applications accepted.

## ALLIANT INTERNATIONAL UNIVERSITY–SACRAMENTO, Sacramento, CA 95833

**General Information** Independent, coed, graduate-only institution. *Graduate housing:* On-campus housing not available.

**GRADUATE UNITS**

**California School of Forensic Studies** Electronic applications accepted.

**California School of Professional Psychology** *Program availability:* Part-time. Electronic applications accepted.

**Shirley M. Hufstedler School of Education** Electronic applications accepted.

## ALLIANT INTERNATIONAL UNIVERSITY - SAN DIEGO, San Diego, CA 92131

**General Information** Independent, coed, university. *Graduate housing:* Room and/or apartments available on a first-come, first-served basis to single students; on-campus housing not available to married students.

**GRADUATE UNITS**

**California School of Management and Leadership** Students: 81 full-time (32 women), 89 part-time (33 women). Average age 31. *Faculty:* 6 full-time (2 women), 28 part-time/adjunct (13 women). Expenses: Contact institution. *Financial support:* Teaching assistantships, career-related internships or fieldwork, and Federal Work-Study available. Financial award application deadline: 3/1; financial award applicants required to submit FAFSA. In 2019, 64 master's awarded. *Program availability:* Part-time, evening/weekend. *Application deadline:* For fall admission, 3/1 priority date for domestic and international students. Applications are processed on a rolling basis. *Application fee:* $65. Electronic applications accepted. *Application Contact:* Alliant International University Central Contact Center, 866-679-3032, Fax: 858-635-4555, E-mail: admissions@alliant.edu. *Dean,* Dr. Rachna Kumar, 858-635-4495, Fax: 858-635-4739, E-mail: admissions@alliant.edu.

***Business Administration Programs*** Students: 61 full-time (27 women), 56 part-time (22 women). Average age 29. *Faculty:* 4 full-time (2 women), 12 part-time/adjunct (5 women). Expenses: Contact institution. *Financial support:* Teaching assistantships, career-related internships or fieldwork, Federal Work-Study, and scholarships/grants available. Financial award application deadline: 3/15; financial award applicants required to submit FAFSA. In 2019, 64 master's awarded. *Program availability:* Part-time, evening/weekend, 100% online, blended/hybrid learning. *Application deadline:* For fall admission, 3/1 priority date for domestic and international students; for spring admission, 11/1 priority date for domestic and international students. Applications are processed on a rolling basis. *Application fee:* $65. Electronic applications accepted. *Application Contact:* Alliant International University Central Contact Center, 866-679-3032, Fax: 858-635-4555, E-mail: admissions@alliant.edu. *Program Director,* Dr. Rachna Kumar, 858-635-4551, Fax: 855-635-4739, E-mail: admissions@alliant.edu.

**California School of Professional Psychology** *Program availability:* Part-time.

***Organizational Psychology Division*** *Program availability:* Part-time, evening/weekend. Electronic applications accepted.

**Shirley M. Hufstedler School of Education** *Program availability:* Part-time, evening/weekend, online learning. Electronic applications accepted.

## ALLIANT INTERNATIONAL UNIVERSITY–SAN FRANCISCO, San Francisco, CA 94133

**General Information** Independent, coed, graduate-only institution. *Graduate housing:* On-campus housing not available.

**GRADUATE UNITS**

**California School of Forensic Studies**

**California School of Professional Psychology** Electronic applications accepted.

***Organizational Psychology Division*** *Program availability:* Part-time, evening/weekend. Electronic applications accepted.

**San Francisco Law School** *Program availability:* Part-time, evening/weekend. Electronic applications accepted.

**Shirley M. Hufstedler School of Education** *Program availability:* Part-time, evening/weekend, online learning. Electronic applications accepted.

## ALVERNIA UNIVERSITY, Reading, PA 19607-1799

**General Information** Independent-religious, coed, comprehensive institution. *Graduate housing:* On-campus housing not available.

**GRADUATE UNITS**

**School of Graduate Studies** *Program availability:* Part-time, evening/weekend. Electronic applications accepted.

## ALVERNO COLLEGE, Milwaukee, WI 53234-3922

**General Information** Independent-religious, Undergraduate: women only; graduate: coed, comprehensive institution. *Enrollment:* 1,743 graduate, professional, and undergraduate students; 370 full-time matriculated graduate/professional students (327 women), 264 part-time matriculated graduate/professional students (238 women). *Enrollment by degree level:* 440 master's, 5 doctoral, 189 other advanced degrees. *Graduate faculty:* 22 full-time (17 women), 49 part-time/adjunct (42 women). *Graduate housing:* Room and/or apartments available on a first-come, first-served basis to single students; on-campus housing not available to married students. Typical cost: $2000 per year. *Student services:* Campus employment opportunities, campus safety program, career counseling, child daycare facilities, exercise/wellness program, free psychological counseling, low-cost health insurance, multicultural affairs office, services for students with disabilities. *Library facilities:* Alverno College Library. *Collection:* Books: 58,739 (physical), 182,187 (digital/electronic); Serial titles: 823 (physical), 27,896 (digital/electronic); Databases: 66. Weekly public service hours: 85.

**Computer facilities:** 646 computers available on campus for general student use. A campuswide network can be accessed. Online class registration is available.
Website: http://www.alverno.edu/

**General Application Contact:** Katie Kipp, Assistant Director, Graduate and Adult Admissions, 414-382-6045, Fax: 414-382-6354, E-mail: katie.kipp@alverno.edu.

**GRADUATE UNITS**

**JoAnn McGrath School of Nursing and Health Professions** Students: 117 full-time (110 women), 139 part-time (129 women); includes 68 minority (32 Black or African American, non-Hispanic/Latino; 8 Asian, non-Hispanic/Latino; 24 Hispanic/Latino; 4 Two or more races, non-Hispanic/Latino), 1 international. Average age 36. 94 applicants, 95% accepted, 60 enrolled. *Faculty:* 7 full-time (all women), 10 part-time/adjunct (8 women). Expenses: Contact institution. *Financial support:* In 2019–20, 4 students received support. Federal Work-Study and scholarships/grants available. Support available to part-time students. Financial award applicants required to submit FAFSA. In 2019, 51 master's, 3 doctorates awarded. *Program availability:* Part-time, evening/weekend, 100% online, blended/hybrid learning. *Application deadline:* For fall admission, 7/15 priority date for domestic and international students; for spring admission, 12/15 priority date for domestic and international students. Applications are processed on a rolling basis. Electronic applications accepted. *Application Contact:* Janet Stikel, Director of Admissions, 414-382-6112, Fax: 414-382-6354, E-mail: janet.stikel@alverno.edu. *Dean,* Patti Varga, 414-382-6303, Fax: 414-382-6354, E-mail: patti.varga@alverno.edu.

**School of Professional Studies - Business Division** Students: 28 full-time (27 women), 4 part-time (2 women); includes 16 minority (9 Black or African American, non-Hispanic/Latino; 1 American Indian or Alaska Native, non-Hispanic/Latino; 5 Hispanic/Latino; 1 Two or more races, non-Hispanic/Latino), 2 international. Average age 35. 22 applicants, 100% accepted, 17 enrolled. *Faculty:* 2 full-time (1 woman), 1 part-time/adjunct (0 women). Expenses: Contact institution. *Financial support:* In 2019–20, 1 student received support. Federal Work-Study and scholarships/grants available. Support available to part-time students. Financial award applicants required to submit FAFSA. In 2019, 33 master's awarded. *Program availability:* Part-time, evening/weekend. *Application deadline:* For fall admission, 7/15 priority date for domestic and international students; for spring admission, 12/15 priority date for domestic and international students. Applications are processed on a rolling basis. Electronic applications accepted. *Application Contact:* Angel Brown, Graduate and Adult Admissions Counselor, 414-382-6110, Fax: 414-382-6354, E-mail: angel.brown@alverno.edu. *Dean, School of Professional Studies,* Dr. Patricia Luebke, 414-382-6368, E-mail: patricia.luebke@alverno.edu.

**School of Professional Studies - Education Division** Students: 112 full-time (88 women), 106 part-time (93 women); includes 84 minority (40 Black or African American, non-Hispanic/Latino; 1 American Indian or Alaska Native, non-Hispanic/Latino; 9 Asian, non-Hispanic/Latino; 29 Hispanic/Latino; 5 Two or more races, non-Hispanic/Latino), 1 international. Average age 32. 79 applicants, 100% accepted, 73 enrolled. *Faculty:* 6 full-time (3 women), 28 part-time/adjunct (25 women). Expenses: Contact institution. *Financial support:* In 2019–20, 5 students received support. Federal Work-Study and scholarships/grants available. Support available to part-time students. Financial award applicants required to submit FAFSA. In 2019, 52 master's awarded. *Program availability:* Part-time, evening/weekend, 100% online, blended/hybrid learning. *Application deadline:* For fall admission, 7/15 priority date for domestic and international students; for spring admission, 12/15 priority date for domestic and international students. Applications are processed on a rolling basis. Electronic applications accepted. *Application Contact:* Katie Kipp, Assistant Director, Graduate and Adult Admissions, 414-382-6045, Fax: 414-382-6354, E-mail: katie.kipp@alverno.edu. *Dean, School of Professional Studies,* Dr. Patricia Luebke, 414-382-6368, Fax: 414-382-6354, E-mail: patricia.luebke@alverno.edu.

**School of Professional Studies - Psychology** Students: 113 full-time (102 women), 10 part-time (9 women); includes 45 minority (23 Black or African American, non-Hispanic/Latino; 2 Asian, non-Hispanic/Latino; 17 Hispanic/Latino; 3 Two or more races, non-Hispanic/Latino), 1 international. Average age 33. 65 applicants, 89% accepted, 39 enrolled. *Faculty:* 4 full-time (all women). Expenses: Contact institution. *Financial support:* Federal Work-Study and scholarships/grants available. Support available to part-time students. Financial award applicants required to submit FAFSA. In 2019, 25 master's awarded. *Program availability:* Part-time, evening/weekend. *Application deadline:* For fall admission, 7/15 priority date for domestic and international students; for spring admission, 12/15 priority date for domestic and international students. Applications are processed on a rolling basis. Electronic applications accepted. *Application Contact:* Annie Barrett, Graduate, Adult, and Transfer Admissions Counselor, 414-382-6113, Fax: 414-382-6354, E-mail: annie.barrett@alverno.edu. *Dean, School of Professional Studies,* Dr. Patricia Luebke, 414-382-6368, Fax: 414-382-6354, E-mail: patricia.luebke@alverno.edu.

## AMBERTON UNIVERSITY, Garland, TX 75041-5595

**General Information** Independent-religious, coed, upper-level institution. *Graduate housing:* On-campus housing not available.

**GRADUATE UNITS**

**Graduate School** *Program availability:* Part-time, evening/weekend.

## AMBROSE UNIVERSITY, Calgary, AB T3H 0L5, Canada

**General Information** Independent-religious, coed, comprehensive institution. *Graduate housing:* Room and/or apartments available on a first-come, first-served basis to single students; on-campus housing not available to married students. Housing application deadline: 6/15.

**GRADUATE UNITS**

**Ambrose Seminary** *Program availability:* Part-time, blended/hybrid learning. Electronic applications accepted.

## AMERICAN ACADEMY OF ACUPUNCTURE AND ORIENTAL MEDICINE, Roseville, MN 55113

**General Information** Proprietary, coed, graduate-only institution.

**GRADUATE UNITS**

**Graduate Programs**

## AMERICAN BAPTIST SEMINARY OF THE WEST, Berkeley, CA 94704-3029

**General Information** Independent-religious, coed, graduate-only institution. *Graduate housing:* Rooms and/or apartments available on a first-come, first-served basis to single and married students. Housing application deadline: 5/1.

**GRADUATE UNITS**

**Graduate and Professional Programs** *Program availability:* Part-time, evening/weekend, online learning. Electronic applications accepted.

## AMERICAN BUSINESS & TECHNOLOGY UNIVERSITY, Saint Joseph, MO 64506

**General Information** Proprietary, coed, comprehensive institution.

**GRADUATE UNITS**

**Programs in Business Administration** *Program availability:* Online learning.

## AMERICAN COLLEGE DUBLIN, Dublin 2, Ireland

**General Information** Independent, coed, comprehensive institution.

GRADUATE UNITS
**Graduate Programs**

## AMERICAN COLLEGE OF ACUPUNCTURE AND ORIENTAL MEDICINE, Houston, TX 77063

**General Information** Proprietary, coed, graduate-only institution. *Research affiliation:* Montrose Clinic (HIV/AIDS research and treatment), Rice University Wellness Center (student and staff care), Baylor College of Medicine (acupuncture for osteoarthritis of the knee), Memorial Herman Healthcare System, Tianjing Hospital, China (traditional Chinese medicine).

GRADUATE UNITS
**Graduate Studies** *Program availability:* Part-time.

## AMERICAN COLLEGE OF EDUCATION, Indianapolis, IN 46204

**General Information** Proprietary, coed, graduate-only institution.

GRADUATE UNITS
**Graduate Programs**

## THE AMERICAN COLLEGE OF FINANCIAL SERVICES, Bryn Mawr, PA 19010-2105

**General Information** Independent, coed, graduate-only institution. *Graduate housing:* On-campus housing not available.

GRADUATE UNITS
**Graduate Programs** *Program availability:* Part-time, evening/weekend, online learning. Electronic applications accepted.

## AMERICAN COLLEGE OF HEALTHCARE SCIENCES, Portland, OR 97239-3719

**General Information** Independent, coed, comprehensive institution. *Graduate housing:* On-campus housing not available.

GRADUATE UNITS
**Graduate Programs** *Program availability:* Part-time, evening/weekend, online learning.

## AMERICAN COLLEGE OF THESSALONIKI, 55535 Pylaia, Greece

**General Information** Independent, coed, comprehensive institution. *Enrollment:* 607 graduate, professional, and undergraduate students; 60 full-time matriculated graduate/professional students (30 women), 30 part-time matriculated graduate/professional students (15 women). *Enrollment by degree level:* 90 master's. *Graduate faculty:* 5 full-time (1 woman), 15 part-time/adjunct (5 women). *Tuition:* Full-time 10,000 euros; part-time 5000 euros per credit. *Required fees:* 10,000 euros; 5000 euros per credit. Tuition and fees vary according to campus/location and program. *Graduate housing:* Room and/or apartments available on a first-come, first-served basis to single students; on-campus housing not available to married students. Typical cost: 1500 euros per year. Room charges vary according to campus/location. Housing application deadline: 9/15. *Student services:* Campus employment opportunities, career counseling, free psychological counseling, international student services, low-cost health insurance, multicultural affairs office, writing training. *Library facilities:* Bissell Library plus 1 other. *Collection:* Books: 28,605 (physical), 201,768 (digital/electronic); Serial titles: 22 (physical), 72,165 (digital/electronic); Databases: 33. Weekly public service hours: 54; students can reserve study rooms.

**Computer facilities:** 165 computers available on campus for general student use. A campuswide network can be accessed.
Website: http://www.act.edu/

**General Application Contact:** Roula Lebetli, Director of Student Recruitment, 30-310-398238, E-mail: rleb@act.edu.

GRADUATE UNITS
**Department of Business Administration** Students: 60 full-time (30 women), 30 part-time (15 women). Average age 26. 100 applicants, 50% accepted, 45 enrolled. *Faculty:* 5 full-time (1 woman), 15 part-time/adjunct (5 women). Expenses: Contact institution. *Financial support:* Fellowships, scholarships/grants, and tuition waivers (full and partial) available. Support available to part-time students. Financial award application deadline: 9/15. In 2019, 30 master's awarded. *Program availability:* Part-time, evening/weekend. *Application deadline:* For fall admission, 9/30 priority date for domestic students; for spring admission, 2/18 priority date for domestic students. Applications are processed on a rolling basis. *Application fee:* 30 euros. Electronic applications accepted. *Application Contact:* Roula Lebetli, Director of Student Recruitment, 30-310-398238, E-mail: rleb@act.edu. *Chair, Business Division,* Dr. Nikolaos Hourvouliades, 30-310-398385, E-mail: hourvoul@act.edu.

## AMERICAN CONSERVATORY THEATER, San Francisco, CA 94108-5800

**General Information** Independent, coed, graduate-only institution. *Graduate housing:* On-campus housing not available.

GRADUATE UNITS
**Program in Acting**

## AMERICAN FILM INSTITUTE CONSERVATORY, Los Angeles, CA 90027-1657

**General Information** Independent, coed, graduate-only institution. *Graduate housing:* On-campus housing not available.

GRADUATE UNITS
**Graduate Program** Electronic applications accepted.

## AMERICAN GRADUATE SCHOOL IN PARIS, F-75006 Paris, France

**General Information** Independent, coed, graduate-only institution. *Enrollment by degree level:* 19 master's, 11 doctoral, 1 other advanced degree. *Graduate faculty:* 3 full-time (1 woman), 8 part-time/adjunct (2 women). *Tuition:* Full-time 19,117 euros; part-time 2667 euros per unit. *Required fees:* 150 euros. One-time fee: 300 euros full-time; 100 euros part-time. *Graduate housing:* On-campus housing not available. *Library facilities:* AGS Library. *Collection:* Students can reserve study rooms.
Website: http://www.ags.edu/

**General Application Contact:** Corentine Chaillet, Administrative manager, (33) 1-47-20-00-94, E-mail: admissions@ags.edu.

GRADUATE UNITS
**Program in International Relations and Diplomacy**

## AMERICAN GRADUATE UNIVERSITY, Covina, CA 91724

**General Information** Proprietary, coed, graduate-only institution. *Enrollment by degree level:* 748 master's, 62 other advanced degrees. *Graduate faculty:* 15 part-time/adjunct (3 women). *Tuition:* Part-time $325 per credit hour. Tuition and fees vary according to program. *Graduate housing:* On-campus housing not available. *Library facilities:* American Graduate University Library. *Research affiliation:* Library and Information Resources Network.

**Computer facilities:** Online class registration is available.
Website: http://www.agu.edu/

**General Application Contact:** Laurie Mejia, Director of Admissions, 626-966-4576 Ext. 1007, Fax: 626-915-1709, E-mail: lauriemejia@agu.edu.

GRADUATE UNITS
**Program in Acquisition Management** *Program availability:* Part-time, online learning. Electronic applications accepted.
**Program in Business Administration** *Program availability:* Part-time, online learning. Electronic applications accepted.
**Program in Contract Management** *Program availability:* Part-time, online learning. Electronic applications accepted.
**Program in Supply Chain Management** *Program availability:* Part-time, online learning.

## AMERICAN INSTITUTE OF ALTERNATIVE MEDICINE, Columbus, OH 43229

**General Information** Proprietary, coed.

GRADUATE UNITS
**School of Acupuncture**

## AMERICAN INTERCONTINENTAL UNIVERSITY ATLANTA, Atlanta, GA 30328

**General Information** Proprietary, coed, comprehensive institution. *Graduate housing:* On-campus housing not available.

GRADUATE UNITS
**Program in Global Technology Management** *Program availability:* Part-time, evening/weekend, online learning. Electronic applications accepted.
**Program in Information Technology** *Program availability:* Part-time, evening/weekend. Electronic applications accepted.

## AMERICAN INTERCONTINENTAL UNIVERSITY HOUSTON, Houston, TX 77042

**General Information** Proprietary, coed, comprehensive institution.

GRADUATE UNITS
**School of Business**

## AMERICAN INTERCONTINENTAL UNIVERSITY ONLINE, Schaumburg, IL 60173

**General Information** Proprietary, coed, comprehensive institution.

GRADUATE UNITS
**Program in Business Administration** *Program availability:* Evening/weekend, online learning. Electronic applications accepted.
**Program in Education** *Program availability:* Evening/weekend, online learning. Electronic applications accepted.
**Program in Information Technology** *Program availability:* Evening/weekend, online learning. Electronic applications accepted.

## AMERICAN INTERNATIONAL COLLEGE, Springfield, MA 01109-3189

**General Information** Independent, coed, comprehensive institution. *Graduate housing:* Room and/or apartments available on a first-come, first-served basis to single students; on-campus housing not available to married students. Housing application deadline: 8/15.

GRADUATE UNITS
**School of Business, Arts and Sciences** *Program availability:* Part-time, evening/weekend.
**School of Education** *Program availability:* Evening/weekend. Electronic applications accepted.
***Low Residency Programs*** *Program availability:* Evening/weekend.
**School of Health Sciences** *Program availability:* Part-time, 100% online. Electronic applications accepted.

## AMERICAN JEWISH UNIVERSITY, Bel Air, CA 90077-1599

**General Information** Independent-religious, coed, graduate-only institution. *Graduate housing:* Rooms and/or apartments available on a first-come, first-served basis to single and married students. Housing application deadline: 6/1.

GRADUATE UNITS
**Graduate School of Education**
**Graduate School of Nonprofit Management** *Program availability:* Part-time, evening/weekend.
**Ziegler School of Rabbinic Studies**

## AMERICAN MUSEUM OF NATURAL HISTORY–RICHARD GILDER GRADUATE SCHOOL, New York, NY 10024

**General Information** Independent, coed, graduate-only institution.

GRADUATE UNITS
**Program in Comparative Biology**

## AMERICAN NATIONAL UNIVERSITY - ROANOKE VALLEY, Salem, VA 24153

**General Information** Proprietary, coed, comprehensive institution.

GRADUATE UNITS
**Program in Business Administration**

## AMERICAN PUBLIC UNIVERSITY SYSTEM, Charles Town, WV 25414

**General Information** Proprietary, coed, comprehensive institution. CGS member. *Enrollment:* 45,249 graduate, professional, and undergraduate students; 461 full-time matriculated graduate/professional students (193 women), 7,322 part-time matriculated graduate/professional students (3,127 women). *Enrollment by degree level:* 7,395 master's, 70 doctoral, 317 other advanced degrees. *Graduate housing:* On-campus housing not available. *Student services:* Career counseling, international student services, services for students with disabilities. *Library facilities:* APUS Online Library.

**Computer facilities:** Online class registration is available.
Website: http://www.apus.edu/

**GRADUATE UNITS**

**AMU/APU Graduate Programs** Students: 461 full-time (193 women), 7,322 part-time (3,127 women); includes 3,089 minority (1,404 Black or African American, non-Hispanic/Latino; 30 American Indian or Alaska Native, non-Hispanic/Latino; 210 Asian, non-Hispanic/Latino; 753 Hispanic/Latino; 445 Native Hawaiian or other Pacific Islander, non-Hispanic/Latino; 247 Two or more races, non-Hispanic/Latino), 117 international. Average age 37. Expenses: Contact institution. *Financial support:* Scholarships/grants available. Financial award applicants required to submit FAFSA. In 2019, 2,681 master's awarded. *Program availability:* Part-time, evening/weekend, online only, 100% online. *Application deadline:* Applications are processed on a rolling basis. Electronic applications accepted. *Application Contact:* Yoci Deal, Associate Vice President, Graduate and International Admissions, 877-468-6268, Fax: 304-724-3764, E-mail: info@apus.edu. *President*, Dr. Wallace Boston, 877-468-6268, Fax: 304-728-2348, E-mail: president@apus.edu.

## AMERICAN SENTINEL UNIVERSITY, Aurora, CO 80014

**General Information** Proprietary, coed, comprehensive institution.

**GRADUATE UNITS**

**Graduate Programs** *Program availability:* Part-time, evening/weekend, online learning. Electronic applications accepted.

## AMERICAN UNIVERSITY, Washington, DC 20016-8001

**General Information** Independent-religious, coed, university. CGS member. *Graduate housing:* On-campus housing not available.

**GRADUATE UNITS**

**College of Arts and Sciences** *Program availability:* Part-time, evening/weekend, 100% online, blended/hybrid learning. Electronic applications accepted.

***Critical Race, Gender, and Culture Studies***

**Kogod School of Business** *Program availability:* Part-time, evening/weekend, 100% online, blended/hybrid learning. Electronic applications accepted.

**School of Communication** *Program availability:* Part-time, evening/weekend, 100% online. Electronic applications accepted.

***Division of Communication Studies*** Electronic applications accepted.

***Division of Journalism*** *Program availability:* Part-time, evening/weekend. Electronic applications accepted.

***Division of Public Communication*** *Program availability:* Part-time, evening/weekend, 100% online. Electronic applications accepted.

***Film and Media Arts Division*** *Program availability:* Part-time, evening/weekend. Electronic applications accepted.

**School of Education** *Program availability:* Part-time, evening/weekend, 100% online. Electronic applications accepted.

**School of International Service** *Program availability:* Part-time, evening/weekend, 100% online, blended/hybrid learning. Electronic applications accepted.

**School of Professional and Extended Studies** *Program availability:* Part-time, evening/weekend, 100% online, blended/hybrid learning. Electronic applications accepted.

**School of Public Affairs** *Program availability:* Part-time, evening/weekend, 100% online, blended/hybrid learning. Electronic applications accepted.

**Washington College of Law** *Program availability:* Part-time, evening/weekend, 100% online, blended/hybrid learning. Electronic applications accepted.

## AMERICAN UNIVERSITY IN BULGARIA, Blagoevgrad 2700, Bulgaria

**General Information** Independent, coed, comprehensive institution.

**GRADUATE UNITS**

**Executive MBA Program**

## THE AMERICAN UNIVERSITY IN CAIRO, 11835 New Cairo, Egypt

**General Information** Independent, coed, comprehensive institution. CGS member. *Graduate housing:* Room and/or apartments available on a first-come, first-served basis to single students; on-campus housing not available to married students.

**GRADUATE UNITS**

**Graduate School of Education** *Program availability:* Part-time, evening/weekend. Electronic applications accepted.

**School of Business** *Program availability:* Part-time, evening/weekend. Electronic applications accepted.

**School of Global Affairs and Public Policy** *Program availability:* Part-time, evening/weekend. Electronic applications accepted.

**School of Humanities and Social Sciences** *Program availability:* Part-time, evening/weekend. Electronic applications accepted.

**School of Sciences and Engineering** *Program availability:* Part-time, evening/weekend. Electronic applications accepted.

## THE AMERICAN UNIVERSITY IN DUBAI, Dubai, United Arab Emirates

**General Information** Proprietary, coed, comprehensive institution. *Graduate housing:* Room and/or apartments available on a first-come, first-served basis to single students; on-campus housing not available to married students. Housing application deadline: 7/31.

**GRADUATE UNITS**

**Graduate Programs** *Program availability:* Part-time, evening/weekend. Electronic applications accepted.

## AMERICAN UNIVERSITY OF ARMENIA, Yerevan 3750198, Armenia

**General Information** Independent, coed, graduate-only institution. *Enrollment by degree level:* 427 master's, 13 other advanced degrees. *Graduate faculty:* 25 full-time (7 women), 44 part-time/adjunct (14 women). *Tuition:* Full-time $3100; part-time $165 per credit. Tuition and fees vary according to program. *Graduate housing:* Room and/or apartments available on a first-come, first-served basis to single students; on-campus housing not available to married students. Typical cost: $1700 per year. Room charges vary according to housing facility selected. Housing application deadline: 6/1. *Student services:* Campus employment opportunities, campus safety program, career counseling, exercise/wellness program, free psychological counseling, international student services, services for students with disabilities, teacher training, writing training. *Library facilities:* AGBU Papazian Library plus 1 other. *Collection:* Books: 39,109 (physical), 186,459 (digital/electronic); Databases: 237,480. Students can reserve study rooms. *Research affiliation:* Samsung (cryptography), Volkswagen Foundation (cryptography), Mentor Graphics (data compression algorithms), IBM (big data and data analytics), Johns Hopkins University Bloomberg School of Public Health (public health), Institut de Medecine Sociale et Preventive, Universite de Genève (Geneva, Switzerland) (tobacco control/health education).

**Computer facilities:** 137 computers available on campus for general student use. Online class registration is available.
Website: http://www.aua.am/

**General Application Contact:** Karine Satamian, Admissions and Recruitment Officer, +374 60 61 27 50, E-mail: admissions@aua.am.

**GRADUATE UNITS**

**Graduate Programs** *Program availability:* Part-time, evening/weekend.

## AMERICAN UNIVERSITY OF BEIRUT, 107 2020 Beirut, Lebanon

**General Information** Independent, coed, university. CGS member. *Enrollment:* 9,497 graduate, professional, and undergraduate students; 1,277 full-time matriculated graduate/professional students (717 women), 872 part-time matriculated graduate/professional students (568 women). *Enrollment by degree level:* 1,540 master's, 168 doctoral, 441 other advanced degrees. *Graduate faculty:* 574 full-time (216 women), 18 part-time/adjunct (3 women). *Tuition:* Full-time $18,288; part-time $1016 per credit. *Required fees:* $917. Tuition and fees vary according to course load and program. *Graduate housing:* Room and/or apartments available on a first-come, first-served basis to single students; on-campus housing not available to married students. Typical cost: $6152 per year. Room charges vary according to campus/location. Housing application deadline: 6/30. *Student services:* Campus employment opportunities, campus safety program, career counseling, exercise/wellness program, free psychological counseling, grant writing training, international student services, low-cost health insurance, services for students with disabilities, teacher training, writing training. *Library facilities:* Jafet Library plus 3 others. *Collection:* Books: 400,000 (physical), 1.1 million (digital/electronic); Serial titles: 5,000 (physical), 140,000 (digital/electronic); Databases: 350. Weekly public service hours: 107. *Research affiliation:* Qatar University (history and archeology), Ford Foundation (health promotion and community health), The University of Texas MD Anderson Cancer Center (medicine), Tech Hub s.a.l. (electrical and computer engineering), Open Society Foundations (public policy), UN Children's Fund (UNICEF) (nutrition and food sciences).

**Computer facilities:** Computer purchase and lease plans are available. 2,450 computers available on campus for general student use. A campuswide network can be accessed. Online class registration is available.
Website: http://www.aub.edu.lb/

**General Application Contact:** Dr. Antoine Sabbagh, Director, Admissions Office and Financial Aid Office, 1-350000 Ext. 2594, Fax: 1-750775, E-mail: as21@aub.edu.lb.

**GRADUATE UNITS**

**Graduate Programs** Students: 1,277 full-time (717 women), 872 part-time (568 women). Average age 26. 2,273 applicants, 57% accepted, 664 enrolled. *Faculty:* 574 full-time (216 women), 18 part-time/adjunct (3 women). Expenses: Contact institution. *Financial support:* In 2019–20, 426 students received support, including 1,473 research assistantships (averaging $5,856 per year); scholarships/grants, health care benefits, and unspecified assistantships also available. Financial award application deadline: 12/20; financial award applicants required to submit CSS PROFILE. *Program availability:* Part-time, 100% online. *Application deadline:* For fall admission, 3/18 for domestic and international students; for spring admission, 11/5 for domestic and international students; for summer admission, 3/18 for domestic and international students. Applications are processed on a rolling basis. *Application fee:* $50. Electronic applications accepted. *Application Contact:* Dr. Antoine Sabbagh, Director, Admissions Office and Financial Aid Office, 1-350000 Ext. 2594, Fax: 1-750775, E-mail: as21@aub.edu.lb. *Associate Provost*, Prof. Zaher Dawy, 1-374374 Ext. 3538, E-mail: zd03@aub.edu.lb.

***Faculty of Agricultural and Food Sciences*** Students: 57 full-time (46 women), 67 part-time (51 women); includes 7 minority (all Black or African American, non-Hispanic/Latino). Average age 26. 263 applicants, 54% accepted, 31 enrolled. *Faculty:* 29 full-time (8 women). Expenses: Contact institution. *Financial support:* In 2019–20, 122 fellowships with full and partial tuition reimbursements (averaging $4,440 per year), 20 research assistantships with full and partial tuition reimbursements (averaging $5,440 per year) were awarded; scholarships/grants, health care benefits, and unspecified assistantships also available. Financial award application deadline: 2/2. *Program availability:* Part-time. *Application deadline:* For fall admission, 3/18 for domestic and international students; for spring admission, 11/5 for domestic and international students. *Application fee:* $50. Electronic applications accepted. *Application Contact:* Tharwat Haddad, Student Records Officer, 1-343002 Ext. 4424, Fax: 1-343002, E-mail: thhaddad@aub.edu.lb. *Dean of Faculty of Agricultural and Food Sciences*, Rabi Hassan Mohtar, 1-350000 Ext. 4400, Fax: 1-744460, E-mail: mohtar@aub.edu.lb.

***Faculty of Health Sciences*** Students: 58 full-time (49 women), 81 part-time (72 women). Average age 27. 425 applicants, 44% accepted, 46 enrolled. *Faculty:* 31 full-time (18 women), 9 part-time/adjunct (3 women). Expenses: Contact institution. *Financial support:* In 2019–20, 73 students received support, including 4 fellowships with full and partial tuition reimbursements available (averaging $15,000 per year), 19 research assistantships with full and partial tuition reimbursements available (averaging $555 per year), 3 teaching assistantships with partial tuition reimbursements available (averaging $725 per year); scholarships/grants and unspecified assistantships also available. Financial award application deadline: 3/18. *Program availability:* Part-time. *Application deadline:* For fall admission, 3/18 for domestic and international students; for spring admission, 11/18 for domestic and international students. *Application fee:* $50. Electronic applications accepted. *Application Contact:* Lama El Kadi, Administrative Coordinator, 1-350000 Ext. 4687, E-mail: le19@aub.edu.lb. *Professor and Dean*, Prof. Iman Adel Nuwayhid, 1-759683 Ext. 4600, Fax: 1-744470, E-mail: nuwayhid@aub.edu.lb.

***Faculty of Medicine*** Students: 704 full-time (407 women). 460 applicants, 49% accepted, 170 enrolled. *Faculty:* 332 full-time (111 women), 61 part-time/adjunct (6 women). Expenses: Contact institution. *Financial support:* Fellowships, research assistantships, teaching assistantships, and tuition waivers available. *Program availability:* Part-time. *Application deadline:* Applications are processed on a rolling basis. *Application fee:* $75. Electronic applications accepted. *Application Contact:* Bradley Jon Tucker, Vice Provost and Registrar, 1-350000 Ext. 2594, Fax: 1-750775, E-mail: bt17@aub.edu.lb. *Interim Dean*, Dr. Ghazi Zaatari, 1-350000 Ext. 4700, Fax: 1-744489, E-mail: zaatari@aub.edu.lb.

***Maroun Semaan Faculty of Engineering and Architecture*** Students: 390 full-time (196 women), 100 part-time (38 women). Average age 28. 392 applicants, 55% accepted, 99 enrolled. *Faculty:* 113 full-time (27 women), 101 part-time/adjunct (36 women). Expenses: Contact institution. *Financial support:* In 2019–20, 85 fellowships with full tuition reimbursements (averaging $16,080 per year), 97 research assistantships with full and partial tuition reimbursements (averaging $5,280 per year), 93 teaching assistantships with full and partial tuition reimbursements (averaging $1,804 per year) were awarded; scholarships/grants, tuition waivers (full and partial), and unspecified assistantships also available. Financial award application deadline: 4/4. *Program availability:* Part-time, 100% online. *Application deadline:* For fall admission, 3/18 for domestic and international students; for spring admission, 11/5 for domestic and international students; for summer admission, 3/18 for domestic and international students. Applications are processed on a rolling basis. *Application fee:* $50. Electronic applications accepted. *Application Contact:* Dr. Antoine Sabbagh, Director, Admissions Office, 1-374374 Ext. 2590, Fax: 1-750775, E-mail: as21@aub.edu.lb. *Dean*, Prof. Alan Shehade, 1-374374 Ext. 3400, Fax: 1-744462, E-mail: as20@aub.edu.lb.

***Rafic Hariri School of Nursing*** Students: 10 full-time (8 women), 51 part-time (41 women). Average age 27. 32 applicants, 81% accepted, 16 enrolled. *Faculty:* 12 full-time (all women), 23 part-time/adjunct (18 women). Expenses: Contact institution. *Financial support:* In 2019–20, 12 students received support. Fellowships, research assistantships, teaching assistantships, tuition waivers, and unspecified assistantships available. Financial award application deadline: 4/3. *Program availability:* Part-time, blended/hybrid learning. *Application deadline:* For fall admission, 3/18 for domestic students. Applications are processed on a rolling basis. *Application fee:* $50. Electronic applications accepted. *Application Contact:* Nisrine Ghalayini, Administrative Assistant, 1-350000 Ext. 5951, Fax: 1-744476, E-mail: ng28@aub.edu.lb. *Interim Dean*, Dr. Laila Farhood, 1-350000 Ext. 5953, Fax: 1-744476, E-mail: lf00@aub.edu.lb.

***Suliman S. Olayan School of Business*** Students: 89 full-time (30 women), 156 part-time (83 women); includes 3 minority (all Black or African American, non-Hispanic/Latino). Average age 26. 589 applicants, 57% accepted, 245 enrolled. *Faculty:* 60 full-time (19 women), 20 part-time/adjunct (8 women). Expenses: Contact institution. *Financial support:* In 2019–20, 76 students received support, including 1 research assistantship (averaging $19,000 per year), 56 teaching assistantships (averaging $19,900 per year); fellowships and tuition waivers also available. Financial award application deadline: 3/15. *Program availability:* Part-time, online learning. *Application deadline:* For fall admission, 3/15 for domestic and international students. Applications are processed on a rolling basis. *Application fee:* $50. Electronic applications accepted. *Application Contact:* Maya El Helou, Director of graduate programs, 1-350000 Ext. 3955, Fax: 1-750214, E-mail: helou@aub.edu.lb. *Dean and Professor*, Dr. Steve Harvey, 1-350000 Ext. 3934, Fax: 1-750214, E-mail: sh146@aub.edu.lb.

## AMERICAN UNIVERSITY OF HEALTH SCIENCES, Signal Hill, CA 90755

**General Information** Proprietary, coed, comprehensive institution.

**GRADUATE UNITS**

**School of Clinical Research**

## THE AMERICAN UNIVERSITY OF PARIS, 75007 Paris, France

**General Information** Independent, coed, comprehensive institution. *Graduate housing:* Room and/or apartments available on a first-come, first-served basis to single students; on-campus housing not available to married students.

**GRADUATE UNITS**

**Graduate Programs** Electronic applications accepted.

## AMERICAN UNIVERSITY OF PUERTO RICO - BAYAMON, Bayamon, PR 00960-2037

**General Information** Independent, coed, comprehensive institution. *Graduate housing:* On-campus housing not available.

**GRADUATE UNITS**

**Program in Criminal Justice** *Program availability:* Part-time, evening/weekend.

**Program in Education** *Program availability:* Part-time, evening/weekend.

## THE AMERICAN UNIVERSITY OF ROME, 00153 Rome, Italy

**General Information** Independent, coed, comprehensive institution. *Research affiliation:* ARCA - Association for Research into Crimes against Art (art crime prevention), ENFSI - European Network of Forensic Science Institutes (forensic archaeology), Conservation Science in Cultural Heritage.

**GRADUATE UNITS**

**Graduate School** Electronic applications accepted.

## AMERICAN UNIVERSITY OF SHARJAH, Sharjah, United Arab Emirates

**General Information** Independent, coed, comprehensive institution. *Graduate housing:* Room and/or apartments available on a first-come, first-served basis to single students; on-campus housing not available to married students. Housing application deadline: 8/16. *Research affiliation:* Emirates Foundation (philanthropy), International Atomic Energy Agency (energy), National Research Foundation, Mohammed Bin Rashid Space Center (space), Advanced Technology Investment Company (technology and investment), Qatar National Research Foundation.

**GRADUATE UNITS**

**Graduate Programs** *Program availability:* Part-time, evening/weekend. Electronic applications accepted.

## AMRIDGE UNIVERSITY, Montgomery, AL 36117

**General Information** Independent-religious, coed, university. *Graduate housing:* On-campus housing not available.

**GRADUATE UNITS**

**Graduate and Professional Programs** *Program availability:* Part-time, evening/weekend, online learning. Electronic applications accepted.

## ANABAPTIST MENNONITE BIBLICAL SEMINARY, Elkhart, IN 46517-1999

**General Information** Independent-religious, coed, graduate-only institution. *Graduate housing:* Rooms and/or apartments available on a first-come, first-served basis to single and married students. Housing application deadline: 8/1.

**GRADUATE UNITS**

**Graduate and Professional Programs** *Program availability:* Part-time, 100% online, blended/hybrid learning. Electronic applications accepted.

## ANAHEIM UNIVERSITY, Anaheim, CA 92806-5150

**General Information** Proprietary, coed, graduate-only institution.

**GRADUATE UNITS**

**Master of Fine Arts in Digital Film Making**

**Program in Teaching English to Speakers of Other Languages** *Program availability:* Part-time, evening/weekend, online only, 100% online. Electronic applications accepted.

**Programs in Business Administration** *Program availability:* Part-time, evening/weekend, online only, 100% online. Electronic applications accepted.

## ANDERSON UNIVERSITY, Anderson, IN 46012

**General Information** Independent-religious, coed, comprehensive institution. *Graduate housing:* Room and/or apartments available to single students; on-campus housing not available to married students. Housing application deadline: 6/1.

**GRADUATE UNITS**

**Falls School of Business**

**School of Education**

**School of Theology** *Program availability:* Part-time.

## ANDERSON UNIVERSITY, Anderson, SC 29621

**General Information** Independent-religious, coed, comprehensive institution. *Enrollment:* 3,497 graduate, professional, and undergraduate students; 455 full-time matriculated graduate/professional students (248 women), 97 part-time matriculated graduate/professional students (44 women). *Enrollment by degree level:* 486 master's, 66 doctoral. *Graduate housing:* Room and/or apartments available on a first-come, first-served basis to single students; on-campus housing not available to married students. Typical cost: $7380 per year. *Student services:* Campus employment opportunities, campus safety program, career counseling, exercise/wellness program, multicultural affairs office, teacher training, writing training. *Library facilities:* Thrift Library. *Collection:* Books: 90,729 (physical), 99,204 (digital/electronic); Serial titles: 14,268 (physical), 174,052 (digital/electronic); Databases: 200. Weekly public service hours: 88; students can reserve study rooms.

**Computer facilities:** 192 computers available on campus for general student use. A campuswide network can be accessed. Online class registration is available.
Website: http://www.andersonuniversity.edu/

**General Application Contact:** Chesley Tench, Director of Post-Traditional Admission, 864-231-5000, E-mail: ctench@andersonuniversity.edu.

**GRADUATE UNITS**

**Clamp Divinity School** Expenses: Contact institution. *Financial support:* Scholarships/grants and tuition waivers available. Financial award application deadline: 3/1; financial award applicants required to submit FAFSA. *Program availability:* Part-time, online only, 100% online, blended/hybrid learning. *Application Contact:* Dr. Ben Brammer, Senior Recruiter, 864-2312039, E-mail: bbrammer@andersonuniversity.edu. *Dean*, Dr. Michael Duduit, 864-328-1809, E-mail: ministry@andersonuniversity.edu.

**College of Business** Expenses: Contact institution. *Financial support:* Scholarships/grants and tuition waivers available. Financial award application deadline: 3/1; financial award applicants required to submit FAFSA. *Application deadline:* Applications are processed on a rolling basis. Electronic applications accepted. *Application Contact:* Sharon Vargo, Graduate Admission Counselor, 864-231-2000, E-mail: svargo@andersonuniversity.edu. *Dean*, Steve Nail, 864-MBA-6000.

**College of Education** Expenses: Contact institution. *Financial support:* Scholarships/grants and tuition waivers available. Financial award application deadline: 3/1; financial award applicants required to submit FAFSA. *Program availability:* 100% online. *Application Contact:* Dr. Mark Butler, Dean, 864-231-2042. *Dean*, Dr. Mark Butler, 864-231-2042.

**College of Health Professions** Expenses: Contact institution. *Financial support:* Scholarships/grants available. *Program availability:* Online learning. *Application deadline:* Applications are processed on a rolling basis. Electronic applications accepted. *Application Contact:* Dr. Donald M. Peace, Dean, 864-231-5513, E-mail: dpeace@andersonuniversity.edu. *Dean*, Dr. Donald M. Peace, 864-231-5513, E-mail: dpeace@andersonuniversity.edu.

**Command College of South Carolina** Expenses: Contact institution. *Financial support:* Scholarships/grants available. Financial award application deadline: 3/1; financial award applicants required to submit FAFSA. *Program availability:* Blended/hybrid learning. *Application deadline:* Applications are processed on a rolling basis. Electronic applications accepted.

**South Carolina School of the Arts** Expenses: Contact institution. *Financial support:* Scholarships/grants available. *Program availability:* Online learning. *Application Contact:* David Larson, Dean, 864-231-2002, E-mail: dlarson@andersonuniversity.edu. *Dean*, David Larson, 864-231-2002, E-mail: dlarson@andersonuniversity.edu.

## ANDREWS UNIVERSITY, Berrien Springs, MI 49104

**General Information** Independent-religious, coed, university. CGS member. *Enrollment:* 3,412 graduate, professional, and undergraduate students; 875 full-time matriculated graduate/professional students (348 women), 788 part-time matriculated graduate/professional students (275 women). *Enrollment by degree level:* 1,066 master's, 565 doctoral, 32 other advanced degrees. *Graduate faculty:* 168 full-time (62 women), 32 part-time/adjunct (11 women). *Graduate housing:* Rooms and/or apartments available on a first-come, first-served basis to single and married students. Typical cost: $2520 per year for single students; $3250 per year for married students. *Student services:* Campus employment opportunities, campus safety program, career counseling, child daycare facilities, exercise/wellness program, free psychological counseling, international student services, low-cost health insurance, multicultural affairs office, teacher training. *Library facilities:* James White Library plus 2 others. *Collection:* Books: 882,326 (physical), 743,147 (digital/electronic); Serial titles: 218,638 (physical), 198,545 (digital/electronic); Databases: 216. *Research affiliation:* RAND Corporation (drug abuse), Argonne National Laboratory (physics), Deutches Electronen Synchroton (physics).

**Computer facilities:** Computer purchase and lease plans are available. 100 computers available on campus for general student use. A campuswide network can be accessed. Online class registration, degree audit are available.
Website: http://www.andrews.edu/

**General Application Contact:** Jillian Panigot, Supervisor of Graduate Admission, 800-253-2874, Fax: 269-471-3228, E-mail: graduate@andrews.edu.

**GRADUATE UNITS**

**College of Health and Human Services** Students: 198 full-time (142 women), 142 part-time (82 women); includes 130 minority (48 Black or African American, non-Hispanic/Latino; 1 American Indian or Alaska Native, non-Hispanic/Latino; 42 Asian, non-Hispanic/Latino; 36 Hispanic/Latino; 3 Two or more races, non-Hispanic/Latino), 58 international. Average age 32. *Faculty:* 13 full-time (10 women), 11 part-time/adjunct (5 women). Expenses: Contact institution. *Financial support:* Research assistantships, Federal Work-Study, institutionally sponsored loans, and scholarships/grants available. In 2019, 37 master's, 50 doctorates, 14 other advanced degrees awarded. *Application deadline:* Applications are processed on a rolling basis. *Application fee:* $60. Electronic applications accepted. *Application Contact:* Jillian Panigot, Supervisor of Graduate Admission, 800-253-2874, Fax: 269-471-3228, E-mail: graduate@andrews.edu. *Dean*, Dr. Emmanuel Rudatsikira, 269-471-6649, E-mail: rudatsikira@andrews.edu.

***School of Architecture and Interior Design*** Students: 13 full-time (9 women), 1 (woman) part-time; includes 8 minority (4 Black or African American, non-Hispanic/Latino; 1 Asian, non-Hispanic/Latino; 3 Hispanic/Latino), 4 international. Average age 24. *Faculty:* 9 full-time (3 women), 1 (woman) part-time/adjunct. Expenses: Contact institution. *Financial support:* Research assistantships, Federal Work-Study, institutionally sponsored loans, scholarships/grants, and health care benefits available. In 2019, 14 master's awarded. *Application deadline:* Applications are processed on a rolling basis. *Application fee:* $60. Electronic applications accepted. *Application Contact:* Jillian Panigot, Supervisor of Graduate Admission, 800-253-2874, Fax: 269-471-6321, E-mail: graduate@andrews.edu. *Dean*, Ariel Solis, 269-471-6003.

**School of Graduate Studies** Students: 875 full-time (348 women), 788 part-time (275 women); includes 741 minority (321 Black or African American, non-Hispanic/Latino; 4 American Indian or Alaska Native, non-Hispanic/Latino; 104 Asian, non-Hispanic/Latino; 284 Hispanic/Latino; 11 Native Hawaiian or other Pacific Islander, non-Hispanic/Latino; 17 Two or more races, non-Hispanic/Latino), 475 international. Average age 37. 1,127 applicants, 76% accepted, 390 enrolled. *Faculty:* 168 full-time (62 women), 32 part-time/adjunct (11 women). Expenses: Contact institution. *Financial support:* Fellowships, research assistantships, teaching assistantships, career-related internships or fieldwork, Federal Work-Study, institutionally sponsored loans, scholarships/grants, tuition waivers (partial), and unspecified assistantships available. Support available to part-time students. Financial award applicants required to submit FAFSA. In 2019, 298 master's, 108 doctorates, 23 other advanced degrees awarded. *Program availability:* Part-time, evening/weekend, online learning. *Application deadline:* Applications are processed on a rolling basis. *Application fee:* $60. Electronic applications accepted. *Application Contact:* Jillian Panagot, Director University Admissions, 800-253-2874, Fax: 269-471-6246, E-mail: graduate@andrews.edu. *Dean*, Dr. Alayne Thorpe, 269-471-3440.

***College of Arts and Sciences*** Students: 54 full-time (37 women), 46 part-time (26 women); includes 32 minority (16 Black or African American, non-Hispanic/Latino; 2 Asian, non-Hispanic/Latino; 13 Hispanic/Latino; 1 Two or more races, non-Hispanic/Latino), 47 international. Average age 32. *Faculty:* 76 full-time (31 women), 3 part-time/adjunct (1 woman). Expenses: Contact institution. *Financial support:* Fellowships, research assistantships, teaching assistantships, career-related internships or fieldwork, Federal Work-Study, and institutionally sponsored loans available. Financial award applicants required to submit FAFSA. In 2019, 38 master's awarded. *Program availability:* Part-time, evening/weekend. *Application deadline:* Applications are processed on a rolling basis. *Application fee:* $60. Electronic applications accepted. *Application Contact:* Jillian Panagot, Director, University Admissions, 800-253-2874, Fax: 269-471-6321, E-mail: graduate@andrews.edu. *Dean*, Dr. Amy Rosenthal, 269-471-3411.

***College of Education and International Services*** Students: 143 full-time (98 women), 106 part-time (66 women); includes 95 minority (57 Black or African American, non-Hispanic/Latino; 5 Asian, non-Hispanic/Latino; 30 Hispanic/Latino; 3 Two or more races, non-Hispanic/Latino), 80 international. Average age 41. *Faculty:* 21 full-time (9 women), 5 part-time/adjunct (2 women). Expenses: Contact institution. *Financial support:* Fellowships, research assistantships, teaching assistantships, career-related internships or fieldwork, Federal Work-Study, institutionally sponsored loans, scholarships/grants, and tuition waivers (partial) available. Support available to part-time students. In 2019, 30 master's, 17 doctorates, 8 other advanced degrees awarded. *Program availability:* Part-time. *Application deadline:* Applications are processed on a rolling basis. *Application fee:* $60. Electronic applications accepted. *Application Contact:* Jillian Panigot, Director, University Admissions, 800-253-2874, Fax: 269-471-6321, E-mail: graduate@andrews.edu. *Dean*, Dr. Alayne Thorpe, 269-471-3464.

***College of Professions*** Students: 32 full-time (19 women), 38 part-time (17 women); includes 21 minority (7 Black or African American, non-Hispanic/Latino; 6 Asian, non-Hispanic/Latino; 7 Hispanic/Latino; 1 Native Hawaiian or other Pacific Islander, non-Hispanic/Latino), 35 international. Average age 30. *Faculty:* 8 full-time (3 women). Expenses: Contact institution. *Financial support:* Fellowships, research assistantships, teaching assistantships, Federal Work-Study, and scholarships/grants available. In 2019, 22 master's awarded. *Program availability:* Part-time. *Application deadline:* For fall admission, 8/15 for domestic students. Applications are processed on a rolling basis. *Application fee:* $60. Electronic applications accepted. *Application Contact:* Jillian Panigot, Director, University Admissions, 800-253-2874, Fax: 269-471-6321, E-mail: graduate@andrews.edu. *Dean*, Dr. Ralph Trecartin, 269-471-3632.

***Seventh-day Adventist Theological Seminary*** Students: 448 full-time (52 women), 456 part-time (84 women); includes 463 minority (193 Black or African American, non-Hispanic/Latino; 3 American Indian or Alaska Native, non-Hispanic/Latino; 49 Asian, non-Hispanic/Latino; 198 Hispanic/Latino; 10 Native Hawaiian or other Pacific Islander, non-Hispanic/Latino; 10 Two or more races, non-Hispanic/Latino), 255 international. Average age 40. *Faculty:* 40 full-time (5 women), 12 part-time/adjunct (2 women). Expenses: Contact institution. *Financial support:* Fellowships, research assistantships, teaching assistantships, career-related internships or fieldwork, Federal Work-Study, and institutionally sponsored loans available. In 2019, 171 master's, 41 doctorates, 1 other advanced degree awarded. *Application deadline:* Applications are processed on a rolling basis. *Application fee:* $60. *Application Contact:* Jillian Panigot, Director of Graduate Admissions, 800-253-2874, Fax: 269-471-6321. *Dean*, Dr. Jiri Moskala, 269-471-3537.

## ANGELO STATE UNIVERSITY, San Angelo, TX 76909

**General Information** State-supported, coed, comprehensive institution. *Graduate housing:* Room and/or apartments available on a first-come, first-served basis to single students; on-campus housing not available to married students. *Research affiliation:* Purina (animal nutrition), Zinpro Corporation (animal nutrition), Texas Space Consortium (space research and technology), TASCO (animal nutrition), Mannatech, Inc. (nutrition).

**GRADUATE UNITS**

**College of Graduate Studies and Research** *Program availability:* Part-time, evening/weekend, online learning. Electronic applications accepted.

***Archer College of Health and Human Services***

***College of Arts and Humanities*** *Program availability:* Part-time, evening/weekend. Electronic applications accepted.

***College of Education*** *Program availability:* Part-time, evening/weekend. Electronic applications accepted.

***College of Science and Engineering*** *Program availability:* Part-time, evening/weekend. Electronic applications accepted.

***Norris-Vincent College of Business*** *Program availability:* Part-time, evening/weekend. Electronic applications accepted.

## ANNA MARIA COLLEGE, Paxton, MA 01612

**General Information** Independent-religious, coed, comprehensive institution. *Graduate housing:* On-campus housing not available.

**GRADUATE UNITS**

**Graduate Division** *Program availability:* Part-time, evening/weekend. Electronic applications accepted.

## ANTIOCH UNIVERSITY LOS ANGELES, Culver City, CA 90230

**General Information** Independent, coed, upper-level institution. *Enrollment:* 614 full-time matriculated graduate/professional students (447 women), 99 part-time matriculated graduate/professional students (82 women). *Enrollment by degree level:* 692 master's, 3 other advanced degrees. *Graduate faculty:* 21 full-time (10 women), 91 part-time/adjunct (56 women). *Tuition:* Full-time $29,992; part-time $17,996 per credit hour. *Graduate housing:* On-campus housing not available. *Student services:* Campus employment opportunities, career counseling, grant writing training, international student services, low-cost health insurance, services for students with disabilities, writing training.

**Computer facilities:** A campuswide network can be accessed from off campus. Online class registration is available.
Website: http://www.antioch.edu/los-angeles/

**General Application Contact:** Information Contact, 310-578-1090, Fax: 310-822-4824, E-mail: admissions@antiochla.edu.

**GRADUATE UNITS**

**Program in Creative Writing & Communication**

**Program in Education** Students: 34 full-time (28 women), 24 part-time (16 women); includes 28 minority (12 Black or African American, non-Hispanic/Latino; 1 Asian, non-Hispanic/Latino; 13 Hispanic/Latino; 2 Two or more races, non-Hispanic/Latino), 1 international. Average age 34. 19 applicants, 63% accepted, 9 enrolled. *Faculty:* 2 full-time (1 woman), 11 part-time/adjunct (5 women). Expenses: Contact institution. *Financial support:* Career-related internships or fieldwork, Federal Work-Study, and scholarships/grants available. Support available to part-time students. Financial award application deadline: 3/24; financial award applicants required to submit CSS PROFILE or FAFSA. In 2019, 24 master's awarded. *Program availability:* Evening/weekend. *Application deadline:* For fall admission, 5/4 priority date for domestic students. Applications are processed on a rolling basis. *Application fee:* $60. *Application Contact:* Jessica Wiltgen, Director of Admissions, 310-578-1080 Ext. 110, E-mail: admissions.aula@antioch.edu. *Chair*, Dr. J. Cynthia McDermott, E-mail: cmcdermott@antioch.edu.

**Program in Leadership, Management and Business** Students: 14 full-time (12 women); includes 10 minority (3 Black or African American, non-Hispanic/Latino; 5 Hispanic/Latino; 1 Native Hawaiian or other Pacific Islander, non-Hispanic/Latino; 1 Two or more races, non-Hispanic/Latino). Average age 33. 14 applicants, 64% accepted, 8 enrolled. *Faculty:* 3 full-time (1 woman). Expenses: Contact institution. *Financial support:* Career-related internships or fieldwork, Federal Work-Study, and scholarships/grants available. Support available to part-time students. Financial award application deadline: 3/24; financial award applicants required to submit CSS PROFILE or FAFSA. In 2019, 16 master's awarded. *Program availability:* Part-time, evening/weekend, online learning. *Application deadline:* For fall admission, 8/4 for domestic students; for winter admission, 11/3 for domestic students; for spring admission, 2/2 for domestic students. *Application Contact:* Information Contact, 310-578-1090, Fax: 310-822-4824, E-mail: admissions@antiochla.edu. *Chair*, Dr. David Norgard, 310-578-1080 Ext. 292, E-mail: dnorgard@antioch.edu.

**Program in Psychology** Students: 456 full-time (322 women), 45 part-time (37 women); includes 136 minority (23 Black or African American, non-Hispanic/Latino; 2 American Indian or Alaska Native, non-Hispanic/Latino; 24 Asian, non-Hispanic/Latino; 62 Hispanic/Latino; 25 Two or more races, non-Hispanic/Latino), 5 international. Average age 36. 169 applicants, 70% accepted, 112 enrolled. *Faculty:* 12 full-time (5 women), 52 part-time/adjunct (31 women). Expenses: Contact institution. *Financial support:* Career-related internships or fieldwork, Federal Work-Study, scholarships/grants, and traineeships available. Support available to part-time students. Financial award application deadline: 3/24; financial award applicants required to submit FAFSA. In 2019, 182 master's awarded. *Program availability:* Part-time. *Application deadline:* For fall admission, 8/4 priority date for domestic students; for winter admission, 11/3 priority date for domestic students; for spring admission, 2/4 priority date for domestic students. Applications are processed on a rolling basis. *Application fee:* $60. *Application Contact:* Information Contact, 310-578-1090, Fax: 310-822-4824, E-mail: admissions@antiochla.edu. *Chair*, Joy Turek, 310-578-1080 Ext. 306, Fax: 310-822-4824, E-mail: joy_turek@antiochla.edu.

**Program in Urban Sustainability** Students: 17 full-time (14 women), 4 part-time (3 women); includes 7 minority (3 Black or African American, non-Hispanic/Latino; 1 Asian, non-Hispanic/Latino; 3 Hispanic/Latino). Average age 43. 9 applicants, 67% accepted, 6 enrolled. *Faculty:* 2 full-time (1 woman), 4 part-time/adjunct (2 women). Expenses: Contact institution. In 2019, 9 master's awarded. *Application Contact:* Information Contact, 310-578-1090, Fax: 310-822-4824, E-mail: admissions@antiochla.edu. *Chair*, Dr. Adonia Lugo, 310-578-1080 Ext. 287, E-mail: alugo@antioch.edu.

## ANTIOCH UNIVERSITY NEW ENGLAND, Keene, NH 03431-3552

**General Information** Independent, coed, graduate-only institution. *Enrollment by degree level:* 625 master's, 232 doctoral, 4 other advanced degrees. *Graduate faculty:*

45 full-time (23 women), 66 part-time/adjunct (42 women). *Graduate housing:* On-campus housing not available. *Student services:* Campus employment opportunities, career counseling, international student services, multicultural affairs office, services for students with disabilities, teacher training, writing training. *Library facilities:* AUNE Library. *Research affiliation:* Cheshire Medical Center Cardiac Rehabilitation Program (clinical psychology), Northeast Foundation for Children (education), Pine Hill Waldorf School (education), Harris Center for Conservation Education (environmental studies).

**Computer facilities:** 25 computers available on campus for general student use. Online class registration is available.
Website: http://www.antioch.edu/new-england/

**General Application Contact:** Laura Andrews, Director of Admissions, 800-552-8380, Fax: 603-357-3122, E-mail: admissions.ane@antioch.edu.

**GRADUATE UNITS**

**Graduate School** *Program availability:* Evening/weekend. Electronic applications accepted.

## ANTIOCH UNIVERSITY SANTA BARBARA, Santa Barbara, CA 93101-1581

**General Information** Independent, coed, upper-level institution. *Enrollment:* 322 graduate, professional, and undergraduate students; 221 full-time matriculated graduate/professional students (168 women), 39 part-time matriculated graduate/professional students (24 women). *Enrollment by degree level:* 200 master's, 60 doctoral, 4 other advanced degrees. *Graduate faculty:* 5 full-time (3 women), 49 part-time/adjunct (32 women). *Tuition:* Full-time $15,936. *Required fees:* $100. *Graduate housing:* On-campus housing not available. *Student services:* Campus employment opportunities, international student services, services for students with disabilities, writing training. *Library facilities:* Sage Library.

**Computer facilities:** 16 computers available on campus for general student use. A campuswide network can be accessed. Online class registration is available.
Website: http://www.antioch.edu/santa-barbara/

**GRADUATE UNITS**

**Degrees in Leadership, Management & Business** Students: 21 full-time (14 women), 2 part-time (both women); includes 8 minority (all Hispanic/Latino), 5 international. Average age 34. 12 applicants, 58% accepted, 7 enrolled. *Faculty:* 5 part-time/adjunct (1 woman). Expenses: Contact institution. In 2019, 12 master's awarded. *Program availability:* Part-time. *Application deadline:* For fall admission, 9/1 for domestic students; for winter admission, 12/1 for domestic students; for spring admission, 3/1 for domestic students; for summer admission, 6/1 for domestic students. Applications are processed on a rolling basis. *Application fee:* $50. Electronic applications accepted. *Application Contact:* Dr. Anna Kwong, Program Chair MBA, E-mail: akwong@antioch.edu. *Program Chair MBA*, Dr. Anna Kwong, E-mail: akwong@antioch.edu.

**Program in Education/Teacher Credentialing** Students: 25 full-time (20 women), 11 part-time (10 women); includes 17 minority (1 Black or African American, non-Hispanic/Latino; 15 Hispanic/Latino; 1 Two or more races, non-Hispanic/Latino), 2 international. Average age 34. 12 applicants, 100% accepted, 9 enrolled. *Faculty:* 1 (woman) full-time, 9 part-time/adjunct (8 women). Expenses: Contact institution. In 2019, 21 master's awarded. *Program availability:* Part-time. *Application deadline:* Applications are processed on a rolling basis. *Application fee:* $60. Electronic applications accepted. *Application Contact:* Dr. Jacqueline Reid, Director, E-mail: jreid@antioch.edu. *Director*, Dr. Jacqueline Reid, E-mail: jreid@antioch.edu.

**Program in Writing and Contemporary Media** Students: 13 full-time (8 women), 1 (woman) part-time; includes 4 minority (2 Black or African American, non-Hispanic/Latino; 1 American Indian or Alaska Native, non-Hispanic/Latino; 1 Native Hawaiian or other Pacific Islander, non-Hispanic/Latino). Average age 35. *Faculty:* 1 full-time, 5 part-time/adjunct (4 women). Expenses: Contact institution. In 2019, 22 master's awarded. *Program availability:* Part-time. *Application Contact:* Ross Brown, Program Director, E-mail: rbrown@antioch.edu. *Program Director*, Ross Brown, E-mail: rbrown@antioch.edu.

**Psychology** Students: 162 full-time (126 women), 25 part-time (11 women); includes 49 minority (3 Black or African American, non-Hispanic/Latino; 2 Asian, non-Hispanic/Latino; 37 Hispanic/Latino; 7 Two or more races, non-Hispanic/Latino), 12 international. Average age 36. 113 applicants, 61% accepted, 54 enrolled. *Faculty:* 3 full-time (2 women), 30 part-time/adjunct (19 women). Expenses: Contact institution. In 2019, 57 master's, 16 doctorates awarded. *Application deadline:* Applications are processed on a rolling basis. *Application fee:* $60. Electronic applications accepted. *Application Contact:* Dr. Sandra Kenny, Chair, 805-962-8179 Ext. 5116, Fax: 805-962-4786, E-mail: skenny@antioch.edu. *Chair*, Dr. Sandra Kenny, 805-962-8179 Ext. 5116, Fax: 805-962-4786, E-mail: skenny@antioch.edu.

## ANTIOCH UNIVERSITY SEATTLE, Seattle, WA 98121

**General Information** Independent, coed, university. *Enrollment:* 407 full-time matriculated graduate/professional students (341 women), 171 part-time matriculated graduate/professional students (142 women). *Enrollment by degree level:* 494 master's, 86 doctoral. *Graduate faculty:* 44 full-time (33 women), 40 part-time/adjunct (31 women). *Tuition:* Full-time $18,604. *Required fees:* $75. *Graduate housing:* On-campus housing not available. *Student services:* Campus employment opportunities, career counseling, free psychological counseling, international student services, services for students with disabilities, teacher training, writing training. *Library facilities:* Antioch Seattle Library. *Collection:* Books: 8,425 (physical), 264,631 (digital/electronic); Serial titles: 40,950 (digital/electronic); Databases: 222.
Website: http://www.antioch.edu/seattle/

**General Application Contact:** Mensima Biney, University Campus Admissions DirectorRecruitment and Admissions Director, E-mail: mbiney@antioch.edu.

**GRADUATE UNITS**

**Program in Clinical Psychology** Students: 347 full-time (295 women), 147 part-time (121 women); includes 92 minority (13 Black or African American, non-Hispanic/Latino; 1 American Indian or Alaska Native, non-Hispanic/Latino; 26 Asian, non-Hispanic/Latino; 35 Hispanic/Latino; 17 Two or more races, non-Hispanic/Latino), 10 international. Average age 40. 83 applicants, 54% accepted, 16 enrolled. *Faculty:* 34 full-time (23 women), 26 part-time/adjunct (21 women). Expenses: Contact institution. *Financial support:* Fellowships, research assistantships with tuition reimbursements, Federal Work-Study, scholarships/grants, and unspecified assistantships available. Financial award applicants required to submit FAFSA. In 2019, 14 doctorates awarded. *Program availability:* Part-time, evening/weekend. *Application deadline:* For fall admission, 9/1 for domestic students; for winter admission, 12/1 for domestic students; for spring admission, 3/1 for domestic students; for summer admission, 6/1 for domestic students. Applications are processed on a rolling basis. *Application fee:* $50. Electronic applications accepted. *Application Contact:* Dana Waters, Associate Chair, 206-268-4865, E-mail: dwaters@antioch.edu. *Associate Chair*, Dana Waters, 206-268-4865, E-mail: dwaters@antioch.edu.

**Program in Counseling, Therapy and Wellness** Students: 150 full-time (129 women), 56 part-time (47 women); includes 37 minority (6 Black or African American, non-Hispanic/Latino; 10 Asian, non-Hispanic/Latino; 13 Hispanic/Latino; 8 Two or more races, non-Hispanic/Latino). Average age 35. 223 applicants, 32% accepted, 69 enrolled. *Faculty:* 34 full-time (23 women), 26 part-time/adjunct (21 women). Expenses: Contact institution. In 2019, 88 master's awarded. *Program availability:* Part-time, evening/weekend. *Application deadline:* For fall admission, 9/1 for domestic students; for winter admission, 12/1 for domestic students; for spring admission, 3/1 for domestic students; for summer admission, 6/1 for domestic students. Applications are processed on a rolling basis. *Application fee:* $50. Electronic applications accepted. *Application Contact:* Kathrine Fort, Chair & Core Faculty, Clinical Mental Health CounselingChair & Core F, 206-268-4875, E-mail: kfort@antioch.edu. *Chair & Core Faculty, Clinical Mental Health CounselingChair & Core F*, Kathrine Fort, 206-268-4875, E-mail: kfort@antioch.edu.

**Program in Education** Students: 60 full-time (46 women), 24 part-time (21 women); includes 20 minority (8 Black or African American, non-Hispanic/Latino; 1 American Indian or Alaska Native, non-Hispanic/Latino; 2 Asian, non-Hispanic/Latino; 4 Hispanic/Latino; 5 Two or more races, non-Hispanic/Latino), 2 international. Average age 36. 15 applicants, 100% accepted, 13 enrolled. *Faculty:* 9 full-time (all women), 6 part-time/adjunct (all women). Expenses: Contact institution. *Financial support:* Research assistantships, Federal Work-Study, scholarships/grants, and unspecified assistantships available. Financial award application deadline: 6/15. *Program availability:* Part-time, evening/weekend. *Application deadline:* Applications are processed on a rolling basis. *Application fee:* $50. *Application Contact:* Sue Byers, Director, E-mail: sbyers@antioch.edu. *Director*, Sue Byers, E-mail: sbyers@antioch.edu.

## AOMA GRADUATE SCHOOL OF INTEGRATIVE MEDICINE, Austin, TX 78757

**General Information** Proprietary, coed, graduate-only institution. *Enrollment by degree level:* 127 master's, 20 doctoral. *Graduate faculty:* 12 full-time (4 women), 29 part-time/adjunct (18 women). *Graduate housing:* On-campus housing not available. *Student services:* Campus employment opportunities, campus safety program, career counseling, exercise/wellness program, international student services, services for students with disabilities. *Library facilities:* AOMA Library. *Collection:* Books: 4,768 (physical); Serial titles: 1,389 (physical). Weekly public service hours: 59; students can reserve study rooms.

**Computer facilities:** 8 computers available on campus for general student use. A campuswide network can be accessed. Online class registration, X are available.
Website: http://www.aoma.edu/

**General Application Contact:** Brian Becker, Director of Admissions, 512-492-3017, Fax: 512-454-7001, E-mail: admissions@aoma.edu.

**GRADUATE UNITS**

**Doctor of Acupuncture and Oriental Medicine Program** Electronic applications accepted.

**Master of Acupuncture and Oriental Medicine Program** Electronic applications accepted.

## APEX SCHOOL OF THEOLOGY, Durham, NC 27703

**General Information** Independent-religious, coed, comprehensive institution. *Graduate housing:* On-campus housing not available.

**GRADUATE UNITS**

**Graduate Programs**

## APOLLOS UNIVERSITY, Great Falls, MT 59401

**General Information** Proprietary, coed, comprehensive institution.

**GRADUATE UNITS**

**School of Business and Management**

## APPALACHIAN BIBLE COLLEGE, Mount Hope, WV 25880

**General Information** Independent-religious, coed, comprehensive institution. *Enrollment:* 262 graduate, professional, and undergraduate students; 2 part-time matriculated graduate/professional students (1 woman). *Enrollment by degree level:* 2 master's. *Graduate faculty:* 3 part-time/adjunct (0 women). *Graduate housing:* Rooms and/or apartments available on a first-come, first-served basis to single and married students. Housing application deadline: 1/1. *Library facilities:* John Van Pufflen Library.

**Computer facilities:** 15 computers available on campus for general student use. A campuswide network can be accessed. 1 available.
Website: http://www.abc.edu/

**General Application Contact:** Benjamin Cale, Director of Admissions, 304-877-6428 Ext. 311, Fax: 304-877-5082, E-mail: admissions@abc.edu.

**GRADUATE UNITS**

**Graduate Program** *Program availability:* Part-time, online learning. Electronic applications accepted.

## APPALACHIAN COLLEGE OF PHARMACY, Oakwood, VA 24631

**General Information** Independent, coed, graduate-only institution.

**GRADUATE UNITS**

**Doctor of Pharmacy Program**

## APPALACHIAN SCHOOL OF LAW, Grundy, VA 24614

**General Information** Independent, coed, graduate-only institution. *Graduate housing:* On-campus housing not available.

**GRADUATE UNITS**

**Professional Program in Law** Electronic applications accepted.

## APPALACHIAN STATE UNIVERSITY, Boone, NC 28608

**General Information** State-supported, coed, comprehensive institution. CGS member. *Graduate housing:* On-campus housing not available.

**GRADUATE UNITS**

**Cratis D. Williams School of Graduate Studies** *Program availability:* Part-time, evening/weekend, 100% online, blended/hybrid learning. Electronic applications accepted.

***Center for Appalachian Studies*** *Program availability:* Part-time. Electronic applications accepted.

***School of Music*** *Program availability:* Part-time. Electronic applications accepted.

## AQUINAS COLLEGE, Grand Rapids, MI 49506

**General Information** Independent-religious, coed, comprehensive institution. *Enrollment:* 1,600 graduate, professional, and undergraduate students; 30 full-time matriculated graduate/professional students (22 women), 114 part-time matriculated graduate/professional students (90 women). *Enrollment by degree level:* 144 master's. *Graduate faculty:* 15 full-time (11 women), 24 part-time/adjunct (14 women). *Tuition:* Part-time $593 per credit. *Required fees:* $120; $120 per unit. *Graduate housing:* On-campus housing not available. *Student services:* Campus employment opportunities, campus safety program, career counseling, exercise/wellness program, free psychological counseling, multicultural affairs office, services for students with disabilities, teacher training, writing training. *Library facilities:* Grace Hauenstein Library plus 1 other. *Collection:* Books: 85,348 (physical), 196,003 (digital/electronic); Serial titles: 231 (physical); Databases: 85. Weekly public service hours: 90; students can reserve study rooms.

**Computer facilities:** Computer purchase and lease plans are available. 210 computers available on campus for general student use. A campuswide network can be accessed. Online class registration is available.
Website: http://www.aquinas.edu/

**General Application Contact:** Lynn Atkins-Rykert, Graduate Programs Coordinator, 616-632-2924, Fax: 616-732-4465, E-mail: atkinlyn@aquinas.edu.

**GRADUATE UNITS**

**Master in the Art of Counseling**

**School of Education** Students: 10 full-time (7 women), 78 part-time (69 women); includes 12 minority (2 Black or African American, non-Hispanic/Latino; 2 American Indian or Alaska Native, non-Hispanic/Latino; 1 Asian, non-Hispanic/Latino; 6 Hispanic/Latino; 1 Two or more races, non-Hispanic/Latino). Average age 37. *Faculty:* 7 full-time (all women), 18 part-time/adjunct (13 women). Expenses: Contact institution. *Financial support:* In 2019–20, 22 students received support. Scholarships/grants available. Support available to part-time students. Financial award application deadline: 3/15. In 2019, 16 master's awarded. *Program availability:* Part-time, evening/weekend. *Application deadline:* Applications are processed on a rolling basis. Electronic applications accepted. *Application Contact:* Michele Mazurek, Certification Officer, Data Records Specialist, 616-632-2427, E-mail: michele.mazurek@aquinas.edu. *Dean*, Dr. Susan English, 616-632-2800, Fax: 616-732-4465, E-mail: englisus@aquinas.edu.

**School of Management** Students: 12 full-time (9 women), 29 part-time (17 women); includes 5 minority (1 Asian, non-Hispanic/Latino; 4 Hispanic/Latino), 2 international. Average age 31. *Faculty:* 4 full-time (1 woman), 5 part-time/adjunct (0 women). Expenses: Contact institution. *Financial support:* Scholarships/grants available. Support available to part-time students. Financial award application deadline: 3/15; financial award applicants required to submit FAFSA. In 2019, 16 master's awarded. *Program availability:* Part-time, evening/weekend. *Application deadline:* Applications are processed on a rolling basis. Electronic applications accepted. *Application Contact:* Lynn Atkins-Rykert, Program Coordinator, 616-632-2925, Fax: 616-732-4489, E-mail: atkinlyn@aquinas.edu. *Interim Director of the Graduate Management Program*, Dr. Linda Hagan, 616-632-2193, Fax: 616-732-4489, E-mail: lmh010@aquinas.edu.

## AQUINAS COLLEGE, Nashville, TN 37205-2005

**General Information** Independent-religious, coed, comprehensive institution. *Graduate housing:* On-campus housing not available.

**GRADUATE UNITS**

**School of Education**

## AQUINAS INSTITUTE OF THEOLOGY, St. Louis, MO 63108

**General Information** Independent-religious, coed, graduate-only institution. *Graduate housing:* On-campus housing not available.

**GRADUATE UNITS**

**Graduate and Professional Programs** *Program availability:* Part-time, evening/weekend, online learning.

## ARCADIA UNIVERSITY, Glenside, PA 19038-3295

**General Information** Independent-religious, coed, comprehensive institution. CGS member. *Enrollment:* 3,465 graduate, professional, and undergraduate students; 479 full-time matriculated graduate/professional students (382 women), 742 part-time matriculated graduate/professional students (548 women). *Enrollment by degree level:* 567 master's, 572 doctoral, 82 other advanced degrees. Tuition and fees vary according to course load and program. *Graduate housing:* On-campus housing not available. *Student services:* Campus safety program, career counseling, free psychological counseling, international student services, low-cost health insurance, multicultural affairs office, services for students with disabilities, writing training. *Library facilities:* Bette E. Landman Library. *Collection:* Students can reserve study rooms.

**Computer facilities:** A campuswide network can be accessed. Online class registration is available.
Website: http://www.arcadia.edu/

**General Application Contact:** Information Contact, 215-572-2910, Fax: 215-572-4049, E-mail: admiss@arcadia.edu.

**GRADUATE UNITS**

**College of Arts and Sciences** Students: 86 full-time (72 women), 69 part-time (53 women); includes 35 minority (25 Black or African American, non-Hispanic/Latino; 3 Asian, non-Hispanic/Latino; 3 Hispanic/Latino; 4 Two or more races, non-Hispanic/Latino), 3 international. Expenses: Contact institution. In 2019, 72 master's awarded. *Application Contact:* Information Contact, 215-572-2910, Fax: 215-572-4049, E-mail: admiss@arcadia.edu. *Dean, College of Arts and Sciences*, Rebecca Kohn, 215-572-2108.

**College of Health Sciences** Students: 359 full-time (280 women), 406 part-time (289 women); includes 130 minority (8 Black or African American, non-Hispanic/Latino; 1 American Indian or Alaska Native, non-Hispanic/Latino; 103 Asian, non-Hispanic/Latino; 11 Hispanic/Latino; 1 Native Hawaiian or other Pacific Islander, non-Hispanic/Latino; 6 Two or more races, non-Hispanic/Latino), 126 international. Expenses: Contact institution. In 2019, 141 master's, 313 doctorates awarded. *Program availability:* Online learning. *Application Contact:* Information Contact, 215-572-2910, Fax: 215-572-4049, E-mail: admiss@arcadia.edu. *Dean*, Rebecca Craik, 215-572-2143, E-mail: craikr@arcadia.edu.

**Program in Business Administration** Students: 1 (woman) full-time, 7 part-time (3 women); includes 3 minority (2 Black or African American, non-Hispanic/Latino; 1 Hispanic/Latino), 1 international. *Faculty:* 10 full-time (5 women). Expenses: Contact institution. In 2019, 26 master's awarded. *Program availability:* Part-time, evening/weekend. *Application fee:* $25. *Application Contact:* Office of Enrollment Management, 215-572-2910, Fax: 215-572-4049, E-mail: admiss@arcadia.edu. *Executive Director*, Dr. Thomas M. Brinker, 215-572-4039.

**School of Education** Students: 32 full-time (28 women), 260 part-time (202 women); includes 66 minority (45 Black or African American, non-Hispanic/Latino; 11 Asian, non-Hispanic/Latino; 5 Hispanic/Latino; 5 Two or more races, non-Hispanic/Latino), 2 international. *Faculty:* 13 full-time (9 women). Expenses: Contact institution. *Financial support:* Career-related internships or fieldwork, tuition waivers (partial), and unspecified assistantships available. In 2019, 148 master's, 8 doctorates, 163 CASs awarded. *Program availability:* Part-time, evening/weekend, online learning. *Application deadline:* Applications are processed on a rolling basis. *Application fee:* $25. Electronic applications accepted. *Application Contact:* 215-572-2925, Fax: 215-572-2126, E-mail: grad@arcadia.edu. *Chair*, Kimberly Dean, 215-572-8629.

## ARIZONA SCHOOL OF ACUPUNCTURE AND ORIENTAL MEDICINE, Tucson, AZ 85712

**General Information** Proprietary, coed, graduate-only institution.

**GRADUATE UNITS**

**Graduate Programs**

## ARIZONA STATE UNIVERSITY AT TEMPE, Tempe, AZ 85287

**General Information** State-supported, coed, university. CGS member. *Graduate housing:* Room and/or apartments available to single students; on-campus housing not available to married students. *Research affiliation:* Arizona Public Service (electrical, computer and energy engineering), Banner Health (health, biomedical, and life sciences), Honeywell (mechanical and aerospace engineering), Mayo Clinic (healthcare, biomedical informatics), Raytheon Corporation (computer science and engineering), Translational Genomics Research Institute (TGen) (biomedicine).

**GRADUATE UNITS**

**College of Health Solutions**

***School of Nutrition and Health Promotion***

**College of Liberal Arts and Sciences** *Program availability:* Part-time, online learning. Electronic applications accepted.

***Hugh Downs School of Human Communication*** *Program availability:* Evening/weekend. Electronic applications accepted.

***School of Earth and Space Exploration*** Electronic applications accepted.

***School of Geographical Sciences and Urban Planning*** Electronic applications accepted.

***School of Historical, Philosophical and Religious Studies*** *Program availability:* Part-time. Electronic applications accepted.

***School of Human Evolution and Social Change*** Electronic applications accepted.

***School of International Letters and Cultures*** Electronic applications accepted.

***School of Life Sciences*** Electronic applications accepted.

***School of Mathematical and Statistical Sciences*** *Program availability:* Part-time. Electronic applications accepted.

***School of Politics and Global Studies*** *Program availability:* Part-time. Electronic applications accepted.

***School of Social and Family Dynamics*** Electronic applications accepted.

***School of Social Transformation*** *Program availability:* Part-time. Electronic applications accepted.

**College of Nursing and Health Innovation** *Program availability:* Online learning. Electronic applications accepted.

**College of Public Programs** *Program availability:* Part-time, evening/weekend, online learning. Electronic applications accepted.

***School of Community Resources and Development*** *Program availability:* Part-time, evening/weekend. Electronic applications accepted.

***School of Criminology and Criminal Justice*** *Program availability:* Part-time, evening/weekend, online learning. Electronic applications accepted.

***School of Public Affairs*** *Program availability:* Part-time, evening/weekend. Electronic applications accepted.

***School of Social Work*** *Program availability:* Part-time. Electronic applications accepted.

**Graduate College** *Program availability:* Part-time, evening/weekend, online learning. Electronic applications accepted.

**Herberger Institute for Design and the Arts** Electronic applications accepted.

***The Design School*** Electronic applications accepted.

***School of Art*** Electronic applications accepted.

***School of Arts, Media and Engineering*** Electronic applications accepted.

***School of Film, Dance and Theatre*** Electronic applications accepted.

***School of Music*** Electronic applications accepted.

**Ira A. Fulton Schools of Engineering** *Program availability:* Part-time, evening/weekend, online learning. Electronic applications accepted.

***The Polytechnic School*** *Program availability:* Part-time, evening/weekend. Electronic applications accepted.

***School of Biological and Health Systems Engineering*** *Program availability:* Part-time, evening/weekend. Electronic applications accepted.

***School of Computing, Informatics, and Decision Systems Engineering*** *Program availability:* Part-time, evening/weekend, online learning. Electronic applications accepted.

***School of Electrical, Computer and Energy Engineering*** *Program availability:* Part-time, evening/weekend, online learning. Electronic applications accepted.

***School of Sustainable Engineering and the Built Environment*** *Program availability:* Part-time, evening/weekend, online learning. Electronic applications accepted.

**Mary Lou Fulton Teachers College** *Program availability:* Part-time, evening/weekend, online learning. Electronic applications accepted.

**New College of Interdisciplinary Arts and Sciences** *Program availability:* Part-time, evening/weekend. Electronic applications accepted.

**Sandra Day O'Connor College of Law** Students: 811 full-time (396 women); includes 197 minority (16 Black or African American, non-Hispanic/Latino; 19 American Indian or Alaska Native, non-Hispanic/Latino; 35 Asian, non-Hispanic/Latino; 87 Hispanic/Latino; 2 Native Hawaiian or other Pacific Islander, non-Hispanic/Latino; 38 Two or more races, non-Hispanic/Latino), 22 international. 3,710 applicants, 29% accepted, 272 enrolled. *Faculty:* 67 full-time (27 women), 138 part-time/adjunct (37 women). Expenses: Contact institution. *Financial support:* In 2019–20, 648 students received support. Institutionally sponsored loans and scholarships/grants available. Financial award application deadline: 3/15; financial award applicants required to submit FAFSA. In 2019, 282 doctorates awarded. *Application deadline:* For fall admission, 3/1 priority date for domestic and international students. Applications are processed on a rolling basis. Electronic applications accepted. *Application Contact:* Chitra Damania, Director, 480-965-1474, Fax: 480-727-7930, E-mail: law.admissions@asu.edu. *Dean/Professor,* Douglas Sylvester, 480-965-6188, Fax: 480-965-6521, E-mail: douglas.sylvester@asu.edu.

**School of Letters and Sciences** *Program availability:* Part-time, evening/weekend, online learning. Electronic applications accepted.

**School of Sustainability** *Program availability:* Part-time, evening/weekend. Electronic applications accepted.

**Thunderbird School of Global Management** *Program availability:* Online learning.

**Walter Cronkite School of Journalism and Mass Communication** Electronic applications accepted.

**W. P. Carey School of Business** *Program availability:* Part-time, evening/weekend, online learning. Electronic applications accepted.

***Morrison School of Agribusiness*** *Program availability:* Part-time, evening/weekend. Electronic applications accepted.

***School of Accountancy*** *Program availability:* Part-time, evening/weekend. Electronic applications accepted.

## ARKANSAS COLLEGES OF HEALTH EDUCATION, Fort Smith, AR 72916

**General Information** Independent, coed, graduate-only institution.

**GRADUATE UNITS**

**Arkansas College of Osteopathic Medicine**

**Program in Biomedicine**

## ARKANSAS STATE UNIVERSITY, State University, AR 72467

**General Information** State-supported, coed, comprehensive institution. CGS member. *Graduate housing:* Rooms and/or apartments available on a first-come, first-served basis to single and married students. *Research affiliation:* Oak Ridge Associated Universities (scientific research and education development), Applied Biotechnologies Institute (recombinant proteins), Biostrategies, LLC (biotechnology), Infinite Enzymes (plant biotechnology), Nature West (physical, engineering, and life sciences), GeneCoMe (biotechnology).

**GRADUATE UNITS**

**Graduate School** *Program availability:* Part-time, online learning. Electronic applications accepted.

***College of Agriculture and Technology*** *Program availability:* Part-time. Electronic applications accepted.

***College of Business*** *Program availability:* Part-time, evening/weekend. Electronic applications accepted.

***College of Education and Behavioral Science*** *Program availability:* Part-time, online learning. Electronic applications accepted.

***College of Engineering*** *Program availability:* Part-time. Electronic applications accepted.

***College of Fine Arts*** *Program availability:* Part-time. Electronic applications accepted.

***College of Humanities and Social Sciences*** *Program availability:* Part-time. Electronic applications accepted.

***College of Media and Communication*** *Program availability:* Part-time. Electronic applications accepted.

***College of Nursing and Health Professions*** *Program availability:* Part-time. Electronic applications accepted.

***College of Sciences and Mathematics*** *Program availability:* Part-time. Electronic applications accepted.

## ARKANSAS TECH UNIVERSITY, Russellville, AR 72801

**General Information** State-supported, coed, comprehensive institution. CGS member. *Enrollment:* 11,829 graduate, professional, and undergraduate students; 149 full-time matriculated graduate/professional students (74 women), 650 part-time matriculated graduate/professional students (470 women). *Enrollment by degree level:* 746 master's, 33 doctoral, 20 other advanced degrees. *Graduate faculty:* 76 full-time (30 women), 13 part-time/adjunct (10 women). *International tuition:* $14,016 full-time. *Tuition, area resident:* Full-time $7008; part-time $292 per credit hour. Tuition, state resident: full-time $7008; part-time $292 per credit hour. Tuition, nonresident: full-time $14,016; part-time $584 per credit hour. *Required fees:* $343 per term. *Graduate housing:* Room and/or apartments available on a first-come, first-served basis to single students; on-campus housing not available to married students. Typical cost: $7967 (including board). Housing application deadline: 8/1. *Student services:* Campus employment opportunities, campus safety program, career counseling, exercise/wellness program, free psychological counseling, international student services, low-cost health insurance, multicultural affairs office, services for students with disabilities, teacher training. *Library facilities:* Ross Pendergraft Library and Technology Center. *Collection:* Books: 156,543 (physical), 459,680 (digital/electronic); Serial titles: 6,649 (physical), 86,255 (digital/electronic); Databases: 336. Students can reserve study rooms.

**Computer facilities:** Computer purchase and lease plans are available. 1,168 computers available on campus for general student use. A campuswide network can be accessed. Online class registration is available.
Website: http://www.atu.edu/

**General Application Contact:** Dr. Richard Schoephoerster, Dean of Graduate College and Research, 479-968-0398, Fax: 479-964-0542, E-mail: gradcollege@atu.edu.

**GRADUATE UNITS**

**College of Arts and Humanities** Students: 32 full-time (19 women), 102 part-time (70 women); includes 22 minority (5 Black or African American, non-Hispanic/Latino; 1 American Indian or Alaska Native, non-Hispanic/Latino; 1 Asian, non-Hispanic/Latino; 12 Hispanic/Latino; 3 Two or more races, non-Hispanic/Latino), 9 international. Average age 32. Expenses: Contact institution. *Financial support:* In 2019–20, research assistantships with full and partial tuition reimbursements (averaging $4,800 per year), teaching assistantships with full and partial tuition reimbursements (averaging $4,800 per year) were awarded; career-related internships or fieldwork, Federal Work-Study, scholarships/grants, health care benefits, and unspecified assistantships also available. Support available to part-time students. Financial award application deadline: 4/15; financial award applicants required to submit FAFSA. In 2019, 89 master's awarded. *Program availability:* Part-time, 100% online, blended/hybrid learning. *Application deadline:* For fall admission, 3/1 priority date for domestic students, 5/1 priority date for international students; for spring admission, 10/1 priority date for domestic and international students. Applications are processed on a rolling basis. *Application fee:* $40 ($90 for international students). Electronic applications accepted. *Application Contact:* Dr. Richard Schoephoerster, Dean of Graduate College and Research, 479-968-0398, Fax: 479-964-0542, E-mail: gradcollege@atu.edu. *Dean of College of Arts and Humanities,* Dr. Jeffrey Cass, 479-968-0274, Fax: 479-964-0812, E-mail: jcass@atu.edu.

**College of Business** Students: 7 full-time (3 women), 57 part-time (36 women); includes 12 minority (4 Black or African American, non-Hispanic/Latino; 1 Asian, non-Hispanic/Latino; 3 Hispanic/Latino; 4 Two or more races, non-Hispanic/Latino), 1 international. Average age 30. Expenses: Contact institution. *Financial support:* In 2019–20, research assistantships with full and partial tuition reimbursements (averaging $4,800 per year), teaching assistantships with full and partial tuition reimbursements (averaging $4,800 per year) were awarded; career-related internships or fieldwork, Federal Work-Study, scholarships/grants, health care benefits, and unspecified assistantships also available. Support available to part-time students. Financial award application deadline: 4/15; financial award applicants required to submit FAFSA. In 2019, 2 master's awarded. *Program availability:* Part-time, evening/weekend, 100% online, blended/hybrid learning. *Application deadline:* For fall admission, 3/1 priority date for domestic students, 5/1 priority date for international students; for spring admission, 10/1 priority date for domestic and international students. Applications are processed on a rolling basis. *Application fee:* $40 ($90 for international students). Electronic applications accepted. *Application Contact:* Dr. Richard Shoephoerster, Dean of Graduate College and Research, 479-968-0398, Fax: 479-964-0542, E-mail: gradcollege@atu.edu. *Interim Dean,* Dr. Kevin Mason, 479-968-0498, E-mail: kmason@atu.edu.

**College of Education** Students: 66 full-time (39 women), 393 part-time (305 women); includes 86 minority (52 Black or African American, non-Hispanic/Latino; 3 American Indian or Alaska Native, non-Hispanic/Latino; 1 Asian, non-Hispanic/Latino; 15 Hispanic/Latino; 15 Two or more races, non-Hispanic/Latino), 4 international. Average age 34. Expenses: Contact institution. *Financial support:* In 2019–20, research assistantships with full and partial tuition reimbursements (averaging $4,800 per year), teaching assistantships with full and partial tuition reimbursements (averaging $4,800 per year) were awarded; career-related internships or fieldwork, Federal Work-Study, scholarships/grants, health care benefits, and unspecified assistantships also available. Support available to part-time students. Financial award application deadline: 4/15; financial award applicants required to submit FAFSA. In 2019, 162 master's, 21 doctorates, 50 other advanced degrees awarded. *Program availability:* Part-time, evening/weekend, 100% online, blended/hybrid learning. *Application deadline:* For fall admission, 3/1 priority date for domestic students, 5/1 priority date for international students; for spring admission, 10/1 priority date for domestic and international students. Applications are processed on a rolling basis. *Application fee:* $40 ($90 for international students). Electronic applications accepted. *Application Contact:* Dr. Richard Schoephoerster, Dean of Graduate College and Research, 479-968-0398, Fax: 479-964-0542, E-mail: gradcollege@atu.edu. *Dean,* Dr. Linda Bean, 479-964-3217, E-mail: lbean@atu.edu.

**College of Engineering and Applied Sciences** Students: 38 full-time (11 women), 45 part-time (22 women); includes 13 minority (10 Black or African American, non-Hispanic/Latino; 1 Asian, non-Hispanic/Latino; 1 Hispanic/Latino; 1 Two or more races, non-Hispanic/Latino), 24 international. Average age 32. Expenses: Contact institution. *Financial support:* In 2019–20, research assistantships with full and partial tuition reimbursements (averaging $4,800 per year), teaching assistantships with full and partial tuition reimbursements (averaging $4,800 per year) were awarded; career-related internships or fieldwork, Federal Work-Study, scholarships/grants, health care benefits, and unspecified assistantships also available. Support available to part-time students. Financial award application deadline: 4/15; financial award applicants required to submit FAFSA. In 2019, 26 master's awarded. *Program availability:* Part-time, evening/weekend, 100% online, blended/hybrid learning. *Application deadline:* For fall admission, 3/1 priority date for domestic students, 5/1 priority date for international students; for spring admission, 10/1 priority date for domestic and international students. Applications are processed on a rolling basis. *Application fee:* $40 ($90 for international students). Electronic applications accepted. *Application Contact:* Dr. Richard Schoephoerster, Dean of Graduate College and Research, 479-968-0398, Fax: 479-964-0542, E-mail: gradcollege@atu.edu. *Dean,* Dr. Judy Cezeaux, 479-968-0353, E-mail: jcezeaux@atu.edu.

**College of Natural and Health Sciences** Students: 6 full-time (2 women), 53 part-time (37 women); includes 7 minority (5 Black or African American, non-Hispanic/Latino; 1 Asian, non-Hispanic/Latino; 1 Hispanic/Latino). Average age 35. Expenses: Contact institution. *Financial support:* In 2019–20, research assistantships with full and partial tuition reimbursements (averaging $4,800 per year), teaching assistantships with full and partial tuition reimbursements (averaging $4,800 per year) were awarded; career-related internships or fieldwork, Federal Work-Study, scholarships/grants, health care benefits, and unspecified assistantships also available. Support available to part-time students. Financial award application deadline: 4/15; financial award applicants required to submit FAFSA. In 2019, 15 master's awarded. *Program availability:* Part-time, evening/weekend, 100% online, blended/hybrid learning. *Application deadline:* For fall admission, 3/1 priority date for domestic students, 5/1 priority date for international students; for spring admission, 10/1 priority date for domestic and international students. Applications are processed on a rolling basis. *Application fee:* $40 ($90 for international students). Electronic applications accepted. *Application Contact:* Dr. Richard Schoephoerster, Dean of Graduate College and Research, 479-968-0398, Fax: 479-964-0542, E-mail: gradcollege@atu.edu. *Dean,* Dr. Jeff Robertson, 479-968-0498, E-mail: jrobertson@atu.edu.

## ARLINGTON BAPTIST UNIVERSITY, Arlington, TX 76012-3425

**General Information** Independent-religious, coed, comprehensive institution.

**GRADUATE UNITS**

**Program in Biblical and Theological Studies** Electronic applications accepted.

**Program in Education**

## ART ACADEMY OF CINCINNATI, Cincinnati, OH 45202

**General Information** Independent, coed, comprehensive institution. *Graduate housing:* Rooms and/or apartments available on a first-come, first-served basis to single and married students. Housing application deadline: 5/1.

**GRADUATE UNITS**

**Program in Art Education** *Program availability:* Part-time. Electronic applications accepted.

## ARTCENTER COLLEGE OF DESIGN, Pasadena, CA 91103

**General Information** Independent, coed, comprehensive institution. *Graduate housing:* On-campus housing not available.

**GRADUATE UNITS**
**Graduate Art Program**
**Graduate Environmental Design Program**
**Graduate Film Program**
**Graduate Graphic Design Program**
**Graduate Industrial Design Program**
**Graduate Media Design Practices Program**
**Graduate Transportation Systems and Design Program**

## THE ART INSTITUTE OF DALLAS, A BRANCH OF MIAMI INTERNATIONAL UNIVERSITY OF ART & DESIGN, Dallas, TX 75231-5993

**General Information** Proprietary, coed, comprehensive institution.

**GRADUATE UNITS**
**Program in Design and Media Management**

## ASBURY THEOLOGICAL SEMINARY, Wilmore, KY 40390-1199

**General Information** Independent-religious, coed, primarily men, graduate-only institution. *Graduate housing:* Rooms and/or apartments available on a first-come, first-served basis to single and married students. Housing application deadline: 8/15.

**GRADUATE UNITS**
**Graduate and Professional Programs** *Program availability:* Part-time, online learning. Electronic applications accepted.

## ASBURY UNIVERSITY, Wilmore, KY 40390-1198

**General Information** Independent-religious, coed, comprehensive institution. *Enrollment:* 10 full-time matriculated graduate/professional students (8 women), 206 part-time matriculated graduate/professional students (106 women). *Enrollment by degree level:* 216 master's. *Graduate faculty:* 24 full-time (10 women), 16 part-time/adjunct (7 women). *Graduate housing:* On-campus housing not available. *Library facilities:* Kinlaw Library. *Collection:* Books: 157,131 (physical), 168,625 (digital/electronic); Serial titles: 442 (physical), 37,780 (digital/electronic); Databases: 60. Weekly public service hours: 88; students can reserve study rooms.

**Computer facilities:** Computer purchase and lease plans are available. 250 computers available on campus for general student use. A campuswide network can be accessed from student residence rooms and from off campus. Online class registration is available.
Website: http://www.asbury.edu/

**General Application Contact:** Macy Williams, Graduate Education Admissions & Recruitment Coordinator, 859-858-3511 Ext. 2502, Fax: 859-858-3921, E-mail: macy.williams@asbury.edu.

**GRADUATE UNITS**
**Graduate Business** Students: 6 full-time (4 women), 30 part-time (15 women); includes 9 minority (3 Black or African American, non-Hispanic/Latino; 1 Asian, non-Hispanic/Latino; 4 Hispanic/Latino; 1 Two or more races, non-Hispanic/Latino), 1 international. Average age 36. 21 applicants, 62% accepted, 10 enrolled. *Faculty:* 7 full-time (2 women), 4 part-time/adjunct. Expenses: Contact institution. *Financial support:* In 2019–20, 4 teaching assistantships (averaging $10,000 per year) were awarded; research assistantships, Federal Work-Study, and tuition waivers (full and partial) also available. Financial award application deadline: 12/1. *Program availability:* Part-time, evening/weekend, online only, 100% online. *Application deadline:* For fall admission, 8/3 for domestic and international students; for spring admission, 12/14 for domestic and international students; for summer admission, 4/30 for domestic and international students. Applications are processed on a rolling basis. Electronic applications accepted. *Application Contact:* Cindy Dean, MBA, Director of Graduate Studies, Dayton School of Business, 859-858-3511 Ext. 2214, E-mail: cindy.dean@asbury.edu. *Dean, Dayton School of Business*, Mike Kane, Ph.D., 859-858-3511 Ext. 2215, E-mail: mike.kane@asbury.edu.

**Graduate Communication Arts** Students: 3 full-time (all women), 43 part-time (14 women); includes 5 minority (2 Black or African American, non-Hispanic/Latino; 3 Hispanic/Latino), 2 international. Average age 35. 32 applicants, 78% accepted, 20 enrolled. *Faculty:* 8 full-time (3 women), 4 part-time/adjunct (2 women). Expenses: Contact institution. *Financial support:* In 2019–20, 25 students received support, including 2 research assistantships with partial tuition reimbursements available (averaging $5,355 per year), 2 teaching assistantships with partial tuition reimbursements available (averaging $5,355 per year); scholarships/grants and unspecified assistantships also available. Financial award applicants required to submit FAFSA. *Program availability:* Part-time, online only, The courses are delivered online; a few are available in seat, as well. There are one or two courses which require in person work, depending on the program. *Application deadline:* Applications are processed on a rolling basis. Electronic applications accepted. *Application Contact:* Johnie Dean, D.M.A., Coordinator of Graduate Studies, 859-858-5318 Ext. 2502, E-mail: johnie.dean@asbury.edu. *Dean, School of Communication Arts*, Jim Owens, Ph.D., 859-858-3511 Ext. 2387, E-mail: jim.owens@asbury.edu.

**Graduate Education** Students: 1 (woman) full-time, 124 part-time (73 women); includes 13 minority (10 Black or African American, non-Hispanic/Latino; 2 Hispanic/Latino; 1 Two or more races, non-Hispanic/Latino). Average age 36. 136 applicants, 49% accepted, 55 enrolled. *Faculty:* 9 full-time (6 women), 8 part-time/adjunct (5 women). Expenses: Contact institution. *Financial support:* In 2019–20, 84 students received support. Federal Work-Study, scholarships/grants, and Discount to identified cohorts available. Financial award application deadline: 12/1; financial award applicants required to submit FAFSA. *Program availability:* Part-time-only, online only, All courses offered online Clinical experiences in P-12 schools. *Application deadline:* Applications are processed on a rolling basis. Electronic applications accepted. *Application Contact:* Macy Williams, Graduate Education Admissions & Recruitment Coordinator, 859-858-3511 Ext. 2502, E-mail: macy.williams@asbury.edu. *Dean, School of Education*, Sharon G. Bixler, Ph.D., 859-858-3511 Ext. 2208, E-mail: sharon.bixler@asbury.edu.

**School of Graduate and Professional Studies** *Program availability:* Part-time. Electronic applications accepted.

## ASHLAND THEOLOGICAL SEMINARY, Ashland, OH 44805

**General Information** Independent-religious, coed, graduate-only institution. *Graduate housing:* Rooms and/or apartments available on a first-come, first-served basis to single and married students. Housing application deadline: 8/30. *Research affiliation:* Tel Gezer Excavation and Publication Program (archaeological studies), Tyndale House, Cambridge England (faculty study and research).

**GRADUATE UNITS**
**Graduate Programs** *Program availability:* Part-time. Electronic applications accepted.

## ASHLAND UNIVERSITY, Ashland, OH 44805-3702

**General Information** Independent-religious, coed, comprehensive institution. *Enrollment:* 7,260 graduate, professional, and undergraduate students; 947 full-time matriculated graduate/professional students (576 women), 862 part-time matriculated graduate/professional students (536 women). *Enrollment by degree level:* 1,272 master's, 98 doctoral, 281 other advanced degrees. *Graduate faculty:* 53 full-time (29 women), 133 part-time/adjunct (67 women). *Tuition:* Full-time $10,800; part-time $5400 per credit hour. *Required fees:* $720; $360 per credit hour. *Graduate housing:* Room and/or apartments available on a first-come, first-served basis to single students; on-campus housing not available to married students. Typical cost: $5250 per year ($9980 including board). Room and board charges vary according to board plan, campus/location and housing facility selected. Housing application deadline: 8/31. *Student services:* Campus employment opportunities, campus safety program, career counseling, exercise/wellness program, free psychological counseling, international student services, low-cost health insurance, multicultural affairs office, services for students with disabilities, teacher training, writing training. *Library facilities:* Ashland University Library plus 2 others. *Collection:* Books: 223,607 (physical), 255,789 (digital/electronic); Serial titles: 1,070 (physical), 114,001 (digital/electronic); Databases: 200. Weekly public service hours: 102; students can reserve study rooms. *Research affiliation:* Teacher Quality Project (TQP) (education).

**Computer facilities:** Computer purchase and lease plans are available. 760 computers available on campus for general student use. A campuswide network can be accessed. Online class registration is available.
Website: http://www.ashland.edu/

**General Application Contact:** Bernie Bannin, Director, Graduate, Online, and Adult Admissions, 419-289-5291, E-mail: grad-admissions@ashland.edu.

**GRADUATE UNITS**
**College of Arts and Sciences** Electronic applications accepted.

**Dauch College of Business and Economics** *Program availability:* Part-time, evening/weekend, 100% online, blended/hybrid learning. Electronic applications accepted.

**Dwight Schar College of Education** *Program availability:* Part-time. Electronic applications accepted.

**Dwight Schar College of Nursing and Health Sciences** *Program availability:* 100% online, blended/hybrid learning. Electronic applications accepted.

## ASHWORTH COLLEGE, Norcross, GA 30092

**General Information** Proprietary, coed, comprehensive institution.

**GRADUATE UNITS**
**Graduate Programs**

## ASPEN UNIVERSITY, Denver, CO 80246-1930

**General Information** Independent, coed, comprehensive institution. *Graduate housing:* On-campus housing not available.

**GRADUATE UNITS**
**Program in Business Administration** *Program availability:* Part-time, evening/weekend, online only, 100% online. Electronic applications accepted.

**Program in Information Technology** *Program availability:* Part-time, evening/weekend, online only, 100% online. Electronic applications accepted.

**Program in Nursing** *Program availability:* Part-time, evening/weekend, online only, 100% online. Electronic applications accepted.

**Programs in Information Management** *Program availability:* Part-time, evening/weekend, online only, 100% online. Electronic applications accepted.

## ASSEMBLIES OF GOD THEOLOGICAL SEMINARY, Springfield, MO 65802

**General Information** Independent-religious, coed, graduate-only institution. *Enrollment by degree level:* 102 master's, 181 doctoral. *Graduate faculty:* 12 full-time (3 women), 15 part-time/adjunct (4 women). *Graduate housing:* On-campus housing not available. *Student services:* Campus employment opportunities, campus safety program, career counseling, exercise/wellness program, free psychological counseling, international student services, services for students with disabilities, writing training. *Library facilities:* Cordas C. Burnett Library plus 1 other.

**Computer facilities:** A campuswide network can be accessed from student residence rooms and from off campus. Online class registration is available.
Website: http://www.agts.edu/

**General Application Contact:** Nik White, Seminary Enrollment Coordinator, 417-268-1000, Fax: 417-268-1030, E-mail: info@agts.edu.

**GRADUATE UNITS**
**Graduate and Professional Programs** Students: 136 full-time (37 women), 147 part-time (40 women); includes 71 minority (24 Black or African American, non-Hispanic/Latino; 6 American Indian or Alaska Native, non-Hispanic/Latino; 7 Asian, non-Hispanic/Latino; 22 Hispanic/Latino; 7 Native Hawaiian or other Pacific Islander, non-Hispanic/Latino; 5 Two or more races, non-Hispanic/Latino), 14 international. Average age 46. 62 applicants, 100% accepted, 42 enrolled. *Faculty:* 12 full-time (3 women), 15 part-time/adjunct (4 women). Expenses: Contact institution. *Financial support:* Career-related internships or fieldwork and scholarships/grants available. Support available to part-time students. Financial award application deadline: 7/15; financial award applicants required to submit FAFSA. In 2019, 37 master's, 25 doctorates awarded. *Program availability:* Part-time, evening/weekend, 100% online. *Application deadline:* For fall admission, 7/1 priority date for domestic students, 6/1 priority date for international students; for spring admission, 12/1 priority date for domestic students, 11/1 priority date for international students. Applications are processed on a rolling basis. *Application fee:* $75. Electronic applications accepted. *Application Contact:* Nik White, Seminary Enrollment Coordinator, 417-268-1000, Fax: 417-268-1030, E-mail: info@agts.edu. *Dean*, Dr. Timothy A. Hager, 417-268-1000, Fax: 417-268-1001.

## ASSUMPTION UNIVERSITY, Worcester, MA 01609-1296

**General Information** Independent-religious, coed, comprehensive institution. *Enrollment:* 2,376 graduate, professional, and undergraduate students; 165 full-time matriculated graduate/professional students (107 women), 220 part-time matriculated graduate/professional students (157 women). *Enrollment by degree level:* 357 master's, 28 other advanced degrees. *Graduate faculty:* 20 full-time (10 women), 57 part-time/adjunct (32 women). *Tuition:* Full-time $12,690; part-time $705 per credit. *Required fees:* $70 per term. *Graduate housing:* On-campus housing not available. *Student services:* Campus employment opportunities, campus safety program, career counseling, exercise/wellness program, international student services, low-cost health insurance, multicultural affairs office, services for students with disabilities, teacher training. *Library facilities:* Emmanuel d'Alzon Library. *Collection:* Books: 127,617 (physical), 171,058 (digital/electronic); Serial titles: 1,830 (physical), 43,143 (digital/electronic); Databases: 75. Weekly public service hours: 102; students can reserve study rooms.

**Computer facilities:** Computer purchase and lease plans are available. 361 computers available on campus for general student use. A campuswide network can be accessed. Online class registration is available.
Website: http://www.assumption.edu/

**General Application Contact:** Karen Stoyanoff, Director of Recruitment for Graduate Enrollment, 508-767-7442, Fax: 508-799-4412, E-mail: graduate@assumption.edu.

**GRADUATE UNITS**

**Addiction Counseling Program** *Program availability:* Part-time, evening/weekend. Electronic applications accepted.
**Applied Behavior Analysis Program** *Program availability:* Part-time, evening/weekend. Electronic applications accepted.
**Business Studies Program** *Program availability:* Part-time, evening/weekend. Electronic applications accepted.
**Clinical Counseling Psychology Program** *Program availability:* Part-time, evening/weekend. Electronic applications accepted.
**Health Advocacy Program** *Program availability:* Part-time, evening/weekend, online only, 100% online. Electronic applications accepted.
**Healthcare Management Program** *Program availability:* Part-time, evening/weekend, online only, 100% online, blended/hybrid learning. Electronic applications accepted.
**Physician Assistant Studies Program**
**Rehabilitation Counseling Program** *Program availability:* Part-time, evening/weekend, blended/hybrid learning. Electronic applications accepted.
**Resiliency in the Helping Professions Program** *Program availability:* Part-time, evening/weekend.
**School Counseling Program** *Program availability:* Part-time, evening/weekend. Electronic applications accepted.
**Special Education Program** *Program availability:* Part-time, evening/weekend. Electronic applications accepted.
**Special Ops: Service Members, Veterans, and their Families Program**

## ATHABASCA UNIVERSITY, Athabasca, AB T9S 3A3, Canada

**General Information** Province-supported, coed, comprehensive institution. *Enrollment:* 4,556 part-time matriculated graduate/professional students (3,470 women). *Enrollment by degree level:* 3,987 master's, 83 doctoral, 486 other advanced degrees. *Graduate faculty:* 184 full-time (83 women), 66 part-time/adjunct (40 women). *Graduate housing:* On-campus housing not available. *Student services:* Career counseling, international student services, services for students with disabilities, writing training. *Library facilities:* Athabasca University Library. *Research affiliation:* SAP (software), IBM (software).

**Computer facilities:** Computer purchase and lease plans are available. 28 computers available on campus for general student use. A campuswide network can be accessed. Online class registration is available.
Website: http://www.athabascau.ca/

**General Application Contact:** Information Contact, 800-788-9041, Fax: 780-675-6174.

**GRADUATE UNITS**

**Centre for Distance Education** *Program availability:* Part-time, online learning. Electronic applications accepted.
**Centre for Interdisciplinary Studies** *Program availability:* Part-time, evening/weekend, online learning. Electronic applications accepted.
**Faculty of Business** *Program availability:* Part-time, evening/weekend, online learning. Electronic applications accepted.
**Faculty of Health Disciplines** *Program availability:* Part-time, online learning. Electronic applications accepted.
**Faculty of Science and Technology** *Program availability:* Part-time, online learning. Electronic applications accepted.
**Program in Counseling**

## THE ATHENAEUM OF OHIO, Cincinnati, OH 45230-5900

**General Information** Independent-religious, coed, graduate-only institution. *Graduate housing:* On-campus housing not available.

**GRADUATE UNITS**

**Graduate Programs** *Program availability:* Part-time, evening/weekend.

## ATHENS STATE UNIVERSITY, Athens, AL 35611

**General Information** State-supported, coed, upper-level institution. *Graduate housing:* On-campus housing not available.

**GRADUATE UNITS**

**Graduate Programs**

## ATLANTA'S JOHN MARSHALL LAW SCHOOL, Atlanta, GA 30309

**General Information** Private, coed, graduate-only institution.

**GRADUATE UNITS**

**JD and LL M Programs** *Program availability:* Part-time, evening/weekend, online learning. Electronic applications accepted.

## ATLANTIC INSTITUTE OF ORIENTAL MEDICINE, Fort Lauderdale, FL 33301

**General Information** Independent, coed, graduate-only institution. *Enrollment by degree level:* 107 master's, 38 doctoral. *Graduate faculty:* 7 full-time (1 woman), 15 part-time/adjunct (6 women). *Tuition:* Full-time $17,000; part-time $15,000 per year. *Required fees:* $250. One-time fee: $150. *Graduate housing:* On-campus housing not available. *Student services:* Campus employment opportunities, campus safety program, career counseling, exercise/wellness program, international student services, services for students with disabilities. *Collection:* Books: 3,986 (physical). Weekly public service hours: 50.

**Computer facilities:** 4 computers available on campus for general student use. A campuswide network can be accessed. Online class registration is available.
Website: http://www.atom.edu/

**General Application Contact:** Karen Gemignani, Admissions Counselor, 954-763-9840 Ext. 213, Fax: 954-763-9844, E-mail: admissions@atom.edu.

**GRADUATE UNITS**

**Graduate Program** *Program availability:* Evening/weekend.

## ATLANTIC SCHOOL OF THEOLOGY, Halifax, NS B3H 3B5, Canada

**General Information** Independent, coed, graduate-only institution. *Enrollment by degree level:* 81 master's, 44 other advanced degrees. *Graduate faculty:* 10 full-time, 12 part-time/adjunct. *Required fees:* $7000 Canadian dollars; $700 Canadian dollars per course. *Graduate housing:* Rooms and/or apartments available on a first-come, first-served basis to single and married students. Typical cost: $650 Canadian dollars per year for single students; $850 Canadian dollars per year for married students. Housing application deadline: 6/1. *Student services:* Campus employment opportunities, career counseling, low-cost health insurance, writing training. *Library facilities:* Atlantic School of Theology Library. *Collection:* Weekly public service hours: 40.

**Computer facilities:** 3 computers available on campus for general student use.
Website: http://www.astheology.ns.ca/

**General Application Contact:** Cynthia Thomson, Registrar, 902-425-3691, Fax: 902-492-4048, E-mail: registrar@astheology.ns.ca.

**GRADUATE UNITS**

**Graduate and Professional Programs** *Program availability:* Part-time, online learning.

## ATLANTIC UNIVERSITY, Virginia Beach, VA 23451-2061

**General Information** Independent, coed, primarily women, graduate-only institution. *Graduate housing:* On-campus housing not available.

**GRADUATE UNITS**

**Program in Integrated Imagery: Regression Hypnosis** *Program availability:* Blended/hybrid learning. Electronic applications accepted.
**Program in Mindful Leadership** *Program availability:* Online learning.
**Program in Transpersonal Psychology** *Program availability:* Part-time, evening/weekend, online learning. Electronic applications accepted.
**Spiritual Guidance Mentor Program** *Program availability:* Online learning. Electronic applications accepted.

## ATLANTIC UNIVERSITY COLLEGE, Guaynabo, PR 00970

**General Information** Independent, coed, comprehensive institution.

**GRADUATE UNITS**

**Program in Graphic Arts** *Program availability:* Part-time.

## ATLANTIS UNIVERSITY, Miami, FL 33132

**General Information** Proprietary, coed, comprehensive institution.

**GRADUATE UNITS**

**School of Business**
**School of Computer Science and Information Technology**
**School of Engineering**
**School of Health Care**

## A.T. STILL UNIVERSITY, Kirksville, MO 63501

**General Information** Independent, coed, graduate-only institution. *Enrollment by degree level:* 818 master's, 2,840 doctoral, 199 other advanced degrees. *Graduate faculty:* 246 full-time (117 women), 482 part-time/adjunct (258 women). *Graduate housing:* Rooms and/or apartments available on a first-come, first-served basis to single and married students. Typical cost: $5640 (including board) for single students; $5640 (including board) for married students. Room and board charges vary according to board plan. Housing application deadline: 6/15. *Student services:* Campus employment opportunities, campus safety program, career counseling, exercise/wellness program, free psychological counseling, multicultural affairs office, services for students with disabilities, writing training. *Library facilities:* A.T. Still Memorial Library plus 1 other. *Collection:* Books: 12,000 (physical), 263,000 (digital/electronic); Serial titles: 1,242 (physical), 23,000 (digital/electronic); Databases: 86. Weekly public service hours: 120. *Research affiliation:* Diers Medical Systems (biomechanics, posture and osteopathic clinical research), University of Missouri, Columbia (osteopathic clinical research), Translational Genomics Research Institute (TGen) (genetics research), Truman State University (osteopathic clinical research), Arizona State University (clinical/translational research/bioengineering), Fresenius University of Applied Sciences, Germany (osteopathic clinical research).

**Computer facilities:** 45 computers available on campus for general student use. A campuswide network can be accessed from student residence rooms and from off campus.
Website: http://www.atsu.edu/

**General Application Contact:** Donna Sparks, Director, Admissions Processing, 660-626-2117, Fax: 660-626-2969, E-mail: admissions@atsu.edu.

**GRADUATE UNITS**

**Arizona School of Dentistry & Oral Health** Students: 314 full-time (169 women); includes 163 minority (9 Black or African American, non-Hispanic/Latino; 2 American Indian or Alaska Native, non-Hispanic/Latino; 107 Asian, non-Hispanic/Latino; 17 Hispanic/Latino; 1 Native Hawaiian or other Pacific Islander, non-Hispanic/Latino; 27 Two or more races, non-Hispanic/Latino), 3 international. Average age 28. 2,323 applicants, 7% accepted, 77 enrolled. *Faculty:* 130 full-time (87 women), 90 part-time/adjunct (32 women). Expenses: Contact institution. *Financial support:* In 2019–20, 61 students received support. Federal Work-Study and scholarships/grants available. Financial award application deadline: 6/1; financial award applicants required to submit FAFSA. In 2019, 5 master's, 74 doctorates, 1 other advanced degree awarded. *Application deadline:* For fall admission, 11/15 for domestic and international students; for summer admission, 11/15 for domestic and international students. Applications are processed on a rolling basis. *Application fee:* $70. Electronic applications accepted. *Application Contact:* Donna Sparks, Director, Admissions Processing, 660-626-2117, Fax: 660-626-2969, E-mail: admissions@atsu.edu. *Dean,* Dr. Robert Trombly, 480-248-8105, Fax: 623-223-7063, E-mail: rtrombly@atsu.edu.

**Arizona School of Health Sciences** Students: 736 full-time (528 women), 289 part-time (195 women); includes 315 minority (53 Black or African American, non-Hispanic/Latino; 7 American Indian or Alaska Native, non-Hispanic/Latino; 94 Asian, non-Hispanic/Latino; 134 Hispanic/Latino; 2 Native Hawaiian or other Pacific Islander, non-Hispanic/Latino; 25 Two or more races, non-Hispanic/Latino), 79 international. Average age 32. 4,387 applicants, 20% accepted, 514 enrolled. *Faculty:* 94 full-time (74 women), 203 part-time/adjunct (145 women). Expenses: Contact institution. *Financial support:* In 2019–20, 170 students received support. Federal Work-Study and scholarships/grants available. Financial award application deadline: 6/1; financial award applicants required to submit FAFSA. In 2019, 153 master's, 344 doctorates, 2 other advanced degrees awarded. *Program availability:* Part-time, evening/weekend, online only, 100% online, blended/hybrid learning. *Application deadline:* For fall admission, 7/7 for domestic and international students; for winter admission, 10/3 for domestic and international students; for spring admission, 1/16 for domestic and international students; for summer admission, 4/17 for domestic and international students. Applications are processed on a rolling basis. *Application fee:* $70. *Application Contact:* Donna Sparks, Director, Admissions Processing, 660-626-2117, Fax: 660-626-2969, E-mail: admissions@atsu.edu. *Dean*, Dr. Ann Lee Burch, 480-219-6061, E-mail: aburch@atsu.edu.

**College of Graduate Health Studies** Students: 601 full-time (406 women), 532 part-time (331 women); includes 457 minority (197 Black or African American, non-Hispanic/Latino; 15 American Indian or Alaska Native, non-Hispanic/Latino; 114 Asian, non-Hispanic/Latino; 105 Hispanic/Latino; 3 Native Hawaiian or other Pacific Islander, non-Hispanic/Latino; 23 Two or more races, non-Hispanic/Latino), 30 international. Average age 36. 339 applicants, 73% accepted, 217 enrolled. *Faculty:* 49 full-time (36 women), 109 part-time/adjunct (66 women). Expenses: Contact institution. *Financial support:* In 2019–20, 13 students received support. Scholarships/grants available. Financial award applicants required to submit FAFSA. In 2019, 175 master's, 100 doctorates, 118 other advanced degrees awarded. *Program availability:* Part-time, evening/weekend, online only, 100% online, blended/hybrid learning. *Application deadline:* For fall admission, 6/24 for domestic and international students; for winter admission, 9/9 for domestic and international students; for spring admission, 12/9 for domestic and international students; for summer admission, 3/2 for domestic and international students. Applications are processed on a rolling basis. *Application fee:* $70. Electronic applications accepted. *Application Contact:* Amie Waldemer, Associate Director, Online Admissions, 480-219-6146, E-mail: awaldemer@atsu.edu. *Dean*, Dr. Donald Altman, 480-219-6008, Fax: 660-626-2826, E-mail: daltman@atsu.edu.

**Kirksville College of Osteopathic Medicine** Students: 710 full-time (311 women), 10 part-time (3 women); includes 143 minority (17 Black or African American, non-Hispanic/Latino; 46 Asian, non-Hispanic/Latino; 41 Hispanic/Latino; 1 Native Hawaiian or other Pacific Islander, non-Hispanic/Latino; 38 Two or more races, non-Hispanic/Latino). Average age 27. 4,388 applicants, 9% accepted, 180 enrolled. *Faculty:* 147 full-time (95 women), 61 part-time/adjunct (23 women). Expenses: Contact institution. *Financial support:* In 2019–20, 194 students received support, including 10 fellowships with full tuition reimbursements available (averaging $58,290 per year); Federal Work-Study and scholarships/grants also available. Financial award application deadline: 6/1; financial award applicants required to submit FAFSA. In 2019, 7 master's, 173 doctorates awarded. *Application deadline:* For fall admission, 2/1 for domestic students; for summer admission, 2/1 for domestic students. Applications are processed on a rolling basis. *Application fee:* $70. Electronic applications accepted. *Application Contact:* Donna Sparks, Director, Admissions Processing, 660-626-2117, Fax: 660-626-2969, E-mail: admissions@atsu.edu. *Dean*, Dr. Margaret Wilson, 660-626-2354, Fax: 660-626-2080, E-mail: mwilson@atsu.edu.

**Missouri School of Dentistry & Oral Health** Students: 185 full-time (87 women); includes 57 minority (1 Black or African American, non-Hispanic/Latino; 38 Asian, non-Hispanic/Latino; 11 Hispanic/Latino; 7 Two or more races, non-Hispanic/Latino). Average age 27. 1,308 applicants, 13% accepted, 62 enrolled. *Faculty:* 48 full-time (23 women), 35 part-time/adjunct (10 women). Expenses: Contact institution. *Financial support:* In 2019–20, 37 students received support. Federal Work-Study and scholarships/grants available. Financial award application deadline: 6/1; financial award applicants required to submit FAFSA. In 2019, 42 doctorates awarded. *Application deadline:* For fall admission, 12/1 for domestic students; for summer admission, 12/1 for domestic students. Applications are processed on a rolling basis. *Application fee:* $70. Electronic applications accepted. *Application Contact:* Donna Sparks, Director, Admissions Processing, 660-626-2237, Fax: 660-626-2969, E-mail: admissions@atsu.edu. *Dean*, Dr. Dwight McLeod, 660-626-2842, Fax: 660-626-2969, E-mail: dmcleod@atsu.edu.

**School of Osteopathic Medicine in Arizona** Students: 480 full-time (276 women); includes 249 minority (9 Black or African American, non-Hispanic/Latino; 163 Asian, non-Hispanic/Latino; 33 Hispanic/Latino; 3 Native Hawaiian or other Pacific Islander, non-Hispanic/Latino; 41 Two or more races, non-Hispanic/Latino). Average age 27. 5,597 applicants, 7% accepted, 161 enrolled. *Faculty:* 49 full-time (26 women), 74 part-time/adjunct (21 women). Expenses: Contact institution. *Financial support:* In 2019–20, 71 students received support, including 1 fellowship with full tuition reimbursement available (averaging $59,802 per year); Federal Work-Study and scholarships/grants also available. Financial award application deadline: 6/1; financial award applicants required to submit FAFSA. In 2019, 104 doctorates awarded. *Application deadline:* For fall admission, 3/1 for domestic students; for summer admission, 3/1 for domestic students. Applications are processed on a rolling basis. *Application fee:* $70. Electronic applications accepted. *Application Contact:* Donna Sparks, Director, Admissions Processing, 660-626-2117, Fax: 660-626-2969, E-mail: admissions@atsu.edu. *Dean*, Dr. Jeffrey Morgan, 480-265-8017, Fax: 480-219-6159, E-mail: jeffreymorgan@atsu.edu.

## AUBURN UNIVERSITY, Auburn University, AL 36849

**General Information** State-supported, coed, university. *Enrollment:* 30,460 graduate, professional, and undergraduate students; 3,337 full-time matriculated graduate/professional students (1,926 women), 2,391 part-time matriculated graduate/professional students (1,119 women). *Enrollment by degree level:* 2,620 master's, 2,946 doctoral, 162 other advanced degrees. *Graduate faculty:* 1,321 full-time (540 women), 160 part-time/adjunct (70 women). *International tuition:* $29,744 full-time. *Tuition, area resident:* Full-time $9828; part-time $546 per credit hour. Tuition, state resident: full-time $9828; part-time $546 per credit hour. Tuition, nonresident: full-time $29,484; part-time $1638 per credit hour. Tuition and fees vary according to course load, program and reciprocity agreements. *Graduate housing:* On-campus housing not available. *Student services:* Campus employment opportunities, campus safety program, career counseling, exercise/wellness program, free psychological counseling, international student services, low-cost health insurance, multicultural affairs office, services for students with disabilities, teacher training, writing training. *Library facilities:* R. B. Draughon Library plus 3 others. *Collection:* Books: 4.6 million (physical), 1 million (digital/electronic); Serial titles: 76,345 (physical), 94,890 (digital/electronic); Databases: 245. Study areas open 24 hours, 5–7 days a week. *Research affiliation:* National Center of Excellence for Airliner Cabin Environmental Research (aerospace, polymer and fibers engineering), National Textile Center Consortium (polymer and fibers engineering), National Asphalt Pavement Association (asphalt technology, civil engineering), Consortium for Vehicle Electronics (mechanical and automotive engineering, electrical engineering), Tay-Sachs Gene Therapy Consortium (veterinary medicine, clinical sciences), Higher Education Consortium for Special Education (special and rehabilitative education).

**Computer facilities:** Computer purchase and lease plans are available. 1,722 computers available on campus for general student use. A campuswide network can be accessed. Online class registration, bursar payments, course materials are available. Website: http://www.auburn.edu/

**General Application Contact:** Dr. George Flowers, Dean of the Graduate School, 334-844-2125, E-mail: flowegt@auburn.edu.

**GRADUATE UNITS**

**College of Veterinary Medicine** Students: 531 full-time (426 women), 49 part-time (32 women); includes 53 minority (11 Black or African American, non-Hispanic/Latino; 1 American Indian or Alaska Native, non-Hispanic/Latino; 10 Asian, non-Hispanic/Latino; 26 Hispanic/Latino; 5 Two or more races, non-Hispanic/Latino), 51 international. Average age 27. 1,130 applicants, 17% accepted, 144 enrolled. *Faculty:* 113 full-time (47 women), 3 part-time/adjunct (2 women). Expenses: Contact institution. *Financial support:* In 2019–20, 47 fellowships with full tuition reimbursements (averaging $3,553 per year), 29 research assistantships with partial tuition reimbursements (averaging $20,042 per year), 63 teaching assistantships with partial tuition reimbursements (averaging $29,618 per year) were awarded; Federal Work-Study also available. Support available to part-time students. Financial award application deadline: 3/15; financial award applicants required to submit FAFSA. In 2019, 18 master's, 124 doctorates awarded. *Program availability:* Part-time. *Application deadline:* For spring admission, 9/15 for domestic and international students. Applications are processed on a rolling basis. *Application fee:* $60 ($70 for international students). Electronic applications accepted. *Application Contact:* Dr. George Flowers, Interim Dean of the Graduate School, 334-844-4700. *Dean*, Dr. Calvin M. Johnson, 334-844-2650.

**Graduate School** Students: 3,337 full-time (1,926 women), 2,391 part-time (1,119 women); includes 913 minority (441 Black or African American, non-Hispanic/Latino; 15 American Indian or Alaska Native, non-Hispanic/Latino; 161 Asian, non-Hispanic/Latino; 213 Hispanic/Latino; 5 Native Hawaiian or other Pacific Islander, non-Hispanic/Latino; 78 Two or more races, non-Hispanic/Latino), 1,197 international. Average age 30. 4,664 applicants, 54% accepted, 1,733 enrolled. *Faculty:* 1,321 full-time (540 women), 160 part-time/adjunct (70 women). Expenses: Contact institution. *Financial support:* In 2019–20, 2,002 fellowships with tuition reimbursements, 1,108 research assistantships with tuition reimbursements (averaging $17,557 per year), 856 teaching assistantships (averaging $20,594 per year) were awarded; career-related internships or fieldwork, Federal Work-Study, scholarships/grants, and unspecified assistantships also available. Support available to part-time students. Financial award application deadline: 3/15; financial award applicants required to submit FAFSA. In 2019, 1,373 master's, 521 doctorates, 285 other advanced degrees awarded. *Program availability:* Part-time, evening/weekend. *Application deadline:* Applications are processed on a rolling basis. *Application fee:* $60 ($70 for international students). Electronic applications accepted. *Application Contact:* Dr. George Flowers, Dean, 334-844-2125, E-mail: flowegt@auburn.edu. *Dean*, Dr. George Flowers, 334-844-2125, E-mail: flowegt@auburn.edu.

***College of Agriculture*** Students: 127 full-time (58 women), 173 part-time (77 women); includes 23 minority (3 Black or African American, non-Hispanic/Latino; 1 American Indian or Alaska Native, non-Hispanic/Latino; 6 Asian, non-Hispanic/Latino; 10 Hispanic/Latino; 3 Two or more races, non-Hispanic/Latino), 102 international. Average age 29. 170 applicants, 54% accepted, 77 enrolled. *Faculty:* 126 full-time (34 women), 2 part-time/adjunct (0 women). Expenses: Contact institution. *Financial support:* In 2019–20, 133 fellowships with tuition reimbursements (averaging $3,845 per year), 206 research assistantships with tuition reimbursements (averaging $17,715 per year) were awarded; teaching assistantships and Federal Work-Study also available. Support available to part-time students. Financial award application deadline: 3/1; financial award applicants required to submit FAFSA. In 2019, 69 master's, 27 doctorates awarded. *Program availability:* Part-time. *Application deadline:* Applications are processed on a rolling basis. *Application fee:* $60 ($70 for international students). Electronic applications accepted. *Application Contact:* Dr. George Flowers, Dean of the Graduate School, 334-844-2125. *Dean*, Paul Patterson, 334-844-3254.

***College of Architecture, Design, and Construction*** Students: 73 full-time (35 women), 106 part-time (21 women); includes 35 minority (18 Black or African American, non-Hispanic/Latino; 1 American Indian or Alaska Native, non-Hispanic/Latino; 5 Asian, non-Hispanic/Latino; 10 Hispanic/Latino; 1 Native Hawaiian or other Pacific Islander, non-Hispanic/Latino), 42 international. Average age 34. 170 applicants, 81% accepted, 87 enrolled. *Faculty:* 71 full-time (20 women), 15 part-time/adjunct (4 women). Expenses: Contact institution. *Financial support:* In 2019–20, 11 fellowships with full tuition reimbursements (averaging $3,845 per year) were awarded; Federal Work-Study, scholarships/grants, and unspecified assistantships also available. Support available to part-time students. Financial award application deadline: 3/15; financial award applicants required to submit FAFSA. In 2019, 68 master's awarded. *Program availability:* Part-time. *Application deadline:* Applications are processed on a rolling basis. *Application fee:* $60 ($70 for international students). Electronic applications accepted. *Application Contact:* Dr. George Flowers, Dean of the Graduate School, 334-844-2125. *Dean/Chair*, Dr. Vini Nathan, 334-844-4529, E-mail: vzn0007@auburn.edu.

***College of Education*** Students: 395 full-time (289 women), 513 part-time (346 women); includes 260 minority (190 Black or African American, non-Hispanic/Latino; 1 American Indian or Alaska Native, non-Hispanic/Latino; 4 Asian, non-Hispanic/Latino; 43 Hispanic/Latino; 2 Native Hawaiian or other Pacific Islander, non-Hispanic/Latino; 20 Two or more races, non-Hispanic/Latino), 56 international. Average age 34. 693 applicants, 62% accepted, 265 enrolled. *Faculty:* 116 full-time (76 women), 31 part-time/adjunct (21 women). Expenses: Contact institution. *Financial support:* In 2019–20, 518 fellowships with tuition reimbursements (averaging $2,457 per year), 67 research assistantships with tuition reimbursements (averaging $15,555 per year), 93 teaching assistantships with tuition reimbursements (averaging $16,241 per year) were awarded; career-related internships or fieldwork and Federal Work-Study also available. Support available to part-time students. Financial award application deadline: 3/15; financial award applicants required to submit FAFSA. In 2019, 287 master's, 63 doctorates, 95 other advanced degrees awarded. *Program availability:* Part-time. *Application deadline:* For fall admission, 6/15 priority date for domestic and international students; for spring admission, 10/15 priority date for domestic and international students; for summer admission, 3/15 priority date for domestic and international students. Applications are processed on a rolling basis. *Application fee:* $60 ($70 for international students). Electronic applications accepted. *Application Contact:* Dr. George Flowers, Dean of the Graduate School, 334-844-2125. *Dean & Wayne T. Smith Distinguished Professor*, Dr. Betty Lou Whitford, 334-844-4446, E-mail: blw0017@auburn.edu.

***College of Human Sciences*** Students: 77 full-time (57 women), 56 part-time (43 women); includes 22 minority (8 Black or African American, non-Hispanic/Latino; 1 American Indian or Alaska Native, non-Hispanic/Latino; 6 Asian, non-Hispanic/Latino; 5 Hispanic/Latino; 1 Native Hawaiian or other Pacific Islander, non-Hispanic/Latino; 1 Two or more races, non-Hispanic/Latino), 32 international. Average age 30. 141 applicants, 43% accepted, 34 enrolled. *Faculty:* 64 full-time (42 women), 1 (woman) part-time/adjunct. Expenses: Contact institution. *Financial support:* In 2019–20, 90 fellowships with tuition reimbursements, 59 research assistantships with tuition reimbursements (averaging $16,925 per year), 34 teaching assistantships with tuition reimbursements (averaging $16,415 per year) were awarded; career-related internships or fieldwork and Federal Work-Study also available. Support available to part-time students. Financial award application deadline: 3/15; financial award applicants required to submit FAFSA. In 2019, 28 master's, 7 doctorates, 16 other advanced degrees awarded. *Program availability:* Part-time. *Application deadline:* Applications are processed on a rolling basis. *Application fee:* $60 ($70 for international students). Electronic applications accepted. *Application Contact:* Dr. George Flowers, Dean of the Graduate School, 334-844-2125. *Dean,* Dr. Susan Hubbard, 334-844-3790, E-mail: hubbasg@auburn.edu.

***College of Liberal Arts*** Students: 344 full-time (235 women), 166 part-time (96 women); includes 91 minority (51 Black or African American, non-Hispanic/Latino; 2 American Indian or Alaska Native, non-Hispanic/Latino; 7 Asian, non-Hispanic/Latino; 24 Hispanic/Latino; 7 Two or more races, non-Hispanic/Latino), 95 international. Average age 30. 872 applicants, 29% accepted, 154 enrolled. *Faculty:* 307 full-time (169 women), 49 part-time/adjunct (25 women). Expenses: Contact institution. *Financial support:* In 2019–20, 155 fellowships with tuition reimbursements, 87 research assistantships with tuition reimbursements (averaging $14,809 per year), 168 teaching assistantships with tuition reimbursements (averaging $19,651 per year) were awarded; career-related internships or fieldwork and Federal Work-Study also available. Support available to part-time students. Financial award application deadline: 3/15; financial award applicants required to submit FAFSA. In 2019, 160 master's, 24 doctorates, 37 other advanced degrees awarded. *Program availability:* Part-time. *Application deadline:* Applications are processed on a rolling basis. *Application fee:* $60 ($70 for international students). Electronic applications accepted. *Application Contact:* Dr. George Flowers, Dean of the Graduate School, 334-844-2125. *Dean,* Dr. Joe Aistrup, 334-844-2183.

***College of Sciences and Mathematics*** Students: 236 full-time (102 women), 180 part-time (78 women); includes 59 minority (21 Black or African American, non-Hispanic/Latino; 1 American Indian or Alaska Native, non-Hispanic/Latino; 11 Asian, non-Hispanic/Latino; 14 Hispanic/Latino; 12 Two or more races, non-Hispanic/Latino), 171 international. Average age 29. 328 applicants, 52% accepted, 101 enrolled. *Faculty:* 172 full-time (52 women), 36 part-time/adjunct (11 women). Expenses: Contact institution. *Financial support:* In 2019–20, 145 fellowships with tuition reimbursements, 97 research assistantships with tuition reimbursements (averaging $23,823 per year), 248 teaching assistantships with tuition reimbursements (averaging $27,269 per year) were awarded; career-related internships or fieldwork and Federal Work-Study also available. Support available to part-time students. Financial award application deadline: 3/15; financial award applicants required to submit FAFSA. In 2019, 74 master's, 33 doctorates awarded. *Program availability:* Part-time. *Application deadline:* Applications are processed on a rolling basis. *Application fee:* $60 ($70 for international students). Electronic applications accepted. *Application Contact:* Dr. George Flowers, Dean of the Graduate School, 334-844-2125. *Dean,* Dr. Nicholas J. Giordano, 334-844-5737, E-mail: njg0003@auburn.edu.

***Raymond J. Harbert College of Business*** Students: 261 full-time (114 women), 528 part-time (181 women); includes 123 minority (39 Black or African American, non-Hispanic/Latino; 3 American Indian or Alaska Native, non-Hispanic/Latino; 35 Asian, non-Hispanic/Latino; 34 Hispanic/Latino; 12 Two or more races, non-Hispanic/Latino), 30 international. Average age 33. 734 applicants, 62% accepted, 188 enrolled. *Faculty:* 89 full-time (26 women), 19 part-time/adjunct (7 women). Expenses: Contact institution. *Financial support:* In 2019–20, 86 fellowships with full tuition reimbursements (averaging $26,667 per year), 25 research assistantships with partial tuition reimbursements (averaging $21,495 per year), 17 teaching assistantships with partial tuition reimbursements (averaging $31,648 per year) were awarded; career-related internships or fieldwork and Federal Work-Study also available. Support available to part-time students. Financial award application deadline: 3/15; financial award applicants required to submit FAFSA. In 2019, 335 master's, 6 doctorates awarded. *Program availability:* Part-time. *Application deadline:* Applications are processed on a rolling basis. *Application fee:* $60 ($70 for international students). Electronic applications accepted. *Application Contact:* Dr. George Flowers, Dean of the Graduate School, 334-844-2125. *Dean,* Dr. Annette R. Ranft, 334-844-4832, E-mail: HarbertDean@auburn.edu.

***Samuel Ginn College of Engineering*** Students: 585 full-time (155 women), 418 part-time (97 women); includes 92 minority (33 Black or African American, non-Hispanic/Latino; 1 American Indian or Alaska Native, non-Hispanic/Latino; 23 Asian, non-Hispanic/Latino; 28 Hispanic/Latino; 7 Two or more races, non-Hispanic/Latino), 537 international. Average age 29. 1,028 applicants, 53% accepted, 215 enrolled. *Faculty:* 185 full-time (18 women), 16 part-time/adjunct (2 women). Expenses: Contact institution. *Financial support:* In 2019–20, 68 research assistantships (averaging $15,750 per year), 18 teaching assistantships (averaging $10,182 per year) were awarded; fellowships and Federal Work-Study also available. Support available to part-time students. Financial award application deadline: 3/15; financial award applicants required to submit FAFSA. In 2019, 229 master's, 70 doctorates, 20 other advanced degrees awarded. *Program availability:* Part-time. *Application deadline:* For fall admission, 3/31 priority date for domestic and international students; for spring admission, 9/30 priority date for domestic and international students. Applications are processed on a rolling basis. *Application fee:* $60 ($70 for international students). Electronic applications accepted. *Application Contact:* Dr. George Flowers, Dean of the Graduate School, 334-844-2125. *Dean,* Dr. Christopher Roberts, 334-844-2308, E-mail: robercr@auburn.edu.

***School of Forestry and Wildlife Sciences*** Students: 50 full-time (18 women), 49 part-time (20 women); includes 11 minority (2 Black or African American, non-Hispanic/Latino; 3 Asian, non-Hispanic/Latino; 4 Hispanic/Latino; 2 Two or more races, non-Hispanic/Latino), 33 international. Average age 32. 65 applicants, 74% accepted, 30 enrolled. *Faculty:* 29 full-time (9 women), 2 part-time/adjunct (1 woman). Expenses: Contact institution. *Financial support:* In 2019–20, 50 fellowships (averaging $33,448 per year), 48 research assistantships (averaging $17,638 per year) were awarded; teaching assistantships and Federal Work-Study also available. Support available to part-time students. Financial award application deadline: 3/15; financial award applicants required to submit FAFSA. In 2019, 14 master's, 4 doctorates awarded. *Program availability:* Part-time. *Application deadline:* Applications are processed on a rolling basis. *Application fee:* $60 ($70 for international students). Electronic applications accepted. *Application Contact:* Dr. George Flowers, Dean of the Graduate School, 334-844-2125. *Dean,* Dr. Janaki R.R. Alavalapati, 334-844-1004, Fax: 334-844-1084, E-mail: jra0024@auburn.edu.

***School of Nursing*** Students: 13 full-time (all women), 132 part-time (117 women); includes 13 minority (7 Black or African American, non-Hispanic/Latino; 1 American Indian or Alaska Native, non-Hispanic/Latino; 2 Asian, non-Hispanic/Latino; 1 Hispanic/Latino; 2 Two or more races, non-Hispanic/Latino), 1 international. Average age 34. 88 applicants, 85% accepted, 58 enrolled. *Faculty:* 30 full-time (27 women), 1 (woman) part-time/adjunct. Expenses: Contact institution. *Financial support:* In 2019–20, 28 fellowships (averaging $28,714 per year), 2 teaching assistantships (averaging $9,696 per year) were awarded; scholarships/grants also available. Financial award application deadline: 3/15; financial award applicants required to submit FAFSA. In 2019, 78 master's awarded. *Program availability:* Part-time. *Application deadline:* For fall admission, 6/1 priority date for domestic and international students; for spring admission, 10/1 priority date for domestic and international students; for summer admission, 3/1 priority date for domestic and international students. *Application fee:* $60 ($70 for international students). Electronic applications accepted. *Application Contact:* Dr. George Flowers, Dean of the Graduate School, 334-844-4700, E-mail: gradadm@auburn.edu. *Dean,* Dr. Gregg E. Newschwander, 334-844-3658, E-mail: gen0002@auburn.edu.

**Harrison School of Pharmacy** Students: 638 full-time (419 women), 15 part-time (7 women); includes 130 minority (58 Black or African American, non-Hispanic/Latino; 2 American Indian or Alaska Native, non-Hispanic/Latino; 49 Asian, non-Hispanic/Latino; 13 Hispanic/Latino; 1 Native Hawaiian or other Pacific Islander, non-Hispanic/Latino; 7 Two or more races, non-Hispanic/Latino), 45 international. Average age 26. 421 applicants, 65% accepted, 158 enrolled. *Faculty:* 58 full-time (34 women), 1 (woman) part-time/adjunct. Expenses: Contact institution. *Financial support:* In 2019–20, 56 fellowships, 29 research assistantships (averaging $21,361 per year), 15 teaching assistantships (averaging $21,267 per year) were awarded; Federal Work-Study also available. Support available to part-time students. Financial award application deadline: 3/15; financial award applicants required to submit FAFSA. In 2019, 3 master's, 154 doctorates awarded. *Program availability:* Part-time. *Application deadline:* For fall admission, 1/15 for domestic and international students. *Application fee:* $60 ($70 for international students). Electronic applications accepted. *Application Contact:* Dr. George Flowers, Dean of the Graduate School, 334-844-2125. *Dean,* Dr. Richard Hansen, 334-844-8307.

## AUBURN UNIVERSITY AT MONTGOMERY, Montgomery, AL 36124-4023

**General Information** State-supported, coed, comprehensive institution. *Enrollment:* 5,188 graduate, professional, and undergraduate students; 259 full-time matriculated graduate/professional students (153 women), 406 part-time matriculated graduate/professional students (281 women). *Enrollment by degree level:* 574 master's, 19 doctoral, 72 other advanced degrees. *Graduate faculty:* 87 full-time (38 women), 19 part-time/adjunct (11 women). *International tuition:* $17,046 full-time. *Tuition, area resident:* Full-time $7578; part-time $421 per credit hour. Tuition, state resident: full-time $7578; part-time $421 per credit hour. Tuition, nonresident: full-time $17,046; part-time $947 per credit hour. *Required fees:* $868. *Graduate housing:* Rooms and/or apartments available on a first-come, first-served basis to single and married students. Typical cost: $4580 per year ($7268 including board) for single students. Housing application deadline: 5/1. *Student services:* Campus employment opportunities, campus safety program, career counseling, exercise/wellness program, free psychological counseling, international student services, low-cost health insurance, multicultural affairs office, services for students with disabilities. *Library facilities:* Auburn University at Montgomery Library. *Collection:* Books: 343,407 (physical), 1.2 million (digital/electronic). Weekly public service hours: 84; students can reserve study rooms.

**Computer facilities:** 500 computers available on campus for general student use. A campuswide network can be accessed. Online class registration is available.
Website: http://www.aum.edu/

**General Application Contact:** Ashley Warren, Administrative Coordinator, Provost's Office, 334-244-3623, Fax: 334-244-3947, E-mail: awarren3@aum.edu.

**GRADUATE UNITS**

**College of Business** Students: 48 full-time (23 women), 106 part-time (61 women); includes 43 minority (36 Black or African American, non-Hispanic/Latino; 5 Asian, non-Hispanic/Latino; 2 Two or more races, non-Hispanic/Latino), 30 international. Average age 28. 174 applicants, 82% accepted, 119 enrolled. *Faculty:* 12 full-time (6 women), 2 part-time/adjunct (1 woman). Expenses: Contact institution. *Financial support:* Research assistantships, career-related internships or fieldwork, and scholarships/grants available. Support available to part-time students. Financial award application deadline: 3/1; financial award applicants required to submit FAFSA. In 2019, 37 master's awarded. *Program availability:* Part-time, evening/weekend, 100% online. *Application deadline:* For fall admission, 7/15 for international students; for spring admission, 11/15 for international students; for summer admission, 4/15 for international students. Applications are processed on a rolling basis. *Application fee:* $25 ($0 for international students). Electronic applications accepted. *Application Contact:* Ashley Warren, Graduate Admissions Coordinator, 334-244-3623, E-mail: awarren3@aum.edu. *Dean,* Dr. Ross Dickens, 334-244-3476, Fax: 334-244-3792, E-mail: rdickens@aum.edu.

***School of Accountancy*** Students: 11 full-time (7 women), 57 part-time (32 women); includes 13 minority (10 Black or African American, non-Hispanic/Latino; 3 Asian, non-Hispanic/Latino), 5 international. Average age 28. 35 applicants, 91% accepted, 29 enrolled. *Faculty:* 4 full-time (3 women), 1 (woman) part-time/adjunct. Expenses: Contact institution. *Financial support:* Scholarships/grants available. Financial award applicants required to submit FAFSA. In 2019, 15 master's awarded. *Program availability:* Part-time. *Application deadline:* Applications are processed on a rolling basis. *Application fee:* $25 ($0 for international students). Electronic applications accepted. *Application Contact:* Rhonda Seay, Graduate Advisor, 334-244-3115, E-mail: rseay@aum.edu. *Director,* Dr. Scott Lane, 334-244-3227, E-mail: slane2@aum.edu.

**College of Education** Students: 120 full-time (82 women), 136 part-time (108 women); includes 117 minority (106 Black or African American, non-Hispanic/Latino; 1 American Indian or Alaska Native, non-Hispanic/Latino; 4 Asian, non-Hispanic/Latino; 5 Hispanic/Latino; 1 Two or more races, non-Hispanic/Latino), 2 international. Average age 33. 212 applicants, 80% accepted, 132 enrolled. *Faculty:* 24 full-time (15 women), 9 part-time/adjunct (4 women). Expenses: Contact institution. *Financial support:* Teaching assistantships, career-related internships or fieldwork, and scholarships/grants available. Support available to part-time students. Financial award application deadline: 3/1; financial award applicants required to submit FAFSA. In 2019, 62 master's, 21 Ed Ss awarded. *Program availability:* Part-time, evening/weekend, 100% online, blended/hybrid learning. *Application deadline:* For fall admission, 7/1 for international students; for spring admission, 11/1 for international students; for summer admission, 4/15 for international students. Applications are processed on a rolling basis. *Application fee:* $25. Electronic applications accepted. *Application Contact:* Dr. Kellie Shumack, Associate Dean/Graduate Coordinator, 334-244-3737, E-mail: kshumack@aum.edu. *Dean,* Dr. Sheila Austin, 334-244-3413, E-mail: saustin1@aum.edu.

**College of Liberal Arts & Social Sciences** Students: 48 full-time (26 women), 107 part-time (65 women); includes 66 minority (59 Black or African American, non-

Hispanic/Latino; 4 Asian, non-Hispanic/Latino; 3 Hispanic/Latino), 12 international. Average age 33. 101 applicants, 95% accepted, 71 enrolled. *Faculty:* 45 full-time (22 women), 5 part-time/adjunct (2 women). Expenses: Contact institution. *Financial support:* Application deadline: 3/1; applicants required to submit FAFSA. *Program availability:* Part-time. *Application deadline:* For fall admission, 7/15 for international students; for spring admission, 11/15 for international students; for summer admission, 4/15 for international students. Applications are processed on a rolling basis. *Application fee:* $25 ($0 for international students). Electronic applications accepted. *Application Contact:* Ashley Warren, Administrative Coordinator, Provost's Office, 334-244-3623, Fax: 334-244-3947, E-mail: awarren3@aum.edu. *Dean,* Dr. Andrew McMichael, 334-2443929, E-mail: amcmich1@aum.edu.

**College of Nursing and Health Sciences** Students: 37 part-time (32 women); includes 13 minority (all Black or African American, non-Hispanic/Latino). Average age 36. 56 applicants, 46% accepted, 22 enrolled. *Faculty:* 3 full-time (all women), 4 part-time/adjunct (all women). Expenses: Contact institution. *Financial support:* Application deadline: 3/1. *Program availability:* Part-time, evening/weekend, 100% online, blended/hybrid learning. *Application deadline:* For fall admission, 7/1 for domestic students; for spring admission, 10/1 for domestic students; for summer admission, 3/1 for domestic students. Applications are processed on a rolling basis. *Application fee:* $25 ($0 for international students). Electronic applications accepted. *Application Contact:* Christy Dearden, Senior Administrative Associate, 334-244-3658, E-mail: cdearden@aum.edu. *Dean,* Dr. Jean Leuner, 334-244-3658, E-mail: jleuner@aum.edu.

**College of Sciences** Students: 40 full-time (22 women), 20 part-time (15 women); includes 12 minority (6 Black or African American, non-Hispanic/Latino; 2 Asian, non-Hispanic/Latino; 3 Hispanic/Latino; 1 Two or more races, non-Hispanic/Latino), 30 international. Average age 28. 160 applicants, 92% accepted, 38 enrolled. *Faculty:* 14 full-time (3 women), 1 (woman) part-time/adjunct. Expenses: Contact institution. *Financial support:* Teaching assistantships and scholarships/grants available. Support available to part-time students. Financial award application deadline: 3/1; financial award applicants required to submit FAFSA. *Program availability:* Part-time, 100% online, blended/hybrid learning. *Application deadline:* For fall admission, 7/15 for international students; for spring admission, 11/15 for international students; for summer admission, 4/15 for international students. Applications are processed on a rolling basis. *Application fee:* $25. Electronic applications accepted. *Application Contact:* Ashley Warren, Administrative Coordinator, Provost's Office, 334-244-3623, Fax: 334-244-3947, E-mail: awarren3@aum.edu. *Interim Dean,* Dr. Matthew Ragland, 334-244-31388, E-mail: mragland@aum.edu.

***Department of Mathematics and Computer Science*** Students: 11 full-time (4 women), 10 international. Average age 24. 61 applicants, 97% accepted, 9 enrolled. *Faculty:* 6 full-time (0 women). Expenses: Contact institution. *Financial support:* Teaching assistantships available. Financial award application deadline: 3/1; financial award applicants required to submit FAFSA. In 2019, 10 master's awarded. *Application deadline:* For fall admission, 7/15 for international students; for spring admission, 11/15 for international students; for summer admission, 4/15 for international students. Applications are processed on a rolling basis. *Application fee:* $25 ($0 for international students). Electronic applications accepted. *Application Contact:* Dr. Luis Cueva-Parra, Associate Dean, 334-244-3321, Fax: 334-244-3826, E-mail: lcuevapa@aum.edu. *Chair,* Dr. Yi Wang, 334-244-3318, Fax: 334-244-3826, E-mail: ywang2@aum.edu.

## AUGSBURG UNIVERSITY, Minneapolis, MN 55454-1351

**General Information** Independent-religious, coed, comprehensive institution. *Graduate housing:* On-campus housing not available.

**GRADUATE UNITS**

**Program in Business Administration** *Program availability:* Evening/weekend. Electronic applications accepted.

**Program in Education** *Program availability:* Part-time, evening/weekend. Electronic applications accepted.

**Program in Leadership** *Program availability:* Part-time, evening/weekend.

**Program in Physician Assistant Studies**

**Program in Social Work** *Program availability:* Part-time, evening/weekend.

**Programs in Nursing**

## AUGUSTANA UNIVERSITY, Sioux Falls, SD 57197

**General Information** Independent-religious, coed, comprehensive institution. *Graduate housing:* Rooms and/or apartments available on a first-come, first-served basis to single and married students. Housing application deadline: 9/1. *Research affiliation:* Binghamton University, State University of New York (chemistry), Sanford Underground Science and Engineering Lab (physics), J.R. Macdonald Laboratory (physics), NASA (computer science), Labratori Nazionalidd Gran Sasso, Italy (physics), Sanford Research (biology, biochemistry, genetic counseling).

**GRADUATE UNITS**

**Augustana-Sanford Genetic Counseling Program** Electronic applications accepted.

**MA in Education Program** *Program availability:* Part-time-only, evening/weekend, online only, 100% online. Electronic applications accepted.

**Master of Professional Accountancy Program** *Program availability:* Part-time. Electronic applications accepted.

**Sports Administration and Leadership Program** *Program availability:* Part-time. Electronic applications accepted.

## AUGUSTA UNIVERSITY, Augusta, GA 30912

**General Information** State-supported, coed, university. CGS member. *Graduate housing:* Rooms and/or apartments available on a first-come, first-served basis to single and married students. *Research affiliation:* Georgia Cancer Coalition (cancer research programs), Advanced Technology Development Center (biotechnology transfer), Medical College of Georgia Research Institute, Inc. (biomedical research), Georgia Center of Innovation for Life Sciences (research commercialization and economic development), Georgia Research Alliance (science and technology development).

**GRADUATE UNITS**

**College of Allied Health Sciences** *Program availability:* Online learning.

**College of Education** *Program availability:* Part-time, evening/weekend.

**College of Nursing**

**College of Science and Mathematics**

**The Dental College of Georgia** Electronic applications accepted.

**Hull College of Business** *Program availability:* Part-time, evening/weekend.

**Medical College of Georgia**

**Program in Biochemistry and Cancer Biology** Electronic applications accepted.

**Program in Cellular Biology and Anatomy**

**Program in Genomic Medicine** Electronic applications accepted.

**Program in Molecular Medicine** Electronic applications accepted.

**Program in Neuroscience** Electronic applications accepted.

**Program in Oral Biology** *Program availability:* Part-time. Electronic applications accepted.

**Program in Pharmacology** Electronic applications accepted.

**Program in Physiology** Electronic applications accepted.

**Program in Vascular Biology**

## AURORA UNIVERSITY, Aurora, IL 60506-4892

**General Information** Independent, coed, comprehensive institution. *Enrollment:* 6,246 graduate, professional, and undergraduate students; 919 full-time matriculated graduate/professional students (764 women), 1,217 part-time matriculated graduate/professional students (931 women). *Enrollment by degree level:* 1,827 master's, 270 doctoral, 39 other advanced degrees. *Graduate faculty:* 38 full-time (18 women), 187 part-time/adjunct (144 women). *Tuition:* Full-time $12,600; part-time $600 per credit hour. Tuition and fees vary according to degree level, campus/location and program. *Graduate housing:* On-campus housing not available. *Student services:* Campus employment opportunities, campus safety program, career counseling, exercise/wellness program, free psychological counseling, international student services, multicultural affairs office, services for students with disabilities, teacher training, writing training. *Library facilities:* Charles B. Phillips Library plus 1 other. *Collection:* Books: 24,587 (physical), 197,381 (digital/electronic); Serial titles: 2 (physical), 55,369 (digital/electronic); Databases: 63. Weekly public service hours: 99; students can reserve study rooms.

**Computer facilities:** 193 computers available on campus for general student use. A campuswide network can be accessed. Online class registration, learning management system are available.
Website: http://www.aurora.edu/

**General Application Contact:** Jason Harmon, Dean of Adult and Graduate Studies, 630-9478955, E-mail: jharmon@aurora.edu.

**GRADUATE UNITS**

**Dunham School of Business and Public Policy** Students: 160 full-time (98 women), 182 part-time (119 women); includes 134 minority (56 Black or African American, non-Hispanic/Latino; 9 Asian, non-Hispanic/Latino; 64 Hispanic/Latino; 5 Two or more races, non-Hispanic/Latino). Average age 31. 277 applicants, 95% accepted, 134 enrolled. *Faculty:* 11 full-time (3 women), 30 part-time/adjunct (15 women). Expenses: Contact institution. *Financial support:* In 2019–20, 66 students received support. Federal Work-Study, scholarships/grants, and unspecified assistantships available. Financial award applicants required to submit FAFSA. In 2019, 162 master's awarded. *Program availability:* Part-time, 100% online, blended/hybrid learning. *Application deadline:* For fall admission, 6/1 for international students; for spring admission, 10/1 for international students. Applications are processed on a rolling basis. Electronic applications accepted. *Application Contact:* Jason Harmon, Dean of Adult and Graduate Studies, 630-9478955, E-mail: AUadmission@aurora.edu. *Dean, School of Business and Policy,* Dr. Toby Arquette, 630-844-5614, E-mail: tarquett@aurora.edu.

**School of Arts and Sciences** Students: 7 full-time (2 women), 48 part-time (32 women); includes 6 minority (1 Black or African American, non-Hispanic/Latino; 1 Asian, non-Hispanic/Latino; 3 Hispanic/Latino; 1 Two or more races, non-Hispanic/Latino). Average age 35. 21 applicants, 100% accepted, 12 enrolled. *Faculty:* 2 full-time (1 woman), 8 part-time/adjunct (4 women). Expenses: Contact institution. *Financial support:* Federal Work-Study, scholarships/grants, and unspecified assistantships available. Financial award applicants required to submit FAFSA. In 2019, 30 master's awarded. *Program availability:* Part-time, evening/weekend, 100% online. *Application deadline:* For fall admission, 6/1 for international students; for spring admission, 10/1 for international students. Applications are processed on a rolling basis. Electronic applications accepted. *Application Contact:* Jason Harmon, Dean of Adult and Graduate Studies, 630-947-8955, E-mail: AUadmission@aurora.edu. *Dean, School of Arts and Sciences,* Dr. Karol Dean, 630-8447585, E-mail: kdean@aurora.edu.

**School of Education and Human Performance** Students: 43 full-time (34 women), 564 part-time (407 women); includes 123 minority (31 Black or African American, non-Hispanic/Latino; 10 Asian, non-Hispanic/Latino; 68 Hispanic/Latino; 1 Native Hawaiian or other Pacific Islander, non-Hispanic/Latino; 13 Two or more races, non-Hispanic/Latino), 2 international. Average age 37. 291 applicants, 98% accepted, 136 enrolled. *Faculty:* 13 full-time (5 women), 36 part-time/adjunct (20 women). Expenses: Contact institution. *Financial support:* In 2019–20, 28 students received support. Federal Work-Study, scholarships/grants, and unspecified assistantships available. Financial award applicants required to submit FAFSA. In 2019, 133 master's, 27 doctorates awarded. *Program availability:* Part-time, evening/weekend, 100% online. *Application deadline:* For fall admission, 6/1 for international students; for spring admission, 10/1 for international students. Applications are processed on a rolling basis. Electronic applications accepted. *Application Contact:* Jason Harmon, Dean of Adult and Graduate Studies, 630-947-8955, E-mail: AUadmission@aurora.edu. *Dean, School of Education and Human Performance,* Dr. Jen Buckley, 630-844-1542, Fax: 630-844-6155, E-mail: jbuckley@aurora.edu.

**School of Social Work** Students: 709 full-time (630 women), 423 part-time (373 women); includes 380 minority (166 Black or African American, non-Hispanic/Latino; 2 American Indian or Alaska Native, non-Hispanic/Latino; 19 Asian, non-Hispanic/Latino; 174 Hispanic/Latino; 19 Two or more races, non-Hispanic/Latino), 2 international. Average age 37. 696 applicants, 100% accepted, 455 enrolled. *Faculty:* 12 full-time (9 women), 113 part-time/adjunct (105 women). Expenses: Contact institution. *Financial support:* In 2019–20, 373 students received support. Federal Work-Study, scholarships/grants, and unspecified assistantships available. Financial award applicants required to submit FAFSA. In 2019, 492 master's, 8 doctorates awarded. *Program availability:* Part-time, evening/weekend, 100% online, blended/hybrid learning. *Application deadline:* For fall admission, 6/1 for international students; for spring admission, 10/1 for international students. Applications are processed on a rolling basis. Electronic applications accepted. *Application Contact:* Jason Harmon, Dean of Adult and Graduate Studies, 630-947-8955, E-mail: AUadmission@aurora.edu. *Dean, School of Social Work,* Dr. Brenda Barnwell, 630-947-8933, E-mail: bbarnwel@aurora.edu.

## AUSTIN COLLEGE, Sherman, TX 75090-4400

**General Information** Independent-religious, coed, comprehensive institution. *Enrollment:* 1,314 graduate, professional, and undergraduate students; 20 full-time matriculated graduate/professional students (16 women). *Enrollment by degree level:* 20 master's. *Graduate faculty:* 4 full-time (all women), 1 (woman) part-time/adjunct. *Graduate housing:* Room and/or apartments available on a first-come, first-served basis to single students; on-campus housing not available to married students. *Student* *services:* Campus employment opportunities, career counseling, free psychological counseling, teacher training. *Library facilities:* Abell Library. *Collection:* Books: 227,390 (physical). Study areas open 24 hours, 5–7 days a week; students can reserve study rooms.

**Computer facilities:** 160 computers available on campus for general student use. A campuswide network can be accessed. Online class registration is available.
Website: http://www.austincollege.edu/

**General Application Contact:** Shanda Husers, Administrative Assistant, Certification Officer, 903-813-2327, E-mail: shusers@austincollege.edu.

**GRADUATE UNITS**

**Austin Teacher Program** Average age 23. Expenses: Contact institution. *Financial support:* Career-related internships or fieldwork, Federal Work-Study, scholarships/grants, and unspecified assistantships available. Support available to part-time students. Financial award application deadline: 4/1; financial award applicants required to submit FAFSA. In 2019, 13 master's awarded. *Program availability:* Part-time. *Application deadline:* For fall admission, 5/1 priority date for domestic students; for spring admission, 1/15 priority date for domestic students. Applications are processed on a rolling basis. *Application fee:* $35. Electronic applications accepted. *Application Contact:* Administrative Assistant, 903-813-2327. *Department Chair*, Julia Shahid, 903-813-2457, E-mail: jshahid@austincollege.edu.

## AUSTIN GRADUATE SCHOOL OF THEOLOGY, Austin, TX 78752

**General Information** Independent-religious, coed, upper-level institution. *Graduate housing:* On-campus housing not available.

## AUSTIN PEAY STATE UNIVERSITY, Clarksville, TN 37044

**General Information** State-supported, coed, comprehensive institution. CGS member. *Graduate housing:* Rooms and/or apartments available on a first-come, first-served basis to single and married students.

**GRADUATE UNITS**

**College of Graduate Studies** Students: 315 full-time (184 women), 728 part-time (508 women); includes 265 minority (156 Black or African American, non-Hispanic/Latino; 1 American Indian or Alaska Native, non-Hispanic/Latino; 15 Asian, non-Hispanic/Latino; 33 Hispanic/Latino; 2 Native Hawaiian or other Pacific Islander, non-Hispanic/Latino; 58 Two or more races, non-Hispanic/Latino), 71 international. Average age 32. 500 applicants, 90% accepted, 309 enrolled. *Faculty:* 138 full-time (65 women), 28 part-time/adjunct (16 women). Expenses: Contact institution. *Financial support:* In 2019–20, 136 students received support, including 136 research assistantships with full tuition reimbursements available (averaging $5,184 per year); career-related internships or fieldwork, Federal Work-Study, institutionally sponsored loans, scholarships/grants, and unspecified assistantships also available. Support available to part-time students. Financial award application deadline: 7/1; financial award applicants required to submit FAFSA. In 2019, 416 master's, 9 other advanced degrees awarded. *Program availability:* Part-time, evening/weekend, online learning. *Application deadline:* For fall admission, 8/5 priority date for domestic students. Applications are processed on a rolling basis. *Application fee:* $45 ($55 for international students). Electronic applications accepted. *Application Contact:* Megan Mitchell, Director of Graduate Admissions and Recruitment, 931-221-6189, Fax: 931-221-7641, E-mail: mitchellm@apsu.edu. *Associate Provost of Research and Dean of the College of Graduate Studies*, Dr. Chad Brooks, 931-221-7415, Fax: 931-221-7641, E-mail: brooksc@apsu.edu.

***College of Arts and Letters*** Students: 43 full-time (22 women), 88 part-time (51 women); includes 32 minority (19 Black or African American, non-Hispanic/Latino; 1 American Indian or Alaska Native, non-Hispanic/Latino; 1 Asian, non-Hispanic/Latino; 2 Hispanic/Latino; 9 Two or more races, non-Hispanic/Latino), 2 international. Average age 32. 61 applicants, 89% accepted, 42 enrolled. *Faculty:* 46 full-time (18 women), 7 part-time/adjunct (4 women). Expenses: Contact institution. *Financial support:* Research assistantships with full tuition reimbursements, teaching assistantships, career-related internships or fieldwork, Federal Work-Study, institutionally sponsored loans, scholarships/grants, and unspecified assistantships available. Support available to part-time students. Financial award application deadline: 7/1; financial award applicants required to submit FAFSA. In 2019, 53 master's awarded. *Program availability:* Part-time, evening/weekend, online learning. *Application deadline:* For fall admission, 8/5 priority date for domestic students. Applications are processed on a rolling basis. *Application fee:* $45 ($55 for international students). Electronic applications accepted. *Application Contact:* Megan Mitchell, Coordinator of Graduate Admissions, 931-221-6189, Fax: 931-221-7641, E-mail: mitchellm@apsu.edu. *Interim Dean*, Dr. Barry Jones, 931-221-7330, Fax: 931-221-1024, E-mail: jonesb@apsu.edu.

***College of Behavioral and Health Sciences*** Students: 127 full-time (96 women), 291 part-time (230 women); includes 130 minority (80 Black or African American, non-Hispanic/Latino; 5 Asian, non-Hispanic/Latino; 17 Hispanic/Latino; 1 Native Hawaiian or other Pacific Islander, non-Hispanic/Latino; 27 Two or more races, non-Hispanic/Latino), 3 international. Average age 32. 184 applicants, 87% accepted, 128 enrolled. *Faculty:* 31 full-time (20 women), 11 part-time/adjunct (8 women). Expenses: Contact institution. *Financial support:* Research assistantships with full tuition reimbursements, career-related internships or fieldwork, Federal Work-Study, institutionally sponsored loans, scholarships/grants, and unspecified assistantships available. Support available to part-time students. Financial award application deadline: 7/1; financial award applicants required to submit FAFSA. In 2019, 170 master's awarded. *Program availability:* Part-time, evening/weekend, online learning. *Application deadline:* For fall admission, 8/5 priority date for domestic students. Applications are processed on a rolling basis. *Application fee:* $45 ($55 for international students). Electronic applications accepted. *Application Contact:* Megan Mitchell, Coordinator of Graduate Admissions, 931-221-6189, Fax: 931-221-7641, E-mail: mitchellm@apsu.edu. *Dean*, Dr. Tucker Brown, 931-2217725, E-mail: brownt@apsu.edu.

***College of Business*** Students: 14 full-time (4 women), 38 part-time (22 women); includes 16 minority (10 Black or African American, non-Hispanic/Latino; 1 Asian, non-Hispanic/Latino; 2 Hispanic/Latino; 1 Native Hawaiian or other Pacific Islander, non-Hispanic/Latino; 2 Two or more races, non-Hispanic/Latino). Average age 33. 23 applicants, 83% accepted, 15 enrolled. *Faculty:* 4 full-time (2 women). Expenses: Contact institution. *Financial support:* Research assistantships with full tuition reimbursements, career-related internships or fieldwork, Federal Work-Study, institutionally sponsored loans, scholarships/grants, and unspecified assistantships available. Support available to part-time students. Financial award application deadline: 7/1; financial award applicants required to submit FAFSA. In 2019, 32 master's awarded. *Program availability:* Part-time, evening/weekend, online learning. *Application deadline:* For fall admission, 8/5 priority date for domestic students. Applications are processed on a rolling basis. *Application fee:* $45 ($55 for international students). Electronic applications accepted. *Application Contact:* Megan Mitchell, Coordinator of Graduate Admissions, 931-221-6189, Fax: 931-221-7641, E-mail: mitchellm@apsu.edu. *Dean*, Dr. Mickey Hepner, 931-221-7675, Fax: 931-221-7355, E-mail: hepnerm@apsu.edu.

***College of Education*** Students: 50 full-time (38 women), 201 part-time (160 women); includes 49 minority (28 Black or African American, non-Hispanic/Latino; 4 Asian, non-Hispanic/Latino; 7 Hispanic/Latino; 10 Two or more races, non-Hispanic/Latino), 2 international. Average age 33. 88 applicants, 95% accepted, 62 enrolled. *Faculty:* 23 full-time (17 women), 5 part-time/adjunct (4 women). Expenses: Contact institution. *Financial support:* Research assistantships with full tuition reimbursements, career-related internships or fieldwork, Federal Work-Study, institutionally sponsored loans, scholarships/grants, and unspecified assistantships available. Support available to part-time students. Financial award application deadline: 7/1; financial award applicants required to submit FAFSA. In 2019, 106 master's, 9 Ed Ss awarded. *Program availability:* Part-time, evening/weekend, online learning. *Application deadline:* For fall admission, 8/5 priority date for domestic students. Applications are processed on a rolling basis. *Application fee:* $45 ($55 for international students). Electronic applications accepted. *Application Contact:* Megan Mitchell, Coordinator of Graduate Admissions, 931-221-6189, Fax: 931-221-7641, E-mail: mitchellm@apsu.edu. *Dean*, Dr. Prentice Chandler, 931-221-7511, Fax: 931-221-1292, E-mail: chandlerp@apsu.edu.

***College of Science, Technology, Engineering and Mathematics*** Students: 81 full-time (24 women), 110 part-time (45 women); includes 38 minority (19 Black or African American, non-Hispanic/Latino; 4 Asian, non-Hispanic/Latino; 5 Hispanic/Latino; 10 Two or more races, non-Hispanic/Latino), 64 international. Average age 31. 144 applicants, 92% accepted, 62 enrolled. *Faculty:* 34 full-time (8 women), 5 part-time/adjunct (0 women). Expenses: Contact institution. *Financial support:* Research assistantships with full tuition reimbursements, career-related internships or fieldwork, Federal Work-Study, institutionally sponsored loans, scholarships/grants, and unspecified assistantships available. Support available to part-time students. Financial award application deadline: 7/1; financial award applicants required to submit FAFSA. In 2019, 42 master's awarded. *Program availability:* Part-time, online learning. *Application deadline:* For fall admission, 8/5 priority date for domestic students. Applications are processed on a rolling basis. *Application fee:* $45 ($55 for international students). Electronic applications accepted. *Application Contact:* Megan Mitchell, Coordinator of Graduate Admissions, 931-221-6189, Fax: 931-221-7641, E-mail: mitchellm@apsu.edu. *Dean*, Dr. Karen Meisch, 931-221-7780, Fax: 931-221-7984, E-mail: meischk@apsu.edu.

## AUSTIN PRESBYTERIAN THEOLOGICAL SEMINARY, Austin, TX 78705-5797

**General Information** Independent-religious, coed, graduate-only institution. *Enrollment by degree level:* 123 master's, 27 doctoral. *Graduate faculty:* 21 full-time (6 women), 10 part-time/adjunct (3 women). *Tuition:* Full-time $13,980; part-time $6990 per credit. *Required fees:* $170; $170. *Graduate housing:* Rooms and/or apartments available on a first-come, first-served basis to single and married students. Typical cost: $3650 per year ($3650 including board) for single students; $9050 per year ($9050 including board) for married students. Room and board charges vary according to housing facility selected. Housing application deadline: 5/31. *Student services:* Campus employment opportunities, campus safety program, career counseling, free psychological counseling, international student services, services for students with disabilities, writing training. *Library facilities:* Stitt Library. *Collection:* Books: 109,766 (physical), 312,522 (digital/electronic); Serial titles: 1,007 (physical), 47,945 (digital/electronic); Databases: 97. Weekly public service hours: 37.

**Computer facilities:** 20 computers available on campus for general student use.
Website: http://www.austinseminary.edu/

**General Application Contact:** Rev. JD Herrera, Vice President for Enrollment Management, 512-404-4827, Fax: 512-472-7089, E-mail: admissions@austinseminary.edu.

**GRADUATE UNITS**

**Graduate and Professional Programs** Electronic applications accepted.

## AVE MARIA SCHOOL OF LAW, Naples, FL 34119

**General Information** Independent-religious, coed, graduate-only institution. *Enrollment by degree level:* 269 doctoral. *Graduate faculty:* 25 full-time (10 women), 18 part-time/adjunct (11 women). *Tuition:* Full-time $39,450. *Required fees:* $2256. *Graduate housing:* Rooms and/or apartments available on a first-come, first-served basis to single and married students. Typical cost: $11,349 per year ($14,562 including board) for single students; $11,349 per year ($14,562 including board) for married students. Housing application deadline: 4/15. *Student services:* Campus employment opportunities, campus safety program, career counseling, exercise/wellness program, international student services, services for students with disabilities, writing training. *Library facilities:* Veterans Memorial Law Library. *Collection:* Books: 53,471 (physical), 48,624 (digital/electronic); Serial titles: 2,330 (physical), 29,769 (digital/electronic); Databases: 206. Weekly public service hours: 168; study areas open 24 hours, 5–7 days a week; students can reserve study rooms.

**Computer facilities:** 20 computers available on campus for general student use. A campuswide network can be accessed from student residence rooms and from off campus. Online class registration is available.
Website: http://www.avemarialaw.edu/

**General Application Contact:** Claire T. O'Keefe, Associate Dean of Admissions and Student Engagement, 239-687-5423, Fax: 239-352-2890, E-mail: info@avemarialaw.edu.

**GRADUATE UNITS**

**Professional Program** Students: 269 full-time (153 women); includes 82 minority (16 Black or African American, non-Hispanic/Latino; 3 American Indian or Alaska Native, non-Hispanic/Latino; 4 Asian, non-Hispanic/Latino; 57 Hispanic/Latino; 1 Native Hawaiian or other Pacific Islander, non-Hispanic/Latino; 1 Two or more races, non-Hispanic/Latino), 5 international. Average age 26. 602 applicants, 54% accepted, 109 enrolled. *Faculty:* 25 full-time (10 women), 18 part-time/adjunct (11 women). Expenses: Contact institution. *Financial support:* In 2019–20, 238 students received support. Career-related internships or fieldwork, Federal Work-Study, and scholarships/grants available. Financial award application deadline: 6/30; financial award applicants required to submit FAFSA. In 2019, 66 doctorates awarded. *Application deadline:* For fall admission, 7/15 priority date for domestic and international students. Applications are processed on a rolling basis. Electronic applications accepted. *Application Contact:* Claire T. O'Keefe, Associate Dean of Admissions and Student Engagement, 239-687-5423, Fax: 239-352-2890, E-mail: info@avemarialaw.edu. *President/Dean*, Kevin Cieply, 239-687-5300, E-mail: kcieply@avemarialaw.edu.

## AVE MARIA UNIVERSITY, Ave Maria, FL 34142

**General Information** Independent-religious, coed, comprehensive institution. *Graduate housing:* Room and/or apartments available on a first-come, first-served basis to single students; on-campus housing not available to married students. Housing application deadline: 7/15.

**GRADUATE UNITS**

**Graduate Programs**

## AVERETT UNIVERSITY, Danville, VA 24541-3692

**General Information** Independent-religious, coed, comprehensive institution. *Enrollment:* 903 graduate, professional, and undergraduate students; 195 full-time matriculated graduate/professional students (135 women), 72 part-time matriculated graduate/professional students (48 women). *Enrollment by degree level:* 267 master's. *Graduate faculty:* 7 full-time (6 women), 38 part-time/adjunct (21 women). Tuition and fees vary according to program. *Graduate housing:* On-campus housing not available. *Student services:* Campus employment opportunities, campus safety program, career counseling, free psychological counseling, services for students with disabilities, teacher training, writing training. *Library facilities:* Mary B. Blount Library. *Collection:* Books: 86,432 (physical), 313,632 (digital/electronic); Serial titles: 98 (physical), 35,069 (digital/electronic); Databases: 160. Weekly public service hours: 81; students can reserve study rooms.

**Computer facilities:** 150 computers available on campus for general student use. A campuswide network can be accessed. Online class registration is available. Website: http://www.averett.edu/

**General Application Contact:** Christy Davis, Assistant Director of Admissions, 434-791-7133, E-mail: cdavis@averett.edu.

**GRADUATE UNITS**

**Graduate Nursing Program**

**Master in Education Program** Students: 106 full-time (86 women), 32 part-time (21 women); includes 36 minority (30 Black or African American, non-Hispanic/Latino; 2 American Indian or Alaska Native, non-Hispanic/Latino; 2 Hispanic/Latino; 2 Native Hawaiian or other Pacific Islander, non-Hispanic/Latino). Average age 36. 95 applicants, 61% accepted, 41 enrolled. *Faculty:* 2 full-time (both women), 20 part-time/adjunct (15 women). Expenses: Contact institution. *Financial support:* Application deadline: 3/1; applicants required to submit FAFSA. In 2019, 52 master's awarded. *Program availability:* Part-time, online only, 100% online. *Application deadline:* Applications are processed on a rolling basis. Electronic applications accepted. *Application Contact:* Christy Davis, Assistant Director of Admissions, 434-791-7133, E-mail: cdavis@averett.edu. *Chair of the Education Department; Director of Teacher Education*, Dr. Nancy Riddell, 434-791-5741, Fax: 434-791-5020, E-mail: nriddell@averett.edu.

**Master of Accountancy Program** Students: 6 full-time (2 women); includes 1 minority (Black or African American, non-Hispanic/Latino). Average age 25. 5 applicants, 100% accepted, 4 enrolled. *Faculty:* 1 (woman) full-time. Expenses: Contact institution. *Financial support:* Application deadline: 3/1; applicants required to submit FAFSA. In 2019, 2 master's awarded. *Program availability:* Part-time. *Application deadline:* Applications are processed on a rolling basis. Electronic applications accepted. *Application Contact:* Christy Davis, Assistant Director of Admissions, 434-791-7133, E-mail: cdavis@averett.edu. *Director of the Master in Accountancy Program*, Dr. Peggy C. Wright, 434-791-7118, E-mail: pwright@averett.edu.

**Master of Business Administration Program** Students: 65 full-time (38 women), 36 part-time (24 women); includes 29 minority (26 Black or African American, non-Hispanic/Latino; 1 American Indian or Alaska Native, non-Hispanic/Latino; 1 Hispanic/Latino; 1 Two or more races, non-Hispanic/Latino). Average age 32. 70 applicants, 86% accepted, 41 enrolled. *Faculty:* 2 full-time (1 woman), 12 part-time/adjunct (3 women). Expenses: Contact institution. *Financial support:* Application deadline: 3/1; applicants required to submit FAFSA. In 2019, 62 master's awarded. *Program availability:* Part-time. *Application deadline:* Applications are processed on a rolling basis. Electronic applications accepted. *Application Contact:* Christy Davis, Assistant Director of Admissions, 434-791-7133, E-mail: cdavis@averett.edu. *Chair, Business Department*, Dr. Peggy C. Wright, 434-791-7118, E-mail: pwright@averett.edu.

**Master of Science in Applied Data Analytics Program** Students: 6 full-time (3 women), 1 part-time (0 women); includes 1 minority (Black or African American, non-Hispanic/Latino), 1 international. Average age 38. 12 applicants, 67% accepted, 3 enrolled. *Faculty:* 1 (woman) full-time, 3 part-time/adjunct (2 women). Expenses: Contact institution. *Financial support:* Application deadline: 3/1; applicants required to submit FAFSA. *Program availability:* Part-time. *Application Contact:* Christy Davis, Assistant Director of Admissions, 434-791-7133, E-mail: cdavis@averett.edu. *Chair of Business Department*, Dr. Peggy Wright, 434-791-7118, E-mail: pwright@averett.edu.

**Master of Science in Criminal Justice Leadership and Administration Program** Students: 5 full-time (0 women), 2 part-time (both women); includes 4 minority (all Black or African American, non-Hispanic/Latino). Average age 38. 15 applicants, 40% accepted, 4 enrolled. *Faculty:* 2 full-time (both women), 4 part-time/adjunct (2 women). Expenses: Contact institution. *Financial support:* Application deadline: 3/1; applicants required to submit FAFSA. *Program availability:* Part-time. *Application deadline:* Applications are processed on a rolling basis. Electronic applications accepted. *Application Contact:* Christy Davis, Assistant Director of Admissions, 434-791-7133, E-mail: cdavis@averett.edu. *Non-Traditional Criminal Justice Program Director*, Dr. James Hodgson, 434-7916881, E-mail: jhodgson@averett.edu.

## AVILA UNIVERSITY, Kansas City, MO 64145-1698

**General Information** Independent-religious, coed, comprehensive institution. *Enrollment:* 1,529 graduate, professional, and undergraduate students; 282 full-time matriculated graduate/professional students (207 women), 93 part-time matriculated graduate/professional students (72 women). *Enrollment by degree level:* 327 master's, 39 other advanced degrees. *Graduate faculty:* 16 full-time (12 women), 32 part-time/adjunct (17 women). Tuition and fees vary according to program. *Graduate housing:* Room and/or apartments available on a first-come, first-served basis to single students; on-campus housing not available to married students. Typical cost: $3450 per year ($6750 including board). Room and board charges vary according to board plan and housing facility selected. *Student services:* Campus employment opportunities, campus safety program, career counseling, child daycare facilities, exercise/wellness program, free psychological counseling, international student services, low-cost health insurance, multicultural affairs office, services for students with disabilities, teacher training, writing training. *Library facilities:* Hooley-Bundshu Library plus 1 other. *Collection:* Books: 39,963 (physical), 309,288 (digital/electronic); Serial titles: 205 (physical), 389,497 (digital/electronic); Databases: 72. Weekly public service hours: 91; students can reserve study rooms.

**Computer facilities:** 141 computers available on campus for general student use. A campuswide network can be accessed. Online class registration, laptop checkout through library are available.
Website: http://www.avila.edu/

**General Application Contact:** Jesse Reinert, Admission Representative, 816-501-2483, E-mail: jessie.reinert@avila.edu.

**GRADUATE UNITS**

**Department of Psychology** Students: 90 full-time (73 women), 20 part-time (17 women); includes 39 minority (23 Black or African American, non-Hispanic/Latino; 1 American Indian or Alaska Native, non-Hispanic/Latino; 3 Asian, non-Hispanic/Latino; 6 Hispanic/Latino; 6 Two or more races, non-Hispanic/Latino), 2 international. Average age 33. 117 applicants, 55% accepted, 52 enrolled. *Faculty:* 6 full-time (all women), 7 part-time/adjunct (4 women). Expenses: Contact institution. *Financial support:* In 2019–20, 12 students received support, including 4 research assistantships with partial tuition reimbursements available; career-related internships or fieldwork, scholarships/grants, and unspecified assistantships also available. Support available to part-time students. Financial award applicants required to submit FAFSA. In 2019, 27 master's awarded. *Program availability:* Part-time. *Application deadline:* Applications are processed on a rolling basis. Electronic applications accepted. *Application Contact:* Heather Nobl, Graduate Admissions Advisor, 816-501-2969, E-mail: gradpsych@avila.edu. *Director of Graduate Psychology Enrollment Management*, Phil Gebauer, 816-501-0419, Fax: 816-501-2455, E-mail: philip.gebauer@avila.edu.

**School of Business** Students: 40 full-time (23 women), 20 part-time (13 women); includes 14 minority (10 Black or African American, non-Hispanic/Latino; 2 Hispanic/Latino; 2 Two or more races, non-Hispanic/Latino), 17 international. Average age 32. 31 applicants, 32% accepted, 6 enrolled. *Faculty:* 6 full-time (2 women), 8 part-time/adjunct (3 women). Expenses: Contact institution. *Financial support:* In 2019–20, 15 students received support. Career-related internships or fieldwork and scholarships/grants available. Support available to part-time students. Financial award applicants required to submit FAFSA. In 2019, 29 master's awarded. *Program availability:* Part-time, evening/weekend. *Application deadline:* For fall admission, 7/30 priority date for domestic and international students; for winter admission, 11/30 priority date for domestic and international students; for spring admission, 2/28 priority date for domestic and international students; for summer admission, 6/1 priority date for domestic and international students. Applications are processed on a rolling basis. Electronic applications accepted. *Application Contact:* Dr. Wendy Acker, Chair, 816-501-3798, E-mail: wendy.acker@avila.edu. *Chair*, Dr. Wendy L. Acker, 816-501-3720, Fax: 816-501-2463, E-mail: wendy.acker@avila.edu.

**School of Education** Students: 63 full-time (49 women), 21 part-time (17 women); includes 18 minority (10 Black or African American, non-Hispanic/Latino; 2 Asian, non-Hispanic/Latino; 4 Hispanic/Latino; 2 Two or more races, non-Hispanic/Latino), 2 international. Average age 36. 43 applicants, 60% accepted, 16 enrolled. *Faculty:* 4 full-time (all women), 1 (woman) part-time/adjunct. Expenses: Contact institution. *Financial support:* In 2019–20, 12 students received support. Unspecified assistantships available. Financial award applicants required to submit FAFSA. In 2019, 28 master's awarded. *Program availability:* Part-time, evening/weekend, online learning. *Application deadline:* Applications are processed on a rolling basis. Electronic applications accepted. *Application Contact:* Cory Roup, Graduate Education Enrollment and Academic Advisor, 816-501-2464, E-mail: cory.roup@avila.edu. *Director of Graduate Education*, Dr. Stacy Keith, 816-501-2446, Fax: 816-501-2915, E-mail: stacy.keith@avila.edu.

**School of Professional Studies** Students: 74 full-time (56 women), 32 part-time (25 women); includes 38 minority (31 Black or African American, non-Hispanic/Latino; 4 Hispanic/Latino; 1 Native Hawaiian or other Pacific Islander, non-Hispanic/Latino; 2 Two or more races, non-Hispanic/Latino), 6 international. Average age 37. 55 applicants, 40% accepted, 20 enrolled. *Faculty:* 16 part-time/adjunct (9 women). Expenses: Contact institution. *Financial support:* In 2019–20, 12 students received support. Unspecified assistantships available. Support available to part-time students. Financial award applicants required to submit FAFSA. In 2019, 44 master's awarded. *Program availability:* Part-time-only, evening/weekend, 100% online, blended/hybrid learning. *Application deadline:* Applications are processed on a rolling basis. Electronic applications accepted. *Application Contact:* Ann Dorrell, Graduate Admission Advisor, 816-501-2482, Fax: 816-941-4650, E-mail: advantage@avila.edu. *Coordinator*, Sarah Sullivan, 816-501-0429, Fax: 816-941-4650, E-mail: advantage@avila.edu.

## AZUSA PACIFIC UNIVERSITY, Azusa, CA 91702-7000

**General Information** Independent-religious, coed, university. CGS member. *Graduate housing:* On-campus housing not available.

**GRADUATE UNITS**

**Azusa Pacific Seminary** *Program availability:* Part-time, evening/weekend.

**College of Liberal Arts and Sciences** *Program availability:* Part-time, evening/weekend, online learning.

***Haggard Graduate School of Theology***

**College of Music and the Arts** *Program availability:* Part-time, evening/weekend.

**School of Behavioral and Applied Sciences**

**School of Business and Management** *Program availability:* Part-time, evening/weekend.

**School of Education** *Program availability:* Part-time, evening/weekend.

**School of Nursing** *Program availability:* Part-time, evening/weekend.

**University College** *Program availability:* Online learning.

## BABEL UNIVERSITY PROFESSIONAL SCHOOL OF TRANSLATION, Honolulu, HI 96815

**General Information** Proprietary, coed, primarily women, graduate-only institution. *Graduate housing:* On-campus housing not available.

**GRADUATE UNITS**

**Program in Translation** *Program availability:* Part-time, evening/weekend, online learning.

## BABSON COLLEGE, Babson Park, MA 02457-0310

**General Information** Independent, coed, comprehensive institution. *Graduate housing:* Rooms and/or apartments available on a first-come, first-served basis to single and married students. Housing application deadline: 5/1.

**GRADUATE UNITS**

**F. W. Olin Graduate School of Business** *Program availability:* Part-time, evening/weekend, online learning. Electronic applications accepted.

## BAKER COLLEGE CENTER FOR GRADUATE STUDIES–ONLINE, Flint, MI 48507

**General Information** Independent, coed, graduate-only institution. *Graduate housing:* On-campus housing not available.

**GRADUATE UNITS**

**Graduate Programs** *Program availability:* Part-time, evening/weekend, online learning. Electronic applications accepted.

## BAKER UNIVERSITY, Baldwin City, KS 66006-0065

**General Information** Independent-religious, coed, comprehensive institution. *Graduate housing:* On-campus housing not available.

**GRADUATE UNITS**

**School of Education** *Program availability:* Part-time, evening/weekend, 100% online. Electronic applications accepted.

**School of Professional and Graduate Studies** *Program availability:* Part-time, evening/weekend, 100% online.

## BAKKE GRADUATE UNIVERSITY, Dallas, TX 75243-7039

**General Information** Independent-religious, coed, primarily men, graduate-only institution. *Graduate housing:* On-campus housing not available.

**GRADUATE UNITS**

**Programs in Pastoral Ministry and Business** *Program availability:* Part-time, online learning. Electronic applications accepted.

## BALDWIN WALLACE UNIVERSITY, Berea, OH 44017-2088

**General Information** Independent-religious, coed, comprehensive institution. *Enrollment:* 3,504 graduate, professional, and undergraduate students; 354 full-time matriculated graduate/professional students (250 women), 176 part-time matriculated graduate/professional students (123 women). *Enrollment by degree level:* 510 master's, 20 other advanced degrees. *Graduate faculty:* 54 full-time (28 women), 36 part-time/adjunct (12 women). *Graduate housing:* Rooms and/or apartments available on a first-come, first-served basis to single and married students. Typical cost: $3447 per year for single students; $3447 per year for married students. *Student services:* Campus employment opportunities, campus safety program, career counseling, free psychological counseling, international student services, multicultural affairs office, services for students with disabilities, teacher training, writing training. *Library facilities:* Ritter Library plus 2 others. *Collection:* Books: 104,636 (physical), 501,982 (digital/electronic); Serial titles: 145 (physical), 91,949 (digital/electronic); Databases: 265. Weekly public service hours: 90; study areas open 24 hours, 5–7 days a week; students can reserve study rooms. *Research affiliation:* Cuyahoga Community College (early childhood education), Berea City Schools (co-teaching models), Head Start Programs (early childhood education).

**Computer facilities:** 409 computers available on campus for general student use. A campuswide network can be accessed. Online class registration is available.
Website: http://www.bw.edu/

**General Application Contact:** Kate Glaser, Associate Director of Admission, Graduate and Professional Studies, 440-826-8022, Fax: 440-826-3830, E-mail: admission@bw.edu.

**GRADUATE UNITS**

**Graduate Programs** Students: 354 full-time (250 women), 176 part-time (123 women); includes 84 minority (46 Black or African American, non-Hispanic/Latino; 18 Asian, non-Hispanic/Latino; 15 Hispanic/Latino; 5 Two or more races, non-Hispanic/Latino), 6 international. Average age 32. *Faculty:* 54 full-time (28 women), 36 part-time/adjunct (12 women). Expenses: Contact institution. In 2019, 285 master's awarded. *Program availability:* Part-time, evening/weekend, 100% online, blended/hybrid learning. *Application deadline:* Applications are processed on a rolling basis. *Application fee:* $25. Electronic applications accepted. *Application Contact:* Kate Glaser, Associate Director of Admission, Graduate and Professional Studies, 440-826-2222, Fax: 440-826-3830, E-mail: admission@bw.edu. *Provost, Academic Affairs,* Stephen D. Stahl, 440-826-2251, Fax: 440-826-2329, E-mail: sstahl@bw.edu.

***School of Business*** Students: 142 full-time (70 women), 74 part-time (39 women); includes 38 minority (20 Black or African American, non-Hispanic/Latino; 8 Asian, non-Hispanic/Latino; 8 Hispanic/Latino; 2 Two or more races, non-Hispanic/Latino), 4 international. Average age 34. 130 applicants, 62% accepted, 47 enrolled. *Faculty:* 25 full-time (9 women), 15 part-time/adjunct (2 women). Expenses: Contact institution. *Financial support:* In 2019–20, 24 students received support. Scholarships/grants and tuition discounts available. Financial award applicants required to submit FAFSA. In 2019, 169 master's awarded. *Program availability:* Part-time, evening/weekend, Multi-modal - student can choose to take some or all classes online. *Application deadline:* For fall admission, 7/25 priority date for domestic students, 4/30 priority date for international students; for spring admission, 12/15 priority date for domestic students, 9/30 priority date for international students; for summer admission, 4/15 for domestic students. Applications are processed on a rolling basis. Electronic applications accepted. *Application Contact:* Laura Spencer, Graduate Business Admission Specialist, 440-826-2191, Fax: 440-826-3868, E-mail: lspencer@bw.edu. *Dean of School of Business,* Dr. Frank C. Braun, 440-826-3566, Fax: 440-826-3868, E-mail: fbraun@bw.edu.

***School of Education*** Students: 79 full-time (63 women), 89 part-time (73 women); includes 20 minority (14 Black or African American, non-Hispanic/Latino; 2 Asian, non-Hispanic/Latino; 3 Hispanic/Latino; 1 Two or more races, non-Hispanic/Latino). Average age 32. 92 applicants, 59% accepted, 47 enrolled. *Faculty:* 10 full-time (6 women), 12 part-time/adjunct (3 women). Expenses: Contact institution. *Financial support:* Career-related internships or fieldwork available. Financial award applicants required to submit FAFSA. In 2019, 56 master's awarded. *Program availability:* Part-time, evening/weekend, 100% online, blended/hybrid learning. *Application deadline:* For fall admission, 8/15 priority date for domestic students; for spring admission, 12/15 priority date for domestic students. Applications are processed on a rolling basis. *Application fee:* $25. Electronic applications accepted. *Application Contact:* Kate Glaser, Associate Director of Admission for Graduate and Professional Studies, 440-826-8016, Fax: 440-826-3830, E-mail: kglaser@bw.edu. *Interim Dean of EDU/HSC/HPE,* Michael J Smith, 440-826-3137, Fax: 440-826-3779, E-mail: mjsmith@bw.edu.

## BALL STATE UNIVERSITY, Muncie, IN 47306

**General Information** State-supported, coed, university. CGS member. *Enrollment:* 22,510 graduate, professional, and undergraduate students; 1,163 full-time matriculated graduate/professional students (810 women), 4,365 part-time matriculated graduate/professional students (3,522 women). *Enrollment by degree level:* 4,880 master's, 348 doctoral, 300 other advanced degrees. *Graduate faculty:* 474 full-time (237 women), 125 part-time/adjunct (89 women). *Tuition, area resident:* Full-time $7506; part-time $417 per credit hour. Tuition, nonresident: full-time $20,610; part-time $1145 per credit hour. *Required fees:* $2126. Tuition and fees vary according to course load, campus/location and program. *Graduate housing:* Rooms and/or apartments available on a first-come, first-served basis to single and married students. Housing application deadline: 6/1. *Student services:* Campus employment opportunities, campus safety program, career counseling, child daycare facilities, exercise/wellness program, free psychological counseling, grant writing training, international student services, low-cost health insurance, multicultural affairs office, services for students with disabilities, teacher training, writing training. *Library facilities:* Bracken Library plus 2 others. *Collection:* Books: 822,983 (physical), 15,244 (digital/electronic); Serial titles: 13,599 (physical), 103,640 (digital/electronic); Databases: 296. Weekly public service hours: 123; students can reserve study rooms. *Research affiliation:* DowAgro (biochemistry), Lilly Company (biochemistry), Cisco (networking, information management), Element (biochemistry), ConforMIS (biomechanics), Monell (chemistry).

**Computer facilities:** Computer purchase and lease plans are available. 578 computers available on campus for general student use. A campuswide network can be accessed. Online class registration, room reservations, testing and test results, manage and pay tuition, order/buy textbooks, request room repairs, order transcripts, manage meal plan, manage and prepay long distance service, undergraduate degree progress report are available.
Website: http://www.bsu.edu/

**General Application Contact:** Dr. Adam Beach, Dean of the Graduate School, 765-285-1300, Fax: 765-285-1994, E-mail: arbeach@bsu.edu.

**GRADUATE UNITS**

**Graduate School** *Program availability:* Part-time, evening/weekend, 100% online, blended/hybrid learning. Electronic applications accepted.

***College of Architecture and Planning*** *Program availability:* Part-time. Electronic applications accepted.

***College of Communication, Information, and Media*** *Program availability:* Part-time, 100% online, blended/hybrid learning. Electronic applications accepted.

***College of Fine Arts*** *Program availability:* Part-time. Electronic applications accepted.

***College of Health*** *Program availability:* Part-time, evening/weekend, 100% online. Electronic applications accepted.

***College of Sciences and Humanities*** *Program availability:* Part-time, 100% online, blended/hybrid learning. Electronic applications accepted.

***Miller College of Business*** *Program availability:* Part-time, evening/weekend, 100% online, blended/hybrid learning. Electronic applications accepted.

***Teachers College*** *Program availability:* Part-time, evening/weekend, 100% online, blended/hybrid learning. Electronic applications accepted.

## BANK STREET COLLEGE OF EDUCATION, New York, NY 10025

**General Information** Independent, coed, graduate-only institution. *Research affiliation:* Annenberg Institute (education), Stanford University (education), Educational Development Center (education), Mathematica Policy Research, Inc. (education), Center for Teaching Quality (education).

**GRADUATE UNITS**

**Graduate School** Electronic applications accepted.

## BAPTIST BIBLE COLLEGE, Springfield, MO 65803-3498

**General Information** Independent-religious, coed, comprehensive institution. *Graduate housing:* Rooms and/or apartments available on a first-come, first-served basis to single and married students.

**GRADUATE UNITS**

**Graduate and Professional Programs** *Program availability:* Part-time. Electronic applications accepted.

## THE BAPTIST COLLEGE OF FLORIDA, Graceville, FL 32440

**General Information** Independent-religious, coed, comprehensive institution. *Enrollment:* 452 graduate, professional, and undergraduate students; 33 full-time matriculated graduate/professional students (6 women). *Enrollment by degree level:* 33 master's. *Graduate faculty:* 13 full-time (2 women). *Tuition:* Full-time $4320; part-time $360 per credit hour. *Graduate housing:* Rooms and/or apartments available on a first-come, first-served basis to single and married students. Typical cost: $4196 (including board) for single students; $3500 per year for married students. Housing application deadline: 8/10. *Student services:* Campus employment opportunities, campus safety program, exercise/wellness program, free psychological counseling, services for students with disabilities, writing training. *Library facilities:* Ida J. MacMillan Library plus 1 other. *Collection:* Books: 87,455 (physical), 1,794 (digital/electronic); Serial titles: 50 (physical); Databases: 17. Weekly public service hours: 66.

**Computer facilities:** 25 computers available on campus for general student use. A campuswide network can be accessed. Online class registration is available.
Website: http://www.baptistcollege.edu/

**General Application Contact:** Sandra Richards, Director of Student Life and Marketing, 850-263-3261 Ext. 415, E-mail: skrichards@baptistcollege.edu.

**GRADUATE UNITS**

**Graduate Programs** Students: 33 full-time (6 women); includes 2 minority (1 Black or African American, non-Hispanic/Latino; 1 Hispanic/Latino). Average age 28. 10 applicants, 100% accepted, 10 enrolled. *Faculty:* 13 full-time (2 women). Expenses: Contact institution. *Financial support:* In 2019–20, 2 students received support. Applicants required to submit FAFSA. In 2019, 3 master's awarded. *Program availability:* Part-time, 100% online, blended/hybrid learning. *Application deadline:* For fall admission, 8/10 for domestic and international students; for spring admission, 1/20 for domestic and international students. Applications are processed on a rolling basis. *Application fee:* $25. Electronic applications accepted. *Application Contact:* Sandra Richards, Director of Student Life and Marketing, 850-263-3261 Ext. 415, Fax: 850-263-9026, E-mail: skrichards@baptistcollege.edu. *Academic Dean,* Dr. Robin Jumper, 850-263-3261 Ext. 425, Fax: 850-263-2141, E-mail: grjumper@baptistcollege.edu.

## BAPTIST MISSIONARY ASSOCIATION THEOLOGICAL SEMINARY, Jacksonville, TX 75766-5407

**General Information** Independent-religious, coed, primarily men, comprehensive institution. *Graduate housing:* Rooms and/or apartments available on a first-come, first-served basis to single and married students. Housing application deadline: 6/1.

**GRADUATE UNITS**

**Graduate and Professional Programs** *Program availability:* Part-time. Electronic applications accepted.

## BARCLAY COLLEGE, Haviland, KS 67059-0288

**General Information** Independent-religious, coed, comprehensive institution.

**GRADUATE UNITS**

**Master of Arts Program** *Program availability:* Online learning. Electronic applications accepted.

## BARD COLLEGE, Annandale-on-Hudson, NY 12504

**General Information** Independent, coed, comprehensive institution. *Graduate housing:* On-campus housing not available.

**GRADUATE UNITS**

**Bard Center for Environmental Policy** *Program availability:* Part-time. Electronic applications accepted.

**Center for Curatorial Studies** Electronic applications accepted.

**Conservatory of Music**

***The Conductors Institute***

**International Center of Photography**

**Levy Economics Institute**

**Longy School of Music of Bard College** *Program availability:* Part-time. Electronic applications accepted.

**Master of Arts in Teaching Program** *Program availability:* Part-time. Electronic applications accepted.

**Milton Avery Graduate School of the Arts** Electronic applications accepted.

## BARD GRADUATE CENTER, New York, NY 10024-3602

**General Information** Independent, coed, primarily women, graduate-only institution. *Graduate housing:* Rooms and/or apartments available on a first-come, first-served basis to single and married students. Housing application deadline: 4/1. *Research affiliation:* Association of Research Institutes in Art History, Metropolitan Museum of Art, Brooklyn Museum, American Museum of Natural History, Museum of Arts and Design, The Frick Collection.

**GRADUATE UNITS**

**Graduate Studies** *Program availability:* Part-time.

## BARRY UNIVERSITY, Miami Shores, FL 33161-6695

**General Information** Independent-religious, coed, university. *Graduate housing:* On-campus housing not available. *Research affiliation:* Baxter Corporation (immunology, diagnostics), Coulter Corporation (immunology, cytology), Cordis Corporation (cardiac product development), Diamedix (immunological diagnostics), Noven Pharmaceutical, Sano Pharmaceuticals.

**GRADUATE UNITS**

**Andreas School of Business** *Program availability:* Part-time, evening/weekend. Electronic applications accepted.

**College of Arts and Sciences** *Program availability:* Part-time, evening/weekend. Electronic applications accepted.

**College of Health Sciences** *Program availability:* Part-time, evening/weekend. Electronic applications accepted.

**Dwayne O. Andreas School of Law**

**Ellen Whiteside McDonnell School of Social Work** *Program availability:* Part-time, evening/weekend. Electronic applications accepted.

**Physician Assistant Program** Electronic applications accepted.

**School of Adult and Continuing Education** *Program availability:* Part-time, evening/weekend. Electronic applications accepted.

***Division of Nursing*** *Program availability:* Part-time, evening/weekend. Electronic applications accepted.

**School of Education** *Program availability:* Part-time, evening/weekend, online learning. Electronic applications accepted.

**School of Human Performance and Leisure Sciences** *Program availability:* Part-time, evening/weekend. Electronic applications accepted.

**School of Podiatric Medicine** Electronic applications accepted.

## BARTON COLLEGE, Wilson, NC 27893-7000

**General Information** Independent-religious, coed, comprehensive institution. *Enrollment:* 1,059 graduate, professional, and undergraduate students; 43 full-time matriculated graduate/professional students (29 women), 53 part-time matriculated graduate/professional students (44 women). *Enrollment by degree level:* 64 master's, 32 other advanced degrees. *Graduate faculty:* 11 full-time (6 women), 2 part-time/adjunct (1 woman). *Graduate housing:* Room and/or apartments available on a first-come, first-served basis to single students; on-campus housing not available to married students. *Student services:* Campus employment opportunities, career counseling, exercise/wellness program, free psychological counseling, services for students with disabilities. *Library facilities:* Willis N. Hackney Library. *Collection:* Books: 129,303 (physical), 503,101 (digital/electronic); Serial titles: 6 (physical), 888,612 (digital/electronic); Databases: 332. Weekly public service hours: 95.

**Computer facilities:** A campuswide network can be accessed. Online class registration is available.
Website: http://www.barton.edu/

**GRADUATE UNITS**

**Program in Business Administration in Strategic Leadership** Students: 24 full-time (13 women); includes 12 minority (9 Black or African American, non-Hispanic/Latino; 2 Hispanic/Latino; 1 Two or more races, non-Hispanic/Latino), 2 international. Average age 36. 2 applicants, 50% accepted, 1 enrolled. *Faculty:* 3 full-time (2 women). Expenses: Contact institution. *Program availability:* Evening/weekend. *Application deadline:* For fall admission, 8/1 for domestic students. Electronic applications accepted. *Application Contact:* Dr. Karen Palasek, Director of MBA Studies, 252-399-6420, E-mail: kpalasek@barton.edu. *Director of MBA Studies*, Dr. Karen Palasek, 252-399-6420, E-mail: kpalasek@barton.edu.

**Program in Criminology and Criminal Justice Sciences** Students: 7 full-time (5 women); includes 2 minority (both Black or African American, non-Hispanic/Latino). Average age 28. *Faculty:* 3 full-time. Expenses: Contact institution. *Program availability:* Part-time, evening/weekend. *Application deadline:* Applications are processed on a rolling basis. Electronic applications accepted. *Application Contact:* Dr. Richard Groskin, Distinguished Professor of Criminology and Criminal Justice Sciences, 252-399-6428, E-mail: rgroskin@barton.edu. *Distinguished Professor of Criminology and Criminal Justice Sciences*, Dr. Richard Groskin, 252-399-6428, E-mail: rgroskin@barton.edu.

**Program in Elementary Education** Electronic applications accepted.

**Program in Nursing** Students: 10 full-time (9 women), 2 part-time (both women); includes 6 minority (all Black or African American, non-Hispanic/Latino). Average age 40. 11 applicants, 73% accepted, 7 enrolled. *Faculty:* 2 full-time (both women), 1 (woman) part-time/adjunct. Expenses: Contact institution. *Program availability:* Part-time, evening/weekend, online only, 100% online. *Application deadline:* Applications are processed on a rolling basis. Electronic applications accepted. *Application Contact:* Dr. Frances Thumberg.

**Program in School Administration** Students: 2 full-time (both women), 19 part-time (14 women); includes 10 minority (all Black or African American, non-Hispanic/Latino). Average age 38. 13 applicants, 85% accepted, 8 enrolled. *Faculty:* 2 full-time (1 woman), 1 part-time/adjunct. Expenses: Contact institution. *Program availability:* Part-time, evening/weekend. *Application deadline:* Applications are processed on a rolling basis. Electronic applications accepted. *Application Contact:* Dr. John F. Boldt, Coordinator of Master of School Administration Program, E-mail: jboldt@barton.edu. *Coordinator of Master of School Administration Program*, Dr. John F. Boldt, E-mail: jboldt@barton.edu.

## BARUCH COLLEGE OF THE CITY UNIVERSITY OF NEW YORK, New York, NY 10010-5585

**General Information** State and locally supported, coed, comprehensive institution. *Graduate housing:* On-campus housing not available.

**GRADUATE UNITS**

**Austin W. Marxe School of Public and International Affairs** *Program availability:* Part-time, evening/weekend. Electronic applications accepted.

**Weissman School of Arts and Sciences** *Program availability:* Part-time, evening/weekend. Electronic applications accepted.

**Zicklin School of Business** *Program availability:* Part-time, evening/weekend. Electronic applications accepted.

## BASTYR UNIVERSITY, Kenmore, WA 98028-4966

**General Information** Independent, coed, upper-level institution. *Graduate housing:* Room and/or apartments available on a first-come, first-served basis to single students; on-campus housing not available to married students. Housing application deadline: 5/1. *Research affiliation:* University of Washington (health), Fred Hutchinson Cancer Research Center (oncology), Seattle Cancer Care Alliance (oncology), Benaroya Research Institute at Virginia Mason (health).

**GRADUATE UNITS**

**School of Natural Health Arts and Sciences** *Program availability:* Part-time.

**School of Naturopathic Medicine** *Program availability:* Part-time. Electronic applications accepted.

**School of Traditional World Medicines** *Program availability:* Evening/weekend. Electronic applications accepted.

## BAYAMÓN CENTRAL UNIVERSITY, Bayamón, PR 00960-1725

**General Information** Independent-religious, coed, comprehensive institution. *Graduate housing:* On-campus housing not available.

**GRADUATE UNITS**

**Graduate Programs** *Program availability:* Part-time, evening/weekend.

## BAY ATLANTIC UNIVERSITY, Washington, DC 20005

**General Information** University.

## BAYLOR COLLEGE OF MEDICINE, Houston, TX 77030-3498

**General Information** Independent, coed, graduate-only institution. CGS member. *Graduate housing:* On-campus housing not available. *Research affiliation:* Veterans Affairs Medical Center (biomedical research), Texas Children's Hospital (pediatric biomedical research), St. Luke's Episcopal Hospital (biomedical research), National Space Biomedical Research Institute (biomedical research), Harris Health System (biomedical research), Children's Nutrition Research Center (pediatric nutrition).

**GRADUATE UNITS**

**Graduate School of Biomedical Sciences** Electronic applications accepted.

**Medical School** Electronic applications accepted.

**School of Health Professions** Electronic applications accepted.

## BAYLOR UNIVERSITY, Waco, TX 76798

**General Information** Independent-religious, coed, university. CGS member. *Enrollment:* 18,033 graduate, professional, and undergraduate students; 3,054 full-time matriculated graduate/professional students (1,721 women), 990 part-time matriculated graduate/professional students (608 women). *Enrollment by degree level:* 2,004 master's, 2,020 doctoral, 20 other advanced degrees. *Graduate faculty:* 789. *Graduate housing:* Rooms and/or apartments available on a first-come, first-served basis to single and married students. *Student services:* Campus employment opportunities, campus safety program, career counseling, exercise/wellness program, free psychological counseling, international student services, low-cost health insurance, multicultural affairs office, services for students with disabilities. *Library facilities:* Moody Memorial Library plus 8 others. *Research affiliation:* Sandia National Laboratories (physics), Zyvex Corporation (physics), OXiGENE, Inc. (pharmaceuticals), Brookhaven National Laboratory (physics), Fermi National Accelerator Laboratory (physics), National Center for Supercomputing Applications (physics).

**Computer facilities:** Computer purchase and lease plans are available. A campuswide network can be accessed. Online class registration is available.
Website: http://www.baylor.edu/

**General Application Contact:** Tosah Hendrickson, Admissions Coordinator, 254-710-3588, Fax: 254-710-3870.

**GRADUATE UNITS**

**Diana R. Garland School of Social Work** *Program availability:* Part-time, blended/hybrid learning. Electronic applications accepted.

**George W. Truett Theological Seminary** *Program availability:* Part-time. Electronic applications accepted.

**Graduate School** Students: 3,096 full-time (1,776 women); includes 1,058 minority (257 Black or African American, non-Hispanic/Latino; 11 American Indian or Alaska Native, non-Hispanic/Latino; 281 Asian, non-Hispanic/Latino; 391 Hispanic/Latino; 1 Native Hawaiian or other Pacific Islander, non-Hispanic/Latino; 117 Two or more races, non-Hispanic/Latino), 247 international. Average age 25. 3,716 applicants, 48% accepted, 1,429 enrolled. Expenses: Contact institution. *Financial support:* Fellowships, research assistantships, teaching assistantships, Federal Work-Study, scholarships/grants, health care benefits, tuition waivers, and unspecified assistantships available. Support available to part-time students. Financial award applicants required to submit FAFSA. In

2019, 159 doctorates awarded. *Program availability:* Part-time, evening/weekend, 100% online, blended/hybrid learning. *Application fee:* $50. Electronic applications accepted. *Application Contact:* Tosha Hendrickson, Admissions and Recruitment Director, 254-710-3588, Fax: 254-710-3870, E-mail: tosha_hendrickson@baylor.edu. *Dean and Vice Provost*, Dr. Larry Lyon, 254-710-3588, Fax: 254-710-3870, E-mail: larry_lyon@baylor.edu.

***College of Arts and Sciences*** *Program availability:* Part-time, evening/weekend. Electronic applications accepted.

***Hankamer School of Business*** Students: 389 full-time (171 women), 261 part-time (98 women); includes 190 minority (42 Black or African American, non-Hispanic/Latino; 42 Asian, non-Hispanic/Latino; 79 Hispanic/Latino; 27 Two or more races, non-Hispanic/Latino), 35 international. 107 applicants, 48% accepted, 41 enrolled. Expenses: Contact institution. *Financial support:* Scholarships/grants and unspecified assistantships available. Financial award application deadline: 4/15. In 2019, 388 master's awarded. *Program availability:* Part-time, evening/weekend, 100% online. *Application deadline:* For fall admission, 7/15 for domestic students, 4/15 for international students; for spring admission, 12/15 for domestic students, 10/15 for international students; for summer admission, 6/15 for domestic students, 2/15 for international students. Applications are processed on a rolling basis. *Application fee:* $50. Electronic applications accepted. *Application Contact:* Laurie Wilson, Director, Graduate Business Programs, 254-710-4163, Fax: 254-710-1066, E-mail: laurie_wilson@baylor.edu. *Associate Dean of Graduate Business Programs*, Dr. Timothy Kayworth, 254-710-4751, Fax: 254-710-1066, E-mail: Timothy_Kayworth@baylor.edu.

***Louise Herrington School of Nursing*** *Program availability:* Part-time, online only, Online with on campus immersions. Electronic applications accepted.

***Robbins College of Health and Human Sciences*** Students: 496 full-time (477 women), 115 part-time (100 women); includes 272 minority (65 Black or African American, non-Hispanic/Latino; 4 American Indian or Alaska Native, non-Hispanic/Latino; 30 Asian, non-Hispanic/Latino; 135 Hispanic/Latino; 38 Two or more races, non-Hispanic/Latino), 19 international. *Faculty:* 83 full-time (51 women). Expenses: Contact institution. *Financial support:* Research assistantships, Federal Work-Study, and unspecified assistantships available. Financial award application deadline: 2/15; financial award applicants required to submit FAFSA. In 2019, 99 master's, 60 doctorates awarded. *Program availability:* Part-time. *Application deadline:* Applications are processed on a rolling basis. *Application fee:* $50. Electronic applications accepted. *Application Contact:* Lori McNamara, Graduate Admissions Coordinator, 254-710-3588, Fax: 254-710-3870, E-mail: lori_mcnamara@baylor.edu. *Associate Dean*, Dr. Denny Kramer, 254-710-4178, Fax: 254-710-3699, E-mail: Denny_Kramer@baylor.edu.

***School of Education*** Students: 165 full-time (107 women), 282 part-time (224 women); includes 179 minority (91 Black or African American, non-Hispanic/Latino; 3 American Indian or Alaska Native, non-Hispanic/Latino; 9 Asian, non-Hispanic/Latino; 59 Hispanic/Latino; 17 Two or more races, non-Hispanic/Latino), 12 international. 461 applicants, 44% accepted, 128 enrolled. *Faculty:* 43 full-time (23 women). Expenses: Contact institution. *Financial support:* In 2019–20, 141 students received support, including 96 research assistantships with full tuition reimbursements available (averaging $22,000 per year); teaching assistantships, scholarships/grants, health care benefits, and unspecified assistantships also available. Financial award application deadline: 2/15; financial award applicants required to submit FAFSA. In 2019, 65 master's, 8 doctorates, 3 other advanced degrees awarded. *Program availability:* Part-time, evening/weekend. *Application deadline:* For fall admission, 2/1 priority date for domestic students; for spring admission, 12/1 for domestic students; for summer admission, 5/1 for domestic students. *Application fee:* $50. *Application Contact:* Terrill Saxon, Associate Dean for Graduate Studies and Research, E-mail: terrill_saxon@baylor.edu. *Dean*, Shanna Hagan-Burke, E-mail: shanna_hagan-burke@baylor.edu.

***School of Engineering and Computer Science*** Students: 108 full-time (22 women), 12 part-time (1 woman); includes 15 minority (1 Black or African American, non-Hispanic/Latino; 1 American Indian or Alaska Native, non-Hispanic/Latino; 5 Asian, non-Hispanic/Latino; 6 Hispanic/Latino; 2 Two or more races, non-Hispanic/Latino), 53 international. Expenses: Contact institution. In 2019, 18 master's, 4 doctorates awarded. *Application Contact:* Dr. Michael W. Thompson, Assoc Dean for Undergrad Programs, 254-710-4129, Fax: 254-710-3010, E-mail: Michael_W_Thompson@baylor.edu. *Dean*, Dr. Dennis L. O'Neal, PhD, 254-710-3895, Fax: 254-710-3839, E-mail: dennis_oneal@baylor.edu.

***School of Music*** Students: 27 full-time (9 women), 44 part-time (21 women); includes 13 minority (2 Black or African American, non-Hispanic/Latino; 9 Hispanic/Latino; 2 Two or more races, non-Hispanic/Latino), 13 international. Average age 26. 88 applicants, 67% accepted, 33 enrolled. *Faculty:* 57 full-time (23 women), 6 part-time/adjunct (4 women). Expenses: Contact institution. *Financial support:* In 2019–20, 66 students received support, including 16 teaching assistantships with full tuition reimbursements available (averaging $7,546 per year); Federal Work-Study, scholarships/grants, and unspecified assistantships also available. Financial award application deadline: 2/15. In 2019, 23 master's, 2 doctorates awarded. *Application deadline:* For fall admission, 2/15 for domestic and international students; for spring admission, 10/15 for domestic and international students. *Application fee:* $80. Electronic applications accepted. *Application Contact:* Melinda G. Coats, Administrative Associate for Graduate and Academic Studies, 254-710-2360, Fax: 254-710-1491, E-mail: melinda_coats@baylor.edu. *Associate Dean for Graduate Studies*, Dr. Timothy McKinney, 254-710-6498, Fax: 254-710-1191, E-mail: Timothy_McKinney@baylor.edu.

**School of Law** Electronic applications accepted.

## BAY PATH UNIVERSITY, Longmeadow, MA 01106-2292

**General Information** Independent, Undergraduate: women only; graduate: coed, comprehensive institution. *Enrollment:* 524 full-time matriculated graduate/professional students (457 women), 978 part-time matriculated graduate/professional students (838 women). *Graduate housing:* Room and/or apartments available on a first-come, first-served basis to single students; on-campus housing not available to married students. *Student services:* Campus employment opportunities, campus safety program, career counseling, exercise/wellness program, free psychological counseling, international student services, low-cost health insurance, multicultural affairs office, services for students with disabilities. *Library facilities:* Hatch Library. *Collection:* Books: 52,565 (physical), 408,000 (digital/electronic); Serial titles: 80 (physical), 55,000 (digital/electronic); Databases: 110. Weekly public service hours: 86; students can reserve study rooms.

**Computer facilities:** 235 computers available on campus for general student use. A campuswide network can be accessed from student residence rooms and from off campus. Online class registration is available.
Website: http://www.baypath.edu/

**General Application Contact:** Sheryl Kosakowski, Executive Director of Graduate Admissions, 413-565-1075, Fax: 413-565-1250, E-mail: skosakowski@baypath.edu.

**GRADUATE UNITS**

**Doctorate Program in Nursing Practice**

**Doctorate Program in Occupational Therapy**

**Program in Accounting** *Program availability:* Part-time, online only, 100% online. Electronic applications accepted.

**Program in Applied Behavior Analysis** *Program availability:* Part-time, blended/hybrid learning. Electronic applications accepted.

**Program in Applied Data Science** *Program availability:* Part-time, 100% online. Electronic applications accepted.

**Program in Applied Laboratory Science and Operations** *Program availability:* Part-time, evening/weekend. Electronic applications accepted.

**Program in Clinical Mental Health Counseling** *Program availability:* Part-time, blended/hybrid learning. Electronic applications accepted.

**Program in Communications** *Program availability:* Part-time, evening/weekend, 100% online, blended/hybrid learning. Electronic applications accepted.

**Program in Communications and Information Management** *Program availability:* Part-time, evening/weekend, 100% online. Electronic applications accepted.

**Program in Creative Nonfiction** *Program availability:* Part-time, evening/weekend, online only, 100% online. Electronic applications accepted.

**Program in Cybersecurity Management** *Program availability:* Part-time, evening/weekend, online only, 100% online. Electronic applications accepted.

**Program in Developmental Psychology** *Program availability:* Part-time, 100% online. Electronic applications accepted.

**Program in Education** *Program availability:* Part-time, 100% online. Electronic applications accepted.

**Program in Entrepreneurial Thinking and Innovative Practices** *Program availability:* Part-time, 100% online. Electronic applications accepted.

**Program in Genetic Counseling** *Program availability:* Evening/weekend, blended/hybrid learning. Electronic applications accepted.

**Program in Healthcare Management** *Program availability:* Part-time, online only, 100% online. Electronic applications accepted.

**Program in Higher Education Administration** *Program availability:* Part-time, online only, 100% online. Electronic applications accepted.

**Program in Higher Education Leadership and Organizational Studies**

**Program in Information Management** *Program availability:* Part-time, 100% online. Electronic applications accepted.

**Program in Leadership and Negotiation** *Program availability:* Part-time, 100% online, blended/hybrid learning. Electronic applications accepted.

**Program in Nonprofit Management and Philanthropy** *Program availability:* Part-time, 100% online. Electronic applications accepted.

**Program in Nursing**

**Program in Occupational Therapy** *Program availability:* Part-time. Electronic applications accepted.

**Program in Physician Assistant Studies** Electronic applications accepted.

**Program in Public Health**

**Program in Strategic Fundraising and Philanthropy** *Program availability:* Part-time, 100% online. Electronic applications accepted.

## BECKER COLLEGE, Worcester, MA 01609

**General Information** Independent, coed, comprehensive institution.

**GRADUATE UNITS**

**Program in Mental Health Counseling** Electronic applications accepted.

## BELHAVEN UNIVERSITY, Jackson, MS 39202-1789

**General Information** Independent-religious, coed, comprehensive institution. *Enrollment:* 4,560 graduate, professional, and undergraduate students; 268 full-time matriculated graduate/professional students (134 women), 1,938 part-time matriculated graduate/professional students (1,473 women). *Enrollment by degree level:* 2,061 master's, 86 doctoral, 57 other advanced degrees. *Graduate faculty:* 11 full-time (7 women), 61 part-time/adjunct (25 women). *Required fees:* $575; $575 per credit. *Graduate housing:* On-campus housing not available. *Student services:* Career counseling, free psychological counseling. *Library facilities:* Warren A. Hood Library plus 1 other. *Collection:* Books: 42,425 (physical), 106,114 (digital/electronic); Serial titles: 160 (physical), 75,718 (digital/electronic); Databases: 96. Weekly public service hours: 104; students can reserve study rooms.

**Computer facilities:** 36 computers available on campus for general student use. A campuswide network can be accessed. Online class registration is available.
Website: http://www.belhaven.edu/

**General Application Contact:** Suzanne Sullivan, Assistant Vice President for Jackson and Online, 601-968-5940, E-mail: ssullivan@belhaven.edu.

**GRADUATE UNITS**

**School of Business** Average age 35. 574 applicants, 75% accepted, 306 enrolled. Expenses: Contact institution. *Financial support:* Applicants required to submit FAFSA. In 2019, 326 master's awarded. *Program availability:* Part-time, evening/weekend, 100% online. *Application deadline:* Applications are processed on a rolling basis. *Application fee:* $25. Electronic applications accepted. *Application Contact:* Dr. Audrey Kelleher, Vice President of Adult and Graduate Marketing and Development, 407-804-1424, Fax: 407-620-5210, E-mail: akelleher@belhaven.edu. *Dean*, Dr. Ralph Mason, 601-968-8949, Fax: 601-968-8951, E-mail: cmason@belhaven.edu.

**School of Education** Students: 11 full-time (7 women), 452 part-time (360 women); includes 262 minority (244 Black or African American, non-Hispanic/Latino; 1 American Indian or Alaska Native, non-Hispanic/Latino; 3 Asian, non-Hispanic/Latino; 3 Hispanic/Latino; 11 Two or more races, non-Hispanic/Latino), 1 international. Average age 36. 299 applicants, 49% accepted, 103 enrolled. *Faculty:* 8 full-time (6 women), 24 part-time/adjunct (20 women). Expenses: Contact institution. *Financial support:* Applicants required to submit FAFSA. In 2019, 65 master's, 5 other advanced degrees awarded. *Program availability:* Part-time, evening/weekend, 100% online, blended/hybrid learning. *Application deadline:* Applications are processed on a rolling basis. *Application fee:* $25. Electronic applications accepted. *Application Contact:* Sean Kirnan, Assistant Vice President for Adult and Graduate Enrollment and Student

Services, 601-968-8727, Fax: 601-968-5953, E-mail: gradadmission@belhaven.edu. *Dean*, Dr. David Hand, 601-965-7020, E-mail: dhand@belhaven.edu.

## BELLARMINE UNIVERSITY, Louisville, KY 40205

**General Information** Independent-religious, coed, comprehensive institution. *Enrollment:* 3,331 graduate, professional, and undergraduate students; 476 full-time matriculated graduate/professional students (286 women), 409 part-time matriculated graduate/professional students (294 women). *Enrollment by degree level:* 369 master's, 347 doctoral, 169 other advanced degrees. *Graduate faculty:* 98 full-time (62 women), 60 part-time/adjunct (39 women). Tuition and fees vary according to degree level and program. *Graduate housing:* Rooms and/or apartments available on a first-come, first-served basis to single and married students. Typical cost: $4410 per year ($9030 including board) for single students. Housing application deadline: 5/1. *Student services:* Campus employment opportunities, campus safety program, career counseling, exercise/wellness program, free psychological counseling, international student services, multicultural affairs office, services for students with disabilities, teacher training, writing training. *Library facilities:* W. L. Lyons Brown Library. *Collection:* Books: 104,478 (physical), 311,091 (digital/electronic); Serial titles: 176 (physical), 73,917 (digital/electronic); Databases: 126. Weekly public service hours: 140; study areas open 24 hours, 5–7 days a week.

**Computer facilities:** 440 computers available on campus for general student use. A campuswide network can be accessed. Online class registration, mobile app are available.
Website: http://www.bellarmine.edu/

**General Application Contact:** Dr. Sara Pettingill, Dean of Graduate Admission, 502-272-8401, Fax: 502-272-8002, E-mail: spettingill@bellarmine.edu.

**GRADUATE UNITS**

**Annsley Frazier Thornton School of Education** Students: 25 full-time (15 women), 183 part-time (132 women); includes 69 minority (49 Black or African American, non-Hispanic/Latino; 7 Asian, non-Hispanic/Latino; 6 Hispanic/Latino; 7 Two or more races, non-Hispanic/Latino), 1 international. Average age 35. 166 applicants, 54% accepted, 79 enrolled. *Faculty:* 23 full-time (15 women), 12 part-time/adjunct (11 women). Expenses: Contact institution. *Financial support:* Scholarships/grants available. Financial award applicants required to submit FAFSA. In 2019, 74 master's, 12 doctorates, 10 other advanced degrees awarded. *Program availability:* Part-time, evening/weekend. *Application deadline:* For fall admission, 8/1 priority date for domestic and international students; for spring admission, 12/1 priority date for domestic and international students; for summer admission, 4/10 priority date for domestic and international students. Applications are processed on a rolling basis. *Application fee:* $40. Electronic applications accepted. *Application Contact:* Sarah Schuble, Assistant Director of Graduate Student Enrollment, 502-272-8271, Fax: 502-272-8002, E-mail: sschuble@bellarmine.edu. *Dean*, Dr. Elizabeth Dinkins, 502-272-7958, Fax: 502-272-8189, E-mail: edinkins@bellarmine.edu.

**College of Health Professions** Students: 29 part-time (23 women); includes 5 minority (3 Black or African American, non-Hispanic/Latino; 2 Asian, non-Hispanic/Latino). Average age 35. 16 applicants, 69% accepted, 9 enrolled. *Faculty:* 10 full-time (7 women). Expenses: Contact institution. *Financial support:* Career-related internships or fieldwork and scholarships/grants available. Support available to part-time students. Financial award applicants required to submit FAFSA. In 2019, 6 master's awarded. *Program availability:* Part-time, evening/weekend, 100% online, blended/hybrid learning. *Application deadline:* Applications are processed on a rolling basis. *Application fee:* $40. Electronic applications accepted. *Application Contact:* Dr. Sara Pettingill, Dean of Graduate Admission, 502-272-8401, Fax: 502-272-8002, E-mail: spettingill@bellarmine.edu. *Vice Provost*, Dr. Mark Wiegand, E-mail: mwiegand@bellarmine.edu.

***Donna and Allan Lansing School of Nursing and Clinical Sciences*** Students: 142 full-time (104 women), 128 part-time (105 women); includes 55 minority (24 Black or African American, non-Hispanic/Latino; 1 American Indian or Alaska Native, non-Hispanic/Latino; 15 Asian, non-Hispanic/Latino; 10 Hispanic/Latino; 5 Two or more races, non-Hispanic/Latino), 10 international. Average age 30. 348 applicants, 82% accepted, 172 enrolled. *Faculty:* 19 full-time (15 women), 7 part-time/adjunct (all women). Expenses: Contact institution. *Financial support:* Career-related internships or fieldwork and scholarships/grants available. Financial award applicants required to submit FAFSA. In 2019, 29 master's, 4 doctorates awarded. *Program availability:* Part-time, evening/weekend. *Application deadline:* Applications are processed on a rolling basis. *Application fee:* $40. Electronic applications accepted. *Application Contact:* Julie Armstrong-Binnix, Health Science Recruiter, 800-274-4723 Ext. 8364, E-mail: julieab@bellarmine.edu. *Dean*, Dr. Nancy York, 502-272-8639, E-mail: nyork@bellarmine.edu.

***School of Movement and Rehabilitation Sciences*** Students: 220 full-time (134 women), 1 (woman) part-time; includes 29 minority (8 Black or African American, non-Hispanic/Latino; 6 Asian, non-Hispanic/Latino; 6 Hispanic/Latino; 9 Two or more races, non-Hispanic/Latino), 1 international. Average age 24. 522 applicants, 29% accepted, 75 enrolled. *Faculty:* 28 full-time (20 women), 30 part-time/adjunct (21 women). Expenses: Contact institution. *Financial support:* Applicants required to submit FAFSA. In 2019, 4 master's, 67 doctorates awarded. *Program availability:* Part-time. *Application deadline:* Applications are processed on a rolling basis. *Application fee:* $40. Electronic applications accepted. *Application Contact:* Dr. Sara Pettingill, Dean of Graduate Admission, 502-272-8401, Fax: 502-272-8002, E-mail: spettingill@bellarmine.edu. *Dean*, Dr. Tony Brosky, 502-272-8375, E-mail: jbrosky@bellarmine.edu.

**School of Communication** Students: 10 full-time (5 women), 14 part-time (11 women); includes 4 minority (3 Black or African American, non-Hispanic/Latino; 1 Two or more races, non-Hispanic/Latino), 5 international. Average age 23. 36 applicants, 53% accepted, 14 enrolled. *Faculty:* 5 full-time (2 women). Expenses: Contact institution. *Financial support:* Scholarships/grants available. Financial award applicants required to submit FAFSA. In 2019, 32 master's awarded. *Program availability:* Part-time, evening/weekend. *Application deadline:* Applications are processed on a rolling basis. *Application fee:* $40. Electronic applications accepted. *Application Contact:* Dr. Sara Pettingill, Dean of Graduate Admission, 502-272-8401, Fax: 502-272-8002, E-mail: spettingill@bellarmine.edu. *Dean*, Dr. Mary O. Huff, 502-272-8359, E-mail: mhuff@bellarmine.edu.

**W. Fielding Rubel School of Business** Students: 80 full-time (29 women), 54 part-time (22 women); includes 23 minority (10 Black or African American, non-Hispanic/Latino; 3 Asian, non-Hispanic/Latino; 6 Hispanic/Latino; 1 Native Hawaiian or other Pacific Islander, non-Hispanic/Latino; 3 Two or more races, non-Hispanic/Latino), 4 international. Average age 29. 70 applicants, 83% accepted, 43 enrolled. *Faculty:* 13 full-time (4 women), 3 part-time/adjunct (0 women). Expenses: Contact institution. *Financial support:* Career-related internships or fieldwork, scholarships/grants, and unspecified assistantships available. Support available to part-time students. Financial award applicants required to submit FAFSA. In 2019, 73 master's awarded. *Program availability:* Part-time, evening/weekend. *Application deadline:* Applications are processed on a rolling basis. *Application fee:* $40. Electronic applications accepted. *Application Contact:* Dr. Sara Pettingill, Dean of Graduate Admission, 800-274-4723 Ext. 8258, Fax: 502-272-8002, E-mail: spettingill@bellarmine.edu. *Dean*, Dr. Natasha Munshi, 502-272-7443, E-mail: nmunshi@bellarmine.edu.

## BELLEVUE UNIVERSITY, Bellevue, NE 68005-3098

**General Information** Independent, coed, comprehensive institution. *Graduate housing:* Room and/or apartments available on a first-come, first-served basis to single students; on-campus housing not available to married students.

**GRADUATE UNITS**

**Graduate School** *Program availability:* Part-time, evening/weekend, online learning.

***College of Arts and Sciences*** *Program availability:* Online learning.

***College of Business***

***College of Information Technology***

***College of Professional Studies***

## BELLIN COLLEGE, Green Bay, WI 54305

**General Information** Independent, coed, primarily women, comprehensive institution. *Enrollment:* 13 full-time matriculated graduate/professional students (12 women), 29 part-time matriculated graduate/professional students (27 women). *Enrollment by degree level:* 42 master's. *Graduate faculty:* 10 part-time/adjunct (all women). *Graduate housing:* On-campus housing not available. *Library facilities:* Phil and Betsy Hendrickson Library. *Collection:* Weekly public service hours: 63; students can reserve study rooms.

**Computer facilities:** 41 computers available on campus for general student use. A campuswide network can be accessed from off campus.
Website: http://www.bellincollege.edu/

**General Application Contact:** Ann Wasmund, Administrative Assistant, 920-433-6628, Fax: 920-433-1921, E-mail: ann.wasmund@bellincollege.edu.

**GRADUATE UNITS**

**School of Nursing**

## BELMONT UNIVERSITY, Nashville, TN 37212

**General Information** Independent-religious, coed, university. *Enrollment:* 8,428 graduate, professional, and undergraduate students; 1,535 full-time matriculated graduate/professional students (1,037 women), 85 part-time matriculated graduate/professional students (51 women). *Enrollment by degree level:* 637 master's, 982 doctoral. *Graduate faculty:* 163 full-time (79 women), 89 part-time/adjunct (41 women). *Graduate housing:* On-campus housing not available. *Student services:* Campus employment opportunities, campus safety program, career counseling, exercise/wellness program, free psychological counseling, international student services, low-cost health insurance, multicultural affairs office, services for students with disabilities. *Library facilities:* Lila D. Bunch Library plus 1 other. *Collection:* Books: 208,565 (physical), 242,722 (digital/electronic); Serial titles: 1,107 (physical), 83,897 (digital/electronic); Databases: 344. Weekly public service hours: 127; students can reserve study rooms.

**Computer facilities:** Computer purchase and lease plans are available. 500 computers available on campus for general student use. A campuswide network can be accessed. Online class registration, individual student information via course management system are available.
Website: http://www.belmont.edu/

**General Application Contact:** Dr. Chris Gage, Associate Provost and Dean of Enrollment Services, 615-460-6785, Fax: 615-460-5434, E-mail: Chris.Gage@belmont.edu.

**GRADUATE UNITS**

**College of Health Sciences** Students: 416 full-time (362 women), 8 part-time (7 women); includes 36 minority (7 Black or African American, non-Hispanic/Latino; 12 Asian, non-Hispanic/Latino; 9 Hispanic/Latino; 8 Two or more races, non-Hispanic/Latino). Average age 26. *Faculty:* 26 full-time (20 women), 30 part-time/adjunct (21 women). Expenses: Contact institution. *Financial support:* Teaching assistantships with full tuition reimbursements, career-related internships or fieldwork, scholarships/grants, and traineeships available. Financial award application deadline: 3/1; financial award applicants required to submit FAFSA. *Program availability:* Part-time, blended/hybrid learning. *Application deadline:* Applications are processed on a rolling basis. *Application fee:* $50. Electronic applications accepted. *Application Contact:* Bill Nichols, Director of Enrollment Services, 615-460-6107, E-mail: bill.nichols@belmont.edu. *Dean*, Dr. Cathy Taylor, 615-460-6916, Fax: 615-460-6750.

**College of Law** Students: 336 full-time (202 women), 1 part-time (0 women); includes 36 minority (14 Black or African American, non-Hispanic/Latino; 1 American Indian or Alaska Native, non-Hispanic/Latino; 5 Asian, non-Hispanic/Latino; 15 Hispanic/Latino; 1 Two or more races, non-Hispanic/Latino), 1 international. Average age 26. *Faculty:* 17 full-time (7 women), 16 part-time/adjunct (5 women). Expenses: Contact institution. *Financial support:* In 2019–20, 180 students received support. Career-related internships or fieldwork and scholarships/grants available. Financial award application deadline: 12/1; financial award applicants required to submit FAFSA. In 2019, 82 doctorates awarded. *Application deadline:* For fall admission, 7/15 priority date for domestic and international students. Applications are processed on a rolling basis. *Application fee:* $50. Electronic applications accepted. *Application Contact:* Drew Ford, Recruiting Coordinator, 615-460-8250, Fax: 615-460-8250, E-mail: drew.ford@belmont.edu. *Dean*, Judge Alberto R. Gonzales, 615-460-8259, E-mail: alberto.gonzales@belmont.edu.

**College of Pharmacy** Students: 354 full-time (242 women); includes 120 minority (50 Black or African American, non-Hispanic/Latino; 1 American Indian or Alaska Native, non-Hispanic/Latino; 41 Asian, non-Hispanic/Latino; 18 Hispanic/Latino; 10 Two or more races, non-Hispanic/Latino), 3 international. Average age 25. *Faculty:* 29 full-time (16 women), 4 part-time/adjunct (2 women). Expenses: Contact institution. *Financial support:* In 2019–20, 112 students received support. Career-related internships or fieldwork and scholarships/grants available. Financial award application deadline: 12/1; financial award applicants required to submit FAFSA. In 2019, 67 doctorates awarded. *Application deadline:* For fall admission, 8/31 priority date for domestic students; for spring admission, 3/1 for domestic students. Applications are processed on a rolling basis. *Application fee:* $50. Electronic applications accepted. *Application Contact:* Dr. David Gregory, Dean, 615-460-6746, Fax: 615-460-6741, E-mail: david.gregory@belmont.edu. *Dean*, Dr. David Gregory, 615-460-6746, Fax: 615-460-6741, E-mail: david.gregory@belmont.edu.

**Jack C. Massey Graduate School of Business** Students: 175 full-time (77 women), 30 part-time (16 women); includes 24 minority (8 Black or African American, non-Hispanic/Latino; 7 Asian, non-Hispanic/Latino; 7 Hispanic/Latino; 2 Two or more races, non-Hispanic/Latino), 6 international. Average age 30. *Faculty:* 29 full-time (9 women), 7 part-time/adjunct (3 women). Expenses: Contact institution. *Financial support:* In 2019–20, 86 students received support. Scholarships/grants, tuition waivers (partial), and unspecified assistantships available. Financial award application deadline: 7/1; financial award applicants required to submit FAFSA. In 2019, 110 master's awarded. *Program availability:* Part-time, evening/weekend. *Application deadline:* For fall admission, 7/1 for domestic and international students; for spring admission, 11/1 for domestic and international students. Applications are processed on a rolling basis. *Application fee:* $50. Electronic applications accepted. *Application Contact:* Dr. Sarah Gardial, Dean, 615-460-6480, Fax: 615-460-6455, E-mail: Sarah.Gardial@belmont.edu. *Dean,* Dr. Sarah Gardial, 615-460-6480, Fax: 615-460-6455, E-mail: Sarah.Gardial@belmont.edu.

**Program in Audio Engineering Technology**

**Program in Education**

**Program in Music**

## BEMIDJI STATE UNIVERSITY, Bemidji, MN 56601-2699

**General Information** State-supported, coed, comprehensive institution. CGS member. *Graduate housing:* Room and/or apartments available on a first-come, first-served basis to single students; on-campus housing not available to married students. Housing application deadline: 8/1. *Research affiliation:* National Interscholastic Athletic Administrators Association, Sanford Research, Mossy Oak, Bass Pro Shops.

**GRADUATE UNITS**

**School of Graduate Studies** *Program availability:* Part-time, online learning. Electronic applications accepted.

## BENEDICTINE COLLEGE, Atchison, KS 66002-1499

**General Information** Independent-religious, coed, comprehensive institution. *Graduate housing:* Room and/or apartments available on a first-come, first-served basis to single students; on-campus housing not available to married students.

**GRADUATE UNITS**

**Master of Arts in Education Program** *Program availability:* Part-time, evening/weekend. Electronic applications accepted.

**Master of Arts in School Leadership Program** *Program availability:* Part-time, evening/weekend. Electronic applications accepted.

**Master of Business Administration Program** *Program availability:* Part-time, evening/weekend. Electronic applications accepted.

## BENEDICTINE UNIVERSITY, Lisle, IL 60532

**General Information** Independent-religious, coed, comprehensive institution. *Graduate housing:* On-campus housing not available.

**GRADUATE UNITS**

**Graduate Programs** *Program availability:* Part-time, evening/weekend, online learning. Electronic applications accepted.

## BENNINGTON COLLEGE, Bennington, VT 05201

**General Information** Independent, coed, comprehensive institution. *Enrollment:* 830 graduate, professional, and undergraduate students; 118 full-time matriculated graduate/professional students (92 women), 13 part-time matriculated graduate/professional students (12 women). *Enrollment by degree level:* 118 master's, 13 other advanced degrees. *Graduate faculty:* 35 full-time (16 women), 19 part-time/adjunct (10 women). *Graduate housing:* Room and/or apartments available on a first-come, first-served basis to single students; on-campus housing not available to married students. *Student services:* Campus employment opportunities, campus safety program, career counseling, exercise/wellness program, free psychological counseling, grant writing training, international student services, low-cost health insurance, services for students with disabilities, teacher training, writing training. *Library facilities:* Crossett Library plus 1 other. *Collection:* Books: 94,505 (physical), 194,000 (digital/electronic); Serial titles: 299 (physical), 28,186 (digital/electronic); Databases: 50. Weekly public service hours: 126; students can reserve study rooms.

**Computer facilities:** 130 computers available on campus for general student use. A campuswide network can be accessed. Online class registration is available.
Website: http://www.bennington.edu/

**General Application Contact:** Carter Strong, Senior Assistant Director of Admissions, 802-440-4312, Fax: 802-440-4320, E-mail: admissions@bennington.edu.

**GRADUATE UNITS**

**Graduate Programs** *Program availability:* Part-time, online learning.

## BENTLEY UNIVERSITY, Waltham, MA 02452-4705

**General Information** Independent, coed, comprehensive institution. *Enrollment:* 5,314 graduate, professional, and undergraduate students; 557 full-time matriculated graduate/professional students (316 women), 520 part-time matriculated graduate/professional students (264 women). *Enrollment by degree level:* 1,046 master's, 25 doctoral, 6 other advanced degrees. *Graduate faculty:* 105 full-time (40 women), 17 part-time/adjunct (5 women). *Graduate housing:* On-campus housing not available. *Student services:* Campus employment opportunities, campus safety program, career counseling, exercise/wellness program, free psychological counseling, international student services, low-cost health insurance, multicultural affairs office, services for students with disabilities. *Library facilities:* Bentley Library. *Collection:* Books: 153,308 (physical), 238,717 (digital/electronic); Serial titles: 2,442 (physical), 115,861 (digital/electronic); Databases: 108. Weekly public service hours: 110; students can reserve study rooms.

**Computer facilities:** Computer purchase and lease plans are available. 3,730 computers available on campus for general student use. A campuswide network can be accessed. Online class registration, grade checking; online admission; blackboard; resume review; student employment; interlibary loan; free software are available.
Website: http://www.bentley.edu/

**General Application Contact:** Office of Graduate Admissions, 781-891-2108, E-mail: applygrad@bentley.edu.

**GRADUATE UNITS**

**Graduate Certificate Programs** *Faculty:* 105 full-time (40 women), 17 part-time/adjunct (5 women). Expenses: Contact institution. *Program availability:* Part-time, evening/weekend, 100% online, blended/hybrid learning. *Application deadline:* For fall admission, 8/25 for domestic and international students; for spring admission, 1/5 for domestic and international students. Applications are processed on a rolling basis. *Application Contact:* Office of Graduate Admissions, 781-891-2108, E-mail: applygrad@bentley.edu.

**McCallum Graduate School of Business** Students: 557 full-time (316 women), 520 part-time (264 women); includes 180 minority (45 Black or African American, non-Hispanic/Latino; 2 American Indian or Alaska Native, non-Hispanic/Latino; 79 Asian, non-Hispanic/Latino; 41 Hispanic/Latino; 13 Two or more races, non-Hispanic/Latino), 380 international. Average age 28. 1,652 applicants, 62% accepted, 415 enrolled. *Faculty:* 105 full-time (40 women), 17 part-time/adjunct (5 women). Expenses: Contact institution. *Financial support:* In 2019–20, 435 students received support. Scholarships/grants, tuition waivers (partial), and unspecified assistantships available. Financial award application deadline: 6/1; financial award applicants required to submit FAFSA. In 2019, 564 master's, 6 doctorates, 60 other advanced degrees awarded. *Program availability:* Part-time, evening/weekend, 100% online, blended/hybrid learning. *Application deadline:* For fall admission, 8/1 for domestic students, 7/1 for international students; for spring admission, 12/15 for domestic students, 11/1 for international students. Applications are processed on a rolling basis. *Application fee:* $150. Electronic applications accepted. *Application Contact:* Office of Graduate Admissions, 781-891-2108, E-mail: applygrad@bentley.edu. *Dean of Business and Professor,* William Read, 781-891-2525, E-mail: wread@bentley.edu.

## BERGIN UNIVERSITY OF CANINE STUDIES, Rohnert Park, CA 94928

**General Information** Independent, coed, comprehensive institution. *Graduate housing:* On-campus housing not available.

**GRADUATE UNITS**

**Program in Canine Life Sciences** *Program availability:* Online learning.

## BERKELEY COLLEGE–WOODLAND PARK CAMPUS, Woodland Park, NJ 07424

**General Information** Proprietary, coed, comprehensive institution.

**GRADUATE UNITS**

**MBA Program**

## BERKLEE COLLEGE OF MUSIC, Boston, MA 02215-3693

**General Information** Independent, coed, comprehensive institution. *Enrollment:* 6,999 graduate, professional, and undergraduate students; 444 full-time matriculated graduate/professional students (228 women), 3 part-time matriculated graduate/professional students (1 woman). *Enrollment by degree level:* 363 master's, 84 other advanced degrees. *Graduate faculty:* 38 full-time (17 women), 72 part-time/adjunct (26 women). *Tuition:* Full-time $50,742. *Required fees:* $1340; $1340 per unit. Tuition and fees vary according to campus/location and program. *Graduate housing:* On-campus housing not available. *Student services:* Campus employment opportunities, campus safety program, career counseling, exercise/wellness program, free psychological counseling, grant writing training, international student services, low-cost health insurance, multicultural affairs office, services for students with disabilities, teacher training, writing training. *Library facilities:* The Stan Getz Media Center and Library.

**Computer facilities:** Computer purchase and lease plans are available. A campuswide network can be accessed from student residence rooms. Online class registration is available.
Website: http://www.berklee.edu/

**GRADUATE UNITS**

**Berklee Graduate Programs** Students: 212 full-time (94 women), 1 part-time (0 women); includes 40 minority (11 Black or African American, non-Hispanic/Latino; 7 Asian, non-Hispanic/Latino; 17 Hispanic/Latino; 5 Two or more races, non-Hispanic/Latino), 123 international. Average age 27. 683 applicants, 39% accepted, 167 enrolled. *Faculty:* 18 full-time (6 women), 46 part-time/adjunct (11 women). Expenses: Contact institution. *Financial support:* Fellowships with full and partial tuition reimbursements, research assistantships, career-related internships or fieldwork, scholarships/grants, and tuition waivers (full and partial) available. Support available to part-time students. Financial award application deadline: 1/15; financial award applicants required to submit CSS PROFILE or FAFSA. In 2019, 141 master's awarded. *Program availability:* Part-time. *Application deadline:* For fall admission, 1/15 for domestic and international students. *Application fee:* 150 euros for international students. Electronic applications accepted. *Application Contact:* Office of Admissions, 617-747-2221, E-mail: admissions@berklee.edu. *Associate Vice President for Academic Affairs,* Rob Lagueux, PhD, 617-747-6908, E-mail: rlagueux@berklee.edu.

**The Boston Conservatory at Berklee** Students: 232 full-time (134 women), 2 part-time (1 woman); includes 45 minority (10 Black or African American, non-Hispanic/Latino; 2 American Indian or Alaska Native, non-Hispanic/Latino; 8 Asian, non-Hispanic/Latino; 10 Hispanic/Latino; 15 Two or more races, non-Hispanic/Latino), 92 international. Average age 26. 769 applicants, 38% accepted, 110 enrolled. *Faculty:* 20 full-time (11 women), 26 part-time/adjunct (15 women). Expenses: Contact institution. *Financial support:* Research assistantships, teaching assistantships, and scholarships/grants available. Financial award application deadline: 12/1; financial award applicants required to submit FAFSA. In 2019, 117 master's, 14 other advanced degrees awarded. *Program availability:* Part-time. *Application deadline:* For fall admission, 12/1 for domestic and international students. *Application fee:* $150. Electronic applications accepted. *Application Contact:* Director of Admissions, 617-912-9153, Fax: 617-912-9217, E-mail: admissions@bostonconservatory.edu. *Associate Vice President, Academic Affairs,* Robert Lagueux, PhD, 617-747-6908, E-mail: rlagueux@berklee.edu.

## BERRY COLLEGE, Mount Berry, GA 30149

**General Information** Independent-religious, coed, comprehensive institution. *Enrollment:* 2,034 graduate, professional, and undergraduate students; 37 full-time matriculated graduate/professional students (20 women), 54 part-time matriculated graduate/professional students (28 women). *Enrollment by degree level:* 8 master's, 6 other advanced degrees. *Graduate faculty:* 5 full-time (0 women), 9 part-time/adjunct (6 women). *Tuition:* Part-time $670 per credit hour. Tuition and fees vary according to program. *Graduate housing:* On-campus housing not available. *Student services:* Campus employment opportunities, campus safety program, career counseling, child daycare facilities, exercise/wellness program, free psychological counseling, international student services, low-cost health insurance, multicultural affairs office, services for students with disabilities, teacher training, writing training. *Library facilities:* Memorial Library plus 1 other. *Collection:* Books: 229,531 (physical), 1.1 million (digital/electronic); Serial titles: 6,932 (physical), 86,384 (digital/electronic); Databases: 223. Weekly public service hours: 100; students can reserve study rooms. *Research affiliation:* Georgia Professional Standards Commission (education), Koch Foundation (business and economics), South Rome Early Learning Center (education), Marcus

Autism Center (psychology and education), South Rome Development Corporation (education), Rome-Floyd County Commission on Children and Youth (education and psychology).

**Computer facilities:** 200 computers available on campus for general student use. A campuswide network can be accessed. Online class registration is available. Website: http://www.berry.edu/

**General Application Contact:** Glenn Getchell, Director of Admissions and Enrollment Engagement, 706-236-2215, Fax: 706-290-2178, E-mail: admissions@berry.edu.

**GRADUATE UNITS**

**Graduate Programs** Students: 37 full-time (20 women), 54 part-time (28 women); includes 11 minority (5 Black or African American, non-Hispanic/Latino; 2 Hispanic/Latino; 4 Two or more races, non-Hispanic/Latino), 1 international. Average age 36. *Faculty:* 5 full-time (0 women), 9 part-time/adjunct (6 women). Expenses: Contact institution. *Financial support:* In 2019–20, 24 students received support, including 9 research assistantships with full tuition reimbursements available (averaging $9,827 per year); scholarships/grants, tuition waivers (partial), and unspecified assistantships also available. Support available to part-time students. Financial award application deadline: 3/1; financial award applicants required to submit FAFSA. In 2019, 20 master's, 48 other advanced degrees awarded. *Program availability:* Part-time, evening/weekend. *Application deadline:* For fall admission, 7/24 for domestic students, 5/1 for international students; for spring admission, 12/1 for domestic students, 2/1 for international students. Applications are processed on a rolling basis. *Application fee:* $25 ($30 for international students). Electronic applications accepted. *Application Contact:* Admissions, 706-236-2215, Fax: 706-290-2178, E-mail: admissions@berry.edu. *Provost*, Dr. Mary K Boyd, 706-236-2216, Fax: 706-290-2179, E-mail: provostoffice@berry.edu.

***Campbell School of Business*** Students: 5 full-time (1 woman), 33 part-time (12 women); includes 3 minority (2 Black or African American, non-Hispanic/Latino; 1 Two or more races, non-Hispanic/Latino), 1 international. Average age 32. *Faculty:* 3 full-time (0 women), 2 part-time/adjunct (1 woman). Expenses: Contact institution. *Financial support:* In 2019–20, 21 students received support, including 9 research assistantships with full tuition reimbursements available (averaging $9,827 per year); scholarships/grants, tuition waivers (partial), and unspecified assistantships also available. Support available to part-time students. Financial award application deadline: 3/1; financial award applicants required to submit FAFSA. In 2019, 16 master's awarded. *Program availability:* Part-time, evening/weekend. *Application deadline:* For fall admission, 7/24 for domestic students; for spring admission, 12/1 for domestic students. Applications are processed on a rolling basis. *Application fee:* $25 ($30 for international students). Electronic applications accepted. *Application Contact:* Admissions, 706-236-2215, Fax: 706-290-2178, E-mail: admissions@berry.edu. *Dean*, Dr. Joyce Heames, 706-236-2233, Fax: 706-802-6728, E-mail: jheames@berry.edu.

## BETHANY COLLEGE, Bethany, WV 26032

**General Information** Independent-religious, coed, comprehensive institution. *Graduate housing:* Room and/or apartments available on a first-come, first-served basis to single students; on-campus housing not available to married students.

**GRADUATE UNITS**

**Master of Arts in Teaching Program** *Program availability:* Part-time. Electronic applications accepted.

## BETHANY GLOBAL UNIVERSITY, Bloomington, MN 55438

**General Information** Independent-religious, coed, comprehensive institution. *Graduate housing:* On-campus housing not available.

**GRADUATE UNITS**

**Bethany Global University Graduate Studies** Students: 2 full-time (0 women), 27 part-time (10 women); includes 4 minority (all Black or African American, non-Hispanic/Latino), 8 international. Average age 38. 7 applicants, 100% accepted, 6 enrolled. *Faculty:* 1 (woman) full-time, 7 part-time/adjunct (1 woman). Expenses: Contact institution. *Program availability:* Part-time, evening/weekend, online only, 100% online. *Application deadline:* Applications are processed on a rolling basis. *Application fee:* $40. Electronic applications accepted. *Application Contact:* Malaina Ortiz, Associate Director of Recruitment, 952-222-0092, E-mail: malaina.ortiz@bethanygu.edu. *Dean of Graduate Studies*, Elisabeth Wilson, E-mail: elisabeth.wilson@bethanygu.edu.

## BETHANY THEOLOGICAL SEMINARY, Richmond, IN 47374-4019

**General Information** Independent-religious, coed, graduate-only institution. *Graduate housing:* On-campus housing not available.

**GRADUATE UNITS**

**Graduate and Professional Programs** *Program availability:* Part-time, online learning.

## BETHEL SEMINARY, St. Paul, MN 55112-6998

**General Information** Independent-religious, coed, graduate-only institution. *Graduate housing:* On-campus housing not available.

**GRADUATE UNITS**

**Graduate and Professional Programs** *Program availability:* Part-time, evening/weekend, 100% online, blended/hybrid learning. Electronic applications accepted.

## BETHEL UNIVERSITY, Mishawaka, IN 46545-5591

**General Information** Independent-religious, coed, comprehensive institution. *Graduate housing:* On-campus housing not available.

**GRADUATE UNITS**

**Adult and Graduate Programs** *Program availability:* Part-time, evening/weekend, 100% online, blended/hybrid learning. Electronic applications accepted.

## BETHEL UNIVERSITY, St. Paul, MN 55112-6999

**General Information** Independent-religious, coed, comprehensive institution. *Graduate housing:* On-campus housing not available.

**GRADUATE UNITS**

**Graduate School** Students: 428 full-time (318 women), 825 part-time (482 women); includes 245 minority (95 Black or African American, non-Hispanic/Latino; 13 American Indian or Alaska Native, non-Hispanic/Latino; 52 Asian, non-Hispanic/Latino; 50 Hispanic/Latino; 2 Native Hawaiian or other Pacific Islander, non-Hispanic/Latino; 33 Two or more races, non-Hispanic/Latino), 28 international. Average age 38. 810 applicants, 45% accepted, 256 enrolled. *Faculty:* 36 full-time (24 women), 112 part-time/adjunct (73 women). Expenses: Contact institution. *Financial support:* Teaching assistantships, career-related internships or fieldwork, and scholarships/grants available. Support available to part-time students. Financial award applicants required to submit FAFSA. In 2019, 320 master's, 34 doctorates, 112 other advanced degrees awarded. *Program availability:* Part-time, evening/weekend, 100% online, blended/hybrid learning. *Application deadline:* Applications are processed on a rolling basis. Electronic applications accepted. *Application Contact:* Director of Admissions, 651-635-8000, Fax: 651-635-8004, E-mail: gs@bethel.edu. *Associate Provost*, Dr. Randy Bergen, 651-635-8000, Fax: 651-635-8004, E-mail: r-bergen@bethel.edu.

## BETHEL UNIVERSITY, McKenzie, TN 38201

**General Information** Independent-religious, coed, comprehensive institution. *Graduate housing:* Room and/or apartments available on a first-come, first-served basis to single students; on-campus housing not available to married students. Housing application deadline: 7/31.

**GRADUATE UNITS**

**Graduate Programs** *Program availability:* Part-time, evening/weekend.

## BETHESDA UNIVERSITY, Anaheim, CA 92801

**General Information** Independent-religious, coed, comprehensive institution.

**GRADUATE UNITS**

**Graduate and Professional Programs**

## BETH HAMEDRASH SHAAREI YOSHER INSTITUTE, Brooklyn, NY 11204

**General Information** Independent-religious, men only, comprehensive institution.

**GRADUATE UNITS**

**Graduate Programs**

## BETH HATALMUD RABBINICAL COLLEGE, Brooklyn, NY 11214

**General Information** Independent-religious, men only, comprehensive institution.

**GRADUATE UNITS**

**Graduate Programs**

## BETHLEHEM COLLEGE & SEMINARY, Minneapolis, MN 55415

**General Information** Independent-religious, coed, comprehensive institution. *Graduate housing:* On-campus housing not available.

**GRADUATE UNITS**

**Graduate and Professional Programs**

## BETH MEDRASH GOVOHA, Lakewood, NJ 08701-2797

**General Information** Independent-religious, men only, comprehensive institution.

**GRADUATE UNITS**

**Graduate Programs**

## BETHUNE-COOKMAN UNIVERSITY, Daytona Beach, FL 32114-3099

**General Information** Independent-religious, coed, comprehensive institution.

**GRADUATE UNITS**

**School of Graduate Studies** *Program availability:* Online learning. Electronic applications accepted.

## BEULAH HEIGHTS UNIVERSITY, Atlanta, GA 30316

**General Information** Independent-religious, coed, comprehensive institution.

**GRADUATE UNITS**

**Graduate School** Electronic applications accepted.

## BEXLEY SEABURY SEMINARY, Chicago, IL 60637

**General Information** Independent-religious, coed, graduate-only institution. *Graduate housing:* On-campus housing not available.

**GRADUATE UNITS**

**Graduate Programs** *Program availability:* Part-time.

## BINGHAMTON UNIVERSITY, STATE UNIVERSITY OF NEW YORK, Binghamton, NY 13902-6000

**General Information** State-supported, coed, university. CGS member. *Graduate housing:* Room and/or apartments available on a first-come, first-served basis to single students; on-campus housing not available to married students. *Research affiliation:* United Health Services Hospitals (health care, engineering), Mount Sinai Hospital (health care, engineering), Lockheed Martin Corporation (engineering, management, mathematics), Matco Company (engineering), IBM (engineering), Universal Instruments (engineering).

**GRADUATE UNITS**

**Graduate School** *Program availability:* Part-time, evening/weekend, online learning. Electronic applications accepted.

***College of Community and Public Affairs*** *Program availability:* Part-time, evening/weekend. Electronic applications accepted.

***Decker School of Nursing*** *Program availability:* Part-time, evening/weekend. Electronic applications accepted.

***Harpur College of Arts and Sciences*** *Program availability:* Part-time, evening/weekend. Electronic applications accepted.

***School of Management*** *Program availability:* Part-time, evening/weekend. Electronic applications accepted.

***School of Pharmacy and Pharmaceutical Sciences***

***Thomas J. Watson School of Engineering and Applied Science*** *Program availability:* Part-time, evening/weekend, online learning. Electronic applications accepted.

## BIOLA UNIVERSITY, La Mirada, CA 90639-0001

**General Information** Independent-religious, coed, university. *Graduate housing:* Rooms and/or apartments available on a first-come, first-served basis to single and married students.

**GRADUATE UNITS**

**Cook School of Intercultural Studies** Students: 108 full-time (55 women), 154 part-time (86 women); includes 77 minority (11 Black or African American, non-Hispanic/Latino; 1 American Indian or Alaska Native, non-Hispanic/Latino; 43 Asian, non-Hispanic/Latino; 19 Hispanic/Latino; 3 Two or more races, non-Hispanic/Latino), 67 international. Average age 35. 142 applicants, 63% accepted, 52 enrolled. *Faculty:* 19. Expenses: Contact institution. *Financial support:* Scholarships/grants available. Support available to part-time students. Financial award applicants required to submit FAFSA. In 2019, 37 master's, 14 doctorates awarded. *Program availability:* Part-time, 100% online.

*Application deadline:* For fall admission, 7/1 for domestic students, 6/1 for international students; for spring admission, 11/1 for domestic students; for summer admission, 5/1 for domestic students. Applications are processed on a rolling basis. *Application fee:* $65. Electronic applications accepted. *Application Contact:* Graduate Admissions Office, 562-903-4752, E-mail: graduate.admissions@biola.edu. *Dean*, Dr. Bulus Y. Galadima, 562-903-4844.

**Crowell School of Business** Students: 42 full-time (20 women), 60 part-time (33 women); includes 45 minority (6 Black or African American, non-Hispanic/Latino; 16 Asian, non-Hispanic/Latino; 20 Hispanic/Latino; 3 Two or more races, non-Hispanic/Latino), 15 international. Average age 31. 103 applicants, 64% accepted, 44 enrolled. *Faculty:* 11. Expenses: Contact institution. *Financial support:* Scholarships/grants available. Support available to part-time students. Financial award applicants required to submit FAFSA. In 2019, 45 master's awarded. *Program availability:* Part-time, evening/weekend. *Application deadline:* For fall admission, 7/1 priority date for domestic students, 6/1 priority date for international students; for spring admission, 11/1 for domestic students. Applications are processed on a rolling basis. *Application fee:* $65. Electronic applications accepted. *Application Contact:* Christina Gramenz, MBA Coordinator, 562-777-4015, E-mail: mba@biola.edu. *Dean*, Dr. Gary Lindblad, 562-777-4015, Fax: 562-906-4545, E-mail: mba@biola.edu.

**Rosemead School of Psychology** Students: 115 full-time (94 women), 48 part-time (43 women); includes 48 minority (2 Black or African American, non-Hispanic/Latino; 1 American Indian or Alaska Native, non-Hispanic/Latino; 24 Asian, non-Hispanic/Latino; 16 Hispanic/Latino; 1 Native Hawaiian or other Pacific Islander, non-Hispanic/Latino; 4 Two or more races, non-Hispanic/Latino), 51 international. Average age 30. 126 applicants, 46% accepted, 34 enrolled. *Faculty:* 23. Expenses: Contact institution. *Financial support:* Scholarships/grants and unspecified assistantships available. Financial award applicants required to submit FAFSA. In 2019, 29 doctorates awarded. *Application deadline:* For fall admission, 12/1 priority date for domestic students, 12/1 for international students. *Application fee:* $65. Electronic applications accepted. *Application Contact:* Nicholas Perry, Graduate Admissions Counselor, 562-903-4752, E-mail: graduate.admissions@biola.edu. *Dean*, Dr. Tamara Anderson, 562-903-4867, Fax: 562-903-4864.

**School of Education** Students: 76 full-time (66 women), 170 part-time (134 women); includes 116 minority (4 Black or African American, non-Hispanic/Latino; 55 Asian, non-Hispanic/Latino; 46 Hispanic/Latino; 1 Native Hawaiian or other Pacific Islander, non-Hispanic/Latino; 10 Two or more races, non-Hispanic/Latino), 13 international. Average age 29. 267 applicants, 76% accepted, 144 enrolled. *Faculty:* 15. Expenses: Contact institution. *Financial support:* Scholarships/grants available. Support available to part-time students. Financial award applicants required to submit FAFSA. In 2019, 98 master's awarded. *Program availability:* Part-time, evening/weekend, online learning. *Application deadline:* For fall admission, 7/1 for domestic students, 6/1 for international students; for spring admission, 11/1 for domestic students, 10/1 for international students; for summer admission, 4/1 for domestic students. Applications are processed on a rolling basis. *Application fee:* $65. Electronic applications accepted. *Application Contact:* Graduate Admissions Office, 562-903-4752, E-mail: graduate.admissions@biola.edu. *Dean*, Dr. June Hetzel, 562-903-4715.

**Talbot School of Theology** Students: 461 full-time (116 women), 768 part-time (228 women); includes 489 minority (54 Black or African American, non-Hispanic/Latino; 1 American Indian or Alaska Native, non-Hispanic/Latino; 303 Asian, non-Hispanic/Latino; 96 Hispanic/Latino; 3 Native Hawaiian or other Pacific Islander, non-Hispanic/Latino; 32 Two or more races, non-Hispanic/Latino), 162 international. Average age 38. 745 applicants, 70% accepted, 320 enrolled. Expenses: Contact institution. *Financial support:* Scholarships/grants and unspecified assistantships available. Support available to part-time students. Financial award applicants required to submit FAFSA. In 2019, 235 master's, 24 doctorates awarded. *Program availability:* Part-time, evening/weekend. *Application deadline:* For fall admission, 7/1 for domestic students, 6/1 for international students; for spring admission, 11/1 for domestic students. Applications are processed on a rolling basis. *Application fee:* $65. Electronic applications accepted. *Application Contact:* Graduate Admissions Office, 562-903-4752, E-mail: graduate.admissions@biola.edu. *Dean*, Dr. Clint Arnold, 562-903-4816, Fax: 562-903-4748.

## BISHOP'S UNIVERSITY, Sherbrooke, QC J1M 1Z7, Canada

**General Information** Province-supported, coed, comprehensive institution. *Graduate housing:* Room and/or apartments available on a first-come, first-served basis to single students; on-campus housing not available to married students. Housing application deadline: 7/1.

**GRADUATE UNITS**

**School of Education** *Program availability:* Part-time, online learning.

## BLACK HILLS STATE UNIVERSITY, Spearfish, SD 57799

**General Information** State-supported, coed, comprehensive institution. *Graduate housing:* Room and/or apartments available on a first-come, first-served basis to single students; on-campus housing not available to married students. Housing application deadline: 4/1.

**GRADUATE UNITS**

**Graduate Studies** *Program availability:* Part-time, evening/weekend, online learning. Electronic applications accepted.

## BLESSING-RIEMAN COLLEGE OF NURSING & HEALTH SCIENCES, Quincy, IL 62305-7005

**General Information** Independent, coed, primarily women, comprehensive institution. *Enrollment:* 17 part-time matriculated graduate/professional students (16 women). *Enrollment by degree level:* 17 master's. *Graduate faculty:* 8 full-time (all women). *Graduate housing:* On-campus housing not available. *Student services:* Campus safety program, services for students with disabilities. *Library facilities:* Blessing Health Professions Library plus 1 other.

**Computer facilities:** 28 computers available on campus for general student use. A campuswide network can be accessed.
Website: http://www.brcn.edu/

**General Application Contact:** Kevin Williams, Admissions Counselor, 217-228-5520 Ext. 6958, Fax: 217-223-1781, E-mail: williamsk@brcn.edu.

**GRADUATE UNITS**

**Master of Science in Nursing Program** *Program availability:* Part-time-only, evening/weekend, online only, 100% online. Electronic applications accepted.

## BLOOMFIELD COLLEGE, Bloomfield, NJ 07003-9981

**General Information** Independent-religious, coed, comprehensive institution. *Enrollment:* 13 full-time matriculated graduate/professional students (11 women), 3 part-time matriculated graduate/professional students (all women). *Enrollment by degree level:* 12 master's, 4 other advanced degrees. *Graduate faculty:* 7 full-time (4 women), 11 part-time/adjunct (7 women). *Tuition:* Full-time $17,640; part-time $11,760 per unit. *Graduate housing:* On-campus housing not available. *Student services:* Campus employment opportunities, campus safety program, career counseling, exercise/wellness program, free psychological counseling, international student services, low-cost health insurance, multicultural affairs office, services for students with disabilities, teacher training, writing training. *Library facilities:* Bloomfield College Library plus 1 other. *Collection:* Books: 63,000 (physical), 127,000 (digital/electronic); Serial titles: 45 (physical); Databases: 50. Weekly public service hours: 92.

**Computer facilities:** 390 computers available on campus for general student use. A campuswide network can be accessed from student residence rooms and from off campus. Online class registration is available.
Website: http://www.bloomfield.edu/

**General Application Contact:** Kevin Cavanagh, Vice President for Enrollment Management, 973-748-9000, E-mail: kevin_cavanagh@bloomfield.edu.

**GRADUATE UNITS**

**Program in Accounting**

## BLOOMSBURG UNIVERSITY OF PENNSYLVANIA, Bloomsburg, PA 17815-1301

**General Information** State-supported, coed, comprehensive institution. *Graduate housing:* Room and/or apartments available on a first-come, first-served basis to single students; on-campus housing not available to married students. *Research affiliation:* Consortium of Big Ten Universities Research and Training Reactors (physics), Melanoma Research Fund (biology), Merck & Company, Inc. (biology), Marine Science Consortium (biology).

**GRADUATE UNITS**

**School of Graduate Studies** *Program availability:* Part-time, evening/weekend. Electronic applications accepted.

***College of Education*** *Program availability:* Part-time. Electronic applications accepted.

***College of Science and Technology*** Electronic applications accepted.

***Zeigler College of Business*** *Program availability:* Part-time, evening/weekend. Electronic applications accepted.

## BLUEFIELD COLLEGE, Bluefield, VA 24605-1799

**General Information** Independent-religious, coed, comprehensive institution. *Graduate housing:* On-campus housing not available.

**GRADUATE UNITS**

**School of Education** *Program availability:* Part-time, online only, 100% online. Electronic applications accepted.

## BLUE MOUNTAIN COLLEGE, Blue Mountain, MS 38610

**General Information** Independent-religious, coed, comprehensive institution. *Enrollment:* 4 full-time matriculated graduate/professional students (all women), 4 part-time matriculated graduate/professional students (2 women). *Enrollment by degree level:* 8 master's. *Graduate faculty:* 4 full-time (3 women), 1 part-time/adjunct. *Tuition:* Full-time $470; part-time $470 per credit hour. *Graduate housing:* Room and/or apartments available on a first-come, first-served basis to single students; on-campus housing not available to married students. Typical cost: $1250 per year ($2400 including board). Housing application deadline: 7/1. *Student services:* Campus employment opportunities, campus safety program, exercise/wellness program, international student services, services for students with disabilities, teacher training. *Library facilities:* Guyton Library plus 1 other. *Collection:* Books: 41,725 (physical), 35,897 (digital/electronic); Serial titles: 143 (physical); Databases: 24. Weekly public service hours: 70.

**Computer facilities:** 95 computers available on campus for general student use. A campuswide network can be accessed from student residence rooms.
Website: http://www.bmc.edu/

**General Application Contact:** Jean Harrington, Administrative Assistant, Department of Education, 662-685-4771 Ext. 238, Fax: 662-815-2919, E-mail: jharrington@bmc.edu.

**GRADUATE UNITS**

**Program in Elementary Education** *Program availability:* Part-time, evening/weekend. Electronic applications accepted.

**Program in Literacy/Reading (K-12)** *Program availability:* Part-time, evening/weekend. Electronic applications accepted.

**Program in Secondary Education - Biology** *Program availability:* Part-time, evening/weekend. Electronic applications accepted.

## BLUFFTON UNIVERSITY, Bluffton, OH 45817

**General Information** Independent-religious, coed, comprehensive institution. *Enrollment:* 768 graduate, professional, and undergraduate students; 43 full-time matriculated graduate/professional students (28 women), 6 part-time matriculated graduate/professional students (3 women). *Enrollment by degree level:* 49 master's. *Graduate faculty:* 6 full-time (4 women), 6 part-time/adjunct (1 woman). *Tuition:* Full-time $6900; part-time $3450 per credit hour. *Required fees:* $200; $200 per credit hour. Tuition and fees vary according to program. *Graduate housing:* On-campus housing not available. *Student services:* Campus employment opportunities, career counseling, exercise/wellness program, free psychological counseling, international student services, multicultural affairs office, services for students with disabilities, writing training. *Library facilities:* Musselman Library plus 1 other. *Collection:* Books: 73,648 (physical), 283,031 (digital/electronic); Serial titles: 1,001 (physical), 46,672 (digital/electronic); Databases: 258. Weekly public service hours: 74; students can reserve study rooms.

**Computer facilities:** 175 computers available on campus for general student use. A campuswide network can be accessed. Online class registration is available.
Website: http://www.bluffton.edu/

**General Application Contact:** Shelby Koenig, Enrollment Counselor for Graduate Program, 419-358-3684, E-mail: admissions@bluffton.edu.

**GRADUATE UNITS**

**Graduate Programs in Business** *Program availability:* Evening/weekend, blended/hybrid learning, videoconference. Electronic applications accepted.

**Programs in Education** Students: 14 full-time (13 women), 5 part-time (3 women); includes 2 minority (1 Hispanic/Latino; 1 Two or more races, non-Hispanic/Latino). Average age 31. *Faculty:* 2 full-time (both women), 1 part-time/adjunct. Expenses: Contact institution. *Financial support:* In 2019–20, 2 students received support. Unspecified assistantships available. Financial award application deadline: 5/1. In 2019,

8 master's awarded. *Program availability:* Part-time, 100% online, blended/hybrid learning, videoconference. *Application deadline:* For fall admission, 8/15 priority date for domestic students, 6/15 priority date for international students; for spring admission, 12/15 priority date for domestic students, 9/15 priority date for international students. Applications are processed on a rolling basis. Electronic applications accepted. *Application Contact:* Shelby Koenig, Enrollment Counselor for Graduate Program, 419-358-3022, E-mail: koenigs@bluffton.edu. *Director of Graduate Programs in Education,* Dr. Amy K. Mullins, 419-358-3457, E-mail: mullinsa@bluffton.edu.

## BOB JONES UNIVERSITY, Greenville, SC 29614

**General Information** Independent-religious, coed, university.

**GRADUATE UNITS**

**Graduate Programs**

## BOISE STATE UNIVERSITY, Boise, ID 83725-0399

**General Information** State-supported, coed, university. CGS member. *Enrollment:* 26,272 graduate, professional, and undergraduate students; 1,059 full-time matriculated graduate/professional students (609 women), 1,653 part-time matriculated graduate/professional students (985 women). *Enrollment by degree level:* 1,922 master's, 281 doctoral, 509 other advanced degrees. *Graduate faculty:* 457. *International tuition:* $24,030 full-time. *Tuition, area resident:* Full-time $7110; part-time $470 per credit hour. Tuition, state resident: full-time $7110; part-time $470 per credit hour. Tuition, nonresident: full-time $24,030; part-time $827 per credit hour. *Required fees:* $2536. Tuition and fees vary according to course load and program. *Graduate housing:* Rooms and/or apartments available on a first-come, first-served basis to single and married students. Typical cost: $6377 per year ($4400 including board) for single students. Room and board charges vary according to board plan and housing facility selected. Housing application deadline: 6/1. *Student services:* Campus employment opportunities, campus safety program, career counseling, child daycare facilities, exercise/wellness program, free psychological counseling, grant writing training, international student services, low-cost health insurance, multicultural affairs office, services for students with disabilities, teacher training, writing training. *Library facilities:* Albertson's Library plus 1 other. *Collection:* Books: 644,899 (physical), 60,977 (digital/electronic); Serial titles: 112,213 (digital/electronic); Databases: 303. Weekly public service hours: 115; study areas open 24 hours, 5–7 days a week; students can reserve study rooms. *Research affiliation:* Federal Aviation Administration (airliner cabin environment research), Lee Pesky Learning Center (elementary mathematics education), Prewitt & Associates, Inc. (C-130 drop zones), Bechtel BWXT Idaho, LLC (energy policy analysis), Argonne National Laboratory (energy policy analysis), American Chemical Society (petroleum research).

**Computer facilities:** 900 computers available on campus for general student use. A campuswide network can be accessed. Online class registration is available. Website: http://www.boisestate.edu/

**General Application Contact:** Melissa Krancer, Graduate Recruiting Specialist, 208-426-4326, Fax: 208-426-2789, E-mail: melissakrancer@boisestate.edu.

**GRADUATE UNITS**

**College of Arts and Sciences** Students: 267 full-time (143 women), 126 part-time (65 women). Expenses: Contact institution. *Financial support:* Research assistantships, teaching assistantships, scholarships/grants, and unspecified assistantships available. Financial award applicants required to submit FAFSA. *Program availability:* Part-time. *Application deadline:* For fall admission, 5/1 for domestic and international students. Electronic applications accepted. *Application Contact:* Dr. Leslie Durham, Interim Dean, 208-426-1414, Fax: 208-426-3006. *Interim Dean,* Dr. Leslie Durham, 208-426-1414, Fax: 208-426-3006.

**College of Business and Economics** Students: 180 full-time (66 women), 331 part-time (127 women); includes 58 minority (15 Black or African American, non-Hispanic/Latino; 1 American Indian or Alaska Native, non-Hispanic/Latino; 19 Asian, non-Hispanic/Latino; 19 Hispanic/Latino; 4 Two or more races, non-Hispanic/Latino), 17 international. Expenses: Contact institution. *Financial support:* Research assistantships, scholarships/grants, and unspecified assistantships available. Financial award applicants required to submit FAFSA. *Program availability:* Part-time, online learning. *Application deadline:* Applications are processed on a rolling basis. *Application fee:* $65. Electronic applications accepted. *Application Contact:* Dr. Mark Bannister, Dean, 208-426-1125, E-mail: markbannister724@boisestate.edu. *Dean,* Dr. Mark Bannister, 208-426-1125, E-mail: markbannister724@boisestate.edu.

**College of Education** Students: 133 full-time (106 women), 581 part-time (424 women); includes 90 minority (14 Black or African American, non-Hispanic/Latino; 1 American Indian or Alaska Native, non-Hispanic/Latino; 13 Asian, non-Hispanic/Latino; 45 Hispanic/Latino; 1 Native Hawaiian or other Pacific Islander, non-Hispanic/Latino; 16 Two or more races, non-Hispanic/Latino), 12 international. Expenses: Contact institution. *Financial support:* Teaching assistantships, scholarships/grants, and unspecified assistantships available. Financial award applicants required to submit FAFSA. *Program availability:* Part-time, 100% online, blended/hybrid learning. Electronic applications accepted. *Application Contact:* Dr. Jennifer Snow, Interim Dean, 208-426-1611, E-mail: jennifersnow@boisestate.edu. *Interim Dean,* Dr. Jennifer Snow, 208-426-1611, E-mail: jennifersnow@boisestate.edu.

**College of Engineering** Students: 173 full-time (53 women), 234 part-time (117 women); includes 48 minority (10 Black or African American, non-Hispanic/Latino; 2 American Indian or Alaska Native, non-Hispanic/Latino; 15 Asian, non-Hispanic/Latino; 13 Hispanic/Latino; 1 Native Hawaiian or other Pacific Islander, non-Hispanic/Latino; 7 Two or more races, non-Hispanic/Latino), 100 international. Expenses: Contact institution. *Financial support:* Research assistantships, teaching assistantships with partial tuition reimbursements, scholarships/grants, and unspecified assistantships available. Financial award applicants required to submit FAFSA. *Program availability:* Part-time, online learning. Electronic applications accepted. *Application Contact:* Hao Chen, Program Coordinator, 208-426-1020, E-mail: haochen@boisestate.edu. *Dean,* Dr. JoAnn Lighty, 208-426-4844, E-mail: joannlighty@boisestate.edu.

***Micron School of Materials Science and Engineering*** Students: 53 full-time (17 women), 11 part-time (3 women); includes 14 minority (1 Black or African American, non-Hispanic/Latino; 3 Asian, non-Hispanic/Latino; 7 Hispanic/Latino; 3 Two or more races, non-Hispanic/Latino), 9 international. Expenses: Contact institution. *Financial support:* Research assistantships, scholarships/grants, and unspecified assistantships available. Financial award applicants required to submit FAFSA. Electronic applications accepted. *Application Contact:* Jessica Economy, Academic Program Manager, 208-426-4896, E-mail: msegrad@boisestate.edu. *Director,* Dr. Will Hughes, 208-426-4859, E-mail: willhughes@boisestate.edu.

**College of Health Sciences** Students: 12 full-time (10 women); includes 1 minority (Black or African American, non-Hispanic/Latino). Average age 35. Expenses: Contact institution. *Financial support:* Applicants required to submit FAFSA. Electronic applications accepted. *Application Contact:* Alicia Anderson, Project Director, 208-426-2425, E-mail: aliciaanderson@boisestate.edu. *Dean,* Dr. Tim Dunnagan, 208-426-4150, E-mail: timdunnagan@boisestate.edu.

***School of Nursing*** Students: 1 (woman) full-time, 91 part-time (73 women); includes 8 minority (4 Black or African American, non-Hispanic/Latino; 3 Asian, non-Hispanic/Latino; 1 Native Hawaiian or other Pacific Islander, non-Hispanic/Latino). Expenses: Contact institution. *Financial support:* Applicants required to submit FAFSA. Electronic applications accepted. *Application Contact:* Dr. Nancy Loftus, Program Coordinator, 208-426-3819, E-mail: nancyloftus@boisestate.edu. *Director,* Dr. Ann Hubbert, 208-426-3404, E-mail: annhubbert@boisestate.edu.

***School of Social Work*** Students: 319 full-time (288 women), 132 part-time (120 women); includes 52 minority (27 Black or African American, non-Hispanic/Latino; 5 American Indian or Alaska Native, non-Hispanic/Latino; 7 Asian, non-Hispanic/Latino; 12 Hispanic/Latino; 1 Native Hawaiian or other Pacific Islander, non-Hispanic/Latino), 1 international. Average age 34. Expenses: Contact institution. *Financial support:* Applicants required to submit FAFSA. Electronic applications accepted. *Application Contact:* Dr. Cynthia Sanders, Program Coordinator, 208-426-1780, E-mail: cynthiasanders@boisestate.edu. *Director,* Dr. Randy Magen, 208-426-1789, E-mail: randymagen@boisestate.edu.

**School of Public Service** Students: 12 full-time (5 women), 11 part-time (5 women); includes 4 minority (1 Asian, non-Hispanic/Latino; 2 Hispanic/Latino; 1 Two or more races, non-Hispanic/Latino), 4 international. Expenses: Contact institution. *Financial support:* Research assistantships, scholarships/grants, and unspecified assistantships available. Financial award applicants required to submit FAFSA. Electronic applications accepted. *Application Contact:* Dr. Andrew Giacomazzi, Interim Dean, 208-426-1368, E-mail: agiacom@boisestate.edu. *Interim Dean,* Dr. Andrew Giacomazzi, 208-426-1368, E-mail: agiacom@boisestate.edu.

## BORICUA COLLEGE, New York, NY 10032-1560

**General Information** Independent, coed, comprehensive institution. *Enrollment:* 89 full-time matriculated graduate/professional students (79 women). *Enrollment by degree level:* 89 master's. *Graduate faculty:* 4 full-time (1 woman), 4 part-time/adjunct (all women). *Tuition:* Full-time $11,000. One-time fee: $100 full-time. *Student services:* Career counseling, teacher training. *Library facilities:* Boricua College Library plus 1 other.

**Computer facilities:** 120 computers available on campus for general student use. Website: http://www.boricuacollege.edu/

**General Application Contact:** Teofilo Santiago, Director of Admissions, 347-964-8680 Ext. 364, E-mail: tsantiago@boricuacollege.edu.

**GRADUATE UNITS**

**Program in Human Services** *Program availability:* Evening/weekend.

**Program in TESOL Education (K-12)** *Program availability:* Evening/weekend.

## BOSTON ARCHITECTURAL COLLEGE, Boston, MA 02115-2795

**General Information** Independent, coed, comprehensive institution.

**GRADUATE UNITS**

**Graduate Programs** Electronic applications accepted.

## BOSTON COLLEGE, Chestnut Hill, MA 02467-3800

**General Information** Independent-religious, coed, university. CGS member. *Graduate housing:* On-campus housing not available.

**GRADUATE UNITS**

**Carroll School of Management** *Program availability:* Part-time, evening/weekend. Electronic applications accepted.

**Law School** Electronic applications accepted.

**Lynch School of Education and Human Development** *Program availability:* Part-time, 100% online. Electronic applications accepted.

**Morrissey Graduate School of Arts and Sciences** Students: 734 full-time (304 women), 40 part-time (24 women). 2,111 applicants, 25% accepted, 214 enrolled. *Faculty:* 497 full-time (167 women). Expenses: Contact institution. *Financial support:* In 2019–20, fellowships with full and partial tuition reimbursements (averaging $23,400 per year), research assistantships with full and partial tuition reimbursements (averaging $23,400 per year), teaching assistantships with full and partial tuition reimbursements (averaging $23,400 per year) were awarded; career-related internships or fieldwork, Federal Work-Study, scholarships/grants, health care benefits, tuition waivers (full and partial), and unspecified assistantships also available. Support available to part-time students. Financial award application deadline: 3/1; financial award applicants required to submit FAFSA. In 2019, 120 master's, 90 doctorates awarded. *Program availability:* Part-time. *Application deadline:* For fall admission, 1/2 priority date for domestic and international students. *Application fee:* $75. Electronic applications accepted. *Application Contact:* Robert V. Howe, Associate Dean, 617-552-3265, Fax: 617-552-3700, E-mail: hower@bc.edu. *Dean,* Dr. Gregory Kalscheur, 617-552-6850, E-mail: gregory.kalscheur@bc.edu.

**School of Social Work** *Program availability:* Part-time. Electronic applications accepted.

**School of Theology and Ministry** *Program availability:* Part-time. Electronic applications accepted.

**William F. Connell School of Nursing** Students: 228 full-time (200 women), 82 part-time (71 women); includes 54 minority (10 Black or African American, non-Hispanic/Latino; 18 Asian, non-Hispanic/Latino; 20 Hispanic/Latino; 6 Two or more races, non-Hispanic/Latino), 7 international. Average age 28. 360 applicants, 56% accepted, 93 enrolled. *Faculty:* 56 full-time (50 women). Expenses: Contact institution. *Financial support:* In 2019–20, 135 students received support, including 12 fellowships with full tuition reimbursements available (averaging $24,504 per year), 29 teaching assistantships (averaging $4,380 per year); scholarships/grants, health care benefits, tuition waivers (partial), and unspecified assistantships also available. Support available to part-time students. Financial award application deadline: 4/18; financial award applicants required to submit FAFSA. In 2019, 107 master's, 7 doctorates awarded. *Program availability:* Part-time. *Application deadline:* For fall admission, 3/15 for domestic and international students; for spring admission, 9/30 for domestic and international students. *Application fee:* $40. Electronic applications accepted. *Application Contact:* Sean Sendall, Assistant Dean, Graduate Enrollment and Data Analytics, 617-552-4745, Fax: 617-552-2121, E-mail: sean.sendall@bc.edu. *Dean,* Dr. Susan Gennaro, 617-552-4251, Fax: 617-552-0931, E-mail: susan.gennaro@bc.edu.

**BOSTON GRADUATE SCHOOL OF PSYCHOANALYSIS, Brookline, MA 02446-4602**

**General Information** Independent, coed, graduate-only institution. *Graduate housing:* On-campus housing not available. *Research affiliation:* Boston Institute for Psychotherapy (psychotherapy).

**GRADUATE UNITS**

**BGSP-New Jersey**

**CAGS and Certificate Programs** *Program availability:* Part-time.

**Doctoral Programs** *Program availability:* Part-time.

**Master's Programs** *Program availability:* Part-time.

**New York Graduate School of Psychoanalysis** *Program availability:* Part-time.

**BOSTON UNIVERSITY, Boston, MA 02215**

**General Information** Independent, coed, university. CGS member. *Enrollment:* 33,720 graduate, professional, and undergraduate students; 10,619 full-time matriculated graduate/professional students (6,021 women), 5,026 part-time matriculated graduate/professional students (2,921 women). *Enrollment by degree level:* 6,057 master's, 687 doctoral, 67 other advanced degrees. *Graduate housing:* On-campus housing not available. *Student services:* Campus employment opportunities, campus safety program, career counseling, child daycare facilities, exercise/wellness program, free psychological counseling, international student services, low-cost health insurance, services for students with disabilities, writing training. *Library facilities:* Mugar Memorial Library plus 20 others. *Collection:* Books: 1.2 million (physical), 2.6 million (digital/electronic); Serial titles: 294,676 (physical), 126,184 (digital/electronic); Databases: 783. Weekly public service hours: 119; students can reserve study rooms. *Research affiliation:* NASA-Ames Research Center, Society for the Preservation of New England Antiquities, Massachusetts Historical Society, Woods Hole Oceanographic Institution-Marine Biological Laboratory.

**Computer facilities:** Computer purchase and lease plans are available. 250 computers available on campus for general student use. A campuswide network can be accessed. Online class registration, research and educational networks are available.
Website: http://www.bu.edu/

**GRADUATE UNITS**

**College of Communication** Students: 460 full-time (367 women), 39 part-time (30 women); includes 48 minority (18 Black or African American, non-Hispanic/Latino; 10 Asian, non-Hispanic/Latino; 15 Hispanic/Latino; 5 Two or more races, non-Hispanic/Latino), 315 international. Average age 24. 1,338 applicants, 59% accepted, 314 enrolled. *Faculty:* 67 full-time, 73 part-time/adjunct. Expenses: Contact institution. *Financial support:* In 2019–20, 175 students received support, including 35 research assistantships (averaging $12,000 per year), 99 teaching assistantships (averaging $12,000 per year); career-related internships or fieldwork, Federal Work-Study, institutionally sponsored loans, scholarships/grants, health care benefits, and unspecified assistantships also available. Support available to part-time students. Financial award application deadline: 5/1; financial award applicants required to submit FAFSA. In 2019, 235 master's awarded. *Program availability:* Part-time. *Application deadline:* For fall admission, 5/1 for domestic and international students. Applications are processed on a rolling basis. *Application fee:* $95. Electronic applications accepted. *Application Contact:* Kayla Ring, Assistant Director, Graduate Affairs, 617-353-3481, E-mail: comgrad@bu.edu. *Dean*, Mariette DiChristina, 617-353-3450, Fax: 617-358-0399, E-mail: comdean@bu.edu.

***Division of Emerging Media Studies*** Students: 48 full-time (39 women), 2 part-time (both women); includes 4 minority (1 Asian, non-Hispanic/Latino; 2 Hispanic/Latino; 1 Two or more races, non-Hispanic/Latino), 34 international. Average age 25. 180 applicants, 56% accepted, 35 enrolled. *Faculty:* 4 full-time (1 woman). Expenses: Contact institution. *Financial support:* In 2019–20, 3 fellowships with full tuition reimbursements were awarded; research assistantships, teaching assistantships, career-related internships or fieldwork, Federal Work-Study, scholarships/grants, health care benefits, and unspecified assistantships also available. Financial award application deadline: 5/1; financial award applicants required to submit FAFSA. In 2019, 24 master's awarded. *Program availability:* Part-time. *Application deadline:* For fall admission, 5/1 for domestic and international students. Applications are processed on a rolling basis. *Application fee:* $95. Electronic applications accepted. *Application Contact:* Jackie Cummings, Admission and Financial Aid Counselor, 617-353-3481, E-mail: comgrad@bu.edu. *Professor of Emerging Media/Chair of the Division of Emerging Media Studies*, Dr. James Katz, 617-353-7733, E-mail: dems@bu.edu.

**College of Engineering** Students: 849 full-time (282 women), 177 part-time (44 women); includes 151 minority (12 Black or African American, non-Hispanic/Latino; 83 Asian, non-Hispanic/Latino; 33 Hispanic/Latino; 23 Two or more races, non-Hispanic/Latino), 536 international. Average age 25. 4,014 applicants, 39% accepted, 348 enrolled. *Faculty:* 112 full-time (12 women), 9 part-time/adjunct (1 woman). Expenses: Contact institution. *Financial support:* In 2019–20, 458 students received support, including 115 fellowships with full tuition reimbursements available (averaging $33,000 per year), 246 research assistantships with full tuition reimbursements available (averaging $33,000 per year), 7 teaching assistantships with full tuition reimbursements available (averaging $22,000 per year); scholarships/grants and unspecified assistantships also available. Support available to part-time students. Financial award application deadline: 1/15; financial award applicants required to submit FAFSA. In 2019, 327 master's, 59 doctorates awarded. *Program availability:* Part-time, blended/hybrid learning. *Application deadline:* For fall admission, 12/15 for domestic and international students; for spring admission, 10/1 for domestic and international students. *Application fee:* $95. Electronic applications accepted. *Application Contact:* Andrew Butler, Assistant Director, Enrollment Operations, 617-353-9760, E-mail: enggrad@bu.edu. *Dean*, Dr. Kenneth R. Lutchen, 617-353-2800, Fax: 617-358-3468, E-mail: klutch@bu.edu.

**College of Fine Arts** Students: 769 full-time (451 women), 11 part-time (4 women); includes 114 minority (26 Black or African American, non-Hispanic/Latino; 3 American Indian or Alaska Native, non-Hispanic/Latino; 27 Asian, non-Hispanic/Latino; 36 Hispanic/Latino; 1 Native Hawaiian or other Pacific Islander, non-Hispanic/Latino; 21 Two or more races, non-Hispanic/Latino), 167 international. Average age 31. 1,239 applicants, 36% accepted, 212 enrolled. Expenses: Contact institution. *Financial support:* In 2019–20, 217 students received support. Fellowships, teaching assistantships, Federal Work-Study, scholarships/grants, health care benefits, and unspecified assistantships available. Support available to part-time students. Financial award application deadline: 12/1. In 2019, 253 master's, 43 doctorates, 6 other advanced degrees awarded. *Program availability:* Part-time, 100% online. *Application deadline:* For fall admission, 12/1 for domestic and international students. *Application fee:* $95. Electronic applications accepted. *Application Contact:* Mark Krone, Assistant Director of Graduate Affairs, 617-353-3350, E-mail: arts@bu.edu. *Dean*, Harvey Young, 617-353-3350.

***School of Music*** Students: 248 full-time (129 women), 7 part-time (3 women); includes 30 minority (4 Black or African American, non-Hispanic/Latino; 2 American Indian or Alaska Native, non-Hispanic/Latino; 9 Asian, non-Hispanic/Latino; 8 Hispanic/Latino; 7 Two or more races, non-Hispanic/Latino), 108 international. Average age 26. 830 applicants, 38% accepted, 100 enrolled. *Faculty:* 36 full-time, 21 part-time/adjunct. Expenses: Contact institution. *Financial support:* In 2019–20, 175 teaching assistantships (averaging $3,500 per year) were awarded; fellowships, scholarships/grants, and unspecified assistantships also available. Financial award application deadline: 12/1. In 2019, 53 master's, 26 doctorates awarded. *Program availability:* Part-time, 100% online. *Application deadline:* For fall admission, 12/1 priority date for domestic and international students. *Application fee:* $95. Electronic applications accepted. *Application Contact:* Laura Conyers, Director of Admissions, 617-353-3341, E-mail: arts@bu.edu. *Director*, Gregory Melchor-Barz, 617-353-3341, Fax: 617-353-7455, E-mail: cfamusic@bu.edu.

***School of Theatre*** Students: 52 full-time (34 women), 2 part-time (0 women); includes 5 minority (1 Black or African American, non-Hispanic/Latino; 2 Asian, non-Hispanic/Latino; 2 Two or more races, non-Hispanic/Latino), 4 international. Average age 28. 139 applicants, 20% accepted, 19 enrolled. *Faculty:* 16 full-time, 9 part-time/adjunct. Expenses: Contact institution. *Financial support:* In 2019–20, 16 students received support, including 16 teaching assistantships (averaging $3,000 per year); scholarships/grants, unspecified assistantships, and stipends also available. Financial award application deadline: 2/1. In 2019, 13 master's awarded. *Program availability:* Part-time. *Application deadline:* For fall admission, 2/1 priority date for domestic and international students. *Application fee:* $95. Electronic applications accepted. *Application Contact:* McCaela Donovan, Assistant Director, School of Theatre, 617-353-3390, E-mail: mccaela@bu.edu. *Director*, Susan Mickey, 617-353-3390.

***School of Visual Arts*** Students: 145 full-time (121 women); includes 23 minority (4 Black or African American, non-Hispanic/Latino; 1 American Indian or Alaska Native, non-Hispanic/Latino; 7 Asian, non-Hispanic/Latino; 10 Hispanic/Latino; 1 Two or more races, non-Hispanic/Latino), 37 international. Average age 30. 270 applicants, 56% accepted, 49 enrolled. *Faculty:* 17 full-time, 4 part-time/adjunct. Expenses: Contact institution. *Financial support:* In 2019–20, 36 students received support. Fellowships, teaching assistantships, scholarships/grants, and unspecified assistantships available. Financial award application deadline: 2/1. In 2019, 13 master's awarded. *Application deadline:* For fall admission, 2/1 for domestic and international students. Applications are processed on a rolling basis. *Application fee:* $95. *Application Contact:* Jessica Caccamo, Assistant Director of Admissions, 617-353-3371, E-mail: visuarts@bu.edu. *Director*, Dana Clancy, 617-353-3371.

**College of Health and Rehabilitation Sciences: Sargent College** Students: 443 full-time (350 women), 90 part-time (82 women); includes 128 minority (12 Black or African American, non-Hispanic/Latino; 64 Asian, non-Hispanic/Latino; 35 Hispanic/Latino; 1 Native Hawaiian or other Pacific Islander, non-Hispanic/Latino; 16 Two or more races, non-Hispanic/Latino), 43 international. Average age 26. 1,536 applicants, 31% accepted, 168 enrolled. *Faculty:* 58 full-time (44 women), 27 part-time/adjunct (18 women). Expenses: Contact institution. *Financial support:* Research assistantships, teaching assistantships, career-related internships or fieldwork, Federal Work-Study, institutionally sponsored loans, scholarships/grants, and health care benefits available. Support available to part-time students. Financial award applicants required to submit FAFSA. In 2019, 73 master's, 96 doctorates awarded. *Program availability:* Blended/hybrid learning. *Application fee:* $95. Electronic applications accepted. *Application Contact:* Sharon Sankey, Assistant Dean, Student Services, 617-353-2713, Fax: 617-353-7500, E-mail: ssankey@bu.edu. *Dean*, Dr. Christopher Moore, 617-353-2705, Fax: 617-353-7500, E-mail: mooreca@bu.edu.

**Graduate School of Arts and Sciences** Students: 1,838 full-time (891 women), 243 part-time (121 women); includes 209 minority (28 Black or African American, non-Hispanic/Latino; 1 American Indian or Alaska Native, non-Hispanic/Latino; 73 Asian, non-Hispanic/Latino; 81 Hispanic/Latino; 1 Native Hawaiian or other Pacific Islander, non-Hispanic/Latino; 25 Two or more races, non-Hispanic/Latino), 1,072 international. Average age 25. 10,160 applicants, 29% accepted, 642 enrolled. Expenses: Contact institution. *Financial support:* In 2019–20, 1,439 students received support, including 220 fellowships with full tuition reimbursements available (averaging $23,340 per year), 415 research assistantships with full tuition reimbursements available (averaging $23,340 per year), 500 teaching assistantships with full tuition reimbursements available (averaging $23,340 per year); career-related internships or fieldwork, Federal Work-Study, scholarships/grants, traineeships, health care benefits, and unspecified assistantships also available. In 2019, 522 master's, 172 doctorates awarded. *Application deadline:* For fall admission, 1/15 priority date for domestic and international students; for spring admission, 10/15 priority date for domestic and international students. *Application fee:* $95. Electronic applications accepted. *Application Contact:* Martin Gastmann, Assistant Director of Admissions and Financial Aid, 617-353-2696, Fax: 617-358-5492, E-mail: grs@bu.edu. *Associate Dean*, Dr. Malika Jeffries-EL, 617-353-2696, Fax: 617-358-5492.

***Editorial Institute*** Students: 5 full-time (4 women), 4 part-time (2 women); includes 2 minority (1 Hispanic/Latino; 1 Two or more races, non-Hispanic/Latino). Average age 34. Expenses: Contact institution. *Financial support:* In 2019–20, 7 students received support, including 1 fellowship with full tuition reimbursement available (averaging $6,000 per year), 1 research assistantship with full tuition reimbursement available (averaging $23,340 per year), 2 teaching assistantships with full tuition reimbursements available (averaging $23,340 per year); Federal Work-Study, scholarships/grants, and health care benefits also available. *Application fee:* $95. *Application Contact:* Ellen Wrigley, Administrative Assistant, 617-353-6631, Fax: 617-353-6917, E-mail: ellen@bu.edu. *Director*, Archie Burnett, 617-353-6631, E-mail: burnetta@bu.edu.

***Frederick S. Pardee School of Global Studies*** Students: 70 full-time (43 women), 13 part-time (7 women); includes 14 minority (3 Black or African American, non-Hispanic/Latino; 3 Asian, non-Hispanic/Latino; 7 Hispanic/Latino; 1 Two or more races, non-Hispanic/Latino), 28 international. Average age 25. 296 applicants, 76% accepted, 39 enrolled. *Faculty:* 33 full-time (8 women), 10 part-time/adjunct (4 women). Expenses: Contact institution. *Financial support:* In 2019–20, 60 students received support. Federal Work-Study, scholarships/grants, and unspecified assistantships available. Financial award application deadline: 1/18. In 2019, 54 master's awarded. *Application deadline:* For fall admission, 1/18 priority date for domestic and international students; for spring admission, 11/1 for domestic and international students. Applications are processed on a rolling basis. *Application fee:* $95. Electronic applications accepted. *Application Contact:* Holly Emery, Graduate Admissions Administrator, 617-358-8625, Fax: 617-353-9290, E-mail: psgsgrad@

bu.edu. *Dean,* Adil Najam, 617-358-0988, Fax: 617-358-7238, E-mail: anajam@bu.edu.

**Metropolitan College** Students: 945 full-time (448 women), 1,901 part-time (841 women); includes 514 minority (126 Black or African American, non-Hispanic/Latino; 3 American Indian or Alaska Native, non-Hispanic/Latino; 230 Asian, non-Hispanic/Latino; 128 Hispanic/Latino; 27 Two or more races, non-Hispanic/Latino), 1,396 international. Average age 29. 3,868 applicants, 75% accepted, 1,049 enrolled. *Faculty:* 52 full-time (15 women), 207 part-time/adjunct (46 women). Expenses: Contact institution. *Financial support:* In 2019–20, 44 research assistantships (averaging $8,400 per year), 36 teaching assistantships (averaging $5,000 per year) were awarded; career-related internships or fieldwork, scholarships/grants, and unspecified assistantships also available. Support available to part-time students. Financial award applicants required to submit FAFSA. In 2019, 1,357 master's awarded. *Program availability:* Part-time, evening/weekend, 100% online, blended/hybrid learning. *Application deadline:* For fall admission, 8/1 priority date for domestic students, 6/1 priority date for international students; for spring admission, 12/1 priority date for domestic students, 11/15 priority date for international students; for summer admission, 4/1 priority date for domestic students, 3/1 priority date for international students. Applications are processed on a rolling basis. *Application fee:* $85. Electronic applications accepted. *Application Contact:* Enrollment Services, 617-353-6000, E-mail: met@bu.edu. *Dean,* Dr. Tanya Zlateva, 617-353-3010, Fax: 617-353-6066, E-mail: met@bu.edu.

**Questrom School of Business** Students: 740 full-time (348 women), 644 part-time (309 women); includes 246 minority (42 Black or African American, non-Hispanic/Latino; 1 American Indian or Alaska Native, non-Hispanic/Latino; 127 Asian, non-Hispanic/Latino; 61 Hispanic/Latino; 15 Two or more races, non-Hispanic/Latino), 507 international. Average age 28. 838 applicants, 48% accepted, 129 enrolled. *Faculty:* 85 full-time (23 women), 28 part-time/adjunct (10 women). Expenses: Contact institution. *Financial support:* Career-related internships or fieldwork, Federal Work-Study, institutionally sponsored loans, scholarships/grants, and tuition waivers (partial) available. Support available to part-time students. Financial award applicants required to submit FAFSA. In 2019, 593 master's, 2 doctorates awarded. *Program availability:* Part-time, evening/weekend, 100% online. *Application deadline:* For fall admission, 3/16 for domestic and international students; for spring admission, 11/6 for domestic and international students. *Application fee:* $125. Electronic applications accepted. *Application Contact:* Meredith C. Siegel, Assistant Dean, Graduate Admissions Office, 617-353-2670, Fax: 617-353-7368, E-mail: mba@bu.edu. *Allen Questrom Professor & Dean,* Susan Fournier, 617-353-9720, Fax: 617-353-5581, E-mail: fournism@bu.edu.

**School of Hospitality Administration** Students: 43 full-time (29 women), 4 part-time (all women); includes 5 minority (4 Asian, non-Hispanic/Latino; 1 Hispanic/Latino), 36 international. Average age 26. *Faculty:* 9 full-time, 17 part-time/adjunct. Expenses: Contact institution. *Financial support:* In 2019–20, 43 students received support. Scholarships/grants and unspecified assistantships available. Financial award application deadline: 2/1; financial award applicants required to submit FAFSA. In 2019, 44 master's awarded. *Program availability:* Part-time, evening/weekend. *Application deadline:* For fall admission, 2/1 priority date for domestic and international students. Applications are processed on a rolling basis. *Application fee:* $95. Electronic applications accepted. *Application Contact:* Micah Sieber, Senior Director of Academic Programs, 617-353-1011, E-mail: shagrad@bu.edu. *Dean,* Dr. Arun Upneja, 617-353-3261, E-mail: aupneja@bu.edu.

**School of Law** Students: 941 full-time (573 women), 83 part-time (45 women); includes 236 minority (35 Black or African American, non-Hispanic/Latino; 1 American Indian or Alaska Native, non-Hispanic/Latino; 63 Asian, non-Hispanic/Latino; 103 Hispanic/Latino; 34 Two or more races, non-Hispanic/Latino), 211 international. Average age 26. 5,812 applicants, 23% accepted, 233 enrolled. *Faculty:* 73 full-time (35 women), 91 part-time/adjunct (30 women). Expenses: Contact institution. *Financial support:* In 2019–20, 935 students received support. Career-related internships or fieldwork, Federal Work-Study, institutionally sponsored loans, scholarships/grants, and resident assistantships available. Financial award application deadline: 3/1; financial award applicants required to submit FAFSA. In 2019, 539 master's awarded. *Program availability:* Part-time, evening/weekend, 100% online, blended/hybrid learning. *Application deadline:* For fall admission, 4/1 for domestic and international students. Applications are processed on a rolling basis. *Application fee:* $85. Electronic applications accepted. *Application Contact:* Alissa Leonard, Director of Admissions and Financial Aid, 617-353-3100, Fax: 617-353-0578, E-mail: bulawadm@bu.edu. *Dean,* Dr. Angela I. Onwuachi-Willig, 617-353-3112, Fax: 617-358-4706, E-mail: lawdean@bu.edu.

**School of Medicine** Students: 1,531 full-time (884 women), 150 part-time (87 women); includes 699 minority (67 Black or African American, non-Hispanic/Latino; 395 Asian, non-Hispanic/Latino; 171 Hispanic/Latino; 3 Native Hawaiian or other Pacific Islander, non-Hispanic/Latino; 63 Two or more races, non-Hispanic/Latino), 129 international. Average age 25. Expenses: Contact institution. *Financial support:* In 2019–20, 379 students received support. Institutionally sponsored loans and scholarships/grants available. Support available to part-time students. Financial award application deadline: 2/1; financial award applicants required to submit CSS PROFILE or FAFSA. In 2019, 549 master's, 33 doctorates awarded. *Program availability:* Part-time, evening/weekend. *Application Contact:* Dr. Kristen Goodell, Associate Dean/Director of Admissions, 617-414-4465, E-mail: kgoodell@bu.edu. *Dean,* Dr. Karen H. Antman, 617-638-5300.

***Graduate Medical Sciences*** Students: 846 full-time (533 women), 121 part-time (69 women); includes 345 minority (38 Black or African American, non-Hispanic/Latino; 187 Asian, non-Hispanic/Latino; 85 Hispanic/Latino; 2 Native Hawaiian or other Pacific Islander, non-Hispanic/Latino; 33 Two or more races, non-Hispanic/Latino), 89 international. Average age 25. *Faculty:* 287 full-time (130 women), 31 part-time/adjunct (13 women). Expenses: Contact institution. *Financial support:* Fellowships, research assistantships, teaching assistantships, Federal Work-Study, scholarships/grants, and traineeships available. Financial award applicants required to submit FAFSA. *Program availability:* Part-time. *Application deadline:* For fall admission, 1/31 for domestic and international students; for spring admission, 10/15 for domestic and international students. *Application fee:* $95. Electronic applications accepted. *Application Contact:* GMS Admissions Office, 617-358-9518, Fax: 617-358-2913, E-mail: gmsbusm@bu.edu. *Associate Provost,* Dr. Deborah Stearns-Kurosawa, 617-358-9553, E-mail: dstearns@bu.edu.

**School of Public Health** Students: 540 full-time (455 women), 327 part-time (265 women); includes 280 minority (69 Black or African American, non-Hispanic/Latino; 1 American Indian or Alaska Native, non-Hispanic/Latino; 111 Asian, non-Hispanic/Latino; 73 Hispanic/Latino; 26 Two or more races, non-Hispanic/Latino), 116 international. Average age 26. 2,298 applicants, 65% accepted, 266 enrolled. *Faculty:* 115 full-time, 190 part-time/adjunct. Expenses: Contact institution. *Financial support:* In 2019–20, 871 students received support. Federal Work-Study, institutionally sponsored loans, and scholarships/grants available. Financial award application deadline: 5/1; financial award applicants required to submit FAFSA. In 2019, 542 master's, 13 doctorates awarded. *Program availability:* Part-time, evening/weekend, 100% online, blended/hybrid learning. *Application deadline:* For fall admission, 1/15 priority date for domestic and international students; for spring admission, 1/1 priority date for domestic students, 10/15 priority date for international students. Applications are processed on a rolling basis. *Application fee:* $140. Electronic applications accepted. *Application Contact:* Ann Marie Larese, Senior Director of Admissions, 617-358-2470, Fax: 617-358-3248, E-mail: asksph@bu.edu. *Dean,* Dr. Sandro Galea, 617-358-3301, E-mail: asksph@bu.edu.

**School of Social Work** Students: 209 full-time (177 women), 708 part-time (642 women); includes 270 minority (74 Black or African American, non-Hispanic/Latino; 2 American Indian or Alaska Native, non-Hispanic/Latino; 52 Asian, non-Hispanic/Latino; 109 Hispanic/Latino; 1 Native Hawaiian or other Pacific Islander, non-Hispanic/Latino; 32 Two or more races, non-Hispanic/Latino), 8 international. Average age 30. 1,252 applicants, 68% accepted, 334 enrolled. *Faculty:* 32 full-time (22 women), 37 part-time/adjunct (29 women). Expenses: Contact institution. *Financial support:* In 2019–20, 108 students received support. Federal Work-Study and scholarships/grants available. Support available to part-time students. Financial award application deadline: 2/1; financial award applicants required to submit FAFSA. In 2019, 322 master's, 2 doctorates awarded. *Program availability:* Part-time, evening/weekend, 100% online, blended/hybrid learning. *Application deadline:* For fall admission, 2/8 for domestic students, 1/7 for international students. *Application fee:* $95. Electronic applications accepted. *Application Contact:* Julie Billings, Graduate Admissions Specialist, 617-353-1212, Fax: 617-353-5612, E-mail: jbilling@bu.edu. *Dean,* Dr. Jorge Delva, 617-353-3760, Fax: 617-353-5612.

**Wheelock College of Education and Human Development** Students: 278 full-time (228 women), 548 part-time (410 women); includes 189 minority (52 Black or African American, non-Hispanic/Latino; 51 Asian, non-Hispanic/Latino; 59 Hispanic/Latino; 27 Two or more races, non-Hispanic/Latino), 72 international. Average age 27. 1,372 applicants, 64% accepted, 340 enrolled. *Faculty:* 89 full-time (60 women), 66 part-time/adjunct (54 women). Expenses: Contact institution. *Financial support:* In 2019–20, 37 fellowships with full tuition reimbursements (averaging $23,340 per year), 29 research assistantships with partial tuition reimbursements (averaging $11,500 per year), 86 teaching assistantships with partial tuition reimbursements (averaging $8,000 per year) were awarded; career-related internships or fieldwork, Federal Work-Study, scholarships/grants, health care benefits, and unspecified assistantships also available. Support available to part-time students. Financial award application deadline: 5/1; financial award applicants required to submit FAFSA. In 2019, 504 master's, 12 doctorates, 5 other advanced degrees awarded. *Program availability:* Part-time, evening/weekend, 100% online. *Application deadline:* For fall admission, 1/15 priority date for domestic and international students; for spring admission, 9/15 priority date for domestic and international students. Applications are processed on a rolling basis. *Application fee:* $95. Electronic applications accepted. *Application Contact:* Julia Cocca, Director of Graduate Enrollment, 617-353-4237, E-mail: whegrad@bu.edu. *Interim Dean,* Dr. David J. Chard, 617-353-3213.

## BOWIE STATE UNIVERSITY, Bowie, MD 20715-9465

**General Information** State-supported, coed, comprehensive institution. CGS member. *Enrollment:* 475 full-time matriculated graduate/professional students (323 women), 469 part-time matriculated graduate/professional students (330 women). *Enrollment by degree level:* 885 master's, 59 doctoral. *Graduate faculty:* 61 full-time (33 women), 64 part-time/adjunct (25 women). *International tuition:* $18,806 full-time. *Tuition, area resident:* Full-time $11,942; part-time $423 per credit hour. Tuition, state resident: full-time $11,942; part-time $423 per credit hour. Tuition, nonresident: full-time $18,806; part-time $709 per credit hour. *Required fees:* $1106; $1106 per semester. $553 per semester. *Graduate housing:* Room and/or apartments available on a first-come, first-served basis to single students; on-campus housing not available to married students. Typical cost: $11,476 (including board). Housing application deadline: 8/1. *Student services:* Campus employment opportunities, campus safety program, career counseling, exercise/wellness program, free psychological counseling, international student services, low-cost health insurance, services for students with disabilities, teacher training, writing training. *Library facilities:* Thurgood Marshall Library. *Collection:* Students can reserve study rooms.

**Computer facilities:** 3,950 computers available on campus for general student use. A campuswide network can be accessed from student residence rooms and from off campus. Online class registration is available.
Website: http://www.bowiestate.edu/

**General Application Contact:** Dr. Cosmas Nwkeafor, Interim Dean, 301-860-3406, Fax: 301-860-3414, E-mail: graduatestudiesandresearch@bowiestate.edu.

**GRADUATE UNITS**

**Graduate Programs** *Program availability:* Part-time, evening/weekend. Electronic applications accepted.

## BOWLING GREEN STATE UNIVERSITY, Bowling Green, OH 43403

**General Information** State-supported, coed, university. CGS member. *Graduate housing:* Rooms and/or apartments available to single and married students. *Research affiliation:* Spectra Group, Inc. (photoscience).

**GRADUATE UNITS**

**Graduate College** *Program availability:* Part-time, evening/weekend. Electronic applications accepted.

***College of Arts and Sciences*** *Program availability:* Part-time. Electronic applications accepted.

***College of Business*** *Program availability:* Part-time, evening/weekend. Electronic applications accepted.

***College of Education and Human Development*** *Program availability:* Part-time, evening/weekend. Electronic applications accepted.

***College of Health and Human Services*** *Program availability:* Part-time, evening/weekend. Electronic applications accepted.

***College of Musical Arts*** *Program availability:* Part-time. Electronic applications accepted.

***College of Technology*** *Program availability:* Part-time. Electronic applications accepted.

***Interdisciplinary Studies*** *Program availability:* Part-time. Electronic applications accepted.

## BRADLEY UNIVERSITY, Peoria, IL 61625-0002

**General Information** Independent, coed, comprehensive institution. CGS member. *Enrollment:* 5,882 graduate, professional, and undergraduate students; 311 full-time matriculated graduate/professional students (209 women), 958 part-time matriculated graduate/professional students (774 women). *Enrollment by degree level:* 807 master's, 387 doctoral, 75 other advanced degrees. *Graduate faculty:* 199 full-time (85 women), 48 part-time/adjunct (36 women). *Tuition:* Part-time $930 per credit hour. *Graduate* *housing:* On-campus housing not available. *Student services:* Campus employment opportunities, campus safety program, career counseling, exercise/wellness program, free psychological counseling, international student services, low-cost health insurance, multicultural affairs office, services for students with disabilities, teacher training. *Library facilities:* Cullom-Davis Library. *Collection:* Weekly public service hours: 129; students can reserve study rooms. *Research affiliation:* Illinois Manufacturing Extension Center, Northern Research Laboratory, Peoria School of Medicine, Caterpillar, Inc., Ford Motor Credit/Visteon.

**Computer facilities:** Computer purchase and lease plans are available. 80 computers available on campus for general student use. A campuswide network can be accessed from student residence rooms and from off campus. Online class registration, online directory, catalog, library materials and other resources are available.
Website: http://www.bradley.edu/

**General Application Contact:** Rachel Webb, Director of On-Campus Graduate Admissions andand International Student and Scholar Services, 309-677-2375, Fax: 309-677-3343, E-mail: rkwebb@bradley.edu.

**GRADUATE UNITS**

**The Graduate School** Students: 311 full-time (209 women), 958 part-time (774 women); includes 344 minority (185 Black or African American, non-Hispanic/Latino; 17 American Indian or Alaska Native, non-Hispanic/Latino; 52 Asian, non-Hispanic/Latino; 70 Hispanic/Latino; 2 Native Hawaiian or other Pacific Islander, non-Hispanic/Latino; 18 Two or more races, non-Hispanic/Latino), 98 international. Average age 35. 1,237 applicants, 93% accepted, 314 enrolled. *Faculty:* 199 full-time (85 women), 48 part-time/adjunct (36 women). Expenses: Contact institution. *Financial support:* In 2019–20, 235 students received support, including 5 fellowships with full tuition reimbursements available (averaging $13,350 per year), 78 research assistantships with full and partial tuition reimbursements available (averaging $8,073 per year); career-related internships or fieldwork, institutionally sponsored loans, scholarships/grants, tuition waivers (full and partial), and unspecified assistantships also available. Support available to part-time students. Financial award application deadline: 4/1. In 2019, 228 master's, 43 doctorates, 6 other advanced degrees awarded. *Program availability:* Part-time, evening/weekend, 100% online, blended/hybrid learning. *Application deadline:* For fall admission, 5/15 priority date for domestic and international students; for spring admission, 10/15 priority date for domestic and international students. Applications are processed on a rolling basis. *Application fee:* $40 ($50 for international students). Electronic applications accepted. *Application Contact:* Rachel Webb, Director of On-Campus Graduate Admissions and International Student and Scholar Services, 309-677-2375, E-mail: rkwebb@bradley.edu. *Dean,* Dr. Jeffrey Bakken, 309-677-2375, E-mail: jbakken@bradley.edu.

***Caterpillar College of Engineering and Technology*** Students: 30 full-time (7 women), 22 part-time (3 women); includes 2 minority (both Black or African American, non-Hispanic/Latino), 46 international. Average age 27. 128 applicants, 58% accepted, 14 enrolled. *Faculty:* 45 full-time (6 women), 1 part-time/adjunct (0 women). Expenses: Contact institution. *Financial support:* In 2019–20, 23 students received support, including 8 teaching assistantships with full and partial tuition reimbursements available (averaging $4,847 per year); research assistantships, institutionally sponsored loans, scholarships/grants, tuition waivers (full and partial), and unspecified assistantships also available. Support available to part-time students. Financial award application deadline: 4/1. In 2019, 34 master's awarded. *Program availability:* Part-time, evening/weekend. *Application deadline:* For fall admission, 5/15 priority date for domestic and international students; for spring admission, 10/15 priority date for domestic and international students. Applications are processed on a rolling basis. *Application fee:* $40 ($50 for international students). Electronic applications accepted. *Application Contact:* Rachel Webb, Director of On-Campus Graduate Admissions and International Student and Scholar Services, 309-677-2375, E-mail: rkwebb@bradley.edu. *Dean,* Lex Akers, 309-677-2721, E-mail: lakers@bradley.edu.

***College of Education and Health Sciences*** Students: 231 full-time (179 women), 886 part-time (750 women); includes 329 minority (179 Black or African American, non-Hispanic/Latino; 16 American Indian or Alaska Native, non-Hispanic/Latino; 49 Asian, non-Hispanic/Latino; 67 Hispanic/Latino; 2 Native Hawaiian or other Pacific Islander, non-Hispanic/Latino; 16 Two or more races, non-Hispanic/Latino), 23 international. Average age 35. 369 applicants, 76% accepted, 191 enrolled. *Faculty:* 54 full-time (40 women), 42 part-time/adjunct (34 women). Expenses: Contact institution. *Financial support:* In 2019–20, 40 students received support, including 20 research assistantships with full and partial tuition reimbursements available (averaging $14,778 per year); fellowships, career-related internships or fieldwork, institutionally sponsored loans, scholarships/grants, tuition waivers (full and partial), and unspecified assistantships also available. Support available to part-time students. Financial award application deadline: 4/1. In 2019, 135 master's, 44 doctorates awarded. *Program availability:* Part-time, evening/weekend, 100% online, blended/hybrid learning. *Application deadline:* For fall admission, 5/15 priority date for domestic students, 5/15 for international students; for spring admission, 10/15 priority date for domestic students, 10/15 for international students. Applications are processed on a rolling basis. *Application fee:* $40 ($50 for international students). Electronic applications accepted. *Application Contact:* Rachel Webb, Director of On-Campus Graduate Admissions and International Student and Scholar Services, 309-677-2375, E-mail: rkwebb@bradley.edu. *Interim Dean,* Dr. Molly Cluskey, 309-677-3181, E-mail: mcluskey@bradley.edu.

***College of Liberal Arts and Sciences*** Students: 28 full-time (14 women), 21 part-time (13 women); includes 5 minority (1 Black or African American, non-Hispanic/Latino; 2 Asian, non-Hispanic/Latino; 2 Hispanic/Latino), 26 international. Average age 28. 91 applicants, 62% accepted, 19 enrolled. *Faculty:* 53 full-time (24 women), 1 part-time/adjunct. Expenses: Contact institution. *Financial support:* In 2019–20, 12 students received support, including 3 research assistantships with partial tuition reimbursements available (averaging $5,580 per year), 7 teaching assistantships with partial tuition reimbursements available (averaging $4,185 per year); career-related internships or fieldwork, institutionally sponsored loans, scholarships/grants, tuition waivers (partial), and unspecified assistantships also available. Support available to part-time students. Financial award application deadline: 4/1. In 2019, 19 master's awarded. *Program availability:* Part-time, evening/weekend. *Application deadline:* For fall admission, 5/15 priority date for domestic and international students; for spring admission, 10/15 priority date for domestic and international students. Applications are processed on a rolling basis. *Application fee:* $40 ($50 for international students). Electronic applications accepted. *Application Contact:* Rachel Webb, Director of On-Campus Graduate Admissions and International Student and Scholar Services, 309-677-2375, E-mail: rkwebb@bradley.edu. *Dean,* Dr. Christopher Jones, 309-677-2380, E-mail: cmjones@bradley.edu.

***Foster College of Business*** Students: 18 full-time (7 women), 27 part-time (6 women); includes 7 minority (3 Black or African American, non-Hispanic/Latino; 1 Asian, non-Hispanic/Latino; 1 Hispanic/Latino; 2 Two or more races, non-Hispanic/Latino), 3 international. Average age 30. 42 applicants, 64% accepted, 14 enrolled. *Faculty:* 34 full-time (10 women), 4 part-time/adjunct (2 women). Expenses: Contact institution. *Financial support:* In 2019–20, 18 students received support, including 5 teaching assistantships with full tuition reimbursements available (averaging $13,104 per year); research assistantships, career-related internships or fieldwork, scholarships/grants, tuition waivers (full), and unspecified assistantships also available. Support available to part-time students. Financial award application deadline: 4/1. In 2019, 47 master's awarded. *Program availability:* Part-time, evening/weekend. *Application deadline:* For fall admission, 5/15 priority date for domestic and international students; for spring admission, 10/15 priority date for domestic and international students. Applications are processed on a rolling basis. *Application fee:* $40 ($50 for international students). Electronic applications accepted. *Application Contact:* Rachel Webb, Director of On-Campus Graduate Admissions and International Student and Scholar Services, 309-677-2375, E-mail: rkwebb@bradley.edu. *Interim Dean and Associate Professor, Marketing,* Dr. Matthew O'Brien, 309-677-2255, E-mail: mobrien@bradley.edu.

***Slane College of Communications and Fine Arts*** Students: 4 full-time (2 women), 2 part-time (both women); includes 1 minority (American Indian or Alaska Native, non-Hispanic/Latino). Average age 42. 3 applicants, 33% accepted. *Faculty:* 13 full-time (5 women). Expenses: Contact institution. *Financial support:* In 2019–20, 2 students received support. Teaching assistantships, scholarships/grants, tuition waivers (partial), and unspecified assistantships available. Support available to part-time students. Financial award application deadline: 4/1. In 2019, 6 master's awarded. *Program availability:* Part-time, evening/weekend. *Application deadline:* For fall admission, 4/1 priority date for domestic students, 4/11 priority date for international students; for spring admission, 11/1 priority date for domestic and international students. Applications are processed on a rolling basis. *Application fee:* $40 ($50 for international students). Electronic applications accepted. *Application Contact:* Rachel Webb, Director of On-Campus Graduate Admissions and International Student and Scholar Services, 309-677-2375, E-mail: rkwebb@bradley.edu. *Dean,* Dr. Jeffrey Huberman, 309-677-2360.

## BRANDEIS UNIVERSITY, Waltham, MA 02454-9110

**General Information** Independent, coed, university. CGS member. *Enrollment:* 5,825 graduate, professional, and undergraduate students; 1,494 full-time matriculated graduate/professional students (841 women), 487 part-time matriculated graduate/professional students (286 women). *Enrollment by degree level:* 1,367 master's, 580 doctoral, 34 other advanced degrees. *Graduate faculty:* 361 full-time (156 women), 208 part-time/adjunct (88 women). *Graduate housing:* On-campus housing not available. *Student services:* Campus employment opportunities, career counseling, exercise/wellness program, free psychological counseling, grant writing training, international student services, low-cost health insurance, multicultural affairs office, services for students with disabilities, teacher training, writing training. *Library facilities:* Brandeis Library plus 1 other. *Collection:* Books: 1 million (physical), 1.1 million (digital/electronic); Serial titles: 11,942 (physical), 49,626 (digital/electronic); Databases: 641. Students can reserve study rooms.

**Computer facilities:** Computer purchase and lease plans are available. 130 computers available on campus for general student use. A campuswide network can be accessed from student residence rooms and from off campus. Online class registration, educational software are available.
Website: http://www.brandeis.edu/

**General Application Contact:** Emily Goldberg, Department Coordinator, 781-736-3410, E-mail: gradschool@brandeis.edu.

**GRADUATE UNITS**

**Brandeis International Business School** Students: 517 full-time (284 women), 1 part-time (0 women); includes 17 minority (3 Black or African American, non-Hispanic/Latino; 2 American Indian or Alaska Native, non-Hispanic/Latino; 5 Asian, non-Hispanic/Latino; 5 Hispanic/Latino; 2 Two or more races, non-Hispanic/Latino), 476 international. Average age 25. 2,438 applicants, 49% accepted, 265 enrolled. *Faculty:* 43 full-time (17 women), 38 part-time/adjunct (9 women). Expenses: Contact institution. *Financial support:* In 2019–20, 141 students received support. Health care benefits and scholarships (averaging $31,449 annually) available. Financial award application deadline: 4/15. In 2019, 224 master's, 3 doctorates awarded. *Application deadline:* For fall admission, 11/1 for domestic students, 11/1 priority date for international students; for winter admission, 1/15 for domestic students, 1/15 priority date for international students; for spring admission, 3/15 for domestic students, 3/15 priority date for international students; for summer admission, 4/15 for domestic and international students. *Application fee:* $100. Electronic applications accepted. *Application Contact:* Kelly Sugrue, Assistant Dean of Admissions, 781-736-2252, Fax: 781-736-2263, E-mail: globaladmissions@brandeis.edu. *Dean,* Kathryn Graddy, 781-736-8616, E-mail: kgraddy@brandeis.edu.

**Graduate School of Arts and Sciences** Students: 764 full-time (384 women), 73 part-time (53 women); includes 136 minority (15 Black or African American, non-Hispanic/Latino; 2 American Indian or Alaska Native, non-Hispanic/Latino; 47 Asian, non-Hispanic/Latino; 50 Hispanic/Latino; 22 Two or more races, non-Hispanic/Latino), 270 international. Average age 28. 2,902 applicants, 30% accepted, 298 enrolled. *Faculty:* 381 full-time (173 women), 171 part-time/adjunct (80 women). Expenses: Contact institution. *Financial support:* Fellowships with full and partial tuition reimbursements, research assistantships with full and partial tuition reimbursements, teaching assistantships with partial tuition reimbursements, and scholarships/grants available. Support available to part-time students. In 2019, 214 master's, 60 doctorates awarded. *Program availability:* Part-time. *Application deadline:* Applications are processed on a rolling basis. *Application fee:* $75. Electronic applications accepted. *Application Contact:* Emily Goldberg, Department Coordinator, 781-736-3410, Fax: 781-736-3412, E-mail: gradschool@brandeis.edu. *Dean,* Dr. Eric Chasalow, 781-736-3410, Fax: 781-736-3412, E-mail: gradschool@brandeis.edu.

**The Heller School for Social Policy and Management** *Program availability:* Part-time. Electronic applications accepted.

**Rabb School of Continuing Studies, Division of Graduate Professional Studies** *Program availability:* Part-time-only. Electronic applications accepted.

## BRANDMAN UNIVERSITY, Irvine, CA 92618

**General Information** Independent, coed, comprehensive institution.

**GRADUATE UNITS**

**Marybelle and S. Paul Musco School of Nursing and Health Professions**

**School of Arts and Sciences**

**School of Business and Professional Studies**

**School of Education**

## BRANDON UNIVERSITY, Brandon, MB R7A 6A9, Canada

**General Information** Province-supported, coed, comprehensive institution. *Graduate housing:* Room and/or apartments available on a first-come, first-served basis to single students; on-campus housing not available to married students.

**GRADUATE UNITS**

**Department of Rural Development** Electronic applications accepted.

**Faculty of Education**

**School of Music** *Program availability:* Part-time. Electronic applications accepted.

## BRENAU UNIVERSITY, Gainesville, GA 30501

**General Information** Independent, coed, primarily women, comprehensive institution. *Enrollment:* 2,817 graduate, professional, and undergraduate students; 443 full-time matriculated graduate/professional students (344 women), 621 part-time matriculated graduate/professional students (521 women). *Enrollment by degree level:* 811 master's, 180 doctoral, 73 other advanced degrees. *Graduate faculty:* 70 full-time (50 women), 60 part-time/adjunct (43 women). *Tuition:* Full-time $7339.65; part-time $3685.36 per year. *Required fees:* $740 per semester. Tuition and fees vary according to course load, degree level and program. *Graduate housing:* Room and/or apartments available on a first-come, first-served basis to single students; on-campus housing not available to married students. Typical cost: $12,500 (including board). *Student services:* Campus employment opportunities, career counseling, child daycare facilities, exercise/wellness program, international student services, services for students with disabilities. *Library facilities:* Brenau Trustee Library. *Collection:* Books: 82,519 (physical), 647,881 (digital/electronic); Serial titles: 178 (physical), 87,285 (digital/electronic); Databases: 167. Weekly public service hours: 76; students can reserve study rooms.

**Computer facilities:** 157 computers available on campus for general student use. A campuswide network can be accessed from student residence rooms and from off campus. Online class registration is available.
Website: http://www.brenau.edu/

**General Application Contact:** Gale Starich, Dean of Graduate Admissions, 678-707-5016, E-mail: gstarich@brenau.edu.

**GRADUATE UNITS**

**Sydney O. Smith Graduate School** Students: 443 full-time (344 women), 621 part-time (521 women); includes 485 minority (368 Black or African American, non-Hispanic/Latino; 4 American Indian or Alaska Native, non-Hispanic/Latino; 30 Asian, non-Hispanic/Latino; 63 Hispanic/Latino; 3 Native Hawaiian or other Pacific Islander, non-Hispanic/Latino; 17 Two or more races, non-Hispanic/Latino), 11 international. Average age 33. Expenses: Contact institution. *Financial support:* In 2019–20, 21 students received support. Scholarships/grants available. Financial award applicants required to submit FAFSA. *Application Contact:* Nathan Goss, Assistant Vice President for Recruitment, 770-534-6162, E-mail: ngoss@brenau.edu. *Dean,* Dr. Gale Starich, 770-718-5305.

***College of Business & Communication*** Students: 53 full-time (38 women), 361 part-time (274 women); includes 240 minority (209 Black or African American, non-Hispanic/Latino; 2 American Indian or Alaska Native, non-Hispanic/Latino; 6 Asian, non-Hispanic/Latino; 21 Hispanic/Latino; 2 Two or more races, non-Hispanic/Latino), 7 international. Average age 36. 211 applicants, 64% accepted, 90 enrolled. *Faculty:* 17 full-time (7 women), 31 part-time/adjunct (15 women). Expenses: Contact institution. *Financial support:* In 2019–20, 7 students received support. Scholarships/grants available. Financial award applicants required to submit FAFSA. In 2019, 158 master's awarded. *Program availability:* Part-time, evening/weekend, 100% online. *Application deadline:* Applications are processed on a rolling basis. *Application fee:* $35. Electronic applications accepted. *Application Contact:* Nathan Goss, Assistant Vice President for Recruitment, 770-534-6162, E-mail: ngoss@brenau.edu. *Dean,* Dr. Suzanne Erickson, 770-531-3174, Fax: 770-537-4701, E-mail: serickson@brenau.edu.

***College of Education*** Students: 68 full-time (63 women), 45 part-time (44 women); includes 59 minority (54 Black or African American, non-Hispanic/Latino; 4 Hispanic/Latino; 1 Native Hawaiian or other Pacific Islander, non-Hispanic/Latino), 1 international. Average age 38. 206 applicants, 26% accepted, 48 enrolled. *Faculty:* 13 full-time (11 women), 37 part-time/adjunct (31 women). Expenses: Contact institution. *Financial support:* Scholarships/grants available. Support available to part-time students. Financial award applicants required to submit FAFSA. In 2019, 31 master's, 6 other advanced degrees awarded. *Program availability:* Evening/weekend, 100% online, blended/hybrid learning. *Application deadline:* Applications are processed on a rolling basis. *Application fee:* $35. Electronic applications accepted. *Application Contact:* Nathan Goss, Assistant Vice President for Recruitment, 770-534-6162, E-mail: ngoss@brenau.edu. *Dean,* Dr. Eugene Williams, 770-531-3172, Fax: 770-718-5329, E-mail: ewilliams4@brenau.edu.

***College of Fine Arts and Humanities*** Students: 1 (woman) full-time, 6 part-time (all women); includes 3 minority (1 Black or African American, non-Hispanic/Latino; 2 Hispanic/Latino). Average age 37. 8 applicants, 50% accepted, 1 enrolled. *Faculty:* 3 full-time (2 women). Expenses: Contact institution. *Financial support:* Applicants required to submit FAFSA. In 2019, 10 master's awarded. *Program availability:* Part-time, evening/weekend. *Application deadline:* Applications are processed on a rolling basis. *Application fee:* $35. Electronic applications accepted. *Application Contact:* Nathan Goss, Assistant Vice President for Recruitment, 770-534-6162, Fax: 770-718-5338. *Dean, College of Fine Arts & Humanities,* Dr. Andrea Birch, 770-718-5325, E-mail: abirch@brenau.edu.

***Ivester College of Health Sciences*** Students: 321 full-time (242 women), 209 part-time (197 women); includes 177 minority (104 Black or African American, non-Hispanic/Latino; 2 American Indian or Alaska Native, non-Hispanic/Latino; 24 Asian, non-Hispanic/Latino; 36 Hispanic/Latino; 2 Native Hawaiian or other Pacific Islander, non-Hispanic/Latino; 9 Two or more races, non-Hispanic/Latino), 3 international. Average age 29. 517 applicants, 47% accepted, 110 enrolled. *Faculty:* 34 full-time (26 women), 11 part-time/adjunct (10 women). Expenses: Contact institution. *Financial support:* In 2019–20, 11 students received support. Scholarships/grants available. Financial award applicants required to submit FAFSA. In 2019, 174 master's awarded. *Program availability:* Part-time, evening/weekend, 100% online, blended/hybrid learning. *Application deadline:* Applications are processed on a rolling basis. *Application fee:* $35. Electronic applications accepted. *Application Contact:* Nathan Goss, Assistant Vice President for Recruitment, 770-534-6162, E-mail: ngoss@brenau.edu. *Dean,* Dr. Gale Starich, 777-718-5305, Fax: 770-297-5929, E-mail: gstarich@brenau.edu.

## BRESCIA UNIVERSITY, Owensboro, KY 42301-3023

**General Information** Independent-religious, coed, comprehensive institution. *Graduate housing:* Room and/or apartments available on a first-come, first-served basis to single students; on-campus housing not available to married students.

**GRADUATE UNITS**

**Program in Business Administration** *Program availability:* Part-time, evening/weekend. Electronic applications accepted.

**Program in Management** *Program availability:* Part-time, evening/weekend.

**Program in Social Work** *Program availability:* Online learning. Electronic applications accepted.

**Program in Teacher Leadership** *Program availability:* Part-time, evening/weekend. Electronic applications accepted.

## BRIAR CLIFF UNIVERSITY, Sioux City, IA 51104-0100

**General Information** Independent-religious, coed, comprehensive institution. *Graduate housing:* Room and/or apartments available on a first-come, first-served basis to single students; on-campus housing not available to married students. Housing application deadline: 6/1.

**GRADUATE UNITS**

**Graduate Nursing Programs** *Program availability:* Part-time, online only, 100% online, blended/hybrid learning. Electronic applications accepted.

## BRIDGEWATER COLLEGE, Bridgewater, VA 22812-1599

**General Information** Independent-religious, coed, comprehensive institution.

**GRADUATE UNITS**

**Program in Athletic Training** Electronic applications accepted.

## BRIDGEWATER STATE UNIVERSITY, Bridgewater, MA 02325

**General Information** State-supported, coed, comprehensive institution. CGS member. *Graduate housing:* On-campus housing not available.

**GRADUATE UNITS**

**College of Graduate Studies** *Program availability:* Part-time, evening/weekend.

***Bartlett College of Science and Mathematics***

***College of Education and Allied Studies*** *Program availability:* Part-time, evening/weekend.

***College of Humanities and Social Sciences*** *Program availability:* Part-time, evening/weekend.

***Ricciardi College of Business*** *Program availability:* Part-time, evening/weekend.

## BRIERCREST SEMINARY, Caronport, SK S0H 0S0, Canada

**General Information** Independent-religious, coed, graduate-only institution. *Graduate housing:* Rooms and/or apartments guaranteed to single students and available on a first-come, first-served basis to married students.

**GRADUATE UNITS**

**Graduate Programs** *Program availability:* Part-time.

## BRIGHAM YOUNG UNIVERSITY, Provo, UT 84602-1001

**General Information** Independent-religious, coed, university. CGS member. *Graduate housing:* Rooms and/or apartments available on a first-come, first-served basis to single and married students. Housing application deadline: 2/1.

**GRADUATE UNITS**

**Graduate Studies** Students: 1,411 full-time (627 women), 303 part-time (158 women); includes 308 minority (19 Black or African American, non-Hispanic/Latino; 39 American Indian or Alaska Native, non-Hispanic/Latino; 126 Asian, non-Hispanic/Latino; 80 Hispanic/Latino; 15 Native Hawaiian or other Pacific Islander, non-Hispanic/Latino; 29 Two or more races, non-Hispanic/Latino), 146 international. Average age 31. 1,433 applicants, 48% accepted, 577 enrolled. *Faculty:* 826 full-time (163 women), 43 part-time/adjunct (17 women). Expenses: Contact institution. *Financial support:* In 2019–20, 1,509 students received support, including 127 fellowships with full and partial tuition reimbursements available (averaging $137,943 per year), 1,049 research assistantships with full and partial tuition reimbursements available (averaging $261,921 per year), 722 teaching assistantships with full and partial tuition reimbursements available (averaging $234,331 per year); career-related internships or fieldwork, institutionally sponsored loans, scholarships/grants, health care benefits, and tuition waivers (full and partial) also available. Support available to part-time students. Financial award applicants required to submit FAFSA. *Program availability:* Part-time, evening/weekend. *Application deadline:* For fall admission, 12/1 priority date for domestic and international students; for winter admission, 6/30 priority date for domestic and international students; for spring admission, 1/15 priority date for domestic and international students; for summer admission, 2/1 for domestic and international students. Applications are processed on a rolling basis. *Application fee:* $50. Electronic applications accepted. *Application Contact:* Logan Gillette, Director of Graduate Admissions and Recruitment, 801-422-7308, E-mail: logangillette@byu.edu. *Dean,* Dr. Logan Gillette, 801-422-7308, Fax: 801-422-0089, E-mail: logan_gillette@byu.edu.

***BYU Marriott School of Business*** Students: 264 full-time (140 women), 186 part-time (79 women); includes 46 minority (5 Black or African American, non-Hispanic/Latino; 1 American Indian or Alaska Native, non-Hispanic/Latino; 13 Asian, non-Hispanic/Latino; 17 Hispanic/Latino; 10 Native Hawaiian or other Pacific Islander, non-Hispanic/Latino). Average age 32. 488 applicants, 66% accepted, 265 enrolled. *Faculty:* 113 full-time (15 women), 33 part-time/adjunct (2 women). Expenses: Contact institution. *Financial support:* In 2019–20, 12 students received support, including 15 research assistantships (averaging $3,000 per year), 25 teaching assistantships (averaging $3,000 per year); career-related internships or fieldwork, institutionally sponsored loans, and scholarships/grants also available. Financial award applicants required to submit FAFSA. In 2019, 280 master's awarded. *Program availability:* Part-time, evening/weekend. *Application fee:* $50. Electronic applications accepted. *Application Contact:* Logan Gillette, Director of Graduate Admissions and Recruitment, 801-422-7308, E-mail: logangillette@byu.edu. *Dean,* Dr. Lee Perry, 801-422-4121, Fax: 801-422-4501.

***College of Family, Home, and Social Sciences*** Students: 183 full-time (131 women); includes 31 minority (5 Black or African American, non-Hispanic/Latino; 3 American Indian or Alaska Native, non-Hispanic/Latino; 11 Asian, non-Hispanic/Latino; 7 Hispanic/Latino; 2 Native Hawaiian or other Pacific Islander, non-Hispanic/Latino; 3 Two or more races, non-Hispanic/Latino), 6 international. Average age 27. 356 applicants, 31% accepted, 82 enrolled. *Faculty:* 95 full-time (26 women), 20 part-time/adjunct (10 women). Expenses: Contact institution. *Financial support:* In 2019–20, 183 students received support, including 86 fellowships with full and partial tuition reimbursements available (averaging $4,519 per year), 125 research assistantships with full and partial tuition reimbursements available (averaging $62,884 per year), 40 teaching assistantships with full and partial tuition reimbursements available (averaging $46,200 per year); career-related internships or fieldwork, institutionally sponsored loans, scholarships/grants, tuition waivers (partial), unspecified assistantships, and administrative aides, paid field practicum, AmeriCorps education awards also available. Financial award application deadline: 3/27; financial award applicants required to submit FAFSA. In 2019, 70 master's, 10 doctorates awarded. *Application deadline:* For fall admission, 1/15 for domestic and international students. *Application fee:* $50. Electronic applications accepted. *Application Contact:* Adviser, 801-422-4541, Fax: 801-378-5238, E-mail: gradstudies@byu.edu. *Dean*, Dr. Benjamin M. Ogles, 801-422-2083, Fax: 801-422-2084, E-mail: ben_ogles@byu.edu.

***College of Fine Arts and Communications*** Students: 69 full-time (45 women), 38 part-time (24 women); includes 22 minority (2 Black or African American, non-Hispanic/Latino; 1 American Indian or Alaska Native, non-Hispanic/Latino; 9 Asian, non-Hispanic/Latino; 8 Hispanic/Latino; 1 Native Hawaiian or other Pacific Islander, non-Hispanic/Latino; 1 Two or more races, non-Hispanic/Latino). Average age 30. 95 applicants, 59% accepted, 48 enrolled. *Faculty:* 83 full-time (14 women). Expenses: Contact institution. *Financial support:* In 2019–20, 46 students received support, including 3 research assistantships (averaging $1,000 per year), 54 teaching assistantships with full and partial tuition reimbursements available (averaging $2,000 per year); career-related internships or fieldwork, institutionally sponsored loans, scholarships/grants, tuition waivers (partial), unspecified assistantships, and supplementary awards also available. Support available to part-time students. Financial award applicants required to submit FAFSA. In 2019, 33 master's awarded. *Application deadline:* Applications are processed on a rolling basis. *Application fee:* $50. Electronic applications accepted. *Application Contact:* Logan Gillette, Director of Graduate Admissions and Recruitment, 801-422-7308, E-mail: logangillette@byu.edu. *Dean*, Edward E. Adams, 801-422-8271, Fax: 801-422-0253, E-mail: francie_jenson@byu.edu.

***College of Humanities*** Students: 159 full-time (111 women), 21 part-time (17 women); includes 41 minority (1 Black or African American, non-Hispanic/Latino; 2 American Indian or Alaska Native, non-Hispanic/Latino; 15 Asian, non-Hispanic/Latino; 20 Hispanic/Latino; 3 Native Hawaiian or other Pacific Islander, non-Hispanic/Latino). Average age 31. 137 applicants, 66% accepted, 72 enrolled. *Faculty:* 163 full-time (45 women), 2 part-time/adjunct (0 women). Expenses: Contact institution. *Financial support:* In 2019–20, 181 students received support, including 1 fellowship with full and partial tuition reimbursement available (averaging $7,200 per year), 56 research assistantships with full and partial tuition reimbursements available (averaging $9,521 per year), 177 teaching assistantships with full and partial tuition reimbursements available (averaging $21,076 per year); career-related internships or fieldwork, institutionally sponsored loans, scholarships/grants, and student instructorships, travel money for conference presentations also available. Financial award application deadline: 2/1. In 2019, 64 master's awarded. *Application deadline:* For fall admission, 1/15 for domestic and international students. *Application fee:* $50. Electronic applications accepted. *Application Contact:* Adviser, 801-422-4541, Fax: 801-378-5238, E-mail: gradstudies@byu.edu. *Dean*, Scott J. Miller, 801-422-2779, Fax: 801-422-0308, E-mail: scott_miller@byu.edu.

***College of Life Sciences*** Students: 198 full-time (115 women), 54 part-time (11 women); includes 64 minority (3 Black or African American, non-Hispanic/Latino; 27 American Indian or Alaska Native, non-Hispanic/Latino; 11 Asian, non-Hispanic/Latino; 16 Hispanic/Latino; 6 Native Hawaiian or other Pacific Islander, non-Hispanic/Latino; 1 Two or more races, non-Hispanic/Latino), 16 international. Average age 29. 158 applicants, 64% accepted, 76 enrolled. *Faculty:* 143 full-time (35 women), 5 part-time/adjunct (2 women). Expenses: Contact institution. *Financial support:* In 2019–20, 171 students received support, including 2 fellowships with full and partial tuition reimbursements available (averaging $37,200 per year), 183 research assistantships with full and partial tuition reimbursements available (averaging $45,058 per year), 102 teaching assistantships with full and partial tuition reimbursements available (averaging $30,471 per year); career-related internships or fieldwork, institutionally sponsored loans, scholarships/grants, health care benefits, tuition waivers (full and partial), and unspecified assistantships also available. Financial award application deadline: 2/1; financial award applicants required to submit FAFSA. In 2019, 55 master's, 13 doctorates awarded. *Application deadline:* For fall admission, 2/1 for domestic and international students; for winter admission, 2/1 for international students. *Application fee:* $50. Electronic applications accepted. *Application Contact:* Sue Pratley, Application Contact, 801-422-3963, Fax: 801-422-0050, E-mail: sue_pratley@byu.edu. *Dean*, James P. Porter, 801-422-3963, Fax: 801-422-0050, E-mail: james_porter@byu.edu.

***College of Nursing*** Students: 30 full-time (26 women); includes 5 minority (1 Black or African American, non-Hispanic/Latino; 1 American Indian or Alaska Native, non-Hispanic/Latino; 2 Asian, non-Hispanic/Latino; 1 Hispanic/Latino), 1 international. Average age 33. 30 applicants, 50% accepted, 15 enrolled. *Faculty:* 16 full-time (9 women). Expenses: Contact institution. *Financial support:* In 2019–20, 30 students received support, including 1 research assistantship (averaging $6,000 per year); teaching assistantships, career-related internships or fieldwork, and scholarships/grants also available. Financial award application deadline: 8/13; financial award applicants required to submit FAFSA. In 2019, 15 master's awarded. *Application deadline:* For spring admission, 12/1 for domestic and international students. *Application fee:* $50. Electronic applications accepted. *Application Contact:* Cherie Top, Graduate Secretary, 801-422-4142, Fax: 801-422-0538, E-mail: cherie-top@byu.edu. *Dean*, Dr. Beth Luthy, 801-422-6683, Fax: 801-422-0536, E-mail: beth-luthy@byu.edu.

***College of Physical and Mathematical Sciences*** Students: 331 full-time (87 women), 46 part-time (15 women); includes 91 minority (5 Black or African American, non-Hispanic/Latino; 61 Asian, non-Hispanic/Latino; 13 Hispanic/Latino; 1 Native Hawaiian or other Pacific Islander, non-Hispanic/Latino; 11 Two or more races, non-Hispanic/Latino), 57 international. Average age 28. 208 applicants, 59% accepted, 94 enrolled. *Faculty:* 162 full-time (17 women), 2 part-time/adjunct (0 women). Expenses: Contact institution. *Financial support:* In 2019–20, 251 students received support, including 22 fellowships with full and partial tuition reimbursements available (averaging $73,000 per year), 187 research assistantships with full and partial tuition reimbursements available (averaging $94,832 per year), 176 teaching assistantships with full and partial tuition reimbursements available (averaging $93,894 per year); career-related internships or fieldwork, institutionally sponsored loans, scholarships/grants, health care benefits, tuition waivers (full and partial), and unspecified assistantships also available. Support available to part-time students. Financial award applicants required to submit CSS PROFILE or FAFSA. In 2019, 73 master's, 34 doctorates awarded. *Program availability:* Part-time. *Application deadline:* For fall admission, 2/1 for domestic and international students. Applications are processed on a rolling basis. *Application fee:* $50. Electronic applications accepted. *Application Contact:* Michelle Prososki, Executive Secretary, 801-422-2290, E-mail: michelle_prososki@byu.edu. *Dean*, Dr. Shane Reese, 801-422-9250, E-mail: shane_reese@byu.edu.

***David O. McKay School of Education*** Students: 141 full-time (101 women), 144 part-time (91 women); includes 39 minority (3 Black or African American, non-Hispanic/Latino; 6 American Indian or Alaska Native, non-Hispanic/Latino; 14 Asian, non-Hispanic/Latino; 14 Hispanic/Latino; 2 Native Hawaiian or other Pacific Islander, non-Hispanic/Latino), 8 international. Average age 34. 288 applicants, 44% accepted, 119 enrolled. *Faculty:* 76 full-time (22 women), 10 part-time/adjunct (2 women). Expenses: Contact institution. *Financial support:* In 2019–20, 217 students received support, including 135 research assistantships (averaging $29,900 per year), 37 teaching assistantships (averaging $26,950 per year); career-related internships or fieldwork, institutionally sponsored loans, scholarships/grants, health care benefits, tuition waivers, and unspecified assistantships also available. Support available to part-time students. Financial award applicants required to submit FAFSA. In 2019, 55 master's, 13 doctorates, 18 other advanced degrees awarded. *Application fee:* $50. Electronic applications accepted. *Application Contact:* Brandan Beerli, Director, Education Student Services, 801-422-9199, Fax: 801-422-0195. *Dean*, Dr. Mary Anne Prater, 801-422-1592, Fax: 801-422-0200, E-mail: prater@byu.edu.

***Ira A. Fulton College of Engineering*** Students: 330 full-time (37 women); includes 20 minority (5 Asian, non-Hispanic/Latino; 2 Hispanic/Latino; 13 Two or more races, non-Hispanic/Latino), 59 international. Average age 28. 191 applicants, 45% accepted, 86 enrolled. *Faculty:* 104 full-time (4 women), 2 part-time/adjunct (1 woman). Expenses: Contact institution. *Financial support:* In 2019–20, 486 students received support, including 16 fellowships with full and partial tuition reimbursements available (averaging $23,224 per year), 360 research assistantships with full and partial tuition reimbursements available (averaging $18,726 per year), 136 teaching assistantships with full and partial tuition reimbursements available (averaging $13,740 per year); scholarships/grants and health care benefits also available. Financial award application deadline: 1/1; financial award applicants required to submit FAFSA. In 2019, 102 master's, 24 doctorates awarded. *Application deadline:* For fall admission, 1/15 for domestic and international students; for winter admission, 6/15 for domestic and international students; for spring admission, 2/5 for domestic and international students; for summer admission, 2/5 for domestic and international students. *Application fee:* $50. Electronic applications accepted. *Application Contact:* Claire A. DeWitt, Adviser, 801-422-4541, Fax: 801-422-0270, E-mail: gradstudies@byu.edu. *Dean*, Dr. Michael A. Jensen, 801-422-5736, Fax: 801-422-0218, E-mail: college@et.byu.edu.

***J. Reuben Clark Law School*** Students: 336 full-time (143 women); includes 54 minority (5 Black or African American, non-Hispanic/Latino; 3 American Indian or Alaska Native, non-Hispanic/Latino; 7 Asian, non-Hispanic/Latino; 18 Hispanic/Latino; 4 Native Hawaiian or other Pacific Islander, non-Hispanic/Latino; 17 Two or more races, non-Hispanic/Latino), 7 international. Average age 28. 458 applicants, 41% accepted, 119 enrolled. *Faculty:* 31 full-time (12 women), 26 part-time/adjunct (6 women). Expenses: Contact institution. *Financial support:* In 2019–20, 298 students received support, including 6 fellowships (averaging $40,000 per year); scholarships/grants and Student employment also available. Financial award application deadline: 6/30; financial award applicants required to submit FAFSA. In 2019, 5 master's, 138 doctorates awarded. *Application deadline:* For fall admission, 6/30 for domestic and international students. Applications are processed on a rolling basis. Electronic applications accepted. *Application Contact:* Jillyn Comstock, Admissions Coordinator, 801-422-4356, Fax: 801-422-0389, E-mail: comstockj@law.byu.edu. *Dean*, D. Gordon Smith, 801-422-6383, Fax: 801-422-0389, E-mail: smithg@law.byu.edu.

## BRITE DIVINITY SCHOOL, Fort Worth, TX 76109

**General Information** Independent-religious, coed, graduate-only institution. *Graduate housing:* Rooms and/or apartments available on a first-come, first-served basis to single and married students. Housing application deadline: 4/1.

**GRADUATE UNITS**

**Graduate and Professional Programs** *Program availability:* Part-time, evening/weekend.

## BROADVIEW UNIVERSITY–WEST JORDAN, West Jordan, UT 84088

**General Information** Proprietary, coed, comprehensive institution.

**GRADUATE UNITS**

**Graduate Programs**

## BROCK UNIVERSITY, St. Catharines, ON L2S 3A1, Canada

**General Information** Province-supported, coed, university. *Graduate housing:* Room and/or apartments available on a first-come, first-served basis to single students; on-campus housing not available to married students. *Research affiliation:* Fly Fishing Canada/Trout Unlimited Canada (fisheries management), Henry Ford Health Centre (cancer epidemiology), Registered Nurses Association of Ontario (nursing best practices), Canadian Honey Council (agriculture, therapeutic product development).

**GRADUATE UNITS**

**Faculty of Graduate Studies** *Program availability:* Part-time, evening/weekend. Electronic applications accepted.

***Faculty of Applied Health Sciences*** Electronic applications accepted.

***Faculty of Business*** *Program availability:* Part-time. Electronic applications accepted.

***Faculty of Education*** *Program availability:* Part-time, evening/weekend. Electronic applications accepted.

***Faculty of Humanities*** *Program availability:* Part-time. Electronic applications accepted.

***Faculty of Mathematics and Science*** *Program availability:* Part-time. Electronic applications accepted.

***Faculty of Social Sciences*** *Program availability:* Part-time. Electronic applications accepted.

## BROOKLINE COLLEGE - PHOENIX CAMPUS, Phoenix, AZ 85021

**General Information** Proprietary, coed, comprehensive institution.

**GRADUATE UNITS**

**Nursing Programs** *Program availability:* Part-time, online learning.

## BROOKLYN COLLEGE OF THE CITY UNIVERSITY OF NEW YORK, Brooklyn, NY 11210-2889

**General Information** State and locally supported, coed, comprehensive institution. *Graduate housing:* Room and/or apartments available on a first-come, first-served basis to single students; on-campus housing not available to married students. *Research affiliation:* Biothera Inc. (biology), Silicon Valley Community Foundation (computer and information science), Jessie Smith Noyes Foundation (sustainability), Sloan-Kettering Memorial Cancer Center (health/biology), Community Health Care Association of New York State (health and nutrition sciences), Welfare Research Inc. (education).

**GRADUATE UNITS**

**School of Business** *Program availability:* Part-time, evening/weekend. Electronic applications accepted.

**School of Education** *Program availability:* Part-time, evening/weekend. Electronic applications accepted.

**School of Humanities and Social Sciences** *Program availability:* Part-time, evening/weekend. Electronic applications accepted.

**School of Natural and Behavioral Sciences** *Program availability:* Part-time, evening/weekend. Electronic applications accepted.

**School of Visual, Media and Performing Arts** *Program availability:* Part-time, evening/weekend. Electronic applications accepted.

***Conservatory of Music*** *Program availability:* Part-time. Electronic applications accepted.

## BROOKLYN LAW SCHOOL, Brooklyn, NY 11201-3798

**General Information** Independent, coed, graduate-only institution. *Graduate housing:* Rooms and/or apartments available to single students and guaranteed to married students. Housing application deadline: 5/1.

**GRADUATE UNITS**

**Graduate and Professional Programs** *Program availability:* Part-time, evening/weekend. Electronic applications accepted.

## BROWN UNIVERSITY, Providence, RI 02912

**General Information** Independent, coed, university. CGS member. *Graduate housing:* Room and/or apartments available to single students; on-campus housing not available to married students. *Research affiliation:* Woods Hole Oceanographic Institution-Marine Biological Laboratory, Rhode Island Reactor, International Center for Numismatic Studies, Meeting Street School.

**GRADUATE UNITS**

**Graduate School** *Program availability:* Part-time.

***A. Alfred Taubman Center for Public Policy and American Institutions***

***Division of Applied Mathematics***

***Division of Biology and Medicine*** *Program availability:* Part-time. Electronic applications accepted.

***Joukowsky Institute for Archaeology and the Ancient World***

***School of Engineering***

**National Institutes of Health Sponsored Programs**

## BRYAN COLLEGE, Dayton, TN 37321

**General Information** Independent-religious, coed, comprehensive institution. *Enrollment:* 1,489 graduate, professional, and undergraduate students; 192 full-time matriculated graduate/professional students (107 women), 35 part-time matriculated graduate/professional students (19 women). *Enrollment by degree level:* 227 master's. *Graduate faculty:* 1 full-time (0 women), 17 part-time/adjunct (8 women). *Tuition:* Full-time $10,710; part-time $595 per credit hour. *Required fees:* $65 per term. One-time fee: $250. Tuition and fees vary according to program. *Graduate housing:* On-campus housing not available. *Student services:* Career counseling, free psychological counseling, services for students with disabilities. *Library facilities:* Bryan College Library. *Collection:* Books: 64,993 (physical), 350,219 (digital/electronic); Serial titles: 48 (physical), 85,938 (digital/electronic). Weekly public service hours: 83; students can reserve study rooms.

**Computer facilities:** 109 computers available on campus for general student use. A campuswide network can be accessed. Online class registration, campus-wide wi-fi are available.
Website: http://www.bryan.edu/

**General Application Contact:** Mandi K. Sullivan, Director of Academic Programs, 423-634-9880, E-mail: mandi.sullivan@bryan.edu.

**GRADUATE UNITS**

**MBA Program** Students: 137 full-time (72 women), 26 part-time (11 women). 70 applicants, 100% accepted, 70 enrolled. *Faculty:* 1 full-time (0 women), 13 part-time/adjunct (5 women). Expenses: Contact institution. *Financial support:* Scholarships/grants available. Financial award applicants required to submit FAFSA. In 2019, 28 master's awarded. *Program availability:* Part-time, evening/weekend, online only, 100% online. *Application deadline:* For fall admission, 9/1 for domestic and international students; for winter admission, 11/15 for domestic and international students; for spring admission, 2/1 for domestic and international students; for summer admission, 6/1 for domestic and international students. Applications are processed on a rolling basis. Electronic applications accepted. *Application Contact:* Mandi K Sullivan, Director of Academic Programs, 423-664-9880, E-mail: mandi.sullivan@bryan.edu. *Dean of Adult and Graduate Studies*, Dr. Adina Scruggs, 423-775-7121, E-mail: adina.scruggs@bryan.edu.

**Program in Master of Art in Human Services (MAHS)** Students: 1 (woman) full-time, 3 part-time (all women). 3 applicants, 100% accepted, 3 enrolled. *Faculty:* 2 part-time/adjunct (1 woman). Expenses: Contact institution. *Financial support:* Scholarships/grants available. Financial award applicants required to submit FAFSA. *Program availability:* Part-time, evening/weekend, online only, 100% online. *Application deadline:* Applications are processed on a rolling basis. Electronic applications accepted. *Application Contact:* Mandi K. Sullivan, Director of Academic Programs, 423-634-9880, E-mail: mandi.sullivan@bryan.edu. *Dean School of Professional Studies*, Dr. Adina Scruggs, 423-775-7121, E-mail: adina.scruggs@bryan.edu.

**Program in Master of Education (MEd)** Students: 53 full-time (41 women), 7 part-time (all women). 10 applicants, 100% accepted, 10 enrolled. *Faculty:* 4 part-time/adjunct (all women). Expenses: Contact institution. *Financial support:* Scholarships/grants available. Financial award applicants required to submit FAFSA. *Program availability:* Part-time, evening/weekend, online only, 100% online. *Application deadline:* Applications are processed on a rolling basis. Electronic applications accepted. *Application Contact:* Mandi K. Sullivan, Director of Academic Programs, 423-634-9880, E-mail: mandi.sullivan@bryan.edu. *Dean School of Professional Studies*, Dr. Adina Scruggs, 423-775-7121, E-mail: adina.scruggs@bryan.edu.

## BRYAN COLLEGE OF HEALTH SCIENCES, Lincoln, NE 68506

**General Information** Independent, coed, comprehensive institution. CGS member.

**GRADUATE UNITS**

**School of Nurse Anesthesia**

## BRYANT UNIVERSITY, Smithfield, RI 02917

**General Information** Independent, coed, comprehensive institution. *Enrollment:* 3,640 graduate, professional, and undergraduate students; 202 full-time matriculated graduate/professional students (125 women), 178 part-time matriculated graduate/professional students (98 women). *Enrollment by degree level:* 380 master's. *Graduate faculty:* 38 full-time (12 women), 12 part-time/adjunct (7 women). *Tuition:* Full-time $40,428; part-time $1118 per credit hour. Part-time tuition and fees vary according to course load, degree level and program. *Graduate housing:* Room and/or apartments available on a first-come, first-served basis to single students; on-campus housing not available to married students. Typical cost: $11,436 per year ($17,740 including board). Room and board charges vary according to board plan and housing facility selected. Housing application deadline: 8/1. *Student services:* Campus employment opportunities, campus safety program, career counseling, exercise/wellness program, free psychological counseling, international student services, low-cost health insurance, multicultural affairs office, services for students with disabilities, teacher training, writing training. *Library facilities:* Douglas and Judith Krupp Library plus 1 other. *Collection:* Books: 134,668 (physical), 351,966 (digital/electronic); Serial titles: 5,018 (physical), 43,931 (digital/electronic); Databases: 68. Weekly public service hours: 110; students can reserve study rooms.

**Computer facilities:** 526 computers available on campus for general student use. A campuswide network can be accessed. Online class registration, e-mail, online library, student Web hosts are available.
Website: http://www.bryant.edu/

**General Application Contact:** Jamie Grenon, Director, Graduate Programs, 401-232-6707, E-mail: graduateprograms@bryant.edu.

**GRADUATE UNITS**

**College of Arts and Sciences** *Program availability:* Part-time, evening/weekend. Electronic applications accepted.

**Graduate School of Business** *Program availability:* Part-time, evening/weekend, 100% online. Electronic applications accepted.

**School of Health Sciences** Electronic applications accepted.

## BRYAN UNIVERSITY, Springfield, MO 65804

**General Information** Proprietary, coed, comprehensive institution.

**GRADUATE UNITS**

**Program in Business Administration** *Program availability:* Online learning.

## BRYN ATHYN COLLEGE OF THE NEW CHURCH, Bryn Athyn, PA 19009-0717

**General Information** Independent-religious, coed, comprehensive institution. *Enrollment:* 318 graduate, professional, and undergraduate students; 7 full-time matriculated graduate/professional students, 19 part-time matriculated graduate/professional students (13 women). *Enrollment by degree level:* 26 master's. *Graduate housing:* Room and/or apartments available on a first-come, first-served basis to single students; on-campus housing not available to married students. Typical cost: $1000 per year ($12,606 including board). Housing application deadline: 1/31. *Student services:* Campus employment opportunities, career counseling, free psychological counseling, international student services, low-cost health insurance, teacher training. *Library facilities:* Swedenborg Library plus 1 other. *Collection:* Books: 70,742 (physical), 252 (digital/electronic); Serial titles: 834 (physical), 74 (digital/electronic); Databases: 13.

**Computer facilities:** 18 computers available on campus for general student use. A campuswide network can be accessed. Online class registration is available.
Website: http://www.brynathyn.edu/

**General Application Contact:** Andrew Dibb, Dean, 267-502-2640, E-mail: andrew.dibb@ancts.org.

**GRADUATE UNITS**

**Academy of the New Church Theological School** Students: 7 full-time (0 women), 19 part-time (13 women), 10 international. Average age 37. 26 applicants, 100% accepted, 9 enrolled. *Faculty:* 12. Expenses: Contact institution. *Financial support:* In 2019–20, 7 students received support. Career-related internships or fieldwork, Federal Work-Study, and institutionally sponsored loans available. Financial award application deadline: 1/31. In 2019, 6 master's awarded. *Program availability:* Part-time, online learning. *Application deadline:* For fall admission, 1/31 for domestic students. Applications are processed on a rolling basis. *Application Contact:* Andrew Dibb, Dean, 267-502-2640, E-mail: andrew.dibb@ancts.org. *Dean*, Andrew Dibb, 267-502-2640, E-mail: andrew.dibb@ancts.org.

## BRYN MAWR COLLEGE, Bryn Mawr, PA 19010-2899

**General Information** Independent, Undergraduate: women only; graduate: coed, comprehensive institution. CGS member. *Graduate housing:* On-campus housing not available.

**GRADUATE UNITS**

**Graduate School of Arts and Sciences** *Program availability:* Part-time. Electronic applications accepted.

**Graduate School of Social Work and Social Research** *Program availability:* Part-time, evening/weekend. Electronic applications accepted.

## BUCKNELL UNIVERSITY, Lewisburg, PA 17837

**General Information** Independent, coed, comprehensive institution. CGS member. *Graduate housing:* On-campus housing not available.

**GRADUATE UNITS**

**Graduate Studies** *Program availability:* Part-time.

***College of Arts and Sciences*** *Program availability:* Part-time.

***College of Engineering*** *Program availability:* Part-time.

## BUENA VISTA UNIVERSITY, Storm Lake, IA 50588

**General Information** Independent-religious, coed, comprehensive institution. *Graduate housing:* Room and/or apartments available on a first-come, first-served basis to single students; on-campus housing not available to married students. Housing application deadline: 5/1.

**GRADUATE UNITS**

**School of Education** *Program availability:* Part-time, evening/weekend, online learning. Electronic applications accepted.

## BUFFALO STATE COLLEGE, STATE UNIVERSITY OF NEW YORK, Buffalo, NY 14222-1095

**General Information** State-supported, coed, comprehensive institution. CGS member. *Graduate housing:* Room and/or apartments available on a first-come, first-served basis to single students; on-campus housing not available to married students. Housing application deadline: 8/15. *Research affiliation:* Friends of Buffalo River, Research Institute on Addictions at the University of Buffalo, Roswell Park Memorial Institute, Hauptman-Woodward Medical Research Institute, Ecology and Environment Corporation, Phillip Morris Foundation.

**GRADUATE UNITS**

**The Graduate School** *Program availability:* Part-time, evening/weekend, online learning.

***School of Arts and Humanities*** *Program availability:* Part-time, evening/weekend.

***School of Education*** *Program availability:* Part-time, evening/weekend, online learning.

***School of Natural and Social Sciences*** *Program availability:* Part-time, evening/weekend.

***School of the Professions***

## BURRELL COLLEGE OF OSTEOPATHIC MEDICINE, Las Cruces, NM 88001

**General Information** Proprietary, coed, graduate-only institution.

**GRADUATE UNITS**

**Graduate Program**

## BUSHNELL UNIVERSITY, Eugene, OR 97401-3745

**General Information** Independent-religious, coed, comprehensive institution. *Graduate housing:* On-campus housing not available.

**GRADUATE UNITS**

**School of Business and Management** *Program availability:* Part-time, evening/weekend, online only, 100% online. Electronic applications accepted.

**School of Education and Counseling** *Program availability:* Part-time, evening/weekend, online learning. Electronic applications accepted.

## BUTLER UNIVERSITY, Indianapolis, IN 46208-3485

**General Information** Independent, coed, comprehensive institution. *Enrollment:* 5,515 graduate, professional, and undergraduate students; 436 full-time matriculated graduate/professional students (280 women), 378 part-time matriculated graduate/professional students (228 women). *Enrollment by degree level:* 540 master's, 205 doctoral, 69 other advanced degrees. *Graduate faculty:* 66 full-time (26 women), 33 part-time/adjunct (19 women). *Tuition:* Full-time $22,742; part-time $979 per credit hour. Tuition and fees vary according to course level and program. *Graduate housing:* Room and/or apartments available on a first-come, first-served basis to single students; on-campus housing not available to married students. Typical cost: $6950 per year ($14,380 including board). Room and board charges vary according to board plan, campus/location and housing facility selected. Housing application deadline: 8/1. *Student services:* Campus employment opportunities, campus safety program, career counseling, exercise/wellness program, free psychological counseling, international student services, low-cost health insurance, multicultural affairs office, services for students with disabilities. *Library facilities:* Irwin Library plus 2 others. *Collection:* Books: 175,278 (physical), 540,672 (digital/electronic); Serial titles: 5,310 (physical), 94,125 (digital/electronic); Databases: 338. Weekly public service hours: 106; students can reserve study rooms.

**Computer facilities:** Computer purchase and lease plans are available. 490 computers available on campus for general student use. A campuswide network can be accessed. Online class registration is available.
Website: http://www.butler.edu/

**General Application Contact:** Diane Dubord, Graduate Student Services Specialist, 317-940-8107, Fax: 317-940-8250, E-mail: ddubord@butler.edu.

**GRADUATE UNITS**

**College of Education** Students: 13 full-time (12 women), 168 part-time (139 women); includes 15 minority (6 Black or African American, non-Hispanic/Latino; 3 Asian, non-Hispanic/Latino; 3 Hispanic/Latino; 3 Two or more races, non-Hispanic/Latino), 1 international. Average age 35. 84 applicants, 58% accepted, 24 enrolled. *Faculty:* 8 full-time (5 women), 10 part-time/adjunct (9 women). Expenses: Contact institution. *Financial support:* In 2019–20, 54 students received support. Scholarships/grants, tuition waivers (full and partial), and unspecified assistantships available. Financial award applicants required to submit FAFSA. In 2019, 52 master's, 48 other advanced degrees awarded. *Program availability:* Evening/weekend. *Application deadline:* For fall admission, 2/1 for domestic and international students; for spring admission, 11/1 for domestic and international students; for summer admission, 4/1 for domestic and international students. Applications are processed on a rolling basis. Electronic applications accepted. *Application Contact:* Dr. Nick Abel, Chair, Graduate Graduate Learning and Teacher Teams, 317-940-9577, Fax: 317-940-6481, E-mail: nabel@butler.edu. *Dean,* Dr. Brooke Elizabeth Kandel-Ciasco, 317-940-9490, Fax: 317-940-6491, E-mail: bkandel@butler.edu.

**College of Liberal Arts and Sciences** Students: 6 full-time (2 women), 54 part-time (37 women); includes 8 minority (3 Black or African American, non-Hispanic/Latino; 3 Hispanic/Latino; 2 Two or more races, non-Hispanic/Latino), 1 international. Average age 34. 68 applicants, 60% accepted, 23 enrolled. *Faculty:* 7 full-time (4 women), 2 part-time/adjunct (1 woman). Expenses: Contact institution. *Financial support:* In 2019–20, 36 students received support. Scholarships/grants, tuition waivers (full and partial), and unspecified assistantships available. Financial award applicants required to submit FAFSA. In 2019, 11 master's awarded. *Program availability:* Part-time, evening/weekend. *Application deadline:* For fall admission, 2/15 for domestic and international students; for spring admission, 9/15 for domestic and international students. Applications are processed on a rolling basis. Electronic applications accepted. *Application Contact:* Diane Dubord, Graduate Student Services Specialist, 317-940-8107, Fax: 317-940-8250, E-mail: ddubord@butler.edu. *Chair,* Dr. Lee Albert Garver, 317-940-9859, E-mail: lgarver@butler.edu.

**College of Pharmacy and Health Sciences** Students: 358 full-time (245 women), 2 part-time (0 women); includes 42 minority (1 Black or African American, non-Hispanic/Latino; 23 Asian, non-Hispanic/Latino; 12 Hispanic/Latino; 6 Two or more races, non-Hispanic/Latino), 4 international. Average age 24. 441 applicants, 17% accepted, 76 enrolled. *Faculty:* 14 full-time (8 women). Expenses: Contact institution. *Financial support:* In 2019–20, 4 students received support. Scholarships/grants, tuition waivers (full and partial), and unspecified assistantships available. Financial award applicants required to submit FAFSA. In 2019, 77 master's, 106 doctorates awarded. *Program availability:* Part-time, evening/weekend, 100% online. *Application deadline:* For fall admission, 4/1 for domestic and international students. Electronic applications accepted. *Application Contact:* Katie Clarizio, Academic Program Coordinator, 317-940-9297, E-mail: kclarizio@butler.edu. *Dean,* Dr. Robert Soltis, 317-940-9322, E-mail: rsoltis@butler.edu.

**Jordan College of the Arts** Students: 20 full-time (9 women), 26 part-time (13 women); includes 6 minority (2 Black or African American, non-Hispanic/Latino; 1 Asian, non-Hispanic/Latino; 2 Hispanic/Latino; 1 Two or more races, non-Hispanic/Latino), 1 international. Average age 27. 43 applicants, 63% accepted, 19 enrolled. *Faculty:* 18 full-time (4 women), 12 part-time/adjunct (7 women). Expenses: Contact institution. *Financial support:* In 2019–20, 21 students received support. Scholarships/grants, tuition waivers (full and partial), and unspecified assistantships available. Financial award applicants required to submit FAFSA. In 2019, 13 master's awarded. *Program availability:* Part-time, evening/weekend, blended/hybrid learning. *Application deadline:* For fall admission, 2/1 for domestic and international students; for spring admission, 12/15 for domestic and international students; for summer admission, 4/15 for domestic and international students. Applications are processed on a rolling basis. Electronic applications accepted. *Application Contact:* Dr. Nicholas Dean Johnson, Director of Graduate Studies, 317-9409064, E-mail: ndjohns1@butler.edu. *Director - School of Music,* David Patrick Murray, 317-940-9988, Fax: 317-9409658, E-mail: dmurray@butler.edu.

**Lacy School of Business** Students: 39 full-time (12 women), 128 part-time (39 women); includes 18 minority (2 Black or African American, non-Hispanic/Latino; 1 American Indian or Alaska Native, non-Hispanic/Latino; 5 Asian, non-Hispanic/Latino; 7 Hispanic/Latino; 3 Two or more races, non-Hispanic/Latino), 8 international. Average age 31. 149 applicants, 66% accepted, 55 enrolled. *Faculty:* 19 full-time (5 women), 9 part-time/adjunct (2 women). Expenses: Contact institution. *Financial support:* In 2019–20, 17 students received support. Scholarships/grants, tuition waivers (full and partial), and unspecified assistantships available. Financial award applicants required to submit FAFSA. In 2019, 79 master's awarded. *Program availability:* Part-time, evening/weekend, 100% online, blended/hybrid learning. *Application deadline:* For fall admission, 8/1 for domestic and international students; for spring admission, 12/1 for domestic and international students; for summer admission, 4/1 for domestic and international students. Applications are processed on a rolling basis. Electronic applications accepted. *Application Contact:* Michelle Worthington, Graduate Programs Admissions Assistant, 317-940-8107, E-mail: mworthin@butler.edu. *Graduate Programs Director,* Marietta Stalcup, 317-940-6842, E-mail: mastalcu@butler.edu.

## BYZANTINE CATHOLIC SEMINARY OF SAINTS CYRIL AND METHODIUS, Pittsburgh, PA 15214

**General Information** Independent-religious, coed, graduate-only institution.

**GRADUATE UNITS**

**Graduate and Professional Programs**

## CABARRUS COLLEGE OF HEALTH SCIENCES, Concord, NC 28025

**General Information** Independent, coed, primarily women, comprehensive institution.

**GRADUATE UNITS**

**Program in Occupational Therapy**

## CABRINI UNIVERSITY, Radnor, PA 19087

**General Information** Independent-religious, coed, comprehensive institution. *Graduate housing:* On-campus housing not available.

**GRADUATE UNITS**

**Academic Affairs** *Program availability:* Part-time, evening/weekend. Electronic applications accepted.

## CAIRN UNIVERSITY, Langhorne, PA 19047-2990

**General Information** Independent-religious, coed, comprehensive institution. *Graduate housing:* Rooms and/or apartments available on a first-come, first-served basis to single and married students.

**GRADUATE UNITS**

**Department of Counseling** *Program availability:* Part-time, evening/weekend. Electronic applications accepted.

**School of Business** *Program availability:* Part-time, evening/weekend, 100% online, blended/hybrid learning. Electronic applications accepted.

**School of Divinity** *Program availability:* Part-time, evening/weekend, 100% online, blended/hybrid learning. Electronic applications accepted.

**School of Education** *Program availability:* Part-time, evening/weekend, 100% online, blended/hybrid learning. Electronic applications accepted.

## CALDWELL UNIVERSITY, Caldwell, NJ 07006-6195

**General Information** Independent-religious, coed, comprehensive institution. CGS member. *Enrollment:* 2,200 graduate, professional, and undergraduate students; 104 full-time matriculated graduate/professional students (90 women), 387 part-time matriculated graduate/professional students (293 women). *Enrollment by degree level:* 330 master's, 60 doctoral, 101 other advanced degrees. *Graduate faculty:* 28 full-time (16 women), 45 part-time/adjunct (28 women). *Tuition:* Full-time $995; part-time $995 per credit hour. *Required fees:* $235 per semester. Tuition and fees vary according to program. *Graduate housing:* Room and/or apartments available on a first-come, first-served basis to single students; on-campus housing not available to married students. Typical cost: $12,415 (including board). Room and board charges vary according to housing facility selected. Housing application deadline: 5/1. *Student services:* Campus employment opportunities, campus safety program, career counseling, free psychological counseling, international student services, services for students with disabilities, teacher training, writing training. *Library facilities:* Jennings Library. *Collection:* Books: 145,000 (physical), 210,323 (digital/electronic); Serial titles: 120 (physical), 78,630 (digital/electronic); Databases: 67. Students can reserve study rooms.

**Computer facilities:** 52 computers available on campus for general student use. A campuswide network can be accessed. Online class registration is available.
Website: http://www.caldwell.edu/

**General Application Contact:** Tom Disch, Senior Graduate Admissions Counselor, 973-618-3544, Fax: 973-618-3640, E-mail: graduate@caldwell.edu.

**GRADUATE UNITS**

**Department of Applied Behavior Analysis** *Program availability:* Part-time. Electronic applications accepted.

**School of Business and Computer Science** *Program availability:* Part-time. Electronic applications accepted.

**School of Education** *Program availability:* Part-time, evening/weekend. Electronic applications accepted.

**School of Psychology and Counseling** *Program availability:* Part-time. Electronic applications accepted.

## CALIFORNIA BAPTIST UNIVERSITY, Riverside, CA 92504-3206

**General Information** Independent-religious, coed, comprehensive institution. *Enrollment:* 11,045 graduate, professional, and undergraduate students; 1,621 full-time matriculated graduate/professional students (1,176 women), 1,234 part-time matriculated graduate/professional students (844 women). *Enrollment by degree level:* 2,664 master's, 191 doctoral. *Graduate faculty:* 188 full-time (97 women), 119 part-time/adjunct (71 women). *Tuition:* Full-time $12,600; part-time $700 per unit. *Required fees:* $730; $360 per unit. Full-time tuition and fees vary according to course load and program. *Graduate housing:* On-campus housing not available. *Student services:* Campus employment opportunities, campus safety program, career counseling, exercise/wellness program, free psychological counseling, international student services, low-cost health insurance, services for students with disabilities, teacher training, writing training. *Library facilities:* Annie Gabriel Library. *Collection:* Books: 126,845 (physical), 280,092 (digital/electronic); Serial titles: 15,127 (physical), 45,466 (digital/electronic); Databases: 105. Weekly public service hours: 101; students can reserve study rooms.

**Computer facilities:** Computer purchase and lease plans are available. 279 computers available on campus for general student use. A campuswide network can be accessed. Online class registration, online course evaluations are available.
Website: http://www.calbaptist.edu/

**General Application Contact:** Alma Salazar, Director of Graduate Admissions, 951-552-8086, Fax: 951-552-8700, E-mail: graduateadmissions@calbaptist.edu.

**GRADUATE UNITS**

**Doctor of Nursing Practice Program** *Program availability:* Part-time. Electronic applications accepted.

**Program in Accounting** *Program availability:* Part-time, evening/weekend, online only, 100% online. Electronic applications accepted.

**Program in Applied Mathematics** *Program availability:* Part-time. Electronic applications accepted.

**Program in Architecture** Electronic applications accepted.

**Program in Athletic Training** *Program availability:* Part-time. Electronic applications accepted.

**Program in Business Administration** *Program availability:* Part-time, evening/weekend, 100% online, blended/hybrid learning. Electronic applications accepted.

**Program in Communication** *Program availability:* Part-time, evening/weekend, online only, 100% online, blended/hybrid learning. Electronic applications accepted.

**Program in Counseling Ministry** *Program availability:* Part-time. Electronic applications accepted.

**Program in Counseling Ministry and Counseling Psychology (Dual Master's)** *Program availability:* Part-time. Electronic applications accepted.

**Program in Counseling Psychology** *Program availability:* Part-time, evening/weekend, 100% online, blended/hybrid learning. Electronic applications accepted.

**Program in Education** *Program availability:* Part-time, evening/weekend, 100% online, blended/hybrid learning. Electronic applications accepted.

**Program in English** *Program availability:* Part-time. Electronic applications accepted.

**Program in Forensic Psychology** *Program availability:* Part-time. Electronic applications accepted.

**Program in Higher Education Leadership and Student Development** *Program availability:* Part-time. Electronic applications accepted.

**Program in Kinesiology** *Program availability:* Part-time, evening/weekend, 100% online, blended/hybrid learning. Electronic applications accepted.

**Program in Leadership and Organizational Studies** *Program availability:* Part-time. Electronic applications accepted.

**Program in Music** *Program availability:* Part-time. Electronic applications accepted.

**Program in Nursing** *Program availability:* Part-time. Electronic applications accepted.

**Program in Organizational Leadership** *Program availability:* Part-time, evening/weekend, 100% online, blended/hybrid learning. Electronic applications accepted.

**Program in Physician Assistant Studies** *Program availability:* Part-time. Electronic applications accepted.

**Program in Public Administration** *Program availability:* Part-time, evening/weekend, online only, 100% online, blended/hybrid learning. Electronic applications accepted.

**Program in Public Health** *Program availability:* Part-time, evening/weekend, 100% online, blended/hybrid learning. Electronic applications accepted.

**Program in School Counseling** *Program availability:* Part-time. Electronic applications accepted.

**Program in School Psychology** *Program availability:* Part-time. Electronic applications accepted.

**Program in Social Work** *Program availability:* Part-time. Electronic applications accepted.

**Program in Speech Language Pathology** *Program availability:* Part-time. Electronic applications accepted.

## CALIFORNIA COAST UNIVERSITY, Santa Ana, CA 92701

**General Information** Proprietary, coed, comprehensive institution.

**GRADUATE UNITS**

**School of Administration and Management** *Program availability:* Online learning. Electronic applications accepted.

**School of Behavioral Science** *Program availability:* Online learning.

**School of Criminal Justice**

**School of Education** *Program availability:* Online learning.

## CALIFORNIA COLLEGE OF THE ARTS, San Francisco, CA 94107

**General Information** Independent, coed, comprehensive institution. *Enrollment:* 424 full-time matriculated graduate/professional students (271 women), 23 part-time matriculated graduate/professional students (13 women). *Enrollment by degree level:* 447 master's. *Graduate faculty:* 65 full-time (36 women), 102 part-time/adjunct (48 women). *Graduate housing:* Room and/or apartments available on a first-come, first-served basis to single students; on-campus housing not available to married students. Housing application deadline: 5/15. *Student services:* Campus employment opportunities, campus safety program, career counseling, exercise/wellness program, free psychological counseling, grant writing training, international student services, low-cost health insurance, multicultural affairs office, services for students with disabilities, writing training. *Library facilities:* Meyer Library plus 1 other.

**Computer facilities:** Computer purchase and lease plans are available. 400 computers available on campus for general student use. A campuswide network can be accessed from student residence rooms and from off campus. Online class registration, online course evaluations, learning management system, media applications, software training, print payments are available.
Website: http://www.cca.edu/

**General Application Contact:** David Murray, Director of Graduate Admissions, 415-703-9533, Fax: 415-703-9539, E-mail: graduateprograms@cca.edu.

**GRADUATE UNITS**

**Graduate Programs** *Program availability:* Part-time. Electronic applications accepted.

## CALIFORNIA HEALTH SCIENCES UNIVERSITY, Clovis, CA 93612

**General Information** Proprietary, coed, graduate-only institution.

**GRADUATE UNITS**

**College of Pharmacy**

## CALIFORNIA INSTITUTE OF ADVANCED MANAGEMENT, El Monte, CA 91731

**General Information** Private, coed, graduate-only institution.

**GRADUATE UNITS**

**The MBA Program**

## CALIFORNIA INSTITUTE OF TECHNOLOGY, Pasadena, CA 91125-0001

**General Information** Independent, coed, university. CGS member. *Graduate housing:* Rooms and/or apartments available on a first-come, first-served basis to single students and available to married students. Housing application deadline: 5/1. *Research affiliation:* Scripps Institute of Oceanography, Stanford Linear Accelerator Center (high-energy physics), European Center for Nuclear Research (high-energy physics), National Science Foundation Center for Research in Parallel Computing, Cosmic Gravitational Waves Observatory (laser interferometer gravitational waves).

**GRADUATE UNITS**

**Division of Biology and Biological Engineering** Electronic applications accepted.

**Division of Chemistry and Chemical Engineering** Electronic applications accepted.

**Division of Engineering and Applied Science** Electronic applications accepted.

**Division of Geological and Planetary Sciences** Electronic applications accepted.

**Division of Physics, Mathematics and Astronomy**

**Division of the Humanities and Social Sciences** Electronic applications accepted.

## CALIFORNIA INSTITUTE OF THE ARTS, Valencia, CA 91355-2340

**General Information** Independent, coed, comprehensive institution. *Graduate housing:* Room and/or apartments available on a first-come, first-served basis to single students; on-campus housing not available to married students. Housing application deadline: 7/1.

**GRADUATE UNITS**

**The Herb Alpert School of Music** *Program availability:* Part-time. Electronic applications accepted.

**School of Art** Electronic applications accepted.

**School of Critical Studies**

**School of Film/Video** Electronic applications accepted.

**School of Theater** Electronic applications accepted.

**The Sharon Disney Lund School of Dance**

## CALIFORNIA INTERCONTINENTAL UNIVERSITY, Irvine, CA 92614

**General Information** Proprietary, coed, comprehensive institution.

**GRADUATE UNITS**

**Hollywood College of the Entertainment Industry**

**School of Business**

**School of Healthcare**

**School of Information Technology**

## CALIFORNIA INTERNATIONAL BUSINESS UNIVERSITY, San Diego, CA 92101

**General Information** Independent, coed, graduate-only institution.

**GRADUATE UNITS**

**Graduate Programs**

## CALIFORNIA LUTHERAN UNIVERSITY, Thousand Oaks, CA 91360-2787

**General Information** Independent-religious, coed, comprehensive institution. CGS member. *Graduate housing:* Room and/or apartments available on a first-come, first-served basis to single students; on-campus housing not available to married students.

**GRADUATE UNITS**

**Graduate Studies** *Program availability:* Part-time, evening/weekend. Electronic applications accepted.

***Graduate School of Education*** *Program availability:* Part-time, evening/weekend. Electronic applications accepted.

***Pacific Lutheran Theological Seminary*** *Program availability:* Part-time. Electronic applications accepted.

***School of Management*** *Program availability:* Part-time, evening/weekend, 100% online, blended/hybrid learning. Electronic applications accepted.

## CALIFORNIA MIRAMAR UNIVERSITY, San Diego, CA 92108

**General Information** Proprietary, coed, comprehensive institution.

**GRADUATE UNITS**

**Program in Business Administration**

**Program in Strategic Leadership**

**Program in Taxation and Trade for Executives**

**Program in Telecommunications Management**

## CALIFORNIA NORTHSTATE UNIVERSITY, Elk Grove, CA 95757

**General Information** Proprietary, coed, comprehensive institution.

**GRADUATE UNITS**

**College of Medicine**

**College of Pharmacy**

## CALIFORNIA POLYTECHNIC STATE UNIVERSITY, SAN LUIS OBISPO, San Luis Obispo, CA 93407

**General Information** State-supported, coed, comprehensive institution. CGS member. *Enrollment:* 21,242 graduate, professional, and undergraduate students; 559 full-time matriculated graduate/professional students (273 women), 208 part-time matriculated graduate/professional students (86 women). *Enrollment by degree level:* 767 master's. *Graduate faculty:* 167 full-time (52 women), 22 part-time/adjunct (12 women). Tuition, state resident: full-time $7176; part-time $4164 per year. Tuition, nonresident: full-time $18,690; part-time $8916 per year. *Required fees:* $4206; $3185 per unit. $1061 per term. *Graduate housing:* Room and/or apartments available on a first-come, first-served basis to single students; on-campus housing not available to married students. *Student services:* Campus employment opportunities, campus safety program, career counseling, child daycare facilities, exercise/wellness program, free psychological counseling, grant writing training, international student services, low-cost health insurance, multicultural affairs office, services for students with disabilities, teacher training, writing training. *Library facilities:* Robert E. Kennedy Library.

**Computer facilities:** A campuswide network can be accessed. Online class registration is available.
Website: http://www.calpoly.edu/

**General Application Contact:** Dr. James Maraviglia, Associate Vice Provost for Marketing and Enrollment Development, 805-756-2311, Fax: 805-756-5400, E-mail: admissions@calpoly.edu.

**GRADUATE UNITS**

**College of Agriculture, Food and Environmental Sciences** *Program availability:* Part-time. Electronic applications accepted.

**College of Architecture and Environmental Design** *Program availability:* Part-time. Electronic applications accepted.

**College of Engineering** *Program availability:* Part-time. Electronic applications accepted.

**College of Liberal Arts** *Program availability:* Part-time.

**College of Science and Mathematics** *Program availability:* Part-time. Electronic applications accepted.

***School of Education*** *Program availability:* Part-time, evening/weekend. Electronic applications accepted.

**Orfalea College of Business** Electronic applications accepted.

## CALIFORNIA STATE POLYTECHNIC UNIVERSITY, POMONA, Pomona, CA 91768-2557

**General Information** State-supported, coed, comprehensive institution. *Enrollment:* 27,915 graduate, professional, and undergraduate students; 595 full-time matriculated graduate/professional students (303 women), 736 part-time matriculated graduate/professional students (326 women). *Enrollment by degree level:* 1,295 master's, 36 doctoral. *Graduate faculty:* 638 full-time (268 women), 814 part-time/adjunct (354 women). *International tuition:* $16,680 full-time. *Tuition, area resident:* Full-time $7176. Tuition, state resident: full-time $7176. Tuition, nonresident: full-time $16,680. *Required fees:* $1654. *Graduate housing:* Room and/or apartments available on a first-come, first-served basis to single students; on-campus housing not available to married students. Housing application deadline: 5/1. *Student services:* Campus employment opportunities, campus safety program, career counseling, child daycare facilities, free psychological counseling, international student services, low-cost health insurance, multicultural affairs office, services for students with disabilities. *Library facilities:* University Library. *Collection:* Books: 517,449 (physical), 314,565 (digital/electronic); Serial titles: 14,240 (physical), 66,509 (digital/electronic); Databases: 197. Weekly public service hours: 92; study areas open 24 hours, 5–7 days a week; students can reserve study rooms.

**Computer facilities:** Computer purchase and lease plans are available. 2,117 computers available on campus for general student use. A campuswide network can be accessed.
Website: http://www.cpp.edu/

**General Application Contact:** Brandon Tuck, Interim Director, Admissions and Enrollment Planning, 909-869-3310, E-mail: hbtuck@cpp.edu.

**GRADUATE UNITS**

**Ed D Program in Educational Leadership** *Program availability:* Part-time, evening/weekend. Electronic applications accepted.

**John T. Lyle Center for Regenerative Studies** *Program availability:* Part-time. Electronic applications accepted.

**Master of Science in Business Administration Program** *Program availability:* Part-time, evening/weekend. Electronic applications accepted.

**Master's Programs in Education** *Program availability:* Part-time, evening/weekend. Electronic applications accepted.

**MBA Program** *Program availability:* Part-time, evening/weekend. Electronic applications accepted.

**Program in Accountancy** *Program availability:* Part-time, evening/weekend. Electronic applications accepted.

**Program in Agriculture** *Program availability:* Part-time, evening/weekend. Electronic applications accepted.

**Program in Architecture** *Program availability:* Part-time, evening/weekend. Electronic applications accepted.

**Program in Biological Sciences** *Program availability:* Part-time, evening/weekend. Electronic applications accepted.

**Program in Chemistry** *Program availability:* Part-time, evening/weekend. Electronic applications accepted.

**Program in Civil Engineering** *Program availability:* Part-time, evening/weekend. Electronic applications accepted.

**Program in Computer Science** *Program availability:* Part-time, evening/weekend. Electronic applications accepted.

**Program in Economics** *Program availability:* Part-time, evening/weekend. Electronic applications accepted.

**Program in Electrical Engineering** *Program availability:* Part-time, evening/weekend. Electronic applications accepted.

**Program in Engineering** *Program availability:* Part-time, evening/weekend. Electronic applications accepted.

**Program in Engineering Management** *Program availability:* Part-time, evening/weekend. Electronic applications accepted.

**Program in English** *Program availability:* Part-time, evening/weekend. Electronic applications accepted.

**Program in Geology** *Program availability:* Part-time, evening/weekend. Electronic applications accepted.

**Program in History** *Program availability:* Part-time, evening/weekend. Electronic applications accepted.

**Program in Hospitality Management** *Program availability:* Part-time, evening/weekend. Electronic applications accepted.

**Program in Interior Architecture** *Program availability:* Part-time, evening/weekend. Electronic applications accepted.

**Program in Kinesiology** *Program availability:* Part-time, evening/weekend. Electronic applications accepted.

**Program in Landscape Architecture** *Program availability:* Part-time, evening/weekend. Electronic applications accepted.

**Program in Mathematics** *Program availability:* Part-time, evening/weekend. Electronic applications accepted.

**Program in Mechanical Engineering** *Program availability:* Part-time, evening/weekend. Electronic applications accepted.

**Program in Psychology** *Program availability:* Part-time, evening/weekend. Electronic applications accepted.

**Program in Public Administration** *Program availability:* Part-time, evening/weekend. Electronic applications accepted.

**Program in Systems Engineering** *Program availability:* Part-time, evening/weekend. Electronic applications accepted.

**Program in Urban and Regional Planning** *Program availability:* Part-time, evening/weekend. Electronic applications accepted.

## CALIFORNIA STATE UNIVERSITY, BAKERSFIELD, Bakersfield, CA 93311

**General Information** State-supported, coed, comprehensive institution. *Graduate housing:* Room and/or apartments available on a first-come, first-served basis to single students; on-campus housing not available to married students. Housing application deadline: 7/15.

**GRADUATE UNITS**

**Division of Graduate Studies**

## CALIFORNIA STATE UNIVERSITY CHANNEL ISLANDS, Camarillo, CA 93012

**General Information** State-supported, coed, comprehensive institution. *Enrollment:* 400 matriculated graduate/professional students. *Enrollment by degree level:* 400 master's. *Graduate housing:* Room and/or apartments available on a first-come, first-served basis to single students; on-campus housing not available to married students. Typical cost: $7040 per year. Housing application deadline: 6/1. *Student services:* Campus employment opportunities, campus safety program, career counseling, exercise/wellness program, grant writing training, international student services, low-cost health insurance, multicultural affairs office, services for students with disabilities, teacher training, writing training. *Library facilities:* John Spoor Broome Library at Channel Islands.
Website: http://www.csuci.edu/

**GRADUATE UNITS**

**Extended University and International Programs** Students: 203 full-time (65 women); includes 86 minority (3 Black or African American, non-Hispanic/Latino; 1 American Indian or Alaska Native, non-Hispanic/Latino; 29 Asian, non-Hispanic/Latino; 46 Hispanic/Latino; 7 Two or more races, non-Hispanic/Latino). 134 applicants, 75% accepted, 78 enrolled. Expenses: Contact institution. *Financial support:* Career-related internships or fieldwork and scholarships/grants available. Financial award applicants required to submit FAFSA. *Program availability:* Part-time, evening/weekend. *Application deadline:* For fall admission, 6/1 for domestic students; for spring admission, 11/1 for domestic students. *Application fee:* $70. Electronic applications accepted. *Application Contact:* Andrew Conley, Graduate Programs Recruiter, 805-437-2652, E-mail: andrew.conley@csuci.edu. *Director of Enrollment, Outreach, and Student Affairs,* Daniel Banyai, 805-437-2651, E-mail: daniel.banyai@csuci.edu.

## CALIFORNIA STATE UNIVERSITY, CHICO, Chico, CA 95929-0722

**General Information** State-supported, coed, comprehensive institution. CGS member. *Enrollment:* 17,014 graduate, professional, and undergraduate students. *Enrollment by degree level:* 1,068 master's. *Graduate housing:* Room and/or apartments available on a first-come, first-served basis to single students; on-campus housing not available to married students. *Student services:* Campus employment opportunities, campus safety program, career counseling, child daycare facilities, exercise/wellness program, free psychological counseling, grant writing training, international student services, low-cost health insurance, multicultural affairs office, services for students with disabilities, teacher training, writing training. *Library facilities:* Meriam Library plus 1 other. *Collection:* Books: 809,358 (physical), 310,706 (digital/electronic); Serial titles: 72,683 (physical). Study areas open 24 hours, 5–7 days a week; students can reserve study rooms. *Research affiliation:* Sierra Nevada Brewery (nutrition, food sciences, agriculture), Lawrence Livermore Labs - Inspection and Surveillance Robots (engineering and computer science), California Department of Transportation Pavement Preservation and Recycling (engineering, computer science, construction management), U.S. Navy Office of Naval Research (engineering), Verizon Wireless/Samsung (business).

**Computer facilities:** Computer purchase and lease plans are available. 1,328 computers available on campus for general student use. A campuswide network can be accessed from student residence rooms and from off campus. Online class registration, student account information, calendar, transcripts are available.
Website: http://www.csuchico.edu/

**General Application Contact:** Micah Lehner, Admissions Counselor, 530-898-6880, Fax: 530-898-3342, E-mail: graduatestudies@csuchico.edu.

**GRADUATE UNITS**

**Office of Graduate Studies** *Program availability:* Part-time, 100% online, blended/hybrid learning. Electronic applications accepted.

***College of Agriculture*** Electronic applications accepted.

***College of Behavioral and Social Sciences*** Electronic applications accepted.

***College of Business*** *Program availability:* Part-time. Electronic applications accepted.

***College of Communication and Education*** *Program availability:* Part-time. Electronic applications accepted.

***College of Engineering, Computer Science, and Construction Management*** *Program availability:* Part-time, online learning. Electronic applications accepted.

***College of Humanities and Fine Arts*** Electronic applications accepted.

***College of Natural Sciences*** *Program availability:* Part-time. Electronic applications accepted.

## CALIFORNIA STATE UNIVERSITY, DOMINGUEZ HILLS, Carson, CA 90747-0001

**General Information** State-supported, coed, comprehensive institution. CGS member. *Graduate housing:* Rooms and/or apartments available on a first-come, first-served basis to single and married students. Housing application deadline: 4/15. *Research affiliation:* Los Angeles Biomedical Research Institute at Harbor UCLA Medical Center (biomedical science), Hewlett Packard (catalyst initiative grants).

**GRADUATE UNITS**

**College of Arts and Humanities** *Program availability:* Part-time, evening/weekend, 100% online.

**College of Business Administration and Public Policy** *Program availability:* Part-time, evening/weekend, online learning.

**College of Education** *Program availability:* Part-time, evening/weekend.

***Division of Graduate Education*** *Program availability:* Part-time, evening/weekend.

***Division of Teacher Education*** *Program availability:* Part-time, evening/weekend.

**College of Extended and International Education** *Program availability:* Part-time, evening/weekend, online learning. Electronic applications accepted.

**College of Health, Human Services and Nursing** Electronic applications accepted.

**College of Natural and Behavioral Sciences**

## CALIFORNIA STATE UNIVERSITY, EAST BAY, Hayward, CA 94542-3000

**General Information** State-supported, coed, comprehensive institution. *Graduate housing:* On-campus housing not available. *Research affiliation:* Bayer USA Foundation (STEM), Chevron (STEM), Hearst Foundation (STEM), NASA (earth and environmental sciences), Irvine Foundation (education: teacher preparation), Carnegie Foundation (statistics for non-STEM majors).

**GRADUATE UNITS**

**Office of Graduate Studies** *Program availability:* Part-time, evening/weekend, online learning. Electronic applications accepted.

***College of Business and Economics*** *Program availability:* Part-time, evening/weekend, online learning. Electronic applications accepted.

***College of Education and Allied Studies*** *Program availability:* Part-time, evening/weekend, online learning. Electronic applications accepted.

***College of Letters, Arts, and Social Sciences*** *Program availability:* Part-time, evening/weekend, online learning. Electronic applications accepted.

***College of Science*** *Program availability:* Part-time, evening/weekend. Electronic applications accepted.

## CALIFORNIA STATE UNIVERSITY, FRESNO, Fresno, CA 93740-8027

**General Information** State-supported, coed, comprehensive institution. CGS member. *Enrollment:* 24,139 graduate, professional, and undergraduate students; 1,366 full-time matriculated graduate/professional students (950 women), 701 part-time matriculated graduate/professional students (429 women). *Enrollment by degree level:* 1,838 master's, 229 doctoral, 12 other advanced degrees. *Graduate faculty:* 799 full-time, 682 part-time/adjunct. Tuition, state resident: full-time $4012; part-time $2506 per semester. *Graduate housing:* Room and/or apartments available on a first-come, first-served basis to single students; on-campus housing not available to married students. Housing application deadline: 4/1. *Student services:* Campus employment opportunities, campus safety program, career counseling, child daycare facilities, exercise/wellness program, free psychological counseling, grant writing training, international student services, low-cost health insurance, multicultural affairs office, services for students with disabilities, teacher training, writing training. *Library facilities:* Henry Madden Library. *Research affiliation:* Coleman Foundation (administration), Starburst Foundation (engineering), Garabedian Foundation (agribusiness), California Endowment (arts and humanities).

**Computer facilities:** A campuswide network can be accessed. Online class registration is available.
Website: http://www.csufresno.edu/

**General Application Contact:** Rodrigo Gomez, Outreach Specialist, 559-278-2448, E-mail: rodrigog@csufresno.edu.

**GRADUATE UNITS**

**Division of Research and Graduate Studies** *Program availability:* Part-time, evening/weekend. Electronic applications accepted.

***College of Arts and Humanities*** *Program availability:* Part-time, evening/weekend. Electronic applications accepted.

***College of Health and Human Services*** *Program availability:* Part-time, evening/weekend. Electronic applications accepted.

***College of Science and Mathematics*** *Program availability:* Part-time, evening/weekend. Electronic applications accepted.

***College of Social Sciences*** *Program availability:* Part-time, evening/weekend. Electronic applications accepted.

***Craig School of Business*** *Program availability:* Part-time, blended/hybrid learning. Electronic applications accepted.

***Jordan College of Agricultural Sciences and Technology*** *Program availability:* Part-time, evening/weekend. Electronic applications accepted.

***Kremen School of Education and Human Development*** *Program availability:* Part-time, evening/weekend. Electronic applications accepted.

***Lyles College of Engineering*** *Program availability:* Part-time, evening/weekend. Electronic applications accepted.

## CALIFORNIA STATE UNIVERSITY, FULLERTON, Fullerton, CA 92831-3599

**General Information** State-supported, coed, comprehensive institution. CGS member. *Graduate housing:* Rooms and/or apartments available on a first-come, first-served basis to single and married students. Housing application deadline: 6/30. *Research affiliation:* U.S. Department of Interior (desert studies), County of Orange (demographic research), Department of Literacy and Reading Education, SchoolsFirst Federal Credit Union (creativity and critical thinking), California Office of Historic Preservation and the State Historic Resources Commission (South Central coastal information).

**GRADUATE UNITS**

**Graduate Studies** *Program availability:* Part-time, evening/weekend, online learning. Electronic applications accepted.

***College of Business and Economics*** *Program availability:* Part-time. Electronic applications accepted.

***College of Communications*** *Program availability:* Part-time.

***College of Education***

***College of Engineering and Computer Science*** *Program availability:* Part-time.

***College of Health and Human Development*** *Program availability:* Part-time.

***College of Humanities and Social Sciences*** *Program availability:* Part-time.

***College of Natural Science and Mathematics*** *Program availability:* Part-time.

***College of the Arts*** *Program availability:* Part-time.

## CALIFORNIA STATE UNIVERSITY, LONG BEACH, Long Beach, CA 90840

**General Information** State-supported, coed, comprehensive institution. *Graduate housing:* Room and/or apartments available on a first-come, first-served basis to single students; on-campus housing not available to married students. Housing application deadline: 5/1. *Research affiliation:* Boeing (aerospace engineering and manufacturing).

**GRADUATE UNITS**

**Graduate Studies** *Program availability:* Part-time, evening/weekend, online learning. Electronic applications accepted.

***College of Business*** *Program availability:* Part-time, evening/weekend. Electronic applications accepted.

***College of Education*** *Program availability:* Part-time, evening/weekend. Electronic applications accepted.

***College of Engineering*** *Program availability:* Part-time, evening/weekend. Electronic applications accepted.

***College of Health and Human Services*** *Program availability:* Part-time, evening/weekend, online learning. Electronic applications accepted.

***College of Liberal Arts*** *Program availability:* Part-time, evening/weekend. Electronic applications accepted.

***College of Natural Sciences and Mathematics*** *Program availability:* Part-time. Electronic applications accepted.

***College of the Arts*** *Program availability:* Part-time. Electronic applications accepted.

## CALIFORNIA STATE UNIVERSITY, LOS ANGELES, Los Angeles, CA 90032-8530

**General Information** State-supported, coed, comprehensive institution. CGS member. *Enrollment:* 26,360 graduate, professional, and undergraduate students; 2,355 full-time matriculated graduate/professional students (1,574 women), 1,380 part-time matriculated graduate/professional students (831 women). *Enrollment by degree level:* 2,767 master's, 94 doctoral, 874 other advanced degrees. *Graduate faculty:* 180 full-time (107 women), 125 part-time/adjunct (79 women). *International tuition:* $14,304 full-time. *Tuition, area resident:* Full-time $7176; part-time $4164 per year. Tuition, state resident: full-time $7176; part-time $4164 per year. Tuition, nonresident: full-time $14,304; part-time $8916 per year. *Required fees:* $1037.76; $1037.76 per unit. Tuition and fees vary according to degree level and program. *Graduate housing:* Room and/or apartments available on a first-come, first-served basis to single students; on-campus housing not available to married students. Typical cost: $11,520 per year ($15,653 including board). Room and board charges vary according to board plan, campus/location and housing facility selected. Housing application deadline: 7/2. *Student services:* Campus employment opportunities, career counseling, child daycare facilities, free psychological counseling, international student services, low-cost health insurance, multicultural affairs office, services for students with disabilities, writing training. *Library facilities:* John F. Kennedy Memorial Library. *Collection:* Books: 537,271 (physical), 86,220 (digital/electronic); Serial titles: 7,843 (physical), 83,822 (digital/electronic); Databases: 230. Weekly public service hours: 99. *Research affiliation:* NASA (engineering), General Motors (engineering).

**Computer facilities:** 1,500 computers available on campus for general student use. A campuswide network can be accessed. Online class registration is available.
Website: http://www.calstatela.edu/

**General Application Contact:** Dr. Karin A. Elliot-Brown, Interim Dean, 323-343-3820, Fax: 323-343-5653, E-mail: kbrown5@calstatela.edu.

**GRADUATE UNITS**

**Graduate Studies** *Program availability:* Part-time, evening/weekend. Electronic applications accepted.

***Charter College of Education*** *Program availability:* Part-time, evening/weekend. Electronic applications accepted.

***College of Arts and Letters*** *Program availability:* Part-time, evening/weekend. Electronic applications accepted.

***College of Business and Economics*** *Program availability:* Part-time, evening/weekend. Electronic applications accepted.

***College of Engineering, Computer Science, and Technology*** *Program availability:* Part-time, evening/weekend. Electronic applications accepted.

***College of Health and Human Services*** *Program availability:* Part-time, evening/weekend. Electronic applications accepted.

***College of Natural and Social Sciences*** *Program availability:* Part-time, evening/weekend.

## CALIFORNIA STATE UNIVERSITY MARITIME ACADEMY, Vallejo, CA 94590

**General Information** State-supported, coed, comprehensive institution. *Enrollment:* 942 graduate, professional, and undergraduate students; 31 full-time matriculated graduate/professional students (7 women). *Enrollment by degree level:* 31 master's. *Graduate faculty:* 19 part-time/adjunct (4 women). *Graduate housing:* On-campus housing not available. *Student services:* Campus employment opportunities, career counseling, services for students with disabilities, writing training.

**Computer facilities:** A campuswide network can be accessed. Online class registration is available.
Website: http://www.csum.edu/

**General Application Contact:** Kathy Arnold, Graduate Program Coordinator, 707-654-1271, Fax: 707-654-1158, E-mail: karnold@csum.edu.

**GRADUATE UNITS**

**Graduate Studies** *Program availability:* Evening/weekend, online only, 100% online. Electronic applications accepted.

## CALIFORNIA STATE UNIVERSITY, MONTEREY BAY, Seaside, CA 93955-8001

**General Information** State-supported, coed, comprehensive institution. *Graduate housing:* Rooms and/or apartments available on a first-come, first-served basis to single and married students.

**GRADUATE UNITS**

**College of Business** *Program availability:* Part-time, evening/weekend, online learning. Electronic applications accepted.

**College of Education** *Program availability:* Part-time, evening/weekend. Electronic applications accepted.

**College of Health Sciences and Human Services** *Program availability:* Part-time. Electronic applications accepted.

**College of Science** *Program availability:* Part-time. Electronic applications accepted.

***School of Computing and Design*** Electronic applications accepted.

## CALIFORNIA STATE UNIVERSITY, NORTHRIDGE, Northridge, CA 91330

**General Information** State-supported, coed, comprehensive institution. *Enrollment:* 38,391 graduate, professional, and undergraduate students; 1,597 full-time matriculated graduate/professional students (1,073 women), 1,338 part-time matriculated graduate/professional students (810 women). *Enrollment by degree level:* 2,776 master's, 159 doctoral. *Graduate faculty:* 771 full-time (372 women), 1,622 part-time/adjunct (801 women). *Graduate housing:* Rooms and/or apartments available on a first-come, first-served basis to single and married students. *Student services:* Campus employment opportunities, campus safety program, career counseling, child daycare facilities, free psychological counseling, international student services, low-cost health insurance, multicultural affairs office, services for students with disabilities, teacher training. *Library facilities:* Oviatt Library plus 1 other. *Collection:* Students can reserve study rooms. *Research affiliation:* Haagen Company (archaeology), Northridge Hospital (biology), Warner Center Institute (child care), Jet Propulsion Laboratory (engineering), Hughes Aircraft Corporation (engineering), California Institute of Technology (science).

**Computer facilities:** A campuswide network can be accessed from student residence rooms and from off campus. Online class registration is available.
Website: http://www.csun.edu/

**General Application Contact:** Dr. Crist Khachikian, Associate Vice President, 818-677-2138, E-mail: graduate.studies@csun.edu.

**GRADUATE UNITS**

**Graduate Studies** Students: 1,597 full-time (1,073 women), 1,338 part-time (810 women); includes 1,547 minority (107 Black or African American, non-Hispanic/Latino; 5 American Indian or Alaska Native, non-Hispanic/Latino; 310 Asian, non-Hispanic/Latino; 1,034 Hispanic/Latino; 7 Native Hawaiian or other Pacific Islander, non-Hispanic/Latino; 84 Two or more races, non-Hispanic/Latino), 237 international. Average age 30. 5,150 applicants, 41% accepted, 1,106 enrolled. *Faculty:* 771 full-time (372 women), 1,622 part-time/adjunct (801 women). Expenses: Contact institution. *Financial support:* Fellowships, research assistantships, teaching assistantships, career-related internships or fieldwork, Federal Work-Study, institutionally sponsored loans, scholarships/grants, tuition waivers (partial), and unspecified assistantships available. Support available to part-time students. Financial award applicants required to submit FAFSA. In 2019, 256 master's awarded. *Program availability:* Part-time, evening/weekend. *Application deadline:* For fall admission, 3/31 for domestic students; for spring admission, 10/31 for domestic students. Applications are processed on a rolling basis. Electronic applications accepted. *Application Contact:* 818-677-3755. *Assistant Vice President, Graduate Studies,* Amy Levin Levin, 818-677-2138, E-mail: graduate.studies@csun.edu.

***College of Engineering and Computer Science*** *Program availability:* Part-time, evening/weekend.

***College of Health and Human Development*** *Program availability:* Part-time, evening/weekend.

***College of Humanities*** Students: 88 full-time (62 women), 106 part-time (66 women); includes 79 minority (3 Black or African American, non-Hispanic/Latino; 2 American Indian or Alaska Native, non-Hispanic/Latino; 14 Asian, non-Hispanic/Latino; 56 Hispanic/Latino; 4 Two or more races, non-Hispanic/Latino), 11 international. Average age 33. 205 applicants, 76% accepted, 77 enrolled. *Faculty:* 106 full-time (58 women), 231 part-time/adjunct (140 women). Expenses: Contact institution. *Financial support:* Teaching assistantships and Federal Work-Study available. Support available to part-time students. Financial award application deadline: 3/1. In 2019, 83 master's awarded. *Program availability:* Part-time, evening/weekend. *Application deadline:* For fall admission, 11/30 for domestic students. *Application fee:* $55. *Application Contact:* Jackie E. Stallcup, Dr., Interim Dean, 818-677-3301. *Interim Dean,* Jackie E. Stallcup, Dr., 818-677-3301.

***College of Science and Mathematics*** *Program availability:* Part-time, evening/weekend.

***College of Social and Behavioral Sciences*** *Program availability:* Part-time, evening/weekend.

***David Nazarian College of Business and Economics*** *Program availability:* Part-time.

***Michael D. Eisner College of Education*** *Program availability:* Part-time, evening/weekend.

***Mike Curb College of Arts, Media, and Communication*** *Program availability:* Part-time, evening/weekend.

***Tseng College***

## CALIFORNIA STATE UNIVERSITY, SACRAMENTO, Sacramento, CA 95819

**General Information** State-supported, coed, comprehensive institution. CGS member. *Enrollment:* 31,156 graduate, professional, and undergraduate students; 1,298 full-time matriculated graduate/professional students (821 women), 1,005 part-time matriculated graduate/professional students (565 women). *Enrollment by degree level:* 2,146 master's, 157 doctoral. *Graduate housing:* Room and/or apartments available on a first-come, first-served basis to single students; on-campus housing not available to married students. *Student services:* Campus employment opportunities, career counseling, child daycare facilities, free psychological counseling, grant writing training, international student services, low-cost health insurance, multicultural affairs office, services for students with disabilities, teacher training, writing training. *Library facilities:* California State University, Sacramento Library. *Collection:* Students can reserve study rooms.

**Computer facilities:** Computer purchase and lease plans are available. A campuswide network can be accessed. Online class registration, online transcripts are available.
Website: http://www.csus.edu/

**General Application Contact:** Dr. Chevelle Newsome, Dean of Graduate Admissions, 916-278-6470, Fax: 916-278-5669, E-mail: cnewsome@skymail.csus.edu.

**GRADUATE UNITS**

**College of Arts and Letters** Students: 104 full-time (66 women), 133 part-time (67 women); includes 67 minority (9 Black or African American, non-Hispanic/Latino; 3 American Indian or Alaska Native, non-Hispanic/Latino; 6 Asian, non-Hispanic/Latino; 49 Hispanic/Latino), 5 international. Average age 31. 148 applicants, 64% accepted, 69 enrolled. Expenses: Contact institution. *Financial support:* Teaching assistantships, career-related internships or fieldwork, Federal Work-Study, and scholarships/grants available. Support available to part-time students. Financial award application deadline: 3/1; financial award applicants required to submit FAFSA. In 2019, 60 master's awarded. *Program availability:* Part-time, evening/weekend. *Application deadline:* For fall admission, 3/1 for domestic students, 2/1 for international students; for spring admission, 9/15 for domestic students, 8/15 for international students. Applications are processed on a rolling basis. *Application fee:* $70. Electronic applications accepted. *Application Contact:* Jose Martinez, Graduate Admissions Supervisor, 916-278-7871, E-mail: martinj@skymail.csus.edu. *Dean,* Dr. Sheree Meyer, 916-278-6502.

**College of Business Administration** Students: 165 full-time (90 women), 223 part-time (102 women); includes 157 minority (18 Black or African American, non-Hispanic/Latino; 2 American Indian or Alaska Native, non-Hispanic/Latino; 86 Asian, non-Hispanic/Latino; 48 Hispanic/Latino; 3 Native Hawaiian or other Pacific Islander, non-Hispanic/Latino), 29 international. Average age 34. 232 applicants, 63% accepted, 100 enrolled. Expenses: Contact institution. *Financial support:* Teaching assistantships, career-related internships or fieldwork, Federal Work-Study, and scholarships/grants available. Support available to part-time students. Financial award application deadline: 3/1; financial award applicants required to submit FAFSA. In 2019, 121 master's awarded. *Program availability:* Part-time, evening/weekend, 100% online, blended/hybrid learning. *Application deadline:* For fall admission, 2/1 for domestic students, 1/1 for international students; for spring admission, 9/15 for domestic students, 8/15 for international students. Applications are processed on a rolling basis. *Application fee:* $70. Electronic applications accepted. *Application Contact:* Jose Martinez, Graduate Admissions Supervisor, 916-278-7871, E-mail: martinj@skymail.csus.edu. *Dean,* Dr. Pierre A. Balthazard, 916-278-6578, Fax: 916-278-5793, E-mail: cba@csus.edu.

**College of Education** Students: 514 full-time (399 women), 168 part-time (132 women); includes 370 minority (63 Black or African American, non-Hispanic/Latino; 12 American Indian or Alaska Native, non-Hispanic/Latino; 99 Asian, non-Hispanic/Latino; 192 Hispanic/Latino; 4 Native Hawaiian or other Pacific Islander, non-Hispanic/Latino), 8 international. Average age 32. 704 applicants, 49% accepted, 265 enrolled. Expenses: Contact institution. *Financial support:* Teaching assistantships, career-related internships or fieldwork, and Federal Work-Study available. Support available to part-time students. Financial award application deadline: 3/1; financial award applicants required to submit FAFSA. In 2019, 128 master's, 25 doctorates, 18 other advanced degrees awarded. *Program availability:* Part-time, evening/weekend, blended/hybrid learning. *Application deadline:* For fall admission, 3/1 for domestic students, 2/1 for international students. Applications are processed on a rolling basis. *Application fee:* $70. Electronic applications accepted. *Application Contact:* Jose Martinez, Graduate Admissions Supervisor, 916-278-6470, E-mail: martinj@skymail.csus.edu. *Dean,* Dr. Alexander Sidorkin, 916-278-6639, E-mail: sidorkin@csus.edu.

**College of Engineering and Computer Science** Students: 228 full-time (85 women), 175 part-time (55 women); includes 92 minority (14 Black or African American, non-Hispanic/Latino; 1 American Indian or Alaska Native, non-Hispanic/Latino; 49 Asian, non-Hispanic/Latino; 24 Hispanic/Latino; 4 Native Hawaiian or other Pacific Islander, non-Hispanic/Latino), 211 international. Average age 28. 641 applicants, 44% accepted, 92 enrolled. Expenses: Contact institution. *Financial support:* Teaching assistantships, career-related internships or fieldwork, Federal Work-Study, and scholarships/grants available. Support available to part-time students. Financial award application deadline: 3/1; financial award applicants required to submit FAFSA. In 2019, 106 master's awarded. *Program availability:* Part-time, evening/weekend. *Application deadline:* For fall admission, 3/1 for domestic students, 2/1 for international students. Applications are processed on a rolling basis. *Application fee:* $70. Electronic applications accepted. *Application Contact:* Jose Martinez, Graduate Admissions Supervisor, 916-278-7871, E-mail: martinj@skymail.csus.edu. *Dean,* Dr. Lorenzo M. Smith, 916-278-6127, Fax: 916-278-5949, E-mail: lsmith@csus.edu.

**College of Health and Human Services** *Program availability:* Part-time, evening/weekend. Electronic applications accepted.

***Division of Criminal Justice*** Students: 2 full-time (0 women), 25 part-time (17 women); includes 15 minority (2 Black or African American, non-Hispanic/Latino; 5 Asian, non-Hispanic/Latino; 7 Hispanic/Latino; 1 Native Hawaiian or other Pacific Islander, non-Hispanic/Latino). Average age 27. 36 applicants, 61% accepted, 17 enrolled. Expenses: Contact institution. *Financial support:* Teaching assistantships, career-related internships or fieldwork, Federal Work-Study, and scholarships/grants available. Support available to part-time students. Financial award application deadline: 3/1; financial award applicants required to submit FAFSA. In 2019, 6 master's awarded. *Program availability:* Part-time. *Application deadline:* For fall admission, 3/1 for domestic students, 2/1 for international students. Applications are processed on a rolling basis. *Application fee:* $70. Electronic applications accepted. *Application Contact:* Jose Martinez, Graduate Admissions Supervisor, 916-278-6470, E-mail: martinj@skymail.csus.edu. *Chair,* Dr. Ernest Uwazie, 916-278-6282, E-mail: uwazieee@csus.edu.

***Division of Social Work*** *Program availability:* Part-time, evening/weekend. Electronic applications accepted.

***School of Nursing*** Students: 72 full-time (64 women), 100 part-time (95 women); includes 64 minority (8 Black or African American, non-Hispanic/Latino; 1 American Indian or Alaska Native, non-Hispanic/Latino; 24 Asian, non-Hispanic/Latino; 29 Hispanic/Latino; 2 Native Hawaiian or other Pacific Islander, non-Hispanic/Latino). Average age 38. 40 applicants, 85% accepted, 16 enrolled. Expenses: Contact institution. *Financial support:* Teaching assistantships, career-related internships or fieldwork, Federal Work-Study, and scholarships/grants available. Support available to part-time students. Financial award application deadline: 3/1; financial award applicants required to submit FAFSA. In 2019, 56 master's awarded. *Program availability:* Part-time. *Application deadline:* For fall admission, 3/1 for domestic and international students; for spring admission, 12/1 for domestic students, 11/1 for international students. Applications are processed on a rolling basis. *Application fee:* $70. Electronic applications accepted. *Application Contact:* Jose Martinez, Graduate Admissions Supervisor, 916-278-6470, E-mail: martinj@skymail.csus.edu. *Chair*, Dr. Tanya Altmann, 916-278-1504, E-mail: altmannt@csus.edu.

**College of Natural Sciences and Mathematics** Students: 44 full-time (15 women), 49 part-time (16 women); includes 29 minority (2 American Indian or Alaska Native, non-Hispanic/Latino; 18 Asian, non-Hispanic/Latino; 8 Hispanic/Latino; 1 Native Hawaiian or other Pacific Islander, non-Hispanic/Latino), 1 international. Average age 31. 108 applicants, 50% accepted, 50 enrolled. Expenses: Contact institution. *Financial support:* Teaching assistantships, career-related internships or fieldwork, Federal Work-Study, and scholarships/grants available. Support available to part-time students. Financial award application deadline: 3/1; financial award applicants required to submit FAFSA. In 2019, 23 master's awarded. *Program availability:* Part-time. *Application deadline:* For fall admission, 3/1 for domestic students, 2/1 for international students. Applications are processed on a rolling basis. *Application fee:* $70. Electronic applications accepted. *Application Contact:* Jose Martinez, Graduate Admissions Supervisor, 916-278-7871, E-mail: martinj@skymail.csus.edu. *Dean*, Dr. Jill Trainer, 916-278-4655, E-mail: jill.trainer@csus.edu.

**College of Social Sciences and Interdisciplinary Studies** Students: 55 full-time (35 women), 82 part-time (49 women); includes 48 minority (6 Black or African American, non-Hispanic/Latino; 2 American Indian or Alaska Native, non-Hispanic/Latino; 13 Asian, non-Hispanic/Latino; 25 Hispanic/Latino; 2 Native Hawaiian or other Pacific Islander, non-Hispanic/Latino), 3 international. Average age 30. 141 applicants, 46% accepted, 36 enrolled. Expenses: Contact institution. *Financial support:* Teaching assistantships, career-related internships or fieldwork, Federal Work-Study, and scholarships/grants available. Support available to part-time students. Financial award application deadline: 3/1; financial award applicants required to submit FAFSA. In 2019, 28 master's awarded. *Program availability:* Part-time. *Application deadline:* For fall admission, 3/1 for domestic students, 2/1 for international students. Applications are processed on a rolling basis. *Application fee:* $70. Electronic applications accepted. *Application Contact:* Jose Martinez, Graduate Admissions Supervisor, 916-278-7871, E-mail: martinj@skymail.csus.edu. *Interim Dean*, Dr. Ted Lascher, 916-278-6504, Fax: 916-278-4678, E-mail: tedl@csus.edu.

## CALIFORNIA STATE UNIVERSITY, SAN BERNARDINO, San Bernardino, CA 92407

**General Information** State-supported, coed, comprehensive institution. CGS member. *Enrollment:* 20,311 graduate, professional, and undergraduate students; 769 full-time matriculated graduate/professional students (567 women), 1,063 part-time matriculated graduate/professional students (672 women). *Enrollment by degree level:* 1,688 master's, 68 doctoral. *Graduate faculty:* 136 full-time (62 women), 93 part-time/adjunct (59 women). *Graduate housing:* Room and/or apartments available on a first-come, first-served basis to single students; on-campus housing not available to married students. Typical cost: $6725 (including board). *Student services:* Campus employment opportunities, campus safety program, career counseling, child daycare facilities, exercise/wellness program, free psychological counseling, international student services, low-cost health insurance, multicultural affairs office, services for students with disabilities, teacher training. *Library facilities:* Pfau Library.

**Computer facilities:** Computer purchase and lease plans are available. A campuswide network can be accessed. Online class registration is available.
Website: http://www.csusb.edu/

**General Application Contact:** Dr. Dorota Huizinga, Dean of Graduate Studies, 909-537-5058, Fax: 909-537-5078, E-mail: dorota.huizinga@csusb.edu.

**GRADUATE UNITS**

**Graduate Studies** Students: 769 full-time (567 women), 1,063 part-time (672 women); includes 1,163 minority (134 Black or African American, non-Hispanic/Latino; 6 American Indian or Alaska Native, non-Hispanic/Latino; 99 Asian, non-Hispanic/Latino; 873 Hispanic/Latino; 4 Native Hawaiian or other Pacific Islander, non-Hispanic/Latino; 47 Two or more races, non-Hispanic/Latino), 133 international. Average age 32. 1,727 applicants, 59% accepted, 679 enrolled. *Faculty:* 136 full-time (62 women), 93 part-time/adjunct (59 women). Expenses: Contact institution. In 2019, 751 master's, 19 doctorates awarded. *Program availability:* Part-time, evening/weekend. *Application deadline:* For fall admission, 7/17 for domestic students. *Application fee:* $55. *Application Contact:* Rachel Beech, Associate Vice President, 909-537-5188, E-mail: rachel.beech@csusb.edu. *Dean*, Dr. Dorota Huizinga, 909-537-5058, Fax: 909-537-5078, E-mail: dorota.huizinga@csusb.edu.

***College of Arts and Letters*** Students: 46 full-time (22 women), 81 part-time (56 women); includes 83 minority (12 Black or African American, non-Hispanic/Latino; 4 Asian, non-Hispanic/Latino; 63 Hispanic/Latino; 4 Two or more races, non-Hispanic/Latino), 4 international. Average age 33. 80 applicants, 73% accepted, 47 enrolled. *Faculty:* 19 full-time (15 women), 1 (woman) part-time/adjunct. Expenses: Contact institution. *Financial support:* Application deadline: 3/1. In 2019, 47 master's awarded. *Program availability:* Part-time, evening/weekend. *Application deadline:* For fall admission, 7/17 priority date for domestic students. Applications are processed on a rolling basis. *Application fee:* $55. Electronic applications accepted. *Application Contact:* Dr. Dorota Huizinga, Dean of Graduate Studies, 909-537-3064, Fax: 909-537-5078, E-mail: dorota.huizinga@csusb.edu. *Dean*, Dr. Rueyling Chuang, 909-537-5800, E-mail: rchuang@csusb.edu.

***College of Business and Public Administration*** Students: 112 full-time (61 women), 447 part-time (238 women); includes 339 minority (44 Black or African American, non-Hispanic/Latino; 2 American Indian or Alaska Native, non-Hispanic/Latino; 42 Asian, non-Hispanic/Latino; 238 Hispanic/Latino; 2 Native Hawaiian or other Pacific Islander, non-Hispanic/Latino; 11 Two or more races, non-Hispanic/Latino), 69 international. Average age 32. 494 applicants, 70% accepted, 199 enrolled. *Faculty:* 20 full-time (5 women), 20 part-time/adjunct (7 women). Expenses: Contact institution. *Financial support:* Application deadline: 3/1. In 2019, 253 master's awarded. *Program availability:* Part-time, evening/weekend. *Application deadline:* For fall admission, 7/17 for domestic students. Applications are processed on a rolling basis. *Application fee:* $55. *Application Contact:* Dr. Dorota Huizinga, Dean of Graduate Studies, 909-537-3064, Fax: 909-537-5078, E-mail: dorota.huizinga@csusb.edu. *Dean*, Dr. Lawrence C. Rose, 909-537-3703, E-mail: lrose@csusb.edu.

***College of Education*** Students: 326 full-time (265 women), 281 part-time (158 women); includes 378 minority (33 Black or African American, non-Hispanic/Latino; 2 American Indian or Alaska Native, non-Hispanic/Latino; 34 Asian, non-Hispanic/Latino; 293 Hispanic/Latino; 2 Native Hawaiian or other Pacific Islander, non-Hispanic/Latino; 14 Two or more races, non-Hispanic/Latino), 32 international. Average age 35. 353 applicants, 81% accepted, 231 enrolled. *Faculty:* 30 full-time (19 women), 50 part-time/adjunct (35 women). Expenses: Contact institution. In 2019, 211 master's, 19 doctorates awarded. *Program availability:* Part-time, evening/weekend. *Application deadline:* For fall admission, 7/17 for domestic students. *Application fee:* $55. *Application Contact:* Dr. Dorota Huizinga, Dean of Graduate Studies, 909-537-3604, E-mail: dorota.huizinga@csusb.edu. *Dean*, Dr. Chinaka DomNwachukwu, 909-537-5645, E-mail: Chinaka.domnwachukwu@csusb.edu.

***College of Natural Sciences*** Students: 50 full-time (30 women), 129 part-time (59 women); includes 111 minority (15 Black or African American, non-Hispanic/Latino; 10 Asian, non-Hispanic/Latino; 83 Hispanic/Latino; 3 Two or more races, non-Hispanic/Latino), 21 international. Average age 29. 284 applicants, 41% accepted, 59 enrolled. *Faculty:* 31 full-time (12 women), 7 part-time/adjunct (3 women). Expenses: Contact institution. *Financial support:* Fellowships, research assistantships, and teaching assistantships available. In 2019, 78 master's awarded. *Program availability:* Part-time. *Application fee:* $55. *Application Contact:* Dr. Dorota Huizinga, Dean of Graduate Studies, 909-537-3064, E-mail: dorota.huizinga@csusb.edu. *Interim Dean*, Dr. Sally McGill, 909-537-3304, Fax: 909-537-7005, E-mail: smcgill@csusb.edu.

***College of Social and Behavioral Sciences*** Students: 233 full-time (187 women), 121 part-time (67 women); includes 248 minority (29 Black or African American, non-Hispanic/Latino; 1 American Indian or Alaska Native, non-Hispanic/Latino; 9 Asian, non-Hispanic/Latino; 194 Hispanic/Latino; 15 Two or more races, non-Hispanic/Latino), 7 international. Average age 30. 515 applicants, 41% accepted, 143 enrolled. *Faculty:* 36 full-time (11 women), 15 part-time/adjunct (13 women). Expenses: Contact institution. *Financial support:* Career-related internships or fieldwork, Federal Work-Study, institutionally sponsored loans, and unspecified assistantships available. Support available to part-time students. In 2019, 162 master's awarded. *Program availability:* Part-time, evening/weekend. *Application deadline:* For fall admission, 7/17 for domestic students. *Application fee:* $55. *Application Contact:* Dr. Dorota Huizinga, Dean of Graduate Studies, 909-537-3064, E-mail: dorota.huizinga@csusb.edu. *Dean*, Dr. Rafik Mohamed, 909-537-7500, Fax: 909-537-7107, E-mail: rafik.mohamed@csusb.edu.

## CALIFORNIA STATE UNIVERSITY, SAN MARCOS, San Marcos, CA 92096-0001

**General Information** State-supported, coed, comprehensive institution. *Enrollment:* 14,519 graduate, professional, and undergraduate students; 268 full-time matriculated graduate/professional students (144 women), 154 part-time matriculated graduate/professional students (95 women). *Enrollment by degree level:* 422 master's. *Graduate faculty:* 292 full-time (148 women), 608 part-time/adjunct (304 women). *International tuition:* $18,640 full-time. *Tuition, area resident:* Full-time $7176. Tuition, state resident: full-time $7176. Tuition, nonresident: full-time $18,640. *Required fees:* $1960. *Graduate housing:* Room and/or apartments available on a first-come, first-served basis to single students; on-campus housing not available to married students. Housing application deadline: 10/1. *Student services:* Campus employment opportunities, campus safety program, career counseling, child daycare facilities, exercise/wellness program, free psychological counseling, international student services, low-cost health insurance, multicultural affairs office, services for students with disabilities, teacher training, writing training. *Library facilities:* Kellogg Library. *Collection:* Books: 215,402 (physical), 268,189 (digital/electronic); Serial titles: 3,130 (physical), 81,643 (digital/electronic); Databases: 100. Weekly public service hours: 100; students can reserve study rooms.

**Computer facilities:** A campuswide network can be accessed. Online class registration is available.
Website: http://www.csusm.edu/

**General Application Contact:** Dr. Charles De Leone, Interim Dean of Office of Graduate Studies and Research, 760-750-8045, Fax: 760-750-4066, E-mail: gradstudies@csusm.edu.

**GRADUATE UNITS**

***School of Education*** *Program availability:* Part-time, evening/weekend.

***School of Nursing***

**College of Humanities, Arts, Behavioral and Social Sciences** *Program availability:* Part-time, evening/weekend. Electronic applications accepted.

**College of Science and Mathematics**

**Program in Biotechnology**

## CALIFORNIA STATE UNIVERSITY, STANISLAUS, Turlock, CA 95382

**General Information** State-supported, coed, comprehensive institution. CGS member. *Graduate housing:* Room and/or apartments available on a first-come, first-served basis to single students; on-campus housing not available to married students. Housing application deadline: 7/15. *Research affiliation:* California Campus Compact-Carnegie Fellowship Program (teaching development for faculty), Valley Mountain Regional Center (development disability), Friends of Turlock Library, EDAW, Inc. (environmental sustainable development), Mathematical Association of America (mathematics), Kaiser Permanente (health care).

**GRADUATE UNITS**

**College of Business Administration** *Program availability:* Part-time, evening/weekend.

**College of Education, Kinesiology and Social Work** *Program availability:* Part-time, evening/weekend.

**College of Natural Sciences**

**College of Science**

**College of the Arts, Humanities and Social Sciences**

## CALIFORNIA UNIVERSITY OF MANAGEMENT AND SCIENCES, Anaheim, CA 92801

**General Information** Independent, coed, comprehensive institution.

**GRADUATE UNITS**

**Graduate Programs**

## CALIFORNIA UNIVERSITY OF PENNSYLVANIA, California, PA 15419-1394

**General Information** State-supported, coed, comprehensive institution. CGS member. *Enrollment:* 7,312 graduate, professional, and undergraduate students; 748 full-time matriculated graduate/professional students (512 women), 1,238 part-time matriculated graduate/professional students (797 women). *Enrollment by degree level:* 1,617 master's, 126 doctoral, 235 other advanced degrees. *Graduate faculty:* 43 full-time (26 women), 109 part-time/adjunct (48 women). *Tuition, area resident:* Full-time $9288; part-time $516 per credit. Tuition, state resident: full-time $9288; part-time $516 per credit. Tuition, nonresident: full-time $13,932; part-time $774 per credit. *Required fees:* $3631; $291.13 per credit. Part-time tuition and fees vary according to course load. *Graduate housing:* Room and/or apartments available on a first-come, first-served basis to single students; on-campus housing not available to married students. Typical cost: $7200 per year ($10,594 including board). Room and board charges vary according to housing facility selected. *Student services:* Campus employment opportunities, campus safety program, career counseling, child daycare facilities, exercise/wellness program, free psychological counseling, international student services, low-cost health insurance, multicultural affairs office, services for students with disabilities, teacher training, writing training. *Library facilities:* Manderino Library. *Collection:* Students can reserve study rooms. *Research affiliation:* The Center for Rural Pennsylvania (agriculture), The Technology Collaborative (robotics), International Technical Education Association (curricular development), National Collegiate Athletic Association (NCAA) (tobacco use), Gettysburg Travel Council (travel and tourism), NASA.

**Computer facilities:** 1,300 computers available on campus for general student use. Online class registration is available.
Website: http://www.calu.edu/

**General Application Contact:** Nicole Popielarcheck, Assistant Director of Graduate Admissions and Recruitment, 724-938-4029, Fax: 724-938-5712, E-mail: popielarcheck@calu.edu.

**GRADUATE UNITS**

**School of Graduate Studies and Research** *Program availability:* Part-time, evening/weekend, 100% online. Electronic applications accepted.

***College of Education and Human Services*** *Program availability:* Part-time, evening/weekend, online learning. Electronic applications accepted.

***College of Liberal Arts*** *Program availability:* Part-time, evening/weekend. Electronic applications accepted.

***Eberly College of Science and Technology*** *Program availability:* Part-time, evening/weekend, online learning. Electronic applications accepted.

## CALIFORNIA WESTERN SCHOOL OF LAW, San Diego, CA 92101-3090

**General Information** Independent, coed, graduate-only institution. *Graduate housing:* On-campus housing not available.

**GRADUATE UNITS**

**Graduate and Professional Programs** *Program availability:* Part-time. Electronic applications accepted.

## CALUMET COLLEGE OF SAINT JOSEPH, Whiting, IN 46394-2195

**General Information** Independent-religious, coed, comprehensive institution.

**GRADUATE UNITS**

**Program in Leadership in Teaching**

**Program in Public Safety Administration**

**Program in Quality Assurance**

## CALVARY UNIVERSITY, Kansas City, MO 64147

**General Information** Independent-religious, coed, comprehensive institution. *Graduate housing:* Rooms and/or apartments available on a first-come, first-served basis to single and married students.

**GRADUATE UNITS**

**Graduate School and Seminary** *Program availability:* Part-time, evening/weekend. Electronic applications accepted.

## CALVIN COLLEGE, Grand Rapids, MI 49546-4388

**General Information** Independent-religious, coed, comprehensive institution. *Graduate housing:* Room and/or apartments available on a first-come, first-served basis to single students; on-campus housing not available to married students. Housing application deadline: 4/1.

**GRADUATE UNITS**

**Graduate Programs in Education** *Program availability:* Part-time. Electronic applications accepted.

**Program in Accounting** *Program availability:* Part-time.

**Program in Speech Pathology**

## CALVIN THEOLOGICAL SEMINARY, Grand Rapids, MI 49546-4387

**General Information** Independent-religious, coed, graduate-only institution. *Graduate housing:* Rooms and/or apartments available on a first-come, first-served basis to single and married students. Housing application deadline: 4/1.

**GRADUATE UNITS**

**Graduate and Professional Programs** *Program availability:* Part-time. Electronic applications accepted.

## CAMBRIDGE COLLEGE, Boston, MA 02129

**General Information** Independent, coed, comprehensive institution. *Graduate housing:* On-campus housing not available.

**GRADUATE UNITS**

**School of Education** *Program availability:* Part-time, evening/weekend, online learning. Electronic applications accepted.

**School of Management** *Program availability:* Part-time, evening/weekend, 100% online, blended/hybrid learning. Electronic applications accepted.

**School of Psychology and Counseling** *Program availability:* Part-time, evening/weekend. Electronic applications accepted.

## CAMERON UNIVERSITY, Lawton, OK 73505-6377

**General Information** State-supported, coed, comprehensive institution. *Graduate housing:* Room and/or apartments available on a first-come, first-served basis to single students; on-campus housing not available to married students. *Research affiliation:* Army Research Institute (human factors), Advanced Systems Technology, Inc. (informational systems), Dynamics Research Corporation (multimedia systems), Eagle Systems, Inc. (multimedia systems), Halliburton (energy systems), Telos OK, LLC (simulations).

**GRADUATE UNITS**

**Office of Graduate Studies** *Program availability:* Part-time, evening/weekend, online learning. Electronic applications accepted.

## CAMPBELLSVILLE UNIVERSITY, Campbellsville, KY 42718-2799

**General Information** Independent-religious, coed, comprehensive institution. *Enrollment:* 13,744 graduate, professional, and undergraduate students; 7,300 full-time matriculated graduate/professional students (2,277 women), 361 part-time matriculated graduate/professional students (193 women). *Enrollment by degree level:* 7,643 master's, 18 doctoral. *Graduate faculty:* 117 full-time (59 women), 121 part-time/adjunct (73 women). *Tuition:* Full-time $9181; part-time $399 per credit hour. *Required fees:* $75 per term. Part-time tuition and fees vary according to course load, degree level, campus/location and program. *Graduate housing:* Room and/or apartments available on a first-come, first-served basis to single students; on-campus housing not available to married students. Typical cost: $8000 (including board). Room and board charges vary according to campus/location and housing facility selected. Housing application deadline: 6/30. *Student services:* Campus employment opportunities, campus safety program, career counseling, exercise/wellness program, international student services, services for students with disabilities, teacher training, writing training. *Library facilities:* Montgomery Library. *Collection:* Books: 128,057 (physical), 1.3 million (digital/electronic); Serial titles: 178,330 (digital/electronic); Databases: 150. Weekly public service hours: 77; students can reserve study rooms.

**Computer facilities:** 250 computers available on campus for general student use. A campuswide network can be accessed. Online class registration is available.
Website: http://www.campbellsville.edu/

**General Application Contact:** Monica Bamwine, Assistant Director of Graduate Admissions, 270-789-5221, Fax: 270-789-5071, E-mail: mkbamwine@campbellsville.edu.

**GRADUATE UNITS**

**Carver School of Social Work** *Program availability:* Part-time, evening/weekend, 100% online, blended/hybrid learning. Electronic applications accepted.

**College of Arts and Sciences** *Program availability:* Part-time, evening/weekend, 100% online, blended/hybrid learning. Electronic applications accepted.

**School of Business, Economics, and Technology** *Program availability:* Part-time, evening/weekend, 100% online, blended/hybrid learning. Electronic applications accepted.

**School of Education** Students: 181 full-time (144 women), 66 part-time (54 women); includes 21 minority (16 Black or African American, non-Hispanic/Latino; 1 American Indian or Alaska Native, non-Hispanic/Latino; 3 Hispanic/Latino; 1 Two or more races, non-Hispanic/Latino). Average age 34. 295 applicants, 37% accepted, 90 enrolled. *Faculty:* 22 full-time (16 women), 11 part-time/adjunct (4 women). Expenses: Contact institution. *Financial support:* Unspecified assistantships available. Financial award applicants required to submit FAFSA. In 2019, 67 master's awarded. *Program availability:* Part-time, evening/weekend, 100% online, blended/hybrid learning. *Application deadline:* For fall admission, 8/15 for domestic students; for spring admission, 12/15 for domestic students; for summer admission, 4/15 for domestic students. Applications are processed on a rolling basis. *Application fee:* $25. Electronic applications accepted. *Application Contact:* Monica Bamwine, Director of Graduate Admissions, 270-789-5221, Fax: 270-789-5071, E-mail: mkbamwine@campbellsville.edu. *Dean of School of Education,* Dr. Lisa Allen, 270-789-5344, Fax: 270-789-5206, E-mail: lsallen@campbellsville.edu.

**School of Music** *Program availability:* Part-time, 100% online, blended/hybrid learning. Electronic applications accepted.

**School of Theology** *Program availability:* Part-time, evening/weekend, 100% online, blended/hybrid learning. Electronic applications accepted.

## CAMPBELL UNIVERSITY, Buies Creek, NC 27506

**General Information** Independent-religious, coed, university. *Graduate housing:* Rooms and/or apartments available on a first-come, first-served basis to single and married students. Housing application deadline: 6/2.

**GRADUATE UNITS**

**Graduate and Professional Programs** *Program availability:* Part-time, evening/weekend.

***College of Pharmacy and Health Sciences*** *Program availability:* Part-time, evening/weekend. Electronic applications accepted.

***Divinity School***

***Jerry M. Wallace School of Osteopathic Medicine***

***Lundy-Fetterman School of Business*** *Program availability:* Part-time, evening/weekend.

***Norman Adrian Wiggins School of Law*** Electronic applications accepted.

***School of Education*** *Program availability:* Part-time, evening/weekend.

## CANADIAN COLLEGE OF NATUROPATHIC MEDICINE, Toronto, ON M2K 1E2, Canada

**General Information** Independent, coed, primarily women, graduate-only institution. *Graduate housing:* Room and/or apartments available on a first-come, first-served basis to single students; on-campus housing not available to married students. Housing application deadline: 4/30. *Research affiliation:* Ottawa Regional Cancer Centre, McMaster University, University of Oxford, Hospital for Sick Children, Mayo Clinic, Johns Hopkins University.

**GRADUATE UNITS**

**Doctor of Naturopathy Program** Electronic applications accepted.

## CANADIAN MEMORIAL CHIROPRACTIC COLLEGE, Toronto, ON M2H 3J1, Canada

**General Information** Independent, coed, graduate-only institution. *Graduate housing:* On-campus housing not available. *Research affiliation:* University of Waterloo, University of Calgary, University of Toronto.

**GRADUATE UNITS**

**Certificate Programs**

**Professional Program**

## CANADIAN SOUTHERN BAPTIST SEMINARY, Cochrane, AB T4C 2G1, Canada

**General Information** Independent-religious, coed, graduate-only institution. *Graduate housing:* Rooms and/or apartments available on a first-come, first-served basis to single and married students. Housing application deadline: 7/1.

**GRADUATE UNITS**

**Graduate Programs** *Program availability:* Part-time, 100% online, blended/hybrid learning.

## CANISIUS COLLEGE, Buffalo, NY 14208-1098

**General Information** Independent-religious, coed, comprehensive institution. *Enrollment:* 3,102 graduate, professional, and undergraduate students; 393 full-time matriculated graduate/professional students (225 women), 483 part-time matriculated graduate/professional students (291 women). *Enrollment by degree level:* 815 master's, 61 other advanced degrees. *Graduate faculty:* 58 full-time (20 women), 131 part-time/adjunct (84 women). *Tuition:* Part-time $900 per credit. *Required fees:* $25 per credit hour. $65 per term. Part-time tuition and fees vary according to course load and program. *Graduate housing:* Room and/or apartments available on a first-come, first-served basis to single students; on-campus housing not available to married students. Housing application deadline: 5/1. *Student services:* Campus employment opportunities, campus safety program, career counseling, exercise/wellness program, free psychological counseling, international student services, multicultural affairs office, services for students with disabilities, teacher training. *Library facilities:* Andrew L. Bouwhuis Library plus 1 other. *Collection:* Books: 237,419 (physical), 2.1 million (digital/electronic); Serial titles: 3,003 (physical), 354,766 (digital/electronic); Databases: 110. Weekly public service hours: 110; students can reserve study rooms. *Research affiliation:* Eduventures (enrollment management).

**Computer facilities:** Computer purchase and lease plans are available. 700 computers available on campus for general student use. A campuswide network can be accessed. Online class registration, online accounts are available.
Website: http://www.canisius.edu/

**General Application Contact:** Lauren M. Kicak, Associate Director of Graduate Admissions, 716-888-2109, Fax: 716-888-3290, E-mail: kicakl@canisius.edu.

**GRADUATE UNITS**

**Graduate Division** Students: 393 full-time (225 women), 483 part-time (291 women); includes 150 minority (76 Black or African American, non-Hispanic/Latino; 2 American Indian or Alaska Native, non-Hispanic/Latino; 13 Asian, non-Hispanic/Latino; 35 Hispanic/Latino; 24 Two or more races, non-Hispanic/Latino), 28 international. Average age 29. 620 applicants, 82% accepted, 293 enrolled. *Faculty:* 58 full-time (20 women), 131 part-time/adjunct (84 women). Expenses: Contact institution. *Financial support:* Career-related internships or fieldwork, Federal Work-Study, scholarships/grants, tuition waivers (partial), and unspecified assistantships available. Support available to part-time students. Financial award application deadline: 4/30; financial award applicants required to submit FAFSA. In 2019, 493 master's awarded. *Program availability:* Part-time, evening/weekend, 100% online, blended/hybrid learning. *Application deadline:* Applications are processed on a rolling basis. Electronic applications accepted. *Application Contact:* Lauren M. Kicak, Associate Director of Graduate Admissions, 716-888-2109, Fax: 716-888-3290, E-mail: kicakl@canisius.edu. *Vice President for Academic Affairs*, Dr. Sara R. Morris, 716-888-2121, Fax: 716-888-2125, E-mail: morriss@canisius.edu.

***College of Arts and Sciences*** Students: 28 full-time (20 women), 48 part-time (32 women); includes 14 minority (2 Black or African American, non-Hispanic/Latino; 2 American Indian or Alaska Native, non-Hispanic/Latino; 2 Asian, non-Hispanic/Latino; 4 Hispanic/Latino; 4 Two or more races, non-Hispanic/Latino). Average age 33. 117 applicants, 52% accepted, 37 enrolled. *Faculty:* 16 full-time (7 women), 13 part-time/adjunct (7 women). Expenses: Contact institution. *Financial support:* Career-related internships or fieldwork, Federal Work-Study, scholarships/grants, tuition waivers (partial), and unspecified assistantships available. Support available to part-time students. Financial award application deadline: 4/30; financial award applicants required to submit FAFSA. In 2019, 30 master's awarded. *Program availability:* Part-time, evening/weekend, 100% online, blended/hybrid learning. *Application deadline:* Applications are processed on a rolling basis. Electronic applications accepted. *Application Contact:* Dr. Thomas A. Chambers, Dean of the College of Arts and Sciences, 716-888-2150, Fax: 716-888-3211, E-mail: chambe27@canisius.edu. *Dean of the College of Arts and Sciences*, Dr. Thomas A. Chambers, 716-888-2150, Fax: 716-888-3211, E-mail: chambe27@canisius.edu.

***Richard J. Wehle School of Business*** Students: 112 full-time (43 women), 113 part-time (45 women); includes 1,026 minority (1,012 Black or African American, non-Hispanic/Latino; 4 Asian, non-Hispanic/Latino; 6 Hispanic/Latino; 4 Two or more races, non-Hispanic/Latino), 11 international. Average age 28. 172 applicants, 87% accepted, 110 enrolled. *Faculty:* 32 full-time (9 women), 16 part-time/adjunct (5 women). Expenses: Contact institution. *Financial support:* Career-related internships or fieldwork, Federal Work-Study, scholarships/grants, tuition waivers (partial), and unspecified assistantships available. Support available to part-time students. Financial award application deadline: 4/30; financial award applicants required to submit FAFSA. In 2019, 151 master's awarded. *Program availability:* Part-time, evening/weekend. *Application deadline:* For fall admission, 7/1 priority date for domestic students; for spring admission, 11/1 priority date for domestic students. Applications are processed on a rolling basis. Electronic applications accepted. *Application Contact:* Dr. Denise M. Rotondo, Dean, 716-888-2164, Fax: 716-888-2145, E-mail: rotondod@canisius.edu. *Dean*, Dr. Denise M. Rotondo, 716-888-2164, Fax: 716-888-2145, E-mail: rotondod@canisius.edu.

***School of Education and Human Services*** Students: 253 full-time (162 women), 322 part-time (214 women); includes 110 minority (62 Black or African American, non-Hispanic/Latino; 7 Asian, non-Hispanic/Latino; 25 Hispanic/Latino; 16 Two or more races, non-Hispanic/Latino), 17 international. Average age 29. 444 applicants, 87% accepted, 234 enrolled. *Faculty:* 31 full-time (13 women), 111 part-time/adjunct (70 women). Expenses: Contact institution. *Financial support:* Career-related internships or fieldwork, Federal Work-Study, scholarships/grants, tuition waivers (partial), and unspecified assistantships available. Support available to part-time students. Financial award application deadline: 4/30; financial award applicants required to submit FAFSA. In 2019, 305 master's awarded. *Program availability:* Part-time, evening/weekend, 100% online, blended/hybrid learning. *Application deadline:* Applications are processed on a rolling basis. Electronic applications accepted. *Application Contact:* Lauren M Kicak, Associate Director of Graduate Admissions, 716-888-2109, Fax: 716-888-3290, E-mail: kicakl@canisius.edu. *Dean*, Dr. Nancy V. Wallace, 716-888-3205, Fax: 716-888-3164, E-mail: wallacen@canisius.edu.

## CAPE BRETON UNIVERSITY, Sydney, NS B1P 6L2, Canada

**General Information** Province-supported, coed, comprehensive institution. *Graduate housing:* Room and/or apartments available on a first-come, first-served basis to single students; on-campus housing not available to married students. Housing application deadline: 3/31. *Research affiliation:* Hyperspectral Data International (marine remote sensing), Sable Offshore Energy, Inc. (petroleum resources), Fortress Louisbourg National Historic Park (museum/heritage projects), Dynagen Industrial Mine Technology (mining industry equipment), Atlantic Geomatics (computer networking and software development), Advanced Glazing, Limited (transparent insulation).

**GRADUATE UNITS**

**Shannon School of Business** *Program availability:* Part-time. Electronic applications accepted.

## CAPELLA UNIVERSITY, Minneapolis, MN 55402

**General Information** Proprietary, coed, upper-level institution. CGS member.

**GRADUATE UNITS**

**Harold Abel School of Social and Behavioral Science** *Program availability:* Part-time, evening/weekend, online learning. Electronic applications accepted.

**School of Business and Technology** *Program availability:* Part-time, evening/weekend, online learning. Electronic applications accepted.

**School of Education** *Program availability:* Part-time, evening/weekend, online learning. Electronic applications accepted.

**School of Public Service Leadership**

## CAPITAL UNIVERSITY, Columbus, OH 43209-2394

**General Information** Independent-religious, coed, comprehensive institution. *Graduate housing:* On-campus housing not available.

**GRADUATE UNITS**

**Conservatory of Music** *Program availability:* Part-time. Electronic applications accepted.

**Law School** *Program availability:* Part-time, evening/weekend. Electronic applications accepted.

**School of Management** *Program availability:* Part-time, evening/weekend. Electronic applications accepted.

**School of Nursing** *Program availability:* Part-time, evening/weekend.

**Trinity Lutheran Seminary** *Program availability:* Part-time. Electronic applications accepted.

## CAPITOL TECHNOLOGY UNIVERSITY, Laurel, MD 20708-9759

**General Information** Independent, coed, comprehensive institution. *Graduate housing:* On-campus housing not available.

**GRADUATE UNITS**

**Graduate Programs** *Program availability:* Part-time, evening/weekend, online learning. Electronic applications accepted.

## CARDINAL STRITCH UNIVERSITY, Milwaukee, WI 53217-3985

**General Information** Independent-religious, coed, university. *Enrollment:* 1,796 graduate, professional, and undergraduate students; 136 full-time matriculated graduate/professional students (102 women), 512 part-time matriculated graduate/professional students (364 women). *Enrollment by degree level:* 541 master's, 107 doctoral. Tuition and fees vary according to course load, degree level and program. *Graduate housing:* Room and/or apartments available on a first-come, first-served basis to single students; on-campus housing not available to married students. *Student services:* Campus employment opportunities, career counseling, exercise/wellness program, free psychological counseling, international student services, multicultural affairs office, services for students with disabilities, teacher training, writing training. *Library facilities:* Cardinal Stritch University Library. *Collection:* Books: 121,982 (physical), 212,458 (digital/electronic); Serial titles: 648 (physical), 45 (digital/electronic); Databases: 70. Weekly public service hours: 90; students can reserve study rooms.

**Computer facilities:** Computer purchase and lease plans are available. 458 computers available on campus for general student use. A campuswide network can be accessed. Online class registration is available.
Website: http://www.stritch.edu/

**General Application Contact:** Susan Slonac, Senior Director of Adult, Graduate & Professional Studies Admissions, 800-347-8822 Ext. 4062, E-mail: admissions@stritch.edu.

**GRADUATE UNITS**

**College of Arts and Sciences** *Program availability:* Part-time, evening/weekend. Electronic applications accepted.

**College of Business and Management** *Program availability:* Part-time, evening/weekend, 100% online, blended/hybrid learning. Electronic applications accepted.

**Ruth S. Coleman College of Nursing and Health Sciences** *Program availability:* Part-time, evening/weekend. Electronic applications accepted.

## CAREY THEOLOGICAL COLLEGE, Vancouver, BC V6T 1J6, Canada

**General Information** Independent-religious, coed, graduate-only institution. *Graduate housing:* Rooms and/or apartments available on a first-come, first-served basis to single and married students. Housing application deadline: 5/31.

**GRADUATE UNITS**

**Graduate Programs** *Program availability:* Part-time. Electronic applications accepted.

## CARIBBEAN UNIVERSITY, Bayamón, PR 00960-0493

**General Information** Independent, coed, comprehensive institution.

**GRADUATE UNITS**

**Graduate School**

## CARLETON UNIVERSITY, Ottawa, ON K1S 5B6, Canada

**General Information** Province-supported, coed, university. *Graduate housing:* Room and/or apartments guaranteed to single students; on-campus housing not available to married students. Housing application deadline: 5/31.

**GRADUATE UNITS**

**Faculty of Graduate Studies** *Program availability:* Part-time, evening/weekend. Electronic applications accepted.

***Faculty of Arts and Social Sciences*** *Program availability:* Part-time, evening/weekend.
***Faculty of Business***
***Faculty of Engineering and Design***
***Faculty of Public Affairs and Management*** *Program availability:* Part-time.
***Faculty of Science*** *Program availability:* Part-time, evening/weekend.

## CARLOW UNIVERSITY, Pittsburgh, PA 15213-3165

**General Information** Independent-religious, coed, primarily women, comprehensive institution. *Enrollment:* 2,022 graduate, professional, and undergraduate students; 531 full-time matriculated graduate/professional students (449 women), 191 part-time matriculated graduate/professional students (176 women). *Enrollment by degree level:* 631 master's, 75 doctoral, 20 other advanced degrees. *Graduate faculty:* 34 full-time, 38 part-time/adjunct. *Tuition:* Full-time $13,666; part-time $902 per credit hour. *Required fees:* $15; $15 per credit. Tuition and fees vary according to degree level and program. *Graduate housing:* Room and/or apartments available on a first-come, first-served basis to single students; on-campus housing not available to married students. *Student services:* Campus employment opportunities, campus safety program, career counseling, exercise/wellness program, free psychological counseling, international student services, multicultural affairs office, services for students with disabilities, teacher training, writing training. *Library facilities:* Grace Library.

**Computer facilities:** A campuswide network can be accessed. Online class registration is available.
Website: http://www.carlow.edu/

**General Application Contact:** Wendy Phillips, Director, Graduate Admissions, 412-578-8861, Fax: 412-578-6321, E-mail: gradstudies@carlow.edu.

**GRADUATE UNITS**

**College of Health and Wellness** Students: 187 full-time (165 women), 92 part-time (89 women); includes 27 minority (17 Black or African American, non-Hispanic/Latino; 5 Asian, non-Hispanic/Latino; 1 Hispanic/Latino; 4 Two or more races, non-Hispanic/Latino). Average age 34. 95 applicants, 100% accepted, 62 enrolled. Expenses: Contact institution. *Financial support:* Application deadline: 4/1; applicants required to submit FAFSA. In 2019, 103 master's, 16 doctorates, 2 other advanced degrees awarded. *Program availability:* Part-time, evening/weekend, 100% online, blended/hybrid learning, low-residency. *Application deadline:* For fall admission, 6/15 priority date for domestic and international students; for spring admission, 11/15 priority date for domestic and international students. Applications are processed on a rolling basis. Electronic applications accepted. *Application Contact:* Dr. Lynn George, Dean, 412-578-6115, Fax: 412-578-6114. *Dean,* Dr. Lynn George, 412-578-6115, Fax: 412-578-6114.

**College of Leadership and Social Change** Students: 257 full-time (213 women), 58 part-time (49 women); includes 87 minority (65 Black or African American, non-Hispanic/Latino; 5 Asian, non-Hispanic/Latino; 7 Hispanic/Latino; 10 Two or more races, non-Hispanic/Latino), 1 international. Average age 32. 179 applicants, 91% accepted, 111 enrolled. Expenses: Contact institution. *Financial support:* Application deadline: 4/1; applicants required to submit FAFSA. *Program availability:* Part-time, evening/weekend, 100% online, blended/hybrid learning. *Application deadline:* Applications are processed on a rolling basis. Electronic applications accepted. *Application Contact:* Wendy Phillips, Director, Graduate Admissions, 412-578-8861, Fax: 412-578-6321, E-mail: gradstudies@carlow.edu.

**College of Learning and Innovation** Students: 87 full-time (71 women), 41 part-time (38 women); includes 21 minority (11 Black or African American, non-Hispanic/Latino; 5 Asian, non-Hispanic/Latino; 5 Two or more races, non-Hispanic/Latino), 2 international. Average age 35. 57 applicants, 100% accepted, 42 enrolled. Expenses: Contact institution. *Financial support:* Application deadline: 4/1; applicants required to submit FAFSA. In 2019, 58 master's, 6 other advanced degrees awarded. *Program availability:* Part-time, evening/weekend, 100% online, blended/hybrid learning, low-residency. *Application deadline:* Applications are processed on a rolling basis. Electronic applications accepted. *Application Contact:* Dr. Matthew Gordley, Dean, 412-578-6262, E-mail: megordley@carlow.edu. *Dean,* Dr. Matthew Gordley, 412-578-6262, E-mail: megordley@carlow.edu.

## CARNEGIE MELLON UNIVERSITY, Pittsburgh, PA 15213-3891

**General Information** Independent, coed, university. CGS member. *Graduate housing:* On-campus housing not available. *Research affiliation:* National Census Data Research Center (public policy), Robotics Engineering Consortium (computer science and engineering), Software Engineering Institute (computer science and engineering), Carnegie Bosch Institute for Applied Studies in International Management (business and management), Pittsburgh Supercomputer Center.

**GRADUATE UNITS**

**Carnegie Institute of Technology** *Program availability:* Part-time, evening/weekend.
***Information Networking Institute***
**Center for the Neural Basis of Cognition**
**College of Fine Arts** *Program availability:* Part-time. Electronic applications accepted.
***School of Architecture***
***School of Art***
***School of Design***
***School of Drama***
***School of Music*** *Program availability:* Part-time.
**Dietrich College of Humanities and Social Sciences** *Program availability:* Part-time. Electronic applications accepted.
**Heinz College** *Program availability:* Part-time, evening/weekend. Electronic applications accepted.
**Heinz College Australia**
***School of Information Systems and Management***
***School of Public Policy and Management***
**Joint CMU-Pitt PhD Program in Computational Biology**
**Mellon College of Science** *Program availability:* Part-time. Electronic applications accepted.
**School of Computer Science**
***Language Technologies Institute***
***Robotics Institute***
**Tepper School of Business** *Program availability:* Part-time.

## CAROLINA CHRISTIAN COLLEGE, Winston-Salem, NC 27102-0777

**General Information** Independent-religious, coed, comprehensive institution.

**GRADUATE UNITS**

**Program in Religious Education**

## CARROLL UNIVERSITY, Waukesha, WI 53186-5593

**General Information** Independent-religious, coed, comprehensive institution. *Graduate housing:* On-campus housing not available.

**GRADUATE UNITS**

**Graduate Programs in Education** *Program availability:* Part-time, evening/weekend. Electronic applications accepted.
**Program in Business Administration** *Program availability:* Part-time. Electronic applications accepted.
**Program in Exercise Physiology**
**Program in Occupational Therapy**
**Program in Physical Therapy**
**Program in Physician Assistant Studies**
**Program in Software Engineering** *Program availability:* Part-time, evening/weekend. Electronic applications accepted.

## CARSON-NEWMAN UNIVERSITY, Jefferson City, TN 37760

**General Information** Independent-religious, coed, comprehensive institution. *Enrollment:* 2,560 graduate, professional, and undergraduate students; 176 full-time matriculated graduate/professional students (92 women), 671 part-time matriculated graduate/professional students (518 women). *Enrollment by degree level:* 638 master's, 184 doctoral, 25 other advanced degrees. *Graduate faculty:* 39 full-time (22 women), 35 part-time/adjunct (25 women). *Tuition:* Full-time $500. *Required fees:* $675; $375 per credit hour. $125 per term. Tuition and fees vary according to class time, course level, course load, degree level, campus/location and program. *Graduate housing:* Room and/or apartments available on a first-come, first-served basis to single students; on-campus housing not available to married students. Typical cost: $2990 per year ($8150 including board). Housing application deadline: 7/15. *Student services:* Campus employment opportunities, campus safety program, career counseling, free psychological counseling, international student services, low-cost health insurance, services for students with disabilities. *Library facilities:* Stephens-Burnett Library plus 3 others. *Collection:* Study areas open 24 hours, 5–7 days a week; students can reserve study rooms.

**Computer facilities:** 200 computers available on campus for general student use. A campuswide network can be accessed from student residence rooms and from off campus. Online class registration is available.
Website: http://www.cn.edu/

**General Application Contact:** Nilma Stewart, Graduate Admissions and Services Adviser, 865-471-3230, Fax: 865-471-3875, E-mail: adults@cn.edu.

**GRADUATE UNITS**

**Program in Applied Theology** Students: 8 part-time (3 women); includes 1 minority (Black or African American, non-Hispanic/Latino). Average age 42. 2 applicants, 100% accepted, 2 enrolled. *Faculty:* 1 full-time (0 women), 1 (woman) part-time/adjunct. Expenses: Contact institution. *Financial support:* Federal Work-Study and tuition waivers (full and partial) available. Financial award applicants required to submit FAFSA. In 2019, 3 master's awarded. *Program availability:* Part-time, evening/weekend. *Application deadline:* For fall admission, 7/15 priority date for domestic students. Applications are processed on a rolling basis. *Application fee:* $50. *Application Contact:* Nilma Stewart, Graduate Admissions and Services Adviser, 865-473-3468, Fax: 865-471-3875, E-mail: adults@cn.edu. *Dean, School of Religion,* Dr. David E. Crutchley, 865-471-3277, E-mail: dcruthley@cn.edu.

**Program in Business Administration** Students: 97 full-time (37 women), 41 part-time (23 women); includes 19 minority (14 Black or African American, non-Hispanic/Latino; 1 Asian, non-Hispanic/Latino; 3 Hispanic/Latino; 1 Two or more races, non-Hispanic/Latino), 18 international. Average age 30. 68 applicants, 100% accepted, 49 enrolled. *Faculty:* 6 full-time (2 women), 7 part-time/adjunct (3 women). Expenses: Contact institution. *Program availability:* Part-time, evening/weekend. *Application Contact:* Nilma Stewart, Graduate Admissions and Services Adviser, 865-471-3230, Fax: 865-471-3875, E-mail: adults@cn.edu. *Director of the MBA Program,* Philip Bailey, 865-471-7174, E-mail: pbailey@cn.edu.

**Program in Counseling** Students: 42 full-time (36 women), 19 part-time (17 women); includes 5 minority (2 Black or African American, non-Hispanic/Latino; 2 American Indian or Alaska Native, non-Hispanic/Latino; 1 Hispanic/Latino), 2 international. Average age 30. 19 applicants, 100% accepted, 15 enrolled. *Faculty:* 4 full-time (3 women), 3 part-time/adjunct (2 women). Expenses: Contact institution. *Program availability:* Part-time, evening/weekend. *Application Contact:* Nilma Stewart, Graduate Admissions and Services Adviser, 865-471-3230, Fax: 865-471-3875, E-mail: adults@cn.edu.

**Program in Education** Students: 29 full-time (16 women), 442 part-time (334 women); includes 50 minority (33 Black or African American, non-Hispanic/Latino; 1 American Indian or Alaska Native, non-Hispanic/Latino; 1 Asian, non-Hispanic/Latino; 9 Hispanic/Latino; 6 Two or more races, non-Hispanic/Latino), 12 international. Average age 35. 249 applicants, 100% accepted, 213 enrolled. *Faculty:* 19 full-time (11 women), 18 part-time/adjunct (14 women). Expenses: Contact institution. *Financial support:* Federal Work-Study and unspecified assistantships available. Financial award applicants required to submit FAFSA. In 2019, 171 master's awarded. *Program availability:* Part-time, evening/weekend, 100% online, blended/hybrid learning. *Application deadline:* For fall admission, 7/15 priority date for domestic students. Applications are processed on a rolling basis. *Application fee:* $50. Electronic applications accepted. *Application Contact:* Nilma Stewart, Graduate Admissions and Services Adviser, 865-471-3230, Fax: 865-471-3875, E-mail: adults@cn.edu. *Chair,* Dr. Kim Hawkins, 865-471-3314, E-mail: khawkins@cn.edu.

**Program in Nursing** Students: 7 full-time (2 women), 158 part-time (139 women); includes 17 minority (10 Black or African American, non-Hispanic/Latino; 1 American Indian or Alaska Native, non-Hispanic/Latino; 2 Asian, non-Hispanic/Latino; 3 Hispanic/Latino; 1 Two or more races, non-Hispanic/Latino), 1 international. Average age 37. 85 applicants, 100% accepted, 59 enrolled. *Faculty:* 8 full-time (6 women), 5 part-time/adjunct (all women). Expenses: Contact institution. *Application Contact:* Nilma Stewart, Graduate Admissions and Services Adviser, 865-471-3230, Fax: 865-471-3875, E-mail: adults@cn.edu.

**Program in Social Entrepreneurship** Students: 1 (woman) full-time, 2 part-time (1 woman), 1 international. Average age 38. *Faculty:* 1 full-time (0 women), 1 part-time/adjunct (0 women). Expenses: Contact institution. *Program availability:* Part-time, evening/weekend. *Application Contact:* Nilma Stewart, Graduate Admissions and Services Adviser, 865-471-3230, Fax: 865-471-3875, E-mail: adults@cn.edu. *Department Chair,* Dr. Laura Wadlington, 865-471-3270, E-mail: lwadlington@cn.edu.

## CARTHAGE COLLEGE, Kenosha, WI 53140

**General Information** Independent-religious, coed, comprehensive institution. *Graduate housing:* On-campus housing not available.

**GRADUATE UNITS**

**Division of Teacher Education** *Program availability:* Part-time, evening/weekend.

## CASE WESTERN RESERVE UNIVERSITY, Cleveland, OH 44106

**General Information** Independent, coed, university. CGS member. *Enrollment:* 11,874 graduate, professional, and undergraduate students. *Enrollment by degree level:* 3,492 master's, 3,071 doctoral, 43 other advanced degrees. *Graduate housing:* On-campus housing not available. *Student services:* Campus employment opportunities, campus safety program, career counseling, exercise/wellness program, free psychological counseling, grant writing training, international student services, low-cost health insurance, multicultural affairs office, services for students with disabilities, teacher training, writing training. *Library facilities:* Kelvin Smith Library plus 6 others. *Collection:* Books: 4 million (physical), 1.5 million (digital/electronic); Serial titles: 65,046 (physical); Databases: 470. Study areas open 24 hours, 5–7 days a week; students can reserve study rooms. *Research affiliation:* Bayer Materials Science (wind materials research), Cleveland Clinic Foundation (biomedical science), Johnson and Johnson Services, Inc. (human health), Cleveland Botanical Garden (plant sciences and ecology), Swagelok Company (surface analysis and materials technology), University Hospitals of Cleveland (biomedical science).

**Computer facilities:** Computer purchase and lease plans are available. 357 computers available on campus for general student use. A campuswide network can be accessed. Online class registration, software library, online reference databases, electronic books and journals, research computing, training are available.
Website: http://www.case.edu/

**GRADUATE UNITS**

**Frances Payne Bolton School of Nursing** Students: 280 full-time (236 women), 189 part-time (151 women); includes 115 minority (49 Black or African American, non-Hispanic/Latino; 1 American Indian or Alaska Native, non-Hispanic/Latino; 32 Asian, non-Hispanic/Latino; 24 Hispanic/Latino; 9 Two or more races, non-Hispanic/Latino), 33 international. Average age 34. 288 applicants, 65% accepted, 108 enrolled. *Faculty:* 63 full-time (51 women), 9 part-time/adjunct (8 women). Expenses: Contact institution. *Financial support:* In 2019–20, 418 students received support, including 3 fellowships with full tuition reimbursements available (averaging $39,428 per year), 3 research assistantships with partial tuition reimbursements available (averaging $17,064 per year), 49 teaching assistantships with partial tuition reimbursements available (averaging $17,064 per year); scholarships/grants, traineeships, and nurse faculty loan program also available. Financial award application deadline: 5/15; financial award applicants required to submit FAFSA. In 2019, 122 master's, 57 doctorates awarded. *Program availability:* Part-time. *Application deadline:* For fall admission, 3/1 for domestic and international students; for spring admission, 10/1 for domestic and international students; for summer admission, 3/1 for domestic and international students. Applications are processed on a rolling basis. *Application fee:* $75. Electronic applications accepted. *Application Contact:* Jackie Tepale, Admissions Coordinator, Graduate Programs, 216-368-5253, Fax: 216-368-3542, E-mail: yyd@case.edu. *Dean/Professor*, Dr. Carol M Musil, 216-368-2545, Fax: 216-368-3542, E-mail: cmm4@case.edu.

**Jack, Joseph and Morton Mandel School of Applied Social Sciences** Students: 447 full-time (392 women), 101 part-time (83 women); includes 187 minority (118 Black or African American, non-Hispanic/Latino; 17 Asian, non-Hispanic/Latino; 31 Hispanic/Latino; 1 Native Hawaiian or other Pacific Islander, non-Hispanic/Latino; 20 Two or more races, non-Hispanic/Latino), 15 international. Average age 32. Expenses: Contact institution. *Financial support:* In 2019–20, 548 students received support, including 548 fellowships with full tuition reimbursements available (averaging $12,500 per year); research assistantships, career-related internships or fieldwork, Federal Work-Study, institutionally sponsored loans, scholarships/grants, tuition waivers (partial), and paid field placements (for MSSA students) also available. Support available to part-time students. Financial award application deadline: 4/15; financial award applicants required to submit FAFSA. In 2019, 184 master's, 3 doctorates awarded. *Program availability:* Part-time, evening/weekend, 100% online. *Application deadline:* For fall admission, 4/15 for domestic and international students; for spring admission, 12/15 for domestic students; for summer admission, 3/15 for domestic students. Applications are processed on a rolling basis. Electronic applications accepted. *Application Contact:* Richard Sigg, Director of Recruitment and Enrollment, 216-368-1655, E-mail: richard.sigg@case.edu. *Dean*, Dr. Grover Cleveland Gilmore, 216-368-2256, E-mail: msassdean@case.edu.

**School of Dental Medicine** Electronic applications accepted.

**School of Graduate Studies** Students: 2,120 full-time (1,079 women), 369 part-time (204 women); includes 633 minority (157 Black or African American, non-Hispanic/Latino; 2 American Indian or Alaska Native, non-Hispanic/Latino; 273 Asian, non-Hispanic/Latino; 140 Hispanic/Latino; 1 Native Hawaiian or other Pacific Islander, non-Hispanic/Latino; 60 Two or more races, non-Hispanic/Latino), 730 international. Average age 28. 3,613 applicants, 53% accepted, 804 enrolled. *Faculty:* 3,555 full-time (1,384 women). Expenses: Contact institution. *Financial support:* Fellowships with tuition reimbursements, research assistantships with tuition reimbursements, teaching assistantships with tuition reimbursements, career-related internships or fieldwork, Federal Work-Study, institutionally sponsored loans, scholarships/grants, traineeships, health care benefits, tuition waivers (full and partial), and unspecified assistantships available. Support available to part-time students. Financial award applicants required to submit CSS PROFILE or FAFSA. In 2019, 682 master's, 192 doctorates awarded. *Program availability:* Part-time, evening/weekend, online learning. *Application deadline:* For fall admission, 3/1 for domestic students; for spring admission, 11/1 for domestic students. *Application fee:* $50. Electronic applications accepted. *Application Contact:* Dr. Charles E. Rozek, Associate Professor and Dean of the School of Graduate Studies and Vice Provost, 216-368-4390, Fax: 216-368-4250, E-mail: charles.rozek@case.edu. *Associate Professor and Dean of the School of Graduate Studies and Vice Provost*, Dr. Charles E. Rozek, 216-368-4390, Fax: 216-368-4250, E-mail: charles.rozek@case.edu.

***Case School of Engineering*** *Program availability:* Part-time, evening/weekend, 100% online, blended/hybrid learning. Electronic applications accepted.

**School of Law** Electronic applications accepted.

**School of Medicine** *Program availability:* Part-time.

***Graduate Programs in Medicine*** *Program availability:* Part-time. Electronic applications accepted.

**Weatherhead School of Management** *Program availability:* Part-time, evening/weekend. Electronic applications accepted.

***Mandel Center for Nonprofit Organizations***

## CASTLETON UNIVERSITY, Castleton, VT 05735

**General Information** State-supported, coed, comprehensive institution. *Graduate housing:* Room and/or apartments available on a first-come, first-served basis to single students; on-campus housing not available to married students. Housing application deadline: 5/19.

**GRADUATE UNITS**

**Division of Graduate Studies** *Program availability:* Part-time, evening/weekend.

## CATAWBA COLLEGE, Salisbury, NC 28144-2488

**General Information** Independent-religious, coed, comprehensive institution. *Graduate housing:* On-campus housing not available.

**GRADUATE UNITS**

**Department of Teacher Education** *Program availability:* Part-time-only. Electronic applications accepted.

## CATHOLIC DISTANCE UNIVERSITY, Charles Town, WV 25414

**General Information** Independent-religious, coed, graduate-only institution. *Graduate housing:* On-campus housing not available.

**GRADUATE UNITS**

**Graduate Programs** *Program availability:* Part-time, evening/weekend, online learning.

## CATHOLIC THEOLOGICAL UNION, Chicago, IL 60615-5698

**General Information** Independent-religious, coed, graduate-only institution. *Graduate housing:* Rooms and/or apartments available on a first-come, first-served basis to single and married students. Housing application deadline: 7/1.

**GRADUATE UNITS**

**Graduate and Professional Programs** *Program availability:* Part-time, evening/weekend.

## THE CATHOLIC UNIVERSITY OF AMERICA, Washington, DC 20064

**General Information** Independent-religious, coed, university. CGS member. *Enrollment:* 5,771 graduate, professional, and undergraduate students. *Enrollment by degree level:* 1,331 master's, 1,188 doctoral, 105 other advanced degrees. *Graduate housing:* Room and/or apartments available on a first-come, first-served basis to single students; on-campus housing not available to married students. Housing application deadline: 5/15. *Student services:* Campus employment opportunities, campus safety program, career counseling, free psychological counseling, international student services, low-cost health insurance, multicultural affairs office, services for students with disabilities, teacher training, writing training. *Library facilities:* Mullen Library plus 1 other. *Collection:* Books: 754,067 (physical), 357,968 (digital/electronic); Serial titles: 14,610 (physical), 129,482 (digital/electronic); Databases: 232. Weekly public service hours: 97. *Research affiliation:* EnergySolutions (waste vitrification research), National Rehabilitation Hospital (rehabilitation engineering research), Samsung (building environmental control), Space Telescope Science Institute (astronomy and space physics research), Better Way Foundation (early childhood education), Eco-Convergence Group, Inc. (concrete materials research).

**Computer facilities:** 542 computers available on campus for general student use. A campuswide network can be accessed. Online class registration is available.
Website: http://www.catholic.edu/

**General Application Contact:** Dr. Steven Brown, Vice Provost and Dean of Graduate Studies, 202-319-5057, Fax: 202-319-6533, E-mail: cua-admissions@cua.edu.

**GRADUATE UNITS**

**Benjamin T. Rome School of Music** Students: 41 full-time (31 women), 85 part-time (55 women); includes 39 minority (10 Black or African American, non-Hispanic/Latino; 12 Asian, non-Hispanic/Latino; 10 Hispanic/Latino; 7 Two or more races, non-Hispanic/Latino), 27 international. Average age 32. 105 applicants, 64% accepted, 26 enrolled. *Faculty:* 31 full-time (9 women), 67 part-time/adjunct (48 women). Expenses: Contact institution. *Financial support:* Fellowships, research assistantships, teaching assistantships, Federal Work-Study, scholarships/grants, tuition waivers (full and partial), and unspecified assistantships available. Financial award application deadline: 2/1; financial award applicants required to submit FAFSA. In 2019, 16 master's, 11 doctorates awarded. *Program availability:* Part-time. *Application deadline:* For fall admission, 7/15 priority date for domestic students, 7/1 for international students; for spring admission, 11/15 priority date for domestic students, 11/1 for international students. Applications are processed on a rolling basis. *Application fee:* $55. Electronic applications accepted. *Application Contact:* Dr. Steven Brown, Director of Graduate Admissions, 202-319-5247, Fax: 202-319-6174, E-mail: cua-graduatestudies@cua.edu. *Dean*, Jacqueline Leary-Warsaw, 202-319-5417, Fax: 202-319-6280, E-mail: cua-music@cua.edu.

**Busch School of Business and Economics** Students: 91 full-time (27 women), 68 part-time (37 women); includes 65 minority (37 Black or African American, non-Hispanic/Latino; 2 American Indian or Alaska Native, non-Hispanic/Latino; 8 Asian, non-Hispanic/Latino; 11 Hispanic/Latino; 7 Two or more races, non-Hispanic/Latino), 26 international. Average age 32. 131 applicants, 88% accepted, 90 enrolled. *Faculty:* 25 full-time (3 women), 19 part-time/adjunct (12 women). Expenses: Contact institution. *Financial support:* Fellowships, research assistantships, teaching assistantships, Federal Work-Study, scholarships/grants, tuition waivers (full and partial), and unspecified assistantships available. Financial award application deadline: 2/1; financial award applicants required to submit FAFSA. In 2019, 81 master's awarded. *Program availability:* Part-time. *Application deadline:* For fall admission, 7/15 priority date for domestic students, 7/1 for international students; for spring admission, 11/15 priority date for domestic students, 11/1 for international students. Applications are processed on a rolling basis. *Application fee:* $55. Electronic applications accepted. *Application Contact:* Dr. Steven Brown, Director of Graduate Admissions, 202-319-5057, Fax: 202-319-6533, E-mail: cua-admissions@cua.edu. *Dean*, Dr. Andrew Abela, 202-319-6130, E-mail: DeanAbela@cua.edu.

**Columbus School of Law** Students: 275 full-time (168 women), 125 part-time (70 women); includes 69 minority (22 Black or African American, non-Hispanic/Latino; 1 American Indian or Alaska Native, non-Hispanic/Latino; 3 Asian, non-Hispanic/Latino; 38 Hispanic/Latino; 5 Two or more races, non-Hispanic/Latino), 9 international. Average age 28. 1,220 applicants, 46% accepted, 155 enrolled. *Faculty:* 32 full-time (16 women), 29 part-time/adjunct (14 women). Expenses: Contact institution. *Financial support:* In 2019–20, 330 students received support. Career-related internships or fieldwork, Federal Work-Study, institutionally sponsored loans, and scholarships/grants available. Support available to part-time students. Financial award application deadline: 8/15; financial award applicants required to submit FAFSA. In 2019, 5 master's, 103 doctorates awarded. *Program availability:* Part-time, evening/weekend. *Application* *deadline:* For fall admission, 3/16 priority date for domestic students, 3/16 for international students. Applications are processed on a rolling basis. *Application fee:* $65. Electronic applications accepted. *Application Contact:* Shani J. P. Butts, Assistant Dean of Admissions, 202-319-5151, Fax: 202-319-4462, E-mail: butts@law.edu. *Dean*, Stephen C. Payne, 202-319-5139, Fax: 202-319-5473.

**Metropolitan School of Professional Studies** Students: 32 full-time (17 women), 73 part-time (43 women); includes 57 minority (39 Black or African American, non-Hispanic/Latino; 4 Asian, non-Hispanic/Latino; 10 Hispanic/Latino; 4 Two or more races, non-Hispanic/Latino), 18 international. Average age 35. 78 applicants, 79% accepted, 34 enrolled. *Faculty:* 22 part-time/adjunct (13 women). Expenses: Contact institution. *Financial support:* Scholarships/grants available. Financial award application deadline: 3/15; financial award applicants required to submit FAFSA. In 2019, 32 master's awarded. *Program availability:* Part-time, evening/weekend, 100% online. *Application deadline:* For fall admission, 7/15 priority date for domestic students, 7/1 for international students; for spring admission, 11/15 priority date for domestic students, 11/1 for international students. Applications are processed on a rolling basis. *Application fee:* $55. Electronic applications accepted. *Application Contact:* Dr. Steven Brown, Director of Graduate Admissions, 202-319-5057, Fax: 202-319-6533, E-mail: cua-admissions@cua.edu. *Dean*, Dr. Vince Kiernan, 202-319-5256, Fax: 202-319-6260, E-mail: kiernan@cua.edu.

**National Catholic School of Social Service** Students: 139 full-time (115 women), 232 part-time (197 women); includes 189 minority (122 Black or African American, non-Hispanic/Latino; 7 Asian, non-Hispanic/Latino; 33 Hispanic/Latino; 1 Native Hawaiian or other Pacific Islander, non-Hispanic/Latino; 26 Two or more races, non-Hispanic/Latino), 11 international. Average age 36. 215 applicants, 72% accepted, 81 enrolled. *Faculty:* 15 full-time (11 women), 27 part-time/adjunct (25 women). Expenses: Contact institution. *Financial support:* Fellowships, research assistantships, teaching assistantships, Federal Work-Study, scholarships/grants, tuition waivers (full and partial), and unspecified assistantships available. Financial award application deadline: 3/15; financial award applicants required to submit FAFSA. In 2019, 191 master's, 7 doctorates awarded. *Program availability:* Part-time, 100% online. *Application deadline:* For fall admission, 7/15 priority date for domestic students, 7/1 for international students; for spring admission, 11/15 priority date for domestic students, 11/1 for international students. Applications are processed on a rolling basis. *Application fee:* $60. Electronic applications accepted. *Application Contact:* Dr. Steven Brown, Director of Graduate Admissions, 202-319-5057, Fax: 202-319-6533, E-mail: cua-admissions@cua.edu. *Dean*, Dr. Marie Raber, 202-319-5472, Fax: 202-319-5093, E-mail: raber@cua.edu.

**School of Architecture and Planning** *Program availability:* Part-time. Electronic applications accepted.

**School of Arts and Sciences** Students: 125 full-time (88 women), 329 part-time (190 women); includes 95 minority (24 Black or African American, non-Hispanic/Latino; 13 Asian, non-Hispanic/Latino; 21 Hispanic/Latino; 37 Two or more races, non-Hispanic/Latino), 94 international. Average age 32. 455 applicants, 56% accepted, 103 enrolled. *Faculty:* 138 full-time (61 women), 63 part-time/adjunct (42 women). Expenses: Contact institution. *Financial support:* Fellowships, research assistantships, teaching assistantships, Federal Work-Study, scholarships/grants, tuition waivers (full and partial), and unspecified assistantships available. Financial award application deadline: 2/1; financial award applicants required to submit FAFSA. In 2019, 122 master's, 45 doctorates awarded. *Program availability:* Part-time. *Application deadline:* For fall admission, 2/1 priority date for domestic students, 7/1 for international students; for spring admission, 11/15 priority date for domestic students, 11/1 for international students. Applications are processed on a rolling basis. *Application fee:* $55. Electronic applications accepted. *Application Contact:* Dr. Steven Brown, Director of Graduate Admissions, 202-319-5057, Fax: 202-319-6533, E-mail: cua-admissions@cua.edu. *Dean*, Dr. Thomas W. Smith, 202-319-5115, Fax: 202-319-4463, E-mail: artsandsciences@cua.edu.

**School of Canon Law** Students: 26 full-time (3 women), 63 part-time (9 women); includes 19 minority (5 Black or African American, non-Hispanic/Latino; 7 Asian, non-Hispanic/Latino; 3 Hispanic/Latino; 4 Two or more races, non-Hispanic/Latino), 10 international. Average age 40. 57 applicants, 88% accepted, 41 enrolled. *Faculty:* 5 full-time (1 woman), 2 part-time/adjunct (0 women). Expenses: Contact institution. *Financial support:* Fellowships, research assistantships, teaching assistantships, Federal Work-Study, scholarships/grants, tuition waivers (full and partial), and unspecified assistantships available. Financial award application deadline: 2/1; financial award applicants required to submit FAFSA. In 2019, 19 master's, 1 doctorate awarded. *Program availability:* Part-time. *Application deadline:* For fall admission, 7/15 priority date for domestic students, 7/1 for international students; for spring admission, 11/15 priority date for domestic students, 11/1 for international students. Applications are processed on a rolling basis. *Application fee:* $55. Electronic applications accepted. *Application Contact:* Dr. Steven Brown, Director of Graduate Admissions, 202-319-5057, Fax: 202-319-6533, E-mail: cua-admissions@cua.edu. *Dean*, Msgr. Ronny Jenkins, 202-319-5492, Fax: 202-319-4187, E-mail: cua-canonlaw@cua.edu.

**School of Engineering** Students: 70 full-time (26 women), 161 part-time (58 women); includes 50 minority (18 Black or African American, non-Hispanic/Latino; 9 Asian, non-Hispanic/Latino; 7 Hispanic/Latino; 16 Two or more races, non-Hispanic/Latino), 114 international. Average age 31. 224 applicants, 77% accepted, 74 enrolled. *Faculty:* 33 full-time (2 women), 31 part-time/adjunct (21 women). Expenses: Contact institution. *Financial support:* Fellowships, research assistantships, teaching assistantships, Federal Work-Study, scholarships/grants, tuition waivers (full and partial), and unspecified assistantships available. Financial award application deadline: 2/1; financial award applicants required to submit FAFSA. In 2019, 73 master's, 13 doctorates awarded. *Program availability:* Part-time. *Application deadline:* For fall admission, 7/15 priority date for domestic students, 7/1 for international students; for spring admission, 11/15 priority date for domestic students, 11/1 for international students. Applications are processed on a rolling basis. *Application fee:* $55. Electronic applications accepted. *Application Contact:* Dr. Steven Brown, Director of Graduate Admissions, 202-319-5057, Fax: 202-319-6533, E-mail: cua-admissions@cua.edu. *Dean*, Dr. John Judge, 202-319-5127, Fax: 202-319-4499, E-mail: judge@cua.edu.

**School of Nursing** Students: 20 full-time (18 women), 125 part-time (115 women); includes 41 minority (28 Black or African American, non-Hispanic/Latino; 4 Asian, non-Hispanic/Latino; 4 Hispanic/Latino; 5 Two or more races, non-Hispanic/Latino), 7 international. Average age 42. 79 applicants, 78% accepted, 26 enrolled. *Faculty:* 22 full-time (21 women), 32 part-time/adjunct (31 women). Expenses: Contact institution. *Financial support:* Fellowships, research assistantships, teaching assistantships, Federal Work-Study, scholarships/grants, tuition waivers (full and partial), and unspecified assistantships available. Financial award application deadline: 2/1; financial award applicants required to submit FAFSA. In 2019, 15 master's, 1 doctorate, 2 other advanced degrees awarded. *Program availability:* Part-time, 100% online. *Application deadline:* For fall admission, 7/15 priority date for domestic students, 7/1 for international students; for spring admission, 11/15 priority date for domestic students, 11/1 for international students. Applications are processed on a rolling basis. *Application fee:* $55. Electronic applications accepted. *Application Contact:* Dr. Steven Brown, Director of Graduate Admissions, 202-319-5057, Fax: 202-319-6533, E-mail: cua-admissions@cua.edu. *Dean*, Dr. Patricia McMullen, 202-319-5403, Fax: 202-319-6485, E-mail: mcmullep@cua.edu.

**School of Philosophy** Students: 44 full-time (7 women), 53 part-time (19 women); includes 19 minority (2 Black or African American, non-Hispanic/Latino; 6 Asian, non-Hispanic/Latino; 5 Hispanic/Latino; 6 Two or more races, non-Hispanic/Latino), 8 international. Average age 31. 76 applicants, 37% accepted, 22 enrolled. *Faculty:* 23 full-time (4 women), 4 part-time/adjunct (3 women). Expenses: Contact institution. *Financial support:* Fellowships, research assistantships, teaching assistantships, Federal Work-Study, scholarships/grants, tuition waivers (full and partial), and unspecified assistantships available. Financial award application deadline: 2/1; financial award applicants required to submit FAFSA. In 2019, 14 master's, 10 doctorates awarded. *Program availability:* Part-time. *Application deadline:* For fall admission, 7/15 priority date for domestic students, 7/1 for international students; for spring admission, 11/15 priority date for domestic students, 11/1 for international students. Applications are processed on a rolling basis. *Application fee:* $55. Electronic applications accepted. *Application Contact:* Dr. Steven Brown, Director of Graduate Admissions, 202-319-5057, Fax: 202-319-6533, E-mail: cua-admissions@cua.edu. *Dean*, Dr. John McCarthy, 202-319-6649, Fax: 202-319-4731, E-mail: mccartjc@cua.edu.

**School of Theology and Religious Studies** Students: 156 full-time (13 women), 167 part-time (69 women); includes 72 minority (13 Black or African American, non-Hispanic/Latino; 1 American Indian or Alaska Native, non-Hispanic/Latino; 13 Asian, non-Hispanic/Latino; 22 Hispanic/Latino; 23 Two or more races, non-Hispanic/Latino), 51 international. Average age 36. 178 applicants, 60% accepted, 67 enrolled. *Faculty:* 39 full-time (5 women), 12 part-time/adjunct (5 women). Expenses: Contact institution. *Financial support:* Fellowships, research assistantships, teaching assistantships, Federal Work-Study, scholarships/grants, tuition waivers (full and partial), and unspecified assistantships available. Financial award application deadline: 2/1; financial award applicants required to submit FAFSA. In 2019, 56 master's, 27 doctorates awarded. *Program availability:* Part-time. *Application deadline:* For fall admission, 7/15 priority date for domestic students, 7/1 for international students; for spring admission, 11/15 priority date for domestic students, 11/1 for international students. Applications are processed on a rolling basis. *Application fee:* $55. Electronic applications accepted. *Application Contact:* Dr. Steven Brown, Director of Graduate Admissions, 202-319-5057, Fax: 202-319-6533, E-mail: cua-admissions@cua.edu. *Dean*, Very Rev. Mark Morozowich, 202-319-5684, Fax: 202-319-4967, E-mail: morozowich@cua.edu.

## CEDAR CREST COLLEGE, Allentown, PA 18104-6196

**General Information** Independent-religious, coed, primarily women, comprehensive institution. *Graduate housing:* On-campus housing not available.

**GRADUATE UNITS**

**Department of Education** *Program availability:* Part-time, evening/weekend, 100% online, blended/hybrid learning. Electronic applications accepted.

**Dietetic Internship Certificate Program** *Program availability:* Part-time, evening/weekend, blended/hybrid learning. Electronic applications accepted.

**Program in Art Therapy** *Program availability:* Part-time, evening/weekend, blended/hybrid learning. Electronic applications accepted.

**Program in Business Administration** *Program availability:* Part-time, evening/weekend, blended/hybrid learning. Electronic applications accepted.

**Program in Creative Writing** *Program availability:* Part-time, evening/weekend, blended/hybrid learning. Electronic applications accepted.

**Program in Forensic Science** Electronic applications accepted.

**School of Nursing** *Program availability:* Part-time. Electronic applications accepted.

## CEDARS-SINAI MEDICAL CENTER, Los Angeles, CA 90048

**General Information** Independent, coed, graduate-only institution. *Graduate housing:* On-campus housing not available.

**GRADUATE UNITS**

**Graduate Programs** Electronic applications accepted.

## CEDARVILLE UNIVERSITY, Cedarville, OH 45314

**General Information** Independent-religious, coed, comprehensive institution. *Enrollment:* 4,302 graduate, professional, and undergraduate students; 378 full-time matriculated graduate/professional students (221 women), 45 part-time matriculated graduate/professional students (23 women). *Enrollment by degree level:* 254 master's, 183 doctoral, 13 other advanced degrees. *Graduate faculty:* 52 full-time (19 women), 21 part-time/adjunct (13 women). *Tuition:* Full-time $12,594; part-time $566 per credit hour. One-time fee: $100. Tuition and fees vary according to course load and program. *Graduate housing:* On-campus housing not available. *Student services:* Campus employment opportunities, campus safety program, career counseling, exercise/wellness program, free psychological counseling, low-cost health insurance, multicultural affairs office, services for students with disabilities, writing training. *Library facilities:* Centennial Library. *Collection:* Books: 185,920 (physical), 154,475 (digital/electronic); Serial titles: 619 (physical), 26,884 (digital/electronic); Databases: 200. Weekly public service hours: 91; students can reserve study rooms.

**Computer facilities:** 2,300 computers available on campus for general student use. A campuswide network can be accessed. Online class registration, over 75 software packages are available.
Website: http://www.cedarville.edu/

**General Application Contact:** Jim Amstutz, Director of Graduate Admissions and Student Success, 937-766-8000, Fax: 937-766-7575, E-mail: amstutzj@cedarville.edu.

**GRADUATE UNITS**

**Graduate Programs** Students: 378 full-time (221 women), 45 part-time (23 women); includes 76 minority (46 Black or African American, non-Hispanic/Latino; 2 American Indian or Alaska Native, non-Hispanic/Latino; 22 Asian, non-Hispanic/Latino; 1 Hispanic/Latino; 5 Two or more races, non-Hispanic/Latino), 2 international. Average age 26. 398 applicants, 70% accepted, 172 enrolled. *Faculty:* 52 full-time (19 women), 21 part-time/adjunct (13 women). Expenses: Contact institution. *Financial support:* Scholarships/grants and unspecified assistantships available. Support available to part-time students. Financial award application deadline: 1/30; financial award applicants required to submit FAFSA. In 2019, 74 master's, 34 doctorates awarded. *Program availability:* Part-time, evening/weekend, 100% online, blended/hybrid learning. *Application deadline:* For fall admission, 5/1 priority date for domestic and international students; for spring admission, 11/1 priority date for domestic and international students. Applications are processed on a rolling basis. Electronic applications accepted. *Application Contact:* Alexis McKay, Graduate Admissions Counselor, 937-766-8000,

E-mail: amckay@cedarville.edu. *Dean of Graduate Studies*, Dr. Janice Supplee, 937-766-8000, E-mail: suppleej@cedarville.edu.

## CENTENARY COLLEGE OF LOUISIANA, Shreveport, LA 71104

**General Information** Independent-religious, coed, comprehensive institution. *Graduate housing:* Room and/or apartments available on a first-come, first-served basis to single students; on-campus housing not available to married students.

**GRADUATE UNITS**

**Graduate Programs** *Program availability:* Part-time, evening/weekend.

***Frost School of Business*** *Program availability:* Part-time, evening/weekend.

## CENTENARY UNIVERSITY, Hackettstown, NJ 07840-2100

**General Information** Independent-religious, coed, comprehensive institution. *Graduate housing:* Room and/or apartments available on a first-come, first-served basis to single students; on-campus housing not available to married students. Housing application deadline: 6/1.

**GRADUATE UNITS**

**Program in Business Administration** *Program availability:* Part-time, evening/weekend, online learning.

**Program in Counseling Psychology** *Program availability:* Part-time, evening/weekend, online learning.

**Program in Education** *Program availability:* Part-time, evening/weekend, online learning.

**Program in Professional Accounting** *Program availability:* Part-time, evening/weekend, online learning.

## CENTRAL BAPTIST THEOLOGICAL SEMINARY, Shawnee, KS 66226

**General Information** Independent-religious, coed, graduate-only institution. *Graduate housing:* On-campus housing not available.

**GRADUATE UNITS**

**Graduate and Professional Programs** *Program availability:* Part-time. Electronic applications accepted.

## CENTRAL CONNECTICUT STATE UNIVERSITY, New Britain, CT 06050-4010

**General Information** State-supported, coed, comprehensive institution. *Graduate housing:* Room and/or apartments available on a first-come, first-served basis to single students; on-campus housing not available to married students. Housing application deadline: 5/1.

**GRADUATE UNITS**

**School of Graduate Studies** *Program availability:* Part-time, evening/weekend, 100% online. Electronic applications accepted.

***College of Liberal Arts and Social Sciences*** *Program availability:* Part-time, evening/weekend. Electronic applications accepted.

***School of Business*** *Program availability:* Part-time, evening/weekend. Electronic applications accepted.

***School of Education and Professional Studies*** *Program availability:* Part-time, evening/weekend. Electronic applications accepted.

***School of Engineering, Science and Technology*** *Program availability:* Part-time, evening/weekend, 100% online. Electronic applications accepted.

## CENTRAL EUROPEAN UNIVERSITY, H-1051 Budapest, Hungary

**General Information** Independent, coed, graduate-only institution. CGS member. *Graduate housing:* Room and/or apartments guaranteed to single students; on-campus housing not available to married students. Housing application deadline: 2/4. *Research affiliation:* Institute of Human Sciences Vienna (social sciences), Open Society Institute (social sciences), Alfréd Rényi Institute of Mathematics.

**GRADUATE UNITS**

**Center for Network Science** Electronic applications accepted.

**Department of Cognitive Science** Electronic applications accepted.

**Department of Economics** *Program availability:* Part-time. Electronic applications accepted.

**Department of Environmental Sciences and Policy** *Program availability:* Part-time. Electronic applications accepted.

**Department of Gender Studies** Electronic applications accepted.

**Department of History** Electronic applications accepted.

**Department of International Relations** Electronic applications accepted.

**Department of Legal Studies** Electronic applications accepted.

**Department of Mathematics and its Applications** Electronic applications accepted.

**Department of Medieval Studies** Electronic applications accepted.

**Department of Philosophy** Electronic applications accepted.

**Department of Political Science** Electronic applications accepted.

**Department of Sociology and Social Anthropology** Electronic applications accepted.

**Nationalism Studies Program** Electronic applications accepted.

**School of Public Policy** Electronic applications accepted.

## CENTRAL METHODIST UNIVERSITY, Fayette, MO 65248-1198

**General Information** Independent-religious, coed, comprehensive institution. *Graduate housing:* Rooms and/or apartments available on a first-come, first-served basis to single and married students.

**GRADUATE UNITS**

**College of Graduate and Extended Studies** *Program availability:* Part-time, evening/weekend, online learning. Electronic applications accepted.

## CENTRAL MICHIGAN UNIVERSITY, Mount Pleasant, MI 48859

**General Information** State-supported, coed, university. CGS member. *Enrollment:* 19,431 graduate, professional, and undergraduate students; 1,667 full-time matriculated graduate/professional students (970 women), 2,913 part-time matriculated graduate/professional students (1,682 women). *Enrollment by degree level:* 3,474 master's, 1,038 doctoral, 68 other advanced degrees. *Graduate faculty:* 392 full-time (168 women), 158 part-time/adjunct (63 women). *International tuition:* $16,110 full-time. *Tuition, area resident:* Full-time $12,267; part-time $8178 per year. Tuition, state resident: full-time $12,267; part-time $8178 per year. Tuition, nonresident: full-time $12,267; part-time $8178 per year. *Required fees:* $225 per semester. Tuition and fees vary according to degree level and program. *Graduate housing:* Rooms and/or apartments available on a first-come, first-served basis to single and married students. Typical cost: $5726 per year for single students; $6218 per year for married students. Room charges vary according to board plan, campus/location and housing facility selected. *Student services:* Campus employment opportunities, campus safety program, career counseling, exercise/wellness program, free psychological counseling, grant writing training, international student services, multicultural affairs office, services for students with disabilities, teacher training, writing training. *Library facilities:* Charles V. Park Library. *Collection:* Books: 895,460 (physical), 709,885 (digital/electronic); Serial titles: 2,156 (physical), 114,678 (digital/electronic); Databases: 336. Weekly public service hours: 101; students can reserve study rooms. *Research affiliation:* IBM (information technology), Dendritic Nanotechnologies, Inc. (chemistry, physics), Dow Corning Corporation (silicon-based technology), Dow Chemical Company (chemicals and plastics), SAS Business Analytics (business analysis), SAP (information technology).

**Computer facilities:** Computer purchase and lease plans are available. 490 computers available on campus for general student use. A campuswide network can be accessed from student residence rooms and from off campus. Online class registration, learning management system are available.
Website: http://www.cmich.edu/

**General Application Contact:** Ryan Griffus, Graduate Student Recruiting, 989-774-1808, Fax: 989-774-3232, E-mail: griff1rp@cmich.edu.

**GRADUATE UNITS**

**Central Michigan University Global Campus** *Program availability:* Part-time, evening/weekend, online learning. Electronic applications accepted.

**College of Graduate Studies** *Program availability:* Part-time, evening/weekend, online learning. Electronic applications accepted.

***College of Business Administration*** *Program availability:* Part-time, evening/weekend. Electronic applications accepted.

***College of Education and Human Services*** *Program availability:* Part-time, evening/weekend. Electronic applications accepted.

***College of Liberal Arts and Social Sciences*** *Program availability:* Part-time, evening/weekend. Electronic applications accepted.

***College of Medicine***

***College of Science and Engineering*** *Program availability:* Part-time, evening/weekend. Electronic applications accepted.

***College of the Arts and Media*** *Program availability:* Part-time. Electronic applications accepted.

***The Herbert H. and Grace A. Dow College of Health Professions*** *Program availability:* Part-time. Electronic applications accepted.

## CENTRAL PENN COLLEGE, Summerdale, PA 17093-0309

**General Information** Proprietary, coed, comprehensive institution.

**GRADUATE UNITS**

**Graduate Programs** *Program availability:* Evening/weekend.

## CENTRAL WASHINGTON UNIVERSITY, Ellensburg, WA 98926

**General Information** State-supported, coed, comprehensive institution. CGS member. *Graduate housing:* Rooms and/or apartments available on a first-come, first-served basis to single and married students. *Research affiliation:* Associated Western Universities (science and engineering), East-West Center (Pacific area studies), Jet Propulsion Laboratory (engineering).

**GRADUATE UNITS**

**School of Graduate Studies and Research** *Program availability:* Part-time, evening/weekend. Electronic applications accepted.

***College of Arts and Humanities*** *Program availability:* Part-time. Electronic applications accepted.

***College of Education and Professional Studies*** *Program availability:* Part-time. Electronic applications accepted.

***College of the Sciences*** *Program availability:* Part-time, evening/weekend. Electronic applications accepted.

## CENTRAL YESHIVA TOMCHEI TMIMIM-LUBAVITCH, Brooklyn, NY 11230

**General Information** Independent-religious, men only, comprehensive institution.

**General Application Contact:** Information Contact, 718-434-0784.

**GRADUATE UNITS**

**Graduate Programs** Expenses: Contact institution. *Application Contact:* Information Contact, 718-434-0784.

## CENTRO DE ESTUDIOS AVANZADOS DE PUERTO RICO Y EL CARIBE, Old San Juan, PR 00902-3970

**General Information** Independent, coed, graduate-only institution. *Graduate housing:* On-campus housing not available. *Research affiliation:* Museo de las Americas, Museo Hombre Dominicano, Archivo General, Museo Universidad del Turabo.

**GRADUATE UNITS**

**Graduate Program in Puerto Rican and Caribbean Studies** *Program availability:* Part-time, evening/weekend.

## CHADRON STATE COLLEGE, Chadron, NE 69337

**General Information** State-supported, coed, comprehensive institution. *Graduate housing:* Rooms and/or apartments available on a first-come, first-served basis to single and married students. Housing application deadline: 6/1.

**GRADUATE UNITS**

**School of Professional and Graduate Studies** *Program availability:* Part-time, evening/weekend, online learning. Electronic applications accepted.

## CHAMINADE UNIVERSITY OF HONOLULU, Honolulu, HI 96816-1578

**General Information** Independent-religious, coed, comprehensive institution. *Enrollment:* 1,675 graduate, professional, and undergraduate students; 277 full-time matriculated graduate/professional students (201 women), 212 part-time matriculated graduate/professional students (141 women). *Enrollment by degree level:* 489 master's. *Graduate faculty:* 23 full-time (8 women), 39 part-time/adjunct (22 women). *Graduate housing:* On-campus housing not available. *Student services:* Campus safety program, career counseling, free psychological counseling, international student services, services for students with disabilities, teacher training, writing training. *Library facilities:*

Sullivan Library. *Collection:* Books: 49,737 (physical), 149,162 (digital/electronic); Serial titles: 112 (physical), 27,423 (digital/electronic); Databases: 97.

**Computer facilities:** 200 computers available on campus for general student use. A campuswide network can be accessed. Online class registration is available.
Website: http://www.chaminade.edu/

**GRADUATE UNITS**

**Graduate** Students: 277 full-time (201 women), 212 part-time (141 women); includes 325 minority (17 Black or African American, non-Hispanic/Latino; 6 American Indian or Alaska Native, non-Hispanic/Latino; 163 Asian, non-Hispanic/Latino; 23 Hispanic/Latino; 97 Native Hawaiian or other Pacific Islander, non-Hispanic/Latino; 19 Two or more races, non-Hispanic/Latino), 8 international. Average age 33. 175 applicants, 85% accepted, 105 enrolled. *Faculty:* 23 full-time (8 women), 39 part-time/adjunct (22 women). Expenses: Contact institution. *Financial support:* Applicants required to submit FAFSA. In 2019, 200 master's awarded. *Program availability:* Part-time, evening/weekend, 100% online, blended/hybrid learning. *Application deadline:* Applications are processed on a rolling basis. *Application fee:* $40. Electronic applications accepted.

## CHAMPLAIN COLLEGE, Burlington, VT 05402-0670

**General Information** Independent, coed, comprehensive institution. *Graduate housing:* Rooms and/or apartments available on a first-come, first-served basis to single and married students.

**GRADUATE UNITS**

**Graduate Studies** *Program availability:* Part-time, online learning. Electronic applications accepted.

## CHAPMAN UNIVERSITY, Orange, CA 92866

**General Information** Independent-religious, coed, comprehensive institution. CGS member. *Enrollment:* 1,814 full-time matriculated graduate/professional students (1,112 women), 527 part-time matriculated graduate/professional students (318 women). *Enrollment by degree level:* 1,197 master's, 1,142 doctoral, 2 other advanced degrees. *Graduate faculty:* 367 full-time (156 women), 372 part-time/adjunct (173 women). *Graduate housing:* Room and/or apartments available on a first-come, first-served basis to single students; on-campus housing not available to married students. Typical cost: $2392 (including board). Room and board charges vary according to board plan and housing facility selected. Housing application deadline: 6/1. *Student services:* Campus employment opportunities, campus safety program, career counseling, exercise/wellness program, free psychological counseling, grant writing training, international student services, low-cost health insurance, multicultural affairs office, services for students with disabilities, teacher training, writing training. *Library facilities:* Leatherby Libraries plus 1 other. *Collection:* Books: 308,474 (physical), 222,717 (digital/electronic); Serial titles: 228 (physical), 86,066 (digital/electronic); Databases: 299. Weekly public service hours: 127; students can reserve study rooms. *Research affiliation:* National Science Foundation (science, engineering), National Endowment for the Arts (NEA) (art), U.S. Department of Education (DOE) (education), U.S. Geological Survey (USGS) (earth sciences), U.S. Department of Agriculture (USDA) (agriculture, food, nutrition).

**Computer facilities:** Computer purchase and lease plans are available. A campuswide network can be accessed. Online class registration is available.
Website: http://www.chapman.edu/

**General Application Contact:** Eva Yen, Director of Graduate Admissions, 888-CU-APPLY, Fax: 714-997-6713, E-mail: eyen@chapman.edu.

**GRADUATE UNITS**

**The College of Performing Arts** Students: 1 part-time. Average age 23. 1 applicant, 100% accepted, 1 enrolled. Expenses: Contact institution. *Program availability:* Part-time. *Application deadline:* Applications are processed on a rolling basis. *Application fee:* $60. Electronic applications accepted. *Application Contact:* Melissa Liberman, Admission Counselor, 714-628-2847, Fax: 714-997-6713, E-mail: liberman@chapman.edu.

**Crean College of Health and Behavioral Sciences** Students: 283 full-time (189 women), 191 part-time (115 women); includes 228 minority (5 Black or African American, non-Hispanic/Latino; 124 Asian, non-Hispanic/Latino; 69 Hispanic/Latino; 30 Two or more races, non-Hispanic/Latino), 7 international. Average age 27. 2,532 applicants, 10% accepted, 182 enrolled. *Faculty:* 35 full-time (25 women), 9 part-time/adjunct (7 women). Expenses: Contact institution. *Financial support:* Fellowships and scholarships/grants available. Financial award application deadline: 4/15; financial award applicants required to submit FAFSA. In 2019, 63 master's, 57 doctorates awarded. *Application fee:* $60. Electronic applications accepted. *Application Contact:* Howard Ying, 714-516-5020, E-mail: hying@chapman.edu. *Dean*, Dr. Janeen Hill, 714-628-7223, E-mail: jhill@chapman.edu.

**Dale E. Fowler School of Law** Students: 453 full-time (269 women), 39 part-time (19 women); includes 209 minority (10 Black or African American, non-Hispanic/Latino; 54 Asian, non-Hispanic/Latino; 113 Hispanic/Latino; 32 Two or more races, non-Hispanic/Latino), 14 international. Average age 27. 1,743 applicants, 34% accepted, 146 enrolled. *Faculty:* 41 full-time (17 women), 35 part-time/adjunct (12 women). Expenses: Contact institution. *Financial support:* Fellowships, Federal Work-Study, and scholarships/grants available. Financial award application deadline: 4/15; financial award applicants required to submit FAFSA. In 2019, 17 master's, 171 doctorates awarded. *Program availability:* Part-time. *Application deadline:* For fall admission, 4/15 priority date for domestic students. Applications are processed on a rolling basis. Electronic applications accepted. *Application Contact:* Justin Cruz, Assistant Dean of Admissions and Diversity Initiatives, 714-628-2594, E-mail: lawadmission@chapman.edu. *Dean*, Matthew J. Parlow, 714-628-2678, E-mail: parlow@chapman.edu.

**Dodge College of Film and Media Arts** Students: 290 full-time (137 women), 5 part-time (3 women); includes 81 minority (14 Black or African American, non-Hispanic/Latino; 21 Asian, non-Hispanic/Latino; 24 Hispanic/Latino; 1 Native Hawaiian or other Pacific Islander, non-Hispanic/Latino; 21 Two or more races, non-Hispanic/Latino), 132 international. Average age 26. 669 applicants, 44% accepted, 117 enrolled. *Faculty:* 53 full-time (16 women), 110 part-time/adjunct (36 women). Expenses: Contact institution. *Financial support:* Fellowships, Federal Work-Study, and scholarships/grants available. Financial award applicants required to submit FAFSA. In 2019, 100 master's awarded. *Application deadline:* For fall admission, 12/1 for domestic students. *Application fee:* $60. Electronic applications accepted. *Application Contact:* Priscilla Campos, Associate Director of Admissions, 714-997-6996, E-mail: pcampos@chapman.edu. *Dean*, Stephen Galloway, 714-997-6715, E-mail: sgalloway@chapman.edu.

**Donna Ford Attallah College of Educational Studies** Students: 145 full-time (127 women), 179 part-time (136 women); includes 178 minority (8 Black or African American, non-Hispanic/Latino; 1 American Indian or Alaska Native, non-Hispanic/Latino; 41 Asian, non-Hispanic/Latino; 117 Hispanic/Latino; 11 Two or more races, non-Hispanic/Latino), 16 international. Average age 28. 333 applicants, 61% accepted, 143 enrolled. *Faculty:* 33 full-time (19 women), 49 part-time/adjunct (36 women). Expenses: Contact institution. *Financial support:* Fellowships and scholarships/grants available. Financial award applicants required to submit FAFSA. In 2019, 153 master's, 11 doctorates awarded. *Program availability:* Part-time, evening/weekend. *Application deadline:* Applications are processed on a rolling basis. *Application fee:* $60. Electronic applications accepted. *Application Contact:* Shannon McCance, Graduate Admission Counselor, 714-516-5236, E-mail: smccance@chapman.edu. *Interim Dean*, Dr. Roxanne Greitz Miller, 714-997-6781, E-mail: rgmiller@chapman.edu.

**The George L. Argyros School of Business and Economics** Students: 136 full-time (55 women), 75 part-time (36 women); includes 86 minority (4 Black or African American, non-Hispanic/Latino; 38 Asian, non-Hispanic/Latino; 35 Hispanic/Latino; 1 Native Hawaiian or other Pacific Islander, non-Hispanic/Latino; 8 Two or more races, non-Hispanic/Latino), 43 international. Average age 30. 218 applicants, 75% accepted, 84 enrolled. *Faculty:* 73 full-time (17 women), 38 part-time/adjunct (10 women). Expenses: Contact institution. *Financial support:* Fellowships, Federal Work-Study, and scholarships/grants available. Financial award applicants required to submit FAFSA. In 2019, 127 master's awarded. *Program availability:* Part-time, evening/weekend. *Application fee:* $60. Electronic applications accepted. *Application Contact:* Jim Dusserre, Assistant Director, Graduate Business Programs, 714-744-7694, E-mail: dusserre@chapman.edu. *Dean*, Dr. Thomas A Turk, 714-997-6819, E-mail: turk@chapman.edu.

**Schmid College of Science and Technology** Students: 49 full-time (18 women), 59 part-time (28 women); includes 28 minority (3 Black or African American, non-Hispanic/Latino; 13 Asian, non-Hispanic/Latino; 9 Hispanic/Latino; 3 Two or more races, non-Hispanic/Latino), 8 international. Average age 28. 99 applicants, 65% accepted, 28 enrolled. *Faculty:* 16 full-time (5 women), 12 part-time/adjunct (10 women). Expenses: Contact institution. In 2019, 47 master's, 5 doctorates awarded. *Program availability:* Part-time, evening/weekend. *Application fee:* $60. Electronic applications accepted. *Application Contact:* Dr. Jason Keller, Interim Dean, 714-289-2072, E-mail: jkeller@chapman.edu. *Interim Dean*, Dr. Jason Keller, 714-289-2072, E-mail: jkeller@chapman.edu.

**School of Communication** Students: 8 full-time (6 women), 9 part-time (7 women); includes 5 minority (2 Asian, non-Hispanic/Latino; 2 Hispanic/Latino; 1 Two or more races, non-Hispanic/Latino). Average age 28. 24 applicants, 75% accepted, 12 enrolled. *Faculty:* 21 full-time (14 women), 7 part-time/adjunct (1 woman). Expenses: Contact institution. *Financial support:* Fellowships, research assistantships, Federal Work-Study, scholarships/grants, and unspecified assistantships available. Financial award applicants required to submit FAFSA. In 2019, 6 master's awarded. *Program availability:* Evening/weekend. *Application deadline:* For fall admission, 1/15 priority date for domestic students. *Application fee:* $60. Electronic applications accepted. *Application Contact:* Shannon McCance, Admission Counselor, 714-997-6711, E-mail: smccance@chapman.edu. *Dean*, Dr. Lisa Sparks, 714-744-7088, E-mail: ditommas@chapman.edu.

**School of Pharmacy** Students: 310 full-time (196 women), 6 part-time (5 women); includes 234 minority (14 Black or African American, non-Hispanic/Latino; 1 American Indian or Alaska Native, non-Hispanic/Latino; 187 Asian, non-Hispanic/Latino; 24 Hispanic/Latino; 8 Two or more races, non-Hispanic/Latino), 17 international. Average age 26. *Faculty:* 44 full-time (22 women), 5 part-time/adjunct (1 woman). Expenses: Contact institution. *Financial support:* Fellowships, research assistantships, Federal Work-Study, and scholarships/grants available. In 2019, 17 master's, 72 doctorates awarded. *Application deadline:* Applications are processed on a rolling basis. Electronic applications accepted. *Application Contact:* Rocke DeMark, Associate Dean of Student and Academic Affairs, 714-516-516-5460, E-mail: pharmacyadmissions@chapman.edu. *Dean*, Ronald P. Jordan, 714-516-5486, E-mail: rpjordan@chapman.edu.

**Wilkinson College of Arts, Humanities, and Social Sciences** Students: 71 full-time (49 women), 35 part-time (18 women); includes 43 minority (5 Black or African American, non-Hispanic/Latino; 1 American Indian or Alaska Native, non-Hispanic/Latino; 8 Asian, non-Hispanic/Latino; 23 Hispanic/Latino; 6 Two or more races, non-Hispanic/Latino), 10 international. Average age 29. 154 applicants, 82% accepted, 40 enrolled. *Faculty:* 34 full-time (13 women), 48 part-time/adjunct (26 women). Expenses: Contact institution. In 2019, 32 master's awarded. *Program availability:* Part-time, evening/weekend. *Application fee:* $60. Electronic applications accepted. *Application Contact:* Dr. Jennifer D. Keene, Dean, 714-997-6947, E-mail: keene@chapman.edu. *Dean*, Dr. Jennifer D. Keene, 714-997-6947, E-mail: keene@chapman.edu.

**See Display on page 311 and Close-Up on page 629.**

## CHARLES R. DREW UNIVERSITY OF MEDICINE AND SCIENCE, Los Angeles, CA 90059

**General Information** Independent, coed, comprehensive institution. *Graduate housing:* On-campus housing not available.

**GRADUATE UNITS**

**College of Science and Health**

**Professional Program in Medicine**

## CHARLESTON SCHOOL OF LAW, Charleston, SC 29403

**General Information** Proprietary, coed, graduate-only institution. *Enrollment by degree level:* 612 doctoral. *Graduate faculty:* 23 full-time (12 women), 61 part-time/adjunct (24 women). *Tuition:* Full-time $41,100. *Required fees:* $1034. *Graduate housing:* On-campus housing not available. *Student services:* Campus employment opportunities, campus safety program, career counseling, free psychological counseling, services for students with disabilities, writing training. *Library facilities:* Sol Blatt Jr. Law Library. *Collection:* Books: 7,342 (physical), 344,940 (digital/electronic). Weekly public service hours: 105; students can reserve study rooms.

**Computer facilities:** A campuswide network can be accessed. Online class registration is available.
Website: http://www.charlestonlaw.edu/

**General Application Contact:** Jacqueline B. Bell, Associate Dean of Admission and Financial Aid, 843-377-2143, Fax: 843-329-4091, E-mail: info@charlestonlaw.edu.

**GRADUATE UNITS**

**Graduate and Professional Programs** Electronic applications accepted.

## CHARLESTON SOUTHERN UNIVERSITY, Charleston, SC 29423-8087

**General Information** Independent-religious, coed, comprehensive institution. *Enrollment:* 124 full-time matriculated graduate/professional students (100 women), 469 part-time matriculated graduate/professional students (277 women). *Enrollment by degree level:* 529 master's, 64 doctoral. *Graduate faculty:* 12 full-time (6 women), 10 part-time/adjunct (3 women). *Graduate housing:* Room and/or apartments available on a first-come, first-served basis to single students; on-campus housing not available to married students. Typical cost: $10,400 (including board). Room and board charges vary according to housing facility selected. *Student services:* Campus employment opportunities, campus safety program, career counseling, free psychological counseling, international student services, services for students with disabilities, writing training. *Library facilities:* L. Mendel Rivers Library plus 1 other. *Collection:* Books: 117,095 (physical), 303,641 (digital/electronic); Serial titles: 4,761 (physical), 53,688 (digital/electronic); Databases: 177. Weekly public service hours: 83; students can reserve study rooms. *Research affiliation:* Waccamaw Regional Planning and Development Council (economic forecasting), Metro Charleston Chamber of Commerce (economic forecasting), Santee Lynches Council of Governments (economic forecasting).

**Computer facilities:** 250 computers available on campus for general student use. A campuswide network can be accessed from student residence rooms and from off campus. Online class registration, online course work are available.
Website: http://www.charlestonsouthern.edu/

**General Application Contact:** Janie Cogdill, Graduate Enrollment Counselor, 843-863-7050, Fax: 843-863-7070, E-mail: jcogdill@csuniv.edu.

**GRADUATE UNITS**

**College of Business** *Program availability:* Part-time, evening/weekend. Electronic applications accepted.

**College of Education** *Program availability:* Part-time, evening/weekend. Electronic applications accepted.

**Department of Criminal Justice** *Program availability:* Part-time, evening/weekend, online learning. Electronic applications accepted.

## CHARLOTTE CHRISTIAN COLLEGE AND THEOLOGICAL SEMINARY, Charlotte, NC 28205

**General Information** Independent-religious, coed, comprehensive institution. *Graduate housing:* On-campus housing not available.

**GRADUATE UNITS**

**Graduate Program** *Program availability:* Part-time, evening/weekend. Electronic applications accepted.

## CHARTER COLLEGE, Vancouver, WA 98683

**General Information** Proprietary, coed, comprehensive institution.

**GRADUATE UNITS**

**Program in Business Administration** *Program availability:* Online learning.

## CHARTER OAK STATE COLLEGE, New Britain, CT 06053-2142

**General Information** State-supported, coed, comprehensive institution. *Graduate housing:* On-campus housing not available.

**GRADUATE UNITS**

**Program in Organizational Effectiveness and Leadership** *Program availability:* Part-time, evening/weekend, online only, 100% online. Electronic applications accepted.

## CHATHAM UNIVERSITY, Pittsburgh, PA 15232-2826

**General Information** Independent, coed, primarily women, university. CGS member. *Enrollment:* 2,437 graduate, professional, and undergraduate students; 706 full-time matriculated graduate/professional students (562 women), 323 part-time matriculated graduate/professional students (254 women). *Enrollment by degree level:* 703 master's, 326 doctoral. *Graduate faculty:* 108 full-time (74 women), 92 part-time/adjunct (66 women). *Tuition:* Part-time $1017 per credit. *Required fees:* $30 per credit. Tuition and fees vary according to program. *Graduate housing:* On-campus housing not available. *Student services:* Campus employment opportunities, campus safety program, career counseling, exercise/wellness program, free psychological counseling, international student services, low-cost health insurance, services for students with disabilities, teacher training, writing training. *Library facilities:* Jennie King Mellon Library. *Collection:* Books: 97,602 (physical), 788,185 (digital/electronic); Serial titles: 585 (physical), 86,930 (digital/electronic); Databases: 70. Weekly public service hours: 99; study areas open 24 hours, 5–7 days a week; students can reserve study rooms.

**Computer facilities:** Computer purchase and lease plans are available. 202 computers available on campus for general student use. A campuswide network can be accessed. Online class registration is available.
Website: http://www.chatham.edu/

**General Application Contact:** Rachel Fiscus, Graduate Admissions Recruiter, 412-365-1141, Fax: 412-365-1609, E-mail: r.fiscus@chatham.edu.

**GRADUATE UNITS**

**Nursing Programs** *Program availability:* Online learning. Electronic applications accepted.

**Program in Accounting** *Program availability:* Part-time, evening/weekend. Electronic applications accepted.

**Program in Biology** *Program availability:* Part-time. Electronic applications accepted.

**Program in Business Administration** Students: 16 full-time (12 women), 24 part-time (17 women); includes 7 minority (2 Black or African American, non-Hispanic/Latino; 1 Asian, non-Hispanic/Latino; 2 Hispanic/Latino; 2 Two or more races, non-Hispanic/Latino), 7 international. Average age 28. 75 applicants, 29% accepted, 10 enrolled. *Faculty:* 1 full-time (0 women), 12 part-time/adjunct (3 women). Expenses: Contact institution. *Financial support:* Applicants required to submit FAFSA. In 2019, 20 master's awarded. *Program availability:* Part-time, evening/weekend. *Application deadline:* For fall admission, 4/1 for domestic and international students; for spring admission, 11/1 for domestic students, 10/1 for international students. Applications are processed on a rolling basis. *Application fee:* $45. Electronic applications accepted. *Application Contact:* Melanie Jo Elmer, Assistant Director of Graduate Admission, 412-365-1394, Fax: 412-365-1609, E-mail: gradadmissions@chatham.edu. *Director of Business and Entrepreneurship Program*, Dr. Rachel Chung, 412-365-2433.

**Program in Communication** *Program availability:* Part-time, online learning. Electronic applications accepted.

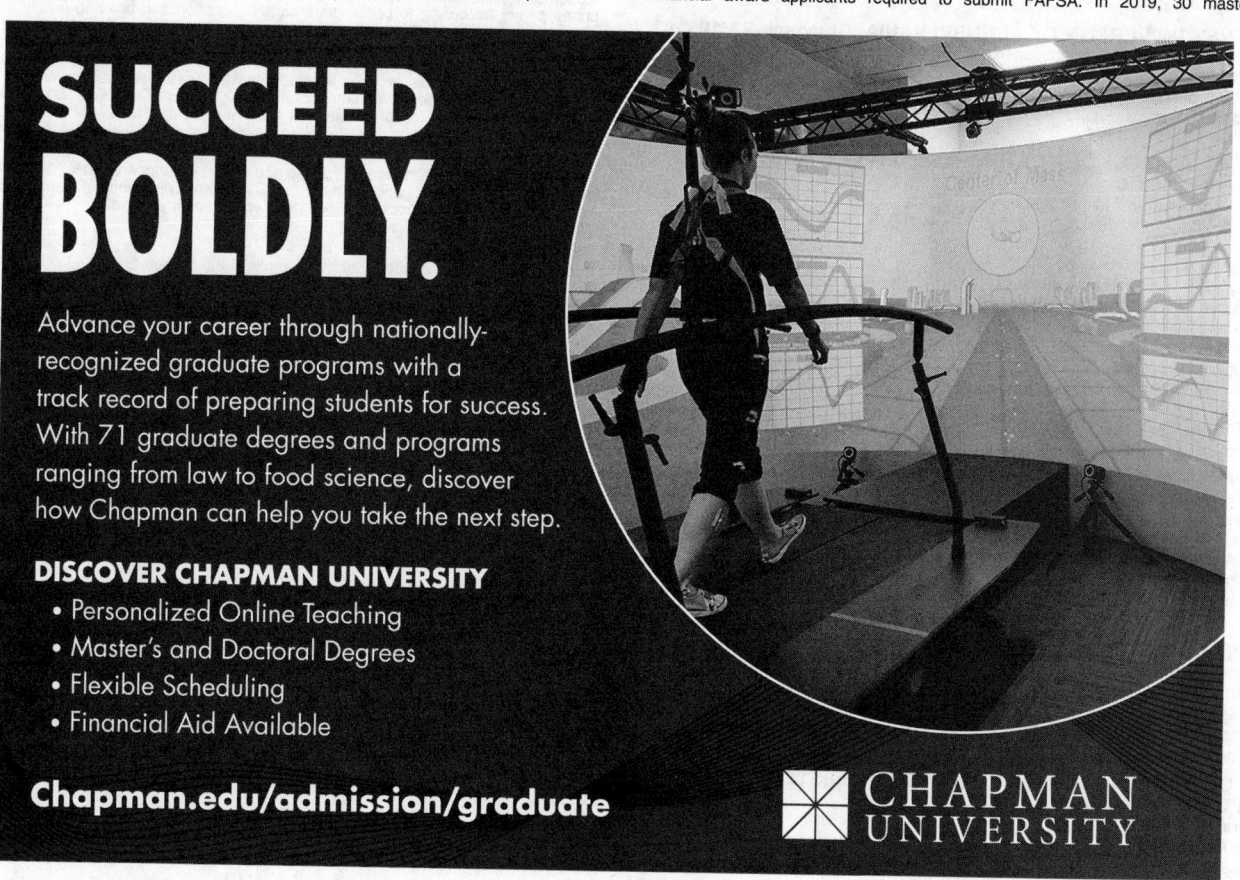

**Program in Counseling Psychology** Students: 93 full-time (79 women), 56 part-time (44 women); includes 29 minority (16 Black or African American, non-Hispanic/Latino; 4 Asian, non-Hispanic/Latino; 6 Hispanic/Latino; 3 Two or more races, non-Hispanic/Latino), 2 international. Average age 29. 172 applicants, 46% accepted, 54 enrolled. *Faculty:* 13 full-time (8 women), 21 part-time/adjunct (17 women). Expenses: Contact institution. *Financial support:* Career-related internships or fieldwork available. Financial award applicants required to submit FAFSA. In 2019, 30 master's, 7 doctorates awarded. *Program availability:* Part-time, evening/weekend. *Application deadline:* For fall admission, 4/1 priority date for domestic and international students; for spring admission, 11/1 for domestic students, 10/1 for international students. Applications are processed on a rolling basis. *Application fee:* $45. Electronic applications accepted. *Application Contact:* Melanie Elmer, Assistant Director of Graduate Admission, 412-365-1394, Fax: 412-365-1609, E-mail: gradadmissions@chatham.edu. *Director*, Dr. Mary Jo Loughran, 412-365-2783, Fax: 412-365-1505, E-mail: mloughran@chatham.edu.

**Program in Education** Students: 20 full-time (19 women), 4 part-time (all women); includes 6 minority (5 Black or African American, non-Hispanic/Latino; 1 Hispanic/Latino). Average age 30. 39 applicants, 41% accepted, 8 enrolled. *Faculty:* 3 full-time (all women), 14 part-time/adjunct (12 women). Expenses: Contact institution. *Financial support:* Career-related internships or fieldwork available. Financial award applicants required to submit FAFSA. In 2019, 20 master's awarded. *Application deadline:* For fall admission, 4/1 priority date for domestic and international students; for spring admission, 11/1 priority date for domestic students, 10/1 priority date for international students. Applications are processed on a rolling basis. *Application fee:* $45. Electronic applications accepted. *Application Contact:* Melanie Jo Elmer, Assistant Director of Graduate Admission, 412-365-1394, Fax: 412-365-1609, E-mail: gradadmissions@chatham.edu. *Chair and Program Director*, Kristin Harty, 412-365-2769, E-mail: kharty@chatham.edu.

**Program in Film and Digital Technology** *Program availability:* Part-time, evening/weekend. Electronic applications accepted.

**Program in Healthcare Informatics** *Program availability:* Online learning.

**Program in Interior Architecture** *Program availability:* Part-time, evening/weekend, online learning. Electronic applications accepted.

**Program in Occupational Therapy** Electronic applications accepted.

**Program in Physical Therapy** Students: 113 full-time (73 women), 5 part-time (2 women); includes 8 minority (1 Black or African American, non-Hispanic/Latino; 4 Asian, non-Hispanic/Latino; 2 Hispanic/Latino; 1 Two or more races, non-Hispanic/Latino). Average age 24. 368 applicants, 25% accepted, 40 enrolled. *Faculty:* 8 full-time (5 women). Expenses: Contact institution. *Financial support:* Career-related internships or fieldwork available. Financial award applicants required to submit FAFSA. In 2019, 37 doctorates awarded. *Application deadline:* For fall admission, 12/1 priority date for domestic and international students. *Application fee:* $45. Electronic applications accepted. *Application Contact:* Melanie Jo Elmer, Assistant Director of Graduate Admission, 412-365-1394, Fax: 412-365-1609, E-mail: gradadmissions@chatham.edu. *Chair and Program Director*, Dr. Joseph Schreiber, 412-365-1358, Fax: 412-365-1505, E-mail: jschreiber@chatham.edu.

**Program in Physician Assistant Studies** Electronic applications accepted.

**Program in Writing** *Program availability:* Part-time, evening/weekend, online learning. Electronic applications accepted.

## CHESTNUT HILL COLLEGE, Philadelphia, PA 19118-2693

**General Information** Independent-religious, coed, comprehensive institution. *Graduate housing:* On-campus housing not available.

**GRADUATE UNITS**

**School of Graduate Studies** *Program availability:* Part-time, evening/weekend. Electronic applications accepted.

***Division of Psychology*** *Program availability:* Part-time, evening/weekend.

## CHEYNEY UNIVERSITY OF PENNSYLVANIA, Cheyney, PA 19319

**General Information** State-supported, coed, comprehensive institution. *Graduate housing:* On-campus housing not available.

**GRADUATE UNITS**

**Graduate Programs** *Program availability:* Part-time, evening/weekend. Electronic applications accepted.

## THE CHICAGO SCHOOL OF PROFESSIONAL PSYCHOLOGY, Chicago, IL 60610

**General Information** Independent, coed, primarily women, graduate-only institution. CGS member. *Graduate housing:* On-campus housing not available.

**GRADUATE UNITS**

**Program in Applied Behavior Analysis**

**Program in Business Psychology**

**Program in Clinical Forensic Psychology**

**Program in Clinical Mental Health Counseling** *Program availability:* Part-time.

**Program in Clinical Psychology** Electronic applications accepted.

**Program in Forensic Psychology**

**Program in Industrial and Organizational Psychology** *Program availability:* Part-time, evening/weekend.

**Program in School Psychology** *Program availability:* Part-time.

## THE CHICAGO SCHOOL OF PROFESSIONAL PSYCHOLOGY AT DOWNTOWN LOS ANGELES, Los Angeles, CA 90017

**General Information** Independent, coed, graduate-only institution.

**GRADUATE UNITS**

**Program in Applied Behavior Analysis**

**Program in Clinical Forensic Psychology**

**Program in Clinical Psychology**

**Program in Industrial and Organizational Psychology**

## THE CHICAGO SCHOOL OF PROFESSIONAL PSYCHOLOGY AT IRVINE, Irvine, CA 92612

**General Information** Independent, coed, graduate-only institution.

**GRADUATE UNITS**

**Program in Clinical Forensic Psychology**

**Program in Marital and Family Therapy**

**Program in Psychology**

## THE CHICAGO SCHOOL OF PROFESSIONAL PSYCHOLOGY AT SAN DIEGO, San Diego, CA 92101

**General Information** Independent, coed, graduate-only institution.

**GRADUATE UNITS**

**Graduate Programs**

## THE CHICAGO SCHOOL OF PROFESSIONAL PSYCHOLOGY AT WASHINGTON DC, Washington, DC 20005

**General Information** Independent, coed.

**GRADUATE UNITS**

**Program in School Psychology** *Program availability:* Part-time.

## THE CHICAGO SCHOOL OF PROFESSIONAL PSYCHOLOGY AT XAVIER UNIVERSITY OF LOUISIANA, New Orleans, LA 70125

**General Information** Independent, coed, graduate-only institution.

**GRADUATE UNITS**

**Graduate Program**

## THE CHICAGO SCHOOL OF PROFESSIONAL PSYCHOLOGY: ONLINE, Chicago, IL 60654

**General Information** Independent, coed, graduate-only institution. *Graduate housing:* On-campus housing not available.

**GRADUATE UNITS**

**PhD Program in Organizational Leadership**

**Program in Applied Industrial and Organizational Psychology**

**Program in Clinical Psychopharmacology** *Program availability:* Online learning.

**Program in Forensic Psychology**

**Program in Health Services Administration** *Program availability:* Online learning.

**Program in International Psychology**

**Program in Psychology**

## CHICAGO STATE UNIVERSITY, Chicago, IL 60628

**General Information** State-supported, coed, comprehensive institution. *Graduate housing:* Room and/or apartments available on a first-come, first-served basis to single students; on-campus housing not available to married students.

**GRADUATE UNITS**

**College of Pharmacy**

**School of Graduate and Professional Studies** *Program availability:* Part-time, evening/weekend. Electronic applications accepted.

***College of Arts and Sciences*** *Program availability:* Part-time, evening/weekend.

***College of Education*** *Program availability:* Part-time.

***College of Health Sciences***

## CHICAGO THEOLOGICAL SEMINARY, Chicago, IL 60637-1507

**General Information** Independent-religious, coed, graduate-only institution. *Graduate housing:* On-campus housing not available.

**GRADUATE UNITS**

**Graduate and Professional Programs** *Program availability:* Part-time.

## CHOWAN UNIVERSITY, Murfreesboro, NC 27855

**General Information** Independent-religious, coed, comprehensive institution. *Tuition:* Full-time $7200; part-time $410 per credit hour. *Graduate housing:* Room and/or apartments guaranteed to single students; on-campus housing not available to married students. Typical cost: $10,690 per year ($11,200 including board). Room and board charges vary according to board plan, campus/location and housing facility selected. Housing application deadline: 8/1. *Student services:* Campus employment opportunities, campus safety program, career counseling, exercise/wellness program, free psychological counseling, international student services, low-cost health insurance, multicultural affairs office, services for students with disabilities, teacher training, writing training. *Library facilities:* Whitaker Library plus 1 other. *Collection:* Books: 163,497 (physical), 405,678 (digital/electronic); Serial titles: 1,310 (physical), 69,556 (digital/electronic); Databases: 135. Weekly public service hours: 84; students can reserve study rooms.

**Computer facilities:** Computer purchase and lease plans are available. 251 computers available on campus for general student use. A campuswide network can be accessed from student residence rooms. Online class registration is available.
Website: http://www.chowan.edu/

**GRADUATE UNITS**

**School of Graduate Studies** Electronic applications accepted.

## CHRISTENDOM COLLEGE, Front Royal, VA 22630-5103

**General Information** Independent-religious, coed, comprehensive institution. *Graduate housing:* On-campus housing not available.

**GRADUATE UNITS**

**Graduate School of Theology** *Program availability:* Part-time, evening/weekend, 100% online, blended/hybrid learning. Electronic applications accepted.

## CHRISTIAN BROTHERS UNIVERSITY, Memphis, TN 38104-5581

**General Information** Independent-religious, coed, comprehensive institution. *Graduate housing:* On-campus housing not available.

**GRADUATE UNITS**

**School of Arts** *Program availability:* Part-time, evening/weekend.

**School of Business** *Program availability:* Part-time, evening/weekend.

**School of Engineering** *Program availability:* Part-time, evening/weekend, online learning.

**School of Sciences**

## CHRISTIAN THEOLOGICAL SEMINARY, Indianapolis, IN 46208-3301

**General Information** Independent-religious, coed, graduate-only institution. *Graduate housing:* Rooms and/or apartments available on a first-come, first-served basis to single and married students.

**GRADUATE UNITS**

**Graduate and Professional Programs** *Program availability:* Part-time. Electronic applications accepted.

## CHRISTIE'S EDUCATION, New York, NY 10020

**General Information** Proprietary, coed, primarily women, graduate-only institution. *Graduate housing:* On-campus housing not available.

**GRADUATE UNITS**

**Certificate Program in Art Business** Electronic applications accepted.

**Certificate Program in Modern and Contemporary Art in New York** *Program availability:* Part-time.
**MA Program in Art, Law and Business**
**MA Program in Modern and Contemporary Art and the Market** *Program availability:* Part-time.

## CHRISTOPHER NEWPORT UNIVERSITY, Newport News, VA 23606-3072

**General Information** State-supported, coed, comprehensive institution. *Enrollment:* 4,919 graduate, professional, and undergraduate students; 63 full-time matriculated graduate/professional students (43 women), 19 part-time matriculated graduate/professional students (6 women). *Enrollment by degree level:* 82 master's. *Graduate faculty:* 19 full-time (6 women), 17 part-time/adjunct (13 women). *International tuition:* $16,686 full-time. *Tuition, area resident:* Full-time $7578; part-time $421 per credit hour. Tuition, state resident: full-time $7578; part-time $421 per credit hour. Tuition, nonresident: full-time $16,686; part-time $927 per credit hour. *Required fees:* $4428; $246 per credit hour. Tuition and fees vary according to course load and program. *Graduate housing:* On-campus housing not available. *Student services:* Campus employment opportunities, career counseling, exercise/wellness program, multicultural affairs office, services for students with disabilities, teacher training. *Library facilities:* Paul and Rosemary Trible Library. *Collection:* Books: 217,255 (physical), 846,460 (digital/electronic); Serial titles: 745 (physical), 63,227 (digital/electronic); Databases: 282. Weekly public service hours: 101; study areas open 24 hours, 5–7 days a week; students can reserve study rooms. *Research affiliation:* Thomas Jefferson National Accelerator Facility (instrument and nuclear physics), Langley Research Center, Center for Distance Learning (flow visualization), National Science Foundation (science).

**Computer facilities:** 540 computers available on campus for general student use. A campuswide network can be accessed. Online class registration is available.
Website: http://www.cnu.edu/

**General Application Contact:** Zena Mageras, Graduate Admissions, 757-594-8585, E-mail: gradadmit@cnu.edu.

**GRADUATE UNITS**

**Graduate Studies** *Program availability:* Part-time. Electronic applications accepted.

## CHRIST THE KING SEMINARY, East Aurora, NY 14052

**General Information** Independent-religious, coed, graduate-only institution. *Graduate housing:* On-campus housing not available.

**GRADUATE UNITS**

**Graduate and Professional Programs** *Program availability:* Part-time, evening/weekend.

## CHURCH DIVINITY SCHOOL OF THE PACIFIC, Berkeley, CA 94709-1217

**General Information** Independent-religious, coed, graduate-only institution. *Graduate housing:* Rooms and/or apartments available on a first-come, first-served basis to single and married students. Housing application deadline: 5/1.

**GRADUATE UNITS**

**Graduate and Professional Programs** *Program availability:* Part-time. Electronic applications accepted.

## CINCINNATI CHRISTIAN UNIVERSITY, Cincinnati, OH 45204-3200

**General Information** Independent-religious, coed, comprehensive institution. *Graduate housing:* On-campus housing not available.

**GRADUATE UNITS**

**Graduate School** *Program availability:* Part-time. Electronic applications accepted.

## THE CITADEL, THE MILITARY COLLEGE OF SOUTH CAROLINA, Charleston, SC 29409

**General Information** State-supported, coed, primarily men, comprehensive institution. *Graduate housing:* On-campus housing not available.

**GRADUATE UNITS**

**Citadel Graduate College** *Program availability:* Part-time, evening/weekend, 100% online, blended/hybrid learning. Electronic applications accepted.

***School of Engineering*** *Program availability:* Part-time, evening/weekend. Electronic applications accepted.

***School of Humanities and Social Sciences*** *Program availability:* Part-time, evening/weekend, 100% online, blended/hybrid learning. Electronic applications accepted.

***School of Science and Mathematics*** *Program availability:* Part-time, evening/weekend. Electronic applications accepted.

***Tommy and Victoria Baker School of Business*** *Program availability:* Part-time, evening/weekend, 100% online, blended/hybrid learning. Electronic applications accepted.

***Zucker Family School of Education*** Students: 37 full-time (27 women), 166 part-time (128 women); includes 55 minority (42 Black or African American, non-Hispanic/Latino; 1 Asian, non-Hispanic/Latino; 8 Hispanic/Latino; 4 Two or more races, non-Hispanic/Latino). *Faculty:* 16 full-time (10 women), 10 part-time/adjunct (7 women). Expenses: Contact institution. *Financial support:* In 2019–20, 21,283 students received support. Federal Work-Study, scholarships/grants, tuition waivers (partial), and Athletics available. Financial award applicants required to submit FAFSA. In 2019, 120 master's, 27 other advanced degrees awarded. *Program availability:* Part-time, evening/weekend, 100% online, blended/hybrid learning. *Application deadline:* Applications are processed on a rolling basis. *Application fee:* $40. Electronic applications accepted. *Application Contact:* Carl Hill, Assistant Director of Enrollment Management, 843-953-6808, Fax: 843-953-7630, E-mail: chill9@citadel.edu. *Zucker Family School of Education Dean,* Evan Ortlieb, 843-953-5097, Fax: 843-953-7258, E-mail: eortlieb@citadel.edu.

## CITY COLLEGE OF THE CITY UNIVERSITY OF NEW YORK, New York, NY 10031-9198

**General Information** State and locally supported, coed, comprehensive institution. CGS member. *Graduate housing:* Room and/or apartments available on a first-come, first-served basis to single students; on-campus housing not available to married students. *Research affiliation:* New York Center for Biological Structures, Lucent Laboratories (engineering), Hospital for Joint Diseases (biomedical engineering), Museum of Natural History.

**GRADUATE UNITS**

**Graduate School** *Program availability:* Part-time, evening/weekend.

***The Bernard and Anne Spitzer School of Architecture*** *Program availability:* Part-time.

***Colin Powell School for Civic and Global Leadership*** *Program availability:* Part-time. Electronic applications accepted.

***Division of Humanities and the Arts*** *Program availability:* Part-time. Electronic applications accepted.

***Division of Science*** *Program availability:* Part-time. Electronic applications accepted.

***Grove School of Engineering*** *Program availability:* Part-time.

***School of Education*** *Program availability:* Part-time, evening/weekend.

## CITY UNIVERSITY OF NEW YORK SCHOOL OF LAW, Long Island City, NY 11101-4356

**General Information** State and locally supported, coed, graduate-only institution. *Enrollment by degree level:* 622 doctoral. *Graduate faculty:* 64 full-time (42 women), 31 part-time/adjunct (20 women). *Tuition, area resident:* Full-time $7725; part-time $5305 per semester. Tuition, nonresident: full-time $12,820; part-time $8815 per semester. *Required fees:* $174 per semester. Tuition and fees vary according to program. *Graduate housing:* On-campus housing not available. *Student services:* Campus employment opportunities, campus safety program, career counseling, exercise/wellness program, free psychological counseling, services for students with disabilities, writing training. *Library facilities:* CUNY School of Law Library. *Collection:* Books: 860,513 (digital/electronic); Serial titles: 1,931 (physical), 149,128 (digital/electronic); Databases: 384. Weekly public service hours: 61; study areas open 24 hours, 5–7 days a week.

**Computer facilities:** 105 computers available on campus for general student use. Online class registration is available.
Website: http://www.law.cuny.edu/

**General Application Contact:** Degna P. Levister, Assistant Dean of Admissions and Enrollment Management, 718-340-4210, Fax: 718-340-4435, E-mail: admissions@law.cuny.edu.

**GRADUATE UNITS**

**Professional Program** Students: 417 full-time (254 women), 161 part-time (94 women); includes 297 minority (68 Black or African American, non-Hispanic/Latino; 54 Asian, non-Hispanic/Latino; 135 Hispanic/Latino; 1 Native Hawaiian or other Pacific Islander, non-Hispanic/Latino; 39 Two or more races, non-Hispanic/Latino), 16 international. Average age 29. 1,606 applicants, 38% accepted, 205 enrolled. *Faculty:* 51 full-time (37 women), 28 part-time/adjunct (14 women). Expenses: Contact institution. *Financial support:* In 2019–20, 175 students received support, including 53 fellowships (averaging $15,578 per year), 33 research assistantships (averaging $1,200 per year); Federal Work-Study, scholarships/grants, tuition waivers (full and partial), and unspecified assistantships also available. Support available to part-time students. Financial award application deadline: 7/15; financial award applicants required to submit FAFSA. In 2019, 165 doctorates awarded. *Program availability:* Part-time, evening/weekend. *Application deadline:* For fall admission, 5/15 priority date for domestic students. Applications are processed on a rolling basis. *Application fee:* $60. Electronic applications accepted. *Application Contact:* Degna P. Levister, Assistant Dean of Admissions and Enrollment Management, 718-340-4210, Fax: 718-340-4435, E-mail: admissions@law.cuny.edu. *Dean/Professor of Law,* Mary Lu Bilek, 718-340-4201, Fax: 718-340-4482.

## CITY UNIVERSITY OF SEATTLE, Seattle, WA 98121

**General Information** Independent, coed, comprehensive institution. *Graduate housing:* Room and/or apartments available on a first-come, first-served basis to single students; on-campus housing not available to married students.

**GRADUATE UNITS**

**Graduate Division** *Program availability:* Part-time, evening/weekend, online learning. Electronic applications accepted.

***Albright School of Education*** *Program availability:* Part-time, evening/weekend, online learning. Electronic applications accepted.

***Division of Arts and Sciences*** *Program availability:* Part-time, evening/weekend, online learning. Electronic applications accepted.

***Division of Doctoral Studies*** *Program availability:* Online learning.

***School of Management*** *Program availability:* Part-time, evening/weekend, online learning. Electronic applications accepted.

## CITY VISION UNIVERSITY, Kansas City, MO 64109-1845

**General Information** Independent-religious, coed, comprehensive institution.

**GRADUATE UNITS**

**Program in Technology and Ministry** *Program availability:* Online learning.

## CLAFLIN UNIVERSITY, Orangeburg, SC 29115

**General Information** Independent-religious, coed, comprehensive institution. *Graduate housing:* Room and/or apartments available on a first-come, first-served basis to single students; on-campus housing not available to married students. Housing application deadline: 4/15.

**GRADUATE UNITS**

**Graduate Programs** *Program availability:* Part-time.

## CLAREMONT GRADUATE UNIVERSITY, Claremont, CA 91711-6160

**General Information** Independent, coed, graduate-only institution. CGS member. *Graduate housing:* Rooms and/or apartments available on a first-come, first-served basis to single and married students. Housing application deadline: 5/15. *Research affiliation:* Claremont School of Theology (religion), Rancho Santa Ana Botanic Garden (botany, native plants).

**GRADUATE UNITS**

**Graduate Programs** *Program availability:* Part-time, evening/weekend. Electronic applications accepted.

***Center for Information Systems and Technology*** *Program availability:* Part-time. Electronic applications accepted.

***Institute of Mathematical Sciences*** *Program availability:* Part-time. Electronic applications accepted.

***Peter F. Drucker and Masatoshi Ito Graduate School of Management*** *Program availability:* Part-time. Electronic applications accepted.

***School of Arts and Humanities*** *Program availability:* Part-time. Electronic applications accepted.

***School of Community and Global Health*** Electronic applications accepted.

***School of Educational Studies*** *Program availability:* Part-time. Electronic applications accepted.

***School of Social Science, Policy and Evaluation***

## CLAREMONT LINCOLN UNIVERSITY, Claremont, CA 91711

**General Information** Independent, coed, graduate-only institution.

**GRADUATE UNITS**

**Graduate Programs**

## CLAREMONT SCHOOL OF THEOLOGY, Claremont, CA 91711-3199

**General Information** Independent-religious, coed, graduate-only institution. *Graduate housing:* Rooms and/or apartments available on a first-come, first-served basis to single students and guaranteed to married students. Housing application deadline: 5/1. *Research affiliation:* Moore Multicultural Resource and Research Center, Institute for Antiquity and Christianity, Center for Process Studies, National United Methodist Native American Center, Center for Pacific and Asian-American Ministries, Ancient Biblical Manuscript Center.

**GRADUATE UNITS**

**Graduate and Professional Programs** *Program availability:* Part-time. Electronic applications accepted.

## CLARION UNIVERSITY OF PENNSYLVANIA, Clarion, PA 16214

**General Information** State-supported, coed, comprehensive institution. *Enrollment:* 4,869 graduate, professional, and undergraduate students; 230 full-time matriculated graduate/professional students (194 women), 680 part-time matriculated graduate/professional students (532 women). *Enrollment by degree level:* 889 master's, 21 doctoral. *Graduate faculty:* 64 full-time (39 women), 25 part-time/adjunct (20 women). *Tuition, area resident:* Part-time $516 per credit hour. Tuition, state resident: part-time $516 per credit hour. Tuition, nonresident: part-time $557 per credit hour. *Required fees:* $161 per credit hour. One-time fee: $50 part-time. Tuition and fees vary according to degree level, campus/location and program. *Graduate housing:* Room and/or apartments available on a first-come, first-served basis to single students; on-campus housing not available to married students. Typical cost: $14,068 (including board). Room and board charges vary according to board plan, campus/location and housing facility selected. *Student services:* Campus employment opportunities, campus safety program, career counseling, child daycare facilities, exercise/wellness program, international student services, multicultural affairs office, services for students with disabilities, teacher training, writing training. *Library facilities:* Carlson Library plus 1 other. *Collection:* Books: 444,818 (physical), 348,037 (digital/electronic); Serial titles: 179 (physical), 57,405 (digital/electronic); Databases: 102. Weekly public service hours: 94; students can reserve study rooms.

**Computer facilities:** 950 computers available on campus for general student use. A campuswide network can be accessed from student residence rooms and from off campus. Online class registration, Online Learning Management System, web-based personal disk space, other online student services (financial aid, billing etc.) are available.
Website: http://www.clarion.edu/

**General Application Contact:** Susan Staub, Graduate Admissions Counselor, 814-393-2337, Fax: 814-393-2722, E-mail: gradstudies@clarion.edu.

**GRADUATE UNITS**

**College of Business Administration and Information Sciences**

**College of Health Sciences & Human Services** Students: 189 full-time (164 women), 86 part-time (76 women); includes 26 minority (10 Black or African American, non-Hispanic/Latino; 1 American Indian or Alaska Native, non-Hispanic/Latino; 3 Asian, non-Hispanic/Latino; 8 Hispanic/Latino; 4 Two or more races, non-Hispanic/Latino). Average age 31. 324 applicants, 38% accepted, 119 enrolled. *Faculty:* 20 full-time (17 women), 8 part-time/adjunct (6 women). Expenses: Contact institution. *Financial support:* Federal Work-Study and scholarships/grants available. Financial award application deadline: 3/1; financial award applicants required to submit FAFSA. In 2019, 101 master's, 15 doctorates awarded. *Application deadline:* Applications are processed on a rolling basis. *Application fee:* $40. Electronic applications accepted. *Application Contact:* Susan Staub, Graduate Admissions Counselor, 814-393-2337, Fax: 814-393-2722, E-mail: gradstudies@clarion.edu. *Dean of the College of Health Sciences & Human Services*, Dr. Jeffery Allen, 814-393-2163, E-mail: jallen@clarion.edu.

**School of Education**

## CLARK ATLANTA UNIVERSITY, Atlanta, GA 30314

**General Information** Independent-religious, coed, university. CGS member. *Graduate housing:* Room and/or apartments available on a first-come, first-served basis to single students; on-campus housing not available to married students. Housing application deadline: 6/1.

**GRADUATE UNITS**

**School of Arts and Sciences** *Program availability:* Part-time.

**School of Business Administration** *Program availability:* Part-time. Electronic applications accepted.

**School of Education** *Program availability:* Part-time, evening/weekend. Electronic applications accepted.

**School of Social Work** *Program availability:* Part-time. Electronic applications accepted.

## CLARKE UNIVERSITY, Dubuque, IA 52001-3198

**General Information** Independent-religious, coed, comprehensive institution. *Graduate housing:* On-campus housing not available.

**GRADUATE UNITS**

**Department of Nursing and Health** *Program availability:* Part-time. Electronic applications accepted.

**Department of Social Work** *Program availability:* Part-time, evening/weekend. Electronic applications accepted.

**Graduate Business Programs** *Program availability:* Part-time, evening/weekend, blended/hybrid learning. Electronic applications accepted.

**Physical Therapy Program** Electronic applications accepted.

**Program in Education** *Program availability:* Part-time, 100% online, blended/hybrid learning. Electronic applications accepted.

## CLARKSON COLLEGE, Omaha, NE 68131-2739

**General Information** Independent, coed, primarily women, comprehensive institution. *Graduate housing:* Room and/or apartments available on a first-come, first-served basis to single students; on-campus housing not available to married students. Housing application deadline: 6/30.

**GRADUATE UNITS**

**Master of Science in Nursing Program** *Program availability:* Part-time, evening/weekend, online learning. Electronic applications accepted.

**Program in Health Care Administration** *Program availability:* Part-time, evening/weekend, online learning. Electronic applications accepted.

## CLARKSON UNIVERSITY, Potsdam, NY 13699

**General Information** Independent, coed, university. CGS member. *Enrollment:* 4,301 graduate, professional, and undergraduate students; 593 full-time matriculated graduate/professional students (288 women), 547 part-time matriculated graduate/professional students (204 women). *Enrollment by degree level:* 864 master's, 242 doctoral, 34 other advanced degrees. *Graduate faculty:* 237 full-time (81 women), 132 part-time/adjunct (47 women). *Tuition:* Full-time $24,984; part-time $1388 per credit hour. *Required fees:* $225. Tuition and fees vary according to campus/location and program. *Graduate housing:* On-campus housing not available. *Student services:* Campus employment opportunities, campus safety program, career counseling, free psychological counseling, international student services, low-cost health insurance, multicultural affairs office, services for students with disabilities, teacher training. *Library facilities:* Harriet Call Burnap Memorial Library plus 1 other. *Collection:* Books: 119,380 (physical), 246,291 (digital/electronic); Serial titles: 7,688 (physical), 48,712 (digital/electronic); Databases: 190. Weekly public service hours: 76; study areas open 24 hours, 5–7 days a week. *Research affiliation:* Trudeau Institute (biomedical sciences).

**Computer facilities:** 350 computers available on campus for general student use. A campuswide network can be accessed. Online class registration is available.
Website: http://www.clarkson.edu/

**General Application Contact:** Daniel Capogna, Director of Graduate Admissions & Recruitment, 518-631-9910, E-mail: graduate@clarkson.edu.

**GRADUATE UNITS**

**David D. Reh School of Business** Students: 98 full-time (45 women), 108 part-time (54 women); includes 32 minority (9 Black or African American, non-Hispanic/Latino; 1 American Indian or Alaska Native, non-Hispanic/Latino; 13 Asian, non-Hispanic/Latino; 5 Hispanic/Latino; 4 Two or more races, non-Hispanic/Latino), 18 international. *Faculty:* 61 full-time (19 women), 21 part-time/adjunct (6 women). Expenses: Contact institution. In 2019, 103 master's awarded. *Application Contact:* Daniel Capogna, Director of Graduate Admissions & Recruitment, 518-631-9910, E-mail: graduate@clarkson.edu. *Dean of the Reh of School Business / Dorf Chair in Entrepreneurship and Innovation*, Dr. Augustine Lado, 315-268-6608, E-mail: alado@clarkson.edu.

**Department of Bioethics** Students: 3 full-time (2 women), 26 part-time (19 women); includes 6 minority (1 Black or African American, non-Hispanic/Latino; 2 Asian, non-Hispanic/Latino; 2 Hispanic/Latino; 1 Two or more races, non-Hispanic/Latino), 14 international. 20 applicants, 90% accepted, 15 enrolled. *Faculty:* 5 part-time/adjunct (2 women). Expenses: Contact institution. *Financial support:* Scholarships/grants available. In 2019, 18 master's, 6 other advanced degrees awarded. *Program availability:* Part-time, evening/weekend, 100% online, blended/hybrid learning. *Application deadline:* Applications are processed on a rolling basis. *Application fee:* $50. Electronic applications accepted. *Application Contact:* Daniel Capogna, Director of Graduate Admissions and Recruitment, 518-631-9910, E-mail: dcapogna@clarkson.edu. *Assistant Professor of Operations & Information Systems*, Jane Oppenlander, 518-631-9905, E-mail: joppenla@clarkson.edu.

**Institute for a Sustainable Environment** Students: 22 full-time (12 women); includes 1 minority (Hispanic/Latino), 8 international. *Faculty:* 1 full-time (0 women), 9 part-time/adjunct (5 women). Expenses: Contact institution. In 2019, 5 master's, 1 doctorate awarded. *Application Contact:* Daniel Capogna, Director of Graduate Admissions & Recruitment, 518-631-9910, E-mail: graduate@clarkson.edu. *Director of the Institute for a Sustainable Environment*, Dr. Susan Powers, 315-268-6542, E-mail: spowers@clarkson.edu.

**Lewis School of Health Sciences** Students: 181 full-time (137 women); includes 33 minority (8 Black or African American, non-Hispanic/Latino; 1 American Indian or Alaska Native, non-Hispanic/Latino; 15 Asian, non-Hispanic/Latino; 5 Hispanic/Latino; 4 Two or more races, non-Hispanic/Latino), 4 international. *Faculty:* 22 full-time (16 women), 16 part-time/adjunct (10 women). Expenses: Contact institution. In 2019, 45 master's, 20 doctorates awarded. *Application Contact:* Daniel Capogna, Director of Graduate Admissions & Recruitment, 518-631-9910, E-mail: dcapogna@clarkson.edu. *Interim Dean of Arts & Sciences / Professor of Biology*, Dr. Tom Langen, 315-268-7933, E-mail: cthorpe@clarkson.edu.

**Program in Data Analytics** Students: 25 full-time (4 women), 17 part-time (9 women); includes 6 minority (4 Asian, non-Hispanic/Latino; 1 Hispanic/Latino; 1 Two or more races, non-Hispanic/Latino), 15 international. 83 applicants, 77% accepted, 15 enrolled. Expenses: Contact institution. *Financial support:* Scholarships/grants and unspecified assistantships available. In 2019, 12 master's awarded. *Program availability:* Part-time, evening/weekend, 100% online. *Application deadline:* Applications are processed on a rolling basis. *Application fee:* $50. Electronic applications accepted. *Application Contact:* Daniel Capogna, Director of Graduate Admissions, 518-631-9910, E-mail: graduate@clarkson.edu. *Professor of Operations & Information Systems / Director of Business Analytics*, Boris Jukic, 315-268-3884, E-mail: bjukic@clarkson.edu.

**Program in Education** Students: 32 full-time (23 women), 44 part-time (31 women); includes 17 minority (7 Black or African American, non-Hispanic/Latino; 5 Asian, non-Hispanic/Latino; 5 Hispanic/Latino), 15 international. 96 applicants, 82% accepted, 64 enrolled. *Faculty:* 6 full-time (all women), 14 part-time/adjunct (5 women). Expenses: Contact institution. *Financial support:* Scholarships/grants available. In 2019, 24 master's awarded. *Application deadline:* Applications are processed on a rolling basis. *Application fee:* $50. Electronic applications accepted. *Application Contact:* Daniel Capogna, Director of Graduate Admissions & Recruitment, 518-631-9910, E-mail: graduate@clarkson.edu. *Associate Professor / Chair of Education / Associate Director of Institute for STEM Education*, Catherine Snyder, 518-631-9870, E-mail: csnyder@clarkson.edu.

**Program in Engineering Management** Students: 211 part-time (54 women); includes 38 minority (8 Black or African American, non-Hispanic/Latino; 15 Asian, non-Hispanic/Latino; 11 Hispanic/Latino; 4 Two or more races, non-Hispanic/Latino), 19 international. 57 applicants, 98% accepted, 56 enrolled. *Faculty:* 7 part-time/adjunct (1 woman). Expenses: Contact institution. *Financial support:* Scholarships/grants available. In 2019, 62 master's awarded. *Program availability:* Part-time-only, evening/weekend, blended/hybrid learning. *Application deadline:* Applications are processed on a rolling basis. *Application fee:* $50. Electronic applications accepted. *Application Contact:* Daniel Capogna, Director of Graduate Admissions & Recruitment, 518-631-9910, E-mail: graduate@clarkson.edu. *Associate Dean of Engineering,* Hugo Irizarry-Quinones, 518-631-9881, E-mail: hirizarr@clarkson.edu.

**School of Arts and Sciences** Students: 100 full-time (36 women), 8 part-time (1 woman); includes 7 minority (1 Black or African American, non-Hispanic/Latino; 4 Asian, non-Hispanic/Latino; 1 Native Hawaiian or other Pacific Islander, non-Hispanic/Latino; 1 Two or more races, non-Hispanic/Latino), 53 international. *Faculty:* 49 full-time (15 women), 10 part-time/adjunct (5 women). Expenses: Contact institution. In 2019, 16 master's, 19 doctorates awarded. *Application Contact:* Daniel Capogna, Director of Graduate Admissions & Recruitment, 518-631-9910, E-mail: graduate@clarkson.edu. *Interim Dean of Arts and Sciences,* Dr. Charles Thorpe, 315-268-6544, E-mail: cthorpe@clarkson.edu.

**Wallace H. Coulter School of Engineering** Students: 132 full-time (29 women), 117 part-time (22 women); includes 27 minority (2 Black or African American, non-Hispanic/Latino; 1 American Indian or Alaska Native, non-Hispanic/Latino; 12 Asian, non-Hispanic/Latino; 6 Hispanic/Latino; 6 Two or more races, non-Hispanic/Latino), 83 international. *Faculty:* 70 full-time (12 women), 21 part-time/adjunct (5 women). Expenses: Contact institution. In 2019, 63 master's, 19 doctorates, 45 other advanced degrees awarded. *Application Contact:* Daniel Capogna, Director of Graduate Admissions & Recruitment, 518-631-9910, E-mail: graduate@clarkson.edu. *Dean of Engineering,* Dr. William Jemison, 315-268-6446, E-mail: wjemison@clarkson.edu.

## CLARKS SUMMIT UNIVERSITY, South Abington Township, PA 18411

**General Information** Independent-religious, coed, comprehensive institution. *Graduate housing:* Room and/or apartments available on a first-come, first-served basis to single students; on-campus housing not available to married students.

**GRADUATE UNITS**

**Baptist Bible Seminary** *Program availability:* Part-time, evening/weekend, online learning. Electronic applications accepted.

**Online Master's Programs** *Program availability:* Part-time, evening/weekend, online learning.

## CLARK UNIVERSITY, Worcester, MA 01610-1477

**General Information** Independent, coed, university. CGS member. *Enrollment:* 3,122 graduate, professional, and undergraduate students; 871 full-time matriculated graduate/professional students (408 women), 180 part-time matriculated graduate/professional students (61 women). *Enrollment by degree level:* 808 master's, 213 doctoral, 30 other advanced degrees. *Graduate faculty:* 209 full-time (93 women), 142 part-time/adjunct (65 women). *Tuition:* Full-time $47,650; part-time $4765 per course. *Required fees:* $1850. *Graduate housing:* Rooms and/or apartments available on a first-come, first-served basis to single and married students. *Student services:* Campus employment opportunities, campus safety program, career counseling, exercise/wellness program, free psychological counseling, grant writing training, international student services, low-cost health insurance, multicultural affairs office, services for students with disabilities, teacher training, writing training. *Library facilities:* Robert Hutchings Goddard Library plus 8 others. *Collection:* Students can reserve study rooms. *Research affiliation:* Worcester Area Computation Center, Worcester Foundation for Experimental Biology, Massachusetts Biotechnology Research Institute.

**Computer facilities:** A campuswide network can be accessed from student residence rooms and from off campus. Online class registration, online course support are available.
Website: http://www.clarku.edu/

**General Application Contact:** Jeremiah Czub, Director of Graduate Admissions, 508-793-7676, Fax: 508-793-8834, E-mail: jczub@clarku.edu.

**GRADUATE UNITS**

**Graduate School** Students: 871 full-time (408 women), 180 part-time (61 women); includes 120 minority (36 Black or African American, non-Hispanic/Latino; 30 Asian, non-Hispanic/Latino; 41 Hispanic/Latino; 13 Two or more races, non-Hispanic/Latino), 549 international. Average age 28. 2,048 applicants, 72% accepted, 388 enrolled. *Faculty:* 209 full-time (93 women), 142 part-time/adjunct (65 women). Expenses: Contact institution. *Financial support:* In 2019–20, 10 fellowships with tuition reimbursements (averaging $17,000 per year), 39 research assistantships with tuition reimbursements (averaging $17,000 per year), 84 teaching assistantships with tuition reimbursements (averaging $17,000 per year) were awarded; career-related internships or fieldwork, Federal Work-Study, institutionally sponsored loans, scholarships/grants, and tuition waivers (full and partial) also available. Support available to part-time students. In 2019, 491 master's, 38 doctorates awarded. *Program availability:* Part-time, evening/weekend. *Application deadline:* Applications are processed on a rolling basis. *Application fee:* $75. Electronic applications accepted. *Application Contact:* Jerry Czub, Director of Graduate Admission, 508-793-7373, E-mail: gradadmissions@clarku.edu. *Associate Provost and Dean of Graduate Studies,* Dr. Yuko Aoyama, 508-793-7403.

***Adam Institute for Urban Teaching and School Practice*** Electronic applications accepted.

***Graduate School of Management*** *Program availability:* Part-time, evening/weekend. Electronic applications accepted.

***Gustav H. Carlson School of Chemistry*** Students: 11 full-time (4 women); includes 1 minority (Hispanic/Latino), 8 international. Average age 27. 75 applicants, 23% accepted, 10 enrolled. *Faculty:* 9 full-time (1 woman). Expenses: Contact institution. *Financial support:* Fellowships, research assistantships, teaching assistantships, and tuition waivers (full) available. *Application deadline:* For fall admission, 1/15 priority date for domestic students. *Application fee:* $75. Electronic applications accepted. *Application Contact:* Rene Baril, Managerial Secretary, 508-793-7130, Fax: 528-793-7117, E-mail: mbaril@clarku.edu. *Chair,* Dr. Shuanghong Huo, 508-793-7533, E-mail: shuo@clarku.edu.

***Hiatt School of Psychology*** Students: 44 full-time (34 women), 2 part-time (both women); includes 12 minority (4 Black or African American, non-Hispanic/Latino; 4 Asian, non-Hispanic/Latino; 4 Hispanic/Latino), 9 international. Average age 28. 272 applicants, 6% accepted, 6 enrolled. *Faculty:* 17 full-time (12 women), 2 part-time/adjunct (both women). Expenses: Contact institution. *Financial support:* Fellowships, research assistantships, teaching assistantships, career-related internships or fieldwork, and tuition waivers (full and partial) available. In 2019, 5 doctorates awarded. *Application deadline:* For fall admission, 12/15 priority date for domestic and international students. *Application fee:* $75. Electronic applications accepted. *Application Contact:* Dr. James Cordova, Chair, 508-793-7268, E-mail: jcordova@clarku.edu. *Chair,* Dr. James Cordova, 508-793-7268, E-mail: jcordova@clarku.edu.

***School of Geography*** Students: 58 full-time (35 women); includes 6 minority (1 Black or African American, non-Hispanic/Latino; 3 Asian, non-Hispanic/Latino; 2 Hispanic/Latino), 26 international. Average age 32. 135 applicants, 13% accepted, 9 enrolled. *Faculty:* 19 full-time (7 women), 3 part-time/adjunct (2 women). Expenses: Contact institution. *Financial support:* Fellowships, research assistantships, teaching assistantships, career-related internships or fieldwork, and tuition waivers (full) available. In 2019, 11 doctorates awarded. *Application deadline:* For fall admission, 12/31 priority date for domestic and international students. *Application fee:* $75. Electronic applications accepted. *Application Contact:* Dr. Deb Martin, Director, 508-793-7104, E-mail: dmartin@clarku.edu. *Director,* Dr. Deb Martin, 508-793-7104, E-mail: dmartin@clarku.edu.

***School of Professional Studies*** *Program availability:* Part-time, evening/weekend. Electronic applications accepted.

## CLAYTON STATE UNIVERSITY, Morrow, GA 30260-0285

**General Information** State-supported, coed, comprehensive institution. *Graduate housing:* On-campus housing not available.

**GRADUATE UNITS**

**School of Graduate Studies** Electronic applications accepted.

***College of Arts and Sciences***

***College of Business***

***College of Health***

***College of Information and Mathematical Sciences***

## CLEARY UNIVERSITY, Howell, MI 48843

**General Information** Independent, coed, comprehensive institution. *Graduate housing:* On-campus housing not available.

**GRADUATE UNITS**

**Online Program in Business Administration** *Program availability:* Part-time, evening/weekend, online learning. Electronic applications accepted.

## CLEMSON UNIVERSITY, Clemson, SC 29634

**General Information** State-supported, coed, university. CGS member. *Enrollment:* 25,822 graduate, professional, and undergraduate students; 3,129 full-time matriculated graduate/professional students (1,323 women), 2,498 part-time matriculated graduate/professional students (1,512 women). *Enrollment by degree level:* 3,603 master's, 1,626 doctoral, 103 other advanced degrees. *Graduate faculty:* 1,562 full-time (610 women), 126 part-time/adjunct (44 women). *International tuition:* $22,050 full-time. *Tuition, area resident:* Full-time $10,600; part-time $8688 per semester. Tuition, state resident: full-time $10,600; part-time $8688 per semester. Tuition, nonresident: full-time $22,050; part-time $17,412 per semester. *Required fees:* $1196; $617 per semester. $617 per semester. Tuition and fees vary according to course load, degree level, campus/location and program. *Graduate housing:* On-campus housing not available. *Student services:* Campus employment opportunities, campus safety program, career counseling, child daycare facilities, exercise/wellness program, free psychological counseling, grant writing training, international student services, low-cost health insurance, multicultural affairs office, services for students with disabilities, teacher training, writing training. *Library facilities:* Robert Muldrow Cooper Library plus 1 other. *Collection:* Study areas open 24 hours, 5–7 days a week; students can reserve study rooms. *Research affiliation:* Greenville Hospital System (biological sciences), South Carolina Universities Research and Education Foundation (energy), Oak Ridge National Laboratory (materials science, physics), BMW (automotive, electrical and mechanical engineering), Savannah National Research Lab (energy), Fluor Corporation (supply chain logistics).

**Computer facilities:** Computer purchase and lease plans are available. 1,250 computers available on campus for general student use. A campuswide network can be accessed. Online class registration is available.
Website: http://www.clemson.edu/

**General Application Contact:** Kathleen Costello, Director of Admissions and Recruitment, 864-656-2561, E-mail: kcostel@clemson.edu.

**GRADUATE UNITS**

**Graduate School** Average age 30. 7,269 applicants, 64% accepted, 2,679 enrolled. Expenses: Contact institution. *Financial support:* In 2019–20, 2,172 students received support, including 223 fellowships with partial tuition reimbursements available (averaging $3,546 per year), 649 research assistantships with partial tuition reimbursements available (averaging $17,404 per year), 809 teaching assistantships with partial tuition reimbursements available (averaging $17,447 per year); career-related internships or fieldwork and unspecified assistantships also available. Support available to part-time students. In 2019, 1,418 master's, 239 doctorates, 153 other advanced degrees awarded. *Program availability:* Part-time, evening/weekend, 100% online, blended/hybrid learning. *Application deadline:* For fall admission, 4/15 for international students; for spring admission, 10/15 for international students. Applications are processed on a rolling basis. *Application fee:* $80 ($90 for international students). Electronic applications accepted. *Application Contact:* Kathleen Costello, Director of Graduate Admissions and Recruitment, 864-656-2561, E-mail: kcostel@clemson.edu. *Interim Dean,* Dr. David Fleming, 864-656-2878, E-mail: dflemin@clemson.edu.

***College of Agriculture, Forestry and Life Sciences*** Average age 29. 315 applicants, 66% accepted, 169 enrolled. Expenses: Contact institution. *Financial support:* In 2019–20, 173 students received support, including 20 fellowships with partial tuition reimbursements available (averaging $4,325 per year), 98 research assistantships with partial tuition reimbursements available (averaging $15,374 per year), 44 teaching assistantships with partial tuition reimbursements available (averaging $12,880 per year); career-related internships or fieldwork and unspecified assistantships also available. In 2019, 66 master's, 20 doctorates awarded. *Program availability:* 100% online, blended/hybrid learning. *Application deadline:* For fall admission, 4/15 for international students; for winter admission, 10/15 for international students. Applications are processed on a rolling basis. *Application fee:* $80 ($90 for international students). Electronic applications accepted. *Application Contact:* Dr. Paula Agudelo, Associate Dean for Research and Graduate Studies, 864-656-2810, E-mail: pagudel@clemson.edu. *Dean,* Dr. Keith Belli, 864-656-3013, E-mail: caflsdean-l@clemson.edu.

***College of Architecture, Arts, and Humanities*** Average age 29. 478 applicants, 78% accepted, 173 enrolled. Expenses: Contact institution. *Financial support:* In 2019–20, 273 students received support, including 64 fellowships with partial tuition reimbursements available (averaging $2,015 per year), 29 research assistantships with partial tuition reimbursements available (averaging $4,415 per year), 77 teaching assistantships with partial tuition reimbursements available (averaging $16,393 per year); career-related internships or fieldwork and unspecified assistantships also available. In 2019, 148 master's, 11 doctorates, 9 other advanced degrees awarded. *Program availability:* Part-time, 100% online. *Application deadline:* For fall admission, 4/15 for international students; for spring admission, 10/15 for international students. Applications are processed on a rolling basis. *Application fee:* $80 ($90 for international students). Electronic applications accepted. *Application Contact:* Dr. James Spencer, Associate Dean for Research and Graduate Studies, 864-656-0377, E-mail: jhspenc@clemson.edu. *Dean,* Dr. Richard Goodstein, 864-656-3084, E-mail: regst@clemson.edu.

***College of Behavioral, Social and Health Sciences*** Students: 234 full-time (176 women), 368 part-time (251 women); includes 94 minority (52 Black or African American, non-Hispanic/Latino; 11 Asian, non-Hispanic/Latino; 20 Hispanic/Latino; 2 Native Hawaiian or other Pacific Islander, non-Hispanic/Latino; 9 Two or more races, non-Hispanic/Latino), 51 international. Average age 32. 646 applicants, 59% accepted, 241 enrolled. *Faculty:* 207 full-time (122 women), 9 part-time/adjunct (3 women). Expenses: Contact institution. *Financial support:* In 2019–20, 218 students received support, including 12 fellowships with full and partial tuition reimbursements available (averaging $9,500 per year), 31 research assistantships with full and partial tuition reimbursements available (averaging $16,340 per year), 156 teaching assistantships with full and partial tuition reimbursements available (averaging $12,571 per year); career-related internships or fieldwork and unspecified assistantships also available. In 2019, 185 master's, 29 doctorates, 46 other advanced degrees awarded. *Application Contact:* Dr. Rachel Mayo, Interim Associate Dean of Research and Graduate Studies, 864-656-7435, E-mail: rmayo@clemson.edu. *Dean,* Dr. Leslie Hossfeld, 864-656-7640, E-mail: lhossfe@clemson.edu.

***College of Business*** Students: 317 full-time (151 women), 442 part-time (152 women); includes 117 minority (49 Black or African American, non-Hispanic/Latino; 6 American Indian or Alaska Native, non-Hispanic/Latino; 19 Asian, non-Hispanic/Latino; 28 Hispanic/Latino; 2 Native Hawaiian or other Pacific Islander, non-Hispanic/Latino; 13 Two or more races, non-Hispanic/Latino), 75 international. Average age 31. 873 applicants, 80% accepted, 440 enrolled. Expenses: Contact institution. *Financial support:* In 2019–20, 128 students received support, including 17 fellowships with partial tuition reimbursements available (averaging $4,118 per year), 8 research assistantships with partial tuition reimbursements available (averaging $20,790 per year), 31 teaching assistantships with partial tuition reimbursements available (averaging $19,975 per year); career-related internships or fieldwork and unspecified assistantships also available. In 2019, 333 master's, 16 doctorates awarded. *Program availability:* Part-time, evening/weekend, 100% online. *Application deadline:* For fall admission, 4/15 for international students; for spring admission, 10/15 for international students. Applications are processed on a rolling basis. *Application fee:* $80 ($90 for international students). Electronic applications accepted. *Application Contact:* Dr. Gregory Pickett, Senior Associate Dean, 864-656-3975, E-mail: pgregor@clemson.edu. *Dean,* Wendy York, 864-656-3178, E-mail: BIZDEAN@clemson.edu.

***College of Education*** *Program availability:* Part-time, evening/weekend, 100% online. Electronic applications accepted.

***College of Engineering, Computing and Applied Sciences*** Students: 1,364 full-time (335 women), 282 part-time (67 women); includes 124 minority (38 Black or African American, non-Hispanic/Latino; 1 American Indian or Alaska Native, non-Hispanic/Latino; 36 Asian, non-Hispanic/Latino; 30 Hispanic/Latino; 1 Native Hawaiian or other Pacific Islander, non-Hispanic/Latino; 18 Two or more races, non-Hispanic/Latino), 969 international. Average age 26. 2,751 applicants, 60% accepted, 679 enrolled. *Faculty:* 292 full-time (61 women), 13 part-time/adjunct (5 women). Expenses: Contact institution. *Financial support:* In 2019–20, 982 students received support, including 116 fellowships with full and partial tuition reimbursements available (averaging $9,990 per year), 402 research assistantships with full and partial tuition reimbursements available (averaging $21,740 per year), 225 teaching assistantships with full and partial tuition reimbursements available (averaging $20,686 per year); career-related internships or fieldwork and unspecified assistantships also available. In 2019, 392 master's, 87 doctorates, 59 other advanced degrees awarded. *Application Contact:* Dr. Douglas Hirt, Associate Dean for Research and Graduate Studies, 864-656-3201, E-mail: hirtd@clemson.edu. *Dean,* Dr. Anand Gramopadhye, 864-656-3200, E-mail: agrampo@clemson.edu.

***College of Science*** Students: 401 full-time (178 women), 229 part-time (151 women); includes 68 minority (12 Black or African American, non-Hispanic/Latino; 2 American Indian or Alaska Native, non-Hispanic/Latino; 10 Asian, non-Hispanic/Latino; 28 Hispanic/Latino; 1 Native Hawaiian or other Pacific Islander, non-Hispanic/Latino; 15 Two or more races, non-Hispanic/Latino), 157 international. Average age 32. 638 applicants, 63% accepted, 204 enrolled. *Faculty:* 223 full-time (74 women), 9 part-time/adjunct (2 women). Expenses: Contact institution. *Financial support:* In 2019–20, 523 students received support, including 37 fellowships with full and partial tuition reimbursements available (averaging $7,233 per year), 136 research assistantships with full and partial tuition reimbursements available (averaging $25,415 per year), 325 teaching assistantships with full and partial tuition reimbursements available (averaging $24,500 per year); career-related internships or fieldwork and unspecified assistantships also available. In 2019, 148 master's, 45 doctorates awarded. *Application Contact:* Dr. Stephen Creager, Interim Associate Dean of Graduate Education, Space Optimization and Faculty Mentoring, 864-656-4995, E-mail: screage@clemson.edu. *Founding Dean,* Dr. Cynthia Young, 864-656-3642, E-mail: sciencedean@clemson.edu.

## CLEVELAND INSTITUTE OF MUSIC, Cleveland, OH 44106-1776

**General Information** Independent, coed, comprehensive institution. *Enrollment:* 141 full-time matriculated graduate/professional students (78 women), 2 part-time matriculated graduate/professional students. *Enrollment by degree level:* 108 master's, 6 doctoral, 29 other advanced degrees. *Graduate faculty:* 29 full-time (12 women), 75 part-time/adjunct (22 women). *Tuition:* Full-time $40,000; part-time $1967 per credit hour. *Required fees:* $4336; $4336 per unit. One-time fee: $250 full-time. *Graduate housing:* Room and/or apartments available on a first-come, first-served basis to single students; on-campus housing not available to married students. Housing application deadline: 6/1. *Student services:* Campus employment opportunities, campus safety program, career counseling, free psychological counseling, international student services, low-cost health insurance, multicultural affairs office, services for students with disabilities, writing training. *Library facilities:* Cleveland Institute of Music Library.

**Computer facilities:** Computer purchase and lease plans are available. A campuswide network can be accessed from student residence rooms and from off campus.
Website: http://www.cim.edu/

**General Application Contact:** Rachel Kunce, Assistant Director of Admissions, 216-795-3107, E-mail: admission@cim.edu.

**GRADUATE UNITS**

**Graduate Programs** Students: 151 full-time (88 women), 7 part-time (4 women); includes 26 minority (4 Black or African American, non-Hispanic/Latino; 14 Asian, non-Hispanic/Latino; 8 Hispanic/Latino), 39 international. Average age 24. 1,041 applicants, 32% accepted, 115 enrolled. *Faculty:* 29 full-time (12 women), 75 part-time/adjunct (22 women). Expenses: Contact institution. *Financial support:* In 2019–20, 142 students received support. Federal Work-Study, scholarships/grants, and unspecified assistantships available. Financial award application deadline: 2/1; financial award applicants required to submit CSS PROFILE or FAFSA. In 2019, 53 master's, 5 doctorates, 14 ADs awarded. *Application deadline:* For fall admission, 12/1 for domestic and international students. *Application fee:* $110. Electronic applications accepted. *Application Contact:* E. William Fay, Director of Admissions, 216-795-3107, E-mail: cimadmission@po.cwru.edu. *President,* David Cerone, 216-791-5000.

## CLEVELAND STATE UNIVERSITY, Cleveland, OH 44115

**General Information** State-supported, coed, university. CGS member. *Enrollment:* 16,943 graduate, professional, and undergraduate students; 1,920 full-time matriculated graduate/professional students (1,179 women), 2,159 part-time matriculated graduate/professional students (1,326 women). *Enrollment by degree level:* 2,607 master's, 823 doctoral, 416 other advanced degrees. *Graduate faculty:* 273 full-time (125 women), 316 part-time/adjunct (162 women). *International tuition:* $19,316 full-time. Tuition, state resident: full-time $10,215; part-time $6810 per credit hour. Tuition, nonresident: full-time $17,496; part-time $11,664 per credit hour. Tuition and fees vary according to degree level and program. *Graduate housing:* Room and/or apartments available on a first-come, first-served basis to single students; on-campus housing not available to married students. Typical cost: $8790 per year ($12,268 including board). Housing application deadline: 7/15. *Student services:* Campus employment opportunities, campus safety program, career counseling, exercise/wellness program, international student services, low-cost health insurance, multicultural affairs office, services for students with disabilities, teacher training, writing training. *Library facilities:* Michael Schwartz Library plus 1 other. *Collection:* Books: 770,460 (physical), 476,174 (digital/electronic); Serial titles: 8,279 (physical), 55,456 (digital/electronic); Databases: 733. Students can reserve study rooms. *Research affiliation:* Cleveland Clinic Foundation, Metro Health System.

**Computer facilities:** Computer purchase and lease plans are available. 736 computers available on campus for general student use. A campuswide network can be accessed. Online class registration, each general purpose computer lab has a scanner and printer, students are allowed free black and white printing up to 2,000 pages per semester are available.
Website: http://www.csuohio.edu/

**General Application Contact:** Tonita May, Coordinator, Graduate Student Services, 216-687-3625, Fax: 216-875-9933, E-mail: t.l.may59@csuohio.edu.

**GRADUATE UNITS**

**Cleveland-Marshall College of Law** Average age 28. 711 applicants, 44% accepted, 118 enrolled. Expenses: Contact institution. *Financial support:* In 2019–20, 198 students received support, including 17 fellowships (averaging $2,500 per year), 34 research assistantships, 7 teaching assistantships with partial tuition reimbursements available (averaging $6,700 per year); career-related internships or fieldwork, Federal Work-Study, scholarships/grants, and unspecified assistantships also available. Support available to part-time students. Financial award application deadline: 5/1; financial award applicants required to submit FAFSA. In 2019, 11 master's, 88 doctorates, 2 Certificates awarded. *Program availability:* Part-time, evening/weekend. *Application deadline:* For fall admission, 5/1 for domestic and international students. Applications are processed on a rolling basis. Electronic applications accepted. *Application Contact:* Christopher Lucak, Assistant Dean for Admission and Financial Aid, 216-687-4692, Fax: 216-687-6881, E-mail: law.admissions@csuohio.edu. *Dean,* Lee Fisher, 216-687-2300, Fax: 216-687-6881, E-mail: lee.fisher@csuohio.edu.

**College of Graduate Studies** Students: 1,532 full-time (983 women), 1,904 part-time (1,172 women); includes 831 minority (519 Black or African American, non-Hispanic/Latino; 6 American Indian or Alaska Native, non-Hispanic/Latino; 98 Asian, non-Hispanic/Latino; 136 Hispanic/Latino; 1 Native Hawaiian or other Pacific Islander, non-Hispanic/Latino; 71 Two or more races, non-Hispanic/Latino), 483 international. Average age 30. 4,931 applicants, 46% accepted, 966 enrolled. *Faculty:* 469 full-time (224 women), 216 part-time/adjunct (102 women). Expenses: Contact institution. *Financial support:* In 2019–20, 306 research assistantships with tuition reimbursements (averaging $3,480 per year), 123 teaching assistantships with tuition reimbursements (averaging $3,480 per year) were awarded; career-related internships or fieldwork, scholarships/grants, tuition waivers (full and partial), and unspecified assistantships also available. Financial award applicants required to submit FAFSA. In 2019, 1,235 master's, 47 doctorates, 38 other advanced degrees awarded. *Program availability:* Part-time, evening/weekend, 100% online, blended/hybrid learning. *Application deadline:* For fall admission, 7/1 priority date for domestic students, 5/15 priority date for international students; for spring admission, 11/15 priority date for domestic students, 11/1 priority date for international students; for summer admission, 4/1 for domestic students, 3/15 for international students. Applications are processed on a rolling basis. *Application fee:* $30. Electronic applications accepted. *Application Contact:* Dianne C. Oloff, Graduate Student Services Specialist, 216-523-7572, Fax: 216-875-9933, E-mail: d.oloff@csuohio.edu. *Dean, College of Graduate Studies,* Dr. Jianping Zhu, 216-687-3595, Fax: 216-875-9933, E-mail: j.zhu94@csuohio.edu.

***College of Education and Human Services*** Students: 217 full-time (175 women), 738 part-time (553 women); includes 323 minority (233 Black or African American, non-Hispanic/Latino; 3 American Indian or Alaska Native, non-Hispanic/Latino; 11 Asian, non-Hispanic/Latino; 41 Hispanic/Latino; 1 Native Hawaiian or other Pacific Islander, non-Hispanic/Latino; 34 Two or more races, non-Hispanic/Latino), 33 international. Average age 34. 487 applicants, 58% accepted, 178 enrolled. *Faculty:* 86 full-time (60 women), 106 part-time/adjunct (81 women). Expenses: Contact institution. *Financial support:* In 2019–20, 64 students received support, including 38 research assistantships with full tuition reimbursements available (averaging $6,960 per year), 2 teaching assistantships with full tuition reimbursements available (averaging $7,800 per year); career-related internships or fieldwork, Federal Work-Study, scholarships/grants, tuition waivers (partial), and unspecified assistantships also available. Support available to part-time students. Financial award application deadline: 8/1; financial award applicants required to submit FAFSA. In 2019, 288 master's, 8 doctorates, 1 other advanced degree awarded. *Program availability:* Part-time, evening/weekend, 100% online, blended/hybrid learning. *Application deadline:* For fall admission, 7/1 priority date for domestic students, 5/15 for international students; for spring admission, 11/15 priority date for domestic students, 11/1 for international students; for summer admission, 4/1 for domestic students, 3/15 for international students. Applications are processed on a rolling basis. *Application fee:* $30. Electronic applications accepted. *Application Contact:* Patricia Sokolowski,

Office Coordinator/Assistant to the Dean, 216-523-7143, Fax: 216-687-5415, E-mail: p.sokolowski@csuohio.edu. *Dean*, Dr. Sajit Zachariah, 216-523-7143, Fax: 216-687-5415, E-mail: sajit.zachariah@csuohio.edu.

***College of Liberal Arts and Social Sciences*** *Program availability:* Part-time, evening/weekend. Electronic applications accepted.

***College of Sciences and Health Professions*** *Program availability:* Part-time, evening/weekend, online learning. Electronic applications accepted.

***Fenn College of Engineering*** Students: 202 full-time (60 women), 153 part-time (41 women); includes 34 minority (7 Black or African American, non-Hispanic/Latino; 17 Asian, non-Hispanic/Latino; 6 Hispanic/Latino; 4 Two or more races, non-Hispanic/Latino), 169 international. Average age 26. 1,037 applicants, 48% accepted, 143 enrolled. *Faculty:* 54 full-time (5 women), 12 part-time/adjunct (0 women). Expenses: Contact institution. *Financial support:* Fellowships, research assistantships, teaching assistantships, career-related internships or fieldwork, institutionally sponsored loans, scholarships/grants, tuition waivers (full and partial), and unspecified assistantships available. Support available to part-time students. Financial award application deadline: 3/30; financial award applicants required to submit FAFSA. In 2019, 157 master's, 8 doctorates awarded. *Program availability:* Part-time, evening/weekend. *Application deadline:* Applications are processed on a rolling basis. *Application fee:* $30. Electronic applications accepted. *Application Contact:* Deborah L. Brown, Interim Assistant Director, Graduate Admissions, 216-523-7572, Fax: 216-687-9214, E-mail: d.l.brown@csuohio.edu. *Associate Dean*, Dr. Paul P. Lin, 216-687-2556, Fax: 216-687-9280, E-mail: p.lin@csuohio.edu.

***Maxine Goodman Levin College of Urban Affairs*** *Program availability:* Part-time, evening/weekend. Electronic applications accepted.

***Monte Ahuja College of Business*** Students: 282 full-time (124 women), 536 part-time (264 women); includes 168 minority (86 Black or African American, non-Hispanic/Latino; 37 Asian, non-Hispanic/Latino; 27 Hispanic/Latino; 18 Two or more races, non-Hispanic/Latino), 109 international. Average age 29. 1,052 applicants, 46% accepted, 258 enrolled. *Faculty:* 48 full-time (16 women), 33 part-time/adjunct (12 women). Expenses: Contact institution. *Financial support:* In 2019–20, 110 students received support, including 26 research assistantships with full tuition reimbursements available (averaging $6,960 per year), 1 teaching assistantship with full tuition reimbursement available (averaging $7,800 per year); career-related internships or fieldwork, scholarships/grants, tuition waivers (full), and unspecified assistantships also available. Financial award application deadline: 5/15; financial award applicants required to submit FAFSA. In 2019, 337 master's, 5 doctorates awarded. *Program availability:* Part-time, evening/weekend, 100% online, blended/hybrid learning. *Application deadline:* For fall admission, 7/1 priority date for domestic students, 5/15 for international students; for spring admission, 11/15 priority date for domestic students, 11/1 for international students; for summer admission, 4/1 for domestic students, 3/15 for international students. Applications are processed on a rolling basis. *Application fee:* $30. Electronic applications accepted. *Application Contact:* Kenneth Dippong, Director, Student Services, 216-523-7545, Fax: 216-687-9354, E-mail: k.dippong@csuohio.edu. *Dean*, Dr. Sanjay Putrevu, 216-687-3786, Fax: 216-687-9354, E-mail: s.putrevu@csuohio.edu.

***School of Nursing*** *Program availability:* Part-time, 100% online. Electronic applications accepted.

## CLEVELAND UNIVERSITY–KANSAS CITY, Overland Park, KS 66210

**General Information** Independent, coed, comprehensive institution. *Graduate housing:* On-campus housing not available.

**GRADUATE UNITS**

**Doctor of Chiropractic Program** *Program availability:* Part-time. Electronic applications accepted.

**Program in Health Education and Promotion** *Program availability:* Part-time. Electronic applications accepted.

## COASTAL CAROLINA UNIVERSITY, Conway, SC 29528-6054

**General Information** State-supported, coed, comprehensive institution. *Enrollment:* 10,484 graduate, professional, and undergraduate students; 202 full-time matriculated graduate/professional students (102 women), 378 part-time matriculated graduate/professional students (271 women). *Enrollment by degree level:* 509 master's, 46 doctoral, 25 other advanced degrees. *Graduate faculty:* 88 full-time (41 women), 26 part-time/adjunct (18 women). *International tuition:* $19,836 full-time. *Tuition, area resident:* Full-time $10,764; part-time $598 per credit hour. Tuition, state resident: full-time $10,764; part-time $598 per credit hour. Tuition, nonresident: full-time $19,836; part-time $1102 per credit hour. *Required fees:* $90; $5 per credit hour. *Graduate housing:* Room and/or apartments available on a first-come, first-served basis to single students; on-campus housing not available to married students. Typical cost: $5440 per year ($9290 including board). Room and board charges vary according to board plan and housing facility selected. Housing application deadline: 5/1. *Student services:* Campus employment opportunities, campus safety program, career counseling, child daycare facilities, exercise/wellness program, free psychological counseling, grant writing training, international student services, multicultural affairs office, services for students with disabilities, teacher training, writing training. *Library facilities:* Kimbel Library. *Collection:* Books: 129,696 (physical), 433,254 (digital/electronic); Serial titles: 622 (physical), 79,146 (digital/electronic); Databases: 213. Weekly public service hours: 168; study areas open 24 hours, 5–7 days a week; students can reserve study rooms.

**Computer facilities:** Computer purchase and lease plans are available. 1,577 computers available on campus for general student use. A campuswide network can be accessed. Online class registration is available.
Website: http://www.coastal.edu/

**General Application Contact:** Dr. Robert Young, Interim Dean, College of Graduate Studies and Research, 843-349-2277, Fax: 843-349-6444, E-mail: ryoung@coastal.edu.

**GRADUATE UNITS**

**E. Craig Wall, Sr. College of Business Administration** Students: 53 full-time (23 women), 60 part-time (38 women); includes 24 minority (18 Black or African American, non-Hispanic/Latino; 3 Hispanic/Latino; 3 Two or more races, non-Hispanic/Latino), 5 international. Average age 29. 109 applicants, 74% accepted, 60 enrolled. *Faculty:* 14 full-time (6 women), 1 part-time/adjunct (0 women). Expenses: Contact institution. *Financial support:* Fellowships, research assistantships, teaching assistantships, and tuition waivers available. Financial award application deadline: 3/1; financial award applicants required to submit FAFSA. In 2019, 61 master's awarded. *Program availability:* Part-time, evening/weekend, 100% online, blended/hybrid learning. *Application deadline:* For fall admission, 6/15 priority date for domestic and international students; for spring admission, 11/15 priority date for domestic and international students; for summer admission, 4/15 priority date for domestic and international students. Applications are processed on a rolling basis. *Application fee:* $45. Electronic applications accepted. *Application Contact:* Dr. James O. Luken, Interim Dean, College of Graduate Studies and Research, 843-349-2277, Fax: 843-349-6444, E-mail: ryoung@coastal.edu. *Associate Dean/Professor/Director of Graduate Programs and Executive Education*, Dr. Mark Mitchell, 843-349-2392, Fax: 843-349-2455, E-mail: mmitchel@coastal.edu.

**Gupta College of Science** Students: 55 full-time (30 women), 35 part-time (13 women); includes 15 minority (10 Black or African American, non-Hispanic/Latino; 4 Hispanic/Latino; 1 Two or more races, non-Hispanic/Latino), 13 international. Average age 27. 88 applicants, 68% accepted, 35 enrolled. *Faculty:* 29 full-time (10 women), 3 part-time/adjunct (1 woman). Expenses: Contact institution. *Financial support:* Fellowships, research assistantships, teaching assistantships, and tuition waivers available. Financial award application deadline: 3/1; financial award applicants required to submit FAFSA. In 2019, 45 master's awarded. *Program availability:* Part-time, evening/weekend, 100% online. *Application deadline:* For fall admission, 1/15 priority date for domestic and international students; for spring admission, 11/1 priority date for domestic and international students. Applications are processed on a rolling basis. *Application fee:* $45. Electronic applications accepted. *Application Contact:* Dr. Robert Young, Interim Dean, College of Graduate Studies and Research, 843-349-2277, Fax: 843-349-6444, E-mail: ryoung@coastal.edu. *Dean/Vice President for Emerging Initiatives*, Dr. Michael H. Roberts, 843-349-2282, Fax: 843-349-2545, E-mail: mroberts@coastal.edu.

**Spadoni College of Education** Students: 52 full-time (27 women), 262 part-time (207 women); includes 56 minority (41 Black or African American, non-Hispanic/Latino; 2 American Indian or Alaska Native, non-Hispanic/Latino; 2 Asian, non-Hispanic/Latino; 6 Hispanic/Latino; 5 Two or more races, non-Hispanic/Latino). Average age 33. 280 applicants, 77% accepted, 135 enrolled. *Faculty:* 16 full-time (11 women), 20 part-time/adjunct (15 women). Expenses: Contact institution. *Financial support:* Fellowships, research assistantships, teaching assistantships, and tuition waivers available. Financial award application deadline: 3/1; financial award applicants required to submit FAFSA. In 2019, 176 master's, 19 other advanced degrees awarded. *Program availability:* Part-time, evening/weekend, 100% online, blended/hybrid learning. *Application deadline:* For fall admission, 6/1 priority date for domestic and international students; for spring admission, 11/1 priority date for domestic and international students; for summer admission, 5/1 priority date for domestic and international students. Applications are processed on a rolling basis. *Application fee:* $45. Electronic applications accepted. *Application Contact:* Dr. Robert Young, Interim Dean, College of Graduate Studies and Research, 843-349-2277, Fax: 843-349-6444, E-mail: ryoung@coastal.edu. *Dean/Vice President for Online Education and Teaching Excellence*, Dr. Edward Jadallah, 843-349-2773, Fax: 843-349-2106, E-mail: ejadalla@coastal.edu.

**Thomas W. and Robin W. Edwards College of Humanities and Fine Arts** Students: 42 full-time (22 women), 21 part-time (13 women); includes 16 minority (9 Black or African American, non-Hispanic/Latino; 2 Asian, non-Hispanic/Latino; 2 Hispanic/Latino; 3 Two or more races, non-Hispanic/Latino), 1 international. Average age 31. 55 applicants, 85% accepted, 30 enrolled. *Faculty:* 28 full-time (14 women), 2 part-time/adjunct (both women). Expenses: Contact institution. *Financial support:* Fellowships, research assistantships, teaching assistantships, and tuition waivers available. Financial award application deadline: 3/1; financial award applicants required to submit FAFSA. In 2019, 18 master's awarded. *Program availability:* Part-time, evening/weekend. *Application deadline:* For fall admission, 5/1 priority date for domestic and international students; for spring admission, 11/15 priority date for domestic and international students. Applications are processed on a rolling basis. *Application fee:* $45. Electronic applications accepted. *Application Contact:* Dr. James O. Luken, Interim Dean, College of Graduate Studies and Research, 843-349-2277, Fax: 843-349-6444, E-mail: ryoung@coastal.edu. *Dean*, Dr. Daniel J. Ennis, 843-349-2691, E-mail: bornholdt@coastal.edu.

## COGSWELL POLYTECHNICAL COLLEGE, San Jose, CA 95134

**General Information** Proprietary, coed, comprehensive institution.

**GRADUATE UNITS**

**Program in Entrepreneurship and Innovation**

## COKER COLLEGE, Hartsville, SC 29550

**General Information** Independent, coed, comprehensive institution. *Graduate housing:* On-campus housing not available.

**GRADUATE UNITS**

**Graduate Programs** *Program availability:* Part-time, 100% online. Electronic applications accepted.

## THE COLBURN SCHOOL CONSERVATORY OF MUSIC, Los Angeles, CA 90012

**General Information** Independent, coed, comprehensive institution. *Enrollment:* 66 full-time matriculated graduate/professional students (26 women). *Enrollment by degree level:* 24 master's, 42 other advanced degrees. *Required fees:* $5905. *Student services:* Campus employment opportunities, low-cost health insurance. *Library facilities:* Colburn School Library.

**Computer facilities:** 12 computers available on campus for general student use. A campuswide network can be accessed from student residence rooms.
Website: http://www.colburnschool.edu/

**GRADUATE UNITS**

**Graduate Programs**

## COLD SPRING HARBOR LABORATORY, Cold Spring Harbor, NY 11724

**General Information** Independent, coed, graduate-only institution. *Enrollment by degree level:* 44 doctoral. *Graduate housing:* Rooms and/or apartments guaranteed to single students and available on a first-come, first-served basis to married students. Housing application deadline: 8/1. *Student services:* Campus safety program, career counseling, child daycare facilities, exercise/wellness program, free psychological counseling, grant writing training, international student services, low-cost health insurance, multicultural affairs office, services for students with disabilities, teacher training, writing training. *Library facilities:* Cold Spring Harbor Laboratory Library. *Collection:* Study areas open 24 hours, 5–7 days a week; students can reserve study rooms.

**Computer facilities:** A campuswide network can be accessed from student residence rooms and from off campus.
Website: http://www.cshl.edu/gradschool/

**General Application Contact:** Kimberly Creteur, Admissions and Recruitment Manager, 516-367-6890, Fax: 516-367-6919, E-mail: gradschool@cshl.edu.

**GRADUATE UNITS**

**School of Biological Sciences** Students: 44 full-time (22 women); includes 7 minority (1 Black or African American, non-Hispanic/Latino; 2 Asian, non-Hispanic/Latino; 3 Hispanic/Latino; 1 Two or more races, non-Hispanic/Latino), 22 international. Average age 27. 202 applicants, 13% accepted, 8 enrolled. *Faculty:* 55 full-time (11 women). Expenses: Contact institution. *Financial support:* In 2019–20, 44 students received support, including 44 fellowships with full tuition reimbursements available (averaging $34,000 per year); scholarships/grants, traineeships, health care benefits, and tuition waivers (full) also available. Financial award application deadline: 12/1. In 2019, 9 doctorates awarded. *Application deadline:* For fall admission, 12/1 for domestic and international students. *Application fee:* $60. Electronic applications accepted. *Application Contact:* Dr. Alexander Gann, Dean, 516-367-6890. *Dean,* Dr. Alexander Gann, 516-367-6890.

## COLGATE ROCHESTER CROZER DIVINITY SCHOOL, Rochester, NY 14620-2530

**General Information** Independent-religious, coed, graduate-only institution. *Graduate housing:* On-campus housing not available.

**GRADUATE UNITS**

**Graduate and Professional Programs** *Program availability:* Part-time, evening/weekend. Electronic applications accepted.

## COLGATE UNIVERSITY, Hamilton, NY 13346-1386

**General Information** Independent, coed, comprehensive institution. *Graduate housing:* On-campus housing not available.

**GRADUATE UNITS**

**Master of Arts in Teaching Program**

## COLLÊGE DOMINICAIN DE PHILOSOPHIE ET DE THÊOLOGIE, Ottawa, ON K1R 7G3, Canada

**General Information** Independent-religious, coed, university. *Enrollment:* 37 full-time matriculated graduate/professional students (3 women). *Enrollment by degree level:* 16 master's, 21 doctoral. *Graduate faculty:* 11 full-time (1 woman), 4 part-time/adjunct. *International tuition:* $19,680 Canadian dollars full-time. *Tuition, area resident:* Full-time $7032 Canadian dollars; part-time $147 Canadian dollars per credit hour. Tuition, Canadian resident: part-time $375 Canadian dollars per credit hour. One-time fee: $165 Canadian dollars full-time. Full-time tuition and fees vary according to class time, course level, course load, degree level, campus/location, program and student level. *Graduate housing:* Room and/or apartments available on a first-come, first-served basis to single students; on-campus housing not available to married students. Typical cost: $1100 Canadian dollars (including board). Room and board charges vary according to campus/location. Housing application deadline: 9/30. *Student services:* Campus safety program. *Library facilities:* Bibliothéque du College Dominicain.

**Computer facilities:** 4 computers available on campus for general student use. Website: http://www.collegedominicain.ca/

**General Application Contact:** Caroline Vandergoten, Registrar, 613-233-3696 Ext. 310, Fax: 613-233-6064, E-mail: registrar@dominicanu.ca.

**GRADUATE UNITS**

**Graduate Programs** *Program availability:* Part-time, evening/weekend.

***Faculty of Philosophy***

***Faculty of Theology*** *Program availability:* Part-time, evening/weekend.

## COLLEGE FOR CREATIVE STUDIES, Detroit, MI 48202-4034

**General Information** Independent, coed, comprehensive institution.

**GRADUATE UNITS**

**Graduate Programs**

## COLLEGE FOR FINANCIAL PLANNING, Centennial, CO 80112

**General Information** Proprietary, coed, primarily men, graduate-only institution. *Enrollment by degree level:* 176 master's, 6,011 other advanced degrees. *Graduate faculty:* 14 full-time (4 women), 17 part-time/adjunct (3 women). *Tuition:* Full-time $7000; part-time $467 per credit hour. *Graduate housing:* On-campus housing not available. *Student services:* Services for students with disabilities. *Library facilities:* College Library. *Collection:* Books: 190,000 (digital/electronic); Databases: 12. Study areas open 24 hours, 5–7 days a week.

**Computer facilities:** A campuswide network can be accessed. Online class registration is available.
Website: http://www.cffp.edu/

**General Application Contact:** Alicia Christensen, Director of Enrollment, 303-220-4835, Fax: 303-220-1810, E-mail: alicia.christensen@cffp.edu.

**GRADUATE UNITS**

**Graduate Programs** Students: 6,187 full-time, 3,035 part-time. *Faculty:* 14 full-time (4 women), 17 part-time/adjunct (3 women). Expenses: Contact institution. *Program availability:* Part-time, evening/weekend, online only, 100% online. *Application deadline:* Applications are processed on a rolling basis. Electronic applications accepted. *Application Contact:* Alicia Christensen, Director of Enrollment, 303-220-4835, Fax: 303-220-1810, E-mail: alicia.christensen@cffp.edu. *President,* Dirk Pantone, 303-220-4970, E-mail: dirk.pantone@cffp.edu.

## COLLEGE OF CHARLESTON, Charleston, SC 29424-0001

**General Information** State-supported, coed, comprehensive institution. CGS member. *Graduate housing:* On-campus housing not available. *Research affiliation:* Oak Ridge Associated Universities (science), South Carolina Department of Natural Resources, Marine Resources Division (marine biology, environmental studies), National Institute of Standards and Technology (NIST) (marine biology, environmental studies), National Oceanic and Atmospheric Administration (NOAA) (marine biology, environmental studies), U.S. Department of Agriculture (USDA) (environmental studies), South Carolina Aquarium (marine biology, environmental studies).

**GRADUATE UNITS**

**Graduate School** *Program availability:* Part-time, evening/weekend. Electronic applications accepted.

***School of Business*** Electronic applications accepted.

***School of Education, Health, and Human Performance*** *Program availability:* Part-time, evening/weekend. Electronic applications accepted.

***School of Humanities and Social Sciences*** *Program availability:* Part-time, evening/weekend. Electronic applications accepted.

***School of Sciences and Mathematics*** *Program availability:* Part-time, evening/weekend. Electronic applications accepted.

***School of the Arts***

## COLLEGE OF EMMANUEL AND ST. CHAD, Saskatoon, SK S7N 0W6, Canada

**General Information** Independent-religious, coed, graduate-only institution. *Graduate housing:* Room and/or apartments available to single students; on-campus housing not available to married students. Housing application deadline: 6/15.

**GRADUATE UNITS**

**Bachelor of Theology Program** *Program availability:* Part-time, online learning.

**Graduate Programs** *Program availability:* Part-time.

## THE COLLEGE OF IDAHO, Caldwell, ID 83605

**General Information** Independent, coed, comprehensive institution. *Graduate housing:* Room and/or apartments available on a first-come, first-served basis to single students; on-campus housing not available to married students. Housing application deadline: 5/1.

**GRADUATE UNITS**

**Department of Education**

## COLLEGE OF MOUNT SAINT VINCENT, Riverdale, NY 10471-1093

**General Information** Independent, coed, comprehensive institution. *Graduate housing:* On-campus housing not available.

**GRADUATE UNITS**

**School of Professional and Graduate Studies**

## THE COLLEGE OF NEW JERSEY, Ewing, NJ 08628

**General Information** State-supported, coed, comprehensive institution. CGS member.

**GRADUATE UNITS**

**Office of Graduate and Advancing Education** *Program availability:* Part-time, evening/weekend. Electronic applications accepted.

***School of Education*** *Program availability:* Part-time, evening/weekend. Electronic applications accepted.

***School of Humanities and Social Sciences*** *Program availability:* Part-time. Electronic applications accepted.

***School of Nursing, Health, and Exercise Science*** *Program availability:* Part-time. Electronic applications accepted.

**School of Engineering**

## THE COLLEGE OF NEW ROCHELLE, New Rochelle, NY 10805-2308

**General Information** Independent, coed, comprehensive institution. *Graduate housing:* On-campus housing not available.

**GRADUATE UNITS**

**Graduate School** *Program availability:* Part-time, evening/weekend. Electronic applications accepted.

***Division of Art and Communication Studies*** *Program availability:* Part-time, evening/weekend.

***Division of Education*** *Program availability:* Part-time, evening/weekend. Electronic applications accepted.

***Division of Human Services*** *Program availability:* Part-time, evening/weekend. Electronic applications accepted.

## COLLEGE OF SAINT ELIZABETH, Morristown, NJ 07960-6989

**General Information** Independent-religious, coed, comprehensive institution. *Graduate housing:* Room and/or apartments available on a first-come, first-served basis to single students; on-campus housing not available to married students. Housing application deadline: 7/1. *Research affiliation:* National Figure Skating Association (sports nutrition), National Institute of Mental Health (NIMH) (mental health service), Cornell University/The University of Texas at Houston (food biotechnology (attitude research)).

**GRADUATE UNITS**

**Department of Business Administration and Management** *Program availability:* Part-time. Electronic applications accepted.

**Department of Educational Leadership** *Program availability:* Part-time. Electronic applications accepted.

**Department of Foods and Nutrition** *Program availability:* Part-time, blended/hybrid learning. Electronic applications accepted.

**Department of Nursing** *Program availability:* Part-time. Electronic applications accepted.

**Department of Psychology** *Program availability:* Part-time. Electronic applications accepted.

**Department of Theology and Philosophy** *Program availability:* Part-time. Electronic applications accepted.

**Health Administration Program** *Program availability:* Part-time. Electronic applications accepted.

**Program in Applied Behavior Analysis** *Program availability:* Part-time. Electronic applications accepted.

**Program in Data Analytics** *Program availability:* Part-time. Electronic applications accepted.

**Program in Education** *Program availability:* Part-time. Electronic applications accepted.

**Program in Justice Administration and Public Service** *Program availability:* Part-time, 100% online, blended/hybrid learning. Electronic applications accepted.

**Program in Public Health** *Program availability:* Part-time. Electronic applications accepted.

**Program in Social Media Design and Management** *Program availability:* Part-time. Electronic applications accepted.

## COLLEGE OF SAINT MARY, Omaha, NE 68106

**General Information** Independent-religious, women only, comprehensive institution.

**GRADUATE UNITS**

**Program in Education** *Program availability:* Part-time.

**Program in Health Professions Education** *Program availability:* Part-time.

**Program in Nursing** *Program availability:* Part-time.

**Program in Occupational Therapy**

**Program in Organizational Leadership** *Program availability:* Part-time, evening/weekend. Electronic applications accepted.

**Program in Teaching** *Program availability:* Evening/weekend.

## THE COLLEGE OF SAINT ROSE, Albany, NY 12203-1419

**General Information** Independent, coed, comprehensive institution. CGS member. *Enrollment:* 4,004 graduate, professional, and undergraduate students; 430 full-time matriculated graduate/professional students (342 women), 1,135 part-time matriculated graduate/professional students (866 women). *Enrollment by degree level:* 642 master's, 923 other advanced degrees. *Graduate faculty:* 59 full-time (35 women), 90 part-time/adjunct (50 women). *Tuition:* Full-time $14,382; part-time $799 per credit hour. *Required fees:* $954; $698. Tuition and fees vary according to course load. *Graduate housing:* On-campus housing not available. *Student services:* Campus employment opportunities, campus safety program, career counseling, child daycare facilities, exercise/wellness program, free psychological counseling, international student services, multicultural affairs office, services for students with disabilities, teacher training, writing training. *Library facilities:* Neil Hellman Library plus 2 others. *Collection:* Books: 241,000 (physical), 225,846 (digital/electronic); Serial titles: 1,201 (physical), 10 (digital/electronic); Databases: 104. Weekly public service hours: 73; students can reserve study rooms.

**Computer facilities:** 822 computers available on campus for general student use. A campuswide network can be accessed. Online class registration is available. Website: http://www.strose.edu/

**General Application Contact:** Daniel Gallagher, Assistant Vice President for Graduate Recruitment and Enrollment, 518-454-5143, Fax: 518-458-5479, E-mail: grad@strose.edu.

**GRADUATE UNITS**

**Graduate Studies** Students: 430 full-time (342 women), 1,135 part-time (866 women); includes 512 minority (220 Black or African American, non-Hispanic/Latino; 2 American Indian or Alaska Native, non-Hispanic/Latino; 49 Asian, non-Hispanic/Latino; 105 Hispanic/Latino; 136 Two or more races, non-Hispanic/Latino), 56 international. Average age 33. 1,097 applicants, 70% accepted, 481 enrolled. *Faculty:* 59 full-time (35 women), 90 part-time/adjunct (50 women). Expenses: Contact institution. *Financial support:* In 2019–20, 333 students received support. Career-related internships or fieldwork, scholarships/grants, tuition waivers (partial), and unspecified assistantships available. Support available to part-time students. Financial award application deadline: 4/15. In 2019, 390 master's, 775 other advanced degrees awarded. *Program availability:* Part-time, evening/weekend, 100% online, blended/hybrid learning. *Application deadline:* For fall admission, 4/1 priority date for domestic and international students; for spring admission, 10/15 priority date for domestic and international students; for summer admission, 3/15 priority date for domestic and international students. Applications are processed on a rolling basis. *Application fee:* $40. Electronic applications accepted. *Application Contact:* Daniel Gallagher, Assistant Vice President for Recruitment and Enrollment, 518-485-3390, Fax: 518-458-5479, E-mail: grad@strose.edu. *Associate Provost for Graduate and Professional Programs*, Margaret McLane, 518-4853334, E-mail: mclanem@strose.edu.

***Huether School of Business*** Students: 59 full-time (27 women), 56 part-time (24 women); includes 26 minority (12 Black or African American, non-Hispanic/Latino; 6 Asian, non-Hispanic/Latino; 4 Hispanic/Latino; 4 Two or more races, non-Hispanic/Latino), 17 international. Average age 29. 68 applicants, 87% accepted, 36 enrolled. *Faculty:* 14 full-time (4 women), 5 part-time/adjunct (1 woman). Expenses: Contact institution. *Financial support:* Career-related internships or fieldwork, scholarships/grants, tuition waivers (partial), and unspecified assistantships available. Support available to part-time students. Financial award application deadline: 4/15. In 2019, 55 master's, 8 other advanced degrees awarded. *Program availability:* Part-time, evening/weekend. *Application deadline:* For fall admission, 4/1 priority date for domestic and international students; for spring admission, 10/15 priority date for domestic and international students; for summer admission, 3/15 priority date for domestic and international students. Applications are processed on a rolling basis. *Application fee:* $40. Electronic applications accepted. *Application Contact:* Daniel Gallagher, Assistant Vice President for Graduate Recruitment and Enrollment, 518-485-3390, Fax: 518-458-5479, E-mail: grad@strose.edu. *Dean*, Rajarshi Aroskar, 518-454-5272, E-mail: aroskarr@strose.edu.

***School of Mathematics and Sciences*** Students: 57 full-time (42 women), 48 part-time (26 women); includes 24 minority (8 Black or African American, non-Hispanic/Latino; 9 Asian, non-Hispanic/Latino; 4 Hispanic/Latino; 3 Two or more races, non-Hispanic/Latino), 34 international. Average age 30. 114 applicants, 84% accepted, 45 enrolled. *Faculty:* 16 full-time (11 women), 3 part-time/adjunct (0 women). Expenses: Contact institution. *Financial support:* Career-related internships or fieldwork, scholarships/grants, tuition waivers (partial), and unspecified assistantships available. Support available to part-time students. Financial award application deadline: 4/15. In 2019, 41 master's, 3 other advanced degrees awarded. *Program availability:* Part-time, evening/weekend, blended/hybrid learning. *Application deadline:* For fall admission, 4/1 priority date for domestic and international students; for spring admission, 10/15 priority date for domestic and international students; for summer admission, 3/15 priority date for domestic and international students. Applications are processed on a rolling basis. *Application fee:* $40. Electronic applications accepted. *Application Contact:* Daniel Gallagher, Assistant Vice President for Graduate Recruitment and Enrollment, 518-485-3390, Fax: 518-458-5479, E-mail: grad@strose.edu. *Dean*, Dr. Ian MacDonald, 518-458-5396, E-mail: macdonai@strose.edu.

***Thelma P. Lally School of Education*** Students: 314 full-time (273 women), 1,031 part-time (816 women); includes 462 minority (200 Black or African American, non-Hispanic/Latino; 2 American Indian or Alaska Native, non-Hispanic/Latino; 34 Asian, non-Hispanic/Latino; 97 Hispanic/Latino; 129 Two or more races, non-Hispanic/Latino), 5 international. Average age 33. 834 applicants, 66% accepted, 400 enrolled. *Faculty:* 31 full-time (21 women), 82 part-time/adjunct (49 women). Expenses: Contact institution. *Financial support:* Career-related internships or fieldwork, scholarships/grants, tuition waivers (partial), and unspecified assistantships available. Support available to part-time students. Financial award application deadline: 4/15. In 2019, 257 master's, 759 other advanced degrees awarded. *Program availability:* Part-time, evening/weekend, 100% online. *Application deadline:* For fall admission, 4/1 priority date for domestic and international students; for spring admission, 10/15 priority date for domestic and international students; for summer admission, 3/15 priority date for domestic and international students. Applications are processed on a rolling basis. *Application fee:* $40. Electronic applications accepted. *Application Contact:* Daniel Gallagher, Assistant Vice President for Graduate Recruitment and Enrollment, 518-454-5136, Fax: 518-458-5479, E-mail: grad@strose.edu. *Interim Dean*, Dr. Theresa Ward, 518-454-5125.

## THE COLLEGE OF ST. SCHOLASTICA, Duluth, MN 55811-4199

**General Information** Independent-religious, coed, comprehensive institution. *Graduate housing:* On-campus housing not available.

**GRADUATE UNITS**

**Graduate Studies** *Program availability:* Part-time, evening/weekend, online learning. Electronic applications accepted.

## COLLEGE OF STATEN ISLAND OF THE CITY UNIVERSITY OF NEW YORK, Staten Island, NY 10314-6600

**General Information** State and locally supported, coed, comprehensive institution. *Enrollment:* 12,782 graduate, professional, and undergraduate students. *Enrollment by degree level:* 795 master's, 67 doctoral, 59 other advanced degrees. *International tuition:* $20,520 full-time. *Tuition, area resident:* Full-time $11,090; part-time $470 per credit. Tuition, state resident: full-time $11,090; part-time $470 per credit. Tuition, nonresident: full-time $20,520; part-time $855 per credit. *Required fees:* $559; $181 per semester. Tuition and fees vary according to program. *Graduate housing:* Room and/or apartments available on a first-come, first-served basis to single students; on-campus housing not available to married students. *Student services:* Career counseling, child daycare facilities, free psychological counseling, international student services, services for students with disabilities. *Library facilities:* College of Staten Island Library. *Collection:* Books: 203,120 (physical), 569,514 (digital/electronic); Serial titles: 1,771 (physical), 121,194 (digital/electronic); Databases: 161. Weekly public service hours: 84; students can reserve study rooms. *Research affiliation:* Alfred P. Sloan Foundation, Craig H. Neilson Foundation, Northfield Bank Foundation, Simons Foundation, Eurasia Foundation, Richmond Foundation Bank.

**Computer facilities:** 1,875 computers available on campus for general student use. A campuswide network can be accessed from off campus. Online class registration is available.
Website: http://www.csi.cuny.edu/

**General Application Contact:** Sasha Spence, Associate Director for Graduate Recruitment and Admissions, 718-982-2019, Fax: 718-982-2500, E-mail: sasha.spence@csi.cuny.edu.

**GRADUATE UNITS**

**Graduate Programs** 951 applicants, 49% accepted, 324 enrolled. Expenses: Contact institution. *Application Contact:* Sasha Spence, Associate Director for Graduate Admissions, 718-982-2019, Fax: 718-982-2500, E-mail: sasha.spence@csi.cuny.edu. *Provost/Senior Vice President for Academic Affairs*, Dr. J Michael Parrish, 718-982-2440, Fax: 718-982-2442, E-mail: provost@csi.cuny.edu.

***Division of Humanities and Social Sciences*** Expenses: Contact institution. *Application Contact:* Sasha Spence, Associate Director for Graduate Admissions, 718-982-2019, Fax: 718-982-2500, E-mail: sasha.spence@csi.cuny.edu. *Dean of Humanities and Social Sciences*, Dr. Sarolta Takacs, 718-982-2315, Fax: 718-982-2316, E-mail: sarolta.takacs@csi.cuny.edu.

***Division of Science and Technology*** Expenses: Contact institution. *Application Contact:* Sasha Spence, Associate Director for Graduate Admissions, 718-982-2019, Fax: 718-982-2500, E-mail: sasha.spence@csi.cuny.edu. *Dean*, Dr. Michael Cavagnero, 718-982-2430, E-mail: michael.cavagnero@csi.cuny.edu.

***Lucille and Jay Chazanoff School of Business*** Expenses: Contact institution. *Application Contact:* Sasha Spence, Associate Director for Graduate Admissions, 718-982-2019, Fax: 718-982-2500, E-mail: sasha.spence@csi.cuny.edu. *Dean of School of Business*, Dr. Susan L. Holak, 718-982-2920, Fax: 718-982-3183, E-mail: susan.holak@csi.cuny.edu.

***School of Education*** Expenses: Contact institution. *Application Contact:* Sasha Spence, Associate Director for Graduate Admissions, 718-982-2019, Fax: 718-982-2500, E-mail: sasha.spence@csi.cuny.edu. *Dean of School of Education*, Dr. Kenneth Gold, 718-982-3737, Fax: 718-982-3743, E-mail: kenneth.gold@csi.cuny.edu.

***School of Health Sciences*** Expenses: Contact institution. *Application Contact:* Sasha Spence, Associate Director for Graduate Admissions, 718-982-2019, Fax: 718-982-2500, E-mail: sasha.spence@csi.cuny.edu. *Dean of School of Health Sciences*, Dr. Marcus C. Tye, 718-982-3690, E-mail: marcus.tye@csi.cuny.edu.

## COLLEGE OF THE ATLANTIC, Bar Harbor, ME 04609-1198

**General Information** Independent, coed, comprehensive institution. *Graduate housing:* Room and/or apartments available to single students; on-campus housing not available to married students. Housing application deadline: 6/1. *Research affiliation:* Acadia National Park, National Park Service (research management, environmental education), Mount Desert Island Biological Laboratory, Jackson Laboratory (genetics), Society for Human Ecology (ecological decision making in society).

**GRADUATE UNITS**

**Program in Human Ecology**

## COLORADO CHRISTIAN UNIVERSITY, Lakewood, CO 80226

**General Information** Independent-religious, coed, comprehensive institution. *Graduate housing:* On-campus housing not available.

**GRADUATE UNITS**

**Program in Business Administration** *Program availability:* Part-time, evening/weekend, online learning. Electronic applications accepted.

**Program in Counseling** *Program availability:* Part-time, evening/weekend. Electronic applications accepted.

**Program in Curriculum and Instruction** *Program availability:* Part-time, evening/weekend. Electronic applications accepted.

## THE COLORADO COLLEGE, Colorado Springs, CO 80903-3294

**General Information** Independent, coed, comprehensive institution. *Graduate housing:* On-campus housing not available.

**GRADUATE UNITS**

**Education Department** Electronic applications accepted.

## COLORADO MESA UNIVERSITY, Grand Junction, CO 81501-3122

**General Information** State-supported, coed, comprehensive institution. *Graduate housing:* Room and/or apartments available on a first-come, first-served basis to single students; on-campus housing not available to married students. Housing application deadline: 8/1.

**GRADUATE UNITS**

**Center for Teacher Education** *Program availability:* Part-time. Electronic applications accepted.

**Department of Business** *Program availability:* Part-time, evening/weekend. Electronic applications accepted.

**Department of Health Sciences** *Program availability:* Part-time, evening/weekend, 100% online, blended/hybrid learning. Electronic applications accepted.

## COLORADO SCHOOL OF MINES, Golden, CO 80401-1887

**General Information** State-supported, coed, university. CGS member. *Enrollment:* 6,605 graduate, professional, and undergraduate students; 1,200 full-time matriculated graduate/professional students (374 women), 252 part-time matriculated graduate/professional students (194 women). *Enrollment by degree level:* 783 master's, 653 doctoral, 16 other advanced degrees. *Graduate faculty:* 454 full-time (149 women), 250 part-time/adjunct (83 women). *International tuition:* $37,350 full-time. Tuition, state resident: full-time $16,650; part-time $925 per credit hour. Tuition, nonresident: full-time $37,350; part-time $2075 per credit hour. *Required fees:* $2412. *Graduate housing:* Rooms and/or apartments available on a first-come, first-served basis to single and married students. Housing application deadline: 5/1. *Student services:* Campus employment opportunities, campus safety program, career counseling, exercise/wellness program, free psychological counseling, international student services, low-cost health insurance, multicultural affairs office, services for students with disabilities, teacher training, writing training. *Library facilities:* Arthur Lakes Library. *Collection:* Books: 406,665 (physical), 822,340 (digital/electronic); Serial titles: 1,768 (physical), 116,813 (digital/electronic); Databases: 168. Weekly public service hours: 107; students can reserve study rooms.

**Computer facilities:** Computer purchase and lease plans are available. 1,000 computers available on campus for general student use. A campuswide network can be accessed. Online class registration is available.
Website: http://www.mines.edu/

**General Application Contact:** Angel Dotson, Graduate Admissions Coordinator, 303-273-3348, E-mail: grad-app@mines.edu.

**GRADUATE UNITS**

**Office of Graduate Studies** *Program availability:* Part-time. Electronic applications accepted.

## COLORADO SCHOOL OF TRADITIONAL CHINESE MEDICINE, Denver, CO 80206-2127

**General Information** Independent, coed, graduate-only institution. *Enrollment by degree level:* 89 master's. *Graduate faculty:* 52 part-time/adjunct (24 women). *Tuition:* Full-time $20,200. *Required fees:* $540. *Graduate housing:* On-campus housing not available. *Student services:* Campus employment opportunities, campus safety program, exercise/wellness program. *Library facilities:* CSTCM Library. *Collection:* Books: 8,000 (physical), 200 (digital/electronic). Weekly public service hours: 24.

**Computer facilities:** 4 computers available on campus for general student use. Online class registration, X are available.
Website: http://www.cstcm.edu/

**General Application Contact:** Chris Duxbury-Edwards, Recruiting Director, 303-329-6355 Ext. 21, Fax: 303-388-8165, E-mail: recruiting@cstcm.edu.

**GRADUATE UNITS**

**Graduate Programs**

## COLORADO STATE UNIVERSITY, Fort Collins, CO 80523

**General Information** State-supported, coed, university. CGS member. *Enrollment:* 33,996 graduate, professional, and undergraduate students; 2,728 full-time matriculated graduate/professional students (1,691 women), 4,348 part-time matriculated graduate/professional students (2,186 women). *Enrollment by degree level:* 4,493 master's, 2,372 doctoral, 211 other advanced degrees. *Graduate faculty:* 1,119 full-time (464 women), 225 part-time/adjunct (106 women). *International tuition:* $25,791 full-time. Tuition, state resident: full-time $10,520; part-time $5844 per credit hour. Tuition, nonresident: full-time $25,791; part-time $14,328 per credit hour. *Required fees:* $2512.80. Part-time tuition and fees vary according to course level, course load, degree level, program and student level. *Graduate housing:* Rooms and/or apartments available on a first-come, first-served basis to single and married students. Typical cost: $7182 per year ($11,439 including board) for single students. Room and board charges vary according to board plan and housing facility selected. *Student services:* Campus employment opportunities, campus safety program, career counseling, child daycare facilities, exercise/wellness program, free psychological counseling, grant writing training, international student services, low-cost health insurance, multicultural affairs office, services for students with disabilities, teacher training, writing training. *Library facilities:* William E. Morgan Library plus 1 other. *Collection:* Books: 1.2 million (physical), 1.1 million (digital/electronic); Serial titles: 45,581 (physical), 104,097 (digital/electronic); Databases: 345. Weekly public service hours: 108; study areas open 24 hours, 5–7 days a week; students can reserve study rooms. *Research affiliation:* U.S. Department of Commerce/National Oceanic and Atmospheric Administration (NOAA) Joint Institutes (meteorological satellite imagery), Natural Resources Research Center/Agencies of U.S. Departments of Agriculture (USDA) and Interior (infectious disease), National Center for Genetic Resources Preservation (genetic resources of crops), National Wildlife Research Center (interactions of wild animals and society), National Centers for Atmospheric Research (climate, meteorology), Solix (algae-produced biofuels).

**Computer facilities:** Computer purchase and lease plans are available. 2,000 computers available on campus for general student use. A campuswide network can be accessed from student residence rooms and from off campus. Online class registration, personalized portal services including transcripts and financials (billing, financial aid) are available.
Website: http://www.colostate.edu/

**General Application Contact:** Sandra Dailey, Academic Progress and Special Admissions Coordinator, Graduate School, 970-491-6817, Fax: 970-491-2194, E-mail: gradschool@colostate.edu.

**GRADUATE UNITS**

**College of Agricultural Sciences** Students: 102 full-time (59 women), 189 part-time (110 women); includes 27 minority (1 Black or African American, non-Hispanic/Latino; 3 American Indian or Alaska Native, non-Hispanic/Latino; 4 Asian, non-Hispanic/Latino; 8 Hispanic/Latino; 11 Two or more races, non-Hispanic/Latino), 69 international. Average age 31. 247 applicants, 51% accepted, 90 enrolled. *Faculty:* 95 full-time (33 women), 13 part-time/adjunct (8 women). Expenses: Contact institution. *Financial support:* In 2019–20, 112 research assistantships with tuition reimbursements (averaging $22,685 per year), 38 teaching assistantships (averaging $18,136 per year) were awarded; fellowships with full tuition reimbursements, Federal Work-Study, scholarships/grants, tuition waivers (full and partial), and unspecified assistantships also available. Financial award application deadline: 1/15; financial award applicants required to submit FAFSA. In 2019, 72 master's, 19 doctorates awarded. *Program availability:* Part-time, evening/weekend, 100% online, blended/hybrid learning. *Application fee:* $60 ($70 for international students). Electronic applications accepted. *Application Contact:* Administrative Assistant, 970-491-7401, Fax: 970-491-4895. *Dean,* Dr. James Pritchett, 970-491-6274, Fax: 970-491-4895, E-mail: james.pritchett@colostate.edu.

**College of Business** Average age 34. 644 applicants, 73% accepted, 318 enrolled. Expenses: Contact institution. *Financial support:* In 2019–20, 62 fellowships with partial tuition reimbursements (averaging $7,128 per year), 1 research assistantship with partial tuition reimbursement (averaging $7,128 per year) were awarded; career-related internships or fieldwork, scholarships/grants, and unspecified assistantships also available. In 2019, 441 master's awarded. *Program availability:* Part-time, evening/weekend, 100% online, blended/hybrid learning. *Application deadline:* Applications are processed on a rolling basis. *Application fee:* $60 ($70 for international students). Electronic applications accepted. *Application Contact:* Graduate Programs Admissions Contact, 970-491-4622, E-mail: cobgradinfo@colostate.edu. *Dean,* Dr. Beth Walker, 970-491-6471, E-mail: beth.walker@colostate.edu.

**College of Health and Human Sciences** Students: 396 full-time (334 women), 709 part-time (531 women); includes 256 minority (47 Black or African American, non-Hispanic/Latino; 5 American Indian or Alaska Native, non-Hispanic/Latino; 34 Asian, non-Hispanic/Latino; 122 Hispanic/Latino; 1 Native Hawaiian or other Pacific Islander, non-Hispanic/Latino; 47 Two or more races, non-Hispanic/Latino), 33 international. Average age 30. 1,377 applicants, 28% accepted, 215 enrolled. *Faculty:* 109 full-time (80 women), 33 part-time/adjunct (22 women). Expenses: Contact institution. *Financial support:* In 2019–20, 13 fellowships with full tuition reimbursements (averaging $9,215 per year), 61 research assistantships with tuition reimbursements (averaging $14,731 per year), 63 teaching assistantships with tuition reimbursements (averaging $12,985 per year) were awarded; Federal Work-Study, scholarships/grants, and unspecified assistantships also available. In 2019, 339 master's, 30 doctorates awarded. *Program availability:* Part-time, evening/weekend, 100% online, blended/hybrid learning. *Application fee:* $60 ($70 for international students). Electronic applications accepted. *Application Contact:* Patricia Davies, Associate Dean for Research and Graduate Programs, 970-491-7294, Fax: 970-491-7859, E-mail: patricia.davies@colostate.edu. *Dean,* Dr. Lise Youngblade, 970-491-5841, Fax: 970-491-7859, E-mail: lise.youngblade@colostate.edu.

***School of Education*** Students: 76 full-time (58 women), 495 part-time (349 women); includes 175 minority (39 Black or African American, non-Hispanic/Latino; 4 American Indian or Alaska Native, non-Hispanic/Latino; 20 Asian, non-Hispanic/Latino; 81 Hispanic/Latino; 1 Native Hawaiian or other Pacific Islander, non-Hispanic/Latino; 30 Two or more races, non-Hispanic/Latino), 13 international. Average age 37. 405 applicants, 24% accepted, 79 enrolled. *Faculty:* 33 full-time (24 women), 14 part-time/adjunct (8 women). Expenses: Contact institution. *Financial support:* In 2019–20, 4 students received support, including 1 fellowship with full and partial tuition reimbursement available (averaging $2,200 per year), 8 research assistantships with full and partial tuition reimbursements available (averaging $12,376 per year), 3 teaching assistantships with full and partial tuition reimbursements available (averaging $15,210 per year); career-related internships or fieldwork, Federal Work-Study, scholarships/grants, and unspecified assistantships also available. Financial award applicants required to submit FAFSA. In 2019, 173 master's, 22 doctorates awarded. *Program availability:* Part-time, online only, 100% online, blended/hybrid learning, Face-to-face learning offered off-site. *Application deadline:* Applications are processed on a rolling basis. *Application fee:* $60 ($70 for international students). Electronic applications accepted. *Application Contact:* Kelli Clark, Graduate Programs Coordinator, 970-491-2093, Fax: 970-491-1317, E-mail: kelli.clark@colostate.edu. *Professor and Director,* Dr. Susan C. Faircloth, 970-491-6316, Fax: 970-491-1317, E-mail: susan.faircloth@colostate.edu.

***School of Social Work*** Students: 94 full-time (84 women), 146 part-time (127 women); includes 45 minority (7 Black or African American, non-Hispanic/Latino; 1 American Indian or Alaska Native, non-Hispanic/Latino; 6 Asian, non-Hispanic/Latino; 25 Hispanic/Latino; 6 Two or more races, non-Hispanic/Latino), 3 international. Average age 33. 132 applicants, 68% accepted, 41 enrolled. *Faculty:* 10 full-time (9 women), 7 part-time/adjunct (6 women). Expenses: Contact institution. *Financial support:* In 2019–20, 4 fellowships (averaging $9,506 per year), 9 research assistantships (averaging $11,830 per year) were awarded; teaching assistantships and scholarships/grants also available. In 2019, 55 master's, 1 doctorate awarded. *Program availability:* Part-time, blended/hybrid learning. *Application deadline:* For fall admission, 12/31 for domestic and international students; for spring admission, 5/31 for domestic and international students; for summer admission, 12/31 for domestic and international students. *Application fee:* $60 ($70 for international students). Electronic applications accepted. *Application Contact:* Timothy Frank, Graduate Program Coordinator, 970-491-2536, Fax: 970-491-7280, E-mail: timothy.frank@colostate.edu. *Interim Director,* Dr. David MacPhee, 970-491-2378, Fax: 970-491-7280, E-mail: sswinfo@colostate.edu.

**College of Liberal Arts** *Program availability:* Part-time. Electronic applications accepted.

***LEAP Institute for the Arts*** *Program availability:* Part-time, evening/weekend, 100% online. Electronic applications accepted.

***School of Music, Theatre and Dance*** *Program availability:* Part-time. Electronic applications accepted.

**College of Natural Sciences** Students: 346 full-time (159 women), 639 part-time (262 women); includes 133 minority (8 Black or African American, non-Hispanic/Latino; 2 American Indian or Alaska Native, non-Hispanic/Latino; 31 Asian, non-Hispanic/Latino; 67 Hispanic/Latino; 25 Two or more races, non-Hispanic/Latino), 182 international. Average age 28. 2,110 applicants, 19% accepted, 269 enrolled. *Faculty:* 208 full-time (75 women), 30 part-time/adjunct (11 women). Expenses: Contact institution. *Financial support:* In 2019–20, 7 fellowships (averaging $15,366 per year), 196 research assistantships with full and partial tuition reimbursements (averaging $23,206 per year), 399 teaching assistantships with full and partial tuition reimbursements (averaging $20,387 per year) were awarded; scholarships/grants and unspecified assistantships also available. In 2019, 175 master's, 73 doctorates awarded. *Program availability:* Part-time, 100% online, blended/hybrid learning. *Application fee:* $60 ($70 for international students). Electronic applications accepted. *Application Contact:* Dr. Simon Tavener, Associate Dean for Academics, 970-491-1300, Fax: 970-491-6639, E-mail: cns@colostate.edu. *Dean,* Dr. Janice Nerger, 970-491-1300, Fax: 970-491-6639, E-mail: janice.nerger@colostate.edu.

**College of Veterinary Medicine and Biomedical Sciences** Students: 833 full-time (658 women), 161 part-time (104 women); includes 189 minority (7 Black or African American, non-Hispanic/Latino; 3 American Indian or Alaska Native, non-Hispanic/Latino; 41 Asian, non-Hispanic/Latino; 100 Hispanic/Latino; 38 Two or more races, non-Hispanic/Latino), 47 international. Average age 28. 2,777 applicants, 15%

accepted, 343 enrolled. *Faculty:* 235 full-time (116 women), 31 part-time/adjunct (19 women). Expenses: Contact institution. *Financial support:* In 2019–20, 80 research assistantships with tuition reimbursements (averaging $25,038 per year), 21 teaching assistantships with tuition reimbursements (averaging $20,805 per year) were awarded; fellowships with full tuition reimbursements, career-related internships or fieldwork, scholarships/grants, traineeships, health care benefits, and unspecified assistantships also available. In 2019, 174 master's, 27 doctorates awarded. *Application fee:* $60 ($70 for international students). Electronic applications accepted. *Application Contact:* Graduate Program Coordinator. *Dean*, Dr. Mark Stetter, 970-491-7051, E-mail: mark.stetter@colostate.edu.

**Interdisciplinary College** Electronic applications accepted.

***School of Global Environmental Sustainability*** *Program availability:* Part-time-only, online only, 100% online. Electronic applications accepted.

**Walter Scott, Jr. College of Engineering** Students: 317 full-time (85 women), 669 part-time (149 women); includes 133 minority (32 Black or African American, non-Hispanic/Latino; 1 American Indian or Alaska Native, non-Hispanic/Latino; 33 Asian, non-Hispanic/Latino; 54 Hispanic/Latino; 13 Two or more races, non-Hispanic/Latino), 311 international. Average age 30. 1,206 applicants, 38% accepted, 234 enrolled. *Faculty:* 188 full-time (49 women), 40 part-time/adjunct (9 women). Expenses: Contact institution. *Financial support:* In 2019–20, 294 research assistantships (averaging $24,920 per year), 69 teaching assistantships (averaging $17,643 per year) were awarded; scholarships/grants, traineeships, health care benefits, and unspecified assistantships also available. In 2019, 206 master's, 60 doctorates awarded. *Program availability:* Part-time, evening/weekend, 100% online, blended/hybrid learning. *Application fee:* $60 ($70 for international students). Electronic applications accepted. *Application Contact:* Dr. Anthony Marchese, Associate Dean of Academic and Student Affairs, 970-491-6220, Fax: 970-491-3429, E-mail: anthony.marchese@colostate.edu. *Dean*, Dr. David McLean, 970-491-3366, E-mail: david.mclean@colostate.edu.

***School of Biomedical Engineering*** *Program availability:* Part-time, online learning. Electronic applications accepted.

**Warner College of Natural Resources** Students: 96 full-time (53 women), 412 part-time (243 women); includes 69 minority (5 Black or African American, non-Hispanic/Latino; 5 American Indian or Alaska Native, non-Hispanic/Latino; 8 Asian, non-Hispanic/Latino; 35 Hispanic/Latino; 16 Two or more races, non-Hispanic/Latino), 29 international. Average age 31. 472 applicants, 45% accepted, 148 enrolled. *Faculty:* 89 full-time (33 women), 33 part-time/adjunct (9 women). Expenses: Contact institution. *Financial support:* In 2019–20, 2 fellowships (averaging $26,250 per year), 74 research assistantships (averaging $24,360 per year), 47 teaching assistantships (averaging $15,867 per year) were awarded; career-related internships or fieldwork, Federal Work-Study, scholarships/grants, and unspecified assistantships also available. In 2019, 163 master's, 11 doctorates awarded. *Program availability:* Part-time, evening/weekend, 100% online, blended/hybrid learning. *Application fee:* $60 ($70 for international students). Electronic applications accepted. *Application Contact:* Dr. Rich Conant, Associate Dean for Academic Affairs, 970-491-1919, Fax: 970-491-0279, E-mail: conant@nrel.colostate.edu. *Dean and Professor*, John P. Hayes, 970-491-6675, Fax: 970-491-0279, E-mail: wcnr_deans_office@mail.colostate.edu.

## COLORADO STATE UNIVERSITY–GLOBAL CAMPUS, Greenwood Village, CO 80111

**General Information** State-supported, coed, comprehensive institution.

**GRADUATE UNITS**

**Graduate Programs** *Program availability:* Online learning.

## COLORADO STATE UNIVERSITY-PUEBLO, Pueblo, CO 81001-4901

**General Information** State-supported, coed, comprehensive institution. *Graduate housing:* Room and/or apartments available on a first-come, first-served basis to single students; on-campus housing not available to married students. Housing application deadline: 8/1.

**GRADUATE UNITS**

**College of Education, Engineering and Professional Studies** *Program availability:* Part-time, evening/weekend. Electronic applications accepted.

**College of Science and Mathematics** *Program availability:* Part-time, evening/weekend.

**Malik and Seeme Hasan School of Business** *Program availability:* Part-time, evening/weekend.

## COLORADO TECHNICAL UNIVERSITY AURORA, Aurora, CO 80014

**General Information** Proprietary, coed, comprehensive institution. *Graduate housing:* On-campus housing not available.

**GRADUATE UNITS**

**Program in Computer Engineering**

**Program in Computer Science** *Program availability:* Part-time, evening/weekend.

**Program in Electrical Engineering**

**Program in Information Science**

**Program in Systems Engineering**

**Programs in Business Administration and Management** *Program availability:* Part-time, evening/weekend.

## COLORADO TECHNICAL UNIVERSITY COLORADO SPRINGS, Colorado Springs, CO 80907

**General Information** Proprietary, coed, university. *Graduate housing:* On-campus housing not available.

**GRADUATE UNITS**

**Graduate Studies** *Program availability:* Part-time, evening/weekend.

## COLUMBIA COLLEGE, Columbia, MO 65216-0002

**General Information** Independent-religious, coed, comprehensive institution. *Enrollment:* 1,152 graduate, professional, and undergraduate students; 77 full-time matriculated graduate/professional students (45 women), 450 part-time matriculated graduate/professional students (291 women). *Enrollment by degree level:* 527 master's. *Graduate faculty:* 12 full-time (5 women), 75 part-time/adjunct (36 women). *Tuition:* Full-time $11,760; part-time $490 per credit hour. Tuition and fees vary according to reciprocity agreements. *Graduate housing:* Room and/or apartments available on a first-come, first-served basis to single students; on-campus housing not available to married students. Typical cost: $5300 per year ($9200 including board). Room and board charges vary according to board plan and housing facility selected. Housing application deadline: 7/6. *Student services:* Campus employment opportunities, campus safety program, career counseling, exercise/wellness program, free psychological counseling, international student services, low-cost health insurance, services for students with disabilities, teacher training, writing training. *Library facilities:* J. W. and Lois Stafford Library. *Collection:* Books: 61,551 (physical), 246,591 (digital/electronic); Serial titles: 84 (physical), 16,729 (digital/electronic); Databases: 74. Weekly public service hours: 94; students can reserve study rooms.

**Computer facilities:** Computer purchase and lease plans are available. 220 computers available on campus for general student use. A campuswide network can be accessed. Online class registration is available.
Website: http://www.ccis.edu/

**General Application Contact:** Admissions Contact Center, 573-875-7515, Fax: 573-875-7506, E-mail: admissions@ccis.edu.

**GRADUATE UNITS**

**Master of Arts in Teaching Program** Students: 11 full-time (8 women), 53 part-time (42 women); includes 14 minority (7 Black or African American, non-Hispanic/Latino; 2 Asian, non-Hispanic/Latino; 2 Hispanic/Latino; 3 Two or more races, non-Hispanic/Latino). Average age 35. 105 applicants, 83% accepted, 47 enrolled. *Faculty:* 5 full-time (4 women), 23 part-time/adjunct (18 women). Expenses: Contact institution. *Financial support:* In 2019–20, 54 students received support. Scholarships/grants, tuition waivers (full and partial), and unspecified assistantships available. Financial award application deadline: 3/15; financial award applicants required to submit FAFSA. In 2019, 51 master's awarded. *Program availability:* Part-time, evening/weekend, 100% online, blended/hybrid learning. *Application deadline:* For fall admission, 8/9 priority date for domestic and international students; for spring admission, 12/27 priority date for domestic and international students. Applications are processed on a rolling basis. Electronic applications accepted. *Application Contact:* Admissions Contact Center, 573-875-7515, Fax: 573-875-7506, E-mail: admissions@ccis.edu. *Dean of School of Humanities, Arts and Social Sciences*, Dr. Lisa Ford-Brown, 573-875-7570, E-mail: labrown@ccis.edu.

**Master of Business Administration Program** Students: 50 full-time (27 women), 302 part-time (189 women); includes 110 minority (55 Black or African American, non-Hispanic/Latino; 1 American Indian or Alaska Native, non-Hispanic/Latino; 10 Asian, non-Hispanic/Latino; 24 Hispanic/Latino; 1 Native Hawaiian or other Pacific Islander, non-Hispanic/Latino; 19 Two or more races, non-Hispanic/Latino), 30 international. Average age 36. 332 applicants, 92% accepted, 98 enrolled. *Faculty:* 4 full-time (0 women), 43 part-time/adjunct (14 women). Expenses: Contact institution. *Financial support:* In 2019–20, 103 students received support. Scholarships/grants, tuition waivers (full and partial), and unspecified assistantships available. Financial award application deadline: 3/1; financial award applicants required to submit FAFSA. In 2019, 180 master's awarded. *Program availability:* Part-time, evening/weekend, 100% online, blended/hybrid learning. *Application deadline:* For fall admission, 8/9 priority date for domestic and international students; for spring admission, 12/27 priority date for domestic and international students. Applications are processed on a rolling basis. Electronic applications accepted. *Application Contact:* Stephanie Johnson, Associate Vice President for Recruiting & Admissions Division, 573-875-7352, Fax: 573-875-7506, E-mail: sjohnson@ccis.edu. *Dean of Robert W. Plaster School of Business Administration*, Dr. Raj Sachdev, 573-876-1124, E-mail: rsachdev@ccis.edu.

**Master of Education in Educational Leadership Program** Students: 8 full-time (7 women), 27 part-time (23 women); includes 5 minority (2 Black or African American, non-Hispanic/Latino; 2 Hispanic/Latino; 1 Two or more races, non-Hispanic/Latino). Average age 36. 12 applicants, 100% accepted, 7 enrolled. *Faculty:* 5 full-time (4 women), 15 part-time/adjunct (12 women). Expenses: Contact institution. *Financial support:* In 2019–20, 34 students received support. Scholarships/grants, tuition waivers (full and partial), and unspecified assistantships available. Financial award application deadline: 3/1; financial award applicants required to submit FAFSA. In 2019, 24 master's awarded. *Program availability:* Part-time, evening/weekend, 100% online, blended/hybrid learning. *Application deadline:* For fall admission, 8/9 priority date for domestic and international students; for spring admission, 12/27 priority date for domestic and international students. Applications are processed on a rolling basis. Electronic applications accepted. *Application Contact:* Stephanie Johnson, Associate Vice President for Recruiting and Admissions Division, 573-875-7352, Fax: 573-875-7506, E-mail: sjohnson@ccis.edu. *Dean of the School of Humanities, Arts and Social Sciences*, Dr. Lisa Ford-Brown, 573-875-7570, E-mail: labrown@ccis.edu.

**Master of Science in Criminal Justice Program** Students: 2 full-time (1 woman), 59 part-time (31 women); includes 26 minority (15 Black or African American, non-Hispanic/Latino; 1 American Indian or Alaska Native, non-Hispanic/Latino; 5 Hispanic/Latino; 5 Two or more races, non-Hispanic/Latino). Average age 39. 72 applicants, 79% accepted, 15 enrolled. *Faculty:* 2 full-time (0 women), 21 part-time/adjunct (12 women). Expenses: Contact institution. *Financial support:* In 2019–20, 14 students received support. Scholarships/grants, tuition waivers (full and partial), and unspecified assistantships available. Financial award application deadline: 3/1; financial award applicants required to submit FAFSA. In 2019, 44 master's awarded. *Program availability:* Part-time, evening/weekend, 100% online, blended/hybrid learning. *Application deadline:* For fall admission, 8/9 priority date for domestic and international students; for spring admission, 12/27 priority date for domestic and international students. Applications are processed on a rolling basis. Electronic applications accepted. *Application Contact:* Stephanie Johnson, Associate Vice President for Recruiting and Admissions Division, 573-875-7352, Fax: 573-875-7506, E-mail: sgjohnson@ccis.edu. *Dean of the School of Humanities, Arts and Social Sciences*, Dr. Lisa Ford-Brown, 573-875-7570, E-mail: labrown@ccis.edu.

## COLUMBIA COLLEGE, Columbia, SC 29203-5998

**General Information** Independent-religious, coed, primarily women, comprehensive institution. *Enrollment:* 1,243 graduate, professional, and undergraduate students; 127 full-time matriculated graduate/professional students (95 women), 15 part-time matriculated graduate/professional students (13 women). *Enrollment by degree level:* 142 master's. *Graduate faculty:* 7 full-time (5 women), 16 part-time/adjunct (7 women). *Tuition:* Full-time $10,080; part-time $480 per semester hour. *Graduate housing:* On-campus housing not available. *Student services:* Campus safety program, career counseling, free psychological counseling, multicultural affairs office, services for students with disabilities. *Library facilities:* J. Edens Drake Library. *Collection:* Books: 128,000 (physical), 92 (digital/electronic); Serial titles: 310 (physical); Databases: 84. Weekly public service hours: 70; students can reserve study rooms.

**Computer facilities:** Computer purchase and lease plans are available. 165 computers available on campus for general student use. A campuswide network can be accessed. Online class registration is available.
Website: http://www.columbiasc.edu/

**General Application Contact:** Myles Hacking, Associate Dean of Admissions, 803-786-3419, Fax: 803-786-3674, E-mail: mhacking@columbiasc.edu.

**GRADUATE UNITS**

**Graduate Programs** *Program availability:* Part-time, evening/weekend. Electronic applications accepted.

***Education Division*** *Program availability:* Part-time, evening/weekend, online learning. Electronic applications accepted.

## COLUMBIA COLLEGE CHICAGO, Chicago, IL 60605-1996

**General Information** Independent, coed, comprehensive institution. CGS member. *Graduate housing:* Room and/or apartments available on a first-come, first-served basis to single students; on-campus housing not available to married students. Housing application deadline: 5/1.

**GRADUATE UNITS**

**School of Graduate Studies** *Program availability:* Part-time, evening/weekend. Electronic applications accepted.

## COLUMBIA COLLEGE OF NURSING, Glendale, WI 53212

**General Information** Independent, coed, primarily women, upper-level institution.

**GRADUATE UNITS**

**Graduate Program**

## COLUMBIA INTERNATIONAL UNIVERSITY, Columbia, SC 29203

**General Information** Independent-religious, coed, university. *Graduate housing:* Rooms and/or apartments available on a first-come, first-served basis to single and married students. Housing application deadline: 8/1.

**GRADUATE UNITS**

**Columbia Graduate School** *Program availability:* Part-time, evening/weekend, online learning. Electronic applications accepted.

**Seminary and School of Ministry** *Program availability:* Part-time, evening/weekend. Electronic applications accepted.

## COLUMBIA SOUTHERN UNIVERSITY, Orange Beach, AL 36561

**General Information** Proprietary, coed, comprehensive institution. *Graduate housing:* On-campus housing not available.

**GRADUATE UNITS**

**College of Safety and Emergency Services** *Program availability:* Part-time, evening/weekend, online learning. Electronic applications accepted.

**DBA Program** *Program availability:* Part-time, evening/weekend, online learning. Electronic applications accepted.

**MBA Program** *Program availability:* Part-time, evening/weekend, online learning. Electronic applications accepted.

**Program in Organizational Leadership**

## COLUMBIA THEOLOGICAL SEMINARY, Decatur, GA 30031-0520

**General Information** Independent-religious, coed, graduate-only institution. *Graduate housing:* Rooms and/or apartments available on a first-come, first-served basis to single students and available to married students. Housing application deadline: 4/30.

**GRADUATE UNITS**

**Graduate and Professional Programs**

## COLUMBIA UNIVERSITY, New York, NY 10027

**General Information** Independent, coed, university. CGS member. *Enrollment by degree level:* 16,858 master's, 4,855 doctoral, 571 other advanced degrees. *Graduate faculty:* 4,352 full-time (1,938 women), 2,304 part-time/adjunct (1,101 women). *Tuition:* Full-time $47,600; part-time $1880 per credit. One-time fee: $105. *Graduate housing:* Rooms and/or apartments available to single and married students. Housing application deadline: 10/15. *Student services:* Campus employment opportunities, campus safety program, career counseling, free psychological counseling, international student services, low-cost health insurance, multicultural affairs office, services for students with disabilities, writing training. *Library facilities:* Butler plus 18 others. *Collection:* Books: 11.7 million (physical), 2.8 million (digital/electronic); Databases: 787. Weekly public service hours: 86; study areas open 24 hours, 5–7 days a week; students can reserve study rooms. *Research affiliation:* Brookhaven National Laboratory, New York Botanical Gardens, American Museum of Natural History, Marine Biological Laboratory, Goddard Space Flight Center, Long Island Biological Laboratory.

**Computer facilities:** 460 computers available on campus for general student use. A campuswide network can be accessed. Online class registration is available.
Website: http://www.columbia.edu/

**General Application Contact:** General Information, 212-854-1754.

**GRADUATE UNITS**

**College of Dental Medicine**

**College of Physicians and Surgeons** *Program availability:* Part-time.

***Institute of Human Nutrition*** *Program availability:* Part-time. Electronic applications accepted.

**Columbia School of Social Work** *Program availability:* 100% online, blended/hybrid learning. Electronic applications accepted.

**Columbia University Mailman School of Public Health** Students: 1,055 full-time (833 women), 511 part-time (366 women); includes 585 minority (94 Black or African American, non-Hispanic/Latino; 4 American Indian or Alaska Native, non-Hispanic/Latino; 298 Asian, non-Hispanic/Latino; 141 Hispanic/Latino; 2 Native Hawaiian or other Pacific Islander, non-Hispanic/Latino; 46 Two or more races, non-Hispanic/Latino), 354 international. Average age 27. 3,081 applicants, 65% accepted, 730 enrolled. Expenses: Contact institution. *Financial support:* Fellowships, research assistantships, teaching assistantships, career-related internships or fieldwork, Federal Work-Study, and traineeships available. Support available to part-time students. Financial award application deadline: 2/1; financial award applicants required to submit FAFSA. In 2019, 597 master's, 29 doctorates awarded. *Program availability:* Part-time, evening/weekend. *Application deadline:* For fall admission, 12/1 priority date for domestic and international students. *Application fee:* $120. Electronic applications accepted. *Application Contact:* Clare Norton, Associate Dean for Enrollment Management, 212-305-8698, Fax: 212-342-1861, E-mail: ph-admit@columbia.edu. *Dean/Professor*, Dr. Linda P. Fried, 212-305-9300, Fax: 212-305-9342, E-mail: lpfried@columbia.edu.

**Fu Foundation School of Engineering and Applied Science** *Program availability:* Part-time, 100% online. Electronic applications accepted.

***Data Science Institute*** *Program availability:* Part-time.

**Graduate School of Architecture, Planning, and Preservation**

**Graduate School of Arts and Sciences** Students: 3,506 full-time (1,844 women), 208 part-time (121 women); includes 864 minority (110 Black or African American, non-Hispanic/Latino; 5 American Indian or Alaska Native, non-Hispanic/Latino; 416 Asian, non-Hispanic/Latino; 147 Hispanic/Latino; 6 Native Hawaiian or other Pacific Islander, non-Hispanic/Latino; 180 Two or more races, non-Hispanic/Latino), 2,065 international. 14,545 applicants, 25% accepted, 1,429 enrolled. Expenses: Contact institution. *Financial support:* Fellowships, research assistantships, teaching assistantships, career-related internships or fieldwork, Federal Work-Study, institutionally sponsored loans, scholarships/grants, traineeships, health care benefits, tuition waivers, and unspecified assistantships available. Support available to part-time students. Financial award application deadline: 12/15. In 2019, 1,262 master's, 363 doctorates awarded. *Program availability:* Part-time. *Application fee:* $115. Electronic applications accepted. *Application Contact:* GSAS Office of Admissions, 212-854-6729, E-mail: gsas-admissions@columbia.edu. *Dean of the Graduate School of Arts and Sciences and Vice President for Graduate Education*, Dr. Carlos J. Alonso, 212-854-2861, E-mail: gsas-dean@columbia.edu.

**Graduate School of Business** Electronic applications accepted.

**Graduate School of Journalism** *Program availability:* Part-time.

**School of International and Public Affairs** *Program availability:* Part-time, evening/weekend. Electronic applications accepted.

**School of Law** Electronic applications accepted.

**School of Nursing** Electronic applications accepted.

**School of Professional Studies** *Program availability:* Part-time, evening/weekend. Electronic applications accepted.

**School of the Arts** *Program availability:* Part-time. Electronic applications accepted.

**South Asia Institute** *Program availability:* Part-time. Electronic applications accepted.

## COLUMBUS COLLEGE OF ART & DESIGN, Columbus, OH 43215-1758

**General Information** Independent, coed, comprehensive institution. *Graduate housing:* Rooms and/or apartments available on a first-come, first-served basis to single and married students. Housing application deadline: 5/1.

**GRADUATE UNITS**

**Graduate Programs** *Program availability:* Part-time. Electronic applications accepted.

## COLUMBUS STATE UNIVERSITY, Columbus, GA 31907-5645

**General Information** State-supported, coed, comprehensive institution. CGS member. *Enrollment:* 7,877 graduate, professional, and undergraduate students; 437 full-time matriculated graduate/professional students (274 women), 898 part-time matriculated graduate/professional students (593 women). *Enrollment by degree level:* 1,099 master's, 160 doctoral, 57 other advanced degrees. *Graduate faculty:* 116 full-time (55 women), 67 part-time/adjunct (37 women). *International tuition:* $817 full-time. *Tuition, area resident:* Full-time $210; part-time $210 per credit hour. Tuition, state resident: full-time $210; part-time $210 per credit hour. Tuition, nonresident: full-time $817; part-time $817 per credit hour. *Required fees:* $802.50. Tuition and fees vary according to course load, degree level and program. *Graduate housing:* Rooms and/or apartments available on a first-come, first-served basis to single and married students. Housing application deadline: 6/30. *Student services:* Campus employment opportunities, campus safety program, career counseling, exercise/wellness program, free psychological counseling, international student services, low-cost health insurance, multicultural affairs office, services for students with disabilities, teacher training, writing training. *Library facilities:* Simon Schwob Memorial Library plus 1 other. *Collection:* Books: 379,660 (physical); Serial titles: 1,103 (physical).

**Computer facilities:** 3,053 computers available on campus for general student use. A campuswide network can be accessed. Online class registration is available.
Website: http://www.columbusstate.edu/

**General Application Contact:** Catrina Smith-Edmond, Assistant Director for Graduate and Global Admission, 706-507-8800, Fax: 706-568-5091, E-mail: smithedmond_catrina@columbusstate.edu.

**GRADUATE UNITS**

**Graduate Studies** *Program availability:* Part-time, evening/weekend, 100% online, blended/hybrid learning. Electronic applications accepted.

***College of Education and Health Professions*** *Program availability:* Part-time, evening/weekend, 100% online, blended/hybrid learning. Electronic applications accepted.

***College of Letters and Sciences*** *Program availability:* Part-time, evening/weekend, 100% online, blended/hybrid learning. Electronic applications accepted.

***College of the Arts*** *Program availability:* Part-time, evening/weekend. Electronic applications accepted.

***Turner College of Business*** *Program availability:* Part-time, evening/weekend, 100% online, blended/hybrid learning. Electronic applications accepted.

## CONCORDIA COLLEGE, Moorhead, MN 56562

**General Information** Independent-religious, coed, comprehensive institution.

**GRADUATE UNITS**

**Program in Education**

## CONCORDIA COLLEGE–NEW YORK, Bronxville, NY 10708-1998

**General Information** Independent-religious, coed, comprehensive institution.

**GRADUATE UNITS**

**Program in Business Leadership**

**Program in Childhood Special Education**

## CONCORDIA LUTHERAN SEMINARY, Edmonton, AB T5B 4E3, Canada

**General Information** Independent-religious, coed, primarily men, graduate-only institution. *Graduate housing:* On-campus housing not available.

**GRADUATE UNITS**

**Graduate and Professional Programs** *Program availability:* Part-time.

## CONCORDIA SEMINARY, St. Louis, MO 63105-3199

**General Information** Independent-religious, coed, primarily men, graduate-only institution. *Graduate housing:* Rooms and/or apartments guaranteed to single students and available to married students. Housing application deadline: 3/4. *Research affiliation:* Center for Reformation Research, Concordia Historical Institute.

**GRADUATE UNITS**

**Graduate Programs**

## CONCORDIA THEOLOGICAL SEMINARY, Fort Wayne, IN 46825-4996

**General Information** Independent-religious, coed, primarily men, graduate-only institution. *Graduate housing:* Room and/or apartments available to single students; on-campus housing not available to married students.

**GRADUATE UNITS**

**Graduate and Professional Programs** *Program availability:* Part-time.

## CONCORDIA UNIVERSITY, Montréal, QC H3G 1M8, Canada

**General Information** Province-supported, coed, university. CGS member. *Graduate housing:* Room and/or apartments available on a first-come, first-served basis to single students; on-campus housing not available to married students. *Research affiliation:* Canadian Rural Revitalization Foundation (sociology), Blue Metropolis Literary Series (English), Canadian Journalism Project (journalism), Centre de Recherche en Plasturgie et Composites (CREPEC) (mechanical and industrial engineering), Centre de Recherche Informatique de Montreal (CRIM) (computer science), Center d'experise et de services en application Multimedia (multimedia).

**GRADUATE UNITS**

**School of Graduate Studies** *Program availability:* Part-time, evening/weekend.

***Faculty of Arts and Science***

***Faculty of Engineering and Computer Science***

***Faculty of Fine Arts*** *Program availability:* Part-time.

***John Molson School of Business*** *Program availability:* Part-time, evening/weekend. Electronic applications accepted.

## CONCORDIA UNIVERSITY ANN ARBOR, Ann Arbor, MI 48105-2797

**General Information** Independent-religious, coed, comprehensive institution. *Graduate housing:* On-campus housing not available.

**GRADUATE UNITS**

**Graduate Programs** *Program availability:* Part-time, evening/weekend. Electronic applications accepted.

## CONCORDIA UNIVERSITY CHICAGO, River Forest, IL 60305-1499

**General Information** Independent-religious, coed, comprehensive institution. CGS member. *Graduate housing:* Rooms and/or apartments available on a first-come, first-served basis to single and married students.

**GRADUATE UNITS**

**College of Graduate Studies**

***College of Business*** *Program availability:* Part-time, evening/weekend, online learning.

## CONCORDIA UNIVERSITY IRVINE, Irvine, CA 92612-3299

**General Information** Independent-religious, coed, comprehensive institution. *Graduate housing:* Room and/or apartments available on a first-come, first-served basis to single students; on-campus housing not available to married students. Housing application deadline: 6/1.

**GRADUATE UNITS**

**School of Arts and Sciences** *Program availability:* Part-time, evening/weekend, online learning. Electronic applications accepted.

**School of Business** *Program availability:* Part-time, evening/weekend. Electronic applications accepted.

**School of Education** *Program availability:* Part-time, evening/weekend, online learning. Electronic applications accepted.

**School of Professional Studies**

**School of Theology** *Program availability:* Part-time, evening/weekend. Electronic applications accepted.

## CONCORDIA UNIVERSITY, NEBRASKA, Seward, NE 68434

**General Information** Independent-religious, coed, comprehensive institution. *Graduate housing:* Rooms and/or apartments available on a first-come, first-served basis to single and married students.

**GRADUATE UNITS**

**Graduate Programs in Education** *Program availability:* Part-time, evening/weekend. Electronic applications accepted.

**Program in Computer Science** *Program availability:* Online learning.

## CONCORDIA UNIVERSITY OF EDMONTON, Edmonton, AB T5B 4E4, Canada

**General Information** Independent-religious, coed, comprehensive institution.

**GRADUATE UNITS**

**Program in Biblical and Christian Studies**

**Program in Information Systems Security Management**

## CONCORDIA UNIVERSITY, ST. PAUL, St. Paul, MN 55104-5494

**General Information** Independent-religious, coed, comprehensive institution. CGS member. *Enrollment:* 5,139 graduate, professional, and undergraduate students; 1,850 full-time matriculated graduate/professional students (1,309 women), 162 part-time matriculated graduate/professional students (113 women). *Enrollment by degree level:* 1,714 master's, 169 doctoral, 129 other advanced degrees. *Graduate faculty:* 47 full-time (27 women), 145 part-time/adjunct (83 women). *Tuition:* Full-time $9000; part-time $475 per credit. Tuition and fees vary according to degree level and program. *Graduate housing:* Rooms and/or apartments available on a first-come, first-served basis to single and married students. Typical cost: $9200 (including board) for single students; $9200 (including board) for married students. Housing application deadline: 6/1. *Student services:* Campus employment opportunities, campus safety program, career counseling, exercise/wellness program, international student services, multicultural affairs office, services for students with disabilities, teacher training, writing training. *Library facilities:* Library Technology Center. *Collection:* Books: 84,956 (physical), 218,505 (digital/electronic); Serial titles: 622 (physical), 40,440 (digital/electronic); Databases: 160. Weekly public service hours: 74; students can reserve study rooms.

**Computer facilities:** 10 computers available on campus for general student use. A campuswide network can be accessed. Online class registration is available.
Website: http://www.csp.edu/

**General Application Contact:** Amber Faletti, Director of Enrollment Management, 651-641-8230, Fax: 651-603-6320, E-mail: faletti@csp.edu.

**GRADUATE UNITS**

**College of Business and Technology** *Program availability:* Part-time, evening/weekend, 100% online, blended/hybrid learning. Electronic applications accepted.

**College of Education** *Program availability:* Part-time, evening/weekend, 100% online, blended/hybrid learning. Electronic applications accepted.

**College of Health and Science** *Program availability:* Part-time, evening/weekend, 100% online, blended/hybrid learning. Electronic applications accepted.

**College of Humanities and Social Sciences** *Program availability:* Part-time, evening/weekend, 100% online, blended/hybrid learning. Electronic applications accepted.

## CONCORDIA UNIVERSITY TEXAS, Austin, TX 78726

**General Information** Independent-religious, coed, comprehensive institution.

**GRADUATE UNITS**

**College of Education** *Program availability:* Part-time, evening/weekend.

## CONCORDIA UNIVERSITY WISCONSIN, Mequon, WI 53097-2402

**General Information** Independent-religious, coed, comprehensive institution. *Graduate housing:* Room and/or apartments available to single students; on-campus housing not available to married students. Housing application deadline: 8/1.

**GRADUATE UNITS**

**Graduate Programs** *Program availability:* Part-time, evening/weekend, online learning. Electronic applications accepted.

***Batterman School of Business***

***School of Arts and Sciences***

***School of Education*** *Program availability:* Part-time, evening/weekend, online learning.

***School of Health Professions***

***School of Nursing*** *Program availability:* Online learning.

***School of Pharmacy***

## CONCORD LAW SCHOOL, Los Angeles, CA 90024

**General Information** Proprietary, coed, graduate-only institution.

**GRADUATE UNITS**

**Program in Law** *Program availability:* Part-time, evening/weekend, online learning. Electronic applications accepted.

## CONCORD UNIVERSITY, Athens, WV 24712-1000

**General Information** State-supported, coed, comprehensive institution. *Enrollment:* 1,886 graduate, professional, and undergraduate students; 97 full-time matriculated graduate/professional students (76 women), 219 part-time matriculated graduate/professional students (178 women). *Enrollment by degree level:* 286 master's, 30 other advanced degrees. *Graduate faculty:* 22 full-time (14 women), 3 part-time/adjunct (all women). *Tuition, area resident:* Full-time $481; part-time $481 per credit hour. Tuition, state resident: full-time $481; part-time $481 per credit hour. Tuition, nonresident: full-time $481; part-time $481 per credit hour. *Graduate housing:* Room and/or apartments available on a first-come, first-served basis to single students; on-campus housing not available to married students. *Student services:* Campus employment opportunities, career counseling, child daycare facilities, free psychological counseling, international student services, multicultural affairs office, services for students with disabilities, teacher training. *Library facilities:* J. Frank Marsh Library. *Collection:* Books: 165,290 (physical), 190,000 (digital/electronic); Serial titles: 60 (physical); Databases: 17. Weekly public service hours: 77; study areas open 24 hours, 5–7 days a week; students can reserve study rooms.

**Computer facilities:** 350 computers available on campus for general student use. A campuswide network can be accessed. Online class registration is available.
Website: http://www.concord.edu/

**General Application Contact:** Debra Moore, Special Events Assistant, 304-384-5113, E-mail: dlm@concord.edu.

**GRADUATE UNITS**

**Graduate Studies** *Program availability:* Part-time, evening/weekend, 100% online. Electronic applications accepted.

## CONSERVATORIO DE MUSICA DE PUERTO RICO, San Juan, PR 00907

**General Information** Commonwealth-supported, coed, comprehensive institution.

**GRADUATE UNITS**

**Program in Musical Performance**

**Program in Music Education**

## CONVERSE COLLEGE, Spartanburg, SC 29302

**General Information** Independent, Undergraduate: women only; graduate: coed, comprehensive institution. *Graduate housing:* Room and/or apartments available to single students; on-campus housing not available to married students.

**GRADUATE UNITS**

**Education Specialist Program** *Program availability:* Part-time. Electronic applications accepted.

**Petrie School of Music** *Program availability:* Part-time, evening/weekend. Electronic applications accepted.

**Program in Art Education**

**Program in Creative Writing**

**Program in Educational Administration and Supervision** Electronic applications accepted.

**Program in Elementary Education** *Program availability:* Part-time. Electronic applications accepted.

**Program in Gifted Education** *Program availability:* Part-time. Electronic applications accepted.

**Program in Liberal Arts**

**Program in Marriage and Family Therapy**

**Program in Middle Level Education**

**Program in Secondary Education** *Program availability:* Part-time. Electronic applications accepted.

**Program in Special Education** *Program availability:* Part-time. Electronic applications accepted.

## THE CONWAY SCHOOL, Conway, MA 01341-0179

**General Information** Independent, coed, graduate-only institution. *Enrollment by degree level:* 17 master's. *Graduate faculty:* 2 full-time (1 woman), 10 part-time/adjunct (6 women). *Graduate housing:* On-campus housing not available. *Student services:* Campus safety program, career counseling, international student services. *Collection:* Books: 4,000 (physical). Study areas open 24 hours, 5–7 days a week; students can reserve study rooms.

**Computer facilities:** 2 computers available on campus for general student use. A campuswide network can be accessed.
Website: http://www.csld.edu/

**General Application Contact:** Kate Cholakis, Director of Admissions, 413-369-4044, E-mail: admissions@csld.edu.

**GRADUATE UNITS**

**Program in Ecological Design**

## COOPER UNION FOR THE ADVANCEMENT OF SCIENCE AND ART, New York, NY 10003-7120

**General Information** Independent, coed, comprehensive institution. *Graduate housing:* On-campus housing not available. *Research affiliation:* National Science Foundation, National Institutes of Health, Defense Advanced Research Projects Agency, Naval Postgraduate School, U.S. Department of Homeland Security, U.S. Department of Defense.

**GRADUATE UNITS**

**Albert Nerken School of Engineering** *Program availability:* Part-time. Electronic applications accepted.

**Irwin S. Chanin School of Architecture** Electronic applications accepted.

## COPPIN STATE UNIVERSITY, Baltimore, MD 21216-3698

**General Information** State-supported, coed, comprehensive institution. CGS member. *Graduate housing:* On-campus housing not available.

**GRADUATE UNITS**

**School of Graduate Studies** *Program availability:* Part-time, evening/weekend, online learning.

***College of Behavioral and Social Sciences*** *Program availability:* Part-time, evening/weekend.

***Helene Fuld School of Nursing*** *Program availability:* Part-time, evening/weekend.

***School of Education*** *Program availability:* Part-time, evening/weekend, online learning.

## CORBAN UNIVERSITY, Salem, OR 97301-9392

**General Information** Independent-religious, coed, comprehensive institution.

**GRADUATE UNITS**

**Graduate School**

***School of Ministry*** *Program availability:* Part-time, evening/weekend.

## CORNELL UNIVERSITY, Ithaca, NY 14853

**General Information** Independent, coed, university. CGS member. *Graduate housing:* Rooms and/or apartments available on a first-come, first-served basis to single and married students. Housing application deadline: 7/1. *Research affiliation:* Brookhaven National Laboratory (physics, biology, medicine, chemistry, energy, engineering, environmental science), Fermi National Accelerator Laboratory, Boyce Thompson Institute for Plant Research (plant research).

**GRADUATE UNITS**

**College of Veterinary Medicine** Students: 442 full-time (362 women); includes 136 minority (11 Black or African American, non-Hispanic/Latino; 5 American Indian or Alaska Native, non-Hispanic/Latino; 48 Asian, non-Hispanic/Latino; 47 Hispanic/Latino; 2 Native Hawaiian or other Pacific Islander, non-Hispanic/Latino; 23 Two or more races, non-Hispanic/Latino), 8 international. Average age 25. 1,147 applicants, 16% accepted, 110 enrolled. *Faculty:* 212 full-time (105 women). Expenses: Contact institution. *Financial support:* In 2019–20, 296 students received support. Federal Work-Study, institutionally sponsored loans, and scholarships/grants available. Financial award application deadline: 2/15; financial award applicants required to submit CSS PROFILE or FAFSA. In 2019, 96 doctorates awarded. *Application deadline:* For fall admission, 9/15 for domestic and international students. Electronic applications accepted. *Application Contact:* Jennifer A. Mailey, Director of Admissions, 607-253-3700, Fax: 607-253-3709, E-mail: jam333@cornell.edu. *Dean*, Dr. Lorin Warnick, 607-253-3771, Fax: 607-253-3701.

**Cornell Law School** Electronic applications accepted.

**Graduate School** Electronic applications accepted.

***Field of Hotel Administration*** Electronic applications accepted.

***Graduate Field in the Law School*** Electronic applications accepted.

***Graduate Field of Management*** Electronic applications accepted.

**Samuel Curtis Johnson Graduate School of Management** Students: 564 full-time (193 women); includes 138 minority (26 Black or African American, non-Hispanic/Latino; 74 Asian, non-Hispanic/Latino; 17 Hispanic/Latino; 21 Two or more races, non-Hispanic/Latino), 165 international. Average age 28. 1,535 applicants, 38% accepted, 282 enrolled. *Faculty:* 66 full-time (18 women), 20 part-time/adjunct (10 women). Expenses: Contact institution. *Financial support:* Fellowships, research assistantships, Federal Work-Study, institutionally sponsored loans, scholarships/grants, and tuition waivers (full and partial) available. Financial award applicants required to submit FAFSA. In 2019, 282 master's awarded. *Application deadline:* For fall admission, 10/8 for domestic and international students; for winter admission, 1/5 for domestic and international students; for spring admission, 4/8 for domestic and international students. *Application fee:* $200. Electronic applications accepted. *Application Contact:* Admissions Office, 607-255-4526, Fax: 607-255-0065, E-mail: mba@johnson.cornell.edu. *Dean*, Dr. Mark Nelson, 607-255-6418, E-mail: dean@johnson.cornell.edu.

## CORNERSTONE UNIVERSITY, Grand Rapids, MI 49525-5897

**General Information** Independent-religious, coed, comprehensive institution. *Graduate housing:* Rooms and/or apartments available on a first-come, first-served basis to single and married students.

**GRADUATE UNITS**

**Graduate Programs** *Program availability:* Part-time, online learning. Electronic applications accepted.

## COVENANT COLLEGE, Lookout Mountain, GA 30750

**General Information** Independent-religious, coed, comprehensive institution. *Graduate housing:* Room and/or apartments available on a first-come, first-served basis to single students; on-campus housing not available to married students. Housing application deadline: 5/1.

**GRADUATE UNITS**

**Program in Education** *Program availability:* Part-time.

## COVENANT THEOLOGICAL SEMINARY, St. Louis, MO 63141-8697

**General Information** Independent-religious, coed, graduate-only institution. *Graduate housing:* Rooms and/or apartments available on a first-come, first-served basis to single and married students.

**GRADUATE UNITS**

**Graduate and Professional Programs** *Program availability:* Part-time, evening/weekend, online learning. Electronic applications accepted.

## COX COLLEGE, Springfield, MO 65802

**General Information** Independent, coed, primarily women, comprehensive institution.

**GRADUATE UNITS**

**Program in Occupational Therapy**

**Programs in Nursing** Electronic applications accepted.

## CRANBROOK ACADEMY OF ART, Bloomfield Hills, MI 48303-0801

**General Information** Independent, coed, graduate-only institution. *Graduate housing:* Room and/or apartments available on a first-come, first-served basis to single students; on-campus housing not available to married students. Housing application deadline: 4/1.

**GRADUATE UNITS**

**Program in Architecture** Electronic applications accepted.

**Program in Fine Arts** Electronic applications accepted.

## CRANDALL UNIVERSITY, Moncton, NB E1C 9L7, Canada

**General Information** Independent-religious, coed, comprehensive institution.

**GRADUATE UNITS**

**Graduate Programs**

## CREIGHTON UNIVERSITY, Omaha, NE 68178-0001

**General Information** Independent-religious, coed, university. CGS member. *Enrollment:* 8,821 graduate, professional, and undergraduate students; 2,903 full-time matriculated graduate/professional students (1,731 women), 1,451 part-time matriculated graduate/professional students (955 women). *Enrollment by degree level:* 947 master's, 3,240 doctoral, 167 other advanced degrees. *Graduate faculty:* 807 full-time (366 women). *Graduate housing:* Rooms and/or apartments available on a first-come, first-served basis to single and married students. Housing application deadline: 5/1. *Student services:* Campus employment opportunities, campus safety program, career counseling, child daycare facilities, exercise/wellness program, free psychological counseling, grant writing training, international student services, low-cost health insurance, multicultural affairs office, services for students with disabilities, teacher training, writing training. *Library facilities:* Reinert Alumni Memorial Library plus 2 others. *Collection:* Books: 345,198 (physical), 515,607 (digital/electronic); Serial titles: 4,297 (physical), 69,034 (digital/electronic); Databases: 380. Weekly public service hours: 112; study areas open 24 hours, 5–7 days a week. *Research affiliation:* U.S. Department of Education (DOE) (student support services), National Institutes of Health (asthma), U.S. Department of Commerce (atmospheric science), National Science Foundation (business and education).

**Computer facilities:** Computer purchase and lease plans are available. 565 computers available on campus for general student use. A campuswide network can be accessed. Online class registration, financial aid information are available.
Website: http://www.creighton.edu/

**General Application Contact:** Lindsay Johnson, Director of Graduate and Adult Recruitment, 402-280-2703, Fax: 402-280-2423, E-mail: gradschool@creighton.edu.

**GRADUATE UNITS**

**College of Nursing** *Program availability:* Part-time, blended/hybrid learning. Electronic applications accepted.

**Graduate School** Students: 331 full-time (200 women), 1,120 part-time (658 women); includes 188 minority (88 Black or African American, non-Hispanic/Latino; 14 American Indian or Alaska Native, non-Hispanic/Latino; 44 Asian, non-Hispanic/Latino; 33 Hispanic/Latino; 5 Native Hawaiian or other Pacific Islander, non-Hispanic/Latino; 4 Two or more races, non-Hispanic/Latino), 88 international. Average age 36. 1,009 applicants, 57% accepted, 317 enrolled. *Faculty:* 323 full-time (119 women). Expenses: Contact institution. *Financial support:* In 2019–20, fellowships with tuition reimbursements (averaging $23,000 per year), research assistantships with tuition reimbursements (averaging $15,700 per year), teaching assistantships with tuition reimbursements (averaging $15,700 per year) were awarded; career-related internships or fieldwork, institutionally sponsored loans, scholarships/grants, tuition waivers (partial), and unspecified assistantships also available. Support available to part-time students. Financial award application deadline: 3/1; financial award applicants required to submit FAFSA. In 2019, 458 master's, 93 doctorates awarded. *Program availability:* Part-time, evening/weekend, 100% online, blended/hybrid learning. *Application deadline:* For fall admission, 3/1 priority date for domestic and international students; for winter admission, 10/1 for domestic students, 7/1 for international students; for spring admission, 4/1 for domestic students, 10/1 for international students. Applications are processed on a rolling basis. *Application fee:* $50. Electronic applications accepted. *Application Contact:* Lindsay Johnson, Director of Graduate and Adult Recruitment, 402-280-2703, Fax: 402-280-2423, E-mail: gradschool@creighton.edu. *Dean*, Dr. Gail M. Jensen, 402-280-2424, Fax: 402-280-2423, E-mail: gjensen@creighton.edu.

***College of Arts and Sciences*** *Program availability:* Part-time, 100% online, blended/hybrid learning. Electronic applications accepted.

***Heider College of Business*** Students: 66 full-time (28 women), 324 part-time (113 women); includes 64 minority (21 Black or African American, non-Hispanic/Latino; 1 American Indian or Alaska Native, non-Hispanic/Latino; 18 Asian, non-Hispanic/Latino; 21 Hispanic/Latino; 1 Native Hawaiian or other Pacific Islander, non-Hispanic/Latino; 2 Two or more races, non-Hispanic/Latino), 22 international. Average age 33. 231 applicants, 79% accepted, 111 enrolled. *Faculty:* 33 full-time (10 women), 22 part-time/adjunct (3 women). Expenses: Contact institution. *Financial support:* In 2019–20, 10 fellowships with partial tuition reimbursements (averaging $8,448 per year) were awarded; career-related internships or fieldwork, tuition waivers (partial), and unspecified assistantships also available. Financial award application deadline: 3/1. In 2019, 179 master's, 4 doctorates awarded. *Program* *availability:* Part-time, evening/weekend, 100% online, blended/hybrid learning. *Application deadline:* For fall admission, 7/1 priority date for domestic students, 3/1 for international students; for winter admission, 10/1 priority date for domestic students, 7/1 for international students; for spring admission, 4/1 priority date for domestic students, 10/1 for international students; for summer admission, 5/1 for domestic and international students. Applications are processed on a rolling basis. *Application fee:* $50. Electronic applications accepted. *Application Contact:* Chris Karasek, Assistant Dean, 402-280-2829, Fax: 402-280-2172, E-mail: chriskarasek@creighton.edu. *Associate Dean for Faculty and Academics*, Dr. Deborah Wells, 402-280-2841, E-mail: deborahwells@creighton.edu.

**School of Dentistry**

**School of Law** *Program availability:* Part-time. Electronic applications accepted.

**School of Medicine** Electronic applications accepted.

**School of Pharmacy and Health Professions** *Program availability:* Online learning. Electronic applications accepted.

## CRISWELL COLLEGE, Dallas, TX 75246-1537

**General Information** Independent-religious, coed, comprehensive institution. *Graduate housing:* On-campus housing not available.

**GRADUATE UNITS**

**Graduate School of the Bible** *Program availability:* Part-time. Electronic applications accepted.

## CROWN COLLEGE, St. Bonifacius, MN 55375-9001

**General Information** Independent-religious, coed, comprehensive institution. *Graduate housing:* Room and/or apartments available on a first-come, first-served basis to married students; on-campus housing not available to single students. Housing application deadline: 7/1.

**GRADUATE UNITS**

**Adult and Graduate Studies** *Program availability:* Part-time, evening/weekend, online learning. Electronic applications accepted.

## CULVER-STOCKTON COLLEGE, Canton, MO 63435-1299

**General Information** Independent-religious, coed, comprehensive institution.

**GRADUATE UNITS**

**MBA Program**

## CUMBERLAND UNIVERSITY, Lebanon, TN 37087

**General Information** Independent, coed, comprehensive institution. *Graduate housing:* Room and/or apartments available on a first-come, first-served basis to single students; on-campus housing not available to married students.

**GRADUATE UNITS**

**Program in Business Administration** *Program availability:* Part-time, evening/weekend.

**Program in Education** *Program availability:* Part-time, evening/weekend, online learning.

**Program in Public Service Administration** *Program availability:* Part-time, evening/weekend.

## CUNY CRAIG NEWMARK GRADUATE SCHOOL OF JOURNALISM, New York, NY 10018

**General Information** City-supported, coed, graduate-only institution.

**GRADUATE UNITS**

**Graduate Program** Electronic applications accepted.

## CURRY COLLEGE, Milton, MA 02186-9984

**General Information** Independent, coed, comprehensive institution. *Graduate housing:* On-campus housing not available. *Research affiliation:* Literacy Centers/GED Programs.

**GRADUATE UNITS**

**Graduate Studies** *Program availability:* Part-time, evening/weekend.

## CURTIS INSTITUTE OF MUSIC, Philadelphia, PA 19103-6107

**General Information** Independent, coed, comprehensive institution. *Graduate housing:* On-campus housing not available.

**GRADUATE UNITS**

**Graduate Studies**

## DAEMEN COLLEGE, Amherst, NY 14226-3592

**General Information** Independent, coed, comprehensive institution. *Graduate housing:* Room and/or apartments available on a first-come, first-served basis to single students; on-campus housing not available to married students. Housing application deadline: 8/31.

**GRADUATE UNITS**

**Applied Behavior Analysis Programs**

**Athletic Training Programs**

**Education Programs** *Program availability:* Part-time. Electronic applications accepted.

**International Business Program** *Program availability:* Part-time, evening/weekend. Electronic applications accepted.

**Leadership and Innovation Programs** *Program availability:* Part-time-only, evening/weekend. Electronic applications accepted.

**Nursing Programs** *Program availability:* Part-time. Electronic applications accepted.

**Paralegal Certificate Programs**

**Physical Therapy Programs** Electronic applications accepted.

**Physician Assistant Programs** Electronic applications accepted.

**Public Health Programs** *Program availability:* Part-time, evening/weekend. Electronic applications accepted.

**Social Work Programs** *Program availability:* Part-time, 100% online, blended/hybrid learning. Electronic applications accepted.

## DAKOTA STATE UNIVERSITY, Madison, SD 57042-1799

**General Information** State-supported, coed, comprehensive institution. CGS member. *Enrollment:* 3,268 graduate, professional, and undergraduate students; 79 full-time matriculated graduate/professional students (14 women), 328 part-time matriculated graduate/professional students (93 women). *Enrollment by degree level:* 250 master's, 140 doctoral, 17 other advanced degrees. *Graduate faculty:* 35 full-time (9 women), 4 part-time/adjunct (3 women). *International tuition:* $14,784 full-time. *Tuition, area resident:* Full-time $7919. Tuition, state resident: full-time $7919. Tuition, nonresident: full-time $14,784. *Required fees:* $961. *Graduate housing:* Room and/or apartments available on a first-come, first-served basis to single students; on-campus housing not available to married students. *Student services:* Campus employment opportunities, campus safety program, career counseling, exercise/wellness program, free psychological counseling, grant writing training, international student services, low-cost health insurance, multicultural affairs office, services for students with disabilities, teacher training, writing training. *Library facilities:* Karl E. Mundt Library & Learning Commons plus 1 other. *Collection:* Books: 38,709 (physical), 261,118 (digital/electronic); Serial titles: 174 (physical); Databases: 124. Weekly public service hours: 85. *Research affiliation:* East River Electric (Computer Science), Raven Industries (Information Security), South Dakota Networks (SDN) (Information Security), SD Attorney General (Digital Forensics), SD Dept of Health (Healthcare), NSF EPSCoR (Data Science).

**Computer facilities:** 80 computers available on campus for general student use. A campuswide network can be accessed. Online class registration is available. Website: http://www.dsu.edu/

**General Application Contact:** Erin Blankespoor, Senior Secretary, Office of Graduate Studies, 605-256-5799, E-mail: erin.blankespoor@dsu.edu.

**GRADUATE UNITS**

**Beacom College of Computer and Cyber Sciences** Students: 44 full-time (5 women), 127 part-time (26 women); includes 43 minority (17 Black or African American, non-Hispanic/Latino; 2 American Indian or Alaska Native, non-Hispanic/Latino; 11 Asian, non-Hispanic/Latino; 9 Hispanic/Latino; 2 Native Hawaiian or other Pacific Islander, non-Hispanic/Latino; 2 Two or more races, non-Hispanic/Latino), 9 international. Average age 35. 205 applicants, 30% accepted, 56 enrolled. *Faculty:* 18 full-time (2 women), 1 part-time/adjunct (0 women). Expenses: Contact institution. *Financial support:* Fellowships, career-related internships or fieldwork, Federal Work-Study, scholarships/grants, unspecified assistantships, and Administrative Assistantships available. Support available to part-time students. Financial award applicants required to submit FAFSA. In 2019, 19 master's, 7 doctorates, 5 other advanced degrees awarded. *Program availability:* Part-time, evening/weekend, online learning. *Application deadline:* For fall admission, 6/15 for domestic students, 4/15 for international students; for spring admission, 11/15 for domestic students, 9/15 priority date for international students; for summer admission, 4/15 for domestic and international students. Applications are processed on a rolling basis. *Application fee:* $35. *Application Contact:* Erin Blankespoor, Senior Secretary, Office of Graduate Studies, 605-256-5799, E-mail: erin.blankespoor@dsu.edu. *Dean, Beacom College of Computer and Cyber Science*, Dr. Pat Engebretson, 605-256-5798, E-mail: pat.engebretson@dsu.edu.

**College of Business and Information Systems** Students: 35 full-time (8 women), 177 part-time (51 women); includes 58 minority (23 Black or African American, non-Hispanic/Latino; 6 American Indian or Alaska Native, non-Hispanic/Latino; 18 Asian, non-Hispanic/Latino; 10 Hispanic/Latino; 1 Two or more races, non-Hispanic/Latino), 45 international. Average age 38. 230 applicants, 34% accepted, 70 enrolled. *Faculty:* 23 full-time (8 women), 1 (woman) part-time/adjunct. Expenses: Contact institution. *Financial support:* Fellowships, career-related internships or fieldwork, Federal Work-Study, scholarships/grants, unspecified assistantships, and Administrative Assistantships available. Support available to part-time students. Financial award applicants required to submit FAFSA. In 2019, 49 master's, 2 doctorates, 13 other advanced degrees awarded. *Program availability:* Part-time, evening/weekend, 100% online, blended/hybrid learning. *Application deadline:* For fall admission, 6/15 for domestic students, 4/15 for international students; for spring admission, 11/15 for domestic students, 9/15 priority date for international students; for summer admission, 4/15 for domestic and international students. Applications are processed on a rolling basis. *Application fee:* $35. *Application Contact:* Erin Blankespoor, Senior Secretary, Office of Graduate Studies, 605-256-5799, E-mail: erin.blankespoor@dsu.edu. *Dean of College of Business and Information Systems*, Dr. Dorine Bennett, 605-256-5176, E-mail: dorine.bennett@dsu.edu.

**College of Education** Students: 1 (woman) full-time, 26 part-time (17 women). Average age 32. 5 applicants, 100% accepted, 3 enrolled. *Faculty:* 2 full-time (1 woman), 2 part-time/adjunct (both women). Expenses: Contact institution. *Financial support:* Fellowships, career-related internships or fieldwork, Federal Work-Study, scholarships/grants, unspecified assistantships, and administrative assistantships available. Support available to part-time students. Financial award applicants required to submit FAFSA. In 2019, 6 master's awarded. *Program availability:* Part-time-only, evening/weekend, online only, 100% online. *Application deadline:* For fall admission, 6/15 for domestic students; for spring admission, 11/15 for domestic students; for summer admission, 4/15 for domestic students. Applications are processed on a rolling basis. *Application fee:* $35. Electronic applications accepted. *Application Contact:* Dr. Kevin Smith, MSET Program Coordinator, 605-256-5175, Fax: 605-256-7300, E-mail: kevin.smith@dsu.edu. *Dean of College of Education*, Dr. Crystal Pauli, 605-256-5799.

## DAKOTA WESLEYAN UNIVERSITY, Mitchell, SD 57301-4398

**General Information** Independent-religious, coed, comprehensive institution. *Enrollment:* 60 full-time matriculated graduate/professional students (35 women), 16 part-time matriculated graduate/professional students (10 women). *Enrollment by degree level:* 50 master's, 26 other advanced degrees. *Graduate faculty:* 14 part-time/adjunct (8 women). *Tuition:* Full-time $375; part-time $375 per credit hour. Tuition and fees vary according to program. *Graduate housing:* Room and/or apartments available on a first-come, first-served basis to single students; on-campus housing not available to married students. Typical cost: $7300 (including board). *Student services:* Campus employment opportunities, career counseling, services for students with disabilities, teacher training, writing training. *Library facilities:* George and Eleanor McGovern Library plus 1 other.

**Computer facilities:** 100 computers available on campus for general student use. A campuswide network can be accessed from student residence rooms and from off campus. Online class registration, portal, course management system are available. Website: http://www.dwu.edu/

**General Application Contact:** Missy Leuthold, Adult and Online Enrollment Coordinator, 605-995-2650, Fax: 605-995-2699, E-mail: admissions@dwv.edu.

**GRADUATE UNITS**

**Program in Education** *Program availability:* Part-time, evening/weekend, online only, 100% online. Electronic applications accepted.

## DALHOUSIE UNIVERSITY, Halifax, NS B3H 4R2, Canada

**General Information** Province-supported, coed, university. *Graduate housing:* Rooms and/or apartments available on a first-come, first-served basis to single and married students. Housing application deadline: 8/1.

**GRADUATE UNITS**

**Faculty of Agriculture** *Program availability:* Part-time.

**Faculty of Architecture and Planning** Electronic applications accepted.
***School of Planning*** Electronic applications accepted.
**Faculty of Arts and Social Sciences** *Program availability:* Part-time. Electronic applications accepted.
***Fountain School of Performing Arts*** Electronic applications accepted.
**Faculty of Computer Science** Electronic applications accepted.
**Faculty of Dentistry**
**Faculty of Engineering**
***School of Biomedical Engineering*** Electronic applications accepted.
**Faculty of Graduate Studies** *Program availability:* Part-time, online learning. Electronic applications accepted.
***Schulich School of Law*** *Program availability:* Part-time. Electronic applications accepted.
**Faculty of Health** *Program availability:* Part-time, online learning.
***School of Communication Sciences and Disorders*** Electronic applications accepted.
***School of Health Administration*** *Program availability:* Part-time, online learning. Electronic applications accepted.
***School of Health and Human Performance*** *Program availability:* Part-time. Electronic applications accepted.
***School of Nursing*** *Program availability:* Part-time, online learning. Electronic applications accepted.
***School of Occupational Therapy*** *Program availability:* Part-time, evening/weekend, online learning. Electronic applications accepted.
***School of Physiotherapy*** Electronic applications accepted.
***School of Social Work*** *Program availability:* Part-time, online learning. Electronic applications accepted.
**Faculty of Management** *Program availability:* Part-time. Electronic applications accepted.
***Centre for Advanced Management Education*** *Program availability:* Part-time, online learning. Electronic applications accepted.
***Rowe School of Business*** *Program availability:* Part-time. Electronic applications accepted.
***School for Resource and Environmental Studies*** *Program availability:* Part-time. Electronic applications accepted.
***School of Information Management*** *Program availability:* Part-time. Electronic applications accepted.
***School of Public Administration*** *Program availability:* Part-time. Electronic applications accepted.
**Faculty of Medicine** Electronic applications accepted.
**Faculty of Science** Electronic applications accepted.

## DALLAS BAPTIST UNIVERSITY, Dallas, TX 75211-9299

**General Information** Independent-religious, coed, comprehensive institution. *Enrollment:* 4,487 graduate, professional, and undergraduate students; 695 full-time matriculated graduate/professional students (432 women), 904 part-time matriculated graduate/professional students (561 women). *Enrollment by degree level:* 1,310 master's, 289 doctoral. *Graduate faculty:* 81 full-time (32 women), 194 part-time/adjunct (83 women). *Tuition:* Full-time $18,072; part-time $1004 per credit hour. *Required fees:* $1100; $550 per semester. Tuition and fees vary according to course level and degree level. *Graduate housing:* Room and/or apartments available on a first-come, first-served basis to single students; on-campus housing not available to married students. Typical cost: $4015 per year ($8226 including board). Room and board charges vary according to board plan and housing facility selected. *Student services:* Campus employment opportunities, campus safety program, career counseling, free psychological counseling, international student services, low-cost health insurance, services for students with disabilities, writing training. *Library facilities:* Vance Memorial Library plus 3 others. *Collection:* Books: 250,441 (physical), 151,333 (digital/electronic); Serial titles: 582 (physical), 48,819 (digital/electronic); Databases: 203. Weekly public service hours: 108.

**Computer facilities:** 214 computers available on campus for general student use. A campuswide network can be accessed. Online class registration is available.
Website: http://www.dbu.edu/

**General Application Contact:** Richard Nassar, Assistant VP for Graduate Affairs, 214-333-6801, Fax: 214-333-5579, E-mail: graduate@dbu.edu.

**GRADUATE UNITS**

**College of Business** Expenses: Contact institution. *Program availability:* Part-time, evening/weekend, online learning. *Application deadline:* Applications are processed on a rolling basis. Electronic applications accepted. *Application Contact:* Dr. Sandra Reid, Chair of Graduate Business Programs, 214-333-6860, E-mail: sandra@dbu.edu. *Dean*, Dr. Jeff Johnson, 214-333-5759, E-mail: graduate@dbu.edu.

**College of Fine Arts** Expenses: Contact institution. *Program availability:* Part-time, evening/weekend. *Application fee:* $25. *Application Contact:* Carter Willis, Program Director, 214-333-5867, E-mail: carterw@dbu.edu. *Dean*, Dr. Wes Moore, 214-333-5316, E-mail: wesm@dbu.edu.

**College of Humanities and Social Sciences** Expenses: Contact institution. *Application Contact:* Dr. Mary Becerril, Program Director, 214-333-5265, Fax: 214-333-6819, E-mail: maryb@dbu.edu. *Dean*, Dr. Rob Sullivan, 214-333-5238.

**Dorothy M. Bush College of Education** Expenses: Contact institution. *Program availability:* Part-time, evening/weekend, online learning. *Application deadline:* Applications are processed on a rolling basis. *Application fee:* $25. Electronic applications accepted. *Application Contact:* Dr. DeAnna Jenkins, Dean, 214-333-5413, E-mail: graduate@dbu.edu. *Dean*, Dr. DeAnna Jenkins, 214-333-5413, E-mail: graduate@dbu.edu.

**Gary Cook School of Leadership** Expenses: Contact institution. *Program availability:* Part-time, evening/weekend. *Application deadline:* Applications are processed on a rolling basis. *Application fee:* $25. Electronic applications accepted. *Application Contact:* Dr. Jack Goodyear, Dean, 214-333-5595, Fax: 214-333-6955, E-mail: jackg@dbu.edu. *Dean*, Dr. Jack Goodyear, 214-333-5595, Fax: 214-333-6955, E-mail: jackg@dbu.edu.

**Graduate School of Ministry** Expenses: Contact institution. *Program availability:* Part-time, evening/weekend, online learning. *Application deadline:* Applications are processed on a rolling basis. *Application fee:* $25. Electronic applications accepted. *Application Contact:* Dr. Shelly Melia, Associate Dean, 214-333-5943, Fax: 214-333-5673, E-mail: shelly@dbu.edu. *Dean*, Dr. Robert R. Brooks, 214-333-5390, Fax: 214-333-5673, E-mail: bobb@dbu.edu.

**Liberal Arts Program** Expenses: Contact institution. *Program availability:* Part-time, evening/weekend, online learning. *Application deadline:* Applications are processed on a rolling basis. *Application fee:* $25. Electronic applications accepted. *Application Contact:* Jared Ingram, Director, 214-333-5584, E-mail: jaredi@dbu.edu. *Director*, Jared Ingram, 214-333-5584, E-mail: jaredi@dbu.edu.

**Professional Development Program** Expenses: Contact institution. *Program availability:* Part-time, evening/weekend, online learning. *Application deadline:* Applications are processed on a rolling basis. *Application fee:* $25. Electronic applications accepted. *Application Contact:* Jared Ingram, Program Director, 214-333-5584, E-mail: jaredi@dbu.edu. *Program Director*, Jared Ingram, 214-333-5584, E-mail: jaredi@dbu.edu.

## DALLAS INTERNATIONAL UNIVERSITY, Dallas, TX 75236

**General Information** Independent, coed, comprehensive institution.

**GRADUATE UNITS**

**Graduate Programs** *Program availability:* Part-time. Electronic applications accepted.

## DALLAS THEOLOGICAL SEMINARY, Dallas, TX 75204-6499

**General Information** Independent, coed, graduate-only institution. *Graduate housing:* Rooms and/or apartments available on a first-come, first-served basis to single and married students.

**GRADUATE UNITS**

**Graduate Programs** *Program availability:* Part-time, online learning. Electronic applications accepted.

## DANIEL MORGAN GRADUATE SCHOOL OF NATIONAL SECURITY, Washington, DC 20036

**General Information** Independent, coed, graduate-only institution.

**GRADUATE UNITS**

**Graduate Programs**

## DAOIST TRADITIONS COLLEGE OF CHINESE MEDICAL ARTS, Asheville, NC 28801

**General Information** Proprietary, coed, graduate-only institution.

**GRADUATE UNITS**

**Graduate Programs**

## DARTMOUTH COLLEGE, Hanover, NH 03755

**General Information** Independent, coed, university. CGS member. *Graduate housing:* Rooms and/or apartments available on a first-come, first-served basis to single and married students. Housing application deadline: 5/15.

**GRADUATE UNITS**

**Dartmouth Engineering - Thayer School of Engineering** Students: 219 full-time (75 women); includes 25 minority (2 Black or African American, non-Hispanic/Latino; 14 Asian, non-Hispanic/Latino; 4 Hispanic/Latino; 5 Two or more races, non-Hispanic/Latino), 124 international. Average age 26. 698 applicants, 22% accepted, 86 enrolled. *Faculty:* 54 full-time (10 women), 17 part-time/adjunct (2 women). Expenses: Contact institution. *Financial support:* In 2019–20, 27 fellowships with full tuition reimbursements (averaging $28,320 per year), 81 research assistantships with full tuition reimbursements (averaging $28,320 per year), 13 teaching assistantships with partial tuition reimbursements (averaging $8,640 per year) were awarded; career-related internships or fieldwork, institutionally sponsored loans, scholarships/grants, and tuition waivers (full and partial) also available. Financial award application deadline: 2/15; financial award applicants required to submit CSS PROFILE. In 2019, 65 master's, 22 doctorates awarded. *Application deadline:* For fall admission, 1/1 priority date for domestic and international students. Applications are processed on a rolling basis. *Application fee:* $45. Electronic applications accepted. *Application Contact:* Candace S. Potter, Graduate Admissions & Financial Aid Administrator, 603-646-3844, Fax: 603-646-1620, E-mail: candace.s.potter@dartmouth.edu. *Dean*, Dr. Alexis R. Abramson, 603-646-2238, Fax: 603-646-2580, E-mail: Alexis.R.Abramson@Dartmouth.edu.

**The Dartmouth Institute** *Program availability:* Part-time.
**Geisel School of Medicine** Electronic applications accepted.
**Guarini School of Graduate and Advanced Studies** Electronic applications accepted.
***Institute for Quantitative Biomedical Sciences*** Electronic applications accepted.
**Program in Experimental and Molecular Medicine** Electronic applications accepted.
**Tuck School of Business at Dartmouth** Electronic applications accepted.

## DAVENPORT UNIVERSITY, Grand Rapids, MI 49512

**General Information** Independent, coed, comprehensive institution. *Graduate housing:* Room and/or apartments available on a first-come, first-served basis to single students; on-campus housing not available to married students. *Research affiliation:* Human Synergistic Center for Applied Research, Inc. (leadership, organizational culture, strategy).

**GRADUATE UNITS**

**Sneden Graduate School** *Program availability:* Evening/weekend. Electronic applications accepted.

## DEFIANCE COLLEGE, Defiance, OH 43512-1610

**General Information** Independent-religious, coed, comprehensive institution. *Graduate housing:* On-campus housing not available.

**GRADUATE UNITS**

**Program in Business Administration** *Program availability:* Part-time, evening/weekend. Electronic applications accepted.

**Program in Education** *Program availability:* Part-time-only. Electronic applications accepted.

## DELAWARE STATE UNIVERSITY, Dover, DE 19901-2277

**General Information** State-supported, coed, university. *Graduate housing:* Room and/or apartments available on a first-come, first-served basis to single students; on-campus housing not available to married students.

**GRADUATE UNITS**

**Graduate Programs** *Program availability:* Part-time, evening/weekend.
***College of Business*** *Program availability:* Part-time, evening/weekend. Electronic applications accepted.
***College of Education, Health and Public Policy*** *Program availability:* Part-time, evening/weekend. Electronic applications accepted.

## DELAWARE VALLEY UNIVERSITY, Doylestown, PA 18901-2697

**General Information** Independent, coed, comprehensive institution. *Graduate housing:* On-campus housing not available.

**GRADUATE UNITS**

**MBA Program** *Program availability:* Part-time, evening/weekend, online learning. Electronic applications accepted.

**Program in Counseling Psychology**

**Program in Criminal Justice**

**Program in Educational Leadership** *Program availability:* Part-time, evening/weekend.

## DELL'ARTE INTERNATIONAL SCHOOL OF PHYSICAL THEATRE, Blue Lake, CA 95525

**General Information** Independent, coed, graduate-only institution. *Graduate housing:* Rooms and/or apartments available on a first-come, first-served basis to single and married students.

**GRADUATE UNITS**

**MFA Program** Electronic applications accepted.

## DELTA STATE UNIVERSITY, Cleveland, MS 38733-0001

**General Information** State-supported, coed, comprehensive institution. *Enrollment:* 3,751 graduate, professional, and undergraduate students; 256 full-time matriculated graduate/professional students (169 women), 368 part-time matriculated graduate/professional students (245 women). *Enrollment by degree level:* 549 master's, 74 doctoral, 1 other advanced degree. *Graduate faculty:* 71 full-time (43 women), 25 part-time/adjunct (15 women). *International tuition:* $7501 full-time. *Tuition, area resident:* Full-time $7501; part-time $417 per credit hour. Tuition, state resident: full-time $7501; part-time $417 per credit hour. Tuition, nonresident: full-time $7501; part-time $417 per credit hour. *Required fees:* $170; $9.45 per credit hour. $9.45 per semester. *Graduate housing:* Rooms and/or apartments available on a first-come, first-served basis to single and married students. Typical cost: $4530 per year ($7908 including board) for single students; $4710 per year ($11,466 including board) for married students. Room and board charges vary according to board plan and housing facility selected. *Student services:* Campus employment opportunities, campus safety program, career counseling, exercise/wellness program, free psychological counseling, grant writing training, international student services, services for students with disabilities, teacher training, writing training. *Library facilities:* Roberts-LaForge Library plus 1 other. *Collection:* Books: 327,724 (physical), 72,046 (digital/electronic); Serial titles: 920 (physical), 24,376 (digital/electronic); Databases: 83. Weekly public service hours: 75; students can reserve study rooms.

**Computer facilities:** Computer purchase and lease plans are available. 533 computers available on campus for general student use. A campuswide network can be accessed. Online class registration is available.
Website: http://www.deltastate.edu/

**General Application Contact:** Cayce Friesenhahn, Coordinator of Graduate Admissions, 662-846-4875, Fax: 662-846-4313, E-mail: cfriesenhahn@deltastate.edu.

**GRADUATE UNITS**

**Graduate Programs** *Program availability:* Part-time, evening/weekend, 100% online, blended/hybrid learning. Electronic applications accepted.

***College of Arts and Sciences*** *Program availability:* Part-time.

***College of Business*** *Program availability:* Part-time, evening/weekend, online learning.

***College of Education*** *Program availability:* Part-time, evening/weekend.

***Robert E. Smith School of Nursing*** *Program availability:* Part-time. Electronic applications accepted.

## DENVER SEMINARY, Littleton, CO 80120

**General Information** Independent-religious, coed, graduate-only institution. *Graduate housing:* Rooms and/or apartments available on a first-come, first-served basis to single and married students. Housing application deadline: 6/1.

**GRADUATE UNITS**

**Graduate and Professional Programs** *Program availability:* Part-time, evening/weekend, online learning. Electronic applications accepted.

## DEPAUL UNIVERSITY, Chicago, IL 60604-2287

**General Information** Independent-religious, coed, university. CGS member. *Graduate housing:* Room and/or apartments available on a first-come, first-served basis to single students; on-campus housing not available to married students. *Research affiliation:* Civic Federation (public services), Metro Chicago Information Center (public services), International Institute of Higher Studies in the Criminal Sciences (law).

**GRADUATE UNITS**

**College of Communication** *Program availability:* Part-time, evening/weekend. Electronic applications accepted.

**College of Computing and Digital Media** *Program availability:* Part-time, evening/weekend, online learning. Electronic applications accepted.

**College of Education** *Program availability:* Part-time, evening/weekend, online learning. Electronic applications accepted.

**College of Law** *Program availability:* Part-time, evening/weekend. Electronic applications accepted.

**College of Liberal Arts and Social Sciences** *Program availability:* Part-time, evening/weekend, online learning. Electronic applications accepted.

**College of Science and Health** Electronic applications accepted.

**Kellstadt Graduate School of Business** *Program availability:* Part-time, evening/weekend, online learning. Electronic applications accepted.

**School for New Learning** *Program availability:* Part-time, evening/weekend. Electronic applications accepted.

**School of Music** *Program availability:* Part-time, evening/weekend. Electronic applications accepted.

**The Theatre School** Electronic applications accepted.

## DEREE - THE AMERICAN COLLEGE OF GREECE, GR-153-42 Aghia Paraskevi, Athens, Greece

**General Information** Independent, coed, comprehensive institution. *Library facilities:* John S. Bailey Library plus 1 other. *Collection:* Books: 120,714 (physical), 394,458 (digital/electronic). Weekly public service hours: 72; students can reserve study rooms.

**Computer facilities:** A campuswide network can be accessed. Online class registration, learning management system are available.
Website: http://www.acg.edu/

**GRADUATE UNITS**

**Graduate Programs**

## DESALES UNIVERSITY, Center Valley, PA 18034-9568

**General Information** Independent-religious, coed, comprehensive institution. *Enrollment:* 3,460 graduate, professional, and undergraduate students; 430 full-time matriculated graduate/professional students (299 women), 538 part-time matriculated graduate/professional students (334 women). *Enrollment by degree level:* 874 master's, 88 doctoral, 17 other advanced degrees. *Graduate faculty:* 30 full-time (20 women), 54 part-time/adjunct (21 women). *Tuition:* Full-time $855; part-time $855 per credit hour. Tuition and fees vary according to program. *Graduate housing:* Room and/or apartments available on a first-come, first-served basis to single students; on-campus housing not available to married students. Typical cost: $13,000 (including board). Housing application deadline: 3/15. *Student services:* Campus safety program, career counseling, free psychological counseling, international student services, low-cost health insurance, multicultural affairs office, services for students with disabilities, teacher training. *Library facilities:* Trexler Library. *Collection:* Books: 110,400 (physical), 190,317 (digital/electronic); Serial titles: 155 (physical), 17,260 (digital/electronic); Databases: 52. Weekly public service hours: 102; students can reserve study rooms.

**Computer facilities:** 245 computers available on campus for general student use. A campuswide network can be accessed. Online class registration is available.
Website: http://www.desales.edu/

**General Application Contact:** Julia Ferraro, Director of Graduate Admissions, 610-282-1100 Ext. 1768, E-mail: gradadmissions@desales.edu.

**GRADUATE UNITS**

**Division of Business** Students: 66 full-time (37 women), 278 part-time (149 women); includes 70 minority (18 Black or African American, non-Hispanic/Latino; 1 American Indian or Alaska Native, non-Hispanic/Latino; 14 Asian, non-Hispanic/Latino; 29 Hispanic/Latino; 8 Two or more races, non-Hispanic/Latino), 2 international. Average age 35. 242 applicants, 60% accepted, 143 enrolled. *Faculty:* 16 full-time (9 women), 21 part-time/adjunct (6 women). Expenses: Contact institution. *Financial support:* Applicants required to submit FAFSA. In 2019, 108 master's awarded. *Program availability:* Part-time, evening/weekend, 100% online, blended/hybrid learning. *Application deadline:* Applications are processed on a rolling basis. *Application fee:* $50. Electronic applications accepted. *Application Contact:* Julia Ferraro, Director of Graduate Admissions, 610-282-1100 Ext. 1768, E-mail: gradadmissions@desales.edu. *Division Head, Division of Business,* Dr. Christopher R. Cocozza, 610-282-1100 Ext. 1446, E-mail: Christopher.Cocozza@desales.edu.

**Division of Healthcare** Students: 294 full-time (219 women), 128 part-time (109 women); includes 71 minority (20 Black or African American, non-Hispanic/Latino; 1 American Indian or Alaska Native, non-Hispanic/Latino; 15 Asian, non-Hispanic/Latino; 30 Hispanic/Latino; 5 Two or more races, non-Hispanic/Latino). Average age 28. 2,666 applicants, 6% accepted, 142 enrolled. *Faculty:* 31 full-time (23 women), 12 part-time/adjunct (9 women). Expenses: Contact institution. *Financial support:* Applicants required to submit FAFSA. In 2019, 115 master's, 30 doctorates awarded. *Program availability:* Part-time. *Application deadline:* Applications are processed on a rolling basis. *Application fee:* $50. Electronic applications accepted. *Application Contact:* Julia Ferraro, Director of Graduate Admissions, 610-282-1100 Ext. 1768, E-mail: gradadmissions@desales.edu. *Dean of Graduate Education,* Ronald Nordone, 610-282-1100 Ext. 1289, E-mail: ronald.nordone@desales.edu.

**Division of Liberal Arts and Social Sciences** Students: 68 full-time (43 women), 115 part-time (72 women); includes 34 minority (8 Black or African American, non-Hispanic/Latino; 1 Asian, non-Hispanic/Latino; 19 Hispanic/Latino; 1 Native Hawaiian or other Pacific Islander, non-Hispanic/Latino; 5 Two or more races, non-Hispanic/Latino), 1 international. Average age 33. 135 applicants, 48% accepted, 63 enrolled. *Faculty:* 5 full-time (3 women), 15 part-time/adjunct (9 women). Expenses: Contact institution. *Financial support:* Applicants required to submit FAFSA. In 2019, 49 master's awarded. *Program availability:* Part-time, 100% online, blended/hybrid learning. *Application deadline:* Applications are processed on a rolling basis. *Application fee:* $50. Electronic applications accepted. *Application Contact:* Julia Ferraro, Director of Graduate Admissions, 610-282-1100 Ext. 1768, E-mail: gradadmissions@desales.edu. *Dean of Graduate Education,* Ronald Nordone, 610-282-1100 Ext. 1289, E-mail: ronald.nordone@desales.edu.

**Division of Science and Mathematics** Students: 2 full-time (0 women), 17 part-time (4 women); includes 3 minority (2 Asian, non-Hispanic/Latino; 1 Two or more races, non-Hispanic/Latino). Average age 36. 15 applicants, 60% accepted, 9 enrolled. *Faculty:* 2 full-time (both women), 5 part-time/adjunct (1 woman). Expenses: Contact institution. *Financial support:* Applicants required to submit FAFSA. In 2019, 6 master's awarded. *Program availability:* Part-time, evening/weekend, 100% online, blended/hybrid learning. *Application deadline:* Applications are processed on a rolling basis. *Application fee:* $50. Electronic applications accepted. *Application Contact:* Julia Ferraro, Director of Graduate Admissions, 610-282-1100 Ext. 1768, E-mail: gradadmissions@desales.edu. *Dean of Graduate Studies,* Dr. Ronald Nordone, 610-282-1100 Ext. 1289, E-mail: Ronald.Nordone@desale.edu.

## DES MOINES UNIVERSITY, Des Moines, IA 50312-4104

**General Information** Independent, coed, graduate-only institution. *Graduate housing:* On-campus housing not available.

**GRADUATE UNITS**

**College of Health Sciences** *Program availability:* Part-time, evening/weekend. Electronic applications accepted.

**College of Osteopathic Medicine** Electronic applications accepted.

**College of Podiatric Medicine and Surgery** Electronic applications accepted.

## DEVRY COLLEGE OF NEW YORK–MIDTOWN MANHATTAN CAMPUS, New York, NY 10016

**General Information** Proprietary, coed, comprehensive institution.

**GRADUATE UNITS**

**Keller Graduate School of Management**

## DEVRY UNIVERSITY–ALPHARETTA CAMPUS, Alpharetta, GA 30009

**General Information** Proprietary, coed, comprehensive institution.

**GRADUATE UNITS**

**Keller Graduate School of Management**

**DEVRY UNIVERSITY–ARLINGTON CAMPUS, Arlington, VA 22202**
**General Information** Proprietary, coed, comprehensive institution.
**GRADUATE UNITS**
**Keller Graduate School of Management**

**DEVRY UNIVERSITY–CHARLOTTE CAMPUS, Charlotte, NC 28273**
**General Information** Proprietary, coed, comprehensive institution.
**GRADUATE UNITS**
**Keller Graduate School of Management**

**DEVRY UNIVERSITY–CHESAPEAKE CAMPUS, Chesapeake, VA 23320**
**General Information** Proprietary, coed, comprehensive institution.
**GRADUATE UNITS**
**Keller Graduate School of Management**

**DEVRY UNIVERSITY–CHICAGO CAMPUS, Chicago, IL 60618**
**General Information** Proprietary, coed, comprehensive institution.
**GRADUATE UNITS**
**Keller Graduate School of Management**

**DEVRY UNIVERSITY–CHICAGO LOOP CAMPUS, Chicago, IL 60606**
**General Information** Proprietary, coed, comprehensive institution.
**GRADUATE UNITS**
**Keller Graduate School of Management**

**DEVRY UNIVERSITY–CINCINNATI CAMPUS, Cincinnati, OH 45249**
**General Information** Proprietary, coed, comprehensive institution.
**GRADUATE UNITS**
**Keller Graduate School of Management**

**DEVRY UNIVERSITY–COLUMBUS CAMPUS, Columbus, OH 43209**
**General Information** Proprietary, coed, comprehensive institution.
**GRADUATE UNITS**
**Keller Graduate School of Management**

**DEVRY UNIVERSITY–DECATUR CAMPUS, Decatur, GA 30030**
**General Information** Proprietary, coed, comprehensive institution.
**GRADUATE UNITS**
**Keller Graduate School of Management**

**DEVRY UNIVERSITY–FOLSOM CAMPUS, Folsom, CA 95630**
**General Information** Proprietary, coed, comprehensive institution.
**GRADUATE UNITS**
**Graduate Programs**

**DEVRY UNIVERSITY–FREMONT CAMPUS, Fremont, CA 94555**
**General Information** Proprietary, coed, comprehensive institution.
**GRADUATE UNITS**
**Keller Graduate School of Management**

**DEVRY UNIVERSITY–FT. WASHINGTON CAMPUS, Fort Washington, PA 19034**
**General Information** Proprietary, coed, comprehensive institution.
**GRADUATE UNITS**
**Keller Graduate School of Management**

**DEVRY UNIVERSITY–HENDERSON CAMPUS, Henderson, NV 89074**
**General Information** Proprietary, coed, comprehensive institution.
**GRADUATE UNITS**
**Keller Graduate School of Management**

**DEVRY UNIVERSITY–IRVING CAMPUS, Irving, TX 75063**
**General Information** Proprietary, coed, comprehensive institution.
**GRADUATE UNITS**
**Keller Graduate School of Management**

**DEVRY UNIVERSITY–JACKSONVILLE CAMPUS, Jacksonville, FL 32256**
**General Information** Proprietary, coed, comprehensive institution.
**GRADUATE UNITS**
**Keller Graduate School of Management**

**DEVRY UNIVERSITY–LONG BEACH CAMPUS, Long Beach, CA 90806**
**General Information** Proprietary, coed, comprehensive institution.
**GRADUATE UNITS**
**Keller Graduate School of Management**

**DEVRY UNIVERSITY–MIRAMAR CAMPUS, Miramar, FL 33027**
**General Information** Proprietary, coed, comprehensive institution.
**GRADUATE UNITS**
**Keller Graduate School of Management**

**DEVRY UNIVERSITY–MORRISVILLE CAMPUS, Morrisville, NC 27560**
**General Information** Proprietary, coed, comprehensive institution.
**GRADUATE UNITS**
**Keller Graduate School of Management**

**DEVRY UNIVERSITY–NASHVILLE CAMPUS, Nashville, TN 37211**
**General Information** Proprietary, coed, comprehensive institution.
**GRADUATE UNITS**
**Keller Graduate School of Management**

**DEVRY UNIVERSITY–NORTH BRUNSWICK CAMPUS, North Brunswick, NJ 08902**
**General Information** Proprietary, coed, comprehensive institution.
**GRADUATE UNITS**
**Keller Graduate School of Management**

**DEVRY UNIVERSITY ONLINE, Addison, IL 60101**
**General Information** Proprietary, coed, comprehensive institution.
**GRADUATE UNITS**
**Keller Graduate School of Management**

**DEVRY UNIVERSITY–ORLANDO CAMPUS, Orlando, FL 32819**
**General Information** Proprietary, coed, comprehensive institution.
**GRADUATE UNITS**
**Keller Graduate School of Management**

**DEVRY UNIVERSITY–PHOENIX CAMPUS, Phoenix, AZ 85021**
**General Information** Proprietary, coed, comprehensive institution.
**GRADUATE UNITS**
**Keller Graduate School of Management**

**DEVRY UNIVERSITY–POMONA CAMPUS, Pomona, CA 91768**
**General Information** Proprietary, coed, comprehensive institution.
**GRADUATE UNITS**
**Keller Graduate School of Management**

**DEVRY UNIVERSITY–SAN DIEGO CAMPUS, San Diego, CA 92108**
**General Information** Proprietary, coed, comprehensive institution.
**GRADUATE UNITS**
**Keller Graduate School of Management**

**DEVRY UNIVERSITY–SEVEN HILLS CAMPUS, Seven Hills, OH 44131**
**General Information** Proprietary, coed, comprehensive institution.
**GRADUATE UNITS**
**Keller Graduate School of Management**

**DEVRY UNIVERSITY–TINLEY PARK CAMPUS, Tinley Park, IL 60477**
**General Information** Proprietary, coed, comprehensive institution.
**GRADUATE UNITS**
**Keller Graduate School of Management**

**DICKINSON STATE UNIVERSITY, Dickinson, ND 58601-4896**
**General Information** State-supported, coed, comprehensive institution. *Enrollment:* 1,350 graduate, professional, and undergraduate students; 7 full-time matriculated graduate/professional students (6 women), 22 part-time matriculated graduate/professional students (12 women). *Enrollment by degree level:* 27 master's. *Graduate faculty:* 4 full-time (3 women), 1 (woman) part-time/adjunct. *International tuition:* $8417 full-time. *Tuition, area resident:* Full-time $8417; part-time $323.72 per credit hour. Tuition, state resident: full-time $8417; part-time $323.72 per credit hour. Tuition, nonresident: full-time $8417; part-time $323.72 per credit hour. *Required fees:* $12.54; $12.54 per credit hour. *Graduate housing:* Room and/or apartments available on a first-come, first-served basis to single students; on-campus housing not available to married students. Typical cost: $3448 per year ($7686 including board). Room and board charges vary according to board plan, campus/location and housing facility selected. Housing application deadline: 7/1. *Student services:* Campus employment opportunities, campus safety program, career counseling, exercise/wellness program, grant writing training, international student services, multicultural affairs office, services for students with disabilities, writing training. *Library facilities:* Stoxen Library plus 1 other. *Collection:* Books: 73,995 (physical), 26,601 (digital/electronic); Serial titles: 282 (physical), 126,440 (digital/electronic); Databases: 91. Weekly public service hours: 56.

**Computer facilities:** 274 computers available on campus for general student use. A campuswide network can be accessed. Online class registration is available. Website: http://www.dickinsonstate.edu/

**General Application Contact:** Megan Robinson, Assistant Director, 701-483-2164, E-mail: megan.robinson@dickinsonstate.edu.

**GRADUATE UNITS**
**Department of Teacher Education** *Program availability:* Part-time, blended/hybrid learning. Electronic applications accepted.

**DIGIPEN INSTITUTE OF TECHNOLOGY, Redmond, WA 98052**
**General Information** Proprietary, coed, comprehensive institution. *Enrollment:* 1,173 graduate, professional, and undergraduate students; 61 full-time matriculated graduate/professional students (13 women), 29 part-time matriculated graduate/professional students (6 women). *Enrollment by degree level:* 90 master's. *Tuition:* Full-time $27,000; part-time $1125 per credit. *Required fees:* $200; $200 per unit. *Graduate housing:* Room and/or apartments available on a first-come, first-served basis to single students; on-campus housing not available to married students. Housing application deadline: 7/16. *Student services:* Campus employment opportunities, career counseling, free psychological counseling, international student services, multicultural affairs office, services for students with disabilities. *Library facilities:* DigiPen Library. *Collection:* Books: 5,045 (physical), 239,473 (digital/electronic); Serial titles: 457 (physical), 7,111 (digital/electronic); Databases: 15. Weekly public service hours: 84. *Research affiliation:* NorthWest Research Associates (NWRA) (atmospheric modeling), Andretti Autosport (software development), Boeing (simulations), Lotus Formula 1 (software development).

**Computer facilities:** 1,068 computers available on campus for general student use. A campuswide network can be accessed. Online class registration is available. Website: http://www.digipen.edu/

**General Application Contact:** Emily Kirby, Director of Admissions, 425-629-4862, Fax: 425-558-0378, E-mail: ekirby@digipen.edu.

**GRADUATE UNITS**
**Graduate Programs** *Program availability:* Part-time. Electronic applications accepted.

## DIVINE MERCY UNIVERSITY, Arlington, VA 30327

**General Information** Independent-religious, coed, graduate-only institution.

**GRADUATE UNITS**

**Institute for the Psychological Sciences** *Program availability:* Part-time.

**School of Counseling** *Program availability:* Online learning.

## DOANE UNIVERSITY, Crete, NE 68333-2430

**General Information** Independent-religious, coed, comprehensive institution. *Enrollment:* 506 full-time matriculated graduate/professional students (349 women), 565 part-time matriculated graduate/professional students (440 women). *Enrollment by degree level:* 943 master's, 86 doctoral, 42 other advanced degrees. *Graduate faculty:* 15 full-time (10 women), 102 part-time/adjunct (70 women). *Graduate housing:* On-campus housing not available. *Student services:* Career counseling, teacher training. *Library facilities:* Perkins Library plus 1 other. *Collection:* Study areas open 24 hours, 5–7 days a week; students can reserve study rooms.

**Computer facilities:** Computer purchase and lease plans are available. 250 computers available on campus for general student use. A campuswide network can be accessed. Online class registration is available.
Website: http://www.doane.edu/

**GRADUATE UNITS**

**Program in Counseling** *Program availability:* Evening/weekend. Electronic applications accepted.

**Program in Education** *Program availability:* Part-time, evening/weekend. Electronic applications accepted.

**Program in Management** *Program availability:* Part-time, evening/weekend. Electronic applications accepted.

## DOMINICAN COLLEGE, Orangeburg, NY 10962-1210

**General Information** Independent, coed, comprehensive institution. *Enrollment:* 1,868 graduate, professional, and undergraduate students; 201 full-time matriculated graduate/professional students (149 women), 290 part-time matriculated graduate/professional students (226 women). *Enrollment by degree level:* 275 master's, 216 doctoral. *Graduate faculty:* 24 full-time (14 women), 20 part-time/adjunct (16 women). *Tuition:* Part-time $965 per credit. *Required fees:* $200 per semester. One-time fee: $200. Tuition and fees vary according to course load, degree level and program. *Graduate housing:* Room and/or apartments available on a first-come, first-served basis to single students; on-campus housing not available to married students. Housing application deadline: 5/1. *Student services:* Campus employment opportunities, campus safety program, career counseling, free psychological counseling, services for students with disabilities, teacher training. *Library facilities:* Sullivan Library plus 1 other. *Collection:* Books: 74,226 (physical), 117,187 (digital/electronic); Serial titles: 610 (physical), 75,067 (digital/electronic); Databases: 85. Weekly public service hours: 89; students can reserve study rooms.

**Computer facilities:** 150 computers available on campus for general student use. A campuswide network can be accessed. Online class registration, Web portal, learning management system are available.
Website: http://www.dc.edu/

**General Application Contact:** Ashley Scales, Assistant Director of Graduate Admissions, 845-848-7908, Fax: 845-365-3150, E-mail: graduate.admissions@dc.edu.

**GRADUATE UNITS**

**Division of Allied Health** *Program availability:* Part-time, evening/weekend, online learning. Electronic applications accepted.

**Division of Nursing** Students: 29 full-time (24 women), 95 part-time (85 women); includes 71 minority (35 Black or African American, non-Hispanic/Latino; 17 Asian, non-Hispanic/Latino; 19 Hispanic/Latino). Average age 38. *Faculty:* 5 full-time (all women), 12 part-time/adjunct (8 women). Expenses: Contact institution. *Financial support:* Scholarships/grants available. Financial award application deadline: 1/1; financial award applicants required to submit FAFSA. In 2019, 36 master's, 10 doctorates awarded. *Program availability:* Part-time, evening/weekend. *Application deadline:* For fall admission, 3/29 priority date for domestic students; for summer admission, 12/15 priority date for domestic students. Applications are processed on a rolling basis. *Application fee:* $50. Electronic applications accepted. *Application Contact:* Ashley Scales, Assistant Director of Graduate Admissions, 845-848-7908, Fax: 845-365-3150, E-mail: admissions@dc.edu. *Director, Master of Science FNP and DNP Programs,* Dr. Lynne Weissman, 845-848-6026, Fax: 845-398-4891, E-mail: lynne.weissman@dc.edu.

**Division of Teacher Education** Students: 13 full-time (10 women), 55 part-time (51 women); includes 15 minority (4 Black or African American, non-Hispanic/Latino; 1 Asian, non-Hispanic/Latino; 9 Hispanic/Latino; 1 Two or more races, non-Hispanic/Latino). Average age 33. *Faculty:* 3 full-time (2 women), 5 part-time/adjunct (all women). Expenses: Contact institution. *Financial support:* Scholarships/grants available. Financial award application deadline: 1/1; financial award applicants required to submit FAFSA. In 2019, 24 master's awarded. *Program availability:* Part-time, evening/weekend. *Application deadline:* For fall admission, 8/1 for domestic students, 6/1 for international students. Applications are processed on a rolling basis. *Application fee:* $50. Electronic applications accepted. *Application Contact:* Ashley Scales, Assistant Director of Graduate Admissions, 845-848-7908 Ext. 15, Fax: 845-365-3150, E-mail: admissions@dc.edu. *Director,* Dr. Mike Kelly, 845-848-4090, Fax: 845-359-7802, E-mail: mike.kelly@dc.edu.

**Master's in Organizational Leadership** Students: 5 full-time (all women), 5 part-time (3 women); includes 5 minority (all Hispanic/Latino). Average age 36. *Faculty:* 5 full-time (3 women). Expenses: Contact institution. *Financial support:* Scholarships/grants available. Financial award application deadline: 1/1; financial award applicants required to submit FAFSA. *Program availability:* Part-time, online only, 100% online. *Application deadline:* Applications are processed on a rolling basis. *Application fee:* $50. Electronic applications accepted. *Application Contact:* Ashley Scales, Assistant Director of Graduate Admissions, 845-848-7908, Fax: 845-365-3150, E-mail: graduate.admissions@dc.edu.

**MBA Program** Students: 1 (woman) full-time, 15 part-time (11 women); includes 8 minority (3 Black or African American, non-Hispanic/Latino; 4 Hispanic/Latino; 1 Native Hawaiian or other Pacific Islander, non-Hispanic/Latino), 1 international. Average age 35. 28 applicants, 16 enrolled. *Faculty:* 3 full-time (1 woman), 4 part-time/adjunct (2 women). Expenses: Contact institution. *Financial support:* Scholarships/grants available. Financial award application deadline: 1/1; financial award applicants required to submit FAFSA. In 2019, 10 master's awarded. *Program availability:* Part-time, evening/weekend. *Application deadline:* Applications are processed on a rolling basis. *Application fee:* $50. Electronic applications accepted. *Application Contact:* Christina Lifshey, Assistant Director of Graduate Admissions, 845-848-7908, Fax: 845-365-3150, E-mail: admissions@dc.edu. *MBA Director,* Ken Mias, 845-848-4102, E-mail: ken.mias@dc.edu.

## DOMINICAN HOUSE OF STUDIES, PONTIFICAL FACULTY OF THE IMMACULATE CONCEPTION, Washington, DC 20017-1585

**General Information** Independent-religious, coed, primarily men, graduate-only institution. *Enrollment by degree level:* 90 master's. *Graduate faculty:* 19 full-time (1 woman), 2 part-time/adjunct (1 woman). *Graduate housing:* On-campus housing not available. *Student services:* Campus employment opportunities, career counseling, international student services. *Library facilities:* Dominican Theological Library. *Collection:* Books: 77,000 (physical); Serial titles: 219 (physical), 18 (digital/electronic); Databases: 6. Weekly public service hours: 61; students can reserve study rooms. *Research affiliation:* Washington Theological Consortium (theology, ecumenism), The Thomist (theology).

**Computer facilities:** 8 computers available on campus for general student use.
Website: http://www.dhs.edu/

**General Application Contact:** Audrey Quade, Registrar and Accreditation Liaison, 202-495-3836, Fax: 202-495-3873, E-mail: registrar@dhs.edu.

**GRADUATE UNITS**

**Graduate and Professional Programs in Theology** Students: 75 full-time (7 women), 9 part-time (3 women); includes 2 minority (both Asian, non-Hispanic/Latino), 13 international. Average age 33. 36 applicants, 100% accepted, 33 enrolled. *Faculty:* 18 full-time (1 woman), 6 part-time/adjunct (3 women). Expenses: Contact institution. *Financial support:* In 2019–20, 3 students received support. Career-related internships or fieldwork and Federal Work-Study available. Support available to part-time students. Financial award application deadline: 6/30; financial award applicants required to submit FAFSA. In 2019, 32 master's awarded. *Program availability:* Part-time. *Application deadline:* For fall admission, 7/1 for domestic and international students; for spring admission, 12/1 for domestic and international students. Applications are processed on a rolling basis. *Application fee:* $150. Electronic applications accepted. *Application Contact:* Audrey Quade, Registrar & Accreditation Liaison, 202-495-3836, Fax: 202-495-3873, E-mail: registrar@dhs.edu. *Vice-President/Academic Dean,* Rev. Thomas Petri, OP, 202-495-3832, Fax: 202-495-3873, E-mail: dean@dhs.edu.

## DOMINICAN SCHOOL OF PHILOSOPHY AND THEOLOGY, Berkeley, CA 94708

**General Information** Independent-religious, coed, graduate-only institution. *Graduate housing:* Rooms and/or apartments available on a first-come, first-served basis to single and married students. Housing application deadline: 5/1.

**GRADUATE UNITS**

**Graduate Programs** *Program availability:* Part-time. Electronic applications accepted.

## DOMINICAN UNIVERSITY, River Forest, IL 60305-1099

**General Information** Independent-religious, coed, comprehensive institution. *Enrollment:* 3,029 graduate, professional, and undergraduate students; 313 full-time matriculated graduate/professional students (257 women), 414 part-time matriculated graduate/professional students (305 women). *Enrollment by degree level:* 711 master's, 16 doctoral. *Graduate faculty:* 46 full-time (30 women), 84 part-time/adjunct (60 women). *Tuition:* Full-time $25,500; part-time $850 per credit. *Required fees:* $840; $23 per credit. $75 per term. One-time fee: $25. Tuition and fees vary according to degree level and program. *Graduate housing:* Room and/or apartments available on a first-come, first-served basis to single students; on-campus housing not available to married students. Typical cost: $5709 (including board). Room and board charges vary according to housing facility selected. Housing application deadline: 7/1. *Student services:* Campus employment opportunities, campus safety program, career counseling, child daycare facilities, exercise/wellness program, free psychological counseling, international student services, low-cost health insurance, multicultural affairs office, services for students with disabilities, teacher training, writing training. *Library facilities:* Rebecca Crown Library. *Collection:* Books: 247,967 (physical), 9,389 (digital/electronic); Serial titles: 280 (physical), 53,047 (digital/electronic); Databases: 114. Weekly public service hours: 100; students can reserve study rooms.

**Computer facilities:** Computer purchase and lease plans are available. 550 computers available on campus for general student use. A campuswide network can be accessed. Online class registration is available.
Website: http://www.dom.edu/

**General Application Contact:** Catherine Galarza-Espino, Coordinator of Graduate Marketing and Recruitment, 708-524-6983, E-mail: cgalarza@dom.edu.

**GRADUATE UNITS**

**Brennan School of Business** Students: 45 full-time (30 women), 52 part-time (29 women); includes 32 minority (6 Black or African American, non-Hispanic/Latino; 2 Asian, non-Hispanic/Latino; 23 Hispanic/Latino; 1 Two or more races, non-Hispanic/Latino), 15 international. Average age 29. 52 applicants, 96% accepted, 32 enrolled. *Faculty:* 20 full-time (10 women), 15 part-time/adjunct (4 women). Expenses: Contact institution. *Financial support:* Research assistantships, career-related internships or fieldwork, scholarships/grants, tuition waivers (partial), and unspecified assistantships available. Financial award application deadline: 3/1; financial award applicants required to submit FAFSA. In 2019, 82 master's awarded. *Program availability:* Part-time, evening/weekend, 100% online, blended/hybrid learning. *Application deadline:* Applications are processed on a rolling basis. *Application fee:* $25. Electronic applications accepted. *Application Contact:* Dr. Kathleen Odell, Associate Dean, Brennan School of Business, 708-488-5394, Fax: 708-524-6939, E-mail: kodell@dom.edu. *Dean,* Dr. Roberto Curci, 708-524-6321, Fax: 708-524-6939, E-mail: rcurci@dom.edu.

**School of Education** *Program availability:* Part-time, evening/weekend, 100% online, blended/hybrid learning.

**School of Information Studies** Students: 56 full-time (44 women), 162 part-time (121 women); includes 60 minority (22 Black or African American, non-Hispanic/Latino; 7 Asian, non-Hispanic/Latino; 30 Hispanic/Latino; 1 Two or more races, non-Hispanic/Latino), 4 international. Average age 32. 87 applicants, 100% accepted, 67 enrolled. Expenses: Contact institution. *Financial support:* Fellowships, research assistantships, career-related internships or fieldwork, scholarships/grants, and unspecified assistantships available. Support available to part-time students. Financial award application deadline: 4/15; financial award applicants required to submit FAFSA. In 2019, 84 master's, 1 doctorate awarded. *Program availability:* Part-time, evening/weekend, 100% online, blended/hybrid learning. *Application deadline:* For fall admission, 6/1 priority date for domestic students; for winter admission, 3/1 priority date for domestic students; for spring admission, 10/1 priority date for domestic students. Applications are processed on a rolling basis. *Application fee:* $25. *Application Contact:*

Catherine Galarza-Espino, Coordinator of Graduate Marketing and Recruiting, 708-524-6983, E-mail: cgalarza@dom.edu. *Director*, Dr. Kate Marek, 708-524-6648, Fax: 708-524-6657, E-mail: kmarek@dom.edu.

**School of Social Work** *Program availability:* Part-time. Electronic applications accepted.

## DOMINICAN UNIVERSITY OF CALIFORNIA, San Rafael, CA 94901-2298

**General Information** Independent-religious, coed, comprehensive institution. *Enrollment:* 1,879 graduate, professional, and undergraduate students; 307 full-time matriculated graduate/professional students (244 women), 108 part-time matriculated graduate/professional students (83 women). *Enrollment by degree level:* 415 master's. *Graduate faculty:* 45 full-time (26 women), 33 part-time/adjunct (22 women). *Required fees:* $360 per semester. Tuition and fees vary according to course load and program. *Graduate housing:* On-campus housing not available. *Student services:* Campus employment opportunities, career counseling, exercise/wellness program, free psychological counseling, international student services, low-cost health insurance, services for students with disabilities. *Library facilities:* Archbishop Alemany Library. *Collection:* Books: 118,725 (physical), 2 million (digital/electronic); Serial titles: 85 (physical), 45,000 (digital/electronic); Databases: 86.

**Computer facilities:** 195 computers available on campus for general student use. A campuswide network can be accessed. Online class registration, office software are available.
Website: http://www.dominican.edu/

**General Application Contact:** Graduate Admissions, 415-485-3280, Fax: 415-485-3214, E-mail: gradmissions@dominican.edu.

**GRADUATE UNITS**

**Barowsky School of Business** Students: 18 full-time (8 women), 30 part-time (20 women); includes 20 minority (2 Black or African American, non-Hispanic/Latino; 6 Asian, non-Hispanic/Latino; 8 Hispanic/Latino; 4 Two or more races, non-Hispanic/Latino), 3 international. Average age 34. 34 applicants, 94% accepted, 23 enrolled. *Faculty:* 9 full-time (2 women), 2 part-time/adjunct (0 women). Expenses: Contact institution. *Financial support:* Scholarships/grants available. Support available to part-time students. Financial award application deadline: 3/2; financial award applicants required to submit FAFSA. In 2019, 29 master's awarded. *Program availability:* Part-time, evening/weekend. *Application deadline:* For fall admission, 5/15 priority date for domestic and international students; for spring admission, 11/15 priority date for domestic and international students. Applications are processed on a rolling basis. Electronic applications accepted. *Application Contact:* Office of Graduate Admissions, 415-485-3280, Fax: 415-485-3214, E-mail: graduate@dominican.edu. *Dean*, Yung-Jae Lee, 415-458-3786, E-mail: yung-jae.lee@dominican.edu.

**Programs in Education plus Teacher Preparation** *Program availability:* Part-time, evening/weekend. Electronic applications accepted.

**School of Health and Natural Sciences** Students: 264 full-time (217 women), 31 part-time (26 women); includes 132 minority (9 Black or African American, non-Hispanic/Latino; 2 American Indian or Alaska Native, non-Hispanic/Latino; 58 Asian, non-Hispanic/Latino; 51 Hispanic/Latino; 1 Native Hawaiian or other Pacific Islander, non-Hispanic/Latino; 11 Two or more races, non-Hispanic/Latino), 4 international. Average age 31. 757 applicants, 22% accepted, 105 enrolled. *Faculty:* 24 full-time (16 women), 23 part-time/adjunct (17 women). Expenses: Contact institution. *Financial support:* Career-related internships or fieldwork and scholarships/grants available. Financial award application deadline: 3/2; financial award applicants required to submit FAFSA. In 2019, 80 master's awarded. *Application deadline:* For fall admission, 3/15 for domestic and international students. Applications are processed on a rolling basis. Electronic applications accepted. *Application Contact:* Allyse Rudolph, Associate Director of Graduate Admissions, 415-585-3221, Fax: 415-485-3214, E-mail: graduate@dominican.edu. *Dean*, Dr. Ruth Ramsey, 415-257-1393, E-mail: ruth.ramsey@dominican.edu.

**School of Liberal Arts and Education** Students: 25 full-time (19 women), 47 part-time (37 women); includes 19 minority (1 Black or African American, non-Hispanic/Latino; 6 Asian, non-Hispanic/Latino; 6 Hispanic/Latino; 6 Two or more races, non-Hispanic/Latino). Average age 37. 35 applicants, 57% accepted, 15 enrolled. *Faculty:* 4 full-time (2 women), 1 (woman) part-time/adjunct. Expenses: Contact institution. *Financial support:* Scholarships/grants available. Support available to part-time students. Financial award application deadline: 3/2; financial award applicants required to submit FAFSA. In 2019, 39 master's awarded. *Program availability:* Part-time, evening/weekend. *Application deadline:* For fall admission, 5/15 for domestic and international students; for spring admission, 11/15 for domestic and international students. Applications are processed on a rolling basis. Electronic applications accepted. *Application Contact:* Allyse Rudolph, Associate Director of Graduate Admissions, 415-585-3221, E-mail: graduate@dominican.edu. *Dean*, Gigi Gokcek, 415-482-2427, E-mail: gigi.gokcek@dominican.edu.

## DONGGUK UNIVERSITY LOS ANGELES, Los Angeles, CA 90020

**General Information** Independent, coed, graduate-only institution. *Graduate housing:* On-campus housing not available.

**GRADUATE UNITS**

**Program in Oriental Medicine** *Program availability:* Part-time, evening/weekend.

## DORDT UNIVERSITY, Sioux Center, IA 51250-1697

**General Information** Independent-religious, coed, comprehensive institution. *Graduate housing:* Rooms and/or apartments available to single and married students.

**GRADUATE UNITS**

**Program in Education** *Program availability:* Part-time, online learning. Electronic applications accepted.

## DRAGON RISES COLLEGE OF ORIENTAL MEDICINE, Gainesville, FL 32601

**General Information** Proprietary, coed, graduate-only institution. *Enrollment by degree level:* 29 master's. *Graduate faculty:* 1 full-time (0 women), 12 part-time/adjunct (7 women). *Tuition:* Full-time $11,200. *Required fees:* $460. *Graduate housing:* On-campus housing not available. *Student services:* Career counseling, exercise/wellness program, free psychological counseling. *Library facilities:* Ewa Hammer Library plus 1 other. *Collection:* Books: 1,743 (physical), 559 (digital/electronic); Serial titles: 89 (physical). Weekly public service hours: 20.

**Computer facilities:** 2 computers available on campus for general student use.
Website: http://www.dragonrises.edu/

**General Application Contact:** Chantay Moxley, Director of Admissions, 352-372-4851, Fax: 352-244-0003, E-mail: admissions@dragonrises.edu.

**GRADUATE UNITS**

**Graduate Program** Electronic applications accepted.

## DRAKE UNIVERSITY, Des Moines, IA 50311-4516

**General Information** Independent, coed, university. *Enrollment:* 4,884 graduate, professional, and undergraduate students; 937 full-time matriculated graduate/professional students (603 women), 993 part-time matriculated graduate/professional students (701 women). *Enrollment by degree level:* 846 master's, 939 doctoral, 145 other advanced degrees. *Graduate faculty:* 107 full-time (60 women), 70 part-time/adjunct (43 women). *Tuition:* Full-time $19,300; part-time $625 per credit hour. Tuition and fees vary according to degree level, program and student level. *Graduate housing:* Room and/or apartments available on a first-come, first-served basis to single students; on-campus housing not available to married students. Housing application deadline: 8/1. *Student services:* Campus employment opportunities, campus safety program, career counseling, exercise/wellness program, free psychological counseling, international student services, low-cost health insurance, services for students with disabilities, teacher training, writing training. *Library facilities:* Cowles Library plus 1 other. *Collection:* Study areas open 24 hours, 5–7 days a week; students can reserve study rooms. *Research affiliation:* NASA through Iowa State University of Science and Technology (arts and sciences), Albertson's Inc. (pharmacy), U.S. Department of Agriculture (USDA) (agriculture), U.S. Department of Education (DOE) (education), Iowa Department of Education (education), National Science Foundation (biology, physics).

**Computer facilities:** A campuswide network can be accessed. Online class registration is available.
Website: http://www.drake.edu/

**General Application Contact:** Jennifer Reitano, Director, Graduate Student Programs, 515-271-2188, Fax: 515-271-2831, E-mail: jennifer.reitano@drake.edu.

**GRADUATE UNITS**

**College of Business and Public Administration** Students: 29 full-time (18 women), 217 part-time (126 women); includes 33 minority (7 Black or African American, non-Hispanic/Latino; 1 American Indian or Alaska Native, non-Hispanic/Latino; 4 Asian, non-Hispanic/Latino; 15 Hispanic/Latino; 6 Two or more races, non-Hispanic/Latino), 13 international. Average age 33. Expenses: Contact institution. *Financial support:* Fellowships with tuition reimbursements, teaching assistantships, career-related internships or fieldwork, and institutionally sponsored loans available. Support available to part-time students. Financial award application deadline: 3/1; financial award applicants required to submit FAFSA. In 2019, 123 master's awarded. *Program availability:* Part-time, evening/weekend, 100% online, blended/hybrid learning. *Application deadline:* For fall admission, 8/15 priority date for domestic students; for winter admission, 12/20 priority date for domestic students; for spring admission, 12/1 priority date for domestic students. Applications are processed on a rolling basis. *Application fee:* $25. Electronic applications accepted. *Application Contact:* Danette Kenne, Assistant Dean, 515-271-2188, Fax: 515-271-4518, E-mail: cbpa.gradprograms@drake.edu. *Dean*, Dr. Daniel J. Connolly, 515-271-2872, Fax: 515-271-4518, E-mail: daniel.connolly@drake.edu.

**College of Pharmacy and Health Sciences** Students: 464 full-time (337 women), 3 part-time (1 woman); includes 74 minority (3 Black or African American, non-Hispanic/Latino; 46 Asian, non-Hispanic/Latino; 17 Hispanic/Latino; 8 Two or more races, non-Hispanic/Latino), 7 international. Average age 23. Expenses: Contact institution. *Financial support:* Teaching assistantships, career-related internships or fieldwork, Federal Work-Study, institutionally sponsored loans, and scholarships/grants available. Support available to part-time students. Financial award application deadline: 3/1; financial award applicants required to submit FAFSA. In 2019, 130 doctorates awarded. *Application deadline:* For fall admission, 2/1 priority date for domestic students. *Application fee:* $135. Electronic applications accepted. *Application Contact:* Dr. Renae Chesnut, Dean, 515-271-3018, Fax: 515-271-4171, E-mail: renae.chesnut@drake.edu. *Dean*, Dr. Renae Chesnut, 515-271-3018, Fax: 515-271-4171, E-mail: renae.chesnut@drake.edu.

**Law School** Students: 314 full-time (148 women), 48 part-time (31 women); includes 44 minority (17 Black or African American, non-Hispanic/Latino; 6 Asian, non-Hispanic/Latino; 13 Hispanic/Latino; 8 Two or more races, non-Hispanic/Latino), 7 international. Average age 27. Expenses: Contact institution. *Financial support:* Research assistantships, teaching assistantships, career-related internships or fieldwork, Federal Work-Study, institutionally sponsored loans, scholarships/grants, and tuition waivers (full and partial) available. Support available to part-time students. Financial award application deadline: 3/1; financial award applicants required to submit FAFSA. In 2019, 8 master's, 107 doctorates awarded. *Program availability:* Part-time. *Application deadline:* For fall admission, 4/1 priority date for domestic and international students. Applications are processed on a rolling basis. *Application fee:* $40. Electronic applications accepted. *Application Contact:* Kara Blanchard, Assistant Dean for Admission and Financial Aid, 515-271-2953, Fax: 515-271-2530, E-mail: kara.blanchard@drake.edu. *Dean*, Jerry Anderson, 515-271-2658, Fax: 515-271-4118, E-mail: jerry.anderson@drake.edu.

**School of Education** Students: 99 full-time (78 women), 666 part-time (500 women); includes 76 minority (33 Black or African American, non-Hispanic/Latino; 11 Asian, non-Hispanic/Latino; 21 Hispanic/Latino; 11 Two or more races, non-Hispanic/Latino), 2 international. Average age 35. Expenses: Contact institution. *Financial support:* Research assistantships, career-related internships or fieldwork, and unspecified assistantships available. Support available to part-time students. In 2019, 212 master's, 30 doctorates awarded. *Program availability:* Part-time, evening/weekend, 100% online, blended/hybrid learning. *Application deadline:* For fall admission, 7/1 priority date for domestic students, 6/1 priority date for international students; for spring admission, 11/1 priority date for domestic students, 10/1 priority date for international students. Applications are processed on a rolling basis. *Application fee:* $25. Electronic applications accepted. *Application Contact:* Dr. Ryan Wise, Dean, 515-271-3829, E-mail: ryan.wise@drake.edu. *Dean*, Dr. Ryan Wise, 515-271-3829, E-mail: ryan.wise@drake.edu.

**School of Journalism and Mass Communication** *Program availability:* Part-time, evening/weekend, 100% online, blended/hybrid learning.

## DREW UNIVERSITY, Madison, NJ 07940-1493

**General Information** Independent-religious, coed, university. CGS member. *Enrollment:* 2,319 graduate, professional, and undergraduate students; 294 full-time matriculated graduate/professional students (148 women), 306 part-time matriculated graduate/professional students (173 women). *Enrollment by degree level:* 313 master's, 283 doctoral, 4 other advanced degrees. *Graduate faculty:* 22 full-time (12 women), 43 part-time/adjunct (20 women). *Graduate housing:* Rooms and/or apartments available on a first-come, first-served basis to single and married students. Housing application deadline: 7/1. *Student services:* Campus employment opportunities, campus safety program, career counseling, child daycare facilities, exercise/wellness program, free psychological counseling, international student services, low-cost health insurance, multicultural affairs office, services for students with disabilities, teacher training, writing training. *Library facilities:* Rose Memorial Library plus 1 other. *Collection:* Books: 448,828 (physical), 279,468 (digital/electronic); Serial titles: 6,550 (physical), 138,582 (digital/electronic); Databases: 207. Weekly public service hours: 108; students can reserve study rooms. *Research affiliation:* Center for Research Libraries (humanities), Dana Rise Institute (science), St. Barnabas Medical Center (medical humanities), Overlook Hospital (medical humanities), Methodist Archives (religion).

**Computer facilities:** Computer purchase and lease plans are available. 95 computers available on campus for general student use. A campuswide network can be accessed. Online class registration is available.
Website: http://www.drew.edu/

**General Application Contact:** Kevin Miller, Executive Director of Graduate Admissions, 973-408-3111, E-mail: kmiller@drew.edu.

**GRADUATE UNITS**

**Caspersen School of Graduate Studies** *Program availability:* Part-time, evening/weekend. Electronic applications accepted.

**Theological School** Students: 204 full-time (100 women), 147 part-time (66 women); includes 137 minority (95 Black or African American, non-Hispanic/Latino; 3 American Indian or Alaska Native, non-Hispanic/Latino; 12 Asian, non-Hispanic/Latino; 16 Hispanic/Latino; 2 Native Hawaiian or other Pacific Islander, non-Hispanic/Latino; 9 Two or more races, non-Hispanic/Latino), 92 international. Average age 42. 226 applicants, 70% accepted, 84 enrolled. *Faculty:* 19 full-time (9 women), 20 part-time/adjunct (7 women). Expenses: Contact institution. *Financial support:* Fellowships, career-related internships or fieldwork, Federal Work-Study, institutionally sponsored loans, and scholarships/grants available. Support available to part-time students. Financial award application deadline: 2/15; financial award applicants required to submit FAFSA. In 2019, 29 master's, 27 doctorates awarded. *Program availability:* Part-time, blended/hybrid learning. *Application deadline:* For fall admission, 8/1 for domestic students, 4/1 for international students; for spring admission, 12/1 for domestic students, 10/1 for international students. Applications are processed on a rolling basis. *Application fee:* $35. Electronic applications accepted. *Application Contact:* Rev. Dr. Kevin D. Miller, Executive Director of Graduate Admissions, 973-408-3109, E-mail: kmiller@drew.edu. *Acting Dean of the Theological School*, Dr. Melanie Johnson-DeBaufre, 973-408-3255, E-mail: mjjohnso@drew.edu.

## DREXEL UNIVERSITY, Philadelphia, PA 19104-2875

**General Information** Independent, coed, university. CGS member. *Graduate housing:* Room and/or apartments available on a first-come, first-served basis to single students; on-campus housing not available to married students. Housing application deadline: 1/9.

**GRADUATE UNITS**

**College of Arts and Sciences** *Program availability:* Part-time, evening/weekend. Electronic applications accepted.

**College of Computing and Informatics** *Program availability:* Part-time, evening/weekend, 100% online. Electronic applications accepted.

**College of Engineering** *Program availability:* Part-time, evening/weekend. Electronic applications accepted.

**College of Medicine** *Program availability:* Part-time. Electronic applications accepted.

***Biomedical Graduate Programs*** *Program availability:* Part-time. Electronic applications accepted.

**College of Nursing and Health Professions** *Program availability:* Part-time, evening/weekend. Electronic applications accepted.

***Division of Graduate Nursing*** Electronic applications accepted.

**Dornsife School of Public Health** Electronic applications accepted.

**Goodwin College of Professional Studies**

***School of Education*** *Program availability:* Part-time, evening/weekend, online learning. Electronic applications accepted.

***School of Technology and Professional Studies*** *Program availability:* Part-time, evening/weekend. Electronic applications accepted.

**LeBow College of Business** *Program availability:* Part-time, evening/weekend. Electronic applications accepted.

**School of Biomedical Engineering, Science and Health Systems** Electronic applications accepted.

**Thomas R. Kline School of Law**

**Westphal College of Media Arts and Design** *Program availability:* Part-time, evening/weekend. Electronic applications accepted.

## DRURY UNIVERSITY, Springfield, MO 65802

**General Information** Independent, coed, comprehensive institution. *Enrollment:* 1,743 graduate, professional, and undergraduate students; 265 full-time matriculated graduate/professional students (200 women). *Enrollment by degree level:* 256 master's, 9 other advanced degrees. *Graduate faculty:* 18 full-time (10 women), 10 part-time/adjunct (6 women). *Graduate housing:* On-campus housing not available. *Student services:* Campus employment opportunities, campus safety program, career counseling, grant writing training, international student services, multicultural affairs office, services for students with disabilities, teacher training, writing training. *Library facilities:* F. W. Olin Library plus 1 other. *Collection:* Books: 146,057 (physical), 250,440 (digital/electronic); Serial titles: 309 (digital/electronic); Databases: 46. Students can reserve study rooms. *Research affiliation:* Yale University (child development).

**Computer facilities:** 400 computers available on campus for general student use. A campuswide network can be accessed. Online class registration, digital imaging lab, online bill payment/student information are available.
Website: http://www.drury.edu/

**General Application Contact:** Regina Waters, Associate Provost of Adult, Online, and Graduate Education, 417-873-7530, E-mail: grad@drury.edu.

**GRADUATE UNITS**

**Business Ventures Certificate Program** Expenses: Contact institution. *Financial support:* Application deadline: 6/30; applicants required to submit FAFSA. *Program availability:* Part-time, evening/weekend, online only, 100% online, blended/hybrid learning. *Application deadline:* For fall admission, 8/10 priority date for domestic and international students; for spring admission, 1/8 priority date for domestic and international students; for summer admission, 5/26 priority date for domestic and international students. Applications are processed on a rolling basis. *Application fee:* $25. Electronic applications accepted. *Application Contact:* Dr. Robin Soster, Program Director, 417-873-7612, E-mail: rsoster@drury.edu. *Program Director*, Dr. Robin Soster, 417-873-7612, E-mail: rsoster@drury.edu.

**Cybersecurity Leadership Certificate Program** Students: 3 full-time (2 women); includes 1 minority (American Indian or Alaska Native, non-Hispanic/Latino). Average age 44. 3 applicants, 100% accepted, 3 enrolled. *Faculty:* 1 full-time (0 women), 2 part-time/adjunct (1 woman). Expenses: Contact institution. *Financial support:* Career-related internships or fieldwork available. Financial award application deadline: 6/30; financial award applicants required to submit FAFSA. *Program availability:* Part-time, evening/weekend, blended/hybrid learning. *Application deadline:* For fall admission, 8/10 priority date for domestic and international students; for spring admission, 1/8 priority date for domestic and international students; for summer admission, 5/26 priority date for domestic and international students. Applications are processed on a rolling basis. *Application fee:* $25. Electronic applications accepted. *Application Contact:* Dr. Robin Soster, Director, 417-873-7612, E-mail: rsoster@drury.edu. *Director*, Dr. Robin Soster, 417-873-7612, E-mail: rsoster@drury.edu.

**Data Leadership Certificate Program** Expenses: Contact institution. *Financial support:* Application deadline: 6/30; applicants required to submit FAFSA. *Program availability:* Part-time, evening/weekend, online only, 100% online. *Application deadline:* For fall admission, 8/10 priority date for domestic and international students; for spring admission, 1/8 priority date for domestic and international students; for summer admission, 5/26 priority date for domestic and international students. Applications are processed on a rolling basis. *Application fee:* $25. Electronic applications accepted. *Application Contact:* Dr. Lori Slater, Program Director, 417-873-7267, E-mail: lslater002@drury.edu. *Program Director*, Dr. Lori Slater, 417-873-7267, E-mail: lslater002@drury.edu.

**Dyslexia Certificate Program** Expenses: Contact institution. *Financial support:* Application deadline: 6/30; applicants required to submit FAFSA. *Program availability:* Part-time, evening/weekend, online only, 100% online. *Application deadline:* For fall admission, 8/10 for domestic and international students; for spring admission, 1/8 for domestic and international students; for summer admission, 5/26 for domestic and international students. Applications are processed on a rolling basis. *Application fee:* $25. Electronic applications accepted. *Application Contact:* Asikaa Cosgrove, Program Director, 417-873-7806, E-mail: asikaa@drury.edu. *Program Director*, Asikaa Cosgrove, 417-873-7806, E-mail: asikaa@drury.edu.

**Instructional Technology Leadership Program** Expenses: Contact institution. *Financial support:* Application deadline: 6/30; applicants required to submit FAFSA. *Program availability:* Part-time, evening/weekend, online only, 100% online. *Application deadline:* For fall admission, 8/10 priority date for domestic and international students; for spring admission, 1/8 priority date for domestic and international students; for summer admission, 5/26 priority date for domestic and international students. Applications are processed on a rolling basis. *Application fee:* $25. Electronic applications accepted. *Application Contact:* Dr. Asikaa Cosgrove, Program Director, E-mail: acosgrov@drury.edu. *Program Director*, Dr. Asikaa Cosgrove, E-mail: acosgrov@drury.edu.

**Master in Business Administration** Students: 34 full-time (16 women). Average age 25. 21 applicants, 81% accepted, 14 enrolled. *Faculty:* 5 full-time (3 women). Expenses: Contact institution. *Financial support:* In 2019–20, 1 student received support. Career-related internships or fieldwork, scholarships/grants, and unspecified assistantships available. Financial award application deadline: 6/30; financial award applicants required to submit FAFSA. In 2019, 17 master's awarded. *Program availability:* Part-time, evening/weekend, 100% online, blended/hybrid learning. *Application deadline:* For fall admission, 8/10 priority date for domestic and international students; for spring admission, 1/8 priority date for domestic and international students; for summer admission, 5/29 priority date for domestic and international students. Applications are processed on a rolling basis. *Application fee:* $25. Electronic applications accepted. *Application Contact:* Dr. Robin Soster, Director, MBA Program, 417-873-7612, E-mail: rsoster@drury.edu. *Director, MBA Program*, Dr. Robin Soster, 417-873-7612, E-mail: rsoster@drury.edu.

**Master in Education Program** Students: 173 full-time (136 women). Average age 34. 66 applicants, 52% accepted, 32 enrolled. *Faculty:* 10 full-time (6 women), 8 part-time/adjunct (6 women). Expenses: Contact institution. *Financial support:* In 2019–20, 4 students received support. Career-related internships or fieldwork, scholarships/grants, and unspecified assistantships available. Financial award application deadline: 6/30; financial award applicants required to submit FAFSA. In 2019, 38 master's awarded. *Program availability:* Part-time, evening/weekend, 100% online, blended/hybrid learning. *Application deadline:* For fall admission, 8/10 priority date for domestic and international students; for spring admission, 1/8 priority date for domestic and international students; for summer admission, 5/26 priority date for domestic and international students. Applications are processed on a rolling basis. *Application fee:* $25. Electronic applications accepted. *Application Contact:* Dr. Asikaa Cosgrove, Director, Master in Education Program, 417-873-7806, E-mail: acosgrov@drury.edu. *Director, Master in Education Program*, Dr. Asikaa Cosgrove, 417-873-7806, E-mail: acosgrov@drury.edu.

**Master in Integrative Leadership Program** Expenses: Contact institution. *Financial support:* Career-related internships or fieldwork, scholarships/grants, and unspecified assistantships available. Financial award application deadline: 6/30; financial award applicants required to submit FAFSA. *Program availability:* Part-time, evening/weekend, 100% online. *Application deadline:* For fall admission, 8/10 priority date for domestic and international students; for spring admission, 1/8 priority date for domestic and international students; for summer admission, 6/26 priority date for domestic and international students. Applications are processed on a rolling basis. *Application fee:* $25. Electronic applications accepted. *Application Contact:* Lori Slater, Program Director, 417-873-7267, E-mail: lslater002@drury.edu. *Program Director*, Lori Slater, 417-873-7267, E-mail: lslater002@drury.edu.

**Master in Public Service and Safety Leadership Program** Expenses: Contact institution. *Financial support:* Scholarships/grants and unspecified assistantships available. Financial award application deadline: 6/30; financial award applicants required to submit FAFSA. *Program availability:* Part-time, evening/weekend, online only, 100% online. *Application deadline:* For fall admission, 8/10 priority date for domestic and international students; for spring admission, 1/8 priority date for domestic and international students; for summer admission, 5/26 priority date for domestic and international students. Applications are processed on a rolling basis. *Application fee:* $25. Electronic applications accepted. *Application Contact:* Lori Slater, Program Director, 417-873-7267, E-mail: lslater002@drury.edu. *Program Director*, Lori Slater, 417-873-7267, E-mail: lslater002@drury.edu.

**Master of Arts in Communication Program** Students: 14 full-time (8 women); includes 5 minority (4 Black or African American, non-Hispanic/Latino; 1 Asian, non-Hispanic/Latino). Average age 29. 16 applicants, 94% accepted, 12 enrolled. *Faculty:* 3 full-time (1 woman), 2 part-time/adjunct (0 women). Expenses: Contact institution. *Financial support:* Career-related internships or fieldwork, scholarships/grants, and unspecified assistantships available. Financial award application deadline: 6/30; financial award applicants required to submit FAFSA. In 2019, 8 master's awarded. *Program availability:* Part-time, evening/weekend. *Application deadline:* For fall admission, 8/10 priority date for domestic and international students; for spring admission, 1/8 priority date for domestic and international students; for summer admission, 5/26 priority date for domestic and international students. Applications are processed on a rolling basis. *Application fee:* $25. Electronic applications accepted. *Application Contact:* Dr. Charles Taylor, Program Director, 417-873-7391, E-mail: ctaylor@drury.edu. *Program Director*, Dr. Charles Taylor, 417-873-7391, E-mail: ctaylor@drury.edu.

**Master of Nonprofit and Civic Leadership Program** Students: 21 full-time (17 women); includes 4 minority (all Two or more races, non-Hispanic/Latino). Average age 27. 15 applicants, 67% accepted, 8 enrolled. *Faculty:* 3 full-time (1 woman), 2 part-time/adjunct (0 women). Expenses: Contact institution. *Financial support:* Career-related internships or fieldwork, institutionally sponsored loans, scholarships/grants, and unspecified assistantships available. Financial award application deadline: 6/30; financial award applicants required to submit FAFSA. In 2019, 7 master's awarded. *Program availability:* Part-time, evening/weekend. *Application deadline:* For fall admission, 8/10 for domestic and international students; for spring admission, 1/8 for domestic and international students; for summer admission, 5/24 for domestic and international students. Applications are processed on a rolling basis. *Application fee:* $25. Electronic applications accepted. *Application Contact:* Dr. Charles Taylor, Director, 417-873-7391, E-mail: ctaylor@drury.edu. *Director*, Dr. Charles Taylor, 417-873-7391, E-mail: ctaylor@drury.edu.

**Nonprofit Leadership Certificate Program** Students: 6 full-time (all women). Average age 39. 10 applicants, 70% accepted, 6 enrolled. *Faculty:* 1 full-time, 3 part-time/adjunct. Expenses: Contact institution. *Financial support:* Career-related internships or fieldwork available. Financial award application deadline: 6/30; financial award applicants required to submit FAFSA. *Program availability:* Part-time, evening/weekend, 100% online, blended/hybrid learning. *Application deadline:* For fall admission, 8/10 for domestic and international students; for spring admission, 1/8 for domestic and international students; for summer admission, 5/26 for domestic and international students. Applications are processed on a rolling basis. *Application fee:* $25. Electronic applications accepted. *Application Contact:* Charles Taylor, Program Director, 417-873-7391, E-mail: ctayor@drury.edu. *Program Director*, Charles Taylor, 417-873-7391, E-mail: ctayor@drury.edu.

**Public Safety Leadership Certificate Program** Expenses: Contact institution. *Financial support:* Unspecified assistantships available. Financial award application deadline: 6/30; financial award applicants required to submit FAFSA. *Program availability:* Part-time, evening/weekend, online only, 100% online. *Application deadline:* For fall admission, 8/10 priority date for domestic and international students; for spring admission, 1/8 priority date for domestic and international students; for summer admission, 5/26 priority date for domestic and international students. Applications are processed on a rolling basis. *Application fee:* $25. Electronic applications accepted. *Application Contact:* Lori Slater, 417-873-7267, E-mail: lslater002@drury.edu.

## DUKE UNIVERSITY, Durham, NC 27708

**General Information** Independent-religious, coed, university. CGS member. *Graduate housing:* Rooms and/or apartments available on a first-come, first-served basis to single and married students. Housing application deadline: 5/8. *Research affiliation:* Highlands Biological Station, U.S. Forest Sciences Laboratory, Organization for Tropical Studies.

**GRADUATE UNITS**

**Divinity School** *Program availability:* Part-time, online learning. Electronic applications accepted.

**The Fuqua School of Business** Students: 1,823 full-time (782 women); includes 427 minority (87 Black or African American, non-Hispanic/Latino; 6 American Indian or Alaska Native, non-Hispanic/Latino; 226 Asian, non-Hispanic/Latino; 78 Hispanic/Latino; 4 Native Hawaiian or other Pacific Islander, non-Hispanic/Latino; 26 Two or more races, non-Hispanic/Latino), 634 international. Average age 29. *Faculty:* 99 full-time (20 women), 56 part-time/adjunct (13 women). Expenses: Contact institution. *Financial support:* Applicants required to submit FAFSA. In 2019, 1,029 master's, 16 doctorates awarded. *Program availability:* Part-time, 100% online. Electronic applications accepted. *Application Contact:* Shari Hubert, Associate Dean, Office of Admissions, Fax: 919-681-8026, E-mail: admissions-info@fuqua.duke.edu. *Dean*, William Boulding, 919-660-7822.

**Graduate School** *Program availability:* Part-time, evening/weekend. Electronic applications accepted.

***Division of Earth and Ocean Sciences*** *Program availability:* Part-time. Electronic applications accepted.

***Duke Global Health Institute***

***Pratt School of Engineering*** *Program availability:* Part-time, online learning.

**Nicholas School of the Environment** Students: 350 full-time (234 women); includes 50 minority (7 Black or African American, non-Hispanic/Latino; 4 American Indian or Alaska Native, non-Hispanic/Latino; 26 Asian, non-Hispanic/Latino; 11 Hispanic/Latino; 2 Native Hawaiian or other Pacific Islander, non-Hispanic/Latino), 72 international. Average age 27. 404 applicants, 84% accepted, 151 enrolled. *Faculty:* 50. Expenses: Contact institution. *Financial support:* Research assistantships, career-related internships or fieldwork, Federal Work-Study, institutionally sponsored loans, scholarships/grants, and unspecified assistantships available. Financial award application deadline: 12/15; financial award applicants required to submit CSS PROFILE or FAFSA. In 2019, 167 master's awarded. *Application deadline:* For fall admission, 12/15 priority date for domestic and international students. *Application fee:* $400. Electronic applications accepted. *Application Contact:* Benjamin Spain, Associate Director of Enrollment Services, 919-613-8063, E-mail: admissions@nicholas.duke.edu. *Associate Dean, Student Services*, Sherri Nevius, 919-613-8063, E-mail: sherri.nevius@duke.edu.

**Sanford School of Public Policy** Electronic applications accepted.

**School of Law** Students: 819. *Faculty:* 96 full-time (40 women), 98 part-time/adjunct (39 women). Expenses: Contact institution. *Financial support:* Institutionally sponsored loans, scholarships/grants, and unspecified assistantships available. Financial award application deadline: 3/15; financial award applicants required to submit FAFSA. *Application deadline:* For fall admission, 2/15 for domestic and international students. Applications are processed on a rolling basis. *Application fee:* $70. Electronic applications accepted. *Application Contact:* William J. Hoye, Associate Dean for Admissions and Student Affairs, 919-613-7020, Fax: 919-613-7257, E-mail: hoye@law.duke.edu. *Dean/Professor of Law*, Kerry Abrams, 919-613-7001, Fax: 919-613-7158.

**School of Medicine**

***Doctor of Physical Therapy*** Electronic applications accepted.

**School of Nursing** Students: 666 full-time (601 women), 157 part-time (139 women); includes 193 minority (61 Black or African American, non-Hispanic/Latino; 4 American Indian or Alaska Native, non-Hispanic/Latino; 57 Asian, non-Hispanic/Latino; 49 Hispanic/Latino; 1 Native Hawaiian or other Pacific Islander, non-Hispanic/Latino; 21 Two or more races, non-Hispanic/Latino), 8 international. Average age 34. 761 applicants, 33% accepted, 149 enrolled. *Faculty:* 48 full-time (40 women), 32 part-time/adjunct (28 women). Expenses: Contact institution. *Financial support:* Institutionally sponsored loans, scholarships/grants, and traineeships available. Support available to part-time students. Financial award applicants required to submit FAFSA. In 2019, 213 master's, 74 doctorates, 18 other advanced degrees awarded. *Program availability:* Part-time, evening/weekend, online with on-campus intensives. *Application deadline:* For fall admission, 12/1 for domestic and international students; for spring admission, 5/1 for domestic and international students. *Application fee:* $50. Electronic applications accepted. *Application Contact:* Dr. Ernie Rushing, Director of Admissions and Recruitment, 919-668-6274, Fax: 919-668-4693, E-mail: ernie.rushing@dm.duke.edu. *Dean/Vice Chancellor for Nursing Affairs/Associate Vice President for Academic Affairs for Nursing*, Dr. Marion E. Broome, 919-684-9446, Fax: 919-684-9414, E-mail: marion.broome@duke.edu.

## DUNLAP-STONE UNIVERSITY, Phoenix, AZ 85024

**General Information** Proprietary, coed, comprehensive institution.

**GRADUATE UNITS**

**Graduate Law Center**

## DUQUESNE UNIVERSITY, Pittsburgh, PA 15282-0001

**General Information** Independent-religious, coed, university. CGS member. *Graduate housing:* Rooms and/or apartments available on a first-come, first-served basis to single and married students. Housing application deadline: 5/1.

**GRADUATE UNITS**

**Bayer School of Natural and Environmental Sciences** *Program availability:* Part-time. Electronic applications accepted.

**Biomedical Engineering Program**

**Graduate School of Liberal Arts** *Program availability:* Part-time, evening/weekend, 100% online, blended/hybrid learning. Electronic applications accepted.

***Center for Healthcare Ethics*** *Program availability:* Part-time, 100% online. Electronic applications accepted.

**John G. Rangos, Sr. School of Health Sciences** *Program availability:* Part-time, minimal on-campus study. Electronic applications accepted.

**Mary Pappert School of Music** *Program availability:* Part-time. Electronic applications accepted.

**Palumbo-Donahue School of Business** *Program availability:* Part-time, evening/weekend, 100% online, blended/hybrid learning. Electronic applications accepted.

**Post-Baccalaureate Pre-Medical and Health Professions Program** Electronic applications accepted.

**School of Education** *Program availability:* Part-time, evening/weekend, 100% online, blended/hybrid learning. Electronic applications accepted.

**School of Law** *Program availability:* Part-time, evening/weekend. Electronic applications accepted.

**School of Nursing** *Program availability:* Part-time, evening/weekend, online only, 100% online. Electronic applications accepted.

**School of Pharmacy** *Program availability:* Evening/weekend. Electronic applications accepted.

***Graduate School of Pharmaceutical Sciences*** Electronic applications accepted.

## D'YOUVILLE COLLEGE, Buffalo, NY 14201-1084

**General Information** Independent, coed, comprehensive institution. *Graduate housing:* Room and/or apartments available on a first-come, first-served basis to single students. Housing application deadline: 8/1.

**GRADUATE UNITS**

**Department of Business** *Program availability:* Part-time, evening/weekend. Electronic applications accepted.

**Department of Chiropractic** Electronic applications accepted.

**Department of Dietetics** Electronic applications accepted.

**Department of Education** *Program availability:* Part-time, evening/weekend. Electronic applications accepted.

**Department of Health Services Administration** *Program availability:* Part-time, evening/weekend. Electronic applications accepted.

**Department of Physical Therapy** *Program availability:* Part-time, online learning. Electronic applications accepted.

**Occupational Therapy Department** Electronic applications accepted.

**Physician Assistant Department** Electronic applications accepted.

**Program in Anatomy**

**School of Nursing** *Program availability:* Part-time. Electronic applications accepted.

**School of Pharmacy** Electronic applications accepted.

## EARLHAM COLLEGE, Richmond, IN 47374-4095

**General Information** Independent-religious, coed, comprehensive institution. *Graduate housing:* On-campus housing not available.

**GRADUATE UNITS**

**Graduate Programs**

## EARLHAM SCHOOL OF RELIGION, Richmond, IN 47374-5360

**General Information** Independent-religious, coed, graduate-only institution. *Enrollment by degree level:* 57 master's, 1 other advanced degree. *Graduate housing:* On-campus housing not available. *Student services:* Campus employment opportunities, campus safety program, career counseling, exercise/wellness program, international student services, teacher training, writing training. *Library facilities:* Lilly Library plus 2 others. *Collection:* Books: 351,561 (physical); Serial titles: 292 (physical). Weekly public service hours: 112; students can reserve study rooms.

**Computer facilities:** 125 computers available on campus for general student use. A campuswide network can be accessed. Online class registration is available.
Website: http://www.esr.earlham.edu/

**General Application Contact:** Julie Dishman, Director of Recruitment and Admissions, 765-983-1523, Fax: 765-983-1688, E-mail: dishmju@earlham.edu.

**GRADUATE UNITS**

**Graduate Programs** Students: 17 full-time (9 women), 18 part-time (11 women); includes 2 minority (both Black or African American, non-Hispanic/Latino). Average age

38. *Faculty:* 8 full-time (2 women), 2 part-time/adjunct (1 woman). Expenses: Contact institution. *Financial support:* Scholarships/grants and tuition waivers (full and partial) available. Financial award application deadline: 4/15; financial award applicants required to submit FAFSA. *Program availability:* Part-time, blended/hybrid learning. *Application deadline:* For fall admission, 6/15 priority date for domestic students; for winter admission, 11/15 priority date for domestic students. Applications are processed on a rolling basis. *Application fee:* $35. Electronic applications accepted. *Application Contact:* Julie Dishman, Director of Recruitment and Admissions, 765-983-1523, Fax: 765-983-1688, E-mail: dishmju@earlham.edu. *Dean,* Matt Hisrich, 800-432-1377, Fax: 765-983-1688, E-mail: hisrima@earlham.edu.

## EAST CAROLINA UNIVERSITY, Greenville, NC 27858-4353

**General Information** State-supported, coed, university. CGS member. *Enrollment:* 28,651 graduate, professional, and undergraduate students; 2,537 full-time matriculated graduate/professional students (1,693 women), 2,739 part-time matriculated graduate/professional students (1,843 women). *Enrollment by degree level:* 3,602 master's, 1,293 doctoral, 381 other advanced degrees. *Graduate faculty:* 1,022 full-time (472 women), 64 part-time/adjunct (36 women). *International tuition:* $17,898 full-time. *Tuition, area resident:* Full-time $4749; part-time $185 per credit hour. Tuition, state resident: full-time $4749; part-time $185 per credit hour. Tuition, nonresident: full-time $17,898; part-time $864 per credit hour. *Required fees:* $2787. *Graduate housing:* Room and/or apartments available on a first-come, first-served basis to single students; on-campus housing not available to married students. Typical cost: $5520 per year ($9712 including board). Housing application deadline: 5/1. *Student services:* Campus employment opportunities, campus safety program, career counseling, exercise/wellness program, free psychological counseling, grant writing training, international student services, low-cost health insurance, multicultural affairs office, services for students with disabilities, teacher training, writing training. *Library facilities:* Joyner Library plus 2 others. *Collection:* Books: 1 million (physical), 911,157 (digital/electronic); Serial titles: 8,079 (physical), 112,386 (digital/electronic); Databases: 452. Weekly public service hours: 142; study areas open 24 hours, 5–7 days a week; students can reserve study rooms.

**Computer facilities:** Computer purchase and lease plans are available. 2,760 computers available on campus for general student use. A campuswide network can be accessed. Online class registration is available.
Website: http://www.ecu.edu/

**General Application Contact:** Heidi Terry, Assistant Dean for Admissions and Enrollment Management, 252-328-5400, Fax: 252-328-6071, E-mail: gradschool@ecu.edu.

**GRADUATE UNITS**

**Brody School of Medicine** Expenses: Contact institution. *Financial support:* Fellowships, institutionally sponsored loans, and unspecified assistantships available. Financial award application deadline: 6/1. *Program availability:* Part-time, online learning. *Application Contact:* Graduate School Admissions, 252-328-6012, Fax: 252-328-6071, E-mail: gradschool@ecu.edu.

***Office of Research and Graduate Studies*** Students: 102 full-time (44 women), 1 part-time (0 women); includes 16 minority (4 Black or African American, non-Hispanic/Latino; 7 Asian, non-Hispanic/Latino; 4 Hispanic/Latino; 1 Two or more races, non-Hispanic/Latino), 13 international. Average age 28. 83 applicants, 40% accepted, 20 enrolled. Expenses: Contact institution. *Financial support:* Fellowships available. Financial award application deadline: 6/1. In 2019, 3 master's, 10 doctorates awarded. *Application deadline:* For fall admission, 8/15 for domestic students; for spring admission, 12/20 for domestic students. Applications are processed on a rolling basis. *Application fee:* $75. Electronic applications accepted. *Application Contact:* Dr. Russ Price, Associate Dean, 252-744-9346, E-mail: pricest17@ecu.edu. *Associate Dean,* Dr. Russ Price, 252-744-9346, E-mail: pricest17@ecu.edu.

**Graduate School** Expenses: Contact institution. *Financial support:* Application deadline: 3/1; applicants required to submit FAFSA. *Program availability:* Part-time, evening/weekend, online learning. *Application deadline:* For fall admission, 8/15 for domestic students, 2/1 for international students; for spring admission, 12/20 for domestic students, 10/1 for international students; for summer admission, 5/5 for domestic students. *Application Contact:* Graduate School Admissions, 252-328-6012, Fax: 252-328-6071, E-mail: gradschool@ecu.edu. *Dean,* Dr. Paul Gemperline, 252-328-6073, E-mail: gemperlinep@ecu.edu.

***College of Allied Health Sciences*** Expenses: Contact institution. *Financial support:* Application deadline: 3/1. *Program availability:* Part-time, evening/weekend, online learning. *Application deadline:* For fall admission, 2/1 for domestic and international students; for spring admission, 9/1 for domestic students, 10/1 for international students. *Application Contact:* Graduate School Admissions, 252-328-6012, Fax: 252-328-6071, E-mail: gradschool@ecu.edu. *Dean,* Dr. Robert F Orlikoff, 252-744-6010.

***College of Business*** Expenses: Contact institution. *Financial support:* Application deadline: 3/1. *Program availability:* Part-time, evening/weekend. *Application deadline:* For fall admission, 6/1 priority date for domestic students, 2/1 for international students; for spring admission, 11/15 for domestic students, 10/1 for international students; for summer admission, 3/15 for domestic students. *Application Contact:* Graduate School Admissions, 252-328-6012, Fax: 252-328-6071, E-mail: gradschool@ecu.edu. *Dean,* Dr. Paul Schwager, 252-328-6966, E-mail: schwagerp@ecu.edu.

***College of Education*** Expenses: Contact institution. *Financial support:* Application deadline: 6/1. *Program availability:* Part-time, evening/weekend, online learning. *Application deadline:* For fall admission, 8/15 for domestic students, 2/1 for international students; for spring admission, 12/20 for domestic students, 10/1 for international students. *Application Contact:* Graduate School Admissions, 252-328-6012, Fax: 252-328-6071, E-mail: gradschool@ecu.edu. *Dean,* Dr. Art Rouse, 252-328-6060, Fax: 252-328-4219, E-mail: rousew@ecu.edu.

***College of Engineering and Technology*** Expenses: Contact institution. *Financial support:* Application deadline: 6/1. *Program availability:* Part-time, evening/weekend, online learning. *Application deadline:* For fall admission, 6/1 priority date for domestic students. *Application Contact:* Graduate School Admissions, 252-328-6012, Fax: 252-328-6071, E-mail: gradschool@ecu.edu. *Dean,* Dr. Harry Ploehn, 252-328-9600, E-mail: ploehnh17@ecu.edu.

***College of Fine Arts and Communication*** Expenses: Contact institution. *Application Contact:* Graduate School Admissions, 252-328-6012, Fax: 252-328-6071, E-mail: gradschool@ecu.edu. *Dean,* J. Christopher Buddo, 252-328-1282, E-mail: buddoj@ecu.edu.

***College of Health and Human Performance*** Expenses: Contact institution. *Financial support:* Application deadline: 6/1. *Program availability:* Part-time, evening/weekend. *Application deadline:* For fall admission, 6/1 priority date for domestic students. *Application Contact:* Graduate School Admissions, 252-328-6012, Fax: 252-328-6071, E-mail: gradschool@ecu.edu. *Dean,* Dr. Ansia Zvonkovic, 252-328-4630, E-mail: zvonkovic@ecu.edu.

***College of Nursing*** Expenses: Contact institution. *Financial support:* Application deadline: 6/1. *Program availability:* Part-time. *Application deadline:* For fall admission, 3/15 priority date for domestic students; for spring admission, 10/15 priority date for domestic students. *Application Contact:* Graduate School Admissions, 252-328-6012, Fax: 252-328-6071, E-mail: gradschool@ecu.edu. *Dean,* Dr. Sylvia T Brown, 252-744-6372, E-mail: brownsy@ecu.edu.

***Thomas Harriot College of Arts and Sciences*** Expenses: Contact institution. *Financial support:* Application deadline: 3/1. *Program availability:* Part-time, evening/weekend, online learning. *Application deadline:* For fall admission, 8/15 priority date for domestic students, 2/1 priority date for international students; for spring admission, 12/20 priority date for domestic students, 10/1 priority date for international students. *Application Contact:* Graduate School Admissions, 252-328-6012, Fax: 252-328-6071, E-mail: gradschool@ecu.edu. *interim Dean,* Dr. Allison S Danell, 252-328-6249, E-mail: danella@ecu.edu.

**School of Dental Medicine** Expenses: Contact institution. *Application deadline:* For fall admission, 6/30 for domestic students. *Application Contact:* Graduate School Admissions, 252-328-6012, Fax: 252-328-6071, E-mail: gradschool@ecu.edu. *Dean,* Dr. Greg Chadwick, 252-737-7703.

## EAST CENTRAL UNIVERSITY, Ada, OK 74820

**General Information** State-supported, coed, comprehensive institution. *Graduate housing:* On-campus housing not available.

**GRADUATE UNITS**

**School of Graduate Studies** *Program availability:* Part-time, evening/weekend. Electronic applications accepted.

## EASTERN CONNECTICUT STATE UNIVERSITY, Willimantic, CT 06226-2295

**General Information** State-supported, coed, comprehensive institution. *Graduate housing:* Room and/or apartments available on a first-come, first-served basis to single students; on-campus housing not available to married students. Housing application deadline: 4/3. *Research affiliation:* Spencer Foundation (early childhood education), CEEDAR Center (early childhood, physical education, elementary education, secondary education).

**GRADUATE UNITS**

**School of Education and Professional Studies/Graduate Division** *Program availability:* Part-time, evening/weekend. Electronic applications accepted.

## EASTERN ILLINOIS UNIVERSITY, Charleston, IL 61920

**General Information** State-supported, coed, comprehensive institution. CGS member. *Graduate housing:* Rooms and/or apartments available on a first-come, first-served basis to single and married students.

**GRADUATE UNITS**

**Graduate School** *Program availability:* Part-time, evening/weekend, 100% online, blended/hybrid learning. Electronic applications accepted.

***College of Education*** *Program availability:* Part-time, evening/weekend. Electronic applications accepted.

***College of Health and Human Services*** *Program availability:* Part-time, online learning.

***College of Liberal Arts and Sciences*** *Program availability:* Part-time, evening/weekend, 100% online, blended/hybrid learning. Electronic applications accepted.

***Lumpkin College of Business and Technology*** *Program availability:* Part-time, evening/weekend, online learning. Electronic applications accepted.

## EASTERN KENTUCKY UNIVERSITY, Richmond, KY 40475-3102

**General Information** State-supported, coed, comprehensive institution. CGS member. *Graduate housing:* Rooms and/or apartments guaranteed to single students and available to married students.

**GRADUATE UNITS**

**The Graduate School** *Program availability:* Part-time, evening/weekend, online learning. Electronic applications accepted.

***College of Arts and Sciences*** *Program availability:* Part-time, evening/weekend.

***College of Business and Technology*** *Program availability:* Part-time.

***College of Education*** *Program availability:* Part-time, online learning.

***College of Health Sciences*** *Program availability:* Part-time.

***College of Justice and Safety*** *Program availability:* Part-time.

## EASTERN MENNONITE UNIVERSITY, Harrisonburg, VA 22802-2462

**General Information** Independent-religious, coed, comprehensive institution. *Enrollment:* 1,360 graduate, professional, and undergraduate students; 114 full-time matriculated graduate/professional students (74 women), 178 part-time matriculated graduate/professional students (130 women). *Enrollment by degree level:* 263 master's, 5 doctoral, 24 other advanced degrees. *Graduate faculty:* 39 full-time (20 women), 35 part-time/adjunct (18 women). *Graduate housing:* Rooms and/or apartments available on a first-come, first-served basis to single and married students. Housing application deadline: 4/15. *Student services:* Campus employment opportunities, campus safety program, career counseling, exercise/wellness program, free psychological counseling, international student services, low-cost health insurance, multicultural affairs office, services for students with disabilities, teacher training, writing training. *Library facilities:* Sadie Hartzler Library. *Collection:* Books: 138,611 (physical), 256,672 (digital/electronic); Serial titles: 2,076 (physical), 70,423 (digital/electronic); Databases: 161. Weekly public service hours: 92.

**Computer facilities:** 100 computers available on campus for general student use. A campuswide network can be accessed. Online class registration is available.
Website: http://www.emu.edu/

**General Application Contact:** Shirley Ewald, Assistant to the Dean of Graduate Studies, 540-432-4026, Fax: 540-432-4444, E-mail: shirley.ewald@emu.edu.

**GRADUATE UNITS**

**Eastern Mennonite Seminary** *Program availability:* Part-time.

**Master of Arts in Counseling Program** *Program availability:* Part-time. Electronic applications accepted.

**Program in Biomedicine** Electronic applications accepted.

**Program in Business Administration** *Program availability:* Part-time, evening/weekend. Electronic applications accepted.

**Program in Conflict Transformation** *Program availability:* Part-time. Electronic applications accepted.

**Program in Nursing** *Program availability:* Part-time, online learning.

**Program in Organizational Leadership**

**Program in Teacher Education** *Program availability:* Part-time. Electronic applications accepted.

## EASTERN MICHIGAN UNIVERSITY, Ypsilanti, MI 48197

**General Information** State-supported, coed, comprehensive institution. CGS member. *Enrollment:* 18,833 graduate, professional, and undergraduate students; 884 full-time matriculated graduate/professional students (595 women), 2,052 part-time matriculated graduate/professional students (1,334 women). *Enrollment by degree level:* 2,411 master's, 186 doctoral, 339 other advanced degrees. *Graduate faculty:* 604 full-time (298 women). *Graduate housing:* Room and/or apartments available on a first-come, first-served basis to single students; on-campus housing not available to married students. Typical cost: $10,696 (including board). *Student services:* Campus employment opportunities, campus safety program, career counseling, child daycare facilities, exercise/wellness program, free psychological counseling, grant writing training, international student services, low-cost health insurance, multicultural affairs office, services for students with disabilities, teacher training, writing training. *Library facilities:* Bruce T. Halle Library. *Research affiliation:* 3M Corporation (coatings research), Toyota Motor Company (coatings research), Beckers-Fusion (coatings research), Dima-Shield (coatings research), Signal Medical Corporation (textiles research), TRACO (coatings research).

**Computer facilities:** 1,600 computers available on campus for general student use. A campuswide network can be accessed from student residence rooms. Online class registration is available.
Website: http://www.emich.edu/

**General Application Contact:** Graduate Admissions, 734-487-2400, Fax: 734-487-6559, E-mail: graduate.admissions@emich.edu.

**GRADUATE UNITS**

**Graduate School** Students: 884 full-time (595 women), 2,052 part-time (1,334 women); includes 786 minority (375 Black or African American, non-Hispanic/Latino; 8 American Indian or Alaska Native, non-Hispanic/Latino; 89 Asian, non-Hispanic/Latino; 204 Hispanic/Latino; 1 Native Hawaiian or other Pacific Islander, non-Hispanic/Latino; 109 Two or more races, non-Hispanic/Latino), 188 international. Average age 32. 2,534 applicants, 56% accepted, 796 enrolled. *Faculty:* 604 full-time (298 women). Expenses: Contact institution. *Financial support:* Fellowships, research assistantships with full tuition reimbursements, teaching assistantships with full tuition reimbursements, career-related internships or fieldwork, Federal Work-Study, institutionally sponsored loans, scholarships/grants, tuition waivers (partial), and unspecified assistantships available. Support available to part-time students. Financial award applicants required to submit FAFSA. In 2019, 1,074 master's, 42 doctorates, 110 other advanced degrees awarded. *Program availability:* Part-time, evening/weekend, online learning. *Application deadline:* For fall admission, 5/15 priority date for domestic students, 2/15 priority date for international students; for winter admission, 10/15 priority date for domestic students, 9/1 priority date for international students; for summer admission, 3/15 priority date for domestic students, 3/1 priority date for international students. Applications are processed on a rolling basis. *Application fee:* $45. Electronic applications accepted.

***Academic and Student Affairs Division*** Students: 4 full-time (3 women), 25 part-time (20 women); includes 8 minority (3 Black or African American, non-Hispanic/Latino; 1 American Indian or Alaska Native, non-Hispanic/Latino; 2 Asian, non-Hispanic/Latino; 1 Hispanic/Latino; 1 Two or more races, non-Hispanic/Latino), 3 international. Average age 37. 56 applicants, 77% accepted, 19 enrolled. *Faculty:* 2 full-time (1 woman). Expenses: Contact institution. In 2019, 1 master's awarded. *Application fee:* $45. *Application Contact:* Graduate Admissions, 734-487-2400, Fax: 734-487-6559, E-mail: graduate.admissions@emich.edu. *Interim Dean*, Dr. Wade Tornquist, 734-487-0042, Fax: 734-487-0050, E-mail: wade.tornquist@emich.edu.

***College of Arts and Sciences*** Students: 211 full-time (140 women), 451 part-time (283 women); includes 152 minority (56 Black or African American, non-Hispanic/Latino; 2 American Indian or Alaska Native, non-Hispanic/Latino; 11 Asian, non-Hispanic/Latino; 52 Hispanic/Latino; 31 Two or more races, non-Hispanic/Latino), 67 international. Average age 31. 733 applicants, 56% accepted, 208 enrolled. *Faculty:* 319 full-time (141 women). Expenses: Contact institution. *Financial support:* Fellowships, research assistantships with full tuition reimbursements, teaching assistantships with full tuition reimbursements, career-related internships or fieldwork, Federal Work-Study, institutionally sponsored loans, and tuition waivers (partial) available. Support available to part-time students. Financial award applicants required to submit FAFSA. In 2019, 265 master's, 7 doctorates, 24 other advanced degrees awarded. *Program availability:* Part-time, evening/weekend. *Application deadline:* Applications are processed on a rolling basis. *Application fee:* $45. *Application Contact:* Dr. Dana Heller, Dean, 734-487-4344, Fax: 734-485-9592, E-mail: dheller@emich.edu. *Dean*, Dr. Dana Heller, 734-487-4344, Fax: 734-485-9592, E-mail: dheller@emich.edu.

***College of Business*** Students: 129 full-time (74 women), 386 part-time (212 women); includes 167 minority (88 Black or African American, non-Hispanic/Latino; 1 American Indian or Alaska Native, non-Hispanic/Latino; 20 Asian, non-Hispanic/Latino; 40 Hispanic/Latino; 18 Two or more races, non-Hispanic/Latino), 36 international. Average age 31. 334 applicants, 64% accepted, 121 enrolled. *Faculty:* 70 full-time (27 women). Expenses: Contact institution. *Financial support:* Fellowships, research assistantships with full tuition reimbursements, teaching assistantships with full tuition reimbursements, career-related internships or fieldwork, Federal Work-Study, institutionally sponsored loans, traineeships, tuition waivers (partial), and unspecified assistantships available. Support available to part-time students. Financial award applicants required to submit FAFSA. In 2019, 229 master's, 30 other advanced degrees awarded. *Program availability:* Part-time, evening/weekend, online learning. *Application deadline:* Applications are processed on a rolling basis. *Application fee:* $45. *Application Contact:* K. Michelle Henry, Director, Graduate Business Programs, 734-487-4444, Fax: 734-483-1316, E-mail: cob.graduate@emich.edu. *Dean*, Dr. Kenneth Lord, 734-487-4140, Fax: 734-487-7099, E-mail: cob_dean@emich.edu.

***College of Education*** Students: 184 full-time (146 women), 649 part-time (492 women); includes 221 minority (120 Black or African American, non-Hispanic/Latino; 12 Asian, non-Hispanic/Latino; 57 Hispanic/Latino; 32 Two or more races, non-Hispanic/Latino), 9 international. Average age 34. 607 applicants, 59% accepted, 226 enrolled. *Faculty:* 54 full-time (35 women). Expenses: Contact institution. *Financial support:* Fellowships, research assistantships with full tuition reimbursements, teaching assistantships with full tuition reimbursements, career-related internships or fieldwork, Federal Work-Study, institutionally sponsored loans, scholarships/grants, tuition waivers (partial), and unspecified assistantships available. Support available to part-time students. Financial award applicants required to submit FAFSA. In 2019, 232 master's, 27 doctorates, 32 other advanced degrees awarded. *Program availability:* Part-time, evening/weekend, online learning. *Application deadline:* Applications are processed on a rolling basis. *Application fee:* $45. *Application Contact:* Dr. Michael Sayler, Dean, 734-487-1414, Fax: 734-484-6471, E-mail: msayler@emich.edu. *Dean*, Dr. Michael Sayler, 734-487-1414, Fax: 734-484-6471, E-mail: msayler@emich.edu.

***College of Engineering and Technology*** Students: 66 full-time (28 women), 211 part-time (73 women); includes 59 minority (28 Black or African American, non-Hispanic/Latino; 1 American Indian or Alaska Native, non-Hispanic/Latino; 13 Asian, non-Hispanic/Latino; 8 Hispanic/Latino; 9 Two or more races, non-Hispanic/Latino), 55 international. Average age 35. 256 applicants, 50% accepted, 58 enrolled. *Faculty:* 51 full-time (13 women). Expenses: Contact institution. *Financial support:* Fellowships, research assistantships with full tuition reimbursements, teaching assistantships with full tuition reimbursements, career-related internships or fieldwork, Federal Work-Study, institutionally sponsored loans, scholarships/grants, tuition waivers (partial), and unspecified assistantships available. Support available to part-time students. Financial award applicants required to submit FAFSA. In 2019, 91 master's, 8 doctorates, 2 other advanced degrees awarded. *Program availability:* Part-time, evening/weekend, online learning. *Application deadline:* For fall admission, 5/15 priority date for domestic students, 2/15 priority date for international students; for winter admission, 10/15 priority date for domestic students, 9/1 priority date for international students; for summer admission, 3/15 priority date for domestic students, 3/1 priority date for international students. Applications are processed on a rolling basis. *Application fee:* $45. *Application Contact:* Dr. Mohamad Qatu, Dean, 734-487-0354, Fax: 734-487-0843, E-mail: mqatu@emich.edu. *Dean*, Dr. Mohamad Qatu, 734-487-0354, Fax: 734-487-0843, E-mail: mqatu@emich.edu.

***College of Health and Human Services*** Students: 290 full-time (204 women), 330 part-time (254 women); includes 179 minority (80 Black or African American, non-Hispanic/Latino; 3 American Indian or Alaska Native, non-Hispanic/Latino; 31 Asian, non-Hispanic/Latino; 46 Hispanic/Latino; 1 Native Hawaiian or other Pacific Islander, non-Hispanic/Latino; 18 Two or more races, non-Hispanic/Latino), 18 international. Average age 30. 548 applicants, 50% accepted, 164 enrolled. *Faculty:* 108 full-time (81 women). Expenses: Contact institution. *Financial support:* Fellowships, research assistantships with full tuition reimbursements, teaching assistantships with full tuition reimbursements, career-related internships or fieldwork, Federal Work-Study, institutionally sponsored loans, scholarships/grants, tuition waivers (partial), and unspecified assistantships available. Support available to part-time students. Financial award applicants required to submit FAFSA. In 2019, 256 master's, 22 other advanced degrees awarded. *Program availability:* Part-time, evening/weekend, online learning. *Application deadline:* For fall admission, 5/15 priority date for domestic students, 2/15 priority date for international students; for winter admission, 10/15 priority date for domestic students, 9/1 priority date for international students; for summer admission, 3/15 priority date for domestic students, 3/1 priority date for international students. Applications are processed on a rolling basis. *Application fee:* $45. *Application Contact:* Dr. Murali Nair, Dean, 734-487-0077, Fax: 734-487-8536, E-mail: mnair@emich.edu. *Dean*, Dr. Murali Nair, 734-487-0077, Fax: 734-487-8536, E-mail: mnair@emich.edu.

## EASTERN NAZARENE COLLEGE, Quincy, MA 02170

**General Information** Independent-religious, coed, comprehensive institution. *Graduate housing:* Rooms and/or apartments available to single students and available on a first-come, first-served basis to married students.

**GRADUATE UNITS**

**Adult and Graduate Studies** *Program availability:* Part-time, evening/weekend.

***Division of Teacher Education*** *Program availability:* Part-time, evening/weekend.

## EASTERN NEW MEXICO UNIVERSITY, Portales, NM 88130

**General Information** State-supported, coed, comprehensive institution. *Enrollment:* 5,694 graduate, professional, and undergraduate students; 313 full-time matriculated graduate/professional students (242 women), 908 part-time matriculated graduate/professional students (661 women). *Enrollment by degree level:* 898 master's, 323 other advanced degrees. *Graduate faculty:* 70 full-time (27 women), 4 part-time/adjunct (2 women). *International tuition:* $7007 full-time. *Tuition, area resident:* Full-time $5283; part-time $389.25 per credit hour. Tuition, state resident: full-time $5283; part-time $389.25 per credit hour. Tuition, nonresident: full-time $7007; part-time $389.25 per credit hour. *Required fees:* $36; $35 per semester. One-time fee: $25. *Graduate housing:* Rooms and/or apartments available on a first-come, first-served basis to single and married students. Housing application deadline: 8/1. *Student services:* Campus employment opportunities, campus safety program, career counseling, child daycare facilities, exercise/wellness program, free psychological counseling, international student services, low-cost health insurance, multicultural affairs office, services for students with disabilities, writing training. *Library facilities:* Golden Student Success Center plus 1 other. *Research affiliation:* National Institutes of Health.

**Computer facilities:** 453 computers available on campus for general student use. A campuswide network can be accessed. Online class registration is available.
Website: http://www.enmu.edu/

**General Application Contact:** Dr. John Montgomery, Dean, Graduate School, 575-562-2147, Fax: 575-562-2500, E-mail: john.montgomery@enmu.edu.

**GRADUATE UNITS**

**Graduate School** *Program availability:* Part-time, evening/weekend, online learning. Electronic applications accepted.

***College of Business*** *Program availability:* Part-time, evening/weekend, online learning. Electronic applications accepted.

***College of Education and Technology*** *Program availability:* Part-time, online learning. Electronic applications accepted.

***College of Fine Arts*** *Program availability:* Part-time, online learning. Electronic applications accepted.

***College of Liberal Arts and Sciences*** *Program availability:* Part-time, evening/weekend, online learning. Electronic applications accepted.

## EASTERN OREGON UNIVERSITY, La Grande, OR 97850-2899

**General Information** State-supported, coed, comprehensive institution. *Enrollment:* 3,067 graduate, professional, and undergraduate students; 77 full-time matriculated graduate/professional students (44 women), 89 part-time matriculated graduate/professional students (69 women). *Enrollment by degree level:* 166 master's. *Graduate faculty:* 22 full-time (13 women), 14 part-time/adjunct (9 women). *International* *tuition:* $17,118 full-time. *Tuition, area resident:* Full-time $13,572; part-time $377 per credit hour. Tuition, state resident: full-time $13,572; part-time $377 per credit hour. Tuition, nonresident: full-time $17,118; part-time $475.50 per credit hour. *Required fees:* $1569; $336 per term. Tuition and fees vary according to course load. *Graduate housing:* Room and/or apartments available on a first-come, first-served basis to single students; on-campus housing not available to married students. Typical cost: $6800 per year ($10,850 including board). Room and board charges vary according to board plan and housing facility selected. *Student services:* Campus employment opportunities, campus safety program, career counseling, exercise/wellness program, free psychological counseling, international student services, multicultural affairs office, services for students with disabilities, writing training. *Library facilities:* Pierce Library. *Collection:* Books: 356,951 (physical), 66,379 (digital/electronic); Serial titles: 392 (physical), 145 (digital/electronic); Databases: 139. Weekly public service hours: 90; students can reserve study rooms.

**Computer facilities:** Computer purchase and lease plans are available. A campuswide network can be accessed. Online class registration is available.
Website: http://www.eou.edu/

**General Application Contact:** Janet Frye, Administrative Program Assistant, 541-962-3772, Fax: 541-962-3701, E-mail: jfrye@eou.edu.

**GRADUATE UNITS**

**Master of Arts in Teaching Program** Students: 39 full-time (23 women), 2 part-time (1 woman); includes 5 minority (1 Black or African American, non-Hispanic/Latino; 1 Hispanic/Latino; 3 Two or more races, non-Hispanic/Latino). Average age 30. *Faculty:* 8 full-time (5 women), 4 part-time/adjunct (2 women). Expenses: Contact institution. *Financial support:* In 2019–20, 21 students received support. Federal Work-Study, institutionally sponsored loans, scholarships/grants, and tuition waivers (full and partial) available. Support available to part-time students. In 2019, 47 master's awarded. *Application deadline:* For fall admission, 3/1 for domestic students. Applications are processed on a rolling basis. Electronic applications accepted. *Application Contact:* Janet Frye, Administrative Support, MAT/MS Graduate Admission, 541-962-3772, Fax: 541-962-3701, E-mail: jfrye@eou.edu. *Dean of College of Business and Education,* Dr. Matt Seimears, 541-962-3399, Fax: 541-962-3701, E-mail: mseimears@eou.edu.

**Master of Fine Arts in Creative Writing** Expenses: Contact institution. *Application Contact:* Janet Frye, Administrative Program Assistant, 541-962-3772, Fax: 541-962-3701, E-mail: jfrye@eou.edu.

**Master of Science Program** Students: 8 full-time (6 women), 55 part-time (45 women); includes 8 minority (1 Black or African American, non-Hispanic/Latino; 1 Asian, non-Hispanic/Latino; 3 Hispanic/Latino; 3 Two or more races, non-Hispanic/Latino), 1 international. Average age 38. *Faculty:* 12 full-time (8 women), 5 part-time/adjunct (2 women). Expenses: Contact institution. *Financial support:* In 2019–20, 12 students received support. Federal Work-Study, scholarships/grants, and tuition waivers (full and partial) available. Support available to part-time students. In 2019, 16 master's awarded. *Program availability:* Part-time, online only, 100% online. *Application deadline:* Applications are processed on a rolling basis. Electronic applications accepted. *Application Contact:* Janet Frye, Administrative Support, MAT/MS Graduate Admission, 541-962-3772, Fax: 541-962-3701, E-mail: jfrye@eou.edu. *Dean of College of Business and Education,* Dr. Matt Seimears, 541-962-3399, Fax: 541-962-3701, E-mail: mseimears@eou.edu.

**Program in Business Administration** Students: 30 full-time (15 women), 24 part-time (16 women); includes 17 minority (1 American Indian or Alaska Native, non-Hispanic/Latino; 2 Asian, non-Hispanic/Latino; 11 Hispanic/Latino; 3 Two or more races, non-Hispanic/Latino), 7 international. Average age 34. *Faculty:* 6 full-time (2 women), 1 (woman) part-time/adjunct. Expenses: Contact institution. *Financial support:* In 2019–20, 14 students received support. Federal Work-Study, scholarships/grants, and tuition waivers (full and partial) available. Support available to part-time students. In 2019, 44 master's awarded. *Program availability:* Part-time, online only, 100% online. *Application deadline:* For fall admission, 5/15 priority date for domestic students. Applications are processed on a rolling basis. Electronic applications accepted. *Application Contact:* Kristin Johnson, Graduate Pre-Admission Advisor, 541-962-3529, Fax: 541-962-3701, E-mail: kristin.johnson@eou.edu. *Chair of Curriculum/Business Faculty,* Laura Gow-Hogge, 541-962-3721, E-mail: lgow@eou.edu.

**Program in Master of Fine Arts Creative Writing**

## EASTERN SCHOOL OF ACUPUNCTURE AND TRADITIONAL MEDICINE, Montclair, NJ 07042-3551

**General Information** Proprietary, graduate-only institution.

**GRADUATE UNITS**

**Acupuncture Program**

## EASTERN UNIVERSITY, St. Davids, PA 19087-3696

**General Information** Independent-religious, coed, university. *Enrollment:* 3,100 graduate, professional, and undergraduate students; 319 full-time matriculated graduate/professional students (226 women), 679 part-time matriculated graduate/professional students (469 women). *Enrollment by degree level:* 789 master's, 169 doctoral, 40 other advanced degrees. *Graduate housing:* Room and/or apartments available on a first-come, first-served basis to single students; on-campus housing not available to married students. *Student services:* Campus employment opportunities, career counseling, international student services, low-cost health insurance, services for students with disabilities. *Library facilities:* Warner Memorial Library plus 1 other. *Collection:* Books: 150,192 (physical), 604,592 (digital/electronic); Serial titles: 60 (physical), 44,003 (digital/electronic); Databases: 176. Weekly public service hours: 85; students can reserve study rooms.

**Computer facilities:** 68 computers available on campus for general student use. A campuswide network can be accessed. Online class registration, BRIGHTSPACE are available.
Website: http://www.eastern.edu/

**General Application Contact:** Katelyn Ambrose, Director of Enrollment, 800-452-0996, E-mail: gpsadmissions@eastern.edu.

**GRADUATE UNITS**

**Graduate Education Programs** Students: 54 full-time (45 women), 149 part-time (134 women); includes 75 minority (54 Black or African American, non-Hispanic/Latino; 3 Asian, non-Hispanic/Latino; 15 Hispanic/Latino; 3 Two or more races, non-Hispanic/Latino). Average age 33. Expenses: Contact institution. In 2019, 89 master's, 10 other advanced degrees awarded. *Program availability:* Part-time, evening/weekend, online learning. *Application deadline:* Applications are processed on a rolling basis. *Application fee:* $35. Electronic applications accepted. *Application Contact:* Michael Dziedziak, Executive Director of Enrollment, 800-452-0996, E-mail: gpsadmissions@eastern.edu. *Executive Director of Enrollment,* Michael Dziedziak, 800-452-0996, E-mail: gpsadmissions@eastern.edu.

**Graduate Programs in Business and Leadership** Students: 104 full-time (75 women), 182 part-time (109 women); includes 108 minority (73 Black or African American, non-Hispanic/Latino; 1 American Indian or Alaska Native, non-Hispanic/Latino; 10 Asian, non-Hispanic/Latino; 16 Hispanic/Latino; 8 Two or more races, non-Hispanic/Latino), 28 international. Average age 38. Expenses: Contact institution. *Financial support:* Applicants required to submit FAFSA. In 2019, 95 master's awarded. *Program availability:* Part-time, evening/weekend, online learning. *Application deadline:* Applications are processed on a rolling basis. *Application fee:* $35. Electronic applications accepted. *Application Contact:* Michael Dziedziak, Executive Director of Enrollment, 800-452-0996, E-mail: gpsadmissions@eastern.edu. *Executive Director of Enrollment,* Michael Dziedziak, 800-452-0996, E-mail: gpsadmissions@eastern.edu.

**Health and Sciences**

**Palmer Theological Seminary** Students: 55 full-time (23 women), 169 part-time (69 women); includes 144 minority (61 Black or African American, non-Hispanic/Latino; 2 Asian, non-Hispanic/Latino; 16 Hispanic/Latino; 65 Two or more races, non-Hispanic/Latino), 5 international. Average age 46. Expenses: Contact institution. In 2019, 68 master's awarded. *Program availability:* Part-time, online learning. *Application deadline:* Applications are processed on a rolling basis. *Application fee:* $30. Electronic applications accepted. *Application Contact:* Michael Dziedziak, Executive Director of Enrollment, 800-452-0996, E-mail: semadmis@eastern.edu. *Executive Director of Enrollment,* Michael Dziedziak, 800-452-0996, E-mail: semadmis@eastern.edu.

**Templeton Honors College** Students: 9 part-time (6 women); includes 1 minority (Hispanic/Latino). Average age 34. Expenses: Contact institution. *Application Contact:* Michael Dziedziak, Executive Director of Enrollment, 800-452-0996, E-mail: gpsadmissions@eastern.edu.

## EASTERN VIRGINIA MEDICAL SCHOOL, Norfolk, VA 23501-1980

**General Information** Independent, coed, graduate-only institution. *Graduate housing:* On-campus housing not available.

**GRADUATE UNITS**

**Biotechnology Program** Electronic applications accepted.

**Doctoral Program in Biomedical Sciences** Electronic applications accepted.

**Graduate Art Therapy and Counseling Program** Electronic applications accepted.

**Master of Physician Assistant Program** Electronic applications accepted.

**Master of Public Health Program** *Program availability:* Evening/weekend. Electronic applications accepted.

**Master of Surgical Assisting Program** Electronic applications accepted.

**Master's Program in Biomedical Sciences Research** Electronic applications accepted.

**Master's Program in Clinical Embryology and Andrology** *Program availability:* Online learning. Electronic applications accepted.

**Medical Master's Program in Biomedical Sciences** Electronic applications accepted.

**Ophthalmic Technology Program** Electronic applications accepted.

**Professional Program in Medicine** Electronic applications accepted.

**The Virginia Consortium Program in Clinical Psychology**

## EASTERN WASHINGTON UNIVERSITY, Cheney, WA 99004-2431

**General Information** State-supported, coed, comprehensive institution. CGS member. *Enrollment:* 12,325 graduate, professional, and undergraduate students; 1,299 full-time matriculated graduate/professional students (954 women), 126 part-time matriculated graduate/professional students (19 women). *Enrollment by degree level:* 1,309 master's, 116 doctoral. *Graduate faculty:* 237 full-time (148 women). *Graduate housing:* Room and/or apartments available on a first-come, first-served basis to single students; on-campus housing not available to married students. Typical cost: $13,026 (including board). Housing application deadline: 5/1. *Student services:* Campus employment opportunities, campus safety program, career counseling, child daycare facilities, exercise/wellness program, free psychological counseling, international student services, low-cost health insurance, multicultural affairs office, services for students with disabilities, teacher training, writing training. *Library facilities:* John F. Kennedy Library. *Collection:* Students can reserve study rooms.

**Computer facilities:** Computer purchase and lease plans are available. A campuswide network can be accessed. Online class registration, network disk storage; discounted software; laptops, still and video cameras, projectors for checkout; print credit; black white laser, color laser, and color photo options, large format print service are available.
Website: http://www.ewu.edu/

**General Application Contact:** Roberta Brooke, Director of Graduate Programs, 509-359-6297, Fax: 509-359-6044, E-mail: gradprograms@ewu.edu.

**GRADUATE UNITS**

**Graduate Studies** Students: 1,301 full-time (955 women), 376 part-time (270 women); includes 91 minority (13 Black or African American, non-Hispanic/Latino; 14 American Indian or Alaska Native, non-Hispanic/Latino; 15 Asian, non-Hispanic/Latino; 49 Hispanic/Latino), 11 international. Average age 35. 1,429 applicants, 48% accepted, 553 enrolled. *Faculty:* 236 full-time (148 women). Expenses: Contact institution. *Financial support:* Teaching assistantships with partial tuition reimbursements, career-related internships or fieldwork, Federal Work-Study, institutionally sponsored loans, scholarships/grants, health care benefits, tuition waivers (full and partial), and unspecified assistantships available. Support available to part-time students. Financial award application deadline: 2/1. In 2019, 371 master's, 37 doctorates, 33 other advanced degrees awarded. *Program availability:* Part-time, evening/weekend. *Application deadline:* For fall admission, 9/1 for domestic students; for winter admission, 12/1 for domestic students; for spring admission, 3/1 for domestic students; for summer admission, 6/1 for domestic students. Applications are processed on a rolling basis. *Application fee:* $75. Electronic applications accepted. *Application Contact:* Roberta Brooke, Executive Director of Graduate Department, 509-359-6566, E-mail: rbrooke@ewu.edu. *Executive Director of Graduate Department,* Roberta Brooke, 509-359-6566, E-mail: rbrooke@ewu.edu.

***College of Arts, Letters and Education*** Students: 363 full-time (278 women), 116 part-time (82 women); includes 23 minority (3 Black or African American, non-Hispanic/Latino; 3 American Indian or Alaska Native, non-Hispanic/Latino; 3 Asian, non-Hispanic/Latino; 14 Hispanic/Latino), 2 international. Average age 36. 309 applicants, 73% accepted, 167 enrolled. *Faculty:* 53 full-time (35 women). Expenses: Contact institution. *Financial support:* Teaching assistantships with partial tuition reimbursements, career-related internships or fieldwork, Federal Work-Study, institutionally sponsored loans, scholarships/grants, health care benefits, tuition waivers (partial), and unspecified assistantships available. Support available to part-time students. Financial award application deadline: 2/1; financial award applicants required to submit FAFSA. In 2019, 76 master's awarded. *Program availability:* Part-time. *Application deadline:* Applications are processed on a rolling basis. *Application fee:* $75. Electronic applications accepted. *Application Contact:* Kathy White, Advisor/Recruiter for Graduate Studies, 509-359-2491, Fax: 509-359-6044, E-mail: gradprograms@ewu.edu. *Dean*, Dr. Pete Porter, E-mail: pporter@ewu.edu.

***College of Business and Public Administration*** Students: 173 full-time (96 women), 68 part-time (42 women); includes 25 minority (4 Black or African American, non-Hispanic/Latino; 2 American Indian or Alaska Native, non-Hispanic/Latino; 5 Asian, non-Hispanic/Latino; 14 Hispanic/Latino), 3 international. Average age 33. 235 applicants, 75% accepted, 140 enrolled. *Faculty:* 16 full-time (6 women). Expenses: Contact institution. *Financial support:* In 2019–20, 9 students received support. Teaching assistantships with partial tuition reimbursements available, career-related internships or fieldwork, Federal Work-Study, institutionally sponsored loans, scholarships/grants, health care benefits, tuition waivers (partial), and unspecified assistantships available. Support available to part-time students. Financial award application deadline: 2/1. In 2019, 78 master's awarded. *Program availability:* Part-time, evening/weekend. *Application deadline:* For fall admission, 4/1 priority date for domestic students; for spring admission, 1/15 for domestic students. Applications are processed on a rolling basis. *Application fee:* $75. Electronic applications accepted. *Application Contact:* Dr. Shuming Bai, Associate Dean, 509-828-1202, E-mail: sbai@ewu.edu. *Interim Dean, College of Business and Public Administration*, Dr. Ahmad Tootoonchi, 509-828-1224, Fax: 509-828-1274, E-mail: tootoonchi@ewu.edu.

***College of Health Science and Public Health*** Students: 296 full-time (222 women), 36 part-time (26 women); includes 12 minority (2 Black or African American, non-Hispanic/Latino; 2 American Indian or Alaska Native, non-Hispanic/Latino; 3 Asian, non-Hispanic/Latino; 5 Hispanic/Latino), 4 international. Average age 29. 604 applicants, 18% accepted, 99 enrolled. *Faculty:* 54 full-time (38 women). Expenses: Contact institution. *Financial support:* Teaching assistantships with partial tuition reimbursements, career-related internships or fieldwork, Federal Work-Study, institutionally sponsored loans, scholarships/grants, health care benefits, tuition waivers (partial), and unspecified assistantships available. Support available to part-time students. Financial award application deadline: 2/1; financial award applicants required to submit FAFSA. In 2019, 110 master's awarded. *Program availability:* Part-time. *Application deadline:* Applications are processed on a rolling basis. *Application fee:* $75. Electronic applications accepted. *Application Contact:* Kathy White, Advisor/Recruiter for Graduate Studies, 509-359-2491, Fax: 509-359-6044, E-mail: gradprograms@ewu.edu. *Dean*, Dr. Laureen OHanlon, 509-359-1456, E-mail: lohanlon@ewu.edu.

***College of Science, Technology, Engineering and Mathematics*** Students: 35 full-time (16 women), 9 part-time (4 women); includes 1 minority (American Indian or Alaska Native, non-Hispanic/Latino), 2 international. Average age 30. 37 applicants, 70% accepted, 19 enrolled. *Faculty:* 26 full-time (10 women). Expenses: Contact institution. *Financial support:* Teaching assistantships and unspecified assistantships available. Financial award application deadline: 2/15; financial award applicants required to submit FAFSA. In 2019, 13 master's awarded. *Program availability:* Part-time. *Application fee:* $75. Electronic applications accepted. *Application Contact:* Kathy White, Advisor/Recruiter for Graduate Studies, 509-359-2491, Fax: 509-359-6044, E-mail: gradprograms@ewu.edu. *Dean*, Dr. David Bowman, 509-359-6244, Fax: 509-359-6950, E-mail: dbowman@ewu.edu.

***College of Social Sciences*** Students: 433 full-time (343 women), 148 part-time (116 women); includes 35 minority (4 Black or African American, non-Hispanic/Latino; 7 American Indian or Alaska Native, non-Hispanic/Latino; 5 Asian, non-Hispanic/Latino; 19 Hispanic/Latino), 14 international. Average age 34. 275 applicants, 53% accepted, 125 enrolled. *Faculty:* 87 full-time (59 women). Expenses: Contact institution. *Financial support:* Research assistantships, teaching assistantships with partial tuition reimbursements, career-related internships or fieldwork, Federal Work-Study, institutionally sponsored loans, scholarships/grants, health care benefits, tuition waivers (partial), and unspecified assistantships available. Support available to part-time students. Financial award application deadline: 2/1; financial award applicants required to submit FAFSA. In 2019, 131 master's, 15 other advanced degrees awarded. *Program availability:* Part-time, evening/weekend. *Application deadline:* Applications are processed on a rolling basis. *Application fee:* $75. Electronic applications accepted. *Application Contact:* Kathy White, Advisor/Recruiter for Graduate Studies, 509-359-6297, Fax: 509-359-6044, E-mail: gradprograms@ewu.edu. *Dean*, Dr. Jonathan Anderson, 509-359-6707, E-mail: janderson@ewu.edu.

## EAST STROUDSBURG UNIVERSITY OF PENNSYLVANIA, East Stroudsburg, PA 18301-2999

**General Information** State-supported, coed, comprehensive institution. *Graduate housing:* Room and/or apartments available on a first-come, first-served basis to single students; on-campus housing not available to married students. Housing application deadline: 6/1.

**GRADUATE UNITS**

**Graduate and Extended Studies** *Program availability:* Part-time, evening/weekend, 100% online, blended/hybrid learning. Electronic applications accepted.

***College of Arts and Sciences*** *Program availability:* Part-time, evening/weekend. Electronic applications accepted.

***College of Business and Management*** *Program availability:* Part-time, evening/weekend, online learning. Electronic applications accepted.

***College of Education*** *Program availability:* Part-time, evening/weekend, online learning. Electronic applications accepted.

***College of Health Sciences*** *Program availability:* Part-time, evening/weekend, online learning. Electronic applications accepted.

## EAST TENNESSEE STATE UNIVERSITY, Johnson City, TN 37614

**General Information** State-supported, coed, university. CGS member. *Graduate housing:* Rooms and/or apartments available on a first-come, first-served basis to single and married students. Housing application deadline: 8/1. *Research affiliation:* Puckett Institute (education), Cyberonics (biomedical science), Mountain Home VA Medical Center (clinical and biomedical science), Mountain States Health Alliance; Wellmont Health System; State of Franklin Healthcare Associates (clinical, nursing, and biomedical science), Oak Ridge National Laboratory (biomedical physical science and computer science), Frontier Health, Inc./Cherokee Health Systems (clinical and education).

**GRADUATE UNITS**

**Bill Gatton College of Pharmacy** *Program availability:* Part-time. Electronic applications accepted.

**College of Graduate and Continuing Studies** Expenses: Contact institution. *Financial support:* Fellowships with tuition reimbursements, research assistantships with tuition reimbursements, and teaching assistantships with tuition reimbursements available. Financial award applicants required to submit FAFSA. *Program availability:* Part-time. *Application fee:* $55 ($65 for international students). Electronic applications accepted. *Application Contact:* Dr. Sharon McGee, Dean, 423-439-4221, Fax: 423-439-5624, E-mail: gradschool@etsu.edu. *Dean*, Dr. Sharon McGee, 423-439-4221, Fax: 423-439-5624, E-mail: gradschool@etsu.edu.

***Clemmer College*** Students: 270 full-time (164 women), 353 part-time (266 women); includes 70 minority (42 Black or African American, non-Hispanic/Latino; 1 American Indian or Alaska Native, non-Hispanic/Latino; 7 Asian, non-Hispanic/Latino; 7 Hispanic/Latino; 13 Two or more races, non-Hispanic/Latino), 29 international. Expenses: Contact institution. *Financial support:* Fellowships with full tuition reimbursements, research assistantships with full tuition reimbursements, teaching assistantships with full tuition reimbursements, career-related internships or fieldwork, institutionally sponsored loans, scholarships/grants, and unspecified assistantships available. Financial award application deadline: 7/1; financial award applicants required to submit FAFSA. In 2019, 186 master's, 32 doctorates, 32 other advanced degrees awarded. *Application fee:* $55 ($65 for international students). Electronic applications accepted. *Application Contact:* School of Graduate Studies, 423-439-4221, Fax: 423-439-5624, E-mail: gradsch@etsu.edu. *Dean*, Dr. Janna L. Scarborough, 423-439-7616, Fax: 423-439-7560, E-mail: scarboro@etsu.edu.

***College of Arts and Sciences*** Students: 279 full-time (155 women), 84 part-time (53 women); includes 39 minority (18 Black or African American, non-Hispanic/Latino; 1 Asian, non-Hispanic/Latino; 3 Hispanic/Latino; 17 Two or more races, non-Hispanic/Latino), 56 international. Expenses: Contact institution. *Financial support:* Research assistantships with tuition reimbursements, teaching assistantships with tuition reimbursements, career-related internships or fieldwork, and unspecified assistantships available. Financial award application deadline: 7/1; financial award applicants required to submit FAFSA. In 2019, 127 master's, 6 doctorates, 8 other advanced degrees awarded. *Program availability:* Part-time. *Application fee:* $55 ($65 for international students). Electronic applications accepted. *Application Contact:* School of Graduate Studies, 423-439-4221, Fax: 423-439-5624, E-mail: gradschool@etsu.edu. *Dean*, Dr. Gordon K. Anderson, 423-439-5671, Fax: 423-439-4645, E-mail: andersgk@etsu.edu.

***College of Business and Technology*** Students: 121 full-time (43 women), 76 part-time (40 women); includes 24 minority (10 Black or African American, non-Hispanic/Latino; 3 Asian, non-Hispanic/Latino; 2 Hispanic/Latino; 9 Two or more races, non-Hispanic/Latino), 33 international. Expenses: Contact institution. *Financial support:* Research assistantships with tuition reimbursements and teaching assistantships with tuition reimbursements available. Financial award application deadline: 7/1; financial award applicants required to submit FAFSA. In 2019, 123 master's, 3 other advanced degrees awarded. *Application fee:* $55 ($65 for international students). Electronic applications accepted. *Application Contact:* School of Graduate Studies, 423-439-4221, Fax: 423-439-5624, E-mail: gradsch@etsu.edu. *Dean*, Dr. Dennis Depew, 423-439-4289, Fax: 423-439-5274, E-mail: depewd@etsu.edu.

***College of Clinical and Rehabilitative Health Sciences*** Students: 318 full-time (246 women), 105 part-time (91 women); includes 35 minority (11 Black or African American, non-Hispanic/Latino; 4 Asian, non-Hispanic/Latino; 9 Hispanic/Latino; 11 Two or more races, non-Hispanic/Latino), 3 international. Expenses: Contact institution. *Financial support:* Research assistantships with tuition reimbursements and teaching assistantships with tuition reimbursements available. In 2019, 96 master's, 45 doctorates awarded. *Application fee:* $55 ($65 for international students). Electronic applications accepted. *Application Contact:* School of Graduate Studies, 423-439-4221, Fax: 423-439-5624, E-mail: gradsch@etsu.edu. *Dean*, Dr. Don Samples, 423-439-7454, Fax: 423-439-4240, E-mail: carhs@etsu.edu.

***College of Nursing*** Students: 196 full-time (163 women), 234 part-time (211 women); includes 36 minority (21 Black or African American, non-Hispanic/Latino; 1 Asian, non-Hispanic/Latino; 3 Hispanic/Latino; 11 Two or more races, non-Hispanic/Latino). Expenses: Contact institution. *Financial support:* Research assistantships with tuition reimbursements, teaching assistantships, career-related internships or fieldwork, scholarships/grants, and unspecified assistantships available. Financial award applicants required to submit FAFSA. In 2019, 114 master's, 22 doctorates, 3 other advanced degrees awarded. *Program availability:* Part-time, evening/weekend, online learning. *Application fee:* $55 ($65 for international students). Electronic applications accepted. *Application Contact:* Dr. Myra Clark, Director of Graduate Programs, 423-439-4396, Fax: 423-439-4100, E-mail: clarkml2@etsu.edu. *Dean*, Dr. Wendy Nehring, 423-439-7051, Fax: 423-439-4543, E-mail: nursing@etsu.edu.

***College of Public Health*** Expenses: Contact institution. *Financial support:* Research assistantships with tuition reimbursements, teaching assistantships with tuition reimbursements, career-related internships or fieldwork, scholarships/grants, and unspecified assistantships available. Financial award applicants required to submit FAFSA. In 2019, 64 master's, 2 doctorates, 27 other advanced degrees awarded. *Program availability:* Part-time, online learning. *Application fee:* $55 ($65 for international students). Electronic applications accepted. *Application Contact:* Dr. Randy Wykoff, Dean, 423-439-4243, Fax: 423-439-5238, E-mail: wykoff@etsu.edu. *Dean*, Dr. Randy Wykoff, 423-439-4243, Fax: 423-439-5238, E-mail: wykoff@etsu.edu.

**Quillen College of Medicine** *Program availability:* Part-time. Electronic applications accepted.

## EAST TEXAS BAPTIST UNIVERSITY, Marshall, TX 75670-1498

**General Information** Independent-religious, coed, comprehensive institution. *Enrollment:* 1,593 graduate, professional, and undergraduate students; 39 full-time matriculated graduate/professional students (19 women), 83 part-time matriculated graduate/professional students (42 women). *Enrollment by degree level:* 122 master's. *Graduate faculty:* 11 full-time (4 women), 12 part-time/adjunct (5 women). *Graduate housing:* Room and/or apartments available on a first-come, first-served basis to single students; on-campus housing not available to married students. Typical cost: $9460 (including board). Room and board charges vary according to board plan and housing facility selected. *Student services:* Campus employment opportunities, campus safety program, career counseling, free psychological counseling, international student services, services for students with disabilities, teacher training, writing training. *Library facilities:* Mamye Jarrett Library. *Collection:* Books: 96,495 (physical), 478,599 (digital/electronic); Serial titles: 403 (physical), 43,364 (digital/electronic); Databases: 175. Weekly public service hours: 88; students can reserve study rooms.

**Computer facilities:** 301 computers available on campus for general student use. A campuswide network can be accessed. Online class registration is available. Website: http://www.etbu.edu/

**General Application Contact:** Den Murley, Director of Graduate Admissions, 903-923-2079, Fax: 903-934-8115, E-mail: gradadmissions@etbu.edu.

**GRADUATE UNITS**

**Master of Arts in Clinical Mental Health Counseling** Students: 5 full-time (3 women), 15 part-time (all women); includes 11 minority (8 Black or African American, non-Hispanic/Latino; 1 American Indian or Alaska Native, non-Hispanic/Latino; 2 Hispanic/Latino). Average age 32. 11 applicants, 73% accepted, 6 enrolled. *Faculty:* 3 full-time (2 women). Expenses: Contact institution. *Financial support:* In 2019–20, 4 students received support. Scholarships/grants, unspecified assistantships, and staff grants available. Financial award applicants required to submit FAFSA. In 2019, 11 master's awarded. *Program availability:* Part-time, evening/weekend. *Application deadline:* For fall admission, 8/13 for domestic students; for spring admission, 1/7 for domestic students; for summer admission, 5/5 for domestic students. Applications are processed on a rolling basis. *Application fee:* $50. Electronic applications accepted. *Application Contact:* Den Murley, Director of Graduate Admissions, 903-923-2079, Fax: 903-934-8115, E-mail: gradadmissions@etbu.edu. *Director*, Dr. Allen Appiah-Boateng, 903-923-2318, E-mail: gradadmissions@etbu.edu.

**Master of Business Administration** Students: 19 full-time (8 women), 13 part-time (6 women); includes 15 minority (13 Black or African American, non-Hispanic/Latino; 1 Hispanic/Latino; 1 Two or more races, non-Hispanic/Latino). Average age 32. 17 applicants, 41% accepted, 6 enrolled. *Faculty:* 4 part-time/adjunct (0 women). Expenses: Contact institution. *Financial support:* In 2019–20, 18 students received support. Federal Work-Study, scholarships/grants, unspecified assistantships, and staff grants available. Financial award applicants required to submit FAFSA. In 2019, 14 master's awarded. *Program availability:* Part-time, evening/weekend, online only, 100% online. *Application deadline:* For fall admission, 8/13 for domestic students; for spring admission, 1/7 for domestic students; for summer admission, 5/5 for domestic students. Applications are processed on a rolling basis. *Application fee:* $50. Electronic applications accepted. *Application Contact:* Den Murley, Director of Graduate Admissions, 903-923-2079, Fax: 903-934-8115, E-mail: dmurley@etbu.edu. *Director of Graduate Admissions*, Den Murley, 903-923-2079, Fax: 903-934-8115, E-mail: dmurley@etbu.edu.

**Master of Science in Kinesiology** Students: 5 full-time (3 women), 12 part-time (3 women); includes 2 minority (both Black or African American, non-Hispanic/Latino). Average age 24. 11 applicants, 73% accepted, 7 enrolled. *Faculty:* 3 full-time (1 woman). Expenses: Contact institution. *Financial support:* In 2019–20, 15 students received support. Federal Work-Study, scholarships/grants, unspecified assistantships, and staff grants available. Financial award applicants required to submit FAFSA. In 2019, 5 master's awarded. *Program availability:* Part-time, evening/weekend. *Application deadline:* For fall admission, 8/13 for domestic students; for spring admission, 1/7 for domestic students; for summer admission, 5/5 for domestic students. Applications are processed on a rolling basis. *Application fee:* $50. Electronic applications accepted. *Application Contact:* Den Murley, Director of Graduate Admissions, 903-923-2079, Fax: 903-934-8115, E-mail: gradadmissions@etbu.edu. *Dean, Frank S. Groner School of Professional Studies*, Dr. Joseph D. Brown, 903-923-2270, Fax: 903-935-4318, E-mail: jbrown@etbu.edu.

**School of Christian Studies** Students: 10 full-time (5 women), 15 part-time (3 women); includes 5 minority (4 Black or African American, non-Hispanic/Latino; 1 Hispanic/Latino). Average age 26. 9 applicants, 89% accepted, 8 enrolled. *Faculty:* 2 full-time (0 women), 4 part-time/adjunct (2 women). Expenses: Contact institution. *Financial support:* In 2019–20, 24 students received support. Federal Work-Study, scholarships/grants, unspecified assistantships, and staff grants available. Financial award applicants required to submit FAFSA. In 2019, 4 master's awarded. *Program availability:* Part-time, evening/weekend, online only, 100% online. *Application deadline:* For fall admission, 8/13 for domestic students; for spring admission, 1/7 for domestic students; for summer admission, 5/5 for domestic students. Applications are processed on a rolling basis. *Application fee:* $50. Electronic applications accepted. *Application Contact:* Den Murley, Director of Graduate Admissions, 903-923-2079, Fax: 903-934-8115, E-mail: gradadmissions@etbu.edu. *Director*, Dr. Scott Stevens, 903-923-2178, Fax: 903-923-2077, E-mail: sstevens@etbu.edu.

**School of Education** Students: 28 part-time (15 women); includes 11 minority (7 Black or African American, non-Hispanic/Latino; 1 Hispanic/Latino; 3 Two or more races, non-Hispanic/Latino). Average age 28. 21 applicants, 62% accepted, 13 enrolled. *Faculty:* 3 full-time (1 woman), 4 part-time/adjunct (3 women). Expenses: Contact institution. *Financial support:* In 2019–20, 11 students received support. Federal Work-Study, scholarships/grants, unspecified assistantships, and staff grants available. Financial award applicants required to submit FAFSA. In 2019, 17 master's awarded. *Program availability:* Part-time, evening/weekend, 100% online, blended/hybrid learning. *Application deadline:* For fall admission, 8/13 for domestic students; for spring admission, 1/7 for domestic students; for summer admission, 5/5 for domestic students. Applications are processed on a rolling basis. *Application fee:* $50. Electronic applications accepted. *Application Contact:* Den Murley, Director of Graduate Admissions, 903-923-2079, Fax: 903-934-8115, E-mail: gradadmissions@etbu.edu. *Director*, Dr. PJ Winters, 903-923-2276, Fax: 903-935-4318, E-mail: med@etbu.edu.

## EAST WEST COLLEGE OF NATURAL MEDICINE, Sarasota, FL 34234

**General Information** Proprietary, coed, graduate-only institution.

**GRADUATE UNITS**

**Graduate Programs**

## ECCLESIA COLLEGE, Springdale, AR 72762

**General Information** Independent-religious, coed, comprehensive institution.

**GRADUATE UNITS**

**Graduate School** *Program availability:* Online learning.

## EC-COUNCIL UNIVERSITY, Albuquerque, NM 87109

**General Information** Proprietary, coed, upper-level institution. *Enrollment by degree level:* 155 master's. *Graduate faculty:* 28 part-time/adjunct (9 women). *Graduate housing:* On-campus housing not available.
Website: http://www.eccu.edu/

**General Application Contact:** David Valdez, Academic Advisor, 505-922-2886, Fax: 505-856-8267, E-mail: david.valdez@eccu.edu.

**GRADUATE UNITS**

**Master of Science in Cyber Security Program** *Program availability:* Part-time, online only, 100% online. Electronic applications accepted.

## ECOLE HÔTELIÈRE DE LAUSANNE, CH-1000 Lausanne 25, Switzerland

**General Information** Independent, coed, comprehensive institution.

**GRADUATE UNITS**

**Program in Hospitality Administration**

## ECPI UNIVERSITY, Virginia Beach, VA 23462

**General Information** Proprietary, coed, comprehensive institution. *Enrollment:* 24,881 graduate, professional, and undergraduate students; 345 full-time matriculated graduate/professional students (173 women). *Enrollment by degree level:* 345 master's. *Graduate faculty:* 24 full-time (8 women), 18 part-time/adjunct (8 women). *Tuition:* Full-time $12,960; part-time $6480 per semester. Full-time tuition and fees vary according to program. *Student services:* Campus employment opportunities, career counseling, international student services, services for students with disabilities. *Library facilities:* ECPI-Virginia Beach Campus Library plus 13 others. *Collection:* Books: 17,128 (physical), 197,849 (digital/electronic); Serial titles: 79 (physical); Databases: 81. Weekly public service hours: 62; students can reserve study rooms.

**Computer facilities:** Computer purchase and lease plans are available. 6,500 computers available on campus for general student use. A campuswide network can be accessed. Online class registration is available.
Website: http://www.ecpi.edu/

**GRADUATE UNITS**

**Graduate Programs** Students: 345 full-time (173 women); includes 157 minority (91 Black or African American, non-Hispanic/Latino; 5 American Indian or Alaska Native, non-Hispanic/Latino; 24 Asian, non-Hispanic/Latino; 25 Hispanic/Latino; 2 Native Hawaiian or other Pacific Islander, non-Hispanic/Latino; 10 Two or more races, non-Hispanic/Latino), 11 international. Average age 35. *Faculty:* 17 full-time (8 women), 25 part-time/adjunct (7 women). Expenses: Contact institution. *Financial support:* In 2019–20, 155 students received support. Career-related internships or fieldwork, Federal Work-Study, institutionally sponsored loans, and scholarships/grants available. Financial award applicants required to submit FAFSA. In 2019, 128 master's awarded. *Program availability:* Part-time, evening/weekend, 100% online, blended/hybrid learning.

## ECUMENICAL THEOLOGICAL SEMINARY, Detroit, MI 48201

**General Information** Independent-religious, coed, graduate-only institution. *Graduate housing:* On-campus housing not available.

**GRADUATE UNITS**

**Professional Program**

**Program in Ministry**

## EDEN THEOLOGICAL SEMINARY, St. Louis, MO 63119-3192

**General Information** Independent-religious, coed, graduate-only institution. *Graduate housing:* Rooms and/or apartments available on a first-come, first-served basis to single and married students. Housing application deadline: 7/30.

**GRADUATE UNITS**

**Graduate and Professional Programs** Electronic applications accepted.

## EDGEWOOD COLLEGE, Madison, WI 53711-1997

**General Information** Independent-religious, coed, comprehensive institution. *Enrollment:* 2,038 graduate, professional, and undergraduate students; 347 full-time matriculated graduate/professional students (252 women), 199 part-time matriculated graduate/professional students (122 women). *Enrollment by degree level:* 412 master's, 134 doctoral. *Tuition:* Part-time $997 per credit. *Graduate housing:* On-campus housing not available. *Student services:* Campus employment opportunities, campus safety program, career counseling, exercise/wellness program, free psychological counseling, international student services, low-cost health insurance, multicultural affairs office, services for students with disabilities, teacher training, writing training. *Library facilities:* Oscar Rennebohm Library. *Collection:* Books: 73,015 (physical), 200,204 (digital/electronic); Serial titles: 65 (physical), 38,100 (digital/electronic); Databases: 87. Weekly public service hours: 98; students can reserve study rooms.

**Computer facilities:** Computer purchase and lease plans are available. 180 computers available on campus for general student use. A campuswide network can be accessed. Online class registration is available.
Website: http://www.edgewood.edu/

**General Application Contact:** Joann Eastman, Admissions Counselor, 608-663-3297, Fax: 608-663-2214, E-mail: gps@edgewood.edu.

**GRADUATE UNITS**

**Division of Education** Students: 201 full-time (141 women), 141 part-time (97 women); includes 71 minority (24 Black or African American, non-Hispanic/Latino; 8 Asian, non-Hispanic/Latino; 31 Hispanic/Latino; 1 Native Hawaiian or other Pacific Islander, non-Hispanic/Latino; 7 Two or more races, non-Hispanic/Latino), 23 international. Average age 37. *Faculty:* 13 full-time (9 women), 15 part-time/adjunct (10 women). Expenses: Contact institution. *Financial support:* Applicants required to submit FAFSA. In 2019, 70 master's, 28 doctorates awarded. *Program availability:* Part-time, evening/weekend. *Application deadline:* For fall admission, 8/15 for domestic students, 5/1 for international students; for spring admission, 1/8 for domestic students, 11/1 for international students. Applications are processed on a rolling basis. *Application fee:* $30. Electronic applications accepted. *Application Contact:* Joann Eastman, Admissions Counselor, 608-663-3250, Fax: 608-663-2214, E-mail: gps@edgewood.edu. *Dean*, Dr. Timothy D. Slekar, 608-663-2293, E-mail: tslekar@edgewood.edu.

**Henry Predolin School of Nursing** Expenses: Contact institution. *Application deadline:* For fall admission, 8/15 priority date for domestic students, 5/1 for international students; for spring admission, 1/8 priority date for domestic students, 11/1 for international students. Applications are processed on a rolling basis. *Application fee:* $30. Electronic applications accepted. *Application Contact:* Dr. Margaret Noreuil, Dean, 608-663-2820, Fax: 608-663-3291, E-mail: mnoreuil@edgewood.edu. *Dean*, Dr. Margaret Noreuil, 608-663-2820, Fax: 608-663-3291, E-mail: mnoreuil@edgewood.edu.

**Program in Social Innovation and Sustainability Leadership** Students: 11 full-time (8 women), 6 part-time (4 women); includes 3 minority (1 Black or African American, non-Hispanic/Latino; 1 Asian, non-Hispanic/Latino; 1 Hispanic/Latino), 1 international. Average age 33. 15 applicants, 100% accepted, 12 enrolled. *Faculty:* 1 full-time (0 women), 2 part-time/adjunct (1 woman). Expenses: Contact institution. *Financial support:* In 2019–20, 14 students received support. Scholarships/grants available. Support available to part-time students. Financial award application deadline: 5/1; financial award applicants required to submit FAFSA. In 2019, 8 master's awarded. *Program availability:* Part-time, evening/weekend. *Application deadline:* For fall admission, 7/1 for domestic students. *Application fee:* $30. *Application Contact:* Joann Eastman, Assistant Director of Graduate Admissions, 608-663-3250, E-mail: jeastman@edgewood.edu. *Director*, Dr. Stephan Gilchrist, 608-663-6991, E-mail: sgilchrist@edgewood.edu.

**School of Business** Students: 82 full-time (42 women), 33 part-time (12 women); includes 18 minority (4 Black or African American, non-Hispanic/Latino; 3 Asian, non-

Hispanic/Latino; 6 Hispanic/Latino; 5 Two or more races, non-Hispanic/Latino), 14 international. Average age 27. Expenses: Contact institution. *Financial support:* Career-related internships or fieldwork and scholarships/grants available. *Program availability:* Part-time, evening/weekend. *Application deadline:* For fall admission, 8/15 for domestic students, 5/1 for international students; for spring admission, 1/8 for domestic students, 11/1 for international students. Applications are processed on a rolling basis. *Application fee:* $30. Electronic applications accepted. *Application Contact:* Joann Eastman, Admissions Counselor, 608-663-3297, Fax: 608-663-2214, E-mail: gps@edgewood.edu.

## EDINBORO UNIVERSITY OF PENNSYLVANIA, Edinboro, PA 16444

**General Information** State-supported, coed, comprehensive institution. *Enrollment:* 4,646 graduate, professional, and undergraduate students; 645 full-time matriculated graduate/professional students (537 women), 599 part-time matriculated graduate/professional students (491 women). *Enrollment by degree level:* 1,137 master's, 27 doctoral, 80 other advanced degrees. *Graduate faculty:* 75 full-time (53 women), 31 part-time/adjunct (19 women). *International tuition:* $16,850 full-time. *Tuition, area resident:* Full-time $11,261; part-time $625.60 per credit. Tuition, state resident: full-time $11,261; part-time $625.60 per credit. Tuition, nonresident: full-time $16,850; part-time $936.10 per credit. *Required fees:* $57.75 per credit. *Graduate housing:* Room and/or apartments available on a first-come, first-served basis to single students; on-campus housing not available to married students. *Student services:* Campus employment opportunities, campus safety program, career counseling, exercise/wellness program, free psychological counseling, international student services, low-cost health insurance, multicultural affairs office, services for students with disabilities, teacher training. *Library facilities:* Baron-Forness Library plus 1 other. *Collection:* Books: 310,014 (physical), 456,241 (digital/electronic); Serial titles: 73 (physical), 78,643 (digital/electronic); Databases: 113. Weekly public service hours: 90; study areas open 24 hours, 5–7 days a week; students can reserve study rooms. *Research affiliation:* Arts Erie (art), State Higher Education Executive Officers Association (education and learning), Preventative Aftercare, Inc. (social work), CampusEAI (computing), Northwest Institute of Research (training and education), College Board (disability education).

**Computer facilities:** A campuswide network can be accessed. Online class registration, new students receive technology instruction during orientation, 24-hour computer lab, some software are available.
Website: http://www.edinboro.edu/

**General Application Contact:** Dr. Lake Erinn, Executive Director of Graduate Studies, 814-732-2856, Fax: 814-732-2611, E-mail: lakee@edinboro.edu.

**GRADUATE UNITS**

**Department of Art** Students: 21 full-time (15 women), 29 part-time (26 women); includes 4 minority (2 Asian, non-Hispanic/Latino; 2 Hispanic/Latino). Average age 31. 39 applicants, 44% accepted, 16 enrolled. *Faculty:* 11 full-time (5 women), 1 part-time/adjunct. Expenses: Contact institution. *Financial support:* In 2019–20, 19 students received support. Research assistantships with tuition reimbursements available, Federal Work-Study, scholarships/grants, and unspecified assistantships available. Financial award application deadline: 2/15; financial award applicants required to submit FAFSA. In 2019, 13 master's awarded. *Program availability:* Evening/weekend. *Application deadline:* Applications are processed on a rolling basis. *Application fee:* $30. Electronic applications accepted. *Application Contact:* Suzanne Proulx, Chairperson, 814-732-1184, E-mail: sproulx@edinboro.edu. *Chairperson*, Suzanne Proulx, 814-732-1184, E-mail: sproulx@edinboro.edu.

**Department of Communication, Journalism and Media** Students: 24 full-time (13 women), 6 part-time (all women); includes 7 minority (5 Black or African American, non-Hispanic/Latino; 2 Hispanic/Latino), 3 international. Average age 26. 25 applicants, 64% accepted, 12 enrolled. *Faculty:* 4 full-time (2 women). Expenses: Contact institution. *Financial support:* In 2019–20, 21 students received support. Research assistantships with tuition reimbursements available, career-related internships or fieldwork, Federal Work-Study, scholarships/grants, and unspecified assistantships available. Support available to part-time students. Financial award application deadline: 2/15; financial award applicants required to submit FAFSA. In 2019, 14 master's awarded. *Program availability:* Part-time, evening/weekend. *Application deadline:* Applications are processed on a rolling basis. *Application fee:* $30. Electronic applications accepted. *Application Contact:* Dr. Melissa Gibson, Graduate program Head, 814-732-1592, E-mail: mgibson@edinboro.edu. *Graduate program Head*, Dr. Melissa Gibson, 814-732-1592, E-mail: mgibson@edinboro.edu.

**Department of Communication Sciences and Disorders** Students: 40 full-time (39 women); includes 5 minority (3 Asian, non-Hispanic/Latino; 1 Native Hawaiian or other Pacific Islander, non-Hispanic/Latino; 1 Two or more races, non-Hispanic/Latino). Average age 25. 161 applicants, 12% accepted, 15 enrolled. *Faculty:* 5 full-time (3 women), 4 part-time/adjunct (all women). Expenses: Contact institution. *Financial support:* In 2019–20, 28 students received support. Research assistantships with tuition reimbursements available, career-related internships or fieldwork, Federal Work-Study, scholarships/grants, and unspecified assistantships available. Support available to part-time students. Financial award application deadline: 2/15; financial award applicants required to submit FAFSA. In 2019, 25 master's awarded. *Program availability:* Part-time, evening/weekend. *Application deadline:* Applications are processed on a rolling basis. *Application fee:* $30. Electronic applications accepted. *Application Contact:* Craig Coleman, Chairperson, 814-732-1407, E-mail: ccoleman@edinboro.edu. *Chairperson*, Craig Coleman, 814-732-1407, E-mail: ccoleman@edinboro.edu.

**Department of Counseling, School Psychology and Special Education** Students: 180 full-time (146 women), 215 part-time (186 women); includes 42 minority (18 Black or African American, non-Hispanic/Latino; 2 American Indian or Alaska Native, non-Hispanic/Latino; 4 Asian, non-Hispanic/Latino; 12 Hispanic/Latino; 1 Native Hawaiian or other Pacific Islander, non-Hispanic/Latino; 5 Two or more races, non-Hispanic/Latino), 3 international. Average age 31. 197 applicants, 63% accepted, 71 enrolled. *Faculty:* 19 full-time (13 women), 2 part-time/adjunct (1 woman). Expenses: Contact institution. *Financial support:* In 2019–20, 35 students received support. Research assistantships with tuition reimbursements available, career-related internships or fieldwork, Federal Work-Study, scholarships/grants, and unspecified assistantships available. Support available to part-time students. Financial award application deadline: 2/15; financial award applicants required to submit FAFSA. In 2019, 87 master's, 8 other advanced degrees awarded. *Program availability:* Part-time, evening/weekend. *Application deadline:* Applications are processed on a rolling basis. *Application fee:* $30. Electronic applications accepted. *Application Contact:* Dr. Penelope Orr, Chairperson, 814-732-1684, E-mail: porr@edinboro.edu. *Chairperson*, Dr. Penelope Orr, 814-732-1684, E-mail: porr@edinboro.edu.

**Department of Early Childhood and Reading** Students: 28 full-time (27 women), 84 part-time (81 women); includes 1 minority (Hispanic/Latino). Average age 31. 25 applicants, 72% accepted, 13 enrolled. *Faculty:* 6 full-time (all women), 1 (woman) part-time/adjunct. Expenses: Contact institution. *Financial support:* In 2019–20, 8 students received support. Research assistantships with tuition reimbursements available, career-related internships or fieldwork, Federal Work-Study, scholarships/grants, and unspecified assistantships available. Support available to part-time students. Financial award application deadline: 2/15; financial award applicants required to submit FAFSA. In 2019, 70 master's, 1 other advanced degree awarded. *Program availability:* Part-time, evening/weekend. *Application deadline:* Applications are processed on a rolling basis. *Application fee:* $30. Electronic applications accepted. *Application Contact:* Dr. Mary Melvin, Chairperson, 814-732-2154, E-mail: mmelvin@edinboro.edu. *Chairperson*, Dr. Mary Melvin, 814-732-2154, E-mail: mmelvin@edinboro.edu.

**Department of Middle and Secondary Education and Educational Leadership** Students: 40 full-time (27 women), 114 part-time (72 women); includes 8 minority (2 Black or African American, non-Hispanic/Latino; 1 American Indian or Alaska Native, non-Hispanic/Latino; 1 Asian, non-Hispanic/Latino; 4 Hispanic/Latino). Average age 32. 40 applicants, 78% accepted, 13 enrolled. *Faculty:* 5 full-time (3 women), 4 part-time/adjunct (3 women). Expenses: Contact institution. *Financial support:* In 2019–20, 13 students received support. Research assistantships with tuition reimbursements available, career-related internships or fieldwork, Federal Work-Study, scholarships/grants, and unspecified assistantships available. Support available to part-time students. Financial award application deadline: 2/15; financial award applicants required to submit FAFSA. In 2019, 54 master's awarded. *Program availability:* Part-time, evening/weekend. *Application deadline:* Applications are processed on a rolling basis. *Application fee:* $30. Electronic applications accepted. *Application Contact:* Dr. Whitney Wesley, Chair, 814-732-1519, E-mail: wwesley@edinboro.edu. *Chair*, Dr. Whitney Wesley, 814-732-1519, E-mail: wwesley@edinboro.edu.

**Department of Nursing** Students: 105 part-time (85 women); includes 9 minority (4 Black or African American, non-Hispanic/Latino; 2 Asian, non-Hispanic/Latino; 3 Hispanic/Latino). Average age 37. 57 applicants, 100% accepted, 57 enrolled. *Faculty:* 6 full-time (5 women), 1 (woman) part-time/adjunct. Expenses: Contact institution. *Financial support:* Application deadline: 2/15; applicants required to submit FAFSA. *Program availability:* Part-time, evening/weekend. *Application fee:* $40. Electronic applications accepted. *Application Contact:* Dr. Victoria Hedderick, Chair, 814-732-1655, E-mail: vhedderick@edinboro.edu. *Chair*, Dr. Victoria Hedderick, 814-732-1655, E-mail: vhedderick@edinboro.edu.

**Department of Social Work** Students: 297 full-time (265 women), 38 part-time (33 women); includes 54 minority (38 Black or African American, non-Hispanic/Latino; 1 American Indian or Alaska Native, non-Hispanic/Latino; 2 Asian, non-Hispanic/Latino; 13 Hispanic/Latino), 1 international. Average age 30. 170 applicants, 71% accepted, 81 enrolled. *Faculty:* 17 full-time (15 women), 12 part-time/adjunct (8 women). Expenses: Contact institution. *Financial support:* In 2019–20, 16 students received support. Research assistantships with tuition reimbursements available, career-related internships or fieldwork, Federal Work-Study, scholarships/grants, and unspecified assistantships available. Support available to part-time students. Financial award application deadline: 2/15; financial award applicants required to submit FAFSA. In 2019, 182 master's awarded. *Program availability:* Evening/weekend. *Application deadline:* Applications are processed on a rolling basis. *Application fee:* $30. Electronic applications accepted. *Application Contact:* Dr. William Koehler, Chairperson, 814-732-1973, E-mail: wkoehler@edinboro.edu. *Chairperson*, Dr. William Koehler, 814-732-1973, E-mail: wkoehler@edinboro.edu.

**Graduate Studies in Business** Students: 14 full-time (4 women), 8 part-time (2 women); includes 3 minority (2 Black or African American, non-Hispanic/Latino; 1 Hispanic/Latino), 2 international. Average age 30. 19 applicants, 79% accepted, 9 enrolled. *Faculty:* 2 full-time (1 woman), 2 part-time/adjunct. Expenses: Contact institution. *Financial support:* In 2019–20, 6 students received support. Unspecified assistantships available. Financial award applicants required to submit FAFSA. *Application fee:* $30. *Application Contact:* Christine Billen, Chairperson, 814-732-2058, E-mail: cmccallum@edinboro.edu. *Chairperson*, Christine Billen, 814-732-2058, E-mail: cmccallum@edinboro.edu.

## EDP UNIVERSITY OF PUERTO RICO–SAN SEBASTIAN, San Sebastian, PR 00685

**General Information** Independent, coed, comprehensive institution.

**GRADUATE UNITS**

**Graduate School**

## EDWARD VIA COLLEGE OF OSTEOPATHIC MEDICINE–CAROLINAS CAMPUS, Spartanburg, SC 29303

**General Information** Independent, coed, graduate-only institution.

**GRADUATE UNITS**

**Graduate Program**

## EDWARD VIA COLLEGE OF OSTEOPATHIC MEDICINE–VIRGINIA CAMPUS, Blacksburg, VA 24060

**General Information** Independent, coed, graduate-only institution. *Research affiliation:* Virginia Polytechnic Institute and State University (biomedical research).

**GRADUATE UNITS**

**Graduate Program**

## EICAR THE INTERNATIONAL FILM SCHOOL OF PARIS, La Plaine Saint Denis, France

**General Information** Coed.

**GRADUATE UNITS**

**Master of Fine Arts in Film Making Cinematography**
**Master of Fine Arts in Film Making Directing**
**Master of Fine Arts in Film Making Editing**
**Master of Fine Arts in Film Making Production**
**Master of Fine Arts in Film Making Screenwriting**

## ELIZABETH CITY STATE UNIVERSITY, Elizabeth City, NC 27909-7806

**General Information** State-supported, coed, comprehensive institution. CGS member. *Graduate housing:* Room and/or apartments available on a first-come, first-served basis to single students; on-campus housing not available to married students. Housing application deadline: 5/31.

**GRADUATE UNITS**

**Department of Education, Psychology and Health** *Program availability:* Part-time, evening/weekend. Electronic applications accepted.

**Department of Mathematics and Computer Science** *Program availability:* Part-time, evening/weekend. Electronic applications accepted.

**Master of Science in Biology Program** *Program availability:* Part-time, evening/weekend. Electronic applications accepted.

## ELIZABETHTOWN COLLEGE, Elizabethtown, PA 17022-2298

**General Information** Independent-religious, coed, comprehensive institution.

**GRADUATE UNITS**

**Department of Occupational Therapy**

## ELMEZZI GRADUATE SCHOOL OF MOLECULAR MEDICINE, Manhasset, NY 11030

**General Information** Independent, coed, graduate-only institution. *Graduate housing:* On-campus housing not available. *Research affiliation:* Feinstein Institute for Medical Research (biomedical research), North Shore Long Island Jewish Health System (medicine).

**GRADUATE UNITS**

**Graduate Program**

## ELMHURST UNIVERSITY, Elmhurst, IL 60126-3296

**General Information** Independent-religious, coed, comprehensive institution. *Enrollment:* 164 full-time matriculated graduate/professional students (140 women), 398 part-time matriculated graduate/professional students (238 women). *Enrollment by degree level:* 562 master's. *Graduate faculty:* 38 full-time (27 women), 37 part-time/adjunct (21 women). *Graduate housing:* On-campus housing not available. *Student services:* Campus employment opportunities, campus safety program, career counseling, exercise/wellness program, free psychological counseling, international student services, low-cost health insurance, multicultural affairs office, services for students with disabilities, teacher training, writing training. *Library facilities:* Buehler Library.

**Computer facilities:** 800 computers available on campus for general student use. A campuswide network can be accessed. Online class registration is available.
Website: http://www.elmhurst.edu/

**General Application Contact:** Timothy J. Panfil, Senior Director, Graduate Admission and Enrollment Management, 630-617-3400 Ext. 3256, Fax: 630-617-6471, E-mail: panfilt@elmhurst.edu.

**GRADUATE UNITS**

**Graduate Programs** Students: 164 full-time (140 women), 398 part-time (238 women); includes 119 minority (22 Black or African American, non-Hispanic/Latino; 1 American Indian or Alaska Native, non-Hispanic/Latino; 31 Asian, non-Hispanic/Latino; 61 Hispanic/Latino; 4 Two or more races, non-Hispanic/Latino), 11 international. Average age 30. 1,918 applicants, 25% accepted, 262 enrolled. *Faculty:* 38 full-time (27 women), 37 part-time/adjunct (21 women). Expenses: Contact institution. *Financial support:* In 2019–20, 281 students received support. Fellowships, scholarships/grants, and unspecified assistantships available. Support available to part-time students. Financial award applicants required to submit FAFSA. In 2019, 281 master's awarded. *Program availability:* Part-time, evening/weekend, 100% online, blended/hybrid learning. *Application deadline:* For fall admission, 7/1 priority date for domestic and international students; for spring admission, 12/1 priority date for domestic students; for summer admission, 4/1 priority date for domestic students. Applications are processed on a rolling basis. Electronic applications accepted. *Application Contact:* Timothy J. Panfil, Senior Director of Graduate Admission and Enrollment Management, 630-617-3300 Ext. 3256, Fax: 630-617-6471, E-mail: panfilt@elmhurst.edu. *Vice President for Admission*, Dr. Timothy Ricordati, 630-617-3089, E-mail: timothy.ricordati@elmhurst.edu.

## ELMS COLLEGE, Chicopee, MA 01013-2839

**General Information** Independent-religious, coed, comprehensive institution. *Graduate housing:* On-campus housing not available.

**GRADUATE UNITS**

**Division of Business** Students: 38 part-time (22 women); includes 5 minority (3 Black or African American, non-Hispanic/Latino; 1 Asian, non-Hispanic/Latino; 1 Hispanic/Latino), 4 international. Average age 34. 11 applicants, 64% accepted, 7 enrolled. *Faculty:* 3 full-time (all women), 7 part-time/adjunct (4 women). Expenses: Contact institution. *Financial support:* Applicants required to submit FAFSA. In 2019, 25 master's awarded. *Program availability:* Part-time, evening/weekend. *Application deadline:* Applications are processed on a rolling basis. Electronic applications accepted. *Application Contact:* Nancy Davis, Director, Office of Graduate and Continuing Education Admissions, 413-265-2456, E-mail: grad@elms.edu. *MBA Program Director*, Kim Kenney-Rockwal, 413-265-2572, E-mail: kenneyrockwalk@elms.edu.

**Division of Education** Students: 6 full-time (4 women), 98 part-time (81 women); includes 13 minority (1 Black or African American, non-Hispanic/Latino; 2 Asian, non-Hispanic/Latino; 10 Hispanic/Latino). Average age 34. 39 applicants, 74% accepted, 28 enrolled. *Faculty:* 3 full-time (all women), 11 part-time/adjunct (10 women). Expenses: Contact institution. *Financial support:* In 2019–20, 2 teaching assistantships with partial tuition reimbursements were awarded. Financial award applicants required to submit FAFSA. In 2019, 51 master's, 2 other advanced degrees awarded. *Program availability:* Part-time, evening/weekend. *Application deadline:* For fall admission, 7/1 priority date for domestic students; for spring admission, 11/1 priority date for domestic students. Applications are processed on a rolling basis. Electronic applications accepted. *Application Contact:* Nancy Davis, Director, Office of Graduate and Continuing Education Admissions, 413-265-2456, E-mail: grad@elms.edu. *Chair, Division of Education*, Dr. Meredith Bertrand, 413-265-2521, E-mail: bertrandm@elms.edu.

**Division of Natural Sciences, Mathematics and Technology** Students: 21 full-time (14 women), 1 (woman) part-time; includes 3 minority (2 Black or African American, non-Hispanic/Latino; 1 Asian, non-Hispanic/Latino). Average age 27. 38 applicants, 79% accepted, 12 enrolled. *Faculty:* 6 full-time (3 women), 4 part-time/adjunct (1 woman). Expenses: Contact institution. *Financial support:* Applicants required to submit FAFSA. In 2019, 24 master's awarded. *Application deadline:* Applications are processed on a rolling basis. Electronic applications accepted. *Application Contact:* Nancy Davis, Director, Office of Graduate and Continuing Education Admissions, 413-265-2456, E-mail: grad@elms.edu. *Co-Chair, Division of Natural Sciences and Mathematics*, Dr. Beryl Hoffman, 413-265-2216, E-mail: hoffmanb@elms.edu.

**Division of Social Sciences** Students: 12 part-time (11 women); includes 1 minority (Hispanic/Latino). Average age 30. 13 applicants, 85% accepted, 11 enrolled. *Faculty:* 2 full-time (1 woman), 3 part-time/adjunct (2 women). Expenses: Contact institution. *Financial support:* Applicants required to submit FAFSA. In 2019, 8 master's, 1 other advanced degree awarded. *Program availability:* Part-time. *Application deadline:* Applications are processed on a rolling basis. Electronic applications accepted. *Application Contact:* Nancy Davis, Director, Office of Graduate and Continuing Education Admissions, 413-265-2456, E-mail: grad@elms.edu. *Chair, Division of Social Sciences*, Dr. Jennifer Rivers, 413-265-2422, E-mail: riversj@elms.edu.

**Religious Studies Department** Students: 2 full-time (both women), 4 part-time (2 women). Average age 51. 2 applicants, 100% accepted, 2 enrolled. *Faculty:* 5 full-time (1 woman), 3 part-time/adjunct (1 woman). Expenses: Contact institution. *Financial support:* Applicants required to submit FAFSA. In 2019, 4 master's awarded. *Program availability:* Part-time, evening/weekend. *Application deadline:* For fall admission, 7/1 priority date for domestic students; for spring admission, 11/1 priority date for domestic students. Applications are processed on a rolling basis. Electronic applications accepted. *Application Contact:* Nancy Davis, Director, Office of Graduate and Continuing Education Admissions, 413-265-2456, E-mail: grad@elms.edu. *Chair, Division of Humanities and Fine Arts*, Dr. Tom Cerasulo, 413-265-2345, E-mail: cerasulot@elms.edu.

**School of Nursing** Students: 13 full-time (11 women), 97 part-time (91 women); includes 8 minority (4 Black or African American, non-Hispanic/Latino; 2 Hispanic/Latino; 2 Two or more races, non-Hispanic/Latino). Average age 38. 39 applicants, 87% accepted, 27 enrolled. *Faculty:* 3 full-time (2 women), 2 part-time/adjunct (both women). Expenses: Contact institution. *Financial support:* Applicants required to submit FAFSA. In 2019, 4 master's, 20 doctorates awarded. *Program availability:* Part-time, evening/weekend. *Application deadline:* For fall admission, 7/1 priority date for domestic students; for spring admission, 11/1 priority date for domestic students. Applications are processed on a rolling basis. Electronic applications accepted. *Application Contact:* Nancy Davis, Director, Office of Graduate and Continuing Education Admissions, 413-265-2456, E-mail: grad@elms.edu. *Dean, School of Nursing*, Dr. Kathleen Scoble, 413-265-2204, E-mail: scoblek@elms.edu.

## ELON UNIVERSITY, Elon, NC 27244-2010

**General Information** Independent-religious, coed, comprehensive institution. *Enrollment:* 7,088 graduate, professional, and undergraduate students; 705 full-time matriculated graduate/professional students (456 women), 106 part-time matriculated graduate/professional students (66 women). *Enrollment by degree level:* 296 master's, 515 doctoral. *Graduate faculty:* 94 full-time (48 women), 55 part-time/adjunct (31 women). *Graduate housing:* On-campus housing not available. *Student services:* Campus employment opportunities, campus safety program, career counseling, exercise/wellness program, free psychological counseling, international student services, low-cost health insurance, multicultural affairs office, services for students with disabilities, teacher training, writing training. *Library facilities:* Carol Grotnes Belk. *Collection:* Books: 195,196 (physical), 1.3 million (digital/electronic); Serial titles: 149 (physical), 64,648 (digital/electronic); Databases: 272. Weekly public service hours: 143; study areas open 24 hours, 5–7 days a week; students can reserve study rooms.

**Computer facilities:** Computer purchase and lease plans are available. 1,200 computers available on campus for general student use. A campuswide network can be accessed. Online class registration is available.
Website: http://www.elon.edu/

**General Application Contact:** Art Fadde, Director of Graduate Admissions, 800-334-8448 Ext. 3, Fax: 336-278-7699, E-mail: afadde@elon.edu.

**GRADUATE UNITS**

**Master in Higher Education Program** Students: 26 full-time (19 women); includes 8 minority (5 Black or African American, non-Hispanic/Latino; 1 Hispanic/Latino; 2 Two or more races, non-Hispanic/Latino). Average age 23. 75 applicants, 23% accepted, 12 enrolled. *Faculty:* 1 (woman) full-time, 13 part-time/adjunct (5 women). Expenses: Contact institution. *Application deadline:* For fall admission, 1/4 for domestic students. *Application fee:* $60. *Application Contact:* Art Fadde, Director of Graduate Admissions, 800-334-8448 Ext. 3, Fax: 336-278-7699, E-mail: afadde@elon.edu. *Dean of the School of Education*, Dr. Ann Bullock, 336-278-5900, E-mail: abullock9@elon.edu.

**Program in Business Administration** Students: 57 full-time (26 women), 69 part-time (33 women); includes 35 minority (27 Black or African American, non-Hispanic/Latino; 4 Asian, non-Hispanic/Latino; 4 Hispanic/Latino), 3 international. Average age 31. 111 applicants, 82% accepted, 67 enrolled. *Faculty:* 27 full-time (10 women), 7 part-time/adjunct (5 women). Expenses: Contact institution. *Financial support:* Applicants required to submit FAFSA. In 2019, 55 master's awarded. *Program availability:* Part-time, evening/weekend. *Application deadline:* For fall admission, 8/15 priority date for domestic students; for spring admission, 2/15 priority date for domestic students. Applications are processed on a rolling basis. *Application fee:* $60. Electronic applications accepted. *Application Contact:* Art Fadde, Director of Graduate Admissions, 800-334-8448 Ext. 3, Fax: 336-278-7699, E-mail: afadde@elon.edu. *Associate Dean of the Love School of Business/Associate Professor of Economics*, Dr. Jen Platania, 336-278-5938, E-mail: jplatania@elon.edu.

**Program in Education** Students: 37 part-time (33 women); includes 15 minority (7 Black or African American, non-Hispanic/Latino; 2 Asian, non-Hispanic/Latino; 5 Hispanic/Latino; 1 Two or more races, non-Hispanic/Latino), 1 international. Average age 37. 38 applicants, 82% accepted, 30 enrolled. *Faculty:* 7 full-time (4 women), 4 part-time/adjunct (all women). Expenses: Contact institution. *Financial support:* Applicants required to submit FAFSA. In 2019, 5 master's awarded. *Program availability:* Part-time. *Application deadline:* For fall admission, 5/1 for domestic students. Applications are processed on a rolling basis. *Application fee:* $60. Electronic applications accepted. *Application Contact:* Art Fadde, Director of Graduate Admissions, 800-334-8448 Ext. 3, Fax: 336-278-7699, E-mail: afadde@elon.edu. *Dean of the School of Education/Professor*, Dr. Ann Bullock, 336-278-5900, E-mail: abullock9@elon.edu.

**Program in Interactive Media** Students: 32 full-time (22 women); includes 21 minority (19 Black or African American, non-Hispanic/Latino; 1 Asian, non-Hispanic/Latino; 1 Hispanic/Latino). Average age 23. 44 applicants, 91% accepted, 31 enrolled. *Faculty:* 8 full-time (2 women), 1 (woman) part-time/adjunct. Expenses: Contact institution. *Financial support:* Applicants required to submit FAFSA. In 2019, 28 master's awarded. *Application deadline:* For fall admission, 5/1 priority date for domestic students. Applications are processed on a rolling basis. *Application fee:* $60. Electronic applications accepted. *Application Contact:* Art Fadde, Director of Graduate Admissions, 800-334-8448 Ext. 3, Fax: 336-278-7699, E-mail: afadde@elon.edu. *Dean of the School of Communications*, Dr. Rochelle Ford, 336-278-5724, E-mail: rford9@elon.edu.

**Program in Law** Students: 376 full-time (231 women); includes 86 minority (63 Black or African American, non-Hispanic/Latino; 2 American Indian or Alaska Native, non-Hispanic/Latino; 20 Hispanic/Latino; 1 Two or more races, non-Hispanic/Latino). Average age 25. 800 applicants, 47% accepted, 144 enrolled. *Faculty:* 31 full-time (17 women), 14 part-time/adjunct (5 women). Expenses: Contact institution. *Financial support:* Applicants required to submit FAFSA. In 2019, 103 doctorates awarded. *Application deadline:* For fall admission, 7/15 for domestic students; for spring admission, 1/10 priority date for domestic students. Applications are processed on a rolling basis. Electronic applications accepted. *Application Contact:* Alan Woodlief,

Associate Dean of School of Law/Director of Law School Admissions, 336-279-9203, E-mail: awoodlief@elon.edu. *Dean*, Dr. Luke Bierman, 336-279-9201, E-mail: lbierman@elon.edu.

**Program in Physical Therapy** Students: 139 full-time (98 women); includes 20 minority (7 Black or African American, non-Hispanic/Latino; 3 Asian, non-Hispanic/Latino; 4 Hispanic/Latino; 6 Two or more races, non-Hispanic/Latino), 2 international. Average age 25. 814 applicants, 12% accepted, 46 enrolled. *Faculty:* 13 full-time (8 women), 14 part-time/adjunct (9 women). Expenses: Contact institution. *Financial support:* Applicants required to submit FAFSA. In 2019, 46 doctorates awarded. *Application deadline:* For fall admission, 11/1 for domestic students; for winter admission, 1/10 priority date for domestic students. Applications are processed on a rolling basis. Electronic applications accepted. *Application Contact:* Art Fadde, Director of Graduate Admissions, 800-334-8448 Ext. 3, Fax: 336-278-7699, E-mail: afadde@elon.edu. *Dean of the School of Health Sciences*, Dr. Becky Neiduski, 336-278-6350, E-mail: bneiduski@elon.edu.

**Program in Physician Assistant Studies** Students: 75 full-time (60 women); includes 15 minority (2 Black or African American, non-Hispanic/Latino; 1 American Indian or Alaska Native, non-Hispanic/Latino; 3 Asian, non-Hispanic/Latino; 8 Hispanic/Latino; 1 Two or more races, non-Hispanic/Latino). Average age 27. 1,739 applicants, 4% accepted, 38 enrolled. *Faculty:* 7 full-time (6 women), 2 part-time/adjunct (both women). Expenses: Contact institution. *Financial support:* Applicants required to submit FAFSA. In 2019, 38 master's awarded. *Application deadline:* For spring admission, 11/1 for domestic students. Applications are processed on a rolling basis. Electronic applications accepted. *Application Contact:* Art Fadde, Director of Graduate Admissions, 800-334-8448 Ext. 3, Fax: 336-278-7699, E-mail: afadde@elon.edu. *Dean of the School of Health Sciences*, Dr. Becky Neiduski, 336-278-6350, E-mail: bneiduski@elon.edu.

## EMBRY-RIDDLE AERONAUTICAL UNIVERSITY–DAYTONA, Daytona Beach, FL 32114-3900

**General Information** Independent, coed, university. *Graduate housing:* On-campus housing not available. *Research affiliation:* United Space Alliance, SpaceX, The Boeing Company, Honeywell, Virgin Galactic, NASA.

**GRADUATE UNITS**

**College of Business** Electronic applications accepted.

**Department of Aerospace Engineering** Electronic applications accepted.

**Department of Civil Engineering** Electronic applications accepted.

**Department of Electrical, Computer, Software and Systems Engineering** Electronic applications accepted.

**Department of Human Factors and Behavioral Neurobiology** Electronic applications accepted.

**Department of Mechanical Engineering** Electronic applications accepted.

**Department of Physical Sciences** Electronic applications accepted.

**Program in Unmanned and Autonomous Systems Engineering** Electronic applications accepted.

**School of Graduate Studies** Electronic applications accepted.

## EMBRY-RIDDLE AERONAUTICAL UNIVERSITY–PRESCOTT, Prescott, AZ 86301-3720

**General Information** Independent, coed, comprehensive institution. *Graduate housing:* On-campus housing not available. *Research affiliation:* Boeing/Intelligent Light/Pointwise (CFD analysis on aerospace vehicles and energy systems), University of Alaska, Anchorage (development of field deployed multi-spectral computer vision systems), NASA (optimization ideas for aircraft design), Federal Aviation Administration (human factors, air traffic control interoperability, air traffic management, low-altitude operations, wake separation and noise reduction), NATO Modelling & Simulation Centre of Excellence (operational requirements, training and interoperability), Flight Research Inc. (production of world-class training and curriculum programs for aircraft loss-of-control situations).

**GRADUATE UNITS**

**Behavioral and Safety Sciences Department** Electronic applications accepted.

**Security and Intelligence Program** Electronic applications accepted.

## EMBRY-RIDDLE AERONAUTICAL UNIVERSITY–WORLDWIDE, Daytona Beach, FL 32114-3900

**General Information** Independent, coed, comprehensive institution. *Graduate housing:* On-campus housing not available. *Research affiliation:* The Society for Protective Coatings and Honda Aircraft (creation of standards for training and certification program for higher paint quality).

**GRADUATE UNITS**

**Department of Aeronautics, Graduate Studies** *Program availability:* Part-time, evening/weekend, 100% online. Electronic applications accepted.

**Department of Business Administration** *Program availability:* Part-time, evening/weekend, online only, EagleVision Classroom (between classrooms), EagleVision Home (faculty and students at home), and a blend of Classroom or Home. Electronic applications accepted.

**Department of Decision Sciences** *Program availability:* Part-time, evening/weekend, EagleVision Classroom (between classrooms), EagleVision Home (faculty and students at home), and a blend of Classroom or Home. Electronic applications accepted.

**Department of Engineering and Technology** *Program availability:* Part-time, evening/weekend, 100% online, blended/hybrid learning. Electronic applications accepted.

**Department of Security and Emergency Services** *Program availability:* Part-time, evening/weekend, EagleVision Classroom (between classrooms), EagleVision Home (faculty and students at home), and a blend of Classroom or Home. Electronic applications accepted.

**Department of Technology Management** *Program availability:* Part-time, evening/weekend, EagleVision Classroom (between classrooms), EagleVision Home (faculty and students at home), and a blend of Classroom or Home. Electronic applications accepted.

## EMERSON COLLEGE, Boston, MA 02116-4624

**General Information** Independent, coed, comprehensive institution. *Enrollment:* 817 full-time matriculated graduate/professional students (649 women), 244 part-time matriculated graduate/professional students (199 women). *Enrollment by degree level:* 1,061 master's. *Tuition:* Full-time $1296; part-time $1296 per credit. *Graduate housing:* On-campus housing not available. *Student services:* Campus employment opportunities, campus safety program, career counseling, exercise/wellness program, free psychological counseling, grant writing training, international student services, low-cost health insurance, multicultural affairs office, services for students with disabilities, writing training. *Library facilities:* Iwasaki Library plus 1 other. *Collection:* Books: 336,669 (physical), 2,484 (digital/electronic); Serial titles: 67,760 (digital/electronic); Databases: 125. Weekly public service hours: 93; students can reserve study rooms.

**Computer facilities:** Computer purchase and lease plans are available. 480 computers available on campus for general student use. A campuswide network can be accessed from student residence rooms and from off campus. Online class registration is available.
Website: http://www.emerson.edu/

**General Application Contact:** Office of Graduate Admission, 617-824-8610, Fax: 617-824-8614, E-mail: gradadmission@emerson.edu.

**GRADUATE UNITS**

**Graduate Studies** *Program availability:* Part-time, evening/weekend. Electronic applications accepted.

## EMILY CARR UNIVERSITY OF ART + DESIGN, Vancouver, BC V6H 3R9, Canada

**General Information** Province-supported, coed, comprehensive institution. *Enrollment:* 85 full-time matriculated graduate/professional students (60 women), 20 part-time matriculated graduate/professional students (16 women). *Enrollment by degree level:* 105 master's. *Graduate faculty:* 20 full-time (10 women), 30 part-time/adjunct (15 women). *Graduate housing:* On-campus housing not available. *Student services:* Campus employment opportunities, campus safety program, career counseling, free psychological counseling, grant writing training, international student services, low-cost health insurance, services for students with disabilities, teacher training, writing training. *Research affiliation:* Children's Hospital, Vancouver BC (health care research), Aldrich Pears and Associates (experience design), Kodak Communications Group (interaction design), Donat Group (e-learning), Paperny Films (television and film production), Fuel Cell Research Centre, National Research Council (clean technology).

**Computer facilities:** Computer purchase and lease plans are available. A campuswide network can be accessed from off campus. Online class registration is available.
Website: http://www.ecuad.ca/

**General Application Contact:** Lee Gilad, Graduate Recruitment Coordinator, 604-604 844 3086, E-mail: masters@ecuad.ca.

**GRADUATE UNITS**

**Program in Applied Arts** Electronic applications accepted.

**Program in Digital Media** Electronic applications accepted.

## EMMANUEL COLLEGE, Boston, MA 02115

**General Information** Independent-religious, coed, comprehensive institution. *Enrollment:* 2,222 graduate, professional, and undergraduate students; 9 full-time matriculated graduate/professional students (8 women), 86 part-time matriculated graduate/professional students (68 women). *Enrollment by degree level:* 90 master's, 5 other advanced degrees. *Graduate faculty:* 2 full-time (both women), 21 part-time/adjunct (14 women). *Graduate housing:* On-campus housing not available. *Student services:* Campus safety program, career counseling, exercise/wellness program, multicultural affairs office, services for students with disabilities, writing training. *Library facilities:* Cardinal Cushing Library/Learning Commons. *Collection:* Books: 63,625 (physical), 265,865 (digital/electronic); Serial titles: 70 (physical), 83,504 (digital/electronic); Databases: 61. Weekly public service hours: 108; students can reserve study rooms.

**Computer facilities:** 284 computers available on campus for general student use. A campuswide network can be accessed. Online class registration, Online learning management system (Canvas). Online Office productivity tools (Office 365). are available.
Website: http://www.emmanuel.edu/

**General Application Contact:** Helen Muterperl, Director of Graduate and Professional Programs, 617-735-9700, Fax: 617-507-0434, E-mail: gpp@emmanuel.edu.

**GRADUATE UNITS**

**Graduate and Professional Programs** Students: 9 full-time (8 women), 86 part-time (68 women); includes 17 minority (8 Black or African American, non-Hispanic/Latino; 3 Asian, non-Hispanic/Latino; 4 Hispanic/Latino; 2 Two or more races, non-Hispanic/Latino). Average age 33. 88 applicants, 33% accepted, 18 enrolled. *Faculty:* 2 full-time (both women), 21 part-time/adjunct (14 women). Expenses: Contact institution. *Financial support:* Application deadline: 2/15; applicants required to submit FAFSA. In 2019, 58 master's, 6 other advanced degrees awarded. *Program availability:* Part-time, evening/weekend, blended/hybrid learning. *Application deadline:* Applications are processed on a rolling basis. Electronic applications accepted. *Application Contact:* Helen Muterperl, Director of Graduate and Professional Programs, 617-735-9700, Fax: 617-507-0434, E-mail: gpp@emmanuel.edu. *Dean of Academic Administration and Graduate and Professional Programs*, Cindy O'Callaghan, 617-735-9700, E-mail: gpp@emmanuel.edu.

## EMORY & HENRY COLLEGE, Emory, VA 24327-0947

**General Information** Independent-religious, coed, comprehensive institution. *Graduate housing:* Room and/or apartments available on a first-come, first-served basis to single students; on-campus housing not available to married students.

**GRADUATE UNITS**

**Graduate Programs** *Program availability:* Part-time. Electronic applications accepted.

## EMORY UNIVERSITY, Atlanta, GA 30322-1100

**General Information** Independent-religious, coed, university. CGS member. *Graduate housing:* Rooms and/or apartments available on a first-come, first-served basis to single and married students. *Research affiliation:* Bill and Melinda Gates Foundation, Children's Pediatric Research Trust, International AIDS Vaccine Initiative, Garden City Group, Georgia Cancer Coalition, The Wistar Institute.

**GRADUATE UNITS**

**Candler School of Theology** *Program availability:* Part-time. Electronic applications accepted.

**Goizueta Business School** *Program availability:* Part-time, evening/weekend. Electronic applications accepted.

**Laney Graduate School** Electronic applications accepted.

***Division of Biological and Biomedical Sciences*** Electronic applications accepted.

***Division of Educational Studies*** Electronic applications accepted.

***Division of Religion*** Electronic applications accepted.

***Emory Center for Ethics*** Electronic applications accepted.

***Graduate Institute of the Liberal Arts*** Electronic applications accepted.

**Nell Hodgson Woodruff School of Nursing** *Program availability:* Part-time. Electronic applications accepted.

**Rollins School of Public Health** *Program availability:* Part-time, evening/weekend, online learning. Electronic applications accepted.

**School of Law** Electronic applications accepted.

**School of Medicine** Electronic applications accepted.

## EMPEROR'S COLLEGE OF TRADITIONAL ORIENTAL MEDICINE, Santa Monica, CA 90403

**General Information** Private, coed, graduate-only institution. *Graduate housing:* On-campus housing not available. *Research affiliation:* Lotus Herbs (herbs), LA Free Clinic (herbs), UCLA Ashe Center (student health).

**GRADUATE UNITS**

**Graduate Programs** *Program availability:* Part-time, evening/weekend.

## EMPIRE COLLEGE, Santa Rosa, CA 95403

**General Information** Proprietary, coed.

**GRADUATE UNITS**

**School of Law**

## EMPORIA STATE UNIVERSITY, Emporia, KS 66801-5415

**General Information** State-supported, coed, comprehensive institution. CGS member. *Enrollment:* 5,877 graduate, professional, and undergraduate students; 405 full-time matriculated graduate/professional students (263 women), 1,456 part-time matriculated graduate/professional students (1,018 women). *Enrollment by degree level:* 1,843 master's, 18 doctoral. *Graduate faculty:* 206 full-time (98 women), 23 part-time/adjunct (14 women). *International tuition:* $20,128 full-time. *Tuition, area resident:* Full-time $6394; part-time $266.41 per credit hour. Tuition, state resident: full-time $6394; part-time $266.41 per credit hour. Tuition, nonresident: full-time $20,128; part-time $828.66 per credit hour. *Required fees:* $2183; $90.95 per credit hour. Tuition and fees vary according to campus/location and program. *Graduate housing:* Room and/or apartments available on a first-come, first-served basis to single students; on-campus housing not available to married students. Typical cost: $5680 per year ($9408 including board). Housing application deadline: 8/1. *Student services:* Campus employment opportunities, career counseling, child daycare facilities, exercise/wellness program, free psychological counseling, grant writing training, international student services, low-cost health insurance, multicultural affairs office, services for students with disabilities, teacher training, writing training. *Library facilities:* William Allen White Library plus 1 other. *Collection:* Books: 389,595 (physical), 153,016 (digital/electronic); Serial titles: 35,153 (physical), 278 (digital/electronic); Databases: 97. Weekly public service hours: 79; study areas open 24 hours, 5–7 days a week; students can reserve study rooms.

**Computer facilities:** 410 computers available on campus for general student use. A campuswide network can be accessed from student residence rooms and from off campus. Online class registration is available.
Website: http://www.emporia.edu/

**General Application Contact:** Kerri Jackson, Recruitment and Development Specialist, 800-950-GRAD, Fax: 620-341-5403, E-mail: kjacks20@emporia.edu.

**GRADUATE UNITS**

**Department of Biological Sciences** *Program availability:* Part-time. Electronic applications accepted.

**Department of Health, Physical Education and Recreation** *Program availability:* Part-time, 100% online. Electronic applications accepted.

**Department of Instructional Design and Technology** *Program availability:* Part-time, online only, 100% online. Electronic applications accepted.

**Department of Mathematics and Economics** *Program availability:* Part-time, evening/weekend, online only, 100% online. Electronic applications accepted.

**Department of Music** *Program availability:* Part-time. Electronic applications accepted.

**Department of Physical Sciences** *Program availability:* Part-time, online learning. Electronic applications accepted.

**Program in Accountancy** *Program availability:* Part-time, 100% online, blended/hybrid learning. Electronic applications accepted.

**Program in Art Therapy** *Program availability:* Part-time. Electronic applications accepted.

**Program in Business Administration** *Program availability:* Part-time, evening/weekend, blended/hybrid learning. Electronic applications accepted.

**Program in Clinical Counseling** *Program availability:* Part-time. Electronic applications accepted.

**Program in Clinical Psychology** *Program availability:* Part-time. Electronic applications accepted.

**Program in Curriculum and Instruction** *Program availability:* Part-time, online only, 100% online. Electronic applications accepted.

**Program in Early Childhood Education** *Program availability:* Part-time, online learning. Electronic applications accepted.

**Program in Educational Administration** *Program availability:* Part-time. Electronic applications accepted.

**Program in English** *Program availability:* Part-time.

**Program in Forensic Science** *Program availability:* Part-time. Electronic applications accepted.

**Program in History** *Program availability:* Part-time. Electronic applications accepted.

**Program in Instructional Specialist** *Program availability:* Part-time. Electronic applications accepted.

**Program in Psychology** *Program availability:* Part-time. Electronic applications accepted.

**Program in Rehabilitation Counseling** *Program availability:* Part-time. Electronic applications accepted.

**Program in School Counseling** *Program availability:* Part-time. Electronic applications accepted.

**Program in School Psychology** *Program availability:* Part-time. Electronic applications accepted.

**Program in Special Education** *Program availability:* Part-time. Electronic applications accepted.

**Program in Teaching** *Program availability:* Part-time, online learning.

**Program in Teaching English to Speakers of Other Languages** *Program availability:* Part-time. Electronic applications accepted.

**School of Library and Information Management** *Program availability:* Part-time, evening/weekend, online learning. Electronic applications accepted.

## ENDICOTT COLLEGE, Beverly, MA 01915-2096

**General Information** Independent, coed, comprehensive institution. *Enrollment:* 5,082 graduate, professional, and undergraduate students; 448 full-time matriculated graduate/professional students (312 women), 814 part-time matriculated graduate/professional students (615 women). *Enrollment by degree level:* 1,131 master's, 85 doctoral, 46 other advanced degrees. *Graduate faculty:* 25 full-time (19 women), 233 part-time/adjunct (134 women). *Graduate housing:* On-campus housing not available. *Student services:* Campus employment opportunities, campus safety program, career counseling, free psychological counseling, international student services, low-cost health insurance, multicultural affairs office, services for students with disabilities, teacher training, writing training. *Library facilities:* Diane M. Halle Library. *Collection:* Books: 112,262 (physical), 189,985 (digital/electronic); Serial titles: 26 (physical), 145,447 (digital/electronic); Databases: 152. Weekly public service hours: 97; students can reserve study rooms. *Research affiliation:* Peabody Essex Museum (history), North Shore Consortium (special needs).

**Computer facilities:** Computer purchase and lease plans are available. 350 computers available on campus for general student use. A campuswide network can be accessed. Online class registration is available.
Website: http://www.endicott.edu/

**General Application Contact:** Ian Menchini, Director, Graduate Enrollment and Advising, 978-232-5292, E-mail: imenchin@endicott.edu.

**GRADUATE UNITS**

**Endicott College School of Arts and Sciences** Students: 16 full-time (7 women), 14 part-time (4 women); includes 5 minority (3 Black or African American, non-Hispanic/Latino; 2 Hispanic/Latino). Average age 29. 23 applicants, 74% accepted, 14 enrolled. *Faculty:* 2 full-time (1 woman), 17 part-time/adjunct (4 women). Expenses: Contact institution. *Financial support:* Applicants required to submit FAFSA. *Program availability:* Part-time, evening/weekend, 100% online. *Application deadline:* Applications are processed on a rolling basis. *Application fee:* $50. Electronic applications accepted. *Application Contact:* Ian Menchini, Director, Graduate Enrollment and Advising, 978-232-5292, E-mail: imenchin@endicott.edu. *Dean, School of Arts and Sciences,* Dr. Gene Wong, 978-232-2311, E-mail: gwong@endicott.edu.

**School of Business** Students: 118 full-time (50 women), 105 part-time (45 women); includes 39 minority (14 Black or African American, non-Hispanic/Latino; 1 American Indian or Alaska Native, non-Hispanic/Latino; 8 Asian, non-Hispanic/Latino; 13 Hispanic/Latino; 3 Two or more races, non-Hispanic/Latino), 21 international. Average age 32. 116 applicants, 76% accepted, 74 enrolled. *Faculty:* 4 full-time (3 women), 45 part-time/adjunct (10 women). Expenses: Contact institution. *Financial support:* Applicants required to submit FAFSA. *Program availability:* Part-time, evening/weekend, 100% online, blended/hybrid learning. *Application deadline:* Applications are processed on a rolling basis. *Application fee:* $50. Electronic applications accepted. *Application Contact:* Ian Menchini, Director, Graduate Enrollment and Advising, 978-232-5292, E-mail: imenchin@endicott.edu. *Dean of Business,* Michael Paige, 978-232-2259, E-mail: mpaige@endicott.edu.

**School of Education**

**School of Nursing** Students: 20 full-time (19 women), 71 part-time (70 women); includes 11 minority (5 Black or African American, non-Hispanic/Latino; 3 Asian, non-Hispanic/Latino; 2 Hispanic/Latino; 1 Two or more races, non-Hispanic/Latino). Average age 37. 32 applicants, 41% accepted, 12 enrolled. *Faculty:* 4 full-time (all women), 18 part-time/adjunct (13 women). Expenses: Contact institution. *Financial support:* Applicants required to submit FAFSA. *Program availability:* Part-time, evening/weekend, blended/hybrid learning. *Application deadline:* Applications are processed on a rolling basis. *Application fee:* $50. Electronic applications accepted. *Application Contact:* Ian Menchini, Director, Graduate Enrollment and Advising, 978-232-5292, E-mail: imenchin@endicott.edu. *Dean, School of Nursing,* Nancy Meedzan, DNP, RN, CNE, 978-232-2389, E-mail: nmeedzan@endicott.edu.

**School of Performing and Visual Arts** Students: 14 full-time (12 women), 2 part-time (1 woman); includes 3 minority (all Asian, non-Hispanic/Latino). Average age 32. 9 applicants, 33% accepted, 2 enrolled. *Faculty:* 1 (woman) full-time, 12 part-time/adjunct (8 women). Expenses: Contact institution. *Financial support:* Applicants required to submit FAFSA. *Program availability:* Part-time, evening/weekend. *Application deadline:* Applications are processed on a rolling basis. *Application fee:* $50. Electronic applications accepted. *Application Contact:* Ian Menchini, Director, Graduate Enrollment and Advising, 978-232-5292, E-mail: imenchin@endicott.edu. *Dean,* Mark Towner, 978-232-2166, E-mail: mtowner@endicott.edu.

**School of Sport Science and Fitness Studies**

**Van Loan School of Graduate and Professional Studies** *Program availability:* Part-time, evening/weekend, 100% online, blended/hybrid learning. Electronic applications accepted.

## EPIC BIBLE COLLEGE, Sacramento, CA 95841

**General Information** Independent-religious, coed, comprehensive institution.

**GRADUATE UNITS**

**Graduate School**

## ERIKSON INSTITUTE, Chicago, IL 60654

**General Information** Independent, coed, primarily women, graduate-only institution.

**GRADUATE UNITS**

**Academic Programs** *Program availability:* Part-time, evening/weekend.

## ERSKINE THEOLOGICAL SEMINARY, Due West, SC 29639-0668

**General Information** Independent-religious, coed, graduate-only institution. *Graduate housing:* Room and/or apartments available on a first-come, first-served basis to single students; on-campus housing not available to married students. Housing application deadline: 6/1.

**GRADUATE UNITS**

**Graduate and Professional Programs** *Program availability:* Part-time, evening/weekend. Electronic applications accepted.

## EVANGELICAL SEMINARY, Myerstown, PA 17067-1212

**General Information** Independent-religious, coed, graduate-only institution. *Graduate housing:* Rooms and/or apartments available on a first-come, first-served basis to single and married students. Housing application deadline: 6/1.

**GRADUATE UNITS**

**Graduate and Professional Programs** *Program availability:* Part-time, online learning.

## EVANGELICAL SEMINARY OF PUERTO RICO, San Juan, PR 00925-2207

**General Information** Independent-religious, coed, graduate-only institution. *Graduate housing:* Rooms and/or apartments available on a first-come, first-served basis to single and married students. Housing application deadline: 12/15.

**GRADUATE UNITS**

**Graduate and Professional Programs** *Program availability:* Part-time.

## EVANGEL UNIVERSITY, Springfield, MO 65802

**General Information** Independent-religious, coed, comprehensive institution. *Graduate housing:* Room and/or apartments available on a first-come, first-served basis to single students; on-campus housing not available to married students.

**GRADUATE UNITS**

**Department of Behavioral and Social Sciences** *Program availability:* Part-time. Electronic applications accepted.

**Department of Education** *Program availability:* Part-time, evening/weekend, 100% online, blended/hybrid learning. Electronic applications accepted.

**Doctor of Education in Educational Leadership, Curriculum, and Instruction Program** *Program availability:* Part-time, evening/weekend. Electronic applications accepted.

**Organizational Leadership Program** *Program availability:* Part-time, evening/weekend, 100% online, blended/hybrid learning. Electronic applications accepted.

**School Counseling Program** *Program availability:* Part-time, evening/weekend. Electronic applications accepted.

## EVERGLADES UNIVERSITY, Boca Raton, FL 33431

**General Information** Independent, coed, comprehensive institution. *Graduate housing:* On-campus housing not available.

**GRADUATE UNITS**

**Graduate Programs** *Program availability:* Part-time, evening/weekend, 100% online. Electronic applications accepted.

## THE EVERGREEN STATE COLLEGE, Olympia, WA 98505

**General Information** State-supported, coed, comprehensive institution. *Enrollment:* 2,854 graduate, professional, and undergraduate students; 172 full-time matriculated graduate/professional students (114 women), 106 part-time matriculated graduate/professional students (76 women). *Enrollment by degree level:* 278 master's. *Graduate faculty:* 16 full-time (12 women), 13 part-time/adjunct (6 women). *Tuition, area resident:* Full-time $10,950; part-time $365 per credit. Tuition, state resident: full-time $10,950; part-time $365 per credit. Tuition, nonresident: full-time $24,975; part-time $832 per credit. *Required fees:* $794.25; $9.25 per credit. $163 per quarter. Tuition and fees vary according to course load. *Graduate housing:* Rooms and/or apartments available on a first-come, first-served basis to single and married students. Typical cost: $8943 per year ($12,363 including board) for single students; $8943 per year ($12,363 including board) for married students. Room and board charges vary according to board plan, campus/location and housing facility selected. Housing application deadline: 5/1. *Student services:* Campus employment opportunities, campus safety program, career counseling, child daycare facilities, free psychological counseling, grant writing training, international student services, multicultural affairs office, services for students with disabilities, teacher training, writing training. *Library facilities:* Daniel J. Evans Library. *Collection:* Books: 378,212 (physical), 240,620 (digital/electronic); Serial titles: 2,504 (physical), 126,748 (digital/electronic); Databases: 103. Weekly public service hours: 77; students can reserve study rooms. *Research affiliation:* Washington State Institute for Public Policy (public policy).

**Computer facilities:** 556 computers available on campus for general student use. A campuswide network can be accessed. Online class registration, online payment, student accounts history, financial aid records, academic history, housing application, evaluations are available.
Website: http://www.evergreen.edu/

**General Application Contact:** Admissions, 360-867-6170, E-mail: admissions@evergreen.edu.

**GRADUATE UNITS**

**Graduate Programs** Students: 172 full-time (114 women), 106 part-time (30 women); includes 73 minority (15 Black or African American, non-Hispanic/Latino; 16 American Indian or Alaska Native, non-Hispanic/Latino; 4 Asian, non-Hispanic/Latino; 31 Hispanic/Latino; 2 Native Hawaiian or other Pacific Islander, non-Hispanic/Latino; 5 Two or more races, non-Hispanic/Latino), 1 international. Average age 34. 183 applicants, 86% accepted, 111 enrolled. *Faculty:* 12 full-time (6 women), 14 part-time/adjunct (9 women). Expenses: Contact institution. *Financial support:* In 2019–20, 142 students received support, including 46 fellowships with partial tuition reimbursements available (averaging $1,595 per year); career-related internships or fieldwork, Federal Work-Study, institutionally sponsored loans, scholarships/grants, health care benefits, and tuition waivers (partial) also available. Support available to part-time students. Financial award application deadline: 4/20; financial award applicants required to submit FAFSA. In 2019, 117 master's awarded. *Program availability:* Part-time, evening/weekend. *Application deadline:* For fall admission, 2/1 priority date for domestic and international students. Applications are processed on a rolling basis. *Application fee:* $50. Electronic applications accepted. *Application Contact:* Amanda Mobbs, Graduate Admission Coordinator, 360-867-6856, E-mail: graduateadmissions@evergreen.edu. *Vice President and Provost,* Dr. Jennifer Drake, 360-867-6400, Fax: 360-867-6745, E-mail: drakej@evergreen.edu.

## EXCELSIOR COLLEGE, Albany, NY 12203-5159

**General Information** Independent, coed, comprehensive institution. *Enrollment:* 23,501 graduate, professional, and undergraduate students; 2,445 part-time matriculated graduate/professional students (1,121 women). *Enrollment by degree level:* 2,443 master's, 2 other advanced degrees. *Graduate faculty:* 39 part-time/adjunct (19 women). *Tuition:* Part-time $645 per credit. *Required fees:* $265 per unit. *Student services:* Career counseling, services for students with disabilities, writing training. *Library facilities:* Excelsior College Library.

**Computer facilities:** A campuswide network can be accessed. Online class registration is available.
Website: http://www.excelsior.edu/

**General Application Contact:** Admissions, 518-464-8500, Fax: 518-464-8777, E-mail: admissions@excelsior.edu.

## FAIRFIELD UNIVERSITY, Fairfield, CT 06824

**General Information** Independent-religious, coed, comprehensive institution. *Enrollment:* 5,349 graduate, professional, and undergraduate students; 445 full-time matriculated graduate/professional students (314 women), 601 part-time matriculated graduate/professional students (425 women). *Enrollment by degree level:* 818 master's, 145 doctoral, 83 other advanced degrees. *Graduate faculty:* 105 full-time (60 women), 79 part-time/adjunct (42 women). *Tuition:* Full-time $850; part-time $850 per credit. *Required fees:* $230; $230 per unit. $115 per semester. Tuition and fees vary according to program. *Graduate housing:* On-campus housing not available. *Student services:* Campus employment opportunities, campus safety program, career counseling, child daycare facilities, exercise/wellness program, free psychological counseling, international student services, low-cost health insurance, multicultural affairs office, services for students with disabilities, teacher training, writing training. *Library facilities:* DiMenna-Nyselius Library. *Collection:* Books: 311,985 (physical), 1 million (digital/electronic); Serial titles: 86,612 (digital/electronic); Databases: 209. Weekly public service hours: 104; study areas open 24 hours, 5–7 days a week; students can reserve study rooms.

**Computer facilities:** Computer purchase and lease plans are available. 150 computers available on campus for general student use. A campuswide network can be accessed. Online class registration is available.
Website: http://www.fairfield.edu/

**General Application Contact:** Melanie Rogers, Director of Graduate Admission, 203-254-4184, Fax: 203-254-4073, E-mail: gradadmis@fairfield.edu.

**GRADUATE UNITS**

**College of Arts and Sciences** Students: 64 full-time (44 women), 84 part-time (48 women); includes 35 minority (9 Black or African American, non-Hispanic/Latino; 1 American Indian or Alaska Native, non-Hispanic/Latino; 1 Asian, non-Hispanic/Latino; 21 Hispanic/Latino; 3 Two or more races, non-Hispanic/Latino), 7 international. Average age 36. 98 applicants, 68% accepted, 64 enrolled. *Faculty:* 35 full-time (19 women), 19 part-time/adjunct (10 women). Expenses: Contact institution. *Financial support:* In 2019–20, 11 students received support. Scholarships/grants and unspecified assistantships available. Financial award applicants required to submit FAFSA. In 2019, 38 master's awarded. *Program availability:* Part-time, evening/weekend, online learning. *Application deadline:* For fall admission, 5/15 for international students; for spring admission, 10/15 for international students. Applications are processed on a rolling basis. *Application fee:* $60. Electronic applications accepted. *Application Contact:* Melanie Rogers, Director of Graduate Admission, 203-254-4184, Fax: 203-254-4073, E-mail: gradadmis@fairfield.edu. *Dean,* Dr. Richard Greenwald, 203-254-4000 Ext. 2221, Fax: 203-254-4119, E-mail: rgreenwald@fairfield.edu.

**Dolan School of Business** Students: 120 full-time (57 women), 67 part-time (27 women); includes 20 minority (3 Black or African American, non-Hispanic/Latino; 1 American Indian or Alaska Native, non-Hispanic/Latino; 3 Asian, non-Hispanic/Latino; 11 Hispanic/Latino; 2 Two or more races, non-Hispanic/Latino), 33 international. Average age 26. 123 applicants, 56% accepted, 64 enrolled. *Faculty:* 18 full-time (6 women), 6 part-time/adjunct (2 women). Expenses: Contact institution. *Financial support:* In 2019–20, 31 students received support. Scholarships/grants and unspecified assistantships available. Financial award applicants required to submit FAFSA. In 2019, 93 master's awarded. *Program availability:* Part-time, evening/weekend. *Application deadline:* For fall admission, 5/15 for international students; for spring admission, 10/15 for international students. Applications are processed on a rolling basis. *Application fee:* $60. Electronic applications accepted. *Application Contact:* Melanie Rogers, Director of Graduate Admission, 203-254-4184, Fax: 203-254-4073, E-mail: gradadmis@fairfield.edu. *Dean,* Dr. Zhan Li, 203-254-4070, Fax: 203-254-4105, E-mail: zli2@fairfield.edu.

**Graduate School of Education and Allied Professions** Students: 169 full-time (149 women), 227 part-time (187 women); includes 96 minority (21 Black or African American, non-Hispanic/Latino; 8 Asian, non-Hispanic/Latino; 60 Hispanic/Latino; 7 Two or more races, non-Hispanic/Latino), 1 international. Average age 31. 194 applicants, 60% accepted, 101 enrolled. *Faculty:* 24 full-time (18 women), 28 part-time/adjunct (20 women). Expenses: Contact institution. *Financial support:* In 2019–20, 34 students received support. Career-related internships or fieldwork and unspecified assistantships available. Support available to part-time students. Financial award applicants required to submit FAFSA. In 2019, 136 master's, 28 other advanced degrees awarded. *Program availability:* Part-time, evening/weekend. *Application deadline:* For fall admission, 2/15 for international students; for spring admission, 10/1 for international students. *Application fee:* $60. Electronic applications accepted. *Application Contact:* Melanie Rogers, Director of Graduate Admission, 203-254-4184, Fax: 203-254-4073, E-mail: gradadmis@fairfield.edu. *Dean,* Dr. Laurie Grupp, 203-254-4250, Fax: 203-254-4241, E-mail: lgrupp@fairfield.edu.

**Marion Peckham Egan School of Nursing and Health Studies** Students: 56 full-time (49 women), 165 part-time (149 women); includes 62 minority (24 Black or African American, non-Hispanic/Latino; 12 Asian, non-Hispanic/Latino; 25 Hispanic/Latino; 1 Two or more races, non-Hispanic/Latino). Average age 33. 129 applicants, 56% accepted, 62 enrolled. *Faculty:* 13 full-time (all women), 12 part-time/adjunct (9 women). Expenses: Contact institution. *Financial support:* In 2019–20, 45 students received support. Scholarships/grants and unspecified assistantships available. Financial award applicants required to submit FAFSA. In 2019, 26 master's, 36 doctorates awarded. *Program availability:* Part-time, evening/weekend. *Application deadline:* For fall admission, 5/15 for international students; for spring admission, 10/15 for international students. Applications are processed on a rolling basis. *Application fee:* $60. Electronic applications accepted. *Application Contact:* Melanie Rogers, Director of Graduate Admission, 203-254-4184, Fax: 203-254-4073, E-mail: gradadmis@fairfield.edu. *Dean,* Dr. Meredith Wallace Kazer, 203-254-4000 Ext. 2701, Fax: 203-254-4126, E-mail: mkazer@fairfield.edu.

**School of Engineering** Students: 46 full-time (24 women), 57 part-time (10 women); includes 23 minority (5 Black or African American, non-Hispanic/Latino; 9 Asian, non-Hispanic/Latino; 9 Hispanic/Latino), 33 international. Average age 29. 68 applicants, 62% accepted, 30 enrolled. *Faculty:* 10 full-time (2 women), 15 part-time/adjunct (1 woman). Expenses: Contact institution. *Financial support:* In 2019–20, 20 students received support. Scholarships/grants and unspecified assistantships available. Financial award applicants required to submit FAFSA. In 2019, 100 master's awarded. *Program availability:* Part-time, evening/weekend. *Application deadline:* For fall admission, 5/15 for international students; for spring admission, 10/15 for international students. Applications are processed on a rolling basis. *Application fee:* $60. Electronic applications accepted. *Application Contact:* Melanie Rogers, Director of Graduate Admission, 203-254-4184, Fax: 203-254-4073, E-mail: gradadmis@fairfield.edu. *Dean,* Richard Heist, 203-254-4147, Fax: 203-254-4013, E-mail: rheist@fairfield.edu.

## FAIRLEIGH DICKINSON UNIVERSITY, FLORHAM CAMPUS, Madison, NJ 07940-1099

**General Information** Independent, coed, comprehensive institution. *Graduate housing:* Room and/or apartments available on a first-come, first-served basis to single students; on-campus housing not available to married students. Housing application deadline: 5/1.

**GRADUATE UNITS**

**Anthony J. Petrocelli College of Continuing Studies**
***International School of Hospitality and Tourism Management***
***Public Administration Institute***
***School of Administrative Science***
**Maxwell Becton College of Arts and Sciences**
**School of Pharmacy**
**Silberman College of Business** *Program availability:* Part-time, evening/weekend.
***Center for Human Resource Management Studies***
**University College: Arts, Sciences, and Professional Studies**
***The Henry P. Becton School of Nursing and Allied Health*** *Program availability:* Part-time, evening/weekend.
***Peter Sammartino School of Education***

## FAIRLEIGH DICKINSON UNIVERSITY, METROPOLITAN CAMPUS, Teaneck, NJ 07666-1914

**General Information** Independent, coed, university. *Graduate housing:* Room and/or apartments available on a first-come, first-served basis to single students; on-campus housing not available to married students. Housing application deadline: 5/1.

**GRADUATE UNITS**

**Anthony J. Petrocelli College of Continuing Studies**
***International School of Hospitality and Tourism Management***
***Public Administration Institute***
***School of Administrative Science***
**Silberman College of Business**
***Center for Human Resources Management Studies***
**University College: Arts, Sciences, and Professional Studies**
***Henry P. Becton School of Nursing and Allied Health***
***Peter Sammartino School of Education*** *Program availability:* Part-time.
***School of Art and Media Studies***
***School of Computer Sciences and Engineering***
***School of Criminal Justice and Legal Studies***
***School of History, Political and International Studies***
***School of Natural Sciences***
***School of Psychology***

## FAIRMONT STATE UNIVERSITY, Fairmont, WV 26554

**General Information** State-supported, coed, comprehensive institution. CGS member. *Graduate housing:* Room and/or apartments available on a first-come, first-served basis to single students; on-campus housing not available to married students.

**GRADUATE UNITS**

**Program in Business Administration** *Program availability:* Part-time, evening/weekend. Electronic applications accepted.
**Program in Criminal Justice** *Program availability:* Part-time, evening/weekend, 100% online. Electronic applications accepted.
**Programs in Education** *Program availability:* Part-time, evening/weekend, 100% online. Electronic applications accepted.

## FAITH BAPTIST BIBLE COLLEGE AND THEOLOGICAL SEMINARY, Ankeny, IA 50023

**General Information** Independent-religious, coed, comprehensive institution. *Graduate housing:* Rooms and/or apartments available on a first-come, first-served basis to single and married students. Housing application deadline: 8/1.

**GRADUATE UNITS**

**Graduate Program** *Program availability:* Part-time. Electronic applications accepted.

## FAITH INTERNATIONAL UNIVERSITY, Tacoma, WA 98407

**General Information** Independent-religious, coed, comprehensive institution. *Enrollment by degree level:* 125 master's, 45 doctoral. *Graduate faculty:* 11 full-time (2 women), 14 part-time/adjunct (1 woman). *Tuition:* Full-time $7000; part-time $1000 per quarter. *Required fees:* $450; $150 per quarter. Tuition and fees vary according to degree level and student's religious affiliation. *Student services:* Campus safety program, career counseling, free psychological counseling, international student services, services for students with disabilities.
Website: http://www.faithseminary.edu/

**General Application Contact:** Dr. Michael J. Adams, President, 253-752-2020 Ext. 111, Fax: 253-759-1790, E-mail: mjadams@faithseminary.edu.

**GRADUATE UNITS**

**Graduate and Professional Programs** *Program availability:* Part-time, evening/weekend, online learning.

## FAITH THEOLOGICAL SEMINARY, Baltimore, MD 21212

**General Information** Independent-religious, coed, comprehensive institution.

**GRADUATE UNITS**

**Graduate Programs**

## FARMINGDALE STATE COLLEGE, Farmingdale, NY 11735

**General Information** State-supported, coed, comprehensive institution.

**GRADUATE UNITS**

**Program in Technology Management**

## FASHION INSTITUTE OF TECHNOLOGY, New York, NY 10001-5992

**General Information** State and locally supported, coed, primarily women, comprehensive institution. *Graduate housing:* Room and/or apartments available on a first-come, first-served basis to single students; on-campus housing not available to married students. *Research affiliation:* Exhibition Designers and Producers Association (exhibition design), Society for Environmental Graphic Design (exhibition design), Lolita S. A. (global fashion management), IDEO (design and management innovation), Grove Dictionary of Art, Oxford University Press (costume history).

**GRADUATE UNITS**

**School of Graduate Studies** *Program availability:* Part-time, evening/weekend. Electronic applications accepted.

## FAULKNER UNIVERSITY, Montgomery, AL 36109-3398

**General Information** Independent-religious, coed, university. *Graduate housing:* On-campus housing not available.

**GRADUATE UNITS**

**Alabama Christian College of Arts and Sciences** *Program availability:* Part-time, evening/weekend, 100% online, blended/hybrid learning. Electronic applications accepted.
**College of Biblical Studies** *Program availability:* Part-time, evening/weekend, 100% online, blended/hybrid learning, synchronous online/on-ground. Electronic applications accepted.
**College of Education** *Program availability:* Part-time, evening/weekend, 100% online, blended/hybrid learning. Electronic applications accepted.
**Harris College of Business and Executive Education** *Program availability:* Part-time, evening/weekend, 100% online, blended/hybrid learning. Electronic applications accepted.
**Thomas Goode Jones School of Law** Electronic applications accepted.

## FAYETTEVILLE STATE UNIVERSITY, Fayetteville, NC 28301-4298

**General Information** State-supported, coed, comprehensive institution. *Enrollment:* 6,551 graduate, professional, and undergraduate students; 368 full-time matriculated graduate/professional students (258 women), 539 part-time matriculated graduate/professional students (315 women). *Enrollment by degree level:* 679 master's, 92 doctoral, 136 other advanced degrees. *Graduate faculty:* 50 full-time (23 women), 26 part-time/adjunct (15 women). *Graduate housing:* On-campus housing not available. *Student services:* Campus employment opportunities, career counseling, child daycare facilities, free psychological counseling, low-cost health insurance, services for students with disabilities. *Library facilities:* Charles W. Chestnut Library. *Collection:* Books: 231,506 (physical), 299,552 (digital/electronic); Serial titles: 8,727 (physical), 56,051 (digital/electronic); Databases: 442. Weekly public service hours: 97; students can reserve study rooms. *Research affiliation:* Research Triangle Park.

**Computer facilities:** Computer purchase and lease plans are available. 600 computers available on campus for general student use. A campuswide network can be accessed. Online class registration is available.
Website: http://www.uncfsu.edu/

**General Application Contact:** Melissa Wells, Assistant Director of Admissions, 910-672-1412, Fax: 910-672-2600, E-mail: mwells@uncfsu.edu.

**GRADUATE UNITS**

**Graduate School** *Program availability:* Part-time, evening/weekend. Electronic applications accepted.

## FELICIAN UNIVERSITY, Lodi, NJ 07644-2117

**General Information** Independent-religious, coed, comprehensive institution. *Graduate housing:* Room and/or apartments available on a first-come, first-served basis to single students; on-campus housing not available to married students. Housing application deadline: 5/1.

**GRADUATE UNITS**

**Doctor of Nursing Practice Program** *Program availability:* Evening/weekend, online only, 100% online, blended/hybrid learning. Electronic applications accepted.
**Master of Science in Nursing Program** *Program availability:* Evening/weekend, online only, 100% online, blended/hybrid learning. Electronic applications accepted.
**Program in Business** *Program availability:* Part-time-only, evening/weekend, online learning. Electronic applications accepted.
**Program in Counseling Psychology** *Program availability:* Part-time, evening/weekend. Electronic applications accepted.
**Program in Education** *Program availability:* Part-time, evening/weekend. Electronic applications accepted.
**Program in Health Care Administration** *Program availability:* Part-time, evening/weekend. Electronic applications accepted.
**Program in Religious Education** *Program availability:* Part-time, evening/weekend, online only, 100% online. Electronic applications accepted.

## FERRIS STATE UNIVERSITY, Big Rapids, MI 49307

**General Information** State-supported, coed, comprehensive institution. CGS member. *Enrollment:* 12,472 graduate, professional, and undergraduate students; 898 full-time matriculated graduate/professional students (538 women), 359 part-time matriculated graduate/professional students (265 women). *Enrollment by degree level:* 542 master's, 679 doctoral, 90 other advanced degrees. *Graduate faculty:* 134 full-time (74 women), 154 part-time/adjunct (78 women). Tuition and fees vary according to degree level, program and student level. *Graduate housing:* Rooms and/or apartments available on a first-come, first-served basis to single and married students. *Student services:* Campus employment opportunities, campus safety program, career counseling, child daycare facilities, exercise/wellness program, free psychological counseling, international student services, low-cost health insurance, multicultural affairs office, services for students with disabilities, teacher training. *Library facilities:* Ferris Library for Information, Technology and Education. *Collection:* Books: 181,270 (physical), 483,402 (digital/electronic); Serial titles: 5,430 (physical), 325,776 (digital/electronic); Databases: 170. Weekly public service hours: 93; students can reserve study rooms. *Research affiliation:* Allergan-Hydron (optometry), Bausch & Lomb (optometry), Ciba Vision (optometry), American Education Research Association (education), Vistakon-Johnson & Johnson (optometry).

**Computer facilities:** 1,751 computers available on campus for general student use. A campuswide network can be accessed. Online class registration is available.
Website: http://www.ferris.edu/

**General Application Contact:** Dr. Kristen Salomonson, Dean, Enrollment Services/Director, Admissions and Records, 231-591-2100, Fax: 231-591-3944, E-mail: admissions@ferris.edu.

**GRADUATE UNITS**

**College of Arts and Sciences** Students: 48 full-time (45 women), 43 part-time (39 women); includes 12 minority (3 Black or African American, non-Hispanic/Latino; 5 Hispanic/Latino; 1 Native Hawaiian or other Pacific Islander, non-Hispanic/Latino; 3 Two or more races, non-Hispanic/Latino). Average age 29. 63 applicants, 94% accepted, 44 enrolled. *Faculty:* 6 full-time (5 women), 2 part-time/adjunct (both women). Expenses: Contact institution. *Financial support:* In 2019–20, 11 students received support. Federal Work-Study and scholarships/grants available. Financial award applicants required to submit FAFSA. In 2019, 33 master's awarded. *Program availability:* Part-time, evening/weekend. *Application deadline:* For fall admission, 12/1 priority date for domestic and international students; for winter admission, 3/15 for domestic and international students. *Application fee:* $0 ($30 for international students). Electronic applications accepted. *Application Contact:* Dr. Janet Vizina-Roubal, MSW, MSW Program Director, 231-357-2816, E-mail: janetvizinaroubal@ferris.edu. *Department Chair*, Dr. Michael Berghoef, PhD, E-mail: MichaelBerghoef@ferris.edu.

**College of Business** Students: 11 full-time (6 women), 73 part-time (34 women); includes 9 minority (2 Black or African American, non-Hispanic/Latino; 1 Asian, non-Hispanic/Latino; 4 Hispanic/Latino; 2 Two or more races, non-Hispanic/Latino), 1 international. Average age 33. 30 applicants, 90% accepted, 21 enrolled. *Faculty:* 19 full-time (6 women), 2 part-time/adjunct (1 woman). Expenses: Contact institution. *Financial support:* In 2019–20, 15 students received support. Career-related internships or fieldwork, Federal Work-Study, scholarships/grants, and unspecified assistantships available. Support available to part-time students. Financial award applicants required to submit FAFSA. In 2019, 50 master's awarded. *Program availability:* Part-time, evening/weekend, online only, 100% online, blended/hybrid learning. *Application deadline:* For fall admission, 6/15 priority date for domestic students, 6/15 for international students; for spring admission, 10/15 priority date for domestic and international students; for summer admission, 2/15 priority date for domestic and international students. Applications are processed on a rolling basis. *Application fee:* $0 ($30 for international students). Electronic applications accepted. *Application Contact:* Dr. Greg Gogolin, Professor, 231-591-3159, Fax: 231-591-3521, E-mail: greggogolin@ferris.edu. *College of Business Dean*, Dr. David Nicol, 231-591-2168, Fax: 231-591-3521, E-mail: davidnicol@ferris.edu.

**College of Education and Human Services** Students: 7 full-time (5 women), 73 part-time (42 women); includes 16 minority (11 Black or African American, non-Hispanic/Latino; 4 Hispanic/Latino; 1 Two or more races, non-Hispanic/Latino), 1 international. Average age 31. 42 applicants, 95% accepted, 33 enrolled. *Faculty:* 14 full-time (5 women), 1 (woman) part-time/adjunct. Expenses: Contact institution. *Financial support:* In 2019–20, 12 students received support, including 4 research assistantships (averaging $4,407 per year); career-related internships or fieldwork, Federal Work-Study, scholarships/grants, and unspecified assistantships also available. Support available to part-time students. Financial award applicants required to submit FAFSA. In 2019, 31 master's awarded. *Program availability:* Part-time, evening/weekend, blended/hybrid learning. *Application deadline:* For fall admission, 7/1 priority date for domestic and international students; for winter admission, 12/15 priority date for domestic and international students; for spring admission, 11/1 priority date for domestic and international students; for summer admission, 3/1 priority date for domestic and international students. Applications are processed on a rolling basis. *Application fee:* $0 ($30 for international students). Electronic applications accepted. *Application Contact:* Dr. Kristen Salomonson, Dean, Enrollment Services/Director, Admissions and Records, 231-591-2100, Fax: 231-591-3944, E-mail: admissions@ferris.edu. *Interim Dean*, Leonard Johnson, 231-591-3648, Fax: 231-592-3792, E-mail: LeonardJohnson@ferris.edu.

***School of Criminal Justice*** Students: 6 full-time (4 women), 39 part-time (22 women); includes 13 minority (9 Black or African American, non-Hispanic/Latino; 3 Hispanic/Latino; 1 Two or more races, non-Hispanic/Latino). Average age 31. 21 applicants, 100% accepted, 18 enrolled. *Faculty:* 8 full-time (2 women). Expenses: Contact institution. *Financial support:* In 2019–20, 5 students received support, including 4 research assistantships (averaging $4,407 per year); Federal Work-Study and unspecified assistantships also available. Support available to part-time students. Financial award applicants required to submit FAFSA. In 2019, 19 master's awarded. *Program availability:* Part-time, evening/weekend. *Application deadline:* For fall admission, 8/15 for domestic students; for winter admission, 12/15 for domestic students; for spring admission, 3/15 for domestic students. Applications are processed on a rolling basis. *Application fee:* $0 ($30 for international students). Electronic applications accepted. *Application Contact:* Sara P. Rasmussen, Secretary, 231-591-3652, Fax: 231-591-3792, E-mail: sararasmussen@ferris.edu. *Professor/Graduate Program Coordinator*, Dr. Nancy L. Hogan, 231-591-2664, Fax: 231-591-3792, E-mail: hogann@ferris.edu.

***School of Education*** Students: 1 (woman) full-time, 34 part-time (20 women); includes 3 minority (2 Black or African American, non-Hispanic/Latino; 1 Hispanic/Latino), 1 international. Average age 30. 21 applicants, 90% accepted, 15 enrolled. *Faculty:* 6 full-time (3 women), 1 (woman) part-time/adjunct. Expenses: Contact institution. *Financial support:* In 2019–20, 7 students received support. Career-related internships or fieldwork available. Support available to part-time students. Financial award applicants required to submit FAFSA. In 2019, 12 master's awarded. *Program availability:* Part-time, evening/weekend, blended/hybrid learning. *Application deadline:* For fall admission, 7/1 priority date for domestic and international students; for spring admission, 11/1 priority date for domestic and international students; for summer admission, 3/1 priority date for domestic and international students. Applications are processed on a rolling basis. *Application fee:* $0 ($30 for international students). Electronic applications accepted. *Application Contact:* Liza Ing, Graduate Program Coordinator, 231-591-5362, Fax: 231-591-2043, E-mail: lizaIng@ferris.edu. *Interim Dean*, Leonard Johnson, 231-591-3648, Fax: 231-591-2043, E-mail: LeonardJohnson@ferris.edu.

**College of Health Professions** Students: 37 full-time (31 women), 133 part-time (123 women); includes 34 minority (10 Black or African American, non-Hispanic/Latino; 8 American Indian or Alaska Native, non-Hispanic/Latino; 7 Asian, non-Hispanic/Latino; 4 Hispanic/Latino; 5 Two or more races, non-Hispanic/Latino). Average age 34. 56 applicants, 95% accepted, 43 enrolled. *Faculty:* 16 full-time (13 women), 1 (woman) part-time/adjunct. Expenses: Contact institution. *Financial support:* In 2019–20, 14 students received support. Career-related internships or fieldwork and scholarships/grants available. Financial award application deadline: 4/15; financial award applicants required to submit FAFSA. In 2019, 36 master's awarded. *Program availability:* Part-time, evening/weekend, 100% online. *Application deadline:* For fall admission, 4/15 priority date for domestic students; for spring admission, 10/15 for domestic students; for summer admission, 4/1 for domestic and international students. Applications are processed on a rolling basis. *Application fee:* $0 ($30 for international students). Electronic applications accepted. *Application Contact:* Dr. Kristen Salomonson, Dean of Enrollment Services and Director of Admissions and Records, 231-591-3963, Fax: 231-591-3179, E-mail: kristensalomonson@ferris.edu. *Dean*, Dr. Lincoln Gibbs, 231-591-2273, E-mail: LincolnGibbs@ferris.edu.

***School of Nursing*** Students: 103 part-time (95 women); includes 14 minority (2 Black or African American, non-Hispanic/Latino; 6 American Indian or Alaska Native, non-Hispanic/Latino; 4 Hispanic/Latino; 2 Two or more races, non-Hispanic/Latino). Average age 38. 31 applicants, 97% accepted, 24 enrolled. *Faculty:* 7 full-time (all women), 1 (woman) part-time/adjunct. Expenses: Contact institution. *Financial support:* In 2019–20, 7 students received support. Career-related internships or fieldwork and scholarships/grants available. Financial award application deadline: 4/15; financial award applicants required to submit FAFSA. In 2019, 24 master's awarded. *Program availability:* Part-time, evening/weekend, online only, 100% online. *Application deadline:* For fall admission, 4/15 priority date for domestic and international students; for spring admission, 10/15 for domestic and international students. Electronic applications accepted. *Application Contact:* Dr. Sharon Colley, MSN Program Coordinator, 231-591-2288, Fax: 231-591-2325, E-mail: colleys@ferris.edu. *Chair, School of Nursing*, Dr. Wendy Lenon, 231-591-2267, Fax: 231-591-2325, E-mail: WendyLenon@ferris.edu.

**College of Pharmacy** Students: 517 full-time (285 women), 16 part-time (10 women); includes 50 minority (4 Black or African American, non-Hispanic/Latino; 2 American Indian or Alaska Native, non-Hispanic/Latino; 21 Asian, non-Hispanic/Latino; 16 Hispanic/Latino; 7 Two or more races, non-Hispanic/Latino), 11 international. Average age 24. 280 applicants, 62% accepted, 119 enrolled. *Faculty:* 43 full-time (26 women), 3 part-time/adjunct (2 women). Expenses: Contact institution. *Financial support:* In 2019–20, 150 students received support. Career-related internships or fieldwork, Federal Work-Study, institutionally sponsored loans, and scholarships/grants available. Financial award application deadline: 4/15; financial award applicants required to submit FAFSA. In 2019, 149 doctorates awarded. *Application deadline:* For fall admission, 3/1 for domestic and international students. Applications are processed on a rolling basis. *Application fee:* $175. Electronic applications accepted. *Application Contact:* Tara M. Lee, Director of Admissions, 231-591-2249, Fax: 231-591-3829, E-mail: leet@ferris.edu. *Dean*, Dr. Stephen Durst, 231-591-2254, Fax: 231-591-3829, E-mail: dursts@ferris.edu.

**Extended and International Operations** Students: 87 full-time (51 women), 3 part-time (2 women); includes 41 minority (27 Black or African American, non-Hispanic/Latino; 3 American Indian or Alaska Native, non-Hispanic/Latino; 1 Asian, non-Hispanic/Latino; 8 Hispanic/Latino; 2 Two or more races, non-Hispanic/Latino). Average age 46. 31 applicants, 90% accepted, 23 enrolled. *Faculty:* 24 part-time/adjunct (16 women). Expenses: Contact institution. *Financial support:* In 2019–20, 12 students received support, including 7 teaching assistantships (averaging $1,000 per year). Financial award applicants required to submit FAFSA. In 2019, 29 doctorates awarded. *Program availability:* Evening/weekend, blended/hybrid learning. *Application deadline:* For summer admission, 4/12 for domestic students. Applications are processed on a rolling basis. Electronic applications accepted. *Application Contact:* Megan Biller, DCCL Assistand Director, 231-591-2710, Fax: 231-591-3539, E-mail: meganbiller@ferris.edu. *DCCL Director*, Dr. Roberta Teahen, 231-591-2710, E-mail: robertateahen@ferris.edu.

**Kendall College of Art and Design** Students: 46 full-time (25 women), 18 part-time (15 women); includes 10 minority (1 Black or African American, non-Hispanic/Latino; 1 American Indian or Alaska Native, non-Hispanic/Latino; 6 Hispanic/Latino; 2 Two or more races, non-Hispanic/Latino), 8 international. Average age 33. 28 applicants, 82% accepted, 19 enrolled. *Faculty:* 16 full-time (9 women), 6 part-time/adjunct (3 women). Expenses: Contact institution. *Financial support:* In 2019–20, 46 students received support, including 46 fellowships (averaging $11,736 per year); scholarships/grants and unspecified assistantships also available. Financial award application deadline: 2/1; financial award applicants required to submit FAFSA. In 2019, 14 master's awarded. *Application deadline:* For fall admission, 2/1 priority date for domestic and international students; for spring admission, 10/15 priority date for domestic and international students. Applications are processed on a rolling basis. *Application fee:* $0 ($30 for international students). Electronic applications accepted. *Application Contact:* Thomas Post, Graduate Recruitment Specialist, 616-451-2787, Fax: 616-831-9689, E-mail: thomaspost@ferris.edu. *President*, Tara McCrackin, 616-451-2787.

**Michigan College of Optometry** Students: 146 full-time (90 women); includes 6 minority (1 Asian, non-Hispanic/Latino; 4 Hispanic/Latino; 1 Two or more races, non-Hispanic/Latino), 10 international. Average age 24. 225 applicants, 30% accepted, 38 enrolled. *Faculty:* 19 full-time (9 women), 115 part-time/adjunct (52 women). Expenses: Contact institution. *Financial support:* In 2019–20, 13 students received support. Career-related internships or fieldwork, Federal Work-Study, and scholarships/grants available. Financial award application deadline: 2/1; financial award applicants required to submit FAFSA. In 2019, 35 doctorates awarded. *Application deadline:* For fall admission, 2/1 for domestic and international students. Applications are processed on a rolling basis. *Application fee:* $175. Electronic applications accepted. *Application Contact:* Amy Parks, Health College Administrative Specialist, 231-591-3703, Fax: 231-591-2394, E-mail: amyparks@ferris.edu. *Dean*, Dr. David Damari, 231-591-3706, Fax: 231-591-2394, E-mail: damarid@ferris.edu.

## FIELDING GRADUATE UNIVERSITY, Santa Barbara, CA 93105-3814

**General Information** Independent, coed, graduate-only institution. CGS member. *Graduate housing:* On-campus housing not available.

**GRADUATE UNITS**

**Graduate Programs** *Program availability:* Part-time, evening/weekend, 100% online, blended/hybrid learning. Electronic applications accepted.

***School of Leadership*** Students: 221 full-time (160 women), 132 part-time (97 women); includes 174 minority (74 Black or African American, non-Hispanic/Latino; 23 American Indian or Alaska Native, non-Hispanic/Latino; 23 Asian, non-Hispanic/Latino; 34 Hispanic/Latino; 2 Native Hawaiian or other Pacific Islander, non-Hispanic/Latino; 18 Two or more races, non-Hispanic/Latino), 5 international. Average age 50. 90 applicants, 96% accepted, 51 enrolled. *Faculty:* 22 full-time (12 women), 51 part-time/adjunct (31 women). Expenses: Contact institution. *Financial support:* In 2019–20, 71 students received support. Research assistantships, teaching assistantships, and scholarships/grants available. Support available to part-time students. Financial award applicants required to submit FAFSA. In 2019, 7 master's, 41 doctorates, 45 other advanced degrees awarded. *Program availability:* Part-time, evening/weekend, 100% online, blended/hybrid learning. *Application deadline:* For fall admission, 7/15 for domestic and international students; for spring admission, 10/24 for domestic and international students; for summer admission, 2/18 for domestic and international students. *Application fee:* $75. Electronic applications accepted. *Application Contact:* Enrollment Coordinator, 800-340-1099 Ext. 4098, Fax: 805-687-9793, E-mail: admissions@fielding.edu.

***School of Psychology*** *Program availability:* Part-time, evening/weekend, 100% online, blended/hybrid learning. Electronic applications accepted.

## FISHER COLLEGE, Boston, MA 02116-1500

**General Information** Independent, coed, comprehensive institution. *Graduate housing:* Room and/or apartments available on a first-come, first-served basis to single students; on-campus housing not available to married students. Housing application deadline: 8/1.

**GRADUATE UNITS**

**Master of Business Administration Program** *Program availability:* Part-time, evening/weekend, online only, 100% online. Electronic applications accepted.

## FISK UNIVERSITY, Nashville, TN 37208-3051

**General Information** Independent-religious, coed, comprehensive institution. *Graduate housing:* Rooms and/or apartments available on a first-come, first-served basis to single and married students. Housing application deadline: 4/6. *Research affiliation:* Oak Ridge Associated Universities (physics).

**GRADUATE UNITS**

**Division of Graduate Studies** *Program availability:* Part-time. Electronic applications accepted.

## FITCHBURG STATE UNIVERSITY, Fitchburg, MA 01420-2697

**General Information** State-supported, coed, comprehensive institution. *Graduate housing:* On-campus housing not available.

**GRADUATE UNITS**

**Division of Graduate and Continuing Education** *Program availability:* Part-time, evening/weekend, online learning. Electronic applications accepted.

## FIVE BRANCHES UNIVERSITY, Santa Cruz, CA 95062

**General Information** Independent, coed, graduate-only institution. *Graduate housing:* On-campus housing not available. *Research affiliation:* Highland Hospital (healthcare).

**GRADUATE UNITS**

**Graduate School of Traditional Chinese Medicine** Electronic applications accepted.

## FIVE TOWNS COLLEGE, Dix Hills, NY 11746-6055

**General Information** Independent, coed, comprehensive institution. *Graduate housing:* Room and/or apartments available on a first-come, first-served basis to single students; on-campus housing not available to married students.

**GRADUATE UNITS**

**Graduate Programs** *Program availability:* Part-time. Electronic applications accepted.

## FLAGLER COLLEGE, St. Augustine, FL 32085-1027

**General Information** Independent, coed, comprehensive institution. *Library facilities:* Proctor Library. *Collection:* Books: 93,031 (physical), 252,378 (digital/electronic); Serial titles: 76 (physical), 47,031 (digital/electronic); Databases: 49. Weekly public service hours: 96; students can reserve study rooms.

**Computer facilities:** A campuswide network can be accessed from student residence rooms and from off campus.
Website: http://www.flagler.edu/

**GRADUATE UNITS**

**Program in Deaf Education** Expenses: Contact institution. *Application Contact:* Dr. Margaret H. Finnegan, Coordinator, 904-819-6250, E-mail: finnegmh@flagler.edu. *Coordinator*, Dr. Margaret H. Finnegan, 904-819-6250, E-mail: finnegmh@flagler.edu.

## FLORIDA AGRICULTURAL AND MECHANICAL UNIVERSITY, Tallahassee, FL 32307-3200

**General Information** State-supported, coed, university. CGS member. *Graduate housing:* Rooms and/or apartments available on a first-come, first-served basis to single and married students. Housing application deadline: 6/1. *Research affiliation:* Boeing (aerospace science), Minority Health Professions Foundation (health science), Pfizer, Inc.

**GRADUATE UNITS**

**College of Law** *Program availability:* Part-time, evening/weekend.

**Division of Graduate Studies, Research, and Continuing Education** *Program availability:* Part-time, evening/weekend.

***College of Education*** *Program availability:* Part-time, evening/weekend.

***College of Pharmacy and Pharmaceutical Sciences***

***College of Science and Technology***

***College of Social Sciences, Arts and Humanities*** *Program availability:* Part-time.

***FAMU-FSU College of Engineering***

***School of Allied Health Sciences***

***School of Architecture*** *Program availability:* Part-time.

***School of Business and Industry***

***School of Journalism and Graphic Communication***

***School of Nursing***

**School of the Environment** Electronic applications accepted.

## FLORIDA ATLANTIC UNIVERSITY, Boca Raton, FL 33431-0991

**General Information** State-supported, coed, university. CGS member. *Enrollment:* 30,061 graduate, professional, and undergraduate students; 2,168 full-time matriculated graduate/professional students (1,239 women), 2,772 part-time matriculated graduate/professional students (1,754 women). *Enrollment by degree level:* 3,661 master's, 1,236 doctoral, 43 other advanced degrees. *Graduate faculty:* 703 full-time (277 women), 61 part-time/adjunct (32 women). *Tuition:* Full-time $20,536; part-time $371.82 per credit hour. Tuition and fees vary according to program. *Graduate housing:* Room and/or apartments available on a first-come, first-served basis to single students; on-campus housing not available to married students. Typical cost: $8320 per year ($12,030 including board). *Library facilities:* S. E. Wimberly Library plus 2 others. *Collection:* Books: 1 million (physical), 1.3 million (digital/electronic); Serial titles: 29,365 (physical), 104,949 (digital/electronic); Databases: 487. Weekly public service hours: 134; study areas open 24 hours, 5–7 days a week. *Research affiliation:* Max Planck Florida Institute for Neuroscience (neuroscience), The Vaccine and Gene Institute of Florida (biomedical sciences), Torrey Pines Institute for Molecular Studies (medical research), The Scripps Research Institute (biomedical sciences).

**Computer facilities:** 1,350 computers available on campus for general student use. A campuswide network can be accessed. Online class registration is available.
Website: http://www.fau.edu/

**General Application Contact:** Jordan Hession, Assistant Director, Graduate Orientation and Admissions, 561-297-1213, Fax: 561-297-1212, E-mail: jhession@fau.edu.

**GRADUATE UNITS**

**Charles E. Schmidt College of Medicine** Students: 286 full-time (146 women), 31 part-time (18 women); includes 139 minority (27 Black or African American, non-Hispanic/Latino; 1 American Indian or Alaska Native, non-Hispanic/Latino; 53 Asian, non-Hispanic/Latino; 52 Hispanic/Latino; 6 Two or more races, non-Hispanic/Latino), 2 international. Average age 25. 3,233 applicants, 4% accepted, 87 enrolled. *Faculty:* 35 full-time (13 women), 1 part-time/adjunct (0 women). Expenses: Contact institution. *Financial support:* Fellowships and research assistantships available. Financial award applicants required to submit FAFSA. In 2019, 30 master's, 55 doctorates awarded. *Program availability:* Part-time. *Application deadline:* For fall admission, 5/1 for domestic students, 3/15 for international students; for spring admission, 10/1 for domestic and international students. *Application fee:* $30. Electronic applications accepted. *Application Contact:* Marc Kantorow, Assistant Dean, Graduate Programs, 561-297-2142, E-mail: mkantoro@health.fau.edu. *Assistant Dean, Graduate Programs*, Marc Kantorow, 561-297-2142, E-mail: mkantoro@health.fau.edu.

**Charles E. Schmidt College of Science** Students: 258 full-time (135 women), 216 part-time (99 women); includes 119 minority (22 Black or African American, non-Hispanic/Latino; 14 Asian, non-Hispanic/Latino; 64 Hispanic/Latino; 19 Two or more races, non-Hispanic/Latino), 82 international. Average age 29. 386 applicants, 41% accepted, 136 enrolled. *Faculty:* 185 full-time (56 women), 9 part-time/adjunct (2 women). Expenses: Contact institution. *Financial support:* Fellowships with partial tuition reimbursements, research assistantships with partial tuition reimbursements, teaching assistantships with partial tuition reimbursements, career-related internships or fieldwork, Federal Work-Study, institutionally sponsored loans, scholarships/grants, tuition waivers (partial), and unspecified assistantships available. Financial award applicants required to submit FAFSA. In 2019, 94 master's, 46 doctorates awarded. *Program availability:* Part-time. *Application deadline:* For fall admission, 6/1 for domestic students, 2/15 for international students; for spring admission, 11/1 for domestic students, 8/15 for international students. Applications are processed on a rolling basis. *Application fee:* $30. Electronic applications accepted. *Application Contact:* Ata Sarejedini, Dean, 561-297-3301, E-mail: ata@fau.edu. *Dean*, Ata Sarejedini, 561-297-3301, E-mail: ata@fau.edu.

***Center for Complex Systems and Brain Sciences*** Students: 6 full-time (4 women), 7 part-time (0 women); includes 3 minority (1 Black or African American, non-Hispanic/Latino; 2 Two or more races, non-Hispanic/Latino), 2 international. Average age 31. 8 applicants, 13% accepted, 1 enrolled. *Faculty:* 1 full-time (0 women). Expenses: Contact institution. *Financial support:* Fellowships with full tuition reimbursements, research assistantships with partial tuition reimbursements, teaching assistantships with partial tuition reimbursements, Federal Work-Study, and traineeships available. In 2019, 3 doctorates awarded. *Application deadline:* For fall admission, 1/15 priority date for domestic and international students. *Application fee:* $30. *Application Contact:* Keyla Thamsten, Assistant Director, Academic Support Services, 561-297-2231, E-mail: thamsten@fau.edu. *Assistant Director, Academic Support Services*, Keyla Thamsten, 561-297-2231, E-mail: thamsten@fau.edu.

**Christine E. Lynn College of Nursing** Students: 75 full-time (66 women), 396 part-time (366 women); includes 272 minority (151 Black or African American, non-Hispanic/Latino; 24 Asian, non-Hispanic/Latino; 81 Hispanic/Latino; 16 Two or more races, non-Hispanic/Latino), 14 international. Average age 36. 515 applicants, 31% accepted, 131 enrolled. *Faculty:* 37 full-time (35 women), 16 part-time/adjunct (15 women). Expenses: Contact institution. *Financial support:* Research assistantships with partial tuition reimbursements, teaching assistantships with partial tuition reimbursements, career-related internships or fieldwork, Federal Work-Study, institutionally sponsored loans, scholarships/grants, and traineeships available. Support available to part-time students. In 2019, 155 master's, 33 doctorates awarded. *Program availability:* Part-time. *Application deadline:* For fall admission, 6/1 for domestic students, 2/15 for international students; for spring admission, 10/1 for domestic students, 7/15 for international students. Applications are processed on a rolling basis. *Application fee:* $30. *Application Contact:* Safiya A George Damida, Dean, 561-297-3206, E-mail: sgeorge@health.fau.edu. *Dean*, Safiya A George Damida, 561-297-3206, E-mail: sgeorge@health.fau.edu.

**College for Design and Social Inquiry** Students: 212 full-time (171 women), 240 part-time (181 women); includes 246 minority (115 Black or African American, non-Hispanic/Latino; 1 American Indian or Alaska Native, non-Hispanic/Latino; 11 Asian, non-Hispanic/Latino; 100 Hispanic/Latino; 1 Native Hawaiian or other Pacific Islander, non-Hispanic/Latino; 18 Two or more races, non-Hispanic/Latino), 13 international. Average age 31. 510 applicants, 53% accepted, 234 enrolled. *Faculty:* 43 full-time (15 women), 1 part-time/adjunct (0 women). Expenses: Contact institution. *Financial support:* Fellowships with partial tuition reimbursements, research assistantships with partial tuition reimbursements, teaching assistantships with partial tuition reimbursements, career-related internships or fieldwork, Federal Work-Study, and institutionally sponsored loans available. Support available to part-time students. Financial award application deadline: 4/1. In 2019, 171 master's, 8 doctorates awarded. *Program availability:* Part-time, evening/weekend. *Application deadline:* For fall admission, 5/1 for domestic students, 2/15 for international students; for spring admission, 11/1 for domestic students, 7/15 for international students. Applications are processed on a rolling basis. *Application fee:* $30. *Application Contact:* Dr. Naelys Luna, Interim Dean, 561-297-2056, E-mail: ndiaz10@fau.edu. *Interim Dean*, Dr. Naelys Luna, 561-297-2056, E-mail: ndiaz10@fau.edu.

***Phyllis and Harvey Sandler School of Social Work*** Students: 158 full-time (134 women), 144 part-time (124 women); includes 163 minority (76 Black or African American, non-Hispanic/Latino; 1 American Indian or Alaska Native, non-Hispanic/Latino; 5 Asian, non-Hispanic/Latino; 68 Hispanic/Latino; 1 Native Hawaiian or other Pacific Islander, non-Hispanic/Latino; 12 Two or more races, non-Hispanic/Latino), 4 international. Average age 31. 346 applicants, 57% accepted, 178 enrolled. *Faculty:* 13 full-time (8 women). Expenses: Contact institution. *Financial support:* Fellowships, research assistantships, career-related internships or fieldwork, Federal Work-Study, institutionally sponsored loans, and tuition waivers (partial) available. Financial award application deadline: 4/1. In 2019, 125 master's, 5 doctorates awarded. *Program availability:* Part-time, evening/weekend. *Application deadline:* For fall admission, 5/1 priority date for domestic students, 2/15 for international students. Applications are processed on a rolling basis. *Application fee:* $30. *Application Contact:* Joy McClellan, Program Coordinator, 561-297-3234, E-mail: jmcclel2@fau.edu. *Program Coordinator*, Joy McClellan, 561-297-3234, E-mail: jmcclel2@fau.edu.

***School of Criminology and Criminal Justice*** Students: 18 full-time (15 women), 21 part-time (20 women); includes 28 minority (13 Black or African American, non-Hispanic/Latino; 1 Asian, non-Hispanic/Latino; 12 Hispanic/Latino; 2 Two or more races, non-Hispanic/Latino), 1 international. Average age 27. 74 applicants, 31% accepted, 19 enrolled. *Faculty:* 8 full-time (2 women). Expenses: Contact institution. *Financial support:* Research assistantships, institutionally sponsored loans, scholarships/grants, and unspecified assistantships available. Financial award application deadline: 4/1. In 2019, 10 master's awarded. *Program availability:* Part-time, evening/weekend, online learning. *Application deadline:* For fall admission, 5/1 priority date for domestic students, 2/15 for international students; for spring admission, 11/1 priority date for domestic students, 7/15 for international students. Applications are processed on a rolling basis. *Application fee:* $30. Electronic applications accepted. *Application Contact:* Dawn Lynette Rothe, Director, 561-297-3173, E-mail: rothed@fau.edu. *Director*, Dawn Lynette Rothe, 561-297-3173, E-mail: rothed@fau.edu.

***School of Public Administration*** Students: 14 full-time (9 women), 56 part-time (32 women); includes 36 minority (16 Black or African American, non-Hispanic/Latino; 4 Asian, non-Hispanic/Latino; 13 Hispanic/Latino; 3 Two or more races, non-Hispanic/Latino), 5 international. Average age 36. 51 applicants, 45% accepted, 17 enrolled. *Faculty:* 11 full-time (4 women), 1 part-time/adjunct (0 women). Expenses: Contact institution. *Financial support:* Fellowships with full tuition reimbursements, research assistantships with partial tuition reimbursements, teaching assistantships with partial tuition reimbursements, career-related internships or fieldwork, Federal Work-Study, institutionally sponsored loans, and tuition waivers (partial) available. Support available to part-time students. Financial award application deadline: 4/1. In 2019, 27 master's, 3 doctorates awarded. *Program availability:* Part-time, evening/weekend. *Application deadline:* For fall admission, 5/1 priority date for domestic students, 2/15 for international students; for spring admission, 11/1 for domestic students, 7/15 for international students. Applications are processed on a rolling basis. *Application fee:* $30. *Application Contact:* Leslie Leip, Program Coordinator, 561-297-4153, E-mail: lleip@fau.edu. *Program Coordinator*, Leslie Leip, 561-297-4153, E-mail: lleip@fau.edu.

***School of Urban and Regional Planning*** Students: 22 full-time (13 women), 19 part-time (5 women); includes 19 minority (10 Black or African American, non-Hispanic/Latino; 1 Asian, non-Hispanic/Latino; 7 Hispanic/Latino; 1 Two or more races, non-Hispanic/Latino), 3 international. Average age 27. 39 applicants, 64% accepted, 20 enrolled. *Faculty:* 5 full-time (1 woman). Expenses: Contact institution. *Financial support:* Fellowships with full tuition reimbursements, research assistantships, career-related internships or fieldwork, Federal Work-Study, institutionally sponsored loans, and tuition waivers (partial) available. Financial award application deadline: 4/1. In 2019, 9 master's awarded. *Program availability:* Part-time, evening/weekend. *Application deadline:* For fall admission, 5/1 priority date for domestic students, 2/15 for international students; for spring admission, 11/1 priority date for domestic students, 7/15 for international students. Applications are processed on a rolling basis. *Application fee:* $30.

**College of Business** Students: 692 full-time (341 women), 1,062 part-time (589 women); includes 894 minority (280 Black or African American, non-Hispanic/Latino; 4 American Indian or Alaska Native, non-Hispanic/Latino; 85 Asian, non-Hispanic/Latino; 455 Hispanic/Latino; 4 Native Hawaiian or other Pacific Islander, non-Hispanic/Latino; 66 Two or more races, non-Hispanic/Latino), 101 international. Average age 32. 1,141 applicants, 69% accepted, 634 enrolled. *Faculty:* 100 full-time (34 women), 2 part-time/adjunct (0 women). Expenses: Contact institution. *Financial support:* Fellowships with partial tuition reimbursements, research assistantships with partial tuition reimbursements, teaching assistantships with full tuition reimbursements, career-related internships or fieldwork, Federal Work-Study, institutionally sponsored loans, tuition waivers (full and partial), and unspecified assistantships available. Support available to part-time students. Financial award application deadline: 3/1. In 2019, 709 master's, 7 doctorates awarded. *Program availability:* Part-time, evening/weekend, online learning. *Application deadline:* For fall admission, 5/1 priority date for domestic students, 2/15 priority date for international students; for spring admission, 4/1 priority date for domestic students, 1/15 priority date for international students. Applications are processed on a rolling basis. *Application fee:* $30. *Application Contact:* Daniel Gropper, Dean, 561-297-3635, E-mail: dgropper@fau.edu. *Dean*, Daniel Gropper, 561-297-3635, E-mail: dgropper@fau.edu.

***School of Accounting*** Students: 142 full-time (70 women), 435 part-time (256 women); includes 304 minority (55 Black or African American, non-Hispanic/Latino; 1 American Indian or Alaska Native, non-Hispanic/Latino; 29 Asian, non-Hispanic/Latino; 201 Hispanic/Latino; 1 Native Hawaiian or other Pacific Islander, non-Hispanic/Latino; 17 Two or more races, non-Hispanic/Latino), 23 international. Average age 31. 410 applicants, 60% accepted, 212 enrolled. *Faculty:* 15 full-time (5 women), 2 part-time/adjunct (0 women). Expenses: Contact institution. *Financial support:* Fellowships, research assistantships with partial tuition reimbursements, teaching assistantships, career-related internships or fieldwork, Federal Work-Study, institutionally sponsored loans, scholarships/grants, and tuition waivers (partial) available. Support available to part-time students. Financial award application deadline: 3/1. In 2019, 265 master's awarded. *Program availability:* Part-time, evening/weekend, online learning. *Application deadline:* For fall admission, 7/1 priority date for domestic students, 2/15 priority date for international students; for spring admission, 11/1 priority date for domestic students, 7/15 priority date for international students. Applications are processed on a rolling basis. *Application fee:* $30. *Application Contact:* George Young, Director, 561-297-3638, E-mail: soa@fau.edu. *Director*, George Young, 561-297-3638, E-mail: soa@fau.edu.

**College of Education** Students: 259 full-time (211 women), 506 part-time (386 women); includes 341 minority (174 Black or African American, non-Hispanic/Latino; 16 Asian, non-Hispanic/Latino; 134 Hispanic/Latino; 17 Two or more races, non-Hispanic/Latino), 15 international. Average age 34. 828 applicants, 38% accepted, 251 enrolled. *Faculty:* 82 full-time (47 women), 23 part-time/adjunct (10 women). Expenses: Contact institution. *Financial support:* Fellowships with partial tuition reimbursements, research assistantships with partial tuition reimbursements, teaching assistantships with partial tuition reimbursements, career-related internships or fieldwork, Federal Work-Study, and unspecified assistantships available. In 2019, 206 master's, 29 doctorates, 26 other advanced degrees awarded. *Program availability:* Part-time, evening/weekend. *Application deadline:* For fall admission, 5/1 for domestic students. Applications are processed on a rolling basis. *Application fee:* $30. Electronic applications accepted. *Application Contact:* Dr. Stephen Silverman, Dean, 561-297-3357, E-mail: silverman@fau.edu. *Dean*, Dr. Stephen Silverman, 561-297-3357, E-mail: silverman@fau.edu.

**College of Engineering and Computer Science** Students: 172 full-time (43 women), 209 part-time (48 women); includes 127 minority (26 Black or African American, non-Hispanic/Latino; 27 Asian, non-Hispanic/Latino; 65 Hispanic/Latino; 9 Two or more races, non-Hispanic/Latino), 115 international. Average age 31. 357 applicants, 53% accepted, 134 enrolled. *Faculty:* 75 full-time (9 women), 1 part-time/adjunct (0 women). Expenses: Contact institution. *Financial support:* Fellowships, research assistantships with partial tuition reimbursements, teaching assistantships with partial tuition reimbursements, career-related internships or fieldwork, Federal Work-Study, and unspecified assistantships available. Support available to part-time students. Financial award applicants required to submit FAFSA. In 2019, 120 master's, 24 doctorates awarded. *Program availability:* Part-time, evening/weekend, online learning. *Application deadline:* For fall admission, 7/1 for domestic students, 2/15 for international students; for spring admission, 11/1 for domestic students, 7/15 for international students. Applications are processed on a rolling basis. *Application fee:* $30. *Application Contact:* Dr. Stella Batalama, Dean, 561-297-3426, E-mail: sbatalama@fau.edu. *Dean*, Dr. Stella Batalama, 561-297-3426, E-mail: sbatalama@fau.edu.

**Dorothy F. Schmidt College of Arts and Letters** Students: 214 full-time (126 women), 112 part-time (67 women); includes 144 minority (44 Black or African American, non-Hispanic/Latino; 6 Asian, non-Hispanic/Latino; 79 Hispanic/Latino; 15 Two or more races, non-Hispanic/Latino), 29 international. Average age 33. 292 applicants, 52% accepted, 107 enrolled. *Faculty:* 146 full-time (68 women), 8 part-time/adjunct (5 women). Expenses: Contact institution. *Financial support:* Fellowships with partial tuition reimbursements, research assistantships, teaching assistantships, career-related internships or fieldwork, Federal Work-Study, institutionally sponsored loans, and tuition waivers (partial) available. Support available to part-time students. In 2019, 96 master's, 9 doctorates awarded. *Program availability:* Part-time. *Application deadline:* For fall admission, 6/1 priority date for domestic students. Applications are processed on a rolling basis. *Application fee:* $30. Electronic applications accepted. *Application Contact:* Michael Horswell, Dean, 561-297-3803, E-mail: horswell@fau.edu. *Dean*, Michael Horswell, 561-297-3803, E-mail: horswell@fau.edu.

***Center for Women, Gender and Sexuality Studies*** Students: 7 full-time (6 women), 1 (woman) part-time; includes 5 minority (1 Black or African American, non-Hispanic/Latino; 4 Hispanic/Latino). Average age 24. 3 applicants, 100% accepted, 3 enrolled. *Faculty:* 2 full-time (both women). Expenses: Contact institution. *Financial support:* Fellowships, teaching assistantships, career-related internships or fieldwork, Federal Work-Study, institutionally sponsored loans, scholarships/grants, and unspecified assistantships available. Support available to part-time students. Financial award applicants required to submit FAFSA. In 2019, 4 master's awarded. *Program availability:* Part-time. *Application deadline:* For fall admission, 7/1 for domestic students, 2/15 for international students; for spring admission, 11/1 for domestic students, 7/15 for international students. Applications are processed on a rolling basis. *Application fee:* $30. Electronic applications accepted. *Application Contact:* William Trapani, Director, 561-297-2051, E-mail: wtrapan1@fau.edu. *Director*, William Trapani, 561-297-2051, E-mail: wtrapan1@fau.edu.

***School of Communication and Multimedia Studies*** Students: 30 full-time (19 women), 13 part-time (5 women); includes 22 minority (9 Black or African American, non-Hispanic/Latino; 1 Asian, non-Hispanic/Latino; 6 Hispanic/Latino; 6 Two or more races, non-Hispanic/Latino), 7 international. Average age 30. 32 applicants, 66% accepted, 19 enrolled. *Faculty:* 23 full-time (9 women). Expenses: Contact institution. *Financial support:* Teaching assistantships with partial tuition reimbursements, Federal Work-Study, institutionally sponsored loans, scholarships/grants, and unspecified assistantships available. Support available to part-time students. Financial award application deadline: 3/1; financial award applicants required to submit FAFSA. In 2019, 8 master's awarded. *Program availability:* Part-time. *Application deadline:* For fall admission, 7/1 priority date for domestic students, 4/1 for international students; for spring admission, 11/1 for domestic students, 10/1 for international students. Applications are processed on a rolling basis. *Application fee:* $30. Electronic applications accepted. *Application Contact:* Dr. Stephen Charbonneau, Graduate Director, 561-297-3856, Fax: 561-297-2615, E-mail: scharbo1@fau.edu. *Director*, Dr. Carol Bishop Mills, 561-297-0042, Fax: 561-297-2615, E-mail: millsc@fau.edu.

## FLORIDA COASTAL SCHOOL OF LAW, Jacksonville, FL 32256

**General Information** Proprietary, coed, graduate-only institution.

**GRADUATE UNITS**

**Professional Program** *Program availability:* Part-time. Electronic applications accepted.

## FLORIDA COLLEGE OF INTEGRATIVE MEDICINE, Orlando, FL 32809

**General Information** Proprietary, coed, graduate-only institution. *Graduate housing:* On-campus housing not available.

**GRADUATE UNITS**

**Graduate Program** *Program availability:* Evening/weekend. Electronic applications accepted.

## FLORIDA GULF COAST UNIVERSITY, Fort Myers, FL 33965-6565

**General Information** State-supported, coed, comprehensive institution. CGS member. *Enrollment:* 15,026 graduate, professional, and undergraduate students; 508 full-time matriculated graduate/professional students (372 women), 642 part-time matriculated graduate/professional students (433 women). *Enrollment by degree level:* 936 master's, 214 doctoral. *Graduate faculty:* 507 full-time (223 women), 448 part-time/adjunct (248 women). *International tuition:* $28,169 full-time. *Tuition, area resident:* Full-time $6974; part-time $4350 per credit hour. Tuition, state resident: full-time $6974; part-time $4350 per credit hour. Tuition, nonresident: full-time $28,169; part-time $17,595 per credit hour. *Required fees:* $2027; $1267 per credit hour. $507 per semester. Tuition and fees vary according to course load. *Graduate housing:* Room and/or apartments available on a first-come, first-served basis to single students; on-campus housing not available to married students. Typical cost: $4820 per year ($8580 including board). Room and board charges vary according to board plan and housing facility selected. Housing application deadline: 4/1. *Student services:* Campus employment opportunities, campus safety program, career counseling, child daycare facilities, exercise/wellness program, free psychological counseling, international student services, low-cost health insurance, multicultural affairs office, services for students with disabilities, teacher training, writing training. *Library facilities:* Library Services plus 1 other. *Collection:* Books: 242,131 (physical), 126,942 (digital/electronic); Serial titles: 128,865 (digital/electronic); Databases: 389. Students can reserve study rooms. *Research affiliation:* Department of Education (education), Small Business Administration (business), Department of Commerce, U.S. Fish and Wildlife Service (biological sciences), Florida Department of Environmental Protection (biological sciences), National Institute of Standards and Technology.

**Computer facilities:** Computer purchase and lease plans are available. 1,029 computers available on campus for general student use. A campuswide network can be accessed. Online class registration, online admissions and advising are available. Website: http://www.fgcu.edu/

**General Application Contact:** Shannon Acosta, Graduate Studies Admissions, 239-590-7027, E-mail: sacosta@fgcu.edu.

**GRADUATE UNITS**

**College of Arts and Sciences** *Program availability:* Part-time, blended/hybrid learning. Electronic applications accepted.

**College of Education** *Program availability:* Part-time, evening/weekend, online learning. Electronic applications accepted.

**Elaine Nicpon Marieb College of Health and Human Services** *Program availability:* Part-time, evening/weekend, online learning. Electronic applications accepted.

**Lutgert College of Business** *Program availability:* Part-time, evening/weekend. Electronic applications accepted.

## FLORIDA INSTITUTE OF TECHNOLOGY, Melbourne, FL 32901-6975

**General Information** Independent, coed, university. *Graduate housing:* Room and/or apartments available on a first-come, first-served basis to single students; on-campus housing not available to married students. Housing application deadline: 6/1. *Research affiliation:* Boeing (digital signal processing aeronautics), Siemens (mechanical and aerospace engineering), General Electric-Harris (software testing), IBM (software technology, information assurance), Microsoft Corporation (simulation software development), Lockheed Martin Corporation (biological sciences).

**GRADUATE UNITS**

**Aberdeen Education Center (Maryland)** *Program availability:* Part-time, evening/weekend. Electronic applications accepted.

**Aberdeen Education Center (Maryland)**

**College of Aeronautics** *Program availability:* Part-time, evening/weekend, 100% online. Electronic applications accepted.

**College of Engineering and Science** *Program availability:* Part-time. Electronic applications accepted.

**College of Psychology and Liberal Arts** *Program availability:* Part-time, evening/weekend, 100% online. Electronic applications accepted.

**Eglin Education Center (Florida)** *Program availability:* Part-time, evening/weekend. Electronic applications accepted.

**Fort Lee Education Center (Virginia)** *Program availability:* Part-time, evening/weekend. Electronic applications accepted.

**Hampton Roads Education Center (Virginia)**

**Nathan M. Bisk College of Business** *Program availability:* Part-time. Electronic applications accepted.

**National Capital Region (Quantico) Education Center (Virginia)**

**Orlando Education Center (Florida)** *Program availability:* Part-time, evening/weekend. Electronic applications accepted.

**Redstone/Huntsville Education Center (Alabama)** *Program availability:* Part-time, evening/weekend. Electronic applications accepted.

**Southern Maryland Education Center** *Program availability:* Part-time, evening/weekend. Electronic applications accepted.

**Spaceport Education Center (Florida)** *Program availability:* Part-time, evening/weekend. Electronic applications accepted.

## FLORIDA INTERNATIONAL UNIVERSITY, Miami, FL 33199

**General Information** State-supported, coed, university. CGS member. *Enrollment:* 58,827 graduate, professional, and undergraduate students; 6,888 full-time matriculated graduate/professional students (4,097 women), 2,111 part-time matriculated graduate/professional students (1,241 women). *Enrollment by degree level:* 5,960 master's, 3,039 doctoral. *Graduate faculty:* 1,240 full-time (538 women), 1,184 part-time/adjunct (560 women). *Tuition, area resident:* Full-time $8912; part-time $446 per credit hour. Tuition, state resident: full-time $8912; part-time $446 per credit hour. Tuition, nonresident: full-time $21,393; part-time $992 per credit hour. *Required fees:* $2194. *Graduate housing:* Room and/or apartments available on a first-come, first-served basis to single students; on-campus housing not available to married students. Typical cost: $850 per year ($3692 including board). *Student services:* Campus employment opportunities, campus safety program, career counseling, child daycare facilities, exercise/wellness program, free psychological counseling, international student services, low-cost health insurance, multicultural affairs office, services for students with disabilities, writing training. *Library facilities:* Steven and Dorothea Green Library plus 4 others. *Collection:* Books: 1.2 million (physical), 473,816 (digital/electronic); Serial titles: 59,835 (physical), 115,482 (digital/electronic); Databases: 820. Weekly public service hours: 112; students can reserve study rooms. *Research affiliation:* National Institute of Justice (law), National Science Foundation (biological sciences), Howard Hughes Medical Institute (physics), National Institute of Child Health and Human Development (social work), Boeing (mechanical engineering), American Heart Association (biomedical engineering).

**Computer facilities:** A campuswide network can be accessed. Online class registration, online financial and cashier's information; financial, campus maps information available on cell phones are available.
Website: http://www.fiu.edu/

**General Application Contact:** Nanett Rojas, Assistant Director of Graduate Admissions, 305-348-7442, Fax: 305-348-7441, E-mail: gradadm@fiu.edu.

**GRADUATE UNITS**

**Chaplin School of Hospitality and Tourism Management** Students: 164 full-time (117 women), 90 part-time (60 women); includes 110 minority (33 Black or African American, non-Hispanic/Latino; 7 Asian, non-Hispanic/Latino; 65 Hispanic/Latino; 5 Two or more races, non-Hispanic/Latino), 114 international. Average age 27. 191 applicants, 81% accepted, 115 enrolled. *Faculty:* 27 full-time (7 women), 37 part-time/adjunct (12 women). Expenses: Contact institution. *Financial support:* Institutionally sponsored loans and scholarships/grants available. Financial award application deadline: 3/1; financial award applicants required to submit FAFSA. In 2019, 167 master's awarded. *Program availability:* Part-time, evening/weekend, online learning. *Application deadline:* For fall admission, 6/1 for domestic students, 4/1 for international students; for spring admission, 10/1 for domestic students, 9/1 for international students. Applications are processed on a rolling basis. *Application fee:* $30. Electronic applications accepted. *Application Contact:* Nanett Rojas, Manager, Admissions Operations, 305-348-7464, Fax: 305-348-7441, E-mail: gradadm@fiu.edu. *Dean*, Dr. Michael Cheng, 305-919-4506, E-mail: michael.cheng@fiu.edu.

**Chapman Graduate School of Business** Students: 1,605 full-time (891 women), 528 part-time (275 women); includes 1,601 minority (306 Black or African American, non-Hispanic/Latino; 2 American Indian or Alaska Native, non-Hispanic/Latino; 65 Asian, non-Hispanic/Latino; 1,180 Hispanic/Latino; 2 Native Hawaiian or other Pacific Islander, non-Hispanic/Latino; 46 Two or more races, non-Hispanic/Latino), 248 international. Average age 31. 2,563 applicants, 50% accepted, 898 enrolled. *Faculty:* 135 full-time (50 women), 124 part-time/adjunct (37 women). Expenses: Contact institution. *Financial support:* Institutionally sponsored loans and scholarships/grants available. Financial award application deadline: 3/1; financial award applicants required to submit FAFSA. In 2019, 1,214 master's, 12 doctorates awarded. *Program availability:* Part-time, evening/weekend. *Application deadline:* For fall admission, 6/1 for domestic students, 4/1 for international students; for spring admission, 10/1 for domestic students, 9/1 for international students. Applications are processed on a rolling basis. *Application fee:* $30. Electronic applications accepted. *Application Contact:* Nanett Rojas, Manager, Admissions Operations, 305-348-7464, Fax: 305-348-7441, E-mail: gradadm@fiu.edu. *Dean*, Dr. Joanne Li, 305-348-2751, Fax: 305-919-5478, E-mail: joanne.li@fiu.edu.

***Hollo School of Real Estate*** Students: 102 full-time (25 women), 10 part-time (5 women); includes 66 minority (20 Black or African American, non-Hispanic/Latino; 2 Asian, non-Hispanic/Latino; 41 Hispanic/Latino; 3 Two or more races, non-Hispanic/Latino), 14 international. Average age 35. 164 applicants, 71% accepted, 77 enrolled. *Faculty:* 5 full-time (1 woman), 3 part-time/adjunct (0 women). Expenses: Contact institution. *Financial support:* Institutionally sponsored loans and scholarships/grants available. Financial award application deadline: 3/1; financial award applicants required to submit FAFSA. In 2019, 68 master's awarded. *Program availability:* Part-time, evening/weekend. *Application deadline:* For fall admission, 4/1 for domestic and international students. *Application fee:* $30. Electronic applications accepted. *Application Contact:* Nanett Rojas, Manager, Admissions Operations, 305-348-7464, Fax: 305-348-7441, E-mail: gradadm@fiu.edu. *Director*, Eli Beracha, 305-779-7898, E-mail: eli.beracha@fiu.edu.

***School of Accounting*** Students: 68 full-time (37 women), 13 part-time (3 women); includes 71 minority (1 Black or African American, non-Hispanic/Latino; 5 Asian, non-Hispanic/Latino; 64 Hispanic/Latino; 1 Two or more races, non-Hispanic/Latino), 2 international. Average age 27. 169 applicants, 49% accepted, 61 enrolled. *Faculty:* 27 full-time (12 women), 12 part-time/adjunct (1 woman). Expenses: Contact institution. *Financial support:* Institutionally sponsored loans and scholarships/grants available. Financial award application deadline: 3/1; financial award applicants required to submit FAFSA. In 2019, 102 master's awarded. *Program availability:* Part-time, evening/weekend. *Application deadline:* For fall admission, 6/1 for domestic students, 4/1 for international students; for spring admission, 10/1 for domestic students, 9/1 for international students. Applications are processed on a rolling basis. *Application fee:* $30. Electronic applications accepted. *Application Contact:* Nanett Rojas, Manager, Admissions Operations, 305-348-7464, Fax: 305-348-7441, E-mail: gradadm@fiu.edu. *Director*, Clark Wheatley, 305-348-4209, Fax: 305-348-2914, E-mail: Clark.Wheatley@fiu.edu.

**College of Arts, Sciences, and Education** Students: 1,094 full-time (746 women), 426 part-time (313 women); includes 997 minority (215 Black or African American, non-Hispanic/Latino; 2 American Indian or Alaska Native, non-Hispanic/Latino; 37 Asian, non-Hispanic/Latino; 699 Hispanic/Latino; 44 Two or more races, non-Hispanic/Latino), 170 international. Average age 30. 1,443 applicants, 40% accepted, 406 enrolled. *Faculty:* 412 full-time (191 women), 316 part-time/adjunct (185 women). Expenses: Contact institution. *Financial support:* Career-related internships or fieldwork, Federal Work-Study, institutionally sponsored loans, and scholarships/grants available. Financial award application deadline: 3/1; financial award applicants required to submit FAFSA. In 2019, 443 master's, 84 doctorates awarded. *Program availability:* Part-time, evening/weekend. *Application deadline:* For fall admission, 6/1 for domestic students, 4/1 for international students; for spring admission, 10/1 for domestic students, 9/1 for international students. Applications are processed on a rolling basis. *Application fee:* $30. Electronic applications accepted. *Application Contact:* Nanett Rojas, Manager, Admissions Operations, 305-348-7464, Fax: 305-348-7441, E-mail: gradadm@fiu.edu. *Dean*, Dr. Michael Heithaus, 305-348-2866, Fax: 305-348-4172, E-mail: casdean@fiu.edu.

**College of Communication, Architecture and The Arts** Students: 412 full-time (273 women), 127 part-time (85 women); includes 397 minority (42 Black or African American, non-Hispanic/Latino; 7 Asian, non-Hispanic/Latino; 336 Hispanic/Latino; 12 Two or more races, non-Hispanic/Latino), 74 international. Average age 28. 306 applicants, 60% accepted, 114 enrolled. *Faculty:* 102 full-time (43 women), 173 part-time/adjunct (94 women). Expenses: Contact institution. *Financial support:* Institutionally sponsored loans and scholarships/grants available. Financial award application deadline: 3/1; financial award applicants required to submit FAFSA. In 2019, 266 master's awarded. *Program availability:* Part-time, evening/weekend. *Application deadline:* For fall admission, 6/1 for domestic students, 4/1 for international students; for spring admission, 10/1 for domestic students, 9/1 for international students. Applications are processed on a rolling basis. *Application fee:* $30. Electronic applications accepted. *Application Contact:* Nanett Rojas, Manager, Admissions Operations, 305-348-7464, Fax: 305-348-7441, E-mail: gradadm@fiu.edu. *Dean*, Dr. Brian Schriner, 305-348-3176, Fax: 305-348-6716, E-mail: schriner@fiu.edu.

***School of Communication and Journalism*** Students: 85 full-time (68 women), 76 part-time (59 women); includes 117 minority (20 Black or African American, non-Hispanic/Latino; 2 Asian, non-Hispanic/Latino; 88 Hispanic/Latino; 7 Two or more races, non-Hispanic/Latino), 22 international. Average age 28. 120 applicants, 75% accepted, 63 enrolled. *Faculty:* 30 full-time (22 women), 71 part-time/adjunct (42 women). Expenses: Contact institution. *Financial support:* Institutionally sponsored loans and scholarships/grants available. Financial award application deadline: 3/1; financial award applicants required to submit FAFSA. In 2019, 107 master's awarded. *Program availability:* Part-time, evening/weekend. *Application deadline:* For fall admission, 6/1 for domestic students, 4/1 for international students; for spring admission, 10/1 for domestic students, 9/1 for international students. Applications are processed on a rolling basis. *Application fee:* $30. Electronic applications accepted. *Application Contact:* Nanett Rojas, Manager, Admissions Operations, 305-348-7464, Fax: 305-348-7441, E-mail: gradadm@fiu.edu. *Chair*, Dr. Aileen Izquierdo, 305-919-5795, E-mail: aileen.izquierdo@fiu.edu.

***School of Music*** Students: 28 full-time (12 women), 17 part-time (5 women); includes 33 minority (4 Black or African American, non-Hispanic/Latino; 28 Hispanic/Latino; 1 Two or more races, non-Hispanic/Latino), 6 international. Average age 33. 33 applicants, 67% accepted, 15 enrolled. *Faculty:* 25 full-time (5 women), 36 part-time/adjunct (14 women). Expenses: Contact institution. *Financial support:* Institutionally sponsored loans and scholarships/grants available. Financial award application deadline: 3/1; financial award applicants required to submit FAFSA. In 2019, 12 master's awarded. *Program availability:* Part-time, evening/weekend. *Application deadline:* For fall admission, 6/1 for domestic students, 4/1 for international students; for spring admission, 10/1 for domestic students, 9/1 for international students. Applications are processed on a rolling basis. *Application fee:* $30. Electronic applications accepted. *Application Contact:* Nanett Rojas, Manager, Admissions Operations, 305-348-7464, Fax: 305-348-7441, E-mail: gradadm@fiu.edu. *Program Director*, Joel Galand, 305-348-7078, E-mail: Joel.Galand@fiu.edu.

**College of Engineering and Computing** Students: 690 full-time (190 women), 378 part-time (103 women); includes 471 minority (67 Black or African American, non-Hispanic/Latino; 1 American Indian or Alaska Native, non-Hispanic/Latino; 35 Asian, non-Hispanic/Latino; 347 Hispanic/Latino; 1 Native Hawaiian or other Pacific Islander, non-Hispanic/Latino; 20 Two or more races, non-Hispanic/Latino), 515 international. Average age 29. 1,218 applicants, 52% accepted, 310 enrolled. *Faculty:* 152 full-time

(30 women), 90 part-time/adjunct (14 women). Expenses: Contact institution. *Financial support:* Career-related internships or fieldwork, Federal Work-Study, institutionally sponsored loans, scholarships/grants, and unspecified assistantships available. Financial award application deadline: 3/1; financial award applicants required to submit FAFSA. In 2019, 274 master's, 46 doctorates awarded. *Program availability:* Part-time, evening/weekend, online learning. *Application deadline:* For fall admission, 6/1 for domestic students, 4/1 for international students; for spring admission, 10/1 for domestic students, 9/1 for international students. Applications are processed on a rolling basis. *Application fee:* $30. Electronic applications accepted. *Application Contact:* Nanett Rojas, Manager, Admissions Operations, 305-348-7464, Fax: 305-348-7441, E-mail: gradadm@fiu.edu. *Dean*, Dr. John Volakis, 305-348-0273, Fax: 305-348-0127, E-mail: grad_eng@fiu.edu.

**School of Computing and Information Sciences** Students: 162 full-time (39 women), 140 part-time (26 women); includes 160 minority (11 Black or African American, non-Hispanic/Latino; 1 American Indian or Alaska Native, non-Hispanic/Latino; 9 Asian, non-Hispanic/Latino; 132 Hispanic/Latino; 7 Two or more races, non-Hispanic/Latino), 120 international. Average age 30. 360 applicants, 49% accepted, 73 enrolled. *Faculty:* 53 full-time (14 women), 33 part-time/adjunct (9 women). Expenses: Contact institution. *Financial support:* Research assistantships, teaching assistantships, institutionally sponsored loans, scholarships/grants, and unspecified assistantships available. Financial award application deadline: 3/1; financial award applicants required to submit FAFSA. In 2019, 89 master's, 13 doctorates awarded. *Program availability:* Part-time, evening/weekend. *Application deadline:* For fall admission, 6/1 for domestic students, 4/1 for international students; for spring admission, 10/1 for domestic students, 9/1 for international students. Applications are processed on a rolling basis. *Application fee:* $30. Electronic applications accepted. *Application Contact:* Nanett Rojas, Manager, Admissions Operations, 305-348-7464, Fax: 305-348-7441, E-mail: gradadm@fiu.edu. *Director*, Dr. Sundararaj S. Iyengar, 305-348-3947, Fax: 305-348-3549, E-mail: sundararaj.iyengar@fiu.edu.

***School of Construction*** Average age 31. 102 applicants, 30% accepted, 11 enrolled. Expenses: Contact institution. *Financial support:* In 2019–20, 5 students received support. Institutionally sponsored loans, scholarships/grants, and unspecified assistantships available. Financial award application deadline: 3/1; financial award applicants required to submit FAFSA. In 2019, 37 master's awarded. *Program availability:* Part-time, evening/weekend. *Application deadline:* For fall admission, 6/1 for domestic students, 4/1 for international students; for spring admission, 10/1 for domestic students, 9/1 for international students. Applications are processed on a rolling basis. *Application fee:* $30. Electronic applications accepted. *Application Contact:* Nanett Rojas, Manager, Admissions Operations, 305-348-7464, Fax: 305-348-7441, E-mail: gradadm@fiu.edu. *Director*, Dr. Irtishad Ahmad, 305-348-3172, Fax: 305-348-6255, E-mail: ahmadi@fiu.edu.

**College of Law** Students: 498 full-time (282 women), 18 part-time (11 women); includes 317 minority (30 Black or African American, non-Hispanic/Latino; 3 American Indian or Alaska Native, non-Hispanic/Latino; 9 Asian, non-Hispanic/Latino; 265 Hispanic/Latino; 10 Two or more races, non-Hispanic/Latino), 27 international. Average age 27. 1,841 applicants, 30% accepted, 223 enrolled. *Faculty:* 28 full-time (14 women), 43 part-time/adjunct (9 women). Expenses: Contact institution. *Financial support:* Application deadline: 3/1; applicants required to submit FAFSA. In 2019, 42 master's, 143 doctorates awarded. *Program availability:* Part-time, evening/weekend. *Application deadline:* For fall admission, 5/1 for domestic and international students. Applications are processed on a rolling basis. *Application fee:* $20. Electronic applications accepted. *Application Contact:* Nannett Rojas, Manager Admissions Operations, 305-348-7464, Fax: 305-348-7441, E-mail: gradadm@fiu.edu. *Dean*, Dr. Antony Page, 305-348-1118, Fax: 305-348-1159, E-mail: antony.page@fiu.edu.

**Herbert Wertheim College of Medicine** Students: 632 full-time (366 women), 1 (woman) part-time; includes 416 minority (41 Black or African American, non-Hispanic/Latino; 112 Asian, non-Hispanic/Latino; 235 Hispanic/Latino; 28 Two or more races, non-Hispanic/Latino), 7 international. Average age 26. 5,124 applicants, 4% accepted, 171 enrolled. *Faculty:* 75 full-time (36 women), 76 part-time/adjunct (23 women). Expenses: Contact institution. *Financial support:* Institutionally sponsored loans and scholarships/grants available. Financial award application deadline: 3/1; financial award applicants required to submit FAFSA. In 2019, 44 master's, 124 doctorates awarded. *Application deadline:* For fall admission, 12/15 for domestic students. *Application fee:* $160. Electronic applications accepted. *Application Contact:* Cristina M. Arabatzis, Assistant Director of Admissions, 305-348-0639, Fax: 305-348-0650, E-mail: carabatz@fiu.edu. *Dean*, Dr. Robert Sackstein, E-mail: med.admissions@fiu.edu.

**Nicole Wertheim College of Nursing and Health Sciences** Students: 849 full-time (631 women), 156 part-time (123 women); includes 774 minority (187 Black or African American, non-Hispanic/Latino; 1 American Indian or Alaska Native, non-Hispanic/Latino; 60 Asian, non-Hispanic/Latino; 503 Hispanic/Latino; 4 Native Hawaiian or other Pacific Islander, non-Hispanic/Latino; 19 Two or more races, non-Hispanic/Latino), 15 international. Average age 29. 1,257 applicants, 27% accepted, 290 enrolled. *Faculty:* 68 full-time (52 women), 133 part-time/adjunct (92 women). Expenses: Contact institution. *Financial support:* Career-related internships or fieldwork, Federal Work-Study, institutionally sponsored loans, and scholarships/grants available. Financial award application deadline: 3/1; financial award applicants required to submit FAFSA. In 2019, 321 master's, 100 doctorates awarded. *Program availability:* Part-time, evening/weekend. *Application fee:* $30. Electronic applications accepted. *Application Contact:* Nanett Rojas, Manager, Admissions Operations, 305-348-7464, Fax: 305-348-7441, E-mail: gradadm@fiu.edu. *Dean*, Dr. Ora Strickland, 305-348-0407, E-mail: olstrick@fiu.edu.

**Robert Stempel College of Public Health and Social Work** Students: 415 full-time (302 women), 145 part-time (119 women); includes 415 minority (109 Black or African American, non-Hispanic/Latino; 1 American Indian or Alaska Native, non-Hispanic/Latino; 23 Asian, non-Hispanic/Latino; 268 Hispanic/Latino; 14 Two or more races, non-Hispanic/Latino), 51 international. Average age 30. 517 applicants, 64% accepted, 167 enrolled. *Faculty:* 61 full-time (38 women), 32 part-time/adjunct (20 women). Expenses: Contact institution. *Financial support:* Institutionally sponsored loans, scholarships/grants, and unspecified assistantships available. Financial award application deadline: 3/1; financial award applicants required to submit FAFSA. In 2019, 236 master's, 22 doctorates awarded. *Program availability:* Part-time, evening/weekend, online learning. *Application deadline:* For fall admission, 6/1 for domestic students, 4/1 for international students; for spring admission, 10/1 for domestic students, 9/1 for international students. Applications are processed on a rolling basis. *Application fee:* $30. Electronic applications accepted. *Application Contact:* Nanett Rojas, Manager, Admissions Operations, 305-348-7464, Fax: 305-348-7441, E-mail: gradadm@fiu.edu. *Dean*, Dr. Tomas Guilarte, 305-348-1158, Fax: 305-348-1691, E-mail: tomas.guilarte@fiu.edu.

***School of Social Work*** Students: 121 full-time (108 women), 36 part-time (31 women); includes 126 minority (33 Black or African American, non-Hispanic/Latino; 1 Asian, non-Hispanic/Latino; 85 Hispanic/Latino; 7 Two or more races, non-Hispanic/Latino), 4 international. Average age 29. 108 applicants, 41% accepted, 32 enrolled. *Faculty:* 18 full-time (12 women), 12 part-time/adjunct (5 women). Expenses: Contact institution. *Financial support:* Institutionally sponsored loans and scholarships/grants available. Financial award application deadline: 3/1; financial award applicants required to submit FAFSA. In 2019, 83 master's, 2 doctorates awarded. *Program availability:* Part-time, evening/weekend. *Application deadline:* For fall admission, 6/1 for domestic students, 4/1 for international students; for spring admission, 10/1 for domestic students, 9/1 for international students. Applications are processed on a rolling basis. *Application fee:* $30. Electronic applications accepted. *Application Contact:* Nanett Rojas, Manager, Admissions Operations, 305-348-7464, Fax: 305-348-7441, E-mail: gradadm@fiu.edu. *Director*, Dr. Shanna Burke, 305-348-7462, E-mail: shanna.burke@fiu.edu.

**Steven J. Green School of International and Public Affairs** Students: 529 full-time (299 women), 242 part-time (151 women); includes 541 minority (120 Black or African American, non-Hispanic/Latino; 19 Asian, non-Hispanic/Latino; 384 Hispanic/Latino; 18 Two or more races, non-Hispanic/Latino), 113 international. Average age 31. 622 applicants, 57% accepted, 242 enrolled. *Faculty:* 174 full-time (73 women), 186 part-time/adjunct (79 women). Expenses: Contact institution. *Financial support:* Career-related internships or fieldwork, Federal Work-Study, institutionally sponsored loans, and scholarships/grants available. Financial award application deadline: 3/1; financial award applicants required to submit FAFSA. In 2019, 210 master's, 46 doctorates awarded. *Program availability:* Part-time, evening/weekend. *Application deadline:* For fall admission, 6/1 for domestic students, 4/1 for international students; for winter admission, 10/1 for domestic students, 9/1 for international students. Applications are processed on a rolling basis. *Application fee:* $30. Electronic applications accepted. *Application Contact:* Nanett Rojas, Manager, Admissions Operations, 305-348-7464, Fax: 305-348-7441, E-mail: gradadm@fiu.edu. *Dean*, Dr. John F. Stack, Jr., 305-348-7266, Fax: 305-348-1013, E-mail: john.stack@fiu.edu.

## FLORIDA MEMORIAL UNIVERSITY, Miami-Dade, FL 33054

**General Information** Independent-religious, coed, comprehensive institution.

**GRADUATE UNITS**

**School of Business** *Program availability:* Part-time.

**School of Education**

## FLORIDA NATIONAL UNIVERSITY, Hialeah, FL 33012

**General Information** Proprietary, coed, comprehensive institution. *Enrollment:* 3,981 graduate, professional, and undergraduate students; 51 full-time matriculated graduate/professional students (29 women), 222 part-time matriculated graduate/professional students (162 women). *Enrollment by degree level:* 273 master's. *Graduate faculty:* 19 full-time (10 women), 16 part-time/adjunct (10 women). *Tuition:* Full-time $16,200; part-time $8100 per year. *Required fees:* $488; $488. *Student services:* Campus employment opportunities, campus safety program, career counseling, child daycare facilities, international student services. *Library facilities:* Hialeah Campus Library plus 1 other. *Collection:* Books: 2,479 (physical), 171,052 (digital/electronic); Serial titles: 19 (physical), 1,900 (digital/electronic); Databases: 32. Weekly public service hours: 78; students can reserve study rooms.

**Computer facilities:** 356 computers available on campus for general student use. A campuswide network can be accessed. Online class registration is available. Website: http://www.fnu.edu/

**General Application Contact:** Virginia Rabelo, Admissions Supervisor, 305-821-3333 Ext. 1016, Fax: 305-362-0595, E-mail: vrabelo@fnu.edu.

**GRADUATE UNITS**

**Program in Business Administration** Students: 23 full-time (15 women), 18 part-time (7 women); includes 37 minority (4 Black or African American, non-Hispanic/Latino; 1 American Indian or Alaska Native, non-Hispanic/Latino; 32 Hispanic/Latino), 1 international. Average age 35. 14 applicants, 100% accepted, 14 enrolled. *Faculty:* 3 full-time (1 woman), 5 part-time/adjunct (2 women). Expenses: Contact institution. *Financial support:* Federal Work-Study, institutionally sponsored loans, scholarships/grants, and tuition waivers (full and partial) available. Financial award applicants required to submit FAFSA. In 2019, 13 master's awarded. *Program availability:* Part-time, online only, blended/hybrid learning. *Application deadline:* Applications are processed on a rolling basis. Electronic applications accepted. *Application Contact:* Dr. Ernesto Gonzalez, Business and Economics Department Head, 305-821- 3333 Ext. 1170, Fax: 305-362-0595, E-mail: egonzalez@fnu.edu. *Business and Economics Division Head*, Dr. James Bullen, 305-821-3333 Ext. 1163, Fax: 305-362-0595, E-mail: jbullen@fnu.edu.

**Program in Health Services Administration** Students: 9 full-time (4 women), 5 part-time (4 women); includes 12 minority (1 Black or African American, non-Hispanic/Latino; 11 Hispanic/Latino). Average age 35. 4 applicants, 100% accepted, 4 enrolled. *Faculty:* 3 full-time (1 woman), 1 (woman) part-time/adjunct. Expenses: Contact institution. *Financial support:* Scholarships/grants available. Financial award applicants required to submit FAFSA. In 2019, 12 master's awarded. *Program availability:* Part-time, evening/weekend, 100% online, blended/hybrid learning. *Application deadline:* Applications are processed on a rolling basis. Electronic applications accepted. *Application Contact:* Dr. Loreto Almonte, Allied Health Division Head, 305-821-3333 Ext. 1074, Fax: 305-362-0595, E-mail: lalmonte@fnu.edu. *Allied Health Division Head*, Dr. Loreto Almonte, 305-821-3333 Ext. 1074, Fax: 305-362-0595, E-mail: lalmonte@fnu.edu.

**Program in Nursing** Students: 14 full-time (10 women), 204 part-time (151 women); includes 213 minority (21 Black or African American, non-Hispanic/Latino; 1 Asian, non-Hispanic/Latino; 191 Hispanic/Latino). Average age 40. 54 applicants, 100% accepted, 54 enrolled. *Faculty:* 6 full-time (4 women), 9 part-time/adjunct (7 women). Expenses: Contact institution. *Financial support:* Scholarships/grants available. In 2019, 53 master's awarded. *Program availability:* 100% online, blended/hybrid learning. *Application Contact:* Dr. Lydie Janvier, Master of Science in Nursing Program Director, 305-821-3333 Ext. 1056, Fax: 305-362-0595, E-mail: ljanvier@fnu.edu. *Master of Science in Nursing Program Director*, Dr. Lydie Janvier, 305-821-3333 Ext. 1056, Fax: 305-362-0595, E-mail: ljanvier@fnu.edu.

## FLORIDA POLYTECHNIC UNIVERSITY, Lakeland, FL 33805

**General Information** State-supported, coed, comprehensive institution.

**GRADUATE UNITS**

**Graduate Programs**

## FLORIDA SOUTHERN COLLEGE, Lakeland, FL 33801-5698

**General Information** Independent-religious, coed, comprehensive institution. *Enrollment:* 3,305 graduate, professional, and undergraduate students; 401 full-time matriculated graduate/professional students (300 women), 149 part-time matriculated graduate/professional students (104 women). *Enrollment by degree level:* 300 master's, 242 doctoral, 9 other advanced degrees. *Graduate faculty:* 34 full-time (20 women), 22 part-time/adjunct (17 women). *Tuition:* Full-time $14,400; part-time $600 per credit. *Required fees:* $150; $75 per unit. $25 per semester. *Graduate housing:* On-campus housing not available. *Student services:* Campus employment opportunities, campus safety program, career counseling, exercise/wellness program, free psychological counseling, international student services, multicultural affairs office, services for students with disabilities, teacher training. *Library facilities:* Roux Library plus 1 other. *Collection:* Books: 160,667 (physical), 167,731 (digital/electronic); Serial titles: 22 (physical), 97,772 (digital/electronic); Databases: 118. Weekly public service hours: 104; study areas open 24 hours, 5–7 days a week; students can reserve study rooms.

**Computer facilities:** Computer purchase and lease plans are available. 490 computers available on campus for general student use. A campuswide network can be accessed. Online class registration, campus portal are available.
Website: http://www.flsouthern.edu/

**General Application Contact:** Kristen Pinner, Director of Adult and Graduate Admission, 863-680-4205, Fax: 863-680-3872, E-mail: evening@flsouthern.edu.

**GRADUATE UNITS**

**Program in Accounting** Students: 16 full-time (5 women), 8 part-time (4 women); includes 4 minority (1 Black or African American, non-Hispanic/Latino; 1 Asian, non-Hispanic/Latino; 2 Hispanic/Latino), 1 international. Average age 30. 11 applicants, 100% accepted, 9 enrolled. *Faculty:* 4 full-time (2 women). Expenses: Contact institution. *Financial support:* In 2019–20, 1 student received support. Federal Work-Study, unspecified assistantships, and employee tuition grants, athletic scholarships for students still eligible available. Financial award application deadline: 8/20; financial award applicants required to submit FAFSA. In 2019, 17 master's awarded. *Program availability:* Part-time, evening/weekend, blended/hybrid learning. *Application deadline:* For fall admission, 6/1 priority date for domestic and international students; for spring admission, 11/1 priority date for domestic and international students. Applications are processed on a rolling basis. Electronic applications accepted. *Application Contact:* Kamalie Dodson, Associate Director, Adult and Graduate Admission (MBA MAcc), 863-680-5022, Fax: 863-680-3872, E-mail: kdodson2@flsouthern.edu. *MAcc Director,* Dr. William Quilliam, 863-680-4279, E-mail: wquilliam@flsouthern.edu.

**Program in Business Administration** Students: 56 full-time (28 women), 13 part-time (3 women); includes 17 minority (6 Black or African American, non-Hispanic/Latino; 1 American Indian or Alaska Native, non-Hispanic/Latino; 3 Asian, non-Hispanic/Latino; 5 Hispanic/Latino; 2 Two or more races, non-Hispanic/Latino), 10 international. Average age 31. 33 applicants, 100% accepted, 21 enrolled. *Faculty:* 6 full-time (2 women). Expenses: Contact institution. *Financial support:* In 2019–20, 11 students received support. Scholarships/grants, unspecified assistantships, and employee tuition grants, athletic scholarships for students still eligible available. Financial award application deadline: 8/20; financial award applicants required to submit FAFSA. In 2019, 39 master's awarded. *Program availability:* Part-time, evening/weekend, 100% online, blended/hybrid learning. *Application deadline:* For fall admission, 6/1 priority date for domestic and international students; for spring admission, 11/1 priority date for domestic and international students. Applications are processed on a rolling basis. Electronic applications accepted. *Application Contact:* Kamalie Dodson, Associate Director of Adult and Graduate Admission (MBA MAcc), 863-680-5022, Fax: 863-680-3872, E-mail: kdodson2@flsouthern.edu. *Program Director,* Krista Lewellyn, 863-680-4285, Fax: 863-680-4355, E-mail: klewellyn@flsouthern.edu.

**Program in Physical Therapy** Students: 24 full-time (10 women); includes 9 minority (4 Black or African American, non-Hispanic/Latino; 3 Asian, non-Hispanic/Latino; 1 Hispanic/Latino; 1 Two or more races, non-Hispanic/Latino). Average age 24. 72 applicants, 44% accepted, 24 enrolled. *Faculty:* 7 full-time (4 women). Expenses: Contact institution. *Application Contact:* Miriam Vega-Rodriguez, Accreditation Support Coordinator, 863-680-4717, E-mail: mvegarodriguez@flsouthern.edu. *Dean and Program Director,* Dr. Nancy A Nuzzo, 863-680-5126, E-mail: nnuzzo@flsouthern.edu.

**School of Education** Students: 159 full-time (125 women), 126 part-time (96 women); includes 91 minority (49 Black or African American, non-Hispanic/Latino; 2 American Indian or Alaska Native, non-Hispanic/Latino; 1 Asian, non-Hispanic/Latino; 31 Hispanic/Latino; 2 Native Hawaiian or other Pacific Islander, non-Hispanic/Latino; 6 Two or more races, non-Hispanic/Latino), 2 international. Average age 41. 48 applicants, 100% accepted, 33 enrolled. *Faculty:* 12 full-time (7 women), 21 part-time/adjunct (16 women). Expenses: Contact institution. *Financial support:* In 2019–20, 4 students received support. Application deadline: 8/20; applicants required to submit FAFSA. In 2019, 38 master's, 4 doctorates awarded. *Program availability:* Part-time, evening/weekend, 100% online, blended/hybrid learning. *Application deadline:* For fall admission, 8/15 priority date for domestic and international students; for spring admission, 12/1 priority date for domestic and international students; for summer admission, 4/1 priority date for domestic and international students. Applications are processed on a rolling basis. Electronic applications accepted. *Application Contact:* Kelly Levin, Admission Counselor and Advisor for Education, 863-680-4914, Fax: 863-680-3872, E-mail: klevin@flsouthern.edu. *Dean,* Dr. Victoria Giordano, 863-680-4172, Fax: 863-680-4102, E-mail: vgiordano@flsouthern.edu.

**School of Nursing and Health Sciences** Students: 145 full-time (131 women), 1 (woman) part-time; includes 70 minority (30 Black or African American, non-Hispanic/Latino; 11 Asian, non-Hispanic/Latino; 25 Hispanic/Latino; 4 Two or more races, non-Hispanic/Latino), 1 international. Average age 39. 81 applicants, 89% accepted, 50 enrolled. *Faculty:* 6 full-time (all women), 1 (woman) part-time/adjunct. Expenses: Contact institution. *Financial support:* In 2019–20, 1 student received support. Employee tuition grants, athletic scholarships for students still eligible available. Financial award application deadline: 8/20; financial award applicants required to submit FAFSA. In 2019, 53 master's awarded. *Program availability:* Part-time, The Nurse Educator MSN degree concentration and NE postmasters certificate are fully online. The Nursing Administrative Leadership MSN degree concentration is delivered in blended/hybrid format. *Application deadline:* For fall admission, 6/1 for domestic and international students; for spring admission, 10/1 for domestic and international students. Applications are processed on a rolling basis. Electronic applications accepted. *Application Contact:* Kimberly Smith, Admission Counselor and Advisor for Nursing, 863-680-3090, Fax: 863-680-3872, E-mail: ksmith@flsouthern.edu. *Dean,* Dr. Linda Comer, 863-680-3951, Fax: 863-680-3860, E-mail: lcomer@flsouthern.edu.

## FLORIDA STATE UNIVERSITY, Tallahassee, FL 32306

**General Information** State-supported, coed, university. CGS member. *Graduate housing:* Room and/or apartments available on a first-come, first-served basis to single students; on-campus housing not available to married students. Housing application deadline: 5/1. *Research affiliation:* University Corporation for Atmospheric Research (atmospheric research), Oak Ridge National Laboratory (materials science), Southeastern Universities Research Association (energy), University Research Association (energy), Bruker, Inc. (nuclear magnetic resonance), Oak Ridge Associated Universities (education, environmental assessment).

**GRADUATE UNITS**

**College of Law** *Program availability:* Part-time, 100% online. Electronic applications accepted.

**College of Medicine** Students: 472 full-time (269 women), 8 part-time (6 women); includes 202 minority (51 Black or African American, non-Hispanic/Latino; 60 Asian, non-Hispanic/Latino; 38 Hispanic/Latino; 53 Two or more races, non-Hispanic/Latino). Average age 26. 7,313 applicants, 2% accepted, 120 enrolled. *Faculty:* 177 full-time (93 women), 68 part-time/adjunct (26 women). Expenses: Contact institution. *Financial support:* In 2019–20, 136 students received support. Scholarships/grants and tuition waivers (partial) available. Financial award application deadline: 6/30; financial award applicants required to submit FAFSA. *Application deadline:* Applications are processed on a rolling basis. *Application fee:* $30. Electronic applications accepted. *Application Contact:* Davalda Bellot, Admissions Officer, 850-644-7904, Fax: 850-645-2846, E-mail: medadmissions@med.fsu.edu. *Dean,* Dr. John Patrick Fogarty, MD, 850-644-1346, Fax: 850-645-1420, E-mail: john.fogarty@med.fsu.edu.

***Division of Research and Graduate Programs*** Students: 48 full-time (30 women), 1 (woman) part-time; includes 7 minority (2 Black or African American, non-Hispanic/Latino; 1 Asian, non-Hispanic/Latino; 4 Two or more races, non-Hispanic/Latino), 12 international. Average age 27. 42 applicants, 33% accepted, 8 enrolled. *Faculty:* 31 full-time (8 women). Expenses: Contact institution. *Financial support:* In 2019–20, 34 students received support, including 34 research assistantships with full tuition reimbursements available (averaging $30,485 per year); tuition waivers (full) also available. Financial award application deadline: 12/1. In 2019, 4 doctorates awarded. *Application deadline:* For fall admission, 12/1 for domestic and international students. *Application fee:* $30. Electronic applications accepted. *Application Contact:* Robin Ryan, Academic Program Specialist, 850-645-6420, Fax: 850-644-5781, E-mail: robin.ryan@med.fsu.edu. *Senior Associate Dean for Research and Graduate Programs,* Dr. Jeffrey N. Joyce, 850-644-2190, Fax: 850-644-9399, E-mail: jeffrey.joyce@med.fsu.edu.

**The Graduate School** *Program availability:* Part-time, evening/weekend, 100% online, blended/hybrid learning. Electronic applications accepted.

***College of Arts and Sciences*** Students: 1,644 full-time (942 women), 153 part-time (76 women); includes 248 minority (39 Black or African American, non-Hispanic/Latino; 53 Asian, non-Hispanic/Latino; 113 Hispanic/Latino; 1 Native Hawaiian or other Pacific Islander, non-Hispanic/Latino; 42 Two or more races, non-Hispanic/Latino), 578 international. Average age 29. 17 applicants, 71% accepted, 9 enrolled. *Faculty:* 588 full-time, 8 part-time/adjunct. Expenses: Contact institution. *Financial support:* In 2019–20, 18 students received support, including 2 research assistantships with full tuition reimbursements available (averaging $14,500 per year), 16 teaching assistantships with full tuition reimbursements available (averaging $14,500 per year); fellowships, career-related internships or fieldwork, institutionally sponsored loans, scholarships/grants, traineeships, health care benefits, and unspecified assistantships also available. Support available to part-time students. Financial award application deadline: 3/15; financial award applicants required to submit FAFSA. In 2019, 292 master's, 181 doctorates awarded. *Program availability:* Part-time. *Application deadline:* For fall admission, 2/1 for domestic and international students. *Application fee:* $30. Electronic applications accepted. *Application Contact:* Scott McLemore, MAI, Academic Program Specialist, 850-644-4281, E-mail: smclemore@fsu.edu. *Dean,* Dr. Sam Huckaba, 850-644-1081.

***College of Business*** Students: 210 full-time (84 women), 450 part-time (160 women); includes 184 minority (34 Black or African American, non-Hispanic/Latino; 1 American Indian or Alaska Native, non-Hispanic/Latino; 32 Asian, non-Hispanic/Latino; 95 Hispanic/Latino; 22 Two or more races, non-Hispanic/Latino), 24 international. Average age 31. 490 applicants, 42% accepted, 145 enrolled. *Faculty:* 33 full-time (8 women). Expenses: Contact institution. *Financial support:* In 2019–20, 146 students received support, including 40 fellowships (averaging $1,500 per year), 77 research assistantships with full tuition reimbursements available (averaging $20,000 per year), 43 teaching assistantships with full tuition reimbursements available (averaging $20,000 per year); career-related internships or fieldwork, scholarships/grants, health care benefits, tuition waivers (full and partial), and unspecified assistantships also available. Support available to part-time students. Financial award application deadline: 1/1; financial award applicants required to submit FAFSA. In 2019, 329 master's, 16 doctorates awarded. *Program availability:* Part-time, 100% online. *Application deadline:* For fall admission, 6/1 for domestic and international students; for spring admission, 10/1 for domestic and international students; for summer admission, 3/1 for domestic and international students. Applications are processed on a rolling basis. *Application fee:* $30. Electronic applications accepted. *Application Contact:* Jennifer Clark, Director, 850-644-6458, E-mail: gradprograms@business.fsu.edu. *Dean,* Dr. Michael Hartline, 850-644-4405, Fax: 850-644-0915, E-mail: mhartline@business.fsu.edu.

***College of Communication and Information*** Students: 196 full-time (147 women), 518 part-time (380 women); includes 287 minority (74 Black or African American, non-Hispanic/Latino; 2 American Indian or Alaska Native, non-Hispanic/Latino; 32 Asian, non-Hispanic/Latino; 121 Hispanic/Latino; 1 Native Hawaiian or other Pacific Islander, non-Hispanic/Latino; 57 Two or more races, non-Hispanic/Latino), 33 international. Average age 26. 922 applicants, 42% accepted, 222 enrolled. *Faculty:* 72 full-time (45 women), 14 part-time/adjunct (7 women). Expenses: Contact institution. *Financial support:* In 2019–20, 298 students received support, including 3 fellowships with full tuition reimbursements available (averaging $21,000 per year), 52 research assistantships with full tuition reimbursements available (averaging $14,425 per year), 165 teaching assistantships with full tuition reimbursements available (averaging $11,412 per year); career-related internships or fieldwork, Federal Work-Study, institutionally sponsored loans, scholarships/grants, health care benefits, tuition waivers (full and partial), and unspecified assistantships also available. Support available to part-time students. Financial award application deadline: 1/1; financial award applicants required to submit FAFSA. In 2019, 223 master's, 11 doctorates, 1 other advanced degree awarded. *Program availability:* Part-time, evening/weekend, 100% online, blended/hybrid learning. *Application deadline:* For fall admission, 1/15 for domestic and international students; for spring admission, 11/1 for domestic and international students; for summer admission, 3/1 for domestic and international students. Applications are processed on a rolling basis. *Application fee:* $30. Electronic applications accepted. *Application Contact:* Betsy Crawford, Development and Recruiting Coordinator, 850-645-9661, Fax: 850-644-0611, E-mail:

betsy.crawford@cci.fsu.edu. *Dean*, Dr. Lawrence C. Dennis, 850-644-9698, Fax: 850-644-0611, E-mail: larry.dennis@cci.fsu.edu.

***College of Criminology and Criminal Justice*** *Program availability:* Part-time, 100% online. Electronic applications accepted.

***College of Education*** *Program availability:* Part-time, evening/weekend, blended/hybrid learning, asynchronous, minimal on-campus study. Electronic applications accepted.

***College of Fine Arts*** Students: 258 full-time (201 women), 35 part-time (25 women); includes 98 minority (22 Black or African American, non-Hispanic/Latino; 1 American Indian or Alaska Native, non-Hispanic/Latino; 11 Asian, non-Hispanic/Latino; 43 Hispanic/Latino; 21 Two or more races, non-Hispanic/Latino), 9 international. Average age 27. 387 applicants, 89% accepted. *Faculty:* 67 full-time (40 women), 17 part-time/adjunct (12 women). Expenses: Contact institution. *Financial support:* In 2019–20, 265 students received support, including 5 fellowships with partial tuition reimbursements available (averaging $18,000 per year), 90 research assistantships with partial tuition reimbursements available (averaging $4,957 per year), 78 teaching assistantships with partial tuition reimbursements available (averaging $8,001 per year); career-related internships or fieldwork, Federal Work-Study, institutionally sponsored loans, scholarships/grants, and unspecified assistantships also available. Support available to part-time students. Financial award application deadline: 4/15; financial award applicants required to submit FAFSA. In 2019, 91 master's, 14 doctorates awarded. *Program availability:* Part-time. *Application deadline:* For fall admission, 7/1 priority date for domestic students; for spring admission, 11/1 priority date for domestic students. Applications are processed on a rolling basis. *Application fee:* $30. Electronic applications accepted. *Application Contact:* Jermaine Williams, Assistant Director for Graduate Admissions, 850-644-7145, Fax: 850-644-0197, E-mail: jawilliams@fsu.edu. *Dean*, James Frazier, 850-664-5244, Fax: 850-644-2604, E-mail: jfrazier@fsu.edu.

***College of Human Sciences*** Students: 107 full-time (71 women), 23 part-time (16 women); includes 28 minority (9 Black or African American, non-Hispanic/Latino; 5 Asian, non-Hispanic/Latino; 1 Hispanic/Latino; 13 Two or more races, non-Hispanic/Latino), 15 international. 157 applicants, 58% accepted, 43 enrolled. *Faculty:* 42 full-time (22 women). Expenses: Contact institution. *Financial support:* In 2019–20, 101 students received support, including 21 research assistantships with full tuition reimbursements available (averaging $23,664 per year), 63 teaching assistantships with full tuition reimbursements available (averaging $23,664 per year); career-related internships or fieldwork, Federal Work-Study, scholarships/grants, and unspecified assistantships also available. Financial award application deadline: 1/15; financial award applicants required to submit FAFSA. In 2019, 20 master's, 15 doctorates awarded. *Program availability:* Part-time. *Application deadline:* For fall admission, 4/1 for domestic and international students; for spring admission, 10/1 for domestic and international students. Applications are processed on a rolling basis. *Application fee:* $30. Electronic applications accepted. *Application Contact:* Tara L. Hartman, Academic Program Specialist, 850-644-7221, E-mail: thartman@fsu.edu. *Dean*, Dr. Michael D. Delp, 850-644-1281, E-mail: mdelp@fsu.edu.

***College of Motion Picture Arts*** Students: 64 full-time (33 women); includes 20 minority (10 Black or African American, non-Hispanic/Latino; 1 American Indian or Alaska Native, non-Hispanic/Latino; 4 Asian, non-Hispanic/Latino; 3 Hispanic/Latino; 2 Two or more races, non-Hispanic/Latino), 14 international. Average age 25. 217 applicants, 15% accepted, 32 enrolled. *Faculty:* 28 full-time (8 women), 3 part-time/adjunct (1 woman). Expenses: Contact institution. *Financial support:* In 2019–20, 20 students received support, including 20 teaching assistantships with partial tuition reimbursements available (averaging $5,500 per year); institutionally sponsored loans, tuition waivers, and unspecified assistantships also available. Financial award application deadline: 7/1; financial award applicants required to submit FAFSA. In 2019, 30 master's awarded. *Application deadline:* For fall admission, 12/1 for domestic and international students. *Application fee:* $30. Electronic applications accepted. *Application Contact:* Paige Roberts, Head of Admissions, 850-644-8524, Fax: 850-644-2626, E-mail: proberts@fsu.edu. *Dean*, Reb Braddock, 850-644-8712, Fax: 850-644-2626.

***College of Music*** Students: 355 full-time (169 women); includes 94 minority (30 Black or African American, non-Hispanic/Latino; 1 American Indian or Alaska Native, non-Hispanic/Latino; 29 Asian, non-Hispanic/Latino; 33 Hispanic/Latino; 1 Native Hawaiian or other Pacific Islander, non-Hispanic/Latino). Average age 26. 789 applicants, 44% accepted, 153 enrolled. *Faculty:* 77 full-time (28 women). Expenses: Contact institution. *Financial support:* In 2019–20, 235 students received support, including 2 fellowships with full tuition reimbursements available (averaging $15,000 per year), 14 research assistantships with full and partial tuition reimbursements available (averaging $7,400 per year), 201 teaching assistantships with full and partial tuition reimbursements available (averaging $7,400 per year); career-related internships or fieldwork, scholarships/grants, tuition waivers (full and partial), and unspecified assistantships also available. Support available to part-time students. Financial award application deadline: 2/28; financial award applicants required to submit FAFSA. In 2019, 98 master's, 36 doctorates awarded. *Program availability:* Part-time. *Application deadline:* For fall admission, 7/1 for domestic and international students; for spring admission, 11/1 for domestic and international students; for summer admission, 3/1 for domestic students. Applications are processed on a rolling basis. *Application fee:* $30. Electronic applications accepted. *Application Contact:* Kristopher Watson, Director of Admissions, 850-645-2126, Fax: 850-644-2033, E-mail: krwatson@fsu.edu. *Dean*, Dr. Patricia Flowers, 850-644-4361, Fax: 850-644-2033, E-mail: pjflowers@fsu.edu.

***College of Nursing*** Students: 66 full-time (59 women), 72 part-time (63 women); includes 61 minority (32 Black or African American, non-Hispanic/Latino; 1 American Indian or Alaska Native, non-Hispanic/Latino; 5 Asian, non-Hispanic/Latino; 20 Hispanic/Latino; 3 Two or more races, non-Hispanic/Latino). Average age 40. 156 applicants, 39% accepted, 54 enrolled. *Faculty:* 31 full-time (27 women), 10 part-time/adjunct (9 women). Expenses: Contact institution. *Financial support:* In 2019–20, 27 students received support, including fellowships with partial tuition reimbursements available (averaging $6,300 per year), research assistantships with partial tuition reimbursements available (averaging $3,000 per year), 3 teaching assistantships with partial tuition reimbursements available (averaging $3,000 per year); career-related internships or fieldwork, Federal Work-Study, institutionally sponsored loans, scholarships/grants, traineeships, and tuition waivers (partial) also available. Financial award application deadline: 4/1; financial award applicants required to submit FAFSA. In 2019, 24 doctorates awarded. *Program availability:* Part-time, online only, 100% online. *Application deadline:* For fall admission, 3/1 for domestic and international students. *Application fee:* $30. Electronic applications accepted. *Application Contact:* Carlos Urrutia, Assistant Director for Student Services, 850-644-5638, Fax: 850-645-7249, E-mail: currutia@fsu.edu. *Interim Dean*, Dr. Laurie Grubbs, 850-644-6846, Fax: 850-644-7660, E-mail: lgrubbs@fsu.edu.

***College of Social Sciences and Public Policy*** Students: 423 full-time (213 women), 196 part-time (102 women); includes 222 minority (78 Black or African American, non-Hispanic/Latino; 1 American Indian or Alaska Native, non-Hispanic/Latino; 18 Asian, non-Hispanic/Latino; 85 Hispanic/Latino; 40 Two or more races, non-Hispanic/Latino), 92 international. Average age 29. 907 applicants, 48% accepted, 231 enrolled. *Faculty:* 134 full-time (47 women), 44 part-time/adjunct (7 women). Expenses: Contact institution. *Financial support:* In 2019–20, 116 students received support, including 33 fellowships with full tuition reimbursements available (averaging $21,828 per year), 19 research assistantships with full tuition reimbursements available (averaging $13,487 per year), 97 teaching assistantships with full tuition reimbursements available (averaging $18,710 per year); career-related internships or fieldwork, Federal Work-Study, institutionally sponsored loans, scholarships/grants, health care benefits, tuition waivers (full and partial), and unspecified assistantships also available. Support available to part-time students. Financial award application deadline: 1/15; financial award applicants required to submit FAFSA. In 2019, 237 master's, 37 doctorates awarded. *Program availability:* Part-time, evening/weekend. *Application deadline:* For fall admission, 7/1 priority date for domestic and international students; for spring admission, 11/1 priority date for domestic and international students; for summer admission, 3/1 priority date for domestic and international students. Applications are processed on a rolling basis. *Application fee:* $30. Electronic applications accepted. *Application Contact:* Jermaine Williams, Assistant Director for Graduate Admissions, 850-644-7145, Fax: 850-644-0197, E-mail: jawilliams@fsu.edu. *Dean*, Dr. Timothy Chapin, 850-644-5488, Fax: 850-645-4923, E-mail: tchapin@fsu.edu.

***College of Social Work*** Students: 260 full-time (27 women), 523 part-time (457 women); includes 302 minority (146 Black or African American, non-Hispanic/Latino; 1 American Indian or Alaska Native, non-Hispanic/Latino; 8 Asian, non-Hispanic/Latino; 108 Hispanic/Latino; 39 Two or more races, non-Hispanic/Latino), 2 international. Average age 32. 609 applicants, 45% accepted, 239 enrolled. *Faculty:* 34 full-time (22 women), 13 part-time/adjunct (9 women). Expenses: Contact institution. *Financial support:* In 2019–20, 111 students received support, including 20 research assistantships with full tuition reimbursements available, 7 teaching assistantships with full tuition reimbursements available; fellowships with full tuition reimbursements available, career-related internships or fieldwork, scholarships/grants, health care benefits, tuition waivers (full and partial), and unspecified assistantships also available. Financial award application deadline: 5/1; financial award applicants required to submit FAFSA. In 2019, 219 master's, 1 doctorate awarded. *Program availability:* Part-time, 100% online coursework with face to face internship requirements. *Application deadline:* For fall admission, 5/1 for domestic and international students; for spring admission, 10/1 for domestic and international students; for summer admission, 3/1 for domestic and international students. Applications are processed on a rolling basis. *Application fee:* $30. Electronic applications accepted. *Application Contact:* Dana DeBoer, Coordinator of MSW Admissions, 800-378-9550, Fax: 850-644-9591, E-mail: ddeboer2@admin.fsu.edu. *Dean*, Dr. James Clark, 850-644-4752, Fax: 850-644-9750, E-mail: jclark5@fsu.edu.

***FAMU-FSU College of Engineering*** Students: 258 full-time (62 women), 68 part-time (17 women); includes 57 minority (33 Black or African American, non-Hispanic/Latino; 2 Asian, non-Hispanic/Latino; 13 Hispanic/Latino; 9 Two or more races, non-Hispanic/Latino), 176 international. Average age 29. 692 applicants, 44% accepted, 101 enrolled. *Faculty:* 92 full-time (16 women). Expenses: Contact institution. *Financial support:* In 2019–20, 261 students received support, including 22 fellowships with full tuition reimbursements available, 135 research assistantships with full tuition reimbursements available, 104 teaching assistantships with full tuition reimbursements available; career-related internships or fieldwork, scholarships/grants, tuition waivers (full), and unspecified assistantships also available. Financial award application deadline: 1/15; financial award applicants required to submit FAFSA. In 2019, 78 master's, 31 doctorates awarded. *Program availability:* Part-time, 100% online. *Application deadline:* For fall admission, 7/1 for domestic and international students; for spring admission, 11/1 for domestic and international students; for summer admission, 3/1 for domestic and international students. Applications are processed on a rolling basis. *Application fee:* $30. Electronic applications accepted. *Application Contact:* Deborah Gautier, Director, Graduate Studies, 850-410-6613, E-mail: gradstudies@eng.famu.fsu.edu. *Dean/Professor*, Dr. John Murray Gibson, 850-410-6161, Fax: 850-410-6546, E-mail: dean@eng.famu.fsu.edu.

## FONTBONNE UNIVERSITY, St. Louis, MO 63105-3098

**General Information** Independent-religious, coed, comprehensive institution. *Enrollment:* 1,199 graduate, professional, and undergraduate students; 140 full-time matriculated graduate/professional students (107 women), 185 part-time matriculated graduate/professional students (139 women). *Enrollment by degree level:* 313 master's, 12 doctoral. *Graduate faculty:* 26 full-time (18 women), 21 part-time/adjunct (11 women). *Tuition:* Full-time $6975; part-time $775 per credit hour. *Required fees:* $225; $25 per credit hour. Tuition and fees vary according to degree level and program. *Graduate housing:* Room and/or apartments available on a first-come, first-served basis to single students; on-campus housing not available to married students. Typical cost: $5320 per year ($10,280 including board). Room and board charges vary according to board plan and housing facility selected. Housing application deadline: 5/1. *Student services:* Campus employment opportunities, career counseling, exercise/wellness program, free psychological counseling, international student services, multicultural affairs office, services for students with disabilities. *Library facilities:* The Jack C. Taylor Library at Fontbonne University plus 1 other. *Collection:* Books: 63,109 (physical), 247,354 (digital/electronic); Serial titles: 73 (physical), 78,918 (digital/electronic); Databases: 35.

**Computer facilities:** 215 computers available on campus for general student use. A campuswide network can be accessed. Online class registration is available. Website: http://www.fontbonne.edu/

**General Application Contact:** Maria Buckel, Interim Vice President for Enrollment Management, 314-862-3456, E-mail: fbyou@fontbonne.edu.

**GRADUATE UNITS**

**Graduate Programs** *Program availability:* Part-time, evening/weekend, online learning. Electronic applications accepted.

## FORDHAM UNIVERSITY, New York, NY 10458

**General Information** Independent-religious, coed, university. CGS member. *Enrollment:* 16,972 graduate, professional, and undergraduate students. *Enrollment by degree level:* 514 master's, 349 doctoral, 20 other advanced degrees. *Graduate housing:* Room and/or apartments available on a first-come, first-served basis to single students; on-campus housing not available to married students. Housing application deadline: 4/10. *Student services:* Campus employment opportunities, campus safety program, career counseling, free psychological counseling, international student services, low-cost health insurance, services for students with disabilities, teacher training, writing training. *Library facilities:* Walsh Library plus 3 others. *Collection:* Books: 1.1 million (physical), 1.3 million (digital/electronic); Serial titles: 16,326 (physical), 94,307 (digital/electronic); Databases: 444. Weekly public service hours: 105; study areas open 24 hours, 5–7 days a week; students can reserve study rooms. *Research affiliation:* Equator Initiative/United Nations Development Programme, Folger Shakespeare Library, New York Botanical Gardens, New York Ocean Science Library, Wildlife Conservation Society, Memorial Sloan-Kettering Cancer Center.

**Computer facilities:** Computer purchase and lease plans are available. 2,600 computers available on campus for general student use. A campuswide network can be accessed. Online class registration, Video Streaming; IP TV Channels; Mobile Apps for University Services; Maker Spaces; University Supplied Software, WebEX Video Conferencing are available.
Website: http://www.fordham.edu/

**General Application Contact:** Office of Admission, 718-817-1000.

**GRADUATE UNITS**

**Gabelli School of Business** Students: 1,038 full-time, 503 part-time; includes 227 minority (57 Black or African American, non-Hispanic/Latino; 1 American Indian or Alaska Native, non-Hispanic/Latino; 65 Asian, non-Hispanic/Latino; 91 Hispanic/Latino; 1 Native Hawaiian or other Pacific Islander, non-Hispanic/Latino; 12 Two or more races, non-Hispanic/Latino), 985 international. Average age 27. 4,250 applicants, 62% accepted, 764 enrolled. *Faculty:* 130 full-time (49 women), 73 part-time/adjunct (12 women). Expenses: Contact institution. *Financial support:* Career-related internships or fieldwork, institutionally sponsored loans, scholarships/grants, and unspecified assistantships available. Support available to part-time students. Financial award application deadline: 6/5; financial award applicants required to submit FAFSA. In 2019, 899 master's awarded. *Program availability:* Part-time, evening/weekend, 100% online, blended/hybrid learning. *Application deadline:* For fall admission, 11/15 for domestic and international students; for winter admission, 1/10 for domestic students, 1/1 for international students; for spring admission, 5/15 for domestic students, 3/1 for international students; for summer admission, 7/10 for domestic students, 6/5 for international students. *Application fee:* $130. Electronic applications accepted. *Application Contact:* Lawrence Mur'ray, Senior Assistant Dean of Graduate Admissions and Advising, 212-636-6200, Fax: 212-636-7076, E-mail: admissionsgb@fordham.edu. *Dean,* Dr. Donna Rapaccioli, 212-636-6165, Fax: 212-307-1779, E-mail: rapaccioli@fordham.edu.

**Graduate School of Arts and Sciences** Students: 609 full-time (298 women), 190 part-time (88 women); includes 167 minority (45 Black or African American, non-Hispanic/Latino; 4 American Indian or Alaska Native, non-Hispanic/Latino; 46 Asian, non-Hispanic/Latino; 71 Hispanic/Latino; 1 Native Hawaiian or other Pacific Islander, non-Hispanic/Latino), 181 international. Average age 31. 2,197 applicants, 36% accepted, 296 enrolled. *Faculty:* 249 full-time (81 women). Expenses: Contact institution. *Financial support:* In 2019–20, 29 fellowships with tuition reimbursements (averaging $22,844 per year), 106 research assistantships with tuition reimbursements (averaging $16,516 per year), 280 teaching assistantships with tuition reimbursements (averaging $19,927 per year) were awarded; career-related internships or fieldwork, Federal Work-Study, institutionally sponsored loans, scholarships/grants, health care benefits, tuition waivers (full and partial), and unspecified assistantships also available. Support available to part-time students. Financial award application deadline: 1/4; financial award applicants required to submit FAFSA. In 2019, 205 master's, 56 doctorates, 58 other advanced degrees awarded. *Program availability:* Part-time, evening/weekend. *Application deadline:* For fall admission, 1/4 priority date for domestic and international students; for spring admission, 10/31 for domestic and international students. Applications are processed on a rolling basis. *Application fee:* $70. Electronic applications accepted. *Application Contact:* Garrett Marino, Director of Graduate Admissions, 718-817-4419, Fax: 718-817-3566, E-mail: gmarino10@fordham.edu. *Dean,* Dr. Melissa Labonte, 718-817-4400, Fax: 718-817-4474, E-mail: labonte@fordham.edu.

***Program in Ethics and Society*** Average age 34. 30 applicants, 87% accepted, 10 enrolled. Expenses: Contact institution. *Financial support:* In 2019–20, 1 student received support. Teaching assistantships, Federal Work-Study, institutionally sponsored loans, scholarships/grants, tuition waivers (partial), and unspecified assistantships available. Financial award application deadline: 1/4. In 2019, 7 master's awarded. *Program availability:* Part-time. *Application deadline:* For fall admission, 1/4 priority date for domestic students; for spring admission, 10/31 for domestic students. Applications are processed on a rolling basis. *Application fee:* $70. Electronic applications accepted. *Application Contact:* Garrett Marino, Director of Graduate Admissions, 718-817-4419, Fax: 718-817-3566, E-mail: gmarino10@fordham.edu. *Interim Director of Academic Programs, Fordham University Center for Ethics Education,* Rimah Jaber, 718-817-0927, E-mail: rjaber@fordham.edu.

***Program in Medieval Studies*** Average age 27. 17 applicants, 82% accepted, 3 enrolled. Expenses: Contact institution. *Financial support:* In 2019–20, 4 students received support. Institutionally sponsored loans, tuition waivers (full and partial), and unspecified assistantships available. Financial award application deadline: 1/4; financial award applicants required to submit FAFSA. In 2019, 6 master's awarded. *Program availability:* Part-time, evening/weekend. *Application deadline:* For fall admission, 1/4 priority date for domestic students; for spring admission, 11/1 for domestic students. Applications are processed on a rolling basis. *Application fee:* $70. Electronic applications accepted. *Application Contact:* Garrett Marino, Director of Graduate Admissions, 718-817-4419, Fax: 718-817-3566, E-mail: gmarino10@fordham.edu. *Director,* Dr. Susanne Hafner, 718-817-4655, E-mail: hafner@fordham.edu.

**Graduate School of Education** *Program availability:* Part-time, evening/weekend. Electronic applications accepted.

***Division of Curriculum and Teaching*** *Program availability:* Part-time, evening/weekend. Electronic applications accepted.

***Division of Educational Leadership, Administration and Policy*** *Program availability:* Part-time, evening/weekend. Electronic applications accepted.

***Division of Psychological and Educational Services*** *Program availability:* Part-time, evening/weekend. Electronic applications accepted.

**Graduate School of Religion and Religious Education** Students: 126 full-time (66 women), 72 part-time (37 women); includes 51 minority (19 Black or African American, non-Hispanic/Latino; 9 Asian, non-Hispanic/Latino; 20 Hispanic/Latino; 3 Two or more races, non-Hispanic/Latino), 34 international. Average age 41. 85 applicants, 76% accepted, 55 enrolled. *Faculty:* 11 full-time (4 women), 16 part-time/adjunct (11 women). Expenses: Contact institution. *Financial support:* In 2019–20, 140 students received support, including 8 research assistantships with partial tuition reimbursements available (averaging $10,800 per year); scholarships/grants, tuition waivers (partial), and unspecified assistantships also available. Support available to part-time students. Financial award application deadline: 8/1; financial award applicants required to submit FAFSA. In 2019, 48 master's, 12 doctorates, 10 other advanced degrees awarded. *Program availability:* Part-time, evening/weekend, 100% online, blended/hybrid learning. *Application deadline:* For fall admission, 7/1 priority date for domestic students, 5/1 priority date for international students; for spring admission, 12/1 priority date for domestic students, 10/1 priority date for international students. Applications are processed on a rolling basis. *Application fee:* $100. Electronic applications accepted. *Application Contact:* Dr. Lois D'Amore, Director of Admissions and Student Life, 718-817-4800, Fax: 718-817-3352, E-mail: ldamore@fordham.edu. *Dean,* Faustino M. Cruz, SM, 718-817-4800, Fax: 718-817-3352, E-mail: fcruz16@fordham.edu.

**Graduate School of Social Service** Students: 1,026 full-time (891 women), 636 part-time (560 women); includes 1,081 minority (577 Black or African American, non-Hispanic/Latino; 3 American Indian or Alaska Native, non-Hispanic/Latino; 52 Asian, non-Hispanic/Latino; 411 Hispanic/Latino; 7 Native Hawaiian or other Pacific Islander, non-Hispanic/Latino; 31 Two or more races, non-Hispanic/Latino), 24 international. Average age 32. *Faculty:* 37 full-time (25 women), 106 part-time/adjunct (29 women). Expenses: Contact institution. *Financial support:* In 2019–20, 838 students received support, including 39 research assistantships with partial tuition reimbursements available (averaging $1,980 per year); fellowships with partial tuition reimbursements available, career-related internships or fieldwork, Federal Work-Study, scholarships/grants, tuition waivers (partial), and unspecified assistantships also available. Support available to part-time students. Financial award application deadline: 2/1. In 2019, 697 master's, 5 doctorates awarded. *Program availability:* Part-time, evening/weekend, 100% online, blended/hybrid learning. *Application deadline:* For fall admission, 2/1 for domestic students; for spring admission, 11/1 for domestic students; for summer admission, 1/1 for domestic students. Applications are processed on a rolling basis. *Application fee:* $60. Electronic applications accepted. *Application Contact:* Melba Remice, Assistant Dean of Admissions, 212-636-6600, Fax: 212-636-6613, E-mail: gssadmission@fordham.edu. *Dean,* Dr. Debra McPhee, 212-636-6616, E-mail: dmcphee1@fordham.edu.

**School of Law** *Program availability:* Part-time, evening/weekend. Electronic applications accepted.

## FORT HAYS STATE UNIVERSITY, Hays, KS 67601-4099

**General Information** State-supported, coed, comprehensive institution. CGS member. *Graduate housing:* Rooms and/or apartments available to single and married students. Housing application deadline: 8/1.

**GRADUATE UNITS**

**Graduate School** *Program availability:* Part-time. Electronic applications accepted.

***College of Arts, Humanities, and Social Sciences*** *Program availability:* Part-time. Electronic applications accepted.

***College of Education*** *Program availability:* Part-time. Electronic applications accepted.

***College of Health and Behavioral Sciences*** *Program availability:* Part-time. Electronic applications accepted.

***Peter Werth College of Science, Technology and Mathematics***

***W.R. and Yvonne Robbins College of Business and Entrepreneurship*** *Program availability:* Part-time. Electronic applications accepted.

## FORT LEWIS COLLEGE, Durango, CO 81301-3999

**General Information** State-supported, coed, comprehensive institution. *Enrollment:* 3,308 graduate, professional, and undergraduate students; 9 full-time matriculated graduate/professional students (5 women), 70 part-time matriculated graduate/professional students (55 women). *Enrollment by degree level:* 79 master's. *Graduate faculty:* 10 full-time (8 women), 3 part-time/adjunct (all women). *International tuition:* $8496 full-time. *Tuition, area resident:* Full-time $8496; part-time $6372 per credit. Tuition, state resident: full-time $8496; part-time $6372 per credit. Tuition, nonresident: full-time $8496; part-time $6372 per credit. *Required fees:* $1452; $1089 per credit. One-time fee: $50. Tuition and fees vary according to course load. *Graduate housing:* Rooms and/or apartments available on a first-come, first-served basis to single and married students. Typical cost: $0 per year ($0 including board) for single students; $0 per year ($0 including board) for married students. Room and board charges vary according to board plan, campus/location and housing facility selected. Housing application deadline: 8/24. *Student services:* Campus employment opportunities, campus safety program, career counseling, child daycare facilities, exercise/wellness program, free psychological counseling, international student services, low-cost health insurance, multicultural affairs office, services for students with disabilities, writing training. *Library facilities:* John F. Reed Library plus 1 other. *Collection:* Books: 117,854 (physical), 217,517 (digital/electronic); Serial titles: 3 (physical), 138,779 (digital/electronic); Databases: 72. Weekly public service hours: 80; study areas open 24 hours, 5–7 days a week; students can reserve study rooms.

**Computer facilities:** 935 computers available on campus for general student use. A campuswide network can be accessed from student residence rooms and from off campus. Online class registration is available.
Website: http://www.fortlewis.edu/

**General Application Contact:** Melissa Stordeur, Graduate Studies Coordinator, 970-247-7097, E-mail: mjstordeur@fortlewis.edu.

**GRADUATE UNITS**

**Program in Teacher Leadership**

## FORT VALLEY STATE UNIVERSITY, Fort Valley, GA 31030

**General Information** State-supported, coed, comprehensive institution. *Graduate housing:* Room and/or apartments available on a first-come, first-served basis to single students; on-campus housing not available to married students. Housing application deadline: 7/1.

**GRADUATE UNITS**

**College of Graduate Studies and Extended Education** *Program availability:* Part-time.

## FRAMINGHAM STATE UNIVERSITY, Framingham, MA 01701-9101

**General Information** State-supported, coed, comprehensive institution. *Graduate housing:* On-campus housing not available.

**GRADUATE UNITS**

**Graduate Studies** *Program availability:* Part-time, evening/weekend, online learning.

## FRANCISCAN MISSIONARIES OF OUR LADY UNIVERSITY, Baton Rouge, LA 70808

**General Information** Independent-religious, coed, comprehensive institution. *Graduate housing:* On-campus housing not available.

**GRADUATE UNITS**

**School of Health Professions**

**School of Nursing**

## FRANCISCAN SCHOOL OF THEOLOGY, Oceanside, CA 92057

**General Information** Independent-religious, coed, graduate-only institution. *Graduate housing:* Rooms and/or apartments available on a first-come, first-served basis to single and married students. Housing application deadline: 5/15.

**GRADUATE UNITS**

**Graduate and Professional Programs** *Program availability:* Part-time.

## FRANCISCAN UNIVERSITY OF STEUBENVILLE, Steubenville, OH 43952-1763

**General Information** Independent-religious, coed, comprehensive institution. *Graduate housing:* On-campus housing not available.

**GRADUATE UNITS**

**Graduate Programs** *Program availability:* Part-time, evening/weekend, online learning. Electronic applications accepted.

## FRANCIS MARION UNIVERSITY, Florence, SC 29502-0547

**General Information** State-supported, coed, comprehensive institution. *Enrollment:* 4,240 graduate, professional, and undergraduate students; 176 full-time matriculated graduate/professional students (146 women), 254 part-time matriculated graduate/professional students (220 women). *Enrollment by degree level:* 410 master's, 8 doctoral, 12 other advanced degrees. *Graduate faculty:* 35 full-time (29 women), 7 part-time/adjunct (5 women). *International tuition:* $21,224 full-time. *Tuition, area resident:* Full-time $10,612; part-time $530.60 per credit hour. Tuition, state resident: full-time $10,612; part-time $530.60 per credit hour. Tuition, nonresident: full-time $21,224; part-time $1061.20 per credit hour. *Required fees:* $312; $156 per credit hour. $332 per semester. Tuition and fees vary according to program. *Graduate housing:* Room and/or apartments available on a first-come, first-served basis to single students; on-campus housing not available to married students. Typical cost: $4490 per year ($8211 including board). Room and board charges vary according to board plan and housing facility selected. *Student services:* Campus employment opportunities, campus safety program, career counseling, child daycare facilities, exercise/wellness program, free psychological counseling, international student services, multicultural affairs office, services for students with disabilities, writing training. *Library facilities:* James A. Rogers Library. *Collection:* Books: 289,630 (physical), 343,000 (digital/electronic); Serial titles: 179 (physical), 34,999 (digital/electronic); Databases: 147. Weekly public service hours: 86.

**Computer facilities:** 141 computers available on campus for general student use. A campuswide network can be accessed. Online class registration, Learning management system are available.
Website: http://www.fmarion.edu/

**General Application Contact:** Brandon Funk, Admissions Counselor, 843-661-1231, Fax: 843-661-4635, E-mail: bfunk@fmarion.edu.

**GRADUATE UNITS**

**Graduate Programs** *Program availability:* Part-time, evening/weekend. Electronic applications accepted.

***School of Business*** *Program availability:* Part-time, evening/weekend.

***School of Education*** *Program availability:* Part-time.

## FRANKLIN COLLEGE, Franklin, IN 46131

**General Information** Independent-religious, coed, comprehensive institution.

**GRADUATE UNITS**

**Program in Athletic Training**

## FRANKLIN PIERCE UNIVERSITY, Rindge, NH 03461-0060

**General Information** Independent, coed, comprehensive institution. *Graduate housing:* On-campus housing not available.

**GRADUATE UNITS**

**Graduate and Professional Studies** *Program availability:* Part-time, 100% online, blended/hybrid learning. Electronic applications accepted.

## FRANKLIN UNIVERSITY, Columbus, OH 43215-5399

**General Information** Independent, coed, comprehensive institution. *Graduate housing:* On-campus housing not available.

**GRADUATE UNITS**

**Accounting Program** *Program availability:* Online learning.

**Computer Science Program** *Program availability:* Part-time, evening/weekend. Electronic applications accepted.

**Criminal Justice Administration Program**

**Instructional Design and Learning Technology Program**

**Marketing and Communication Program** *Program availability:* Part-time, evening/weekend. Electronic applications accepted.

**MBA Program** *Program availability:* Part-time, evening/weekend, online learning. Electronic applications accepted.

## FRANKLIN UNIVERSITY SWITZERLAND, CH-6924 Sorengo, Switzerland

**General Information** Independent, coed, comprehensive institution. *Enrollment:* 6 full-time matriculated graduate/professional students (1 woman), 2 part-time matriculated graduate/professional students (1 woman). *Enrollment by degree level:* 8 master's. *Graduate faculty:* 2 full-time (both women), 16 part-time/adjunct (5 women). *Tuition:* Full-time 25,000 Swiss francs. *Required fees:* 1500 Swiss francs. *Graduate housing:* Room and/or apartments available on a first-come, first-served basis to single students; on-campus housing not available to married students. Typical cost: 11,060 Swiss francs per year. Room charges vary according to housing facility selected. Housing application deadline: 6/15. *Student services:* Campus employment opportunities, campus safety program, career counseling, exercise/wellness program, free psychological counseling, international student services, low-cost health insurance, multicultural affairs office, services for students with disabilities, writing training. *Library facilities:* David R. Grace Library plus 2 others.

**Computer facilities:** A campuswide network can be accessed. Online class registration, Live@EDU skydrive, learning management system, office online collaboration tools, LAN Storage space, student access to academic/financial records and portal available in student lounge and libraries are available.
Website: http://www.fus.edu/

**General Application Contact:** Sara Diviani, Admission Counselor, 41-91-986-3613, E-mail: sdiviani@fus.edu.

## FREDERICK S. PARDEE RAND GRADUATE SCHOOL, Santa Monica, CA 90407-2138

**General Information** Independent, coed, graduate-only institution. *Graduate housing:* On-campus housing not available. *Research affiliation:* RAND Corporation (not-for-profit research).

**GRADUATE UNITS**

**Program in Policy Analysis** Electronic applications accepted.

## FREED-HARDEMAN UNIVERSITY, Henderson, TN 38340-2399

**General Information** Independent-religious, coed, comprehensive institution. *Graduate housing:* Room and/or apartments available on a first-come, first-served basis to single students; on-campus housing not available to married students. Housing application deadline: 8/22.

**GRADUATE UNITS**

**Program in Business Administration** *Program availability:* Part-time, evening/weekend, online learning.

**Program in Counseling** *Program availability:* Part-time, evening/weekend.

**Program in Education** *Program availability:* Part-time, evening/weekend.

**School of Biblical Studies** *Program availability:* Part-time.

## FRESNO PACIFIC UNIVERSITY, Fresno, CA 93702-4709

**General Information** Independent-religious, coed, comprehensive institution. *Graduate housing:* Rooms and/or apartments available on a first-come, first-served basis to single and married students. Housing application deadline: 4/20.

**GRADUATE UNITS**

**Biblical Seminary** *Program availability:* Part-time, online learning.

**Graduate Programs** *Program availability:* Part-time, evening/weekend. Electronic applications accepted.

***School of Education*** *Program availability:* Part-time, evening/weekend. Electronic applications accepted.

## FRIENDS UNIVERSITY, Wichita, KS 67213

**General Information** Independent-religious, coed, comprehensive institution.

**GRADUATE UNITS**

**Graduate School** *Program availability:* Part-time, evening/weekend, online learning. Electronic applications accepted.

## FRONTIER NURSING UNIVERSITY, Versailes, KY 40383

**General Information** Independent, coed, primarily women, graduate-only institution.

**GRADUATE UNITS**

**Graduate Programs**

## FROSTBURG STATE UNIVERSITY, Frostburg, MD 21532-1099

**General Information** State-supported, coed, comprehensive institution. *Graduate housing:* Room and/or apartments available to single students; on-campus housing not available to married students. Housing application deadline: 6/1.

**GRADUATE UNITS**

**College of Business** *Program availability:* Part-time, evening/weekend. Electronic applications accepted.

**College of Education** *Program availability:* Part-time, evening/weekend. Electronic applications accepted.

**College of Liberal Arts and Sciences** *Program availability:* Part-time, evening/weekend. Electronic applications accepted.

## FULLER THEOLOGICAL SEMINARY, Pasadena, CA 91182

**General Information** Independent-religious, coed, graduate-only institution. *Graduate housing:* Rooms and/or apartments available on a first-come, first-served basis to single and married students.

**GRADUATE UNITS**

**Graduate Programs**

## FULL SAIL UNIVERSITY, Winter Park, FL 32792-7437

**General Information** Proprietary, coed, primarily men, comprehensive institution. *Graduate housing:* On-campus housing not available.

**GRADUATE UNITS**

**Creative Writing Master of Fine Arts Program - Online** *Program availability:* Online learning.

**Education Media Design and Technology Master of Science Program - Online** *Program availability:* Online learning.

**Entertainment Business Master of Science Program - Campus**

**Entertainment Business Master of Science Program - Online** *Program availability:* Online learning.

**Game Design Master of Science Program - Campus**

**Internet Marketing Master of Science Program - Online** *Program availability:* Online learning.

**Media Design Master of Fine Arts Program - Online** *Program availability:* Online learning.

**New Media Journalism Master of Arts Program - Online**

## FURMAN UNIVERSITY, Greenville, SC 29613

**General Information** Independent, coed, comprehensive institution. CGS member. *Enrollment:* 2,728 graduate, professional, and undergraduate students; 58 full-time matriculated graduate/professional students (47 women), 82 part-time matriculated graduate/professional students (67 women). *Enrollment by degree level:* 140 master's, 10 other advanced degrees. *Graduate faculty:* 18 full-time (12 women), 9 part-time/adjunct (3 women). *Tuition:* Full-time $8750; part-time $415 per credit. *Graduate housing:* On-campus housing not available. *Student services:* Campus employment opportunities, campus safety program, career counseling, child daycare facilities, exercise/wellness program, free psychological counseling, international student services, multicultural affairs office, services for students with disabilities, teacher training. *Library facilities:* James Buchanan Duke Library plus 3 others. *Collection:* Books: 366,124 (physical), 1.1 million (digital/electronic); Serial titles: 501 (physical), 752,337 (digital/electronic); Databases: 496. Study areas open 24 hours, 5–7 days a week.

**Computer facilities:** Computer purchase and lease plans are available. 500 computers available on campus for general student use. A campuswide network can be accessed. Online class registration is available.
Website: http://www.furman.edu/

**General Application Contact:** Dr. Troy M. Terry, Executive Director of Graduate and Evening Studies, 864-294-2213, Fax: 864-294-3579, E-mail: troy.terry@furman.edu.

**GRADUATE UNITS**

**Community Engaged Medicine** Students: 12 full-time (9 women); includes 4 minority (3 Black or African American, non-Hispanic/Latino; 1 Asian, non-Hispanic/Latino), 1 international. Average age 23. *Faculty:* 4 full-time (all women). Expenses: Contact institution. *Financial support:* Application deadline: 4/15; applicants required to submit FAFSA. *Application deadline:* For summer admission, 4/15 for domestic students, 4/1 for international students. Applications are processed on a rolling basis. *Application fee:* $85. Electronic applications accepted. *Application Contact:* Dr. Victoria Turgeon, Executive Director of Graduate and Evening Studies, 864-294-3791, E-mail: victoria.turgeon@furman.edu. *Executive Director of Graduate and Evening Studies*, Dr. Troy M. Terry, 864-294-2213, Fax: 864-294-3579, E-mail: troy.terry@furman.edu.

**Department of Chemistry** Students: 7 full-time (5 women); includes 2 minority (1 Asian, non-Hispanic/Latino; 1 Hispanic/Latino). Average age 22. *Faculty:* 8 full-time (5 women). Expenses: Contact institution. *Financial support:* In 2019–20, 10 students received support, including 10 fellowships with full tuition reimbursements available (averaging $8,700 per year); scholarships/grants also available. In 2019, 2 master's awarded. *Program availability:* Part-time. *Application deadline:* Applications are processed on a rolling basis. Electronic applications accepted. *Application Contact:* Dr. Laura Lee Wright, Professor, 864-294-3375, Fax: 864-294-3559, E-mail: laura.wright@furman.edu. *Professor and Department Chair*, Dr. Timothy Wayne Hanks, 864-294-3372, Fax: 864-294-3559, E-mail: tim.hanks@furman.edu.

**Department of Education** Students: 28 full-time (25 women), 82 part-time (67 women); includes 15 minority (8 Black or African American, non-Hispanic/Latino; 1 American Indian or Alaska Native, non-Hispanic/Latino; 2 Asian, non-Hispanic/Latino; 4 Hispanic/Latino). Average age 35. 12 applicants, 100% accepted, 12 enrolled. *Faculty:* 8 full-time (5 women), 1 (woman) part-time/adjunct. Expenses: Contact institution. *Financial support:* Application deadline: 7/15; applicants required to submit FAFSA. In 2019, 51 master's, 13 other advanced degrees awarded. *Program availability:* Part-time-only. *Application deadline:* For fall admission, 7/1 for domestic students, 6/15 for international students; for spring admission, 11/1 for domestic students, 10/15 for international students; for summer admission, 5/1 for domestic students, 4/15 for international students. Applications are processed on a rolling basis. *Application fee:* $55. Electronic applications accepted. *Application Contact:* Dr. Troy M. Terry, Executive Director of Graduate and Evening Studies, 864-294-2213, Fax: 864-294-3579, E-mail: troy.terry@furman.edu. *Head*, Dr. Nelly Hecker, 864-294-3385.

**Graduate Division** *Program availability:* Part-time, online learning.

## FUTURE GENERATIONS UNIVERSITY, Franklin, WV 26807

**General Information** Independent, coed, graduate-only institution. *Graduate housing:* On-campus housing not available.

**GRADUATE UNITS**

**Program in Applied Community Change** *Program availability:* Blended/hybrid learning. Electronic applications accepted.

## GALLAUDET UNIVERSITY, Washington, DC 20002-3625

**General Information** Independent, coed, university. CGS member. *Enrollment:* 1,485 graduate, professional, and undergraduate students; 267 full-time matriculated graduate/professional students (208 women), 139 part-time matriculated graduate/professional students (95 women). *Enrollment by degree level:* 241 master's, 137 doctoral, 28 other advanced degrees. *Graduate faculty:* 95 full-time (38 women). *Tuition:* Full-time $18,180; part-time $688 per credit. *Required fees:* $526; $526. Tuition and fees vary according to course load. *Graduate housing:* Rooms and/or apartments available on a first-come, first-served basis to single and married students. Housing application deadline: 4/1. *Student services:* Campus employment opportunities, campus safety program, career counseling, exercise/wellness program, free psychological counseling, grant writing training, international student services, low-cost health insurance, multicultural affairs office, services for students with disabilities, teacher training, writing training. *Library facilities:* Merrill Learning Center. *Collection:* Books: 121,359 (physical), 547,506 (digital/electronic); Serial titles: 4,142 (physical), 71,930 (digital/electronic); Databases: 79. Weekly public service hours: 90; students can reserve study rooms. *Research affiliation:* National Science Foundation/Howard University (linguistics, visual language and visual learning, integrated quantum materials), Maryland Sea Grant/University of Maryland/National Oceanic and Atmospheric Administration (NOAA) (advanced recruitment and retention in geosciences), U.S. Department of Education/Vcom3D Inc. (signing math dictionaries with mouth morphemes; accessibility and usability technologies for deaf and hard of hearing), Spencer Foundation (deaf legal discourse), University of Wisconsin-Madison/U.S. Department of Education (DOE) (telecommunications access), University of California Los Angeles/National Institutes of Health (cancer genetics).

**Computer facilities:** 400 computers available on campus for general student use. A campuswide network can be accessed from student residence rooms and from off campus. Online class registration is available.
Website: http://www.gallaudet.edu/

**General Application Contact:** Heidi Zornes-Foster, Senior Graduate Admissions Counselor, 202-651-5436, Fax: 202-651-5295, E-mail: graduate.school@gallaudet.edu.

**GRADUATE UNITS**

**The Graduate School** Students: 267 full-time (208 women), 139 part-time (95 women); includes 120 minority (38 Black or African American, non-Hispanic/Latino; 20 Asian, non-Hispanic/Latino; 44 Hispanic/Latino; 18 Two or more races, non-Hispanic/Latino), 19 international. Average age 30. 484 applicants, 50% accepted, 162 enrolled. *Faculty:* 101 full-time (70 women). Expenses: Contact institution. *Financial support:* In 2019–20, 50 students received support. Fellowships, research assistantships, teaching assistantships, career-related internships or fieldwork, Federal Work-Study, scholarships/grants, tuition waivers (partial), and unspecified assistantships available. Support available to part-time students. Financial award application deadline: 7/1; financial award applicants required to submit FAFSA. In 2019, 138 master's, 25 doctorates, 14 other advanced degrees awarded. *Program availability:* Part-time. *Application deadline:* For fall admission, 2/15 for domestic students. Applications are processed on a rolling basis. *Application fee:* $75. Electronic applications accepted. *Application Contact:* Heidi Zornes-Foster, Senior Graduate Admissions Counselor, 202-650-5436, Fax: 202-651-5295, E-mail: graduate.school@gallaudet.edu. *Dean, Graduate School and Continuing Studies*, Dr. Gaurav Mathur, 202-250-2380, Fax: 202-651-5027, E-mail: gaurav.mathur@gallaudet.edu.

## GANNON UNIVERSITY, Erie, PA 16541-0001

**General Information** Independent-religious, coed, university. *Graduate housing:* Rooms and/or apartments available on a first-come, first-served basis to single and married students. *Research affiliation:* GE Global Research (nanotechnology), LifeLink Technologies (postural stability of flooring), Erie Insurance, Precision Rehabilitation Manufacturing (software development), AirBorn (PPS software enhancer).

**GRADUATE UNITS**

**School of Graduate Studies** *Program availability:* Part-time, evening/weekend, 100% online, blended/hybrid learning. Electronic applications accepted.

***College of Engineering and Business*** *Program availability:* Part-time, evening/weekend, 100% online, blended/hybrid learning. Electronic applications accepted.

***College of Humanities, Education, and Social Sciences*** *Program availability:* Part-time, evening/weekend, 100% online, blended/hybrid learning. Electronic applications accepted.

***Morosky College of Health Professions and Sciences*** *Program availability:* Part-time, evening/weekend, 100% online. Electronic applications accepted.

## GARDNER-WEBB UNIVERSITY, Boiling Springs, NC 28017

**General Information** Independent-religious, coed, university. *Enrollment:* 3,550 graduate, professional, and undergraduate students; 310 full-time matriculated graduate/professional students (189 women), 1,212 part-time matriculated graduate/professional students (890 women). *Enrollment by degree level:* 1,037 master's, 446 doctoral, 39 other advanced degrees. *Graduate faculty:* 69 full-time (38 women), 67 part-time/adjunct (44 women). *Graduate housing:* Room and/or apartments available on a first-come, first-served basis to single students; on-campus housing not available to married students. Typical cost: $2630 per year ($5195 including board). Room and board charges vary according to board plan and housing facility selected. *Student services:* Campus employment opportunities, campus safety program, career counseling, exercise/wellness program, free psychological counseling, international student services, low-cost health insurance, services for students with disabilities, teacher training, writing training. *Library facilities:* Dover Memorial Library plus 1 other.

**Computer facilities:** Computer purchase and lease plans are available. 121 computers available on campus for general student use. A campuswide network can be accessed. Online class registration, 1 are available.
Website: http://www.gardner-webb.edu/

**General Application Contact:** Office of Graduate Admissions, 877-498-4723, Fax: 704-406-3895, E-mail: gradinfo@gardner-webb.edu.

**GRADUATE UNITS**

**Graduate School** Students: 310 full-time (189 women), 1,212 part-time (890 women); includes 550 minority (476 Black or African American, non-Hispanic/Latino; 8 American Indian or Alaska Native, non-Hispanic/Latino; 19 Asian, non-Hispanic/Latino; 36 Hispanic/Latino; 11 Two or more races, non-Hispanic/Latino), 3 international. Average age 27. 1,420 applicants, 56% accepted, 127 enrolled. *Faculty:* 70 full-time (38 women), 66 part-time/adjunct (44 women). Expenses: Contact institution. *Financial support:* Unspecified assistantships available. In 2019, 341 master's, 102 doctorates awarded. *Program availability:* Part-time, evening/weekend, 100% online, blended/hybrid learning. *Application deadline:* Applications are processed on a rolling basis. Electronic applications accepted. *Application Contact:* Michael Utsman, Office of Graduate Admissions, 704-406-4490, Fax: 704-406-3972, E-mail: gradinfo@gardner-webb.edu. *Dean*, Dr. Sydney Brown, 704-406-3019, E-mail: gradschool@gardner-webb.edu.

**Graduate School of Business** *Program availability:* Part-time, evening/weekend, online learning. Electronic applications accepted.

***School of Education*** *Program availability:* Part-time, evening/weekend. Electronic applications accepted.

***School of Nursing*** *Program availability:* Part-time, online learning.

***School of Psychology*** *Program availability:* Part-time, evening/weekend. Electronic applications accepted.

**School of Divinity** *Program availability:* Part-time. Electronic applications accepted.

## GARRETT-EVANGELICAL THEOLOGICAL SEMINARY, Evanston, IL 60201-3298

**General Information** Independent-religious, coed, graduate-only institution. *Graduate housing:* Rooms and/or apartments guaranteed to single students and available to married students. Housing application deadline: 4/1.

**GRADUATE UNITS**

**Graduate and Professional Programs** *Program availability:* Part-time. Electronic applications accepted.

## GATEWAY SEMINARY, Ontario, CA 91761-8642

**General Information** Independent-religious, coed, graduate-only institution. *Graduate housing:* Rooms and/or apartments available on a first-come, first-served basis to single and married students. Housing application deadline: 6/15.

**GRADUATE UNITS**

**Graduate and Professional Programs** *Program availability:* Part-time, evening/weekend. Electronic applications accepted.

## GEISINGER COMMONWEALTH SCHOOL OF MEDICINE, Scranton, PA 18509

**General Information** Independent, coed, graduate-only institution.

**GRADUATE UNITS**

**Graduate Programs in Medicine** *Program availability:* Part-time, evening/weekend. Electronic applications accepted.

**Professional Program in Medicine**

## THE GENERAL THEOLOGICAL SEMINARY, New York, NY 10011-4977

**General Information** Independent-religious, coed, graduate-only institution. *Graduate housing:* Rooms and/or apartments available to single and married students. Housing application deadline: 6/1.

**GRADUATE UNITS**

**Graduate and Professional Programs** *Program availability:* Part-time, evening/weekend.

## GENEVA COLLEGE, Beaver Falls, PA 15010-3599

**General Information** Independent-religious, coed, comprehensive institution. *Enrollment:* 1,432 graduate, professional, and undergraduate students; 143 full-time matriculated graduate/professional students (88 women), 38 part-time matriculated graduate/professional students (24 women). *Enrollment by degree level:* 181 master's. *Graduate faculty:* 12 full-time (3 women), 24 part-time/adjunct (12 women). *Tuition:* Full-time $27,324; part-time $662 per credit. *Required fees:* $200 per term. Tuition and fees vary according to course load and program. *Graduate housing:* On-campus housing not available. *Student services:* Campus employment opportunities, campus safety program, career counseling, free psychological counseling, international student services, low-cost health insurance, multicultural affairs office, services for students with disabilities, teacher training. *Library facilities:* McCartney Library plus 3 others. *Collection:* Books: 140,157 (physical), 12,739 (digital/electronic); Serial titles: 30,449 (physical); Databases: 54. Weekly public service hours: 84. *Research affiliation:* INOVA Fairfax Hospital (cardiovascular science).

**Computer facilities:** 150 computers available on campus for general student use. A campuswide network can be accessed. Online class registration is available.
Website: http://www.geneva.edu/

**General Application Contact:** Information Contact, 724-846-5100.

**GRADUATE UNITS**

**Master of Arts in Counseling Program** Students: 26 full-time (20 women), 22 part-time (17 women); includes 11 minority (9 Black or African American, non-Hispanic/Latino; 1 Asian, non-Hispanic/Latino; 1 Two or more races, non-Hispanic/Latino), 1 international. Average age 33. 24 applicants, 63% accepted, 14 enrolled. *Faculty:* 4 full-time (1 woman), 5 part-time/adjunct (2 women). Expenses: Contact institution. *Financial support:* Research assistantships, teaching assistantships, career-related internships or fieldwork, and unspecified assistantships available. Financial award application deadline: 8/1; financial award applicants required to submit FAFSA. In 2019, 34 master's awarded. *Program availability:* Part-time, evening/weekend, online only, 100% online, blended/hybrid learning. *Application deadline:* For fall admission, 9/1 for domestic students; for spring admission, 1/10 for domestic students. Applications are processed on a rolling basis. Electronic applications accepted. *Application Contact:* Marina Frazier, Graduate Program Manager, 724-847-6697, E-mail: counseling@geneva.edu. *Program Director,* Dr. Shannan Shiderly, 724-847-6649, Fax: 724-847-6101, E-mail: slshider@geneva.edu.

**Master of Arts in Higher Education Program** Students: 34 full-time (21 women), 3 part-time (2 women); includes 4 minority (1 Black or African American, non-Hispanic/Latino; 1 Asian, non-Hispanic/Latino; 1 Hispanic/Latino; 1 Two or more races, non-Hispanic/Latino), 2 international. Average age 25. 34 applicants, 62% accepted, 15 enrolled. *Faculty:* 2 full-time (0 women), 7 part-time/adjunct (4 women). Expenses: Contact institution. *Financial support:* Unspecified assistantships available. Financial award application deadline: 8/1; financial award applicants required to submit FAFSA. In 2019, 18 master's awarded. *Program availability:* Part-time, evening/weekend, blended/hybrid learning. *Application deadline:* Applications are processed on a rolling basis. Electronic applications accepted. *Application Contact:* Allison Davis, Assistant Director, 724-847-6510, Fax: 724-847-6696, E-mail: hed@geneva.edu. *Program Director,* Dr. Keith Martel, 724-847-6884, Fax: 724-847-6107, E-mail: hed@geneva.edu.

**Master of Education in Curriculum and Instruction** Students: 1 (woman) full-time, all international. Average age 25. 4 applicants, 50% accepted, 1 enrolled. *Faculty:* 3 part-time/adjunct (all women). Expenses: Contact institution. *Program availability:* Part-time, evening/weekend. *Application deadline:* Applications are processed on a rolling basis. Electronic applications accepted. *Application Contact:* Information Contact, 724-846-5100.

**Master of Education with School Counseling Certification**

**Masters Program in Cybersecurity** Students: 4 full-time (0 women), 5 part-time (0 women). Average age 37. 8 applicants, 38% accepted, 1 enrolled. *Faculty:* 1 full-time (0 women). Expenses: Contact institution. *Program availability:* Part-time, evening/weekend, blended/hybrid learning. *Application deadline:* For fall admission, 9/1 for domestic students; for spring admission, 1/10 for domestic students. Applications are processed on a rolling basis. Electronic applications accepted. *Application Contact:* Marina Frazier, Assistant to Counseling and Cybersecurity Programs, 724-847-6697, E-mail: msfrazie@geneva.edu. *Department Chair - Computer Science and Cybersecurity,* Dr. Gordon P. Richards, 724-8476718, E-mail: grichards@geneva.edu.

**Program in Business Administration** Students: 25 full-time (12 women), 7 part-time (5 women); includes 8 minority (3 Black or African American, non-Hispanic/Latino; 1 American Indian or Alaska Native, non-Hispanic/Latino; 1 Asian, non-Hispanic/Latino; 2 Hispanic/Latino; 1 Two or more races, non-Hispanic/Latino), 1 international. Average age 35. 18 applicants, 39% accepted, 3 enrolled. *Faculty:* 6 full-time (2 women), 4 part-time/adjunct (0 women). Expenses: Contact institution. *Financial support:* Scholarships/grants available. Financial award application deadline: 8/1; financial award applicants required to submit FAFSA. In 2019, 17 master's awarded. *Program availability:* Part-time, evening/weekend, 100% online, blended/hybrid learning. *Application deadline:* For fall admission, 3/1 priority date for domestic students; for spring admission, 11/1 priority date for domestic students. Applications are processed on a rolling basis. Electronic applications accepted. *Application Contact:* Dr. Christen Adels, Director of the MBA Program, 724-847-6658, E-mail: csadels@geneva.edu. *Director of the MBA Program,* Dr. Christen Adels, 724-847-6658, E-mail: csadels@geneva.edu.

**Program in Leadership Studies** Students: 13 full-time (11 women), 2 part-time (both women); includes 7 minority (5 Black or African American, non-Hispanic/Latino; 2 Two or more races, non-Hispanic/Latino). Average age 46. 14 applicants, 57% accepted, 2 enrolled. *Faculty:* 4 part-time/adjunct (3 women). Expenses: Contact institution. *Financial support:* Scholarships/grants available. Financial award application deadline: 8/1; financial award applicants required to submit FAFSA. In 2019, 16 master's awarded. *Program availability:* Part-time, evening/weekend, online only, 100% online. *Application deadline:* For fall admission, 9/21 for domestic students; for spring admission, 2/23 for domestic students; for summer admission, 7/22 for domestic students. Applications are processed on a rolling basis. Electronic applications accepted. *Application Contact:* Graduate Enrollment Representative, 800-576-3111, Fax: 724-847-6839, E-mail: msls@geneva.edu. *Dean of Graduate, Adult and Online Programs,* John D. Gallo, 800-576-3111, Fax: 724-847-6839, E-mail: msls@geneva.edu.

## GEORGE FOX UNIVERSITY, Newberg, OR 97132-2697

**General Information** Independent-religious, coed, university. *Enrollment:* 3,899 graduate, professional, and undergraduate students; 652 full-time matriculated graduate/professional students (451 women), 761 part-time matriculated graduate/professional students (470 women). *Enrollment by degree level:* 707 master's, 503 doctoral, 203 other advanced degrees. *Graduate faculty:* 58 full-time (25 women), 79 part-time/adjunct (39 women). *Graduate housing:* On-campus housing not available. *Student services:* Campus employment opportunities, career counseling, international student services, low-cost health insurance, services for students with disabilities, writing training. *Library facilities:* Murdock Learning Resource Center plus 1 other. *Collection:* Weekly public service hours: 93; study areas open 24 hours, 5–7 days a week; students can reserve study rooms.

**Computer facilities:** A campuswide network can be accessed from student residence rooms and from off campus. Online class registration, online acceptance of financial aid are available.
Website: http://www.georgefox.edu/

**General Application Contact:** John Regier, Director for Graduate Admissions, E-mail: admissions@georgefox.edu.

**GRADUATE UNITS**

**College of Business** *Program availability:* Part-time, evening/weekend, online learning. Electronic applications accepted.

**College of Education**

**Portland Seminary** *Program availability:* Part-time, evening/weekend, online learning. Electronic applications accepted.

**Program in Clinical Psychology** Electronic applications accepted.

**Program in Physical Therapy** Electronic applications accepted.

**School of Social Work**

## GEORGE MASON UNIVERSITY, Fairfax, VA 22030

**General Information** State-supported, coed, university. CGS member. *Graduate housing:* Room and/or apartments available on a first-come, first-served basis to single students; on-campus housing not available to married students. Housing application deadline: 5/1. *Research affiliation:* Science Applications International Corporation (science and technology), Lockheed Martin Corporation (science and technology), Inova Health System (health care and medical research), CIT Center for Innovative Technology (nonprofit technology company), Alion Science and Technology Corporation (science and technology research), Northrop Grumman Corporation (high-tech communication technology).

**GRADUATE UNITS**

**Antonin Scalia Law School** Students: 425 full-time (214 women), 116 part-time (49 women); includes 102 minority (8 Black or African American, non-Hispanic/Latino; 1 American Indian or Alaska Native, non-Hispanic/Latino; 32 Asian, non-Hispanic/Latino; 38 Hispanic/Latino; 23 Two or more races, non-Hispanic/Latino), 4 international. Average age 29. 2,964 applicants, 21% accepted, 139 enrolled. *Faculty:* 58 full-time (14 women), 157 part-time/adjunct (41 women). Expenses: Contact institution. *Financial support:* In 2019–20, 451 students received support, including 1 fellowship with full tuition reimbursement available; research assistantships, teaching assistantships, career-related internships or fieldwork, scholarships/grants, and tuition waivers (full and partial) also available. Support available to part-time students. Financial award applicants required to submit FAFSA. In 2019, 165 doctorates awarded. *Program availability:* Part-time, evening/weekend. *Application deadline:* For fall admission, 6/15 for domestic and international students. Applications are processed on a rolling basis. Electronic applications accepted. *Application Contact:* Sabrina A. Huffman, Director of Admissions, 703-993-8010, Fax: 703-993-8088, E-mail: lawadmit@gmu.edu. *Dean,* Henry N. Butler, 703-993-8644, Fax: 703-993-8088.

**College of Education and Human Development** *Program availability:* Part-time, evening/weekend, 100% online, blended/hybrid learning. Electronic applications accepted.

**College of Health and Human Services** *Program availability:* Part-time, evening/weekend, 100% online, blended/hybrid learning. Electronic applications accepted.

***School of Nursing*** *Program availability:* Part-time, evening/weekend, blended/hybrid learning. Electronic applications accepted.

**College of Humanities and Social Sciences** *Program availability:* Part-time, evening/weekend. Electronic applications accepted.

**College of Science** *Program availability:* Part-time, evening/weekend, 100% online. Electronic applications accepted.

***School of Systems Biology*** Electronic applications accepted.

**College of Visual and Performing Arts** *Program availability:* Part-time, evening/weekend. Electronic applications accepted.

***School of Music*** Electronic applications accepted.

**Schar School of Policy and Government** *Program availability:* Part-time, evening/weekend, 100% online. Electronic applications accepted.

**School for Conflict Analysis and Resolution** *Program availability:* Part-time, evening/weekend, blended/hybrid learning. Electronic applications accepted.

**School of Business** *Program availability:* Part-time, evening/weekend, 100% online. Electronic applications accepted.

**Volgenau School of Engineering** *Program availability:* Part-time, evening/weekend, 100% online. Electronic applications accepted.

## GEORGETOWN COLLEGE, Georgetown, KY 40324-1696

**General Information** Independent-religious, coed, comprehensive institution. *Graduate housing:* On-campus housing not available.

**GRADUATE UNITS**

**Department of Education** *Program availability:* Part-time.

## GEORGETOWN UNIVERSITY, Washington, DC 20057

**General Information** Independent-religious, coed, university. CGS member. *Graduate housing:* On-campus housing not available.

**GRADUATE UNITS**

**Graduate School of Arts and Sciences**

***McDonough School of Business***

***School of Continuing Studies***

***School of Nursing and Health Studies***

***Walsh School of Foreign Service***

**Law Center** *Program availability:* Part-time, evening/weekend.

**Master of Arts in Learning and Design Program** *Program availability:* Part-time, evening/weekend. Electronic applications accepted.

**McCourt School of Public Policy** Students: 243 full-time (148 women), 25 part-time (16 women); includes 65 minority (24 Black or African American, non-Hispanic/Latino; 16 Asian, non-Hispanic/Latino; 15 Hispanic/Latino; 10 Two or more races, non-Hispanic/Latino), 78 international. 1,353 applicants, 78% accepted, 268 enrolled. *Faculty:* 35 full-time (14 women), 35 part-time/adjunct (16 women). Expenses: Contact institution. *Financial support:* In 2019–20, 230 students received support, including 5 fellowships with full tuition reimbursements available (averaging $10,000 per year), 40 research assistantships, 60 teaching assistantships; career-related internships or fieldwork, scholarships/grants, and unspecified assistantships also available. Support available to part-time students. Financial award application deadline: 1/15; financial award applicants required to submit FAFSA. *Program availability:* Part-time. *Application deadline:* For fall admission, 1/15 priority date for domestic and international students; for summer admission, 1/15 priority date for domestic students, 1/17 priority date for international students. *Application fee:* $90. Electronic applications accepted. *Application Contact:* Julie Ito, Director of Admissions, 202-687-0678, E-mail: mccourtadmissions@georgetown.edu. *Dean, McCourt School of Public Policy,* Dr. Maria Cancian, 202-687-6163, E-mail: mcancian@georgetown.edu.

**School of Medicine**

## THE GEORGE WASHINGTON UNIVERSITY, Washington, DC 20052

**General Information** Independent, coed, university. CGS member. *Graduate housing:* Room and/or apartments available on a first-come, first-served basis to single students; on-campus housing not available to married students. *Research affiliation:* Goddard Space Flight Center (radar modeling analysis, space systems technologies), Library of Congress, Smithsonian Institution, National Institutes of Health (biostatistics), NASA Langley Research Center (aeroacoustics, aeronautics, astronautics), Children's Hospital National Medical Center.

**GRADUATE UNITS**

**College of Professional Studies**

***Graduate School of Political Management*** Electronic applications accepted.

**Columbian College of Arts and Sciences** *Program availability:* Part-time, evening/weekend. Electronic applications accepted.

***Institute for Biomedical Sciences*** *Program availability:* Part-time, evening/weekend. Electronic applications accepted.

***School of Media and Public Affairs*** Electronic applications accepted.

***Trachtenberg School of Public Policy and Public Administration*** Students: 184 full-time (104 women), 235 part-time (150 women); includes 127 minority (50 Black or African American, non-Hispanic/Latino; 2 American Indian or Alaska Native, non-Hispanic/Latino; 22 Asian, non-Hispanic/Latino; 42 Hispanic/Latino; 11 Two or more races, non-Hispanic/Latino), 45 international. Average age 26. 1,015 applicants, 63% accepted, 164 enrolled. *Faculty:* 13 full-time (7 women), 20 part-time/adjunct (8 women). Expenses: Contact institution. *Financial support:* In 2019–20, 57 students received support. Fellowships, research assistantships, teaching assistantships, Federal Work-Study, scholarships/grants, health care benefits, and unspecified assistantships available. Support available to part-time students. Financial award application deadline: 1/15; financial award applicants required to submit FAFSA. In 2019, 135 master's, 16 doctorates awarded. *Program availability:* Part-time, evening/weekend, online learning. *Application deadline:* For fall admission, 1/15 priority date for domestic and international students; for spring admission, 10/1 priority date for domestic students, 10/1 for international students. *Application fee:* $80. Electronic applications accepted. *Application Contact:* Lindsey A. Duble-Dice, Director of Graduate Admissions and Recruitment, 202-994-8569, Fax: 202-994-6792, E-mail: ldubledice@gwu.edu. *Director,* Dr. Mary Tschirhart, 202-994-2006, Fax: 202-994-6792, E-mail: marytschirhart@gwu.edu.

**Elliott School of International Affairs** *Program availability:* Part-time. Electronic applications accepted.

**Graduate School of Education and Human Development** *Program availability:* Part-time, evening/weekend, online learning. Electronic applications accepted.

**Law School** *Program availability:* Part-time, evening/weekend.

**Milken Institute School of Public Health** *Program availability:* Part-time, evening/weekend.

**School of Business** *Program availability:* Part-time, evening/weekend, online learning. Electronic applications accepted.

**School of Engineering and Applied Science** *Program availability:* Part-time, evening/weekend.

**School of Medicine and Health Sciences**

**School of Nursing**

## GEORGIA CAMPUS–PHILADELPHIA COLLEGE OF OSTEOPATHIC MEDICINE, Suwanee, GA 30024

**General Information** Independent, coed, graduate-only institution. *Graduate housing:* On-campus housing not available.

**GRADUATE UNITS**

**Doctor of Osteopathic Medicine Program** Electronic applications accepted.

**Doctor of Physical Therapy Program**

**School of Pharmacy** Electronic applications accepted.

## GEORGIA COLLEGE & STATE UNIVERSITY, Milledgeville, GA 31061

**General Information** State-supported, coed, comprehensive institution. *Enrollment:* 7,031 graduate, professional, and undergraduate students; 327 full-time matriculated graduate/professional students (214 women), 822 part-time matriculated graduate/professional students (571 women). *Enrollment by degree level:* 1,021 master's, 37 doctoral, 91 other advanced degrees. *Graduate faculty:* 334 full-time (188 women). Tuition and fees vary according to course load, degree level, campus/location and program. *Graduate housing:* Room and/or apartments available on a first-come, first-served basis to single students; on-campus housing not available to married students. Typical cost: $7222 per year ($13,052 including board). Room and board charges vary according to board plan, campus/location and housing facility selected. Housing application deadline: 5/1. *Student services:* Campus employment opportunities, campus safety program, career counseling, free psychological counseling, grant writing training, international student services, low-cost health insurance, multicultural affairs office, services for students with disabilities, teacher training, writing training. *Library facilities:* Ina Dillard Russell Library plus 1 other. *Collection:* Books: 168,723 (physical), 720,251 (digital/electronic); Serial titles: 4,076 (physical), 170,730 (digital/electronic); Databases: 360. Weekly public service hours: 102; students can reserve study rooms.

**Computer facilities:** 900 computers available on campus for general student use. A campuswide network can be accessed from student residence rooms and from off campus. Online class registration is available.
Website: http://www.gcsu.edu/

**General Application Contact:** Kate Marshall, Graduate Admissions Coordinator, 478-445-1184, Fax: 478-445-1336, E-mail: grad-admit@gcsu.edu.

**GRADUATE UNITS**

**The Graduate School** Students: 327 full-time (214 women), 822 part-time (571 women); includes 351 minority (276 Black or African American, non-Hispanic/Latino; 2 American Indian or Alaska Native, non-Hispanic/Latino; 14 Asian, non-Hispanic/Latino; 45 Hispanic/Latino; 14 Two or more races, non-Hispanic/Latino), 12 international. Average age 33. 463 applicants, 92% accepted, 349 enrolled. Expenses: Contact institution. *Financial support:* In 2019–20, 117 students received support. Unspecified assistantships available. Financial award application deadline: 7/1; financial award applicants required to submit FAFSA. In 2019, 384 master's, 8 doctorates, 89 other advanced degrees awarded. *Program availability:* Part-time, evening/weekend, 100% online, blended/hybrid learning. *Application fee:* $40. Electronic applications accepted. *Application Contact:* Kate Marshall, Graduate Admissions Coordinator, 478-445-1184, Fax: 478-445-1336, E-mail: grad-admit@gcsu.edu. *Associate Provost of Academic Affairs and Director of The Graduate School,* Dr. Holley Roberts, 478-445-3340, Fax: 478-445-5151, E-mail: holley.roberts@gcsu.edu.

***College of Arts and Sciences*** Students: 62 full-time (41 women), 141 part-time (88 women); includes 65 minority (53 Black or African American, non-Hispanic/Latino; 2 Asian, non-Hispanic/Latino; 9 Hispanic/Latino; 1 Two or more races, non-Hispanic/Latino), 3 international. Average age 30. 100 applicants, 86% accepted, 61 enrolled. *Faculty:* 193 full-time (95 women). Expenses: Contact institution. *Financial support:* In 2019–20, 56 students received support. Unspecified assistantships available. Support available to part-time students. Financial award application deadline: 7/1; financial award applicants required to submit FAFSA. In 2019, 50 master's awarded. *Program availability:* Part-time, evening/weekend, 100% online, blended/hybrid learning. *Application deadline:* For fall admission, 7/1 priority date for domestic students, 4/1 priority date for international students; for spring admission, 11/1 priority date for domestic students, 9/1 priority date for international students; for summer admission, 4/1 priority date for domestic students. Applications are processed on a rolling basis. *Application fee:* $40. Electronic applications accepted. *Application Contact:* Kate Marshall, Graduate Admissions Coordinator, 478-445-1184, Fax: 478-445-1336, E-mail: grad-admit@gcsu.edu. *Dean, College of Arts & Sciences,* Dr. Eric Tenbus, 478-445-4441, E-mail: eric.tenbus@gcsu.edu.

***College of Health Sciences*** Students: 71 full-time (49 women), 187 part-time (161 women); includes 83 minority (62 Black or African American, non-Hispanic/Latino; 5 Asian, non-Hispanic/Latino; 12 Hispanic/Latino; 4 Two or more races, non-Hispanic/Latino), 2 international. Average age 35. 83 applicants, 98% accepted, 69 enrolled. *Faculty:* 51 full-time (39 women). Expenses: Contact institution. *Financial support:* In 2019–20, 28 students received support. Unspecified assistantships available. Financial award applicants required to submit FAFSA. In 2019, 53 master's, 8 doctorates, 10 other advanced degrees awarded. *Program availability:* Part-time, evening/weekend, 100% online, blended/hybrid learning. *Application fee:* $40. Electronic applications accepted. *Application Contact:* Kate Marshall, Graduate Admissions Coordinator, 478-445-1184, Fax: 478-445-1336, E-mail: grad-admit@gcsu.edu. *Dean,* Dr. Sheri noviello, 478-445-4092, Fax: 478-445-1913, E-mail: sheri.noviello@gcsu.edu.

***The John H. Lounsbury College of Education*** Students: 148 full-time (105 women), 344 part-time (265 women); includes 154 minority (132 Black or African American, non-Hispanic/Latino; 2 American Indian or Alaska Native, non-Hispanic/Latino; 1 Asian, non-Hispanic/Latino; 15 Hispanic/Latino; 4 Two or more races, non-Hispanic/Latino). Average age 32. 163 applicants, 84% accepted, 122 enrolled. *Faculty:* 30 full-time (25 women). Expenses: Contact institution. *Financial support:* In 2019–20, 9 students received support. Unspecified assistantships available. Financial award application deadline: 3/1; financial award applicants required to submit FAFSA. In 2019, 163 master's, 79 other advanced degrees awarded. *Program availability:* Evening/weekend, 100% online, blended/hybrid learning. *Application deadline:* Applications are processed on a rolling basis. *Application fee:* $40. Electronic applications accepted. *Application Contact:* Shanda Brand, Graduate Admissions Advisor, 478-445-1383, Fax: 478-445-6582, E-mail: shanda.brand@gcsu.edu. *Dean, College of Education,* Dr. Joseph Peters, 478-445-2518, Fax: 478-445-6582, E-mail: joseph.peters@gcsu.edu.

***The J. Whitney Bunting School of Business*** Students: 45 full-time (19 women), 149 part-time (57 women); includes 49 minority (29 Black or African American, non-Hispanic/Latino; 6 Asian, non-Hispanic/Latino; 9 Hispanic/Latino; 5 Two or more races, non-Hispanic/Latino), 7 international. Average age 32. 127 applicants, 94% accepted, 97 enrolled. *Faculty:* 51 full-time (21 women). Expenses: Contact institution. *Financial support:* In 2019–20, 21 students received support. Unspecified assistantships available. Financial award application deadline: 7/1; financial award applicants required to submit FAFSA. In 2019, 121 master's awarded. *Program availability:* Part-time, evening/weekend, 100% online, blended/hybrid learning, Accounting program is face to face. *Application deadline:* For fall admission, 7/1 priority date for domestic students, 4/1 priority date for international students; for spring admission, 11/1 priority date for domestic students, 8/1 priority date for international students; for summer admission, 4/1 priority date for domestic students. Applications are processed on a rolling basis. *Application fee:* $40. Electronic applications accepted. *Application Contact:* Lynn Hanson, Director of Graduate Programs, 478-445-5115, E-mail: lynn.hanson@gcsu.edu. *Dean, School of Business,* Dr. Dale Young, 478-445-5497, E-mail: dael.young@gcsu.edu.

## GEORGIA INSTITUTE OF TECHNOLOGY, Atlanta, GA 30332-0001

**General Information** State-supported, coed, university. CGS member. *Enrollment:* 36,490 graduate, professional, and undergraduate students; 6,367 full-time matriculated graduate/professional students (2,065 women), 1,306 part-time matriculated graduate/professional students (364 women). *Enrollment by degree level:* 4,125 master's, 3,548 doctoral, 2 other advanced degrees. *Graduate faculty:* 1,018 full-time (223 women), 76 part-time/adjunct (22 women). *International tuition:* $29,140 full-time. *Tuition, area resident:* Full-time $14,064; part-time $586 per credit hour. Tuition, state resident: full-time $14,064; part-time $586 per credit hour. Tuition, nonresident: full-time $29,140; part-time $1215 per credit hour. *Required fees:* $2024; $840 per semester. $2096. Tuition and fees vary according to course load. *Graduate housing:* Rooms and/or apartments available on a first-come, first-served basis to single and married students. Typical cost: $9658 per year ($14,830 including board) for single students; $11,916 per year for married students. Room and board charges vary according to housing facility selected. Housing application deadline: 5/1. *Student services:* Campus employment opportunities, campus safety program, career counseling, child daycare facilities, exercise/wellness program, free psychological counseling, grant writing training, international student services, low-cost health insurance, multicultural affairs office, services for students with disabilities, teacher training, writing training. *Library facilities:* Georgia Institute of Technology Library plus 1 other. *Collection:* Books: 909,730 (physical), 1 million (digital/electronic); Serial titles: 12,999 (physical), 29,621 (digital/electronic); Databases: 336. Weekly public service hours: 168; study areas open 24 hours, 5–7 days a week; students can reserve study rooms. *Research affiliation:* Oak Ridge National Laboratory (energy, health, environment), Children's Healthcare of Atlanta (pediatric biomedical and device research), Georgia State University (brain imaging), Southeastern Universities Research Association (high-energy physics), Emory University Medical School (biomedical engineering), Zoo Atlanta (environmental design, environmental psychology).

**Computer facilities:** 2,500 computers available on campus for general student use. A campuswide network can be accessed. Online class registration, access to a virtual lab environment from a personal device or GT computer are available.
Website: http://www.gatech.edu/

**General Application Contact:** Marla Bruner, Director of Graduate Studies, 404-894-1610, Fax: 404-894-1609, E-mail: gradinfo@mail.gatech.edu.

**GRADUATE UNITS**

**Graduate Studies** Students: 6,367 full-time (2,065 women), 1,308 part-time (365 women); includes 1,630 minority (306 Black or African American, non-Hispanic/Latino; 4 American Indian or Alaska Native, non-Hispanic/Latino; 796 Asian, non-Hispanic/Latino; 359 Hispanic/Latino; 1 Native Hawaiian or other Pacific Islander, non-Hispanic/Latino; 164 Two or more races, non-Hispanic/Latino), 3,458 international. Average age 27. 19,209 applicants, 29% accepted, 2,496 enrolled. *Faculty:* 1,018 full-time (223 women), 76 part-time/adjunct (22 women). Expenses: Contact institution. *Financial support:* Fellowships, research assistantships, teaching assistantships, career-related internships or fieldwork, Federal Work-Study, institutionally sponsored loans, traineeships, tuition waivers (full and partial), and unspecified assistantships available. Support available to part-time students. Financial award application deadline: 7/1; financial award applicants required to submit FAFSA. *Program availability:* Part-time, evening/weekend, 100% online. *Application deadline:* Applications are processed on a rolling basis. *Application fee:* $75 ($85 for international students). Electronic applications accepted. *Application Contact:* Marla S. Bruner, Director, Graduate Studies, 404-894-1610, E-mail: gradinfo@gatech.edu. *Director, Graduate Studies,* Marla S. Bruner, 404-894-1610, E-mail: gradinfo@gatech.edu.

***College of Computing*** Students: 204 full-time (64 women), 13 part-time (2 women); includes 59 minority (5 Black or African American, non-Hispanic/Latino; 49 Asian, non-Hispanic/Latino; 3 Hispanic/Latino; 2 Two or more races, non-Hispanic/Latino), 124 international. Average age 24. 377 applicants, 97% accepted, 208 enrolled. *Faculty:* 6 full-time (1 woman). Expenses: Contact institution. *Financial support:* Fellowships, research assistantships, teaching assistantships, career-related internships or fieldwork, Federal Work-Study, institutionally sponsored loans, tuition waivers (full and partial), and unspecified assistantships available. Support available to part-time students. Financial award application deadline: 7/1; financial award applicants required to submit FAFSA. In 2019, 308 master's, 45 doctorates awarded. *Program availability:* Part-time, 100% online. *Application fee:* $75 ($85 for international students). Electronic applications accepted. *Application Contact:* Marla Bruner, Director of Graduate Studies, 404-894-1610, E-mail: gradinfo@mail.gatech.edu. *Dean,* Charles Isbell, 404-894-3152, Fax: 404-894-9846, E-mail: isbell@cc.gatech.edu.

***College of Design*** Electronic applications accepted.

***College of Engineering*** Students: 93 part-time (24 women); includes 26 minority (5 Black or African American, non-Hispanic/Latino; 3 Asian, non-Hispanic/Latino; 15 Hispanic/Latino; 3 Two or more races, non-Hispanic/Latino), 6 international. Average age 35. 74 applicants, 82% accepted, 49 enrolled. *Faculty:* 3 full-time (1 woman). Expenses: Contact institution. *Financial support:* Fellowships, research assistantships, teaching assistantships, career-related internships or fieldwork, Federal Work-Study, institutionally sponsored loans, tuition waivers (full and partial), and unspecified assistantships available. Support available to part-time students. Financial award application deadline: 7/1; financial award applicants required to submit FAFSA. In 2019, 37 master's awarded. *Program availability:* Part-time, 100% online. *Application deadline:* Applications are processed on a rolling basis. *Application fee:* $75 ($85 for international students). Electronic applications accepted. *Application Contact:* Marla Bruner, Director of Graduate Studies, 404-894-1610, Fax: 404-894-1609, E-mail: gradinfo@mail.gatech.edu. *Dean,* Steven McLaughlin, 404-894-3350, Fax: 404-894-0168, E-mail: steve.mclaughlin@coe.gatech.edu.

***College of Sciences*** *Faculty:* 3 full-time (1 woman). Expenses: Contact institution. *Financial support:* Fellowships, research assistantships, teaching assistantships, career-related internships or fieldwork, Federal Work-Study, institutionally sponsored loans, tuition waivers (full and partial), and unspecified assistantships available. Support available to part-time students. Financial award application deadline: 7/1; financial award applicants required to submit FAFSA. *Program availability:* Part-time. *Application deadline:* Applications are processed on a rolling basis. *Application fee:* $75 ($85 for international students). Electronic applications accepted. *Application Contact:* Marla Bruner, Director of Graduate Studies, 404-894-1610, Fax: 404-894-1609, E-mail: gradinfo@mail.gatech.edu. *Dean,* Susan Lozier, 404-894-3300, Fax: 404-894-7466, E-mail: susan.lozier@gatech.edu.

***Ivan Allen College of Liberal Arts*** Students: 15 full-time (11 women), 1 part-time; includes 8 minority (1 Black or African American, non-Hispanic/Latino; 3 Asian, non-Hispanic/Latino; 2 Hispanic/Latino; 2 Two or more races, non-Hispanic/Latino), 2 international. Average age 26. 26 applicants, 73% accepted, 16 enrolled. *Faculty:* 2 full-time (1 woman). Expenses: Contact institution. *Financial support:* Fellowships, research assistantships, teaching assistantships, career-related internships or fieldwork, Federal Work-Study, institutionally sponsored loans, tuition waivers (full and partial), and unspecified assistantships available. Support available to part-time students. Financial award application deadline: 7/1; financial award applicants required to submit FAFSA. *Program availability:* Part-time. *Application deadline:* Applications are processed on a rolling basis. *Application fee:* $75 ($85 for international students). Electronic applications accepted. *Application Contact:* Marla Bruner, Director of Graduate Studies, 404-894-1610, Fax: 404-894-1609, E-mail: gradinfo@mail.gatech.edu. *Dean,* Kaye Husbands Fealing, 404-894-2601, Fax: 404-894-8573, E-mail: dean@iac.gatech.edu.

***Scheller College of Business*** Students: 585 full-time (218 women), 250 part-time (88 women); includes 285 minority (89 Black or African American, non-Hispanic/Latino; 1 American Indian or Alaska Native, non-Hispanic/Latino; 121 Asian, non-Hispanic/Latino; 57 Hispanic/Latino; 17 Two or more races, non-Hispanic/Latino), 126 international. Average age 32. 1,707 applicants, 32% accepted, 322 enrolled. *Faculty:* 76 full-time (17 women), 4 part-time/adjunct (1 woman). Expenses: Contact institution. *Financial support:* In 2019–20, 1 fellowship, 6 teaching assistantships were awarded; research assistantships, career-related internships or fieldwork, Federal Work-Study, institutionally sponsored loans, tuition waivers (full and partial), and unspecified assistantships also available. Support available to part-time students. Financial award application deadline: 7/1; financial award applicants required to submit FAFSA. In 2019, 380 master's, 9 doctorates awarded. *Program availability:* Part-time, evening/weekend. *Application deadline:* For fall admission, 3/15 for domestic students, 1/15 for international students. Applications are processed on a rolling basis. *Application fee:* $75 ($85 for international students). Electronic applications accepted. *Application Contact:* Marla Bruner, Director of Graduate Studies, 404-894-1610, Fax: 404-894-1609, E-mail: gradinfo@mail.gatech.edu. *Dean,* Maryam Alavi, 404-894.2600, Fax: 404-894.6030, E-mail: maryam.alavi@scheller.gatech.edu.

## GEORGIAN COURT UNIVERSITY, Lakewood, NJ 08701-2697

**General Information** Independent-religious, coed, comprehensive institution. *Enrollment:* 2,411 graduate, professional, and undergraduate students; 149 full-time matriculated graduate/professional students (122 women), 521 part-time matriculated graduate/professional students (408 women). *Enrollment by degree level:* 670 master's. *Graduate housing:* Room and/or apartments available on a first-come, first-served basis to single students; on-campus housing not available to married students. Typical cost: $1293 per year ($5404 including board). Housing application deadline: 5/1. *Student services:* Campus employment opportunities, campus safety program, career counseling, exercise/wellness program, free psychological counseling, low-cost health insurance, services for students with disabilities, teacher training. *Library facilities:* The Sister Mary Joseph Cunningham Library. *Collection:* Books: 532,946 (physical), 167,764 (digital/electronic); Serial titles: 57,032 (physical), 53,706 (digital/electronic); Databases: 111. Weekly public service hours: 85; students can reserve study rooms.

**Computer facilities:** 228 computers available on campus for general student use. A campuswide network can be accessed. Online class registration is available.
Website: http://www.georgian.edu/

**General Application Contact:** Patrick Givens, Director of Graduate and Professional Studies Admissions, 732-987-2736, Fax: 732-987-2000, E-mail: gps@georgian.edu.

**GRADUATE UNITS**

**School of Arts and Sciences** Students: 90 full-time (80 women), 71 part-time (59 women); includes 26 minority (8 Black or African American, non-Hispanic/Latino; 2 Asian, non-Hispanic/Latino; 14 Hispanic/Latino; 2 Two or more races, non-Hispanic/Latino), 1 international. Average age 32. 138 applicants, 58% accepted, 57 enrolled. *Faculty:* 19 full-time (11 women), 7 part-time/adjunct (3 women). Expenses: Contact institution. *Financial support:* Scholarships/grants, health care benefits, and unspecified assistantships available. Financial award application deadline: 4/15; financial award applicants required to submit FAFSA. In 2019, 68 master's, 19 other advanced degrees awarded. *Program availability:* Part-time, evening/weekend. *Application deadline:* For fall admission, 8/15 for domestic students, 5/1 for international students; for spring admission, 1/15 for domestic students, 10/1 for international students. Applications are processed on a rolling basis. *Application fee:* $40. Electronic applications accepted. *Application Contact:* Dr. Mary Chinery, Dean, 732-987-2493, Fax: 732-987-2007, E-mail: mchinery@georgian.edu. *Dean,* Dr. Mary Chinery, 732-987-2493, Fax: 732-987-2007, E-mail: mchinery@georgian.edu.

**School of Business and Digital Media** Students: 22 full-time (9 women), 21 part-time (14 women); includes 13 minority (5 Black or African American, non-Hispanic/Latino; 1 Asian, non-Hispanic/Latino; 6 Hispanic/Latino; 1 Native Hawaiian or other Pacific Islander, non-Hispanic/Latino), 1 international. Average age 28. 37 applicants, 57% accepted, 15 enrolled. *Faculty:* 7 full-time (3 women), 5 part-time/adjunct (2 women). Expenses: Contact institution. *Financial support:* Scholarships/grants, health care benefits, and unspecified assistantships available. Financial award application deadline: 4/15; financial award applicants required to submit FAFSA. In 2019, 23 master's, 3 other advanced degrees awarded. *Program availability:* Part-time, evening/weekend. *Application deadline:* For fall admission, 8/15 for domestic students, 5/1 for international students; for spring admission, 1/15 for domestic students, 10/1 for international students. Applications are processed on a rolling basis. *Application fee:* $40. Electronic applications accepted. *Application Contact:* Dr. Jennifer Edmonds, Dean School of Business and Digital Media, 732-987-2662, Fax: 732-987-2024, E-mail: jedmonds@georgian.edu. *Dean School of Business and Digital Media,* Dr. Jennifer Edmonds, 732-987-2662, Fax: 732-987-2024, E-mail: jedmonds@georgian.edu.

**School of Education** Students: 33 full-time (26 women), 372 part-time (299 women); includes 84 minority (34 Black or African American, non-Hispanic/Latino; 1 American Indian or Alaska Native, non-Hispanic/Latino; 11 Asian, non-Hispanic/Latino; 36 Hispanic/Latino; 2 Two or more races, non-Hispanic/Latino). Average age 36. 320 applicants, 67% accepted, 153 enrolled. *Faculty:* 8 full-time (5 women), 32 part-time/adjunct (20 women). Expenses: Contact institution. *Financial support:* Scholarships/grants, health care benefits, and unspecified assistantships available. Financial award application deadline: 4/15; financial award applicants required to submit FAFSA. In 2019, 152 master's, 4 other advanced degrees awarded. *Program availability:* Part-time, evening/weekend. *Application deadline:* For fall admission, 8/15 priority date for domestic students, 5/1 for international students; for spring admission, 1/15 priority date for domestic students, 10/1 for international students. Applications are processed on a rolling basis. *Application fee:* $40. Electronic applications accepted. *Application Contact:* Dr. Amuhelang Magaya, Dean of School of Education, 732-987-2786, Fax: 732-987-2025, E-mail: amagaya@georgian.edu. *Dean of School of Education,* Dr. Amuhelang Magaya, 732-987-2786, Fax: 732-987-2025, E-mail: amagaya@georgian.edu.

## GEORGIA SOUTHERN UNIVERSITY, Statesboro, GA 30458

**General Information** State-supported, coed, university. CGS member. *Enrollment:* 26,054 graduate, professional, and undergraduate students; 1,353 full-time matriculated graduate/professional students (945 women), 1,971 part-time matriculated graduate/professional students (1,437 women). *Enrollment by degree level:* 2,300 master's, 657 doctoral, 367 other advanced degrees. *Graduate faculty:* 934 full-time (408 women), 52 part-time/adjunct (28 women). *International tuition:* $19,890 full-time. *Tuition, area resident:* Full-time $4986; part-time $277 per credit hour. Tuition, nonresident: full-time $19,890; part-time $1105 per credit hour. *Required fees:* $2114; $1057 per semester. $1057 per semester. Tuition and fees vary according to course load, campus/location and program. *Graduate housing:* Room and/or apartments available on a first-come, first-served basis to single students; on-campus housing not available to married students. Housing application deadline: 5/1. *Student services:* Campus employment opportunities, campus safety program, career counseling, exercise/wellness program, free psychological counseling, grant writing training, international student services, low-cost health insurance, multicultural affairs office, services for students with disabilities, teacher training, writing training. *Library facilities:*

Henderson Library. *Collection:* Books: 649,104 (physical), 656,518 (digital/electronic); Serial titles: 15,006 (physical), 104,711 (digital/electronic); Databases: 325. Weekly public service hours: 143; study areas open 24 hours, 5–7 days a week; students can reserve study rooms. *Research affiliation:* Oak Ridge National Laboratory (physical sciences), Mount Desert Island Biological Laboratory (marine biology), Space Telescope Science Institute (astronomy, physics), St. Catherine's Island Foundation (marine science, life sciences), Skidaway Institute of Oceanography (marine sciences).

**Computer facilities:** Computer purchase and lease plans are available. 3,743 computers available on campus for general student use. A campuswide network can be accessed. Online class registration, online degree audit, online career services, and online healthcare are available.
Website: http://www.georgiasouthern.edu/

**General Application Contact:** Naronda C. Wright, Office of Graduate Admissions, 912-478-5384, Fax: 912-478-0740, E-mail: gradadmissions@georgiasouthern.edu.

**GRADUATE UNITS**

***Jack N. Averitt College of Graduate Studies*** Students: 1,353 full-time (945 women), 1,971 part-time (1,437 women); includes 1,053 minority (755 Black or African American, non-Hispanic/Latino; 4 American Indian or Alaska Native, non-Hispanic/Latino; 61 Asian, non-Hispanic/Latino; 150 Hispanic/Latino; 2 Native Hawaiian or other Pacific Islander, non-Hispanic/Latino; 81 Two or more races, non-Hispanic/Latino), 180 international. Average age 32. 1,861 applicants, 75% accepted, 829 enrolled. *Faculty:* 934 full-time (408 women), 52 part-time/adjunct (28 women). Expenses: Contact institution. *Financial support:* In 2019–20, 884 students received support, including 40 research assistantships with partial tuition reimbursements available (averaging $7,750 per year), 215 teaching assistantships with partial tuition reimbursements available (averaging $7,750 per year); career-related internships or fieldwork, Federal Work-Study, scholarships/grants, traineeships, tuition waivers (partial), unspecified assistantships, and doctoral stipends also available. Support available to part-time students. Financial award application deadline: 4/15; financial award applicants required to submit FAFSA. In 2019, 1,121 master's, 84 doctorates, 99 other advanced degrees awarded. *Program availability:* Part-time, evening/weekend, 100% online, blended/hybrid learning. *Application deadline:* For fall admission, 4/1 priority date for domestic and international students; for spring admission, 10/1 priority date for domestic and international students; for summer admission, 4/1 for domestic students. Applications are processed on a rolling basis. *Application fee:* $50. Electronic applications accepted. *Application Contact:* Naronda C. Wright, Graduate Admissions Specialist, 912-478-5384, Fax: 912-478-0740, E-mail: gradadmissions@georgiasouthern.edu. *Dean, Jack N. Averitt College of Graduate Studies,* Dr. Ashley Walker Colquitt, 912-478-0851, Fax: 912-478-8642, E-mail: awalker@georgiasouthern.edu.

***Allen E. Paulson College of Engineering and Computing*** Students: 77 full-time (11 women), 49 part-time (11 women); includes 32 minority (16 Black or African American, non-Hispanic/Latino; 5 Asian, non-Hispanic/Latino; 9 Hispanic/Latino; 2 Two or more races, non-Hispanic/Latino), 50 international. Average age 28. 156 applicants, 75% accepted, 40 enrolled. *Faculty:* 92 full-time (9 women), 1 part-time/adjunct (0 women). Expenses: Contact institution. *Financial support:* In 2019–20, 84 students received support, including 3 research assistantships with full tuition reimbursements available (averaging $7,750 per year), 4 teaching assistantships with full tuition reimbursements available (averaging $7,750 per year); Federal Work-Study, scholarships/grants, tuition waivers (full), and unspecified assistantships also available. Financial award applicants required to submit FAFSA. In 2019, 53 master's, 1 other advanced degree awarded. *Program availability:* Part-time, blended/hybrid learning. *Application deadline:* For fall admission, 3/1 priority date for domestic students, 6/1 for international students; for spring admission, 10/1 priority date for domestic students, 10/1 for international students. Applications are processed on a rolling basis. *Application fee:* $50. Electronic applications accepted. *Application Contact:* Dr. Mohammad S. Davoud, Dean, 912-478-8046, E-mail: mdavoud@georgiasouthern.edu. *Dean,* Dr. Mohammad S. Davoud, 912-478-8046, E-mail: mdavoud@georgiasouthern.edu.

***College of Arts and Humanities*** Students: 98 full-time (69 women), 68 part-time (46 women); includes 50 minority (27 Black or African American, non-Hispanic/Latino; 1 Asian, non-Hispanic/Latino; 15 Hispanic/Latino; 7 Two or more races, non-Hispanic/Latino), 14 international. Average age 31. 104 applicants, 94% accepted, 63 enrolled. *Faculty:* 204 full-time (88 women), 5 part-time/adjunct (0 women). Expenses: Contact institution. *Financial support:* In 2019–20, 80 students received support, including 72 fellowships with full tuition reimbursements available (averaging $7,750 per year), 10 research assistantships with full tuition reimbursements available (averaging $7,750 per year), 26 teaching assistantships with full tuition reimbursements available (averaging $7,750 per year); career-related internships or fieldwork, Federal Work-Study, scholarships/grants, tuition waivers (full), and unspecified assistantships also available. Support available to part-time students. Financial award application deadline: 4/15; financial award applicants required to submit FAFSA. In 2019, 56 master's awarded. *Program availability:* Part-time. *Application deadline:* For fall admission, 3/1 priority date for domestic and international students; for spring admission, 10/1 priority date for domestic students, 10/1 for international students. Applications are processed on a rolling basis. *Application fee:* $50. Electronic applications accepted. *Dean,* Dr. Curtis Ricker, 912-478-2527, Fax: 912-478-5346, E-mail: cricker@georgiasouthern.edu.

***College of Behavioral and Social Sciences*** Students: 121 full-time (74 women), 38 part-time (22 women); includes 56 minority (34 Black or African American, non-Hispanic/Latino; 4 Asian, non-Hispanic/Latino; 15 Hispanic/Latino; 3 Two or more races, non-Hispanic/Latino), 6 international. Average age 27. 86 applicants, 81% accepted, 55 enrolled. *Faculty:* 109 full-time (61 women), 4 part-time/adjunct (all women). Expenses: Contact institution. *Financial support:* In 2019–20, 92 students received support, including 7 research assistantships with full tuition reimbursements available (averaging $8,000 per year), 7 teaching assistantships with full tuition reimbursements available (averaging $8,000 per year); unspecified assistantships also available. Financial award application deadline: 4/15; financial award applicants required to submit FAFSA. In 2019, 36 master's, 1 other advanced degree awarded. *Program availability:* Part-time. *Application deadline:* For fall admission, 12/15 for domestic students; for spring admission, 11/15 for domestic students. Applications are processed on a rolling basis. *Application fee:* $50. Electronic applications accepted. *Application Contact:* Naronda C. Wright, Graduate Admissions Specialist, 912-478-8626, Fax: 912-478-0740, E-mail: gradadmissions@georgiasouthern.edu. *Dean,* Dr. Ryan Schroeder, 912-478-8641, E-mail: jkraft@georgiasouthern.edu.

***College of Education*** Students: 462 full-time (395 women), 1,246 part-time (1,015 women); includes 517 minority (402 Black or African American, non-Hispanic/Latino; 2 American Indian or Alaska Native, non-Hispanic/Latino; 17 Asian, non-Hispanic/Latino; 62 Hispanic/Latino; 2 Native Hawaiian or other Pacific Islander, non-Hispanic/Latino; 32 Two or more races, non-Hispanic/Latino), 6 international. Average age 33. 563 applicants, 85% accepted, 295 enrolled. *Faculty:* 99 full-time (72 women), 29 part-time/adjunct (15 women). Expenses: Contact institution. *Financial support:* In 2019–20, 159 students received support, including 1 teaching assistantship with full tuition reimbursement available (averaging $7,750 per year); research assistantships with partial tuition reimbursements available, career-related internships or fieldwork, scholarships/grants, and unspecified assistantships also available. Financial award application deadline: 4/15; financial award applicants required to submit FAFSA. In 2019, 446 master's, 24 doctorates, 71 other advanced degrees awarded. *Program availability:* Part-time, evening/weekend, 100% online, blended/hybrid learning. *Application deadline:* For fall admission, 3/1 priority date for domestic and international students; for spring admission, 10/1 priority date for domestic students, 10/1 for international students. Applications are processed on a rolling basis. *Application fee:* $50. Electronic applications accepted. *Application Contact:* Dr. Lydia Cross, Director, Graduate Academic Services Center, 912-478-1447, E-mail: gasc@georgiasouthern.edu. *Dean,* Dr. Thomas Koballa, 912-478-5648, Fax: 912-478-5093, E-mail: tkoballa@georgiasouthern.edu.

***College of Science and Mathematics*** Students: 79 full-time (43 women), 19 part-time (9 women); includes 16 minority (7 Black or African American, non-Hispanic/Latino; 2 American Indian or Alaska Native, non-Hispanic/Latino; 4 Hispanic/Latino; 3 Two or more races, non-Hispanic/Latino), 26 international. Average age 27. 63 applicants, 78% accepted, 39 enrolled. *Faculty:* 180 full-time (62 women), 3 part-time/adjunct (1 woman). Expenses: Contact institution. *Financial support:* In 2019–20, 93 students received support, including 4 fellowships with full tuition reimbursements available (averaging $7,750 per year), 22 research assistantships with full tuition reimbursements available (averaging $7,750 per year), 79 teaching assistantships with full tuition reimbursements available (averaging $7,750 per year); career-related internships or fieldwork, Federal Work-Study, scholarships/grants, tuition waivers (full), and unspecified assistantships also available. Support available to part-time students. Financial award application deadline: 4/15; financial award applicants required to submit FAFSA. In 2019, 48 master's awarded. *Program availability:* Part-time. *Application deadline:* For fall admission, 3/1 priority date for domestic and international students; for spring admission, 10/1 priority date for domestic students, 10/1 for international students. Applications are processed on a rolling basis. *Application fee:* $50. Electronic applications accepted. *Application Contact:* 912-478-5384, E-mail: gradadmissions@georgiasouthern.edu. *Dean,* Dr. Delana Gajdosik-Nivens, 912-478-5132, Fax: 912-478-0836, E-mail: dnivens@georgiasouthern.edu.

***Jiann-Ping Hsu College of Public Health*** Students: 142 full-time (105 women), 88 part-time (62 women); includes 132 minority (100 Black or African American, non-Hispanic/Latino; 10 Asian, non-Hispanic/Latino; 8 Hispanic/Latino; 14 Two or more races, non-Hispanic/Latino), 46 international. Average age 32. 195 applicants, 85% accepted, 59 enrolled. *Faculty:* 42 full-time (22 women), 1 (woman) part-time/adjunct. Expenses: Contact institution. *Financial support:* In 2019–20, 94 students received support, including 53 fellowships with full tuition reimbursements available (averaging $7,750 per year), 3 research assistantships with full tuition reimbursements available (averaging $7,750 per year), 1 teaching assistantship with full tuition reimbursement available (averaging $7,750 per year); scholarships/grants, tuition waivers (full), and unspecified assistantships also available. Financial award application deadline: 6/30; financial award applicants required to submit FAFSA. In 2019, 90 master's, 14 doctorates awarded. *Program availability:* Part-time. *Application deadline:* For fall admission, 1/31 priority date for domestic and international students. Applications are processed on a rolling basis. *Application fee:* $135. Electronic applications accepted. *Application Contact:* Monica H Brister, Academic Services Coordinator, 912-478-2674, Fax: 912-4782479, E-mail: mbrister@georgiasouthern.edu. *Dean,* Dr. Stuart H Tedders, 912-478-2674, Fax: 912-478-5811, E-mail: stedders@georgiasouthern.edu.

***Parker College of Business*** Students: 100 full-time (55 women), 201 part-time (94 women); includes 87 minority (59 Black or African American, non-Hispanic/Latino; 12 Asian, non-Hispanic/Latino; 11 Hispanic/Latino; 5 Two or more races, non-Hispanic/Latino), 23 international. Average age 30. 214 applicants, 92% accepted, 125 enrolled. *Faculty:* 96 full-time (23 women), 1 part-time/adjunct (0 women). Expenses: Contact institution. *Financial support:* In 2019–20, 59 students received support. Research assistantships with partial tuition reimbursements available, teaching assistantships with partial tuition reimbursements available, career-related internships or fieldwork, Federal Work-Study, scholarships/grants, tuition waivers (partial), and unspecified assistantships available. Support available to part-time students. Financial award application deadline: 4/15; financial award applicants required to submit FAFSA. In 2019, 182 master's, 1 doctorate, 6 other advanced degrees awarded. *Program availability:* Part-time, evening/weekend, 100% online. *Application deadline:* For fall admission, 3/1 priority date for domestic and international students; for spring admission, 10/1 priority date for domestic students, 10/1 for international students. Applications are processed on a rolling basis. *Application fee:* $50. Electronic applications accepted. *Dean,* Dr. Allen Amason, 912-478-2622, Fax: 912-478-0292, E-mail: aamason@georgiasouthern.edu.

***Waters College of Health Professions*** Students: 274 full-time (193 women), 262 part-time (178 women); includes 163 minority (110 Black or African American, non-Hispanic/Latino; 12 Asian, non-Hispanic/Latino; 26 Hispanic/Latino; 15 Two or more races, non-Hispanic/Latino), 9 international. Average age 29. 380 applicants, 56% accepted, 153 enrolled. *Faculty:* 99 full-time (63 women), 8 part-time/adjunct (7 women). Expenses: Contact institution. *Financial support:* In 2019–20, 223 students received support, including 24 fellowships with full tuition reimbursements available (averaging $7,750 per year), 9 research assistantships with full tuition reimbursements available (averaging $7,750 per year), 33 teaching assistantships with full tuition reimbursements available (averaging $7,750 per year); career-related internships or fieldwork, Federal Work-Study, scholarships/grants, traineeships, and unspecified assistantships also available. Support available to part-time students. Financial award application deadline: 4/15; financial award applicants required to submit FAFSA. In 2019, 173 master's, 39 doctorates, 19 other advanced degrees awarded. *Program availability:* Part-time, evening/weekend, 100% online, blended/hybrid learning. *Application deadline:* For fall admission, 3/1 priority date for domestic students, 3/1 for international students; for spring admission, 10/1 priority date for domestic students, 10/1 for international students. Applications are processed on a rolling basis. *Application fee:* $50. Electronic applications accepted. *Dean,* Dr. Barry Joyner, 912-478-5322, Fax: 912-478-5349, E-mail: joyner@georgiasouthern.edu.

## GEORGIA SOUTHWESTERN STATE UNIVERSITY, Americus, GA 31709-4693

**General Information** State-supported, coed, comprehensive institution. *Enrollment:* 2,950 graduate, professional, and undergraduate students; 264 full-time matriculated graduate/professional students (240 women), 186 part-time matriculated graduate/professional students (145 women). *Enrollment by degree level:* 293 master's, 157 other advanced degrees. *Graduate faculty:* 42 full-time (24 women), 15 part-time/adjunct (13 women). *Tuition, area resident:* Full-time $3492; part-time $194 per credit hour. Tuition, state resident: full-time $3492; part-time $194 per credit hour. Tuition, nonresident: full-time $13,806; part-time $767 per credit hour. *Required fees:* $1400. Tuition and fees vary according to course load, campus/location and program. *Graduate housing:* Room and/or apartments available on a first-come, first-served basis to single students; on-campus housing not available to married students. Typical cost: $5480 per year ($9650 including board). Room and board charges vary according to board plan and housing facility selected. *Student services:* Campus safety program, exercise/wellness program, low-cost health insurance, services for students with disabilities. *Library facilities:* James Earl Carter Library. *Collection:* Books: 204,602 (physical), 76,482 (digital/electronic); Serial titles: 12,000 (physical), 861 (digital/electronic); Databases: 257. Weekly public service hours: 72; students can reserve study rooms.

**Computer facilities:** A campuswide network can be accessed. Online class registration is available.
Website: http://www.gsw.edu/

**General Application Contact:** Office of Graduate Admissions, 800-338-0082, Fax: 229-931-2983, E-mail: graduateadmissions@gsw.edu.

**GRADUATE UNITS**

**College of Business and Computing** Students: 6 full-time (3 women), 55 part-time (39 women); includes 22 minority (13 Black or African American, non-Hispanic/Latino; 4 Asian, non-Hispanic/Latino; 4 Hispanic/Latino; 1 Two or more races, non-Hispanic/Latino), 1 international. Average age 35. 46 applicants, 48% accepted, 16 enrolled. *Faculty:* 13 full-time (7 women), 2 part-time/adjunct (1 woman). Expenses: Contact institution. *Financial support:* Application deadline: 6/1; applicants required to submit FAFSA. In 2019, 30 master's awarded. *Program availability:* Part-time, online only, 100% online. *Application deadline:* For fall admission, 6/30 for domestic students; for spring admission, 11/30 for domestic students; for summer admission, 4/30 for domestic students. Applications are processed on a rolling basis. *Application fee:* $25. Electronic applications accepted. *Application Contact:* Office of Graduate Admissions, 800-338-0082, Fax: 229-931-2983, E-mail: graduateadmissions@gsw.edu. *Interim Dean*, Dr. Gaynor Cheokas, 229-931-2090.

**College of Education** Students: 236 full-time (222 women), 10 part-time (all women); includes 66 minority (60 Black or African American, non-Hispanic/Latino; 6 Hispanic/Latino), 2 international. Average age 35. *Faculty:* 16 full-time (8 women), 7 part-time/adjunct (all women). Expenses: Contact institution. *Financial support:* Application deadline: 6/1; applicants required to submit FAFSA. In 2019, 101 master's, 105 Ed Ss awarded. *Application deadline:* For summer admission, 4/15 for domestic students. *Application fee:* $25. Electronic applications accepted. *Application Contact:* Office of Graduate Admissions, 800-338-0082, Fax: 229-931-2983, E-mail: graduateadmissions@gsw.edu. *Dean*, Dr. Rachel Abbott, 229-931-2145.

**College of Nursing and Health Sciences** Students: 18 full-time (14 women), 104 part-time (91 women); includes 45 minority (31 Black or African American, non-Hispanic/Latino; 1 American Indian or Alaska Native, non-Hispanic/Latino; 4 Asian, non-Hispanic/Latino; 3 Hispanic/Latino; 6 Two or more races, non-Hispanic/Latino). Average age 36. 96 applicants, 45% accepted, 24 enrolled. *Faculty:* 9 full-time (all women), 5 part-time/adjunct (all women). Expenses: Contact institution. *Financial support:* Application deadline: 6/1; applicants required to submit FAFSA. In 2019, 53 master's awarded. *Program availability:* Part-time, online only, all theory courses are offered online. *Application fee:* $25. Electronic applications accepted. *Application Contact:* Office of Graduate Admissions, 800-338-0082, Fax: 229-931-2983, E-mail: graduateadmissions@gsw.edu. *Dean*, Dr. Sandra Daniel, 229-931-2275.

**Department of Computer Science** Students: 4 full-time (1 woman), 17 part-time (5 women); includes 8 minority (5 Black or African American, non-Hispanic/Latino; 2 Asian, non-Hispanic/Latino; 1 Hispanic/Latino), 7 international. Average age 36. 34 applicants, 38% accepted, 11 enrolled. *Faculty:* 4 full-time (0 women), 1 part-time/adjunct (0 women). Expenses: Contact institution. *Financial support:* Application deadline: 6/1; applicants required to submit FAFSA. In 2019, 4 master's awarded. *Program availability:* Part-time, online only, 100% online. *Application deadline:* For fall admission, 6/30 for domestic students; for spring admission, 11/30 for domestic students; for summer admission, 4/30 for domestic students. Applications are processed on a rolling basis. *Application fee:* $25. Electronic applications accepted. *Application Contact:* Office of Graduate Admissions, 800-338-0082, Fax: 229-931-2983, E-mail: graduateadmissions@gsw.edu.

## GEORGIA STATE UNIVERSITY, Atlanta, GA 30302-3083

**General Information** State-supported, coed, university. CGS member. *Enrollment:* 35,059 graduate, professional, and undergraduate students; 4,945 full-time matriculated graduate/professional students (2,999 women), 1,918 part-time matriculated graduate/professional students (1,242 women). *Enrollment by degree level:* 3,441 master's, 2,525 doctoral, 108 other advanced degrees. *Graduate faculty:* 855 full-time (381 women), 124 part-time/adjunct (64 women). *International tuition:* $22,662 full-time. *Tuition, area resident:* Full-time $7164; part-time $398 per credit hour. Tuition, state resident: full-time $7164; part-time $398 per credit hour. Tuition, nonresident: full-time $22,662; part-time $1259 per credit hour. *Required fees:* $2128; $312 per credit hour. Tuition and fees vary according to course load and program. *Graduate housing:* Rooms and/or apartments available on a first-come, first-served basis to single and married students. Typical cost: $12,634 per year ($16,576 including board) for single students; $12,634 per year ($16,576 including board) for married students. Room and board charges vary according to board plan, campus/location and housing facility selected. *Student services:* Campus safety program, career counseling, child daycare facilities, exercise/wellness program, international student services, services for students with disabilities. *Library facilities:* University Library plus 6 others. *Collection:* Books: 1.9 million (physical), 1.3 million (digital/electronic); Serial titles: 36,191 (physical), 246,459 (digital/electronic). Students can reserve study rooms. *Research affiliation:* Cerro Tololo Interamerican Observatory (astronomy), Research Atlanta, Inc. (policy studies), Oak Ridge National Laboratory (environmental policy), Lowell Observatory (astronomy), Brookhaven National Laboratory (physics), Argonne National Laboratory, Advanced Photon Source (crystallography).

**Computer facilities:** 2,059 computers available on campus for general student use. A campuswide network can be accessed. Online class registration is available.
Website: http://www.gsu.edu/

**GRADUATE UNITS**

**Andrew Young School of Policy Studies** Students: 398 full-time (265 women), 133 part-time (96 women); includes 243 minority (177 Black or African American, non-Hispanic/Latino; 17 Asian, non-Hispanic/Latino; 34 Hispanic/Latino; 15 Two or more races, non-Hispanic/Latino), 106 international. Average age 30. 814 applicants, 54% accepted, 185 enrolled. *Faculty:* 59 full-time (22 women), 7 part-time/adjunct (3 women). Expenses: Contact institution. *Financial support:* Unspecified assistantships available. Financial award application deadline: 2/15; financial award applicants required to submit FAFSA. In 2019, 170 master's, 12 doctorates, 8 other advanced degrees awarded. *Program availability:* Part-time, evening/weekend. *Application deadline:* For fall admission, 1/15 for domestic and international students. *Application fee:* $50. Electronic applications accepted. *Application Contact:* Dr. Sally Wallace, Dean, 404-413-0000, Fax: 404-413-0004. *Dean*, Dr. Sally Wallace, 404-413-0000, Fax: 404-413-0004.

***School of Social Work*** Students: 118 full-time (105 women), 19 part-time (18 women); includes 91 minority (76 Black or African American, non-Hispanic/Latino; 3 Asian, non-Hispanic/Latino; 9 Hispanic/Latino; 3 Two or more races, non-Hispanic/Latino). Average age 30. 183 applicants, 56% accepted, 47 enrolled. *Faculty:* 12 full-time (8 women), 4 part-time/adjunct (2 women). Expenses: Contact institution. *Financial support:* In 2019–20, research assistantships with tuition reimbursements (averaging $4,000 per year), teaching assistantships with tuition reimbursements (averaging $4,000 per year) were awarded; career-related internships or fieldwork, institutionally sponsored loans, scholarships/grants, tuition waivers, and unspecified assistantships also available. Financial award application deadline: 2/1; financial award applicants required to submit FAFSA. In 2019, 62 master's awarded. *Program availability:* Part-time. *Application deadline:* For fall admission, 2/1 priority date for domestic and international students. *Application fee:* $50. Electronic applications accepted. *Application Contact:* Brian Bride, Director of School of Social Work, 404-413-1052, Fax: 404-413-1075, E-mail: bbride@gsu.edu. *Director of School of Social Work*, Brian Bride, 404-413-1052, Fax: 404-413-1075, E-mail: bbride@gsu.edu.

**Byrdine F. Lewis School of Nursing** Students: 388 full-time (290 women), 155 part-time (135 women); includes 217 minority (130 Black or African American, non-Hispanic/Latino; 47 Asian, non-Hispanic/Latino; 26 Hispanic/Latino; 14 Two or more races, non-Hispanic/Latino), 45 international. Average age 32. 480 applicants, 50% accepted, 164 enrolled. *Faculty:* 57 full-time (40 women), 5 part-time/adjunct (4 women). Expenses: Contact institution. *Financial support:* In 2019–20, research assistantships with tuition reimbursements (averaging $1,666 per year), teaching assistantships with tuition reimbursements (averaging $1,920 per year) were awarded; scholarships/grants, tuition waivers (full and partial), and unspecified assistantships also available. Support available to part-time students. Financial award application deadline: 8/1; financial award applicants required to submit FAFSA. In 2019, 158 master's, 64 doctorates, 20 other advanced degrees awarded. *Program availability:* Part-time, blended/hybrid learning. *Application deadline:* For fall admission, 2/1 priority date for domestic and international students; for spring admission, 9/15 for domestic and international students. Applications are processed on a rolling basis. *Application fee:* $50. Electronic applications accepted. *Application Contact:* Huanbiao Mo, Dean of Nursing. *Dean of Nursing*, Huanbiao Mo.

***Division of Nutrition*** Students: 44 full-time (38 women); includes 17 minority (10 Black or African American, non-Hispanic/Latino; 2 Asian, non-Hispanic/Latino; 4 Hispanic/Latino; 1 Two or more races, non-Hispanic/Latino). Average age 29. 45 applicants, 58% accepted, 23 enrolled. *Faculty:* 9 full-time (7 women), 1 (woman) part-time/adjunct. Expenses: Contact institution. *Financial support:* In 2019–20, research assistantships with tuition reimbursements (averaging $1,647 per year), teaching assistantships with full tuition reimbursements (averaging $2,666 per year) were awarded. Financial award application deadline: 4/1. In 2019, 23 master's awarded. *Program availability:* Part-time. *Application deadline:* For fall admission, 5/15 for domestic and international students; for spring admission, 10/1 for domestic and international students. *Application fee:* $50. Electronic applications accepted. *Application Contact:* Dr. Anita Nucci, Associate Professor and Graduate Program Director, 404-413-1234, Fax: 404-413-1228, E-mail: anucci@gsu.edu. *Associate Professor and Graduate Program Director*, Dr. Anita Nucci, 404-413-1234, Fax: 404-413-1228, E-mail: anucci@gsu.edu.

***Division of Physical Therapy*** Students: 124 full-time (82 women), 1 (woman) part-time; includes 37 minority (12 Black or African American, non-Hispanic/Latino; 15 Asian, non-Hispanic/Latino; 5 Hispanic/Latino; 5 Two or more races, non-Hispanic/Latino). Average age 26. *Faculty:* 11 full-time (5 women), 1 (woman) part-time/adjunct. Expenses: Contact institution. *Financial support:* In 2019–20, research assistantships with full tuition reimbursements (averaging $2,000 per year), teaching assistantships with full tuition reimbursements (averaging $2,000 per year) were awarded; scholarships/grants, tuition waivers (partial), and unspecified assistantships also available. Financial award application deadline: 4/1; financial award applicants required to submit FAFSA. In 2019, 39 doctorates awarded. *Application deadline:* For fall admission, 11/15 for domestic and international students. *Application fee:* $50. Electronic applications accepted. *Application Contact:* Dr. Sujay Galen, Chair, 404-413-1243, Fax: 404-413-1230, E-mail: sgalen@gsu.edu. *Chair*, Dr. Sujay Galen, 404-413-1243, Fax: 404-413-1230, E-mail: sgalen@gsu.edu.

***Division of Respiratory Therapy*** Students: 62 full-time (22 women), 7 part-time (5 women); includes 17 minority (7 Black or African American, non-Hispanic/Latino; 7 Asian, non-Hispanic/Latino; 2 Hispanic/Latino; 1 Two or more races, non-Hispanic/Latino), 44 international. Average age 32. 81 applicants, 64% accepted, 29 enrolled. *Faculty:* 8 full-time (3 women). Expenses: Contact institution. *Financial support:* In 2019–20, research assistantships with full tuition reimbursements (averaging $2,000 per year), teaching assistantships with full tuition reimbursements (averaging $2,000 per year) were awarded; scholarships/grants and unspecified assistantships also available. Financial award application deadline: 6/1; financial award applicants required to submit FAFSA. In 2019, 20 master's awarded. *Application deadline:* For fall admission, 5/1 for domestic and international students; for spring admission, 9/15 for domestic and international students. *Application fee:* $50. Electronic applications accepted. *Application Contact:* Dr. Douglas Gardenhire, Department Head, 404-413-1270, Fax: 404-413-1230, E-mail: dgardenhire@gsu.edu. *Department Head*, Dr. Douglas Gardenhire, 404-413-1270, Fax: 404-413-1230, E-mail: dgardenhire@gsu.edu.

**College of Arts** Students: 178 full-time (94 women), 38 part-time (20 women); includes 77 minority (34 Black or African American, non-Hispanic/Latino; 7 Asian, non-Hispanic/Latino; 18 Hispanic/Latino; 1 Native Hawaiian or other Pacific Islander, non-Hispanic/Latino; 17 Two or more races, non-Hispanic/Latino), 31 international. Average age 31. 296 applicants, 44% accepted, 84 enrolled. *Faculty:* 76 full-time (32 women), 11 part-time/adjunct (3 women). Expenses: Contact institution. *Application Contact:* Dr. Wade Weast.

**College of Arts and Sciences** Students: 1,500 full-time (850 women), 350 part-time (202 women); includes 601 minority (329 Black or African American, non-Hispanic/Latino; 1 American Indian or Alaska Native, non-Hispanic/Latino; 108 Asian, non-Hispanic/Latino; 102 Hispanic/Latino; 2 Native Hawaiian or other Pacific Islander, non-Hispanic/Latino; 59 Two or more races, non-Hispanic/Latino), 528 international. Average age 31. 2,206 applicants, 41% accepted, 464 enrolled. *Faculty:* 366 full-time (149 women), 17 part-time/adjunct (7 women). Expenses: Contact institution. *Financial* *support:* Fellowships with tuition reimbursements, research assistantships with tuition reimbursements, teaching assistantships with tuition reimbursements, career-related internships or fieldwork, scholarships/grants, health care benefits, tuition waivers (partial), and unspecified assistantships available. Support available to part-time students. Financial award application deadline: 4/15; financial award applicants required to submit FAFSA. In 2019, 421 master's, 132 doctorates, 37 other advanced degrees awarded. *Program availability:* Part-time, evening/weekend. *Application deadline:* For fall admission, 7/1 for domestic and international students; for spring admission, 11/15 for domestic and international students. *Application fee:* $50. Electronic applications accepted. *Application Contact:* Amber Amari, Assistant Dean for Graduate Programs, 404-413-5037, E-mail: aamari@gsu.edu. *Dean,* Dr. Sara Rosen, 404-413-5114, Fax: 404-413-5117, E-mail: rosen@gsu.edu.

***Gerontology Institute*** Students: 22 full-time (19 women), 14 part-time (10 women); includes 17 minority (14 Black or African American, non-Hispanic/Latino; 2 Asian, non-Hispanic/Latino; 1 Hispanic/Latino), 7 international. Average age 42. 20 applicants, 85% accepted, 14 enrolled. *Faculty:* 4 full-time (all women), 1 (woman) part-time/adjunct. Expenses: Contact institution. *Financial support:* In 2019–20, research assistantships with full tuition reimbursements (averaging $6,000 per year) were awarded; career-related internships or fieldwork, scholarships/grants, and unspecified assistantships also available. Financial award application deadline: 4/15; financial award applicants required to submit FAFSA. In 2019, 15 master's, 2 other advanced degrees awarded. *Program availability:* Part-time. *Application deadline:* For fall admission, 4/15 for domestic and international students; for spring admission, 10/15 for domestic and international students. Applications are processed on a rolling basis. *Application fee:* $50. Electronic applications accepted. *Application Contact:* Dr. Candace L. Kemp, Director of Graduate Studies, 404-413-5210, Fax: 404-413-5219, E-mail: ckemp@gsu.edu. *Director,* Dr. Elizabeth O. Burgess, 404-413-5210, Fax: 404-413-5219, E-mail: eburgess@gsu.edu.

***Institute for Women's, Gender, and Sexuality Studies*** Students: 15 full-time (all women), 5 part-time (all women); includes 10 minority (8 Black or African American, non-Hispanic/Latino; 2 Hispanic/Latino), 3 international. Average age 31. 31 applicants, 61% accepted, 9 enrolled. *Faculty:* 6 full-time (all women). Expenses: Contact institution. *Financial support:* In 2019–20, research assistantships with full tuition reimbursements (averaging $7,000 per year), teaching assistantships with full tuition reimbursements (averaging $7,500 per year) were awarded; career-related internships or fieldwork, health care benefits, and unspecified assistantships also available. Financial award application deadline: 2/15. In 2019, 4 master's, 3 other advanced degrees awarded. *Program availability:* Part-time. *Application deadline:* For fall admission, 2/15 for domestic and international students. *Application fee:* $50. Electronic applications accepted. *Application Contact:* Dr. Megan Sinnott, Director of Graduate Studies, Fax: 404-413-6585, E-mail: megansinnott@gsu.edu.

***Neuroscience Institute*** Students: 61 full-time (37 women), 2 part-time (1 woman); includes 19 minority (4 Black or African American, non-Hispanic/Latino; 6 Asian, non-Hispanic/Latino; 8 Hispanic/Latino; 1 Two or more races, non-Hispanic/Latino), 10 international. Average age 29. 64 applicants, 44% accepted, 20 enrolled. *Faculty:* 19 full-time (8 women). Expenses: Contact institution. *Financial support:* In 2019–20, fellowships (averaging $22,000 per year), research assistantships (averaging $22,000 per year) were awarded. Financial award applicants required to submit FAFSA. In 2019, 6 doctorates awarded. *Application deadline:* For fall admission, 12/10 for domestic and international students. *Application fee:* $50. Electronic applications accepted. *Application Contact:* Dr. Laura L. Carruth, Director of Graduate Studies, 404-413-5340, E-mail: lcarruth@gsu.edu.

***Ernest G. Welch School of Art and Design*** Students: 54 full-time (37 women), 9 part-time (7 women); includes 17 minority (8 Black or African American, non-Hispanic/Latino; 1 Asian, non-Hispanic/Latino; 3 Hispanic/Latino; 1 Native Hawaiian or other Pacific Islander, non-Hispanic/Latino; 4 Two or more races, non-Hispanic/Latino), 7 international. Average age 34. 136 applicants, 28% accepted, 25 enrolled. *Faculty:* 24 full-time (13 women), 1 (woman) part-time/adjunct. Expenses: Contact institution. *Financial support:* In 2019–20, fellowships with full tuition reimbursements (averaging $11,000 per year), research assistantships with full tuition reimbursements (averaging $6,000 per year), teaching assistantships with full tuition reimbursements (averaging $7,000 per year) were awarded; scholarships/grants and unspecified assistantships also available. Financial award application deadline: 4/15; financial award applicants required to submit FAFSA. In 2019, 27 master's awarded. *Application deadline:* For fall admission, 1/6 for domestic and international students; for spring admission, 1/15 priority date for domestic and international students. *Application fee:* $50. Electronic applications accepted. *Application Contact:* Michael White, Director, Welch School of Art and Design, 404-413-5228, E-mail: mwhite@gsu.edu. *Director, Welch School of Art and Design,* Michael White, 404-413-5228, E-mail: mwhite@gsu.edu.

***School of Film, Media, and Theater*** Students: 56 full-time (23 women), 16 part-time (6 women); includes 32 minority (14 Black or African American, non-Hispanic/Latino; 1 Asian, non-Hispanic/Latino; 11 Hispanic/Latino; 6 Two or more races, non-Hispanic/Latino), 7 international. Average age 34. 79 applicants, 42% accepted, 23 enrolled. *Faculty:* 17 full-time (7 women). Expenses: Contact institution. *Application Contact:* Karin Smoot, Graduate Coordinator, E-mail: ksmoot@gsu.edu.

***School of Music*** Students: 68 full-time (34 women), 13 part-time (7 women); includes 28 minority (12 Black or African American, non-Hispanic/Latino; 5 Asian, non-Hispanic/Latino; 4 Hispanic/Latino; 7 Two or more races, non-Hispanic/Latino), 17 international. Average age 28. 81 applicants, 73% accepted, 36 enrolled. *Faculty:* 35 full-time (12 women), 10 part-time/adjunct (2 women). Expenses: Contact institution.

**College of Education and Human Development** Students: 830 full-time (614 women), 582 part-time (164 women); includes 778 minority (560 Black or African American, non-Hispanic/Latino; 1 American Indian or Alaska Native, non-Hispanic/Latino; 65 Asian, non-Hispanic/Latino; 94 Hispanic/Latino; 58 Two or more races, non-Hispanic/Latino), 38 international. Average age 32. 1,059 applicants, 48% accepted, 354 enrolled. *Faculty:* 111 full-time (70 women), 47 part-time/adjunct (38 women). Expenses: Contact institution. *Financial support:* In 2019–20, fellowships with full tuition reimbursements (averaging $25,000 per year), research assistantships with tuition reimbursements (averaging $4,867 per year), teaching assistantships with tuition reimbursements (averaging $4,683 per year) were awarded; career-related internships or fieldwork, Federal Work-Study, scholarships/grants, tuition waivers (partial), and unspecified assistantships also available. Support available to part-time students. Financial award applicants required to submit FAFSA. In 2019, 433 master's, 63 doctorates, 13 other advanced degrees awarded. *Program availability:* Part-time, evening/weekend, online learning. *Application fee:* $50. Electronic applications accepted. *Application Contact:* Nancy Keita, Assistant Dean for Student Services, 404-413-8001, E-mail: nkeita@gsu.edu. *Dean,* Dr. Paul A. Alberto, 404-413-8100, Fax: 404-413-8103, E-mail: palberto@gsu.edu.

**College of Law** Students: 512 full-time (259 women), 170 part-time (97 women); includes 204 minority (93 Black or African American, non-Hispanic/Latino; 2 American Indian or Alaska Native, non-Hispanic/Latino; 38 Asian, non-Hispanic/Latino; 53 Hispanic/Latino; 18 Two or more races, non-Hispanic/Latino), 11 international. Average age 27. 1,048 applicants, 51% accepted, 237 enrolled. *Faculty:* 56 full-time (33 women), 10 part-time/adjunct (4 women). Expenses: Contact institution. *Financial support:* In 2019–20, research assistantships with tuition reimbursements (averaging $2,500 per year), teaching assistantships (averaging $2,500 per year) were awarded; scholarships/grants, tuition waivers, and unspecified assistantships also available. Financial award application deadline: 4/1; financial award applicants required to submit FAFSA. In 2019, 200 doctorates awarded. *Program availability:* Part-time, evening/weekend. *Application deadline:* For fall admission, 3/15 for domestic students, 3/15 priority date for international students. Applications are processed on a rolling basis. *Application fee:* $50. Electronic applications accepted. *Application Contact:* Dr. Monique McCarthy, Senior Director of Admissions, 404-413-9004, Fax: 404-413-9203, E-mail: mmccarthy18@gsu.edu. *Interim Dean, College of Law,* Dr. Leslie E. Wolf, 404-413-9035, Fax: 404-413-9227, E-mail: lwolf@gsu.edu.

**J. Mack Robinson College of Business** Students: 856 full-time (421 women), 376 part-time (186 women); includes 507 minority (258 Black or African American, non-Hispanic/Latino; 2 American Indian or Alaska Native, non-Hispanic/Latino; 155 Asian, non-Hispanic/Latino; 57 Hispanic/Latino; 35 Two or more races, non-Hispanic/Latino), 374 international. Average age 31. 1,767 applicants, 52% accepted, 503 enrolled. *Faculty:* 85 full-time (16 women), 20 part-time/adjunct (2 women). Expenses: Contact institution. *Financial support:* Research assistantships, teaching assistantships, scholarships/grants, tuition waivers, and unspecified assistantships available. Financial award applicants required to submit FAFSA. In 2019, 544 master's, 31 doctorates, 32 other advanced degrees awarded. *Program availability:* Part-time, evening/weekend. *Application deadline:* For fall admission, 5/1 priority date for domestic students, 2/1 priority date for international students; for spring admission, 9/15 priority date for domestic students, 4/1 priority date for international students. Applications are processed on a rolling basis. *Application fee:* $50. Electronic applications accepted. *Application Contact:* Toby McChesney, Assistant Dean for Graduate Recruiting and Student Services, 404-413-7167, Fax: 404-413-7162, E-mail: rcbgradadmissions@gsu.edu. *Dean of the J. Mack Robinson College of Business,* Dr. Richard D. Phillips, 404-413-7000, Fax: 404-413-7035, E-mail: rphillips@gsu.edu.

***Institute of Health Administration*** Students: 37 full-time (18 women), 38 part-time (25 women); includes 37 minority (18 Black or African American, non-Hispanic/Latino; 11 Asian, non-Hispanic/Latino; 4 Hispanic/Latino; 4 Two or more races, non-Hispanic/Latino), 11 international. Average age 31. 57 applicants, 47% accepted, 19 enrolled. *Faculty:* 4 full-time (1 woman). Expenses: Contact institution. *Financial support:* Research assistantships, teaching assistantships, scholarships/grants, tuition waivers, and unspecified assistantships available. In 2019, 26 master's awarded. *Program availability:* Part-time, evening/weekend. *Application deadline:* For fall admission, 5/1 priority date for domestic students, 2/1 priority date for international students; for spring admission, 9/15 priority date for domestic students, 4/1 priority date for international students. Applications are processed on a rolling basis. *Application fee:* $50. Electronic applications accepted. *Application Contact:* Toby McChesney, Assistant Dean for Graduate Recruiting and Student Services, 404-413-7167, Fax: 404-413-7162, E-mail: rcbgradadmissions@gsu.edu. *Chair in Health Administration/Director of the Institute of Health,* Dr. Andrew T. Sumner, 404-413-7630, Fax: 404-413-7631.

***Institute of International Business*** Students: 14 full-time (10 women), 1 part-time (0 women); includes 3 minority (2 Asian, non-Hispanic/Latino; 1 Hispanic/Latino), 9 international. Average age 29. 39 applicants, 62% accepted, 15 enrolled. *Faculty:* 5 full-time (3 women). Expenses: Contact institution. *Financial support:* Research assistantships, teaching assistantships, scholarships/grants, tuition waivers (partial), and unspecified assistantships available. Financial award application deadline: 5/1. In 2019, 18 master's awarded. *Program availability:* Part-time, evening/weekend. *Application deadline:* For fall admission, 5/1 priority date for domestic students, 2/1 priority date for international students; for spring admission, 9/15 priority date for domestic students, 5/1 priority date for international students. Applications are processed on a rolling basis. *Application fee:* $50. Electronic applications accepted. *Application Contact:* Toby McChesney, Assistant Dean for Graduate Recruiting and Student Services, 404-413-7167, Fax: 404-413-7162, E-mail: rcbgradadmissions@gsu.edu. *Professor/Director of the Institute of International Business,* Dr. Daniel Bello, 404-413-7275, Fax: 404-413-7276.

***School of Accountancy*** Students: 108 full-time (69 women), 110 part-time (68 women); includes 126 minority (58 Black or African American, non-Hispanic/Latino; 41 Asian, non-Hispanic/Latino; 19 Hispanic/Latino; 8 Two or more races, non-Hispanic/Latino), 28 international. Average age 31. 183 applicants, 64% accepted, 82 enrolled. *Faculty:* 8 full-time (3 women), 10 part-time/adjunct (0 women). Expenses: Contact institution. *Financial support:* Research assistantships, teaching assistantships, scholarships/grants, tuition waivers, and unspecified assistantships available. Financial award applicants required to submit FAFSA. In 2019, 122 master's, 2 doctorates awarded. *Program availability:* Part-time, evening/weekend. *Application deadline:* For fall admission, 5/1 priority date for domestic students, 2/1 priority date for international students; for spring admission, 9/15 priority date for domestic students, 4/1 priority date for international students. Applications are processed on a rolling basis. *Application fee:* $50. Electronic applications accepted. *Application Contact:* Toby McChesney, Assistant Dean for Graduate Recruiting and Student Services, 404-413-7167, Fax: 404-413-7162, E-mail: rcbgradadmissions@gsu.edu. *Director of the School of Accountancy,* Dr. Douglas E. Stevens, 404-413-7212, Fax: 404-413-7203, E-mail: dstevens11@gsu.edu.

**School of Public Health** Students: 233 full-time (175 women), 101 part-time (80 women); includes 196 minority (126 Black or African American, non-Hispanic/Latino; 31 Asian, non-Hispanic/Latino; 24 Hispanic/Latino; 15 Two or more races, non-Hispanic/Latino), 38 international. Average age 29. 405 applicants, 60% accepted, 122 enrolled. *Faculty:* 30 full-time (16 women), 7 part-time/adjunct (3 women). Expenses: Contact institution. *Financial support:* In 2019–20, fellowships (averaging $2,500 per year), research assistantships with full tuition reimbursements (averaging $22,000 per year), teaching assistantships with full tuition reimbursements (averaging $22,000 per year) were awarded; career-related internships or fieldwork, scholarships/grants, health care benefits, unspecified assistantships, and out-of-state tuition waivers also available. In 2019, 105 master's, 9 doctorates, 9 other advanced degrees awarded. *Program availability:* Part-time. *Application deadline:* For fall admission, 2/1 for domestic and international students; for spring admission, 10/1 for domestic and international students. *Application fee:* $50. Electronic applications accepted. *Application Contact:* Dr. Rodney Lyn.

## GERSTNER SLOAN KETTERING GRADUATE SCHOOL OF BIOMEDICAL SCIENCES, New York, NY 10021

**General Information** Independent, coed, graduate-only institution. *Enrollment by degree level:* 77 doctoral. *Graduate faculty:* 128 full-time (27 women). *Graduate housing:* Rooms and/or apartments guaranteed to single and married students. Typical cost: $11,052 per year for single students. Housing application deadline: 5/5. *Student services:* Campus employment opportunities, campus safety program, career counseling, child daycare facilities, exercise/wellness program, free psychological counseling, grant writing training, international student services, low-cost health insurance, multicultural affairs office, services for students with disabilities, writing training. *Library facilities:* Memorial Sloan Kettering Cancer Center Library. *Collection:* Books: 3,863 (physical), 24,373 (digital/electronic); Serial titles: 507 (physical), 6,816 (digital/electronic); Databases: 150. Weekly public service hours: 53; students can reserve study rooms. *Research affiliation:* Memorial Sloan-Kettering Cancer Center (biomedical sciences).

**Computer facilities:** 74 computers available on campus for general student use. A campuswide network can be accessed from student residence rooms and from off campus. Online class registration is available.
Website: https://www.sloankettering.edu/gerstner

**General Application Contact:** Julie Masen, Main Office, 646-888-6639, Fax: 646-422-2351, E-mail: gradstudies@sloankettering.edu.

**GRADUATE UNITS**

**Program in Cancer Biology** Electronic applications accepted.

## GLION INSTITUTE OF HIGHER EDUCATION, CH-1823 Glion-sur-Montreux, Switzerland

**General Information** Proprietary, coed, comprehensive institution.

**GRADUATE UNITS**

**Graduate Programs** *Program availability:* Evening/weekend.

## GLOBAL UNIVERSITY, Springfield, MO 65804

**General Information** Independent-religious, coed, comprehensive institution. *Graduate housing:* On-campus housing not available.

**GRADUATE UNITS**

**Graduate School of Theology** *Program availability:* Part-time, evening/weekend, online learning. Electronic applications accepted.

## GODDARD COLLEGE, Plainfield, VT 05667-9432

**General Information** Independent, coed, comprehensive institution. *Graduate housing:* On-campus housing not available.

**GRADUATE UNITS**

**Graduate Division** *Program availability:* Part-time, online learning. Electronic applications accepted.

## GOLDEN GATE UNIVERSITY, San Francisco, CA 94105-2968

**General Information** Independent, coed, university. *Graduate housing:* On-campus housing not available.

**GRADUATE UNITS**

**Ageno School of Business** *Program availability:* Part-time, evening/weekend. Electronic applications accepted.

**School of Accounting** *Program availability:* Part-time, evening/weekend. Electronic applications accepted.

**School of Law** *Program availability:* Part-time, evening/weekend. Electronic applications accepted.

**School of Taxation** *Program availability:* Part-time, evening/weekend. Electronic applications accepted.

## GOLDEY-BEACOM COLLEGE, Wilmington, DE 19808-1999

**General Information** Independent, coed, comprehensive institution. *Graduate housing:* Room and/or apartments available on a first-come, first-served basis to single students; on-campus housing not available to married students.

**GRADUATE UNITS**

**Graduate Program** *Program availability:* Part-time, evening/weekend. Electronic applications accepted.

## GOLDFARB SCHOOL OF NURSING AT BARNES-JEWISH COLLEGE, St. Louis, MO 63110

**General Information** Independent, coed, primarily women, comprehensive institution. *Graduate housing:* On-campus housing not available.

**GRADUATE UNITS**

**Graduate Programs** *Program availability:* Part-time, online learning.

## GONZAGA UNIVERSITY, Spokane, WA 99258

**General Information** Independent-religious, coed, university. *Graduate housing:* Rooms and/or apartments available on a first-come, first-served basis to single and married students. Housing application deadline: 5/1.

**GRADUATE UNITS**

**College of Arts and Sciences** *Program availability:* Part-time, blended/hybrid learning. Electronic applications accepted.

**English Language Center** *Program availability:* Part-time. Electronic applications accepted.

**School of Business Administration** *Program availability:* Part-time, evening/weekend. Electronic applications accepted.

**School of Education** *Program availability:* Part-time, evening/weekend, 100% online, blended/hybrid learning. Electronic applications accepted.

**School of Engineering and Applied Science** *Program availability:* Part-time-only, evening/weekend, online only, 100% online. Electronic applications accepted.

**School of Law** *Program availability:* Part-time. Electronic applications accepted.

**School of Leadership Studies** *Program availability:* Part-time, evening/weekend, 100% online, blended/hybrid learning, immersion weekends. Electronic applications accepted.

**School of Nursing and Human Physiology** *Program availability:* Part-time, evening/weekend, 100% online, immersion weekends. Electronic applications accepted.

## GORDON COLLEGE, Wenham, MA 01984-1899

**General Information** Independent-religious, coed, comprehensive institution. *Graduate housing:* Room and/or apartments available on a first-come, first-served basis to single students; on-campus housing not available to married students. Housing application deadline: 6/15. *Research affiliation:* National Association for Music Education (music education), Feierabend Association for Music Education (early childhood music education), American Choral Directors Association (choral music education), Embracing the New Music Educators Association (mentoring for new music teaching professionals).

**GRADUATE UNITS**

**Graduate Education Program** *Program availability:* Part-time, evening/weekend.

**Graduate Financial Analysis Program** *Program availability:* Part-time, evening/weekend. Electronic applications accepted.

**Graduate Leadership Program**

**Graduate Music Education Program** *Program availability:* Part-time.

## GORDON-CONWELL THEOLOGICAL SEMINARY, South Hamilton, MA 01982-2395

**General Information** Independent-religious, coed, graduate-only institution. *Graduate housing:* Rooms and/or apartments available to single and married students. Housing application deadline: 4/1.

**GRADUATE UNITS**

**Graduate and Professional Programs** *Program availability:* Part-time, evening/weekend.

## GOSHEN COLLEGE, Goshen, IN 46526-4794

**General Information** Independent-religious, coed, comprehensive institution. *Enrollment:* 907 graduate, professional, and undergraduate students; 75 full-time matriculated graduate/professional students (64 women), 6 part-time matriculated graduate/professional students (all women). *Enrollment by degree level:* 81 master's. *Graduate faculty:* 14 full-time (6 women). *Tuition:* Full-time $9100; part-time $650 per credit hour. Tuition and fees vary according to degree level and program. *Graduate housing:* On-campus housing not available. *Student services:* Child daycare facilities, exercise/wellness program, international student services, multicultural affairs office, services for students with disabilities, writing training. *Library facilities:* The Harold and Wilma Good Library plus 1 other. *Collection:* Books: 188,371 (physical), 243,626 (digital/electronic); Serial titles: 3,196 (physical), 13,072 (digital/electronic); Databases: 72. Weekly public service hours: 89; students can reserve study rooms.

**Computer facilities:** 160 computers available on campus for general student use. A campuswide network can be accessed. Online class registration is available.
Website: http://www.goshen.edu/

**General Application Contact:** Richard Warren, Admissions Counselor for Graduate and Continuing Studies, 574-535-7458, Fax: 574-535-7245, E-mail: rwarren@goshen.edu.

**GRADUATE UNITS**

**Graduate Program in Nursing** Students: 56 full-time (51 women), 5 part-time (all women); includes 11 minority (3 Black or African American, non-Hispanic/Latino; 2 Asian, non-Hispanic/Latino; 5 Hispanic/Latino; 1 Two or more races, non-Hispanic/Latino). Average age 35. 22 applicants, 100% accepted, 22 enrolled. *Faculty:* 7 full-time (5 women). Expenses: Contact institution. *Financial support:* In 2019–20, 7 students received support. Scholarships/grants available. In 2019, 21 master's awarded. *Program availability:* Part-time, evening/weekend. *Application deadline:* For fall admission, 3/15 priority date for domestic students. Applications are processed on a rolling basis. *Application fee:* $25. Electronic applications accepted. *Application Contact:* Ruth Stoltzfus, Director, 574-535-7973, E-mail: ruthas@goshen.edu. *Director,* Ruth Stoltzfus, 574-535-7973, E-mail: ruthas@goshen.edu.

**Merry Lea Environmental Learning Center** Students: 10 full-time (9 women), 1 (woman) part-time, 1 international. Average age 24. 8 applicants, 100% accepted, 8 enrolled. *Faculty:* 5 full-time (0 women). Expenses: Contact institution. *Financial support:* Application deadline: 9/10. In 2019, 11 master's awarded. *Application deadline:* For fall admission, 3/30 for domestic students. Applications are processed on a rolling basis. *Application fee:* $25. Electronic applications accepted. *Application Contact:* Dr. David Ostergren, Director of the Graduate Program in Environmental Education, 260-799-5869, E-mail: daveo@goshen.edu. *Executive Director,* Dr. Jason Martin, 260-799-5869, E-mail: jmmartin@goshen.edu.

## GOUCHER COLLEGE, Baltimore, MD 21204-2794

**General Information** Independent, coed, comprehensive institution. *Graduate housing:* On-campus housing not available. *Research affiliation:* Sheppard-Pratt Hospital (education).

**GRADUATE UNITS**

**Graduate Programs in Education** *Program availability:* Part-time, evening/weekend. Electronic applications accepted.

**MA and MFA Programs** *Program availability:* Part-time, evening/weekend, blended/hybrid learning. Electronic applications accepted.

**Post-Baccalaureate Premedical Program** Electronic applications accepted.

## GOVERNORS STATE UNIVERSITY, University Park, IL 60484

**General Information** State-supported, coed, university. CGS member. *Enrollment:* 4,854 graduate, professional, and undergraduate students; 647 full-time matriculated graduate/professional students (452 women), 936 part-time matriculated graduate/professional students (246 women). *Enrollment by degree level:* 1,367 master's, 216 doctoral. *Graduate faculty:* 230 full-time (133 women), 290 part-time/adjunct (105 women). *International tuition:* $16,944 full-time. *Tuition, area resident:* Full-time $8472; part-time $353 per credit hour. Tuition, state resident: full-time $8472; part-time $353 per credit hour. Tuition, nonresident: full-time $16,944; part-time $706 per credit hour. *Required fees:* $2520; $105 per credit hour. $38 per term. Tuition and fees vary according to course load, degree level and program. *Graduate housing:* Rooms and/or apartments available on a first-come, first-served basis to single and married students. Typical cost: $7181 per year ($10,181 including board) for single students; $7181 per year ($10,181 including board) for married students. Room and board charges vary according to board plan and housing facility selected. Housing application deadline: 6/1. *Student services:* Campus employment opportunities, career counseling, child daycare facilities, exercise/wellness program, international student services, multicultural affairs office, services for students with disabilities, writing training. *Library facilities:* Governors State University Library. *Collection:* Books: 260,817 (physical), 388,203 (digital/electronic); Serial titles: 9,808 (physical), 11,430 (digital/electronic); Databases: 170. Weekly public service hours: 75; students can reserve study rooms.

**Computer facilities:** 670 computers available on campus for general student use. A campuswide network can be accessed. Online class registration, student portal are available.
Website: http://www.govst.edu/

**General Application Contact:** Paul McGuinness, Associate Vice President Enrollment Management, 708-534-5000 Ext. 7308, E-mail: pmcguinness@govst.edu.

**GRADUATE UNITS**

**College of Arts and Sciences** Students: 107 full-time (43 women), 184 part-time (112 women); includes 140 minority (108 Black or African American, non-Hispanic/Latino; 2 Asian, non-Hispanic/Latino; 26 Hispanic/Latino; 4 Two or more races, non-Hispanic/Latino), 63 international. Average age 35. 456 applicants, 68% accepted, 76 enrolled. *Faculty:* 96 full-time (47 women), 97 part-time/adjunct (52 women). Expenses: Contact institution. *Financial support:* Federal Work-Study and unspecified assistantships available. Financial award application deadline: 5/1; financial award applicants required to submit FAFSA. In 2019, 41 master's awarded. *Program availability:* Part-time. *Application deadline:* For fall admission, 4/1 for domestic students. Applications are processed on a rolling basis. *Application fee:* $50. Electronic applications accepted. *Application Contact:* Paul McGuinness, Associate Vice President Enrollment Management, 708-534-5000 Ext. 7308, E-mail: pmcguinness@govst.edu. *Dean, College of Arts and Sciences/Dean, Graduate Studies*, Andrae Marak, 708-534-5000 Ext. 4589, E-mail: amarak@govst.edu.

**College of Business** Students: 47 full-time (21 women), 110 part-time (62 women); includes 78 minority (49 Black or African American, non-Hispanic/Latino; 8 Asian, non-Hispanic/Latino; 19 Hispanic/Latino; 2 Two or more races, non-Hispanic/Latino), 9 international. Average age 35. 124 applicants, 56% accepted, 51 enrolled. *Faculty:* 26 full-time (8 women), 34 part-time/adjunct (12 women). Expenses: Contact institution. *Financial support:* Federal Work-Study and unspecified assistantships available. Financial award application deadline: 5/1; financial award applicants required to submit FAFSA. In 2019, 33 master's awarded. *Program availability:* Part-time. *Application deadline:* For fall admission, 4/1 for domestic students. Applications are processed on a rolling basis. *Application fee:* $50. Electronic applications accepted. *Application Contact:* Paul McGuinness, Associate Vice President, Enrollment Management, 708-534-5000 Ext. 7308, E-mail: pmcguinness@govst.edu. *Dean, College of Business*, Jun Zhao, 708-534-5000 Ext. 4953, E-mail: jzhao@govst.edu.

**College of Education** Students: 159 full-time (126 women), 262 part-time (207 women); includes 244 minority (181 Black or African American, non-Hispanic/Latino; 3 Asian, non-Hispanic/Latino; 44 Hispanic/Latino; 16 Two or more races, non-Hispanic/Latino), 4 international. Average age 38. 267 applicants, 54% accepted, 125 enrolled. *Faculty:* 44 full-time (28 women), 76 part-time/adjunct (56 women). Expenses: Contact institution. *Financial support:* Federal Work-Study and unspecified assistantships available. Financial award application deadline: 5/1; financial award applicants required to submit FAFSA. In 2019, 103 master's, 10 doctorates awarded. *Program availability:* Part-time. *Application deadline:* For fall admission, 4/1 for domestic students. Applications are processed on a rolling basis. *Application fee:* $50. Electronic applications accepted. *Application Contact:* Paul McGuinness, Associate Vice President, Enrollment Management/Director, Admissions, 708-534-5000 Ext. 7308, E-mail: pmcguinness@govst.edu. *Dean, College of Education*, Shannon Dermer, 708-534-5000 Ext. 8396, E-mail: sdermer@govst.edu.

**College of Health and Human Services** Students: 334 full-time (260 women), 319 part-time (267 women); includes 345 minority (227 Black or African American, non-Hispanic/Latino; 39 Asian, non-Hispanic/Latino; 64 Hispanic/Latino; 15 Two or more races, non-Hispanic/Latino), 10 international. Average age 32. 473 applicants, 37% accepted, 133 enrolled. *Faculty:* 58 full-time (47 women), 82 part-time/adjunct (65 women). Expenses: Contact institution. *Financial support:* Federal Work-Study and unspecified assistantships available. Financial award application deadline: 5/1; financial award applicants required to submit FAFSA. In 2019, 196 master's, 42 doctorates awarded. *Program availability:* Part-time. *Application deadline:* For fall admission, 4/1 for domestic students. Applications are processed on a rolling basis. *Application fee:* $50. Electronic applications accepted. *Application Contact:* Paul McGuinness, Associate Vice President Enrollment Management, 708-534-5000 Ext. 7308, E-mail: pmcguinness@govst.edu. *Dean, College of Health and Human Services*, Catherine Balthazar, 708-534-5000 Ext. 4592, E-mail: cbalthazar@govst.edu.

## GRACE COLLEGE, Winona Lake, IN 46590-1294

**General Information** Independent-religious, coed, comprehensive institution. *Graduate housing:* On-campus housing not available.

**GRADUATE UNITS**

**Department of Graduate Counseling** *Program availability:* Part-time. Electronic applications accepted.

## GRACE COLLEGE OF DIVINITY, Fayetteville, NC 28314

**General Information** Independent-religious, coed, comprehensive institution. *Enrollment by degree level:* 32 master's, 5 doctoral, 1 other advanced degree. *Graduate faculty:* 3 full-time (1 woman), 6 part-time/adjunct (1 woman). *Tuition:* Full-time $5040; part-time $280 per credit hour. *Required fees:* $110; $110 per unit. $50 per semester. One-time fee: $10. Tuition and fees vary according to degree level. *Graduate housing:* On-campus housing not available. *Student services:* Free psychological counseling, international student services, services for students with disabilities, writing training.
Website: http://www.gcd.edu/

**General Application Contact:** Frank R Brazell, Director of Enrollment Management, 910-2212224, E-mail: admissions@gcd.edu.

**GRADUATE UNITS**

**Graduate Program**

## GRACELAND UNIVERSITY, Lamoni, IA 50140

**General Information** Independent-religious, coed, comprehensive institution. *Graduate housing:* On-campus housing not available.

**GRADUATE UNITS**

**Community of Christ Seminary** *Program availability:* Evening/weekend. Electronic applications accepted.

**Gleazer School of Education** *Program availability:* Part-time, 100% online. Electronic applications accepted.

**School of Nursing** *Program availability:* Part-time, online only, 100% online. Electronic applications accepted.

## GRACE MISSION UNIVERSITY, Fullerton, CA 92833

**General Information** Independent, coed, comprehensive institution.

**GRADUATE UNITS**

**Graduate School**

## GRACE SCHOOL OF THEOLOGY, Conroe, TX 77384-4894

**General Information** Independent, coed, comprehensive institution.

**GRADUATE UNITS**

**Graduate Programs**

## GRACE THEOLOGICAL SEMINARY, Winona Lake, IN 46590-9907

**General Information** Independent-religious, coed, primarily men, graduate-only institution. *Graduate housing:* On-campus housing not available.

**GRADUATE UNITS**

**Graduate and Professional Programs** *Program availability:* Part-time, online learning. Electronic applications accepted.

## THE GRADUATE CENTER, CITY UNIVERSITY OF NEW YORK, New York, NY 10016-4039

**General Information** State and locally supported, coed, graduate-only institution. CGS member. *Graduate housing:* Rooms and/or apartments available to single and married students. Housing application deadline: 5/1. *Research affiliation:* American Museum of Natural History (anthropology), Roche Institute of Molecular Biology (biological sciences), New York Botanical Gardens (biological sciences).

**GRADUATE UNITS**

**Graduate Studies** Electronic applications accepted.

## GRADUATE THEOLOGICAL UNION, Berkeley, CA 94709-1212

**General Information** Independent-religious, coed, graduate-only institution. *Graduate housing:* Rooms and/or apartments available on a first-come, first-served basis to single and married students. Housing application deadline: 6/1.

**GRADUATE UNITS**

**Graduate Programs** Electronic applications accepted.

## GRAMBLING STATE UNIVERSITY, Grambling, LA 71245

**General Information** State-supported, coed, university. CGS member. *Graduate housing:* On-campus housing not available. *Research affiliation:* U.S. Department of Defense (cyberspace technology, materials and manufacturing), National Institutes of Justice (technology and equipment in forensic science), U.S. Department of Housing and Urban Development (HUD) (housing preservation in low-income areas), National Science Foundation (science and engineering), NASA (aeronautics research), National Institutes of Health (biomedical sciences).

**GRADUATE UNITS**

**School of Graduate Studies and Research** *Program availability:* Part-time, evening/weekend. Electronic applications accepted.

***College of Arts and Sciences*** *Program availability:* Part-time. Electronic applications accepted.

***College of Education*** *Program availability:* Part-time, evening/weekend. Electronic applications accepted.

***College of Professional Studies*** *Program availability:* Part-time. Electronic applications accepted.

## GRAND CANYON UNIVERSITY, Phoenix, AZ 85017-1097

**General Information** Independent-religious, coed, comprehensive institution. *Graduate housing:* Rooms and/or apartments available on a first-come, first-served basis to single and married students.

**GRADUATE UNITS**

**Colangelo College of Business** *Program availability:* Part-time, evening/weekend, online learning. Electronic applications accepted.

**College of Doctoral Studies**

**College of Education** *Program availability:* Part-time, evening/weekend, online learning. Electronic applications accepted.

**College of Nursing and Health Care Professions** *Program availability:* Part-time, evening/weekend, online learning.

## GRAND RAPIDS THEOLOGICAL SEMINARY OF CORNERSTONE UNIVERSITY, Grand Rapids, MI 49525-5897

**General Information** Independent-religious, coed, graduate-only institution. *Graduate housing:* Rooms and/or apartments available on a first-come, first-served basis to single and married students. Housing application deadline: 6/1.

**GRADUATE UNITS**

**Graduate Programs** *Program availability:* Part-time, evening/weekend, 100% online, blended/hybrid learning. Electronic applications accepted.

## GRAND VALLEY STATE UNIVERSITY, Allendale, MI 49401-9403

**General Information** State-supported, coed, comprehensive institution. CGS member. *Enrollment:* 24,033 graduate, professional, and undergraduate students; 1,381 full-time matriculated graduate/professional students (1,025 women), 1,433 part-time matriculated graduate/professional students (979 women). *Enrollment by degree level:* 2,542 master's, 248 doctoral, 24 other advanced degrees. *Graduate faculty:* 307 full-time (159 women), 96 part-time/adjunct (58 women). *International tuition:* $12,654 full-time. Tuition, state resident: full-time $12,654; part-time $3515 per credit hour. Tuition, nonresident: full-time $12,654; part-time $3515 per credit hour. Tuition and fees vary according to degree level and program. *Graduate housing:* Rooms and/or apartments available on a first-come, first-served basis to single and married students. Housing application deadline: 2/1. *Student services:* Campus employment opportunities, campus safety program, career counseling, child daycare facilities, exercise/wellness program, free psychological counseling, grant writing training, international student services, low-cost health insurance, multicultural affairs office, services for students with disabilities, teacher training, writing training. *Library facilities:* Mary Idema Pew Library Learning and Information Commons plus 5 others. *Collection:* Books: 527,588 (physical), 1 million (digital/electronic). Students can reserve study rooms. *Research affiliation:* Van Andel Institute (life sciences/medical research), Spectrum Health (medical research), Elkins Innovations (life sciences), Progressive AE (water quality).

**Computer facilities:** 2,600 computers available on campus for general student use. A campuswide network can be accessed. Online class registration, transcript, degree audit, credit card payments are available.
Website: http://www.gvsu.edu/

**General Application Contact:** Tracey James-Heer, Associate Director of Admissions, 616-331-2025, Fax: 616-331-2000, E-mail: james-ht@gvsu.edu.

**GRADUATE UNITS**

**Brooks College of Interdisciplinary Studies**

**College of Community and Public Service** Students: 248 full-time (212 women), 238 part-time (186 women); includes 88 minority (31 Black or African American, non-Hispanic/Latino; 5 American Indian or Alaska Native, non-Hispanic/Latino; 7 Asian, non-Hispanic/Latino; 33 Hispanic/Latino; 12 Two or more races, non-Hispanic/Latino), 18 international. Average age 28. 284 applicants, 93% accepted, 135 enrolled. *Faculty:* 28 full-time (15 women), 23 part-time/adjunct (13 women). Expenses: Contact institution. *Financial support:* In 2019–20, 95 students received support, including 61 fellowships, 36 research assistantships with full and partial tuition reimbursements available (averaging $8,000 per year); teaching assistantships, career-related internships or fieldwork, Federal Work-Study, institutionally sponsored loans, scholarships/grants, and unspecified assistantships also available. Financial award application deadline: 5/1. In 2019, 220 master's awarded. *Program availability:* Part-time, evening/weekend. *Application deadline:* For fall admission, 5/1 priority date for domestic students; for winter admission, 11/1 priority date for domestic students; for spring admission, 4/10 priority date for domestic students. Applications are processed on a rolling basis. *Application fee:* $30. Electronic applications accepted. *Application Contact:* Tracey James-Heer, Associate Director of Admissions, 616-331-2025, Fax: 616-331-2000, E-mail: james-ht@gvsu.edu. *Dean*, Dr. George Grant, 616-331-6850, E-mail: grantg@gvsu.edu.

***School of Criminal Justice*** Students: 11 full-time (9 women), 9 part-time (7 women); includes 6 minority (2 Black or African American, non-Hispanic/Latino; 4 Hispanic/Latino), 1 international. Average age 28. 18 applicants, 89% accepted, 8 enrolled. *Faculty:* 4 full-time (2 women). Expenses: Contact institution. *Financial support:* In 2019–20, 6 students received support, including 2 fellowships, 6 research assistantships with full and partial tuition reimbursements available (averaging $4,000 per year); career-related internships or fieldwork, Federal Work-Study, scholarships/grants, and unspecified assistantships also available. Financial award application deadline: 5/1. In 2019, 3 master's awarded. *Program availability:* Part-time, evening/weekend. *Application deadline:* For fall admission, 5/1 priority date for domestic students; for winter admission, 11/1 priority date for domestic students; for spring admission, 4/1 priority date for domestic students. Applications are processed on a rolling basis. *Application fee:* $30. Electronic applications accepted. *Application Contact:* Dr. Tonisha Jones, Graduate Program Director/Recruiting Contact, 616-331-7187, Fax: 616-331-7155, E-mail: jontonis@gvsu.edu. *Director*, Dr. Patrick Gerkin, 616-331-7130, Fax: 616-331-7155, E-mail: gerkinp@gvsu.edu.

***School of Public, Nonprofit and Health Administration*** Students: 29 full-time (20 women), 72 part-time (47 women); includes 11 minority (6 Black or African American, non-Hispanic/Latino; 2 American Indian or Alaska Native, non-Hispanic/Latino; 2 Asian, non-Hispanic/Latino; 1 Hispanic/Latino), 5 international. Average age 29. 68 applicants, 88% accepted, 23 enrolled. *Faculty:* 9 full-time (3 women), 6 part-time/adjunct (2 women). Expenses: Contact institution. *Financial support:* In 2019–20, 26 students received support, including 16 fellowships, 8 research assistantships with full and partial tuition reimbursements available (averaging $4,000 per year); career-related internships or fieldwork, Federal Work-Study, scholarships/grants, and unspecified assistantships also available. Financial award application deadline: 5/1. In 2019, 40 master's awarded. *Program availability:* Part-time, evening/weekend. *Application deadline:* For fall admission, 6/1 priority date for domestic students; for winter admission, 11/1 priority date for domestic students; for spring admission, 4/1 priority date for domestic students. Applications are processed on a rolling basis. *Application fee:* $30. Electronic applications accepted. *Application Contact:* Dr. Davia Downey, Graduate Program Director/Recruiting Contact, 616-331-6681, Fax: 616-331-7120, E-mail: downeyd@gvsu.edu. *Director*, Dr. Richard Jelier, 616-331-6575, Fax: 616-331-7120, E-mail: jelierr@gvsu.edu.

***School of Social Work*** Students: 169 full-time (154 women), 111 part-time (100 women); includes 57 minority (18 Black or African American, non-Hispanic/Latino; 3 American Indian or Alaska Native, non-Hispanic/Latino; 4 Asian, non-Hispanic/Latino; 25 Hispanic/Latino; 7 Two or more races, non-Hispanic/Latino), 2 international. Average age 28. 151 applicants, 95% accepted, 85 enrolled. *Faculty:* 15 full-time (10 women), 17 part-time/adjunct (11 women). Expenses: Contact institution. *Financial support:* In 2019–20, 51 students received support, including 37 fellowships, 17 research assistantships with full and partial tuition reimbursements available (averaging $4,000 per year); career-related internships or fieldwork, Federal Work-Study, institutionally sponsored loans, and unspecified assistantships also available. In 2019, 151 master's awarded. *Program availability:* Part-time. *Application deadline:* For fall admission, 5/1 priority date for domestic students; for winter admission, 10/1 priority date for domestic students; for spring admission, 3/15 priority date for domestic students. Applications are processed on a rolling basis. *Application fee:* $30. Electronic applications accepted. *Application Contact:* Dr. Cray Mulder, Graduate Program Director/Recruiting Contact, 616-331-6596, Fax: 616-331-6570, E-mail: muldercra@gvsu.edu. *Chair*, Dr. Scott Berlin, 616-331-6556, Fax: 616-331-6570, E-mail: berlins@gvsu.edu.

**College of Education** Students: 132 full-time (80 women), 689 part-time (534 women); includes 105 minority (51 Black or African American, non-Hispanic/Latino; 2 American Indian or Alaska Native, non-Hispanic/Latino; 8 Asian, non-Hispanic/Latino; 33 Hispanic/Latino; 11 Two or more races, non-Hispanic/Latino), 7 international. Average age 33. 253 applicants, 95% accepted, 106 enrolled. *Faculty:* 42 full-time (25 women), 17 part-time/adjunct (11 women). Expenses: Contact institution. *Financial support:* In 2019–20, 237 students received support, including 184 fellowships, 5 research assistantships with full and partial tuition reimbursements available (averaging $8,000 per year); career-related internships or fieldwork, Federal Work-Study, scholarships/grants, and unspecified assistantships also available. In 2019, 271 master's, 9 Ed Ss awarded. *Program availability:* Part-time, evening/weekend, 100% online. *Application deadline:* Applications are processed on a rolling basis. *Application fee:* $30. Electronic applications accepted. *Application Contact:* Annukka Thelen, Director, Student Information and Services Center, 616-331-6650, Fax: 616-331-6217, E-mail: thelenant@gvsu.edu. *Dean*, Dr. Sherril Soman, 616-331-2987, Fax: 616-331-6515, E-mail: somans@gvsu.edu.

**College of Health Professions** Students: 672 full-time (554 women), 40 part-time (37 women); includes 75 minority (18 Black or African American, non-Hispanic/Latino; 1 American Indian or Alaska Native, non-Hispanic/Latino; 17 Asian, non-Hispanic/Latino; 22 Hispanic/Latino; 17 Two or more races, non-Hispanic/Latino), 9 international. Average age 25. 1,196 applicants, 34% accepted, 292 enrolled. *Faculty:* 61 full-time (49 women), 17 part-time/adjunct (14 women). Expenses: Contact institution. *Financial support:* In 2019–20, 122 students received support, including 84 fellowships, 46 research assistantships with full and partial tuition reimbursements available (averaging $8,000 per year); career-related internships or fieldwork, Federal Work-Study, institutionally sponsored loans, and scholarships/grants also available. Financial award application deadline: 2/15. In 2019, 221 master's, 60 doctorates awarded. *Application deadline:* For winter admission, 1/15 priority date for domestic and international students. Applications are processed on a rolling basis. Electronic applications accepted. *Application Contact:* Darlene Zwart, Student Services Coordinator, 616-331-3958, E-mail: zwartda@gvsu.edu. *Dean*, Dr. Roy Olsson, 616-331-3356, Fax: 616-331-3350, E-mail: olssonr@gvsu.edu.

**College of Liberal Arts and Sciences** Students: 135 full-time (84 women), 127 part-time (85 women); includes 35 minority (13 Black or African American, non-Hispanic/Latino; 2 American Indian or Alaska Native, non-Hispanic/Latino; 2 Asian, non-Hispanic/Latino; 7 Hispanic/Latino; 11 Two or more races, non-Hispanic/Latino), 25 international. Average age 27. 207 applicants, 83% accepted, 92 enrolled. *Faculty:* 95 full-time (40 women), 7 part-time/adjunct (3 women). Expenses: Contact institution. *Financial support:* In 2019–20, 116 students received support, including 41 fellowships; research assistantships, career-related internships or fieldwork, Federal Work-Study, institutionally sponsored loans, scholarships/grants, and unspecified assistantships also available. In 2019, 97 master's, 12 other advanced degrees awarded. *Program availability:* Part-time, evening/weekend. *Application deadline:* Applications are processed on a rolling basis. *Application fee:* $30. Electronic applications accepted. *Application Contact:* Betty Schaner, Assistant Dean of Advising and Student Services, 616-331-2495, Fax: 616-331-3675, E-mail: schanerb@gvsu.edu. *Dean*, Dr. Frederick Antczak, 616-331-2495, Fax: 616-331-3675, E-mail: antczakf@gvsu.edu.

***School of Communications*** Students: 15 full-time (9 women), 26 part-time (18 women); includes 14 minority (8 Black or African American, non-Hispanic/Latino; 2 Hispanic/Latino; 4 Two or more races, non-Hispanic/Latino), 4 international. Average age 29. 33 applicants, 100% accepted, 14 enrolled. *Faculty:* 2 full-time (0 women), 1 part-time/adjunct (0 women). Expenses: Contact institution. *Financial support:* In 2019–20, 13 students received support, including 9 fellowships, 1 research assistantship with full and partial tuition reimbursement available (averaging $8,000 per year); career-related internships or fieldwork, Federal Work-Study, and institutionally sponsored loans also available. Support available to part-time students. Financial award application deadline: 4/15. In 2019, 22 master's awarded. *Program availability:* Part-time, evening/weekend. *Application deadline:* For fall admission, 8/15 priority date for domestic students; for winter admission, 12/15 priority date for domestic students; for spring admission, 4/15 priority date for domestic students. Applications are processed on a rolling basis. *Application fee:* $30. Electronic applications accepted. *Application Contact:* Dr. Alex Nesterenko, Graduate Program Director, 616-331-3667, Fax: 616-331-2700, E-mail: nesterea@gvsu.edu. *Department Director*, Dr. Richard Besel, 616-331-8045, Fax: 616-331-2700, E-mail: beselri@gvsu.edu.

**Kirkhof College of Nursing** Students: 55 full-time (47 women), 21 part-time (19 women); includes 12 minority (5 Black or African American, non-Hispanic/Latino; 4 Asian, non-Hispanic/Latino; 2 Hispanic/Latino; 1 Two or more races, non-Hispanic/Latino), 1 international. Average age 32. 33 applicants, 94% accepted, 21 enrolled. *Faculty:* 14 full-time (all women), 4 part-time/adjunct (3 women). Expenses: Contact institution. *Financial support:* In 2019–20, 39 students received support, including 14 fellowships, 20 research assistantships with partial tuition reimbursements available (averaging $4,000 per year); career-related internships or fieldwork, Federal Work-Study, institutionally sponsored loans, and traineeships also available. Financial award application deadline: 2/15. In 2019, 7 master's, 49 doctorates awarded. *Program availability:* Part-time. *Application deadline:* For fall admission, 3/15 priority date for domestic students. Applications are processed on a rolling basis. *Application fee:* $30. Electronic applications accepted. *Application Contact:* Dr. Katherine Moran, Graduate Program Director, 616-331-5458, Fax: 616-331-2510, E-mail: morakath@gvsu.edu. *Dean*, Dr. Cynthia McCurren, 616-331-3558, Fax: 616-331-2510, E-mail: mccurrec@gvsu.edu.

**Padnos College of Engineering and Computing** Students: 67 full-time (22 women), 123 part-time (31 women); includes 25 minority (3 Black or African American, non-Hispanic/Latino; 13 Asian, non-Hispanic/Latino; 7 Hispanic/Latino; 2 Two or more races, non-Hispanic/Latino), 65 international. Average age 28. 206 applicants, 73% accepted, 34 enrolled. *Faculty:* 36 full-time (6 women), 1 part-time/adjunct (0 women). Expenses: Contact institution. *Financial support:* In 2019–20, 69 students received support, including 18 fellowships, 56 research assistantships with full and partial tuition reimbursements available (averaging $8,000 per year); unspecified assistantships also available. In 2019, 71 master's awarded. *Program availability:* Part-time. *Application deadline:* For fall admission, 2/1 for domestic students. Applications are processed on a rolling basis. *Application fee:* $30. Electronic applications accepted. *Application Contact:* Sara Wheeler, Director, Advising Center, 616-331-6025, Fax: 616-331-6770, E-mail: wheelesa@gvsu.edu. *Dean*, Dr. Paul Plotkowski, 616-331-6260, Fax: 616-331-6770, E-mail: plotkowp@gvsu.edu.

***School of Computing and Information Systems*** Students: 11 full-time (4 women), 52 part-time (9 women); includes 12 minority (2 Black or African American, non-Hispanic/Latino; 5 Asian, non-Hispanic/Latino; 4 Hispanic/Latino; 1 Two or more races, non-Hispanic/Latino), 12 international. Average age 30. 31 applicants, 58% accepted, 6 enrolled. *Faculty:* 10 full-time (0 women). Expenses: Contact institution. *Financial support:* In 2019–20, 13 students received support, including 6 fellowships, 5 research assistantships with full and partial tuition reimbursements available (averaging $8,000 per year). In 2019, 23 master's awarded. *Program availability:* Part-time, evening/weekend. *Application deadline:* For fall admission, 6/1 for international students; for winter admission, 9/1 for international students. Applications are processed on a rolling basis. *Application fee:* $30. Electronic applications accepted. *Application Contact:* Dr. D. Robert Adams, Graduate Program Director, 616-331-3885, Fax: 616-331-2144, E-mail: adamsr@gvsu.edu. *Director*, Dr. Paul Leidig, 616-331-2060, Fax: 616-331-2144, E-mail: leidigp@gvsu.edu.

***School of Engineering*** Students: 23 full-time (2 women), 35 part-time (5 women); includes 4 minority (2 Asian, non-Hispanic/Latino; 1 Hispanic/Latino; 1 Two or more races, non-Hispanic/Latino), 25 international. Average age 27. 46 applicants, 78% accepted, 10 enrolled. *Faculty:* 22 full-time (6 women), 1 part-time/adjunct (0 women). Expenses: Contact institution. *Financial support:* In 2019–20, 40 students received support, including 8 fellowships, 34 research assistantships with full and partial tuition reimbursements available (averaging $4,000 per year); career-related internships or fieldwork, Federal Work-Study, institutionally sponsored loans, scholarships/grants, and unspecified assistantships also available. In 2019, 32 master's awarded. *Program availability:* Part-time, evening/weekend. *Application deadline:* Applications are processed on a rolling basis. *Application fee:* $30. Electronic applications accepted. *Application Contact:* Dr. Shabbir Choudhuri, Graduate Program Director, 616-331-6845, Fax: 616-331-7215, E-mail: choudhus@gvsu.edu. *Director*, Dr. Wael Mokhtar, 616-331-6015, Fax: 616-331-7215, E-mail: mokhtarw@gvsu.edu.

**Seidman College of Business** Students: 81 full-time (35 women), 184 part-time (77 women); includes 46 minority (4 Black or African American, non-Hispanic/Latino; 3 American Indian or Alaska Native, non-Hispanic/Latino; 15 Asian, non-Hispanic/Latino; 15 Hispanic/Latino; 9 Two or more races, non-Hispanic/Latino), 13 international.

Average age 31. 74 applicants, 89% accepted, 25 enrolled. *Faculty:* 26 full-time (7 women), 10 part-time/adjunct (1 woman). Expenses: Contact institution. *Financial support:* In 2019–20, 50 students received support, including 36 fellowships, 19 research assistantships; Federal Work-Study, institutionally sponsored loans, and unspecified assistantships also available. Support available to part-time students. Financial award application deadline: 2/15; financial award applicants required to submit FAFSA. In 2019, 111 master's awarded. *Program availability:* Part-time, evening/weekend. *Application deadline:* For fall admission, 8/1 priority date for domestic students, 5/1 priority date for international students; for winter admission, 12/1 priority date for domestic students, 11/1 priority date for international students; for spring admission, 4/1 priority date for domestic students, 3/1 priority date for international students. Applications are processed on a rolling basis. *Application fee:* $30. Electronic applications accepted. *Application Contact:* Koleta Moore, Assistant Dean of Student Engagement, Graduate Program Operations, 616-331-7400, Fax: 616-331-7389, E-mail: moorekol@gvsu.edu. *Dean,* Dr. Diana Lawson, 616-331-7385, Fax: 616-331-7380, E-mail: lawsond1@gvsu.edu.

## GRAND VIEW UNIVERSITY, Des Moines, IA 50316-1599

**General Information** Independent-religious, coed, comprehensive institution.

**GRADUATE UNITS**

**Graduate Studies** *Program availability:* Part-time, evening/weekend. Electronic applications accepted.

## GRANITE STATE COLLEGE, Concord, NH 03301

**General Information** State and locally supported, coed, comprehensive institution. *Enrollment:* 2,005 graduate, professional, and undergraduate students; 20 full-time matriculated graduate/professional students (15 women), 114 part-time matriculated graduate/professional students (75 women). *Enrollment by degree level:* 134 master's. *Graduate faculty:* 5 full-time (all women), 31 part-time/adjunct (15 women). *International tuition:* $10,620 full-time. *Tuition, area resident:* Full-time $9684; part-time $538 per credit. Tuition, state resident: full-time $9684; part-time $538 per credit. Tuition, nonresident: full-time $10,620; part-time $590 per credit. *Graduate housing:* On-campus housing not available. *Student services:* Campus employment opportunities, campus safety program, career counseling, free psychological counseling, services for students with disabilities, writing training. *Library facilities:* GSC Library and Information Commons. *Collection:* Books: 400,000 (digital/electronic); Serial titles: 900 (digital/electronic); Databases: 22. Weekly public service hours: 160.

**Computer facilities:** 120 computers available on campus for general student use. A campuswide network can be accessed. Online class registration is available.
Website: http://www.granite.edu/

**General Application Contact:** Ana Gonzalez, Program Director, Graduate Studies, 603-822-5433, E-mail: gsc.graduatestudies@granite.edu.

**GRADUATE UNITS**

**Master's Program in Health Care Management** Students: 5 full-time (4 women), 11 part-time (8 women); includes 4 minority (3 Black or African American, non-Hispanic/Latino; 1 Hispanic/Latino). Average age 37. 5 applicants, 80% accepted, 4 enrolled. *Faculty:* 2 part-time/adjunct (both women). Expenses: Contact institution. *Financial support:* In 2019–20, 9 students received support. Federal Work-Study and National Guard course waivers available. Financial award applicants required to submit FAFSA. *Program availability:* Part-time, evening/weekend, 100% online, blended/hybrid learning. *Application deadline:* Applications are processed on a rolling basis. Electronic applications accepted. *Application Contact:* Ana Gonzalez, Program Coordinator, Academic Affairs, Graduate Studies, 603-513-1334, Fax: 603-513-1387, E-mail: gsc.graduatestudies@granite.edu. *Dean of Graduate Studies and Academic Effectiveness,* Carina Self, 603-822-5440, E-mail: carina.self@granite.edu.

**MS in Instruction and Leadership Program** Students: 1 (woman) full-time, 17 part-time (14 women); includes 4 minority (3 Hispanic/Latino; 1 Two or more races, non-Hispanic/Latino). Average age 40. 7 applicants, 100% accepted, 3 enrolled. *Faculty:* 2 part-time/adjunct (both women). Expenses: Contact institution. *Financial support:* In 2019–20, 2 students received support. Federal Work-Study and National Guard course waiver available. Financial award applicants required to submit FAFSA. In 2019, 16 master's awarded. *Program availability:* Part-time, evening/weekend, 100% online, blended/hybrid learning. *Application deadline:* Applications are processed on a rolling basis. Electronic applications accepted. *Application Contact:* Ana Gonzalez, Program Coordinator, Academic Affairs, Graduate Studies, 603-513-1334, Fax: 603-513-1387, E-mail: gsc.graduatestudies@granite.edd. *Dean of Graduate Studies and Academic Effectiveness,* Dr. Carina Self, 603-822-5440, E-mail: carina.self@granite.edu.

**MS in Leadership Program** Students: 10 full-time (8 women), 55 part-time (36 women); includes 4 minority (1 Black or African American, non-Hispanic/Latino; 3 Hispanic/Latino). Average age 40. 13 applicants, 100% accepted, 11 enrolled. *Faculty:* 1 (woman) full-time, 10 part-time/adjunct (3 women). Expenses: Contact institution. *Financial support:* In 2019–20, 45 students received support. Federal Work-Study and National Guard course waivers available. Financial award applicants required to submit FAFSA. In 2019, 13 master's awarded. *Program availability:* Part-time, evening/weekend, 100% online, blended/hybrid learning. *Application deadline:* Applications are processed on a rolling basis. Electronic applications accepted. *Application Contact:* Ana Gonzalez, Program Coordinator, Academic Affairs, Graduate Studies, 603-513-1334, Fax: 603-513-1387, E-mail: gsc.graduatestudies@granite.edu. *Dean of Graduate Studies and Academic Effectiveness,* Dr. Carina Self, 603-822-5440, E-mail: carina.self@granite.edu.

**MS in Project Management Program** Students: 3 full-time (1 woman), 17 part-time (5 women); includes 2 minority (both Two or more races, non-Hispanic/Latino). Average age 41. 7 applicants, 71% accepted, 3 enrolled. *Faculty:* 1 (woman) full-time, 3 part-time/adjunct (all women). Expenses: Contact institution. *Financial support:* In 2019–20, 13 students received support. Federal Work-Study and National Guard course waivers available. Financial award applicants required to submit FAFSA. In 2019, 16 master's awarded. *Program availability:* Part-time, evening/weekend, 100% online, blended/hybrid learning. *Application deadline:* Applications are processed on a rolling basis. Electronic applications accepted. *Application Contact:* Ana Gonzalez, Program Coordinator, Academic Affairs, Graduate Studies, 603-822-5433, Fax: 603-513-1387, E-mail: gsc.graduatestudies@granite.edu. *Dean of Graduate Studies and Academic Effectiveness,* Dr. Carina Self, 603-822-5440, E-mail: carina.self@granite.edu.

**MS Program in Nursing** Students: 6 full-time (all women), 1 (woman) part-time. Average age 44. 8 applicants, 88% accepted, 7 enrolled. *Faculty:* 2 full-time (both women), 5 part-time/adjunct (all women). Expenses: Contact institution. *Financial support:* In 2019–20, 5 students received support. Federal Work-Study and National Guard course waiver available. Financial award applicants required to submit FAFSA. *Program availability:* Part-time, evening/weekend, 100% online, blended/hybrid learning. *Application deadline:* Applications are processed on a rolling basis. Electronic applications accepted. *Application Contact:* Ana Gonzalez, Administrative Assistant, Office of Graduate Studies, 603-513-1334, Fax: 603-513-1387, E-mail: gsc.graduatestudies@granite.edu. *Dean of Graduate Studies and Academic Effectiveness,* Dr. Carina Self, 603-822-5440, E-mail: carina.self@granite.edu.

## GRANTHAM UNIVERSITY, Lenexa, KS 66219

**General Information** Proprietary, coed, comprehensive institution. *Enrollment:* 850 full-time matriculated graduate/professional students (419 women), 333 part-time matriculated graduate/professional students (155 women). *Enrollment by degree level:* 1,140 master's, 36 other advanced degrees. *Student services:* Career counseling, services for students with disabilities, writing training. *Library facilities:* Grantham Online Library.

**Computer facilities:** Online class registration is available.
Website: http://www.grantham.edu/

**General Application Contact:** Adam Wright, Associate VP of Admissions, 800-955-2527 Ext. 4430, E-mail: admissions@grantham.edu.

**GRADUATE UNITS**

**College of Arts and Sciences** Students: 33 full-time (13 women), 31 part-time (11 women); includes 29 minority (18 Black or African American, non-Hispanic/Latino; 1 American Indian or Alaska Native, non-Hispanic/Latino; 1 Asian, non-Hispanic/Latino; 1 Hispanic/Latino; 1 Native Hawaiian or other Pacific Islander, non-Hispanic/Latino; 7 Two or more races, non-Hispanic/Latino). Average age 39. 35 applicants, 91% accepted, 29 enrolled. *Faculty:* 22 full-time (all women), 346 part-time/adjunct (266 women). Expenses: Contact institution. *Financial support:* Applicants required to submit FAFSA. *Program availability:* Part-time, online only, 100% online. Electronic applications accepted. *Application Contact:* Adam Wright, Associate VP, Enrollment Services, 800-955-2527 Ext. 803, Fax: 877-3044467, E-mail: admissions@grantham.edu. *Dean, College of Business, Management, and Economics; Dean, College of Humanities and Social Science,* Bill Allen, Ph D., 816-500-9206, E-mail: WAllen9@Grantham.EDU.

**College of Engineering and Computer Science** Students: 118 full-time (28 women), 45 part-time (11 women); includes 94 minority (55 Black or African American, non-Hispanic/Latino; 8 Asian, non-Hispanic/Latino; 19 Hispanic/Latino; 1 Native Hawaiian or other Pacific Islander, non-Hispanic/Latino; 11 Two or more races, non-Hispanic/Latino). Average age 40. 20 applicants, 95% accepted, 17 enrolled. Expenses: Contact institution. *Financial support:* Scholarships/grants available. Financial award applicants required to submit FAFSA. In 2019, 96 master's awarded. *Program availability:* Part-time, evening/weekend, online only, 100% online. *Application deadline:* Applications are processed on a rolling basis. Electronic applications accepted. *Application Contact:* Lauren Cook, Director of Admissions, 800-955-2527 Ext. 803, Fax: 877-304-4467, E-mail: admissions@grantham.edu. *Dean of the College of Engineering and Computer Science,* Dr. Nancy Miller, 913-309-4738, Fax: 855-681-5201, E-mail: nmiller@grantham.edu.

**College of Nursing and Allied Health** Students: 180 full-time (135 women), 61 part-time (47 women); includes 124 minority (71 Black or African American, non-Hispanic/Latino; 1 American Indian or Alaska Native, non-Hispanic/Latino; 17 Asian, non-Hispanic/Latino; 17 Hispanic/Latino; 1 Native Hawaiian or other Pacific Islander, non-Hispanic/Latino; 17 Two or more races, non-Hispanic/Latino). Average age 40. 53 applicants, 89% accepted, 37 enrolled. Expenses: Contact institution. *Financial support:* Scholarships/grants available. Financial award applicants required to submit FAFSA. In 2019, 100 master's awarded. *Program availability:* Part-time, evening/weekend, online only, 100% online. *Application deadline:* Applications are processed on a rolling basis. Electronic applications accepted. *Application Contact:* Adam Wright, Associate VP, Enrollment Services, 800-955-2527 Ext. 803, Fax: 877-304-4467, E-mail: admissions@grantham.edu. *Dean of the College of Nursing and the School of Allied Health changing to College of Health Professions,* Dr. Cheryl Rules, 913-309-4783, Fax: 844-897-6490, E-mail: crules@grantham.edu.

**Mark Skousen School of Business** Students: 515 full-time (243 women), 193 part-time (84 women); includes 364 minority (225 Black or African American, non-Hispanic/Latino; 4 American Indian or Alaska Native, non-Hispanic/Latino; 14 Asian, non-Hispanic/Latino; 59 Hispanic/Latino; 2 Native Hawaiian or other Pacific Islander, non-Hispanic/Latino; 60 Two or more races, non-Hispanic/Latino). Average age 40. 111 applicants, 93% accepted, 92 enrolled. Expenses: Contact institution. *Financial support:* Scholarships/grants available. Financial award applicants required to submit FAFSA. In 2019, 324 master's awarded. *Program availability:* Part-time, evening/weekend, online only, 100% online. *Application deadline:* Applications are processed on a rolling basis. Electronic applications accepted. *Application Contact:* Adam Wright, Associate VP, Enrollment Services, 800-955-2527 Ext. 803, Fax: 877-304-4467, E-mail: admissions@grantham.edu. *Dean of the College of Business, Management, and Economics,* Dr. Bill Allen, 800-9552527, E-mail: wallen9@grantham.edu.

## GRATZ COLLEGE, Melrose Park, PA 19027

**General Information** Independent-religious, coed, graduate-only institution. *Graduate housing:* On-campus housing not available.

**GRADUATE UNITS**

**Graduate Programs** *Program availability:* Part-time, evening/weekend, online learning.

## GREENSBORO COLLEGE, Greensboro, NC 27401-1875

**General Information** Independent-religious, coed, comprehensive institution. *Graduate housing:* Rooms and/or apartments guaranteed to single students and available on a first-come, first-served basis to married students. Housing application deadline: 6/1.

**GRADUATE UNITS**

**Program in Education** *Program availability:* Part-time, evening/weekend. Electronic applications accepted.

**Program in Teaching English to Speakers of Other Languages** *Program availability:* Part-time, evening/weekend. Electronic applications accepted.

**Program in Theology, Ethics and Culture**

## GREENVILLE UNIVERSITY, Greenville, IL 62246-0159

**General Information** Independent-religious, coed, comprehensive institution. *Graduate housing:* On-campus housing not available.

**GRADUATE UNITS**

**Program in Education** Electronic applications accepted.

**Program in Leadership and Ministry** *Program availability:* Part-time. Electronic applications accepted.

## GUILFORD COLLEGE, Greensboro, NC 27410-4173

**General Information** Independent-religious, coed, comprehensive institution. *Enrollment:* 1,541 graduate, professional, and undergraduate students; 5 full-time matriculated graduate/professional students (3 women), 4 part-time matriculated graduate/professional students (3 women). *Enrollment by degree level:* 9 master's. *Graduate faculty:* 2 full-time (1 woman), 2 part-time/adjunct (both women). *Tuition:* Part-time $600 per credit. *Student services:* Campus safety program, career counseling, exercise/wellness program, free psychological counseling, multicultural affairs office, services for students with disabilities, writing training. *Library facilities:* Hege Library. *Collection:* Books: 126,217 (physical), 632,861 (digital/electronic); Serial titles: 1,315 (physical), 61,103 (digital/electronic); Databases: 159. Weekly public service hours: 91; students can reserve study rooms.

**Computer facilities:** 275 computers available on campus for general student use. A campuswide network can be accessed. Online class registration, network storage are available.
Website: http://www.guilford.edu/

**General Application Contact:** Kyle Wooden, Director of Admissions, 336-3162000, E-mail: admissions@guilford.edu.

**GRADUATE UNITS**

**Master in Criminal Justice** Students: 4 full-time (2 women), 2 part-time (1 woman); includes 2 minority (both Black or African American, non-Hispanic/Latino). Average age 31. 6 applicants, 100% accepted, 6 enrolled. *Faculty:* 2 full-time (1 woman), 1 (woman) part-time/adjunct. Expenses: Contact institution. *Financial support:* Applicants required to submit FAFSA. *Program availability:* Part-time, evening/weekend. *Application deadline:* Applications are processed on a rolling basis. *Application fee:* $75. Electronic applications accepted. *Application Contact:* Will Pizio, Coordinator, 336-316-2418, E-mail: wpizio@guilford.edu. *Coordinator,* Will Pizio, 336-316-2418, E-mail: wpizio@guilford.edu.

## GWYNEDD MERCY UNIVERSITY, Gwynedd Valley, PA 19437-0901

**General Information** Independent-religious, coed, comprehensive institution. *Enrollment:* 2,990 graduate, professional, and undergraduate students; 696 full-time matriculated graduate/professional students (531 women), 91 part-time matriculated graduate/professional students (72 women). *Enrollment by degree level:* 529 master's, 196 doctoral, 52 other advanced degrees. *Graduate faculty:* 10 full-time (8 women), 146 part-time/adjunct (89 women). *Tuition:* Full-time $10,800; part-time $600 per credit. *Required fees:* $17 per credit. Tuition and fees vary according to program. *Graduate housing:* On-campus housing not available. *Student services:* Campus employment opportunities, campus safety program, career counseling, exercise/wellness program, free psychological counseling, international student services, low-cost health insurance, services for students with disabilities, teacher training, writing training. *Library facilities:* Keiss Library plus 1 other. *Collection:* Books: 85,778 (physical), 180,000 (digital/electronic); Serial titles: 21 (physical), 111,480 (digital/electronic); Databases: 46. Weekly public service hours: 76; students can reserve study rooms.

**Computer facilities:** 200 computers available on campus for general student use. A campuswide network can be accessed. Online class registration is available.
Website: http://www.gmercyu.edu/

**General Application Contact:** Admission Counselor, 866-660-0113, E-mail: accelerate@gmercyu.edu.

**GRADUATE UNITS**

**Frances M. Maguire School of Nursing and Health Professions** Students: 52 full-time (47 women), 58 part-time (52 women); includes 28 minority (17 Black or African American, non-Hispanic/Latino; 9 Asian, non-Hispanic/Latino; 2 Hispanic/Latino). Average age 33. 35 applicants, 43% accepted, 14 enrolled. *Faculty:* 4 full-time (all women), 1 (woman) part-time/adjunct. Expenses: Contact institution. *Financial support:* Scholarships/grants, traineeships, and unspecified assistantships available. Financial award application deadline: 4/15. In 2019, 26 master's awarded. *Program availability:* Part-time, blended/hybrid learning. *Application deadline:* For fall admission, 4/15 for domestic and international students. Applications are processed on a rolling basis. Electronic applications accepted. *Application Contact:* Mary Hermann, Associate Dean, 215-646-7300, E-mail: herman.m@gmercyu.edu. *Dean,* Dr. Ann Phalen, 215-646-7300 Ext. 539, Fax: 215-641-5517, E-mail: phalen.a@gmercyu.edu.

## HALLMARK UNIVERSITY, San Antonio, TX 78230

**General Information** Independent, coed, comprehensive institution. *Graduate housing:* On-campus housing not available.

**GRADUATE UNITS**

**School of Business**

## HAMLINE UNIVERSITY, St. Paul, MN 55104-1284

**General Information** Independent-religious, coed, comprehensive institution. *Graduate housing:* Rooms and/or apartments available on a first-come, first-served basis to single and married students. *Research affiliation:* Minnesota Women Elected Officials.

**GRADUATE UNITS**

**College of Liberal Arts** *Program availability:* Part-time, evening/weekend. Electronic applications accepted.

**School of Business** *Program availability:* Part-time, evening/weekend, blended/hybrid learning. Electronic applications accepted.

**School of Education** *Program availability:* Part-time, evening/weekend, 100% online, blended/hybrid learning. Electronic applications accepted.

## HAMPTON UNIVERSITY, Hampton, VA 23668

**General Information** Independent, coed, comprehensive institution. CGS member. *Enrollment:* 4,619 graduate, professional, and undergraduate students; 310 full-time matriculated graduate/professional students (201 women), 98 part-time matriculated graduate/professional students (68 women). *Enrollment by degree level:* 210 master's, 194 doctoral, 4 other advanced degrees. *Graduate housing:* Room and/or apartments available on a first-come, first-served basis to single students; on-campus housing not available to married students. Typical cost: $6754 per year. Housing application deadline: 6/1. *Student services:* Campus employment opportunities, campus safety program, career counseling, child daycare facilities, exercise/wellness program, free psychological counseling, international student services, services for students with disabilities, teacher training, writing training. *Library facilities:* William R. and Norma B. Harvey Library plus 4 others. *Collection:* Books: 327,841 (physical), 113,623 (digital/electronic); Serial titles: 4,783 (physical), 55,592 (digital/electronic); Databases: 145. Study areas open 24 hours, 5–7 days a week; students can reserve study rooms. *Research affiliation:* NASA (Atmospheric and Planetary Sciences), NASA (Atmospheric and Planetary Sciences, Engineering), National Oceanic and Atmospheric Administration (NOAA) (Atmospheric, Planetary, Marine & Environmental Sciences), Thomas Jefferson National Accelerator Lab (Physics, Medical Physics), L'Oreal (Dermatology, Cancer Research), The Cancer Action Coalition of Virginia (Biology, Nursing, Pharmacy, Medical Physics, Biochemistry & Chemistry).

**Computer facilities:** Computer purchase and lease plans are available. 1,500 computers available on campus for general student use. A campuswide network can be accessed. Online class registration, learning management system are available.
Website: http://www.hamptonu.edu/

**General Application Contact:** Dr. Michelle Penn-Marshall, Dean, Graduate College, 757-727-5454, E-mail: hugrad@hamptonu.edu.

**GRADUATE UNITS**

**Program in Business Administration** Students: 34 full-time (19 women), 15 part-time (6 women); includes 44 minority (43 Black or African American, non-Hispanic/Latino; 1 Hispanic/Latino), 3 international. Average age 29. 27 applicants, 41% accepted, 11 enrolled. Expenses: Contact institution. *Financial support:* Research assistantships, teaching assistantships, career-related internships or fieldwork, Federal Work-Study, institutionally sponsored loans, scholarships/grants, health care benefits, tuition waivers, unspecified assistantships, and stipends available. Support available to part-time students. Financial award application deadline: 6/30; financial award applicants required to submit FAFSA. In 2019, 21 master's, 3 doctorates awarded. *Program availability:* Part-time, online learning. *Application deadline:* For fall admission, 6/1 priority date for domestic students, 4/1 priority date for international students; for spring admission, 11/1 priority date for domestic students, 9/1 priority date for international students; for summer admission, 4/1 priority date for domestic students, 2/1 priority date for international students. Applications are processed on a rolling basis. *Application fee:* $35. Electronic applications accepted. *Application Contact:* Dr. Ziette Hayes, Dean, School of Business, 757-727-5361. *Dean, School of Business,* Dr. Ziette Hayes, 757-727-5361.

**School of Liberal Arts and Education** Students: 91 full-time (53 women), 51 part-time (37 women); includes 133 minority (131 Black or African American, non-Hispanic/Latino; 1 Asian, non-Hispanic/Latino; 1 Native Hawaiian or other Pacific Islander, non-Hispanic/Latino), 2 international. Average age 35. 73 applicants, 56% accepted, 34 enrolled. Expenses: Contact institution. *Financial support:* Fellowships, research assistantships, teaching assistantships, career-related internships or fieldwork, Federal Work-Study, institutionally sponsored loans, and scholarships/grants available. Support available to part-time students. Financial award application deadline: 5/1; financial award applicants required to submit FAFSA. In 2019, 31 master's, 4 doctorates, 5 other advanced degrees awarded. *Program availability:* Part-time, evening/weekend. *Application deadline:* For fall admission, 6/1 priority date for domestic students, 4/1 priority date for international students; for winter admission, 9/1 priority date for international students; for spring admission, 11/1 for domestic students; for summer admission, 4/15 for domestic students, 2/1 priority date for international students. Applications are processed on a rolling basis. *Application fee:* $35. Electronic applications accepted. *Application Contact:* Dr. Michelle Penn-Marshall, Dean, Graduate College, 757-727-5454, E-mail: hugrad@hamptonu.edu. *Dean,* Dr. Linda Malone-Colon, 757-727-5400.

**School of Nursing** Students: 3 full-time (all women), 13 part-time (12 women); includes 15 minority (all Black or African American, non-Hispanic/Latino). Average age 49. 4 applicants, 25% accepted. Expenses: Contact institution. *Financial support:* In 2019–20, 2 students received support. Fellowships, research assistantships, teaching assistantships, career-related internships or fieldwork, Federal Work-Study, institutionally sponsored loans, and scholarships/grants available. Support available to part-time students. Financial award application deadline: 6/30; financial award applicants required to submit FAFSA. In 2019, 3 master's, 5 doctorates awarded. *Program availability:* Part-time, online learning. *Application deadline:* For fall admission, 6/1 priority date for domestic students, 4/1 priority date for international students; for spring admission, 11/1 priority date for domestic students, 9/1 priority date for international students; for summer admission, 4/1 priority date for domestic students, 2/1 priority date for international students. Applications are processed on a rolling basis. *Application fee:* $35. Electronic applications accepted. *Application Contact:* Dr. Shevellanie Lott, Dean, 757-727-5654, E-mail: shevellanie.lott@hamptonu.edu. *Dean,* Dr. Shevellanie Lott, 757-727-5654, E-mail: shevellanie.lott@hamptonu.edu.

**School of Science** Students: 182 full-time (126 women), 17 part-time (11 women); includes 142 minority (121 Black or African American, non-Hispanic/Latino; 2 American Indian or Alaska Native, non-Hispanic/Latino; 10 Asian, non-Hispanic/Latino; 6 Hispanic/Latino; 3 Native Hawaiian or other Pacific Islander, non-Hispanic/Latino), 20 international. Average age 28. 173 applicants, 32% accepted, 37 enrolled. Expenses: Contact institution. *Financial support:* Fellowships, research assistantships, teaching assistantships, career-related internships or fieldwork, Federal Work-Study, institutionally sponsored loans, scholarships/grants, and stipends available. Support available to part-time students. Financial award application deadline: 6/30; financial award applicants required to submit FAFSA. In 2019, 74 master's, 3 doctorates awarded. *Program availability:* Part-time, evening/weekend, online learning. *Application deadline:* For fall admission, 6/1 for domestic students, 4/1 for international students; for winter admission, 11/1 for domestic students, 9/1 for international students; for spring admission, 11/1 for domestic students; for summer admission, 4/1 for domestic students, 2/1 for international students. Applications are processed on a rolling basis. *Application fee:* $35. Electronic applications accepted. *Application Contact:* Dr. Calvin Lowe, Dean, 757-722-5239. *Dean,* Dr. Calvin Lowe, 757-722-5239.

## HANNIBAL-LAGRANGE UNIVERSITY, Hannibal, MO 63401-1999

**General Information** Independent-religious, coed, comprehensive institution.

**GRADUATE UNITS**

**Program in Education** *Program availability:* Part-time, evening/weekend.

## HARDING SCHOOL OF THEOLOGY, Memphis, TN 38117-5499

**General Information** Independent-religious, coed, primarily men, graduate-only institution. *Enrollment by degree level:* 91 master's, 11 doctoral. *Graduate faculty:* 6 full-time (0 women), 2 part-time/adjunct (1 woman). *Tuition:* Full-time $12,240; part-time $8160 per semester hour. *Required fees:* $306; $204 per semester hour. $324 per semester. Tuition and fees vary according to degree level. *Graduate housing:* Rooms and/or apartments available on a first-come, first-served basis to single and married students. Typical cost: $300 per year for single students; $570 per year for married students. Room charges vary according to housing facility selected. *Student services:* Career counseling, low-cost health insurance. *Library facilities:* L.M. Graves Memorial Library. *Collection:* Books: 112,000 (physical); Serial titles: 28,000 (physical); Databases: 62. Weekly public service hours: 63; students can reserve study rooms.

**Computer facilities:** 20 computers available on campus for general student use. A campuswide network can be accessed from student residence rooms. Online class registration, X are available.
Website: http://hst.edu/

**General Application Contact:** Dr. Matt R. Carter, Director of Admissions, 901-761-1356, Fax: 901-761-1358, E-mail: mrcarter@harding.edu.

**GRADUATE UNITS**

**Graduate Programs** *Program availability:* Part-time, online learning. Electronic applications accepted.

## HARDING UNIVERSITY, Searcy, AR 72149-0001

**General Information** Independent-religious, coed, university. *Enrollment:* 5,121 graduate, professional, and undergraduate students; 600 full-time matriculated graduate/professional students (400 women), 500 part-time matriculated graduate/professional students (287 women). *Enrollment by degree level:* 565 master's, 437 doctoral, 98 other advanced degrees. *Graduate faculty:* 68 full-time (24 women), 26 part-time/adjunct (19 women). *Graduate housing:* Rooms and/or apartments available on a first-come, first-served basis to single and married students. *Student services:* Campus employment opportunities, campus safety program, career counseling, exercise/wellness program, free psychological counseling, international student services, services for students with disabilities, writing training. *Library facilities:* Brackett Library plus 1 other. *Collection:* Books: 178,520 (physical), 222,895 (digital/electronic); Serial titles: 464 (physical), 86,289 (digital/electronic); Databases: 188. Weekly public service hours: 88; students can reserve study rooms.

**Computer facilities:** 512 computers available on campus for general student use. A campuswide network can be accessed. Online class registration is available.
Website: http://www.harding.edu/

**GRADUATE UNITS**

**Cannon-Clary College of Education** Students: 109 full-time (69 women), 289 part-time (201 women); includes 63 minority (35 Black or African American, non-Hispanic/Latino; 3 American Indian or Alaska Native, non-Hispanic/Latino; 2 Asian, non-Hispanic/Latino; 14 Hispanic/Latino; 9 Two or more races, non-Hispanic/Latino), 8 international. Average age 34. 115 applicants, 85% accepted, 98 enrolled. *Faculty:* 14 full-time (4 women), 14 part-time/adjunct (12 women). Expenses: Contact institution. *Financial support:* In 2019–20, 33 students received support. Unspecified assistantships available. In 2019, 138 master's, 24 other advanced degrees awarded. *Program availability:* Part-time, evening/weekend. *Application deadline:* For fall admission, 8/1 for domestic and international students; for spring admission, 1/1 for domestic and international students. Applications are processed on a rolling basis. *Application fee:* $35. *Application Contact:* Information Contact, 501-279-4315, E-mail: gradstudiesedu@harding.edu. *Chair,* Dr. Clara Carroll, 501-279-4501, Fax: 501-279-4083, E-mail: ccarroll@harding.edu.

**College of Allied Health** Students: 254 full-time (179 women), 2 part-time (both women); includes 39 minority (10 Black or African American, non-Hispanic/Latino; 2 American Indian or Alaska Native, non-Hispanic/Latino; 14 Asian, non-Hispanic/Latino; 10 Hispanic/Latino; 3 Two or more races, non-Hispanic/Latino). Average age 26. 1,055 applicants, 12% accepted, 85 enrolled. *Faculty:* 14 full-time (4 women). Expenses: Contact institution. *Financial support:* In 2019–20, 6 students received support. In 2019, 54 master's, 31 doctorates awarded. *Application Contact:* Dr. Julie Hixson-Wallace, Vice Provost, 501-279-5205, Fax: 501-279-5192, E-mail: jahixson@harding.edu.

**College of Bible and Ministry** Students: 2 part-time (0 women); includes 1 minority (Black or African American, non-Hispanic/Latino). Average age 48. *Faculty:* 2 full-time (0 women). Expenses: Contact institution. *Financial support:* In 2019–20, 2 students received support. Scholarships/grants and unspecified assistantships available. Financial award applicants required to submit FAFSA. In 2019, 2 master's awarded. *Program availability:* Part-time, online learning. *Application Contact:* Dr. Monte Cox, Dean, 501-279-4448, Fax: 501-279-4042, E-mail: mcox@harding.edu. *Dean,* Dr. Monte Cox, 501-279-4448, Fax: 501-279-4042, E-mail: mcox@harding.edu.

**College of Pharmacy** Students: 172 full-time (119 women), 9 part-time (5 women); includes 41 minority (22 Black or African American, non-Hispanic/Latino; 16 Asian, non-Hispanic/Latino; 3 Hispanic/Latino), 2 international. Average age 27. 143 applicants, 24% accepted, 35 enrolled. *Faculty:* 16 full-time (11 women). Expenses: Contact institution. *Financial support:* In 2019–20, 35 students received support. Scholarships/grants available. Financial award applicants required to submit FAFSA. In 2019, 48 doctorates awarded. *Application deadline:* For fall admission, 3/1 priority date for domestic and international students. Applications are processed on a rolling basis. *Application fee:* $50. Electronic applications accepted. *Application Contact:* Carol Jones, Director of Admissions, 501-279-5523, Fax: 501-279-5525, E-mail: ccjones@harding.edu. *Dean,* Dr. Jeff Mercer, 501-279-5205, Fax: 501-279-5525, E-mail: jmercer@harding.edu.

**Paul R. Carter College of Business Administration** Students: 12 full-time (5 women), 43 part-time (19 women); includes 11 minority (5 Black or African American, non-Hispanic/Latino; 3 Asian, non-Hispanic/Latino; 2 Hispanic/Latino; 1 Two or more races, non-Hispanic/Latino), 2 international. Average age 34. 19 applicants, 95% accepted, 18 enrolled. *Faculty:* 3 part-time/adjunct (1 woman). Expenses: Contact institution. *Financial support:* Unspecified assistantships available. Financial award application deadline: 7/30; financial award applicants required to submit FAFSA. In 2019, 48 master's awarded. *Program availability:* Part-time, evening/weekend, 100% online. *Application deadline:* For fall admission, 8/1 priority date for domestic and international students; for spring admission, 12/1 priority date for domestic and international students. Applications are processed on a rolling basis. *Application fee:* $40.

## HARDIN-SIMMONS UNIVERSITY, Abilene, TX 79698-0001

**General Information** Independent-religious, coed, comprehensive institution. *Graduate housing:* Rooms and/or apartments available on a first-come, first-served basis to single and married students.

**GRADUATE UNITS**

**Graduate School** *Program availability:* Part-time. Electronic applications accepted.

***College of Fine Arts*** *Program availability:* Part-time. Electronic applications accepted.

***College of Human Sciences and Educational Studies*** *Program availability:* Part-time. Electronic applications accepted.

***Cynthia Ann Parker College of Liberal Arts*** *Program availability:* Part-time. Electronic applications accepted.

***Holland School of Sciences and Mathematics*** *Program availability:* Part-time. Electronic applications accepted.

***Kelley College of Business*** *Program availability:* Part-time. Electronic applications accepted.

***Logsdon Seminary*** *Program availability:* Part-time, evening/weekend. Electronic applications accepted.

***Patty Hanks Shelton School of Nursing*** *Program availability:* Part-time. Electronic applications accepted.

## HARRISBURG UNIVERSITY OF SCIENCE AND TECHNOLOGY, Harrisburg, PA 17101

**General Information** Independent, coed, comprehensive institution. *Enrollment:* 3,418 full-time matriculated graduate/professional students (1,610 women), 167 part-time matriculated graduate/professional students (81 women). *Enrollment by degree level:* 3,529 master's, 56 doctoral. *Graduate faculty:* 32 full-time (3 women), 43 part-time/adjunct (12 women). *Tuition:* Full-time $15,900; part-time $7950 per credit hour. *Graduate housing:* On-campus housing not available. *Student services:* Campus employment opportunities, career counseling, international student services. *Library facilities:* Information Commons. *Collection:* Books: 4,130 (physical), 26 (digital/electronic); Serial titles: 103 (physical), 126 (digital/electronic); Databases: 24. Study areas open 24 hours, 5–7 days a week. *Research affiliation:* MistIQ Technologies (data analytics), WildFig Data Company (data analytics).

**Computer facilities:** Computer purchase and lease plans are available. 10 computers available on campus for general student use. A campuswide network can be accessed from student residence rooms and from off campus.
Website: http://www.HarrisburgU.edu/

**General Application Contact:** Steven Infanti, AVP, Graduate Admissions, 717-901-5146, E-mail: Masters@HarrisburgU.edu.

**GRADUATE UNITS**

**Learning Technologies and Media Systems Program** *Program availability:* Part-time, evening/weekend. Electronic applications accepted.

**Program in Human-Centered Interaction Design**

**Program in Information Systems Engineering and Management** *Program availability:* Part-time, evening/weekend. Electronic applications accepted.

**Program in Project Management** *Program availability:* Part-time, evening/weekend. Electronic applications accepted.

**Program in Techpreneurship**

## HARRISON MIDDLETON UNIVERSITY, Tempe, AZ 85282

**General Information** Independent, coed, graduate-only institution.

**GRADUATE UNITS**

**Graduate Program** *Program availability:* Part-time, evening/weekend, online learning. Electronic applications accepted.

## HARTFORD SEMINARY, Hartford, CT 06105-2279

**General Information** Independent-religious, coed, graduate-only institution. *Graduate housing:* Rooms and/or apartments available on a first-come, first-served basis to single and married students. Housing application deadline: 7/15.

**GRADUATE UNITS**

**Graduate Programs** *Program availability:* Part-time, evening/weekend, online learning.

## HARVARD UNIVERSITY, Cambridge, MA 02138

**General Information** Independent, coed, university. CGS member. *Enrollment:* 12,990 full-time matriculated graduate/professional students (6,631 women), 581 part-time matriculated graduate/professional students (303 women). *Enrollment by degree level:* 6,185 master's, 7,352 doctoral, 34 other advanced degrees. *Graduate faculty:* 2,096 full-time (758 women), 411 part-time/adjunct (159 women). *Graduate housing:* Rooms and/or apartments available on a first-come, first-served basis to single and married students. *Student services:* Campus employment opportunities, campus safety program, career counseling, child daycare facilities, exercise/wellness program, free psychological counseling, grant writing training, international student services, low-cost health insurance, multicultural affairs office, services for students with disabilities, teacher training, writing training. *Library facilities:* Widener Library. *Research affiliation:* Woods Hole Oceanographic Institution (biology).

**Computer facilities:** Computer purchase and lease plans are available. 605 computers available on campus for general student use. A campuswide network can be accessed. Online class registration is available.
Website: http://www.harvard.edu/

**GRADUATE UNITS**

**Cyprus International Institute for the Environment and Public Health in Association with Harvard School of Public Health** Electronic applications accepted.

**Extension School** *Program availability:* Part-time, evening/weekend.

**Graduate School of Arts and Sciences** Electronic applications accepted.

***Division of Medical Sciences***

***Harvard John A. Paulson School of Engineering and Applied Sciences*** *Program availability:* Part-time. Electronic applications accepted.

**Graduate School of Design** Electronic applications accepted.

**Harvard Business School**

**Harvard Divinity School** Electronic applications accepted.

**Harvard Graduate School of Education** *Program availability:* Part-time. Electronic applications accepted.

**Harvard Medical School** Electronic applications accepted.

**Harvard T.H. Chan School of Public Health** Students: 797 full-time (526 women), 318 part-time (163 women); includes 279 minority (48 Black or African American, non-Hispanic/Latino; 2 American Indian or Alaska Native, non-Hispanic/Latino; 144 Asian, non-Hispanic/Latino; 52 Hispanic/Latino; 1 Native Hawaiian or other Pacific Islander, non-Hispanic/Latino; 32 Two or more races, non-Hispanic/Latino), 473 international. Average age 29. 2,231 applicants, 42% accepted, 643 enrolled. *Faculty:* 407 full-time (154 women), 133 part-time/adjunct (52 women). Expenses: Contact institution. *Financial support:* Fellowships, research assistantships, teaching assistantships, career-related internships or fieldwork, Federal Work-Study, scholarships/grants, traineeships, and unspecified assistantships available. Support available to part-time students. Financial award application deadline: 2/15; financial award applicants required to submit FAFSA. In 2019, 550 master's, 102 doctorates awarded. *Program availability:* Part-time. *Application deadline:* For fall admission, 12/1 for domestic and international students. *Application fee:* $140. Electronic applications accepted. *Application Contact:* Vincent W. James, Director of Admissions, 617-432-1031, Fax: 617-432-7080, E-mail: admissions@hsph.harvard.edu. *Director of Admissions,* Vincent James, 617-432-1031, E-mail: admissions@hsph.harvard.edu.

**John F. Kennedy School of Government** Electronic applications accepted.

**Law School**

**School of Dental Medicine** Electronic applications accepted.

## HASTINGS COLLEGE, Hastings, NE 68901

**General Information** Independent-religious, coed, comprehensive institution. *Graduate housing:* On-campus housing not available.

**GRADUATE UNITS**

**Department of Teacher Education** *Program availability:* Part-time. Electronic applications accepted.

## HAWAII PACIFIC UNIVERSITY, Honolulu, HI 96813

**General Information** Independent, coed, comprehensive institution. *Enrollment by degree level:* 551 master's, 6 doctoral, 23 other advanced degrees. *Graduate faculty:* 130 full-time (61 women), 157 part-time/adjunct (76 women). *Tuition:* Full-time $18,000; part-time $1125 per credit. *Required fees:* $213; $38 per semester. *Graduate housing:* Room and/or apartments available on a first-come, first-served basis to single students; on-campus housing not available to married students. Typical cost: $5850 per year ($9100 including board). Room and board charges vary according to board plan and housing facility selected. Housing application deadline: 8/1. *Student services:* Campus employment opportunities, campus safety program, career counseling, exercise/wellness program, free psychological counseling, international student services, low-cost health insurance, multicultural affairs office, services for students with disabilities, writing training. *Library facilities:* Meader Library plus 2 others. *Collection:* Books: 103,021 (physical), 191,075 (digital/electronic); Serial titles: 64 (physical), 4,520 (digital/electronic); Databases: 101. Students can reserve study rooms. *Research affiliation:* Oceanic Institute (marine science).

**Computer facilities:** 200 computers available on campus for general student use. A campuswide network can be accessed from student residence rooms and from off campus. Online class registration is available.
Website: http://www.hpu.edu/

**General Application Contact:** Danny Lam, Assistant Director of Graduate Admissions, 808-544-1135, E-mail: graduate@hpu.edu.

**GRADUATE UNITS**

**College of Business** Students: 40 full-time (16 women), 74 part-time (34 women); includes 50 minority (4 Black or African American, non-Hispanic/Latino; 17 Asian, non-Hispanic/Latino; 13 Hispanic/Latino; 1 Native Hawaiian or other Pacific Islander, non-Hispanic/Latino; 15 Two or more races, non-Hispanic/Latino), 18 international. Average age 34. 118 applicants, 77% accepted, 61 enrolled. *Faculty:* 16 full-time (6 women), 6 part-time/adjunct (0 women). Expenses: Contact institution. *Financial support:* In 2019–20, 29 students received support. Research assistantships, teaching assistantships, career-related internships or fieldwork, Federal Work-Study, scholarships/grants, tuition waivers (partial), and unspecified assistantships available. Financial award application deadline: 3/1; financial award applicants required to submit FAFSA. In 2019, 116 master's awarded. *Program availability:* Part-time, evening/weekend, 100% online, blended/hybrid learning. *Application deadline:* For fall admission, 1/15 priority date for domestic students; for spring admission, 10/15 priority date for domestic students. Applications are processed on a rolling basis. *Application fee:* $50. Electronic applications accepted. *Application Contact:* Danny Lam, Assistant Director of Graduate Admissions, 808-544-1135, E-mail: graduate@hpu.edu. *Dean,* Mani Sehgal, 808-544-0275, E-mail: msehgal@hpu.edu.

**College of Health and Society** *Program availability:* Part-time, evening/weekend, 100% online, blended/hybrid learning. Electronic applications accepted.

**College of Liberal Arts** *Program availability:* Part-time, evening/weekend. Electronic applications accepted.

**College of Natural and Computational Sciences** *Program availability:* Part-time. Electronic applications accepted.

**College of Professional Studies** *Program availability:* Part-time, evening/weekend, 100% online, blended/hybrid learning. Electronic applications accepted.

## HAZELDEN BETTY FORD GRADUATE SCHOOL OF ADDICTION STUDIES, Center City, MN 55012

**General Information** Independent, coed, graduate-only institution. CGS member. *Graduate housing:* On-campus housing not available.

**GRADUATE UNITS**

**Graduate Programs** *Program availability:* Part-time.

## HEBREW COLLEGE, Newton Centre, MA 02459

**General Information** Independent-religious, coed, graduate-only institution. *Graduate housing:* On-campus housing not available.

**GRADUATE UNITS**

**Cantor Educator Program**

**Program in Jewish Studies** *Program availability:* Part-time, evening/weekend, online learning.

**Rabbinical School**

**Shoolman Graduate School of Jewish Education** *Program availability:* Part-time, evening/weekend, online learning.

## HEBREW UNION COLLEGE–JEWISH INSTITUTE OF RELIGION, New York, NY 10012-1186

**General Information** Independent-religious, coed, graduate-only institution. *Graduate housing:* On-campus housing not available.

**GRADUATE UNITS**

**Rabbinical School**

**School of Education** *Program availability:* Part-time.

**School of Graduate Studies** *Program availability:* Part-time.

**School of Jewish Nonprofit Management**

**School of Sacred Music**

## HEC MONTREAL, Montréal, QC H3T 2A7, Canada

**General Information** Province-supported, coed, comprehensive institution. *Graduate housing:* Rooms and/or apartments available on a first-come, first-served basis to single students and guaranteed to married students. *Research affiliation:* CIRANO (Centre for Interuniversity Research and Analysis of Organizations) (research and transfer), ACFAS (Association Francophone Pour Le Savoir), PROMPT (Financement de la RD en TIC), CRIAQ (Consortium of Synergetic Research and Innovation in Aerospace) (aerospace), UNIVALOR (Valorisation de la recherche universitaire et le transfert technologique).

**GRADUATE UNITS**

**School of Business Administration** Electronic applications accepted.

## HEIDELBERG UNIVERSITY, Tiffin, OH 44883-2462

**General Information** Independent-religious, coed, comprehensive institution. *Enrollment:* 93 full-time matriculated graduate/professional students (54 women), 78 part-time matriculated graduate/professional students (54 women). *Enrollment by degree level:* 171 master's. *Graduate faculty:* 12 full-time (9 women), 15 part-time/adjunct (8 women). *Tuition:* Full-time $15,580; part-time $744 per credit hour. One-time fee: $240. *Graduate housing:* On-campus housing not available. *Student services:* Campus employment opportunities, campus safety program, career counseling, exercise/wellness program, free psychological counseling, international student services, multicultural affairs office, services for students with disabilities, teacher training, writing training. *Library facilities:* Beeghly Library plus 1 other. *Collection:* Books: 86,891 (physical), 279,499 (digital/electronic); Serial titles: 1,293 (physical), 61,058 (digital/electronic); Databases: 198. Weekly public service hours: 83.

**Computer facilities:** 125 computers available on campus for general student use. A campuswide network can be accessed from student residence rooms and from off campus. Online class registration is available.
Website: http://www.heidelberg.edu/

**General Application Contact:** Katie Zeyen, Graduate Admissions Coordinator, 419-448-2602, Fax: 419-448-2565, E-mail: kzeyen@heidelberg.edu.

**GRADUATE UNITS**

**Master of Arts in Counseling Program** Students: 47 full-time (36 women), 23 part-time (18 women). 43 applicants, 88% accepted, 21 enrolled. Expenses: Contact institution. *Financial support:* Unspecified assistantships available. Financial award applicants required to submit FAFSA. In 2019, 7 master's awarded. *Program availability:* Part-time, evening/weekend. *Application deadline:* For fall admission, 8/15 for domestic students, 6/1 for international students; for spring admission, 12/3 for domestic students, 11/1 for international students; for summer admission, 5/1 for domestic students, 4/1 for international students. Applications are processed on a rolling basis. Electronic applications accepted. *Application Contact:* Katie Zeyen, Graduate Admissions Coordinator, 419-448-2602, Fax: 419-448-2565, E-mail: kzeyen@heidelberg.edu. *Director of Graduate Studies in Counseling,* Dr. Marjorie Shavers, 419-448-2308, E-mail: mshavers@heidelberg.edu.

**Master of Business Administration Program** Students: 45 full-time (17 women), 12 part-time (4 women). 66 applicants, 77% accepted, 35 enrolled. Expenses: Contact institution. *Financial support:* In 2019–20, 26 students received support. Scholarships/grants and unspecified assistantships available. Financial award applicants required to submit FAFSA. In 2019, 21 master's awarded. *Program availability:* Part-time, evening/weekend. *Application deadline:* For fall admission, 6/1 for domestic and international students; for spring admission, 12/3 for domestic students, 12/1 for international students; for summer admission, 5/15 for domestic students, 4/1 for international students. Applications are processed on a rolling basis. Electronic applications accepted. *Application Contact:* Katie Zeyen, Graduate Admissions Coordinator, 419-448-2602, Fax: 419-448-2565, E-mail: kzeyen@heidelberg.edu. *Dean of Business and Technology,* Dr. Scott Johnson, 419-448-2284, E-mail: sjohnson@heidelberg.edu.

**Master of Music Education Program** Expenses: Contact institution. *Financial support:* Unspecified assistantships available. Financial award applicants required to submit FAFSA. *Program availability:* Part-time. *Application deadline:* For fall admission, 6/1 for domestic students. Applications are processed on a rolling basis. Electronic applications accepted. *Application Contact:* Katie Zeyen, Graduate Studies Coordinator, 419-448-2602, Fax: 419-448-2565, E-mail: kzeyen@heidelberg.edu. *Director,* Dr. Carol Dusdieker, 419-448-2080, E-mail: cdusdiek@heidelberg.edu.

## HENDERSON STATE UNIVERSITY, Arkadelphia, AR 71999-0001

**General Information** State-supported, coed, comprehensive institution. CGS member. *Graduate housing:* Room and/or apartments available on a first-come, first-served basis to single students; on-campus housing not available to married students. Housing application deadline: 8/1.

**GRADUATE UNITS**

**Graduate Studies** *Program availability:* Part-time, 100% online.

***Ellis College of Arts and Sciences*** *Program availability:* Part-time.

***School of Business*** *Program availability:* Part-time, 100% online.

***Teachers College*** *Program availability:* Part-time, 100% online.

## HENDRIX COLLEGE, Conway, AR 72032

**General Information** Independent-religious, coed, comprehensive institution. *Graduate housing:* Room and/or apartments available on a first-come, first-served basis to single students. Housing application deadline: 6/1.

**GRADUATE UNITS**

**Program in Accounting** *Program availability:* Part-time.

## HENLEY-PUTNAM SCHOOL OF STRATEGIC SECURITY, Rapid City, SD 57701

**General Information** Proprietary, coed, comprehensive institution.

**GRADUATE UNITS**

**Doctorate Program in Strategic Security** *Program availability:* Part-time, online learning.

**Master of Science Program in Intelligence Management** *Program availability:* Part-time, online learning.

**Master of Science Program in Strategic Security and Protection Management** *Program availability:* Part-time, online learning.

**Master of Science Program in Terrorism and Counterterrorism Studies** *Program availability:* Part-time, online learning.

## HERITAGE CHRISTIAN UNIVERSITY, Florence, AL 35630

**General Information** Independent-religious, coed, primarily men, comprehensive institution.

**GRADUATE UNITS**

**Graduate Programs**

## HERITAGE COLLEGE AND SEMINARY, Cambridge, ON N3C 3T2, Canada

**General Information** Independent-religious, coed, comprehensive institution. *Graduate housing:* Room and/or apartments available on a first-come, first-served basis to single students; on-campus housing not available to married students. Housing application deadline: 5/31.

**GRADUATE UNITS**
**Graduate and Professional Programs**

## HERITAGE UNIVERSITY, Toppenish, WA 98948-9599

**General Information** Independent, coed, comprehensive institution. *Graduate housing:* On-campus housing not available.

**GRADUATE UNITS**
**Graduate Programs in Education** *Program availability:* Part-time, evening/weekend.

## HERZING UNIVERSITY ONLINE, Menomonee Falls, WI 53051

**General Information** Independent, coed, comprehensive institution. CGS member.

**GRADUATE UNITS**
**Program in Business Administration** *Program availability:* Online learning.
**Program in Nursing** *Program availability:* Online learning.

## HIGH POINT UNIVERSITY, High Point, NC 27268

**General Information** Independent-religious, coed, university. *Graduate housing:* On-campus housing not available.

**GRADUATE UNITS**
**Norcross Graduate School** *Program availability:* Part-time, evening/weekend. Electronic applications accepted.

## HIGH TECH HIGH GRADUATE SCHOOL OF EDUCATION, San Diego, CA 92106

**General Information** Private, coed, graduate-only institution.

**GRADUATE UNITS**
**Program in Educational Leadership** *Program availability:* Part-time.

## HILBERT COLLEGE, Hamburg, NY 14075-1597

**General Information** Independent-religious, coed, comprehensive institution. *Graduate housing:* On-campus housing not available.

**GRADUATE UNITS**
**Program in Criminal Justice Administration** *Program availability:* Evening/weekend. Electronic applications accepted.
**Program in Public Administration** *Program availability:* Evening/weekend. Electronic applications accepted.

## HILLSDALE COLLEGE, Hillsdale, MI 49242-1298

**General Information** Independent, coed, comprehensive institution. *Enrollment:* 1,526 graduate, professional, and undergraduate students; 40 full-time matriculated graduate/professional students (10 women), 18 part-time matriculated graduate/professional students (6 women). *Enrollment by degree level:* 28 master's, 30 doctoral. *Graduate faculty:* 11 full-time. *Tuition:* Full-time $24,370; part-time $1340 per credit hour. *Required fees:* $560; $560 per unit. One-time fee: $25. *Graduate housing:* Room and/or apartments available to single students; on-campus housing not available to married students. Typical cost: $5640 per year ($11,390 including board). Room and board charges vary according to board plan and housing facility selected. Housing application deadline: 12/15. *Student services:* Campus employment opportunities, campus safety program, career counseling, exercise/wellness program, free psychological counseling, services for students with disabilities, writing training. *Library facilities:* Michael Alex Mossey Library. *Collection:* Books: 227,424 (physical), 868,409 (digital/electronic); Serial titles: 172 (physical), 154,317 (digital/electronic); Databases: 122.

**Computer facilities:** 345 computers available on campus for general student use. A campuswide network can be accessed from student residence rooms and from off campus. Online class registration is available.
Website: http://www.hillsdale.edu/

**General Application Contact:** Mariel Stauff, Graduate Program Coordinator, 517-607-2483, E-mail: gradschool@hillsdale.edu.

**GRADUATE UNITS**
**Van Andel Graduate School of Statesmanship** Students: 40 full-time (10 women), 11 part-time (3 women). Average age 28. 49 applicants, 37% accepted, 14 enrolled. *Faculty:* 11 full-time. Expenses: Contact institution. *Financial support:* In 2019–20, 51 students received support, including 30 fellowships with full tuition reimbursements available (averaging $20,000 per year), 35 research assistantships with full tuition reimbursements available (averaging $4,143 per year); institutionally sponsored loans, scholarships/grants, and unspecified assistantships also available. Financial award application deadline: 12/15. In 2019, 13 master's, 3 doctorates awarded. *Application deadline:* For fall admission, 12/15 priority date for domestic and international students; for spring admission, 10/15 for domestic and international students. *Application fee:* $25. Electronic applications accepted. *Application Contact:* Mariel Stauff, Graduate Program Coordinator, 517-607-2483, E-mail: gradschool@hillsdale.edu. *Dean*, Dr. Ronald J. Pestritto, 517-607-2483, E-mail: gradschool@hillsdale.edu.

## HIRAM COLLEGE, Hiram, OH 44234

**General Information** Independent, coed, comprehensive institution.

**GRADUATE UNITS**
**Graduate Studies** *Program availability:* Part-time, evening/weekend.

## HODGES UNIVERSITY, Naples, FL 34119

**General Information** Independent, coed, comprehensive institution. *Graduate housing:* On-campus housing not available.

**GRADUATE UNITS**
**Graduate Programs** *Program availability:* Part-time, evening/weekend, 100% online, blended/hybrid learning. Electronic applications accepted.

## HOFSTRA UNIVERSITY, Hempstead, NY 11549

**General Information** Independent, coed, university. CGS member. *Enrollment:* 10,804 graduate, professional, and undergraduate students; 2,968 full-time matriculated graduate/professional students (1,781 women), 1,167 part-time matriculated graduate/professional students (785 women). *Enrollment by degree level:* 2,513 master's, 1,504 doctoral, 118 other advanced degrees. *Graduate faculty:* 243 full-time (123 women), 332 part-time/adjunct (176 women). *Tuition:* Full-time $25,164; part-time $1398 per credit. *Required fees:* $580; $165 per semester. Tuition and fees vary according to course load, degree level and program. *Graduate housing:* Room and/or apartments available on a first-come, first-served basis to single students; on-campus housing not available to married students. Typical cost: $17,716 per year ($22,456 including board). Housing application deadline: 5/1. *Student services:* Campus employment opportunities, campus safety program, career counseling, child daycare facilities, exercise/wellness program, free psychological counseling, grant writing training, international student services, multicultural affairs office, services for students with disabilities, teacher training, writing training. *Library facilities:* Axinn Library plus 2 others. *Collection:* Books: 852,704 (physical), 232,970 (digital/electronic); Serial titles: 13,004 (physical), 207,565 (digital/electronic); Databases: 441. Weekly public service hours: 110; study areas open 24 hours, 5–7 days a week; students can reserve study rooms.

**Computer facilities:** Computer purchase and lease plans are available. 1,536 computers available on campus for general student use. A campuswide network can be accessed. Online class registration, Emergency alert system, online course management system, online card services balance update, online e-portfolio, software tutoring, support for specific tech-enhanced assignments, repair and rebuilding-after-virus services, and printing services are available.
Website: http://www.hofstra.edu/

**General Application Contact:** Sunil Samuel, Assistant Vice President of Admissions, 516-463-4723, Fax: 516-463-4664, E-mail: graduateadmission@hofstra.edu.

**GRADUATE UNITS**
**College of Liberal Arts and Sciences** Students: 269 full-time (193 women), 49 part-time (31 women); includes 70 minority (13 Black or African American, non-Hispanic/Latino; 1 American Indian or Alaska Native, non-Hispanic/Latino; 15 Asian, non-Hispanic/Latino; 35 Hispanic/Latino; 6 Two or more races, non-Hispanic/Latino), 33 international. Average age 27. 531 applicants, 47% accepted, 110 enrolled. *Faculty:* 46 full-time (18 women), 44 part-time/adjunct (21 women). Expenses: Contact institution. *Financial support:* In 2019–20, 240 students received support, including 175 fellowships with full and partial tuition reimbursements available (averaging $7,176 per year), 4 research assistantships with full and partial tuition reimbursements available (averaging $5,531 per year); career-related internships or fieldwork, Federal Work-Study, institutionally sponsored loans, scholarships/grants, traineeships, tuition waivers (full and partial), unspecified assistantships, and scholarships and endowed scholarships also available. Support available to part-time students. Financial award applicants required to submit FAFSA. In 2019, 97 master's, 33 doctorates awarded. *Program availability:* Part-time, evening/weekend. *Application deadline:* Applications are processed on a rolling basis. *Application fee:* $75. Electronic applications accepted. *Application Contact:* Sunil Samuel, Assistant Vice President of Admissions, 516-463-4723, Fax: 516-463-4664, E-mail: graduateadmission@hofstra.edu. *Dean*, Dr. Benjamin Rifkin, 516-463-5411, Fax: 516-463-4861, E-mail: benjamin.rifkin@hofstra.edu.

**Donald and Barbara Zucker School of Medicine at Hofstra/Northwell** Students: 429 full-time (197 women); includes 195 minority (26 Black or African American, non-Hispanic/Latino; 108 Asian, non-Hispanic/Latino; 46 Hispanic/Latino; 4 Native Hawaiian or other Pacific Islander, non-Hispanic/Latino; 11 Two or more races, non-Hispanic/Latino), 2 international. Average age 25. 5,330 applicants, 7% accepted, 104 enrolled. *Faculty:* 20 full-time (13 women), 15 part-time/adjunct (10 women). Expenses: Contact institution. *Financial support:* In 2019–20, 352 students received support, including 347 fellowships with full and partial tuition reimbursements available (averaging $26,261 per year); research assistantships with full and partial tuition reimbursements available, career-related internships or fieldwork, Federal Work-Study, institutionally sponsored loans, scholarships/grants, tuition waivers (full and partial), unspecified assistantships, and scholarships and endowed scholarships also available. Support available to part-time students. Financial award applicants required to submit FAFSA. In 2019, 98 doctorates awarded. *Application deadline:* For fall admission, 12/1 priority date for domestic students. Applications are processed on a rolling basis. *Application fee:* $100. Electronic applications accepted. *Application Contact:* Sunil Samuel, Assistant Vice President of Admissions, 516-463-4723, Fax: 516-463-4664. *Dean*, Dr. Lawrence Smith, 516-463-7517, Fax: 516-463-7543, E-mail: lawrence.smith@hofstra.edu.

**Frank G. Zarb School of Business** Students: 451 full-time (187 women), 274 part-time (126 women); includes 215 minority (45 Black or African American, non-Hispanic/Latino; 2 American Indian or Alaska Native, non-Hispanic/Latino; 87 Asian, non-Hispanic/Latino; 72 Hispanic/Latino; 3 Native Hawaiian or other Pacific Islander, non-Hispanic/Latino; 6 Two or more races, non-Hispanic/Latino), 228 international. Average age 29. 1,129 applicants, 75% accepted, 259 enrolled. *Faculty:* 43 full-time (13 women), 24 part-time/adjunct (4 women). Expenses: Contact institution. *Financial support:* In 2019–20, 220 students received support, including 185 fellowships with full and partial tuition reimbursements available (averaging $5,649 per year), 7 research assistantships with full and partial tuition reimbursements available (averaging $7,705 per year); career-related internships or fieldwork, Federal Work-Study, institutionally sponsored loans, scholarships/grants, tuition waivers (full and partial), unspecified assistantships, and scholarships and endowed scholarships also available. Support available to part-time students. Financial award applicants required to submit FAFSA. In 2019, 375 master's awarded. *Program availability:* Part-time, evening/weekend, online only, blended/hybrid learning. *Application deadline:* Applications are processed on a rolling basis. *Application fee:* $75. Electronic applications accepted. *Application Contact:* Sunil Samuel, Assistant Vice President of Admissions, 516-463-4723, Fax: 516-463-4664, E-mail: graduateadmission@hofstra.edu. *Dean*, Dr. Janet Lenaghan, 516-463-6574, Fax: 516-463-5268, E-mail: janet.a.lenaghan@hofstra.edu.

**Fred DeMatteis School of Engineering and Applied Sciences** Students: 26 full-time (7 women), 34 part-time (7 women); includes 19 minority (3 Black or African American, non-Hispanic/Latino; 1 American Indian or Alaska Native, non-Hispanic/Latino; 6 Asian, non-Hispanic/Latino; 8 Hispanic/Latino; 1 Native Hawaiian or other Pacific Islander, non-Hispanic/Latino), 19 international. Average age 28. 107 applicants, 63% accepted, 26 enrolled. *Faculty:* 8 full-time (2 women), 6 part-time/adjunct (0 women). Expenses: Contact institution. *Financial support:* In 2019–20, 29 students received support, including 22 fellowships with full and partial tuition reimbursements available (averaging $3,686 per year), 2 research assistantships with full and partial tuition reimbursements available (averaging $6,675 per year); career-related internships or fieldwork, Federal Work-Study, institutionally sponsored loans, scholarships/grants, tuition waivers (full and partial), unspecified assistantships, and scholarships and endowed scholarships also available. Support available to part-time students. Financial award applicants required to submit FAFSA. In 2019, 17 master's awarded. *Program availability:* Part-time, evening/weekend, blended/hybrid learning. *Application deadline:* Applications are processed on a rolling basis. *Application fee:* $75. Electronic applications accepted. *Application Contact:* Sunil Samuel, Assistant Vice President of Admissions, 516-463-4723, Fax: 516-463-4664, E-mail: graduateadmission@hofstra.edu. *Dean*, Dr. Sina Rabbany, 516-463-6672, E-mail: sina.y.rabbany@hofstra.edu.

**Hofstra Northwell School of Nursing and Physician Assistant Studies** Students: 211 full-time (156 women), 159 part-time (138 women); includes 127 minority (24 Black or African American, non-Hispanic/Latino; 2 American Indian or Alaska Native, non-Hispanic/Latino; 53 Asian, non-Hispanic/Latino; 45 Hispanic/Latino; 2 Native Hawaiian or other Pacific Islander, non-Hispanic/Latino; 1 Two or more races, non-Hispanic/Latino), 1 international. Average age 29. 2,339 applicants, 8% accepted, 144 enrolled. *Faculty:* 15 full-time (13 women), 24 part-time/adjunct (17 women). Expenses: Contact institution. *Financial support:* In 2019–20, 67 students received support, including 16 fellowships with full and partial tuition reimbursements available (averaging $8,034 per year); research assistantships with full and partial tuition reimbursements available, career-related internships or fieldwork, Federal Work-Study, institutionally sponsored loans, scholarships/grants, traineeships, tuition waivers (full and partial), unspecified assistantships, and scholarships and endowed scholarships also available. Support available to part-time students. Financial award applicants required to submit FAFSA. In 2019, 91 master's awarded. *Application deadline:* For fall admission, 10/1 for domestic students. *Application fee:* $75. Electronic applications accepted. *Application Contact:* Sunil Samuel, Assistant Vice President of Admissions, 516-463-4723, Fax: 516-463-4664, E-mail: graduateadmission@hofstra.edu. *Dean*, Kathleen Gallo, 516-463-7475, Fax: 516-463-7495, E-mail: kathleen.gallo@hofstra.edu.

**Lawrence Herbert School of Communication** Students: 47 full-time (27 women), 17 part-time (12 women); includes 35 minority (22 Black or African American, non-Hispanic/Latino; 2 American Indian or Alaska Native, non-Hispanic/Latino; 2 Asian, non-Hispanic/Latino; 9 Hispanic/Latino), 6 international. Average age 28. 73 applicants, 75% accepted, 23 enrolled. *Faculty:* 7 full-time (3 women), 11 part-time/adjunct (6 women). Expenses: Contact institution. *Financial support:* In 2019–20, 29 students received support, including 23 fellowships with full and partial tuition reimbursements available (averaging $3,783 per year); research assistantships with full and partial tuition reimbursements available, career-related internships or fieldwork, Federal Work-Study, institutionally sponsored loans, scholarships/grants, tuition waivers (full and partial), unspecified assistantships, and scholarships and endowed scholarships also available. Support available to part-time students. Financial award applicants required to submit FAFSA. In 2019, 28 master's awarded. *Program availability:* Part-time, evening/weekend. *Application deadline:* Applications are processed on a rolling basis. *Application fee:* $75. Electronic applications accepted. *Application Contact:* Sunil Samuel, Assistant Vice President of Admissions, 516-463-4723, Fax: 516-463-4664, E-mail: graduateadmission@hofstra.edu. *Dean*, Mark Lukasiewicz, 516-463-5213, E-mail: Mark.Lukasiewicz@hofstra.edu.

**Maurice A. Deane School of Law** Students: 768 full-time (401 women), 119 part-time (83 women); includes 200 minority (56 Black or African American, non-Hispanic/Latino; 3 American Indian or Alaska Native, non-Hispanic/Latino; 42 Asian, non-Hispanic/Latino; 91 Hispanic/Latino; 4 Native Hawaiian or other Pacific Islander, non-Hispanic/Latino; 4 Two or more races, non-Hispanic/Latino), 14 international. Average age 27. 2,993 applicants, 49% accepted, 312 enrolled. *Faculty:* 45 full-time (24 women), 86 part-time/adjunct (34 women). Expenses: Contact institution. *Financial support:* In 2019–20, 690 students received support, including 669 fellowships with full and partial tuition reimbursements available (averaging $33,308 per year), 1 research assistantship with full and partial tuition reimbursement available (averaging $6,750 per year); career-related internships or fieldwork, Federal Work-Study, institutionally sponsored loans, scholarships/grants, tuition waivers (full and partial), unspecified assistantships, and scholarships and endowed scholarships also available. Support available to part-time students. Financial award applicants required to submit FAFSA. In 2019, 48 master's, 217 doctorates awarded. *Program availability:* Part-time, 100% online. *Application deadline:* For fall admission, 4/15 priority date for domestic and international students. Applications are processed on a rolling basis. Electronic applications accepted. *Application Contact:* Sunil Samuel, Assistant Vice President of Admissions, 516-463-4723, Fax: 516-463-4664. *Dean*, Gail Prudenti, 516-463-4068, E-mail: gail.prudenti@hofstra.edu.

**School of Education** Students: 240 full-time (179 women), 316 part-time (234 women); includes 149 minority (55 Black or African American, non-Hispanic/Latino; 3 American Indian or Alaska Native, non-Hispanic/Latino; 20 Asian, non-Hispanic/Latino; 64 Hispanic/Latino; 7 Two or more races, non-Hispanic/Latino), 6 international. Average age 30. 422 applicants, 86% accepted, 222 enrolled. *Faculty:* 25 full-time (16 women), 52 part-time/adjunct (41 women). Expenses: Contact institution. *Financial support:* In 2019–20, 275 students received support, including 155 fellowships with full and partial tuition reimbursements available (averaging $4,689 per year), 14 research assistantships with full and partial tuition reimbursements available (averaging $5,077 per year); career-related internships or fieldwork, Federal Work-Study, institutionally sponsored loans, scholarships/grants, traineeships, tuition waivers (full and partial), unspecified assistantships, and scholarships and endowed scholarships also available. Support available to part-time students. Financial award applicants required to submit FAFSA. In 2019, 216 master's, 30 doctorates, 64 other advanced degrees awarded. *Program availability:* Part-time, evening/weekend, online only, blended/hybrid learning. *Application deadline:* Applications are processed on a rolling basis. *Application fee:* $75. Electronic applications accepted. *Application Contact:* Sunil Samuel, Assistant Vice President of Admissions, 516-463-4723, Fax: 516-463-4664, E-mail: graduateadmission@hofstra.edu. *Dean*, Dr. Benjamin Rifkin, 516-463-5411, Fax: 516-463-4861, E-mail: benjamin.rifkin@hofstra.edu.

**School of Health Professions and Human Services** Students: 527 full-time (434 women), 199 part-time (154 women); includes 276 minority (95 Black or African American, non-Hispanic/Latino; 3 American Indian or Alaska Native, non-Hispanic/Latino; 86 Asian, non-Hispanic/Latino; 78 Hispanic/Latino; 7 Native Hawaiian or other Pacific Islander, non-Hispanic/Latino; 7 Two or more races, non-Hispanic/Latino), 31 international. Average age 28. 1,227 applicants, 57% accepted, 256 enrolled. *Faculty:* 34 full-time (21 women), 70 part-time/adjunct (43 women). Expenses: Contact institution. *Financial support:* In 2019–20, 289 students received support, including 179 fellowships with full and partial tuition reimbursements available (averaging $3,937 per year), 16 research assistantships with full and partial tuition reimbursements available (averaging $6,770 per year); career-related internships or fieldwork, Federal Work-Study, institutionally sponsored loans, scholarships/grants, traineeships, tuition waivers (full and partial), unspecified assistantships, and scholarships and endowed scholarships also available. Support available to part-time students. Financial award applicants required to submit FAFSA. In 2019, 275 master's, 7 doctorates, 6 other advanced degrees awarded. *Program availability:* Part-time, evening/weekend. *Application deadline:* Applications are processed on a rolling basis. *Application fee:* $75. Electronic applications accepted. *Application Contact:* Sunil Samuel, Assistant Vice President of Admissions, 516-463-4723, Fax: 516-463-4664, E-mail: graduateadmission@hofstra.edu. *Dean*, Dr. Holly Seirup, 516-463-5301, Fax: 516-463-5317, E-mail: holly.j.seirup@hofstra.edu.

## HOLLINS UNIVERSITY, Roanoke, VA 24020

**General Information** Independent, Undergraduate: women only; graduate: coed, comprehensive institution. *Enrollment:* 798 graduate, professional, and undergraduate students; 50 full-time matriculated graduate/professional students (39 women), 77 part-time matriculated graduate/professional students (67 women). *Enrollment by degree level:* 127 master's, 2 other advanced degrees. *Graduate faculty:* 17 full-time (9 women), 31 part-time/adjunct (11 women). *Graduate housing:* On-campus housing not available. *Student services:* Campus safety program, career counseling, services for students with disabilities, teacher training, writing training. *Library facilities:* Wyndham Robertson Library plus 1 other. *Collection:* Books: 211,223 (physical), 288,069 (digital/electronic); Serial titles: 1,250 (physical), 64,491 (digital/electronic); Databases: 142. Weekly public service hours: 94.

**Computer facilities:** 102 computers available on campus for general student use. A campuswide network can be accessed. Online class registration is available.
Website: http://www.hollins.edu/

**General Application Contact:** Cathy S. Koon, Manager of Graduate Services, 540-362-6326, Fax: 540-362-6288, E-mail: ckoon@hollins.edu.

**GRADUATE UNITS**

**Graduate Programs** *Program availability:* 100% online, blended/hybrid learning. Electronic applications accepted.

## HOLMES INSTITUTE, Golden, CO 80401

**General Information** Independent-religious, coed, graduate-only institution. *Graduate housing:* On-campus housing not available.

**GRADUATE UNITS**

**Graduate Program** *Program availability:* Online learning.

## HOLY APOSTLES COLLEGE AND SEMINARY, Cromwell, CT 06416-2005

**General Information** Independent-religious, coed, comprehensive institution. *Enrollment:* 603 graduate, professional, and undergraduate students; 165 full-time matriculated graduate/professional students (40 women), 236 part-time matriculated graduate/professional students (80 women). *Enrollment by degree level:* 383 master's, 18 other advanced degrees. *Graduate faculty:* 10 full-time (3 women), 16 part-time/adjunct (5 women). *Tuition:* Full-time $4320; part-time $2160 per credit. *Required fees:* $80; $80 per credit. $40 per semester. One-time fee: $150. *Graduate housing:* On-campus housing not available. *Student services:* Free psychological counseling, writing training. *Library facilities:* Holy Apostles College and Seminary Library. *Collection:* Books: 60,000 (physical); Serial titles: 145 (physical), 32 (digital/electronic); Databases: 5. Weekly public service hours: 70.

**Computer facilities:** 10 computers available on campus for general student use. A campuswide network can be accessed. Online class registration is available.
Website: http://www.holyapostles.edu/

**General Application Contact:** Dr. Elizabeth Rex, Director of Graduate Admission, 860-632-3066, Fax: 860-632-3075, E-mail: registrar@holyapostles.edu.

**GRADUATE UNITS**

**Department of Theology** *Program availability:* Part-time, evening/weekend, online learning. Electronic applications accepted.

## HOLY CROSS GREEK ORTHODOX SCHOOL OF THEOLOGY, Brookline, MA 02445-7496

**General Information** Independent-religious, coed, primarily men, graduate-only institution. *Graduate housing:* Rooms and/or apartments available on a first-come, first-served basis to single and married students.

**GRADUATE UNITS**

**Theological Programs** *Program availability:* Part-time.

## HOLY FAMILY UNIVERSITY, Philadelphia, PA 19114

**General Information** Independent-religious, coed, comprehensive institution. *Graduate housing:* On-campus housing not available.

**GRADUATE UNITS**

**Graduate and Professional Programs** *Program availability:* Part-time, evening/weekend. Electronic applications accepted.

***School of Arts and Sciences*** *Program availability:* Part-time, evening/weekend. Electronic applications accepted.

***School of Business Administration*** *Program availability:* Part-time, evening/weekend. Electronic applications accepted.

***School of Education*** *Program availability:* Part-time, evening/weekend. Electronic applications accepted.

***School of Nursing and Allied Health Professions*** *Program availability:* Part-time, evening/weekend. Electronic applications accepted.

## HOLY NAMES UNIVERSITY, Oakland, CA 94619-1699

**General Information** Independent-religious, coed, comprehensive institution. *Graduate housing:* Room and/or apartments available on a first-come, first-served basis to single students; on-campus housing not available to married students. Housing application deadline: 8/15.

**GRADUATE UNITS**

**Graduate Division** *Program availability:* Part-time, evening/weekend. Electronic applications accepted.

## HOOD COLLEGE, Frederick, MD 21701-8575

**General Information** Independent, coed, comprehensive institution. CGS member. *Graduate housing:* On-campus housing not available. *Research affiliation:* U.S. Department of Agriculture (USDA) (biomedical science and environmental biology), United States Army Medical Research Institute of Infectious Diseases (USAMRIID) (biomedical science), National Cancer Institute (biomedical science).

**GRADUATE UNITS**

**Graduate School** *Program availability:* Part-time, evening/weekend. Electronic applications accepted.

## HOOD THEOLOGICAL SEMINARY, Salisbury, NC 28144

**General Information** Independent-religious, coed, graduate-only institution. *Enrollment by degree level:* 79 master's, 48 doctoral. *Graduate faculty:* 8 full-time (3 women), 8 part-time/adjunct (1 woman). *Tuition:* Full-time $17,160; part-time $7920 per credit hour. *Required fees:* $700; $520 per credit hour. $260 per semester. Full-time tuition and fees vary according to course level, course load and program. *Graduate housing:* Rooms and/or apartments available on a first-come, first-served basis to single and married students. Typical cost: $4000 per year ($5056 including board) for single students; $4000 per year ($5056 including board) for married students. Housing application deadline: 8/15. *Student services:* Campus employment opportunities, writing training. *Library facilities:* Hood Theological Seminary Library. *Collection:* Books: 30,000 (physical); Databases: 3. Weekly public service hours: 48; students can reserve study rooms.

**Computer facilities:** 7 computers available on campus for general student use. A campuswide network can be accessed from student residence rooms and from off campus. Online class registration is available.
Website: http://www.hoodseminary.edu/

**General Application Contact:** Reginald Boyd, Jr., Director of Recruitment and Admissions, 704-636-6455, Fax: 704-636-7685, E-mail: admissions@hoodseminary.edu.

**GRADUATE UNITS**

**Graduate and Professional Programs** *Program availability:* Part-time, evening/weekend, online learning.

## HOPE INTERNATIONAL UNIVERSITY, Fullerton, CA 92831-3138

**General Information** Independent-religious, coed, comprehensive institution. *Graduate housing:* Room and/or apartments available on a first-come, first-served basis to single students; on-campus housing not available to married students. Housing application deadline: 7/1.

**GRADUATE UNITS**

**School of Graduate and Professional Studies** *Program availability:* Part-time, evening/weekend, online learning. Electronic applications accepted.

## HOUGHTON COLLEGE, Houghton, NY 14744

**General Information** Independent-religious, coed, comprehensive institution. *Graduate housing:* On-campus housing not available.

**GRADUATE UNITS**

**Greatbatch School of Music** Electronic applications accepted.

## HOUSTON BAPTIST UNIVERSITY, Houston, TX 77074-3298

**General Information** Independent-religious, coed, comprehensive institution. *Graduate housing:* Rooms and/or apartments available on a first-come, first-served basis to single and married students. Housing application deadline: 4/1.

**GRADUATE UNITS**

**Archie W. Dunham College of Business** *Program availability:* Part-time, evening/weekend, 100% online. Electronic applications accepted.

**College of Education and Behavioral Sciences** *Program availability:* Part-time, evening/weekend, 100% online. Electronic applications accepted.

**School of Christian Thought** *Program availability:* Part-time, evening/weekend. Electronic applications accepted.

**School of Fine Arts** *Program availability:* Part-time, evening/weekend. Electronic applications accepted.

**School of Humanities** *Program availability:* Part-time, evening/weekend. Electronic applications accepted.

**School of Nursing and Allied Health** *Program availability:* Part-time, evening/weekend, online only, 100% online. Electronic applications accepted.

## HOUSTON GRADUATE SCHOOL OF THEOLOGY, Houston, TX 77092

**General Information** Independent-religious, coed, graduate-only institution. *Graduate housing:* On-campus housing not available.

**GRADUATE UNITS**

**Graduate Programs** *Program availability:* Part-time, evening/weekend.

## HOWARD PAYNE UNIVERSITY, Brownwood, TX 76801-2715

**General Information** Independent-religious, coed, comprehensive institution. *Graduate housing:* Room and/or apartments available on a first-come, first-served basis to single students; on-campus housing not available to married students.

**GRADUATE UNITS**

**Program in Business Administration** *Program availability:* Part-time, evening/weekend. Electronic applications accepted.

**Program in Criminal Justice** *Program availability:* Part-time, evening/weekend, online only, 100% online. Electronic applications accepted.

**Program in Instructional Leadership** *Program availability:* Part-time, evening/weekend, online only. Electronic applications accepted.

**Program in Sport and Wellness Leadership** *Program availability:* Part-time. Electronic applications accepted.

**Program in Theology and Ministry** *Program availability:* Part-time. Electronic applications accepted.

**Program in Youth Ministry** *Program availability:* Part-time. Electronic applications accepted.

## HOWARD UNIVERSITY, Washington, DC 20059-0002

**General Information** Independent, coed, university. CGS member. *Graduate housing:* Rooms and/or apartments available on a first-come, first-served basis to single and married students. Housing application deadline: 4/1. *Research affiliation:* Ewing Marion Kauffman Foundation (science education), The Tokyo Foundation (women's studies, international affairs), National Oceanic and Atmospheric Administration (NOAA) (atmospheric science and nanotechnology), National Institute of Mental Health (NIMH) (genomics), Akilu Lamma Institute of Pathobiology (HIV/AIDS infection, water resources development, population movement), Labor Research Laboratories and Medical Center in Benin City, Nigeria (infectious diseases).

**GRADUATE UNITS**

**Cathy Hughes School of Communications** *Program availability:* Part-time, evening/weekend. Electronic applications accepted.

***Department of Communication, Culture and Media Studies*** *Program availability:* Part-time, evening/weekend. Electronic applications accepted.

**College of Dentistry**

**College of Engineering, Architecture, and Computer Sciences** *Program availability:* Part-time. Electronic applications accepted.

***School of Engineering and Computer Science*** *Program availability:* Part-time. Electronic applications accepted.

**College of Medicine**

**College of Nursing and Allied Health Sciences** *Program availability:* Part-time. Electronic applications accepted.

***Division of Allied Health Sciences***

***Division of Nursing*** *Program availability:* Part-time.

**College of Pharmacy** *Program availability:* Online learning. Electronic applications accepted.

**Graduate School** *Program availability:* Part-time, evening/weekend. Electronic applications accepted.

***Division of Fine Arts*** *Program availability:* Part-time.

**School of Business** *Program availability:* Part-time, evening/weekend, online learning.

**School of Divinity** *Program availability:* Part-time, evening/weekend. Electronic applications accepted.

**School of Education** Electronic applications accepted.

**School of Law** Electronic applications accepted.

**School of Social Work** *Program availability:* Part-time. Electronic applications accepted.

## HULT INTERNATIONAL BUSINESS SCHOOL, Cambridge, MA 02141

**General Information** Independent, coed, comprehensive institution. *Graduate housing:* On-campus housing not available.

**GRADUATE UNITS**

**Graduate Programs** Electronic applications accepted.

## HUMBOLDT STATE UNIVERSITY, Arcata, CA 95521-8299

**General Information** State-supported, coed, comprehensive institution. *Enrollment:* 6,983 graduate, professional, and undergraduate students; 277 full-time matriculated graduate/professional students (191 women), 266 part-time matriculated graduate/professional students (180 women). *Enrollment by degree level:* 543 master's. *Graduate faculty:* 142 full-time (71 women), 178 part-time/adjunct (118 women). Tuition, state resident: full-time $7176; part-time $4164 per term. *Required fees:* $2120; $1672 per term. *Graduate housing:* Room and/or apartments available on a first-come, first-served basis to single students; on-campus housing not available to married students. Typical cost: $6638 per year ($13,562 including board). Room and board charges vary according to board plan, campus/location and housing facility selected. Housing application deadline: 3/1. *Student services:* Campus employment opportunities, campus safety program, career counseling, child daycare facilities, exercise/wellness program, free psychological counseling, international student services, low-cost health insurance, multicultural affairs office, services for students with disabilities, teacher training. *Library facilities:* Humbolot State University Library. *Collection:* Books: 733,134 (physical), 165,816 (digital/electronic); Serial titles: 91,453 (physical), 190 (digital/electronic); Databases: 204. Weekly public service hours: 100; students can reserve study rooms. *Research affiliation:* McIntire-Stennis (forestry), National Sea Grant, U.S. Fish and Wildlife Service-Wildlife Field Station, Redwood Sciences Laboratory of the Pacific Southwest Forest and Range Experiment Station, California Cooperative Fisheries Research Unit.

**Computer facilities:** Computer purchase and lease plans are available. A campuswide network can be accessed. Online class registration is available.
Website: http://www.humboldt.edu/

**General Application Contact:** Cynthia Werner, Admissions Coordinator, 707-826-6250, E-mail: apply@humboldt.edu.

**GRADUATE UNITS**

**Academic Programs** Students: 277 full-time (191 women), 266 part-time (180 women); includes 166 minority (4 Black or African American, non-Hispanic/Latino; 25 American Indian or Alaska Native, non-Hispanic/Latino; 16 Asian, non-Hispanic/Latino; 89 Hispanic/Latino; 32 Two or more races, non-Hispanic/Latino), 10 international. Average age 29. 441 applicants, 55% accepted, 178 enrolled. *Faculty:* 142 full-time (71 women), 178 part-time/adjunct (118 women). Expenses: Contact institution. *Financial support:* Fellowships, research assistantships, teaching assistantships, career-related internships or fieldwork, Federal Work-Study, and institutionally sponsored loans available. Support available to part-time students. Financial award application deadline: 3/1; financial award applicants required to submit FAFSA. In 2019, 223 master's awarded. *Program availability:* Part-time, evening/weekend. *Application deadline:* Applications are processed on a rolling basis. *Application fee:* $55. Electronic applications accepted. *Application Contact:* Terri Fisher, Graduate Coordinator, 707-826-5194, E-mail: terri.fisher@humboldt.edu. *Vice Provost*, Dr. Mary Oling-Sisay, 707-826-3722.

***College of Arts, Humanities, and Social Sciences*** Students: 34 full-time (27 women), 61 part-time (47 women); includes 28 minority (6 American Indian or Alaska Native, non-Hispanic/Latino; 3 Asian, non-Hispanic/Latino; 14 Hispanic/Latino; 5 Two or more races, non-Hispanic/Latino). Average age 32. 56 applicants, 80% accepted, 24 enrolled. *Faculty:* 27 full-time (19 women), 30 part-time/adjunct (24 women). Expenses: Contact institution. *Financial support:* Fellowships, teaching assistantships, career-related internships or fieldwork, Federal Work-Study, and institutionally sponsored loans available. Support available to part-time students. Financial award application deadline: 3/1; financial award applicants required to submit FAFSA. In 2019, 33 master's awarded. *Program availability:* Part-time. *Application deadline:* Applications are processed on a rolling basis. *Application fee:* $55. Electronic applications accepted. *Application Contact:* Cynthia Werner, Graduate Admissions Office Coordinator, 707-826 Ext. 6250, E-mail: cw7001@humboldt.edu. *Dean*, Dr. Rosamel Benavides-Garb, 707-826-4491, Fax: 707-826-4498, E-mail: rsb1@humboldt.edu.

***College of Natural Resources and Sciences*** Students: 85 full-time (48 women), 89 part-time (43 women); includes 38 minority (3 American Indian or Alaska Native, non-Hispanic/Latino; 7 Asian, non-Hispanic/Latino; 18 Hispanic/Latino; 10 Two or more races, non-Hispanic/Latino), 6 international. Average age 29. 133 applicants, 47% accepted, 52 enrolled. *Faculty:* 64 full-time (24 women), 52 part-time/adjunct (27 women). Expenses: Contact institution. *Financial support:* Fellowships, career-related internships or fieldwork, and Federal Work-Study available. Support available to part-time students. Financial award application deadline: 3/1; financial award applicants required to submit FAFSA. In 2019, 42 master's awarded. *Program availability:* Part-time. *Application deadline:* Applications are processed on a rolling basis. *Application fee:* $55. *Application Contact:* Dr. Dale Oliver, Dean, 707-826-3256, E-mail: dale.oliver@humboldt.edu. *Dean*, Dr. Dale Oliver, 707-826-3256, E-mail: dale.oliver@humboldt.edu.

***College of Professional Studies*** Students: 158 full-time (116 women), 116 part-time (90 women); includes 100 minority (4 Black or African American, non-Hispanic/Latino; 16 American Indian or Alaska Native, non-Hispanic/Latino; 6 Asian, non-Hispanic/Latino; 57 Hispanic/Latino; 17 Two or more races, non-Hispanic/Latino), 4 international. Average age 32. 252 applicants, 53% accepted, 102 enrolled. *Faculty:* 51 full-time (28 women), 96 part-time/adjunct (67 women). Expenses: Contact institution. *Financial support:* Fellowships, teaching assistantships, career-related internships or fieldwork, Federal Work-Study, and institutionally sponsored loans available. Support available to part-time students. Financial award application deadline: 3/1; financial award applicants required to submit FAFSA. In 2019, 148 master's awarded. *Program availability:* Part-time, evening/weekend. *Application deadline:* Applications are processed on a rolling basis. *Application fee:* $55. *Application Contact:* Dr. Shawna Young, Dean, 707-826-3961, Fax: 707-826-3963, E-mail: shy4@humboldt.edu. *Dean*, Dr. Shawna Young, 707-826-3961, Fax: 707-826-3963, E-mail: shy4@humboldt.edu.

## HUMPHREYS UNIVERSITY, Stockton, CA 95207-3896

**General Information** Independent, coed, comprehensive institution. *Enrollment:* 28 full-time matriculated graduate/professional students (23 women), 61 part-time matriculated graduate/professional students (49 women). *Enrollment by degree level:* 89 master's, 71 doctoral. *Graduate faculty:* 3 full-time (0 women), 17 part-time/adjunct (6 women). *Tuition:* Full-time $19,800; part-time $15,255 per unit. One-time fee: $40. Tuition and fees vary according to course load, degree level and program. *Graduate housing:* On-campus housing not available. *Student services:* Campus employment opportunities, career counseling, international student services, teacher training. *Library facilities:* Humphreys College Library plus 1 other.

**Computer facilities:** 40 computers available on campus for general student use. Website: http://www.humphreys.edu/

**General Application Contact:** Santa Lopez-Minatre, Admission Counselor, 209-478-0800, Fax: 209-234-3114, E-mail: santa.lopez@humphreys.edu.

GRADUATE UNITS

**Drivon School of Law** Students: 72 part-time (40 women); includes 39 minority (6 Black or African American, non-Hispanic/Latino; 1 Asian, non-Hispanic/Latino; 31 Hispanic/Latino; 1 Native Hawaiian or other Pacific Islander, non-Hispanic/Latino). Average age 30. 20 applicants, 55% accepted, 11 enrolled. *Faculty:* 1 full-time (0 women), 10 part-time/adjunct (1 woman). Expenses: Contact institution. *Financial support:* In 2019–20, 58 students received support. Federal Work-Study and Federal Loans available. Financial award application deadline: 3/2; financial award applicants required to submit FAFSA. In 2019, 40 doctorates awarded. *Program availability:* Part-time-only, evening/weekend. *Application deadline:* For fall admission, 8/28 priority date for domestic students; for winter admission, 12/4 priority date for domestic students; for summer admission, 6/6 priority date for domestic students. Applications are processed on a rolling basis. *Application fee:* $40. Electronic applications accepted. *Application Contact:* Santa Lopez-Minatre, Admission Counselor, 209-478-0800 Ext. 3147, Fax: 209-243-3114, E-mail: santa.lopez-minatre@humphreys.edu. *Law Registrar*, Wendy A. Campigli, 209-2352905 Ext. 3171, Fax: 209-320-0639, E-mail: wcampigli@humphreys.edu.

## HUNTER COLLEGE OF THE CITY UNIVERSITY OF NEW YORK, New York, NY 10065-5085

**General Information** State and locally supported, coed, comprehensive institution. *Graduate housing:* Room and/or apartments available on a first-come, first-served basis to single students; on-campus housing not available to married students. *Research affiliation:* Mount Sinai Medical Center, Bellevue Hospital Center, Cornell University Medical Center, New York Hospital.

GRADUATE UNITS

**Graduate School** *Program availability:* Part-time, evening/weekend.

***Hunter-Bellevue School of Nursing*** *Program availability:* Part-time.

***School of Arts and Sciences*** *Program availability:* Part-time, evening/weekend.

***School of Education*** *Program availability:* Part-time, evening/weekend. Electronic applications accepted.

***School of Health Professions*** *Program availability:* Part-time, evening/weekend.

***School of Urban Public Health*** *Program availability:* Part-time.

***Silberman School of Social Work***

## HUNTINGTON UNIVERSITY, Huntington, IN 46750-1299

**General Information** Independent-religious, coed, comprehensive institution. *Graduate housing:* On-campus housing not available. *Research affiliation:* Link Institute (youth ministry).

GRADUATE UNITS

**Graduate School** *Program availability:* Part-time, online learning. Electronic applications accepted.

## HUNTINGTON UNIVERSITY OF HEALTH SCIENCES, Knoxville, TN 37918

**General Information** Proprietary, coed, comprehensive institution.

GRADUATE UNITS

**Program in Nutrition** *Program availability:* Part-time, evening/weekend, online learning. Electronic applications accepted.

## HUNTSVILLE BIBLE COLLEGE, Huntsville, AL 35811-1632

**General Information** Independent, coed, comprehensive institution.

GRADUATE UNITS

**Program in Ministry**

## HUSSON UNIVERSITY, Bangor, ME 04401-2999

**General Information** Independent, coed, comprehensive institution. *Graduate housing:* Room and/or apartments available on a first-come, first-served basis to single students; on-campus housing not available to married students. Housing application deadline: 6/1.

GRADUATE UNITS

**Doctorate in Physical Therapy Program** Electronic applications accepted.

**Graduate Nursing Program** *Program availability:* Part-time, evening/weekend. Electronic applications accepted.

**Graduate Programs in Counseling and Human Relations** *Program availability:* Part-time, evening/weekend. Electronic applications accepted.

**Master of Business Administration Program** *Program availability:* Part-time, evening/weekend, 100% online, blended/hybrid learning. Electronic applications accepted.

**Master of Science in Criminal Justice Administration Program** *Program availability:* Part-time, evening/weekend. Electronic applications accepted.

**School of Pharmacy** Electronic applications accepted.

## HUSTON-TILLOTSON UNIVERSITY, Austin, TX 78702-2795

**General Information** Independent-religious, coed, comprehensive institution.

GRADUATE UNITS

**Graduate Programs**

## ICAHN SCHOOL OF MEDICINE AT MOUNT SINAI, New York, NY 10029-6504

**General Information** Independent, coed, graduate-only institution. *Graduate housing:* Rooms and/or apartments guaranteed to single and married students. Housing application deadline: 6/1.

GRADUATE UNITS

**The Bioethics Program**

**Department of Medical Education** Electronic applications accepted.

**Graduate School of Biomedical Sciences** Electronic applications accepted.

## IDAHO STATE UNIVERSITY, Pocatello, ID 83209

**General Information** State-supported, coed, university. CGS member. *Graduate housing:* Rooms and/or apartments available on a first-come, first-served basis to single and married students. Housing application deadline: 5/1. *Research affiliation:* S.M. Stoller Corporation (ecology, waste management), ON Semiconductor (computer sciences, environmental management), Inland Northwest Research Alliance (INRA) (science), J.R. Simplot Company (plant sciences, environmental studies), Bechtel BWXT Idaho, LLC (environmental management, nuclear sciences), Environmental Science and Research Foundation (waste management, ecology).

GRADUATE UNITS

**Graduate School** *Program availability:* Part-time. Electronic applications accepted.

***College of Arts and Letters*** *Program availability:* Part-time. Electronic applications accepted.

***College of Business*** *Program availability:* Part-time. Electronic applications accepted.

***College of Education*** *Program availability:* Part-time. Electronic applications accepted.

***College of Health Professions*** *Program availability:* Part-time. Electronic applications accepted.

***College of Nursing*** *Program availability:* Part-time. Electronic applications accepted.

***College of Pharmacy*** *Program availability:* Part-time. Electronic applications accepted.

***College of Rehabilitation and Communication Sciences***

***College of Science and Engineering*** *Program availability:* Part-time. Electronic applications accepted.

## IGLOBAL UNIVERSITY, Vienna, VA 22182

**General Information** Proprietary, coed, comprehensive institution.

GRADUATE UNITS

**Graduate Programs**

## ILIFF SCHOOL OF THEOLOGY, Denver, CO 80210-4798

**General Information** Independent-religious, coed, graduate-only institution. *Graduate housing:* Rooms and/or apartments available on a first-come, first-served basis to single and married students.

GRADUATE UNITS

**Graduate and Professional Programs** *Program availability:* Part-time, evening/weekend. Electronic applications accepted.

## ILLINOIS COLLEGE, Jacksonville, IL 62650-2299

**General Information** Independent-religious, coed, comprehensive institution. *Graduate housing:* On-campus housing not available.

## ILLINOIS COLLEGE OF OPTOMETRY, Chicago, IL 60616-3878

**General Information** Independent, coed, graduate-only institution. *Graduate housing:* Rooms and/or apartments available on a first-come, first-served basis to single and married students. Housing application deadline: 6/1. *Research affiliation:* Rush University (cataract development), University of Chicago (vision science), University of Illinois at Chicago (neuropharmacology), Vision Service Plan (pediatric optometry), Ciba Vision (contact lenses).

GRADUATE UNITS

**Professional Program** Electronic applications accepted.

## ILLINOIS INSTITUTE OF TECHNOLOGY, Chicago, IL 60616

**General Information** Independent, coed, university. CGS member. *Graduate housing:* Rooms and/or apartments available on a first-come, first-served basis to single and married students. Housing application deadline: 6/1.

GRADUATE UNITS

**Chicago-Kent College of Law** Students: 609 full-time (307 women), 112 part-time (58 women); includes 207 minority (37 Black or African American, non-Hispanic/Latino; 2 American Indian or Alaska Native, non-Hispanic/Latino; 47 Asian, non-Hispanic/Latino; 96 Hispanic/Latino; 25 Two or more races, non-Hispanic/Latino), 29 international. Average age 27. 2,676 applicants, 55% accepted, 282 enrolled. *Faculty:* 56 full-time (22 women), 117 part-time/adjunct (22 women). Expenses: Contact institution. *Financial support:* In 2019–20, 742 students received support. Career-related internships or fieldwork, Federal Work-Study, institutionally sponsored loans, scholarships/grants, and tuition waivers (full) available. Support available to part-time students. Financial award application deadline: 3/15; financial award applicants required to submit FAFSA. In 2019, 106 master's, 286 doctorates awarded. *Program availability:* Part-time, evening/weekend. *Application deadline:* For fall admission, 3/15 priority date for domestic students, 2/1 priority date for international students. Applications are processed on a rolling basis. *Application fee:* $0 ($75 for international students). Electronic applications accepted. *Application Contact:* Nicole Vilches, Assistant Dean, 312-906-5020, Fax: 312-906-5274, E-mail: admissions@kentlaw.iit.edu. *Dean*, Anita K. Krug, 312-906-5010, Fax: 312-906-5335, E-mail: akrug2@kentlaw.iit.edu.

**Graduate College** *Program availability:* Part-time, evening/weekend, online learning. Electronic applications accepted.

***Armour College of Engineering*** *Program availability:* Part-time, evening/weekend, online learning. Electronic applications accepted.

***College of Architecture*** *Program availability:* Part-time. Electronic applications accepted.

***College of Science*** *Program availability:* Part-time, evening/weekend, online learning. Electronic applications accepted.

***Institute of Design*** *Program availability:* Part-time. Electronic applications accepted.

***Lewis College of Human Sciences***

***School of Applied Technology*** *Program availability:* Part-time, evening/weekend, online learning. Electronic applications accepted.

**Stuart School of Business** *Program availability:* Part-time, evening/weekend. Electronic applications accepted.

## ILLINOIS STATE UNIVERSITY, Normal, IL 61790

**General Information** State-supported, coed, university. CGS member. *Enrollment:* 20,878 graduate, professional, and undergraduate students; 1,364 full-time matriculated graduate/professional students (830 women), 1,148 part-time matriculated graduate/professional students (797 women). *Enrollment by degree level:* 1,927 master's, 468 doctoral, 117 other advanced degrees. *Graduate faculty:* 911 full-time (476 women), 461 part-time/adjunct (290 women). *Tuition, area resident:* Full-time $7956; part-time $9767 per year. Tuition, nonresident: full-time $9233; part-time $17,592 per year. *Required fees:* $1797. *Graduate housing:* Rooms and/or apartments available on a first-come, first-served basis to single and married students. Housing application deadline: 5/1. *Student services:* Campus employment opportunities, campus safety program, career counseling, child daycare facilities, exercise/wellness program, free psychological counseling, international student services, low-cost health insurance, multicultural affairs office, services for students with disabilities, teacher training, writing training. *Library facilities:* Milner Library. *Collection:* Books: 1.4 million (physical), 190,817 (digital/electronic); Serial titles: 141,304 (digital/electronic); Databases: 284. Students can reserve study rooms.

**Computer facilities:** Computer purchase and lease plans are available. 2,500 computers available on campus for general student use. A campuswide network can be accessed. Online class registration is available.
Website: http://www.illinoisstate.edu/

**General Application Contact:** Dr. Noelle Selkow, Interim Director of Graduate Studies, 309-438-2583, Fax: 309-438-7912, E-mail: gradinfo@ilstu.edu.

**GRADUATE UNITS**

**Graduate School** Students: 1,375 full-time (838 women), 1,253 part-time (865 women). Average age 31. 2,164 applicants, 68% accepted, 771 enrolled. *Faculty:* 911 full-time (476 women), 461 part-time/adjunct (290 women). Expenses: Contact institution. *Financial support:* In 2019–20, 242 research assistantships, 455 teaching assistantships were awarded; fellowships, career-related internships or fieldwork, Federal Work-Study, institutionally sponsored loans, tuition waivers (full and partial), and unspecified assistantships also available. Support available to part-time students. Financial award application deadline: 4/1. In 2019, 730 master's, 65 doctorates, 136 other advanced degrees awarded. *Program availability:* Part-time. *Application deadline:* Applications are processed on a rolling basis. *Application fee:* $50. Electronic applications accepted. *Application Contact:* Dr. Noelle Selkow, Interim Director of Graduate Studies, 309-438-2583, Fax: 309-438-7912, E-mail: gradinfo@ilstu.edu. *Interim Director of Graduate Studies*, Dr. Noelle Selkow, 309-438-2583, Fax: 309-438-7912, E-mail: gradinfo@ilstu.edu.

***College of Applied Science and Technology*** Students: 275 full-time (161 women), 104 part-time (56 women). Average age 27. 435 applicants, 67% accepted, 134 enrolled. *Faculty:* 153 full-time (79 women), 91 part-time/adjunct (40 women). Expenses: Contact institution. *Financial support:* In 2019–20, 51 research assistantships, 65 teaching assistantships were awarded; fellowships, career-related internships or fieldwork, Federal Work-Study, institutionally sponsored loans, tuition waivers (full and partial), and unspecified assistantships also available. Support available to part-time students. Financial award application deadline: 4/1. In 2019, 155 master's, 66 other advanced degrees awarded. *Program availability:* Part-time. *Application deadline:* Applications are processed on a rolling basis. *Application fee:* $50. *Application Contact:* Dr. Todd McLoda, Dean, 309-438-7602, E-mail: tamclod@IllinoisState.edu. *Dean*, Dr. Todd McLoda, 309-438-7602, E-mail: tamclod@IllinoisState.edu.

***College of Arts and Sciences*** Students: 617 full-time (435 women), 224 part-time (139 women). Average age 27. 893 applicants, 56% accepted, 236 enrolled. *Faculty:* 387 full-time (176 women), 122 part-time/adjunct (78 women). Expenses: Contact institution. *Financial support:* In 2019–20, 104 research assistantships, 308 teaching assistantships were awarded; career-related internships or fieldwork, Federal Work-Study, institutionally sponsored loans, tuition waivers (full and partial), and unspecified assistantships also available. Support available to part-time students. Financial award application deadline: 4/1. In 2019, 251 master's, 25 doctorates, 25 other advanced degrees awarded. *Program availability:* Part-time. *Application deadline:* Applications are processed on a rolling basis. *Application fee:* $50. *Application Contact:* Dr. Noelle Selkow, Interim Director of Graduate Studies, 309-438-2583, Fax: 309-438-7912, E-mail: gradinfo@ilstu.edu. *Interim Dean*, Dr. Diane Zosky, 309-438-5669, E-mail: dlzosky@IllinoisState.edu.

***College of Business*** Students: 190 full-time (87 women), 76 part-time (44 women). Average age 28. 180 applicants, 82% accepted, 71 enrolled. *Faculty:* 104 full-time (39 women), 27 part-time/adjunct (4 women). Expenses: Contact institution. *Financial support:* In 2019–20, 14 research assistantships were awarded; career-related internships or fieldwork, Federal Work-Study, institutionally sponsored loans, and tuition waivers (full and partial) also available. Support available to part-time students. Financial award application deadline: 4/1. In 2019, 99 master's awarded. *Program availability:* Part-time. *Application deadline:* Applications are processed on a rolling basis. *Application fee:* $50. *Application Contact:* Dr. Noelle Selkow, Interim Director of Graduate Studies, 309-438-2583, Fax: 309-438-7912, E-mail: gradinfo@ilstu.edu. *Dean of the College of Business*, Dr. Ajay Samant, 309-438-2251, E-mail: asamant@IllinoisState.edu.

***College of Education*** Students: 63 full-time (41 women), 593 part-time (436 women). Average age 35. 269 applicants, 82% accepted, 149 enrolled. *Faculty:* 112 full-time (87 women), 123 part-time/adjunct (95 women). Expenses: Contact institution. *Financial support:* In 2019–20, 33 research assistantships were awarded; career-related internships or fieldwork, Federal Work-Study, institutionally sponsored loans, tuition waivers (full and partial), and unspecified assistantships also available. Support available to part-time students. Financial award application deadline: 4/1. In 2019, 131 master's, 29 doctorates, 45 other advanced degrees awarded. *Program availability:* Part-time. *Application deadline:* Applications are processed on a rolling basis. *Application fee:* $50. *Application Contact:* Dr. Noelle Selkow, Interim Director of Graduate Studies, 309-438-2583, Fax: 309-438-7912, E-mail: gradinfo@ilstu.edu. *Dean of College of Education*, Kevin Laudner, 309-438-2453, E-mail: klaudne@ilstu.edu.

***Mennonite College of Nursing*** Students: 12 full-time (9 women), 118 part-time (102 women). Average age 37. 46 applicants, 83% accepted, 16 enrolled. *Faculty:* 41 full-time (39 women), 47 part-time/adjunct (40 women). Expenses: Contact institution. *Financial support:* In 2019–20, 5 teaching assistantships were awarded. In 2019, 32 master's, 11 doctorates awarded. *Application fee:* $50. *Application Contact:* Dr. Noelle Selkow, Interim Director of Graduate Studies, 309-438-2583, Fax: 309-438-7912, E-mail: gradinfor@ilstu.edu. *Dean of Mennonite College of Nursing*, Dr. Judy Neubrander, 309-438-2174, E-mail: jlneubr@IllinoisState.edu.

***Wonsook Kim College of Fine Arts*** Students: 114 full-time (65 women), 33 part-time (20 women). Average age 28. 150 applicants, 65% accepted, 59 enrolled. *Faculty:* 113 full-time (55 women), 37 part-time/adjunct (20 women). Expenses: Contact institution. *Financial support:* In 2019–20, 78 teaching assistantships were awarded; career-related internships or fieldwork, Federal Work-Study, institutionally sponsored loans, tuition waivers (full and partial), and unspecified assistantships also available. Support available to part-time students. Financial award application deadline: 4/1. In 2019, 62 master's awarded. *Program availability:* Part-time. *Application deadline:* Applications are processed on a rolling basis. *Application fee:* $50. *Application Contact:* Dr. Noelle Selkow, Interim Director of Graduate Studies, 309-438-2583, Fax: 309-438-7912, E-mail: gradinfo@ilstu.edu. *Dean of the College of Fine Arts*, Dr. Jean M.K. Miller, 309-438-8321, E-mail: jmmill5@ilstu.edu.

## IMMACULATA UNIVERSITY, Immaculata, PA 19345

**General Information** Independent-religious, coed, university. CGS member. *Graduate housing:* Rooms and/or apartments available on a first-come, first-served basis to single and married students.

**GRADUATE UNITS**

**College of Graduate Studies** *Program availability:* Part-time, evening/weekend. Electronic applications accepted.

***Division of Nursing*** *Program availability:* Part-time, evening/weekend.

## INDEPENDENCE UNIVERSITY, Salt Lake City, UT 84107

**General Information** Proprietary, coed, comprehensive institution. *Graduate housing:* On-campus housing not available.

**GRADUATE UNITS**

**Program in Business Administration**

**Program in Business Administration in Health Care** *Program availability:* Part-time, evening/weekend, online learning.

**Program in Health Care Administration** *Program availability:* Part-time, evening/weekend, online learning.

**Program in Health Services** *Program availability:* Part-time, evening/weekend, online learning.

**Program in Nursing**

**Program in Public Health** *Program availability:* Part-time, evening/weekend, online learning.

## INDIANA STATE UNIVERSITY, Terre Haute, IN 47809

**General Information** State-supported, coed, university. CGS member. *Graduate housing:* Rooms and/or apartments available on a first-come, first-served basis to single and married students. Housing application deadline: 4/18. *Research affiliation:* Indiana Space Grant (remote sensing), Indiana University School of Medicine (cancer and Lupus research), Cranberry Lake Biological Station (psychosocial impacts of cancer), Boston Museum of Science (remote sensing, biology), Great Lakes Northern Forest Cooperative Ecosystem Study Unit (biology, life sciences).

**GRADUATE UNITS**

**College of Graduate and Professional Studies** *Program availability:* Part-time, evening/weekend, online learning. Electronic applications accepted.

***Bayh College of Education*** *Program availability:* Part-time, evening/weekend. Electronic applications accepted.

***College of Arts and Sciences*** *Program availability:* Part-time, evening/weekend. Electronic applications accepted.

***College of Health and Human Services*** Electronic applications accepted.

***College of Technology*** Electronic applications accepted.

***Scott College of Business*** *Program availability:* Part-time, evening/weekend. Electronic applications accepted.

## INDIANA TECH, Fort Wayne, IN 46803-1297

**General Information** Independent, coed, comprehensive institution. *Graduate housing:* Room and/or apartments available on a first-come, first-served basis to single students; on-campus housing not available to married students. Housing application deadline: 8/15.

**GRADUATE UNITS**

**Program in Business Administration** *Program availability:* Part-time, evening/weekend, online learning. Electronic applications accepted.

**Program in Engineering Management** *Program availability:* Part-time, evening/weekend, online only, 100% online. Electronic applications accepted.

**Program in Global Leadership** *Program availability:* Part-time, evening/weekend, online only, 100% online. Electronic applications accepted.

**Program in Management** *Program availability:* Part-time, evening/weekend, 100% online. Electronic applications accepted.

**Program in Organizational Leadership** *Program availability:* Part-time, evening/weekend, online only, 100% online. Electronic applications accepted.

**Program in Psychology**

## INDIANA UNIVERSITY BLOOMINGTON, Bloomington, IN 47405-7000

**General Information** State-supported, coed, university. CGS member. *Graduate housing:* Rooms and/or apartments available to single and married students. Housing application deadline: 5/11.

**GRADUATE UNITS**

**Jacobs School of Music** Electronic applications accepted.

**Kelley School of Business** Electronic applications accepted.

**Maurer School of Law** Electronic applications accepted.

**School of Education** *Program availability:* Part-time, 100% online, blended/hybrid learning. Electronic applications accepted.

**School of Informatics, Computing, and Engineering** *Program availability:* Part-time, online learning. Electronic applications accepted.

**School of Optometry** Electronic applications accepted.

**School of Public and Environmental Affairs** *Program availability:* Part-time, 100% online, blended/hybrid learning. Electronic applications accepted.

**School of Public Health** *Program availability:* Part-time, online learning. Electronic applications accepted.

**University Graduate School** *Program availability:* Part-time. Electronic applications accepted.

***College of Arts and Sciences*** *Program availability:* Part-time. Electronic applications accepted.

## INDIANA UNIVERSITY EAST, Richmond, IN 47374-1289

**General Information** State-supported, coed, comprehensive institution.

**GRADUATE UNITS**

**School of Education**

**School of Nursing**

**School of Social Work**

## INDIANA UNIVERSITY KOKOMO, Kokomo, IN 46902-9003

**General Information** State-supported, coed, comprehensive institution. *Graduate housing:* On-campus housing not available.

**GRADUATE UNITS**

**Department of Public Administration and Health Management** *Program availability:* Part-time, evening/weekend. Electronic applications accepted.

**School of Business** *Program availability:* Part-time, evening/weekend. Electronic applications accepted.

**School of Nursing** Electronic applications accepted.

## INDIANA UNIVERSITY NORTHWEST, Gary, IN 46408-1197

**General Information** State-supported, coed, comprehensive institution. *Graduate housing:* On-campus housing not available.

**GRADUATE UNITS**

**College of Arts and Sciences** *Program availability:* Part-time, evening/weekend. Electronic applications accepted.

**School of Business and Economics** *Program availability:* Part-time, evening/weekend. Electronic applications accepted.

**School of Education** *Program availability:* Part-time, evening/weekend. Electronic applications accepted.

**School of Public and Environmental Affairs** *Program availability:* Part-time. Electronic applications accepted.

**School of Social Work** *Program availability:* Part-time, evening/weekend. Electronic applications accepted.

## INDIANA UNIVERSITY OF PENNSYLVANIA, Indiana, PA 15705

**General Information** State-supported, coed, university. CGS member. *Enrollment:* 10,302 graduate, professional, and undergraduate students; 817 full-time matriculated graduate/professional students (493 women), 1,252 part-time matriculated graduate/professional students (793 women). *Enrollment by degree level:* 1,178 master's, 827 doctoral, 64 other advanced degrees. *Graduate faculty:* 210 full-time (94 women), 20 part-time/adjunct (15 women). *Tuition, area resident:* Full-time $9288; part-time $516 per credit. Tuition, nonresident: full-time $13,932; part-time $774 per credit. *Required fees:* $4454. One-time fee: $115 full-time. Tuition and fees vary according to course load and program. *Graduate housing:* Room and/or apartments available on a first-come, first-served basis to single students; on-campus housing not available to married students. Typical cost: $10,530 per year ($14,150 including board). Room and board charges vary according to board plan. *Student services:* Campus employment opportunities, campus safety program, career counseling, child daycare facilities, free psychological counseling, grant writing training, international student services, low-cost health insurance, multicultural affairs office, services for students with disabilities, writing training. *Library facilities:* Stapleton Library plus 1 other. *Collection:* Books: 501,766 (physical), 712,755 (digital/electronic); Serial titles: 125,395 (physical), 148,271 (digital/electronic); Databases: 261. Weekly public service hours: 116; study areas open 24 hours, 5–7 days a week; students can reserve study rooms.

**Computer facilities:** Computer purchase and lease plans are available. 2,363 computers available on campus for general student use. A campuswide network can be accessed. Online class registration is available.
Website: http://www.iup.edu/

**General Application Contact:** Amber Dworek, Director, Graduate Admissions, 724-357-2222, E-mail: graduate-admissions@iup.edu.

**GRADUATE UNITS**

**School of Graduate Studies and Research** Students: 817 full-time (493 women), 1,252 part-time (793 women); includes 273 minority (145 Black or African American, non-Hispanic/Latino; 4 American Indian or Alaska Native, non-Hispanic/Latino; 32 Asian, non-Hispanic/Latino; 52 Hispanic/Latino; 40 Two or more races, non-Hispanic/Latino), 353 international. Average age 33. 1,732 applicants, 78% accepted, 866 enrolled. *Faculty:* 210 full-time (94 women), 20 part-time/adjunct (15 women). Expenses: Contact institution. *Financial support:* In 2019–20, 181 fellowships (averaging $1,152 per year), 484 research assistantships with tuition reimbursements (averaging $4,335 per year), 26 teaching assistantships with partial tuition reimbursements (averaging $20,080 per year) were awarded; career-related internships or fieldwork, Federal Work-Study, scholarships/grants, tuition waivers (full and partial), and unspecified assistantships also available. Support available to part-time students. Financial award application deadline: 4/15; financial award applicants required to submit FAFSA. In 2019, 637 master's, 109 doctorates, 27 other advanced degrees awarded. *Program availability:* Part-time, evening/weekend, 100% online, blended/hybrid learning. *Application deadline:* Applications are processed on a rolling basis. *Application fee:* $50. Electronic applications accepted. *Application Contact:* Amber Dworek, Director of Graduate Admissions, 724-357-2222, E-mail: a.m.dworek@iup.edu. *Dean School of Graduate Studies and Research*, Randy Martin, 724-357-4511, E-mail: rmartin@iup.edu.

***College of Education and Communications*** Students: 266 full-time (202 women), 405 part-time (277 women); includes 100 minority (54 Black or African American, non-Hispanic/Latino; 6 Asian, non-Hispanic/Latino; 18 Hispanic/Latino; 1 Native Hawaiian or other Pacific Islander, non-Hispanic/Latino; 21 Two or more races, non-Hispanic/Latino), 17 international. Average age 33. 579 applicants, 72% accepted, 277 enrolled. *Faculty:* 47 full-time (32 women), 13 part-time/adjunct (11 women). Expenses: Contact institution. *Financial support:* In 2019–20, 56 fellowships (averaging $627 per year), 151 research assistantships with tuition reimbursements (averaging $4,291 per year), 9 teaching assistantships with tuition reimbursements (averaging $24,340 per year) were awarded; career-related internships or fieldwork, Federal Work-Study, scholarships/grants, and unspecified assistantships also available. Support available to part-time students. Financial award application deadline: 4/15; financial award applicants required to submit FAFSA. In 2019, 151 master's, 35 doctorates, 15 other advanced degrees awarded. *Program availability:* Part-time, evening/weekend. *Application deadline:* Applications are processed on a rolling basis. *Application fee:* $50. Electronic applications accepted. *Application Contact:* Paula Stossel, Assistant Dean for Administration, 724-357-4511, Fax: 724-357-4862, E-mail: graduate-admissions@iup.edu. *Dean*, Dr. Lara Luetkehans, 724-357-2480, Fax: 724-357-5595.

***College of Fine Arts*** Students: 17 full-time (8 women), 22 part-time (10 women); includes 2 minority (both Hispanic/Latino), 5 international. Average age 30. 37 applicants, 97% accepted, 19 enrolled. *Faculty:* 18 full-time (7 women), 2 part-time/adjunct (1 woman). Expenses: Contact institution. *Financial support:* In 2019–20, 2 fellowships with full tuition reimbursements (averaging $500 per year), 19 research assistantships with tuition reimbursements (averaging $4,734 per year) were awarded; career-related internships or fieldwork, Federal Work-Study, scholarships/grants, and unspecified assistantships also available. Support available to part-time students. Financial award application deadline: 4/15; financial award applicants required to submit FAFSA. In 2019, 17 master's awarded. *Program availability:* Part-time. *Application deadline:* Applications are processed on a rolling basis. *Application fee:* $50. Electronic applications accepted. *Application Contact:* Dr. Susan Palmisano, Graduate Coordinator, 724-357-2536, E-mail: palmisan@iup.edu. *Dean*, Curtis A. Scheib, 724-357-2397, Fax: 724-357-7778, E-mail: Curtis.Scheib@iup.edu.

***College of Health and Human Services*** Students: 157 full-time (103 women), 332 part-time (218 women); includes 70 minority (49 Black or African American, non-Hispanic/Latino; 2 American Indian or Alaska Native, non-Hispanic/Latino; 5 Asian, non-Hispanic/Latino; 7 Hispanic/Latino; 7 Two or more races, non-Hispanic/Latino), 23 international. Average age 33. 349 applicants, 95% accepted, 216 enrolled. *Faculty:* 40 full-time (19 women), 1 (woman) part-time/adjunct. Expenses: Contact institution. *Financial support:* In 2019–20, 21 fellowships (averaging $743 per year), 100 research assistantships with tuition reimbursements (averaging $3,880 per year), 3 teaching assistantships with partial tuition reimbursements (averaging $25,035 per year) were awarded; career-related internships or fieldwork, Federal Work-Study, scholarships/grants, and unspecified assistantships also available. Support available to part-time students. Financial award application deadline: 4/15; financial award applicants required to submit FAFSA. In 2019, 194 master's, 14 doctorates, 12 other advanced degrees awarded. *Program availability:* Part-time, evening/weekend, 100% online, blended/hybrid learning. *Application deadline:* Applications are processed on a rolling basis. *Application fee:* $50. Electronic applications accepted. *Application Contact:* Amber Dworek, Director of Graduate Admissions, 724-357-222, E-mail: graduate-admissions@iup.edu. *Dean*, Dr. Sylvia Gaiko, 724-357-2555, E-mail: sgaiko@iup.edu.

***College of Humanities and Social Sciences*** Students: 119 full-time (58 women), 298 part-time (182 women); includes 67 minority (33 Black or African American, non-Hispanic/Latino; 2 American Indian or Alaska Native, non-Hispanic/Latino; 12 Asian, non-Hispanic/Latino; 14 Hispanic/Latino; 6 Two or more races, non-Hispanic/Latino), 82 international. Average age 36. 308 applicants, 79% accepted, 113 enrolled. *Faculty:* 45 full-time (21 women), 2 part-time/adjunct (0 women). Expenses: Contact institution. *Financial support:* In 2019–20, 33 fellowships (averaging $3,142 per year), 97 research assistantships with tuition reimbursements (averaging $3,960 per year), 9 teaching assistantships with partial tuition reimbursements (averaging $12,518 per year) were awarded; career-related internships or fieldwork, Federal Work-Study, scholarships/grants, and unspecified assistantships also available. Support available to part-time students. Financial award application deadline: 4/15; financial award applicants required to submit FAFSA. In 2019, 41 master's, 47 doctorates awarded. *Program availability:* Part-time, evening/weekend. *Application deadline:* Applications are processed on a rolling basis. *Application fee:* $50. Electronic applications accepted. *Application Contact:* Amber Dworek, Director of Graduate Admissions, 724-357-222, E-mail: graduate-admissions@iup.edu. *Dean*, Dr. Yaw Asamoah, 724-357-5764, E-mail: osebo@iup.edu.

***College of Natural Sciences and Mathematics*** Students: 75 full-time (43 women), 72 part-time (52 women); includes 20 minority (5 Black or African American, non-Hispanic/Latino; 6 Asian, non-Hispanic/Latino; 7 Hispanic/Latino; 2 Two or more races, non-Hispanic/Latino), 12 international. Average age 28. 234 applicants, 47% accepted, 56 enrolled. *Faculty:* 33 full-time (11 women). Expenses: Contact institution. *Financial support:* In 2019–20, 38 fellowships (averaging $1,168 per year), 67 research assistantships with tuition reimbursements (averaging $7,584 per year), 3 teaching assistantships with tuition reimbursements (averaging $25,035 per year) were awarded; career-related internships or fieldwork, Federal Work-Study, scholarships/grants, and unspecified assistantships also available. Support available to part-time students. Financial award application deadline: 4/15; financial award applicants required to submit FAFSA. In 2019, 46 master's, 13 doctorates awarded. *Program availability:* Part-time. *Application deadline:* Applications are processed on a rolling basis. *Application fee:* $50. Electronic applications accepted. *Application Contact:* Amber Dworek, Director of Graduate Admissions, 724-357-2222, E-mail: graduate-admissions@iup.edu. *Dean*, Dr. Deanne Snavely, 724-357-2609, Fax: 724-357-5700, E-mail: snavely@iup.edu.

***Eberly College of Business and Information Technology*** Students: 178 full-time (72 women), 138 part-time (62 women); includes 23 minority (12 Black or African American, non-Hispanic/Latino; 4 Asian, non-Hispanic/Latino; 3 Hispanic/Latino; 4 Two or more races, non-Hispanic/Latino), 203 international. Average age 29. 203 applicants, 98% accepted, 156 enrolled. *Faculty:* 27 full-time (4 women), 1 (woman) part-time/adjunct. Expenses: Contact institution. *Financial support:* In 2019–20, 31 fellowships (averaging $281 per year), 50 research assistantships with full and partial tuition reimbursements (averaging $1,596 per year) were awarded; career-related internships or fieldwork, Federal Work-Study, scholarships/grants, and unspecified assistantships also available. Support available to part-time students. Financial award application deadline: 4/15; financial award applicants required to submit FAFSA. In 2019, 188 master's awarded. *Program availability:* Part-time, evening/weekend. *Application deadline:* Applications are processed on a rolling basis. *Application fee:* $50. Electronic applications accepted. *Application Contact:* Amber Dworek, Director of Graduate Admissions, 724-357-2222, E-mail: graduate-admissions@iup.edu. *Dean*, Dr. Robert Camp, 724-357-7889, E-mail: bobcamp@iup.edu.

## INDIANA UNIVERSITY-PURDUE UNIVERSITY INDIANAPOLIS, Indianapolis, IN 46202

**General Information** State-supported, coed, university. *Graduate housing:* Rooms and/or apartments available on a first-come, first-served basis to single and married students. Housing application deadline: 3/15.

**GRADUATE UNITS**

**Herron School of Art and Design** Electronic applications accepted.

**Indiana University School of Medicine**

***Stark Neurosciences Research Institute***

**Kelley School of Business**
**Lilly Family School of Philanthropy**
**Richard M. Fairbanks School of Public Health**
**Robert H. McKinney School of Law** *Program availability:* Part-time. Electronic applications accepted.
**School of Dentistry** Electronic applications accepted.
**School of Education** *Program availability:* Part-time, evening/weekend. Electronic applications accepted.
**School of Engineering and Technology** *Program availability:* Part-time, evening/weekend. Electronic applications accepted.
**School of Health and Rehabilitation Sciences** *Program availability:* Part-time, evening/weekend. Electronic applications accepted.
**School of Informatics and Computing** *Program availability:* Part-time, evening/weekend. Electronic applications accepted.
**School of Liberal Arts**
**School of Nursing** *Program availability:* Part-time, blended/hybrid learning. Electronic applications accepted.
**School of Physical Education and Tourism Management** Electronic applications accepted.
**School of Public and Environmental Affairs** *Program availability:* Part-time, evening/weekend, online learning. Electronic applications accepted.
**School of Science** *Program availability:* Part-time, evening/weekend. Electronic applications accepted.
**School of Social Work** *Program availability:* Part-time, evening/weekend.

## INDIANA UNIVERSITY SOUTH BEND, South Bend, IN 46615

**General Information** State-supported, coed, comprehensive institution. *Graduate housing:* On-campus housing not available.

**GRADUATE UNITS**
**College of Liberal Arts and Sciences** *Program availability:* Part-time, evening/weekend.
**Ernestine M. Raclin School of the Arts** *Program availability:* Part-time. Electronic applications accepted.
**Judd Leighton School of Business and Economics** *Program availability:* Part-time, evening/weekend. Electronic applications accepted.
**School of Education** *Program availability:* Part-time, evening/weekend. Electronic applications accepted.
**School of Social Work** *Program availability:* Part-time, evening/weekend.
**Vera Z. Dwyer College of Health Sciences**
***School of Nursing*** *Program availability:* Part-time, evening/weekend.

## INDIANA UNIVERSITY SOUTHEAST, New Albany, IN 47150-6405

**General Information** State-supported, coed, comprehensive institution. *Graduate housing:* On-campus housing not available.

**GRADUATE UNITS**
**Master of Interdisciplinary Studies Program** *Program availability:* Part-time. Electronic applications accepted.
**School of Business** *Program availability:* Part-time. Electronic applications accepted.
**School of Education** *Program availability:* Part-time, evening/weekend. Electronic applications accepted.

## INDIANA WESLEYAN UNIVERSITY, Marion, IN 46953-4974

**General Information** Independent-religious, coed, comprehensive institution. *Graduate housing:* On-campus housing not available. *Research affiliation:* Eli Lilly and Company.

**GRADUATE UNITS**
**College of Adult and Professional Studies** *Program availability:* Part-time, evening/weekend, online learning. Electronic applications accepted.
***School of Educational Leadership*** *Program availability:* Part-time, evening/weekend, online learning. Electronic applications accepted.
**Graduate School** *Program availability:* Part-time, evening/weekend, online learning. Electronic applications accepted.
***College of Arts and Sciences*** *Program availability:* Part-time. Electronic applications accepted.
***School of Health Sciences***
***School of Nursing*** *Program availability:* Part-time, online learning.
***Wesley Seminary***

## INSTITUTE FOR CHRISTIAN STUDIES, Toronto, ON M5S 2E6, Canada

**General Information** Independent-religious, coed, graduate-only institution. *Graduate housing:* On-campus housing not available.

**GRADUATE UNITS**
**Graduate Programs** *Program availability:* Part-time, online learning.

## INSTITUTE FOR CLINICAL SOCIAL WORK, Chicago, IL 60601

**General Information** Independent, coed, primarily women, graduate-only institution. *Graduate housing:* On-campus housing not available.

**GRADUATE UNITS**
**Graduate Programs** *Program availability:* Part-time.

## INSTITUTE FOR DOCTORAL STUDIES IN THE VISUAL ARTS, Portland, ME 04102

**General Information** Independent, coed, graduate-only institution. *Enrollment by degree level:* 60 doctoral. *Graduate faculty:* 3 full-time, 7 part-time/adjunct. *Tuition:* Full-time $42,600.
Website: https://www.idsva.edu/

**General Application Contact:** Molly Davis, Director of Administration/Director of Admissions, 207-771-8887, E-mail: info@idsva.edu.

**GRADUATE UNITS**
**PhD Program in Visual Art: Philosophy, Aesthetics, and Art Theory** *Program availability:* Blended/hybrid learning. Electronic applications accepted.

## INSTITUTE OF AMERICAN INDIAN ARTS, Santa Fe, NM 87508

**General Information** Federally supported, coed, comprehensive institution. *Graduate housing:* On-campus housing not available.

**GRADUATE UNITS**
**Low Residency MFA in Creative Writing Program** *Program availability:* Low-residency. Electronic applications accepted.

## INSTITUTE OF CLINICAL ACUPUNCTURE AND ORIENTAL MEDICINE, Honolulu, HI 96817

**General Information** Proprietary, coed, graduate-only institution.

**GRADUATE UNITS**
**Program in Oriental Medicine**

## INSTITUTE OF PUBLIC ADMINISTRATION, Dublin 4, Ireland

**General Information** Proprietary, coed, comprehensive institution.

**GRADUATE UNITS**
**Programs in Public Administration**

## INSTITUTE OF TAOIST EDUCATION AND ACUPUNCTURE, Louisville, CO 80027

**General Information** Independent, coed, graduate-only institution.

**GRADUATE UNITS**
**Graduate Program**

## THE INSTITUTE OF WORLD POLITICS, Washington, DC 20036

**General Information** Independent, coed, graduate-only institution. *Graduate housing:* On-campus housing not available.

**GRADUATE UNITS**
**Graduate Programs in National Security, Intelligence, and International Affairs** *Program availability:* Part-time, evening/weekend. Electronic applications accepted.

## INSTITUT FRANCO-EUROPÉEN DE CHIROPRAXIE, 94200, France

**General Information** Independent, coed, graduate-only institution.

**GRADUATE UNITS**
**Professional Program**

## INSTITUTO CENTROAMERICANO DE ADMINISTRACION DE EMPRESAS, La Garita, Alajuela, Costa Rica

**General Information** Independent, coed, graduate-only institution. *Graduate housing:* Rooms and/or apartments guaranteed to single students and available to married students. *Research affiliation:* Tropical Agricultural Research and Higher Education Center (agribusiness), Harvard Institute for International Development (macroeconomics and environment), Earth University (agribusiness), Inter-American Institute for Cooperation on Agriculture (agribusiness), David Rockefeller Center for Latin American Studies (competitiveness), Zamarano (agribusiness).

**GRADUATE UNITS**
**Graduate Programs** Electronic applications accepted.

## INSTITUTO TECNOLÓGICO Y DE ESTUDIOS SUPERIORES DE MONTERREY, CAMPUS CENTRAL DE VERACRUZ, 94500 Córdoba, Veracruz, Mexico

**General Information** Independent, coed, comprehensive institution.

**GRADUATE UNITS**
**Graduate Programs** *Program availability:* Part-time, evening/weekend, online learning. Electronic applications accepted.

## INSTITUTO TECNOLÓGICO Y DE ESTUDIOS SUPERIORES DE MONTERREY, CAMPUS CHIAPAS, 29000 Tuxtla Gutiérrez, Chiapas, Mexico

**General Information** Independent, coed, comprehensive institution.

## INSTITUTO TECNOLÓGICO Y DE ESTUDIOS SUPERIORES DE MONTERREY, CAMPUS CHIHUAHUA, 31300 Chihuahua, Chihuahua, Mexico

**General Information** Independent, coed, comprehensive institution.

**GRADUATE UNITS**
**Graduate Programs**

## INSTITUTO TECNOLÓGICO Y DE ESTUDIOS SUPERIORES DE MONTERREY, CAMPUS CIUDAD DE MÉXICO, 14380 Ciudad de Mexico, DF, Mexico

**General Information** Independent, coed, comprehensive institution. *Graduate housing:* On-campus housing not available. *Research affiliation:* McGill University (management), Concordia University (business and management), Eli Lilly S. A. de C. U. (technological development), Ford Motor Company (industrial organizations), German Research Center on Artificial Intelligence (informatics), Brent University (telecommunications).

**GRADUATE UNITS**
**School of Business Administration** *Program availability:* Part-time, evening/weekend, online learning.
**School of Design, Engineering and Architecture** *Program availability:* Part-time, evening/weekend, online learning.
**School of Humanities and Social Sciences** *Program availability:* Part-time, evening/weekend.
**Virtual University Division** *Program availability:* Part-time, evening/weekend, online learning.

## INSTITUTO TECNOLÓGICO Y DE ESTUDIOS SUPERIORES DE MONTERREY, CAMPUS CIUDAD JUÁREZ, 32320 Ciudad Juárez, Chihuahua, Mexico

**General Information** Independent, coed, comprehensive institution.

**GRADUATE UNITS**
**Program in Administration of Information Technology**
**Program in Applied Public Management**
**Program in Business Administration** *Program availability:* Part-time, online learning.
**Program in Education**
**Program in Educational Administration**
**Program in Educational Innovation**

**Program in Educational Technology**
**Program in Electronic Commerce**
**Program in Humanistic Studies**
**Program in Quality Management**

## INSTITUTO TECNOLÓGICO Y DE ESTUDIOS SUPERIORES DE MONTERREY, CAMPUS CIUDAD OBREGÓN, 85000 Ciudad Obregón, Sonora, Mexico

**General Information** Independent, coed, comprehensive institution.

**GRADUATE UNITS**
**Program in Administration**
**Program in Administration of Information Technology**
**Program in Administration of Telecommunications**
**Program in Engineering**
**Program in Finance**
**Program in International Relations**
**Program in Marketing Technology**
**Programs in Education**

## INSTITUTO TECNOLOGICO Y DE ESTUDIOS SUPERIORES DE MONTERREY, CAMPUS COLIMA, 28010 Colima, Colima, Mexico

**General Information** Independent, coed, comprehensive institution.

## INSTITUTO TECNOLÓGICO Y DE ESTUDIOS SUPERIORES DE MONTERREY, CAMPUS CUERNAVACA, 62000 Temixco, Morelos, Mexico

**General Information** Independent, coed, comprehensive institution.

**GRADUATE UNITS**
**Programs in Business Administration**
**Programs in Information Science**

## INSTITUTO TECNOLÓGICO Y DE ESTUDIOS SUPERIORES DE MONTERREY, CAMPUS ESTADO DE MÉXICO, Estado de Mexico 52926, Mexico

**General Information** Independent, coed, comprehensive institution. *Graduate housing:* On-campus housing not available. *Research affiliation:* Texas Instruments (semiconductors), Sony Electronics (new products), Kaltex (quality control), Transportadora San Marcos, S. A. de C. V. (quality control), Microsoft Visual Studio (computer science).

**GRADUATE UNITS**
**Professional and Graduate Division** *Program availability:* Part-time, online learning.

## INSTITUTO TECNOLÓGICO Y DE ESTUDIOS SUPERIORES DE MONTERREY, CAMPUS GUADALAJARA, 45140 Zapopan, Jalisco, Mexico

**General Information** Independent, coed, comprehensive institution. *Graduate housing:* Rooms and/or apartments available to single and married students. Housing application deadline: 8/30.

**GRADUATE UNITS**
**Program in Business Administration** *Program availability:* Part-time, evening/weekend, online learning.
**Program in Finance**

## INSTITUTO TECNOLÓGICO Y DE ESTUDIOS SUPERIORES DE MONTERREY, CAMPUS HIDALGO, 42090 Pachuca, Hidalgo, Mexico

**General Information** Independent, coed, comprehensive institution.

## INSTITUTO TECNOLÓGICO Y DE ESTUDIOS SUPERIORES DE MONTERREY, CAMPUS IRAPUATO, 36660 Irapuato, Guanajuato, Mexico

**General Information** Independent, coed, comprehensive institution.

**GRADUATE UNITS**
**Graduate Programs**

## INSTITUTO TECNOLÓGICO Y DE ESTUDIOS SUPERIORES DE MONTERREY, CAMPUS LAGUNA, 27250 Torreón, Coahuila, Mexico

**General Information** Independent, coed, comprehensive institution. *Graduate housing:* On-campus housing not available.

**GRADUATE UNITS**
**Graduate School** *Program availability:* Part-time.

## INSTITUTO TECNOLÓGICO Y DE ESTUDIOS SUPERIORES DE MONTERREY, CAMPUS LEÓN, 37120 León, Guanajuato, Mexico

**General Information** Independent, coed, comprehensive institution.

**GRADUATE UNITS**
**Program in Business Administration** *Program availability:* Part-time.

## INSTITUTO TECNOLÓGICO Y DE ESTUDIOS SUPERIORES DE MONTERREY, CAMPUS MONTERREY, 64849 Monterrey, Nuevo León, Mexico

**General Information** Independent, coed, comprehensive institution. *Graduate housing:* Room and/or apartments available to single students; on-campus housing not available to married students. *Research affiliation:* IBM de Mexico (computer science), Southwest Research Institute (environment), Hylsa (steel), Vitro (glass products), Cydsa (petrochemicals), Cemex (cement).

**GRADUATE UNITS**
**Graduate and Research Division** *Program availability:* Part-time, evening/weekend.
**Graduate School of Business Administration and Leadership** *Program availability:* Part-time.

## INSTITUTO TECNOLÓGICO Y DE ESTUDIOS SUPERIORES DE MONTERREY, CAMPUS QUERÉTARO, 76130 Querétaro, Querétaro, Mexico

**General Information** Independent, coed, comprehensive institution. *Graduate housing:* Room and/or apartments guaranteed to single students; on-campus housing not available to married students. Housing application deadline: 6/15. *Research affiliation:* Transmisiones y Equipos Mecanicos (manufacturing design).

**GRADUATE UNITS**
**School of Business**

## INSTITUTO TECNOLÓGICO Y DE ESTUDIOS SUPERIORES DE MONTERREY, CAMPUS SALTILLO, 25270 Saltillo, Coahuila, Mexico

**General Information** Independent, coed, comprehensive institution.

## INSTITUTO TECNOLÓGICO Y DE ESTUDIOS SUPERIORES DE MONTERREY, CAMPUS SAN LUIS POTOSÍ, 78140 San Luis Potosí, SLP, Mexico

**General Information** Independent, coed, comprehensive institution.

## INSTITUTO TECNOLÓGICO Y DE ESTUDIOS SUPERIORES DE MONTERREY, CAMPUS SINALOA, 80800 Culiacán, Sinaloa, Mexico

**General Information** Independent, coed, comprehensive institution.

## INSTITUTO TECNOLÓGICO Y DE ESTUDIOS SUPERIORES DE MONTERREY, CAMPUS SONORA NORTE, 83000 Hermosillo, Sonora, Mexico

**General Information** Independent, coed, comprehensive institution. *Graduate housing:* On-campus housing not available. *Research affiliation:* National Council for Science and Technology (engineering).

**GRADUATE UNITS**
**Program in Business**
**Program in Education**
**Program in Technological Information Management**

## INSTITUTO TECNOLÓGICO Y DE ESTUDIOS SUPERIORES DE MONTERREY, CAMPUS TAMPICO, 89120 Altimira, Tamaulipas, Mexico

**General Information** Independent, coed, comprehensive institution.

## INSTITUTO TECNOLÓGICO Y DE ESTUDIOS SUPERIORES DE MONTERREY, CAMPUS TOLUCA, 50252 Toluca, Estado de Mexico, Mexico

**General Information** Independent, coed, comprehensive institution.

**GRADUATE UNITS**
**Graduate Programs** *Program availability:* Part-time, evening/weekend.

## INSTITUTO TECNOLÓGICO Y DE ESTUDIOS SUPERIORES DE MONTERREY, CAMPUS ZACATECAS, 98000 Zacatecas, Zacatecas, Mexico

**General Information** Independent, coed, comprehensive institution.

## INTER AMERICAN UNIVERSITY OF PUERTO RICO, AGUADILLA CAMPUS, Aguadilla, PR 00605

**General Information** Independent, coed, comprehensive institution. *Enrollment:* 3,903 graduate, professional, and undergraduate students; 172 full-time matriculated graduate/professional students (112 women), 23 part-time matriculated graduate/professional students (16 women). *Enrollment by degree level:* 195 master's. *Graduate faculty:* 6 full-time (all women), 10 part-time/adjunct (5 women). *Tuition:* Full-time $3870; part-time $645 per trimester. *Required fees:* $235 per trimester. Tuition and fees vary according to course load. *Student services:* Career counseling, services for students with disabilities. *Library facilities:* Manuel Mendez Ballester Information Access Center. *Collection:* Books: 62,162 (physical), 249,610 (digital/electronic); Serial titles: 100 (physical); Databases: 75. Weekly public service hours: 80; students can reserve study rooms.

**Computer facilities:** 861 computers available on campus for general student use. A campuswide network can be accessed from off campus. Online class registration is available.
Website: http://www.aguadilla.inter.edu/

**General Application Contact:** Doris Perez, Admission Director, 787-891-0925 Ext. 2740, Fax: 787-882-3020, E-mail: dperez@aguadilla.inter.edu.

**GRADUATE UNITS**
**Graduate School** Students: 172 full-time (112 women), 23 part-time (16 women); all minorities (all Hispanic/Latino). Average age 30. 102 applicants, 63% accepted, 59 enrolled. *Faculty:* 6 full-time (all women), 10 part-time/adjunct (5 women). Expenses: Contact institution. *Program availability:* Part-time, evening/weekend. *Application fee:* $31. Electronic applications accepted. *Application Contact:* Doris Perez, Admission Director, 787-891-0925 Ext. 2740, Fax: 787-882-3020, E-mail: dperez@aguadilla.inter.edu. *Chancellor*, Dr. Elie Agesilas, 787-891-0925 Ext. 2236, Fax: 787-882-3020, E-mail: eagesila@aguadilla.inter.edu.

## INTER AMERICAN UNIVERSITY OF PUERTO RICO, ARECIBO CAMPUS, Arecibo, PR 00614-4050

**General Information** Independent, coed, comprehensive institution.

**GRADUATE UNITS**
**Program in Anesthesia**
**Program in Business Administration**
**Program in Nursing**
**Programs in Education**

## INTER AMERICAN UNIVERSITY OF PUERTO RICO, BARRANQUITAS CAMPUS, Barranquitas, PR 00794

**General Information** Independent, coed, comprehensive institution. *Graduate housing:* On-campus housing not available.

GRADUATE UNITS
**Business Administration Program** *Program availability:* Part-time, evening/weekend. Electronic applications accepted.
**Program in Biotechnology** *Program availability:* Part-time, evening/weekend. Electronic applications accepted.
**Program in Criminal Justice** *Program availability:* Evening/weekend. Electronic applications accepted.
**Program in Education** *Program availability:* Part-time, evening/weekend. Electronic applications accepted.
**Program in Nursing** *Program availability:* Part-time, evening/weekend. Electronic applications accepted.

## INTER AMERICAN UNIVERSITY OF PUERTO RICO, BAYAMÓN CAMPUS, Bayamón, PR 00957

**General Information** Independent, coed, comprehensive institution. *Enrollment:* 4,500 graduate, professional, and undergraduate students; 91 full-time matriculated graduate/professional students (63 women), 15 part-time matriculated graduate/professional students (9 women). *Enrollment by degree level:* 106 master's. *Graduate faculty:* 10 full-time (3 women), 3 part-time/adjunct (all women). *Tuition:* Full-time $3870; part-time $1935 per year. *Required fees:* $735; $642 per unit. *Graduate housing:* Room and/or apartments available on a first-come, first-served basis to single students; on-campus housing not available to married students. Typical cost: $4000 per year ($8464 including board). *Student services:* Career counseling, free psychological counseling, international student services, services for students with disabilities. *Library facilities:* Centro de Acceso a la Informacion plus 1 other. *Collection:* Books: 27,751 (physical), 250,984 (digital/electronic); Serial titles: 104 (physical), 2 (digital/electronic); Databases: 67. Weekly public service hours: 79; students can reserve study rooms. *Research affiliation:* Bayamon Central University.

**Computer facilities:** 730 computers available on campus for general student use. A campuswide network can be accessed. Online class registration is available. Website: http://bayamon.inter.edu/

**General Application Contact:** Aurelis Baez, Director of Students Services, 787-279-1912 Ext. 2017, Fax: 787-279-2205, E-mail: abaez@bayamon.inter.edu.

GRADUATE UNITS
**Graduate School** *Program availability:* Part-time, evening/weekend.

## INTER AMERICAN UNIVERSITY OF PUERTO RICO, FAJARDO CAMPUS, Fajardo, PR 00738-7003

**General Information** Independent, coed, comprehensive institution. *Graduate housing:* On-campus housing not available.

GRADUATE UNITS
**Graduate Programs** *Program availability:* Online learning.

## INTER AMERICAN UNIVERSITY OF PUERTO RICO, GUAYAMA CAMPUS, Guayama, PR 00785

**General Information** Independent, coed, comprehensive institution.

GRADUATE UNITS
**Department of Business Administration**
**Department of Education and Social Sciences** *Program availability:* Part-time. Electronic applications accepted.
**Department of Natural and Applied Sciences**

## INTER AMERICAN UNIVERSITY OF PUERTO RICO, METROPOLITAN CAMPUS, San Juan, PR 00919-1293

**General Information** Independent, coed, comprehensive institution. CGS member. *Graduate housing:* On-campus housing not available. *Research affiliation:* Innovation Technology (electronics).

GRADUATE UNITS
**Graduate Programs** *Program availability:* Part-time, evening/weekend. Electronic applications accepted.

## INTER AMERICAN UNIVERSITY OF PUERTO RICO, PONCE CAMPUS, Mercedita, PR 00715-1602

**General Information** Independent, coed, comprehensive institution.

GRADUATE UNITS
**Graduate School**

## INTER AMERICAN UNIVERSITY OF PUERTO RICO, SAN GERMÁN CAMPUS, San Germán, PR 00683-5008

**General Information** Independent, coed, university. *Graduate housing:* Rooms and/or apartments available on a first-come, first-served basis to single and married students. Housing application deadline: 6/15.

GRADUATE UNITS
**Graduate Studies Center** *Program availability:* Part-time, evening/weekend.

## INTER AMERICAN UNIVERSITY OF PUERTO RICO SCHOOL OF LAW, San Juan, PR 00936-8351

**General Information** Independent, coed, graduate-only institution.

GRADUATE UNITS
**Professional Program** *Program availability:* Part-time, evening/weekend.

## INTER AMERICAN UNIVERSITY OF PUERTO RICO SCHOOL OF OPTOMETRY, Bayamón, PR 00957

**General Information** Independent, coed, graduate-only institution. *Graduate housing:* Room and/or apartments available on a first-come, first-served basis to single students; on-campus housing not available to married students.

GRADUATE UNITS
**Professional Program** Electronic applications accepted.

## INTERDENOMINATIONAL THEOLOGICAL CENTER, Atlanta, GA 30314-4112

**General Information** Independent-religious, coed, graduate-only institution. *Graduate housing:* Room and/or apartments available on a first-come, first-served basis to single students; on-campus housing not available to married students. Housing application deadline: 8/1. *Research affiliation:* Atlanta University Center, Inc., Columbia Theological Seminary Library, Candler School of Theology Library, Emory University Library.

GRADUATE UNITS
**Graduate and Professional Programs** *Program availability:* Part-time, evening/weekend, blended/hybrid learning. Electronic applications accepted.

## INTERIOR DESIGNERS INSTITUTE, Newport Beach, CA 92660

**General Information** Proprietary, coed, comprehensive institution.

GRADUATE UNITS
**Graduate Program**

## INTERNATIONAL BAPTIST COLLEGE AND SEMINARY, Chandler, AZ 85286

**General Information** Independent-religious, coed, comprehensive institution. *Graduate housing:* Room and/or apartments available on a first-come, first-served basis to single students; on-campus housing not available to married students.

GRADUATE UNITS
**Program in Biblical Studies**
**Program in Education**
**Program in Ministry**

## INTERNATIONAL INSTITUTE FOR RESTORATIVE PRACTICES, Bethlehem, PA 18018

**General Information** Independent, coed, graduate-only institution. CGS member.

GRADUATE UNITS
**Graduate Programs** *Program availability:* Online learning.

## INTERNATIONAL TECHNOLOGICAL UNIVERSITY, San Jose, CA 95134

**General Information** Independent, coed, graduate-only institution. CGS member. *Research affiliation:* Linux Works, Inc. (software), @Channel (software), New Trends Technology, Inc. (hardware), Pico Turbo, Inc. (hardware).

GRADUATE UNITS
**Program in Business Administration** *Program availability:* Part-time, evening/weekend. Electronic applications accepted.
**Program in Computer Engineering** *Program availability:* Part-time, evening/weekend. Electronic applications accepted.
**Program in Digital Arts** *Program availability:* Part-time. Electronic applications accepted.
**Program in Electrical Engineering** *Program availability:* Part-time, evening/weekend. Electronic applications accepted.
**Program in Engineering Management** *Program availability:* Part-time, evening/weekend. Electronic applications accepted.
**Program in Software Engineering** *Program availability:* Part-time, evening/weekend. Electronic applications accepted.

## INTERNATIONAL UNIVERSITY IN GENEVA, CH-1215 Geneva 15, Switzerland

**General Information** Private, coed, comprehensive institution. *Graduate housing:* Room and/or apartments available on a first-come, first-served basis to single students; on-campus housing not available to married students. Housing application deadline: 7/31.

GRADUATE UNITS
**Business Programs** *Program availability:* Part-time, evening/weekend. Electronic applications accepted.
**Leadership Programs** Electronic applications accepted.

## THE INTERNATIONAL UNIVERSITY OF MONACO, MC-98000 Principality of Monaco, Monaco

**General Information** Independent, coed, comprehensive institution. *Graduate housing:* Rooms and/or apartments guaranteed to single and married students. *Research affiliation:* Alpstar (hedge funds).

GRADUATE UNITS
**Graduate Programs** *Program availability:* Part-time. Electronic applications accepted.

## IONA COLLEGE, New Rochelle, NY 10801-1890

**General Information** Independent-religious, coed, comprehensive institution. *Enrollment:* 3,613 graduate, professional, and undergraduate students. *Enrollment by degree level:* 639 master's. *Graduate housing:* On-campus housing not available. *Student services:* Campus employment opportunities, campus safety program, career counseling, exercise/wellness program, free psychological counseling, international student services, multicultural affairs office, services for students with disabilities, writing training. *Library facilities:* Ryan Library plus 1 other. *Collection:* Books: 265,074 (physical), 329,090 (digital/electronic); Serial titles: 112 (physical), 347 (digital/electronic); Databases: 84. Weekly public service hours: 101; students can reserve study rooms. *Research affiliation:* IBM (teacher preparation).

**Computer facilities:** Computer purchase and lease plans are available. A campuswide network can be accessed. Online class registration, bill payment are available. Website: http://www.iona.edu/

**General Application Contact:** Katelyn Brunck, Associate Director of Graduate Admissions, 914-633-2451, Fax: 914-633-2277, E-mail: kbrunck@iona.edu.

GRADUATE UNITS
**School of Arts and Science** Students: 232 full-time (202 women), 112 part-time (71 women); includes 146 minority (43 Black or African American, non-Hispanic/Latino; 17 Asian, non-Hispanic/Latino; 75 Hispanic/Latino; 1 Native Hawaiian or other Pacific Islander, non-Hispanic/Latino; 10 Two or more races, non-Hispanic/Latino), 6 international. Average age 25. 376 applicants, 90% accepted, 131 enrolled. *Faculty:* 60 full-time (33 women), 46 part-time/adjunct (23 women). Expenses: Contact institution. *Financial support:* In 2019–20, 10 students received support. Tuition waivers (partial) and unspecified assistantships available. Support available to part-time students. Financial award application deadline: 4/15; financial award applicants required to submit FAFSA. In 2019, 125 master's, 26 other advanced degrees awarded. *Program availability:* Part-time, evening/weekend. *Application deadline:* For fall admission, 8/1 priority date for domestic students, 5/1 priority date for international students; for winter admission, 12/1 priority date for domestic students, 8/1 priority date for international students; for spring admission, 1/1 priority date for domestic students, 9/1 priority date for international students; for summer admission, 5/1 priority date for domestic students, 1/1 priority date for international students. Applications are processed on a rolling basis.

Electronic applications accepted. *Application Contact:* Dr. Katherine Zaromatidis, Director of Graduate Studies, School of Arts and Science, 914-633-2375, E-mail: kzaromatidis@iona.edu. *Dean, School of Arts and Science*, Joseph Stabile, PhD, 914-633-2253, Fax: 914-633-2023, E-mail: jstabile@iona.edu.

**School of Business** Students: 103 full-time (46 women), 183 part-time (89 women); includes 100 minority (33 Black or African American, non-Hispanic/Latino; 1 American Indian or Alaska Native, non-Hispanic/Latino; 10 Asian, non-Hispanic/Latino; 51 Hispanic/Latino; 5 Two or more races, non-Hispanic/Latino), 11 international. Average age 27. 156 applicants, 97% accepted, 75 enrolled. *Faculty:* 40 full-time (16 women), 20 part-time/adjunct (8 women). Expenses: Contact institution. *Financial support:* In 2019–20, 162 students received support. Scholarships/grants, tuition waivers (partial), and unspecified assistantships available. Support available to part-time students. Financial award application deadline: 4/15; financial award applicants required to submit FAFSA. In 2019, 183 master's, 96 other advanced degrees awarded. *Program availability:* Part-time, evening/weekend, 100% online, blended/hybrid learning. *Application deadline:* For fall admission, 8/15 priority date for domestic students, 8/1 priority date for international students; for winter admission, 11/15 priority date for domestic students, 11/1 priority date for international students; for spring admission, 2/15 priority date for domestic students, 2/1 priority date for international students; for summer admission, 5/15 priority date for domestic students, 5/1 priority date for international students. Applications are processed on a rolling basis. Electronic applications accepted. *Application Contact:* Kimberly Kelly, Director of Graduate Business Admissions, 914-633-2271, Fax: 914-633-2012, E-mail: kkelly@iona.edu. *Interim Dean of the School of Business*, Richard Highfield, PhD, 914-633-2789, Fax: 914-637-2708, E-mail: rhighfield@iona.edu.

## IOWA STATE UNIVERSITY OF SCIENCE AND TECHNOLOGY, Ames, IA 50011

**General Information** State-supported, coed, university. CGS member. *Graduate housing:* Rooms and/or apartments available on a first-come, first-served basis to single and married students. Housing application deadline: 6/15. *Research affiliation:* National Veterinary Services Laboratories, National Animal Disease Center, National Soil Tilth Laboratory, North Central Regional Center for Rural Development, U.S. Department of Energy-Ames Laboratory.

**GRADUATE UNITS**

**Bioinformatics and Computational Biology Program** Electronic applications accepted.

**Department of Accounting** Electronic applications accepted.

**Department of Aerospace Engineering and Engineering Mechanics** Electronic applications accepted.

**Department of Agricultural Education and Studies** Electronic applications accepted.

**Department of Agronomy** Electronic applications accepted.

**Department of Animal Science** Electronic applications accepted.

**Department of Anthropology** Electronic applications accepted.

**Department of Apparel, Events, and Hospitality Management** *Program availability:* Online learning. Electronic applications accepted.

**Department of Architecture** Electronic applications accepted.

**Department of Biomedical Sciences** Electronic applications accepted.

**Department of Chemical and Biological Engineering** Electronic applications accepted.

**Department of Chemistry** Electronic applications accepted.

**Department of Civil and Construction Engineering** Electronic applications accepted.

**Department of Community and Regional Planning** Electronic applications accepted.

**Department of Computer Science** Electronic applications accepted.

**Department of Economics** Electronic applications accepted.

**Department of Education** Electronic applications accepted.

**Department of Educational Leadership and Policy Studies** Electronic applications accepted.

**Department of Electrical and Computer Engineering** Electronic applications accepted.

**Department of English** Electronic applications accepted.

**Department of Entomology** Electronic applications accepted.

**Department of Food Science and Human Nutrition** Electronic applications accepted.

**Department of Geological and Atmospheric Sciences** Electronic applications accepted.

**Department of History** Electronic applications accepted.

**Department of Horticulture** Electronic applications accepted.

**Department of Human Development and Family Studies** Electronic applications accepted.

**Department of Industrial and Manufacturing Systems Engineering** Electronic applications accepted.

**Department of Kinesiology** Electronic applications accepted.

**Department of Landscape Architecture** *Program availability:* Part-time. Electronic applications accepted.

**Department of Materials Science and Engineering** Electronic applications accepted.

**Department of Mathematics** Electronic applications accepted.

**Department of Mechanical Engineering** Electronic applications accepted.

**Department of Natural Resource Ecology and Management** Electronic applications accepted.

**Department of Physics and Astronomy** Electronic applications accepted.

**Department of Plant Pathology** Electronic applications accepted.

**Department of Political Science** Electronic applications accepted.

**Department of Psychology** Electronic applications accepted.

**Department of Sociology** Electronic applications accepted.

**Department of Statistics** Electronic applications accepted.

**Department of Veterinary Clinical Sciences** Electronic applications accepted.

**Department of Veterinary Diagnostic and Production Animal Medicine** Electronic applications accepted.

**Department of Veterinary Microbiology and Preventive Medicine** Electronic applications accepted.

**Department of Veterinary Pathology** Electronic applications accepted.

**Greenlee School of Journalism and Communication** Electronic applications accepted.

**Program in Agricultural and Biosystems Engineering** Electronic applications accepted.

**Program in Agricultural Economics** Electronic applications accepted.

**Program in Agricultural Meteorology** Electronic applications accepted.

**Program in Analytical Chemistry** Electronic applications accepted.

**Program in Animal Breeding and Genetics** Electronic applications accepted.

**Program in Animal Physiology** Electronic applications accepted.

**Program in Apparel, Merchandising, and Design** Electronic applications accepted.

**Program in Applied Linguistics and Technology** Electronic applications accepted.

**Program in Applied Mathematics** Electronic applications accepted.

**Program in Applied Physics** Electronic applications accepted.

**Program in Astrophysics**

**Program in Biophysics** Electronic applications accepted.

**Program in Biorenewable Resources and Technology** Electronic applications accepted.

**Program in Business Administration** Electronic applications accepted.

**Program in Business Analytics** *Program availability:* Online learning.

**Program in Business and Technology** Electronic applications accepted.

**Program in Computer Engineering** Electronic applications accepted.

**Program in Condensed Matter Physics** Electronic applications accepted.

**Program in Creative Writing and Environment** Electronic applications accepted.

**Program in Crop Production and Physiology** Electronic applications accepted.

**Program in Diet and Exercise** Electronic applications accepted.

**Program in Earth Science** Electronic applications accepted.

**Program in Ecology and Evolutionary Biology** Electronic applications accepted.

**Program in Engineering Mechanics** Electronic applications accepted.

**Program in Environmental Sciences** Electronic applications accepted.

**Program in Family and Consumer Sciences** Electronic applications accepted.

**Program in Finance**

**Program in Fisheries Biology** Electronic applications accepted.

**Program in Forestry** Electronic applications accepted.

**Program in Genetics** Electronic applications accepted.

**Program in Graphic Design** Electronic applications accepted.

**Program in High Energy Physics** Electronic applications accepted.

**Program in Human-Computer Interaction** Electronic applications accepted.

**Program in Immunobiology** Electronic applications accepted.

**Program in Industrial Agriculture and Technology** Electronic applications accepted.

**Program in Industrial Design** Electronic applications accepted.

**Program in Information Assurance** Electronic applications accepted.

**Program in Information Systems** Electronic applications accepted.

**Program in Inorganic Chemistry** Electronic applications accepted.

**Program in Integrated Visual Arts**

**Program in Interdisciplinary Graduate Studies** Electronic applications accepted.

**Program in Interior Design** Electronic applications accepted.

**Program in Meat Science** Electronic applications accepted.

**Program in Meteorology** Electronic applications accepted.

**Program in Microbiology** Electronic applications accepted.

**Program in Molecular, Cellular, and Developmental Biology** Electronic applications accepted.

**Program in Neuroscience** Electronic applications accepted.

**Program in Nuclear Physics** Electronic applications accepted.

**Program in Nutritional Sciences** Electronic applications accepted.

**Program in Organic Chemistry** Electronic applications accepted.

**Program in Physical Chemistry** Electronic applications accepted.

**Program in Plant Biology** Electronic applications accepted.

**Program in Plant Breeding** Electronic applications accepted.

**Program in Rhetoric and Professional Communication** Electronic applications accepted.

**Program in Rhetoric, Composition, and Professional Communication** Electronic applications accepted.

**Program in Rural Sociology** Electronic applications accepted.

**Program in School Mathematics** Electronic applications accepted.

**Program in Science Education** Electronic applications accepted.

**Program in Seed Technology and Business** Electronic applications accepted.

**Program in Soil Science** Electronic applications accepted.

**Program in Sustainable Agriculture** Electronic applications accepted.

**Program in Systems Engineering** Electronic applications accepted.

**Program in Teaching English as a Second Language/Applied Linguistics** Electronic applications accepted.

**Program in Toxicology** Electronic applications accepted.

**Program in Transportation** Electronic applications accepted.

**Rural, Agricultural, Technological, and Environmental History Program** Electronic applications accepted.

## IOWA WESLEYAN UNIVERSITY, Mount Pleasant, IA 52641-1398

**General Information** Independent-religious, coed, comprehensive institution. *Enrollment:* 29 full-time matriculated graduate/professional students (14 women). *Enrollment by degree level:* 29 master's. *Graduate faculty:* 1 full-time, 7 part-time/adjunct (5 women). *Tuition:* Full-time $8910; part-time $4455 per credit hour. *Required fees:* $1000. Tuition and fees vary according to program. *Graduate housing:* On-campus housing not available. *Student services:* Campus employment opportunities, career counseling, free psychological counseling. *Library facilities:* Chadwick Library plus 1 other. *Collection:* Books: 93,754 (physical), 3,338 (digital/electronic); Serial titles: 2,169 (physical), 4,827 (digital/electronic); Databases: 32. Weekly public service hours: 80; students can reserve study rooms.

**Computer facilities:** 97 computers available on campus for general student use. A campuswide network can be accessed from student residence rooms.
Website: http://www.iw.edu/

**General Application Contact:** Tiffany Hill, Online Enrollment Advisor, 319-385-6208, E-mail: online@iw.edu.

## IRELL & MANELLA GRADUATE SCHOOL OF BIOLOGICAL SCIENCES, Duarte, CA 91010

**General Information** Independent, coed, graduate-only institution. *Graduate housing:* Room and/or apartments available on a first-come, first-served basis to single students; on-campus housing not available to married students. Housing application deadline: 7/31.

**GRADUATE UNITS**

**Graduate Program** Electronic applications accepted.

## ITHACA COLLEGE, Ithaca, NY 14850

**General Information** Independent, coed, comprehensive institution. *Enrollment:* 6,266 graduate, professional, and undergraduate students; 348 full-time matriculated graduate/professional students (269 women), 65 part-time matriculated graduate/professional students (36 women). *Enrollment by degree level:* 245 master's, 168 doctoral. *Graduate faculty:* 162 full-time (78 women), 4 part-time/adjunct (all women). *Graduate housing:* On-campus housing not available. *Student services:* Campus employment opportunities, campus safety program, career counseling, exercise/wellness program, free psychological counseling, international student services, low-cost health insurance, multicultural affairs office, services for students with disabilities, teacher training, writing training. *Library facilities:* Ithaca College Library. *Collection:* Books: 303,169 (physical), 194,765 (digital/electronic); Serial titles: 577 (physical), 73,113 (digital/electronic); Databases: 151. Weekly public service hours: 148; study areas open 24 hours, 5–7 days a week. *Research affiliation:* NASA (physics and astronomy), National Science Foundation (mathematics), National Institutes of Health (exercise and sport sciences), U.S. Department of Health and Human Services/National Institutes of Health (biology).

**Computer facilities:** 700 computers available on campus for general student use. A campuswide network can be accessed. Online class registration is available. Website: http://www.ithaca.edu/

**General Application Contact:** Nicole Eversley Bradwell, Director, Office of Admission, 800-429-4274, Fax: 607-274-1263, E-mail: admission@ithaca.edu.

**GRADUATE UNITS**

**Roy H. Park School of Communications** Students: 12 part-time (6 women); includes 3 minority (2 Black or African American, non-Hispanic/Latino; 1 Two or more races, non-Hispanic/Latino), 1 international. Average age 38. 30 applicants, 87% accepted, 10 enrolled. *Faculty:* 12 full-time (3 women). Expenses: Contact institution. *Financial support:* In 2019–20, 12 students received support, including 11 fellowships (averaging $8,221 per year); Federal Work-Study and scholarships/grants also available. Support available to part-time students. Financial award application deadline: 3/1; financial award applicants required to submit FAFSA. In 2019, 13 master's awarded. *Program availability:* Part-time. *Application deadline:* For fall admission, 2/1 for domestic and international students. Applications are processed on a rolling basis. *Application fee:* $40. Electronic applications accepted. *Application Contact:* Nicole Eversley Bradwell, Director, Office of Admission, 800-429-4274, Fax: 607-274-1263, E-mail: admission@ithaca.edu. *Interim Dean, School of Communications*, Dr. Jack Powers, 607-274-1862, E-mail: jpowers@ithaca.edu.

**School of Business** Students: 29 full-time (12 women), 2 part-time (0 women); includes 5 minority (2 Black or African American, non-Hispanic/Latino; 2 Asian, non-Hispanic/Latino; 1 Hispanic/Latino), 2 international. Average age 23. 41 applicants, 76% accepted, 29 enrolled. *Faculty:* 13 full-time (6 women). Expenses: Contact institution. *Financial support:* In 2019–20, 17 students received support, including 13 fellowships (averaging $12,385 per year); Federal Work-Study and scholarships/grants also available. Support available to part-time students. Financial award application deadline: 3/1; financial award applicants required to submit FAFSA. In 2019, 26 master's awarded. *Program availability:* Part-time. *Application deadline:* For fall admission, 5/15 for domestic and international students; for spring admission, 11/1 for domestic and international students. Applications are processed on a rolling basis. *Application fee:* $40. Electronic applications accepted. *Application Contact:* Nicole Eversley Bradwell, Director, Office of Admission, 800-429-4274, E-mail: admission@ithaca.edu. *Interim Dean, School of Business*, Dr. Alka Bramhandkar, E-mail: abramhandkar@ithaca.edu.

**School of Health Sciences and Human Performance** Students: 284 full-time (230 women), 22 part-time (16 women); includes 40 minority (4 Black or African American, non-Hispanic/Latino; 14 Asian, non-Hispanic/Latino; 13 Hispanic/Latino; 9 Two or more races, non-Hispanic/Latino), 4 international. Average age 23. 280 applicants, 64% accepted, 173 enrolled. *Faculty:* 56 full-time (37 women), 1 (woman) part-time/adjunct. Expenses: Contact institution. *Financial support:* In 2019–20, 205 students received support, including 62 research assistantships (averaging $12,603 per year); Federal Work-Study and scholarships/grants also available. Support available to part-time students. Financial award application deadline: 3/1; financial award applicants required to submit FAFSA. In 2019, 95 master's, 82 doctorates awarded. *Program availability:* Part-time. *Application deadline:* Applications are processed on a rolling basis. *Application fee:* $40. Electronic applications accepted. *Application Contact:* Nicole Eversley Bradwell, Director, Office of Admission, 607-800-429-4274, Fax: 607-274-1263, E-mail: admission@ithaca.edu. *Dean, School of Health Sciences and Human Performance*, Dr. Linda Petrosino, 607-274-3237, Fax: 607-274-1263, E-mail: lpetrosino@ithaca.edu.

**School of Humanities and Sciences** Students: 26 full-time (21 women). Average age 26. 32 applicants, 91% accepted, 25 enrolled. *Faculty:* 12 full-time (7 women). Expenses: Contact institution. *Financial support:* In 2019–20, 24 students received support, including 24 teaching assistantships (averaging $11,296 per year); Federal Work-Study and scholarships/grants also available. Support available to part-time students. Financial award application deadline: 3/1; financial award applicants required to submit FAFSA. In 2019, 18 master's awarded. *Application deadline:* For fall admission, 3/19 for domestic and international students. Applications are processed on a rolling basis. *Application fee:* $40. Electronic applications accepted. *Application Contact:* Nicole Eversley Bradwell, Director, Office of Admission, 800-429-4274274-3124, Fax: 607-274-1263, E-mail: admission@ithaca.edu. *Dean, School of Humanities and Sciences*, Dr. Melanie Stein, 607-274-3102, E-mail: mstein2@ithaca.edu.

**School of Music** Students: 9 full-time (6 women), 29 part-time (14 women); includes 8 minority (1 Black or African American, non-Hispanic/Latino; 4 Asian, non-Hispanic/Latino; 3 Hispanic/Latino), 9 international. Average age 24. 114 applicants, 46% accepted, 16 enrolled. *Faculty:* 69 full-time (25 women), 3 part-time/adjunct (all women). Expenses: Contact institution. *Financial support:* In 2019–20, 37 students received support, including 37 teaching assistantships (averaging $10,451 per year); Federal Work-Study and scholarships/grants also available. Support available to part-time students. Financial award application deadline: 3/1; financial award applicants required to submit FAFSA. In 2019, 23 master's awarded. *Program availability:* Part-time. *Application deadline:* For fall admission, 12/1 for domestic and international students. Applications are processed on a rolling basis. *Application fee:* $40. Electronic applications accepted. *Application Contact:* Nicole Eversley Bradwell, Director, Office of Admission, 800-429-4274, Fax: 607-274-1263, E-mail: admission@ithaca.edu. *Interim Dean, School of Music*, Dr. Keith Kaiser, 607-274-1938, E-mail: kaiser@ithaca.edu.

## JACKSON STATE UNIVERSITY, Jackson, MS 39217

**General Information** State-supported, coed, university. CGS member. *Graduate housing:* Room and/or apartments available on a first-come, first-served basis to single students; on-campus housing not available to married students. Housing application deadline: 7/15. *Research affiliation:* Lawrence A. Berkeley Laboratories (biology, chemistry), U.S. Department of Energy (biology), National Science Foundation (biology, chemistry), Environmental Protection Agency, Oak Ridge Associated Universities (science), Raytheon Systems Company (computer science).

**GRADUATE UNITS**

**Graduate School** *Program availability:* Part-time, evening/weekend, online only, 100% online, blended/hybrid learning. Electronic applications accepted.

***College of Business*** *Program availability:* Part-time, evening/weekend. Electronic applications accepted.

***College of Education and Human Development*** *Program availability:* Part-time, evening/weekend, 100% online, blended/hybrid learning. Electronic applications accepted.

***College of Liberal Arts*** *Program availability:* Part-time, evening/weekend. Electronic applications accepted.

***College of Public Service***

***College of Science, Engineering and Technology*** *Program availability:* Part-time, evening/weekend.

***School of Public Health***

## JACKSONVILLE STATE UNIVERSITY, Jacksonville, AL 36265-1602

**General Information** State-supported, coed, comprehensive institution. *Graduate housing:* Rooms and/or apartments available on a first-come, first-served basis to single and married students.

**GRADUATE UNITS**

**Graduate Studies** *Program availability:* Part-time, evening/weekend, 100% online, blended/hybrid learning. Electronic applications accepted.

***School of Arts and Humanities***

***School of Business and Industry*** *Program availability:* Part-time, evening/weekend, 100% online, blended/hybrid learning. Electronic applications accepted.

***School of Education*** *Program availability:* Part-time, evening/weekend, 100% online, blended/hybrid learning. Electronic applications accepted.

***School of Human Services and Social Sciences***

***School of Science*** *Program availability:* Part-time, evening/weekend, 100% online, blended/hybrid learning.

## JACKSONVILLE UNIVERSITY, Jacksonville, FL 32211

**General Information** Independent, coed, comprehensive institution. *Enrollment:* 4,164 graduate, professional, and undergraduate students; 440 full-time matriculated graduate/professional students (302 women), 790 part-time matriculated graduate/professional students (586 women). *Enrollment by degree level:* 975 master's, 227 doctoral, 28 other advanced degrees. *Graduate faculty:* 69 full-time (35 women), 78 part-time/adjunct (43 women). *Graduate housing:* Room and/or apartments available on a first-come, first-served basis to single students; on-campus housing not available to married students. Housing application deadline: 8/1. *Student services:* Campus employment opportunities, campus safety program, career counseling, exercise/wellness program, free psychological counseling, international student services, low-cost health insurance, multicultural affairs office, services for students with disabilities, teacher training, writing training. *Library facilities:* Carl S. Swisher Library. *Collection:* Books: 187,294 (physical), 268,187 (digital/electronic); Serial titles: 7,434 (physical), 55,516 (digital/electronic); Databases: 69. Weekly public service hours: 88; students can reserve study rooms.

**Computer facilities:** Computer purchase and lease plans are available. 400 computers available on campus for general student use. A campuswide network can be accessed. Online class registration, learning management systems are available. Website: http://www.ju.edu/

**General Application Contact:** Kristen Kirkendall, Associate Director of Graduate Admissions and Communication, 904-256-7169, E-mail: kgreene8@ju.edu.

**GRADUATE UNITS**

**Brooks Rehabilitation College of Healthcare Sciences** Students: 280 full-time (217 women), 507 part-time (430 women); includes 240 minority (123 Black or African American, non-Hispanic/Latino; 4 American Indian or Alaska Native, non-Hispanic/Latino; 34 Asian, non-Hispanic/Latino; 61 Hispanic/Latino; 1 Native Hawaiian or other Pacific Islander, non-Hispanic/Latino; 17 Two or more races, non-Hispanic/Latino), 14 international. Average age 36. 631 applicants, 42% accepted, 153 enrolled. Expenses: Contact institution. *Financial support:* Fellowships, Federal Work-Study, institutionally sponsored loans, scholarships/grants, and health care benefits available. Support available to part-time students. Financial award application deadline: 3/15; financial award applicants required to submit FAFSA. In 2019, 337 master's, 15 doctorates awarded. *Program availability:* Part-time, 100% online, blended/hybrid learning. *Application deadline:* Applications are processed on a rolling basis. *Application fee:* $50. Electronic applications accepted. *Application Contact:* Kristen Kirkendall, Associate Director of Graduate Admissions and Communications, 904-256-7169, E-mail: kgreene8@ju.edu. *Dean, Brooks Rehabilitation College of Healthcare Sciences*, Dr. Mark Tillman, 904-256-7977, E-mail: mtillma3@ju.edu.

**Keigwin School of Nursing** Students: 49 full-time (39 women), 463 part-time (406 women); includes 153 minority (85 Black or African American, non-Hispanic/Latino; 2 American Indian or Alaska Native, non-Hispanic/Latino; 22 Asian, non-Hispanic/Latino; 32 Hispanic/Latino; 1 Native Hawaiian or other Pacific Islander, non-Hispanic/Latino; 11 Two or more races, non-Hispanic/Latino), 1 international. Average age 39. 203 applicants, 39% accepted, 67 enrolled. Expenses: Contact institution. *Financial support:* Federal Work-Study, institutionally sponsored loans, scholarships/grants, and health care benefits available. Support available to part-time students. Financial award application deadline: 3/15; financial award applicants required to submit FAFSA. In 2019, 215 master's, 15 doctorates awarded. *Program availability:* Part-time, 100% online, blended/hybrid learning. *Application deadline:* Applications are processed on a rolling basis. *Application fee:* $50. Electronic applications accepted. *Application Contact:* Kristen Kirkendall, Associate Director of Graduate Admissions and Communications, 904-256-7169, E-mail: kgreene8@

ju.edu. *Director, Graduate Nursing Programs/Associate Professor*, Dr. Hilary Morgan, 904-256-7601, E-mail: hmorgan@ju.edu.

***School of Applied Health Sciences*** Students: 187 full-time (160 women), 38 part-time (21 women); includes 73 minority (37 Black or African American, non-Hispanic/Latino; 2 American Indian or Alaska Native, non-Hispanic/Latino; 10 Asian, non-Hispanic/Latino; 19 Hispanic/Latino; 5 Two or more races, non-Hispanic/Latino), 8 international. Average age 29. 428 applicants, 43% accepted, 86 enrolled. Expenses: Contact institution. *Financial support:* Federal Work-Study, institutionally sponsored loans, scholarships/grants, and health care benefits available. Support available to part-time students. Financial award application deadline: 3/15; financial award applicants required to submit FAFSA. In 2019, 114 master's awarded. *Program availability:* Part-time, 100% online, blended/hybrid learning. *Application deadline:* Applications are processed on a rolling basis. *Application fee:* $50. Electronic applications accepted. *Application Contact:* Pam Adrian, Assistant Director of Enrollment and Advising, 904-256-7245, E-mail: padrian@ju.edu. *Dean, Brooks Rehabilitation College of Healthcare Sciences*, Dr. Mark Tillman, 904-256-7977, E-mail: mtillma3@ju.edu.

***School of Orthodontics*** Students: 44 full-time (18 women), 6 part-time (3 women); includes 14 minority (1 Black or African American, non-Hispanic/Latino; 2 Asian, non-Hispanic/Latino; 10 Hispanic/Latino; 1 Two or more races, non-Hispanic/Latino), 5 international. Average age 34. Expenses: Contact institution. *Financial support:* Fellowships, scholarships/grants, and health care benefits available. Financial award application deadline: 3/15; financial award applicants required to submit FAFSA. In 2019, 8 other advanced degrees awarded. *Application deadline:* For fall admission, 9/14 priority date for domestic students, 9/14 for international students. Applications are processed on a rolling basis. *Application fee:* $175. Electronic applications accepted. *Application Contact:* Sharon Frazier, Executive Operations Coordinator, 904-256-7847, Fax: 904-256-7847, E-mail: juorthoadmissions@ju.edu. *Program Director & Clinical Associate Professor*, Dr. James Toruten, 904-256-7850, E-mail: jtroute@ju.edu.

**College of Arts and Sciences** Students: 28 full-time (20 women), 76 part-time (52 women); includes 40 minority (26 Black or African American, non-Hispanic/Latino; 1 Asian, non-Hispanic/Latino; 6 Hispanic/Latino; 7 Two or more races, non-Hispanic/Latino), 1 international. Average age 34. Expenses: Contact institution. *Financial support:* Research assistantships, teaching assistantships, institutionally sponsored loans, scholarships/grants, and health care benefits available. Support available to part-time students. Financial award application deadline: 3/15; financial award applicants required to submit FAFSA. In 2019, 30 master's awarded. *Program availability:* Evening/weekend. *Application deadline:* For fall admission, 2/15 priority date for domestic and international students. Applications are processed on a rolling basis. *Application fee:* $50. Electronic applications accepted. *Application Contact:* Joel Walker, Assistant Director of Graduate Admissions, 904-256-7428, E-mail: jwalker28@ju.edu. *Dean for the College of Arts and Sciences*, Dr. Matthew Corrigan, 904-256-7101, E-mail: mcorrig2@ju.edu.

***Marine Science Research Institute*** Students: 10 full-time (6 women), 18 part-time (14 women); includes 4 minority (2 Black or African American, non-Hispanic/Latino; 1 Hispanic/Latino; 1 Two or more races, non-Hispanic/Latino). Average age 27. 17 applicants, 71% accepted, 9 enrolled. Expenses: Contact institution. *Financial support:* Teaching assistantships, career-related internships or fieldwork, scholarships/grants, tuition waivers, and unspecified assistantships available. Support available to part-time students. Financial award application deadline: 3/1. In 2019, 6 master's awarded. *Program availability:* Part-time. *Application deadline:* For fall admission, 2/1 priority date for domestic students, 2/1 for international students. Applications are processed on a rolling basis. *Application fee:* $50. Electronic applications accepted. *Application Contact:* Joel Walker, Assistant Director of Graduate Admissions, 904-256-7428, E-mail: jwalker28@ju.edu. *Executive Director*, Dr. A. Quinton White, Jr., 904-256-7100, E-mail: qwhite@ju.edu.

**College of Fine Arts** Students: 12 full-time (9 women), 21 part-time (17 women); includes 3 minority (2 Black or African American, non-Hispanic/Latino; 1 Hispanic/Latino). Average age 37. 30 applicants, 70% accepted, 14 enrolled. Expenses: Contact institution. *Financial support:* Fellowships, institutionally sponsored loans, scholarships/grants, and health care benefits available. Support available to part-time students. Financial award application deadline: 3/1; financial award applicants required to submit FAFSA. In 2019, 21 master's awarded. *Program availability:* Blended/hybrid learning. *Application deadline:* Applications are processed on a rolling basis. *Application fee:* $50. Electronic applications accepted. *Application Contact:* Kyrstin Creswell, Assistant Director of Graduate Admissions, 904-256-7002, E-mail: kcreswe@ju.edu. *Dean of Fine Arts/Associate Professor of Music*, Dr. Timothy Snyder, 904-256-7377, E-mail: tsnyder2@ju.edu.

**Davis College of Business** Students: 120 full-time (56 women), 186 part-time (87 women); includes 93 minority (53 Black or African American, non-Hispanic/Latino; 1 American Indian or Alaska Native, non-Hispanic/Latino; 9 Asian, non-Hispanic/Latino; 23 Hispanic/Latino; 1 Native Hawaiian or other Pacific Islander, non-Hispanic/Latino; 6 Two or more races, non-Hispanic/Latino), 35 international. Average age 35. 169 applicants, 56% accepted, 72 enrolled. *Faculty:* 39 full-time (14 women), 13 part-time/adjunct (4 women). Expenses: Contact institution. *Financial support:* In 2019–20, 4 students received support. Scholarships/grants, health care benefits, and unspecified assistantships available. Financial award application deadline: 6/30; financial award applicants required to submit FAFSA. In 2019, 136 master's, 8 doctorates awarded. *Program availability:* Part-time, evening/weekend, 100% online. *Application deadline:* Applications are processed on a rolling basis. *Application fee:* $50. Electronic applications accepted. *Application Contact:* Benjamin Southern, Assistant Director of Admissions, 904-256-7293, E-mail: bsouthe@ju.edu. *Dean*, Dr. Barbara Ritter, 904-256-7430, E-mail: britter1@ju.edu.

**Public Policy Institute** Students: 13 full-time (9 women), 39 part-time (24 women); includes 22 minority (15 Black or African American, non-Hispanic/Latino; 1 Asian, non-Hispanic/Latino; 3 Hispanic/Latino; 3 Two or more races, non-Hispanic/Latino). Average age 36. 40 applicants, 68% accepted, 22 enrolled. *Faculty:* 6 full-time (1 woman), 15 part-time/adjunct (3 women). Expenses: Contact institution. *Financial support:* Fellowships, career-related internships or fieldwork, Federal Work-Study, scholarships/grants, and unspecified assistantships available. Support available to part-time students. Financial award application deadline: 4/1; financial award applicants required to submit FAFSA. In 2019, 14 master's awarded. *Program availability:* Part-time, evening/weekend. *Application deadline:* For fall admission, 2/15 priority date for domestic students, 2/15 for international students. Applications are processed on a rolling basis. *Application fee:* $50. Electronic applications accepted. *Application Contact:* Fowler Martens, Administrative Associate, 904-256-7053, E-mail: fmarten@ju.edu. *Director of Public Policy Institute*, Dr. Richard A. Mullaney, 904-256-7342, E-mail: rmullan1@ju.edu.

## JAMES MADISON UNIVERSITY, Harrisonburg, VA 22807

**General Information** State-supported, coed, comprehensive institution. CGS member. *Enrollment:* 21,820 graduate, professional, and undergraduate students; 1,045 full-time matriculated graduate/professional students (774 women), 673 part-time matriculated graduate/professional students (458 women). *Enrollment by degree level:* 1,444 master's, 197 doctoral, 77 other advanced degrees. *Graduate faculty:* 802. *Graduate housing:* On-campus housing not available. *Student services:* Campus employment opportunities, campus safety program, career counseling, exercise/wellness program, free psychological counseling, international student services, multicultural affairs office, services for students with disabilities, teacher training, writing training. *Library facilities:* Carrier Library plus 2 others. *Collection:* Students can reserve study rooms. *Research affiliation:* National Institute of Standards and Technology (NIST) through George Mason University (network risk assessment), National Oceanic and Atmospheric Administration (NOAA) (applied meteorological research), National Science Foundation (development of a detector array for Compton Scattering using polarized beams and targets; quantitative skills in biology).

**Computer facilities:** Computer purchase and lease plans are available. A campuswide network can be accessed. Online class registration is available.
Website: http://www.jmu.edu/

**General Application Contact:** John Burgess, Interim Dean, The Graduate School, 540-568-4213, Fax: 540-568-7860, E-mail: grad@jmu.edu.

**GRADUATE UNITS**

**The Graduate School** Students: 1,045 full-time (774 women), 673 part-time (458 women); includes 286 minority (103 Black or African American, non-Hispanic/Latino; 1 American Indian or Alaska Native, non-Hispanic/Latino; 58 Asian, non-Hispanic/Latino; 82 Hispanic/Latino; 42 Two or more races, non-Hispanic/Latino), 58 international. Average age 30. 2,121 applicants, 51% accepted, 727 enrolled. *Faculty:* 802. Expenses: Contact institution. *Financial support:* In 2019–20, 422 students received support, including fellowships with full tuition reimbursements available (averaging $7,911 per year), 39 teaching assistantships with full tuition reimbursements available (averaging $9,284 per year); research assistantships, career-related internships or fieldwork, Federal Work-Study, tuition waivers, unspecified assistantships, and athletic assistantships (averaging $9284), doctoral assistantships (stipend varies) also available. Financial award application deadline: 3/1; financial award applicants required to submit FAFSA. In 2019, 716 master's, 37 doctorates, 29 other advanced degrees awarded. *Program availability:* Part-time, evening/weekend, 100% online, blended/hybrid learning. *Application fee:* $60. Electronic applications accepted. *Application Contact:* Lynette D. Michael, Director of Graduate Admissions, 540-568-6131 Ext. 6395, Fax: 540-568-7860, E-mail: michaeld@jmu.edu. *Interim Dean, The Graduate School*, John Burgess, 540-568-4213, Fax: 540-568-7860, E-mail: grad@jmu.edu.

***College of Arts and Letters*** Students: 102 full-time (65 women), 32 part-time (22 women); includes 27 minority (12 Black or African American, non-Hispanic/Latino; 3 Asian, non-Hispanic/Latino; 6 Hispanic/Latino; 6 Two or more races, non-Hispanic/Latino), 6 international. Average age 30. *Faculty:* 136. Expenses: Contact institution. *Financial support:* In 2019–20, 72 students received support, including 19 teaching assistantships with full tuition reimbursements available (averaging $9,284 per year); fellowships and Federal Work-Study also available. Financial award application deadline: 3/1; financial award applicants required to submit FAFSA. In 2019, 55 master's awarded. *Program availability:* Part-time. *Application fee:* $60. Electronic applications accepted. *Application Contact:* Lynette D. Michael, Director of Graduate Admissions, 540-568-6131 Ext. 6395, Fax: 540-568-7860, E-mail: michaeld@jmu.edu. *Dean*, Dr. David K. Jeffrey, 540-568-7044.

***College of Business*** Students: 98 full-time (39 women), 123 part-time (58 women); includes 35 minority (11 Black or African American, non-Hispanic/Latino; 8 Asian, non-Hispanic/Latino; 13 Hispanic/Latino; 3 Two or more races, non-Hispanic/Latino), 17 international. Average age 30. *Faculty:* 58. Expenses: Contact institution. *Financial support:* In 2019–20, 31 students received support. Fellowships, career-related internships or fieldwork, Federal Work-Study, and assistantships (averaging $7911), 6 doctoral assistantships, 1 service assistantship available. Financial award application deadline: 3/1; financial award applicants required to submit FAFSA. In 2019, 117 master's, 4 doctorates awarded. *Program availability:* Part-time, evening/weekend, blended/hybrid learning. *Application fee:* $60. Electronic applications accepted. *Application Contact:* Lynette D. Michael, Director of Graduate Admissions, 540-568-6395, Fax: 540-568-7860, E-mail: michaeld@jmu.edu. *Dean*, Dr. Mary A. Gowan, 540-568-3254, E-mail: gowanma@jmu.edu.

***College of Education*** Students: 276 full-time (235 women), 212 part-time (157 women); includes 69 minority (16 Black or African American, non-Hispanic/Latino; 1 American Indian or Alaska Native, non-Hispanic/Latino; 11 Asian, non-Hispanic/Latino; 31 Hispanic/Latino; 10 Two or more races, non-Hispanic/Latino), 3 international. Average age 30. *Faculty:* 130. Expenses: Contact institution. *Financial support:* In 2019–20, 34 students received support. Teaching assistantships, career-related internships or fieldwork, Federal Work-Study, and assistantships (averaging $7911) available. Financial award application deadline: 3/1; financial award applicants required to submit FAFSA. In 2019, 312 master's awarded. *Program availability:* Part-time, evening/weekend, 100% online, blended/hybrid learning. *Application fee:* $60. Electronic applications accepted. *Application Contact:* Lynette D. Michael, Director of Graduate Admissions, 540-568-6131 Ext. 6395, Fax: 540-568-7860, E-mail: michaeld@jmu.edu. *Dean*, Dr. Phillip M. Wishon, 540-568-6572, E-mail: wishonpm@jmu.edu.

***College of Health and Behavioral Studies*** Students: 451 full-time (367 women), 145 part-time (132 women); includes 101 minority (36 Black or African American, non-Hispanic/Latino; 25 Asian, non-Hispanic/Latino; 23 Hispanic/Latino; 17 Two or more races, non-Hispanic/Latino), 10 international. Average age 30. *Faculty:* 227. Expenses: Contact institution. *Financial support:* In 2019–20, 192 students received support, including 17 teaching assistantships with full tuition reimbursements available (averaging $9,284 per year); career-related internships or fieldwork, Federal Work-Study, unspecified assistantships, and athletic assistantships (averaging $8837), service assistantships (averaging $7530), doctoral assistantships also available. Financial award application deadline: 3/1; financial award applicants required to submit FAFSA. In 2019, 152 master's, 19 doctorates, 10 other advanced degrees awarded. *Program availability:* Part-time, evening/weekend, 100% online, blended/hybrid learning. *Application fee:* $60. Electronic applications accepted. *Application Contact:* Lynette D. Michael, Director of Graduate Admissions, 540-568-6131 Ext. 6395, Fax: 540-568-7860, E-mail: michaeld@jmu.edu. *Dean*, Dr. Sharon E. Lovell, 540-568-2705, Fax: 540-568-2747, E-mail: lovellse@jmu.edu.

***College of Integrated Science and Engineering*** Students: 3 full-time (1 woman), 55 part-time (11 women); includes 14 minority (8 Black or African American, non-Hispanic/Latino; 3 Asian, non-Hispanic/Latino; 3 Hispanic/Latino), 3 international.

Average age 30. *Faculty:* 76. Expenses: Contact institution. *Financial support:* In 2019–20, 2 students received support. Career-related internships or fieldwork, Federal Work-Study, and assistantships (averaging $7911) available. Financial award application deadline: 3/1; financial award applicants required to submit FAFSA. In 2019, 19 master's awarded. *Program availability:* Part-time, evening/weekend, 100% online, blended/hybrid learning, study abroad. *Application fee:* $60. Electronic applications accepted. *Application Contact:* Lynette D. Michael, Director of Graduate Admissions, 540-568-6395, Fax: 540-568-7860, E-mail: michaeld@jmu.edu. *Dean*, Dr. Robert A. Kolvoord, 540-568-2752, E-mail: kolvoora@jmu.edu.

***College of Science and Mathematics*** Students: 16 full-time (10 women), 31 part-time (21 women); includes 9 minority (2 Black or African American, non-Hispanic/Latino; 2 Asian, non-Hispanic/Latino; 2 Hispanic/Latino; 3 Two or more races, non-Hispanic/Latino). Average age 30. *Faculty:* 69. Expenses: Contact institution. *Financial support:* In 2019–20, 16 students received support. Fellowships, Federal Work-Study, and assistantships (averaging $7911) available. Financial award application deadline: 3/1; financial award applicants required to submit FAFSA. In 2019, 12 master's awarded. *Program availability:* Part-time. *Application fee:* $60. Electronic applications accepted. *Application Contact:* Lynette D. Michael, Director of Graduate Admissions, 540-568-6131 Ext. 6395, Fax: 540-568-7860, E-mail: michaeld@jmu.edu. *Dean*, Dr. David F. Brakke, 540-568-3508, E-mail: brakkedf@jmu.edu.

***College of Visual and Performing Arts*** Students: 55 full-time (33 women), 22 part-time (10 women); includes 8 minority (3 Black or African American, non-Hispanic/Latino; 2 Asian, non-Hispanic/Latino; 2 Hispanic/Latino; 1 Two or more races, non-Hispanic/Latino), 19 international. Average age 30. *Faculty:* 89. Expenses: Contact institution. *Financial support:* In 2019–20, 44 students received support, including 3 teaching assistantships with full tuition reimbursements available (averaging $9,284 per year); fellowships, Federal Work-Study, and assistantships (averaging $7911), 17 doctoral assistantships (stipend varies) also available. Financial award application deadline: 3/1; financial award applicants required to submit FAFSA. In 2019, 11 master's, 6 doctorates awarded. *Program availability:* Part-time. *Application fee:* $60. Electronic applications accepted. *Application Contact:* Lynette D. Michael, Director of Graduate Admissions and Student Records, 540-568-6131 Ext. 6395, Fax: 540-568-7860, E-mail: michaeld@jmu.edu. *Dean*, Dr. George Sparks, 540-568-6247, E-mail: sparksge@jmu.edu.

## JEFFERSON COLLEGE OF HEALTH SCIENCES, Roanoke, VA 24013

**General Information** Independent, coed, comprehensive institution. *Graduate housing:* Room and/or apartments available on a first-come, first-served basis to single students; on-campus housing not available to married students. *Research affiliation:* Carilion Clinic (hospital and medical services), Virginia Polytechnic Institute and State University/Carilion Medical School (medicine).

**GRADUATE UNITS**

**Program in Nursing** *Program availability:* Part-time. Electronic applications accepted.

**Program in Occupational Therapy** *Program availability:* Part-time. Electronic applications accepted.

**Program in Physician Assistant** Electronic applications accepted.

## THE JEWISH THEOLOGICAL SEMINARY, New York, NY 10027-4649

**General Information** Independent-religious, coed, university. *Graduate housing:* Rooms and/or apartments available on a first-come, first-served basis to single and married students. Housing application deadline: 5/15.

**GRADUATE UNITS**

**The Graduate School** *Program availability:* Part-time.

**H. L. Miller Cantorial School and College of Jewish Music**

**The Rabbinical School**

**William Davidson Graduate School of Jewish Education** *Program availability:* Part-time, online learning.

## JOHN BROWN UNIVERSITY, Siloam Springs, AR 72761-2121

**General Information** Independent-religious, coed, comprehensive institution. *Enrollment:* 2,150 graduate, professional, and undergraduate students; 215 full-time matriculated graduate/professional students (162 women), 457 part-time matriculated graduate/professional students (289 women). *Enrollment by degree level:* 668 master's, 4 other advanced degrees. *Graduate faculty:* 13 full-time (4 women), 53 part-time/adjunct (17 women). *Graduate housing:* Rooms and/or apartments available on a first-come, first-served basis to single and married students. *Student services:* Campus employment opportunities, career counseling, exercise/wellness program, free psychological counseling, international student services, services for students with disabilities, teacher training. *Library facilities:* Arutunoff Learning Resource Center plus 4 others. *Collection:* Books: 105,116 (physical), 329,913 (digital/electronic); Serial titles: 1,032 (physical), 67,078 (digital/electronic); Databases: 144. Weekly public service hours: 110; students can reserve study rooms.

**Computer facilities:** 250 computers available on campus for general student use. A campuswide network can be accessed. Online class registration is available.
Website: http://www.jbu.edu/

**General Application Contact:** Kent Shaffer, Graduate Admissions Representative, 800-528-4723, E-mail: kents@jbu.edu.

**GRADUATE UNITS**

**Graduate Counseling Programs** *Program availability:* Part-time, evening/weekend. Electronic applications accepted.

**Graduate Education Programs** *Program availability:* Part-time, evening/weekend. Electronic applications accepted.

**Soderquist College of Business** *Program availability:* Part-time, evening/weekend, online only, 100% online, blended/hybrid learning. Electronic applications accepted.

## JOHN CABOT UNIVERSITY, Rome 00165, Italy

**General Information** Independent, coed, comprehensive institution. *Graduate housing:* On-campus housing not available.

**GRADUATE UNITS**

**John Cabot University - Graduate School** Electronic applications accepted.

## JOHN CARROLL UNIVERSITY, University Heights, OH 44118

**General Information** Independent-religious, coed, comprehensive institution. CGS member. *Enrollment:* 3,506 graduate, professional, and undergraduate students; 250 full-time matriculated graduate/professional students (175 women), 239 part-time matriculated graduate/professional students (154 women). *Enrollment by degree level:* 462 master's, 27 other advanced degrees. *Graduate faculty:* 34 full-time (12 women), 38 part-time/adjunct (24 women). *Graduate housing:* On-campus housing not available. *Student services:* Campus employment opportunities, campus safety program, career counseling, exercise/wellness program, free psychological counseling, grant writing training, international student services, multicultural affairs office, services for students with disabilities, teacher training, writing training. *Library facilities:* Grasselli Library. *Collection:* Books: 309,993 (physical), 670,707 (digital/electronic); Serial titles: 278 (physical), 90,378 (digital/electronic); Databases: 308. Weekly public service hours: 111; students can reserve study rooms.

**Computer facilities:** Computer purchase and lease plans are available. 396 computers available on campus for general student use. A campuswide network can be accessed. Online class registration, advising system; course management site (Canvas); online financial aid and billing; online housing selection are available.
Website: http://www.jcu.edu/

**General Application Contact:** Dr. Rebecca E. Drenovsky, Dean of Graduate Studies, 216-397-4284, E-mail: rdrenovsky@jcu.edu.

**GRADUATE UNITS**

**Graduate School** Students: 250 full-time (175 women), 239 part-time (154 women); includes 64 minority (36 Black or African American, non-Hispanic/Latino; 2 American Indian or Alaska Native, non-Hispanic/Latino; 9 Asian, non-Hispanic/Latino; 11 Hispanic/Latino; 6 Two or more races, non-Hispanic/Latino), 20 international. 216 applicants, 77% accepted, 118 enrolled. *Faculty:* 34 full-time (12 women), 38 part-time/adjunct (24 women). Expenses: Contact institution. *Financial support:* Research assistantships, teaching assistantships, scholarships/grants, and unspecified assistantships available. Support available to part-time students. Financial award applicants required to submit FAFSA. In 2019, 193 master's, 11 other advanced degrees awarded. *Program availability:* Part-time, evening/weekend, online learning. *Application deadline:* Applications are processed on a rolling basis. Electronic applications accepted. *Application Contact:* Colleen K. Sommerfeld, Assistant Dean for Graduate Admission & Retention, 216-397-4902, Fax: 216-397-1835, E-mail: csommerfeld@jcu.edu. *Dean of Graduate Studies*, Dr. Rebecca E. Drenovsky, 216-397-4284, Fax: 216-397-1835, E-mail: rdrenovsky@jcu.edu.

***John M. and Mary Jo Boler College of Business*** Students: 78 full-time (37 women), 76 part-time (35 women); includes 14 minority (7 Black or African American, non-Hispanic/Latino; 2 Asian, non-Hispanic/Latino; 1 Hispanic/Latino; 4 Two or more races, non-Hispanic/Latino), 15 international. *Faculty:* 10 full-time (1 woman), 10 part-time/adjunct (2 women). Expenses: Contact institution. *Financial support:* Fellowships, scholarships/grants, and unspecified assistantships available. Financial award applicants required to submit FAFSA. *Program availability:* Part-time, evening/weekend, online learning. *Application deadline:* For fall admission, 8/1 priority date for domestic and international students; for spring admission, 12/1 priority date for domestic and international students; for summer admission, 4/1 priority date for domestic and international students. Applications are processed on a rolling basis. Electronic applications accepted. *Application Contact:* Dr. Walter Simmons, Associate Dean, Boler College of Business, 216-397-4659, Fax: 216-397-1833, E-mail: gradadmit@jcu.edu. *Dean, Boler College of Business*, Dr. Alan R. Miciak, 216-397-4391, Fax: 216-397-1833.

## JOHN F. KENNEDY UNIVERSITY, Pleasant Hill, CA 94523-4817

**General Information** Independent, coed, primarily women, upper-level institution. *Graduate housing:* On-campus housing not available.

**GRADUATE UNITS**

**College of Business and Professional Studies** *Program availability:* Part-time, evening/weekend, online learning.

**College of Law** *Program availability:* Part-time, evening/weekend, blended/hybrid learning.

**College of Psychology** *Program availability:* Part-time, evening/weekend.

## JOHN JAY COLLEGE OF CRIMINAL JUSTICE OF THE CITY UNIVERSITY OF NEW YORK, New York, NY 10019

**General Information** State and locally supported, coed, comprehensive institution. CGS member. *Graduate housing:* On-campus housing not available. *Research affiliation:* The Fire Science Institute, The Institute For Criminal Justice Ethics, Criminal Justice Center, Criminal Justice Research and Evaluation Center, Center on Violence and Human Survival, Center for Dispute Resolution.

**GRADUATE UNITS**

**Graduate Studies** *Program availability:* Part-time, evening/weekend.

## JOHN PATRICK UNIVERSITY OF HEALTH AND APPLIED SCIENCES, South Bend, IN 46601

**General Information** Proprietary, coed, comprehensive institution.

**GRADUATE UNITS**

**Graduate Programs**

## JOHN PAUL THE GREAT CATHOLIC UNIVERSITY, Escondido, CA 92025

**General Information** Independent-religious, coed, comprehensive institution.

**GRADUATE UNITS**

**School of Theology**

## JOHNS HOPKINS UNIVERSITY, Baltimore, MD 21218

**General Information** Independent, coed, university. CGS member. *Enrollment:* 9,044 full-time matriculated graduate/professional students (5,042 women), 10,865 part-time matriculated graduate/professional students (5,533 women). *Enrollment by degree level:* 15,536 master's, 4,299 doctoral, 74 other advanced degrees. *Graduate faculty:* 4,908 full-time (2,229 women). *Graduate housing:* On-campus housing not available. *Student services:* Campus employment opportunities, campus safety program, career counseling, exercise/wellness program, free psychological counseling, grant writing training, international student services, low-cost health insurance, multicultural affairs office, services for students with disabilities, teacher training, writing training. *Library facilities:* The Sheridan Libraries plus 2 others. *Collection:* Books: 2.4 million (physical), 1.8 million (digital/electronic); Serial titles: 52,559 (physical), 171,703 (digital/electronic); Databases: 836. Study areas open 24 hours, 5–7 days a week; students can reserve study rooms. *Research affiliation:* Carnegie Institution of Washington (biological sciences), SmithKline Beecham (asthma and allergy), Bristol-Myers Squibb (human nutrition), Howard Hughes Medical Institute (biomedical sciences), Space Telescope Science Institute (astronomy), General Electric Company (GE) (medical technology).

**Computer facilities:** Computer purchase and lease plans are available. 200 computers available on campus for general student use. A campuswide network can be accessed from student residence rooms and from off campus. Online class registration is available.
Website: http://www.jhu.edu/

**GRADUATE UNITS**

**Advanced Academic Programs** *Program availability:* Part-time, evening/weekend, online learning. Electronic applications accepted.

**Bloomberg School of Public Health** *Program availability:* Part-time, 100% online, blended/hybrid learning. Electronic applications accepted.

***Master of Bioethics Program*** *Program availability:* Part-time. Electronic applications accepted.

**Carey Business School** *Program availability:* Part-time, evening/weekend, online only, blended/hybrid learning, on-site residency requirement. Electronic applications accepted.

**Engineering Program for Professionals** *Program availability:* Part-time, evening/weekend, 100% online, blended/hybrid learning. Electronic applications accepted.

**G. W. C. Whiting School of Engineering** Electronic applications accepted.

**National Institutes of Health Sponsored Programs** Electronic applications accepted.

**Peabody Conservatory** Electronic applications accepted.

**Program in Molecular Biophysics**

**School of Advanced International Studies** *Program availability:* Evening/weekend. Electronic applications accepted.

**School of Education** *Program availability:* Part-time, evening/weekend, 100% online, blended/hybrid learning. Electronic applications accepted.

**School of Medicine** Electronic applications accepted.

***Graduate Programs in Medicine*** Electronic applications accepted.

**School of Nursing** Students: 588 full-time (513 women), 320 part-time (293 women); includes 351 minority (103 Black or African American, non-Hispanic/Latino; 2 American Indian or Alaska Native, non-Hispanic/Latino; 134 Asian, non-Hispanic/Latino; 80 Hispanic/Latino; 2 Native Hawaiian or other Pacific Islander, non-Hispanic/Latino; 30 Two or more races, non-Hispanic/Latino), 12 international. 1,159 applicants, 57% accepted, 404 enrolled. *Faculty:* 79 full-time (68 women), 31 part-time/adjunct (28 women). Expenses: Contact institution. *Financial support:* In 2019–20, 736 students received support, including 42 fellowships with full and partial tuition reimbursements available (averaging $5,000 per year), 21 research assistantships with full tuition reimbursements available (averaging $8,000 per year), 14 teaching assistantships (averaging $3,000 per year); Federal Work-Study, scholarships/grants, and tuition waivers (full and partial) also available. Support available to part-time students. Financial award application deadline: 3/1; financial award applicants required to submit FAFSA. In 2019, 316 master's, 56 doctorates, 39 other advanced degrees awarded. *Program availability:* Part-time, 100% online, blended/hybrid learning. *Application deadline:* For fall admission, 11/1 priority date for domestic and international students; for spring admission, 7/1 priority date for domestic and international students; for summer admission, 11/1 priority date for domestic and international students. *Application fee:* $75. Electronic applications accepted. *Application Contact:* Cathy Wilson, Director of Admissions, 410-955-7548, Fax: 410-614-7086, E-mail: jhuson@jhu.edu. *Dean,* Dr. Patricia M. Davidson, 410-955-7544, Fax: 410-955-4890, E-mail: sondeansoffice@jhu.edu.

**Zanvyl Krieger School of Arts and Sciences** Electronic applications accepted.

## JOHNSON & WALES UNIVERSITY, Providence, RI 02903-3703

**General Information** Independent, coed, comprehensive institution. *Graduate housing:* On-campus housing not available. *Research affiliation:* Consortium of Rhode Island Academic and Research Libraries, Association of Institutional Research.

**GRADUATE UNITS**

**Graduate Studies** *Program availability:* Part-time, evening/weekend.

## JOHNSON C. SMITH UNIVERSITY, Charlotte, NC 28216-5398

**General Information** Independent, coed, comprehensive institution. *Graduate housing:* Room and/or apartments available on a first-come, first-served basis to single students; on-campus housing not available to married students.

**GRADUATE UNITS**

**Program in Social Work** *Program availability:* Part-time, evening/weekend. Electronic applications accepted.

## JOHNSON UNIVERSITY, Knoxville, TN 37998-1001

**General Information** Independent-religious, coed, comprehensive institution. *Enrollment:* 1,086 graduate, professional, and undergraduate students; 116 full-time matriculated graduate/professional students (56 women), 196 part-time matriculated graduate/professional students (91 women). *Enrollment by degree level:* 209 master's, 103 doctoral. *Graduate faculty:* 17 full-time (6 women), 44 part-time/adjunct (15 women). *Tuition:* Full-time $9285; part-time $515 per credit hour. *Required fees:* $700; $700. Tuition and fees vary according to degree level and program. *Graduate housing:* Rooms and/or apartments available on a first-come, first-served basis to single and married students. Typical cost: $5370 per year ($9310 including board) for single students; $7500 per year ($10,175 including board) for married students. Room and board charges vary according to board plan and housing facility selected. Housing application deadline: 8/1. *Student services:* Campus employment opportunities, career counseling, child daycare facilities, exercise/wellness program, free psychological counseling, multicultural affairs office, services for students with disabilities, teacher training, writing training. *Library facilities:* Glass Memorial Library plus 1 other. *Collection:* Weekly public service hours: 80.

**Computer facilities:** A campuswide network can be accessed. Online class registration is available.
Website: http://www.johnsonu.edu/

**General Application Contact:** Lisa Tarwater, Director of Graduate Admissions, 865-251-3400, Fax: 865-251-2336, E-mail: ltarwater@johnsonu.edu.

**GRADUATE UNITS**

**Graduate and Professional Programs** Students: 116 full-time (56 women), 196 part-time (91 women); includes 40 minority (23 Black or African American, non-Hispanic/Latino; 1 American Indian or Alaska Native, non-Hispanic/Latino; 4 Asian, non-Hispanic/Latino; 6 Hispanic/Latino; 6 Two or more races, non-Hispanic/Latino), 31 international. Average age 36. *Faculty:* 26 full-time (10 women), 32 part-time/adjunct (9 women). Expenses: Contact institution. *Financial support:* Scholarships/grants available. Financial award application deadline: 4/15; financial award applicants required to submit FAFSA. In 2019, 87 master's, 6 doctorates, 14 other advanced degrees awarded. *Program availability:* Part-time, 100% online, blended/hybrid learning. *Application deadline:* For fall admission, 7/1 for domestic students; for spring admission, 11/1 for domestic students; for summer admission, 4/1 for domestic students. *Application fee:* $50. Electronic applications accepted. *Application Contact:* Lisa Tarwater, Chief Admissions Officer, 865-251-3400, E-mail: ltarwater@johnsonu.edu. *Chief Admissions Officer,* Lisa Tarwater, 865-251-3400, E-mail: ltarwater@johnsonu.edu.

## JOHNSON UNIVERSITY FLORIDA, Kissimmee, FL 34744-5301

**General Information** Independent-religious, coed, comprehensive institution.

**GRADUATE UNITS**

**Program in Strategic Ministry** *Program availability:* Online learning.

## JOSE MARIA VARGAS UNIVERSITY, Pembroke Pines, FL 33026

**General Information** Proprietary, coed, comprehensive institution.

**GRADUATE UNITS**

**Program in Preschool Education**

## THE JUDGE ADVOCATE GENERAL'S SCHOOL, U.S. ARMY, Charlottesville, VA 22903-1781

**General Information** Federally supported, coed, primarily men, graduate-only institution. *Graduate housing:* On-campus housing not available.

**GRADUATE UNITS**

**Graduate Programs**

## JUDSON UNIVERSITY, Elgin, IL 60123-1498

**General Information** Independent-religious, coed, comprehensive institution. *Enrollment:* 1,233 graduate, professional, and undergraduate students; 144 full-time matriculated graduate/professional students (105 women), 43 part-time matriculated graduate/professional students (33 women). *Enrollment by degree level:* 146 master's, 35 doctoral, 6 other advanced degrees. *Graduate faculty:* 23 full-time (14 women), 47 part-time/adjunct (20 women). *Required fees:* $250. One-time fee: $125 full-time. *Graduate housing:* Rooms and/or apartments available on a first-come, first-served basis to single and married students. Typical cost: $10,290 (including board) for single students. Housing application deadline: 8/1. *Student services:* Campus employment opportunities, campus safety program, career counseling, exercise/wellness program, free psychological counseling, international student services, low-cost health insurance, multicultural affairs office, services for students with disabilities, writing training. *Library facilities:* Benjamin P. Browne Library. *Collection:* Books: 121,582 (physical), 6,280 (digital/electronic); Serial titles: 154 (physical), 55,984 (digital/electronic); Databases: 53. Weekly public service hours: 71; students can reserve study rooms.

**Computer facilities:** 140 computers available on campus for general student use. A campuswide network can be accessed. Online class registration is available.
Website: http://www.judsonu.edu/

**General Application Contact:** Maria Aguirre, Student Academic Advisor, 847-628-1160, E-mail: maguirre@judsonu.edu.

**GRADUATE UNITS**

**Doctor of Education in Literacy Program** Students: 12 full-time (11 women), 23 part-time (21 women); includes 1 minority (Hispanic/Latino). Average age 46. 11 applicants, 100% accepted, 11 enrolled. *Faculty:* 4 full-time (all women), 10 part-time/adjunct (8 women). Expenses: Contact institution. *Financial support:* Teaching assistantships available. Financial award application deadline: 11/15; financial award applicants required to submit FAFSA. In 2019, 9 doctorates awarded. *Application deadline:* For fall admission, 11/15 for domestic and international students. *Application fee:* $200. *Application Contact:* Brenda Buckley-Hughes, Co-Director, 847-628-1060, E-mail: bbuckley-hughes@judsonu.edu. *Co-Director,* Dr. Brenda Buckley-Hughes, 847-628-1060, E-mail: bbuckley-hughes@judsonu.edu.

**Master of Architecture Program** Students: 11 full-time (4 women), 1 part-time (0 women); includes 10 minority (all Hispanic/Latino). Average age 24. 12 applicants, 100% accepted, 12 enrolled. *Faculty:* 4 full-time (0 women), 2 part-time/adjunct (0 women). Expenses: Contact institution. *Financial support:* In 2019–20, 9 students received support. Fellowships, research assistantships, teaching assistantships, scholarships/grants, and 8 assistantships available. Financial award application deadline: 5/1; financial award applicants required to submit FAFSA. In 2019, 18 master's awarded. *Program availability:* Part-time. *Application deadline:* For fall admission, 2/15 priority date for domestic and international students; for winter admission, 11/15 for domestic students; for spring admission, 11/15 for domestic and international students. Applications are processed on a rolling basis. *Application fee:* $100. Electronic applications accepted. *Application Contact:* Annelise Pollard, Admissions Representative, 847-628-2519, E-mail: annelise.pollard@judsonu.edu. *Interim Chair,* Dr. Curtis Sartor, 847-628-1017, E-mail: csartor@judsonu.edu.

**Master of Arts in Clinical Mental Health Counseling Program** Students: 44 full-time (38 women), 2 part-time (both women); includes 12 minority (10 Black or African American, non-Hispanic/Latino; 1 Asian, non-Hispanic/Latino; 1 Hispanic/Latino). Average age 39. 58 applicants, 53% accepted, 9 enrolled. *Faculty:* 6 full-time (4 women), 8 part-time/adjunct (5 women). Expenses: Contact institution. *Financial support:* Unspecified assistantships available. In 2019, 19 master's awarded. *Program availability:* Evening/weekend. *Application deadline:* Applications are processed on a rolling basis. *Application fee:* $35. Electronic applications accepted. *Application Contact:* Kim Surin, Enrollment Manager, 847-628-5033, E-mail: kim.surin@info.judsonu.edu. *Program Director,* Dr. Amber Randolph, 847-628-1544, E-mail: amber.randolph@judsonu.edu.

**Master of Arts in Human Services Administration** Students: 9 full-time (all women), 2 part-time (1 woman); includes 7 minority (4 Black or African American, non-Hispanic/Latino; 3 Hispanic/Latino). Average age 42. 9 applicants, 22% accepted, 1 enrolled. *Faculty:* 2 full-time (both women), 2 part-time/adjunct (1 woman). Expenses: Contact institution. *Financial support:* Unspecified assistantships available. In 2019, 6 master's awarded. *Program availability:* Evening/weekend. *Application deadline:* Applications are processed on a rolling basis. *Application fee:* $35. Electronic applications accepted. *Application Contact:* Kim Surin, Enrollment Manager, 847-628-5033, E-mail: kim.surin@info.judsonu.edu.

**Master of Arts in Organizational Leadership** Students: 18 full-time (11 women), 2 part-time (1 woman); includes 7 minority (4 Black or African American, non-Hispanic/Latino; 1 Asian, non-Hispanic/Latino; 2 Hispanic/Latino). Average age 32. 26 applicants, 65% accepted, 7 enrolled. *Faculty:* 3 full-time (all women), 11 part-time/adjunct (10 women). Expenses: Contact institution. *Financial support:* Institutionally sponsored loans and unspecified assistantships available. Financial award applicants required to submit FAFSA. In 2019, 9 master's awarded. *Program availability:*

Part-time, evening/weekend, 100% online, blended/hybrid learning. *Application deadline:* Applications are processed on a rolling basis. *Application fee:* $35. Electronic applications accepted. *Application Contact:* Kim Surin, Enrollment Manager, 847-628-5033, E-mail: kim.surin@info.judsonu.edu. *Chair*, Karen Love, 847-628-1524, E-mail: klove@judsonu.edu.

**Master of Business Administration Program** Students: 34 full-time (19 women), 8 part-time (5 women); includes 18 minority (7 Black or African American, non-Hispanic/Latino; 1 Asian, non-Hispanic/Latino; 10 Hispanic/Latino), 1 international. Average age 35. 39 applicants, 54% accepted, 8 enrolled. *Faculty:* 2 full-time (0 women), 6 part-time/adjunct (0 women). Expenses: Contact institution. *Financial support:* In 2019–20, 6 teaching assistantships were awarded; tuition waivers (partial) also available. Financial award applicants required to submit FAFSA. In 2019, 29 master's awarded. *Program availability:* Evening/weekend, 100% online. *Application deadline:* Applications are processed on a rolling basis. *Application fee:* $35. Electronic applications accepted. *Application Contact:* Kim Surin, Enrollment Manager, 847-628-5033, E-mail: kim.surin@info.judsonu.edu. *Chair*, John C. Boggs, 847-628-1041, E-mail: john.boggs@judsonu.edu.

**Master of Education in Literacy Program** Students: 6 full-time (all women); includes 1 minority (Hispanic/Latino). Average age 30. 6 applicants, 100% accepted, 6 enrolled. *Faculty:* 1 (woman) full-time, 4 part-time/adjunct (all women). Expenses: Contact institution. *Financial support:* Tuition discounts available. Financial award application deadline: 4/15; financial award applicants required to submit FAFSA. In 2019, 11 master's awarded. *Application deadline:* For fall admission, 4/15 for domestic and international students. Applications are processed on a rolling basis. *Application fee:* $55. *Application Contact:* Dr. Kristy Piebenga, Director, 847-628-1086, E-mail: kristy.piebenga@judsonu.edu. *Director*, Dr. Kristy Piebenga, 847-628-1086, E-mail: kristy.piebenga@judsonu.edu.

**Master of Leadership in Ministry Program** Students: 6 full-time (4 women), 3 part-time (1 woman). Average age 33. 3 applicants, 100% accepted. *Faculty:* 1 full-time (0 women), 4 part-time/adjunct (1 woman). Expenses: Contact institution. *Financial support:* In 2019–20, 5 students received support. Scholarships/grants and tuition waivers available. Financial award application deadline: 8/15; financial award applicants required to submit FAFSA. In 2019, 6 master's awarded. *Program availability:* Evening/weekend, online only, blended/hybrid learning. *Application deadline:* Applications are processed on a rolling basis. *Application fee:* $35. Electronic applications accepted. *Application Contact:* Dr. David Sanders, Director, 847-628-1052, E-mail: dsanders@judsonu.edu. *Director*, Dr. David Sanders, 847-628-1052, E-mail: dsanders@judsonu.edu.

## THE JUILLIARD SCHOOL, New York, NY 10023-6588

**General Information** Independent, coed, comprehensive institution. *Graduate housing:* Room and/or apartments available on a first-come, first-served basis to single students; on-campus housing not available to married students. Housing application deadline: 5/15.

**GRADUATE UNITS**

**Graduate Programs** Electronic applications accepted.

## JUNIATA COLLEGE, Huntingdon, PA 16652-2119

**General Information** Independent-religious, coed, comprehensive institution. *Graduate housing:* On-campus housing not available.

**GRADUATE UNITS**

**Department of Accounting, Business, and Economics**

## KANSAS CITY UNIVERSITY OF MEDICINE AND BIOSCIENCES, Kansas City, MO 64106-1453

**General Information** Independent, coed, graduate-only institution. CGS member. *Graduate housing:* On-campus housing not available. *Research affiliation:* Boehringer Ingelheim (HIV/AIDS), Mylanta-Bertek (hypertension), Covance (hypertension), Novartis Pharmaceuticals (Chronic Obstructive Pulmonary Disease (COPD)).

**GRADUATE UNITS**

**College of Biosciences** *Program availability:* Part-time.

**College of Osteopathic Medicine**

## KANSAS STATE UNIVERSITY, Manhattan, KS 66506

**General Information** State-supported, coed, university. CGS member. *Graduate housing:* Rooms and/or apartments available on a first-come, first-served basis to single and married students. Housing application deadline: 2/1. *Research affiliation:* Visteon Corporation, Midwest Research Institute, NASA-Research Center, U.S. Grain Marketing Research Laboratory.

**GRADUATE UNITS**

**Graduate School** *Program availability:* Part-time, evening/weekend, online learning. Electronic applications accepted.

***College of Agriculture*** *Program availability:* Part-time, online learning. Electronic applications accepted.

***College of Architecture, Planning and Design*** *Program availability:* Part-time. Electronic applications accepted.

***College of Arts and Sciences*** *Program availability:* Part-time, online learning. Electronic applications accepted.

***College of Business*** *Program availability:* Part-time. Electronic applications accepted.

***College of Education*** *Program availability:* Part-time, evening/weekend, online learning. Electronic applications accepted.

***College of Engineering*** *Program availability:* Part-time, online learning. Electronic applications accepted.

***College of Human Ecology*** *Program availability:* Part-time, online learning. Electronic applications accepted.

***College of Technology and Aviation*** *Program availability:* Part-time, evening/weekend, 100% online. Electronic applications accepted.

***College of Veterinary Medicine*** Electronic applications accepted.

***School of Applied and Interdisciplinary Studies*** *Program availability:* Part-time, 100% online, blended/hybrid learning. Electronic applications accepted.

## KANSAS WESLEYAN UNIVERSITY, Salina, KS 67401-6196

**General Information** Independent-religious, coed, comprehensive institution. *Graduate housing:* Rooms and/or apartments available to single and married students.

**GRADUATE UNITS**

**Program in Business Administration** *Program availability:* Part-time, evening/weekend.

## KEAN UNIVERSITY, Union, NJ 07083

**General Information** State-supported, coed, university. *Enrollment:* 14,309 graduate, professional, and undergraduate students; 1,018 full-time matriculated graduate/professional students (787 women), 790 part-time matriculated graduate/professional students (596 women). *Enrollment by degree level:* 1,569 master's, 201 doctoral, 38 other advanced degrees. *Graduate faculty:* 260 full-time (140 women). Tuition, state resident: full-time $15,326; part-time $748 per credit. Tuition, nonresident: full-time $20,288; part-time $902 per credit. *Required fees:* $2149.50; $91.25 per credit. Tuition and fees vary according to course level, course load, degree level and program. *Graduate housing:* Room and/or apartments available on a first-come, first-served basis to single students; on-campus housing not available to married students. Typical cost: $6265 per year. Room charges vary according to board plan and housing facility selected. Housing application deadline: 5/1. *Student services:* Campus employment opportunities, campus safety program, career counseling, child daycare facilities, exercise/wellness program, free psychological counseling, grant writing training, international student services, low-cost health insurance, services for students with disabilities, teacher training, writing training. *Library facilities:* Nancy Thompson Library. *Collection:* Books: 172,411 (physical), 12,565 (digital/electronic); Serial titles: 55,488 (digital/electronic); Databases: 235. Weekly public service hours: 106; students can reserve study rooms. *Research affiliation:* Robert Wood Johnson Foundation (the effect of tobacco control policy), Institute of Vertebrate Paleontology and Paleoanthropology (paleoanthropology), Shodor Foundation (intelligent Internet search engines for science research and education), New Jersey Institute of Technology (partitioning to support auditing and extending the UMLS), National Bureau of Economic Research (alcoholic advertising and youth).

**Computer facilities:** 1,700 computers available on campus for general student use. A campuswide network can be accessed. Online class registration is available. Website: http://www.kean.edu/

**General Application Contact:** Helen Ramirez, Associate Director, 908-737-7137, E-mail: hramirez@kean.edu.

**GRADUATE UNITS**

**College of Business and Public Management** Average age 31. 119 applicants, 95% accepted, 72 enrolled. Expenses: Contact institution. *Financial support:* Federal Work-Study, scholarships/grants, and unspecified assistantships available. Financial award applicants required to submit FAFSA. In 2019, 94 master's awarded. *Program availability:* Part-time. *Application deadline:* For fall admission, 6/30 for domestic and international students; for spring admission, 12/1 for domestic and international students. Applications are processed on a rolling basis. *Application fee:* $75. Electronic applications accepted. *Application Contact:* Pedro Lopes, Admissions Counselor, 908-737-7100, E-mail: gradadmissions@kean.edu. *Dean*, Dr. Jin Wang, 908-737-4700, Fax: 908-737-4755, E-mail: cbpm@kean.edu.

**College of Education** Students: 53 full-time (33 women), 151 part-time (122 women); includes 85 minority (30 Black or African American, non-Hispanic/Latino; 16 Asian, non-Hispanic/Latino; 38 Hispanic/Latino; 1 Two or more races, non-Hispanic/Latino), 5 international. Average age 31. 122 applicants, 100% accepted, 87 enrolled. *Faculty:* 51 full-time (34 women). Expenses: Contact institution. *Financial support:* Scholarships/grants and unspecified assistantships available. Financial award applicants required to submit FAFSA. In 2019, 59 master's awarded. *Program availability:* Part-time. *Application deadline:* For fall admission, 6/30 for domestic and international students; for spring admission, 12/1 for domestic and international students. Applications are processed on a rolling basis. *Application fee:* $75. Electronic applications accepted. *Application Contact:* Amy Clark, Graduate Admissions, 908-737-7100, E-mail: gradadmissions@kean.edu.

**College of Liberal Arts** Students: 171 full-time (147 women), 115 part-time (89 women); includes 162 minority (71 Black or African American, non-Hispanic/Latino; 13 Asian, non-Hispanic/Latino; 76 Hispanic/Latino; 2 Two or more races, non-Hispanic/Latino), 7 international. Average age 29. 190 applicants, 80% accepted, 108 enrolled. *Faculty:* 91 full-time (52 women). Expenses: Contact institution. *Financial support:* Scholarships/grants and unspecified assistantships available. Financial award applicants required to submit FAFSA. In 2019, 97 master's awarded. *Program availability:* Part-time. *Application deadline:* For fall admission, 6/30 for domestic and international students; for spring admission, 12/1 for domestic and international students. Applications are processed on a rolling basis. *Application fee:* $75. Electronic applications accepted. *Application Contact:* Amy Clark, Program Assistant, 908-737-7100, E-mail: gradadmissions@kean.edu. *Acting Dean*, Dr. Jonathan Mercantini, 908-737-0430, Fax: 908-737-0435, E-mail: jmercant@kean.edu.

**College of Science, Mathematics and Technology** Students: 13 full-time (3 women), 3 part-time (1 woman); includes 6 minority (2 Black or African American, non-Hispanic/Latino; 1 Asian, non-Hispanic/Latino; 2 Hispanic/Latino; 1 Two or more races, non-Hispanic/Latino), 7 international. Average age 28. 20 applicants, 70% accepted, 6 enrolled. *Faculty:* 28 full-time (10 women). Expenses: Contact institution. *Financial support:* Scholarships/grants and unspecified assistantships available. Financial award applicants required to submit FAFSA. In 2019, 9 master's awarded. *Program availability:* Part-time. *Application deadline:* For fall admission, 6/30 for domestic and international students; for spring admission, 12/1 for domestic and international students. Applications are processed on a rolling basis. *Application fee:* $75. Electronic applications accepted. *Application Contact:* Pedro Lopes, Admissions Counselor, 908-737-7100, E-mail: gradadmissions@kean.edu. *Dean*, Dr. George Chang, 908-737-3600, Fax: 908-737-3606, E-mail: gchang@kean.edu.

**Michael Graves College** Students: 10 full-time (4 women); includes 4 minority (2 Black or African American, non-Hispanic/Latino; 2 Hispanic/Latino). Average age 24. 15 applicants, 100% accepted, 10 enrolled. *Faculty:* 3 full-time. Expenses: Contact institution. *Financial support:* Scholarships/grants and unspecified assistantships available. Financial award applicants required to submit FAFSA. *Application fee:* $75. Electronic applications accepted. *Application Contact:* Helen Ramirez, Associate Director, 908-737-7137, E-mail: hramirez@kean.edu.

**Nathan Weiss Graduate College** Students: 610 full-time (505 women), 406 part-time (320 women); includes 443 minority (206 Black or African American, non-Hispanic/Latino; 3 American Indian or Alaska Native, non-Hispanic/Latino; 35 Asian, non-Hispanic/Latino; 184 Hispanic/Latino; 2 Native Hawaiian or other Pacific Islander, non-Hispanic/Latino; 13 Two or more races, non-Hispanic/Latino), 6 international. Average age 31. 1,369 applicants, 33% accepted, 223 enrolled. *Faculty:* 52 full-time (37 women). Expenses: Contact institution. *Financial support:* Scholarships/grants and unspecified assistantships available. Financial award applicants required to submit FAFSA. In 2019, 324 master's, 42 doctorates, 10 other advanced degrees awarded. *Program availability:* Part-time. *Application deadline:* For fall admission, 6/1 for domestic and international students; for spring admission, 12/1 for domestic and international students. Applications are processed on a rolling basis. *Application fee:* $75. Electronic applications accepted. *Application Contact:* Ann-Marie Kay, Associate Director,

Graduate Admissions, 908-737-7100, E-mail: grad-adm@kean.edu. *Dean*, Dr. Jeffrey Beck, 908-737-5902, Fax: 908-737-5905, E-mail: jbeck@kean.edu.

**New Jersey Center for Science, Technology and Mathematics** Students: 25 full-time (15 women), 6 part-time (4 women); includes 14 minority (8 Black or African American, non-Hispanic/Latino; 2 Asian, non-Hispanic/Latino; 3 Hispanic/Latino; 1 Two or more races, non-Hispanic/Latino), 2 international. Average age 25. 10 applicants, 100% accepted, 5 enrolled. *Faculty:* 9 full-time (1 woman). Expenses: Contact institution. *Financial support:* Scholarships/grants and unspecified assistantships available. Financial award applicants required to submit FAFSA. In 2019, 28 master's awarded. *Application deadline:* For fall admission, 6/30 for domestic and international students; for spring admission, 12/1 for domestic and international students. Applications are processed on a rolling basis. *Application fee:* $75. Electronic applications accepted. *Application Contact:* Pedro Lopes, Admissions Counselor, 908-737-7100, E-mail: gradcoordinatorcdd@kean.edu. *Dean*, Dr. Keith Bostian, 908-737-7200, E-mail: kbostian@kean.edu.

## KECK GRADUATE INSTITUTE, Claremont, CA 91711

**General Information** Independent, coed, graduate-only institution. CGS member. *Graduate housing:* Rooms and/or apartments available on a first-come, first-served basis to single and married students. Housing application deadline: 7/1.

**GRADUATE UNITS**

**Henry E. Riggs School of Applied Life Sciences**

**Minerva Schools at KGI** Expenses: Contact institution. In 2019, 3 master's awarded. *Program availability:* Part-time-only. *Application deadline:* For fall admission, 10/1 for domestic and international students; for winter admission, 2/1 for domestic and international students; for spring admission, 4/1 for domestic and international students; for summer admission, 5/15 for domestic and international students. Applications are processed on a rolling basis. Electronic applications accepted. *Application Contact:* Samantha Maskey, Admissions Program Manager, E-mail: samantha@minervaproject.com. *Dean of Graduate Studies*, Dr. Joshua Fost, E-mail: jfost@minerva.kgi.edu.

**School of Pharmacy and Health Sciences**

## KEENE STATE COLLEGE, Keene, NH 03435

**General Information** State-supported, coed, comprehensive institution. *Enrollment:* 3,528 graduate, professional, and undergraduate students; 22 full-time matriculated graduate/professional students (17 women), 52 part-time matriculated graduate/professional students (27 women). *Enrollment by degree level:* 70 master's, 4 other advanced degrees. *Graduate faculty:* 8 full-time (4 women), 10 part-time/adjunct (5 women). Tuition, state resident: full-time $9720; part-time $540 per credit. Tuition, nonresident: full-time $10,620; part-time $590 per credit. *Required fees:* $2052; $114 per credit. Tuition and fees vary according to course load. *Graduate housing:* Room and/or apartments available on a first-come, first-served basis to single students; on-campus housing not available to married students. Typical cost: $7542 per year ($11,560 including board). Room and board charges vary according to board plan and housing facility selected. Housing application deadline: 5/1. *Student services:* Campus employment opportunities, campus safety program, career counseling, exercise/wellness program, free psychological counseling, grant writing training, international student services, multicultural affairs office, services for students with disabilities, teacher training, writing training. *Library facilities:* Mason Library. *Collection:* Books: 209,007 (physical), 251,658 (digital/electronic); Serial titles: 135 (physical), 63,840 (digital/electronic); Databases: 90. Weekly public service hours: 102; students can reserve study rooms.

**Computer facilities:** Computer purchase and lease plans are available. 600 computers available on campus for general student use. A campuswide network can be accessed. Online class registration, Web conferencing are available.
Website: http://www.keene.edu/

**General Application Contact:** Robert Baker, Director of Continuing Education, 603-358-2338, E-mail: graduatestudies@keene.edu.

**GRADUATE UNITS**

**The School of Arts, Education, and Humanities** Students: 18 full-time (17 women), 23 part-time (16 women); includes 2 minority (1 Hispanic/Latino; 1 Two or more races, non-Hispanic/Latino). Average age 27. 7 applicants, 57% accepted, 4 enrolled. *Faculty:* 7 full-time (3 women), 7 part-time/adjunct (4 women). Expenses: Contact institution. *Financial support:* In 2019–20, 18 students received support. Career-related internships or fieldwork, Federal Work-Study, institutionally sponsored loans, scholarships/grants, and unspecified assistantships available. Support available to part-time students. Financial award application deadline: 3/1; financial award applicants required to submit FAFSA. *Program availability:* Part-time, evening/weekend. *Application deadline:* For fall admission, 4/1 for domestic and international students; for spring admission, 11/1 for domestic and international students; for summer admission, 3/1 for domestic and international students. Applications are processed on a rolling basis. *Application fee:* $50. Electronic applications accepted. *Application Contact:* Robert Baker, Director of Continuing Education, 603-358-2338, E-mail: graduatestudies@keene.edu. *Dean of Arts, Education, and Humanities*, Dr. Kirsti A. Sandy, 603-358-2772, E-mail: ksandy@keene.edu.

**The School of Sciences, Sustainability, and Health** Students: 4 full-time (0 women), 29 part-time (11 women); includes 5 minority (1 Asian, non-Hispanic/Latino; 2 Hispanic/Latino; 2 Two or more races, non-Hispanic/Latino). Average age 32. 23 applicants, 74% accepted, 15 enrolled. *Faculty:* 1 (woman) full-time, 3 part-time/adjunct (1 woman). Expenses: Contact institution. *Financial support:* In 2019–20, 7 students received support. Career-related internships or fieldwork, Federal Work-Study, institutionally sponsored loans, scholarships/grants, and unspecified assistantships available. Support available to part-time students. Financial award application deadline: 3/1; financial award applicants required to submit FAFSA. *Program availability:* Part-time, evening/weekend, online only, 100% online, blended/hybrid learning, Internship. *Application deadline:* For fall admission, 4/1 for domestic and international students; for spring admission, 11/1 for domestic and international students; for summer admission, 3/1 for domestic and international students. Applications are processed on a rolling basis. *Application fee:* $50. Electronic applications accepted. *Application Contact:* Robert Baker, Director of Continuing Education, 603-358-2338, E-mail: graduatestudies@keene.edu. *Dean of Sciences, Sustainability and Health*, Dr. Karrie Kalich, 603-358-2544, E-mail: kkalich@keene.edu.

## KEHILATH YAKOV RABBINICAL SEMINARY, Ossining, NY 10562

**General Information** Independent-religious, men only, comprehensive institution.

**GRADUATE UNITS**

**Graduate Programs**

## KEISER UNIVERSITY, Fort Lauderdale, FL 33309

**General Information** Independent, coed, university.

**GRADUATE UNITS**

**Doctor of Business Administration Program**

**Ed S in Educational Leadership Program**

**Ed S in Instructional Design and Technology Program**

**Joint MS Ed/MBA Program**

**MA in Criminal Justice Program** *Program availability:* Part-time, online learning.

**MA in Homeland Security Program**

**Master of Accountancy Program**

**Master of Business Administration Program** *Program availability:* Part-time, online learning.

**Master of Science in Education Program** *Program availability:* Part-time, online learning.

**Master of Science in Nursing Program**

**MS in Information Security Program**

**MS in Information Technology Leadership Program**

**MS in Occupational Therapy Program**

**MS in Organizational Leadership Program**

**MS in Organizational Psychology Program**

**MS in Physician Assistant Program**

**MS in Psychology Program**

**Nurse Anesthesia Programs**

**PhD in Educational Leadership Program**

**PhD in Industrial and Organizational Psychology Program**

**PhD in Instructional Design and Technology Program**

**PhD in Psychology Program**

## KENNESAW STATE UNIVERSITY, Kennesaw, GA 30144

**General Information** State-supported, coed, comprehensive institution. CGS member. *Enrollment:* 37,807 graduate, professional, and undergraduate students; 1,034 full-time matriculated graduate/professional students (650 women), 2,274 part-time matriculated graduate/professional students (1,360 women). *Enrollment by degree level:* 2,405 master's, 242 doctoral, 661 other advanced degrees. *International tuition:* $25,584 full-time. *Tuition, area resident:* Full-time $7104; part-time $296 per credit hour. Tuition, state resident: full-time $7104; part-time $296 per credit hour. Tuition, nonresident: full-time $25,584; part-time $1066 per credit hour. *Required fees:* $2006; $1706 per unit. $853 per semester. *Graduate housing:* Room and/or apartments available on a first-come, first-served basis to single students; on-campus housing not available to married students. Typical cost: $7200 per year ($12,947 including board). *Student services:* Campus employment opportunities, campus safety program, career counseling, exercise/wellness program, free psychological counseling, international student services, low-cost health insurance, multicultural affairs office, services for students with disabilities, teacher training, writing training. *Library facilities:* Kennesaw State University Library System plus 2 others. *Collection:* Books: 378,276 (physical), 656,005 (digital/electronic); Serial titles: 1,273 (physical), 115,672 (digital/electronic); Databases: 476. Students can reserve study rooms.

**Computer facilities:** Computer purchase and lease plans are available. 4,500 computers available on campus for general student use. A campuswide network can be accessed. Online class registration is available.
Website: http://www.kennesaw.edu/

**General Application Contact:** Admissions Counselor, 470-578-4377, Fax: 470-578-9172, E-mail: ksugrad@kennesaw.edu.

**GRADUATE UNITS**

**Analytics and Data Science Institute** Students: 20 full-time (10 women), 3 part-time (0 women); includes 3 minority (1 Black or African American, non-Hispanic/Latino; 2 Asian, non-Hispanic/Latino), 12 international. Average age 33. 49 applicants, 16% accepted, 6 enrolled. Expenses: Contact institution. *Financial support:* In 2019–20, 5 research assistantships with full and partial tuition reimbursements (averaging $36,000 per year) were awarded. In 2019, 3 doctorates awarded. *Application deadline:* For fall admission, 2/1 for domestic and international students. *Application fee:* $60. Electronic applications accepted. *Application Contact:* Admissions Counselor, 470-578-4377, Fax: 470-578-9172, E-mail: ksugrad@kennesaw.edu. *Program Director*, Sherrill Hayes, 470-578-6499, E-mail: shayes32@kennesaw.edu.

**Bagwell College of Education** Students: 186 full-time (161 women), 909 part-time (701 women); includes 316 minority (236 Black or African American, non-Hispanic/Latino; 1 American Indian or Alaska Native, non-Hispanic/Latino; 22 Asian, non-Hispanic/Latino; 44 Hispanic/Latino; 2 Native Hawaiian or other Pacific Islander, non-Hispanic/Latino; 11 Two or more races, non-Hispanic/Latino), 1 international. Average age 36. 456 applicants, 72% accepted, 272 enrolled. Expenses: Contact institution. *Financial support:* Research assistantships with tuition reimbursements, Federal Work-Study, and unspecified assistantships available. Support available to part-time students. Financial award application deadline: 4/1; financial award applicants required to submit FAFSA. In 2019, 197 master's, 27 doctorates, 191 other advanced degrees awarded. *Program availability:* Part-time, 100% online, blended/hybrid learning. *Application deadline:* For fall admission, 7/1 for domestic and international students; for spring admission, 11/1 for domestic and international students; for summer admission, 4/1 for domestic and international students. Applications are processed on a rolling basis. *Application fee:* $60. Electronic applications accepted. *Application Contact:* Admission Counselor, 470-578-4377, Fax: 470-578-9172, E-mail: ksugrad@kennesaw.edu. *Dean*, Cynthia Reed, 470-578-6117, Fax: 470-578-6567.

**Coles College of Business** Students: 143 full-time (76 women), 525 part-time (273 women); includes 291 minority (182 Black or African American, non-Hispanic/Latino; 1 American Indian or Alaska Native, non-Hispanic/Latino; 55 Asian, non-Hispanic/Latino; 41 Hispanic/Latino; 12 Two or more races, non-Hispanic/Latino), 26 international. Average age 36. 521 applicants, 76% accepted, 302 enrolled. Expenses: Contact institution. *Financial support:* Application deadline: 4/1; applicants required to submit FAFSA. In 2019, 265 master's, 12 doctorates awarded. *Program availability:* Part-time, evening/weekend, 100% online. *Application deadline:* For fall admission, 7/1 for domestic and international students; for spring admission, 11/1 for domestic and international students; for summer admission, 4/1 for domestic and international students. Applications are processed on a rolling basis. *Application fee:* $60. Electronic applications accepted. *Application Contact:* Admissions Counselor, 470-578-4377, Fax: 470-578-9172, E-mail: ksugrad@kennesaw.edu. *Dean*, Dr. Robin Cheramie, 470-578-6425, E-mail: rcheram1@kennesaw.edu.

**College of Architecture and Construction Management** Students: 6 full-time (2 women), 9 part-time (4 women); includes 9 minority (6 Black or African American, non-Hispanic/Latino; 2 Asian, non-Hispanic/Latino; 1 Hispanic/Latino), 2 international. Average age 35. 6 applicants, 67% accepted, 4 enrolled. Expenses: Contact institution. *Financial support:* Applicants required to submit FAFSA. In 2019, 5 master's awarded. *Program availability:* Part-time, evening/weekend. *Application deadline:* For fall admission, 7/1 priority date for domestic students, 5/1 priority date for international students; for spring admission, 11/1 priority date for domestic students, 9/1 priority date for international students. Applications are processed on a rolling basis. *Application fee:* $60. Electronic applications accepted. *Application Contact:* Admission Counselor, 470-578-4377, Fax: 470-578-9172, E-mail: ksugrad@kennesaw.edu.

**College of Computing and Software Engineering** Students: 171 full-time (85 women), 240 part-time (72 women); includes 180 minority (89 Black or African American, non-Hispanic/Latino; 1 American Indian or Alaska Native, non-Hispanic/Latino; 59 Asian, non-Hispanic/Latino; 21 Hispanic/Latino; 10 Two or more races, non-Hispanic/Latino), 102 international. Average age 32. 117 applicants, 88% accepted, 71 enrolled. Expenses: Contact institution. *Financial support:* Applicants required to submit FAFSA. In 2019, 150 master's awarded. *Program availability:* Part-time, evening/weekend, blended/hybrid learning. *Application deadline:* For fall admission, 7/1 priority date for domestic students, 5/1 priority date for international students; for spring admission, 11/1 priority date for domestic students, 9/1 priority date for international students; for summer admission, 4/1 priority date for domestic students, 3/1 priority date for international students. Applications are processed on a rolling basis. *Application fee:* $60. Electronic applications accepted. *Application Contact:* Admission Counselor, 470-578-4377, Fax: 470-578-9172, E-mail: ksugrad@kennesaw.edu. *Dean*, Dr. Jon Preston, 470-578-5572, E-mail: jprest20@kennesaw.edu.

**College of Humanities and Social Sciences** Students: 151 full-time (98 women), 188 part-time (128 women); includes 147 minority (105 Black or African American, non-Hispanic/Latino; 11 Asian, non-Hispanic/Latino; 23 Hispanic/Latino; 8 Two or more races, non-Hispanic/Latino), 18 international. Average age 35. 185 applicants, 85% accepted, 110 enrolled. Expenses: Contact institution. *Financial support:* Applicants required to submit FAFSA. In 2019, 92 master's, 9 doctorates awarded. *Program availability:* Part-time, evening/weekend, 100% online. *Application deadline:* For fall admission, 6/1 priority date for domestic and international students; for spring admission, 10/1 priority date for domestic and international students. Applications are processed on a rolling basis. *Application fee:* $60. Electronic applications accepted. *Application Contact:* Admissions Counselor, 470-578-4377, Fax: 470-578-9172, E-mail: ksugrad@kennesaw.edu.

**College of Science and Mathematics** Students: 75 full-time (34 women), 30 part-time (18 women); includes 34 minority (20 Black or African American, non-Hispanic/Latino; 5 Asian, non-Hispanic/Latino; 6 Hispanic/Latino; 3 Two or more races, non-Hispanic/Latino), 3 international. Average age 30. 102 applicants, 70% accepted, 54 enrolled. Expenses: Contact institution. *Financial support:* Applicants required to submit FAFSA. In 2019, 32 master's awarded. *Program availability:* Part-time, 100% online, blended/hybrid learning. *Application deadline:* For fall admission, 6/1 for domestic and international students; for spring admission, 10/1 for domestic and international students. Applications are processed on a rolling basis. *Application fee:* $60. Electronic applications accepted. *Application Contact:* Admissions Counselor, 470-578-4377, Fax: 470-578-9172, E-mail: ksugrad@kennesaw.edu.

**Southern Polytechnic College of Engineering and Engineering Technology** Students: 30 full-time (9 women), 192 part-time (50 women); includes 90 minority (42 Black or African American, non-Hispanic/Latino; 20 Asian, non-Hispanic/Latino; 24 Hispanic/Latino; 4 Two or more races, non-Hispanic/Latino), 10 international. Average age 35. 88 applicants, 95% accepted, 58 enrolled. Expenses: Contact institution. *Financial support:* Applicants required to submit FAFSA. In 2019, 52 master's awarded. *Program availability:* Part-time, evening/weekend, online learning. *Application deadline:* For fall admission, 7/1 priority date for domestic and international students; for spring admission, 11/1 priority date for domestic and international students. Applications are processed on a rolling basis. *Application fee:* $60. Electronic applications accepted. *Application Contact:* Admissions Counselor, 470-578-4377, E-mail: ksugrad@kennesaw.edu.

**WellStar College of Health and Human Services** Students: 185 full-time (155 women), 74 part-time (60 women); includes 87 minority (55 Black or African American, non-Hispanic/Latino; 10 Asian, non-Hispanic/Latino; 12 Hispanic/Latino; 1 Native Hawaiian or other Pacific Islander, non-Hispanic/Latino; 9 Two or more races, non-Hispanic/Latino), 5 international. Average age 31. 258 applicants, 70% accepted, 125 enrolled. Expenses: Contact institution. *Financial support:* Applicants required to submit FAFSA. In 2019, 94 master's, 2 doctorates awarded. *Program availability:* Part-time, evening/weekend, online learning. *Application deadline:* For fall admission, 6/1 for domestic and international students. *Application fee:* $60. Electronic applications accepted. *Application Contact:* Admissions Counselor, 470-578-4377, Fax: 470-578-9172, E-mail: ksugrad@kennesaw.edu.

## KENRICK-GLENNON SEMINARY, St. Louis, MO 63119-4330

**General Information** Independent-religious, men only, graduate-only institution. *Graduate housing:* Room and/or apartments available to single students; on-campus housing not available to married students.

**GRADUATE UNITS**

**Graduate and Professional Programs**

## KENT STATE UNIVERSITY, Kent, OH 44242-0001

**General Information** State-supported, coed, university. CGS member. *Enrollment:* 27,716 graduate, professional, and undergraduate students. *Enrollment by degree level:* 3,542 master's, 1,633 doctoral, 152 other advanced degrees. *Graduate housing:* Room and/or apartments available on a first-come, first-served basis to single students; on-campus housing not available to married students. *Student services:* Campus employment opportunities, campus safety program, career counseling, child daycare facilities, exercise/wellness program, free psychological counseling, grant writing training, international student services, low-cost health insurance, multicultural affairs office, services for students with disabilities, teacher training, writing training. *Library facilities:* Kent State University Main Library plus 4 others. *Collection:* Books: 3 million (physical), 1.2 million (digital/electronic); Serial titles: 35,857 (physical), 14,996 (digital/electronic); Databases: 355. Weekly public service hours: 146; study areas open 24 hours, 5–7 days a week; students can reserve study rooms.

**Computer facilities:** Computer purchase and lease plans are available. A campuswide network can be accessed. Online class registration is available.
Website: http://www.kent.edu/

**General Application Contact:** Lana Whitehead, Director of Graduate Admissions, 330-672-6336, E-mail: lwhiteh2@kent.edu.

**GRADUATE UNITS**

**College of Aeronautics and Engineering** Students: 15 full-time (5 women), 21 part-time (3 women); includes 4 minority (3 Black or African American, non-Hispanic/Latino; 1 Hispanic/Latino), 12 international. Average age 31. 65 applicants, 54% accepted, 15 enrolled. *Faculty:* 11 full-time (2 women), 3 part-time/adjunct (2 women). Expenses: Contact institution. *Financial support:* Research assistantships, teaching assistantships, career-related internships or fieldwork, Federal Work-Study, scholarships/grants, and unspecified assistantships available. Financial award application deadline: 2/1; financial award applicants required to submit FAFSA. In 2019, 31 master's awarded. *Program availability:* Part-time, 100% online. *Application deadline:* For fall admission, 7/23 for domestic and international students; for spring admission, 12/14 for domestic and international students; for summer admission, 4/30 for domestic and international students. Applications are processed on a rolling basis. *Application fee:* $45 ($70 for international students). Electronic applications accepted. *Application Contact:* Richard Mangrum, Ed.D., Coordinator, Graduate Program, 330-672-1933, E-mail: rmangrum@kent.edu. *Dean and Professor*, Christina Bloebaum, Ph.D., 330-672-2892, E-mail: cbloebau@kent.edu.

**College of Architecture and Environmental Design** Students: 62 full-time (29 women), 12 part-time (9 women); includes 8 minority (3 Black or African American, non-Hispanic/Latino; 1 Asian, non-Hispanic/Latino; 2 Hispanic/Latino; 2 Two or more races, non-Hispanic/Latino), 11 international. Average age 26. 149 applicants, 87% accepted, 69 enrolled. *Faculty:* 19 full-time (5 women), 9 part-time/adjunct (3 women). Expenses: Contact institution. *Financial support:* Research assistantships with full tuition reimbursements, teaching assistantships with full tuition reimbursements, Federal Work-Study, scholarships/grants, and unspecified assistantships available. Financial award application deadline: 2/1; financial award applicants required to submit FAFSA. In 2019, 66 master's awarded. *Program availability:* Part-time. *Application deadline:* For fall admission, 1/15 for domestic students; for spring admission, 6/1 for domestic students. Applications are processed on a rolling basis. *Application fee:* $45 ($70 for international students). Electronic applications accepted. *Application Contact:* Bill Willoughby, Associate Dean, 330-672-2917, E-mail: wwilloug@kenk.edu. *Dean*, Mark Mistur, 330-672-2917, E-mail: mmistur1@kent.edu.

**College of Arts and Sciences** Students: 858 full-time (440 women), 263 part-time (153 women); includes 112 minority (37 Black or African American, non-Hispanic/Latino; 1 American Indian or Alaska Native, non-Hispanic/Latino; 27 Asian, non-Hispanic/Latino; 27 Hispanic/Latino; 20 Two or more races, non-Hispanic/Latino), 378 international. Average age 31. 1,444 applicants, 47% accepted, 284 enrolled. *Faculty:* 266 full-time (93 women), 24 part-time/adjunct (11 women). Expenses: Contact institution. *Financial support:* Fellowships with full tuition reimbursements, research assistantships with full tuition reimbursements, teaching assistantships with full tuition reimbursements, career-related internships or fieldwork, Federal Work-Study, scholarships/grants, and unspecified assistantships available. Financial award application deadline: 2/1; financial award applicants required to submit FAFSA. In 2019, 223 master's, 94 doctorates awarded. *Program availability:* Part-time, 100% online. *Application deadline:* Applications are processed on a rolling basis. *Application fee:* $45 ($70 for international students). Electronic applications accepted. *Application Contact:* Matthew Minichillo, Assistant Dean, Academic & Student Services, 330-672-8972, E-mail: mminichi@kent.edu. *Interim Dean, College of Arts & Sciences*, Dr. Mandy Munro-Stasiuk, 330-672-2045, E-mail: mmunrost@kent.edu.

***School of Biomedical Sciences*** Students: 73 full-time (48 women), 2 part-time (1 woman); includes 9 minority (2 Black or African American, non-Hispanic/Latino; 1 Asian, non-Hispanic/Latino; 3 Hispanic/Latino; 3 Two or more races, non-Hispanic/Latino), 53 international. Average age 29. 78 applicants, 17% accepted, 9 enrolled. *Faculty:* 17 full-time (8 women). Expenses: Contact institution. *Financial support:* Research assistantships with full tuition reimbursements, teaching assistantships, health care benefits, and unspecified assistantships available. Financial award application deadline: 1/1. In 2019, 2 master's, 5 doctorates awarded. *Application deadline:* For fall admission, 1/1 for domestic students, 12/15 for international students. Applications are processed on a rolling basis. *Application fee:* $45 ($70 for international students). Electronic applications accepted. *Application Contact:* School of Biomedical Sciences, 330-6722263, Fax: 330-6729391. *Director, School of Biomedical Sciences*, Dr. Ernest J. Freeman, 330-672-2363, E-mail: efreema2@kent.edu.

**College of Business Administration** Students: 197 full-time (85 women), 69 part-time (32 women); includes 29 minority (13 Black or African American, non-Hispanic/Latino; 4 Asian, non-Hispanic/Latino; 1 Hispanic/Latino; 11 Two or more races, non-Hispanic/Latino), 83 international. Average age 31. 325 applicants, 68% accepted, 130 enrolled. *Faculty:* 41 full-time (15 women), 6 part-time/adjunct (3 women). Expenses: Contact institution. *Financial support:* In 2019–20, 13 research assistantships with full tuition reimbursements (averaging $5,200 per year), 35 teaching assistantships with full tuition reimbursements (averaging $23,000 per year) were awarded; fellowships with full tuition reimbursements, career-related internships or fieldwork, Federal Work-Study, health care benefits, and unspecified assistantships also available. Financial award applicants required to submit FAFSA. In 2019, 98 master's, 8 doctorates awarded. *Program availability:* Part-time, evening/weekend, online learning. *Application fee:* $45 ($70 for international students). Electronic applications accepted. *Application Contact:* Roberto E. Chavez, Director, Graduate Programs, 330-672-2282, Fax: 330-672-7303, E-mail: gradbus@kent.edu. *Associate Dean for Graduate Programs*, Dr. Cathy L.Z. Dubois, 330-672-1103, E-mail: cdubois@kent.edu.

**College of Communication and Information** Students: 215 full-time (165 women), 547 part-time (392 women); includes 115 minority (48 Black or African American, non-Hispanic/Latino; 20 Asian, non-Hispanic/Latino; 30 Hispanic/Latino; 1 Native Hawaiian or other Pacific Islander, non-Hispanic/Latino; 16 Two or more races, non-Hispanic/Latino), 24 international. Average age 32. 339 applicants, 90% accepted, 187 enrolled. *Faculty:* 48 full-time (35 women), 41 part-time/adjunct (17 women). Expenses: Contact institution. *Financial support:* Fellowships with full tuition reimbursements, research assistantships with full tuition reimbursements, teaching assistantships with full tuition reimbursements, career-related internships or fieldwork, Federal Work-Study, scholarships/grants, and unspecified assistantships available. Financial award application deadline: 3/1. In 2019, 363 master's awarded. *Program availability:* Part-time, 100% online. *Application deadline:* For fall admission, 1/1 for domestic and international students. Applications are processed on a rolling basis. *Application fee:* $45 ($70 for international students). Electronic applications accepted. *Application Contact:* Nzinga Hart, Graduate Academic Program Coordinator, 330-672-2502, E-mail: nbodden@kent.edu. *Professor and Dean*, Amy Reynolds, Ph.D., 330-672-2950, E-mail: areyno24@kent.edu.

***School of Communication Studies*** Students: 8 full-time (7 women), 5 part-time (3 women); includes 3 minority (all Black or African American, non-Hispanic/Latino), 3 international. Average age 29. 18 applicants, 83% accepted, 7 enrolled. *Faculty:* 6 full-time (5 women). Expenses: Contact institution. *Financial support:* Research assistantships with full tuition reimbursements, teaching assistantships with full tuition reimbursements, career-related internships or fieldwork, and unspecified assistantships available. Financial award application deadline: 1/15. In 2019, 9 master's awarded. *Program availability:* Part-time. *Application deadline:* For fall admission, 1/15 for domestic students, 12/20 for international students; for spring admission, 11/15 for domestic students, 10/20 for international students. Applications are processed on a rolling basis. *Application fee:* $45 ($70 for international students). Electronic applications accepted. *Application Contact:* Dr. Elizabeth E. Graham, Director & Professor, 330-672-2659, E-mail: egraha18@kent.edu. *Director & Professor*, Dr. Elizabeth E. Graham, 330-672-2659, E-mail: egraha18@kent.edu.

***School of Emerging Media and Technology*** Students: 7 full-time (5 women), 20 part-time (4 women); includes 5 minority (1 Black or African American, non-Hispanic/Latino; 1 Asian, non-Hispanic/Latino; 1 Hispanic/Latino; 2 Two or more races, non-Hispanic/Latino), 6 international. Average age 35. 35 applicants, 77% accepted, 8 enrolled. *Faculty:* 1 (woman) full-time, 5 part-time/adjunct (2 women). Expenses: Contact institution. *Financial support:* Career-related internships or fieldwork and scholarships/grants available. In 2019, 35 master's awarded. *Program availability:* Part-time, 100% online. *Application deadline:* For fall admission, 7/1 for domestic students, 5/15 for international students; for spring admission, 11/15 for domestic students, 10/1 for international students; for summer admission, 4/15 for domestic students, 3/15 for international students. Applications are processed on a rolling basis. *Application fee:* $45 ($70 for international students). Electronic applications accepted. *Application Contact:* Tang Tang, Professor/Graduate Coordinator, 330-672-1132, E-mail: ttang2@kent.edu. *Dean*, Dr. Amy Reynolds, Ph.D., 330-672-2950, E-mail: areyno24@kent.edu.

***School of Information*** Students: 148 full-time (120 women), 372 part-time (274 women); includes 89 minority (34 Black or African American, non-Hispanic/Latino; 16 Asian, non-Hispanic/Latino; 26 Hispanic/Latino; 13 Two or more races, non-Hispanic/Latino), 2 international. Average age 32. 211 applicants, 100% accepted, 142 enrolled. *Faculty:* 16 full-time (13 women), 26 part-time/adjunct (12 women). Expenses: Contact institution. *Financial support:* Fellowships with full tuition reimbursements, research assistantships with full tuition reimbursements, teaching assistantships with full tuition reimbursements, scholarships/grants, and unspecified assistantships available. Financial award application deadline: 3/1. In 2019, 32 master's awarded. *Program availability:* Part-time, 100% online. *Application deadline:* For fall admission, 3/15 priority date for domestic students, 3/15 for international students; for spring admission, 9/15 priority date for domestic students, 9/15 for international students; for summer admission, 1/15 priority date for domestic students, 1/15 for international students. Applications are processed on a rolling basis. *Application fee:* $45 ($70 for international students). Electronic applications accepted. *Application Contact:* Dr. Kendra Albright, Ph.D., Director and Professor, 330-672-8535, E-mail: kalbrig7@kent.edu. *Director and Professor*, Dr. Kendra Albright, Ph.D., 330-672-8535, E-mail: kalbrig7@kent.edu.

***School of Media and Journalism*** Students: 11 full-time (8 women), 35 part-time (22 women); includes 3 minority (all Black or African American, non-Hispanic/Latino), 3 international. Average age 34. 18 applicants, 78% accepted, 10 enrolled. *Faculty:* 7 full-time (6 women), 5 part-time/adjunct (2 women). Expenses: Contact institution. *Financial support:* Research assistantships with full tuition reimbursements, teaching assistantships with full tuition reimbursements, scholarships/grants, and unspecified assistantships available. Financial award application deadline: 3/1. In 2019, 40 master's awarded. *Program availability:* Part-time, 100% online. *Application deadline:* For fall admission, 7/1 for domestic and international students. Applications are processed on a rolling basis. *Application fee:* $45 ($70 for international students). Electronic applications accepted. *Application Contact:* Tang Tang, Graduate Coordinator/Professor, 330-672-1132, E-mail: ttang2@kent.edu. *Interim Director and Professor*, Jeff Fruit, 330-672-2572, E-mail: jmc@kent.edu.

***School of Visual Communication Design*** Students: 20 full-time (10 women), 11 part-time (6 women); includes 6 minority (3 Black or African American, non-Hispanic/Latino; 2 Asian, non-Hispanic/Latino; 1 Two or more races, non-Hispanic/Latino), 5 international. Average age 31. 29 applicants, 66% accepted, 9 enrolled. *Faculty:* 9 full-time (4 women), 5 part-time/adjunct (1 woman). Expenses: Contact institution. *Financial support:* Scholarships/grants and unspecified assistantships available. Financial award application deadline: 3/5; financial award applicants required to submit FAFSA. In 2019, 4 master's awarded. *Program availability:* Part-time. *Application deadline:* For fall admission, 3/1 for domestic and international students; for spring admission, 10/1 for domestic and international students. Applications are processed on a rolling basis. *Application fee:* $45 ($70 for international students). Electronic applications accepted. *Application Contact:* Ken Visocky O'Grady, Graduate Coordinator and Professor, 330-672-1353, E-mail: kogrady@kent.edu. *Director*, Dr. Daniel Alenquer, 330-672-7856, E-mail: dalenque@kent.edu.

**College of Education, Health and Human Services** *Program availability:* Part-time, evening/weekend, online learning. Electronic applications accepted.

***School of Foundations, Leadership and Administration*** Electronic applications accepted.

***School of Health Sciences*** *Program availability:* Part-time, evening/weekend. Electronic applications accepted.

***School of Lifespan Development and Educational Sciences*** *Program availability:* Part-time, evening/weekend. Electronic applications accepted.

***School of Teaching, Learning and Curriculum Studies*** *Program availability:* Part-time, evening/weekend. Electronic applications accepted.

**College of Nursing** Students: 138 full-time (123 women), 522 part-time (464 women); includes 80 minority (41 Black or African American, non-Hispanic/Latino; 16 Asian, non-Hispanic/Latino; 9 Hispanic/Latino; 1 Native Hawaiian or other Pacific Islander, non-Hispanic/Latino; 13 Two or more races, non-Hispanic/Latino), 7 international. Average age 35. 303 applicants, 68% accepted, 154 enrolled. *Faculty:* 28 full-time (26 women), 15 part-time/adjunct (13 women). Expenses: Contact institution. *Financial support:* Federal Work-Study and scholarships/grants available. Financial award application deadline: 2/1. In 2019, 156 master's, 8 doctorates awarded. *Program availability:* Part-time, online learning. *Application deadline:* For fall admission, 3/1 for domestic and international students; for spring admission, 10/1 for domestic and international students. Applications are processed on a rolling basis. *Application fee:* $45 ($70 for international students). Electronic applications accepted. *Application Contact:* Dr. Wendy A. Umberger, Ph.D., Associate Dean for Graduate Programs/Professor, 330-672-8813, E-mail: wlewando@kent.edu. *Dean*, Dr. Barbara Broome, Ph.D., 330-672-3777, E-mail: bbroome1@kent.edu.

**College of Podiatric Medicine** Electronic applications accepted.

**College of Public Health** Students: 136 full-time (98 women), 158 part-time (129 women); includes 71 minority (45 Black or African American, non-Hispanic/Latino; 12 Asian, non-Hispanic/Latino; 8 Hispanic/Latino; 6 Two or more races, non-Hispanic/Latino), 40 international. Average age 31. 187 applicants, 79% accepted, 85 enrolled. *Faculty:* 23 full-time (12 women), 4 part-time/adjunct (1 woman). Expenses: Contact institution. *Financial support:* Career-related internships or fieldwork, Federal Work-Study, scholarships/grants, and unspecified assistantships available. In 2019, 93 master's, 7 doctorates awarded. *Program availability:* Part-time, 100% online. *Application deadline:* For fall admission, 6/15 for domestic and international students; for spring admission, 10/15 for domestic and international students; for summer admission, 3/15 for domestic and international students. Applications are processed on a rolling basis. *Application fee:* $45 ($70 for international students). Electronic applications accepted. *Application Contact:* Dr. Jeffrey S. Hallam, Professor/Associate Dean for Research and Graduate Studies, 330-672-0679, E-mail: jhallam1@kent.edu. *Dean and Professor of Health Policy and Management*, Dr. Sonia Alemagno, 330-672-6500, E-mail: salemagn@kent.edu.

**College of the Arts** Students: 123 full-time (73 women), 213 part-time (142 women); includes 31 minority (18 Black or African American, non-Hispanic/Latino; 1 Asian, non-Hispanic/Latino; 6 Hispanic/Latino; 1 Native Hawaiian or other Pacific Islander, non-Hispanic/Latino; 5 Two or more races, non-Hispanic/Latino), 39 international. Average age 31. 204 applicants, 79% accepted, 110 enrolled. *Faculty:* 81 full-time (42 women), 30 part-time/adjunct (19 women). Expenses: Contact institution. *Financial support:* Research assistantships, teaching assistantships with full tuition reimbursements, scholarships/grants, and unspecified assistantships available. Financial award application deadline: 2/2. In 2019, 115 master's, 4 doctorates awarded. *Program availability:* Part-time, 100% online. *Application deadline:* For fall admission, 2/1 priority date for domestic and international students; for spring admission, 10/15 for domestic and international students. Applications are processed on a rolling basis. *Application fee:* $45 ($70 for international students). Electronic applications accepted. *Application Contact:* Yuko Kurahashi, Professor of Theatre, Graduate Coordinator, 330-672-9483, E-mail: ykurahas@kent.edu. *Dean and Professor*, Dr. John R. Crawford-Spinelli, 330-672-2760, E-mail: jcrawfo1@kent.edu.

***Hugh A. Glauser School of Music*** Students: 57 full-time (28 women), 186 part-time (118 women); includes 21 minority (12 Black or African American, non-Hispanic/Latino; 1 Asian, non-Hispanic/Latino; 4 Hispanic/Latino; 1 Native Hawaiian or other Pacific Islander, non-Hispanic/Latino; 3 Two or more races, non-Hispanic/Latino), 30 international. Average age 31. 106 applicants, 90% accepted, 68 enrolled. *Faculty:* 36 full-time (12 women), 23 part-time/adjunct (15 women). Expenses: Contact institution. *Financial support:* Teaching assistantships with full and partial tuition reimbursements, scholarships/grants, and unspecified assistantships available. Financial award application deadline: 3/1. In 2019, 94 master's, 4 doctorates awarded. *Program availability:* Part-time, 100% online. *Application deadline:* Applications are processed on a rolling basis. *Application fee:* $45 ($70 for international students). Electronic applications accepted. *Application Contact:* Michael Chunn, Graduate Coordinator/Trumpet Professor, 330-672-9234, Fax: 330-672-7837, E-mail: mchunn@kent.edu. *Director, Hugh A. Glausser School of Music*, Kent McWilliams, 330-672-2172, E-mail: kmcwill2@kent.edu.

***School of Art*** Students: 36 full-time (27 women), 24 part-time (22 women); includes 4 minority (3 Black or African American, non-Hispanic/Latino; 1 Hispanic/Latino), 2 international. Average age 30. 52 applicants, 67% accepted, 20 enrolled. *Faculty:* 22 full-time (13 women), 5 part-time/adjunct (4 women). Expenses: Contact institution. *Financial support:* Career-related internships or fieldwork, scholarships/grants, and unspecified assistantships available. Financial award application deadline: 3/1. In 2019, 15 master's awarded. *Program availability:* Part-time, 100% online, blended/hybrid learning. *Application deadline:* For fall admission, 2/2 priority date for domestic students, 2/2 for international students; for spring admission, 10/15 for domestic and international students. Applications are processed on a rolling basis. *Application fee:* $45 ($70 for international students). Electronic applications accepted. *Application Contact:* Peter Christian Johnson, Graduate Coordinator and Associate Professor Ceramics, 330-672-3360, E-mail: pjohns35@kent.edu. *Director*, Marie Bukowski, 330-672-2192, E-mail: mbukows1@kent.edu.

***School of Fashion Design and Merchandising*** Students: 30 full-time (18 women), 3 part-time (2 women); includes 6 minority (3 Black or African American, non-Hispanic/Latino; 1 Hispanic/Latino; 2 Two or more races, non-Hispanic/Latino), 7 international. Average age 26. 28 applicants, 61% accepted, 10 enrolled. *Faculty:* 11 full-time (9 women). Expenses: Contact institution. *Financial support:* Career-related internships or fieldwork, health care benefits, and unspecified assistantships available. Financial award application deadline: 2/1. *Application deadline:* For fall admission, 2/1 priority date for domestic students, 2/1 for international students. Applications are processed on a rolling basis. *Application fee:* $45 ($70 for international students). Electronic applications accepted. *Application Contact:* Jihyun Kim-Vick, Graduate Program Coordinator & Professor, 330-672-1473, E-mail: jkim55@kent.edu. *Director and Professor*, Dr. Louise Valentine, Ph.D., 330-672-2838, E-mail: lvalent9@kent.edu.

***School of Theatre and Dance*** Students: 17 full-time (6 women), 1 part-time (0 women); includes 2 minority (1 Black or African American, non-Hispanic/Latino; 1 Two or more races, non-Hispanic/Latino), 2 international. Average age 36. 10 applicants, 80% accepted, 7 enrolled. *Faculty:* 12 full-time (8 women), 2 part-time/adjunct (0 women). Expenses: Contact institution. *Financial support:* Teaching assistantships with full tuition reimbursements, career-related internships or fieldwork, Federal Work-Study, scholarships/grants, and unspecified assistantships available. Financial award application deadline: 5/1. In 2019, 6 master's awarded. *Program availability:* Part-time. *Application deadline:* Applications are processed on a rolling basis. *Application fee:* $45 ($70 for international students). Electronic applications accepted. *Application Contact:* Yuko Kurahashi, Graduate Coordinator and Associate Professor of Theatre, 330-672-9483, E-mail: ykurahas@kent.edu. *Director and Associate Professor*, Eric van Baars, 330-672-0102, E-mail: fvanbaar@kent.edu.

## KENT STATE UNIVERSITY AT STARK, Canton, OH 44720-7599

**General Information** State-supported, coed, comprehensive institution.

**GRADUATE UNITS**

**Graduate School of Education, Health and Human Services**

**Professional MBA Program**

## KENTUCKY CHRISTIAN UNIVERSITY, Grayson, KY 41143-2205

**General Information** Independent-religious, coed, comprehensive institution. *Graduate housing:* Rooms and/or apartments available on a first-come, first-served basis to single and married students.

**GRADUATE UNITS**

**Graduate School** *Program availability:* Part-time. Electronic applications accepted.

## KENTUCKY STATE UNIVERSITY, Frankfort, KY 40601

**General Information** State-related, coed, comprehensive institution. *Graduate housing:* Room and/or apartments available on a first-come, first-served basis to single students; on-campus housing not available to married students. Housing application deadline: 6/1. *Research affiliation:* National Science Foundation (Brain Neuron simulation; Promoting STEM minority), Verison (Innovative learning program), NASA (Signal processing simulation), Alltech (Aquaculture), Alltech (aquaculture nutrition).

**GRADUATE UNITS**

**Program in Aquaculture** *Program availability:* Evening/weekend. Electronic applications accepted.

**Program in Business Administration** *Program availability:* Part-time, evening/weekend. Electronic applications accepted.

**Program in Computer Science Technology** *Program availability:* Evening/weekend. Electronic applications accepted.

**Program in Environmental Studies** *Program availability:* Evening/weekend. Electronic applications accepted.

**Program in Interdisciplinary Behavioral Science** *Program availability:* Part-time, evening/weekend. Electronic applications accepted.

**Program in Nursing Practice** Electronic applications accepted.

**Program in Public Administration** *Program availability:* Evening/weekend. Electronic applications accepted.

**Program in Special Education** *Program availability:* Evening/weekend, online only, blended/hybrid learning. Electronic applications accepted.

## KETTERING COLLEGE, Kettering, OH 45429-1299

**General Information** Independent-religious, coed, primarily women, comprehensive institution.

**GRADUATE UNITS**

**Program in Occupational Therapy**

**Program in Physician Assistant Studies**

## KETTERING UNIVERSITY, Flint, MI 48504

**General Information** Independent, coed, comprehensive institution. CGS member. *Graduate housing:* Rooms and/or apartments available on a first-come, first-served basis to single students and available to married students. Housing application deadline: 7/15. *Research affiliation:* McLaren Foundation (orthopedic surgery biomechanics), Shin-Estu Chemical Company (atmospheric plasma technology), Broad-Ocean Technologies (electric vehicle battery systems), Landaal Packaging Systems (space utilization and process flow of operations), Mahindra Tractor Assembly, dba Mahindra GenZe (electric power and control boards), TRW (crash safety).

**GRADUATE UNITS**

**Graduate School** *Program availability:* Part-time, evening/weekend, online learning. Electronic applications accepted.

## KEUKA COLLEGE, Keuka Park, NY 14478

**General Information** Independent-religious, coed, comprehensive institution. *Enrollment:* 1,777 graduate, professional, and undergraduate students; 125 full-time matriculated graduate/professional students (101 women), 123 part-time matriculated graduate/professional students (101 women). *Enrollment by degree level:* 239 master's, 9 other advanced degrees. *Graduate faculty:* 29 full-time (20 women), 124 part-time/adjunct (50 women). *Graduate housing:* Room and/or apartments available on a first-come, first-served basis to single students; on-campus housing not available to married students. Housing application deadline: 5/1. *Student services:* Campus safety program, career counseling, exercise/wellness program, free psychological counseling, grant writing training, international student services, low-cost health insurance, multicultural affairs office, services for students with disabilities, teacher training, writing training. *Library facilities:* Lightner Library plus 1 other. *Collection:* Books: 78,791 (physical), 13,006 (digital/electronic); Serial titles: 391 (physical), 80 (digital/electronic); Databases: 82. Weekly public service hours: 96.

**Computer facilities:** Computer purchase and lease plans are available. 185 computers available on campus for general student use. A campuswide network can be accessed from student residence rooms and from off campus. Online class registration, phone app for cancellations are available.
Website: http://www.keuka.edu/

**General Application Contact:** Megan Perkins, Director of Admissions, 315-279-5254, Fax: 315-279-5386, E-mail: admissions@keuka.edu.

**GRADUATE UNITS**

**Program in Childhood Education/Literacy** Electronic applications accepted.

**Program in Management** *Program availability:* Part-time, evening/weekend, 100% online, blended/hybrid learning.

**Program in Nursing** Electronic applications accepted.

**Program in Occupational Therapy** Students: 34 full-time (32 women); includes 2 minority (1 Asian, non-Hispanic/Latino; 1 Hispanic/Latino). Average age 22. *Faculty:* 4 full-time (3 women). Expenses: Contact institution. *Financial support:* Research assistantships, scholarships/grants, and tuition waivers (full and partial) available. Financial award applicants required to submit FAFSA. In 2019, 33 master's awarded. *Application deadline:* For fall admission, 8/15 priority date for domestic students; for winter admission, 12/15 priority date for domestic students; for spring admission, 4/15 priority date for domestic students. Applications are processed on a rolling basis. *Application fee:* $50. Electronic applications accepted. *Application Contact:* Keuka College Admissions Office, 315-279-5254, Fax: 315-279-5386, E-mail: admissions@keuka.edu. *Division Chair of Occupational Therapy*, Dr. Christopher Alterio, 315-279-5483, Fax: 315-279-5439, E-mail: calterio1@keuka.edu.

**Program in Social Work** Students: 42 full-time (39 women); includes 13 minority (11 Black or African American, non-Hispanic/Latino; 1 Hispanic/Latino; 1 Two or more races, non-Hispanic/Latino). Average age 37. *Faculty:* 5 full-time (4 women), 6 part-time/adjunct (5 women). Expenses: Contact institution. *Financial support:* Fellowships with tuition reimbursements, research assistantships with tuition reimbursements, teaching assistantships with tuition reimbursements, scholarships/grants, and tuition waivers (full and partial) available. Financial award applicants required to submit FAFSA. In 2019, 34 master's awarded. *Program availability:* Part-time, evening/weekend. *Application deadline:* For fall admission, 8/15 for domestic students; for winter admission, 12/15 for domestic students; for spring admission, 4/15 for domestic students. Applications are processed on a rolling basis. *Application fee:* $50. Electronic applications accepted. *Application Contact:* Keuka College Admissions Office, 315-279-5254, Fax: 315-279-5386, E-mail: admissions@keuka.edu. *Division Chair*, Dr. Jason McKinney, 315-279-5434, E-mail: jmckinney@keuka.edu.

## KEYSTONE COLLEGE, La Plume, PA 18440

**General Information** Independent, coed, comprehensive institution. *Enrollment:* 1,364 graduate, professional, and undergraduate students; 24 full-time matriculated graduate/professional students (16 women), 52 part-time matriculated graduate/professional students (43 women). *Enrollment by degree level:* 76 master's. *Tuition:* Part-time $650 per credit. One-time fee: $100. Tuition and fees vary according to program. *Graduate housing:* On-campus housing not available. *Student services:* Campus employment opportunities, campus safety program, career counseling, exercise/wellness program, free psychological counseling, international student services, multicultural affairs office, services for students with disabilities, writing training. *Library facilities:* Miller Library.

**Computer facilities:** 100 computers available on campus for general student use. A campuswide network can be accessed. Online class registration is available.
Website: http://www.keystone.edu/

**General Application Contact:** Jennifer Sekol, Director of Admissions, 570-945-8117, Fax: 570-945-7916, E-mail: jennifer.sekol@keystone.edu.

**GRADUATE UNITS**

**Master's in Business Administration** Students: 38. Expenses: Contact institution. *Financial support:* Unspecified assistantships available. Financial award applicants required to submit FAFSA. *Program availability:* Part-time, online only, 100% online. *Application deadline:* For fall admission, 8/1 for domestic students; for spring admission, 3/1 for domestic students; for summer admission, 7/1 for domestic students. Applications are processed on a rolling basis. Electronic applications accepted. *Application Contact:* Sarah Louzon, Admissions Counselor, 570-945-8126, Fax: 570-945-7916, E-mail: sarah.louzon@keystone.edu. *Associate Professor/Coordinator of MBA Program*, Dr. Dana Harris, 570-945-8421, E-mail: dana.harris@keystone.edu.

**Master's in Early Childhood Education Leadership** Students: 23. Expenses: Contact institution. *Financial support:* Unspecified assistantships available. Financial award applicants required to submit FAFSA. *Program availability:* Part-time, blended/hybrid learning. *Application deadline:* For fall admission, 8/1 for domestic students; for spring admission, 1/1 for domestic students; for summer admission, 5/1 for domestic students. Applications are processed on a rolling basis. Electronic applications accepted. *Application Contact:* Jennifer Sekol, Director of Admissions, 570-945-8117, Fax: 570-945-7916, E-mail: jennifer.sekol@keystone.edu. *Professor*, Heather Shanks-McElroy, PhD, 570-945-8475, E-mail: heather.mcelroy@keystone.edu.

**MS Program in Criminal Justice** Expenses: Contact institution. *Application Contact:* Jennifer Sekol, Director of Admissions, 570-945-8117, Fax: 570-945-7916, E-mail: jennifer.sekol@keystone.edu.

**Program in Accountancy** *Program availability:* Part-time, online only, 100% online. Electronic applications accepted.

## KING'S COLLEGE, Wilkes-Barre, PA 18711-0801

**General Information** Independent-religious, coed, comprehensive institution. *Graduate housing:* On-campus housing not available.

**GRADUATE UNITS**

**Program in Education** *Program availability:* Part-time, evening/weekend.

**Program in Physician Assistant Studies** Electronic applications accepted.

**William G. McGowan School of Business** *Program availability:* Part-time.

## THE KING'S UNIVERSITY, Southlake, TX 76092

**General Information** Independent-religious, coed, comprehensive institution.

**GRADUATE UNITS**

**Graduate and Professional Programs**

## KINGSWOOD UNIVERSITY, Sussex, NB E4E 5L2, Canada

**General Information** Independent-religious, coed, comprehensive institution. *Enrollment:* 8 full-time matriculated graduate/professional students (3 women), 6 part-time matriculated graduate/professional students (2 women). *Enrollment by degree level:* 14 master's. *Graduate faculty:* 1 full-time (0 women), 1 part-time/adjunct (0 women). *Tuition:* Part-time $370 Canadian dollars per credit hour. One-time fee: $160 Canadian dollars full-time. *Graduate housing:* On-campus housing not available. *Library facilities:* The Earle and Marion Trouten Library.

**Computer facilities:** 8 computers available on campus for general student use. A campuswide network can be accessed from student residence rooms and from off campus.
Website: http://www.kingswood.edu/

**General Application Contact:** Enrolment Office, 506-432-4422, Fax: 506-432-4442, E-mail: enrolment@kingswood.edu.

**GRADUATE UNITS**

**Program in Pastoral Theology**

## KING UNIVERSITY, Bristol, TN 37620-2699

**General Information** Independent-religious, coed, comprehensive institution. *Enrollment:* 1,974 graduate, professional, and undergraduate students; 302 full-time matriculated graduate/professional students (212 women), 55 part-time matriculated graduate/professional students (42 women). *Enrollment by degree level:* 338 master's, 11 doctoral, 8 other advanced degrees. *Graduate faculty:* 29 full-time (17 women), 24 part-time/adjunct (19 women). *Tuition:* Full-time $10,890; part-time $605 per semester hour. *Required fees:* $100 per course. *Graduate housing:* Room and/or apartments available on a first-come, first-served basis to single students; on-campus housing not available to married students. Typical cost: $2466 per year ($4712 including board). Housing application deadline: 8/18. *Student services:* Campus employment opportunities, campus safety program, career counseling, exercise/wellness program, free psychological counseling, international student services, services for students with disabilities, writing training. *Library facilities:* E. W. King Library plus 3 others. *Collection:* Books: 79,129 (physical), 212,133 (digital/electronic); Serial titles: 179 (physical); Databases: 95. Weekly public service hours: 85.

**Computer facilities:** 90 computers available on campus for general student use. A campuswide network can be accessed. Online class registration, Student Portal are available.
Website: http://www.king.edu/

**General Application Contact:** Ashley Hartless, Interim Director of Enrollment Management Adult, Graduate and Professional Studies/Tri Cities, 276-964-7471, Fax: 423-652-4727, E-mail: ajhartless@king.edu.

**GRADUATE UNITS**

**School of Business, Economics, and Technology** Students: 154 full-time (89 women), 14 part-time (11 women); includes 24 minority (17 Black or African American, non-Hispanic/Latino; 3 Asian, non-Hispanic/Latino; 4 Hispanic/Latino), 6 international. Average age 33. 127 applicants, 96% accepted, 60 enrolled. *Faculty:* 12 full-time (3 women), 8 part-time/adjunct (4 women). Expenses: Contact institution. *Financial support:* Unspecified assistantships available. Financial award applicants required to submit FAFSA. In 2019, 103 master's awarded. *Program availability:* Part-time, evening/weekend, 100% online, blended/hybrid learning. *Application deadline:* Applications are processed on a rolling basis. *Application fee:* $50. Electronic applications accepted. *Application Contact:* Nancy Beverly, Territory Manager/Enrollment Counselor, 423-341-9495, Fax: 423-652-4727, E-mail: nmbeverly@king.edu. *Dean, School of Business, Economics and Technology*, Dr. Mark Pate, 423-652-4814, E-mail: mjpate@king.edu.

**School of Education** Students: 33 full-time (20 women), 5 part-time (3 women); includes 4 minority (3 Black or African American, non-Hispanic/Latino; 1 Hispanic/Latino), 1 international. Average age 38. 27 applicants, 100% accepted, 7 enrolled. *Faculty:* 4 full-time (3 women), 5 part-time/adjunct (4 women). Expenses: Contact institution. *Financial support:* Unspecified assistantships available. Financial award applicants required to submit FAFSA. *Program availability:* Part-time, evening/weekend, 100% online, blended/hybrid learning. *Application deadline:* Applications are processed on a rolling basis. *Application fee:* $50. Electronic applications accepted. *Application Contact:* Ashley Hartless, Interim Director of Enrollment Management Adult, Graduate and Professional Studies/Tri Cities, 276-964-7471, Fax: 423-652-4727, E-mail: ajhartless@king.edu. *Dean, School of Education*, Dr. Donna Watson, 423-652-4843, E-mail: dhwatson@king.edu.

**School of Nursing** Students: 115 full-time (103 women), 35 part-time (28 women); includes 12 minority (9 Black or African American, non-Hispanic/Latino; 1 Asian, non-Hispanic/Latino; 1 Hispanic/Latino; 1 Native Hawaiian or other Pacific Islander, non-Hispanic/Latino). Average age 37. 141 applicants, 96% accepted, 63 enrolled. *Faculty:* 13 full-time (12 women), 4 part-time/adjunct (2 women). Expenses: Contact institution. *Financial support:* Unspecified assistantships available. Financial award applicants required to submit FAFSA. In 2019, 89 master's, 1 doctorate, 6 other advanced degrees awarded. *Program availability:* Part-time, evening/weekend, 100% online, blended/hybrid learning. *Application deadline:* Applications are processed on a rolling basis. *Application fee:* $50. Electronic applications accepted. *Application Contact:* Natalie Blankenship, Territory Manager/Enrollment Counselor, 652-652-4159, Fax: 652-652-4727, E-mail: nblankenship@king.edu. *Dean, School of Nursing*, Dr. Tracy Slemp, 423-652-6335, E-mail: tjslemp@king.edu.

## KNOX COLLEGE, Toronto, ON M5S 2E6, Canada

**General Information** Independent-religious, coed, graduate-only institution. *Enrollment by degree level:* 72 master's, 37 doctoral, 12 other advanced degrees. *Graduate faculty:* 9 full-time (3 women), 10 part-time/adjunct (3 women). *Graduate housing:* Rooms and/or apartments available on a first-come, first-served basis to single students and available to married students. Housing application deadline: 8/1. *Student services:* Campus employment opportunities, free psychological counseling, international student services, low-cost health insurance, services for students with disabilities, writing training. *Library facilities:* Caven Library plus 42 others.

**Computer facilities:** 10 computers available on campus for general student use. Online class registration is available.
Website: http://www.knox.utoronto.ca/

**General Application Contact:** Megan Shin, Recruitment Officer and Admissions Counsellor, 416-978-5306, Fax: 416-971-2758, E-mail: megan.shin@utoronto.ca.

**GRADUATE UNITS**

**College of Theology** *Program availability:* Part-time.

## KNOX THEOLOGICAL SEMINARY, Fort Lauderdale, FL 33308

**General Information** Independent-religious, coed, primarily men, graduate-only institution. *Graduate housing:* On-campus housing not available.

**GRADUATE UNITS**

**Graduate Programs** *Program availability:* Part-time, blended/hybrid learning.

## KUTZTOWN UNIVERSITY OF PENNSYLVANIA, Kutztown, PA 19530-0730

**General Information** State-supported, coed, comprehensive institution. CGS member. *Enrollment:* 8,199 graduate, professional, and undergraduate students; 318 full-time matriculated graduate/professional students (240 women), 653 part-time matriculated graduate/professional students (517 women). *Enrollment by degree level:* 862 master's, 55 doctoral, 54 other advanced degrees. *Graduate faculty:* 99 full-time (64 women), 10 part-time/adjunct (6 women). *Tuition, area resident:* Full-time $9288; part-time $515 per credit. Tuition, state resident: full-time $9288. Tuition, nonresident: full-time $13,932; part-time $774 per credit. *Required fees:* $1688; $94 per credit. *Graduate housing:* Room and/or apartments available on a first-come, first-served basis to single students; on-campus housing not available to married students. Typical cost: $3990 per year. Housing application deadline: 5/1. *Student services:* Campus employment opportunities, campus safety program, career counseling, exercise/wellness program, free psychological counseling, international student services, low-cost health insurance, multicultural affairs office, services for students with disabilities. *Library facilities:* Rohrbach Library. *Collection:* Books: 313,503 (physical), 436,634 (digital/electronic); Serial titles: 892 (physical), 32,486 (digital/electronic); Databases: 145. Weekly public service hours: 96; students can reserve study rooms.

**Computer facilities:** Computer purchase and lease plans are available. 1,075 computers available on campus for general student use. A campuswide network can be accessed. Online class registration is available.
Website: http://www.kutztown.edu/

**General Application Contact:** Kelly Hish, Admissions Clerk, 610-683-4190, Fax: 610-683-1375, E-mail: graduate@kutztown.edu.

**GRADUATE UNITS**

**College of Business** Students: 16 full-time (7 women), 25 part-time (13 women); includes 3 minority (2 Black or African American, non-Hispanic/Latino; 1 Hispanic/Latino), 3 international. Average age 33. 40 applicants, 83% accepted, 13 enrolled. *Faculty:* 5 full-time (2 women). Expenses: Contact institution. *Financial support:* Career-related internships or fieldwork, Federal Work-Study, and unspecified assistantships available. Financial award application deadline: 3/1; financial award applicants required to submit FAFSA. In 2019, 6 master's awarded. *Program availability:* Part-time, evening/weekend, 100% online, blended/hybrid learning. *Application deadline:* For fall admission, 8/1 priority date for domestic and international students; for spring admission, 12/1 priority date for domestic and international students. Applications are processed on a rolling basis. *Application fee:* $35. Electronic applications accepted. *Application Contact:* Dr. Anne Carroll, Dean, 610-683-4575, Fax: 610-683-4573, E-mail: acarroll@kutztown.edu. *Dean*, Dr. Anne Carroll, 610-683-4575, Fax: 610-683-4573, E-mail: acarroll@kutztown.edu.

**College of Education** Students: 188 full-time (148 women), 431 part-time (355 women); includes 96 minority (27 Black or African American, non-Hispanic/Latino; 7 Asian, non-Hispanic/Latino; 43 Hispanic/Latino; 19 Two or more races, non-Hispanic/Latino), 3 international. Average age 31. 339 applicants, 81% accepted, 176 enrolled. *Faculty:* 36 full-time (28 women), 7 part-time/adjunct (4 women). Expenses: Contact institution. *Financial support:* Career-related internships or fieldwork, Federal Work-Study, and unspecified assistantships available. Financial award application deadline: 3/1; financial award applicants required to submit FAFSA. In 2019, 167 master's awarded. *Program availability:* Part-time, evening/weekend, 100% online, blended/hybrid learning. *Application deadline:* For fall admission, 8/1 for domestic and international students; for spring admission, 12/1 for domestic and international students. *Application fee:* $35. Electronic applications accepted. *Application Contact:* Dr. John Ward, Dean, 610-683-4253, Fax: 610-683-4255, E-mail: ward@kutztown.edu. *Dean*, Dr. John Ward, 610-683-4253, Fax: 610-683-4255, E-mail: ward@kutztown.edu.

**College of Liberal Arts and Sciences** Students: 92 full-time (67 women), 88 part-time (65 women); includes 48 minority (22 Black or African American, non-Hispanic/Latino; 2 Asian, non-Hispanic/Latino; 17 Hispanic/Latino; 1 Native Hawaiian or other Pacific Islander, non-Hispanic/Latino; 6 Two or more races, non-Hispanic/Latino), 2 international. Average age 30. 172 applicants, 83% accepted, 86 enrolled. *Faculty:* 40 full-time (21 women). Expenses: Contact institution. *Financial support:* Career-related internships or fieldwork, Federal Work-Study, and unspecified assistantships available. Financial award application deadline: 3/1; financial award applicants required to submit FAFSA. In 2019, 60 master's, 3 doctorates awarded. *Program availability:* Part-time, evening/weekend. *Application deadline:* For fall admission, 8/1 for domestic and international students; for spring admission, 12/1 for domestic and international students. *Application fee:* $35. Electronic applications accepted. *Application Contact:* Dr. David Beougher, Dean, 610-683-4305, Fax: 610-683-4633, E-mail: clas@kutztown.edu. *Dean*, Dr. David Beougher, 610-683-4305, Fax: 610-683-4633, E-mail: clas@kutztown.edu.

**College of Visual and Performing Arts** Students: 22 full-time (18 women), 109 part-time (84 women); includes 13 minority (2 Black or African American, non-Hispanic/Latino; 1 Asian, non-Hispanic/Latino; 6 Hispanic/Latino; 4 Two or more races, non-Hispanic/Latino). Average age 31. 76 applicants, 89% accepted, 44 enrolled. *Faculty:* 18 full-time (13 women), 3 part-time/adjunct (2 women). Expenses: Contact institution. *Financial support:* Career-related internships or fieldwork, Federal Work-Study, institutionally sponsored loans, and unspecified assistantships available. Financial award application deadline: 3/1; financial award applicants required to submit FAFSA. In 2019, 36 master's awarded. *Program availability:* Part-time. *Application deadline:* For fall admission, 8/1 for domestic and international students; for spring admission, 12/1 for domestic and international students. *Application fee:* $35. Electronic applications accepted. *Application Contact:* Dr. Michelle Kiec, Dean, 610-683-4500, Fax: 610-683-4547, E-mail: kiec@kutztown.edu. *Dean*, Dr. Michelle Kiec, 610-683-4500, Fax: 610-683-4547, E-mail: kiec@kutztown.edu.

## LAGRANGE COLLEGE, LaGrange, GA 30240-2999

**General Information** Independent-religious, coed, comprehensive institution. *Graduate housing:* Room and/or apartments available on a first-come, first-served basis to single students; on-campus housing not available to married students. Housing application deadline: 5/1.

**GRADUATE UNITS**

**Graduate Programs** *Program availability:* Part-time, evening/weekend. Electronic applications accepted.

**Program in Strength and Conditioning**

## LAGUNA COLLEGE OF ART & DESIGN, Laguna Beach, CA 92651-1136

**General Information** Independent, coed, comprehensive institution.

**GRADUATE UNITS**

**Graduate Program** Electronic applications accepted.

## LAKE ERIE COLLEGE, Painesville, OH 44077-3389

**General Information** Independent, coed, comprehensive institution. *Graduate housing:* On-campus housing not available.

**GRADUATE UNITS**

**School of Business** *Program availability:* Part-time, evening/weekend. Electronic applications accepted.

**School of Education and Professional Studies** *Program availability:* Part-time, evening/weekend. Electronic applications accepted.

## LAKE ERIE COLLEGE OF OSTEOPATHIC MEDICINE, Erie, PA 16509-1025

**General Information** Independent, coed, graduate-only institution. *Graduate housing:* On-campus housing not available. *Research affiliation:* West Virginia University (neurology), Neuro Structural Research Laboratories (neurology), Cornelli Consulting (CORCON) (neurology), University of Maryland (neurology), Duke University (neurology).

**GRADUATE UNITS**

**Professional Programs** Electronic applications accepted.

## LAKE FOREST COLLEGE, Lake Forest, IL 60045

**General Information** Independent, coed, comprehensive institution. *Enrollment:* 1,512 graduate, professional, and undergraduate students; 14 full-time matriculated graduate/professional students (10 women), 10 part-time matriculated graduate/professional students (6 women). *Enrollment by degree level:* 24 master's. *Graduate faculty:* 11 full-time (6 women), 9 part-time/adjunct (6 women). *Tuition:* Full-time $29,600; part-time $3200 per course. *Graduate housing:* On-campus housing not available. *Student services:* Campus safety program, career counseling, exercise/wellness program, grant writing training, multicultural affairs office, teacher training, writing training. *Library facilities:* Donnelley and Lee Library. *Collection:* Books: 199,540 (physical), 213,024 (digital/electronic); Serial titles: 86,824 (physical). Study areas open 24 hours, 5–7 days a week; students can reserve study rooms. *Research affiliation:* Argonne National Laboratory (physics), Merck & Company, Inc., Chicago History Museum (Chicago history), Lake Forest Hospital (genomes), The Art Institute of Chicago (Asian art), Newberry Library (medieval and Renaissance history, American West).

**Computer facilities:** Computer purchase and lease plans are available. 400 computers available on campus for general student use. A campuswide network can be accessed.

Online class registration, file storage are available.
Website: http://www.lakeforest.edu/

**General Application Contact:** Prof. Carol Gayle, Associate Director, Graduate Program in Liberal Studies, 847-735-5083, Fax: 847-735-6291, E-mail: gayle@lakeforest.edu.

**GRADUATE UNITS**

**Graduate Program in Liberal Studies** Students: 24 part-time (14 women). Average age 45. 10 applicants, 80% accepted, 3 enrolled. *Faculty:* 10 full-time (4 women). Expenses: Contact institution. *Financial support:* In 2019–20, 2 students received support. Partial tuition grants (for full-time teachers) available. In 2019, 5 master's awarded. *Program availability:* Part-time, evening/weekend. *Application deadline:* For fall admission, 8/15 priority date for domestic students, 7/15 priority date for international students; for spring admission, 12/15 priority date for domestic students, 11/15 priority date for international students. Applications are processed on a rolling basis. *Application fee:* $30. Electronic applications accepted. *Application Contact:* Prof. Carol Gayle, Associate Director, 847-735-5083, Fax: 847-735-6291, E-mail: gayle@lakeforest.edu. *Director,* Prof. D. L. LeMahieu, 847-735-5133, Fax: 847-735-6291, E-mail: lemahieu@lakeforest.edu.

**Master of Arts in Teaching Program**

## LAKE FOREST GRADUATE SCHOOL OF MANAGEMENT, Lake Forest, IL 60045

**General Information** Independent, coed, graduate-only institution. *Graduate housing:* On-campus housing not available.

**GRADUATE UNITS**

**The Immersion MBA Program (iMBA)** *Program availability:* Online learning.

**The Leadership MBA Program** *Program availability:* Part-time, evening/weekend. Electronic applications accepted.

## LAKEHEAD UNIVERSITY, Thunder Bay, ON P7B 5E1, Canada

**General Information** Province-supported, coed, comprehensive institution. *Graduate housing:* Rooms and/or apartments available to single students and available on a first-come, first-served basis to married students. Housing application deadline: 3/10. *Research affiliation:* Falcon Bridge (biology), Placer Dome (biology), Centre for Northern Forest Ecosystem Research (biology, forestry, tourism), Thunder Bay Regional Cancer Centre (psychosocial oncology), Bowater Inc. (chemistry, engineering).

**GRADUATE UNITS**

**Graduate Studies** *Program availability:* Part-time, evening/weekend.

***Faculty of Education*** *Program availability:* Part-time, evening/weekend.

***Faculty of Engineering*** *Program availability:* Part-time.

***Faculty of Natural Resources Management*** *Program availability:* Part-time.

***Faculty of Social Sciences and Humanities*** *Program availability:* Part-time, evening/weekend.

***School of Kinesiology*** *Program availability:* Part-time.

***School of Mathematical Sciences*** *Program availability:* Part-time, evening/weekend.

***School of Social Work*** *Program availability:* Part-time.

## LAKELAND UNIVERSITY, Plymouth, WI 53073

**General Information** Independent-religious, coed, comprehensive institution. *Enrollment:* 109 part-time matriculated graduate/professional students (68 women). *Enrollment by degree level:* 111 master's, 23 doctoral. *Graduate faculty:* 16 part-time/adjunct (1 woman). *Tuition:* Part-time $3232 per unit. *Graduate housing:* Room and/or apartments guaranteed to single students; on-campus housing not available to married students. Typical cost: $4636 per year. Room charges vary according to campus/location. Housing application deadline: 1/17. *Student services:* Campus employment opportunities, campus safety program, career counseling, child daycare facilities, writing training. *Library facilities:* Esch Memorial Library.

**Computer facilities:** Computer purchase and lease plans are available. 157 computers available on campus for general student use. A campuswide network can be accessed from student residence rooms and from off campus. Online class registration is available.
Website: http://www.lakeland.edu/

**General Application Contact:** Rebecca Hagan, Graduate Program Coordinator, 920-565-1256, Fax: 920-565-1206.

**GRADUATE UNITS**

**Graduate Studies Division** Students: 23,809 part-time (368 women); includes 341 minority (1 Black or African American, non-Hispanic/Latino; 340 Hispanic/Latino), 342 international. Average age 30. 283 applicants, 10% accepted. *Faculty:* 4,233 full-time (4,230 women), 1,449 part-time/adjunct (1,434 women). Expenses: Contact institution. *Financial support:* Fellowships, teaching assistantships, and Federal Work-Study available. Financial award applicants required to submit CSS PROFILE. In 2019, 23 master's awarded. *Application deadline:* Applications are processed on a rolling basis. *Application fee:* $25. Electronic applications accepted. *Application Contact:* Rebecca Hagan, Graduate Program Coordinator, 920-565-1256, Fax: 920-565-1206. *Head,* Suzanne Sellars, 920-565-1256.

## LAMAR UNIVERSITY, Beaumont, TX 77710

**General Information** State-supported, coed, university. CGS member. *Enrollment:* 15,460 graduate, professional, and undergraduate students; 613 full-time matriculated graduate/professional students (418 women), 5,069 part-time matriculated graduate/professional students (3,851 women). *Enrollment by degree level:* 5,128 master's, 348 doctoral, 206 other advanced degrees. *Graduate faculty:* 464 full-time (213 women), 133 part-time/adjunct (89 women). *International tuition:* $13,920 full-time. *Tuition, area resident:* Full-time $6324; part-time $351 per credit. Tuition, state resident: full-time $6324; part-time $351 per credit. Tuition, nonresident: full-time $13,920; part-time $773 per credit. *Required fees:* $2462; $327 per credit. Tuition and fees vary according to course load, campus/location and reciprocity agreements. *Graduate housing:* Rooms and/or apartments available on a first-come, first-served basis to single and married students. Typical cost: $5868 per year ($9158 including board) for single students. *Student services:* Campus employment opportunities, campus safety program, career counseling, exercise/wellness program, free psychological counseling, grant writing training, international student services, low-cost health insurance, multicultural affairs office, services for students with disabilities, teacher training, writing training. *Library facilities:* Mary and John Gray Library plus 1 other. *Collection:* Books: 410,300 (physical), 115,699 (digital/electronic); Serial titles: 29,473 (physical), 47,431 (digital/electronic); Databases: 140. Weekly public service hours: 90; students can reserve study rooms. *Research affiliation:* Grants Resource Center, National Council of Research Administrators, BASF.

**Computer facilities:** 1,104 computers available on campus for general student use. A campuswide network can be accessed. Online class registration is available.
Website: http://www.lamar.edu/

**General Application Contact:** Celeste Contreas, Director, Admissions and Recruitment, 409-880-7870, Fax: 409-880-8180, E-mail: gradadmissions@lamar.edu.

**GRADUATE UNITS**

**College of Graduate Studies** Students: 613 full-time (418 women), 5,069 part-time (3,851 women); includes 2,523 minority (1,201 Black or African American, non-Hispanic/Latino; 16 American Indian or Alaska Native, non-Hispanic/Latino; 129 Asian, non-Hispanic/Latino; 1,049 Hispanic/Latino; 4 Native Hawaiian or other Pacific Islander, non-Hispanic/Latino; 124 Two or more races, non-Hispanic/Latino), 281 international. Average age 36. 6,345 applicants, 79% accepted, 1,604 enrolled. *Faculty:* 161 full-time (80 women), 45 part-time/adjunct (35 women). Expenses: Contact institution. *Financial support:* In 2019–20, 459 students received support. Fellowships with partial tuition reimbursements available, research assistantships, teaching assistantships, career-related internships or fieldwork, Federal Work-Study, institutionally sponsored loans, scholarships/grants, and tuition waivers (partial) available. Support available to part-time students. Financial award applicants required to submit FAFSA. In 2019, 2,058 master's, 89 doctorates, 877 other advanced degrees awarded. *Program availability:* Part-time, evening/weekend. *Application deadline:* Applications are processed on a rolling basis. *Application fee:* $25 ($50 for international students). Electronic applications accepted. *Application Contact:* Celeste Contreras, Director, Admissions, 409-880-8888, Fax: 409-880-7419, E-mail: gradmissions@lamar.edu. *Dean,* Dr. William E. Harn, 409-880-8229, Fax: 409-880-1723, E-mail: lugradstudies@lamar.edu.

***College of Arts and Sciences*** Students: 117 full-time (61 women), 339 part-time (231 women); includes 185 minority (85 Black or African American, non-Hispanic/Latino; 2 American Indian or Alaska Native, non-Hispanic/Latino; 18 Asian, non-Hispanic/Latino; 70 Hispanic/Latino; 10 Two or more races, non-Hispanic/Latino), 86 international. Average age 33. 518 applicants, 79% accepted, 118 enrolled. *Faculty:* 205 full-time (97 women), 47 part-time/adjunct (32 women). Expenses: Contact institution. *Financial support:* In 2019–20, 95 students received support. Fellowships, research assistantships, teaching assistantships with tuition reimbursements available, career-related internships or fieldwork, Federal Work-Study, institutionally sponsored loans, scholarships/grants, and tuition waivers (partial) available. Support available to part-time students. Financial award applicants required to submit FAFSA. In 2019, 173 master's awarded. *Program availability:* Part-time, evening/weekend. *Application deadline:* Applications are processed on a rolling basis. *Application fee:* $25 ($50 for international students). Electronic applications accepted. *Application Contact:* Celeste Contreras, Director, Admissions, 409-880-8888, E-mail: gradmissions@lamar.edu. *Dean,* Dr. Lynn Maurer, 409-880-8508, Fax: 409-880-8007.

***College of Business*** Students: 23 full-time (15 women), 351 part-time (191 women); includes 158 minority (73 Black or African American, non-Hispanic/Latino; 1 American Indian or Alaska Native, non-Hispanic/Latino; 25 Asian, non-Hispanic/Latino; 44 Hispanic/Latino; 15 Two or more races, non-Hispanic/Latino), 32 international. Average age 34. 394 applicants, 81% accepted, 130 enrolled. *Faculty:* 47 full-time (14 women), 9 part-time/adjunct (5 women). Expenses: Contact institution. *Financial support:* In 2019–20, 43 students received support. Fellowships with tuition reimbursements available, research assistantships with partial tuition reimbursements available, career-related internships or fieldwork, Federal Work-Study, institutionally sponsored loans, scholarships/grants, and tuition waivers (partial) available. Support available to part-time students. Financial award applicants required to submit FAFSA. In 2019, 114 master's awarded. *Program availability:* Part-time, evening/weekend. *Application deadline:* Applications are processed on a rolling basis. *Application fee:* $25 ($50 for international students). Electronic applications accepted. *Application Contact:* Celeste Contreas, Director, Admissions and Academic Services, 409-880-8888, Fax: 409-880-7419, E-mail: gradmissions@lamar.edu. *Dean,* Dr. Dan French, 409-880-8603, Fax: 409-880-8088, E-mail: dan.french@lamar.edu.

***College of Education and Human Development*** Students: 250 full-time (224 women), 4,239 part-time (3,373 women); includes 2,094 minority (1,025 Black or African American, non-Hispanic/Latino; 12 American Indian or Alaska Native, non-Hispanic/Latino; 65 Asian, non-Hispanic/Latino; 893 Hispanic/Latino; 4 Native Hawaiian or other Pacific Islander, non-Hispanic/Latino; 95 Two or more races, non-Hispanic/Latino), 10 international. Average age 37. 4,881 applicants, 81% accepted, 1,253 enrolled. *Faculty:* 80 full-time (57 women), 43 part-time/adjunct (34 women). Expenses: Contact institution. *Financial support:* In 2019–20, 124 students received support. Fellowships, research assistantships, teaching assistantships, career-related internships or fieldwork, Federal Work-Study, institutionally sponsored loans, and scholarships/grants available. Support available to part-time students. Financial award applicants required to submit FAFSA. In 2019, 1,626 master's, 61 doctorates, 876 other advanced degrees awarded. *Program availability:* Part-time, evening/weekend, online learning. *Application deadline:* Applications are processed on a rolling basis. *Application fee:* $25 ($50 for international students). Electronic applications accepted. *Application Contact:* Celeste Contreas, Director, Admissions and Academic Services, 409-880-8888, Fax: 409-880-7419, E-mail: gradmissions@lamar.edu. *Dean,* Dr. Robert Spina, 409-880-8661.

***College of Engineering*** Students: 108 full-time (14 women), 91 part-time (21 women); includes 32 minority (3 Black or African American, non-Hispanic/Latino; 1 American Indian or Alaska Native, non-Hispanic/Latino; 13 Asian, non-Hispanic/Latino; 13 Hispanic/Latino; 2 Two or more races, non-Hispanic/Latino), 144 international. Average age 29. 288 applicants, 82% accepted, 47 enrolled. *Faculty:* 50 full-time (7 women), 4 part-time/adjunct (1 woman). Expenses: Contact institution. *Financial support:* In 2019–20, 14 students received support. Fellowships with partial tuition reimbursements available, research assistantships with partial tuition reimbursements available, teaching assistantships with partial tuition reimbursements available, career-related internships or fieldwork, Federal Work-Study, institutionally sponsored loans, scholarships/grants, tuition waivers (full and partial), and laboratory assistantships available. Support available to part-time students. Financial award applicants required to submit FAFSA. In 2019, 107 master's, 15 doctorates awarded. *Program availability:* Part-time, evening/weekend. *Application deadline:* Applications are processed on a rolling basis. *Application fee:* $25 ($50 for international students). Electronic applications accepted. *Application Contact:* Celeste Contreas, Director, Admissions and Academic Services, 409-880-8888, Fax: 409-880-7419, E-mail: gradmissions@lamar.edu. *Dean,* Dr. Brian Craig, 409-880-8784, Fax: 409-880-2197.

***College of Fine Arts and Communication*** Students: 115 full-time (104 women), 49 part-time (35 women); includes 54 minority (15 Black or African American, non-Hispanic/Latino; 8 Asian, non-Hispanic/Latino; 29 Hispanic/Latino; 2 Two or more races, non-Hispanic/Latino), 9 international. Average age 28. 264 applicants, 33% accepted, 56 enrolled. *Faculty:* 78 full-time (36 women), 30 part-time/adjunct (17 women). Expenses: Contact institution. *Financial support:* In 2019–20, 129 students received support. Fellowships, research assistantships, teaching assistantships, career-related internships or fieldwork, Federal Work-Study, institutionally sponsored loans, and tuition waivers (partial) available. Support available to part-time students. Financial award applicants required to submit FAFSA. In 2019, 38 master's, 13 doctorates awarded. *Program availability:* Part-time, evening/weekend. *Application deadline:* Applications are processed on a rolling basis. *Application fee:* $25 ($50 for international students). Electronic applications accepted. *Application Contact:* Celeste Contreas, Director, Admissions and Academic Services, 409-880-8888, Fax: 409-880-7419, E-mail: gradmissions@lamar.edu. *Dean,* Dr. Derina Holtzhausen, 409-880-8137, Fax: 409-880-2286.

## LANCASTER BIBLE COLLEGE, Lancaster, PA 17601

**General Information** Independent-religious, coed, comprehensive institution. *Enrollment:* 2,122 graduate, professional, and undergraduate students; 255 full-time matriculated graduate/professional students (99 women), 119 part-time matriculated graduate/professional students (58 women). *Enrollment by degree level:* 313 master's, 61 doctoral. *Graduate faculty:* 8 full-time (1 woman), 5 part-time/adjunct (1 woman). *Graduate housing:* On-campus housing not available. *Student services:* Campus employment opportunities, career counseling, international student services. *Library facilities:* Lancaster Bible College Library.

**Computer facilities:** 50 computers available on campus for general student use. A campuswide network can be accessed from student residence rooms.
Website: http://www.lbc.edu/

**General Application Contact:** Steve Bowers, Recruitment and Admissions Counselor, 717-560-8297, Fax: 717-560-8236, E-mail: sbowers@lbc.edu.

**GRADUATE UNITS**

**Capital Bible Seminary** *Program availability:* Part-time, evening/weekend.

**Graduate School** *Program availability:* Part-time, evening/weekend.

## LANCASTER THEOLOGICAL SEMINARY, Lancaster, PA 17603-2812

**General Information** Independent-religious, coed, graduate-only institution. *Graduate housing:* Rooms and/or apartments available on a first-come, first-served basis to single and married students. Housing application deadline: 8/1.

**GRADUATE UNITS**

**Graduate and Professional Programs**

## LANDER UNIVERSITY, Greenwood, SC 29649-2099

**General Information** State-supported, coed, comprehensive institution. *Graduate housing:* Room and/or apartments available on a first-come, first-served basis to single students; on-campus housing not available to married students.

**GRADUATE UNITS**

**Graduate Studies** *Program availability:* Part-time, online learning. Electronic applications accepted.

## LANGSTON UNIVERSITY, Langston, OK 73050

**General Information** State-supported, coed, comprehensive institution. CGS member. *Graduate housing:* Rooms and/or apartments available on a first-come, first-served basis to single and married students.

**GRADUATE UNITS**

**School of Education and Behavioral Sciences** *Program availability:* Part-time.

**School of Physical Therapy**

## LA ROCHE UNIVERSITY, Pittsburgh, PA 15237-5898

**General Information** Independent-religious, coed, comprehensive institution. *Enrollment:* 1,401 graduate, professional, and undergraduate students; 75 full-time matriculated graduate/professional students (48 women), 85 part-time matriculated graduate/professional students (60 women). *Enrollment by degree level:* 153 master's, 1 doctoral, 6 other advanced degrees. *Graduate faculty:* 10 full-time (all women), 18 part-time/adjunct (10 women). *Tuition:* Full-time $20,520; part-time $760 per credit hour. *Required fees:* $80; $40 per semester. *Graduate housing:* On-campus housing not available. *Student services:* Campus employment opportunities, career counseling, free psychological counseling, international student services, low-cost health insurance, multicultural affairs office, services for students with disabilities. *Library facilities:* John J. Wright Library plus 1 other. *Collection:* Books: 80,000 (physical), 276,600 (digital/electronic); Serial titles: 770 (physical), 28 (digital/electronic); Databases: 55.

**Computer facilities:** Computer purchase and lease plans are available. 200 computers available on campus for general student use. A campuswide network can be accessed. Online class registration is available.
Website: http://www.laroche.edu/

**General Application Contact:** Erin Pottgen, Assistant Director, Graduate Admissions, 412-847-2509, Fax: 412-536-1283, E-mail: erin.pottgen@laroche.edu.

**GRADUATE UNITS**

**Doctoral Program of Nurse Anesthesia Practice** Students: 1 (woman) full-time. Average age 36. 1 applicant, 100% accepted, 1 enrolled. *Faculty:* 1 (woman) full-time, 1 (woman) part-time/adjunct. Expenses: Contact institution. *Application Contact:* Erin Pottgen, Assistant Director, Graduate Admissions, 412-847-2509, Fax: 412-536-1283, E-mail: erin.pottgen@laroche.edu. *Associate Vice President for Academic Affairs and Dean of Graduate Studies & Adult Education,* Dr. Rosemary McCarthy, PhD, 412-536-1173, E-mail: rosemary.mccarthy@laroche.edu.

**Program in Education** Students: 3 part-time (all women). Average age 40. 2 applicants, 100% accepted, 1 enrolled. *Faculty:* 1 (woman) full-time, 1 part-time/adjunct. Expenses: Contact institution. *Program availability:* Part-time. *Application Contact:* Erin Pottgen, Assistant Director, Graduate Admissions, 412-847-2509, Fax: 412-536-1283, E-mail: erin.pottgen@laroche.edu. *Professor, Education Department Chair,* Dr. Kathryn Silvis, 412-536-1297, E-mail: kathryn.silvis@laroche.edu.

**Program in Information Systems** Students: 8 full-time (4 women), 13 part-time (6 women), 15 international. Average age 30. 68 applicants, 74% accepted, 7 enrolled. *Faculty:* 2 full-time (both women), 2 part-time/adjunct (0 women). Expenses: Contact institution. *Program availability:* Part-time, evening/weekend. *Application Contact:* Erin Pottgen, Assistant Director, Graduate Admissions, 412-847-2509, Fax: 412-536-1283, E-mail: erin.pottgen@laroche.edu. *Assistant Professor, Information Systems Graduate Program Chair,* Dr. Cristina Bahm, Ph.D., 412-536-1192, E-mail: cristina.bahm@laroche.edu.

**School of Graduate Studies and Adult Education** Students: 75 full-time (48 women), 85 part-time (60 women); includes 10 minority (3 Black or African American, non-Hispanic/Latino; 3 Asian, non-Hispanic/Latino; 3 Hispanic/Latino; 1 Native Hawaiian or other Pacific Islander, non-Hispanic/Latino), 37 international. Average age 31. 198 applicants, 74% accepted, 53 enrolled. *Faculty:* 10 full-time (all women), 19 part-time/adjunct (11 women). Expenses: Contact institution. *Financial support:* Unspecified assistantships available. Financial award application deadline: 3/31; financial award applicants required to submit FAFSA. In 2019, 54 master's, 2 doctorates awarded. *Program availability:* Part-time, evening/weekend, 100% online. *Application deadline:* For fall admission, 8/15 for domestic and international students; for spring admission, 12/15 for domestic and international students. Applications are processed on a rolling basis. *Application fee:* $50. Electronic applications accepted. *Application Contact:* Erin Pottgen, Assistant Director, Graduate Admissions, 412-847-2509, Fax: 412-536-1283, E-mail: erin.pottgen@laroche.edu. *Dean,* Dr. Rosemary McCarthy, 412-536-1193, Fax: 412-536-1763, E-mail: rosemary.mccarthy@laroche.edu.

## LA SALLE UNIVERSITY, Philadelphia, PA 19141-1199

**General Information** Independent-religious, coed, comprehensive institution. CGS member. *Enrollment:* 240 full-time matriculated graduate/professional students (183 women), 1,028 part-time matriculated graduate/professional students (674 women). *Enrollment by degree level:* 1,064 master's, 204 doctoral. *Graduate faculty:* 26 full-time (15 women), 87 part-time/adjunct (56 women). *Tuition:* Full-time $25,060. *Required fees:* $570. *Graduate housing:* Room and/or apartments available on a first-come, first-served basis to single students; on-campus housing not available to married students. *Student services:* Campus employment opportunities, campus safety program, career counseling, exercise/wellness program, free psychological counseling, international student services, multicultural affairs office, services for students with disabilities, teacher training, writing training. *Library facilities:* Connelly Library. *Collection:* Books: 314,203 (physical), 819,865 (digital/electronic); Serial titles: 2,982 (physical), 139,962 (digital/electronic); Databases: 88. Weekly public service hours: 96; students can reserve study rooms.

**Computer facilities:** 1,100 computers available on campus for general student use. A campuswide network can be accessed from student residence rooms and from off campus. Online class registration, course management system are available.
Website: http://www.lasalle.edu/

**General Application Contact:** Dr. LeeAnn Cardaciotto, Interim Chair, Graduate Advisory Committee, 215-951-1270, E-mail: cardaciotto@lasalle.edu.

**GRADUATE UNITS**

**School of Arts and Sciences** *Program availability:* Part-time, evening/weekend, 100% online, blended/hybrid learning. Electronic applications accepted.

***Hispanic Institute*** *Program availability:* Part-time, evening/weekend. Electronic applications accepted.

**School of Business** *Program availability:* Part-time, evening/weekend, 100% online, blended/hybrid learning. Electronic applications accepted.

**School of Nursing and Health Sciences** *Program availability:* Part-time, evening/weekend. Electronic applications accepted.

## LASELL COLLEGE, Newton, MA 02466-2709

**General Information** Independent, coed, comprehensive institution. *Enrollment:* 2,090 graduate, professional, and undergraduate students; 159 full-time matriculated graduate/professional students (86 women), 292 part-time matriculated graduate/professional students (167 women). *Enrollment by degree level:* 446 master's, 5 other advanced degrees. *Graduate faculty:* 25 full-time (13 women), 42 part-time/adjunct (24 women). *Tuition:* Part-time $600 per credit. *Required fees:* $40 per semester. *Graduate housing:* Room and/or apartments available on a first-come, first-served basis to single students; on-campus housing not available to married students. Typical cost: $9450 (including board). Room and board charges vary according to housing facility selected. Housing application deadline: 8/15. *Student services:* Campus employment opportunities, career counseling, exercise/wellness program, international student services, multicultural affairs office, services for students with disabilities. *Library facilities:* Brennan Library. *Collection:* Books: 34,031 (physical), 70,716 (digital/electronic); Serial titles: 60 (physical), 83,985 (digital/electronic); Databases: 107. Weekly public service hours: 83; students can reserve study rooms. *Research affiliation:* Lasell Village (education).

**Computer facilities:** Computer purchase and lease plans are available. 219 computers available on campus for general student use. A campuswide network can be accessed. Online class registration, online tutoring are available.
Website: http://www.lasell.edu/

**General Application Contact:** Adrienne Franciosi, Assistant Vice President of Graduate and Professional Studies, 617-243-2400, Fax: 617-243-2450, E-mail: gradinfo@lasell.edu.

**GRADUATE UNITS**

**Graduate and Professional Studies in Athletic Training**

**Graduate and Professional Studies in Communication** Students: 25 full-time (18 women), 34 part-time (27 women); includes 10 minority (7 Black or African American, non-Hispanic/Latino; 3 Hispanic/Latino), 15 international. Average age 31. 40 applicants, 48% accepted, 14 enrolled. *Faculty:* 3 full-time (2 women), 10 part-time/adjunct (4 women). Expenses: Contact institution. *Financial support:* Federal Work-Study, scholarships/grants, and tuition discounts available. Support available to part-time students. Financial award application deadline: 8/31; financial award applicants required to submit FAFSA. In 2019, 34 master's, 2 other advanced degrees awarded. *Program availability:* Part-time, evening/weekend, 100% online, blended/hybrid learning. *Application deadline:* For fall admission, 8/31 priority date for domestic students, 6/30 priority date for international students; for spring admission, 12/31 priority date for domestic students, 10/31 priority date for international students. Applications are processed on a rolling basis. Electronic applications accepted. *Application Contact:* Adrienne Franciosi, Assistant Vice President of Graduate and Professional Studies, 617-243-2214, Fax: 617-243-2450, E-mail: gradinfo@lasell.edu. *Vice President of Graduate and Professional Studies,* Chrystal Porter, 617-243-2083, Fax: 617-243-2450, E-mail: gradinfo@lasell.edu.

**Graduate and Professional Studies in Criminal Justice** Students: 28 full-time (5 women), 71 part-time (21 women); includes 27 minority (9 Black or African American, non-Hispanic/Latino; 2 Asian, non-Hispanic/Latino; 13 Hispanic/Latino; 3 Two or more races, non-Hispanic/Latino). Average age 33. 38 applicants, 63% accepted, 17 enrolled. *Faculty:* 6 full-time (3 women), 1 part-time/adjunct (0 women). Expenses: Contact institution. *Financial support:* Federal Work-Study, scholarships/grants, and tuition discounts available. Support available to part-time students. Financial award application deadline: 8/31; financial award applicants required to submit FAFSA. In 2019, 33 master's awarded. *Program availability:* Part-time, evening/weekend, online only, 100% online. *Application deadline:* For fall admission, 8/31 priority date for domestic students, 6/30 priority date for international students; for spring admission, 12/31 priority date for domestic students, 10/31 priority date for international students. Applications are processed on a rolling basis. Electronic applications accepted. *Application Contact:*

Adrienne Franciosi, Assistant Vice President of Graduate and Professional Studies, 617-243-2214, Fax: 617-243-2450, E-mail: gradinfo@lasell.edu. *Vice President of Graduate and Professional Studies*, Chrystal Porter, 617-243-2083, Fax: 617-243-2450, E-mail: gradinfo@lasell.edu.

**Graduate and Professional Studies in Education** Students: 13 full-time (all women), 36 part-time (29 women); includes 3 minority (2 Black or African American, non-Hispanic/Latino; 1 Two or more races, non-Hispanic/Latino). Average age 28. 18 applicants, 72% accepted, 10 enrolled. *Faculty:* 5 full-time (4 women), 12 part-time/adjunct (10 women). Expenses: Contact institution. *Financial support:* Federal Work-Study, scholarships/grants, and tuition discounts available. Support available to part-time students. Financial award application deadline: 8/31; financial award applicants required to submit FAFSA. In 2019, 22 master's awarded. *Program availability:* Part-time-only, evening/weekend, blended/hybrid learning. *Application deadline:* For fall admission, 8/31 priority date for domestic students, 6/30 priority date for international students; for spring admission, 12/31 priority date for domestic students, 10/31 priority date for international students. Applications are processed on a rolling basis. Electronic applications accepted. *Application Contact:* Adrienne Franciosi, Assistant Vice President of Graduate and Professional Studies, 617-243-2214, Fax: 617-243-2450, E-mail: gradinfo@lasell.edu. *Vice President of Graduate and Professional Studies*, Chrystal Porter, 617-243-2083, Fax: 617-243-2450, E-mail: gradinfo@lasell.edu.

**Graduate and Professional Studies in Management** Students: 58 full-time (33 women), 84 part-time (54 women); includes 29 minority (15 Black or African American, non-Hispanic/Latino; 2 Asian, non-Hispanic/Latino; 9 Hispanic/Latino; 3 Two or more races, non-Hispanic/Latino), 21 international. Average age 30. 141 applicants, 40% accepted, 34 enrolled. *Faculty:* 3 full-time (1 woman), 14 part-time/adjunct (7 women). Expenses: Contact institution. *Financial support:* Federal Work-Study, scholarships/grants, and tuition discounts available. Support available to part-time students. Financial award application deadline: 8/31; financial award applicants required to submit FAFSA. In 2019, 73 master's, 1 other advanced degree awarded. *Program availability:* Part-time, evening/weekend, 100% online, blended/hybrid learning. *Application deadline:* For fall admission, 8/31 priority date for domestic students, 6/30 priority date for international students; for spring admission, 12/31 priority date for domestic students, 10/31 priority date for international students. Applications are processed on a rolling basis. Electronic applications accepted. *Application Contact:* Adrienne Franciosi, Assistant Vice President of Graduate and Professional Studies, 617-243-2214, Fax: 617-243-2450, E-mail: gradinfo@lasell.edu. *Vice President of Graduate and Professional Studies*, Chrystal Porter, 617-243-2083, Fax: 617-243-2450, E-mail: gradinfo@lasell.edu.

**Graduate and Professional Studies in Nutrition for Human Performance**

**Graduate and Professional Studies in Rehabilitation Science** Students: 15 full-time (10 women), 12 part-time (10 women); includes 5 minority (3 Black or African American, non-Hispanic/Latino; 2 Hispanic/Latino), 1 international. Average age 28. 22 applicants, 41% accepted, 5 enrolled. *Faculty:* 3 full-time (1 woman), 3 part-time/adjunct (2 women). Expenses: Contact institution. *Financial support:* Federal Work-Study, scholarships/grants, and tuition discounts available. Support available to part-time students. Financial award application deadline: 8/31; financial award applicants required to submit FAFSA. In 2019, 6 master's awarded. *Program availability:* Part-time, evening/weekend, online only, 100% online. *Application deadline:* For fall admission, 8/31 priority date for domestic students, 6/30 priority date for international students; for spring admission, 12/31 priority date for domestic students, 10/31 priority date for international students. Applications are processed on a rolling basis. Electronic applications accepted. *Application Contact:* Adrienne Franciosi, Assistant Vice President of Graduate and Professional Studies, 617-243-2214, Fax: 617-243-2450, E-mail: gradinfo@lasell.edu. *Vice President of Graduate and Professional Studies*, Chrystal Porter, 617-243-2083, Fax: 617-243-2450, E-mail: gradinfo@lasell.edu.

**Graduate and Professional Studies in Sport Management** Students: 12 full-time (1 woman), 41 part-time (14 women); includes 15 minority (8 Black or African American, non-Hispanic/Latino; 4 Hispanic/Latino; 3 Two or more races, non-Hispanic/Latino). Average age 30. 33 applicants, 64% accepted, 14 enrolled. *Faculty:* 5 full-time (1 woman), 1 part-time/adjunct (0 women). Expenses: Contact institution. *Financial support:* Federal Work-Study, scholarships/grants, and tuition discounts available. Support available to part-time students. Financial award application deadline: 8/31; financial award applicants required to submit FAFSA. In 2019, 22 master's awarded. *Program availability:* Part-time, evening/weekend, online only, 100% online. *Application deadline:* For fall admission, 8/31 priority date for domestic students, 6/30 priority date for international students; for spring admission, 12/31 priority date for domestic students, 10/31 priority date for international students. Applications are processed on a rolling basis. Electronic applications accepted. *Application Contact:* Adrienne Franciosi, Assistant Vice President of Graduate and Professional Studies, 617-243-2214, Fax: 617-243-2450, E-mail: gradinfo@lasell.edu. *Vice President of Graduate and Professional Studies*, Chrystal Porter, 617-243-2083, Fax: 617-243-2450, E-mail: gradinfo@lasell.edu.

## LA SIERRA UNIVERSITY, Riverside, CA 92505

**General Information** Independent-religious, coed, comprehensive institution. CGS member. *Graduate housing:* Rooms and/or apartments available on a first-come, first-served basis to single students and available to married students.

**GRADUATE UNITS**

**College of Arts and Sciences** *Program availability:* Part-time.

**School of Business and Management**

**School of Education** *Program availability:* Part-time, evening/weekend.

**School of Religion** *Program availability:* Part-time.

## LAURENTIAN UNIVERSITY, Sudbury, ON P3E 2C6, Canada

**General Information** Province-supported, coed, comprehensive institution. *Graduate housing:* Rooms and/or apartments available on a first-come, first-served basis to single and married students.

**GRADUATE UNITS**

**School of Graduate Studies and Research** *Program availability:* Part-time, evening/weekend.

***School of Commerce and Administration*** *Program availability:* Part-time, evening/weekend.

***School of Engineering*** *Program availability:* Part-time.

***School of Social Work*** *Program availability:* Part-time.

## LAWRENCE TECHNOLOGICAL UNIVERSITY, Southfield, MI 48075-1058

**General Information** Independent, coed, university. *Enrollment:* 2,848 graduate, professional, and undergraduate students; 26 full-time matriculated graduate/professional students (10 women), 686 part-time matriculated graduate/professional students (231 women). *Enrollment by degree level:* 684 master's, 16 doctoral, 12 other advanced degrees. *Graduate faculty:* 46 full-time (8 women), 41 part-time/adjunct (9 women). *Tuition:* Full-time $16,618; part-time $8309 per year. *Required fees:* $600; $600. *Graduate housing:* Rooms and/or apartments available on a first-come, first-served basis to single and married students. Typical cost: $9060 per year ($12,340 including board) for single students; $9060 per year ($12,340 including board) for married students. Housing application deadline: 5/1. *Student services:* Campus employment opportunities, campus safety program, career counseling, exercise/wellness program, free psychological counseling, international student services, low-cost health insurance, multicultural affairs office, services for students with disabilities, writing training. *Library facilities:* Lawrence Technological University Library plus 1 other. *Collection:* Books: 119,278 (physical), 597,667 (digital/electronic); Serial titles: 85,850 (digital/electronic); Databases: 171. Weekly public service hours: 73; students can reserve study rooms. *Research affiliation:* Ford Motor Company (engineering), Clinton River Watershed Council (storm water analysis), Detroit Economic Growth Association (Great Lakes Shoreline Cities Green Infrastructure Project), Hyundai-KIA America Technical Center, Inc. (improvement of built-in hands-free cell phone performance), Johnson Controls Battery Group, Inc. (vehicle system power management testing), Meijer Foundation (engineering).

**Computer facilities:** Computer purchase and lease plans are available. 52 computers available on campus for general student use. A campuswide network can be accessed. Online class registration, degree audit, Canvas/Blackboard, Banner (student information), personal websites, document collection, Handshake, Placement, Mapworks advising are available.
Website: http://www.ltu.edu/

**General Application Contact:** Jane Rohrback, Director of Admissions, 248-204-3160, Fax: 248-204-2228, E-mail: admissions@ltu.edu.

**GRADUATE UNITS**

**College of Architecture and Design** Students: 6 full-time (3 women), 149 part-time (70 women); includes 18 minority (7 Black or African American, non-Hispanic/Latino; 3 Asian, non-Hispanic/Latino; 6 Hispanic/Latino; 2 Two or more races, non-Hispanic/Latino), 21 international. Average age 30. 214 applicants, 84% accepted, 94 enrolled. *Faculty:* 10 full-time (1 woman), 7 part-time/adjunct (4 women). Expenses: Contact institution. *Financial support:* In 2019–20, 39 students received support, including 8 research assistantships with partial tuition reimbursements available (averaging $6,000 per year); career-related internships or fieldwork, scholarships/grants, and unspecified assistantships also available. Financial award application deadline: 4/1; financial award applicants required to submit FAFSA. In 2019, 54 master's awarded. *Program availability:* Part-time, evening/weekend. *Application deadline:* For fall admission, 5/24 for international students; for spring admission, 10/13 for international students; for summer admission, 2/18 for international students. Applications are processed on a rolling basis. *Application fee:* $50. Electronic applications accepted. *Application Contact:* Jane Rohrback, Director of Admissions, 248-204-3160, Fax: 248-204-2228, E-mail: admissions@ltu.edu. *Dean/Professor*, Prof. Karl Daubmann, 248-204-2805, E-mail: archdean@ltu.edu.

**College of Arts and Sciences** Students: 1 (woman) full-time, 25 part-time (15 women); includes 6 minority (3 Black or African American, non-Hispanic/Latino; 2 Asian, non-Hispanic/Latino; 1 Hispanic/Latino), 6 international. Average age 34. 50 applicants, 68% accepted, 3 enrolled. *Faculty:* 5 full-time (2 women), 2 part-time/adjunct (1 woman). Expenses: Contact institution. *Financial support:* In 2019–20, 4 students received support. Scholarships/grants and tuition reduction available. Financial award application deadline: 4/1; financial award applicants required to submit FAFSA. In 2019, 14 master's, 4 other advanced degrees awarded. *Program availability:* Part-time, evening/weekend. *Application deadline:* For fall admission, 5/24 for international students; for spring admission, 10/13 for international students; for summer admission, 2/18 for international students. Applications are processed on a rolling basis. *Application fee:* $50. Electronic applications accepted. *Application Contact:* Jane Rohrback, Director of Admissions, 248-204-3160, Fax: 248-204-2228, E-mail: admissions@ltu.edu. *Interim Dean*, Glen Bauer, 248-204-3532, Fax: 248-204-3518, E-mail: scidean@ltu.edu.

**College of Engineering** Students: 14 full-time (5 women), 286 part-time (54 women); includes 26 minority (13 Black or African American, non-Hispanic/Latino; 8 Asian, non-Hispanic/Latino; 3 Hispanic/Latino; 2 Two or more races, non-Hispanic/Latino), 150 international. Average age 29. 384 applicants, 58% accepted, 74 enrolled. *Faculty:* 23 full-time (2 women), 20 part-time/adjunct (1 woman). Expenses: Contact institution. *Financial support:* In 2019–20, 21 students received support. Unspecified assistantships available. Financial award application deadline: 4/1; financial award applicants required to submit FAFSA. In 2019, 223 master's, 7 doctorates awarded. *Program availability:* Part-time, evening/weekend. *Application deadline:* For fall admission, 5/24 for international students; for spring admission, 10/13 for international students; for summer admission, 2/18 for international students. Applications are processed on a rolling basis. *Application fee:* $50. Electronic applications accepted. *Application Contact:* Jane Rohrback, Director of Admissions, 248-204-3160, Fax: 248-204-2228, E-mail: admissions@ltu.edu. *Dean*, Dr. Nabil Grace, 248-204-2500, Fax: 248-204-2509, E-mail: engrdean@ltu.edu.

**College of Management** Students: 5 full-time (1 woman), 226 part-time (92 women); includes 51 minority (28 Black or African American, non-Hispanic/Latino; 1 American Indian or Alaska Native, non-Hispanic/Latino; 11 Asian, non-Hispanic/Latino; 6 Hispanic/Latino; 1 Native Hawaiian or other Pacific Islander, non-Hispanic/Latino; 4 Two or more races, non-Hispanic/Latino), 45 international. Average age 33. 123 applicants, 58% accepted, 49 enrolled. *Faculty:* 9 full-time (3 women), 12 part-time/adjunct (3 women). Expenses: Contact institution. *Financial support:* In 2019–20, 25 students received support, including 8 research assistantships with partial tuition reimbursements available (averaging $3,360 per year); career-related internships or fieldwork, unspecified assistantships, and corporate tuition incentives also available. Financial award application deadline: 4/1; financial award applicants required to submit FAFSA. In 2019, 96 master's, 3 doctorates, 9 other advanced degrees awarded. *Program availability:* Part-time, evening/weekend, 100% online. *Application deadline:* For fall admission, 5/24 for international students; for spring admission, 10/13 for international students; for summer admission, 2/18 for international students. Applications are processed on a rolling basis. *Application fee:* $50. Electronic applications accepted. *Application Contact:* Jane Rohrback, Director of Admissions, 248-204-3160, Fax: 248-204-2228, E-mail: admissions@ltu.edu. *Dean*, Dr. Bahman Mirshab, 248-204-3050, E-mail: mgtdean@ltu.edu.

## LEBANESE AMERICAN UNIVERSITY, Beirut, Lebanon

**General Information** Private, coed, comprehensive institution.

**GRADUATE UNITS**

**School of Arts and Sciences**

**School of Business**

**School of Pharmacy**

## LEBANON VALLEY COLLEGE, Annville, PA 17003-1400

**General Information** Independent-religious, coed, comprehensive institution. *Graduate housing:* Room and/or apartments available on a first-come, first-served basis to single students; on-campus housing not available to married students. Housing application deadline: 3/3.

**GRADUATE UNITS**

**Program in Athletic Training** Electronic applications accepted.

**Program in Business Administration** *Program availability:* Part-time, evening/weekend. Electronic applications accepted.

**Program in Music Education** *Program availability:* Part-time-only, evening/weekend. Electronic applications accepted.

**Program in Physical Therapy** Electronic applications accepted.

**Program in Science Education** *Program availability:* Part-time-only, evening/weekend, 100% online, blended/hybrid learning. Electronic applications accepted.

**Program in Speech-Language Pathology**

## LEE UNIVERSITY, Cleveland, TN 37320-3450

**General Information** Independent-religious, coed, comprehensive institution. *Enrollment:* 5,189 graduate, professional, and undergraduate students; 176 full-time matriculated graduate/professional students (116 women), 284 part-time matriculated graduate/professional students (139 women). *Enrollment by degree level:* 447 master's, 13 doctoral. *Graduate faculty:* 60 full-time (22 women), 29 part-time/adjunct (11 women). *Tuition:* Full-time $13,590; part-time $755 per credit hour. *Required fees:* $25. Tuition and fees vary according to program. *Graduate housing:* Rooms and/or apartments available on a first-come, first-served basis to single and married students. Typical cost: $4575 per year ($8325 including board) for single students; $7320 per year ($3450 including board) for married students. Room and board charges vary according to board plan and housing facility selected. Housing application deadline: 9/1. *Student services:* Campus employment opportunities, campus safety program, career counseling, exercise/wellness program, free psychological counseling, international student services, services for students with disabilities, teacher training, writing training. *Library facilities:* William G. Squires Library plus 2 others. *Collection:* Books: 149,928 (physical), 439,290 (digital/electronic); Serial titles: 244 (physical), 97,212 (digital/electronic); Databases: 136. Weekly public service hours: 93; students can reserve study rooms.

**Computer facilities:** 460 computers available on campus for general student use. A campuswide network can be accessed from student residence rooms and from off campus. Online class registration is available.
Website: http://www.leeuniversity.edu/

**General Application Contact:** Jeffery McGirt, Director of Graduate Enrollment, 423-614-8691, Fax: 423-614-8317, E-mail: jmcgirt@leeuniversity.edu.

**GRADUATE UNITS**

**Graduate Studies in Counseling** Students: 80 full-time (65 women), 31 part-time (24 women); includes 20 minority (6 Black or African American, non-Hispanic/Latino; 10 Hispanic/Latino; 4 Two or more races, non-Hispanic/Latino), 4 international. Average age 29. 60 applicants, 77% accepted, 36 enrolled. *Faculty:* 7 full-time (4 women), 3 part-time/adjunct (1 woman). Expenses: Contact institution. *Financial support:* In 2019–20, 48 students received support. Career-related internships or fieldwork, Federal Work-Study, institutionally sponsored loans, scholarships/grants, and unspecified assistantships available. Financial award application deadline: 3/1; financial award applicants required to submit FAFSA. In 2019, 47 master's awarded. *Program availability:* Part-time, 100% online. *Application deadline:* For fall admission, 4/1 priority date for domestic and international students; for spring admission, 11/1 priority date for domestic and international students. Applications are processed on a rolling basis. *Application fee:* $25. Electronic applications accepted. *Application Contact:* Jeffery McGirt, Director of Graduate Enrollment, 423-614-8691, Fax: 423-614-8317, E-mail: jmcgirt@leeuniversity.edu. *Director,* Dr. Heather Quagliana, 423-614-8359, Fax: 423-614-8124, E-mail: heatherlewis@leeuniversity.edu.

**MBA Program** Students: 12 full-time (4 women), 68 part-time (32 women); includes 10 minority (3 Black or African American, non-Hispanic/Latino; 2 Asian, non-Hispanic/Latino; 2 Hispanic/Latino; 3 Two or more races, non-Hispanic/Latino), 8 international. Average age 28. 43 applicants, 91% accepted, 33 enrolled. *Faculty:* 4 full-time (1 woman). Expenses: Contact institution. *Financial support:* In 2019–20, 39 students received support. Scholarships/grants available. Financial award application deadline: 3/1; financial award applicants required to submit FAFSA. In 2019, 27 master's awarded. *Program availability:* Part-time, evening/weekend, 100% online. *Application deadline:* For fall admission, 4/1 priority date for domestic and international students; for spring admission, 10/1 priority date for domestic and international students. Applications are processed on a rolling basis. *Application fee:* $25. Electronic applications accepted. *Application Contact:* Jeffery McGirt, Director of Graduate Enrollment, 423-614-8691, Fax: 423-614-8317, E-mail: jmcgirt@leeuniversity.edu. *Director,* Dr. Shane Griffith, 423-614-8694, E-mail: mba@leeuniversity.edu.

**Program in Education** Students: 24 full-time (15 women), 72 part-time (46 women); includes 14 minority (8 Black or African American, non-Hispanic/Latino; 1 Hispanic/Latino; 5 Two or more races, non-Hispanic/Latino), 1 international. Average age 29. 44 applicants, 86% accepted, 33 enrolled. *Faculty:* 13 full-time (5 women), 9 part-time/adjunct (6 women). Expenses: Contact institution. *Financial support:* In 2019–20, 40 students received support. Career-related internships or fieldwork, Federal Work-Study, institutionally sponsored loans, scholarships/grants, and unspecified assistantships available. Financial award application deadline: 3/1; financial award applicants required to submit FAFSA. In 2019, 60 master's, 3 other advanced degrees awarded. *Program availability:* Part-time. *Application deadline:* For fall admission, 6/1 priority date for domestic and international students; for spring admission, 11/1 priority date for domestic and international students; for summer admission, 4/1 priority date for domestic and international students. Applications are processed on a rolling basis. *Application fee:* $25. Electronic applications accepted. *Application Contact:* Jeffery McGirt, Director of Graduate Enrollment, 423-614-8691, Fax: 423-614-8317, E-mail: jmcgirt@leeuniversity.edu. *Director,* Dr. William Kamm, 423-614-8544, E-mail: wkamm@leeuniversity.edu.

**Program in Music** Students: 16 full-time (7 women), 8 part-time (3 women); includes 2 minority (1 Black or African American, non-Hispanic/Latino; 1 Asian, non-Hispanic/Latino), 6 international. Average age 28. 20 applicants, 100% accepted, 13 enrolled. *Faculty:* 20 full-time (5 women), 9 part-time/adjunct (4 women). Expenses: Contact institution. *Financial support:* In 2019–20, 32 students received support. Career-related internships or fieldwork, Federal Work-Study, institutionally sponsored loans, scholarships/grants, and unspecified assistantships available. Financial award application deadline: 3/1; financial award applicants required to submit FAFSA. In 2019, 12 master's awarded. *Program availability:* Part-time, online only, 100% online. *Application deadline:* For fall admission, 4/1 priority date for domestic and international students; for spring admission, 10/1 priority date for domestic and international students. Applications are processed on a rolling basis. *Application fee:* $25. Electronic applications accepted. *Application Contact:* Jeffery McGirt, Director of Graduate Enrollment, 423-614-8691, Fax: 423-614-8317, E-mail: jmcgirt@leeuniversity.edu. *Director,* Dr. Ron Brendle, 423-614-8240, Fax: 423-614-8245, E-mail: gradmusic@leeuniversity.edu.

**Programs in Religion** Students: 32 full-time (13 women), 104 part-time (33 women); includes 74 minority (10 Black or African American, non-Hispanic/Latino; 60 Hispanic/Latino; 4 Two or more races, non-Hispanic/Latino), 5 international. Average age 38. 43 applicants, 79% accepted, 24 enrolled. *Faculty:* 12 full-time (3 women), 8 part-time/adjunct (0 women). Expenses: Contact institution. *Financial support:* In 2019–20, 39 students received support, including 12 teaching assistantships (averaging $2,046 per year); career-related internships or fieldwork, Federal Work-Study, institutionally sponsored loans, scholarships/grants, and unspecified assistantships also available. Financial award application deadline: 3/1; financial award applicants required to submit FAFSA. In 2019, 15 master's awarded. *Program availability:* Part-time, 100% online. *Application deadline:* For fall admission, 4/1 priority date for domestic and international students; for spring admission, 10/1 priority date for domestic and international students. Applications are processed on a rolling basis. *Application fee:* $25. Electronic applications accepted. *Application Contact:* Jeffery McGirt, Director of Graduate Enrollment, 423-614-8691, Fax: 423-614-8317, E-mail: jmcgirt@leeuniversity.edu. *Director,* Dr. Lisa Long, 423-303-5100, E-mail: llong@leeuniversity.edu.

**School of Nursing** Students: 12 full-time (all women), 1 (woman) part-time; includes 4 minority (1 American Indian or Alaska Native, non-Hispanic/Latino; 1 Hispanic/Latino; 2 Two or more races, non-Hispanic/Latino). Average age 25. 15 applicants, 87% accepted, 10 enrolled. *Faculty:* 8 full-time (7 women). Expenses: Contact institution. *Financial support:* In 2019–20, 12 students received support. Scholarships/grants available. Financial award application deadline: 3/1; financial award applicants required to submit FAFSA. *Program availability:* Part-time. *Application deadline:* For fall admission, 4/1 priority date for domestic and international students; for spring admission, 11/1 priority date for domestic and international students. Applications are processed on a rolling basis. *Application fee:* $25. Electronic applications accepted. *Application Contact:* Dr. Jeffery McGirt, Director of Graduate Enrollment, 423-614-8691, Fax: 423-614-8317, E-mail: jmcgirt@leeuniversity.edu. *Dean, School of Nursing,* Dr. Sara Campbell, 423-614-8526.

## LEHIGH UNIVERSITY, Bethlehem, PA 18015

**General Information** Independent, coed, university. CGS member. *Enrollment:* 6,953 graduate, professional, and undergraduate students; 1,022 full-time matriculated graduate/professional students (409 women), 624 part-time matriculated graduate/professional students (308 women). *Enrollment by degree level:* 958 master's, 678 doctoral, 10 other advanced degrees. *Graduate faculty:* 350 full-time (102 women), 39 part-time/adjunct (22 women). *Graduate housing:* Rooms and/or apartments available on a first-come, first-served basis to single and married students. *Student services:* Campus employment opportunities, campus safety program, career counseling, child daycare facilities, exercise/wellness program, free psychological counseling, international student services, low-cost health insurance, multicultural affairs office, services for students with disabilities, teacher training, writing training. *Library facilities:* E. W. Fairchild-Martindale Library plus 1 other. *Collection:* Books: 739,278 (physical), 471,889 (digital/electronic); Serial titles: 7,595 (physical), 60,385 (digital/electronic); Databases: 209. Weekly public service hours: 83; students can reserve study rooms.

**Computer facilities:** Computer purchase and lease plans are available. 437 computers available on campus for general student use. A campuswide network can be accessed from student residence rooms and from off campus. Online class registration is available.
Website: http://www.lehigh.edu/

**GRADUATE UNITS**

**College of Arts and Sciences** Students: 253 full-time (122 women), 74 part-time (40 women); includes 39 minority (6 Black or African American, non-Hispanic/Latino; 1 American Indian or Alaska Native, non-Hispanic/Latino; 10 Asian, non-Hispanic/Latino; 19 Hispanic/Latino; 3 Two or more races, non-Hispanic/Latino), 80 international. Average age 28. 479 applicants, 47% accepted, 106 enrolled. *Faculty:* 151 full-time (55 women), 6 part-time/adjunct (3 women). Expenses: Contact institution. *Financial support:* Application deadline: 1/1. In 2019, 67 master's, 32 doctorates awarded. *Program availability:* Part-time, online learning. *Application deadline:* For fall admission, 7/1 for domestic students, 7/15 for international students; for spring admission, 12/1 for domestic and international students. *Application fee:* $75. Electronic applications accepted. *Application Contact:* Tyler Frey, Administrative Clerk, 610-758-4281, Fax: 610-758-6232, E-mail: trf218@lehigh.edu. *Associate Dean of Graduate Studies,* R Michael Burger, 610-758-4282, Fax: 610-758-6232, E-mail: rmb206@lehigh.edu.

**College of Business** Students: 104 full-time (49 women), 175 part-time (49 women); includes 37 minority (5 Black or African American, non-Hispanic/Latino; 18 Asian, non-Hispanic/Latino; 11 Hispanic/Latino; 1 Native Hawaiian or other Pacific Islander, non-Hispanic/Latino; 2 Two or more races, non-Hispanic/Latino), 79 international. Average age 31. 455 applicants, 59% accepted, 102 enrolled. *Faculty:* 44 full-time (5 women), 2 part-time/adjunct (1 woman). Expenses: Contact institution. *Financial support:* In 2019–20, 11 fellowships with partial tuition reimbursements, 1 research assistantship with full tuition reimbursement (averaging $20,600 per year), 15 teaching assistantships with full tuition reimbursements (averaging $20,600 per year) were awarded; scholarships/grants and unspecified assistantships also available. Support available to part-time students. Financial award application deadline: 1/15. In 2019, 143 master's, 5 doctorates awarded. *Program availability:* Part-time, evening/weekend, synchronous with live classroom. *Application deadline:* For fall admission, 7/15 for domestic students, 5/1 for international students; for spring admission, 12/1 for domestic and international students. *Application fee:* $75. *Application Contact:* Mary Theresa Taglang, Director of Recruitment and Admissions, 610-758-4386, Fax: 610-758-5283, E-mail: mtt4@lehigh.edu. *Dean,* Georgette Chapman-Phillips, 610-758-6725, Fax: 610-758-4499, E-mail: gcp214@lehigh.edu.

**College of Education** Students: 135 full-time (114 women), 251 part-time (169 women); includes 62 minority (13 Black or African American, non-Hispanic/Latino; 14 Asian, non-Hispanic/Latino; 31 Hispanic/Latino; 2 Native Hawaiian or other Pacific Islander, non-

Hispanic/Latino; 2 Two or more races, non-Hispanic/Latino), 37 international. Average age 31. 318 applicants, 43% accepted, 83 enrolled. *Faculty:* 33 full-time (22 women), 33 part-time/adjunct (23 women). Expenses: Contact institution. *Financial support:* In 2019–20, 127 students received support, including 3 fellowships with tuition reimbursements available (averaging $27,125 per year), 38 research assistantships with full and partial tuition reimbursements available (averaging $13,210 per year); scholarships/grants and unspecified assistantships also available. Financial award application deadline: 3/1. In 2019, 101 master's, 9 doctorates, 5 other advanced degrees awarded. *Program availability:* Part-time, online only, 100% online, blended/hybrid learning. *Application deadline:* For fall admission, 12/1 for domestic and international students; for spring admission, 12/15 for domestic and international students; for summer admission, 5/1 for domestic students, 5/15 for international students. Applications are processed on a rolling basis. *Application fee:* $65. Electronic applications accepted. *Application Contact:* Jaime Kardos, Assoc Dir Admissions, Recruiting & Graduate Programs, 610-758-5857, Fax: 610-758-6223, E-mail: jsk419@lehigh.edu. *Dean*, Dr. William Gaudelli, 610-758-3221, Fax: 610-758-6223, E-mail: wig318@lehigh.edu.

**P.C. Rossin College of Engineering and Applied Science** Students: 654 full-time (174 women), 124 part-time (50 women); includes 58 minority (10 Black or African American, non-Hispanic/Latino; 24 Asian, non-Hispanic/Latino; 20 Hispanic/Latino; 1 Native Hawaiian or other Pacific Islander, non-Hispanic/Latino; 3 Two or more races, non-Hispanic/Latino), 387 international. Average age 27. 1,501 applicants, 40% accepted, 184 enrolled. *Faculty:* 134 full-time (24 women), 9 part-time/adjunct (1 woman). Expenses: Contact institution. *Financial support:* In 2019–20, 48 fellowships with tuition reimbursements (averaging $22,050 per year), 129 research assistantships with tuition reimbursements (averaging $29,400 per year), 50 teaching assistantships with tuition reimbursements (averaging $22,050 per year) were awarded; tuition waivers (full and partial) and unspecified assistantships also available. Financial award application deadline: 1/15. In 2019, 205 master's, 55 doctorates, 5 other advanced degrees awarded. *Program availability:* Part-time, 100% online, blended/hybrid learning. *Application deadline:* For fall admission, 7/15 for domestic students; for spring admission, 12/1 for domestic students. *Application fee:* $75. Electronic applications accepted. *Application Contact:* Brianne Lisk, Manager of Graduate Programs, 610-758-6310, Fax: 610-758-5623, E-mail: brie.lisk@lehigh.edu. *Dean*, Dr. Stephen P. DeWeerth, 610-758-5308, Fax: 610-758-5623, E-mail: steve.deweerth@lehigh.edu.

***Center for Polymer Science and Engineering*** Students: 6 full-time (4 women), 32 part-time (13 women); includes 13 minority (4 Black or African American, non-Hispanic/Latino; 5 Asian, non-Hispanic/Latino; 4 Hispanic/Latino), 3 international. Average age 31. 28 applicants, 43% accepted, 7 enrolled. *Faculty:* 5 full-time (3 women). Expenses: Contact institution. *Financial support:* In 2019–20, 1 research assistantship with full tuition reimbursement (averaging $11,025 per year), 1 teaching assistantship with full tuition reimbursement (averaging $11,025 per year) were awarded; health care benefits also available. Financial award application deadline: 1/15. In 2019, 9 master's awarded. *Program availability:* Part-time, evening/weekend, 100% online, blended/hybrid learning. *Application deadline:* For fall admission, 7/15 for domestic students, 1/15 for international students; for spring admission, 12/1 for domestic and international students; for summer admission, 4/30 for domestic and international students. Applications are processed on a rolling basis. *Application fee:* $75. Electronic applications accepted. *Application Contact:* James E. Roberts, Chair, Polymer Education Committee, 610-758-4841, Fax: 610-758-6536, E-mail: jer1@lehigh.edu. *Director*, Dr. Raymond A. Pearson, 610-758-3857, Fax: 610-758-3526, E-mail: rp02@lehigh.edu.

## LEHMAN COLLEGE OF THE CITY UNIVERSITY OF NEW YORK, Bronx, NY 10468-1589

**General Information** State and locally supported, coed, comprehensive institution. *Enrollment:* 15,143 graduate, professional, and undergraduate students; 198 full-time matriculated graduate/professional students (146 women), 1,943 part-time matriculated graduate/professional students (1,363 women). *Enrollment by degree level:* 2,141 master's. *Tuition, area resident:* Full-time $5545; part-time $470 per credit. Tuition, nonresident: part-time $855 per credit. *Required fees:* $240. *Graduate housing:* On-campus housing not available. *Student services:* Campus employment opportunities, campus safety program, career counseling, child daycare facilities, exercise/wellness program, international student services, low-cost health insurance, services for students with disabilities, teacher training. *Library facilities:* Leonard Lief Library plus 1 other. *Collection:* Books: 362,674 (physical), 378,426 (digital/electronic); Serial titles: 299,414 (physical), 100,000 (digital/electronic). Weekly public service hours: 40; students can reserve study rooms. *Research affiliation:* New York Botanical Gardens, Montefiore Hospital and Medical Center.

**Computer facilities:** 800 computers available on campus for general student use. A campuswide network can be accessed. Online class registration is available.
Website: http://www.lehman.cuny.edu/

**General Application Contact:** Laurie Austin, Director of Admissions and Recruitment, 718-960-8706, Fax: 718-960-8172.

**GRADUATE UNITS**

**School of Arts and Humanities** *Program availability:* Part-time, evening/weekend.

**School of Education** *Program availability:* Part-time, evening/weekend.

**School of Health Sciences, Human Services and Nursing**

**School of Natural and Social Sciences** *Program availability:* Part-time, evening/weekend.

## LE MOYNE COLLEGE, Syracuse, NY 13214

**General Information** Independent-religious, coed, comprehensive institution. *Enrollment:* 3,326 graduate, professional, and undergraduate students; 290 full-time matriculated graduate/professional students (220 women), 248 part-time matriculated graduate/professional students (160 women). *Enrollment by degree level:* 467 master's, 10 doctoral, 61 other advanced degrees. *Graduate faculty:* 35 full-time (19 women), 36 part-time/adjunct (22 women). *Tuition:* Full-time $13,482; part-time $749 per credit hour. *Required fees:* $75 per semester. Tuition and fees vary according to degree level and program. *Graduate housing:* On-campus housing not available. *Student services:* Campus employment opportunities, campus safety program, career counseling, exercise/wellness program, free psychological counseling, international student services, low-cost health insurance, multicultural affairs office, services for students with disabilities, teacher training, writing training. *Library facilities:* Noreen Reale Falcone Library. *Collection:* Books: 264,034 (physical), 228,586 (digital/electronic); Serial titles: 1,371 (physical), 107,697 (digital/electronic); Databases: 251. Weekly public service hours: 110; study areas open 24 hours, 5–7 days a week; students can reserve study rooms. *Research affiliation:* Blue Highway, Inc. (medical technology).

**Computer facilities:** 315 computers available on campus for general student use. A campuswide network can be accessed from student residence rooms and from off campus. Online class registration, ECHO (campus-wide portal), some virtual access from off campus are available.
Website: http://www.lemoyne.edu/

**General Application Contact:** Teresa M. Renn, Director of Graduate Admission, 315-445-5444, Fax: 315-445-6092, E-mail: GradAdmission@lemoyne.edu.

**GRADUATE UNITS**

**Department of Education** Students: 27 full-time (21 women), 127 part-time (83 women); includes 16 minority (6 Black or African American, non-Hispanic/Latino; 1 American Indian or Alaska Native, non-Hispanic/Latino; 2 Asian, non-Hispanic/Latino; 6 Hispanic/Latino; 1 Two or more races, non-Hispanic/Latino), 1 international. Average age 34. 155 applicants, 88% accepted, 117 enrolled. *Faculty:* 8 full-time (5 women), 15 part-time/adjunct (10 women). Expenses: Contact institution. *Financial support:* In 2019–20, 37 students received support. Career-related internships or fieldwork, Federal Work-Study, scholarships/grants, and health care benefits available. Support available to part-time students. Financial award applicants required to submit FAFSA. In 2019, 66 master's, 39 CASs awarded. *Program availability:* Part-time, evening/weekend. *Application deadline:* For fall admission, 4/1 priority date for domestic and international students; for spring admission, 10/1 priority date for domestic and international students; for summer admission, 3/1 priority date for domestic and international students. Applications are processed on a rolling basis. Electronic applications accepted. *Application Contact:* Teresa M. Renn, Director of Graduate Admission, 315-445-5444, Fax: 315-445-6092, E-mail: GradEducation@lemoyne.edu. *Chair, Department of Education*, Dr. Stephen C. Fleury, 315-445-4376, Fax: 315-445-4744, E-mail: fleurysc@lemoyne.edu.

**Department of Nursing** Students: 18 full-time (17 women), 57 part-time (52 women); includes 7 minority (1 Black or African American, non-Hispanic/Latino; 1 Asian, non-Hispanic/Latino; 4 Hispanic/Latino; 1 Two or more races, non-Hispanic/Latino). Average age 31. 43 applicants, 84% accepted, 32 enrolled. *Faculty:* 4 full-time (all women), 6 part-time/adjunct (4 women). Expenses: Contact institution. *Financial support:* In 2019–20, 1 student received support. Career-related internships or fieldwork, Federal Work-Study, scholarships/grants, health care benefits, and unspecified assistantships available. Support available to part-time students. Financial award applicants required to submit FAFSA. In 2019, 33 master's, 3 other advanced degrees awarded. *Program availability:* Part-time, evening/weekend. *Application deadline:* For fall admission, 4/1 priority date for domestic students, 4/1 for international students; for spring admission, 11/1 priority date for domestic students, 11/1 for international students; for summer admission, 5/1 priority date for domestic students, 5/1 for international students. Applications are processed on a rolling basis. Electronic applications accepted. *Application Contact:* Teresa M. Renn, Director of Graduate Admission, 315-445-5444, Fax: 315-445-6092, E-mail: GradAdmission@lemoyne.edu. *Professor - Chair of Nursing*, Catherine A. Brownell, 315-445-5426, Fax: 315-445-6024, E-mail: nursing@lemoyne.edu.

**Department of Occupational Therapy** Students: 58 full-time (57 women), 1 part-time; includes 13 minority (4 Black or African American, non-Hispanic/Latino; 6 Asian, non-Hispanic/Latino; 2 Hispanic/Latino; 1 Native Hawaiian or other Pacific Islander, non-Hispanic/Latino). Average age 24. 78 applicants, 65% accepted, 22 enrolled. *Faculty:* 4 full-time (all women), 2 part-time/adjunct (1 woman). Expenses: Contact institution. *Financial support:* Career-related internships or fieldwork, Federal Work-Study, scholarships/grants, and health care benefits available. Financial award applicants required to submit FAFSA. In 2019, 39 master's awarded. *Application deadline:* For fall admission, 4/1 for domestic and international students. Applications are processed on a rolling basis. *Application fee:* $150. Electronic applications accepted. *Application Contact:* Teresa M. Renn, Director of Graduate Admission, 315-445-5444, Fax: 315-445-6092, E-mail: GradEducation@lemoyne.edu. *Chair and Assistant Professor*, Caitlin O. Esposito, 315-445-5432, E-mail: occupationaltherapy@lemoyne.edu.

**Department of Physician Assistant Studies** Students: 133 full-time (103 women), 1 (woman) part-time; includes 15 minority (3 Black or African American, non-Hispanic/Latino; 8 Asian, non-Hispanic/Latino; 4 Hispanic/Latino). Average age 25. 1,127 applicants, 7% accepted, 75 enrolled. *Faculty:* 4 full-time (2 women), 3 part-time/adjunct (all women). Expenses: Contact institution. *Financial support:* In 2019–20, 17 students received support. Career-related internships or fieldwork, Federal Work-Study, scholarships/grants, and health care benefits available. Financial award applicants required to submit FAFSA. In 2019, 67 master's awarded. *Application deadline:* For fall admission, 10/1 for domestic and international students. *Application fee:* $179. Electronic applications accepted. *Application Contact:* Teresa M. Renn, Director of Graduate Admission, 315-445-5444, Fax: 315-445-6092, E-mail: GradEducation@lemoyne.edu. *Program Director, Department of Physician Assistant Studies*, Elizabeth W. Mercer, 315-445-4745, Fax: 315-445-4602, E-mail: physassist@lemoyne.edu.

**Madden School of Business** Students: 46 full-time (16 women), 56 part-time (20 women); includes 13 minority (3 Black or African American, non-Hispanic/Latino; 2 Asian, non-Hispanic/Latino; 5 Hispanic/Latino; 3 Two or more races, non-Hispanic/Latino), 6 international. Average age 26. 95 applicants, 85% accepted, 65 enrolled. *Faculty:* 14 full-time (4 women), 8 part-time/adjunct (2 women). Expenses: Contact institution. *Financial support:* In 2019–20, 45 students received support. Career-related internships or fieldwork, Federal Work-Study, scholarships/grants, and health care benefits available. Support available to part-time students. Financial award applicants required to submit FAFSA. In 2019, 62 master's awarded. *Program availability:* Part-time, evening/weekend. *Application deadline:* For fall admission, 8/1 for domestic students, 8/1 priority date for international students; for spring admission, 10/15 priority date for domestic and international students; for summer admission, 4/1 priority date for domestic and international students. Applications are processed on a rolling basis. Electronic applications accepted. *Application Contact:* Teresa M. Renn, Director of Graduate Admission, 315-445-5444, Fax: 315-445-6092, E-mail: GradAdmission@lemoyne.edu. *Dean of Madden School of Business*, James Joseph, 315-445-4280, Fax: 315-445-4787, E-mail: josepjae@lemoyne.edu.

**Program in Arts Administration** Students: 8 full-time (6 women), 6 part-time (4 women); includes 4 minority (2 Black or African American, non-Hispanic/Latino; 1 Hispanic/Latino; 1 Two or more races, non-Hispanic/Latino). Average age 26. 16 applicants, 88% accepted, 13 enrolled. *Faculty:* 1 full-time (0 women), 2 part-time/adjunct (both women). Expenses: Contact institution. *Financial support:* In 2019–20, 8 students received support. Career-related internships or fieldwork, Federal Work-Study, scholarships/grants, and health care benefits available. Support available to part-time students. Financial award applicants required to submit FAFSA. In 2019, 7 master's awarded. *Program availability:* Part-time, evening/weekend. *Application deadline:* For fall admission, 3/1 priority date for domestic and international students; for spring admission, 11/1 priority date for domestic and international students; for summer admission, 4/1 priority date for domestic and international students. Applications are processed on a rolling basis. Electronic applications accepted. *Application Contact:* Travis Newton, Director of Graduate Admission, 315-445-4201, E-mail: artsadmin@lemoyne.edu. *Associate Professor and Director of Arts Administration,* Travis Newton, 315-445-4201, E-mail: newtontm@lemoyne.edu.

## LENOIR-RHYNE UNIVERSITY, Hickory, NC 28601

**General Information** Independent-religious, coed, comprehensive institution. *Graduate housing:* Room and/or apartments available on a first-come, first-served basis to single students; on-campus housing not available to married students. Housing application deadline: 5/1.

**GRADUATE UNITS**

**Graduate Programs** *Program availability:* Part-time, evening/weekend, online learning. Electronic applications accepted.

***Charles M. Snipes School of Business*** *Program availability:* Part-time, evening/weekend, online learning. Electronic applications accepted.

***Lutheran Theological Southern Seminary*** *Program availability:* Part-time.

***School of Arts and Letters*** Electronic applications accepted.

***School of Counseling and Human Services*** *Program availability:* Part-time, evening/weekend. Electronic applications accepted.

***School of Education*** *Program availability:* Part-time, evening/weekend, online learning. Electronic applications accepted.

***School of Health, Exercise and Sport Science*** *Program availability:* Part-time.

***School of Natural Sciences*** *Program availability:* Part-time, evening/weekend, online learning. Electronic applications accepted.

***School of Nursing*** *Program availability:* Online only. Electronic applications accepted.

***School of Occupational Therapy***

***School of Physician Assistant Studies***

## LESLEY UNIVERSITY, Cambridge, MA 02138-2790

**General Information** Independent, coed, primarily women, comprehensive institution. *Graduate housing:* Room and/or apartments available to single students; on-campus housing not available to married students. *Research affiliation:* TERC (education research and development).

**GRADUATE UNITS**

**College of Art and Design** *Program availability:* Part-time. Electronic applications accepted.

**Graduate School of Arts and Social Sciences** *Program availability:* Part-time, online learning. Electronic applications accepted.

**Graduate School of Education** *Program availability:* Part-time, evening/weekend, online learning. Electronic applications accepted.

## LES ROCHES INTERNATIONAL SCHOOL OF HOTEL MANAGEMENT, CH-3975 Bluche, Switzerland

**General Information** Private, coed, comprehensive institution.

**GRADUATE UNITS**

**Program in Hospitality Management**

## LETOURNEAU UNIVERSITY, Longview, TX 75607-7001

**General Information** Independent-religious, coed, comprehensive institution. *Enrollment:* 3,150 graduate, professional, and undergraduate students; 45 full-time matriculated graduate/professional students (34 women), 243 part-time matriculated graduate/professional students (186 women). *Enrollment by degree level:* 288 master's. *Graduate housing:* Rooms and/or apartments available on a first-come, first-served basis to single and married students. Typical cost: $15,810 (including board) for single students; $15,810 (including board) for married students. *Student services:* Campus employment opportunities, campus safety program, career counseling, exercise/wellness program, free psychological counseling, international student services, low-cost health insurance, multicultural affairs office, services for students with disabilities, writing training. *Library facilities:* Margaret Estes Library plus 1 other. *Collection:* Books: 31,156 (physical), 287,976 (digital/electronic); Serial titles: 53,534 (digital/electronic); Databases: 106. Weekly public service hours: 93; students can reserve study rooms.

**Computer facilities:** Computer purchase and lease plans are available. A campuswide network can be accessed. Online class registration is available.
Website: http://www.letu.edu/

**GRADUATE UNITS**

**Graduate Programs** Students: 45 full-time (34 women), 243 part-time (186 women); includes 142 minority (89 Black or African American, non-Hispanic/Latino; 1 Asian, non-Hispanic/Latino; 26 Hispanic/Latino; 26 Two or more races, non-Hispanic/Latino), 2 international. Average age 37. Expenses: Contact institution. *Financial support:* Unspecified assistantships and employee tuition waivers and institutionally sponsored loans available. Financial award applicants required to submit FAFSA. In 2019, 143 master's awarded. *Program availability:* Part-time, 100% online, blended/hybrid learning. *Application deadline:* Applications are processed on a rolling basis. Electronic applications accepted.

## LEWIS & CLARK COLLEGE, Portland, OR 97219-7899

**General Information** Independent, coed, comprehensive institution. *Graduate housing:* On-campus housing not available.

**GRADUATE UNITS**

**Graduate School of Education and Counseling** *Program availability:* Part-time, evening/weekend. Electronic applications accepted.

**Lewis & Clark Law School** *Program availability:* Part-time, evening/weekend. Electronic applications accepted.

## LEWIS UNIVERSITY, Romeoville, IL 60446

**General Information** Independent-religious, coed, comprehensive institution. CGS member. *Enrollment:* 6,359 graduate, professional, and undergraduate students; 494 full-time matriculated graduate/professional students (329 women), 1,416 part-time matriculated graduate/professional students (972 women). *Enrollment by degree level:* 1,876 master's, 65 doctoral. *Graduate housing:* Room and/or apartments available on a first-come, first-served basis to single students; on-campus housing not available to married students. Housing application deadline: 7/1. *Student services:* Campus employment opportunities, campus safety program, career counseling, exercise/wellness program, free psychological counseling, international student services, low-cost health insurance, multicultural affairs office, services for students with disabilities, teacher training, writing training. *Library facilities:* Lewis University Library. *Collection:* Books: 91,369 (physical), 267,351 (digital/electronic); Serial titles: 1,143 (physical), 117,860 (digital/electronic); Databases: 76. Weekly public service hours: 98; students can reserve study rooms.

**Computer facilities:** A campuswide network can be accessed from student residence rooms and from off campus. Online class registration, online help desk, online billing, online financial aid, online payments, online admission application, online housing application, online application for graduation, online Blackboard course management system, online tutoring are available.
Website: http://www.lewisu.edu/

**General Application Contact:** Dr. Leslie Jacobson, Director, Graduate Admission, 815-836-5610, E-mail: grad@lewisu.edu.

**GRADUATE UNITS**

**College of Aviation, Science and Technology** Students: 89 full-time (26 women), 255 part-time (77 women); includes 101 minority (23 Black or African American, non-Hispanic/Latino; 32 Asian, non-Hispanic/Latino; 31 Hispanic/Latino; 3 Native Hawaiian or other Pacific Islander, non-Hispanic/Latino; 12 Two or more races, non-Hispanic/Latino), 36 international. Average age 32. Expenses: Contact institution. *Financial support:* Unspecified assistantships available. Financial award applicants required to submit FAFSA. *Program availability:* Part-time, 100% online, blended/hybrid learning.

**College of Business** Students: 139 full-time (85 women), 329 part-time (216 women); includes 188 minority (82 Black or African American, non-Hispanic/Latino; 22 Asian, non-Hispanic/Latino; 74 Hispanic/Latino; 10 Two or more races, non-Hispanic/Latino), 32 international. Average age 33. Expenses: Contact institution. *Financial support:* Federal Work-Study and unspecified assistantships available. Financial award application deadline: 5/1; financial award applicants required to submit FAFSA. *Program availability:* Part-time, evening/weekend, 100% online, blended/hybrid learning. *Application deadline:* For fall admission, 5/1 priority date for international students; for spring admission, 11/15 priority date for international students. Applications are processed on a rolling basis. *Application fee:* $40. Electronic applications accepted. *Application Contact:* Office of Graduate Admission, 815-836-5610, E-mail: grad@lewisu.edu. *Dean,* Dr. Ryan Butt.

**College of Education and Social Sciences** Students: 207 full-time (168 women), 367 part-time (257 women); includes 173 minority (58 Black or African American, non-Hispanic/Latino; 1 American Indian or Alaska Native, non-Hispanic/Latino; 6 Asian, non-Hispanic/Latino; 99 Hispanic/Latino; 1 Native Hawaiian or other Pacific Islander, non-Hispanic/Latino; 8 Two or more races, non-Hispanic/Latino), 11 international. Average age 32. Expenses: Contact institution. *Application deadline:* Applications are processed on a rolling basis. Electronic applications accepted. *Application Contact:* Dr. Leslie Jacobson, Director, Graduate Admission, 815-836-5610, E-mail: grad@lewisu.edu.

**College of Nursing and Health Sciences** Students: 59 full-time (50 women), 465 part-time (422 women); includes 141 minority (25 Black or African American, non-Hispanic/Latino; 48 Asian, non-Hispanic/Latino; 58 Hispanic/Latino; 10 Two or more races, non-Hispanic/Latino), 2 international. Average age 35. Expenses: Contact institution. *Financial support:* Federal Work-Study and unspecified assistantships available. *Program availability:* Part-time, evening/weekend, online learning. *Application fee:* $40. *Application Contact:* Dr. Leslie Jacobson, Director, Graduate Admission, 815-836-5610, E-mail: grad@lewisu.edu.

## LEXINGTON THEOLOGICAL SEMINARY, Lexington, KY 40508-3218

**General Information** Independent-religious, coed, graduate-only institution. *Enrollment by degree level:* 87 master's, 11 doctoral. *Graduate faculty:* 3 full-time (2 women), 34 part-time/adjunct (18 women). *Tuition:* Full-time $480. *Required fees:* $360. Tuition and fees vary according to program. *Graduate housing:* On-campus housing not available. *Student services:* Campus employment opportunities, career counseling, international student services, services for students with disabilities, writing training. *Library facilities:* Bosworth Memorial Library plus 1 other. *Collection:* Books: 92,871 (physical), 512,369 (digital/electronic); Serial titles: 1,286 (physical), 53,877 (digital/electronic); Databases: 188. Weekly public service hours: 40.

**Computer facilities:** A campuswide network can be accessed. Online class registration, X are available.
Website: http://www.lextheo.edu/

**General Application Contact:** Rev. Carole Devine, Director of Admissions, 859-280-1249, Fax: 859-281-6042, E-mail: cdevine@lextheo.edu.

**GRADUATE UNITS**

**Graduate and Professional Programs** *Program availability:* Part-time, evening/weekend.

## LIBERTY UNIVERSITY, Lynchburg, VA 24515

**General Information** Independent-religious, coed, comprehensive institution. *Enrollment:* 18,114 full-time matriculated graduate/professional students (11,207 women), 20,146 part-time matriculated graduate/professional students (12,026 women). *Enrollment by degree level:* 28,004 master's, 9,136 doctoral, 1,120 other advanced degrees. *Tuition:* Full-time $545; part-time $410 per credit hour. One-time fee: $50. *Graduate housing:* Room and/or apartments available on a first-come, first-served basis to single students; on-campus housing not available to married students. *Student services:* Campus employment opportunities, career counseling, exercise/wellness program, free psychological counseling, international student services, multicultural affairs office, services for students with disabilities, writing training. *Library facilities:* Jerry Falwell Library plus 2 others. *Collection:* Books: 336,202 (physical), 978,080 (digital/electronic); Serial titles: 2,987 (physical), 156,971 (digital/electronic); Databases: 451. Weekly public service hours: 100; students can reserve study rooms.

**Computer facilities:** 1,640 computers available on campus for general student use. A campuswide network can be accessed. Online class registration is available.
Website: http://www.liberty.edu/

**General Application Contact:** Chris Jones, Director of Admissions, 877-298-9617, Fax: 434-522-0430, E-mail: admissions@liberty.edu.

**GRADUATE UNITS**

**College of Arts and Sciences** Students: 382 full-time (203 women), 499 part-time (272 women); includes 161 minority (82 Black or African American, non-Hispanic/Latino; 4 American Indian or Alaska Native, non-Hispanic/Latino; 4 Asian, non-Hispanic/Latino; 43 Hispanic/Latino; 1 Native Hawaiian or other Pacific Islander, non-Hispanic/Latino; 27 Two or more races, non-Hispanic/Latino), 9 international. Average age 38. 1,716 applicants, 32% accepted, 320 enrolled. Expenses: Contact institution. *Financial support:* In 2019–20, 659 students received support. Teaching assistantships with tuition reimbursements available and Federal Work-Study available. In 2019, 253 master's awarded. *Program availability:* Part-time, online learning. *Application deadline:* For fall admission, 6/1 for domestic students; for spring admission, 11/1 for domestic students. Applications are processed on a rolling basis. *Application fee:* $50. Electronic applications accepted. *Application Contact:* Chris Jones, Director of Admissions, 434-592-3966, Fax: 434-522-0430, E-mail: gradadmissions@liberty.edu. *Dean*, Dr. Roger Schultz, 434-592-4031, Fax: 434-522-0430, E-mail: rschultz@liberty.edu.

**College of Osteopathic Medicine** Students: 604 full-time (280 women), 6 part-time (1 woman); includes 135 minority (14 Black or African American, non-Hispanic/Latino; 1 American Indian or Alaska Native, non-Hispanic/Latino; 82 Asian, non-Hispanic/Latino; 22 Hispanic/Latino; 16 Two or more races, non-Hispanic/Latino), 23 international. Average age 27. 2,282 applicants, 7% accepted, 152 enrolled. Expenses: Contact institution. *Financial support:* In 2019–20, 167 students received support. Teaching assistantships and Federal Work-Study available. In 2019, 126 doctorates awarded. *Application deadline:* Applications are processed on a rolling basis. Electronic applications accepted. *Application Contact:* Jay Bridge, Director of Admissions, 800-424-9595, Fax: 800-628-7977, E-mail: gradadmissions@liberty.edu. *Dean*, Dr. Peter A. Bell, 434-592-6515.

**Helms School of Government** Students: 1,143 full-time (565 women), 572 part-time (408 women); includes 795 minority (499 Black or African American, non-Hispanic/Latino; 16 American Indian or Alaska Native, non-Hispanic/Latino; 23 Asian, non-Hispanic/Latino; 162 Hispanic/Latino; 7 Native Hawaiian or other Pacific Islander, non-Hispanic/Latino; 88 Two or more races, non-Hispanic/Latino), 27 international. Average age 35. 3,017 applicants, 44% accepted, 728 enrolled. Expenses: Contact institution. *Financial support:* In 2019–20, 808 students received support. Teaching assistantships and Federal Work-Study available. In 2019, 415 master's awarded. *Program availability:* Part-time, online learning. *Application deadline:* Applications are processed on a rolling basis. *Application fee:* $50. Electronic applications accepted. *Application Contact:* Jay Bridge, Director of Admissions, 800-424-9595, Fax: 800-628-7977, E-mail: gradadmissions@liberty.edu. *Dean*, Ron Miller, 434-592-4986, E-mail: govtdean@liberty.edu.

**School of Behavioral Sciences** Students: 3,786 full-time (3,065 women), 5,193 part-time (4,081 women); includes 2,733 minority (1,967 Black or African American, non-Hispanic/Latino; 48 American Indian or Alaska Native, non-Hispanic/Latino; 103 Asian, non-Hispanic/Latino; 349 Hispanic/Latino; 19 Native Hawaiian or other Pacific Islander, non-Hispanic/Latino; 247 Two or more races, non-Hispanic/Latino), 133 international. Average age 38. 13,324 applicants, 28% accepted, 2,163 enrolled. Expenses: Contact institution. *Financial support:* In 2019–20, 1,003 students received support. Teaching assistantships and Federal Work-Study available. Financial award applicants required to submit FAFSA. In 2019, 2,322 master's, 19 doctorates, 112 other advanced degrees awarded. *Program availability:* Part-time, online learning. *Application deadline:* Applications are processed on a rolling basis. *Application fee:* $50. Electronic applications accepted. *Application Contact:* Jay Bridge, Director of Admissions, 800-424-9595, Fax: 800-628-7977, E-mail: gradadmissions@liberty.edu. *Dean, School of Behavioral Services*, Dr. Kenyon Knapp, E-mail: kcknapp@liberty.edu.

**School of Business** Students: 3,187 full-time (1,641 women), 4,818 part-time (2,180 women); includes 2,429 minority (1,588 Black or African American, non-Hispanic/Latino; 36 American Indian or Alaska Native, non-Hispanic/Latino; 176 Asian, non-Hispanic/Latino; 397 Hispanic/Latino; 21 Native Hawaiian or other Pacific Islander, non-Hispanic/Latino; 211 Two or more races, non-Hispanic/Latino), 171 international. Average age 36. 8,665 applicants, 42% accepted, 1,753 enrolled. Expenses: Contact institution. *Financial support:* In 2019–20, 990 students received support. Teaching assistantships and Federal Work-Study available. Financial award applicants required to submit FAFSA. In 2019, 2,008 master's, 28 doctorates awarded. *Program availability:* Part-time, online learning. *Application deadline:* Applications are processed on a rolling basis. *Application fee:* $50. Electronic applications accepted. *Application Contact:* Jay Bridge, Director of Graduate Admissions, 800-424-9595, Fax: 800-628-7977, E-mail: gradadmissions@liberty.edu. *Dean*, Dr. Dave Bratt, 434-592-7321, E-mail: dabrat@liberty.edu.

**School Of Communication & the Arts** Students: 335 full-time (235 women), 331 part-time (204 women); includes 190 minority (114 Black or African American, non-Hispanic/Latino; 2 American Indian or Alaska Native, non-Hispanic/Latino; 18 Asian, non-Hispanic/Latino; 24 Hispanic/Latino; 1 Native Hawaiian or other Pacific Islander, non-Hispanic/Latino; 31 Two or more races, non-Hispanic/Latino), 19 international. Average age 33. 1,223 applicants, 40% accepted, 242 enrolled. Expenses: Contact institution. *Financial support:* In 2019–20, 882 students received support. Federal Work-Study and unspecified assistantships available. Financial award applicants required to submit FAFSA. In 2019, 146 master's awarded. *Program availability:* Part-time. *Application deadline:* For fall admission, 6/1 for domestic students; for spring admission, 11/1 for domestic students. Applications are processed on a rolling basis. *Application fee:* $50. Electronic applications accepted. *Application Contact:* Dr. Jay Bridge, Director of OnlineAdmissions, 800-4249505, E-mail: gradadmissions@liberty.edu. *Residential Dean*, Dr. Scott Hayes, E-mail: smhayes@liberty.edu.

**School of Divinity** Students: 2,691 full-time (814 women), 2,570 part-time (732 women); includes 1,484 minority (1,046 Black or African American, non-Hispanic/Latino; 33 American Indian or Alaska Native, non-Hispanic/Latino; 120 Asian, non-Hispanic/Latino; 167 Hispanic/Latino; 8 Native Hawaiian or other Pacific Islander, non-Hispanic/Latino; 110 Two or more races, non-Hispanic/Latino), 101 international. Average age 43. 4,508 applicants, 34% accepted, 952 enrolled. Expenses: Contact institution. *Financial support:* Teaching assistantships with tuition reimbursements, career-related internships or fieldwork, and Federal Work-Study available. Financial award applicants required to submit FAFSA. In 2019, 1,251 master's, 71 doctorates awarded. *Program availability:* Part-time, online learning. *Application deadline:* For fall admission, 6/1 for domestic students; for spring admission, 11/1 for domestic students. Applications are processed on a rolling basis. *Application fee:* $50. Electronic applications accepted. *Application Contact:* Jay Bridge, Director of Graduate Admissions, 800-424-9595, Fax: 800-628-7977, E-mail: gradadmissions@liberty.edu. *Interim Dean, School of Divinity*, Dr. Troy Temple, E-mail: divinity@liberty.edu.

**School of Education** Students: 4,441 full-time (3,342 women), 3,629 part-time (2,729 women); includes 2,319 minority (1,676 Black or African American, non-Hispanic/Latino; 46 American Indian or Alaska Native, non-Hispanic/Latino; 99 Asian, non-Hispanic/Latino; 241 Hispanic/Latino; 16 Native Hawaiian or other Pacific Islander, non-Hispanic/Latino; 241 Two or more races, non-Hispanic/Latino), 87 international. Average age 38. 8,200 applicants, 40% accepted, 1,715 enrolled. Expenses: Contact institution. *Financial support:* In 2019–20, 265 students received support. Federal Work-Study and tuition waivers (partial) available. In 2019, 1,026 master's, 200 doctorates, 426 other advanced degrees awarded. *Program availability:* Part-time, online learning. *Application deadline:* For fall admission, 6/1 for domestic students; for spring admission, 11/1 for domestic students. Applications are processed on a rolling basis. *Application fee:* $50. Electronic applications accepted. *Application Contact:* Jay Bridge, Director of Graduate Admissions, 800-424-9595, Fax: 800-628-7977, E-mail: gradadmissions@liberty.edu. *Dean*, Dr. Deanna Keith, 434-582-2417, E-mail: dkeith@liberty.edu.

**School of Health Sciences** Students: 820 full-time (588 women), 889 part-time (612 women); includes 611 minority (402 Black or African American, non-Hispanic/Latino; 10 American Indian or Alaska Native, non-Hispanic/Latino; 43 Asian, non-Hispanic/Latino; 85 Hispanic/Latino; 1 Native Hawaiian or other Pacific Islander, non-Hispanic/Latino; 70 Two or more races, non-Hispanic/Latino), 67 international. Average age 32. 2,610 applicants, 33% accepted, 406 enrolled. Expenses: Contact institution. *Financial support:* In 2019–20, 918 students received support. Federal Work-Study available. Financial award applicants required to submit FAFSA. In 2019, 445 master's awarded. *Program availability:* Part-time, online learning. *Application fee:* $50. *Application Contact:* Jay Bridge, Director of Admissions, 800-424-9595, Fax: 800-628-7977, E-mail: gradadmissions@liberty.edu. *Dean*, Dr. Ralph Linstra.

**School of Law** Students: 299 full-time (145 women), 154 part-time (89 women); includes 119 minority (58 Black or African American, non-Hispanic/Latino; 3 American Indian or Alaska Native, non-Hispanic/Latino; 10 Asian, non-Hispanic/Latino; 33 Hispanic/Latino; 1 Native Hawaiian or other Pacific Islander, non-Hispanic/Latino; 14 Two or more races, non-Hispanic/Latino), 11 international. Average age 33. 428 applicants, 52% accepted, 158 enrolled. Expenses: Contact institution. *Financial support:* In 2019–20, 208 students received support. Federal Work-Study available. Financial award applicants required to submit FAFSA. *Program availability:* Online learning. *Application deadline:* For fall admission, 6/1 for domestic students. *Application Contact:* Joleen Thaxton, Assistant Director of Admissions, 434-592-5300, Fax: 434-592-5400, E-mail: lawadmissions@liberty.edu. *Dean*, B. Keith Faulkner, 434-592-5300, Fax: 434-592-5400, E-mail: law@liberty.edu.

**School of Music** Students: 147 full-time (72 women), 220 part-time (103 women); includes 104 minority (61 Black or African American, non-Hispanic/Latino; 1 American Indian or Alaska Native, non-Hispanic/Latino; 15 Asian, non-Hispanic/Latino; 21 Hispanic/Latino; 6 Two or more races, non-Hispanic/Latino), 17 international. Average age 37. 537 applicants, 30% accepted, 89 enrolled. Expenses: Contact institution. *Financial support:* In 2019–20, 619 students received support. Federal Work-Study available. Financial award applicants required to submit FAFSA. In 2019, 44 master's, 11 doctorates awarded. *Program availability:* Part-time, online learning. *Application deadline:* Applications are processed on a rolling basis. *Application fee:* $50. Electronic applications accepted. *Application Contact:* Jay Bridge, Director of Admissions, 800-424-9595, Fax: 800-628-7977, E-mail: gradadmissions@liberty.edu. *Dean*, Dr. Stephen W. Müller,, 434-5823459, E-mail: swmuller@liberty.edu.

**School of Nursing** Students: 279 full-time (257 women), 505 part-time (449 women); includes 170 minority (118 Black or African American, non-Hispanic/Latino; 2 American Indian or Alaska Native, non-Hispanic/Latino; 19 Asian, non-Hispanic/Latino; 25 Hispanic/Latino; 6 Two or more races, non-Hispanic/Latino), 11 international. Average age 39. 1,154 applicants, 27% accepted, 171 enrolled. Expenses: Contact institution. *Financial support:* In 2019–20, 128 students received support. Federal Work-Study available. Financial award applicants required to submit FAFSA. In 2019, 138 master's, 26 doctorates awarded. *Program availability:* Part-time, online learning. *Application deadline:* Applications are processed on a rolling basis. *Application fee:* $50. Electronic applications accepted. *Application Contact:* Jay Bridge, Director of Admissions, 800-424-9595, Fax: 800-628-7977, E-mail: gradadmissions@liberty.edu. *Dean*, Dr. Shanna Akers, 434-592-3618, E-mail: lusondean@liberty.edu.

## LIFE CHIROPRACTIC COLLEGE WEST, Hayward, CA 94545

**General Information** Independent, coed, graduate-only institution. *Graduate housing:* On-campus housing not available. *Research affiliation:* National Center for Complimentary Medicine, National Center for Complementary and Alternative Medicine/University Cancer Research Fund, Advanced Orthogonality, San Jose State University, University of Calgary.

**GRADUATE UNITS**

**Professional Program** Electronic applications accepted.

## LIFE UNIVERSITY, Marietta, GA 30060-2903

**General Information** Independent, coed, comprehensive institution. *Enrollment:* 2,728 graduate, professional, and undergraduate students; 1,673 full-time matriculated graduate/professional students (834 women), 175 part-time matriculated graduate/professional students (78 women). *Enrollment by degree level:* 195 master's, 1,653 doctoral. *Graduate faculty:* 93 full-time (36 women), 32 part-time/adjunct (16 women). *Tuition:* Full-time $28,425; part-time $8235 per year. *Required fees:* $1491. *Graduate housing:* Rooms and/or apartments available on a first-come, first-served basis to single and married students. Typical cost: $6400 per year ($14,400 including board) for single students. Room and board charges vary according to housing facility selected. *Student services:* Campus employment opportunities, campus safety program, career counseling, exercise/wellness program, free psychological counseling, international student services, services for students with disabilities. *Library facilities:* Library & Learning Services. *Collection:* Books: 33,771 (physical), 39,225 (digital/electronic); Serial titles: 66 (physical), 31,104 (digital/electronic); Databases: 25. Weekly public service hours: 98; students can reserve study rooms.

**Computer facilities:** A campuswide network can be accessed. Online class registration is available.
Website: http://www.life.edu/

**General Application Contact:** Keith Jordon, Director of Graduate & Undergraduate Enrollment, 800-543-3202, Fax: 770-426-2895, E-mail: keith.jordan@life.edu.

**GRADUATE UNITS**

**College of Chiropractic** Students: 1,552 full-time (712 women), 99 part-time (50 women); includes 576 minority (207 Black or African American, non-Hispanic/Latino; 17 American Indian or Alaska Native, non-Hispanic/Latino; 62 Asian, non-Hispanic/Latino; 290 Hispanic/Latino), 66 international. Average age 28. *Faculty:* 83 full-time (32 women), 22 part-time/adjunct (6 women). Expenses: Contact institution. *Financial support:* Research assistantships, Federal Work-Study, institutionally sponsored loans, scholarships/grants, and tuition waivers (partial) available. Support available to part-time students. Financial award application deadline: 9/1; financial award applicants required to submit FAFSA. In 2019, 353 doctorates awarded. *Application deadline:* For fall admission, 8/1 for domestic students; for winter admission, 11/1 for domestic students; for spring admission, 3/1 for domestic students; for summer admission, 7/1 for domestic students. Applications are processed on a rolling basis. *Application fee:* $50. Electronic applications accepted. *Application Contact:* Charmaine Townsend, Director of Chiropractic Enrollment, 678-331 4382, Fax: 770-426-2895, E-mail: charmaine.edwards@life.edu. *Dean*, Dr. Leslie King, 770-426-2713, E-mail: lesliek@life.edu.

**College of Graduate and Undergraduate Studies** *Program availability:* Part-time, 100% online, blended/hybrid learning. Electronic applications accepted.

## LIM COLLEGE, New York, NY 10022-5268

**General Information** Proprietary, coed, primarily women, comprehensive institution. *Graduate housing:* Room and/or apartments available on a first-come, first-served basis to single students; on-campus housing not available to married students.

**GRADUATE UNITS**

**MPS Program** *Program availability:* Part-time, 100% online. Electronic applications accepted.

## LIMESTONE COLLEGE, Gaffney, SC 29340-3799

**General Information** Independent, coed, comprehensive institution. *Enrollment:* 2,219 graduate, professional, and undergraduate students; 51 full-time matriculated graduate/professional students (20 women), 34 part-time matriculated graduate/professional students (21 women). *Enrollment by degree level:* 85 master's. *Graduate faculty:* 11 full-time (5 women), 2 part-time/adjunct (0 women). *Tuition:* Full-time $9925; part-time $7720 per credit hour. *Required fees:* $150 per degree program. One-time fee: $150. Tuition and fees vary according to course load and program. *Graduate housing:* On-campus housing not available. *Student services:* Campus employment opportunities, campus safety program, career counseling, free psychological counseling, international student services, services for students with disabilities, writing training. *Library facilities:* A. J. Eastwood Library plus 1 other. *Collection:* Books: 67,000 (physical), 239,537 (digital/electronic); Serial titles: 111 (physical), 482,082 (digital/electronic); Databases: 156. Weekly public service hours: 70.

**Computer facilities:** 137 computers available on campus for general student use. A campuswide network can be accessed. Online class registration is available.
Website: http://www.limestone.edu/

**General Application Contact:** Adair Haynes, Director of Graduate Studies in Enrollment and Admissions, 800-795-7151 Ext. 4370, Fax: 864-487-8706, E-mail: ahaynes@limestone.edu.

**GRADUATE UNITS**

**MBA Program** Students: 51 full-time (20 women), 34 part-time (21 women); includes 39 minority (36 Black or African American, non-Hispanic/Latino; 2 Asian, non-Hispanic/Latino; 1 Two or more races, non-Hispanic/Latino), 6 international. Average age 36. 71 applicants, 34% accepted, 11 enrolled. *Faculty:* 10 full-time (4 women), 2 part-time/adjunct (0 women). Expenses: Contact institution. *Financial support:* Scholarships/grants available. Financial award application deadline: 6/15; financial award applicants required to submit FAFSA. In 2019, 30 master's awarded. *Program availability:* Part-time, evening/weekend, online only, 100% online, but there are three 1-hour group dynamics classes offered during weekends between semesters. *Application deadline:* For fall admission, 8/1 priority date for domestic and international students; for winter admission, 12/12 priority date for domestic and international students; for spring admission, 4/1 priority date for domestic and international students. Applications are processed on a rolling basis. *Application fee:* $25. Electronic applications accepted. *Application Contact:* Adair Hudson, Director of Graduate Studies in Enrollment and Admissions, 800-795-7151 Ext. 4370, Fax: 864-467-8706, E-mail: ahaynes@limestone.edu. *Director of Graduate Studies in Enrollment and Admissions*, Adair Hudson, 864-488-4370, Fax: 864-487-8706, E-mail: ahudson@limestone.edu.

## LINCOLN CHRISTIAN SEMINARY, Lincoln, IL 62656-2167

**General Information** Independent-religious, coed, graduate-only institution. *Graduate housing:* Rooms and/or apartments available on a first-come, first-served basis to single and married students.

**GRADUATE UNITS**

**Graduate and Professional Programs** *Program availability:* Part-time. Electronic applications accepted.

## LINCOLN CHRISTIAN UNIVERSITY, Lincoln, IL 62656-2167

**General Information** Independent-religious, coed, comprehensive institution. *Graduate housing:* Rooms and/or apartments available on a first-come, first-served basis to single and married students. Housing application deadline: 8/15.

**GRADUATE UNITS**

**Graduate Programs** *Program availability:* Online learning.

## LINCOLN MEMORIAL UNIVERSITY, Harrogate, TN 37752-1901

**General Information** Independent, coed, university. *Graduate housing:* Rooms and/or apartments available on a first-come, first-served basis to single and married students.

**GRADUATE UNITS**

**Carter and Moyers School of Education** *Program availability:* Part-time, evening/weekend, online learning.

**Caylor School of Nursing** *Program availability:* Part-time.

**College of Veterinary Medicine**

**DeBusk College of Osteopathic Medicine**

**Duncan School of Law** *Program availability:* Part-time. Electronic applications accepted.

**School of Business** *Program availability:* Part-time, evening/weekend.

## LINCOLN UNIVERSITY, Oakland, CA 94612

**General Information** Independent, coed, comprehensive institution. *Enrollment:* 362 full-time matriculated graduate/professional students (152 women), 28 part-time matriculated graduate/professional students (14 women). *Enrollment by degree level:* 384 master's, 6 doctoral. *Graduate faculty:* 19 full-time (3 women), 16 part-time/adjunct (4 women). *Tuition:* Full-time $8460; part-time $510 per unit. *Required fees:* $215 per semester. Tuition and fees vary according to course level, course load, degree level and program. *Student services:* Campus employment opportunities, career counseling, international student services, writing training. *Library facilities:* Lincoln University Library. *Collection:* Books: 14,400 (physical), 128,000 (digital/electronic); Serial titles: 350 (physical), 5,050 (digital/electronic); Databases: 19.

**Computer facilities:** 39 computers available on campus for general student use. A campuswide network can be accessed.
Website: http://www.lincolnuca.edu/

**General Application Contact:** Peggy Au, Director of Admissions and Records, 510-628-8010, Fax: 510-628-8012, E-mail: admissions@lincolnuca.edu.

**GRADUATE UNITS**

**Graduate Studies** *Program availability:* Part-time. Electronic applications accepted.

## LINCOLN UNIVERSITY, Jefferson City, MO 65101

**General Information** State-supported, coed, comprehensive institution. *Enrollment:* 2,436 graduate, professional, and undergraduate students; 37 full-time matriculated graduate/professional students (23 women), 52 part-time matriculated graduate/professional students (25 women). *Enrollment by degree level:* 82 master's, 7 other advanced degrees. *International tuition:* $886 full-time. *Tuition, area resident:* Full-time $511; part-time $511 per credit hour. Tuition, state resident: full-time $511; part-time $511 per credit hour. Tuition, nonresident: full-time $886; part-time $886 per credit hour. *Required fees:* $20; $20 per credit hour. $381.10 per semester. *Graduate housing:* Room and/or apartments available on a first-come, first-served basis to single students; on-campus housing not available to married students. Typical cost: $2297 per year ($4074 including board). Housing application deadline: 7/1. *Student services:* Campus employment opportunities, career counseling, international student services, services for students with disabilities. *Library facilities:* Inman E. Page Library. *Collection:* Books: 117,765 (physical), 225,904 (digital/electronic); Serial titles: 1,301 (physical), 19,000 (digital/electronic); Databases: 50. Weekly public service hours: 84. *Research affiliation:* National Science Foundation (STEM research), Ceres Trust (agriculture), Missouri Department of Agriculture (agriculture), Center for Rural Affairs (sustainable agriculture), U.S. Department of Education (DOE) (defense, government), U.S. Department of Agriculture (USDA) (agriculture, government).

**Computer facilities:** Computer purchase and lease plans are available. 365 computers available on campus for general student use. A campuswide network can be accessed. Online class registration is available.
Website: http://www.lincolnu.edu/

**General Application Contact:** Dr. Benjamin Arnold, Assistant Vice President of Academic Affairs, 573-681-5247, Fax: 573-681-5106, E-mail: gradschool@lincolnu.edu.

**GRADUATE UNITS**

**Graduate Studies** Students: 47 full-time (33 women), 62 part-time (35 women); includes 42 minority (39 Black or African American, non-Hispanic/Latino; 1 American Indian or Alaska Native, non-Hispanic/Latino; 1 Asian, non-Hispanic/Latino; 1 Native Hawaiian or other Pacific Islander, non-Hispanic/Latino), 13 international. Average age 33. Expenses: Contact institution. *Financial support:* In 2019–20, 8 fellowships (averaging $4,017 per year), 6 research assistantships (averaging $18,500 per year) were awarded; Federal Work-Study, scholarships/grants, and unspecified assistantships also available. Support available to part-time students. Financial award application deadline: 3/1; financial award applicants required to submit FAFSA. In 2019, 32 master's awarded. *Program availability:* Part-time, evening/weekend, 100% online, blended/hybrid learning. *Application deadline:* For fall admission, 7/1 priority date for domestic students, 5/1 priority date for international students; for spring admission, 11/1 priority date for domestic students, 10/1 priority date for international students; for summer admission, 6/1 priority date for domestic students. Applications are processed on a rolling basis. *Application fee:* $30. Electronic applications accepted. *Application Contact:* James Kendall, Graduate Admission Coordinator/Recruiter, 573-681-5150, Fax: 573-681-5106, E-mail: gradschool@lincolnu.edu. *Assistant Vice President of Academic Affairs*, Dr. Benjamin Arnold, 573-681-5247, Fax: 573-681-5106, E-mail: gradschool@lincolnu.edu.

## LINCOLN UNIVERSITY, Lincoln University, PA 19352

**General Information** State-related, coed, comprehensive institution. *Enrollment:* 2,241 graduate, professional, and undergraduate students; 149 full-time matriculated graduate/professional students (115 women), 47 part-time matriculated graduate/professional students (30 women). *Enrollment by degree level:* 196 master's. *Graduate faculty:* 8 full-time (4 women), 20 part-time/adjunct (10 women). *Tuition, area resident:* Full-time $10,106; part-time $511 per credit hour. Tuition, state resident: full-time $10,106; part-time $511 per credit hour. Tuition, nonresident: full-time $17,636; part-time $886 per credit hour. *Required fees:* $1237; $59.50 per credit hour. One-time fee: $204. *Graduate housing:* On-campus housing not available. *Student services:* Campus employment opportunities, career counseling, free psychological counseling, international student services, low-cost health insurance, teacher training. *Library facilities:* Langston Hughes Memorial Library. *Collection:* Books: 177,538 (physical), 133,000 (digital/electronic); Serial titles: 37,382 (physical). Weekly public service hours: 96; study areas open 24 hours, 5–7 days a week; students can reserve study rooms. *Research affiliation:* The Treatment Research Institute (addictive disorders).

**Computer facilities:** 600 computers available on campus for general student use. A campuswide network can be accessed. Online class registration is available.
Website: http://www.lincoln.edu/

**General Application Contact:** Jernice Lea, Director, University City Student Services and Admissions, 215-590-8231, Fax: 215-387-3859, E-mail: jlea@lincoln.edu.

**GRADUATE UNITS**

**School of Adult and Continuing Education** Students: 149 full-time (115 women), 47 part-time (30 women); includes 177 minority (170 Black or African American, non-Hispanic/Latino; 5 Hispanic/Latino; 2 Two or more races, non-Hispanic/Latino), 2 international. Average age 34. 156 applicants, 51% accepted, 53 enrolled. *Faculty:* 8 full-time (4 women), 20 part-time/adjunct (10 women). Expenses: Contact institution. *Financial support:* In 2019–20, 2 students received support. Scholarships/grants available. Financial award application deadline: 4/1; financial award applicants required to submit FAFSA. In 2019, 105 master's awarded. *Program availability:* Part-time, evening/weekend. *Application deadline:* For fall admission, 8/19 for domestic and international students; for spring admission, 12/30 for domestic and international students. Applications are processed on a rolling basis. *Application fee:* $50. Electronic applications accepted. *Application Contact:* Jernice Lea, Director, Student Services and Admissions, 215-590-8231, Fax: 215-387-3859, E-mail: jlea@lincoln.edu. *Dean of Faculty*, Dr. Patricia Joseph, 484-365-7659, E-mail: joseph@lincoln.edu.

## LINDENWOOD UNIVERSITY, St. Charles, MO 63301-1695

**General Information** Independent-religious, coed, comprehensive institution. *Enrollment:* 8,406 graduate, professional, and undergraduate students; 1,137 full-time matriculated graduate/professional students (747 women), 1,601 part-time matriculated graduate/professional students (1,183 women). *Enrollment by degree level:* 2,382 master's, 231 doctoral, 125 other advanced degrees. *Graduate faculty:* 101 full-time (54 women), 270 part-time/adjunct (133 women). *Tuition:* Full-time $8910; part-time $495 per credit. Tuition and fees vary according to course load, degree level and program. *Graduate housing:* Rooms and/or apartments available on a first-come, first-served basis to single and married students. Housing application deadline: 8/26. *Student services:* Campus employment opportunities, campus safety program, career counseling, exercise/wellness program, free psychological counseling, international student services, services for students with disabilities, teacher training, writing training. *Library facilities:* Library and Academic Resource Center plus 1 other. *Collection:* Books: 74,272 (physical), 268,719 (digital/electronic); Serial titles: 132 (physical), 102 (digital/electronic); Databases: 141. Students can reserve study rooms.

**Computer facilities:** 231 computers available on campus for general student use. A campuswide network can be accessed. Online class registration is available.
Website: http://www.lindenwood.edu/

**General Application Contact:** Kara Schilli, Assistant Vice President University Admissions, 636-949-4349, Fax: 636-949-4109, E-mail: adultadmissions@lindenwood.edu.

**GRADUATE UNITS**

**Graduate Programs** Students: 1,137 full-time (747 women), 1,601 part-time (1,183 women); includes 719 minority (544 Black or African American, non-Hispanic/Latino; 12 American Indian or Alaska Native, non-Hispanic/Latino; 14 Asian, non-Hispanic/Latino; 76 Hispanic/Latino; 3 Native Hawaiian or other Pacific Islander, non-Hispanic/Latino; 70 Two or more races, non-Hispanic/Latino), 102 international. Average age 35. 1,365 applicants, 56% accepted, 550 enrolled. *Faculty:* 101 full-time (54 women), 270 part-time/adjunct (133 women). Expenses: Contact institution. *Financial support:* In 2019–20, 661 students received support. Career-related internships or fieldwork, Federal Work-Study, institutionally sponsored loans, scholarships/grants, tuition waivers (full), and unspecified assistantships available. Financial award application deadline: 6/30; financial award applicants required to submit FAFSA. In 2019, 1,063 master's, 60 doctorates, 77 other advanced degrees awarded. *Program availability:* Part-time, evening/weekend, 100% online, blended/hybrid learning. *Application deadline:* For fall admission, 8/9 priority date for domestic students, 6/1 priority date for international students; for spring admission, 12/20 priority date for domestic students, 11/1 priority date for international students; for summer admission, 5/15 priority date for domestic students, 3/27 priority date for international students. Applications are processed on a rolling basis. *Application fee:* $0 ($100 for international students). Electronic applications accepted. *Application Contact:* Kara Schilli, Assistant Vice President, University Admissions, 636-949-4349, Fax: 636-949-4109, E-mail: KSchilli@lindenwood.edu. *Provost/Senior Vice President Academic Affairs*, Dr. Mark Arant, 636-949-4912, Fax: 636-949-4912, E-mail: MArant@lindenwood.edu.

***Plaster School of Business and Entrepreneurship*** Students: 240 full-time (138 women), 274 part-time (168 women); includes 150 minority (113 Black or African American, non-Hispanic/Latino; 2 American Indian or Alaska Native, non-Hispanic/Latino; 6 Asian, non-Hispanic/Latino; 12 Hispanic/Latino; 1 Native Hawaiian or other Pacific Islander, non-Hispanic/Latino; 16 Two or more races, non-Hispanic/Latino), 44 international. Average age 31. 415 applicants, 54% accepted, 151 enrolled. *Faculty:* 20 full-time (9 women), 46 part-time/adjunct (15 women). Expenses: Contact institution. *Financial support:* In 2019–20, 257 students received support. Career-related internships or fieldwork, Federal Work-Study, institutionally sponsored loans, scholarships/grants, tuition waivers (partial), and unspecified assistantships available. Financial award application deadline: 6/30; financial award applicants required to submit FAFSA. In 2019, 230 master's awarded. *Program availability:* Part-time, evening/weekend, 100% online. *Application deadline:* For fall admission, 8/9 priority date for domestic students, 6/1 priority date for international students; for winter admission, 12/20 priority date for domestic students, 11/1 priority date for international students; for spring admission, 2/28 priority date for domestic students, 1/3 priority date for international students; for summer admission, 5/15 priority date for domestic students, 3/27 priority date for international students. Applications are processed on a rolling basis. *Application fee:* $0 ($100 for international students). Electronic applications accepted. *Application Contact:* Kara Schilli, Assistant Vice President, University Admissions, 636-949-4349, Fax: 636-949-4109, E-mail: adultadmissions@lindenwood.edu. *Interim Dean, School of Business and Entrepreneurship*, Molly Hudgins, JD, 636-949-4192, E-mail: rellis@lindenwood.edu.

***School of Accelerated Degree Programs*** Students: 408 full-time (262 women), 60 part-time (40 women); includes 149 minority (111 Black or African American, non-Hispanic/Latino; 2 American Indian or Alaska Native, non-Hispanic/Latino; 2 Asian, non-Hispanic/Latino; 18 Hispanic/Latino; 1 Native Hawaiian or other Pacific Islander, non-Hispanic/Latino; 15 Two or more races, non-Hispanic/Latino), 33 international. Average age 39. 268 applicants, 46% accepted, 99 enrolled. *Faculty:* 11 full-time (6 women), 66 part-time/adjunct (23 women). Expenses: Contact institution. *Financial support:* In 2019–20, 145 students received support. Career-related internships or fieldwork, institutionally sponsored loans, scholarships/grants, tuition waivers (partial), and unspecified assistantships available. Financial award application deadline: 6/30; financial award applicants required to submit FAFSA. In 2019, 347 master's awarded. *Program availability:* Part-time, evening/weekend, 100% online. *Application deadline:* For fall admission, 9/30 priority date for domestic and international students; for winter admission, 1/6 priority date for domestic and international students; for spring admission, 4/6 priority date for domestic and international students; for summer admission, 7/8 priority date for domestic and international students. Applications are processed on a rolling basis. *Application fee:* $0 ($100 for international students). Electronic applications accepted. *Application Contact:* Kara Schilli, Assistant Vice President, University Admissions, 636-949-4349, Fax: 636-949-4109, E-mail: adultadmissions@lindenwood.edu. *Dean, Accelerated Degree Programs*, Dr. Gina Ganahl, 636-949-4501, Fax: 636-949-4505, E-mail: gganahl@lindenwood.edu.

***School of Arts, Media, and Communications*** Students: 64 full-time (42 women), 76 part-time (57 women); includes 43 minority (20 Black or African American, non-Hispanic/Latino; 13 Hispanic/Latino; 10 Two or more races, non-Hispanic/Latino), 8 international. Average age 33. 145 applicants, 46% accepted, 56 enrolled. *Faculty:* 20 full-time (5 women), 15 part-time/adjunct (6 women). Expenses: Contact institution. *Financial support:* In 2019–20, 23 students received support. Career-related internships or fieldwork, institutionally sponsored loans, scholarships/grants, tuition waivers (partial), and unspecified assistantships available. Financial award application deadline: 6/30; financial award applicants required to submit FAFSA. In 2019, 11 master's awarded. *Program availability:* Part-time, 100% online. *Application deadline:* For fall admission, 8/9 priority date for domestic students, 6/1 priority date for international students; for spring admission, 12/20 for domestic students, 11/1 priority date for international students; for summer admission, 5/15 priority date for domestic students, 3/27 priority date for international students. Applications are processed on a rolling basis. *Application fee:* $0 ($100 for international students). Electronic applications accepted. *Application Contact:* Kara Schilli, Assistant Vice President, University Admissions, 636-949-4349, Fax: 636-949-4109, E-mail: adultadmissions@lindenwood.edu. *Dean, School of Arts, Media, and Communications*, Dr. Jason Lively, 636-949-4164, Fax: 636-949-4910, E-mail: JLively@lindenwood.edu.

***School of Education*** Students: 391 full-time (287 women), 1,149 part-time (889 women); includes 358 minority (284 Black or African American, non-Hispanic/Latino; 8 American Indian or Alaska Native, non-Hispanic/Latino; 6 Asian, non-Hispanic/Latino; 32 Hispanic/Latino; 28 Two or more races, non-Hispanic/Latino), 11 international. Average age 35. 465 applicants, 71% accepted, 229 enrolled. *Faculty:* 39 full-time (28 women), 133 part-time/adjunct (83 women). Expenses: Contact institution. *Financial support:* In 2019–20, 198 students received support. Career-related internships or fieldwork, Federal Work-Study, institutionally sponsored loans, scholarships/grants, tuition waivers (partial), and unspecified assistantships available. Financial award application deadline: 6/30; financial award applicants required to submit FAFSA. In 2019, 432 master's, 60 doctorates, 77 other advanced degrees awarded. *Program availability:* Part-time, evening/weekend, 100% online, blended/hybrid learning. *Application deadline:* For fall admission, 8/9 priority date for domestic students, 6/1 priority date for international students; for spring admission, 12/20 priority date for domestic students, 11/1 priority date for international students; for summer admission, 5/15 priority date for domestic students, 3/27 priority date for international students. Applications are processed on a rolling basis. *Application fee:* $0 ($100 for international students). Electronic applications accepted. *Application Contact:* Kara Schilli, Assistant Vice President, University Admissions, 636-949-4349, Fax: 636-949-4109, E-mail: adultadmissions@lindenwood.edu. *Dean, School of Education*, Dr. Anthony Scheffler, 636-949-4618, Fax: 636-949-4197, E-mail: ascheffler@lindenwood.edu.

***School of Health Sciences*** Students: 22 full-time (11 women), 25 part-time (18 women); includes 5 minority (3 Black or African American, non-Hispanic/Latino; 1 Hispanic/Latino; 1 Native Hawaiian or other Pacific Islander, non-Hispanic/Latino), 6 international. Average age 30. 43 applicants, 37% accepted, 12 enrolled. *Faculty:* 8 full-time (3 women), 8 part-time/adjunct (5 women). Expenses: Contact institution. *Financial support:* In 2019–20, 25 students received support. Career-related internships or fieldwork, Federal Work-Study, institutionally sponsored loans, scholarships/grants, tuition waivers (partial), and unspecified assistantships available. Financial award application deadline: 6/30; financial award applicants required to submit FAFSA. In 2019, 31 master's awarded. *Program availability:* Part-time, blended/hybrid learning. *Application deadline:* For fall admission, 8/9 priority date for domestic students, 6/1 priority date for international students; for spring admission, 12/20 priority date for domestic students, 11/1 priority date for international students; for summer admission, 5/15 priority date for domestic students, 3/27 priority date for international students. Applications are processed on a rolling basis. *Application fee:* $0 ($100 for international students). Electronic applications accepted. *Application Contact:* Kara Schilli, Assistant Vice President, University Admissions, 636-949-4349, Fax: 636-949-4109, E-mail: adultadmissions@lindenwood.edu. *Dean, School of Health Sciences*, Dr. Cynthia Schroeder, 636-949-4318, E-mail: cschroeder@lindenwood.edu.

## LINDENWOOD UNIVERSITY–BELLEVILLE, Belleville, IL 62226

**General Information** Independent-religious, coed, comprehensive institution.

**GRADUATE UNITS**

**Graduate Programs**

## LINDSEY WILSON COLLEGE, Columbia, KY 42728

**General Information** Independent-religious, coed, comprehensive institution. *Graduate housing:* Rooms and/or apartments available on a first-come, first-served basis to single and married students.

**GRADUATE UNITS**

**Division of Education** *Program availability:* Online learning.

**Louisville Center for Design** *Program availability:* Online learning.

**School of Professional Counseling** *Program availability:* Part-time, evening/weekend, online learning.

## LIPSCOMB UNIVERSITY, Nashville, TN 37204-3951

**General Information** Independent-religious, coed, university. CGS member. *Graduate housing:* Room and/or apartments available on a first-come, first-served basis to single students; on-campus housing not available to married students. Housing application deadline: 7/15.

**GRADUATE UNITS**

**College of Business** *Program availability:* Part-time, evening/weekend. Electronic applications accepted.

**College of Computing and Technology** *Program availability:* Part-time, evening/weekend. Electronic applications accepted.

**College of Education** *Program availability:* Part-time, evening/weekend, 100% online. Electronic applications accepted.

**College of Pharmacy** Electronic applications accepted.

**Department of Psychology, Counseling, and Family Science** *Program availability:* Part-time, evening/weekend. Electronic applications accepted.

**Hazelip School of Theology** *Program availability:* Part-time, evening/weekend, online learning. Electronic applications accepted.

**Institute for Conflict Management** *Program availability:* Part-time, evening/weekend. Electronic applications accepted.

**Institute for Sustainable Practice** *Program availability:* Part-time, evening/weekend, online learning. Electronic applications accepted.

**Nelson and Sue Andrews Institute for Civic Leadership** *Program availability:* Part-time, evening/weekend. Electronic applications accepted.

**Program in Biomolecular Science** *Program availability:* Part-time, evening/weekend. Electronic applications accepted.

**Program in Exercise and Nutrition Science** *Program availability:* Part-time, evening/weekend. Electronic applications accepted.

**Program in Film and Creative Media** *Program availability:* Part-time, evening/weekend. Electronic applications accepted.

**Program in Organizational Leadership** *Program availability:* Part-time, online only, blended/hybrid learning. Electronic applications accepted.

**School of Public Policy** Electronic applications accepted.

## LOCK HAVEN UNIVERSITY OF PENNSYLVANIA, Lock Haven, PA 17745-2390

**General Information** State-supported, coed, comprehensive institution. *Graduate housing:* Room and/or apartments available on a first-come, first-served basis to single students; on-campus housing not available to married students. Housing application deadline: 6/1.

**GRADUATE UNITS**

**College of Liberal Arts and Education** *Program availability:* Part-time, evening/weekend, online learning. Electronic applications accepted.

**College of Natural, Behavioral and Health Sciences** Electronic applications accepted.

**The Stephen Poorman College of Business, Information Systems, and Human Services** *Program availability:* Online learning. Electronic applications accepted.

## LOGAN UNIVERSITY, Chesterfield, MO 63017

**General Information** Independent, coed, upper-level institution. *Graduate housing:* On-campus housing not available. *Research affiliation:* BTE-Multi-Cervical Unit (cervical spine analysis), Cadwell (electrophysiological diagnosis), Standard Process (nutrition and lipid management), Biofreeze (topical analgesics), Foot Levelers, Inc. (orthotics).

**GRADUATE UNITS**

**College of Chiropractic** Electronic applications accepted.

**College of Health Sciences** *Program availability:* Part-time, online only, 100% online. Electronic applications accepted.

## LOGOS EVANGELICAL SEMINARY, El Monte, CA 91731

**General Information** Independent-religious, coed, graduate-only institution. *Graduate faculty:* 14 full-time (7 women), 29 part-time/adjunct (8 women). *Tuition:* Full-time $10,410; part-time $4364 per unit. *Required fees:* $100 per semester. *Graduate housing:* Rooms and/or apartments available on a first-come, first-served basis to single and married students. Typical cost: $12,300 per year for single students; $15,480 per year for married students. Housing application deadline: 7/15. *Student services:* Campus employment opportunities, campus safety program, career counseling, international student services, low-cost health insurance. *Library facilities:* Logos Library plus 1 other. *Collection:* Books: 63,467 (physical), 38,708 (digital/electronic); Serial titles: 162 (physical), 7 (digital/electronic); Databases: 10. Weekly public service hours: 64; students can reserve study rooms.

**Computer facilities:** 12 computers available on campus for general student use. A campuswide network can be accessed from student residence rooms and from off campus. Online class registration, X are available.
Website: http://www.les.edu/language/en/

**General Application Contact:** Carrie Zhou, Admission Officer, 626-571-5110 Ext. 112, E-mail: admission@les.edu.

**GRADUATE UNITS**

**Graduate Programs** *Program availability:* Part-time, 100% online, blended/hybrid learning. Electronic applications accepted.

## LOMA LINDA UNIVERSITY, Loma Linda, CA 92350

**General Information** Independent-religious, coed, university. CGS member. *Graduate housing:* Room and/or apartments available on a first-come, first-served basis to single students; on-campus housing not available to married students. *Research affiliation:* City of Hope Hospital (cancer research), Children's Hospital Los Angeles (cancer research), Children's Hospital Orange County (cancer research).

**GRADUATE UNITS**

**School of Allied Health Professions** Electronic applications accepted.

**School of Behavioral Health** Electronic applications accepted.

**School of Dentistry**

**School of Medicine**

**School of Nursing** *Program availability:* Part-time. Electronic applications accepted.

**School of Pharmacy**

**School of Public Health** *Program availability:* Part-time. Electronic applications accepted.

**School of Religion** Electronic applications accepted.

## LONDON METROPOLITAN UNIVERSITY, London N7 8DB, United Kingdom

**General Information** Private, coed, university.

**GRADUATE UNITS**

**Graduate Programs**

## LONG ISLAND UNIVERSITY - BRENTWOOD CAMPUS, Brentwood, NY 11717

**General Information** Independent, coed, upper-level institution. *Graduate housing:* On-campus housing not available.

**GRADUATE UNITS**

**Graduate Programs** *Program availability:* Part-time. Electronic applications accepted.

## LONG ISLAND UNIVERSITY - BROOKLYN, Brooklyn, NY 11201-8423

**General Information** Independent, coed, university. *Graduate housing:* Room and/or apartments available on a first-come, first-served basis to single students; on-campus housing not available to married students. Housing application deadline: 5/1. *Research affiliation:* California Table Grape Commission (pharmacy), Latitude Pharmaceuticals, Inc. (pharmacy), National Institute for Pharmaceutical Technology and Education (pharmacy), Natoli Engineering Company (pharmacy), Onconova Therapeutics, Inc. (pharmacy), Simcyp Limited (pharmacy).

**GRADUATE UNITS**

**Arnold and Marie Schwartz College of Pharmacy and Health Sciences** *Program availability:* Part-time. Electronic applications accepted.

**Harriet Rothkopf Heilbrunn School of Nursing** *Program availability:* Part-time, evening/weekend, blended/hybrid learning. Electronic applications accepted.

**Richard L. Conolly College of Liberal Arts and Sciences** *Program availability:* Part-time. Electronic applications accepted.

**School of Business, Public Administration and Information Sciences** *Program availability:* Part-time, evening/weekend. Electronic applications accepted.

**School of Education** *Program availability:* Part-time, evening/weekend, 100% online. Electronic applications accepted.

**School of Health Professions** Electronic applications accepted.

## LONG ISLAND UNIVERSITY - HUDSON, Purchase, NY 10577

**General Information** Independent, coed, graduate-only institution. *Graduate housing:* On-campus housing not available.

**GRADUATE UNITS**

**Graduate School** *Program availability:* Part-time, evening/weekend. Electronic applications accepted.

## LONG ISLAND UNIVERSITY - POST, Brookville, NY 11548-1300

**General Information** Independent, coed, university. *Graduate housing:* Room and/or apartments available on a first-come, first-served basis to single students; on-campus housing not available to married students. Housing application deadline: 5/1. *Research affiliation:* Structure-ase Inc. (biology).

**GRADUATE UNITS**

**College of Arts, Communications and Design** Electronic applications accepted.

**College of Education, Information and Technology** *Program availability:* Part-time, 100% online, blended/hybrid learning. Electronic applications accepted.

**College of Liberal Arts and Sciences** *Program availability:* Part-time, evening/weekend, blended/hybrid learning. Electronic applications accepted.

**College of Management** *Program availability:* Part-time, evening/weekend, blended/hybrid learning. Electronic applications accepted.

**School of Health Professions and Nursing** *Program availability:* Part-time, blended/hybrid learning. Electronic applications accepted.

## LONG ISLAND UNIVERSITY - RIVERHEAD, Riverhead, NY 11901

**General Information** Independent, coed, graduate-only institution. *Graduate housing:* On-campus housing not available.

**GRADUATE UNITS**

**Graduate Programs** *Program availability:* Part-time. Electronic applications accepted.

## LONGWOOD UNIVERSITY, Farmville, VA 23909

**General Information** State-supported, coed, comprehensive institution. CGS member. *Graduate housing:* On-campus housing not available.

**GRADUATE UNITS**

**College of Graduate and Professional Studies** *Program availability:* Part-time, evening/weekend. Electronic applications accepted.

***College of Business and Economics*** *Program availability:* Part-time, online only, 100% online. Electronic applications accepted.

***College of Education and Human Services*** *Program availability:* Part-time, evening/weekend. Electronic applications accepted.

## LORAS COLLEGE, Dubuque, IA 52004-0178

**General Information** Independent-religious, coed, comprehensive institution. *Graduate housing:* On-campus housing not available.

**GRADUATE UNITS**

**Graduate Division** *Program availability:* Part-time, evening/weekend.

## LOUISIANA COLLEGE, Pineville, LA 71359-0001

**General Information** Independent-religious, coed, comprehensive institution.

**GRADUATE UNITS**

**Graduate Programs**

## LOUISIANA STATE UNIVERSITY AND AGRICULTURAL & MECHANICAL COLLEGE, Baton Rouge, LA 70803

**General Information** State-supported, coed, university. CGS member. *Graduate housing:* Rooms and/or apartments available on a first-come, first-served basis to single and married students. Housing application deadline: 3/15. *Research affiliation:* Arctic Research Consortium of the U.S., Organization for Tropical Studies, Coalition for Academic Scientific Computing, Albert Einstein Institute, Inter-University Consortium for Political and Social Research, Laser Interferometer Gravitational Wave Observatory.

**GRADUATE UNITS**

**Graduate School** *Program availability:* Part-time, evening/weekend. Electronic applications accepted.

***College of Agriculture***

***College of Art and Design***

***College of Engineering***

***College of Humanities and Social Sciences***

***College of Human Sciences and Education***

***College of Music and Dramatic Arts***

***College of Science***

***E. J. Ourso College of Business***

***Manship School of Mass Communication***

***School of the Coast and Environment***

**Paul M. Hebert Law Center** Students: 582 full-time (295 women); includes 127 minority (64 Black or African American, non-Hispanic/Latino; 2 American Indian or Alaska Native, non-Hispanic/Latino; 8 Asian, non-Hispanic/Latino; 41 Hispanic/Latino; 12 Two or more races, non-Hispanic/Latino), 10 international. Average age 26. 966 applicants, 56% accepted, 206 enrolled. *Faculty:* 38 full-time (16 women), 22 part-time/adjunct (2 women). Expenses: Contact institution. *Financial support:* In 2019–20, 532 students received support. Scholarships/grants and tuition waivers (full and partial) available. Financial award application deadline: 7/1; financial award applicants required to submit FAFSA. In 2019, 11 master's awarded. *Application deadline:* For fall admission, 3/1 priority date for domestic and international students. Applications are processed on a rolling basis. *Application fee:* $50. Electronic applications accepted. *Application Contact:* Jake T. Henry, III, Director of Admissions, 225-578-8646, Fax: 225-578-8647, E-mail: jakeh@lsu.edu. *Interim Dean*, Lee Ann Lockridge, 225-578-8491, Fax: 225-578-8202, E-mail: lockridge@lsu.edu.

**School of Veterinary Medicine**

## LOUISIANA STATE UNIVERSITY HEALTH SCIENCES CENTER, New Orleans, LA 70112-2223

**General Information** State-supported, coed, university. CGS member. *Enrollment:* 2,804 graduate, professional, and undergraduate students; 1,780 full-time matriculated graduate/professional students (1,054 women), 103 part-time matriculated graduate/professional students (83 women). *Graduate faculty:* 906 full-time (404 women). *Graduate housing:* Rooms and/or apartments available on a first-come, first-served basis to single and married students. Housing application deadline: 5/1. *Student services:* Campus safety program, exercise/wellness program, free psychological counseling, grant writing training, international student services, low-cost health insurance, multicultural affairs office, services for students with disabilities, teacher training, writing training. *Library facilities:* John P. Ische Library plus 2 others. *Collection:* Books: 61,199 (physical); Serial titles: 4,968 (physical), 3,068 (digital/electronic); Databases: 204. Weekly public service hours: 97; study areas open 24 hours, 5–7 days a week.

**Computer facilities:** Computer purchase and lease plans are available. 120 computers available on campus for general student use. A campuswide network can be accessed. Online class registration is available.
Website: http://www.lsuhsc.edu/

**General Application Contact:** Leigh Smith-Vaniz, Coordinator of Student Affairs, 504-568-2211, Fax: 504-568-5588, E-mail: lsmi30@lsuhsc.edu.

**GRADUATE UNITS**

**School of Allied Health Professions** Average age 25. 1,032 applicants, 14% accepted, 141 enrolled. Expenses: Contact institution. *Financial support:* Work assistantships available. Financial award application deadline: 4/15; financial award applicants required to submit FAFSA. In 2019, 104 master's, 44 doctorates awarded. *Application deadline:* For fall admission, 4/15 priority date for domestic students; for spring admission, 1/15 priority date for domestic students. *Application fee:* $150. Electronic applications accepted. *Application Contact:* Yudialys Delgado Cazanas, Student Affairs Director, 504-568-4253, Fax: 504-568-3185, E-mail: ydelga@lsuhsc.edu. *Dean*, Dr. Jimmy M. Cairo, 504-556-3400, Fax: 504-568-4249, E-mail: jcairo@lsuhsc.edu.

**School of Dentistry**

**School of Graduate Studies in New Orleans** Students: 76 full-time (44 women); includes 17 minority (5 Black or African American, non-Hispanic/Latino; 6 Asian, non-Hispanic/Latino; 4 Hispanic/Latino; 2 Two or more races, non-Hispanic/Latino), 8 international. Average age 26. 85 applicants, 19% accepted, 12 enrolled. *Faculty:* 159 full-time (45 women). Expenses: Contact institution. *Financial support:* In 2019–20, 70 students received support. Tuition waivers (full) and unspecified assistantships available. Financial award application deadline: 4/1. In 2019, 13 doctorates awarded. *Application deadline:* For fall admission, 4/1 for domestic and international students. Applications are processed on a rolling basis. *Application fee:* $30. Electronic applications accepted. *Application Contact:* Leigh Smith-Vaniz, Coordinator of Student Affairs, 504-568-2211, Fax: 504-568-5588, E-mail: lsmi30@lsuhsc.edu. *Dean*, Dr. Joseph M. Moerschbaecher, III, 504-568-2211, Fax: 504-568-2361.

**School of Medicine in New Orleans** Electronic applications accepted.

**School of Nursing** Students: 182 full-time (127 women), 70 part-time (59 women); includes 82 minority (52 Black or African American, non-Hispanic/Latino; 2 American Indian or Alaska Native, non-Hispanic/Latino; 14 Asian, non-Hispanic/Latino; 14 Hispanic/Latino), 1 international. Average age 34. 34 applicants, 62% accepted, 21 enrolled. *Faculty:* 25 full-time (21 women), 25 part-time/adjunct (13 women). Expenses: Contact institution. *Financial support:* In 2019–20, 20 students received support. Institutionally sponsored loans, scholarships/grants, unspecified assistantships, and DNS Scholars Program available. Financial award application deadline: 4/15; financial award applicants required to submit FAFSA. In 2019, 72 doctorates awarded. *Program availability:* Part-time. *Application deadline:* For fall admission, 6/1 priority date for domestic and international students; for spring admission, 10/1 priority date for domestic and international students; for summer admission, 3/1 priority date for domestic and international students. Applications are processed on a rolling basis. *Application fee:* $100. Electronic applications accepted. *Application Contact:* Tracie Gravolet, Director, Office of Student Affairs, 504-568-4114, Fax: 504-568-5711, E-mail: tgravo@lsuhsc.edu. *Dean*, Dr. Demetrius James Porche, 504-568-4106, Fax: 504-599-0573, E-mail: dporch@lsuhsc.edu.

**School of Public Health** *Program availability:* Part-time. Electronic applications accepted.

## LOUISIANA STATE UNIVERSITY HEALTH SCIENCES CENTER AT SHREVEPORT, Shreveport, LA 71130-3932

**General Information** State-supported, coed, university. *Research affiliation:* Pennington Biomedical Research Center (metabolic disorders/obesity).

**GRADUATE UNITS**

**Department of Biochemistry and Molecular Biology** Electronic applications accepted.

**Department of Cellular Biology and Anatomy**

**Department of Microbiology and Immunology** Electronic applications accepted.

**Department of Molecular and Cellular Physiology**

**Department of Pharmacology, Toxicology and Neuroscience**

**Master of Science in Biomedical Sciences Program**

**School of Medicine**

## LOUISIANA STATE UNIVERSITY IN SHREVEPORT, Shreveport, LA 71115-2399

**General Information** State-supported, coed, comprehensive institution. *Research affiliation:* Micromanufacturing Institute (manufacturing technology), U.S. Department of Agriculture (USDA) (crop science), Louisiana Manufacturing Science Center (robotics), Biomedical Research Institute, Cotton, Incorporated (plant physiology).

**GRADUATE UNITS**

**College of Arts and Sciences** *Program availability:* Part-time, evening/weekend, 100% online. Electronic applications accepted.

**College of Business, Education, and Human Development** *Program availability:* Part-time. Electronic applications accepted.

## LOUISIANA TECH UNIVERSITY, Ruston, LA 71272

**General Information** State-supported, coed, university. *Enrollment:* 23,306 graduate, professional, and undergraduate students; 732 full-time matriculated graduate/professional students (396 women), 489 part-time matriculated graduate/professional students (304 women). *Enrollment by degree level:* 706 master's, 317 doctoral, 198 other advanced degrees. *Graduate faculty:* 269 full-time (92 women), 15 part-time/adjunct (7 women). *International tuition:* $13,333 full-time. *Tuition, area resident:* Full-time $6592; part-time $400 per credit. Tuition, state resident: full-time $6592; part-time $400 per credit. Tuition, nonresident: full-time $13,333; part-time $681 per credit. *Required fees:* $3011; $3011 per unit. *Graduate housing:* Rooms and/or apartments available on a first-come, first-served basis to single and married students. Typical cost: $6000 per year ($10,155 including board) for single students. Room and board charges vary according to board plan and housing facility selected. Housing application deadline: 1/15. *Student services:* Campus employment opportunities, career counseling, exercise/wellness program, free psychological counseling, international student services, low-cost health insurance, multicultural affairs office, services for students with disabilities. *Library facilities:* Prescott Memorial Library.

**Computer facilities:** A campuswide network can be accessed from student residence rooms and from off campus.
Website: http://www.latech.edu/

**General Application Contact:** Dr. Ramu Ramachandran, Dean of the Graduate School, 318-257-2924, Fax: 318-257-4487, E-mail: ramu@latech.edu.

**GRADUATE UNITS**

**Graduate School** *Program availability:* Part-time, evening/weekend. Electronic applications accepted.

***College of Applied and Natural Sciences*** *Program availability:* Part-time. Electronic applications accepted.

***College of Business*** *Program availability:* Part-time, evening/weekend, 100% online, blended/hybrid learning. Electronic applications accepted.

***College of Education*** *Program availability:* Part-time. Electronic applications accepted.

***College of Engineering and Science*** *Program availability:* Part-time-only. Electronic applications accepted.

***College of Liberal Arts*** *Program availability:* Part-time. Electronic applications accepted.

## LOUISVILLE PRESBYTERIAN THEOLOGICAL SEMINARY, Louisville, KY 40205-1798

**General Information** Independent-religious, coed, graduate-only institution. *Enrollment by degree level:* 103 master's, 49 doctoral. *Graduate faculty:* 17 full-time (8 women), 12 part-time/adjunct (6 women). *Tuition:* Full-time $11,502; part-time $426 per credit hour. *Required fees:* $336; $336 per semester. $168 per semester. *Graduate housing:* Rooms and/or apartments available on a first-come, first-served basis to single and married students. Typical cost: $4941 per year for single students; $6084 per year for married students. Room charges vary according to housing facility selected. Housing application deadline: 4/15. *Student services:* Campus employment opportunities, career counseling, international student services, services for students with disabilities, writing training. *Library facilities:* E.M. White Library. *Collection:* Books: 171,766 (physical), 11,301 (digital/electronic); Serial titles: 1,276 (physical), 2,954 (digital/electronic); Databases: 45. Students can reserve study rooms. *Research affiliation:* Louisville Institute (American religion).

**Computer facilities:** 22 computers available on campus for general student use.
Website: http://www.lpts.edu/

**General Application Contact:** Rev. Sandra Moon, Director of Admissions, 502-895-3411 Ext. 371, Fax: 502-895-1096, E-mail: smoon@lpts.edu.

**GRADUATE UNITS**

**Graduate and Professional Programs** Students: 94 full-time (58 women), 58 part-time (37 women); includes 58 minority (44 Black or African American, non-Hispanic/Latino; 4 Asian, non-Hispanic/Latino; 6 Hispanic/Latino; 1 Native Hawaiian or other Pacific Islander, non-Hispanic/Latino; 3 Two or more races, non-Hispanic/Latino), 2 international. Average age 41. *Faculty:* 17 full-time (8 women), 12 part-time/adjunct (6 women). Expenses: Contact institution. *Financial support:* Career-related internships or fieldwork, Federal Work-Study, institutionally sponsored loans, and scholarships/grants available. Financial award application deadline: 2/1. In 2019, 25 master's, 10 doctorates awarded. *Program availability:* Part-time. *Application deadline:* For fall admission, 6/1 priority date for domestic students, 2/1 priority date for international students; for spring admission, 3/4 priority date for domestic students. Applications are processed on a rolling basis. *Application fee:* $50. Electronic applications accepted. *Application Contact:* Rev. Sandra Moon, Director of Admissions, 502-895-3411, Fax: 502-895-1096, E-mail: smoon@lpts.edu. *Dean*, Dr. Debra Mumford, 502-895-3411, Fax: 502-895-1096, E-mail: dmumford@lpts.edu.

## LOURDES UNIVERSITY, Sylvania, OH 43560-2898

**General Information** Independent-religious, coed, comprehensive institution. *Graduate housing:* Rooms and/or apartments available to single and married students. Housing application deadline: 5/1.

**GRADUATE UNITS**

**Graduate School** *Program availability:* Evening/weekend.

## LOYOLA MARYMOUNT UNIVERSITY, Los Angeles, CA 90045

**General Information** Independent-religious, coed, comprehensive institution. CGS member. *Enrollment:* 9,822 graduate, professional, and undergraduate students; 2,144 full-time matriculated graduate/professional students (1,314 women), 438 part-time matriculated graduate/professional students (229 women). *Enrollment by degree level:* 1,492 master's, 1,090 doctoral. *Graduate faculty:* 259 full-time (113 women), 270 part-time/adjunct (141 women). *Graduate housing:* Room and/or apartments available on a first-come, first-served basis to single students; on-campus housing not available to married students. Typical cost: $11,158 per year ($13,000 including board). Room and board charges vary according to campus/location. *Student services:* Campus employment opportunities, career counseling, child daycare facilities, exercise/wellness program, free psychological counseling, international student services, low-cost health insurance, multicultural affairs office, services for students with disabilities, teacher training. *Library facilities:* William H. Hannon Library. *Collection:* Study areas open 24 hours, 5–7 days a week; students can reserve study rooms.

**Computer facilities:** Computer purchase and lease plans are available. 820 computers available on campus for general student use. A campuswide network can be accessed. Online class registration is available.
Website: http://www.lmu.edu/

**General Application Contact:** Ammar Dalal, Assistant Vice Provost for Graduate Enrollment, 310-338-2721, Fax: 310-338-6086, E-mail: graduateadmission@lmu.edu.

**GRADUATE UNITS**

**Bellarmine College of Liberal Arts** Students: 135 full-time (71 women), 27 part-time (14 women); includes 73 minority (10 Black or African American, non-Hispanic/Latino; 1 American Indian or Alaska Native, non-Hispanic/Latino; 10 Asian, non-Hispanic/Latino; 46 Hispanic/Latino; 1 Native Hawaiian or other Pacific Islander, non-Hispanic/Latino; 5 Two or more races, non-Hispanic/Latino), 23 international. Average age 39. 157 applicants, 80% accepted, 67 enrolled. *Faculty:* 45 full-time (19 women), 9 part-time/adjunct (5 women). Expenses: Contact institution. *Financial support:* Research assistantships, teaching assistantships, Federal Work-Study, scholarships/grants, and unspecified assistantships available. Support available to part-time students. Financial award application deadline: 5/1; financial award applicants required to submit FAFSA. In 2019, 54 master's awarded. *Program availability:* Part-time, evening/weekend. *Application fee:* $50. Electronic applications accepted. *Application Contact:* Ammar Dalal, Assistant Vice Provost for Graduate Enrollment, 310-338-2721, Fax: 310-338-6086, E-mail: graduateadmission@lmu.edu. *Dean, Bellarmine College of Liberal Arts*, Dr. Robbin D. Crabtree, 310-338-2716, E-mail: robbin.crabtree@lmu.edu.

**College of Business Administration** Students: 116 full-time (57 women), 1 (woman) part-time; includes 53 minority (8 Black or African American, non-Hispanic/Latino; 15 Asian, non-Hispanic/Latino; 28 Hispanic/Latino; 2 Two or more races, non-Hispanic/Latino), 24 international. Average age 30. 191 applicants, 66% accepted, 56 enrolled. *Faculty:* 47 full-time (9 women), 14 part-time/adjunct (4 women). Expenses:

Contact institution. *Financial support:* Research assistantships, career-related internships or fieldwork, institutionally sponsored loans, scholarships/grants, and unspecified assistantships available. Support available to part-time students. Financial award application deadline: 5/1; financial award applicants required to submit FAFSA. In 2019, 71 master's awarded. *Program availability:* Part-time. *Application deadline:* Applications are processed on a rolling basis. *Application fee:* $50. Electronic applications accepted. *Application Contact:* Ammar Dalal, Assistant Vice Provost for Graduate Enrollment, 310-338-2721, Fax: 310-338-6086, E-mail: graduateadmission@lmu.edu. *Dean, College of Business Administration*, Dr. Dayle Smith, 310-338-7504, E-mail: dayle.Smith@lmu.edu.

**College of Communication and Fine Arts** Students: 58 full-time (54 women); includes 27 minority (1 Black or African American, non-Hispanic/Latino; 9 Asian, non-Hispanic/Latino; 16 Hispanic/Latino; 1 Two or more races, non-Hispanic/Latino), 2 international. Average age 32. 55 applicants, 75% accepted, 34 enrolled. *Faculty:* 11 full-time (7 women), 12 part-time/adjunct (11 women). Expenses: Contact institution. *Financial support:* Research assistantships, career-related internships or fieldwork, institutionally sponsored loans, scholarships/grants, and unspecified assistantships available. Financial award application deadline: 5/1; financial award applicants required to submit FAFSA. In 2019, 23 master's awarded. *Application fee:* $50. Electronic applications accepted. *Application Contact:* Ammar Dalal, Assistant Vice Provost for Graduate Enrollment, 310-338-2721, Fax: 310-338-6086, E-mail: graduateadmission@lmu.edu. *Dean, College of Communication and Fine Arts*, Dr. Bryant Keith Alexander, 310-338-7430, E-mail: bryantkeithalexander@lmu.edu.

**Frank R. Seaver College of Science and Engineering** Students: 95 full-time (30 women), 31 part-time (9 women); includes 61 minority (7 Black or African American, non-Hispanic/Latino; 14 Asian, non-Hispanic/Latino; 31 Hispanic/Latino; 1 Native Hawaiian or other Pacific Islander, non-Hispanic/Latino; 8 Two or more races, non-Hispanic/Latino), 37 international. Average age 28. 168 applicants, 77% accepted, 55 enrolled. *Faculty:* 20 full-time (5 women), 14 part-time/adjunct (2 women). Expenses: Contact institution. *Financial support:* Research assistantships, Federal Work-Study, scholarships/grants, unspecified assistantships, and laboratory assistantships available. Support available to part-time students. Financial award application deadline: 5/1; financial award applicants required to submit FAFSA. In 2019, 54 master's awarded. *Program availability:* Part-time. *Application deadline:* Applications are processed on a rolling basis. *Application fee:* $50. Electronic applications accepted. *Application Contact:* Ammar Dalal, Assistant Vice Provost for Graduate Enrollment, 310-338-2721, Fax: 310-338-6086, E-mail: graduateadmission@lmu.edu. *Dean, Frank R. Seaver College of Science and Engineering*, Dr. Tina Choe, 310-338-2834, E-mail: tina.choe@lmu.edu.

**Loyola Law School Los Angeles** Students: 932 full-time (515 women), 180 part-time (83 women); includes 471 minority (42 Black or African American, non-Hispanic/Latino; 1 American Indian or Alaska Native, non-Hispanic/Latino; 124 Asian, non-Hispanic/Latino; 241 Hispanic/Latino; 2 Native Hawaiian or other Pacific Islander, non-Hispanic/Latino; 61 Two or more races, non-Hispanic/Latino), 69 international. Average age 27. 3,802 applicants, 33% accepted, 324 enrolled. *Faculty:* 65 full-time (33 women), 120 part-time/adjunct (47 women). Expenses: Contact institution. *Financial support:* In 2019–20, 645 students received support, including 40 research assistantships (averaging $1,823 per year); career-related internships or fieldwork, Federal Work-Study, and scholarships/grants also available. Support available to part-time students. Financial award application deadline: 3/15; financial award applicants required to submit FAFSA. In 2019, 62 master's, 322 doctorates awarded. *Program availability:* Part-time, evening/weekend, 100% online, blended/hybrid learning. *Application deadline:* For fall admission, 2/1 priority date for domestic and international students. Applications are processed on a rolling basis. *Application fee:* $65 ($0 for international students). Electronic applications accepted. *Application Contact:* Jannell Lundy Roberts, Senior Assistant Dean, Admissions and Enrollment Services, 213-736-1074, Fax: 213-736-6523, E-mail: admissions@lls.edu. *Dean*, Michael Waterstone, 213-736-2243, Fax: 213-487-6736, E-mail: michael.waterstone@lls.edu.

**School of Education** Students: 630 full-time (488 women), 168 part-time (111 women); includes 507 minority (54 Black or African American, non-Hispanic/Latino; 68 Asian, non-Hispanic/Latino; 351 Hispanic/Latino; 1 Native Hawaiian or other Pacific Islander, non-Hispanic/Latino; 33 Two or more races, non-Hispanic/Latino), 36 international. Average age 29. 465 applicants, 68% accepted, 236 enrolled. *Faculty:* 38 full-time (26 women), 116 part-time/adjunct (79 women). Expenses: Contact institution. *Financial support:* Research assistantships, teaching assistantships, institutionally sponsored loans, scholarships/grants, and unspecified assistantships available. Support available to part-time students. Financial award application deadline: 5/1; financial award applicants required to submit FAFSA. In 2019, 466 master's, 20 doctorates awarded. *Program availability:* Part-time, evening/weekend. *Application fee:* $50. Electronic applications accepted. *Application Contact:* Ammar Dalal, Assistant Vice Provost for Graduate Enrollment, 310-338-2721, Fax: 310-338-6086, E-mail: graduateadmission@lmu.edu. *Dean, School of Education*, Dr. Michelle D Young, E-mail: Michelle.Young@lmu.edu.

**School of Film and Television** Students: 203 full-time (111 women), 8 part-time (0 women); includes 88 minority (40 Black or African American, non-Hispanic/Latino; 10 Asian, non-Hispanic/Latino; 26 Hispanic/Latino; 12 Two or more races, non-Hispanic/Latino), 49 international. Average age 26. 356 applicants, 56% accepted, 79 enrolled. *Faculty:* 31 full-time (13 women), 36 part-time/adjunct (12 women). Expenses: Contact institution. *Financial support:* Research assistantships, teaching assistantships, career-related internships or fieldwork, and scholarships/grants available. Support available to part-time students. Financial award application deadline: 12/4; financial award applicants required to submit FAFSA. In 2019, 49 master's awarded. *Application fee:* $50. Electronic applications accepted. *Application Contact:* Ammar Dalal, Assistant Vice Provost for Graduate Enrollment, 310-338-2721, Fax: 310-338-6086, E-mail: graduateadmission@lmu.edu. *Dean, School of Film and Television*, Peggy M. Rajski, 310-338-5800, E-mail: Peggy.Rajski@lmu.edu.

## LOYOLA UNIVERSITY CHICAGO, Chicago, IL 60660

**General Information** Independent-religious, coed, university. CGS member. *Enrollment:* 17,159 graduate, professional, and undergraduate students; 3,772 full-time matriculated graduate/professional students (2,474 women), 1,227 part-time matriculated graduate/professional students (881 women). *Enrollment by degree level:* 2,689 master's, 2,123 doctoral, 187 other advanced degrees. *Tuition:* Full-time $18,540; part-time $1033 per credit hour. *Required fees:* $904; $230 per credit hour. *Graduate housing:* Rooms and/or apartments available on a first-come, first-served basis to single and married students. Typical cost: $14,780 (including board) for single students. Housing application deadline: 5/1. *Student services:* Campus employment opportunities, campus safety program, career counseling, exercise/wellness program, free psychological counseling, international student services, low-cost health insurance, multicultural affairs office, services for students with disabilities, teacher training, writing training. *Library facilities:* Cudahy Library plus 7 others. *Collection:* Books: 916,582 (physical), 810,385 (digital/electronic); Serial titles: 2,078 (physical), 97,083 (digital/electronic); Databases: 553. Weekly public service hours: 144; study areas open 24 hours, 5–7 days a week; students can reserve study rooms. *Research affiliation:* Chicago Transformational Teacher Institutes (math and science education reform), Chicagoland Lutheran Education Foundation Literacy Program (literacy professional development program for K-8 teachers), Chicago Public Schools (evaluation of dual language education initiative), Field Museum (digital learning), Big Shoulders Foundation (internal evaluation of professional development for middle grades Catholic Archdiocese science teachers).

**Computer facilities:** Computer purchase and lease plans are available. 1,300 computers available on campus for general student use. A campuswide network can be accessed. Online class registration is available.
Website: http://www.luc.edu/

**General Application Contact:** Jill Schur, Director, Graduate Enrollment Management, 312-915-8902, E-mail: gradinfo@luc.edu.

**GRADUATE UNITS**

**Graduate School** Students: 821 full-time (489 women), 235 part-time (136 women); includes 305 minority (80 Black or African American, non-Hispanic/Latino; 2 American Indian or Alaska Native, non-Hispanic/Latino; 88 Asian, non-Hispanic/Latino; 107 Hispanic/Latino; 2 Native Hawaiian or other Pacific Islander, non-Hispanic/Latino; 26 Two or more races, non-Hispanic/Latino), 96 international. Average age 32. 1,427 applicants, 38% accepted, 232 enrolled. Expenses: Contact institution. *Financial support:* Fellowships with full tuition reimbursements, research assistantships with full tuition reimbursements, teaching assistantships with tuition reimbursements, career-related internships or fieldwork, Federal Work-Study, institutionally sponsored loans, scholarships/grants, and unspecified assistantships available. Support available to part-time students. Financial award application deadline: 2/1; financial award applicants required to submit FAFSA. In 2019, 366 master's, 86 doctorates, 14 other advanced degrees awarded. *Program availability:* Part-time, evening/weekend, 100% online, blended/hybrid learning. *Application deadline:* Applications are processed on a rolling basis. *Application fee:* $50. Electronic applications accepted. *Application Contact:* Jill Schur, Director of Graduate Enrollment Management, 312-915-8902, E-mail: gradinfo@luc.edu. *Dean*, Dr. Thomas Regan, 773-508-3505, Fax: 773-508-3514, E-mail: tregan1@luc.edu.

***Marcella Niehoff School of Nursing*** Students: 182 full-time (168 women), 198 part-time (175 women); includes 95 minority (26 Black or African American, non-Hispanic/Latino; 29 Asian, non-Hispanic/Latino; 37 Hispanic/Latino; 3 Two or more races, non-Hispanic/Latino), 7 international. Average age 35. 148 applicants, 59% accepted, 54 enrolled. *Faculty:* 36 full-time (32 women), 18 part-time/adjunct (16 women). Expenses: Contact institution. *Financial support:* In 2019–20, 53 students received support, including 3 research assistantships with full tuition reimbursements available (averaging $18,000 per year), 1 teaching assistantship with full tuition reimbursement available (averaging $18,000 per year); scholarships/grants, unspecified assistantships, and Nurse Faculty Loan Program also available. Financial award application deadline: 5/1; financial award applicants required to submit FAFSA. In 2019, 84 master's, 16 doctorates, 27 other advanced degrees awarded. *Program availability:* Part-time, blended/hybrid learning. *Application deadline:* For fall admission, 7/1 priority date for domestic and international students; for spring admission, 12/1 priority date for domestic and international students; for summer admission, 4/1 priority date for domestic and international students. Applications are processed on a rolling basis. Electronic applications accepted. *Application Contact:* Glenda Runnels, Enrollment Advisor, 708-216-3751, Fax: 708-216-9555, E-mail: grunnels@luc.edu. *Dean and Professor*, Dr. Lorna Finnegan, 708-216-5448, Fax: 708-216-9555, E-mail: lornaf@luc.edu.

***Neiswanger Institute for Bioethics*** Students: 26 full-time (17 women), 91 part-time (53 women); includes 21 minority (7 Black or African American, non-Hispanic/Latino; 2 American Indian or Alaska Native, non-Hispanic/Latino; 4 Asian, non-Hispanic/Latino; 7 Hispanic/Latino; 1 Two or more races, non-Hispanic/Latino). Average age 47. 43 applicants, 72% accepted, 25 enrolled. *Faculty:* 8 full-time (5 women), 6 part-time/adjunct (2 women). Expenses: Contact institution. *Financial support:* In 2019–20, 93 students received support. Institutionally sponsored loans and scholarships/grants available. Financial award applicants required to submit FAFSA. In 2019, 33 master's, 11 doctorates, 8 other advanced degrees awarded. *Program availability:* Part-time, online only, 100% online, blended/hybrid learning. *Application deadline:* For fall admission, 8/1 for domestic and international students; for spring admission, 1/5 for domestic and international students; for summer admission, 5/1 for domestic and international students. *Application Contact:* Robbin Hiller, Coordinator, Bioethics Education, 708-321-9219, Fax: 708-327-9209, E-mail: rhiller@luc.edu. *Coordinator, Bioethics Education*, Robbin Hiller, 708-327-9212, Fax: 708-327-9209, E-mail: rhiller@luc.edu.

***School of Communication*** Students: 50 full-time (34 women), 13 part-time (11 women); includes 18 minority (9 Black or African American, non-Hispanic/Latino; 2 Asian, non-Hispanic/Latino; 6 Hispanic/Latino; 1 Two or more races, non-Hispanic/Latino), 18 international. Average age 29. 100 applicants, 56% accepted, 29 enrolled. Expenses: Contact institution. *Financial support:* Career-related internships or fieldwork and scholarships/grants available. Financial award applicants required to submit FAFSA. In 2019, 17 master's awarded. *Program availability:* Part-time, evening/weekend. *Application deadline:* Applications are processed on a rolling basis. Electronic applications accepted. *Application Contact:* Maria Villanueva, Associate Director of GPEM Operations, E-mail: mvilla2@luc.edu. *Dean*, Dr. Hong Cheng, 312-915-6548, E-mail: hcheng5@luc.edu.

**Institute of Pastoral Studies** Students: 72 full-time (45 women), 130 part-time (90 women); includes 55 minority (14 Black or African American, non-Hispanic/Latino; 9 Asian, non-Hispanic/Latino; 28 Hispanic/Latino; 4 Two or more races, non-Hispanic/Latino), 21 international. Average age 45. 90 applicants, 79% accepted, 49 enrolled. *Faculty:* 9 full-time (3 women), 20 part-time/adjunct (7 women). Expenses: Contact institution. *Financial support:* In 2019–20, 111 students received support. Career-related internships or fieldwork, Federal Work-Study, scholarships/grants, and unspecified assistantships available. Support available to part-time students. Financial award application deadline: 3/15. In 2019, 48 master's, 8 other advanced degrees awarded. *Program availability:* Part-time, evening/weekend, 100% online, blended/hybrid learning. *Application deadline:* Applications are processed on a rolling basis. *Application fee:* $50. Electronic applications accepted. *Application Contact:* Dr. Peter L Jones, Interim Dean, 312-915-7400, Fax: 312-915-7504, E-mail: pjones5@luc.edu. *Interim Dean*, Dr. Peter L Jones, 312-915-7400, Fax: 312-915-7504, E-mail: pjones5@luc.edu.

**Parkinson School of Health Sciences and Public Health** Expenses: Contact institution. *Application Contact:* Jill Schur, Director, Graduate Enrollment Management, 312-915-8902, E-mail: gradinfo@luc.edu.

**Quinlan School of Business** *Program availability:* Part-time, evening/weekend. Electronic applications accepted.

**School of Education** Students: 308 full-time (237 women), 182 part-time (135 women); includes 188 minority (71 Black or African American, non-Hispanic/Latino; 29 Asian, non-Hispanic/Latino; 73 Hispanic/Latino; 1 Native Hawaiian or other Pacific Islander, non-Hispanic/Latino; 14 Two or more races, non-Hispanic/Latino), 20 international. Average age 31. 608 applicants, 63% accepted, 146 enrolled. *Faculty:* 49 full-time (32 women), 69 part-time/adjunct (50 women). Expenses: Contact institution. *Financial support:* In 2019–20, 293 students received support, including 120 fellowships with partial tuition reimbursements available, 80 research assistantships with full tuition reimbursements available (averaging $14,000 per year), 93 teaching assistantships (averaging $4,000 per year); career-related internships or fieldwork, Federal Work-Study, institutionally sponsored loans, scholarships/grants, traineeships, health care benefits, and unspecified assistantships also available. Support available to part-time students. Financial award application deadline: 2/1; financial award applicants required to submit FAFSA. In 2019, 174 master's, 45 doctorates, 19 other advanced degrees awarded. *Program availability:* Part-time, evening/weekend. *Application deadline:* For fall admission, 11/1 for domestic and international students; for winter admission, 12/1 for domestic and international students; for spring admission, 3/1 for domestic and international students. *Application fee:* $50. Electronic applications accepted. *Application Contact:* Dr. Siobhan Cafferty, Program Chair, 312-915-7002, E-mail: scaffer@luc.edu. *Dean,* Dr. Malik Henfield, 312-915-7002, E-mail: mhenfield@luc.edu.

**School of Law** Students: 906 full-time (558 women), 232 part-time (172 women); includes 373 minority (129 Black or African American, non-Hispanic/Latino; 63 Asian, non-Hispanic/Latino; 132 Hispanic/Latino; 1 Native Hawaiian or other Pacific Islander, non-Hispanic/Latino; 48 Two or more races, non-Hispanic/Latino), 34 international. Average age 36. 3,092 applicants, 45% accepted, 366 enrolled. *Faculty:* 69 full-time (36 women), 306 part-time/adjunct (148 women). Expenses: Contact institution. *Financial support:* In 2019–20, 598 students received support, including 67 fellowships; research assistantships, Federal Work-Study, scholarships/grants, and health care benefits also available. Financial award application deadline: 3/1; financial award applicants required to submit FAFSA. In 2019, 159 master's, 197 doctorates, 155 Certificates awarded. *Program availability:* Part-time, evening/weekend, 100% online, blended/hybrid learning. *Application deadline:* For fall admission, 4/1 for domestic and international students. Applications are processed on a rolling basis. Electronic applications accepted. *Application Contact:* Jill Schur, Director, Graduate Enrollment Management, 312-915-8902, E-mail: gradinfo@luc.edu. *Associate Dean for Administration, Law School,* Dr. James Faught, JD, 312-915-7131, Fax: 312-915-6911, E-mail: law-admissions@luc.edu.

**School of Social Work** *Program availability:* Part-time.

## LOYOLA UNIVERSITY MARYLAND, Baltimore, MD 21210-2699

**General Information** Independent-religious, coed, university. CGS member. *Enrollment:* 5,473 graduate, professional, and undergraduate students; 423 full-time matriculated graduate/professional students (331 women), 1,041 part-time matriculated graduate/professional students (714 women). *Enrollment by degree level:* 1,356 master's, 62 doctoral, 46 other advanced degrees. *Graduate faculty:* 116 full-time (70 women), 58 part-time/adjunct (33 women). *Graduate housing:* On-campus housing not available. *Student services:* Campus employment opportunities, campus safety program, career counseling, exercise/wellness program, free psychological counseling, international student services, low-cost health insurance, multicultural affairs office, services for students with disabilities. *Library facilities:* Loyola/Notre Dame Library plus 1 other. *Collection:* Books: 314,146 (physical), 46,721 (digital/electronic); Serial titles: 56,315 (physical), 183 (digital/electronic); Databases: 118. Weekly public service hours: 107; students can reserve study rooms.

**Computer facilities:** Computer purchase and lease plans are available. 528 computers available on campus for general student use. A campuswide network can be accessed. Online class registration, unlimited wireless access across entire campus are available. Website: http://www.loyola.edu/

**General Application Contact:** Maureen Bush, Executive Director, Graduate Admissions, 410-617-5020, Fax: 410-617-2002, E-mail: graduate@loyola.edu.

### GRADUATE UNITS

**Graduate Programs** Students: 423 full-time (331 women), 1,041 part-time (714 women); includes 442 minority (248 Black or African American, non-Hispanic/Latino; 72 Asian, non-Hispanic/Latino; 89 Hispanic/Latino; 33 Two or more races, non-Hispanic/Latino), 17 international. Average age 31. 2,170 applicants, 57% accepted, 934 enrolled. *Faculty:* 116 full-time (70 women), 58 part-time/adjunct (33 women). Expenses: Contact institution. *Financial support:* Scholarships/grants and unspecified assistantships available. Financial award application deadline: 4/15; financial award applicants required to submit FAFSA. In 2019, 802 master's, 21 doctorates, 1 other advanced degree awarded. *Program availability:* Part-time, evening/weekend. *Application deadline:* For fall admission, 3/1 for domestic and international students. Applications are processed on a rolling basis. *Application fee:* $60. Electronic applications accepted. *Application Contact:* Maureen Bush, Executive Director, Graduate Admissions, 410-617-5020, Fax: 410-617-2002, E-mail: graduate@loyola.edu. *Dean for Graduate Studies,* Dr. Elissa Derrickson, 410-617-5547, E-mail: ederrickson@loyola.edu.

***Loyola College of Arts and Sciences*** Students: 250 full-time (222 women), 164 part-time (103 women); includes 118 minority (51 Black or African American, non-Hispanic/Latino; 31 Asian, non-Hispanic/Latino; 31 Hispanic/Latino; 5 Two or more races, non-Hispanic/Latino), 8 international. Average age 30. 765 applicants, 48% accepted, 127 enrolled. *Faculty:* 64 full-time (37 women), 28 part-time/adjunct (18 women). Expenses: Contact institution. *Financial support:* Scholarships/grants and unspecified assistantships available. Financial award application deadline: 4/15; financial award applicants required to submit FAFSA. In 2019, 187 master's, 21 doctorates, 1 other advanced degree awarded. *Program availability:* Part-time, evening/weekend. *Application deadline:* For fall admission, 8/1 for domestic students; for spring admission, 12/1 for domestic students. *Application fee:* $60. Electronic applications accepted. *Application Contact:* Office of Graduate Admission, 410-617-5020, E-mail: graduate@loyola.edu. *Dean, College of Arts and Sciences,* Stephen Fowl, 410-617-2327, E-mail: sfowl@loyola.edu.

***School of Education*** Students: 101 full-time (79 women), 598 part-time (504 women); includes 238 minority (165 Black or African American, non-Hispanic/Latino; 23 Asian, non-Hispanic/Latino; 32 Hispanic/Latino; 18 Two or more races, non-Hispanic/Latino), 6 international. Average age 32. 484 applicants, 56% accepted, 181 enrolled. *Faculty:* 34 full-time (27 women), 25 part-time/adjunct (15 women). Expenses: Contact institution. *Financial support:* Research assistantships, scholarships/grants, and unspecified assistantships available. Financial award application deadline: 4/15; financial award applicants required to submit FAFSA. In 2019, 409 master's awarded. *Program availability:* Part-time, evening/weekend. *Application deadline:* For fall admission, 7/15 for domestic students, 4/1 for international students; for spring admission, 11/15 for domestic students; for summer admission, 4/1 for domestic students. Applications are processed on a rolling basis. *Application fee:* $60. Electronic applications accepted. *Application Contact:* Office of Graduate Admission, 410-617-5020, E-mail: graduate@loyola.edu. *Dean, School of Education,* Dr. Joshua Smith, 410-617-5343, E-mail: jssmith2@loyola.edu.

***Sellinger School of Business*** Students: 72 full-time (30 women), 279 part-time (107 women); includes 86 minority (32 Black or African American, non-Hispanic/Latino; 18 Asian, non-Hispanic/Latino; 26 Hispanic/Latino; 10 Two or more races, non-Hispanic/Latino), 3 international. Average age 30. 148 applicants, 97% accepted, 118 enrolled. *Faculty:* 18 full-time (6 women), 5 part-time/adjunct (0 women). Expenses: Contact institution. *Financial support:* Scholarships/grants available. Financial award application deadline: 4/15; financial award applicants required to submit FAFSA. In 2019, 206 master's awarded. *Program availability:* Part-time, evening/weekend. *Application deadline:* For fall admission, 8/1 priority date for domestic students, 4/1 for international students; for winter admission, 12/1 priority date for domestic students; for spring admission, 5/1 priority date for domestic students. Applications are processed on a rolling basis. *Application fee:* $60. Electronic applications accepted. *Application Contact:* Office of Graduate Business Programs, 410-617-5067. *Dean,* Kathleen A. Getz, 410-617-2301, E-mail: kgetz@loyola.edu.

## LOYOLA UNIVERSITY NEW ORLEANS, New Orleans, LA 70118-6195

**General Information** Independent-religious, coed, comprehensive institution. *Enrollment:* 4,384 graduate, professional, and undergraduate students; 626 full-time matriculated graduate/professional students (395 women), 569 part-time matriculated graduate/professional students (436 women). *Enrollment by degree level:* 583 master's, 608 doctoral, 4 other advanced degrees. *Graduate faculty:* 86 full-time (46 women), 65 part-time/adjunct (27 women). *Tuition:* Full-time $818; part-time $818 per credit hour. *Required fees:* $380 per semester. Tuition and fees vary according to course load, degree level and program. *Graduate housing:* Rooms and/or apartments available on a first-come, first-served basis to single students and available to married students. Typical cost: $7688 per year ($13,606 including board) for single students. Room and board charges vary according to board plan and housing facility selected. Housing application deadline: 5/1. *Student services:* Campus employment opportunities, campus safety program, career counseling, child daycare facilities, exercise/wellness program, free psychological counseling, international student services, low-cost health insurance, multicultural affairs office, services for students with disabilities. *Library facilities:* Monroe Library plus 1 other. *Collection:* Books: 363,298 (physical), 59,595 (digital/electronic); Serial titles: 1,385 (physical), 277,557 (digital/electronic); Databases: 129. Weekly public service hours: 114; students can reserve study rooms. *Research affiliation:* New Orleans Museum of Art (communications, history, visual arts).

**Computer facilities:** Computer purchase and lease plans are available. 525 computers available on campus for general student use. A campuswide network can be accessed. Online class registration is available.
Website: http://www.loyno.edu/

**General Application Contact:** Tharren Poplion, Assistant Director, Admissions, 504-865-3240, E-mail: poplion@loyno.edu.

### GRADUATE UNITS

**College of Arts and Sciences** Students: 16 full-time (12 women), 45 part-time (33 women); includes 31 minority (26 Black or African American, non-Hispanic/Latino; 5 Hispanic/Latino). Average age 32. 53 applicants, 58% accepted, 29 enrolled. *Faculty:* 4 full-time (3 women), 4 part-time/adjunct (3 women). Expenses: Contact institution. *Financial support:* Research assistantships, teaching assistantships, career-related internships or fieldwork, Federal Work-Study, scholarships/grants, and tuition waivers (partial) available. Support available to part-time students. Financial award application deadline: 5/1; financial award applicants required to submit FAFSA. In 2019, 12 master's awarded. *Program availability:* Part-time, evening/weekend. *Application fee:* $20. Electronic applications accepted. *Application Contact:* Tharren Poplion, Assistant Director, Admissions, 504-865-3240, E-mail: poplion@loyno.edu. *Interim Dean,* Uriel Quesada, 504-865-3049, Fax: 504-865-2059, E-mail: uquesada@loyno.edu.

**College of Law** Students: 454 full-time (260 women), 72 part-time (35 women); includes 188 minority (82 Black or African American, non-Hispanic/Latino; 10 American Indian or Alaska Native, non-Hispanic/Latino; 21 Asian, non-Hispanic/Latino; 71 Hispanic/Latino; 1 Native Hawaiian or other Pacific Islander, non-Hispanic/Latino; 3 Two or more races, non-Hispanic/Latino), 5 international. Average age 27. 855 applicants, 62% accepted, 172 enrolled. *Faculty:* 40 full-time (18 women), 25 part-time/adjunct (6 women). Expenses: Contact institution. *Financial support:* In 2019–20, 314 students received support. Scholarships/grants available. Financial award applicants required to submit FAFSA. In 2019, 4 master's, 148 doctorates awarded. *Program availability:* Part-time, evening/weekend. *Application deadline:* For fall admission, 8/1 priority date for domestic and international students. Applications are processed on a rolling basis. Electronic applications accepted. *Application Contact:* Kimberly Jones, Director of Law Admissions, 504-861-5575, Fax: 504-861-5772, E-mail: ladmit@loyno.edu. *Dean,* Madeleine Landrieu, 504-861-5760, Fax: 504-861-5677, E-mail: landrieu@loyno.edu.

**College of Music and Media** Students: 15 full-time (6 women), 31 part-time (24 women); includes 16 minority (7 Black or African American, non-Hispanic/Latino; 6 Hispanic/Latino; 3 Two or more races, non-Hispanic/Latino). Average age 28. 43 applicants, 93% accepted, 26 enrolled. *Faculty:* 13 full-time (6 women), 17 part-time/adjunct (7 women). Expenses: Contact institution. *Financial support:* In 2019–20, 43 students received support. Career-related internships or fieldwork, Federal Work-Study, institutionally sponsored loans, scholarships/grants, unspecified assistantships, and talent-based music scholarships available. Support available to part-time students. Financial award application deadline: 5/1; financial award applicants required to submit FAFSA. In 2019, 14 master's awarded. *Program availability:* Part-time. *Application deadline:* For fall admission, 8/15 priority date for domestic and international students; for spring admission, 1/1 priority date for domestic and international students. Applications are processed on a rolling basis. *Application fee:* $20. Electronic applications accepted. *Application Contact:* Dr. Kern Maass, Dean, 504-865-3039, Fax: 504-865-2852, E-mail: kdmaass@loyno.edu. *Dean,* Dr. Kern Maass, 504-865-3039, Fax: 504-865-2852, E-mail: kdmaass@loyno.edu.

**College of Nursing and Health** Students: 126 full-time (113 women), 347 part-time (301 women); includes 125 minority (78 Black or African American, non-Hispanic/Latino; 4 American Indian or Alaska Native, non-Hispanic/Latino; 8 Asian, non-Hispanic/Latino; 32 Hispanic/Latino; 2 Native Hawaiian or other Pacific Islander, non-Hispanic/Latino; 1

Two or more races, non-Hispanic/Latino), 4 international. Average age 39. 309 applicants, 72% accepted, 97 enrolled. *Faculty:* 22 full-time (17 women), 12 part-time/adjunct (9 women). Expenses: Contact institution. In 2019, 134 master's, 19 doctorates awarded. *Program availability:* Part-time. *Application deadline:* Applications are processed on a rolling basis. Electronic applications accepted. *Application Contact:* Tharren Poplion, Assistant Director, Admissions, 504-865-3240, E-mail: poplion@loyno.edu. *Dean*, Dr. Laurie Ann Ferguson, 504-865-2880, E-mail: ferguson@loyno.edu.

***Loyola Institute for Ministry*** Students: 6 full-time (all women), 85 part-time (67 women); includes 22 minority (7 Black or African American, non-Hispanic/Latino; 1 American Indian or Alaska Native, non-Hispanic/Latino; 4 Asian, non-Hispanic/Latino; 9 Hispanic/Latino; 1 Two or more races, non-Hispanic/Latino), 1 international. Average age 47. 50 applicants, 86% accepted, 10 enrolled. *Faculty:* 2 full-time (1 woman), 4 part-time/adjunct (3 women). Expenses: Contact institution. *Financial support:* In 2019–20, 37 students received support. Career-related internships or fieldwork, scholarships/grants, health care benefits, and tuition waivers (partial) available. Support available to part-time students. Financial award application deadline: 5/1; financial award applicants required to submit FAFSA. In 2019, 26 master's awarded. *Program availability:* Part-time, evening/weekend, online learning. *Application deadline:* For fall admission, 8/15 for domestic and international students; for spring admission, 1/1 for domestic and international students. Applications are processed on a rolling basis. *Application fee:* $20. Electronic applications accepted. *Application Contact:* Diane Blair, Manager of Admissions, 504-865-3728, Fax: 504-865-2066, E-mail: lim@loyno.edu. *Director*, Dr. Tom Ryan, 504-865-2069, Fax: 504-865-2066, E-mail: tfryan@loyno.edu.

***School of Nursing*** Students: 78 full-time (74 women), 222 part-time (198 women); includes 86 minority (62 Black or African American, non-Hispanic/Latino; 3 American Indian or Alaska Native, non-Hispanic/Latino; 4 Asian, non-Hispanic/Latino; 15 Hispanic/Latino; 2 Native Hawaiian or other Pacific Islander, non-Hispanic/Latino). Average age 39. 209 applicants, 70% accepted, 60 enrolled. *Faculty:* 15 full-time (13 women), 5 part-time/adjunct (4 women). Expenses: Contact institution. *Financial support:* Traineeships and Incumbent Workers Training Program grants available. Financial award application deadline: 5/1; financial award applicants required to submit FAFSA. In 2019, 89 master's, 19 doctorates awarded. *Program availability:* Part-time, online only, 100% online. *Application deadline:* For fall admission, 7/15 priority date for domestic students; for spring admission, 11/15 priority date for domestic students; for summer admission, 4/15 priority date for domestic students. Applications are processed on a rolling basis. Electronic applications accepted. *Application Contact:* Jennifer Brackett, SON Office Manager & Admissions Coordinator, 504-865-2823, Fax: 504-865-3254, E-mail: edwadswo@loyno.edu. *Dean and Director*, Dr. Laurie Anne Ferguson, 504-865-2880, Fax: 504-865-3254, E-mail: nursing@loyno.edu.

**Joseph A. Butt, S.J., College of Business** Students: 15 full-time (4 women), 74 part-time (43 women); includes 40 minority (22 Black or African American, non-Hispanic/Latino; 2 American Indian or Alaska Native, non-Hispanic/Latino; 2 Asian, non-Hispanic/Latino; 12 Hispanic/Latino; 2 Two or more races, non-Hispanic/Latino), 3 international. Average age 35. 79 applicants, 92% accepted, 43 enrolled. *Faculty:* 7 full-time (2 women), 7 part-time/adjunct (2 women). Expenses: Contact institution. *Financial support:* Research assistantships, scholarships/grants, tuition waivers (partial), and unspecified assistantships available. Financial award application deadline: 5/1; financial award applicants required to submit FAFSA. In 2019, 22 master's awarded. *Program availability:* Part-time, evening/weekend, online learning. *Application deadline:* For fall admission, 6/15 priority date for domestic students, 5/15 priority date for international students; for spring admission, 11/15 priority date for domestic students, 10/15 priority date for international students. Applications are processed on a rolling basis. *Application fee:* $50. Electronic applications accepted. *Application Contact:* Christina Morales, MBA Director, 504-864-7960, Fax: 504-864-7970, E-mail: mba@loyno.edu. *Dean*, Dr. Michael L Capella, 504-864-7990, Fax: 504-864-7970, E-mail: mba@loyno.edu.

## LUBBOCK CHRISTIAN UNIVERSITY, Lubbock, TX 79407-2099

**General Information** Independent-religious, coed, comprehensive institution. *Graduate housing:* Rooms and/or apartments available to single and married students. Housing application deadline: 8/15.

**GRADUATE UNITS**

**Graduate Biblical Studies** *Program availability:* Part-time.

## LUTHERAN SCHOOL OF THEOLOGY AT CHICAGO, Chicago, IL 60615-5199

**General Information** Independent-religious, coed, graduate-only institution. *Graduate housing:* Rooms and/or apartments available on a first-come, first-served basis to single and married students. Housing application deadline: 5/15. *Research affiliation:* Chicago Center for Public Ministry, Zygon Center for Religion and Science.

**GRADUATE UNITS**

**Graduate and Professional Programs** *Program availability:* Part-time.

## LUTHERAN THEOLOGICAL SEMINARY SASKATOON, Saskatoon, SK S7N 0X3, Canada

**General Information** Independent-religious, coed, graduate-only institution. *Graduate housing:* Room and/or apartments available to single students; on-campus housing not available to married students. Housing application deadline: 4/30.

**GRADUATE UNITS**

**Graduate and Professional Programs** *Program availability:* Part-time.

## LUTHER RICE COLLEGE & SEMINARY, Lithonia, GA 30038-2454

**General Information** Independent-religious, coed, comprehensive institution. *Graduate housing:* On-campus housing not available.

**GRADUATE UNITS**

**Graduate Programs** *Program availability:* Part-time, evening/weekend, online learning. Electronic applications accepted.

## LUTHER SEMINARY, St. Paul, MN 55108-1445

**General Information** Independent-religious, coed, graduate-only institution. *Graduate housing:* Rooms and/or apartments available on a first-come, first-served basis to single and married students.

**GRADUATE UNITS**

**Graduate and Professional Programs** *Program availability:* Part-time, online learning. Electronic applications accepted.

## LYNN UNIVERSITY, Boca Raton, FL 33431-5598

**General Information** Independent, coed, comprehensive institution. *Enrollment:* 3,247 graduate, professional, and undergraduate students; 415 full-time matriculated graduate/professional students (265 women), 410 part-time matriculated graduate/professional students (233 women). *Enrollment by degree level:* 724 master's, 76 doctoral, 25 other advanced degrees. *Graduate faculty:* 69 full-time (30 women), 30 part-time/adjunct (17 women). *Tuition:* Full-time $17,760; part-time $740 per credit. One-time fee: $100. Tuition and fees vary according to class time, course load and degree level. *Graduate housing:* On-campus housing not available. *Student services:* Campus employment opportunities, campus safety program, career counseling, exercise/wellness program, free psychological counseling, international student services, low-cost health insurance, multicultural affairs office, services for students with disabilities. *Library facilities:* Eugene M. and Christine E. Lynn Library. *Collection:* Books: 47,403 (physical), 406,452 (digital/electronic); Serial titles: 1,603 (physical), 71,094 (digital/electronic); Databases: 125. Weekly public service hours: 96; students can reserve study rooms.

**Computer facilities:** Computer purchase and lease plans are available. 150 computers available on campus for general student use. A campuswide network can be accessed. Online class registration is available.
Website: http://www.lynn.edu/

**General Application Contact:** Steven Pruitt, Assistant Director of Graduate Admissions, 561-237-7834, Fax: 561-237-7100, E-mail: admission@lynn.edu.

**GRADUATE UNITS**

**College of Arts and Sciences** Students: 98 full-time (81 women), 55 part-time (33 women); includes 57 minority (23 Black or African American, non-Hispanic/Latino; 1 American Indian or Alaska Native, non-Hispanic/Latino; 28 Hispanic/Latino; 2 Native Hawaiian or other Pacific Islander, non-Hispanic/Latino; 3 Two or more races, non-Hispanic/Latino), 9 international. Average age 32. 126 applicants, 77% accepted, 69 enrolled. *Faculty:* 15 full-time (7 women), 12 part-time/adjunct (7 women). Expenses: Contact institution. *Financial support:* In 2019–20, 42 students received support. Career-related internships or fieldwork, Federal Work-Study, scholarships/grants, tuition waivers (full and partial), and unspecified assistantships available. Support available to part-time students. Financial award application deadline: 3/1; financial award applicants required to submit FAFSA. In 2019, 37 master's awarded. *Program availability:* Part-time, evening/weekend, 100% online, blended/hybrid learning. *Application deadline:* For fall admission, 8/10 for domestic students, 7/31 for international students; for spring admission, 12/18 for domestic students, 12/2 for international students; for summer admission, 4/12 for domestic students, 4/2 for international students. Applications are processed on a rolling basis. *Application fee:* $45. Electronic applications accepted. *Application Contact:* Steven Pruitt, Director of Graduate and Online Admission, 561-237-7834, Fax: 561-237-7100, E-mail: admissionpm@lynn.edu. *Dean, College of Arts and Sciences*, Dr. Gary Villa, 561-237-7025, E-mail: gvilla@lynn.edu.

**College of Business and Management** Students: 223 full-time (121 women), 202 part-time (105 women); includes 108 minority (53 Black or African American, non-Hispanic/Latino; 1 American Indian or Alaska Native, non-Hispanic/Latino; 12 Asian, non-Hispanic/Latino; 40 Hispanic/Latino; 2 Two or more races, non-Hispanic/Latino), 116 international. Average age 31. 269 applicants, 91% accepted, 160 enrolled. *Faculty:* 25 full-time (11 women), 11 part-time/adjunct (4 women). Expenses: Contact institution. *Financial support:* In 2019–20, 127 students received support. Career-related internships or fieldwork, Federal Work-Study, scholarships/grants, tuition waivers (full and partial), and unspecified assistantships available. Support available to part-time students. Financial award application deadline: 3/1; financial award applicants required to submit FAFSA. In 2019, 270 master's awarded. *Program availability:* Part-time, evening/weekend, 100% online, blended/hybrid learning. *Application deadline:* For fall admission, 8/10 for domestic students, 7/31 for international students; for spring admission, 12/18 for domestic students, 12/2 for international students; for summer admission, 4/12 for domestic students, 4/2 for international students. Applications are processed on a rolling basis. *Application fee:* $45. Electronic applications accepted. *Application Contact:* Steven Pruitt, Director of Graduate and Undergraduate Evening Admission, 561-237-7834, Fax: 561-237-7100, E-mail: spruitt@lynn.edu. *Dean of the College of Business and Management*, Dr. RT Good, 561-237-7458, E-mail: rgood@lynn.edu.

**Conservatory of Music** Students: 24 full-time (13 women), 25 part-time (8 women); includes 11 minority (3 Asian, non-Hispanic/Latino; 8 Hispanic/Latino), 23 international. Average age 26. 59 applicants, 44% accepted, 26 enrolled. *Faculty:* 6 full-time (2 women), 1 part-time/adjunct (0 women). Expenses: Contact institution. *Financial support:* In 2019–20, 49 students received support. Career-related internships or fieldwork, Federal Work-Study, scholarships/grants, tuition waivers (full and partial), and unspecified assistantships available. Support available to part-time students. Financial award application deadline: 3/1; financial award applicants required to submit FAFSA. In 2019, 17 master's, 13 Certificates awarded. *Program availability:* Part-time, evening/weekend. *Application deadline:* For fall admission, 8/10 for domestic students, 7/31 for international students; for spring admission, 12/18 for domestic students, 12/2 for international students; for summer admission, 4/12 for domestic students, 4/2 for international students. Applications are processed on a rolling basis. *Application fee:* $50. Electronic applications accepted. *Application Contact:* Steven Pruitt, Director of Graduate Admissions, 561-237-7834, Fax: 561-237-7100, E-mail: admission@lynn.edu. *Dean*, Dr. Jon Robertson, 561-237-7702, Fax: 561-237-9002, E-mail: jrobertson@lynn.edu.

**Donald E. and Helen L. Ross College of Education** Students: 42 full-time (35 women), 96 part-time (71 women); includes 48 minority (34 Black or African American, non-Hispanic/Latino; 13 Hispanic/Latino; 1 Two or more races, non-Hispanic/Latino), 7 international. Average age 38. 39 applicants, 95% accepted, 25 enrolled. *Faculty:* 6 full-time (4 women), 3 part-time/adjunct (all women). Expenses: Contact institution. *Financial support:* In 2019–20, 89 students received support. Career-related internships or fieldwork, Federal Work-Study, scholarships/grants, tuition waivers (full and partial), and unspecified assistantships available. Support available to part-time students. Financial award application deadline: 3/1; financial award applicants required to submit FAFSA. In 2019, 11 master's, 17 doctorates awarded. *Program availability:* Part-time, evening/weekend, 100% online, blended/hybrid learning. *Application deadline:* For fall admission, 8/10 for domestic students, 7/31 for international students; for spring admission, 12/18 for domestic students, 12/2 for international students; for summer admission, 4/12 for domestic students, 4/2 for international students. Applications are processed on a rolling basis. *Application fee:* $45. Electronic applications accepted. *Application Contact:* Steven Pruitt, Director of Graduate and Undergraduate Evening Admission, 561-237-7834, Fax: 561-237-7100, E-mail: spruitt@lynn.edu. *Dean, College of Education*, Dr. Kathleen Weigel, 561-237-7441, E-mail: kweigel@lynn.edu.

**Eugene M. and Christine E. Lynn College of Communication and Design** Students: 28 full-time (15 women), 32 part-time (16 women); includes 15 minority (8 Black or

African American, non-Hispanic/Latino; 6 Hispanic/Latino; 1 Two or more races, non-Hispanic/Latino), 19 international. Average age 28. 36 applicants, 92% accepted, 20 enrolled. *Faculty:* 17 full-time (6 women), 3 part-time/adjunct (2 women). Expenses: Contact institution. *Financial support:* In 2019–20, 15 students received support. Career-related internships or fieldwork, Federal Work-Study, scholarships/grants, tuition waivers (full and partial), and unspecified assistantships available. Support available to part-time students. Financial award application deadline: 3/1; financial award applicants required to submit FAFSA. In 2019, 30 master's awarded. *Program availability:* Part-time, evening/weekend. *Application deadline:* For fall admission, 8/10 for domestic students, 7/31 for international students; for spring admission, 12/18 for domestic students, 12/2 for international students; for summer admission, 4/12 for domestic students, 4/2 for international students. Applications are processed on a rolling basis. *Application fee:* $45. Electronic applications accepted. *Application Contact:* Steven Pruitt, Director of Graduate Admission, 561-237-7834, Fax: 561-237-7100, E-mail: admission@lynn.edu. *Dean*, Dr. David L. Jaffe, 561-237-7099, Fax: 561-237-7097, E-mail: djaffe@lynn.edu.

## MAASTRICHT SCHOOL OF MANAGEMENT, 6201 BE Maastricht, Netherlands

**General Information** Private, coed, graduate-only institution.

**GRADUATE UNITS**

**Graduate Programs**

## MACHZIKEI HADATH RABBINICAL COLLEGE, Brooklyn, NY 11204-1805

**General Information** Independent-religious, men only, comprehensive institution. *Graduate housing:* Room and/or apartments available to single students; on-campus housing not available to married students.

**GRADUATE UNITS**

**Graduate Programs**

## MADONNA UNIVERSITY, Livonia, MI 48150-1173

**General Information** Independent-religious, coed, comprehensive institution. *Enrollment:* 3,044 graduate, professional, and undergraduate students; 138 full-time matriculated graduate/professional students (108 women), 403 part-time matriculated graduate/professional students (309 women). *Enrollment by degree level:* 478 master's, 44 doctoral, 19 other advanced degrees. *Graduate faculty:* 35 full-time (28 women), 45 part-time/adjunct (32 women). *Tuition:* Full-time $15,930; part-time $885 per credit hour. Tuition and fees vary according to degree level and program. *Graduate housing:* Room and/or apartments available on a first-come, first-served basis to single students; on-campus housing not available to married students. Typical cost: $6500 per year ($11,450 including board). Room and board charges vary according to board plan and housing facility selected. Housing application deadline: 3/31. *Student services:* Campus employment opportunities, campus safety program, free psychological counseling, international student services, low-cost health insurance, services for students with disabilities, writing training. *Library facilities:* Madonna University Library. *Collection:* Books: 71,562 (physical), 181,927 (digital/electronic); Serial titles: 190 (physical), 70,781 (digital/electronic); Databases: 130. Weekly public service hours: 100; students can reserve study rooms.

**Computer facilities:** Computer purchase and lease plans are available. 205 computers available on campus for general student use. A campuswide network can be accessed. Online class registration, online payments, online statements, online unofficial transcripts are available.
Website: http://www.madonna.edu/

**General Application Contact:** Sarah Gombar, Director of Graduate Admissions, 734-432-5341, Fax: 734-432-5862, E-mail: sgombar@madonna.edu.

**GRADUATE UNITS**

**Department of Psychology** *Program availability:* Part-time, evening/weekend. Electronic applications accepted.

**Program in Health Services** *Program availability:* Part-time. Electronic applications accepted.

**Program in Hospice** *Program availability:* Part-time, evening/weekend. Electronic applications accepted.

**Program in Liberal Studies**

**Program in Nursing** *Program availability:* Part-time. Electronic applications accepted.

**Program in Religious Studies**

**Program in Social Work**

**Program in Teaching English to Speakers of Other Languages** *Program availability:* Part-time, evening/weekend. Electronic applications accepted.

**Programs in Education** *Program availability:* Part-time, evening/weekend. Electronic applications accepted.

**School of Business** *Program availability:* Part-time, evening/weekend, online learning. Electronic applications accepted.

## MAHARISHI INTERNATIONAL UNIVERSITY, Fairfield, IA 52557

**General Information** Independent, coed, university. *Graduate housing:* Room and/or apartments guaranteed to single students; on-campus housing not available to married students. Housing application deadline: 8/1. *Research affiliation:* National Institutes of Health (stress reduction/disease prevention), U.S. Department of Defense (therapy/education/PTSD in veterans), Columbia University Medical Center (natural medicine and prevention), Institute of Noetic Sciences (psychophysiological correlates of consciousness), San Diego VA Healthcare System (veterans' health/PTSD stress reduction), Howard University Medical Center (stress reduction/hypertension prevention).

**GRADUATE UNITS**

**Graduate Studies** *Program availability:* Evening/weekend, online learning. Electronic applications accepted.

## MAINE COLLEGE OF ART, Portland, ME 04101

**General Information** Independent, coed, comprehensive institution. *Enrollment:* 19 full-time matriculated graduate/professional students (13 women). *Enrollment by degree level:* 19 master's, 16 other advanced degrees. *Graduate faculty:* 9 full-time (4 women), 18 part-time/adjunct (13 women). *Tuition:* Full-time $36,850. *Required fees:* $1280. One-time fee: $50 full-time. *Graduate housing:* Room and/or apartments available on a first-come, first-served basis to single students; on-campus housing not available to married students. Typical cost: $11,120 per year ($15,240 including board). Housing application deadline: 5/1. *Student services:* Campus employment opportunities, career counseling, free psychological counseling, grant writing training, low-cost health insurance, services for students with disabilities, writing training. *Library facilities:* Joanne Waxman Library.

**Computer facilities:** 85 computers available on campus for general student use. A campuswide network can be accessed from student residence rooms and from off campus. Invoices, transcripts available.
Website: http://www.meca.edu/

**General Application Contact:** Rachel Katz, Administrative Director, Graduate Programs, 207-699-5030, Fax: 207-772-5069, E-mail: mfa@meca.edu.

**GRADUATE UNITS**

**Program in Studio Art** Students: 38 full-time (24 women). 105 applicants, 67% accepted, 23 enrolled. *Faculty:* 8 full-time (5 women), 7 part-time/adjunct (5 women). Expenses: Contact institution. *Financial support:* In 2019–20, 13 teaching assistantships with partial tuition reimbursements (averaging $3,000 per year) were awarded; Federal Work-Study, scholarships/grants, and resident advisor positions also available. Financial award application deadline: 3/1; financial award applicants required to submit FAFSA. In 2019, 20 master's awarded. *Application deadline:* For fall admission, 2/22 for domestic students; for summer admission, 2/22 priority date for domestic students, 2/22 for international students. Applications are processed on a rolling basis. *Application fee:* $50 ($70 for international students). Electronic applications accepted. *Application Contact:* Joel Tsui, Graduate Admissions Counselor, 207-699-5021, Fax: 207-775-5069, E-mail: joel.tsui-staff@meca.edu. *Administrative Director, Graduate Programs*, Rachel Katz, 207-699-5030, Fax: 207-775-5069, E-mail: rkatz@meca.edu.

## MAINE MARITIME ACADEMY, Castine, ME 04420

**General Information** State-supported, coed, primarily men, comprehensive institution. *Graduate housing:* Rooms and/or apartments available on a first-come, first-served basis to single and married students. Housing application deadline: 4/15.

**GRADUATE UNITS**

**Loeb-Sullivan School of International Business and Logistics** *Program availability:* Part-time, 100% online. Electronic applications accepted.

## MALONE UNIVERSITY, Canton, OH 44709

**General Information** Independent-religious, coed, comprehensive institution. *Enrollment:* 1,561 graduate, professional, and undergraduate students; 75 full-time matriculated graduate/professional students (43 women), 366 part-time matriculated graduate/professional students (252 women). *Enrollment by degree level:* 441 master's. *Graduate faculty:* 39 full-time (24 women), 41 part-time/adjunct (28 women). *Graduate housing:* Room and/or apartments available on a first-come, first-served basis to single students; on-campus housing not available to married students. *Student services:* Exercise/wellness program, multicultural affairs office, services for students with disabilities. *Library facilities:* Everett L. Cattell Library plus 1 other. *Collection:* Books: 169,479 (physical), 312,753 (digital/electronic); Serial titles: 2,035 (physical), 39,854 (digital/electronic); Databases: 176. Weekly public service hours: 82; study areas open 24 hours, 5–7 days a week.

**Computer facilities:** Computer purchase and lease plans are available. 220 computers available on campus for general student use. A campuswide network can be accessed. Online class registration, online advising, online financial aid information, and online credit card payments are available.
Website: http://www.malone.edu/

**General Application Contact:** Graduate and Professional Studies, E-mail: gps@malone.edu.

**GRADUATE UNITS**

**Graduate Program in Business** Students: 20 full-time (4 women), 68 part-time (32 women); includes 10 minority (5 Black or African American, non-Hispanic/Latino; 5 Hispanic/Latino), 2 international. Average age 35. *Faculty:* 8 full-time (3 women), 2 part-time/adjunct (1 woman). Expenses: Contact institution. *Financial support:* Unspecified assistantships available. In 2019, 36 master's awarded. *Program availability:* Part-time, evening/weekend, online learning. *Application deadline:* Applications are processed on a rolling basis. *Application Contact:* Dr. Mike Ophardt, Director, 330-471-8179, Fax: 330-471-8563, E-mail: mophardt@malone.edu. *Director*, Dr. Mike Ophardt, 330-471-8179, Fax: 330-471-8563, E-mail: mophardt@malone.edu.

**Graduate Program in Counseling and Human Development** Students: 29 full-time (21 women), 84 part-time (66 women); includes 16 minority (8 Black or African American, non-Hispanic/Latino; 1 American Indian or Alaska Native, non-Hispanic/Latino; 1 Asian, non-Hispanic/Latino; 4 Hispanic/Latino; 2 Two or more races, non-Hispanic/Latino). Average age 33. *Faculty:* 4 full-time (all women), 7 part-time/adjunct (5 women). Expenses: Contact institution. *Financial support:* Unspecified assistantships available. Financial award applicants required to submit FAFSA. *Program availability:* Part-time, evening/weekend, 100% online, blended/hybrid learning. *Application deadline:* Applications are processed on a rolling basis. *Application Contact:* Dr. Kara Kaelber, Director, 330-471-8508, Fax: 330-471-8343, E-mail: kkaelber@malone.edu. *Director*, Dr. Kara Kaelber, 330-471-8508, Fax: 330-471-8343, E-mail: kkaelber@malone.edu.

**Graduate Program in Nursing** Students: 30 part-time (24 women). Average age 30. *Faculty:* 10 full-time (all women), 14 part-time/adjunct (13 women). Expenses: Contact institution. *Financial support:* Unspecified assistantships available. In 2019, 26 master's awarded. *Program availability:* Part-time, evening/weekend. *Application deadline:* Applications are processed on a rolling basis. *Application Contact:* Dr. Sheri Hartman, Director, 330-471-8330, Fax: 330-471-8607, E-mail: shartman@malone.edu. *Director*, Dr. Sheri Hartman, 330-471-8330, Fax: 330-471-8607, E-mail: shartman@malone.edu.

**Graduate Program in Organizational Leadership** Students: 13 full-time (9 women), 57 part-time (36 women); includes 6 minority (all Black or African American, non-Hispanic/Latino). Average age 38. *Faculty:* 4 full-time (2 women), 3 part-time/adjunct (0 women). Expenses: Contact institution. *Financial support:* Unspecified assistantships available. Financial award applicants required to submit FAFSA. In 2019, 21 master's awarded. *Program availability:* Part-time, evening/weekend, 100% online, blended/hybrid learning. *Application deadline:* Applications are processed on a rolling basis. *Application Contact:* Dr. Mike Ophardt, Director, 330-471-8179, Fax: 330-471-8563, E-mail: mophardt@malone.edu. *Director*, Dr. Mike Ophardt, 330-471-8179, Fax: 330-471-8563, E-mail: mophardt@malone.edu.

## MANCHESTER UNIVERSITY, North Manchester, IN 46962-1225

**General Information** Independent-religious, coed, comprehensive institution. *Graduate housing:* On-campus housing not available.

**GRADUATE UNITS**

**Doctor of Pharmacy Program** Electronic applications accepted.

**Master of Athletic Training Program** Electronic applications accepted.

**Master of Science in Pharmacogenomics Program** *Program availability:* Part-time, 100% online, blended/hybrid learning. Electronic applications accepted.

## MANHATTAN COLLEGE, Riverdale, NY 10471

**General Information** Independent-religious, coed, comprehensive institution. *Enrollment:* 4,058 graduate, professional, and undergraduate students; 11 full-time matriculated graduate/professional students (9 women), 2 part-time matriculated graduate/professional students (both women). *Enrollment by degree level:* 13 master's. *Graduate faculty:* 4 full-time (0 women), 1 part-time/adjunct (0 women). *Graduate housing:* Rooms and/or apartments available on a first-come, first-served basis to single and married students. *Student services:* Career counseling, free psychological counseling, low-cost health insurance, services for students with disabilities. *Library facilities:* Mary Alice and Tom OMalley Library. *Collection:* Books: 259,987 (physical), 191,706 (digital/electronic); Serial titles: 379 (physical), 186,500 (digital/electronic). Weekly public service hours: 168; study areas open 24 hours, 5–7 days a week.

**Computer facilities:** 450 computers available on campus for general student use. A campuswide network can be accessed. Online class registration, course management system, degree audit/planning tool, campus card access are available.
Website: http://www.manhattan.edu/

**General Application Contact:** Colette Geary, Vice President for Enrollment Management, 718-862-7199, Fax: 718-862-8019, E-mail: cgeary01@manhattan.edu.

**GRADUATE UNITS**

**Graduate Programs** *Program availability:* Part-time, evening/weekend.

***School of Business*** Students: 43 full-time (23 women), 26 part-time (12 women). Average age 25. *Faculty:* 35 full-time (19 women), 2 part-time/adjunct (1 woman). Expenses: Contact institution. *Financial support:* Research assistantships, career-related internships or fieldwork, scholarships/grants, and unspecified assistantships available. In 2019, 42 master's awarded. *Program availability:* Part-time, 100% online, blended/hybrid learning. *Application deadline:* For fall admission, 8/1 for domestic and international students; for spring admission, 1/1 for domestic and international students; for summer admission, 4/1 for domestic and international students. Applications are processed on a rolling basis. *Application fee:* $75. Electronic applications accepted. *Application Contact:* Dr. Marc Waldman, MBA Program Director, 718-862-3856, E-mail: marc.waldman@manhattan.edu. *Dean,* Dr. Donald Gibson, 718-862-7440, Fax: 718-862-8032, E-mail: dgibson01@manhattan.edu.

***School of Continuing and Professional Studies*** Students: 71 full-time (34 women), 25 part-time (10 women); includes 37 minority (14 Black or African American, non-Hispanic/Latino; 4 Asian, non-Hispanic/Latino; 17 Hispanic/Latino; 2 Two or more races, non-Hispanic/Latino). Average age 35. 37 applicants, 89% accepted, 14 enrolled. *Faculty:* 13 part-time/adjunct (8 women). Expenses: Contact institution. *Financial support:* Fellowships, research assistantships, teaching assistantships, and tuition waivers available. Financial award application deadline: 2/15; financial award applicants required to submit FAFSA. In 2019, 43 master's awarded. *Program availability:* Part-time, evening/weekend, 100% online, blended/hybrid learning. *Application deadline:* For fall admission, 8/1 for domestic students; for spring admission, 11/15 for domestic students. Applications are processed on a rolling basis. *Application fee:* $75. Electronic applications accepted. *Application Contact:* Dr. Steven Goss, Dean, 718-862-7862, E-mail: sgoss01@manhattan.edu. *Dean,* Dr. Steven Goss, 718-862-7862, E-mail: sgoss01@manhattan.edu.

***School of Education and Health*** *Program availability:* Part-time, evening/weekend, online learning.

***School of Engineering*** *Program availability:* Part-time, evening/weekend.

***School of Science***

## MANHATTAN SCHOOL OF MUSIC, New York, NY 10027-4698

**General Information** Independent, coed, comprehensive institution. *Graduate housing:* Room and/or apartments available on a first-come, first-served basis to single students; on-campus housing not available to married students. Housing application deadline: 5/1.

**GRADUATE UNITS**

**Graduate Programs** Electronic applications accepted.

**Professional Studies Certificate Program** Electronic applications accepted.

## MANHATTANVILLE COLLEGE, Purchase, NY 10577-2132

**General Information** Independent, coed, comprehensive institution. *Enrollment:* 2,535 graduate, professional, and undergraduate students; 339 full-time matriculated graduate/professional students (218 women), 502 part-time matriculated graduate/professional students (360 women). *Enrollment by degree level:* 660 master's, 116 doctoral, 65 other advanced degrees. *Graduate faculty:* 25 full-time (16 women), 109 part-time/adjunct (61 women). *Tuition:* Full-time $16,830; part-time $935 per credit. *Required fees:* $90; $45 per term. $45 per term. One-time fee: $40. Tuition and fees vary according to course load, degree level and program. *Graduate housing:* Rooms and/or apartments available on a first-come, first-served basis to single and married students. Typical cost: $10,850 per year ($16,690 including board) for single students; $10,850 per year ($16,690 including board) for married students. Room and board charges vary according to board plan. Housing application deadline: 7/1. *Student services:* Campus employment opportunities, campus safety program, career counseling, exercise/wellness program, free psychological counseling, grant writing training, international student services, low-cost health insurance, multicultural affairs office, services for students with disabilities, teacher training, writing training. *Library facilities:* Manhattanville College Library. *Collection:* Books: 191,679 (physical), 182,461 (digital/electronic); Serial titles: 924 (physical), 63,053 (digital/electronic); Databases: 119. Weekly public service hours: 109; study areas open 24 hours, 5–7 days a week.

**Computer facilities:** 125 computers available on campus for general student use. A campuswide network can be accessed from student residence rooms and from off campus. Online class registration, Mobile Apps are available.
Website: http://www.mville.edu/

**General Application Contact:** Brian Sondey, Director of Graduate Admissions, 914-323-1490, Fax: 914-694-1732, E-mail: Brian.Sondey@mville.edu.

**GRADUATE UNITS**

**Master of Fine Arts in Creative Writing Program** Students: 10 full-time (6 women), 14 part-time (8 women); includes 3 minority (1 Black or African American, non-Hispanic/Latino; 1 Asian, non-Hispanic/Latino; 1 Hispanic/Latino). Average age 37. 18 applicants, 89% accepted, 12 enrolled. *Faculty:* 5 part-time/adjunct (3 women). Expenses: Contact institution. *Financial support:* In 2019–20, 19 students received support, including 4 fellowships with partial tuition reimbursements available (averaging $14,220 per year); scholarships/grants, tuition waivers (partial), and unspecified assistantships also available. Financial award application deadline: 3/15; financial award applicants required to submit FAFSA. In 2019, 6 master's awarded. *Program availability:* Part-time, evening/weekend. *Application deadline:* Applications are processed on a rolling basis. *Application fee:* $40. Electronic applications accepted. *Application Contact:* Brian Sondey, Director of Graduate Admissions, 914-323-1490, Fax: 914-694-1732, E-mail: Brian.Sondey@mville.edu. *Program Director,* Lori Soderlind, 914-323-5239, E-mail: Lori.Soderlind@mville.edu.

**School of Education** Students: 248 full-time (161 women), 457 part-time (338 women); includes 141 minority (43 Black or African American, non-Hispanic/Latino; 2 American Indian or Alaska Native, non-Hispanic/Latino; 14 Asian, non-Hispanic/Latino; 72 Hispanic/Latino; 4 Native Hawaiian or other Pacific Islander, non-Hispanic/Latino; 6 Two or more races, non-Hispanic/Latino), 2 international. Average age 32. 249 applicants, 86% accepted, 177 enrolled. *Faculty:* 25 full-time (16 women), 83 part-time/adjunct (53 women). Expenses: Contact institution. *Financial support:* In 2019–20, 420 students received support, including 2 teaching assistantships with partial tuition reimbursements available (averaging $5,000 per year); scholarships/grants, tuition waivers (partial), and unspecified assistantships also available. Support available to part-time students. Financial award application deadline: 3/15; financial award applicants required to submit FAFSA. In 2019, 213 master's, 19 doctorates, 27 other advanced degrees awarded. *Program availability:* Part-time, evening/weekend. *Application deadline:* Applications are processed on a rolling basis. *Application fee:* $75. Electronic applications accepted. *Application Contact:* Alissa Wilson, Director, SOE Graduate Enrollment Management, 914-323-3150, E-mail: Alissa.Wilson@mville.edu. *Dean,* Dr. Shelley Wepner, 914-323-3153, Fax: 914-323-5493, E-mail: Shelly.Wepner@mville.edu.

**School of Professional Studies** Students: 81 full-time (51 women), 30 part-time (13 women); includes 40 minority (10 Black or African American, non-Hispanic/Latino; 1 Asian, non-Hispanic/Latino; 25 Hispanic/Latino; 4 Two or more races, non-Hispanic/Latino), 9 international. Average age 29. 57 applicants, 91% accepted, 35 enrolled. *Faculty:* 23 part-time/adjunct (5 women). Expenses: Contact institution. *Financial support:* In 2019–20, 44 students received support. Scholarships/grants and unspecified assistantships available. Support available to part-time students. Financial award applicants required to submit FAFSA. In 2019, 51 master's, 2 other advanced degrees awarded. *Program availability:* Part-time, evening/weekend. *Application deadline:* Applications are processed on a rolling basis. *Application fee:* $75. Electronic applications accepted. *Application Contact:* Jean Mann, Program Director, 914-323-5419, E-mail: Jean.Mann@mville.edu. *Associate Dean,* Laura Persky, 914-323-5188, E-mail: Laura.Persky@mville.edu.

## MANSFIELD UNIVERSITY OF PENNSYLVANIA, Mansfield, PA 16933

**General Information** State-supported, coed, comprehensive institution. *Graduate housing:* Room and/or apartments available on a first-come, first-served basis to single students; on-campus housing not available to married students.

**GRADUATE UNITS**

**Graduate Studies** *Program availability:* Part-time, evening/weekend, online learning. Electronic applications accepted.

## MAPLE SPRINGS BAPTIST BIBLE COLLEGE AND SEMINARY, Capitol Heights, MD 20743

**General Information** Independent-religious, coed, comprehensive institution. *Enrollment:* 14 full-time matriculated graduate/professional students (7 women), 48 part-time matriculated graduate/professional students (26 women). *Graduate faculty:* 5 full-time (1 woman), 14 part-time/adjunct (7 women). *Tuition:* Part-time $300 per credit. *Graduate housing:* On-campus housing not available. *Student services:* Career counseling, free psychological counseling. *Library facilities:* Maple Springs Baptist Bible College and Seminary Library plus 1 other.
Website: http://www.msbbcs.edu/

**General Application Contact:** Anthony E. Broadnax, Registrar and Director of Admissions and Records, 301-736-3631.

**GRADUATE UNITS**

**Graduate and Professional Programs** Expenses: Contact institution. In 2019, 10 master's, 1 doctorate awarded. *Application fee:* $40. *Application Contact:* Anthony E. Broadnax, Registrar and Director of Admissions and Records, 301-736-3631.

## MARANATHA BAPTIST UNIVERSITY, Watertown, WI 53094

**General Information** Independent-religious, coed, comprehensive institution. *Enrollment:* 979 graduate, professional, and undergraduate students; 33 full-time matriculated graduate/professional students (9 women), 180 part-time matriculated graduate/professional students (84 women). *Enrollment by degree level:* 225 master's, 10 doctoral. *Graduate faculty:* 5 full-time (1 woman), 25 part-time/adjunct (6 women). *Tuition:* Full-time $5940; part-time $3960 per credit. *Required fees:* $25 per credit. Tuition and fees vary according to degree level and program. *Graduate housing:* Room and/or apartments available to single students; on-campus housing not available to married students. Typical cost: $6550 (including board). *Student services:* Campus employment opportunities, campus safety program, child daycare facilities, teacher training. *Library facilities:* Cedarholm Library and Resource Center. *Collection:* Students can reserve study rooms.

**Computer facilities:** A campuswide network can be accessed. Online class registration is available.
Website: http://www.mbu.edu/

**General Application Contact:** Dr. Jim Harrison, Director of Admissions, 920-206-2327, Fax: 920-261-9109, E-mail: admissions@mbu.edu.

**GRADUATE UNITS**

**Doctor of Ministry Program** Students: 10 part-time (0 women); includes 1 minority (Two or more races, non-Hispanic/Latino), 1 international. Average age 46. *Faculty:* 4 full-time (0 women), 5 part-time/adjunct (0 women). Expenses: Contact institution. *Financial support:* Scholarships/grants available. Financial award applicants required to submit FAFSA. In 2019, 1 doctorate awarded. *Program availability:* Part-time, evening/weekend, online only, 100% online, blended/hybrid learning. *Application Contact:* Dr. Jim Harrison, Director of Admissions, 920-206-2327, Fax: 920-261-9109, E-mail: admissions@mbbc.edu. *Dean of the Seminary,* Mark Herbster, E-mail: mark.herbster@mbu.edu.

**Master of Arts in English Bible Program** *Program availability:* Part-time, 100% online.

**Master of Arts in Intercultural Studies Program** *Program availability:* Part-time.

**Master of Divinity Program** *Program availability:* Part-time.

**Program in Biblical Counseling** *Program availability:* Part-time.

**Program in Biblical Studies** *Program availability:* Part-time.

**Program in Organizational Leadership**

**Program in Teaching and Learning** *Program availability:* Part-time, evening/weekend, 100% online.

## MARCONI INTERNATIONAL UNIVERSITY, Miami, FL 33132

**General Information** Proprietary, coed, comprehensive institution.

**GRADUATE UNITS**

**Graduate Programs**

## MARIAN UNIVERSITY, Indianapolis, IN 46222-1997

**General Information** Independent-religious, coed, comprehensive institution. *Graduate housing:* On-campus housing not available.

**GRADUATE UNITS**

**College of Osteopathic Medicine** Electronic applications accepted.

**Educators College** *Program availability:* Part-time, evening/weekend, 100% online. Electronic applications accepted.

**Leighton School of Nursing** *Program availability:* Part-time. Electronic applications accepted.

**Master of Science in Counseling Program** *Program availability:* Part-time. Electronic applications accepted.

## MARIAN UNIVERSITY, Fond du Lac, WI 54935-4699

**General Information** Independent-religious, coed, comprehensive institution. *Graduate housing:* On-campus housing not available.

**GRADUATE UNITS**

**School of Business and Public Safety** *Program availability:* Part-time, evening/weekend. Electronic applications accepted.

**School of Education** *Program availability:* Part-time, evening/weekend, online learning.

**School of Nursing and Health Professions** *Program availability:* Part-time, evening/weekend. Electronic applications accepted.

## MARIETTA COLLEGE, Marietta, OH 45750-4000

**General Information** Independent, coed, comprehensive institution. *Enrollment:* 1,145 graduate, professional, and undergraduate students; 75 full-time matriculated graduate/professional students (61 women), 1 part-time matriculated graduate/professional student. *Enrollment by degree level:* 76 master's. *Graduate faculty:* 11 full-time (5 women). *Tuition:* Part-time $790 per credit hour. Tuition and fees vary according to program. *Graduate housing:* On-campus housing not available. *Student services:* Campus safety program, career counseling, free psychological counseling, international student services, services for students with disabilities, teacher training, writing training. *Library facilities:* Legacy Library. *Collection:* Books: 183,103 (physical), 137,587 (digital/electronic); Serial titles: 230 (physical), 15,786 (digital/electronic); Databases: 186. Weekly public service hours: 95; students can reserve study rooms.

**Computer facilities:** 475 computers available on campus for general student use. A campuswide network can be accessed. Online class registration is available. Website: http://www.marietta.edu/

**General Application Contact:** Scot Schaeffer, Vice President for Enrollment Management, 740-376-4503, E-mail: sjs005@marietta.edu.

**GRADUATE UNITS**

**Master of Arts in Psychology** Students: 1 part-time. Average age 24. *Faculty:* 3 full-time (2 women). Expenses: Contact institution. *Financial support:* Unspecified assistantships available. In 2019, 3 master's awarded. *Program availability:* Part-time. *Application deadline:* Applications are processed on a rolling basis. *Application fee:* $25. *Application Contact:* Dr. Mary Barnas, Director, 740-376-4766, E-mail: barnasm@marietta.edu. *Director*, Dr. Mary Barnas, 740-376-4766, E-mail: barnasm@marietta.edu.

**Program in Clinical Mental Health Counseling** *Faculty:* 2 full-time (1 woman). Expenses: Contact institution. *Financial support:* Career-related internships or fieldwork and unspecified assistantships available. *Application Contact:* Scot Schaeffer, Vice President for Enrollment Management, 740-376-4503, E-mail: sjs005@marietta.edu. *Assistant Professor/Director of Clinical Mental Health Counseling*, Michael Williams, 740-376 Ext. 4595, E-mail: maw013@marietta.edu.

**Program in Physician Assistant Studies** Students: 70 full-time (58 women); includes 5 minority (2 Black or African American, non-Hispanic/Latino; 2 Asian, non-Hispanic/Latino; 1 Hispanic/Latino). Average age 25. 1,085 applicants, 6% accepted, 36 enrolled. *Faculty:* 7 full-time (2 women). Expenses: Contact institution. *Financial support:* Scholarships/grants available. In 2019, 35 master's awarded. *Application deadline:* For fall admission, 11/1 for domestic students. Electronic applications accepted. *Application Contact:* Lori Hart, Administrative Coordinator, 740-376-4458, E-mail: lori.hart@marietta.edu. *Director*, Miranda Collins, 740-376-4953, E-mail: miranda.collins@marietta.edu.

## MARIST COLLEGE, Poughkeepsie, NY 12601-1387

**General Information** Independent, coed, comprehensive institution. *Graduate housing:* On-campus housing not available. *Research affiliation:* Center for Advanced Brain Imaging Psychology (psychology), New York State Office of Technology and Academic Research (NYSTAR) (technology), Hudson Valley Technology Development Corporation (HVTDC) (technology), Hudson River Psychiatric Center (psychology), St. Francis Hospital, Dutchess County Community Mental Health Center (mental health).

**GRADUATE UNITS**

**Graduate Programs** *Program availability:* Part-time, evening/weekend, online learning. Electronic applications accepted.

***School of Communication and the Arts*** *Program availability:* Part-time, online learning. Electronic applications accepted.

***School of Computer Science and Mathematics*** *Program availability:* Part-time, evening/weekend, online learning. Electronic applications accepted.

***School of Management*** *Program availability:* Part-time, evening/weekend, online learning. Electronic applications accepted.

***School of Science***

***School of Social and Behavioral Sciences*** *Program availability:* Part-time, evening/weekend. Electronic applications accepted.

## MARLBORO COLLEGE, Marlboro, VT 05344

**General Information** Independent, coed, comprehensive institution. *Graduate housing:* On-campus housing not available.

**GRADUATE UNITS**

**Graduate and Professional Studies** *Program availability:* Part-time, evening/weekend, blended/hybrid learning. Electronic applications accepted.

## MARQUETTE UNIVERSITY, Milwaukee, WI 53201-1881

**General Information** Independent-religious, coed, university. CGS member. *Graduate housing:* Rooms and/or apartments available on a first-come, first-served basis to single and married students. *Research affiliation:* Shriners Hospital for Children in Chicago, Rehabilitation Institute of Chicago, Froedtert Memorial Lutheran Hospital, Children's Hospital of Wisconsin, Blood Center of Wisconsin, Department of Orthopedic Surgery, Medical College of Wisconsin.

**GRADUATE UNITS**

**Graduate School** *Program availability:* Part-time, evening/weekend, online learning. Electronic applications accepted.

***College of Arts and Sciences*** *Program availability:* Part-time. Electronic applications accepted.

***College of Communication*** *Program availability:* Part-time, evening/weekend. Electronic applications accepted.

***College of Education*** *Program availability:* Part-time.

***College of Engineering*** *Program availability:* Part-time, evening/weekend. Electronic applications accepted.

***College of Health Sciences*** Electronic applications accepted.

***College of Nursing*** Electronic applications accepted.

**Graduate School of Management** *Program availability:* Part-time, evening/weekend. Electronic applications accepted.

**Law School** *Program availability:* Part-time, evening/weekend. Electronic applications accepted.

**School of Dentistry**

## MARSHALL B. KETCHUM UNIVERSITY, Fullerton, CA 92831-1615

**General Information** Independent, coed, graduate-only institution. *Graduate housing:* On-campus housing not available. *Research affiliation:* Alcon Laboratories (ophthalmic products), Essilor (spectacle lenses), Allergan (ophthalmic products).

**GRADUATE UNITS**

**Graduate and Professional Programs** Electronic applications accepted.

## MARSHALL UNIVERSITY, Huntington, WV 25755

**General Information** State-supported, coed, university. *Graduate housing:* Rooms and/or apartments available on a first-come, first-served basis to single and married students. *Research affiliation:* Bayer Corporation, Kanawha Valley Local Port District, Greenbrier County Commission, Dominion Power, Wyeth-Ayerst (clinical pharmaceutical study).

**GRADUATE UNITS**

**Academic Affairs Division** *Program availability:* Part-time, evening/weekend.

***College of Arts and Media*** *Program availability:* Evening/weekend.

***College of Business*** *Program availability:* Part-time, evening/weekend.

***College of Education and Professional Development*** *Program availability:* Part-time, evening/weekend. Electronic applications accepted.

***College of Health Professions***

***College of Information Technology and Engineering*** *Program availability:* Part-time, evening/weekend.

***College of Liberal Arts*** *Program availability:* Evening/weekend.

***College of Science***

***Forensic Science Center***

***School of Pharmacy***

**Joan C. Edwards School of Medicine** Electronic applications accepted.

## MARS HILL UNIVERSITY, Mars Hill, NC 28754

**General Information** Independent-religious, coed, comprehensive institution.

**GRADUATE UNITS**

**Adult and Graduate Studies**

## MARTIN LUTHER COLLEGE, New Ulm, MN 56073

**General Information** Independent-religious, coed, comprehensive institution. *Enrollment:* 993 graduate, professional, and undergraduate students; 1 full-time matriculated graduate/professional student, 82 part-time matriculated graduate/professional students (24 women). *Enrollment by degree level:* 83 master's. *Graduate faculty:* 12 full-time (2 women), 34 part-time/adjunct (9 women). *Tuition:* Part-time $315 per credit. *Graduate housing:* On-campus housing not available. *Library facilities:* Martin Luther College Library.

**Computer facilities:** A campuswide network can be accessed. Website: http://www.mlc-wels.edu/

**General Application Contact:** Dr. John E. Meyer, Director of Graduate Studies, 507-354-8221 Ext. 398, Fax: 507-354-8225, E-mail: meyerjd@mlc-wels.edu.

**GRADUATE UNITS**

**Graduate Studies** Students: 1 full-time (0 women), 82 part-time (24 women), 2 international. Average age 38. 39 applicants, 100% accepted, 37 enrolled. *Faculty:* 12 full-time (2 women), 34 part-time/adjunct (9 women). Expenses: Contact institution. *Financial support:* In 2019–20, 1 student received support. Scholarships/grants available. Financial award application deadline: 9/1. In 2019, 23 master's awarded. *Program availability:* Part-time, evening/weekend, online only, 100% online. *Application deadline:* Applications are processed on a rolling basis. *Application fee:* $35. Electronic applications accepted. *Application Contact:* Dr. John E. Meyer, Director of Graduate Studies, 507-354-8221 Ext. 398, E-mail: meyerjd@mlc-wels.edu. *Director of Graduate Studies*, Dr. John E. Meyer, 507-354-8221 Ext. 398, E-mail: meyerjd@mlc-wels.edu.

## MARTIN UNIVERSITY, Indianapolis, IN 46218-3867

**General Information** Independent, coed, comprehensive institution. *Graduate housing:* On-campus housing not available.

**GRADUATE UNITS**

**Division of Psychology** *Program availability:* Part-time, evening/weekend.

**Graduate School of Urban Ministry** *Program availability:* Part-time, evening/weekend.

## MARY BALDWIN UNIVERSITY, Staunton, VA 24401-3610

**General Information** Independent, coed, primarily women, comprehensive institution. *Graduate housing:* On-campus housing not available.

**GRADUATE UNITS**

**Graduate Studies** *Program availability:* Part-time, evening/weekend, online learning.

## MARYLAND INSTITUTE COLLEGE OF ART, Baltimore, MD 21217

**General Information** Independent, coed, comprehensive institution. *Enrollment:* 367 full-time matriculated graduate/professional students (241 women). *Enrollment by degree level:* 299 master's, 68 other advanced degrees. *Graduate faculty:* 26 full-time (18 women), 56 part-time/adjunct (23 women). *Tuition:* Full-time $50,160. One-time fee: $150 full-time. Full-time tuition and fees vary according to degree level. *Graduate housing:* Room and/or apartments available on a first-come, first-served basis to single students; on-campus housing not available to married students. Housing application deadline: 6/15. *Student services:* Campus employment opportunities, campus safety program, career counseling, exercise/wellness program, free psychological counseling, grant writing training, international student services, low-cost health insurance, multicultural affairs office, services for students with disabilities, teacher training, writing training. *Library facilities:* Decker Library. *Collection:* Books: 76,337 (physical), 191,873 (digital/electronic); Serial titles: 407 (physical); Databases: 41. Weekly public service hours: 70; students can reserve study rooms.

**Computer facilities:** 750 computers available on campus for general student use. A campuswide network can be accessed from student residence rooms and from off campus. Online class registration, Campus Portal, online gallery space, Behance image portfolio system, Google Apps, Lynda.com web-based training, network storage space, personal websites, online software training tutorials, Canvas learning management system, printing services are available.
Website: http://www.mica.edu/

**General Application Contact:** Chris D. Harring, Director of Graduate Admission, 410-225-2256, Fax: 410-225-5275, E-mail: graduate@mica.edu.

**GRADUATE UNITS**

**Graduate Studies** Students: 367 full-time (241 women); includes 86 minority (16 Black or African American, non-Hispanic/Latino; 1 American Indian or Alaska Native, non-Hispanic/Latino; 28 Asian, non-Hispanic/Latino; 18 Hispanic/Latino; 1 Native Hawaiian or other Pacific Islander, non-Hispanic/Latino; 22 Two or more races, non-Hispanic/Latino), 46 international. Average age 27. 1,100 applicants, 36% accepted, 215 enrolled. *Faculty:* 26 full-time (18 women), 56 part-time/adjunct (23 women). Expenses: Contact institution. *Financial support:* In 2019–20, 303 students received support, including 367 fellowships (averaging $11,000 per year), 328 teaching assistantships (averaging $3,200 per year); career-related internships or fieldwork and scholarships/grants also available. Financial award application deadline: 1/15; financial award applicants required to submit FAFSA. In 2019, 175 master's, 23 other advanced degrees awarded. *Program availability:* Part-time, online learning. *Application deadline:* For fall admission, 1/15 for domestic and international students. *Application fee:* $75. Electronic applications accepted. *Application Contact:* Chris D. Harring, Director of Graduate Admission, 410-225-2256, Fax: 410-225-5275, E-mail: graduate@mica.edu. *Vice Provost for Graduate Studies and Research,* Stacey Salazar, 410-225-5274, Fax: 410-225-5275, E-mail: graduate@mica.edu.

***LeRoy E. Hoffberger School of Painting*** Students: 20 full-time (12 women); includes 4 minority (1 Black or African American, non-Hispanic/Latino; 1 Asian, non-Hispanic/Latino; 1 Hispanic/Latino; 1 Two or more races, non-Hispanic/Latino), 4 international. Average age 27. 200 applicants, 10% accepted, 10 enrolled. *Faculty:* 1 (woman) full-time, 2 part-time/adjunct (0 women). Expenses: Contact institution. *Financial support:* In 2019–20, 20 students received support, including 20 fellowships (averaging $13,000 per year), 20 teaching assistantships (averaging $3,200 per year); career-related internships or fieldwork and scholarships/grants also available. Financial award application deadline: 1/15; financial award applicants required to submit FAFSA. In 2019, 10 master's awarded. *Application deadline:* For fall admission, 1/15 for domestic and international students. *Application fee:* $75. Electronic applications accepted. *Application Contact:* Chris D. Harring, Director of Graduate Admission, 410-225-2256, Fax: 410-225-5275, E-mail: graduate@mica.edu. *Director,* Joan Waltemath, 410-225-5274, Fax: 410-225-5275, E-mail: graduate@mica.edu.

***Mount Royal School of Art*** Electronic applications accepted.

***Rinehart School of Sculpture*** Electronic applications accepted.

## MARYLAND UNIVERSITY OF INTEGRATIVE HEALTH, Laurel, MD 20723

**General Information** Independent, coed, primarily women, graduate-only institution. *Graduate housing:* On-campus housing not available. *Research affiliation:* Food as Medicine, Georgetown University School of Complementary and Alternative Medicine, Natural Gourmet Institute, Institute for Integrative Nutrition.

**GRADUATE UNITS**

**Program in Herbal Medicine**

**Program in Naturopathic Medicine**

**Programs in Acupuncture and Oriental Medicine**

**Programs in Health and Wellness Coaching**

**Programs in Health Promotion and Yoga Therapy**

**Programs in Nutrition**

## MARYMOUNT CALIFORNIA UNIVERSITY, Rancho Palos Verdes, CA 90275-6299

**General Information** Independent-religious, coed, comprehensive institution.

**GRADUATE UNITS**

**Program in Business Administration**

**Program in Community Psychology**

**Program in Leadership and Global Development**

## MARYMOUNT UNIVERSITY, Arlington, VA 22207-4299

**General Information** Independent-religious, coed, comprehensive institution. *Enrollment:* 3,363 graduate, professional, and undergraduate students; 688 full-time matriculated graduate/professional students (520 women), 503 part-time matriculated graduate/professional students (334 women). *Enrollment by degree level:* 978 master's, 199 doctoral, 14 other advanced degrees. *Graduate faculty:* 73 full-time (56 women), 63 part-time/adjunct (37 women). *Tuition:* Part-time $1050 per credit. *Required fees:* $22 per credit. One-time fee: $270 part-time. Tuition and fees vary according to program. *Graduate housing:* Rooms and/or apartments available on a first-come, first-served basis to single and married students. Typical cost: $7500 per year for single students; $7500 per year for married students. Room charges vary according to housing facility selected. Housing application deadline: 5/1. *Student services:* Campus employment opportunities, campus safety program, career counseling, free psychological counseling, international student services, low-cost health insurance, services for students with disabilities, teacher training. *Library facilities:* Emerson C. Reinsch Library plus 1 other. *Collection:* Weekly public service hours: 104; students can reserve study rooms.

**Computer facilities:** 270 computers available on campus for general student use. A campuswide network can be accessed. Online class registration, online drive space are available.
Website: http://www.marymount.edu/

**General Application Contact:** Fiona McDonnell, Administrative Assistant, 703-284-5901, E-mail: gadmissi@marymount.edu.

**GRADUATE UNITS**

**Malek School of Health Professions** Students: 175 full-time (119 women), 50 part-time (42 women); includes 54 minority (16 Black or African American, non-Hispanic/Latino; 14 Asian, non-Hispanic/Latino; 14 Hispanic/Latino; 10 Two or more races, non-Hispanic/Latino), 37 international. Average age 29. 473 applicants, 55% accepted, 81 enrolled. *Faculty:* 15 full-time (14 women), 19 part-time/adjunct (13 women). Expenses: Contact institution. *Financial support:* In 2019–20, 28 students received support. Research assistantships, teaching assistantships, career-related internships or fieldwork, scholarships/grants, and unspecified assistantships available. Support available to part-time students. Financial award application deadline: 3/1; financial award applicants required to submit FAFSA. In 2019, 27 master's, 45 doctorates, 1 other advanced degree awarded. *Program availability:* Part-time, evening/weekend. *Application deadline:* For fall admission, 3/1 priority date for domestic and international students; for spring admission, 11/1 priority date for domestic and international students. Applications are processed on a rolling basis. *Application fee:* $40. Electronic applications accepted. *Application Contact:* Fiona McDonnell, Administrative Assistant, 703-284-5901, E-mail: gadmissi@marymount.edu. *Interim Dean,* Dr. Michelle Walter-Edwards, 703-284-1580, Fax: 703-284-3819, E-mail: michelle.walters-edwards@marymount.edu.

**School of Business and Technology** Students: 154 full-time (85 women), 255 part-time (126 women); includes 204 minority (91 Black or African American, non-Hispanic/Latino; 1 American Indian or Alaska Native, non-Hispanic/Latino; 56 Asian, non-Hispanic/Latino; 42 Hispanic/Latino; 2 Native Hawaiian or other Pacific Islander, non-Hispanic/Latino; 12 Two or more races, non-Hispanic/Latino), 81 international. Average age 33. 310 applicants, 95% accepted, 132 enrolled. *Faculty:* 19 full-time (11 women), 21 part-time/adjunct (5 women). Expenses: Contact institution. *Financial support:* In 2019–20, 54 students received support. Research assistantships, teaching assistantships, career-related internships or fieldwork, scholarships/grants, and unspecified assistantships available. Support available to part-time students. Financial award application deadline: 3/1; financial award applicants required to submit FAFSA. In 2019, 118 master's, 10 other advanced degrees awarded. *Program availability:* Part-time, evening/weekend, 100% online, blended/hybrid learning. *Application deadline:* For fall admission, 7/16 priority date for domestic and international students; for spring admission, 11/16 priority date for domestic and international students; for summer admission, 4/16 priority date for domestic and international students. Applications are processed on a rolling basis. *Application fee:* $40. Electronic applications accepted. *Application Contact:* Fiona McDonnell, Administrative Assistant, 703-284-5901, E-mail: gadmissi@marymount.edu. *Interim Dean,* Jonathan Aberman, 703-284-5910, Fax: 703-527-3830, E-mail: jonathan.aberman@marymount.edu.

**School of Design, Arts, and Humanities** Students: 44 full-time (42 women), 42 part-time (36 women); includes 26 minority (16 Black or African American, non-Hispanic/Latino; 5 Asian, non-Hispanic/Latino; 4 Hispanic/Latino; 1 Two or more races, non-Hispanic/Latino), 18 international. Average age 36. 35 applicants, 89% accepted, 17 enrolled. *Faculty:* 14 full-time (10 women), 6 part-time/adjunct (5 women). Expenses: Contact institution. *Financial support:* In 2019–20, 12 students received support. Research assistantships, teaching assistantships, career-related internships or fieldwork, scholarships/grants, and unspecified assistantships available. Support available to part-time students. Financial award application deadline: 3/1; financial award applicants required to submit FAFSA. In 2019, 30 master's awarded. *Program availability:* Part-time, evening/weekend. *Application deadline:* For fall admission, 7/16 priority date for domestic and international students; for spring admission, 11/16 priority date for domestic and international students; for summer admission, 4/16 priority date for domestic and international students. Applications are processed on a rolling basis. *Application fee:* $40. Electronic applications accepted. *Application Contact:* Fiona McDonnell, Administrative Assistant, 703-284-5901, E-mail: gadmissi@marymount.edu. *Dean,* Dr. Christina Clark, 703-284-1560, Fax: 703-284-3859, E-mail: christina.clark@marymount.edu.

**School of Sciences, Mathematics, and Education** Students: 315 full-time (274 women), 156 part-time (130 women); includes 138 minority (47 Black or African American, non-Hispanic/Latino; 2 American Indian or Alaska Native, non-Hispanic/Latino; 17 Asian, non-Hispanic/Latino; 58 Hispanic/Latino; 1 Native Hawaiian or other Pacific Islander, non-Hispanic/Latino; 13 Two or more races, non-Hispanic/Latino), 10 international. Average age 28. 369 applicants, 93% accepted, 179 enrolled. *Faculty:* 26 full-time (22 women), 17 part-time/adjunct (14 women). Expenses: Contact institution. *Financial support:* In 2019–20, 97 students received support. Research assistantships, teaching assistantships, career-related internships or fieldwork, scholarships/grants, and unspecified assistantships available. Support available to part-time students. Financial award application deadline: 3/1; financial award applicants required to submit FAFSA. In 2019, 183 master's awarded. *Program availability:* Part-time, evening/weekend. *Application deadline:* For fall admission, 1/15 priority date for domestic and international students; for spring admission, 11/16 for domestic students, 11/16 priority date for international students. Applications are processed on a rolling basis. *Application fee:* $40. Electronic applications accepted. *Application Contact:* Fiona McDonnell, Administrative Assistant, 703-284-5901, E-mail: gadmissi@marymount.edu. *Dean,* Dr. Catherine Wehlburg, 703-284-1620, Fax: 703-284-1631, E-mail: catherine.wehlburg@marymount.edu.

## MARYVILLE UNIVERSITY OF SAINT LOUIS, St. Louis, MO 63141-7299

**General Information** Independent, coed, university. *Enrollment:* 10,013 graduate, professional, and undergraduate students; 701 full-time matriculated graduate/professional students (481 women), 4,858 part-time matriculated graduate/professional students (3,865 women). *Enrollment by degree level:* 4,119 master's, 738 doctoral, 702 other advanced degrees. *Graduate faculty:* 94 full-time (70 women), 376 part-time/adjunct (245 women). *Tuition:* Full-time $26,070; part-time $714 per credit hour. *Required fees:* $450 per semester. *Graduate housing:* Room and/or apartments available on a first-come, first-served basis to single students; on-campus housing not available to married students. Typical cost: $7800 per year ($10,300 including board). Room and board charges vary according to board plan and housing facility selected. Housing application deadline: 5/1. *Student services:* Campus employment opportunities, campus safety program, career counseling, exercise/wellness program, free psychological counseling, international student services, low-cost health insurance, multicultural affairs office, services for students with disabilities, teacher training, writing training. *Library facilities:* University Library. *Collection:* Books: 59,710 (physical), 290,347 (digital/electronic); Serial titles: 189 (physical), 70,563 (digital/electronic); Databases: 141. Weekly public service hours: 105; study areas open 24 hours, 5–7 days a week. *Research affiliation:* Monsanto Fund (STEM, computer coding), Southwestern Bell Foundation (secondary education curriculum and teacher education).

**Computer facilities:** 570 computers available on campus for general student use. A campuswide network can be accessed. Online class registration, specialized software, university catalog are available.
Website: http://www.maryville.edu/

**General Application Contact:** Jeannie DeLuca, Director of Admissions and Advising for Online Programs, 314-529-9355, Fax: 314-529-9927, E-mail: jdeluca@maryville.edu.

**GRADUATE UNITS**

**College of Arts and Sciences** Students: 48 full-time (30 women), 79 part-time (52 women); includes 33 minority (11 Black or African American, non-Hispanic/Latino; 9 Asian, non-Hispanic/Latino; 10 Hispanic/Latino; 3 Two or more races, non-Hispanic/Latino), 45 international. Average age 32. *Faculty:* 10 full-time (5 women), 14 part-time/adjunct (6 women). Expenses: Contact institution. *Financial support:* Application deadline: 4/1; applicants required to submit FAFSA. In 2019, 55 master's awarded. *Program availability:* Part-time. *Application deadline:* Applications are processed on a rolling basis. Electronic applications accepted. *Application Contact:* Shani Lenore-Jenkins, Vice President of Enrollment, 314-529-9359, E-mail: slenore@maryville.edu. *Dean*, Jennifer Yukna, 314-529-6858, Fax: 314-529-9965, E-mail: jyukna@maryville.edu.

**The John E. Simon School of Business** Students: 315 full-time (155 women), 738 part-time (344 women); includes 329 minority (186 Black or African American, non-Hispanic/Latino; 5 American Indian or Alaska Native, non-Hispanic/Latino; 48 Asian, non-Hispanic/Latino; 60 Hispanic/Latino; 30 Two or more races, non-Hispanic/Latino), 38 international. Average age 34. *Faculty:* 3 full-time (0 women), 107 part-time/adjunct (28 women). Expenses: Contact institution. *Financial support:* Career-related internships or fieldwork, Federal Work-Study, tuition waivers (partial), and campus employment available. Financial award application deadline: 4/1; financial award applicants required to submit FAFSA. In 2019, 388 master's awarded. *Program availability:* Part-time, 100% online, blended/hybrid learning. *Application deadline:* Applications are processed on a rolling basis. Electronic applications accepted. *Application Contact:* Chris Gourdine, Assistant Dean Business Administration, 314-529-6861, Fax: 314-529-9975, E-mail: cgourdine@maryville.edu. *Associate Academic Vice President/Interim Dean*, Tammy Gocial, 314-529-9401, Fax: 314-529-9975, E-mail: tgocial@maryville.edu.

**Myrtle E. and Earl E. Walker College of Health Professions** Students: 323 full-time (284 women), 3,726 part-time (3,242 women); includes 1,113 minority (565 Black or African American, non-Hispanic/Latino; 41 American Indian or Alaska Native, non-Hispanic/Latino; 177 Asian, non-Hispanic/Latino; 235 Hispanic/Latino; 95 Two or more races, non-Hispanic/Latino), 9 international. Average age 36. *Faculty:* 56 full-time (48 women), 229 part-time/adjunct (197 women). Expenses: Contact institution. *Financial support:* Career-related internships or fieldwork, Federal Work-Study, and campus employment available. Financial award application deadline: 4/1; financial award applicants required to submit FAFSA. In 2019, 1,109 master's, 91 doctorates awarded. *Program availability:* Part-time, 100% online, blended/hybrid learning. *Application deadline:* Applications are processed on a rolling basis. Electronic applications accepted. *Application Contact:* Jeannie DeLuca, Director of Admissions and Advising, 314-529-9355, Fax: 314-529-9927, E-mail: jdeluca@maryville.edu. *Dean*, Michelle Jenkins-Unterberg, 314-529-9590, Fax: 314-529-9495, E-mail: munterberg@maryville.edu.

***The Catherine McAuley School of Nursing*** Students: 103 full-time (91 women), 3,493 part-time (3,050 women); includes 1,039 minority (530 Black or African American, non-Hispanic/Latino; 41 American Indian or Alaska Native, non-Hispanic/Latino; 157 Asian, non-Hispanic/Latino; 221 Hispanic/Latino; 90 Two or more races, non-Hispanic/Latino), 9 international. Average age 37. *Faculty:* 14 full-time (all women), 131 part-time/adjunct (114 women). Expenses: Contact institution. *Financial support:* Federal Work-Study and campus employment available. Support available to part-time students. Financial award application deadline: 4/1; financial award applicants required to submit FAFSA. In 2019, 1,012 master's, 54 doctorates awarded. *Program availability:* 100% online, blended/hybrid learning. *Application deadline:* Applications are processed on a rolling basis. Electronic applications accepted. *Application Contact:* Jeannie DeLuca, Director of Admissions and Advising, 314-929-9355, Fax: 314-529-9927, E-mail: jdeluca@maryville.edu. *Assistant Dean Nursing*, Karla Larson, 314-529-6856, Fax: 314-529-9139, E-mail: klarson@maryville.edu.

**School of Education** Students: 42 full-time (12 women), 314 part-time (227 women); includes 103 minority (81 Black or African American, non-Hispanic/Latino; 5 Asian, non-Hispanic/Latino; 12 Hispanic/Latino; 5 Two or more races, non-Hispanic/Latino), 1 international. Average age 39. *Faculty:* 25 full-time (17 women), 26 part-time/adjunct (14 women). Expenses: Contact institution. *Financial support:* Career-related internships or fieldwork, Federal Work-Study, tuition waivers (partial), and professional educator discounts available. Financial award application deadline: 4/1; financial award applicants required to submit FAFSA. In 2019, 31 master's, 76 doctorates awarded. *Program availability:* Part-time, 100% online, blended/hybrid learning. *Application deadline:* Applications are processed on a rolling basis. Electronic applications accepted. *Application Contact:* Stacey Ruffin, Director of Clinical Experiences & Partnerships, 314-529-9542, Fax: 314-529-9921, E-mail: sruffin@maryville.edu. *Dean*, Dr. Maschael Schappe, 314-529-9670, Fax: 314-529-9921, E-mail: mschappe@maryville.edu.

## MARYWOOD UNIVERSITY, Scranton, PA 18509-1598

**General Information** Independent-religious, coed, comprehensive institution. *Enrollment:* 2,679 graduate, professional, and undergraduate students; 723 full-time matriculated graduate/professional students (576 women), 138 part-time matriculated graduate/professional students (101 women). *Enrollment by degree level:* 741 master's, 92 doctoral, 28 other advanced degrees. *Graduate housing:* Room and/or apartments available on a first-come, first-served basis to single students; on-campus housing not available to married students. *Student services:* Campus employment opportunities, campus safety program, career counseling, exercise/wellness program, free psychological counseling, grant writing training, international student services, low-cost health insurance, multicultural affairs office, services for students with disabilities, teacher training, writing training. *Library facilities:* Learning Commons plus 2 others. *Collection:* Books: 185,509 (physical), 225,884 (digital/electronic); Serial titles: 62 (physical), 44,458 (digital/electronic); Databases: 62. Weekly public service hours: 99; students can reserve study rooms.

**Computer facilities:** 359 computers available on campus for general student use. A campuswide network can be accessed. Online class registration, degree audit, student account management, financial aid self-service, student planning are available.
Website: http://www.marywood.edu/

**General Application Contact:** Jay Yander, Director of Graduate and International Admissions, 570-3486234, Fax: 570-961-4763, E-mail: gograd@marywood.edu.

**GRADUATE UNITS**

**Academic Affairs** *Program availability:* Part-time, evening/weekend, online learning. Electronic applications accepted.

***Center for Interdisciplinary Studies*** *Program availability:* Part-time. Electronic applications accepted.

***College of Health and Human Services*** *Program availability:* Part-time, online learning. Electronic applications accepted.

***Insalaco College of Creative and Performing Arts*** *Program availability:* Part-time. Electronic applications accepted.

***Munley College of Liberal Arts and Sciences*** *Program availability:* Part-time, online learning. Electronic applications accepted.

***Reap College of Education and Human Development*** *Program availability:* Part-time.

***School of Architecture*** *Program availability:* Part-time. Electronic applications accepted.

## MASSACHUSETTS COLLEGE OF ART AND DESIGN, Boston, MA 02115-5882

**General Information** State-supported, coed, comprehensive institution. *Enrollment:* 2,065 graduate, professional, and undergraduate students; 96 full-time matriculated graduate/professional students (57 women), 44 part-time matriculated graduate/professional students (31 women). *Enrollment by degree level:* 128 master's, 12 other advanced degrees. *Graduate faculty:* 2 full-time (both women), 60 part-time/adjunct (27 women). Tuition, state resident: part-time $400 per credit. Tuition, nonresident: part-time $400 per credit. *Required fees:* $400 per credit. Tuition and fees vary according to course load and program. *Graduate housing:* Room and/or apartments available on a first-come, first-served basis to single students; on-campus housing not available to married students. Typical cost: $10,592 per year. Housing application deadline: 5/1. *Student services:* Campus employment opportunities, campus safety program, career counseling, exercise/wellness program, free psychological counseling, international student services, low-cost health insurance, multicultural affairs office, services for students with disabilities, teacher training, writing training. *Library facilities:* Morton R. Godine Library.

**Computer facilities:** Computer purchase and lease plans are available. 370 computers available on campus for general student use. A campuswide network can be accessed from student residence rooms and from off campus. Online class registration is available.
Website: http://www.massart.edu/

**General Application Contact:** Stacy Petersen, Associate Director of Graduate Admissions and Operations, 617-879-7238, E-mail: gradadmissions@massart.edu.

**GRADUATE UNITS**

**Graduate Programs** Students: 96 full-time (57 women), 44 part-time (31 women); includes 30 minority (4 Black or African American, non-Hispanic/Latino; 7 Asian, non-Hispanic/Latino; 13 Hispanic/Latino; 1 Native Hawaiian or other Pacific Islander, non-Hispanic/Latino; 5 Two or more races, non-Hispanic/Latino), 35 international. 303 applicants, 54% accepted, 72 enrolled. *Faculty:* 2 full-time (both women), 60 part-time/adjunct (27 women). Expenses: Contact institution. *Financial support:* In 2019–20, 48 students received support, including 2 research assistantships (averaging $2,180 per year), 47 teaching assistantships (averaging $2,180 per year); career-related internships or fieldwork, scholarships/grants, unspecified assistantships, and adjunct co-teaching positions also available. Support available to part-time students. Financial award application deadline: 1/20; financial award applicants required to submit FAFSA. In 2019, 58 master's, 8 other advanced degrees awarded. *Application deadline:* For fall admission, 1/20 priority date for domestic and international students; for summer admission, 1/20 priority date for domestic and international students. *Application fee:* $90. Electronic applications accepted. *Application Contact:* Stacey Petersen, Associate Director of Graduate Admissions and Operations, 617-879-7238, E-mail: gradadmissions@massart.edu. *Dean of Graduate Studies*, Lucinda Bliss, 617-879-7157, E-mail: lbliss@massart.edu.

## MASSACHUSETTS COLLEGE OF LIBERAL ARTS, North Adams, MA 01247-4100

**General Information** State-supported, coed, comprehensive institution. *Graduate housing:* On-campus housing not available.

**GRADUATE UNITS**

**Graduate Programs** *Program availability:* Part-time, evening/weekend.

## MASSACHUSETTS INSTITUTE OF TECHNOLOGY, Cambridge, MA 02139-4307

**General Information** Independent, coed, university. CGS member. *Graduate housing:* Rooms and/or apartments available to single and married students. Housing application deadline: 5/15. *Research affiliation:* Novartis Pharmaceuticals (pharmaceutical manufacturing), Singapore National Research Foundation (infectious diseases, environmental sensing, biosystems, urban transportation, low power electronics), Woods Hole Oceanographic Institution (applied ocean science and engineering), Broad Institute (genomics and biomedical research), Whitehead Institute for Biomedical Research (developmental biology), Eni S.p.A (renewable energy), Woods Hole Oceanographic Institute (applied ocean science and engineering), Broad Institute (genomics and biomedical research), Whitehead Institute for Biomedical Research (developmental biology).

**GRADUATE UNITS**

**MIT Sloan School of Management** Expenses: Contact institution. *Financial support:* Fellowships with tuition reimbursements, research assistantships with tuition reimbursements, teaching assistantships with tuition reimbursements, Federal Work-Study, institutionally sponsored loans, scholarships/grants, health care benefits, and unspecified assistantships available. Support available to part-time students. Electronic applications accepted. *Application Contact:* Rod Garcia, Director of Admissions, 617-253-5434, Fax: 617-253-6405, E-mail: mbaadmissions@sloan.mit.edu. *Dean*, David C. Schmittlein, 617-253-2804, Fax: 617-258-6617, E-mail: dschmitt@mit.edu.

**Operations Research Center** Electronic applications accepted.

**School of Architecture and Planning** Electronic applications accepted.

***Center for Real Estate*** Electronic applications accepted.

**School of Engineering** Electronic applications accepted.
***Institute for Data, Systems, and Society*** Electronic applications accepted.
**School of Humanities, Arts, and Social Sciences** Electronic applications accepted.
**School of Science** Electronic applications accepted.

## MASSACHUSETTS MARITIME ACADEMY, Buzzards Bay, MA 02532-1803

**General Information** State-supported, coed, comprehensive institution. *Graduate housing:* On-campus housing not available.

GRADUATE UNITS

**Master's in Maritime Business Management Program** Students: 50 full-time (20 women); includes 10 minority (3 Black or African American, non-Hispanic/Latino; 2 Asian, non-Hispanic/Latino; 5 Hispanic/Latino). Average age 35. 24 applicants, 63% accepted, 14 enrolled. *Faculty:* 13 full-time (5 women). Expenses: Contact institution. *Financial support:* Application deadline: 10/10; applicants required to submit FAFSA. *Program availability:* Part-time, evening/weekend, 100% online, blended/hybrid learning. *Application deadline:* Applications are processed on a rolling basis. Electronic applications accepted. *Application Contact:* Anna Woringer, Staff Assistant, 508-830-5019, E-mail: dce@maritime.edu. *Graduate Dean*, Dr. James McDonald, 617-8305096 Ext. 5096, E-mail: jmcdonald@maritme.edu.

**Program in Emergency Management** *Program availability:* Evening/weekend. Electronic applications accepted.

**Program in Facilities Management** *Program availability:* Evening/weekend. Electronic applications accepted.

## MASSACHUSETTS SCHOOL OF LAW AT ANDOVER, Andover, MA 01810

**General Information** Independent, coed, graduate-only institution. *Graduate housing:* On-campus housing not available.

GRADUATE UNITS

**Professional Program** *Program availability:* Part-time, evening/weekend. Electronic applications accepted.

## THE MASTER'S UNIVERSITY, Santa Clarita, CA 91321-1200

**General Information** Independent-religious, coed, comprehensive institution. *Graduate housing:* On-campus housing not available.

GRADUATE UNITS

**The Master's Seminary** *Program availability:* Part-time.

## MAYO CLINIC ALIX SCHOOL OF MEDICINE, Rochester, MN 55905

**General Information** Independent, coed, graduate-only institution. *Graduate housing:* On-campus housing not available.

GRADUATE UNITS

**Professional Program** Electronic applications accepted.

## MAYO CLINIC GRADUATE SCHOOL OF BIOMEDICAL SCIENCES, Rochester, MN 55905

**General Information** Independent, coed, graduate-only institution. *Enrollment by degree level:* 202 doctoral. *Graduate faculty:* 341 full-time (78 women). *Graduate housing:* On-campus housing not available. *Student services:* Campus safety program, career counseling, exercise/wellness program, free psychological counseling, grant writing training, international student services, low-cost health insurance, multicultural affairs office, services for students with disabilities, writing training. *Library facilities:* Mayo Clinic Libraries plus 11 others. *Collection:* Books: 400,000 (digital/electronic); Databases: 4,300. Study areas open 24 hours, 5–7 days a week; students can reserve study rooms.

**Computer facilities:** Online class registration is available.
Website: https://college.mayo.edu/academics/biomedical-research-training/

**General Application Contact:** Sarah E. Giese, PhD Admissions Coordinator, 507-538-1160, Fax: 507-293-0838, E-mail: phd.training@mayo.edu.

GRADUATE UNITS

**Program in Biochemistry and Molecular Biology** Electronic applications accepted.
**Program in Biomedical Engineering and Physiology** Electronic applications accepted.
**Program in Clinical and Translational Science** Electronic applications accepted.
**Program in Immunology** Electronic applications accepted.
**Program in Molecular Pharmacology and Experimental Therapeutics** Electronic applications accepted.
**Program in Neuroscience** Electronic applications accepted.
**Program in Virology and Gene Therapy** Electronic applications accepted.

## MAYO CLINIC SCHOOL OF HEALTH SCIENCES, Rochester, MN 55905

**General Information** Independent, coed, graduate-only institution. *Enrollment:* 253 full-time matriculated graduate/professional students (158 women). *Enrollment by degree level:* 346 doctoral. *Graduate faculty:* 20 full-time (11 women). *Student services:* Campus employment opportunities, campus safety program, career counseling, exercise/wellness program, free psychological counseling, international student services, multicultural affairs office, services for students with disabilities, teacher training, writing training. *Library facilities:* Venables Health Sciences Library plus 3 others. *Collection:* Study areas open 24 hours, 5–7 days a week; students can reserve study rooms.

**Computer facilities:** Online class registration is available.
Website: http://www.mayo.edu/mayo-clinic-school-of-health-sciences

**General Application Contact:** Kammi Englund, Education Coordinator, 507-284-3678, Fax: 507-284-0656, E-mail: englund.kammi@mayo.edu.

GRADUATE UNITS

**Doctor of Nurse Anesthesia Practice Program** Electronic applications accepted.
**Program in Physical Therapy** Electronic applications accepted.

## MCCORMICK THEOLOGICAL SEMINARY, Chicago, IL 60615

**General Information** Independent-religious, coed, graduate-only institution. *Graduate housing:* Rooms and/or apartments available on a first-come, first-served basis to single and married students. Housing application deadline: 7/1.

GRADUATE UNITS

**Graduate and Professional Programs** *Program availability:* Part-time, evening/weekend.

## MCDANIEL COLLEGE, Westminster, MD 21157-4390

**General Information** Independent, coed, comprehensive institution. *Graduate housing:* On-campus housing not available.

GRADUATE UNITS

**Graduate and Professional Studies** *Program availability:* Part-time, evening/weekend, 100% online, blended/hybrid learning. Electronic applications accepted.

## MCGILL UNIVERSITY, Montréal, QC H3A 2T5, Canada

**General Information** Province-supported, coed, university. CGS member. *Graduate housing:* Room and/or apartments available to married students; on-campus housing not available to single students.

GRADUATE UNITS

**Faculty of Graduate and Postdoctoral Studies**
***Desautels Faculty of Management***
***Faculty of Agricultural and Environmental Sciences***
***Faculty of Arts***
***Faculty of Dentistry***
***Faculty of Education***
***Faculty of Engineering***
***Faculty of Law***
***Faculty of Medicine***
***Faculty of Religious Studies***
***Faculty of Science***
***Schulich School of Music***
**Max Bell School of Public Policy**
**Professional Program in Dentistry** Electronic applications accepted.
**Professional Program in Medicine**

## MCKENDREE UNIVERSITY, Lebanon, IL 62254-1299

**General Information** Independent-religious, coed, university. *Graduate housing:* On-campus housing not available.

GRADUATE UNITS

**Graduate Programs** *Program availability:* Part-time, evening/weekend. Electronic applications accepted.

## MCMASTER UNIVERSITY, Hamilton, ON L8S 4M2, Canada

**General Information** Province-supported, coed, university. CGS member. *Graduate housing:* Room and/or apartments available to single students; on-campus housing not available to married students. Housing application deadline: 6/30. *Research affiliation:* Commonwealth Development (telecommunications), Canadian Centre for Inland Waters (chemical and civil engineering).

GRADUATE UNITS

**Faculty of Health Sciences** *Program availability:* Part-time, online learning.
**McMaster Divinity College** *Program availability:* Part-time.
**School of Graduate Studies** *Program availability:* Part-time.
***DeGroote School of Business*** *Program availability:* Part-time.
***Faculty of Engineering*** *Program availability:* Part-time.
***Faculty of Humanities*** *Program availability:* Part-time, evening/weekend.
***Faculty of Science*** *Program availability:* Part-time, evening/weekend.
***Faculty of Social Sciences*** *Program availability:* Part-time, evening/weekend.

## MCMURRY UNIVERSITY, Abilene, TX 79697

**General Information** Independent-religious, coed, comprehensive institution.

GRADUATE UNITS

**Graduate Studies**

## MCNEESE STATE UNIVERSITY, Lake Charles, LA 70609

**General Information** State-supported, coed, comprehensive institution. *Graduate housing:* Room and/or apartments available on a first-come, first-served basis to single students. Housing application deadline: 8/15.

GRADUATE UNITS

**Doré School of Graduate Studies** *Program availability:* Part-time, evening/weekend.
***Burton College of Education*** *Program availability:* Part-time, evening/weekend.
***College of Business*** *Program availability:* Part-time, evening/weekend.
***College of Engineering and Computer Science*** *Program availability:* Part-time, evening/weekend.
***College of Liberal Arts*** *Program availability:* Part-time, evening/weekend.
***College of Nursing and Health Professions***
***College of Science and Agriculture*** *Program availability:* Part-time, evening/weekend.

## MCPHERSON COLLEGE, McPherson, KS 67460-1402

**General Information** Independent-religious, coed, comprehensive institution. *Graduate housing:* On-campus housing not available.

GRADUATE UNITS

**Program in Education**

## MCPHS UNIVERSITY, Boston, MA 02115-5896

**General Information** Independent, coed, university. *Graduate housing:* Room and/or apartments available on a first-come, first-served basis to single students; on-campus housing not available to married students. Housing application deadline: 5/1. *Research affiliation:* Cephrim Biosciences, Inc. (pharmaceutics), Center for Analytical Science (analytical medicinal chemistry).

GRADUATE UNITS

**Graduate Studies** *Program availability:* Part-time.
**New England School of Acupuncture** *Program availability:* Part-time.
**School of Optometry**
**School of Pharmacy–Worcester/Manchester**
**School of Physical Therapy**

## MEADVILLE LOMBARD THEOLOGICAL SCHOOL, Chicago, IL 60637-1602

**General Information** Independent-religious, coed, graduate-only institution. *Graduate housing:* Rooms and/or apartments available on a first-come, first-served basis to single and married students. Housing application deadline: 3/15.

**GRADUATE UNITS**

**Graduate and Professional Programs** *Program availability:* Part-time, online learning.

## MEDAILLE COLLEGE, Buffalo, NY 14214-2695

**General Information** Independent, coed, comprehensive institution. *Graduate housing:* Rooms and/or apartments available on a first-come, first-served basis to single and married students. Housing application deadline: 8/15.

**GRADUATE UNITS**

**Program in Business Administration - Amherst** *Program availability:* Evening/weekend. Electronic applications accepted.

**Program in Business Administration - Rochester** *Program availability:* Evening/weekend.

**Program in Education** *Program availability:* Part-time, evening/weekend. Electronic applications accepted.

**Programs in Psychology** *Program availability:* Part-time, evening/weekend. Electronic applications accepted.

## MEDICAL COLLEGE OF WISCONSIN, Milwaukee, WI 53226-0509

**General Information** Independent, coed, graduate-only institution. CGS member. *Enrollment by degree level:* 108 master's, 1,347 doctoral, 22 other advanced degrees. *Graduate faculty:* 1,739 full-time (674 women), 344 part-time/adjunct (191 women). *Tuition:* Full-time $55,130; part-time $1056 per credit. *Required fees:* $555.50. One-time fee: $72 full-time; $50 part-time. Tuition and fees vary according to degree level and program. *Graduate housing:* On-campus housing not available. *Student services:* Campus employment opportunities, campus safety program, career counseling, exercise/wellness program, free psychological counseling, grant writing training, international student services, low-cost health insurance, multicultural affairs office, services for students with disabilities. *Library facilities:* Todd Wehr Library plus 2 others. *Collection:* Books: 49,825 (physical), 13,488 (digital/electronic); Serial titles: 7 (physical), 12,661 (digital/electronic); Databases: 74. Study areas open 24 hours, 5–7 days a week; students can reserve study rooms. *Research affiliation:* General Electric Medical Systems (biophysics, radiology).

**Computer facilities:** 250 computers available on campus for general student use. A campuswide network can be accessed from off campus. Online class registration is available.
Website: http://www.mcw.edu/

**General Application Contact:** Anthony Perez, Associate Director - Graduate School, 414-955-8218, Fax: 414-955-6555, E-mail: anperez@mcw.edu.

**GRADUATE UNITS**

**Graduate School** Students: 241 full-time (136 women), 68 part-time (46 women); includes 47 minority (15 Black or African American, non-Hispanic/Latino; 1 American Indian or Alaska Native, non-Hispanic/Latino; 13 Asian, non-Hispanic/Latino; 14 Hispanic/Latino; 4 Two or more races, non-Hispanic/Latino), 75 international. Average age 29. 353 applicants, 49% accepted, 82 enrolled. Expenses: Contact institution. *Financial support:* In 2019–20, 226 students received support, including 177 research assistantships with full tuition reimbursements available (averaging $30,480 per year); career-related internships or fieldwork, Federal Work-Study, institutionally sponsored loans, scholarships/grants, traineeships, health care benefits, unspecified assistantships, and full tuition scholarship plus cost of living stipend (for all full-time PhD seekers) also available. Financial award application deadline: 2/15; financial award applicants required to submit FAFSA. In 2019, 44 master's, 35 doctorates, 4 other advanced degrees awarded. *Program availability:* Part-time, evening/weekend, 100% online. *Application deadline:* For fall admission, 1/15 priority date for domestic students, 1/15 for international students; for spring admission, 12/1 priority date for domestic students, 12/1 for international students. Applications are processed on a rolling basis. *Application fee:* $50. Electronic applications accepted. *Application Contact:* Anthony Perez, Associate Director - Graduate School, 414-9554407, E-mail: anperez@mcw.edu. *Dean*, Dr. Ravindra P. Misra, 414-955-8218, Fax: 414-955-6555, E-mail: gradschool@mcw.edu.

***Center for Bioethics and Medical Humanities*** Students: 5 full-time (2 women), 12 part-time (all women); includes 2 minority (1 Black or African American, non-Hispanic/Latino; 1 Two or more races, non-Hispanic/Latino). Average age 35. 16 applicants, 63% accepted, 8 enrolled. Expenses: Contact institution. *Financial support:* Available to part-time students. Application deadline: 2/15; applicants required to submit FAFSA. In 2019, 6 master's, 3 other advanced degrees awarded. *Program availability:* Part-time. *Application deadline:* For fall admission, 1/15 priority date for domestic students. Applications are processed on a rolling basis. *Application fee:* $50. Electronic applications accepted. *Application Contact:* Recruitment Office, 414-955-4402, Fax: 414-955-6555, E-mail: gradschoolrecruit@mcw.edu.

***Medical Scientist Training Program*** Students: 53 full-time (25 women); includes 12 minority (1 Black or African American, non-Hispanic/Latino; 7 Asian, non-Hispanic/Latino; 1 Hispanic/Latino; 3 Two or more races, non-Hispanic/Latino), 6 international. Average age 27. 6 applicants, 100% accepted, 6 enrolled. Expenses: Contact institution. *Financial support:* Applicants required to submit FAFSA. *Application deadline:* For fall admission, 12/1 for domestic and international students. *Application fee:* $50. *Application Contact:* Dr. Joseph T. Barbieri, Director, 414-456-8412, E-mail: jtb01@mcw.edu. *Director*, Dr. Joseph T. Barbieri, 414-456-8412, E-mail: jtb01@mcw.edu.

**Interdisciplinary Program in Biomedical Sciences** Students: 40 full-time (26 women); includes 2 minority (1 Black or African American, non-Hispanic/Latino; 1 Hispanic/Latino), 15 international. Average age 25. 99 applicants, 42% accepted, 20 enrolled. Expenses: Contact institution. *Financial support:* In 2019–20, 40 students received support, including fellowships with full tuition reimbursements available (averaging $30,000 per year), research assistantships with full tuition reimbursements available (averaging $30,000 per year); tuition waivers (full) and unspecified assistantships also available. Financial award application deadline: 2/1; financial award applicants required to submit FAFSA. *Application deadline:* For fall admission, 12/15 priority date for domestic students. Applications are processed on a rolling basis. *Application fee:* $50. Electronic applications accepted. *Application Contact:* Dr. Joseph C. Besharse, Director, 414-955-8063, Fax: 414-955-6517, E-mail: biomed@mcw.edu. *Director*, Dr. Joseph C. Besharse, 414-955-8063, Fax: 414-955-6517, E-mail: biomed@mcw.edu.

**Medical School** Students: 1,022 full-time (511 women), 3 part-time (1 woman); includes 291 minority (43 Black or African American, non-Hispanic/Latino; 1 American Indian or Alaska Native, non-Hispanic/Latino; 130 Asian, non-Hispanic/Latino; 78 Hispanic/Latino; 3 Native Hawaiian or other Pacific Islander, non-Hispanic/Latino; 36 Two or more races, non-Hispanic/Latino), 35 international. Average age 26. Expenses: Contact institution. *Financial support:* Fellowships, career-related internships or fieldwork, and institutionally sponsored loans available. Financial award application deadline: 2/1; financial award applicants required to submit FAFSA. In 2019, 12 master's, 229 doctorates awarded. *Program availability:* Part-time. *Application deadline:* For fall admission, 1/15 for domestic and international students. *Application fee:* $50. Electronic applications accepted. *Application Contact:* Registrar, 414-456-8733. *Provost/Executive Vice President/Dean*, Joseph E. Kerschner, MD, 414-955-8739.

**Pharmacy School** Students: 142 full-time (79 women), 1 part-time (0 women); includes 33 minority (2 Black or African American, non-Hispanic/Latino; 21 Asian, non-Hispanic/Latino; 5 Hispanic/Latino; 1 Native Hawaiian or other Pacific Islander, non-Hispanic/Latino; 4 Two or more races, non-Hispanic/Latino), 1 international. Average age 26. 156 applicants, 51% accepted, 49 enrolled. Expenses: Contact institution. *Financial support:* Applicants required to submit FAFSA. *Application deadline:* For fall admission, 6/1 for domestic students. Applications are processed on a rolling basis. *Application fee:* $175. Electronic applications accepted. *Application Contact:* Dr. George E. MacKinnon, III, Dean, 414-955-7476, E-mail: gmackinnon@mcw.edu. *Dean*, Dr. George E. MacKinnon, III, 414-955-7476, E-mail: gmackinnon@mcw.edu.

## MEDICAL UNIVERSITY OF SOUTH CAROLINA, Charleston, SC 29425

**General Information** State-supported, coed, upper-level institution. CGS member. *Research affiliation:* Novartis Pharmaceuticals (cancer), Boston Scientific Corporation (cardiovascular diseases), Genentech (Alzheimer's disease), AstraZeneca (cancer/cardiovascular diseases), Merck & Company, Inc. (neuroscience), Eli Lilly and Company (substance abuse).

**GRADUATE UNITS**

**College of Dental Medicine** Electronic applications accepted.

**College of Graduate Studies** Electronic applications accepted.

***Division of Biostatistics and Epidemiology*** Electronic applications accepted.

***South Carolina Clinical and Translational Research Institute*** *Program availability:* Online learning. Electronic applications accepted.

**College of Health Professions** *Program availability:* Part-time. Electronic applications accepted.

**College of Medicine** Electronic applications accepted.

**College of Nursing** *Program availability:* Part-time, online learning. Electronic applications accepted.

**South Carolina College of Pharmacy** Electronic applications accepted.

## MEHARRY MEDICAL COLLEGE, Nashville, TN 37208-9989

**General Information** Independent-religious, coed, graduate-only institution. CGS member. *Graduate faculty:* 273 full-time (69 women), 46 part-time/adjunct (11 women). *Graduate housing:* Rooms and/or apartments available on a first-come, first-served basis to single and married students. *Student services:* Campus employment opportunities, campus safety program, career counseling, child daycare facilities, exercise/wellness program, free psychological counseling, international student services, low-cost health insurance. *Library facilities:* Meharry Medical College Library.

**Computer facilities:** 100 computers available on campus for general student use.
Website: http://www.mmc.edu/

**General Application Contact:** April Curry, Director of Admissions and Recruitment, 615-327-6453, Fax: 615-327-6228, E-mail: acurry@mmc.edu.

**GRADUATE UNITS**

**School of Dentistry** Expenses: Contact institution. *Financial support:* Career-related internships or fieldwork, Federal Work-Study, and institutionally sponsored loans available. Financial award application deadline: 4/15; financial award applicants required to submit FAFSA. *Application deadline:* For winter admission, 1/15 for domestic and international students. Applications are processed on a rolling basis. *Application fee:* $65. *Application Contact:* Cherae M. Farmer-Dixon, DDS, Dean, 615-327-6207, E-mail: cdixon@mmc.edu. *Dean*, Cherae M. Farmer-Dixon, DDS, 615-327-6207, E-mail: cdixon@mmc.edu.

**School of Graduate Studies** Expenses: Contact institution. *Financial support:* Fellowships, research assistantships, teaching assistantships, career-related internships or fieldwork, Federal Work-Study, institutionally sponsored loans, scholarships/grants, and tuition waivers (full) available. Support available to part-time students. Financial award applicants required to submit FAFSA. *Program availability:* Online learning. *Application deadline:* For fall admission, 6/1 for domestic students. Applications are processed on a rolling basis. *Application fee:* $65. Electronic applications accepted. *Application Contact:* Dr. LaMonica Stewart, Interim Associate Dean, 615-327-6533, Fax: 615-321-2933, E-mail: lstewart@mmc.edu. *Interim Dean*, Dr. Evangeline Delores Motley-Johnson, 615-327-6533, Fax: 615-321-2933, E-mail: emotley@mmc.edu.

***Division of Public Health Practice*** Expenses: Contact institution. *Financial support:* Career-related internships or fieldwork, Federal Work-Study, institutionally sponsored loans, and scholarships/grants available. Support available to part-time students. Financial award application deadline: 7/15; financial award applicants required to submit FAFSA. *Program availability:* Part-time, evening/weekend. *Application deadline:* For fall admission, 6/1 for domestic students. Applications are processed on a rolling basis. *Application fee:* $65. *Application Contact:* Kimberlee Wyche-Etheridge, MD,MPH, Interim Program Director, 615-327-6675, E-mail: ketheridge@mmc.edu. *Senior Associate Dean*, Stephanie Bailey, MD, 615-327-6069, E-mail: sbailey@mmc.edu.

**School of Medicine** Expenses: Contact institution. *Financial support:* Federal Work-Study, institutionally sponsored loans, and tuition waivers (partial) available. Financial award applicants required to submit FAFSA. *Application deadline:* For fall admission, 12/15 for domestic students. Applications are processed on a rolling basis. *Application fee:* $65. Electronic applications accepted. *Application Contact:* Dr. Theodora Pinnock, Associate Dean of Student Affairs & Admissions, 615-327-6057, E-mail: tpinnock@mmc.edu. *Interim Dean*, Dr. Digna Forbes, 615-327-6204, E-mail: dforbes@mmc.edu.

## MELBOURNE BUSINESS SCHOOL, Carlton, Victoria 3053, Australia

**General Information** Independent, coed, graduate-only institution.

**GRADUATE UNITS**

**Graduate Programs**

## MEMORIAL UNIVERSITY OF NEWFOUNDLAND, St. John's, NL A1C 5S7, Canada

**General Information** Province-supported, coed, university. CGS member. *Graduate housing:* Rooms and/or apartments available on a first-come, first-served basis to single and married students. *Research affiliation:* Eastern Regional Health Authority (health research).

**GRADUATE UNITS**

**Faculty of Medicine** *Program availability:* Part-time, online learning. Electronic applications accepted.

***Graduate Programs in Medicine*** *Program availability:* Part-time. Electronic applications accepted.

**School of Graduate Studies** *Program availability:* Part-time, evening/weekend, 100% online, blended/hybrid learning. Electronic applications accepted.

***Faculty of Business Administration*** *Program availability:* Part-time. Electronic applications accepted.

***Faculty of Education*** *Program availability:* Part-time. Electronic applications accepted.

***Faculty of Engineering and Applied Science*** *Program availability:* Part-time. Electronic applications accepted.

***School of Human Kinetics and Recreation*** *Program availability:* Part-time. Electronic applications accepted.

***School of Music*** Electronic applications accepted.

***School of Nursing*** *Program availability:* Part-time. Electronic applications accepted.

***School of Pharmacy*** *Program availability:* Part-time. Electronic applications accepted.

***School of Social Work*** Electronic applications accepted.

## MEMPHIS THEOLOGICAL SEMINARY, Memphis, TN 38104-4395

**General Information** Independent-religious, coed, graduate-only institution. *Graduate housing:* Rooms and/or apartments available on a first-come, first-served basis to single and married students. Housing application deadline: 7/15. *Research affiliation:* Lilly Foundation (technology, religion), Wabash Center for Teaching and Learning (theology, religion).

**GRADUATE UNITS**

**Graduate and Professional Programs** *Program availability:* Part-time.

## MERCER UNIVERSITY, Macon, GA 31207

**General Information** Independent-religious, coed, university. *Enrollment:* 7,276 graduate, professional, and undergraduate students; 2,791 full-time matriculated graduate/professional students (1,801 women), 1,061 part-time matriculated graduate/professional students (762 women). *Enrollment by degree level:* 1,915 master's, 1,885 doctoral, 53 other advanced degrees. *Graduate faculty:* 224 full-time (103 women), 122 part-time/adjunct (72 women). Tuition and fees vary according to degree level, campus/location and program. *Graduate housing:* On-campus housing not available. *Student services:* Campus employment opportunities, campus safety program, career counseling, exercise/wellness program, free psychological counseling, international student services, low-cost health insurance, services for students with disabilities. *Library facilities:* Jack Tarver Library plus 3 others. *Collection:* Study areas open 24 hours, 5–7 days a week; students can reserve study rooms. *Research affiliation:* Memorial Health Care (medical research), Piedmont (medical research), Total Therapeutic Management (pharmaceuticals), The Coca Cola Company (pharmaceutical research), Georgia Neurological Institute (medical research), Medical Center of Central Georgia (medical research).

**Computer facilities:** A campuswide network can be accessed. Online class registration is available.
Website: http://www.mercer.edu/

**General Application Contact:** Tracey M. Wofford, Director of Graduate Admissions, 678-547-6422, Fax: 678-547-6422, E-mail: wofford_tm@mercer.edu.

**GRADUATE UNITS**

**Graduate Studies, Cecil B. Day Campus** Students: 1,603 full-time (1,175 women), 920 part-time (683 women); includes 1,387 minority (968 Black or African American, non-Hispanic/Latino; 4 American Indian or Alaska Native, non-Hispanic/Latino; 271 Asian, non-Hispanic/Latino; 112 Hispanic/Latino; 2 Native Hawaiian or other Pacific Islander, non-Hispanic/Latino; 30 Two or more races, non-Hispanic/Latino), 114 international. Average age 31. *Faculty:* 148 full-time (90 women), 102 part-time/adjunct (77 women). Expenses: Contact institution. *Financial support:* In 2019–20, 372 students received support. Teaching assistantships, career-related internships or fieldwork, Federal Work-Study, and scholarships/grants available. Support available to part-time students. Financial award applicants required to submit FAFSA. In 2019, 724 master's, 234 doctorates, 14 other advanced degrees awarded. *Program availability:* Part-time, evening/weekend, 100% online, blended/hybrid learning. *Application Contact:* Tracey M. Wofford, Director of Admissions, 678-547-6422, E-mail: wofford_tm@mercer.edu. *Provost*, Dr. Scott Davis, 478-301-2110, E-mail: davis_ds@mercer.edu.

***College of Health Professions*** Students: 360 full-time (292 women), 74 part-time (58 women); includes 171 minority (100 Black or African American, non-Hispanic/Latino; 36 Asian, non-Hispanic/Latino; 31 Hispanic/Latino; 4 Two or more races, non-Hispanic/Latino), 10 international. Average age 26. *Faculty:* 17 full-time (13 women), 17 part-time/adjunct (10 women). Expenses: Contact institution. *Financial support:* Federal Work-Study, traineeships, and unspecified assistantships available. In 2019, 141 master's, 51 doctorates awarded. *Application Contact:* Laura Ellison, Director of Admissions and Student Affairs, 678-547-6391, E-mail: ellison_la@mercer.edu. *Dean/Clinical Professor*, Dr. Lisa Lundquist, 678-547-6308, E-mail: lundquist_lm@mercer.edu.

***College of Pharmacy*** Students: 573 full-time (388 women), 3 part-time (2 women); includes 366 minority (164 Black or African American, non-Hispanic/Latino; 168 Asian, non-Hispanic/Latino; 22 Hispanic/Latino; 12 Two or more races, non-Hispanic/Latino), 49 international. Average age 26. 677 applicants, 48% accepted, 152 enrolled. *Faculty:* 22 full-time (16 women), 15 part-time/adjunct (6 women). Expenses: Contact institution. *Financial support:* In 2019–20, 238 students received support, including 10 research assistantships with full tuition reimbursements available (averaging $15,000 per year), 35 teaching assistantships with full tuition reimbursements available (averaging $15,000 per year); Federal Work-Study, scholarships/grants, and tuition waivers (full) also available. Financial award application deadline: 5/1; financial award applicants required to submit FAFSA. In 2019, 144 doctorates awarded. *Application deadline:* For fall admission, 6/3 for domestic and international students. Applications are processed on a rolling basis. Electronic applications accepted. *Application Contact:* Jordana S. Berry, Director of Admissions, 678-547-6182, Fax: 678-547-6518, E-mail: berry_js@mercer.edu. *Dean*, Dr. Brian L. Crabtree, 678-547-6306, Fax: 678-547-6315, E-mail: crabtree_bl@mercer.edu.

***College of Professional Advancement*** Students: 193 full-time (156 women), 277 part-time (225 women); includes 260 minority (211 Black or African American, non-Hispanic/Latino; 2 American Indian or Alaska Native, non-Hispanic/Latino; 23 Asian, non-Hispanic/Latino; 19 Hispanic/Latino; 5 Two or more races, non-Hispanic/Latino), 3 international. Average age 32. 300 applicants, 45% accepted, 114 enrolled. *Faculty:* 19 full-time (11 women), 34 part-time/adjunct (30 women). Expenses: Contact institution. *Financial support:* In 2019–20, 32 students received support. Federal Work-Study, scholarships/grants, and unspecified assistantships available. Financial award applicants required to submit FAFSA. In 2019, 183 master's, 7 doctorates awarded. *Program availability:* Part-time, evening/weekend, 100% online, blended/hybrid learning. *Application deadline:* For fall admission, 7/1 priority date for domestic and international students; for spring admission, 11/1 priority date for domestic and international students; for summer admission, 4/1 priority date for domestic and international students. *Application fee:* $35. Electronic applications accepted. *Application Contact:* Theatis Anderson, Asst VP for Enrollment Management, 678-547-6421, E-mail: anderson_t@mercer.edu. *Dean*, Dr. Priscilla R. Danheiser, 678-547-6028, Fax: 678-547-6008, E-mail: danheiser_p@mercer.edu.

***Georgia Baptist College of Nursing*** Students: 69 full-time (64 women), 45 part-time (41 women); includes 61 minority (42 Black or African American, non-Hispanic/Latino; 12 Asian, non-Hispanic/Latino; 4 Hispanic/Latino; 1 Native Hawaiian or other Pacific Islander, non-Hispanic/Latino; 2 Two or more races, non-Hispanic/Latino), 1 international. Average age 35. 92 applicants, 75% accepted, 57 enrolled. *Faculty:* 26 full-time (23 women), 13 part-time/adjunct (11 women). Expenses: Contact institution. *Financial support:* In 2019–20, 23 students received support, including 1 research assistantship with partial tuition reimbursement available (averaging $10,500 per year); scholarships/grants also available. Financial award application deadline: 6/30; financial award applicants required to submit FAFSA. In 2019, 14 master's, 10 doctorates awarded. *Program availability:* Part-time, blended/hybrid learning. *Application deadline:* For fall admission, 7/1 for domestic students; for spring admission, 12/1 for domestic students; for summer admission, 4/15 for domestic students. Applications are processed on a rolling basis. *Application fee:* $50. Electronic applications accepted. *Application Contact:* Janda Anderson, Director of Admissions, 678-547-6700, Fax: 678-547-6794, E-mail: anderson_j@mercer.edu. *Dean/Professor*, Dr. Linda Streit, 678-547-6793, Fax: 678-547-6796, E-mail: streit_la@mercer.edu.

***James and Carolyn McAfee School of Theology*** Students: 53 full-time (34 women), 81 part-time (37 women); includes 77 minority (68 Black or African American, non-Hispanic/Latino; 1 Asian, non-Hispanic/Latino; 7 Hispanic/Latino; 1 Two or more races, non-Hispanic/Latino). Average age 41. 107 applicants, 51% accepted, 38 enrolled. *Faculty:* 9 full-time (4 women), 4 part-time/adjunct (2 women). Expenses: Contact institution. *Financial support:* In 2019–20, 50 students received support, including 2 fellowships with full tuition reimbursements available (averaging $3,000 per year); career-related internships or fieldwork, Federal Work-Study, scholarships/grants, and stipends also available. Support available to part-time students. Financial award application deadline: 1/15; financial award applicants required to submit FAFSA. In 2019, 43 master's, 7 doctorates awarded. *Program availability:* Part-time, 100% online. *Application deadline:* For fall admission, 6/15 priority date for domestic and international students; for spring admission, 11/15 priority date for domestic and international students. Applications are processed on a rolling basis. *Application fee:* $50. Electronic applications accepted. *Application Contact:* Nathan Cost, Director of Admissions, 678-547-6451, E-mail: cost_na@mercer.edu. *Interim Dean*, Dr. C. Gregory DeLoach, 678-547-6620, E-mail: deloach_cg@mercer.edu.

***Stetson-Hatcher School of Business (Atlanta)*** Students: 177 full-time (92 women), 155 part-time (97 women); includes 160 minority (122 Black or African American, non-Hispanic/Latino; 2 American Indian or Alaska Native, non-Hispanic/Latino; 22 Asian, non-Hispanic/Latino; 12 Hispanic/Latino; 2 Two or more races, non-Hispanic/Latino), 46 international. Average age 32. 207 applicants, 77% accepted, 110 enrolled. *Faculty:* 18 full-time (8 women), 4 part-time/adjunct (3 women). Expenses: Contact institution. *Financial support:* In 2019–20, 25 students received support. Federal Work-Study and tuition discounts available. Financial award application deadline: 5/1; financial award applicants required to submit FAFSA. In 2019, 216 master's awarded. *Program availability:* Part-time, evening/weekend, 100% online, blended/hybrid learning. *Application deadline:* For fall admission, 6/15 priority date for domestic and international students; for spring admission, 11/1 priority date for domestic and international students; for summer admission, 3/15 priority date for domestic and international students. Applications are processed on a rolling basis. *Application fee:* $50 ($100 for international students). Electronic applications accepted. *Application Contact:* Mat Edmunds, Director of Admissions, Atlanta, 678-547-63147, Fax: 678-547-6160, E-mail: edmunds_mp@mercer.edu. *Dean*, Dr. Julie Petherbridge, 678-547-6010, Fax: 678-547-6337, E-mail: petherbrid_j@mercer.edu.

***Tift College of Education (Atlanta)*** Students: 169 full-time (143 women), 288 part-time (225 women); includes 289 minority (258 Black or African American, non-Hispanic/Latino; 9 Asian, non-Hispanic/Latino; 17 Hispanic/Latino; 1 Native Hawaiian or other Pacific Islander, non-Hispanic/Latino; 4 Two or more races, non-Hispanic/Latino), 5 international. Average age 35. *Faculty:* 35 full-time (26 women), 32 part-time/adjunct (28 women). Expenses: Contact institution. *Financial support:* Federal Work-Study and unspecified assistantships available. Support available to part-time students. Financial award application deadline: 5/1; financial award applicants required to submit FAFSA. In 2019, 126 master's, 15 doctorates, 14 other advanced degrees awarded. *Program availability:* Part-time, evening/weekend. *Application deadline:* For fall admission, 8/1 for domestic and international students; for spring admission, 12/1 for domestic and international students; for summer admission, 5/1 for domestic and international students. Applications are processed on a rolling basis. *Application fee:* $25 ($50 for international students). Electronic applications accepted. *Application Contact:* Dr. Thomas R Koballa, Jr, Dean, 678-547-6333, E-mail: koballa_tr@mercer.edu. *Dean*, Dr. Thomas R Koballa, Jr, 678-547-6333, E-mail: koballa_tr@mercer.edu.

**Graduate Studies, Macon Campus** Students: 165 full-time (72 women), 186 part-time (113 women); includes 151 minority (112 Black or African American, non-Hispanic/Latino; 19 Asian, non-Hispanic/Latino; 17 Hispanic/Latino; 1 Native Hawaiian or other Pacific Islander, non-Hispanic/Latino; 2 Two or more races, non-Hispanic/Latino), 8 international. Average age 29. *Faculty:* 103 full-time (43 women), 22 part-time/adjunct (8 women). Expenses: Contact institution. *Financial support:* Career-related internships or fieldwork, Federal Work-Study, and institutionally sponsored loans available. Financial award applicants required to submit FAFSA. In 2019, 154 master's, 4 doctorates awarded. *Program availability:* Part-time, evening/weekend, online learning. *Application deadline:* Applications are processed on a rolling basis. Electronic applications accepted. *Application Contact:* Tracey M. Wofford, Director of Graduate Admissions, 678-547-6422, E-mail: wofford_tm@mercer.edu. *Interim Dean of Graduate Studies/Professor of Mathematics,* Keith Howard, 478-301-5983, E-mail: howard_ke@mercer.edu.

***School of Engineering*** Students: 38 full-time (10 women), 51 part-time (20 women); includes 22 minority (5 Black or African American, non-Hispanic/Latino; 11 Asian, non-Hispanic/Latino; 4 Hispanic/Latino; 2 Two or more races, non-Hispanic/Latino), 2 international. Average age 26. *Faculty:* 27 full-time (9 women), 2 part-time/adjunct (0 women). Expenses: Contact institution. *Financial support:* Federal Work-Study available. Financial award applicants required to submit FAFSA. In 2019, 70 master's awarded. *Program availability:* Part-time-only, evening/weekend, online learning. *Application deadline:* For fall admission, 4/1 priority date for domestic and international students; for spring admission, 11/1 priority date for domestic and international students. Applications are processed on a rolling basis. *Application fee:* $75. *Application Contact:* Dr. Sinjae Hyun, Program Director, 478-301-2214, Fax: 478-301-5593, E-mail: hyun_s@mercer.edu. *Dean,* Dr. Laura W. Lackey, 478-301-4106, Fax: 478-301-5593, E-mail: lackey_l@mercer.edu.

***Stetson-Hatcher School of Business (Macon)*** Students: 61 full-time (24 women), 30 part-time (10 women); includes 26 minority (16 Black or African American, non-Hispanic/Latino; 4 Asian, non-Hispanic/Latino; 5 Hispanic/Latino; 1 Two or more races, non-Hispanic/Latino), 1 international. Average age 28. 69 applicants, 78% accepted, 27 enrolled. *Faculty:* 6 full-time (3 women), 2 part-time/adjunct (0 women). Expenses: Contact institution. *Financial support:* Unspecified assistantships and employee tuition waivers available. In 2019, 43 master's awarded. *Program availability:* Part-time, evening/weekend. *Application deadline:* For fall admission, 8/1 for domestic students; for spring admission, 12/1 for domestic students; for summer admission, 5/1 for domestic students. Applications are processed on a rolling basis. *Application fee:* $50 ($100 for international students). Electronic applications accepted. *Application Contact:* Jamie Lineberry, Director of Graduate Admissions, 478-301-2835, Fax: 478-301-2635, E-mail: macon_ba@mercer.edu. *Interim Dean,* Dr. Julie Petherbridge, 678-547-6010, E-mail: petherbrid_j@mercer.edu.

***Tift College of Education (Macon)*** Students: 44 full-time (26 women), 39 part-time (26 women); includes 44 minority (37 Black or African American, non-Hispanic/Latino; 2 Asian, non-Hispanic/Latino; 4 Hispanic/Latino; 1 Native Hawaiian or other Pacific Islander, non-Hispanic/Latino), 2 international. Average age 30. *Faculty:* 9 full-time (7 women), 2 part-time/adjunct (1 woman). Expenses: Contact institution. *Financial support:* Federal Work-Study, institutionally sponsored loans, and unspecified assistantships available. Support available to part-time students. Financial award application deadline: 5/1; financial award applicants required to submit FAFSA. In 2019, 34 master's, 4 doctorates awarded. *Program availability:* Part-time, evening/weekend, 100% online, blended/hybrid learning. *Application deadline:* For fall admission, 8/1 for domestic and international students; for spring admission, 12/1 for domestic and international students. Applications are processed on a rolling basis. *Application fee:* $35. Electronic applications accepted. *Application Contact:* Tracey Wofford, Director of Graduate Admissions, 678-547-6084, E-mail: wofford_tm@mercer.edu. *Dean,* Dr. Thomas R. Koballa, Jr, 678-547-6333, E-mail: koballa_tr@mercer.edu.

***Townsend School of Music*** Students: 10 full-time (4 women), 1 (woman) part-time; includes 1 minority (Hispanic/Latino), 1 international. Average age 25. 25 applicants, 48% accepted, 9 enrolled. *Faculty:* 12 full-time (4 women), 2 part-time/adjunct (1 woman). Expenses: Contact institution. *Financial support:* In 2019–20, 14 students received support. Tuition waivers (full) and unspecified assistantships available. Financial award application deadline: 6/1; financial award applicants required to submit FAFSA. In 2019, 2 master's awarded. *Application deadline:* For fall admission, 6/1 for domestic students, 5/1 for international students. Applications are processed on a rolling basis. *Application fee:* $100. *Application Contact:* Dr. Richard G. Kosowski, Director of Graduate Studies, 478-301-4167, E-mail: kosowski_rg@mercer.edu. *Director of Graduate Studies,* Dr. Richard G. Kosowski, 478-301-4167, Fax: 478-301-5633, E-mail: kosowski_rg@mercer.edu.

**Mercer University School of Law** Students: 388 full-time (206 women); includes 88 minority (48 Black or African American, non-Hispanic/Latino; 15 Asian, non-Hispanic/Latino; 20 Hispanic/Latino; 5 Two or more races, non-Hispanic/Latino), 2 international. Average age 25. 788 applicants, 52% accepted, 122 enrolled. *Faculty:* 29 full-time (11 women), 22 part-time/adjunct (6 women). Expenses: Contact institution. *Financial support:* In 2019–20, 325 students received support, including 14 fellowships (averaging $3,714 per year), 35 research assistantships (averaging $277 per year); career-related internships or fieldwork, Federal Work-Study, institutionally sponsored loans, scholarships/grants, and institutional work-study also available. Support available to part-time students. Financial award application deadline: 4/1; financial award applicants required to submit FAFSA. In 2019, 130 doctorates awarded. *Application deadline:* For fall admission, 3/15 priority date for domestic students. Applications are processed on a rolling basis. Electronic applications accepted. *Application Contact:* Lindsey Stewert, Director of Admissions & Financial Aid, 478-301-5001, Fax: 478-301-2989, E-mail: stewart_l@law.mercer.edu. *Dean,* Cathy Cox, 478-301-2602, Fax: 478-301-2101, E-mail: cox_c@law.mercer.edu.

**School of Medicine** Students: 586 full-time (307 women), 11 part-time (9 women); includes 193 minority (59 Black or African American, non-Hispanic/Latino; 1 American Indian or Alaska Native, non-Hispanic/Latino; 93 Asian, non-Hispanic/Latino; 29 Hispanic/Latino; 11 Two or more races, non-Hispanic/Latino). Average age 25. 1,060 applicants, 24% accepted, 174 enrolled. Expenses: Contact institution. *Financial support:* Institutionally sponsored loans available. Financial award application deadline: 4/1; financial award applicants required to submit FAFSA. In 2019, 63 master's, 108 doctorates awarded. *Application deadline:* For fall admission, 1/15 for domestic students, 10/1 for international students. Applications are processed on a rolling basis. *Application fee:* $50 ($150 for international students). *Application Contact:* Ariel Morgan, Assistant Director for Admission, 478-301-5425, Fax: 478-301-2547, E-mail: morgan_ac@mercer.edu. *Dean,* Dr. Jean Sumner, 478-301-5571, Fax: 478-301-2547, E-mail: sumner_jr@mercer.edu.

## MERCY COLLEGE, Dobbs Ferry, NY 10522-1189

**General Information** Independent-religious, coed, comprehensive institution. CGS member. *Enrollment:* 10,557 graduate, professional, and undergraduate students; 1,131 full-time matriculated graduate/professional students (840 women), 1,217 part-time matriculated graduate/professional students (989 women). *Enrollment by degree level:* 2,130 master's, 119 doctoral, 99 other advanced degrees. *Graduate faculty:* 79 full-time (55 women), 147 part-time/adjunct (86 women). *Tuition:* Full-time $16,146; part-time $897 per credit. *Required fees:* $332; $166 per semester. Tuition and fees vary according to course load and program. *Graduate housing:* Room and/or apartments available on a first-come, first-served basis to single students; on-campus housing not available to married students. Typical cost: $5450 per year. Room charges vary according to board plan and housing facility selected. *Student services:* Campus employment opportunities, campus safety program, career counseling, exercise/wellness program, free psychological counseling, international student services, services for students with disabilities, teacher training, writing training. *Library facilities:* Mercy College Library plus 3 others. *Collection:* Books: 71,778 (physical), 74,320 (digital/electronic); Serial titles: 29 (physical), 60,580 (digital/electronic); Databases: 43. Students can reserve study rooms.

**Computer facilities:** Computer purchase and lease plans are available. 1,000 computers available on campus for general student use. A campuswide network can be accessed. Online class registration is available.
Website: http://www.mercy.edu/

**General Application Contact:** Allison Gurdineer, Executive Director of Admissions, 877-637-2946, Fax: 914-674-7382, E-mail: admissions@mercy.edu.

**GRADUATE UNITS**

**School of Business** Students: 328 full-time (190 women), 120 part-time (78 women); includes 321 minority (128 Black or African American, non-Hispanic/Latino; 2 American Indian or Alaska Native, non-Hispanic/Latino; 26 Asian, non-Hispanic/Latino; 156 Hispanic/Latino; 1 Native Hawaiian or other Pacific Islander, non-Hispanic/Latino; 8 Two or more races, non-Hispanic/Latino), 28 international. Average age 32. 378 applicants, 67% accepted, 154 enrolled. Expenses: Contact institution. *Financial support:* Career-related internships or fieldwork, Federal Work-Study, scholarships/grants, and unspecified assistantships available. Support available to part-time students. Financial award applicants required to submit FAFSA. In 2019, 234 master's awarded. *Program availability:* Part-time, evening/weekend, 100% online, blended/hybrid learning. *Application deadline:* Applications are processed on a rolling basis. *Application fee:* $40. Electronic applications accepted. *Application Contact:* Allison Gurdineer, Executive Director of Admissions, 877-637-2946, Fax: 914-674-7382, E-mail: admissions@mercy.edu. *Dean, School of Business,* Dr. Lloyd Gibson, 914-674-7159, Fax: 914-674-7493, E-mail: lgibson@mercy.edu.

**School of Education** Students: 195 full-time (165 women), 429 part-time (367 women); includes 328 minority (95 Black or African American, non-Hispanic/Latino; 1 American Indian or Alaska Native, non-Hispanic/Latino; 26 Asian, non-Hispanic/Latino; 195 Hispanic/Latino; 2 Native Hawaiian or other Pacific Islander, non-Hispanic/Latino; 9 Two or more races, non-Hispanic/Latino). Average age 33. 779 applicants, 67% accepted, 248 enrolled. Expenses: Contact institution. *Financial support:* Career-related internships or fieldwork, Federal Work-Study, scholarships/grants, and unspecified assistantships available. Support available to part-time students. Financial award applicants required to submit FAFSA. In 2019, 234 master's, 55 other advanced degrees awarded. *Program availability:* Part-time, evening/weekend, 100% online, blended/hybrid learning. *Application deadline:* Applications are processed on a rolling basis. *Application fee:* $40. Electronic applications accepted. *Application Contact:* Allison Gurdineer, Executive Director of Admissions, 877-637-2946, Fax: 914-674-7382, E-mail: admissions@mercy.edu. *Interim Dean, School of Education,* Dr. Eric Martone, 914-674-7618, Fax: 914-674-7352, E-mail: emartone@mercy.edu.

**School of Health and Natural Sciences** Students: 353 full-time (273 women), 295 part-time (256 women); includes 334 minority (123 Black or African American, non-Hispanic/Latino; 78 Asian, non-Hispanic/Latino; 105 Hispanic/Latino; 3 Native Hawaiian or other Pacific Islander, non-Hispanic/Latino; 25 Two or more races, non-Hispanic/Latino), 5 international. Average age 32. 1,012 applicants, 35% accepted, 241 enrolled. Expenses: Contact institution. *Financial support:* Career-related internships or fieldwork, Federal Work-Study, scholarships/grants, and unspecified assistantships available. Support available to part-time students. Financial award applicants required to submit FAFSA. In 2019, 194 master's, 31 doctorates awarded. *Program availability:* Part-time, evening/weekend, 100% online, blended/hybrid learning. *Application deadline:* Applications are processed on a rolling basis. *Application fee:* $40. Electronic applications accepted. *Application Contact:* Allison Gurdineer, Executive Director of Admissions, 877-637-2946, Fax: 914-674-7382, E-mail: admissions@mercy.edu. *Dean, School of Health and Natural Sciences,* Dr. Joan Toglia, 914-674-7746, E-mail: jtoglia@mercy.edu.

**School of Liberal Arts** Students: 21 full-time (7 women), 78 part-time (42 women); includes 46 minority (20 Black or African American, non-Hispanic/Latino; 6 Asian, non-Hispanic/Latino; 17 Hispanic/Latino; 3 Two or more races, non-Hispanic/Latino), 3 international. Average age 34. 58 applicants, 57% accepted, 24 enrolled. Expenses: Contact institution. *Financial support:* Career-related internships or fieldwork, Federal Work-Study, scholarships/grants, and unspecified assistantships available. Support available to part-time students. Financial award applicants required to submit FAFSA. In 2019, 35 master's awarded. *Program availability:* Part-time, evening/weekend, 100% online, blended/hybrid learning. *Application deadline:* Applications are processed on a rolling basis. *Application fee:* $40. Electronic applications accepted. *Application Contact:* Allison Gurdineer, Executive Director of Admissions, 877-637-2946, Fax: 914-674-7382, E-mail: admissions@mercy.edu. *Dean, School of Liberal Arts,* Dr. Peter West, 914-674-3033, Fax: 914-674-7518, E-mail: pwest@mercy.edu.

**School of Social and Behavioral Sciences** Students: 234 full-time (205 women), 295 part-time (246 women); includes 387 minority (187 Black or African American, non-Hispanic/Latino; 6 Asian, non-Hispanic/Latino; 187 Hispanic/Latino; 2 Native Hawaiian or other Pacific Islander, non-Hispanic/Latino; 5 Two or more races, non-Hispanic/Latino), 5 international. Average age 33. 677 applicants, 62% accepted, 205 enrolled. Expenses: Contact institution. *Financial support:* Career-related internships or fieldwork, Federal Work-Study, scholarships/grants, and unspecified assistantships available. Support available to part-time students. Financial award applicants required to submit FAFSA. In 2019, 171 master's awarded. *Program availability:* Part-time, evening/weekend, 100% online, blended/hybrid learning. *Application deadline:* Applications are processed on a rolling basis. *Application fee:* $40. Electronic applications accepted. *Application Contact:* Allison Gurdineer, Executive Director of Admissions, 877-637-2946, Fax: 914-674-7382, E-mail: admissions@mercy.edu. *Interim Dean, School of Social and Behavioral Sciences,* Dr. Diana Juetter, 914-674-7546, E-mail: djuettner@mercy.edu.

## MERCY COLLEGE OF OHIO, Toledo, OH 43604

**General Information** Independent-religious, coed, primarily women, comprehensive institution. *Enrollment:* 1,560 graduate, professional, and undergraduate students; 60 part-time matriculated graduate/professional students (52 women). *Enrollment by degree level:* 60 master's. *Tuition:* Part-time $649 per credit hour. *Required fees:* $450 per term. One-time fee: $250 part-time. Tuition and fees vary according to program. *Graduate housing:* On-campus housing not available. *Student services:* Career counseling, free psychological counseling, low-cost health insurance, multicultural affairs office, services for students with disabilities, writing training. *Library facilities:* Mercy College of Ohio Library. *Collection:* Books: 7,081 (physical), 98,167 (digital/electronic); Serial titles: 334 (physical), 82,313 (digital/electronic); Databases: 59. Weekly public service hours: 57; students can reserve study rooms.

**Computer facilities:** 125 computers available on campus for general student use. A campuswide network can be accessed. Online class registration is available.
Website: http://www.mercycollege.edu/

**General Application Contact:** Admission office, 888-8063729, E-mail: admissions@mercycollege.edu.

**GRADUATE UNITS**

**Program in Health Administration** Students: 45 part-time (39 women). 43 applicants, 44% accepted, 14 enrolled. *Faculty:* 1 full-time, 14 part-time/adjunct. Expenses: Contact institution. *Financial support:* Tuition discounts for alumni and Bon Secours/Mercy Health Employees available. Financial award applicants required to submit FAFSA. *Program availability:* Part-time-only, online only, 100% online, Practicum may be required based on student prior experience. *Application deadline:* Applications are processed on a rolling basis. Electronic applications accepted. *Application Contact:* Amy Mergen, Director of Enrollment Management, 888-806-3729, E-mail: admissions@mercycollege.edu. *Dean Health Sciences; Program Director: Master of Health Administration,* Dr. Kimberly Watson, 419-251-1852, E-mail: kim.watson@mercycollege.edu.

**Program in Nursing** Students: 15 part-time (13 women). 22 applicants, 50% accepted, 5 enrolled. *Faculty:* 1 (woman) full-time, 8 part-time/adjunct (7 women). Expenses: Contact institution. *Financial support:* Scholarships/grants and Tuition discounts for alumni and Bon Secours/Mercy Health Employees available. Financial award applicants required to submit FAFSA. In 2019, 10 master's awarded. *Program availability:* Part-time-only, online only, 100% online, Practicum Experiences: 140 hours total. *Application deadline:* Applications are processed on a rolling basis. Electronic applications accepted. *Application Contact:* Amy Mergen, Director of Enrollment Management, 888-806-3729, E-mail: admissions@mercycollege.edu. *MSN Program Director,* Dr. Deborah Karns, 419-251-1718, E-mail: deborah.karns@mercycollege.edu.

## MERCYHURST UNIVERSITY, Erie, PA 16546

**General Information** Independent-religious, coed, comprehensive institution. *Graduate housing:* On-campus housing not available.

**GRADUATE UNITS**

**Graduate Studies** *Program availability:* Part-time, evening/weekend. Electronic applications accepted.

## MEREDITH COLLEGE, Raleigh, NC 27607-5298

**General Information** Independent, Undergraduate: women only; graduate: coed, comprehensive institution. *Graduate housing:* On-campus housing not available.

**GRADUATE UNITS**

**School of Business** Students: 3 full-time (all women), 63 part-time (52 women); includes 22 minority (15 Black or African American, non-Hispanic/Latino; 1 Asian, non-Hispanic/Latino; 5 Hispanic/Latino; 1 Two or more races, non-Hispanic/Latino), 3 international. Average age 34. Expenses: Contact institution. *Financial support:* Career-related internships or fieldwork, institutionally sponsored loans, scholarships/grants, and tuition waivers (partial) available. Support available to part-time students. Financial award application deadline: 2/15; financial award applicants required to submit FAFSA. In 2019, 32 master's awarded. *Program availability:* Part-time, evening/weekend. *Application deadline:* For fall admission, 7/1 priority date for domestic and international students; for spring admission, 11/1 priority date for domestic and international students. Applications are processed on a rolling basis. *Application fee:* $50. Electronic applications accepted. *Application Contact:* Kristie Ogilvie, Dean, 919-760-8432, Fax: 919-760-8470. *Dean,* Kristie Ogilvie, 919-760-8432, Fax: 919-760-8470.

**School of Education, Health and Human Sciences** Students: 63 full-time (58 women), 88 part-time (84 women); includes 34 minority (14 Black or African American, non-Hispanic/Latino; 1 American Indian or Alaska Native, non-Hispanic/Latino; 11 Asian, non-Hispanic/Latino; 6 Hispanic/Latino; 2 Two or more races, non-Hispanic/Latino), 3 international. Average age 28. Expenses: Contact institution. *Financial support:* Career-related internships or fieldwork, institutionally sponsored loans, and tuition waivers (partial) available. Support available to part-time students. Financial award application deadline: 2/15; financial award applicants required to submit FAFSA. In 2019, 48 master's, 41 other advanced degrees awarded. *Program availability:* Part-time, evening/weekend. *Application deadline:* For fall admission, 7/1 priority date for domestic students; for spring admission, 11/1 priority date for domestic students. Applications are processed on a rolling basis. *Application fee:* $50. Electronic applications accepted. *Application Contact:* Dr. Monica McKinney, Graduate Program Manager, 919-760-8056, Fax: 919-760-2303, E-mail: mckinneym@meredith.edu. *Graduate Program Manager,* Dr. Monica McKinney, 919-760-8056, Fax: 919-760-2303, E-mail: mckinneym@meredith.edu.

## MERRIMACK COLLEGE, North Andover, MA 01845-5800

**General Information** Independent-religious, coed, comprehensive institution. CGS member. *Graduate housing:* On-campus housing not available.

**GRADUATE UNITS**

**Girard School of Business** *Program availability:* Part-time, evening/weekend, 100% online. Electronic applications accepted.

**School of Education and Social Policy** *Program availability:* Part-time, evening/weekend, 100% online courses with immersion events and in-classroom practicum close to home. Electronic applications accepted.

**School of Health Sciences** *Program availability:* Part-time, evening/weekend. Electronic applications accepted.

**School of Liberal Arts** *Program availability:* Part-time, evening/weekend. Electronic applications accepted.

**School of Science and Engineering** *Program availability:* Part-time, evening/weekend, 100% online. Electronic applications accepted.

## MESIVTA OF EASTERN PARKWAY–YESHIVA ZICHRON MEILECH, Brooklyn, NY 11218-5559

**General Information** Independent-religious, men only, comprehensive institution. *Enrollment:* 5 full-time matriculated graduate/professional students (2 women), 5,539 part-time matriculated graduate/professional students (5,534 women). *Enrollment by degree level:* 461 master's, 832 doctoral, 23 other advanced degrees. *Graduate faculty:* 57 full-time (53 women), 539 part-time/adjunct (5 women). *Tuition:* Full-time $9450; part-time $9450 per year. *Required fees:* $44; $2 per unit. *Student services:* Campus safety program, child daycare facilities, services for students with disabilities.

**General Application Contact:** Information Contact, 718-438-1002.

**GRADUATE UNITS**

**Graduate Programs** Students: 398 full-time (55 women), 70 part-time (4 women); includes 729 minority (54 Black or African American, non-Hispanic/Latino; 77 American Indian or Alaska Native, non-Hispanic/Latino; 542 Asian, non-Hispanic/Latino; 53 Hispanic/Latino; 3 Native Hawaiian or other Pacific Islander, non-Hispanic/Latino), 2 international. Average age 44. 3,324 applicants, 2% accepted, 3 enrolled. *Faculty:* 5,165 full-time (5,132 women), 5 part-time/adjunct (1 woman). Expenses: Contact institution. *Financial support:* Fellowships and research assistantships available. Financial award application deadline: 12/17; financial award applicants required to submit CSS PROFILE or FAFSA. *Application deadline:* For fall admission, 1/16 for domestic students; for spring admission, 3/19 for domestic students. Applications are processed on a rolling basis. *Application fee:* $21. Electronic applications accepted. *Application Contact:* Information Contact, 718-438-1002. *Director,* Dr. Jane Douglas, 551-4948843, E-mail: jdoug@yomama.com.

## MESIVTA TORAH VODAATH RABBINICAL SEMINARY, Brooklyn, NY 11218-5299

**General Information** Independent-religious, men only, comprehensive institution. *Enrollment:* 16 full-time matriculated graduate/professional students (12 women), 167 part-time matriculated graduate/professional students (123 women). *Enrollment by degree level:* 55 master's, 665 doctoral, 48 other advanced degrees. Full-time tuition and fees vary according to class time. *Graduate housing:* Rooms and/or apartments available on a first-come, first-served basis to single and married students. *Student services:* Campus employment opportunities, campus safety program, international student services.
Website: http://www.torahvodaath.org/

**General Application Contact:** Information Contact, 718-941-8000.

## MESIVTHA TIFERETH JERUSALEM OF AMERICA, New York, NY 10002-6301

**General Information** Independent-religious, men only, comprehensive institution. *Enrollment:* 8 full-time matriculated graduate/professional students (4 women), 4 part-time matriculated graduate/professional students (2 women). *Enrollment by degree level:* 13 master's, 14 doctoral, 15 other advanced degrees. *Graduate faculty:* 3 full-time (1 woman), 2,275 part-time/adjunct (2,231 women). *Tuition:* Full-time $11,250; part-time $11,250 per year. Full-time tuition and fees vary according to class time. *Graduate housing:* Room and/or apartments available to married students; on-campus housing not available to single students. Housing application deadline: 12/23. *Student services:* Campus safety program, child daycare facilities, free psychological counseling, international student services, multicultural affairs office.

**General Application Contact:** Information Contact, 212-964-2830.

**GRADUATE UNITS**

**Graduate Programs** Students: 6 full-time (2 women), 546 part-time (12 women); includes 3,914 minority (54 Black or African American, non-Hispanic/Latino; 6 American Indian or Alaska Native, non-Hispanic/Latino; 425 Asian, non-Hispanic/Latino; 4 Hispanic/Latino; 3,423 Native Hawaiian or other Pacific Islander, non-Hispanic/Latino; 2 Two or more races, non-Hispanic/Latino), 2 international. Average age 22. 14 applicants, 14% accepted, 1 enrolled. *Faculty:* 6 full-time (2 women), 17 part-time/adjunct (12 women). Expenses: Contact institution. *Financial support:* Fellowships available. Financial award application deadline: 2/2; financial award applicants required to submit CSS PROFILE. *Program availability:* Part-time-only. *Application deadline:* Applications are processed on a rolling basis. *Application fee:* $55. Electronic applications accepted. *Application Contact:* Information Contact, 212-964-2830. *Director,* James Charles, 510-4456678, E-mail: jc@yomama.com.

## MESSIAH UNIVERSITY, Mechanicsburg, PA 17055

**General Information** Independent-religious, coed, comprehensive institution.

**GRADUATE UNITS**

**Program in Business and Leadership** *Program availability:* Online learning.

**Program in Conducting** *Program availability:* Part-time, online learning. Electronic applications accepted.

**Program in Counseling** *Program availability:* Part-time, online learning. Electronic applications accepted.

**Program in Education** *Program availability:* Part-time, online learning. Electronic applications accepted.

**Program in Higher Education** *Program availability:* Part-time. Electronic applications accepted.

**Program in Nursing**

## METHODIST THEOLOGICAL SCHOOL IN OHIO, Delaware, OH 43015-8004

**General Information** Independent-religious, coed, graduate-only institution. *Graduate housing:* Rooms and/or apartments available on a first-come, first-served basis to single students and available to married students. Housing application deadline: 8/15.

**GRADUATE UNITS**

**Graduate and Professional Programs** *Program availability:* Part-time.

## METHODIST UNIVERSITY, Fayetteville, NC 28311-1498

**General Information** Independent-religious, coed, comprehensive institution. *Graduate housing:* Room and/or apartments available on a first-come, first-served basis to single students; on-campus housing not available to married students. Housing application deadline: 6/1.

**GRADUATE UNITS**

**School of Graduate Studies** *Program availability:* Part-time, evening/weekend. Electronic applications accepted.

## METROPOLITAN COLLEGE OF NEW YORK, New York, NY 10006

**General Information** Independent, coed, comprehensive institution. *Graduate housing:* On-campus housing not available. *Research affiliation:* U.S. Department of Homeland Security (homeland security), U.S. Federal Emergency Management Administration (higher education).

**GRADUATE UNITS**

**Program in Business Administration** *Program availability:* Evening/weekend. Electronic applications accepted.

**Program in Childhood/Special Education** Electronic applications accepted.

**Program in Public Administration** *Program availability:* Evening/weekend. Electronic applications accepted.

## METROPOLITAN STATE UNIVERSITY, St. Paul, MN 55106-5000

**General Information** State-supported, coed, comprehensive institution. *Graduate housing:* On-campus housing not available.

**GRADUATE UNITS**
**College of Community Studies and Public Affairs**
**College of Liberal Arts** *Program availability:* Part-time, evening/weekend. Electronic applications accepted.
**College of Management** *Program availability:* Part-time, evening/weekend. Electronic applications accepted.
**College of Nursing and Health Sciences** *Program availability:* Part-time.
**College of Sciences**
**School of Law Enforcement and Criminal Justice** *Program availability:* Part-time, evening/weekend. Electronic applications accepted.
**School of Urban Education**

## METROPOLITAN STATE UNIVERSITY OF DENVER, Denver, CO 80204

**General Information** State-supported, coed, comprehensive institution. CGS member.
**GRADUATE UNITS**
**College of Letters, Arts and Sciences**
**School of Business**
**School of Education**

## MGH INSTITUTE OF HEALTH PROFESSIONS, Boston, MA 02129

**General Information** Independent, coed, primarily women, graduate-only institution. *Graduate housing:* On-campus housing not available. *Research affiliation:* Health and Disability Research Institute, Boston University (efficacy of a post-rehabilitation exercise intervention in patients after hip fracture), Eunice Kennedy Shriver National Institute of Child and Health Development (dyadic intervention for women at risk for postpartum depression and their infants), National Institutes of Health (postnatal parental depression, family dynamics in early parenting), Robert Wood Johnson Foundation (mother-infant intervention for the prevention of postpartum depression and associated mother-infant relationship dysfunction), U.S. Department of Defense (robotic nursing assistant to H-star technology), The American Academy of Nursing/John W. Hartford Foundation (building academic geriatric nursing capacity).
**GRADUATE UNITS**
**School of Health and Rehabilitation Sciences** *Program availability:* Part-time. Electronic applications accepted.
**School of Nursing** Electronic applications accepted.

## MIAMI INTERNATIONAL UNIVERSITY OF ART & DESIGN, Miami, FL 33132-1418

**General Information** Proprietary, coed, comprehensive institution.
**GRADUATE UNITS**
**Program in Design and Media Management**
**Program in Film** *Program availability:* Online learning.

## MIAMI REGIONAL UNIVERSITY, Miami Springs, FL 33166

**General Information** Proprietary, coed, comprehensive institution.
**GRADUATE UNITS**
**School of Nursing and Health Sciences**

## MIAMI UNIVERSITY, Oxford, OH 45056

**General Information** State-related, coed, university. CGS member. *Graduate housing:* Room and/or apartments available on a first-come, first-served basis to single students; on-campus housing not available to married students.
**GRADUATE UNITS**
**College of Arts and Science** *Program availability:* Part-time.
**College of Creative Arts**
**College of Education, Health and Society**
**College of Engineering and Computing**
**Farmer School of Business**

## MICHIGAN SCHOOL OF PSYCHOLOGY, Farmington Hills, MI 48334

**General Information** Independent, coed, graduate-only institution. *Enrollment by degree level:* 107 master's, 78 doctoral. *Graduate faculty:* 14 full-time (7 women), 16 part-time/adjunct (11 women). *Tuition:* Full-time $40,000; part-time $15,000 per year. *Required fees:* $2265; $780 per semester. $260 per semester. One-time fee: $75. Tuition and fees vary according to course load, degree level and program. *Graduate housing:* On-campus housing not available. *Student services:* Campus employment opportunities, campus safety program, international student services, multicultural affairs office, services for students with disabilities, writing training. *Library facilities:* Moustakas Johnson Library plus 1 other. *Collection:* Books: 7,247 (physical), 4,299 (digital/electronic); Serial titles: 2 (physical); Databases: 70. Weekly public service hours: 49.

**Computer facilities:** 40 computers available on campus for general student use. A campuswide network can be accessed. Online class registration is available.
Website: https://msp.edu/

**General Application Contact:** Carrie Pyeatt, Coordinator of Admissions and Student Engagement, 248-476-1122 Ext. 117, Fax: 248-476-1125, E-mail: cpyeatt@msp.edu.
**GRADUATE UNITS**
**MA and Psy D Programs in Clinical Psychology** Students: 125 full-time (97 women), 60 part-time (43 women); includes 47 minority (29 Black or African American, non-Hispanic/Latino; 3 Asian, non-Hispanic/Latino; 6 Hispanic/Latino; 9 Two or more races, non-Hispanic/Latino). Average age 30. 205 applicants, 54% accepted, 86 enrolled. *Faculty:* 14 full-time (7 women), 16 part-time/adjunct (11 women). Expenses: Contact institution. *Financial support:* In 2019–20, 12 students received support, including 1 research assistantship (averaging $8,566 per year), 5 teaching assistantships (averaging $14,436 per year); institutionally sponsored loans, scholarships/grants, and unspecified assistantships also available. Financial award application deadline: 8/30; financial award applicants required to submit FAFSA. In 2019, 61 master's, 13 doctorates awarded. *Program availability:* Part-time, evening/weekend. *Application deadline:* For fall admission, 2/15 for domestic students. *Application fee:* $75. Electronic applications accepted. *Application Contact:* Carrie Pyeatt, Coordinator of Admissions and Student Engagement, 248-476-1122 Ext. 117, Fax: 248-476-1125, E-mail: cpyeatt@msp.edu. *Program Director,* Dr. Shannon Chavez-Korell, 248-476-1122, Fax: 248-476-1125.

## MICHIGAN STATE UNIVERSITY, East Lansing, MI 48824

**General Information** State-supported, coed, university. CGS member. *Graduate housing:* Rooms and/or apartments available on a first-come, first-served basis to single and married students. *Research affiliation:* Argonne National Laboratory (high-energy physics and structural biology), Association of Sea Grant Programs (fresh water ecosystems), Fraunhofer Center (manufacturing), Michigan Economic Development Corporation (life sciences, homeland security, automotive technologies), Oak Ridge Associated Universities (scientific research and education), Southern Astrophysical Research (SOAR) Telescope (astronomy).
**GRADUATE UNITS**
**College of Human Medicine**
**College of Osteopathic Medicine**
**College of Veterinary Medicine**
**The Graduate School** *Program availability:* Part-time, evening/weekend, online learning. Electronic applications accepted.
***College of Agriculture and Natural Resources***
***College of Arts and Letters*** Electronic applications accepted.
***College of Communication Arts and Sciences***
***College of Education*** Electronic applications accepted.
***College of Engineering*** *Program availability:* Part-time. Electronic applications accepted.
***College of Music*** Electronic applications accepted.
***College of Natural Science*** Electronic applications accepted.
***College of Nursing*** *Program availability:* Part-time, online learning. Electronic applications accepted.
***College of Social Science*** Electronic applications accepted.
***Eli Broad College of Business*** *Program availability:* Evening/weekend. Electronic applications accepted.
**National Superconducting Cyclotron Laboratory**

## MICHIGAN STATE UNIVERSITY COLLEGE OF LAW, East Lansing, MI 48824-1300

**General Information** Independent, coed, graduate-only institution. *Enrollment by degree level:* 78 master's, 698 doctoral. *Graduate faculty:* 45 full-time (20 women). *Tuition:* Full-time $45,600. *Required fees:* $37. *Graduate housing:* Rooms and/or apartments available on a first-come, first-served basis to single and married students. Typical cost: $8310 per year ($13,862 including board) for single students; $9040 per year ($15,188 including board) for married students. Room and board charges vary according to board plan and housing facility selected. Housing application deadline: 5/1. *Student services:* Campus employment opportunities, campus safety program, career counseling, exercise/wellness program, international student services, low-cost health insurance, multicultural affairs office, services for students with disabilities, writing training. *Library facilities:* John F. Schaefer Law Library plus 2 others. *Collection:* Books: 118,955 (physical), 50,042 (digital/electronic); Serial titles: 3,378 (physical), 281,266 (digital/electronic); Databases: 31. Weekly public service hours: 71; students can reserve study rooms.

**Computer facilities:** 60 computers available on campus for general student use. A campuswide network can be accessed from student residence rooms and from off campus. Online class registration, X are available.
Website: http://www.law.msu.edu/

**General Application Contact:** Ian McInnis, Director of Admissions, 517-432-6949, Fax: 517-432-6801, E-mail: ian.mcinnis@law.msu.edu.
**GRADUATE UNITS**
**Graduate and Professional Programs** *Program availability:* Part-time. Electronic applications accepted.

## MICHIGAN TECHNOLOGICAL UNIVERSITY, Houghton, MI 49931

**General Information** State-supported, coed, university. CGS member. *Enrollment:* 7,041 graduate, professional, and undergraduate students; 947 full-time matriculated graduate/professional students (287 women), 299 part-time matriculated graduate/professional students (88 women). *Enrollment by degree level:* 731 master's, 503 doctoral, 12 other advanced degrees. *Graduate faculty:* 443 full-time (122 women), 154 part-time/adjunct (35 women). *International tuition:* $19,206 full-time. *Tuition, area resident:* Full-time $19,206; part-time $1067 per credit. Tuition, state resident: full-time $19,206; part-time $1067 per credit. Tuition, nonresident: full-time $19,206; part-time $1067 per credit. *Required fees:* $248; $248 per unit. $124 per semester. Tuition and fees vary according to course load and program. *Graduate housing:* Room and/or apartments available on a first-come, first-served basis to single students; on-campus housing not available to married students. Typical cost: $4620 per year ($9487 including board). Room and board charges vary according to board plan and housing facility selected. *Student services:* Campus employment opportunities, campus safety program, career counseling, child daycare facilities, exercise/wellness program, free psychological counseling, grant writing training, international student services, low-cost health insurance, multicultural affairs office, services for students with disabilities, teacher training, writing training. *Library facilities:* J. R. Van Pelt and John and Ruanne Opie Library. *Collection:* Books: 372,479 (physical), 295,187 (digital/electronic); Serial titles: 14,193 (physical), 74,714 (digital/electronic); Databases: 183. Weekly public service hours: 105; study areas open 24 hours, 5–7 days a week; students can reserve study rooms. *Research affiliation:* Ariens Company (Materials testing), E3 Sparkplugs (Automotive technology design), Faurecia Emissions Control Technologies (Emissions Testing), Osmose Inc (Materials Testing), Nostrum Energy LLC (Control system design).

**Computer facilities:** 1,079 computers available on campus for general student use. A campuswide network can be accessed. Online class registration is available.
Website: http://www.mtu.edu/

**General Application Contact:** Ashli Wells, Assistant Director of Graduate Enrollment Services, 906-487-2328, Fax: 906-487-2284, E-mail: gradadms@mtu.edu.
**GRADUATE UNITS**
**Graduate School** Students: 947 full-time (287 women), 299 part-time (88 women); includes 64 minority (20 Black or African American, non-Hispanic/Latino; 4 American Indian or Alaska Native, non-Hispanic/Latino; 13 Asian, non-Hispanic/Latino; 8 Hispanic/Latino; 19 Two or more races, non-Hispanic/Latino), 684 international. Average age 28. 4,531 applicants, 35% accepted, 423 enrolled. *Faculty:* 443 full-time (122 women), 154 part-time/adjunct (35 women). Expenses: Contact institution. *Financial support:* In 2019–20, 869 students received support, including 107 fellowships with tuition reimbursements available (averaging $16,590 per year), 215 research assistantships with tuition reimbursements available (averaging $16,590 per year), 218

teaching assistantships with tuition reimbursements available (averaging $16,590 per year); career-related internships or fieldwork, Federal Work-Study, scholarships/grants, traineeships, health care benefits, unspecified assistantships, and cooperative program also available. Financial award applicants required to submit FAFSA. In 2019, 448 master's, 86 doctorates, 59 other advanced degrees awarded. *Program availability:* Part-time, 100% online, blended/hybrid learning. *Application deadline:* Applications are processed on a rolling basis. Electronic applications accepted. *Application Contact:* Ashli Wells, Assistant Director of Graduate Enrollment Services, 906-487-3513, Fax: 906-487-2284, E-mail: aesniego@mtu.edu. *Dean of the Graduate School*, Dr. Will H Cantrell, 906-487-2326, Fax: 906-487-2284, E-mail: cantrell@mtu.edu.

***College of Business*** Students: 34 full-time (13 women), 13 part-time (7 women); includes 5 minority (3 Black or African American, non-Hispanic/Latino; 1 Asian, non-Hispanic/Latino; 1 Hispanic/Latino), 8 international. Average age 28. 162 applicants, 27% accepted, 30 enrolled. *Faculty:* 24 full-time (8 women), 1 part-time/adjunct. Expenses: Contact institution. *Financial support:* In 2019–20, 23 students received support, including 4 fellowships with tuition reimbursements available (averaging $16,590 per year), 1 teaching assistantship with tuition reimbursement available (averaging $16,590 per year); health care benefits and unspecified assistantships also available. Financial award application deadline: 4/1; financial award applicants required to submit FAFSA. In 2019, 55 master's awarded. *Program availability:* Part-time, evening/weekend. *Application deadline:* For fall admission, 7/1 for domestic and international students; for spring admission, 12/1 for domestic and international students. Applications are processed on a rolling basis. Electronic applications accepted. *Application Contact:* Ashli Wells, Assistant Director of Graduate Enrollment Services, 906-487-3513, Fax: 906-487-2284, E-mail: gradadms@mtu.edu. *Dean*, Dr. Dean Johnson, 906-487-2668, Fax: 906-487-1863, E-mail: dean@mtu.edu.

***College of Computing*** Students: 48 full-time (10 women), 10 part-time (6 women); includes 2 minority (1 Asian, non-Hispanic/Latino; 1 Two or more races, non-Hispanic/Latino), 32 international. Average age 27. 613 applicants, 27% accepted, 19 enrolled. *Faculty:* 33 full-time (7 women), 4 part-time/adjunct. Expenses: Contact institution. *Financial support:* In 2019–20, 44 students received support, including 2 fellowships with tuition reimbursements available (averaging $16,590 per year), 15 research assistantships with tuition reimbursements available (averaging $16,590 per year), 14 teaching assistantships with tuition reimbursements available (averaging $16,590 per year); career-related internships or fieldwork, Federal Work-Study, scholarships/grants, and health care benefits also available. Financial award applicants required to submit FAFSA. *Program availability:* Part-time, 100% online, blended/hybrid learning. *Application deadline:* Applications are processed on a rolling basis. Electronic applications accepted. *Application Contact:* Denise Landsberg, Advisor, 906-487-3643, Fax: 906-487-2283, E-mail: dllandsb@mtu.edu. *Dean*, Dr. Adrienne R. Minerick, 906-487-2209, Fax: 906-487-2283, E-mail: minerick@mtu.edu.

***College of Engineering*** Students: 549 full-time (116 women), 163 part-time (35 women); includes 24 minority (7 Black or African American, non-Hispanic/Latino; 7 Asian, non-Hispanic/Latino; 5 Hispanic/Latino; 5 Two or more races, non-Hispanic/Latino), 473 international. Average age 27. 2,262 applicants, 40% accepted, 230 enrolled. *Faculty:* 247 full-time (42 women), 93 part-time/adjunct (19 women). Expenses: Contact institution. *Financial support:* In 2019–20, 497 students received support, including 58 fellowships with tuition reimbursements available (averaging $16,590 per year), 119 research assistantships with tuition reimbursements available (averaging $16,590 per year), 76 teaching assistantships with tuition reimbursements available (averaging $16,590 per year); career-related internships or fieldwork, Federal Work-Study, scholarships/grants, health care benefits, unspecified assistantships, and cooperative program also available. Financial award applicants required to submit FAFSA. In 2019, 269 master's, 46 doctorates, 20 other advanced degrees awarded. *Program availability:* Part-time, 100% online, blended/hybrid learning. *Application deadline:* Applications are processed on a rolling basis. Electronic applications accepted. *Application Contact:* Ashli Wells, Assistant Director of Graduate Enrollment Services, 906-487-3513, Fax: 906-487-2284, E-mail: gradadms@mtu.edu. *Dean*, Dr. Janet Callahan, 906-487-2005, E-mail: callahan@mtu.edu.

***College of Forest Resources and Environmental Science*** Students: 51 full-time (21 women), 15 part-time (7 women); includes 3 minority (1 Black or African American, non-Hispanic/Latino; 2 Two or more races, non-Hispanic/Latino), 11 international. Average age 30. 130 applicants, 35% accepted, 25 enrolled. *Faculty:* 43 full-time (10 women), 20 part-time/adjunct (9 women). Expenses: Contact institution. *Financial support:* In 2019–20, 49 students received support, including 7 fellowships with tuition reimbursements available (averaging $16,590 per year), 24 research assistantships with tuition reimbursements available (averaging $16,590 per year), 3 teaching assistantships with tuition reimbursements available (averaging $16,590 per year); career-related internships or fieldwork, Federal Work-Study, scholarships/grants, health care benefits, unspecified assistantships, and cooperative program also available. Financial award applicants required to submit FAFSA. In 2019, 22 master's, 2 doctorates awarded. *Program availability:* Part-time. *Application deadline:* Applications are processed on a rolling basis. Electronic applications accepted. *Application Contact:* Dr. Audrey L. Mayer, Graduate Director/Professor, 906-487-3448, Fax: 906-487-2915, E-mail: almayer@mtu.edu. *Dean*, Dr. Andrew J. Storer, 906-487-3470, Fax: 906-487-2915, E-mail: storer@mtu.edu.

***College of Sciences and Arts*** Students: 208 full-time (107 women), 79 part-time (32 women); includes 23 minority (6 Black or African American, non-Hispanic/Latino; 3 American Indian or Alaska Native, non-Hispanic/Latino; 3 Asian, non-Hispanic/Latino; 2 Hispanic/Latino; 9 Two or more races, non-Hispanic/Latino), 118 international. Average age 31. 889 applicants, 33% accepted, 94 enrolled. *Faculty:* 228 full-time (88 women), 56 part-time/adjunct (13 women). Expenses: Contact institution. *Financial support:* In 2019–20, 202 students received support, including 27 fellowships with tuition reimbursements available (averaging $16,590 per year), 43 research assistantships with tuition reimbursements available (averaging $16,590 per year), 114 teaching assistantships with tuition reimbursements available (averaging $16,590 per year); career-related internships or fieldwork, Federal Work-Study, scholarships/grants, traineeships, health care benefits, unspecified assistantships, and cooperative program also available. Financial award applicants required to submit FAFSA. In 2019, 53 master's, 27 doctorates, 3 other advanced degrees awarded. *Program availability:* Part-time, blended/hybrid learning. *Application deadline:* For fall admission, 4/1 for domestic and international students; for spring admission, 9/1 for domestic and international students. Applications are processed on a rolling basis. Electronic applications accepted. *Application Contact:* Ashli Wells, Assistant Director of Graduate Enrollment Services, 906-487-3513, Fax: 906-487-2284, E-mail: aesniego@mtu.edu. *Dean*, Dr. David Hemmer, 906-487-2156, Fax: 906-487-3347, E-mail: djhemmer@mtu.edu.

## MID-AMERICA BAPTIST THEOLOGICAL SEMINARY, Cordova, TN 38016

**General Information** Independent-religious, men only, comprehensive institution. *Graduate housing:* Rooms and/or apartments available on a first-come, first-served basis to single and married students. Housing application deadline: 7/31.

**GRADUATE UNITS**

**Graduate and Professional Programs** Electronic applications accepted.

## MID-AMERICA BAPTIST THEOLOGICAL SEMINARY NORTHEAST BRANCH, Schenectady, NY 12303-3463

**General Information** Independent-religious, coed, primarily men, graduate-only institution. *Graduate housing:* Rooms and/or apartments available on a first-come, first-served basis to single and married students.

**GRADUATE UNITS**

**Program in Theology** *Program availability:* Part-time, evening/weekend. Electronic applications accepted.

## MID-AMERICA CHRISTIAN UNIVERSITY, Oklahoma City, OK 73170-4504

**General Information** Independent-religious, coed, comprehensive institution.

**GRADUATE UNITS**

**Program in Business Administration**
**Program in Counseling**
**Program in Leadership**
**Program in Public Administration**

## MIDAMERICA NAZARENE UNIVERSITY, Olathe, KS 66062-1899

**General Information** Independent-religious, coed, comprehensive institution. *Enrollment:* 1,909 graduate, professional, and undergraduate students; 94 full-time matriculated graduate/professional students (73 women), 332 part-time matriculated graduate/professional students (261 women). *Enrollment by degree level:* 388 master's, 38 other advanced degrees. *Tuition:* Part-time $506 per credit hour. *Required fees:* $34 per credit hour. Tuition and fees vary according to program. *Graduate housing:* On-campus housing not available. *Student services:* Campus employment opportunities, campus safety program, exercise/wellness program, free psychological counseling, international student services, services for students with disabilities, teacher training. *Library facilities:* Mabee Library. *Collection:* Books: 69,432 (physical), 197,000 (digital/electronic); Serial titles: 133 (digital/electronic); Databases: 39. Weekly public service hours: 83; study areas open 24 hours, 5–7 days a week; students can reserve study rooms.

**Computer facilities:** 142 computers available on campus for general student use. A campuswide network can be accessed. Online class registration is available.
Website: http://www.mnu.edu/

**GRADUATE UNITS**

**Professional and Graduate Studies in Education** Students: 45 part-time (39 women); includes 3 minority (1 Black or African American, non-Hispanic/Latino; 1 American Indian or Alaska Native, non-Hispanic/Latino; 1 Asian, non-Hispanic/Latino). Average age 34. 59 applicants, 58% accepted, 22 enrolled. Expenses: Contact institution. *Financial support:* Scholarships/grants available. Financial award applicants required to submit FAFSA. In 2019, 41 master's awarded. *Program availability:* Part-time, online only, 100% online. *Application deadline:* For fall admission, 8/6 for domestic students; for spring admission, 12/15 for domestic students; for summer admission, 5/7 for domestic students. Applications are processed on a rolling basis. Electronic applications accepted. *Application Contact:* Glenna Murray, Administrative Assistant, 913-971-3292, Fax: 913-971-3002, E-mail: gkmurray@mnu.edu. *Chair*, Dr. Martin Dunlap, 913-971-3517, Fax: 913-971-3407, E-mail: mhdunlap@mnu.edu.

**School of Behavioral Sciences and Counseling** Students: 64 full-time (52 women), 143 part-time (113 women); includes 33 minority (20 Black or African American, non-Hispanic/Latino; 2 American Indian or Alaska Native, non-Hispanic/Latino; 2 Asian, non-Hispanic/Latino; 8 Hispanic/Latino; 1 Two or more races, non-Hispanic/Latino), 1 international. Average age 34. 131 applicants, 73% accepted, 84 enrolled. *Faculty:* 7 full-time (2 women), 14 part-time/adjunct (9 women). Expenses: Contact institution. *Financial support:* Applicants required to submit FAFSA. In 2019, 50 master's awarded. *Program availability:* 100% online. *Application deadline:* For winter admission, 2/15 for domestic and international students; for spring admission, 4/1 for domestic and international students. Electronic applications accepted. *Application Contact:* Jeanne Blades, Administrative Assistant, 913-971-3730, E-mail: jmblades@mnu.edu. *Dean, School of Behavioral Sciences and Counseling*, Dr. Todd Frye, 913-971-3449, Fax: 913-971-3402, E-mail: tmfrye@mnu.edu.

**School of Business** Students: 1 full-time (0 women), 64 part-time (34 women); includes 16 minority (6 Black or African American, non-Hispanic/Latino; 1 American Indian or Alaska Native, non-Hispanic/Latino; 7 Hispanic/Latino; 2 Native Hawaiian or other Pacific Islander, non-Hispanic/Latino), 4 international. Average age 36. 94 applicants, 32% accepted, 25 enrolled. Expenses: Contact institution. *Financial support:* Scholarships/grants and unspecified assistantships available. Financial award applicants required to submit FAFSA. In 2019, 48 master's awarded. *Program availability:* Part-time, evening/weekend, 100% online, blended/hybrid learning. *Application deadline:* Applications are processed on a rolling basis. Electronic applications accepted. *Application Contact:* Kathy Adamson, Administrative Assistant, 913-971-3862, E-mail: kadamson@mnu.edu. *Dean of Graduate Studies in Management*, Dr. Yorton Clark, 913-971-3578, Fax: 913-791-3409, E-mail: yclark@mnu.edu.

**School of Nursing and Health Science** Students: 14 full-time (12 women), 79 part-time (74 women); includes 12 minority (10 Black or African American, non-Hispanic/Latino; 1 American Indian or Alaska Native, non-Hispanic/Latino; 1 Hispanic/Latino), 2 international. Average age 38. 87 applicants, 39% accepted, 14 enrolled. *Faculty:* 5 full-time (all women), 9 part-time/adjunct (7 women). Expenses: Contact institution. *Financial support:* Unspecified assistantships available. Financial award applicants required to submit FAFSA. In 2019, 39 master's awarded. *Program availability:* Part-time, evening/weekend, 100% online. *Application deadline:* Applications are processed on a rolling basis. Electronic applications accepted. *Application Contact:* JoVonda Merrell, Compliance Coordinator, 913-971-3844, E-mail: jkmerrell@mnu.edu. *Dean*, Dr. Karen Wiegman, 913-971-3839, E-mail: kdwiegman@mnu.edu.

## MID-AMERICA REFORMED SEMINARY, Dyer, IN 46311

**General Information** Independent-religious, men only, graduate-only institution.

**GRADUATE UNITS**
**Graduate Programs**

## MIDDLEBURY COLLEGE, Middlebury, VT 05753-6002

**General Information** Independent, coed, comprehensive institution. *Enrollment:* 2,674 graduate, professional, and undergraduate students; 47 part-time matriculated graduate/professional students (39 women). *Enrollment by degree level:* 47 master's. *Graduate housing:* Room and/or apartments guaranteed to single students; on-campus housing not available to married students. *Student services:* Campus safety program, career counseling, free psychological counseling, international student services, services for students with disabilities, teacher training. *Library facilities:* Davis Family Library plus 2 others. *Collection:* Weekly public service hours: 112; students can reserve study rooms.

**Computer facilities:** Computer purchase and lease plans are available. A campuswide network can be accessed from student residence rooms and from off campus. Online class registration, personal Web pages, file servers are available.
Website: http://www.middlebury.edu/

**General Application Contact:** Admissions Office, 802-443-3000, Fax: 802-443-2056, E-mail: admissions@middlebury.edu.

**GRADUATE UNITS**

**Language Schools** Students: 77 part-time (14 women). Expenses: Contact institution. *Financial support:* Fellowships and scholarships/grants available. Financial award applicants required to submit FAFSA. In 2019, 114 master's, 5 doctorates awarded. *Application deadline:* For summer admission, 5/1 for domestic and international students. Applications are processed on a rolling basis. *Application fee:* $75. Electronic applications accepted. *Application Contact:* Kara Gennarelli, Technical and Lead Coordinator, Language Schools Office, 802-443-5727, Fax: 802-443-2075, E-mail: languages@middlebury.edu. *Dean*, Dr. Stephen B. Snyder, 802-443-5979, Fax: 802-443-2075, E-mail: ssnyder@middlebury.edu.

***Arabic School*** Expenses: Contact institution. *Financial support:* Fellowships and scholarships/grants available. Financial award application deadline: 3/14; financial award applicants required to submit FAFSA. In 2019, 4 master's awarded. *Application deadline:* For summer admission, 5/1 for domestic and international students. Applications are processed on a rolling basis. *Application fee:* $75. Electronic applications accepted. *Application Contact:* Barbara Walter, Coordinator, 802-443-5230, Fax: 802-443-2075, E-mail: bwalter@middlebury.edu. *Director*, Dr. Mahmoud Abdalla, 802-443-5230, Fax: 802-443-2075, E-mail: mabdalla@miis.edu.

***Chinese School*** Expenses: Contact institution. *Financial support:* Fellowships and scholarships/grants available. Financial award application deadline: 3/15; financial award applicants required to submit FAFSA. In 2019, 7 master's awarded. *Application deadline:* Applications are processed on a rolling basis. *Application fee:* $75. Electronic applications accepted. *Application Contact:* Mimi Clark, Coordinator, 802-443-5520, Fax: 802-443-2075, E-mail: chineseschool@middlebury.edu. *Director*, Cecilia Chang, 802-443-5520, Fax: 802-443-3510, E-mail: cchang@middlebury.edu.

***French School*** Expenses: Contact institution. *Financial support:* Fellowships and scholarships/grants available. Financial award application deadline: 3/10; financial award applicants required to submit FAFSA. In 2019, 27 master's, 4 doctorates awarded. *Application deadline:* Applications are processed on a rolling basis. *Application fee:* $75. Electronic applications accepted. *Application Contact:* Sheila Schwaneflugel, Coordinator, 802-443-5526, Fax: 802-443-2075, E-mail: sschwaneflugel@middlebury.edu. *Director*, Armelle Crouzieres-Ingenthron, 802-443-2427, Fax: 802-443-2075, E-mail: crouzier@middlebury.edu.

***German School*** Expenses: Contact institution. *Financial support:* Fellowships and scholarships/grants available. Financial award application deadline: 3/9; financial award applicants required to submit FAFSA. In 2019, 4 master's awarded. *Application deadline:* Applications are processed on a rolling basis. *Application fee:* $75. Electronic applications accepted. *Application Contact:* Christina Ellison, Coordinator, 802-443-5203, Fax: 802-443-2075, E-mail: germanschool@middlebury.edu. *Director*, Dr. Bettina Matthias, 802-443-3527, Fax: 802-443-2075, E-mail: bmatthia@middlebury.edu.

***Hebrew School*** Students: 77 part-time (63 women). Expenses: Contact institution. *Financial support:* Fellowships and scholarships/grants available. Financial award application deadline: 3/28; financial award applicants required to submit FAFSA. In 2019, 15 master's awarded. *Program availability:* Blended/hybrid learning. *Application deadline:* Applications are processed on a rolling basis. *Application fee:* $75. Electronic applications accepted. *Application Contact:* Vardit Ringvald, Director, 802-443-3574, E-mail: vringval@middlebury.edu. *Director*, Vardit Ringvald, 802-443-3574, E-mail: vringval@middlebury.edu.

***Italian School*** Expenses: Contact institution. *Financial support:* Fellowships and scholarships/grants available. Financial award application deadline: 3/10; financial award applicants required to submit FAFSA. In 2019, 12 master's, 1 doctorate awarded. *Application deadline:* Applications are processed on a rolling basis. *Application fee:* $75. Electronic applications accepted. *Application Contact:* Joseph Tamagni, Coordinator, 802-443-5727, Fax: 802-443-2075, E-mail: italianschool@middlebury.edu. *Director*, Dr. Antonio Vitti, 802-443-5727, Fax: 802-443-2075, E-mail: acvitti@middlebury.edu.

***Russian School*** Expenses: Contact institution. *Financial support:* Fellowships and scholarships/grants available. Financial award application deadline: 3/14; financial award applicants required to submit FAFSA. In 2019, 5 master's awarded. *Application deadline:* Applications are processed on a rolling basis. *Application fee:* $75. Electronic applications accepted. *Application Contact:* Oliver Carling, Coordinator, 802-443-2006, Fax: 802-443-2075, E-mail: ocarling@middlebury.edu. *Director*, Dr. Jason Merrill, 802-443-5230, Fax: 802-443-2075, E-mail: jmerrill@middlebury.edu.

***Spanish School*** Expenses: Contact institution. *Financial support:* Fellowships and scholarships/grants available. Financial award application deadline: 3/8; financial award applicants required to submit FAFSA. In 2019, 40 master's awarded. *Application deadline:* Applications are processed on a rolling basis. *Application fee:* $75. Electronic applications accepted. *Application Contact:* Audrey LaRock, Coordinator, 802-443-5539, Fax: 802-443-2075, E-mail: larock@middlebury.edu. *Director*, Dr. Jacobo Sefami, 802-443-5539, Fax: 802-443-2075, E-mail: jsefami@middlebury.edu.

**Middlebury Bread Loaf School of English** *Program availability:* Part-time. Electronic applications accepted.

## MIDDLEBURY INSTITUTE OF INTERNATIONAL STUDIES AT MONTEREY, Monterey, CA 93940-2691

**General Information** Independent, coed, graduate-only institution. *Graduate housing:* On-campus housing not available.

**GRADUATE UNITS**

**Graduate School of International Policy and Management** Electronic applications accepted.

**Graduate School of Translation, Interpretation and Language Education** Electronic applications accepted.

## MIDDLE GEORGIA STATE UNIVERSITY, Macon, GA 31206

**General Information** State-supported, coed, comprehensive institution.

**GRADUATE UNITS**
**Office of Graduate Studies**

## MIDDLE TENNESSEE SCHOOL OF ANESTHESIA, Madison, TN 37116

**General Information** Independent-religious, coed, graduate-only institution. *Enrollment by degree level:* 216 doctoral. *Graduate faculty:* 6 full-time (2 women), 13 part-time/adjunct (4 women). *Tuition:* Full-time $30,000. *Graduate housing:* On-campus housing not available. *Library facilities:* Nelda F. Ackerman Learning Resource Center. *Collection:* Study areas open 24 hours, 5–7 days a week.

**Computer facilities:** 11 computers available on campus for general student use. A campuswide network can be accessed from off campus.
Website: http://www.mtsa.edu/

**General Application Contact:** Lyndsey Steen, Coordinator, Admissions & Recruitment, 615-868-6503, Fax: 615-732-7662, E-mail: lyndsey.steen@mtsa.edu.

## MIDDLE TENNESSEE STATE UNIVERSITY, Murfreesboro, TN 37132

**General Information** State-supported, coed, university. CGS member. *Graduate housing:* Rooms and/or apartments available on a first-come, first-served basis to single and married students.

**GRADUATE UNITS**

**College of Graduate Studies** *Program availability:* Part-time, evening/weekend, online learning. Electronic applications accepted.

***College of Basic and Applied Sciences*** *Program availability:* Part-time, evening/weekend, online learning. Electronic applications accepted.

***College of Behavioral and Health Sciences*** Electronic applications accepted.

***College of Education*** *Program availability:* Part-time, evening/weekend, online learning. Electronic applications accepted.

***College of Liberal Arts*** *Program availability:* Part-time, evening/weekend, online learning. Electronic applications accepted.

***College of Mass Communication*** *Program availability:* Part-time, evening/weekend, online learning. Electronic applications accepted.

***Jennings A. Jones College of Business*** *Program availability:* Part-time, evening/weekend, online learning. Electronic applications accepted.

***University College*** *Program availability:* Part-time, evening/weekend, online learning.

## MIDWAY UNIVERSITY, Midway, KY 40347-1120

**General Information** Independent-religious, coed, comprehensive institution. *Graduate housing:* On-campus housing not available.

**GRADUATE UNITS**
**Graduate Programs**

## MIDWEST COLLEGE OF ORIENTAL MEDICINE, Racine, WI 53403-9747

**General Information** Proprietary, coed, graduate-only institution. *Enrollment by degree level:* 223 master's, 34 other advanced degrees. *Graduate faculty:* 7 full-time (3 women), 32 part-time/adjunct (14 women). *Tuition:* Full-time $1160; part-time $1160 per course. *Required fees:* $570; $570 per course. $190 per quarter. One-time fee: $65. *Graduate housing:* On-campus housing not available. *Student services:* Career counseling, international student services, writing training. *Library facilities:* Main library plus 1 other. *Collection:* Weekly public service hours: 40. *Research affiliation:* Guangzhou University of Traditional Chinese Medicine (pharmacology).

**Computer facilities:** 12 computers available on campus for general student use.
Website: http://www.acupuncture.edu/

**General Application Contact:** Pam L. Taylor, Administrative Coordinator, 800-593-2320, Fax: 262-554-7475, E-mail: pamelalt@sbcglobal.net.

**GRADUATE UNITS**

**Graduate Programs** *Program availability:* Part-time, evening/weekend.

**Graduate Programs-Chicago** *Program availability:* Part-time, evening/weekend.

## MIDWESTERN BAPTIST THEOLOGICAL SEMINARY, Kansas City, MO 64118-4697

**General Information** Independent-religious, coed, graduate-only institution. *Graduate housing:* Rooms and/or apartments guaranteed to single and married students.

**GRADUATE UNITS**

**Graduate and Professional Programs** *Program availability:* Part-time, online learning. Electronic applications accepted.

## MIDWESTERN STATE UNIVERSITY, Wichita Falls, TX 76308

**General Information** State-supported, coed, comprehensive institution. CGS member. *Graduate housing:* Rooms and/or apartments available on a first-come, first-served basis to single and married students.

**GRADUATE UNITS**

**Billie Doris McAda Graduate School** *Program availability:* Part-time, evening/weekend. Electronic applications accepted.

***College of Science and Mathematics*** *Program availability:* Part-time, evening/weekend. Electronic applications accepted.

***Dillard College of Business Administration*** *Program availability:* Part-time, evening/weekend. Electronic applications accepted.

***Prothro-Yeager College of Humanities and Social Sciences*** *Program availability:* Part-time, evening/weekend. Electronic applications accepted.

***Robert D. and Carol Gunn College of Health Sciences and Human Services*** *Program availability:* Part-time, evening/weekend. Electronic applications accepted.

***West College of Education*** *Program availability:* Part-time, evening/weekend. Electronic applications accepted.

## MIDWESTERN UNIVERSITY, DOWNERS GROVE CAMPUS, Downers Grove, IL 60515-1235

**General Information** Independent, coed, graduate-only institution. *Graduate housing:* Rooms and/or apartments available on a first-come, first-served basis to single and married students.

**GRADUATE UNITS**

**Chicago College of Optometry**

**Chicago College of Osteopathic Medicine**

**Chicago College of Pharmacy** *Program availability:* Part-time, online learning.

**College of Dental Medicine-Illinois**

**College of Graduate Studies**

**College of Health Sciences, Illinois Campus**

## MIDWESTERN UNIVERSITY, GLENDALE CAMPUS, Glendale, AZ 85308

**General Information** Independent, coed, graduate-only institution. *Graduate housing:* Rooms and/or apartments available on a first-come, first-served basis to single and married students.

**GRADUATE UNITS**

**Arizona College of Optometry**

**Arizona College of Osteopathic Medicine** Electronic applications accepted.

**College of Dental Medicine**

**College of Health Sciences, Arizona Campus** *Program availability:* Part-time.

**College of Pharmacy-Glendale**

**College of Veterinary Medicine**

## MIDWEST UNIVERSITY, Wentzville, MO 63385

**General Information** Independent-religious, coed, university. *Graduate housing:* Rooms and/or apartments available on a first-come, first-served basis to single and married students. Housing application deadline: 1/21.

**GRADUATE UNITS**

**Graduate Programs** *Program availability:* Part-time, online learning.

## MIDWIVES COLLEGE OF UTAH, Salt Lake City, UT 84106

**General Information** Independent, women only, comprehensive institution. *Graduate housing:* On-campus housing not available.

**GRADUATE UNITS**

**Graduate Program** *Program availability:* Part-time. Electronic applications accepted.

## MILLENNIA ATLANTIC UNIVERSITY, Doral, FL 33178

**General Information** Proprietary, coed, comprehensive institution.

**GRADUATE UNITS**

**Graduate Programs** *Program availability:* Online learning.

## MILLERSVILLE UNIVERSITY OF PENNSYLVANIA, Millersville, PA 17551-0302

**General Information** State-supported, coed, university. CGS member. *Enrollment:* 7,802 graduate, professional, and undergraduate students; 187 full-time matriculated graduate/professional students (138 women), 659 part-time matriculated graduate/professional students (476 women). *Enrollment by degree level:* 772 master's, 54 doctoral, 20 other advanced degrees. *Graduate faculty:* 90 full-time (56 women), 50 part-time/adjunct (33 women). *Tuition, area resident:* Part-time $516 per credit. Tuition, state resident: part-time $516 per credit. Tuition, nonresident: part-time $774 per credit. *Required fees:* $118.75 per credit. Tuition and fees vary according to course load, degree level and program. *Graduate housing:* Room and/or apartments available on a first-come, first-served basis to single students; on-campus housing not available to married students. Typical cost: $8780 per year ($12,980 including board). Room and board charges vary according to board plan and housing facility selected. *Student services:* Campus employment opportunities, campus safety program, career counseling, exercise/wellness program, free psychological counseling, grant writing training, international student services, multicultural affairs office, services for students with disabilities, teacher training, writing training. *Library facilities:* The Francine G. McNairy Library and Learning Forum at Ganser Hall. *Collection:* Books: 265,170 (physical), 58,096 (digital/electronic); Serial titles: 4,575 (physical), 230,749 (digital/electronic); Databases: 179. Weekly public service hours: 94; students can reserve study rooms. *Research affiliation:* Chincoteague Bay Field Station for the Marine Science Consortium (Biology).

**Computer facilities:** 430 computers available on campus for general student use. A campuswide network can be accessed. Online class registration is available. Website: http://www.millersville.edu/

**General Application Contact:** Dr. James A. Delle, Acting Dean of College of Graduate Studies and Adult Learning/Associate Provost, Academic Administration, 717-871-7462, E-mail: james.delle@millersville.edu.

**GRADUATE UNITS**

***College of Graduate Studies and Adult Learning*** Students: 187 full-time (138 women), 659 part-time (476 women); includes 125 minority (43 Black or African American, non-Hispanic/Latino; 18 Asian, non-Hispanic/Latino; 51 Hispanic/Latino; 13 Two or more races, non-Hispanic/Latino), 4 international. Average age 32. 400 applicants, 89% accepted, 257 enrolled. *Faculty:* 90 full-time (56 women), 50 part-time/adjunct (33 women). Expenses: Contact institution. *Financial support:* In 2019–20, 132 students received support. Scholarships/grants and unspecified assistantships available. Financial award application deadline: 3/15; financial award applicants required to submit FAFSA. In 2019, 280 master's, 7 doctorates, 27 other advanced degrees awarded. *Program availability:* Part-time. *Application fee:* $40. Electronic applications accepted. *Application Contact:* Chad E. Baker, Director of Graduate Admissions and Recruitment, 717-871-7644, E-mail: chad.baker@millersville.edu. *Acting Dean of College of Graduate Studies and Adult Learning/Associate Provost, Academic Administration,* Dr. James A. Delle, 717-871-7462, E-mail: James.Delle@millersville.edu.

***College of Arts, Humanities and Social Sciences*** Students: 6 full-time (4 women), 41 part-time (27 women); includes 7 minority (1 Asian, non-Hispanic/Latino; 6 Hispanic/Latino). Average age 32. 22 applicants, 91% accepted, 11 enrolled. *Faculty:* 20 full-time (14 women), 1 (woman) part-time/adjunct. Expenses: Contact institution. *Financial support:* In 2019–20, 9 students received support. Scholarships/grants and unspecified assistantships available. Financial award application deadline: 3/15; financial award applicants required to submit FAFSA. In 2019, 20 master's awarded. *Program availability:* Part-time. *Application deadline:* Applications are processed on a rolling basis. *Application fee:* $40. Electronic applications accepted. *Application Contact:* Dr. James A. Delle, Acting Dean of College of Graduate Studies and Adult Learning/Associate Provost, Academic Administration, 717-871-7462, E-mail: James.Delle@millersville.edu. *Interim Dean,* Dr. Orlando J. Perez, 717-871-5631, Fax: 717-871-7947, E-mail: orlando.perez@millersville.edu.

***College of Education and Human Services*** Students: 159 full-time (127 women), 406 part-time (320 women); includes 78 minority (30 Black or African American, non-Hispanic/Latino; 9 Asian, non-Hispanic/Latino; 32 Hispanic/Latino; 7 Two or more races, non-Hispanic/Latino), 2 international. Average age 31. 292 applicants, 90% accepted, 191 enrolled. *Faculty:* 51 full-time (35 women), 31 part-time/adjunct (22 women). Expenses: Contact institution. *Financial support:* In 2019–20, 95 students received support. Scholarships/grants and unspecified assistantships available. Financial award application deadline: 3/15; financial award applicants required to submit FAFSA. In 2019, 193 master's, 7 doctorates awarded. *Program availability:* Part-time, evening/weekend, 100% online, blended/hybrid learning, The DSW coursework is 100% online and students attend weekend residency at start of each semester. *Application fee:* $40. Electronic applications accepted. *Application Contact:* Dr. James A. Delle, Acting Dean of College of Graduate Studies and Adult Learning/Associate Provost, Academic Administration, 717-871-7462, E-mail: James.Delle@millersville.edu. *Dean,* Dr. George Drake, 717-871-7333, E-mail: george.drake@millersville.edu.

***College of Science and Technology*** Students: 22 full-time (7 women), 212 part-time (129 women); includes 40 minority (13 Black or African American, non-Hispanic/Latino; 8 Asian, non-Hispanic/Latino; 13 Hispanic/Latino; 6 Two or more races, non-Hispanic/Latino), 2 international. Average age 35. 86 applicants, 84% accepted, 55 enrolled. *Faculty:* 19 full-time (7 women), 18 part-time/adjunct (10 women). Expenses: Contact institution. *Financial support:* In 2019–20, 28 students received support. Scholarships/grants and unspecified assistantships available. Financial award application deadline: 3/15; financial award applicants required to submit FAFSA. In 2019, 67 master's awarded. *Program availability:* Part-time, online only, 100% online. *Application fee:* $40. Electronic applications accepted. *Application Contact:* Dr. James A. Delle, Acting Dean of Graduate Studies and Adult Learning/Associate Provost, Academic Administration, 717-871-7462, E-mail: James.Delle@millersville.edu. *Dean, College of Science and Technology,* Dr. Michael Jackson, 717-871-4292, E-mail: michael.jackson@millersville.edu.

## MILLIGAN UNIVERSITY, Milligan College, TN 37682

**General Information** Independent-religious, coed, comprehensive institution. *Enrollment:* 1,310 graduate, professional, and undergraduate students; 302 full-time matriculated graduate/professional students (185 women), 126 part-time matriculated graduate/professional students (67 women). *Enrollment by degree level:* 391 master's, 29 doctoral, 8 other advanced degrees. *Graduate faculty:* 49 full-time (22 women), 18 part-time/adjunct (5 women). *Graduate housing:* Rooms and/or apartments available on a first-come, first-served basis to single and married students. Housing application deadline: 4/1. *Student services:* Campus employment opportunities, campus safety program, career counseling, exercise/wellness program, free psychological counseling, international student services, multicultural affairs office, services for students with disabilities, teacher training, writing training. *Library facilities:* P. H. Welshimer Memorial Library plus 1 other. *Collection:* Books: 173,100 (physical), 284,410 (digital/electronic); Serial titles: 610 (physical), 36,590 (digital/electronic); Databases: 96. Weekly public service hours: 89; students can reserve study rooms.

**Computer facilities:** 102 computers available on campus for general student use. A campuswide network can be accessed. Online class registration is available. Website: http://www.milligan.edu/

**General Application Contact:** Pam Smith, Operations Assistant, 423-461-8482, Fax: 423-461-8789, E-mail: pbsmith@milligan.edu.

**GRADUATE UNITS**

**Area of Business Administration** Students: 48 full-time (21 women); includes 2 minority (1 Asian, non-Hispanic/Latino; 1 Two or more races, non-Hispanic/Latino), 2 international. Average age 33. 55 applicants, 98% accepted, 34 enrolled. *Faculty:* 4 full-time (0 women), 3 part-time/adjunct (1 woman). Expenses: Contact institution. *Financial support:* Scholarships/grants available. Financial award application deadline: 12/1; financial award applicants required to submit FAFSA. In 2019, 33 master's awarded. *Application deadline:* For fall admission, 8/1 for domestic students, 6/1 for international students; for spring admission, 1/15 for domestic students, 12/1 for international students. Applications are processed on a rolling basis. *Application fee:* $30. Electronic applications accepted. *Application Contact:* Rebecca Banton, Graduate Admissions Recruiter, Business Area, 423-461-8662, Fax: 423-461-8789, E-mail: rbbanton@milligan.edu. *Area Chair of Business,* Dr. David Campbell, 423-461-8674, Fax: 423-461-8677, E-mail: dacampbell@milligan.edu.

**Area of Computer Science** Students: 2 full-time (0 women), 8 part-time (3 women). Average age 38. 11 applicants, 100% accepted, 8 enrolled. *Faculty:* 4 full-time (3 women). Expenses: Contact institution. *Financial support:* Scholarships/grants available. Financial award application deadline: 12/1; financial award applicants required to submit FAFSA. *Application deadline:* For fall admission, 8/1 for domestic students, 6/1 for international students; for spring admission, 1/15 for domestic students, 12/1 for international students. Applications are processed on a rolling basis. *Application fee:* $30. Electronic applications accepted. *Application Contact:* Rebecca Banton, Graduate Admissions Recruiter, Business Area, 423-461-8662, Fax: 423-461-8789, E-mail: RBBanton@Milligan.edu. *MSIS Program Director, Professor of Information Systems,* Dr. Teresa Carter, 423-461-8411, E-mail: TACarter@Milligan.edu.

**Area of Counselor Education Programs** Students: 24 full-time (20 women), 4 part-time (3 women); includes 2 minority (1 Black or African American, non-Hispanic/Latino; 1 Two or more races, non-Hispanic/Latino). Average age 30. 33 applicants, 67% accepted, 16 enrolled. *Faculty:* 3 full-time (all women), 2 part-time/adjunct (1 woman). Expenses: Contact institution. *Financial support:* Scholarships/grants available. Financial award application deadline: 12/1; financial award applicants required to submit FAFSA. In 2019, 15 master's awarded. *Program availability:* Part-time. *Application deadline:* For fall admission, 8/1 for domestic students, 6/1 for international students. Applications are processed on a rolling basis. *Application fee:* $30. Electronic applications accepted. *Application Contact:* Stacy Shankle, Graduate Admissions Recruiter, Healthcare Programs, 423-461-8424, Fax: 423-461-8789, E-mail: srshankle@milligan.edu. *Director of Master of Science in Counseling Program,* Dr. Rebecca Sapp, 423-461-3071, E-mail: rlsapp@milligan.edu.

**Area of Education** Students: 42 full-time (27 women), 12 part-time (9 women); includes 1 minority (Hispanic/Latino). Average age 32. 47 applicants, 74% accepted, 34 enrolled. *Faculty:* 6 full-time (4 women), 2 part-time/adjunct (0 women). Expenses: Contact institution. *Financial support:* Scholarships/grants available. Financial award application deadline: 12/1; financial award applicants required to submit FAFSA. In 2019, 12 master's, 8 doctorates awarded. *Program availability:* Part-time, 100% online, blended/hybrid learning. *Application deadline:* For fall admission, 8/1 priority date for domestic students, 6/1 for international students; for spring admission, 11/15 priority date for domestic students, 12/1 for international students; for summer admission, 4/1 for domestic students. Applications are processed on a rolling basis. *Application fee:* $30. Electronic applications accepted. *Application Contact:* Melissa Dillow, Graduate Admissions Recruiter, Education, 423-461-8306, Fax: 423-461-8982, E-mail: msdillow@milligan.edu. *Area Chair of Education,* Dr. Angela Hilton-Prillhart, 423-461-8769, Fax: 423-461-3103, E-mail: anhilton-prillhart@milligan.edu.

**Area of Humane Learning** Students: 4 full-time (1 woman), 1 part-time (0 women). Average age 27. 5 applicants, 80% accepted, 3 enrolled. *Faculty:* 7 full-time (2 women), 1 part-time/adjunct (0 women). Expenses: Contact institution. *Financial support:* Scholarships/grants available. Financial award application deadline: 12/1; financial award applicants required to submit FAFSA. *Program availability:* Part-time. *Application deadline:* For fall admission, 8/1 for domestic students, 6/1 for international students. Applications are processed on a rolling basis. *Application fee:* $30. Electronic applications accepted. *Application Contact:* Pam Smith, Operations Assistant, 423-461-8482, Fax: 423-461-8789, E-mail: pbsmith@milligan.edu. *MAH Program Director; Associate Professor of English and Composition,* Dr. Heather Hoover, 423-461-8944, E-mail: HHoover@Milligan.edu.

**Area of Physician Assistant Studies** Students: 49 full-time (32 women); includes 3 minority (1 Black or African American, non-Hispanic/Latino; 1 Asian, non-Hispanic/Latino; 1 Two or more races, non-Hispanic/Latino). Average age 28. 226 applicants, 21% accepted, 26 enrolled. *Faculty:* 6 full-time (3 women), 4 part-time/adjunct (3 women). Expenses: Contact institution. *Financial support:* Scholarships/grants available. Financial award application deadline: 12/1; financial award applicants required to submit FAFSA. *Application deadline:* For spring admission, 9/1 for domestic students. *Application fee:* $120. Electronic applications accepted. *Application Contact:* Rebekah Bess, Program Secretary, 423-461-1557, Fax: 423-461-1518, E-mail: rbess@milligan.edu. *Area Chair and Director,* Andrew Hull, 423-461-1558, Fax: 423-461-1518, E-mail: awhull@milligan.edu.

**Emmanuel Christian Seminary at Milligan College** Students: 70 full-time (28 women), 70 part-time (26 women); includes 19 minority (9 Black or African American, non-Hispanic/Latino; 3 American Indian or Alaska Native, non-Hispanic/Latino; 2 Asian, non-Hispanic/Latino; 5 Hispanic/Latino), 8 international. Average age 34. 109 applicants, 90% accepted, 64 enrolled. *Faculty:* 12 full-time (1 woman), 5 part-time/adjunct (0 women). Expenses: Contact institution. *Financial support:* Scholarships/grants and unspecified assistantships available. Financial award application deadline: 12/1; financial award applicants required to submit FAFSA. In 2019, 21 master's, 3 doctorates awarded. *Program availability:* Part-time, blended/hybrid learning. *Application deadline:* For fall admission, 8/1 for domestic students, 6/1 for international students; for spring admission, 12/15 for domestic students, 8/1 for international students. Applications are processed on a rolling basis. *Application fee:* $30. Electronic applications accepted. *Application Contact:* Lauren Gullett, Director of Admissions and Recruitment for Emmanuel Christian Seminary, 423-461-1535, Fax: 423-926-6198, E-mail: lwgullett@milligan.edu. *Academic Dean, Emmanuel Christian Seminary,* Dr. Rollin Ramsaran, 423-461-1524, Fax: 423-926-6198, E-mail: raramsaran@milligan.edu.

**Program in Occupational Therapy** Students: 63 full-time (56 women), 31 part-time (26 women); includes 5 minority (1 Black or African American, non-Hispanic/Latino; 3 Hispanic/Latino; 1 Two or more races, non-Hispanic/Latino). Average age 25. 163 applicants, 44% accepted, 32 enrolled. *Faculty:* 5 full-time (4 women), 4 part-time/adjunct (3 women). Expenses: Contact institution. *Financial support:* Career-related internships or fieldwork and institutionally sponsored loans available. Financial award application deadline: 4/15; financial award applicants required to submit FAFSA. In 2019, 32 master's awarded. *Application deadline:* For spring admission, 11/15 for domestic and international students. *Application fee:* $120. Electronic applications accepted. *Application Contact:* Kristia Brown, Office Manager and Admissions Representative, 423-975-8010, Fax: 423-975-8019, E-mail: lkbrown@milligan.edu. *Program Director and Area Chair of Occupational Therapy;,* Dr. Christy Isbell, 423-461-1548, Fax: 423-975-8019, E-mail: cisbell@milligan.edu.

## MILLIKIN UNIVERSITY, Decatur, IL 62522-2084

**General Information** Independent-religious, coed, comprehensive institution. *Enrollment:* 2,083 graduate, professional, and undergraduate students; 69 full-time matriculated graduate/professional students (43 women), 19 part-time matriculated graduate/professional students (13 women). *Enrollment by degree level:* 45 master's, 43 doctoral. *Graduate faculty:* 22 full-time (16 women), 24 part-time/adjunct (13 women). Tuition and fees vary according to course load, degree level and program. *Graduate housing:* Room and/or apartments available on a first-come, first-served basis to single students; on-campus housing not available to married students. *Student services:* Campus employment opportunities, career counseling, exercise/wellness program, grant writing training, international student services, multicultural affairs office, services for students with disabilities, writing training. *Library facilities:* Staley Library. *Collection:* Books: 125,046 (physical), 29,809 (digital/electronic); Serial titles: 543 (physical), 45 (digital/electronic); Databases: 50. Weekly public service hours: 87; students can reserve study rooms.

**Computer facilities:** 135 computers available on campus for general student use. A campuswide network can be accessed. Online class registration, online degree audit, online financials (view and pay bills, financial aid) are available.
Website: http://www.millikin.edu/

**General Application Contact:** Marianne Taylor, Director of Graduate Admission, 217-420-6771, Fax: 217-425-4669, E-mail: mgtaylor@millikin.edu.

**GRADUATE UNITS**

**School of Nursing** Students: 45 full-time (31 women), 17 part-time (12 women); includes 19 minority (11 Black or African American, non-Hispanic/Latino; 4 Asian, non-Hispanic/Latino; 4 Hispanic/Latino), 1 international. Average age 31. 129 applicants, 35% accepted, 19 enrolled. *Faculty:* 18 full-time (15 women), 8 part-time/adjunct (7 women). Expenses: Contact institution. *Financial support:* Traineeships and unspecified assistantships available. Financial award applicants required to submit FAFSA. In 2019, 5 master's, 14 doctorates awarded. *Program availability:* Part-time. *Application deadline:* For winter admission, 1/15 priority date for domestic and international students; for summer admission, 1/15 priority date for domestic and international students. Applications are processed on a rolling basis. Electronic applications accepted. *Application Contact:* Marianne Taylor, Director, Graduate Admission, 217-420-6771, Fax: 217-425-4669, E-mail: mgtaylor@millikin.edu. *Interim Director,* Dr. Elizabeth Gephart, 217-424-6397, E-mail: egephart@millikin.edu.

**Tabor School of Business** Students: 24 full-time (12 women), 2 part-time (1 woman); includes 6 minority (4 Black or African American, non-Hispanic/Latino; 1 Asian, non-Hispanic/Latino; 1 Hispanic/Latino), 3 international. Average age 30. 47 applicants, 77% accepted, 25 enrolled. *Faculty:* 5 full-time (2 women), 15 part-time/adjunct (6 women). Expenses: Contact institution. *Financial support:* In 2019–20, 21 students received support, including 6 research assistantships with partial tuition reimbursements available (averaging $6,000 per year), 4 teaching assistantships with partial tuition reimbursements available (averaging $6,000 per year); scholarships/grants and tuition waivers (full) also available. Financial award applicants required to submit FAFSA. In 2019, 22 master's awarded. *Program availability:* Evening/weekend. *Application deadline:* For fall admission, 6/1 priority date for domestic students, 4/1 priority date for international students; for spring admission, 11/1 priority date for domestic students, 8/1 priority date for international students. Applications are processed on a rolling basis. Electronic applications accepted. *Application Contact:* Marianne Taylor, Director, Graduate Admission, 217-420-6771, Fax: 217-424-6286, E-mail: mgtaylor@millikin.edu. *Dean,* Dr. Najiba Benabess, 217-420-6762, E-mail: nbenabess@millikin.edu.

## MILLSAPS COLLEGE, Jackson, MS 39210

**General Information** Independent-religious, coed, comprehensive institution. *Graduate housing:* Room and/or apartments available to single students; on-campus housing not available to married students. Housing application deadline: 6/1. *Research affiliation:* Downtown Jackson Partners Group (real estate development), Oxbow Ventures (commercialization of renewable energy), Midtown Partners (economic development).

**GRADUATE UNITS**

**Else School of Management** Students: 42 full-time (16 women), 22 part-time (6 women); includes 8 minority (5 Black or African American, non-Hispanic/Latino; 1 American Indian or Alaska Native, non-Hispanic/Latino; 1 Asian, non-Hispanic/Latino; 1 Hispanic/Latino), 2 international. Average age 24. 55 applicants, 76% accepted, 35 enrolled. *Faculty:* 12 full-time (5 women), 6 part-time/adjunct (2 women). Expenses: Contact institution. *Financial support:* In 2019–20, 41 students received support. Career-related internships or fieldwork, Federal Work-Study, scholarships/grants, and tuition waivers available. Support available to part-time students. Financial award application deadline: 4/15; financial award applicants required to submit FAFSA. In 2019, 57 master's awarded. *Program availability:* Part-time, evening/weekend. *Application deadline:* For fall admission, 7/1 priority date for domestic students; for spring admission, 11/15 priority date for domestic students. Applications are processed on a rolling basis. Electronic applications accepted. *Application Contact:* Christine Rials, Director of Graduate Business Admissions, 601-974-1253, E-mail: mbamacc@millsaps.edu. *Dean,* Dr. Kimberly G. Burke, 601-974-1250, Fax: 601-974-1260.

## MILLS COLLEGE, Oakland, CA 94613-1000

**General Information** Independent, Undergraduate: women only; graduate: coed, comprehensive institution. *Graduate housing:* Rooms and/or apartments available on a first-come, first-served basis to single and married students. Housing application deadline: 6/15.

**GRADUATE UNITS**

**Graduate Studies** *Program availability:* Part-time, evening/weekend. Electronic applications accepted.

***Lorry I. Lokey Graduate School of Business*** *Program availability:* Part-time.

***School of Education*** *Program availability:* Part-time, evening/weekend. Electronic applications accepted.

## MILWAUKEE SCHOOL OF ENGINEERING, Milwaukee, WI 53202-3109

**General Information** Independent, coed, primarily men, comprehensive institution. *Graduate housing:* Rooms and/or apartments available on a first-come, first-served basis to single and married students. Housing application deadline: 7/1. *Research affiliation:* Keen Foundation (entrepreneurship and engineering education), National Fluid Power Association (hydraulics and pneumatics), 3dMD (biomolecular modeling), National Additine Manufacturing Innovation Institute (rapid prototyping), Caterpillar, Inc. (electrohydraulics), Clinical Translational Science Institute (medical and healthcare innovation and transfer).

**GRADUATE UNITS**

**MBA in STEM Leadership Program** *Program availability:* Part-time, evening/weekend. Electronic applications accepted.

**MBA Program in Education Leadership** *Program availability:* Part-time, evening/weekend. Electronic applications accepted.

**MS Program in Architectural Engineering** *Program availability:* Part-time, evening/weekend. Electronic applications accepted.

**MS Program in Civil Engineering** *Program availability:* Part-time, evening/weekend. Electronic applications accepted.

**MS Program in Engineering** *Program availability:* Part-time, evening/weekend. Electronic applications accepted.

**MS Program in Engineering Management** *Program availability:* Part-time, evening/weekend. Electronic applications accepted.

**MS Program in Marketing and Export Management** *Program availability:* Part-time, evening/weekend. Electronic applications accepted.

**MS Program in New Product Management** *Program availability:* Part-time, evening/weekend. Electronic applications accepted.

**MS Program in Nursing - Leadership and Management** *Program availability:* Part-time, evening/weekend, 100% online, blended/hybrid learning. Electronic applications accepted.

**MS Program in Perfusion** Electronic applications accepted.

**Program in Business Administration** *Program availability:* Part-time, evening/weekend, 100% online, blended/hybrid learning. Electronic applications accepted.

## MINNEAPOLIS COLLEGE OF ART AND DESIGN, Minneapolis, MN 55404-4347

**General Information** Independent, coed, comprehensive institution. *Enrollment:* 796 graduate, professional, and undergraduate students; 67 full-time matriculated graduate/professional students (45 women), 15 part-time matriculated graduate/professional students (12 women). *Enrollment by degree level:* 82 master's, 5 other advanced degrees. *Graduate faculty:* 42 full-time (19 women). *Tuition:* Full-time $41,344. *Required fees:* $450. One-time fee: $300 full-time. *Graduate housing:* On-campus housing not available. *Student services:* Campus employment opportunities, campus safety program, career counseling, exercise/wellness program, free psychological counseling, grant writing training, international student services, low-cost health insurance, services for students with disabilities, teacher training, writing training.

*Library facilities:* MCAD Library. *Collection:* Books: 50,000 (physical), 145,000 (digital/electronic); Serial titles: 329 (physical); Databases: 8.

**Computer facilities:** Computer purchase and lease plans are available. A campuswide network can be accessed. Online class registration is available.
Website: http://www.mcad.edu/

**General Application Contact:** Melissa Huybrecht, Vice President, Enrollment Management, 612-874-3764, E-mail: mhuybrecht@mcad.edu.

**GRADUATE UNITS**

**Master of Arts in Graphic and Web Design** 22 applicants, 82% accepted, 14 enrolled. Expenses: Contact institution. *Financial support:* Career-related internships or fieldwork available. Support available to part-time students. Financial award application deadline: 3/15; financial award applicants required to submit FAFSA. *Program availability:* Part-time, evening/weekend. *Application deadline:* For fall admission, 4/1 priority date for domestic and international students; for spring admission, 11/1 priority date for domestic and international students. Applications are processed on a rolling basis. *Application fee:* $50. Electronic applications accepted. *Application Contact:* Mary Kazura, Director of Admissions, 612-874-3668, E-mail: mkazura@mcad.edu. *Director, Master of Arts in Graphic and Web Design*, Lafe Smith, E-mail: lsmith257@mcad.edu.

**Master of Arts in Sustainable Design** 11 applicants, 82% accepted, 6 enrolled. Expenses: Contact institution. *Financial support:* Career-related internships or fieldwork available. Support available to part-time students. Financial award application deadline: 3/15; financial award applicants required to submit FAFSA. *Program availability:* Part-time, evening/weekend. *Application deadline:* For fall admission, 4/1 priority date for domestic and international students; for spring admission, 11/1 priority date for domestic and international students. Applications are processed on a rolling basis. *Application fee:* $50. Electronic applications accepted. *Application Contact:* Mary Kazura, Director of Admissions, 612-8743668, E-mail: mkazura@mcad.edu. *Director, Sustainable Design Program*, Denise DeLuca, 612-8722915, E-mail: denise_deluca@mcad.edu.

**Master of Fine Arts in Visual Studies** 86 applicants, 44% accepted, 9 enrolled. Expenses: Contact institution. *Financial support:* In 2019–20, 15 teaching assistantships (averaging $6,000 per year) were awarded; career-related internships or fieldwork, Federal Work-Study, scholarships/grants, and unspecified assistantships also available. Support available to part-time students. Financial award application deadline: 3/15; financial award applicants required to submit FAFSA. *Program availability:* Part-time. *Application deadline:* For fall admission, 2/1 for domestic and international students. *Application fee:* $50. Electronic applications accepted. *Application Contact:* Mary Kazura, Director of Admissions, 612-874-3668, Fax: 612-874-3701, E-mail: mkazura@mcad.edu. *Director, MFA Program*, Ellen Mueller, 612-874-3629, E-mail: emueller@mcad.edu.

## MINNESOTA STATE UNIVERSITY MANKATO, Mankato, MN 56001

**General Information** State-supported, coed, university. CGS member. *Graduate housing:* Room and/or apartments available on a first-come, first-served basis to single students; on-campus housing not available to married students.

**GRADUATE UNITS**

**College of Graduate Studies and Research** *Program availability:* Part-time, online learning. Electronic applications accepted.

***College of Allied Health and Nursing*** *Program availability:* Part-time. Electronic applications accepted.

***College of Arts and Humanities*** *Program availability:* Part-time, evening/weekend.

***College of Business*** Electronic applications accepted.

***College of Education*** *Program availability:* Part-time, evening/weekend. Electronic applications accepted.

***College of Science, Engineering and Technology*** *Program availability:* Part-time. Electronic applications accepted.

***College of Social and Behavioral Sciences*** *Program availability:* Part-time. Electronic applications accepted.

## MINNESOTA STATE UNIVERSITY MOORHEAD, Moorhead, MN 56563

**General Information** State-supported, coed, comprehensive institution. CGS member. *Enrollment:* 201 full-time matriculated graduate/professional students (161 women), 636 part-time matriculated graduate/professional students (459 women). *Enrollment by degree level:* 664 master's, 61 doctoral, 112 other advanced degrees. *Graduate housing:* Room and/or apartments available on a first-come, first-served basis to single students; on-campus housing not available to married students. *Student services:* Campus employment opportunities, campus safety program, career counseling, child daycare facilities, exercise/wellness program, free psychological counseling, grant writing training, international student services, low-cost health insurance, multicultural affairs office, services for students with disabilities, teacher training. *Library facilities:* Livingston Lord Library plus 1 other. *Collection:* Books: 326,187 (physical), 20,401 (digital/electronic); Serial titles: 1,634 (physical), 18,041 (digital/electronic); Databases: 84. Weekly public service hours: 79. *Research affiliation:* West Central Minnesota Business Innovation Center.

**Computer facilities:** Computer purchase and lease plans are available. 1,500 computers available on campus for general student use. A campuswide network can be accessed from student residence rooms and from off campus. Online class registration is available.
Website: http://www.mnstate.edu/

**General Application Contact:** Karla Wenger, Office Manager, 218-477-2344, Fax: 218-477-2344, E-mail: wengerk@mnstate.edu.

**GRADUATE UNITS**

**Graduate and Extended Learning** Students: 201 full-time (161 women), 636 part-time (459 women). Average age 33. 346 applicants, 63% accepted. Expenses: Contact institution. *Financial support:* Federal Work-Study and unspecified assistantships available. Financial award application deadline: 10/1; financial award applicants required to submit FAFSA. In 2019, 263 master's, 29 other advanced degrees awarded. *Program availability:* Part-time, evening/weekend, 100% online, blended/hybrid learning. *Application deadline:* Applications are processed on a rolling basis. *Application fee:* $35. Electronic applications accepted. *Application Contact:* Karla Wenger, Office Manager, 218-236-2344, Fax: 218-236-2482, E-mail: wengerk@mnstate.edu. *Interim Dean of Graduate and Extended Learning*, Dr. Lisa Karch, 218-477-2699, Fax: 218-236-2482, E-mail: lisa.karch@mnstate.edu.

***College of Arts & Humanities*** Students: 1 (woman) full-time, 5 part-time (3 women). Average age 41. 5 applicants, 80% accepted. Expenses: Contact institution. *Financial support:* Federal Work-Study and unspecified assistantships available. Financial award application deadline: 10/1; financial award applicants required to submit FAFSA. In 2019, 7 master's awarded. *Program availability:* Part-time, evening/weekend. *Application deadline:* For fall admission, 4/15 for domestic students; for spring admission, 11/15 for domestic students; for summer admission, 4/15 for domestic students. Applications are processed on a rolling basis. *Application fee:* $35. Electronic applications accepted. *Application Contact:* Karla Wenger, Office Manager, 218-477-2344, Fax: 218-477-2482, E-mail: wengerk@mnstate.edu. *Dean*, Dr. Earnest Lamb, 218-477-2815, E-mail: earnest.lamb@mnstate.edu.

***College of Business and Innovation*** Students: 22 full-time (12 women), 28 part-time (13 women). Average age 30. 33 applicants, 73% accepted. *Faculty:* 13. Expenses: Contact institution. *Financial support:* Federal Work-Study and unspecified assistantships available. Financial award application deadline: 10/1; financial award applicants required to submit FAFSA. In 2019, 26 master's awarded. *Program availability:* Part-time, evening/weekend, 100% online, blended/hybrid learning. *Application deadline:* For fall admission, 4/15 for domestic students; for spring admission, 11/15 for domestic students; for summer admission, 4/15 for domestic students. Applications are processed on a rolling basis. *Application fee:* $35. Electronic applications accepted. *Application Contact:* Karla Wenger, Office Manager, 218-477-2344, E-mail: wengerk@mnstate.edu. *Interim Dean*, Joshua Behl, 218-477-2667, E-mail: joshua.behl@mnstate.edu.

***College of Education and Human Services*** Students: 148 full-time (122 women), 484 part-time (353 women). Average age 33. 231 applicants, 63% accepted. Expenses: Contact institution. *Financial support:* Federal Work-Study and unspecified assistantships available. Financial award application deadline: 10/1; financial award applicants required to submit FAFSA. In 2019, 190 master's, 18 other advanced degrees awarded. *Program availability:* Part-time, evening/weekend, 100% online, blended/hybrid learning. *Application deadline:* For fall admission, 7/1 priority date for domestic students; for spring admission, 11/15 priority date for domestic students; for summer admission, 2/15 for domestic students. Applications are processed on a rolling basis. *Application fee:* $35. Electronic applications accepted. *Application Contact:* Karla Wenger, Office Manager, 218-477-2344, Fax: 218-477-2482, E-mail: wengerk@mnstate.edu. *Dean*, Dr. Ok-Hee Lee, 218-477-2095, E-mail: okheelee@mnstate.edu.

***College of Science, Health and the Environment*** Students: 30 full-time (26 women), 120 part-time (91 women). Average age 33. 77 applicants, 57% accepted. Expenses: Contact institution. *Financial support:* Federal Work-Study and unspecified assistantships available. Financial award application deadline: 10/1; financial award applicants required to submit FAFSA. In 2019, 40 master's, 11 other advanced degrees awarded. *Program availability:* Part-time, evening/weekend, 100% online, blended/hybrid learning. *Application deadline:* Applications are processed on a rolling basis. *Application fee:* $35. Electronic applications accepted. *Application Contact:* Karla Wenger, Office Manager, 218-477-2344, Fax: 218-477-2482, E-mail: wengerk@mnstate.edu. *Interim Dean*, Dr. Elizabeth Nawrot, 218-477-5892, E-mail: nawrot@mnstate.edu.

## MINOT STATE UNIVERSITY, Minot, ND 58707-0002

**General Information** State-supported, coed, comprehensive institution. *Graduate housing:* Rooms and/or apartments available on a first-come, first-served basis to single and married students. Housing application deadline: 6/30. *Research affiliation:* Rural Crime and Justice Center (criminal justice research), North Dakota Center for Persons with Disabilities (NDCPD).

**GRADUATE UNITS**

**Graduate School** *Program availability:* Part-time, 100% online, blended/hybrid learning. Electronic applications accepted.

## MIRRER YESHIVA CENTRAL INSTITUTE, Brooklyn, NY 11223-2010

**General Information** Independent-religious, men only, comprehensive institution.

**General Application Contact:** Information Contact, 718-645-0536.

**GRADUATE UNITS**

**Graduate Programs**

## MISERICORDIA UNIVERSITY, Dallas, PA 18612-1098

**General Information** Independent-religious, coed, comprehensive institution. *Graduate housing:* On-campus housing not available.

**GRADUATE UNITS**

**College of Business** *Program availability:* Part-time, evening/weekend. Electronic applications accepted.

**College of Health Sciences and Education** *Program availability:* Part-time, evening/weekend. Electronic applications accepted.

## MISSIO SEMINARY, Hatfield, PA 19440-2499

**General Information** Independent-religious, coed, graduate-only institution. *Graduate housing:* On-campus housing not available. *Research affiliation:* Christian Counseling and Education Foundation (psychology).

**GRADUATE UNITS**

**Graduate and Professional Programs** *Program availability:* Part-time, evening/weekend. Electronic applications accepted.

## MISSISSIPPI COLLEGE, Clinton, MS 39058

**General Information** Independent-religious, coed, comprehensive institution. *Graduate housing:* Room and/or apartments available on a first-come, first-served basis to single students; on-campus housing not available to married students. Housing application deadline: 8/15. *Research affiliation:* Gulf Coast Research Laboratory (marine biology).

**GRADUATE UNITS**

**Graduate School** *Program availability:* Part-time, evening/weekend, online learning. Electronic applications accepted.

***College of Arts and Sciences*** *Program availability:* Part-time, evening/weekend. Electronic applications accepted.

***School of Business*** *Program availability:* Part-time, evening/weekend. Electronic applications accepted.

***School of Education*** *Program availability:* Part-time, evening/weekend, online learning. Electronic applications accepted.

**School of Law** Electronic applications accepted.

## MISSISSIPPI STATE UNIVERSITY, Mississippi State, MS 39762

**General Information** State-supported, coed, university. CGS member. *Enrollment:* 22,226 graduate, professional, and undergraduate students; 1,834 full-time matriculated graduate/professional students (1,037 women), 1,526 part-time matriculated graduate/professional students (716 women). *Enrollment by degree level:* 1,810 master's, 1,501 doctoral, 49 other advanced degrees. *Graduate faculty:* 809 full-time (262 women), 22 part-time/adjunct (6 women). *Tuition, area resident:* Full-time $8880; part-time $456 per credit hour. Tuition, state resident: full-time $8880. Tuition, nonresident: full-time $23,840; part-time $1236 per credit hour. *Required fees:* $110; $11.12 per credit hour. Tuition and fees vary according to course load. *Graduate housing:* Room and/or apartments available on a first-come, first-served basis to single students; on-campus housing not available to married students. Typical cost: $6440 per year. Room charges vary according to board plan and housing facility selected. Housing application deadline: 4/1. *Student services:* Campus employment opportunities, campus safety program, career counseling, child daycare facilities, exercise/wellness program, free psychological counseling, grant writing training, international student services, low-cost health insurance, multicultural affairs office, services for students with disabilities, teacher training, writing training. *Library facilities:* Mitchell Memorial Library plus 2 others. *Collection:* Books: 2.8 million (physical), 73,631 (digital/electronic); Serial titles: 1,509 (physical), 295,495 (digital/electronic); Databases: 393. Weekly public service hours: 110; students can reserve study rooms. *Research affiliation:* Mississippi Research Consortium (interdisciplinary research), Southeastern Universities Research Association (interdisciplinary research), Oak Ridge Associated Universities (interdisciplinary energy-related research), Mississippi Research and Technology Park (interdisciplinary engineering), Mississippi Mineral Resources Institute (geology sciences and engineering), NASA-Stennis Space Center (interdisciplinary research).

**Computer facilities:** A campuswide network can be accessed. Online class registration is available.
Website: http://www.msstate.edu/

**General Application Contact:** Forest Sparks, Admissions Manager, 662-325-7400, Fax: 662-325-1967, E-mail: grad@grad.msstate.edu.

**GRADUATE UNITS**

**Bagley College of Engineering** Students: 329 full-time (109 women), 352 part-time (75 women); includes 108 minority (37 Black or African American, non-Hispanic/Latino; 35 Asian, non-Hispanic/Latino; 30 Hispanic/Latino; 6 Two or more races, non-Hispanic/Latino), 218 international. Average age 31. 509 applicants, 57% accepted, 122 enrolled. *Faculty:* 100 full-time (15 women), 7 part-time/adjunct (2 women). Expenses: Contact institution. *Financial support:* In 2019–20, 179 research assistantships with full tuition reimbursements (averaging $17,054 per year), 60 teaching assistantships with full tuition reimbursements (averaging $15,495 per year) were awarded; Federal Work-Study, institutionally sponsored loans, scholarships/grants, and unspecified assistantships also available. Financial award application deadline: 4/1; financial award applicants required to submit FAFSA. In 2019, 117 master's, 47 doctorates awarded. *Program availability:* Part-time, 100% online. *Application deadline:* For fall admission, 7/1 for domestic students, 5/1 for international students; for spring admission, 11/1 for domestic students, 9/1 for international students. Applications are processed on a rolling basis. *Application fee:* $60 ($80 for international students). Electronic applications accepted. *Application Contact:* Angie Campbell, Admissions and Enrollment Assistant, 662-325-9514, E-mail: acampbell@grad.msstate.edu. *Dean*, Dr. Jason Keith, 662-325-7183, Fax: 662-325-8573, E-mail: keith@bagley.msstate.edu.

***Dave C. Swalm School of Chemical Engineering*** Students: 21 full-time (8 women), 3 part-time (0 women); includes 2 minority (both Asian, non-Hispanic/Latino), 17 international. Average age 29. 9 applicants, 67% accepted, 2 enrolled. *Faculty:* 10 full-time (2 women). Expenses: Contact institution. *Financial support:* In 2019–20, 15 research assistantships with full tuition reimbursements (averaging $17,952 per year), 2 teaching assistantships with full tuition reimbursements (averaging $15,705 per year) were awarded; Federal Work-Study, institutionally sponsored loans, and unspecified assistantships also available. Financial award application deadline: 4/1; financial award applicants required to submit FAFSA. In 2019, 3 doctorates awarded. *Application deadline:* For fall admission, 4/1 priority date for domestic students, 5/1 for international students; for spring admission, 8/1 priority date for domestic students, 9/1 for international students. Applications are processed on a rolling basis. *Application fee:* $60 ($80 for international students). Electronic applications accepted. *Application Contact:* Angie Campbell, Admissions and Enrollment Assistant, 662-325-9514, E-mail: acampbell@grad.msstate.edu. *Director/Earnest W. Deavenport Jr. Chair*, Dr. Bill Elmore, 662-325-2480, Fax: 662-325-2482, E-mail: elmore@che.msstate.edu.

**College of Agriculture and Life Sciences** Students: 235 full-time (134 women), 168 part-time (94 women); includes 42 minority (25 Black or African American, non-Hispanic/Latino; 2 American Indian or Alaska Native, non-Hispanic/Latino; 1 Asian, non-Hispanic/Latino; 11 Hispanic/Latino; 3 Two or more races, non-Hispanic/Latino), 82 international. Average age 30. 181 applicants, 56% accepted, 77 enrolled. *Faculty:* 185 full-time (50 women), 1 part-time/adjunct (0 women). Expenses: Contact institution. *Financial support:* In 2019–20, 161 research assistantships with full tuition reimbursements (averaging $15,119 per year), 13 teaching assistantships with full tuition reimbursements (averaging $13,410 per year) were awarded; career-related internships or fieldwork, Federal Work-Study, institutionally sponsored loans, scholarships/grants, tuition waivers (partial), and unspecified assistantships also available. Financial award application deadline: 4/1; financial award applicants required to submit FAFSA. In 2019, 76 master's, 27 doctorates awarded. *Program availability:* Blended/hybrid learning. *Application deadline:* For fall admission, 7/1 for domestic students, 5/1 for international students; for spring admission, 11/1 for domestic students, 9/1 for international students. Applications are processed on a rolling basis. *Application fee:* $60 ($80 for international students). Electronic applications accepted. *Application Contact:* Nathan Drake, Manager, Graduate Programs, 662-325-7394, Fax: 662-325-1967, E-mail: ndrake@grad.msstate.edu. *Dean of Agriculture and Life Sciences/Director of Mississippi Agricultural and Forestry Experiment Station*, Dr. George Hopper, 662-325-2953, Fax: 662-325-8580, E-mail: dean@cfr.msstate.edu.

***School of Human Sciences*** Students: 26 full-time (21 women), 62 part-time (46 women); includes 16 minority (12 Black or African American, non-Hispanic/Latino; 1 American Indian or Alaska Native, non-Hispanic/Latino; 1 Hispanic/Latino; 2 Two or more races, non-Hispanic/Latino), 4 international. Average age 34. 26 applicants, 69% accepted, 16 enrolled. *Faculty:* 21 full-time (11 women). Expenses: Contact institution. *Financial support:* In 2019–20, 15 research assistantships (averaging $12,541 per year) were awarded; Federal Work-Study, institutionally sponsored loans, and unspecified assistantships also available. Financial award application deadline: 4/1; financial award applicants required to submit FAFSA. In 2019, 12 master's, 4 doctorates awarded. *Program availability:* Part-time. *Application deadline:* For fall admission, 7/1 for domestic students, 5/1 for international students; for spring admission, 11/1 for domestic students, 9/1 for international students. Applications are processed on a rolling basis. *Application fee:* $60 ($80 for international students). Electronic applications accepted. *Application Contact:* Ryan King, Admissions and Enrollment Assistant, 662-325-8951, E-mail: rjk101@grad.msstate.edu. *Professor and Director*, Dr. Michael Newman, 662-325-2950, E-mail: mnewman@humansci.msstate.edu.

**College of Arts and Sciences** Students: 424 full-time (204 women), 330 part-time (164 women); includes 112 minority (51 Black or African American, non-Hispanic/Latino; 1 American Indian or Alaska Native, non-Hispanic/Latino; 11 Asian, non-Hispanic/Latino; 37 Hispanic/Latino; 2 Native Hawaiian or other Pacific Islander, non-Hispanic/Latino; 10 Two or more races, non-Hispanic/Latino), 163 international. Average age 30. 597 applicants, 53% accepted, 211 enrolled. *Faculty:* 243 full-time (92 women), 4 part-time/adjunct (0 women). Expenses: Contact institution. *Financial support:* In 2019–20, 47 research assistantships with full tuition reimbursements (averaging $16,278 per year), 322 teaching assistantships with full tuition reimbursements (averaging $14,652 per year) were awarded; Federal Work-Study, institutionally sponsored loans, scholarships/grants, tuition waivers (partial), and unspecified assistantships also available. Financial award application deadline: 4/1; financial award applicants required to submit FAFSA. In 2019, 169 master's, 21 doctorates awarded. *Program availability:* Part-time, evening/weekend. *Application deadline:* For fall admission, 7/1 for domestic students, 5/1 for international students; for spring admission, 11/1 for domestic students, 9/1 for international students. Applications are processed on a rolling basis. *Application fee:* $60 ($80 for international students). Electronic applications accepted. *Application Contact:* Nathan Drake, Manager, Graduate Programs, 662-325-7394, E-mail: ndrake@msstate.edu. *Dean and Professor*, Dr. Rick Travis, 662-325-2646, Fax: 662-325-8740, E-mail: rtravis@deanas.msstate.edu.

**College of Business** Students: 109 full-time (44 women), 223 part-time (76 women); includes 44 minority (24 Black or African American, non-Hispanic/Latino; 3 American Indian or Alaska Native, non-Hispanic/Latino; 5 Asian, non-Hispanic/Latino; 9 Hispanic/Latino; 3 Two or more races, non-Hispanic/Latino), 23 international. Average age 31. 181 applicants, 46% accepted, 55 enrolled. *Faculty:* 57 full-time (14 women), 3 part-time/adjunct (0 women). Expenses: Contact institution. *Financial support:* In 2019–20, 3 research assistantships (averaging $11,861 per year), 45 teaching assistantships (averaging $13,317 per year) were awarded; career-related internships or fieldwork, Federal Work-Study, institutionally sponsored loans, scholarships/grants, and unspecified assistantships also available. Financial award application deadline: 4/1; financial award applicants required to submit FAFSA. In 2019, 181 master's, 3 doctorates awarded. *Program availability:* Part-time, evening/weekend, blended/hybrid learning. *Application deadline:* For fall admission, 3/1 priority date for domestic students, 5/1 for international students; for spring admission, 11/1 for domestic students, 9/1 for international students. Applications are processed on a rolling basis. *Application fee:* $60 ($80 for international students). Electronic applications accepted. *Application Contact:* Nathan Drake, Manager, Graduate Programs, 662-325-7394, E-mail: ndrake@grad.msstate.edu. *Dean and Professor*, Dr. Sharon Oswald, 662-325-2580, Fax: 662-325-2410, E-mail: slo49@msstate.edu.

***Adkerson School of Accountancy*** Students: 41 full-time (21 women), 1 (woman) part-time; includes 3 minority (2 Black or African American, non-Hispanic/Latino; 1 Asian, non-Hispanic/Latino), 1 international. Average age 23. 21 applicants, 81% accepted, 13 enrolled. *Faculty:* 12 full-time (2 women), 1 part-time/adjunct (0 women). Expenses: Contact institution. *Financial support:* Career-related internships or fieldwork, Federal Work-Study, institutionally sponsored loans, scholarships/grants, and unspecified assistantships available. Support available to part-time students. Financial award application deadline: 4/1; financial award applicants required to submit FAFSA. In 2019, 64 master's awarded. *Application deadline:* For fall admission, 7/1 for domestic students, 5/1 for international students; for spring admission, 11/1 for domestic students, 9/1 for international students. Applications are processed on a rolling basis. *Application fee:* $60 ($80 for international students). Electronic applications accepted. *Application Contact:* Robbie Salters, Admissions and Enrollment Management Assistant and Coordinator, 662-325-5188, E-mail: rsalters@grad.msstate.edu. *Professor and Director*, Dr. Shawn Mauldin, 662-325-3710, Fax: 662-325-1646, E-mail: smauldin@business.msstate.edu.

**College of Education** Students: 258 full-time (173 women), 390 part-time (278 women); includes 228 minority (194 Black or African American, non-Hispanic/Latino; 1 American Indian or Alaska Native, non-Hispanic/Latino; 3 Asian, non-Hispanic/Latino; 16 Hispanic/Latino; 14 Two or more races, non-Hispanic/Latino), 17 international. Average age 32. 288 applicants, 72% accepted, 156 enrolled. *Faculty:* 85 full-time (45 women), 3 part-time/adjunct (all women). Expenses: Contact institution. *Financial support:* In 2019–20, 14 research assistantships (averaging $10,694 per year), 22 teaching assistantships (averaging $9,862 per year) were awarded; career-related internships or fieldwork, Federal Work-Study, institutionally sponsored loans, scholarships/grants, and unspecified assistantships also available. Financial award application deadline: 4/1; financial award applicants required to submit FAFSA. In 2019, 208 master's, 31 doctorates, 26 other advanced degrees awarded. *Program availability:* Part-time, evening/weekend, blended/hybrid learning. *Application deadline:* For fall admission, 7/1 for domestic students, 5/1 for international students; for spring admission, 11/1 for domestic students, 9/1 for international students. Applications are processed on a rolling basis. *Application fee:* $60 ($80 for international students). Electronic applications accepted. *Application Contact:* Nathan Drake, Manager, Graduate Programs, 662-325-7394, E-mail: ndrake@grad.msstate.edu. *Dean*, Dr. Richard Blackbourn, 662-325-3717, Fax: 662-325-8784, E-mail: rlb277@msstate.edu.

**College of Forest Resources** Students: 83 full-time (42 women), 34 part-time (10 women); includes 7 minority (4 Black or African American, non-Hispanic/Latino; 1 Hispanic/Latino; 2 Two or more races, non-Hispanic/Latino), 30 international. Average age 29. 45 applicants, 60% accepted, 26 enrolled. *Faculty:* 54 full-time (10 women), 2 part-time/adjunct (0 women). Expenses: Contact institution. *Financial support:* In 2019–20, 82 research assistantships with full tuition reimbursements (averaging $16,037 per year) were awarded; career-related internships or fieldwork, Federal Work-Study, institutionally sponsored loans, and unspecified assistantships also available. Financial award application deadline: 4/1; financial award applicants required to submit FAFSA. In 2019, 27 master's, 16 doctorates awarded. *Program availability:* Part-time. *Application deadline:* For fall admission, 7/1 for domestic students, 5/1 for international students; for spring admission, 11/1 for domestic students, 9/1 for international students. Applications are processed on a rolling basis. *Application fee:* $60 ($80 for international students). Electronic applications accepted. *Application Contact:* Nathan Drake, Manager, Graduate Programs, 662-325-7394, E-mail: ndrake@grad.msstate.edu. *Dean*, Dr. George Hopper, 662-325-2953, Fax: 662-325-8726, E-mail: ghopper@cfr.msstate.edu.

**College of Veterinary Medicine** Students: 396 full-time (331 women), 29 part-time (19 women); includes 39 minority (6 Black or African American, non-Hispanic/Latino; 1 American Indian or Alaska Native, non-Hispanic/Latino; 8 Asian, non-Hispanic/Latino; 20 Hispanic/Latino; 4 Two or more races, non-Hispanic/Latino), 11 international. Average age 26. 1,125 applicants, 9% accepted, 103 enrolled. *Faculty:* 64 full-time (29 women), 2 part-time/adjunct (1 woman). Expenses: Contact institution. *Financial support:* In 2019–20, 235 students received support, including 21 research assistantships with full tuition reimbursements available (averaging $17,458 per year);

fellowships also available. Financial award application deadline: 6/30; financial award applicants required to submit CSS PROFILE or FAFSA. In 2019, 11 master's, 7 doctorates awarded. *Application deadline:* For fall admission, 9/15 for domestic and international students. *Application fee:* $60 ($80 for international students). Electronic applications accepted. *Application Contact:* Jennifer Burns, Academic Affairs Manager, 662-325-1078, Fax: 663-325-1027, E-mail: jenny.burns@msstate.edu. *Dean,* Dr. Kent H. Hoblet, 662-325-1131, Fax: 662-325-1498, E-mail: hoblet@cvm.msstate.edu.

## MISSISSIPPI UNIVERSITY FOR WOMEN, Columbus, MS 39701-9998

**General Information** State-supported, coed, comprehensive institution. *Graduate housing:* Rooms and/or apartments available on a first-come, first-served basis to single and married students.

**GRADUATE UNITS**

**Graduate School** *Program availability:* Part-time.

***College of Education and Human Sciences*** *Program availability:* Part-time.

***College of Nursing and Health Sciences*** *Program availability:* Part-time.

## MISSISSIPPI VALLEY STATE UNIVERSITY, Itta Bena, MS 38941-1400

**General Information** State-supported, coed, comprehensive institution. *Graduate housing:* On-campus housing not available.

**GRADUATE UNITS**

**College of Education** *Program availability:* Part-time, evening/weekend.

**Department of Criminal Justice** *Program availability:* Part-time, evening/weekend, 100% online. Electronic applications accepted.

**Department of Natural Sciences and Environmental Health** *Program availability:* Part-time, evening/weekend.

## MISSOURI BAPTIST UNIVERSITY, St. Louis, MO 63141-8660

**General Information** Independent-religious, coed, comprehensive institution.

**GRADUATE UNITS**

**Graduate Programs**

## MISSOURI SOUTHERN STATE UNIVERSITY, Joplin, MO 64801-1595

**General Information** State-supported, coed, comprehensive institution.

**GRADUATE UNITS**

**Program in Business Administration** *Program availability:* Online learning.

**Program in Criminal Justice Administration** *Program availability:* Online learning.

**Program in Dental Hygiene** *Program availability:* Part-time. Electronic applications accepted.

**Program in Early Childhood Education**

**Program in Instructional Technology**

**Program in Nursing** *Program availability:* Part-time. Electronic applications accepted.

**Program in Teaching**

## MISSOURI STATE UNIVERSITY, Springfield, MO 65897

**General Information** State-supported, coed, comprehensive institution. CGS member. *Enrollment:* 23,453 graduate, professional, and undergraduate students; 1,569 full-time matriculated graduate/professional students (977 women), 1,839 part-time matriculated graduate/professional students (1,149 women). *Enrollment by degree level:* 2,724 master's, 371 doctoral, 311 other advanced degrees. *Graduate faculty:* 759 full-time (375 women), 384 part-time/adjunct (213 women). *International tuition:* $5240 full-time. *Tuition, area resident:* Full-time $2600; part-time $1735 per credit hour. Tuition, nonresident: full-time $5240; part-time $3495 per credit hour. *Required fees:* $530; $438 per credit hour. Tuition and fees vary according to class time, course level, course load, degree level, campus/location and program. *Graduate housing:* Rooms and/or apartments available on a first-come, first-served basis to single and married students. Typical cost: $9660 (including board) for single students; $9660 (including board) for married students. Room and board charges vary according to board plan, campus/location and housing facility selected. Housing application deadline: 10/31. *Student services:* Campus employment opportunities, campus safety program, career counseling, child daycare facilities, exercise/wellness program, free psychological counseling, grant writing training, international student services, multicultural affairs office, services for students with disabilities, teacher training, writing training. *Library facilities:* Meyer Library. *Collection:* Students can reserve study rooms.

**Computer facilities:** A campuswide network can be accessed. Online class registration is available.
Website: http://www.missouristate.edu/

**General Application Contact:** Lakan Drinker, Director, Graduate Enrollment Management, 417-836-5330, Fax: 417-836-6200, E-mail: graduateadmissions@missouristate.edu.

**GRADUATE UNITS**

**Graduate College** *Program availability:* Part-time, 100% online, blended/hybrid learning. Electronic applications accepted.

***College of Arts and Letters*** *Program availability:* Part-time, evening/weekend, 100% online, blended/hybrid learning. Electronic applications accepted.

***College of Business*** *Program availability:* Part-time, evening/weekend, 100% online, blended/hybrid learning. Electronic applications accepted.

***College of Education*** *Program availability:* Part-time. Electronic applications accepted.

***College of Health and Human Services*** *Program availability:* Part-time. Electronic applications accepted.

***College of Humanities and Public Affairs*** *Program availability:* Part-time. Electronic applications accepted.

***College of Natural and Applied Sciences*** *Program availability:* Part-time, evening/weekend. Electronic applications accepted.

***Darr College of Agriculture*** *Program availability:* Part-time. Electronic applications accepted.

## MISSOURI UNIVERSITY OF SCIENCE AND TECHNOLOGY, Rolla, MO 65409

**General Information** State-supported, coed, university. CGS member. *Enrollment:* 8,096 graduate, professional, and undergraduate students; 920 full-time matriculated graduate/professional students (203 women), 714 part-time matriculated graduate/professional students (162 women). *Enrollment by degree level:* 663 master's, 677 doctoral, 294 other advanced degrees. *Graduate faculty:* 289 full-time (72 women), 17 part-time/adjunct (1 woman). *International tuition:* $22,169 full-time. Tuition, state resident: full-time $7839; part-time $435.50 per credit hour. Tuition, nonresident: full-time $22,169; part-time $1231.60 per credit hour. *Required fees:* $649.76. One-time fee: $119. Tuition and fees vary according to course load and program. *Graduate housing:* Room and/or apartments available on a first-come, first-served basis to single students; on-campus housing not available to married students. *Student services:* Campus employment opportunities, campus safety program, career counseling, exercise/wellness program, free psychological counseling, grant writing training, international student services, low-cost health insurance, multicultural affairs office, services for students with disabilities, teacher training, writing training. *Library facilities:* Curtis Laws Wilson Library. *Collection:* Books: 305,834 (physical), 447,868 (digital/electronic); Serial titles: 14,178 (physical), 79,586 (digital/electronic); Databases: 180. Weekly public service hours: 112; students can reserve study rooms. *Research affiliation:* Cisco (material research), Honeywell (material research and additive manufacturing), Caterpillar, Inc. (mining and nuclear engineering), Idaho National Laboratory (material research), Hussmann Corporation (mining and nuclear engineering), Samsung (material research).

**Computer facilities:** Computer purchase and lease plans are available. 980 computers available on campus for general student use. A campuswide network can be accessed. Online class registration is available.
Website: http://www.mst.edu/

**General Application Contact:** Adrienne Neckermann, Manager, Office of Graduate Studies, 573-341-7712, E-mail: neckermanna@mst.edu.

**GRADUATE UNITS**

**Department of Biological Sciences** Students: 10 full-time (6 women), 6 part-time (5 women); includes 1 minority (Hispanic/Latino), 6 international. Average age 28. 19 applicants, 68% accepted, 7 enrolled. *Faculty:* 10 full-time (3 women). Expenses: Contact institution. *Financial support:* In 2019–20, 6 research assistantships (averaging $1,810 per year), 1 teaching assistantship (averaging $1,814 per year) were awarded; institutionally sponsored loans and unspecified assistantships also available. In 2019, 8 master's awarded. *Application fee:* $50. *Application Contact:* Debbie Schwertz, Admissions Coordinator, 573-341-6013, Fax: 573-341-6271, E-mail: schwertz@mst.edu. *Chair,* Dr. David Duvernell, 573-341-6988, Fax: 573-341-4821, E-mail: duvernelld@mst.edu.

**Department of Business and Information Technology** Electronic applications accepted.

**Department of Chemical and Biochemical Engineering** Electronic applications accepted.

**Department of Chemistry** Electronic applications accepted.

**Department of Civil, Architectural, and Environmental Engineering** *Program availability:* Part-time, evening/weekend. Electronic applications accepted.

**Department of Computer Science** *Program availability:* Part-time. Electronic applications accepted.

**Department of Electrical and Computer Engineering** *Program availability:* Part-time, evening/weekend. Electronic applications accepted.

**Department of Engineering Management and Systems Engineering** Electronic applications accepted.

**Department of English and Technical Communication**

**Department of Geosciences and Geological and Petroleum Engineering** *Program availability:* Part-time. Electronic applications accepted.

**Department of Materials Science and Engineering** Electronic applications accepted.

**Department of Mathematics and Statistics** Electronic applications accepted.

**Department of Mechanical and Aerospace Engineering** *Program availability:* Part-time, evening/weekend. Electronic applications accepted.

**Department of Mining and Nuclear Engineering** Electronic applications accepted.

**Department of Physics** Electronic applications accepted.

**Department of Psychological Science**

**Program in Geotechnics**

## MISSOURI VALLEY COLLEGE, Marshall, MO 65340-3197

**General Information** Independent-religious, coed, comprehensive institution.

**GRADUATE UNITS**

**Graduate Studies**

## MISSOURI WESTERN STATE UNIVERSITY, St. Joseph, MO 64507-2294

**General Information** State-supported, coed, comprehensive institution. CGS member. *Enrollment:* 65 full-time matriculated graduate/professional students (32 women), 182 part-time matriculated graduate/professional students (123 women). *Enrollment by degree level:* 232 master's, 15 other advanced degrees. *Graduate faculty:* 44 full-time (24 women), 8 part-time/adjunct (5 women). Tuition, state resident: full-time $6469.02; part-time $359.39 per credit hour. Tuition, nonresident: full-time $11,581; part-time $643.39 per credit hour. *Required fees:* $345.20; $99.10 per credit hour. Tuition and fees vary according to course load, campus/location and program. *Graduate housing:* Room and/or apartments available on a first-come, first-served basis to single students; on-campus housing not available to married students. Typical cost: $5756 per year ($9672 including board). Room and board charges vary according to board plan and housing facility selected. *Student services:* Campus employment opportunities, campus safety program, career counseling, child daycare facilities, exercise/wellness program, free psychological counseling, international student services, low-cost health insurance, multicultural affairs office, services for students with disabilities, writing training. *Library facilities:* Missouri Western State University Library. *Collection:* Books: 166,649 (physical), 215,083 (digital/electronic); Serial titles: 1,585 (physical), 57,298 (digital/electronic); Databases: 65.

**Computer facilities:** Computer purchase and lease plans are available. A campuswide network can be accessed from student residence rooms and from off campus. Online class registration, personal online storage are available.
Website: http://www.missouriwestern.edu/

**General Application Contact:** Dr. Susan Bashinski, Dean of the Graduate School, 816-271-4394, Fax: 816-271-4525, E-mail: graduate@missouriwestern.edu.

**GRADUATE UNITS**

**CyberSecurity** Students: 4 full-time (1 woman), 1 part-time (0 women); includes 1 minority (Asian, non-Hispanic/Latino), 4 international. Average age 26. 11 applicants, 9% accepted, 1 enrolled. Expenses: Contact institution. *Financial support:* Scholarships/grants and unspecified assistantships available. Support available to part-time students. In 2019, 6 master's awarded. *Program availability:* Part-time. *Application deadline:* For fall admission, 7/15 for domestic and international students; for spring admission, 11/1 for domestic and international students; for summer admission, 4/29 for domestic and international students. Applications are processed on a rolling basis. *Application fee:* $45 ($50 for international students). Electronic applications accepted. *Application Contact:* Dr. Susan Bashinski, Dean of the Graduate School, 816-271-4394, Fax: 816-271-4525, E-mail: graduate@missouriwestern.edu. *Assistant Professor*, Dr. Yipkei Kwok, 816-271-4523, E-mail: ykwok@missouriwestern.edu.

**Program in Applied Science** Students: 24 full-time (10 women), 21 part-time (5 women); includes 11 minority (3 Black or African American, non-Hispanic/Latino; 1 American Indian or Alaska Native, non-Hispanic/Latino; 1 Hispanic/Latino; 6 Two or more races, non-Hispanic/Latino), 8 international. Average age 26. 19 applicants, 89% accepted, 15 enrolled. Expenses: Contact institution. *Financial support:* Scholarships/grants and unspecified assistantships available. Support available to part-time students. In 2019, 18 master's awarded. *Program availability:* Part-time. *Application deadline:* For fall admission, 7/15 for domestic and international students; for spring admission, 11/1 for domestic and international students; for summer admission, 4/29 for domestic and international students. Applications are processed on a rolling basis. *Application fee:* $45 ($50 for international students). Electronic applications accepted. *Application Contact:* Dr. Susan Bashinski, Dean of the Graduate School, 816-271-4394, Fax: 816-271-4525, E-mail: graduate@missouriwestern.edu. *Dean of the Graduate School*, Dr. Susan Bashinski, 816-271-4394, Fax: 816-271-4525, E-mail: graduate@missouriwestern.edu.

**Program in Assessment** Students: 47 part-time (45 women); includes 6 minority (1 Black or African American, non-Hispanic/Latino; 2 American Indian or Alaska Native, non-Hispanic/Latino; 2 Asian, non-Hispanic/Latino; 1 Two or more races, non-Hispanic/Latino). Average age 36. 33 applicants, 100% accepted, 28 enrolled. Expenses: Contact institution. *Financial support:* Scholarships/grants and unspecified assistantships available. Support available to part-time students. In 2019, 11 master's, 2 other advanced degrees awarded. *Program availability:* Part-time. *Application deadline:* For fall admission, 7/15 for domestic and international students; for spring admission, 11/1 for domestic and international students; for summer admission, 4/29 for domestic and international students. Applications are processed on a rolling basis. *Application fee:* $45 ($50 for international students). Electronic applications accepted. *Application Contact:* Dr. Susan Bashinski, Dean of Graduate Programs, 816-271-4394, E-mail: graduate@missouriwestern.edu. *Dean of Graduate Programs*, Dr. Susan Bashinski, 816-271-4394, E-mail: graduate@missouriwestern.edu.

**Program in Business Administration** Students: 26 full-time (12 women), 62 part-time (30 women); includes 10 minority (3 Black or African American, non-Hispanic/Latino; 1 American Indian or Alaska Native, non-Hispanic/Latino; 3 Asian, non-Hispanic/Latino; 1 Hispanic/Latino; 2 Two or more races, non-Hispanic/Latino), 5 international. Average age 33. 45 applicants, 93% accepted, 35 enrolled. Expenses: Contact institution. *Financial support:* Scholarships/grants and unspecified assistantships available. Support available to part-time students. In 2019, 26 master's awarded. *Program availability:* Part-time, 100% online. *Application deadline:* For fall admission, 7/15 for domestic and international students; for spring admission, 11/1 for domestic and international students; for summer admission, 4/29 for domestic and international students. Applications are processed on a rolling basis. *Application fee:* $45 ($50 for international students). Electronic applications accepted. *Application Contact:* Dr. Susan Bashinski, Dean of the Graduate School, 816-271-4394, Fax: 816-271-4525, E-mail: graduate@missouriwestern.edu. *Dean of the College of Business & Professional Studies*, Dr. Logan Jones, 816-271-4286, E-mail: jones@missouriwestern.edu.

**Program in Forensic Investigations** Students: 8 full-time (6 women), 10 part-time (5 women); includes 5 minority (1 Black or African American, non-Hispanic/Latino; 2 Asian, non-Hispanic/Latino; 2 Two or more races, non-Hispanic/Latino), 1 international. Average age 25. 18 applicants, 83% accepted, 10 enrolled. Expenses: Contact institution. *Financial support:* Scholarships/grants and unspecified assistantships available. Support available to part-time students. In 2019, 7 master's awarded. *Program availability:* Part-time. *Application deadline:* For fall admission, 7/15 for domestic and international students; for spring admission, 11/1 for domestic and international students; for summer admission, 4/29 for domestic and international students. Applications are processed on a rolling basis. *Application fee:* $45 ($50 for international students). Electronic applications accepted. *Application Contact:* Dr. Monty Smith, Forensics Graduate Program Director, 816-271-4434, E-mail: msmith84@missouriwestern.edu. *Forensics Graduate Program Director*, Dr. Monty Smith, 816-271-4434, E-mail: msmith84@missouriwestern.edu.

**Program in Nursing** Students: 2 full-time (both women), 29 part-time (all women); includes 3 minority (1 Black or African American, non-Hispanic/Latino; 1 Asian, non-Hispanic/Latino; 1 Hispanic/Latino), 1 international. Average age 37. 13 applicants, 100% accepted, 12 enrolled. Expenses: Contact institution. *Financial support:* Scholarships/grants and unspecified assistantships available. Support available to part-time students. In 2019, 12 master's, 1 other advanced degree awarded. *Program availability:* Part-time. *Application deadline:* For fall admission, 7/15 for domestic and international students; for spring admission, 11/1 for domestic and international students; for summer admission, 4/29 for domestic and international students. Applications are processed on a rolling basis. *Application fee:* $45 ($50 for international students). Electronic applications accepted. *Application Contact:* Dr. Jacklyn Gentry, MSN Program Director and Assistant Professor, 816-271-4415, E-mail: jgentry8@missouriwestern.edu. *MSN Program Director and Assistant Professor*, Dr. Jacklyn Gentry, 816-271-4415, E-mail: jgentry8@missouriwestern.edu.

## MITCHELL HAMLINE SCHOOL OF LAW, Saint Paul, MN 55105-3076

**General Information** Independent, coed, graduate-only institution.

**GRADUATE UNITS**

**Graduate and Professional Programs** *Program availability:* Part-time, evening/weekend, blended/hybrid learning. Electronic applications accepted.

## MOLLOY COLLEGE, Rockville Centre, NY 11571-5002

**General Information** Independent, coed, comprehensive institution. *Enrollment:* 5,113 graduate, professional, and undergraduate students; 319 full-time matriculated graduate/professional students (246 women), 1,059 part-time matriculated graduate/professional students (868 women). *Enrollment by degree level:* 1,157 master's, 136 doctoral, 103 other advanced degrees. *Graduate faculty:* 81 full-time (64 women), 50 part-time/adjunct (35 women). *Tuition:* Full-time $21,510; part-time $1195 per credit hour. *Required fees:* $1100. Tuition and fees vary according to course load, degree level and program. *Graduate housing:* On-campus housing not available. *Student services:* Campus employment opportunities, campus safety program, career counseling, free psychological counseling, international student services, low-cost health insurance, services for students with disabilities, teacher training, writing training. *Library facilities:* James Edward Tobin Library plus 1 other. *Collection:* Books: 27,612 (physical), 255,591 (digital/electronic); Serial titles: 24 (physical), 63,761 (digital/electronic); Databases: 206.

**Computer facilities:** 887 computers available on campus for general student use. A campuswide network can be accessed. Online class registration is available.
Website: http://www.molloy.edu/

**General Application Contact:** Faye Hood, Assistant Director for Admissions, 516-323-4009, E-mail: fhood@molloy.edu.

**GRADUATE UNITS**

**Criminal Justice Program** Students: 9 full-time (5 women), 11 part-time (7 women); includes 10 minority (7 Black or African American, non-Hispanic/Latino; 2 Hispanic/Latino; 1 Native Hawaiian or other Pacific Islander, non-Hispanic/Latino). Average age 31. 11 applicants, 45% accepted, 3 enrolled. *Faculty:* 4 full-time (2 women), 2 part-time/adjunct (0 women). Expenses: Contact institution. *Financial support:* Application deadline: 3/1; applicants required to submit FAFSA. In 2019, 12 master's awarded. *Program availability:* Part-time, evening/weekend. *Application deadline:* Applications are processed on a rolling basis. *Application fee:* $60. Electronic applications accepted. *Application Contact:* Faye Hood, Assistant Director for Admissions, 516-323-4009, E-mail: fhood@molloy.edu. *Associate Dean/Graduate Program Director*, Dr. John Eterno, 516-323-3804, E-mail: crj@molloy.edu.

**Graduate Business Program** Students: 76 full-time (36 women), 175 part-time (101 women); includes 105 minority (36 Black or African American, non-Hispanic/Latino; 1 American Indian or Alaska Native, non-Hispanic/Latino; 22 Asian, non-Hispanic/Latino; 37 Hispanic/Latino; 1 Native Hawaiian or other Pacific Islander, non-Hispanic/Latino; 8 Two or more races, non-Hispanic/Latino), 1 international. Average age 31. 97 applicants, 72% accepted, 63 enrolled. *Faculty:* 11 full-time (3 women), 7 part-time/adjunct (4 women). Expenses: Contact institution. *Financial support:* Application deadline: 3/1; applicants required to submit FAFSA. In 2019, 103 master's awarded. *Program availability:* Part-time, evening/weekend, online only, 100% online, blended/hybrid learning. *Application deadline:* Applications are processed on a rolling basis. *Application fee:* $60. Electronic applications accepted. *Application Contact:* Faye Hood, Assistant Director for Admissions, 516-323-4009, E-mail: fhood@molloy.edu. *Assistant Vice President for Academic Affairs*, Dr. Barbara Schmidt, 516-323-3015, E-mail: MBAdean@molloy.edu.

**Graduate Education Program** Students: 97 full-time (76 women), 260 part-time (209 women); includes 92 minority (23 Black or African American, non-Hispanic/Latino; 9 Asian, non-Hispanic/Latino; 55 Hispanic/Latino; 5 Two or more races, non-Hispanic/Latino), 1 international. Average age 31. 176 applicants, 69% accepted, 106 enrolled. *Faculty:* 21 full-time (18 women), 20 part-time/adjunct (16 women). Expenses: Contact institution. *Financial support:* Application deadline: 3/1; applicants required to submit FAFSA. In 2019, 129 master's awarded. *Program availability:* Part-time, evening/weekend. *Application deadline:* Applications are processed on a rolling basis. *Application fee:* $60. Electronic applications accepted. *Application Contact:* Faye Hood, Assistant Director for Admissions, 516-323-4009, E-mail: fhood@molloy.edu. *Associate Dean and Director of Graduate Education Program*, Dr. Audra Cerruto, 516-323-3116, E-mail: acerruto@molloy.edu.

**Graduate Music Therapy Program** Students: 20 full-time (17 women), 10 part-time (7 women); includes 11 minority (1 Black or African American, non-Hispanic/Latino; 2 Asian, non-Hispanic/Latino; 7 Hispanic/Latino; 1 Two or more races, non-Hispanic/Latino), 8 international. Average age 29. 12 applicants, 50% accepted, 2 enrolled. *Faculty:* 5 full-time (4 women), 5 part-time/adjunct (3 women). Expenses: Contact institution. *Financial support:* Application deadline: 3/1; applicants required to submit FAFSA. In 2019, 12 master's awarded. *Program availability:* Part-time, evening/weekend. *Application deadline:* Applications are processed on a rolling basis. *Application fee:* $60. Electronic applications accepted. *Application Contact:* Faye Hood, Assistant Director for Admissions, 516-323-4009, E-mail: fhood@molloy.edu. *Associate Dean, Director of Graduate Music Therapy*, Suzanne Sorel, 516-323-3322, E-mail: ssorel@molloy.edu.

**Graduate Nursing Program** Students: 18 full-time (17 women), 573 part-time (520 women); includes 340 minority (181 Black or African American, non-Hispanic/Latino; 2 American Indian or Alaska Native, non-Hispanic/Latino; 100 Asian, non-Hispanic/Latino; 42 Hispanic/Latino; 5 Native Hawaiian or other Pacific Islander, non-Hispanic/Latino; 10 Two or more races, non-Hispanic/Latino), 3 international. Average age 38. 332 applicants, 60% accepted, 149 enrolled. *Faculty:* 30 full-time (28 women), 10 part-time/adjunct (6 women). Expenses: Contact institution. *Financial support:* Application deadline: 3/1; applicants required to submit FAFSA. In 2019, 136 master's, 12 doctorates, 22 other advanced degrees awarded. *Program availability:* Part-time, evening/weekend. *Application deadline:* Applications are processed on a rolling basis. *Application fee:* $60. Electronic applications accepted. *Application Contact:* Faye Hood, Assistant Director for Admissions, 516-323-4009, E-mail: fhood@molloy.edu. *Dean, The Barbara H. Hagan School of Nursing*, Dr. Marcia R. Gardner, 516-323-3651, E-mail: mgardner@molloy.edu.

**Graduate Speech-Language Pathology Program** Students: 85 full-time (83 women); includes 27 minority (7 Black or African American, non-Hispanic/Latino; 1 Asian, non-Hispanic/Latino; 16 Hispanic/Latino; 3 Two or more races, non-Hispanic/Latino). Average age 24. 193 applicants, 47% accepted, 42 enrolled. *Faculty:* 7 full-time (all women), 5 part-time/adjunct (all women). Expenses: Contact institution. *Financial support:* Application deadline: 3/1; applicants required to submit FAFSA. In 2019, 42 master's awarded. *Program availability:* Part-time, evening/weekend. *Application deadline:* Applications are processed on a rolling basis. *Application fee:* $60. Electronic applications accepted. *Application Contact:* Faye Hood, Assistant Director for Admissions, 516-323-4009, E-mail: fhood@molloy.edu. *Associate Dean, Communication Sciences and Disorders*, Dr. Susan Alimonti, 516-323-3517, E-mail: salimonti@molloy.edu.

**Program in Clinical Mental Health Counseling** Students: 14 full-time (12 women), 30 part-time (24 women); includes 14 minority (7 Black or African American, non-Hispanic/Latino; 1 Asian, non-Hispanic/Latino; 5 Hispanic/Latino; 1 Two or more races, non-Hispanic/Latino). Average age 33. 33 applicants, 45% accepted, 14 enrolled. *Faculty:* 3 full-time (2 women), 1 (woman) part-time/adjunct. Expenses: Contact institution. *Financial support:* Application deadline: 3/1; applicants required to submit FAFSA. In 2019, 13 master's awarded. *Program availability:* Part-time-only, evening/weekend. *Application deadline:* Applications are processed on a rolling basis. *Application fee:* $60. Electronic applications accepted. *Application Contact:* Faye Hood, Assistant Director for Admissions, 516-323-4009, E-mail: fhood@molloy.edu. *Associate Dean and Director, Master of Science Program Department of Clinical Mental Health Counseling*, Dr. Laura B. Kestemberg, 516-323-3842, E-mail: lkestemberg@molloy.edu.

## MONMOUTH UNIVERSITY, West Long Branch, NJ 07764-1898

**General Information** Independent, coed, comprehensive institution. CGS member. *Enrollment:* 6,371 graduate, professional, and undergraduate students; 611 full-time matriculated graduate/professional students (458 women), 879 part-time matriculated graduate/professional students (686 women). *Enrollment by degree level:* 1,304 master's, 82 doctoral, 104 other advanced degrees. *Graduate faculty:* 128 full-time (74 women), 78 part-time/adjunct (51 women). *Tuition:* Full-time $22,194; part-time $14,796 per credit. *Required fees:* $712; $178 per semester. $178 per semester. Tuition and fees vary according to course load. *Graduate housing:* Room and/or apartments available on a first-come, first-served basis to single students; on-campus housing not available to married students. *Student services:* Campus employment opportunities, campus safety program, career counseling, exercise/wellness program, free psychological counseling, international student services, low-cost health insurance, multicultural affairs office, services for students with disabilities, teacher training, writing training. *Library facilities:* Murry and Leonie Guggenheim Memorial Library at Monmouth University. *Collection:* Books: 269,305 (physical), 51,043 (digital/electronic); Serial titles: 1,072 (physical), 95,057 (digital/electronic); Databases: 232. Weekly public service hours: 96; students can reserve study rooms. *Research affiliation:* The Nature Conservancy, Ecotrust (healthy oceans and coastal communities), National Institute of Standards and Technology (NIST), National Oceanic and Atmospheric Administration (NOAA), Substance Abuse and Mental Health Services Administration (SAMHSA) (campus suicide prevention), Gordon and Betty Moore Foundation (environmental conservation, patient care).

**Computer facilities:** Computer purchase and lease plans are available. 1,000 computers available on campus for general student use. A campuswide network can be accessed. Online class registration is available.
Website: http://www.monmouth.edu/

**General Application Contact:** Lauren Vento-Cifelli, Associate Vice President of Undergraduate and Graduate Admission, 732-571-3562, Fax: 732-263-5123, E-mail: gradadm@monmouth.edu.

**GRADUATE UNITS**

**Graduate Studies** *Program availability:* Part-time, evening/weekend, 100% online, blended/hybrid learning. Electronic applications accepted.

***Leon Hess Business School*** Students: 76 full-time (39 women), 90 part-time (41 women); includes 16 minority (2 Black or African American, non-Hispanic/Latino; 6 Asian, non-Hispanic/Latino; 8 Hispanic/Latino), 9 international. Average age 32. *Faculty:* 23 full-time (6 women), 6 part-time/adjunct (0 women). Expenses: Contact institution. *Financial support:* In 2019–20, 189 students received support. Research assistantships, teaching assistantships, scholarships/grants, and unspecified assistantships available. Support available to part-time students. Financial award applicants required to submit FAFSA. In 2019, 79 master's, 1 other advanced degree awarded. *Program availability:* Part-time, evening/weekend. *Application deadline:* For fall admission, 7/15 priority date for domestic students, 6/1 for international students; for spring admission, 12/1 priority date for domestic students, 11/1 for international students; for summer admission, 5/1 for domestic students. Applications are processed on a rolling basis. *Application fee:* $50. Electronic applications accepted. *Application Contact:* Laurie Kuhn, Associate Director of Graduate Admission, 732-571-3452, Fax: 732-263-5123, E-mail: gradadm@monmouth.edu. *MBA Program Director*, Dr. Susan Gupta, 732-571-3639, Fax: 732-263-5517, E-mail: sgupta@monmouth.edu.

***Marjorie K. Unterberg School of Nursing and Health Studies*** Students: 1 (woman) full-time, 284 part-time (261 women); includes 108 minority (37 Black or African American, non-Hispanic/Latino; 38 Asian, non-Hispanic/Latino; 32 Hispanic/Latino; 1 Two or more races, non-Hispanic/Latino). Average age 39. *Faculty:* 13 full-time (all women), 9 part-time/adjunct (8 women). Expenses: Contact institution. *Financial support:* In 2019–20, 251 students received support. Research assistantships, teaching assistantships, scholarships/grants, and unspecified assistantships available. Support available to part-time students. Financial award applicants required to submit FAFSA. In 2019, 100 master's, 14 doctorates, 10 other advanced degrees awarded. *Program availability:* Part-time, evening/weekend, 100% online, blended/hybrid learning. *Application deadline:* For fall admission, 7/15 priority date for domestic students, 6/1 for international students; for spring admission, 12/1 priority date for domestic students, 11/1 for international students; for summer admission, 5/1 for domestic students. Applications are processed on a rolling basis. *Application fee:* $50. Electronic applications accepted. *Application Contact:* Laurie Kuhn, Associate Director of Graduate Admission, 732-571-3452, Fax: 732-263-5123, E-mail: gradadm@monmouth.edu. *Dean*, Dr. Ann Marie Mauro, 732-571-3443, Fax: 732-263-5131, E-mail: amauro@monmouth.edu.

***School of Education*** Students: 168 full-time (144 women), 225 part-time (197 women); includes 66 minority (20 Black or African American, non-Hispanic/Latino; 6 Asian, non-Hispanic/Latino; 37 Hispanic/Latino; 3 Two or more races, non-Hispanic/Latino), 2 international. Average age 30. *Faculty:* 28 full-time (19 women), 34 part-time/adjunct (25 women). Expenses: Contact institution. *Financial support:* In 2019–20, 337 students received support. Research assistantships, teaching assistantships, scholarships/grants, and unspecified assistantships available. Support available to part-time students. Financial award applicants required to submit FAFSA. In 2019, 108 master's, 9 other advanced degrees awarded. *Program availability:* Part-time, evening/weekend, 100% online, blended/hybrid learning. *Application deadline:* For fall admission, 7/15 priority date for domestic students, 7/1 for international students; for spring admission, 12/1 priority date for domestic students, 11/1 for international students; for summer admission, 5/1 for domestic students. Applications are processed on a rolling basis. *Application fee:* $50. Electronic applications accepted. *Application Contact:* Kirsten Sneeringer, Graduate Admission Counselor, 732-571-3452, Fax: 732-263-5123, E-mail: gradadm@monmouth.edu. *Dean*, Dr. John E. Henning, 732-263-5513, Fax: 732-263-5277, E-mail: kodonnel@monmouth.edu.

***School of Social Work*** Students: 96 full-time (85 women), 75 part-time (68 women); includes 65 minority (39 Black or African American, non-Hispanic/Latino; 2 American Indian or Alaska Native, non-Hispanic/Latino; 3 Asian, non-Hispanic/Latino; 17 Hispanic/Latino; 4 Two or more races, non-Hispanic/Latino), 2 international. Average age 31. *Faculty:* 13 full-time (9 women), 11 part-time/adjunct (10 women). Expenses: Contact institution. *Financial support:* In 2019–20, 159 students received support. Research assistantships, teaching assistantships, scholarships/grants, and unspecified assistantships available. Support available to part-time students. Financial award applicants required to submit FAFSA. In 2019, 91 master's, 2 other advanced degrees awarded. *Program availability:* Part-time, evening/weekend. *Application deadline:* For fall admission, 3/15 for domestic and international students. Applications are processed on a rolling basis. *Application fee:* $50. Electronic applications accepted. *Application Contact:* Kevin New, Graduate Admission Counselor, 732-571-3452, Fax: 732-263-5123, E-mail: gradm@monmouth.edu. *Program Director*, Dr. Elena Mazza, 732-263-5373, Fax: 732-263-5217, E-mail: emazza@monmouth.edu.

## MONROE COLLEGE, Bronx, NY 10468

**General Information** Proprietary, coed, comprehensive institution. *Graduate housing:* Rooms and/or apartments available on a first-come, first-served basis to single and married students. Housing application deadline: 5/1.

**GRADUATE UNITS**

**King Graduate School** *Program availability:* Online learning.

## MONTANA STATE UNIVERSITY, Bozeman, MT 59717

**General Information** State-supported, coed, university. CGS member. *Graduate housing:* Rooms and/or apartments available on a first-come, first-served basis to single and married students. *Research affiliation:* Phillips Environmental (microbial technology), Microvision (information transmission systems), LigoCyte Pharmaceuticals, Inc. (pharmaceuticals), Eli Lilly and Company (antifungal technology), S2 Corporation (instrumentation), ILX Lightwave (laser diodes, electro-optical test equipment).

**GRADUATE UNITS**

**The Graduate School** *Program availability:* Part-time, online learning. Electronic applications accepted.

***College of Agriculture*** *Program availability:* Part-time, online learning. Electronic applications accepted.

***College of Arts and Architecture*** *Program availability:* Part-time. Electronic applications accepted.

***College of Business*** *Program availability:* Part-time. Electronic applications accepted.

***College of Education, Health, and Human Development*** *Program availability:* Part-time, online learning. Electronic applications accepted.

***College of Engineering*** *Program availability:* Part-time. Electronic applications accepted.

***College of Letters and Science*** *Program availability:* Part-time, online learning. Electronic applications accepted.

***College of Nursing*** *Program availability:* Part-time, online learning. Electronic applications accepted.

## MONTANA STATE UNIVERSITY BILLINGS, Billings, MT 59101

**General Information** State-supported, coed, comprehensive institution. *Graduate housing:* Rooms and/or apartments available on a first-come, first-served basis to single and married students. Housing application deadline: 5/1.

**GRADUATE UNITS**

**College of Allied Health Professions** *Program availability:* Part-time, evening/weekend, 100% online, blended/hybrid learning. Electronic applications accepted.

**College of Arts and Sciences** *Program availability:* Part-time, 100% online, blended/hybrid learning. Electronic applications accepted.

**College of Education** *Program availability:* Part-time, 100% online, blended/hybrid learning. Electronic applications accepted.

## MONTANA STATE UNIVERSITY–NORTHERN, Havre, MT 59501-7751

**General Information** State-supported, coed, comprehensive institution. *Graduate housing:* Rooms and/or apartments available on a first-come, first-served basis to single students and available to married students. Housing application deadline: 8/22.

**GRADUATE UNITS**

**Graduate Programs** *Program availability:* Part-time, evening/weekend, online learning. Electronic applications accepted.

## MONTANA TECHNOLOGICAL UNIVERSITY, Butte, MT 59701-8997

**General Information** State-supported, coed, comprehensive institution. CGS member. *Enrollment:* 2,421 graduate, professional, and undergraduate students; 72 full-time matriculated graduate/professional students (25 women), 141 part-time matriculated graduate/professional students (53 women). *Enrollment by degree level:* 196 master's, 17 doctoral, 3 other advanced degrees. *Graduate faculty:* 138 full-time (49 women), 78 part-time/adjunct (35 women). *Graduate housing:* Rooms and/or apartments available on a first-come, first-served basis to single and married students. Housing application deadline: 7/1. *Student services:* Campus employment opportunities, campus safety program, career counseling, exercise/wellness program, free psychological counseling, grant writing training, international student services, low-cost health insurance, multicultural affairs office, services for students with disabilities, writing training. *Library facilities:* Montana Tech Library. *Collection:* Books: 57,343 (physical), 549,676 (digital/electronic); Serial titles: 1,862 (physical), 84,127 (digital/electronic); Databases: 146. Weekly public service hours: 80; students can reserve study rooms. *Research affiliation:* Edison Welding Institute (fuel cell design), Montana Resources, Inc. (mine reclamation and revegetation), QualTech, Inc. (battery monitor technology), Newmont Mining (mining and mineral processing), Stillwater Mining (mineral production and training), NorthWestern Energy (electric efficiency).

**Computer facilities:** 660 computers available on campus for general student use. A campuswide network can be accessed. Online class registration is available.
Website: http://www.mtech.edu/

**General Application Contact:** Daniel Stirling, Graduate School Program Manager, 406-496-4304, Fax: 406-496-4710, E-mail: gradschool@mtech.edu.

**GRADUATE UNITS**

**Department of Environmental Engineering** Students: 8 full-time (2 women); includes 1 minority (Black or African American, non-Hispanic/Latino). Average age 26. 4 applicants, 100% accepted, 4 enrolled. *Faculty:* 7 full-time (2 women). Expenses: Contact institution. *Financial support:* In 2019–20, 3 students received support, including 4 teaching assistantships with partial tuition reimbursements available (averaging $4,000 per year); research assistantships with full tuition reimbursements available, career-related internships or fieldwork, tuition waivers (full and partial), and unspecified assistantships also available. Financial award application deadline: 4/1; financial award applicants required to submit FAFSA. In 2019, 3 master's awarded. *Program availability:* Part-time. *Application deadline:* For fall admission, 4/1 priority date for domestic students, 3/1 priority date for international students; for spring admission, 10/1 priority date for domestic students, 6/1 priority date for international students. Applications are processed on a rolling basis. *Application fee:* $50. Electronic applications accepted. *Application Contact:* Daniel Stirling, Administrator, Graduate School, 406-496-4304, Fax: 406-496-4710, E-mail: gradschool@mtech.edu. *Head*, Dr. Kumar Ganesan, 406-496-4239, Fax: 406-496-4650, E-mail: kganesan@mtech.edu.

**Department of General Engineering** Students: 9 full-time (0 women), 1 part-time (0 women), 1 international. Average age 25. 6 applicants, 67% accepted, 3 enrolled. *Faculty:* 9 full-time (1 woman), 4 part-time/adjunct (0 women). Expenses: Contact institution. *Financial support:* In 2019–20, 9 students received support, including 11 teaching assistantships with partial tuition reimbursements available (averaging $3,500 per year); research assistantships with partial tuition reimbursements available, career-related internships or fieldwork, tuition waivers (full and partial), and unspecified assistantships also available. Financial award application deadline: 4/1; financial award applicants required to submit FAFSA. In 2019, 8 master's awarded. *Program availability:* Part-time. *Application deadline:* For fall admission, 4/1 priority date for domestic students, 3/1 priority date for international students; for spring admission, 10/1 priority date for domestic students, 6/1 priority date for international students. Applications are processed on a rolling basis. *Application fee:* $50. Electronic applications accepted. *Application Contact:* Daniel Stirling, Administrator, Graduate School, 406-496-4304, Fax: 406-496-4710, E-mail: gradschool@mtech.edu. *Department Head,* Dr. Jack Skinner, 406-496-4460, Fax: 406-496-4650, E-mail: JSkinner@mtech.edu.

**Department of Industrial Hygiene** Students: 19 full-time (13 women), 90 part-time (34 women); includes 15 minority (4 Black or African American, non-Hispanic/Latino; 1 American Indian or Alaska Native, non-Hispanic/Latino; 1 Asian, non-Hispanic/Latino; 8 Hispanic/Latino; 1 Native Hawaiian or other Pacific Islander, non-Hispanic/Latino), 4 international. 30 applicants, 70% accepted, 19 enrolled. *Faculty:* 9 full-time (4 women). Expenses: Contact institution. *Financial support:* In 2019–20, 15 students received support, including 9 teaching assistantships with partial tuition reimbursements available (averaging $2,400 per year); research assistantships with partial tuition reimbursements available, career-related internships or fieldwork, institutionally sponsored loans, and tuition waivers (full and partial) also available. Financial award application deadline: 4/1; financial award applicants required to submit FAFSA. In 2019, 23 master's awarded. *Program availability:* Part-time, online learning. *Application deadline:* For fall admission, 4/1 priority date for domestic students; for spring admission, 10/1 priority date for domestic students. Applications are processed on a rolling basis. *Application fee:* $50. Electronic applications accepted. *Application Contact:* Daniel Stirling, Administrator, Graduate School, 406-496-4304, Fax: 406-496-4710, E-mail: gradschool@mtech.edu. *Head,* Dr. Terry Spear, 406-496-4445, Fax: 406-496-4650, E-mail: tspear@mtech.edu.

**Department of Metallurgical/Mineral Processing Engineering** Students: 7 full-time (1 woman), 3 international. Average age 27. 4 applicants, 75% accepted, 3 enrolled. *Faculty:* 6 full-time (0 women). Expenses: Contact institution. *Financial support:* In 2019–20, 4 students received support, including 2 teaching assistantships with partial tuition reimbursements available (averaging $5,000 per year); research assistantships with partial tuition reimbursements available, career-related internships or fieldwork, tuition waivers (full and partial), and unspecified assistantships also available. Financial award application deadline: 4/1; financial award applicants required to submit FAFSA. In 2019, 2 master's awarded. *Program availability:* Part-time. *Application deadline:* For fall admission, 4/1 priority date for domestic students, 3/1 priority date for international students; for spring admission, 10/1 priority date for domestic students, 6/1 priority date for international students. Applications are processed on a rolling basis. *Application fee:* $50. Electronic applications accepted. *Application Contact:* Daniel Stirling, Administrator, Graduate School, 406-496-4304, Fax: 406-496-4710, E-mail: gradschool@mtech.edu. *Department Head,* Dr. Jerry Downey, 406-496-4578, Fax: 406-496-4664, E-mail: jdowney@mtech.edu.

**Department of Petroleum Engineering** Students: 4 full-time (0 women), 1 international. Average age 26. 15 applicants, 20% accepted, 1 enrolled. *Faculty:* 5 full-time (1 woman), 1 part-time/adjunct (0 women). Expenses: Contact institution. *Financial support:* In 2019–20, 6 students received support, including 5 teaching assistantships with partial tuition reimbursements available (averaging $4,800 per year); research assistantships, career-related internships or fieldwork, institutionally sponsored loans, tuition waivers (full and partial), and unspecified assistantships also available. Financial award application deadline: 4/1; financial award applicants required to submit FAFSA. In 2019, 3 master's awarded. *Program availability:* Part-time, evening/weekend. *Application deadline:* For fall admission, 4/1 priority date for domestic students, 3/1 priority date for international students; for spring admission, 10/1 priority date for domestic students, 6/1 priority date for international students. Applications are processed on a rolling basis. *Application fee:* $50. Electronic applications accepted. *Application Contact:* Daniel Stirling, Administrator, Graduate School, 406-496-4304, Fax: 406-496-4710, E-mail: gradschool@mtech.edu. *Head,* Dr. Todd Hoffman, 406-496-4753, Fax: 406-496-4417, E-mail: thoffman@mtech.edu.

**Electrical Engineering Program** Students: 4 full-time (0 women), 3 part-time (0 women), 2 international. Average age 28. 5 applicants, 60% accepted, 2 enrolled. *Faculty:* 4 full-time (0 women). Expenses: Contact institution. *Financial support:* In 2019–20, 3 students received support, including 5 teaching assistantships with partial tuition reimbursements available (averaging $4,000 per year); research assistantships with full tuition reimbursements available, career-related internships or fieldwork, tuition waivers (full and partial), and unspecified assistantships also available. Financial award application deadline: 4/1. In 2019, 4 master's awarded. *Program availability:* Part-time. *Application deadline:* For fall admission, 4/1 priority date for domestic students, 3/1 priority date for international students; for spring admission, 10/1 priority date for domestic students, 6/1 priority date for international students. Applications are processed on a rolling basis. *Application fee:* $50. Electronic applications accepted. *Application Contact:* Daniel Stirling, Administrator, Graduate School, 406-496-4304, Fax: 406-496-4710, E-mail: gradschool@mtech.edu. *Professor,* Dr. Matthew Donnelly, 406-496-4846, Fax: 406-496-4849, E-mail: mdonnelly@mtech.edu.

**Geosciences Programs** Students: 24 full-time (6 women), 1 part-time (0 women); includes 1 minority (Hispanic/Latino), 2 international. Average age 28. 27 applicants, 52% accepted, 11 enrolled. *Faculty:* 18 full-time (5 women), 6 part-time/adjunct (2 women). Expenses: Contact institution. *Financial support:* In 2019–20, 15 students received support, including 10 teaching assistantships with partial tuition reimbursements available (averaging $5,000 per year); research assistantships with partial tuition reimbursements available, career-related internships or fieldwork, tuition waivers (full and partial), and unspecified assistantships also available. Financial award application deadline: 4/1; financial award applicants required to submit FAFSA. In 2019, 13 master's awarded. *Program availability:* Part-time. *Application deadline:* For fall admission, 4/1 priority date for domestic students, 3/1 priority date for international students; for spring admission, 10/1 priority date for domestic students, 7/1 priority date for international students. Applications are processed on a rolling basis. *Application fee:* $50. Electronic applications accepted. *Application Contact:* Daniel Stirling, Administrator, Graduate School, 406-496-4304, Fax: 406-496-4710, E-mail: gradschool@mtech.edu. *Department Head,* Dr. Glenn Shaw, 406-496-4809, Fax: 406-496-4260, E-mail: gshaw@mtech.edu.

**Health Care Informatics Program** Students: 1 part-time (0 women). Average age 42. *Faculty:* 4 full-time (2 women). Expenses: Contact institution. *Financial support:* Scholarships/grants available. Financial award application deadline: 4/1; financial award applicants required to submit FAFSA. In 2019, 3 Certificates awarded. *Program availability:* Part-time, evening/weekend, online learning. *Application deadline:* For fall admission, 4/1 priority date for domestic students, 3/1 priority date for international students; for spring admission, 10/1 priority date for domestic students, 6/1 priority date for international students. Applications are processed on a rolling basis. *Application fee:* $50. Electronic applications accepted. *Application Contact:* Daniel Stirling, Administrator, Graduate School, 406-496-4304, Fax: 406-496-4710, E-mail: gradschool@mtech.edu. *Department Head,* Dr. Charie Faught, 406-496-4884, Fax: 406-496-4435, E-mail: cfaught@mtech.edu.

**Interdisciplinary Program** Students: 5 full-time (4 women), 2 part-time (1 woman); includes 2 minority (1 Black or African American, non-Hispanic/Latino; 1 American Indian or Alaska Native, non-Hispanic/Latino), 1 international. Average age 28. 5 applicants, 80% accepted, 3 enrolled. *Faculty:* 9 full-time (5 women), 4 part-time/adjunct (2 women). Expenses: Contact institution. *Financial support:* In 2019–20, 3 students received support. Research assistantships, teaching assistantships, career-related internships or fieldwork, tuition waivers (full and partial), and unspecified assistantships available. In 2019, 3 master's awarded. *Program availability:* Part-time. *Application deadline:* For fall admission, 4/1 for domestic students, 3/1 priority date for international students; for spring admission, 10/1 for domestic students, 6/1 priority date for international students. *Application fee:* $50. *Application Contact:* Daniel Stirling, Administrator, Graduate School, 406-496-4304, Fax: 406-496-4710, E-mail: gradschool@mtech.edu. *Vice Chancellor of Research/Dean of the Graduate School,* Dr. Beverly Hartline, 406-496-4456, E-mail: graduatedean@mtech.edu.

**Materials Science Ph.D.** Students: 16 full-time (4 women), 1 (woman) part-time; includes 1 minority (Black or African American, non-Hispanic/Latino), 4 international. Average age 32. 10 applicants, 40% accepted, 4 enrolled. *Faculty:* 14 full-time (4 women), 4 part-time/adjunct (1 woman). Expenses: Contact institution. *Financial support:* In 2019–20, 4 research assistantships with full tuition reimbursements (averaging $24,000 per year) were awarded; teaching assistantships, Federal Work-Study, health care benefits, tuition waivers (full), and unspecified assistantships also available. Financial award application deadline: 4/1; financial award applicants required to submit FAFSA. In 2019, 2 doctorates awarded. *Application deadline:* For fall admission, 4/1 for domestic students, 6/1 for international students; for spring admission, 9/1 for domestic and international students. *Application fee:* $50. *Application Contact:* Daniel Stirling, Administrator, Graduate School, 406-496-4304, Fax: 406-496-4723, E-mail: gradschool@mtech.edu. *Professor, Metallurgical and Materials Engineering,* Dr. Jerry Downey, 406-496-4578, Fax: 406-496-4723, E-mail: jdowney@mtech.edu.

**Mining Engineering Program** Students: 5 full-time (3 women), 3 international. Average age 26. 8 applicants, 75% accepted, 3 enrolled. *Faculty:* 4 full-time (0 women). Expenses: Contact institution. *Financial support:* In 2019–20, 2 students received support, including 2 teaching assistantships with partial tuition reimbursements available (averaging $4,000 per year); research assistantships, career-related internships or fieldwork, tuition waivers (full and partial), and unspecified assistantships also available. Financial award application deadline: 4/1; financial award applicants required to submit FAFSA. In 2019, 4 master's awarded. *Program availability:* Part-time. *Application deadline:* For fall admission, 4/1 priority date for domestic students, 3/1 priority date for international students; for spring admission, 10/1 priority date for domestic students, 6/1 priority date for international students. Applications are processed on a rolling basis. *Application fee:* $50. Electronic applications accepted. *Application Contact:* Daniel Stirling, Administrator, Graduate School, 406-496-4304, Fax: 406-496-4710, E-mail: gradschool@mtech.edu. *Department Head,* Dr. Scott Rosenthal, 406-496-4867, Fax: 406-496-4260, E-mail: srosenthal@mtech.edu.

**Project Engineering and Management Program** Students: 5 part-time (1 woman). Average age 36. 6 applicants, 83% accepted, 4 enrolled. *Faculty:* 1 full-time (0 women), 8 part-time/adjunct (2 women). Expenses: Contact institution. *Financial support:* Application deadline: 4/1; applicants required to submit FAFSA. In 2019, 4 master's awarded. *Program availability:* Part-time, evening/weekend, online learning. *Application deadline:* For fall admission, 4/1 priority date for domestic students, 3/1 priority date for international students; for spring admission, 10/1 priority date for domestic students, 8/1 priority date for international students. Applications are processed on a rolling basis. *Application fee:* $50. Electronic applications accepted. *Application Contact:* Daniel Stirling, Administrator, Graduate School, 406-496-4304, Fax: 406-496-4710, E-mail: gradschoo@mtech.edu. *Director,* Dr. Kumar Ganesan, 406-496-4239, Fax: 406-496-4650, E-mail: kganesan@mtech.edu.

## MONTCLAIR STATE UNIVERSITY, Montclair, NJ 07043-1624

**General Information** State-supported, coed, university. CGS member. *Graduate housing:* Room and/or apartments available on a first-come, first-served basis to single students; on-campus housing not available to married students. Housing application deadline: 3/1. *Research affiliation:* Spencer Foundation (education improvement), The International Society for Optical Engineering (optics and photonics), Deafness Research Foundation (hearing science).

**GRADUATE UNITS**

**The Graduate School** *Program availability:* Part-time, evening/weekend. Electronic applications accepted.

***College of Education and Human Services*** *Program availability:* Part-time, evening/weekend. Electronic applications accepted.

***College of Humanities and Social Sciences*** *Program availability:* Part-time, evening/weekend. Electronic applications accepted.

***College of Science and Mathematics*** *Program availability:* Part-time, evening/weekend. Electronic applications accepted.

***College of the Arts*** *Program availability:* Part-time, evening/weekend. Electronic applications accepted.

***Feliciano School of Business*** *Program availability:* Part-time, evening/weekend. Electronic applications accepted.

## MONTREAT COLLEGE, Montreat, NC 28757-1267

**General Information** Independent-religious, coed, comprehensive institution. *Graduate housing:* On-campus housing not available.

**GRADUATE UNITS**

**School of Professional and Adult Studies** *Program availability:* Part-time, evening/weekend, online learning. Electronic applications accepted.

## MOODY BIBLE INSTITUTE, Chicago, IL 60610-3284

**General Information** Independent-religious, coed, comprehensive institution. *Graduate housing:* Rooms and/or apartments guaranteed to single students and available on a first-come, first-served basis to married students. Housing application deadline: 6/1.

**GRADUATE UNITS**

**Graduate School** *Program availability:* Part-time.

## MOODY THEOLOGICAL SEMINARY–MICHIGAN, Plymouth, MI 48170

**General Information** Independent-religious, coed, graduate-only institution. *Graduate housing:* On-campus housing not available.

**GRADUATE UNITS**

**Graduate Programs** *Program availability:* Part-time, evening/weekend.

## MOORE COLLEGE OF ART & DESIGN, Philadelphia, PA 19103

**General Information** Independent, Undergraduate: women only; graduate: coed, comprehensive institution.

**GRADUATE UNITS**

**Program in Art Education** *Program availability:* Part-time.

**Program in Community Practice**

**Program in Interior Design** *Program availability:* Evening/weekend.

**Program in Social Engagement** *Program availability:* Part-time.

**Program in Studio Art**

## MORAVIAN COLLEGE, Bethlehem, PA 18018-6650

**General Information** Independent-religious, coed, comprehensive institution. *Enrollment:* 2,595 graduate, professional, and undergraduate students; 127 full-time matriculated graduate/professional students (96 women), 318 part-time matriculated graduate/professional students (235 women). *Enrollment by degree level:* 342 master's, 23 doctoral, 64 other advanced degrees. *Graduate faculty:* 14 full-time (11 women), 16 part-time/adjunct (7 women). *Tuition:* Full-time $16,848; part-time $2808 per course. *Required fees:* $90; $45 per semester. Tuition and fees vary according to program. *Graduate housing:* On-campus housing not available. *Student services:* Campus employment opportunities, campus safety program, career counseling, exercise/wellness program, free psychological counseling, international student services, multicultural affairs office, services for students with disabilities, teacher training, writing training. *Library facilities:* Reeves Library. *Collection:* Books: 225,810 (physical), 288,179 (digital/electronic); Serial titles: 164 (physical), 5,827 (digital/electronic); Databases: 67. Weekly public service hours: 86.

**Computer facilities:** Computer purchase and lease plans are available. 230 computers available on campus for general student use. A campuswide network can be accessed. Online class registration is available.
Website: http://www.moravian.edu/

**General Application Contact:** Scott Dams, VP for Enrollment and Marketing, 610-861-1400, E-mail: graduate@moravian.edu.

**GRADUATE UNITS**

**Graduate and Continuing Studies** Students: 127 full-time (96 women), 318 part-time (235 women); includes 65 minority (14 Black or African American, non-Hispanic/Latino; 1 American Indian or Alaska Native, non-Hispanic/Latino; 13 Asian, non-Hispanic/Latino; 35 Hispanic/Latino; 1 Native Hawaiian or other Pacific Islander, non-Hispanic/Latino; 1 Two or more races, non-Hispanic/Latino), 3 international. Average age 32. 725 applicants, 60% accepted, 295 enrolled. *Faculty:* 14 full-time (11 women), 16 part-time/adjunct (7 women). Expenses: Contact institution. *Financial support:* Applicants required to submit FAFSA. In 2019, 92 master's awarded. *Program availability:* Part-time, evening/weekend, 100% online, blended/hybrid learning. *Application deadline:* For fall admission, 8/1 priority date for domestic and international students; for spring admission, 1/1 priority date for domestic and international students; for summer admission, 5/1 priority date for domestic and international students. Applications are processed on a rolling basis. Electronic applications accepted. *Application Contact:* Scott Dams, VP of Enrollment and Marketing, 610-861-1400, Fax: 610-861-1466, E-mail: graduate@moravian.edu. *VP of Enrollment and Marketing,* Scott Dams, 610-861-1400, Fax: 610-861-1466, E-mail: graduate@moravian.edu.

***Helen S. Breidegam School of Nursing*** Students: 5 full-time (4 women), 103 part-time (95 women); includes 19 minority (4 Black or African American, non-Hispanic/Latino; 8 Asian, non-Hispanic/Latino; 7 Hispanic/Latino), 1 international. Average age 37. 131 applicants, 69% accepted, 85 enrolled. *Faculty:* 2 full-time (both women), 3 part-time/adjunct (2 women). Expenses: Contact institution. *Financial support:* Applicants required to submit FAFSA. In 2019, 25 master's awarded. *Program availability:* Part-time, evening/weekend. *Application deadline:* For fall admission, 8/1 priority date for domestic and international students; for spring admission, 1/1 priority date for domestic and international students; for summer admission, 5/1 priority date for domestic and international students. Applications are processed on a rolling basis. Electronic applications accepted. *Application Contact:* Caroline Bechtel, Student Experience Mentor, 610-861-1400, Fax: 610-861-1466, E-mail: graduate@moravian.edu.

## MORAVIAN THEOLOGICAL SEMINARY, Bethlehem, PA 18018-6614

**General Information** Independent-religious, coed, graduate-only institution. *Enrollment by degree level:* 61 master's, 12 other advanced degrees. *Graduate faculty:* 9 full-time (4 women), 1 (woman) part-time/adjunct. *Tuition:* Full-time $680; part-time $680 per credit hour. *Required fees:* $430; $430 per term. $215 per term. *Graduate housing:* Rooms and/or apartments available on a first-come, first-served basis to single and married students. Typical cost: $865 per year for single students; $865 per year for married students. Housing application deadline: 7/31. *Student services:* Campus employment opportunities, campus safety program, exercise/wellness program, international student services, low-cost health insurance, multicultural affairs office, services for students with disabilities, writing training. *Library facilities:* Reeves Library. *Collection:* Books: 192,017 (physical), 137,800 (digital/electronic); Serial titles: 6,082 (physical), 2,168 (digital/electronic); Databases: 62. Weekly public service hours: 100; students can reserve study rooms.

**Computer facilities:** 227 computers available on campus for general student use. A campuswide network can be accessed from student residence rooms and from off campus. Online class registration is available.
Website: http://www.moravianseminary.edu/

**General Application Contact:** Rev. Randy D'Angelo, Director of Seminary Enrollment, 610-861-1512, Fax: 610-861-1569, E-mail: dangelor@moravian.edu.

**GRADUATE UNITS**

**Graduate and Certificate Programs** Students: 14 full-time (8 women), 62 part-time (45 women); includes 14 minority (2 Black or African American, non-Hispanic/Latino; 11 Hispanic/Latino; 1 Two or more races, non-Hispanic/Latino), 2 international. Average age 44. 124 applicants, 14% accepted, 16 enrolled. *Faculty:* 9 full-time (4 women), 1 (woman) part-time/adjunct. Expenses: Contact institution. *Financial support:* In 2019–20, 46 students received support. Career-related internships or fieldwork, Federal Work-Study, and scholarships/grants available. Support available to part-time students. Financial award application deadline: 7/15; financial award applicants required to submit FAFSA. In 2019, 13 master's, 1 other advanced degree awarded. *Program availability:* Part-time. *Application deadline:* For fall admission, 7/15 for domestic students, 4/1 priority date for international students; for spring admission, 11/15 for domestic students, 9/1 priority date for international students. Applications are processed on a rolling basis. *Application fee:* $50. Electronic applications accepted. *Application Contact:* Rev. Randy L. D'Angelo, Director of Seminary Enrollment, 610-861-1512, Fax: 610-861-1569, E-mail: dangelor@moravian.edu. *Dean and Vice President,* Rev. Dr. Frank L. Crouch, 610-861-1516, E-mail: crouchf@moravian.edu.

## MOREHEAD STATE UNIVERSITY, Morehead, KY 40351

**General Information** State-supported, coed, comprehensive institution. *Enrollment:* 9,660 graduate, professional, and undergraduate students; 205 full-time matriculated graduate/professional students (122 women), 491 part-time matriculated graduate/professional students (331 women). *Enrollment by degree level:* 547 master's, 74 doctoral, 75 other advanced degrees. *Graduate faculty:* 157 full-time (76 women), 33 part-time/adjunct (15 women). *Tuition, area resident:* Part-time $570 per credit hour. Tuition, state resident: part-time $570 per credit hour. Tuition, nonresident: part-time $570 per credit hour. *Required fees:* $14 per credit hour. *Graduate housing:* Room and/or apartments available on a first-come, first-served basis to single students; on-campus housing not available to married students. Typical cost: $2650 per year ($4850 including board). Room and board charges vary according to board plan and housing facility selected. *Student services:* Campus employment opportunities, campus safety program, career counseling, exercise/wellness program, free psychological counseling, grant writing training, international student services, low-cost health insurance, multicultural affairs office, services for students with disabilities, teacher training, writing training. *Library facilities:* Camden Carroll Library. *Collection:* Books: 347,507 (physical), 215,552 (digital/electronic); Serial titles: 52,680 (physical), 104,203 (digital/electronic); Databases: 159. Students can reserve study rooms.

**Computer facilities:** 950 computers available on campus for general student use. A campuswide network can be accessed. Online class registration is available.
Website: http://www.moreheadstate.edu/

**General Application Contact:** Susan Maxey, Director of Graduate School/ Certification Officer, 606-7832317, Fax: 606-7835061, E-mail: s.maxey@moreheadstate.edu.

**GRADUATE UNITS**

**Graduate School** Students: 205 full-time (122 women), 491 part-time (331 women); includes 84 minority (49 Black or African American, non-Hispanic/Latino; 1 American Indian or Alaska Native, non-Hispanic/Latino; 4 Asian, non-Hispanic/Latino; 15 Hispanic/Latino; 15 Two or more races, non-Hispanic/Latino), 16 international. 367 applicants, 72% accepted, 145 enrolled. *Faculty:* 157 full-time (76 women), 33 part-time/adjunct (15 women). Expenses: Contact institution. *Financial support:* In 2019–20, 180 students received support, including 79 research assistantships (averaging $10,000 per year), 42 teaching assistantships (averaging $10,000 per year); career-related internships or fieldwork and unspecified assistantships also available. Financial award applicants required to submit FAFSA. In 2019, 279 master's, 20 other advanced degrees awarded. *Program availability:* Part-time, evening/weekend, 100% online, blended/hybrid learning. *Application deadline:* For fall admission, 8/1 priority date for domestic and international students; for spring admission, 12/1 priority date for domestic and international students. Applications are processed on a rolling basis. *Application fee:* $30. Electronic applications accepted. *Application Contact:* Michelle Emrick, Graduate Admissions Specialist, 606-783-5204, E-mail: m.emrick@moreheadstate.edu. *Director for Graduate and Undergraduate Programs/Certifications,* Dr. Susan Maxey, 606-783-2317, Fax: 606-783-5061, E-mail: s.maxey@moreheadstate.edu.

***Caudill College of Arts, Humanities and Social Sciences*** Students: 50 full-time (29 women), 62 part-time (44 women); includes 12 minority (7 Black or African American, non-Hispanic/Latino; 3 Hispanic/Latino; 2 Two or more races, non-Hispanic/Latino), 2 international. 97 applicants, 72% accepted, 39 enrolled. *Faculty:* 58 full-time (28 women), 6 part-time/adjunct (3 women). Expenses: Contact institution. *Financial support:* In 2019–20, 14 research assistantships (averaging $10,000 per year), 13 teaching assistantships (averaging $10,000 per year) were awarded; career-related internships or fieldwork, Federal Work-Study, and unspecified assistantships also available. Financial award application deadline: 3/15; financial award applicants required to submit FAFSA. In 2019, 45 master's awarded. *Program availability:* Part-time, 100% online, blended/hybrid learning. *Application deadline:* For fall admission, 8/1 priority date for domestic and international students; for spring admission, 12/1 priority date for domestic and international students. Applications are processed on a rolling basis. *Application fee:* $30. Electronic applications accepted. *Application Contact:* Dr. Scott Davison, Dean, 606-7832273, E-mail: s.davison@moreheadstate.edu. *Dean,* Dr. Scott Davison, 606-7832273, E-mail: s.davison@moreheadstate.edu.

***College of Science*** Students: 49 full-time (35 women), 35 part-time (29 women); includes 10 minority (4 Black or African American, non-Hispanic/Latino; 1 Hispanic/Latino; 5 Two or more races, non-Hispanic/Latino). 60 applicants, 68% accepted, 29 enrolled. *Faculty:* 47 full-time (21 women), 6 part-time/adjunct (3 women). Expenses: Contact institution. *Financial support:* Research assistantships, teaching assistantships, career-related internships or fieldwork, and unspecified assistantships available. Financial award applicants required to submit FAFSA. In 2019, 24 master's awarded. *Program availability:* Part-time, evening/weekend. *Application deadline:* Applications are processed on a rolling basis. *Application fee:* $30. Electronic applications accepted. *Application Contact:* Dr. Wayne Creger Miller, Dean, 606-7832158, E-mail: w.miller@moreheadstate.edu. *Dean,* Dr. Wayne Creger Miller, 606-7832158, E-mail: w.miller@moreheadstate.edu.

***Elmer R. Smith College of Business and Technology*** Students: 49 full-time (14 women), 109 part-time (55 women); includes 17 minority (6 Black or African American, non-Hispanic/Latino; 4 Asian, non-Hispanic/Latino; 6 Hispanic/Latino; 1 Two or more races, non-Hispanic/Latino), 14 international. 96 applicants, 71% accepted, 28 enrolled. *Faculty:* 29 full-time (10 women), 7 part-time/adjunct (2 women). Expenses: Contact institution. *Financial support:* Research assistantships, teaching assistantships, career-related internships or fieldwork, and unspecified assistantships available. Financial award applicants required to submit FAFSA. In 2019, 66 master's awarded. *Program availability:* Part-time, evening/weekend, 100% online, blended/hybrid learning. *Application deadline:* Applications are processed on a rolling basis. *Application fee:* $30. Electronic applications accepted. *Application Contact:* Dr. Johnathan Kyle Nelson, Dean, Elmer R Smith School of Business & Technology, 606-783-2090, E-mail: j.nelson@moreheadstate.edu. *Dean, Elmer R Smith School of Business & Technology,* Dr. Johnathan Kyle Nelson, 606-783-2090, E-mail: j.nelson@moreheadstate.edu.

***Ernst & Sara Lane Volgenau College of Education*** Students: 59 full-time (46 women), 279 part-time (197 women); includes 43 minority (32 Black or African American, non-Hispanic/Latino; 1 American Indian or Alaska Native, non-Hispanic/Latino; 4 Hispanic/Latino; 6 Two or more races, non-Hispanic/Latino). 114 applicants, 74% accepted, 49 enrolled. *Faculty:* 23 full-time (17 women), 14 part-time/adjunct (7 women). Expenses: Contact institution. *Financial support:* Research assistantships, teaching assistantships, career-related internships or fieldwork, Federal Work-Study, and unspecified assistantships available. Financial award applicants required to submit FAFSA. In 2019, 144 master's, 20 other advanced degrees awarded. *Program availability:* Part-time, evening/weekend. *Application deadline:* For fall admission, 8/1 priority date for domestic and international students; for spring admission, 12/1 priority date for domestic and international students. Applications are processed on a rolling basis. *Application fee:* $30. Electronic applications accepted. *Application Contact:* Dr. Antony D. Norman, Dean, 606-7832162, E-mail: adnorman@moreheadstate.edu. *Dean*, Dr. Antony D. Norman, 606-7832162, E-mail: adnorman@moreheadstate.edu.

## MOREHOUSE SCHOOL OF MEDICINE, Atlanta, GA 30310-1495

**General Information** Independent, coed, graduate-only institution. CGS member. *Enrollment by degree level:* 147 master's, 446 doctoral. *Graduate faculty:* 240 full-time (129 women), 69 part-time/adjunct (40 women). *Graduate housing:* On-campus housing not available. *Student services:* Campus employment opportunities, career counseling, exercise/wellness program, free psychological counseling, international student services. *Library facilities:* MSM Library. *Research affiliation:* Merck & Company, Inc. (hypotension), CareStat (renal insufficiency), Wyeth (helicobacter pylori study), Bristol-Myers Squibb (pharmacokinetics), Parke-Davis (cardiovascular risk factors), NitroMel, Inc. (heart failure).

**Computer facilities:** Online class registration is available.
Website: http://www.msm.edu/

**General Application Contact:** Director of Admissions, 404-752-1650, Fax: 404-752-1512.

**GRADUATE UNITS**

**Graduate Programs in Biomedical Sciences** Electronic applications accepted.

**Master of Public Health Program** *Program availability:* Part-time. Electronic applications accepted.

**Master of Science in Clinical Research Program** *Program availability:* Part-time. Electronic applications accepted.

**Professional Program** Electronic applications accepted.

## MORGAN STATE UNIVERSITY, Baltimore, MD 21251

**General Information** State-supported, coed, university. CGS member. *Enrollment:* 7,005 graduate, professional, and undergraduate students; 999 full-time matriculated graduate/professional students (651 women), 303 part-time matriculated graduate/professional students (185 women). *Enrollment by degree level:* 677 master's, 596 doctoral, 29 other advanced degrees. *Graduate faculty:* 467 full-time (210 women), 223 part-time/adjunct (112 women). Tuition, state resident: full-time $455; part-time $455 per credit hour. Tuition, nonresident: full-time $894; part-time $894 per credit hour. *Required fees:* $82; $82 per credit hour. *Graduate housing:* On-campus housing not available. *Student services:* Campus employment opportunities, campus safety program, career counseling, child daycare facilities, free psychological counseling, grant writing training, international student services, low-cost health insurance, services for students with disabilities, teacher training, writing training. *Library facilities:* Earl S Richardson Library. *Collection:* Books: 399,671 (physical), 60,730 (digital/electronic); Serial titles: 1,994 (physical). Weekly public service hours: 97; students can reserve study rooms.

**Computer facilities:** A campuswide network can be accessed. Online class registration is available.
Website: http://www.morgan.edu/

**General Application Contact:** Dr. Jahmaine Smith, Director, Graduate Admissions, 443-885-3185, Fax: 443-885-8226, E-mail: gradapply@morgan.edu.

**GRADUATE UNITS**

**School of Graduate Studies** Students: 999 full-time (651 women), 303 part-time (185 women); includes 1,029 minority (907 Black or African American, non-Hispanic/Latino; 30 Asian, non-Hispanic/Latino; 50 Hispanic/Latino; 42 Two or more races, non-Hispanic/Latino), 152 international. Average age 37. 742 applicants, 79% accepted, 290 enrolled. *Faculty:* 467 full-time (210 women), 223 part-time/adjunct (112 women). Expenses: Contact institution. *Financial support:* In 2019–20, 307 students received support. Fellowships with full and partial tuition reimbursements available, research assistantships with full and partial tuition reimbursements available, teaching assistantships with full and partial tuition reimbursements available, career-related internships or fieldwork, Federal Work-Study, scholarships/grants, tuition waivers (full and partial), and unspecified assistantships available. Support available to part-time students. Financial award application deadline: 2/1. In 2019, 248 master's, 71 doctorates, 1 other advanced degree awarded. *Program availability:* Part-time, evening/weekend, 100% online. *Application deadline:* For fall admission, 2/1 priority date for domestic and international students; for spring admission, 10/1 priority date for domestic and international students. Applications are processed on a rolling basis. *Application fee:* $50 ($70 for international students). Electronic applications accepted. *Application Contact:* Paul Voos, Assistant Dean, 443-885-3185, Fax: 443-885-8226, E-mail: paul.voos@morgan.edu. *Dean*, Dr. Mark Garrison, 443-885-3185, Fax: 443-885-8226, E-mail: mark.garrisonr@morgan.edu.

***Clarence M. Mitchell, Jr. School of Engineering*** Students: 113 full-time (34 women), 24 part-time (4 women); includes 88 minority (75 Black or African American, non-Hispanic/Latino; 8 Asian, non-Hispanic/Latino; 2 Hispanic/Latino; 3 Two or more races, non-Hispanic/Latino), 36 international. Average age 35. 78 applicants, 83% accepted, 26 enrolled. *Faculty:* 35 full-time (8 women), 19 part-time/adjunct (4 women). Expenses: Contact institution. *Financial support:* In 2019–20, 35 students received support. Fellowships with full and partial tuition reimbursements available, research assistantships with full and partial tuition reimbursements available, teaching assistantships with full and partial tuition reimbursements available, career-related internships or fieldwork, scholarships/grants, and unspecified assistantships available. Financial award application deadline: 2/1. In 2019, 23 master's, 11 doctorates awarded. *Program availability:* Part-time, evening/weekend. *Application deadline:* For fall admission, 2/1 priority date for domestic students; for spring admission, 10/1 priority date for domestic students. Applications are processed on a rolling basis. *Application fee:* $50 ($70 for international students). Electronic applications accepted. *Application Contact:* Dr. Jahmaine Smith, Director of Admissions, 443-885-3185, Fax: 443-885-8226, E-mail: gradapply@morgan.edu. *Interim Dean*, Dr. Craig Scott, 443-885-3231, E-mail: craig.scott@morgan.edu.

***Earl G. Graves School of Business and Management*** Students: 93 full-time (51 women), 41 part-time (15 women); includes 86 minority (77 Black or African American, non-Hispanic/Latino; 2 Asian, non-Hispanic/Latino; 2 Hispanic/Latino; 5 Two or more races, non-Hispanic/Latino), 40 international. Average age 34. 114 applicants, 59% accepted, 28 enrolled. *Faculty:* 61 full-time (27 women), 20 part-time/adjunct (5 women). Expenses: Contact institution. *Financial support:* In 2019–20, 75 students received support. Fellowships with full tuition reimbursements available, research assistantships with full tuition reimbursements available, teaching assistantships with full tuition reimbursements available, career-related internships or fieldwork, Federal Work-Study, scholarships/grants, tuition waivers (full and partial), and unspecified assistantships available. Support available to part-time students. Financial award application deadline: 2/1. In 2019, 52 master's, 2 doctorates awarded. *Program availability:* Part-time, evening/weekend, 100% online. *Application deadline:* For fall admission, 4/1 for domestic and international students. Applications are processed on a rolling basis. *Application fee:* $50 ($70 for international students). Electronic applications accepted. *Application Contact:* Dr. Jahmaine Smith, Director of Admissions, 443-885-3185, Fax: 443-885-8226, E-mail: gradapply@morgan.edu. *Dean*, Dr. Fikru Boghossian, 443-885-3609, E-mail: fikru.boghossian@morgan.edu.

***James H. Gilliam Jr College of Liberal Arts*** Students: 95 full-time (63 women), 22 part-time (18 women); includes 93 minority (81 Black or African American, non-Hispanic/Latino; 7 Hispanic/Latino; 5 Two or more races, non-Hispanic/Latino), 13 international. Average age 36. 49 applicants, 80% accepted, 19 enrolled. *Faculty:* 128 full-time (62 women), 37 part-time/adjunct (13 women). Expenses: Contact institution. *Financial support:* In 2019–20, 32 students received support. Fellowships with full and partial tuition reimbursements available, research assistantships with full and partial tuition reimbursements available, teaching assistantships with full and partial tuition reimbursements available, career-related internships or fieldwork, scholarships/grants, tuition waivers (full and partial), and unspecified assistantships available. Support available to part-time students. Financial award application deadline: 2/1. In 2019, 30 master's, 5 doctorates awarded. *Program availability:* Part-time, evening/weekend. *Application deadline:* For fall admission, 2/1 priority date for domestic students, 4/1 for international students; for spring admission, 11/15 priority date for domestic students, 10/1 for international students. Applications are processed on a rolling basis. *Application fee:* $50 ($70 for international students). Electronic applications accepted. *Application Contact:* Jahmaine Smith, Director of Admissions, 443-885-3185, Fax: 443-885-8226, E-mail: Jahmaine.smith@morgan.edu. *Dean*, Dr. M'bare N'gom, 443-885-3090, E-mail: mbare.ngom@morgan.edu.

***School of Architecture and Planning*** Students: 53 full-time (27 women), 23 part-time (16 women); includes 47 minority (33 Black or African American, non-Hispanic/Latino; 6 Asian, non-Hispanic/Latino; 6 Hispanic/Latino; 2 Two or more races, non-Hispanic/Latino), 3 international. Average age 33. 34 applicants, 88% accepted, 15 enrolled. *Faculty:* 30 full-time (11 women), 22 part-time/adjunct (7 women). Expenses: Contact institution. *Financial support:* In 2019–20, 10 students received support. Fellowships with full tuition reimbursements available, research assistantships with full tuition reimbursements available, teaching assistantships with full tuition reimbursements available, career-related internships or fieldwork, Federal Work-Study, scholarships/grants, tuition waivers (full and partial), and unspecified assistantships available. Support available to part-time students. Financial award application deadline: 2/1. In 2019, 25 master's awarded. *Program availability:* Part-time, evening/weekend, 100% online. *Application deadline:* For fall admission, 5/1 for domestic students, 4/1 for international students; for spring admission, 11/15 for domestic students, 10/1 for international students. Applications are processed on a rolling basis. *Application fee:* $50 ($70 for international students). Electronic applications accepted. *Application Contact:* Dr. Jahmaine Smith, Director of Admissions, 443-885-3185, Fax: 443-885-8226, E-mail: gradapply@morgan.edu. *Dean*, Dr. Mary Anne Akers, 443-885-3225, Fax: 443-885-8233, E-mail: maryanne.akers@morgan.edu.

***School of Community Health and Policy*** Students: 91 full-time (77 women), 25 part-time (19 women); includes 99 minority (94 Black or African American, non-Hispanic/Latino; 2 Asian, non-Hispanic/Latino; 1 Hispanic/Latino; 2 Two or more races, non-Hispanic/Latino), 12 international. Average age 36. 63 applicants, 67% accepted, 14 enrolled. *Faculty:* 28 full-time (19 women), 24 part-time/adjunct (19 women). Expenses: Contact institution. *Financial support:* In 2019–20, 36 students received support. Fellowships with full and partial tuition reimbursements available, research assistantships with full and partial tuition reimbursements available, teaching assistantships with full and partial tuition reimbursements available, career-related internships or fieldwork, Federal Work-Study, scholarships/grants, tuition waivers (full and partial), and unspecified assistantships available. Support available to part-time students. Financial award application deadline: 2/1. In 2019, 19 master's, 6 doctorates awarded. *Program availability:* Part-time, evening/weekend, 100% online. *Application deadline:* For fall admission, 4/15 for domestic students, 4/1 for international students. Applications are processed on a rolling basis. *Application fee:* $50 ($70 for international students). Electronic applications accepted. *Application Contact:* Dr. Jahmine Smith, Director of Admissions, 443-885-3185, Fax: 443-885-8226, E-mail: gradapply@morgan.edu. *Dean*, Dr. Kim Dobson Sydnor, 443-885-3560, E-mail: kim.sydnor@morgan.edu.

***School of Computer, Mathematical, and Natural Sciences*** Students: 64 full-time (33 women), 10 part-time (3 women); includes 38 minority (31 Black or African American, non-Hispanic/Latino; 3 Asian, non-Hispanic/Latino; 2 Hispanic/Latino; 2 Two or more races, non-Hispanic/Latino), 27 international. Average agé 34. 38 applicants, 84% accepted, 10 enrolled. *Faculty:* 100 full-time (32 women), 24 part-time/adjunct (9 women). Expenses: Contact institution. *Financial support:* In 2019–20, 29 students received support. Fellowships with full and partial tuition reimbursements available, research assistantships with full and partial tuition reimbursements available, teaching assistantships with full and partial tuition reimbursements available, career-related internships or fieldwork, Federal Work-Study, scholarships/grants, tuition waivers (full and partial), and unspecified assistantships available. Support available to part-time students. Financial award application deadline: 2/1. In 2019, 4 master's, 1 doctorate awarded. *Program availability:* Part-time, evening/weekend. *Application deadline:* For fall admission, 2/1 priority date for domestic students, 4/15 for international students; for spring admission, 10/1 priority date for domestic students, 10/1 for international students. Applications are processed on a rolling basis. *Application fee:* $50 ($70 for international students). Electronic applications accepted. *Application Contact:* Dr. Jahmaine Smith, Director of Admissions, 443-885-3185, Fax: 443-885-8226, E-mail: gradapply@morgan.edu. *Interim Dean*, Dr. Hongtao Yu, 443-885-4515, E-mail: Hongtao.Yu@morgan.edu.

***School of Education and Urban Studies*** Students: 275 full-time (194 women), 104 part-time (72 women); includes 325 minority (288 Black or African American, non-Hispanic/Latino; 7 Asian, non-Hispanic/Latino; 18 Hispanic/Latino; 12 Two or more races, non-Hispanic/Latino), 18 international. Average age 43. 108 applicants, 83% accepted, 57 enrolled. *Faculty:* 36 full-time (23 women), 30 part-time/adjunct (18 women). Expenses: Contact institution. *Financial support:* In 2019–20, 62 students received support. Fellowships with full and partial tuition reimbursements available, research assistantships with full and partial tuition reimbursements available, teaching assistantships with full and partial tuition reimbursements available, Federal Work-Study, institutionally sponsored loans, and tuition waivers (full and partial) available. Financial award application deadline: 2/1. In 2019, 20 master's, 38 doctorates awarded. *Program availability:* Part-time, evening/weekend, 100% online. *Application deadline:* For fall admission, 2/1 priority date for domestic students, 4/15 for international students; for spring admission, 10/1 priority date for domestic students, 4/15 for international students. Applications are processed on a rolling basis. *Application fee:* $50 ($70 for international students). Electronic applications accepted. *Application Contact:* Dr. Jahmaine Smith, Director of Admissions, 443-885-3185, Fax: 443-885-8226, E-mail: gradapply@morgan.edu. *Dean*, Dr. Glenda Prime, 443-885-3385, Fax: 443-885-8240, E-mail: glenda.prime@morgan.edu.

***School of Global Journalism and Communication*** Students: 12 full-time (7 women), 4 part-time (3 women); includes 15 minority (13 Black or African American, non-Hispanic/Latino; 2 Hispanic/Latino), 1 international. Average age 30. 8 applicants, 75% accepted, 4 enrolled. *Faculty:* 8 full-time (3 women), 3 part-time/adjunct (0 women). Expenses: Contact institution. *Financial support:* In 2019–20, 5 students received support. Fellowships with full and partial tuition reimbursements available, research assistantships with full and partial tuition reimbursements available, teaching assistantships with full and partial tuition reimbursements available, career-related internships or fieldwork, Federal Work-Study, institutionally sponsored loans, scholarships/grants, tuition waivers (full and partial), and unspecified assistantships available. Support available to part-time students. Financial award application deadline: 2/1. In 2019, 5 master's awarded. *Program availability:* Part-time, evening/weekend. *Application deadline:* For fall admission, 2/2 priority date for domestic students, 4/15 for international students. Applications are processed on a rolling basis. *Application fee:* $50 ($70 for international students). Electronic applications accepted. *Application Contact:* Dr. Jahmaine Smith, Director of Admissions, 443-885-3185, Fax: 443-885-8226, E-mail: gradapply@morgan.edu. *Dean*, DeWayne Wickham, 443-885-3330, Fax: 443-885-8322.

***School of Social Work*** Students: 193 full-time (163 women), 31 part-time (24 women); includes 216 minority (198 Black or African American, non-Hispanic/Latino; 2 Asian, non-Hispanic/Latino; 7 Hispanic/Latino; 9 Two or more races, non-Hispanic/Latino), 2 international. Average age 33. 175 applicants, 85% accepted, 83 enrolled. *Faculty:* 17 full-time (11 women), 28 part-time/adjunct (25 women). Expenses: Contact institution. *Financial support:* In 2019–20, 22 students received support. Fellowships with full and partial tuition reimbursements available, research assistantships with full and partial tuition reimbursements available, teaching assistantships with full and partial tuition reimbursements available, career-related internships or fieldwork, Federal Work-Study, scholarships/grants, tuition waivers (full and partial), and unspecified assistantships available. Financial award application deadline: 2/1. In 2019, 69 master's awarded. *Program availability:* Part-time, evening/weekend, online only, 100% online. *Application deadline:* For fall admission, 2/1 priority date for domestic students, 4/15 for international students. Applications are processed on a rolling basis. *Application fee:* $50 ($70 for international students). Electronic applications accepted. *Application Contact:* Dr. Jahmaine Smith, Director of Graduate Admissions, 443-885-3185, Fax: 443-885-8226, E-mail: gradapply@morgan.edu. *Dean*, Dr. Anna McPhatter, 443-885-4126, E-mail: anna.mcphatter@morgan.edu.

## MORNINGSIDE COLLEGE, Sioux City, IA 51106

**General Information** Independent-religious, coed, comprehensive institution. *Graduate housing:* On-campus housing not available. *Research affiliation:* Iowa Public Service Company (biology, chemistry, physics).

**GRADUATE UNITS**

**Graduate Programs** *Program availability:* Part-time, evening/weekend, online only, 100% online. Electronic applications accepted.

***Nylen School of Nursing*** *Program availability:* Part-time, online only, 100% online. Electronic applications accepted.

***Sharon Walker School of Education*** *Program availability:* Part-time, online only, 100% online. Electronic applications accepted.

## MOUNT ALLISON UNIVERSITY, Sackville, NB E4L 1E4, Canada

**General Information** Province-supported, coed, comprehensive institution. *Graduate housing:* Room and/or apartments guaranteed to single students; on-campus housing not available to married students. Housing application deadline: 8/31. *Research affiliation:* Atlantic Cancer Institute (medical research), Moncton Hospital (medical research), Huntsman Marine Science Centre (marine biology).

**GRADUATE UNITS**

**Department of Biology**

**Department of Chemistry and Biochemistry**

## MOUNT ALOYSIUS COLLEGE, Cresson, PA 16630-1999

**General Information** Independent-religious, coed, comprehensive institution. *Graduate housing:* On-campus housing not available. *Student services:* Campus employment opportunities, campus safety program, career counseling, child daycare facilities, exercise/wellness program, free psychological counseling, international student services, services for students with disabilities, writing training. *Library facilities:* Mount Aloysius College Library.

**Computer facilities:** Computer purchase and lease plans are available. A campuswide network can be accessed. Online class registration is available.
Website: http://www.mtaloy.edu/

**General Application Contact:** Matthew P. Bodenschatz, Director of Graduate and Continuing Education Admissions, 814-886-6556, Fax: 814-886-6441, E-mail: mbodenschatz@mtaloy.edu.

**GRADUATE UNITS**

**Program in Business Administration** Expenses: Contact institution. *Financial support:* Unspecified assistantships available. Financial award applicants required to submit FAFSA. *Program availability:* Part-time, evening/weekend. *Application deadline:* For fall admission, 8/1 for domestic students; for spring admission, 12/1 for domestic students. Applications are processed on a rolling basis. *Application fee:* $30. Electronic applications accepted. *Application Contact:* Matthew P. Bodenschatz, Director of Graduate and Continuing Education Admissions, 814-886-6556, Fax: 814-886-6441, E-mail: mbodenschatz@mtaloy.edu.

**Program in Community Counseling** Expenses: Contact institution. *Financial support:* Unspecified assistantships available. Financial award applicants required to submit FAFSA. *Program availability:* Evening/weekend. *Application deadline:* For fall admission, 8/1 for domestic students; for spring admission, 12/1 for domestic students. Applications are processed on a rolling basis. *Application fee:* $30. Electronic applications accepted. *Application Contact:* Matthew P. Bodenschatz, Director of Graduate and Continuing Education Admissions, 814-886-6556, Fax: 814-886-6441, E-mail: mbodenschatz@mtaloy.edu.

## MOUNT ANGEL SEMINARY, Saint Benedict, OR 97373

**General Information** Independent-religious, Undergraduate: men only; graduate: coed, comprehensive institution. *Enrollment:* 80 full-time matriculated graduate/professional students (5 women), 21 part-time matriculated graduate/professional students (13 women). *Graduate housing:* On-campus housing not available. *Student services:* Free psychological counseling, international student services, low-cost health insurance, writing training. *Library facilities:* Mount Angel Abbey Library.
Website: http://www.mountangelabbey.org/seminary/

**General Application Contact:** Very Rev. Patrick Brennan, President-Rector, 503-845-3951.

**GRADUATE UNITS**

**Program in Theology** Average age 54. 86 applicants, 100% accepted. Expenses: Contact institution. *Financial support:* Career-related internships or fieldwork available. *Program availability:* Part-time. *Application deadline:* For fall admission, 7/15 for domestic students. Applications are processed on a rolling basis. *Application fee:* $25. *Application Contact:* Very Rev. Patrick Brennan, President-Rector, 503-845-3951. *Dean*, Rev. Ernest Skublics, 503-845-3951.

## MOUNT CARMEL COLLEGE OF NURSING, Columbus, OH 43222

**General Information** Independent, coed, primarily women, comprehensive institution. *Enrollment:* 946 graduate, professional, and undergraduate students; 103 full-time matriculated graduate/professional students (84 women), 107 part-time matriculated graduate/professional students (93 women). *Enrollment by degree level:* 198 master's, 2 doctoral, 10 other advanced degrees. *Graduate faculty:* 6 full-time (all women), 10 part-time/adjunct (9 women). *Tuition:* Full-time $27,936; part-time $27,936 per year. *Required fees:* $360. *Graduate housing:* Rooms and/or apartments available on a first-come, first-served basis to single and married students. Typical cost: $5000 per year for single students; $5000 per year for married students. Housing application deadline: 7/1. *Student services:* Free psychological counseling, multicultural affairs office, services for students with disabilities, teacher training, writing training. *Library facilities:* The Mount Carmel Health Sciences Library plus 1 other. *Collection:* Books: 8,109 (physical), 400,726 (digital/electronic); Serial titles: 682 (physical), 32,726 (digital/electronic); Databases: 179. Weekly public service hours: 61; study areas open 24 hours, 5–7 days a week; students can reserve study rooms.

**Computer facilities:** 55 computers available on campus for general student use. A campuswide network can be accessed. Online class registration is available.
Website: http://www.mccn.edu/

**General Application Contact:** Dr. Kim Campbell, Director of Recruitment and Admissions, 614-234-5144, Fax: 614-234-5427, E-mail: kcampbell@mccn.edu.

**GRADUATE UNITS**

**Nursing Program** Students: 101 full-time (82 women), 109 part-time (95 women); includes 43 minority (27 Black or African American, non-Hispanic/Latino; 4 Asian, non-Hispanic/Latino; 5 Hispanic/Latino; 7 Two or more races, non-Hispanic/Latino). Average age 32. 133 applicants, 84% accepted, 95 enrolled. *Faculty:* 6 full-time (all women), 10 part-time/adjunct (9 women). Expenses: Contact institution. *Financial support:* In 2019–20, 13 students received support. Institutionally sponsored loans and scholarships/grants available. Financial award application deadline: 3/1; financial award applicants required to submit FAFSA. In 2019, 66 master's, 2 doctorates awarded. *Program availability:* Part-time. *Application deadline:* For fall admission, 2/1 priority date for domestic students; for spring admission, 11/1 priority date for domestic students. Applications are processed on a rolling basis. *Application fee:* $30. Electronic applications accepted. *Application Contact:* Dr. Kim Campbell, Director of Recruitment and Admissions, 614-234-5144, Fax: 614-234-5427, E-mail: kcampbell@mccn.edu. *Interim Associate Dean Graduate Studies*, Dr. Jami Nininger, 614-234-1777, Fax: 614-234-2875, E-mail: jnininger@mccn.edu.

## MOUNT HOLYOKE COLLEGE, South Hadley, MA 01075

**General Information** Independent, women only, comprehensive institution. *Enrollment:* 2,335 graduate, professional, and undergraduate students; 19 full-time matriculated graduate/professional students (17 women), 91 part-time matriculated graduate/professional students (79 women). *Enrollment by degree level:* 110 master's. *Graduate faculty:* 48 part-time/adjunct (38 women). *Tuition:* Full-time $775; part-time $775 per credit. One-time fee: $150 full-time. *Graduate housing:* On-campus housing not available. *Student services:* Campus employment opportunities, campus safety program, career counseling, exercise/wellness program, free psychological counseling, international student services, multicultural affairs office, services for students with disabilities, teacher training, writing training. *Library facilities:* Williston Memorial Library plus 2 others. *Collection:* Weekly public service hours: 115; students can reserve study rooms.

**Computer facilities:** Computer purchase and lease plans are available. 392 computers available on campus for general student use. A campuswide network can be accessed from student residence rooms and from off campus. Online class registration, personal Web pages are available.
Website: http://www.mtholyoke.edu/

**General Application Contact:** Dr. Tiffany Espinosa, Executive Director of Professional and Graduate Education, 413-538-3478, Fax: 413-538-3098, E-mail: tespinos@mtholyoke.edu.

**GRADUATE UNITS**

**Professional and Graduate Education (PaGE)** Students: 19 full-time (17 women), 91 part-time (79 women); includes 21 minority (5 Black or African American, non-Hispanic/Latino; 2 Asian, non-Hispanic/Latino; 13 Hispanic/Latino; 1 Two or more races, non-Hispanic/Latino), 8 international. Average age 35. 89 applicants, 94% accepted, 65 enrolled. *Faculty:* 59 part-time/adjunct (49 women). Expenses: Contact institution. *Financial support:* In 2019–20, 99 students received support, including 5 fellowships with partial tuition reimbursements available (averaging $3,390 per year); scholarships/grants and unspecified assistantships also available. In 2019, 67 master's awarded. *Program availability:* Part-time, evening/weekend, blended/hybrid learning. *Application deadline:* For fall admission, 8/1 priority date for domestic and international students; for winter admission, 12/1 priority date for domestic and international students; for spring admission, 1/15 priority date for domestic and international students; for summer admission, 5/15 priority date for domestic and international students. Applications are processed on a rolling basis. *Application fee:* $50. Electronic applications accepted. *Application Contact:* Dr. Tiffany Espinosa, Executive Director of Professional and Graduate Education, 413-538-3478, Fax: 413-538-3098, E-mail: tespinos@mtholyoke.edu. *Executive Director of Professional and Graduate Education,* Dr. Tiffany Espinosa, 413-538-3478, Fax: 413-538-3098, E-mail: tespinos@mtholyoke.edu.

## MOUNT MARTY UNIVERSITY, Yankton, SD 57078-3724

**General Information** Independent-religious, coed, comprehensive institution. *Graduate housing:* On-campus housing not available.

**GRADUATE UNITS**

**Graduate Studies Division** Electronic applications accepted.

## MOUNT MARY UNIVERSITY, Milwaukee, WI 53222-4597

**General Information** Independent-religious, Undergraduate: women only; graduate: coed, comprehensive institution. CGS member. *Graduate housing:* Room and/or apartments available on a first-come, first-served basis to single students; on-campus housing not available to married students.

**GRADUATE UNITS**

**Graduate Programs** *Program availability:* Part-time, evening/weekend, 100% online, blended/hybrid learning. Electronic applications accepted.

## MOUNT MERCY UNIVERSITY, Cedar Rapids, IA 52402-4797

**General Information** Independent-religious, coed, comprehensive institution.

**GRADUATE UNITS**

**Program in Business Administration** *Program availability:* Evening/weekend. Electronic applications accepted.

**Program in Criminal Justice** *Program availability:* Evening/weekend, online learning.

**Program in Education** Electronic applications accepted.

**Program in Marriage and Family Therapy** *Program availability:* Evening/weekend.

**Program in Nursing** *Program availability:* Evening/weekend.

**Program in Strategic Leadership** *Program availability:* Evening/weekend.

## MOUNT ST. JOSEPH UNIVERSITY, Cincinnati, OH 45233-1670

**General Information** Independent-religious, coed, comprehensive institution. CGS member. *Graduate housing:* Room and/or apartments available on a first-come, first-served basis to single students; on-campus housing not available to married students. Housing application deadline: 4/1.

**GRADUATE UNITS**

**Doctor of Nursing Practice Program** *Program availability:* Part-time-only. Electronic applications accepted.

**Graduate Education Program** *Program availability:* Part-time, evening/weekend, 100% online, blended/hybrid learning. Electronic applications accepted.

**Graduate Program in Religious Studies** *Program availability:* Part-time, evening/weekend. Electronic applications accepted.

**Master of Business Administration Program** *Program availability:* Part-time, evening/weekend. Electronic applications accepted.

**Master of Science in Nursing Program** *Program availability:* Part-time. Electronic applications accepted.

**Master of Science in Organizational Leadership Program** *Program availability:* Part-time, evening/weekend. Electronic applications accepted.

**Master's Graduate Entry-Level into Nursing (MAGELIN) Program** Electronic applications accepted.

**Physical Therapy Program** Electronic applications accepted.

## MOUNT SAINT MARY COLLEGE, Newburgh, NY 12550-3494

**General Information** Independent, coed, comprehensive institution. *Enrollment:* 2,236 graduate, professional, and undergraduate students; 58 full-time matriculated graduate/professional students (34 women), 294 part-time matriculated graduate/professional students (249 women). *Enrollment by degree level:* 333 master's, 19 other advanced degrees. *Graduate faculty:* 20 full-time (15 women), 21 part-time/adjunct (15 women). *Tuition:* Full-time $15,192; part-time $844 per credit. *Required fees:* $180; $90 per semester. *Graduate housing:* Room and/or apartments guaranteed to single students; on-campus housing not available to married students. Typical cost: $10,264 per year ($16,938 including board). Housing application deadline: 5/1. *Student services:* Campus employment opportunities, campus safety program, career counseling, free psychological counseling, international student services, services for students with disabilities. *Library facilities:* Kaplan Family Library and Learning Center. *Collection:* Books: 74,074 (physical), 5,894 (digital/electronic); Serial titles: 188 (physical), 78,175 (digital/electronic); Databases: 91. Students can reserve study rooms.

**Computer facilities:** Computer purchase and lease plans are available. 470 computers available on campus for general student use. A campuswide network can be accessed. Online class registration is available.
Website: http://www.msmc.edu/

**General Application Contact:** Eileen Bardney, Director of Admissions, 845-569-3254, Fax: 845-569-3438, E-mail: Eileen.Bardney@msmc.edu.

**GRADUATE UNITS**

**Division of Education** Students: 23 full-time (16 women), 83 part-time (64 women); includes 13 minority (1 Black or African American, non-Hispanic/Latino; 1 Asian, non-Hispanic/Latino; 10 Hispanic/Latino; 1 Native Hawaiian or other Pacific Islander, non-Hispanic/Latino). Average age 29. 45 applicants, 58% accepted, 23 enrolled. *Faculty:* 7 full-time (6 women), 6 part-time/adjunct (4 women). Expenses: Contact institution. *Financial support:* In 2019–20, 18 students received support. Institutionally sponsored loans, scholarships/grants, and unspecified assistantships available. Financial award application deadline: 4/15; financial award applicants required to submit FAFSA. In 2019, 28 master's awarded. *Program availability:* Part-time, evening/weekend. *Application deadline:* Applications are processed on a rolling basis. *Application fee:* $45. Electronic applications accepted. *Application Contact:* Eileen Bardney, Director of Admissions, 845-569-3254, Fax: 845-569-3438, E-mail: graduateadmissions@msmc.edu. *Graduate Coordinator,* Dr. Rebecca Norman, 845-569-3431, Fax: 845-569-3551, E-mail: Rebecca.Norman@msmc.edu.

**School of Business** Students: 34 full-time (17 women), 25 part-time (14 women); includes 14 minority (1 Black or African American, non-Hispanic/Latino; 13 Hispanic/Latino). Average age 30. 18 applicants, 100% accepted, 11 enrolled. *Faculty:* 7 full-time (3 women), 4 part-time/adjunct (1 woman). Expenses: Contact institution. *Financial support:* In 2019–20, 14 students received support. Scholarships/grants and unspecified assistantships available. Financial award application deadline: 4/15; financial award applicants required to submit FAFSA. In 2019, 48 master's awarded. *Program availability:* Part-time, evening/weekend. *Application deadline:* Applications are processed on a rolling basis. *Application fee:* $45. Electronic applications accepted. *Application Contact:* Eileen Bardney, Director of Admissions, 845-569-3254, Fax: 845-569-3438, E-mail: GraduateAdmissions@msmc.edu. *Graduate Program Coordinator,* Michael Fox, 845-569-3122, Fax: 845-569-3885, E-mail: Michael.Fox@msmc.edu.

**School of Nursing** Students: 1 (woman) full-time, 186 part-time (171 women); includes 36 minority (16 Black or African American, non-Hispanic/Latino; 1 American Indian or Alaska Native, non-Hispanic/Latino; 5 Asian, non-Hispanic/Latino; 11 Hispanic/Latino; 1 Native Hawaiian or other Pacific Islander, non-Hispanic/Latino; 2 Two or more races, non-Hispanic/Latino), 1 international. Average age 37. 37 applicants, 84% accepted, 22 enrolled. *Faculty:* 6 full-time (all women), 11 part-time/adjunct (10 women). Expenses: Contact institution. *Financial support:* In 2019–20, 10 students received support. Scholarships/grants and unspecified assistantships available. Financial award application deadline: 4/15; financial award applicants required to submit FAFSA. In 2019, 33 master's, 4 other advanced degrees awarded. *Program availability:* Part-time, evening/weekend, blended/hybrid learning. *Application deadline:* For fall admission, 6/3 priority date for domestic students; for spring admission, 10/31 priority date for domestic students. Applications are processed on a rolling basis. *Application fee:* $45. Electronic applications accepted. *Application Contact:* Eileen Bardney, Director of Admissions, 845-569-3254, Fax: 845-569-3438, E-mail: GraduateAdmissions@msmc.edu. *Graduate Coordinator,* Christine Berte, 845-569-3141, Fax: 845-562-6762, E-mail: christine.berte@msmc.edu.

## MOUNT SAINT MARY'S UNIVERSITY, Los Angeles, CA 90049

**General Information** Independent-religious, coed, primarily women, comprehensive institution. CGS member. *Enrollment:* 689 full-time matriculated graduate/professional students (569 women), 178 part-time matriculated graduate/professional students (143 women). *Enrollment by degree level:* 515 master's, 92 doctoral, 260 other advanced degrees. *Graduate faculty:* 41 full-time (33 women), 159 part-time/adjunct (118 women). *Tuition:* Full-time $18,648; part-time $9324 per year. *Required fees:* $540; $540 per unit. *Graduate housing:* Room and/or apartments available on a first-come, first-served basis to single students; on-campus housing not available to married students. *Student services:* Campus employment opportunities, career counseling, exercise/wellness program, free psychological counseling, low-cost health insurance, services for students with disabilities, writing training. *Library facilities:* Charles Willard Coe Library plus 1 other. *Collection:* Books: 88,758 (physical), 396,855 (digital/electronic); Serial titles: 168 (physical), 39,316 (digital/electronic); Databases: 215. Weekly public service hours: 91; study areas open 24 hours, 5–7 days a week. *Research affiliation:* John Tracy Clinic (education - deaf and hard of hearing teacher preparation).

**Computer facilities:** 170 computers available on campus for general student use. A campuswide network can be accessed from student residence rooms and from off campus. Online class registration is available.
Website: http://www.msmu.edu/

**General Application Contact:** Albert Ramos, Director of Graduate Admissions, 213-477-2800, Fax: 213-477-2797, E-mail: gradprograms@msmu.edu.

**GRADUATE UNITS**

**Graduate Division** *Program availability:* Part-time, evening/weekend. Electronic applications accepted.

## MOUNT ST. MARY'S UNIVERSITY, Emmitsburg, MD 21727-7799

**General Information** Independent-religious, coed, comprehensive institution. *Enrollment:* 2,362 graduate, professional, and undergraduate students; 218 full-time matriculated graduate/professional students (34 women), 245 part-time matriculated graduate/professional students (145 women). *Enrollment by degree level:* 440 master's, 23 other advanced degrees. *Graduate housing:* Room and/or apartments available on a first-come, first-served basis to single students; on-campus housing not available to married students. *Student services:* Campus employment opportunities, campus safety program, career counseling, exercise/wellness program, free psychological counseling, international student services, low-cost health insurance, multicultural affairs office, services for students with disabilities, teacher training, writing training. *Library facilities:* Phillips Library. *Collection:* Books: 149,042 (physical), 3 million (digital/electronic); Serial titles: 170 (physical), 21,747 (digital/electronic); Databases: 133.

**Computer facilities:** 80 computers available on campus for general student use. A campuswide network can be accessed. Online class registration, tuition payment, course management system are available.
Website: http://www.msmary.edu/

**GRADUATE UNITS**

**Graduate Seminary** Students: 150 full-time, 2 part-time (0 women); includes 11 minority (3 Black or African American, non-Hispanic/Latino; 1 American Indian or Alaska Native, non-Hispanic/Latino; 3 Asian, non-Hispanic/Latino; 4 Hispanic/Latino), 19 international. Expenses: Contact institution. *Financial support:* Applicants required to submit FAFSA. In 2019, 22 master's awarded. *Application deadline:* For fall admission, 8/1 for domestic and international students. *Application Contact:* Susan Nield, Seminary Admissions, 301-447-7423, Fax: 301-447-7402, E-mail: nield@msmary.edu. *Vice President/Rector,* Rev. Andrew R. Baker, 301-447-5295, Fax: 301-447-5636, E-mail: baker@msmary.edu.

**Program in Biotechnology and Management** Students: 4 full-time (2 women), 13 part-time (8 women); includes 4 minority (1 Black or African American, non-Hispanic/Latino; 2 Hispanic/Latino; 1 Two or more races, non-Hispanic/Latino). Expenses: Contact institution. *Financial support:* Unspecified assistantships available. Financial award applicants required to submit FAFSA. In 2019, 5 master's awarded. *Program availability:* Part-time-only, evening/weekend. *Application deadline:* Applications are processed on a rolling basis. Electronic applications accepted.

**Program in Business Administration** Students: 33 full-time (14 women), 103 part-time (44 women); includes 35 minority (14 Black or African American, non-Hispanic/Latino; 2 American Indian or Alaska Native, non-Hispanic/Latino; 6 Asian, non-Hispanic/Latino; 8 Hispanic/Latino; 5 Two or more races, non-Hispanic/Latino), 4 international. Expenses: Contact institution. *Financial support:* Career-related internships or fieldwork and unspecified assistantships available. Financial award applicants required to submit FAFSA. In 2019, 84 master's awarded. *Program availability:* Part-time, evening/weekend. *Application deadline:* Applications are processed on a rolling basis. Electronic applications accepted.

**Program in Education** Students: 23 full-time (15 women), 89 part-time (70 women); includes 19 minority (6 Black or African American, non-Hispanic/Latino; 1 American Indian or Alaska Native, non-Hispanic/Latino; 2 Asian, non-Hispanic/Latino; 8 Hispanic/Latino; 1 Native Hawaiian or other Pacific Islander, non-Hispanic/Latino; 1 Two or more races, non-Hispanic/Latino). Expenses: Contact institution. *Financial support:* Unspecified assistantships available. Financial award applicants required to submit FAFSA. In 2019, 48 master's awarded. *Application deadline:* Applications are processed on a rolling basis. Electronic applications accepted.

**Program in Health Administration** Students: 2 full-time (1 woman), 22 part-time (16 women); includes 10 minority (7 Black or African American, non-Hispanic/Latino; 1 Asian, non-Hispanic/Latino; 1 Hispanic/Latino; 1 Two or more races, non-Hispanic/Latino), 1 international. Expenses: Contact institution. *Financial support:* Unspecified assistantships available. Financial award applicants required to submit FAFSA. In 2019, 18 master's awarded. *Program availability:* Part-time, evening/weekend. *Application deadline:* Applications are processed on a rolling basis. Electronic applications accepted.

**Program in Philosophical Studies** Students: 2 part-time (both women); includes 1 minority (Black or African American, non-Hispanic/Latino). Expenses: Contact institution. *Financial support:* Unspecified assistantships available. Financial award applicants required to submit FAFSA. In 2019, 3 master's awarded. *Program availability:* Part-time. *Application deadline:* For fall admission, 8/1 for domestic students; for spring admission, 12/1 for domestic students.

**Program in Sport Management** Students: 6 full-time (2 women), 14 part-time (5 women); includes 6 minority (3 Black or African American, non-Hispanic/Latino; 1 Hispanic/Latino; 2 Two or more races, non-Hispanic/Latino). Expenses: Contact institution. *Financial support:* Unspecified assistantships available. Financial award applicants required to submit FAFSA. In 2019, 15 master's awarded. *Program availability:* Part-time, evening/weekend. *Application deadline:* Applications are processed on a rolling basis. Electronic applications accepted.

## MOUNT SAINT VINCENT UNIVERSITY, Halifax, NS B3M 2J6, Canada

**General Information** Province-supported, coed, primarily women, comprehensive institution. *Graduate housing:* Room and/or apartments available on a first-come, first-served basis to single students; on-campus housing not available to married students. Housing application deadline: 5/15.

**GRADUATE UNITS**

**Graduate Programs** *Program availability:* Part-time, evening/weekend, online learning. Electronic applications accepted.

***Faculty of Education*** *Program availability:* Part-time, evening/weekend, online learning. Electronic applications accepted.

## MOUNT VERNON NAZARENE UNIVERSITY, Mount Vernon, OH 43050-9500

**General Information** Independent-religious, coed, comprehensive institution. *Graduate housing:* On-campus housing not available.

**GRADUATE UNITS**

**Department of Education** *Program availability:* Part-time, evening/weekend.

**Program in Management** *Program availability:* Part-time, evening/weekend.

**Program in Ministry** *Program availability:* Part-time, evening/weekend.

## MULTNOMAH UNIVERSITY, Portland, OR 97220-5898

**General Information** Independent-religious, coed, comprehensive institution. *Graduate housing:* Room and/or apartments available on a first-come, first-served basis to single students; on-campus housing not available to married students. Housing application deadline: 7/15.

**GRADUATE UNITS**

**Graduate Programs** *Program availability:* Part-time, evening/weekend. Electronic applications accepted.

**Multnomah Biblical Seminary** *Program availability:* Part-time.

## MURRAY STATE UNIVERSITY, Murray, KY 42071

**General Information** State-supported, coed, university. *Graduate housing:* Rooms and/or apartments available on a first-come, first-served basis to single and married students.

**GRADUATE UNITS**

**Arthur J. Bauernfeind College of Business** *Program availability:* Part-time, evening/weekend, 100% online, blended/hybrid learning. Electronic applications accepted.

**College of Education and Human Services** *Program availability:* Part-time, evening/weekend, 100% online, blended/hybrid learning. Electronic applications accepted.

***Center for Communication Disorders*** *Program availability:* Part-time. Electronic applications accepted.

**College of Humanities and Fine Arts** *Program availability:* Part-time, evening/weekend, 100% online, blended/hybrid learning. Electronic applications accepted.

**Hutson School of Agriculture** *Program availability:* Part-time, 100% online, blended/hybrid learning. Electronic applications accepted.

**Jesse D. Jones College of Science, Engineering and Technology** *Program availability:* Part-time, evening/weekend, 100% online, blended/hybrid learning. Electronic applications accepted.

***Institute of Engineering*** *Program availability:* Part-time. Electronic applications accepted.

**School of Nursing and Health Professions** *Program availability:* Part-time, evening/weekend, 100% online, blended/hybrid learning. Electronic applications accepted.

## MUSKINGUM UNIVERSITY, New Concord, OH 43762

**General Information** Independent-religious, coed, comprehensive institution. *Enrollment:* 2,369 graduate, professional, and undergraduate students; 162 matriculated graduate/professional students. *Enrollment by degree level:* 162 master's. *Graduate faculty:* 19. *Graduate housing:* On-campus housing not available. *Student services:* Child daycare facilities, exercise/wellness program, grant writing training, international student services, multicultural affairs office. *Library facilities:* Roberta A. Smith Library. *Collection:* Books: 101,051 (physical), 412,702 (digital/electronic); Serial titles: 1,085 (physical), 72,557 (digital/electronic); Databases: 285. Weekly public service hours: 89; students can reserve study rooms.

**Computer facilities:** 303 computers available on campus for general student use. A campuswide network can be accessed. Online class registration is available.
Website: http://www.muskingum.edu/

**General Application Contact:** Dr. Rolf G. Schmitz, Director of Graduate Studies, 614-826-8037.

**GRADUATE UNITS**

**Graduate Programs in Education** Students: 162. *Faculty:* 19. Expenses: Contact institution. *Financial support:* Scholarships/grants available. *Program availability:* Part-time. *Application deadline:* Applications are processed on a rolling basis. *Application fee:* $20. *Application Contact:* Dr. Rolf G. Schmitz, Director of Graduate Studies, 614-826-8037. *Director of Graduate Studies,* Dr. Rolf G. Schmitz, 614-826-8037.

## NAROPA UNIVERSITY, Boulder, CO 80302-6697

**General Information** Independent, coed, comprehensive institution. *Graduate housing:* Room and/or apartments available on a first-come, first-served basis to single students; on-campus housing not available to married students. Housing application deadline: 7/1.

**GRADUATE UNITS**

**Graduate Programs** *Program availability:* Part-time, blended/hybrid learning. Electronic applications accepted.

## NASHOTAH HOUSE THEOLOGICAL SEMINARY, Nashotah, WI 53058-9793

**General Information** Independent-religious, coed, primarily men, graduate-only institution. *Graduate housing:* Rooms and/or apartments available on a first-come, first-served basis to single and married students. Housing application deadline: 5/1.

**GRADUATE UNITS**

**Graduate Programs** *Program availability:* Part-time. Electronic applications accepted.

## NATIONAL AMERICAN UNIVERSITY, Austin, TX 78731

**General Information** Proprietary, coed, graduate-only institution.

**GRADUATE UNITS**

**Roueche Graduate Center** *Program availability:* Part-time, evening/weekend, online learning. Electronic applications accepted.

## NATIONAL COLLEGE OF MIDWIFERY, Taos, NM 87571

**General Information** Independent, women only, comprehensive institution.

**GRADUATE UNITS**

**Graduate Programs** *Program availability:* Part-time, evening/weekend, online learning. Electronic applications accepted.

## NATIONAL DEFENSE UNIVERSITY, Washington, DC 20319-5066

**General Information** Federally supported, coed, graduate-only institution. *Graduate housing:* On-campus housing not available.

**GRADUATE UNITS**

**College of International Security Affairs** *Program availability:* Part-time, evening/weekend.

**The Dwight D. Eisenhower School for National Security and Resource Strategy**

**Joint Advanced Warfighting School**

**National War College**

## NATIONAL INTELLIGENCE UNIVERSITY, Washington, DC 20340-5100

**General Information** Federally supported, coed, upper-level institution. *Graduate housing:* On-campus housing not available.

**GRADUATE UNITS**

**Graduate Program** *Program availability:* Part-time, evening/weekend.

## NATIONAL LOUIS UNIVERSITY, Chicago, IL 60603

**General Information** Independent, coed, university.

**GRADUATE UNITS**

**College of Arts and Sciences** *Program availability:* Part-time, evening/weekend, online learning. Electronic applications accepted.

**College of Management and Business** *Program availability:* Part-time, evening/weekend.

**National College of Education** *Program availability:* Part-time, evening/weekend.

## NATIONAL PARALEGAL COLLEGE, Phoenix, AZ 85014

**General Information** Proprietary, coed, comprehensive institution. *Library facilities:* Jones eGlobal Library. *Collection:* Books: 27,803 (digital/electronic); Databases: 56. Weekly public service hours: 168.

**Computer facilities:** Online class registration is available.
Website: http://nationalparalegal.edu/

**General Application Contact:** Dana Luxsenburg, Registrar, 800-371-6105, E-mail: dana@nationalparalegal.edu.

**GRADUATE UNITS**

**Graduate Programs** *Program availability:* Part-time. Electronic applications accepted.

## NATIONAL TEST PILOT SCHOOL, Mojave, CA 93502-0658

**General Information** Independent, coed, graduate-only institution.

**GRADUATE UNITS**

**National Flight Institute**

## NATIONAL UNIVERSITY, La Jolla, CA 92037-1011

**General Information** Independent, coed, comprehensive institution. CGS member. *Enrollment:* 16,930 graduate, professional, and undergraduate students; 6,762 full-time matriculated graduate/professional students (4,617 women), 1,492 part-time matriculated graduate/professional students (969 women). *Enrollment by degree level:* 8,154 master's, 100 other advanced degrees. *Graduate faculty:* 113 full-time (57 women), 529 part-time/adjunct (281 women). *Tuition:* Full-time $442; part-time $442 per unit. *Graduate housing:* On-campus housing not available. *Student services:* Campus employment opportunities, campus safety program, career counseling, international student services, services for students with disabilities, teacher training, writing training. *Library facilities:* National University Library. *Collection:* Books: 201,123 (physical), 368,486 (digital/electronic); Serial titles: 3,050 (physical), 95,256 (digital/electronic); Databases: 190. Weekly public service hours: 72; students can reserve study rooms.

**Computer facilities:** 2,800 computers available on campus for general student use. A campuswide network can be accessed from off campus. Online class registration is available.
Website: http://www.nu.edu/

**General Application Contact:** Brandon Jouganatos, Vice President for Enrollment Services, 800-628-8648, E-mail: advisor@nu.edu.

**GRADUATE UNITS**

**College of Letters and Sciences** *Program availability:* Part-time, evening/weekend, 100% online, blended/hybrid learning. Electronic applications accepted.

**Sanford College of Education** *Program availability:* Part-time, evening/weekend, 100% online, blended/hybrid learning. Electronic applications accepted.

**School of Business and Management** *Program availability:* Part-time, evening/weekend, 100% online, blended/hybrid learning. Electronic applications accepted.

**School of Engineering and Computing** *Program availability:* Part-time, evening/weekend, 100% online, blended/hybrid learning. Electronic applications accepted.

**School of Health and Human Services** *Program availability:* Part-time, evening/weekend, 100% online, blended/hybrid learning. Electronic applications accepted.

**School of Professional Studies** *Program availability:* Part-time, evening/weekend, 100% online, blended/hybrid learning. Electronic applications accepted.

## NATIONAL UNIVERSITY COLLEGE, Bayamón, PR 00960

**General Information** Proprietary, coed, comprehensive institution.

**GRADUATE UNITS**

**Graduate Programs**

## NATIONAL UNIVERSITY OF HEALTH SCIENCES, Lombard, IL 60148-4583

**General Information** Independent, coed, graduate-only institution. *Graduate housing:* Rooms and/or apartments available on a first-come, first-served basis to single and married students. *Research affiliation:* University of Illinois at Chicago (public health), Canadian Memorial Chiropractic College (mechanisms of CAM), Cox Technic F/D Enterprise LLC (mechanisms of CAM), Logan Chiropractic College (behavior research), Foot Levelers, Inc. (orthotics/biomechanics), Auburn University (mechanisms of CAM).

**GRADUATE UNITS**

**Graduate Programs**

## NATIONAL UNIVERSITY OF NATURAL MEDICINE, Portland, OR 97201

**General Information** Independent, coed, primarily women, graduate-only institution. *Enrollment by degree level:* 137 master's, 316 doctoral. *Graduate faculty:* 29 full-time (15 women), 131 part-time/adjunct (87 women). *Tuition:* Part-time $464 per credit hour. *Graduate housing:* On-campus housing not available. *Student services:* Campus employment opportunities, campus safety program, career counseling, free psychological counseling, international student services, multicultural affairs office, services for students with disabilities. *Library facilities:* NUNM Library. *Collection:* Books: 17,377 (physical), 3,732 (digital/electronic); Serial titles: 16,784 (digital/electronic); Databases: 21. Weekly public service hours: 67. *Research affiliation:* Metagenics, Inc. (effects of methylation diet, nutrition supplements), Divinia Water (product safety and tolerability, case reports, water).

**Computer facilities:** 29 computers available on campus for general student use. A campuswide network can be accessed from off campus. Online class registration is available.
Website: http://www.nunm.edu/

**General Application Contact:** Ryan Hollister, Director of Admissions, 503-552-1665, Fax: 503-499-0027, E-mail: admissions@nunm.edu.

**GRADUATE UNITS**

**College of Classical Chinese Medicine** Students: 70 full-time (55 women), 22 part-time (15 women); includes 21 minority (4 Black or African American, non-Hispanic/Latino; 7 Asian, non-Hispanic/Latino; 5 Hispanic/Latino; 5 Two or more races, non-Hispanic/Latino), 2 international. Average age 33. 45 applicants, 78% accepted, 23 enrolled. Expenses: Contact institution. *Financial support:* Federal Work-Study and scholarships/grants available. Financial award application deadline: 2/15; financial award applicants required to submit FAFSA. In 2019, 21 master's, 13 doctorates awarded. *Application deadline:* For fall and winter admission, 5/1 priority date for domestic and international students. Applications are processed on a rolling basis. *Application fee:* $75. Electronic applications accepted. *Application Contact:* Ryan Hollister, Director of Admissions, 503-552-1665, Fax: 503-499-0027, E-mail: admissions@numn.edu. *Program Director of Chinese Medicine*, Andrew McIntyre, LAc, 503-552-1775, Fax: 503-499-0027, E-mail: admissions@nunm.edu.

**College of Naturopathic Medicine** Students: 247 full-time (210 women), 16 part-time (12 women); includes 67 minority (3 Black or African American, non-Hispanic/Latino; 3 American Indian or Alaska Native, non-Hispanic/Latino; 21 Asian, non-Hispanic/Latino; 22 Hispanic/Latino; 1 Native Hawaiian or other Pacific Islander, non-Hispanic/Latino; 17 Two or more races, non-Hispanic/Latino), 5 international. Average age 30. 113 applicants, 79% accepted, 55 enrolled. Expenses: Contact institution. *Financial support:* Federal Work-Study and scholarships/grants available. Financial award application deadline: 2/15; financial award applicants required to submit FAFSA. In 2019, 89 doctorates awarded. *Application deadline:* For fall admission, 5/1 priority date for domestic and international students. Applications are processed on a rolling basis. *Application fee:* $75. Electronic applications accepted. *Application Contact:* Ryan Hollister, Director of Admissions, 503-552-1665, Fax: 503-499-0027, E-mail: admissions@numn.edu. *Interim Program Director of Naturopathic Medicine*, Kelly Baltazar, ND, DC, MS, 503-503.552.1696, Fax: 503-499-0027, E-mail: admissions@nunm.edu.

**School of Undergraduate and Graduate Studies** Students: 92 full-time (83 women), 6 part-time (all women); includes 13 minority (1 Black or African American, non-Hispanic/Latino; 4 Asian, non-Hispanic/Latino; 3 Hispanic/Latino; 5 Two or more races, non-Hispanic/Latino). Average age 31. 114 applicants, 88% accepted, 60 enrolled. Expenses: Contact institution. *Financial support:* Federal Work-Study and scholarships/grants available. Financial award application deadline: 2/15; financial award applicants required to submit FAFSA. In 2019, 72 master's awarded. *Program availability:* 100% online. *Application deadline:* For fall admission, 5/1 for domestic and international students. Applications are processed on a rolling basis. *Application fee:* $75. Electronic applications accepted. *Application Contact:* Ryan Hollister, Director of Admissions, 503-552-1665, Fax: 503-499-0027, E-mail: admissions@numn.edu. *Program Director - School of Undergraduate and Graduate Studies*, Dr. Tim Irving, 503-552-1660, Fax: 503-499-0027, E-mail: admission@nunm.edu.

## NAVAJO TECHNICAL UNIVERSITY, Crownpoint, NM 87313

**General Information** Independent, coed, comprehensive institution.

**GRADUATE UNITS**

**Program in Dine Studies**

## NAVAL POSTGRADUATE SCHOOL, Monterey, CA 93943

**General Information** Federally supported, coed, graduate-only institution. *Graduate housing:* Rooms and/or apartments available to single and married students. *Research affiliation:* U.S. Department of Homeland Security, National Reconnaissance Office, National Oceanic and Atmospheric Administration (NOAA), National Security Agency, Federal Law Enforcement Training.

**GRADUATE UNITS**

**Departments and Academic Groups** *Program availability:* Part-time, online learning.

***Graduate School of Business and Public Policy*** *Program availability:* Part-time, online learning.

## NAVAL WAR COLLEGE, Newport, RI 02841-1207

**General Information** Federally supported, coed, primarily men, graduate-only institution.

**GRADUATE UNITS**

**Program in National Security and Strategic Studies**

## NAZARENE THEOLOGICAL SEMINARY, Kansas City, MO 64131-1263

**General Information** Independent-religious, coed, graduate-only institution. *Graduate housing:* Rooms and/or apartments available on a first-come, first-served basis to single and married students. *Research affiliation:* University of Missouri-Kansas City (religious studies).

**GRADUATE UNITS**

**Graduate and Professional Programs** *Program availability:* Part-time. Electronic applications accepted.

## NAZARETH COLLEGE OF ROCHESTER, Rochester, NY 14618

**General Information** Independent, coed, comprehensive institution. CGS member. *Graduate housing:* Room and/or apartments available on a first-come, first-served basis to single students; on-campus housing not available to married students. Housing application deadline: 5/15.

**GRADUATE UNITS**

**Graduate Studies** *Program availability:* Part-time, evening/weekend.

## NEBRASKA METHODIST COLLEGE, Omaha, NE 68114

**General Information** Independent-religious, coed, comprehensive institution. *Graduate housing:* Rooms and/or apartments available on a first-come, first-served basis to single students and available to married students. Housing application deadline: 4/1.

**GRADUATE UNITS**

**Program in Healthcare Operations Management** *Program availability:* Part-time, evening/weekend, online learning.

**Program in Health Promotion Management** *Program availability:* Part-time, evening/weekend, online learning.

**Program in Nursing** *Program availability:* Evening/weekend, online learning.

**Program in Occupational Therapy**

## NEBRASKA WESLEYAN UNIVERSITY, Lincoln, NE 68504-2796

**General Information** Independent-religious, coed, comprehensive institution. *Enrollment:* 2,044 graduate, professional, and undergraduate students; 22 full-time matriculated graduate/professional students (15 women), 180 part-time matriculated graduate/professional students (136 women). *Enrollment by degree level:* 202 master's. *Graduate faculty:* 15 full-time (11 women), 18 part-time/adjunct (7 women). *Tuition:* Full-time $5388; part-time $499 per credit hour. One-time fee: $120. Tuition and fees vary according to program. *Graduate housing:* Room and/or apartments available on a first-come, first-served basis to single students; on-campus housing not available to married students. Typical cost: $9000 (including board). *Student services:* Career counseling, multicultural affairs office, services for students with disabilities. *Library facilities:* Cochrane Woods Library. *Collection:* Books: 148,110 (physical), 191,524 (digital/electronic); Serial titles: 1,573 (physical), 18,736 (digital/electronic); Databases: 48. Weekly public service hours: 98; students can reserve study rooms.

**Computer facilities:** 360 computers available on campus for general student use. A campuswide network can be accessed. Online class registration is available.
Website: http://www.nebrwesleyan.edu/

**General Application Contact:** Graduate, Adult and Transfer Admissions Office, 402-465-2329, Fax: 402-465-2179, E-mail: adultadmissions@nebrwesleyan.edu.

**GRADUATE UNITS**

**MSN/MBA Joint Degree Program** Students: 12 full-time (9 women), 39 part-time (36 women); includes 5 minority (2 Black or African American, non-Hispanic/Latino; 1 Asian, non-Hispanic/Latino; 1 Hispanic/Latino; 1 Two or more races, non-Hispanic/Latino). Average age 39. 8 applicants, 50% accepted, 4 enrolled. *Faculty:* 13 full-time (10 women), 15 part-time/adjunct (7 women). Expenses: Contact institution. *Program availability:* Part-time, evening/weekend. *Application deadline:* Applications are processed on a rolling basis. Electronic applications accepted. *Application Contact:* Graduate, Adult and Transfer Admissions Office, 402-465-2329, Fax: 402-465-2179, E-mail: adultadmissions@nebrwesleyan.edu.

**Program in Business Administration** Students: 9 full-time (4 women), 69 part-time (34 women); includes 7 minority (1 Asian, non-Hispanic/Latino; 4 Hispanic/Latino; 1 Native Hawaiian or other Pacific Islander, non-Hispanic/Latino; 1 Two or more races, non-Hispanic/Latino). Average age 35. 17 applicants, 76% accepted, 12 enrolled. *Faculty:* 7 full-time (4 women), 7 part-time/adjunct (2 women). Expenses: Contact institution. *Program availability:* Part-time, evening/weekend. *Application deadline:* Applications are processed on a rolling basis. Electronic applications accepted. *Application Contact:* Graduate, Adult and Transfer Admissions Office, 402-465-2329, Fax: 402-465-2179, E-mail: adultadmissions@nebrwesleyan.edu. *MBA Program Director*, Dr. Tami Thompson, 402-465-2200, E-mail: tthompso@nebrwesleyan.edu.

**Program in Education** Students: 19 part-time (15 women). Average age 31. 13 applicants, 38% accepted, 4 enrolled. *Faculty:* 2 full-time (1 woman), 3 part-time/adjunct (0 women). Expenses: Contact institution. *Program availability:* Part-time, evening/weekend. *Application deadline:* Applications are processed on a rolling basis. Electronic applications accepted. *Application Contact:* Graduate, Adult and Transfer Admissions Office, 402-465-2329, Fax: 402-465-2179, E-mail: adultadmissions@nebrwesleyan.edu. *Education Department Chair*, Dr. Randal Ernst, 402-465-2310, E-mail: rernst2@nebrwesleyan.edu.

**Program in Nursing** Students: 1 (woman) full-time, 50 part-time (48 women); includes 3 minority (1 Hispanic/Latino; 2 Two or more races, non-Hispanic/Latino), 1 international. Average age 42. 12 applicants, 75% accepted, 9 enrolled. *Faculty:* 6 full-time (all women), 9 part-time/adjunct (4 women). Expenses: Contact institution. In 2019, 21 master's awarded. *Program availability:* Part-time. *Application deadline:* Applications are processed on a rolling basis. Electronic applications accepted. *Application Contact:* Graduate, Adult and Transfer Admissions, 402-465-2329, Fax: 402-465-2179, E-mail: adultadmissions@nebrwesleyan.edu. *Nursing Department Chair,* Charlotte Liggett, 402-465-7521, E-mail: cliggett@nebrwesleyan.edu.

## NER ISRAEL RABBINICAL COLLEGE, Baltimore, MD 21208

**General Information** Independent-religious, men only, comprehensive institution. *Graduate housing:* Rooms and/or apartments guaranteed to single students and available on a first-come, first-served basis to married students.

**GRADUATE UNITS**

**Graduate Programs**

## NER ISRAEL YESHIVA COLLEGE OF TORONTO, Thornhill, ON L4J 8A7, Canada

**General Information** Independent-religious, men only, comprehensive institution. Website: http://www.neryisroel.info/

**General Application Contact:** Matej, Information Contact, 905-731-1224.

**GRADUATE UNITS**

**Graduate Programs**

## NEUMANN UNIVERSITY, Aston, PA 19014-1298

**General Information** Independent-religious, coed, comprehensive institution. *Graduate housing:* On-campus housing not available.

**GRADUATE UNITS**

**Graduate Program in Education** *Program availability:* Part-time, evening/weekend, 100% online, blended/hybrid learning. Electronic applications accepted.

**Graduate Program in Nursing** *Program availability:* Part-time, evening/weekend. Electronic applications accepted.

**Graduate Programs in Business and Information Management** *Program availability:* Part-time, evening/weekend. Electronic applications accepted.

**Program in Educational Leadership** *Program availability:* Part-time, evening/weekend. Electronic applications accepted.

**Program in Organizational and Strategic Leadership** *Program availability:* Part-time, evening/weekend, 100% online, blended/hybrid learning. Electronic applications accepted.

**Program in Pastoral Clinical Mental Health Counseling** *Program availability:* Part-time, evening/weekend. Electronic applications accepted.

**Program in Physical Therapy** *Program availability:* Evening/weekend. Electronic applications accepted.

## NEW BRUNSWICK THEOLOGICAL SEMINARY, New Brunswick, NJ 08901-1196

**General Information** Independent-religious, coed, graduate-only institution. *Graduate housing:* Rooms and/or apartments available on a first-come, first-served basis to single and married students. Housing application deadline: 6/30.

**GRADUATE UNITS**

**Graduate and Professional Programs** *Program availability:* Part-time, evening/weekend. Electronic applications accepted.

## NEW CHARTER UNIVERSITY, Salt Lake City, UT 84101

**General Information** Proprietary, coed, comprehensive institution. *Enrollment:* 35 graduate, professional, and undergraduate students; 13 part-time matriculated graduate/professional students (9 women). *Enrollment by degree level:* 13 master's. *Graduate faculty:* 12 part-time/adjunct (7 women). *Graduate housing:* On-campus housing not available.

**Computer facilities:** A campuswide network can be accessed.
Website: http://www.new.edu/

**General Application Contact:** Stephen Mann, Admissions Advisor, 801-515-3085, Fax: 801-855-5922, E-mail: smann@new.edu.

**GRADUATE UNITS**

**College of Business** *Program availability:* Part-time, evening/weekend, online only, 100% online. Electronic applications accepted.

## NEW COLLEGE OF FLORIDA, Sarasota, FL 34243

**General Information** State-supported, coed, comprehensive institution.

**GRADUATE UNITS**

**Program in Data Science**

## NEW ENGLAND COLLEGE, Henniker, NH 03242-3293

**General Information** Independent, coed, comprehensive institution. *Graduate housing:* Room and/or apartments available on a first-come, first-served basis to single students; on-campus housing not available to married students. Housing application deadline: 5/1.

**GRADUATE UNITS**

**Program in Community Mental Health Counseling** *Program availability:* Part-time, evening/weekend.

**Program in Education** *Program availability:* Part-time, evening/weekend.

**Program in Management** *Program availability:* Part-time, evening/weekend. Electronic applications accepted.

**Program in Public Policy** *Program availability:* Part-time, evening/weekend, online learning. Electronic applications accepted.

**Program in Sports and Recreation Management: Coaching**

**Programs in Writing** *Program availability:* Part-time, evening/weekend. Electronic applications accepted.

## NEW ENGLAND COLLEGE OF BUSINESS AND FINANCE, Boston, MA 02111-2645

**General Information** Independent, coed, primarily women, comprehensive institution.

**GRADUATE UNITS**

**Program in Business Ethics and Compliance** *Program availability:* Online learning.

**Program in Finance** *Program availability:* Online learning.

**Program in Quality Systems Management**

## NEW ENGLAND COLLEGE OF OPTOMETRY, Boston, MA 02115-1100

**General Information** Independent, coed, graduate-only institution. *Enrollment by degree level:* 456 doctoral. *Graduate faculty:* 37 full-time (18 women), 28 part-time/adjunct (13 women). *Graduate housing:* On-campus housing not available. *Student services:* Campus employment opportunities, career counseling, free psychological counseling, international student services, low-cost health insurance. *Research affiliation:* Vistakon-Johnson & Johnson (contact lenses), Boston University School of Medicine (vision science).

**Computer facilities:** 31 computers available on campus for general student use.
Website: http://www.neco.edu/

**General Application Contact:** Dr. Taline Farra, Assistant Dean and Director of Admissions, 617-587-5580, Fax: 617-587-5550, E-mail: farrat@neco.edu.

**GRADUATE UNITS**

**Graduate and Professional Programs** 815 applicants, 40% accepted, 138 enrolled. Expenses: Contact institution. *Financial support:* In 2019–20, 357 students received support, including 12 research assistantships (averaging $5,193 per year); career-related internships or fieldwork, Federal Work-Study, institutionally sponsored loans, and scholarships/grants also available. Financial award application deadline: 4/1; financial award applicants required to submit FAFSA. In 2019, 115 doctorates awarded. *Application deadline:* For fall admission, 3/31 for domestic students. Applications are processed on a rolling basis. *Application fee:* $40. Electronic applications accepted. *Application Contact:* Kristen Tobin, Director of Admissions, 617-587-5580, Fax: 617-587-5550, E-mail: tobink@neco.edu.

## NEW ENGLAND CONSERVATORY OF MUSIC, Boston, MA 02115-5000

**General Information** Independent, coed, comprehensive institution. *Enrollment:* 323 full-time matriculated graduate/professional students (157 women), 23 part-time matriculated graduate/professional students (10 women). *Enrollment by degree level:* 262 master's, 36 doctoral, 48 other advanced degrees. *Graduate faculty:* 92 full-time (31 women), 106 part-time/adjunct (37 women). *Tuition:* Full-time $49,580; part-time $3180 per credit. *Required fees:* $880. *Graduate housing:* Room and/or apartments available on a first-come, first-served basis to single students; on-campus housing not available to married students. Typical cost: $16,500 (including board). Room and board charges vary according to housing facility selected. Housing application deadline: 4/15. *Student services:* Campus employment opportunities, campus safety program, career counseling, exercise/wellness program, free psychological counseling, grant writing training, international student services, low-cost health insurance, services for students with disabilities, writing training. *Library facilities:* Spaulding Library plus 3 others. *Collection:* Books: 103,097 (physical), 248,432 (digital/electronic); Serial titles: 161 (physical), 98 (digital/electronic); Databases: 109. Weekly public service hours: 85.

**Computer facilities:** 70 computers available on campus for general student use. A campuswide network can be accessed. Online class registration is available.
Website: http://necmusic.edu/

**General Application Contact:** Alex Powell, Dean for Admissions and Financial Aid, 617-585-1101, Fax: 617-585-1115, E-mail: alex.powell@necmusic.edu.

**GRADUATE UNITS**

**Graduate Program in Music** Students: 323 full-time (157 women), 23 part-time (10 women); includes 58 minority (8 Black or African American, non-Hispanic/Latino; 27 Asian, non-Hispanic/Latino; 9 Hispanic/Latino; 14 Two or more races, non-Hispanic/Latino), 152 international. Average age 23. 1,301 applicants, 33% accepted, 168 enrolled. *Faculty:* 92 full-time (31 women), 106 part-time/adjunct (37 women). Expenses: Contact institution. *Financial support:* Fellowships with partial tuition reimbursements, teaching assistantships, Federal Work-Study, scholarships/grants, and tuition waivers (partial) available. Support available to part-time students. Financial award application deadline: 12/1; financial award applicants required to submit FAFSA. In 2019, 147 master's, 10 doctorates awarded. *Application deadline:* For fall admission, 12/1 priority date for domestic and international students; for spring admission, 10/15 for domestic and international students. Applications are processed on a rolling basis. *Application fee:* $115. Electronic applications accepted. *Application Contact:* Alex Powell, Dean of Admissions and Financial Aid, 617-585-1101, Fax: 617-585-1115, E-mail: alex.powell@newenglandconservatory.edu. *Vice President and Provost,* Novak, 617-585-1308, Fax: 617-585-1303, E-mail: tom.novak@necmusic.edu.

## NEW ENGLAND INSTITUTE OF TECHNOLOGY, East Greenwich, RI 02818

**General Information** Independent, coed, comprehensive institution. *Enrollment:* 2,498 graduate, professional, and undergraduate students; 153 full-time matriculated graduate/professional students (103 women), 31 part-time matriculated graduate/professional students (20 women). *Enrollment by degree level:* 184 master's, 6 doctoral. *Graduate faculty:* 13 full-time (9 women), 6 part-time/adjunct (4 women). *Graduate housing:* On-campus housing not available. *Student services:* Campus safety program, career counseling, exercise/wellness program. *Library facilities:* New England Institute of Technology Library. *Collection:* Books: 46,560 (physical), 27,542 (digital/electronic); Serial titles: 314 (physical), 92,156 (digital/electronic); Databases: 64. Weekly public service hours: 70; students can reserve study rooms.

**Computer facilities:** 1,300 computers available on campus for general student use. A campuswide network can be accessed from off campus. Online class registration is available.
Website: http://www.neit.edu/

**General Application Contact:** Tim Reardon, Vice President for Enrollment Management and Marketing, 800-736-7744, Fax: 401-886-0859, E-mail: treardon@neit.edu.

**GRADUATE UNITS**

**Post-Professional Doctorate of Occupational Therapy**

**Program in Construction Management** Students: 22 full-time (8 women), 3 part-time (2 women); includes 7 minority (3 Black or African American, non-Hispanic/Latino; 1 American Indian or Alaska Native, non-Hispanic/Latino; 1 Asian, non-Hispanic/Latino; 2 Hispanic/Latino). Average age 32. *Faculty:* 2 part-time/adjunct (1 woman). Expenses: Contact institution. In 2019, 8 master's awarded. *Program availability:* Part-time, evening/weekend, online only, 100% online, blended/hybrid learning. *Application deadline:* Applications are processed on a rolling basis. *Application fee:* $50. Electronic applications accepted. *Application Contact:* Tim Reardon, Vice President of Enrollment Management and Marketing, 401-739-5000, Fax: 401-886-0859, E-mail: treardon@neit.edu. *Senior Vice President and Provost,* Dr. Douglas H. Sherman, 401-739-5000 Ext. 3481, Fax: 401-886-0859, E-mail: dsherman@neit.edu.

**Program in Cybersecurity Defense** Students: 5 full-time (1 woman); includes 3 minority (2 Black or African American, non-Hispanic/Latino; 1 Asian, non-Hispanic/Latino). Average age 30. Expenses: Contact institution. *Program availability:* Part-time, evening/weekend, 100% online, blended/hybrid learning. *Application deadline:* Applications are processed on a rolling basis. *Application fee:* $50. Electronic applications accepted. *Application Contact:* Tim Reardon, Vice President for Enrollment Management and Marketing, 800-736-7744 Ext. 3411, Fax: 401-886-0868, E-mail: treardon@neit.edu. *Senior Vice President and Provost,* Dr. Douglas H Sherman, 401-739-5000, Fax: 401-886-0859, E-mail: dsherman@neit.edu.

**Program in Engineering Management** Students: 6 full-time (0 women), 3 part-time (0 women); includes 4 minority (3 Black or African American, non-Hispanic/Latino; 1 Hispanic/Latino). Average age 30. Expenses: Contact institution. In 2019, 6 master's awarded. *Program availability:* Part-time, evening/weekend, 100% online, blended/hybrid learning. *Application deadline:* Applications are processed on a rolling basis. *Application fee:* $50. Electronic applications accepted. *Application Contact:* Tim Reardon, Vice President of Enrollment Management and Marketing, 401-739-5000, Fax: 401-886-0859, E-mail: treardon@neit.edu. *Senior Vice President and Provost,* Dr. Douglas H. Sherman, 401-739-5000 Ext. 3481, Fax: 401-886-0859, E-mail: dsherman@neit.edu.

**Program in Information Technology** Students: 9 full-time (3 women), 8 part-time (1 woman); includes 3 minority (2 Black or African American, non-Hispanic/Latino; 1 Asian, non-Hispanic/Latino). Average age 39. *Faculty:* 2 full-time, 1 part-time/adjunct. Expenses: Contact institution. In 2019, 14 master's awarded. *Program availability:* Part-time, evening/weekend, 100% online, blended/hybrid learning. *Application deadline:* Applications are processed on a rolling basis. *Application fee:* $50. Electronic applications accepted. *Application Contact:* Tim Reardon, Vice President of Enrollment Management and Marketing, 401-739-5000, Fax: 401-886-0859, E-mail: treardon@neit.edu. *Senior Vice President and Provost,* Dr. Douglas H. Sherman, 401-739-5000 Ext. 3481, Fax: 401-886-0859, E-mail: dsherman@neit.edu.

**Program in Nursing** Students: 7 full-time (5 women), 5 part-time (all women); includes 1 minority (Two or more races, non-Hispanic/Latino). Average age 35. Expenses: Contact institution. *Program availability:* Part-time, evening/weekend, 100% online, blended/hybrid learning. *Application deadline:* Applications are processed on a rolling basis. *Application fee:* $50. Electronic applications accepted. *Application Contact:* Tim Reardon, Vice President for Enrollment Management and Marketing, 800-736-7744, Fax: 401-886-0859, E-mail: treardon@neit.edu. *Senior Vice President and Provost,* Dr. Douglas H Sherman, 401-739-5000, Fax: 401-886-0859, E-mail: dsherman@neit.edu.

**Program in Occupational Therapy** Students: 89 full-time (75 women), 6 part-time (all women); includes 14 minority (2 Black or African American, non-Hispanic/Latino; 5 Asian, non-Hispanic/Latino; 2 Hispanic/Latino; 5 Two or more races, non-Hispanic/Latino). Average age 30. Expenses: Contact institution. In 2019, 25 master's awarded. *Program availability:* Part-time, evening/weekend, 100% online, blended/hybrid learning. *Application deadline:* Applications are processed on a rolling basis. *Application fee:* $50. Electronic applications accepted. *Application Contact:* Tim Reardon, Vice President for Enrollment Management and Marketing, 800-736-7744, Fax: 401-886-0859, E-mail: treardon@neit.edu. *Senior Vice President and Provost,* Dr. Douglas H. Sherman, 401-739-5000 Ext. 3481, Fax: 401-886-0859, E-mail: dsherman@neit.edu.

**Program in Public Health** Students: 15 full-time (11 women), 6 part-time (all women); includes 5 minority (3 Black or African American, non-Hispanic/Latino; 1 Hispanic/Latino; 1 Two or more races, non-Hispanic/Latino). Average age 32. Expenses: Contact institution. In 2019, 2 master's awarded. *Program availability:* Part-time, evening/weekend, online only, 100% online, blended/hybrid learning. *Application deadline:* Applications are processed on a rolling basis. *Application fee:* $50. Electronic applications accepted. *Application Contact:* Tim Reardon, Vice President for Enrollment Management and Marketing, 401-739-5000, Fax: 401-886-0859, E-mail: treardon@neit.edu. *Senior Vice President and Provost,* Dr. Douglas H. Sherman, 401-739-5000 Ext. 3481, Fax: 401-886-0859, E-mail: dsherman@neit.edu.

## NEW ENGLAND LAW - BOSTON, Boston, MA 02116-5687

**General Information** Independent, coed, graduate-only institution. *Graduate housing:* On-campus housing not available.

**GRADUATE UNITS**

**Graduate Programs** *Program availability:* Part-time, evening/weekend. Electronic applications accepted.

## NEW HAMPSHIRE INSTITUTE OF ART, Manchester, NH 03104

**General Information** Independent, coed, comprehensive institution. *Graduate housing:* Room and/or apartments available on a first-come, first-served basis to single students; on-campus housing not available to married students. Housing application deadline: 6/15.

**GRADUATE UNITS**

**Graduate Studies** Electronic applications accepted.

## NEW JERSEY CITY UNIVERSITY, Jersey City, NJ 07305-1597

**General Information** State-supported, coed, comprehensive institution. *Graduate housing:* On-campus housing not available.

**GRADUATE UNITS**

**College of Professional Studies** *Program availability:* Part-time, evening/weekend.

**Debra Cannon Partridge Wolfe College of Education** *Program availability:* Part-time, evening/weekend.

**Graduate Studies and Continuing Education** *Program availability:* Part-time, evening/weekend, online learning.

**School of Business** *Program availability:* Part-time, evening/weekend.

**William J. Maxwell College of Arts and Sciences** *Program availability:* Part-time, evening/weekend.

## NEW JERSEY INSTITUTE OF TECHNOLOGY, Newark, NJ 07102

**General Information** State-supported, coed, university. CGS member. *Enrollment:* 11,518 graduate, professional, and undergraduate students; 1,601 full-time matriculated graduate/professional students (529 women), 1,123 part-time matriculated graduate/professional students (311 women). *Enrollment by degree level:* 2,130 master's, 524 doctoral, 70 other advanced degrees. *Graduate faculty:* 462 full-time (108 women), 416 part-time/adjunct (109 women). *Tuition, area resident:* Part-time $1122 per credit hour. Tuition, state resident: part-time $1122 per credit hour. Tuition, nonresident: part-time $1613 per credit hour. *Graduate housing:* Room and/or apartments available on a first-come, first-served basis to single students; on-campus housing not available to married students. Housing application deadline: 3/31. *Student services:* Campus employment opportunities, campus safety program, career counseling, exercise/wellness program, free psychological counseling, grant writing training, international student services, low-cost health insurance, multicultural affairs office, services for students with disabilities, teacher training, writing training. *Library facilities:* Van Houten Library plus 1 other. *Collection:* Books: 140,063 (physical), 168,865 (digital/electronic); Serial titles: 54 (physical), 60,525 (digital/electronic); Databases: 37. Weekly public service hours: 111; students can reserve study rooms. *Research affiliation:* UT-Battele, LLC c/o ORNL, Brookhaven National Laboratory, Booz Allen Hamilton, Inc., The Wistar Institute, EPRI - Electronic Power Research Institute, ExxonMobil.

**Computer facilities:** Computer purchase and lease plans are available. 1,938 computers available on campus for general student use. A campuswide network can be accessed. Online class registration is available.
Website: http://www.njit.edu/

**General Application Contact:** Stephen Eck, Executive Director of University Admissions, 973-596-3300, Fax: 973-596-3461, E-mail: admissions@njit.edu.

**GRADUATE UNITS**

**College of Science and Liberal Arts** Students: 197 full-time (80 women), 58 part-time (14 women); includes 58 minority (18 Black or African American, non-Hispanic/Latino; 22 Asian, non-Hispanic/Latino; 16 Hispanic/Latino; 2 Two or more races, non-Hispanic/Latino), 130 international. Average age 29. 401 applicants, 63% accepted, 73 enrolled. *Faculty:* 159 full-time (42 women), 156 part-time/adjunct (61 women). Expenses: Contact institution. *Financial support:* In 2019–20, 147 students received support, including 13 fellowships with full tuition reimbursements available (averaging $24,000 per year), 41 research assistantships with full tuition reimbursements available (averaging $24,000 per year), 87 teaching assistantships with full tuition reimbursements available (averaging $24,000 per year); scholarships/grants, traineeships, health care benefits, and unspecified assistantships also available. Financial award application deadline: 1/15. In 2019, 54 master's, 10 doctorates, 1 other advanced degree awarded. *Program availability:* Part-time, evening/weekend. *Application deadline:* For fall admission, 6/1 priority date for domestic students, 5/1 priority date for international students; for spring admission, 11/15 priority date for domestic and international students. Applications are processed on a rolling basis. *Application fee:* $75. Electronic applications accepted. *Application Contact:* Stephen Eck, Director of Admissions, 973-596-3300, Fax: 973-596-3461, E-mail: admissions@njit.edu. *Dean,* Dr. Kevin Belfield, 973-596-3676, Fax: 973-565-0586, E-mail: kevin.d.belfield@njit.edu.

**J. Robert and Barbara A. Hillier College of Architecture and Design** Students: 51 full-time (33 women), 2 part-time (1 woman); includes 13 minority (1 Black or African American, non-Hispanic/Latino; 1 Asian, non-Hispanic/Latino; 8 Hispanic/Latino; 3 Two or more races, non-Hispanic/Latino), 19 international. Average age 29. 71 applicants, 63% accepted, 20 enrolled. *Faculty:* 24 full-time (9 women), 35 part-time/adjunct (16 women). Expenses: Contact institution. *Financial support:* In 2019–20, 36 students received support, including fellowships with full tuition reimbursements available (averaging $24,000 per year), 1 research assistantship with full tuition reimbursement available (averaging $24,000 per year), 7 teaching assistantships with full tuition reimbursements available (averaging $24,000 per year); career-related internships or fieldwork, Federal Work-Study, scholarships/grants, traineeships, unspecified assistantships, and studio assistantships (1 averaging $10,000) also available. Financial award application deadline: 1/15. In 2019, 27 master's awarded. *Program availability:* Part-time, evening/weekend. *Application deadline:* For fall admission, 6/1 priority date for domestic students, 5/1 priority date for international students; for spring admission, 11/15 priority date for domestic and international students. Applications are processed on a rolling basis. *Application fee:* $75. Electronic applications accepted. *Application Contact:* Stephen Eck, Executive Director of University Admissions, 973-596-3300, Fax: 973-596-3461, E-mail: admissions@njit.edu. *Dean,* Dr. Branko Kolarevic, 973-596-3080, E-mail: branko.r.kolarevic@njit.edu.

**Martin Tuchman School of Management** Students: 148 full-time (43 women), 141 part-time (78 women); includes 146 minority (41 Black or African American, non-Hispanic/Latino; 55 Asian, non-Hispanic/Latino; 42 Hispanic/Latino; 8 Two or more races, non-Hispanic/Latino), 42 international. Average age 30. 336 applicants, 73% accepted, 91 enrolled. *Faculty:* 35 full-time (9 women), 27 part-time/adjunct (7 women). Expenses: Contact institution. *Financial support:* In 2019–20, 57 students received support, including 8 fellowships with full tuition reimbursements available (averaging $24,000 per year), 7 research assistantships with full tuition reimbursements available (averaging $24,000 per year), 13 teaching assistantships with full tuition reimbursements available (averaging $24,000 per year); career-related internships or fieldwork, Federal Work-Study, scholarships/grants, and unspecified assistantships also available. Financial award application deadline: 1/15. In 2019, 67 master's, 9 other advanced degrees awarded. *Program availability:* Part-time, evening/weekend. *Application deadline:* For fall admission, 6/1 priority date for domestic students, 5/1 priority date for international students; for spring admission, 11/15 priority date for domestic and international students. Applications are processed on a rolling basis. *Application fee:* $75. Electronic applications accepted. *Application Contact:* Stephen Eck, Executive Director of University Admissions, 973-596-3300, Fax: 973-596-3461, E-mail: admissions@njit.edu. *Dean,* Dr. Oya Tukel, 973-596-3248, Fax: 973-596-3074, E-mail: oya.i.tukel@njit.edu.

**Newark College of Engineering** Students: 576 full-time (161 women), 528 part-time (111 women); includes 366 minority (61 Black or African American, non-Hispanic/Latino; 1 American Indian or Alaska Native, non-Hispanic/Latino; 166 Asian, non-Hispanic/Latino; 115 Hispanic/Latino; 23 Two or more races, non-Hispanic/Latino), 450 international. Average age 28. 2,053 applicants, 67% accepted, 338 enrolled. *Faculty:* 151 full-time (29 women), 135 part-time/adjunct (15 women). Expenses: Contact institution. *Financial support:* In 2019–20, 352 students received support, including 33 fellowships with full tuition reimbursements available (averaging $24,000 per year), 89 research assistantships with full tuition reimbursements available (averaging $24,000 per year), 112 teaching assistantships with full tuition reimbursements available (averaging $24,000 per year); career-related internships or fieldwork, Federal Work-Study, scholarships/grants, and unspecified assistantships also available. Financial award application deadline: 1/15. In 2019, 474 master's, 30 doctorates awarded. *Program availability:* Part-time, evening/weekend. *Application deadline:* For fall admission, 6/1 priority date for domestic students, 5/1 priority date for international students; for spring admission, 11/15 priority date for domestic and international students. Applications are processed on a rolling basis. *Application fee:* $75. Electronic applications accepted. *Application Contact:* Stephen Eck, Executive Director of University Admissions, 973-596-3300, Fax: 973-596-3461, E-mail: admissions@njit.edu. *Dean,* Dr. Moshe Kam, 973-596-5534, Fax: 973-596-2316, E-mail: moshe.kam@njit.edu.

**Ying Wu College of Computing** Students: 668 full-time (210 women), 290 part-time (81 women); includes 277 minority (46 Black or African American, non-Hispanic/Latino;

1 American Indian or Alaska Native, non-Hispanic/Latino; 161 Asian, non-Hispanic/Latino; 53 Hispanic/Latino; 16 Two or more races, non-Hispanic/Latino), 565 international. Average age 27. 2,671 applicants, 62% accepted, 360 enrolled. *Faculty:* 78 full-time (16 women), 63 part-time/adjunct (10 women). Expenses: Contact institution. *Financial support:* In 2019–20, 383 students received support, including 8 fellowships with full tuition reimbursements available, 34 research assistantships with full tuition reimbursements available (averaging $24,000 per year), 57 teaching assistantships with full tuition reimbursements available (averaging $24,000 per year); career-related internships or fieldwork, Federal Work-Study, scholarships/grants, and unspecified assistantships also available. Financial award application deadline: 1/15. In 2019, 407 master's, 5 doctorates, 12 other advanced degrees awarded. *Program availability:* Part-time, evening/weekend. *Application deadline:* For fall admission, 6/1 priority date for domestic students, 5/1 priority date for international students; for spring admission, 11/15 priority date for domestic and international students. Applications are processed on a rolling basis. *Application fee:* $75. Electronic applications accepted. *Application Contact:* Stephen Eck, Executive Director of University Admissions, 973-596-3300, Fax: 973-596-3461, E-mail: admissions@njit.edu. *Dean*, Dr. Craig Gotsman, 973-596-3366, Fax: 973-596-5777, E-mail: craig.gotsman@njit.edu.

## NEWMAN THEOLOGICAL COLLEGE, Edmonton, AB T6V 1H3, Canada

**General Information** Independent-religious, coed, graduate-only institution. *Enrollment:* 35 full-time matriculated graduate/professional students (6 women), 199 part-time matriculated graduate/professional students (122 women). *Enrollment by degree level:* 123 master's, 3 other advanced degrees. *Graduate faculty:* 14 full-time (3 women), 8 part-time/adjunct (2 women). *Tuition:* Full-time $6900 Canadian dollars; part-time $690 Canadian dollars per course. *Required fees:* $310 Canadian dollars; $190 Canadian dollars per unit. $95 Canadian dollars per semester. One-time fee: $45 Canadian dollars. Tuition and fees vary according to course load. *Graduate housing:* On-campus housing not available. *Student services:* Campus employment opportunities, career counseling, free psychological counseling, services for students with disabilities. *Library facilities:* Sopchyshyn Family Library. *Collection:* Books: 72,000 (physical); Serial titles: 181 (physical); Databases: 13. Weekly public service hours: 45; students can reserve study rooms.

**Computer facilities:** 5 computers available on campus for general student use. Website: http://www.newman.edu/

**General Application Contact:** Maria Saulnier, Registrar, 780-392-2451, Fax: 780-462-4013, E-mail: registrar@newman.edu.

**GRADUATE UNITS**

**Religious Education Programs** Students: 1 (woman) full-time, 87 part-time (68 women). Average age 40. 40 applicants, 100% accepted, 40 enrolled. *Faculty:* 2 full-time (1 woman), 4 part-time/adjunct (1 woman). Expenses: Contact institution. *Financial support:* In 2019–20, 9 students received support. Tuition bursaries available. Support available to part-time students. Financial award application deadline: 5/31. In 2019, 25 master's awarded. *Program availability:* Part-time, blended/hybrid learning. *Application deadline:* For fall admission, 8/19 priority date for domestic students, 2/19 priority date for international students; for winter admission, 11/20 priority date for domestic students; for spring admission, 2/19 priority date for domestic students. Applications are processed on a rolling basis. *Application fee:* $45 ($250 for international students). *Application Contact:* Maria Saulnier, Registrar, 780-392-2451, Fax: 780-462-4013, E-mail: registrar@newman.edu. *Director*, Sandra Talarico, 780-392-2450 Ext. 2214, Fax: 780-462-4013, E-mail: sandra.talarico@newman.edu.

**Theology Programs** Students: 27 full-time (4 women), 9 part-time (5 women). Average age 30. 19 applicants, 100% accepted, 18 enrolled. *Faculty:* 14 full-time (3 women), 5 part-time/adjunct (1 woman). Expenses: Contact institution. *Financial support:* In 2019–20, 6 students received support. Tuition bursaries available. Support available to part-time students. Financial award application deadline: 5/31. In 2019, 7 master's awarded. *Program availability:* Part-time, 100% online. *Application deadline:* For fall admission, 8/19 priority date for domestic students, 2/19 priority date for international students; for winter admission, 11/20 priority date for domestic students; for spring admission, 2/19 priority date for domestic students. Applications are processed on a rolling basis. *Application fee:* $45 ($250 for international students). *Application Contact:* Maria Saulnier, Registrar, 780-392-2451, Fax: 780-462-4013, E-mail: registrar@newman.edu. *Academic Dean/Vice President*, Dr. Ryan Topping, 780-392-2450 Ext. 2444, Fax: 780-462-4013, E-mail: ryan.topping@newman.edu.

## NEWMAN UNIVERSITY, Wichita, KS 67213-2097

**General Information** Independent-religious, coed, comprehensive institution. *Graduate housing:* Rooms and/or apartments available on a first-come, first-served basis to single and married students. Housing application deadline: 8/1.

**GRADUATE UNITS**

**Graduate Theology Program** *Program availability:* Part-time, online learning.

**Master of Science in Education Program** *Program availability:* Part-time, evening/weekend, online learning. Electronic applications accepted.

**MBA Program** *Program availability:* Part-time. Electronic applications accepted.

**School of Nursing and Allied Health** Electronic applications accepted.

**School of Social Work** *Program availability:* Online learning.

## NEW MEXICO HIGHLANDS UNIVERSITY, Las Vegas, NM 87701

**General Information** State-supported, coed, comprehensive institution. CGS member. *Graduate housing:* Rooms and/or apartments guaranteed to single and married students. *Research affiliation:* Spectra Gases, Inc. (chemistry), Los Alamos National Laboratory (chemistry), Sigma Aldrich (chemistry).

**GRADUATE UNITS**

**Graduate Studies** *Program availability:* Part-time.

***College of Arts and Sciences*** *Program availability:* Part-time. Electronic applications accepted.

***Facundo Valdez School of Social Work*** *Program availability:* Part-time.

***School of Business, Media and Technology***

***School of Education*** *Program availability:* Part-time.

## NEW MEXICO INSTITUTE OF MINING AND TECHNOLOGY, Socorro, NM 87801

**General Information** State-supported, coed, university. CGS member. *Graduate housing:* Rooms and/or apartments available on a first-come, first-served basis to single and married students. Housing application deadline: 6/1. *Research affiliation:* Gas Technology Institute (natural gas recovery), Optical Surface Technologies LLC (custom optical components), National Center for Atmospheric Research (atmosphere research), National Radio Astronomy Observatory (astronomy), Joint Center for Materials Research (materials engineering, metallurgy).

**GRADUATE UNITS**

**Center for Graduate Studies** Electronic applications accepted.

## NEW MEXICO STATE UNIVERSITY, Las Cruces, NM 88003-8001

**General Information** State-supported, coed, university. CGS member. *Enrollment:* 14,296 graduate, professional, and undergraduate students; 1,278 full-time matriculated graduate/professional students (695 women), 857 part-time matriculated graduate/professional students (529 women). *Enrollment by degree level:* 1,467 master's, 633 doctoral, 35 other advanced degrees. *Graduate faculty:* 500 full-time (203 women), 59 part-time/adjunct (39 women). *Graduate housing:* Rooms and/or apartments available on a first-come, first-served basis to single and married students. Typical cost: $6244 per year ($7544 including board) for single students; $9720 per year ($11,020 including board) for married students. Housing application deadline: 7/1. *Student services:* Campus employment opportunities, campus safety program, career counseling, child daycare facilities, exercise/wellness program, free psychological counseling, grant writing training, international student services, low-cost health insurance, multicultural affairs office, services for students with disabilities, teacher training, writing training. *Library facilities:* New Mexico State University Library - Zuhl plus 1 other. *Collection:* Books: 1.2 million (physical), 160,068 (digital/electronic); Serial titles: 23,730 (physical), 135,113 (digital/electronic); Databases: 410. Weekly public service hours: 112; students can reserve study rooms. *Research affiliation:* Sandia National Laboratories (energy research, computation), NASA (STEM education research), Fred Hutchinson Cancer Research Center (cancer research), U.S. Air Force Research Laboratory (AFRL) (space weather, high energy research), U.S. Bureau of Land Management (BLM) (resource management research), Los Alamos National Laboratory (energy research, environmental sciences, information sciences).

**Computer facilities:** Computer purchase and lease plans are available. 708 computers available on campus for general student use. A campuswide network can be accessed. Online class registration, antivirus software; student portal online with file share/storage space, student employee clock-in, payments system, hardware rentals, short-term tablet checkout, software discounts are available.
Website: http://www.nmsu.edu/

**General Application Contact:** Dr. Luis Cifuentes, Dean, 575-646-5746, Fax: 575-646-7758, E-mail: gradinfo@nmsu.edu.

**GRADUATE UNITS**

**College of Agricultural, Consumer and Environmental Sciences** Students: 140 full-time (91 women), 68 part-time (41 women); includes 72 minority (3 Black or African American, non-Hispanic/Latino; 2 American Indian or Alaska Native, non-Hispanic/Latino; 6 Asian, non-Hispanic/Latino; 58 Hispanic/Latino; 3 Two or more races, non-Hispanic/Latino), 32 international. Average age 29. 121 applicants, 67% accepted, 56 enrolled. *Faculty:* 74 full-time (25 women), 3 part-time/adjunct (1 woman). Expenses: Contact institution. *Financial support:* In 2019–20, 208 students received support, including 3 fellowships (averaging $4,844 per year), 73 research assistantships (averaging $20,501 per year), 58 teaching assistantships (averaging $14,657 per year); career-related internships or fieldwork, Federal Work-Study, scholarships/grants, traineeships, health care benefits, and unspecified assistantships also available. Support available to part-time students. Financial award application deadline: 3/1. In 2019, 63 master's, 4 doctorates awarded. *Program availability:* Part-time. *Application deadline:* For fall admission, 8/15 for domestic and international students; for spring admission, 12/15 for domestic and international students; for summer admission, 5/15 for domestic and international students. Applications are processed on a rolling basis. *Application fee:* $40 ($50 for international students). Electronic applications accepted. *Application Contact:* Dr. Donald Conner, Associate Dean, 575-646-1109, Fax: 575-646-5975, E-mail: deconner@nmsu.edu. *Dean*, Dr. Rolando A. Flores, 575-646-3748, Fax: 575-646-5975, E-mail: agdean@nmsu.edu.

**College of Arts and Sciences** Students: 459 full-time (219 women), 188 part-time (95 women); includes 259 minority (22 Black or African American, non-Hispanic/Latino; 5 American Indian or Alaska Native, non-Hispanic/Latino; 32 Asian, non-Hispanic/Latino; 181 Hispanic/Latino; 19 Two or more races, non-Hispanic/Latino), 155 international. Average age 31. 688 applicants, 57% accepted, 166 enrolled. *Faculty:* 211 full-time (83 women), 10 part-time/adjunct (6 women). Expenses: Contact institution. *Financial support:* In 2019–20, 450 students received support, including 31 fellowships (averaging $4,433 per year), 97 research assistantships (averaging $17,452 per year), 290 teaching assistantships (averaging $17,146 per year); career-related internships or fieldwork, Federal Work-Study, scholarships/grants, traineeships, health care benefits, and unspecified assistantships also available. Support available to part-time students. Financial award application deadline: 3/1. In 2019, 178 master's, 40 doctorates, 21 other advanced degrees awarded. *Program availability:* Part-time, online learning. *Application fee:* $40 ($50 for international students). Electronic applications accepted. *Application Contact:* Dr. James Murphy, Associate Dean, 575-646-3500, Fax: 575-646-6799, E-mail: murphy@nmsu.edu. *Dean*, Dr. Enrico Pontelli, 575-646-3500, Fax: 575-646-6799, E-mail: epontell@nmsu.edu.

**College of Business** Students: 88 full-time (42 women), 74 part-time (38 women); includes 84 minority (4 Black or African American, non-Hispanic/Latino; 1 American Indian or Alaska Native, non-Hispanic/Latino; 7 Asian, non-Hispanic/Latino; 71 Hispanic/Latino; 1 Two or more races, non-Hispanic/Latino), 38 international. Average age 33. 203 applicants, 73% accepted, 55 enrolled. *Faculty:* 52 full-time (13 women). Expenses: Contact institution. *Financial support:* In 2019–20, 86 students received support, including 1 fellowship (averaging $4,844 per year), 2 research assistantships (averaging $18,582 per year), 42 teaching assistantships (averaging $18,361 per year); career-related internships or fieldwork, Federal Work-Study, scholarships/grants, traineeships, health care benefits, and unspecified assistantships also available. Support available to part-time students. Financial award application deadline: 3/1. In 2019, 100 master's, 15 doctorates, 15 other advanced degrees awarded. *Program availability:* Part-time, 100% online. *Application deadline:* For fall admission, 7/1 priority date for domestic students; for spring admission, 11/1 for domestic students. Applications are processed on a rolling basis. *Application fee:* $40 ($50 for international students). Electronic applications accepted. *Application Contact:* Graduate Admissions, 575-646-3121, E-mail: admissions@nmsu.edu. *Dean*, Dr. James Hoffman, 575-646-2821, Fax: 575-646-6155, E-mail: jhoffman@nmsu.edu.

**College of Education** Students: 232 full-time (177 women), 361 part-time (270 women); includes 349 minority (20 Black or African American, non-Hispanic/Latino; 9 American Indian or Alaska Native, non-Hispanic/Latino; 14 Asian, non-Hispanic/Latino; 287 Hispanic/Latino; 2 Native Hawaiian or other Pacific Islander, non-Hispanic/Latino; 17 Two or more races, non-Hispanic/Latino), 25 international. Average age 36. 419 applicants, 56% accepted, 172 enrolled. *Faculty:* 60 full-time (42 women), 23 part-time/adjunct (18 women). Expenses: Contact institution. *Financial support:* In 2019–20,

296 students received support, including 14 fellowships (averaging $4,844 per year), 26 research assistantships (averaging $12,990 per year), 50 teaching assistantships (averaging $14,358 per year); career-related internships or fieldwork, Federal Work-Study, scholarships/grants, traineeships, health care benefits, and unspecified assistantships also available. Support available to part-time students. Financial award application deadline: 3/1. In 2019, 156 master's, 29 doctorates, 26 other advanced degrees awarded. *Program availability:* Part-time-only, evening/weekend, blended/hybrid learning. *Application deadline:* For fall admission, 3/15 for international students; for spring admission, 10/15 for international students. Applications are processed on a rolling basis. *Application fee:* $40 ($50 for international students). Electronic applications accepted. *Application Contact:* Dr. David Rutledge, Graduate Education Advising, 575-646-5411, Fax: 575-646-6032, E-mail: rutledge@nmsu.edu. *Interim Dean*, Dr. Susan Brown, 575-646-5858, Fax: 575-646-6032, E-mail: susanbro@nmsu.edu.

**College of Engineering** Students: 212 full-time (51 women), 82 part-time (21 women); includes 98 minority (5 Black or African American, non-Hispanic/Latino; 1 American Indian or Alaska Native, non-Hispanic/Latino; 13 Asian, non-Hispanic/Latino; 70 Hispanic/Latino; 9 Two or more races, non-Hispanic/Latino), 117 international. Average age 30. 220 applicants, 63% accepted, 57 enrolled. *Faculty:* 63 full-time (11 women), 4 part-time/adjunct (0 women). Expenses: Contact institution. *Financial support:* In 2019–20, 228 students received support, including 13 fellowships (averaging $3,752 per year), 94 research assistantships (averaging $15,692 per year), 59 teaching assistantships (averaging $13,560 per year); career-related internships or fieldwork, Federal Work-Study, scholarships/grants, traineeships, health care benefits, and unspecified assistantships also available. Support available to part-time students. Financial award application deadline: 3/1. In 2019, 112 master's, 21 doctorates, 6 other advanced degrees awarded. *Program availability:* Part-time, online learning. *Application deadline:* For fall admission, 7/1 priority date for domestic students; for spring admission, 11/1 for domestic students. Applications are processed on a rolling basis. *Application fee:* $40 ($50 for international students). Electronic applications accepted. *Application Contact:* Graduate Admissions, 575-646-3121, E-mail: admissions@nmsu.edu. *Dean*, Dr. Lakshmi Reddi, 575-646-7234, Fax: 575-646-3549, E-mail: engrdean@nmsu.edu.

***Klipsch School of Electrical and Computer Engineering*** Students: 53 full-time (12 women), 39 part-time (9 women); includes 31 minority (3 Black or African American, non-Hispanic/Latino; 7 Asian, non-Hispanic/Latino; 19 Hispanic/Latino; 2 Two or more races, non-Hispanic/Latino), 29 international. Average age 31. 57 applicants, 65% accepted, 19 enrolled. *Faculty:* 19 full-time (2 women). Expenses: Contact institution. *Financial support:* In 2019–20, 58 students received support, including 29 research assistantships (averaging $15,554 per year), 14 teaching assistantships (averaging $12,445 per year); career-related internships or fieldwork, Federal Work-Study, scholarships/grants, traineeships, health care benefits, and unspecified assistantships also available. Support available to part-time students. Financial award application deadline: 3/1. In 2019, 25 master's, 7 doctorates, 5 other advanced degrees awarded. *Program availability:* Part-time, evening/weekend, 100% online. *Application deadline:* For fall admission, 3/1 priority date for domestic and international students; for spring admission, 8/1 priority date for domestic and international students. Applications are processed on a rolling basis. *Application fee:* $40 ($50 for international students). Electronic applications accepted. *Application Contact:* Dr. Steven Stochaj, Interim Department Head, 575-646-3115, Fax: 575-646-1435, E-mail: sstochaj@nmsu.edu. *Interim Department Head*, Dr. Steven Stochaj, 575-646-3115, Fax: 575-646-1435, E-mail: sstochaj@nmsu.edu.

**College of Health and Social Services** Students: 138 full-time (106 women), 78 part-time (65 women); includes 123 minority (12 Black or African American, non-Hispanic/Latino; 7 American Indian or Alaska Native, non-Hispanic/Latino; 5 Asian, non-Hispanic/Latino; 93 Hispanic/Latino; 6 Two or more races, non-Hispanic/Latino), 11 international. Average age 32. 274 applicants, 86% accepted, 97 enrolled. *Faculty:* 37 full-time (29 women), 19 part-time/adjunct (14 women). Expenses: Contact institution. *Financial support:* In 2019–20, 99 students received support, including 1 fellowship (averaging $4,844 per year), 11 research assistantships (averaging $10,091 per year), 18 teaching assistantships (averaging $11,146 per year); career-related internships or fieldwork, Federal Work-Study, scholarships/grants, traineeships, health care benefits, and unspecified assistantships also available. Support available to part-time students. Financial award application deadline: 3/1. In 2019, 74 master's, 20 doctorates, 9 other advanced degrees awarded. *Program availability:* Part-time, evening/weekend, online learning. *Application deadline:* For fall admission, 7/1 priority date for domestic students. Applications are processed on a rolling basis. *Application fee:* $40 ($50 for international students). Electronic applications accepted. *Application Contact:* Graduate Admissions, 575-646-3121, E-mail: admissions@nmsu.edu. *Dean*, Dr. Sonya Cooper, 575-646-3526, Fax: 575-646-6166, E-mail: socooper@nmsu.edu.

***School of Nursing*** Students: 29. 57 applicants, 98% accepted. *Faculty:* 12 full-time (all women). Expenses: Contact institution. *Financial support:* In 2019–20, 7 teaching assistantships (averaging $10,499 per year) were awarded; career-related internships or fieldwork, Federal Work-Study, scholarships/grants, traineeships, health care benefits, and unspecified assistantships also available. Support available to part-time students. Financial award application deadline: 3/1. In 2019, 4 master's, 20 doctorates, 5 other advanced degrees awarded. *Program availability:* Part-time, blended/hybrid learning. *Application deadline:* For fall admission, 2/1 priority date for domestic students, 2/1 for international students. *Application fee:* $40 ($50 for international students). Electronic applications accepted. *Application Contact:* Alyce Kolenovsky, Academic Advisor, 575-646-3812, Fax: 575-646-2167, E-mail: nursing@nmsu.edu. *Director*, Dr. Alexa Doig, 575-646-3812, Fax: 575-646-2167, E-mail: adoig@nmsu.edu.

***School of Social Work*** Students: 98 full-time (77 women), 12 part-time (10 women); includes 69 minority (8 Black or African American, non-Hispanic/Latino; 1 American Indian or Alaska Native, non-Hispanic/Latino; 1 Asian, non-Hispanic/Latino; 57 Hispanic/Latino; 2 Two or more races, non-Hispanic/Latino), 2 international. Average age 31. 108 applicants, 78% accepted, 41 enrolled. *Faculty:* 12 full-time (8 women), 15 part-time/adjunct (11 women). Expenses: Contact institution. *Financial support:* In 2019–20, 57 students received support, including 7 research assistantships (averaging $9,049 per year), 1 teaching assistantship (averaging $9,081 per year); career-related internships or fieldwork, Federal Work-Study, scholarships/grants, traineeships, health care benefits, and unspecified assistantships also available. Support available to part-time students. Financial award application deadline: 3/1. In 2019, 47 master's awarded. *Program availability:* Part-time, blended/hybrid learning. *Application deadline:* For fall admission, 1/16 priority date for domestic students, 2/16 priority date for international students. Applications are processed on a rolling basis. *Application fee:* $40 ($50 for international students). Electronic applications accepted. *Application Contact:* MSW Program Coordinator, 575-646-2143, Fax: 575-646-4116, E-mail: socwork@nmsu.edu. *Interim Department Head*, Dr. Loui Reyes, 575-646-4820, Fax: 575-646-4116, E-mail: louireye@nmsu.edu.

**Graduate School** Students: 36 full-time (23 women), 19 part-time (6 women); includes 18 minority (1 American Indian or Alaska Native, non-Hispanic/Latino; 3 Asian, non-Hispanic/Latino; 14 Hispanic/Latino), 18 international. Average age 35. 33 applicants, 64% accepted, 6 enrolled. *Faculty:* 3 full-time (0 women). Expenses: Contact institution. *Financial support:* In 2019–20, 38 students received support, including 3 fellowships (averaging $4,844 per year), 10 research assistantships (averaging $21,436 per year), 3 teaching assistantships (averaging $18,302 per year); career-related internships or fieldwork, Federal Work-Study, scholarships/grants, traineeships, health care benefits, and unspecified assistantships also available. Support available to part-time students. Financial award application deadline: 3/1. In 2019, 4 master's, 5 doctorates awarded. *Program availability:* Part-time, evening/weekend, online learning. *Application fee:* $40 ($50 for international students). Electronic applications accepted. *Application Contact:* Graduate Admissions, 575-646-3121, E-mail: admissions@nmsu.edu. *Dean*, Dr. Luis Cifuentes, 575-646-5746, Fax: 575-646-7758, E-mail: gradinfo@nmsu.edu.

## NEW ORLEANS BAPTIST THEOLOGICAL SEMINARY, New Orleans, LA 70126-4858

**General Information** Independent-religious, coed, primarily men, comprehensive institution. *Graduate housing:* Rooms and/or apartments available to single and married students.

**GRADUATE UNITS**

**Graduate and Professional Programs** *Program availability:* Evening/weekend.

***Division of Biblical Studies***

***Division of Christian Education Ministries*** *Program availability:* Evening/weekend, online learning.

***Division of Church Music Ministries*** *Program availability:* Online learning.

***Division of Pastoral Ministries*** *Program availability:* Online learning.

***Division of Theological and Historical Studies*** *Program availability:* Online learning.

## NEW SAINT ANDREWS COLLEGE, Moscow, ID 83843

**General Information** Independent-religious, coed, comprehensive institution. *Enrollment:* 158 graduate, professional, and undergraduate students; 27 full-time matriculated graduate/professional students (13 women), 3 part-time matriculated graduate/professional students (1 woman). *Enrollment by degree level:* 30 master's. *Graduate faculty:* 1 full-time (0 women), 13 part-time/adjunct (1 woman). *Tuition:* Full-time $8800; part-time $550 per credit. *Graduate housing:* On-campus housing not available. *Student services:* Campus employment opportunities, career counseling, international student services. *Library facilities:* Tyndale Library plus 1 other. *Collection:* Students can reserve study rooms.

**Computer facilities:** 4 computers available on campus for general student use. A campuswide network can be accessed. Online class registration is available.
Website: http://www.nsa.edu/

**General Application Contact:** Brenda Schlect, Director of Admissions, 208-882-1566 Ext. 113, Fax: 208-882-4293, E-mail: admissions@nsa.edu.

**GRADUATE UNITS**

**Graduate School** *Program availability:* Part-time, blended/hybrid learning. Electronic applications accepted.

## THE NEW SCHOOL, New York, NY 10011

**General Information** Independent, coed, university. *Enrollment by degree level:* 2,445 master's, 439 doctoral, 115 other advanced degrees. *Graduate faculty:* 428 full-time (217 women), 884 part-time/adjunct (456 women). *Tuition:* Full-time $46,710; part-time $1952 per credit hour. *Required fees:* $1216; $608 per semester. $608 per summer. One-time fee: $50. Tuition and fees vary according to program. *Graduate housing:* Room and/or apartments available on a first-come, first-served basis to single students; on-campus housing not available to married students. Typical cost: $20,080 per year ($23,400 including board). Room and board charges vary according to board plan, campus/location and housing facility selected. Housing application deadline: 5/8. *Student services:* Campus employment opportunities, campus safety program, career counseling, exercise/wellness program, free psychological counseling, grant writing training, international student services, low-cost health insurance, multicultural affairs office, services for students with disabilities, writing training. *Research affiliation:* The Goldman Sachs Group, Inc., Siemens, Raytheon Corporation, National Geospatial-Intelligence Agency, Environmental Systems Research Institute, Dow Jones & Company, Inc.
Website: http://www.newschool.edu/

**General Application Contact:** Erin Stine, Assistant Vice President, 212-229-8989 Ext. 4020, E-mail: stinee@newschool.edu.

**GRADUATE UNITS**

**College of Performing Arts** Students: 405 full-time (256 women), 4 part-time (0 women); includes 72 minority (24 Black or African American, non-Hispanic/Latino; 17 Asian, non-Hispanic/Latino; 26 Hispanic/Latino; 5 Two or more races, non-Hispanic/Latino), 207 international. Average age 26. 1,062 applicants, 44% accepted, 409 enrolled. *Faculty:* 9 full-time (3 women), 480 part-time/adjunct. Expenses: Contact institution. *Financial support:* In 2019–20, 389 students received support, including 5 fellowships (averaging $2,247 per year), 5 teaching assistantships (averaging $6,554 per year); career-related internships or fieldwork and scholarships/grants also available. Support available to part-time students. Financial award application deadline: 2/1; financial award applicants required to submit FAFSA. In 2019, 115 master's, 27 other advanced degrees awarded. *Program availability:* Part-time. *Application deadline:* For fall admission, 1/15 priority date for domestic and international students; for spring admission, 10/15 priority date for domestic and international students. Applications are processed on a rolling basis. *Application fee:* $50. Electronic applications accepted. *Application Contact:* Amanda Hosking, Director of Admission, College of Performing Arts, 212-229-5150, E-mail: copaadmissions@newschool.edu. *Executive Dean, College of Performing Arts*, Richard Kessler, 212-580-0210 Ext. 4848, E-mail: richardkessler@newschool.edu.

***Mannes School of Music*** Students: 315 full-time (200 women), 3 part-time (0 women); includes 35 minority (4 Black or African American, non-Hispanic/Latino; 17 Asian, non-Hispanic/Latino; 10 Hispanic/Latino; 4 Two or more races, non-Hispanic/Latino), 192 international. Average age 25. 894 applicants, 44% accepted, 318 enrolled. *Faculty:* 9 full-time (4 women), 128 part-time/adjunct (53 women). Expenses: Contact institution. *Financial support:* In 2019–20, 303 students received support, including 4 fellowships (averaging $4,994 per year), 4 research assistantships (averaging $2,887 per year), 4 teaching assistantships (averaging $7,022 per year); career-related internships or fieldwork, Federal Work-Study, scholarships/grants, and unspecified assistantships also available. Support available to part-time students. Financial award application deadline: 2/1; financial award applicants required to submit FAFSA. In

2019, 103 master's, 27 Advanced Diplomas awarded. *Program availability:* Part-time. *Application deadline:* For fall admission, 12/1 priority date for domestic and international students; for spring admission, 10/15 priority date for domestic and international students. Applications are processed on a rolling basis. *Application fee:* $50. Electronic applications accepted. *Application Contact:* Amanda Hosking, Director of Admission, College of Performing Arts, 212-229-5150 Ext. 4805, E-mail: performingarts@newschool.edu. *Executive Dean, College of Performing Arts,* Richard Kessler, 212-580-0210 Ext. 4848, E-mail: richardkessler@newschool.edu.

***School of Drama*** Students: 63 full-time (37 women); includes 30 minority (17 Black or African American, non-Hispanic/Latino; 12 Hispanic/Latino; 1 Two or more races, non-Hispanic/Latino), 8 international. Average age 28. 131 applicants, 24% accepted, 25 enrolled. *Faculty:* 6 full-time (0 women), 141 part-time/adjunct. Expenses: Contact institution. *Financial support:* In 2019–20, 60 students received support, including 1 fellowship (averaging $6,243 per year), 1 teaching assistantship (averaging $4,682 per year); career-related internships or fieldwork, Federal Work-Study, scholarships/grants, and unspecified assistantships also available. Support available to part-time students. Financial award application deadline: 2/1; financial award applicants required to submit FAFSA. In 2019, 18 master's awarded. *Program availability:* Part-time. *Application deadline:* For fall admission, 12/1 priority date for domestic and international students; for spring admission, 1/15 for domestic students, 1/15 priority date for international students. Applications are processed on a rolling basis. *Application fee:* $50. Electronic applications accepted. *Application Contact:* Marlon Meikle, Assistant Director of Admissions, College of Performing Arts, 212-229-5859 Ext. 4828, E-mail: performingarts@newschool.edu. *Dean, School of Drama,* Pippin Parker, 212-229-5859 Ext. 2636, E-mail: parkerp@newschool.edu.

**The New School for Social Research** Students: 637 full-time (344 women), 105 part-time (67 women); includes 123 minority (26 Black or African American, non-Hispanic/Latino; 25 Asian, non-Hispanic/Latino; 56 Hispanic/Latino; 1 Native Hawaiian or other Pacific Islander, non-Hispanic/Latino; 15 Two or more races, non-Hispanic/Latino), 283 international. Average age 31. 832 applicants, 72% accepted, 166 enrolled. *Faculty:* 99 full-time (58 women). Expenses: Contact institution. *Financial support:* In 2019–20, 587 students received support, including 79 fellowships (averaging $6,866 per year), 157 research assistantships (averaging $5,006 per year), 150 teaching assistantships with full and partial tuition reimbursements available (averaging $7,736 per year); career-related internships or fieldwork, Federal Work-Study, scholarships/grants, and tuition waivers (full and partial) also available. Support available to part-time students. Financial award application deadline: 2/1; financial award applicants required to submit FAFSA. In 2019, 247 master's, 53 doctorates awarded. *Program availability:* Part-time. *Application deadline:* For fall admission, 6/15 priority date for domestic and international students; for spring admission, 10/15 priority date for domestic and international students. Applications are processed on a rolling basis. *Application fee:* $50. Electronic applications accepted. *Application Contact:* Mérida Gasbarro, Director of Graduate Admission, 212-229-5600 Ext. 1108, E-mail: escandom@newschool.edu. *Dean, The New School for Social Research,* Dr. William Milberg, 212-229-5777, E-mail: milbergw@newschool.edu.

**Parsons Paris** Students: 41 full-time (38 women), 4 part-time (all women); includes 7 minority (4 Black or African American, non-Hispanic/Latino; 1 Asian, non-Hispanic/Latino; 2 Hispanic/Latino), 22 international. Average age 26. 36 applicants, 78% accepted, 15 enrolled. *Faculty:* 5 full-time (2 women), 46 part-time/adjunct (31 women). Expenses: Contact institution. *Financial support:* In 2019–20, 29 students received support. Career-related internships or fieldwork and scholarships/grants available. Financial award application deadline: 2/1; financial award applicants required to submit FAFSA. In 2019, 13 master's awarded. *Program availability:* Part-time. *Application deadline:* For fall admission, 1/1 priority date for domestic and international students. Applications are processed on a rolling basis. *Application fee:* $50. Electronic applications accepted. *Application Contact:* Mike Fakih, Director of Admissions, Parsons Paris, 33 176 21 76 67, E-mail: thinkparsonsparis@newschool.edu. *Dean,* Florence Leclerc-Dickler, 33-176217661, E-mail: leclercf@newschool.edu.

**Parsons School of Design** Students: 885 full-time (673 women), 71 part-time (53 women); includes 194 minority (48 Black or African American, non-Hispanic/Latino; 66 Asian, non-Hispanic/Latino; 61 Hispanic/Latino; 2 Native Hawaiian or other Pacific Islander, non-Hispanic/Latino; 17 Two or more races, non-Hispanic/Latino), 537 international. Average age 27. 2,440 applicants, 44% accepted, 453 enrolled. *Faculty:* 171 full-time (85 women), 235 part-time/adjunct. Expenses: Contact institution. *Financial support:* In 2019–20, 599 students received support, including 1 fellowship (averaging $2,081 per year), 145 research assistantships (averaging $2,809 per year), 78 teaching assistantships (averaging $5,514 per year); career-related internships or fieldwork, Federal Work-Study, scholarships/grants, unspecified assistantships, and travel funding; tuition waivers for students who are also New School employees also available. Support available to part-time students. Financial award application deadline: 2/1; financial award applicants required to submit FAFSA. In 2019, 457 master's awarded. *Program availability:* Part-time. *Application deadline:* For fall admission, 1/1 priority date for domestic and international students; for summer admission, 1/1 priority date for domestic and international students. Applications are processed on a rolling basis. *Application fee:* $50. Electronic applications accepted. *Application Contact:* Simone Varadian, Senior Director I, 212-229-5150 Ext. 4117, E-mail: thinkparsonsgrad@newschool.edu. *Executive Dean, Parsons School of Design,* Dr. Rachel Schreiber, 212-229-8950 Ext. 4393, E-mail: schreibr@newschool.edu.

**Schools of Public Engagement** Students: 658 full-time (487 women), 234 part-time (169 women); includes 294 minority (118 Black or African American, non-Hispanic/Latino; 37 Asian, non-Hispanic/Latino; 115 Hispanic/Latino; 1 Native Hawaiian or other Pacific Islander, non-Hispanic/Latino; 23 Two or more races, non-Hispanic/Latino), 225 international. Average age 29. 963 applicants, 88% accepted, 342 enrolled. *Faculty:* 94 full-time, 141 part-time/adjunct. Expenses: Contact institution. *Financial support:* In 2019–20, 731 students received support, including 17 fellowships (averaging $5,342 per year), 91 research assistantships (averaging $4,686 per year), 32 teaching assistantships (averaging $5,284 per year); career-related internships or fieldwork, Federal Work-Study, scholarships/grants, and unspecified assistantships also available. Support available to part-time students. Financial award application deadline: 2/1; financial award applicants required to submit FAFSA. In 2019, 384 master's, 4 doctorates, 37 other advanced degrees awarded. *Program availability:* Part-time, 100% online. *Application deadline:* For fall admission, 1/15 priority date for domestic and international students; for spring admission, 10/15 priority date for domestic and international students. Applications are processed on a rolling basis. *Application fee:* $50. Electronic applications accepted. *Application Contact:* Merida Gasbarro, Director of Graduate Admission, 212-229-5600 Ext. 1108, E-mail: escandom@newschool.edu. *Executive Dean, Schools of Public Engagement,* Mary Watson, 212-229-5613 Ext. 2130, E-mail: watsonm@newschool.edu.

## NEWSCHOOL OF ARCHITECTURE AND DESIGN, San Diego, CA 92101-6634

**General Information** Proprietary, coed, primarily men, comprehensive institution. *Research affiliation:* Academy of Neuroscience for Architecture (neuroscience and architecture).

**GRADUATE UNITS**

**Program in Architecture** *Program availability:* Part-time, online learning.

**Program in Construction Management** *Program availability:* Part-time, online learning. Electronic applications accepted.

## NEW YORK ACADEMY OF ART, New York, NY 10013-2911

**General Information** Independent, coed, graduate-only institution. *Graduate housing:* On-campus housing not available.

**GRADUATE UNITS**

**Master of Fine Arts Program** Electronic applications accepted.

## NEW YORK CHIROPRACTIC COLLEGE, Seneca Falls, NY 13148-0800

**General Information** Independent, coed, graduate-only institution. *Graduate housing:* Rooms and/or apartments available on a first-come, first-served basis to single and married students. *Research affiliation:* Foot Levelers, Inc. (orthotics research), Atrium Innovations (nutrition), Nimmo Education Foundation (muscle physiology).

**GRADUATE UNITS**

**Doctor of Chiropractic Program** Electronic applications accepted.

**Finger Lakes School of Acupuncture and Oriental Medicine** Electronic applications accepted.

**Program in Applied Clinical Nutrition** *Program availability:* Part-time, evening/weekend. Electronic applications accepted.

**Program in Clinical Anatomy** Electronic applications accepted.

**Program in Human Anatomy and Physiology Instruction** *Program availability:* Online learning.

## NEW YORK COLLEGE OF HEALTH PROFESSIONS, Syosset, NY 11791-4413

**General Information** Independent, coed, comprehensive institution. *Graduate housing:* On-campus housing not available. *Research affiliation:* North Shore Hospital (acupuncture).

**GRADUATE UNITS**

**Graduate School of Oriental Medicine** *Program availability:* Part-time.

## NEW YORK COLLEGE OF PODIATRIC MEDICINE, New York, NY 10035

**General Information** Independent, coed, graduate-only institution. *Graduate housing:* Rooms and/or apartments available on a first-come, first-served basis to single and married students. Housing application deadline: 8/15. *Research affiliation:* Cyberlogics (ultrasound use), Novartis Pharmaceuticals (fungal diseases of nail), Prescription Dispensing Laboratories (topical verapamil), Anodyne Corporation (light energy applications).

**GRADUATE UNITS**

**Professional Program**

## NEW YORK COLLEGE OF TRADITIONAL CHINESE MEDICINE, Mineola, NY 11501

**General Information** Independent, coed, graduate-only institution.

**GRADUATE UNITS**

**Graduate Programs**

## NEW YORK FILM ACADEMY, Burbank, CA 91505

**General Information** Independent, coed, comprehensive institution.

**GRADUATE UNITS**

**Program in Filmmaking–Los Angeles**

**Program in Filmmaking–South Beach, Florida**

## NEW YORK INSTITUTE OF TECHNOLOGY, Old Westbury, NY 11568-8000

**General Information** Independent, coed, comprehensive institution. *Enrollment:* 7,230 graduate, professional, and undergraduate students; 2,930 full-time matriculated graduate/professional students (1,436 women), 559 part-time matriculated graduate/professional students (313 women). *Enrollment by degree level:* 1,592 master's, 1,848 doctoral, 49 other advanced degrees. *Graduate faculty:* 232 full-time (99 women), 236 part-time/adjunct (90 women). *Tuition:* Full-time $23,760; part-time $1320 per credit. *Required fees:* $260; $220 per unit. Full-time tuition and fees vary according to degree level and program. Part-time tuition and fees vary according to course load and program. *Graduate housing:* Room and/or apartments available on a first-come, first-served basis to single students; on-campus housing not available to married students. Typical cost: $9500 per year ($14,470 including board). Room and board charges vary according to campus/location and housing facility selected. *Student services:* Campus employment opportunities, campus safety program, career counseling, free psychological counseling, international student services, low-cost health insurance, services for students with disabilities, teacher training, writing training. *Library facilities:* George and Gertrude Wisser Memorial Library plus 3 others. *Collection:* Books: 75,647 (physical), 83,169 (digital/electronic); Serial titles: 2,421 (physical), 93,810 (digital/electronic). Weekly public service hours: 78; students can reserve study rooms.

**Computer facilities:** A campuswide network can be accessed. Online class registration is available.
Website: http://www.nyit.edu/

**General Application Contact:** Alice Dolitsky, Director, Graduate Admissions, 800-345-6948, Fax: 516-686-1116, E-mail: grad@nyit.edu.

**GRADUATE UNITS**

**College of Arts and Sciences** *Program availability:* Part-time, evening/weekend, 100% online, blended/hybrid learning. Electronic applications accepted.

**College of Engineering and Computing Sciences** *Program availability:* Part-time, evening/weekend, 100% online, blended/hybrid learning. Electronic applications accepted.

**College of Osteopathic Medicine** Students: 1,734 full-time (827 women); includes 814 minority (68 Black or African American, non-Hispanic/Latino; 627 Asian, non-Hispanic/Latino; 81 Hispanic/Latino; 38 Two or more races, non-Hispanic/Latino). Average age 27. 7,140 applicants, 13% accepted, 435 enrolled. *Faculty:* 94 full-time (44 women), 36 part-time/adjunct (16 women). Expenses: Contact institution. *Financial support:* In 2019–20, 690 students received support. Federal Work-Study and scholarships/grants available. Financial award application deadline: 2/15; financial award applicants required to submit FAFSA. *Application deadline:* For fall admission, 3/1 for domestic students. Applications are processed on a rolling basis. *Application fee:* $80. Electronic applications accepted. *Application Contact:* Carol Zerah, Director, Admissions, 516-686-3997, E-mail: comadm@nyit.edu. *Dean*, Dr. Jerry Balentine, 516-686-3999, Fax: 516-686-3830, E-mail: Jerry.Balentine@nyit.edu.

**School of Architecture and Design** *Program availability:* Part-time. Electronic applications accepted.

**School of Health Professions** *Program availability:* Part-time, evening/weekend, 100% online. Electronic applications accepted.

**School of Management** *Program availability:* Part-time. Electronic applications accepted.

## NEW YORK LAW SCHOOL, New York, NY 10013

**General Information** Independent, coed, graduate-only institution. *Enrollment by degree level:* 22 master's, 1,080 doctoral. *Graduate faculty:* 55 full-time (26 women), 80 part-time/adjunct (25 women). *Tuition:* Full-time $52,552; part-time $40,464 per year. *Required fees:* $1830; $1328 per unit. Tuition and fees vary according to course load and degree level. *Graduate housing:* Room and/or apartments available on a first-come, first-served basis to single students; on-campus housing not available to married students. Typical cost: $23,436 per year. Housing application deadline: 7/1. *Student services:* Campus employment opportunities, campus safety program, career counseling, exercise/wellness program, free psychological counseling, international student services, low-cost health insurance, multicultural affairs office, services for students with disabilities, writing training. *Library facilities:* The Mendik Library. *Collection:* Books: 280,368 (physical), 161 (digital/electronic); Serial titles: 5,529 (physical), 247,039 (digital/electronic); Databases: 140. Weekly public service hours: 93.

**Computer facilities:** 70 computers available on campus for general student use. A campuswide network can be accessed. Online class registration is available.
Website: http://www.nyls.edu/

**General Application Contact:** Ella Mae Estrada, Associate Dean for Enrollment Management, Financial Aid and Diversity Initiatives, 212-431-2888, Fax: 212-966-1522, E-mail: admissions@nyls.edu.

**GRADUATE UNITS**

**Graduate Programs** Students: 874 full-time (516 women), 228 part-time (119 women); includes 323 minority (52 Black or African American, non-Hispanic/Latino; 77 Asian, non-Hispanic/Latino; 158 Hispanic/Latino; 2 Native Hawaiian or other Pacific Islander, non-Hispanic/Latino; 34 Two or more races, non-Hispanic/Latino), 33 international. Average age 26. 2,913 applicants, 50% accepted, 394 enrolled. *Faculty:* 55 full-time (26 women), 80 part-time/adjunct (25 women). Expenses: Contact institution. *Financial support:* In 2019–20, 779 students received support, including 95 fellowships (averaging $4,200 per year), 24 research assistantships (averaging $5,000 per year), 8 teaching assistantships (averaging $5,000 per year); career-related internships or fieldwork, Federal Work-Study, and scholarships/grants also available. Support available to part-time students. Financial award application deadline: 7/1; financial award applicants required to submit FAFSA. In 2019, 14 master's, 272 doctorates awarded. *Program availability:* Part-time, evening/weekend. *Application deadline:* For fall admission, 7/1 priority date for domestic and international students. Applications are processed on a rolling basis. Electronic applications accepted. *Application Contact:* Ella Mae Estrada, Associate Dean for Enrollment Management, Financial Aid and Diversity Initiatives, 212-431-2888, Fax: 212-966-1522, E-mail: admissions@nyls.edu. *Dean and President*, Anthony W. Crowell, 212-431-2840, Fax: 212-219-3752, E-mail: anthony.crowell@nyls.edu.

## NEW YORK MEDICAL COLLEGE, Valhalla, NY 10595

**General Information** Independent, coed, graduate-only institution. CGS member. *Enrollment by degree level:* 211 master's, 1,049 doctoral, 39 other advanced degrees. *Graduate faculty:* 1,077 full-time (439 women), 1,023 part-time/adjunct (373 women). *Tuition:* Full-time $54,580; part-time $1195 per credit. *Required fees:* $500; $500. Tuition and fees vary according to course load and program. *Graduate housing:* Rooms and/or apartments available on a first-come, first-served basis to single and married students. Typical cost: $10,800 per year for single students; $17,000 per year for married students. Room charges vary according to housing facility selected. *Student services:* Campus employment opportunities, campus safety program, career counseling, exercise/wellness program, free psychological counseling, international student services, low-cost health insurance, multicultural affairs office, services for students with disabilities, writing training. *Library facilities:* Health Sciences Library plus 2 others. *Collection:* Books: 27,361 (physical), 30,040 (digital/electronic); Serial titles: 530 (physical), 21,101 (digital/electronic); Databases: 231. Weekly public service hours: 83; study areas open 24 hours, 5–7 days a week; students can reserve study rooms. *Research affiliation:* Westchester Medical Center (biomedical research), Metropolitan Hospital (biomedical research), Westchester Institute for Human Development (biomedical research), Columbia University College of Physicians and Surgeons (neurosciences), Seattle Children's Hospital (pediatric pulmonary disease), Touro College & University System (biomedical research).

**Computer facilities:** 52 computers available on campus for general student use. A campuswide network can be accessed from student residence rooms and from off campus. Online class registration is available.
Website: http://www.nymc.edu/

**General Application Contact:** James Demaio, Director, School of Medicine Admissions, 914-594-4507, Fax: 914-594-4613, E-mail: mdadmit@nymc.edu.

**GRADUATE UNITS**

**Graduate School of Basic Medical Sciences** Students: 141 full-time (90 women), 17 part-time (3 women); includes 68 minority (16 Black or African American, non-Hispanic/Latino; 32 Asian, non-Hispanic/Latino; 15 Hispanic/Latino; 1 Native Hawaiian or other Pacific Islander, non-Hispanic/Latino; 4 Two or more races, non-Hispanic/Latino), 19 international. Average age 26. 351 applicants, 62% accepted, 86 enrolled. *Faculty:* 98 full-time (24 women). Expenses: Contact institution. *Financial support:* In 2019–20, 400 students received support. Federal Work-Study, scholarships/grants, unspecified assistantships, and Student Federal Loans available. Financial award application deadline: 4/30; financial award applicants required to submit FAFSA. In 2019, 28 master's, 5 doctorates awarded. *Program availability:* Part-time, evening/weekend. *Application deadline:* For fall admission, 6/1 priority date for domestic students, 5/1 priority date for international students. Applications are processed on a rolling basis. *Application fee:* $75 ($100 for international students). Electronic applications accepted. *Application Contact:* Valerie Romeo-Messana, Director of Admissions, 914-594-4110, Fax: 914-594-4944, E-mail: v_romeomessana@nymc.edu. *Dean*, Dr. Marina K Holz, 914-594-4110, Fax: 914-594-4944, E-mail: mholz@nymc.edu.

**School of Health Sciences and Practice** Students: 230 full-time (171 women), 292 part-time (207 women); includes 204 minority (73 Black or African American, non-Hispanic/Latino; 4 American Indian or Alaska Native, non-Hispanic/Latino; 59 Asian, non-Hispanic/Latino; 54 Hispanic/Latino; 1 Native Hawaiian or other Pacific Islander, non-Hispanic/Latino; 13 Two or more races, non-Hispanic/Latino), 35 international. Average age 29. 790 applicants, 61% accepted, 162 enrolled. *Faculty:* 47 full-time (34 women), 203 part-time/adjunct (125 women). Expenses: Contact institution. *Financial support:* In 2019–20, 18 students received support. Federal Work-Study, scholarships/grants, unspecified assistantships, and Federal student loans available. Financial award application deadline: 4/30; financial award applicants required to submit FAFSA. In 2019, 113 master's, 47 doctorates awarded. *Program availability:* Part-time, evening/weekend, 100% online, blended/hybrid learning. *Application deadline:* For fall admission, 8/1 for domestic students, 4/15 for international students; for spring admission, 12/1 for domestic students; for summer admission, 5/1 for domestic students, 4/15 for international students. Applications are processed on a rolling basis. *Application fee:* $128 ($120 for international students). Electronic applications accepted. *Application Contact:* Irene Bundziak, Assistant to Director of Admissions, 914-594-4905, E-mail: irene_bundziak@nymc.edu. *Vice Dean*, Ben Johnson, PhD, 914-594-4531, E-mail: bjohnson23@nymc.edu.

**School of Medicine** Students: 862 full-time (493 women); includes 376 minority (54 Black or African American, non-Hispanic/Latino; 220 Asian, non-Hispanic/Latino; 77 Hispanic/Latino; 25 Two or more races, non-Hispanic/Latino), 8 international. Average age 26. 12,845 applicants, 4% accepted, 215 enrolled. *Faculty:* 1,077 full-time (439 women), 1,023 part-time/adjunct (373 women). Expenses: Contact institution. *Financial support:* In 2019–20, 404 students received support. Federal Work-Study, institutionally sponsored loans, scholarships/grants, unspecified assistantships, and Federal Student Loans available. Financial award application deadline: 4/30; financial award applicants required to submit FAFSA. In 2019, 200 doctorates awarded. *Application deadline:* For fall admission, 1/31 for domestic and international students. Applications are processed on a rolling basis. *Application fee:* $130. Electronic applications accepted. *Application Contact:* James DeMaio, Director of Admissions, 914-594-4507, Fax: 914-594-4613, E-mail: mdadmit@nymc.edu. *Senior Associate Dean for Medical Education*, Jennifer Koestler, MD, 914-594-4500, E-mail: jennifer_koestler@nymc.edu.

## NEW YORK SCHOOL OF INTERIOR DESIGN, New York, NY 10021-5110

**General Information** Independent, coed, primarily women, comprehensive institution. *Graduate housing:* Room and/or apartments available on a first-come, first-served basis to single students; on-campus housing not available to married students. Housing application deadline: 5/1. *Research affiliation:* Metropolitan New York Library Council-Research Consortium.

**GRADUATE UNITS**

**Program in Healthcare Interior Design** Electronic applications accepted.

**Program in Interior Design (Post-Professional Level)** Electronic applications accepted.

**Program in Interior Design (Professional-Level)** Electronic applications accepted.

**Program in Interior Lighting Design** Electronic applications accepted.

**Program in Sustainable Interior Environments** Electronic applications accepted.

## NEW YORK STUDIO SCHOOL OF DRAWING, PAINTING AND SCULPTURE, New York, NY 10011

**General Information** Independent, coed, comprehensive institution. *Enrollment by degree level:* 25 master's, 21 other advanced degrees. *Graduate faculty:* 4 full-time (3 women), 23 part-time/adjunct (12 women). *Tuition:* Full-time $25,375. *Graduate housing:* On-campus housing not available. *Student services:* Campus employment opportunities, career counseling, international student services, services for students with disabilities, writing training.
Website: http://www.nyss.org/

**General Application Contact:** Amber Duntley, Registrar, 212-673-6466 Ext. 129, E-mail: aduntley@nyss.org.

**GRADUATE UNITS**

**Certificate Program**

**MFA Program**

## NEW YORK THEOLOGICAL SEMINARY, New York, NY 10115

**General Information** Independent-religious, coed, graduate-only institution. *Graduate housing:* On-campus housing not available. *Research affiliation:* Goldwater Memorial Hospital, Institutes of Religion and Health, Lutheran Medical Center, Postgraduate Center for Mental Health, Bellevue Hospital Center.

**GRADUATE UNITS**

**Graduate and Professional Programs** *Program availability:* Part-time.

## NEW YORK UNIVERSITY, New York, NY 10012-1019

**General Information** Independent, coed, university. CGS member. *Graduate housing:* Room and/or apartments available on a first-come, first-served basis to single students; on-campus housing not available to married students. Housing application deadline: 5/1. *Research affiliation:* Research Network on Opening Governance, MacArthur Foundation (technology management and innovation), Data Science Environments Program, Gordon and Betty Moore Foundation (data science), Center for the Study of Complex Malaria in India, National Institutes of Health (biology), Training in Systems and Integrative Neuroscience, National Institutes of Health (neural science).

**GRADUATE UNITS**

**College of Dentistry** Electronic applications accepted.

**College of Global Public Health** *Program availability:* Part-time, online learning. Electronic applications accepted.

**Gallatin School of Individualized Study** *Program availability:* Part-time, evening/weekend. Electronic applications accepted.

**Graduate School of Arts and Science** *Program availability:* Part-time, evening/weekend. Electronic applications accepted.

***Arthur L. Carter Journalism Institute*** *Program availability:* Part-time.

***Center for European Studies*** Electronic applications accepted.

***Center for French Civilization and Culture*** *Program availability:* Part-time, evening/weekend.

***Center for Latin American and Caribbean Studies*** *Program availability:* Part-time.

***Center for Neural Science***

***Courant Institute of Mathematical Sciences*** *Program availability:* Part-time, evening/weekend.

***Hagop Kevorkian Center for Near Eastern Studies*** *Program availability:* Part-time, evening/weekend.

***Institute for Law and Society***

***Institute for the Study of the Ancient World*** Electronic applications accepted.

***Institute of Fine Arts*** *Program availability:* Part-time.

**Leonard N. Stern School of Business** *Program availability:* Part-time, evening/weekend. Electronic applications accepted.

**Rory Meyers College of Nursing** *Program availability:* Part-time, evening/weekend. Electronic applications accepted.

**School of Law** *Program availability:* Part-time, blended/hybrid learning. Electronic applications accepted.

**School of Medicine** Electronic applications accepted.

***Sackler Institute of Graduate Biomedical Sciences*** Electronic applications accepted.

**School of Professional Studies** *Program availability:* Part-time, evening/weekend, 100% online, blended/hybrid learning. Electronic applications accepted.

***Center for Applied Liberal Arts*** *Program availability:* Part-time, evening/weekend, 100% online, blended/hybrid learning. Electronic applications accepted.

***Center for Global Affairs*** *Program availability:* Part-time, evening/weekend. Electronic applications accepted.

***Center for Publishing*** *Program availability:* Part-time, evening/weekend. Electronic applications accepted.

***Division of Programs in Business*** *Program availability:* Part-time, evening/weekend, 100% online, blended/hybrid learning. Electronic applications accepted.

***Jonathan M. Tisch Center of Hospitality*** *Program availability:* Part-time, evening/weekend. Electronic applications accepted.

***Preston Robert Tisch Institute for Global Sport*** *Program availability:* Part-time, evening/weekend. Electronic applications accepted.

***Schack Institute of Real Estate*** *Program availability:* Part-time, evening/weekend. Electronic applications accepted.

**Silver School of Social Work** *Program availability:* Part-time, evening/weekend. Electronic applications accepted.

**Steinhardt School of Culture, Education, and Human Development** *Program availability:* Part-time. Electronic applications accepted.

**Tandon School of Engineering** *Program availability:* Part-time, 100% online, blended/hybrid learning. Electronic applications accepted.

**Tisch School of the Arts** Electronic applications accepted.

***Game Center*** Electronic applications accepted.

***Kanbar Institute of Film and Television*** Electronic applications accepted.

**Wagner Graduate School of Public Service** *Program availability:* Part-time. Electronic applications accepted.

## NIAGARA UNIVERSITY, Niagara University, NY 14109

**General Information** Independent-religious, coed, comprehensive institution. *Graduate housing:* Room and/or apartments available to single students; on-campus housing not available to married students. Housing application deadline: 8/1. *Research affiliation:* Roswell Park Memorial Institute.

**GRADUATE UNITS**

**Graduate Division of Arts and Sciences** *Program availability:* Part-time. Electronic applications accepted.

**Graduate Division of Business Administration** *Program availability:* Part-time, evening/weekend, 100% online, blended/hybrid learning. Electronic applications accepted.

**Graduate Division of Education** *Program availability:* Part-time, evening/weekend, 100% online, blended/hybrid learning. Electronic applications accepted.

## NICHOLLS STATE UNIVERSITY, Thibodaux, LA 70310

**General Information** State-supported, coed, comprehensive institution. *Graduate housing:* Rooms and/or apartments available on a first-come, first-served basis to single and married students. Housing application deadline: 4/15.

**GRADUATE UNITS**

**Graduate Studies** *Program availability:* Part-time, evening/weekend, online learning.

***College of Arts and Sciences*** *Program availability:* Part-time, evening/weekend. Electronic applications accepted.

***College of Business Administration*** *Program availability:* Part-time, evening/weekend. Electronic applications accepted.

***College of Education*** *Program availability:* Part-time, evening/weekend. Electronic applications accepted.

***College of Nursing and Allied Health***

## NICHOLS COLLEGE, Dudley, MA 01571-5000

**General Information** Independent, coed, comprehensive institution. *Graduate housing:* On-campus housing not available.

**GRADUATE UNITS**

**Graduate and Professional Studies** *Program availability:* Part-time, evening/weekend, online learning. Electronic applications accepted.

## NIPISSING UNIVERSITY, North Bay, ON P1B 8L7, Canada

**General Information** Province-supported, coed, comprehensive institution. *Graduate housing:* Room and/or apartments available to single students; on-campus housing not available to married students. Housing application deadline: 6/13. *Research affiliation:* Tembec (forestry restoration), Metals in the Human Environment Research Network (MITHE-RN) (assessing environmental pollutants on aquatic ecosystems), Canada Space Agency (CSA) and MacDonald, Dettwiler and Associates Ltd. (MDA–RADARSAT-2) (remote sensing), Education Quality and Accountability Office (EQAO) (assessing educational quality), Ontario Association of Deans of Education (OADE) (assessing pre-service practicum processes).

**GRADUATE UNITS**

**Faculty of Education** *Program availability:* Part-time, evening/weekend.

## NORFOLK STATE UNIVERSITY, Norfolk, VA 23504

**General Information** State-supported, coed, comprehensive institution. CGS member. *Graduate housing:* Room and/or apartments available to single students; on-campus housing not available to married students. Housing application deadline: 3/1. *Research affiliation:* U.S. Department of Energy/NASA (fundamental and applied research studies), NASA Langley Research Center (aerospace applications, lidar application), National Science Foundation (fundamental and applied research studies), U.S. Department of Education (DOE) (Title III projects, No Child Left Behind initiative), University of Virginia's Integrative Graduate Education and Research Traineeship (IGERT) (science and engineering interactions with matter), Applied Research Center (technology transfer).

**GRADUATE UNITS**

**School of Graduate Studies** *Program availability:* Part-time. Electronic applications accepted.

***Ethelyn R. Strong School of Social Work*** *Program availability:* Part-time.

***School of Education*** *Program availability:* Part-time.

***School of Liberal Arts*** *Program availability:* Part-time.

***School of Science and Technology***

## NORTH AMERICAN UNIVERSITY, Stafford, TX 77477

**General Information** Independent, coed, comprehensive institution.

**GRADUATE UNITS**

**Program in Educational Leadership**

## NORTH CAROLINA AGRICULTURAL AND TECHNICAL STATE UNIVERSITY, Greensboro, NC 27411

**General Information** State-supported, coed, university. CGS member. *Graduate housing:* Room and/or apartments available on a first-come, first-served basis to single students; on-campus housing not available to married students. Housing application deadline: 5/8. *Research affiliation:* North Carolina Biotechnology Research Center (biotechnology), Boeing (aerospace engineering), Northrop Grumman Corporation (high performance computing), Research Triangle Institute (environmental protection, advanced technology), Rockwell, Inc. (avionics technology, communications technology), Honeywell (industrial automation control).

**GRADUATE UNITS**

**The Graduate College** *Program availability:* Part-time, evening/weekend. Electronic applications accepted.

***College of Agriculture and Environmental Sciences*** *Program availability:* Part-time, evening/weekend.

***College of Arts, Humanities, and Social Sciences*** *Program availability:* Part-time, evening/weekend.

***College of Business and Economics***

***College of Education*** *Program availability:* Part-time, evening/weekend.

***College of Engineering*** *Program availability:* Part-time.

***College of Health and Human Sciences***

***College of Science and Technology*** *Program availability:* Part-time, evening/weekend.

## NORTH CAROLINA CENTRAL UNIVERSITY, Durham, NC 27707-3129

**General Information** State-supported, coed, comprehensive institution. CGS member. *Graduate housing:* Room and/or apartments available on a first-come, first-served basis to single students; on-campus housing not available to married students. Housing application deadline: 7/1.

**GRADUATE UNITS**

**College of Arts and Sciences**

**College of Behavioral and Social Sciences**

**School of Business** *Program availability:* Part-time, evening/weekend.

**School of Education** *Program availability:* Part-time, evening/weekend.

**School of Law** *Program availability:* Part-time, evening/weekend.

**School of Library and Information Sciences** *Program availability:* Part-time, evening/weekend.

## NORTH CAROLINA STATE UNIVERSITY, Raleigh, NC 27695

**General Information** State-supported, coed, university. CGS member. *Graduate housing:* Rooms and/or apartments available on a first-come, first-served basis to single and married students. *Research affiliation:* Triangle Universities Nuclear Laboratory, Research Triangle Institute, Highlands Biological Station, National Humanities Center, Microelectronics Center of North Carolina, North Carolina-Japan Center.

**GRADUATE UNITS**

**College of Veterinary Medicine** *Program availability:* Part-time. Electronic applications accepted.

**Graduate School** *Program availability:* Part-time, evening/weekend, online learning. Electronic applications accepted.

***College of Agriculture and Life Sciences*** *Program availability:* Part-time. Electronic applications accepted.

***College of Design*** *Program availability:* Part-time. Electronic applications accepted.

***College of Education*** *Program availability:* Part-time. Electronic applications accepted.

***College of Engineering*** *Program availability:* Part-time. Electronic applications accepted.

***College of Humanities and Social Sciences*** *Program availability:* Part-time, evening/weekend. Electronic applications accepted.

***College of Natural Resources*** *Program availability:* Part-time. Electronic applications accepted.

***College of Sciences*** *Program availability:* Part-time. Electronic applications accepted.

***Poole College of Management*** *Program availability:* Part-time. Electronic applications accepted.

***Wilson College of Textiles*** *Program availability:* Part-time, evening/weekend, online learning. Electronic applications accepted.

## NORTH CENTRAL COLLEGE, Naperville, IL 60566-7063

**General Information** Independent-religious, coed, comprehensive institution. CGS member. *Graduate housing:* Room and/or apartments available on a first-come, first-served basis to single students; on-campus housing not available to married students. Housing application deadline: 4/15.

**GRADUATE UNITS**

**School of Graduate and Professional Studies** *Program availability:* Part-time, evening/weekend. Electronic applications accepted.

## NORTHCENTRAL UNIVERSITY, San Diego, CA 92106

**General Information** Proprietary, coed, upper-level institution. CGS member. *Enrollment:* 10,698 graduate, professional, and undergraduate students; 4,759 full-time matriculated graduate/professional students (2,997 women), 5,939 part-time matriculated graduate/professional students (3,987 women). *Enrollment by degree level:* 4,009 master's, 6,206 doctoral, 454 other advanced degrees. *Graduate faculty:* 119 full-time (77 women), 379 part-time/adjunct (195 women). *Tuition:* Part-time $1053 per credit. *Required fees:* $95 per course. Full-time tuition and fees vary according to degree level and program. *Graduate housing:* On-campus housing not available. *Student services:* Services for students with disabilities, writing training. *Library facilities:* Northcentral University Library (Virtual). *Collection:* Weekly public service hours: 79. *Research affiliation:* Coalition for Research to Practice (mental health services; aligning academic training with workforce demands).

**Computer facilities:** Online class registration is available.
Website: http://www.ncu.edu/

**General Application Contact:** Enrollment Advisor, 866-776-0331, Fax: 928-541-7817, E-mail: admissions@ncu.edu.

**GRADUATE UNITS**

**Graduate Studies** *Program availability:* Part-time, evening/weekend, online only, 100% online. Electronic applications accepted.

## NORTH DAKOTA STATE UNIVERSITY, Fargo, ND 58102

**General Information** State-supported, coed, university. CGS member. *Enrollment:* 13,173 graduate, professional, and undergraduate students; 622 full-time matriculated graduate/professional students (312 women), 1,210 part-time matriculated graduate/professional students (597 women). *Enrollment by degree level:* 1,038 master's, 766 doctoral, 28 other advanced degrees. Tuition and fees vary according to program and reciprocity agreements. *Student services:* Campus employment opportunities, campus safety program, career counseling, child daycare facilities, exercise/wellness program, free psychological counseling, grant writing training, international student services, low-cost health insurance, multicultural affairs office, services for students with disabilities, teacher training, writing training. *Library facilities:* North Dakota State University Library plus 6 others. *Collection:* Books: 662,884 (physical), 162,977 (digital/electronic); Serial titles: 171,924 (physical), 99,565 (digital/electronic); Databases: 232. Weekly public service hours: 93; students can reserve study rooms. *Research affiliation:* U.S. Department of Agriculture (USDA), Metabolism and Radiation Laboratory.

**Computer facilities:** Computer purchase and lease plans are available. 601 computers available on campus for general student use. A campuswide network can be accessed. Online class registration, online course content (e.g., learning management system, lecture capture video recordings) are available.
Website: http://www.ndsu.edu/

**General Application Contact:** Neely Benton, Student Recruitment Coordinator, 701-231-8476, Fax: 701-231-6524, E-mail: neely.benton@ndsu.edu.

**GRADUATE UNITS**

**College of Graduate and Interdisciplinary Studies** *Program availability:* Part-time, evening/weekend, 100% online, blended/hybrid learning. Electronic applications accepted.

***College of Agriculture, Food Systems, and Natural Resources*** *Program availability:* Part-time. Electronic applications accepted.

***College of Arts, Humanities and Social Sciences*** *Program availability:* Part-time, evening/weekend. Electronic applications accepted.

***College of Business*** *Program availability:* Part-time, evening/weekend. Electronic applications accepted.

***College of Engineering*** *Program availability:* Part-time. Electronic applications accepted.

***College of Health Professions*** *Program availability:* Part-time. Electronic applications accepted.

***College of Human Development and Education*** *Program availability:* Part-time, evening/weekend, online learning. Electronic applications accepted.

***College of Science and Mathematics*** *Program availability:* Part-time. Electronic applications accepted.

## NORTHEASTERN ILLINOIS UNIVERSITY, Chicago, IL 60625-4699

**General Information** State-supported, coed, comprehensive institution. *Graduate housing:* Room and/or apartments available to single students; on-campus housing not available to married students. *Research affiliation:* Advocate Health Care Network (health care cost containment), Lutheran General Hospital (clinical cardiology), Advocate Medical Group (health care outcomes research).

**GRADUATE UNITS**

**College of Graduate Studies and Research** *Program availability:* Part-time, evening/weekend. Electronic applications accepted.

***College of Arts and Sciences*** *Program availability:* Part-time, evening/weekend. Electronic applications accepted.

***College of Business and Management*** *Program availability:* Part-time, evening/weekend. Electronic applications accepted.

***Daniel L. Goodwin College of Education*** *Program availability:* Part-time, evening/weekend. Electronic applications accepted.

## NORTHEASTERN SEMINARY AT ROBERTS WESLEYAN COLLEGE, Rochester, NY 14624

**General Information** Independent-religious, coed, graduate-only institution. *Graduate housing:* On-campus housing not available.

**GRADUATE UNITS**

**Graduate and Professional Programs** *Program availability:* Part-time, evening/weekend, 100% online, blended/hybrid learning. Electronic applications accepted.

## NORTHEASTERN STATE UNIVERSITY, Tahlequah, OK 74464-2399

**General Information** State-supported, coed, comprehensive institution. *Enrollment:* 7,496 graduate, professional, and undergraduate students; 498 full-time matriculated graduate/professional students (359 women), 608 part-time matriculated graduate/professional students (455 women). *Enrollment by degree level:* 993 master's, 113 doctoral. *Graduate faculty:* 120 full-time (59 women), 19 part-time/adjunct (14 women). *Tuition, area resident:* Full-time $250; part-time $250 per credit hour. Tuition, state resident: full-time $250; part-time $250 per credit hour. Tuition, nonresident: full-time $556; part-time $555.50 per credit hour. *Required fees:* $33.40 per credit hour. *Graduate housing:* Rooms and/or apartments available on a first-come, first-served basis to single and married students. Typical cost: $1600 per year ($2590 including board) for single students; $1600 per year ($2590 including board) for married students. Housing application deadline: 6/1. *Student services:* Campus employment opportunities, campus safety program, career counseling, exercise/wellness program, free psychological counseling, international student services, low-cost health insurance, multicultural affairs office, services for students with disabilities, teacher training, writing training. *Library facilities:* John Vaughn Library plus 1 other. *Collection:* Books: 344,747 (physical), 71,226 (digital/electronic); Serial titles: 11,698 (physical), 34,336 (digital/electronic); Databases: 252. Weekly public service hours: 114.

**Computer facilities:** Computer purchase and lease plans are available. 1,160 computers available on campus for general student use. A campuswide network can be accessed. Online class registration is available.
Website: http://www.nsuok.edu/

**General Application Contact:** Josh McCollum, Graduate Coordinator, Advising and Admissions, 918-444-2093, E-mail: mccolluj@nsuok.edu.

**GRADUATE UNITS**

**College of Business and Technology** Students: 45 full-time (25 women), 130 part-time (79 women); includes 91 minority (10 Black or African American, non-Hispanic/Latino; 29 American Indian or Alaska Native, non-Hispanic/Latino; 6 Asian, non-Hispanic/Latino; 8 Hispanic/Latino; 38 Two or more races, non-Hispanic/Latino), 7 international. Average age 33. *Faculty:* 17 full-time (4 women), 2 part-time/adjunct (1 woman). Expenses: Contact institution. *Financial support:* Teaching assistantships and Federal Work-Study available. Financial award application deadline: 3/1. In 2019, 38 master's awarded. *Program availability:* Part-time, evening/weekend. *Application deadline:* For fall admission, 6/1 priority date for domestic students. Applications are processed on a rolling basis. *Application fee:* $0 ($25 for international students). Electronic applications accepted. *Application Contact:* Josh McCollum, Graduate Coordinator, 918-444-2093, E-mail: mccolluj@nsuok.edu. *Dean,* Dr. Janet Buzzard, 918-444-2900, E-mail: buzzardj@nsuok.edu.

**College of Education** Students: 141 full-time (105 women), 322 part-time (262 women); includes 184 minority (24 Black or African American, non-Hispanic/Latino; 65 American Indian or Alaska Native, non-Hispanic/Latino; 6 Asian, non-Hispanic/Latino; 14 Hispanic/Latino; 75 Two or more races, non-Hispanic/Latino), 5 international. Average age 34. *Faculty:* 33 full-time (24 women), 10 part-time/adjunct (7 women). Expenses: Contact institution. *Financial support:* Teaching assistantships, career-related internships or fieldwork, and Federal Work-Study available. Financial award application deadline: 3/1. In 2019, 160 master's awarded. *Program availability:* Part-time, evening/weekend. *Application deadline:* For fall admission, 6/1 priority date for domestic students. Applications are processed on a rolling basis. *Application fee:* $25. Electronic applications accepted. *Application Contact:* Josh McCollum, Graduate Coordinator, 918-444-2093, E-mail: mccolluj@nsuok.edu. *Dean of the College of Education,* Dr. Vanessa Anton, 918-444-3700, Fax: 918-458-2351, E-mail: anton@nsuok.edu.

**College of Liberal Arts** Students: 75 full-time (52 women), 65 part-time (42 women); includes 77 minority (13 Black or African American, non-Hispanic/Latino; 29 American Indian or Alaska Native, non-Hispanic/Latino; 1 Asian, non-Hispanic/Latino; 6 Hispanic/Latino; 2 Native Hawaiian or other Pacific Islander, non-Hispanic/Latino; 26 Two or more races, non-Hispanic/Latino). Average age 35. *Faculty:* 34 full-time (16 women). Expenses: Contact institution. *Financial support:* Teaching assistantships and Federal Work-Study available. Financial award application deadline: 3/1. In 2019, 28 master's awarded. *Program availability:* Part-time, evening/weekend. *Application deadline:* For fall admission, 6/1 priority date for domestic students. Applications are processed on a rolling basis. *Application fee:* $25. Electronic applications accepted. *Application Contact:* Josh McCollum, Graduate Coordinator, 918-444-2093, E-mail: mccolluj@nsuok.edu. *Dean of Liberal Arts,* Dr. Mike Chanslor, 918-444-3600, Fax: 918-458-2348, E-mail: cola@nsuok.edu.

**College of Science and Health Professions** Students: 124 full-time (113 women), 91 part-time (72 women); includes 72 minority (5 Black or African American, non-Hispanic/Latino; 30 American Indian or Alaska Native, non-Hispanic/Latino; 3 Asian, non-Hispanic/Latino; 12 Hispanic/Latino; 22 Two or more races, non-Hispanic/Latino), 1 international. Average age 32. *Faculty:* 22 full-time (10 women), 7 part-time/adjunct (6 women). Expenses: Contact institution. In 2019, 88 master's awarded. *Application deadline:* Applications are processed on a rolling basis. *Application fee:* $25. Electronic applications accepted. *Application Contact:* Josh McCollum, Graduate Coordinator, 918-444-2093, E-mail: mccolluj@nsuok.edu. *Dean,* Dr. Pamela Hathorn, 918-444-3800, E-mail: hathorn@nsuok.edu.

**Oklahoma College of Optometry** Students: 113 full-time (64 women); includes 28 minority (1 Black or African American, non-Hispanic/Latino; 4 American Indian or Alaska Native, non-Hispanic/Latino; 8 Asian, non-Hispanic/Latino; 3 Hispanic/Latino; 12 Two or more races, non-Hispanic/Latino). Average age 25. *Faculty:* 15 full-time (6 women). Expenses: Contact institution. *Financial support:* Federal Work-Study, institutionally sponsored loans, scholarships/grants, tuition waivers (partial), and residencies available. Financial award application deadline: 5/1; financial award applicants required to submit FAFSA. In 2019, 27 doctorates awarded. *Application deadline:* For fall admission, 2/1 for domestic students. Applications are processed on a rolling basis. *Application fee:* $45. Electronic applications accepted. *Application Contact:* Sandy Medearis, Optometric Student and Alumni Services Director, 918-444-4006, Fax: 918-458-2104, E-mail: medearis@nsuok.edu. *Dean of Oklahoma College of Optometry,* Dr. Douglas Penisten, 918-444-4025, E-mail: penisten@nsuok.edu.

## NORTHEASTERN UNIVERSITY, Boston, MA 02115-5096

**General Information** Independent, coed, university. CGS member. *Enrollment:* 27,391 graduate, professional, and undergraduate students; 8,221 full-time matriculated graduate/professional students (3,427 women), 734 part-time matriculated graduate/professional students (329 women). *Enrollment by degree level:* 6,365 master's, 2,552 doctoral, 38 other advanced degrees. *Graduate faculty:* 1,352 full-time (578 women), 470 part-time/adjunct (234 women). *Graduate housing:* Room and/or apartments available on a first-come, first-served basis to single students; on-campus housing not available to married students. Housing application deadline: 5/31. *Student services:* Campus employment opportunities, campus safety program, career counseling, child daycare facilities, exercise/wellness program, free psychological counseling, grant writing training, international student services, low-cost health insurance, multicultural affairs office, services for students with disabilities, teacher training. *Library facilities:* Snell Library plus 1 other. *Collection:* Books: 525,602 (physical), 1.1 million (digital/electronic). Study areas open 24 hours, 5–7 days a week; students can reserve study rooms. *Research affiliation:* Jobs for America's Graduates (labor studies), Cytyc Corporation (medical technology), BBN Technologies (information technology), Analog Devices, Inc. (electronics), General Electric Company (GE) (engineering).

**Computer facilities:** Computer purchase and lease plans are available. A campuswide network can be accessed. Online class registration is available.
Website: http://www.northeastern.edu/

**GRADUATE UNITS**

**Bouvé College of Health Sciences** *Program availability:* Part-time, evening/weekend, online learning. Electronic applications accepted.

**College of Arts, Media and Design** Electronic applications accepted.

**College of Computer and Information Science** *Program availability:* Part-time, evening/weekend. Electronic applications accepted.

**College of Engineering** *Program availability:* Part-time, online learning. Electronic applications accepted.

**College of Professional Studies** Students: 5,699 part-time (3,305 women). *Faculty:* 85 full-time (53 women), 892 part-time/adjunct (379 women). Expenses: Contact institution. *Financial support:* Applicants required to submit FAFSA. In 2019, 1,787 master's awarded. *Program availability:* Part-time, evening/weekend, 100% online, blended/hybrid learning. *Application deadline:* Applications are processed on a rolling basis. Electronic applications accepted. *Application Contact:* Dr. Mary Loeffelholz, Dean of the College of Professional Studies, 617-373-6060. *Dean of the College of Professional Studies,* Dr. Mary Loeffelholz, 617-373-6060.

**College of Science** *Program availability:* Part-time. Electronic applications accepted.

**College of Social Sciences and Humanities** *Program availability:* Online learning. Electronic applications accepted.

**D'Amore-McKim School of Business** *Program availability:* Part-time, evening/weekend, online learning. Electronic applications accepted.

**School of Law** *Program availability:* Online learning. Electronic applications accepted.

## NORTHEAST OHIO MEDICAL UNIVERSITY, Rootstown, OH 44272-0095

**General Information** State-supported, coed, graduate-only institution. *Enrollment by degree level:* 40 master's, 914 doctoral, 5 other advanced degrees. *Graduate faculty:* 182 full-time (74 women), 2,641 part-time/adjunct (1,033 women). Full-time tuition and fees vary according to course level, course load, degree level, program and student level. *Graduate housing:* On-campus housing not available. *Student services:* Campus employment opportunities, campus safety program, career counseling, exercise/wellness program, free psychological counseling, grant writing training, low-cost health insurance, multicultural affairs office, services for students with disabilities. *Library facilities:* Aneal Mohan Kohli Academic and Information Technology Center. *Collection:* Books: 4,400 (physical), 197,809 (digital/electronic); Serial titles: 30,618 (digital/electronic); Databases: 175. Weekly public service hours: 64; study areas open 24 hours, 5–7 days a week. *Research affiliation:* American Heart Association (physiology, biochemistry), National Science Foundation (anatomy), National Institutes of Health (anatomy, biochemistry, immunology, neurobiology, microbiology), Summa Health Systems (orthopedics, anatomy), Margaret Clark Morgan Foundation (schizophrenia, mental illness), Austen BioInnovation Institute in Akron (pharmacology, drug delivery, biotechnology, community health).

**Computer facilities:** 50 computers available on campus for general student use. A campuswide network can be accessed. Online class registration is available.
Website: http://www.neomed.edu/

**General Application Contact:** James Barrett, Sr. Executive Director, Strategic Enrollment Initiative, 330-325-6274, E-mail: admission@neomed.edu.

**GRADUATE UNITS**

**College of Graduate Studies** Students: 24 full-time (12 women), 28 part-time (15 women); includes 21 minority (2 Black or African American, non-Hispanic/Latino; 10 Asian, non-Hispanic/Latino; 5 Hispanic/Latino; 4 Two or more races, non-Hispanic/Latino). Average age 26. 31 applicants, 97% accepted, 21 enrolled. *Faculty:* 126 part-time/adjunct (62 women). Expenses: Contact institution. *Financial support:* In 2019–20, 6 students received support. Scholarships/grants and tuition waivers (full and partial) available. Financial award application deadline: 3/15; financial award applicants required to submit FAFSA. In 2019, 15 master's, 13 other advanced degrees awarded. *Program availability:* Part-time, evening/weekend, 100% online, blended/hybrid learning. *Application deadline:* For fall admission, 7/17 for domestic students. Applications are processed on a rolling basis. *Application fee:* $95. Electronic applications accepted. *Application Contact:* Dr. Steven Schmidt, Dean, 330-325-6290. *Dean,* Dr. Steven Schmidt, 330-325-6290.

**College of Medicine** Students: 586 full-time (313 women); includes 286 minority (19 Black or African American, non-Hispanic/Latino; 224 Asian, non-Hispanic/Latino; 15 Hispanic/Latino; 28 Two or more races, non-Hispanic/Latino). Average age 24. 4,069 applicants, 5% accepted, 151 enrolled. *Faculty:* 137 full-time (53 women), 1,984 part-time/adjunct (652 women). Expenses: Contact institution. *Financial support:* In 2019–20, 185 students received support. Institutionally sponsored loans, scholarships/grants, tuition waivers, and Service Scholarships/Forgivable Loans available. Financial award application deadline: 3/15; financial award applicants required to submit FAFSA. In 2019, 154 doctorates awarded. *Application deadline:* For fall admission, 8/1 priority date for domestic students; for winter admission, 10/1 for domestic students. Applications are processed on a rolling basis. *Application fee:* $95. Electronic applications accepted. *Application Contact:* James Barrett, Sr. Executive Director, Strategic Enrollment Initiative, 330-325-6274, E-mail: admission@neomed.edu. *Dean,* Dr. Elisabeth H. Young, 330-325-6122, Fax: 330-325-5941, E-mail: eyoung1@neomed.edu.

**College of Pharmacy** Students: 340 full-time (202 women); includes 88 minority (32 Black or African American, non-Hispanic/Latino; 36 Asian, non-Hispanic/Latino; 10 Hispanic/Latino; 10 Two or more races, non-Hispanic/Latino). Average age 26. 479 applicants, 35% accepted, 92 enrolled. *Faculty:* 45 full-time (21 women), 620 part-time/adjunct (356 women). Expenses: Contact institution. *Financial support:* In 2019–20, 100 students received support. Scholarships/grants available. Financial award application deadline: 3/15; financial award applicants required to submit FAFSA. In 2019, 67 doctorates awarded. *Application deadline:* For fall admission, 6/1 for domestic students. Applications are processed on a rolling basis. *Application fee:* $175. Electronic applications accepted. *Application Contact:* James Barrett, Sr. Executive Director, Strategic Enrollment Initiative, 330-325-6274, E-mail: admission@neomed.edu. *Dean,* Dr. Richard Kasmer, Pharm.D., J.D., 330-325-6461, Fax: 330-325-5951, E-mail: rkasmer@neomed.edu.

## NORTHERN ARIZONA UNIVERSITY, Flagstaff, AZ 86011

**General Information** State-supported, coed, university. CGS member. *Graduate housing:* Rooms and/or apartments available on a first-come, first-served basis to single and married students. Housing application deadline: 5/1. *Research affiliation:* W.L. Gore and Associates, Inc. (biomedical engineering), Museum of Northern Arizona (anthropology), Lowell Observatory (physics and astronomy), Rocky Mountain Forest and Range Experiment Station (forestry), U.S. Naval Observatory (physics and astronomy), U.S. Geological Survey (USGS) (geology).

**GRADUATE UNITS**

**College of Arts and Letters** *Program availability:* Part-time, 100% online, blended/hybrid learning. Electronic applications accepted.

***School of Music*** *Program availability:* Part-time. Electronic applications accepted.

**College of Education** *Program availability:* Part-time, 100% online, blended/hybrid learning. Electronic applications accepted.

**College of Engineering, Informatics, and Applied Sciences**

**College of Environment, Forestry, and Natural Sciences** *Program availability:* Part-time, 100% online, blended/hybrid learning. Electronic applications accepted.

***Center for Science Teaching and Learning*** *Program availability:* Part-time, 100% online, blended/hybrid learning. Electronic applications accepted.

***School of Earth Sciences and Environmental Sustainability*** *Program availability:* Part-time. Electronic applications accepted.

***School of Forestry*** *Program availability:* Part-time. Electronic applications accepted.

**College of Health and Human Services** *Program availability:* Part-time, 100% online, blended/hybrid learning. Electronic applications accepted.

***School of Nursing*** *Program availability:* Part-time, 100% online, blended/hybrid learning. Electronic applications accepted.

**College of Social and Behavioral Sciences** *Program availability:* Part-time, 100% online, blended/hybrid learning. Electronic applications accepted.

***Institute for Human Development*** *Program availability:* Part-time. Electronic applications accepted.

***School of Communication*** *Program availability:* Part-time, 100% online, blended/hybrid learning. Electronic applications accepted.

**Office of the Provost** *Program availability:* Part-time, blended/hybrid learning. Electronic applications accepted.

**Online, Statewide and Education Innovation**

**The W. A. Franke College of Business** *Program availability:* Part-time, 100% online, blended/hybrid learning. Electronic applications accepted.

## NORTHERN ILLINOIS UNIVERSITY, De Kalb, IL 60115-2854

**General Information** State-supported, coed, university. CGS member. *Enrollment:* 16,609 graduate, professional, and undergraduate students; 1,965 full-time matriculated graduate/professional students (1,042 women), 2,513 part-time matriculated graduate/professional students (1,522 women). *Enrollment by degree level:* 3,473 master's, 945 doctoral, 60 other advanced degrees. *Graduate faculty:* 672 full-time (248 women), 66 part-time/adjunct (17 women). *Graduate housing:* Rooms and/or apartments available on a first-come, first-served basis to single and married students. *Student services:* Campus employment opportunities, campus safety program, career counseling, child daycare facilities, exercise/wellness program, free psychological counseling, grant writing training, international student services, low-cost health insurance, services for students with disabilities, teacher training, writing training. *Library facilities:* Founders Memorial Library plus 4 others. *Collection:* Books: 1.8 million (physical), 750,000 (digital/electronic); Serial titles: 1,227 (physical), 83,137 (digital/electronic); Databases: 314. Weekly public service hours: 100; students can reserve study rooms. *Research affiliation:* Field Museum of Natural History, Burpee Museum of Natural History, Argonne National Laboratory, Fermi National Accelerator Laboratory.

**Computer facilities:** 1,500 computers available on campus for general student use. A campuswide network can be accessed. Online class registration is available.
Website: http://www.niu.edu/

**General Application Contact:** Dr. Bradley G. Bond, Dean, Graduate School, 815-753-0395, Fax: 815-753-6366, E-mail: gradsch@niu.edu.

**GRADUATE UNITS**

**College of Law** Students: 245 full-time (112 women), 29 part-time (18 women); includes 56 minority (22 Black or African American, non-Hispanic/Latino; 1 American Indian or Alaska Native, non-Hispanic/Latino; 7 Asian, non-Hispanic/Latino; 21 Hispanic/Latino; 1 Native Hawaiian or other Pacific Islander, non-Hispanic/Latino; 4 Two or more races, non-Hispanic/Latino), 2 international. Average age 27. 695 applicants, 58% accepted, 115 enrolled. *Faculty:* 22 full-time (11 women). Expenses: Contact institution. *Financial support:* In 2019–20, 8 teaching assistantships were awarded; research assistantships, career-related internships or fieldwork, Federal Work-Study, tuition waivers (full and partial), and unspecified assistantships also available. Support available to part-time students. Financial award application deadline: 3/1; financial award applicants required to submit FAFSA. In 2019, 85 doctorates awarded. *Program availability:* Part-time. *Application deadline:* For fall admission, 4/1 priority date for domestic and international students. Applications are processed on a rolling basis. Electronic applications accepted. *Application Contact:* Kellie Martial, Acting Director of Admissions, 815-753-8595, Fax: 815-753-5680, E-mail: law-admit@niu.edu. *Dean,* Cassandra L Hill, 815-753-1068, Fax: 815-753-8552, E-mail: law-admit@niu.edu.

**Graduate School** Students: 1,720 full-time (930 women), 2,484 part-time (1,504 women); includes 1,024 minority (290 Black or African American, non-Hispanic/Latino; 6 American Indian or Alaska Native, non-Hispanic/Latino; 209 Asian, non-Hispanic/Latino; 416 Hispanic/Latino; 103 Two or more races, non-Hispanic/Latino), 684 international. Average age 32. 3,063 applicants, 62% accepted, 711 enrolled. *Faculty:* 672 full-time (248 women), 66 part-time/adjunct (17 women). Expenses: Contact institution. *Financial support:* In 2019–20, 419 research assistantships with full tuition reimbursements, 802 teaching assistantships with full tuition reimbursements were awarded; fellowships with full tuition reimbursements, career-related internships or fieldwork, Federal Work-Study, scholarships/grants, tuition waivers (full), and staff assistantships also available. Support available to part-time students. Financial award applicants required to submit FAFSA. In 2019, 1,344 master's, 152 doctorates, 27 other advanced degrees awarded. *Program availability:* Part-time, evening/weekend, online learning. *Application deadline:* For fall admission, 8/1 for domestic students, 5/1 for international students; for spring admission, 12/1 for domestic students, 10/1 for international students. Applications are processed on a rolling basis. *Application fee:* $40. Electronic applications accepted. *Application Contact:* Graduate School Information, 815-753-0395, E-mail: gradsch@niu.edu. *Dean,* Dr. Bradley G. Bond, 815-753-9403, Fax: 815-753-6366, E-mail: bbond@niu.edu.

***College of Business*** Students: 347 full-time (158 women), 419 part-time (167 women); includes 851 minority (50 Black or African American, non-Hispanic/Latino; 1 American Indian or Alaska Native, non-Hispanic/Latino; 700 Asian, non-Hispanic/Latino; 80

Hispanic/Latino; 20 Two or more races, non-Hispanic/Latino), 175 international. Average age 30. 519 applicants, 86% accepted, 114 enrolled. *Faculty:* 53 full-time (17 women), 3 part-time/adjunct (0 women). Expenses: Contact institution. *Financial support:* In 2019–20, 39 research assistantships with full tuition reimbursements, 55 teaching assistantships with full tuition reimbursements were awarded; fellowships with full tuition reimbursements, career-related internships or fieldwork, Federal Work-Study, scholarships/grants, tuition waivers (full), and unspecified assistantships also available. Support available to part-time students. Financial award applicants required to submit FAFSA. In 2019, 430 master's awarded. *Program availability:* Part-time, evening/weekend. *Application deadline:* For fall admission, 6/1 for domestic students, 5/1 for international students; for spring admission, 11/1 for domestic students, 10/1 for international students. Applications are processed on a rolling basis. *Application fee:* $40. Electronic applications accepted. *Application Contact:* Office of Graduate Studies in Business, 815-753-6301. *Dean*, Balaji Rajagopalan, 815-753-6225, Fax: 815-753-5305, E-mail: brajagopalan@niu.edu.

***College of Education*** Students: 343 full-time (233 women), 852 part-time (598 women); includes 337 minority (129 Black or African American, non-Hispanic/Latino; 2 American Indian or Alaska Native, non-Hispanic/Latino; 50 Asian, non-Hispanic/Latino; 122 Hispanic/Latino; 34 Two or more races, non-Hispanic/Latino), 74 international. Average age 36. 485 applicants, 78% accepted, 211 enrolled. *Faculty:* 110 full-time (66 women), 5 part-time/adjunct (3 women). Expenses: Contact institution. *Financial support:* In 2019–20, 35 research assistantships with full tuition reimbursements, 63 teaching assistantships with full tuition reimbursements were awarded; fellowships with full tuition reimbursements, career-related internships or fieldwork, Federal Work-Study, scholarships/grants, tuition waivers (full), and staff assistantships also available. Support available to part-time students. Financial award applicants required to submit FAFSA. In 2019, 359 master's, 45 doctorates, 19 other advanced degrees awarded. *Program availability:* Part-time, evening/weekend, online learning. *Application deadline:* For fall admission, 6/1 for domestic students, 5/1 for international students; for spring admission, 11/1 for domestic students, 10/1 for international students. Applications are processed on a rolling basis. *Application fee:* $40. Electronic applications accepted. *Application Contact:* Graduate School Office, 815-753-0395, E-mail: gradsch@niu.edu. *Dean*, Laurie Elish-Piper, 815-753-1949, Fax: 851-753-2100.

***College of Engineering and Engineering Technology*** Students: 125 full-time (32 women), 138 part-time (23 women); includes 36 minority (4 Black or African American, non-Hispanic/Latino; 14 Asian, non-Hispanic/Latino; 12 Hispanic/Latino; 6 Two or more races, non-Hispanic/Latino), 140 international. Average age 28. 274 applicants, 66% accepted, 55 enrolled. *Faculty:* 36 full-time (2 women), 2 part-time/adjunct (0 women). Expenses: Contact institution. *Financial support:* In 2019–20, 48 research assistantships with full tuition reimbursements, 90 teaching assistantships with full tuition reimbursements were awarded; fellowships with full tuition reimbursements, career-related internships or fieldwork, Federal Work-Study, scholarships/grants, tuition waivers (full), and unspecified assistantships also available. Support available to part-time students. Financial award applicants required to submit FAFSA. In 2019, 128 master's awarded. *Program availability:* Part-time, evening/weekend. *Application deadline:* For fall admission, 6/1 for domestic students, 5/1 for international students; for spring admission, 11/1 for domestic students, 10/1 for international students. Applications are processed on a rolling basis. *Application fee:* $40. Electronic applications accepted. *Application Contact:* Graduate School Office, 815-753-0395, E-mail: gradsch@niu.edu. *Dean*, Dr. Donald R Peterson, 815-753-1281, Fax: 815-753-1310, E-mail: drpeterson@niu.edu.

***College of Health and Human Sciences*** Students: 284 full-time (218 women), 284 part-time (237 women); includes 168 minority (47 Black or African American, non-Hispanic/Latino; 2 American Indian or Alaska Native, non-Hispanic/Latino; 33 Asian, non-Hispanic/Latino; 70 Hispanic/Latino; 16 Two or more races, non-Hispanic/Latino), 12 international. Average age 31. 511 applicants, 51% accepted, 100 enrolled. *Faculty:* 46 full-time (37 women), 5 part-time/adjunct (3 women). Expenses: Contact institution. *Financial support:* In 2019–20, 68 research assistantships with full tuition reimbursements, 50 teaching assistantships with full tuition reimbursements were awarded; fellowships with full tuition reimbursements, career-related internships or fieldwork, Federal Work-Study, scholarships/grants, tuition waivers (full), and staff assistantships also available. Support available to part-time students. Financial award applicants required to submit FAFSA. In 2019, 107 master's, 42 doctorates awarded. *Program availability:* Part-time, evening/weekend. *Application deadline:* For fall admission, 6/1 for domestic students, 5/1 for international students; for spring admission, 11/1 for domestic students, 10/1 for international students. Applications are processed on a rolling basis. *Application fee:* $40. Electronic applications accepted. *Application Contact:* Graduate School Office, 815-753-0395, E-mail: gradsch@niu.edu. *Dean*, Dr. Derryl Block, 815-753-6157.

***College of Liberal Arts and Sciences*** Students: 503 full-time (226 women), 333 part-time (169 women); includes 127 minority (29 Black or African American, non-Hispanic/Latino; 21 Asian, non-Hispanic/Latino; 62 Hispanic/Latino; 15 Two or more races, non-Hispanic/Latino), 234 international. Average age 30. 1,126 applicants, 50% accepted, 191 enrolled. *Faculty:* 342 full-time (99 women), 36 part-time/adjunct (7 women). Expenses: Contact institution. *Financial support:* In 2019–20, 129 research assistantships with full tuition reimbursements, 418 teaching assistantships with full tuition reimbursements were awarded; fellowships with full tuition reimbursements, career-related internships or fieldwork, Federal Work-Study, scholarships/grants, tuition waivers (full), and unspecified assistantships also available. Support available to part-time students. Financial award applicants required to submit FAFSA. In 2019, 254 master's, 64 doctorates awarded. *Program availability:* Part-time, evening/weekend. *Application deadline:* For fall admission, 6/1 for domestic students, 5/1 for international students; for spring admission, 11/1 for domestic students, 10/1 for international students. Applications are processed on a rolling basis. *Application fee:* $40. Electronic applications accepted. *Application Contact:* Graduate School Office, 815-753-0395, E-mail: gradsch@niu.edu. *Dean*, Dr. Bob Brinkmann, 815-753-1061, Fax: 815-753-7950.

***College of Visual and Performing Arts*** Students: 93 full-time (46 women), 63 part-time (34 women); includes 30 minority (6 Black or African American, non-Hispanic/Latino; 6 Asian, non-Hispanic/Latino; 13 Hispanic/Latino; 5 Two or more races, non-Hispanic/Latino), 38 international. Average age 29. 135 applicants, 68% accepted, 43 enrolled. *Faculty:* 85 full-time (27 women), 15 part-time/adjunct (4 women). Expenses: Contact institution. *Financial support:* In 2019–20, 29 research assistantships with full tuition reimbursements, 73 teaching assistantships with full tuition reimbursements were awarded; fellowships with full tuition reimbursements, career-related internships or fieldwork, Federal Work-Study, scholarships/grants, tuition waivers (full), and staff assistantships also available. Support available to part-time students. Financial award applicants required to submit FAFSA. In 2019, 65 master's, 8 other advanced degrees awarded. *Program availability:* Part-time, evening/weekend. *Application deadline:* For fall admission, 5/1 for international students; for spring admission, 10/1 for international students. Applications are processed on a rolling basis. *Application fee:* $40. Electronic applications accepted. *Application Contact:* Graduate School Office, 815-753-0395, E-mail: gradsch@niu.edu. *Dean*, Dr. Paul Kassel, 815-753-1138, Fax: 815-753-8372, E-mail: pkassel@niu.edu.

## NORTHERN KENTUCKY UNIVERSITY, Highland Heights, KY 41099

**General Information** State-supported, coed, comprehensive institution. CGS member. *Graduate housing:* Room and/or apartments available on a first-come, first-served basis to single students; on-campus housing not available to married students. Housing application deadline: 5/1.

**GRADUATE UNITS**

**Office of Graduate Programs** *Program availability:* Part-time, evening/weekend, online learning. Electronic applications accepted.

***College of Arts and Sciences*** *Program availability:* Part-time, evening/weekend, online learning. Electronic applications accepted.

***College of Business*** *Program availability:* Part-time, evening/weekend. Electronic applications accepted.

***College of Education and Human Services*** *Program availability:* Part-time, evening/weekend. Electronic applications accepted.

***College of Informatics*** *Program availability:* Part-time, evening/weekend. Electronic applications accepted.

***School of Nursing and Health Professions*** *Program availability:* Part-time, evening/weekend, online learning. Electronic applications accepted.

**Salmon P. Chase College of Law** Students: 285 full-time (150 women), 114 part-time (57 women); includes 49 minority (23 Black or African American, non-Hispanic/Latino; 1 American Indian or Alaska Native, non-Hispanic/Latino; 6 Asian, non-Hispanic/Latino; 18 Hispanic/Latino; 1 Two or more races, non-Hispanic/Latino). Average age 27. 506 applicants, 68% accepted, 130 enrolled. *Faculty:* 26 full-time (9 women), 32 part-time/adjunct (8 women). Expenses: Contact institution. *Financial support:* Fellowships, research assistantships, career-related internships or fieldwork, Federal Work-Study, scholarships/grants, and unspecified assistantships available. Support available to part-time students. Financial award application deadline: 3/1; financial award applicants required to submit FAFSA. In 2019, 132 doctorates awarded. *Program availability:* Part-time, evening/weekend. *Application deadline:* For fall admission, 4/1 priority date for domestic and international students; for summer admission, 3/15 priority date for domestic students, 3/15 for international students. Applications are processed on a rolling basis. *Application fee:* $40. Electronic applications accepted. *Application Contact:* Ashley Siemer, Director of Student Affairs and Enrollment Management, 859-572-5841, E-mail: graya4@nku.edu. *Dean*, Judith Daar, 859-572-5781, E-mail: daarj1@nku.edu.

## NORTHERN MICHIGAN UNIVERSITY, Marquette, MI 49855-5301

**General Information** State-supported, coed, comprehensive institution. CGS member. *Graduate housing:* Rooms and/or apartments available on a first-come, first-served basis to single and married students. Housing application deadline: 7/15.

**GRADUATE UNITS**

**Office of Graduate Education and Research** *Program availability:* Part-time, evening/weekend, online learning. Electronic applications accepted.

***College of Arts and Sciences*** *Program availability:* Part-time, online learning. Electronic applications accepted.

***College of Business*** Expenses: Contact institution. *Financial support:* Research assistantships with full tuition reimbursements, career-related internships or fieldwork, scholarships/grants, traineeships, and unspecified assistantships available. Support available to part-time students. Financial award application deadline: 3/1; financial award applicants required to submit FAFSA. *Program availability:* Part-time, evening/weekend, blended/hybrid learning. *Application deadline:* For fall admission, 7/1 for domestic students; for winter admission, 11/15 for domestic students; for summer admission, 5/1 for domestic students. Applications are processed on a rolling basis. *Application fee:* $50. Electronic applications accepted. *Application Contact:* Dr. Stacy Boyer-Davis, MBA Director, Assistant Department Head, Extended Learning Scholar, Assistant Professor, 906-227-1805, E-mail: sboyerda@nmu.edu. *Dean*, Carol W. Johnson, 906-227-2970, E-mail: carjohns@nmu.edu.

***College of Health Sciences and Professional Studies*** *Program availability:* Part-time.

## NORTHERN SEMINARY, Lombard, IL 60148-5698

**General Information** Independent-religious, coed, primarily men, graduate-only institution. *Graduate housing:* On-campus housing not available.

**GRADUATE UNITS**

**Graduate and Professional Programs** *Program availability:* Part-time, evening/weekend. Electronic applications accepted.

## NORTHERN STATE UNIVERSITY, Aberdeen, SD 57401-7198

**General Information** State-supported, coed, comprehensive institution. *Enrollment:* 3,427 graduate, professional, and undergraduate students; 38 full-time matriculated graduate/professional students (23 women), 121 part-time matriculated graduate/professional students (78 women). *Enrollment by degree level:* 159 master's. *Graduate faculty:* 28 full-time (17 women), 3 part-time/adjunct (2 women). *International tuition:* $7392 full-time. *Tuition, area resident:* Full-time $5939; part-time $5939 per year. Tuition, state resident: full-time $8816; part-time $8816 per year. Tuition, nonresident: full-time $11,088; part-time $11,088 per year. *Required fees:* $484; $242. *Graduate housing:* Room and/or apartments available on a first-come, first-served basis to single students; on-campus housing not available to married students. Typical cost: $4818 per year ($9042 including board). Room and board charges vary according to board plan and housing facility selected. Housing application deadline: 8/1. *Student services:* Campus employment opportunities, campus safety program, career counseling, exercise/wellness program, free psychological counseling, international student services, multicultural affairs office, services for students with disabilities, teacher training, writing training. *Library facilities:* Beulah Williams Library. *Collection:* Books: 156,950 (physical), 15,000 (digital/electronic); Serial titles: 7,000 (physical), 250 (digital/electronic); Databases: 80. Weekly public service hours: 90; students can reserve study rooms. *Research affiliation:* AASCU–Grants Resource Center.

**Computer facilities:** 130 computers available on campus for general student use. A campuswide network can be accessed. Online class registration is available. Website: http://www.northern.edu/

**General Application Contact:** Tammy K. Griffith, Program Assistant, 605-626-2558, Fax: 605-626-7190, E-mail: tammy.griffith@northern.edu.

**GRADUATE UNITS**

**MME Program in Music Education** Students: 28 part-time (18 women); includes 3 minority (all Black or African American, non-Hispanic/Latino). Average age 31. 23 applicants, 83% accepted, 14 enrolled. *Faculty:* 7 full-time (3 women). Expenses: Contact institution. *Financial support:* Institutionally sponsored loans and scholarships/grants available. Support available to part-time students. Financial award application deadline: 3/1; financial award applicants required to submit FAFSA. In 2019, 10 master's awarded. *Program availability:* Part-time, online learning. *Application deadline:* Applications are processed on a rolling basis. *Application fee:* $35. Electronic applications accepted. *Application Contact:* Tammy Giffith, Program Assistant, 605-626-2558, Fax: 605-626-7190, E-mail: tammy.griffith@northern.edu. *Dean of Fine Arts,* Dr. Kenneth Boulton, 605-626-2500, Fax: 605-626-2263, E-mail: kenneth.boulton@northern.edu.

**MS Ed Program in Counseling** Students: 21 full-time (16 women), 2 part-time (1 woman); includes 4 minority (1 American Indian or Alaska Native, non-Hispanic/Latino; 1 Hispanic/Latino; 2 Two or more races, non-Hispanic/Latino), 1 international. Average age 29. 17 applicants, 47% accepted, 8 enrolled. *Faculty:* 5 full-time (all women). Expenses: Contact institution. *Financial support:* In 2019–20, 11 students received support, including 5 teaching assistantships with partial tuition reimbursements available (averaging $7,764 per year); career-related internships or fieldwork, Federal Work-Study, institutionally sponsored loans, scholarships/grants, and unspecified assistantships also available. Support available to part-time students. Financial award application deadline: 3/1; financial award applicants required to submit FAFSA. In 2019, 12 master's awarded. *Program availability:* Part-time, online learning. *Application deadline:* For fall admission, 8/15 for domestic and international students; for spring admission, 12/15 for domestic and international students. Applications are processed on a rolling basis. *Application fee:* $35. Electronic applications accepted. *Application Contact:* Tammy K. Griffith, Program Assistant, 605-626-2558, Fax: 605-626-7190, E-mail: tammy.griffith@northern.edu. *Dean of Professional Studies,* Dr. Doug Ohmer, 605-626-2400, Fax: 605-626-2980, E-mail: doug.ohmer@northern.edu.

**MS Ed Program in Educational Studies** Students: 3 full-time (1 woman), 13 part-time (8 women); includes 1 minority (Black or African American, non-Hispanic/Latino), 4 international. Average age 32. 11 applicants, 18% accepted, 1 enrolled. *Faculty:* 16 full-time (10 women), 3 part-time/adjunct (2 women). Expenses: Contact institution. *Financial support:* In 2019–20, 1 student received support, including 3 teaching assistantships (averaging $7,764 per year); career-related internships or fieldwork, Federal Work-Study, institutionally sponsored loans, scholarships/grants, and unspecified assistantships also available. Support available to part-time students. Financial award application deadline: 3/1; financial award applicants required to submit FAFSA. In 2019, 4 master's awarded. *Program availability:* Part-time, blended/hybrid learning. *Application deadline:* Applications are processed on a rolling basis. *Application fee:* $35. Electronic applications accepted. *Application Contact:* Tammy K. Griffith, Program Assistant, 605-626-2558, Fax: 605-626-7190, E-mail: tammy.griffith@northern.edu. *Dean of Professional Studies,* Dr. Doug Ohmer, 605-626-2400, Fax: 605-626-2980, E-mail: doug.ohmer@northern.edu.

**MS Ed Program in Instructional Design in E-learning** Expenses: Contact institution. *Financial support:* Career-related internships or fieldwork, Federal Work-Study, institutionally sponsored loans, scholarships/grants, and unspecified assistantships available. Support available to part-time students. Financial award application deadline: 3/1; financial award applicants required to submit FAFSA. *Program availability:* Part-time, online learning. *Application deadline:* Applications are processed on a rolling basis. *Application fee:* $35. Electronic applications accepted. *Application Contact:* Tammy K. Griffith, Program Assistant, 605-626-2558, Fax: 605-626-7190, E-mail: tammy.griffith@northern.edu. *Dean of Professional Studies,* Dr. Doug Ohmer, 605-626-2400, Fax: 605-626-2980, E-mail: doug.ohmer@northern.edu.

**MS Ed Program in Leadership and Administration** Students: 22 part-time (12 women); includes 1 minority (Native Hawaiian or other Pacific Islander, non-Hispanic/Latino). Average age 31. 23 applicants, 78% accepted, 12 enrolled. *Faculty:* 3 full-time (1 woman). Expenses: Contact institution. *Financial support:* In 2019–20, 1 student received support, including 2 teaching assistantships with partial tuition reimbursements available (averaging $7,764 per year); career-related internships or fieldwork, Federal Work-Study, institutionally sponsored loans, scholarships/grants, and unspecified assistantships also available. Support available to part-time students. Financial award application deadline: 3/1; financial award applicants required to submit FAFSA. In 2019, 10 master's awarded. *Program availability:* Part-time, online learning. *Application deadline:* Applications are processed on a rolling basis. *Application fee:* $35. Electronic applications accepted. *Application Contact:* Tammy K. Griffith, Program Assistant, 605-626-2558, Fax: 605-626-7190, E-mail: tammy.griffith@northern.edu. *Dean of Professional Studies,* Dr. Doug Ohmer, 605-626-2400, Fax: 605-626-2980, E-mail: doug.ohmer@northern.edu.

**MS Ed Program in Sport Performance and Leadership** Students: 14 full-time (6 women), 12 part-time (1 woman); includes 1 minority (Black or African American, non-Hispanic/Latino), 1 international. Average age 24. 28 applicants, 50% accepted, 13 enrolled. *Faculty:* 4 full-time (1 woman). Expenses: Contact institution. *Financial support:* In 2019–20, 16 teaching assistantships (averaging $7,764 per year) were awarded; career-related internships or fieldwork, Federal Work-Study, institutionally sponsored loans, scholarships/grants, and unspecified assistantships also available. Support available to part-time students. Financial award application deadline: 3/1; financial award applicants required to submit FAFSA. In 2019, 9 master's awarded. *Program availability:* Part-time. *Application deadline:* Applications are processed on a rolling basis. *Application fee:* $35. Electronic applications accepted. *Application Contact:* Tammy K. Griffith, Program Assistant, 605-626-2558, Fax: 605-626-7190, E-mail: tammy.griffith@northern.edu. *Dean of Professional Studies,* Dr. Doug Ohmer, 605-626-2400, Fax: 605-626-2980, E-mail: doug.ohmer@northern.edu.

**MS Ed Program in Teaching and Learning** Students: 36 part-time (33 women); includes 1 minority (Two or more races, non-Hispanic/Latino). Average age 33. 6 applicants, 83% accepted, 3 enrolled. *Faculty:* 5 full-time (2 women). Expenses: Contact institution. *Financial support:* In 2019–20, 2 teaching assistantships with partial tuition reimbursements (averaging $7,764 per year) were awarded; career-related internships or fieldwork, Federal Work-Study, institutionally sponsored loans, scholarships/grants, and unspecified assistantships also available. Support available to part-time students. Financial award application deadline: 3/1; financial award applicants required to submit FAFSA. In 2019, 4 master's awarded. *Program availability:* Part-time, online learning. *Application deadline:* Applications are processed on a rolling basis. *Application fee:* $35. Electronic applications accepted. *Application Contact:* Tammy K. Griffith, Program Assistant, 605-626-2558, Fax: 605-626-7190, E-mail: tammy.griffith@northern.edu. *Dean of Professional Studies,* Dr. Doug Ohmer, 605-626-2400, Fax: 605-626-2980, E-mail: doug.ohmer@northern.edu.

**MS Program in Banking and Financial Services** Students: 8 part-time (5 women), 1 international. Average age 30. 4 applicants, 75% accepted, 2 enrolled. *Faculty:* 2 full-time (1 woman). Expenses: Contact institution. *Financial support:* In 2019–20, 2 students received support. Federal Work-Study and institutionally sponsored loans available. Support available to part-time students. Financial award application deadline: 3/1; financial award applicants required to submit FAFSA. In 2019, 3 master's awarded. *Program availability:* Part-time, online learning. *Application deadline:* Applications are processed on a rolling basis. *Application fee:* $35. Electronic applications accepted. *Application Contact:* Tammy K. Griffith, Program Assistant, 605-626-2558, E-mail: gradoff@northern.edu. *Dean of Professional Studies,* Dr. Doug Ohmer, 605-626-2400, Fax: 605-626-2980, E-mail: doug.ohmer@northern.edu.

## NORTHERN VERMONT UNIVERSITY–JOHNSON, Johnson, VT 05656

**General Information** State-supported, coed, comprehensive institution. *Graduate housing:* Rooms and/or apartments available on a first-come, first-served basis to single and married students. Housing application deadline: 3/15.

**GRADUATE UNITS**

**Program in Counseling** *Program availability:* Part-time. Electronic applications accepted.

**Program in Education** *Program availability:* Part-time. Electronic applications accepted.

**Program in Studio Arts** *Program availability:* Part-time, online learning. Electronic applications accepted.

## NORTHERN VERMONT UNIVERSITY–LYNDON, Lyndonville, VT 05851

**General Information** State-supported, coed, comprehensive institution. *Graduate housing:* On-campus housing not available.

**GRADUATE UNITS**

**Graduate Programs in Education** *Program availability:* Part-time, evening/weekend.

## NORTH GREENVILLE UNIVERSITY, Tigerville, SC 29688-1892

**General Information** Independent-religious, coed, comprehensive institution. *Graduate housing:* Room and/or apartments available on a first-come, first-served basis to single students; on-campus housing not available to married students. Housing application deadline: 8/1.

**GRADUATE UNITS**

**T. Walter Brashier Graduate School** *Program availability:* Part-time, evening/weekend, online learning. Electronic applications accepted.

## NORTH PARK THEOLOGICAL SEMINARY, Chicago, IL 60625-4895

**General Information** Independent-religious, coed, graduate-only institution. *Enrollment by degree level:* 225 master's, 40 doctoral, 60 other advanced degrees. *Graduate faculty:* 17 full-time (4 women), 13 part-time/adjunct (3 women). *Graduate housing:* Rooms and/or apartments available on a first-come, first-served basis to single and married students. Housing application deadline: 7/1. *Student services:* Campus employment opportunities, campus safety program, career counseling, free psychological counseling, international student services, multicultural affairs office, writing training. *Library facilities:* Brandel Library. *Research affiliation:* Northside Chicago Theological Institute, Covenant Archives and Historical Society, American Theological Library Association.
Website: http://www.northpark.edu/sem/

**General Application Contact:** Baily Warman Manwatkar, Admission Counselor, 773-244-6229, E-mail: semadmissions@northpark.edu.

**GRADUATE UNITS**

**Graduate and Professional Programs** *Program availability:* Part-time.

## NORTH PARK UNIVERSITY, Chicago, IL 60625-4895

**General Information** Independent-religious, coed, comprehensive institution. *Graduate housing:* Rooms and/or apartments available to single and married students.

**GRADUATE UNITS**

**School of Business and Nonprofit Management** *Program availability:* Part-time, evening/weekend, online learning.

**School of Education**

**School of Music**

**School of Nursing and Health Sciences** *Program availability:* Part-time, evening/weekend.

## NORTHWESTERN COLLEGE, Orange City, IA 51041-1996

**General Information** Independent-religious, coed, comprehensive institution.

**GRADUATE UNITS**

**Program in Education** *Program availability:* Online learning.

## NORTHWESTERN HEALTH SCIENCES UNIVERSITY, Bloomington, MN 55431-1599

**General Information** Independent, coed, graduate-only institution. *Graduate housing:* On-campus housing not available. *Research affiliation:* University of Minnesota, Center for Spirituality and Healing (education research), University of Western States (clinical research), University of Pittsburgh (education research).

**GRADUATE UNITS**

**College of Chiropractic** Electronic applications accepted.

**College of Health and Wellness** Electronic applications accepted.

## NORTHWESTERN OKLAHOMA STATE UNIVERSITY, Alva, OK 73717-2799

**General Information** State-supported, coed, comprehensive institution. *Graduate housing:* Room and/or apartments available to single students; on-campus housing not available to married students.

**GRADUATE UNITS**

**Program in American Studies** *Program availability:* Part-time.

**School of Professional Studies** *Program availability:* Part-time.

## NORTHWESTERN POLYTECHNIC UNIVERSITY, Fremont, CA 94539-7482

**General Information** Independent, coed, comprehensive institution. *Graduate housing:* Room and/or apartments available on a first-come, first-served basis to single students; on-campus housing not available to married students. Housing application deadline: 7/15.

**GRADUATE UNITS**

**School of Business and Information Technology** *Program availability:* Part-time, evening/weekend.

**School of Engineering** *Program availability:* Part-time, evening/weekend.

## NORTHWESTERN STATE UNIVERSITY OF LOUISIANA, Natchitoches, LA 71497

**General Information** State-supported, coed, comprehensive institution. CGS member. *Graduate housing:* Room and/or apartments available on a first-come, first-served basis to single students; on-campus housing not available to married students. Housing application deadline: 3/1. *Research affiliation:* NASA (Strategic Defense Initiative), Central State Hospital, Federal Records and Archives Services.

**GRADUATE UNITS**

**Graduate Studies and Research** *Program availability:* Part-time, evening/weekend, online learning. Electronic applications accepted.

***College of Education and Human Development*** Electronic applications accepted.

***College of Nursing and School of Allied Health*** *Program availability:* Part-time. Electronic applications accepted.

***School of Creative and Performing Arts*** Electronic applications accepted.

## NORTHWESTERN UNIVERSITY, Evanston, IL 60208

**General Information** Independent, coed, university. CGS member. *Graduate housing:* Rooms and/or apartments available on a first-come, first-served basis to single students and available to married students. Housing application deadline: 9/1. *Research affiliation:* Dow Chemical Company (materials science and engineering), E.I. du Pont de Nemours and Company (physics), Exxon Chemical Company (chemical engineering), Ford Motor Company (mechanical engineering), Medtronics, Inc. (cardiology), Amoco Oil Company (materials science and engineering).

**GRADUATE UNITS**

**Feinberg School of Medicine** Electronic applications accepted.

**The Graduate School** *Program availability:* Part-time, evening/weekend. Electronic applications accepted.

***Center for International and Comparative Studies***

***Judd A. and Marjorie Weinberg College of Arts and Sciences*** *Program availability:* Part-time, evening/weekend.

***School of Communication*** *Program availability:* Part-time.

***School of Education and Social Policy*** *Program availability:* Part-time, evening/weekend. Electronic applications accepted.

**Henry and Leigh Bienen School of Music** Electronic applications accepted.

**McCormick School of Engineering and Applied Science** *Program availability:* Part-time, evening/weekend. Electronic applications accepted.

***Segal Design Institute***

**Medill School of Journalism, Media, and Integrated Marketing Communications** Electronic applications accepted.

**Pritzker School of Law** *Program availability:* Part-time, online learning. Electronic applications accepted.

**School of Professional Studies**

## NORTHWEST MISSOURI STATE UNIVERSITY, Maryville, MO 64468-6001

**General Information** State-supported, coed, comprehensive institution. *Enrollment:* 7,104 graduate, professional, and undergraduate students; 462 full-time matriculated graduate/professional students (256 women), 932 part-time matriculated graduate/professional students (614 women). *Enrollment by degree level:* 1,353 master's, 22 doctoral, 19 other advanced degrees. *Graduate faculty:* 150 full-time (52 women). *Tuition, area resident:* Full-time $6003.79; part-time $333.54 per credit hour. Tuition, state resident: full-time $6003.79; part-time $333.54 per credit hour. Tuition, nonresident: full-time $6004; part-time $333.54 per credit hour. *Required fees:* $1018.80; $56.50 per credit hour. Tuition and fees vary according to program. *Graduate housing:* Rooms and/or apartments available on a first-come, first-served basis to single and married students. Typical cost: $6356 per year ($10,106 including board) for single students; $6356 per year ($10,106 including board) for married students. Housing application deadline: 6/1. *Student services:* Campus employment opportunities, campus safety program, career counseling, exercise/wellness program, free psychological counseling, international student services, low-cost health insurance, multicultural affairs office, services for students with disabilities, teacher training, writing training. *Library facilities:* Owens Library. *Collection:* Books: 96,983 (physical), 243,090 (digital/electronic); Serial titles: 5 (physical), 53,342 (digital/electronic); Databases: 137. Weekly public service hours: 95; students can reserve study rooms.

**Computer facilities:** Computer purchase and lease plans are available. 260 computers available on campus for general student use. A campuswide network can be accessed. Online class registration, online courses with library and databases are available. Website: http://www.nwmissouri.edu/

**General Application Contact:** Dr. Gregory Haddock, Dean of Graduate School, 660-562-1145, Fax: 660-562-1096, E-mail: gradsch@nwmissouri.edu.

**GRADUATE UNITS**

**Graduate School** Students: 462 full-time (256 women), 932 part-time (614 women); includes 103 minority (45 Black or African American, non-Hispanic/Latino; 5 American Indian or Alaska Native, non-Hispanic/Latino; 9 Asian, non-Hispanic/Latino; 26 Hispanic/Latino; 3 Native Hawaiian or other Pacific Islander, non-Hispanic/Latino; 15 Two or more races, non-Hispanic/Latino), 279 international. Average age 30. 856 applicants, 73% accepted, 325 enrolled. *Faculty:* 150 full-time (52 women). Expenses: Contact institution. *Financial support:* Research assistantships with full tuition reimbursements, teaching assistantships with full tuition reimbursements, career-related internships or fieldwork, Federal Work-Study, institutionally sponsored loans, scholarships/grants, unspecified assistantships, and administrative assistantships, tutorial assistantships available. Financial award application deadline: 4/1; financial award applicants required to submit FAFSA. In 2019, 435 master's, 25 other advanced degrees awarded. *Program availability:* Part-time, evening/weekend. *Application deadline:* For fall admission, 7/1 for domestic and international students; for spring admission, 11/15 for domestic and international students. Applications are processed on a rolling basis. *Application fee:* $0 ($75 for international students). Electronic applications accepted. *Application Contact:* Cynthia Williams, Executive Secretary, 660-562-1144, Fax: 660-562-1096, E-mail: gradsch@nwmissouri.edu. *Dean*, Dr. Gregory Haddock, 660-562-1145, Fax: 660-562-1096, E-mail: gradsch@nwmissouri.edu.

***College of Arts and Sciences*** Students: 10 full-time (5 women), 47 part-time (23 women); includes 6 minority (2 American Indian or Alaska Native, non-Hispanic/Latino; 1 Asian, non-Hispanic/Latino; 1 Hispanic/Latino; 1 Native Hawaiian or other Pacific Islander, non-Hispanic/Latino; 1 Two or more races, non-Hispanic/Latino), 1 international. Average age 31. 17 applicants, 65% accepted, 9 enrolled. *Faculty:* 18 full-time (8 women). Expenses: Contact institution. *Financial support:* Research assistantships with full tuition reimbursements, teaching assistantships with full tuition reimbursements, and administrative assistantships, tutorial assistantships available. Financial award application deadline: 4/1; financial award applicants required to submit FAFSA. In 2019, 25 master's, 6 other advanced degrees awarded. *Program availability:* Part-time. *Application deadline:* For fall admission, 7/1 for domestic and international students; for spring admission, 11/15 for domestic and international students. Applications are processed on a rolling basis. *Application fee:* $0 ($75 for international students). Electronic applications accepted. *Application Contact:* Dr. Michael Steiner, Associate Provost-UG Studies & Dean, 660-562-1197. *Associate Provost-UG Studies & Dean*, Dr. Michael Steiner, 660-562-1197.

***Melvin and Valorie Booth College of Business and Professional Studies*** Students: 52 full-time (29 women), 237 part-time (127 women); includes 41 minority (19 Black or African American, non-Hispanic/Latino; 7 Asian, non-Hispanic/Latino; 11 Hispanic/Latino; 4 Two or more races, non-Hispanic/Latino), 10 international. Average age 32. 110 applicants, 66% accepted, 63 enrolled. *Faculty:* 10 full-time (5 women). Expenses: Contact institution. *Financial support:* Research assistantships with full tuition reimbursements, teaching assistantships with full tuition reimbursements, career-related internships or fieldwork, unspecified assistantships, and administrative assistantships, tutorial assistantships available. Financial award application deadline: 4/1; financial award applicants required to submit FAFSA. In 2019, 48 master's awarded. *Program availability:* Part-time. *Application deadline:* For fall admission, 7/1 for domestic and international students; for spring admission, 11/15 for domestic and international students; for summer admission, 4/1 for domestic and international students. Applications are processed on a rolling basis. *Application fee:* $0 ($75 for international students). Electronic applications accepted. *Application Contact:* Dr. Steve Ludwig, Director of the Melvin And Valorie Booth School of Business, 660-562-1749, Fax: 660-562-1096, E-mail: sludwig@nwmissouri.edu. *Director of the Melvin And Valorie Booth School of Business*, Dr. Steve Ludwig, 660-562-1749, Fax: 660-562-1096, E-mail: sludwig@nwmissouri.edu.

***School of Agricultural Sciences*** Students: 4 full-time (2 women), 2 part-time (1 woman), 5 international. Average age 24. 12 applicants, 50% accepted, 1 enrolled. *Faculty:* 5 full-time (1 woman). Expenses: Contact institution. *Financial support:* Research assistantships with full tuition reimbursements, teaching assistantships with full tuition reimbursements, and unspecified assistantships available. Financial award application deadline: 4/1; financial award applicants required to submit FAFSA. In 2019, 3 master's awarded. *Program availability:* Part-time. *Application deadline:* For fall admission, 7/1 for domestic and international students; for spring admission, 11/15 for domestic and international students. Applications are processed on a rolling basis. *Application fee:* $0 ($75 for international students). Electronic applications accepted. *Application Contact:* Dr. Rod Barr, Director, 660-562-1620. *Director*, Dr. Rod Barr, 660-562-1620.

***School of Computer Science and Information Systems*** Students: 204 full-time (77 women), 54 part-time (26 women), 257 international. Average age 24. 478 applicants, 72% accepted, 62 enrolled. *Faculty:* 15 full-time (5 women). Expenses: Contact institution. *Financial support:* Research assistantships, teaching assistantships with full tuition reimbursements, and unspecified assistantships available. Financial award application deadline: 4/1; financial award applicants required to submit FAFSA. In 2019, 129 master's awarded. *Program availability:* Part-time. *Application deadline:* Applications are processed on a rolling basis. *Application fee:* $0 ($75 for international students). Electronic applications accepted. *Application Contact:* Dr. Gregory Haddock, Dean of Graduate School, 660-562-1145, Fax: 660-562-1096, E-mail: gradsch@nwmissouri.edu. *Director of School of Computer Science and Information Systems*, Dr. Douglas Hawley, 660-562-1200, Fax: 660-562-1963, E-mail: hawley@nwmissouri.edu.

***School of Education*** Students: 135 full-time (108 women), 548 part-time (407 women); includes 44 minority (18 Black or African American, non-Hispanic/Latino; 3 American Indian or Alaska Native, non-Hispanic/Latino; 1 Asian, non-Hispanic/Latino; 12 Hispanic/Latino; 2 Native Hawaiian or other Pacific Islander, non-Hispanic/Latino; 8 Two or more races, non-Hispanic/Latino), 5 international. Average age 32. 207 applicants, 84% accepted, 172 enrolled. *Faculty:* 29 full-time (19 women). Expenses: Contact institution. *Financial support:* Research assistantships with full tuition reimbursements, teaching assistantships with full tuition reimbursements, and unspecified assistantships available. Financial award application deadline: 4/1; financial award applicants required to submit FAFSA. In 2019, 181 master's, 19 other advanced degrees awarded. *Program availability:* Part-time. *Application deadline:* For fall admission, 7/1 for domestic and international students; for spring admission, 11/15 for domestic and international students. Applications are processed on a rolling basis. *Application fee:* $0 ($75 for international students). Electronic applications accepted. *Application Contact:* Dr. Tim Wall, Director, 660-562-1179, E-mail: timwall@nwmissouri.edu. *Director*, Dr. Tim Wall, 660-562-1179, E-mail: timwall@nwmissouri.edu.

***School of Health Science and Wellness*** Students: 57 full-time (35 women), 22 part-time (16 women); includes 10 minority (8 Black or African American, non-Hispanic/Latino; 2 Hispanic/Latino), 1 international. Average age 25. 30 applicants, 67% accepted, 17 enrolled. *Faculty:* 17 full-time (9 women). Expenses: Contact institution. *Financial support:* Teaching assistantships with full tuition reimbursements and unspecified assistantships available. Financial award application deadline: 4/1; financial award applicants required to submit FAFSA. In 2019, 45 master's awarded. *Program availability:* Part-time. *Application deadline:* For fall admission, 7/1 for domestic and international students; for spring admission, 11/15 for domestic and international students. Applications are processed on a rolling basis. *Application fee:* $0 ($75 for international students). *Application Contact:* Gina Smith, Office Manager, 660-562-1297, Fax: 660-562-1963, E-mail: smigina@nwmissouri.edu. *Director, School of Health Science and Wellness*, Dr. Terry Long, 660-562-1706, Fax: 660-562-1483, E-mail: tlong@nwmissouri.edu.

## NORTHWEST NAZARENE UNIVERSITY, Nampa, ID 83686-5897

**General Information** Independent-religious, coed, comprehensive institution. *Graduate housing:* On-campus housing not available.

**GRADUATE UNITS**

**Graduate Business Programs** *Program availability:* Part-time, evening/weekend, 100% online, blended/hybrid learning, 100% Face-to-face. Electronic applications accepted.

**Graduate Education Program** *Program availability:* Part-time, online only, 100% online, 2-week face-to-face residency (for doctoral programs). Electronic applications accepted.

**NNU Graduate School of Theology** *Program availability:* Part-time, online only, 100% online. Electronic applications accepted.

**Program in Counselor Education** *Program availability:* Part-time, evening/weekend. Electronic applications accepted.

**Program in Nursing** *Program availability:* Part-time, evening/weekend, online only, 100% online, And Residential LABS for FNP. Electronic applications accepted.

**Program in Social Work** *Program availability:* Part-time-only, evening/weekend. Electronic applications accepted.

## NORTHWEST UNIVERSITY, Kirkland, WA 98033

**General Information** Independent-religious, coed, comprehensive institution. *Graduate housing:* Rooms and/or apartments available on a first-come, first-served basis to single and married students.

**GRADUATE UNITS**

**College of Business** *Program availability:* Part-time, evening/weekend. Electronic applications accepted.

**College of Ministry** *Program availability:* Part-time, evening/weekend, online learning. Electronic applications accepted.

**College of Social and Behavioral Sciences** *Program availability:* Evening/weekend.

**School of Education** *Program availability:* Part-time, evening/weekend. Electronic applications accepted.

## NORTHWOOD UNIVERSITY, MICHIGAN CAMPUS, Midland, MI 48640-2398

**General Information** Independent, coed, comprehensive institution. *Enrollment:* 1,522 graduate, professional, and undergraduate students; 41 full-time matriculated graduate/professional students (19 women), 314 part-time matriculated graduate/professional students (164 women). *Enrollment by degree level:* 355 master's. *Graduate faculty:* 3 full-time (0 women), 43 part-time/adjunct (12 women). *Tuition:* Full-time $12,360; part-time $1030 per credit hour. Full-time tuition and fees vary according to program. *Graduate housing:* Rooms and/or apartments guaranteed to single and married students. Typical cost: $5320 per year ($5790 including board) for single students. Housing application deadline: 8/20. *Student services:* Campus employment opportunities, campus safety program, career counseling, exercise/wellness program, free psychological counseling, international student services, low-cost health insurance, multicultural affairs office, services for students with disabilities. *Library facilities:* Strosacker Library. *Collection:* Books: 30,504 (physical); Databases: 26. Weekly public service hours: 89; students can reserve study rooms. *Research affiliation:* Motor & Equipment Manufacturers Association (automotive engineering), Specialized Equipment Manufacturers Association (automotive engineering), Automotive Aftermarket Industry Association (automotive engineering), Automotive Warehouse Distributors Association (automotive engineering).

**Computer facilities:** 215 computers available on campus for general student use. A campuswide network can be accessed. Online class registration is available.
Website: http://www.northwood.edu/

**General Application Contact:** Lucille Pagan, Director of Admissions, Devos, 989-837-4893, Fax: 989-837-4800, E-mail: DeVos@northwood.edu.

**GRADUATE UNITS**

**DeVos Graduate School** Students: 37 full-time (17 women), 275 part-time (136 women); includes 74 minority (48 Black or African American, non-Hispanic/Latino; 1 American Indian or Alaska Native, non-Hispanic/Latino; 1 Asian, non-Hispanic/Latino; 12 Hispanic/Latino; 1 Native Hawaiian or other Pacific Islander, non-Hispanic/Latino; 11 Two or more races, non-Hispanic/Latino), 12 international. Average age 34. 181 applicants, 73% accepted, 115 enrolled. *Faculty:* 6 full-time (1 woman), 8 part-time/adjunct (2 women). Expenses: Contact institution. *Financial support:* In 2019–20, 178 students received support. Scholarships/grants available. Support available to part-time students. In 2019, 240 master's awarded. *Program availability:* Part-time, evening/weekend, 100% online, blended/hybrid learning. *Application deadline:* Applications are processed on a rolling basis. *Application fee:* $50. Electronic applications accepted. *Application Contact:* Lucille Pagan, Director of Admissions, DeVos, 989-837-4893, Fax: 989-837-4800, E-mail: devos@northwood.edu. *Assistant Vice President & Dean*, Dr. Lisa Fairbairn, 989-837-4143, Fax: 989-837-4800, E-mail: fairbair@northwood.edu.

## NORWICH UNIVERSITY, Northfield, VT 05663

**General Information** Independent, coed, comprehensive institution.

**GRADUATE UNITS**

**College of Graduate and Continuing Studies** *Program availability:* Evening/weekend, online only, mostly all online with a week-long residency requirement. Electronic applications accepted.

## NOTRE DAME COLLEGE, South Euclid, OH 44121-4293

**General Information** Independent-religious, coed, comprehensive institution. *Enrollment:* 1,393 graduate, professional, and undergraduate students; 42 full-time matriculated graduate/professional students (32 women), 34 part-time matriculated graduate/professional students (20 women). *Enrollment by degree level:* 76 master's. *Graduate faculty:* 11 full-time (8 women), 8 part-time/adjunct (5 women). *Tuition:* Full-time $590; part-time $590 per credit hour. *Graduate housing:* On-campus housing not available. *Student services:* Campus safety program, career counseling, free psychological counseling, services for students with disabilities, teacher training. *Library facilities:* Clara Fritzsche Library. *Collection:* Books: 40,931 (physical), 194,266 (digital/electronic); Serial titles: 499 (physical), 32,658 (digital/electronic); Databases: 121. Study areas open 24 hours, 5–7 days a week; students can reserve study rooms.

**Computer facilities:** 65 computers available on campus for general student use. A campuswide network can be accessed. Online class registration is available.
Website: http://www.notredamecollege.edu/

**General Application Contact:** Brandy Viol, Assistant Dean of Enrollment, 216-373-6481, Fax: 216-373-0357, E-mail: bviol@ndc.edu.

**GRADUATE UNITS**

**Graduate Programs** Students: 20 full-time (17 women), 83 part-time (59 women); includes 28 minority (12 Black or African American, non-Hispanic/Latino; 2 Hispanic/Latino; 1 Native Hawaiian or other Pacific Islander, non-Hispanic/Latino; 13 Two or more races, non-Hispanic/Latino). Average age 35. *Faculty:* 11 full-time (8 women), 8 part-time/adjunct (5 women). Expenses: Contact institution. *Financial support:* Tuition waivers (full) available. Support available to part-time students. Financial award application deadline: 4/15; financial award applicants required to submit FAFSA. In 2019, 5 master's awarded. *Program availability:* Part-time, evening/weekend, online only, 100% online. *Application deadline:* For fall admission, 8/1 priority date for domestic students; for spring admission, 1/1 for domestic students. Applications are processed on a rolling basis. *Application fee:* $40. *Application Contact:* Brandy Viol, Assistant Dean of Enrollment, 216-373-5350, Fax: 216-373-6330, E-mail: bviol@ndc.edu. *Dean of Online and Graduate Programs*, Florentine Hoelker, 215-373-6469, E-mail: fhoelker@ndc.edu.

## NOTRE DAME OF MARYLAND UNIVERSITY, Baltimore, MD 21210-2476

**General Information** Independent-religious, coed, primarily women, comprehensive institution. *Graduate housing:* On-campus housing not available.

**GRADUATE UNITS**

**Graduate Studies** *Program availability:* Part-time, evening/weekend. Electronic applications accepted.

## NOTRE DAME SEMINARY, New Orleans, LA 70118-4391

**General Information** Independent-religious, coed, primarily men, graduate-only institution. *Graduate housing:* Room and/or apartments guaranteed to single students; on-campus housing not available to married students. Housing application deadline: 7/31.

**GRADUATE UNITS**

**Graduate School of Theology** *Program availability:* Part-time.

## NOVA SOUTHEASTERN UNIVERSITY, Fort Lauderdale, FL 33314-7796

**General Information** Independent, coed, university. *Enrollment:* 20,576 graduate, professional, and undergraduate students; 9,120 full-time matriculated graduate/professional students (6,015 women), 5,685 part-time matriculated graduate/professional students (4,487 women). *Enrollment by degree level:* 7,089 master's, 7,339 doctoral, 377 other advanced degrees. *Graduate faculty:* 830 full-time (456 women), 759 part-time/adjunct (410 women). Tuition and fees vary according to course load, degree level and program. *Graduate housing:* Rooms and/or apartments available on a first-come, first-served basis to single and married students. Typical cost: $10,190 per year ($13,380 including board) for single students. Room and board charges vary according to board plan and housing facility selected. *Student services:* Campus employment opportunities, campus safety program, career counseling, exercise/wellness program, free psychological counseling, international student services, low-cost health insurance, services for students with disabilities, teacher training, writing training. *Library facilities:* Alvin Sherman Library, Research, and Information Technology Center plus 4 others. *Collection:* Books: 498,823 (physical), 379,928 (digital/electronic); Serial titles: 6,035 (physical), 20,738 (digital/electronic); Databases: 577. Study areas open 24 hours, 5–7 days a week; students can reserve study rooms.

**Computer facilities:** 3,000 computers available on campus for general student use. A campuswide network can be accessed from student residence rooms and from off campus. Online class registration is available.
Website: http://www.nova.edu/

**General Application Contact:** Information Contact, 800-541-6682, E-mail: nsuinfo@nsu.nova.edu.

**GRADUATE UNITS**

**Abraham S. Fischler College of Education** Students: 1,228 full-time (946 women), 1,712 part-time (1,395 women); includes 2,286 minority (1,109 Black or African American, non-Hispanic/Latino; 3 American Indian or Alaska Native, non-Hispanic/Latino; 31 Asian, non-Hispanic/Latino; 1,087 Hispanic/Latino; 3 Native Hawaiian or other Pacific Islander, non-Hispanic/Latino; 53 Two or more races, non-Hispanic/Latino), 14 international. Average age 40. 704 applicants, 74% accepted, 429 enrolled. *Faculty:* 41 full-time (27 women), 179 part-time/adjunct (113 women). Expenses: Contact institution. *Financial support:* In 2019–20, 67 students received support. Career-related internships or fieldwork and Federal Work-Study available. Support available to part-time students. Financial award application deadline: 4/15; financial award applicants required to submit FAFSA. In 2019, 423 master's, 434 doctorates, 81 other advanced degrees awarded. *Program availability:* Part-time, evening/weekend, 100% online, blended/hybrid learning. *Application deadline:* Applications are processed on a rolling basis. *Application fee:* $50. Electronic applications accepted. *Application Contact:* Dr. Kimberly Durham, Interim Dean, 954-262-8731, Fax: 954-262-3894, E-mail: durham@nova.edu. *Interim Dean*, Dr. Kimberly Durham, 954-262-8731, Fax: 954-262-3894, E-mail: durham@nova.edu.

**College of Arts, Humanities, and Social Sciences** Students: 201 full-time (157 women), 418 part-time (297 women); includes 365 minority (180 Black or African American, non-Hispanic/Latino; 4 American Indian or Alaska Native, non-Hispanic/Latino; 15 Asian, non-Hispanic/Latino; 141 Hispanic/Latino; 25 Two or more races, non-Hispanic/Latino), 49 international. Average age 37. 303 applicants, 84% accepted, 197 enrolled. *Faculty:* 60 full-time (37 women), 88 part-time/adjunct (65 women). Expenses: Contact institution. *Financial support:* In 2019–20, 170 students received support. Career-related internships or fieldwork, Federal Work-Study, scholarships/grants, and unspecified assistantships available. Financial award application deadline: 4/1; financial award applicants required to submit FAFSA. In 2019, 125 master's, 63 doctorates, 24 other advanced degrees awarded. *Program availability:* Part-time, evening/weekend, 100% online, blended/hybrid learning. *Application deadline:* Applications are processed on a rolling basis. *Application fee:* $50. Electronic applications accepted. *Application Contact:* Marcia Arango, Student Recruitment Coordinator, 954-262-3006, Fax: 954-262-3968, E-mail: marango@nsu.nova.edu. *Dean*, Dr. Honggang Yang, 954-262-3016, Fax: 954-262-3968, E-mail: yangh@nova.edu.

**College of Dental Medicine** Students: 598 full-time (330 women), 8 part-time (3 women); includes 312 minority (15 Black or African American, non-Hispanic/Latino; 84 Asian, non-Hispanic/Latino; 197 Hispanic/Latino; 16 Two or more races, non-Hispanic/Latino), 66 international. Average age 28. 3,207 applicants, 5% accepted, 155 enrolled. *Faculty:* 82 full-time (34 women), 10 part-time/adjunct (1 woman). Expenses: Contact institution. *Financial support:* Application deadline: 4/15; applicants required to submit FAFSA. In 2019, 21 master's, 125 doctorates awarded. *Application deadline:* Applications are processed on a rolling basis. *Application fee:* $50. Electronic applications accepted. *Application Contact:* Audrey Levitt Galga, Assistant Dean, Admissions, Student Affairs and Services, 954-262-7318, E-mail: agalka@nova.edu. *Interim Dean and Professor*, Dr. Steven I. Kaltman, 954-262-7332, Fax: 954-262-3293, E-mail: skaltman@nova.edu.

**College of Engineering and Computing** Students: 206 full-time (67 women), 244 part-time (71 women); includes 229 minority (93 Black or African American, non-Hispanic/Latino; 1 American Indian or Alaska Native, non-Hispanic/Latino; 36 Asian, non-Hispanic/Latino; 84 Hispanic/Latino; 1 Native Hawaiian or other Pacific Islander, non-Hispanic/Latino; 14 Two or more races, non-Hispanic/Latino), 80 international. Average age 40. 212 applicants, 58% accepted, 63 enrolled. *Faculty:* 18 full-time (6 women), 20 part-time/adjunct (4 women). Expenses: Contact institution. *Financial support:* Federal Work-Study, scholarships/grants, and corporate financial support available. Financial award application deadline: 4/15; financial award applicants required to submit FAFSA. In 2019, 142 master's, 41 doctorates awarded. *Program availability:* Part-time, evening/weekend, blended/hybrid learning. *Application deadline:* Applications are processed on a rolling basis. *Application fee:* $50. Electronic applications accepted. *Application Contact:* Nancy Azoulay, Director, Admissions, 954-262-2026, Fax: 954-262-2752, E-mail: azoulayn@nova.edu. *Associate Provost, Dean of Computering and Engineering,* Dr. Meline Kevorkian, 954-262-2063, Fax: 954-262-2752, E-mail: melinek@nova.edu.

**College of Medical Sciences** Students: 51 full-time (31 women); includes 33 minority (3 Black or African American, non-Hispanic/Latino; 11 Asian, non-Hispanic/Latino; 17 Hispanic/Latino; 2 Two or more races, non-Hispanic/Latino), 3 international. Average age 25. 350 applicants, 11% accepted, 40 enrolled. *Faculty:* 36 full-time (18 women), 1 part-time/adjunct (0 women). Expenses: Contact institution. *Financial support:* Application deadline: 4/15; applicants required to submit FAFSA. In 2019, 7 master's awarded. *Program availability:* Part-time. *Application deadline:* Applications are processed on a rolling basis. *Application fee:* $50. *Application Contact:* Dr. Lori B. Dribin, Assistant Dean for Student Affairs, 954-262-1341, Fax: 954-262-1802, E-mail: lorib@nova.edu. *Dean,* Dr. Harold E. Laubach, 954-262-1303, Fax: 954-262-1802, E-mail: harold@nova.edu.

**College of Optometry** Students: 435 full-time (292 women), 5 part-time (all women); includes 228 minority (25 Black or African American, non-Hispanic/Latino; 90 Asian, non-Hispanic/Latino; 90 Hispanic/Latino; 23 Two or more races, non-Hispanic/Latino), 41 international. Average age 28. 636 applicants, 17% accepted, 110 enrolled. *Faculty:* 41 full-time (30 women), 4 part-time/adjunct (2 women). Expenses: Contact institution. *Financial support:* Federal Work-Study, institutionally sponsored loans, and scholarships/grants available. Support available to part-time students. Financial award application deadline: 4/15; financial award applicants required to submit FAFSA. In 2019, 3 master's, 104 doctorates awarded. *Program availability:* Part-time. *Application deadline:* For fall admission, 10/1 for domestic students; for winter admission, 1/1 for domestic students; for spring admission, 4/1 for domestic students; for summer admission, 7/1 for domestic students. Applications are processed on a rolling basis. *Application fee:* $50. Electronic applications accepted. *Application Contact:* Nicole Patterson, Assistant Dean for Student Affairs & Admissions, 954-262-1410, Fax: 954-262-1818, E-mail: npatters@nova.edu. *Dean,* Dr. David Loshin, 954-262-1404, Fax: 954-262-1818, E-mail: loshin@nova.edu.

**College of Pharmacy** Students: 969 full-time (663 women), 16 part-time (11 women); includes 763 minority (64 Black or African American, non-Hispanic/Latino; 114 Asian, non-Hispanic/Latino; 564 Hispanic/Latino; 1 Native Hawaiian or other Pacific Islander, non-Hispanic/Latino; 20 Two or more races, non-Hispanic/Latino), 72 international. Average age 27. 723 applicants, 32% accepted, 230 enrolled. *Faculty:* 51 full-time (29 women), 9 part-time/adjunct (3 women). Expenses: Contact institution. *Financial support:* In 2019–20, 62 students received support, including 12 teaching assistantships with full tuition reimbursements available (averaging $45,465 per year); career-related internships or fieldwork, Federal Work-Study, scholarships/grants, tuition waivers (full), and unspecified assistantships also available. Financial award application deadline: 4/15; financial award applicants required to submit FAFSA. In 2019, 254 doctorates awarded. *Application deadline:* For fall admission, 3/15 for international students. Applications are processed on a rolling basis. *Application fee:* $50. Electronic applications accepted. *Application Contact:* Rose Llanos-Almeida, Assistant Director II, Graduate Admissions, 954-262-1193, Fax: 954-262-2282, E-mail: rllanos@nova.edu. *Dean,* Dr. Michelle Clark, 954-262-1384, Fax: 954-262-2282, E-mail: miclark@nova.edu.

**College of Psychology** Students: 1,263 full-time (1,068 women), 868 part-time (761 women); includes 1,221 minority (368 Black or African American, non-Hispanic/Latino; 3 American Indian or Alaska Native, non-Hispanic/Latino; 111 Asian, non-Hispanic/Latino; 668 Hispanic/Latino; 1 Native Hawaiian or other Pacific Islander, non-Hispanic/Latino; 70 Two or more races, non-Hispanic/Latino), 59 international. Average age 31. 935 applicants, 56% accepted, 375 enrolled. *Faculty:* 72 full-time (34 women), 111 part-time/adjunct (76 women). Expenses: Contact institution. *Financial support:* In 2019–20, 197 students received support, including 15 research assistantships (averaging $5,600 per year), 68 teaching assistantships (averaging $2,000 per year); career-related internships or fieldwork, Federal Work-Study, institutionally sponsored loans, scholarships/grants, and unspecified assistantships also available. Support available to part-time students. Financial award application deadline: 4/15; financial award applicants required to submit FAFSA. In 2019, 400 master's, 72 doctorates, 13 other advanced degrees awarded. *Program availability:* Part-time, 100% online, blended/hybrid learning. *Application deadline:* Applications are processed on a rolling basis. *Application fee:* $50. Electronic applications accepted. *Application Contact:* Gregory Gayle, Director, Recruitment and Admissions, 954-262-5903, Fax: 954-262-3893, E-mail: ggayle1@nova.edu. *Dean,* Dr. Karen Grosby, 954-262-5712, Fax: 954-262-3859, E-mail: grosby@nova.edu.

**Dr. Kiran C. Patel College of Allopathic Medicine** Students: 104 full-time (41 women); includes 42 minority (1 Black or African American, non-Hispanic/Latino; 30 Asian, non-Hispanic/Latino; 8 Hispanic/Latino; 3 Two or more races, non-Hispanic/Latino). Average age 25. *Faculty:* 18 full-time (11 women), 3 part-time/adjunct (2 women). Expenses: Contact institution. *Financial support:* Applicants required to submit FAFSA. Electronic applications accepted. *Application Contact:* Paula Wales, Executive Associate Dean, Academic and Student Affairs/Professor, 954-262-1074, E-mail: pwales@nova.edu. *Dean,* Dr. Johannes Vieweg, MD, 954-262-1501, E-mail: jvieweg@nova.edu.

**Dr. Kiran C. Patel College of Osteopathic Medicine** Students: 1,410 full-time (740 women), 182 part-time (118 women); includes 895 minority (126 Black or African American, non-Hispanic/Latino; 1 American Indian or Alaska Native, non-Hispanic/Latino; 416 Asian, non-Hispanic/Latino; 309 Hispanic/Latino; 1 Native Hawaiian or other Pacific Islander, non-Hispanic/Latino; 42 Two or more races, non-Hispanic/Latino), 70 international. Average age 26. 5,078 applicants, 10% accepted, 495 enrolled. *Faculty:* 73 full-time (43 women), 35 part-time/adjunct (14 women). Expenses: Contact institution. *Financial support:* In 2019–20, 83 students received support, including 24 fellowships with tuition reimbursements available; Federal Work-Study and scholarships/grants also available. Financial award application deadline: 6/1; financial award applicants required to submit FAFSA. In 2019, 117 master's, 233 doctorates, 3 other advanced degrees awarded. *Program availability:* Part-time, 100% online, blended/hybrid learning. *Application deadline:* For fall admission, 1/15 for domestic students. Applications are processed on a rolling basis. *Application fee:* $50. Electronic applications accepted. *Application Contact:* HPD Admissions, 877-640-0218, E-mail: hpdinfo@nova.edu. *Dean,* Elaine M. Wallace, 954-262-1457, Fax: 954-262-2250, E-mail: ewallace@nova.edu.

**Dr. Pallavi Patel College of Health Care Sciences** Students: 1,336 full-time (992 women), 950 part-time (824 women); includes 839 minority (195 Black or African American, non-Hispanic/Latino; 4 American Indian or Alaska Native, non-Hispanic/Latino; 165 Asian, non-Hispanic/Latino; 397 Hispanic/Latino; 3 Native Hawaiian or other Pacific Islander, non-Hispanic/Latino; 75 Two or more races, non-Hispanic/Latino), 26 international. Average age 30. 634 applicants, 28% accepted, 159 enrolled. *Faculty:* 127 full-time (85 women), 107 part-time/adjunct (79 women). Expenses: Contact institution. *Financial support:* Federal Work-Study, institutionally sponsored loans, and scholarships/grants available. Financial award application deadline: 4/15; financial award applicants required to submit FAFSA. In 2019, 613 master's, 261 doctorates awarded. *Program availability:* Part-time, 100% online, blended/hybrid learning. *Application deadline:* Applications are processed on a rolling basis. *Application fee:* $50. Electronic applications accepted. *Application Contact:* Joycelyn Vogt, Director of Admissions and Outreach, 954-262-1200, Fax: 954-262-1181, E-mail: joycelyn.vogt@nova.edu. *Dean,* Dr. Stanley Wilson, 954-262-1203, E-mail: swilson@nova.edu.

**Halmos College of Natural Sciences and Oceanography** Students: 39 full-time (25 women), 118 part-time (88 women); includes 33 minority (11 Black or African American, non-Hispanic/Latino; 6 Asian, non-Hispanic/Latino; 12 Hispanic/Latino; 4 Two or more races, non-Hispanic/Latino), 10 international. Average age 27. 86 applicants, 49% accepted, 26 enrolled. *Faculty:* 63 full-time (16 women), 60 part-time/adjunct (27 women). Expenses: Contact institution. *Financial support:* In 2019–20, 101 students received support, including 6 fellowships with full and partial tuition reimbursements available (averaging $25,000 per year), 40 research assistantships with full and partial tuition reimbursements available (averaging $20,000 per year), 8 teaching assistantships with tuition reimbursements available (averaging $15,000 per year); career-related internships or fieldwork, Federal Work-Study, scholarships/grants, health care benefits, tuition waivers (full and partial), and unspecified assistantships also available. Support available to part-time students. Financial award application deadline: 4/15; financial award applicants required to submit FAFSA. In 2019, 48 master's, 2 doctorates awarded. *Program availability:* Part-time, evening/weekend, blended/hybrid learning. *Application deadline:* Applications are processed on a rolling basis. *Application fee:* $50. Electronic applications accepted. *Application Contact:* Dr. Bernhard Riegl, Chair, Department of Marine and Environmental Sciences, 954-262-3600, Fax: 954-262-4020, E-mail: rieglb@nova.edu. *Dean,* Dr. Richard Dodge, 954-262-3600, Fax: 954-262-4020, E-mail: dodge@nsu.nova.edu.

**H. Wayne Huizenga College of Business and Entrepreneurship** Students: 1,988 full-time (1,145 women), 316 part-time (195 women); includes 1,484 minority (554 Black or African American, non-Hispanic/Latino; 3 American Indian or Alaska Native, non-Hispanic/Latino; 117 Asian, non-Hispanic/Latino; 747 Hispanic/Latino; 4 Native Hawaiian or other Pacific Islander, non-Hispanic/Latino; 59 Two or more races, non-Hispanic/Latino), 254 international. Average age 33. 877 applicants, 57% accepted, 352 enrolled. *Faculty:* 54 full-time (23 women), 38 part-time/adjunct (11 women). Expenses: Contact institution. *Financial support:* In 2019–20, 325 students received support. Federal Work-Study and scholarships/grants available. Support available to part-time students. Financial award application deadline: 4/15; financial award applicants required to submit FAFSA. In 2019, 828 master's awarded. *Program availability:* Part-time, evening/weekend, 100% online, blended/hybrid learning. *Application deadline:* For fall admission, 8/5 priority date for domestic students, 7/29 priority date for international students; for winter admission, 12/16 priority date for domestic students, 12/9 priority date for international students; for summer admission, 4/21 priority date for domestic and international students. Applications are processed on a rolling basis. *Application fee:* $50. Electronic applications accepted. *Application Contact:* Liza Sumulong, Executive Director, 954-262-5119, Fax: 954-262-3822, E-mail: sumulong@nova.edu. *Dean,* Dr. Andrew Rosman, 954-262-5127, E-mail: arosman1@nova.edu.

**Ron and Kathy Assaf College of Nursing** Students: 4 full-time (3 women), 658 part-time (585 women); includes 427 minority (182 Black or African American, non-Hispanic/Latino; 35 Asian, non-Hispanic/Latino; 197 Hispanic/Latino; 13 Two or more races, non-Hispanic/Latino), 3 international. Average age 38. 157 applicants, 93% accepted, 146 enrolled. *Faculty:* 32 full-time (29 women), 34 part-time/adjunct (31 women). Expenses: Contact institution. *Financial support:* Application deadline: 4/15; applicants required to submit FAFSA. In 2019, 184 master's, 12 doctorates awarded. *Program availability:* Part-time, evening/weekend, 100% online, blended/hybrid learning, annual one-week summer institute delivered face-to-face on main campus. *Application deadline:* For fall admission, 8/1 for domestic students, 3/1 for international students; for winter admission, 12/9 for domestic students, 11/1 for international students. Applications are processed on a rolling basis. *Application fee:* $50. Electronic applications accepted. *Application Contact:* Dianna Murphey, Director of Operations, 954-262-1975, E-mail: dgardner1@nova.edu. *Dean,* Dr. Marcella M. Rutherford, 954-262-1963, E-mail: rmarcell@nova.edu.

**Shepard Broad College of Law** Students: 524 full-time (281 women), 342 part-time (249 women); includes 491 minority (134 Black or African American, non-Hispanic/Latino; 2 American Indian or Alaska Native, non-Hispanic/Latino; 22 Asian, non-Hispanic/Latino; 305 Hispanic/Latino; 3 Native Hawaiian or other Pacific Islander, non-Hispanic/Latino; 25 Two or more races, non-Hispanic/Latino), 26 international. Average age 31. 1,382 applicants, 33% accepted, 272 enrolled. *Faculty:* 42 full-time (22 women), 56 part-time/adjunct (30 women). Expenses: Contact institution. *Financial support:* In 2019–20, 211 students received support, including 221 fellowships (averaging $12,000 per year); Federal Work-Study, institutionally sponsored loans, scholarships/grants, and unspecified assistantships also available. Support available to part-time students. Financial award application deadline: 4/15; financial award applicants required to submit FAFSA. In 2019, 57 master's, 234 doctorates awarded. *Program availability:* Part-time, evening/weekend, 100% online, blended/hybrid learning. *Application deadline:* For fall admission, 5/1 priority date for domestic and international students. Applications are processed on a rolling basis. Electronic applications accepted. *Application Contact:* Tanya Hildalgo, Acting Director of Admissions, 954-262-6251, Fax: 954-262-3844, E-mail: tanya.hildalgo@nova.edu. *Dean,* Jon M. Garon, 954-262-6101, Fax: 954-262-2862, E-mail: garon@nova.edu.

## NSCAD UNIVERSITY, Halifax, NS B3J 3J6, Canada

**General Information** Province-supported, coed, comprehensive institution. *Graduate housing:* On-campus housing not available.

**GRADUATE UNITS**

**Program in Fine Arts**

## NYACK COLLEGE, New York, NY 10004

**General Information** Independent-religious, coed, comprehensive institution. *Enrollment:* 1,981 graduate, professional, and undergraduate students; 393 full-time matriculated graduate/professional students (234 women), 551 part-time matriculated graduate/professional students (344 women). *Enrollment by degree level:* 880 master's,

64 doctoral. *Graduate faculty:* 25 full-time (11 women), 49 part-time/adjunct (22 women). *Graduate housing:* Rooms and/or apartments available on a first-come, first-served basis to single and married students. Typical cost: $15,000 (including board) for single students; $15,000 (including board) for married students. Housing application deadline: 9/1. *Student services:* Campus employment opportunities, career counseling, free psychological counseling, international student services, services for students with disabilities, writing training. *Library facilities:* Eastman. *Collection:* Students can reserve study rooms.

**Computer facilities:** 70 computers available on campus for general student use. A campuswide network can be accessed. Online class registration, wireless network throughout the entire campus are available.
Website: http://www.nyack.edu/

**GRADUATE UNITS**

**Alliance Graduate School of Counseling** Students: 62 full-time (56 women), 128 part-time (102 women); includes 157 minority (62 Black or African American, non-Hispanic/Latino; 1 American Indian or Alaska Native, non-Hispanic/Latino; 40 Asian, non-Hispanic/Latino; 48 Hispanic/Latino; 6 Two or more races, non-Hispanic/Latino), 4 international. Average age 37. Expenses: Contact institution. *Financial support:* Career-related internships or fieldwork and scholarships/grants available. Financial award applicants required to submit FAFSA. In 2019, 60 master's awarded. *Program availability:* Part-time, evening/weekend, 100% online, blended/hybrid learning. *Application deadline:* For fall admission, 8/1 for domestic students, 2/15 for international students; for spring admission, 12/15 for domestic students, 7/15 for international students. Applications are processed on a rolling basis. *Application fee:* $30. Electronic applications accepted. *Application Contact:* Dr. Antoinette Gines-Rivera, Director, 646-378-6160. *Director*, Dr. Antoinette Gines-Rivera, 646-378-6160.

**Alliance Theological Seminary** Students: 203 full-time (89 women), 343 part-time (176 women); includes 418 minority (140 Black or African American, non-Hispanic/Latino; 94 Asian, non-Hispanic/Latino; 172 Hispanic/Latino; 1 Native Hawaiian or other Pacific Islander, non-Hispanic/Latino; 11 Two or more races, non-Hispanic/Latino), 40 international. Average age 43. Expenses: Contact institution. *Financial support:* Career-related internships or fieldwork, Federal Work-Study, and scholarships/grants available. Financial award applicants required to submit FAFSA. In 2019, 100 master's, 17 doctorates awarded. *Program availability:* Part-time, evening/weekend, 100% online, blended/hybrid learning. *Application deadline:* Applications are processed on a rolling basis. *Application fee:* $30. Electronic applications accepted. *Application Contact:* Dr. Ronald Walborn, Dean, 845-770-5715, Fax: 845-358-1663. *Dean*, Dr. Ronald Walborn, 845-770-5715, Fax: 845-358-1663.

**College of Bible and Christian Ministry** Expenses: Contact institution. *Financial support:* Applicants required to submit FAFSA. In 2019, 1 master's awarded. *Program availability:* Part-time, evening/weekend, 100% online, blended/hybrid learning. *Application deadline:* Applications are processed on a rolling basis. *Application fee:* $30. Electronic applications accepted. *Application Contact:* Dr. Steven Notley, Director, 646-378-6148, E-mail: steven.notley@nyack.edu. *Director*, Dr. Steven Notley, 646-378-6148, E-mail: steven.notley@nyack.edu.

**School of Business and Leadership** Students: 46 full-time (20 women), 16 part-time (14 women); includes 45 minority (26 Black or African American, non-Hispanic/Latino; 1 Asian, non-Hispanic/Latino; 15 Hispanic/Latino; 3 Two or more races, non-Hispanic/Latino), 5 international. Average age 34. Expenses: Contact institution. *Financial support:* Scholarships/grants available. Financial award applicants required to submit FAFSA. In 2019, 24 master's awarded. *Program availability:* Part-time, evening/weekend, 100% online, blended/hybrid learning. *Application deadline:* Applications are processed on a rolling basis. *Application fee:* $50. Electronic applications accepted. *Application Contact:* Dr. Anita Underwood, Dean, 845-675-4511. *Dean*, Dr. Anita Underwood, 845-675-4511.

**School of Education** Students: 19 full-time (16 women), 24 part-time (22 women); includes 23 minority (8 Black or African American, non-Hispanic/Latino; 4 Asian, non-Hispanic/Latino; 10 Hispanic/Latino; 1 Two or more races, non-Hispanic/Latino), 3 international. Average age 33. Expenses: Contact institution. *Financial support:* Scholarships/grants available. Financial award applicants required to submit FAFSA. In 2019, 20 master's awarded. *Program availability:* Part-time, evening/weekend, 100% online, blended/hybrid learning. *Application deadline:* Applications are processed on a rolling basis. *Application fee:* $30. Electronic applications accepted. *Application Contact:* Dr. JoAnn Looney, Dean, 845-675-4538. *Dean*, Dr. JoAnn Looney, 845-675-4538.

**School of Social Work** Students: 63 full-time (53 women), 37 part-time (29 women); includes 90 minority (54 Black or African American, non-Hispanic/Latino; 4 Asian, non-Hispanic/Latino; 32 Hispanic/Latino), 3 international. Average age 36. Expenses: Contact institution. *Financial support:* Scholarships/grants available. Financial award applicants required to submit FAFSA. In 2019, 26 master's awarded. *Program availability:* Part-time, evening/weekend. *Application deadline:* Applications are processed on a rolling basis. *Application fee:* $45. Electronic applications accepted. *Application Contact:* Dr. Stacey Barker, Director of MSW Program, 646-378-6100 Ext. 7745, E-mail: stacey.barker@nyack.edu. *Director of MSW Program*, Dr. Stacey Barker, 646-378-6100 Ext. 7745, E-mail: stacey.barker@nyack.edu.

## OAKLAND CITY UNIVERSITY, Oakland City, IN 47660-1099

**General Information** Independent-religious, coed, comprehensive institution. *Graduate housing:* Rooms and/or apartments guaranteed to single students and available on a first-come, first-served basis to married students. Housing application deadline: 7/1.

**GRADUATE UNITS**

**Chapman Seminary** *Program availability:* Part-time.

**School of Business** *Program availability:* Part-time, evening/weekend.

**School of Education**

## OAKLAND UNIVERSITY, Rochester, MI 48309-4401

**General Information** State-supported, coed, university. CGS member. *Enrollment:* 19,013 graduate, professional, and undergraduate students; 2,001 full-time matriculated graduate/professional students (1,146 women), 1,405 part-time matriculated graduate/professional students (755 women). *Enrollment by degree level:* 2,085 master's, 1,160 doctoral, 161 other advanced degrees. *Graduate faculty:* 281 full-time (129 women), 87 part-time/adjunct (36 women). *International tuition:* $16,432 full-time. *Tuition, area resident:* Full-time $12,328; part-time $770.50 per credit hour. Tuition, state resident: full-time $12,328; part-time $770.50 per credit hour. Tuition, nonresident: full-time $16,432; part-time $1027 per credit hour. Tuition and fees vary according to degree level and program. *Graduate housing:* Rooms and/or apartments available on a first-come, first-served basis to single and married students. Housing application deadline: 9/1. *Student services:* Campus employment opportunities, campus safety program, career counseling, child daycare facilities, exercise/wellness program, free psychological counseling, international student services, low-cost health insurance, multicultural affairs office, services for students with disabilities. *Library facilities:* Kresge Library plus 1 other. *Collection:* Books: 512,415 (physical), 682,722 (digital/electronic); Serial titles: 3,568 (physical), 71,808 (digital/electronic); Databases: 240. Weekly public service hours: 168; study areas open 24 hours, 5–7 days a week; students can reserve study rooms. *Research affiliation:* Beaumont Hospital Corporation (eye research, nursing), Henry Ford Health Systems (medical physics, health sciences).

**Computer facilities:** A campuswide network can be accessed. Online class registration is available.
Website: http://www.oakland.edu/

**General Application Contact:** Lynn Coughlin, Admissions Coordinator, 248-370-2653, Fax: 248-370-4114, E-mail: coughlin@oakland.edu.

**GRADUATE UNITS**

**Graduate Study and Lifelong Learning** Students: 2,001 full-time (1,146 women), 1,405 part-time (755 women); includes 655 minority (216 Black or African American, non-Hispanic/Latino; 11 American Indian or Alaska Native, non-Hispanic/Latino; 259 Asian, non-Hispanic/Latino; 111 Hispanic/Latino; 58 Two or more races, non-Hispanic/Latino), 564 international. Average age 30. 2,423 applicants, 44% accepted, 870 enrolled. *Faculty:* 281 full-time (129 women), 87 part-time/adjunct (36 women). Expenses: Contact institution. *Financial support:* Fellowships, research assistantships, teaching assistantships, career-related internships or fieldwork, Federal Work-Study, institutionally sponsored loans, and tuition waivers available. Financial award application deadline: 3/1; financial award applicants required to submit FAFSA. In 2019, 812 master's, 243 doctorates, 87 other advanced degrees awarded. *Program availability:* Part-time, 100% online, blended/hybrid learning. *Application deadline:* For fall admission, 7/15 for domestic students, 5/1 for international students; for winter admission, 11/15 for domestic students, 9/1 for international students; for summer admission, 3/1 for domestic students, 1/1 for international students. Applications are processed on a rolling basis. Electronic applications accepted. *Application Contact:* Lynn Coughlin, Graduate Administrator, 248-370-2653, Fax: 248-370-4114, E-mail: coughlin@oakland.edu. *Dean of Graduate Education*, Brandy Randall, PhD, 248-370-3169, Fax: 248-370-4114, E-mail: brandall@oakland.edu.

***College of Arts and Sciences*** Students: 230 full-time (138 women), 129 part-time (75 women); includes 77 minority (31 Black or African American, non-Hispanic/Latino; 1 American Indian or Alaska Native, non-Hispanic/Latino; 23 Asian, non-Hispanic/Latino; 14 Hispanic/Latino; 8 Two or more races, non-Hispanic/Latino), 47 international. Average age 30. 350 applicants, 45% accepted, 118 enrolled. *Faculty:* 96 full-time (38 women), 15 part-time/adjunct (5 women). Expenses: Contact institution. *Financial support:* Fellowships, research assistantships, teaching assistantships, career-related internships or fieldwork, Federal Work-Study, institutionally sponsored loans, and tuition waivers available. Financial award application deadline: 3/1; financial award applicants required to submit FAFSA. In 2019, 95 master's, 12 doctorates, 6 other advanced degrees awarded. *Program availability:* Part-time, 100% online, blended/hybrid learning. *Application deadline:* Applications are processed on a rolling basis. Electronic applications accepted. *Application Contact:* Kevin J. Corcoran, Dean, 248-370-2140, Fax: 248-370-4280, E-mail: corcoran@oakland.edu. *Dean*, Kevin J. Corcoran, 248-370-2140, Fax: 248-370-4280, E-mail: corcoran@oakland.edu.

***School of Business Administration*** Students: 145 full-time (69 women), 269 part-time (106 women); includes 51 minority (14 Black or African American, non-Hispanic/Latino; 25 Asian, non-Hispanic/Latino; 10 Hispanic/Latino; 2 Two or more races, non-Hispanic/Latino), 99 international. Average age 31. 250 applicants, 53% accepted, 127 enrolled. *Faculty:* 32 full-time (12 women), 9 part-time/adjunct (0 women). Expenses: Contact institution. *Financial support:* Career-related internships or fieldwork, Federal Work-Study, institutionally sponsored loans, and tuition waivers (full) available. Financial award application deadline: 3/1; financial award applicants required to submit FAFSA. In 2019, 147 master's, 8 other advanced degrees awarded. *Program availability:* Part-time, evening/weekend. *Application deadline:* For fall admission, 4/15 for domestic students, 5/1 for international students; for winter admission, 11/15 for domestic students, 9/1 for international students; for summer admission, 3/1 for domestic students, 1/1 for international students. Applications are processed on a rolling basis. *Application fee:* $45. Electronic applications accepted. *Application Contact:* Dr. Michael A. Mazzeo, Dean, 248-370-2957, Fax: 248-370-4974, E-mail: mazzeo@oakland.edu. *Dean*, Dr. Michael A. Mazzeo, 248-370-2957, Fax: 248-370-4974, E-mail: mazzeo@oakland.edu.

***School of Education and Human Services*** Students: 400 full-time (312 women), 418 part-time (349 women); includes 167 minority (105 Black or African American, non-Hispanic/Latino; 6 American Indian or Alaska Native, non-Hispanic/Latino; 16 Asian, non-Hispanic/Latino; 25 Hispanic/Latino; 15 Two or more races, non-Hispanic/Latino), 27 international. Average age 34. 532 applicants, 55% accepted, 245 enrolled. *Faculty:* 51 full-time (33 women), 45 part-time/adjunct (30 women). Expenses: Contact institution. *Financial support:* Career-related internships or fieldwork, Federal Work-Study, institutionally sponsored loans, and tuition waivers (full) available. Financial award application deadline: 3/1; financial award applicants required to submit FAFSA. In 2019, 253 master's, 22 doctorates, 57 other advanced degrees awarded. *Program availability:* Part-time, evening/weekend. *Application deadline:* Applications are processed on a rolling basis. *Application fee:* $45. Electronic applications accepted. *Application Contact:* Dr. Jon Margerum-Leys, Dean, 248-370-3045, Fax: 248-370-4202, E-mail: jmargerumleys@oakland.edu. *Dean*, Dr. Jon Margerum-Leys, 248-370-3045, Fax: 248-370-4202, E-mail: jmargerumleys@oakland.edu.

***School of Engineering and Computer Science*** Students: 402 full-time (135 women), 447 part-time (111 women); includes 102 minority (22 Black or African American, non-Hispanic/Latino; 2 American Indian or Alaska Native, non-Hispanic/Latino; 46 Asian, non-Hispanic/Latino; 24 Hispanic/Latino; 8 Two or more races, non-Hispanic/Latino), 369 international. Average age 30. 627 applicants, 51% accepted, 239 enrolled. *Faculty:* 56 full-time (10 women), 15 part-time/adjunct (0 women). Expenses: Contact institution. *Financial support:* Federal Work-Study, institutionally sponsored loans, and tuition waivers (full) available. Financial award application deadline: 3/1; financial award applicants required to submit FAFSA. In 2019, 209 master's, 31 doctorates awarded. *Program availability:* Part-time, evening/weekend. *Application fee:* $45. Electronic applications accepted. *Application Contact:* Dr. Louay M. Chamra, Dean/Professor, 248-370-2217, E-mail: chamra@oakland.edu. *Dean/Professor*, Dr. Louay M. Chamra, 248-370-2217, E-mail: chamra@oakland.edu.

***School of Health Sciences*** Students: 200 full-time (139 women), 49 part-time (32 women); includes 37 minority (11 Black or African American, non-Hispanic/Latino; 1 American Indian or Alaska Native, non-Hispanic/Latino; 12 Asian, non-Hispanic/Latino; 7 Hispanic/Latino; 6 Two or more races, non-Hispanic/Latino), 15 international. Average age 26. 464 applicants, 20% accepted, 73 enrolled. *Faculty:* 23

full-time (14 women), 3 part-time/adjunct (1 woman). Expenses: Contact institution. *Financial support:* Fellowships, Federal Work-Study, institutionally sponsored loans, and tuition waivers (full) available. Financial award application deadline: 3/1; financial award applicants required to submit FAFSA. In 2019, 30 master's, 41 doctorates, 11 other advanced degrees awarded. *Application fee:* $45. Electronic applications accepted. *Application Contact:* Dr. Kevin Ball, Dean/Professor, 248-364-8673, Fax: 248-364-3562, E-mail: kevinball@oakland.edu. *Dean/Professor*, Dr. Kevin Ball, 248-364-8673, Fax: 248-364-3562, E-mail: kevinball@oakland.edu.

**School of Nursing** Students: 139 full-time (103 women), 93 part-time (82 women); includes 35 minority (12 Black or African American, non-Hispanic/Latino; 1 American Indian or Alaska Native, non-Hispanic/Latino; 12 Asian, non-Hispanic/Latino; 6 Hispanic/Latino; 4 Two or more races, non-Hispanic/Latino), 2 international. Average age 33. 200 applicants, 38% accepted, 68 enrolled. *Faculty:* 23 full-time (22 women). Expenses: Contact institution. *Financial support:* Federal Work-Study, institutionally sponsored loans, and tuition waivers (full) available. Financial award application deadline: 3/1; financial award applicants required to submit FAFSA. In 2019, 78 master's, 7 doctorates, 2 other advanced degrees awarded. *Program availability:* Part-time, evening/weekend. *Application fee:* $45. Electronic applications accepted. *Application Contact:* Dr. Judy Didion, Dean, School of Nursing, 248-364-8787, E-mail: jdidion@oakland.edu. *Dean, School of Nursing*, Dr. Judy Didion, 248-364-8787, E-mail: jdidion@oakland.edu.

**School of Music, Theatre and Dance** Students: 8 full-time (3 women), 13 part-time (6 women); includes 4 minority (1 Black or African American, non-Hispanic/Latino; 1 Asian, non-Hispanic/Latino; 1 Hispanic/Latino; 1 Two or more races, non-Hispanic/Latino), 2 international. Average age 33. 19 applicants, 32% accepted, 5 enrolled. *Faculty:* 11 full-time (6 women), 7 part-time/adjunct (4 women). Expenses: Contact institution. *Financial support:* Federal Work-Study, institutionally sponsored loans, and tuition waivers (full) available. Financial award application deadline: 3/1; financial award applicants required to submit FAFSA. In 2019, 25 master's, 1 doctorate awarded. *Application fee:* $45. Electronic applications accepted. *Application Contact:* Jessica Payette, Associate Professor of Music and Musicology/Master's Program Coordinator, 248-370-3148, Fax: 248-370-2041, E-mail: payette@oakland.edu. *Chair/Professor of Music Education/Doctoral Coordinator*, Dr. Jacqueline H. Wiggins, 248-370-2030, Fax: 248-370-2041, E-mail: jwiggins@oakland.edu.

## OAKWOOD UNIVERSITY, Huntsville, AL 35896

**General Information** Independent-religious, coed, comprehensive institution. *Graduate housing:* On-campus housing not available.

**GRADUATE UNITS**

**Program in Pastoral Studies**

## OBERLIN COLLEGE, Oberlin, OH 44074

**General Information** Independent, coed, comprehensive institution. *Graduate housing:* Rooms and/or apartments available on a first-come, first-served basis to single students and available to married students. Housing application deadline: 6/15.

**GRADUATE UNITS**

**Conservatory of Music** Electronic applications accepted.

## OBLATE SCHOOL OF THEOLOGY, San Antonio, TX 78216-6693

**General Information** Independent-religious, coed, graduate-only institution. *Enrollment by degree level:* 127 master's, 15 doctoral. *Graduate faculty:* 21 full-time (5 women), 4 part-time/adjunct (0 women). *Graduate housing:* On-campus housing not available. *Student services:* Campus employment opportunities, international student services, low-cost health insurance, services for students with disabilities, writing training. *Library facilities:* Donald E. O'Shaughnessy Library. *Collection:* Books: 79,000 (physical), 35,000 (digital/electronic); Serial titles: 300 (physical), 25 (digital/electronic); Databases: 15. Weekly public service hours: 71.

**Computer facilities:** 10 computers available on campus for general student use. A campuswide network can be accessed from off campus. X available.
Website: http://www.ost.edu/

**General Application Contact:** Brenda Reyna, Registrar, 210-341-1366 Ext. 226, Fax: 210-341-4519, E-mail: registrar@ost.edu.

**GRADUATE UNITS**

**Graduate and Professional Programs** Students: 89 full-time (9 women), 54 part-time (31 women); includes 77 minority (11 Black or African American, non-Hispanic/Latino; 8 Asian, non-Hispanic/Latino; 57 Hispanic/Latino; 1 Two or more races, non-Hispanic/Latino), 24 international. Average age 39. *Faculty:* 21 full-time (5 women), 4 part-time/adjunct (0 women). Expenses: Contact institution. *Financial support:* In 2019–20, 25 students received support. Scholarships/grants available. Support available to part-time students. Financial award application deadline: 8/15; financial award applicants required to submit FAFSA. In 2019, 24 master's, 1 doctorate awarded. *Program availability:* Part-time, 100% online, blended/hybrid learning. *Application deadline:* For fall admission, 6/30 priority date for domestic and international students; for winter admission, 11/30 for domestic and international students; for spring admission, 11/30 for domestic and international students; for summer admission, 4/30 for domestic and international students. Applications are processed on a rolling basis. *Application fee:* $65. Electronic applications accepted. *Application Contact:* Brenda Reyna, Registrar, 210-341-1366 Ext. 226, Fax: 210-341-4519, E-mail: registrar@ost.edu. *Academic Dean*, Dr. R. Scott Woodward, 210-341-1366, Fax: 210-341-4519, E-mail: rsw@ost.edu.

## OCCIDENTAL COLLEGE, Los Angeles, CA 90041-3314

**General Information** Independent, coed, comprehensive institution. *Graduate housing:* On-campus housing not available.

**GRADUATE UNITS**

**Department of Biology** *Program availability:* Part-time.

## OGLALA LAKOTA COLLEGE, Kyle, SD 57752-0490

**General Information** State and locally supported, coed, comprehensive institution. *Graduate housing:* On-campus housing not available.

**GRADUATE UNITS**

**Graduate Studies** *Program availability:* Part-time, evening/weekend.

## OHIO CHRISTIAN UNIVERSITY, Circleville, OH 43113

**General Information** Independent-religious, coed, comprehensive institution.

**GRADUATE UNITS**

**Graduate Programs**

## OHIO DOMINICAN UNIVERSITY, Columbus, OH 43219-2099

**General Information** Independent-religious, coed, comprehensive institution. *Enrollment:* 1,641 graduate, professional, and undergraduate students; 164 full-time matriculated graduate/professional students (109 women), 331 part-time matriculated graduate/professional students (222 women). *Enrollment by degree level:* 495 master's. *Graduate faculty:* 31 full-time (14 women), 20 part-time/adjunct (5 women). *Tuition:* Full-time $10,800; part-time $600 per credit hour. *Required fees:* $225 per semester. Tuition and fees vary according to program. *Graduate housing:* Room and/or apartments available on a first-come, first-served basis to single students; on-campus housing not available to married students. Typical cost: $11,340 (including board). Room and board charges vary according to board plan, campus/location and housing facility selected. Housing application deadline: 8/20. *Student services:* Campus employment opportunities, campus safety program, career counseling, exercise/wellness program, free psychological counseling, international student services, multicultural affairs office, services for students with disabilities, teacher training, writing training. *Library facilities:* Ohio Dominican Library. *Collection:* Books: 79,322 (physical), 123,948 (digital/electronic); Serial titles: 416 (physical), 10,463 (digital/electronic); Databases: 224. Students can reserve study rooms.

**Computer facilities:** 350 computers available on campus for general student use. A campuswide network can be accessed. Online class registration is available.
Website: http://www.ohiodominican.edu/

**General Application Contact:** John W. Naughton, Vice President of Enrollment and Student Success, 614-251-4721, Fax: 614-251-6654, E-mail: grad@ohiodominican.edu.

**GRADUATE UNITS**

**Division of Arts and Letters** Students: 1 full-time (0 women), 50 part-time (34 women); includes 3 minority (1 Black or African American, non-Hispanic/Latino; 1 Hispanic/Latino; 1 Two or more races, non-Hispanic/Latino). Average age 45. 12 applicants, 100% accepted, 11 enrolled. *Faculty:* 4 full-time (2 women), 2 part-time/adjunct (1 woman). Expenses: Contact institution. In 2019, 13 master's awarded. *Program availability:* Part-time, evening/weekend, 100% online. *Application deadline:* For fall admission, 8/20 for domestic students, 7/15 for international students; for spring admission, 1/3 for domestic students, 12/15 for international students; for summer admission, 6/3 for domestic students, 5/15 for international students. Applications are processed on a rolling basis. *Application fee:* $25. Electronic applications accepted. *Application Contact:* John W. Naughton, Vice President for Enrollment and Student Success, 614-251-4721, Fax: 614-251-6654, E-mail: grad@ohiodominican.edu. *Chair*, Dr. Bruce Gartner, 614-251-4604, Fax: 614-253-3656, E-mail: gartnerb@ohiodominican.edu.

**Division of Business** Students: 60 full-time (35 women), 104 part-time (52 women); includes 41 minority (25 Black or African American, non-Hispanic/Latino; 2 American Indian or Alaska Native, non-Hispanic/Latino; 5 Asian, non-Hispanic/Latino; 3 Hispanic/Latino; 6 Two or more races, non-Hispanic/Latino), 19 international. Average age 30. 103 applicants, 92% accepted, 75 enrolled. *Faculty:* 11 full-time (3 women), 13 part-time/adjunct (2 women). Expenses: Contact institution. In 2019, 70 master's awarded. *Program availability:* Part-time, evening/weekend, 100% online, blended/hybrid learning. *Application deadline:* For fall admission, 8/15 for domestic students, 6/10 for international students; for spring admission, 1/4 for domestic students, 11/2 for international students. Applications are processed on a rolling basis. *Application fee:* $25. Electronic applications accepted. *Application Contact:* John W. Naughton, Vice President for Enrollment and Student Success, 614-251-4721, Fax: 614-251-6654, E-mail: grad@ohiodominican.edu. *Chair*, Dr. Kenneth C. Fah, 614-251-4566, E-mail: fahk@ohiodominican.edu.

**Division of Education** Students: 6 full-time (all women), 127 part-time (97 women); includes 13 minority (6 Black or African American, non-Hispanic/Latino; 1 Asian, non-Hispanic/Latino; 3 Hispanic/Latino; 3 Two or more races, non-Hispanic/Latino), 8 international. Average age 33. 89 applicants, 100% accepted, 69 enrolled. *Faculty:* 8 full-time (5 women), 4 part-time/adjunct (2 women). Expenses: Contact institution. *Financial support:* Tuition discounts (for diocesan teachers) available. Financial award applicants required to submit FAFSA. In 2019, 64 master's awarded. *Program availability:* Part-time, evening/weekend, 100% online, blended/hybrid learning. *Application deadline:* For fall admission, 8/15 for domestic students, 6/10 for international students; for spring admission, 1/4 for domestic students, 11/2 for international students. Applications are processed on a rolling basis. *Application fee:* $25. Electronic applications accepted. *Application Contact:* John W. Naughton, Vice President for Enrollment and Student Success, 614-251-4721, Fax: 614-251-6654, E-mail: grad@ohiodominican.edu. *Chair, Division of Education*, Dr. Marlissa Stauffer, 614-251-4621, E-mail: stauffem@ohiodominican.edu.

**Division of Physician Assistant Studies** Students: 97 full-time (68 women), 50 part-time (39 women); includes 7 minority (1 Asian, non-Hispanic/Latino; 2 Hispanic/Latino; 4 Two or more races, non-Hispanic/Latino), 1 international. Average age 25. 651 applicants, 11% accepted, 50 enrolled. *Faculty:* 7 full-time (4 women), 2 part-time/adjunct (0 women). Expenses: Contact institution. *Financial support:* Applicants required to submit FAFSA. In 2019, 51 master's awarded. *Application deadline:* For fall admission, 10/1 for domestic and international students. Applications are processed on a rolling basis. Electronic applications accepted. *Application Contact:* John W. Naughton, Vice President for Enrollment and Student Success, 614-251-4721, Fax: 614-251-6654, E-mail: grad@ohiodominican.edu. *Program Director*, Prof. Shonna Riedlinger, 614-251-8988, E-mail: riedlins@ohiodominican.edu.

## OHIO NORTHERN UNIVERSITY, Ada, OH 45810-1599

**General Information** Independent-religious, coed, comprehensive institution. *Graduate housing:* Room and/or apartments available on a first-come, first-served basis to single students; on-campus housing not available to married students.

**GRADUATE UNITS**

**Claude W. Pettit College of Law** Electronic applications accepted.

**College of Business**

**Raabe College of Pharmacy**

## THE OHIO STATE UNIVERSITY, Columbus, OH 43210

**General Information** State-supported, coed, university. CGS member. *Graduate housing:* Rooms and/or apartments available on a first-come, first-served basis to single and married students. *Research affiliation:* Transportation Research Center, Midwest Universities Consortium for International Activities, Children's Hospital (pediatrics), Ohio Learning Network (education).

**GRADUATE UNITS**

**College of Dentistry** Electronic applications accepted.

**College of Medicine** Electronic applications accepted.

***School of Health and Rehabilitation Sciences*** *Program availability:* Part-time. Electronic applications accepted.

**College of Optometry** Electronic applications accepted.

**College of Pharmacy** Electronic applications accepted.

**College of Public Health** *Program availability:* Part-time. Electronic applications accepted.

**College of Veterinary Medicine** Electronic applications accepted.

**Graduate School** *Program availability:* Part-time, evening/weekend. Electronic applications accepted.

***Center for Applied Plant Sciences*** Electronic applications accepted.

***Center for Latin American Studies*** Electronic applications accepted.

***Center for Slavic and East European Studies*** Electronic applications accepted.

***College of Arts and Sciences*** *Program availability:* Part-time. Electronic applications accepted.

***College of Education and Human Ecology*** Electronic applications accepted.

***College of Engineering*** *Program availability:* Part-time, evening/weekend. Electronic applications accepted.

***College of Food, Agricultural, and Environmental Sciences*** *Program availability:* Part-time. Electronic applications accepted.

***College of Nursing*** *Program availability:* Part-time. Electronic applications accepted.

***College of Social Work*** *Program availability:* Part-time. Electronic applications accepted.

***East Asian Studies Center*** Electronic applications accepted.

***John Glenn College of Public Affairs*** *Program availability:* Part-time. Electronic applications accepted.

***Max M. Fisher College of Business*** *Program availability:* Part-time, evening/weekend. Electronic applications accepted.

**Moritz College of Law** Electronic applications accepted.

## THE OHIO STATE UNIVERSITY AT LIMA, Lima, OH 45804

**General Information** State-supported, coed, comprehensive institution. *Enrollment:* 982 graduate, professional, and undergraduate students; 1 (woman) part-time matriculated graduate/professional student. *Enrollment by degree level:* 1 master's. *Graduate faculty:* 33. *Graduate housing:* On-campus housing not available. *Student services:* Campus safety program, career counseling, child daycare facilities, exercise/wellness program, free psychological counseling, grant writing training, international student services, low-cost health insurance, multicultural affairs office, services for students with disabilities, teacher training, writing training. *Library facilities:* Lima Campus Library. *Collection:* Books: 69,501 (physical), 1.4 million (digital/electronic); Serial titles: 873 (physical), 76,682 (digital/electronic); Databases: 3,763. Weekly public service hours: 57; students can reserve study rooms.

**Computer facilities:** A campuswide network can be accessed. Online class registration is available.
Website: http://lima.osu.edu/

**General Application Contact:** Graduate and Professional Admissions, 614-292-9444, Fax: 614-292-3895, E-mail: gpadmissions@osu.edu.

**GRADUATE UNITS**

**Graduate Programs** Students: 1 (woman) part-time. *Faculty:* 33. Expenses: Contact institution. *Financial support:* Application deadline: 2/15. *Program availability:* Part-time. *Application deadline:* For fall admission, 4/1 for domestic students, 3/1 for international students; for spring admission, 10/15 for domestic and international students; for summer admission, 4/10 for domestic students, 3/1 for international students. Applications are processed on a rolling basis. *Application fee:* $60 ($70 for international students). Electronic applications accepted. *Application Contact:* Graduate and Professional Admissions, 614-292-9444, Fax: 614-292-3895, E-mail: gpadmissions@osu.edu. *Dean and Director*, Dr. Tim Rehner, 419-995-8600, E-mail: rehner.6@osu.edu.

## THE OHIO STATE UNIVERSITY AT MANSFIELD, Mansfield, OH 44906-1599

**General Information** State-supported, coed, comprehensive institution. *Graduate housing:* On-campus housing not available.

**GRADUATE UNITS**

**Graduate Programs** *Program availability:* Part-time. Electronic applications accepted.

## THE OHIO STATE UNIVERSITY AT MARION, Marion, OH 43302-5695

**General Information** State-supported, coed, comprehensive institution. *Graduate housing:* On-campus housing not available.

**GRADUATE UNITS**

**Graduate Programs** *Program availability:* Part-time. Electronic applications accepted.

## THE OHIO STATE UNIVERSITY AT NEWARK, Newark, OH 43055-1797

**General Information** State-supported, coed, comprehensive institution. *Graduate housing:* Rooms and/or apartments available on a first-come, first-served basis to single and married students.

**GRADUATE UNITS**

**Graduate Programs** *Program availability:* Part-time. Electronic applications accepted.

## OHIO UNIVERSITY, Athens, OH 45701-2979

**General Information** State-supported, coed, university. CGS member. *Graduate housing:* Rooms and/or apartments available on a first-come, first-served basis to single and married students. Housing application deadline: 5/1.

**GRADUATE UNITS**

**Graduate College** *Program availability:* Part-time, evening/weekend, online learning. Electronic applications accepted.

***Center for International Studies*** *Program availability:* Part-time. Electronic applications accepted.

***College of Arts and Sciences*** *Program availability:* Part-time, evening/weekend. Electronic applications accepted.

***College of Business*** *Program availability:* Part-time, evening/weekend, online learning. Electronic applications accepted.

***College of Fine Arts*** *Program availability:* Part-time, evening/weekend, online learning. Electronic applications accepted.

***College of Health Sciences and Professions*** *Program availability:* Part-time, evening/weekend, online learning. Electronic applications accepted.

***Gladys W. and David H. Patton College of Education and Human Services*** *Program availability:* Part-time, evening/weekend. Electronic applications accepted.

***Russ College of Engineering and Technology*** *Program availability:* Part-time. Electronic applications accepted.

***Scripps College of Communication*** *Program availability:* Part-time. Electronic applications accepted.

***Voinovich School of Leadership and Public Affairs*** Electronic applications accepted.

**Heritage College of Osteopathic Medicine** Electronic applications accepted.

## OHIO VALLEY UNIVERSITY, Vienna, WV 26105-8000

**General Information** Independent-religious, coed, comprehensive institution.

**GRADUATE UNITS**

**School of Graduate Education** *Program availability:* Online learning.

## OHR HAMEIR THEOLOGICAL SEMINARY, Cortlandt Manor, NY 10567

**General Information** Independent-religious, men only, comprehensive institution.
Website: http://www.ohrhameir.com/

**General Application Contact:** Information Contact, 914-736-1500.

**GRADUATE UNITS**

**Graduate Programs**

## OKLAHOMA BAPTIST UNIVERSITY, Shawnee, OK 74804

**General Information** Independent-religious, coed, comprehensive institution. *Graduate housing:* Rooms and/or apartments available on a first-come, first-served basis to single and married students. Housing application deadline: 7/31.

**GRADUATE UNITS**

**Master of Business Administration in Transformational Leadership** *Program availability:* Part-time, evening/weekend, 100% online, blended/hybrid learning. Electronic applications accepted.

**Program in Marriage and Family Therapy** *Program availability:* Part-time, evening/weekend. Electronic applications accepted.

**Program in Nursing**

## OKLAHOMA CHRISTIAN UNIVERSITY, Oklahoma City, OK 73136-1100

**General Information** Independent-religious, coed, comprehensive institution. *Graduate housing:* Rooms and/or apartments available on a first-come, first-served basis to single and married students. Housing application deadline: 8/31.

**GRADUATE UNITS**

**Graduate School of Business** *Program availability:* Part-time, 100% online. Electronic applications accepted.

**Graduate School of Engineering and Computer Science** *Program availability:* Part-time. Electronic applications accepted.

**Graduate School of Theology** *Program availability:* Part-time, 100% online, blended/hybrid learning. Electronic applications accepted.

## OKLAHOMA CITY UNIVERSITY, Oklahoma City, OK 73106-1402

**General Information** Independent-religious, coed, comprehensive institution. *Graduate housing:* Rooms and/or apartments available on a first-come, first-served basis to single and married students. Housing application deadline: 6/15.

**GRADUATE UNITS**

**Kramer School of Nursing** *Program availability:* Part-time, evening/weekend, online learning. Electronic applications accepted.

**Meinders School of Business** *Program availability:* Part-time, evening/weekend, 100% online. Electronic applications accepted.

**Petree College of Arts and Sciences** *Program availability:* Part-time, evening/weekend. Electronic applications accepted.

**School of Law** *Program availability:* Part-time, evening/weekend. Electronic applications accepted.

**Wanda L. Bass School of Music** *Program availability:* Part-time. Electronic applications accepted.

## OKLAHOMA STATE UNIVERSITY, Stillwater, OK 74078

**General Information** State-supported, coed, university. CGS member. *Enrollment:* 24,041 graduate, professional, and undergraduate students; 1,580 full-time matriculated graduate/professional students (970 women), 2,437 part-time matriculated graduate/professional students (1,115 women). *Enrollment by degree level:* 2,087 master's, 1,778 doctoral, 152 other advanced degrees. *Graduate faculty:* 885 full-time (315 women), 115 part-time/adjunct (42 women). *International tuition:* $15,775.20 full-time. *Tuition, area resident:* Full-time $4148.10; part-time $2765.40 per credit hour. Tuition, state resident: full-time $4148.10; part-time $2765.40 per credit hour. Tuition, nonresident: full-time $15,775; part-time $10,516.80 per credit hour. *Required fees:* $2196.90; $122.05 per credit hour. Tuition and fees vary according to course load, campus/location and program. *Graduate housing:* Rooms and/or apartments available on a first-come, first-served basis to single and married students. Typical cost: $5096 per year ($9106 including board) for single students; $10,056 per year ($14,066 including board) for married students. Room and board charges vary according to board plan and housing facility selected. *Student services:* Campus employment opportunities, campus safety program, career counseling, exercise/wellness program, free psychological counseling, grant writing training, international student services, low-cost health insurance, multicultural affairs office, services for students with disabilities, teacher training, writing training. *Library facilities:* Edmon Low Library plus 3 others. *Collection:* Books: 1.9 million (physical), 3.2 million (digital/electronic); Serial titles: 71,356 (physical), 130,130 (digital/electronic); Databases: 54. Weekly public service hours: 146; study areas open 24 hours, 5–7 days a week; students can reserve study rooms. *Research affiliation:* Allens, Inc. (horticulture and landscape architecture), General Motors (industrial engineering and management), Simons Foundation (mathematics), Howard Hughes Medical Institute (educational studies), Narramore Christian Foundation (Human Development and Family Science.), LiteCure, LLC (veterinary clinical sciences).

**Computer facilities:** Computer purchase and lease plans are available. 177 computers available on campus for general student use. A campuswide network can be accessed. Online class registration, computer labs are available.
Website: http://www.okstate.edu/

**General Application Contact:** Dr. Sheryl Tucker, Vice Prov/Dean of Graduate College, 405-744-6368, Fax: 405-744-0355, E-mail: gradi@okstate.edu.

**GRADUATE UNITS**

**Center for Veterinary Health Sciences** *Program availability:* Online learning.

**College of Agricultural Science and Natural Resources** Students: 109 full-time (63 women), 284 part-time (146 women); includes 37 minority (10 Black or African American, non-Hispanic/Latino; 4 American Indian or Alaska Native, non-Hispanic/Latino; 1 Asian, non-Hispanic/Latino; 12 Hispanic/Latino; 10 Two or more races, non-Hispanic/Latino), 113 international. Average age 28. 217 applicants, 53% accepted, 88 enrolled. *Faculty:* 169 full-time (42 women), 1 part-time/adjunct (0 women). Expenses: Contact institution. *Financial support:* In 2019–20, 223 research assistantships (averaging $1,557 per year), 63 teaching assistantships (averaging $1,548 per year) were awarded; fellowships, career-related internships or fieldwork, Federal Work-Study, scholarships/grants, health care benefits, tuition waivers (partial), and unspecified assistantships also available. Support available to part-time students. Financial award application deadline: 3/1; financial award applicants required to submit FAFSA. In 2019, 100 master's, 38 doctorates awarded. *Program availability:* Online learning. *Application deadline:* For fall admission, 3/1 priority date for domestic and international students; for spring admission, 8/1 priority date for domestic and international students. Applications are processed on a rolling basis. *Application fee:* $50 ($75 for international students). Electronic applications accepted. *Application Contact:* Kassie Jo Winn-Huizar, Prospective Student Coordinator, 405-744-9464, E-mail: kj.winn_huizar@okstate.edu. *Vice President/Dean*, Dr. Thomas Coon, 405-744-2474, E-mail: thomas.coon@okstate.edu.

**College of Arts and Sciences** Students: 274 full-time (166 women), 529 part-time (226 women); includes 119 minority (18 Black or African American, non-Hispanic/Latino; 14 American Indian or Alaska Native, non-Hispanic/Latino; 18 Asian, non-Hispanic/Latino; 37 Hispanic/Latino; 1 Native Hawaiian or other Pacific Islander, non-Hispanic/Latino; 31 Two or more races, non-Hispanic/Latino), 222 international. Average age 29. 934 applicants, 35% accepted, 221 enrolled. *Faculty:* 327 full-time (112 women), 28 part-time/adjunct (14 women). Expenses: Contact institution. *Financial support:* In 2019–20, 90 research assistantships (averaging $1,994 per year), 529 teaching assistantships (averaging $1,905 per year) were awarded; career-related internships or fieldwork, Federal Work-Study, scholarships/grants, health care benefits, tuition waivers (partial), and unspecified assistantships also available. Support available to part-time students. Financial award application deadline: 3/1; financial award applicants required to submit FAFSA. In 2019, 117 master's, 72 doctorates awarded. *Application deadline:* For fall admission, 3/1 priority date for domestic and international students; for spring admission, 8/1 priority date for domestic and international students. Applications are processed on a rolling basis. *Application fee:* $50 ($75 for international students). Electronic applications accepted. *Application Contact:* Dr. Sheryl Tucker, Dean, 405-744-6368, Fax: 405-744-0355, E-mail: gradi@okstate.edu. *Dean*, Dr. Glen Krutz, 405-744-5663, E-mail: gkrutz@okstate.edu.

***Boone Pickens School of Geology*** Students: 23 full-time (6 women), 42 part-time (10 women); includes 8 minority (1 Black or African American, non-Hispanic/Latino; 2 American Indian or Alaska Native, non-Hispanic/Latino; 1 Asian, non-Hispanic/Latino; 3 Hispanic/Latino; 1 Two or more races, non-Hispanic/Latino), 18 international. Average age 30. 40 applicants, 38% accepted, 13 enrolled. *Faculty:* 15 full-time (4 women), 2 part-time/adjunct (1 woman). Expenses: Contact institution. *Financial support:* In 2019–20, 10 research assistantships (averaging $1,722 per year), 32 teaching assistantships (averaging $1,050 per year) were awarded; career-related internships or fieldwork, Federal Work-Study, scholarships/grants, health care benefits, tuition waivers (partial), and unspecified assistantships also available. Support available to part-time students. Financial award application deadline: 3/1; financial award applicants required to submit FAFSA. In 2019, 15 master's, 9 doctorates awarded. *Application deadline:* For fall admission, 3/1 priority date for international students; for spring admission, 8/1 priority date for international students. Applications are processed on a rolling basis. *Application fee:* $50 ($75 for international students). Electronic applications accepted. *Application Contact:* Dr. Sheryl Tucker, Dean, 405-744-6368, Fax: 405-744-0355, E-mail: gradi@okstate.edu. *Department Head*, Dr. Camelia Knapp, 405-744-6358, Fax: 405-744-7841, E-mail: camelia.knapp@okstate.edu.

***Michael and Anne Greenwood School of Music*** Students: 14 full-time (7 women), 9 part-time (4 women); includes 2 minority (both Hispanic/Latino), 3 international. Average age 25. 47 applicants, 55% accepted, 9 enrolled. *Faculty:* 28 full-time (9 women), 7 part-time/adjunct (2 women). Expenses: Contact institution. *Financial support:* In 2019–20, 22 teaching assistantships (averaging $1,302 per year) were awarded; research assistantships, career-related internships or fieldwork, Federal Work-Study, scholarships/grants, health care benefits, tuition waivers (partial), and unspecified assistantships also available. Support available to part-time students. Financial award application deadline: 3/1; financial award applicants required to submit FAFSA. In 2019, 12 master's awarded. *Application deadline:* For fall admission, 3/1 priority date for international students; for spring admission, 8/1 priority date for international students. Applications are processed on a rolling basis. *Application fee:* $50 ($75 for international students). Electronic applications accepted. *Application Contact:* Dr. Sheryl Tucker, Dean, 405-744-6368, Fax: 405-744-0355, E-mail: gradi@okstate.edu. *Director*, Dr. Jeff Loeffert, 405-744-8997, Fax: 405-744-9324, E-mail: osumusic@okstate.edu.

***School of Media and Strategic Communications*** Students: 14 full-time (12 women), 18 part-time (12 women); includes 8 minority (1 Black or African American, non-Hispanic/Latino; 2 American Indian or Alaska Native, non-Hispanic/Latino; 1 Asian, non-Hispanic/Latino; 1 Hispanic/Latino; 3 Two or more races, non-Hispanic/Latino), 2 international. Average age 25. 21 applicants, 81% accepted, 13 enrolled. *Faculty:* 12 full-time (3 women). Expenses: Contact institution. *Financial support:* In 2019–20, 9 teaching assistantships (averaging $1,791 per year) were awarded; research assistantships, career-related internships or fieldwork, Federal Work-Study, scholarships/grants, health care benefits, tuition waivers (partial), and unspecified assistantships also available. Support available to part-time students. Financial award application deadline: 3/1; financial award applicants required to submit FAFSA. In 2019, 14 master's awarded. *Application deadline:* For fall admission, 3/1 priority date for international students; for spring admission, 8/1 priority date for international students. Applications are processed on a rolling basis. *Application fee:* $50 ($75 for international students). Electronic applications accepted. *Application Contact:* Dr. Sheryl Tucker, Dean, 405-744-6368, Fax: 405-744-0355, E-mail: gradi@okstate.edu. *Director*, Dr. Max Andrews, 405-744-4207, Fax: 405-744-7104, E-mail: max.andrews@okstate.edu.

**College of Education, Health and Aviation** Students: 268 full-time (180 women), 518 part-time (358 women); includes 220 minority (66 Black or African American, non-Hispanic/Latino; 35 American Indian or Alaska Native, non-Hispanic/Latino; 15 Asian, non-Hispanic/Latino; 46 Hispanic/Latino; 58 Two or more races, non-Hispanic/Latino), 45 international. Average age 35. 370 applicants, 70% accepted, 219 enrolled. *Faculty:* 91 full-time (63 women), 25 part-time/adjunct (14 women). Expenses: Contact institution. *Financial support:* In 2019–20, 62 research assistantships (averaging $1,223 per year), 78 teaching assistantships (averaging $1,236 per year) were awarded; career-related internships or fieldwork, Federal Work-Study, scholarships/grants, health care benefits, tuition waivers (partial), and unspecified assistantships also available. Support available to part-time students. Financial award application deadline: 3/1; financial award applicants required to submit FAFSA. In 2019, 148 master's, 60 doctorates awarded. *Program availability:* Part-time, online learning. *Application deadline:* For fall admission, 3/1 priority date for domestic and international students; for spring admission, 8/1 priority date for domestic and international students. Applications are processed on a rolling basis. *Application fee:* $50 ($75 for international students). Electronic applications accepted. *Application Contact:* Dr. Sheryl Tucker, Dean, 405-744-6368, Fax: 405-744-0355, E-mail: gradi@okstate.edu. *Interim Dean*, Dr. Stephan M Wilson, 405.744.9805, E-mail: contact.ehs@okstate.edu.

***Community Health Sciences, Counseling & Counseling Psychology*** Students: 90 full-time (71 women), 36 part-time (26 women); includes 38 minority (7 Black or African American, non-Hispanic/Latino; 5 American Indian or Alaska Native, non-Hispanic/Latino; 5 Asian, non-Hispanic/Latino; 8 Hispanic/Latino; 13 Two or more races, non-Hispanic/Latino), 3 international. Average age 28. 99 applicants, 56% accepted, 48 enrolled. *Faculty:* 18 full-time (12 women), 2 part-time/adjunct (1 woman). Expenses: Contact institution. *Financial support:* In 2019–20, 12 research assistantships (averaging $1,172 per year), 15 teaching assistantships (averaging $1,027 per year) were awarded; career-related internships or fieldwork, Federal Work-Study, scholarships/grants, health care benefits, tuition waivers, and unspecified assistantships also available. Support available to part-time students. Financial award application deadline: 3/1; financial award applicants required to submit FAFSA. *Application fee:* $50 ($75 for international students). *Application Contact:* Dr. Sheryl Tucker, Dean, 405-744-6368, Fax: 405-744-0355, E-mail: gradi@okstate.edu. *Department Head*, Dr. Julie Kock, 405-744-6040, E-mail: julie.koch@okstate.edu.

***Educational Foundations Leadership & Aviation*** Students: 88 full-time (56 women), 274 part-time (178 women); includes 106 minority (32 Black or African American, non-Hispanic/Latino; 17 American Indian or Alaska Native, non-Hispanic/Latino; 6 Asian, non-Hispanic/Latino; 22 Hispanic/Latino; 29 Two or more races, non-Hispanic/Latino), 13 international. Average age 38. 114 applicants, 73% accepted, 73 enrolled. *Faculty:* 23 full-time (16 women), 11 part-time/adjunct (2 women). Expenses: Contact institution. *Financial support:* In 2019–20, 17 research assistantships (averaging $1,326 per year), 16 teaching assistantships (averaging $1,348 per year) were awarded; career-related internships or fieldwork, Federal Work-Study, scholarships/grants, health care benefits, tuition waivers, and unspecified assistantships also available. Support available to part-time students. Financial award application deadline: 3/1; financial award applicants required to submit FAFSA. *Application fee:* $50 ($75 for international students). *Application Contact:* Dr. Sheryl Tucker, Dean, 405-744-6368, Fax: 405-744-0355, E-mail: gradi@okstate.edu. *Department Head*, Dr. Chad Depperschmidt, 405-744-4407, E-mail: chad.depperschmidt@okstate.edu.

***Kinesiology, Applied Health and Recreation*** Students: 39 full-time (16 women), 48 part-time (22 women); includes 22 minority (11 Black or African American, non-Hispanic/Latino; 3 American Indian or Alaska Native, non-Hispanic/Latino; 5 Hispanic/Latino; 3 Two or more races, non-Hispanic/Latino), 5 international. Average age 29. 33 applicants, 85% accepted, 22 enrolled. *Faculty:* 11 full-time (4 women), 1 (woman) part-time/adjunct. Expenses: Contact institution. *Financial support:* In 2019–20, 2 research assistantships (averaging $1,453 per year), 26 teaching assistantships (averaging $1,492 per year) were awarded; career-related internships or fieldwork, Federal Work-Study, scholarships/grants, health care benefits, tuition waivers, and unspecified assistantships also available. Support available to part-time students. Financial award application deadline: 3/1; financial award applicants required to submit FAFSA. *Application fee:* $50 ($75 for international students). *Application Contact:* Dr. Sheryl Tucker, Dean, 405-744-6368, Fax: 405-744-0355, E-mail: gradi@okstate.edu. *Department Head*, Dr. Bert Jacobson, 405-744-7476, E-mail: bert.jacobson@okstate.edu.

***Teaching, Learning & Educational Sciences*** Students: 51 full-time (37 women), 159 part-time (131 women); includes 54 minority (16 Black or African American, non-Hispanic/Latino; 10 American Indian or Alaska Native, non-Hispanic/Latino; 4 Asian, non-Hispanic/Latino; 11 Hispanic/Latino; 13 Two or more races, non-Hispanic/Latino), 24 international. Average age 36. 116 applicants, 83% accepted, 78 enrolled. *Faculty:* 36 full-time (28 women), 9 part-time/adjunct (8 women). Expenses: Contact institution. *Financial support:* In 2019–20, 27 research assistantships (averaging $1,173 per year), 18 teaching assistantships (averaging $970 per year) were awarded; career-related internships or fieldwork, Federal Work-Study, scholarships/grants, health care benefits, tuition waivers, and unspecified assistantships also available. Support available to part-time students. Financial award application deadline: 3/1; financial award applicants required to submit FAFSA. *Application fee:* $50 ($75 for international students). *Application Contact:* Dr. Sheryl Tucker, Dean, 405-744-6368, Fax: 405-744-0355, E-mail: gradi@okstate.edu. *Department Head*, Dr. Shelbie Witte, 405-744-9214, E-mail: shelbie.witte@okstate.edu.

**College of Engineering, Architecture and Technology** Students: 135 full-time (23 women), 377 part-time (58 women); includes 62 minority (7 Black or African American, non-Hispanic/Latino; 9 American Indian or Alaska Native, non-Hispanic/Latino; 13 Asian, non-Hispanic/Latino; 14 Hispanic/Latino; 19 Two or more races, non-Hispanic/Latino), 222 international. Average age 30. 511 applicants, 41% accepted, 149 enrolled. *Faculty:* 127 full-time (16 women), 3 part-time/adjunct (1 woman). Expenses: Contact institution. *Financial support:* In 2019–20, 169 research assistantships (averaging $1,928 per year), 132 teaching assistantships (averaging $1,636 per year) were awarded; career-related internships or fieldwork, Federal Work-Study, scholarships/grants, health care benefits, tuition waivers (partial), and unspecified assistantships also available. Support available to part-time students. Financial award application deadline: 3/1; financial award applicants required to submit FAFSA. In 2019, 122 master's, 35 doctorates awarded. *Program availability:* Online learning. *Application deadline:* For fall admission, 3/1 priority date for domestic and international students; for spring admission, 8/1 priority date for domestic and international students. Applications are processed on a rolling basis. *Application fee:* $50 ($75 for international students). Electronic applications accepted. *Application Contact:* Dr. Sheryl Tucker, Dean, 405-744-6368, Fax: 405-744-0355, E-mail: gradi@okstate.edu. *Dean*, Dr. Paul Tikalsky, 405-744-5140, E-mail: paul.tikalsky@okstate.edu.

***School of Chemical Engineering*** Students: 23 full-time (4 women), 26 part-time (4 women); includes 6 minority (2 American Indian or Alaska Native, non-Hispanic/Latino; 1 Asian, non-Hispanic/Latino; 1 Hispanic/Latino; 2 Two or more races, non-Hispanic/Latino), 30 international. Average age 28. 58 applicants, 29% accepted, 16 enrolled. *Faculty:* 18 full-time (4 women). Expenses: Contact institution. *Financial support:* In 2019–20, 36 research assistantships (averaging $2,164 per year), 10 teaching assistantships (averaging $2,170 per year) were awarded; career-related internships or fieldwork, Federal Work-Study, scholarships/grants, health care benefits, tuition waivers (partial), and unspecified assistantships also available. Support available to part-time students. Financial award application deadline: 3/1; financial award applicants required to submit FAFSA. In 2019, 7 master's, 8 doctorates awarded. *Application deadline:* For fall admission, 3/1 priority date for international students; for spring admission, 8/1 priority date for international students. Applications are processed on a rolling basis. *Application fee:* $50 ($75 for international students). Electronic applications accepted. *Application Contact:* Dr. Sheryl Tucker, Dean, 405-744-6368, Fax: 405-744-0355, E-mail: gradi@okstate.edu. *Continental Resources Chair, Professor and Head*, Dr. Gier Hareland, 405-744-5280, Fax: 405-744-6338.

***School of Civil and Environmental Engineering*** Students: 30 full-time (7 women), 40 part-time (10 women); includes 5 minority (3 American Indian or Alaska Native, non-Hispanic/Latino; 2 Two or more races, non-Hispanic/Latino), 40 international. Average age 28. 47 applicants, 49% accepted, 18 enrolled. *Faculty:* 16 full-time (1 woman), 1 (woman) part-time/adjunct. Expenses: Contact institution. *Financial support:* In 2019–20, 51 research assistantships (averaging $1,915 per year), 1 teaching assistantship (averaging $2,000 per year) were awarded; career-related internships or fieldwork, Federal Work-Study, scholarships/grants, health care benefits, tuition waivers (partial), and unspecified assistantships also available. Support available to part-time students. Financial award application deadline: 3/1; financial award applicants required to submit FAFSA. In 2019, 11 master's, 6 doctorates awarded. *Application deadline:* For fall admission, 3/1 priority date for international students; for spring admission, 8/1 priority date for international students. Applications are processed on a rolling basis. *Application fee:* $50 ($75 for international students). Electronic applications accepted. *Application Contact:* Dr. Sheryl Tucker, Dean, 405-744-6368, Fax: 405-744-0355, E-mail: gradi@okstate.edu. *Department Head*, Dr. Norb Delatte, 405-744-5190, Fax: 405-744-7554, E-mail: norb.delatte@okstate.edu.

***School of Electrical and Computer Engineering*** Students: 15 full-time (0 women), 30 part-time (7 women); includes 5 minority (1 Asian, non-Hispanic/Latino; 2 Hispanic/Latino; 2 Two or more races, non-Hispanic/Latino), 27 international. Average age 29. 81 applicants, 31% accepted, 15 enrolled. *Faculty:* 17 full-time (1 woman). Expenses: Contact institution. *Financial support:* In 2019–20, 9 research assistantships (averaging $2,382 per year), 21 teaching assistantships (averaging $1,860 per year) were awarded; career-related internships or fieldwork, Federal Work-Study, scholarships/grants, health care benefits, tuition waivers (partial), and unspecified assistantships also available. Support available to part-time students. Financial award application deadline: 3/1; financial award applicants required to submit FAFSA. In 2019, 17 master's, 9 doctorates awarded. *Program availability:* Online learning. *Application deadline:* For fall admission, 3/1 priority date for international students; for spring admission, 8/1 priority date for international students. Applications are processed on a rolling basis. *Application fee:* $50 ($75 for international students). Electronic applications accepted. *Application Contact:* Dr. Sheryl Tucker, Vice Prov/Dean/Prof, 405-744-6368, E-mail: igrad@okstate.edu. *Department Head*, Dr. Jeffrey Young, 405-744-5151, Fax: 405-744-9198, E-mail: jl.young@okstate.edu.

***School of Industrial Engineering and Management*** Students: 22 full-time (4 women), 108 part-time (17 women); includes 22 minority (5 Black or African American, non-Hispanic/Latino; 1 American Indian or Alaska Native, non-Hispanic/Latino; 5 Asian, non-Hispanic/Latino; 6 Hispanic/Latino; 5 Two or more races, non-Hispanic/Latino), 43 international. Average age 31. 132 applicants, 43% accepted, 35 enrolled. *Faculty:* 15 full-time (3 women). Expenses: Contact institution. *Financial support:* In 2019–20, 10 research assistantships (averaging $1,757 per year), 25 teaching assistantships (averaging $1,929 per year) were awarded; career-related internships or fieldwork, Federal Work-Study, scholarships/grants, health care benefits, tuition waivers (partial), and unspecified assistantships also available. Support available to part-time students. Financial award application deadline: 3/1; financial award applicants required to submit FAFSA. In 2019, 53 master's, 2 doctorates awarded. *Program availability:* Online learning. *Application deadline:* For fall admission, 3/1 priority date for international students; for spring admission, 8/1 priority date for international students. Applications are processed on a rolling basis. *Application fee:* $50 ($75 for international students). Electronic applications accepted. *Application Contact:* Dr. Sheryl Tucker, Vice Prov/Dean/Prof, 405-744-6368, E-mail: gradi@okstate.edu. *Head*, Dr. Sunderesh Heragu, 405-744-6055, Fax: 405-744-4654, E-mail: sunderesh.heragu@okstate.edu.

***School of Materials Science and Engineering*** Students: 5 full-time (3 women), 15 part-time (2 women); includes 3 minority (1 American Indian or Alaska Native, non-Hispanic/Latino; 2 Two or more races, non-Hispanic/Latino), 9 international. Average age 29. 13 applicants, 38% accepted, 3 enrolled. *Faculty:* 6 full-time (0 women). Expenses: Contact institution. *Financial support:* In 2019–20, 9 teaching assistantships (averaging $1,665 per year) were awarded; research assistantships also available. In 2019, 2 master's awarded. *Application deadline:* For fall admission, 3/1 for domestic students; for spring admission, 8/1 for domestic students. *Application fee:* $50 ($75 for international students). Electronic applications accepted. *Application Contact:* Dr. Sheryl Tucker, Dean, 405-744-6368, Fax: 405-744-0355, E-mail: gradi@okstate.edu. *Head*, Dr. Raman P Singh, 918-594-8155, E-mail: raman.singh@okstate.edu.

***School of Mechanical and Aerospace Engineering*** Students: 26 full-time (2 women), 100 part-time (9 women); includes 12 minority (1 Black or African American, non-Hispanic/Latino; 2 American Indian or Alaska Native, non-Hispanic/Latino; 3 Asian, non-Hispanic/Latino; 1 Hispanic/Latino; 5 Two or more races, non-Hispanic/Latino), 60 international. Average age 26. 134 applicants, 42% accepted, 45 enrolled. *Faculty:* 30 full-time (1 woman), 1 part-time/adjunct (0 women). Expenses: Contact institution. *Financial support:* In 2019–20, 50 research assistantships (averaging $1,745 per year), 49 teaching assistantships (averaging $1,224 per year) were awarded; career-related internships or fieldwork, Federal Work-Study, scholarships/grants, health care benefits, tuition waivers (partial), and unspecified assistantships also available. Support available to part-time students. Financial award application deadline: 3/1; financial award applicants required to submit FAFSA. In 2019, 21 master's, 7 doctorates awarded. *Program availability:* Online learning. *Application deadline:* For fall admission, 3/1 priority date for international students; for spring admission, 8/1 priority date for international students. Applications are processed on a rolling basis. *Application fee:* $50 ($75 for international students). Electronic applications accepted. *Application Contact:* Dr. Charlotte Fore, Manager of Graduate Studies and Research Development, 405-744-5900, Fax: 405-744-7873, E-mail: charlotte.fore@okstate.edu. *Department Head*, Dr. Daniel E. Fisher, 405-744-5900, Fax: 405-744-7873, E-mail: maehead@okstate.edu.

**College of Human Sciences** Students: 61 full-time (47 women), 105 part-time (74 women); includes 32 minority (13 Black or African American, non-Hispanic/Latino; 2 American Indian or Alaska Native, non-Hispanic/Latino; 5 Asian, non-Hispanic/Latino; 6 Hispanic/Latino; 1 Native Hawaiian or other Pacific Islander, non-Hispanic/Latino; 5 Two or more races, non-Hispanic/Latino), 38 international. Average age 30. 127 applicants, 53% accepted, 47 enrolled. *Faculty:* 51 full-time (33 women), 4 part-time/adjunct (3 women). Expenses: Contact institution. *Financial support:* In 2019–20, 35 research assistantships (averaging $1,392 per year), 46 teaching assistantships (averaging $1,255 per year) were awarded; career-related internships or fieldwork, Federal Work-Study, scholarships/grants, health care benefits, tuition waivers (partial), and unspecified assistantships also available. Support available to part-time students. Financial award application deadline: 3/1; financial award applicants required to submit FAFSA. In 2019, 52 master's, 12 doctorates awarded. *Program availability:* Online learning. *Application deadline:* For fall admission, 3/1 priority date for domestic and international students; for spring admission, 8/1 priority date for domestic and international students. Applications are processed on a rolling basis. *Application fee:* $50 ($75 for international students). Electronic applications accepted. *Application Contact:* Dr. Sheryl Tucker, Dean, 405-744-6368, Fax: 405-744-0355, E-mail: gradi@okstate.edu. *Dean*, Dr. Stephan M. Wilson, 405-744-9805, E-mail: contact.ehs@okstate.edu.

***School of Hospitality and Tourism Management*** Students: 12 full-time (3 women), 15 part-time (9 women); includes 3 minority (1 Black or African American, non-Hispanic/Latino; 2 Asian, non-Hispanic/Latino), 22 international. Average age 33. 45 applicants, 53% accepted, 24 enrolled. *Faculty:* 8 full-time (5 women). Expenses: Contact institution. *Financial support:* Research assistantships, teaching assistantships, career-related internships or fieldwork, Federal Work-Study, scholarships/grants, health care benefits, tuition waivers (partial), and unspecified assistantships available. Support available to part-time students. Financial award application deadline: 3/1; financial award applicants required to submit FAFSA. In 2019, 8 master's, 4 doctorates awarded. *Application deadline:* For fall admission, 3/1 priority date for international students; for spring admission, 8/1 priority date for international students. Applications are processed on a rolling basis. *Application fee:* $50 ($75 for international students). Electronic applications accepted. *Application Contact:* Dr. Sheryl Tucker, Vice Prov/Dean/Prof, 405-744-6368, E-mail: gradi@okstate.edu. *Interim Director*, Dr. Li Miao, 405-744-6713, Fax: 405-744-6299, E-mail: htm@okstate.edu.

**Graduate College** Students: 32 full-time (22 women), 203 part-time (114 women); includes 63 minority (12 Black or African American, non-Hispanic/Latino; 19 American Indian or Alaska Native, non-Hispanic/Latino; 12 Asian, non-Hispanic/Latino; 8 Hispanic/Latino; 12 Two or more races, non-Hispanic/Latino), 38 international. Average age 34. 301 applicants, 83% accepted, 173 enrolled. Expenses: Contact institution. *Financial support:* Research assistantships, career-related internships or fieldwork, Federal Work-Study, scholarships/grants, health care benefits, tuition waivers (partial), and unspecified assistantships available. Support available to part-time students. Financial award application deadline: 3/1; financial award applicants required to submit FAFSA. In 2019, 26 master's, 2 doctorates awarded. *Application deadline:* For fall admission, 3/1 priority date for domestic and international students; for spring admission, 8/1 priority date for domestic and international students. Applications are processed on a rolling basis. *Application fee:* $50 ($75 for international students). Electronic applications accepted. *Application Contact:* Dr. Sheryl Tucker, Dean, 405-744-6368, Fax: 405-744-0355, E-mail: gradi@okstate.edu. *Dean*, Dr. Sheryl Tucker, 405-744-6368, Fax: 405-744-0355, E-mail: gradi@okstate.edu.

**School of Global Studies and Partnerships** Students: 25 full-time (17 women), 15 part-time (7 women); includes 7 minority (2 Black or African American, non-Hispanic/Latino; 1 Asian, non-Hispanic/Latino; 2 Hispanic/Latino; 2 Two or more races, non-Hispanic/Latino), 20 international. Average age 28. 1 applicant, 100% accepted, 1 enrolled. Expenses: Contact institution. *Financial support:* Fellowships, research assistantships, teaching assistantships, career-related internships or fieldwork, Federal Work-Study, scholarships/grants, health care benefits, tuition waivers (partial), and unspecified assistantships available. Financial award application deadline: 3/1; financial award applicants required to submit FAFSA. *Program availability:* Online learning. *Application deadline:* For fall admission, 3/1 priority date for domestic and international students; for spring admission, 8/1 priority date for domestic and international students. Applications are processed on a rolling basis. *Application fee:* $50 ($75 for international students). Electronic applications accepted. *Application Contact:* Dr. Sheryl Tucker, Vice Prov/Dean/Prof, 405-744-6368, Fax: 405-744-0355, E-mail: gradi@okstate.edu. *Dean*, Dr. Randy Kulver, 405-744-6606, E-mail: randy.kluver@okstate.edu.

**Spears School of Business** Students: 281 full-time (121 women), 406 part-time (132 women); includes 115 minority (20 Black or African American, non-Hispanic/Latino; 18 American Indian or Alaska Native, non-Hispanic/Latino; 22 Asian, non-Hispanic/Latino; 28 Hispanic/Latino; 1 Native Hawaiian or other Pacific Islander, non-Hispanic/Latino; 26 Two or more races, non-Hispanic/Latino), 177 international. Average age 30. 745 applicants, 45% accepted, 239 enrolled. *Faculty:* 55 full-time (20 women), 53 part-time/adjunct (10 women). Expenses: Contact institution. *Financial support:* In 2019–20, 69 research assistantships (averaging $1,555 per year), 146 teaching assistantships (averaging $1,277 per year) were awarded; career-related internships or fieldwork, Federal Work-Study, scholarships/grants, health care benefits, tuition waivers (partial), and unspecified assistantships also available. Support available to part-time students. Financial award application deadline: 3/1; financial award applicants required to submit FAFSA. In 2019, 293 master's, 18 doctorates awarded. *Program availability:* Part-time, online learning. *Application deadline:* For fall admission, 3/1 priority date for domestic and international students; for spring admission, 8/1 priority date for domestic and international students. Applications are processed on a rolling basis. *Application fee:* $50 ($75 for international students). Electronic applications accepted. *Application Contact:* Dr. Sheryl Tucker, Dean, 405-744-6368, Fax: 405-744-0355, E-mail: gradi@okstate.edu. *Dean*, Dr. Ken Eastman, 405-744-5064, Fax: 405-744-8956, E-mail: ken.eastman@okstate.edu.

***School of Accounting*** Students: 46 full-time (22 women), 16 part-time (9 women); includes 17 minority (2 Black or African American, non-Hispanic/Latino; 3 American Indian or Alaska Native, non-Hispanic/Latino; 2 Asian, non-Hispanic/Latino; 2 Hispanic/Latino; 8 Two or more races, non-Hispanic/Latino), 3 international. Average age 24. 55 applicants, 27% accepted, 5 enrolled. *Faculty:* 9 full-time (5 women), 1 part-time/adjunct (0 women). Expenses: Contact institution. *Financial support:* In 2019–20, 1 research assistantship (averaging $1,134 per year), 24 teaching assistantships (averaging $1,153 per year) were awarded; career-related internships or fieldwork, Federal Work-Study, scholarships/grants, health care benefits, tuition waivers (partial), and unspecified assistantships also available. Support available to part-time students. Financial award application deadline: 3/1; financial award applicants required to submit FAFSA. In 2019, 34 master's, 3 doctorates awarded. *Program availability:* Part-time. *Application deadline:* For fall admission, 3/1 priority date for international students; for spring admission, 8/1 priority date for international students. Applications are processed on a rolling basis. *Application fee:* $50 ($75 for international students). Electronic applications accepted. *Application Contact:* Dr. Sheryl Tucker, Vice Prov/Dean/Prof, 405-744-6386, E-mail: gradi@okstate.edu. *Department Head*, Dr. Audrey Gramling, 405-744-1245, Fax: 405-744-1680, E-mail: audrey.gramling@okstate.edu.

***School of Marketing and International Business*** Students: 67 full-time (23 women), 43 part-time (20 women); includes 13 minority (1 Black or African American, non-Hispanic/Latino; 6 Asian, non-Hispanic/Latino; 4 Hispanic/Latino; 2 Two or more races, non-Hispanic/Latino), 70 international. Average age 29. 198 applicants, 32% accepted, 49 enrolled. *Faculty:* 14 full-time (4 women), 3 part-time/adjunct (0 women). Expenses: Contact institution. *Financial support:* In 2019–20, 29 research assistantships (averaging $1,382 per year), 9 teaching assistantships (averaging $1,169 per year) were awarded; career-related internships or fieldwork, Federal Work-Study, scholarships/grants, health care benefits, tuition waivers (partial), and unspecified assistantships also available. Support available to part-time students. Financial award application deadline: 3/1; financial award applicants required to submit FAFSA. In 2019, 41 master's, 1 doctorate awarded. *Program availability:* Part-time. *Application deadline:* For fall admission, 3/1 priority date for international students; for spring admission, 8/1 priority date for international students. Applications are processed on a rolling basis. *Application fee:* $50 ($75 for international students). Electronic applications accepted. *Application Contact:* Dr. Sheryl Tucker, Vice Prov/Dean/Prof, 405-744-6368, E-mail: gradi@okstate.edu. *Department Head*, Dr. Tom Brown, 405-744-5113, Fax: 405-744-5180, E-mail: tom.brown@okstate.edu.

## OKLAHOMA STATE UNIVERSITY CENTER FOR HEALTH SCIENCES, Tulsa, OK 74107-1898

**General Information** State-supported, coed, graduate-only institution. *Graduate housing:* On-campus housing not available. *Research affiliation:* Viropharma, Inc. (pharmaceutical sciences), Ingenex (pharmaceutical sciences), The Procter & Gamble Company (pharmaceutical sciences), Glaxo-Smith Kline (pharmaceutical sciences), Sun River, Inc. (cognitive rehabilitation), Merck & Company, Inc. (pharmaceutical sciences).

**GRADUATE UNITS**

**College of Osteopathic Medicine** Electronic applications accepted.

**Graduate Program in Forensic Sciences** *Program availability:* Part-time, evening/weekend, 100% online, blended/hybrid learning. Electronic applications accepted.

**Program in Biomedical Sciences** Electronic applications accepted.

**Program in Health Care Administration** *Program availability:* Part-time, evening/weekend, 100% online.

## OKLAHOMA WESLEYAN UNIVERSITY, Bartlesville, OK 74006-6299

**General Information** Independent-religious, coed, comprehensive institution.

**GRADUATE UNITS**

**Professional Studies Division**

## OLD DOMINION UNIVERSITY, Norfolk, VA 23529

**General Information** State-supported, coed, university. CGS member. *Graduate housing:* Room and/or apartments available on a first-come, first-served basis to single students; on-campus housing not available to married students. Housing application deadline: 5/1. *Research affiliation:* Commonwealth Center for Advanced Manufacturing (CCAM) (advanced engineering and manufacturing), Huntington Ingalls Industries (Newport News Shipbuilding) (digital shipbuilding), Thomas Jefferson National Accelerator Facility (high energy physics and laser processing), NASA Langley Research Center (aeronautics and data analytics), Eastern Virginia Medical School (medicine), Virginia Institute of Marine Science (marine science and coastal resilience).

**GRADUATE UNITS**

**College of Arts and Letters** *Program availability:* Part-time, evening/weekend, 100% online. Electronic applications accepted.

**College of Health Sciences** *Program availability:* Part-time, evening/weekend, 100% online, blended/hybrid learning. Electronic applications accepted.

***School of Community and Environmental Health*** Electronic applications accepted.

***School of Dental Hygiene*** *Program availability:* Part-time, evening/weekend, blended/hybrid learning. Electronic applications accepted.

***School of Nursing*** *Program availability:* Part-time, 100% online, blended/hybrid learning. Electronic applications accepted.

***School of Physical Therapy and Athletic Training*** Electronic applications accepted.

**College of Sciences** *Program availability:* Part-time, evening/weekend, 100% online. Electronic applications accepted.

**Darden College of Education** *Program availability:* Part-time, evening/weekend, 100% online, blended/hybrid learning. Electronic applications accepted.

**Frank Batten College of Engineering and Technology** *Program availability:* Part-time, evening/weekend, 100% online, blended/hybrid learning. Electronic applications accepted.

**Strome College of Business** *Program availability:* Part-time, evening/weekend, online learning. Electronic applications accepted.

## OLIVET COLLEGE, Olivet, MI 49076-9701

**General Information** Independent-religious, coed, comprehensive institution.

**GRADUATE UNITS**

**Master of Business Administration in Insurance Program** *Program availability:* Part-time, online only, 100% online, blended/hybrid learning. Electronic applications accepted.

## OLIVET NAZARENE UNIVERSITY, Bourbonnais, IL 60914

**General Information** Independent-religious, coed, comprehensive institution. *Graduate housing:* Room and/or apartments available to single students; on-campus housing not available to married students. Housing application deadline: 8/15.

**GRADUATE UNITS**

**Graduate School** *Program availability:* Part-time, evening/weekend.

***Division of Education*** *Program availability:* Evening/weekend.

***Division of Religion*** *Program availability:* Part-time.

**Program in Organizational Leadership**

## OMEGA GRADUATE SCHOOL, Dayton, TN 37321-6736

**General Information** Independent-religious, coed, graduate-only institution. *Graduate housing:* Rooms and/or apartments guaranteed to single students and available on a first-come, first-served basis to married students.

**GRADUATE UNITS**

**Graduate Programs**

## OPEN UNIVERSITY, Milton Keynes MK7 6AA, United Kingdom

**General Information** Public, coed, comprehensive institution.

**GRADUATE UNITS**

**Graduate Programs**

## ORAL ROBERTS UNIVERSITY, Tulsa, OK 74171

**General Information** Independent-religious, coed, comprehensive institution. *Enrollment:* 4,042 graduate, professional, and undergraduate students; 432 full-time matriculated graduate/professional students (236 women), 131 part-time matriculated graduate/professional students (71 women). *Enrollment by degree level:* 336 master's, 227 doctoral. *Graduate faculty:* 23 full-time (7 women), 19 part-time/adjunct (8 women). *Tuition:* Full-time $11,052; part-time $5526 per year. *Required fees:* $1230; $615 per unit. Tuition and fees vary according to program. *Graduate housing:* Room and/or apartments available on a first-come, first-served basis to single students; on-campus housing not available to married students. Typical cost: $4050 per year ($8650 including board). Room and board charges vary according to board plan and housing facility selected. *Student services:* Campus employment opportunities, campus safety program, career counseling, exercise/wellness program, free psychological counseling, international student services, low-cost health insurance, multicultural affairs office, services for students with disabilities, teacher training, writing training. *Library facilities:* John D. Messick Resources Center.

**Computer facilities:** A campuswide network can be accessed. Online class registration is available.

Website: http://www.oru.edu/

**General Application Contact:** Graduate Enrollment Counselors, 918-495-6161, E-mail: gradadmissions@oru.edu.

**GRADUATE UNITS**

**School of Business** Students: 67 full-time (32 women), 19 part-time (11 women); includes 9 minority (6 Black or African American, non-Hispanic/Latino; 1 American Indian or Alaska Native, non-Hispanic/Latino; 2 Asian, non-Hispanic/Latino), 29 international. Average age 29. 257 applicants, 26% accepted, 46 enrolled. *Faculty:* 7 full-time (0 women), 5 part-time/adjunct (4 women). Expenses: Contact institution. *Financial support:* In 2019–20, 39 students received support. Scholarships/grants and unspecified assistantships available. Financial award application deadline: 6/1; financial award applicants required to submit FAFSA. In 2019, 73 master's awarded. *Program availability:* Part-time, 100% online. *Application deadline:* Applications are processed on a rolling basis. *Application fee:* $35. Electronic applications accepted. *Application Contact:* David Ferreyro, Enrollment Counselor, 918-495-6963, E-mail: dferreyro@oru.edu. *Chair of the Graduate School of Business*, Dr. Marshal Wright, 918-495-6988, E-mail: mwright@oru.edu.

**School of Education** Students: 75 full-time (46 women), 15 part-time (7 women); includes 13 minority (10 Black or African American, non-Hispanic/Latino; 2 American Indian or Alaska Native, non-Hispanic/Latino; 1 Asian, non-Hispanic/Latino), 28 international. Average age 42. 158 applicants, 18% accepted, 23 enrolled. *Faculty:* 7 full-time (2 women), 6 part-time/adjunct (2 women). Expenses: Contact institution. *Financial support:* Fellowships and scholarships/grants available. Financial award application deadline: 3/15. In 2019, 21 master's, 30 doctorates awarded. *Program availability:* Part-time, 100% online. *Application deadline:* Applications are processed on a rolling basis. *Application fee:* $35. Electronic applications accepted. *Application Contact:* Katie Lentz, Enrollment Counselor, 918-495-6553, E-mail: klentz@oru.edu. *Chair of Graduate School of Education*, Dr. Patrick Otto, 918-495-7087, E-mail: jotto@oru.edu.

**School of Theology and Missions** Students: 268 full-time (146 women), 96 part-time (52 women); includes 66 minority (48 Black or African American, non-Hispanic/Latino; 9 American Indian or Alaska Native, non-Hispanic/Latino; 8 Asian, non-Hispanic/Latino; 1 Native Hawaiian or other Pacific Islander, non-Hispanic/Latino), 65 international. Average age 40. 661 applicants, 24% accepted, 136 enrolled. *Faculty:* 17 full-time (2 women). Expenses: Contact institution. *Financial support:* Fellowships and scholarships/grants available. Financial award application deadline: 6/1. In 2019, 113 master's, 19 doctorates awarded. *Program availability:* Part-time, online learning. *Application deadline:* Applications are processed on a rolling basis. *Application fee:* $35. Electronic applications accepted. *Application Contact:* Joe Sims, Enrollment Counselor, 918-495-6618, E-mail: jsims@oru.edu. *Chair*, Dr. Bill Buker, 918-495-6493, E-mail: bbuker@oru.edu.

## OREGON COLLEGE OF ORIENTAL MEDICINE, Portland, OR 97216

**General Information** Independent, coed, graduate-only institution. *Graduate housing:* On-campus housing not available.

**GRADUATE UNITS**

**Graduate Program in Acupuncture and Oriental Medicine** *Program availability:* Part-time.

## OREGON HEALTH & SCIENCE UNIVERSITY, Portland, OR 97239-3098

**General Information** State-related, coed, upper-level institution. CGS member. *Graduate housing:* On-campus housing not available. *Research affiliation:* Oregon Regional Primate Research Center.

**GRADUATE UNITS**

**School of Dentistry** Electronic applications accepted.

**School of Medicine** *Program availability:* Part-time. Electronic applications accepted.

***Graduate Programs in Medicine*** *Program availability:* Part-time. Electronic applications accepted.

**School of Nursing** *Program availability:* Part-time, 100% online, blended/hybrid learning. Electronic applications accepted.

## OREGON INSTITUTE OF TECHNOLOGY, Klamath Falls, OR 97601-8801

**General Information** State-supported, coed, comprehensive institution. *Graduate housing:* Room and/or apartments available on a first-come, first-served basis to single students; on-campus housing not available to married students. Housing application deadline: 3/1.

**GRADUATE UNITS**
**Program in Manufacturing Engineering Technology** *Program availability:* Part-time, online learning. Electronic applications accepted.

## OREGON STATE UNIVERSITY, Corvallis, OR 97331

**General Information** State-supported, coed, university. CGS member. *Graduate housing:* Rooms and/or apartments guaranteed to single students and available on a first-come, first-served basis to married students. Housing application deadline: 5/1. *Research affiliation:* W.M. Keck Foundation (science, engineering), David and Lucille Packard Foundation (science, environmental science), William and Flora Hewlett Foundation (science, engineering), George and Betty Moore Foundation (medical research, science education), Comer Science and Educational Foundation (science).

**GRADUATE UNITS**
**College of Agricultural Sciences** *Program availability:* Part-time, online learning.
**College of Business** *Program availability:* Part-time, blended/hybrid learning.
**College of Earth, Ocean, and Atmospheric Sciences**
**College of Education** *Program availability:* Part-time, 100% online, blended/hybrid learning.
**College of Engineering** *Program availability:* Part-time, 100% online.
**College of Forestry** *Program availability:* Part-time, 100% online.
**College of Liberal Arts** *Program availability:* Part-time.
**College of Pharmacy**
**College of Public Health and Human Sciences** Electronic applications accepted.
**College of Science** *Program availability:* Part-time.
**College of Veterinary Medicine**
**Interdisciplinary/Institutional Programs** *Program availability:* Part-time.

## OREGON STATE UNIVERSITY–CASCADES, Bend, OR 97701

**General Information** State-supported, coed, comprehensive institution.

**GRADUATE UNITS**
**Program in Counseling**
**Program in Education**

## OTIS COLLEGE OF ART AND DESIGN, Los Angeles, CA 90045-9785

**General Information** Independent, coed, comprehensive institution. *Graduate housing:* On-campus housing not available.

**GRADUATE UNITS**
**Program in Fine Arts** Electronic applications accepted.
**Program in Graphic Design** Electronic applications accepted.
**Program in Public Practice** Electronic applications accepted.
**Program in Writing** Electronic applications accepted.

## OTTAWA UNIVERSITY, Ottawa, KS 66067-3399

**General Information** Independent-religious, coed, comprehensive institution. *Graduate housing:* On-campus housing not available.

**GRADUATE UNITS**
**Graduate Studies-Arizona** *Program availability:* Part-time, evening/weekend, online learning. Electronic applications accepted.
**Graduate Studies-International** *Program availability:* Online learning. Electronic applications accepted.
**Graduate Studies-Kansas City** *Program availability:* Part-time, evening/weekend, online learning. Electronic applications accepted.
**Graduate Studies-Wisconsin** *Program availability:* Part-time, evening/weekend, online learning. Electronic applications accepted.

## OTTERBEIN UNIVERSITY, Westerville, OH 43081

**General Information** Independent-religious, coed, comprehensive institution. CGS member. *Graduate housing:* On-campus housing not available.

**GRADUATE UNITS**
**Department of Business, Accounting and Economics** *Program availability:* Part-time, evening/weekend.
**Department of Education**
**Department of Nursing** *Program availability:* Part-time, evening/weekend, online learning.

## OUR LADY OF THE LAKE UNIVERSITY, San Antonio, TX 78207-4689

**General Information** Independent-religious, coed, comprehensive institution. *Graduate housing:* Room and/or apartments available on a first-come, first-served basis to single students; on-campus housing not available to married students. Housing application deadline: 7/15. *Research affiliation:* Texas Higher Education Coordinating Board (teacher quality, education), Texas Regional Collaborative (education).

**GRADUATE UNITS**
**College of Arts and Sciences** *Program availability:* Part-time, evening/weekend. Electronic applications accepted.
**College of Professional Studies** *Program availability:* Part-time, evening/weekend, 100% online, blended/hybrid learning. Electronic applications accepted.
**School of Business and Leadership** *Program availability:* Part-time, evening/weekend, 100% online, blended/hybrid learning. Electronic applications accepted.
**Worden School of Social Service** *Program availability:* Part-time, evening/weekend, 100% online, blended/hybrid learning. Electronic applications accepted.

## PACE UNIVERSITY, New York, NY 10038

**General Information** Independent, coed, university. *Graduate housing:* Room and/or apartments available on a first-come, first-served basis to single students; on-campus housing not available to married students.

**GRADUATE UNITS**
**College of Health Professions** *Program availability:* Part-time. Electronic applications accepted.
***Lienhard School of Nursing*** *Program availability:* Part-time. Electronic applications accepted.
**Dyson College of Arts and Sciences** *Program availability:* Part-time, evening/weekend, 100% online, blended/hybrid learning. Electronic applications accepted.
**Elisabeth Haub School of Law** *Program availability:* Part-time. Electronic applications accepted.
**Lubin School of Business** *Program availability:* Part-time, evening/weekend, blended/hybrid learning. Electronic applications accepted.
**School of Education** *Program availability:* Part-time, evening/weekend, 100% online, blended/hybrid learning. Electronic applications accepted.
**Seidenberg School of Computer Science and Information Systems** *Program availability:* Part-time, evening/weekend, online only, 100% online, blended/hybrid learning. Electronic applications accepted.

## PACIFICA GRADUATE INSTITUTE, Carpinteria, CA 93013

**General Information** Proprietary, coed, graduate-only institution. *Graduate housing:* Rooms and/or apartments guaranteed to single and married students. Housing application deadline: 8/15. *Research affiliation:* Elton B. Stevens Company (EBSCO) (journal management), American Psychological Association (psychology), North California Consortium of Psychology Libraries (psychology).

**GRADUATE UNITS**
**Graduate Programs**

## PACIFIC COLLEGE OF ORIENTAL MEDICINE, San Diego, CA 92108

**General Information** Proprietary, coed, graduate-only institution. *Graduate housing:* On-campus housing not available. *Research affiliation:* National Institutes of Health (complimentary and alternative medicine).

**GRADUATE UNITS**
**Graduate Program** *Program availability:* Part-time, evening/weekend.

## PACIFIC COLLEGE OF ORIENTAL MEDICINE–CHICAGO, Chicago, IL 60601

**General Information** Proprietary, coed, graduate-only institution. *Graduate housing:* On-campus housing not available. *Research affiliation:* Children's Memorial Hospital of Chicago (pediatric research).

**GRADUATE UNITS**
**Graduate Program** *Program availability:* Part-time, evening/weekend.

## PACIFIC COLLEGE OF ORIENTAL MEDICINE-NEW YORK, New York, NY 10010

**General Information** Proprietary, coed, graduate-only institution. *Graduate housing:* On-campus housing not available.

**GRADUATE UNITS**
**Graduate Program** *Program availability:* Part-time, evening/weekend.

## PACIFIC LUTHERAN UNIVERSITY, Tacoma, WA 98447

**General Information** Independent-religious, coed, comprehensive institution. *Graduate housing:* Rooms and/or apartments available on a first-come, first-served basis to single and married students. Housing application deadline: 5/1.

**GRADUATE UNITS**
**Division of Humanities** *Program availability:* Part-time, blended/hybrid learning. Electronic applications accepted.
**Division of Social Sciences** Electronic applications accepted.
**School of Business** *Program availability:* Part-time, evening/weekend. Electronic applications accepted.
**School of Education and Kinesiology** *Program availability:* Part-time, evening/weekend. Electronic applications accepted.
**School of Nursing** Electronic applications accepted.

## PACIFIC NORTHWEST COLLEGE OF ART, Portland, OR 97209

**General Information** Independent, coed, comprehensive institution.

**GRADUATE UNITS**
**Program in Applied Craft and Design**
**Program in Collaborative Design**
**Program in Critical Studies**
**Program in Print Media**
**Program in Visual Studies**

## PACIFIC NORTHWEST UNIVERSITY OF HEALTH SCIENCES, Yakima, WA 98901

**General Information** Independent, coed, graduate-only institution. *Enrollment by degree level:* 576 doctoral. *Graduate faculty:* 27 full-time (11 women), 24 part-time/adjunct (8 women). *Tuition:* Full-time $56,000; part-time $56,000 per degree program. Tuition and fees vary according to program. *Graduate housing:* On-campus housing not available. *Student services:* Campus employment opportunities, campus safety program, career counseling, exercise/wellness program, free psychological counseling. *Library facilities:* PNWU Library. *Collection:* Books: 2,837 (physical), 33,712 (digital/electronic); Serial titles: 70 (physical), 47,729 (digital/electronic); Databases: 14. Weekly public service hours: 73; study areas open 24 hours, 5–7 days a week. *Research affiliation:* Yakima Valley Community Foundation (health care), Arnold P. Gold Foundation (health care), Health Resources and Services Administration (health care).

**Computer facilities:** 2 computers available on campus for general student use. A campuswide network can be accessed from off campus. Online class registration is available.
Website: http://www.pnwu.edu/

**GRADUATE UNITS**
**College of Osteopathic Medicine** Electronic applications accepted.

## PACIFIC OAKS COLLEGE, Pasadena, CA 91103

**General Information** Independent, coed, primarily women, upper-level institution. *Graduate housing:* Room and/or apartments available to single students; on-campus housing not available to married students.

**GRADUATE UNITS**
**Graduate School** *Program availability:* Part-time, evening/weekend, online learning.

### PACIFIC RIM CHRISTIAN UNIVERSITY, Honolulu, HI 96819
**General Information** Independent-religious, coed, comprehensive institution.
**GRADUATE UNITS**
**Program in Christian Ministry**

### PACIFIC SCHOOL OF RELIGION, Berkeley, CA 94709-1323
**General Information** Independent, coed, graduate-only institution. *Graduate housing:* Rooms and/or apartments guaranteed to single and married students. Housing application deadline: 4/1. *Research affiliation:* Center for Women and Religion (women's studies), Center for Ethics and Social Policy (business ethics), Disciples Seminary Foundation (theology), Swedenborgean House of Studies (theology), Bay Area Faith and Health Consortium (public health).
**GRADUATE UNITS**
**Graduate and Professional Programs** *Program availability:* Part-time. Electronic applications accepted.

### PACIFIC STATES UNIVERSITY, Los Angeles, CA 90010
**General Information** Independent, coed, comprehensive institution. *Graduate housing:* Room and/or apartments available on a first-come, first-served basis to single students; on-campus housing not available to married students.
**GRADUATE UNITS**
**College of Business** *Program availability:* Part-time, evening/weekend, online learning.
**College of Computer Science and Information Systems** *Program availability:* Part-time, evening/weekend.

### PACIFIC UNION COLLEGE, Angwin, CA 94508-9707
**General Information** Independent-religious, coed, comprehensive institution. *Graduate housing:* Room and/or apartments available on a first-come, first-served basis to married students; on-campus housing not available to single students.
**GRADUATE UNITS**
**Education Department** *Program availability:* Part-time.

### PACIFIC UNIVERSITY, Forest Grove, OR 97116-1797
**General Information** Independent, coed, comprehensive institution. *Graduate housing:* On-campus housing not available. *Research affiliation:* NEI/PEDIG–JAEB Center of Health Research (amblyopia treatment), BSK, CIBA Vision (contact lenses), Cooper Vision (contact lenses), The Ohio State University/Vistakon-Johnson & Johnson (adolescent and child vision care).
**GRADUATE UNITS**
**College of Business**
**College of Education** *Program availability:* Part-time, evening/weekend. Electronic applications accepted.
**College of Optometry** Electronic applications accepted.
**Healthcare Administration Program**
**Program in Social Work**
**Program in Writing** *Program availability:* Part-time.
**School of Audiology**
**School of Occupational Therapy** Electronic applications accepted.
**School of Pharmacy** Electronic applications accepted.
**School of Physical Therapy** Electronic applications accepted.
**School of Physician Assistant Studies**
**School of Professional Psychology** *Program availability:* Part-time. Electronic applications accepted.

### PALM BEACH ATLANTIC UNIVERSITY, West Palm Beach, FL 33416-4708
**General Information** Independent-religious, coed, comprehensive institution. *Enrollment:* 3,691 graduate, professional, and undergraduate students; 567 full-time matriculated graduate/professional students (403 women), 241 part-time matriculated graduate/professional students (156 women). *Enrollment by degree level:* 439 master's, 369 doctoral. *Graduate faculty:* 36 full-time (17 women), 32 part-time/adjunct (21 women). *Tuition:* Part-time $570 per credit hour. *Required fees:* $580 per unit. Tuition and fees vary according to degree level, campus/location and program. *Graduate housing:* Room and/or apartments available on a first-come, first-served basis to single students; on-campus housing not available to married students. *Student services:* Campus employment opportunities, campus safety program, career counseling, exercise/wellness program, multicultural affairs office, services for students with disabilities, writing training. *Library facilities:* Warren Library plus 1 other. *Collection:* Books: 143,334 (physical), 126,921 (digital/electronic); Serial titles: 114 (physical), 121,795 (digital/electronic); Databases: 143. Weekly public service hours: 100; students can reserve study rooms.
**Computer facilities:** Computer purchase and lease plans are available. 340 computers available on campus for general student use. A campuswide network can be accessed. Online class registration, Center for Writing Excellence; Academic Tutoring are available.
Website: http://www.pba.edu/
**General Application Contact:** Joe Sharp, Director for Evening, Graduate and Online Admission, 888-468-6722, E-mail: grad@pba.edu.
**GRADUATE UNITS**
**Gregory School of Pharmacy** Electronic applications accepted.
**MacArthur School of Leadership** *Program availability:* Part-time, evening/weekend, 100% online, blended/hybrid learning. Electronic applications accepted.
**Rinker School of Business** *Program availability:* Part-time, evening/weekend. Electronic applications accepted.
**School of Education and Behavioral Studies** *Program availability:* Part-time, evening/weekend. Electronic applications accepted.
**School of Ministry** *Program availability:* Part-time. Electronic applications accepted.
**School of Nursing** *Program availability:* Part-time. Electronic applications accepted.

### PALMER COLLEGE OF CHIROPRACTIC, Davenport, IA 52803-5287
**General Information** Independent, coed, comprehensive institution.
**GRADUATE UNITS**
**Division of Graduate Studies** *Program availability:* Part-time. Electronic applications accepted.
**Professional Program** *Program availability:* Part-time. Electronic applications accepted.
**Professional Program–Florida Campus** *Program availability:* Part-time.
**Professional Program–West Campus** *Program availability:* Part-time. Electronic applications accepted.

### PALO ALTO UNIVERSITY, Palo Alto, CA 94304
**General Information** Independent, coed, upper-level institution. *Graduate housing:* On-campus housing not available.
**GRADUATE UNITS**
**MA in Counseling Program** *Program availability:* Part-time, 100% online, blended/hybrid learning. Electronic applications accepted.
**MS in Psychology (PhD Prep) Program** *Program availability:* Part-time, online only, online program with 1-week on-campus intensive. Electronic applications accepted.
**PGSP-Stanford Psy D Consortium Program** Electronic applications accepted.
**PhD in Clinical Psychology Program** Electronic applications accepted.

### PARIS COLLEGE OF ART, 75010 Paris, France
**General Information** Independent, coed, comprehensive institution.
**GRADUATE UNITS**
**Graduate Programs**

### PARKER UNIVERSITY, Dallas, TX 75229-5668
**General Information** Independent, coed, graduate-only institution. *Graduate housing:* On-campus housing not available.
**GRADUATE UNITS**
**Doctor of Chiropractic Program** *Program availability:* Part-time. Electronic applications accepted.

### PARK UNIVERSITY, Parkville, MO 64152-3795
**General Information** Independent, coed, comprehensive institution. CGS member.
**GRADUATE UNITS**
**School of Graduate and Professional Studies** *Program availability:* Part-time, evening/weekend, online learning. Electronic applications accepted.

### PAYNE THEOLOGICAL SEMINARY, Wilberforce, OH 45384-3474
**General Information** Independent-religious, coed, graduate-only institution. *Graduate housing:* Rooms and/or apartments available on a first-come, first-served basis to single and married students. Housing application deadline: 8/15.
**GRADUATE UNITS**
**Program in Theology** *Program availability:* Part-time, evening/weekend, online learning.

### PEIRCE COLLEGE, Philadelphia, PA 19102-4699
**General Information** Independent, coed, primarily women, comprehensive institution.
**GRADUATE UNITS**
**Program in Organizational Leadership and Management**

### PENN STATE ERIE, THE BEHREND COLLEGE, Erie, PA 16563
**General Information** State-related, coed, comprehensive institution. *Graduate housing:* Room and/or apartments available on a first-come, first-served basis to single students; on-campus housing not available to married students.
**GRADUATE UNITS**
**Graduate School** *Program availability:* Part-time. Electronic applications accepted.

### PENN STATE GREAT VALLEY, Malvern, PA 19355-1488
**General Information** State-related, coed, graduate-only institution. *Graduate housing:* On-campus housing not available.
**GRADUATE UNITS**
**Graduate Studies** *Program availability:* Part-time, evening/weekend. Electronic applications accepted.
***Engineering Division***
***Management Division***

### PENN STATE HARRISBURG, Middletown, PA 17057
**General Information** State-related, coed, comprehensive institution. *Graduate housing:* Room and/or apartments available on a first-come, first-served basis to single students; on-campus housing not available to married students.
**GRADUATE UNITS**
**Graduate School** *Program availability:* Part-time, evening/weekend. Electronic applications accepted.
***School of Behavioral Sciences and Education*** *Program availability:* Part-time, evening/weekend.
***School of Business Administration*** *Program availability:* Part-time, evening/weekend.
***School of Humanities*** *Program availability:* Evening/weekend.
***School of Public Affairs***
***School of Science, Engineering and Technology*** *Program availability:* Part-time, evening/weekend.

### PENN STATE HERSHEY MEDICAL CENTER, Hershey, PA 17033-2360
**General Information** State-related, coed, graduate-only institution. *Graduate housing:* Rooms and/or apartments available on a first-come, first-served basis to single and married students.
**GRADUATE UNITS**
**College of Medicine** Electronic applications accepted.
***Graduate School Programs in the Biomedical Sciences*** Electronic applications accepted.

### PENN STATE UNIVERSITY–DICKINSON LAW, Carlisle, PA 17013
**General Information** State-related, coed, graduate-only institution. *Graduate housing:* On-campus housing not available.
**GRADUATE UNITS**
**Graduate and Professional Programs** Electronic applications accepted.

## PENN STATE UNIVERSITY PARK, University Park, PA 16802

**General Information** State-related, coed, university. CGS member. *Graduate housing:* Rooms and/or apartments available on a first-come, first-served basis to single and married students.

**GRADUATE UNITS**

**Graduate School** *Program availability:* Part-time, evening/weekend, online learning. Electronic applications accepted.

***College of Agricultural Sciences*** *Program availability:* Part-time. Electronic applications accepted.

***College of Arts and Architecture*** *Program availability:* Part-time, evening/weekend. Electronic applications accepted.

***College of Earth and Mineral Sciences*** Electronic applications accepted.

***College of Education*** *Program availability:* Part-time, evening/weekend. Electronic applications accepted.

***College of Engineering*** *Program availability:* Part-time, evening/weekend. Electronic applications accepted.

***College of Health and Human Development*** *Program availability:* Part-time, evening/weekend. Electronic applications accepted.

***College of Information Sciences and Technology*** *Program availability:* Part-time, evening/weekend. Electronic applications accepted.

***College of Nursing*** *Program availability:* Part-time, evening/weekend. Electronic applications accepted.

***College of the Liberal Arts*** *Program availability:* Part-time, evening/weekend. Electronic applications accepted.

***Donald P. Bellisario College of Communications*** *Program availability:* Part-time, evening/weekend. Electronic applications accepted.

***Eberly College of Science*** *Program availability:* Part-time, evening/weekend. Electronic applications accepted.

***Intercollege Graduate Programs*** *Program availability:* Part-time, evening/weekend. Electronic applications accepted.

***School of International Affairs*** *Program availability:* Part-time, evening/weekend. Electronic applications accepted.

***Smeal College of Business*** *Program availability:* Part-time, evening/weekend. Electronic applications accepted.

**Penn State Law** Electronic applications accepted.

## PENN STATE YORK, York, PA 17403

**General Information** State-related, coed, comprehensive institution.

**GRADUATE UNITS**

**Graduate School**

## PENNSYLVANIA ACADEMY OF THE FINE ARTS, Philadelphia, PA 19102

**General Information** Independent, coed, comprehensive institution. *Graduate housing:* On-campus housing not available.

**GRADUATE UNITS**

**Division of Graduate Studies** Electronic applications accepted.

## PENNSYLVANIA COLLEGE OF HEALTH SCIENCES, Lancaster, PA 17601

**General Information** Independent, coed, comprehensive institution.

**GRADUATE UNITS**

**Graduate Programs**

## PENSACOLA CHRISTIAN COLLEGE, Pensacola, FL 32503-2267

**General Information** Independent-religious, coed, comprehensive institution.

**GRADUATE UNITS**

**Graduate Studies**

## PENTECOSTAL THEOLOGICAL SEMINARY, Cleveland, TN 37320-3330

**General Information** Independent-religious, coed, graduate-only institution. *Graduate housing:* Rooms and/or apartments available to single and married students.

**GRADUATE UNITS**

**Graduate and Professional Programs** *Program availability:* Part-time.

## PEPPERDINE UNIVERSITY, Malibu, CA 90263

**General Information** Independent-religious, coed, university. *Graduate housing:* Rooms and/or apartments available on a first-come, first-served basis to single and married students.

**GRADUATE UNITS**

**Graduate School of Education and Psychology** *Program availability:* Part-time, evening/weekend, 100% online, blended/hybrid learning. Electronic applications accepted.

**Pepperdine Graziadio Business School** *Program availability:* Part-time, evening/weekend, 100% online. Electronic applications accepted.

**School of Law** Electronic applications accepted.

**School of Public Policy** Electronic applications accepted.

**Seaver College**

## PERU STATE COLLEGE, Peru, NE 68421

**General Information** State-supported, coed, comprehensive institution. *Enrollment:* 219 part-time matriculated graduate/professional students (155 women). *Enrollment by degree level:* 219 master's. *Graduate faculty:* 12 full-time (8 women), 7 part-time/adjunct (5 women). *Tuition, area resident:* Full-time $5625; part-time $375 per credit hour. One-time fee: $75. *Graduate housing:* On-campus housing not available. *Student services:* Campus safety program, career counseling, child daycare facilities, exercise/wellness program, free psychological counseling, low-cost health insurance, services for students with disabilities, teacher training. *Library facilities:* Peru State College Library.

**Computer facilities:** 125 computers available on campus for general student use. A campuswide network can be accessed from student residence rooms. Online class registration is available.
Website: http://www.peru.edu/

**General Application Contact:** Dr. Greg Seay, Dean, Graduate Programs, 402-872-2283, Fax: 402-872-2413, E-mail: gseay@peru.edu.

**GRADUATE UNITS**

**Graduate Programs** *Program availability:* Part-time, online learning.

## PFEIFFER UNIVERSITY, Misenheimer, NC 28109-0960

**General Information** Independent-religious, coed, comprehensive institution. *Graduate housing:* On-campus housing not available.

**GRADUATE UNITS**

**Program in Business Administration** *Program availability:* Part-time, evening/weekend, online learning.

**Program in Elementary Education**

**Program in Health Administration**

**Program in Leadership and Organizational Change**

**Program in Practical Theology** *Program availability:* Part-time, evening/weekend.

## PHILADELPHIA COLLEGE OF OSTEOPATHIC MEDICINE, Philadelphia, PA 19131-1694

**General Information** Independent, coed, graduate-only institution. *Enrollment by degree level:* 449 master's, 1,253 doctoral, 33 other advanced degrees. *Graduate faculty:* 152 full-time (67 women), 1,639 part-time/adjunct (435 women). *Graduate housing:* On-campus housing not available. *Student services:* Campus employment opportunities, campus safety program, career counseling, exercise/wellness program, free psychological counseling, low-cost health insurance, multicultural affairs office, services for students with disabilities, writing training. *Library facilities:* PCOM Library plus 1 other. *Collection:* Study areas open 24 hours, 5–7 days a week; students can reserve study rooms. *Research affiliation:* Intracell (biotechnology inflammation), Proteapex (biotechnology), Novartis Pharmaceuticals (drug development), Theramunex (biotechnology inflammation), Lankenau Institute for Medical Research (cell biology), Cleveland Museum Natural History (developmental biology).

**Computer facilities:** 142 computers available on campus for general student use. A campuswide network can be accessed from student residence rooms and from off campus. Online class registration is available.
Website: http://www.pcom.edu/

**General Application Contact:** Kari A. Shotwell, Director of Admissions, 215-871-6700, Fax: 215-871-6719, E-mail: karis@pcom.edu.

## PHILLIPS GRADUATE UNIVERSITY, Chatsworth, CA 91311

**General Information** Independent, coed, graduate-only institution. *Graduate housing:* On-campus housing not available.

**GRADUATE UNITS**

**Doctoral Program in Organizational Management and Consulting** *Program availability:* Evening/weekend. Electronic applications accepted.

**Master's Program in Psychology** *Program availability:* Evening/weekend. Electronic applications accepted.

## PHILLIPS THEOLOGICAL SEMINARY, Tulsa, OK 74116

**General Information** Independent-religious, coed, graduate-only institution. *Graduate housing:* On-campus housing not available.

**GRADUATE UNITS**

**Programs in Theology** *Program availability:* Part-time, online learning.

## PHOENIX INSTITUTE OF HERBAL MEDICINE & ACUPUNCTURE, Phoenix, AZ 85018

**General Information** Proprietary, coed, graduate-only institution.

**GRADUATE UNITS**

**Graduate Programs**

## PHOENIX SEMINARY, Phoenix, AZ 85018

**General Information** Independent-religious, coed, graduate-only institution.

**GRADUATE UNITS**

**Graduate Programs** *Program availability:* Part-time, evening/weekend.

## PIEDMONT COLLEGE, Demorest, GA 30535

**General Information** Independent-religious, coed, comprehensive institution. *Enrollment:* 2,510 graduate, professional, and undergraduate students; 454 full-time matriculated graduate/professional students (360 women), 773 part-time matriculated graduate/professional students (660 women). *Enrollment by degree level:* 448 master's, 68 doctoral, 711 other advanced degrees. *Tuition:* Full-time $10,134; part-time $563 per credit. *Required fees:* $200 per semester. *Graduate housing:* Room and/or apartments available on a first-come, first-served basis to single students; on-campus housing not available to married students. Typical cost: $6010 per year. *Student services:* Campus employment opportunities, campus safety program, career counseling, exercise/wellness program, services for students with disabilities, teacher training, writing training. *Library facilities:* Arrendale Library plus 1 other. *Collection:* Books: 85,454 (physical), 767,949 (digital/electronic); Serial titles: 63 (physical), 27,219 (digital/electronic); Databases: 250. Students can reserve study rooms.

**Computer facilities:** 225 computers available on campus for general student use. A campuswide network can be accessed. Online class registration is available.
Website: http://www.piedmont.edu/

**General Application Contact:** Kathleen Carter, Director of Graduate Enrollment Management, 706-778-8500 Ext. 1181, Fax: 706-776-0150, E-mail: kanderson@piedmont.edu.

**GRADUATE UNITS**

**School of Business** Students: 24 full-time (12 women), 8 part-time (6 women); includes 7 minority (3 Black or African American, non-Hispanic/Latino; 4 Hispanic/Latino), 1 international. Average age 30. 15 applicants, 67% accepted, 9 enrolled. Expenses: Contact institution. *Financial support:* Federal Work-Study and unspecified assistantships available. Financial award applicants required to submit FAFSA. In 2019, 39 master's awarded. *Program availability:* Part-time, evening/weekend. *Application deadline:* For fall admission, 7/15 for domestic students; for spring admission, 12/1 for domestic students. Applications are processed on a rolling basis. *Application fee:* $50. Electronic applications accepted. *Application Contact:* Kathleen Carter, Director of Graduate Enrollment Management, 706-778-3000, E-mail: kcarter@piedmont.edu. *Dean,* Dr. J. Kerry Waller, 706-778-3000, E-mail: jkwaller@piedmont.edu.

**School of Education** Students: 428 full-time (346 women), 765 part-time (654 women); includes 196 minority (139 Black or African American, non-Hispanic/Latino; 7 American Indian or Alaska Native, non-Hispanic/Latino; 11 Asian, non-Hispanic/Latino; 36 Hispanic/Latino; 2 Native Hawaiian or other Pacific Islander, non-Hispanic/Latino; 1 Two or more races, non-Hispanic/Latino). Average age 37. 434 applicants, 85% accepted, 317 enrolled. Expenses: Contact institution. *Financial support:* Career-related internships or fieldwork, Federal Work-Study, and unspecified assistantships available. Support available to part-time students. Financial award applicants required to submit FAFSA. In 2019, 261 master's, 9 doctorates, 373 other advanced degrees awarded. *Program availability:* Part-time, evening/weekend. *Application deadline:* For fall admission, 7/15 for domestic students; for spring admission, 12/1 for domestic students. Applications are processed on a rolling basis. Electronic applications accepted. *Application Contact:* Kathleen Carter, Director of Graduate Enrollment Management, 706-778-8500 Ext. 1181, Fax: 706-778-0150, E-mail: kanderson@piedmont.edu. *Dean,* Dr. R.D. Nordgren, 706-778-3000 Ext. 1201, Fax: 706-776-9608, E-mail: rdnordgren@piedmont.edu.

## PIEDMONT INTERNATIONAL UNIVERSITY, Winston-Salem, NC 27101-5197

**General Information** Independent-religious, coed, university. *Enrollment:* 124 full-time matriculated graduate/professional students (45 women), 210 part-time matriculated graduate/professional students (43 women). *Enrollment by degree level:* 173 master's, 161 doctoral. *Graduate faculty:* 9 full-time (0 women), 27 part-time/adjunct (5 women). *Tuition:* Full-time $3375; part-time $375 per credit. *Required fees:* $400; $200 per semester. Part-time tuition and fees vary according to program. *Graduate housing:* Room and/or apartments available on a first-come, first-served basis to single students; on-campus housing not available to married students. Typical cost: $4000 (including board). Housing application deadline: 8/1. *Student services:* Campus employment opportunities, campus safety program, career counseling, writing training. *Library facilities:* George Manuel Memorial Library.

**Computer facilities:** 20 computers available on campus for general student use. A campuswide network can be accessed from student residence rooms and from off campus. Online class registration is available.
Website: http://www.piedmontu.edu/

**General Application Contact:** Charles Hall, Asst Director for Enrollment Data and Admissions, 336-714-7933, E-mail: HallC@piedmontu.edu.

**GRADUATE UNITS**

**Graduate School** *Program availability:* Part-time, online learning. Electronic applications accepted.

**Temple Baptist Seminary** *Program availability:* Part-time, evening/weekend, online learning.

## PILLAR COLLEGE, Newark, NJ 07102

**General Information** Independent-religious, coed, comprehensive institution.

**GRADUATE UNITS**

**Program in Counseling**

## PITTSBURGH THEOLOGICAL SEMINARY, Pittsburgh, PA 15206-2596

**General Information** Independent-religious, coed, graduate-only institution. *Graduate housing:* Rooms and/or apartments available on a first-come, first-served basis to single and married students. Housing application deadline: 6/1.

**GRADUATE UNITS**

**Graduate and Professional Programs** *Program availability:* Part-time, evening/weekend. Electronic applications accepted.

## PITTSBURG STATE UNIVERSITY, Pittsburg, KS 66762

**General Information** State-supported, coed, comprehensive institution. *Graduate housing:* Rooms and/or apartments available on a first-come, first-served basis to single and married students. Housing application deadline: 8/15. *Research affiliation:* Cargill, Inc. (vegetable oil).

**GRADUATE UNITS**

**Graduate School** *Program availability:* Part-time, evening/weekend, 100% online, blended/hybrid learning. Electronic applications accepted.

***College of Arts and Sciences*** *Program availability:* Part-time, 100% online, blended/hybrid learning. Electronic applications accepted.

***College of Education*** *Program availability:* Part-time, 100% online, blended/hybrid learning. Electronic applications accepted.

***College of Technology*** *Program availability:* Part-time, 100% online, blended/hybrid learning. Electronic applications accepted.

***Kelce College of Business*** Electronic applications accepted.

## PLYMOUTH STATE UNIVERSITY, Plymouth, NH 03264-1595

**General Information** State-supported, coed, comprehensive institution. *Graduate housing:* Rooms and/or apartments available on a first-come, first-served basis to single students and guaranteed to married students. Housing application deadline: 5/1. *Research affiliation:* Hubbard Brook Experimental Forest (science), New Hampshire Department of Environmental Services (science), White Mountain National Forest (science), National Oceanic and Atmospheric Administration (NOAA) (science).

**GRADUATE UNITS**

**College of Graduate Studies** *Program availability:* Part-time, evening/weekend, online learning.

***Graduate Studies in Business*** *Program availability:* Part-time, evening/weekend, online learning.

***Graduate Studies in Education*** *Program availability:* Part-time, evening/weekend, online learning.

**Program in Historic Preservation**

**Program in Personal and Organizational Wellness**

## POINT LOMA NAZARENE UNIVERSITY, San Diego, CA 92106-2899

**General Information** Independent-religious, coed, comprehensive institution. *Enrollment:* 4,567 graduate, professional, and undergraduate students; 463 full-time matriculated graduate/professional students (358 women), 724 part-time matriculated graduate/professional students (522 women). *Enrollment by degree level:* 1,165 master's, 20 doctoral, 2 other advanced degrees. *Graduate faculty:* 40 full-time (28 women), 125 part-time/adjunct (75 women). Tuition and fees vary according to program. *Graduate housing:* On-campus housing not available. *Student services:* Campus employment opportunities, campus safety program, career counseling, free psychological counseling, international student services, low-cost health insurance, services for students with disabilities, teacher training. *Library facilities:* Ryan Library.

**Computer facilities:** 346 computers available on campus for general student use. A campuswide network can be accessed. Online class registration is available.
Website: http://www.pointloma.edu/

**General Application Contact:** Dana Barger, Director of Recruitment and Admissions, Graduate and Professional Students, 619-329-6799, E-mail: gradinfo@pointloma.edu.

**GRADUATE UNITS**

**College of Extended Learning** Students: 146 full-time (116 women), 15 part-time (14 women); includes 84 minority (9 Black or African American, non-Hispanic/Latino; 1 American Indian or Alaska Native, non-Hispanic/Latino; 9 Asian, non-Hispanic/Latino; 53 Hispanic/Latino; 12 Two or more races, non-Hispanic/Latino), 3 international. Average age 31. 67 applicants, 91% accepted, 58 enrolled. *Faculty:* 1 (woman) full-time, 19 part-time/adjunct (9 women). Expenses: Contact institution. *Financial support:* In 2019–20, 42 students received support. Scholarships/grants available. Financial award applicants required to submit FAFSA. In 2019, 53 master's awarded. *Application fee:* $50. Electronic applications accepted. *Application Contact:* Dana Barger, Director of Recruitment and Admissions, Graduate and Professional Students, 619-329-6799, E-mail: gradinfo@pointloma.edu. *Vice Provost for Graduate and Professional Studies and Dean of Extended Learning,* Dr. Holly Orozco, 619-849-7909, E-mail: HollyOrozco@pointloma.edu.

**Department of Biology** Students: 2 full-time (1 woman), 26 part-time (20 women); includes 9 minority (2 Asian, non-Hispanic/Latino; 5 Hispanic/Latino; 1 Native Hawaiian or other Pacific Islander, non-Hispanic/Latino; 1 Two or more races, non-Hispanic/Latino), 3 international. Average age 34. 6 applicants, 100% accepted, 4 enrolled. *Faculty:* 5 full-time (4 women), 1 part-time/adjunct (0 women). Expenses: Contact institution. *Financial support:* In 2019–20, 2 students received support. Available to part-time students. Applicants required to submit FAFSA. In 2019, 8 master's awarded. *Program availability:* Part-time. *Application deadline:* For fall admission, 7/26 priority date for domestic students; for spring admission, 11/29 priority date for domestic students; for summer admission, 5/23 priority date for domestic students. *Application fee:* $50. Electronic applications accepted. *Application Contact:* Maira Lopes, Enrollment Advisor, 619-948-2885, E-mail: mairalopes@pointloma.edu. *Director of Master's Program in Biology,* Dr. Dianne Anderson, 619-849-2705, E-mail: DianneAnderson@pointloma.edu.

**Department of Kinesiology** Students: 68 full-time (47 women), 15 part-time (6 women); includes 34 minority (3 Black or African American, non-Hispanic/Latino; 3 Asian, non-Hispanic/Latino; 21 Hispanic/Latino; 2 Native Hawaiian or other Pacific Islander, non-Hispanic/Latino; 5 Two or more races, non-Hispanic/Latino), 4 international. Average age 28. 117 applicants, 75% accepted, 61 enrolled. *Faculty:* 7 full-time (4 women), 3 part-time/adjunct (0 women). Expenses: Contact institution. *Financial support:* In 2019–20, 45 students received support. Teaching assistantships, scholarships/grants, and unspecified assistantships available. Financial award applicants required to submit FAFSA. In 2019, 52 master's awarded. *Program availability:* Part-time, 100% online. *Application fee:* $50. Electronic applications accepted. *Application Contact:* Dana Barger, Director of Recruitment and Admissions, Graduate and Professional Students, 619-329-6799, E-mail: gradinfo@pointloma.edu. *Chair,* Dr. Jeff Sullivan, 619-849-2629, E-mail: JeffSullivan@pointloma.edu.

**Fermanian School of Business** Students: 20 full-time (10 women), 81 part-time (44 women); includes 49 minority (4 Black or African American, non-Hispanic/Latino; 1 American Indian or Alaska Native, non-Hispanic/Latino; 10 Asian, non-Hispanic/Latino; 26 Hispanic/Latino; 8 Two or more races, non-Hispanic/Latino), 11 international. Average age 30. 80 applicants, 89% accepted, 49 enrolled. *Faculty:* 9 full-time (3 women), 6 part-time/adjunct (2 women). Expenses: Contact institution. *Financial support:* In 2019–20, 43 students received support. Applicants required to submit FAFSA. In 2019, 73 master's awarded. *Program availability:* Part-time, evening/weekend. *Application deadline:* For fall admission, 7/26 priority date for domestic students; for spring admission, 11/29 priority date for domestic students; for summer admission, 4/2 priority date for domestic students. Applications are processed on a rolling basis. *Application fee:* $50. Electronic applications accepted. *Application Contact:* Dana Barger, Director of Recruitment and Admissions, Graduate and Professional Students, 619-329-6799, E-mail: gradinfo@pointloma.edu. *Associate Dean, Graduate Business,* Dr. Jamie McIlwaine, 619-849-2721, E-mail: JamieMcIlwaine@pointloma.edu.

**School of Education** Students: 223 full-time (181 women), 477 part-time (362 women); includes 366 minority (20 Black or African American, non-Hispanic/Latino; 3 American Indian or Alaska Native, non-Hispanic/Latino; 23 Asian, non-Hispanic/Latino; 278 Hispanic/Latino; 4 Native Hawaiian or other Pacific Islander, non-Hispanic/Latino; 38 Two or more races, non-Hispanic/Latino), 3 international. Average age 32. 208 applicants, 88% accepted, 147 enrolled. *Faculty:* 14 full-time (12 women), 86 part-time/adjunct (58 women). Expenses: Contact institution. *Financial support:* In 2019–20, 181 students received support. Career-related internships or fieldwork and scholarships/grants available. Support available to part-time students. Financial award application deadline: 4/10; financial award applicants required to submit FAFSA. In 2019, 168 master's awarded. *Program availability:* Part-time, evening/weekend. *Application deadline:* For fall admission, 8/4 priority date for domestic students; for spring admission, 12/8 priority date for domestic students; for summer admission, 4/13 priority date for domestic students. Applications are processed on a rolling basis. *Application fee:* $50. Electronic applications accepted. *Application Contact:* Dana Barger, Director of Recruitment and Admissions, Graduate and Professional Students, 619-329-6799, E-mail: gradinfo@pointloma.edu. *Dean,* Dr. Deborah Erickson, 619-563-2864, Fax: 619-849-2579, E-mail: DebErickson@pointloma.edu.

**School of Nursing** Students: 4 full-time (3 women), 71 part-time (60 women); includes 43 minority (7 Black or African American, non-Hispanic/Latino; 14 Asian, non-Hispanic/Latino; 17 Hispanic/Latino; 1 Native Hawaiian or other Pacific Islander, non-Hispanic/Latino; 4 Two or more races, non-Hispanic/Latino). Average age 41. 34 applicants, 100% accepted, 21 enrolled. *Faculty:* 5 full-time (4 women), 7 part-time/adjunct (5 women). Expenses: Contact institution. *Financial support:* In 2019–20, 15 students received support. Scholarships/grants available. Financial award applicants required to submit FAFSA. In 2019, 28 master's awarded. *Program availability:* Part-time. *Application deadline:* For fall admission, 7/5 priority date for domestic students; for spring admission, 11/1 priority date for domestic students; for summer admission, 3/22 priority date for domestic students. Applications are processed on a rolling basis. *Application fee:* $50. Electronic applications accepted. *Application Contact:* Dana Barger, Director of Recruitment and Admissions, Graduate and Professional Students, 619-329-6799, E-mail: gradinfo@pointloma.edu. *Dean of the School of Nursing,* Dr. Barb Taylor, 619-849-7816, E-mail: BarbaraTaylor@pointloma.edu.

**School of Theology and Christian Ministry** Students: 39 part-time (16 women); includes 24 minority (1 Black or African American, non-Hispanic/Latino; 1 Asian, non-Hispanic/Latino; 20 Hispanic/Latino; 2 Two or more races, non-Hispanic/Latino), 5 international. Average age 47. 11 applicants, 82% accepted, 7 enrolled. *Faculty:* 1 full-time (0 women), 3 part-time/adjunct (0 women). Expenses: Contact institution. *Financial support:* In 2019–20, 24 students received support. Scholarships/grants available. Financial award application deadline: 6/5; financial award applicants required to submit FAFSA. In 2019, 4 master's awarded. *Program availability:* Part-time, online only, nine-week quads with eight weeks of online coursework and a one-week intensive. *Application deadline:* For fall admission, 8/30 priority date for domestic students; for spring admission, 4/4 priority date for domestic students; for summer admission, 6/20 priority date for domestic students. Applications are processed on a rolling basis. Electronic applications accepted. *Application Contact:* Dana Barger, Director of Recruitment and Admissions, Graduate and Professional Students, 619-329-6799, E-mail: gradinfo@pointloma.edu. *Dean,* Dr. Mark Maddix, 619-849-7236, E-mail: MarkMaddix@pointloma.edu.

## POINT PARK UNIVERSITY, Pittsburgh, PA 15222-1984

**General Information** Independent, coed, university. CGS member. *Graduate housing:* Room and/or apartments available on a first-come, first-served basis to single students; on-campus housing not available to married students. Housing application deadline: 7/31.

**GRADUATE UNITS**

**Center for Innovative Learning**

**Conservatory of Performing Arts** *Program availability:* Blended/hybrid learning. Electronic applications accepted.

**Rowland School of Business** *Program availability:* Part-time, evening/weekend, 100% online. Electronic applications accepted.

**School of Arts and Sciences** *Program availability:* Part-time, evening/weekend, online learning. Electronic applications accepted.

**School of Communication** *Program availability:* Part-time, evening/weekend. Electronic applications accepted.

## POINT UNIVERSITY, West Point, GA 31833

**General Information** Independent-religious, coed, comprehensive institution. *Enrollment:* 2,389 graduate, professional, and undergraduate students; 8 full-time matriculated graduate/professional students (1 woman), 27 part-time matriculated graduate/professional students (19 women). *Enrollment by degree level:* 49 master's. *Graduate faculty:* 2 full-time (both women), 8 part-time/adjunct (3 women). *Library facilities:* Point University Library plus 1 other.

**Computer facilities:** 115 computers available on campus for general student use. A campuswide network can be accessed. Online class registration is available.
Website: http://point.edu/

**General Application Contact:** Rusty Hassell, Dean of Enrollment Management, 706-385-1503, E-mail: rusty.hassell@point.edu.

**GRADUATE UNITS**

**Graduate Programs** Students: 43 full-time (20 women), 6 part-time (5 women); includes 17 minority (12 Black or African American, non-Hispanic/Latino; 1 American Indian or Alaska Native, non-Hispanic/Latino; 1 Hispanic/Latino; 3 Two or more races, non-Hispanic/Latino), 1 international. Average age 36. *Faculty:* 2 full-time (both women), 8 part-time/adjunct (3 women). Expenses: Contact institution. *Program availability:* Part-time, online only, 100% online. *Application deadline:* Applications are processed on a rolling basis. Electronic applications accepted. *Application Contact:* Rusty Hassell, Dean of Enrollment Management, 706-385-1503, E-mail: rhassell@point.edu.

## POLYTECHNIC UNIVERSITY OF PUERTO RICO, Hato Rey, PR 00918

**General Information** Independent, coed, comprehensive institution. CGS member. *Graduate housing:* On-campus housing not available. *Research affiliation:* University of Missouri (engineering, mathematics and science), University of Puerto Rico, Mayaguez Campus (electrical engineering), Virginia Polytechnic Institute and State University (mechanical and electrical engineering), Naval Research Laboratories (mechanical and electrical engineering), U.S. Department of Energy Laboratories (electrical engineering).

**GRADUATE UNITS**

**Graduate School** *Program availability:* Part-time, evening/weekend.

## POLYTECHNIC UNIVERSITY OF PUERTO RICO, MIAMI CAMPUS, Miami, FL 33166

**General Information** Independent, coed, comprehensive institution.

**GRADUATE UNITS**

**Graduate School** *Program availability:* Part-time, evening/weekend, online learning. Electronic applications accepted.

## POLYTECHNIC UNIVERSITY OF PUERTO RICO, ORLANDO CAMPUS, Orlando, FL 32825

**General Information** Independent, coed, comprehensive institution. *Graduate housing:* On-campus housing not available.

**GRADUATE UNITS**

**Graduate School** *Program availability:* Part-time, evening/weekend, online learning. Electronic applications accepted.

## POLYTECHNIQUE MONTRÉAL, Montréal, QC H3C 3A7, Canada

**General Information** Province-supported, coed, university. *Graduate housing:* Room and/or apartments available on a first-come, first-served basis to single students; on-campus housing not available to married students. Housing application deadline: 2/1. *Research affiliation:* Hydro-Quebec (energy), Bell Canada (telecommunications), Bombardier, Inc. (aircraft and aviation), IBM (computer research), Pratt and Whitney (aircraft and aviation), Ubisoft (video games).

**GRADUATE UNITS**

**Graduate Programs** *Program availability:* Part-time, evening/weekend. Electronic applications accepted.

***Institute of Biomedical Engineering*** *Program availability:* Part-time.

***Institute of Nuclear Engineering***

## PONCE HEALTH SCIENCES UNIVERSITY, Ponce, PR 00732-7004

**General Information** Independent, coed, graduate-only institution. *Research affiliation:* The University of Texas at San Antonio (health disparities, proteomics, bioinformatics), H.L. Moffitt Cancer Center (cancer biology, oncology), Oregon Health & Science University (neurosciences, cancer, inflammation), University of Puerto Rico, Mayaguez Campus (cancer biology, molecular genetics), University of Puerto Rico, Medical Sciences Campus (translational research), University of Maryland–Institute of Human Virology (HIV/AIDS research).

**GRADUATE UNITS**

**DrPH Program in Epidemiology**

**Masters Program in Public Health**

**MD Program**

**MPH Program in Environmental Health**

**MPH Program in Epidemiology**

**MS Program in Medical Sciences**

**MS Program in School Psychology**

**PhD Program in Biomedical Sciences**

**PhD Program in Clinical Psychology**

**Post Graduate Certificate Program in Neuroscience of Learning**

**Professional Certificate Program in Family and Couples Therapy**

**PsyD Program in Clinical Psychology**

## PONTIFICAL CATHOLIC UNIVERSITY OF PUERTO RICO, Ponce, PR 00717-0777

**General Information** Independent-religious, coed, university. *Graduate housing:* Room and/or apartments available to single students; on-campus housing not available to married students. Housing application deadline: 7/15.

**GRADUATE UNITS**

**College of Arts and Humanities** *Program availability:* Part-time, evening/weekend.

**College of Business Administration** *Program availability:* Part-time, evening/weekend.

**College of Education** *Program availability:* Part-time, evening/weekend.

**College of Graduate Studies in Behavioral Science and Community Affairs** *Program availability:* Part-time, evening/weekend.

**College of Sciences** *Program availability:* Part-time, evening/weekend.

***School of Medical Technology***

**School of Law** *Program availability:* Part-time, evening/weekend.

## PONTIFICAL COLLEGE JOSEPHINUM, Columbus, OH 43235

**General Information** Independent-religious, men only, comprehensive institution. *Graduate housing:* Room and/or apartments guaranteed to single students; on-campus housing not available to married students. Housing application deadline: 8/15.

**GRADUATE UNITS**

**School of Theology** *Program availability:* Part-time.

## PONTIFICAL JOHN PAUL II INSTITUTE FOR STUDIES ON MARRIAGE AND FAMILY, Washington, DC 20064

**General Information** Independent-religious, coed, graduate-only institution.

**GRADUATE UNITS**

**Graduate Programs**

## POPE ST. JOHN XXIII NATIONAL SEMINARY, Weston, MA 02493-2618

**General Information** Independent-religious, men only, graduate-only institution. *Graduate housing:* Room and/or apartments available to single students; on-campus housing not available to married students. Housing application deadline: 8/1.

**GRADUATE UNITS**

**Graduate Program**

## PORTLAND STATE UNIVERSITY, Portland, OR 97207-0751

**General Information** State-supported, coed, university. CGS member. *Enrollment:* 26,021 graduate, professional, and undergraduate students; 2,424 full-time matriculated graduate/professional students (1,476 women), 2,303 part-time matriculated graduate/professional students (1,438 women). *Enrollment by degree level:* 3,722 master's, 654 doctoral, 351 other advanced degrees. *Graduate faculty:* 768 full-time (364 women), 586 part-time/adjunct (310 women). *International tuition:* $19,830 full-time. *Tuition, area resident:* Full-time $13,020; part-time $6510 per year. Tuition, state resident: full-time $13,020; part-time $6510 per year. Tuition, nonresident: full-time $19,830; part-time $9915 per year. *Required fees:* $1226. One-time fee: $350. Tuition and fees vary according to course load, program and reciprocity agreements. *Graduate housing:* Rooms and/or apartments available on a first-come, first-served basis to single and married students. Typical cost: $6975 per year ($11,523 including board) for single students; $8520 per year for married students. Room and board charges vary according to board plan, campus/location and housing facility selected. Housing application deadline: 5/1. *Student services:* Campus employment opportunities, campus safety program, career counseling, child daycare facilities, exercise/wellness program, free psychological counseling, international student services, low-cost health insurance, multicultural affairs office, services for students with disabilities, teacher training, writing training. *Library facilities:* Branford P. Millar Library plus 1 other. *Collection:* Books: 1.4 million (physical), 1 million (digital/electronic); Serial titles: 167 (physical), 86,341 (digital/electronic); Databases: 390. Students can reserve study rooms. *Research affiliation:* DesignMedix Inc (chemistry, drug development for infectious diseases), Metron Inc. (computer engineering, advanced mathematical methods), Portland General Electric (electrical engineering), Semiconductor Research Corporation (computer science), Oregon Nanoscience and Microtechnologies Institute (electrical and computer engineering), Tektronix (electrical engineering).

**Computer facilities:** A campuswide network can be accessed. Online class registration is available.
Website: http://www.pdx.edu/

**General Application Contact:** Kelly Doherty, Director of Graduate Admissions, 503-725-5391, Fax: 503-725-3416, E-mail: askogs@pdx.edu.

**GRADUATE UNITS**

**Graduate Studies** Students: 2,424 full-time (1,476 women), 2,303 part-time (1,438 women); includes 1,026 minority (110 Black or African American, non-Hispanic/Latino; 38 American Indian or Alaska Native, non-Hispanic/Latino; 230 Asian, non-Hispanic/Latino; 428 Hispanic/Latino; 15 Native Hawaiian or other Pacific Islander, non-Hispanic/Latino; 205 Two or more races, non-Hispanic/Latino), 568 international. Average age 33. 3,959 applicants, 62% accepted, 1,436 enrolled. *Faculty:* 800 full-time (396 women), 676 part-time/adjunct (378 women). Expenses: Contact institution. *Financial support:* In 2019–20, 177 research assistantships with full and partial tuition reimbursements (averaging $14,612 per year), 381 teaching assistantships with full and partial tuition reimbursements (averaging $13,241 per year) were awarded; fellowships, career-related internships or fieldwork, Federal Work-Study, scholarships/grants, tuition waivers (full and partial), and unspecified assistantships also available. Support available to part-time students. Financial award application deadline: 3/1; financial award applicants required to submit FAFSA. In 2019, 1,655 master's, 83 doctorates awarded. *Program availability:* Part-time, evening/weekend, 100% online, blended/hybrid learning. *Application fee:* $65. Electronic applications accepted. *Application Contact:* Kelly Doherty, Director of Graduate Admissions, 503-725-5391, Fax: 503-725-3416, E-mail: dohertyk@pdx.edu. *Dean of Graduate Studies*, Dr. Rossitza Wooster, 503-725-5258, Fax: 503-725-3416, E-mail: wooster@pdx.edu.

***College of Liberal Arts and Sciences*** Students: 553 full-time (343 women), 333 part-time (181 women); includes 162 minority (4 Black or African American, non-Hispanic/Latino; 4 American Indian or Alaska Native, non-Hispanic/Latino; 34 Asian, non-Hispanic/Latino; 81 Hispanic/Latino; 1 Native Hawaiian or other Pacific Islander, non-Hispanic/Latino; 38 Two or more races, non-Hispanic/Latino), 84 international. Average age 33. 917 applicants, 50% accepted, 235 enrolled. *Faculty:* 311 full-time (140 women), 187 part-time/adjunct (104 women). Expenses: Contact institution. *Financial support:* In 2019–20, 68 research assistantships with full and partial tuition reimbursements (averaging $17,474 per year), 207 teaching assistantships with full and partial tuition reimbursements (averaging $15,597 per year) were awarded; career-related internships or fieldwork, Federal Work-Study, scholarships/grants, health care benefits, tuition waivers (full and partial), and unspecified assistantships also available. Support available to part-time students. Financial award application deadline: 3/1; financial award applicants required to submit FAFSA. In 2019, 249 master's, 26 doctorates awarded. *Program availability:* Part-time. *Application fee:* $65. Electronic applications accepted. *Application Contact:* Dr. Todd Rosenstiel, Associate Dean for Research and Graduate Programs, 503-725-8503, Fax: 503-725-3693, E-mail: rosensti@pdx.edu. *Dean*, Dr. Matt Carlson, 503-725-3514, Fax: 503-725-3693, E-mail: kje2@pdx.edu.

***College of the Arts*** Students: 93 full-time (49 women), 11 part-time (6 women); includes 24 minority (1 Black or African American, non-Hispanic/Latino; 5 Asian, non-Hispanic/Latino; 9 Hispanic/Latino; 9 Two or more races, non-Hispanic/Latino), 11 international. Average age 31. 136 applicants, 71% accepted, 32 enrolled. *Faculty:* 79 full-time (41 women), 136 part-time/adjunct (71 women). Expenses: Contact institution. *Financial support:* In 2019–20, 62 students received support, including 1 research assistantship with full and partial tuition reimbursement available (averaging $7,209 per year), 21 teaching assistantships with full and partial tuition reimbursements available (averaging $7,204 per year); career-related internships or fieldwork, Federal Work-Study, scholarships/grants, and unspecified assistantships also available. Support available to part-time students. Financial award application deadline: 3/1; financial award applicants required to submit FAFSA. In 2019, 26 master's awarded. *Program availability:* Part-time. *Application deadline:* For fall admission, 3/1 for domestic and international students. Applications are processed on a rolling basis. *Application fee:* $65. *Application Contact:* Leroy Bynum, Jr., Dean, 503-725-3105, E-mail: lbynumjr@pdx.edu. *Dean*, Leroy Bynum, Jr., 503-725-3105, E-mail: lbynumjr@pdx.edu.

***College of Urban and Public Affairs*** Students: 228 full-time (140 women), 183 part-time (107 women); includes 90 minority (7 Black or African American, non-Hispanic/Latino; 6 American Indian or Alaska Native, non-Hispanic/Latino; 15 Asian, non-Hispanic/Latino; 38 Hispanic/Latino; 3 Native Hawaiian or other Pacific Islander, non-Hispanic/Latino; 21 Two or more races, non-Hispanic/Latino), 48 international. Average age 34. 393 applicants, 77% accepted, 148 enrolled. *Faculty:* 88 full-time (37 women), 52 part-time/adjunct (20 women). Expenses: Contact institution. *Financial support:* In 2019–20, 46 research assistantships with full and partial tuition reimbursements (averaging $10,426 per year), 33 teaching assistantships with full and partial tuition reimbursements (averaging $8,541 per year) were awarded; fellowships, career-related internships or fieldwork, Federal Work-Study, scholarships/grants, and unspecified assistantships also available. Support available to part-time students. Financial award application deadline: 3/1; financial award applicants required to submit FAFSA. In 2019, 121 master's, 6 doctorates awarded. *Program availability:* Part-time, evening/weekend. *Application fee:* $65. Electronic applications accepted. *Application Contact:* Dr. Sy Adler, Interim Dean, 503-725-4043, Fax: 503-725-5199, E-mail: d3sa@pdx.edu. *Interim Dean*, Dr. Sy Adler, 503-725-4043, Fax: 503-725-5199, E-mail: d3sa@pdx.edu.

***Maseeh College of Engineering and Computer Science*** Students: 388 full-time (120 women), 372 part-time (111 women); includes 135 minority (14 Black or African American, non-Hispanic/Latino; 67 Asian, non-Hispanic/Latino; 31 Hispanic/Latino; 1 Native Hawaiian or other Pacific Islander, non-Hispanic/Latino; 22 Two or more races, non-Hispanic/Latino), 325 international. Average age 31. 585 applicants, 70% accepted, 189 enrolled. *Faculty:* 96 full-time (18 women), 39 part-time/adjunct (3 women). Expenses: Contact institution. *Financial support:* In 2019–20, 181 students received support, including 40 research assistantships (averaging $17,176 per year), 71 teaching assistantships (averaging $11,956 per year); career-related internships or fieldwork, Federal Work-Study, scholarships/grants, and unspecified assistantships also available. Support available to part-time students. Financial award application deadline: 3/1; financial award applicants required to submit FAFSA. In 2019, 308 master's, 25 doctorates awarded. *Program availability:* Part-time, evening/weekend. *Application deadline:* For fall admission, 4/1 for domestic students, 3/1 for international students; for winter admission, 9/1 for domestic and international students; for spring admission, 2/1 for domestic and international students. *Application fee:* $65. *Application Contact:* Dr. Richard Corsi, Dean, 503-725-2816, Fax: 503-725-2825, E-mail: engdean@pdx.edu. *Dean*, Dr. Richard Corsi, 503-725-2816, Fax: 503-725-2825, E-mail: engdean@pdx.edu.

***OHSU-PSU School of Public Health*** Students: 2 full-time (both women), 13 part-time (11 women); includes 4 minority (1 Asian, non-Hispanic/Latino; 1 Native Hawaiian or other Pacific Islander, non-Hispanic/Latino; 2 Two or more races, non-Hispanic/Latino). Average age 40. *Faculty:* 26 full-time (19 women), 15 part-time/adjunct (10 women). Expenses: Contact institution. *Financial support:* In 2019–20, 15 students received support, including 8 research assistantships with full and partial tuition reimbursements available (averaging $11,578 per year); teaching assistantships with full and partial tuition reimbursements available, Federal Work-Study, and unspecified assistantships also available. Financial award applicants required to submit FAFSA. In 2019, 15 master's, 1 doctorate awarded. *Program availability:* Part-time. *Application deadline:* For fall admission, 4/1 for domestic students. *Application fee:* $165. *Application Contact:* Kelly Doherty, Director of Graduate Admissions, 503-725-5391, Fax: 503-725-3416, E-mail: dohertyk@pdx.edu. *Dean*, Dr. David Bangsberg, 503-494-8257.

***The School of Business*** Students: 237 full-time (106 women), 130 part-time (63 women); includes 86 minority (11 Black or African American, non-Hispanic/Latino; 2 American Indian or Alaska Native, non-Hispanic/Latino; 25 Asian, non-Hispanic/Latino; 31 Hispanic/Latino; 2 Native Hawaiian or other Pacific Islander, non-Hispanic/Latino; 15 Two or more races, non-Hispanic/Latino), 50 international. Average age 33. 379 applicants, 73% accepted, 164 enrolled. *Faculty:* 65 full-time (31 women), 75 part-time/adjunct (30 women). Expenses: Contact institution. *Financial support:* Research assistantships, teaching assistantships, career-related internships or fieldwork, Federal Work-Study, scholarships/grants, and unspecified assistantships available. Support available to part-time students. Financial award application deadline: 3/1; financial award applicants required to submit FAFSA. In 2019, 180 master's awarded. *Program availability:* Part-time, evening/weekend. *Application fee:* $65. Electronic applications accepted. *Application Contact:* Dr. Cliff Allen, Dean, 503-725-5053, Fax: 503-725-5850, E-mail: cliffa@pdx.edu. *Dean*, Dr. Cliff Allen, 503-725-5053, Fax: 503-725-5850, E-mail: cliffa@pdx.edu.

***School of Education*** Students: 374 full-time (275 women), 702 part-time (538 women); includes 265 minority (27 Black or African American, non-Hispanic/Latino; 9 American Indian or Alaska Native, non-Hispanic/Latino; 46 Asian, non-Hispanic/Latino; 130 Hispanic/Latino; 5 Native Hawaiian or other Pacific Islander, non-Hispanic/Latino; 48 Two or more races, non-Hispanic/Latino), 25 international. Average age 35. 944 applicants, 58% accepted, 409 enrolled. *Faculty:* 66 full-time (45 women), 114 part-time/adjunct (85 women). Expenses: Contact institution. *Financial support:* In 2019–20, 3 research assistantships with full and partial tuition reimbursements (averaging $8,711 per year) were awarded; teaching assistantships, career-related internships or fieldwork, Federal Work-Study, institutionally sponsored loans, scholarships/grants, and unspecified assistantships also available. Support available to part-time students. Financial award application deadline: 3/1; financial award applicants required to submit FAFSA. In 2019, 460 master's, 12 doctorates awarded. *Program availability:* Part-time, evening/weekend. *Application fee:* $65. Electronic applications accepted. *Application Contact:* Information Contact, 503-725-4619, E-mail: askcoe@pdx.edu. *Dean*, Dr. Marvin Lynn, 503-725-4697, Fax: 503-725-5399, E-mail: mlynn@pdx.edu.

***School of Social Work*** Students: 369 full-time (303 women), 288 part-time (242 women); includes 179 minority (30 Black or African American, non-Hispanic/Latino; 12 American Indian or Alaska Native, non-Hispanic/Latino; 19 Asian, non-Hispanic/Latino; 86 Hispanic/Latino; 2 Native Hawaiian or other Pacific Islander, non-Hispanic/Latino; 30 Two or more races, non-Hispanic/Latino), 7 international. Average age 34. 599 applicants, 64% accepted, 253 enrolled. *Faculty:* 71 full-time (59 women), 75 part-time/adjunct (64 women). Expenses: Contact institution. *Financial support:* In 2019–20, 12 research assistantships with full and partial tuition reimbursements (averaging $11,761 per year), 4 teaching assistantships with full and partial tuition reimbursements (averaging $6,613 per year) were awarded; career-related internships or fieldwork, Federal Work-Study, scholarships/grants, tuition waivers (full and partial), and unspecified assistantships also available. Support available to part-time students. Financial award application deadline: 3/1; financial award applicants required to submit FAFSA. In 2019, 235 master's, 6 doctorates awarded. *Program availability:* Part-time, 100% online, blended/hybrid learning. *Application fee:* $65. Electronic applications accepted. *Application Contact:* Sarah Bradley, Director of MSW Program, 503-725-8028, E-mail: bradles@pdx.edu. *Dean*, Dr. Jose Coll, 503-725-3997, Fax: 503-725-5545, E-mail: Coll@pdx.edu.

## POST UNIVERSITY, Waterbury, CT 06723-2540

**General Information** Independent, coed, comprehensive institution.

**GRADUATE UNITS**

**Program in Business Administration** *Program availability:* Online learning.

**Program in Counseling and Human Services** *Program availability:* Part-time, evening/weekend, online learning.

**Program in Education** *Program availability:* Online learning.

**Program in Public Administration** *Program availability:* Online learning.

## PRAIRIE VIEW A&M UNIVERSITY, Prairie View, TX 77446

**General Information** State-supported, coed, university. *Enrollment:* 9,516 graduate, professional, and undergraduate students; 386 full-time matriculated graduate/professional students (227 women), 445 part-time matriculated graduate/professional students (302 women). *Enrollment by degree level:* 691 master's, 136 doctoral, 4 other advanced degrees. *Graduate faculty:* 111 full-time (41 women), 11 part-time/adjunct (7 women). *International tuition:* $15,439 full-time. *Tuition, area resident:* Full-time $5479.68. Tuition, state resident: full-time $5479.68. Tuition, nonresident: full-time $15,439. *Required fees:* $2149.32. *Graduate housing:* Room and/or apartments available on a first-come, first-served basis to single students; on-campus housing not available to married students. Typical cost: $7558 per year ($8258 including board). Housing application deadline: 4/16. *Student services:* Campus employment opportunities, campus safety program, career counseling, exercise/wellness program, free psychological counseling, grant writing training, international student services, low-cost health insurance, multicultural affairs office, services for students with disabilities, teacher training, writing training. *Library facilities:* John B. Coleman Library plus 3 others. *Collection:* Weekly public service hours: 97; students can reserve study rooms. *Research affiliation:* U.S. Department of Education (DOE) (engineering), U.S. Department of Energy (engineering and sciences), Science and Engineering Alliance, NASA (space radiation on material systems and devices), Sandia National Laboratories (engineering and chemistry), Lawrence Livermore National Laboratory (engineering and sciences).

**Computer facilities:** 3,500 computers available on campus for general student use. A campuswide network can be accessed from student residence rooms and from off campus. Online class registration is available.
Website: http://www.pvamu.edu/

**General Application Contact:** Pauline Walker, Office of Graduate Admissions, 936-261-3521, Fax: 936-261-3529, E-mail: gradadmissions@pvamu.edu.

**GRADUATE UNITS**

**College of Agriculture and Human Sciences** Students: 24 full-time (23 women), 19 part-time (17 women); includes 38 minority (35 Black or African American, non-Hispanic/Latino; 3 Hispanic/Latino), 3 international. Average age 30. 23 applicants, 83% accepted, 14 enrolled. *Faculty:* 7 full-time (4 women). Expenses: Contact institution. *Financial support:* Research assistantships, health care benefits, and unspecified assistantships available. Financial award application deadline: 4/1; financial award applicants required to submit FAFSA. In 2019, 19 master's awarded. *Program availability:* Part-time, evening/weekend. *Application deadline:* For fall admission, 5/1 priority date for domestic and international students; for spring admission, 10/11 priority date for domestic students, 9/1 priority date for international students; for summer admission, 3/1 priority date for domestic students, 2/1 priority date for international students. Applications are processed on a rolling basis. *Application fee:* $50. Electronic applications accepted. *Application Contact:* Pauline Walker, Administrative Assistant II, 936-261-3521, Fax: 936-261-3529, E-mail: gradadmissions@pvamu.edu. *Dean and Director of Land-Grant Programs*, Dr. Gerard D'Souza, 936-261-2212, E-mail: gedsouza@pvamu.edu.

**College of Arts and Sciences** Students: 31 full-time (23 women), 7 part-time (all women); includes 33 minority (31 Black or African American, non-Hispanic/Latino; 1 Hispanic/Latino; 1 Two or more races, non-Hispanic/Latino), 2 international. Average age 31. 27 applicants, 85% accepted, 12 enrolled. *Faculty:* 8 full-time (2 women). Expenses: Contact institution. *Financial support:* Research assistantships, teaching assistantships, career-related internships or fieldwork, Federal Work-Study, institutionally sponsored loans, and tuition waivers (full and partial) available. Support available to part-time students. Financial award application deadline: 4/1; financial award applicants required to submit FAFSA. In 2019, 18 master's awarded. *Program availability:* Part-time, evening/weekend. *Application deadline:* For fall admission, 5/1 priority date for domestic and international students; for spring admission, 10/11 priority date for domestic students, 9/1 priority date for international students; for summer admission, 3/1 priority date for domestic students, 2/1 priority date for international students. Applications are processed on a rolling basis. *Application fee:* $50. Electronic applications accepted. *Application Contact:* Pauline Walker, Administrative Assistant II, Research and Graduate Studies, 936-261-3521, Fax: 936-261-3529, E-mail: gradadmissions@pvamu.edu. *Dean*, Dr. Danny R. Kelley, 936-261-3180, Fax: 936-261-3188, E-mail: drkelley@pvamu.edu.

***Division of Social Work, Behavioral and Political Sciences*** Students: 15 full-time (12 women), 6 part-time (all women); includes 19 minority (all Black or African American, non-Hispanic/Latino), 1 international. Average age 33. 13 applicants, 85% accepted, 10 enrolled. *Faculty:* 3 full-time (1 woman). Expenses: Contact institution. *Financial support:* Application deadline: 4/1; applicants required to submit FAFSA. In 2019, 12 master's awarded. *Program availability:* Part-time, evening/weekend. *Application deadline:* For fall admission, 5/1 priority date for domestic and international students; for spring admission, 10/1 priority date for domestic students, 9/1 priority date for international students; for summer admission, 3/1 priority date for domestic students, 2/1 priority date for international students. Applications are processed on a rolling basis. *Application fee:* $50. Electronic applications accepted. *Application Contact:* Pauline Walker, Administrative Assistant II, Research and Graduate Studies, 936-261-3521, Fax: 936-261-3529, E-mail: gradadmissions@pvamu.edu. *Division Head*, Dr. Walle Engedayehu, 936-261-3202, Fax: 936-261-3229, E-mail: waengedayehu@pvamu.edu.

**College of Business** Students: 59 full-time (40 women), 128 part-time (83 women); includes 170 minority (142 Black or African American, non-Hispanic/Latino; 1 American Indian or Alaska Native, non-Hispanic/Latino; 11 Asian, non-Hispanic/Latino; 13 Hispanic/Latino; 1 Native Hawaiian or other Pacific Islander, non-Hispanic/Latino; 2 Two or more races, non-Hispanic/Latino), 4 international. Average age 30. 97 applicants, 92% accepted, 56 enrolled. *Faculty:* 16 full-time (3 women), 1 part-time/adjunct (0 women). Expenses: Contact institution. *Financial support:* Application deadline: 4/1; applicants required to submit FAFSA. In 2019, 84 master's awarded. *Program availability:* Part-time, evening/weekend. *Application deadline:* For fall admission, 5/1 for domestic students, 5/1 priority date for international students; for spring admission, 10/1 for domestic students, 9/1 priority date for international students; for summer admission, 3/1 for domestic students, 2/1 for international students. Applications are processed on a rolling basis. *Application fee:* $50. Electronic applications accepted. *Application Contact:* Gabriel Crosby, Director, Graduate Programs in Business, 936-261-9217, Fax: 936-261-9232, E-mail: mba@pvamu.edu. *Dean*, Dr. Munir Quddus, 936-261-9200, Fax: 936-261-9241, E-mail: cob@pvamu.edu.

**College of Education** Students: 63 full-time (45 women), 135 part-time (102 women); includes 189 minority (175 Black or African American, non-Hispanic/Latino; 2 Asian, non-Hispanic/Latino; 12 Hispanic/Latino), 6 international. Average age 36. 83 applicants, 81% accepted, 50 enrolled. *Faculty:* 17 full-time (7 women), 2 part-time/adjunct (1 woman). Expenses: Contact institution. *Financial support:* Career-related internships or fieldwork, institutionally sponsored loans, scholarships/grants, and unspecified assistantships available. Support available to part-time students. Financial award application deadline: 4/1; financial award applicants required to submit FAFSA. In 2019, 98 master's, 11 doctorates awarded. *Program availability:* Part-time, evening/weekend, blended/hybrid learning. *Application deadline:* For fall admission, 5/1 priority date for domestic and international students; for spring admission, 10/1 priority date for domestic students, 9/1 priority date for international students; for summer admission, 3/1 priority date for domestic students, 2/1 priority date for international students. Applications are processed on a rolling basis. *Application fee:* $50. Electronic applications accepted. *Application Contact:* Pauline Walker, Administrative Assistant II, Research and Graduate Studies, 936-261-3521, Fax: 936-261-3529, E-mail: gradadmissions@pvamu.edu. *Dean*, Dr. Michael L McFrazier, 936-261-3600 Ext. 2102, Fax: 936-261-3621, E-mail: mlmcFrazier@pvamu.edu.

**College of Engineering** Students: 121 full-time (38 women), 55 part-time (14 women); includes 82 minority (61 Black or African American, non-Hispanic/Latino; 14 Asian, non-Hispanic/Latino; 7 Hispanic/Latino), 77 international. Average age 32. 139 applicants, 84% accepted, 40 enrolled. *Faculty:* 30 full-time (8 women), 1 part-time/adjunct (0 women). Expenses: Contact institution. *Financial support:* In 2019–20, 64 students received support, including 64 research assistantships (averaging $14,400 per year), 8 teaching assistantships (averaging $14,400 per year); career-related internships or fieldwork, institutionally sponsored loans, scholarships/grants, health care benefits, tuition waivers (full), and unspecified assistantships also available. Financial award application deadline: 4/1; financial award applicants required to submit FAFSA. In 2019, 78 master's, 2 doctorates awarded. *Program availability:* Part-time, evening/weekend. *Application deadline:* For fall admission, 5/1 priority date for domestic and international students; for spring admission, 10/1 priority date for domestic students, 9/1 priority date for international students; for summer admission, 3/1 priority date for domestic students, 2/1 priority date for international students. Applications are processed on a rolling basis. *Application fee:* $50. Electronic applications accepted. *Application Contact:* Pauline Walker, Administrative Assistant II, Research and Graduate Studies, 936-261-3521, Fax: 936-261-3529, E-mail: gradadmissions@pvamu.edu. *Dean*, Dr. Pamela H Obiomon, 936-261-9890, Fax: 936-261-9868, E-mail: phobiomon@pvamu.edu.

**College of Juvenile Justice and Psychology** Students: 19 full-time (13 women), 35 part-time (26 women); includes 45 minority (44 Black or African American, non-Hispanic/Latino; 1 Hispanic/Latino), 7 international. Average age 31. 24 applicants, 79% accepted, 19 enrolled. *Faculty:* 11 full-time (5 women), 3 part-time/adjunct (all women). Expenses: Contact institution. *Financial support:* In 2019–20, 26 students received support, including 24 research assistantships with full tuition reimbursements available (averaging $24,000 per year), 8 teaching assistantships with full tuition reimbursements available (averaging $18,000 per year); career-related internships or fieldwork, institutionally sponsored loans, scholarships/grants, health care benefits, tuition waivers (full), and unspecified assistantships also available. Support available to part-time students. Financial award application deadline: 4/1; financial award applicants required to submit FAFSA. In 2019, 6 master's, 4 doctorates awarded. *Program availability:* Part-time, evening/weekend, online only, 100% online, Master's in Juvenile Justice. *Application deadline:* For fall admission, 5/1 priority date for domestic and international students; for spring admission, 10/1 priority date for domestic students, 9/1 priority date for international students; for summer admission, 3/1 priority date for domestic students, 2/1 priority date for international students. Applications are processed on a rolling basis. *Application fee:* $50. Electronic applications accepted. *Application Contact:* Pauline Walker, Executive Secretary, Graduate Program, 936-261-3521, Fax: 936-261-3529, E-mail: gradadmissions@pvamu.edu. *Interim Dean*, Dr. Camille Gibson, 936-261-5265 Ext. 5265, Fax: 936-261-5253, E-mail: cbgibson@pvamu.edu.

**College of Nursing** Students: 39 full-time (30 women), 49 part-time (45 women); includes 82 minority (63 Black or African American, non-Hispanic/Latino; 13 Asian, non-Hispanic/Latino; 6 Hispanic/Latino). Average age 37. 23 applicants, 91% accepted, 18 enrolled. *Faculty:* 8 full-time (7 women), 3 part-time/adjunct (2 women). Expenses: Contact institution. *Financial support:* Career-related internships or fieldwork, Federal Work-Study, institutionally sponsored loans, scholarships/grants, and traineeships available. Support available to part-time students. Financial award application deadline: 4/1; financial award applicants required to submit FAFSA. In 2019, 41 master's, 4 doctorates awarded. *Program availability:* Part-time, evening/weekend. *Application deadline:* For fall admission, 5/1 priority date for domestic and international students; for spring admission, 10/1 priority date for domestic students, 9/1 priority date for international students; for summer admission, 3/1 priority date for domestic students, 2/1 priority date for international students. Applications are processed on a rolling basis. *Application fee:* $50. Electronic applications accepted. *Application Contact:* Dr. Forest Smith, Director of Student Services and Admissions, 713-797-7031, Fax: 713-797-7012, E-mail: fdsmith@pvamu.edu. *Dean*, Dr. Betty N. Adams, 713-797-7009, Fax: 713-797-7013, E-mail: bnadams@pvamu.edu.

**School of Architecture** Students: 30 full-time (15 women), 17 part-time (8 women); includes 39 minority (31 Black or African American, non-Hispanic/Latino; 1 Asian, non-Hispanic/Latino; 7 Hispanic/Latino), 4 international. Average age 31. 21 applicants, 95% accepted, 15 enrolled. *Faculty:* 6 full-time (1 woman), 1 (woman) part-time/adjunct. Expenses: Contact institution. *Financial support:* In 2019–20, 10 students received support, including 5 research assistantships (averaging $14,400 per year); career-related internships or fieldwork, institutionally sponsored loans, scholarships/grants, unspecified assistantships, and out of state waiver- $1000 each also available. Support available to part-time students. Financial award application deadline: 4/1; financial award applicants required to submit FAFSA. In 2019, 29 master's awarded. *Program availability:* Part-time, evening/weekend. *Application deadline:* For fall admission, 5/1 priority date for domestic and international students; for spring admission, 10/1 priority date for domestic students, 9/1 priority date for international students; for summer admission, 3/1 priority date for domestic students, 2/1 priority date for international students. Applications are processed on a rolling basis. *Application fee:* $50. Electronic applications accepted. *Application Contact:* Pauline Walker, Administrative Assistant II, Research and Graduate Studies, 936-261-3521, Fax: 936-261-3529, E-mail: pmwalker@pvamu.edu. *Dean*, Dr. Ikhlas Sabouni, 936-261-9800, Fax: 936-261-2350, E-mail: isabouni@pvamu.edu.

## PRATT INSTITUTE, Brooklyn, NY 11205-3899

**General Information** Independent, coed, comprehensive institution. *Enrollment:* 4,875 graduate, professional, and undergraduate students; 1,199 full-time matriculated graduate/professional students (876 women), 175 part-time matriculated graduate/professional students (138 women). *Enrollment by degree level:* 1,372 master's, 2 other advanced degrees. *Graduate faculty:* 86 full-time (50 women), 543 part-time/adjunct (280 women). *Tuition:* Full-time $33,246; part-time $1847 per credit. *Required fees:* $1980. *Graduate housing:* Room and/or apartments available on a first-come, first-served basis to single students; on-campus housing not available to married students. Typical cost: $22,150 per year ($26,022 including board). Housing application deadline: 5/1. *Student services:* Campus employment opportunities, campus safety program, career counseling, exercise/wellness program, free psychological counseling, grant writing training, international student services, low-cost health insurance, multicultural affairs office, services for students with disabilities, teacher training, writing training. *Library facilities:* Pratt Institute Library. *Research affiliation:* The Procter & Gamble Company (product design), General Motors (transportation), Ford Motor Company (transportation).

**Computer facilities:** A campuswide network can be accessed from student residence rooms and from off campus. Online class registration is available.
Website: http://www.pratt.edu/

**General Application Contact:** Natalie Capannelli, Director of Graduate Admissions, 718-636-3551, Fax: 718-636-3670, E-mail: ncapanne@pratt.edu.

**GRADUATE UNITS**

**School of Architecture** Students: 293 full-time (161 women), 29 part-time (18 women); includes 70 minority (13 Black or African American, non-Hispanic/Latino; 19 Asian, non-Hispanic/Latino; 31 Hispanic/Latino; 7 Two or more races, non-Hispanic/Latino), 154 international. Average age 26. 823 applicants, 86% accepted, 121 enrolled. *Faculty:* 10 full-time (4 women), 232 part-time/adjunct (71 women). Expenses: Contact institution. *Financial support:* Career-related internships or fieldwork, Federal Work-Study, institutionally sponsored loans, scholarships/grants, health care benefits, and unspecified assistantships available. Support available to part-time students. Financial award application deadline: 2/1; financial award applicants required to submit FAFSA. In 2019, 156 master's awarded. *Application deadline:* For fall admission, 1/5 for domestic and international students; for spring admission, 10/1 for domestic and international students. *Application fee:* $50 ($90 for international students). Electronic applications accepted. *Application Contact:* Natalie Capannelli, Director of Graduate Admissions, 718-636-3551, Fax: 718-399-4242, E-mail: ncapanne@pratt.edu. *Dean*, Dr. Harriet Harriss, 718-399-4304, E-mail: hharriss@pratt.edu.

**School of Art** Students: 284 full-time (229 women), 88 part-time (75 women); includes 93 minority (24 Black or African American, non-Hispanic/Latino; 18 Asian, non-Hispanic/Latino; 39 Hispanic/Latino; 12 Two or more races, non-Hispanic/Latino), 163 international. Average age 27. 1,001 applicants, 52% accepted, 169 enrolled. *Faculty:* 27 full-time (15 women), 11 part-time/adjunct (5 women). Expenses: Contact institution. *Financial support:* Career-related internships or fieldwork, Federal Work-Study, institutionally sponsored loans, scholarships/grants, health care benefits, and unspecified assistantships available. Support available to part-time students. Financial award application deadline: 2/1; financial award applicants required to submit FAFSA. In 2019, 150 master's, 2 other advanced degrees awarded. *Program availability:* Part-time. *Application deadline:* For fall admission, 1/5 for domestic and international students; for spring admission, 10/1 for domestic and international students. *Application fee:* $50 ($90 for international students). Electronic applications accepted. *Application Contact:* Natalie Capannelli, Director of Graduate Admissions, 718-636-3551, Fax: 718-399-4242, E-mail: ncapanne@pratt.edu. *Acting Dean*, Jorge Oliver, 718-636-3619, E-mail: joliver6@pratt.edu.

**School of Design** Students: 405 full-time (310 women), 12 part-time (7 women); includes 42 minority (5 Black or African American, non-Hispanic/Latino; 18 Asian, non-

Hispanic/Latino; 12 Hispanic/Latino; 1 Native Hawaiian or other Pacific Islander, non-Hispanic/Latino; 6 Two or more races, non-Hispanic/Latino), 321 international. Average age 24. 987 applicants, 52% accepted, 194 enrolled. *Faculty:* 17 full-time (8 women), 248 part-time/adjunct (111 women). Expenses: Contact institution. *Financial support:* Career-related internships or fieldwork, Federal Work-Study, institutionally sponsored loans, scholarships/grants, health care benefits, and unspecified assistantships available. Support available to part-time students. Financial award application deadline: 2/1; financial award applicants required to submit FAFSA. In 2019, 151 master's awarded. *Program availability:* Part-time. *Application deadline:* For fall admission, 1/5 for domestic and international students; for spring admission, 10/1 for domestic and international students. *Application fee:* $50 ($90 for international students). Electronic applications accepted. *Application Contact:* Natalie Capannelli, Director of Graduate Admissions, 718-636-3551, Fax: 718-636-3670, E-mail: ncapanne@pratt.edu. *Dean, School of Design*, Anita Cooney, 718-687-5744, Fax: 718-636-3410, E-mail: acooney@pratt.edu.

**School of Information** Students: 173 full-time (141 women), 37 part-time (32 women); includes 53 minority (9 Black or African American, non-Hispanic/Latino; 1 American Indian or Alaska Native, non-Hispanic/Latino; 19 Asian, non-Hispanic/Latino; 16 Hispanic/Latino; 8 Two or more races, non-Hispanic/Latino), 66 international. Average age 28. 460 applicants, 62% accepted, 76 enrolled. *Faculty:* 10 full-time (8 women), 21 part-time/adjunct (11 women). Expenses: Contact institution. *Financial support:* Career-related internships or fieldwork, Federal Work-Study, institutionally sponsored loans, scholarships/grants, health care benefits, and unspecified assistantships available. Support available to part-time students. Financial award application deadline: 2/1; financial award applicants required to submit FAFSA. In 2019, 82 master's, 1 other advanced degree awarded. *Program availability:* Part-time. *Application deadline:* For fall admission, 1/5 for domestic and international students; for spring admission, 10/1 for domestic and international students. Applications are processed on a rolling basis. *Application fee:* $50 ($90 for international students). Electronic applications accepted. *Application Contact:* Natalie Capannelli, Director of Graduate Admissions, 718-636-3551, Fax: 718-399-4242, E-mail: ncapanne@pratt.edu. *Dean*, Anthony Cocciolo, 212-647-7702, Fax: 212-367-2492, E-mail: acocciol@pratt.edu.

**School of Liberal Arts and Sciences** Students: 44 full-time (35 women), 9 part-time (6 women); includes 20 minority (7 Black or African American, non-Hispanic/Latino; 1 Asian, non-Hispanic/Latino; 8 Hispanic/Latino; 4 Two or more races, non-Hispanic/Latino), 10 international. Average age 27. 164 applicants, 59% accepted, 16 enrolled. *Faculty:* 22 full-time (15 women), 188 part-time/adjunct (102 women). Expenses: Contact institution. *Financial support:* Career-related internships or fieldwork, Federal Work-Study, institutionally sponsored loans, scholarships/grants, health care benefits, and unspecified assistantships available. Support available to part-time students. Financial award application deadline: 2/1; financial award applicants required to submit FAFSA. In 2019, 36 master's awarded. *Application deadline:* For fall admission, 1/5 for domestic and international students; for spring admission, 10/1 for domestic and international students. *Application fee:* $50 ($90 for international students). Electronic applications accepted. *Application Contact:* Natalie Capannelli, Director of Graduate Admissions, 718-636-3551, Fax: 718-399-4242, E-mail: ncapanne@pratt.edu. *Interim Dean*, Dr. Helio Takai, 718-636-3570, Fax: 718-399-4586, E-mail: htakai@pratt.edu.

## PRESBYTERIAN COLLEGE, Clinton, SC 29325

**General Information** Independent-religious, coed, comprehensive institution. *Graduate housing:* On-campus housing not available.

**GRADUATE UNITS**

**Presbyterian College School of Pharmacy (PCSP)** Electronic applications accepted.

## PRESCOTT COLLEGE, Prescott, AZ 86301

**General Information** Independent, coed, comprehensive institution. *Graduate housing:* Room and/or apartments available on a first-come, first-served basis to single students; on-campus housing not available to married students. Housing application deadline: 5/1. *Research affiliation:* Marshall Foundation (youth and wilderness), U.S. Department of Agriculture (USDA) (agro-ecology), National Park Service (forest health), Packard Foundation (Kino Bay research).

**GRADUATE UNITS**

**Graduate Programs** *Program availability:* Part-time, online learning. Electronic applications accepted.

## PRESIDIO GRADUATE SCHOOL, San Francisco, CA 94129

**General Information** Independent, coed, graduate-only institution.

**GRADUATE UNITS**

**Graduate Programs - San Francisco**

**MBA Programs - Seattle** *Program availability:* Part-time, evening/weekend, blended/hybrid learning. Electronic applications accepted.

## PRINCETON THEOLOGICAL SEMINARY, Princeton, NJ 08542-0803

**General Information** Independent-religious, coed, graduate-only institution. *Graduate housing:* Rooms and/or apartments available on a first-come, first-served basis to single and married students. *Research affiliation:* Center of Theological Inquiry.

**GRADUATE UNITS**

**Graduate and Professional Programs** *Program availability:* Part-time. Electronic applications accepted.

## PRINCETON UNIVERSITY, Princeton, NJ 08544-1019

**General Information** Independent, coed, university. CGS member. *Graduate housing:* Rooms and/or apartments available to single and married students. Housing application deadline: 4/15. *Research affiliation:* Institute for Advanced Study (physics and mathematics), Brookhaven National Laboratory (experimental physics), Textile Research Institute (polymer research), National Oceanic and Atmospheric Administration (NOAA)–GFD Laboratory (weather prediction).

**GRADUATE UNITS**

**Graduate School** Electronic applications accepted.

***Bendheim Center for Finance*** Electronic applications accepted.

***School of Architecture*** Electronic applications accepted.

***School of Engineering and Applied Science*** Electronic applications accepted.

***Woodrow Wilson School of Public and International Affairs*** Electronic applications accepted.

**Princeton Institute for the Science and Technology of Materials (PRISM)**

**Princeton Neuroscience Institute** Electronic applications accepted.

## PROVIDENCE COLLEGE, Providence, RI 02918

**General Information** Independent-religious, coed, comprehensive institution. *Graduate housing:* On-campus housing not available.

**GRADUATE UNITS**

**Department of History** *Program availability:* Part-time, evening/weekend.

**Department of Theology** *Program availability:* Part-time, evening/weekend.

**Program in Counseling** *Program availability:* Part-time, evening/weekend.

**Program in Literacy** *Program availability:* Part-time, evening/weekend.

**Program in Special Education** *Program availability:* Part-time, evening/weekend.

**Program in Teaching Mathematics** *Program availability:* Part-time, evening/weekend.

**Program in Urban Teaching** *Program availability:* Part-time, evening/weekend.

**Programs in Administration** *Program availability:* Part-time, evening/weekend.

**Providence Alliance for Catholic Teachers (PACT) Program**

**School of Business** *Program availability:* Part-time, evening/weekend.

## PROVIDENCE UNIVERSITY COLLEGE & THEOLOGICAL SEMINARY, Otterburne, MB R0A 1G0, Canada

**General Information** Independent-religious, coed, comprehensive institution. *Graduate housing:* Rooms and/or apartments guaranteed to single students and available on a first-come, first-served basis to married students. Housing application deadline: 8/15.

**GRADUATE UNITS**

**Theological Seminary** *Program availability:* Part-time.

## PURCHASE COLLEGE, STATE UNIVERSITY OF NEW YORK, Purchase, NY 10577-1400

**General Information** State-supported, coed, comprehensive institution. *Enrollment:* 4,187 graduate, professional, and undergraduate students; 97 full-time matriculated graduate/professional students (54 women), 9 part-time matriculated graduate/professional students (3 women). *Enrollment by degree level:* 106 master's. *Tuition, area resident:* Full-time $11,310. Tuition, state resident: full-time $11,310. Tuition, nonresident: full-time $23,100. *Required fees:* $1883. *Graduate housing:* Room and/or apartments available on a first-come, first-served basis to single students; on-campus housing not available to married students. Typical cost: $9098 per year. Room charges vary according to board plan and housing facility selected. Housing application deadline: 5/1. *Student services:* Campus employment opportunities, campus safety program, career counseling, child daycare facilities, exercise/wellness program, free psychological counseling, international student services, low-cost health insurance, multicultural affairs office, services for students with disabilities. *Library facilities:* Purchase College Library plus 1 other. *Collection:* Books: 229,091 (physical), 117,469 (digital/electronic); Serial titles: 1,585 (physical), 39 (digital/electronic); Databases: 171. Weekly public service hours: 109; students can reserve study rooms.

**Computer facilities:** 600 computers available on campus for general student use. A campuswide network can be accessed. Online class registration, CNC-routers, 3D printers, laser cutters, vinyl printers, virtual reality lab, fabrication lab, non-liner edit labs for film, music digital audio workstations, 24 and 48 inch plotters for high-quality photographic output, digital embroidery machine are available.
Website: http://www.purchase.edu/

**General Application Contact:** Bea Martin-Ruiz, Admissions Counselor, 914-250-6704, Fax: 914-251-6314, E-mail: admissn@purchase.edu.

**GRADUATE UNITS**

**Conservatory of Music** Students: 53 full-time (22 women), 2 part-time (1 woman); includes 13 minority (2 Black or African American, non-Hispanic/Latino; 5 Asian, non-Hispanic/Latino; 5 Hispanic/Latino; 1 Two or more races, non-Hispanic/Latino), 19 international. Average age 28. 120 applicants, 57% accepted, 21 enrolled. Expenses: Contact institution. *Financial support:* Fellowships, teaching assistantships, career-related internships or fieldwork, Federal Work-Study, scholarships/grants, and tuition waivers (partial) available. Support available to part-time students. Financial award application deadline: 3/15; financial award applicants required to submit FAFSA. *Application deadline:* For fall admission, 1/15 for domestic students; for spring admission, 10/15 for domestic students. Applications are processed on a rolling basis. *Application fee:* $142. Electronic applications accepted. *Application Contact:* Beatriz Martin-Ruiz, Assistant Director of Admissions, 914-251-6304, Fax: 914-251-6316, E-mail: admissn@purchase.edu. *Director*, Jennifer Undercofler, 914-251-6700, Fax: 914-251-6739, E-mail: jennifer.undercofler@purchase.edu.

**School of Art and Design** Students: 17 full-time (12 women); includes 3 minority (2 Asian, non-Hispanic/Latino; 1 Hispanic/Latino), 4 international. Average age 31. 46 applicants, 41% accepted, 8 enrolled. Expenses: Contact institution. *Financial support:* Fellowships, teaching assistantships, Federal Work-Study, scholarships/grants, and tuition waivers (partial) available. Support available to part-time students. Financial award application deadline: 3/15; financial award applicants required to submit FAFSA. *Application deadline:* For fall admission, 2/15 for domestic students. Applications are processed on a rolling basis. *Application fee:* $85. Electronic applications accepted. *Application Contact:* Beatriz Martin-Ruiz, Assistant Director of Admissions, 914-251-6304, Fax: 914-251-6314, E-mail: admissn@purchase.edu. *Director*, Christopher Robbins, 914-251-6750, Fax: 914-251-6793, E-mail: christopher.robbins@purchase.edu.

**School of Humanities** Students: 7 full-time (6 women), 4 part-time (2 women); includes 5 minority (1 Black or African American, non-Hispanic/Latino; 3 Hispanic/Latino; 1 Two or more races, non-Hispanic/Latino). Average age 36. 16 applicants, 88% accepted, 5 enrolled. Expenses: Contact institution. *Financial support:* Fellowships, Federal Work-Study, scholarships/grants, and tuition waivers (partial) available. Support available to part-time students. Financial award application deadline: 3/15; financial award applicants required to submit FAFSA. *Application deadline:* For fall admission, 3/1 for domestic students. *Application fee:* $85. Electronic applications accepted. *Application Contact:* Beatriz Martin-Ruiz, Assistant Director of Admissions, 914-251-6304, Fax: 914-251-6314, E-mail: admissn@purchase.edu. *Chair*, Ross Daly, 914-251-6550.

**School of the Arts** Students: 13 full-time (10 women), 3 part-time; includes 3 minority (1 Black or African American, non-Hispanic/Latino; 2 Hispanic/Latino), 3 international. Average age 29. 18 applicants, 94% accepted, 11 enrolled. Expenses: Contact institution. *Program availability:* Part-time. *Application deadline:* For fall admission, 3/1 for domestic students. Applications are processed on a rolling basis. *Application fee:* $85. Electronic applications accepted. *Application Contact:* Beatriz Martin-Ruiz, 914-251-6304, Fax: 914-251-6314, E-mail: admissn@purchase.edu.

## PURDUE UNIVERSITY, West Lafayette, IN 47907

**General Information** State-supported, coed, university. CGS member. *Enrollment:* 44,551 graduate, professional, and undergraduate students; 6,042 full-time matriculated graduate/professional students (2,351 women), 3,461 part-time matriculated graduate/professional students (1,558 women). *Enrollment by degree level:* 4,596 master's, 4,878 doctoral, 163 other advanced degrees. *Graduate faculty:* 2,003 full-time (653 women), 280 part-time/adjunct (102 women). *Graduate housing:* Rooms and/or apartments available on a first-come, first-served basis to single and married students. Housing application deadline: 3/1. *Student services:* Campus employment opportunities, campus safety program, career counseling, child daycare facilities, exercise/wellness program, free psychological counseling, grant writing training, international student services, low-cost health insurance, multicultural affairs office, services for students with disabilities, teacher training, writing training. *Library facilities:* Purdue University Libraries plus 9 others. *Collection:* Books: 946,376 (physical), 2.5 million (digital/electronic); Serial titles: 44,788 (physical), 136,167 (digital/electronic); Databases: 580. Weekly public service hours: 168; study areas open 24 hours, 5–7 days a week; students can reserve study rooms.

**Computer facilities:** Computer purchase and lease plans are available. 5,237 computers available on campus for general student use. A campuswide network can be accessed. Online class registration is available.
Website: http://www.purdue.edu/

**General Application Contact:** Dyane Roesel, Graduate School Admissions, 765-494-2606, Fax: 765-494-0136, E-mail: gradinfo@purdue.edu.

**GRADUATE UNITS**

**College of Engineering** Students: 3,628. *Faculty:* 513. Expenses: Contact institution. *Financial support:* Fellowships with full and partial tuition reimbursements, research assistantships with full and partial tuition reimbursements, teaching assistantships with full and partial tuition reimbursements, career-related internships or fieldwork, scholarships/grants, health care benefits, and unspecified assistantships available. *Program availability:* Part-time, 100% online, blended/hybrid learning. *Application deadline:* Applications are processed on a rolling basis. *Application fee:* $60 ($75 for international students). Electronic applications accepted. *Application Contact:* Dr. Jacqueline McDermott, Asst Director of Graduate Recruitment and Retention, E-mail: engrgrad@purdue.edu. *Associate Dean for Graduate Education,* Dr. Dana Weinstein, E-mail: engrgrad@purdue.edu.

***Davidson School of Chemical Engineering*** Students: 207. *Faculty:* 29. Expenses: Contact institution. *Financial support:* Fellowships with full and partial tuition reimbursements, research assistantships with full and partial tuition reimbursements, teaching assistantships with full and partial tuition reimbursements, career-related internships or fieldwork, scholarships/grants, health care benefits, and unspecified assistantships available. *Application deadline:* For fall admission, 12/15 for domestic and international students. Applications are processed on a rolling basis. *Application fee:* $60 ($75 for international students). Electronic applications accepted. *Application Contact:* Beverly Johnson, Graduate Program Administrator, 765-494-4057, E-mail: bevjohnson@purdue.edu. *Head of Chemical Engineering/Professor,* Dr. Kim Sangtae, 765-494-3492, E-mail: kim55@purdue.edu.

***Division of Environmental and Ecological Engineering*** Students: 54. *Faculty:* 1. Expenses: Contact institution. *Financial support:* Fellowships with full and partial tuition reimbursements, research assistantships with full and partial tuition reimbursements, teaching assistantships with full and partial tuition reimbursements, career-related internships or fieldwork, scholarships/grants, health care benefits, and unspecified assistantships available. *Application deadline:* For fall admission, 12/15 for domestic and international students; for spring admission, 9/15 for domestic and international students. *Application fee:* $60 ($75 for international students). *Application Contact:* Cresta Cates, Graduate Administrative Assistant, 765-496-0545, E-mail: eeegrad@purdue.edu. *Professor/Head of Environmental and Ecological Engineering,* Dr. John W. Sutherland, 765-496-9697, E-mail: jwsuther@purdue.edu.

***Lyles School of Civil Engineering*** Students: 346. *Faculty:* 59. Expenses: Contact institution. *Financial support:* Fellowships with full and partial tuition reimbursements, research assistantships with full and partial tuition reimbursements, teaching assistantships with full and partial tuition reimbursements, career-related internships or fieldwork, scholarships/grants, health care benefits, and unspecified assistantships available. *Program availability:* Part-time. *Application deadline:* For fall admission, 5/15 priority date for domestic students, 4/15 priority date for international students; for spring admission, 9/15 for domestic and international students. Applications are processed on a rolling basis. *Application fee:* $60 ($75 for international students). Electronic applications accepted. *Application Contact:* Jenny Ricksy, Graduate Administrator, 765-494-2436, E-mail: jricksy@purdue.edu. *Head/Professor,* Dr. Rao Govindaraju, 765-494-2256, E-mail: govind@purdue.edu.

***School of Aeronautics and Astronautics*** Students: 550. *Faculty:* 46. Expenses: Contact institution. *Financial support:* Fellowships with full and partial tuition reimbursements, research assistantships with full and partial tuition reimbursements, teaching assistantships with full and partial tuition reimbursements, career-related internships or fieldwork, scholarships/grants, health care benefits, and unspecified assistantships available. *Program availability:* Part-time, 100% online. *Application deadline:* For fall admission, 12/15 priority date for domestic and international students; for spring admission, 9/15 priority date for domestic and international students. Applications are processed on a rolling basis. *Application fee:* $60 ($75 for international students). Electronic applications accepted. *Application Contact:* Jon Mrozinski, Graduate Administrator, E-mail: jwmrozin@purdue.edu. *Department Head,* Dr. William Crossley, E-mail: crossley@purdue.edu.

***School of Agricultural and Biological Engineering*** Students: 191. *Faculty:* 39. Expenses: Contact institution. *Financial support:* Fellowships with full and partial tuition reimbursements, research assistantships with full and partial tuition reimbursements, teaching assistantships with full and partial tuition reimbursements, career-related internships or fieldwork, scholarships/grants, health care benefits, unspecified assistantships, and instructorships available. *Program availability:* Part-time. *Application deadline:* For fall admission, 12/1 for domestic and international students; for spring admission, 9/1 for domestic and international students. Applications are processed on a rolling basis. *Application fee:* $60 ($75 for international students). Electronic applications accepted. *Application Contact:* Becky Peer, Assistant to Department Head, 765-494-1181, E-mail: peerb@purdue.edu. *Interim Head,* Nathan Mosier, 765-496-2044, E-mail: mosiern@purdue.edu.

***School of Electrical and Computer Engineering*** Students: 668. *Faculty:* 98. Expenses: Contact institution. *Financial support:* Fellowships with full and partial tuition reimbursements, research assistantships with full and partial tuition reimbursements, teaching assistantships with full and partial tuition reimbursements, career-related internships or fieldwork, scholarships/grants, health care benefits, and unspecified assistantships available. *Program availability:* Part-time, online learning. *Application deadline:* For fall admission, 12/15 priority date for domestic and international students; for spring admission, 5/1 for domestic and international students. *Application fee:* $60 ($75 for international students). Electronic applications accepted. *Application Contact:* Debra Bowman, Graduate Admissions, 765-494-3392, E-mail: dbowman1@purdue.edu. *Department Head,* Dimitrios Peroulis, E-mail: dperouli@purdue.edu.

***School of Engineering Education*** Students: 61. *Faculty:* 26. Expenses: Contact institution. *Financial support:* Fellowships with full and partial tuition reimbursements, research assistantships with full and partial tuition reimbursements, teaching assistantships with full and partial tuition reimbursements, career-related internships or fieldwork, scholarships/grants, health care benefits, and unspecified assistantships available. *Application deadline:* For fall admission, 12/15 for domestic and international students; for spring admission, 9/15 for domestic and international students; for summer admission, 12/15 for domestic and international students. Applications are processed on a rolling basis. *Application fee:* $60 ($75 for international students). Electronic applications accepted. *Application Contact:* Loretta McKinniss, Graduate Administrator, 765-494-3331, E-mail: lmckinni@purdue.edu. *Head of the School of Engineering Education,* Dr. Donna Riley, E-mail: riley@purdue.edu.

***School of Industrial Engineering*** Students: 276. *Faculty:* 30. Expenses: Contact institution. *Financial support:* Fellowships with full and partial tuition reimbursements, research assistantships with full and partial tuition reimbursements, teaching assistantships with full and partial tuition reimbursements, scholarships/grants, health care benefits, and unspecified assistantships available. *Program availability:* Part-time, online learning. *Application deadline:* For fall admission, 1/5 for domestic and international students; for spring admission, 9/1 for domestic and international students. Applications are processed on a rolling basis. *Application fee:* $60 ($75 for international students). Electronic applications accepted. *Application Contact:* Anita Park, Graduate Administrator, 765-494-5434, E-mail: apark@purdue.edu. *Head/Professor of Industrial Engineering,* Dr. Abhijit Deshmukh, 765-496-6007, E-mail: abhi@purdue.edu.

***School of Materials Engineering*** Students: 177. *Faculty:* 40. Expenses: Contact institution. *Financial support:* Fellowships with full and partial tuition reimbursements, research assistantships with full and partial tuition reimbursements, teaching assistantships with full and partial tuition reimbursements, career-related internships or fieldwork, scholarships/grants, health care benefits, and unspecified assistantships available. *Program availability:* Part-time. *Application deadline:* For fall admission, 12/15 for domestic and international students; for spring admission, 10/15 for domestic and international students. Applications are processed on a rolling basis. *Application fee:* $60 ($75 for international students). Electronic applications accepted. *Application Contact:* Vicki Kline, 765-494-4103, E-mail: vicline@purdue.edu. *Head and Professor of Materials Engineering,* Dr. David Bahr, 765-494-4100, E-mail: dfbahr@purdue.edu.

***School of Mechanical Engineering*** Students: 624. *Faculty:* 84. Expenses: Contact institution. *Financial support:* Fellowships with full and partial tuition reimbursements, research assistantships with full and partial tuition reimbursements, teaching assistantships with full and partial tuition reimbursements, career-related internships or fieldwork, scholarships/grants, health care benefits, and unspecified assistantships available. *Program availability:* Part-time, online learning. *Application deadline:* For fall admission, 12/15 for domestic and international students; for spring admission, 9/15 for domestic and international students. Applications are processed on a rolling basis. *Application fee:* $60 ($75 for international students). Electronic applications accepted. *Application Contact:* Xiaomin Qian, Graduate Administrator, 765-494-0231, E-mail: xiaomin@purdue.edu. *Department Head,* Eckhard Groll, E-mail: groll@purdue.edu.

***School of Nuclear Engineering*** Students: 49. *Faculty:* 19. Expenses: Contact institution. *Financial support:* Fellowships with full and partial tuition reimbursements, research assistantships with full and partial tuition reimbursements, teaching assistantships with full and partial tuition reimbursements, career-related internships or fieldwork, scholarships/grants, and unspecified assistantships available. Support available to part-time students. *Program availability:* Part-time. *Application deadline:* For fall admission, 5/1 priority date for domestic students, 3/1 priority date for international students; for spring admission, 8/15 for domestic and international students. Applications are processed on a rolling basis. *Application fee:* $60 ($75 for international students). Electronic applications accepted. *Application Contact:* Teresa Luse, Graduate Administrator, E-mail: nuclss@purdue.edu. *Head of the School of Nuclear Engineering,* Dr. Seungjin Kim, 765-494-5742, E-mail: seungjin@purdue.edu.

**College of Pharmacy** Students: 732 full-time (464 women), 13 part-time (6 women); includes 192 minority (27 Black or African American, non-Hispanic/Latino; 3 American Indian or Alaska Native, non-Hispanic/Latino; 116 Asian, non-Hispanic/Latino; 26 Hispanic/Latino; 20 Two or more races, non-Hispanic/Latino), 93 international. Average age 23. 646 applicants, 34% accepted, 171 enrolled. *Faculty:* 65 full-time (28 women), 16 part-time/adjunct (7 women). Expenses: Contact institution. *Financial support:* Fellowships, research assistantships, teaching assistantships, career-related internships or fieldwork, Federal Work-Study, scholarships/grants, and traineeships available. Support available to part-time students. Financial award applicants required to submit FAFSA. In 2019, 4 master's, 19 doctorates, 147 other advanced degrees awarded. *Program availability:* Part-time. *Application deadline:* Applications are processed on a rolling basis. *Application fee:* $60 ($75 for international students). Electronic applications accepted. *Application Contact:* Danzhou Yang, Associate Dean for Research and Graduate Programs, 765-494-1362, E-mail: yangdz@purdue.edu. *Dean,* Eric L. Barker, 765-494-1368, E-mail: barkerel@purdue.edu.

**Graduate School** Students: 6,042 full-time (2,351 women), 3,461 part-time (1,558 women); includes 1,299 minority (279 Black or African American, non-Hispanic/Latino; 15 American Indian or Alaska Native, non-Hispanic/Latino; 456 Asian, non-Hispanic/Latino; 390 Hispanic/Latino; 6 Native Hawaiian or other Pacific Islander, non-Hispanic/Latino; 153 Two or more races, non-Hispanic/Latino), 4,302 international. Average age 29. 16,297 applicants, 35% accepted, 2,465 enrolled. *Faculty:* 1,938 full-time (625 women), 264 part-time/adjunct (95 women). Expenses: Contact institution. *Financial support:* Fellowships with tuition reimbursements, research assistantships with tuition reimbursements, teaching assistantships with tuition reimbursements, career-related internships or fieldwork, scholarships/grants, tuition waivers (full and partial), and instructorships available. Support available to part-time students. Financial award applicants required to submit FAFSA. In 2019, 2,283 master's, 719 doctorates, 216 other advanced degrees awarded. *Program availability:* Part-time, evening/weekend, online learning. *Application deadline:* Applications are processed on a rolling basis. *Application fee:* $60 ($75 for international students). Electronic applications accepted. *Application Contact:* Graduate School Admissions, 765-494-2600, Fax: 765-494-0136, E-mail: gradinfo@purdue.edu. *Dean,* Dr. Linda J. Mason, 765-494-2604, E-mail: lmason@purdue.edu.

***College of Agriculture*** Students: 598 full-time (276 women), 135 part-time (77 women); includes 82 minority (19 Black or African American, non-Hispanic/Latino; 3 American Indian or Alaska Native, non-Hispanic/Latino; 19 Asian, non-Hispanic/Latino; 25

Hispanic/Latino; 1 Native Hawaiian or other Pacific Islander, non-Hispanic/Latino; 15 Two or more races, non-Hispanic/Latino), 328 international. Average age 30. 674 applicants, 35% accepted, 186 enrolled. *Faculty:* 277 full-time (70 women), 49 part-time/adjunct (17 women). Expenses: Contact institution. *Financial support:* Fellowships with tuition reimbursements, research assistantships with tuition reimbursements, teaching assistantships with tuition reimbursements, career-related internships or fieldwork, and tuition waivers (partial) available. Support available to part-time students. Financial award applicants required to submit FAFSA. In 2019, 123 master's, 86 doctorates awarded. *Program availability:* Part-time. *Application deadline:* Applications are processed on a rolling basis. *Application fee:* $60 ($75 for international students). Electronic applications accepted. *Application Contact:* Graduate School Admissions, 765-494-2600, Fax: 765-494-0136, E-mail: gradinfo@purdue.edu. *Dean*, Karen Plaut, 765-494-8391, E-mail: kplaut@purdue.edu.

***College of Education*** Students: 157 full-time (117 women), 554 part-time (425 women); includes 123 minority (34 Black or African American, non-Hispanic/Latino; 1 American Indian or Alaska Native, non-Hispanic/Latino; 33 Asian, non-Hispanic/Latino; 40 Hispanic/Latino; 1 Native Hawaiian or other Pacific Islander, non-Hispanic/Latino; 14 Two or more races, non-Hispanic/Latino), 101 international. Average age 34. 403 applicants, 51% accepted, 182 enrolled. *Faculty:* 64 full-time (45 women), 8 part-time/adjunct (4 women). Expenses: Contact institution. *Financial support:* Fellowships with full tuition reimbursements, research assistantships with full tuition reimbursements, teaching assistantships with full tuition reimbursements, career-related internships or fieldwork, and tuition waivers (full) available. Support available to part-time students. Financial award application deadline: 3/1; financial award applicants required to submit FAFSA. In 2019, 267 master's, 33 doctorates, 17 other advanced degrees awarded. *Program availability:* Part-time, evening/weekend. *Application deadline:* For fall admission, 12/15 for domestic students, 3/1 for international students; for spring admission, 9/15 for domestic students, 8/1 for international students. *Application fee:* $60 ($75 for international students). Electronic applications accepted. *Application Contact:* Graduate School Admissions, 765-494-2600, Fax: 765-494-0136, E-mail: gradinfo@purdue.edu. *Dean*, Dr. Linda J. Mason, 765-494-0245, E-mail: lmason@purdue.edu.

***College of Health and Human Sciences*** Students: 446 full-time (355 women), 221 part-time (173 women); includes 122 minority (38 Black or African American, non-Hispanic/Latino; 2 American Indian or Alaska Native, non-Hispanic/Latino; 35 Asian, non-Hispanic/Latino; 27 Hispanic/Latino; 20 Two or more races, non-Hispanic/Latino), 122 international. Average age 29. 1,069 applicants, 36% accepted, 213 enrolled. *Faculty:* 216 full-time (132 women), 28 part-time/adjunct (19 women). Expenses: Contact institution. *Financial support:* Fellowships, research assistantships, teaching assistantships, and career-related internships or fieldwork available. Support available to part-time students. Financial award applicants required to submit FAFSA. In 2019, 128 master's, 53 doctorates, 17 other advanced degrees awarded. *Program availability:* Part-time. *Application deadline:* Applications are processed on a rolling basis. *Application fee:* $60 ($75 for international students). Electronic applications accepted. *Application Contact:* Graduate School Admissions, 765-494-2600, Fax: 765-494-0136, E-mail: gradinfo@purdue.edu. *Dean*, Dr. Marion K. Underwood, 765-494-8210.

***College of Liberal Arts*** Students: 401 full-time (243 women), 476 part-time (341 women); includes 177 minority (61 Black or African American, non-Hispanic/Latino; 1 American Indian or Alaska Native, non-Hispanic/Latino; 25 Asian, non-Hispanic/Latino; 69 Hispanic/Latino; 1 Native Hawaiian or other Pacific Islander, non-Hispanic/Latino; 20 Two or more races, non-Hispanic/Latino), 149 international. Average age 32. 957 applicants, 35% accepted, 215 enrolled. *Faculty:* 251 full-time (116 women), 23 part-time/adjunct (14 women). Expenses: Contact institution. *Financial support:* Fellowships, research assistantships, teaching assistantships, career-related internships or fieldwork, scholarships/grants, and tuition waivers (full) available. Support available to part-time students. Financial award applicants required to submit FAFSA. In 2019, 345 master's, 77 doctorates awarded. *Program availability:* Part-time, evening/weekend. *Application deadline:* Applications are processed on a rolling basis. *Application fee:* $60 ($75 for international students). Electronic applications accepted. *Application Contact:* Graduate School Admissions, 765-494-2600, Fax: 765-494-0136, E-mail: gradinfo@purdue.edu. *Dean*, David A. Reingold, 765-494-3664, E-mail: reingold@purdue.edu.

***College of Science*** Students: 1,137 full-time (354 women), 224 part-time (62 women); includes 172 minority (28 Black or African American, non-Hispanic/Latino; 2 American Indian or Alaska Native, non-Hispanic/Latino; 63 Asian, non-Hispanic/Latino; 64 Hispanic/Latino; 1 Native Hawaiian or other Pacific Islander, non-Hispanic/Latino; 14 Two or more races, non-Hispanic/Latino), 808 international. Average age 26. 4,119 applicants, 22% accepted, 312 enrolled. *Faculty:* 297 full-time (59 women), 40 part-time/adjunct (14 women). Expenses: Contact institution. *Financial support:* Fellowships with tuition reimbursements, research assistantships with tuition reimbursements, teaching assistantships with tuition reimbursements, career-related internships or fieldwork, and tuition waivers (partial) available. Support available to part-time students. Financial award applicants required to submit FAFSA. In 2019, 131 master's, 151 doctorates, 6 other advanced degrees awarded. *Program availability:* Part-time. *Application fee:* $60 ($75 for international students). Electronic applications accepted. *Application Contact:* Graduate School Admissions, 765-494-2600, Fax: 765-494-0136, E-mail: gradinfo@purdue.edu. *Dean*, Patrick Wolfe, 765-494-1730, E-mail: patrick@purdue.edu.

***Krannert School of Management*** Electronic applications accepted.

***Purdue Polytechnic Institute*** Students: 353 full-time (115 women), 373 part-time (106 women); includes 109 minority (27 Black or African American, non-Hispanic/Latino; 1 American Indian or Alaska Native, non-Hispanic/Latino; 39 Asian, non-Hispanic/Latino; 27 Hispanic/Latino; 2 Native Hawaiian or other Pacific Islander, non-Hispanic/Latino; 13 Two or more races, non-Hispanic/Latino), 314 international. Average age 30. 665 applicants, 53% accepted, 205 enrolled. *Faculty:* 183 full-time (40 women), 16 part-time/adjunct (2 women). Expenses: Contact institution. *Financial support:* In 2019–20, 37 teaching assistantships were awarded; fellowships also available. Support available to part-time students. Financial award applicants required to submit FAFSA. In 2019, 230 master's, 30 doctorates awarded. *Program availability:* Online learning. *Application deadline:* Applications are processed on a rolling basis. *Application fee:* $60 ($75 for international students). Electronic applications accepted. *Application Contact:* Graduate School Admissions, 765-494-2600, Fax: 765-494-0136, E-mail: gradinfo@purdue.edu. *Dean*, Dr. Gary R. Bertoline, 765-494-2552, E-mail: bertoline@purdue.edu.

**School of Veterinary Medicine** *Program availability:* Part-time, evening/weekend.

## PURDUE UNIVERSITY FORT WAYNE, Fort Wayne, IN 46805-1499

**General Information** State-supported, coed, comprehensive institution. *Graduate housing:* Room and/or apartments available on a first-come, first-served basis to single students; on-campus housing not available to married students. *Research affiliation:* Regenstrief Institute, Inc. (nursing), Earthwatch (biology), PHD, Inc. (engineering), Bendix Commercial Vehicle Systems, LLC (engineering, technology, and computer science), Northeast Indiana Fund (education and public policy), Fort Wayne Metals (geosciences).

**GRADUATE UNITS**

**College of Arts and Sciences** *Program availability:* Part-time, evening/weekend.

**College of Engineering, Technology, and Computer Science** *Program availability:* Part-time. Electronic applications accepted.

**College of Health and Human Services** *Program availability:* Part-time. Electronic applications accepted.

**College of Professional Studies** *Program availability:* Part-time.

***School of Education*** *Program availability:* Part-time.

**Doermer School of Business** *Program availability:* Part-time.

## PURDUE UNIVERSITY GLOBAL, Davenport, IA 52807

**General Information** Independent, coed, comprehensive institution.

**GRADUATE UNITS**

**School of Business** *Program availability:* Part-time, evening/weekend, online learning. Electronic applications accepted.

**School of Criminal Justice** *Program availability:* Part-time, evening/weekend, online learning. Electronic applications accepted.

**School of Higher Education Studies** *Program availability:* Part-time, evening/weekend, online learning.

**School of Information Technology** *Program availability:* Part-time, evening/weekend, online learning.

**School of Legal Studies** *Program availability:* Part-time, evening/weekend, online learning.

**School of Nursing** *Program availability:* Part-time, evening/weekend, online learning.

**School of Teacher Education** *Program availability:* Part-time, evening/weekend, online learning.

## PURDUE UNIVERSITY NORTHWEST, Hammond, IN 46323-2094

**General Information** State-supported, coed, comprehensive institution. *Graduate housing:* Room and/or apartments available on a first-come, first-served basis to single students; on-campus housing not available to married students.

**GRADUATE UNITS**

**Graduate Studies Office** *Program availability:* Part-time, evening/weekend, online learning. Electronic applications accepted.

***School of Education***

***School of Engineering, Mathematics, and Science*** *Program availability:* Part-time, evening/weekend, online learning. Electronic applications accepted.

***School of Liberal Arts and Social Sciences*** *Program availability:* Part-time.

***School of Management*** *Program availability:* Part-time, evening/weekend. Electronic applications accepted.

***School of Nursing*** *Program availability:* Part-time, online learning. Electronic applications accepted.

***School of Technology***

## QUEENS COLLEGE OF THE CITY UNIVERSITY OF NEW YORK, Queens, NY 11367-1597

**General Information** State and locally supported, coed, comprehensive institution. *Graduate housing:* Room and/or apartments available on a first-come, first-served basis to single students; on-campus housing not available to married students. *Research affiliation:* Hudson River Foundation (earth and environmental sciences), Consortium for Ocean Leadership (earth and environmental sciences), Institute for New Economic Thinking (economics), Social Explorer (sociology), Wildlife Conservation Society (biology), IBM (computer science).

**GRADUATE UNITS**

**Arts and Humanities Division** *Program availability:* Part-time. Electronic applications accepted.

***Aaron Copland School of Music*** Students: 21 full-time (6 women), 153 part-time (75 women); includes 60 minority (8 Black or African American, non-Hispanic/Latino; 1 American Indian or Alaska Native, non-Hispanic/Latino; 22 Asian, non-Hispanic/Latino; 22 Hispanic/Latino; 7 Two or more races, non-Hispanic/Latino), 33 international. Average age 30. 72 applicants, 63% accepted, 19 enrolled. *Faculty:* 25 full-time (7 women), 74 part-time/adjunct (28 women). Expenses: Contact institution. *Financial support:* In 2019–20, 20 students received support. Career-related internships or fieldwork, Federal Work-Study, institutionally sponsored loans, and scholarships/grants available. Financial award application deadline: 4/1; financial award applicants required to submit FAFSA. In 2019, 50 master's, 5 other advanced degrees awarded. *Program availability:* Part-time. *Application deadline:* For fall admission, 4/1 for domestic students; for spring admission, 11/1 for domestic students. Applications are processed on a rolling basis. *Application fee:* $125. Electronic applications accepted. *Application Contact:* Elizabeth D'Amico-Ramirez, Assistant Director of Graduate Admissions, 718-997-5203, E-mail: elizabeth.damicoramirez@qc.cuny.edu. *Chair*, Michael Lipsey, 718-997-3800, E-mail: Michael.Lipsey@qc.cuny.edu.

**Division of Education** *Program availability:* Part-time, evening/weekend. Electronic applications accepted.

**Mathematics and Natural Sciences Division** *Program availability:* Part-time. Electronic applications accepted.

***School of Earth and Environmental Sciences*** Students: 1 (woman) full-time, 14 part-time (5 women); includes 3 minority (2 Black or African American, non-Hispanic/Latino; 1 Asian, non-Hispanic/Latino), 1 international. Average age 28. 11 applicants, 73% accepted, 6 enrolled. *Faculty:* 14 full-time (4 women), 16 part-time/adjunct (8 women). Expenses: Contact institution. *Financial support:* In 2019–20, 8 students received support, including 8 teaching assistantships (averaging $15,679 per year); career-related internships or fieldwork and unspecified assistantships also available. Financial award application deadline: 4/1; financial award applicants required to submit FAFSA. In 2019, 11 master's awarded. *Program availability:* Part-time, evening/weekend. *Application deadline:* For fall admission, 4/1 for domestic students; for spring admission, 11/1 for domestic students. Applications are processed on a rolling basis. *Application fee:* $125. Electronic applications accepted. *Application Contact:* Dr. Gregory O'Mullan, Graduate Advisor, 718-997-3452, E-mail: gomullan@qc.cuny.edu. *Chair*, Dr. Jeffrey Bird, 718-997-3301, E-mail: jbird@qc.cuny.edu.

**School of Social Sciences** Students: 62 full-time (40 women), 695 part-time (457 women); includes 393 minority (89 Black or African American, non-Hispanic/Latino; 1 American Indian or Alaska Native, non-Hispanic/Latino; 141 Asian, non-Hispanic/Latino; 140 Hispanic/Latino; 2 Native Hawaiian or other Pacific Islander, non-Hispanic/Latino; 20 Two or more races, non-Hispanic/Latino), 42 international. Average age 32. *Faculty:* 177 full-time (73 women), 226 part-time/adjunct (85 women). Expenses: Contact institution. *Financial support:* Career-related internships or fieldwork available. Financial award application deadline: 4/1; financial award applicants required to submit FAFSA. In 2019, 254 master's, 1 other advanced degree awarded. *Program availability:* Part-time, evening/weekend. *Application deadline:* For fall admission, 4/1 for domestic students; for spring admission, 11/1 for domestic students. Applications are processed on a rolling basis. *Application fee:* $125. Electronic applications accepted. *Application Contact:* Elizabeth D'Amico-Ramirez, Assistant Director of Graduate Admissions, 718-997-5203, E-mail: elizabeth.damicoramirez@qc.cuny.edu. *Dean,* Dr. Michael Wolfe, 718-997-5210, E-mail: michael.wolfe@qc.cuny.edu.

***Graduate School of Library and Information Studies*** *Program availability:* Part-time, evening/weekend. Electronic applications accepted.

## QUEEN'S UNIVERSITY AT KINGSTON, Kingston, ON K7L 3N6, Canada

**General Information** Province-supported, coed, university. CGS member. *Graduate housing:* Rooms and/or apartments available to single students and available on a first-come, first-served basis to married students. Housing application deadline: 6/15.

**GRADUATE UNITS**

**Faculty of Law** *Program availability:* Part-time.

**School of Graduate Studies** *Program availability:* Part-time.

***Faculty of Arts and Science*** *Program availability:* Part-time. Electronic applications accepted.

***Faculty of Education*** *Program availability:* Part-time.

***Faculty of Engineering and Applied Science*** *Program availability:* Part-time. Electronic applications accepted.

***Faculty of Health Sciences*** *Program availability:* Part-time. Electronic applications accepted.

***School of Kinesiology and Health Studies*** *Program availability:* Part-time. Electronic applications accepted.

***School of Policy Studies*** *Program availability:* Part-time.

**School of Medicine** Electronic applications accepted.

**Smith School of Business**

## QUEENS UNIVERSITY OF CHARLOTTE, Charlotte, NC 28274-0002

**General Information** Independent-religious, coed, comprehensive institution. *Graduate housing:* On-campus housing not available.

**GRADUATE UNITS**

**College of Arts and Sciences** *Program availability:* Part-time, online learning. Electronic applications accepted.

**Knight School of Communication** *Program availability:* Part-time, evening/weekend, online learning.

**McColl School of Business** *Program availability:* Part-time, evening/weekend, online learning. Electronic applications accepted.

**Presbyterian School of Nursing** Electronic applications accepted.

**Wayland H. Cato, Jr. School of Education** *Program availability:* Part-time, evening/weekend, online learning.

## QUINCY UNIVERSITY, Quincy, IL 62301-2699

**General Information** Independent-religious, coed, comprehensive institution. *Graduate housing:* Room and/or apartments available to single students; on-campus housing not available to married students.

**GRADUATE UNITS**

**Master of Science in Education Counseling Program** *Program availability:* Part-time, evening/weekend. Electronic applications accepted.

**Master of Science in Education Programs** *Program availability:* Part-time, evening/weekend, online learning. Electronic applications accepted.

**MBA Program** *Program availability:* Part-time, evening/weekend, online learning. Electronic applications accepted.

## QUINNIPIAC UNIVERSITY, Hamden, CT 06518-1940

**General Information** Independent, coed, comprehensive institution. *Enrollment:* 933 full-time matriculated graduate/professional students (661 women), 1,119 part-time matriculated graduate/professional students (821 women). *Graduate faculty:* 152 full-time (99 women), 170 part-time/adjunct (96 women). *Tuition:* Part-time $1055 per credit. *Required fees:* $945 per semester. Tuition and fees vary according to course load and program. *Graduate housing:* Room and/or apartments available on a first-come, first-served basis to single students; on-campus housing not available to married students. Typical cost: $14,000 (including board). Room and board charges vary according to housing facility selected. *Student services:* Campus employment opportunities, campus safety program, career counseling, exercise/wellness program, free psychological counseling, international student services, low-cost health insurance, multicultural affairs office, services for students with disabilities. *Library facilities:* Arnold Bernhard Library plus 3 others. *Collection:* Books: 135,000 (physical), 500,000 (digital/electronic); Databases: 190. Weekly public service hours: 93; study areas open 24 hours, 5–7 days a week; students can reserve study rooms.

**Computer facilities:** Computer purchase and lease plans are available. 600 computers available on campus for general student use. A campuswide network can be accessed from student residence rooms and from off campus. Online class registration, e-commerce and Q card for local merchants, food service, dorm card access are available.
Website: http://www.qu.edu/

**General Application Contact:** Katie Ludovico, Senior Associate Director of Graduate Admissions, 800-462-1944, Fax: 203-582-3443, E-mail: graduate@qu.edu.

**GRADUATE UNITS**

**College of Arts and Sciences** *Program availability:* Part-time, evening/weekend. Electronic applications accepted.

**Frank H. Netter MD School of Medicine** Electronic applications accepted.

**School of Business** *Program availability:* Part-time, evening/weekend, 100% online, blended/hybrid learning. Electronic applications accepted.

**School of Communications** *Program availability:* Part-time, evening/weekend, online learning. Electronic applications accepted.

**School of Education** Electronic applications accepted.

**School of Engineering**

**School of Health Sciences** Electronic applications accepted.

**School of Law** *Program availability:* Part-time, evening/weekend. Electronic applications accepted.

**School of Nursing** Electronic applications accepted.

## RABBINICAL ACADEMY MESIVTA RABBI CHAIM BERLIN, Brooklyn, NY 11230-4715

**General Information** Independent-religious, men only, comprehensive institution. *Graduate housing:* Room and/or apartments available to single students; on-campus housing not available to married students. Housing application deadline: 9/30.

**GRADUATE UNITS**

**Graduate Program**

## RABBINICAL COLLEGE BETH SHRAGA, Monsey, NY 10952-3035

**General Information** Independent-religious, men only, comprehensive institution.

**General Application Contact:** Information Contact, 914-356-1980.

**GRADUATE UNITS**

**Graduate Programs**

## RABBINICAL COLLEGE BOBOVER YESHIVA B'NEI ZION, Brooklyn, NY 11219

**General Information** Independent-religious, men only, comprehensive institution. *Graduate housing:* Room and/or apartments available to single students; on-campus housing not available to married students.

**General Application Contact:** B. Grunfew, Information Contact, 718-438-2018.

**GRADUATE UNITS**

**Graduate Programs**

## RABBINICAL COLLEGE OF LONG ISLAND, Long Beach, NY 11561-3305

**General Information** Independent-religious, men only, comprehensive institution.

**GRADUATE UNITS**

**Graduate Programs**

## RABBINICAL SEMINARY OF AMERICA, Flushing, NY 11367

**General Information** Independent-religious, men only, comprehensive institution. *Graduate housing:* Room and/or apartments available to single students; on-campus housing not available to married students. Housing application deadline: 6/15.

**GRADUATE UNITS**

**Graduate Programs**

## RADFORD UNIVERSITY, Radford, VA 24142

**General Information** State-supported, coed, university. CGS member. *Graduate housing:* On-campus housing not available. *Research affiliation:* U.S. Department of Health and Human Services (nursing, psychology), Virginia Department of Social Services (social work), Virginia Department of Education (teacher education and leadership), Verizon Foundation (communication sciences and disorders), National Science Foundation (communication sciences and disorders, nursing, criminal justice, psychology, mathematics, biology, computer science), U.S. Department of Education (DOE) (teacher education and leadership).

**GRADUATE UNITS**

**College of Graduate Studies and Research** *Program availability:* Part-time, evening/weekend, 100% online, blended/hybrid learning. Electronic applications accepted.

***Data and Information Management, MS*** *Program availability:* Part-time. Electronic applications accepted.

## RAMAPO COLLEGE OF NEW JERSEY, Mahwah, NJ 07430-1680

**General Information** State-supported, coed, comprehensive institution. *Graduate housing:* Room and/or apartments available on a first-come, first-served basis to single students; on-campus housing not available to married students. Housing application deadline: 7/1. *Research affiliation:* American Association of State Colleges and Universities, New Jersey Council of Magnet Organizations, Council of Public Liberal Arts Colleges.

**GRADUATE UNITS**

**Master of Arts in Educational Leadership Program** *Program availability:* Part-time. Electronic applications accepted.

**Master of Arts in Special Education Program** *Program availability:* Part-time, evening/weekend. Electronic applications accepted.

**Master of Business Administration Program** *Program availability:* Part-time-only, evening/weekend. Electronic applications accepted.

**Master of Science in Accounting Program** *Program availability:* Part-time. Electronic applications accepted.

**Master of Science in Educational Technology Program** *Program availability:* Part-time, evening/weekend. Electronic applications accepted.

**Master of Science in Nursing Program** *Program availability:* Part-time. Electronic applications accepted.

**Master of Social Work Program** *Program availability:* Part-time. Electronic applications accepted.

## RANDALL UNIVERSITY, Moore, OK 73160-1208

**General Information** Independent-religious, coed, comprehensive institution. *Graduate housing:* Room and/or apartments available on a first-come, first-served basis to single students.

**GRADUATE UNITS**

**Department of Bible Studies** *Program availability:* Part-time, evening/weekend.

## RANDOLPH COLLEGE, Lynchburg, VA 24503

**General Information** Independent-religious, coed, comprehensive institution.

**GRADUATE UNITS**

**Program in Creative Writing**

**Programs in Education**

## RECONSTRUCTIONIST RABBINICAL COLLEGE, Wyncote, PA 19095-1898

**General Information** Independent-religious, coed, graduate-only institution. *Enrollment by degree level:* 35 master's. *Graduate faculty:* 6 full-time (4 women), 12 part-time/adjunct (11 women). *Tuition:* Full-time $26,000. *Graduate housing:* On-campus housing not available. *Student services:* Campus employment opportunities, career counseling, international student services. *Library facilities:* Mordecai M. Kaplan Library.

**Computer facilities:** 20 computers available on campus for general student use. Online class registration is available.
Website: http://www.rrc.edu/

**General Application Contact:** Rabbi Melissa Heller, Director of Admissions and Recruitment, 215-576-0800 Ext. 123, Fax: 215-576-6143, E-mail: mheller@rrc.edu.

**GRADUATE UNITS**

**Graduate Programs** *Program availability:* Part-time.

## REED COLLEGE, Portland, OR 97202-8199

**General Information** Independent, coed, comprehensive institution. *Graduate housing:* On-campus housing not available.

**GRADUATE UNITS**

**Graduate Program in Liberal Studies** Students: 28 part-time (15 women); includes 2 minority (1 Black or African American, non-Hispanic/Latino; 1 American Indian or Alaska Native, non-Hispanic/Latino). Average age 49. 5 applicants, 80% accepted, 4 enrolled. *Faculty:* 9 part-time/adjunct (3 women). Expenses: Contact institution. *Financial support:* In 2019–20, 2 students received support. Scholarships/grants and health care benefits available. Support available to part-time students. Financial award application deadline: 5/1; financial award applicants required to submit CSS PROFILE or FAFSA. In 2019, 4 master's awarded. *Program availability:* Part-time-only, evening/weekend. *Application deadline:* For fall admission, 7/1 priority date for domestic students, 5/1 for international students; for spring admission, 12/1 priority date for domestic students, 9/1 for international students; for summer admission, 4/1 for domestic students, 2/1 for international students. Applications are processed on a rolling basis. *Application fee:* $75. Electronic applications accepted. *Application Contact:* Barbara A. Amen, Director, Graduate Studies, 503-777-7259, Fax: 503-517-7345, E-mail: bamen@reed.edu. *Director, Graduate Studies*, Barbara A. Amen, 503-777-7259, Fax: 503-517-7345, E-mail: bamen@reed.edu.

## REFORMED EPISCOPAL SEMINARY, Blue Bell, PA 19422

**General Information** Independent-religious, coed, graduate-only institution. *Graduate housing:* Room and/or apartments available on a first-come, first-served basis to single students; on-campus housing not available to married students.

**GRADUATE UNITS**

**Graduate Program**

## REFORMED PRESBYTERIAN THEOLOGICAL SEMINARY, Pittsburgh, PA 15208-2594

**General Information** Independent-religious, coed, primarily men, graduate-only institution. *Graduate housing:* Rooms and/or apartments available on a first-come, first-served basis to single and married students.

**GRADUATE UNITS**

**Graduate and Professional Programs** *Program availability:* Part-time, evening/weekend. Electronic applications accepted.

## REFORMED THEOLOGICAL SEMINARY–ATLANTA CAMPUS, Marietta, GA 30067

**General Information** Independent-religious, coed, primarily men, graduate-only institution.

**GRADUATE UNITS**

**Graduate Programs**

## REFORMED THEOLOGICAL SEMINARY–CHARLOTTE CAMPUS, Charlotte, NC 28226-6318

**General Information** Independent-religious, coed, primarily men, graduate-only institution. *Graduate housing:* On-campus housing not available.

**GRADUATE UNITS**

**Graduate and Professional Programs** *Program availability:* Part-time. Electronic applications accepted.

## REFORMED THEOLOGICAL SEMINARY–DALLAS CAMPUS, Dallas, TX 75207

**General Information** Independent-religious, coed, graduate-only institution.

**GRADUATE UNITS**

**Graduate and Professional Programs**

## REFORMED THEOLOGICAL SEMINARY–HOUSTON CAMPUS, Houston, TX 77024

**General Information** Independent-religious, coed, primarily men, graduate-only institution. *Graduate housing:* On-campus housing not available.

**GRADUATE UNITS**

**Graduate Program** Electronic applications accepted.

## REFORMED THEOLOGICAL SEMINARY–JACKSON CAMPUS, Jackson, MS 39209-3004

**General Information** Independent-religious, coed, primarily men, graduate-only institution. *Graduate housing:* Rooms and/or apartments available on a first-come, first-served basis to single and married students.

**GRADUATE UNITS**

**Graduate and Professional Programs**

## REFORMED THEOLOGICAL SEMINARY–ORLANDO CAMPUS, Oviedo, FL 32765

**General Information** Independent-religious, coed, primarily men, graduate-only institution. *Enrollment by degree level:* 276 master's, 63 doctoral, 2 other advanced degrees. *Graduate faculty:* 10 full-time (1 woman), 11 part-time/adjunct (2 women). *Graduate housing:* Rooms and/or apartments available on a first-come, first-served basis to single and married students. *Student services:* Campus employment opportunities, career counseling, free psychological counseling, international student services, writing training. *Library facilities:* RTS Library. *Collection:* Books: 89,941 (physical); Serial titles: 80 (physical). Weekly public service hours: 69.

**Computer facilities:** 6 computers available on campus for general student use. A campuswide network can be accessed. Online class registration is available.
Website: http://rts.edu/orlando/

**General Application Contact:** Caleb T. Burnison, Director of Admissions & Recruitment, 407-278-8830, Fax: 407-366-9425, E-mail: cburnison@rts.edu.

**GRADUATE UNITS**

**Graduate Programs** *Program availability:* Part-time, online learning. Electronic applications accepted.

## REFORMED THEOLOGICAL SEMINARY–WASHINGTON D.C., McLean, VA 22102

**General Information** Independent-religious, coed, primarily men, graduate-only institution. *Enrollment by degree level:* 75 master's, 1 other advanced degree. *Graduate faculty:* 4 full-time (0 women), 6 part-time/adjunct (1 woman). *Tuition:* Full-time $550; part-time $550 per credit. *Required fees:* $200; $200 per term. Tuition and fees vary according to course load. *Graduate housing:* On-campus housing not available. *Student services:* Campus employment opportunities, campus safety program, career counseling, international student services, writing training. *Library facilities:* RTS Library. *Collection:* Books: 7,575 (physical).

**Computer facilities:** 1 computer available on campus for general student use. Online class registration is available.
Website: http://www.rts.edu/washington/

**General Application Contact:** Timo Sazo, Director of Admissions, 703-448-3393 Ext. 5104, Fax: 571-297-8010, E-mail: tsazo@rts.edu.

**GRADUATE UNITS**

**Graduate and Professional Programs** *Program availability:* Part-time, evening/weekend. Electronic applications accepted.

## REFORMED UNIVERSITY, Lawrenceville, GA 30043

**General Information** Independent-religious, coed, comprehensive institution.

**GRADUATE UNITS**

**Graduate Programs**

## REGENT COLLEGE, Vancouver, BC V6T 2E4, Canada

**General Information** Independent-religious, coed, graduate-only institution. *Graduate housing:* On-campus housing not available. *Research affiliation:* University of British Columbia (theology, religion).

**GRADUATE UNITS**

**Program in Theology** *Program availability:* Part-time. Electronic applications accepted.

## REGENT'S UNIVERSITY LONDON, London NW1 4NS, United Kingdom

**General Information** Independent, coed, comprehensive institution.

**GRADUATE UNITS**

**Webster Graduate School** *Program availability:* Part-time.

## REGENT UNIVERSITY, Virginia Beach, VA 23464-9800

**General Information** Independent-religious, coed, comprehensive institution. *Enrollment:* 10,409 graduate, professional, and undergraduate students; 1,968 full-time matriculated graduate/professional students (1,246 women), 3,781 part-time matriculated graduate/professional students (2,427 women). *Enrollment by degree level:* 3,810 master's, 1,868 doctoral, 71 other advanced degrees. *Graduate faculty:* 87 full-time (30 women), 334 part-time/adjunct (134 women). *Required fees:* $1400; $700 per semester. $700 per semester. Tuition and fees vary according to course level, course load, degree level and program. *Graduate housing:* Rooms and/or apartments available on a first-come, first-served basis to single and married students. Typical cost: $9970 per year ($12,490 including board) for single students; $13,580 per year ($16,100 including board) for married students. Room and board charges vary according to board plan and housing facility selected. Housing application deadline: 5/1. *Student services:* Campus employment opportunities, campus safety program, career counseling, exercise/wellness program, free psychological counseling, international student services, low-cost health insurance, services for students with disabilities, teacher training, writing training. *Library facilities:* Regent University Library plus 1 other. *Collection:* Books: 306,180 (physical), 729,410 (digital/electronic); Serial titles: 51,444 (physical), 93,389 (digital/electronic); Databases: 419. Students can reserve study rooms.

**Computer facilities:** 70 computers available on campus for general student use. A campuswide network can be accessed. Online class registration is available.
Website: http://www.regent.edu/

**General Application Contact:** Heidi Cece, Assistant Vice President for Enrollment Management, 800-373-5504, Fax: 757-352-4381, E-mail: admissions@regent.edu.

**GRADUATE UNITS**

**Graduate School** *Program availability:* Part-time, evening/weekend, 100% online, blended/hybrid learning. Electronic applications accepted.

***Robertson School of Government*** Students: 36 full-time (22 women), 159 part-time (89 women); includes 82 minority (52 Black or African American, non-Hispanic/Latino; 2 American Indian or Alaska Native, non-Hispanic/Latino; 2 Asian, non-Hispanic/Latino; 23 Hispanic/Latino; 3 Two or more races, non-Hispanic/Latino), 4 international. Average age 36. 181 applicants, 70% accepted, 75 enrolled. *Faculty:* 5 full-time (1 woman), 19 part-time/adjunct (2 women). Expenses: Contact institution. *Financial support:* In 2019–20, 132 students received support. Career-related internships or fieldwork, scholarships/grants, and unspecified assistantships available. Support available to part-time students. Financial award applicants required to submit FAFSA. In 2019, 58 master's awarded. *Program availability:* Part-time, evening/weekend, 100% online, blended/hybrid learning. *Application deadline:* For fall admission, 5/1 priority date for domestic students; for spring admission, 11/1 priority date for domestic students. Applications are processed on a rolling basis. *Application fee:* $50. Electronic applications accepted. *Application Contact:* Heidi Cece, Assistant Vice President for Enrollment Management, 800-373-5504, Fax: 757-352-4381, E-mail: admissions@regent.edu. *Interim Dean*, Dr. Stephen Perry, 757-352-4082, E-mail: sperry@regent.edu.

***School of Business and Leadership*** Students: 397 full-time (229 women), 828 part-time (474 women); includes 698 minority (531 Black or African American, non-Hispanic/Latino; 5 American Indian or Alaska Native, non-Hispanic/Latino; 35 Asian, non-Hispanic/Latino; 87 Hispanic/Latino; 5 Native Hawaiian or other Pacific Islander, non-Hispanic/Latino; 35 Two or more races, non-Hispanic/Latino), 45 international. Average age 41. 615 applicants, 76% accepted, 275 enrolled. *Faculty:* 9 full-time (2 women), 39 part-time/adjunct (14 women). Expenses: Contact institution. *Financial support:* In 2019–20, 959 students received support. Career-related internships or fieldwork, scholarships/grants, health care benefits, and unspecified assistantships available. Support available to part-time students. Financial award applicants required to submit FAFSA. In 2019, 218 master's, 91 doctorates, 1 other advanced degree awarded. *Program availability:* Part-time, evening/weekend, 100% online, blended/hybrid learning. *Application deadline:* For fall admission, 5/1 priority date for domestic students; for spring admission, 10/1 priority date for domestic students. Applications are processed on a rolling basis. *Application fee:* $50. Electronic applications accepted. *Application Contact:* Heidi Cece, Assistant Vice President for Enrollment Management, 800-373-5504, Fax: 757-352-4381, E-mail: admissions@regent.edu. *Dean*, Dr. Doris Gomez, 757-352-4686, Fax: 757-352-4634, E-mail: dorigom@regent.edu.

***School of Communication and the Arts*** *Program availability:* Part-time, evening/weekend, 100% online, blended/hybrid learning. Electronic applications accepted.

***School of Divinity*** Students: 303 full-time (119 women), 813 part-time (403 women); includes 632 minority (509 Black or African American, non-Hispanic/Latino; 3 American Indian or Alaska Native, non-Hispanic/Latino; 31 Asian, non-Hispanic/Latino; 54 Hispanic/Latino; 2 Native Hawaiian or other Pacific Islander, non-Hispanic/Latino; 33 Two or more races, non-Hispanic/Latino), 16 international. Average age 45. 561 applicants, 66% accepted, 194 enrolled. *Faculty:* 15 full-time (3 women), 58 part-time/adjunct (10 women). Expenses: Contact institution. *Financial support:* In 2019–20, 856 students received support. Career-related internships or fieldwork, scholarships/grants, health care benefits, and unspecified assistantships available. Support available to part-time students. Financial award applicants required to submit FAFSA. In 2019, 168 master's, 13 doctorates awarded. *Program availability:* Part-time, evening/weekend, 100% online, blended/hybrid learning. *Application deadline:* For fall admission, 5/1 priority date for domestic students. Applications are processed on a rolling basis. *Application fee:* $50. Electronic applications accepted. *Application Contact:* Heidi Cece, Assistant Vice President for Enrollment Management, 800-373-5504, Fax: 757-352-4381, E-mail: admissions@regent.edu. *Dean*, Dr. Cornelius Bekker, 757-352-4258, Fax: 757-352-4597, E-mail: clbekker@regent.edu.

***School of Education*** *Program availability:* Part-time, evening/weekend, 100% online, blended/hybrid learning. Electronic applications accepted.

***School of Law*** Students: 378 full-time (230 women), 349 part-time (246 women); includes 311 minority (207 Black or African American, non-Hispanic/Latino; 5 American Indian or Alaska Native, non-Hispanic/Latino; 17 Asian, non-Hispanic/Latino; 56 Hispanic/Latino; 2 Native Hawaiian or other Pacific Islander, non-Hispanic/Latino; 24 Two or more races, non-Hispanic/Latino), 46 international. Average age 35. 680 applicants, 62% accepted, 223 enrolled. *Faculty:* 16 full-time (5 women), 66 part-time/adjunct (22 women). Expenses: Contact institution. *Financial support:* In 2019–20, 582 students received support. Career-related internships or fieldwork, scholarships/grants, health care benefits, and unspecified assistantships available. Support available to part-time students. Financial award applicants required to submit FAFSA. In 2019, 176 master's, 72 doctorates awarded. *Program availability:* Part-time, 100% online, blended/hybrid learning. *Application deadline:* For fall admission, 3/1 for domestic students. Applications are processed on a rolling basis. *Application fee:* $50. Electronic applications accepted. *Application Contact:* Ernie Walton, Assistant Dean of Admissions, 757-352-4315, E-mail: lawschool@regent.edu. *Dean*, Mark Martin, 757-352-4040, Fax: 757-352-4595, E-mail: mmartin@regent.edu.

***School of Psychology and Counseling*** *Program availability:* Part-time, evening/weekend, 100% online, blended/hybrid learning. Electronic applications accepted.

## REGIS COLLEGE, Toronto, ON M5S 2Z5, Canada

**General Information** Independent-religious, coed, graduate-only institution. *Graduate housing:* Room and/or apartments available on a first-come, first-served basis to single students; on-campus housing not available to married students. *Research affiliation:* Lonergan Research Institute (theology/philosophy), Lupina Foundation (research and innovation related to health/society issues).

**GRADUATE UNITS**

**Graduate and Professional Programs**

## REGIS COLLEGE, Weston, MA 02493

**General Information** Independent-religious, coed, comprehensive institution. *Enrollment:* 3,194 graduate, professional, and undergraduate students; 200 full-time matriculated graduate/professional students, 1,900 part-time matriculated graduate/professional students. *Graduate housing:* Room and/or apartments available on a first-come, first-served basis to single students; on-campus housing not available to married students. Typical cost: $16,182 (including board). *Student services:* Campus employment opportunities, campus safety program, career counseling, exercise/wellness program, international student services, low-cost health insurance, multicultural affairs office, services for students with disabilities, teacher training, writing training. *Library facilities:* Regis College Library. *Collection:* Books: 48,867 (physical), 381,876 (digital/electronic); Serial titles: 51 (physical), 1,106 (digital/electronic); Databases: 62. Weekly public service hours: 108. *Research affiliation:* Beth Israel Deaconess Medical Center (nursing), Caritas Norwood Hospital (nursing), Boston Medical Center (nursing), Lahey Clinic Medical Center (nursing).

**Computer facilities:** 196 computers available on campus for general student use. A campuswide network can be accessed. Online class registration, online bills, financial aid award letters and check-in requirements are available.
Website: http://www.regiscollege.edu/

**General Application Contact:** Shelagh Tomaino, Dean of Graduate Admission, 781-768-7330, Fax: 781-768-8218, E-mail: graduatedepartment@regiscollege.edu.

**GRADUATE UNITS**

**Business and Communication** Expenses: Contact institution. *Financial support:* Federal Work-Study and unspecified assistantships available. Financial award applicants required to submit FAFSA. *Program availability:* Part-time, evening/weekend, 100% online, blended/hybrid learning. *Application deadline:* Applications are processed on a rolling basis. *Application fee:* $65. Electronic applications accepted. *Application Contact:* Hillary Lyons, Assistant Director of Graduate Admission, 781-768-7746, E-mail: hillary.lyons@regiscollege.edu. *Dean*, Dr. William Koehler, 781-768-8326, E-mail: william.koehler@regiscollege.edu.

**Department of Education** Expenses: Contact institution. *Financial support:* Federal Work-Study, scholarships/grants, and unspecified assistantships available. Financial award applicants required to submit FAFSA. *Program availability:* Part-time, evening/weekend. *Application deadline:* Applications are processed on a rolling basis. *Application fee:* $65. Electronic applications accepted. *Application Contact:* Dr. Priscilla Boerger, Department Chair/Graduate Program Director, 781-768-7422, E-mail: priscilla.boerger@regiscollege.edu. *Department Chair/Graduate Program Director*, Dr. Priscilla Boerger, 781-768-7422, E-mail: priscilla.boerger@regiscollege.edu.

**Nursing and Health Sciences School** Expenses: Contact institution. *Financial support:* Federal Work-Study, scholarships/grants, and unspecified assistantships available. Support available to part-time students. Financial award applicants required to submit FAFSA. *Program availability:* Part-time, evening/weekend, 100% online, blended/hybrid learning. *Application deadline:* Applications are processed on a rolling basis. *Application fee:* $75. Electronic applications accepted. *Application Contact:* Thomas May, Graduate Admission Counselor, 781-768-7162, E-mail: thomas.may@regiscollege.edu.

## REGIS UNIVERSITY, Denver, CO 80221-1099

**General Information** Independent-religious, coed, comprehensive institution. *Graduate housing:* Room and/or apartments available on a first-come, first-served basis to single students; on-campus housing not available to married students. Housing application deadline: 5/1. *Research affiliation:* Commission for Accelerated Programs, Learning Anytime Anywhere Partnership (Internet-based technology), Transparency by Design (online programs, best practices).

**GRADUATE UNITS**

**College of Business and Economics** *Program availability:* Part-time, evening/weekend, 100% online, blended/hybrid learning. Electronic applications accepted.

**College of Computer and Information Sciences** *Program availability:* Part-time, evening/weekend, 100% online, blended/hybrid learning. Electronic applications accepted.

**College of Contemporary Liberal Studies** *Program availability:* Part-time, evening/weekend, 100% online, blended/hybrid learning. Electronic applications accepted.

**Regis College** *Program availability:* Part-time. Electronic applications accepted.

**Rueckert-Hartman College for Health Professions** *Program availability:* Part-time, evening/weekend, 100% online, blended/hybrid learning. Electronic applications accepted.

## REINHARDT UNIVERSITY, Waleska, GA 30183-2981

**General Information** Independent-religious, coed, comprehensive institution. *Graduate housing:* Room and/or apartments available on a first-come, first-served basis to single students; on-campus housing not available to married students.

**GRADUATE UNITS**

**McCamish School of Business & Sport Studies** *Program availability:* Part-time, evening/weekend, 100% online. Electronic applications accepted.

**Price School of Education** *Program availability:* Part-time. Electronic applications accepted.

**School of Arts & Humanities** *Program availability:* Blended/hybrid learning.

**School of Professional Studies** *Program availability:* Part-time-only, blended/hybrid learning. Electronic applications accepted.

## RELAY GRADUATE SCHOOL OF EDUCATION, New York, NY 10011

**General Information** Independent, coed, graduate-only institution.

**GRADUATE UNITS**

**Graduate Programs** *Program availability:* Online learning.

## RENSSELAER AT HARTFORD, Hartford, CT 06120-2991

**General Information** Independent, coed, graduate-only institution. *Graduate housing:* On-campus housing not available.

**GRADUATE UNITS**

**Department of Computer and Information Science** *Program availability:* Part-time, evening/weekend. Electronic applications accepted.

**Department of Engineering** *Program availability:* Part-time, evening/weekend. Electronic applications accepted.

**Lally School of Management and Technology** *Program availability:* Part-time, evening/weekend, online learning. Electronic applications accepted.

## RENSSELAER POLYTECHNIC INSTITUTE, Troy, NY 12180-3590

**General Information** Independent, coed, university. CGS member. *Enrollment:* 7,617 graduate, professional, and undergraduate students; 1,197 full-time matriculated graduate/professional students (404 women), 181 part-time matriculated graduate/professional students (55 women). *Enrollment by degree level:* 551 master's, 823 doctoral, 4 other advanced degrees. *Graduate faculty:* 477 full-time (120 women), 50 part-time/adjunct (10 women). *Graduate housing:* Rooms and/or apartments available on a first-come, first-served basis to single and married students. *Student services:* Campus employment opportunities, campus safety program, career counseling, exercise/wellness program, free psychological counseling, grant writing training, international student services, low-cost health insurance, multicultural affairs office, services for students with disabilities, teacher training, writing training. *Library facilities:* Folsom Library plus 2 others. *Collection:* Students can reserve study rooms. *Research affiliation:* IBM (high performance computing, advanced modeling and simulation research), Boeing (flow control, computational fluid dynamics), Skidmore, Owings & Merrill (SOM) (built environment (solar concentrators, phytoremediation, integrated hybrid flow control, parametric design)), Mount Sinai School of Medicine (biomedical and clinical research (healthcare analytics, orthopedic-musculoskeletal research, imaging, brain-machine interfaces)), Disney (synthetic characters), General Electric Company (GE) (renewable energy, power electronic, and imaging research).

**Computer facilities:** Computer purchase and lease plans are available. A campuswide network can be accessed. Online class registration, billing, downloadable software, webpages are available.
Website: http://www.rpi.edu/

**General Application Contact:** Jarron Decker, Director of Graduate Admissions, 518-276-6216, Fax: 518-276-4072, E-mail: gradadmissions@rpi.edu.

**GRADUATE UNITS**

**Graduate School** Students: 1,197 full-time (404 women), 181 part-time (55 women); includes 197 minority (25 Black or African American, non-Hispanic/Latino; 2 American Indian or Alaska Native, non-Hispanic/Latino; 77 Asian, non-Hispanic/Latino; 45

Hispanic/Latino; 48 Two or more races, non-Hispanic/Latino), 660 international. Average age 26. 3,197 applicants, 45% accepted, 391 enrolled. *Faculty:* 477 full-time (120 women), 50 part-time/adjunct (10 women). Expenses: Contact institution. *Financial support:* In 2019–20, 968 students received support, including research assistantships with full tuition reimbursements available (averaging $23,000 per year), teaching assistantships with full tuition reimbursements available (averaging $23,000 per year); fellowships with full tuition reimbursements available, scholarships/grants, health care benefits, and tuition waivers (full) also available. Financial award application deadline: 1/1. In 2019, 352 master's, 162 doctorates awarded. *Program availability:* Part-time-only, evening/weekend, online only, 100% online, blended/hybrid learning. *Application deadline:* For fall admission, 1/1 priority date for domestic and international students; for spring admission, 8/15 priority date for domestic and international students. Applications are processed on a rolling basis. *Application fee:* $75. Electronic applications accepted. *Application Contact:* Jarron Decker, Director of Graduate Admissions, 518-276-6216, Fax: 518-276-4072, E-mail: gradadmissions@rpi.edu.

***Lally School of Management*** Students: 168 full-time (80 women), 67 part-time (31 women); includes 25 minority (3 Black or African American, non-Hispanic/Latino; 10 Asian, non-Hispanic/Latino; 7 Hispanic/Latino; 5 Two or more races, non-Hispanic/Latino), 177 international. Average age 24. 1,045 applicants, 46% accepted, 123 enrolled. *Faculty:* 36 full-time (9 women), 5 part-time/adjunct (0 women). Expenses: Contact institution. *Financial support:* In 2019–20, 64 students received support. Scholarships/grants available. Financial award application deadline: 1/1; financial award applicants required to submit FAFSA. In 2019, 123 master's, 6 doctorates awarded. *Program availability:* Part-time. *Application deadline:* For fall admission, 1/1 priority date for domestic and international students. Applications are processed on a rolling basis. *Application fee:* $75. Electronic applications accepted. *Application Contact:* Jarron Decker, Director of Graduate Admissions, 518-276-6216, Fax: 518-276-4072, E-mail: gradadmissions@rpi.edu. *Interim Dean, Lally School of Management*, Dr. Chanaka Edirisinghe, 518-276-3336, E-mail: edirin@rpi.edu.

***School of Architecture*** Students: 44 full-time (14 women), 2 part-time (both women); includes 7 minority (2 Black or African American, non-Hispanic/Latino; 1 Asian, non-Hispanic/Latino; 1 Hispanic/Latino; 3 Two or more races, non-Hispanic/Latino), 16 international. Average age 28. 103 applicants, 78% accepted, 15 enrolled. *Faculty:* 33 full-time (8 women), 13 part-time/adjunct (1 woman). Expenses: Contact institution. *Financial support:* In 2019–20, research assistantships (averaging $23,000 per year), teaching assistantships (averaging $23,000 per year) were awarded; fellowships and scholarships/grants also available. Financial award application deadline: 1/1. In 2019, 25 master's, 5 doctorates awarded. *Application deadline:* For fall admission, 1/1 priority date for domestic and international students; for spring admission, 8/15 for domestic and international students; for summer admission, 1/1 for domestic and international students. Applications are processed on a rolling basis. *Application fee:* $75. Electronic applications accepted. *Application Contact:* Jarron Decker, Director of Graduate Admissions, 518-276-6216, Fax: 518-276-4072, E-mail: gradadmissions@rpi.edu. *Dean, School of Architecture*, Evan Douglis, 518-276-6460, E-mail: douglis@rpi.edu.

***School of Engineering*** Students: 582 full-time (162 women), 95 part-time (16 women); includes 99 minority (12 Black or African American, non-Hispanic/Latino; 1 American Indian or Alaska Native, non-Hispanic/Latino; 40 Asian, non-Hispanic/Latino; 20 Hispanic/Latino; 26 Two or more races, non-Hispanic/Latino), 319 international. Average age 26. 1,367 applicants, 46% accepted, 214 enrolled. *Faculty:* 179 full-time (28 women), 8 part-time/adjunct (0 women). Expenses: Contact institution. *Financial support:* In 2019–20, 462 students received support, including research assistantships (averaging $23,000 per year), teaching assistantships (averaging $23,000 per year); fellowships also available. Financial award application deadline: 1/1. In 2019, 128 master's, 89 doctorates awarded. *Program availability:* Part-time. *Application deadline:* For fall admission, 1/1 priority date for domestic and international students; for spring admission, 8/15 priority date for domestic and international students; for summer admission, 1/1 priority date for domestic and international students. Applications are processed on a rolling basis. *Application fee:* $75. Electronic applications accepted. *Application Contact:* Jarron Decker, Director of Graduate Admissions, 518-276-6216, Fax: 518-276-4072, E-mail: gradadmissions@rpi.edu. *Dean*, Shekhar Garde, 518-276-6298, E-mail: gardes@rpi.edu.

***School of Humanities, Arts, and Social Sciences*** Students: 72 full-time (36 women), 3 part-time (2 women); includes 12 minority (1 Black or African American, non-Hispanic/Latino; 4 Asian, non-Hispanic/Latino; 3 Hispanic/Latino; 4 Two or more races, non-Hispanic/Latino), 20 international. Average age 30. 84 applicants, 40% accepted, 16 enrolled. *Faculty:* 92 full-time (36 women), 12 part-time/adjunct (5 women). Expenses: Contact institution. *Financial support:* In 2019–20, research assistantships (averaging $23,000 per year), teaching assistantships (averaging $23,000 per year) were awarded; fellowships and scholarships/grants also available. Financial award application deadline: 1/1. In 2019, 5 master's, 15 doctorates awarded. *Program availability:* Part-time. *Application deadline:* For fall admission, 1/1 priority date for domestic students, 1/15 priority date for international students; for spring admission, 8/15 priority date for domestic and international students. Applications are processed on a rolling basis. *Application fee:* $75. Electronic applications accepted. *Application Contact:* Jarron Decker, Director of Graduate Admissions, 518-276-6216, Fax: 518-276-4072, E-mail: gradadmissions@rpi.edu. *Associate Dean for Research and Graduate Studies*, Dr. Curtis Bahn, 518-276-6065, E-mail: crb@rpi.edu.

***School of Science*** Students: 331 full-time (112 women), 10 part-time (4 women); includes 54 minority (7 Black or African American, non-Hispanic/Latino; 1 American Indian or Alaska Native, non-Hispanic/Latino; 22 Asian, non-Hispanic/Latino; 14 Hispanic/Latino; 10 Two or more races, non-Hispanic/Latino), 128 international. Average age 26. 890 applicants, 39% accepted, 116 enrolled. *Faculty:* 127 full-time (33 women), 9 part-time/adjunct (4 women). Expenses: Contact institution. *Financial support:* In 2019–20, research assistantships (averaging $23,000 per year), teaching assistantships (averaging $23,000 per year) were awarded; fellowships also available. Financial award application deadline: 1/1. In 2019, 71 master's, 47 doctorates awarded. *Application deadline:* For fall admission, 1/1 priority date for domestic and international students; for spring admission, 8/15 priority date for domestic and international students. Applications are processed on a rolling basis. *Application fee:* $75. Electronic applications accepted. *Application Contact:* Jarron Decker, Director of Graduate Admissions, 518-276-6216, Fax: 518-276-4072, E-mail: gradadmissions@rpi.edu. *Associate Dean, School of Science*, Dr. Christian Wetzel, 518-276-3755, E-mail: wetzel@rpi.edu.

## RESEARCH COLLEGE OF NURSING, Kansas City, MO 64132

**General Information** Independent, coed, primarily women, comprehensive institution. *Enrollment:* 135 part-time matriculated graduate/professional students (113 women). *Enrollment by degree level:* 135 master's. *Graduate faculty:* 9 full-time (all women), 4 part-time/adjunct (2 women). *Tuition:* Part-time $560 per credit hour. *Graduate housing:* Rooms and/or apartments available on a first-come, first-served basis to single and married students. Typical cost: $8400 per year for single students; $8400 per year for married students. Housing application deadline: 1/15. *Library facilities:* Greenlease Library.

**Computer facilities:** 125 computers available on campus for general student use. A campuswide network can be accessed from student residence rooms and from off campus. Online class registration is available.
Website: http://www.researchcollege.edu/

**General Application Contact:** Leslie Burry, Director of Admission, 816-995-2820, Fax: 816-995-2813, E-mail: leslie.burry@researchcollege.edu.

## RESURRECTION UNIVERSITY, Chicago, IL 60622

**General Information** Independent, coed, upper-level institution.

**GRADUATE UNITS**

**Nursing Program**

## RHODE ISLAND COLLEGE, Providence, RI 02908-1991

**General Information** State-supported, coed, comprehensive institution. *Enrollment:* 7,523 graduate, professional, and undergraduate students; 215 full-time matriculated graduate/professional students (164 women), 666 part-time matriculated graduate/professional students (526 women). *Enrollment by degree level:* 684 master's, 62 doctoral, 135 other advanced degrees. *Graduate faculty:* 106 full-time (70 women), 87 part-time/adjunct (66 women). *Tuition, area resident:* Part-time $462 per credit hour. Tuition, state resident: part-time $462 per credit hour. *Required fees:* $720. One-time fee: $140. *Graduate housing:* Room and/or apartments available on a first-come, first-served basis to single students; on-campus housing not available to married students. Housing application deadline: 5/15. *Student services:* Campus employment opportunities, career counseling, free psychological counseling, grant writing training, international student services, low-cost health insurance, multicultural affairs office, services for students with disabilities. *Library facilities:* Adams Library. *Collection:* Books: 306,080 (physical), 302,387 (digital/electronic); Serial titles: 3,081 (physical), 52,652 (digital/electronic); Databases: 123. Weekly public service hours: 80.

**Computer facilities:** Computer purchase and lease plans are available. 250 computers available on campus for general student use. A campuswide network can be accessed. Online class registration is available.
Website: http://www.ric.edu/

**General Application Contact:** Dr. Leslie Schuster, Interim Dean of Graduate Studies, 401-456-9723, E-mail: graduatestudies@ric.edu.

**GRADUATE UNITS**

**School of Graduate Studies** Students: 215 full-time (164 women), 666 part-time (526 women); includes 224 minority (74 Black or African American, non-Hispanic/Latino; 26 Asian, non-Hispanic/Latino; 106 Hispanic/Latino; 2 Native Hawaiian or other Pacific Islander, non-Hispanic/Latino; 16 Two or more races, non-Hispanic/Latino). Average age 33. *Faculty:* 100 full-time (65 women), 76 part-time/adjunct (60 women). Expenses: Contact institution. *Financial support:* Research assistantships, teaching assistantships, career-related internships or fieldwork, Federal Work-Study, traineeships, health care benefits, tuition waivers (full and partial), and unspecified assistantships available. Support available to part-time students. Financial award application deadline: 5/15; financial award applicants required to submit FAFSA. In 2019, 269 master's, 9 doctorates, 36 other advanced degrees awarded. *Program availability:* Part-time, evening/weekend. *Application deadline:* For fall admission, 3/1 priority date for domestic students; for spring admission, 11/1 for domestic students. Applications are processed on a rolling basis. *Application fee:* $50. Electronic applications accepted. *Application Contact:* Graduate Studies, 401-456-8700. *Interim Dean of Graduate Studies*, Dr. Leslie Schuster, 401-456-9723, E-mail: graduatestudies@ric.edu.

***Faculty of Arts and Sciences*** Students: 11 full-time (6 women), 39 part-time (24 women); includes 7 minority (3 Black or African American, non-Hispanic/Latino; 1 Asian, non-Hispanic/Latino; 3 Hispanic/Latino). Average age 30. *Faculty:* 37 full-time (19 women), 1 (woman) part-time/adjunct. Expenses: Contact institution. *Financial support:* Research assistantships with tuition reimbursements, teaching assistantships, career-related internships or fieldwork, Federal Work-Study, scholarships/grants, health care benefits, and unspecified assistantships available. Support available to part-time students. Financial award application deadline: 5/15; financial award applicants required to submit FAFSA. In 2019, 19 master's, 2 other advanced degrees awarded. *Program availability:* Part-time, evening/weekend. *Application deadline:* For fall admission, 3/1 for domestic students; for spring admission, 11/1 for domestic students. Applications are processed on a rolling basis. *Application fee:* $50. Electronic applications accepted. *Application Contact:* Graduate Studies, 401-456-8700, E-mail: graduatestudies@ric.edu. *Dean*, Dr. Earl Simson, 401-456-8106, E-mail: esimson@ric.edu.

***Feinstein School of Education and Human Development*** Students: 84 full-time (63 women), 334 part-time (279 women); includes 73 minority (20 Black or African American, non-Hispanic/Latino; 15 Asian, non-Hispanic/Latino; 30 Hispanic/Latino; 1 Native Hawaiian or other Pacific Islander, non-Hispanic/Latino; 7 Two or more races, non-Hispanic/Latino). Average age 34. *Faculty:* 30 full-time (22 women), 38 part-time/adjunct (29 women). Expenses: Contact institution. *Financial support:* Teaching assistantships, career-related internships or fieldwork, Federal Work-Study, scholarships/grants, health care benefits, and unspecified assistantships available. Support available to part-time students. Financial award application deadline: 5/15; financial award applicants required to submit FAFSA. In 2019, 115 master's, 5 doctorates, 31 other advanced degrees awarded. *Program availability:* Part-time, evening/weekend. *Application deadline:* For fall admission, 3/1 for domestic students; for spring admission, 11/1 for domestic students. Applications are processed on a rolling basis. *Application fee:* $50. Electronic applications accepted. *Application Contact:* Dr. Jeannine Dingus-Eason, Dean, 401-456-8110, E-mail: jdinguseason@ric.edu. *Dean*, Dr. Jeannine Dingus-Eason, 401-456-8110, E-mail: jdinguseason@ric.edu.

***School of Business*** Students: 15 full-time (11 women), 59 part-time (31 women); includes 27 minority (8 Black or African American, non-Hispanic/Latino; 6 Asian, non-Hispanic/Latino; 12 Hispanic/Latino; 1 Two or more races, non-Hispanic/Latino). Average age 33. *Faculty:* 6 full-time (3 women), 7 part-time/adjunct (2 women). Expenses: Contact institution. *Financial support:* Research assistantships, teaching assistantships, Federal Work-Study, scholarships/grants, health care benefits, and unspecified assistantships available. Support available to part-time students. Financial award application deadline: 5/15; financial award applicants required to submit FAFSA. In 2019, 8 master's awarded. *Program availability:* Part-time, evening/weekend. *Application deadline:* For fall admission, 3/1 for domestic students. Applications are processed on a rolling basis. *Application fee:* $50. Electronic applications accepted. *Application Contact:* Alema Karim, Acting Dean, 401-456-8009, E-mail: akarim@ric.edu. *Acting Dean,* Alema Karim, 401-456-8009, E-mail: akarim@ric.edu.

***School of Nursing*** Students: 22 full-time (16 women), 83 part-time (70 women); includes 21 minority (5 Black or African American, non-Hispanic/Latino; 3 Asian, non-Hispanic/Latino; 9 Hispanic/Latino; 1 Native Hawaiian or other Pacific Islander, non-Hispanic/Latino; 3 Two or more races, non-Hispanic/Latino). Average age 36. *Faculty:* 14 full-time (13 women), 16 part-time/adjunct (15 women). Expenses: Contact institution. *Financial support:* Teaching assistantships, Federal Work-Study, scholarships/grants, health care benefits, and unspecified assistantships available. Support available to part-time students. Financial award application deadline: 5/15; financial award applicants required to submit FAFSA. In 2019, 30 master's, 4 doctorates awarded. *Program availability:* Part-time. *Application deadline:* For fall admission, 2/15 for domestic students. Applications are processed on a rolling basis. *Application fee:* $50. Electronic applications accepted. *Application Contact:* Carolynn Masters, Dean, 401-456-8014, E-mail: cmasters@ric.edu. *Dean,* Carolynn Masters, 401-456-8014, E-mail: cmasters@ric.edu.

***School of Social Work*** Students: 98 full-time (80 women), 172 part-time (142 women); includes 111 minority (41 Black or African American, non-Hispanic/Latino; 3 Asian, non-Hispanic/Latino; 60 Hispanic/Latino; 7 Two or more races, non-Hispanic/Latino). Average age 31. *Faculty:* 13 full-time (8 women), 14 part-time/adjunct (13 women). Expenses: Contact institution. *Financial support:* Career-related internships or fieldwork, Federal Work-Study, scholarships/grants, health care benefits, and unspecified assistantships available. Support available to part-time students. Financial award application deadline: 5/15; financial award applicants required to submit FAFSA. In 2019, 97 master's awarded. *Program availability:* Part-time, evening/weekend. *Application deadline:* For fall admission, 2/1 for domestic students. Applications are processed on a rolling basis. *Application fee:* $50. Electronic applications accepted. *Application Contact:* Dr. Jayashree Nimmagadda, Interim Dean, 401-456-8042, E-mail: jnimmagadda@ric.edu. *Interim Dean,* Dr. Jayashree Nimmagadda, 401-456-8042, E-mail: jnimmagadda@ric.edu.

## RHODE ISLAND SCHOOL OF DESIGN, Providence, RI 02903-2784

**General Information** Independent, coed, comprehensive institution. *Enrollment:* 2,500 graduate, professional, and undergraduate students; 491 full-time matriculated graduate/professional students (325 women). *Enrollment by degree level:* 491 master's. *Tuition:* Full-time $51,800. *Required fees:* $1060. *Graduate housing:* Rooms and/or apartments available on a first-come, first-served basis to single and married students. Housing application deadline: 5/15. *Student services:* Campus employment opportunities, campus safety program, career counseling, exercise/wellness program, free psychological counseling, grant writing training, international student services, low-cost health insurance, multicultural affairs office, services for students with disabilities, teacher training, writing training. *Library facilities:* Fleet Library. *Collection:* Books: 132,119 (physical), 196,058 (digital/electronic); Serial titles: 1,669 (physical), 940 (digital/electronic); Databases: 48. Students can reserve study rooms.

**Computer facilities:** Computer purchase and lease plans are available. A campuswide network can be accessed. Online class registration is available.
Website: http://www.risd.edu/

**General Application Contact:** Molly Pettengill, Associate Director for Graduate Recruitment, 401-454-6312, Fax: 401-454-6309, E-mail: admissions@risd.edu.

**GRADUATE UNITS**

**Department of Architecture** Students: 98 full-time (52 women); includes 19 minority (5 Black or African American, non-Hispanic/Latino; 4 Asian, non-Hispanic/Latino; 7 Hispanic/Latino; 3 Two or more races, non-Hispanic/Latino), 42 international. Average age 25. 313 applicants, 68% accepted, 41 enrolled. Expenses: Contact institution. *Financial support:* Fellowships, research assistantships, teaching assistantships, Federal Work-Study, and unspecified assistantships available. Financial award application deadline: 2/1; financial award applicants required to submit FAFSA. In 2019, 28 master's awarded. *Application deadline:* For fall admission, 1/10 for domestic and international students. *Application fee:* $60. Electronic applications accepted. *Application Contact:* Molly Pettengill, Assistant Director for Graduate Recruitment, 401-454-6312, Fax: 401-454-6309, E-mail: mpetteng@risd.edu. *Department Head,* Amy Kulper, 401-454-6281, Fax: 401-454-6299, E-mail: archgrad@risd.edu.

**Department of Ceramics** Students: 9 full-time (5 women); includes 3 minority (1 Black or African American, non-Hispanic/Latino; 2 Asian, non-Hispanic/Latino), 2 international. Average age 27. 24 applicants, 54% accepted, 5 enrolled. Expenses: Contact institution. *Financial support:* Fellowships, research assistantships, teaching assistantships, Federal Work-Study, scholarships/grants, and unspecified assistantships available. Financial award application deadline: 2/1; financial award applicants required to submit FAFSA. In 2019, 6 master's awarded. *Application deadline:* For fall admission, 1/10 for domestic and international students. *Application fee:* $60. Electronic applications accepted. *Application Contact:* Molly Pettengill, Associate Director for Graduate Recruitment, 401-454-6312, Fax: 401-454-6309, E-mail: ceramics@risd.edu. *Department Head and Graduate Coordinator,* Lesley Baker, 401-454-6190, Fax: 401-454-6191, E-mail: ceramics@risd.edu.

**Department of Digital and Media** Students: 19 full-time (14 women); includes 2 minority (both Hispanic/Latino), 11 international. Average age 27. 161 applicants, 17% accepted, 11 enrolled. Expenses: Contact institution. *Financial support:* Fellowships, research assistantships, teaching assistantships, Federal Work-Study, scholarships/grants, and unspecified assistantships available. Financial award application deadline: 2/1; financial award applicants required to submit FAFSA. In 2019, 11 master's awarded. *Application deadline:* For fall admission, 1/10 for domestic and international students. *Application fee:* $60. Electronic applications accepted. *Application Contact:* Molly Pettengill, Associate Director for Graduate Recruitment, 401-454-6312, Fax: 401-454-6309, E-mail: mpetteng@risd.edu. *Department Head and Graduate Program Director,* Shawn Greenlee, 401-454-6139, Fax: 401-277-4966, E-mail: digital@risd.edu.

**Department of Furniture Design** Students: 18 full-time (10 women); includes 2 minority (1 Hispanic/Latino; 1 Two or more races, non-Hispanic/Latino), 11 international. Average age 28. 36 applicants, 50% accepted, 9 enrolled. Expenses: Contact institution. *Financial support:* Fellowships, research assistantships, teaching assistantships, Federal Work-Study, scholarships/grants, and unspecified assistantships available. Financial award application deadline: 2/1; financial award applicants required to submit FAFSA. In 2019, 11 master's awarded. *Application deadline:* For fall admission, 1/10 for domestic and international students. *Application fee:* $60. Electronic applications accepted. *Application Contact:* Molly Pettengill, Associate Director for Graduate Recruitment, 401-454-6312, Fax: 401-454-6309, E-mail: mpetteng@risd.edu. *Department Head,* Chris Specce, 401-454-6102, E-mail: furniture@risd.edu.

**Department of Glass** Students: 6 full-time (5 women); includes 2 minority (1 Asian, non-Hispanic/Latino; 1 Two or more races, non-Hispanic/Latino), 3 international. Average age 28. 5 applicants, 60% accepted, 3 enrolled. Expenses: Contact institution. *Financial support:* Fellowships, research assistantships, teaching assistantships, Federal Work-Study, scholarships/grants, and unspecified assistantships available. Financial award application deadline: 2/1; financial award applicants required to submit FAFSA. In 2019, 5 master's awarded. *Application deadline:* For fall admission, 1/10 for domestic and international students. *Application fee:* $60. Electronic applications accepted. *Application Contact:* Molly Pettengill, Associate Director for Graduate Recruitment, 401-454-6312, Fax: 401-454-6309, E-mail: mpetteng@risd.edu. *Department Head and Graduate Program Director,* Jocelyne Prince, 401-454-6190, Fax: 401-454-6680, E-mail: jprince@risd.edu.

**Department of Graphic Design** Students: 37 full-time (19 women); includes 7 minority (5 Asian, non-Hispanic/Latino; 1 Hispanic/Latino; 1 Two or more races, non-Hispanic/Latino), 13 international. Average age 28. 315 applicants, 9% accepted, 16 enrolled. Expenses: Contact institution. *Financial support:* Fellowships, research assistantships, teaching assistantships, Federal Work-Study, scholarships/grants, and unspecified assistantships available. Financial award application deadline: 2/1; financial award applicants required to submit FAFSA. In 2019, 16 master's awarded. *Application deadline:* For fall admission, 1/10 for domestic and international students. *Application fee:* $60. Electronic applications accepted. *Application Contact:* Molly Pettengill, Associate Director for Graduate Recruitment, 401-454-6312, Fax: 401-454-6309, E-mail: mpetteng@risd.edu. *Department Head,* Lucy Hitchcock, 401-454-6171, Fax: 401-454-6117, E-mail: gd@risd.edu.

**Department of Industrial Design** Students: 50 full-time (24 women); includes 6 minority (4 Asian, non-Hispanic/Latino; 2 Hispanic/Latino), 31 international. Average age 26. 255 applicants, 17% accepted, 9 enrolled. Expenses: Contact institution. *Financial support:* Fellowships, research assistantships, teaching assistantships, Federal Work-Study, scholarships/grants, and unspecified assistantships available. Financial award application deadline: 2/1; financial award applicants required to submit FAFSA. In 2019, 14 master's awarded. *Application deadline:* For fall admission, 1/10 for domestic and international students. *Application fee:* $60. Electronic applications accepted. *Application Contact:* Molly Pettengill, Associate Director for Graduate Recruitment, 401-454-6312, Fax: 401-454-6309, E-mail: mpetteng@risd.edu. *Department Head,* Khipra Nichols, 401-454-6160, Fax: 401-454-6157, E-mail: idgradprogram@risd.edu.

**Department of Interior Architecture** Students: 69 full-time (58 women); includes 3 minority (all Asian, non-Hispanic/Latino), 59 international. Average age 25. 200 applicants, 46% accepted, 37 enrolled. Expenses: Contact institution. *Financial support:* Fellowships, research assistantships, teaching assistantships, Federal Work-Study, scholarships/grants, and unspecified assistantships available. Financial award application deadline: 2/1; financial award applicants required to submit FAFSA. In 2019, 44 master's awarded. *Application deadline:* For fall admission, 1/10 for domestic and international students. *Application fee:* $60. Electronic applications accepted. *Application Contact:* Molly Pettengill, Associate Director for Graduate Recruitment, 401-454-6312, Fax: 401-454-6309, E-mail: mpetteng@risd.edu. *Department Head,* Liliane Wong, 401-454-6272, Fax: 401-277-4962, E-mail: lwong@risd.edu.

**Department of Jewelry and Metalsmithing** Students: 10 full-time (8 women); includes 1 minority (Asian, non-Hispanic/Latino), 6 international. Average age 25. 41 applicants, 24% accepted, 6 enrolled. Expenses: Contact institution. *Financial support:* Fellowships, research assistantships, teaching assistantships, Federal Work-Study, scholarships/grants, and unspecified assistantships available. Financial award application deadline: 2/1; financial award applicants required to submit FAFSA. In 2019, 4 master's awarded. *Application deadline:* For fall admission, 1/10 for domestic and international students. *Application fee:* $60. Electronic applications accepted. *Application Contact:* Molly Pettengill, Associate Director for Graduate Recruitment, 401-454-6312, Fax: 401-454-6309, E-mail: mpetteng@risd.edu. *Department Head,* Tracy Steepy, 401-454-6190, Fax: 401-454-6191, E-mail: jewelry@risd.edu.

**Department of Landscape Architecture** Students: 77 full-time (55 women); includes 1 minority (Asian, non-Hispanic/Latino), 66 international. Average age 24. 144 applicants, 63% accepted, 29 enrolled. Expenses: Contact institution. *Financial support:* Fellowships, research assistantships, teaching assistantships, Federal Work-Study, scholarships/grants, and unspecified assistantships available. Financial award application deadline: 2/1; financial award applicants required to submit FAFSA. In 2019, 26 master's awarded. *Application deadline:* For fall admission, 1/10 for domestic and international students. *Application fee:* $60. Electronic applications accepted. *Application Contact:* Molly Pettengill, Associate Director for Graduate Recruitment, 401-454-6312, Fax: 401-454-6309, E-mail: mpetteng@risd.edu. *Department Head,* Johanna Barthmeier-Payne, 401-454-6282, Fax: 401-454-6299, E-mail: ldardept@risd.edu.

**Department of Painting** Students: 19 full-time (10 women); includes 2 minority (1 Black or African American, non-Hispanic/Latino; 1 Asian, non-Hispanic/Latino), 1 international. Average age 27. 216 applicants, 11% accepted, 9 enrolled. Expenses: Contact institution. *Financial support:* Fellowships, research assistantships, teaching assistantships, Federal Work-Study, scholarships/grants, and unspecified assistantships available. Financial award application deadline: 2/1; financial award applicants required to submit FAFSA. In 2019, 9 master's awarded. *Application deadline:* For fall admission, 1/10 for domestic and international students. *Application fee:* $60. Electronic applications accepted. *Application Contact:* Molly Pettengill, Associate Director for Graduate Recruitment, 401-454-6312, Fax: 401-454-6309, E-mail: mpetteng@risd.edu. *Department Head,* Kevin Zucker, 401-454-6158, Fax: 401-454-6681, E-mail: painting@risd.edu.

**Department of Photography** Students: 14 full-time (10 women); includes 2 minority (both Hispanic/Latino), 4 international. Average age 27. 123 applicants, 17% accepted, 8 enrolled. Expenses: Contact institution. *Financial support:* Fellowships, research assistantships, teaching assistantships, Federal Work-Study, scholarships/grants, and unspecified assistantships available. Financial award application deadline: 2/1; financial award applicants required to submit FAFSA. In 2019, 9 master's awarded. *Application deadline:* For fall admission, 1/10 for domestic and international students. *Application fee:* $60. Electronic applications accepted. *Application Contact:* Molly Pettengill, Associate Director for Graduate Recruitment, 401-454-6312, Fax: 401-454-6309, E-mail: mpetteng@risd.edu. *Department Head,* Steven Smith, 401-454-6122, Fax: 401-454-6385, E-mail: photo@risd.edu.

**Department of Printmaking** Students: 14 full-time (11 women); includes 3 minority (1 Hispanic/Latino; 2 Two or more races, non-Hispanic/Latino), 3 international. Average age 26. 40 applicants, 25% accepted, 6 enrolled. Expenses: Contact institution. *Financial support:* Fellowships, research assistantships, teaching assistantships, Federal Work-Study, scholarships/grants, and unspecified assistantships available. Financial award application deadline: 2/1; financial award applicants required to submit FAFSA. In 2019, 5 master's awarded. *Application deadline:* For fall admission, 1/10 for domestic and international students. *Application fee:* $60. Electronic applications accepted. *Application Contact:* Molly Pettengill, Associate Director for Graduate

Recruitment, 401-454-6312, Fax: 401-454-6309, E-mail: mpetteng@risd.edu. *Department Head*, Cornelia McSheehy, 401-454-6224, Fax: 401-454-6707, E-mail: printmaking@risd.edu.

**Department of Sculpture** Students: 10 full-time (8 women); includes 2 minority (1 Hispanic/Latino; 1 Two or more races, non-Hispanic/Latino), 7 international. Average age 27. 68 applicants, 26% accepted, 5 enrolled. Expenses: Contact institution. *Financial support:* Fellowships, research assistantships, teaching assistantships, Federal Work-Study, scholarships/grants, and unspecified assistantships available. Financial award application deadline: 2/1; financial award applicants required to submit FAFSA. In 2019, 9 master's awarded. *Application deadline:* For fall admission, 1/10 for domestic and international students. *Application fee:* $60. Electronic applications accepted. *Application Contact:* Molly Pettengill, Associate Director for Graduate Recruitment, 401-454-6312, Fax: 401-454-6309, E-mail: mpetteng@risd.edu. *Department Head*, Lisi Raskin, 401-454-6425, Fax: 401-454-6191, E-mail: sculpture@risd.edu.

**Department of Teaching and Learning in Art and Design** Students: 10 full-time (9 women); includes 1 minority (Asian, non-Hispanic/Latino), 2 international. Average age 24. 35 applicants, 69% accepted, 10 enrolled. Expenses: Contact institution. *Financial support:* Fellowships, research assistantships, teaching assistantships, Federal Work-Study, scholarships/grants, and unspecified assistantships available. Financial award application deadline: 2/1; financial award applicants required to submit FAFSA. In 2019, 11 master's awarded. *Application deadline:* For fall admission, 1/10 for domestic and international students. *Application fee:* $60. Electronic applications accepted. *Application Contact:* Molly Pettengill, Associate Director for Graduate Recruitment, 401-454-6312, Fax: 401-454-6309, E-mail: mpetteng@risd.edu. *Department Head and Graduate Program Director*, Paul Sproll, 401-454-6695, Fax: 401-454-6694, E-mail: teachlearn@risd.edu.

**Department of Textiles** Students: 10 full-time (8 women), 8 international. Average age 27. 46 applicants, 22% accepted, 4 enrolled. Expenses: Contact institution. *Financial support:* Fellowships, research assistantships, teaching assistantships, Federal Work-Study, scholarships/grants, and unspecified assistantships available. Financial award application deadline: 2/1; financial award applicants required to submit FAFSA. In 2019, 5 master's awarded. *Application deadline:* For fall admission, 1/10 for domestic and international students. *Application fee:* $60. Electronic applications accepted. *Application Contact:* Molly Pettengill, Associate Director for Graduate Recruitment, 401-454-6312, Fax: 401-454-6309, E-mail: mpetteng@risd.edu. *Department Head*, Mary Anne Friel, 401-427-6967, Fax: 401-277-4883, E-mail: textiles@risd.edu.

## RHODES COLLEGE, Memphis, TN 38112-1690

**General Information** Independent, coed, comprehensive institution. *Enrollment:* 2,010 graduate, professional, and undergraduate students; 26 full-time matriculated graduate/professional students (15 women), 2 part-time matriculated graduate/professional students (both women). *Enrollment by degree level:* 28 master's. *Graduate faculty:* 7 full-time (all women), 2 part-time/adjunct (0 women). *Tuition:* Full-time $48,888. *Required fees:* $310. *Graduate housing:* Room and/or apartments available on a first-come, first-served basis to single students; on-campus housing not available to married students. Typical cost: $11,631 (including board). Room and board charges vary according to board plan. Housing application deadline: 3/1. *Student services:* Campus employment opportunities, campus safety program, career counseling, exercise/wellness program, free psychological counseling, international student services, low-cost health insurance, multicultural affairs office, services for students with disabilities, writing training. *Library facilities:* Paul Barret, Jr. Library. *Collection:* Books: 221,803 (physical), 351,899 (digital/electronic); Serial titles: 16,497 (physical), 92,422 (digital/electronic); Databases: 296. Weekly public service hours: 113.

**Computer facilities:** 1,000 computers available on campus for general student use. A campuswide network can be accessed. Online class registration is available.
Website: http://www.rhodes.edu/

**General Application Contact:** Dr. Kayla Booker, Program Director, 901-843-3568, E-mail: bookerk@rhodes.edu.

**GRADUATE UNITS**

**Department of Business** Students: 17 full-time (8 women); includes 3 minority (1 Black or African American, non-Hispanic/Latino; 2 Two or more races, non-Hispanic/Latino). Average age 22. 17 applicants, 100% accepted, 17 enrolled. *Faculty:* 2 full-time (both women), 2 part-time/adjunct (0 women). Expenses: Contact institution. *Financial support:* In 2019–20, 17 students received support. Career-related internships or fieldwork and scholarships/grants available. Financial award application deadline: 3/1; financial award applicants required to submit FAFSA. In 2019, 18 master's awarded. *Program availability:* Part-time. *Application deadline:* For fall admission, 3/1 for domestic students. Electronic applications accepted. *Application Contact:* Dr. Kayla Booker, Program Director, 901-843-3568, Fax: 901-843-3798, E-mail: bookerk@rhodes.edu.

## RICE UNIVERSITY, Houston, TX 77251-1892

**General Information** Independent, coed, university. CGS member. *Graduate housing:* Rooms and/or apartments available on a first-come, first-served basis to single and married students. Housing application deadline: 7/15. *Research affiliation:* Fermi National Accelerator Laboratory, Los Alamos National Laboratory, Brookhaven National Laboratory, Arecibo Observatory, Houston Area Research Center.

**GRADUATE UNITS**

**Graduate Programs** *Program availability:* Part-time. Electronic applications accepted.

***George R. Brown School of Engineering*** *Program availability:* Part-time. Electronic applications accepted.

***Jesse H. Jones Graduate School of Business*** *Program availability:* Evening/weekend. Electronic applications accepted.

***School of Architecture*** Electronic applications accepted.

***School of Humanities***

***School of Social Sciences***

***Shepherd School of Music***

***Susanne M. Glasscock School of Continuing Studies*** *Program availability:* Part-time, evening/weekend.

***Wiess School of Natural Sciences*** *Program availability:* Part-time. Electronic applications accepted.

***Wiess School–Professional Science Master's Programs***

**Rice Quantum Institute** Electronic applications accepted.

## RICHMOND, THE AMERICAN INTERNATIONAL UNIVERSITY IN LONDON, Richmond, Surrey TW10 6JP, United Kingdom

**General Information** Independent, coed, comprehensive institution. *Graduate housing:* Room and/or apartments available on a first-come, first-served basis to single students; on-campus housing not available to married students. Housing application deadline: 8/1.

**GRADUATE UNITS**

**MA in Art History Program** *Program availability:* Part-time. Electronic applications accepted.

**MA in International Relations Program** *Program availability:* Part-time. Electronic applications accepted.

## RICHMONT GRADUATE UNIVERSITY, Atlanta, GA 30339

**General Information** Independent-religious, coed, graduate-only institution.

**GRADUATE UNITS**

**School of Counseling** *Program availability:* Part-time, evening/weekend. Electronic applications accepted.

**School of Ministry** *Program availability:* Part-time, evening/weekend, 100% online, blended/hybrid learning. Electronic applications accepted.

## RIDER UNIVERSITY, Lawrenceville, NJ 08648-3001

**General Information** Independent, coed, comprehensive institution. *Graduate housing:* Room and/or apartments available on a first-come, first-served basis to single students; on-campus housing not available to married students.

**GRADUATE UNITS**

**College of Business Administration** *Program availability:* Part-time, evening/weekend. Electronic applications accepted.

**College of Continuing Studies**

**College of Education and Human Services** *Program availability:* Part-time, evening/weekend. Electronic applications accepted.

**College of Liberal Arts and Sciences** *Program availability:* Part-time, evening/weekend. Electronic applications accepted.

**School of Fine and Performing Arts**

**Westminster Choir College** Electronic applications accepted.

## RIVIER UNIVERSITY, Nashua, NH 03060

**General Information** Independent-religious, coed, comprehensive institution. *Graduate housing:* On-campus housing not available.

**GRADUATE UNITS**

**School of Graduate Studies** *Program availability:* Part-time. Electronic applications accepted.

***Division of Nursing and Health Professions*** *Program availability:* Part-time, evening/weekend. Electronic applications accepted.

## THE ROBERT E. WEBBER INSTITUTE FOR WORSHIP STUDIES, Jacksonville, FL 32207

**General Information** Independent-religious, coed, graduate-only institution.

**GRADUATE UNITS**

**Doctor of Worship Studies Program**

**Master of Worship Studies Program**

## ROBERT MORRIS UNIVERSITY, Moon Township, PA 15108-1189

**General Information** Independent, coed, university. *Enrollment:* 4,608 graduate, professional, and undergraduate students; 838 part-time matriculated graduate/professional students (477 women). *Enrollment by degree level:* 536 master's, 263 doctoral, 31 other advanced degrees. *Graduate faculty:* 60 full-time (30 women), 19 part-time/adjunct (5 women). *Tuition:* Part-time $995 per credit. *Required fees:* $85 per credit. Part-time tuition and fees vary according to program. *Graduate housing:* On-campus housing not available. *Student services:* Campus employment opportunities, campus safety program, career counseling, exercise/wellness program, international student services, multicultural affairs office, services for students with disabilities, teacher training. *Library facilities:* Robert Morris University Library. *Collection:* Books: 97,693 (physical), 172,931 (digital/electronic); Serial titles: 244 (physical), 47,791 (digital/electronic); Databases: 104. Weekly public service hours: 101; study areas open 24 hours, 5–7 days a week; students can reserve study rooms.

**Computer facilities:** Computer purchase and lease plans are available. 375 computers available on campus for general student use. A campuswide network can be accessed. Online class registration, online payment are available.
Website: http://www.rmu.edu/

**General Application Contact:** Kellie L. Laurenzi, Associate Vice President, 412-397-5200, Fax: 412-397-2425, E-mail: graduateadmissions@rmu.edu.

**GRADUATE UNITS**

**School of Business** Students: 259 part-time (120 women); includes 22 minority (11 Black or African American, non-Hispanic/Latino; 8 Asian, non-Hispanic/Latino; 1 Hispanic/Latino; 2 Two or more races, non-Hispanic/Latino), 10 international. Average age 30. *Faculty:* 15 full-time (8 women), 2 part-time/adjunct (1 woman). Expenses: Contact institution. *Financial support:* Institutionally sponsored loans available. Support available to part-time students. Financial award application deadline: 5/1; financial award applicants required to submit FAFSA. In 2019, 111 master's awarded. *Program availability:* Part-time-only, evening/weekend, 100% online. *Application deadline:* For fall admission, 7/1 priority date for domestic and international students; for spring admission, 11/1 priority date for domestic and international students. Applications are processed on a rolling basis. *Application fee:* $35. Electronic applications accepted. *Application Contact:* Dr. Jodi Potter, Director, MBA Program, 412-397-6387, E-mail: potterj@rmu.edu. *Dean*, Dr. Michelle L. Patrick, 412-397-5445, Fax: 412-397-2585, E-mail: patrick@rmu.edu.

**School of Engineering, Mathematics and Science** Students: 20 part-time (8 women); includes 4 minority (1 Black or African American, non-Hispanic/Latino; 2 Asian, non-Hispanic/Latino; 1 Two or more races, non-Hispanic/Latino), 6 international. Average age 28. *Faculty:* 6 full-time (1 woman), 1 part-time/adjunct (0 women). Expenses: Contact institution. *Financial support:* Federal Work-Study, institutionally sponsored loans, and unspecified assistantships available. Financial award application deadline: 5/1; financial award applicants required to submit FAFSA. In 2019, 20 master's awarded. *Program availability:* Part-time-only, evening/weekend, 100% online. *Application deadline:* For fall admission, 7/1 priority date for domestic and international students; for spring admission, 11/1 priority date for domestic and international students. Applications are processed on a rolling basis. *Application fee:* $35. Electronic applications accepted. *Application Contact:* Kellie Laurenzi, Associate Vice President,

Enrollment Management, 412-397-5200, E-mail: graduateadmissions@rmu.edu. *Dean*, Dr. Maria V. Kalevitch, 412-397-4020, E-mail: kalevitch@rmu.edu.

**School of Informatics, Humanities and Social Sciences** Students: 224 part-time (90 women); includes 46 minority (28 Black or African American, non-Hispanic/Latino; 5 Asian, non-Hispanic/Latino; 9 Hispanic/Latino; 4 Two or more races, non-Hispanic/Latino), 31 international. Average age 35. *Faculty:* 23 full-time (9 women), 11 part-time/adjunct (0 women). Expenses: Contact institution. *Financial support:* Institutionally sponsored loans available. Support available to part-time students. Financial award application deadline: 5/1; financial award applicants required to submit FAFSA. In 2019, 118 master's, 14 doctorates awarded. *Program availability:* Part-time-only, evening/weekend, 100% online. *Application deadline:* For fall admission, 7/1 priority date for domestic and international students; for spring admission, 11/1 priority date for domestic and international students. Applications are processed on a rolling basis. *Application fee:* $35. Electronic applications accepted. *Application Contact:* Kellie Laurenzi, Associate Vice President, Enrollment Management, 412-397-5200, E-mail: graduateadmissions@rmu.edu. *Dean, School of Informatics, Humanities and Social Sciences*, Dr. Amjad Ali, 412-397-3000.

**School of Nursing, Education and Human Studies** Students: 351 part-time (266 women); includes 45 minority (31 Black or African American, non-Hispanic/Latino; 5 Asian, non-Hispanic/Latino; 3 Hispanic/Latino; 1 Native Hawaiian or other Pacific Islander, non-Hispanic/Latino; 5 Two or more races, non-Hispanic/Latino), 5 international. Average age 35. *Faculty:* 16 full-time (13 women), 5 part-time/adjunct (4 women). Expenses: Contact institution. *Financial support:* Federal Work-Study, institutionally sponsored loans, and unspecified assistantships available. Financial award application deadline: 5/1; financial award applicants required to submit FAFSA. In 2019, 52 master's, 69 doctorates awarded. *Program availability:* Part-time-only, evening/weekend, 100% online. *Application deadline:* For fall admission, 7/1 priority date for domestic and international students; for spring admission, 11/1 priority date for domestic and international students. Applications are processed on a rolling basis. *Application fee:* $35. Electronic applications accepted. *Application Contact:* Kellie Laurenzi, Associate Vice President, Enrollment Management, 412-397-5200, E-mail: graduateadmissions@rmu.edu.

**See Display below and Close-Up on page 631.**

## ROBERT MORRIS UNIVERSITY ILLINOIS, Chicago, IL 60605

**General Information** Independent, coed, comprehensive institution. *Graduate housing:* Room and/or apartments available to single students.

**GRADUATE UNITS**

**Morris Graduate School of Management** *Program availability:* Part-time, evening/weekend. Electronic applications accepted.

## ROBERTS WESLEYAN COLLEGE, Rochester, NY 14624-1997

**General Information** Independent-religious, coed, comprehensive institution. *Graduate housing:* Rooms and/or apartments available on a first-come, first-served basis to single and married students.

**GRADUATE UNITS**

**Department of Nursing** *Program availability:* Evening/weekend, online learning. Electronic applications accepted.

**Department of Social Work**

**Graduate Business Programs** *Program availability:* Evening/weekend.

**Graduate Psychology Programs** *Program availability:* Part-time, evening/weekend. Electronic applications accepted.

**Graduate Teacher Education Programs** *Program availability:* Part-time, evening/weekend. Electronic applications accepted.

**Health Administration Programs** *Program availability:* Evening/weekend, online learning.

## ROCHESTER INSTITUTE OF TECHNOLOGY, Rochester, NY 14623-5603

**General Information** Independent, coed, university. CGS member. *Graduate housing:* Rooms and/or apartments available on a first-come, first-served basis to single and married students. *Research affiliation:* Corning Inc. (materials science technology), Harris Corporation (information technology, broadband communications), Toyota Materials Handling N.A. (industrial equipment performance), Hewlett Packard (enterprise information technology), Bausch & Lomb (eye health), Yamaha Corporation (audio and acoustic engineering).

**GRADUATE UNITS**

**Graduate Enrollment Services** *Program availability:* Part-time, evening/weekend, 100% online, blended/hybrid learning. Electronic applications accepted.

***College of Applied Science and Technology*** *Program availability:* Part-time, evening/weekend, 100% online, blended/hybrid learning. Electronic applications accepted.

***College of Health Sciences and Technology*** *Program availability:* Part-time, evening/weekend, 100% online. Electronic applications accepted.

***College of Imaging Arts and Sciences*** *Program availability:* Part-time, 100% online. Electronic applications accepted.

***College of Liberal Arts*** *Program availability:* Part-time, 100% online. Electronic applications accepted.

***College of Science*** *Program availability:* Part-time, evening/weekend, 100% online. Electronic applications accepted.

***Golisano College of Computing and Information Sciences*** *Program availability:* Part-time, evening/weekend, 100% online. Electronic applications accepted.

***Golisano Institute for Sustainability*** *Program availability:* Part-time. Electronic applications accepted.

***Kate Gleason College of Engineering*** *Program availability:* Part-time, evening/weekend, 100% online. Electronic applications accepted.

***National Technical Institute for the Deaf*** *Program availability:* Part-time, evening/weekend, blended/hybrid learning. Electronic applications accepted.

***Saunders College of Business*** *Program availability:* Part-time, evening/weekend, 100% online, blended/hybrid learning. Electronic applications accepted.

***School of Individualized Study*** *Program availability:* Part-time, evening/weekend, 100% online, blended/hybrid learning. Electronic applications accepted.

## ROCHESTER UNIVERSITY, Rochester Hills, MI 48307-2764

**General Information** Independent-religious, coed, comprehensive institution.

**GRADUATE UNITS**

**Center for Missional Leadership**

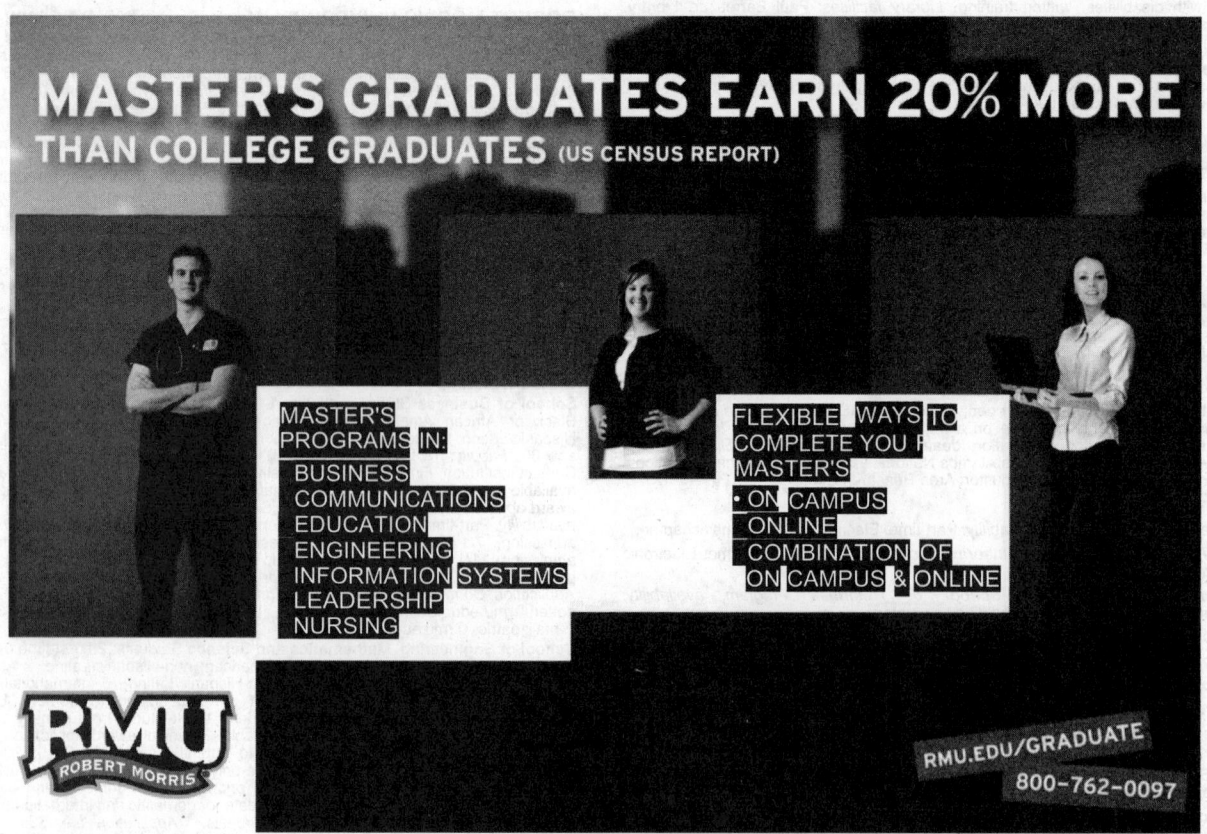

## THE ROCKEFELLER UNIVERSITY, New York, NY 10021-6399

**General Information** Independent, coed, graduate-only institution. CGS member. *Enrollment by degree level:* 14 master's, 234 doctoral. *Graduate faculty:* 74 full-time (13 women). *Graduate housing:* Rooms and/or apartments guaranteed to single and married students. Housing application deadline: 6/1. *Student services:* Campus safety program, career counseling, child daycare facilities, exercise/wellness program, free psychological counseling, grant writing training, low-cost health insurance, services for students with disabilities, teacher training. *Library facilities:* Rita and Frits Markus Library. *Collection:* Books: 44,687 (physical), 199,577 (digital/electronic); Serial titles: 7,204 (digital/electronic); Databases: 22. Weekly public service hours: 40; study areas open 24 hours, 5–7 days a week; students can reserve study rooms.

**Computer facilities:** 32 computers available on campus for general student use. A campuswide network can be accessed from student residence rooms and from off campus. Online class registration is available.
Website: http://www.rockefeller.edu/

**General Application Contact:** Kristen Cullen, Graduate Admissions Administrator/Registrar, 212-327-8086, Fax: 212-327-8505, E-mail: phd@rockefeller.edu.

**GRADUATE UNITS**

**The David Rockefeller Graduate Program in Bioscience** Students: 248 full-time (108 women); includes 60 minority (9 Black or African American, non-Hispanic/Latino; 2 American Indian or Alaska Native, non-Hispanic/Latino; 29 Asian, non-Hispanic/Latino; 19 Hispanic/Latino; 1 Native Hawaiian or other Pacific Islander, non-Hispanic/Latino), 78 international. Average age 28. 1,098 applicants, 7% accepted, 27 enrolled. *Faculty:* 74 full-time (13 women). Expenses: Contact institution. *Financial support:* In 2019–20, 248 students received support, including 248 fellowships with full tuition reimbursements available; institutionally sponsored loans, scholarships/grants, traineeships, and health care benefits also available. In 2019, 9 master's, 30 doctorates awarded. *Application deadline:* For fall and winter admission, 12/1 for domestic and international students. *Application fee:* $50. Electronic applications accepted. *Application Contact:* Kristen Cullen, Graduate Admissions Administrator/Registrar, 212-327-8086, Fax: 212-327-8505, E-mail: phd@rockefeller.edu. *Dean of Graduate and Postgraduate Studies/Vice President*, Dr. Sidney Strickland, 212-327-8086, Fax: 212-327-8505, E-mail: phd@rockefeller.edu.

## ROCKFORD UNIVERSITY, Rockford, IL 61108-2393

**General Information** Independent, coed, comprehensive institution. *Graduate housing:* Room and/or apartments available on a first-come, first-served basis to single students; on-campus housing not available to married students.

**GRADUATE UNITS**

**Graduate Studies** *Program availability:* Part-time, evening/weekend. Electronic applications accepted.

## ROCKHURST UNIVERSITY, Kansas City, MO 64110-2561

**General Information** Independent-religious, coed, comprehensive institution. *Graduate housing:* Room and/or apartments available on a first-come, first-served basis to single students; on-campus housing not available to married students.

**GRADUATE UNITS**

**College of Health and Human Services** *Program availability:* Part-time, evening/weekend.

**Helzberg School of Management** *Program availability:* Part-time, evening/weekend. Electronic applications accepted.

## ROCKY MOUNTAIN COLLEGE, Billings, MT 59102-1796

**General Information** Independent-religious, coed, comprehensive institution. *Enrollment:* 1,000 graduate, professional, and undergraduate students; 116 full-time matriculated graduate/professional students (83 women), 1 part-time matriculated graduate/professional student. *Enrollment by degree level:* 87 master's, 30 doctoral. *Graduate faculty:* 14 full-time (9 women), 2 part-time/adjunct (1 woman). Tuition and fees vary according to program. *Graduate housing:* Rooms and/or apartments available on a first-come, first-served basis to single and married students. *Student services:* Campus employment opportunities, campus safety program, career counseling, free psychological counseling, international student services, services for students with disabilities, teacher training, writing training. *Library facilities:* Paul M. Adams Memorial Library. *Collection:* Books: 47,570 (physical), 172,956 (digital/electronic); Serial titles: 396 (physical), 51,657 (digital/electronic); Databases: 120. Weekly public service hours: 89.

**Computer facilities:** 113 computers available on campus for general student use. A campuswide network can be accessed. Online class registration is available.
Website: http://www.rocky.edu/

**General Application Contact:** Austin Mapston, Dean of Enrollment Services, 406-657-1026, Fax: 406-657-1189, E-mail: admissions@rocky.edu.

**GRADUATE UNITS**

**Program in Accountancy** Students: 1 part-time (0 women). Average age 45. *Faculty:* 2 full-time (0 women). Expenses: Contact institution. *Financial support:* Campus work-study available. Financial award applicants required to submit FAFSA. In 2019, 7 master's awarded. *Program availability:* Part-time-only. *Application deadline:* Applications are processed on a rolling basis. *Application fee:* $35 ($40 for international students). Electronic applications accepted. *Application Contact:* Austin Mapston, Dean of Enrollment Services, 406-657-1026, Fax: 406-657-1189, E-mail: admissions@rocky.edu. *Professor of Business Administration and Economics*, Anthony Piltz, 406-657-1069, E-mail: piltza@rocky.edu.

**Program in Educational Leadership** Students: 14 full-time (7 women). Average age 35. *Faculty:* 1 (woman) full-time. Expenses: Contact institution. *Financial support:* Scholarships/grants available. Financial award applicants required to submit FAFSA. In 2019, 18 master's awarded. *Application deadline:* Applications are processed on a rolling basis. *Application fee:* $35 ($40 for international students). Electronic applications accepted. *Application Contact:* Austin Mapston, Dean of Enrollment Services, 406-657-1026, Fax: 406-657-1189, E-mail: admissions@rocky.edu. *Director of Educational Leadership and Distance Education*, Dr. Stevie Schmitz, 406-657-1134, E-mail: schmitzs@rocky.edu.

**Program in Occupational Therapy** Students: 30 full-time (26 women); includes 7 minority (1 Asian, non-Hispanic/Latino; 3 Hispanic/Latino; 3 Two or more races, non-Hispanic/Latino). Average age 25. *Faculty:* 5 full-time (all women). Expenses: Contact institution. *Financial support:* In 2019–20, 7 students received support. Unspecified assistantships and campus work-study available. Financial award applicants required to submit FAFSA. *Application deadline:* Applications are processed on a rolling basis. *Application fee:* $145. Electronic applications accepted. *Application Contact:* Cody Halverson, Coordinator of Admissions for Health Professions, 406-657-1198, E-mail: halversonc@rocky.edu. *Director*, Dr. Twylla M. Kirchen, 406-657-1165, E-mail: twylla.kirchen@rocky.edu.

**Program in Physician Assistant Studies** Students: 72 full-time (50 women); includes 7 minority (3 Asian, non-Hispanic/Latino; 3 Hispanic/Latino; 1 Two or more races, non-Hispanic/Latino). Average age 27. *Faculty:* 6 full-time (3 women), 2 part-time/adjunct (1 woman). Expenses: Contact institution. *Financial support:* Applicants required to submit FAFSA. In 2019, 36 master's awarded. *Application deadline:* Applications are processed on a rolling basis. *Application fee:* $80. Electronic applications accepted. *Application Contact:* Cody Halverson, Coordinator of Admissions for Health Professions, 406-657-1198, E-mail: halversonc@rocky.edu. *Program Director*, Adam Mattingly, 406-657-1192, E-mail: adam.mattingly@rocky.edu.

## ROCKY MOUNTAIN COLLEGE OF ART + DESIGN, Lakewood, CO 80214

**General Information** Proprietary, coed, comprehensive institution.

**GRADUATE UNITS**

**Program in Education, Leadership + Emerging Technologies** *Program availability:* Online learning.

## ROCKY MOUNTAIN UNIVERSITY OF HEALTH PROFESSIONS, Provo, UT 84606

**General Information** Proprietary, coed, graduate-only institution. *Research affiliation:* Aegis Corporation.

**GRADUATE UNITS**

**Doctor of Nursing Practice Program**

**Doctor of Science Program in Clinical Electrophysiology** *Program availability:* Online learning.

**Program in Occupational Therapy** *Program availability:* Online learning. Electronic applications accepted.

**Program in Physician Assistant Studies**

**Program in Speech-Language Pathology**

**Programs in Physical Therapy**

## ROCKY VISTA UNIVERSITY, Parker, CO 80134

**General Information** Proprietary, coed, graduate-only institution.

**GRADUATE UNITS**

**College of Osteopathic Medicine**

**Program in Biomedical Sciences**

**Program in Physician Assistant Studies**

## ROGERS STATE UNIVERSITY, Claremore, OK 74017-3252

**General Information** State-supported, coed, comprehensive institution. *Enrollment:* 3,614 graduate, professional, and undergraduate students; 18 full-time matriculated graduate/professional students (11 women), 12 part-time matriculated graduate/professional students (7 women). *Enrollment by degree level:* 30 master's. *Tuition, area resident:* Full-time $10,880; part-time $5440 per credit hour. *Graduate housing:* Rooms and/or apartments available on a first-come, first-served basis to single and married students. Typical cost: $5490 per year ($8975 including board) for single students; $5490 per year ($8975 including board) for married students. *Student services:* Campus employment opportunities, career counseling, free psychological counseling, services for students with disabilities. *Library facilities:* Stratton Taylor Library. *Collection:* Books: 80,238 (physical), 298,063 (digital/electronic); Serial titles: 491 (physical), 67,126 (digital/electronic); Databases: 81. Weekly public service hours: 86; students can reserve study rooms.

**Computer facilities:** 251 computers available on campus for general student use. A campuswide network can be accessed. Online class registration, software to support courses are available.
Website: http://www.rsu.edu/

**General Application Contact:** Ronna Hatley, MBA Program Coordinator, 918-343-6819, E-mail: mba@rsu.edu.

**GRADUATE UNITS**

**Program in Business Administration**

## ROGER WILLIAMS UNIVERSITY, Bristol, RI 02809

**General Information** Independent, coed, comprehensive institution. *Enrollment:* 4,838 graduate, professional, and undergraduate students; 180 full-time matriculated graduate/professional students (103 women), 131 part-time matriculated graduate/professional students (65 women). *Enrollment by degree level:* 305 master's, 6 other advanced degrees. *Graduate faculty:* 23 full-time (11 women), 28 part-time/adjunct (12 women). *Tuition:* Full-time $15,768. *Required fees:* $900; $450. *Graduate housing:* On-campus housing not available. *Student services:* Campus employment opportunities, campus safety program, career counseling, exercise/wellness program, free psychological counseling, international student services, low-cost health insurance, services for students with disabilities, teacher training. *Library facilities:* Roger Williams University Library plus 1 other. *Collection:* Books: 188,670 (physical), 173,161 (digital/electronic); Serial titles: 1,391 (physical), 173,161 (digital/electronic); Databases: 300. Weekly public service hours: 111; students can reserve study rooms.

**Computer facilities:** 100 computers available on campus for general student use. A campuswide network can be accessed. Online class registration is available.
Website: http://www.rwu.edu/

**General Application Contact:** Marcus Hanscom, Director of Graduate Admission, 401-254-6200, Fax: 401-254-3557, E-mail: gradadmit@rwu.edu.

**GRADUATE UNITS**

**Feinstein School of Humanities, Arts and Education** Students: 1 full-time (0 women). 9 applicants, 78% accepted, 3 enrolled. Expenses: Contact institution. *Financial support:* Application deadline: 3/15; applicants required to submit FAFSA. In 2019, 7 master's awarded. *Program availability:* Part-time, evening/weekend, online learning. *Application deadline:* Applications are processed on a rolling basis. *Application fee:* $50. Electronic applications accepted. *Application Contact:* Marcus Hanscom, Director of Graduate Admissions, 401-254-3345, Fax: 401-254-3557, E-mail: gradadmit@rwu.edu. *Dean*, Dr. Cynthia Scheinberg, 401-254-3828, E-mail: cscheinberg@rwu.edu.

**Feinstein School of Social and Natural Sciences** Students: 34 full-time (31 women), 1 part-time (0 women); includes 5 minority (1 Black or African American, non-Hispanic/Latino; 1 Asian, non-Hispanic/Latino; 3 Hispanic/Latino). Average age 23. 84 applicants, 57% accepted, 19 enrolled. *Faculty:* 1 (woman) full-time, 1 part-time/adjunct (0 women). Expenses: Contact institution. *Financial support:* In 2019–20, 29 students received support. Scholarships/grants and unspecified assistantships available. Financial award application deadline: 3/15; financial award applicants required to submit FAFSA. In 2019, 22 master's awarded. *Application deadline:* For fall admission, 2/15 for domestic students, 2/1 for international students. *Application fee:* $50. *Application Contact:* Marcus Hanscom, Director of Graduate Admissions, 401-254-3345, Fax: 401-254-3557, E-mail: gradadmit@rwu.edu. *Graduate Program Director*, Alejandro Leguizamo, 401-254-3934, E-mail: aleguizamo@rwu.edu.

**Mario J. Gabelli School of Business** Students: 21 full-time (10 women); includes 1 minority (Hispanic/Latino). Average age 22. 32 applicants, 81% accepted, 22 enrolled. *Faculty:* 3 full-time (1 woman). Expenses: Contact institution. *Financial support:* In 2019–20, 11 students received support. Scholarships/grants and unspecified assistantships available. Financial award application deadline: 3/15; financial award applicants required to submit FAFSA. In 2019, 15 master's awarded. *Application deadline:* Applications are processed on a rolling basis. *Application fee:* $50. Electronic applications accepted. *Application Contact:* Jason Oliver, MBA Program Coordinator, 401-254-3018, E-mail: joliver@rwu.edu. *Dean of School of Business*, Dr. Susan McTiernan, 401-254-3444, E-mail: smctiernan@rwu.edu.

**School of Architecture, Art and Historic Preservation** Students: 97 full-time (46 women), 10 part-time (0 women); includes 15 minority (1 Black or African American, non-Hispanic/Latino; 1 American Indian or Alaska Native, non-Hispanic/Latino; 1 Asian, non-Hispanic/Latino; 8 Hispanic/Latino; 4 Two or more races, non-Hispanic/Latino), 5 international. Average age 23. 97 applicants, 92% accepted, 54 enrolled. *Faculty:* 8 full-time (4 women), 6 part-time/adjunct (1 woman). Expenses: Contact institution. *Financial support:* In 2019–20, 103 students received support. Scholarships/grants and unspecified assistantships available. Financial award application deadline: 3/15; financial award applicants required to submit FAFSA. In 2019, 48 master's awarded. *Program availability:* Part-time. *Application deadline:* For fall admission, 1/15 for domestic students, 5/1 for international students. *Application fee:* $50. Electronic applications accepted. *Application Contact:* Gregory Laramie, Associate Dean, 401-254-3743, E-mail: glaramie@rwu.edu. *Dean*, Stephen White, 401-254-3607, E-mail: swhite@rwu.edu.

**School of Engineering, Computing and Construction Management** Students: 4 full-time (1 woman), 3 part-time (0 women), 2 international. Average age 29. 10 applicants, 100% accepted, 3 enrolled. *Faculty:* 2 full-time. Expenses: Contact institution. *Financial support:* Application deadline: 3/15. *Program availability:* Part-time, blended/hybrid learning. *Application deadline:* Applications are processed on a rolling basis. *Application fee:* $50. Electronic applications accepted. *Application Contact:* Michael Emmer, Assistant Professor of Construction Managemen, 401-254-3964, Fax: 401-254-3557, E-mail: memmer@rwu.edu.

**School of Justice Studies** Students: 24 full-time (15 women), 109 part-time (59 women); includes 31 minority (9 Black or African American, non-Hispanic/Latino; 1 Asian, non-Hispanic/Latino; 17 Hispanic/Latino; 4 Two or more races, non-Hispanic/Latino), 2 international. Average age 34. 94 applicants, 83% accepted, 46 enrolled. *Faculty:* 1 (woman) full-time, 5 part-time/adjunct (0 women). Expenses: Contact institution. *Financial support:* In 2019–20, 8 students received support. Scholarships/grants and unspecified assistantships available. Financial award application deadline: 3/15; financial award applicants required to submit FAFSA. In 2019, 46 master's awarded. *Program availability:* Part-time, evening/weekend, 100% online, blended/hybrid learning. *Application deadline:* Applications are processed on a rolling basis. *Application fee:* $50. Electronic applications accepted. *Application Contact:* Marcus Hanscom, Director of Graduate Admission, 401-254-3345, Fax: 401-254-3557, E-mail: gradadmit@rwu.edu. *Dean and Professor of Criminal Justice*, Dr. Eric Bronson, 401-254-3336, E-mail: ebronson@rwu.edu.

**School of Law** Students: 487 full-time (279 women); includes 134 minority (35 Black or African American, non-Hispanic/Latino; 2 American Indian or Alaska Native, non-Hispanic/Latino; 18 Asian, non-Hispanic/Latino; 67 Hispanic/Latino; 1 Native Hawaiian or other Pacific Islander, non-Hispanic/Latino; 11 Two or more races, non-Hispanic/Latino), 7 international. Average age 27. 946 applicants, 67% accepted, 169 enrolled. *Faculty:* 27 full-time (16 women), 31 part-time/adjunct (14 women). Expenses: Contact institution. *Financial support:* In 2019–20, 255 students received support, including 9 fellowships (averaging $1,739 per year), 51 research assistantships (averaging $931 per year); Federal Work-Study also available. Financial award application deadline: 3/15; financial award applicants required to submit FAFSA. In 2019, 3 master's, 134 doctorates awarded. *Program availability:* Part-time. *Application deadline:* For fall admission, 4/1 priority date for domestic and international students. Applications are processed on a rolling basis. *Application fee:* $60. Electronic applications accepted. *Application Contact:* Michael W. Donnelly-Boylen, Assistant Dean of Admissions, 401-254-4555, Fax: 401-254-4516, E-mail: mdonnelly-boylen@rwu.edu. *Dean*, Gregroy Bowman, 401-254-4500, Fax: 401-254-3525, E-mail: gbowman@rwu.edu.

**University College** Students: 8 part-time (6 women); includes 3 minority (2 Hispanic/Latino; 1 Two or more races, non-Hispanic/Latino). Average age 40. *Faculty:* 2 full-time (1 woman). Expenses: Contact institution. *Program availability:* Part-time, evening/weekend, 100% online, blended/hybrid learning. *Application deadline:* Applications are processed on a rolling basis. Electronic applications accepted. *Application Contact:* Karla Alba, Director of Graduate Admission, 401-254-3705, Fax: 401-254-3557, E-mail: kalba@rwu.edu. *Vice President, University College*, Jamie Scurry, 401-254-3118, E-mail: jscurry@rwu.edu.

## ROLLINS COLLEGE, Winter Park, FL 32789-4499

**General Information** Independent, coed, comprehensive institution. *Enrollment:* 2,662 graduate, professional, and undergraduate students; 278 full-time matriculated graduate/professional students (156 women), 251 part-time matriculated graduate/professional students (156 women). *Enrollment by degree level:* 486 master's, 43 doctoral. *Graduate faculty:* 40 full-time (15 women). *Tuition:* Part-time $2700 per credit hour. Tuition and fees vary according to program. *Graduate housing:* Room and/or apartments available on a first-come, first-served basis to single students; on-campus housing not available to married students. *Student services:* Campus employment opportunities, campus safety program, career counseling, exercise/wellness program, free psychological counseling, international student services, low-cost health insurance, multicultural affairs office, services for students with disabilities, writing training. *Library facilities:* Olin Library. *Collection:* Books: 204,677 (physical), 236,421 (digital/electronic); Serial titles: 117 (physical), 104,688 (digital/electronic); Databases: 107. Weekly public service hours: 96; study areas open 24 hours, 5–7 days a week; students can reserve study rooms.

**Computer facilities:** 254 computers available on campus for general student use. A campuswide network can be accessed. Online class registration is available.
Website: http://www.rollins.edu/

**General Application Contact:** Dr. Faye Tydlaska, Vice President for Enrollment Management and Marketing, 407-646-2161 Ext. 2532, E-mail: eveningadmission@rollins.edu.

**GRADUATE UNITS**

**Crummer Graduate School of Business** Students: 192 full-time (86 women), 111 part-time (52 women); includes 85 minority (15 Black or African American, non-Hispanic/Latino; 19 Asian, non-Hispanic/Latino; 45 Hispanic/Latino; 6 Two or more races, non-Hispanic/Latino), 29 international. Average age 32. *Faculty:* 20 full-time (4 women). Expenses: Contact institution. *Financial support:* Scholarships/grants available. Support available to part-time students. Financial award applicants required to submit FAFSA. In 2019, 175 master's awarded. *Program availability:* Part-time, evening/weekend, online learning. *Application deadline:* Applications are processed on a rolling basis. *Application fee:* $50. Electronic applications accepted. *Application Contact:* Maralyn E. Graham, Admissions Coordinator, 407-646-2405, Fax: 407-646-1550, E-mail: mbaadmissions@rollins.edu. *Dean*, Deborah Crown, 407-646-2249, Fax: 407-646-1550, E-mail: dcrown@rollins.edu.

**Hamilton Holt School** Students: 111 full-time (92 women), 153 part-time (114 women); includes 67 minority (18 Black or African American, non-Hispanic/Latino; 5 Asian, non-Hispanic/Latino; 43 Hispanic/Latino; 1 Two or more races, non-Hispanic/Latino), 12 international. Average age 32. *Faculty:* 14 full-time (6 women), 12 part-time/adjunct (8 women). Expenses: Contact institution. *Financial support:* Scholarships/grants and unspecified assistantships available. Support available to part-time students. Financial award applicants required to submit FAFSA. In 2019, 97 master's awarded. *Program availability:* Part-time, evening/weekend. *Application fee:* $50. *Application Contact:* Director of Admission, 407-691-1781, Fax: 407-646-1551, E-mail: holtadmission@rollins.edu. *Dean*, Dr. Rob Sanders, 407-646-2232, Fax: 407-646-1551, E-mail: rsanders@rollins.edu.

## ROOSEVELT UNIVERSITY, Chicago, IL 60605

**General Information** Independent, coed, comprehensive institution. *Graduate housing:* Room and/or apartments available on a first-come, first-served basis to single students; on-campus housing not available to married students. Housing application deadline: 7/1.

**GRADUATE UNITS**

**Graduate Division** *Program availability:* Part-time, evening/weekend. Electronic applications accepted.

***Chicago College of Performing Arts*** Electronic applications accepted.

***College of Arts and Sciences*** *Program availability:* Part-time, evening/weekend. Electronic applications accepted.

***College of Education*** *Program availability:* Part-time, evening/weekend. Electronic applications accepted.

***College of Pharmacy*** Electronic applications accepted.

***Walter E. Heller College of Business*** *Program availability:* Part-time, evening/weekend. Electronic applications accepted.

## ROSALIND FRANKLIN UNIVERSITY OF MEDICINE AND SCIENCE, North Chicago, IL 60064-3095

**General Information** Independent, coed, graduate-only institution. CGS member. *Graduate housing:* Rooms and/or apartments available on a first-come, first-served basis to single and married students. Housing application deadline: 3/13. *Research affiliation:* Argonne National Laboratory (medical physics), Veterans Administration Hospital (pulmonary medicine).

**GRADUATE UNITS**

**Chicago Medical School**

**College of Health Professions** *Program availability:* Part-time, online learning.

**College of Pharmacy**

**Dr. William M. Scholl College of Podiatric Medicine**

**School of Graduate and Postdoctoral Studies - Interdisciplinary Graduate Program in Biomedical Sciences** Electronic applications accepted.

## ROSE-HULMAN INSTITUTE OF TECHNOLOGY, Terre Haute, IN 47803-3999

**General Information** Independent, coed, primarily men, comprehensive institution. *Enrollment:* 2,038 graduate, professional, and undergraduate students. *Enrollment by degree level:* 57 master's. *Graduate housing:* Room and/or apartments available on a first-come, first-served basis to single students; on-campus housing not available to married students. Typical cost: $10,389 per year ($16,551 including board). *Student services:* Campus employment opportunities, career counseling, exercise/wellness program, free psychological counseling, international student services, low-cost health insurance, multicultural affairs office, services for students with disabilities. *Library facilities:* John A. Logan Library. *Collection:* Books: 28,477 (physical), 552,296 (digital/electronic); Serial titles: 26 (physical), 87,425 (digital/electronic); Databases: 37. Weekly public service hours: 101; students can reserve study rooms.

**Computer facilities:** Computer purchase and lease plans are available. 15 computers available on campus for general student use. A campuswide network can be accessed. Online class registration is available.
Website: http://www.rose-hulman.edu/

**General Application Contact:** Dr. Craig Downing, Associate Dean of Lifelong Learning, 812-877-8822, E-mail: downing@rose-hulman.edu.

**GRADUATE UNITS**

**Graduate Studies** Average age 25. 57 applicants, 60% accepted, 21 enrolled. Expenses: Contact institution. *Financial support:* In 2019–20, 49 students received support. Fellowships, research assistantships, institutionally sponsored loans, scholarships/grants, and tuition waivers (full and partial) available. Financial award application deadline: 2/1; financial award applicants required to submit FAFSA. In 2019, 33 master's awarded. *Program availability:* Part-time. *Application deadline:* For fall admission, 2/1 priority date for domestic and international students; for winter admission, 10/1 for domestic students, 8/1 for international students; for spring admission, 1/15 for domestic students, 11/1 for international students. Applications are processed on a rolling basis. Electronic applications accepted. *Application Contact:* Dr. Craig Downing, Associate Dean of Lifelong Learning, 812-877-8822, E-mail: downing@rose-hulman.edu. *Associate Dean of Lifelong Learning*, Dr. Craig Downing, 812-877-8822, E-mail: downing@rose-hulman.edu.

## ROSEMAN UNIVERSITY OF HEALTH SCIENCES, Henderson, NV 89014

**General Information** Private, coed, graduate-only institution. *Graduate housing:* On-campus housing not available.

**GRADUATE UNITS**

**College of Dental Medicine - Henderson Campus**

**College of Dental Medicine - South Jordan, Utah Campus** Electronic applications accepted.

**College of Pharmacy** Electronic applications accepted.

**MBA Program** *Program availability:* Part-time, evening/weekend.

## ROSEMONT COLLEGE, Rosemont, PA 19010-1699

**General Information** Independent-religious, coed, comprehensive institution. *Graduate housing:* Room and/or apartments available on a first-come, first-served basis to single students; on-campus housing not available to married students. Housing application deadline: 8/1.

**GRADUATE UNITS**

**Schools of Graduate and Professional Studies** *Program availability:* Part-time, evening/weekend, online learning. Electronic applications accepted.

## ROWAN UNIVERSITY, Glassboro, NJ 08028-1701

**General Information** State-supported, coed, comprehensive institution. CGS member. *Enrollment:* 19,618 graduate, professional, and undergraduate students; 1,808 full-time matriculated graduate/professional students (924 women), 1,799 part-time matriculated graduate/professional students (1,162 women). *Enrollment by degree level:* 1,504 master's, 319 doctoral, 1,784 other advanced degrees. *Graduate faculty:* 227 full-time (102 women), 203 part-time/adjunct (93 women). *Tuition, area resident:* Part-time $715.50 per semester hour. Tuition, state resident: part-time $715.50 per semester hour. Tuition, nonresident: part-time $715.50 per semester hour. *Required fees:* $161.55 per semester hour. *Graduate housing:* Room and/or apartments available on a first-come, first-served basis to single students; on-campus housing not available to married students. Housing application deadline: 5/1. *Student services:* Campus employment opportunities, campus safety program, career counseling, child daycare facilities, exercise/wellness program, free psychological counseling, international student services, low-cost health insurance, multicultural affairs office, services for students with disabilities, teacher training, writing training. *Library facilities:* Keith and Shirley Campbell Library plus 4 others. *Collection:* Books: 328,891 (physical), 494,739 (digital/electronic); Serial titles: 129,972 (digital/electronic); Databases: 846. Students can reserve study rooms.

**Computer facilities:** 836 computers available on campus for general student use. A campuswide network can be accessed. Online class registration is available.
Website: http://www.rowan.edu/

**General Application Contact:** Jeffrey Fields, College of Graduate and Continuing Education, 856-256-4747, E-mail: global@rowan.edu.

**GRADUATE UNITS**

**Cooper Medical School**

**Graduate School** *Program availability:* Part-time, evening/weekend. Electronic applications accepted.

***College of Communication and Creative Arts*** *Program availability:* Part-time, evening/weekend. Electronic applications accepted.

***College of Education*** *Program availability:* Part-time, evening/weekend. Electronic applications accepted.

***College of Engineering*** Students: 108 full-time (24 women), 120 part-time (30 women); includes 45 minority (8 Black or African American, non-Hispanic/Latino; 20 Asian, non-Hispanic/Latino; 11 Hispanic/Latino; 6 Two or more races, non-Hispanic/Latino), 82 international. Average age 28. 2,270 applicants, 72% accepted, 547 enrolled. *Faculty:* 46 full-time (10 women), 23 part-time/adjunct (3 women). Expenses: Contact institution. *Financial support:* Career-related internships or fieldwork, Federal Work-Study, and unspecified assistantships available. Support available to part-time students. *Program availability:* Part-time, evening/weekend. *Application deadline:* Applications are processed on a rolling basis. *Application fee:* $65. Electronic applications accepted.

***College of Humanities and Social Sciences***

***College of Performing Arts*** *Program availability:* Part-time, evening/weekend. Electronic applications accepted.

***College of Science and Mathematics*** *Program availability:* Part-time, evening/weekend. Electronic applications accepted.

***Rohrer College of Business*** Students: 68 full-time (31 women), 190 part-time (83 women); includes 60 minority (20 Black or African American, non-Hispanic/Latino; 15 Asian, non-Hispanic/Latino; 19 Hispanic/Latino; 6 Two or more races, non-Hispanic/Latino), 20 international. Average age 30. 2,835 applicants, 65% accepted, 552 enrolled. *Faculty:* 15 full-time (4 women), 16 part-time/adjunct (5 women). Expenses: Contact institution. *Financial support:* Career-related internships or fieldwork, scholarships/grants, health care benefits, and unspecified assistantships available. In 2019, 51 master's awarded. *Program availability:* Part-time, evening/weekend. *Application deadline:* For fall admission, 8/1 for domestic and international students; for spring admission, 12/1 for domestic and international students; for summer admission, 4/1 for domestic and international students. Applications are processed on a rolling basis. *Application fee:* $65. Electronic applications accepted. *Application Contact:* Admissions and Enrollment Services, 856-256-5435, Fax: 856-256-5637, E-mail: cgceadmissions@rowan.edu. *Dean, College of Graduate and Continuing Education,* Dr. Horacio Sosa, 856-256-4747, E-mail: sosa@rowan.edu.

***School of Biomedical Science and Health Professions*** *Program availability:* Part-time, evening/weekend, online learning. Electronic applications accepted.

**School of Osteopathic Medicine** Electronic applications accepted.

## ROYAL MILITARY COLLEGE OF CANADA, Kingston, ON K7K 7B4, Canada

**General Information** Federally supported, coed, university.

**GRADUATE UNITS**

**Division of Graduate Studies** *Program availability:* Part-time, online learning. Electronic applications accepted.

***Continuing Studies*** Electronic applications accepted.

***Faculty of Engineering*** Electronic applications accepted.

***Faculty of Science*** Electronic applications accepted.

## ROYAL ROADS UNIVERSITY, Victoria, BC V9B 5Y2, Canada

**General Information** Province-supported, coed, upper-level institution. *Graduate housing:* Room and/or apartments available on a first-come, first-served basis to single students; on-campus housing not available to married students.

**GRADUATE UNITS**

**Graduate Studies** *Program availability:* Blended/hybrid learning. Electronic applications accepted.

## RUSH UNIVERSITY, Chicago, IL 60612-3832

**General Information** Independent, coed, upper-level institution. CGS member. *Graduate housing:* Rooms and/or apartments available on a first-come, first-served basis to single and married students.

**GRADUATE UNITS**

**College of Health Sciences** Expenses: Contact institution. *Financial support:* Career-related internships or fieldwork, Federal Work-Study, institutionally sponsored loans, and scholarships/grants available. Support available to part-time students. Financial award application deadline: 4/1; financial award applicants required to submit FAFSA. *Program availability:* Part-time. Electronic applications accepted.

**College of Nursing** Students: 410 full-time (350 women), 824 part-time (728 women); includes 307 minority (91 Black or African American, non-Hispanic/Latino; 3 American Indian or Alaska Native, non-Hispanic/Latino; 47 Asian, non-Hispanic/Latino; 146 Hispanic/Latino; 1 Native Hawaiian or other Pacific Islander, non-Hispanic/Latino; 19 Two or more races, non-Hispanic/Latino). Average age 32. 1,130 applicants, 48% accepted, 427 enrolled. *Faculty:* 84 full-time (77 women), 103 part-time/adjunct (94 women). Expenses: Contact institution. *Financial support:* Fellowships, research assistantships, teaching assistantships, Federal Work-Study, scholarships/grants, traineeships, health care benefits, and unspecified assistantships available. Support available to part-time students. Financial award application deadline: 3/1; financial award applicants required to submit FAFSA. In 2019, 168 master's, 193 doctorates, 14 other advanced degrees awarded. *Program availability:* 100% online, blended/hybrid learning. *Application deadline:* Applications are processed on a rolling basis. Electronic applications accepted. *Application Contact:* Office of Admissions, 312-942-7117, E-mail: con_admissions@rush.edu. *Interim Dean,* Dr. Barbara Swanson, 312-942-7117, E-mail: barbara_a_swanson@rush.edu.

**Graduate College** *Program availability:* Part-time. Electronic applications accepted.

***Division of Anatomy and Cell Biology*** Electronic applications accepted.

***Division of Biochemistry*** Electronic applications accepted.

***Division of Immunology and Microbiology***

***Division of Medical Physics*** Electronic applications accepted.

***Division of Neuroscience*** Electronic applications accepted.

***Division of Pharmacology***

**Rush Medical College** Students: 553 full-time (276 women); includes 221 minority (35 Black or African American, non-Hispanic/Latino; 112 Asian, non-Hispanic/Latino; 50 Hispanic/Latino; 24 Two or more races, non-Hispanic/Latino). Average age 26. 9,099 applicants, 3% accepted, 144 enrolled. *Faculty:* 1,634. Expenses: Contact institution. *Financial support:* In 2019–20, 317 students received support. Federal Work-Study, institutionally sponsored loans, and scholarships/grants available. Financial award applicants required to submit FAFSA. In 2019, 120 doctorates awarded. *Application deadline:* For fall admission, 11/1 for domestic students. Applications are processed on a rolling basis. *Application fee:* $100. Electronic applications accepted. *Application Contact:* Dr. Cynthia E. Boyd, Assistant Dean, Admissions and Recruitment, 312-942-6915, E-mail: rmc_admissions@rush.edu. *Assistant Dean, Admissions and Recruitment,* Dr. Cynthia E. Boyd, 312-942-6915, E-mail: rmc_admissions@rush.edu.

## RUTGERS UNIVERSITY - CAMDEN, Camden, NJ 08102-1401

**General Information** State-supported, coed, university. *Graduate housing:* Rooms and/or apartments available to single and married students.

**GRADUATE UNITS**

**Graduate School of Arts and Sciences** *Program availability:* Part-time, evening/weekend. Electronic applications accepted.

**School of Business** *Program availability:* Part-time, evening/weekend. Electronic applications accepted.

**School of Law** *Program availability:* Part-time, evening/weekend. Electronic applications accepted.

**School of Nursing–Camden**

**School of Public Health** *Program availability:* Part-time, evening/weekend. Electronic applications accepted.

## RUTGERS UNIVERSITY - NEWARK, Newark, NJ 07102

**General Information** State-supported, coed, university. CGS member. *Graduate housing:* Room and/or apartments available to single students; on-campus housing not available to married students. Housing application deadline: 5/15.

**GRADUATE UNITS**

**Graduate School** *Program availability:* Part-time, evening/weekend. Electronic applications accepted.

***Division of Global Affairs*** *Program availability:* Part-time, evening/weekend. Electronic applications accepted.

**Graduate School of Biomedical Sciences** *Program availability:* Part-time, evening/weekend. Electronic applications accepted.

***School of Criminal Justice*** Electronic applications accepted.

**New Jersey Medical School** Electronic applications accepted.

**Rutgers Business School–Newark and New Brunswick** *Program availability:* Part-time, evening/weekend. Electronic applications accepted.

**Rutgers School of Dental Medicine** Electronic applications accepted.

**Rutgers School of Nursing** *Program availability:* Part-time. Electronic applications accepted.

**School of Health Related Professions** *Program availability:* Part-time. Electronic applications accepted.

**School of Law** *Program availability:* Part-time, evening/weekend.

**School of Public Health** *Program availability:* Part-time, evening/weekend. Electronic applications accepted.

## RUTGERS UNIVERSITY - NEW BRUNSWICK, Piscataway, NJ 08854-8097

**General Information** State-supported, coed, university. CGS member. *Graduate housing:* Rooms and/or apartments available to single and married students.

**GRADUATE UNITS**

**Edward J. Bloustein School of Planning and Public Policy** *Program availability:* Part-time, evening/weekend, online learning. Electronic applications accepted.

**Ernest Mario School of Pharmacy** Electronic applications accepted.

**Graduate School-New Brunswick** *Program availability:* Part-time, evening/weekend, online learning.

**Graduate School of Applied and Professional Psychology** Electronic applications accepted.

**Graduate School of Biomedical Sciences** Electronic applications accepted.

**Graduate School of Education** *Program availability:* Part-time, evening/weekend. Electronic applications accepted.

**Mason Gross School of the Arts** *Program availability:* Part-time.

**Robert Wood Johnson Medical School** Electronic applications accepted.

**School of Communication and Information** *Program availability:* Part-time, online learning. Electronic applications accepted.

**School of Management and Labor Relations** *Program availability:* Part-time, evening/weekend. Electronic applications accepted.

**School of Public Health** *Program availability:* Part-time, evening/weekend. Electronic applications accepted.

**School of Social Work** *Program availability:* Part-time. Electronic applications accepted.

## RYERSON UNIVERSITY, Toronto, ON M5B 2K3, Canada

**General Information** Province-supported, coed, comprehensive institution. CGS member.

**GRADUATE UNITS**

**School of Graduate Studies**

***Ted Rogers School of Management***

## SACRED HEART MAJOR SEMINARY, Detroit, MI 48206-1799

**General Information** Independent-religious, coed, comprehensive institution. *Graduate housing:* Room and/or apartments guaranteed to single students; on-campus housing not available to married students. Housing application deadline: 8/1.

**GRADUATE UNITS**

**School of Theology** *Program availability:* Part-time, evening/weekend.

## SACRED HEART SEMINARY AND SCHOOL OF THEOLOGY, Hales Corners, WI 53130-0429

**General Information** Independent-religious, coed, primarily men, graduate-only institution. *Graduate housing:* Room and/or apartments guaranteed to single students; on-campus housing not available to married students.

**GRADUATE UNITS**

**Graduate and Professional Programs** *Program availability:* Part-time.

## SACRED HEART UNIVERSITY, Fairfield, CT 06825

**General Information** Independent-religious, coed, comprehensive institution. CGS member. *Graduate housing:* On-campus housing not available.

**GRADUATE UNITS**

**Graduate Programs** *Program availability:* Part-time, evening/weekend, online learning. Electronic applications accepted.

***College of Arts and Sciences*** Electronic applications accepted.

***College of Health Professions*** *Program availability:* Part-time, evening/weekend, 100% online, blended/hybrid learning. Electronic applications accepted.

***College of Nursing*** *Program availability:* Part-time, evening/weekend, 100% online, blended/hybrid learning. Electronic applications accepted.

***Isabelle Farrington College of Education*** *Program availability:* Part-time, evening/weekend. Electronic applications accepted.

***Jack Welch College of Business*** *Program availability:* Part-time, evening/weekend. Electronic applications accepted.

## SAGE GRADUATE SCHOOL, Troy, NY 12180-4115

**General Information** Independent, coed, graduate-only institution. *Enrollment by degree level:* 813 master's, 214 doctoral, 52 other advanced degrees. *Graduate faculty:* 58 full-time (49 women), 55 part-time/adjunct (41 women). *Tuition:* Part-time $730 per credit hour. Tuition and fees vary according to course load, degree level and program. *Graduate housing:* Room and/or apartments available on a first-come, first-served basis to single students; on-campus housing not available to married students. Typical cost: $6654 per year ($13,058 including board). Housing application deadline: 5/1. *Student services:* Career counseling. *Library facilities:* James Wheelock Clark Library plus 1 other. *Collection:* Books: 183,099 (physical), 18,514 (digital/electronic); Serial titles: 223 (physical), 67,117 (digital/electronic); Databases: 97. Weekly public service hours: 65; students can reserve study rooms. *Research affiliation:* Rensselaer Polytechnic Institute (education), St. Peter's Hospital (health care services), University at Albany, State University of New York (public health, health and the environment), Albany Medical College (health care services), National Center for Adaptive Neurotechnologies (NCAN).

**Computer facilities:** 420 computers available on campus for general student use. Online class registration is available.
Website: http://www.sage.edu/

**General Application Contact:** Michael Jones, Senior Associate Director of Graduate Enrollment Management, 518-292-8615, E-mail: orm-sgs@sage.edu.

**GRADUATE UNITS**

**Esteves School of Education** Students: 79 full-time (64 women), 302 part-time (236 women); includes 133 minority (51 Black or African American, non-Hispanic/Latino; 2 American Indian or Alaska Native, non-Hispanic/Latino; 18 Asian, non-Hispanic/Latino; 49 Hispanic/Latino; 13 Two or more races, non-Hispanic/Latino). Average age 33. 482 applicants, 47% accepted, 138 enrolled. *Faculty:* 16 full-time (12 women), 24 part-time/adjunct (16 women). Expenses: Contact institution. *Financial support:* Fellowships, research assistantships, scholarships/grants, and unspecified assistantships available. Financial award application deadline: 3/1; financial award applicants required to submit FAFSA. In 2019, 126 master's, 33 doctorates, 16 other advanced degrees awarded. *Program availability:* Part-time, evening/weekend. *Application deadline:* Applications are processed on a rolling basis. *Application fee:* $30. Electronic applications accepted. *Application Contact:* Michael Jones, SR Associate Director of Graduate Enrollment Management, 518-292-8615, Fax: 518-292-1912, E-mail: jonesm4@sage.edu. *Dean, Esteves School of Education*, Dr. John Pelizza, 518-244-2051, Fax: 518-244-2334, E-mail: pelizj@sage.edu.

**School of Health Sciences** Students: 319 full-time (270 women), 301 part-time (269 women); includes 100 minority (27 Black or African American, non-Hispanic/Latino; 3 American Indian or Alaska Native, non-Hispanic/Latino; 30 Asian, non-Hispanic/Latino; 26 Hispanic/Latino; 14 Two or more races, non-Hispanic/Latino), 7 international. Average age 30. 664 applicants, 45% accepted, 157 enrolled. *Faculty:* 37 full-time (33 women), 27 part-time/adjunct (26 women). Expenses: Contact institution. *Financial support:* Fellowships, research assistantships, scholarships/grants, and unspecified assistantships available. Financial award application deadline: 3/1; financial award applicants required to submit FAFSA. In 2019, 135 master's, 33 doctorates, 54 other advanced degrees awarded. *Program availability:* Part-time, evening/weekend. *Application deadline:* Applications are processed on a rolling basis. *Application fee:* $30. Electronic applications accepted. *Application Contact:* Michael Jones, SR Associate Director of Graduate Enrollment Management, 518-292-8615, Fax: 518-292-1912, E-mail: jonesm4@sage.edu. *Dean, School of Health Sciences*, Dr. Kathleen Kelly, 518-244-2030, E-mail: kellyk5@sage.edu.

**School of Management** Students: 28 full-time (20 women), 50 part-time (30 women); includes 23 minority (10 Black or African American, non-Hispanic/Latino; 1 American Indian or Alaska Native, non-Hispanic/Latino; 3 Asian, non-Hispanic/Latino; 6 Hispanic/Latino; 3 Two or more races, non-Hispanic/Latino), 2 international. Average age 31. 123 applicants, 41% accepted, 24 enrolled. *Faculty:* 5 full-time (3 women), 4 part-time/adjunct (1 woman). Expenses: Contact institution. *Financial support:* Fellowships, research assistantships, and unspecified assistantships available. Financial award application deadline: 3/1; financial award applicants required to submit FAFSA. In 2019, 36 master's awarded. *Program availability:* Part-time, evening/weekend, 100% online, blended/hybrid learning. *Application deadline:* Applications are processed on a rolling basis. *Application fee:* $30. Electronic applications accepted. *Application Contact:* Michael Jones, SR Associate Director of Graduate Enrollment Management, 518-292-8615, Fax: 518-292-1912, E-mail: jonesm4@sage.edu. *Dean, School of Management*, Dr. Kimberly Fredericks, 518-292-1782, Fax: 518-292-1964, E-mail: fredek1@sage.edu.

## SAGINAW VALLEY STATE UNIVERSITY, University Center, MI 48710

**General Information** State-supported, coed, comprehensive institution. *Enrollment:* 8,265 graduate, professional, and undergraduate students; 263 full-time matriculated graduate/professional students (211 women), 495 part-time matriculated graduate/professional students (377 women). *Enrollment by degree level:* 706 master's, 26 doctoral, 26 other advanced degrees. *Graduate faculty:* 68 full-time (46 women), 24 part-time/adjunct (17 women). *Tuition, area resident:* Full-time $11,212; part-time $622.90 per credit hour. Tuition, state resident: full-time $11,212; part-time $622.90 per credit hour. Tuition, nonresident: full-time $11,212; part-time $1253 per credit hour. *Required fees:* $263; $14.60 per credit hour. Tuition and fees vary according to course load, degree level and program. *Graduate housing:* Room and/or apartments available on a first-come, first-served basis to single students; on-campus housing not available to married students. Housing application deadline: 5/1. *Student services:* Campus employment opportunities, career counseling, exercise/wellness program, free psychological counseling, international student services, multicultural affairs office, services for students with disabilities, writing training. *Library facilities:* Zahnow Library. *Collection:* Books: 135,959 (physical), 189,629 (digital/electronic); Serial titles: 430 (physical), 77,436 (digital/electronic); Databases: 125. Weekly public service hours: 92.

**Computer facilities:** Computer purchase and lease plans are available. 424 computers available on campus for general student use. A campuswide network can be accessed. Online class registration is available.
Website: http://www.svsu.edu/

**General Application Contact:** Jenna Briggs, Director, Graduate and International Admissions, 989-964-6096, Fax: 989-964-2788, E-mail: gradadm@svsu.edu.

**GRADUATE UNITS**

**College of Arts and Behavioral Sciences** Students: 20 full-time (10 women), 32 part-time (22 women); includes 10 minority (5 Black or African American, non-Hispanic/Latino; 3 Hispanic/Latino; 2 Two or more races, non-Hispanic/Latino), 7 international. Average age 28. 49 applicants, 67% accepted, 23 enrolled. *Faculty:* 7 full-time (3 women), 1 (woman) part-time/adjunct. Expenses: Contact institution. *Financial support:* Federal Work-Study and scholarships/grants available. Support available to part-time students. Financial award applicants required to submit FAFSA. In 2019, 13 master's awarded. *Program availability:* Part-time, evening/weekend. *Application deadline:* For fall admission, 7/15 for international students; for winter admission, 11/15 for international students; for spring admission, 4/15 for international students. Applications are processed on a rolling basis. *Application fee:* $30 ($90 for international students). Electronic applications accepted. *Application Contact:* Jenna Briggs, Director, Graduate and International Admissions, 989-964-6096, Fax: 989-964-2788, E-mail: gradadm@svsu.edu. *Dean*, Dr. Marc Peretz, 989-964-4062, Fax: 989-964-7232, E-mail: mhp@svsu.edu.

**College of Business and Management** Students: 21 full-time (13 women), 34 part-time (13 women); includes 14 minority (3 Black or African American, non-Hispanic/Latino; 1 Asian, non-Hispanic/Latino; 8 Hispanic/Latino; 2 Two or more races, non-Hispanic/Latino), 16 international. Average age 29. 59 applicants, 69% accepted, 18 enrolled. *Faculty:* 11 full-time (3 women). Expenses: Contact institution. *Financial support:* Federal Work-Study and scholarships/grants available. Support available to part-time students. Financial award application deadline: 4/1; financial award applicants required to submit FAFSA. In 2019, 13 master's awarded. *Program availability:* Part-time, evening/weekend, online only, 100% online, blended/hybrid learning. *Application deadline:* For fall admission, 7/15 for international students; for winter admission, 11/15 for international students; for spring admission, 4/15 for international students. Applications are processed on a rolling basis. *Application fee:* $30 ($90 for international students). Electronic applications accepted. *Application Contact:* Jenna Briggs, Director, Graduate and International Admissions, 989-964-6096, Fax: 989-964-2788, E-mail: gradadm@svsu.edu. *MBA Program Coordinator*, Dr. Mark McCartney, 989-964-4064.

**College of Education** Students: 16 full-time (11 women), 166 part-time (134 women); includes 15 minority (6 Black or African American, non-Hispanic/Latino; 1 Asian, non-Hispanic/Latino; 4 Hispanic/Latino; 4 Two or more races, non-Hispanic/Latino), 12 international. Average age 33. 81 applicants, 90% accepted, 53 enrolled. *Faculty:* 14 full-time (12 women), 12 part-time/adjunct (9 women). Expenses: Contact institution. *Financial support:* Federal Work-Study and scholarships/grants available. Support available to part-time students. Financial award applicants required to submit FAFSA. In 2019, 69 master's, 3 other advanced degrees awarded. *Program availability:* Part-time, evening/weekend, online learning. *Application deadline:* For fall admission, 7/15 for international students; for winter admission, 11/15 for international students; for spring admission, 4/15 for international students. Applications are processed on a rolling basis. *Application fee:* $30 ($90 for international students). Electronic applications accepted. *Application Contact:* Jenna Briggs, Director, Graduate and International Admissions, 989-964-6096, Fax: 989-964-2788, E-mail: gradadm@svsu.edu. *Dean*, Dr. Craig Douglas, 989-964-4057, Fax: 989-964-4563, E-mail: coeconnect@svsu.edu.

**College of Health and Human Services** Students: 199 full-time (175 women), 252 part-time (207 women); includes 61 minority (31 Black or African American, non-

Hispanic/Latino; 4 Asian, non-Hispanic/Latino; 13 Hispanic/Latino; 13 Two or more races, non-Hispanic/Latino), 14 international. Average age 28. 98 applicants, 88% accepted, 70 enrolled. *Faculty:* 31 full-time (28 women), 10 part-time/adjunct (7 women). Expenses: Contact institution. *Financial support:* Federal Work-Study and scholarships/grants available. Support available to part-time students. Financial award application deadline: 4/1; financial award applicants required to submit FAFSA. In 2019, 159 master's, 4 doctorates awarded. *Program availability:* Part-time, evening/weekend. *Application deadline:* For fall admission, 7/15 for international students; for winter admission, 11/15 for international students; for spring admission, 4/15 for international students. Applications are processed on a rolling basis. *Application fee:* $30 ($90 for international students). Electronic applications accepted. *Application Contact:* Jenna Briggs, Director, Graduate and International Admissions, 989-964-6096, Fax: 989-964-2788, E-mail: gradadm@svsu.edu. *Dean,* Dr. Judith Ruland, 989-964-4145, Fax: 989-964-4024, E-mail: jruland@svsu.edu.

**College of Science, Engineering, and Technology** Students: 7 full-time (2 women), 11 part-time (1 woman); includes 2 minority (both Asian, non-Hispanic/Latino), 4 international. Average age 32. 29 applicants, 62% accepted, 4 enrolled. *Faculty:* 6 full-time (1 woman), 1 part-time/adjunct (0 women). Expenses: Contact institution. *Financial support:* Federal Work-Study and scholarships/grants available. Support available to part-time students. Financial award application deadline: 4/1; financial award applicants required to submit FAFSA. In 2019, 4 master's awarded. *Program availability:* Part-time, evening/weekend. *Application deadline:* For fall admission, 7/15 for international students; for winter admission, 11/15 for international students; for spring admission, 4/15 for international students. Applications are processed on a rolling basis. *Application fee:* $30 ($90 for international students). Electronic applications accepted. *Application Contact:* Jenna Briggs, Director, Graduate and International Admissions, 989-964-6096, Fax: 989-964-2788, E-mail: gradadm@svsu.edu. *Program Coordinator,* Dr. Robert Tuttle, 989-964-4144, Fax: 989-964-2717.

## ST. AMBROSE UNIVERSITY, Davenport, IA 52803-2898

**General Information** Independent-religious, coed, comprehensive institution. CGS member. *Graduate housing:* Room and/or apartments available on a first-come, first-served basis to single students; on-campus housing not available to married students. Housing application deadline: 3/1.

**GRADUATE UNITS**

**College of Arts and Sciences** *Program availability:* Part-time, evening/weekend. Electronic applications accepted.

**College of Business** *Program availability:* Part-time, evening/weekend. Electronic applications accepted.

**College of Health and Human Services** *Program availability:* Part-time, evening/weekend, online learning. Electronic applications accepted.

**School of Education** *Program availability:* Part-time, evening/weekend, online learning. Electronic applications accepted.

## ST. ANDREW'S COLLEGE, Saskatoon, SK S7N 0W3, Canada

**General Information** Independent-religious, coed, graduate-only institution.

**GRADUATE UNITS**

**Graduate Programs in Theology**

## ST. ANDREW'S COLLEGE IN WINNIPEG, Winnipeg, MB R3T 2M7, Canada

**General Information** Independent-religious, coed, primarily men, graduate-only institution. *Enrollment by degree level:* 1 master's. *Graduate housing:* Rooms and/or apartments available to single and married students. Housing application deadline: 7/31. *Student services:* Career counseling. *Library facilities:* Main library plus 5 others. Website: http://www.umanitoba.ca/colleges/st_andrews/

**General Application Contact:** Rev. Roman Bozyk, Registrar, 204-474-6514, Fax: 204-474-7629, E-mail: bozykr@ms.umanitoba.ca.

**GRADUATE UNITS**

**Graduate Programs** Students: 1 part-time (0 women). Expenses: Contact institution. *Financial support:* Fellowships, career-related internships or fieldwork, Federal Work-Study, and institutionally sponsored loans available. Support available to part-time students. Financial award application deadline: 7/31. *Application deadline:* For fall admission, 7/31 for domestic students. *Application fee:* $15. *Application Contact:* Rev. Roman Bozyk TEST, Registrar, 204-474-6514, Fax: 204-474-7629, E-mail: bozykr@ms.umanitoba.ca. *Dean TEST,* Rev. S. Jarmus, 204-474-8898.

## SAINT ANTHONY COLLEGE OF NURSING, Rockford, IL 61114

**General Information** Independent-religious, coed, primarily women, upper-level institution. *Enrollment:* 280 graduate, professional, and undergraduate students; 3 full-time matriculated graduate/professional students (all women), 75 part-time matriculated graduate/professional students (69 women). *Enrollment by degree level:* 16 master's, 62 doctoral. *Graduate faculty:* 6 full-time (5 women), 13 part-time/adjunct (11 women). *Tuition:* Full-time $17,712; part-time $984 per credit. *Required fees:* $605; $605 per unit. Tuition and fees vary according to course load. *Graduate housing:* On-campus housing not available. *Student services:* Free psychological counseling. *Library facilities:* Sister Mary Linus Learning Resource Center. *Collection:* Students can reserve study rooms.

**Computer facilities:** A campuswide network can be accessed. Online class registration is available.
Website: http://www.sacn.edu/

**General Application Contact:** Jean Odom, Student Affairs Specialist - Graduate Program, 815-282-7900, Fax: 815-282-7901, E-mail: GradAdmissions@sacn.edu.

**GRADUATE UNITS**

**Graduate Program** Students: 3 full-time (all women), 75 part-time (69 women); includes 13 minority (5 Black or African American, non-Hispanic/Latino; 4 Asian, non-Hispanic/Latino; 4 Hispanic/Latino). Average age 37. *Faculty:* 6 full-time (5 women), 13 part-time/adjunct (11 women). Expenses: Contact institution. *Financial support:* Scholarships/grants available. Financial award applicants required to submit FAFSA. In 2019, 12 master's awarded. *Program availability:* Part-time, evening/weekend. *Application deadline:* For fall admission, 7/1 for domestic students; for spring admission, 12/1 for domestic students; for summer admission, 4/1 for domestic students. Applications are processed on a rolling basis. *Application fee:* $75. Electronic applications accepted. *Application Contact:* Jean Odom, Student Affairs Specialist - Graduate Program, 815-282-7900, Fax: 815-282-7901, E-mail: GradAdmissions@sacn.edu. *Dean, Graduate Affairs & Research,* Dr. Shannon Lizer, 815-282-7900, Fax: 815-282-7901, E-mail: shannonlizer@sacn.edu.

## ST. AUGUSTINE'S SEMINARY OF TORONTO, Scarborough, ON M1M 1M3, Canada

**General Information** Independent-religious, coed, primarily men, graduate-only institution. *Graduate housing:* On-campus housing not available.

**GRADUATE UNITS**

**Graduate and Professional Programs** *Program availability:* Part-time, evening/weekend.

## ST. BERNARD'S SCHOOL OF THEOLOGY AND MINISTRY, Rochester, NY 14618

**General Information** Independent-religious, coed, graduate-only institution. *Graduate housing:* On-campus housing not available. *Research affiliation:* Colgate Rochester Crozer Divinity School.

**GRADUATE UNITS**

**Graduate and Professional Programs** *Program availability:* Part-time, evening/weekend.

## ST. BONAVENTURE UNIVERSITY, St. Bonaventure, NY 14778-2284

**General Information** Independent-religious, coed, comprehensive institution. CGS member. *Enrollment:* 2,422 graduate, professional, and undergraduate students; 121 full-time matriculated graduate/professional students (77 women), 454 part-time matriculated graduate/professional students (291 women). *Enrollment by degree level:* 539 master's, 36 other advanced degrees. *Graduate faculty:* 34 full-time (15 women), 30 part-time/adjunct (17 women). *Tuition:* Full-time $770; part-time $770 per credit hour. *Required fees:* $35; $35 per credit hour. Tuition and fees vary according to course load. *Graduate housing:* Room and/or apartments available on a first-come, first-served basis to single students; on-campus housing not available to married students. Typical cost: $10,200 per year. Room charges vary according to board plan and housing facility selected. Housing application deadline: 3/19. *Student services:* Career counseling, free psychological counseling, international student services, low-cost health insurance, multicultural affairs office. *Library facilities:* Friedsam Memorial Library. *Collection:* Books: 371,691 (physical), 1.6 million (digital/electronic); Serial titles: 253 (physical), 269,989 (digital/electronic); Databases: 64. Weekly public service hours: 109; students can reserve study rooms.

**Computer facilities:** 320 computers available on campus for general student use. A campuswide network can be accessed. Online class registration, Moodle are available.
Website: http://www.sbu.edu/

**General Application Contact:** Matthew Retchless, Director of Graduate Admissions, 716-375-2429, Fax: 716-375-4015, E-mail: gradsch@sbu.edu.

**GRADUATE UNITS**

**School of Graduate Studies** Students: 121 full-time (77 women), 454 part-time (291 women); includes 105 minority (40 Black or African American, non-Hispanic/Latino; 5 American Indian or Alaska Native, non-Hispanic/Latino; 13 Asian, non-Hispanic/Latino; 32 Hispanic/Latino; 1 Native Hawaiian or other Pacific Islander, non-Hispanic/Latino; 14 Two or more races, non-Hispanic/Latino), 9 international. Average age 33. 357 applicants, 93% accepted, 149 enrolled. *Faculty:* 34 full-time (15 women), 31 part-time/adjunct (17 women). Expenses: Contact institution. *Financial support:* In 2019–20, 26 students received support. Scholarships/grants, health care benefits, and unspecified assistantships available. Financial award application deadline: 4/15; financial award applicants required to submit FAFSA. In 2019, 223 master's, 34 other advanced degrees awarded. *Program availability:* Part-time, evening/weekend, 100% online, blended/hybrid learning. *Application deadline:* For fall admission, 3/15 priority date for domestic students, 2/1 priority date for international students; for spring admission, 10/15 priority date for domestic students, 7/1 priority date for international students. Applications are processed on a rolling basis. Electronic applications accepted. *Application Contact:* Matthew Retchless, Director of Graduate Admissions, 716-375-2021, Fax: 716-375-4015, E-mail: gradsch@sbu.edu. *Dean,* Dr. Lisa Buenaventura, 716-375-2394, Fax: 716-375-2360, E-mail: lbuenave@sbu.edu.

***Jandoli School of Communication*** Students: 18 full-time (11 women), 59 part-time (34 women); includes 22 minority (10 Black or African American, non-Hispanic/Latino; 1 American Indian or Alaska Native, non-Hispanic/Latino; 8 Hispanic/Latino; 3 Two or more races, non-Hispanic/Latino), 2 international. Average age 34. 36 applicants, 97% accepted, 16 enrolled. *Faculty:* 5 full-time (3 women), 8 part-time/adjunct (6 women). Expenses: Contact institution. *Financial support:* In 2019–20, 8 students received support. Scholarships/grants, health care benefits, and unspecified assistantships available. Financial award application deadline: 4/15; financial award applicants required to submit FAFSA. In 2019, 46 master's awarded. *Program availability:* Part-time, evening/weekend, online only, 100% online. *Application deadline:* For fall admission, 3/15 priority date for domestic students, 2/1 priority date for international students; for spring admission, 10/15 priority date for domestic students, 7/1 priority date for international students. Applications are processed on a rolling basis. Electronic applications accepted. *Application Contact:* Matthew Retchless, Director of Graduate Admissions, 716-375-2021, Fax: 716-375-4015, E-mail: gradsch@sbu.edu. *Dean,* Aaron Chimbel, 716-375-2040, Fax: 716-375-2588, E-mail: achimbel@sbu.edu.

***School of Arts & Sciences*** Students: 38 part-time (2 women); includes 8 minority (4 Black or African American, non-Hispanic/Latino; 2 Asian, non-Hispanic/Latino; 1 Hispanic/Latino; 1 Two or more races, non-Hispanic/Latino), 2 international. Average age 41. 40 applicants, 80% accepted, 12 enrolled. *Faculty:* 2 part-time/adjunct (0 women). Expenses: Contact institution. *Financial support:* Scholarships/grants and health care benefits available. Financial award application deadline: 4/15; financial award applicants required to submit FAFSA. *Program availability:* Part-time, evening/weekend, online only, 100% online. *Application deadline:* For fall admission, 3/15 for domestic students, 2/1 for international students; for spring admission, 10/15 for domestic students, 7/1 for international students. Applications are processed on a rolling basis. Electronic applications accepted. *Application Contact:* Matthew Retchless, Director of Graduate Admissions, 716-375-2021, Fax: 716-375-4015, E-mail: gradsch@sbu.edu. *Dean,* Dr. David Hilmey, 716-375-2136, Fax: 716-375-7857, E-mail: dhilmey@sbu.edu.

***School of Business*** Students: 47 full-time (19 women), 92 part-time (43 women); includes 14 minority (3 Black or African American, non-Hispanic/Latino; 2 American Indian or Alaska Native, non-Hispanic/Latino; 4 Asian, non-Hispanic/Latino; 4 Hispanic/Latino; 1 Two or more races, non-Hispanic/Latino), 5 international. Average age 28. 88 applicants, 100% accepted, 44 enrolled. *Faculty:* 15 full-time (3 women), 5 part-time/adjunct (3 women). Expenses: Contact institution. *Financial support:* In 2019–20, 9 students received support. Scholarships/grants, health care benefits, and unspecified assistantships available. Financial award application deadline: 4/15;

financial award applicants required to submit FAFSA. In 2019, 126 master's awarded. *Program availability:* Part-time, 100% online. *Application deadline:* For fall admission, 3/15 priority date for domestic students, 2/1 priority date for international students; for spring admission, 10/15 priority date for domestic students, 7/1 priority date for international students. Applications are processed on a rolling basis. Electronic applications accepted. *Application Contact:* Matthew Retchless, Director of Graduate Admissions, 716-375-2021, Fax: 716-375-4015, E-mail: gradsch@sbu.edu. *Dean,* Dr. Matrecia James, 716-375-2200, Fax: 716-372-2191, E-mail: mjames@sbu.edu.

***School of Education*** Students: 56 full-time (47 women), 266 part-time (211 women); includes 61 minority (23 Black or African American, non-Hispanic/Latino; 2 American Indian or Alaska Native, non-Hispanic/Latino; 7 Asian, non-Hispanic/Latino; 19 Hispanic/Latino; 1 Native Hawaiian or other Pacific Islander, non-Hispanic/Latino; 9 Two or more races, non-Hispanic/Latino). Average age 32. 196 applicants, 87% accepted, 77 enrolled. *Faculty:* 13 full-time (9 women), 16 part-time/adjunct (9 women). Expenses: Contact institution. *Financial support:* In 2019–20, 12 students received support. Scholarships/grants, health care benefits, and unspecified assistantships available. Financial award application deadline: 4/15; financial award applicants required to submit FAFSA. In 2019, 49 master's, 33 Adv Cs awarded. *Program availability:* Part-time, evening/weekend, 100% online, blended/hybrid learning. *Application deadline:* For fall admission, 3/15 priority date for domestic students, 2/1 priority date for international students; for spring admission, 10/15 priority date for domestic students, 7/1 priority date for international students. Applications are processed on a rolling basis. Electronic applications accepted. *Application Contact:* Matthew Retchless, Director of Graduate Admissions, 716-375-2021, Fax: 716-375-4015, E-mail: gradsch@sbu.edu. *Dean,* Dr. Lisa Buenaventura, 716-375-2394, Fax: 716-375-2360, E-mail: lbuenave@sbu.edu.

## ST. CATHERINE UNIVERSITY, St. Paul, MN 55105

**General Information** Independent-religious, Undergraduate: women only; graduate: coed, comprehensive institution. CGS member. *Graduate housing:* Rooms and/or apartments available on a first-come, first-served basis to single and married students. Housing application deadline: 5/1.

**GRADUATE UNITS**

**Graduate Programs** *Program availability:* Part-time, evening/weekend, online learning.

## SAINT CHARLES BORROMEO SEMINARY, OVERBROOK, Wynnewood, PA 19096

**General Information** Independent-religious, coed, primarily men, comprehensive institution. *Graduate housing:* Room and/or apartments guaranteed to single students; on-campus housing not available to married students. Housing application deadline: 7/15.

**GRADUATE UNITS**

**School of Theological Studies** *Program availability:* Part-time, evening/weekend.

## ST. CLOUD STATE UNIVERSITY, St. Cloud, MN 56301-4498

**General Information** State-supported, coed, comprehensive institution. CGS member. *Graduate housing:* Room and/or apartments available on a first-come, first-served basis to single students; on-campus housing not available to married students. Housing application deadline: 4/15.

**GRADUATE UNITS**

**School of Graduate Studies** *Program availability:* Part-time, evening/weekend, online learning. Electronic applications accepted.

***College of Liberal Arts***

***College of Science and Engineering*** Electronic applications accepted.

***College of Social Sciences*** *Program availability:* Part-time. Electronic applications accepted.

***Herberger Business School*** *Program availability:* Part-time, evening/weekend. Electronic applications accepted.

***School of Education*** *Program availability:* Part-time, evening/weekend, online learning.

***School of Health and Human Services***

## ST. EDWARD'S UNIVERSITY, Austin, TX 78704

**General Information** Independent-religious, coed, comprehensive institution. *Graduate housing:* On-campus housing not available.

**GRADUATE UNITS**

**Bill Munday School of Business** *Program availability:* Part-time, evening/weekend. Electronic applications accepted.

**School of Behavioral and Social Sciences** Electronic applications accepted.

**School of Education** *Program availability:* Part-time, evening/weekend. Electronic applications accepted.

## ST. FRANCIS COLLEGE, Brooklyn Heights, NY 11201-4398

**General Information** Independent-religious, coed, comprehensive institution.

**GRADUATE UNITS**

**Program in Professional Accountancy**

## SAINT FRANCIS MEDICAL CENTER COLLEGE OF NURSING, Peoria, IL 61603-3783

**General Information** Independent-religious, coed, primarily women, upper-level institution. *Enrollment:* 507 graduate, professional, and undergraduate students; 1 (woman) full-time matriculated graduate/professional student, 188 part-time matriculated graduate/professional students (157 women). *Enrollment by degree level:* 163 master's, 20 doctoral, 5 other advanced degrees. *Graduate faculty:* 12 full-time (all women), 10 part-time/adjunct (all women). *Tuition:* Part-time $705 per credit hour. *Required fees:* $270 per unit. *Graduate housing:* Room and/or apartments available on a first-come, first-served basis to single students; on-campus housing not available to married students. Typical cost: $3900 per year. Housing application deadline: 3/15. *Student services:* Campus safety program, exercise/wellness program, free psychological counseling, multicultural affairs office, writing training. *Library facilities:* Sister Mary Ludgera Pieperbeck Learning and Resource Center plus 1 other. *Collection:* Books: 3,884 (physical), 392 (digital/electronic); Serial titles: 61 (physical); Databases: 64. Students can reserve study rooms.

**Computer facilities:** 62 computers available on campus for general student use. A campuswide network can be accessed. Online class registration is available. Website: http://www.sfmccon.edu/

**General Application Contact:** Dr. Kim A. Mitchell, Dean, Graduate Program, 309-655-2201, Fax: 309-624-8973, E-mail: kim.a.mitchell@osfhealthcare.org.

**GRADUATE UNITS**

**SFMC College of Nursing Graduate Programs** Students: 1 (woman) full-time, 188 part-time (157 women); includes 20 minority (10 Black or African American, non-Hispanic/Latino; 3 Asian, non-Hispanic/Latino; 3 Hispanic/Latino; 4 Two or more races, non-Hispanic/Latino). Average age 40. 54 applicants, 91% accepted, 18 enrolled. *Faculty:* 12 full-time (all women), 10 part-time/adjunct (all women). Expenses: Contact institution. *Financial support:* In 2019–20, 13 students received support. Scholarships/grants available. Support available to part-time students. Financial award application deadline: 6/15; financial award applicants required to submit FAFSA. In 2019, 51 master's, 11 doctorates awarded. *Program availability:* Part-time, online only, 100% online, blended/hybrid learning. *Application deadline:* For fall admission, 6/1 priority date for domestic and international students; for spring admission, 11/15 priority date for domestic and international students. Applications are processed on a rolling basis. *Application fee:* $50. *Application Contact:* Dr. Kim A. Mitchell, Dean, Graduate Program, 309-655-2201, Fax: 309-624-8973, E-mail: kim.a.mitchell@osfhealthcare.org. *President of OSF Colleges of Health Sciences,* Dr. Sandie S Soldwisch, 815-282-7909, Fax: 309-624-8973, E-mail: Sandie.S.Soldwisch@osfhealthcare.org.

## SAINT FRANCIS UNIVERSITY, Loretto, PA 15940-0600

**General Information** Independent-religious, coed, comprehensive institution. *Enrollment:* 2,619 graduate, professional, and undergraduate students; 291 full-time matriculated graduate/professional students (187 women), 249 part-time matriculated graduate/professional students (163 women). *Enrollment by degree level:* 471 master's, 69 doctoral. *Graduate faculty:* 51 full-time (27 women), 13 part-time/adjunct (8 women). Tuition and fees vary according to program. *Graduate housing:* On-campus housing not available. *Student services:* Campus employment opportunities, campus safety program, career counseling, exercise/wellness program, free psychological counseling, low-cost health insurance, multicultural affairs office, services for students with disabilities, writing training. *Library facilities:* Saint Francis University Library. *Collection:* Books: 60,353 (physical), 1.3 million (digital/electronic); Databases: 74.

**Computer facilities:** Computer purchase and lease plans are available. 1,500 computers available on campus for general student use. A campuswide network can be accessed. Online class registration is available. Website: http://www.francis.edu/

**General Application Contact:** Dr. Bobby L Anderson, Associate Dean of Admissions, 814-472-3386, Fax: 814-472-3365, E-mail: banderson@francis.edu.

**GRADUATE UNITS**

**Cancer Care Program** Students: 10 full-time (2 women), 1 (woman) part-time. Average age 23. *Faculty:* 10 full-time (5 women). Expenses: Contact institution. *Financial support:* Unspecified assistantships available. Financial award applicants required to submit FAFSA. In 2019, 3 master's awarded. *Application deadline:* Applications are processed on a rolling basis. *Application fee:* $35. Electronic applications accepted. *Application Contact:* Dr. Peter Raymond Skoner. *Coordinator,* Dr. Stephen LoRusso, 814-472-3853, E-mail: slorusso@francis.edu.

**Department of Occupational Therapy** Students: 41 full-time (37 women); includes 3 minority (2 Black or African American, non-Hispanic/Latino; 1 Asian, non-Hispanic/Latino). Average age 22. 6 applicants, 100% accepted, 3 enrolled. *Faculty:* 6 full-time (5 women). Expenses: Contact institution. In 2019, 39 master's awarded. *Application fee:* $30. Electronic applications accepted. *Application Contact:* Amy Hudkins, Instructor, 814-472-2792, E-mail: ahudkins@francis.edu. *Department Chair,* Dr. Edward Mihelcic, 814-472-2760, E-mail: emihelcic@francis.edu.

**Department of Physical Therapy** Students: 69 full-time (41 women), 1 part-time (0 women); includes 3 minority (2 Asian, non-Hispanic/Latino; 1 Hispanic/Latino). Average age 23. 264 applicants, 16% accepted, 10 enrolled. *Faculty:* 9 full-time (5 women), 2 part-time/adjunct (0 women). Expenses: Contact institution. *Financial support:* Teaching assistantships with partial tuition reimbursements and unspecified assistantships available. Financial award applicants required to submit FAFSA. In 2019, 29 doctorates awarded. *Application deadline:* For winter admission, 1/15 for domestic and international students. *Application fee:* $30. Electronic applications accepted. *Application Contact:* Dr. Ivan J. Mulligan, Chair/Associate Professor, 814-472-3123, Fax: 814-472-3140, E-mail: imulligan@francis.edu. *Chair/Associate Professor,* Dr. Ivan J. Mulligan, 814-472-3123, Fax: 814-472-3140, E-mail: imulligan@francis.edu.

**Department of Physician Assistant Sciences** Students: 59 full-time (46 women); includes 5 minority (all Asian, non-Hispanic/Latino). Average age 24. 64 applicants, 22% accepted, 9 enrolled. *Faculty:* 9 full-time (7 women), 3 part-time/adjunct (2 women). Expenses: Contact institution. *Financial support:* Unspecified assistantships available. Financial award applicants required to submit FAFSA. In 2019, 49 master's awarded. *Application deadline:* For fall admission, 10/1 for domestic and international students. Applications are processed on a rolling basis. *Application fee:* $175. Electronic applications accepted. *Application Contact:* Dr. Carrie Beebout, MPAS Program Director, 814-472-3128, E-mail: cbeebout@francis.edu. *MPAS Program Director,* Dr. Carrie Beebout, 814-472-3128, E-mail: cbeebout@francis.edu.

**Graduate Education Program** Students: 8 full-time (5 women), 85 part-time (50 women); includes 3 minority (2 Black or African American, non-Hispanic/Latino; 1 Native Hawaiian or other Pacific Islander, non-Hispanic/Latino). Average age 36. 14 applicants, 100% accepted, 14 enrolled. *Faculty:* 1 full-time (0 women), 15 part-time/adjunct (9 women). Expenses: Contact institution. *Financial support:* Applicants required to submit FAFSA. In 2019, 27 master's awarded. *Program availability:* Part-time, 100% online, blended/hybrid learning. *Application deadline:* Applications are processed on a rolling basis. *Application fee:* $30. Electronic applications accepted. *Application Contact:* Sherri L. Link, Coordinator, 814-472-3058, Fax: 814-472-3864, E-mail: slink@francis.edu. *Director,* Melissa Peppetti, 814-472-3068, Fax: 814-472-3864, E-mail: mpeppetti@francis.edu.

**Health Science Program** Students: 5 full-time (2 women), 30 part-time (25 women); includes 9 minority (4 Black or African American, non-Hispanic/Latino; 2 Asian, non-Hispanic/Latino; 1 Hispanic/Latino; 2 Two or more races, non-Hispanic/Latino). Average age 36. 7 applicants, 71% accepted, 3 enrolled. *Faculty:* 2 full-time (both women). Expenses: Contact institution. *Financial support:* Available to part-time students. Applicants required to submit FAFSA. In 2019, 34 master's awarded. *Program availability:* Part-time, evening/weekend, 100% online. *Application deadline:* For fall admission, 7/19 for domestic and international students; for spring admission, 11/15 for domestic and international students; for summer admission, 3/22 for domestic and international students. Applications are processed on a rolling basis. *Application fee:* $50. Electronic applications accepted. *Application Contact:* Jean A. Kline, Administrative Assistant, 814-472-3357, Fax: 814-472-3066, E-mail: jkline@francis.edu. *Chair - Public Health/MMS&MHS,* Dr. Theresa Horner, 814-471-1314, E-mail: thorner@francis.edu.

**Medical Science Program** Students: 34 full-time (22 women), 41 part-time (29 women); includes 44 minority (4 Black or African American, non-Hispanic/Latino; 4 Asian, non-Hispanic/Latino; 35 Hispanic/Latino; 1 Native Hawaiian or other Pacific Islander, non-

Hispanic/Latino). Average age 31. 59 applicants, 100% accepted, 57 enrolled. *Faculty:* 2 full-time (both women). Expenses: Contact institution. *Financial support:* Available to part-time students. Applicants required to submit FAFSA. In 2019, 66 master's awarded. *Program availability:* Part-time, evening/weekend, 100% online. *Application deadline:* For fall admission, 6/15 for domestic students; for spring admission, 11/15 for domestic students; for summer admission, 3/15 for domestic students. Applications are processed on a rolling basis. Electronic applications accepted. *Application Contact:* Dr. Theresa Horner, Assistant Professor/Chair - Public Health/MMS, 814-471-1314, E-mail: thorner@francis.edu. *Assistant Professor/Chair - Public Health/MMS,* Dr. Theresa Horner, 814-471-1314, E-mail: thorner@francis.edu.

**Nursing Program** Students: 7 part-time (all women). Average age 44. 9 applicants, 78% accepted, 4 enrolled. *Faculty:* 2 full-time (both women), 4 part-time/adjunct (all women). Expenses: Contact institution. *Financial support:* Applicants required to submit FAFSA. In 2019, 10 master's awarded. *Program availability:* Part-time, online only, blended/hybrid learning. *Application fee:* $30. Electronic applications accepted. *Application Contact:* Dr. Peter Raymond Skoner. *Coordinator,* Dr. Camille Wendekier, RN, 814-472-2843, E-mail: cwendekier@francis.edu.

**Program in Public Health** Students: 7 full-time (6 women), 4 part-time (all women); includes 4 minority (3 Black or African American, non-Hispanic/Latino; 1 Hispanic/Latino). Average age 32. 16 applicants, 94% accepted, 10 enrolled. *Faculty:* 2 part-time/adjunct (both women). Expenses: Contact institution. *Financial support:* Applicants required to submit FAFSA. *Program availability:* Part-time, evening/weekend, online only, 100% online. *Application deadline:* Applications are processed on a rolling basis. *Application fee:* $55. Electronic applications accepted. *Application Contact:* Dr. Theresa Horner, Chair - Public Health/MMS&MHS, 814-471-1314, E-mail: thorner@francis.edu. *Chair - Public Health/MMS&MHS,* Dr. Theresa Horner, 814-471-1314, E-mail: thorner@francis.edu.

**School of Business** Students: 52 full-time (17 women), 76 part-time (44 women); includes 10 minority (8 Black or African American, non-Hispanic/Latino; 1 Native Hawaiian or other Pacific Islander, non-Hispanic/Latino; 1 Two or more races, non-Hispanic/Latino), 1 international. Average age 30. 65 applicants, 77% accepted, 45 enrolled. *Faculty:* 10 full-time (4 women), 13 part-time/adjunct (9 women). Expenses: Contact institution. *Financial support:* Fellowships with partial tuition reimbursements, career-related internships or fieldwork, and unspecified assistantships available. Financial award application deadline: 8/15; financial award applicants required to submit FAFSA. In 2019, 69 master's awarded. *Program availability:* Part-time, evening/weekend, blended/hybrid learning. *Application deadline:* For fall admission, 8/15 priority date for domestic and international students; for spring admission, 12/1 priority date for domestic students, 12/1 for international students. Applications are processed on a rolling basis. *Application fee:* $30. Electronic applications accepted. *Application Contact:* Nicole Marie Bauman, Coordinator, Graduate Business Programs, 814-472-3026, Fax: 814-472-3369, E-mail: nbauman@francis.edu. *Director, Graduate Business Programs,* Dr. Randy L. Frye, 814-472-3041, Fax: 814-472-3174, E-mail: rfrye@francis.edu.

## ST. FRANCIS XAVIER UNIVERSITY, Antigonish, NS B2G 2W5, Canada

**General Information** Independent-religious, coed, comprehensive institution. *Enrollment:* 66 full-time matriculated graduate/professional students (23 women), 689 part-time matriculated graduate/professional students (505 women). *Enrollment by degree level:* 476 master's, 21 doctoral, 258 other advanced degrees. *International tuition:* $3976 Canadian dollars full-time. *Tuition, area resident:* Part-time $1731 Canadian dollars per course. Tuition, province resident: part-time $1731 Canadian dollars per course. Tuition, Canadian resident: part-time $1988 Canadian dollars per course. *Required fees:* $185 Canadian dollars per course. Tuition and fees vary according to course level, course load, degree level and program. *Graduate housing:* Room and/or apartments available on a first-come, first-served basis to single students; on-campus housing not available to married students. Typical cost: $1131 Canadian dollars per year. Room charges vary according to board plan and housing facility selected. *Student services:* Campus employment opportunities, campus safety program, career counseling, child daycare facilities, exercise/wellness program, free psychological counseling, international student services, low-cost health insurance, multicultural affairs office, services for students with disabilities, teacher training, writing training. *Library facilities:* Angus L. Macdonald Library plus 1 other.

**Computer facilities:** 500 computers available on campus for general student use. A campuswide network can be accessed from student residence rooms and from off campus. Online class registration, online financial account, personal network storage, personal Web publishing, WirelessSynch iPods, Smartphones are available.
Website: http://www.stfx.ca/

**General Application Contact:** Dr. Richard Isnor, Associate VP Research & Graduate Studies, Research Services Group, 902-8675036, E-mail: gradstudies@stfx.ca.

**GRADUATE UNITS**

**Graduate Studies** Expenses: Contact institution. *Financial support:* Teaching assistantships and scholarships/grants available. Financial award application deadline: 2/15. *Program availability:* Part-time, online learning. *Application deadline:* For fall admission, 8/1 priority date for domestic students, 5/30 priority date for international students. Applications are processed on a rolling basis. *Application fee:* $40. *Application Contact:* 902-867-2219, Fax: 902-867-2329, E-mail: admit@stfx.ca. *Associate Vice-President, Research and Graduate Studies,* Dr. Richard Isnor, 902-867-2324, Fax: 902-867-2414.

## ST. JOHN FISHER COLLEGE, Rochester, NY 14618-3597

**General Information** Independent-religious, coed, comprehensive institution. *Enrollment:* 3,719 graduate, professional, and undergraduate students; 512 full-time matriculated graduate/professional students (330 women), 448 part-time matriculated graduate/professional students (344 women). *Enrollment by degree level:* 532 master's, 428 doctoral. *Graduate faculty:* 77 full-time (52 women), 14 part-time/adjunct (6 women). *Tuition:* Full-time $975; part-time $1950 per credit hour. *Required fees:* $15. *Graduate housing:* On-campus housing not available. *Student services:* Campus employment opportunities, campus safety program, career counseling, child daycare facilities, exercise/wellness program, free psychological counseling, international student services, low-cost health insurance, multicultural affairs office, services for students with disabilities, teacher training, writing training. *Library facilities:* Charles J. Lavery Library plus 1 other. *Collection:* Books: 138,569 (physical), 297,511 (digital/electronic); Databases: 156. Students can reserve study rooms.

**Computer facilities:** 550 computers available on campus for general student use. A campuswide network can be accessed. Online class registration is available.
Website: http://www.sjfc.edu/

**General Application Contact:** Michelle Gosier, Director of Transfer and Graduate Admissions, 585-385-8064, Fax: 585-385-8344, E-mail: mgosier@sjfc.edu.

**GRADUATE UNITS**

**Ralph C. Wilson Jr. School of Education** Students: 120 full-time (84 women), 76 part-time (58 women); includes 74 minority (60 Black or African American, non-Hispanic/Latino; 1 American Indian or Alaska Native, non-Hispanic/Latino; 3 Asian, non-Hispanic/Latino; 10 Hispanic/Latino), 1 international. Average age 40. 146 applicants, 77% accepted, 85 enrolled. *Faculty:* 19 full-time (14 women), 6 part-time/adjunct (5 women). Expenses: Contact institution. *Financial support:* Scholarships/grants available. Financial award applicants required to submit FAFSA. In 2019, 45 master's, 61 doctorates awarded. *Program availability:* Part-time, evening/weekend. *Application deadline:* Applications are processed on a rolling basis. *Application fee:* $30. Electronic applications accepted. *Application Contact:* Michelle Gosier, Director of Transfer and Graduate Admissions, 585-385-8064, E-mail: mgosier@sjfc.edu. *Interim Dean,* Joellen Maples, 585-899-3727, E-mail: jmaples@sjfc.edu.

**School of Arts and Sciences** Students: 11 full-time (8 women), 12 part-time (6 women); includes 7 minority (2 Black or African American, non-Hispanic/Latino; 3 Asian, non-Hispanic/Latino; 1 Hispanic/Latino; 1 Two or more races, non-Hispanic/Latino). Average age 27. 33 applicants, 67% accepted, 13 enrolled. *Faculty:* 4 full-time (2 women), 2 part-time/adjunct (1 woman). Expenses: Contact institution. *Financial support:* Scholarships/grants available. Financial award applicants required to submit FAFSA. *Program availability:* Part-time, evening/weekend. *Application deadline:* Applications are processed on a rolling basis. *Application fee:* $30. Electronic applications accepted. *Application Contact:* Michelle Gosier, Director of Transfer and Graduate Admissions, 585-385-8064, E-mail: mgosier@sjfc.edu. *Dean,* Ann Marie Fallon, 585-385-8477, E-mail: afallon@sjfc.edu.

**School of Business** Students: 51 full-time (20 women), 53 part-time (20 women); includes 10 minority (2 Black or African American, non-Hispanic/Latino; 7 Asian, non-Hispanic/Latino; 1 Hispanic/Latino), 2 international. Average age 27. 65 applicants, 82% accepted, 33 enrolled. *Faculty:* 7 full-time (2 women), 3 part-time/adjunct (0 women). Expenses: Contact institution. *Financial support:* Scholarships/grants available. Financial award applicants required to submit FAFSA. In 2019, 81 master's awarded. *Program availability:* Part-time, evening/weekend. *Application deadline:* Applications are processed on a rolling basis. *Application fee:* $30. Electronic applications accepted. *Application Contact:* Michelle Gosier, Director of Transfer and Graduate Admissions, 585-385-8064, E-mail: mgosier@sjfc.edu. *Interim Associate Dean,* Carol Wittmeyer, 585-385-8238, E-mail: cwittmeyer@sjfc.edu.

**Wegmans School of Nursing** Students: 52 full-time (48 women), 296 part-time (256 women); includes 49 minority (22 Black or African American, non-Hispanic/Latino; 1 American Indian or Alaska Native, non-Hispanic/Latino; 10 Asian, non-Hispanic/Latino; 11 Hispanic/Latino; 5 Two or more races, non-Hispanic/Latino). Average age 31. 234 applicants, 61% accepted, 94 enrolled. *Faculty:* 24 full-time (21 women), 3 part-time/adjunct (0 women). Expenses: Contact institution. *Financial support:* Scholarships/grants available. Financial award applicants required to submit FAFSA. In 2019, 84 master's, 2 doctorates awarded. *Program availability:* Part-time, evening/weekend. *Application deadline:* Applications are processed on a rolling basis. Electronic applications accepted. *Application Contact:* Michelle Gosier, Director of Transfer and Graduate Admissions, 585-385-8064, E-mail: mgosier@sjfc.edu. *Dean,* Dr. Diane Cooney-Miner, 585-385-8241, Fax: 585-385-8466, E-mail: dcooney-miner@sjfc.edu.

**Wegmans School of Pharmacy** Students: 278 full-time (170 women), 11 part-time (4 women); includes 60 minority (8 Black or African American, non-Hispanic/Latino; 38 Asian, non-Hispanic/Latino; 6 Hispanic/Latino; 8 Two or more races, non-Hispanic/Latino), 3 international. Average age 24. 269 applicants, 43% accepted, 67 enrolled. *Faculty:* 21 full-time (12 women). Expenses: Contact institution. *Financial support:* Scholarships/grants available. Financial award applicants required to submit FAFSA. In 2019, 79 doctorates awarded. *Application deadline:* For fall admission, 3/1 for domestic students. Applications are processed on a rolling basis. *Application fee:* $30. Electronic applications accepted. *Application Contact:* Michelle Gosier, Director of Transfer and Graduate Admissions, 585-385-8064, E-mail: mgosier@sjfc.edu. *Dean,* Dr. Christine Birnie, 585-385-7202, E-mail: cbirnie@sjfc.edu.

## ST. JOHN'S COLLEGE, Annapolis, MD 21401

**General Information** Independent, coed, comprehensive institution. *Graduate housing:* On-campus housing not available.

**GRADUATE UNITS**

**Graduate Institute** *Program availability:* Evening/weekend. Electronic applications accepted.

## ST. JOHN'S COLLEGE, Santa Fe, NM 87505

**General Information** Independent, coed, comprehensive institution. *Graduate housing:* Rooms and/or apartments available on a first-come, first-served basis to single and married students. Housing application deadline: 4/1.

**GRADUATE UNITS**

**Graduate Institute in Liberal Education** *Program availability:* Evening/weekend.

## ST. JOHN'S SEMINARY, Camarillo, CA 93012-2598

**General Information** Independent-religious, coed, primarily men, graduate-only institution. *Graduate housing:* Room and/or apartments guaranteed to single students; on-campus housing not available to married students.

**GRADUATE UNITS**

**Graduate and Professional Programs** *Program availability:* Part-time. Electronic applications accepted.

## SAINT JOHN'S SEMINARY, Brighton, MA 02135

**General Information** Independent-religious, coed, graduate-only institution. *Graduate housing:* Room and/or apartments available to single students; on-campus housing not available to married students. Housing application deadline: 8/1.

**GRADUATE UNITS**

**Graduate Programs**

## SAINT JOHN'S UNIVERSITY, Collegeville, MN 56321

**General Information** Independent-religious, Undergraduate: men only; graduate: coed, comprehensive institution. *Graduate housing:* Rooms and/or apartments available on a first-come, first-served basis to single and married students. *Research affiliation:* Hill Monastic Manuscript Library (monastic studies, liturgy, spirituality), Center for Ecumenical and Cultural Research, Arca Artium (visual and book arts).

**GRADUATE UNITS**

**Saint John's School of Theology and Seminary** *Program availability:* Part-time, online learning. Electronic applications accepted.

## ST. JOHN'S UNIVERSITY, Queens, NY 11439

**General Information** Independent-religious, coed, university. CGS member. *Graduate housing:* Room and/or apartments available on a first-come, first-served basis to single students; on-campus housing not available to married students. Housing application deadline: 5/1. *Research affiliation:* Raybiotech (biotechnology), Amneal Pharmaceuticals (pharmaceutical research), RAND Corporation, Jewish Board of Family and Children's Services (mental health and social services), Merck & Company, Inc. (pharmaceutical research), ABITEC (specialty chemicals).

**GRADUATE UNITS**

**College of Pharmacy and Health Sciences** *Program availability:* Part-time, evening/weekend. Electronic applications accepted.

**College of Professional Studies** Electronic applications accepted.

**Institute for Biotechnology** Electronic applications accepted.

**The Peter J. Tobin College of Business** Electronic applications accepted.

***School of Risk Management, Insurance and Actuarial Science*** Electronic applications accepted.

**St. John's College of Liberal Arts and Sciences** *Program availability:* Part-time, evening/weekend, 100% online, blended/hybrid learning. Electronic applications accepted.

***Division of Library and Information Science*** *Program availability:* Part-time, online only, 100% online. Electronic applications accepted.

***Institute of Asian Studies*** *Program availability:* Part-time, evening/weekend. Electronic applications accepted.

**The School of Education** Electronic applications accepted.

**School of Law** *Program availability:* Part-time, evening/weekend. Electronic applications accepted.

## ST. JOSEPH'S COLLEGE, LONG ISLAND CAMPUS, Patchogue, NY 11772-2399

**General Information** Independent, coed, comprehensive institution. *Enrollment:* 3,959 graduate, professional, and undergraduate students; 112 full-time matriculated graduate/professional students (73 women), 685 part-time matriculated graduate/professional students (533 women). *Enrollment by degree level:* 797 master's, 130 other advanced degrees. *Graduate faculty:* 33 full-time (21 women), 52 part-time/adjunct (25 women). *Tuition:* Full-time $19,350; part-time $1075 per credit. *Required fees:* $410. *Graduate housing:* On-campus housing not available. *Student services:* Campus employment opportunities, campus safety program, career counseling, exercise/wellness program, free psychological counseling, low-cost health insurance, multicultural affairs office, services for students with disabilities, teacher training, writing training. *Library facilities:* Callahan Library plus 1 other. *Collection:* Books: 108,559 (physical), 190,647 (digital/electronic); Serial titles: 224 (physical), 94,744 (digital/electronic); Databases: 126. Weekly public service hours: 80; students can reserve study rooms.

**Computer facilities:** 267 computers available on campus for general student use. A campuswide network can be accessed. Online class registration, library databases, learning management system, course evaluations, print management, virtual application labs, office 365, student suggestion box are available.
Website: http://www.sjcny.edu/

**General Application Contact:** Christina Seifert, Director of Graduate and Professional Studies Admissions, 631-687-4525, E-mail: cseifert@sjcny.edu.

**GRADUATE UNITS**

**Program in Forensic Computing** Students: 7 full-time (4 women), 18 part-time (7 women); includes 9 minority (4 Black or African American, non-Hispanic/Latino; 5 Hispanic/Latino). Average age 28. 18 applicants, 72% accepted, 10 enrolled. *Faculty:* 1 full-time (0 women), 3 part-time/adjunct (1 woman). Expenses: Contact institution. *Financial support:* In 2019–20, 7 students received support. In 2019, 2 master's awarded. *Program availability:* Part-time, evening/weekend. *Application deadline:* Applications are processed on a rolling basis. *Application fee:* $25. Electronic applications accepted. *Application Contact:* Victoria Hong, Director of M.S. in Forensic Computing, Chairperson, Assistant Professor, 631-687-2646, E-mail: vhong@sjcny.edu. *Director of M.S. in Forensic Computing, Chairperson, Assistant Professor*, Victoria Hong, 631-687-2646, E-mail: vhong@sjcny.edu.

**Program in Nursing** Students: 54 part-time (48 women); includes 18 minority (7 Black or African American, non-Hispanic/Latino; 2 Asian, non-Hispanic/Latino; 8 Hispanic/Latino; 1 Two or more races, non-Hispanic/Latino). Average age 38. 57 applicants, 51% accepted, 22 enrolled. *Faculty:* 7 full-time (6 women), 1 (woman) part-time/adjunct. Expenses: Contact institution. *Financial support:* In 2019–20, 33 students received support. In 2019, 14 master's awarded. *Program availability:* Part-time, evening/weekend. *Application deadline:* Applications are processed on a rolling basis. *Application fee:* $25. Electronic applications accepted. *Application Contact:* Dr. Maria Fletcher, RN, Director, Associate Professor, 631-687-5180, E-mail: mfletcher@sjcny.edu. *Director, Associate Professor*, Dr. Maria Fletcher, RN, 631-687-5180, E-mail: mfletcher@sjcny.edu.

**Programs in Business Management and Administration** Students: 45 full-time (22 women), 114 part-time (62 women); includes 35 minority (9 Black or African American, non-Hispanic/Latino; 8 Asian, non-Hispanic/Latino; 17 Hispanic/Latino; 1 Two or more races, non-Hispanic/Latino). Average age 31. 152 applicants, 57% accepted, 51 enrolled. *Faculty:* 10 full-time (4 women), 18 part-time/adjunct (7 women). Expenses: Contact institution. *Financial support:* In 2019–20, 38 students received support. Federal Work-Study available. In 2019, 69 master's awarded. *Program availability:* Part-time, evening/weekend, 100% online, blended/hybrid learning. *Application deadline:* Applications are processed on a rolling basis. *Application fee:* $25. Electronic applications accepted. *Application Contact:* Mary A. Chance, Assistant Professor, Director of Graduate Management Studies, 631-687-1297, E-mail: mchance@sjcny.edu. *Assistant Professor, Director of Graduate Management Studies*, Mary A. Chance, 631-687-1297, E-mail: mchance@sjcny.edu.

**Programs in Education** Students: 28 full-time (23 women), 335 part-time (289 women); includes 46 minority (6 Black or African American, non-Hispanic/Latino; 1 American Indian or Alaska Native, non-Hispanic/Latino; 3 Asian, non-Hispanic/Latino; 27 Hispanic/Latino; 3 Native Hawaiian or other Pacific Islander, non-Hispanic/Latino; 6 Two or more races, non-Hispanic/Latino). Average age 26. 277 applicants, 76% accepted, 152 enrolled. *Faculty:* 14 full-time (10 women), 24 part-time/adjunct (12 women). Expenses: Contact institution. *Financial support:* In 2019–20, 144 students received support. Federal Work-Study available. In 2019, 166 master's awarded. *Program availability:* Part-time, evening/weekend. *Application deadline:* Applications are processed on a rolling basis. *Application fee:* $25. Electronic applications accepted. *Application Contact:* Nancy Gilchriest, Associate Professor and Department Chair, 631-687-1472, E-mail: ngilchriest@sjcny.edu. *Associate Professor and Department Chair*, Nancy Gilchriest, 631-687-1472, E-mail: ngilchriest@sjcny.edu.

***Field in Special Education*** Students: 17 full-time (13 women), 92 part-time (72 women); includes 9 minority (2 Black or African American, non-Hispanic/Latino; 1 Asian, non-Hispanic/Latino; 5 Hispanic/Latino; 1 Two or more races, non-Hispanic/Latino). Average age 25. 89 applicants, 78% accepted, 47 enrolled. *Faculty:* 8 full-time (5 women), 10 part-time/adjunct (3 women). Expenses: Contact institution. *Financial support:* In 2019–20, 37 students received support. Federal Work-Study available. In 2019, 55 master's awarded. *Program availability:* Part-time, evening/weekend. *Application deadline:* Applications are processed on a rolling basis. *Application fee:* $25. Electronic applications accepted. *Application Contact:* Joan Silver, Associate Professor, Director of MA in Childhood and Adolescence Education with an annotation in Severe and Multiple Disabilities, 631-687-1219, E-mail: jsilver@sjcny.edu. *Associate Professor, Director of MA in Childhood and Adolescence Education with an annotation in Severe and Multiple Disabilities*, Joan Silver, 631-687-1219, E-mail: jsilver@sjcny.edu.

***Field of Infant/Toddler Early Childhood Special Education*** Students: 6 full-time (5 women), 133 part-time (122 women); includes 18 minority (3 Black or African American, non-Hispanic/Latino; 1 American Indian or Alaska Native, non-Hispanic/Latino; 10 Hispanic/Latino; 2 Native Hawaiian or other Pacific Islander, non-Hispanic/Latino; 2 Two or more races, non-Hispanic/Latino). Average age 27. 105 applicants, 74% accepted, 59 enrolled. *Faculty:* 4 full-time (all women), 7 part-time/adjunct (all women). Expenses: Contact institution. *Financial support:* In 2019–20, 39 students received support. In 2019, 63 master's awarded. *Program availability:* Part-time, evening/weekend. *Application deadline:* Applications are processed on a rolling basis. *Application fee:* $25. Electronic applications accepted. *Application Contact:* Katherine Granelli, Director of MA in Infant/Toddler Early Childhood Special Education, 631-687-1217, E-mail: kgranelli@sjcny.edu. *Director of MA in Infant/Toddler Early Childhood Special Education*, Katherine Granelli, 631-687-1217, E-mail: kgranelli@sjcny.edu.

***Field of Literacy and Cognition*** Students: 4 full-time (all women), 85 part-time (82 women); includes 12 minority (1 Asian, non-Hispanic/Latino; 8 Hispanic/Latino; 3 Two or more races, non-Hispanic/Latino). Average age 26. 73 applicants, 79% accepted, 43 enrolled. *Faculty:* 1 (woman) part-time/adjunct. Expenses: Contact institution. *Financial support:* In 2019–20, 54 students received support. Federal Work-Study available. In 2019, 36 master's awarded. *Program availability:* Part-time, evening/weekend. *Application deadline:* Applications are processed on a rolling basis. *Application fee:* $25. Electronic applications accepted. *Application Contact:* Karen Megay-Nespoli, Associate Professor, Director of MA in Literacy and Cognition, 631-687-1212, E-mail: kmegay-nespoli@sjcny.edu. *Associate Professor, Director of MA in Literacy and Cognition*, Karen Megay-Nespoli, 631-687-1212, E-mail: kmegay-nespoli@sjcny.edu.

**Programs in Health Care Administration** Students: 2 full-time (1 woman), 19 part-time (14 women); includes 9 minority (2 Black or African American, non-Hispanic/Latino; 1 Asian, non-Hispanic/Latino; 6 Hispanic/Latino). Average age 37. 15 applicants, 27% accepted, 3 enrolled. *Faculty:* 10 full-time (4 women), 18 part-time/adjunct (7 women). Expenses: Contact institution. *Financial support:* In 2019–20, 6 students received support. In 2019, 11 master's awarded. *Program availability:* Part-time, evening/weekend, 100% online, blended/hybrid learning. *Application deadline:* Applications are processed on a rolling basis. *Application fee:* $25. Electronic applications accepted. *Application Contact:* Mary A. Chance, Assistant Professor, Director of Graduate Management Studies, 631-687-1297, E-mail: mchance@sjcny.edu. *Assistant Professor, Director of Graduate Management Studies*, Mary A. Chance, 631-687-1297, E-mail: mchance@sjcny.edu.

**Programs in Management** Students: 30 full-time (23 women), 145 part-time (113 women); includes 66 minority (33 Black or African American, non-Hispanic/Latino; 8 Asian, non-Hispanic/Latino; 23 Hispanic/Latino; 2 Two or more races, non-Hispanic/Latino), 2 international. Average age 35. 193 applicants, 40% accepted, 47 enrolled. *Faculty:* 10 full-time (4 women), 18 part-time/adjunct (7 women). Expenses: Contact institution. *Financial support:* In 2019–20, 25 students received support. In 2019, 44 master's awarded. *Program availability:* Part-time, evening/weekend, 100% online, blended/hybrid learning. *Application deadline:* Applications are processed on a rolling basis. *Application fee:* $25. Electronic applications accepted. *Application Contact:* Mary A. Chance, Assistant Professor, Director of Graduate Management Studies, 631-687-1297, E-mail: mchance@sjcny.edu. *Assistant Professor, Director of Graduate Management Studies*, Mary A. Chance, 631-687-1297, E-mail: mchance@sjcny.edu.

## ST. JOSEPH'S COLLEGE, NEW YORK, Brooklyn, NY 11205-3688

**General Information** Independent, coed, comprehensive institution. *Enrollment:* 1,185 graduate, professional, and undergraduate students; 55 full-time matriculated graduate/professional students (35 women), 163 part-time matriculated graduate/professional students (123 women). *Enrollment by degree level:* 218 master's, 2 other advanced degrees. *Graduate faculty:* 19 full-time (13 women), 21 part-time/adjunct (14 women). *Tuition:* Full-time $19,350; part-time $1075 per credit. *Required fees:* $400. *Graduate housing:* On-campus housing not available. *Student services:* Campus employment opportunities, campus safety program, career counseling, exercise/wellness program, free psychological counseling, low-cost health insurance, multicultural affairs office, services for students with disabilities, teacher training, writing training. *Library facilities:* McEntegart Hall Library plus 1 other. *Collection:* Books: 88,509 (physical), 190,647 (digital/electronic); Serial titles: 41 (physical), 94,561 (digital/electronic); Databases: 126. Weekly public service hours: 83; students can reserve study rooms.

**Computer facilities:** 207 computers available on campus for general student use. A campuswide network can be accessed. Online class registration, library databases, learning management system, course evaluations, print management, virtual application labs, office software, student suggestion box are available.
Website: http://www.sjcny.edu/

**General Application Contact:** Roberto Figueroa, Director of Transfer, Adult, and Graduate Admissions, 718-940-5828, E-mail: rfigueroa@sjcny.edu.

**GRADUATE UNITS**

**Program in Creative Writing** Students: 24 full-time (5 women); includes 9 minority (1 Black or African American, non-Hispanic/Latino; 1 Asian, non-Hispanic/Latino; 4 Hispanic/Latino; 3 Two or more races, non-Hispanic/Latino), 2 international. Average age 30. 49 applicants, 90% accepted, 20 enrolled. *Faculty:* 2 full-time (0 women), 4 part-time/adjunct (2 women). Expenses: Contact institution. *Financial support:* In 2019–20,

24 students received support. In 2019, 2 master's awarded. *Program availability:* Part-time, evening/weekend. *Application deadline:* Applications are processed on a rolling basis. *Application fee:* $25. Electronic applications accepted. *Application Contact:* Lee Clay Johnson, E-mail: ljohnson6@sjcny.edu.

**Program in Forensic Computing** Students: 6 full-time (3 women), 6 part-time (0 women); includes 9 minority (5 Black or African American, non-Hispanic/Latino; 4 Hispanic/Latino). Average age 30. 12 applicants, 83% accepted, 3 enrolled. *Faculty:* 1 full-time (0 women), 1 (woman) part-time/adjunct. Expenses: Contact institution. *Financial support:* In 2019–20, 4 students received support. In 2019, 3 master's awarded. *Program availability:* Part-time, evening/weekend. *Application deadline:* Applications are processed on a rolling basis. *Application fee:* $25. Electronic applications accepted. *Application Contact:* Roberto Figueroa, Director of Transfer, Adult and Graduate Admissions, 718-940-5828, E-mail: rfigueroa@sjcny.edu. *Associate Professor*, Dr. Joseph Pascarella, 718-940-5775, E-mail: jpascarella2@sjcny.edu.

**Program in Nursing** Students: 52 part-time (47 women); includes 43 minority (40 Black or African American, non-Hispanic/Latino; 2 Asian, non-Hispanic/Latino; 1 Two or more races, non-Hispanic/Latino). Average age 43. 49 applicants, 67% accepted, 21 enrolled. *Faculty:* 3 full-time (all women), 2 part-time/adjunct (both women). Expenses: Contact institution. *Financial support:* In 2019–20, 9 students received support. In 2019, 19 master's awarded. *Program availability:* Part-time, evening/weekend. *Application deadline:* Applications are processed on a rolling basis. *Application fee:* $25. Electronic applications accepted. *Application Contact:* Maria Fletcher, Director, Associate Professor, 718-940-5891, E-mail: mfletcher@sjcny.edu. *Director, Associate Professor*, Maria Fletcher, 718-940-5891, E-mail: mfletcher@sjcny.edu.

**Programs in Business Management and Administration** Students: 11 full-time (2 women), 25 part-time (13 women); includes 26 minority (16 Black or African American, non-Hispanic/Latino; 2 Asian, non-Hispanic/Latino; 8 Hispanic/Latino), 1 international. Average age 35. 18 applicants, 61% accepted, 10 enrolled. *Faculty:* 6 full-time (3 women), 11 part-time/adjunct (7 women). Expenses: Contact institution. *Financial support:* In 2019–20, 13 students received support. In 2019, 20 master's awarded. *Program availability:* Part-time, evening/weekend, 100% online, blended/hybrid learning. *Application deadline:* Applications are processed on a rolling basis. *Application fee:* $25. Electronic applications accepted. *Application Contact:* Mary A. Chance, Interim Director and Assistant Professor, 631-687-1297, E-mail: mchance@sjcny.edu. *Interim Director and Assistant Professor*, Mary A. Chance, 631-687-1297, E-mail: mchance@sjcny.edu.

**Programs in Education** Students: 25 part-time (22 women); includes 9 minority (3 Black or African American, non-Hispanic/Latino; 6 Hispanic/Latino). Average age 24. 17 applicants, 76% accepted, 6 enrolled. *Faculty:* 6 full-time (3 women), 11 part-time/adjunct (7 women). Expenses: Contact institution. *Financial support:* In 2019–20, 19 students received support. In 2019, 21 master's awarded. *Program availability:* Part-time, evening/weekend. *Application deadline:* Applications are processed on a rolling basis. *Application fee:* $25. Electronic applications accepted. *Application Contact:* Nancy Gilchriest, Associate Professor, Department Chair, 631-687-1472, E-mail: ngilchriest@sjcny.edu. *Associate Professor, Department Chair*, Nancy Gilchriest, 631-687-1472, E-mail: ngilchriest@sjcny.edu.

***Field of Literacy and Cognition*** Students: 10 part-time (9 women); includes 5 minority (1 Black or African American, non-Hispanic/Latino; 4 Hispanic/Latino). Average age 25. 6 applicants, 83% accepted, 3 enrolled. *Faculty:* 2 full-time (both women), 1 (woman) part-time/adjunct. Expenses: Contact institution. *Financial support:* In 2019–20, 6 students received support. In 2019, 9 master's awarded. *Program availability:* Part-time, evening/weekend. *Application deadline:* Applications are processed on a rolling basis. *Application fee:* $25. Electronic applications accepted. *Application Contact:* Esther Berkowitz, Associate Professor/Director of the Literacy and Cognition Program, 718-940-5692, E-mail: eberkowitz@sjcny.edu. *Associate Professor/Director of the Literacy and Cognition Program*, Esther Berkowitz, 718-940-5692, E-mail: eberkowitz@sjcny.edu.

***Field of Special Education*** Students: 10 part-time (all women); includes 2 minority (both Hispanic/Latino). Average age 23. 10 applicants, 70% accepted, 3 enrolled. *Faculty:* 3 full-time (all women), 1 (woman) part-time/adjunct. Expenses: Contact institution. *Financial support:* In 2019–20, 10 students received support. In 2019, 8 master's awarded. *Program availability:* Part-time, evening/weekend. *Application deadline:* Applications are processed on a rolling basis. *Application fee:* $25. Electronic applications accepted. *Application Contact:* Dr. Sarah Birch, Director of the MA in Childhood and Adolescence Special Education/Assistant Professor, 718-940-5685, E-mail: sbirch@sjcny.edu. *Director of the MA in Childhood and Adolescence Special Education/Assistant Professor*, Dr. Sarah Birch, 718-940-5685, E-mail: sbirch@sjcny.edu.

**Programs in Health Care Administration** Students: 10 part-time (8 women); includes 7 minority (4 Black or African American, non-Hispanic/Latino; 1 Asian, non-Hispanic/Latino; 2 Hispanic/Latino). Average age 39. 2 applicants, 50% accepted. *Faculty:* 6 full-time (3 women), 11 part-time/adjunct (7 women). Expenses: Contact institution. *Financial support:* In 2019–20, 2 students received support. In 2019, 7 master's awarded. *Program availability:* Part-time, evening/weekend, 100% online, blended/hybrid learning. *Application deadline:* Applications are processed on a rolling basis. *Application fee:* $25. Electronic applications accepted. *Application Contact:* Dr. Lauren Pete, Associate Professor and Chair, 718-940-5890, E-mail: lpete@sjcny.edu. *Associate Professor and Chair*, Dr. Lauren Pete, 718-940-5890, E-mail: lpete@sjcny.edu.

***Field in Health Care Management - Health Information Systems*** Students: 7 part-time (6 women); includes 5 minority (3 Black or African American, non-Hispanic/Latino; 1 Asian, non-Hispanic/Latino; 1 Hispanic/Latino). Average age 37. 2 applicants, 50% accepted. *Faculty:* 6 full-time (3 women), 11 part-time/adjunct (7 women). Expenses: Contact institution. *Financial support:* In 2019–20, 1 student received support. In 2019, 5 master's awarded. *Program availability:* Part-time, evening/weekend, 100% online, blended/hybrid learning. *Application deadline:* Applications are processed on a rolling basis. *Application fee:* $25. Electronic applications accepted. *Application Contact:* Dr. Lauren Pete, Chair, 718-940-5890, E-mail: lpete@sjcny.edu. *Chair*, Dr. Lauren Pete, 718-940-5890, E-mail: lpete@sjcny.edu.

**Programs in Management** Students: 14 full-time (11 women), 45 part-time (33 women); includes 45 minority (29 Black or African American, non-Hispanic/Latino; 3 Asian, non-Hispanic/Latino; 13 Hispanic/Latino), 3 international. Average age 35. 54 applicants, 67% accepted, 22 enrolled. *Faculty:* 6 full-time (3 women), 11 part-time/adjunct (7 women). Expenses: Contact institution. *Financial support:* In 2019–20, 5 students received support. In 2019, 26 master's awarded. *Program availability:* Part-time, evening/weekend, 100% online, blended/hybrid learning. *Application deadline:* Applications are processed on a rolling basis. *Application fee:* $25. Electronic applications accepted. *Application Contact:* Sharon Didier, Assistant Chair/Director of Graduate Management Studies/Associate Professor, 718-940-5790, E-mail: sdidier@sjcny.edu. *Assistant Chair/Director of Graduate Management Studies/Associate Professor*, Sharon Didier, 718-940-5790, E-mail: sdidier@sjcny.edu.

***Field in Health Care Management*** Students: 6 full-time (5 women), 20 part-time (14 women); includes 20 minority (11 Black or African American, non-Hispanic/Latino; 1 Asian, non-Hispanic/Latino; 8 Hispanic/Latino), 1 international. Average age 34. 19 applicants, 63% accepted, 7 enrolled. *Faculty:* 6 full-time (3 women), 11 part-time/adjunct (7 women). Expenses: Contact institution. *Financial support:* In 2019–20, 1 student received support. In 2019, 12 master's awarded. *Program availability:* Part-time, evening/weekend, 100% online, blended/hybrid learning. *Application deadline:* Applications are processed on a rolling basis. *Application fee:* $25. Electronic applications accepted. *Application Contact:* Dr. Lauren Pete, Associate Professor/Chair, 718-940-5890, E-mail: lpete@sjcny.edu. *Associate Professor/Chair*, Dr. Lauren Pete, 718-940-5890, E-mail: lpete@sjcny.edu.

***Field in Human Services Management and Leadership*** Students: 1 (woman) full-time, 9 part-time (8 women); includes 8 minority (6 Black or African American, non-Hispanic/Latino; 1 Asian, non-Hispanic/Latino; 1 Hispanic/Latino). Average age 41. 9 applicants, 78% accepted, 3 enrolled. *Faculty:* 2 full-time (both women), 1 part-time/adjunct (0 women). Expenses: Contact institution. *Financial support:* In 2019–20, 2 students received support. In 2019, 8 master's awarded. *Program availability:* Part-time, evening/weekend, 100% online, blended/hybrid learning. *Application deadline:* Applications are processed on a rolling basis. *Application fee:* $25. Electronic applications accepted. *Application Contact:* Sharon Didier, Assistant Chair/Director of Graduate Management Studies/Associate Professor, 718-940-5790, E-mail: sdidier@sjcny.edu. *Assistant Chair/Director of Graduate Management Studies/Associate Professor*, Sharon Didier, 718-940-5790, E-mail: sdidier@sjcny.edu.

## SAINT JOSEPH'S COLLEGE OF MAINE, Standish, ME 04084

**General Information** Independent-religious, coed, comprehensive institution. *Graduate housing:* On-campus housing not available.

**GRADUATE UNITS**

**Master of Accountancy Program** *Program availability:* Part-time, online learning. Electronic applications accepted.

**Master of Arts in Pastoral Theology Program** *Program availability:* Part-time, online learning.

**Master of Business Administration in Leadership Program** *Program availability:* Part-time, online learning.

**Master of Health Administration Program** *Program availability:* Part-time, online learning. Electronic applications accepted.

**Master of Science in Education Program** *Program availability:* Part-time, online learning. Electronic applications accepted.

**Master of Science in Nursing Program** *Program availability:* Part-time, online learning. Electronic applications accepted.

## ST. JOSEPH'S SEMINARY, Yonkers, NY 10704

**General Information** Independent-religious, coed, graduate-only institution. *Graduate housing:* Room and/or apartments guaranteed to single students; on-campus housing not available to married students.

**GRADUATE UNITS**

**Graduate and Professional Programs**

## SAINT JOSEPH'S UNIVERSITY, Philadelphia, PA 19131-1395

**General Information** Independent-religious, coed, comprehensive institution. *Enrollment:* 7,361 graduate, professional, and undergraduate students; 411 full-time matriculated graduate/professional students (250 women), 2,149 part-time matriculated graduate/professional students (1,414 women). *Enrollment by degree level:* 2,393 master's, 70 doctoral, 97 other advanced degrees. *Graduate faculty:* 94 full-time (47 women), 178 part-time/adjunct (83 women). Tuition and fees vary according to course load, degree level and program. *Graduate housing:* Room and/or apartments available on a first-come, first-served basis to single students; on-campus housing not available to married students. Typical cost: $10,240 per year ($15,656 including board). Room and board charges vary according to board plan and housing facility selected. *Student services:* Campus employment opportunities, campus safety program, career counseling, exercise/wellness program, free psychological counseling, international student services, low-cost health insurance, multicultural affairs office, services for students with disabilities, teacher training, writing training. *Library facilities:* Post Learning Commons and Drexel Library. *Collection:* Books: 271,281 (physical), 467,643 (digital/electronic); Serial titles: 3,324 (physical), 76,020 (digital/electronic); Databases: 219. Weekly public service hours: 109; students can reserve study rooms.

**Computer facilities:** Computer purchase and lease plans are available. 900 computers available on campus for general student use. A campuswide network can be accessed. Online class registration is available.
Website: http://www.sju.edu/

**General Application Contact:** Graduate Admissions, 610-660-1101, E-mail: graduate@sju.edu.

**GRADUATE UNITS**

**College of Arts and Sciences** Students: 157 full-time (109 women), 1,251 part-time (943 women); includes 354 minority (231 Black or African American, non-Hispanic/Latino; 1 American Indian or Alaska Native, non-Hispanic/Latino; 44 Asian, non-Hispanic/Latino; 63 Hispanic/Latino; 2 Native Hawaiian or other Pacific Islander, non-Hispanic/Latino; 13 Two or more races, non-Hispanic/Latino), 29 international. Average age 29. 426 applicants, 70% accepted, 242 enrolled. *Faculty:* 26 full-time (15 women), 44 part-time/adjunct (22 women). Expenses: Contact institution. *Financial support:* In 2019–20, 38 students received support. Scholarships/grants and unspecified assistantships available. Financial award application deadline: 5/1; financial award applicants required to submit FAFSA. In 2019, 183 master's, 28 other advanced degrees awarded. *Program availability:* Part-time, evening/weekend, 100% online, blended/hybrid learning. *Application deadline:* For fall admission, 3/15 for international students; for spring admission, 11/1 for international students. Applications are processed on a rolling basis. *Application fee:* $35. Electronic applications accepted. *Application Contact:* Graduate Admissions, 610-660-1101, E-mail: graduate@sju.edu. *Dean*, Dr. Shaily Menon, 610-660-1282, E-mail: graduate@sju.edu.

**Erivan K. Haub School of Business** Students: 206 full-time (104 women), 708 part-time (320 women); includes 205 minority (93 Black or African American, non-Hispanic/Latino; 1 American Indian or Alaska Native, non-Hispanic/Latino; 58 Asian, non-Hispanic/Latino; 43 Hispanic/Latino; 1 Native Hawaiian or other Pacific Islander, non-Hispanic/Latino; 9 Two or more races, non-Hispanic/Latino), 91 international. Average age 31. 569 applicants, 77% accepted, 340 enrolled. *Faculty:* 44 full-time (13 women), 46 part-time/adjunct (8 women). Expenses: Contact institution. *Financial* *support:* In 2019–20, 347 students received support. Scholarships/grants and unspecified assistantships available. Financial award application deadline: 5/1; financial award applicants required to submit FAFSA. In 2019, 428 master's, 1 other advanced degree awarded. *Program availability:* Part-time-only, evening/weekend, 100% online. *Application deadline:* For fall admission, 7/15 priority date for domestic students, 5/15 priority date for international students; for spring admission, 11/15 priority date for domestic students, 10/15 priority date for international students; for summer admission, 4/15 priority date for domestic students, 2/15 priority date for international students. Applications are processed on a rolling basis. *Application fee:* $35. Electronic applications accepted. *Application Contact:* Christine Anderson, Graduate Admissions, 610-660-1692, Fax: 610-660-1599, E-mail: graduate@sju.edu. *Dean,* Dr. Joseph A. DiAngelo, 610-660-1645, Fax: 610-660-1649, E-mail: jodiange@sju.edu.

**School of Health Studies and Education** Students: 133 full-time (101 women), 1,156 part-time (900 women); includes 300 minority (200 Black or African American, non-Hispanic/Latino; 2 American Indian or Alaska Native, non-Hispanic/Latino; 38 Asian, non-Hispanic/Latino; 46 Hispanic/Latino; 1 Native Hawaiian or other Pacific Islander, non-Hispanic/Latino; 13 Two or more races, non-Hispanic/Latino), 48 international. Average age 33. 473 applicants, 88% accepted, 332 enrolled. *Faculty:* 24 full-time (19 women), 88 part-time/adjunct (53 women). Expenses: Contact institution. *Financial support:* In 2019–20, 22 students received support. Scholarships/grants and unspecified assistantships available. Financial award application deadline: 5/1; financial award applicants required to submit FAFSA. *Program availability:* Part-time, evening/weekend, 100% online. *Application deadline:* For fall admission, 7/15 priority date for domestic students, 5/15 priority date for international students; for spring admission, 11/15 priority date for domestic students, 10/15 priority date for international students. Applications are processed on a rolling basis. *Application fee:* $35. Electronic applications accepted. *Application Contact:* Graduate Admissions, 610-660-1101, E-mail: graduate@sju.edu. *Dean,* Dr. Angela McDonald, 610-6601101, E-mail: graduate@sju.edu.

## SAINT LEO UNIVERSITY, Saint Leo, FL 33574-6665

**General Information** Independent-religious, coed, comprehensive institution. *Enrollment:* 5,351 graduate, professional, and undergraduate students; 82 full-time matriculated graduate/professional students (63 women), 3,908 part-time matriculated graduate/professional students (2,514 women). *Enrollment by degree level:* 3,694 master's, 285 doctoral, 11 other advanced degrees. *Graduate faculty:* 98 full-time (39 women), 128 part-time/adjunct (63 women). *Tuition:* Full-time $12,960; part-time $6480 per year. *Required fees:* $150; $75 per unit. Tuition and fees vary according to degree level, campus/location and program. *Graduate housing:* Room and/or apartments available on a first-come, first-served basis to single students; on-campus housing not available to married students. *Student services:* Campus employment opportunities, campus safety program, career counseling, exercise/wellness program, free psychological counseling, international student services, low-cost health insurance, multicultural affairs office, services for students with disabilities, teacher training, writing training. *Library facilities:* Cannon Memorial Library plus 1 other. *Collection:* Books: 91,413 (physical), 403,690 (digital/electronic); Serial titles: 8,106 (physical), 570,461 (digital/electronic); Databases: 121. Weekly public service hours: 112. *Research affiliation:* American Jewish Committee (religion).

**Computer facilities:** Computer purchase and lease plans are available. 150 computers available on campus for general student use. A campuswide network can be accessed. Online class registration is available.
Website: http://www.saintleo.edu/

**General Application Contact:** Saint Leo University Office of Graduate Admissions, 800-707-8846, Fax: 352-588-7873, E-mail: grad.admissions@saintleo.edu.

**GRADUATE UNITS**

**Graduate Studies in Business** Students: 8 full-time (2 women), 1,963 part-time (1,176 women); includes 1,147 minority (580 Black or African American, non-Hispanic/Latino; 8 American Indian or Alaska Native, non-Hispanic/Latino; 43 Asian, non-Hispanic/Latino; 250 Hispanic/Latino; 4 Native Hawaiian or other Pacific Islander, non-Hispanic/Latino; 262 Two or more races, non-Hispanic/Latino), 96 international. Average age 37. 818 applicants, 78% accepted, 424 enrolled. *Faculty:* 51 full-time (15 women), 45 part-time/adjunct (18 women). Expenses: Contact institution. *Financial support:* In 2019–20, 1,510 students received support. Scholarships/grants, unspecified assistantships, and tuition remission for Saint Leo employees and their dependents available. Financial award application deadline: 3/1; financial award applicants required to submit FAFSA. In 2019, 766 master's, 14 doctorates awarded. *Program availability:* Part-time, evening/weekend, 100% online, blended/hybrid learning. *Application deadline:* For fall admission, 7/1 priority date for domestic and international students; for spring admission, 11/12 priority date for domestic students, 11/1 for international students. Applications are processed on a rolling basis. Electronic applications accepted. *Application Contact:* Saint Leo University Office of Graduate Admissions, 800-707-8846, Fax: 352-588-7873, E-mail: grad.admissions@saintleo.edu. *Dean, School of Business,* Dr. Robyn Parker, 352-588-8599, Fax: 352-588-8912, E-mail: mbaslu@saintleo.edu.

**Graduate Studies in Creative Writing** Students: 1 (woman) full-time, 27 part-time (22 women); includes 15 minority (5 Black or African American, non-Hispanic/Latino; 6 Hispanic/Latino; 4 Two or more races, non-Hispanic/Latino). Average age 42. 21 applicants, 71% accepted, 10 enrolled. *Faculty:* 4 full-time (2 women), 1 (woman) part-time/adjunct. Expenses: Contact institution. *Financial support:* In 2019–20, 12 students received support. Tuition remission for Saint Leo employees and their dependents available. Financial award application deadline: 3/1; financial award applicants required to submit FAFSA. In 2019, 14 master's awarded. *Program availability:* Part-time, online only, blended/hybrid learning. *Application deadline:* For fall admission, 7/1 priority date for domestic and international students; for spring admission, 11/1 priority date for domestic and international students. Applications are processed on a rolling basis. Electronic applications accepted. *Application Contact:* Saint Leo University Office of Graduate Admissions, 800-707-8846, Fax: 352-588-7873, E-mail: grad.admissions@saintleo.edu. *Director,* Dr. Steve Kistulentz, 352-588-7218, Fax: 352-588-8300, E-mail: creativewriting@saintleo.edu.

**Graduate Studies in Education** Students: 420 part-time (343 women); includes 193 minority (76 Black or African American, non-Hispanic/Latino; 1 American Indian or Alaska Native, non-Hispanic/Latino; 3 Asian, non-Hispanic/Latino; 48 Hispanic/Latino; 65 Two or more races, non-Hispanic/Latino). Average age 39. 251 applicants, 80% accepted, 119 enrolled. *Faculty:* 8 full-time (7 women), 17 part-time/adjunct (11 women). Expenses: Contact institution. *Financial support:* In 2019–20, 40 students received support. Career-related internships or fieldwork, scholarships/grants, health care benefits, and tuition remission for Saint Leo employees and their dependents available. Financial award application deadline: 3/1; financial award applicants required to submit FAFSA. In 2019, 149 master's, 1 other advanced degree awarded. *Program availability:* Part-time, evening/weekend, 100% online, blended/hybrid learning. *Application deadline:* For fall admission, 7/1 priority date for domestic students, 7/1 for international students; for winter admission, 7/1 for international students; for spring admission, 11/1 priority date for domestic students. Applications are processed on a rolling basis. Electronic applications accepted. *Application Contact:* Saint Leo University Office of Graduate Admissions, 800-707-8846, Fax: 352-588-7873, E-mail: grad.admissions@saintleo.edu. *Director of Graduate Studies in Education,* Dr. Fern Aefsky, 352-588-8309, Fax: 352-588-8861, E-mail: kara.winkler@saintleo.edu.

**Graduate Studies in Human Services Administration** Students: 188 part-time (163 women); includes 153 minority (123 Black or African American, non-Hispanic/Latino; 1 Asian, non-Hispanic/Latino; 8 Hispanic/Latino; 21 Two or more races, non-Hispanic/Latino). Average age 40. 78 applicants, 82% accepted, 51 enrolled. *Faculty:* 4 full-time (all women), 10 part-time/adjunct (8 women). Expenses: Contact institution. *Financial support:* In 2019–20, 40 students received support. Career-related internships or fieldwork, scholarships/grants, health care benefits, and tuition remission for Saint Leo employees and their dependents available. Financial award application deadline: 3/1; financial award applicants required to submit FAFSA. In 2019, 44 master's awarded. *Program availability:* Part-time, evening/weekend, online only, 100% online. *Application deadline:* For fall admission, 7/1 for domestic and international students; for spring admission, 11/1 for domestic and international students. Applications are processed on a rolling basis. Electronic applications accepted. *Application Contact:* Saint Leo University Office of Graduate Admissions, 800-707-8846, Fax: 352-588-7873, E-mail: grad.admissions@saintleo.edu. *Director, Graduate Studies in Human Services Administration,* Dr. Nancy Wood, 352-588-8131, Fax: 352-588-8289, E-mail: nancy.wood@saintleo.edu.

**Graduate Studies in Psychology** Students: 83 part-time (59 women); includes 43 minority (22 Black or African American, non-Hispanic/Latino; 1 Asian, non-Hispanic/Latino; 8 Hispanic/Latino; 12 Two or more races, non-Hispanic/Latino), 1 international. Average age 32. 53 applicants, 62% accepted, 23 enrolled. *Faculty:* 6 full-time (3 women), 4 part-time/adjunct (1 woman). Expenses: Contact institution. *Financial support:* In 2019–20, 16 students received support. Scholarships/grants, health care benefits, and tuition remission for Saint Leo employees and their dependents available. Financial award application deadline: 3/1; financial award applicants required to submit FAFSA. In 2019, 5 master's awarded. *Program availability:* Part-time-only, evening/weekend, online only, 100% online. *Application deadline:* For fall admission, 7/1 priority date for domestic students, 7/1 for international students; for spring admission, 11/1 priority date for domestic students, 11/1 for international students. Applications are processed on a rolling basis. Electronic applications accepted. *Application Contact:* Saint Leo University Office of Graduate Admissions, 800-707-8846, Fax: 352-588-7873, E-mail: grad.admissions@saintleo.edu. *Director, Graduate Studies in Psychology,* Dr. Cathleen Dunn, 352-588-8294, Fax: 352-588-8300.

**Graduate Studies in Public Safety Administration** Students: 1 (woman) full-time, 761 part-time (490 women); includes 466 minority (252 Black or African American, non-Hispanic/Latino; 4 American Indian or Alaska Native, non-Hispanic/Latino; 5 Asian, non-Hispanic/Latino; 94 Hispanic/Latino; 111 Two or more races, non-Hispanic/Latino). Average age 37. 314 applicants, 82% accepted, 173 enrolled. *Faculty:* 10 full-time (4 women), 26 part-time/adjunct (6 women). Expenses: Contact institution. *Financial support:* In 2019–20, 62 students received support. Scholarships/grants, health care benefits, and tuition remission for Saint Leo employees and their dependents available. Financial award application deadline: 3/1; financial award applicants required to submit FAFSA. In 2019, 236 master's, 2 doctorates awarded. *Program availability:* Part-time, evening/weekend, 100% online, blended/hybrid learning. *Application deadline:* For fall admission, 7/1 priority date for domestic and international students; for spring admission, 11/1 priority date for domestic and international students. Applications are processed on a rolling basis. Electronic applications accepted. *Application Contact:* Saint Leo University Office of Graduate Admissions, 800-707-8846, Fax: 352-588-7873, E-mail: grad.admissions@saintleo.edu. *Director of Graduate Studies in Public Safety Administration,* Dr. Robert Diemer, 352-588-8974, Fax: 352-588-8660, E-mail: graduatepublicsafety@saintleo.edu.

**Graduate Studies in Social Work** Students: 69 full-time (58 women), 189 part-time (156 women); includes 156 minority (84 Black or African American, non-Hispanic/Latino; 2 Asian, non-Hispanic/Latino; 40 Hispanic/Latino; 30 Two or more races, non-Hispanic/Latino). Average age 37. 197 applicants, 73% accepted, 92 enrolled. *Faculty:* 8 full-time (6 women), 17 part-time/adjunct (16 women). Expenses: Contact institution. *Financial support:* In 2019–20, 14 students received support. Scholarships/grants, health care benefits, unspecified assistantships, and tuition remission for Saint Leo employees and their dependents available. Financial award application deadline: 3/1. In 2019, 77 master's awarded. *Program availability:* Part-time, online only, blended/hybrid learning. *Application deadline:* For fall admission, 6/1 for domestic and international students. Electronic applications accepted. *Application Contact:* Saint Leo University Office of Graduate Admissions, 800-707-8846, Fax: 352-588-7873, E-mail: grad.admissions@saintleo.edu. *Director of Graduate Studies in Social Work,* Dr. Courtney Wiest, 352-588-8015, Fax: 352-588-8289, E-mail: courtney.wiest@saintleo.edu.

**Graduate Studies in Theology** Students: 3 full-time (1 woman), 239 part-time (78 women); includes 180 minority (22 Black or African American, non-Hispanic/Latino; 1 Asian, non-Hispanic/Latino; 13 Hispanic/Latino; 1 Native Hawaiian or other Pacific Islander, non-Hispanic/Latino; 143 Two or more races, non-Hispanic/Latino). Average age 51. 92 applicants, 93% accepted, 66 enrolled. *Faculty:* 9 full-time (0 women), 9 part-time/adjunct (3 women). Expenses: Contact institution. *Financial support:* In 2019–20, 11 students received support. Fellowships, scholarships/grants, and tuition remission for Saint Leo employees and their dependents available. Financial award application deadline: 3/1; financial award applicants required to submit FAFSA. In 2019, 46 master's, 2 other advanced degrees awarded. *Program availability:* Part-time, evening/weekend, 100% online, blended/hybrid learning. *Application deadline:* For fall admission, 7/1 priority date for domestic and international students; for spring admission, 11/1 priority date for domestic and international students. Applications are processed on a rolling basis. Electronic applications accepted. *Application Contact:* Saint Leo University Office of Graduate Admissions, 800-707-8846, Fax: 352-588-7873, E-mail: grad.admissions@saintleo.edu. *Director, Graduate Theology,* Dr. Randall Woodard, 352-588-8239, Fax: 352-588-8404, E-mail: randall.woodard@saintleo.edu.

## ST. LOUIS COLLEGE OF PHARMACY, St. Louis, MO 63110-1088

**General Information** Independent, coed, comprehensive institution. *Enrollment:* 679 full-time matriculated graduate/professional students (427 women), 25 part-time matriculated graduate/professional students (14 women). *Enrollment by degree level:* 704 doctoral. *Graduate faculty:* 37 full-time (23 women), 43 part-time/adjunct (31 women). *Tuition:* Full-time $37,153; part-time $1161 per credit hour. *Required fees:* $600; $600. Part-time tuition and fees vary according to course load. *Graduate housing:* Room and/or apartments available on a first-come, first-served basis to single students; on-campus housing not available to married students. Typical cost: $8600 per year ($11,890 including board). Room and board charges vary according to board plan and housing facility selected. Housing application deadline: 6/1. *Student services:* Campus employment opportunities, campus safety program, career counseling, exercise/wellness program, free psychological counseling, international student services, low-cost health insurance, multicultural affairs office, services for students with disabilities, writing training. *Library facilities:* O. J. Cloughly Alumni Library. *Collection:* Books: 14,941 (physical), 180,979 (digital/electronic); Serial titles: 445 (physical), 43,334 (digital/electronic); Databases: 62. Weekly public service hours: 101; study areas open 24 hours, 5–7 days a week; students can reserve study rooms. *Research affiliation:* Express Scripts (pharmacy), Strategic Biomedical, Inc.

**Computer facilities:** Computer purchase and lease plans are available. 1,390 computers available on campus for general student use. A campuswide network can be accessed from student residence rooms and from off campus. Online class registration is available.
Website: http://www.stlcop.edu/

**General Application Contact:** Jill Gebke, Director of Admissions, 314-446-8140, Fax: 314-446-8309, E-mail: jill.gebke@stlcop.edu.

**GRADUATE UNITS**

**School of Pharmacy** Students: 679 full-time (427 women), 25 part-time (14 women); includes 248 minority (72 Black or African American, non-Hispanic/Latino; 1 American Indian or Alaska Native, non-Hispanic/Latino; 150 Asian, non-Hispanic/Latino; 15 Hispanic/Latino; 10 Two or more races, non-Hispanic/Latino), 28 international. Average age 25. 292 applicants, 59% accepted, 154 enrolled. *Faculty:* 37 full-time (23 women), 43 part-time/adjunct (31 women). Expenses: Contact institution. *Financial support:* In 2019–20, 389 students received support. Federal Work-Study and scholarships/grants available. Financial award application deadline: 3/15; financial award applicants required to submit FAFSA. In 2019, 241 doctorates awarded. *Application deadline:* For fall admission, 3/1 for domestic and international students. Applications are processed on a rolling basis. *Application fee:* $55. Electronic applications accepted. *Application Contact:* Jill Gebke, Director of Admissions, 314-446-8140, Fax: 314-446-8309, E-mail: jill.gebke@stlcop.edu. *Interim Dean of Pharmacy,* Dr. Brenda Gleason, 314-446-8184.

## SAINT LOUIS UNIVERSITY, St. Louis, MO 63103

**General Information** Independent-religious, coed, university. CGS member. *Graduate housing:* Rooms and/or apartments available to single and married students. Housing application deadline: 5/1. *Research affiliation:* National Center for Atmospheric Research (earth and atmospheric sciences), Argonne National Laboratory (energy, physics, chemistry, mathematics and computer science), Small Business Administration (business, administration and entrepreneurship), Monsanto Chemical Corporation (chemistry), Missouri Botanical Garden (biology, plant science), AT&T Foundation (communication).

**GRADUATE UNITS**

***Center for Advanced Dental Education*** Electronic applications accepted.

***Center for Health Care Ethics*** Electronic applications accepted.

***College for Public Health and Social Justice*** *Program availability:* Part-time.

***College of Arts and Sciences*** *Program availability:* Part-time, evening/weekend. Electronic applications accepted.

***Doisy College of Health Sciences*** *Program availability:* Part-time.

***John Cook School of Business*** *Program availability:* Part-time, evening/weekend. Electronic applications accepted.

***Parks College of Engineering, Aviation, and Technology*** *Program availability:* Part-time, online learning.

***School of Education*** *Program availability:* Part-time. Electronic applications accepted.

***School of Medicine*** Electronic applications accepted.

***School of Nursing*** *Program availability:* Part-time, online learning. Electronic applications accepted.

**School of Law** *Program availability:* Part-time, evening/weekend. Electronic applications accepted.

## SAINT LOUIS UNIVERSITY–MADRID CAMPUS, 28003 Madrid, Spain

**General Information** Independent-religious, coed, comprehensive institution. *Graduate housing:* Room and/or apartments guaranteed to single students. *Research affiliation:* Universidad Autonoma de Madrid (English philology), Pontificia Universidade Catolica do Rio de Janeiro, Sogang University, Korea.

**GRADUATE UNITS**

**Graduate Programs** *Program availability:* Part-time.

## SAINT MARTIN'S UNIVERSITY, Lacey, WA 98503

**General Information** Independent-religious, coed, comprehensive institution. *Enrollment:* 1,609 graduate, professional, and undergraduate students; 74 full-time matriculated graduate/professional students (38 women), 166 part-time matriculated graduate/professional students (98 women). *Enrollment by degree level:* 227 master's, 13 other advanced degrees. *Graduate faculty:* 23 full-time (11 women), 27 part-time/adjunct (13 women). *Tuition:* Full-time $22,950; part-time $15,300 per year. Tuition and fees vary according to course level, course load, degree level, campus/location and program. *Graduate housing:* Room and/or apartments available on a first-come, first-served basis to single students; on-campus housing not available to married students. Housing application deadline: 3/15. *Student services:* Campus employment opportunities, campus safety program, career counseling, exercise/wellness program, free psychological counseling, international student services, low-cost health insurance, multicultural affairs office, services for students with disabilities, writing training. *Library facilities:* O'Grady Library. *Collection:* Weekly public service hours: 88; students can reserve study rooms.

**Computer facilities:** 80 computers available on campus for general student use. A campuswide network can be accessed from student residence rooms. Online class registration is available.
Website: http://www.stmartin.edu/

**General Application Contact:** Chantelle Petrone Marker, Director of Graduate Admissions, 360-412-6128, E-mail: cmarker@stmartin.edu.

**GRADUATE UNITS**

***College of Education*** Students: 37 full-time (20 women), 15 part-time (8 women); includes 8 minority (1 Black or African American, non-Hispanic/Latino; 3 Asian, non-Hispanic/Latino; 4 Hispanic/Latino), 1 international. Average age 33. *Faculty:* 9 full-time (5 women), 11 part-time/adjunct (9 women). Expenses: Contact institution. *Financial support:* Career-related internships or fieldwork, Federal Work-Study, institutionally sponsored loans, and unspecified assistantships available. Support available to part-time students. Financial award application deadline: 3/1; financial award applicants required to submit FAFSA. In 2019, 16 master's awarded. *Program availability:* Part-time, evening/weekend. *Application deadline:* For fall admission, 4/1 priority date for domestic and international students; for spring admission, 11/1 priority date for domestic and international students. Applications are processed on a rolling basis. *Application fee:* $50. Electronic applications accepted. *Application Contact:* Timothy Greer, Graduate Admissions Recruiter, 360-412-6128, E-mail: tgreer@stmartin.edu. *Interim Dean of College of Education and Counseling,* Dr. Jeff Crane, 360-438-4333, Fax: 360-438-4486, E-mail: jcrane@stmartin.edu.

***School of Business*** Students: 35 full-time (14 women), 3 part-time (2 women); includes 18 minority (5 Black or African American, non-Hispanic/Latino; 8 Asian, non-Hispanic/Latino; 5 Hispanic/Latino), 2 international. Average age 33. Expenses: Contact institution. *Financial support:* Career-related internships or fieldwork and scholarships/grants available. Support available to part-time students. Financial award application deadline: 3/1; financial award applicants required to submit FAFSA. In 2019, 32 master's awarded. *Program availability:* Part-time, evening/weekend. *Application deadline:* For fall admission, 7/1 priority date for domestic and international students; for spring admission, 12/1 for domestic students, 12/1 priority date for international students. Applications are processed on a rolling basis. *Application fee:* $50. Electronic applications accepted. *Application Contact:* Timothy Greer, Graduate Admissions Recruiter, 360-412-6128, E-mail: tgreer@stmartin.edu. *Dean, School of Business,* Dr. Chung Lee, 360-438-4564, E-mail: clee@stmartin.edu.

## SAINT MARY-OF-THE-WOODS COLLEGE, Saint Mary of the Woods, IN 47876

**General Information** Independent-religious, coed, primarily women, comprehensive institution. *Enrollment:* 1,094 graduate, professional, and undergraduate students; 205 full-time matriculated graduate/professional students (189 women), 25 part-time matriculated graduate/professional students (all women). *Enrollment by degree level:* 230 master's. *Graduate faculty:* 18 full-time (13 women), 8 part-time/adjunct (7 women). Tuition and fees vary according to course load and program. *Graduate housing:* On-campus housing not available. *Student services:* Campus employment opportunities, campus safety program, career counseling, exercise/wellness program, grant writing training, international student services, services for students with disabilities, writing training. *Library facilities:* Rooney Library.

**Computer facilities:** Computer purchase and lease plans are available. A campuswide network can be accessed.
Website: http://www.smwc.edu/

**General Application Contact:** Crystal Cox, Associate Director of Admissions, 812-535-5263, E-mail: graduate@smwc.edu.

**GRADUATE UNITS**

**Master of Arts in Art Therapy Program** Students: 123 full-time (118 women), 19 part-time (all women); includes 32 minority (7 Black or African American, non-Hispanic/Latino; 1 American Indian or Alaska Native, non-Hispanic/Latino; 2 Asian, non-Hispanic/Latino; 3 Hispanic/Latino; 19 Two or more races, non-Hispanic/Latino), 1 international. Average age 34. 68 applicants, 62% accepted, 32 enrolled. *Faculty:* 5 full-time (all women). Expenses: Contact institution. *Financial support:* In 2019–20, 38 students received support. Scholarships/grants available. Financial award applicants required to submit FAFSA. In 2019, 27 master's awarded. *Program availability:* Part-time. *Application deadline:* For fall admission, 4/30 priority date for domestic and international students; for winter admission, 10/31 priority date for domestic and international students. Applications are processed on a rolling basis. Electronic applications accepted. *Application Contact:* Crystal Cox, Associate Director of Admissions, 812-535-5263, E-mail: graduate@smwc.edu. *Dean of Graduate Therapy and Counseling Programs,* Dr. Tracy Richardson, 812-535-5154, E-mail: trichardson@smwc.edu.

**Master of Arts in Music Therapy Program** Students: 26 full-time (24 women); includes 7 minority (1 Black or African American, non-Hispanic/Latino; 1 Asian, non-Hispanic/Latino; 5 Two or more races, non-Hispanic/Latino). Average age 32. 17 applicants, 47% accepted, 7 enrolled. *Faculty:* 2 full-time (both women), 7 part-time/adjunct (6 women). Expenses: Contact institution. *Financial support:* In 2019–20, 21 students received support. Career-related internships or fieldwork, scholarships/grants, and unspecified assistantships available. Financial award applicants required to submit FAFSA. In 2019, 7 master's awarded. *Program availability:* Part-time, blended/hybrid learning. *Application deadline:* For fall admission, 4/30 priority date for domestic and international students; for winter admission, 10/31 priority date for domestic students, 10/30 priority date for international students. Applications are processed on a rolling basis. Electronic applications accepted. *Application Contact:* Crystal Cox, Associate Director of Admissions, 812-535-5263, E-mail: graduate@smwc.edu. *Dean of Graduate Therapy and Counseling Programs,* Dr. Tracy Richardson, 812-535-5154, E-mail: trichardson@smwc.edu.

**Master of Healthcare Administration Program** Students: 8 full-time (5 women), 1 (woman) part-time; includes 3 minority (1 Black or African American, non-Hispanic/Latino; 2 Two or more races, non-Hispanic/Latino). Average age 33. 7 applicants, 100% accepted, 5 enrolled. *Faculty:* 1 (woman) full-time, 4 part-time/adjunct (all women). Expenses: Contact institution. *Financial support:* In 2019–20, 6 students received support. Scholarships/grants available. Financial award applicants required to submit FAFSA. In 2019, 9 master's awarded. *Program availability:* Part-time. *Application deadline:* Applications are processed on a rolling basis. *Application Contact:* Office of Admissions, 800-926-7692, E-mail: admissions@smwc.edu. *Assistant Professor, Healthcare Administration Program Director,* Dr. Michelle Ruiz, 812-535-5112, E-mail: Michelle.Ruiz@smwc.edu.

**Master of Leadership Development Program** Students: 32 full-time (28 women), 2 part-time (both women); includes 17 minority (2 Black or African American, non-Hispanic/Latino; 15 Two or more races, non-Hispanic/Latino). Average age 36. 218 applicants, 7% accepted, 13 enrolled. *Faculty:* 8 full-time (5 women), 3 part-time/adjunct (2 women). Expenses: Contact institution. *Financial support:* In 2019–20, 27 students received support. Scholarships/grants and unspecified assistantships available. Financial award applicants required to submit FAFSA. In 2019, 19 master's awarded. *Program availability:* Part-time. *Application deadline:* Applications are processed on a rolling basis. Electronic applications accepted. *Application Contact:* Dr. Lamprini Pantazi, Professor of MLD, Director of MLD, 812-535-5232, E-mail: lpantazi@smwc.edu. *Professor of MLD, Director of MLD,* Dr. Lamprini Pantazi, 812-535-5232, E-mail: lpantazi@smwc.edu.

**Master of Science in Nursing Program** Students: 16 full-time (14 women), 1 (woman) part-time; includes 9 minority (all Two or more races, non-Hispanic/Latino). Average age 38. 12 applicants, 100% accepted, 11 enrolled. *Faculty:* 2 full-time (both women). Expenses: Contact institution. *Financial support:* Scholarships/grants available. Financial award applicants required to submit FAFSA. *Application Contact:* Marcia

Miller, Chair, 812-535-5119, E-mail: mmiller5@smwc.edu. *Chair,* Marcia Miller, 812-535-5119, E-mail: mmiller5@smwc.edu.

## SAINT MARY'S COLLEGE, Notre Dame, IN 46556

**General Information** Independent-religious, women only, comprehensive institution. *Enrollment:* 1,580 graduate, professional, and undergraduate students; 63 full-time matriculated graduate/professional students (all women), 65 part-time matriculated graduate/professional students (57 women). *Enrollment by degree level:* 70 master's, 58 doctoral. Tuition and fees vary according to course load, degree level and program. *Graduate housing:* Room and/or apartments available on a first-come, first-served basis to single students; on-campus housing not available to married students. Typical cost: $8070 per year ($13,020 including board). Room and board charges vary according to board plan and housing facility selected. Housing application deadline: 5/1. *Student services:* Campus employment opportunities, campus safety program, career counseling, child daycare facilities, exercise/wellness program, free psychological counseling, international student services, multicultural affairs office, services for students with disabilities, writing training. *Library facilities:* Cushwa-Leighton Library. *Collection:* Books: 154,790 (physical), 170,212 (digital/electronic); Serial titles: 3,122 (physical), 66,162 (digital/electronic); Databases: 99. Weekly public service hours: 54; study areas open 24 hours, 5–7 days a week; students can reserve study rooms.

**Computer facilities:** Computer purchase and lease plans are available. 284 computers available on campus for general student use. A campuswide network can be accessed from student residence rooms and from off campus. Online class registration is available.
Website: http://www.saintmarys.edu/

**General Application Contact:** Melissa Fruscione, Director, Graduate Studies, 574-284-5098, E-mail: mfruscione@saintmarys.edu.

**GRADUATE UNITS**

**Graduate Studies** Students: 67 full-time (65 women), 59 part-time (54 women); includes 33 minority (11 Black or African American, non-Hispanic/Latino; 1 American Indian or Alaska Native, non-Hispanic/Latino; 7 Asian, non-Hispanic/Latino; 6 Hispanic/Latino; 8 Two or more races, non-Hispanic/Latino). Average age 29. 265 applicants, 61% accepted, 50 enrolled. *Faculty:* 27 full-time (0 women). Expenses: Contact institution. *Financial support:* In 2019–20, 13 students received support. Scholarships/grants available. Financial award application deadline: 3/1; financial award applicants required to submit FAFSA. In 2019, 36 master's, 1 doctorate awarded. *Program availability:* Part-time, evening/weekend, Coursework 100% online, including minimal on campus meetings for presentation purposes. *Application deadline:* Applications are processed on a rolling basis. Electronic applications accepted. *Application Contact:* Melissa Fruscione, Director, Graduate Studies, 574-284-5098, E-mail: graduateadmission@saintmarys.edu. *Provost/Senior Vice President,* Titilayo Ufomata, 574-284-4575, E-mail: tufomata@saintmarys.edu.

## SAINT MARY'S COLLEGE OF CALIFORNIA, Moraga, CA 94575

**General Information** Independent-religious, coed, upper-level institution. CGS member. *Graduate housing:* Room and/or apartments available on a first-come, first-served basis to single students; on-campus housing not available to married students. Housing application deadline: 6/1.

**GRADUATE UNITS**

**Kalmanovitz School of Education** *Program availability:* Part-time, evening/weekend.

**School of Economics and Business Administration** *Program availability:* Part-time, evening/weekend.

**School of Liberal Arts** *Program availability:* Part-time.

## ST. MARY'S COLLEGE OF MARYLAND, St. Mary's City, MD 20686-3001

**General Information** State-supported, coed, comprehensive institution. *Enrollment:* 1,513 graduate, professional, and undergraduate students; 21 full-time matriculated graduate/professional students (16 women). *Enrollment by degree level:* 21 master's. *Graduate faculty:* 5 full-time (4 women), 6 part-time/adjunct (5 women). *International tuition:* $16,530 full-time. *Tuition, area resident:* Full-time $16,530. Tuition, state resident: full-time $16,530. Tuition, nonresident: full-time $16,530. *Required fees:* $4706. *Graduate housing:* Room and/or apartments available on a first-come, first-served basis to single students; on-campus housing not available to married students. Housing application deadline: 5/1. *Student services:* Career counseling, exercise/wellness program, free psychological counseling, multicultural affairs office, services for students with disabilities, teacher training, writing training. *Library facilities:* Library, Archives, and Media Center. *Collection:* Books: 118,066 (physical), 12,955 (digital/electronic); Serial titles: 1,077 (physical), 111,374 (digital/electronic); Databases: 108. Weekly public service hours: 96; study areas open 24 hours, 5–7 days a week; students can reserve study rooms.

**Computer facilities:** Computer purchase and lease plans are available. 317 computers available on campus for general student use. A campuswide network can be accessed. Online class registration, learning management system are available.
Website: http://www.smcm.edu/

**General Application Contact:** Dr. Angela Johnson, Director of Teacher Education, 240-895-2065, E-mail: mat@smcm.edu.

**GRADUATE UNITS**

**Department of Educational Studies** Students: 31 full-time (27 women); includes 1 minority (Black or African American, non-Hispanic/Latino). Average age 23. 41 applicants, 95% accepted, 31 enrolled. *Faculty:* 6 full-time (5 women), 3 part-time/adjunct (2 women). Expenses: Contact institution. *Financial support:* In 2019–20, 10 students received support. Scholarships/grants available. Financial award application deadline: 4/1; financial award applicants required to submit FAFSA. In 2019, 29 master's awarded. *Application deadline:* For fall admission, 11/15 priority date for domestic and international students; for spring admission, 1/31 priority date for domestic and international students. Applications are processed on a rolling basis. *Application fee:* $50. Electronic applications accepted. *Application Contact:* Dr. Angela Johnson, Director of Teacher Education, 240-895-2065, E-mail: mat@smcm.edu. *Director of Teacher Education,* Dr. Angela Johnson, 240-895-2065, E-mail: mat@smcm.edu.

## SAINT MARY SEMINARY AND GRADUATE SCHOOL OF THEOLOGY, Wickliffe, OH 44092-2527

**General Information** Independent-religious, coed, primarily men, graduate-only institution. *Graduate housing:* Room and/or apartments available to single students; on-campus housing not available to married students.

**GRADUATE UNITS**

**Graduate and Professional Programs** *Program availability:* Part-time.

## ST. MARY'S SEMINARY AND UNIVERSITY, Baltimore, MD 21210-1994

**General Information** Independent-religious, coed, primarily men, graduate-only institution. *Graduate housing:* Room and/or apartments guaranteed to single students; on-campus housing not available to married students. Housing application deadline: 8/15.

**GRADUATE UNITS**

**Ecumenical Institute of Theology** *Program availability:* Part-time, evening/weekend.

**School of Theology** *Program availability:* Part-time.

## SAINT MARY'S UNIVERSITY, Halifax, NS B3H 3C3, Canada

**General Information** Province-supported, coed, comprehensive institution. *Graduate housing:* Rooms and/or apartments available on a first-come, first-served basis to single students and available to married students.

**GRADUATE UNITS**

**Faculty of Arts** *Program availability:* Part-time, evening/weekend.

**Faculty of Science** *Program availability:* Part-time.

**Sobey School of Business** *Program availability:* Part-time, evening/weekend.

## ST. MARY'S UNIVERSITY, San Antonio, TX 78228

**General Information** Independent-religious, coed, comprehensive institution. CGS member. *Graduate housing:* Room and/or apartments available on a first-come, first-served basis to single students; on-campus housing not available to married students. Housing application deadline: 5/1. *Research affiliation:* Southeast Research Consortium (behavioral science, biomedical engineering, social science).

**GRADUATE UNITS**

**Graduate Studies** *Program availability:* Part-time, evening/weekend, 100% online. Electronic applications accepted.

***Greehey School of Business*** *Program availability:* Part-time, evening/weekend. Electronic applications accepted.

**School of Law** *Program availability:* Part-time.

**School of Science, Engineering and Technology** *Program availability:* Part-time, evening/weekend, blended/hybrid learning. Electronic applications accepted.

## SAINT MARY'S UNIVERSITY OF MINNESOTA, Winona, MN 55987-1399

**General Information** Independent-religious, coed, comprehensive institution. *Enrollment:* 5,548 graduate, professional, and undergraduate students. *Enrollment by degree level:* 3,493 master's, 354 doctoral, 176 other advanced degrees. *Student services:* Campus safety program, services for students with disabilities, teacher training, writing training. *Library facilities:* Fitzgerald Library plus 1 other. *Collection:* Books: 155,417 (physical), 423,045 (digital/electronic); Serial titles: 1,120 (physical), 165,670 (digital/electronic); Databases: 93. Weekly public service hours: 97; students can reserve study rooms.

**Computer facilities:** 200 computers available on campus for general student use. A campuswide network can be accessed. Online class registration is available.
Website: http://www.smumn.edu/

**General Application Contact:** James Callinan, Director of Admission for Graduate and Professional Programs, 612-728-5158, Fax: 612-728-5121, E-mail: jcallina@smumn.edu.

**GRADUATE UNITS**

**Schools of Graduate and Professional Programs** Average age 35. Expenses: Contact institution. *Financial support:* Applicants required to submit FAFSA. In 2019, 1,297 master's, 36 doctorates, 124 other advanced degrees awarded. *Program availability:* Part-time, evening/weekend, 100% online, blended/hybrid learning. *Application deadline:* Applications are processed on a rolling basis. Electronic applications accepted. *Application Contact:* Laura Roy, Director of Admission of Schools of Graduate and Professional Programs, 507-457-8606, Fax: 612-728-5121, E-mail: lroy@smumn.edu. *Provost and Dean of Faculties,* Brian Schmisek, 507-457-1756, E-mail: bschmise@smumn.edu.

***Graduate School of Business and Technology*** Average age 36. Expenses: Contact institution. *Program availability:* Part-time, evening/weekend, 100% online, blended/hybrid learning. *Application deadline:* Applications are processed on a rolling basis. Electronic applications accepted. *Application Contact:* Laurie Roy, Director of Admission of Schools of Graduate and Professional Programs, 507-457-8606, E-mail: lroy@smumn.edu. *Dean,* Dr. Michelle Wieser, 507-457-1451, E-mail: mwieser@smumn.edu.

***Graduate School of Education*** Average age 35. Expenses: Contact institution. *Program availability:* Part-time, evening/weekend, 100% online, blended/hybrid learning. *Application deadline:* Applications are processed on a rolling basis. Electronic applications accepted. *Application Contact:* Laurie Roy, Director of Admission of Schools of Graduate and Professional Programs, 507-457-8606, Fax: 612-728-5121, E-mail: lroy@smumn.edu. *Dean,* Dr. Rebecca Hopkins, 507-457-6620, E-mail: rhopkins@smumn.edu.

***Graduate School of Health and Human Services*** Average age 33. Expenses: Contact institution. *Program availability:* Part-time, evening/weekend, 100% online, blended/hybrid learning. *Application deadline:* Applications are processed on a rolling basis. Electronic applications accepted. *Application Contact:* Laurie Roy, Director of Admission of Schools of Graduate and Professional Programs, 507-313-5564, Fax: 612-728-5121, E-mail: lroy@smumn.edu. *Dean,* Dr. Todd Reinhart, 507-457-1758, E-mail: treinhar@smumn.edu.

## SAINT MEINRAD SCHOOL OF THEOLOGY, Saint Meinrad, IN 47577

**General Information** Independent-religious, coed, primarily men, graduate-only institution. *Enrollment by degree level:* 178 master's. *Graduate faculty:* 17 full-time (2 women), 14 part-time/adjunct (5 women). *Tuition:* Full-time $27,714; part-time $520 per credit hour. *Required fees:* $34 per course. One-time fee: $200. Tuition and fees vary according to program. *Graduate housing:* On-campus housing not available. *Student services:* Campus employment opportunities, campus safety program, exercise/wellness program, free psychological counseling, writing training. *Library facilities:* Archabbey Library. *Collection:* Students can reserve study rooms.

**Computer facilities:** 30 computers available on campus for general student use. A campuswide network can be accessed from student residence rooms and from off campus.
Website: http://www.saintmeinrad.edu/

**General Application Contact:** Dr. John Schlachter, Director of Admissions, 812-357-6142, Fax: 812-357-6816, E-mail: apply@saintmeinrad.edu.

**GRADUATE UNITS**

**Master of Arts (Catholic Philosophical Studies) Program** Students: 32 full-time (0 women); includes 1 minority (Black or African American, non-Hispanic/Latino), 3 international. Average age 28. *Faculty:* 5 full-time, 4 part-time/adjunct (1 woman). Expenses: Contact institution. *Financial support:* Federal Work-Study and scholarships/grants available. Financial award applicants required to submit FAFSA. In 2019, 11 master's awarded. *Application deadline:* For fall admission, 7/1 priority date for domestic and international students; for winter admission, 11/15 for domestic and international students. Applications are processed on a rolling basis. *Application fee:* $30. *Application Contact:* Dr. John Schlachter, Director of Admissions, 812-357-6142, Fax: 812-357-6816, E-mail: jschlachter@saintmeinrad.edu. *Academic Dean,* Dr. Robert Alvis, 812-357-6543, Fax: 812-357-6816, E-mail: ralvis@saintmeinrad.edu.

**Master of Arts (Theology) Program** Students: 6 full-time (2 women), 52 part-time (22 women); includes 6 minority (2 Black or African American, non-Hispanic/Latino; 4 Hispanic/Latino), 3 international. Average age 49. *Faculty:* 16 full-time (1 woman), 14 part-time/adjunct (6 women). Expenses: Contact institution. *Financial support:* Federal Work-Study, institutionally sponsored loans, and scholarships/grants available. Support available to part-time students. Financial award application deadline: 7/1; financial award applicants required to submit FAFSA. In 2019, 20 master's awarded. *Program availability:* Part-time, evening/weekend. *Application deadline:* For fall admission, 7/1 for domestic and international students; for winter admission, 11/15 for domestic and international students. Applications are processed on a rolling basis. *Application fee:* $30. Electronic applications accepted. *Application Contact:* Dr. John Schlachter, Director of Admissions, 812-357-6142, Fax: 812-357-6816, E-mail: apply@saintmeinrad.edu. *Director of Graduate Theology Programs,* Sr. Jeana Visel, OSB, 812-357-6721, Fax: 812-357-6816.

**Master of Divinity Program** Students: 91 full-time (0 women); includes 5 minority (1 Black or African American, non-Hispanic/Latino; 4 Hispanic/Latino), 34 international. Average age 30. *Faculty:* 17 full-time (1 woman), 5 part-time/adjunct (1 woman). Expenses: Contact institution. *Financial support:* Federal Work-Study, institutionally sponsored loans, and scholarships/grants available. Financial award application deadline: 7/31; financial award applicants required to submit FAFSA. In 2019, 18 master's awarded. *Application deadline:* For fall admission, 7/1 priority date for domestic students, 7/1 for international students; for winter admission, 11/15 for domestic and international students. Applications are processed on a rolling basis. *Application Contact:* Dr. John Schlachter, Director of Admissions, 812-357-6142, Fax: 812-357-6816, E-mail: apply@saintmeinrad.edu. *Academic Dean,* Dr. Robert Alvis, 812-357-6543, Fax: 812-357-6816, E-mail: ralvis@saintmeinrad.edu.

## SAINT MICHAEL'S COLLEGE, Colchester, VT 05439

**General Information** Independent-religious, coed, comprehensive institution. *Graduate housing:* On-campus housing not available.

**GRADUATE UNITS**

**Graduate Programs** *Program availability:* Part-time, evening/weekend. Electronic applications accepted.

## ST. NORBERT COLLEGE, De Pere, WI 54115-2099

**General Information** Independent-religious, coed, comprehensive institution. *Enrollment:* 2,081 graduate, professional, and undergraduate students; 26 full-time matriculated graduate/professional students (19 women), 55 part-time matriculated graduate/professional students (27 women). *Enrollment by degree level:* 81 master's. *Graduate faculty:* 28. *Graduate housing:* On-campus housing not available. *Student services:* Campus safety program, career counseling, child daycare facilities, exercise/wellness program, free psychological counseling, international student services, multicultural affairs office, services for students with disabilities, writing training. *Library facilities:* Miriam B. and James J. Mulva Library plus 1 other. *Collection:* Books: 252,444 (physical), 207,312 (digital/electronic); Serial titles: 103,421 (physical), 103,236 (digital/electronic). Weekly public service hours: 116; students can reserve study rooms.

**Computer facilities:** Computer purchase and lease plans are available. 167 computers available on campus for general student use. A campuswide network can be accessed. Online class registration is available.
Website: http://www.snc.edu/

**General Application Contact:** Brenda Busch, Associate Director of Graduate Recruitment, 920-403-3942, Fax: 920-403-4072, E-mail: brenda.busch@snc.edu.

**GRADUATE UNITS**

**Master of Arts in Liberal Studies Program** Students: 7 part-time (5 women); includes 1 minority (Hispanic/Latino). Average age 41. 1 applicant, 100% accepted, 1 enrolled. *Faculty:* 3 full-time (2 women), 2 part-time/adjunct (1 woman). Expenses: Contact institution. *Financial support:* Scholarships/grants available. *Program availability:* Part-time-only, evening/weekend. *Application deadline:* Applications are processed on a rolling basis. *Application fee:* $50. Electronic applications accepted. *Application Contact:* Danielle Wahlen, Program Coordinator, 920-403-3957, E-mail: danielle.wahlen@snc.edu. *Director,* Dr. Howard Ebert, 920-403-3956, E-mail: howard.ebert@snc.edu.

**Master of Business Administration Program** Students: 52 (29 women); includes 4 minority (all American Indian or Alaska Native, non-Hispanic/Latino). Average age 33. 23 applicants, 39% accepted, 9 enrolled. *Faculty:* 11 full-time (2 women), 4 part-time/adjunct (0 women). Expenses: Contact institution. *Financial support:* Application deadline: 1/1; applicants required to submit FAFSA. In 2019, 18 master's awarded. *Program availability:* Part-time-only, evening/weekend. *Application deadline:* For fall admission, 7/31 for domestic students; for winter admission, 12/1 for domestic students; for spring admission, 1/1 for domestic students; for summer admission, 4/15 for domestic students. Applications are processed on a rolling basis. *Application fee:* $50. Electronic applications accepted. *Application Contact:* Brenda Busch, Associate Director of Graduate Recruitment, 920-403-3942, E-mail: brenda.busch@snc.edu. *Dean of the Schneider School of Business and Economics,* Dr. Daniel Heiser, 920-403-3440, E-mail: dan.heiser@snc.edu.

**Master of Theological Studies Program** Students: 22 (12 women); includes 3 minority (2 Hispanic/Latino; 1 Two or more races, non-Hispanic/Latino). Average age 53. 2 applicants, 100% accepted, 2 enrolled. *Faculty:* 6 full-time (3 women), 4 part-time/adjunct (0 women). Expenses: Contact institution. *Financial support:* In 2019–20, 6 students received support. Scholarships/grants available. In 2019, 3 master's awarded. *Program availability:* Part-time-only, evening/weekend. *Application deadline:* Applications are processed on a rolling basis. *Application fee:* $50. Electronic applications accepted. *Application Contact:* Danielle Wahlen, Program Coordinator, 920-403-3957, E-mail: danielle.wahlen@snc.edu. *Director,* Dr. Howard Ebert, 920-403-3956, E-mail: howard.ebert@snc.edu.

## ST. PATRICK'S SEMINARY & UNIVERSITY, Menlo Park, CA 94025-3596

**General Information** Independent-religious, coed, primarily men, graduate-only institution. *Graduate housing:* Room and/or apartments guaranteed to single students; on-campus housing not available to married students. Housing application deadline: 8/15.

**GRADUATE UNITS**

**School of Theology** *Program availability:* Part-time.

## SAINT PAUL SCHOOL OF THEOLOGY, Overland Park, KS 66211

**General Information** Independent-religious, coed, graduate-only institution. *Graduate housing:* Rooms and/or apartments available to single and married students. Housing application deadline: 5/31.

**GRADUATE UNITS**

**Graduate and Professional Programs** *Program availability:* Part-time.

## SAINT PAUL UNIVERSITY, Ottawa, ON K1S 1C4, Canada

**General Information** Province-supported, coed, university. *Graduate housing:* Room and/or apartments available to single students; on-campus housing not available to married students.

**GRADUATE UNITS**

**Faculty of Canon Law** *Program availability:* Part-time.

**Faculty of Human Sciences**

**Faculty of Theology**

## ST. PETER'S SEMINARY, London, ON N6A 3Y1, Canada

**General Information** Independent-religious, coed, primarily men, graduate-only institution.

**GRADUATE UNITS**

**Department of Theology**

## SAINT PETER'S UNIVERSITY, Jersey City, NJ 07306-5997

**General Information** Independent-religious, coed, comprehensive institution. *Graduate housing:* On-campus housing not available.

**GRADUATE UNITS**

**Graduate Business Programs** *Program availability:* Part-time, evening/weekend. Electronic applications accepted.

**Graduate Programs in Education** *Program availability:* Part-time, evening/weekend. Electronic applications accepted.

**Program in Criminal Justice Administration** *Program availability:* Part-time, evening/weekend. Electronic applications accepted.

**Program in Public Administration**

**School of Nursing** *Program availability:* Part-time, evening/weekend. Electronic applications accepted.

## SAINTS CYRIL AND METHODIUS SEMINARY, Orchard Lake, MI 48324

**General Information** Independent-religious, coed, graduate-only institution. *Graduate housing:* Room and/or apartments guaranteed to single students; on-campus housing not available to married students. Housing application deadline: 7/1.

**GRADUATE UNITS**

**Graduate and Professional Programs** *Program availability:* Part-time.

## ST. STEPHEN'S COLLEGE, Edmonton, AB T6G 2J6, Canada

**General Information** Independent-religious, coed, graduate-only institution. *Enrollment by degree level:* 67 master's, 22 doctoral, 11 other advanced degrees. *Graduate faculty:* 1 full-time (0 women), 54 part-time/adjunct (34 women). *Tuition:* Full-time $8294 Canadian dollars; part-time $4858 Canadian dollars per course. *Graduate housing:* On-campus housing not available. *Library facilities:* University of Alberta Library.

**Computer facilities:** 2 computers available on campus for general student use.
Website: http://ststephenscollege.ca/

**General Application Contact:** Shelley Westermann, Registrar, 780-439-7311, Fax: 780-433-8875, E-mail: westerma@ualberta.ca.

**GRADUATE UNITS**

**Programs in Theology** *Program availability:* Part-time, evening/weekend, online learning. Electronic applications accepted.

## ST. THOMAS AQUINAS COLLEGE, Sparkill, NY 10976

**General Information** Independent, coed, comprehensive institution. *Graduate housing:* On-campus housing not available. *Research affiliation:* Lederle Laboratories (science education), Lamont Doherty Laboratories (science education).

**GRADUATE UNITS**

**Division of Business Administration** *Program availability:* Part-time, evening/weekend. Electronic applications accepted.

**Division of Teacher Education** *Program availability:* Part-time, evening/weekend. Electronic applications accepted.

## ST. THOMAS UNIVERSITY - FLORIDA, Miami Gardens, FL 33054-6459

**General Information** Independent-religious, coed, university. *Graduate housing:* Room and/or apartments available on a first-come, first-served basis to single students; on-campus housing not available to married students. Housing application deadline: 7/1.

**GRADUATE UNITS**

**Biscayne College**

**School of Business**

**School of Law** *Program availability:* Online learning. Electronic applications accepted.

**School of Leadership Studies** *Program availability:* Part-time, evening/weekend.

***Institute for Education*** *Program availability:* Part-time, evening/weekend. Electronic applications accepted.

**School of Theology and Ministry**

***Institute for Pastoral Ministries*** *Program availability:* Part-time, evening/weekend. Electronic applications accepted.

## ST. TIKHON'S ORTHODOX THEOLOGICAL SEMINARY, South Canaan, PA 18459

**General Information** Independent-religious, men only, graduate-only institution. *Graduate housing:* Room and/or apartments guaranteed to single students; on-campus housing not available to married students.

GRADUATE UNITS

**Divinity Program** *Program availability:* Part-time.

## SAINT VINCENT COLLEGE, Latrobe, PA 15650-2690

**General Information** Independent-religious, coed, comprehensive institution. *Graduate housing:* Room and/or apartments available on a first-come, first-served basis to single students; on-campus housing not available to married students.

GRADUATE UNITS

**Program in Business**

**Program in Education** *Program availability:* Part-time, evening/weekend.

**Program in Health Science**

## ST. VINCENT DE PAUL REGIONAL SEMINARY, Boynton Beach, FL 33436-4899

**General Information** Independent-religious, coed, primarily men, graduate-only institution. *Graduate housing:* Room and/or apartments guaranteed to single students; on-campus housing not available to married students.

GRADUATE UNITS

**Graduate and Professional Programs** *Program availability:* Part-time.

## SAINT VINCENT SEMINARY, Latrobe, PA 15650-2690

**General Information** Independent-religious, coed, primarily men, graduate-only institution. *Enrollment by degree level:* 49 master's. *Graduate faculty:* 6 full-time (1 woman), 12 part-time/adjunct (2 women). *Tuition:* Full-time $30,178; part-time $1003 per credit. *Graduate housing:* Room and/or apartments guaranteed to single students; on-campus housing not available to married students. Typical cost: $7434 per year ($14,632 including board). Housing application deadline: 8/15. *Student services:* Campus safety program, exercise/wellness program, free psychological counseling, international student services, services for students with disabilities, writing training. *Library facilities:* Latimer Family Library - currently partially under construction.

**Computer facilities:** 150 computers available on campus for general student use. A campuswide network can be accessed from student residence rooms and from off campus. Online class registration is available.
Website: http://www.saintvincentseminary.edu/

**General Application Contact:** Rev. Patrick T. Cronauer, OSB, Academic Dean, 724-805-2324, Fax: 724-805-2880, E-mail: patrick.cronauer@stvincent.edu.

GRADUATE UNITS

**School of Theology** Students: 45 full-time (0 women), 4 part-time (0 women); includes 2 minority (both Asian, non-Hispanic/Latino), 13 international. Average age 34. 13 applicants, 100% accepted, 13 enrolled. *Faculty:* 7 full-time (1 woman), 12 part-time/adjunct (2 women). Expenses: Contact institution. *Financial support:* In 2019–20, 49 students received support. Scholarships/grants available. Support available to part-time students. In 2019, 9 master's awarded. *Program availability:* Part-time, evening/weekend. *Application deadline:* For fall admission, 8/15 priority date for domestic and international students. Applications are processed on a rolling basis. *Application fee:* $45. *Application Contact:* Rev. Patrick T. Cronauer, OSB, Academic Dean, 724-805-2324, Fax: 724-805-2880, E-mail: patrick.cronauer@stvincent.edu. *President/Rector,* Very Rev. Edward M. Mazich, OSB, 724-805-2845, Fax: 724-532-5052, E-mail: edward.mazich@stvincent.edu.

## ST. VLADIMIR'S ORTHODOX THEOLOGICAL SEMINARY, Crestwood, NY 10707-1699

**General Information** Independent-religious, coed, primarily men, graduate-only institution. *Enrollment by degree level:* 65 master's, 12 doctoral. *Graduate faculty:* 7 full-time (1 woman), 22 part-time/adjunct (3 women). *Tuition:* Full-time $12,000; part-time $1500 per course. *Required fees:* $150 per semester. Part-time tuition and fees vary according to course load and program. *Graduate housing:* Rooms and/or apartments available on a first-come, first-served basis to single and married students. Typical cost: $2700 per year ($6700 including board) for single students; $8222 per year for married students. Housing application deadline: 5/1. *Student services:* Exercise/wellness program, international student services, services for students with disabilities, writing training. *Library facilities:* Father Georges Florovsky Library. *Collection:* Books: 200,000 (physical); Serial titles: 330 (physical); Databases: 6. Weekly public service hours: 60.

**Computer facilities:** 5 computers available on campus for general student use.
Website: http://www.svots.edu/

**General Application Contact:** Alexandru Popovici, Academic & Recruitment Advisor, 914-961-8313 Ext. 342, Fax: 914-961-4507, E-mail: admissions@svots.edu.

GRADUATE UNITS

**Graduate School of Theology** Students: 75 full-time (6 women), 2 part-time (0 women); includes 11 minority (1 Black or African American, non-Hispanic/Latino; 9 Asian, non-Hispanic/Latino; 1 Two or more races, non-Hispanic/Latino), 13 international. Average age 29. 41 applicants, 95% accepted, 37 enrolled. *Faculty:* 7 full-time (1 woman), 23 part-time/adjunct (3 women). Expenses: Contact institution. *Financial support:* In 2019–20, 74 students received support. Fellowships, research assistantships, teaching assistantships, and scholarships/grants available. Financial award application deadline: 4/1; financial award applicants required to submit FAFSA. In 2019, 16 master's, 3 doctorates awarded. *Program availability:* Part-time. *Application deadline:* For fall admission, 5/1 priority date for domestic and international students. Applications are processed on a rolling basis. *Application fee:* $75. Electronic applications accepted. *Application Contact:* Gabrielle Russin, Student Affairs Administrator, 914-961-8313 Ext. 348, Fax: 914-961-4507, E-mail: grussin@svots.edu. *President,* Rev. Dr. Chad Hatfield, 914-961-8313 Ext. 323, Fax: 914-961-4507, E-mail: hatfield@svots.edu.

## SAINT XAVIER UNIVERSITY, Chicago, IL 60655-3105

**General Information** Independent-religious, coed, comprehensive institution. CGS member. *Graduate housing:* Room and/or apartments available on a first-come, first-served basis to single students; on-campus housing not available to married students. Housing application deadline: 8/15. *Research affiliation:* Alexian Brothers Hospital, Holy Cross Hospital, Little Company of Mary Hospital, Mercy Center for Health Care Services.

GRADUATE UNITS

**Graduate Studies** *Program availability:* Part-time, evening/weekend. Electronic applications accepted.

***College of Arts and Sciences*** *Program availability:* Part-time, evening/weekend.

***Graham School of Management*** *Program availability:* Part-time, evening/weekend. Electronic applications accepted.

***School of Education*** *Program availability:* Part-time, evening/weekend.

***School of Nursing*** *Program availability:* Part-time, evening/weekend.

## SALEM COLLEGE, Winston-Salem, NC 27101

**General Information** Independent-religious, coed, primarily women, comprehensive institution. *Enrollment:* 85 full-time matriculated graduate/professional students (76 women), 15 part-time matriculated graduate/professional students (14 women). *Enrollment by degree level:* 100 master's. *Graduate faculty:* 6 full-time (all women), 5 part-time/adjunct (all women). *Tuition:* Full-time $2700; part-time $450 per semester hour. *Required fees:* $300. *Graduate housing:* On-campus housing not available. *Student services:* Career counseling, multicultural affairs office, services for students with disabilities, teacher training, writing training. *Library facilities:* Dale H. Gramley Library plus 2 others. *Collection:* Books: 119,591 (physical), 110,764 (digital/electronic); Databases: 123.

**Computer facilities:** Computer purchase and lease plans are available. 54 computers available on campus for general student use. A campuswide network can be accessed from student residence rooms and from off campus. Online class registration is available.
Website: http://www.salem.edu/

**General Application Contact:** Dr. Sheryl Long, Director of Teacher Education & Graduate Studies in Education, 336-721-2658, Fax: 336-917-5384, E-mail: sheryl.long@salem.edu.

GRADUATE UNITS

**Graduate Studies** *Program availability:* Part-time, evening/weekend, online learning. Electronic applications accepted.

## SALEM INTERNATIONAL UNIVERSITY, Salem, WV 26426-0500

**General Information** Independent, coed, comprehensive institution. *Graduate housing:* Rooms and/or apartments available on a first-come, first-served basis to single students and available to married students.

GRADUATE UNITS

**School of Business** *Program availability:* Part-time, online learning. Electronic applications accepted.

**School of Education** *Program availability:* Part-time, evening/weekend, online learning. Electronic applications accepted.

## SALEM STATE UNIVERSITY, Salem, MA 01970-5353

**General Information** State-supported, coed, comprehensive institution. CGS member. *Graduate housing:* On-campus housing not available.

GRADUATE UNITS

**School of Graduate Studies** *Program availability:* Part-time, evening/weekend.

## SALISBURY UNIVERSITY, Salisbury, MD 21801-6837

**General Information** State-supported, coed, comprehensive institution. CGS member. *Enrollment:* 8,617 graduate, professional, and undergraduate students; 525 full-time matriculated graduate/professional students (409 women), 336 part-time matriculated graduate/professional students (265 women). *Enrollment by degree level:* 767 master's, 80 doctoral, 14 other advanced degrees. *Graduate faculty:* 109 full-time (63 women), 52 part-time/adjunct (45 women). *Graduate housing:* On-campus housing not available. *Student services:* Campus employment opportunities, campus safety program, career counseling, exercise/wellness program, free psychological counseling, international student services, multicultural affairs office, services for students with disabilities, teacher training, writing training. *Library facilities:* SU Libraries plus 2 others. *Collection:* Books: 273,282 (physical), 426 (digital/electronic); Serial titles: 652 (physical), 152 (digital/electronic); Databases: 122. Weekly public service hours: 108; students can reserve study rooms. *Research affiliation:* Maryland Department of Labor (program effectiveness and efficiency research), Talbot County Senior Center (market research for demand analysis), Maryland Association of Boards of Education (statewide economic impact analysis for K-12 public education), Trinity Sterile (expansion feasibility and scenario analysis), Town of Annapolis (mixed use development economic impact analysis), Konsyl Pharmaceuticals (compensation research).

**Computer facilities:** 1,000 computers available on campus for general student use. A campuswide network can be accessed. Online class registration, student web hosting, computer repair service, discounted computer hardware and software are available.
Website: http://www.salisbury.edu/

**General Application Contact:** Elizabeth Walk, Graduate Enrollment Management Specialist, 410-548-3546, E-mail: ehwalk@salisbury.edu.

GRADUATE UNITS

**Department of Conflict Analysis and Dispute Resolution** Students: 25 full-time (10 women), 8 part-time (6 women); includes 10 minority (8 Black or African American, non-Hispanic/Latino; 1 Hispanic/Latino; 1 Two or more races, non-Hispanic/Latino), 3 international. Average age 30. 37 applicants, 89% accepted, 21 enrolled. *Faculty:* 6 full-time (1 woman). Expenses: Contact institution. *Financial support:* In 2019–20, 13 students received support, including 5 research assistantships with full tuition reimbursements available (averaging $8,400 per year), 9 teaching assistantships with full tuition reimbursements available (averaging $8,027 per year); career-related internships or fieldwork also available. Support available to part-time students. Financial award application deadline: 3/1; financial award applicants required to submit FAFSA. In 2019, 19 master's awarded. *Program availability:* Part-time, evening/weekend. *Application deadline:* For fall admission, 5/1 priority date for domestic and international students. Applications are processed on a rolling basis. *Application fee:* $65. Electronic applications accepted. *Application Contact:* Dr. Ignaciyas Soosaipillai, Graduate Program Director, 410-543-6435, E-mail: iksoosaipillai@salisbury.edu. *Graduate Program Director,* Dr. Ignaciyas Soosaipillai, 410-543-6435, E-mail: iksoosaipillai@salisbury.edu.

**Department of English** Students: 9 full-time (7 women), 12 part-time (11 women); includes 2 minority (1 Asian, non-Hispanic/Latino; 1 Hispanic/Latino), 2 international. Average age 34. 13 applicants, 92% accepted, 6 enrolled. *Faculty:* 11 full-time (5 women). Expenses: Contact institution. *Financial support:* In 2019–20, 3 students received support, including 8 teaching assistantships with full tuition reimbursements available (averaging $10,250 per year); career-related internships or fieldwork and scholarships/grants also available. Support available to part-time students. Financial award application deadline: 3/1; financial award applicants required to submit FAFSA. In 2019, 14 master's awarded. *Program availability:* Part-time, evening/weekend. *Application deadline:* For fall admission, 8/1 for domestic and international students; for spring admission, 1/1 for domestic and international students. *Application fee:* $65. Electronic applications accepted. *Application Contact:* Dr. John Nieves, Graduate Program Director, 410-677-6511, E-mail: janieves@salisbury.edu. *Graduate Program Director*, Dr. John Nieves, 410-677-6511, E-mail: janieves@salisbury.edu.

**Department of History** Students: 6 full-time (3 women), 5 part-time (2 women); includes 2 minority (both Two or more races, non-Hispanic/Latino). Average age 33. 9 applicants, 89% accepted, 8 enrolled. *Faculty:* 5 full-time (1 woman). Expenses: Contact institution. *Financial support:* In 2019–20, 3 students received support, including 4 research assistantships with full tuition reimbursements available (averaging $8,000 per year); career-related internships or fieldwork and scholarships/grants also available. Support available to part-time students. Financial award application deadline: 3/1; financial award applicants required to submit FAFSA. In 2019, 5 master's awarded. *Program availability:* Part-time, evening/weekend. *Application deadline:* For fall admission, 4/15 priority date for domestic and international students; for spring admission, 11/15 priority date for domestic and international students. Applications are processed on a rolling basis. *Application fee:* $65. Electronic applications accepted. *Application Contact:* Dr. Celine Carayon, Graduate Program Director, 410-677-4601, E-mail: cxcarayon@salisbury.edu. *Graduate Program Director*, Dr. Celine Carayon, 410-677-4601, E-mail: cxcarayon@salisbury.edu.

**Department of Social Work** Students: 349 full-time (307 women), 60 part-time (54 women); includes 113 minority (81 Black or African American, non-Hispanic/Latino; 5 Asian, non-Hispanic/Latino; 9 Hispanic/Latino; 18 Two or more races, non-Hispanic/Latino), 2 international. Average age 31. 350 applicants, 77% accepted, 206 enrolled. *Faculty:* 24 full-time (20 women), 43 part-time/adjunct (38 women). Expenses: Contact institution. *Financial support:* In 2019–20, 21 students received support, including 4 research assistantships with full tuition reimbursements available (averaging $2,750 per year), 4 teaching assistantships with full tuition reimbursements available (averaging $7,120 per year); career-related internships or fieldwork and scholarships/grants also available. Support available to part-time students. Financial award application deadline: 3/1; financial award applicants required to submit FAFSA. In 2019, 169 master's awarded. *Program availability:* Part-time, evening/weekend, 100% online, blended/hybrid learning. *Application deadline:* For fall admission, 1/15 priority date for domestic and international students; for summer admission, 1/15 priority date for domestic and international students. Applications are processed on a rolling basis. *Application fee:* $65. Electronic applications accepted. *Application Contact:* Lindsey Shockley, Admissions Program Specialist, 410-677-5363, E-mail: lrshockley@salisbury.edu. *Graduate Program Director*, Dr. Mary Hylton, 410-677-5346, E-mail: mehylton@salisbury.edu.

**DNP Program** Students: 25 full-time (22 women), 8 part-time (all women); includes 8 minority (5 Black or African American, non-Hispanic/Latino; 1 Hispanic/Latino; 2 Two or more races, non-Hispanic/Latino). Average age 34. 17 applicants, 71% accepted, 8 enrolled. *Faculty:* 14 full-time (13 women), 4 part-time/adjunct (all women). Expenses: Contact institution. *Financial support:* Career-related internships or fieldwork and scholarships/grants available. Support available to part-time students. Financial award application deadline: 3/1; financial award applicants required to submit FAFSA. In 2019, 7 doctorates awarded. *Program availability:* Part-time, evening/weekend, 100% online, blended/hybrid learning. *Application deadline:* For fall admission, 3/1 priority date for domestic and international students. Applications are processed on a rolling basis. *Application fee:* $65. Electronic applications accepted. *Application Contact:* Kristi Jenkins, Administrative Assistant II, 410-548-2242, E-mail: kljenkins@salisbury.edu. *Graduate Program Chair*, Dr. Annette Barnes, 410-546-4380, E-mail: ahbarnes@salisbury.edu.

**MS in Nursing Program** Students: 1 (woman) full-time, 4 part-time (all women); includes 2 minority (1 Asian, non-Hispanic/Latino; 1 Hispanic/Latino). Average age 27. 3 applicants, 100% accepted, 3 enrolled. *Faculty:* 14 full-time (13 women), 4 part-time/adjunct (all women). Expenses: Contact institution. *Financial support:* In 2019–20, 1 student received support, including 1 research assistantship with full tuition reimbursement available (averaging $8,000 per year), 1 teaching assistantship with full tuition reimbursement available (averaging $9,000 per year); career-related internships or fieldwork and scholarships/grants also available. Support available to part-time students. Financial award application deadline: 3/1; financial award applicants required to submit FAFSA. *Program availability:* Part-time, evening/weekend, 100% online, blended/hybrid learning. *Application deadline:* For fall admission, 3/1 priority date for domestic and international students. *Application fee:* $65. Electronic applications accepted. *Application Contact:* Kristi Jenkins, Administrative Assistant II, 410-548-2242, E-mail: kljenkins@salisbury.edu. *Graduate Program Chair*, Dr. Annette Barnes, 410-546-4380, E-mail: ahbarnes@salisbury.edu.

**Perdue School of Business** Students: 28 full-time (11 women), 25 part-time (18 women); includes 5 minority (4 Black or African American, non-Hispanic/Latino; 1 Two or more races, non-Hispanic/Latino), 3 international. Average age 28. 42 applicants, 74% accepted, 24 enrolled. *Faculty:* 6 full-time (1 woman). Expenses: Contact institution. *Financial support:* In 2019–20, 7 students received support, including 10 research assistantships with full tuition reimbursements available (averaging $8,024 per year), 10 teaching assistantships with full tuition reimbursements available (averaging $8,248 per year); career-related internships or fieldwork and scholarships/grants also available. Support available to part-time students. Financial award application deadline: 3/1; financial award applicants required to submit FAFSA. In 2019, 38 master's awarded. *Program availability:* Part-time, evening/weekend, 100% online, blended/hybrid learning. *Application deadline:* For fall admission, 3/1 priority date for domestic and international students. Applications are processed on a rolling basis. *Application fee:* $65. Electronic applications accepted. *Application Contact:* Yvonne Downie Hanley, Graduate Program Director, 410-548-3983, E-mail: yxdownie@salisbury.edu. *Graduate Program Director*, Yvonne Downie Hanley, 410-548-3983, E-mail: yxdownie@salisbury.edu.

**Program in Applied Biology** Students: 5 full-time (3 women), 4 part-time (2 women); includes 2 minority (1 Asian, non-Hispanic/Latino; 1 Native Hawaiian or other Pacific Islander, non-Hispanic/Latino). Average age 24. 2 applicants, 100% accepted, 1 enrolled. *Faculty:* 11 full-time (7 women). Expenses: Contact institution. *Financial support:* In 2019–20, 1 student received support, including 11 teaching assistantships with full tuition reimbursements available (averaging $13,000 per year); career-related internships or fieldwork and scholarships/grants also available. Support available to part-time students. Financial award application deadline: 3/1; financial award applicants required to submit FAFSA. In 2019, 2 master's awarded. *Program availability:* Part-time. *Application deadline:* For fall admission, 3/1 for domestic and international students; for spring admission, 10/1 for domestic and international students. *Application fee:* $65. Electronic applications accepted. *Application Contact:* Dr. Dana Price, Graduate Program Director, 410-543-6498, E-mail: dlprice@salisbury.edu. *Graduate Program Director*, Dr. Dana Price, 410-543-6498, E-mail: dlprice@salisbury.edu.

**Program in Applied Health Physiology** Students: 23 full-time (8 women), 5 part-time (4 women); includes 9 minority (3 Black or African American, non-Hispanic/Latino; 1 Asian, non-Hispanic/Latino; 2 Hispanic/Latino; 3 Two or more races, non-Hispanic/Latino). Average age 25. 26 applicants, 73% accepted, 15 enrolled. *Faculty:* 8 full-time (0 women). Expenses: Contact institution. *Financial support:* In 2019–20, 10 students received support, including 1 research assistantship with full tuition reimbursement available (averaging $8,000 per year), 12 teaching assistantships with full tuition reimbursements available (averaging $8,083 per year); career-related internships or fieldwork and scholarships/grants also available. Support available to part-time students. Financial award application deadline: 3/1; financial award applicants required to submit FAFSA. In 2019, 16 master's awarded. *Application deadline:* For fall admission, 8/1 for domestic and international students; for spring admission, 12/1 for domestic and international students. *Application fee:* $65. Electronic applications accepted. *Application Contact:* Dr. Scott Mazzetti, Graduate Program Chair, 410-677-0151, E-mail: szmazzetti@salisbury.edu. *Graduate Program Chair*, Dr. Scott Mazzetti, 410-677-0151, E-mail: szmazzetti@salisbury.edu.

**Program in Athletic Training** Students: 14 full-time (10 women); includes 8 minority (7 Black or African American, non-Hispanic/Latino; 1 Two or more races, non-Hispanic/Latino), 1 international. Average age 24. 16 applicants, 81% accepted, 5 enrolled. *Faculty:* 3 full-time (2 women). Expenses: Contact institution. *Financial support:* In 2019–20, 1 student received support. Career-related internships or fieldwork and scholarships/grants available. Support available to part-time students. Financial award application deadline: 3/1; financial award applicants required to submit FAFSA. In 2019, 3 master's awarded. *Application deadline:* For summer admission, 3/1 for domestic and international students. Applications are processed on a rolling basis. *Application fee:* $65. Electronic applications accepted. *Application Contact:* Dr. Laura Marinaro, Graduate Program Director, 410-548-3529, E-mail: lmmarinaro@salisbury.edu. *Graduate Program Director*, Dr. Laura Marinaro, 410-548-3529, E-mail: lmmarinaro@salisbury.edu.

**Program in Contemporary Curriculum Theory and Instruction: Literacy** Students: 23 full-time (17 women), 24 part-time (22 women); includes 5 minority (4 Black or African American, non-Hispanic/Latino; 1 Two or more races, non-Hispanic/Latino), 2 international. Average age 42. 16 applicants, 94% accepted, 14 enrolled. *Faculty:* 6 full-time (5 women). Expenses: Contact institution. *Financial support:* In 2019–20, 3 students received support, including 2 teaching assistantships with full tuition reimbursements available (averaging $10,000 per year); career-related internships or fieldwork and scholarships/grants also available. Support available to part-time students. Financial award application deadline: 3/1; financial award applicants required to submit FAFSA. *Program availability:* Part-time, blended/hybrid learning. *Application deadline:* For fall admission, 3/1 priority date for domestic and international students. Applications are processed on a rolling basis. *Application fee:* $65. Electronic applications accepted. *Application Contact:* Dr. Maida Finch, Program Chair, 410-677-0179, E-mail: mafinch@salisbury.edu. *Program Chair*, Dr. Maida Finch, 410-677-0179, E-mail: mafinch@salisbury.edu.

**Program in Curriculum and Instruction** Students: 10 full-time (6 women), 70 part-time (56 women); includes 11 minority (5 Black or African American, non-Hispanic/Latino; 1 Hispanic/Latino; 5 Two or more races, non-Hispanic/Latino). Average age 29. 20 applicants, 70% accepted, 13 enrolled. *Faculty:* 7 full-time (4 women), 1 part-time/adjunct (0 women). Expenses: Contact institution. *Financial support:* In 2019–20, 5 students received support, including 8 teaching assistantships with full tuition reimbursements available (averaging $8,625 per year); career-related internships or fieldwork and scholarships/grants also available. Support available to part-time students. Financial award application deadline: 3/1; financial award applicants required to submit FAFSA. In 2019, 27 master's awarded. *Program availability:* Part-time, evening/weekend. *Application deadline:* For fall admission, 4/1 priority date for domestic and international students; for spring admission, 10/1 priority date for domestic and international students; for summer admission, 4/1 priority date for domestic and international students. Applications are processed on a rolling basis. *Application fee:* $65. Electronic applications accepted. *Application Contact:* Dr. Douglas DeWitt, Graduate Program Director, 410-543-6286, E-mail: dmdewitt@salisbury.edu. *Graduate Program Director*, Dr. Douglas DeWitt, 410-543-6286, E-mail: dmdewitt@salisbury.edu.

**Program in Educational Leadership** Students: 55 part-time (35 women); includes 7 minority (all Black or African American, non-Hispanic/Latino). Average age 30. 24 applicants, 71% accepted, 16 enrolled. *Faculty:* 3 full-time (0 women), 3 part-time/adjunct (2 women). Expenses: Contact institution. *Financial support:* Career-related internships or fieldwork and scholarships/grants available. Support available to part-time students. Financial award application deadline: 3/1; financial award applicants required to submit FAFSA. In 2019, 8 master's awarded. *Program availability:* Part-time, evening/weekend. *Application deadline:* For fall admission, 4/1 priority date for domestic and international students; for spring admission, 10/1 priority date for domestic and international students; for summer admission, 4/1 priority date for domestic and international students. Applications are processed on a rolling basis. *Application fee:* $65. Electronic applications accepted. *Application Contact:* Dr. Douglas DeWitt, Graduate Program Director, 410-543-6286, E-mail: dmdewitt@salisbury.edu. *Graduate Program Director*, Dr. Douglas DeWitt, 410-543-6286, E-mail: dmdewitt@salisbury.edu.

**Program in Geographic Information Systems Management** Students: 3 full-time (1 woman), 10 part-time (2 women); includes 2 minority (both Two or more races, non-Hispanic/Latino). Average age 33. 9 applicants, 89% accepted, 7 enrolled. *Faculty:* 2 full-time (0 women). Expenses: Contact institution. *Financial support:* In 2019–20, 2 students received support, including 2 research assistantships with full tuition reimbursements available (averaging $6,500 per year); career-related internships or fieldwork and scholarships/grants also available. Support available to part-time students. Financial award application deadline: 3/1; financial award applicants required to submit FAFSA. In 2019, 12 master's awarded. *Program availability:* Part-time, evening/weekend, online only, 100% online. *Application deadline:* For fall admission, 8/1 for domestic and international students; for spring admission, 1/3 for domestic and international students; for summer admission, 5/1 for domestic and international students. Applications are processed on a rolling basis. *Application fee:* $65. Electronic applications accepted. *Application Contact:* Dr. Stuart Hamilton, Graduate Program Director, 410-543-6459, E-mail: sehamilton@salisbury.edu. *Graduate Program Director*, Dr. Stuart Hamilton, 410-543-6459, E-mail: sehamilton@salisbury.edu.

**Program in Mathematics Education** Students: 12 part-time (10 women). Average age 27. 2 applicants, 50% accepted, 1 enrolled. *Faculty:* 1 (woman) full-time. Expenses: Contact institution. *Financial support:* Career-related internships or fieldwork and scholarships/grants available. Support available to part-time students. Financial award application deadline: 3/1; financial award applicants required to submit FAFSA. In 2019, 1 master's awarded. *Program availability:* Part-time. *Application deadline:* For fall admission, 8/15 priority date for domestic and international students; for spring admission, 10/1 priority date for domestic and international students. Applications are processed on a rolling basis. *Application fee:* $65. Electronic applications accepted. *Application Contact:* Dr. Jennifer Bergner, Graduate Program Director, 410-677-5429, E-mail: jabergner@salisbury.edu. *Graduate Program Director*, Dr. Jennifer Bergner, 410-677-5429, E-mail: jabergner@salisbury.edu.

**Program in Reading Specialist** Students: 33 part-time (30 women); includes 3 minority (all Asian, non-Hispanic/Latino). Average age 28. 8 applicants, 75% accepted, 5 enrolled. *Faculty:* 2 full-time (1 woman). Expenses: Contact institution. *Financial support:* In 2019–20, 4 students received support. Career-related internships or fieldwork and scholarships/grants available. Support available to part-time students. Financial award application deadline: 3/1; financial award applicants required to submit FAFSA. In 2019, 4 master's awarded. *Program availability:* Part-time, evening/weekend. *Application deadline:* For fall admission, 3/1 priority date for domestic and international students; for spring admission, 10/1 priority date for domestic and international students; for summer admission, 3/1 priority date for domestic and international students. Applications are processed on a rolling basis. *Application fee:* $65. Electronic applications accepted. *Application Contact:* Dr. Joyce Wiencek, Graduate Program Director, 410-543-6288, E-mail: bjwiencek@salisbury.edu. *Graduate Program Director*, Dr. Joyce Wiencek, 410-543-6288, E-mail: bjwiencek@salisbury.edu.

**Program in Teaching** Students: 4 full-time (3 women), 1 (woman) part-time; includes 1 minority (Asian, non-Hispanic/Latino). Average age 27. *Faculty:* 3 full-time (all women), 1 (woman) part-time/adjunct. Expenses: Contact institution. *Financial support:* In 2019–20, 2 students received support, including 2 teaching assistantships with full tuition reimbursements available (averaging $8,000 per year); career-related internships or fieldwork and scholarships/grants also available. Support available to part-time students. Financial award application deadline: 3/1; financial award applicants required to submit FAFSA. In 2019, 5 master's awarded. *Program availability:* Part-time, evening/weekend. *Application deadline:* For winter admission, 10/1 priority date for domestic and international students. *Application fee:* $65. Electronic applications accepted. *Application Contact:* Claire Williams, Program Management Specialist, 410-677-0001, E-mail: clwilliams@salisbury.edu. *Graduate Program Director*, Dr. Starlin Weaver, 410-543-6268, E-mail: sdweaver@salisbury.edu.

## SALUS UNIVERSITY, Elkins Park, PA 19027-1598

**General Information** Independent, coed, graduate-only institution. *Graduate housing:* On-campus housing not available. *Research affiliation:* Dynamis Pharmaceuticals (diabetes research), DakDak (photobiology).

**GRADUATE UNITS**

**College of Education and Rehabilitation** *Program availability:* Part-time, online learning.

**College of Health Sciences** Electronic applications accepted.

**Osborne College of Audiology** Electronic applications accepted.

**Pennsylvania College of Optometry** Electronic applications accepted.

## SALVE REGINA UNIVERSITY, Newport, RI 02840-4192

**General Information** Independent-religious, coed, comprehensive institution. *Graduate housing:* On-campus housing not available.

**GRADUATE UNITS**

**The Newport MFA in Creative Writing Program** Expenses: Contact institution. *Application Contact:* Laurie Reilly, Graduate Admissions Manager, 401-341-2153, Fax: 401-341-2973, E-mail: laurie.reilly@salve.edu.

**Program in Administration of Justice and Homeland Security** Expenses: Contact institution. *Financial support:* Application deadline: 3/1; applicants required to submit FAFSA. *Program availability:* Part-time, evening/weekend, some in-person. *Application deadline:* For fall admission, 7/1 priority date for domestic students, 3/15 priority date for international students; for spring admission, 11/1 priority date for domestic students, 9/5 priority date for international students. Applications are processed on a rolling basis. Electronic applications accepted. *Application Contact:* Laurie Reilly, Graduate Admissions Manager, 401-341-2153, Fax: 401-341-2973, E-mail: laurie.reilly@salve.edu. *Director*, Jeffrey Mace, 401-341-2338, E-mail: jeffrey.mac@salve.edu.

**Program in Applied Behavior Analysis** Expenses: Contact institution. *Financial support:* Application deadline: 3/1; applicants required to submit FAFSA. *Program availability:* Part-time, some fully in person classes offered. *Application deadline:* For fall admission, 8/1 for domestic students; for winter admission, 12/1 for domestic students; for spring admission, 2/1 for domestic students; for summer admission, 4/1 for domestic students. Applications are processed on a rolling basis. Electronic applications accepted. *Application Contact:* Laurie Reilly, Graduate Admissions Manager, 401-341-2153, Fax: 401-341-2973, E-mail: laurie.reilly@salve.edu. *Graduate Program Director*, Dr. Cody Morris, E-mail: cody.morris@salve.edu.

**Program in Business Administration** *Program availability:* Part-time, evening/weekend, online learning. Electronic applications accepted.

**Program in Healthcare Administration and Management** *Program availability:* Part-time, evening/weekend, online learning. Electronic applications accepted.

**Program in Humanities** *Program availability:* Part-time, evening/weekend, online learning. Electronic applications accepted.

**Program in International Relations** *Program availability:* Part-time, evening/weekend, online learning. Electronic applications accepted.

**Program in Management** *Program availability:* Part-time, evening/weekend, online learning. Electronic applications accepted.

**Program in Nursing** Expenses: Contact institution. *Financial support:* Application deadline: 3/1; applicants required to submit FAFSA. *Program availability:* Part-time, evening/weekend, online only, 100% online. *Application deadline:* For fall admission, 7/1 for domestic students, 3/15 priority date for international students; for spring admission, 11/1 for domestic students, 9/15 priority date for international students. Applications are processed on a rolling basis. Electronic applications accepted. *Application Contact:* Laurie Reilly, Graduate Admissions Manager, 401-341-2153, Fax: 401-341-2973, E-mail: laurie.reilly@salve.edu. *Director*, Dr. Sharon Stager, 401-341-3297, E-mail: sharon.stager@salve.edu.

**Program in Rehabilitation Counseling** *Program availability:* Part-time, evening/weekend. Electronic applications accepted.

## SAMFORD UNIVERSITY, Birmingham, AL 35229

**General Information** Independent-religious, coed, university. *Enrollment:* 5,692 graduate, professional, and undergraduate students; 1,832 full-time matriculated graduate/professional students (1,176 women), 240 part-time matriculated graduate/professional students (176 women). *Enrollment by degree level:* 621 master's, 1,427 doctoral, 24 other advanced degrees. *Graduate faculty:* 161 full-time (82 women), 68 part-time/adjunct (34 women). *Tuition:* Full-time $17,754; part-time $862 per credit hour. *Required fees:* $550; $550 per unit. Full-time tuition and fees vary according to course load, program and student level. *Graduate housing:* On-campus housing not available. *Student services:* Campus employment opportunities, campus safety program, career counseling, exercise/wellness program, free psychological counseling, grant writing training, international student services, multicultural affairs office, services for students with disabilities, teacher training, writing training. *Library facilities:* University Library plus 2 others. *Collection:* Books: 569,940 (physical), 389,971 (digital/electronic); Serial titles: 6,045 (physical), 118,182 (digital/electronic); Databases: 302. Weekly public service hours: 99; students can reserve study rooms. *Research affiliation:* Heartland Institute, Beacon Center of Tennessee, Institute for Faith, Work, and Economics, Foundation for Economic Education, Jack Miller Center.

**Computer facilities:** 330 computers available on campus for general student use. A campuswide network can be accessed. Online class registration, free online storage and tech support are available.
Website: http://www.samford.edu/

**General Application Contact:** Brian L. Kennedy, Director of Recruitment, 205-726-4176, Fax: 205-726-2171, E-mail: blkenned@samford.edu.

**GRADUATE UNITS**

**Beeson School of Divinity** Students: 138 full-time (31 women), 15 part-time (8 women); includes 26 minority (24 Black or African American, non-Hispanic/Latino; 1 Asian, non-Hispanic/Latino; 1 Hispanic/Latino), 5 international. Average age 31. 56 applicants, 98% accepted, 27 enrolled. *Faculty:* 14 full-time (2 women), 2 part-time/adjunct (0 women). Expenses: Contact institution. *Financial support:* In 2019–20, 127 students received support, including 6 teaching assistantships (averaging $1,200 per year); Federal Work-Study and scholarships/grants also available. Financial award application deadline: 2/15; financial award applicants required to submit FAFSA. In 2019, 39 master's, 7 doctorates awarded. *Program availability:* Part-time. *Application deadline:* For fall admission, 2/15 for domestic and international students; for spring admission, 10/1 for domestic and international students. *Application fee:* $35. Electronic applications accepted. *Application Contact:* Sherri S. Brown, Director of Admission, 205-726-2066, E-mail: sbrown5@samford.edu. *Dean, Professor of Divinity*, Dr. Douglas A Sweeney, 205-726-2632, E-mail: dsweeney@samford.edu.

**Brock School of Business** Students: 73 full-time (32 women), 25 part-time (14 women); includes 7 minority (5 Black or African American, non-Hispanic/Latino; 1 Hispanic/Latino; 1 Two or more races, non-Hispanic/Latino), 6 international. Average age 27. 38 applicants, 84% accepted, 13 enrolled. *Faculty:* 9 full-time (1 woman), 2 part-time/adjunct (0 women). Expenses: Contact institution. *Financial support:* In 2019–20, 51 students received support. Scholarships/grants available. Financial award application deadline: 2/15; financial award applicants required to submit FAFSA. In 2019, 60 master's awarded. *Program availability:* Part-time, 100% online, blended/hybrid learning. *Application deadline:* For fall admission, 8/1 for domestic and international students; for spring admission, 1/1 for domestic and international students. Applications are processed on a rolling basis. *Application fee:* $35. Electronic applications accepted. *Application Contact:* Elizabeth Gambrell, Associate Director, 205-726-2040, Fax: 205-726-2540, E-mail: eagambre@samford.edu. *Senior Assistant Dean*, Dr. Barbara Cartledge, 205-726-2935, Fax: 205-726-2540, E-mail: bhcartle@samford.edu.

**Cumberland School of Law** Students: 478 full-time (255 women), 8 part-time (5 women); includes 79 minority (53 Black or African American, non-Hispanic/Latino; 3 American Indian or Alaska Native, non-Hispanic/Latino; 5 Asian, non-Hispanic/Latino; 16 Hispanic/Latino; 2 Two or more races, non-Hispanic/Latino), 2 international. Average age 26. 647 applicants, 66% accepted, 166 enrolled. *Faculty:* 17 full-time (6 women), 33 part-time/adjunct (16 women). Expenses: Contact institution. *Financial support:* In 2019–20, 414 students received support. Scholarships/grants available. Financial award application deadline: 3/1; financial award applicants required to submit FAFSA. In 2019, 12 master's, 136 doctorates awarded. *Program availability:* Part-time, 100% online, blended/hybrid learning, Students can take up to a maximum of 15 online hours toward the total for the award of the JD degree. Masters of Law programs are 100% online. *Application deadline:* For spring admission, 6/1 for domestic and international students. Applications are processed on a rolling basis. Electronic applications accepted. *Application Contact:* Whitney Dachelet, Director of Admissions, 205-726-2702, Fax: 205-726-2057, E-mail: wdachele@samford.edu. *Dean and Ethel P. Malugen Professor of Law*, Henry C. Strickland, 205-726-2704, Fax: 205-726-4457, E-mail: hcstrick@samford.edu.

**Howard College of Arts and Sciences** Students: 11 full-time (5 women); includes 3 minority (all Black or African American, non-Hispanic/Latino). Average age 29. 25 applicants, 20% accepted, 5 enrolled. *Faculty:* 8 full-time (3 women), 1 part-time/adjunct (0 women). Expenses: Contact institution. *Financial support:* Career-related internships or fieldwork available. Financial award application deadline: 2/15; financial award applicants required to submit FAFSA. In 2019, 5 master's awarded. *Program availability:* Part-time-only, online only, 100% online. *Application deadline:* Applications are processed on a rolling basis. *Application fee:* $35. Electronic applications accepted. *Application Contact:* David Frings, Assistant Graduate Director, 205-726-4537, E-mail: dmfrings@samford.edu. *Professor and Chair*, Dr. Anthony Scott Overton, 205-726-2944, E-mail: aoverton@samford.edu.

**Ida Moffett School of Nursing** Students: 281 full-time (239 women), 39 part-time (38 women); includes 68 minority (39 Black or African American, non-Hispanic/Latino; 2 American Indian or Alaska Native, non-Hispanic/Latino; 10 Asian, non-Hispanic/Latino; 10 Hispanic/Latino; 1 Native Hawaiian or other Pacific Islander, non-Hispanic/Latino; 6 Two or more races, non-Hispanic/Latino). Average age 35. 59 applicants, 97% accepted, 29 enrolled. *Faculty:* 16 full-time (all women), 3 part-time/adjunct (0 women). Expenses: Contact institution. *Financial support:* In 2019–20, 30 students received support. Application deadline: 2/15; applicants required to submit FAFSA. In 2019, 47 master's, 68 doctorates awarded. *Program availability:* Part-time, evening/weekend, blended/hybrid learning. *Application deadline:* For fall admission, 4/1 for domestic and international students; for spring admission, 8/1 for domestic and international students; for summer admission, 1/1 for domestic and international students. *Application fee:* $50. Electronic applications accepted. *Application Contact:* Allyson Maddox, Director of Graduate Student Services, 205-726-2047, E-mail: amaddox@samford.edu. *Interim Dean and Professor, Ida Moffett School of Nursing*, Dr. Jane S. Martin, 205-726-2760, E-mail: jsmartin@samford.edu.

**McWhorter School of Pharmacy** Students: 461 full-time (300 women), 8 part-time (6 women); includes 102 minority (50 Black or African American, non-Hispanic/Latino; 3 American Indian or Alaska Native, non-Hispanic/Latino; 27 Asian, non-Hispanic/Latino; 18 Hispanic/Latino; 4 Two or more races, non-Hispanic/Latino), 2 international. Average age 24. 331 applicants, 38% accepted, 125 enrolled. *Faculty:* 34 full-time (23 women), 1 part-time/adjunct (0 women). Expenses: Contact institution. *Financial support:* In 2019–20, 243 students received support. Institutionally sponsored loans and scholarships/grants available. Financial award application deadline: 2/15; financial award applicants required to submit FAFSA. In 2019, 123 doctorates awarded. *Application deadline:* For fall admission, 6/1 priority date for domestic and international students. Applications are processed on a rolling basis. Electronic applications accepted. *Application Contact:* Jonathan Parker, MA, EdS, Director of Pharmacy Admissions, 205-726-4242, E-mail: jmparker@samford.edu. *Dean/Professor,* Dr. Michael Crouch, PharmD, BCPS, 205-726-4475, E-mail: mcrouch@samford.edu.

**Orlean Beeson School of Education** Students: 110 full-time (85 women), 125 part-time (87 women); includes 110 minority (98 Black or African American, non-Hispanic/Latino; 3 American Indian or Alaska Native, non-Hispanic/Latino; 1 Asian, non-Hispanic/Latino; 2 Hispanic/Latino; 6 Two or more races, non-Hispanic/Latino). Average age 39. 64 applicants, 81% accepted, 29 enrolled. *Faculty:* 14 full-time (10 women), 13 part-time/adjunct (8 women). Expenses: Contact institution. *Financial support:* In 2019–20, 133 students received support. Scholarships/grants available. Financial award application deadline: 2/15; financial award applicants required to submit FAFSA. In 2019, 61 master's, 17 doctorates, 15 other advanced degrees awarded. *Program availability:* Part-time, evening/weekend, 100% online, blended/hybrid learning. *Application deadline:* For fall admission, 7/15 for domestic and international students; for winter admission, 11/15 for domestic and international students; for spring admission, 11/15 for domestic and international students; for summer admission, 5/15 for domestic and international students. *Application fee:* $35. Electronic applications accepted. *Application Contact:* Brooke Karr, Graduate Admissions Office Coordinator, 205-729-2783, E-mail: kbgilrea@samford.edu. *Dean,* Dr. Anna McEwan, 205-726-2745, E-mail: amcewan@samford.edu.

**School of Health Professions** Students: 193 full-time (152 women), 3 part-time (all women); includes 23 minority (7 Black or African American, non-Hispanic/Latino; 1 American Indian or Alaska Native, non-Hispanic/Latino; 3 Asian, non-Hispanic/Latino; 4 Hispanic/Latino; 8 Two or more races, non-Hispanic/Latino). Average age 24. 897 applicants, 25% accepted, 42 enrolled. *Faculty:* 24 full-time (9 women), 2 part-time/adjunct (both women). Expenses: Contact institution. *Financial support:* In 2019–20, 32 students received support. Scholarships/grants available. Financial award application deadline: 5/1; financial award applicants required to submit FAFSA. In 2019, 52 master's awarded. *Application deadline:* For fall admission, 8/1 for domestic students; for winter admission, 10/1 for domestic students; for spring admission, 1/1 for domestic students. *Application fee:* $120. Electronic applications accepted. *Application Contact:* Dr. Marian Carter, Ed.D., Assistant Dean of Enrollment Management and Student Services, 205-726-2611, E-mail: mwcarter@samford.edu. *Dean of the School of Health Professions,* Dr. Alan Jung, Ph.D., 205-726-2716, E-mail: apjung@samford.edu.

**School of Public Health** Students: 76 full-time (71 women), 16 part-time (14 women); includes 19 minority (14 Black or African American, non-Hispanic/Latino; 1 Asian, non-Hispanic/Latino; 1 Hispanic/Latino; 3 Two or more races, non-Hispanic/Latino). Average age 28. 74 applicants, 78% accepted, 39 enrolled. *Faculty:* 16 full-time (9 women), 5 part-time/adjunct (4 women). Expenses: Contact institution. *Financial support:* In 2019–20, 30 students received support. Scholarships/grants available. Financial award application deadline: 5/1; financial award applicants required to submit FAFSA. In 2019, 51 master's awarded. *Program availability:* Part-time, online only, 100% online. *Application deadline:* For fall admission, 10/1 for domestic students; for winter admission, 12/1 for domestic students; for spring admission, 5/1 for domestic students. Applications are processed on a rolling basis. *Application fee:* $75. Electronic applications accepted. *Application Contact:* Dr. Marian Carter, Ed.D, Assistant Dean of Enrollment Management, 205-726-2611, E-mail: mwcarter@samford.edu. *Dean, School of Public Health,* Dr. Keith Elder, Ph.D., 205-726-4655, E-mail: kelder@samford.edu.

**School of the Arts** Students: 11 full-time (6 women), 1 (woman) part-time; includes 1 minority (Black or African American, non-Hispanic/Latino), 2 international. Average age 26. 17 applicants, 82% accepted, 3 enrolled. *Faculty:* 9 full-time (3 women), 6 part-time/adjunct (4 women). Expenses: Contact institution. *Financial support:* In 2019–20, 11 students received support. Scholarships/grants available. Financial award application deadline: 1/17; financial award applicants required to submit FAFSA. In 2019, 6 master's awarded. *Program availability:* Part-time. *Application deadline:* For fall admission, 1/17 for domestic and international students; for spring admission, 10/18 for domestic and international students. Applications are processed on a rolling basis. *Application fee:* $35. Electronic applications accepted. *Application Contact:* Dr. Mark Lackey, Associate Professor, 205-726-4623, E-mail: mlackey@samford.edu. *Associate Professor,* Dr. Mark Lackey, 205-726-4623, E-mail: mlackey@samford.edu.

## SAM HOUSTON STATE UNIVERSITY, Huntsville, TX 77341

**General Information** State-supported, coed, university. CGS member. *Graduate housing:* Room and/or apartments available on a first-come, first-served basis to single students; on-campus housing not available to married students. Housing application deadline: 8/20. *Research affiliation:* Texas Criminal Justice Division, Texas Department of Corrections, Research Division.

**GRADUATE UNITS**

**College of Business Administration** *Program availability:* Part-time, evening/weekend, online learning. Electronic applications accepted.

**College of Criminal Justice** *Program availability:* Part-time, evening/weekend, online learning. Electronic applications accepted.

**College of Education** *Program availability:* Part-time, evening/weekend, online learning. Electronic applications accepted.

**College of Fine Arts and Mass Communication** *Program availability:* Part-time. Electronic applications accepted.

***School of Music*** *Program availability:* Part-time. Electronic applications accepted.

**College of Health Sciences** *Program availability:* Part-time. Electronic applications accepted.

**College of Humanities and Social Sciences** *Program availability:* Part-time, online learning. Electronic applications accepted.

**College of Sciences** *Program availability:* Part-time, evening/weekend. Electronic applications accepted.

## SAMUEL MERRITT UNIVERSITY, Oakland, CA 94609-3108

**General Information** Independent, coed, primarily women, upper-level institution. *Graduate housing:* On-campus housing not available. *Research affiliation:* Summit Medical Center (nursing).

**GRADUATE UNITS**

**California School of Podiatric Medicine** Electronic applications accepted.

**Department of Occupational Therapy** Electronic applications accepted.

**Department of Physical Therapy** Electronic applications accepted.

**Department of Physician Assistant Studies** Electronic applications accepted.

**School of Nursing** *Program availability:* Part-time, evening/weekend, 100% online, blended/hybrid learning. Electronic applications accepted.

## SAN DIEGO CHRISTIAN COLLEGE, Santee, CA 92071

**General Information** Independent-religious, coed, comprehensive institution.

**GRADUATE UNITS**

**Graduate Programs**

## SAN DIEGO STATE UNIVERSITY, San Diego, CA 92182

**General Information** State-supported, coed, university. CGS member. *Graduate housing:* Room and/or apartments available on a first-come, first-served basis to single students; on-campus housing not available to married students. Housing application deadline: 5/1. *Research affiliation:* Children's Hospital and Research Center (children's health), Robert Wood Johnson Foundation (public health), General Atomics (technical student services), William and Flora Hewlett Foundation (teacher education), American Heart Association (biology), Qualcomm (wireless and telecommunications).

**GRADUATE UNITS**

**Graduate and Research Affairs** *Program availability:* Part-time, evening/weekend. Electronic applications accepted.

***College of Arts and Letters*** *Program availability:* Part-time, evening/weekend. Electronic applications accepted.

***College of Education*** *Program availability:* Part-time, evening/weekend. Electronic applications accepted.

***College of Engineering*** *Program availability:* Part-time, evening/weekend. Electronic applications accepted.

***College of Health and Human Services*** *Program availability:* Part-time, evening/weekend. Electronic applications accepted.

***College of Professional Studies and Fine Arts*** *Program availability:* Part-time.

***College of Sciences*** *Program availability:* Part-time. Electronic applications accepted.

***Fowler College of Business*** *Program availability:* Part-time, evening/weekend. Electronic applications accepted.

## SANFORD BURNHAM PREBYS MEDICAL DISCOVERY INSTITUTE, La Jolla, CA 92037

**General Information** Independent, coed, graduate-only institution.

**GRADUATE UNITS**

**Graduate School of Biomedical Sciences**

## SAN FRANCISCO ART INSTITUTE, San Francisco, CA 94133

**General Information** Independent, coed, comprehensive institution. *Graduate housing:* Room and/or apartments available on a first-come, first-served basis to single students; on-campus housing not available to married students. Housing application deadline: 6/1. *Research affiliation:* Headlands Center for the Arts (multidisciplinary art exhibition), Kadist Art Foundation (contemporary art exhibition), San Francisco Museum of Modern Art (art history, museum studies, contemporary art), Yerba Buena Center for the Arts (art exhibits), Tremaine Foundation (education; art, environment, and learning disabilities), Prelinger Library (library).

**GRADUATE UNITS**

**Master of Arts Programs** Electronic applications accepted.

**Master of Fine Arts Programs** Electronic applications accepted.

## SAN FRANCISCO CONSERVATORY OF MUSIC, San Francisco, CA 94102

**General Information** Independent, coed, comprehensive institution. *Graduate housing:* Rooms and/or apartments available on a first-come, first-served basis to single and married students. Housing application deadline: 5/31.

**GRADUATE UNITS**

**Graduate Division** Electronic applications accepted.

## SAN FRANCISCO STATE UNIVERSITY, San Francisco, CA 94132-1722

**General Information** State-supported, coed, university. *Enrollment:* 28,880 graduate, professional, and undergraduate students; 1,724 full-time matriculated graduate/professional students (1,169 women), 1,035 part-time matriculated graduate/professional students (633 women). *International tuition:* $16,680 full-time. *Tuition, area resident:* Full-time $7176; part-time $4164 per year. Tuition, state resident: full-time $7176; part-time $4164 per year. Tuition, nonresident: full-time $16,680; part-time $396 per unit. *Required fees:* $1524; $1524 per unit. $762 per semester. Tuition and fees vary according to degree level and program. *Graduate housing:* Room and/or apartments available on a first-come, first-served basis to single students; on-campus housing not available to married students. *Student services:* Campus employment opportunities, campus safety program, career counseling, child daycare facilities, exercise/wellness program, free psychological counseling, international student services, low-cost health insurance, multicultural affairs office, services for students with disabilities, teacher training. *Library facilities:* J. Paul Leonard Library. *Collection:* Study areas open 24 hours, 5–7 days a week; students can reserve study rooms.

**Computer facilities:** Computer purchase and lease plans are available. 2,000 computers available on campus for general student use. A campuswide network can be accessed. Online class registration is available.
Website: http://www.sfsu.edu/

**General Application Contact:** Noah Price, Associate Dean of Graduate Studies, 415-405-3506, Fax: 415-405-0340, E-mail: nprice@sfsu.edu.

**GRADUATE UNITS**

**Division of Graduate Studies** Expenses: Contact institution. *Financial support:* Fellowships, research assistantships, teaching assistantships, career-related internships or fieldwork, Federal Work-Study, institutionally sponsored loans, tuition waivers (partial), and unspecified assistantships available. Support available to part-time students. Financial award application deadline: 3/1; financial award applicants required to submit FAFSA. *Program availability:* Part-time, evening/weekend. *Application fee:* $55. *Application Contact:* Noah Price, Associate Dean of Graduate Studies, 415-405-3506, Fax: 415-405-0340, E-mail: nprice@sfsu.edu. *Dean,* Dr. Sophie Clavier, 415-338-2232, Fax: 415-405-0340, E-mail: sclavier@sfsu.edu.

***College of Education*** Expenses: Contact institution. *Application Contact:* Victoria Narkewicz, Executive Assistant, 415-338-2687, Fax: 415-338-6951, E-mail: toria@sfsu.edu. *Dean,* Dr. Cynthia Grutzik, 415-338-2687, Fax: 415-338-6951, E-mail: cgrutzik@sfsu.edu.

***College of Ethnic Studies*** Expenses: Contact institution. *Program availability:* Part-time. *Application Contact:* Dr. Catriona Rueda Esquibel, Associate Dean, 415-338-

1693, Fax: 415-338-1739, E-mail: ktrion@sfsu.edu. *Dean*, Dr. Amy H. Sueyoshi, 415-338-1693, Fax: 415-338-1739, E-mail: ethnicst@sfsu.edu.

**College of Health and Social Sciences** Expenses: Contact institution. *Financial support:* Fellowships, research assistantships, teaching assistantships, career-related internships or fieldwork, Federal Work-Study, institutionally sponsored loans, and unspecified assistantships available. *Program availability:* Part-time. *Application Contact:* Christina Alcantara, Assistant to the Dean, 415-338-3327, Fax: 415-338-0586, E-mail: cba@sfsu.edu. *Dean*, Dr. Alvin Alvarez, 415-338-3326, Fax: 415-338-0586, E-mail: aalvarez@sfsu.edu.

**College of Liberal and Creative Arts** Expenses: Contact institution. *Financial support:* Teaching assistantships, career-related internships or fieldwork, and Federal Work-Study available. *Program availability:* Part-time, evening/weekend. *Application Contact:* Michelle Rashleger, Chief of Staff, 415-405-4281, Fax: 415-338-6159, E-mail: mrash@sfsu.edu. *Dean*, Dr. Andrew Harris, 415-338-1471, Fax: 415-338-6159, E-mail: a1harris@sfsu.edu.

**College of Science and Engineering** Expenses: Contact institution. *Program availability:* Part-time. *Application deadline:* Applications are processed on a rolling basis. Electronic applications accepted. *Application Contact:* Nadia Chan, Executive Assistant to the Dean, 415-338-1571, Fax: 415-338-6136, E-mail: nadiach@sfsu.edu. *Dean*, Dr. Carmen Domingo, 415-338-1571, Fax: 415-338-6136, E-mail: cdomingo@sfsu.edu.

**Lam Family College of Business** Expenses: Contact institution. *Application Contact:* Dr. Denise Kleinrichert, Interim Associate Dean, 415-338-1276, Fax: 415-338-6237, E-mail: dk@sfsu.edu. *Dean*, Dr. Eugene Sivadas, 415-338-3650, Fax: 415-338-6237, E-mail: cobus@sfsu.edu.

## SAN FRANCISCO THEOLOGICAL SEMINARY, San Anselmo, CA 94960

**General Information** Independent-religious, coed, graduate-only institution. *Graduate housing:* Rooms and/or apartments available on a first-come, first-served basis to single and married students. Housing application deadline: 5/1.

**GRADUATE UNITS**

**Graduate and Professional Programs** *Program availability:* Part-time.

## SAN IGNACIO UNIVERSITY, Doral, FL 33178

**General Information** Proprietary, coed, comprehensive institution.

**GRADUATE UNITS**

**Graduate Programs**

## SAN JOAQUIN COLLEGE OF LAW, Clovis, CA 93612-1312

**General Information** Independent, coed, graduate-only institution. *Graduate housing:* On-campus housing not available.

**GRADUATE UNITS**

**Law Program** Expenses: Contact institution. *Financial support:* Career-related internships or fieldwork and Federal Work-Study available. Support available to part-time students. Financial award application deadline: 8/24. *Program availability:* Part-time, evening/weekend. *Application deadline:* For fall admission, 6/30 priority date for domestic students. Applications are processed on a rolling basis. *Application fee:* $40. *Application Contact:* Joyce Morodomi, Registrar/Admissions Officer, 209-323-2100, Fax: 209-323-5566, E-mail: jmorodomi@sjcl.edu. *Associate Dean of Academic Affairs*, Sally Ann Perring, 209-323-2100, Fax: 209-323-5566.

## SAN JOSE STATE UNIVERSITY, San Jose, CA 95192-0001

**General Information** State-supported, coed, comprehensive institution. *Enrollment:* 32,926 graduate, professional, and undergraduate students; 3,747 full-time matriculated graduate/professional students (2,271 women), 4,097 part-time matriculated graduate/professional students (2,572 women). *Enrollment by degree level:* 7,796 master's, 48 doctoral. *Graduate faculty:* 326 full-time (165 women), 235 part-time/adjunct (115 women). *International tuition:* $7176 full-time. *Tuition, area resident:* Full-time $7176; part-time $4164 per credit hour. Tuition, state resident: full-time $7176; part-time $4164 per credit hour. Tuition, nonresident: full-time $7176; part-time $4165 per credit hour. *Required fees:* $2110; $2110. *Graduate housing:* Room and/or apartments available on a first-come, first-served basis to single students; on-campus housing not available to married students. Typical cost: $10,368 per year ($16,248 including board). Room and board charges vary according to board plan and housing facility selected. Housing application deadline: 5/1. *Student services:* Campus employment opportunities, campus safety program, career counseling, child daycare facilities, exercise/wellness program, free psychological counseling, grant writing training, international student services, low-cost health insurance, multicultural affairs office, services for students with disabilities, teacher training, writing training. *Library facilities:* Dr. Martin Luther King Jr. Library plus 1 other. *Collection:* Books: 108,203 (physical), 899,231 (digital/electronic); Serial titles: 170,652 (physical), 170,652 (digital/electronic); Databases: 448. Weekly public service hours: 62; study areas open 24 hours, 5–7 days a week; students can reserve study rooms. *Research affiliation:* Moss Landing Marine Laboratories (oceanography/marine science).

**Computer facilities:** A campuswide network can be accessed. Online class registration is available.

Website: http://www.sjsu.edu/

**General Application Contact:** Christie Wright, Associate Director, Graduate Admissions and Program Evaluation, 408-283-7500, E-mail: admissions@sjsu.edu.

**GRADUATE UNITS**

**EdD Leadership Program** Students: 2 full-time (1 woman), 46 part-time (31 women); includes 31 minority (5 Black or African American, non-Hispanic/Latino; 10 Asian, non-Hispanic/Latino; 16 Hispanic/Latino). Average age 43. 51 applicants, 39% accepted, 20 enrolled. *Faculty:* 1 full-time (0 women), 4 part-time/adjunct (1 woman). Expenses: Contact institution. *Financial support:* In 2019–20, 7 students received support. Scholarships/grants available. Financial award application deadline: 5/1. *Program availability:* Evening/weekend. *Application deadline:* Applications are processed on a rolling basis. *Application fee:* $70. Electronic applications accepted. *Application Contact:* Maria Munoz, Associate Resource Analyst, 408-924-3719, E-mail: Maria.Munoz@sjsu.edu. *Department Chair*, Bradley Porfilio, 408-924-35666, E-mail: bradley.porfilio@sjsu.edu.

**Moss Landing Marine Laboratories** Students: 2 full-time (both women), 14 part-time (8 women); includes 6 minority (3 Asian, non-Hispanic/Latino; 3 Hispanic/Latino). Average age 29. 90 applicants, 37% accepted, 29 enrolled. *Faculty:* 5 full-time (1 woman), 2 part-time/adjunct (1 woman). Expenses: Contact institution. *Financial support:* In 2019–20, 11 students received support, including 1 fellowship (averaging $6,000 per year), 3 research assistantships (averaging $8,763 per year); scholarships/grants also available. Financial award application deadline: 5/1; financial award applicants required to submit FAFSA. In 2019, 5 master's awarded. *Application deadline:* For fall admission, 2/1 for domestic and international students. *Application fee:* $70. Electronic applications accepted. *Application Contact:* Terra Eggink, Graduate Program Specialist, E-mail: gradprog@mlml.calstate.edu. *Director*, James Harvey, 831-771-4434, E-mail: james.harvey@sjsu.edu.

**Program in Anthropology** Students: 15 full-time (9 women), 12 part-time (6 women); includes 16 minority (3 Black or African American, non-Hispanic/Latino; 3 Asian, non-Hispanic/Latino; 10 Hispanic/Latino), 2 international. Average age 30. 16 applicants, 69% accepted, 7 enrolled. *Faculty:* 4 full-time (2 women). Expenses: Contact institution. *Financial support:* In 2019–20, 12 students received support. Scholarships/grants available. Financial award application deadline: 5/15; financial award applicants required to submit FAFSA. In 2019, 9 master's awarded. *Program availability:* Part-time, evening/weekend. *Application deadline:* For fall admission, 7/1 for domestic students, 5/1 for international students. Applications are processed on a rolling basis. *Application fee:* $70. Electronic applications accepted. *Application Contact:* Roberto Gonzalez, Department Chair, 408-924-5715, E-mail: roberto.gonzalez@sjsu.edu. *Department Chair*, Roberto Gonzalez, 408-924-5715, E-mail: roberto.gonzalez@sjsu.edu.

**Program in Applied Data Science**

**Program in Art and Art History**

**Program in Audiology**

**Program in Aviation and Technology** Electronic applications accepted.

**Program in Biological Sciences** *Program availability:* Part-time. Electronic applications accepted.

**Program in Biomedical Engineering** Students: 43 full-time (25 women), 58 part-time (28 women); includes 46 minority (39 Asian, non-Hispanic/Latino; 7 Hispanic/Latino), 28 international. Average age 27. 63 applicants, 70% accepted, 24 enrolled. *Faculty:* 6 full-time (1 woman), 3 part-time/adjunct (0 women). Expenses: Contact institution. *Financial support:* In 2019–20, 18 students received support. Research assistantships, teaching assistantships, and Federal Work-Study available. Financial award application deadline: 5/15; financial award applicants required to submit FAFSA. *Program availability:* Part-time. *Application deadline:* For fall admission, 6/1 for domestic students, 5/1 for international students; for spring admission, 11/1 for domestic students, 2/1 for international students. Applications are processed on a rolling basis. *Application fee:* $70. Electronic applications accepted. *Application Contact:* Dr. Alessandro Bellofiore, Professor, Graduate Coordinator, E-mail: alessandro.bellofiore@sjsu.edu. *Department Chair*, Dr. Guna Selvaduray, 408-924-3874, E-mail: guna.selvaduray@sjsu.edu.

**Program in Business Graduate Programs** Students: 126 full-time (69 women), 206 part-time (96 women); includes 162 minority (13 Black or African American, non-Hispanic/Latino; 105 Asian, non-Hispanic/Latino; 42 Hispanic/Latino; 2 Native Hawaiian or other Pacific Islander, non-Hispanic/Latino), 55 international. Average age 32. 347 applicants, 58% accepted, 154 enrolled. *Faculty:* 16 full-time (8 women), 5 part-time/adjunct (3 women). Expenses: Contact institution. *Financial support:* In 2019–20, 68 students received support, including 1 fellowship (averaging $3,000 per year); scholarships/grants and tuition waivers also available. Financial award application deadline: 5/1; financial award applicants required to submit FAFSA. *Program availability:* Part-time, evening/weekend. *Application deadline:* For fall admission, 5/1 for domestic and international students; for spring admission, 11/1 for domestic and international students. Applications are processed on a rolling basis. *Application fee:* $70. Electronic applications accepted. *Application Contact:* Dr. Michelle Waldron, Graduate Programs Outreach Coordinator, 408-924-3427, E-mail: michelle.waldron@sjsu.edu. *Associate Dean*, Dr. Marco Pagani, 408-924-3477, E-mail: marco.pagani@sjsu.edu.

**Program in Chemical & Materials Engineering** Students: 23 full-time (6 women), 68 part-time (16 women); includes 59 minority (32 Asian, non-Hispanic/Latino; 11 Hispanic/Latino; 16 Two or more races, non-Hispanic/Latino), 16 international. Average age 29. 68 applicants, 72% accepted, 27 enrolled. *Faculty:* 2 full-time (both women), 5 part-time/adjunct (0 women). Expenses: Contact institution. *Financial support:* In 2019–20, 16 students received support, including 1 fellowship (averaging $4,500 per year), 10 research assistantships (averaging $8,000 per year), 6 teaching assistantships (averaging $14,000 per year); scholarships/grants and health care benefits also available. Financial award application deadline: 5/1; financial award applicants required to submit FAFSA. In 2019, 23 master's awarded. *Program availability:* Part-time. *Application deadline:* For fall admission, 7/1 for domestic students, 5/1 for international students; for spring admission, 12/1 for domestic students, 11/1 for international students. Applications are processed on a rolling basis. *Application fee:* $70. Electronic applications accepted. *Application Contact:* Debi Fennern, Administrative Analyst, 408-924-4056, E-mail: debi.fennern@sjsu.edu. *Department Chair*, Dr. Richard Chung, 408-924-3927, E-mail: richard.chung@sjsu.edu.

**Program in Chemistry** Students: 2 full-time (1 woman), 18 part-time (8 women); includes 11 minority (9 Asian, non-Hispanic/Latino; 2 Hispanic/Latino), 1 international. Average age 28. 21 applicants, 24% accepted, 3 enrolled. *Faculty:* 16 full-time (5 women), 1 part-time/adjunct (0 women). Expenses: Contact institution. *Financial support:* In 2019–20, 1 student received support. Scholarships/grants available. Financial award application deadline: 5/1; financial award applicants required to submit FAFSA. In 2019, 4 master's awarded. *Application deadline:* For fall admission, 7/1 for domestic students, 5/1 for international students. Applications are processed on a rolling basis. *Application fee:* $70. Electronic applications accepted. *Application Contact:* Lionelk Cheruzel, Graduate Advisor, 408-924-5283, E-mail: lionel.cheruzel@sjsu.edu. *Department Chair*, Karen Singmaster, 408-924-5000, E-mail: karen.singmaster@sjsu.edu.

**Program in Chicana and Chicano Studies** Students: 7 full-time (6 women), 19 part-time (16 women); includes 21 minority (all Hispanic/Latino), 3 international. Average age 28. 11 applicants, 91% accepted, 9 enrolled. *Faculty:* 7 full-time (3 women). Expenses: Contact institution. *Financial support:* In 2019–20, 10 students received support, including 2 fellowships (averaging $4,625 per year); teaching assistantships and scholarships/grants also available. Financial award applicants required to submit FAFSA. *Program availability:* Part-time, evening/weekend. *Application deadline:* For fall admission, 4/1 priority date for domestic students, 5/1 priority date for international students; for spring admission, 11/1 priority date for domestic students, 10/1 priority date for international students. Applications are processed on a rolling basis. *Application fee:* $70. Electronic applications accepted. *Application Contact:* Dr. Estevan Azcona, Assistant Professor/Graduate Coordinator, 408-924-5837, E-mail: estevan.azcona@sjsu.edu. *Department Chair*, Dr. Magdalena Barrera, 408-924-5583, E-mail: magdalena.barrera@sjsu.edu.

**Program in Child & Adolescent Development** Students: 2 full-time (both women), 9 part-time (all women); includes 5 minority (1 Asian, non-Hispanic/Latino; 4 Hispanic/Latino), 1 international. Average age 28. 17 applicants, 65% accepted, 6 enrolled. *Faculty:* 12 full-time (all women), 1 part-time/adjunct (0 women). Expenses: Contact institution. *Financial support:* In 2019–20, 5 students received support. Research assistantships, teaching assistantships, Federal Work-Study, and scholarships/grants available. Financial award application deadline: 5/1; financial award applicants required to submit FAFSA. In 2019, 9 master's awarded. *Application deadline:* For fall admission, 3/1 for domestic and international students. Applications are processed on a rolling basis. *Application fee:* $70. Electronic applications accepted. *Application Contact:* Bryon McIntyre, Administrative Coordinator, 408-924-3614, Fax: 408-924-3758, E-mail: bryon.mcintyre@sjsu.edu. *Department Chair*, Dr. Emily Slusser, 408-924-3752, Fax: 408-924-3758, E-mail: emily.slusser@sjsu.edu.

**Program in Civil & Environmental Engineering** Electronic applications accepted.

**Program in Communication Studies** Students: 15 full-time (9 women), 22 part-time (14 women); includes 15 minority (9 Asian, non-Hispanic/Latino; 6 Hispanic/Latino), 3 international. Average age 28. 41 applicants, 59% accepted, 17 enrolled. *Faculty:* 6 full-time (3 women), 1 part-time/adjunct (0 women). Expenses: Contact institution. *Financial support:* In 2019–20, 15 students received support, including 1 fellowship (averaging $1,000 per year); scholarships/grants also available. Financial award application deadline: 5/1; financial award applicants required to submit FAFSA. In 2019, 15 master's awarded. *Application deadline:* For fall admission, 6/1 for domestic students, 3/1 for international students. Applications are processed on a rolling basis. *Application fee:* $70. Electronic applications accepted. *Application Contact:* Oona Tatton, Graduate Coordinator, E-mail: oona.hatton@sjsu.edu. *Department Chair*, Anne Marie Todd, 408-924-5391, E-mail: annemarie.todd@sjsu.edu.

**Program in Communicative Disorders and Sciences** Students: 109 full-time (100 women), 1 (woman) part-time; includes 63 minority (3 Black or African American, non-Hispanic/Latino; 37 Asian, non-Hispanic/Latino; 15 Hispanic/Latino; 8 Native Hawaiian or other Pacific Islander, non-Hispanic/Latino), 2 international. Average age 28. 264 applicants, 13% accepted, 35 enrolled. *Faculty:* 8 full-time (7 women), 7 part-time/adjunct (all women). Expenses: Contact institution. *Financial support:* In 2019–20, 57 students received support, including 1 fellowship (averaging $5,250 per year); research assistantships, scholarships/grants, traineeships, and Tutor jobs, student assistants also available. Financial award application deadline: 5/1; financial award applicants required to submit FAFSA. In 2019, 42 master's awarded. *Application deadline:* For fall admission, 2/1 for domestic and international students. Applications are processed on a rolling basis. *Application fee:* $70. Electronic applications accepted. *Application Contact:* Cindy Aubrey, Administrative Support Coordinator, 408-924-3659, E-mail: communicative-disorders-sciences@sjsu.edu. *Department Chair*, Nidhi Mahendra, 408-924-8161, E-mail: nidhi.mahendra@sjsu.edu.

**Program in Computer Engineering** Students: 833 full-time (352 women), 352 part-time (101 women); includes 186 minority (7 Black or African American, non-Hispanic/Latino; 160 Asian, non-Hispanic/Latino; 19 Hispanic/Latino), 922 international. Average age 27. 1,637 applicants, 23% accepted, 224 enrolled. *Faculty:* 14 full-time (5 women), 28 part-time/adjunct (4 women). Expenses: Contact institution. *Financial support:* In 2019–20, 30 students received support. Scholarships/grants available. Financial award application deadline: 5/15; financial award applicants required to submit FAFSA. In 2019, 515 master's awarded. *Application deadline:* For fall admission, 7/1 for domestic students, 5/1 for international students; for spring admission, 12/1 for domestic students, 11/1 for international students. Applications are processed on a rolling basis. *Application fee:* $70. Electronic applications accepted. *Application Contact:* David Bruck, MS Computer Engineering Advisor, E-mail: David.bruck@sjsu.edu. *Department Chair*, Xiao Su, 408-924-7366, E-mail: xiao.su@sjsu.edu.

**Program in Computer Science** Students: 108 full-time (50 women), 48 part-time (12 women); includes 56 minority (51 Asian, non-Hispanic/Latino; 5 Hispanic/Latino), 82 international. Average age 27. 862 applicants, 16% accepted, 62 enrolled. *Faculty:* 12 full-time (3 women), 8 part-time/adjunct (3 women). Expenses: Contact institution. *Financial support:* In 2019–20, 2 fellowships (averaging $1,600 per year) were awarded; teaching assistantships, scholarships/grants, and unspecified assistantships also available. Financial award application deadline: 5/1; financial award applicants required to submit FAFSA. *Program availability:* Part-time, evening/weekend. *Application deadline:* For fall admission, 2/1 for domestic and international students; for spring admission, 10/1 for domestic students. Applications are processed on a rolling basis. *Application fee:* $70. Electronic applications accepted. *Application Contact:* Christopher Pollett, Grad Coordinator, 408-9240-5145, E-mail: chris@pollett.org. *Department Chair*, Melody Moh, 408-924-5088, E-mail: melody.moh@sjsu.edu.

**Program in Counselor Education** Students: 155 full-time (113 women), 30 part-time (22 women); includes 137 minority (10 Black or African American, non-Hispanic/Latino; 24 Asian, non-Hispanic/Latino; 102 Hispanic/Latino; 1 Native Hawaiian or other Pacific Islander, non-Hispanic/Latino), 8 international. Average age 30. 174 applicants, 48% accepted, 58 enrolled. *Faculty:* 4 full-time (3 women), 15 part-time/adjunct (12 women). Expenses: Contact institution. *Financial support:* In 2019–20, 80 students received support, including 1 fellowship (averaging $3,000 per year); career-related internships or fieldwork, scholarships/grants, and tuition waivers (partial) also available. Financial award application deadline: 5/1; financial award applicants required to submit FAFSA. In 2019, 74 master's awarded. *Program availability:* Part-time, evening/weekend. *Application deadline:* For fall admission, 2/1 for domestic and international students; for spring admission, 10/1 for domestic and international students. *Application fee:* $70. Electronic applications accepted. *Application Contact:* Dr. Dolores DeHaro Mena, Department Chair, 408-924-3627, E-mail: dolores.mena@sjsu.edu. *Department Chair*, Dr. Dolores DeHaro Mena, 408-924-3627, E-mail: dolores.mena@sjsu.edu.

**Program in Economics** *Program availability:* Part-time. Electronic applications accepted.

**Program in Educational Leadership** Electronic applications accepted.

**Program in Electrical Engineering** Electronic applications accepted.

**Program in English and Comparative Literature** Students: 14 full-time (6 women), 53 part-time (40 women); includes 21 minority (1 Black or African American, non-Hispanic/Latino; 8 Asian, non-Hispanic/Latino; 12 Hispanic/Latino), 1 international. Average age 35. 44 applicants, 68% accepted, 16 enrolled. *Faculty:* 8 full-time (7 women), 3 part-time/adjunct (1 woman). Expenses: Contact institution. *Financial support:* In 2019–20, 19 students received support, including 2 fellowships (averaging $1,750 per year), 7 research assistantships (averaging $10,000 per year), 15 teaching assistantships with partial tuition reimbursements available (averaging $16,000 per year); scholarships/grants also available. Financial award application deadline: 5/1; financial award applicants required to submit FAFSA. *Program availability:* Part-time, evening/weekend. *Application deadline:* For fall admission, 6/1 for domestic students, 5/1 for international students; for spring admission, 11/1 for domestic and international students. Applications are processed on a rolling basis. *Application fee:* $70. Electronic applications accepted. *Application Contact:* Revathi Krishnaswamy, Graduate Coordinator, 408-924-1384, E-mail: revathi.krishnaswamy@sjsu.edu. *Department Chair*, Noelle Brada-Williams, 408-924-4439, E-mail: noelle.brada-williams@sjsu.edu.

**Program in Environmental Studies** Students: 21 full-time (19 women), 26 part-time (18 women); includes 17 minority (1 Black or African American, non-Hispanic/Latino; 7 Asian, non-Hispanic/Latino; 9 Hispanic/Latino), 4 international. Average age 30. 25 applicants, 68% accepted, 12 enrolled. *Faculty:* 4 full-time (2 women). Expenses: Contact institution. *Financial support:* In 2019–20, 11 students received support. Scholarships/grants available. Financial award application deadline: 5/1; financial award applicants required to submit FAFSA. In 2019, 7 master's awarded. *Application deadline:* For fall admission, 6/1 for domestic students, 5/1 for international students; for spring admission, 11/1 for domestic and international students. Applications are processed on a rolling basis. *Application fee:* $70. Electronic applications accepted. *Application Contact:* Rachel O'Malley, 408-924-5450, E-mail: envstudies-ms@sjsu.edu. *Department Chair*, Lynne Trulio, 408-924-5450, E-mail: envstudies-ms@sjsu.edu.

**Program in Film and Theatre** Electronic applications accepted.

**Program in General Engineering** Students: 21 full-time (11 women), 61 part-time (9 women); includes 37 minority (3 Black or African American, non-Hispanic/Latino; 29 Asian, non-Hispanic/Latino; 5 Hispanic/Latino), 27 international. Average age 32. 23 applicants, 57% accepted, 10 enrolled. *Faculty:* 2 full-time (0 women), 2 part-time/adjunct (1 woman). Expenses: Contact institution. *Financial support:* In 2019–20, 1 student received support. Scholarships/grants available. Financial award application deadline: 5/1; financial award applicants required to submit FAFSA. *Program availability:* Part-time. *Application deadline:* For fall admission, 7/1 for domestic students, 5/1 for international students; for spring admission, 12/1 for domestic students, 11/1 for international students. Applications are processed on a rolling basis. *Application fee:* $70. Electronic applications accepted. *Application Contact:* Ping Hsu, Department Chair, 408-924-3902, E-mail: ping.hsu@sjsu.edu. *Department Chair*, Ping Hsu, 408-924-3902, E-mail: ping.hsu@sjsu.edu.

**Program in Geology** Electronic applications accepted.

**Program in Health Science and Recreation**

**Program in History** Students: 7 full-time (2 women), 32 part-time (12 women); includes 17 minority (6 Asian, non-Hispanic/Latino; 11 Hispanic/Latino). Average age 36. 15 applicants, 87% accepted, 9 enrolled. *Faculty:* 8 full-time (6 women), 2 part-time/adjunct (both women). Expenses: Contact institution. *Financial support:* In 2019–20, 9 students received support. Scholarships/grants and Instructional Student Assistants available. Financial award application deadline: 5/1; financial award applicants required to submit FAFSA. In 2019, 12 master's awarded. *Program availability:* Part-time, evening/weekend. *Application deadline:* For fall admission, 4/1 for domestic and international students; for spring admission, 11/1 for domestic and international students. Applications are processed on a rolling basis. *Application fee:* $70. Electronic applications accepted. *Application Contact:* Libra Hilde, Graduate Advisor, 408-924-5512, Fax: 408-9244-5531, E-mail: libra.hilde@sjsu.edu. *Department Chair*, Glen Gendzel, 408-924-5514, Fax: 408-924-5531, E-mail: glen.gendzel@sjsu.edu.

**Program in Industrial and Systems Engineering** Students: 196 full-time (112 women), 214 part-time (127 women); includes 85 minority (5 Black or African American, non-Hispanic/Latino; 61 Asian, non-Hispanic/Latino; 19 Hispanic/Latino), 262 international. Average age 27. 542 applicants, 39% accepted, 131 enrolled. *Faculty:* 5 full-time (2 women), 9 part-time/adjunct (1 woman). Expenses: Contact institution. *Financial support:* In 2019–20, 24 students received support. Scholarships/grants available. Financial award application deadline: 5/1; financial award applicants required to submit FAFSA. In 2019, 141 master's awarded. *Application deadline:* For fall admission, 6/1 for domestic students, 5/1 for international students; for spring admission, 12/1 for domestic students, 11/1 for international students. Applications are processed on a rolling basis. *Application fee:* $70. Electronic applications accepted. *Application Contact:* Yasser Dessouky, Department Chair, 408-924-4133, E-mail: yasser.dessouky@sjsu.edu. *Department Chair*, Yasser Dessouky, 408-924-4133, E-mail: yasser.dessouky@sjsu.edu.

**Program in Journalism and Mass Communication** Students: 31 full-time (18 women), 6 part-time (5 women); includes 8 minority (2 Asian, non-Hispanic/Latino; 6 Hispanic/Latino), 7 international. 31 applicants, 55% accepted, 12 enrolled. *Faculty:* 13 full-time (6 women). Expenses: Contact institution. *Financial support:* In 2019–20, 1 student received support, including 10 teaching assistantships (averaging $9,728 per year); scholarships/grants and unspecified assistantships also available. Financial award application deadline: 5/1; financial award applicants required to submit FAFSA. In 2019, 7 master's awarded. *Program availability:* Part-time, evening/weekend. *Application deadline:* For fall admission, 6/1 for domestic students, 5/1 for international students; for spring admission, 11/1 for domestic students, 10/1 for international students. Applications are processed on a rolling basis. *Application fee:* $70. Electronic applications accepted. *Application Contact:* Scott Fosdick, PdD, Graduate Coordinator, E-mail: scott.fosdick@sjsu.edu. *School Director*, Phylis West Johnson, 408-924-3249, E-mail: phylis.west@sjsu.edu.

**Program in Justice Studies** *Program availability:* Part-time. Electronic applications accepted.

**Program in Kinesiology** Students: 43 full-time (20 women), 28 part-time (12 women); includes 29 minority (3 Black or African American, non-Hispanic/Latino; 9 Asian, non-Hispanic/Latino; 17 Hispanic/Latino), 7 international. Average age 26. 72 applicants, 82% accepted, 30 enrolled. *Faculty:* 12 full-time (6 women), 4 part-time/adjunct (2 women). Expenses: Contact institution. *Financial support:* In 2019–20, 13 students received support, including 22 teaching assistantships; scholarships/grants also available. Financial award application deadline: 5/1; financial award applicants required to submit FAFSA. In 2019, 34 master's awarded. *Program availability:* Part-time. *Application deadline:* For fall admission, 6/1 for domestic students, 5/1 for international students; for spring admission, 11/1 for domestic students, 10/1 for international students. Applications are processed on a rolling basis. *Application fee:* $70. Electronic applications accepted. *Application Contact:* Dr. Ted Butryn, Professor and Graduate Coordinator, 408-924-3068, E-mail: theodore.butryn@sjsu.edu. *Department Chair*, Dr. Tamar Semerjian, 408-924-3069, E-mail: tamar.semerjian@sjsu.edu.

**Program in Linguistics and Language Development** Students: 18 full-time (14 women), 27 part-time (21 women); includes 19 minority (1 Black or African American, non-Hispanic/Latino; 15 Asian, non-Hispanic/Latino; 3 Hispanic/Latino), 9 international. Average age 35. 26 applicants, 69% accepted, 7 enrolled. *Faculty:* 3 full-time (1 woman), 3 part-time/adjunct (1 woman). Expenses: Contact institution. *Financial support:* In 2019–20, 7 students received support. Scholarships/grants available. Financial award application deadline: 5/15; financial award applicants required to submit FAFSA. In 2019, 18 master's awarded. *Program availability:* Part-time. *Application deadline:* For fall admission, 7/1 for domestic students, 3/1 for international students; for spring admission, 12/1 for domestic students, 11/1 for international students. Applications are processed on a rolling basis. *Application fee:* $70. Electronic applications accepted. *Application Contact:* Stefan Frazier, Department Chair, 408-924-4443, E-mail: stefan.frazier@sjsu.edu. *Department Chair*, Stefan Frazier, 408-924-4443, E-mail: stefan.frazier@sjsu.edu.

**Program in Mathematics and Statistics** Students: 54 full-time (31 women), 39 part-time (22 women); includes 39 minority (2 Black or African American, non-Hispanic/Latino; 24 Asian, non-Hispanic/Latino; 13 Hispanic/Latino), 32 international.

Average age 29. 59 applicants, 47% accepted, 19 enrolled. *Faculty:* 6 full-time (3 women). Expenses: Contact institution. *Financial support:* In 2019–20, 9 students received support. Teaching assistantships, scholarships/grants, and unspecified assistantships available. Financial award application deadline: 5/1; financial award applicants required to submit FAFSA. *Program availability:* Part-time. *Application deadline:* For fall admission, 4/1 for domestic and international students. Applications are processed on a rolling basis. *Application fee:* $70. Electronic applications accepted. *Application Contact:* Steve Crunk, Admissions Coordinator, E-mail: steven.crunk@sjsu.edu. *Department Chair,* Ben Cayco, 408-924-5100, E-mail: bem.cayco@sjsu.edu.

**Program in Mechanical and Aerospace Engineering** Average age 27. 113 applicants, 69% accepted, 51 enrolled. *Faculty:* 15 full-time (4 women), 13 part-time/adjunct (0 women). Expenses: Contact institution. *Financial support:* In 2019–20, 14 teaching assistantships with full and partial tuition reimbursements (averaging $6,400 per year) were awarded; scholarships/grants also available. In 2019, 56 master's awarded. *Program availability:* Part-time, evening/weekend. *Application deadline:* For fall admission, 6/1 for domestic students, 5/1 for international students; for spring admission, 12/1 for domestic students, 11/1 for international students. Applications are processed on a rolling basis. *Application fee:* $150. Electronic applications accepted. *Application Contact:* Dr. Nicole Okamoto, Department Chair, 408-924-4054, E-mail: nicole.okamoto@sjsu.edu. *Department Chair,* Dr. Nicole Okamoto, 408-924-4054, E-mail: nicole.okamoto@sjsu.edu.

**Program in Meteorology and Climate Science** Students: 6 full-time (4 women), 13 part-time (6 women); includes 5 minority (1 Black or African American, non-Hispanic/Latino; 3 Asian, non-Hispanic/Latino; 1 Hispanic/Latino). Average age 28. 11 applicants, 73% accepted, 4 enrolled. *Faculty:* 4 full-time (2 women). Expenses: Contact institution. *Financial support:* In 2019–20, 10 students received support, including 5 fellowships (averaging $5,000 per year), 5 research assistantships with full tuition reimbursements available (averaging $30,000 per year); scholarships/grants also available. Financial award application deadline: 5/1; financial award applicants required to submit FAFSA. In 2019, 5 master's awarded. *Application deadline:* For fall admission, 4/1 for domestic students, 5/1 for international students; for spring admission, 11/1 for domestic and international students. Applications are processed on a rolling basis. *Application fee:* $70. Electronic applications accepted. *Application Contact:* Sen Chiao, Department Chair, 408-924-5204, E-mail: sen.chiao@sjsu.edu. *Department Chair,* Sen Chiao, 408-924-5204, E-mail: sen.chiao@sjsu.edu.

**Program in Music and Dance** Students: 17 full-time (10 women), 15 part-time (9 women); includes 15 minority (12 Asian, non-Hispanic/Latino; 3 Hispanic/Latino), 4 international. Average age 30. 34 applicants, 56% accepted, 15 enrolled. *Faculty:* 9 full-time (5 women), 15 part-time/adjunct (3 women). Expenses: Contact institution. *Financial support:* In 2019–20, 16 students received support, including 5 fellowships (averaging $12,000 per year), 6 teaching assistantships with partial tuition reimbursements available (averaging $4,000 per year); Federal Work-Study, scholarships/grants, and unspecified assistantships also available. Financial award application deadline: 5/1; financial award applicants required to submit FAFSA. *Application deadline:* For fall admission, 5/1 for domestic and international students; for spring admission, 11/1 for domestic and international students; for summer admission, 5/1 for domestic students. Applications are processed on a rolling basis. *Application fee:* $70. Electronic applications accepted. *Application Contact:* Dr. Gordon Haramaki, Director of Graduate Studies, 408-924-4634, Fax: 408-924-4773, E-mail: gordon.haramaki@sjsu.edu. *Director, School of Music and Dance,* Dr. Fred Cohen, 408-924-4677, Fax: 408-924-4773, E-mail: fred.cohen@sjsu.edu.

**Program in Nursing** Students: 21 full-time (17 women), 52 part-time (49 women); includes 45 minority (4 Black or African American, non-Hispanic/Latino; 29 Asian, non-Hispanic/Latino; 12 Hispanic/Latino), 3 international. Average age 37. 30 applicants, 97% accepted, 23 enrolled. *Faculty:* 5 full-time (all women), 3 part-time/adjunct (all women). Expenses: Contact institution. *Financial support:* Application deadline: 5/1; applicants required to submit FAFSA. In 2019, 22 master's awarded. *Application deadline:* For fall admission, 3/1 for domestic students. Applications are processed on a rolling basis. *Application fee:* $70. Electronic applications accepted. *Application Contact:* Karen Wilcox, FNP Program Analyst, 408-924-3153, Fax: 408-924-3135, E-mail: karen.wilcox@sjsu.edu. *Department Chair,* Colleen O'Leary-Kelley, 408-924-1319, Fax: 408-924-3135, E-mail: colleen.oleary-kelley@sjsu.edu.

**Program in Nutrition, Food Science, and Packaging** Students: 25 full-time (20 women), 18 part-time (17 women); includes 19 minority (11 Asian, non-Hispanic/Latino; 8 Hispanic/Latino), 2 international. Average age 32. 51 applicants, 35% accepted, 9 enrolled. *Faculty:* 6 full-time (4 women), 4 part-time/adjunct (3 women). Expenses: Contact institution. *Financial support:* In 2019–20, 8 students received support. Scholarships/grants available. Financial award application deadline: 5/1; financial award applicants required to submit FAFSA. In 2019, 7 master's awarded. *Application deadline:* For fall admission, 2/1 for domestic and international students. Applications are processed on a rolling basis. *Application fee:* $70. Electronic applications accepted. *Application Contact:* Adrianne Widaman, Assistant Professor, E-mail: adrianne.widaman@sjsu.edu. *Department Chair,* Ashwini Wagle, 408-924-3100, E-mail: ashwini.wagle@sjsu.edu.

**Program in Occupational Therapy** Students: 156 full-time (128 women), 79 part-time (68 women); includes 88 minority (59 Asian, non-Hispanic/Latino; 29 Hispanic/Latino), 1 international. Average age 30. 216 applicants, 40% accepted, 76 enrolled. *Faculty:* 9 full-time (7 women), 13 part-time/adjunct (12 women). Expenses: Contact institution. *Financial support:* In 2019–20, 107 students received support, including 3 fellowships (averaging $3,833 per year), 5 research assistantships (averaging $3,800 per year); scholarships/grants also available. Financial award application deadline: 5/1; financial award applicants required to submit FAFSA. In 2019, 74 master's awarded. *Application deadline:* For fall admission, 2/1 for domestic and international students. Applications are processed on a rolling basis. *Application fee:* $70. Electronic applications accepted. *Application Contact:* Dr. Jerilyn "Gigi"? Smith, PhD, OTR/L, FAOTA, Graduate Admissions Coordinator, 408-924-3081, Fax: 408-924-3088, E-mail: gigi.smith@sjsu.edu.

**Program in Philosophy** Students: 4 full-time (1 woman), 13 part-time (1 woman); includes 7 minority (1 Asian, non-Hispanic/Latino; 6 Hispanic/Latino), 2 international. Average age 34. 13 applicants, 77% accepted, 5 enrolled. *Faculty:* 4 full-time (2 women), 2 part-time/adjunct (1 woman). Expenses: Contact institution. *Financial support:* In 2019–20, 7 students received support, including 1 fellowship (averaging $3,000 per year); scholarships/grants also available. Financial award application deadline: 5/1; financial award applicants required to submit FAFSA. In 2019, 7 master's awarded. *Application deadline:* For fall admission, 6/1 for domestic students, 5/1 for international students; for spring admission, 11/1 for domestic and international students. Applications are processed on a rolling basis. *Application fee:* $70. Electronic applications accepted. *Application Contact:* Carlos A. Sanchez, Professor, E-mail: carlos.sanchez@sjsu.edu. *Department Chair,* Janet D. Stemwedel, 408-924-4470, E-mail: janet.stemwedel@sjsu.edu.

**Program in Physics and Astronomy** *Program availability:* Part-time, evening/weekend. Electronic applications accepted.

**Program in Political Science** Students: 23 full-time (14 women), 70 part-time (46 women); includes 59 minority (5 Black or African American, non-Hispanic/Latino; 23 Asian, non-Hispanic/Latino; 29 Hispanic/Latino; 2 Native Hawaiian or other Pacific Islander, non-Hispanic/Latino), 5 international. Average age 31. 56 applicants, 64% accepted, 19 enrolled. *Faculty:* 5 full-time (1 woman), 4 part-time/adjunct (0 women). Expenses: Contact institution. *Financial support:* In 2019–20, 15 students received support, including 2 research assistantships (averaging $1,500 per year); scholarships/grants also available. Financial award application deadline: 5/1; financial award applicants required to submit FAFSA. In 2019, 16 master's awarded. *Program availability:* Part-time, evening/weekend. *Application deadline:* For fall admission, 4/1 for domestic students; for spring admission, 10/1 for domestic students. *Application fee:* $70. Electronic applications accepted. *Application Contact:* Dr. Frances Edwards, MPA Director, 408-806-7937, E-mail: frances.edwards@sjsu.edu. *Department Chair,* Dr. Garrick Percival, 408-924-5553, E-mail: garrick.percival@sjsu.edu.

**Program in Psychology** Students: 51 full-time (44 women), 30 part-time (21 women); includes 37 minority (2 Black or African American, non-Hispanic/Latino; 14 Asian, non-Hispanic/Latino; 21 Hispanic/Latino), 4 international. Average age 27. 184 applicants, 23% accepted, 31 enrolled. *Faculty:* 19 full-time (12 women), 2 part-time/adjunct (1 woman). Expenses: Contact institution. *Financial support:* In 2019–20, 22 students received support, including 1 research assistantship (averaging $500 per year); scholarships/grants also available. Financial award application deadline: 5/1; financial award applicants required to submit FAFSA. In 2019, 35 master's awarded. *Application deadline:* For fall admission, 2/1 for domestic and international students. *Application fee:* $70. Electronic applications accepted. *Application Contact:* Psychology Department, 408-924-5600, E-mail: psychology@sjsu.edu. *Professor and Chair,* Clifton Oyamot, 408-924-5650, E-mail: clifton.oyamot@sjsu.edu.

**Program in Social Work** *Program availability:* Part-time. Electronic applications accepted.

**Program in Special Education** Students: 37 full-time (31 women), 21 part-time (16 women); includes 24 minority (3 Black or African American, non-Hispanic/Latino; 7 Asian, non-Hispanic/Latino; 12 Hispanic/Latino; 2 Two or more races, non-Hispanic/Latino). 95 applicants, 63% accepted, 58 enrolled. *Faculty:* 6 full-time (5 women), 5 part-time/adjunct (all women). Expenses: Contact institution. *Financial support:* In 2019–20, 13 students received support, including 1 fellowship (averaging $4,500 per year); scholarships/grants also available. Financial award application deadline: 5/15; financial award applicants required to submit FAFSA. *Program availability:* Part-time, blended/hybrid learning. *Application deadline:* For fall admission, 7/1 for domestic students, 5/1 for international students; for spring admission, 11/1 for domestic and international students. Applications are processed on a rolling basis. *Application fee:* $70. Electronic applications accepted. *Application Contact:* Peg Hughes, Ph.D., Department Chair, 408-924-3673, Fax: 408-924-3701, E-mail: peg.hughes@sjsu.edu. *Department Chair,* Peg Hughes, Ph.D., 408-924-3673, Fax: 408-924-3701, E-mail: peg.hughes@sjsu.edu.

**Program in Technology**

**Program in Urban and Regional Planning** Students: 53 full-time (26 women), 47 part-time (18 women); includes 35 minority (5 Black or African American, non-Hispanic/Latino; 14 Asian, non-Hispanic/Latino; 16 Hispanic/Latino), 14 international. Average age 31. 58 applicants, 74% accepted, 25 enrolled. *Faculty:* 7 full-time (3 women), 5 part-time/adjunct (1 woman). Expenses: Contact institution. *Financial support:* In 2019–20, 15 students received support, including 3 research assistantships (averaging $4,000 per year); fellowships, Federal Work-Study, and scholarships/grants also available. Support available to part-time students. Financial award application deadline: 5/1; financial award applicants required to submit FAFSA. *Program availability:* Part-time, online only, 100% online, blended/hybrid learning. *Application deadline:* For fall admission, 7/1 for domestic students, 5/1 for international students; for winter admission, 12/1 for domestic students, 11/1 for international students. Applications are processed on a rolling basis. *Application fee:* $70 ($150 for international students). Electronic applications accepted. *Application Contact:* Richard Kos, AICP, Graduate Advisor, 408-924-5882, E-mail: gradadvisor-urbanplanning@sjsu.edu. *Department Chair,* Dr. Laxmi Ramasubramanian, AICP, 408-924-5882, E-mail: laxmi.ramasubramanian@sjsu.edu.

**Program in World Languages and Literature**

**Program Recreation and Leisure Studies**

**School of Information** Students: 489 full-time (383 women), 1,756 part-time (1,430 women); includes 655 minority (74 Black or African American, non-Hispanic/Latino; 164 Asian, non-Hispanic/Latino; 414 Hispanic/Latino; 3 Native Hawaiian or other Pacific Islander, non-Hispanic/Latino), 40 international. Average age 36. 988 applicants, 84% accepted, 601 enrolled. *Faculty:* 26 full-time (20 women), 41 part-time/adjunct (29 women). Expenses: Contact institution. *Financial support:* In 2019–20, 144 students received support. Scholarships/grants available. Financial award application deadline: 5/1; financial award applicants required to submit FAFSA. *Program availability:* Part-time, online only, 100% online. *Application deadline:* For fall admission, 5/1 for domestic students; for spring admission, 12/1 for domestic students. Applications are processed on a rolling basis. *Application fee:* $70. Electronic applications accepted. *Application Contact:* Dr. Linda Main, Interim Director, 408-924-2494, E-mail: linda.main@sjsu.edu. *Interim Director,* Dr. Linda Main, 408-924-2494, E-mail: linda.main@sjsu.edu.

**Teacher Education** Students: 44 full-time (33 women), 11 part-time (10 women); includes 23 minority (11 Asian, non-Hispanic/Latino; 12 Hispanic/Latino), 1 international. Average age 31. 11 applicants, 9% accepted, 1 enrolled. *Faculty:* 5 full-time (4 women), 8 part-time/adjunct (7 women). Expenses: Contact institution. *Financial support:* In 2019–20, 43 students received support. Career-related internships or fieldwork available. Financial award application deadline: 5/1; financial award applicants required to submit FAFSA. In 2019, 115 master's awarded. *Application deadline:* For fall admission, 6/1 for domestic students, 5/1 for international students; for spring admission, 11/1 for domestic students, 10/1 for international students; for summer admission, 4/1 for domestic students, 2/1 for international students. Applications are processed on a rolling basis. *Application fee:* $70. Electronic applications accepted. *Application Contact:* Deb Codiroli, Records Specialist, 408-924-3749. *Chair,* Patty Swanson, E-mail: patricia.swanson@sjsu.edu.

## SAN JUAN BAUTISTA SCHOOL OF MEDICINE, Caguas, PR 00726-4968

**General Information** Independent, coed, graduate-only institution. *Graduate housing:* On-campus housing not available. *Research affiliation:* Universidad Central del Caribe (molecular biology), Fundación de Investigacion de Puerto Rico (clinical and translational research), University of Puerto Rico, Medical Sciences Campus (molecular biology, microbiology, neurosciences, pediatrics, public health), Ponce School of

Medicine and Health Sciences (virology, immunology), Veteran Affairs (clinical research).
**GRADUATE UNITS**
**Graduate and Professional Programs**

## THE SANS TECHNOLOGY INSTITUTE, Bethesda, MD 20814
**General Information** Proprietary, coed, graduate-only institution.
**GRADUATE UNITS**
**Programs in Information Security**

## THE SANTA BARBARA AND VENTURA COLLEGES OF LAW–SANTA BARBARA, Santa Barbara, CA 93101
**General Information** Independent, coed, graduate-only institution.
**GRADUATE UNITS**
**Graduate and Professional Programs**

## THE SANTA BARBARA AND VENTURA COLLEGES OF LAW–VENTURA, Ventura, CA 93003
**General Information** Independent, coed, graduate-only institution.
**GRADUATE UNITS**
**Graduate and Professional Programs**

## SANTA CLARA UNIVERSITY, Santa Clara, CA 95053
**General Information** Independent-religious, coed, university. *Graduate housing:* Rooms and/or apartments available on a first-come, first-served basis to single and married students. Housing application deadline: 3/28.
**GRADUATE UNITS**
**College of Arts and Sciences** *Program availability:* Part-time, online learning. Electronic applications accepted.
**Jesuit School of Theology** *Program availability:* Part-time, online learning. Electronic applications accepted.
**Leavey School of Business** *Program availability:* Part-time, online learning. Electronic applications accepted.
**School of Education and Counseling Psychology** *Program availability:* Part-time, online learning. Electronic applications accepted.
**School of Engineering** *Program availability:* Part-time. Electronic applications accepted.
**School of Law** *Program availability:* Part-time, online learning. Electronic applications accepted.

## SARAH LAWRENCE COLLEGE, Bronxville, NY 10708-5999
**General Information** Independent, coed, comprehensive institution. CGS member. *Graduate housing:* On-campus housing not available. *Research affiliation:* Westchester Medical Center/New York Medical College, New York Hospital–Cornell Medical Center, Albert Einstein College of Medicine, New York University Medical Center, Columbia University Medical Center.
**GRADUATE UNITS**
**Graduate Studies** *Program availability:* Part-time. Electronic applications accepted.

## SAVANNAH COLLEGE OF ART AND DESIGN, Savannah, GA 31402-3146
**General Information** Independent, coed, comprehensive institution. CGS member. *Graduate housing:* Room and/or apartments available on a first-come, first-served basis to single students; on-campus housing not available to married students. Housing application deadline: 4/1.
**GRADUATE UNITS**
**Creative Business Leadership** *Program availability:* Part-time, 100% online. Electronic applications accepted.
**Program in Accessory Design** *Program availability:* Part-time. Electronic applications accepted.
**Program in Advertising** *Program availability:* Part-time. Electronic applications accepted.
**Program in Animation** *Program availability:* Part-time, 100% online. Electronic applications accepted.
**Program in Architectural History** *Program availability:* Part-time. Electronic applications accepted.
**Program in Architecture** *Program availability:* Part-time. Electronic applications accepted.
**Program in Art History** *Program availability:* Part-time. Electronic applications accepted.
**Program in Cinema Studies** *Program availability:* Part-time. Electronic applications accepted.
**Program in Design for Sustainability** *Program availability:* Part-time. Electronic applications accepted.
**Program in Design Management** *Program availability:* Part-time, 100% online. Electronic applications accepted.
**Program in Dramatic Writing** *Program availability:* Part-time. Electronic applications accepted.
**Program in Fashion** *Program availability:* Part-time, 100% online. Electronic applications accepted.
**Program in Fibers** *Program availability:* Part-time. Electronic applications accepted.
**Program in Film and Television** *Program availability:* Part-time. Electronic applications accepted.
**Program in Furniture Design** *Program availability:* Part-time. Electronic applications accepted.
**Program in Graphic Design and Visual Experience** *Program availability:* Part-time, 100% online. Electronic applications accepted.
**Program in Illustration** *Program availability:* Part-time, 100% online. Electronic applications accepted.
**Program in Industrial Design** *Program availability:* Part-time. Electronic applications accepted.
**Program in Interactive Design and Game Development** *Program availability:* Part-time, 100% online. Electronic applications accepted.
**Program in Interior Design** *Program availability:* Part-time, 100% online. Electronic applications accepted.
**Program in Jewelry** *Program availability:* Part-time. Electronic applications accepted.
**Program in Luxury and Fashion Management** *Program availability:* Part-time, 100% online. Electronic applications accepted.
**Program in Motion Media Design** *Program availability:* Part-time, 100% online. Electronic applications accepted.
**Program in Painting** *Program availability:* Part-time, 100% online. Electronic applications accepted.
**Program in Performing Arts** *Program availability:* Part-time. Electronic applications accepted.
**Program in Photography** *Program availability:* Part-time, 100% online. Electronic applications accepted.
**Program in Preservation Design** *Program availability:* Part-time, 100% online. Electronic applications accepted.
**Program in Production Design** *Program availability:* Part-time. Electronic applications accepted.
**Program in Sculpture** *Program availability:* Part-time. Electronic applications accepted.
**Program in Sequential Art** *Program availability:* Part-time. Electronic applications accepted.
**Program in Service Design** *Program availability:* Part-time. Electronic applications accepted.
**Program in Sound Design** *Program availability:* Part-time. Electronic applications accepted.
**Program in Themed Entertainment Design** *Program availability:* Part-time. Electronic applications accepted.
**Program in Urban Design** *Program availability:* Part-time. Electronic applications accepted.
**Program in Visual Effects** *Program availability:* Part-time. Electronic applications accepted.
**Program in Writing** *Program availability:* Part-time, 100% online. Electronic applications accepted.

## SAVANNAH STATE UNIVERSITY, Savannah, GA 31404
**General Information** State-supported, coed, comprehensive institution. CGS member. *Graduate housing:* Room and/or apartments available on a first-come, first-served basis to single students; on-campus housing not available to married students. Housing application deadline: 5/1. *Research affiliation:* Office of Naval Research (ONR) (marine science), Living Marine Resources Cooperative Science Center (LMRCSC) (marine science), National Institute of Mental Health (NIMH) (social work), U.S. Department of Homeland Security (urban studies and planning), Skidaway Institute of Oceanography (marine science), University of Georgia Marine Education Center & Aquarium (marine science).
**GRADUATE UNITS**
**Master of Business Administration Program** *Program availability:* Part-time, evening/weekend. Electronic applications accepted.
**Master of Public Administration Program** *Program availability:* Part-time. Electronic applications accepted.
**Master of Science in Marine Sciences Program** *Program availability:* Part-time. Electronic applications accepted.
**Master of Science in Urban Studies and Planning Program** *Program availability:* Part-time. Electronic applications accepted.
**Master of Social Work Program**

## SAYBROOK UNIVERSITY, San Francisco, CA 94612
**General Information** Independent, coed, graduate-only institution. *Research affiliation:* Rollo May Center for Humanistic Studies.
**GRADUATE UNITS**
**LIOS MA Residential Programs**
**School of Clinical Psychology**
**School of Mind-Body Medicine** Electronic applications accepted.
**School of Organizational Leadership and Transformation**
**School of Psychology and Interdisciplinary Inquiry** *Program availability:* Online learning. Electronic applications accepted.

## SCHILLER INTERNATIONAL UNIVERSITY - HEIDELBERG, 69115 Heidelberg, Germany
**General Information** Independent, coed, comprehensive institution. *Graduate housing:* Room and/or apartments available on a first-come, first-served basis to single students; on-campus housing not available to married students.
**GRADUATE UNITS**
**MBA Programs, Heidelberg, Germany** *Program availability:* Part-time, evening/weekend.

## SCHILLER INTERNATIONAL UNIVERSITY - MADRID, 28002 Madrid, Spain
**General Information** Independent, coed, comprehensive institution. *Graduate housing:* On-campus housing not available.
**GRADUATE UNITS**
**MBA Program, Madrid, Spain** *Program availability:* Part-time.

## SCHILLER INTERNATIONAL UNIVERSITY - PARIS, F-75015 Paris, France
**General Information** Independent, coed, comprehensive institution. *Graduate housing:* On-campus housing not available.
**GRADUATE UNITS**
**MBA Program Paris, France** *Program availability:* Part-time, evening/weekend, online learning.
**Program in International Relations and Diplomacy** *Program availability:* Part-time, evening/weekend.

## SCHILLER INTERNATIONAL UNIVERSITY - TAMPA, Largo, FL 33771
**General Information** Independent, coed, comprehensive institution. *Graduate housing:* Room and/or apartments available on a first-come, first-served basis to single students; on-campus housing not available to married students. Housing application deadline: 8/1.

**GRADUATE UNITS**

**MBA Programs, Florida** *Program availability:* Part-time, evening/weekend, online learning.

## SCHOOL OF ADVANCED AIR AND SPACE STUDIES, Maxwell AFB, AL 36112-6424

**General Information** Federally supported, coed, primarily men, graduate-only institution.

**GRADUATE UNITS**

**Program in Airpower Art and Science**

## SCHOOL OF ARCHITECTURE AT TALIESIN, Scottsdale, AZ 85261-4430

**General Information** Independent, coed, graduate-only institution. *Graduate housing:* Rooms and/or apartments guaranteed to single students and available on a first-come, first-served basis to married students. Housing application deadline: 3/20.

**GRADUATE UNITS**

**Graduate Program** Electronic applications accepted.

## SCHOOL OF THE ART INSTITUTE OF CHICAGO, Chicago, IL 60603-3103

**General Information** Independent, coed, comprehensive institution. *Graduate housing:* Room and/or apartments available on a first-come, first-served basis to single students; on-campus housing not available to married students. Housing application deadline: 8/27.

## SCHOOL OF VISUAL ARTS, New York, NY 10010-3994

**General Information** Proprietary, coed, comprehensive institution. CGS member. *Graduate housing:* Room and/or apartments available on a first-come, first-served basis to single students; on-campus housing not available to married students.

**GRADUATE UNITS**

**Graduate Programs** Electronic applications accepted.

## SCHREINER UNIVERSITY, Kerrville, TX 78028-5697

**General Information** Independent-religious, coed, comprehensive institution. *Enrollment:* 1,342 graduate, professional, and undergraduate students; 65 full-time matriculated graduate/professional students (49 women), 20 part-time matriculated graduate/professional students (14 women). *Enrollment by degree level:* 67 master's, 18 other advanced degrees. *Graduate faculty:* 4 full-time (1 woman), 10 part-time/adjunct (5 women). *Tuition:* Full-time $10,332; part-time $574 per credit hour. *Required fees:* $200; $100 per term. Tuition and fees vary according to course load and program. *Graduate housing:* Room and/or apartments available on a first-come, first-served basis to single students; on-campus housing not available to married students. Typical cost: $7134 per year. Room charges vary according to board plan. *Student services:* Campus employment opportunities, campus safety program, career counseling, exercise/wellness program, free psychological counseling, services for students with disabilities, teacher training. *Library facilities:* W. M. Logan Library. *Collection:* Books: 75,807 (physical), 201,500 (digital/electronic); Serial titles: 45 (physical), 49,182 (digital/electronic); Databases: 104. Weekly public service hours: 30; students can reserve study rooms.

**Computer facilities:** Computer purchase and lease plans are available. 120 computers available on campus for general student use. A campuswide network can be accessed. Online class registration is available.
Website: http://www.schreiner.edu/

**General Application Contact:** Magda Riveros, Graduate Admission Counselor, 830-792-7224, Fax: 830-792-7226, E-mail: gradadmissions@schreiner.edu.

**GRADUATE UNITS**

**Department of Education** Students: 31 full-time (24 women), 2 part-time (1 woman); includes 15 minority (5 Black or African American, non-Hispanic/Latino; 8 Hispanic/Latino; 2 Two or more races, non-Hispanic/Latino). Average age 36. 29 applicants, 93% accepted, 25 enrolled. *Faculty:* 2 full-time (1 woman), 4 part-time/adjunct (3 women). Expenses: Contact institution. *Financial support:* In 2019–20, 31 students received support. Scholarships/grants available. Financial award application deadline: 8/1; financial award applicants required to submit FAFSA. In 2019, 29 master's, 11 Certificates awarded. *Program availability:* Part-time, evening/weekend, online learning. *Application deadline:* For fall admission, 8/1 priority date for domestic students, 8/1 for international students; for spring admission, 12/1 priority date for domestic students, 12/1 for international students; for summer admission, 5/1 priority date for domestic students, 5/1 for international students. Applications are processed on a rolling basis. *Application fee:* $25. Electronic applications accepted. *Application Contact:* Magda Riveros, Graduate Admission Counselor, 830-792-7224, Fax: 830-792-7226, E-mail: MRiveros@schreiner.edu. *Director, Teacher Education,* Dr. Neva Cramer, 830-792-7266, Fax: 830-792-7382, E-mail: nvcramer@schreiner.edu.

**MBA Program** Students: 23 full-time (15 women), 11 part-time (7 women); includes 17 minority (2 Black or African American, non-Hispanic/Latino; 1 Asian, non-Hispanic/Latino; 14 Hispanic/Latino). Average age 30. 45 applicants, 93% accepted, 20 enrolled. *Faculty:* 2 full-time (0 women), 6 part-time/adjunct (2 women). Expenses: Contact institution. *Financial support:* In 2019–20, 31 students received support. Application deadline: 8/1; applicants required to submit FAFSA. In 2019, 30 master's awarded. *Program availability:* Part-time, online only, 100% online. *Application deadline:* For fall admission, 8/1 priority date for domestic students, 8/1 for international students; for spring admission, 12/1 priority date for domestic students, 12/1 for international students; for summer admission, 5/1 priority date for domestic students, 4/1 for international students. Applications are processed on a rolling basis. *Application fee:* $25. Electronic applications accepted. *Application Contact:* Magda Riveros, Graduate Admission Counselor, 800-343-4919, Fax: 830-792-7226, E-mail: MRiveros@schreiner.edu. *Director,* Dr. Mark Woodhull, 830-792-7479.

## THE SCRIPPS RESEARCH INSTITUTE, La Jolla, CA 92037

**General Information** Independent, coed, graduate-only institution. *Graduate housing:* On-campus housing not available.

**GRADUATE UNITS**

**Kellogg School of Science and Technology** Electronic applications accepted.

## SEATTLE INSTITUTE OF EAST ASIAN MEDICINE, Seattle, WA 98115

**General Information** Proprietary, coed, primarily women, graduate-only institution. *Graduate housing:* On-campus housing not available.

**GRADUATE UNITS**

**Graduate Program**

## SEATTLE PACIFIC UNIVERSITY, Seattle, WA 98119-1997

**General Information** Independent-religious, coed, comprehensive institution. *Enrollment:* 3,529 graduate, professional, and undergraduate students; 368 full-time matriculated graduate/professional students (287 women), 410 part-time matriculated graduate/professional students (291 women). *Enrollment by degree level:* 537 master's, 193 doctoral, 48 other advanced degrees. *Graduate housing:* Rooms and/or apartments available on a first-come, first-served basis to single and married students. Housing application deadline: 8/1. *Student services:* Campus employment opportunities, campus safety program, career counseling, exercise/wellness program, free psychological counseling, international student services, low-cost health insurance, multicultural affairs office, services for students with disabilities, teacher training, writing training. *Library facilities:* University Library. *Collection:* Books: 233,157 (physical), 269,170 (digital/electronic); Serial titles: 3,293 (physical), 92,500 (digital/electronic); Databases: 213. *Research affiliation:* Washington Research Center/Gates Foundation (education effectiveness), Fred Hutchinson Cancer Research Center (cancer and tumors), Battelle Research Center (business marketing).

**Computer facilities:** 150 computers available on campus for general student use. A campuswide network can be accessed. Online class registration is available.
Website: http://www.spu.edu/

**GRADUATE UNITS**

**Doctoral Program in Education** Students: 10 part-time (8 women); includes 2 minority (1 Black or African American, non-Hispanic/Latino; 1 Two or more races, non-Hispanic/Latino), 1 international. Average age 46. 8 applicants, 50% accepted, 3 enrolled. Expenses: Contact institution. *Financial support:* Career-related internships or fieldwork available. Financial award applicants required to submit FAFSA. In 2019, 8 doctorates awarded. *Application deadline:* For fall admission, 8/15 for domestic students; for winter admission, 11/15 for domestic students; for spring admission, 2/15 for domestic students; for summer admission, 5/15 for domestic students. Applications are processed on a rolling basis. *Application fee:* $50. *Application Contact:* Nyaradzo Mvududu, Director of Doctoral Programs, 206-281-2551, E-mail: nyaradzo@spu.edu. *Director of Doctoral Programs,* Nyaradzo Mvududu, 206-281-2551, E-mail: nyaradzo@spu.edu.

**Educational Leadership Programs** Students: 4 full-time (2 women), 47 part-time (30 women); includes 12 minority (4 Black or African American, non-Hispanic/Latino; 1 American Indian or Alaska Native, non-Hispanic/Latino; 2 Asian, non-Hispanic/Latino; 4 Hispanic/Latino; 1 Two or more races, non-Hispanic/Latino). Average age 41. 19 applicants, 74% accepted, 10 enrolled. Expenses: Contact institution. *Financial support:* Career-related internships or fieldwork available. Financial award applicants required to submit FAFSA. In 2019, 11 master's awarded. *Program availability:* Part-time, evening/weekend. *Application deadline:* For fall admission, 8/15 priority date for domestic students; for winter admission, 11/15 for domestic students; for spring admission, 2/15 priority date for domestic students; for summer admission, 5/15 for domestic students. Applications are processed on a rolling basis. *Application fee:* $50. Electronic applications accepted. *Application Contact:* The Graduate Center, 206-281-2091. *Chair,* Dr. William Prenevost, 206-281-2370, Fax: 206-281-2756, E-mail: prenew@spu.edu.

**Industrial-Organizational Psychology Program** Students: 53 full-time (39 women), 23 part-time (16 women); includes 24 minority (4 Black or African American, non-Hispanic/Latino; 1 American Indian or Alaska Native, non-Hispanic/Latino; 9 Asian, non-Hispanic/Latino; 6 Hispanic/Latino; 4 Two or more races, non-Hispanic/Latino), 2 international. Average age 28. 67 applicants, 43% accepted, 29 enrolled. Expenses: Contact institution. *Financial support:* Applicants required to submit FAFSA. In 2019, 28 master's, 3 doctorates awarded. *Application deadline:* For fall admission, 12/15 for domestic and international students. *Application fee:* $50. Electronic applications accepted. *Application Contact:* The Graduate Center, 206-281-2091. *Chair,* Dr. Robert B. McKenna, 206-281-2629, E-mail: rmckenna@spu.edu.

**Master of Arts in Management Program** Expenses: Contact institution. *Application deadline:* For fall admission, 8/1 for domestic students, 6/1 for international students; for winter admission, 11/1 for domestic students, 9/1 for international students; for spring admission, 2/1 for domestic students, 12/1 for international students; for summer admission, 5/1 for domestic students. *Application fee:* $50.

**Master of Arts in Teaching Program** Students: 79 full-time (58 women), 68 part-time (46 women); includes 36 minority (2 Black or African American, non-Hispanic/Latino; 1 American Indian or Alaska Native, non-Hispanic/Latino; 7 Asian, non-Hispanic/Latino; 16 Hispanic/Latino; 1 Native Hawaiian or other Pacific Islander, non-Hispanic/Latino; 9 Two or more races, non-Hispanic/Latino), 2 international. Average age 33. 54 applicants, 74% accepted, 28 enrolled. Expenses: Contact institution. *Financial support:* Scholarships/grants available. Financial award applicants required to submit FAFSA. In 2019, 78 master's awarded. *Program availability:* Part-time, evening/weekend. *Application deadline:* For fall admission, 3/15 for domestic students. *Application fee:* $50. Electronic applications accepted. *Application Contact:* Graduate Admission, 206-281-2091.

**Master of Arts in Theology Program** Students: 22 full-time (14 women), 30 part-time (13 women); includes 20 minority (10 Black or African American, non-Hispanic/Latino; 6 Asian, non-Hispanic/Latino; 3 Hispanic/Latino; 1 Native Hawaiian or other Pacific Islander, non-Hispanic/Latino), 3 international. Average age 34. 21 applicants, 52% accepted, 11 enrolled. Expenses: Contact institution. *Financial support:* Application deadline: 4/1; applicants required to submit FAFSA. In 2019, 15 master's awarded. *Application deadline:* For fall admission, 7/31 for domestic students, 6/15 for international students; for winter admission, 11/15 for domestic students; for spring admission, 2/15 for domestic students; for summer admission, 5/1 for domestic students. Applications are processed on a rolling basis. *Application fee:* $50. Electronic applications accepted. *Application Contact:* Dr. Doug Strong, Dean, 206-281-2473, E-mail: dstrong@spu.edu. *Dean,* Dr. Doug Strong, 206-281-2473, E-mail: dstrong@spu.edu.

**Master of Business Administration Program** Students: 3 full-time (2 women), 23 part-time (15 women); includes 8 minority (3 Black or African American, non-Hispanic/Latino; 3 Asian, non-Hispanic/Latino; 1 Hispanic/Latino; 1 Two or more races, non-Hispanic/Latino), 5 international. Average age 33. 18 applicants, 11% accepted, 1 enrolled. Expenses: Contact institution. *Financial support:* Scholarships/grants available. Financial award applicants required to submit FAFSA. In 2019, 19 master's awarded. *Program availability:* Part-time. *Application deadline:* For fall admission, 8/1 for domestic and international students; for winter admission, 11/1 for domestic and international students; for spring admission, 2/1 for domestic and international students. Applications are processed on a rolling basis. *Application fee:* $50. Electronic applications accepted. *Application Contact:* Gary Karns, Associate Dean for Graduate

Studies, 206-281-2948, Fax: 206-281-2733. *Associate Dean for Graduate Studies*, Gary Karns, 206-281-2948, Fax: 206-281-2733.

**Master of Divinity Program** Students: 2 full-time (1 woman), 1 part-time (0 women). Average age 32. 19 applicants, 53% accepted, 10 enrolled. Expenses: Contact institution. *Financial support:* Scholarships/grants available. Financial award applicants required to submit FAFSA. *Application deadline:* For fall admission, 7/31 for domestic students; for winter admission, 11/15 for domestic students; for spring admission, 2/15 for domestic students; for summer admission, 5/1 for domestic students. *Application fee:* $50. *Application Contact:* Dr. Doug Strong, Dean, 206-281-2473, E-mail: dstrong@spu.edu. *Dean*, Dr. Doug Strong, 206-281-2473, E-mail: dstrong@spu.edu.

**Master of Education in Literacy Program** Students: 10 part-time (all women); includes 1 minority (Asian, non-Hispanic/Latino). Average age 34. 3 applicants, 100% accepted, 3 enrolled. Expenses: Contact institution. *Financial support:* Scholarships/grants available. Financial award applicants required to submit FAFSA. In 2019, 6 master's awarded. *Program availability:* Part-time. *Application deadline:* For fall admission, 8/15 for domestic students; for winter admission, 11/15 for domestic students; for spring admission, 2/15 for domestic students; for summer admission, 5/15 for domestic students. Applications are processed on a rolling basis. *Application fee:* $50. Electronic applications accepted. *Application Contact:* The Graduate Center, 206-281-2091. *Chair*, Dr. Scott F. Beers, 206-281-2707, E-mail: sbeers@spu.edu.

**Master of Education in School Counseling Program** Students: 46 full-time (42 women), 34 part-time (26 women); includes 20 minority (1 Black or African American, non-Hispanic/Latino; 10 Asian, non-Hispanic/Latino; 5 Hispanic/Latino; 1 Native Hawaiian or other Pacific Islander, non-Hispanic/Latino; 3 Two or more races, non-Hispanic/Latino), 3 international. Average age 30. 70 applicants, 13% accepted, 9 enrolled. Expenses: Contact institution. *Financial support:* Scholarships/grants available. Financial award applicants required to submit FAFSA. In 2019, 29 master's awarded. *Program availability:* Part-time. *Application deadline:* For fall admission, 4/1 priority date for domestic students; for spring admission, 2/15 priority date for domestic students. *Application fee:* $50. Electronic applications accepted. *Application Contact:* Dr. June Hyun, Chair, 206-281-2671, Fax: 206-281-2756, E-mail: jhyun@spu.edu. *Chair*, Dr. June Hyun, 206-281-2671, Fax: 206-281-2756, E-mail: jhyun@spu.edu.

**Master of Education in Teacher Leadership Program** Students: 28 part-time (24 women); includes 2 minority (both Hispanic/Latino), 2 international. Average age 36. 7 applicants, 57% accepted, 1 enrolled. Expenses: Contact institution. *Financial support:* Applicants required to submit FAFSA. In 2019, 10 master's awarded. *Program availability:* Part-time, evening/weekend. *Application deadline:* For fall admission, 8/15 priority date for domestic students, 7/1 for international students; for winter admission, 11/15 for domestic students; for spring admission, 2/15 for domestic students, 3/1 for international students; for summer admission, 5/15 for domestic students. Applications are processed on a rolling basis. *Application fee:* $50. Electronic applications accepted. *Application Contact:* The Graduate Center, 206-281-2091. *Chair*, Daniel Bishop, 206-281-2593, E-mail: bishod@spu.edu.

**Master of Fine Arts in Creative Writing Program** Students: 1 (woman) full-time, 35 part-time (27 women); includes 4 minority (1 Asian, non-Hispanic/Latino; 2 Hispanic/Latino; 1 Two or more races, non-Hispanic/Latino). Average age 33. 23 applicants, 35% accepted, 8 enrolled. Expenses: Contact institution. *Financial support:* Applicants required to submit FAFSA. In 2019, 11 master's awarded. *Program availability:* Part-time. *Application deadline:* For winter admission, 11/1 for domestic students; for summer admission, 5/1 for domestic students. *Application fee:* $50. Electronic applications accepted. *Application Contact:* The Graduate Center, 206-281-2091. *Director*, Dr. Scott Cairns, 206-281-2109, E-mail: gwolfe@spu.edu.

**Master of Science in Data Analytics in Business** Students: 1 (woman) full-time, 12 part-time (7 women), 9 international. Average age 31. 13 applicants, 69% accepted, 6 enrolled. Expenses: Contact institution. *Application Contact:* Gary Karns, Associate Dean for Graduate Programs, E-mail: gkarns@spu.edu. *Associate Dean for Graduate Programs*, Gary Karns, E-mail: gkarns@spu.edu.

**Master of Science in Information Systems Management Program** Students: 2 full-time (1 woman), 13 part-time (8 women); includes 5 minority (2 Black or African American, non-Hispanic/Latino; 2 Asian, non-Hispanic/Latino; 1 Hispanic/Latino), 9 international. Average age 31. 13 applicants, 15% accepted, 1 enrolled. Expenses: Contact institution. *Financial support:* Applicants required to submit FAFSA. In 2019, 11 master's awarded. *Program availability:* Part-time. *Application deadline:* For fall admission, 8/1 for domestic students, 6/1 for international students; for winter admission, 11/1 for domestic and international students; for spring admission, 2/1 for domestic students, 12/1 for international students; for summer admission, 5/1 for domestic students. Applications are processed on a rolling basis. *Application fee:* $50. Electronic applications accepted. *Application Contact:* Gary Karns, Associate Dean for Graduate Studies, 206-281-2948, Fax: 206-281-2733. *Associate Dean for Graduate Studies*, Gary Karns, 206-281-2948, Fax: 206-281-2733.

**MS in Marriage and Family Therapy Program** Students: 51 full-time (44 women), 12 part-time (9 women); includes 16 minority (3 Black or African American, non-Hispanic/Latino; 6 Asian, non-Hispanic/Latino; 3 Hispanic/Latino; 4 Two or more races, non-Hispanic/Latino), 3 international. Average age 31. 60 applicants, 47% accepted, 27 enrolled. Expenses: Contact institution. *Financial support:* Fellowships and Federal Work-Study available. Financial award applicants required to submit FAFSA. In 2019, 22 master's awarded. *Program availability:* Part-time. *Application deadline:* For fall admission, 1/23 for domestic students, 2/1 for international students. Applications are processed on a rolling basis. *Application fee:* $50. Electronic applications accepted. *Application Contact:* Dr. Scott Edwards, Chair, 206-281-2681, E-mail: sedwards@spu.edu. *Chair*, Dr. Scott Edwards, 206-281-2681, E-mail: sedwards@spu.edu.

**MS in Nursing Program** Students: 42 full-time (38 women), 18 part-time (16 women); includes 28 minority (5 Black or African American, non-Hispanic/Latino; 18 Asian, non-Hispanic/Latino; 5 Hispanic/Latino), 2 international. Average age 33. 59 applicants, 41% accepted. Expenses: Contact institution. *Financial support:* Fellowships and scholarships/grants available. Financial award applicants required to submit FAFSA. In 2019, 10 master's awarded. *Program availability:* Part-time. *Application deadline:* For fall admission, 1/15 priority date for domestic students; for spring admission, 1/15 for domestic students. Applications are processed on a rolling basis. *Application fee:* $50. Electronic applications accepted. *Application Contact:* Dr. Antwinett Lee, Associate Dean, 206-281-2607, E-mail: leea30@spu.edu. *Associate Dean*, Dr. Antwinett Lee, 206-281-2607, E-mail: leea30@spu.edu.

**PhD in Clinical Psychology Program** Students: 48 full-time (36 women), 21 part-time (18 women); includes 21 minority (3 Black or African American, non-Hispanic/Latino; 8 Asian, non-Hispanic/Latino; 7 Hispanic/Latino; 3 Two or more races, non-Hispanic/Latino), 4 international. Average age 28. 91 applicants, 13% accepted, 12 enrolled. Expenses: Contact institution. *Financial support:* Fellowships and scholarships/grants available. Financial award applicants required to submit FAFSA. In 2019, 5 doctorates awarded. *Application deadline:* For fall admission, 12/15 for domestic and international students. Electronic applications accepted. *Application Contact:* Dr. Amy Mezuli, Chair of Clinical Psychology, 206-281-2820, E-mail: mezulis@spu.edu. *Chair of Clinical Psychology*, Dr. Amy Mezuli, 206-281-2820, E-mail: mezulis@spu.edu.

**PhD in Counselor Education Program** Students: 1 (woman) full-time, 3 part-time (all women); includes 1 minority (Two or more races, non-Hispanic/Latino). Average age 35. Expenses: Contact institution. In 2019, 2 doctorates awarded. *Application deadline:* For fall admission, 8/15 for domestic students; for winter admission, 11/15 for domestic students; for spring admission, 2/15 for domestic students; for summer admission, 5/15 for domestic students. *Application fee:* $50. *Application Contact:* Munyi Shea, Chair, 206-281-2369, E-mail: mshea@spu.edu. *Chair*, Munyi Shea, 206-281-2369, E-mail: mshea@spu.edu.

**Program in Digital Education Leadership** Students: 16 part-time (13 women); includes 2 minority (1 Asian, non-Hispanic/Latino; 1 Two or more races, non-Hispanic/Latino). Average age 38. 8 applicants, 100% accepted, 4 enrolled. Expenses: Contact institution. In 2019, 7 master's awarded. *Application deadline:* For fall admission, 9/8 for domestic students. *Application Contact:* Graduate Center, 206-281-2091. *Dean*, Rick Eigenbrood, 206-281-2710, E-mail: eigend@spu.edu.

**Program in Teaching Mathematics and Science** Students: 13 full-time (7 women), 6 part-time (2 women); includes 5 minority (2 Asian, non-Hispanic/Latino; 1 Hispanic/Latino; 2 Two or more races, non-Hispanic/Latino). Average age 34. 27 applicants, 63% accepted, 16 enrolled. Expenses: Contact institution. In 2019, 15 master's awarded. *Application deadline:* For fall admission, 8/15 for domestic students; for winter admission, 11/15 for domestic students; for spring admission, 2/15 for domestic students; for summer admission, 5/15 for domestic students. *Application Contact:* David W. Dento, Graduate Teacher Education Chair, 206-281-2504, E-mail: dentod@spu.edu. *Graduate Teacher Education Chair*, David W. Dento, 206-281-2504, E-mail: dentod@spu.edu.

## THE SEATTLE SCHOOL OF THEOLOGY AND PSYCHOLOGY, Seattle, WA 98121

**General Information** Independent-religious, coed, graduate-only institution.

**GRADUATE UNITS**

**Graduate Programs** *Program availability:* Part-time.

## SEATTLE UNIVERSITY, Seattle, WA 98122-1090

**General Information** Independent-religious, coed, comprehensive institution. *Enrollment:* 7,199 graduate, professional, and undergraduate students. *Enrollment by degree level:* 1,549 master's, 416 doctoral, 657 other advanced degrees. *Graduate housing:* Room and/or apartments available on a first-come, first-served basis to single students; on-campus housing not available to married students. *Student services:* Campus employment opportunities, campus safety program, career counseling, exercise/wellness program, free psychological counseling, international student services, low-cost health insurance, multicultural affairs office, services for students with disabilities, teacher training, writing training. *Library facilities:* Lemieux Library & McGoldrick Learning Commons plus 1 other. *Collection:* Books: 472,572 (physical), 257,641 (digital/electronic); Serial titles: 118,353 (physical), 8,597 (digital/electronic); Databases: 235. Students can reserve study rooms. *Research affiliation:* Swedish Medical Centers (nursing).

**Computer facilities:** Computer purchase and lease plans are available. 467 computers available on campus for general student use. A campuswide network can be accessed. Online class registration is available.
Website: http://www.seattleu.edu/

**General Application Contact:** Janet Shandley, Director of Graduate Admissions, 206-296-5900, Fax: 206-298-5656, E-mail: grad_admissions@seattleu.edu.

**GRADUATE UNITS**

**Albers School of Business and Economics** Average age 30. 454 applicants, 63% accepted, 162 enrolled. Expenses: Contact institution. *Financial support:* In 2019–20, 174 students received support. Fellowships with partial tuition reimbursements available, research assistantships, career-related internships or fieldwork, Federal Work-Study, scholarships/grants, and unspecified assistantships available. Support available to part-time students. Financial award application deadline: 6/1; financial award applicants required to submit FAFSA. In 2019, 254 master's, 66 other advanced degrees awarded. *Program availability:* Part-time, evening/weekend. *Application deadline:* For fall admission, 8/20 priority date for domestic students, 4/1 priority date for international students; for winter admission, 11/20 priority date for domestic students, 9/1 priority date for international students; for spring admission, 2/20 priority date for domestic students, 12/1 priority date for international students; for summer admission, 5/20 priority date for domestic students, 1/1 priority date for international students. Applications are processed on a rolling basis. *Application fee:* $55. Electronic applications accepted. *Application Contact:* Jeff Millard, Assistant Dean of Graduate Programs, 206-296-5700, E-mail: albersgrad@seattleu.edu. *Dean*, Dr. Joseph M. Phillips, Jr., 206-296-5700, Fax: 206-296-5795, E-mail: phillipsj@seattleu.edu.

***Center for Leadership Formation*** Average age 42. 40 applicants, 98% accepted, 31 enrolled. Expenses: Contact institution. *Financial support:* In 2019–20, 17 students received support. Scholarships/grants available. Financial award applicants required to submit FAFSA. In 2019, 25 master's, 16 other advanced degrees awarded. *Program availability:* Evening/weekend. *Application deadline:* Applications are processed on a rolling basis. *Application fee:* $55. Electronic applications accepted. *Application Contact:* Sommer Harrison, Manager, Graduate Programs Outreach, 206-296-2529, E-mail: emba@seattleu.edu. *Associate Dean of Executive Education*, Dr. Marilyn Gist, 206-296-5413, E-mail: gistm@seattleu.edu.

**College of Arts and Sciences** Average age 30. 306 applicants, 71% accepted, 135 enrolled. Expenses: Contact institution. *Financial support:* In 2019–20, 161 students received support. Career-related internships or fieldwork, Federal Work-Study, scholarships/grants, and unspecified assistantships available. Support available to part-time students. Financial award application deadline: 3/15; financial award applicants required to submit FAFSA. In 2019, 169 master's, 10 other advanced degrees awarded. *Program availability:* Part-time, evening/weekend. *Application deadline:* For fall admission, 1/15 for domestic and international students; for winter admission, 10/15 for domestic and international students; for spring admission, 2/15 for domestic and international students. Applications are processed on a rolling basis. *Application fee:* $55. Electronic applications accepted. *Application Contact:* Janet Shandley, Director of Graduate Admissions, 206-296-5900, Fax: 206-298-5656, E-mail: grad_admissions@seattleu.edu. *Dean*, Dr. David Powers, 206-296-5300, E-mail: powersda@seattleu.edu.

***Center for the Study of Sport and Exercise*** Average age 26. 1 applicant, 100% accepted, 1 enrolled. Expenses: Contact institution. *Financial support:* In 2019–20, 20 students received support. Research assistantships and scholarships/grants available. Financial award applicants required to submit FAFSA. In 2019, 22 master's awarded. *Program availability:* Part-time, evening/weekend. *Application deadline:* For fall admission, 2/15 for domestic and international students. *Application fee:* $55.

Electronic applications accepted. *Application Contact:* Janet Shandley, Associate Dean of Graduate Admissions, 206-296-5900, Fax: 206-298-5656, E-mail: grad_admissions@seattleu.edu. *Director,* Dr. Dan Tripps, 206-398-4605, E-mail: trippsd@seattleu.edu.

***Institute of Public Service*** Students: 11 full-time (6 women), 111 part-time (69 women); includes 59 minority (17 Black or African American, non-Hispanic/Latino; 1 American Indian or Alaska Native, non-Hispanic/Latino; 9 Asian, non-Hispanic/Latino; 22 Hispanic/Latino; 1 Native Hawaiian or other Pacific Islander, non-Hispanic/Latino; 9 Two or more races, non-Hispanic/Latino), 1 international. Average age 31. 53 applicants, 91% accepted, 35 enrolled. *Faculty:* 7 full-time (4 women), 3 part-time/adjunct (2 women). Expenses: Contact institution. *Financial support:* In 2019–20, 23 students received support. Career-related internships or fieldwork, Federal Work-Study, and unspecified assistantships available. Support available to part-time students. Financial award applicants required to submit FAFSA. In 2019, 50 master's awarded. *Program availability:* Part-time, evening/weekend. *Application deadline:* For fall admission, 7/20 priority date for domestic students, 7/20 for international students; for winter admission, 10/20 priority date for domestic students, 10/20 for international students; for spring admission, 2/20 priority date for domestic students, 2/20 for international students. Applications are processed on a rolling basis. *Application fee:* $55. Electronic applications accepted. *Application Contact:* Janet Shandley, Associate Dean of Graduate Admissions, 206-296-5900, Fax: 206-298-5656, E-mail: grad_admissions@seattleu.edu. *Interim Director, Institute of Public Service,* Dr. John Collins, 206-296-5442, Fax: 206-296-5997, E-mail: collinsj@seattleu.edu.

**College of Education** Students: 216 full-time (162 women), 192 part-time (156 women); includes 160 minority (28 Black or African American, non-Hispanic/Latino; 4 American Indian or Alaska Native, non-Hispanic/Latino; 55 Asian, non-Hispanic/Latino; 53 Hispanic/Latino; 2 Native Hawaiian or other Pacific Islander, non-Hispanic/Latino; 18 Two or more races, non-Hispanic/Latino), 7 international. Average age 30. 465 applicants, 53% accepted, 148 enrolled. *Faculty:* 30 full-time (17 women), 19 part-time/adjunct (12 women). Expenses: Contact institution. *Financial support:* In 2019–20, 134 students received support. Career-related internships or fieldwork, Federal Work-Study, scholarships/grants, and unspecified assistantships available. Support available to part-time students. Financial award applicants required to submit FAFSA. In 2019, 177 master's, 21 doctorates, 27 other advanced degrees awarded. *Program availability:* Part-time, evening/weekend. *Application deadline:* Applications are processed on a rolling basis. *Application fee:* $55. Electronic applications accepted. *Application Contact:* Janet Shandley, Director of Graduate Admissions, 206-296-5900, Fax: 206-298-5656, E-mail: grad_admissions@seattleu.edu. *Dean,* Dr. Deanna Sands, 206-296-5758, E-mail: sandsd@seattleu.edu.

**College of Nursing** Average age 32. 16 applicants, 88% accepted, 9 enrolled. Expenses: Contact institution. *Financial support:* In 2019–20, 95 students received support. Fellowships, research assistantships, career-related internships or fieldwork, Federal Work-Study, and scholarships/grants available. Support available to part-time students. Financial award applicants required to submit FAFSA. In 2019, 9 doctorates awarded. *Program availability:* Part-time, evening/weekend. *Application deadline:* For fall admission, 7/1 for domestic students. *Application fee:* $55. *Application Contact:* Janet Shandley, Director of Graduate Admissions, 206-296-5900, Fax: 206-298-5656, E-mail: grad_admissions@seattleu.edu. *Dean,* Dr. Kristen Swanson, 206-296-5676.

**College of Science and Engineering** Students: 81 full-time (35 women), 75 part-time (22 women); includes 31 minority (16 Asian, non-Hispanic/Latino; 10 Hispanic/Latino; 5 Two or more races, non-Hispanic/Latino), 67 international. Average age 28. 136 applicants, 57% accepted, 56 enrolled. *Faculty:* 104 full-time (42 women), 15 part-time/adjunct (7 women). Expenses: Contact institution. *Financial support:* In 2019–20, 14 students received support. Career-related internships or fieldwork and Federal Work-Study available. Support available to part-time students. Financial award applicants required to submit FAFSA. In 2019, 32 master's awarded. *Program availability:* Part-time, evening/weekend. *Application deadline:* For fall admission, 7/1 for domestic students. *Application fee:* $55. *Application Contact:* Janet Shandley, Director of Graduate Admissions, 206-296-5900, Fax: 206-298-5656, E-mail: grad_admissions@seattleu.edu. *Dean,* Dr. Michael Quinn, 206-296-5500, Fax: 206-296-2071.

**School of Law** Students: 485 full-time (291 women), 90 part-time (54 women); includes 265 minority (31 Black or African American, non-Hispanic/Latino; 6 American Indian or Alaska Native, non-Hispanic/Latino; 109 Asian, non-Hispanic/Latino; 61 Hispanic/Latino; 6 Native Hawaiian or other Pacific Islander, non-Hispanic/Latino; 52 Two or more races, non-Hispanic/Latino), 6 international. Average age 27. 1,443 applicants, 67% accepted, 215 enrolled. *Faculty:* 46 full-time (24 women), 46 part-time/adjunct (16 women). Expenses: Contact institution. *Financial support:* In 2019–20, 520 students received support. Career-related internships or fieldwork, Federal Work-Study, and scholarships/grants available. Support available to part-time students. Financial award application deadline: 2/15; financial award applicants required to submit FAFSA. In 2019, 300 doctorates awarded. *Program availability:* Part-time, evening/weekend, blended/hybrid learning. *Application deadline:* For fall admission, 3/1 priority date for domestic and international students. Applications are processed on a rolling basis. *Application fee:* $65. Electronic applications accepted. *Application Contact:* Gerald Heppler, Assistant Dean of Admission, 206-398-4205, Fax: 206-398-4058, E-mail: hepplerg@seattleu.edu. *Dean,* Annette E. Clark, 206-398-4300, Fax: 206-398-4310, E-mail: annclark@seattleu.edu.

**School of Theology and Ministry** Students: 37 full-time (31 women), 99 part-time (68 women); includes 46 minority (20 Black or African American, non-Hispanic/Latino; 11 Asian, non-Hispanic/Latino; 7 Hispanic/Latino; 1 Native Hawaiian or other Pacific Islander, non-Hispanic/Latino; 7 Two or more races, non-Hispanic/Latino), 4 international. Average age 41. 38 applicants, 89% accepted, 20 enrolled. *Faculty:* 22 full-time (12 women), 22 part-time/adjunct (14 women). Expenses: Contact institution. *Financial support:* In 2019–20, 78 students received support. Career-related internships or fieldwork, Federal Work-Study, and scholarships/grants available. Support available to part-time students. Financial award application deadline: 6/1; financial award applicants required to submit FAFSA. In 2019, 32 master's, 5 doctorates, 5 other advanced degrees awarded. *Program availability:* Part-time, online learning. *Application deadline:* For fall admission, 6/1 priority date for domestic students, 4/1 for international students. *Application fee:* $55. Electronic applications accepted. *Application Contact:* Colette Meda Casavant, Admissions Coordinator, 206-296-5333, Fax: 206-296-5329, E-mail: casavant@seattleu.edu. *Dean,* Dr. Mark Markuly, 206-296-5330, Fax: 206-296-5329, E-mail: stm@seattleu.edu.

## SELMA UNIVERSITY, Selma, AL 36701-5299

**General Information** Independent-religious, coed, comprehensive institution.

**GRADUATE UNITS**

**Graduate Programs**

## SEMINARY OF THE SOUTHWEST, Austin, TX 78768-2247

**General Information** Independent-religious, coed, graduate-only institution. *Enrollment by degree level:* 127 master's, 3 other advanced degrees. *Graduate faculty:* 12 full-time (6 women), 14 part-time/adjunct (9 women). *Tuition:* Full-time $16,200; part-time $675 per hour. *Required fees:* $513; $317 per degree program. Tuition and fees vary according to program. *Graduate housing:* Rooms and/or apartments available on a first-come, first-served basis to single and married students. Typical cost: $498 per year for single students; $759 per year for married students. Room charges vary according to housing facility selected. Housing application deadline: 8/1. *Student services:* Campus safety program, exercise/wellness program, writing training. *Library facilities:* Booher Library. *Collection:* Books: 119,122 (physical), 178,977 (digital/electronic); Serial titles: 405 (physical), 27,622 (digital/electronic); Databases: 76. Weekly public service hours: 86; students can reserve study rooms.

**Computer facilities:** 8 computers available on campus for general student use. A campuswide network can be accessed from student residence rooms. Online class registration is available.
Website: http://www.ssw.edu/

**General Application Contact:** Hope Benko, Director of Admissions, 512-472-4133, Fax: 512-472-3098, E-mail: hope.benko@ssw.edu.

## SETON HALL UNIVERSITY, South Orange, NJ 07079-2697

**General Information** Independent-religious, coed, university. CGS member. *Graduate housing:* On-campus housing not available.

**GRADUATE UNITS**

**College of Arts and Sciences** *Program availability:* Part-time, evening/weekend, online learning. Electronic applications accepted.

**College of Communication and the Arts** *Program availability:* Part-time, evening/weekend, online learning. Electronic applications accepted.

**College of Education and Human Services** Students: 72 full-time (53 women), 906 part-time (606 women); includes 312 minority (166 Black or African American, non-Hispanic/Latino; 36 Asian, non-Hispanic/Latino; 92 Hispanic/Latino; 3 Native Hawaiian or other Pacific Islander, non-Hispanic/Latino; 15 Two or more races, non-Hispanic/Latino), 23 international. Average age 37. 539 applicants, 61% accepted, 221 enrolled. *Faculty:* 27 full-time (14 women), 25 part-time/adjunct (10 women). Expenses: Contact institution. *Financial support:* In 2019–20, 30 students received support. Fellowships, career-related internships or fieldwork, institutionally sponsored loans, and unspecified assistantships available. Financial award application deadline: 2/1; financial award applicants required to submit FAFSA. In 2019, 122 master's, 53 doctorates, 69 other advanced degrees awarded. *Program availability:* Part-time, evening/weekend, 100% online, blended/hybrid learning. *Application deadline:* Applications are processed on a rolling basis. *Application fee:* $75. Electronic applications accepted. *Application Contact:* Diana Minakakis, Director of Graduate Admissions, 973-275-2824, Fax: 973-275-2187, E-mail: Diana.Minakakis@shu.edu. *Dean,* Dr. Maureen D. Gillette, 973-761-9025, E-mail: maureen.gillette@shu.edu.

**College of Nursing** *Program availability:* Part-time, online learning. Electronic applications accepted.

**Immaculate Conception Seminary School of Theology** *Program availability:* Part-time, evening/weekend. Electronic applications accepted.

**School of Diplomacy and International Relations** *Program availability:* Part-time, evening/weekend, 100% online, blended/hybrid learning. Electronic applications accepted.

**School of Health and Medical Sciences** *Program availability:* Part-time, evening/weekend. Electronic applications accepted.

**School of Law** *Program availability:* Part-time, evening/weekend. Electronic applications accepted.

**School of Medicine**

**Stillman School of Business** Students: 218 full-time (94 women), 354 part-time (140 women); includes 86 minority (28 Black or African American, non-Hispanic/Latino; 16 Asian, non-Hispanic/Latino; 33 Hispanic/Latino; 9 Two or more races, non-Hispanic/Latino), 249 international. Average age 34. 446 applicants, 67% accepted, 173 enrolled. *Faculty:* 33 full-time (5 women), 19 part-time/adjunct (2 women). Expenses: Contact institution. *Financial support:* In 2019–20, 39 students received support, including 15 research assistantships with full tuition reimbursements available (averaging $2,250 per year); career-related internships or fieldwork, scholarships/grants, and unspecified assistantships also available. Financial award application deadline: 6/30; financial award applicants required to submit FAFSA. In 2019, 214 master's awarded. *Program availability:* Part-time, evening/weekend, 100% online, blended/hybrid learning. *Application deadline:* For fall admission, 5/31 priority date for domestic students, 3/31 priority date for international students; for spring admission, 10/31 priority date for domestic students, 9/30 priority date for international students; for summer admission, 4/30 priority date for domestic students, 3/31 priority date for international students. Applications are processed on a rolling basis. *Application fee:* $75. Electronic applications accepted. *Application Contact:* Alfred Ayoub, Director of Graduate Admissions, 973-761-9262, Fax: 973-761-9208, E-mail: alfred.ayoub@shu.edu. *Dean,* Dr. Joyce Strawser, 973-761-9013, Fax: 973-275-2465, E-mail: joyce.strawser@shu.edu.

## SETON HILL UNIVERSITY, Greensburg, PA 15601

**General Information** Independent-religious, coed, comprehensive institution. *Enrollment:* 2,079 graduate, professional, and undergraduate students; 250 full-time matriculated graduate/professional students (173 women), 120 part-time matriculated graduate/professional students (92 women). *Enrollment by degree level:* 370 master's, 3 other advanced degrees. *Graduate faculty:* 14 full-time, 15 part-time/adjunct. *Tuition:* Full-time $29,196; part-time $811 per credit. *Required fees:* $550; $100 per unit. $25 per semester. Tuition and fees vary according to class time, course level, course load, degree level, campus/location, program, reciprocity agreements, student level and student's religious affiliation. *Graduate housing:* Room and/or apartments available on a first-come, first-served basis to single students; on-campus housing not available to married students. Housing application deadline: 7/1. *Student services:* Campus employment opportunities, campus safety program, career counseling, exercise/wellness program, free psychological counseling, international student services, multicultural affairs office, services for students with disabilities, teacher training, writing training. *Library facilities:* Reeves Memorial Library. *Collection:* Books: 72,274 (physical), 127,160 (digital/electronic); Serial titles: 2,919 (physical); Databases: 37. Students can reserve study rooms.

**Computer facilities:** Computer purchase and lease plans are available. 66 computers available on campus for general student use. A campuswide network can be accessed from student residence rooms and from off campus. Online class registration is

available.
Website: http://www.setonhill.edu/

**General Application Contact:** Ellen Monnich, Assistant Director of Graduate Admissions, 724-838-4208, Fax: 724-830-1891, E-mail: gadmit@setonhill.edu.

**GRADUATE UNITS**

**MA Program in Art Therapy** Students: 49. Average age 35. 35 applicants, 57% accepted, 18 enrolled. Expenses: Contact institution. *Financial support:* Federal Work-Study, scholarships/grants, and tuition discounts available. Financial award application deadline: 8/15; financial award applicants required to submit FAFSA. *Program availability:* Part-time. *Application deadline:* For fall admission, 7/1 for domestic and international students; for spring admission, 11/30 for domestic and international students. Applications are processed on a rolling basis. Electronic applications accepted. *Application Contact:* Dr. Julie Barris, Director, Graduate & Adult Studies, E-mail: jbarris@setonhill.edu. *Director, Graduate & Adult Studies,* Dr. Julie Barris, E-mail: jbarris@setonhill.edu.

**Master of Arts Program in Elementary/Middle Level Education** Students: 17. Expenses: Contact institution. *Financial support:* Federal Work-Study, scholarships/grants, and tuition discounts available. Financial award application deadline: 8/15; financial award applicants required to submit FAFSA. *Program availability:* Part-time, evening/weekend, blended/hybrid learning. *Application deadline:* For fall admission, 8/5 for domestic students, 8/1 for international students; for spring admission, 12/10 for domestic students, 12/1 for international students. Applications are processed on a rolling basis. Electronic applications accepted. *Application Contact:* Ellen Monnich, Assistant Director, Graduate & Adult Studies, 724-838-4208, E-mail: monnich@setonhill.edu. *Director, Graduate & Adult Studies,* Julie Barris, 724-838-4208, E-mail: jbarris@setonhill.edu.

**Master of Arts Program in Special Education** Students: 25. Expenses: Contact institution. *Financial support:* Scholarships/grants and tuition discounts available. Support available to part-time students. Financial award application deadline: 8/15; financial award applicants required to submit FAFSA. *Program availability:* Part-time, evening/weekend, 100% online, blended/hybrid learning. *Application deadline:* For fall admission, 8/5 for domestic students, 8/1 for international students; for spring admission, 12/10 for domestic students, 12/1 for international students. Applications are processed on a rolling basis. Electronic applications accepted. *Application Contact:* Ellen Monnich, Assistant Director, Graduate & Adult Studies, 724-838-4208, E-mail: monnich@setonhill.edu. *Director, Graduate & Adult Studies,* Dr. Julie Barris, 724-838-4208, E-mail: jbarris@setonhill.edu.

**Master of Education in Innovative Instruction** Students: 16. Average age 34. 21 applicants, 86% accepted, 17 enrolled. Expenses: Contact institution. *Financial support:* Scholarships/grants, unspecified assistantships, and Tuition Discounts available. Support available to part-time students. Financial award application deadline: 8/15; financial award applicants required to submit FAFSA. *Program availability:* Part-time, evening/weekend. *Application deadline:* For fall admission, 8/10 for domestic students, 8/1 for international students; for spring admission, 12/10 for domestic students, 12/1 for international students. Applications are processed on a rolling basis. Electronic applications accepted. *Application Contact:* Ellen Monnich, Assistant Director, Graduate & Adult Studies, 724-838-4208, E-mail: monnich@setonhill.edu. *Director, Graduate & Adult Studies,* Dr. Julie Barris, 724-838-4208, E-mail: gadmit@setonhill.edu.

**Master of Science Program in Physician Assistant** Students: 56. Expenses: Contact institution. *Financial support:* Application deadline: 8/15; applicants required to submit FAFSA. *Application deadline:* Applications are processed on a rolling basis. Electronic applications accepted. *Application Contact:* Lis Glessner, Enrollment Operations Director, 724-838-4208, E-mail: lglessner@setonhill.edu.

**Master's and Certificate Program in Orthodontics** Students: 27. Expenses: Contact institution. *Financial support:* Application deadline: 5/15; applicants required to submit FAFSA. *Application deadline:* Applications are processed on a rolling basis. Electronic applications accepted.

**MBA Program** Students: 103. Expenses: Contact institution. *Financial support:* Federal Work-Study, scholarships/grants, unspecified assistantships, and tuition discounts available. Financial award application deadline: 8/15; financial award applicants required to submit FAFSA. *Program availability:* Part-time, evening/weekend. *Application deadline:* For fall admission, 8/10 for domestic students, 8/1 for international students; for spring admission, 12/10 for domestic students, 12/1 for international students. Applications are processed on a rolling basis. Electronic applications accepted. *Application Contact:* Ellen Monnich, Assistant Director, Graduate & Adult Studies, 724-838-4208, E-mail: monnich@setonhill.edu. *Associate Professor, Business/MBA Program Director,* Dr. Douglas Nelson, E-mail: dnelson@setonhill.edu.

**MFA Program in Writing Popular Fiction** Students: 64. Expenses: Contact institution. *Financial support:* Scholarships/grants and tuition discounts available. Support available to part-time students. Financial award application deadline: 8/15; financial award applicants required to submit FAFSA. *Program availability:* Part-time. *Application deadline:* For fall admission, 10/1 priority date for domestic students; for spring admission, 3/1 priority date for domestic students. Applications are processed on a rolling basis. Electronic applications accepted. *Application Contact:* Ellen Monnich, Assistant Director Graduate & Adult Studies, 724-838-4208, E-mail: monnich@setonhill.edu. *Associate Professor, English/Program Director, Writing Popular Fiction,* Dr. Nicole Peeler, E-mail: peeler@setonhill.edu.

## SHASTA BIBLE COLLEGE, Redding, CA 96002

**General Information** Independent-religious, coed, comprehensive institution. *Graduate housing:* Rooms and/or apartments available on a first-come, first-served basis to single and married students.

**GRADUATE UNITS**

**Program in Biblical Counseling** *Program availability:* Part-time.

**Program in Christian Ministry** *Program availability:* Part-time, online learning.

**Program in School and Church Administration** *Program availability:* Part-time, evening/weekend.

## SHAWNEE STATE UNIVERSITY, Portsmouth, OH 45662

**General Information** State-supported, coed, comprehensive institution.

**GRADUATE UNITS**

**Program in Curriculum and Instruction**

**Program in Occupational Therapy**

## SHAW UNIVERSITY, Raleigh, NC 27601-2399

**General Information** Independent-religious, coed, comprehensive institution. *Graduate housing:* Room and/or apartments available on a first-come, first-served basis to single students; on-campus housing not available to married students. *Research affiliation:* The Louisville Institute (book writing, theology), Wabash Center (philosophy of religious education), The Society of Biblical Literature (biblical studies), The American Academy of Religion (theology, ethics, Church history, contemporary issues), Society for the Study of Black Religion (African American churches), The Association of Theological Schools (theological research).

**GRADUATE UNITS**

**Department of Education & Child Development** *Program availability:* Part-time, evening/weekend. Electronic applications accepted.

**Divinity School** *Program availability:* Part-time, evening/weekend. Electronic applications accepted.

## SHENANDOAH UNIVERSITY, Winchester, VA 22601-5195

**General Information** Independent-religious, coed, university. *Enrollment:* 3,791 graduate, professional, and undergraduate students; 987 full-time matriculated graduate/professional students (727 women), 729 part-time matriculated graduate/professional students (530 women). *Enrollment by degree level:* 723 master's, 869 doctoral, 124 other advanced degrees. *Graduate faculty:* 68 full-time (44 women), 22 part-time/adjunct (17 women). *Tuition:* Full-time $16,065; part-time $4075 per year. *Required fees:* $1240. Tuition and fees vary according to course load and program. *Graduate housing:* Room and/or apartments available on a first-come, first-served basis to single students; on-campus housing not available to married students. Typical cost: $10,570 (including board). Room and board charges vary according to board plan and housing facility selected. Housing application deadline: 3/1. *Student services:* Campus employment opportunities, campus safety program, career counseling, child daycare facilities, exercise/wellness program, free psychological counseling, international student services, low-cost health insurance, multicultural affairs office, services for students with disabilities, teacher training, writing training. *Library facilities:* Alson H. Smith, Jr. Library plus 1 other. *Collection:* Books: 121,000 (physical), 372,566 (digital/electronic); Serial titles: 1,050 (physical), 66,729 (digital/electronic); Databases: 135. Weekly public service hours: 96; students can reserve study rooms. *Research affiliation:* Inova Center for Personalized Health (pharmacogenomics and precision medicine).

**Computer facilities:** 32 computers available on campus for general student use. A campuswide network can be accessed. Online class registration, online student account information are available.
Website: http://www.su.edu/

**General Application Contact:** Katie Olivo, Associate Director of Admissions, 540-665-5441, Fax: 540-665-4627, E-mail: kolivo@su.edu.

**GRADUATE UNITS**

**College of Arts and Sciences** *Program availability:* Part-time, evening/weekend. Electronic applications accepted.

**Doctor of Pharmacy** Students: 317 full-time (219 women), 2 part-time (both women); includes 54 minority (25 Black or African American, non-Hispanic/Latino; 1 American Indian or Alaska Native, non-Hispanic/Latino; 16 Asian, non-Hispanic/Latino; 7 Hispanic/Latino; 1 Native Hawaiian or other Pacific Islander, non-Hispanic/Latino; 4 Two or more races, non-Hispanic/Latino), 15 international. Average age 26. 260 applicants, 73% accepted, 76 enrolled. *Faculty:* 30 full-time (19 women), 6 part-time/adjunct (3 women). Expenses: Contact institution. *Financial support:* In 2019–20, 18 students received support. Scholarships/grants available. Financial award application deadline: 7/1; financial award applicants required to submit FAFSA. In 2019, 63 doctorates awarded. *Program availability:* Online only, 100% online. *Application deadline:* For fall admission, 6/1 for domestic and international students. Applications are processed on a rolling basis. *Application fee:* $30. Electronic applications accepted. *Application Contact:* Katelyn M Sanders, Pharm.D., Director Admissions Pharmacy Practice, 540-678-4377, Fax: 540-665-1283, E-mail: ksanders@su.edu. *Dean of Pharmacy,* Robert DiCenzo, PhD, 540-665-1280, Fax: 540-665-1283, E-mail: rdicenzo@su.edu.

**Eleanor Wade Custer School of Nursing** Electronic applications accepted.

**School of Business** Students: 54 full-time (36 women), 34 part-time (15 women); includes 13 minority (4 Black or African American, non-Hispanic/Latino; 5 Asian, non-Hispanic/Latino; 3 Hispanic/Latino; 1 Two or more races, non-Hispanic/Latino), 34 international. Average age 32. 57 applicants, 98% accepted, 40 enrolled. *Faculty:* 20 full-time (10 women), 4 part-time/adjunct (2 women). Expenses: Contact institution. *Financial support:* In 2019–20, 20 students received support, including 1 fellowship (averaging $8,010 per year); scholarships/grants, unspecified assistantships, and Institutional work study also available. Financial award application deadline: 7/1; financial award applicants required to submit FAFSA. In 2019, 34 master's, 1 other advanced degree awarded. *Program availability:* Part-time, evening/weekend. *Application deadline:* For fall admission, 7/1 priority date for domestic students, 6/15 priority date for international students; for spring admission, 11/15 priority date for domestic students, 10/15 priority date for international students; for summer admission, 3/1 priority date for domestic and international students. *Application fee:* $30. Electronic applications accepted. *Application Contact:* Katie Olivo, E-mail: kolivo@su.edu. *Dean of School of Business,* Astrid Sheil, Ph.D., 540-545-7253, Fax: 540-665-5437, E-mail: asheil@su.edu.

**School of Education and Leadership** Students: 14 full-time (7 women), 200 part-time (152 women); includes 37 minority (20 Black or African American, non-Hispanic/Latino; 1 American Indian or Alaska Native, non-Hispanic/Latino; 5 Asian, non-Hispanic/Latino; 7 Hispanic/Latino; 4 Two or more races, non-Hispanic/Latino), 3 international. Average age 38. 119 applicants, 100% accepted, 81 enrolled. *Faculty:* 9 full-time (7 women), 48 part-time/adjunct (28 women). Expenses: Contact institution. *Financial support:* In 2019–20, 34 students received support. Scholarships/grants and unspecified assistantships available. Financial award application deadline: 3/1; financial award applicants required to submit FAFSA. In 2019, 64 master's, 5 doctorates, 25 other advanced degrees awarded. *Program availability:* Part-time, evening/weekend. *Application deadline:* For fall admission, 4/1 for domestic and international students. *Application fee:* $30. Electronic applications accepted. *Application Contact:* Andrew Woodall, Assistant Vice President for Admissions and Recruitment, 540-665-4581, Fax: 540-665-4627, E-mail: admit@su.edu. *Director, School of Education and Leadership,* Jill Lindsey, PhD, 540-545-7324, Fax: 540-665-4726, E-mail: jlindsey@su.edu.

**School of Health Professions** Students: 3 full-time (2 women), 25 part-time (20 women); includes 8 minority (4 Black or African American, non-Hispanic/Latino; 2 Asian, non-Hispanic/Latino; 2 Hispanic/Latino). Average age 34. 35 applicants, 97% accepted, 6 enrolled. *Faculty:* 1 (woman) full-time, 2 part-time/adjunct (both women). Expenses: Contact institution. *Financial support:* In 2019–20, 17 students received support, including 1 fellowship (averaging $210 per year); scholarships/grants and Faculty staff grant Public Health Discount (graduate) Valley Health SU Discretionary Award Anatomy and physiology graduate also available. Financial award application deadline: 8/1; financial award applicants required to submit FAFSA. In 2019, 1 other advanced degree awarded. *Program availability:* Part-time, 100% online. *Application deadline:* For fall admission, 8/1 for domestic students; for spring admission, 12/1 for domestic students.

Applications are processed on a rolling basis. *Application fee:* $30. Electronic applications accepted. *Application Contact:* Katie Olivo, Associate Director of Admission, 540-665-5441, Fax: 540-665-4627, E-mail: kolivo@su.edu. *Director,* Michelle Gamber, DrPH, MA, 540-665-5560, Fax: 540-665-5519, E-mail: mgamber@su.edu.

***Division of Athletic Training*** Students: 21 full-time (15 women), 6 part-time (5 women); includes 4 minority (all Black or African American, non-Hispanic/Latino). Average age 24. 35 applicants, 100% accepted, 10 enrolled. *Faculty:* 5 full-time (4 women), 1 (woman) part-time/adjunct. Expenses: Contact institution. *Financial support:* Application deadline: 3/1; applicants required to submit FAFSA. In 2019, 14 master's, 7 other advanced degrees awarded. *Application deadline:* For summer admission, 4/1 priority date for domestic and international students. Applications are processed on a rolling basis. *Application fee:* $85. *Application Contact:* Karen Gross, Administrative Assistant, 540-545-7385, Fax: 540-545-7887, E-mail: kgross@su.edu. *Program Director,* Dr. Rose A. Schmieg, PhD, 540-665-5534, Fax: 540-545-7387, E-mail: rschmieg@su.edu.

***Division of Physical Therapy - Non-Traditional Physical Therapy*** *Program availability:* Minimal on-campus study. Electronic applications accepted.

***Division of Physician Assistant Studies*** Students: 169 full-time (141 women), 1 (woman) part-time; includes 9 minority (1 Black or African American, non-Hispanic/Latino; 3 Asian, non-Hispanic/Latino; 3 Hispanic/Latino; 2 Two or more races, non-Hispanic/Latino), 4 international. Average age 27. 152 applicants, 59% accepted, 61 enrolled. *Faculty:* 9 full-time (7 women), 5 part-time/adjunct (3 women). Expenses: Contact institution. *Financial support:* In 2019–20, 16 students received support. Institutionally sponsored loans and VTAG for Virginia residents, student loans, private sources available. Financial award application deadline: 8/1; financial award applicants required to submit FAFSA. In 2019, 52 master's awarded. *Application deadline:* For fall admission, 10/1 priority date for domestic students, 9/1 priority date for international students. Applications are processed on a rolling basis. *Application fee:* $179. Electronic applications accepted. *Application Contact:* Karen Marie O'Neil, Admissions Coordinator, 540-545-7381, Fax: 540-542-6554, E-mail: pa@su.edu. *Distinguished Professor and Director,* Anthony A. Miller, 540-545-7257, Fax: 540-542-6554, E-mail: amiller@su.edu.

***School of Occupational Therapy*** Students: 106 full-time (95 women), 54 part-time (46 women); includes 7 minority (2 Black or African American, non-Hispanic/Latino; 2 Asian, non-Hispanic/Latino; 3 Hispanic/Latino). Average age 26. 120 applicants, 76% accepted, 53 enrolled. *Faculty:* 6 full-time (all women), 6 part-time/adjunct (all women). Expenses: Contact institution. *Financial support:* In 2019–20, 11 students received support. Scholarships/grants available. Financial award application deadline: 8/1; financial award applicants required to submit FAFSA. In 2019, 51 master's awarded. *Program availability:* 100% online, blended/hybrid learning. *Application deadline:* For fall admission, 10/15 for domestic and international students. *Application fee:* $150. Electronic applications accepted. *Application Contact:* Dr. Alicia Lutman, Associate Professor, 540-665-5563, Fax: 540-665-5564, E-mail: alutman@su.edu. *Division Director, Occupational Therapy,* Dr. Cathy F. Shanholtz, OTD, 540-665-5441, Fax: 540-665-5564, E-mail: cshanhol2@su.edu.

**Shenandoah Conservatory** Students: 73 full-time (51 women), 66 part-time (41 women); includes 24 minority (11 Black or African American, non-Hispanic/Latino; 10 Hispanic/Latino; 3 Two or more races, non-Hispanic/Latino), 18 international. Average age 30. 127 applicants, 84% accepted, 52 enrolled. *Faculty:* 40 full-time (14 women), 15 part-time/adjunct (7 women). Expenses: Contact institution. *Financial support:* In 2019–20, 43 students received support, including 12 teaching assistantships with full tuition reimbursements available (averaging $9,000 per year); tuition waivers (partial) and unspecified assistantships also available. Financial award application deadline: 8/1; financial award applicants required to submit FAFSA. In 2019, 39 master's, 4 doctorates, 8 other advanced degrees awarded. *Program availability:* Part-time, 100% online. *Application deadline:* For fall admission, 1/15 for domestic and international students; for spring admission, 12/1 for domestic and international students; for summer admission, 4/15 for domestic and international students. Applications are processed on a rolling basis. *Application fee:* $30. Electronic applications accepted. *Application Contact:* Andrew Woodall, Executive Director of Recruitment and Advancement, 540-665-4581, Fax: 540-665-4627, E-mail: admit@su.edu. *Dean,* Dr. Michael J. Stepniak, 540-542-6201, Fax: 540-665-5402, E-mail: mstepnia@su.edu.

## SHEPHERDS THEOLOGICAL SEMINARY, Cary, NC 27518

**General Information** Independent-religious, coed, graduate-only institution. *Graduate housing:* On-campus housing not available.

**GRADUATE UNITS**

**Graduate Programs**

## SHEPHERD UNIVERSITY, Shepherdstown, WV 25443

**General Information** State-supported, coed, comprehensive institution.

**GRADUATE UNITS**

**Program in Curriculum and Instruction**

## SHERMAN COLLEGE OF CHIROPRACTIC, Spartanburg, SC 29304-1452

**General Information** Independent, coed, graduate-only institution. *Graduate housing:* Room and/or apartments available to single students. *Research affiliation:* American Public Health Service (chiropractic research), Upper Cervical Research Foundation (chiropractic).

**GRADUATE UNITS**

**Professional Program** Electronic applications accepted.

## SHILOH UNIVERSITY, Kalona, IA 52247

**General Information** Independent, coed, comprehensive institution. *Graduate housing:* On-campus housing not available.

**GRADUATE UNITS**

**Graduate Programs** *Program availability:* Part-time, evening/weekend, online only, 100% online. Electronic applications accepted.

## SHIPPENSBURG UNIVERSITY OF PENNSYLVANIA, Shippensburg, PA 17257-2299

**General Information** State-supported, coed, comprehensive institution. CGS member. *Enrollment:* 6,084 graduate, professional, and undergraduate students; 256 full-time matriculated graduate/professional students (173 women), 472 part-time matriculated graduate/professional students (286 women). *Enrollment by degree level:* 676 master's, 43 doctoral, 9 other advanced degrees. *Graduate faculty:* 128 full-time (51 women), 24 part-time/adjunct (21 women). Tuition, state resident: part-time $516 per credit. Tuition, nonresident: part-time $774 per credit. *Required fees:* $149 per credit. *Graduate housing:* Room and/or apartments guaranteed to single students; on-campus housing not available to married students. Typical cost: $3600 per year. *Student services:* Campus employment opportunities, campus safety program, career counseling, child daycare facilities, exercise/wellness program, free psychological counseling, grant writing training, international student services, low-cost health insurance, multicultural affairs office, services for students with disabilities, teacher training, writing training. *Library facilities:* Ezra Lehman Memorial Library plus 1 other. *Collection:* Books: 360,690 (physical), 539,411 (digital/electronic); Serial titles: 33 (physical), 252 (digital/electronic); Databases: 105. Weekly public service hours: 97.

**Computer facilities:** 1,100 computers available on campus for general student use. A campuswide network can be accessed. Online class registration, personal Web pages are available.
Website: http://www.ship.edu/

**General Application Contact:** Maya T. Mapp, Director of Admissions, 717-477-1231, Fax: 717-477-4016, E-mail: mtmapp@ship.edu.

**GRADUATE UNITS**

**School of Graduate Studies** Students: 256 full-time (173 women), 472 part-time (286 women); includes 111 minority (51 Black or African American, non-Hispanic/Latino; 14 Asian, non-Hispanic/Latino; 33 Hispanic/Latino; 13 Two or more races, non-Hispanic/Latino), 20 international. Average age 32. 777 applicants, 62% accepted, 266 enrolled. *Faculty:* 128 full-time (51 women), 24 part-time/adjunct (21 women). Expenses: Contact institution. *Financial support:* In 2019–20, 174 students received support. Career-related internships or fieldwork, scholarships/grants, unspecified assistantships, and resident hall director and student payroll positions available. Support available to part-time students. Financial award application deadline: 3/1; financial award applicants required to submit FAFSA. In 2019, 298 master's, 12 doctorates awarded. *Program availability:* Part-time, evening/weekend, 100% online, blended/hybrid learning. *Application deadline:* For fall admission, 4/30 for international students; for spring admission, 9/30 for international students. Applications are processed on a rolling basis. *Application fee:* $45. Electronic applications accepted. *Application Contact:* Maya T. Mapp, Director of Admissions, 717-477-1231, Fax: 717-477-4016, E-mail: mtmapp@ship.edu. *Associate Provost and Dean of Graduate Studies,* Dr. Tracy A. Schoolcraft, 717-477-1148, Fax: 717-477-4038, E-mail: tascho@ship.edu.

***College of Arts and Sciences*** Students: 71 full-time (35 women), 75 part-time (43 women); includes 23 minority (14 Black or African American, non-Hispanic/Latino; 3 Asian, non-Hispanic/Latino; 4 Hispanic/Latino; 2 Two or more races, non-Hispanic/Latino), 9 international. Average age 30. 223 applicants, 60% accepted, 56 enrolled. *Faculty:* 67 full-time (23 women), 4 part-time/adjunct (3 women). Expenses: Contact institution. *Financial support:* In 2019–20, 76 students received support. Career-related internships or fieldwork, scholarships/grants, unspecified assistantships, and resident hall director and student payroll positions available. Support available to part-time students. Financial award application deadline: 3/1; financial award applicants required to submit FAFSA. In 2019, 106 master's awarded. *Program availability:* Part-time, evening/weekend. *Application deadline:* For fall admission, 4/30 for international students; for spring admission, 9/30 for international students. Applications are processed on a rolling basis. *Application fee:* $45. Electronic applications accepted. *Application Contact:* Maya T. Mapp, Director of Admissions, 717-477-1231, Fax: 717-477-4016, E-mail: mtmapp@ship.edu. *Dean,* Dr. James H. Mike, 717-477-1151, Fax: 717-477-4026, E-mail: jhmike@ship.edu.

***College of Education and Human Services*** Students: 139 full-time (115 women), 241 part-time (184 women); includes 53 minority (25 Black or African American, non-Hispanic/Latino; 5 Asian, non-Hispanic/Latino; 17 Hispanic/Latino; 6 Two or more races, non-Hispanic/Latino), 3 international. Average age 32. 362 applicants, 65% accepted, 139 enrolled. *Faculty:* 40 full-time (24 women), 20 part-time/adjunct (18 women). Expenses: Contact institution. *Financial support:* In 2019–20, 76 students received support. Career-related internships or fieldwork, scholarships/grants, unspecified assistantships, and resident hall director and student payroll positions available. Support available to part-time students. Financial award application deadline: 3/1; financial award applicants required to submit FAFSA. In 2019, 103 master's, 12 doctorates awarded. *Program availability:* Part-time, evening/weekend, 100% online, blended/hybrid learning. *Application deadline:* For fall admission, 4/30 for international students; for spring admission, 9/30 for international students. Applications are processed on a rolling basis. *Application fee:* $45. Electronic applications accepted. *Application Contact:* Maya T. Mapp, Director of Admissions, 717-477-1231, Fax: 717-477-4016, E-mail: mtmapp@ship.edu. *Dean of the College of Education and Human Services,* Dr. Nicole R. Hill, 717-477-1373, Fax: 717-477-4012, E-mail: nrhill@ship.edu.

***John L. Grove College of Business*** Students: 46 full-time (23 women), 156 part-time (59 women); includes 35 minority (12 Black or African American, non-Hispanic/Latino; 6 Asian, non-Hispanic/Latino; 12 Hispanic/Latino; 5 Two or more races, non-Hispanic/Latino), 8 international. Average age 32. 192 applicants, 58% accepted, 71 enrolled. *Faculty:* 21 full-time (4 women). Expenses: Contact institution. *Financial support:* In 2019–20, 22 students received support. Career-related internships or fieldwork, scholarships/grants, unspecified assistantships, and resident hall director and student payroll positions available. Support available to part-time students. Financial award application deadline: 3/1; financial award applicants required to submit FAFSA. In 2019, 89 master's awarded. *Program availability:* Part-time, evening/weekend, 100% online, blended/hybrid learning. *Application deadline:* For fall admission, 4/30 for international students; for spring admission, 9/30 for international students. Applications are processed on a rolling basis. *Application fee:* $45. Electronic applications accepted. *Application Contact:* Maya T. Mapp, Director of Admissions, 717-477-1231, Fax: 717-477-4016, E-mail: mtmapp@ship.edu. *Dean of the College of Business,* Dr. John G. Kooti, 717-477-1435, Fax: 717-477-4003, E-mail: jgkooti@ship.edu.

## SHORTER UNIVERSITY, Rome, GA 30165

**General Information** Independent-religious, coed, comprehensive institution. *Graduate housing:* Room and/or apartments available on a first-come, first-served basis to single students; on-campus housing not available to married students. Housing application deadline: 3/30.

**GRADUATE UNITS**

**Professional Studies** *Program availability:* Evening/weekend. Electronic applications accepted.

## SH'OR YOSHUV RABBINICAL COLLEGE, Lawrence, NY 11559-1714

**General Information** Independent-religious, men only, comprehensive institution.

**GRADUATE UNITS**
**Graduate Programs**

## SIENA COLLEGE, Loudonville, NY 12211-1462

**General Information** Independent-religious, coed, comprehensive institution. *Graduate housing:* On-campus housing not available.

**GRADUATE UNITS**

**School of Business** *Program availability:* Evening/weekend.

## SIENA HEIGHTS UNIVERSITY, Adrian, MI 49221-1796

**General Information** Independent-religious, coed, comprehensive institution. *Graduate housing:* Rooms and/or apartments available on a first-come, first-served basis to single and married students. Housing application deadline: 5/1.

**GRADUATE UNITS**

**Graduate College** *Program availability:* Part-time, evening/weekend. Electronic applications accepted.

## SIERRA NEVADA COLLEGE, Incline Village, NV 89451

**General Information** Independent, coed, comprehensive institution. *Graduate housing:* On-campus housing not available.

**GRADUATE UNITS**

**Teacher Education Program** *Program availability:* Part-time, evening/weekend, online learning. Electronic applications accepted.

## SIMMONS UNIVERSITY, Boston, MA 02115

**General Information** Independent, Undergraduate: women only; graduate: coed, university. *Enrollment:* 6,635 graduate, professional, and undergraduate students; 1,627 full-time matriculated graduate/professional students (1,414 women), 3,231 part-time matriculated graduate/professional students (2,861 women). *Enrollment by degree level:* 4,498 master's, 243 doctoral, 117 other advanced degrees. *Graduate faculty:* 117 full-time (91 women), 372 part-time/adjunct (327 women). *Tuition:* Full-time $21,654; part-time $1203 per credit. *Required fees:* $164; $164 per unit. Tuition and fees vary according to course load, campus/location and program. *Graduate housing:* On-campus housing not available. *Student services:* Campus employment opportunities, campus safety program, career counseling, exercise/wellness program, free psychological counseling, grant writing training, international student services, low-cost health insurance, multicultural affairs office, services for students with disabilities, writing training. *Library facilities:* Beatley Library. *Collection:* Books: 147,693 (physical), 38,799 (digital/electronic); Serial titles: 50,977 (digital/electronic); Databases: 123. Weekly public service hours: 105; study areas open 24 hours, 5–7 days a week; students can reserve study rooms. *Research affiliation:* Carnegie Corporation of New York (gender equality in higher education in Sub-Saharan African universities), Harvard Medical School (women in academic medicine), Institute for Quantitative Social Science, Harvard University (usability), Boston Children's Hospital (scholarly communication), University College London (cultural heritage and informatics), Oxfam America (gender mainstreaming).

**Computer facilities:** Computer purchase and lease plans are available. 570 computers available on campus for general student use. A campuswide network can be accessed. Online class registration is available.
Website: http://www.simmons.edu/

**General Application Contact:** Kerri Brophy, Vice President of Enrollment Management, E-mail: kerri.brophy@simmons.edu.

**GRADUATE UNITS**

**College of Natural, Behavioral, and Health Sciences** Students: 418 full-time (374 women), 1,868 part-time (1,682 women); includes 477 minority (161 Black or African American, non-Hispanic/Latino; 4 American Indian or Alaska Native, non-Hispanic/Latino; 138 Asian, non-Hispanic/Latino; 124 Hispanic/Latino; 1 Native Hawaiian or other Pacific Islander, non-Hispanic/Latino; 49 Two or more races, non-Hispanic/Latino), 22 international. Average age 32. 1,442 applicants, 62% accepted, 501 enrolled. *Faculty:* 39 full-time (33 women), 194 part-time/adjunct (180 women). Expenses: Contact institution. *Financial support:* In 2019–20, 25 students received support, including 25 fellowships (averaging $3,015 per year); teaching assistantships and scholarships/grants also available. Financial award applicants required to submit FAFSA. In 2019, 630 master's, 39 doctorates awarded. *Program availability:* Part-time. *Application deadline:* For fall admission, 6/1 for international students. Applications are processed on a rolling basis. *Application fee:* $50. Electronic applications accepted. *Application Contact:* Brett DiMarzo, Director of Graduate Admission, 617-521-2651, Fax: 617-521-3137, E-mail: brett.dimarzo@simmons.edu. *Dean*, Dr. Lepaine Sharp-McHenry.

**College of Organizational, Computational, and Information Sciences** Students: 300 full-time (250 women), 530 part-time (452 women); includes 131 minority (19 Black or African American, non-Hispanic/Latino; 31 Asian, non-Hispanic/Latino; 55 Hispanic/Latino; 1 Native Hawaiian or other Pacific Islander, non-Hispanic/Latino; 25 Two or more races, non-Hispanic/Latino), 16 international. Average age 31. 475 applicants, 67% accepted, 274 enrolled. *Faculty:* 32 full-time (19 women), 18 part-time/adjunct (15 women). Expenses: Contact institution. *Financial support:* In 2019–20, 16 students received support, including 6 fellowships (averaging $30,000 per year), 10 teaching assistantships (averaging $20,000 per year); scholarships/grants also available. Financial award applicants required to submit FAFSA. In 2019, 342 master's awarded. *Program availability:* Part-time. *Application deadline:* For fall admission, 7/18 priority date for domestic students; for summer admission, 4/24 priority date for domestic students. Applications are processed on a rolling basis. *Application fee:* $65. Electronic applications accepted. *Application Contact:* Kate Benson, Director, Library Science Admission Office, 617-5212801, E-mail: kate.benson@simmons.edu. *Dean*, Dr. Marie desJardins, E-mail: marie.desjardins@simmons.edu.

**College of Social Sciences, Policy, and Practice** Students: 907 full-time (788 women), 766 part-time (670 women); includes 500 minority (252 Black or African American, non-Hispanic/Latino; 1 American Indian or Alaska Native, non-Hispanic/Latino; 42 Asian, non-Hispanic/Latino; 161 Hispanic/Latino; 44 Two or more races, non-Hispanic/Latino), 5 international. Average age 31. 1,206 applicants, 66% accepted, 434 enrolled. *Faculty:* 36 full-time (30 women), 153 part-time/adjunct (126 women). Expenses: Contact institution. *Financial support:* In 2019–20, 20 students received support, including 17 fellowships (averaging $2,400 per year), 3 teaching assistantships (averaging $2,000 per year); scholarships/grants also available. Support available to part-time students. Financial award applicants required to submit FAFSA. In 2019, 708 master's, 4 doctorates awarded. *Program availability:* Part-time. *Application deadline:* For fall admission, 8/1 for domestic students; for spring admission, 12/15 for domestic students; for summer admission, 5/1 for domestic students. Applications are processed on a rolling basis. *Application fee:* $45. Electronic applications accepted. *Application Contact:* Carlos D. Frontado, Director of Admissions, 617-521-3920, Fax: 617-521-3980, E-mail: ssw@simmons.edu. *Dean*, Dr. Stephanie Berzin, 617-521-2759, E-mail: stephanie.berzin@simmons.edu.

**Gwen Ifill College of Media, Arts, and Humanities** Students: 2 full-time (both women), 67 part-time (57 women); includes 13 minority (3 Black or African American, non-Hispanic/Latino; 4 Asian, non-Hispanic/Latino; 3 Hispanic/Latino; 3 Two or more races, non-Hispanic/Latino), 1 international. Average age 31. 42 applicants, 62% accepted, 23 enrolled. *Faculty:* 10 full-time (9 women), 7 part-time/adjunct (6 women). Expenses: Contact institution. *Financial support:* In 2019–20, 14 students received support, including 1 fellowship (averaging $15,360 per year), 13 teaching assistantships (averaging $2,000 per year); scholarships/grants also available. Financial award applicants required to submit FAFSA. In 2019, 24 master's awarded. *Program availability:* Part-time. *Application deadline:* For fall admission, 8/1 for domestic and international students; for spring admission, 12/15 for domestic and international students; for summer admission, 5/1 for domestic and international students. Applications are processed on a rolling basis. *Application fee:* $35. Electronic applications accepted. *Application Contact:* Patricia Flaherty, Director, Graduate Studies Admission, 617-521-3902, Fax: 617-521-3058, E-mail: gsa@simmons.edu. *Dean*, Dr. Brian Norman, 617-521-2472, E-mail: brian.norman@simmons.edu.

## SIMON FRASER UNIVERSITY, Burnaby, BC V5A 1S6, Canada

**General Information** Province-supported, coed, university. *Graduate housing:* Room and/or apartments available on a first-come, first-served basis to single students; on-campus housing not available to married students. Housing application deadline: 12/1. *Research affiliation:* BC Cancer Agency (health sciences, biomedical sciences, physiology, kinesiology), TRIUMF (physics), Ballard Power Systems (mechatronics), Bamfield Marine Research Station (marine biology, ecology, archaeology).

**GRADUATE UNITS**

**Office of Graduate Studies and Postdoctoral Fellows** *Program availability:* Part-time, evening/weekend, online learning. Electronic applications accepted.

***Faculty of Applied Sciences*** Electronic applications accepted.

***Faculty of Arts and Social Sciences*** *Program availability:* Part-time, evening/weekend. Electronic applications accepted.

***Faculty of Business Administration*** *Program availability:* Online learning.

***Faculty of Communication, Art and Technology***

***Faculty of Education*** Electronic applications accepted.

***Faculty of Environment***

***Faculty of Health Sciences*** Electronic applications accepted.

***Faculty of Science*** Electronic applications accepted.

## SIMPSON COLLEGE, Indianola, IA 50125-1297

**General Information** Independent-religious, coed, comprehensive institution.

**GRADUATE UNITS**

**Department of Education**

**Department of Social Sciences** *Program availability:* Evening/weekend.

## SIMPSON UNIVERSITY, Redding, CA 96003-8606

**General Information** Independent-religious, coed, comprehensive institution. *Graduate housing:* On-campus housing not available.

**GRADUATE UNITS**

**A.W. Tozer Theological Seminary** *Program availability:* Part-time, evening/weekend, 100% online, blended/hybrid learning. Electronic applications accepted.

**School of Education** *Program availability:* Part-time, evening/weekend. Electronic applications accepted.

**School of Graduate Studies** *Program availability:* Evening/weekend, 100% online, blended/hybrid learning. Electronic applications accepted.

## SINTE GLESKA UNIVERSITY, Mission, SD 57555

**General Information** Independent, coed, comprehensive institution. *Graduate housing:* Rooms and/or apartments available on a first-come, first-served basis to single and married students.

**GRADUATE UNITS**

**Graduate Education Program** *Program availability:* Part-time, evening/weekend.

## SIOUX FALLS SEMINARY, Sioux Falls, SD 57105-1599

**General Information** Independent-religious, coed, graduate-only institution. *Graduate housing:* On-campus housing not available.

**GRADUATE UNITS**

**Graduate and Professional Programs** *Program availability:* Part-time.

## SIT GRADUATE INSTITUTE, Brattleboro, VT 05302-0676

**General Information** Independent, coed, graduate-only institution. *Enrollment by degree level:* 100 master's. *Graduate faculty:* 11 full-time (6 women), 6 part-time/adjunct (2 women). *Tuition:* Full-time $43,500; part-time $21,750 per credit. *Graduate housing:* On-campus housing not available. *Student services:* Campus safety program, career counseling, free psychological counseling, international student services, low-cost health insurance, multicultural affairs office, services for students with disabilities, writing training. *Library facilities:* Donald B. Watt Library plus 1 other. *Collection:* Books: 26,120 (physical), 205,276 (digital/electronic); Serial titles: 71 (digital/electronic); Databases: 84.

**Computer facilities:** Online class registration is available.
Website: https://graduate.sit.edu/

**General Application Contact:** Graduate Admissions, 800-336-1616, Fax: 802-258-3500, E-mail: admissions@sit.edu.

**GRADUATE UNITS**

**Graduate Programs** *Program availability:* Part-time, online learning. Electronic applications accepted.

## SITTING BULL COLLEGE, Fort Yates, ND 58538-9701

**General Information** Independent, coed, comprehensive institution. *Enrollment:* 15 full-time matriculated graduate/professional students (13 women). *Enrollment by degree level:* 15 master's. *Graduate faculty:* 7 full-time (0 women). *Tuition:* Full-time $6300; part-time $2100 per year. *Required fees:* $410; $410. *Graduate housing:* Rooms and/or apartments available on a first-come, first-served basis to single and married students. Typical cost: $3000 per year for single students; $5400 per year for married students. Housing application deadline: 4/30. *Student services:* Career counseling, child daycare facilities, exercise/wellness program. *Library facilities:* Sitting Bull College Library.

**Computer facilities:** 16 computers available on campus for general student use. Website: http://www.sittingbull.edu/

**General Application Contact:** Dr. Mafany Mongoh, Science Faculty, 701-854-8051, Fax: 701-854-8197, E-mail: mafany.mongoh@sittingbull.edu.

**GRADUATE UNITS**

**Graduate Programs**

## SLIPPERY ROCK UNIVERSITY OF PENNSYLVANIA, Slippery Rock, PA 16057-1383

**General Information** State-supported, coed, university. *Enrollment:* 8,824 graduate, professional, and undergraduate students. *Enrollment by degree level:* 957 master's, 217 doctoral. *Graduate housing:* Room and/or apartments available on a first-come, first-served basis to single students; on-campus housing not available to married students. Typical cost: $2785 per year. Housing application deadline: 6/1. *Student services:* Campus employment opportunities, campus safety program, career counseling, child daycare facilities, exercise/wellness program, free psychological counseling, international student services, multicultural affairs office, services for students with disabilities, writing training. *Library facilities:* Bailey Library. *Collection:* Weekly public service hours: 98; students can reserve study rooms.

**Computer facilities:** Computer purchase and lease plans are available. 1,654 computers available on campus for general student use. A campuswide network can be accessed from student residence rooms and from off campus. Online class registration is available.
Website: http://www.sru.edu/

**General Application Contact:** Brandi Weber-Mortimer, Director of Graduate Admissions, 724-738-2051, Fax: 724-738-2146, E-mail: graduate.admissions@sru.edu.

**GRADUATE UNITS**

**Graduate Studies (Recruitment)** Students: 546 full-time (388 women), 679 part-time (515 women); includes 105 minority (33 Black or African American, non-Hispanic/Latino; 2 American Indian or Alaska Native, non-Hispanic/Latino; 19 Asian, non-Hispanic/Latino; 28 Hispanic/Latino; 23 Two or more races, non-Hispanic/Latino), 3 international. Average age 29. 1,694 applicants, 53% accepted, 458 enrolled. *Faculty:* 117 full-time (66 women), 19 part-time/adjunct (11 women). Expenses: Contact institution. *Financial support:* In 2019–20, 175 students received support. Career-related internships or fieldwork, Federal Work-Study, institutionally sponsored loans, scholarships/grants, tuition waivers (partial), and unspecified assistantships available. Support available to part-time students. Financial award application deadline: 5/1; financial award applicants required to submit FAFSA. In 2019, 435 master's, 66 doctorates awarded. *Program availability:* Part-time, evening/weekend, 100% online, blended/hybrid learning. *Application deadline:* For fall admission, 1/15 priority date for domestic and international students; for spring admission, 10/1 priority date for domestic students, 9/1 priority date for international students. Applications are processed on a rolling basis. *Application fee:* $25 ($30 for international students). Electronic applications accepted. *Application Contact:* Brandi Weber-Mortimer, Director of Graduate Admissions, 724-738-4340, Fax: 724-738-2146, E-mail: graduate.admissions@sru.edu. *Director of Graduate Admissions*, Brandi Weber-Mortimer, 724-738-4340, Fax: 724-738-2146, E-mail: graduate.admissions@sru.edu.

***College of Business*** Students: 32 full-time (17 women), 38 part-time (19 women); includes 8 minority (4 Black or African American, non-Hispanic/Latino; 2 Hispanic/Latino; 2 Two or more races, non-Hispanic/Latino), 1 international. Average age 28. 88 applicants, 69% accepted, 12 enrolled. *Faculty:* 17 full-time (10 women), 1 part-time/adjunct (0 women). Expenses: Contact institution. *Financial support:* In 2019–20, 12 students received support. Career-related internships or fieldwork, Federal Work-Study, institutionally sponsored loans, scholarships/grants, tuition waivers (partial), and unspecified assistantships available. Support available to part-time students. Financial award application deadline: 5/1; financial award applicants required to submit FAFSA. In 2019, 23 master's awarded. *Program availability:* Part-time, evening/weekend. *Application deadline:* For fall admission, 3/1 priority date for domestic students, 5/1 priority date for international students; for spring admission, 10/1 priority date for domestic students, 9/1 priority date for international students. Applications are processed on a rolling basis. *Application fee:* $25 ($30 for international students). Electronic applications accepted. *Application Contact:* Brandi Weber-Mortimer, Director of Graduate Admissions, 724-738-2051, Fax: 724-738-2146, E-mail: graduate.admissions@sru.edu. *Dean*, Dr. Lawrence Shao, 724-738-2687, Fax: 724-738-4767, E-mail: lawrence.shao@sru.edu.

***College of Education*** Students: 151 full-time (111 women), 427 part-time (371 women); includes 39 minority (10 Black or African American, non-Hispanic/Latino; 1 American Indian or Alaska Native, non-Hispanic/Latino; 4 Asian, non-Hispanic/Latino; 15 Hispanic/Latino; 9 Two or more races, non-Hispanic/Latino), 1 international. Average age 30. 459 applicants, 72% accepted, 177 enrolled. *Faculty:* 40 full-time (22 women), 9 part-time/adjunct (4 women). Expenses: Contact institution. *Financial support:* In 2019–20, 81 students received support. Career-related internships or fieldwork, Federal Work-Study, institutionally sponsored loans, scholarships/grants, tuition waivers (partial), and unspecified assistantships available. Support available to part-time students. Financial award application deadline: 5/1; financial award applicants required to submit FAFSA. In 2019, 258 master's, 12 doctorates awarded. *Program availability:* Part-time, evening/weekend, 100% online. *Application deadline:* For fall admission, 3/1 priority date for domestic students, 5/1 priority date for international students; for spring admission, 10/1 priority date for domestic students, 9/1 priority date for international students. Applications are processed on a rolling basis. *Application fee:* $25 ($30 for international students). Electronic applications accepted. *Application Contact:* Brandi Weber-Mortimer, Director of Graduate Admissions, 724-738-2051, Fax: 724-738-2146, E-mail: graduate.admissions@sru.edu. *Dean*, Dr. A. Keith Dils, 724-738-2007, Fax: 724-738-2880, E-mail: keith.dils@sru.edu.

***College of Health, Engineering, and Science*** Students: 335 full-time (236 women), 110 part-time (63 women); includes 40 minority (11 Black or African American, non-Hispanic/Latino; 12 Asian, non-Hispanic/Latino; 7 Hispanic/Latino; 10 Two or more races, non-Hispanic/Latino), 1 international. Average age 26. 1,004 applicants, 43% accepted, 188 enrolled. *Faculty:* 41 full-time (25 women), 9 part-time/adjunct (2 women). Expenses: Contact institution. *Financial support:* In 2019–20, 71 students received support. Career-related internships or fieldwork, Federal Work-Study, institutionally sponsored loans, scholarships/grants, tuition waivers (partial), and unspecified assistantships available. Support available to part-time students. Financial award application deadline: 5/1; financial award applicants required to submit FAFSA. In 2019, 112 master's, 54 doctorates awarded. *Program availability:* Part-time, evening/weekend, 100% online. *Application deadline:* For fall admission, 3/1 priority date for domestic students, 5/1 priority date for international students; for spring admission, 10/1 priority date for domestic students, 9/1 priority date for international students. Applications are processed on a rolling basis. *Application fee:* $25 ($30 for international students). Electronic applications accepted. *Application Contact:* Brandi Weber-Mortimer, Director of Graduate Admissions, 724-738-2051, Fax: 724-738-2146, E-mail: graduate.admissions@sru.edu. *Dean*, Dr. Michael Zieg, 724-738-4862, Fax: 724-738-2881, E-mail: michael.zieg@sru.edu.

***College of Liberal Arts*** Students: 28 full-time (24 women), 104 part-time (62 women); includes 18 minority (8 Black or African American, non-Hispanic/Latino; 1 American Indian or Alaska Native, non-Hispanic/Latino; 3 Asian, non-Hispanic/Latino; 4 Hispanic/Latino; 2 Two or more races, non-Hispanic/Latino). Average age 32. 119 applicants, 54% accepted, 46 enrolled. *Faculty:* 19 full-time (9 women). Expenses: Contact institution. *Financial support:* In 2019–20, 11 students received support. Career-related internships or fieldwork, Federal Work-Study, institutionally sponsored loans, scholarships/grants, tuition waivers (partial), and unspecified assistantships available. Support available to part-time students. Financial award application deadline: 5/1; financial award applicants required to submit FAFSA. In 2019, 42 master's awarded. *Program availability:* Part-time, evening/weekend, online only, 100% online. *Application deadline:* For fall admission, 3/1 priority date for domestic students, 5/1 priority date for international students; for spring admission, 10/1 priority date for domestic students, 9/1 priority date for international students. Applications are processed on a rolling basis. *Application fee:* $25 ($30 for international students). Electronic applications accepted. *Application Contact:* Brandi Weber-Mortimer, Director of Graduate Admissions, 724-738-2051, Fax: 724-738-2146, E-mail: graduate.admissions@sru.edu. *Dean*, Dr. Dan Bauer, 724-738-4262, Fax: 724-738-2188, E-mail: dan.bauer@sru.edu.

## SMITH COLLEGE, Northampton, MA 01063

**General Information** Independent, Undergraduate: women only; graduate: coed, comprehensive institution. *Enrollment:* 2,894 graduate, professional, and undergraduate students; 344 full-time matriculated graduate/professional students (287 women), 18 part-time matriculated graduate/professional students (13 women). *Enrollment by degree level:* 288 master's, 56 doctoral, 18 other advanced degrees. *Graduate faculty:* 290 full-time (172 women), 17 part-time/adjunct (9 women). *Tuition:* Full-time $36,940; part-time $1690 per credit. *Required fees:* $90. Full-time tuition and fees vary according to course load, degree level and program. *Graduate housing:* Room and/or apartments available on a first-come, first-served basis to single students; on-campus housing not available to married students. Typical cost: $9100 per year ($18,130 including board). Housing application deadline: 5/1. *Student services:* Campus safety program, career counseling, child daycare facilities, exercise/wellness program, international student services, low-cost health insurance, multicultural affairs office, services for students with disabilities, teacher training, writing training. *Library facilities:* Neilson Library.

**Computer facilities:** Computer purchase and lease plans are available. A campuswide network can be accessed. Online class registration is available.
Website: http://www.smith.edu/

**General Application Contact:** Helene Visentin, Dean of the Faculty/Dean for Academic Development, 413-585-3000, Fax: 413-585-3054, E-mail: hvisenti@smith.edu.

**GRADUATE UNITS**

**Graduate and Special Programs** Students: 65 full-time (48 women), 16 part-time (11 women); includes 19 minority (4 Black or African American, non-Hispanic/Latino; 4 Asian, non-Hispanic/Latino; 6 Hispanic/Latino; 5 Two or more races, non-Hispanic/Latino), 13 international. Average age 27. 120 applicants, 55% accepted, 45 enrolled. *Faculty:* 290 full-time (172 women), 17 part-time/adjunct (9 women). Expenses: Contact institution. *Financial support:* In 2019–20, 70 students received support, including 7 fellowships with full tuition reimbursements available, 5 research assistantships with full tuition reimbursements available (averaging $13,850 per year), 7 teaching assistantships with full tuition reimbursements available (averaging $13,850 per year); scholarships/grants, tuition waivers (full and partial), and human resources employee benefit also available. Support available to part-time students. Financial award application deadline: 1/15; financial award applicants required to submit CSS PROFILE or FAFSA. In 2019, 41 master's, 8 other advanced degrees awarded. *Program availability:* Part-time. *Application deadline:* For fall admission, 1/15 for domestic and international students; for spring admission, 12/1 for domestic students. *Application fee:* $60. *Application Contact:* Ruth Morgan, Program Coordinator, 413-585-3050, Fax: 413-585-3054, E-mail: gradstdy@smith.edu. *Director*, Helene Visentin, 413-585-3050, Fax: 413-585-3054, E-mail: hvisenti@smith.edu.

**School for Social Work** Students: 227 full-time (195 women), 42 part-time (37 women); includes 71 minority (23 Black or African American, non-Hispanic/Latino; 2 American Indian or Alaska Native, non-Hispanic/Latino; 17 Asian, non-Hispanic/Latino; 21 Hispanic/Latino; 8 Two or more races, non-Hispanic/Latino). Average age 32. 398 applicants, 50% accepted, 112 enrolled. *Faculty:* 14 full-time (10 women), 105 part-time/adjunct (74 women). Expenses: Contact institution. *Financial support:* In 2019–20, 258 students received support. Research assistantships, career-related internships or fieldwork, and scholarships/grants available. Financial award application deadline: 3/1; financial award applicants required to submit FAFSA. In 2019, 119 master's, 7 doctorates awarded. *Application deadline:* For fall admission, 2/21 for domestic students, 2/15 for international students. Applications are processed on a rolling basis. *Application fee:* $60. Electronic applications accepted. *Application Contact:* Irene Rodriguez Martin, Associate Dean, Graduate Enrollment and Student Services, 413-585-7960, Fax: 413-585-7994, E-mail: imartin@smith.edu. *Dean/Professor*, Dr. Marianne Yoshioka, 413-585-7977, E-mail: myoshioka@smith.edu.

## SOFIA UNIVERSITY, Palo Alto, CA 94303

**General Information** Independent, coed, graduate-only institution. *Graduate housing:* On-campus housing not available.

**GRADUATE UNITS**

**Hybrid: Face-to-Face/Online Programs** *Program availability:* Online learning. Electronic applications accepted.

**Residential Programs** *Program availability:* Part-time, evening/weekend. Electronic applications accepted.

## SOKA UNIVERSITY OF AMERICA, Aliso Viejo, CA 92656

**General Information** Independent, coed, comprehensive institution. *Graduate housing:* Room and/or apartments available to single students; on-campus housing not available to married students.

**GRADUATE UNITS**

**Graduate School** *Program availability:* Evening/weekend.

## SONOMA STATE UNIVERSITY, Rohnert Park, CA 94928-3609

**General Information** State-supported, coed, comprehensive institution. *Graduate housing:* Room and/or apartments available on a first-come, first-served basis to single students; on-campus housing not available to married students. Housing application deadline: 1/1. *Research affiliation:* Biomimetica (bioacoustics, metabolic flux modeling), Gallo Family Vineyards (science), Kenwood Vineyards (science), Natural Industries, Inc. (Sudden Oak Death research), Clean Filtration Technologies (environmental microbiology).

**GRADUATE UNITS**

**Department of English** *Program availability:* Part-time, evening/weekend.

**School of Business and Economics** *Program availability:* Part-time, evening/weekend.

**School of Education** *Program availability:* Part-time, evening/weekend.

**School of Science and Technology** *Program availability:* Part-time.

**School of Social Sciences** *Program availability:* Part-time, evening/weekend.

## SOTHEBY'S INSTITUTE OF ART–LONDON, WC1B 3EE London, United Kingdom

**General Information** Private, coed, graduate-only institution. *Graduate housing:* On-campus housing not available. *Research affiliation:* University of Manchester.

**GRADUATE UNITS**

**Graduate Programs** Electronic applications accepted.

## SOTHEBY'S INSTITUTE OF ART–NEW YORK, New York, NY 10021

**General Information** Proprietary, coed, graduate-only institution. *Graduate housing:* On-campus housing not available.

**GRADUATE UNITS**

**Graduate Programs** Electronic applications accepted.

## SOUTH BAYLO UNIVERSITY, Anaheim, CA 92801-1701

**General Information** Independent, coed, graduate-only institution. *Graduate housing:* On-campus housing not available. *Research affiliation:* University of California Irvine College of Medicine (complimentary and alternative medicine), National Nutritional Foods Association (herbs and nutritional supplements), Henan College of Traditional Chinese Medicine (herbology and acupuncture), Kaiser Permanente (patient care: acupuncture and Oriental medicine), University of Illinois at Chicago (testing of herbal formulations).

**GRADUATE UNITS**

**Program in Oriental Medicine and Acupuncture** *Program availability:* Evening/weekend. Electronic applications accepted.

## SOUTH CAROLINA STATE UNIVERSITY, Orangeburg, SC 29117-0001

**General Information** State-supported, coed, comprehensive institution. *Graduate housing:* Room and/or apartments available on a first-come, first-served basis to single students; on-campus housing not available to married students. Housing application deadline: 7/31.

**GRADUATE UNITS**

**College of Graduate and Professional Studies** *Program availability:* Part-time, evening/weekend. Electronic applications accepted.

***Department of Business Administration*** *Program availability:* Part-time, evening/weekend. Electronic applications accepted.

## SOUTH COLLEGE, Knoxville, TN 37917

**General Information** Proprietary, coed, primarily women, comprehensive institution.

**GRADUATE UNITS**

**Program in Pharmacy**

**Program in Physician Assistant Studies**

## SOUTH DAKOTA SCHOOL OF MINES AND TECHNOLOGY, Rapid City, SD 57701-3995

**General Information** State-supported, coed, university. CGS member. *Graduate housing:* Room and/or apartments available on a first-come, first-served basis to single students; on-campus housing not available to married students. *Research affiliation:* Raven Industries (composite and thin films), Black Hills Power (NDA-Lightning (experimental and data collection)), CalxAqua (filtration media), RESPEC, Inc. (mining and waste storage), HF Webster (cold spray applications), Nanofiber Sperations (cutting edge separation media composed of functionalized nanofibers).

**GRADUATE UNITS**

**Graduate Division** *Program availability:* Part-time. Electronic applications accepted.

***College of Engineering*** *Program availability:* Part-time, online learning. Electronic applications accepted.

***College of Science and Letters*** *Program availability:* Part-time.

## SOUTH DAKOTA STATE UNIVERSITY, Brookings, SD 57007

**General Information** State-supported, coed, university. CGS member. *Graduate housing:* Rooms and/or apartments available to single and married students.

**GRADUATE UNITS**

**Graduate School** *Program availability:* Part-time, evening/weekend, online learning.

***College of Agriculture, Food and Environmental Sciences*** *Program availability:* Part-time.

***College of Arts, Humanities and Social Sciences*** *Program availability:* Part-time.

***College of Education and Human Sciences***

***College of Natural Sciences***

***College of Nursing*** *Program availability:* Part-time, evening/weekend, online learning.

***College of Pharmacy and Allied Health Professions***

***Jerome J. Lohr College of Engineering*** *Program availability:* Part-time.

## SOUTHEASTERN BAPTIST THEOLOGICAL SEMINARY, Wake Forest, NC 27587

**General Information** Independent-religious, coed, comprehensive institution. *Graduate housing:* Rooms and/or apartments available on a first-come, first-served basis to single and married students.

**GRADUATE UNITS**

**Graduate and Professional Programs**

## SOUTHEASTERN LOUISIANA UNIVERSITY, Hammond, LA 70402

**General Information** State-supported, coed, comprehensive institution. *Enrollment:* 14,260 graduate, professional, and undergraduate students; 363 full-time matriculated graduate/professional students (252 women), 512 part-time matriculated graduate/professional students (404 women). *Enrollment by degree level:* 735 master's, 122 doctoral, 18 other advanced degrees. *Graduate faculty:* 160 full-time (87 women), 3 part-time/adjunct (2 women). *International tuition:* $19,162 full-time. *Tuition, area resident:* Full-time $6684; part-time $489 per credit hour. Tuition, state resident: full-time $6684; part-time $489 per credit hour. Tuition, nonresident: full-time $19,162; part-time $1183 per credit hour. *Required fees:* $2124. *Graduate housing:* Room and/or apartments available on a first-come, first-served basis to single students; on-campus housing not available to married students. Typical cost: $3160 per year ($4715 including board). Room and board charges vary according to board plan and housing facility selected. Housing application deadline: 6/15. *Student services:* Campus employment opportunities, campus safety program, career counseling, exercise/wellness program, free psychological counseling, international student services, low-cost health insurance, multicultural affairs office, services for students with disabilities, teacher training, writing training. *Library facilities:* Linus A. Sims Memorial Library plus 1 other. *Collection:* Books: 1.3 million (physical), 513,005 (digital/electronic); Serial titles: 499 (physical), 56,076 (digital/electronic). Students can reserve study rooms. *Research affiliation:* Bradken Manufacturing (steel), Petroleum Research Fund (chemistry), Gaylord Chemical Company (chemical manufacturing), Ochsner Medical Center (medicine), Lake Ponchartrain Basin Foundation (water quality and wetland ecology).

**Computer facilities:** 1,123 computers available on campus for general student use. A campuswide network can be accessed from student residence rooms and from off campus. Online class registration, campus Webmail, student newspaper, transcripts, bookstore are available.
Website: http://www.southeastern.edu/

**General Application Contact:** John Boulahanis, Director of Graduate Studies, 985-549-2610, Fax: 985-549-5882, E-mail: graduatestudies@southeastern.edu.

**GRADUATE UNITS**

**College of Arts, Humanities and Social Sciences** Students: 83 full-time (48 women), 64 part-time (29 women); includes 39 minority (14 Black or African American, non-Hispanic/Latino; 1 American Indian or Alaska Native, non-Hispanic/Latino; 2 Asian, non-Hispanic/Latino; 10 Hispanic/Latino; 1 Native Hawaiian or other Pacific Islander, non-Hispanic/Latino; 11 Two or more races, non-Hispanic/Latino), 5 international. Average age 28. 58 applicants, 98% accepted, 41 enrolled. *Faculty:* 62 full-time (28 women), 1 part-time/adjunct (0 women). Expenses: Contact institution. *Financial support:* In 2019–20, 99 students received support, including 1 fellowship with tuition reimbursement available (averaging $2,500 per year), 30 research assistantships with tuition reimbursements available (averaging $9,623 per year), 21 teaching assistantships with tuition reimbursements available (averaging $9,886 per year); career-related internships or fieldwork, institutionally sponsored loans, traineeships, and unspecified assistantships also available. Financial award application deadline: 5/1; financial award applicants required to submit FAFSA. In 2019, 40 master's awarded. *Program availability:* Part-time, evening/weekend. *Application deadline:* For fall admission, 7/15 priority date for domestic students, 6/1 priority date for international students; for spring admission, 12/1 priority date for domestic students, 10/1 priority date for international students. Applications are processed on a rolling basis. *Application fee:* $20 ($30 for international students). Electronic applications accepted. *Application Contact:* Office of Admissions, 985-549-5637, Fax: 985-549-5822, E-mail: admissions@southeastern.edu. *Dean,* Dr. Karen Fontenot, 985-549-2101, Fax: 985-549-5014, E-mail: ahss@southeastern.edu.

**College of Business** Students: 75 full-time (36 women), 18 part-time (8 women); includes 13 minority (5 Black or African American, non-Hispanic/Latino; 1 American Indian or Alaska Native, non-Hispanic/Latino; 7 Hispanic/Latino), 8 international. Average age 27. 32 applicants, 94% accepted, 24 enrolled. *Faculty:* 15 full-time (2 women). Expenses: Contact institution. *Financial support:* In 2019–20, 56 students received support, including 1 fellowship with tuition reimbursement available (averaging $2,500 per year), 1 research assistantship with tuition reimbursement available (averaging $9,000 per year); career-related internships or fieldwork, institutionally sponsored loans, and unspecified assistantships also available. Financial award application deadline: 5/1; financial award applicants required to submit FAFSA. In 2019, 71 master's awarded. *Program availability:* Part-time, evening/weekend. *Application deadline:* For fall admission, 7/15 priority date for domestic students, 6/1 priority date for international students; for spring admission, 12/1 priority date for domestic students, 10/1 priority date for international students. Applications are processed on a rolling basis. *Application fee:* $20 ($30 for international students). Electronic applications accepted. *Application Contact:* Dr. Antoinette Phillips, Dean, 985-549-2258, Fax: 985-549-5038, E-mail: business@southeastern.edu. *Dean,* Dr. Antoinette Phillips, 985-549-2258, Fax: 985-549-5038, E-mail: business@southeastern.edu.

**College of Education** Students: 6 full-time (4 women), 231 part-time (197 women); includes 73 minority (57 Black or African American, non-Hispanic/Latino; 1 American Indian or Alaska Native, non-Hispanic/Latino; 1 Asian, non-Hispanic/Latino; 6 Hispanic/Latino; 8 Two or more races, non-Hispanic/Latino), 2 international. Average age 38. 54 applicants, 98% accepted, 47 enrolled. *Faculty:* 19 full-time (13 women). Expenses: Contact institution. *Financial support:* In 2019–20, 6 students received support, including 1 fellowship with tuition reimbursement available (averaging $2,500 per year); institutionally sponsored loans, traineeships, and unspecified assistantships also available. Financial award application deadline: 5/1; financial award applicants required to submit FAFSA. In 2019, 49 master's, 7 doctorates awarded. *Program availability:* Part-time. *Application deadline:* For fall admission, 7/15 priority date for domestic students, 6/1 priority date for international students; for spring admission, 12/1 priority date for domestic students, 10/1 priority date for international students. Applications are processed on a rolling basis. *Application fee:* $20 ($30 for international students). Electronic applications accepted. *Application Contact:* Dr. Paula Calderon, Dean, 985-549-2217, Fax: 985-549-2070, E-mail: collegeofeducation@southeastern.edu. *Dean,* Dr. Paula Calderon, 985-549-2217, Fax: 985-549-2070, E-mail: collegeofeducation@southeastern.edu.

**College of Nursing and Health Sciences** Students: 167 full-time (144 women), 191 part-time (168 women); includes 90 minority (48 Black or African American, non-Hispanic/Latino; 4 American Indian or Alaska Native, non-Hispanic/Latino; 2 Asian, non-Hispanic/Latino; 22 Hispanic/Latino; 1 Native Hawaiian or other Pacific Islander, non-Hispanic/Latino; 13 Two or more races, non-Hispanic/Latino), 4 international. Average age 30. 247 applicants, 67% accepted, 77 enrolled. *Faculty:* 42 full-time (36 women), 2 part-time/adjunct (both women). Expenses: Contact institution. *Financial support:* In 2019–20, 113 students received support, including 2 fellowships with tuition reimbursements available (averaging $1,250 per year), 6 research assistantships with tuition reimbursements available (averaging $9,367 per year), 6 teaching assistantships with tuition reimbursements available (averaging $10,700 per year); career-related internships or fieldwork, institutionally sponsored loans, and unspecified assistantships also available. Financial award application deadline: 5/1; financial award applicants required to submit FAFSA. In 2019, 114 master's, 9 doctorates awarded. *Program* *availability:* Part-time, evening/weekend, 100% online. *Application deadline:* For fall admission, 7/15 priority date for domestic students, 6/1 priority date for international students; for spring admission, 12/1 priority date for domestic students, 10/1 priority date for international students. Applications are processed on a rolling basis. *Application fee:* $20 ($30 for international students). Electronic applications accepted. *Application Contact:* Office of Admissions, 985-549-5637, Fax: 985-549-5632, E-mail: admissions@southeastern.edu. *Dean,* Dr. Ann Carruth, 985-549-3772, Fax: 985-549-5179, E-mail: cnhs@southeastern.edu.

***School of Nursing*** Students: 24 full-time (19 women), 127 part-time (116 women); includes 37 minority (23 Black or African American, non-Hispanic/Latino; 1 American Indian or Alaska Native, non-Hispanic/Latino; 2 Asian, non-Hispanic/Latino; 4 Hispanic/Latino; 7 Two or more races, non-Hispanic/Latino). Average age 35. 63 applicants, 49% accepted, 19 enrolled. *Faculty:* 16 full-time (15 women), 1 (woman) part-time/adjunct. Expenses: Contact institution. *Financial support:* Institutionally sponsored loans and unspecified assistantships available. Financial award application deadline: 5/1; financial award applicants required to submit FAFSA. In 2019, 40 master's, 9 doctorates awarded. *Program availability:* Part-time, 100% online. *Application deadline:* For fall admission, 4/1 for domestic and international students; for spring admission, 10/1 for domestic and international students. Applications are processed on a rolling basis. *Application fee:* $20 ($30 for international students). Electronic applications accepted. *Application Contact:* Office of Admissions, 985-549-5637, Fax: 985-549-5632, E-mail: admissions@southeastern.edu. *Department Head, School of Nursing,* Dr. Ken Tillman, 985-549-2156, Fax: 985-549-2869, E-mail: nursing@southeastern.edu.

**College of Science and Technology** Students: 32 full-time (20 women), 8 part-time (2 women); includes 5 minority (1 Black or African American, non-Hispanic/Latino; 1 Asian, non-Hispanic/Latino; 3 Hispanic/Latino), 4 international. Average age 26. 23 applicants, 100% accepted, 15 enrolled. *Faculty:* 22 full-time (8 women). Expenses: Contact institution. *Financial support:* In 2019–20, 37 students received support, including 1 fellowship with tuition reimbursement available (averaging $2,500 per year), 10 research assistantships with tuition reimbursements available (averaging $9,990 per year), 14 teaching assistantships with tuition reimbursements available (averaging $10,721 per year); career-related internships or fieldwork, institutionally sponsored loans, and unspecified assistantships also available. Financial award application deadline: 5/1; financial award applicants required to submit FAFSA. In 2019, 14 master's awarded. *Program availability:* Part-time. *Application deadline:* For fall admission, 7/15 priority date for domestic students, 6/1 priority date for international students; for spring admission, 12/1 priority date for domestic students, 10/1 priority date for international students. Applications are processed on a rolling basis. *Application fee:* $20 ($30 for international students). Electronic applications accepted. *Application Contact:* Office of Admissions, 985-549-5637, Fax: 985-549-5632, E-mail: admissions@southeastern.edu. *Dean,* Dr. Daniel McCarthy, 985-549-2055, Fax: 985-549-3396, E-mail: science@southeastern.edu.

## SOUTHEASTERN OKLAHOMA STATE UNIVERSITY, Durant, OK 74701-0609

**General Information** State-supported, coed, comprehensive institution. *Graduate housing:* Rooms and/or apartments available on a first-come, first-served basis to single and married students. Housing application deadline: 6/15. *Research affiliation:* U.S. Department of the Interior (biological sciences), U.S. Department of Agriculture (USDA) (biological sciences), National Science Foundation (chemistry, computer science, physical sciences), U.S. Fish and Wildlife Service (biological sciences), National Institutes of Health (biological sciences, chemistry, computer science, physical sciences).

**GRADUATE UNITS**

**Department of Aviation Science** *Program availability:* Part-time, evening/weekend. Electronic applications accepted.

**John Massey School of Business** *Program availability:* Part-time, evening/weekend. Electronic applications accepted.

**School of Arts and Sciences** *Program availability:* Part-time, evening/weekend. Electronic applications accepted.

**School of Behavioral Sciences** *Program availability:* Part-time, evening/weekend. Electronic applications accepted.

**School of Education** *Program availability:* Part-time, evening/weekend. Electronic applications accepted.

## SOUTHEASTERN UNIVERSITY, Lakeland, FL 33801-6099

**General Information** Independent-religious, coed, comprehensive institution. *Enrollment:* 8,759 graduate, professional, and undergraduate students; 485 full-time matriculated graduate/professional students (301 women), 681 part-time matriculated graduate/professional students (428 women). *Enrollment by degree level:* 942 master's, 224 doctoral. *Graduate faculty:* 52 full-time (24 women), 24 part-time/adjunct (8 women). *Graduate housing:* On-campus housing not available. *Student services:* Campus employment opportunities, campus safety program, career counseling, exercise/wellness program, international student services, multicultural affairs office, services for students with disabilities, writing training. *Library facilities:* Steelman Library.

**Computer facilities:** 220 computers available on campus for general student use. A campuswide network can be accessed from student residence rooms and from off campus. Online class registration, network programs are available.
Website: http://www.seu.edu/

**GRADUATE UNITS**

**Barnett College of Ministry & Theology** Students: 103 full-time (38 women), 195 part-time (77 women); includes 90 minority (28 Black or African American, non-Hispanic/Latino; 1 American Indian or Alaska Native, non-Hispanic/Latino; 16 Asian, non-Hispanic/Latino; 37 Hispanic/Latino; 2 Native Hawaiian or other Pacific Islander, non-Hispanic/Latino; 6 Two or more races, non-Hispanic/Latino), 4 international. Average age 37. *Faculty:* 30 full-time (5 women), 1 part-time/adjunct (0 women). Expenses: Contact institution. In 2019, 73 master's, 5 doctorates awarded. *Program availability:* Evening/weekend, online learning. *Application fee:* $50. Electronic applications accepted. *Application Contact:* Dr. Alan Ehler, Dean, 863-667-5044, E-mail: ajehler@seu.edu. *Dean,* Dr. Alan Ehler, 863-667-5044, E-mail: ajehler@seu.edu.

**College of Behavioral & Social Sciences** Students: 95 full-time (80 women), 9 part-time (6 women); includes 49 minority (18 Black or African American, non-Hispanic/Latino; 3 Asian, non-Hispanic/Latino; 25 Hispanic/Latino; 1 Native Hawaiian or other Pacific Islander, non-Hispanic/Latino; 2 Two or more races, non-Hispanic/Latino), 1 international. Average age 28. *Faculty:* 17 full-time (12 women). Expenses: Contact institution. In 2019, 50 master's awarded. *Program availability:* Evening/weekend. *Application fee:* $50. Electronic applications accepted. *Application Contact:* Dr. Erica H. Sirrine, Dean, 863-667-5341, E-mail: ehsirrine@seu.edu. *Dean,* Dr. Erica H. Sirrine, 863-667-5341, E-mail: ehsirrine@seu.edu.

**College of Education** Students: 136 full-time (100 women), 311 part-time (248 women); includes 163 minority (84 Black or African American, non-Hispanic/Latino; 1 American Indian or Alaska Native, non-Hispanic/Latino; 8 Asian, non-Hispanic/Latino; 64 Hispanic/Latino; 6 Two or more races, non-Hispanic/Latino), 4 international. Average age 38. *Faculty:* 25 full-time (13 women), 9 part-time/adjunct (7 women). Expenses: Contact institution. In 2019, 105 master's, 18 doctorates awarded. *Application fee:* $50. Electronic applications accepted. *Application Contact:* Dr. James A. Anderson, Dean, 863-667-5366, E-mail: jaanderson2@seu.edu. *Dean,* Dr. James A. Anderson, 863-667-5366, E-mail: jaanderson2@seu.edu.

**Jannetides College of Business & Entrepreneurial Leadership** Students: 127 full-time (61 women), 80 part-time (41 women); includes 78 minority (37 Black or African American, non-Hispanic/Latino; 5 Asian, non-Hispanic/Latino; 34 Hispanic/Latino; 1 Native Hawaiian or other Pacific Islander, non-Hispanic/Latino; 1 Two or more races, non-Hispanic/Latino), 4 international. Average age 33. *Faculty:* 16 full-time (3 women). Expenses: Contact institution. In 2019, 63 master's awarded. *Program availability:* Evening/weekend, online learning. *Application fee:* $50. Electronic applications accepted. *Application Contact:* Dr. Lyle L. Bowlin, Dean, 863-667-5118, E-mail: llbowlin@seu.edu. *Dean,* Dr. Lyle L. Bowlin, 863-667-5118, E-mail: llbowlin@seu.edu.

## SOUTHEAST MISSOURI STATE UNIVERSITY, Cape Girardeau, MO 63701-4799

**General Information** State-supported, coed, comprehensive institution. CGS member. *Enrollment:* 10,637 graduate, professional, and undergraduate students; 451 full-time matriculated graduate/professional students (275 women), 649 part-time matriculated graduate/professional students (465 women). *Enrollment by degree level:* 952 master's, 17 doctoral, 131 other advanced degrees. *Graduate faculty:* 196 full-time (100 women), 9 part-time/adjunct (4 women). *International tuition:* $13,061 full-time. Tuition, state resident: full-time $6989; part-time $291.20 per credit hour. Tuition, nonresident: full-time $13,061; part-time $544.20 per credit hour. *Required fees:* $955; $39.80 per credit hour. Tuition and fees vary according to degree level. *Graduate housing:* Room and/or apartments available on a first-come, first-served basis to single students; on-campus housing not available to married students. Housing application deadline: 12/1. *Student services:* Campus employment opportunities, campus safety program, career counseling, child daycare facilities, exercise/wellness program, free psychological counseling, international student services, multicultural affairs office, services for students with disabilities, teacher training, writing training. *Library facilities:* Kent Library. *Collection:* Books: 380,006 (physical), 263,780 (digital/electronic); Serial titles: 4,163 (physical), 58,594 (digital/electronic); Databases: 159. Weekly public service hours: 92.

**Computer facilities:** 1,550 computers available on campus for general student use. A campuswide network can be accessed. Online class registration is available.
Website: http://www.semo.edu/

**GRADUATE UNITS**

***Harrison College of Business and Computing*** *Program availability:* Part-time, evening/weekend, 100% online. Electronic applications accepted.

## SOUTHERN ADVENTIST UNIVERSITY, Collegedale, TN 37315-0370

**General Information** Independent-religious, coed, comprehensive institution. *Graduate housing:* Rooms and/or apartments available on a first-come, first-served basis to single and married students. Housing application deadline: 7/1.

**GRADUATE UNITS**

**School of Business** *Program availability:* Part-time, evening/weekend, 100% online. Electronic applications accepted.

**School of Computing** *Program availability:* Part-time. Electronic applications accepted.

**School of Education and Psychology** *Program availability:* Part-time, evening/weekend, 100% online, blended/hybrid learning. Electronic applications accepted.

**School of Nursing** *Program availability:* Part-time, 100% online. Electronic applications accepted.

**School of Religion** *Program availability:* Part-time.

**School of Social Work** *Program availability:* Part-time, evening/weekend. Electronic applications accepted.

## SOUTHERN ARKANSAS UNIVERSITY–MAGNOLIA, Magnolia, AR 71753

**General Information** State-supported, coed, comprehensive institution. *Enrollment:* 4,474 graduate, professional, and undergraduate students; 134 full-time matriculated graduate/professional students (80 women), 704 part-time matriculated graduate/professional students (471 women). *Enrollment by degree level:* 838 master's. *Graduate faculty:* 33 full-time (18 women), 29 part-time/adjunct (17 women). *International tuition:* $10,560 full-time. *Tuition, area resident:* Full-time $6720; part-time $3360 per semester. Tuition, state resident: full-time $6720; part-time $3360 per semester. Tuition, nonresident: full-time $10,560; part-time $5280 per semester. *Required fees:* $2046; $1023 $267. One-time fee: $25. Tuition and fees vary according to course load. *Graduate housing:* Rooms and/or apartments available on a first-come, first-served basis to single and married students. Typical cost: $6300 per year ($6745 including board) for single students; $10,680 per year ($11,155 including board) for married students. Room and board charges vary according to board plan, campus/location and housing facility selected. Housing application deadline: 8/1. *Student services:* Campus employment opportunities, campus safety program, career counseling, exercise/wellness program, free psychological counseling, international student services, low-cost health insurance, multicultural affairs office, services for students with disabilities, writing training. *Library facilities:* Magale Library. *Collection:* Books: 149,415 (physical), 14,006 (digital/electronic); Serial titles: 96 (physical), 82 (digital/electronic); Databases: 188. Weekly public service hours: 87.

**Computer facilities:** 199 computers available on campus for general student use. A campuswide network can be accessed. Online class registration is available.
Website: http://www.saumag.edu/

**General Application Contact:** Talia Jett, Admissions Coordinator, School of Graduate Studies, 870-235-5450, Fax: 870-235-5227, E-mail: taliajett@saumag.edu.

**GRADUATE UNITS**

**School of Graduate Studies** Students: 134 full-time (80 women), 704 part-time (471 women); includes 223 minority (158 Black or African American, non-Hispanic/Latino; 5 American Indian or Alaska Native, non-Hispanic/Latino; 19 Asian, non-Hispanic/Latino; 6 Hispanic/Latino; 1 Native Hawaiian or other Pacific Islander, non-Hispanic/Latino; 34 Two or more races, non-Hispanic/Latino), 135 international. Average age 28. 290 applicants, 99% accepted, 149 enrolled. *Faculty:* 33 full-time (18 women), 29 part-time/adjunct (17 women). Expenses: Contact institution. *Financial support:* Career-related internships or fieldwork, Federal Work-Study, scholarships/grants, tuition waivers (full), and unspecified assistantships available. Financial award applicants required to submit FAFSA. In 2019, 177 master's awarded. *Program availability:* Part-time, 100% online, blended/hybrid learning. *Application deadline:* For fall admission, 8/1 for domestic and international students; for spring admission, 12/1 for domestic students, 11/15 for international students; for summer admission, 5/1 for domestic students, 5/10 for international students. Applications are processed on a rolling basis. *Application fee:* $25 ($90 for international students). Electronic applications accepted. *Application Contact:* Talia Jett, Admissions Coordinator, 870-2355450, Fax: 870-235-5227, E-mail: taliajett@saumag.edu. *Dean, School of Graduate Studies*, Dr. Kim Bloss, 870-235-4150, Fax: 870-235-5227, E-mail: kkbloss@saumag.edu.

## THE SOUTHERN BAPTIST THEOLOGICAL SEMINARY, Louisville, KY 40280-0004

**General Information** Independent-religious, coed, comprehensive institution. *Graduate housing:* Rooms and/or apartments available on a first-come, first-served basis to single and married students.

**GRADUATE UNITS**

**Billy Graham School of Missions, Evangelism and Ministry** *Program availability:* Part-time, evening/weekend, online learning.

**School of Theology** *Program availability:* Part-time, evening/weekend, online learning.

## SOUTHERN CALIFORNIA INSTITUTE OF ARCHITECTURE, Los Angeles, CA 90013

**General Information** Independent, coed, comprehensive institution. *Graduate housing:* On-campus housing not available.

**GRADUATE UNITS**

**Center for Advanced Studies**

**Graduate Program in Architecture** Electronic applications accepted.

## SOUTHERN CALIFORNIA SEMINARY, El Cajon, CA 92019

**General Information** Independent-religious, coed, comprehensive institution. *Graduate housing:* Rooms and/or apartments available on a first-come, first-served basis to single and married students.

**GRADUATE UNITS**

**Graduate and Professional Programs** *Program availability:* Part-time, evening/weekend, online learning. Electronic applications accepted.

## SOUTHERN CALIFORNIA UNIVERSITY OF HEALTH SCIENCES, Whittier, CA 90609-1166

**General Information** Independent, coed, graduate-only institution. *Graduate housing:* On-campus housing not available. *Research affiliation:* Samueli Institute (alternative health care), Anton B. Burg Foundation (alternative health care).

**GRADUATE UNITS**

**College of Eastern Medicine** *Program availability:* Part-time, evening/weekend. Electronic applications accepted.

**Los Angeles College of Chiropractic** Electronic applications accepted.

## SOUTHERN COLLEGE OF OPTOMETRY, Memphis, TN 38104-2222

**General Information** Independent, coed, graduate-only institution. *Graduate housing:* On-campus housing not available.

**GRADUATE UNITS**

**Professional Program**

## SOUTHERN CONNECTICUT STATE UNIVERSITY, New Haven, CT 06515-1355

**General Information** State-supported, coed, comprehensive institution. CGS member. *Graduate housing:* Room and/or apartments available on a first-come, first-served basis to single students; on-campus housing not available to married students.

**GRADUATE UNITS**

**School of Graduate Studies** *Program availability:* Part-time, evening/weekend, online learning. Electronic applications accepted.

***School of Arts and Sciences*** Electronic applications accepted.

***School of Business*** *Program availability:* Part-time, evening/weekend. Electronic applications accepted.

***School of Education*** *Program availability:* Part-time. Electronic applications accepted.

***School of Health and Human Services*** *Program availability:* Part-time, evening/weekend. Electronic applications accepted.

## SOUTHERN EVANGELICAL SEMINARY, Matthews, NC 28105

**General Information** Independent-religious, coed, primarily men, graduate-only institution. *Enrollment by degree level:* 118 master's, 36 doctoral. *Graduate faculty:* 8 full-time (0 women), 11 part-time/adjunct (0 women). *Tuition:* Full-time $24,000; part-time $12,000 per year. *Required fees:* $600; $300 per semester. $150 per semester. *Graduate housing:* On-campus housing not available. *Student services:* Campus employment opportunities, international student services, writing training. *Library facilities:* Jamison Library. *Collection:* Books: 60,000 (physical), 60,000 (digital/electronic); Databases: 6. Weekly public service hours: 40.

**Computer facilities:** 5 computers available on campus for general student use. A campuswide network can be accessed from student residence rooms and from off campus. Online class registration is available.
Website: http://www.ses.edu/

**General Application Contact:** Adam Tucker, Director of Recruitment, 704-847-5600 Ext. 211, E-mail: atucker@ses.edu.

**GRADUATE UNITS**

**Graduate Programs** *Program availability:* Part-time, evening/weekend, online learning.

## SOUTHERN ILLINOIS UNIVERSITY CARBONDALE, Carbondale, IL 62901-4701

**General Information** State-supported, coed, university. CGS member. *Graduate housing:* Rooms and/or apartments available on a first-come, first-served basis to single and married students. *Research affiliation:* NASA-Ames Research Center, Argonne National Laboratory.

**GRADUATE UNITS**

**Graduate School** *Program availability:* Part-time.

***College of Agriculture*** *Program availability:* Part-time.

***College of Applied Science*** Electronic applications accepted.

***College of Business and Administration*** *Program availability:* Part-time. Electronic applications accepted.

***College of Education and Human Services*** *Program availability:* Part-time. Electronic applications accepted.

***College of Engineering***

***College of Liberal Arts*** *Program availability:* Part-time.

***College of Mass Communication and Media Arts*** *Program availability:* Part-time.

***College of Science*** *Program availability:* Part-time.

**School of Law** *Program availability:* Part-time. Electronic applications accepted.

## SOUTHERN ILLINOIS UNIVERSITY EDWARDSVILLE, Edwardsville, IL 62026

**General Information** State-supported, coed, university. CGS member. *Graduate housing:* Rooms and/or apartments available on a first-come, first-served basis to single and married students. Housing application deadline: 5/1. *Research affiliation:* Long Island Veterinary Clinic (electrical engineering), SSM DePaul Health Center (nursing), Nurturenergy (mechanical engineering), Tulsa Dental Products (dental medicine), Mallinckrodt (pharmacy), Schlumberger (mechanical engineering).

**GRADUATE UNITS**

**Graduate School** *Program availability:* Part-time, evening/weekend, blended/hybrid learning. Electronic applications accepted.

***College of Arts and Sciences*** *Program availability:* Part-time, evening/weekend, online learning. Electronic applications accepted.

***School of Business*** *Program availability:* Part-time, evening/weekend. Electronic applications accepted.

***School of Education, Health, and Human Behavior*** *Program availability:* Part-time, evening/weekend. Electronic applications accepted.

***School of Engineering*** *Program availability:* Part-time, evening/weekend. Electronic applications accepted.

***School of Nursing*** *Program availability:* Part-time, evening/weekend. Electronic applications accepted.

**School of Dental Medicine** Electronic applications accepted.

**School of Pharmacy** Electronic applications accepted.

## SOUTHERN METHODIST UNIVERSITY, Dallas, TX 75275

**General Information** Independent-religious, coed, university. CGS member. *Graduate housing:* Rooms and/or apartments available on a first-come, first-served basis to single and married students. Housing application deadline: 6/1.

**GRADUATE UNITS**

**Cox School of Business** *Program availability:* Part-time, evening/weekend. Electronic applications accepted.

**Dedman College of Humanities and Sciences** *Program availability:* Part-time, evening/weekend. Electronic applications accepted.

**Dedman School of Law** *Program availability:* Part-time, evening/weekend. Electronic applications accepted.

**Lyle School of Engineering** *Program availability:* Part-time, evening/weekend, online learning.

**Meadows School of the Arts** *Program availability:* Evening/weekend. Electronic applications accepted.

***Division of Art***

***Division of Art History*** *Program availability:* Part-time, evening/weekend.

***Division of Arts Management and Arts Entrepreneurship*** Electronic applications accepted.

***Division of Music*** *Program availability:* Part-time. Electronic applications accepted.

***Division of Theatre*** Electronic applications accepted.

***Temerlin Advertising Institute*** Electronic applications accepted.

**Perkins School of Theology** *Program availability:* Part-time.

**Simmons School of Education and Human Development** *Program availability:* Part-time, evening/weekend.

## SOUTHERN NAZARENE UNIVERSITY, Bethany, OK 73008

**General Information** Independent-religious, coed, comprehensive institution. *Graduate housing:* Rooms and/or apartments available on a first-come, first-served basis to single and married students. Housing application deadline: 8/1.

**GRADUATE UNITS**

**College of Professional and Graduate Studies** *Program availability:* Part-time, evening/weekend. Electronic applications accepted.

***School of Business*** *Program availability:* Part-time, evening/weekend, online learning. Electronic applications accepted.

***School of Kinesiology***

***School of Nursing*** *Program availability:* Part-time, evening/weekend.

## SOUTHERN NEW HAMPSHIRE UNIVERSITY, Manchester, NH 03106-1045

**General Information** Independent, coed, university. *Graduate housing:* Room and/or apartments available on a first-come, first-served basis to single students; on-campus housing not available to married students.

**GRADUATE UNITS**

**Program in Nursing** *Program availability:* Online only, 100% online. Electronic applications accepted.

**School of Arts and Sciences** *Program availability:* Part-time, evening/weekend. Electronic applications accepted.

**School of Business** *Program availability:* Part-time, evening/weekend, online learning. Electronic applications accepted.

**School of Education** *Program availability:* Part-time, evening/weekend, online learning. Electronic applications accepted.

## SOUTHERN OREGON UNIVERSITY, Ashland, OR 97520

**General Information** State-supported, coed, comprehensive institution. *Graduate housing:* Rooms and/or apartments available on a first-come, first-served basis to single and married students. Housing application deadline: 8/1. *Research affiliation:* U.S. Forest Service (biology, ecology studies), U.S. Fish and Wildlife Service (forensics), Oregon Shakespeare Festival (theatre arts), Crater Lake National Park (scientific studies), Bureau of Land Management (ecological studies), Bear Creek Corporation (environmental studies).

**GRADUATE UNITS**

**Graduate Studies** *Program availability:* Part-time, evening/weekend, online learning. Electronic applications accepted.

***Ashland Center for Theatre Studies*** *Program availability:* Part-time. Electronic applications accepted.

***School of Business*** *Program availability:* Part-time, evening/weekend, online learning. Electronic applications accepted.

***School of Education*** *Program availability:* Online learning. Electronic applications accepted.

## SOUTHERN STATES UNIVERSITY, San Diego, CA 92110

**General Information** Proprietary, coed, comprehensive institution.

**GRADUATE UNITS**

**Graduate Programs**

## SOUTHERN UNIVERSITY AND AGRICULTURAL AND MECHANICAL COLLEGE, Baton Rouge, LA 70813

**General Information** State-supported, coed, university. CGS member. *Graduate housing:* Room and/or apartments available on a first-come, first-served basis to single students; on-campus housing not available to married students. Housing application deadline: 6/30. *Research affiliation:* Michigan State University (language screening of African-Americans), University of Georgia (substance abuse prevention), The University of Alabama (diabetes), NASA (drinking water remote sensing, mechanical engineering), Livingston Observatory (gravitational waves, cosmic gravity waves, black waves).

**GRADUATE UNITS**

**College of Business**

**College of Nursing and Allied Health**

***School of Nursing*** *Program availability:* Part-time.

**Graduate School** *Program availability:* Part-time.

***College of Agricultural, Family and Consumer Sciences***

***College of Humanities and Interdisciplinary Studies***

***College of Sciences and Engineering*** *Program availability:* Part-time.

***Nelson Mandela College of Government and Social Sciences***

**Southern University Law Center** *Program availability:* Part-time, evening/weekend. Electronic applications accepted.

## SOUTHERN UNIVERSITY AT NEW ORLEANS, New Orleans, LA 70126-1009

**General Information** State-supported, coed, primarily women, comprehensive institution. *Graduate housing:* Room and/or apartments available on a first-come, first-served basis to single students; on-campus housing not available to married students.

**GRADUATE UNITS**

**School of Graduate Studies** *Program availability:* Part-time, evening/weekend.

## SOUTHERN UTAH UNIVERSITY, Cedar City, UT 84720-2498

**General Information** State-supported, coed, comprehensive institution. *Graduate housing:* Room and/or apartments available on a first-come, first-served basis to single students; on-campus housing not available to married students.

**GRADUATE UNITS**

**Master of Accountancy/MBA Dual Degree Program** *Program availability:* Part-time, online only, 100% online. Electronic applications accepted.

**Program in Accounting** *Program availability:* Part-time, 100% online. Electronic applications accepted.

**Program in Arts Administration** *Program availability:* Part-time, 100% online. Electronic applications accepted.

**Program in Business Administration** *Program availability:* Part-time, 100% online. Electronic applications accepted.

**Program in Communication** *Program availability:* Part-time, 100% online. Electronic applications accepted.

**Program in Cyber Security and Information Assurance** *Program availability:* Part-time, online only, 100% online. Electronic applications accepted.

**Program in Education** *Program availability:* Part-time, 100% online. Electronic applications accepted.

**Program in Interdisciplinary Studies** *Program availability:* 100% online.

**Program in Music** *Program availability:* Part-time, 100% online.

**Program in Public Administration** *Program availability:* Part-time, evening/weekend, 100% online. Electronic applications accepted.

**Program in Sports Conditioning and Performance** *Program availability:* Part-time, online only, three intensive summer courses/clinical workshops on campus for 1-2 weeks. Electronic applications accepted.

## SOUTHERN WESLEYAN UNIVERSITY, Central, SC 29630-1020

**General Information** Independent-religious, coed, comprehensive institution. *Graduate housing:* On-campus housing not available.

**GRADUATE UNITS**

**Program in Business Administration** *Program availability:* Evening/weekend.

**Program in Christian Ministries** *Program availability:* Part-time, evening/weekend.

**Program in Education** *Program availability:* Evening/weekend.

**Program in Management** *Program availability:* Evening/weekend.

## SOUTH FLORIDA BIBLE COLLEGE AND THEOLOGICAL SEMINARY, Deerfield Beach, FL 33442

**General Information** Proprietary, coed, comprehensive institution.

**GRADUATE UNITS**

**Graduate Programs**

## SOUTH TEXAS COLLEGE OF LAW HOUSTON, Houston, TX 77002-7000

**General Information** Independent, coed, graduate-only institution.

**GRADUATE UNITS**

**Professional Program** *Program availability:* Part-time, evening/weekend. Electronic applications accepted.

## SOUTH UNIVERSITY - AUSTIN, Round Rock, TX 78681

**General Information** Independent, coed, comprehensive institution.

**GRADUATE UNITS**

**Program in Business Administration**

**Program in Clinical Mental Health Counseling**

**Program in Information Systems and Technology**

## SOUTH UNIVERSITY - COLUMBIA, Columbia, SC 29203

**General Information** Independent, coed, comprehensive institution.

**GRADUATE UNITS**

**Program in Business Administration**

**Program in Clinical Mental Health Counseling**

**Program in Criminal Justice**

**Program in Healthcare Administration**

**Program in Leadership**

**Program in Nursing**

**Program in Pharmacy**

## SOUTH UNIVERSITY - MONTGOMERY, Montgomery, AL 36116-1120

**General Information** Independent, coed, comprehensive institution.

**GRADUATE UNITS**

**Program in Business Administration**

**Program in Clinical Mental Health Counseling**

**Program in Criminal Justice**

**Program in Healthcare Administration**

**Program in Information Systems and Technology**

**Program in Nursing**

**Program in Public Administration**

## SOUTH UNIVERSITY - RICHMOND, Glen Allen, VA 23060

**General Information** Independent, coed, comprehensive institution.

**GRADUATE UNITS**

**Program in Business Administration**

**Program in Clinical Mental Health Counseling**

**Program in Nursing**

## SOUTH UNIVERSITY - SAVANNAH, Savannah, GA 31406

**General Information** Independent, coed, comprehensive institution.

**GRADUATE UNITS**

**Graduate Programs**

***College of Arts and Sciences***

***College of Business***

***College of Health Professions***

***College of Nursing***

***Doctor of Ministry Program***

***School of Pharmacy***

## SOUTH UNIVERSITY - TAMPA, Tampa, FL 33614

**General Information** Independent, coed, comprehensive institution.

**GRADUATE UNITS**

**Program in Business Administration**

**Program in Criminal Justice**

**Program in Healthcare Administration**

**Program in Information Systems and Technology**

**Program in Nursing**

**Program in Physician Assistant Studies**

## SOUTH UNIVERSITY - VIRGINIA BEACH, Virginia Beach, VA 23452

**General Information** Independent, coed, comprehensive institution.

**GRADUATE UNITS**

**Program in Business Administration**

**Program in Clinical Mental Health Counseling**

**Program in Information Systems and Technology**

**Program in Leadership**

**Program in Nursing**

## SOUTH UNIVERSITY - WEST PALM BEACH, Royal Palm Beach, FL 33411

**General Information** Independent, coed, comprehensive institution.

**GRADUATE UNITS**

**Program in Business Administration**

**Program in Clinical Mental Health Counseling**

**Program in Criminal Justice**

**Program in Information Systems and Technology**

**Program in Nursing**

**Program in Occupational Therapy**

**Program in Public Administration**

## SOUTHWEST ACUPUNCTURE COLLEGE, Santa Fe, NM 87505

**General Information** Private, coed, primarily women, graduate-only institution. *Enrollment by degree level:* 85 master's. *Graduate faculty:* 41 part-time/adjunct (24 women). *Tuition:* Full-time $19,500; part-time $9450 per credit hour. *Required fees:* $300; $300 per semester. Tuition and fees vary according to course load. *Graduate housing:* On-campus housing not available. *Student services:* Campus employment opportunities, services for students with disabilities. *Library facilities:* Southwest Acupuncture College Library plus 2,457 others. *Collection:* Books: 2,457 (physical), 5 (digital/electronic). Weekly public service hours: 45.

**Computer facilities:** 14 computers available on campus for general student use. A campuswide network can be accessed. Online class registration is available. Website: http://www.acupuncturecollege.edu/

**General Application Contact:** Sophia Bungay, Admissions Director, 505-438-8884 Ext. 1009, Fax: 505-438-8883, E-mail: admissions@acupuncturecollege.edu.

**GRADUATE UNITS**

**Master in Acupuncture & Chinese Herbal Medicine** Expenses: Contact institution. *Financial support:* Scholarships/grants available. Financial award applicants required to submit FAFSA. *Program availability:* Part-time. *Application deadline:* For fall admission, 8/1 priority date for domestic and international students; for spring admission, 12/1 priority date for domestic and international students; for summer admission, 4/1 priority date for domestic and international students. Applications are processed on a rolling basis. *Application fee:* $50. Electronic applications accepted. *Application Contact:* Susan Chaney, Academic Dean, 505-438-8884, Fax: 505-438-8883. *Campus Director*, Paul Rossignol, 505-438-8884, Fax: 505-438-8883.

**Master in Acupuncture with a Chinese Herbal Medicine Specilization** Expenses: Contact institution. *Financial support:* Scholarships/grants available. Financial award applicants required to submit FAFSA. In 2019, 2 master's awarded. *Program availability:* Part-time. *Application deadline:* For fall admission, 8/1 priority date for domestic students; for spring admission, 12/1 priority date for domestic students; for summer admission, 4/1 priority date for domestic students. Applications are processed on a rolling basis. *Application fee:* $50. Electronic applications accepted. *Application Contact:* Nate Mohler, Academic Dean, 303-581-9955, Fax: 303-581-9944, E-mail: nate@acupuncturecollege.edu. *Campus Director*, Heather Lang, 303-581-9955, Fax: 303-581-9944, E-mail: boulder@acupuncturecollege.edu.

## SOUTHWEST BAPTIST UNIVERSITY, Bolivar, MO 65613-2597

**General Information** Independent-religious, coed, comprehensive institution. *Graduate housing:* Room and/or apartments available on a first-come, first-served basis to single students; on-campus housing not available to married students.

**GRADUATE UNITS**

**Program in Business** *Program availability:* Part-time, online learning.

**Program in Education** *Program availability:* Part-time.

**Program in Physical Therapy**

## SOUTHWEST COLLEGE OF NATUROPATHIC MEDICINE AND HEALTH SCIENCES, Tempe, AZ 85282

**General Information** Independent, coed, graduate-only institution. *Graduate housing:* On-campus housing not available. *Research affiliation:* Gaia Herbs, Arizona State University, Biodesign Institute (immune modulation, virology, genomics, herbal medicine), Emory University, Aviratek, LLC (antimicrobial botanicals).

**GRADUATE UNITS**

**Doctor of Naturopathic Medicine Program** Electronic applications accepted.

## SOUTHWESTERN ADVENTIST UNIVERSITY, Keene, TX 76059

**General Information** Independent-religious, coed, comprehensive institution. *Graduate housing:* Rooms and/or apartments available on a first-come, first-served basis to single and married students. Housing application deadline: 8/31.

**GRADUATE UNITS**

**Business Administration Department** *Program availability:* Part-time, evening/weekend.

**Education Department** *Program availability:* Part-time, evening/weekend.

## SOUTHWESTERN ASSEMBLIES OF GOD UNIVERSITY, Waxahachie, TX 75165-5735

**General Information** Independent-religious, coed, comprehensive institution. *Graduate housing:* Room and/or apartments guaranteed to single students.

**GRADUATE UNITS**

**Thomas F. Harrison School of Graduate Studies** *Program availability:* Part-time, evening/weekend, online learning. Electronic applications accepted.

## SOUTHWESTERN BAPTIST THEOLOGICAL SEMINARY, Fort Worth, TX 76122-0000

**General Information** Independent-religious, coed, primarily men, graduate-only institution. *Graduate housing:* Rooms and/or apartments available on a first-come, first-served basis to single and married students. *Research affiliation:* Campus Crusade for Christ/Jesus Film Project (evangelical missions), DAWN: Discipling A Whole Nation (evangelical missions).

**GRADUATE UNITS**

**Jack D. Terry School of Church and Family Ministries** *Program availability:* Part-time, evening/weekend. Electronic applications accepted.

**Roy Fish School of Evangelism and Missions**

**School of Church Music** *Program availability:* Part-time. Electronic applications accepted.

**School of Preaching**

**School of Theology** *Program availability:* Part-time, evening/weekend. Electronic applications accepted.

## SOUTHWESTERN CHRISTIAN UNIVERSITY, Bethany, OK 73008-0340

**General Information** Independent-religious, coed, comprehensive institution.

**GRADUATE UNITS**

**Program in Ministry** *Program availability:* Part-time. Electronic applications accepted.

## SOUTHWESTERN COLLEGE, Winfield, KS 67156-2499

**General Information** Independent-religious, coed, comprehensive institution. *Enrollment:* 1,513 graduate, professional, and undergraduate students; 41 full-time matriculated graduate/professional students (18 women), 109 part-time matriculated graduate/professional students (61 women). *Enrollment by degree level:* 106 master's, 43 doctoral, 1 other advanced degree. *Graduate faculty:* 10 full-time (6 women), 30 part-time/adjunct (14 women). *Tuition:* Full-time $12,060; part-time $670 per credit hour. *Required fees:* $60; $30. Tuition and fees vary according to degree level, campus/location and program. *Graduate housing:* Rooms and/or apartments available on a first-come, first-served basis to single and married students. Typical cost: $5000 per year ($9500 including board) for single students; $14,000 per year ($18,500 including board) for married students. Room and board charges vary according to board plan and housing facility selected. *Student services:* Campus employment opportunities, campus safety program, career counseling, free psychological counseling, international student services, services for students with disabilities, teacher training, writing training. *Library facilities:* Harold and Mary Ellen Deets Library. *Collection:* Books: 44,435 (physical), 847,600 (digital/electronic); Serial titles: 3 (physical); Databases: 182. Weekly public service hours: 91; students can reserve study rooms.

**Computer facilities:** Computer purchase and lease plans are available. 45 computers available on campus for general student use. A campuswide network can be accessed. Online class registration, everything in Self-Service and BlackBoard are available. Website: http://www.sckans.edu/

**General Application Contact:** Adam Jenkins, Vice President for Enrollment Management, 620-229-6091, Fax: 620-229-6344, E-mail: adam.jenkins@sckans.edu.

**GRADUATE UNITS**

**Education Programs** Students: 8 full-time (6 women), 75 part-time (50 women); includes 14 minority (3 Black or African American, non-Hispanic/Latino; 2 American Indian or Alaska Native, non-Hispanic/Latino; 1 Asian, non-Hispanic/Latino; 3 Hispanic/Latino; 5 Two or more races, non-Hispanic/Latino), 3 international. Average age 39. 30 applicants, 93% accepted, 23 enrolled. *Faculty:* 6 full-time (5 women), 13 part-time/adjunct (11 women). Expenses: Contact institution. *Financial support:* In 2019–20, 16 students received support. Unspecified assistantships and employee tuition waivers available. Financial award applicants required to submit FAFSA. In 2019, 24 master's, 8 doctorates awarded. *Program availability:* Part-time, 100% online, blended/hybrid learning. *Application deadline:* Applications are processed on a rolling basis. *Application fee:* $40. Electronic applications accepted. *Application Contact:* Jen Caughron, Director of Enrollment Services and Marketing, 888-684-5335 Ext. 3312, Fax: 316-688-5218, E-mail: jennifer.caughron@sckans.edu. *Education Division Chair*, J.K. Campbell, 620-229-6115, E-mail: JK.Campbell@sckans.edu.

**Fifth-Year Graduate Programs** Students: 16 full-time (5 women), 1 (woman) part-time; includes 5 minority (2 Black or African American, non-Hispanic/Latino; 1 American Indian or Alaska Native, non-Hispanic/Latino; 1 Asian, non-Hispanic/Latino; 1 Hispanic/Latino), 4 international. Average age 24. 18 applicants, 56% accepted, 8 enrolled. *Faculty:* 4 full-time (1 woman). Expenses: Contact institution. *Financial support:* In 2019–20, 13 students received support. Fellowships, unspecified assistantships, and employee tuition waivers available. Financial award applicants required to submit FAFSA. In 2019, 9 master's awarded. *Program availability:* Part-time. *Application deadline:* For fall admission, 8/26 for domestic students; for spring admission, 1/21 for domestic students. Applications are processed on a rolling basis. *Application fee:* $25. Electronic applications accepted. *Application Contact:* Adam Jenkins, Vice President for Enrollment Management, 620-229-6091, Fax: 620-229-6344, E-mail: adam.jenkins@sckans.edu. *Professor/Division Chair*, Dr. Kurt Keiser, 620-229-6361, E-mail: kurt.keiser@sckans.edu.

**Professional Studies Programs** Students: 17 full-time (7 women), 33 part-time (10 women); includes 8 minority (5 Black or African American, non-Hispanic/Latino; 1 Asian, non-Hispanic/Latino; 2 Hispanic/Latino). Average age 36. 30 applicants, 93% accepted, 21 enrolled. *Faculty:* 17 part-time/adjunct (3 women). Expenses: Contact institution. *Financial support:* In 2019–20, 7 students received support. Unspecified assistantships and employee tuition waivers available. Financial award applicants required to submit FAFSA. In 2019, 37 master's awarded. *Program availability:* Part-time, online only, 100% online. *Application deadline:* Applications are processed on a rolling basis. *Application fee:* $40. Electronic applications accepted. *Application Contact:* Jen Caughron, Director of Enrollment Services and Marketing, 888-684-5335 Ext. 3312, Fax: 316-688-5218, E-mail: jennifer.caughron@sckans.edu. *Director of Enrollment Services and Marketing*, Jen Caughron, 888-684-5335 Ext. 3312, Fax: 316-688-5218, E-mail: jennifer.caughron@sckans.edu.

## SOUTHWESTERN COLLEGE, Santa Fe, NM 87502-4788

**General Information** Independent, coed, primarily women, graduate-only institution. *Graduate housing:* On-campus housing not available.

**GRADUATE UNITS**

**Program in Art Therapy/Counseling** *Program availability:* Part-time, evening/weekend.

**Program in Counseling** *Program availability:* Part-time, evening/weekend.

**Program in Grief, Loss and Trauma Counseling** *Program availability:* Part-time, evening/weekend, online learning.

**Program in Integral Somatic Psychology**

**Program in Psychodrama and Action Methods**

**Program in Transformational Ecopsychology**

## SOUTHWESTERN LAW SCHOOL, Los Angeles, CA 90010

**General Information** Independent, coed, graduate-only institution. *Enrollment by degree level:* 14 master's, 805 doctoral. *Graduate faculty:* 58 full-time (30 women), 111 part-time/adjunct (46 women). *Tuition:* Full-time $55,312; part-time $36,894 per year. *Required fees:* $200; $200. Tuition and fees vary according to program. *Graduate housing:* Rooms and/or apartments available on a first-come, first-served basis to single and married students. Typical cost: $20,520 (including board) for single students; $20,520 (including board) for married students. Room and board charges vary according to housing facility selected. *Student services:* Campus employment opportunities, campus safety program, career counseling, exercise/wellness program, free psychological counseling, international student services, low-cost health insurance, multicultural affairs office, services for students with disabilities, writing training. *Library facilities:* Leigh H. Taylor Law Library. *Collection:* Books: 85,302 (physical), 313,270 (digital/electronic); Serial titles: 7,570 (physical), 5,700 (digital/electronic); Databases: 159. Weekly public service hours: 102; students can reserve study rooms.

**Computer facilities:** 102 computers available on campus for general student use. A campuswide network can be accessed from student residence rooms. Online class registration is available.
Website: http://www.swlaw.edu/

**General Application Contact:** Lisa Gear, Assistant Dean of Admissions, 213-738-6834, Fax: 213-738-6899, E-mail: admissions@swlaw.edu.

**GRADUATE UNITS**

**Graduate and Professional Programs** Students: 616 full-time (342 women), 203 part-time (127 women); includes 372 minority (50 Black or African American, non-Hispanic/Latino; 75 Asian, non-Hispanic/Latino; 205 Hispanic/Latino; 2 Native Hawaiian or other Pacific Islander, non-Hispanic/Latino; 40 Two or more races, non-Hispanic/Latino), 24 international. Average age 26. 1,900 applicants, 48% accepted, 341 enrolled. *Faculty:* 58 full-time (30 women), 111 part-time/adjunct (46 women). Expenses: Contact institution. *Financial support:* In 2019–20, 554 students received support. Federal Work-Study, institutionally sponsored loans, and scholarships/grants available. Support available to part-time students. Financial award application deadline: 6/1; financial award applicants required to submit FAFSA. In 2019, 8 master's, 199 doctorates awarded. *Program availability:* Part-time, evening/weekend. *Application deadline:* For fall admission, 4/1 for domestic and international students. Applications are processed on a rolling basis. *Application fee:* $60. Electronic applications accepted. *Application Contact:* Lisa Gear, Assistant Dean of Admissions, 213-738-6834, Fax: 213-738-6899, E-mail: admissions@swlaw.edu. *Dean,* Susan Westerberg Prager, 213-738-6710, Fax: 213-383-1688.

## SOUTHWESTERN OKLAHOMA STATE UNIVERSITY, Weatherford, OK 73096-3098

**General Information** State-supported, coed, comprehensive institution. *Graduate housing:* Rooms and/or apartments available on a first-come, first-served basis to single and married students. Housing application deadline: 8/19. *Research affiliation:* Gulf Coast Research Laboratory.

**GRADUATE UNITS**

**College of Arts and Sciences** *Program availability:* Part-time.

**College of Pharmacy**

**College of Professional and Graduate Studies** *Program availability:* Part-time, evening/weekend, online learning.

***Everett Dobson School of Business and Technology*** *Program availability:* Part-time, evening/weekend, online learning.

***School of Behavioral Sciences and Education*** *Program availability:* Part-time, evening/weekend, online learning.

## SOUTHWEST MINNESOTA STATE UNIVERSITY, Marshall, MN 56258

**General Information** State-supported, coed, comprehensive institution. *Graduate housing:* Room and/or apartments available to single students; on-campus housing not available to married students.

**GRADUATE UNITS**

**Department of Business and Public Affairs** *Program availability:* Part-time, evening/weekend, online learning. Electronic applications accepted.

**Department of Education** *Program availability:* Part-time, evening/weekend, online learning.

## SOUTHWEST UNIVERSITY, Kenner, LA 70062

**General Information** Proprietary, coed, comprehensive institution.

**GRADUATE UNITS**

**MBA Program**

**Program in Criminal Justice**

**Program in Management**

**Program in Organizational Management**

## SOUTHWEST UNIVERSITY OF VISUAL ARTS, Tucson, AZ 85716-2505

**General Information** Proprietary, coed, comprehensive institution.

**GRADUATE UNITS**

**MFA Programs**

## SPALDING UNIVERSITY, Louisville, KY 40203-2188

**General Information** Independent-religious, coed, comprehensive institution. CGS member. *Graduate housing:* Room and/or apartments available on a first-come, first-served basis to single students; on-campus housing not available to married students.

**GRADUATE UNITS**

**Graduate Studies** *Program availability:* Part-time, evening/weekend.

***College of Education*** *Program availability:* Part-time, evening/weekend. Electronic applications accepted.

***College of Social Sciences and Humanities*** *Program availability:* Part-time, evening/weekend, online learning.

***Kosair College of Health and Natural Sciences*** *Program availability:* Part-time, evening/weekend.

## SPERTUS INSTITUTE FOR JEWISH LEARNING AND LEADERSHIP, Chicago, IL 60605-1901

**General Information** Independent, coed, graduate-only institution. *Graduate housing:* On-campus housing not available.

**GRADUATE UNITS**

**Program in Jewish Studies** *Program availability:* Part-time, evening/weekend, online learning.

## SPRING ARBOR UNIVERSITY, Spring Arbor, MI 49283-9799

**General Information** Independent-religious, coed, comprehensive institution. *Graduate housing:* Rooms and/or apartments available on a first-come, first-served basis to single and married students. Housing application deadline: 5/1.

**GRADUATE UNITS**

**Gainey School of Business** *Program availability:* Part-time, evening/weekend, online learning.

**School of Arts and Sciences** *Program availability:* Part-time, online learning.

**School of Education** *Program availability:* Part-time, evening/weekend, online learning. Electronic applications accepted.

**School of Human Services** *Program availability:* Part-time, evening/weekend, online learning. Electronic applications accepted.

## SPRINGFIELD COLLEGE, Springfield, MA 01109-3797

**General Information** Independent, coed, comprehensive institution. CGS member. *Graduate housing:* Rooms and/or apartments available on a first-come, first-served basis to single and married students.

**GRADUATE UNITS**

**Graduate Programs** *Program availability:* Part-time, evening/weekend. Electronic applications accepted.

***School of Social Work*** *Program availability:* Part-time, evening/weekend. Electronic applications accepted.

## SPRING HILL COLLEGE, Mobile, AL 36608-1791

**General Information** Independent-religious, coed, comprehensive institution. *Enrollment:* 1,317 graduate, professional, and undergraduate students; 16 full-time matriculated graduate/professional students (8 women), 114 part-time matriculated graduate/professional students (44 women). *Enrollment by degree level:* 104 master's, 26 other advanced degrees. *Graduate faculty:* 15 full-time (8 women), 10 part-time/adjunct (5 women). *Tuition:* Full-time $9270; part-time $515 per credit hour. *Graduate housing:* On-campus housing not available. *Student services:* Campus safety program, career counseling, exercise/wellness program, writing training. *Library facilities:* Marnie and John Burke Memorial Library plus 1 other.

**Computer facilities:** A campuswide network can be accessed. Online class registration is available.
Website: http://www.shc.edu/

**General Application Contact:** Gary Bracken, Vice President of Enrollment Management, 251-380-3038, Fax: 251-460-2186, E-mail: gbracken@shc.edu.

**GRADUATE UNITS**

**Graduate Programs** Students: 16 full-time (8 women), 114 part-time (44 women); includes 31 minority (14 Black or African American, non-Hispanic/Latino; 3 American Indian or Alaska Native, non-Hispanic/Latino; 5 Asian, non-Hispanic/Latino; 6 Hispanic/Latino; 1 Native Hawaiian or other Pacific Islander, non-Hispanic/Latino; 2 Two or more races, non-Hispanic/Latino), 5 international. Average age 40. *Faculty:* 15 full-time (8 women), 10 part-time/adjunct (5 women). Expenses: Contact institution. *Financial support:* Fellowships, research assistantships, teaching assistantships, and tuition waivers available. Financial award applicants required to submit FAFSA. In 2019, 26 master's, 13 other advanced degrees awarded. *Program availability:* Part-time, online learning. *Application deadline:* For fall admission, 8/1 priority date for domestic and international students; for spring admission, 12/1 priority date for domestic and international students. Applications are processed on a rolling basis. *Application fee:* $25 ($35 for international students). Electronic applications accepted. *Application Contact:* Gary Bracken, Vice President of Enrollment Management, 251-380-3038, Fax: 251-460-2186, E-mail: gbracken@shc.edu. *Vice President of Enrollment Management,* Gary Bracken, 251-380-3038, Fax: 251-460-2186, E-mail: gbracken@shc.edu.

## STANBRIDGE UNIVERSITY, Irvine, CA 92612

**General Information** Proprietary, coed, comprehensive institution.

**GRADUATE UNITS**

**Program in Nursing** *Program availability:* Online learning.

**Program in Occupational Therapy**

## STANFORD UNIVERSITY, Stanford, CA 94305-2004

**General Information** Independent, coed, university. CGS member. *Enrollment:* 17,249 graduate, professional, and undergraduate students; 9,090 full-time matriculated graduate/professional students (3,906 women), 300 part-time matriculated graduate/professional students (118 women). *Enrollment by degree level:* 3,496 master's, 5,894 doctoral. *Graduate faculty:* 2,276 full-time (683 women). *Tuition:* Full-time $52,479; part-time $34,110 per unit. *Required fees:* $672; $224 per quarter. Tuition and fees vary according to program and student level. *Graduate housing:* Rooms and/or apartments guaranteed to single and married students. Typical cost: $13,165 per year for single students; $21,015 per year for married students. Housing application deadline: 6/10. *Student services:* Campus employment opportunities, campus safety program, career counseling, child daycare facilities, exercise/wellness program, free psychological counseling, grant writing training, international student services, low-cost health insurance, multicultural affairs office, services for students with disabilities, teacher training, writing training. *Library facilities:* Green Library plus 20 others. *Collection:* Books: 9.5 million (physical), 1.5 million (digital/electronic); Serial titles: 77,000 (physical). Study areas open 24 hours, 5–7 days a week; students can reserve study rooms.

**Computer facilities:** Computer purchase and lease plans are available. 1,000 computers available on campus for general student use. A campuswide network can be accessed. Online class registration is available.
Website: http://www.stanford.edu/

**General Application Contact:** Graduate Admissions, 866-432-7472, Fax: 650-723-8371, E-mail: gradadmissions@stanford.edu.

**GRADUATE UNITS**

**Graduate School of Business** Expenses: Contact institution.

**Graduate School of Education** Expenses: Contact institution.

**Law School** Expenses: Contact institution. *Application Contact:* Graduate Admissions, 866-432-7472, Fax: 650-723-8371, E-mail: gradadmissions@stanford.edu. *Dean,* M. Elizabeth Magill, 650-723-4455, Fax: 650-725-0253, E-mail: emagill@law.stanford.edu.

**School of Earth, Energy and Environmental Sciences** Expenses: Contact institution.

**School of Engineering** Expenses: Contact institution.

***Institute for Computational and Mathematical Engineering*** Expenses: Contact institution.

**School of Humanities and Sciences** Expenses: Contact institution.

***Center for East Asian Studies*** Expenses: Contact institution.

***Center for Russian, East European and Eurasian Studies*** Expenses: Contact institution.

**School of Medicine** Expenses: Contact institution.

***Graduate Programs in Medicine*** Expenses: Contact institution.

***Stanford Center for Biomedical Informatics Research*** Expenses: Contact institution.

## STARR KING SCHOOL FOR THE MINISTRY, Berkeley, CA 94709-1209

**General Information** Independent-religious, coed, graduate-only institution. *Graduate housing:* On-campus housing not available.

**GRADUATE UNITS**

**Professional Program**

## STATE UNIVERSITY OF NEW YORK AT FREDONIA, Fredonia, NY 14063-1136

**General Information** State-supported, coed, comprehensive institution. *Graduate housing:* Room and/or apartments available on a first-come, first-served basis to single students; on-campus housing not available to married students. Housing application deadline: 8/24.

**GRADUATE UNITS**

**College of Education** *Program availability:* Part-time. Electronic applications accepted.

**College of Liberal Arts and Sciences** *Program availability:* Part-time, evening/weekend. Electronic applications accepted.

**School of Music** *Program availability:* Part-time. Electronic applications accepted.

## STATE UNIVERSITY OF NEW YORK AT NEW PALTZ, New Paltz, NY 12561

**General Information** State-supported, coed, comprehensive institution. *Enrollment:* 7,757 graduate, professional, and undergraduate students; 488 full-time matriculated graduate/professional students (355 women), 462 part-time matriculated graduate/professional students (346 women). *Enrollment by degree level:* 950 master's. *Graduate faculty:* 123 full-time (70 women), 54 part-time/adjunct (30 women). *International tuition:* $23,100 full-time. *Tuition, area resident:* Full-time $11,310; part-time $471 per credit. Tuition, state resident: full-time $11,310; part-time $471 per credit. Tuition, nonresident: full-time $23,100; part-time $963 per credit. *Required fees:* $1432; $41.83 per credit. *Graduate housing:* On-campus housing not available. *Student services:* Campus employment opportunities, campus safety program, career counseling, child daycare facilities, free psychological counseling, international student services, low-cost health insurance, services for students with disabilities, teacher training, writing training. *Library facilities:* Sojourner Truth Library. *Collection:* Books: 405,123 (physical), 205,499 (digital/electronic); Serial titles: 7,819 (physical), 113,923 (digital/electronic); Databases: 98. Weekly public service hours: 103; students can reserve study rooms.

**Computer facilities:** 800 computers available on campus for general student use. A campuswide network can be accessed. Online class registration is available.
Website: http://www.newpaltz.edu/

**General Application Contact:** Vika Shock, Director of Graduate Admissions, 845-257-3285, Fax: 845-257-3284, E-mail: gradstudies@newpaltz.edu.

**GRADUATE UNITS**

**Graduate and Extended Learning School** Students: 494 full-time (359 women), 402 part-time (303 women); includes 162 minority (27 Black or African American, non-Hispanic/Latino; 20 Asian, non-Hispanic/Latino; 97 Hispanic/Latino; 1 Native Hawaiian or other Pacific Islander, non-Hispanic/Latino; 17 Two or more races, non-Hispanic/Latino), 75 international. 936 applicants, 50% accepted, 256 enrolled. *Faculty:* 124 full-time (70 women), 56 part-time/adjunct (31 women). Expenses: Contact institution. *Financial support:* In 2019–20, 15 fellowships with partial tuition reimbursements (averaging $1,360 per year), 30 research assistantships with partial tuition reimbursements (averaging $5,000 per year), 40 teaching assistantships with partial tuition reimbursements (averaging $5,000 per year) were awarded; career-related internships or fieldwork, scholarships/grants, traineeships, health care benefits, and unspecified assistantships also available. Financial award application deadline: 8/1; financial award applicants required to submit FAFSA. In 2019, 369 master's, 58 other advanced degrees awarded. *Program availability:* Part-time, evening/weekend. *Application fee:* $50. Electronic applications accepted. *Application Contact:* Vika Shock, Director of Graduate Admissions, 845-257-3285, Fax: 845-257-3284, E-mail: shockv@newpaltz.edu. *Assistant Vice President*, Dr. Shala Mills, 845-257-3947, Fax: 845-257-3284, E-mail: millss@newpaltz.edu.

***School of Business*** Students: 59 full-time (29 women), 43 part-time (25 women); includes 23 minority (3 Black or African American, non-Hispanic/Latino; 6 Asian, non-Hispanic/Latino; 13 Hispanic/Latino; 1 Two or more races, non-Hispanic/Latino), 7 international. 99 applicants, 41% accepted, 26 enrolled. *Faculty:* 13 full-time (4 women), 6 part-time/adjunct (2 women). Expenses: Contact institution. *Financial support:* In 2019–20, 6 research assistantships with partial tuition reimbursements (averaging $5,000 per year), 1 teaching assistantship with partial tuition reimbursement (averaging $5,000 per year) were awarded; scholarships/grants, traineeships, and unspecified assistantships also available. Financial award application deadline: 8/1. In 2019, 66 master's awarded. *Program availability:* Part-time, evening/weekend. *Application deadline:* Applications are processed on a rolling basis. *Application fee:* $50. Electronic applications accepted. *Application Contact:* Aaron Hines, Director of MBA Program, 845-257-2968, E-mail: mba@newpaltz.edu. *Dean*, Dr. Kristin Backhaus, 845-257-2930, E-mail: mba@newpaltz.edu.

***School of Education*** Students: 161 full-time (127 women), 271 part-time (220 women); includes 70 minority (13 Black or African American, non-Hispanic/Latino; 1 Asian, non-Hispanic/Latino; 50 Hispanic/Latino; 6 Two or more races, non-Hispanic/Latino), 2 international. 252 applicants, 65% accepted, 101 enrolled. *Faculty:* 30 full-time (21 women), 27 part-time/adjunct (19 women). Expenses: Contact institution. *Financial support:* Scholarships/grants available. Financial award application deadline: 8/1. In 2019, 157 master's, 58 other advanced degrees awarded. *Program availability:* Part-time, evening/weekend. *Application deadline:* For fall admission, 3/1 for domestic and international students; for spring admission, 10/1 for domestic and international students. *Application fee:* $50. Electronic applications accepted. *Application Contact:* Vika Shock, Director of Graduate Admissions, 845-257-3285, Fax: 845-257-3284, E-mail: gradstudies@newpaltz.edu. *Dean*, Dr. Michael Rosenberg, 845-257-2800, E-mail: schoolofed@newpaltz.edu.

***School of Fine and Performing Arts*** Students: 24 full-time (17 women), 21 part-time (17 women); includes 7 minority (1 Black or African American, non-Hispanic/Latino; 2 Asian, non-Hispanic/Latino; 4 Hispanic/Latino), 4 international. 130 applicants, 47% accepted, 37 enrolled. *Faculty:* 26 full-time (18 women), 8 part-time/adjunct (3 women). Expenses: Contact institution. *Financial support:* In 2019–20, 8 research assistantships with partial tuition reimbursements (averaging $5,000 per year), 7 teaching assistantships with partial tuition reimbursements (averaging $5,000 per year) were awarded; scholarships/grants also available. Financial award application deadline: 8/1. In 2019, 47 master's awarded. *Program availability:* Part-time, evening/weekend. *Application deadline:* For fall admission, 2/15 priority date for domestic students, 2/15 for international students. Applications are processed on a rolling basis. *Application fee:* $50. Electronic applications accepted. *Application Contact:* Vika Shock, Director of Graduate Admissions, 845-257-3286, Fax: 845-257-3284, E-mail: gradstudies@newpaltz.edu. *Dean*, Prof. Jeni Mokren, 845-257-3860, E-mail: mokrenj@newpaltz.edu.

***School of Liberal Arts and Sciences*** Students: 127 full-time (111 women), 71 part-time (51 women); includes 47 minority (7 Black or African American, non-Hispanic/Latino; 5 Asian, non-Hispanic/Latino; 26 Hispanic/Latino; 1 Native Hawaiian or other Pacific Islander, non-Hispanic/Latino; 8 Two or more races, non-Hispanic/Latino). 226 applicants, 47% accepted, 61 enrolled. *Faculty:* 41 full-time (24 women), 7 part-time/adjunct (6 women). Expenses: Contact institution. *Financial support:* In 2019–20, 1 research assistantship with partial tuition reimbursement (averaging $5,000 per year), 28 teaching assistantships with partial tuition reimbursements (averaging $5,000 per year) were awarded. Financial award application deadline: 8/1. In 2019, 73 master's, 5 other advanced degrees awarded. *Program availability:* Part-time, evening/weekend. *Application deadline:* For fall admission, 2/1 for domestic and international students; for spring admission, 11/15 for domestic and international students. Applications are processed on a rolling basis. *Application fee:* $50. Electronic applications accepted. *Application Contact:* Vika Shock, Director of Graduate Admissions, 845-257-3286, E-mail: gradstudies@newpaltz.edu. *Dean*, Dr. Laura Barrett, 845-257-3520, E-mail: barrett@newpaltz.edu.

***School of Science and Engineering*** Students: 15 full-time (5 women), 65 part-time (31 women); includes 7 minority (2 Black or African American, non-Hispanic/Latino; 4 Asian, non-Hispanic/Latino; 1 Hispanic/Latino), 55 international. 183 applicants, 53% accepted, 31 enrolled. *Faculty:* 14 full-time (3 women), 8 part-time/adjunct (1 woman). Expenses: Contact institution. *Financial support:* In 2019–20, 15 fellowships with partial tuition reimbursements (averaging $1,360 per year), 4 teaching assistantships with partial tuition reimbursements (averaging $5,000 per year) were awarded. Financial award application deadline: 8/1. In 2019, 29 master's awarded. *Program availability:* Part-time, evening/weekend. *Application deadline:* For fall admission, 5/15 for domestic and international students; for spring admission, 11/15 for domestic and international students. Applications are processed on a rolling basis. *Application fee:* $50. Electronic applications accepted. *Application Contact:* Vika Shock, Director of Graduate Admission, 845-257-3286, E-mail: gradstudies@newpaltz.edu. *Dean*, Dr. Daniel Freedman, 845-257-3728, E-mail: freedmad@newpaltz.edu.

## STATE UNIVERSITY OF NEW YORK AT OSWEGO, Oswego, NY 13126

**General Information** State-supported, coed, comprehensive institution. CGS member. *Enrollment:* 7,830 graduate, professional, and undergraduate students; 319 full-time matriculated graduate/professional students (209 women), 591 part-time matriculated graduate/professional students (382 women). *Graduate faculty:* 107 full-time (62 women), 54 part-time/adjunct (30 women). *Graduate housing:* Room and/or apartments available on a first-come, first-served basis to single students; on-campus housing not available to married students. Housing application deadline: 4/1. *Student services:* Campus employment opportunities, career counseling, child daycare facilities, exercise/wellness program, free psychological counseling, grant writing training, international student services, low-cost health insurance, services for students with disabilities. *Library facilities:* Penfield Library. *Collection:* Books: 331,049 (physical), 154,207 (digital/electronic); Serial titles: 1,932 (physical), 55,500 (digital/electronic); Databases: 139. Weekly public service hours: 96; study areas open 24 hours, 5–7 days a week; students can reserve study rooms. *Research affiliation:* Intel Corporation (research and education), IBM (research and education), Alcan (research and education), MACTEC (research and education), Entergy (research and education).

**Computer facilities:** Computer purchase and lease plans are available. 1,250 computers available on campus for general student use. A campuswide network can be accessed. Online class registration is available.
Website: http://www.oswego.edu/

**General Application Contact:** Dr. Kristen C Eichhorn, Dean of Graduate Studies, 315-312-3692, Fax: 315-312-3228, E-mail: KRISTEN.EICHHORN@OSWEGO.EDU.

**GRADUATE UNITS**

**Graduate Studies** Students: 319 full-time (209 women), 591 part-time (382 women); includes 158 minority (57 Black or African American, non-Hispanic/Latino; 3 American Indian or Alaska Native, non-Hispanic/Latino; 39 Asian, non-Hispanic/Latino; 44 Hispanic/Latino; 15 Two or more races, non-Hispanic/Latino), 23 international. Average age 30. 970 applicants, 35% accepted, 279 enrolled. *Faculty:* 107 full-time (62 women), 54 part-time/adjunct (30 women). Expenses: Contact institution. *Financial support:* Fellowships with full tuition reimbursements, research assistantships with full tuition reimbursements, teaching assistantships with full and partial tuition reimbursements, career-related internships or fieldwork, Federal Work-Study, institutionally sponsored loans, scholarships/grants, health care benefits, tuition waivers (partial), and unspecified assistantships available. Support available to part-time students. Financial award application deadline: 4/1; financial award applicants required to submit FAFSA. In 2019, 345 master's, 78 other advanced degrees awarded. *Program availability:* Part-time. *Application deadline:* For fall admission, 2/1 for domestic students, 4/15 for international students; for spring admission, 10/1 for domestic students, 11/1 for international students. Applications are processed on a rolling basis. *Application fee:* $65. Electronic applications accepted. *Application Contact:* Sharon Griffin, Graduate Admissions Counselor, 315-312-3504, E-mail: sharon.griffin@oswego.edu. *Dean of Graduate Studies*, Dr. Kristen Eichhorn, 315-312-3692, E-mail: kristen.eichhorn@oswego.edu.

***College of Liberal Arts and Sciences*** Students: 93. Expenses: Contact institution. *Financial support:* Fellowships, research assistantships with partial tuition reimbursements, teaching assistantships with full and partial tuition reimbursements, career-related internships or fieldwork, Federal Work-Study, institutionally sponsored loans, scholarships/grants, health care benefits, tuition waivers (partial), and unspecified assistantships available. Support available to part-time students. Financial award application deadline: 4/1; financial award applicants required to submit FAFSA. In 2019, 30 master's awarded. *Program availability:* Part-time. *Application deadline:* For fall admission, 4/1 priority date for domestic students, 4/1 for international students; for spring admission, 10/1 priority date for domestic students, 10/1 for international students. Applications are processed on a rolling basis. *Application fee:* $65. *Application Contact:* Dr. Kristen Eichhorn, Dean of Graduate Studies, 315-312-3152, E-mail: kristen.eichhorn@oswego.edu. *Dean*, Dr. Kristen Croyle, 315-312-2285, Fax: 315-312-3577, E-mail: clas@oswego.edu.

***School of Business*** Students: 254. Expenses: Contact institution. *Financial support:* Fellowships with full tuition reimbursements, teaching assistantships with partial tuition reimbursements, career-related internships or fieldwork, Federal Work-Study, institutionally sponsored loans, scholarships/grants, health care benefits, tuition waivers (partial), and unspecified assistantships available. Support available to part-time students. Financial award application deadline: 4/1; financial award applicants required to submit FAFSA. In 2019, 145 master's awarded. *Program availability:* Part-time, evening/weekend. *Application deadline:* For fall admission, 4/15 for domestic and international students; for spring admission, 10/1 for domestic students, 11/1 for international students. Applications are processed on a rolling basis. *Application fee:* $65. Electronic applications accepted. *Application Contact:* Dr. Irene Scruton, Assistant Dean and MBA Program Director, 315-312-2911, E-mail: irene.scruton@oswego.edu. *Dean*, Dr. Prabakar Kothandaraman, 315-312-3168, E-mail: pk@oswego.edu.

***School of Communication, Media and the Arts*** Students: 34. Expenses: Contact institution. *Financial support:* Fellowships, research assistantships, teaching assistantships, institutionally sponsored loans, scholarships/grants, and unspecified assistantships available. Support available to part-time students. Financial award application deadline: 4/1; financial award applicants required to submit FAFSA. In 2019, 17 master's awarded. *Application deadline:* Applications are processed on a rolling basis. *Application fee:* $65. Electronic applications accepted. *Application Contact:* Dr. Julie Pretzat, Dean, 315-312-6612, E-mail: julie.pretzat@oswego.edu. *Dean*, Dr. Julie Pretzat, 315-312-6612, E-mail: julie.pretzat@oswego.edu.

***School of Education*** Students: 401. Expenses: Contact institution. *Financial support:* Fellowships with full tuition reimbursements, research assistantships, teaching assistantships with full and partial tuition reimbursements, career-related internships or fieldwork, Federal Work-Study, institutionally sponsored loans, scholarships/grants, health care benefits, and unspecified assistantships available. Support available to part-time students. Financial award application deadline: 4/1; financial award applicants required to submit FAFSA. In 2019, 227 master's awarded. *Program availability:* Part-time. *Application deadline:* For fall admission, 1/15 for domestic and international students; for spring admission, 10/1 for domestic and international students. Applications are processed on a rolling basis. *Application fee:* $65. Electronic applications accepted. *Application Contact:* Dr. Pamela Michel, Dean, 315-312-2102, E-mail: pamela.michel@oswego.edu. *Dean*, Dr. Pamela Michel, 315-312-2102, E-mail: pamela.michel@oswego.edu.

## STATE UNIVERSITY OF NEW YORK AT PLATTSBURGH, Plattsburgh, NY 12901-2681

**General Information** State-supported, coed, comprehensive institution. *Graduate housing:* Room and/or apartments available on a first-come, first-served basis to single students; on-campus housing not available to married students. Housing application deadline: 5/1. *Research affiliation:* New York State Sea Grant (environmental science), Miner Agricultural Research Institute (environmental science).

**GRADUATE UNITS**

**School of Arts and Sciences** *Program availability:* Part-time.

**School of Education, Health, and Human Services** *Program availability:* Part-time.

## STATE UNIVERSITY OF NEW YORK COLLEGE AT CORTLAND, Cortland, NY 13045

**General Information** State-supported, coed, comprehensive institution. *Graduate housing:* Room and/or apartments available on a first-come, first-served basis to single students; on-campus housing not available to married students.

**GRADUATE UNITS**

**Graduate Studies** *Program availability:* Part-time, evening/weekend. Electronic applications accepted.

***School of Arts and Sciences*** *Program availability:* Part-time, evening/weekend.

***School of Education*** *Program availability:* Part-time, evening/weekend.

***School of Professional Studies*** *Program availability:* Part-time, evening/weekend.

## STATE UNIVERSITY OF NEW YORK COLLEGE AT GENESEO, Geneseo, NY 14454-1401

**General Information** State-supported, coed, comprehensive institution. *Enrollment:* 5,344 graduate, professional, and undergraduate students; 48 full-time matriculated graduate/professional students (33 women), 42 part-time matriculated graduate/professional students (34 women). *Enrollment by degree level:* 90 master's. *Graduate faculty:* 10 full-time (7 women), 4 part-time/adjunct (1 woman). *International tuition:* $24,046 full-time. *Tuition, area resident:* Full-time $11,310; part-time $471 per credit hour. Tuition, state resident: full-time $11,310; part-time $471 per credit hour. Tuition, nonresident: full-time $24,046; part-time $963 per credit hour. *Required fees:* $946; $78.10 $39.05. *Graduate housing:* Room and/or apartments available on a first-come, first-served basis to single students; on-campus housing not available to married students. Typical cost: $4727 per year. Room charges vary according to board plan and housing facility selected. Housing application deadline: 5/1. *Student services:* Campus employment opportunities, campus safety program, career counseling, free psychological counseling, grant writing training, international student services, multicultural affairs office, services for students with disabilities, teacher training. *Library facilities:* Milne Library plus 1 other. *Research affiliation:* Rochester City School District/School #19 (education), Avon School District (education), The Community Place of Greater Rochester (reading literacy), Central Library of Rochester (education), The Genesee Valley Educational Partnership (education), Greater Rochester Summer Learning Association (education).

**Computer facilities:** 273 computers available on campus for general student use. A campuswide network can be accessed. Online class registration is available.
Website: http://www.geneseo.edu/

**General Application Contact:** Michael R. George, Graduate Enrollment Coordinator, 585-245-5148, Fax: 585-245-5550, E-mail: georgem@geneseo.edu.

**GRADUATE UNITS**

**Graduate Studies** Students: 48 full-time (33 women), 42 part-time (34 women); includes 7 minority (1 Black or African American, non-Hispanic/Latino; 2 Asian, non-Hispanic/Latino; 2 Hispanic/Latino; 2 Two or more races, non-Hispanic/Latino), 2 international. Average age 25. 96 applicants, 68% accepted, 53 enrolled. *Faculty:* 10 full-time (7 women), 4 part-time/adjunct (1 woman). Expenses: Contact institution. *Financial support:* In 2019–20, 9 students received support. Research assistantships, career-related internships or fieldwork, scholarships/grants, tuition waivers (full and partial), and unspecified assistantships available. Support available to part-time students. Financial award application deadline: 4/1; financial award applicants required to submit FAFSA. In 2019, 64 master's awarded. *Program availability:* Part-time. *Application deadline:* For fall admission, 4/1 priority date for domestic students; for spring admission, 11/1 priority date for domestic students; for summer admission, 4/1 priority date for domestic students. Applications are processed on a rolling basis. *Application fee:* $50. Electronic applications accepted. *Application Contact:* Michael R. George, Graduate Enrollment Coordinator, 585-245-5148, E-mail: georgem@geneseo.edu. *Assistant Provost for Curriculum and Assessment*, Dr. Melanie Blood, 585-245-5531, Fax: 585-245-5032, E-mail: blood@geneseo.edu.

***School of Business*** Students: 19 full-time (7 women), 1 part-time (0 women); includes 1 minority (Asian, non-Hispanic/Latino), 2 international. Average age 23. 42 applicants, 55% accepted, 19 enrolled. *Faculty:* 4 full-time (2 women), 2 part-time/adjunct (0 women). Expenses: Contact institution. *Financial support:* In 2019–20, 1 student received support. Scholarships/grants and Graduate assistantships available. Financial award application deadline: 4/1; financial award applicants required to submit FAFSA. In 2019, 15 master's awarded. *Application deadline:* For fall admission, 6/1 priority date for domestic students. Applications are processed on a rolling basis. *Application fee:* $50. Electronic applications accepted. *Application Contact:* Michael R. George, Director of Graduate Admissions, 585-245-5148, Fax: 585-245-5550, E-mail: georgem@geneseo.edu. *Dean of the School of Business*, Dr. Mary Ellen Zuckerman, 585-245-5123, Fax: 585-245-5467, E-mail: zuckerman@geneseo.edu.

***School of Education*** Students: 29 full-time (26 women), 41 part-time (34 women); includes 6 minority (1 Black or African American, non-Hispanic/Latino; 1 Asian, non-Hispanic/Latino; 2 Hispanic/Latino; 2 Two or more races, non-Hispanic/Latino). Average age 24. 54 applicants, 78% accepted, 34 enrolled. *Faculty:* 6 full-time (5 women), 2 part-time/adjunct (1 woman). Expenses: Contact institution. *Financial support:* In 2019–20, 8 students received support. Fellowships, career-related internships or fieldwork, scholarships/grants, tuition waivers (full and partial), unspecified assistantships, and Graduate assistantships available. Support available to part-time students. Financial award application deadline: 4/1; financial award applicants required to submit FAFSA. In 2019, 49 master's awarded. *Program availability:* Part-time. *Application deadline:* For fall admission, 4/1 priority date for domestic students; for spring admission, 11/1 priority date for domestic students; for summer admission, 4/1 priority date for domestic students. Applications are processed on a rolling basis. *Application fee:* $50. Electronic applications accepted. *Application Contact:* Michael R. George, Director of Graduate Admissions, 585-245-5148, Fax: 585-245-5550, E-mail: georgem@geneseo.edu. *Interim Dean of School of Education*, Dr. Dennis Showers, 585-245-5151, Fax: 585-245-5264, E-mail: showers@geneseo.edu.

## STATE UNIVERSITY OF NEW YORK COLLEGE AT OLD WESTBURY, Old Westbury, NY 11568-0210

**General Information** State-supported, coed, comprehensive institution. *Graduate housing:* Room and/or apartments available on a first-come, first-served basis to single students; on-campus housing not available to married students.

**GRADUATE UNITS**

**Program in Liberal Studies** Students: 5 full-time (1 woman), 4 part-time (3 women); includes 4 minority (1 Black or African American, non-Hispanic/Latino; 1 Asian, non-Hispanic/Latino; 2 Hispanic/Latino). Average age 38. 10 applicants, 80% accepted, 5 enrolled. *Faculty:* 2 full-time (both women). Expenses: Contact institution. *Financial support:* Applicants required to submit FAFSA. In 2019, 1 master's awarded. *Program availability:* Part-time, evening/weekend. *Application deadline:* Applications are processed on a rolling basis. *Application fee:* $50. Electronic applications accepted. *Application Contact:* Philip D'Angelo, Graduate Admissions Office, 516-876-3073, E-mail: enroll@oldwestbury.edu. *Associate Professor, American Studies*, Dr. Amanda Frisken, 516-876-4853, E-mail: friskena@oldwestbury.edu.

**Program in Mental Health Counseling**

**School of Business** *Program availability:* Part-time, evening/weekend. Electronic applications accepted.

**School of Education** *Program availability:* Part-time, evening/weekend.

## STATE UNIVERSITY OF NEW YORK COLLEGE AT ONEONTA, Oneonta, NY 13820-4015

**General Information** State-supported, coed, comprehensive institution. *Graduate housing:* Room and/or apartments available on a first-come, first-served basis to single students; on-campus housing not available to married students. Housing application deadline: 5/1. *Research affiliation:* New York State Historical Association (museum studies (history and science)).

**GRADUATE UNITS**

**Graduate Programs** *Program availability:* Part-time, evening/weekend, online learning.

***Division of Education*** *Program availability:* Part-time, evening/weekend.

## STATE UNIVERSITY OF NEW YORK COLLEGE AT POTSDAM, Potsdam, NY 13676

**General Information** State-supported, coed, comprehensive institution. *Graduate housing:* Room and/or apartments available on a first-come, first-served basis to single students; on-campus housing not available to married students.

**GRADUATE UNITS**

**Crane School of Music** *Program availability:* Part-time. Electronic applications accepted.

**School of Arts and Sciences** *Program availability:* Part-time, evening/weekend. Electronic applications accepted.

**School of Education and Professional Studies** *Program availability:* Online learning. Electronic applications accepted.

## STATE UNIVERSITY OF NEW YORK COLLEGE OF ENVIRONMENTAL SCIENCE AND FORESTRY, Syracuse, NY 13210-2779

**General Information** State-supported, coed, university. CGS member. *Enrollment:* 321 full-time matriculated graduate/professional students (185 women), 56 part-time matriculated graduate/professional students (25 women). *Enrollment by degree level:* 209 master's, 165 doctoral, 3 other advanced degrees. *Graduate faculty:* 129 full-time (44 women), 56 part-time/adjunct (20 women). Tuition, state resident: full-time $11,310; part-time $472 per credit hour. Tuition, nonresident: full-time $23,100; part-time $963 per credit hour. *Required fees:* $1890; $95.21 per credit hour. *Graduate housing:* On-campus housing not available. *Student services:* Campus employment opportunities, campus safety program, career counseling, exercise/wellness program, free psychological counseling, grant writing training, international student services, low-cost health insurance, multicultural affairs office, writing training. *Library facilities:* F. Franklin Moon Library plus 1 other. *Collection:* Books: 57,565 (physical), 444,963 (digital/electronic); Serial titles: 1,568 (physical), 163,166 (digital/electronic); Databases: 181. Weekly public service hours: 97. *Research affiliation:* U.S. Department of Agriculture (USDA) (forest and natural resources management), NASA (remote sensing and GIS), New York State Department of Agriculture and Markets (green infrastructure and food systems), New York State Department of Environmental Conservation (environmental conservation and wildlife management), Honeywell (brownfields remediation), U.S. Department of Commerce (Great Lakes water).

**Computer facilities:** Computer purchase and lease plans are available. 350 computers available on campus for general student use. A campuswide network can be accessed from student residence rooms and from off campus. Online class registration is available.
Website: http://www.esf.edu/

**General Application Contact:** Laura Payne, Administrative Assistant, Office of Instruction and Graduate Studies, 315-470-6599, Fax: 315-470-6978, E-mail: esfgrad@esf.edu.

**GRADUATE UNITS**

**Department of Chemistry** Students: 34 full-time (15 women), 4 part-time (2 women); includes 1 minority (Asian, non-Hispanic/Latino), 12 international. Average age 28. 32 applicants, 59% accepted, 6 enrolled. *Faculty:* 14 full-time (1 woman), 1 part-time/adjunct (0 women). Expenses: Contact institution. *Financial support:* In 2019–20, 12 students received support. Unspecified assistantships available. Financial award application deadline: 6/30; financial award applicants required to submit FAFSA. In 2019, 6 master's, 4 doctorates awarded. *Program availability:* Part-time. *Application deadline:* For fall admission, 2/1 priority date for domestic and international students; for spring admission, 11/1 priority date for domestic and international students. Applications are processed on a rolling basis. *Application fee:* $60. Electronic applications accepted. *Application Contact:* Laura Payne, Administrative Assistant, Office of Instruction and Graduate Studies, 315-470-6599, Fax: 315-470-6978, E-mail: esfgrad@esf.edu. *Chair,* Dr. Avik Chatterjee, 315-470-4747, Fax: 315-470-6855, E-mail: achatter@esf.edu.

**Department of Environmental and Forest Biology** Students: 103 full-time (60 women), 17 part-time (7 women); includes 7 minority (4 American Indian or Alaska Native, non-Hispanic/Latino; 2 Asian, non-Hispanic/Latino; 1 Hispanic/Latino), 13 international. Average age 29. 69 applicants, 45% accepted, 17 enrolled. *Faculty:* 35 full-time (10 women), 4 part-time/adjunct (3 women). Expenses: Contact institution. *Financial support:* In 2019–20, 35 students received support. Unspecified assistantships available. Financial award application deadline: 6/30; financial award applicants required to submit FAFSA. In 2019, 28 master's, 6 doctorates awarded. *Program availability:* Part-time. *Application deadline:* For fall admission, 2/1 priority date for domestic and international students; for spring admission, 11/1 priority date for domestic and international students. Applications are processed on a rolling basis. *Application fee:* $60. Electronic applications accepted. *Application Contact:* Laura Payne, Administrative Assistant Office of Instruction & Graduate Studies, 315-470-6599, E-mail: esfgrad@esf.edu. *Chair,* Dr. Melissa K. Fierke, 315-470-6809, Fax: 315-470-6743, E-mail: mkfierke@esf.edu.

**Department of Environmental Resources Engineering** Students: 22 full-time (13 women), 4 part-time (1 woman); includes 1 minority (Asian, non-Hispanic/Latino), 15 international. Average age 31. 32 applicants, 31% accepted, 7 enrolled. *Faculty:* 9 full-time (1 woman), 3 part-time/adjunct (0 women). Expenses: Contact institution. *Financial support:* In 2019–20, 8 students received support. Unspecified assistantships available. Financial award application deadline: 6/30; financial award applicants required to submit FAFSA. In 2019, 3 master's, 2 doctorates awarded. *Program availability:* Part-time. *Application deadline:* For fall admission, 1/15 priority date for domestic and international students; for spring admission, 11/1 priority date for domestic and international students. Applications are processed on a rolling basis. *Application fee:* $60. Electronic applications accepted. *Application Contact:* Laura Payne, Administrative Assistant, Office of Instruction & Graduate Studies, 315-470-6599, Fax: 315-470-6978, E-mail: esfgrad@esf.edu. *Chair,* Dr. Lindi Quackenbush, 315-470-4727, Fax: 315-470-4710, E-mail: ljquackc@esf.edu.

**Department of Environmental Studies** Students: 9 full-time (all women), 1 (woman) part-time, 1 international. Average age 32. 23 applicants, 83% accepted, 6 enrolled. *Faculty:* 10 full-time (7 women), 3 part-time/adjunct (2 women). Expenses: Contact institution. *Financial support:* In 2019–20, 2 students received support. Unspecified assistantships available. Financial award application deadline: 6/30; financial award applicants required to submit FAFSA. *Program availability:* Part-time. *Application deadline:* Applications are processed on a rolling basis. *Application fee:* $60. Electronic applications accepted. *Application Contact:* Scott Shannon, Administrative Assistant, Office of Instruction & Graduate Studies, 315-470-6599, Fax: 315-470-6978, E-mail: esfgrad@esf.edu. *Chair,* Dr. Bennette Whitmore, 315-470-6636, E-mail: bwhitmor@esf.edu.

**Department of Landscape Architecture** Students: 19 full-time (13 women), 5 international. Average age 27. 21 applicants, 95% accepted, 7 enrolled. *Faculty:* 10 full-time (4 women), 7 part-time/adjunct (5 women). Expenses: Contact institution. *Financial support:* In 2019–20, 10 students received support. Unspecified assistantships available. Financial award application deadline: 6/30; financial award applicants required to submit FAFSA. In 2019, 9 master's awarded. *Program availability:* Part-time. *Application deadline:* For fall admission, 2/1 priority date for domestic and international students; for spring admission, 11/1 priority date for domestic and international students. Applications are processed on a rolling basis. *Application fee:* $60. Electronic applications accepted. *Application Contact:* Scott Shannon, Associate Provost for Instruction/Dean of the Graduate School, 315-470-6599, Fax: 315-470-6978, E-mail: esfgrad@esf.edu. *Chair,* Dr. Douglas Johnston, 315-470-6544, Fax: 315-470-6540, E-mail: dmjohnst@esf.edu.

**Department of Paper and Bioprocess Engineering** Students: 28 full-time (13 women), 3 part-time (0 women); includes 1 minority (Hispanic/Latino), 22 international. Average age 29. 19 applicants, 89% accepted, 10 enrolled. *Faculty:* 13 full-time (2 women), 1 part-time/adjunct (0 women). Expenses: Contact institution. *Financial support:* In 2019–20, 17 students received support. Unspecified assistantships available. Financial award application deadline: 6/30; financial award applicants required to submit FAFSA. In 2019, 5 master's, 2 doctorates awarded. *Program availability:* Part-time. *Application deadline:* For fall admission, 2/1 priority date for domestic and international students; for spring admission, 11/1 priority date for domestic and international students. Applications are processed on a rolling basis. *Application fee:* $60. Electronic applications accepted. *Application Contact:* Laura Payne, Office of Instruction and Graduate Studies, 315-470-6599, Fax: 315-470-6978, E-mail: esfgrad@esf.edu. *Chair,* Dr. Bandaru Ramarao, 315-470-6502, Fax: 315-470-6945, E-mail: bvramara@esf.edu.

**Department of Sustainable Resources Management** Students: 106 full-time (67 women), 18 part-time (12 women); includes 10 minority (2 Black or African American, non-Hispanic/Latino; 4 American Indian or Alaska Native, non-Hispanic/Latino; 3 Asian, non-Hispanic/Latino; 1 Hispanic/Latino), 40 international. Average age 30. 96 applicants, 83% accepted, 39 enrolled. *Faculty:* 33 full-time (8 women), 7 part-time/adjunct (0 women). Expenses: Contact institution. *Financial support:* In 2019–20, 21 students received support. Unspecified assistantships available. Financial award application deadline: 6/30; financial award applicants required to submit FAFSA. In 2019, 13 master's, 3 doctorates awarded. *Program availability:* Part-time. *Application deadline:* For fall admission, 2/1 priority date for domestic and international students; for spring admission, 11/1 priority date for domestic and international students. Applications are processed on a rolling basis. *Application fee:* $60. *Application Contact:* Laura Payne, Office of Instruction & Graduate Studies, 315-470-6599, Fax: 315-470-6978, E-mail: esfgrad@esf.edu. *Chair,* Dr. Christopher Nowak, 315-470-6575, Fax: 315-470-6536, E-mail: canowak@esf.edu.

**Program in Environmental Science** Students: 62 full-time (40 women), 12 part-time (9 women); includes 8 minority (1 Black or African American, non-Hispanic/Latino; 4 American Indian or Alaska Native, non-Hispanic/Latino; 2 Asian, non-Hispanic/Latino; 1 Hispanic/Latino), 28 international. Average age 31. 68 applicants, 84% accepted, 26 enrolled. *Faculty:* 1 full-time (0 women), 1 (woman) part-time/adjunct. Expenses: Contact institution. *Financial support:* In 2019–20, 15 students received support. Unspecified assistantships available. Financial award application deadline: 6/30; financial award applicants required to submit FAFSA. In 2019, 10 master's, 2 doctorates awarded. *Program availability:* Part-time. *Application deadline:* For fall admission, 2/1 priority date for domestic and international students; for spring admission, 11/1 priority date for domestic and international students. Applications are processed on a rolling basis. *Application fee:* $60. Electronic applications accepted. *Application Contact:* Laura Payne, Office of Instruction and Graduate Studies, 315-470-6599, E-mail: esfgrad@esf.edu. *Director of the Division of Environmental Science,* Dr. Russell Briggs, 315-470-6989, Fax: 315-470-6700, E-mail: rdbriggs@esf.edu.

## STATE UNIVERSITY OF NEW YORK COLLEGE OF OPTOMETRY, New York, NY 10036

**General Information** State-supported, coed, graduate-only institution. *Graduate housing:* On-campus housing not available. *Research affiliation:* Schnurmacher Institute for Vision Research (vision science).

**GRADUATE UNITS**

**Graduate Programs** *Program availability:* Part-time.

**Professional Program** Electronic applications accepted.

## STATE UNIVERSITY OF NEW YORK COLLEGE OF TECHNOLOGY AT DELHI, Delhi, NY 13753

**General Information** State-supported, coed, comprehensive institution. *Enrollment:* 3,086 graduate, professional, and undergraduate students; 10 full-time matriculated graduate/professional students (7 women), 77 part-time matriculated graduate/professional students (70 women). *Enrollment by degree level:* 87 master's. *Graduate faculty:* 6 full-time (all women), 2 part-time/adjunct (both women). *International tuition:* $13,570 full-time. *Tuition, area resident:* Full-time $11,310; part-time $471 per credit hour. Tuition, state resident: full-time $11,310; part-time $471 per credit hour. Tuition, nonresident: full-time $13,570; part-time $565 per credit hour. *Required fees:* $420; $21.70 per credit hour. $21.70. *Graduate housing:* On-campus housing not available. *Student services:* Career counseling, international student services, multicultural affairs office, services for students with disabilities. *Library facilities:* Resnick Library. *Collection:* Books: 34,976 (physical), 180,389 (digital/electronic); Serial titles: 98 (physical), 747,277 (digital/electronic); Databases: 72. Weekly public service hours: 93; students can reserve study rooms.

**Computer facilities:** 102 computers available on campus for general student use. A campuswide network can be accessed. Online class registration is available.
Website: http://www.delhi.edu/

**General Application Contact:** Misty Fields, Assistant Director of Admissions, 607-746-4546, E-mail: fieldsmr@delhi.edu.

**GRADUATE UNITS**

**Program in Nursing** Students: 10 full-time (7 women), 77 part-time (70 women); includes 13 minority (7 Black or African American, non-Hispanic/Latino; 2 Asian, non-Hispanic/Latino; 4 Hispanic/Latino). Average age 38. 70 applicants, 71% accepted, 37 enrolled. *Faculty:* 6 full-time (all women), 2 part-time/adjunct (both women). Expenses: Contact institution. *Financial support:* In 2019–20, 4 students received support. Scholarships/grants available. Financial award applicants required to submit FAFSA. In 2019, 15 master's awarded. *Program availability:* Part-time, online only, 100% online. *Application deadline:* For fall admission, 7/15 for domestic and international students; for spring admission, 11/15 for domestic and international students. Applications are processed on a rolling basis. *Application fee:* $75. Electronic applications accepted. *Application Contact:* Misty Fields, Associate Director of Admission, 607-746-4546, E-mail: fieldsmr@delhi.edu. *Dean of the School of Nursing,* Susan Deane, 607-746-4550, Fax: 607-746-4104, E-mail: deanesg@delhi.edu.

## STATE UNIVERSITY OF NEW YORK DOWNSTATE MEDICAL CENTER, Brooklyn, NY 11203-2098

**General Information** State-supported, coed, upper-level institution. *Graduate housing:* Rooms and/or apartments available on a first-come, first-served basis to single and married students. Housing application deadline: 5/29. *Research affiliation:* Brooklyn Veterans Administration Medical Center, Polytechnic Institute of New York University (biomedical engineering).

**GRADUATE UNITS**

**College of Medicine**

**College of Nursing** *Program availability:* Part-time, evening/weekend.

**School of Graduate Studies**

## STATE UNIVERSITY OF NEW YORK EMPIRE STATE COLLEGE, Saratoga Springs, NY 12866-4391

**General Information** State-supported, coed, comprehensive institution. *Graduate housing:* On-campus housing not available.

**GRADUATE UNITS**

**School for Graduate Studies** *Program availability:* Part-time, evening/weekend, online learning. Electronic applications accepted.

## STATE UNIVERSITY OF NEW YORK MARITIME COLLEGE, Throggs Neck, NY 10465-4198

**General Information** State-supported, coed, comprehensive institution. *Enrollment:* 1,734 graduate, professional, and undergraduate students; 165 matriculated graduate/professional students (15 women). *Enrollment by degree level:* 165 master's. *Graduate faculty:* 7 full-time, 12 part-time/adjunct. *Graduate housing:* Room and/or apartments available to single students; on-campus housing not available to married students. *Student services:* Campus employment opportunities, career counseling, international student services, low-cost health insurance. *Library facilities:* Stephen B. Luce Library. *Collection:* Books: 41,000 (physical), 60,567 (digital/electronic); Serial titles: 125 (physical), 323,000 (digital/electronic); Databases: 68. Weekly public service hours: 111; students can reserve study rooms. *Research affiliation:* Port Authority of New York and New Jersey (transportation), Transportation Infrastructure Research Consortium, Transportation Research Board (maritime transportation).

**Computer facilities:** 160 computers available on campus for general student use. A campuswide network can be accessed. Online class registration is available.
Website: http://www.sunymaritime.edu/

**General Application Contact:** Dr. Shmuel Yahalom, Director, 718-409-7285, Fax: 718-409-7359, E-mail: syahalom@sunymaritime.edu.

**GRADUATE UNITS**

**Program in International Transportation Management** *Program availability:* Part-time, evening/weekend.

## STATE UNIVERSITY OF NEW YORK POLYTECHNIC INSTITUTE, Utica, NY 13502

**General Information** State-supported, coed, comprehensive institution. *Graduate housing:* Room and/or apartments available to single students; on-campus housing not available to married students. *Research affiliation:* Griffiss Institute (Innovation and Entrepreneurship), Assured Information Security, Inc. (cyber security), Masconic Research Laboratory (heart research), New West Technologies (mechanical engineering), Air Force Research Laboratory (computer science/systems and signal processing).

**GRADUATE UNITS**

**College of Nanoscale Science and Engineering** Electronic applications accepted.

**MBA Program in Technology Management** *Program availability:* Part-time, 100% online. Electronic applications accepted.

**MS Program in Accountancy**

**MS Program in Transformational Leadership**

**Program in Advanced Technology** Electronic applications accepted.

**Program in Computer and Information Science** *Program availability:* Part-time. Electronic applications accepted.

**Program in Family Nurse Practitioner** *Program availability:* Part-time.

**Program in Information Design and Technology** *Program availability:* Part-time. Electronic applications accepted.

**Program in Network and Computer Security** *Program availability:* Part-time. Electronic applications accepted.

**Program in Nursing Education** *Program availability:* Part-time, 100% online. Electronic applications accepted.

## STATE UNIVERSITY OF NEW YORK UPSTATE MEDICAL UNIVERSITY, Syracuse, NY 13210

**General Information** State-supported, coed, upper-level institution. CGS member. *Graduate housing:* Rooms and/or apartments available on a first-come, first-served basis to single and married students. Housing application deadline: 8/1.

**GRADUATE UNITS**

**College of Graduate Studies** Electronic applications accepted.

**College of Medicine** Electronic applications accepted.

**College of Nursing** *Program availability:* Part-time, online learning. Electronic applications accepted.

**Department of Physical Therapy** *Program availability:* Part-time, evening/weekend, online learning. Electronic applications accepted.

**Program in Medical Technology**

## STEPHEN F. AUSTIN STATE UNIVERSITY, Nacogdoches, TX 75962

**General Information** State-supported, coed, comprehensive institution. *Graduate housing:* Rooms and/or apartments available on a first-come, first-served basis to single students and available to married students. Housing application deadline: 6/1. *Research affiliation:* University Health Center at Tyler (biotechnology, environmental science).

**GRADUATE UNITS**

**Graduate School** *Program availability:* Part-time, evening/weekend, online learning. Electronic applications accepted.

***Arthur Temple College of Forestry and Agriculture***

***College of Fine Arts*** *Program availability:* Part-time.

***College of Liberal and Applied Arts*** *Program availability:* Part-time, evening/weekend.

***College of Sciences and Mathematics*** *Program availability:* Part-time.

***James I. Perkins College of Education*** *Program availability:* Part-time, evening/weekend.

***Nelson Rusche College of Business*** *Program availability:* Part-time, evening/weekend.

## STEPHENS COLLEGE, Columbia, MO 65215-0002

**General Information** Independent, Undergraduate: women only; graduate: coed, comprehensive institution. *Graduate housing:* On-campus housing not available.

**GRADUATE UNITS**

**Division of Graduate and Continuing Studies** *Program availability:* Part-time, evening/weekend, online learning. Electronic applications accepted.

## STETSON UNIVERSITY, DeLand, FL 32723

**General Information** Independent, coed, comprehensive institution. *Enrollment:* 4,429 graduate, professional, and undergraduate students; 1,085 full-time matriculated graduate/professional students (624 women), 154 part-time matriculated graduate/professional students (80 women). *Enrollment by degree level:* 316 master's, 923 doctoral. *Graduate faculty:* 66 full-time (37 women), 73 part-time/adjunct (36 women). *Graduate housing:* Rooms and/or apartments available to single and married students. *Student services:* Campus employment opportunities, career counseling, free psychological counseling, international student services, low-cost health insurance, services for students with disabilities, teacher training, writing training. *Library facilities:* DuPont-Ball Library plus 1 other. *Collection:* Books: 219,200 (physical), 166,549 (digital/electronic); Serial titles: 228 (physical), 186,552 (digital/electronic); Databases: 247. Weekly public service hours: 104; study areas open 24 hours, 5–7 days a week; students can reserve study rooms. *Research affiliation:* New Teacher Center (teacher education), Teacher Prep Inspection-Us, LLC (teacher preparation), Erin Deady, PA (environmental policy and legal affairs).

**Computer facilities:** 600 computers available on campus for general student use. A campuswide network can be accessed. Online class registration is available.
Website: http://www.stetson.edu/

**General Application Contact:** Jamie Vanderlip, Director of Admissions for Graduate, Transfer and Adult Populations, 386-822-7100, Fax: 386-822-7112, E-mail: gradadmissions@stetson.edu.

**GRADUATE UNITS**

**College of Arts and Sciences** Students: 157 full-time (127 women), 7 part-time (6 women); includes 55 minority (16 Black or African American, non-Hispanic/Latino; 3 American Indian or Alaska Native, non-Hispanic/Latino; 21 Hispanic/Latino; 15 Two or more races, non-Hispanic/Latino), 8 international. Average age 33. 95 applicants, 83% accepted, 62 enrolled. *Faculty:* 14 full-time (10 women), 10 part-time/adjunct (7 women). Expenses: Contact institution. *Financial support:* In 2019–20, 70 students received support. Teaching assistantships, career-related internships or fieldwork, Federal Work-Study, scholarships/grants, unspecified assistantships, and tuition waivers (for staff and dependents) available. Support available to part-time students. Financial award applicants required to submit FAFSA. In 2019, 70 master's awarded. *Program availability:* Part-time, evening/weekend. *Application deadline:* For fall admission, 8/1 priority date for domestic students; for spring admission, 1/1 priority date for domestic students; for summer admission, 5/1 priority date for domestic students. Applications are processed on a rolling basis. *Application fee:* $50. Electronic applications accepted. *Application Contact:* Jamie Vanderlip, Director of Admissions for Graduate, Transfer and Adult Populations, 386-822-7100, Fax: 386-822-7112, E-mail: jlvander@stetson.edu. *Dean,* Dr. Elizabeth Skomp, 386-822-7515.

***Division of Education*** Students: 131 full-time (100 women), 6 part-time (5 women); includes 45 minority (19 Black or African American, non-Hispanic/Latino; 3 American Indian or Alaska Native, non-Hispanic/Latino; 16 Hispanic/Latino; 7 Two or more races, non-Hispanic/Latino), 4 international. Average age 32. 84 applicants, 83% accepted, 57 enrolled. *Faculty:* 12 full-time (8 women), 6 part-time/adjunct (5 women). Expenses: Contact institution. *Financial support:* In 2019–20, 60 students received support. Career-related internships or fieldwork, Federal Work-Study, institutionally sponsored loans, scholarships/grants, unspecified assistantships, and tuition waivers (for staff and dependents) available. Support available to part-time students. Financial award applicants required to submit FAFSA. In 2019, 60 master's awarded. *Program availability:* Part-time, evening/weekend. *Application deadline:* For fall admission, 8/1 priority date for domestic students; for spring admission, 1/1 priority date for domestic students; for summer admission, 5/1 priority date for domestic students. Applications are processed on a rolling basis. *Application fee:* $50. Electronic applications accepted. *Application Contact:* Jamie Vanderlip, Director of Admissions for Graduate, Transfer and Adult Programs, 386-822-7100, Fax: 386-822-7112, E-mail: jlvander@stetson.edu. *Dean of the College of Arts and Sciences,* Dr. Elizabeth Skomp, 386-822-7515.

**College of Law** Students: 802 full-time (435 women), 121 part-time (58 women); includes 242 minority (55 Black or African American, non-Hispanic/Latino; 4 American Indian or Alaska Native, non-Hispanic/Latino; 28 Asian, non-Hispanic/Latino; 133 Hispanic/Latino; 22 Two or more races, non-Hispanic/Latino), 26 international. Average age 27. 1,816 applicants, 51% accepted, 322 enrolled. *Faculty:* 41 full-time (24 women), 60 part-time/adjunct (28 women). Expenses: Contact institution. *Financial support:* In 2019–20, 687 students received support, including 50 research assistantships (averaging $1,370 per year), 53 teaching assistantships (averaging $949 per year); career-related internships or fieldwork, Federal Work-Study, scholarships/grants, unspecified assistantships, and tuition waivers (for staff and dependents) also available. Support available to part-time students. Financial award application deadline: 8/15; financial award applicants required to submit FAFSA. In 2019, 28 master's, 263 doctorates awarded. *Program availability:* Part-time, evening/weekend, 100% online. *Application deadline:* For fall admission, 5/15 for domestic and international students. Applications are processed on a rolling basis. *Application fee:* $55. Electronic applications accepted. *Application Contact:* Darren Kettles, Director of Admissions, 727-562-7802, Fax: 727-562-7670, E-mail: lawadmit@law.stetson.edu. *Dean/Professor of Law,* Michele Alexandre, 727-562-7809, Fax: 727-562-7800, E-mail: malexandre@law.stetson.edu.

**School of Business Administration** Students: 134 full-time (77 women), 27 part-time (17 women); includes 41 minority (16 Black or African American, non-Hispanic/Latino; 20 Hispanic/Latino; 5 Two or more races, non-Hispanic/Latino), 10 international. Average age 30. 133 applicants, 94% accepted, 106 enrolled. *Faculty:* 11 full-time (3 women), 3 part-time/adjunct (1 woman). Expenses: Contact institution. *Financial support:* In 2019–20, 78 students received support. Career-related internships or fieldwork, Federal Work-Study, institutionally sponsored loans, scholarships/grants, unspecified assistantships, and tuition waivers (for staff and dependents) available. Support available to part-time students. Financial award applicants required to submit FAFSA. In 2019, 71 master's awarded. *Program availability:* Part-time, evening/weekend. *Application deadline:* For fall admission, 8/1 for domestic students; for spring admission, 12/1 for domestic students; for summer admission, 4/15 for domestic students. Applications are processed on a rolling basis. *Application fee:* $50. Electronic applications accepted. *Application Contact:* Jamie Vanderlip, Director of Admissions for Graduate, Transfer and Adult Programs, 386-822-7100, Fax: 386-822-7112, E-mail: jlvander@stetson.edu. *Dean, School of Business Administration,* Dr. Neal P. Mero, 386-822-7405.

## STEVENS-HENAGER COLLEGE, Salt Lake City, UT 84123

**General Information** Independent, coed, comprehensive institution.

## STEVENS INSTITUTE OF TECHNOLOGY, Hoboken, NJ 07030

**General Information** Independent, coed, university. CGS member. *Enrollment:* 7,283 graduate, professional, and undergraduate students; 2,459 full-time matriculated graduate/professional students (688 women), 1,062 part-time matriculated graduate/professional students (361 women). *Enrollment by degree level:* 3,032 master's, 430 doctoral, 59 other advanced degrees. *Graduate faculty:* 276 full-time (74 women), 168 part-time/adjunct (33 women). *Tuition:* Full-time $52,134. *Required fees:* $1880. Tuition and fees vary according to course load. *Graduate housing:* Room and/or apartments available on a first-come, first-served basis to single students; on-campus housing not available to married students. Typical cost: $15,770 (including board). Room and board charges vary according to board plan. Housing application deadline: 2/1. *Student services:* Campus employment opportunities, campus safety program, career counseling, exercise/wellness program, free psychological counseling, grant writing training, international student services, low-cost health insurance, multicultural affairs office, services for students with disabilities, teacher training, writing training. *Library facilities:* Samuel C. Williams Library. *Collection:* Books: 66,492 (physical), 210,243 (digital/electronic); Serial titles: 898 (physical), 35,353 (digital/electronic); Databases: 71. Students can reserve study rooms. *Research affiliation:* U.S. Department of Homeland Security (secure maritime systems), U.S. Department of Defense (systems engineering), National Science Foundation (nanotechnology and multi-scale systems, secure systems and information assurance), AT&T (intelligent networked systems).

**Computer facilities:** 156 computers available on campus for general student use. A campuswide network can be accessed. Online class registration, online account information, debit dining program, laundry status are available.
Website: http://www.stevens.edu/

**GRADUATE UNITS**

***Charles V. Schaefer Jr. School of Engineering and Science*** Students: 1,352 full-time (319 women), 269 part-time (71 women); includes 141 minority (25 Black or African American, non-Hispanic/Latino; 4 American Indian or Alaska Native, non-Hispanic/Latino; 103 Asian, non-Hispanic/Latino; 9 Hispanic/Latino), 1,148 international. Average age 26. *Faculty:* 159 full-time (36 women), 92 part-time/adjunct

(10 women). Expenses: Contact institution. *Financial support:* Fellowships, research assistantships, teaching assistantships, career-related internships or fieldwork, Federal Work-Study, scholarships/grants, and unspecified assistantships available. Financial award application deadline: 2/15; financial award applicants required to submit FAFSA. In 2019, 718 master's, 39 doctorates, 112 other advanced degrees awarded. *Program availability:* Part-time, evening/weekend, 100% online, blended/hybrid learning. *Application deadline:* For fall admission, 4/15 for domestic and international students; for spring admission, 11/1 for domestic and international students; for summer admission, 5/1 for domestic students. Applications are processed on a rolling basis. *Application fee:* $60. Electronic applications accepted. *Application Contact:* Graduate Admissions, 888-783-8367, Fax: 888-555-1306, E-mail: graduate@stevens.edu. *Dean,* Dr. Jean Zu, 201-216-2833, E-mail: jean.zu@stevens.edu.

***College of Arts and Letters*** Students: 1 full-time (0 women), 1 (woman) part-time, 1 international. Average age 31. *Faculty:* 34 full-time (18 women), 27 part-time/adjunct (13 women). Expenses: Contact institution. *Financial support:* Fellowships, research assistantships, teaching assistantships, career-related internships or fieldwork, Federal Work-Study, scholarships/grants, and unspecified assistantships available. Financial award application deadline: 2/15; financial award applicants required to submit FAFSA. *Program availability:* Part-time, evening/weekend. *Application deadline:* For fall admission, 4/15 for domestic and international students; for spring admission, 11/1 for domestic and international students; for summer admission, 5/1 for domestic students. Applications are processed on a rolling basis. *Application fee:* $60. Electronic applications accepted. *Application Contact:* Graduate Admission, 888-783-8367, Fax: 888-511-1306, E-mail: graduate@stevens.edu. *Dean of CAL,* Dr. Kelland Thomas, 201-216-3728, Fax: 201-216-8245, E-mail: Kelland.Thomas@stevens.edu.

***School of Business*** Students: 827 full-time (299 women), 552 part-time (219 women); includes 182 minority (40 Black or African American, non-Hispanic/Latino; 5 American Indian or Alaska Native, non-Hispanic/Latino; 130 Asian, non-Hispanic/Latino; 6 Hispanic/Latino; 1 Two or more races, non-Hispanic/Latino), 849 international. Average age 29. *Faculty:* 59 full-time (11 women), 30 part-time/adjunct (5 women). Expenses: Contact institution. *Financial support:* Fellowships, research assistantships, teaching assistantships, career-related internships or fieldwork, Federal Work-Study, scholarships/grants, and unspecified assistantships available. Financial award application deadline: 2/15; financial award applicants required to submit FAFSA. In 2019, 651 master's, 7 doctorates, 175 other advanced degrees awarded. *Program availability:* Part-time, evening/weekend, 100% online, blended/hybrid learning. *Application deadline:* For fall admission, 4/1 for domestic and international students; for spring admission, 11/1 for domestic and international students; for summer admission, 5/1 for domestic students. Applications are processed on a rolling basis. *Application fee:* $60. Electronic applications accepted. *Application Contact:* Graduate Admissions, 888-793-8367, Fax: 888-511-1306, E-mail: graduate@stevens.edu. *Dean of SB,* Dr. Gregory Prastacos, 201-216-8366, E-mail: gprastac@stevens.edu.

***School of Systems and Enterprises*** Students: 279 full-time (70 women), 240 part-time (70 women); includes 68 minority (21 Black or African American, non-Hispanic/Latino; 3 American Indian or Alaska Native, non-Hispanic/Latino; 38 Asian, non-Hispanic/Latino; 6 Hispanic/Latino), 241 international. Average age 28. *Faculty:* 22 full-time (8 women), 15 part-time/adjunct (3 women). Expenses: Contact institution. *Financial support:* Fellowships, research assistantships, teaching assistantships, career-related internships or fieldwork, Federal Work-Study, scholarships/grants, and unspecified assistantships available. Financial award application deadline: 2/15; financial award applicants required to submit FAFSA. In 2019, 255 master's, 7 doctorates, 232 other advanced degrees awarded. *Program availability:* Part-time, evening/weekend, 100% online, blended/hybrid learning. *Application deadline:* For fall admission, 4/15 for domestic and international students; for spring admission, 11/1 for domestic and international students; for summer admission, 5/1 for domestic students. Applications are processed on a rolling basis. *Application fee:* $60. Electronic applications accepted. *Application Contact:* Graduate Admissions, 888-783-8367, Fax: 888-511-1306, E-mail: graduate@stevens.edu. *Dean of SSE,* Dr. Yehia Massoud, 201.216.8025, E-mail: yehia.massoud@stevens.edu.

## STEVENSON UNIVERSITY, Stevenson, MD 21153

**General Information** Independent, coed, comprehensive institution. *Enrollment:* 3,579 graduate, professional, and undergraduate students; 74 full-time matriculated graduate/professional students (52 women), 478 part-time matriculated graduate/professional students (390 women). *Enrollment by degree level:* 552 master's. *Graduate faculty:* 8 full-time (5 women), 55 part-time/adjunct (29 women). *Tuition:* Part-time $650.46 per credit. Tuition and fees vary according to program. *Graduate housing:* On-campus housing not available. *Student services:* Campus employment opportunities, career counseling, exercise/wellness program, multicultural affairs office, services for students with disabilities, writing training. *Library facilities:* Stevenson University Learning Resource Center-Greenspring Campus plus 2 others. *Collection:* Books: 60,915 (physical), 383,563 (digital/electronic); Serial titles: 240 (physical), 34,695 (digital/electronic); Databases: 86. Weekly public service hours: 136; students can reserve study rooms.

**Computer facilities:** Computer purchase and lease plans are available. 552 computers available on campus for general student use. A campuswide network can be accessed. Online class registration is available.
Website: http://www.stevenson.edu/

**General Application Contact:** Amanda Millar, Director, SUO Admissions, 443-334-3334, Fax: 443-394-0538, E-mail: amillar@stevenson.edu.

**GRADUATE UNITS**

**Master of Arts in Teaching Program** Students: 13 part-time (10 women); includes 3 minority (2 Black or African American, non-Hispanic/Latino; 1 Two or more races, non-Hispanic/Latino). Average age 31. 14 applicants, 36% accepted, 5 enrolled. *Faculty:* 1 (woman) full-time, 5 part-time/adjunct (4 women). Expenses: Contact institution. *Financial support:* Unspecified assistantships available. Financial award applicants required to submit FAFSA. In 2019, 7 master's awarded. *Program availability:* Part-time, blended/hybrid learning. *Application deadline:* For fall admission, 8/9 priority date for domestic students; for spring admission, 1/11 priority date for domestic students; for summer admission, 5/1 priority date for domestic students. Applications are processed on a rolling basis. Electronic applications accepted. *Application Contact:* Amanda Millar, Director, Admissions, 443-352-4243, Fax: 443-352-4440, E-mail: amillar@stevenson.edu. *Program Coordinator & Assistant Professor Graduate Education,* Dr. Lisa A. Moyer, 443-352-4867, E-mail: lmoyer@steveson.edu.

**Master of Forensic Science** Students: 23 full-time (22 women), 61 part-time (52 women); includes 47 minority (31 Black or African American, non-Hispanic/Latino; 4 Asian, non-Hispanic/Latino; 8 Hispanic/Latino; 4 Two or more races, non-Hispanic/Latino). Average age 28. 53 applicants, 66% accepted, 24 enrolled. *Faculty:* 1 full-time (0 women), 12 part-time/adjunct (5 women). Expenses: Contact institution. *Financial support:* Unspecified assistantships available. Financial award applicants required to submit FAFSA. In 2019, 15 master's awarded. *Program availability:* Part-time. *Application deadline:* For fall admission, 8/9 priority date for domestic students; for spring admission, 1/11 priority date for domestic students; for summer admission, 5/1 priority date for domestic students. Applications are processed on a rolling basis. Electronic applications accepted. *Application Contact:* Amanda Millar, Director, Admissions, 443-333-3334, Fax: 443-394-0538, E-mail: amillar@stevenson.edu. *Department Chair & Professor,* Carolyn Johnson, 443-352-4074, E-mail: CHJOHNSON@stevenson.edu.

**Program in Business and Technology Management** Students: 15 full-time (7 women), 43 part-time (25 women); includes 29 minority (20 Black or African American, non-Hispanic/Latino; 2 Asian, non-Hispanic/Latino; 3 Hispanic/Latino; 4 Two or more races, non-Hispanic/Latino). Average age 30. 21 applicants, 76% accepted, 11 enrolled. *Faculty:* 1 full-time (0 women), 10 part-time/adjunct (2 women). Expenses: Contact institution. *Financial support:* Unspecified assistantships available. Financial award applicants required to submit FAFSA. In 2019, 66 master's awarded. *Program availability:* Part-time, online only, 100% online. *Application deadline:* For fall admission, 8/9 priority date for domestic students; for spring admission, 1/11 priority date for domestic students; for summer admission, 5/1 priority date for domestic students. Applications are processed on a rolling basis. Electronic applications accepted. *Application Contact:* Amanda Millar, Director, Admissions, 443-352-4058, Fax: 443-394-0538, E-mail: amillar@stevenson.edu. *Graduate Program Director,* Steven Engorn, 443-352-4220, Fax: 443-394-0538, E-mail: sengorn@stevenson.edu.

**Program in Communication Studies** Students: 5 full-time (4 women), 18 part-time (15 women); includes 14 minority (12 Black or African American, non-Hispanic/Latino; 1 Asian, non-Hispanic/Latino; 1 Two or more races, non-Hispanic/Latino). Average age 27. 18 applicants, 67% accepted, 5 enrolled. *Faculty:* 1 full-time (0 women), 3 part-time/adjunct (2 women). Expenses: Contact institution. *Financial support:* Unspecified assistantships available. Financial award applicants required to submit FAFSA. In 2019, 11 master's awarded. *Program availability:* Part-time, online only, 100% online, blended/hybrid learning. *Application deadline:* For fall admission, 8/9 priority date for domestic students; for spring admission, 1/11 priority date for domestic students; for summer admission, 5/1 priority date for domestic students. Applications are processed on a rolling basis. Electronic applications accepted. *Application Contact:* Amanda Millar, Director, Admissions, 443-352-4243, Fax: 443-352-4440, E-mail: amillar@stevenson.edu. *Interim Dean Stevenson University Online & Program Coordinator,* Dr. Lee Krahenbuhl, 443-352-5348, E-mail: lkrahenbuhl@stevenson.edu.

**Program in Community-Based Education and Leadership** Students: 8 full-time (6 women), 39 part-time (32 women); includes 18 minority (14 Black or African American, non-Hispanic/Latino; 2 Hispanic/Latino; 2 Two or more races, non-Hispanic/Latino). Average age 34. 26 applicants, 85% accepted, 14 enrolled. *Faculty:* 2 part-time/adjunct (both women). Expenses: Contact institution. *Financial support:* Unspecified assistantships available. Financial award applicants required to submit FAFSA. In 2019, 10 master's awarded. *Program availability:* Part-time, evening/weekend, online only, 100% online. *Application deadline:* For fall admission, 8/9 priority date for domestic students; for spring admission, 1/11 priority date for domestic students; for summer admission, 5/1 priority date for domestic students. Applications are processed on a rolling basis. Electronic applications accepted. *Application Contact:* Amanda Millar, Director, Admissions, 443-334-3334, Fax: 443-394-0538, E-mail: amillar@stevenson.edu. *Program Coordinator,* Dr. Lisa Moyer, 443-352-4867, E-mail: lmoyer@stevenson.edu.

**Program in Crime Scene Investigation** Students: 11 full-time (5 women), 56 part-time (47 women); includes 37 minority (25 Black or African American, non-Hispanic/Latino; 2 American Indian or Alaska Native, non-Hispanic/Latino; 1 Asian, non-Hispanic/Latino; 5 Hispanic/Latino; 4 Two or more races, non-Hispanic/Latino). Average age 28. 40 applicants, 60% accepted, 13 enrolled. Expenses: Contact institution. *Financial support:* Unspecified assistantships available. Financial award applicants required to submit FAFSA. *Program availability:* Part-time, online only, 100% online. *Application deadline:* For fall admission, 8/9 priority date for domestic students; for spring admission, 1/11 priority date for domestic students; for summer admission, 5/1 priority date for domestic students. Applications are processed on a rolling basis. Electronic applications accepted. *Application Contact:* Amanda Millar, Director, SUO Admissions, 443-352-4243, Fax: 443-352-4440, E-mail: amillar@stevenson.edu. *Department Chair & Professor,* Carolyn Johnson, 443-352-4074, E-mail: chjohnson@stevenson.edu.

**Program in Cybersecurity and Digital Forensics** Students: 3 full-time (0 women), 21 part-time (7 women); includes 8 minority (4 Black or African American, non-Hispanic/Latino; 2 Hispanic/Latino; 2 Two or more races, non-Hispanic/Latino). Average age 31. 26 applicants, 50% accepted, 6 enrolled. *Faculty:* 3 part-time/adjunct (2 women). Expenses: Contact institution. *Financial support:* Unspecified assistantships available. Financial award applicants required to submit FAFSA. In 2019, 11 master's awarded. *Program availability:* Part-time, 100% online. *Application deadline:* For fall admission, 8/9 priority date for domestic students; for spring admission, 1/11 priority date for domestic students; for summer admission, 5/1 priority date for domestic students. Applications are processed on a rolling basis. Electronic applications accepted. *Application Contact:* Amanda Millar, Director, Admissions, 443-334-3334, Fax: 443-394-0538, E-mail: amillar@stevenson.edu. *Graduate Program Director,* Steven R. Engorn, 443-352-4074, E-mail: CHJOHNSON@stevenson.edu.

**Program in Forensic Accounting** Students: 3 full-time (all women), 13 part-time (9 women); includes 5 minority (3 Black or African American, non-Hispanic/Latino; 1 Hispanic/Latino; 1 Two or more races, non-Hispanic/Latino). Average age 33. 19 applicants, 42% accepted, 2 enrolled. *Faculty:* 3 part-time/adjunct (0 women). Expenses: Contact institution. *Financial support:* Unspecified assistantships available. Financial award applicants required to submit FAFSA. *Program availability:* Part-time, online only, 100% online. *Application deadline:* For fall admission, 8/9 priority date for domestic students; for spring admission, 1/11 priority date for domestic students; for summer admission, 5/1 priority date for domestic students. Applications are processed on a rolling basis. Electronic applications accepted. *Application Contact:* Amanda Millar, Director, SUO Admissions, 443-352-4243, Fax: 443-352-4440, E-mail: amillar@stevenson.edu. *Department Chair & Professor,* Carolyn Johnson, 443-352-4074, E-mail: chjohnson@stevenson.edu.

**Program in Forensic Investigations** Students: 5 full-time (4 women), 16 part-time (14 women); includes 13 minority (9 Black or African American, non-Hispanic/Latino; 1 Hispanic/Latino; 3 Two or more races, non-Hispanic/Latino). Average age 30. 27 applicants, 59% accepted, 6 enrolled. *Faculty:* 2 part-time/adjunct (0 women). Expenses: Contact institution. *Financial support:* Unspecified assistantships available. Financial award applicants required to submit FAFSA. *Program availability:* Part-time, online only, 100% online. *Application deadline:* For fall admission, 8/9 priority date for domestic students; for spring admission, 1/11 priority date for domestic students; for summer admission, 5/1 priority date for domestic students. Applications are processed on a rolling basis. Electronic applications accepted. *Application Contact:* Amanda Millar, Director, SUO Admissions, 443-352-4243, Fax: 443-352-4440, E-mail: amillar@stevenson.edu. *Department Chair & Professor*, Carolyn Johnson, 443-352-4074, E-mail: chjohnson@stevenson.edu.

**Program in Forensic Studies** Students: 1 (woman) full-time, 19 part-time (14 women); includes 11 minority (6 Black or African American, non-Hispanic/Latino; 1 Asian, non-Hispanic/Latino; 3 Hispanic/Latino; 1 Two or more races, non-Hispanic/Latino). Average age 35. 5 applicants, 40% accepted. *Faculty:* 1 (woman) full-time, 7 part-time/adjunct (3 women). Expenses: Contact institution. *Financial support:* Unspecified assistantships available. Financial award applicants required to submit FAFSA. In 2019, 25 master's awarded. *Program availability:* Part-time, blended/hybrid learning. *Application deadline:* For fall admission, 8/9 priority date for domestic students; for spring admission, 1/11 priority date for domestic students; for summer admission, 5/1 priority date for domestic students. Applications are processed on a rolling basis. Electronic applications accepted. *Application Contact:* Amanda Millar, Director, Admissions, 443-334-3334, Fax: 443-394-0538, E-mail: amillar@stevenson.edu. *Department Chair & Professor*, Carolyn Johnson, 443-352-4074, E-mail: CHJOHNSON@stevenson.edu.

**Program in Healthcare Management** Students: 33 part-time (25 women); includes 13 minority (11 Black or African American, non-Hispanic/Latino; 2 Asian, non-Hispanic/Latino). Average age 35. 19 applicants, 42% accepted, 6 enrolled. *Faculty:* 1 (woman) full-time, 5 part-time/adjunct (4 women). Expenses: Contact institution. *Financial support:* Unspecified assistantships available. Financial award applicants required to submit FAFSA. In 2019, 18 master's awarded. *Program availability:* Part-time, online only, 100% online. *Application deadline:* For fall admission, 8/9 priority date for domestic students; for spring admission, 1/11 priority date for domestic students; for summer admission, 5/1 priority date for domestic students. Applications are processed on a rolling basis. Electronic applications accepted. *Application Contact:* Amanda Millar, Director, Admissions, 443-352-4243, Fax: 443-394-0538, E-mail: amillar@stevenson.edu. *Program Coordinator*, Dr. Sharon Buchbinder, 443-394-9290, Fax: 443-394-0538, E-mail: sbuchbinder@stevenson.edu.

**Program in Nursing** Students: 144 part-time (138 women); includes 33 minority (24 Black or African American, non-Hispanic/Latino; 3 Asian, non-Hispanic/Latino; 4 Hispanic/Latino; 2 Two or more races, non-Hispanic/Latino). Average age 37. 56 applicants, 73% accepted, 30 enrolled. *Faculty:* 2 full-time (both women), 5 part-time/adjunct (all women). Expenses: Contact institution. *Financial support:* Unspecified assistantships available. Financial award applicants required to submit FAFSA. In 2019, 50 master's awarded. *Program availability:* Part-time, blended/hybrid learning. *Application deadline:* For fall admission, 8/9 priority date for domestic students; for spring admission, 1/11 priority date for domestic students; for summer admission, 5/1 priority date for domestic students. Applications are processed on a rolling basis. Electronic applications accepted. *Application Contact:* Amanda Millar, Director, Admissions, 443-352-4243, Fax: 443-394-0538, E-mail: amillar@stevenson.edu. *Associate Dean*, Dr. Judith Feustle, 443-394-9818, Fax: 443-394-0538, E-mail: jfeustle@stevenson.edu.

## STOCKTON UNIVERSITY, Galloway, NJ 08205-9441

**General Information** State-supported, coed, comprehensive institution. CGS member. *Enrollment:* 9,934 graduate, professional, and undergraduate students; 311 full-time matriculated graduate/professional students (239 women), 701 part-time matriculated graduate/professional students (496 women). *Enrollment by degree level:* 707 master's, 189 doctoral, 116 other advanced degrees. *Graduate faculty:* 121 full-time (72 women), 24 part-time/adjunct (17 women). *International tuition:* $1195.96 full-time. *Tuition, area resident:* Full-time $750.92; part-time $78.58 per credit hour. Tuition, state resident: full-time $750.92; part-time $78.58 per credit hour. Tuition, nonresident: full-time $846; part-time $78.58 per credit hour. *Required fees:* $1464; $78.58 per credit hour. One-time fee: $50 full-time. *Graduate housing:* Room and/or apartments available on a first-come, first-served basis to single students; on-campus housing not available to married students. Typical cost: $8396 per year ($12,496 including board). Housing application deadline: 6/1. *Student services:* Campus employment opportunities, campus safety program, career counseling, child daycare facilities, exercise/wellness program, free psychological counseling, grant writing training, international student services, low-cost health insurance, services for students with disabilities, teacher training, writing training. *Library facilities:* Richard E. Bjork Library. *Collection:* Books: 198,696 (physical), 251,566 (digital/electronic); Serial titles: 85 (physical), 91,490 (digital/electronic); Databases: 188. Weekly public service hours: 116. *Research affiliation:* Jewish Foundation (Holocaust studies), Wetlands Institute (marine biology), Aviation Research and Technology Park (aviation research), Nature Conservancy of New Jersey (environmental studies), Association of State Colleges (civic engagement).

**Computer facilities:** 1,879 computers available on campus for general student use. A campuswide network can be accessed from student residence rooms and from off campus. Online class registration is available.
Website: http://www.stockton.edu/

**General Application Contact:** Tara Williams, Assistant Director of Graduate Enrollment Management, 609-626-3640, E-mail: gradschool@stockton.edu.

**GRADUATE UNITS**

**Office of Graduate Studies** Students: 311 full-time (239 women), 701 part-time (496 women); includes 252 minority (80 Black or African American, non-Hispanic/Latino; 2 American Indian or Alaska Native, non-Hispanic/Latino; 46 Asian, non-Hispanic/Latino; 92 Hispanic/Latino; 1 Native Hawaiian or other Pacific Islander, non-Hispanic/Latino; 31 Two or more races, non-Hispanic/Latino), 5 international. Average age 33. 1,546 applicants, 45% accepted, 414 enrolled. *Faculty:* 121 full-time (72 women), 24 part-time/adjunct (17 women). Expenses: Contact institution. *Financial support:* Fellowships, research assistantships, career-related internships or fieldwork, Federal Work-Study, scholarships/grants, and unspecified assistantships available. Support available to part-time students. Financial award application deadline: 3/1; financial award applicants required to submit FAFSA. In 2019, 274 master's, 45 doctorates, 15 other advanced degrees awarded. *Program availability:* Part-time, evening/weekend, 100% online, blended/hybrid learning. *Application deadline:* For fall admission, 7/1 for domestic and international students. Applications are processed on a rolling basis. *Application fee:* $50. Electronic applications accepted. *Application Contact:* Tara Williams, Assistant Director of Graduate Enrollment, 609-626-3640, Fax: 609-626-6050, E-mail: gradschool@stockton.edu. *Director of Graduate Enrollment Management*, AmyBeth Glass, 609-652-4298, E-mail: graduatestudies@stockton.edu.

## STONEHILL COLLEGE, Easton, MA 02357

**General Information** Independent-religious, coed, comprehensive institution. *Graduate housing:* On-campus housing not available.

**GRADUATE UNITS**

**Program in Integrated Marketing Communications**

**Program in Special Education** *Program availability:* Part-time, evening/weekend. Electronic applications accepted.

## STONY BROOK UNIVERSITY, STATE UNIVERSITY OF NEW YORK, Stony Brook, NY 11794

**General Information** State-supported, coed, university. CGS member. *Enrollment:* 26,814 graduate, professional, and undergraduate students; 5,462 full-time matriculated graduate/professional students (2,637 women), 3,178 part-time matriculated graduate/professional students (2,316 women). *Enrollment by degree level:* 4,737 master's, 3,170 doctoral, 733 other advanced degrees. *Graduate faculty:* 1,968 full-time (850 women), 737 part-time/adjunct (384 women). *International tuition:* $23,100 full-time. *Tuition, area resident:* Full-time $11,310; part-time $471 per credit. Tuition, state resident: full-time $11,310; part-time $471 per credit. Tuition, nonresident: full-time $23,100; part-time $963 per credit. *Required fees:* $2247.50. *Graduate housing:* Rooms and/or apartments available to single and married students. Typical cost: $9082 per year ($14,278 including board) for single students. Housing application deadline: 5/1. *Student services:* Campus employment opportunities, campus safety program, career counseling, child daycare facilities, exercise/wellness program, free psychological counseling, grant writing training, international student services, multicultural affairs office, services for students with disabilities, teacher training, writing training. *Library facilities:* Frank Melville, Jr. Memorial Library plus 7 others. *Collection:* Books: 1.8 million (physical), 354,833 (digital/electronic); Serial titles: 1,127 (physical), 170,894 (digital/electronic); Databases: 643. Weekly public service hours: 132; study areas open 24 hours, 5–7 days a week; students can reserve study rooms. *Research affiliation:* Mount Sinai Health System, Veterans Affairs Medical Center, Nassau University Medical Center, Winthrop University Hospital, Cold Spring Harbor Laboratory, Brookhaven National Laboratory.

**Computer facilities:** Computer purchase and lease plans are available. 1,800 computers available on campus for general student use. A campuswide network can be accessed. Online class registration is available.
Website: http://www.stonybrook.edu/

**General Application Contact:** Melissa Jordan, Senior Assistant Dean for Records and Admission, 631-632-9712, Fax: 631-632-7243, E-mail: gradadmissions@stonybrook.edu.

**GRADUATE UNITS**

**Graduate School** Students: 3,379 full-time (1,283 women), 700 part-time (313 women); includes 707 minority (108 Black or African American, non-Hispanic/Latino; 1 American Indian or Alaska Native, non-Hispanic/Latino; 324 Asian, non-Hispanic/Latino; 213 Hispanic/Latino; 1 Native Hawaiian or other Pacific Islander, non-Hispanic/Latino; 60 Two or more races, non-Hispanic/Latino), 1,970 international. Average age 27. 7,306 applicants, 44% accepted, 1,287 enrolled. *Faculty:* 916 full-time (323 women), 304 part-time/adjunct (140 women). Expenses: Contact institution. *Financial support:* In 2019–20, 126 fellowships, 604 research assistantships, 923 teaching assistantships were awarded; career-related internships or fieldwork, Federal Work-Study, institutionally sponsored loans, scholarships/grants, traineeships, health care benefits, tuition waivers (full), and unspecified assistantships also available. In 2019, 1,416 master's, 367 doctorates, 68 other advanced degrees awarded. *Program availability:* Part-time, evening/weekend. *Application deadline:* For fall admission, 1/15 for domestic and international students; for spring admission, 10/1 for domestic and international students. *Application fee:* $100. Electronic applications accepted. *Application Contact:* Melissa Jordan, Assistant Dean for Records and Admission, 631-632-9712, Fax: 631-632-7243, E-mail: gradadmissions@stonybrook.edu. *Dean and Vice Provost*, Dr. Eic Wertheimer, 631-632-7035, Fax: 631-632-7112, E-mail: Eric.Wertheimer@stonybrook.edu.

***College of Arts and Sciences*** Students: 1,533 full-time (680 women), 132 part-time (82 women); includes 301 minority (42 Black or African American, non-Hispanic/Latino; 1 American Indian or Alaska Native, non-Hispanic/Latino; 116 Asian, non-Hispanic/Latino; 110 Hispanic/Latino; 32 Two or more races, non-Hispanic/Latino), 638 international. Average age 28. 2,988 applicants, 35% accepted, 398 enrolled. *Faculty:* 512 full-time (199 women), 144 part-time/adjunct (64 women). Expenses: Contact institution. *Financial support:* In 2019–20, 64 fellowships, 280 research assistantships, 836 teaching assistantships were awarded; career-related internships or fieldwork, Federal Work-Study, scholarships/grants, traineeships, health care benefits, and unspecified assistantships also available. Financial award applicants required to submit FAFSA. In 2019, 272 master's, 231 doctorates, 29 other advanced degrees awarded. *Program availability:* Part-time, evening/weekend. *Application deadline:* For fall admission, 1/15 for domestic students; for spring admission, 10/1 for domestic students. *Application fee:* $100. Electronic applications accepted. *Application Contact:* Melissa Jordan, Senior Assistant Dean for Records and Admission, 631-632-9712, Fax: 631-632-7243, E-mail: melissa.jordan@stonybrook.edu. *Dean*, Dr. Nicole S Sampson, 631-632-6976, Fax: 631-632-6900, E-mail: Nicole.Sampson@stonybrook.edu.

***College of Business*** Students: 241 full-time (114 women), 159 part-time (74 women); includes 119 minority (20 Black or African American, non-Hispanic/Latino; 51 Asian, non-Hispanic/Latino; 40 Hispanic/Latino; 8 Two or more races, non-Hispanic/Latino), 90 international. Average age 27. 382 applicants, 77% accepted, 167 enrolled. *Faculty:* 37 full-time (14 women), 7 part-time/adjunct (3 women). Expenses: Contact institution. *Financial support:* Research assistantships and teaching assistantships available. In 2019, 229 master's, 2 other advanced degrees awarded. *Application deadline:* For fall admission, 12/1 for domestic students, 10/15 priority date for international students; for spring admission, 11/15 for domestic students. *Application fee:* $100. *Application Contact:* Joyce Gibson, Graduate Coordinator, 631-632-7171, Fax: 631-632-8181, E-mail: Joyce.Gibson@stonybrook.edu. *Dean*, Dr. Manuel London, 631-632-7159, E-mail: manuel.london@stonybrook.edu.

***College of Engineering and Applied Sciences*** Students: 1,276 full-time (309 women), 295 part-time (74 women); includes 186 minority (21 Black or African American, non-Hispanic/Latino; 120 Asian, non-Hispanic/Latino; 34 Hispanic/Latino; 11 Two or more races, non-Hispanic/Latino), 1,179 international. Average age 26. 3,500 applicants, 47% accepted, 594 enrolled. *Faculty:* 169 full-time (27 women), 38 part-time/adjunct (8 women). Expenses: Contact institution. *Financial support:* In 2019–20, 24 fellowships, 248 research assistantships, 248 teaching assistantships were awarded; career-related internships or fieldwork also available. In 2019, 743 master's, 109 doctorates, 21 other advanced degrees awarded. *Program availability:* Part-time, evening/weekend. *Application deadline:* For fall admission, 1/15 for domestic students; for spring admission, 10/1 for domestic students. *Application fee:* $100. *Application Contact:* Melissa Jordan, Assistant Dean for Records and Admission, 631-632-9712, Fax: 631-632-7243, E-mail: gradadmissions@stonybrook.edu. *Dean*, Dr. Fotis Sotiropoulos, 631-632-8380, Fax: 631-632-8205, E-mail: fotis.sotiropoulos@stonybrook.edu.

***School of Marine and Atmospheric Sciences*** Students: 111 full-time (53 women), 21 part-time (11 women); includes 12 minority (3 Asian, non-Hispanic/Latino; 6 Hispanic/Latino; 3 Two or more races, non-Hispanic/Latino), 25 international. Average age 28. 135 applicants, 39% accepted, 29 enrolled. *Faculty:* 49 full-time (14 women), 11 part-time/adjunct (4 women). Expenses: Contact institution. *Financial support:* In 2019–20, 10 fellowships, 43 research assistantships, 24 teaching assistantships were awarded; career-related internships or fieldwork and tuition waivers (full) also available. In 2019, 22 master's, 10 doctorates, 6 other advanced degrees awarded. *Application deadline:* For fall admission, 1/15 for domestic students; for spring admission, 10/1 for domestic students. *Application fee:* $100. *Application Contact:* Ginny Clancy, Educational Programs Coordinator, 631-632-8681, Fax: 631-632-8200. *Dean*, Dr. Paul Shepson, 631-632-8700, Fax: 631-632-8820, E-mail: Paul.Shepson@stonybrook.edu.

**School of Journalism** *Faculty:* 11 full-time (4 women), 11 part-time/adjunct (3 women). Expenses: Contact institution. *Financial support:* Teaching assistantships available. In 2019, 2 master's awarded. *Application deadline:* For fall admission, 1/15 for domestic students; for spring admission, 10/1 for domestic students. *Application fee:* $100. *Application Contact:* Maureen Robinson, Coordinator, 631-632-7403, Fax: 631-632-7550, E-mail: maureen.robinson@stonybrook.edu. *Dean*, Dr. Laura Lindenfeld, 631-632-7403, E-mail: laura.lindenfeld@stonybrook.edu.

**School of Professional Development** Students: 226 full-time (148 women), 1,203 part-time (891 women); includes 324 minority (101 Black or African American, non-Hispanic/Latino; 1 American Indian or Alaska Native, non-Hispanic/Latino; 40 Asian, non-Hispanic/Latino; 159 Hispanic/Latino; 2 Native Hawaiian or other Pacific Islander, non-Hispanic/Latino; 21 Two or more races, non-Hispanic/Latino), 5 international. Average age 33. 686 applicants, 88% accepted, 402 enrolled. *Faculty:* 3 full-time (2 women), 104 part-time/adjunct (44 women). Expenses: Contact institution. *Financial support:* Fellowships, research assistantships, teaching assistantships, and career-related internships or fieldwork available. Support available to part-time students. In 2019, 332 master's, 177 other advanced degrees awarded. *Program availability:* Part-time, evening/weekend, online learning. *Application deadline:* For fall admission, 1/15 for domestic students, 6/1 for international students; for spring admission, 10/1 for domestic and international students. Applications are processed on a rolling basis. *Application fee:* $100. *Application Contact:* Linda Varga, Office Manager, 631-632-7050, E-mail: Linda.Varga@stonybrook.edu. *Associate Vice President for Professional Education and Assistant Provost for Engaged Learning*, Patricia Malone, 631-632-7512, Fax: 631-632-9046, E-mail: patricia.malone@stonybrook.edu.

**Stony Brook Medicine** Students: 2,008 full-time (1,295 women), 1,313 part-time (1,143 women); includes 1,244 minority (283 Black or African American, non-Hispanic/Latino; 6 American Indian or Alaska Native, non-Hispanic/Latino; 522 Asian, non-Hispanic/Latino; 359 Hispanic/Latino; 7 Native Hawaiian or other Pacific Islander, non-Hispanic/Latino; 67 Two or more races, non-Hispanic/Latino), 73 international. 9,708 applicants, 21% accepted, 1,332 enrolled. Expenses: Contact institution. *Financial support:* In 2019–20, 28 fellowships, 38 research assistantships were awarded; teaching assistantships also available. In 2019, 919 master's, 288 doctorates, 60 other advanced degrees awarded. *Application deadline:* For fall admission, 1/15 for domestic students; for spring admission, 10/1 for domestic students. *Application fee:* $100. Electronic applications accepted. *Application Contact:* Melissa Jordan, Assistant Dean for Records and Admission, 631-632-9712, Fax: 631-632-7243, E-mail: gradadmissions@stonybrook.edu. *Dean*, Dr. Kenneth Kaushansky, 631-444-8234, E-mail: kenneth.kaushansky@stonybrook.edu.

***Renaissance School of Medicine*** Students: 760 full-time (399 women), 138 part-time (120 women); includes 385 minority (46 Black or African American, non-Hispanic/Latino; 3 American Indian or Alaska Native, non-Hispanic/Latino; 230 Asian, non-Hispanic/Latino; 84 Hispanic/Latino; 1 Native Hawaiian or other Pacific Islander, non-Hispanic/Latino; 21 Two or more races, non-Hispanic/Latino), 54 international. Average age 26. 5,241 applicants, 8% accepted, 136 enrolled. *Faculty:* 964 full-time (465 women), 137 part-time/adjunct (96 women). Expenses: Contact institution. *Financial support:* In 2019–20, 28 fellowships, 33 research assistantships were awarded; teaching assistantships, career-related internships or fieldwork, Federal Work-Study, and tuition waivers (full) also available. In 2019, 65 master's, 141 doctorates awarded. *Application deadline:* For fall admission, 1/15 for domestic students; for spring admission, 10/1 for domestic students. *Application fee:* $100. *Application Contact:* Dr. Jack Fuhrer, Associate Dean of Admissions, 631-444-2113, Fax: 631-444-6032, E-mail: somadmissions@stonybrook.edu. *Dean*, Dr. Kenneth Kaushansky, 631-444-2121, Fax: 631-632-6621, E-mail: kenneth.kaushansky@stonybrook.edu.

***School of Dental Medicine*** Students: 202 full-time (108 women), 3 part-time (all women); includes 81 minority (3 Black or African American, non-Hispanic/Latino; 63 Asian, non-Hispanic/Latino; 10 Hispanic/Latino; 5 Two or more races, non-Hispanic/Latino), 5 international. Average age 25. 1,065 applicants, 12% accepted, 46 enrolled. *Faculty:* 33 full-time (15 women), 75 part-time/adjunct (20 women). Expenses: Contact institution. *Financial support:* Fellowships, research assistantships, teaching assistantships, and Federal Work-Study available. In 2019, 46 doctorates, 8 other advanced degrees awarded. *Application deadline:* For fall admission, 1/15 for domestic students; for spring admission, 10/1 for domestic students. *Application fee:* $100. *Application Contact:* Marguerite Baldwin, Coordinator, 631-632-9189, Fax: 631-632-7130, E-mail: marguerite.baldwin@stonybrook.edu. *Dean*, Dr. Mary R. Truhlar, 631-632-6985, Fax: 631-632-6621, E-mail: mary.truhlar@stonybrookmedicine.edu.

***School of Health Technology and Management*** Students: 605 full-time (417 women), 65 part-time (43 women); includes 225 minority (28 Black or African American, non-Hispanic/Latino; 110 Asian, non-Hispanic/Latino; 73 Hispanic/Latino; 1 Native Hawaiian or other Pacific Islander, non-Hispanic/Latino; 13 Two or more races, non-Hispanic/Latino), 9 international. Average age 26. 1,816 applicants, 21% accepted, 293 enrolled. *Faculty:* 53 full-time (37 women), 54 part-time/adjunct (34 women). Expenses: Contact institution. *Financial support:* Fellowships, research assistantships, teaching assistantships, career-related internships or fieldwork, Federal Work-Study, and institutionally sponsored loans available. Financial award application deadline: 3/15. In 2019, 152 master's, 86 doctorates, 21 other advanced degrees awarded. *Application deadline:* For fall admission, 1/15 for domestic students; for spring admission, 10/1 for domestic students. *Application fee:* $100. *Application Contact:* Jessica M Rotolo, Executive Assistant to the Dean, 631-444-2252, Fax: 631-444-7621, E-mail: jessica.rotolo@stonybrook.edu. *Dean and Professor*, Dr. Stacy Jafee Gropack, 631-444-2252, Fax: 631-444-7621, E-mail: stacy.jaffeegropack@stonybrook.edu.

***School of Nursing*** Students: 16 full-time (15 women), 1,033 part-time (917 women); includes 364 minority (129 Black or African American, non-Hispanic/Latino; 1 American Indian or Alaska Native, non-Hispanic/Latino; 105 Asian, non-Hispanic/Latino; 106 Hispanic/Latino; 3 Native Hawaiian or other Pacific Islander, non-Hispanic/Latino; 20 Two or more races, non-Hispanic/Latino), 2 international. Average age 35. 965 applicants, 57% accepted, 488 enrolled. *Faculty:* 34 full-time (31 women), 49 part-time/adjunct (45 women). Expenses: Contact institution. *Financial support:* Fellowships, research assistantships, teaching assistantships, career-related internships or fieldwork, Federal Work-Study, institutionally sponsored loans, and traineeships available. Financial award application deadline: 3/15. In 2019, 337 master's, 12 doctorates, 23 other advanced degrees awarded. *Program availability:* Blended/hybrid learning. *Application deadline:* For fall admission, 2/27 for domestic students. *Application fee:* $100. Electronic applications accepted. *Application Contact:* Karen Allard, Admissions Coordinator, 631-444-6628, Fax: 631-444-3136, E-mail: karen.allard@stonybrook.edu. *Dean*, Dr. Annette B Wysocki, 631-444-3200, Fax: 631-444-3136, E-mail: annette.wysocki@stonybrook.edu.

***School of Social Welfare*** Students: 425 full-time (356 women), 74 part-time (60 women); includes 189 minority (77 Black or African American, non-Hispanic/Latino; 2 American Indian or Alaska Native, non-Hispanic/Latino; 14 Asian, non-Hispanic/Latino; 86 Hispanic/Latino; 2 Native Hawaiian or other Pacific Islander, non-Hispanic/Latino; 8 Two or more races, non-Hispanic/Latino), 3 international. Average age 30. 406 applicants, 94% accepted, 275 enrolled. *Faculty:* 20 full-time (14 women), 45 part-time/adjunct (33 women). Expenses: Contact institution. *Financial support:* Fellowships, research assistantships, teaching assistantships, career-related internships or fieldwork, Federal Work-Study, and institutionally sponsored loans available. Financial award applicants required to submit FAFSA. In 2019, 285 master's, 3 doctorates awarded. *Program availability:* Part-time. *Application deadline:* For fall admission, 1/15 for domestic students; for spring admission, 10/1 for domestic students. *Application fee:* $100. *Application Contact:* Jamie Weissbach, Coordinator, 631-444-3146, Fax: 631-444-7565, E-mail: jamie.weissbach@stonybrook.edu. *Dean and Assistant Vice President for Social Determinants of Health*, Dr. Jacqueline B. Mondros, 631-444-2139, E-mail: jacqueline.mondros@stonybrook.edu.

**Stony Brook Southampton** Students: 67 full-time (38 women), 55 part-time (41 women); includes 20 minority (6 Black or African American, non-Hispanic/Latino; 9 Asian, non-Hispanic/Latino; 3 Hispanic/Latino; 2 Two or more races, non-Hispanic/Latino), 6 international. Average age 33. 99 applicants, 74% accepted, 38 enrolled. *Faculty:* 19 full-time (10 women), 33 part-time/adjunct (15 women). Expenses: Contact institution. *Financial support:* In 2019–20, 4 teaching assistantships were awarded. In 2019, 30 master's, 3 other advanced degrees awarded. *Application deadline:* For fall admission, 1/15 for domestic students; for spring admission, 10/1 for domestic students. Applications are processed on a rolling basis. *Application fee:* $100. *Application Contact:* Margaret S Grigonis, Administrative Coordinator, 631-632-5028, Fax: 631-982-7318, E-mail: margaret.grigonis@stonybrook.edu. *Associate Provost*, Dr. Robert Reeves, 631-632-5030, Fax: 631-982-7318, E-mail: robert.reeves@stonybrook.edu.

## STRATFORD UNIVERSITY, Baltimore, MD 21202

**General Information** Proprietary, coed, comprehensive institution.

**GRADUATE UNITS**

**Program in International Hospitality Management** *Program availability:* Part-time, evening/weekend, online learning.

## STRATFORD UNIVERSITY, Falls Church, VA 22043

**General Information** Proprietary, coed, comprehensive institution. *Graduate housing:* On-campus housing not available.

**GRADUATE UNITS**

**School of Graduate Studies** *Program availability:* Part-time, evening/weekend, 100% online, blended/hybrid learning. Electronic applications accepted.

## STRAYER UNIVERSITY, Washington, DC 20005-2603

**General Information** Proprietary, coed, comprehensive institution. *Graduate housing:* On-campus housing not available.

**GRADUATE UNITS**

**Graduate Studies** *Program availability:* Part-time, evening/weekend, online learning. Electronic applications accepted.

## SUFFOLK UNIVERSITY, Boston, MA 02108-2770

**General Information** Independent, coed, comprehensive institution. *Enrollment:* 7,288 graduate, professional, and undergraduate students; 1,248 full-time matriculated graduate/professional students (727 women), 1,024 part-time matriculated graduate/professional students (603 women). *Enrollment by degree level:* 1,110 master's, 1,133 doctoral, 29 other advanced degrees. *Graduate faculty:* 164 full-time (77 women), 50 part-time/adjunct (19 women). *Graduate housing:* On-campus housing not available. *Student services:* Campus employment opportunities, campus safety program, career counseling, exercise/wellness program, free psychological counseling, grant writing training, international student services, low-cost health insurance, multicultural affairs office, services for students with disabilities, writing training. *Library facilities:* Mildred Sawyer Library plus 2 others. *Collection:* Books: 128,945 (physical), 296,604 (digital/electronic); Serial titles: 307 (physical), 76,045 (digital/electronic); Databases: 144. Weekly public service hours: 103; students can reserve study rooms.

**Computer facilities:** Computer purchase and lease plans are available. 675 computers available on campus for general student use. A campuswide network can be accessed. Online class registration is available.
Website: http://www.suffolk.edu/

**General Application Contact:** Heather O'Leary, Director of Graduate Admissions, 617-573-8302, Fax: 617-305-1733.

**GRADUATE UNITS**

**College of Arts and Sciences** Students: 141 full-time (125 women), 76 part-time (66 women); includes 32 minority (9 Black or African American, non-Hispanic/Latino; 8 Asian, non-Hispanic/Latino; 12 Hispanic/Latino; 3 Two or more races, non-Hispanic/Latino), 37 international. Average age 27. 521 applicants, 40% accepted, 86 enrolled. *Faculty:* 60 full-time (30 women), 28 part-time/adjunct (13 women). Expenses: Contact institution. *Financial support:* In 2019–20, 164 students received support, including 33 fellowships (averaging $3,218 per year); career-related internships or fieldwork, Federal Work-Study, institutionally sponsored loans, scholarships/grants, and unspecified assistantships also available. Support available to part-time students. Financial award application deadline: 4/1; financial award applicants required to submit FAFSA. In 2019, 97 master's, 6 doctorates, 1 other advanced degree awarded. *Program availability:* Part-time, evening/weekend. *Application deadline:* For fall admission, 3/15 priority date for domestic and international students; for spring admission, 10/15 priority date for domestic students, 10/1 priority date for international students. Applications are processed on a rolling basis. *Application fee:* $50. Electronic applications accepted. *Application Contact:* Mara Marzocchi, Associate Director of Graduate Admissions, 617-

573-8302, Fax: 617-305-1733, E-mail: grad.admission@suffolk.edu. *Dean,* Maria Toyoda, 617-573-8265, Fax: 617-573-8513, E-mail: mtoyada@suffolk.edu.

**Law School** Students: 748 full-time (407 women), 370 part-time (194 women); includes 203 minority (41 Black or African American, non-Hispanic/Latino; 56 Asian, non-Hispanic/Latino; 85 Hispanic/Latino; 2 Native Hawaiian or other Pacific Islander, non-Hispanic/Latino; 19 Two or more races, non-Hispanic/Latino), 48 international. Average age 27. 1,924 applicants, 67% accepted, 364 enrolled. *Faculty:* 47 full-time (21 women), 22 part-time/adjunct (9 women). Expenses: Contact institution. *Financial support:* In 2019–20, 797 students received support. Fellowships, career-related internships or fieldwork, Federal Work-Study, institutionally sponsored loans, and scholarships/grants available. Support available to part-time students. Financial award application deadline: 3/1; financial award applicants required to submit FAFSA. In 2019, 18 master's, 296 doctorates awarded. *Program availability:* Part-time, evening/weekend. *Application deadline:* For fall admission, 4/1 for domestic and international students. Applications are processed on a rolling basis. *Application fee:* $60. Electronic applications accepted. *Application Contact:* Jennifer Bonniwell, Assistant Dean for Admissions and Financial Aid, 617-573-8144, Fax: 617-994-6838, E-mail: lawadm@suffolk.edu. *Dean,* Andrew Perlman, 617-573-8144, Fax: 617-994-6838, E-mail: lawadmin@suffolk.edu.

**New England School of Art and Design** Students: 36 full-time (31 women), 6 part-time (all women); includes 7 minority (2 Black or African American, non-Hispanic/Latino; 2 Asian, non-Hispanic/Latino; 3 Hispanic/Latino), 14 international. Average age 26. 81 applicants, 79% accepted, 25 enrolled. *Faculty:* 2 full-time (1 woman), 2 part-time/adjunct (1 woman). Expenses: Contact institution. *Financial support:* In 2019–20, 36 students received support, including 7 fellowships (averaging $2,829 per year); career-related internships or fieldwork, Federal Work-Study, institutionally sponsored loans, scholarships/grants, and unspecified assistantships also available. Financial award application deadline: 4/1; financial award applicants required to submit FAFSA. In 2019, 20 master's awarded. *Program availability:* Part-time, evening/weekend. *Application deadline:* For fall admission, 3/15 priority date for domestic and international students; for spring admission, 10/15 priority date for domestic and international students. Applications are processed on a rolling basis. *Application fee:* $50. Electronic applications accepted. *Application Contact:* Mara Marzocchi, Associate Director of Graduate Admissions, 617-573-8302, Fax: 617-305-1733, E-mail: grad.admission@suffolk.edu. *Department Chair,* Audrey Goldstein, 617-997-4290, E-mail: agoldstein@suffolk.edu.

**Sawyer Business School** Students: 323 full-time (169 women), 518 part-time (306 women); includes 226 minority (90 Black or African American, non-Hispanic/Latino; 58 Asian, non-Hispanic/Latino; 68 Hispanic/Latino; 10 Two or more races, non-Hispanic/Latino), 236 international. Average age 29. 1,333 applicants, 72% accepted, 352 enrolled. *Faculty:* 49 full-time (21 women), 13 part-time/adjunct (3 women). Expenses: Contact institution. *Financial support:* In 2019–20, 490 students received support, including 24 fellowships (averaging $3,184 per year); career-related internships or fieldwork, Federal Work-Study, institutionally sponsored loans, scholarships/grants, and unspecified assistantships also available. Support available to part-time students. Financial award application deadline: 4/1; financial award applicants required to submit FAFSA. In 2019, 350 master's awarded. *Program availability:* Part-time, evening/weekend, 100% online, blended/hybrid learning. *Application deadline:* For fall admission, 3/15 priority date for domestic and international students; for spring admission, 10/15 for domestic students, 3/15 priority date for international students. Applications are processed on a rolling basis. *Application fee:* $50. Electronic applications accepted. *Application Contact:* Mara Marzocchi, Associate Director of Graduate Admissions, 617-573-8302, Fax: 617-305-1733, E-mail: grad.admission@suffolk.edu. *Dean,* Amy Zeng, 617-573-2665, Fax: 617-573-8704, E-mail: azeng@suffolk.edu.

## SULLIVAN UNIVERSITY, Louisville, KY 40205

**General Information** Proprietary, coed, comprehensive institution. *Enrollment:* 3,323 graduate, professional, and undergraduate students; 481 full-time matriculated graduate/professional students (298 women), 206 part-time matriculated graduate/professional students (111 women). *Enrollment by degree level:* 440 master's, 247 doctoral. *Graduate faculty:* 70 full-time (41 women), 26 part-time/adjunct (12 women). *Tuition:* Full-time $21,120; part-time $660 per quarter hour. One-time fee: $30 full-time. Tuition and fees vary according to course load and degree level. *Graduate housing:* Room and/or apartments available on a first-come, first-served basis to single students; on-campus housing not available to married students. Typical cost: $2970 per year ($4320 including board). *Student services:* Campus employment opportunities, campus safety program, career counseling, exercise/wellness program, international student services, services for students with disabilities, teacher training, writing training. *Library facilities:* Sullivan University Libraries. *Collection:* Books: 52,600 (physical), 67,908 (digital/electronic); Serial titles: 97 (physical), 43,372 (digital/electronic); Databases: 83. Weekly public service hours: 82; students can reserve study rooms.

**Computer facilities:** 93 computers available on campus for general student use. A campuswide network can be accessed. Online class registration is available.
Website: http://www.sullivan.edu/

**GRADUATE UNITS**

**College of Pharmacy**

**School of Business** *Program availability:* Part-time, online learning.

## SUL ROSS STATE UNIVERSITY, Alpine, TX 79832

**General Information** State-supported, coed, comprehensive institution. *Graduate housing:* Rooms and/or apartments available on a first-come, first-served basis to single and married students. *Research affiliation:* Chihuahuan Desert Research Institute (biology, geology), Big Bend National Park (biology, geology).

**GRADUATE UNITS**

**College of Arts and Sciences** *Program availability:* Part-time, evening/weekend.

**College of Professional Studies** *Program availability:* Part-time, evening/weekend.

**Division of Agricultural and Natural Resource Science** *Program availability:* Part-time.

**Rio Grande College of Sul Ross State University** *Program availability:* Part-time, evening/weekend, online learning.

## SUM BIBLE COLLEGE & THEOLOGICAL SEMINARY, Oakland, CA 94603

**General Information** Independent-religious, coed, comprehensive institution.

**GRADUATE UNITS**

**Graduate Programs**

## SUNY BROCKPORT, Brockport, NY 14420-2997

**General Information** State-supported, coed, comprehensive institution. CGS member. *Enrollment:* 7,924 graduate, professional, and undergraduate students; 345 full-time matriculated graduate/professional students (219 women), 1,121 part-time matriculated graduate/professional students (741 women). *Enrollment by degree level:* 1,466 master's. *Graduate faculty:* 138 full-time (74 women), 61 part-time/adjunct (33 women). *Tuition, area resident:* Part-time $471 per credit hour. Tuition, nonresident: part-time $963 per credit hour. *Graduate housing:* On-campus housing not available. *Student services:* Campus employment opportunities, campus safety program, career counseling, child daycare facilities, exercise/wellness program, free psychological counseling, grant writing training, international student services, low-cost health insurance, multicultural affairs office, services for students with disabilities, teacher training, writing training. *Library facilities:* Drake Memorial Library plus 1 other. *Collection:* Books: 395,601 (physical), 376,105 (digital/electronic); Serial titles: 7,162 (physical), 114,760 (digital/electronic); Databases: 502. Weekly public service hours: 103; students can reserve study rooms.

**Computer facilities:** 1,000 computers available on campus for general student use. A campuswide network can be accessed from student residence rooms and from off campus. Online class registration is available.
Website: http://www.brockport.edu/

**General Application Contact:** Danielle A. Welch, Graduate Admissions Counselor, 585-395-2525, Fax: 585-395-2515, E-mail: dwelch@brockport.edu.

**GRADUATE UNITS**

**School of Arts and Sciences** Students: 77 full-time (45 women), 151 part-time (91 women); includes 18 minority (10 Black or African American, non-Hispanic/Latino; 3 Asian, non-Hispanic/Latino; 5 Hispanic/Latino). 129 applicants, 56% accepted, 55 enrolled. *Faculty:* 56 full-time (31 women), 9 part-time/adjunct (5 women). Expenses: Contact institution. *Financial support:* Research assistantships, teaching assistantships, Federal Work-Study, scholarships/grants, and unspecified assistantships available. Support available to part-time students. Financial award applicants required to submit FAFSA. In 2019, 100 master's, 1 other advanced degree awarded. *Program availability:* Part-time. *Application Contact:* Danielle A. Welch, Graduate Admissions Counselor, 585-395-2525, Fax: 585-395-2515. *Dean,* Dr. Jose Maliekal, 585-395-5806, E-mail: jmalieka@brockport.edu.

**School of Business and Management** Students: 48 full-time (30 women), 171 part-time (99 women); includes 21 minority (13 Black or African American, non-Hispanic/Latino; 4 Hispanic/Latino; 4 Native Hawaiian or other Pacific Islander, non-Hispanic/Latino). 131 applicants, 81% accepted, 72 enrolled. *Faculty:* 10 full-time (5 women), 8 part-time/adjunct (1 woman). Expenses: Contact institution. *Financial support:* Career-related internships or fieldwork, Federal Work-Study, scholarships/grants, and unspecified assistantships available. Financial award application deadline: 3/15; financial award applicants required to submit FAFSA. In 2019, 124 master's, 15 other advanced degrees awarded. *Program availability:* Part-time. *Application deadline:* For fall admission, 7/1 priority date for domestic and international students; for spring admission, 12/1 priority date for domestic and international students. *Application fee:* $50. Electronic applications accepted. *Application Contact:* Danielle A. Welch, Graduate Counselor, 585-395-5430, Fax: 585-395-2515, E-mail: dwelch@brockport.edu. *Interim Associate Dean,* Dr. Lerong He, 585-395-5781, Fax: 585-395-2542, E-mail: lhe@brockport.edu.

**School of Education, Health, and Human Services** Students: 198 full-time (128 women), 760 part-time (518 women); includes 54 minority (32 Black or African American, non-Hispanic/Latino; 2 American Indian or Alaska Native, non-Hispanic/Latino; 6 Asian, non-Hispanic/Latino; 14 Hispanic/Latino). 542 applicants, 70% accepted, 290 enrolled. *Faculty:* 43 full-time (24 women), 37 part-time/adjunct (24 women). Expenses: Contact institution. *Financial support:* In 2019–20, 3 teaching assistantships with full tuition reimbursements (averaging $3,000 per year) were awarded; institutionally sponsored loans, scholarships/grants, and unspecified assistantships also available. Financial award applicants required to submit FAFSA. In 2019, 352 master's, 88 other advanced degrees awarded. *Program availability:* Part-time, 100% online. *Application Contact:* Danielle A. Welch, Graduate Admissions Counselor, 585-395-2525, Fax: 585-395-2515. *Dean,* Dr. Thomas Hernandez, 585-395-2510, Fax: 585-395-2172, E-mail: thernandez@brockport.edu.

## SWEDISH INSTITUTE, COLLEGE OF HEALTH SCIENCES, New York, NY 10001-6700

**General Information** Proprietary, coed, comprehensive institution. *Graduate housing:* On-campus housing not available.

**GRADUATE UNITS**

**Graduate Program** *Program availability:* Part-time, evening/weekend.

## SWEET BRIAR COLLEGE, Sweet Briar, VA 24595

**General Information** Independent, women only, comprehensive institution. *Graduate housing:* Room and/or apartments available on a first-come, first-served basis to single students; on-campus housing not available to married students.

**GRADUATE UNITS**

**Department of Education** *Program availability:* Part-time. Electronic applications accepted.

## SYRACUSE UNIVERSITY, Syracuse, NY 13244

**General Information** Independent, coed, university. CGS member. *Graduate housing:* On-campus housing not available. *Research affiliation:* South Side Innovation Center (business incubator and entrepreneurship development), IBM Green Data Center (advanced infrastructure and smarter computing technologies), Institute for Manufacturing Enterprises (promoting learning in manufacturing enterprises through teaching, application, integration, discovery, and service), Syracuse Research Corporation (defense, environmental and intelligence systems), Center of Excellence (environmental and energy systems innovation), Say Yes to Education, Inc. (academic support and funding to high school students).

**GRADUATE UNITS**

**College of Arts and Sciences** *Program availability:* Part-time.

**College of Engineering and Computer Science** *Program availability:* Part-time, evening/weekend. Electronic applications accepted.

**College of Law** *Program availability:* Part-time. Electronic applications accepted.

**College of Visual and Performing Arts** Electronic applications accepted.

**David B. Falk College of Sport and Human Dynamics** *Program availability:* Part-time, evening/weekend. Electronic applications accepted.

**Martin J. Whitman School of Management** *Program availability:* Part-time, 100% online. Electronic applications accepted.

**Maxwell School of Citizenship and Public Affairs** *Program availability:* Part-time, online learning. Electronic applications accepted.

**School of Architecture** Students: 91 full-time (49 women), 68 international. Average age 26. *Faculty:* 41 full-time (15 women), 10 part-time/adjunct (2 women). Expenses: Contact institution. *Financial support:* Fellowships with full tuition reimbursements, teaching assistantships, Federal Work-Study, scholarships/grants, and health care benefits available. Financial award application deadline: 4/15. In 2019, 39 master's awarded. *Application deadline:* For fall admission, 1/3 priority date for domestic and international students. Applications are processed on a rolling basis. *Application fee:* $75. Electronic applications accepted. *Application Contact:* Lauren Mintier, Graduate Program Manager, 315-443-1041, E-mail: lmintier@syr.edu. *Dean, School of Architecture,* Michael Speaks, 315-443-0790, E-mail: maspeaks@syr.edu.

**School of Education** *Program availability:* Part-time. Electronic applications accepted.

**School of Information Studies** *Program availability:* Part-time, evening/weekend, online learning. Electronic applications accepted.

**S. I. Newhouse School of Public Communications** *Program availability:* Online learning. Electronic applications accepted.

## TABOR COLLEGE, Hillsboro, KS 67063

**General Information** Independent-religious, coed, comprehensive institution.

**GRADUATE UNITS**

**Graduate Program**

## TAFT UNIVERSITY SYSTEM, Denver, CO 80246

**General Information** Proprietary, coed, graduate-only institution.

**GRADUATE UNITS**

**The Boyer Graduate School of Education**

**Taft Law School**

**W. Edwards Deming School of Business**

## TALMUDICAL ACADEMY OF NEW JERSEY, Adelphia, NJ 07710

**General Information** Independent-religious, men only, comprehensive institution.

**GRADUATE UNITS**

**Graduate Program**

## TALMUDIC UNIVERSITY, Miami Beach, FL 33140

**General Information** Independent-religious, men only, comprehensive institution. *Graduate housing:* Rooms and/or apartments available on a first-come, first-served basis to single and married students.

**GRADUATE UNITS**

**Program in Talmudic Law**

## TARLETON STATE UNIVERSITY, Stephenville, TX 76402

**General Information** State-supported, coed, comprehensive institution. *Enrollment:* 13,176 graduate, professional, and undergraduate students; 421 full-time matriculated graduate/professional students (289 women), 1,405 part-time matriculated graduate/professional students (924 women). *Enrollment by degree level:* 1,675 master's, 151 doctoral. *Graduate faculty:* 159 full-time (79 women), 34 part-time/adjunct (15 women). Tuition, state resident: part-time $221.73 per credit hour. Tuition, nonresident: part-time $636.73 per credit hour. *Required fees:* $198 per credit hour. $100 per semester. Tuition and fees vary according to degree level. *Graduate housing:* Rooms and/or apartments available on a first-come, first-served basis to single and married students. Housing application deadline: 8/1. *Student services:* Campus employment opportunities, campus safety program, career counseling, child daycare facilities, exercise/wellness program, free psychological counseling, grant writing training, international student services, low-cost health insurance, multicultural affairs office, services for students with disabilities, teacher training, writing training. *Library facilities:* Dick Smith Library plus 1 other. *Collection:* Books: 200,093 (physical), 266,615 (digital/electronic); Serial titles: 3,999 (physical), 158,307 (digital/electronic); Databases: 311. Students can reserve study rooms.

**Computer facilities:** 1,200 computers available on campus for general student use. A campuswide network can be accessed. Online class registration is available. Website: http://www.tarleton.edu/

**General Application Contact:** Wendy Weiss, Graduate Admissions Coordinator, 254-968-9104, Fax: 254-968-9670, E-mail: weiss@tarleton.edu.

**GRADUATE UNITS**

**College of Graduate Studies** Students: 410 full-time (287 women), 1,407 part-time (919 women); includes 586 minority (235 Black or African American, non-Hispanic/Latino; 6 American Indian or Alaska Native, non-Hispanic/Latino; 37 Asian, non-Hispanic/Latino; 255 Hispanic/Latino; 1 Native Hawaiian or other Pacific Islander, non-Hispanic/Latino; 52 Two or more races, non-Hispanic/Latino), 30 international. Average age 32. 1,079 applicants, 79% accepted, 579 enrolled. *Faculty:* 161 full-time (81 women), 36 part-time/adjunct (15 women). Expenses: Contact institution. *Financial support:* Research assistantships, teaching assistantships, career-related internships or fieldwork, Federal Work-Study, institutionally sponsored loans, scholarships/grants, and tuition waivers (partial) available. Support available to part-time students. Financial award application deadline: 5/1; financial award applicants required to submit FAFSA. In 2019, 632 master's, 20 doctorates awarded. *Program availability:* Part-time, evening/weekend, 100% online, blended/hybrid learning. *Application deadline:* For fall admission, 8/15 priority date for domestic students; for spring admission, 1/7 for domestic students. *Application fee:* $50 ($130 for international students). Electronic applications accepted. *Application Contact:* Wendy Weiss, Graduate Admissions Coordinator, 254-968-9104, Fax: 254-968-9670, E-mail: weiss@tarleton.edu. *Dean,* Dr. Credence Baker, 254-968-9420, Fax: 254-968-9670, E-mail: cbaker@tarleton.edu.

***College of Agricultural and Environmental Sciences*** Students: 51 full-time (36 women), 49 part-time (37 women); includes 15 minority (2 Black or African American, non-Hispanic/Latino; 2 Asian, non-Hispanic/Latino; 8 Hispanic/Latino; 3 Two or more races, non-Hispanic/Latino), 1 international. Average age 25. 55 applicants, 73% accepted, 34 enrolled. *Faculty:* 21 full-time (7 women), 3 part-time/adjunct (1 woman). Expenses: Contact institution. *Financial support:* Research assistantships, teaching assistantships, career-related internships or fieldwork, Federal Work-Study, and institutionally sponsored loans available. Support available to part-time students. Financial award application deadline: 5/1; financial award applicants required to submit FAFSA. In 2019, 10 master's awarded. *Program availability:* Part-time, evening/weekend, 100% online, blended/hybrid learning. *Application deadline:* For fall admission, 8/15 priority date for domestic students; for spring admission, 1/7 for domestic students. Applications are processed on a rolling basis. *Application fee:* $50 ($130 for international students). Electronic applications accepted. *Application Contact:* Wendy Weiss, Information Contact, 254-968-9104, Fax: 254-968-9670, E-mail: gradoffice@tarleton.edu. *Dean,* Dr. Steve Damron, 254-968-9227, Fax: 254-968-9655, E-mail: sdamron@tarleton.edu.

***College of Business Administration*** Students: 67 full-time (48 women), 437 part-time (267 women); includes 153 minority (53 Black or African American, non-Hispanic/Latino; 3 American Indian or Alaska Native, non-Hispanic/Latino; 15 Asian, non-Hispanic/Latino; 67 Hispanic/Latino; 1 Native Hawaiian or other Pacific Islander, non-Hispanic/Latino; 14 Two or more races, non-Hispanic/Latino), 15 international. Average age 36. 321 applicants, 74% accepted, 142 enrolled. *Faculty:* 32 full-time (7 women), 4 part-time/adjunct (1 woman). Expenses: Contact institution. *Financial support:* Research assistantships, teaching assistantships, career-related internships or fieldwork, Federal Work-Study, and institutionally sponsored loans available. Support available to part-time students. Financial award application deadline: 5/1; financial award applicants required to submit FAFSA. In 2019, 77 master's awarded. *Program availability:* Part-time, evening/weekend, 100% online, blended/hybrid learning. *Application deadline:* For fall admission, 8/15 priority date for domestic students; for spring admission, 1/7 for domestic students. Applications are processed on a rolling basis. *Application fee:* $50 ($130 for international students). Electronic applications accepted. *Application Contact:* Wendy Weiss, Graduate Admissions Coordinator, 254-968-9104, E-mail: weiss@tarleton.edu. *Dean,* Dr. Chris Shao, 254-968-9350, E-mail: shao@tarleton.edu.

***College of Education*** Students: 155 full-time (106 women), 388 part-time (289 women); includes 173 minority (78 Black or African American, non-Hispanic/Latino; 2 American Indian or Alaska Native, non-Hispanic/Latino; 3 Asian, non-Hispanic/Latino; 81 Hispanic/Latino; 9 Two or more races, non-Hispanic/Latino), 3 international. Average age 38. 196 applicants, 86% accepted, 127 enrolled. *Faculty:* 35 full-time (24 women), 9 part-time/adjunct (6 women). Expenses: Contact institution. *Financial support:* Research assistantships, teaching assistantships with partial tuition reimbursements, career-related internships or fieldwork, Federal Work-Study, institutionally sponsored loans, and tuition waivers available. Support available to part-time students. Financial award application deadline: 5/1; financial award applicants required to submit FAFSA. In 2019, 61 master's, 5 doctorates awarded. *Program availability:* Part-time, evening/weekend, 100% online, blended/hybrid learning. *Application deadline:* For fall admission, 8/15 priority date for domestic students; for spring admission, 1/7 for domestic students. Applications are processed on a rolling basis. *Application fee:* $50 ($130 for international students). Electronic applications accepted. *Application Contact:* Wendy Weiss, Information Contact, 254-968-9104, Fax: 254-968-9670, E-mail: weiss@tarleton.edu. *Dean,* Dr. Kim Rynearson, 254-968-9916, Fax: 254-968-9525, E-mail: rynearson@tarleton.edu.

***College of Health Sciences and Human Services*** Students: 79 full-time (65 women), 205 part-time (174 women); includes 110 minority (45 Black or African American, non-Hispanic/Latino; 1 American Indian or Alaska Native, non-Hispanic/Latino; 8 Asian, non-Hispanic/Latino; 47 Hispanic/Latino; 9 Two or more races, non-Hispanic/Latino), 5 international. Average age 34. 285 applicants, 81% accepted, 161 enrolled. *Faculty:* 22 full-time (17 women), 5 part-time/adjunct (4 women). Expenses: Contact institution. *Financial support:* Research assistantships, teaching assistantships, career-related internships or fieldwork, Federal Work-Study, scholarships/grants, and unspecified assistantships available. Financial award application deadline: 2/15; financial award applicants required to submit FAFSA. In 2019, 4 master's awarded. *Program availability:* Part-time, evening/weekend, 100% online, blended/hybrid learning. *Application deadline:* For fall admission, 8/15 for domestic students, 6/15 for international students; for spring admission, 1/5 for domestic students, 11/15 for international students; for summer admission, 5/1 for domestic students, 4/15 for international students. Applications are processed on a rolling basis. *Application fee:* $50 ($130 for international students). Electronic applications accepted. *Application Contact:* Wendy Weiss, Graduate Admissions Coordinator, 254-968-9104, Fax: 254-968-9670, E-mail: weiss@tarleton.edu. *Dean,* Sally Lewis, 254-968-1692, E-mail: slewis@tarleton.edu.

***College of Liberal and Fine Arts*** Students: 30 full-time (20 women), 254 part-time (127 women); includes 102 minority (45 Black or African American, non-Hispanic/Latino; 5 Asian, non-Hispanic/Latino; 40 Hispanic/Latino; 12 Two or more races, non-Hispanic/Latino), 2 international. Average age 38. 162 applicants, 78% accepted, 82 enrolled. *Faculty:* 31 full-time (18 women), 13 part-time/adjunct (3 women). Expenses: Contact institution. *Financial support:* Research assistantships, teaching assistantships, Federal Work-Study, scholarships/grants, and unspecified assistantships available. Financial award application deadline: 5/1; financial award applicants required to submit FAFSA. In 2019, 24 master's awarded. *Program availability:* Part-time, evening/weekend, 100% online, blended/hybrid learning. *Application deadline:* For fall admission, 8/15 priority date for domestic students; for spring admission, 1/7 for domestic students. Applications are processed on a rolling basis. *Application fee:* $50 ($130 for international students). Electronic applications accepted. *Application Contact:* Wendy Weiss, Information Contact, 254-968-9104, Fax: 254-968-9670, E-mail: weiss@tarleton.edu. *Dean,* Dr. Eric Morrow, 254-968-9141, Fax: 254-968-9784, E-mail: morrow@tarleton.edu.

***College of Science and Technology*** Students: 28 full-time (12 women), 74 part-time (25 women); includes 33 minority (12 Black or African American, non-Hispanic/Latino; 4 Asian, non-Hispanic/Latino; 12 Hispanic/Latino; 5 Two or more races, non-Hispanic/Latino), 4 international. Average age 29. 60 applicants, 77% accepted, 33 enrolled. *Faculty:* 20 full-time (8 women), 2 part-time/adjunct (0 women). Expenses: Contact institution. *Financial support:* Research assistantships, teaching assistantships, career-related internships or fieldwork, Federal Work-Study, and tuition waivers available. Support available to part-time students. Financial award application deadline: 5/1; financial award applicants required to submit FAFSA. In 2019, 11 master's awarded. *Program availability:* Part-time, evening/weekend, 100% online, blended/hybrid learning. *Application deadline:* For fall admission, 8/15 priority date for domestic students; for spring admission, 1/7 for domestic students. Applications are processed on a rolling basis. *Application fee:* $50 ($130 for international students). Electronic applications accepted. *Application Contact:* Wendy Weiss, Information Contact, 254-968-9104, Fax: 254-968-9670, E-mail: weiss@tarleton.edu. *Dean,* Dr. Michael Huggins, 254-968-9781, Fax: 254-968-0549, E-mail: mhuggins@tarleton.edu.

## TAYLOR COLLEGE AND SEMINARY, Edmonton, AB T6J 4T3, Canada

**General Information** Independent-religious, coed, comprehensive institution. *Graduate housing:* Room and/or apartments available on a first-come, first-served basis to single students; on-campus housing not available to married students. Housing application deadline: 8/1.

**GRADUATE UNITS**

**Graduate and Professional Programs** *Program availability:* Part-time, online learning.

## TAYLOR UNIVERSITY, Upland, IN 46989-1001

**General Information** Independent-religious, coed, comprehensive institution. *Graduate housing:* On-campus housing not available.

**GRADUATE UNITS**

**Master of Arts in Higher Education Program** *Program availability:* Part-time.

## TEACHERS COLLEGE, COLUMBIA UNIVERSITY, New York, NY 10027-6696

**General Information** Independent, coed, graduate-only institution. *Enrollment by degree level:* 3,065 master's, 1,213 doctoral, 29 other advanced degrees. *Graduate faculty:* 149 full-time (89 women). *Graduate housing:* Rooms and/or apartments available on a first-come, first-served basis to single and married students. *Library facilities:* Gottesman Library. *Collection:* Students can reserve study rooms.

**Computer facilities:** A campuswide network can be accessed from student residence rooms.
Website: http://www.tc.columbia.edu/

**General Application Contact:** Kelly Sutton-Skinner, Director of Admissions and New Student Enrollment, 212-678-3710, E-mail: admission@tc.columbia.edu.

**GRADUATE UNITS**

**Department of Arts and Humanities** Students: 426 full-time (358 women), 390 part-time (259 women); includes 222 minority (44 Black or African American, non-Hispanic/Latino; 2 American Indian or Alaska Native, non-Hispanic/Latino; 94 Asian, non-Hispanic/Latino; 65 Hispanic/Latino; 17 Two or more races, non-Hispanic/Latino), 252 international. 957 applicants, 66% accepted, 375 enrolled. *Faculty:* 26 full-time (17 women). Expenses: Contact institution. *Application Contact:* Kelly Sutton-Skinner, Director of Admissions and New Student Enrollment, 212-678-3710, E-mail: kms2237@tc.columbia.edu. *Department Chair*, Dr. ZhaoHong Han, E-mail: zhh2@tc.columbia.edu.

**Department of Biobehavioral Sciences** Students: 153 full-time (134 women), 149 part-time (106 women); includes 122 minority (25 Black or African American, non-Hispanic/Latino; 32 Asian, non-Hispanic/Latino; 55 Hispanic/Latino; 10 Two or more races, non-Hispanic/Latino), 37 international. 582 applicants, 51% accepted, 165 enrolled. *Faculty:* 9 full-time (8 women). Expenses: Contact institution. *Application Contact:* Kelly Sutton Skinner, Director of Admission and New Student Enrollment, 212-678-3710, E-mail: kms2237@tc.columbia.edu.

**Department of Counseling and Clinical Psychology** *Program availability:* Part-time.

**Department of Curriculum and Teaching** Students: 156 full-time (143 women), 181 part-time (159 women); includes 109 minority (36 Black or African American, non-Hispanic/Latino; 34 Asian, non-Hispanic/Latino; 31 Hispanic/Latino; 8 Two or more races, non-Hispanic/Latino), 60 international. 329 applicants, 78% accepted, 136 enrolled. *Faculty:* 14 full-time (10 women). Expenses: Contact institution. *Application Contact:* Kelly Sutton-Skinner, Director of Admission and New Student Enrollment, 212-678-3710, E-mail: kms2237@tc.columbia.edu.

**Department of Education Policy and Social Analysis** Students: 89 full-time (71 women), 154 part-time (113 women); includes 91 minority (36 Black or African American, non-Hispanic/Latino; 19 Asian, non-Hispanic/Latino; 29 Hispanic/Latino; 7 Two or more races, non-Hispanic/Latino), 73 international. 433 applicants, 60% accepted, 107 enrolled. *Faculty:* 11 full-time (4 women). Expenses: Contact institution. *Application Contact:* Kelly Sutton-Skinner, Director of Admission and New Student Enrollment, 212-678-3710, E-mail: kms2237@tc.columbia.edu. *Chair*, Dr. Aaron Pallas, 212-678-8119, E-mail: amp155@tc.columbia.edu.

**Department of Health and Behavior Studies** Students: 243 full-time (225 women), 246 part-time (211 women); includes 172 minority (33 Black or African American, non-Hispanic/Latino; 2 American Indian or Alaska Native, non-Hispanic/Latino; 63 Asian, non-Hispanic/Latino; 63 Hispanic/Latino; 11 Two or more races, non-Hispanic/Latino), 67 international. 515 applicants, 68% accepted, 170 enrolled. *Faculty:* 17 full-time (11 women). Expenses: Contact institution. *Application Contact:* Kelly Sutton-Skinner, Director of Admission and New Student Enrollment, E-mail: kms2237@tc.columbia.edu. *Chair*, Dr. Dolores Perin, 212-678-3091, E-mail: dp111@tc.columbia.edu.

**Department of Human Development** Students: 123 full-time (94 women), 129 part-time (91 women); includes 58 minority (12 Black or African American, non-Hispanic/Latino; 32 Asian, non-Hispanic/Latino; 13 Hispanic/Latino; 1 Two or more races, non-Hispanic/Latino), 131 international. 429 applicants, 60% accepted, 108 enrolled. *Faculty:* 10 full-time (4 women). Expenses: Contact institution. *Application Contact:* Kelly Sutton-Skinner, Director of Admission and New Student Enrollment, E-mail: kms2237@tc.columbia.edu. *Chair*, Dr. James Corter, 212-678-3843, E-mail: jec34@tc.columbia.edu.

**Department of International and Transcultural Studies** Students: 94 full-time (75 women), 142 part-time (123 women); includes 79 minority (19 Black or African American, non-Hispanic/Latino; 31 Asian, non-Hispanic/Latino; 25 Hispanic/Latino; 4 Two or more races, non-Hispanic/Latino), 102 international. 312 applicants, 69% accepted, 105 enrolled. *Faculty:* 11 full-time (7 women). Expenses: Contact institution. *Application Contact:* Kelly Sutton Skinner, Director of Admission and New Student Enrollment, E-mail: kms2237@tc.columbia.edu. *Chair*, Prof. Herve Varenne, 212-678-3190, E-mail: varenne@tc.columbia.edu.

**Department of Mathematics, Science and Technology** Students: 166 full-time (124 women), 188 part-time (113 women); includes 122 minority (40 Black or African American, non-Hispanic/Latino; 1 American Indian or Alaska Native, non-Hispanic/Latino; 50 Asian, non-Hispanic/Latino; 23 Hispanic/Latino; 8 Two or more races, non-Hispanic/Latino), 120 international. 476 applicants, 51% accepted, 125 enrolled. *Faculty:* 13 full-time (8 women). Expenses: Contact institution. *Application Contact:* Kelly Sutton Skinner, Director of Admission and New Student Enrollment, 212-678-3710, E-mail: kms2237@tc.columbia.edu. *Chair*, Dr. Erica Walker, 212-678-8246, E-mail: ewalker@tc.edu.

**Department of Organization and Leadership** Students: 272 full-time (178 women), 321 part-time (222 women); includes 239 minority (78 Black or African American, non-Hispanic/Latino; 70 Asian, non-Hispanic/Latino; 71 Hispanic/Latino; 1 Native Hawaiian or other Pacific Islander, non-Hispanic/Latino; 19 Two or more races, non-Hispanic/Latino), 73 international. 761 applicants, 65% accepted, 330 enrolled. *Faculty:* 24 full-time (12 women). Expenses: Contact institution. *Application Contact:* Kelly Sutton-Skinner, Director of Admission and New Student Enrollment, 212-678-3710, E-mail: kms2237@tc.columbia.edu. *Chair*, Prof. Bill Baldwin, 212-678-3043, E-mail: wjb12@tc.columbia.edu.

**Interdisciplinary Programs** Students: 10 full-time (7 women), 18 part-time (12 women); includes 9 minority (2 Black or African American, non-Hispanic/Latino; 3 Asian, non-Hispanic/Latino; 2 Hispanic/Latino; 1 Native Hawaiian or other Pacific Islander, non-Hispanic/Latino; 1 Two or more races, non-Hispanic/Latino), 6 international. 2 applicants, 50% accepted, 1 enrolled. Expenses: Contact institution. *Application Contact:* Kelly Sutton-Skinner, Director of Admissions and New Student Enrollment, E-mail: kms2237@tc.columbia.edu.

## TEACHERS COLLEGE OF SAN JOAQUIN, Stockton, CA 95206

**General Information** Public, coed, graduate-only institution. *Graduate housing:* On-campus housing not available.

**GRADUATE UNITS**

**Master's Program in Education**

## TELSHE YESHIVA - CHICAGO, Chicago, IL 60625-5598

**General Information** Independent-religious, men only, comprehensive institution.

**GRADUATE UNITS**

**Graduate Program**

## TEMPLE UNIVERSITY, Philadelphia, PA 19122-6096

**General Information** State-related, coed, university. CGS member. *Enrollment:* 38,822 graduate, professional, and undergraduate students; 7,287 full-time matriculated graduate/professional students (4,072 women), 2,388 part-time matriculated graduate/professional students (1,396 women). *Enrollment by degree level:* 4,414 master's, 5,080 doctoral, 181 other advanced degrees. *Graduate faculty:* 1,322 full-time (561 women), 786 part-time/adjunct (352 women). *Graduate housing:* Rooms and/or apartments available on a first-come, first-served basis to single and married students. *Student services:* Campus employment opportunities, campus safety program, career counseling, exercise/wellness program, free psychological counseling, grant writing training, international student services, low-cost health insurance, multicultural affairs office, services for students with disabilities, teacher training, writing training. *Library facilities:* Paley Library plus 6 others. *Collection:* Books: 3.4 million (physical), 1.6 million (digital/electronic); Serial titles: 61,478 (physical), 189,776 (digital/electronic); Databases: 773. Students can reserve study rooms.

**Computer facilities:** Computer purchase and lease plans are available. 15,100 computers available on campus for general student use. A campuswide network can be accessed. Online class registration, student accounts, Web hosting are available.
Website: http://www.temple.edu/

**General Application Contact:** Temple University Graduate School, 215-204-1380, E-mail: grad@temple.edu.

**GRADUATE UNITS**

**Beasley School of Law** *Program availability:* Part-time, evening/weekend. Electronic applications accepted.

**Center for the Performing and Cinematic Arts** Students: 310 full-time (194 women), 58 part-time (37 women); includes 67 minority (31 Black or African American, non-Hispanic/Latino; 1 American Indian or Alaska Native, non-Hispanic/Latino; 6 Asian, non-Hispanic/Latino; 15 Hispanic/Latino; 14 Two or more races, non-Hispanic/Latino), 120 international. 597 applicants, 47% accepted, 134 enrolled. *Faculty:* 85 full-time (39 women), 113 part-time/adjunct (45 women). Expenses: Contact institution. *Financial support:* Fellowships, research assistantships, teaching assistantships, Federal Work-Study, scholarships/grants, health care benefits, and unspecified assistantships available. Financial award applicants required to submit FAFSA. In 2019, 93 master's, 20 doctorates awarded. *Program availability:* Part-time, evening/weekend, online learning. *Application fee:* $60. Electronic applications accepted. *Application Contact:* James Short, Assistant Dean, Undergraduate and Graduate Admissions/CPCA, 215-204-8598, E-mail: james.short@temple.edu. *Dean/Vice Provost for the Arts*, Dr. Robert Stroker, 215-204-5004, E-mail: robert.stroker@temple.edu.

***Boyer College of Music and Dance*** Students: 248 full-time (163 women), 54 part-time (35 women); includes 49 minority (24 Black or African American, non-Hispanic/Latino; 5 Asian, non-Hispanic/Latino; 10 Hispanic/Latino; 10 Two or more races, non-Hispanic/Latino), 103 international. 510 applicants, 46% accepted, 108 enrolled. *Faculty:* 51 full-time (24 women), 64 part-time/adjunct (26 women). Expenses: Contact institution. *Financial support:* Fellowships with tuition reimbursements, research assistantships with tuition reimbursements, teaching assistantships with tuition reimbursements, career-related internships or fieldwork, Federal Work-Study, scholarships/grants, health care benefits, and unspecified assistantships available. Financial award application deadline: 3/1; financial award applicants required to submit FAFSA. In 2019, 77 master's, 20 doctorates awarded. *Program availability:* Part-time, evening/weekend, online learning. *Application fee:* $60. Electronic applications accepted. *Application Contact:* James Short, Director of Undergraduate and Graduate Admissions, 215-204-8598, Fax: 215-204-4957, E-mail: james.short@temple.edu. *Dean*, Dr. Robert Stroker, 215-204-5004, Fax: 215-204-4957, E-mail: rstroker@temple.edu.

***School of Theater, Film and Media Arts*** Students: 62 full-time (31 women), 4 part-time (2 women); includes 18 minority (7 Black or African American, non-Hispanic/Latino; 1 American Indian or Alaska Native, non-Hispanic/Latino; 1 Asian, non-Hispanic/Latino; 5 Hispanic/Latino; 4 Two or more races, non-Hispanic/Latino), 17 international. 87 applicants, 53% accepted, 26 enrolled. *Faculty:* 34 full-time (15 women), 49 part-time/adjunct (19 women). Expenses: Contact institution. *Financial support:* Fellowships, teaching assistantships, Federal Work-Study, and health care benefits available. Financial award application deadline: 3/1; financial award applicants required to submit FAFSA. In 2019, 16 master's awarded. *Application fee:* $60. Electronic applications accepted. *Application Contact:* Paury Flowers, Recruitment Coordinator, 215-777-9135, E-mail: pflowers@temple.edu. *Dean/Vice Provost for the Arts*, Dr. Robert Stroker, 215-204-8598, E-mail: robert.stroker@temple.edu.

**College of Education and Human Development** Students: 467 full-time (321 women), 372 part-time (250 women); includes 260 minority (155 Black or African American, non-Hispanic/Latino; 36 Asian, non-Hispanic/Latino; 53 Hispanic/Latino; 1 Native Hawaiian or other Pacific Islander, non-Hispanic/Latino; 15 Two or more races, non-Hispanic/Latino), 30 international. 860 applicants, 58% accepted, 307 enrolled. *Faculty:* 58 full-time (34 women), 87 part-time/adjunct (55 women). Expenses: Contact institution. *Financial support:* Fellowships, Federal Work-Study, scholarships/grants, health care benefits, and unspecified assistantships available. Support available to part-time students. Financial award application deadline: 10/1; financial award applicants required to submit FAFSA. In 2019, 291 master's, 35 doctorates, 51 other advanced degrees awarded. *Program availability:* Part-time, evening/weekend. *Application fee:* $60. Electronic applications accepted. *Application Contact:* Joseph Paris, Assistant Dean of Marketing and Enrollment Management, 215-204-2810, E-mail: educate@temple.edu. *Dean*, Dr. Gregory Anderson, 215-204-8017, Fax: 215-204-5622, E-mail: gregory.anderson@temple.edu.

**College of Engineering** Students: 154 full-time (48 women), 52 part-time (11 women); includes 40 minority (16 Black or African American, non-Hispanic/Latino; 12 Asian, non-Hispanic/Latino; 8 Hispanic/Latino; 4 Two or more races, non-Hispanic/Latino), 99 international. 269 applicants, 53% accepted, 54 enrolled. *Faculty:* 74 full-time (16 women), 56 part-time/adjunct (9 women). Expenses: Contact institution. *Financial support:* In 2019–20, 84 students received support, including 3 fellowships with full tuition reimbursements available (averaging $30,000 per year), research assistantships with full tuition reimbursements available (averaging $19,211 per year), teaching assistantships with full tuition reimbursements available (averaging $19,211 per year). Financial award application deadline: 1/15; financial award applicants required to submit FAFSA. In 2019, 48 master's, 11 doctorates awarded. *Program availability:* Part-time, 100% online, blended/hybrid learning. *Application deadline:* For fall admission, 6/1 priority date for domestic students, 3/1 priority date for international students; for spring admission, 11/1 priority date for domestic students, 8/1 priority date for international students. Applications are processed on a rolling basis. *Application fee:* $60. Electronic applications accepted. *Application Contact:* Colleen Baillie, Director, Enrollment, 215-204-7800, Fax: 215-204-6936, E-mail: gradengr@temple.edu. *Dean*, Dr. Keya Sadeghipour, 215-204-5285.

**College of Liberal Arts** Students: 571 full-time (334 women), 116 part-time (69 women); includes 177 minority (82 Black or African American, non-Hispanic/Latino; 2 American Indian or Alaska Native, non-Hispanic/Latino; 22 Asian, non-Hispanic/Latino; 51 Hispanic/Latino; 20 Two or more races, non-Hispanic/Latino), 84 international. 1,272 applicants, 27% accepted, 169 enrolled. *Faculty:* 287 full-time (125 women), 121 part-time/adjunct (62 women). Expenses: Contact institution. *Financial support:* Fellowships, research assistantships, teaching assistantships, Federal Work-Study, and health care benefits available. Financial award applicants required to submit FAFSA. In 2019, 97 master's, 71 doctorates, 7 other advanced degrees awarded. *Program availability:* Part-time. *Application fee:* $60. Electronic applications accepted. *Application Contact:* Amy Defibaugh, Director, Graduate Affairs, 215-204-8504, E-mail: amy.defibaugh@temple.edu. *Dean*, Richard Deeg, 215-204-7747, Fax: 215-204-5022, E-mail: rdeeg@temple.edu.

**College of Public Health** Students: 698 full-time (541 women), 369 part-time (304 women); includes 340 minority (168 Black or African American, non-Hispanic/Latino; 3 American Indian or Alaska Native, non-Hispanic/Latino; 61 Asian, non-Hispanic/Latino; 74 Hispanic/Latino; 34 Two or more races, non-Hispanic/Latino), 44 international. 1,237 applicants, 50% accepted, 267 enrolled. *Faculty:* 130 full-time (93 women), 48 part-time/adjunct (32 women). Expenses: Contact institution. *Financial support:* Fellowships, research assistantships, teaching assistantships, Federal Work-Study, scholarships/grants, health care benefits, and unspecified assistantships available. Support available to part-time students. Financial award applicants required to submit FAFSA. In 2019, 295 master's, 89 doctorates awarded. *Program availability:* Part-time, evening/weekend, online learning. *Application fee:* $60. *Application Contact:* Michael Usino, Assistant Dean of Admissions, 215-204-5717, E-mail: michael.usino@temple.edu. *Dean*, Laura Siminoff, 215-707-8624, E-mail: laura.siminoff@temple.edu.

***School of Social Work*** Students: 187 full-time (162 women), 108 part-time (97 women); includes 123 minority (84 Black or African American, non-Hispanic/Latino; 2 American Indian or Alaska Native, non-Hispanic/Latino; 5 Asian, non-Hispanic/Latino; 25 Hispanic/Latino; 7 Two or more races, non-Hispanic/Latino), 1 international. 266 applicants, 61% accepted, 70 enrolled. *Faculty:* 17 full-time (13 women), 16 part-time/adjunct (11 women). Expenses: Contact institution. *Financial support:* Career-related internships or fieldwork, Federal Work-Study, and scholarships/grants available. Financial award application deadline: 1/15; financial award applicants required to submit FAFSA. In 2019, 135 master's awarded. *Program availability:* Part-time, evening/weekend, online learning. *Application deadline:* For fall admission, 1/15 priority date for domestic students; for spring admission, 11/1 for domestic students; for summer admission, 1/15 priority date for domestic students. Applications are processed on a rolling basis. *Application fee:* $60. Electronic applications accepted. *Application Contact:* Tre Grue, Assistant Director of Admissions, 215-204-5806, E-mail: tre@temple.edu. *Director of the School of Social Work*, Philip McCallion, 215-204-8137, E-mail: philip.mccallion@temple.edu.

**College of Science and Technology** Students: 413 full-time (152 women), 43 part-time (17 women); includes 65 minority (17 Black or African American, non-Hispanic/Latino; 30 Asian, non-Hispanic/Latino; 16 Hispanic/Latino; 2 Two or more races, non-Hispanic/Latino), 225 international. 534 applicants, 47% accepted, 117 enrolled. *Faculty:* 187 full-time (50 women), 12 part-time/adjunct (1 woman). Expenses: Contact institution. *Financial support:* Fellowships, research assistantships, teaching assistantships, career-related internships or fieldwork, Federal Work-Study, scholarships/grants, health care benefits, and unspecified assistantships available. Support available to part-time students. Financial award applicants required to submit FAFSA. In 2019, 67 master's, 47 doctorates awarded. *Program availability:* Part-time, evening/weekend. *Application fee:* $60. Electronic applications accepted. *Application Contact:* Caitlyn Moynahan, Graduate Admissions Coordinator, 215-204-5295, E-mail: cst.gradinfo@temple.edu. *Dean*, Michael Klein, 215-204-1927, E-mail: cst.dean@temple.edu.

**Fox School of Business** *Program availability:* Part-time, evening/weekend, online learning. Electronic applications accepted.

**Klein College of Media and Communication** Students: 92 full-time (58 women), 28 part-time (17 women); includes 35 minority (23 Black or African American, non-Hispanic/Latino; 3 Asian, non-Hispanic/Latino; 5 Hispanic/Latino; 4 Two or more races, non-Hispanic/Latino), 31 international. 155 applicants, 66% accepted, 48 enrolled. *Faculty:* 74 full-time (39 women), 73 part-time/adjunct (37 women). Expenses: Contact institution. *Financial support:* Fellowships, teaching assistantships, Federal Work-Study, scholarships/grants, health care benefits, unspecified assistantships, and travel award available. Financial award applicants required to submit FAFSA. In 2019, 27 master's, 7 doctorates awarded. *Program availability:* Part-time, evening/weekend, online learning. *Application fee:* $60. Electronic applications accepted. *Application Contact:* Nicole McKenna, Graduate Office Director, 215-204-1497, E-mail: nmckenna@temple.edu. *Dean*, David Boardman, 215-204-8422, Fax: 215-204-4811, E-mail: dboardman@temple.edu.

**Kornberg School of Dentistry** Electronic applications accepted.

**Lewis Katz School of Medicine** Students: 994 full-time (542 women), 24 part-time (19 women); includes 438 minority (108 Black or African American, non-Hispanic/Latino; 186 Asian, non-Hispanic/Latino; 117 Hispanic/Latino; 1 Native Hawaiian or other Pacific Islander, non-Hispanic/Latino; 26 Two or more races, non-Hispanic/Latino), 23 international. 8,346 applicants, 6% accepted, 248 enrolled. *Faculty:* 22 full-time (9 women). Expenses: Contact institution. *Financial support:* Fellowships, research assistantships, Federal Work-Study, institutionally sponsored loans, scholarships/grants, and health care benefits available. Financial award applicants required to submit FAFSA. In 2019, 44 master's, 214 doctorates awarded. *Application fee:* $60. Electronic applications accepted. *Application Contact:* Jacob Ufberg, Associate Dean of Admissions, 215-707-5308, E-mail: medadmissions@temple.edu. *Dean*, Larry R. Kaiser, 215-707-8773, E-mail: sks@temple.edu.

**School of Pharmacy** Students: 596 full-time (331 women), 222 part-time (153 women); includes 369 minority (62 Black or African American, non-Hispanic/Latino; 173 Asian, non-Hispanic/Latino; 23 Hispanic/Latino; 111 Two or more races, non-Hispanic/Latino), 49 international. 550 applicants, 55% accepted, 199 enrolled. *Faculty:* 33 full-time (16 women), 38 part-time/adjunct (15 women). Expenses: Contact institution. *Financial support:* Fellowships, research assistantships, teaching assistantships, Federal Work-Study, and unspecified assistantships available. Financial award application deadline: 3/1; financial award applicants required to submit FAFSA. In 2019, 89 master's, 139 doctorates awarded. *Program availability:* Part-time, evening/weekend, online learning. *Application fee:* $60. Electronic applications accepted. *Application Contact:* Joan Hankins, Director of Admissions, 215-707-4900, E-mail: joan.hankins@temple.edu. *Interim Dean*, Michael Borenstein, 215-707-2976, E-mail: michael.borenstein@temple.edu.

**School of Podiatric Medicine**

**School of Sport, Tourism and Hospitality Management** Students: 137 full-time (66 women), 44 part-time (24 women); includes 41 minority (29 Black or African American, non-Hispanic/Latino; 3 Asian, non-Hispanic/Latino; 7 Hispanic/Latino; 2 Two or more races, non-Hispanic/Latino), 36 international. 208 applicants, 70% accepted, 81 enrolled. *Faculty:* 24 full-time (11 women), 9 part-time/adjunct (3 women). Expenses: Contact institution. *Financial support:* Scholarships/grants, health care benefits, and unspecified assistantships available. Financial award application deadline: 3/1; financial award applicants required to submit FAFSA. In 2019, 95 master's awarded. *Program availability:* Part-time, evening/weekend, online learning. *Application deadline:* For fall admission, 12/15 priority date for domestic students, 3/1 for international students; for spring admission, 11/1 for domestic students, 8/1 for international students. Applications are processed on a rolling basis. *Application fee:* $60. Electronic applications accepted. *Application Contact:* Michelle Rosar, Assistant Director of Graduate Enrollment, 215-204-3315, E-mail: michelle.rosar@temple.edu. *Dean*, Ronald C. Anderson, 215-204-8701, E-mail: sthm@temple.edu.

**Tyler School of Art and Architecture** Students: 204 full-time (147 women), 24 part-time (13 women); includes 42 minority (10 Black or African American, non-Hispanic/Latino; 11 Asian, non-Hispanic/Latino; 15 Hispanic/Latino; 6 Two or more races, non-Hispanic/Latino), 35 international. 353 applicants, 43% accepted, 72 enrolled. *Faculty:* 73 full-time (36 women), 120 part-time/adjunct (57 women). Expenses: Contact institution. *Financial support:* Fellowships with full tuition reimbursements, research assistantships with full tuition reimbursements, teaching assistantships with full tuition reimbursements, Federal Work-Study, institutionally sponsored loans, scholarships/grants, health care benefits, and travel scholarships/grants available. Financial award application deadline: 1/6; financial award applicants required to submit FAFSA. In 2019, 56 master's, 3 doctorates awarded. *Program availability:* Part-time, evening/weekend. *Application fee:* $60. Electronic applications accepted. *Application Contact:* Lauren O'Neill, Director of Admissions, 215-777-9159, E-mail: tyleradmissions@temple.edu. *Dean*, Susan E. Cahan, 215-777-9000, E-mail: tyler@temple.edu.

## TENNESSEE STATE UNIVERSITY, Nashville, TN 37209-1561

**General Information** State-supported, coed, comprehensive institution. CGS member. *Graduate housing:* Rooms and/or apartments available on a first-come, first-served basis to single and married students. Housing application deadline: 8/1.

**GRADUATE UNITS**

**The School of Graduate Studies and Research**

***College of Agriculture, Human and Natural Sciences*** *Program availability:* Part-time, evening/weekend.

***College of Business*** *Program availability:* Part-time, evening/weekend, online learning. Electronic applications accepted.

***College of Education*** *Program availability:* Part-time, evening/weekend.

***College of Engineering*** *Program availability:* Part-time, evening/weekend.

***College of Health Sciences*** *Program availability:* Part-time, evening/weekend. Electronic applications accepted.

***College of Liberal Arts*** *Program availability:* Part-time, evening/weekend. Electronic applications accepted.

***College of Public Service*** *Program availability:* Part-time, evening/weekend.

## TENNESSEE TECHNOLOGICAL UNIVERSITY, Cookeville, TN 38505

**General Information** State-supported, coed, university. CGS member. *Enrollment:* 276 full-time matriculated graduate/professional students (156 women), 888 part-time matriculated graduate/professional students (513 women). *Enrollment by degree level:* 915 master's, 191 doctoral, 58 other advanced degrees. *Graduate faculty:* 341 full-time (62 women). *Tuition, area resident:* Part-time $597 per credit hour. Tuition, state resident: part-time $597 per credit hour. Tuition, nonresident: part-time $1323 per credit hour. *Graduate housing:* Rooms and/or apartments available on a first-come, first-served basis to single and married students. Housing application deadline: 6/1. *Student services:* Campus employment opportunities, campus safety program, career counseling, child daycare facilities, exercise/wellness program, free psychological counseling, international student services, low-cost health insurance, multicultural affairs office, services for students with disabilities, teacher training. *Library facilities:* Angelo and Jennette Volpe Library and Media Center. *Collection:* Books: 235,249 (physical), 267,168 (digital/electronic); Serial titles: 120,118 (physical); Databases: 193. *Research affiliation:* Center for Excellence in Teacher Evaluation, Appalachian Center for Crafts, Center of Excellence in Water Resources, Center of Excellence in Manufacturing Resources, Center of Excellence in Energy Systems Research.

**Computer facilities:** 227 computers available on campus for general student use. A campuswide network can be accessed. Online class registration, 590 additional computers are available for student use in individual departmental labs are available. Website: http://www.tntech.edu/

**General Application Contact:** Shelia K. Kendrick, Coordinator of Graduate Studies, 931-372-3808, Fax: 931-372-3497, E-mail: skendrick@tntech.edu.

**GRADUATE UNITS**

**College of Graduate Studies** Students: 276 full-time (156 women), 888 part-time (513 women); includes 84 minority (34 Black or African American, non-Hispanic/Latino; 1 American Indian or Alaska Native, non-Hispanic/Latino; 16 Asian, non-Hispanic/Latino; 19 Hispanic/Latino; 14 Two or more races, non-Hispanic/Latino), 118 international. 781 applicants, 66% accepted, 329 enrolled. *Faculty:* 341 full-time (62 women). Expenses: Contact institution. *Financial support:* In 2019–20, 354 students received support, including 50 fellowships (averaging $8,000 per year), 143 research assistantships (averaging $6,973 per year), 156 teaching assistantships (averaging $6,213 per year); career-related internships or fieldwork and Federal Work-Study also available. Support available to part-time students. Financial award application deadline: 4/1; financial award applicants required to submit FAFSA. In 2019, 360 master's, 25 doctorates, 64 other advanced degrees awarded. *Program availability:* Part-time, evening/weekend, 100% online, blended/hybrid learning. *Application deadline:* For fall admission, 7/1 for domestic students, 5/1 for international students; for spring admission, 12/1 for domestic students, 10/1 for international students; for summer admission, 5/1 for domestic students, 2/1 for international students. Applications are processed on a rolling basis. *Application fee:* $35 ($40 for international students). Electronic applications accepted. *Application Contact:* Shelia K. Kendrick, Coordinator of Graduate Studies, 931-372-3808, Fax: 931-372-3497, E-mail: skendrick@tntech.edu. *Senior Associate Provost and Dean of Graduate Studies*, Dr. Mark A. Stephens, 931-372-3233, Fax: 931-372-3497, E-mail: mstephens@tntech.edu.

***College of Arts and Sciences*** Students: 25 full-time (11 women), 40 part-time (19 women); includes 2 minority (1 Asian, non-Hispanic/Latino; 1 Two or more races, non-Hispanic/Latino), 3 international. 55 applicants, 85% accepted, 21 enrolled. *Faculty:* 78 full-time (15 women). Expenses: Contact institution. *Financial support:* In 2019–20, 8 research assistantships (averaging $7,600 per year), 45 teaching assistantships (averaging $6,630 per year) were awarded; fellowships and career-related internships or fieldwork also available. Support available to part-time students. Financial award application deadline: 4/1. In 2019, 19 master's awarded. *Program availability:* Part-time. *Application deadline:* For fall admission, 8/1 for domestic students, 5/1 for international students; for spring admission, 12/1 for domestic students, 10/1 for international students; for summer admission, 5/1 for domestic students, 2/1 for international students. Applications are processed on a rolling basis. *Application fee:* $35 ($40 for international students). Electronic applications accepted. *Application Contact:* Shelia K. Kendrick, Coordinator of Graduate Studies, 931-372-3808, Fax: 931-372-3497, E-mail: skendrick@tntech.edu. *Dean*, Dr. Paul Semmes, 931-372-3118, Fax: 931-372-6142, E-mail: psemmes@tntech.edu.

***College of Business*** Students: 43 full-time (21 women), 165 part-time (69 women); includes 24 minority (8 Black or African American, non-Hispanic/Latino; 5 Asian, non-Hispanic/Latino; 8 Hispanic/Latino; 3 Two or more races, non-Hispanic/Latino), 1 international. 175 applicants, 66% accepted, 80 enrolled. *Faculty:* 28 full-time (5 women). Expenses: Contact institution. *Financial support:* In 2019–20, 2 research assistantships (averaging $4,400 per year), 4 teaching assistantships (averaging $4,400 per year) were awarded; fellowships also available. Support available to part-time students. Financial award application deadline: 4/1. In 2019, 101 master's awarded. *Program availability:* Part-time, evening/weekend, online learning. *Application deadline:* For fall admission, 8/1 for domestic students, 5/1 for international students; for spring admission, 12/1 for domestic students, 10/1 for international students; for summer admission, 5/1 for domestic students, 2/1 for international students. Applications are processed on a rolling basis. *Application fee:* $35 ($40 for international students). Electronic applications accepted. *Application Contact:* Shelia K. Kendrick, Coordinator of Graduate Studies, 931-372-3808, Fax: 931-372-3497, E-mail: skendrick@tntech.edu. *Director*, Kate Nicewicz, 931-372-3600, Fax: 931-372-6249, E-mail: knicewicz@tntech.edu.

***College of Education*** Students: 111 full-time (83 women), 284 part-time (213 women); includes 22 minority (7 Black or African American, non-Hispanic/Latino; 2 American Indian or Alaska Native, non-Hispanic/Latino; 3 Asian, non-Hispanic/Latino; 6 Hispanic/Latino; 4 Two or more races, non-Hispanic/Latino), 8 international. 196 applicants, 68% accepted, 109 enrolled. *Faculty:* 58 full-time (16 women). Expenses: Contact institution. *Financial support:* Fellowships, research assistantships, teaching assistantships, and career-related internships or fieldwork available. Support available to part-time students. Financial award application deadline: 4/1. In 2019, 129 master's, 5 doctorates, 36 other advanced degrees awarded. *Program availability:* Part-time, evening/weekend. *Application deadline:* For fall admission, 8/1 for domestic students, 5/1 for international students; for spring admission, 12/1 for domestic students, 10/1 for international students; for summer admission, 5/1 for domestic students, 2/1 for international students. Applications are processed on a rolling basis. *Application fee:* $35 ($40 for international students). Electronic applications accepted. *Application Contact:* Shelia K. Kendrick, Coordinator of Graduate Studies, 931-372-3808, Fax: 931-372-3497, E-mail: skendrick@tntech.edu. *Dean*, Dr. Lisa Zagumny, 931-372-3124, Fax: 931-372-6319, E-mail: lzagumny@tntech.edu.

***College of Engineering*** Students: 58 full-time (10 women), 153 part-time (30 women); includes 8 minority (3 Black or African American, non-Hispanic/Latino; 4 Asian, non-Hispanic/Latino; 1 Hispanic/Latino), 100 international. 205 applicants, 62% accepted, 44 enrolled. *Faculty:* 76 full-time (2 women). Expenses: Contact institution. *Financial support:* Fellowships, research assistantships, teaching assistantships, and career-related internships or fieldwork available. Support available to part-time students. Financial award application deadline: 4/1. In 2019, 32 master's, 15 doctorates awarded. *Program availability:* Part-time. *Application deadline:* For fall admission, 8/1 for domestic students, 5/1 for international students; for spring admission, 12/1 for domestic students, 10/1 for international students. Applications are processed on a rolling basis. *Application fee:* $35 ($40 for international students). Electronic applications accepted. *Application Contact:* Shelia K. Kendrick, Coordinator of Graduate Studies, 931-372-3808, Fax: 931-372-3497, E-mail: skendrick@tntech.edu. *Dean*, Dr. Joseph Slater, 931-372-3172, Fax: 931-372-6172, E-mail: jslater@tntech.edu.

***College of Interdisciplinary Studies*** Students: 17 full-time (12 women), 124 part-time (77 women); includes 19 minority (10 Black or African American, non-Hispanic/Latino; 2 Asian, non-Hispanic/Latino; 3 Hispanic/Latino; 4 Two or more races, non-Hispanic/Latino), 6 international. 70 applicants, 80% accepted, 36 enrolled. Expenses: Contact institution. *Financial support:* Research assistantships and teaching assistantships available. In 2019, 41 master's, 5 doctorates awarded. *Program availability:* Part-time. *Application deadline:* For fall admission, 7/1 for domestic students, 5/1 for international students; for spring admission, 11/1 for domestic students, 10/1 for international students; for summer admission, 5/1 for domestic students, 2/1 for international students. Applications are processed on a rolling basis. *Application fee:* $35 ($40 for international students). Electronic applications accepted. *Application Contact:* Shelia K. Kendrick, Coordinator of Graduate Studies, 931-372-3808, Fax: 931-372-3497, E-mail: skendrick@tntech.edu. *Dean*, Dr. Mike Gotcher, 931-372-6238, E-mail: mgotcher@tntech.edu.

**Whitson-Hester School of Nursing** Students: 22 full-time (19 women), 122 part-time (105 women); includes 10 minority (6 Black or African American, non-Hispanic/Latino; 1 Asian, non-Hispanic/Latino; 1 Hispanic/Latino; 2 Two or more races, non-Hispanic/Latino). 80 applicants, 69% accepted, 39 enrolled. Expenses: Contact institution. *Financial support:* Teaching assistantships available. Financial award application deadline: 4/1. In 2019, 29 master's awarded. *Program availability:* Part-time, evening/weekend, online learning. *Application deadline:* For fall admission, 7/1 for domestic students, 5/1 for international students; for spring admission, 11/1 for domestic students, 10/1 for international students; for summer admission, 5/1 for domestic students, 2/1 for international students. Applications are processed on a rolling basis. *Application fee:* $35 ($40 for international students). Electronic applications accepted. *Application Contact:* Shelia K. Kendrick, Coordinator of Graduate Studies, 931-372-3808, Fax: 931-372-3497, E-mail: skendrick@tntech.edu. *Dean*, Dr. Kim Hanna, 931-372-3547, Fax: 931-372-6244, E-mail: khanna@tntech.edu.

## TENNESSEE WESLEYAN UNIVERSITY, Athens, TN 37303

**General Information** Independent-religious, coed, comprehensive institution. *Graduate housing:* On-campus housing not available.

**GRADUATE UNITS**

**Graduate Programs** *Program availability:* Part-time. Electronic applications accepted.

## TEXAS A&M INTERNATIONAL UNIVERSITY, Laredo, TX 78041

**General Information** State-supported, coed, comprehensive institution. CGS member. *Graduate housing:* Rooms and/or apartments available on a first-come, first-served basis to single and married students.

**GRADUATE UNITS**

**Office of Graduate Studies and Research** *Program availability:* Part-time.

***A.R. Sanchez, Jr. School of Business*** *Program availability:* Part-time, evening/weekend.

***College of Arts and Sciences*** *Program availability:* Part-time, online learning.

***College of Education*** *Program availability:* Part-time, evening/weekend.

***College of Nursing and Health Sciences***

## TEXAS A&M UNIVERSITY, College Station, TX 77843

**General Information** State-supported, coed, university. CGS member. *Graduate housing:* Rooms and/or apartments available on a first-come, first-served basis to single and married students. *Research affiliation:* U.S. Department of Agriculture (USDA) (agriculture), National Science Foundation (geosciences), Joint Oceanographic Institutions, Inc. (geosciences), Texas Department of Transportation (transportation).

**GRADUATE UNITS**

**Bush School of Government and Public Service** Electronic applications accepted.

**College of Agriculture and Life Sciences** Students: 894 full-time (462 women), 242 part-time (123 women); includes 194 minority (34 Black or African American, non-Hispanic/Latino; 3 American Indian or Alaska Native, non-Hispanic/Latino; 23 Asian, non-Hispanic/Latino; 116 Hispanic/Latino; 2 Native Hawaiian or other Pacific Islander, non-Hispanic/Latino; 16 Two or more races, non-Hispanic/Latino), 390 international. Average age 30. 467 applicants, 60% accepted, 207 enrolled. *Faculty:* 342. Expenses: Contact institution. *Financial support:* In 2019–20, 998 students received support, including 138 fellowships with tuition reimbursements available (averaging $12,384 per year), 538 research assistantships with tuition reimbursements available (averaging $13,863 per year), 377 teaching assistantships with tuition reimbursements available (averaging $12,276 per year); career-related internships or fieldwork, institutionally sponsored loans, scholarships/grants, traineeships, health care benefits, and unspecified assistantships also available. Support available to part-time students. Financial award application deadline: 3/15; financial award applicants required to submit FAFSA. In 2019, 195 master's, 146 doctorates awarded. *Program availability:* Part-time, blended/hybrid learning. *Application deadline:* Applications are processed on a rolling basis. *Application fee:* $65 ($90 for international students). Electronic applications accepted. *Application Contact:* Dr. Mary Bryk, Associate Dean for Academic Affairs, 979-847-6180, E-mail: mary.bryk@ag.tamu.edu. *Vice Chancellor and Dean for Agriculture and Life Sciences*, Dr. Patrick Stover, 979-845-4747, E-mail: vcdean@ag.tamu.edu.

**College of Architecture** Students: 388 full-time (195 women), 48 part-time (25 women); includes 92 minority (15 Black or African American, non-Hispanic/Latino; 1 American Indian or Alaska Native, non-Hispanic/Latino; 23 Asian, non-Hispanic/Latino; 53 Hispanic/Latino), 204 international. Average age 28. 396 applicants, 71% accepted, 135 enrolled. *Faculty:* 113. Expenses: Contact institution. *Financial support:* In 2019–20, 355 students received support, including 20 fellowships with tuition reimbursements available (averaging $6,821 per year), 102 research assistantships with tuition reimbursements available (averaging $9,891 per year), 124 teaching assistantships with tuition reimbursements available (averaging $8,775 per year); career-related internships or fieldwork, institutionally sponsored loans, scholarships/grants, traineeships, health care benefits, tuition waivers (full and partial), and unspecified assistantships also available. Support available to part-time students. Financial award application deadline: 3/15; financial award applicants required to submit FAFSA. In 2019, 146 master's, 11 doctorates awarded. *Application deadline:* Applications are processed on a rolling basis. *Application fee:* $65 ($90 for international students). Electronic applications accepted. *Application Contact:* Graduate Admissions, 979-458-0427, E-mail: admissions@tamu.edu. *Dean*, Dr. Jorge Vanegas, 979-845-1223, Fax: 979-845-4491, E-mail: jvanegas@arch.tamu.edu.

**College of Dentistry** Electronic applications accepted.

**College of Education and Human Development** Students: 700 full-time (523 women), 871 part-time (663 women); includes 567 minority (128 Black or African American, non-Hispanic/Latino; 3 American Indian or Alaska Native, non-Hispanic/Latino; 56 Asian, non-Hispanic/Latino; 356 Hispanic/Latino; 2 Native Hawaiian or other Pacific Islander, non-Hispanic/Latino; 22 Two or more races, non-Hispanic/Latino), 133 international. Average age 34. 561 applicants, 66% accepted, 274 enrolled. *Faculty:* 185. Expenses: Contact institution. *Financial support:* In 2019–20, 1,098 students received support, including 28 fellowships with tuition reimbursements available (averaging $11,595 per year), 270 research assistantships with tuition reimbursements available (averaging $13,318 per year), 130 teaching assistantships with tuition reimbursements available (averaging $11,505 per year); career-related internships or fieldwork, institutionally sponsored loans, scholarships/grants, traineeships, health care benefits, tuition waivers (full and partial), and unspecified assistantships also available. Support available to part-time students. Financial award application deadline: 3/15; financial award applicants required to submit FAFSA. In 2019, 533 master's, 83 doctorates awarded. *Program availability:* Part-time, evening/weekend, blended/hybrid learning. *Application deadline:* Applications are processed on a rolling basis. *Application fee:* $65 ($90 for international students). Electronic applications accepted. *Application Contact:* Dr. Beverly Irby, Professor and Associate Dean for Academic Affairs, 979-845-5311, E-mail: beverly.irby@tamu.edu. *Professor and Dean*, Dr. Joyce Alexander, 979-862-6649, E-mail: joycemalexander@tamu.edu.

**College of Engineering** Students: 3,504 full-time (766 women), 703 part-time (129 women); includes 518 minority (66 Black or African American, non-Hispanic/Latino; 1 American Indian or Alaska Native, non-Hispanic/Latino; 187 Asian, non-Hispanic/Latino; 226 Hispanic/Latino; 1 Native Hawaiian or other Pacific Islander, non-Hispanic/Latino; 37 Two or more races, non-Hispanic/Latino), 2,751 international. Average age 28. 7,529 applicants, 38% accepted, 1,197 enrolled. *Faculty:* 606. Expenses: Contact institution. *Financial support:* In 2019–20, 2,943 students received support, including 453 fellowships with tuition reimbursements available (averaging $9,364 per year), 1,641 research assistantships with tuition reimbursements available (averaging $12,128 per year), 675 teaching assistantships with tuition reimbursements available (averaging $14,407 per year); career-related internships or fieldwork, institutionally sponsored loans, scholarships/grants, traineeships, health care benefits, tuition waivers (full and partial), and unspecified assistantships also available. Support available to part-time students. Financial award applicants required to submit FAFSA. In 2019, 1,076 master's, 298 doctorates awarded. *Program availability:* Part-time, online learning. *Application fee:* $65 ($90 for international students). Electronic applications accepted. *Application Contact:* Harry Hogan, Associate Dean for Graduate Programs, 979-845-1538, E-mail: hhogan@tamu.edu. *Dean and Vice Chancellor,* Dr. M. Katherine Banks, 979-845-1321, E-mail: engineeringvcd@tamu.edu.

**College of Geosciences** Students: 253 full-time (107 women), 111 part-time (47 women); includes 74 minority (11 Black or African American, non-Hispanic/Latino; 2 American Indian or Alaska Native, non-Hispanic/Latino; 13 Asian, non-Hispanic/Latino; 42 Hispanic/Latino; 6 Two or more races, non-Hispanic/Latino), 97 international. Average age 31. 315 applicants, 45% accepted, 79 enrolled. *Faculty:* 98. Expenses: Contact institution. *Financial support:* In 2019–20, 276 students received support, including 61 fellowships with tuition reimbursements available (averaging $8,924 per year), 138 research assistantships with tuition reimbursements available (averaging $13,533 per year), 83 teaching assistantships with tuition reimbursements available (averaging $12,091 per year); career-related internships or fieldwork, institutionally sponsored loans, traineeships, health care benefits, tuition waivers (full and partial), and unspecified assistantships also available. Support available to part-time students. Financial award application deadline: 3/15; financial award applicants required to submit FAFSA. In 2019, 59 master's, 27 doctorates awarded. *Program availability:* Part-time, online learning. *Application deadline:* Applications are processed on a rolling basis. *Application fee:* $65 ($90 for international students). Electronic applications accepted. *Application Contact:* Dr. Debbie Thomas, Dean, 979-845-3651, E-mail: dthomas@ocean.tamu.edu. *Dean,* Dr. Debbie Thomas, 979-845-3651, E-mail: dthomas@ocean.tamu.edu.

**College of Liberal Arts** Students: 674 full-time (344 women), 155 part-time (91 women); includes 199 minority (36 Black or African American, non-Hispanic/Latino; 1 American Indian or Alaska Native, non-Hispanic/Latino; 29 Asian, non-Hispanic/Latino; 118 Hispanic/Latino; 15 Two or more races, non-Hispanic/Latino), 289 international. Average age 30. 991 applicants, 41% accepted, 188 enrolled. *Faculty:* 323. Expenses: Contact institution. *Financial support:* In 2019–20, 608 students received support, including 86 fellowships with tuition reimbursements available (averaging $13,585 per year), 153 research assistantships with tuition reimbursements available (averaging $13,829 per year), 358 teaching assistantships with tuition reimbursements available (averaging $15,859 per year); career-related internships or fieldwork, institutionally sponsored loans, scholarships/grants, traineeships, health care benefits, tuition waivers (full and partial), unspecified assistantships, and assistant lecturer positions also available. Support available to part-time students. Financial award application deadline: 3/15; financial award applicants required to submit FAFSA. In 2019, 150 master's, 79 doctorates awarded. *Program availability:* Part-time. *Application fee:* $65 ($90 for international students). Electronic applications accepted. *Application Contact:* Dr. Pamela R. Matthews, Dean, 979-845-5141, Fax: 979-845-5164, E-mail: p-matthews@tamu.edu. *Dean,* Dr. Pamela R. Matthews, 979-845-5141, Fax: 979-845-5164, E-mail: p-matthews@tamu.edu.

**College of Medicine** Electronic applications accepted.

**College of Nursing**

**College of Science** Students: 954 full-time (284 women), 328 part-time (128 women); includes 220 minority (22 Black or African American, non-Hispanic/Latino; 2 American Indian or Alaska Native, non-Hispanic/Latino; 104 Asian, non-Hispanic/Latino; 72 Hispanic/Latino; 1 Native Hawaiian or other Pacific Islander, non-Hispanic/Latino; 19 Two or more races, non-Hispanic/Latino), 521 international. Average age 29. 1,044 applicants, 50% accepted, 269 enrolled. *Faculty:* 306. Expenses: Contact institution. *Financial support:* In 2019–20, 837 students received support, including 105 fellowships with tuition reimbursements available (averaging $15,046 per year), 393 research assistantships with tuition reimbursements available (averaging $14,296 per year), 542 teaching assistantships with tuition reimbursements available (averaging $15,727 per year); career-related internships or fieldwork, institutionally sponsored loans, scholarships/grants, traineeships, health care benefits, tuition waivers (full and partial), and unspecified assistantships also available. Support available to part-time students. Financial award applicants required to submit FAFSA. In 2019, 183 master's, 98 doctorates awarded. *Program availability:* Part-time. *Application fee:* $65 ($90 for international students). *Application Contact:* Mark Zoran, Associate Dean for Graduate Studies, 979-458-8001, Fax: 979-845-6077, E-mail: zoran@science.tamu.edu. *Dean,* Dr. Valen Johnson, 979-845-3141, E-mail: vejohnson@tamu.edu.

**College of Veterinary Medicine and Biomedical Sciences** *Program availability:* Part-time.

**Galveston Campus** Students: 162 full-time (66 women), 39 part-time (19 women); includes 37 minority (6 Black or African American, non-Hispanic/Latino; 11 Asian, non-Hispanic/Latino; 14 Hispanic/Latino; 6 Two or more races, non-Hispanic/Latino), 10 international. Average age 28. 80 applicants, 86% accepted, 45 enrolled. *Faculty:* 61. Expenses: Contact institution. *Financial support:* In 2019–20, 110 students received support, including 2 fellowships with tuition reimbursements available (averaging $24,070 per year), 50 research assistantships with tuition reimbursements available (averaging $10,072 per year), 58 teaching assistantships with tuition reimbursements available (averaging $14,308 per year). In 2019, 72 master's awarded. *Application Contact:* Col. Michael E. Fossum, Chief Operation Officer, E-mail: fossum@tamug.edu. *Chief Operation Officer,* Col. Michael E. Fossum, E-mail: fossum@tamug.edu.

**Irma Lerma Rangel College of Pharmacy** Electronic applications accepted.

**Mays Business School** Electronic applications accepted.

**School of Law**

**School of Public Health** *Program availability:* Part-time, blended/hybrid learning. Electronic applications accepted.

## TEXAS A&M UNIVERSITY–CENTRAL TEXAS, Killeen, TX 76549

**General Information** State-supported, coed, upper-level institution. CGS member.

**GRADUATE UNITS**

**Graduate Studies and Research**

## TEXAS A&M UNIVERSITY–COMMERCE, Commerce, TX 75429

**General Information** State-supported, coed, university. CGS member. *Enrollment:* 11,725 graduate, professional, and undergraduate students; 780 full-time matriculated graduate/professional students (499 women), 2,720 part-time matriculated graduate/professional students (1,850 women). *Enrollment by degree level:* 2,922 master's, 479 doctoral, 99 other advanced degrees. *Graduate faculty:* 227 full-time (101 women), 46 part-time/adjunct (24 women). *International tuition:* $11,232 full-time. *Tuition, area resident:* Full-time $3630; part-time $202 per credit hour. Tuition, state resident: full-time $3630; part-time $202 per credit hour. Tuition, nonresident: full-time $11,232; part-time $624 per credit hour. *Required fees:* $2948. *Graduate housing:* Rooms and/or apartments available on a first-come, first-served basis to single and married students. Typical cost: $5158 per year ($7950 including board) for single students; $5254 per year ($8154 including board) for married students. Room and board charges vary according to board plan and housing facility selected. *Student services:* Campus employment opportunities, campus safety program, career counseling, child daycare facilities, exercise/wellness program, free psychological counseling, grant writing training, international student services, low-cost health insurance, multicultural affairs office, services for students with disabilities, writing training. *Library facilities:* Gee Library. *Collection:* Books: 363,482 (physical), 740,828 (digital/electronic); Serial titles: 14,396 (physical), 123,135 (digital/electronic); Databases: 272. Weekly public service hours: 110; students can reserve study rooms.

**Computer facilities:** A campuswide network can be accessed. Online class registration is available.
Website: http://www.tamuc.edu/

**General Application Contact:** Dayla Burgin, Graduate Student Services Coordinator, 903-886-5134, E-mail: dayla.burgin@tamuc.edu.

**GRADUATE UNITS**

**College of Agricultural Sciences and Natural Resources** Students: 16 full-time (12 women), 34 part-time (21 women); includes 14 minority (1 Black or African American, non-Hispanic/Latino; 6 Hispanic/Latino; 7 Two or more races, non-Hispanic/Latino). Average age 27. 35 applicants, 74% accepted, 19 enrolled. *Faculty:* 9 full-time (1 woman), 1 (woman) part-time/adjunct. Expenses: Contact institution. *Financial support:* In 2019–20, 13 students received support, including 61 research assistantships with partial tuition reimbursements available (averaging $2,685 per year); teaching assistantships with partial tuition reimbursements available, career-related internships or fieldwork, Federal Work-Study, institutionally sponsored loans, scholarships/grants, health care benefits, and unspecified assistantships also available. Financial award application deadline: 5/1; financial award applicants required to submit FAFSA. In 2019, 20 master's awarded. *Program availability:* Part-time, evening/weekend, 100% online, blended/hybrid learning. *Application deadline:* For fall admission, 6/1 priority date for international students; for spring admission, 10/15 priority date for international students; for summer admission, 10/15 priority date for international students. Applications are processed on a rolling basis. *Application fee:* $50 ($75 for international students). Electronic applications accepted. *Application Contact:* Vicky Turner, Doctoral Degree and Special Programs Coordinator, 903-886-5167, E-mail: vicky.turner@tamuc.edu. *Dean,* Dr. Randy Harp, 903-886-5351, Fax: 903-886-5990, E-mail: randy.harp@tamuc.edu.

**College of Business** Students: 351 full-time (211 women), 882 part-time (498 women); includes 548 minority (207 Black or African American, non-Hispanic/Latino; 89 Asian, non-Hispanic/Latino; 208 Hispanic/Latino; 1 Native Hawaiian or other Pacific Islander, non-Hispanic/Latino; 43 Two or more races, non-Hispanic/Latino), 168 international. Average age 33. 759 applicants, 68% accepted, 309 enrolled. *Faculty:* 45 full-time (13 women), 6 part-time/adjunct (1 woman). Expenses: Contact institution. *Financial support:* In 2019–20, 43 students received support, including 58 research assistantships with partial tuition reimbursements available (averaging $3,540 per year); Federal Work-Study, institutionally sponsored loans, scholarships/grants, health care benefits, and unspecified assistantships also available. Financial award application deadline: 5/1; financial award applicants required to submit FAFSA. In 2019, 615 master's awarded. *Program availability:* Part-time, evening/weekend, 100% online, blended/hybrid learning. *Application deadline:* For fall admission, 6/1 priority date for international students; for spring admission, 10/15 priority date for international students; for summer admission, 3/15 priority date for international students. Applications are processed on a rolling basis. *Application fee:* $50 ($75 for international students). Electronic applications accepted. *Application Contact:* Rebecca Stevens, Graduate Student Services Coordinator, 903-468-6049, E-mail: rebecca.stevens@tamuc.edu. *Dean of College of Business,* Dr. Mario Joseph Hayek, 903-886-5191, Fax: 903-886-5650, E-mail: mario.hayek@tamuc.edu.

**College of Education and Human Services** Students: 261 full-time (202 women), 1,180 part-time (943 women); includes 597 minority (300 Black or African American, non-Hispanic/Latino; 8 American Indian or Alaska Native, non-Hispanic/Latino; 30 Asian, non-Hispanic/Latino; 211 Hispanic/Latino; 48 Two or more races, non-Hispanic/Latino), 11 international. Average age 37. 689 applicants, 52% accepted, 291 enrolled. *Faculty:* 88 full-time (52 women), 23 part-time/adjunct (19 women). Expenses: Contact institution. *Financial support:* In 2019–20, 82 students received support, including 109 research assistantships with partial tuition reimbursements available (averaging $3,657 per year), 42 teaching assistantships with partial tuition reimbursements available (averaging $4,705 per year); career-related internships or fieldwork, Federal Work-Study, institutionally sponsored loans, scholarships/grants, health care benefits, and unspecified assistantships also available. Financial award application deadline: 5/1; financial award applicants required to submit FAFSA. In 2019, 527 master's, 64 doctorates awarded. *Program availability:* Part-time, evening/weekend, 100% online, blended/hybrid learning. *Application deadline:* For fall admission, 6/1 priority date for international students; for spring admission, 10/15 priority date for international students; for summer admission, 3/15 priority date for international students. Applications are processed on a rolling basis. *Application fee:* $50 ($75 for international students). Electronic applications accepted. *Application Contact:* Dayla Burgin, Graduate Student Services Coordinator, 903-886-5134, E-mail: dayla.burgin@tamuc.edu. *Dean,* Dr. Kimberly McLeod, 903-886-5181, Fax: 903-886-5905, E-mail: kimberly.mcleod@tamuc.edu.

**College of Humanities, Social Sciences and Arts** Students: 34 full-time (21 women), 427 part-time (302 women); includes 175 minority (66 Black or African American, non-Hispanic/Latino; 1 American Indian or Alaska Native, non-Hispanic/Latino; 13 Asian, non-Hispanic/Latino; 79 Hispanic/Latino; 16 Two or more races, non-Hispanic/Latino), 15 international. Average age 38. 193 applicants, 49% accepted, 78 enrolled. *Faculty:* 49 full-time (28 women), 8 part-time/adjunct (2 women). Expenses: Contact institution. *Financial support:* In 2019–20, 30 students received support, including 18 research assistantships with partial tuition reimbursements available (averaging $3,231 per year), 136 teaching assistantships with partial tuition reimbursements available (averaging $4,053 per year); Federal Work-Study, institutionally sponsored loans, scholarships/grants, health care benefits, and unspecified assistantships also available. Financial award application deadline: 5/1; financial award applicants required to submit FAFSA. In 2019, 122 master's, 6 doctorates awarded. *Program availability:* Part-time. *Application deadline:* For fall admission, 6/1 priority date for international students; for spring admission, 10/15 priority date for international students; for summer admission, 3/15 priority date for international students. Applications are processed on a rolling basis. *Application fee:* $50 ($75 for international students). Electronic applications accepted. *Application Contact:* Rebecca Stevens, Graduate Student Services Coordinator, 903-468-6049, E-mail: rebecca.stevens@tamuc.edu. *Interim Dean,* Dr. William F. Kuracina, 903-886-5166, Fax: 903-886-5774, E-mail: william.kuracina@tamuc.edu.

**College of Innovation and Design** Expenses: Contact institution. *Application Contact:* Kimberly Stringer, Graduate Liaison, 903-468-3066, E-mail: kimberly.stringer@tamuc.edu.

**College of Science and Engineering** Students: 118 full-time (53 women), 197 part-time (86 women); includes 71 minority (18 Black or African American, non-Hispanic/Latino; 1 American Indian or Alaska Native, non-Hispanic/Latino; 12 Asian, non-Hispanic/Latino; 32 Hispanic/Latino; 8 Two or more races, non-Hispanic/Latino), 118 international. Average age 31. 303 applicants, 70% accepted, 99 enrolled. *Faculty:* 38 full-time (7 women), 6 part-time/adjunct (0 women). Expenses: Contact institution. *Financial support:* In 2019–20, 56 students received support, including 47 research assistantships with partial tuition reimbursements available (averaging $3,080 per year), 130 teaching assistantships with partial tuition reimbursements available (averaging $3,359 per year); scholarships/grants, health care benefits, and unspecified assistantships also available. Financial award application deadline: 5/1; financial award applicants required to submit FAFSA. In 2019, 226 master's awarded. *Program availability:* Part-time. *Application deadline:* For fall admission, 6/1 priority date for international students; for spring admission, 10/15 priority date for international students; for summer admission, 3/15 priority date for international students. Applications are processed on a rolling basis. *Application fee:* $50 ($75 for international students). Electronic applications accepted. *Application Contact:* Dayla Burgin, Graduate Student Services Coordinator, 903-886-5134, E-mail: dayla.burgin@tamuc.edu. *Dean,* Dr. Brent L. Donham, 903-886-5321, Fax: 903-886-5199, E-mail: brent.donham@tamuc.edu.

## TEXAS A&M UNIVERSITY–CORPUS CHRISTI, Corpus Christi, TX 78412

**General Information** State-supported, coed, university. CGS member. *Graduate housing:* Room and/or apartments available on a first-come, first-served basis to single students; on-campus housing not available to married students. Housing application deadline: 5/1.

**GRADUATE UNITS**

**College of Graduate Studies** *Program availability:* Part-time, evening/weekend, 100% online, blended/hybrid learning. Electronic applications accepted.

***College of Business*** *Program availability:* Part-time, evening/weekend, 100% online, blended/hybrid learning. Electronic applications accepted.

***College of Education and Human Development*** *Program availability:* Part-time, evening/weekend, blended/hybrid learning. Electronic applications accepted.

***College of Liberal Arts*** *Program availability:* Part-time, evening/weekend. Electronic applications accepted.

***College of Nursing and Health Sciences*** *Program availability:* Part-time, evening/weekend, online only, 100% online. Electronic applications accepted.

***College of Science and Engineering*** *Program availability:* Part-time, evening/weekend. Electronic applications accepted.

## TEXAS A&M UNIVERSITY–KINGSVILLE, Kingsville, TX 78363

**General Information** State-supported, coed, university. *Graduate housing:* Room and/or apartments available on a first-come, first-served basis to single students; on-campus housing not available to married students. Housing application deadline: 8/1. *Research affiliation:* American Chemical Society (chemistry: the use of terminally-functionalized atactic-polypropylene oligomers as supports for catalysis), Texas Citrus Producers Board (agriculture: citrus center grapefruit research), ExxonMobil, East Wildlife Foundation (agriculture: bird populations, deer research), The Brown Foundation (agriculture: invasive grass research), Wildlife Pharmaceuticals, Inc. (agriculture: deer).

**GRADUATE UNITS**

**College of Graduate Studies** *Program availability:* Part-time, online learning. Electronic applications accepted.

***College of Arts and Sciences*** Electronic applications accepted.

***College of Business Administration*** *Program availability:* Online only, 100% online, blended/hybrid learning. Electronic applications accepted.

***College of Education and Human Performance*** *Program availability:* 100% online, blended/hybrid learning. Electronic applications accepted.

***Dick and Mary Lewis Kleberg College of Agriculture, Natural Resources and Human Sciences*** Electronic applications accepted.

***Frank H. Dotterweich College of Engineering*** Electronic applications accepted.

## TEXAS A&M UNIVERSITY–SAN ANTONIO, San Antonio, TX 78224

**General Information** State-supported, coed, comprehensive institution. *Enrollment by degree level:* 666 master's. *Graduate faculty:* 92 full-time (40 women), 12 part-time/adjunct (7 women). *Tuition, area resident:* Full-time $3822; part-time $1068 per semester. *Required fees:* $2146; $1412 per unit. $706 per semester. *Graduate housing:* Room and/or apartments available on a first-come, first-served basis to single students; on-campus housing not available to married students. Typical cost: $7393 per year. Room charges vary according to housing facility selected. *Student services:* Campus employment opportunities, campus safety program, career counseling, exercise/wellness program, free psychological counseling, services for students with disabilities, teacher training, writing training.
Website: http://www.tamusa.edu/

**GRADUATE UNITS**

**Department of Counseling, Health and Kinesiology** *Program availability:* Part-time, evening/weekend, online learning. Electronic applications accepted.

**Department of Educator and Leadership Preparation** *Program availability:* Part-time, evening/weekend, online learning. Electronic applications accepted.

**School of Arts and Sciences** *Program availability:* Part-time, evening/weekend, online learning. Electronic applications accepted.

**School of Business** *Program availability:* Part-time, evening/weekend, online learning. Electronic applications accepted.

## TEXAS A&M UNIVERSITY–TEXARKANA, Texarkana, TX 75503

**General Information** State-supported, coed, comprehensive institution. *Graduate housing:* On-campus housing not available.

**GRADUATE UNITS**

**Graduate Studies and Research** *Program availability:* Part-time, evening/weekend. Electronic applications accepted.

***College of Business*** *Program availability:* Part-time, evening/weekend. Electronic applications accepted.

***College of Education and Liberal Arts*** *Program availability:* Part-time, evening/weekend. Electronic applications accepted.

***College of Health and Behavioral Sciences*** *Program availability:* Part-time, evening/weekend. Electronic applications accepted.

## TEXAS CHIROPRACTIC COLLEGE, Pasadena, TX 77505-1699

**General Information** Independent, coed, graduate-only institution. *Graduate housing:* On-campus housing not available.

**GRADUATE UNITS**

**Professional Program**

## TEXAS CHRISTIAN UNIVERSITY, Fort Worth, TX 76129-0002

**General Information** Independent-religious, coed, university. CGS member. *Enrollment:* 11,024 graduate, professional, and undergraduate students; 1,344 full-time matriculated graduate/professional students (762 women), 134 part-time matriculated graduate/professional students (85 women). *Enrollment by degree level:* 900 master's, 23 doctoral, 50 other advanced degrees. *Graduate faculty:* 430 full-time (193 women), 105 part-time/adjunct (41 women). Full-time tuition and fees vary according to program. *Graduate housing:* Rooms and/or apartments available on a first-come, first-served basis to single and married students. Typical cost: $7705 per year for single students; $15,428 per year for married students. Room charges vary according to housing facility selected. Housing application deadline: 5/1. *Student services:* Campus employment opportunities, campus safety program, career counseling, exercise/wellness program, free psychological counseling, international student services, low-cost health insurance, multicultural affairs office, services for students with disabilities, teacher training, writing training. *Library facilities:* Mary Couts Burnett Library. *Collection:* Books: 1.4 million (physical), 1.4 million (digital/electronic); Serial titles: 11,084 (physical), 154,528 (digital/electronic); Databases: 598. Weekly public service hours: 139; study areas open 24 hours, 5–7 days a week; students can reserve study rooms. *Research affiliation:* Lockheed Martin Corporation (business), Botanical Research Institute of Texas, Inc. (biology, environmental science, ranch management), The University of Texas Southwestern Medical School (health sciences), NextEra (environmental science, wind energy), University of North Texas Health Science Center at Fort Worth (physics, biology), Bell Helicopter (engineering).

**Computer facilities:** 1,400 computers available on campus for general student use. A campuswide network can be accessed. Online class registration is available.
Website: http://www.tcu.edu/

**General Application Contact:** Anita Unger, Admissions, TCU Graduate Studies Office, 817-257-7515, Fax: 817-257-7484, E-mail: frogmail@tcu.edu.

**GRADUATE UNITS**

**AddRan College of Liberal Arts** Students: 205 full-time (99 women), 35 part-time (28 women); includes 79 minority (24 Black or African American, non-Hispanic/Latino; 1 American Indian or Alaska Native, non-Hispanic/Latino; 1 Asian, non-Hispanic/Latino; 44 Hispanic/Latino; 2 Native Hawaiian or other Pacific Islander, non-Hispanic/Latino; 7 Two or more races, non-Hispanic/Latino), 9 international. Average age 33. 162 applicants, 84% accepted, 93 enrolled. *Faculty:* 62 full-time (27 women), 7 part-time/adjunct (1 woman). Expenses: Contact institution. *Financial support:* Fellowships, research assistantships, teaching assistantships, career-related internships or fieldwork, Federal Work-Study, institutionally sponsored loans, traineeships, health care benefits, tuition waivers, and unspecified assistantships available. Support available to part-time students. In 2019, 50 master's, 9 doctorates awarded. *Application Contact:* Admissions, TCU Graduate Studies Office, 817-257-7515, Fax: 817-257-7484, E-mail: frogmail@tcu.edu. *Associate Dean,* Dr. Don M. Coerver, 817-257-6290, Fax: 817-257-7709, E-mail: d.coerver@tcu.edu.

**Bob Schieffer College of Communication** Students: 35 full-time (25 women); includes 6 minority (2 Black or African American, non-Hispanic/Latino; 3 Hispanic/Latino; 1 Native Hawaiian or other Pacific Islander, non-Hispanic/Latino), 3 international. Average age 25. 36 applicants, 78% accepted, 21 enrolled. *Faculty:* 27 full-time (13 women). Expenses: Contact institution. *Financial support:* In 2019–20, 23 students received support, including 20 teaching assistantships with full tuition reimbursements available (averaging $12,500 per year); health care benefits, tuition waivers (full and partial), and unspecified assistantships also available. Financial award application deadline: 2/15. In 2019, 12 master's awarded. *Program availability:* Part-time. *Application deadline:* For fall admission, 2/15 for domestic and international students; for spring admission, 10/15 for domestic and international students. Applications are processed on a rolling basis. *Application fee:* $60. Electronic applications accepted. *Application Contact:* Ashley Tully, Coordinator of Degree of Certification, 817-257-4935, Fax: 817-257-5921, E-mail: A.TULLY@tcu.edu. *Associate Dean,* Dr. Julie O'Neil, 817-257-6966, Fax: 817-257-5921, E-mail: j.oneil@tcu.edu.

**College of Education** Students: 210 full-time (159 women), 36 part-time (25 women); includes 86 minority (35 Black or African American, non-Hispanic/Latino; 1 American Indian or Alaska Native, non-Hispanic/Latino; 7 Asian, non-Hispanic/Latino; 36 Hispanic/Latino; 7 Two or more races, non-Hispanic/Latino), 8 international. Average age 32. 220 applicants, 79% accepted, 97 enrolled. *Faculty:* 30 full-time (22 women), 10 part-time/adjunct (6 women). Expenses: Contact institution. *Financial support:* In 2019–20, 201 students received support, including 1 fellowship with full tuition reimbursement available (averaging $18,500 per year), 9 research assistantships with full tuition reimbursements available (averaging $18,500 per year), 39 teaching assistantships with full tuition reimbursements available (averaging $15,000 per year); career-related internships or fieldwork, scholarships/grants, health care benefits, and unspecified assistantships also available. Support available to part-time students. Financial award application deadline: 2/1. In 2019, 84 master's, 14 doctorates awarded. *Program availability:* Part-time, evening/weekend. *Application deadline:* For fall admission, 2/1 for domestic and international students; for spring admission, 11/16 for domestic and international students; for summer admission, 2/1 for domestic and international students. *Application fee:* $60. Electronic applications accepted. *Application Contact:* Lori Kimball, Graduate Coordinator, 817-257-7661, Fax: 817-257-7466, E-mail: l.kimball@tcu.edu. *Interim Dean,* Dr. Jan Lacina, 817-257-6786, Fax: 817-257-7466, E-mail: j.lacina@tcu.edu.

**College of Fine Arts** Students: 76 full-time (36 women), 5 part-time (2 women); includes 14 minority (1 Black or African American, non-Hispanic/Latino; 2 Asian, non-Hispanic/Latino; 9 Hispanic/Latino; 2 Two or more races, non-Hispanic/Latino), 28 international. Average age 27. 132 applicants, 34% accepted, 31 enrolled. *Faculty:* 62 full-time (20 women), 16 part-time/adjunct (7 women). Expenses: Contact institution. *Financial support:* In 2019–20, 66 students received support, including 88 teaching assistantships with full tuition reimbursements available (averaging $34,120 per year); career-related internships or fieldwork, scholarships/grants, health care benefits, tuition waivers (full and partial), and unspecified assistantships also available. Financial award application deadline: 2/15. In 2019, 30 master's, 7 doctorates awarded. *Application deadline:* For fall admission, 2/1 for domestic and international students; for spring admission, 10/1 for domestic and international students. *Application fee:* $60. Electronic applications accepted. *Application Contact:* Donna Smolik, TCU College of Fine Arts Graduate Office, 817-257-7603, Fax: 817-257-5672, E-mail: cfagradinfo@tcu.edu. *Associate Dean, College of Fine Arts,* Dr. H. Joseph Butler, 817-257-7603, Fax: 817-257-5672, E-mail: cfagradinfo@tcu.edu.

***School of Art*** Students: 21 full-time (13 women); includes 6 minority (2 Asian, non-Hispanic/Latino; 4 Hispanic/Latino), 2 international. Average age 27. 36 applicants, 31% accepted, 9 enrolled. *Faculty:* 12 full-time (6 women), 2 part-time/adjunct (1 woman). Expenses: Contact institution. *Financial support:* In 2019–20, 21 students received support, including 21 teaching assistantships (averaging $10,000 per year); institutionally sponsored loans, scholarships/grants, health care benefits, tuition waivers (full and partial), and unspecified assistantships also available. Financial award application deadline: 2/1. In 2019, 9 master's awarded. *Application deadline:* For fall admission, 2/1 for domestic and international students. *Application fee:* $60. Electronic applications accepted. *Application Contact:* Donna Smolik, TCU College of Fine Arts Graduate Office, 817-257-7603, Fax: 817-257-5672, E-mail: cfagradinfo@tcu.edu. *Director,* Richard Lane, 817-257-7643, E-mail: r.lane@tcu.edu.

***School of Music*** Students: 55 full-time (23 women), 5 part-time (2 women); includes 8 minority (1 Black or African American, non-Hispanic/Latino; 5 Hispanic/Latino; 2 Two or more races, non-Hispanic/Latino), 26 international. Average age 27. 101 applicants, 39% accepted, 27 enrolled. *Faculty:* 44 full-time (10 women), 14 part-time/adjunct (6 women). Expenses: Contact institution. *Financial support:* In 2019–20, 84 students received support, including 54 research assistantships with full tuition reimbursements available (averaging $9,000 per year); career-related internships or fieldwork, institutionally sponsored loans, scholarships/grants, tuition waivers (full and partial), and unspecified assistantships also available. Financial award application deadline: 12/1; financial award applicants required to submit CSS PROFILE or FAFSA. In 2019, 21 master's, 7 doctorates awarded. *Application deadline:* For fall admission, 12/1 for domestic and international students; for spring admission, 9/1 for domestic and international students. *Application fee:* $60. Electronic applications accepted. *Application Contact:* Dr. Joseph Butler, Associate Dean, College of Fine Arts, 817-257-6629, E-mail: h.j.butler@tcu.edu. *Director,* Dr. Richard C. Gipson, 817-257-7602, E-mail: r.gipson@tcu.edu.

**College of Science and Engineering** Average age 27. 179 applicants, 40% accepted, 49 enrolled. Expenses: Contact institution. *Financial support:* In 2019–20, 135 students received support, including 5 fellowships with full tuition reimbursements available (averaging $21,000 per year), 9 research assistantships with full tuition reimbursements available (averaging $21,000 per year), 94 teaching assistantships with full tuition reimbursements available (averaging $20,000 per year); health care benefits, tuition waivers (full and partial), and unspecified assistantships also available. Support available to part-time students. Financial award application deadline: 1/1. In 2019, 47 master's, 16 doctorates awarded. *Program availability:* Part-time. *Application deadline:* For fall admission, 1/1 priority date for domestic and international students; for spring admission, 9/15 priority date for domestic and international students. Applications are processed on a rolling basis. *Application fee:* $60. Electronic applications accepted. *Application Contact:* Sue Dolce, Director of Degree Certification, 817-257-7734, Fax: 817-257-7736, E-mail: s.dolce@tcu.edu. *Senior Associate Dean for Administration and Graduate Programs,* Dr. Magnus Rittby, 817-257-7729, Fax: 817-257-7736, E-mail: m.rittby@tcu.edu.

**Harris College of Nursing and Health Sciences** Students: 345 full-time (259 women), 25 part-time (19 women); includes 96 minority (18 Black or African American, non-Hispanic/Latino; 2 American Indian or Alaska Native, non-Hispanic/Latino; 25 Asian, non-Hispanic/Latino; 40 Hispanic/Latino; 11 Two or more races, non-Hispanic/Latino), 6 international. Average age 31. 628 applicants, 33% accepted, 163 enrolled. *Faculty:* 66 full-time (53 women), 5 part-time/adjunct (2 women). Expenses: Contact institution. *Financial support:* Application deadline: 5/1; applicants required to submit FAFSA. In 2019, 63 master's, 77 doctorates, 12 other advanced degrees awarded. *Program availability:* Part-time, 100% online, blended/hybrid learning. *Application fee:* $60. Electronic applications accepted. *Application Contact:* Debbie Rhea, Associate Dean, 817-257-5263, E-mail: d.rhea@tcu.edu. *Interim Dean,* Dr. Suzy Lockwood, 817-257-6749, E-mail: s.lockwood@tcu.edu.

***Davies School of Communication Sciences and Disorders*** Students: 42 full-time (40 women); includes 11 minority (2 Asian, non-Hispanic/Latino; 8 Hispanic/Latino; 1 Two or more races, non-Hispanic/Latino), 2 international. Average age 24. 212 applicants, 10% accepted, 20 enrolled. *Faculty:* 9 full-time (8 women), 1 part-time/adjunct. Expenses: Contact institution. *Financial support:* In 2019–20, 40 students received support, including 40 research assistantships (averaging $35,000 per year); tuition waivers (partial) and unspecified assistantships also available. Financial award application deadline: 1/15; financial award applicants required to submit FAFSA. In 2019, 19 master's awarded. *Application deadline:* For fall admission, 1/15 for domestic and international students. *Application fee:* $60. Electronic applications accepted. *Application Contact:* Janet Schwartz, Administrative Assistant, 817-257-7620, E-mail: janet.schwartz@tcu.edu. *Director,* Dr. Christopher Watts, 817-257-7620, E-mail: c.watts@tcu.edu.

***School of Nurse Anesthesia*** Students: 208 full-time (135 women); includes 53 minority (7 Black or African American, non-Hispanic/Latino; 1 American Indian or Alaska Native, non-Hispanic/Latino; 19 Asian, non-Hispanic/Latino; 19 Hispanic/Latino; 7 Two or more races, non-Hispanic/Latino). Average age 31. 304 applicants, 35% accepted, 89 enrolled. *Faculty:* 11 full-time (6 women), 2 part-time/adjunct (1 woman). Expenses: Contact institution. *Financial support:* In 2019–20, 3 students received support. Scholarships/grants available. Financial award application deadline: 7/1; financial award applicants required to submit FAFSA. In 2019, 50 doctorates awarded. *Application deadline:* For fall and spring admission, 7/1 for domestic and international students. Applications are processed on a rolling basis. *Application fee:* $70. Electronic applications accepted. *Application Contact:* Kimberly Bowen, Administrative Assistant, 817-257-7887, Fax: 817-257-5472, E-mail: k.k.bowen@tcu.edu. *Director,* Dr. Robyn Ward, 817-257-7887, Fax: 817-257-5472, E-mail: r.ward@tcu.edu.

**Master of Liberal Arts Program** Students: 81 full-time (33 women), 30 part-time (22 women); includes 37 minority (21 Black or African American, non-Hispanic/Latino; 2 American Indian or Alaska Native, non-Hispanic/Latino; 8 Hispanic/Latino; 1 Native Hawaiian or other Pacific Islander, non-Hispanic/Latino; 5 Two or more races, non-Hispanic/Latino), 3 international. Average age 32. 85 applicants, 93% accepted, 57 enrolled. *Faculty:* 5 part-time/adjunct (0 women). Expenses: Contact institution. *Financial support:* In 2019–20, 55 students received support. Scholarships/grants, unspecified assistantships, and employee tuition benefits available. Financial award applicants required to submit FAFSA. In 2019, 33 master's awarded. *Program availability:* Part-time, evening/weekend, 100% online. *Application deadline:* For fall admission, 8/15 for domestic students, 6/1 for international students; for spring admission, 1/15 for domestic students, 11/1 for international students. Applications are processed on a rolling basis. *Application fee:* $60. Electronic applications accepted. *Application Contact:* Ellen Irwin, Administrative Assistant, 817-257-7160, Fax: 817-257-7709, E-mail: e.irwin@tcu.edu. *Associate Dean, AddRan College of Liberal Arts,* Dr. Peter Worthing, 817-257-6656, E-mail: p.worthing@tcu.edu.

**Neeley School of Business** Students: 342 full-time (113 women), 32 part-time (10 women); includes 63 minority (21 Black or African American, non-Hispanic/Latino; 1 American Indian or Alaska Native, non-Hispanic/Latino; 9 Asian, non-Hispanic/Latino; 30 Hispanic/Latino; 2 Two or more races, non-Hispanic/Latino), 24 international. Average age 30. 313 applicants, 95% accepted, 206 enrolled. *Faculty:* 77 full-time (24 women), 13 part-time/adjunct (3 women). Expenses: Contact institution. *Financial support:* Career-related internships or fieldwork, scholarships/grants, and unspecified assistantships available. Financial award application deadline: 4/5; financial award applicants required to submit FAFSA. In 2019, 184 master's awarded. *Program availability:* Part-time, evening/weekend. *Application deadline:* For fall admission, 10/15 priority date for domestic and international students. Applications are processed on a rolling basis. *Application fee:* $100. Electronic applications accepted. *Application Contact:* Graduate Programs Admissions Office, 817-257-7531, E-mail: mbainfo@tcu.edu. *Associate Dean Graduate Programs,* Dr. David Allen, 817-257-7535, E-mail: david.allen@tcu.edu.

## TEXAS HEALTH AND SCIENCE UNIVERSITY, Austin, TX 78704

**General Information** Private, coed, graduate-only institution. *Enrollment by degree level:* 80 master's, 8 doctoral. *Graduate faculty:* 7 full-time (3 women), 2 part-time/adjunct (1 woman). *Tuition:* Full-time $11,780; part-time $3440 per credit. *Required fees:* $292; $146 per credit. $220 per trimester. One-time fee: $72. Tuition and fees vary according to course load and program. *Graduate housing:* On-campus housing not available. *Student services:* Campus employment opportunities, campus safety program, career counseling, international student services, multicultural affairs office, services for students with disabilities. *Library facilities:* Texas Health and Science University Library. *Collection:* Books: 4,202 (physical), 50 (digital/electronic); Serial titles: 41 (physical), 6,300 (digital/electronic); Databases: 4.

**Computer facilities:** 5 computers available on campus for general student use. Online class registration is available.
Website: http://www.thsu.edu/

**General Application Contact:** Alexis Sanftner, Admissions Officer, 512-444-8082, Fax: 512-444-6345, E-mail: admissions@thsu.edu.

**GRADUATE UNITS**

**Graduate Programs** Electronic applications accepted.

## TEXAS LUTHERAN UNIVERSITY, Seguin, TX 78155-5999

**General Information** Independent-religious, coed, comprehensive institution. *Enrollment:* 1,476 graduate, professional, and undergraduate students; 26 full-time matriculated graduate/professional students (11 women), 5 part-time matriculated graduate/professional students (3 women). *Enrollment by degree level:* 31 master's. *Tuition:* Full-time $30,550; part-time $1010 per credit hour. *Required fees:* $310; $310. *Graduate housing:* Rooms and/or apartments available to single students and available on a first-come, first-served basis to married students. Typical cost: $10,440 (including board) for single students; $10,440 (including board) for married students. Room and board charges vary according to board plan and housing facility selected. *Student services:* Campus employment opportunities, career counseling, exercise/wellness program, free psychological counseling, services for students with disabilities. *Library facilities:* Blumberg Memorial Library plus 1 other. *Collection:* Weekly public service hours: 86; students can reserve study rooms.

**Computer facilities:** A campuswide network can be accessed. Online class registration, free printing are available.
Website: http://www.tlu.edu/

**General Application Contact:** Alecia McCain, Director Admissions Recruiting, 830-372-6078, E-mail: amccain@tlu.edu.

**GRADUATE UNITS**

**Program in Accounting** Expenses: Contact institution. *Application Contact:* Fern Garza, Department Chair, 830-372-6096, E-mail: fgarza@tlu.edu. *Department Chair,* Fern Garza, 830-372-6096, E-mail: fgarza@tlu.edu.

## TEXAS SOUTHERN UNIVERSITY, Houston, TX 77004-4584

**General Information** State-supported, coed, university. CGS member. *Graduate housing:* Room and/or apartments available on a first-come, first-served basis to single students; on-campus housing not available to married students. Housing application deadline: 7/15. *Research affiliation:* Environmental Research and Technology Transfer Center (chemistry and environmental toxicology), Institute for International and Immigration Law/Center on Legal Pedagogy (law), Innovative Transportation Research Institute (transportation planning and management), NASA University Research Biotechnology & Environmental Health (biology), Economic Development Center/JP Chase Center for Financial Education (business), Gerald B. Smith Center for Entrepreneurship and Executive Development (business, urban planning and environmental policy).

**GRADUATE UNITS**

**Barbara Jordan-Mickey Leland School of Public Affairs** *Program availability:* Part-time. Electronic applications accepted.

**College of Education** *Program availability:* Part-time, evening/weekend. Electronic applications accepted.

**College of Liberal Arts and Behavioral Sciences** *Program availability:* Part-time, evening/weekend. Electronic applications accepted.

**College of Pharmacy and Health Sciences** *Program availability:* Online learning. Electronic applications accepted.

**Jesse H. Jones School of Business** *Program availability:* Part-time, evening/weekend. Electronic applications accepted.

**School of Science and Technology** *Program availability:* Part-time, evening/weekend. Electronic applications accepted.

**Tavis Smiley School of Communication** *Program availability:* Part-time. Electronic applications accepted.

**Thurgood Marshall School of Law** Electronic applications accepted.

## TEXAS STATE UNIVERSITY, San Marcos, TX 78666

**General Information** State-supported, coed, university. CGS member. *Graduate housing:* Room and/or apartments available on a first-come, first-served basis to single students; on-campus housing not available to married students. Housing application deadline: 7/1. *Research affiliation:* The Ewing Halsell Foundation (education: improving STEM learning), NEC Corporation of America (high-speed data analysis), MicroPower Global Corporation (chip prototype development), Quantum Materials Corporation (material physics), Magellan Pipeline and Bridge (environmental conservation), National Fish and Wildlife Foundation (environmental conservation).

**GRADUATE UNITS**

**The Graduate College** Students: 2,268 full-time (1,493 women), 1,551 part-time (1,040 women); includes 1,478 minority (265 Black or African American, non-Hispanic/Latino; 3 American Indian or Alaska Native, non-Hispanic/Latino; 131 Asian, non-Hispanic/Latino; 983 Hispanic/Latino; 1 Native Hawaiian or other Pacific Islander, non-Hispanic/Latino; 95 Two or more races, non-Hispanic/Latino), 357 international. Average age 30. 4,617 applicants, 46% accepted, 1,354 enrolled. *Faculty:* 893 full-time (429 women), 115 part-time/adjunct (67 women). Expenses: Contact institution. *Financial support:* In 2019–20, 1,411 students received support, including 421 fellowships with partial tuition reimbursements available (averaging $292 per year), 200 research assistantships (averaging $17,675 per year), 792 teaching assistantships (averaging $15,674 per year); career-related internships or fieldwork, Federal Work-Study, institutionally sponsored loans, scholarships/grants, unspecified assistantships, and laboratory instructorships, stipends also available. Support available to part-time students. Financial award application deadline: 1/15; financial award applicants required to submit FAFSA. In 2019, 1,381 master's, 54 doctorates, 41 other advanced degrees awarded. *Program availability:* Part-time, evening/weekend, blended/hybrid learning. *Application deadline:* For fall admission, 1/15 for domestic students, 1/1 for international students; for spring admission, 10/15 for domestic students, 10/1 for international students. Applications are processed on a rolling basis. *Application fee:* $55 ($90 for international students). Electronic applications accepted. *Application Contact:* Dr. Andrea Golato, Dean of Graduate School, 512-245-2581, Fax: 512-245-8365, E-mail: gradcollege@txstate.edu. *Dean,* Dr. Andrea Golato, 512-245-2581, Fax: 512-245-8365, E-mail: gradcollege@txstate.edu.

**College of Applied Arts** Students: 314 full-time (253 women), 231 part-time (170 women); includes 262 minority (59 Black or African American, non-Hispanic/Latino; 1 American Indian or Alaska Native, non-Hispanic/Latino; 12 Asian, non-Hispanic/Latino; 175 Hispanic/Latino; 15 Two or more races, non-Hispanic/Latino), 10 international. Average age 31. 563 applicants, 54% accepted, 226 enrolled. *Faculty:* 87 full-time (50 women), 17 part-time/adjunct (13 women). Expenses: Contact institution. *Financial support:* In 2019–20, 249 students received support, including 37 fellowships with partial tuition reimbursements available (averaging $233 per year), 43 research assistantships (averaging $13,898 per year), 46 teaching assistantships (averaging $16,893 per year); career-related internships or fieldwork, Federal Work-Study, scholarships/grants, and unspecified assistantships also available. Support available to part-time students. Financial award application deadline: 1/15; financial award applicants required to submit FAFSA. In 2019, 259 master's, 2 doctorates awarded. *Program availability:* Part-time, evening/weekend, blended/hybrid learning. *Application deadline:* For fall admission, 2/1 priority date for domestic and international students; for spring admission, 10/15 priority date for domestic students, 10/1 for international students. Applications are processed on a rolling basis. *Application fee:* $55 ($90 for international students). Electronic applications accepted. *Application Contact:* Dr. Andrea Golato, Dean of Graduate School, 512-245-2581, Fax: 512-245-8365, E-mail: gradcollege@txstate.edu. *Dean,* Dr. T. Jaime Chahin, 512-245-3333, Fax: 512-245-3338, E-mail: tc03@txstate.edu.

**College of Education** Students: 525 full-time (407 women), 508 part-time (401 women); includes 446 minority (88 Black or African American, non-Hispanic/Latino; 1 American Indian or Alaska Native, non-Hispanic/Latino; 33 Asian, non-Hispanic/Latino; 303 Hispanic/Latino; 21 Two or more races, non-Hispanic/Latino), 29 international. Average age 31. 1,010 applicants, 55% accepted, 356 enrolled. *Faculty:* 118 full-time (79 women), 33 part-time/adjunct (25 women). Expenses: Contact institution. *Financial support:* In 2019–20, 339 students received support, including 16 fellowships with partial tuition reimbursements available (averaging $331 per year), 68 research assistantships (averaging $19,397 per year), 69 teaching assistantships (averaging $14,475 per year); career-related internships or fieldwork, Federal Work-Study, institutionally sponsored loans, and scholarships/grants also available. Support available to part-time students. Financial award application deadline: 1/15; financial award applicants required to submit FAFSA. In 2019, 409 master's, 30 doctorates awarded. *Program availability:* Part-time, evening/weekend. *Application deadline:* For fall admission, 1/15 priority date for domestic and international students; for spring admission, 10/1 priority date for domestic and international students. Applications are processed on a rolling basis. *Application fee:* $55 ($90 for international students). Electronic applications accepted. *Application Contact:* Dr. Andrea Golato, Dean of Graduate School, 512-245-2581, Fax: 512-245-8365, E-mail: gradcollege@txstate.edu. *Dean,* Dr. Michael O'Malley, 512-245-2150, Fax: 512-245-3158, E-mail: mo20@txstate.edu.

**College of Fine Arts and Communication** Students: 140 full-time (77 women), 58 part-time (34 women); includes 82 minority (14 Black or African American, non-Hispanic/Latino; 2 Asian, non-Hispanic/Latino; 63 Hispanic/Latino; 3 Two or more races, non-Hispanic/Latino), 11 international. Average age 29. 208 applicants, 51% accepted, 76 enrolled. *Faculty:* 125 full-time (59 women), 12 part-time/adjunct (5 women). Expenses: Contact institution. *Financial support:* In 2019–20, 106 students received support, including 58 fellowships with partial tuition reimbursements available (averaging $249 per year), 3 research assistantships (averaging $14,608 per year), 99 teaching assistantships (averaging $12,102 per year); career-related internships or fieldwork, Federal Work-Study, institutionally sponsored loans, scholarships/grants, and unspecified assistantships also available. Support available to part-time students. Financial award application deadline: 1/15; financial award applicants required to submit FAFSA. In 2019, 75 master's awarded. *Program availability:* Part-time, evening/weekend. *Application deadline:* For fall admission, 2/1 priority date for domestic and international students; for spring admission, 10/15 for domestic students, 10/1 for international students; for summer admission, 4/15 for domestic students, 3/15 for international students. Applications are processed on a rolling basis. *Application fee:* $55 ($90 for international students). Electronic applications accepted. *Application Contact:* Dr. Andrea Golato, Dean of Graduate School, 512-245-2581, Fax: 512-245-8365, E-mail: gradcollege@txstate.edu. *Dean of the College of Fine Arts and Communication,* Dr. John Fleming, 512-245-2308, Fax: 512-245-8386, E-mail: jf18@txstate.edu.

**College of Health Professions** Students: 307 full-time (244 women), 110 part-time (84 women); includes 171 minority (45 Black or African American, non-Hispanic/Latino; 22 Asian, non-Hispanic/Latino; 93 Hispanic/Latino; 11 Two or more races, non-Hispanic/Latino), 6 international. Average age 29. 1,226 applicants, 24% accepted, 203 enrolled. *Faculty:* 67 full-time (44 women), 21 part-time/adjunct (13 women). Expenses: Contact institution. *Financial support:* In 2019–20, 175 students received support, including 2 fellowships with partial tuition reimbursements available (averaging $144 per year), 6 research assistantships (averaging $9,883 per year), 35 teaching assistantships (averaging $10,777 per year); career-related internships or fieldwork, Federal Work-Study, institutionally sponsored loans, scholarships/grants, unspecified assistantships, and stipends also available. Support available to part-time students. Financial award application deadline: 1/15; financial award applicants required to submit FAFSA. In 2019, 109 master's awarded. *Program availability:* Part-time. *Application deadline:* For fall admission, 1/15 priority date for domestic and international students; for spring admission, 10/1 for domestic and international students; for summer admission, 10/1 for domestic students, 10/1 priority date for international students. Applications are processed on a rolling basis. *Application fee:* $55 ($90 for international students). Electronic applications accepted. *Application Contact:* Dr. Andrea Golato, Dean of Graduate School, 512-245-2581, Fax: 512-245-8365, E-mail: gradcollege@txstate.edu. *Dean,* Dr. Ruth Welborn, 512-245-3300, Fax: 512-245-3791, E-mail: rw01@txstate.edu.

**College of Liberal Arts** Students: 467 full-time (273 women), 324 part-time (203 women); includes 288 minority (35 Black or African American, non-Hispanic/Latino; 11 Asian, non-Hispanic/Latino; 210 Hispanic/Latino; 32 Two or more races, non-Hispanic/Latino), 39 international. Average age 31. 728 applicants, 50% accepted, 219 enrolled. *Faculty:* 236 full-time (111 women), 22 part-time/adjunct (9 women). Expenses: Contact institution. *Financial support:* In 2019–20, 300 students received support, including 142 fellowships with partial tuition reimbursements available (averaging $355 per year), 20 research assistantships (averaging $13,919 per year), 269 teaching assistantships (averaging $15,462 per year); career-related internships or fieldwork, Federal Work-Study, institutionally sponsored loans, scholarships/grants, and unspecified assistantships also available. Support available to part-time students. Financial award application deadline: 1/15; financial award applicants required to submit FAFSA. In 2019, 240 master's, 9 doctorates awarded. *Program availability:* Part-time, evening/weekend. *Application deadline:* For fall admission, 1/15 priority date for domestic students, 1/1 priority date for international students; for spring admission, 10/15 for domestic students, 10/1 for international students; for summer admission, 4/15 for domestic students, 3/15 for international students. Applications are processed on a rolling basis. *Application fee:* $55 ($90 for international students). Electronic applications accepted. *Application Contact:* Dr. Andrea Golato, Dean of Graduate School, 512-245-2581, Fax: 512-245-8365, E-mail: gradcollege@txstate.edu. *Dean,* Dr. Mary Brennan, 512-245-2317, Fax: 512-245-8291, E-mail: liberalarts@txstate.edu.

**College of Science and Engineering** Students: 382 full-time (177 women), 151 part-time (65 women); includes 115 minority (7 Black or African American, non-Hispanic/Latino; 26 Asian, non-Hispanic/Latino; 72 Hispanic/Latino; 10 Two or more races, non-Hispanic/Latino), 233 international. Average age 29. 590 applicants, 62% accepted, 172 enrolled. *Faculty:* 183 full-time (54 women), 5 part-time/adjunct (0 women). Expenses: Contact institution. *Financial support:* In 2019–20, 146 students received support, including 133 fellowships with partial tuition reimbursements available (averaging $174 per year), 60 research assistantships (averaging $20,615 per year), 246 teaching assistantships (averaging $18,383 per year); career-related internships or fieldwork, Federal Work-Study, institutionally sponsored loans, scholarships/grants, health care benefits, unspecified assistantships, and laboratory instructorships also available. Support available to part-time students. Financial award application deadline: 1/15; financial award applicants required to submit FAFSA. In 2019, 147 master's, 13 doctorates awarded. *Program availability:* Part-time, evening/weekend. *Application deadline:* For fall admission, 1/15 priority date for domestic and international students; for spring admission, 10/15 for domestic students, 10/1 for international students. Applications are processed on a rolling basis. *Application fee:* $55 ($90 for international students). Electronic applications accepted. *Application Contact:* Dr. Andrea Golato, Dean of Graduate School, 512-245-2581, Fax: 512-245-8365, E-mail: gradcollege@txstate.edu. *Dean,* Dr. Christine Hailey, 512-245-2119, Fax: 512-245-8095, E-mail: ceh138@txstate.edu.

**Emmett and Miriam McCoy College of Business Administration** Students: 133 full-time (62 women), 169 part-time (83 women); includes 114 minority (17 Black or African American, non-Hispanic/Latino; 1 American Indian or Alaska Native, non-Hispanic/Latino; 25 Asian, non-Hispanic/Latino; 67 Hispanic/Latino; 1 Native Hawaiian or other Pacific Islander, non-Hispanic/Latino; 3 Two or more races, non-Hispanic/Latino), 29 international. Average age 29. 291 applicants, 49% accepted, 102 enrolled. *Faculty:* 76 full-time (32 women), 3 part-time/adjunct. Expenses: Contact institution. *Financial support:* In 2019–20, 96 students received support, including 24 fellowships with partial tuition reimbursements available (averaging $742 per year), 28 teaching assistantships (averaging $13,620 per year); research assistantships, Federal Work-Study, institutionally sponsored loans, scholarships/grants, health care benefits, and unspecified assistantships also available. Support available to part-time students. Financial award application deadline: 1/15; financial award applicants required to submit FAFSA. In 2019, 142 master's awarded. *Program availability:* Part-time. *Application deadline:* For fall admission, 1/15 priority date for domestic and international students; for spring admission, 10/1 for domestic and international students; for summer admission, 4/1 for domestic students, 3/15 for international students. Applications are processed on a rolling basis. *Application fee:* $55 ($90 for international students). Electronic applications accepted. *Application Contact:* Dr. Andrea Golato, Dean of Graduate School, 512-245-2581, Fax: 512-245-8365, E-mail: gradcollege@txstate.edu. *Dean of the College of Business Administration,* Dr. Denise Smart, 512-245-2311, Fax: 512-245-8375, E-mail: businessgraduate@txstate.edu.

## TEXAS TECH UNIVERSITY, Lubbock, TX 79409

**General Information** State-supported, coed, university. CGS member. *Enrollment:* 38,742 graduate, professional, and undergraduate students; 4,035 full-time matriculated graduate/professional students (1,928 women), 2,295 part-time matriculated graduate/professional students (1,454 women). *Enrollment by degree level:* 3,365 master's, 2,965 doctoral. *Graduate faculty:* 1,571 full-time (640 women), 192 part-time/adjunct (95 women). Tuition, state resident: full-time $7944; part-time $331 per credit hour. Tuition, nonresident: full-time $17,904; part-time $746 per credit hour. *Required fees:* $2556; $55.50 per credit hour. $612 per semester. Tuition and fees vary according to program. *Graduate housing:* Room and/or apartments available on a first-come, first-served basis to single students; on-campus housing not available to married students. Typical cost: $6236 per year ($9772 including board). Room and board charges vary according to board plan and housing facility selected. *Student services:* Campus employment opportunities, campus safety program, career counseling, exercise/wellness program, free psychological counseling, grant writing training, international student services, low-cost health insurance, multicultural affairs office, services for students with disabilities, teacher training, writing training. *Library facilities:* Texas Tech Library plus 3 others. *Collection:* Books: 2.9 million (physical), 160,584 (digital/electronic); Serial titles: 1,464 (physical), 200,332 (digital/electronic); Databases:

405. Weekly public service hours: 146; study areas open 24 hours, 5–7 days a week; students can reserve study rooms. *Research affiliation:* U.S. Department of Education (DOE) (student achievement and preparation for global competitiveness), U.S. Department of Health and Human Services (advances in medicine, public health, and social sciences), U.S. Department of Defense (pulsed power and nanotechnology for defense applications), U.S. Department of Agriculture (USDA) (food safety, development and production in agriculture), U.S. Department of Energy (research and development in wind energy), Bill and Melinda Gates Foundation (education through innovation).

**Computer facilities:** Computer purchase and lease plans are available. 1,934 computers available on campus for general student use. A campuswide network can be accessed. Online class registration, online degree plans, accounts, transcripts, financial aid, course and instructor evaluations, scholarship applications and submissions are available.
Website: http://www.ttu.edu/

**General Application Contact:** Jade Foerster, Director of Admissions, 806-834-5332, Fax: 806-742-4038, E-mail: graduate.admissions@ttu.edu.

**GRADUATE UNITS**

**Graduate School** Students: 3,634 full-time (1,753 women), 2,292 part-time (1,453 women); includes 1,480 minority (317 Black or African American, non-Hispanic/Latino; 11 American Indian or Alaska Native, non-Hispanic/Latino; 149 Asian, non-Hispanic/Latino; 774 Hispanic/Latino; 3 Native Hawaiian or other Pacific Islander, non-Hispanic/Latino; 226 Two or more races, non-Hispanic/Latino), 1,398 international. Average age 31. 4,626 applicants, 59% accepted, 1,855 enrolled. *Faculty:* 1,535 full-time (625 women), 182 part-time/adjunct (92 women). Expenses: Contact institution. *Financial support:* In 2019–20, 4,550 students received support, including 4,098 fellowships (averaging $3,322 per year), 950 research assistantships (averaging $17,680 per year), 1,499 teaching assistantships (averaging $15,506 per year); career-related internships or fieldwork, Federal Work-Study, scholarships/grants, traineeships, health care benefits, and unspecified assistantships also available. Support available to part-time students. Financial award application deadline: 4/15; financial award applicants required to submit FAFSA. In 2019, 1,565 master's, 340 doctorates awarded. *Program availability:* Part-time, evening/weekend, 100% online, blended/hybrid learning. *Application deadline:* For fall admission, 6/1 priority date for domestic students, 1/15 priority date for international students; for spring admission, 9/1 priority date for domestic students, 6/15 priority date for international students. Applications are processed on a rolling basis. *Application fee:* $65. Electronic applications accepted. *Application Contact:* Jade Foerster, Director of Admissions, 806-742-2787, E-mail: graduate.admissions@ttu.edu. *Vice Provost for Graduate and Postdoctoral Affairs/Dean of the Graduate School*, Dr. Mark A. Sheridan, 806-834-5537, Fax: 806-742-1746, E-mail: mark.sheridan@ttu.edu.

***College of Agricultural Sciences and Natural Resources*** Students: 267 full-time (143 women), 130 part-time (75 women); includes 47 minority (6 Black or African American, non-Hispanic/Latino; 2 American Indian or Alaska Native, non-Hispanic/Latino; 5 Asian, non-Hispanic/Latino; 26 Hispanic/Latino; 8 Two or more races, non-Hispanic/Latino), 104 international. Average age 29. 186 applicants, 63% accepted, 90 enrolled. *Faculty:* 116 full-time (40 women), 18 part-time/adjunct (5 women). Expenses: Contact institution. *Financial support:* In 2019–20, 340 students received support, including 274 fellowships (averaging $3,550 per year), 238 research assistantships (averaging $14,408 per year), 27 teaching assistantships (averaging $17,179 per year); scholarships/grants, health care benefits, and unspecified assistantships also available. Support available to part-time students. Financial award application deadline: 4/15; financial award applicants required to submit FAFSA. In 2019, 102 master's, 41 doctorates awarded. *Program availability:* Part-time, 100% online, blended/hybrid learning. *Application deadline:* For fall admission, 6/1 priority date for domestic students, 1/15 priority date for international students; for spring admission, 9/1 priority date for domestic students, 6/15 priority date for international students. Applications are processed on a rolling basis. *Application fee:* $65. Electronic applications accepted. *Application Contact:* Dr. Cindy Akers, Associate Dean for Academic Programs, 806-834-4578, Fax: 806-742-2836, E-mail: cindy.akers@ttu.edu. *Dean*, Dr. William F. Brown, 806-742-2808, Fax: 806-742-2836, E-mail: william.f.brown@ttu.edu.

***College of Architecture*** Students: 67 full-time (30 women), 6 part-time (0 women); includes 38 minority (1 Black or African American, non-Hispanic/Latino; 36 Hispanic/Latino; 1 Two or more races, non-Hispanic/Latino), 6 international. Average age 25. 50 applicants, 72% accepted, 24 enrolled. *Faculty:* 35 full-time (13 women), 14 part-time/adjunct (4 women). Expenses: Contact institution. *Financial support:* In 2019–20, 73 students received support, including 56 fellowships (averaging $3,795 per year), 11 teaching assistantships (averaging $9,155 per year); research assistantships, career-related internships or fieldwork, Federal Work-Study, institutionally sponsored loans, scholarships/grants, traineeships, health care benefits, and unspecified assistantships also available. Support available to part-time students. Financial award application deadline: 2/1; financial award applicants required to submit FAFSA. In 2019, 41 master's awarded. *Program availability:* Part-time. *Application deadline:* For fall admission, 6/1 priority date for domestic students, 1/15 priority date for international students; for spring admission, 9/1 priority date for domestic students, 6/15 priority date for international students. Applications are processed on a rolling basis. *Application fee:* $65. Electronic applications accepted. *Application Contact:* Sarah Hatley, Unit Manager, College Advising, 806-834-5704, Fax: 806-742-1400, E-mail: sarah.hatley@ttu.edu. *Dean*, Prof. James P. Williamson, 806-742-3136, Fax: 806-742-1400, E-mail: james.p.williamson@ttu.edu.

***College of Arts and Sciences*** Students: 1,061 full-time (538 women), 259 part-time (161 women); includes 278 minority (38 Black or African American, non-Hispanic/Latino; 4 American Indian or Alaska Native, non-Hispanic/Latino; 32 Asian, non-Hispanic/Latino; 160 Hispanic/Latino; 2 Native Hawaiian or other Pacific Islander, non-Hispanic/Latino; 42 Two or more races, non-Hispanic/Latino), 413 international. Average age 30. 1,124 applicants, 47% accepted, 344 enrolled. *Faculty:* 509 full-time (185 women), 36 part-time/adjunct (21 women). Expenses: Contact institution. *Financial support:* In 2019–20, 1,149 students received support, including 981 fellowships (averaging $2,464 per year), 228 research assistantships (averaging $17,764 per year), 818 teaching assistantships (averaging $16,017 per year); career-related internships or fieldwork, Federal Work-Study, institutionally sponsored loans, scholarships/grants, traineeships, health care benefits, and unspecified assistantships also available. Support available to part-time students. Financial award application deadline: 12/1; financial award applicants required to submit FAFSA. In 2019, 241 master's, 87 doctorates awarded. *Program availability:* Part-time, evening/weekend, 100% online, blended/hybrid learning. *Application deadline:* For fall admission, 6/1 priority date for domestic students, 1/15 priority date for international students; for spring admission, 9/1 priority date for domestic students, 6/15 priority date for international students. Applications are processed on a rolling basis. *Application fee:* $65. Electronic applications accepted. *Application Contact:* Dr. Jorge Iber, Associate Dean, 806-834-5511, E-mail: jorge.iber@ttu.edu. *Dean*, Dr. W. Brent Lindquist, 806-742-3831, Fax: 806-742-3893, E-mail: brent.lindquist@ttu.edu.

***College of Education*** Students: 320 full-time (232 women), 995 part-time (785 women); includes 443 minority (121 Black or African American, non-Hispanic/Latino; 3 American Indian or Alaska Native, non-Hispanic/Latino; 20 Asian, non-Hispanic/Latino; 226 Hispanic/Latino; 1 Native Hawaiian or other Pacific Islander, non-Hispanic/Latino; 72 Two or more races, non-Hispanic/Latino), 59 international. Average age 37. 629 applicants, 75% accepted, 389 enrolled. *Faculty:* 161 full-time (109 women), 12 part-time/adjunct (10 women). Expenses: Contact institution. *Financial support:* In 2019–20, 784 students received support, including 772 fellowships (averaging $2,786 per year), 86 research assistantships (averaging $12,916 per year), 14 teaching assistantships (averaging $13,312 per year); career-related internships or fieldwork, Federal Work-Study, institutionally sponsored loans, scholarships/grants, traineeships, health care benefits, and unspecified assistantships also available. Support available to part-time students. Financial award application deadline: 2/1; financial award applicants required to submit FAFSA. In 2019, 271 master's, 52 doctorates awarded. *Program availability:* Part-time, evening/weekend. *Application deadline:* For fall admission, 6/1 priority date for domestic students, 1/15 priority date for international students; for spring admission, 9/1 priority date for domestic students, 6/15 priority date for international students. Applications are processed on a rolling basis. *Application fee:* $65. Electronic applications accepted. *Application Contact:* Beth Watson, Coordinator, 806-834-0429, Fax: 806-742-2179, E-mail: beth.watson@ttu.edu. *Dean*, Dr. Jesse Perez Mendez, 806-742-2377, Fax: 806-742-2179, E-mail: jp.mendez@ttu.edu.

***College of Human Sciences*** Students: 287 full-time (178 women), 208 part-time (137 women); includes 134 minority (24 Black or African American, non-Hispanic/Latino; 19 Asian, non-Hispanic/Latino; 68 Hispanic/Latino; 23 Two or more races, non-Hispanic/Latino), 84 international. Average age 31. 296 applicants, 62% accepted, 146 enrolled. *Faculty:* 109 full-time (70 women), 21 part-time/adjunct (15 women). Expenses: Contact institution. *Financial support:* In 2019–20, 334 students received support, including 314 fellowships (averaging $4,687 per year), 73 research assistantships (averaging $14,731 per year), 101 teaching assistantships (averaging $14,139 per year); career-related internships or fieldwork, institutionally sponsored loans, scholarships/grants, and unspecified assistantships also available. Support available to part-time students. Financial award application deadline: 1/15; financial award applicants required to submit FAFSA. In 2019, 132 master's, 38 doctorates awarded. *Program availability:* Part-time, 100% online, blended/hybrid learning. *Application deadline:* For fall admission, 6/1 priority date for domestic students, 1/15 priority date for international students; for spring admission, 9/1 priority date for domestic students, 6/15 priority date for international students. Applications are processed on a rolling basis. *Application fee:* $65. Electronic applications accepted. *Application Contact:* Prof. Mitzi Lauderdale, Associate Dean for Students, 806-834-0529, Fax: 806-742-1849, E-mail: mitzi.lauderdale@ttu.edu. *Interim Dean*, Dr. Tim Dodd, 806-742-3031, Fax: 806-742-1849, E-mail: tim.dodd@ttu.edu.

***College of Media and Communication*** Students: 124 full-time (78 women), 170 part-time (105 women); includes 73 minority (20 Black or African American, non-Hispanic/Latino; 6 Asian, non-Hispanic/Latino; 39 Hispanic/Latino; 8 Two or more races, non-Hispanic/Latino), 23 international. Average age 30. 187 applicants, 64% accepted, 98 enrolled. *Faculty:* 79 full-time (37 women), 14 part-time/adjunct (8 women). Expenses: Contact institution. *Financial support:* In 2019–20, 177 students received support, including 141 fellowships (averaging $4,028 per year), 17 research assistantships (averaging $13,600 per year), 98 teaching assistantships (averaging $11,902 per year); career-related internships or fieldwork, scholarships/grants, and unspecified assistantships also available. Support available to part-time students. Financial award application deadline: 4/15; financial award applicants required to submit FAFSA. In 2019, 109 master's, 6 doctorates awarded. *Program availability:* Part-time, evening/weekend, 100% online, blended/hybrid learning. *Application deadline:* For fall admission, 6/1 priority date for domestic students, 1/15 priority date for international students; for spring admission, 9/1 priority date for domestic students, 6/15 priority date for international students. Applications are processed on a rolling basis. *Application fee:* $65. Electronic applications accepted. *Application Contact:* Elaine Taylor, Graduate Program Administrative, 806-834-7064, Fax: 806-742-1085, E-mail: elaine.taylor@ttu.edu. *Professor and Associate Dean of Graduate Studies*, Dr. Coy Callison, 806-834-5344, E-mail: coy.callison@ttu.edu.

***Edward E. Whitacre Jr. College of Engineering*** Students: 640 full-time (175 women), 205 part-time (35 women); includes 117 minority (24 Black or African American, non-Hispanic/Latino; 27 Asian, non-Hispanic/Latino; 51 Hispanic/Latino; 15 Two or more races, non-Hispanic/Latino), 514 international. Average age 29. 1,036 applicants, 58% accepted, 241 enrolled. *Faculty:* 182 full-time (33 women), 20 part-time/adjunct (5 women). Expenses: Contact institution. *Financial support:* In 2019–20, 683 students received support, including 614 fellowships (averaging $3,437 per year), 268 research assistantships (averaging $23,055 per year), 129 teaching assistantships (averaging $22,516 per year); scholarships/grants, health care benefits, and unspecified assistantships also available. Financial award application deadline: 4/15; financial award applicants required to submit FAFSA. In 2019, 155 master's, 72 doctorates awarded. *Program availability:* Part-time, evening/weekend, 100% online, blended/hybrid learning. *Application deadline:* For fall admission, 6/1 priority date for domestic students, 1/15 priority date for international students; for spring admission, 9/1 priority date for domestic students, 6/15 priority date for international students. Applications are processed on a rolling basis. *Application fee:* $65. Electronic applications accepted. *Application Contact:* Dr. Brandon Weeks, Associate Dean of Research and Graduate Programs, Edward E. Whitacre Jr. College of Engineering, 806-834-7450, Fax: 806-742-3493, E-mail: brandon.weeks@ttu.edu. *Dean, Edward E. Whitacre Jr. College of Engineering*, Dr. Albert Sacco, Jr., 806-742-3451, Fax: 806-742-3493, E-mail: al.sacco-jr@ttu.edu.

***J.T. and Margaret Talkington College of Visual and Performing Arts*** Students: 235 full-time (115 women), 79 part-time (47 women); includes 61 minority (8 Black or African American, non-Hispanic/Latino; 5 Asian, non-Hispanic/Latino; 34 Hispanic/Latino; 14 Two or more races, non-Hispanic/Latino), 70 international. Average age 32. 243 applicants, 60% accepted, 98 enrolled. *Faculty:* 116 full-time (56 women), 16 part-time/adjunct (9 women). Expenses: Contact institution. *Financial support:* In 2019–20, 297 students received support, including 272 fellowships (averaging $3,607 per year), 10 research assistantships (averaging $15,464 per year), 214 teaching assistantships (averaging $10,837 per year); Federal Work-Study, institutionally sponsored loans, scholarships/grants, health care benefits, tuition waivers (partial), unspecified assistantships, and competitive grants to support graduate research also available. Financial award application deadline: 2/1; financial award applicants required to submit FAFSA. In 2019, 59 master's, 28 doctorates awarded. *Program availability:* Part-time. *Application deadline:* For fall admission, 6/1 priority date for domestic students, 1/15 priority date for international students; for spring admission, 9/1 priority date for domestic students, 6/15 priority date for international students. Applications are processed on a rolling basis. *Application fee:* $65. Electronic applications accepted. *Application Contact:* Shannon Samson, Coordinator of Graduate School Recruitment, 806-834-5201, Fax: 806-742-1746, E-mail: gradschool@ttu.edu. *Dean and Professor*, Dr. Noel Zahler, 806-742-0700, Fax: 806-742-0695, E-mail: noel.zahler@ttu.edu.

**Rawls College of Business Administration** Students: 505 full-time (209 women), 251 part-time (87 women); includes 239 minority (50 Black or African American, non-Hispanic/Latino; 2 American Indian or Alaska Native, non-Hispanic/Latino; 39 Asian, non-Hispanic/Latino; 112 Hispanic/Latino; 36 Two or more races, non-Hispanic/Latino), 96 international. Average age 28. 534 applicants, 57% accepted, 229 enrolled. *Faculty:* 90 full-time (20 women). Expenses: Contact institution. *Financial support:* In 2019–20, 373 students received support, including 1 fellowship with full tuition reimbursement available (averaging $34,000 per year), 2 research assistantships with full tuition reimbursements available (averaging $21,742 per year), 57 teaching assistantships with full tuition reimbursements available (averaging $22,750 per year); career-related internships or fieldwork, Federal Work-Study, scholarships/grants, traineeships, health care benefits, and unspecified assistantships also available. Financial award application deadline: 3/1; financial award applicants required to submit FAFSA. In 2019, 415 master's, 10 doctorates awarded. *Program availability:* Part-time, evening/weekend, 100% online, blended/hybrid learning. *Application deadline:* For fall admission, 7/1 priority date for domestic students, 1/15 for international students; for spring admission, 12/1 priority date for domestic students, 6/15 for international students; for summer admission, 5/1 priority date for domestic students, 1/15 for international students. Applications are processed on a rolling basis. *Application fee:* $60. Electronic applications accepted. *Application Contact:* Elisa Dunman, Lead Administrator, Graduate and Professional Programs, 806-834-7772, E-mail: rawlsgrad@ttu.edu. *Dean*, Dr. Margaret Williams, 806-834-2839, Fax: 806-742-1092, E-mail: margaret.l.williams@ttu.edu.

**School of Law** Students: 401 full-time (175 women), 3 part-time (1 woman); includes 126 minority (16 Black or African American, non-Hispanic/Latino; 1 American Indian or Alaska Native, non-Hispanic/Latino; 10 Asian, non-Hispanic/Latino; 64 Hispanic/Latino; 35 Two or more races, non-Hispanic/Latino), 2 international. Average age 25. 1,149 applicants, 44% accepted, 146 enrolled. *Faculty:* 36 full-time (15 women), 10 part-time/adjunct (3 women). Expenses: Contact institution. *Financial support:* In 2019–20, 405 students received support. Federal Work-Study, scholarships/grants, and tutor available. Financial award application deadline: 5/1; financial award applicants required to submit FAFSA. In 2019, 135 doctorates awarded. *Application deadline:* For fall admission, 3/1 priority date for domestic and international students. Applications are processed on a rolling basis. Electronic applications accepted. *Application Contact:* Dean Danielle I. Saavedra, Assistant Dean of Admissions, 806-834-7092, Fax: 806-742-1629, E-mail: admissions.law@ttu.edu. *Dean and W. Frank Newton Professor of Law*, Dean Jack Wade Nowlin, 806-834-1504, Fax: 806-742-1629, E-mail: jack.nowlin@ttu.edu.

## TEXAS TECH UNIVERSITY HEALTH SCIENCES CENTER, Lubbock, TX 79430

**General Information** State-supported, coed, graduate-only institution. *Graduate housing:* On-campus housing not available.

**GRADUATE UNITS**

**Graduate School of Biomedical Sciences** Electronic applications accepted.

**Pharm D Program**

**School of Health Professions** Students: 1,170 full-time (880 women), 302 part-time (203 women); includes 609 minority (138 Black or African American, non-Hispanic/Latino; 9 American Indian or Alaska Native, non-Hispanic/Latino; 111 Asian, non-Hispanic/Latino; 310 Hispanic/Latino; 2 Native Hawaiian or other Pacific Islander, non-Hispanic/Latino; 39 Two or more races, non-Hispanic/Latino), 1 international. Average age 30. 967 applicants, 35% accepted, 320 enrolled. *Faculty:* 81 full-time (43 women), 44 part-time/adjunct (25 women). Expenses: Contact institution. *Financial support:* In 2019–20, 623 students received support. Research assistantships, teaching assistantships, institutionally sponsored loans, scholarships/grants, and health care benefits available. Support available to part-time students. Financial award application deadline: 9/1; financial award applicants required to submit FAFSA. *Program availability:* Part-time, 100% online, blended/hybrid learning. *Application deadline:* Applications are processed on a rolling basis. *Application fee:* $75. Electronic applications accepted. *Application Contact:* Lindsay Johnson, Associate Dean for Admissions and Student Affairs, 806-743-3220, Fax: 806-743-2994, E-mail: health.professions@ttuhsc.edu. *Associate Dean for Admissions and Student Affairs*, Lindsay R. Johnson, 806-743-3220, Fax: 806-743-2994, E-mail: health.professions@ttuhsc.edu.

**School of Medicine** Electronic applications accepted.

**School of Nursing** *Program availability:* Part-time, online learning.

## TEXAS TECH UNIVERSITY HEALTH SCIENCES CENTER EL PASO, El Paso, TX 79905

**General Information** State-supported, coed, comprehensive institution.

**GRADUATE UNITS**

**Gayle Greve Hunt School of Nursing**

**Graduate School of Biomedical Sciences**

**Paul L. Foster School of Medicine**

## TEXAS WESLEYAN UNIVERSITY, Fort Worth, TX 76105

**General Information** Independent-religious, coed, university. *Graduate housing:* Room and/or apartments available on a first-come, first-served basis to single students; on-campus housing not available to married students.

**GRADUATE UNITS**

**Graduate Programs** *Program availability:* Part-time, evening/weekend, 100% online. Electronic applications accepted.

## TEXAS WOMAN'S UNIVERSITY, Denton, TX 76204

**General Information** State-supported, coed, primarily women, university. CGS member. *Enrollment:* 15,826 graduate, professional, and undergraduate students; 2,199 full-time matriculated graduate/professional students (1,953 women), 3,030 part-time matriculated graduate/professional students (2,720 women). *Enrollment by degree level:* 4,147 master's, 976 doctoral, 106 other advanced degrees. *Graduate faculty:* 342 full-time (251 women), 126 part-time/adjunct (92 women). *International tuition:* $12,569.40 full-time. *Tuition, area resident:* Full-time $4973.40; part-time $276.30 per semester hour. Tuition, state resident: full-time $4973.40; part-time $276.30 per semester hour. Tuition, nonresident: full-time $12,569; part-time $698.30 per semester hour. *Required fees:* $2524.30. Tuition and fees vary according to course level, course load, degree level and program. *Graduate housing:* Rooms and/or apartments available on a first-come, first-served basis to single and married students. Typical cost: $7000 per year for single students; $8400 per year for married students. Room charges vary according to board plan. *Student services:* Campus employment opportunities, campus safety program, career counseling, exercise/wellness program, free psychological counseling, grant writing training, international student services, low-cost health insurance, services for students with disabilities, teacher training, writing training. *Library facilities:* Blagg-Huey Library. *Collection:* Books: 389,891 (physical), 551,571 (digital/electronic); Serial titles: 163,695 (physical), 265,681 (digital/electronic); Databases: 306. Weekly public service hours: 116; students can reserve study rooms.

**Computer facilities:** Computer purchase and lease plans are available. 296 computers available on campus for general student use. A campuswide network can be accessed. Online class registration is available.
Website: http://www.twu.edu/

**General Application Contact:** Korie Hawkins, Associate Director of Admissions, Graduate Recruitment, 940-898-3188, Fax: 940-898-3081, E-mail: admissions@twu.edu.

**GRADUATE UNITS**

**Graduate School** Students: 2,199 full-time (1,953 women), 3,030 part-time (2,720 women); includes 2,528 minority (850 Black or African American, non-Hispanic/Latino; 10 American Indian or Alaska Native, non-Hispanic/Latino; 516 Asian, non-Hispanic/Latino; 983 Hispanic/Latino; 2 Native Hawaiian or other Pacific Islander, non-Hispanic/Latino; 167 Two or more races, non-Hispanic/Latino), 158 international. Average age 33. 3,367 applicants, 52% accepted, 1,223 enrolled. *Faculty:* 348 full-time (255 women), 126 part-time/adjunct (92 women). Expenses: Contact institution. *Financial support:* In 2019–20, 1,961 students received support, including 29 research assistantships (averaging $9,454 per year), 261 teaching assistantships (averaging $9,018 per year); career-related internships or fieldwork, scholarships/grants, health care benefits, and unspecified assistantships also available. Support available to part-time students. Financial award application deadline: 3/1; financial award applicants required to submit FAFSA. In 2019, 1,515 master's, 221 doctorates, 218 other advanced degrees awarded. *Program availability:* Part-time, evening/weekend, 100% online, blended/hybrid learning. *Application deadline:* For fall admission, 3/1 priority date for domestic and international students; for spring admission, 11/1 priority date for domestic students, 7/1 priority date for international students; for summer admission, 5/1 priority date for domestic students, 2/1 priority date for international students. Applications are processed on a rolling basis. *Application fee:* $50 ($75 for international students). Electronic applications accepted. *Application Contact:* Korie Hawkins, Associate Director of Admissions, Graduate Recruitment, 940-898-3188, Fax: 940-898-3081, E-mail: admissions@twu.edu. *Interim Dean of Graduate School*, Dr. Claire Sahlin, 940-898-3415, Fax: 940-898-3412, E-mail: gradschool@twu.edu.

***College of Arts and Sciences*** Students: 262 full-time (224 women), 377 part-time (310 women); includes 283 minority (93 Black or African American, non-Hispanic/Latino; 2 American Indian or Alaska Native, non-Hispanic/Latino; 51 Asian, non-Hispanic/Latino; 113 Hispanic/Latino; 24 Two or more races, non-Hispanic/Latino), 46 international. Average age 32. 360 applicants, 61% accepted, 152 enrolled. *Faculty:* 103 full-time (65 women), 19 part-time/adjunct (11 women). Expenses: Contact institution. *Financial support:* In 2019–20, 339 students received support, including 10 research assistantships (averaging $15,379 per year), 167 teaching assistantships (averaging $9,354 per year); career-related internships or fieldwork, scholarships/grants, and unspecified assistantships also available. Support available to part-time students. Financial award application deadline: 3/1; financial award applicants required to submit FAFSA. In 2019, 131 master's, 23 doctorates, 15 other advanced degrees awarded. *Program availability:* Part-time, evening/weekend, 100% online. *Application deadline:* For fall admission, 3/1 priority date for domestic and international students; for spring admission, 11/1 priority date for domestic students, 7/1 priority date for international students; for summer admission, 5/1 priority date for domestic students, 2/1 priority date for international students. Applications are processed on a rolling basis. *Application fee:* $50 ($75 for international students). Electronic applications accepted. *Application Contact:* Korie Hawkins, Associate Director of Admissions, Graduate Recruitment, 940-898-3188, Fax: 940-898-3081, E-mail: admissions@twu.edu. *Dean*, Dr. Abigail Tilton, 940-898-3326, Fax: 940-898-3366, E-mail: cas@twu.edu.

***College of Business*** Students: 537 full-time (471 women), 491 part-time (425 women); includes 715 minority (334 Black or African American, non-Hispanic/Latino; 3 American Indian or Alaska Native, non-Hispanic/Latino; 143 Asian, non-Hispanic/Latino; 198 Hispanic/Latino; 1 Native Hawaiian or other Pacific Islander, non-Hispanic/Latino; 36 Two or more races, non-Hispanic/Latino), 43 international. Average age 33. 461 applicants, 87% accepted, 274 enrolled. *Faculty:* 27 full-time (11 women), 9 part-time/adjunct (4 women). Expenses: Contact institution. *Financial support:* In 2019–20, 249 students received support, including 11 teaching assistantships (averaging $11,180 per year); career-related internships or fieldwork, scholarships/grants, health care benefits, and unspecified assistantships also available. Support available to part-time students. Financial award application deadline: 3/1; financial award applicants required to submit FAFSA. In 2019, 359 master's awarded. *Program availability:* Part-time, 100% online, blended/hybrid learning. *Application deadline:* For fall admission, 3/1 priority date for domestic students, 3/1 for international students; for spring admission, 11/1 priority date for domestic students, 7/1 for international students; for summer admission, 5/1 priority date for domestic students, 2/1 for international students. Applications are processed on a rolling basis. *Application fee:* $50 ($75 for international students). Electronic applications accepted. *Application Contact:* Korie Hawkins, Associate Director of Admissions, Graduate Recruitment, 940-898-3188, Fax: 940-898-3081, E-mail: admissions@twu.edu. *Dean*, Dr. James R. Lumpkin, 940-898-2458, Fax: 940-898-2120, E-mail: mba@twu.edu.

***College of Health Sciences*** Students: 1,004 full-time (885 women), 373 part-time (314 women); includes 534 minority (105 Black or African American, non-Hispanic/Latino; 1 American Indian or Alaska Native, non-Hispanic/Latino; 129 Asian, non-Hispanic/Latino; 254 Hispanic/Latino; 45 Two or more races, non-Hispanic/Latino), 33 international. Average age 29. 1,572 applicants, 28% accepted, 365 enrolled. *Faculty:* 99 full-time (75 women), 19 part-time/adjunct (17 women). Expenses: Contact institution. *Financial support:* In 2019–20, 746 students received support, including 16 research assistantships (averaging $5,198 per year), 53 teaching assistantships (averaging $6,886 per year); career-related internships or fieldwork, scholarships/grants, health care benefits, and unspecified assistantships also available. Support available to part-time students. Financial award application deadline: 3/1; financial award applicants required to submit FAFSA. In 2019, 434 master's, 128 doctorates awarded. *Program availability:* Part-time, evening/weekend, 100% online, blended/hybrid learning. *Application deadline:* For fall admission, 3/1 priority date for domestic and international students; for spring admission, 11/1 priority date for domestic students, 7/1 priority date for international students; for summer admission, 5/1 priority date for domestic students, 2/1 priority date for international students. Applications are processed on a rolling basis. *Application fee:* $50 ($75 for international students). Electronic applications accepted. *Application Contact:* Korie Hawkins, Associate Director of Admissions, Graduate Recruitment, 940-898-3188, Fax: 940-898-3081, E-mail: admissions@twu.edu. *Dean,* Dr. Christopher T. Ray, 940-898-2852, Fax: 940-898-2853.

***College of Nursing*** Students: 42 full-time (40 women), 811 part-time (756 women); includes 481 minority (168 Black or African American, non-Hispanic/Latino; 2 American Indian or Alaska Native, non-Hispanic/Latino; 165 Asian, non-Hispanic/Latino; 118 Hispanic/Latino; 1 Native Hawaiian or other Pacific Islander, non-Hispanic/Latino; 27 Two or more races, non-Hispanic/Latino), 26 international. Average age 36. 435 applicants, 71% accepted, 172 enrolled. *Faculty:* 48 full-time (47 women), 31 part-time/adjunct (24 women). Expenses: Contact institution. *Financial support:* In 2019–20, 212 students received support, including 1 research assistantship, 6 teaching assistantships (averaging $12,029 per year); career-related internships or fieldwork, scholarships/grants, health care benefits, and unspecified assistantships also available. Support available to part-time students. Financial award application deadline: 3/1; financial award applicants required to submit FAFSA. In 2019, 203 master's, 37 doctorates awarded. *Program availability:* Part-time, 100% online, blended/hybrid learning. *Application deadline:* For fall admission, 5/1 for domestic students, 3/1 priority date for international students; for spring admission, 9/15 for domestic students, 7/1 priority date for international students. *Application fee:* $50 ($75 for international students). Electronic applications accepted. *Application Contact:* Korie Hawkins, Associate Director of Admissions, Graduate Recruitment, 940-898-3188, Fax: 940-898-3081, E-mail: admissions@twu.edu. *Dean,* Dr. Rosalie Mainous, 940-898-2401, Fax: 940-898-2437, E-mail: nursing@twu.edu.

***College of Professional Education*** Students: 354 full-time (333 women), 978 part-time (915 women); includes 515 minority (150 Black or African American, non-Hispanic/Latino; 2 American Indian or Alaska Native, non-Hispanic/Latino; 28 Asian, non-Hispanic/Latino; 300 Hispanic/Latino; 35 Two or more races, non-Hispanic/Latino), 10 international. Average age 35. 549 applicants, 68% accepted, 260 enrolled. *Faculty:* 68 full-time (55 women), 47 part-time/adjunct (35 women). Expenses: Contact institution. *Financial support:* In 2019–20, 415 students received support, including 2 research assistantships, 24 teaching assistantships (averaging $9,639 per year); career-related internships or fieldwork, scholarships/grants, health care benefits, and unspecified assistantships also available. Support available to part-time students. Financial award application deadline: 3/1; financial award applicants required to submit FAFSA. In 2019, 388 master's, 33 doctorates, 136 other advanced degrees awarded. *Program availability:* Part-time, evening/weekend, 100% online, blended/hybrid learning. *Application deadline:* For fall admission, 3/1 priority date for domestic and international students; for spring admission, 11/1 priority date for domestic students, 7/1 priority date for international students; for summer admission, 5/1 priority date for domestic students, 2/1 priority date for international students. Applications are processed on a rolling basis. *Application fee:* $50 ($75 for international students). Electronic applications accepted. *Application Contact:* Korie Hawkins, Associate Director of Admissions, Graduate Recruitment, 940-898-3188, Fax: 940-898-3081, E-mail: admissions@twu.edu. *Dean,* Dr. Lisa Huffman, 940-898-2202, Fax: 940-898-2209, E-mail: cope@twu.edu.

## THEOLOGICAL UNIVERSITY OF THE CARIBBEAN, Saint Just, PR 00978-0901

**General Information** Independent-religious, coed, comprehensive institution.

**GRADUATE UNITS**

**Graduate Programs**

## THOMAS COLLEGE, Waterville, ME 04901-5097

**General Information** Independent, coed, comprehensive institution. *Graduate housing:* On-campus housing not available.

**GRADUATE UNITS**

**Graduate School** *Program availability:* Part-time, evening/weekend. Electronic applications accepted.

## THOMAS EDISON STATE UNIVERSITY, Trenton, NJ 08608

**General Information** State-supported, coed, comprehensive institution. *Graduate housing:* On-campus housing not available.

**GRADUATE UNITS**

**Heavin School of Arts and Sciences** *Program availability:* Part-time, online learning. Electronic applications accepted.

**John S. Watson School of Public Service and Continuing Studies** *Program availability:* Part-time, online learning. Electronic applications accepted.

**School of Applied Science and Technology** *Program availability:* Part-time, online learning. Electronic applications accepted.

**School of Business and Management** *Program availability:* Part-time, online learning. Electronic applications accepted.

**W. Cary Edwards School of Nursing** *Program availability:* Part-time, online learning. Electronic applications accepted.

## THOMAS JEFFERSON SCHOOL OF LAW, San Diego, CA 92110-2905

**General Information** Independent, coed, graduate-only institution. *Graduate housing:* Rooms and/or apartments available on a first-come, first-served basis to single and married students. Housing application deadline: 5/1.

**GRADUATE UNITS**

**Graduate and Professional Programs** *Program availability:* Part-time, evening/weekend. Electronic applications accepted.

## THOMAS JEFFERSON UNIVERSITY, Philadelphia, PA 19107

**General Information** Independent, coed, university. CGS member. *Graduate housing:* Rooms and/or apartments available to single and married students. *Research affiliation:* Christiana Care Health Services (biomedical research), Lankenau Institute for Medical Research (biomedical research), A.I. du Pont for Children Nemours (biomedical research), University of Delaware (biomedical research).

**GRADUATE UNITS**

**College of Architecture and the Built Environment**

**Jefferson College of Health Professions** Electronic applications accepted.

**Jefferson College of Life Sciences** *Program availability:* Part-time, evening/weekend. Electronic applications accepted.

**Jefferson College of Nursing** *Program availability:* Part-time, online only, 100% online, blended/hybrid learning. Electronic applications accepted.

**Jefferson College of Pharmacy** Electronic applications accepted.

**Jefferson College of Population Health** *Program availability:* Part-time, evening/weekend, online learning. Electronic applications accepted.

**Jefferson College of Rehabilitation Sciences** *Program availability:* Part-time, evening/weekend, online learning. Electronic applications accepted.

**Kanbar College of Design, Engineering and Commerce** *Program availability:* Part-time. Electronic applications accepted.

**School of Continuing and Professional Studies**

**Sidney Kimmel Medical College** Electronic applications accepted.

## THOMAS MORE UNIVERSITY, Crestview Hills, KY 41017-3495

**General Information** Independent-religious, coed, comprehensive institution. *Graduate housing:* On-campus housing not available.

**GRADUATE UNITS**

**Program in Business Administration** *Program availability:* Evening/weekend, 100% online. Electronic applications accepted.

**Program in Teacher Leader** *Program availability:* Part-time, evening/weekend. Electronic applications accepted.

**Program in Teaching** *Program availability:* Part-time. Electronic applications accepted.

## THOMAS UNIVERSITY, Thomasville, GA 31792-7499

**General Information** Independent, coed, comprehensive institution. *Graduate housing:* Room and/or apartments available on a first-come, first-served basis to single students; on-campus housing not available to married students. Housing application deadline: 8/1.

**GRADUATE UNITS**

**Department of Business Administration** *Program availability:* Part-time. Electronic applications accepted.

**Department of Education** *Program availability:* Part-time. Electronic applications accepted.

**Department of Human Services** *Program availability:* Part-time. Electronic applications accepted.

**Department of Nursing** *Program availability:* Part-time. Electronic applications accepted.

## THOMPSON RIVERS UNIVERSITY, Kamloops, BC V2C 0C8, Canada

**General Information** Province-supported, coed, comprehensive institution. CGS member.

**GRADUATE UNITS**

**Program in Business Administration** *Program availability:* Part-time.

**Program in Education** *Program availability:* Part-time.

**Program in Environmental Science**

**Program in Social Work**

## TIFFIN UNIVERSITY, Tiffin, OH 44883-2161

**General Information** Independent, coed, comprehensive institution. *Graduate housing:* Room and/or apartments available on a first-come, first-served basis to single students; on-campus housing not available to married students. Housing application deadline: 8/1.

**GRADUATE UNITS**

**Program in Business Administration** *Program availability:* Part-time, evening/weekend, online learning. Electronic applications accepted.

**Program in Criminal Justice** *Program availability:* Part-time, evening/weekend, 100% online, blended/hybrid learning. Electronic applications accepted.

**Program in Education** *Program availability:* Part-time, evening/weekend, online only, 100% online, blended/hybrid learning. Electronic applications accepted.

**Program in Humanities** *Program availability:* Part-time, evening/weekend, online only, 100% online, blended/hybrid learning. Electronic applications accepted.

**Program in Psychology** *Program availability:* Part-time, evening/weekend, online only, 100% online. Electronic applications accepted.

## TORONTO SCHOOL OF THEOLOGY, Toronto, ON M5S 2C3, Canada

**General Information** Independent-religious, coed, graduate-only institution. *Enrollment by degree level:* 43 master's, 208 doctoral, 615 other advanced degrees. *Library facilities:* University of Toronto Libraries plus 7 others.
Website: http://www.tst.edu/

**General Application Contact:** David Wagschal, GCTS Administrator, 416-978-4050, Fax: 416-978-7821, E-mail: inquiries@tst.edu.

**GRADUATE UNITS**

**Graduate Centre for Theological Studies** Expenses: Contact institution. *Application deadline:* For fall admission, 12/15 priority date for domestic and international students. Applications are processed on a rolling basis. *Application fee:* $120 Canadian dollars. Electronic applications accepted. *Application Contact:* David Wagschal, Administrator, Graduate Centre for Theological Studies, 416-978-4050, Fax: 416-978-7821, E-mail: inquiries@tst.edu. *Director,* Pamela Couture, 416-978-7822, Fax: 416-978-7821, E-mail: pamela.couture@utoronto.ca.

## TOURO COLLEGE, New York, NY 10010

**General Information** Independent-religious, coed, comprehensive institution. *Enrollment:* 11,631 graduate, professional, and undergraduate students; 3,517 full-time matriculated graduate/professional students (2,115 women), 1,977 part-time matriculated graduate/professional students (1,560 women). *Enrollment by degree level:* 2,907 master's, 2,483 doctoral, 104 other advanced degrees. *Graduate faculty:* 259 full-time (152 women), 453 part-time/adjunct (211 women). *Student services:* Campus employment opportunities, campus safety program, career counseling, exercise/wellness program, free psychological counseling, grant writing training, international student services, low-cost health insurance, services for students with disabilities, teacher training, writing training. *Library facilities:* Touro College Library plus 14 others.

**Computer facilities:** A campuswide network can be accessed. Online class registration is available.
Website: http://www.touro.edu/

**General Application Contact:** Dr. Benjamin Enoma, Director of Admissions, Division of Graduate Studies, 212-463-0400 Ext. 55307, Fax: 212-634-2210, E-mail: benjamin.enoma@touro.edu.

**GRADUATE UNITS**

**College of Pharmacy** Students: 249 full-time (160 women); includes 130 minority (37 Black or African American, non-Hispanic/Latino; 60 Asian, non-Hispanic/Latino; 27 Hispanic/Latino; 6 Two or more races, non-Hispanic/Latino), 8 international. Average age 28. 277 applicants, 41% accepted, 58 enrolled. *Faculty:* 34 full-time (22 women), 3 part-time/adjunct. Expenses: Contact institution. *Financial support:* In 2019–20, 27 students received support, including 2 fellowships (averaging $51,000 per year), 7 research assistantships (averaging $2,000 per year); career-related internships or fieldwork, scholarships/grants, traineeships, and health care benefits also available. Financial award application deadline: 7/15; financial award applicants required to submit FAFSA. *Application deadline:* Applications are processed on a rolling basis. *Application Contact:* Heidi Fuchs, Assistant Dean for Admissions and Enrollment Management, 646-981-4750, E-mail: heidi.fuchs@touro.edu.

**Graduate School of Business** Students: 80 part-time (49 women); includes 47 minority (14 Black or African American, non-Hispanic/Latino; 20 Asian, non-Hispanic/Latino; 10 Hispanic/Latino; 3 Native Hawaiian or other Pacific Islander, non-Hispanic/Latino). Average age 32. 54 applicants, 59% accepted, 24 enrolled. *Faculty:* 1 full-time (0 women), 24 part-time/adjunct (8 women). Expenses: Contact institution. *Financial support:* Career-related internships or fieldwork, scholarships/grants, and unspecified assistantships available. Financial award application deadline: 6/30; financial award applicants required to submit FAFSA. *Program availability:* Part-time, evening/weekend, 100% online, blended/hybrid learning. *Application deadline:* For fall admission, 8/31 priority date for domestic students, 8/15 priority date for international students; for spring admission, 1/15 priority date for domestic and international students; for summer admission, 5/15 priority date for domestic and international students. Applications are processed on a rolling basis. *Application fee:* $65. Electronic applications accepted. *Application Contact:* Celina N. Dark, Administrative Manager, 212-742-8770 Ext. 42420, E-mail: celina.dark@touro.edu. *Dean, Graduate School of Business,* Mary Louise Lo Re, Ph.D., 212-742-8770 Ext. 42430, E-mail: mary.lo-re@touro.edu.

**Graduate School of Technology** Students: 136 full-time (52 women), 34 part-time (15 women); includes 99 minority (22 Black or African American, non-Hispanic/Latino; 55 Asian, non-Hispanic/Latino; 22 Hispanic/Latino), 61 international. Average age 34. 54 applicants, 93% accepted, 29 enrolled. *Faculty:* 9 full-time (1 woman), 25 part-time/adjunct (10 women). Expenses: Contact institution. *Financial support:* Federal Work-Study, scholarships/grants, and unspecified assistantships available. Financial award applicants required to submit FAFSA. In 2019, 46 master's awarded. *Program availability:* Part-time, evening/weekend, 100% online, blended/hybrid learning. *Application deadline:* For fall admission, 8/15 for domestic students, 7/15 for international students; for spring admission, 1/10 for domestic students, 12/15 for international students; for summer admission, 5/28 for domestic students. Applications are processed on a rolling basis. *Application fee:* $50. Electronic applications accepted. *Application Contact:* James David Shafer, Director of Marketing and Recruiting, 212-463-0400 Ext. 55585, E-mail: james.shafer@touro.edu. *Executive Director of Administration,* Robert Grosberg, 202-463-0400 Ext. 55496, E-mail: robert.grosberg@touro.edu.

**Jacob D. Fuchsberg Law Center** Students: 346 full-time (178 women), 156 part-time (81 women); includes 186 minority (46 Black or African American, non-Hispanic/Latino; 40 Asian, non-Hispanic/Latino; 46 Hispanic/Latino; 54 Two or more races, non-Hispanic/Latino), 6 international. Average age 27. 1,229 applicants, 55% accepted, 196 enrolled. *Faculty:* 31 full-time (15 women), 52 part-time/adjunct (19 women). Expenses: Contact institution. *Financial support:* In 2019–20, 400 students received support, including 12 fellowships (averaging $5,600 per year), 15 research assistantships (averaging $4,200 per year), 15 teaching assistantships (averaging $3,500 per year); career-related internships or fieldwork, Federal Work-Study, and scholarships/grants also available. Financial award application deadline: 6/30; financial award applicants required to submit FAFSA. In 2019, 113 doctorates awarded. *Program availability:* Part-time, evening/weekend, blended/hybrid learning. *Application deadline:* For fall admission, 8/10 priority date for domestic students, 5/15 for international students; for spring admission, 12/31 priority date for domestic students; for summer admission, 4/30 for domestic students. Applications are processed on a rolling basis. Electronic applications accepted. *Application Contact:* Dr. Susan Thompson, Director of Enrollment, 631-761-7010, Fax: 631-761-7019, E-mail: sthompso2@tourolaw.edu. *Dean and Professor of Law,* Elena B. Langan, 631-761-7100, Fax: 631-761-7109, E-mail: elangan@tourolaw.edu.

## TOURO UNIVERSITY CALIFORNIA, Vallejo, CA 94592

**General Information** Independent, coed, graduate-only institution. *Graduate housing:* On-campus housing not available. *Research affiliation:* University of California San Francisco (cancer, HIV/AIDS), Genetech (cancer), National Institutes of Health (diabetes, cardiac arrest in teens).

**GRADUATE UNITS**

**Graduate Programs** *Program availability:* Part-time, evening/weekend. Electronic applications accepted.

## TOWSON UNIVERSITY, Towson, MD 21252-0001

**General Information** State-supported, coed, university. CGS member. *Enrollment:* 22,709 graduate, professional, and undergraduate students; 1,017 full-time matriculated graduate/professional students (750 women), 2,049 part-time matriculated graduate/professional students (1,539 women). *Enrollment by degree level:* 2,624 master's, 199 doctoral, 243 other advanced degrees. *Graduate faculty:* 302 full-time (177 women), 106 part-time/adjunct (66 women). *International tuition:* $16,344 full-time. *Tuition, area resident:* Full-time $7920; part-time $439 per credit. Tuition, nonresident: full-time $16,344; part-time $908 per credit. *Required fees:* $2628; $146 per credit. $876 per term. *Graduate housing:* On-campus housing not available. *Student services:* Campus employment opportunities, campus safety program, career counseling, child daycare facilities, exercise/wellness program, free psychological counseling, international student services, low-cost health insurance, multicultural affairs office, services for students with disabilities, writing training. *Library facilities:* Cook Library. *Collection:* Books: 384,697 (physical), 516,920 (digital/electronic); Serial titles: 22,544 (physical), 79,916 (digital/electronic); Databases: 308. Weekly public service hours: 108; study areas open 24 hours, 5–7 days a week; students can reserve study rooms. *Research affiliation:* Exelon Generation Company (biology, mathematics), Prometheus Computing (computer science), Coracias Advance Technology, LLC (computer science), Vesperix Corporation (physics, astronomy and geosciences), Brekford Corporation (computer science), RTR Technologies (computer science).

**Computer facilities:** 4,157 computers available on campus for general student use. A campuswide network can be accessed. Online class registration is available. Website: http://www.towson.edu/

**General Application Contact:** Coverley Beidleman, Assistant Director of Graduate Admissions, 410-704-5630, Fax: 410-704-3030, E-mail: grads@towson.edu.

**GRADUATE UNITS**

**College of Business and Economics** Students: 36 full-time (24 women), 50 part-time (23 women); includes 29 minority (19 Black or African American, non-Hispanic/Latino; 7 Asian, non-Hispanic/Latino; 1 Hispanic/Latino; 2 Two or more races, non-Hispanic/Latino), 11 international. Expenses: Contact institution. *Application deadline:* For fall admission, 1/17 for domestic students, 5/15 for international students; for spring admission, 10/15 for domestic students, 12/1 for international students. Applications are processed on a rolling basis. *Application fee:* $45. Electronic applications accepted. *Application Contact:* Coverley Beidleman, Assistant Director of Graduate Admissions, 410-704-5630, Fax: 410-704-3030, E-mail: cbeidleman@towson.edu. *Dean,* Dr. Shohreh Kaynama, 410-704-3342, E-mail: skaynama@towson.edu.

**College of Education** Students: 96 full-time (67 women), 1,243 part-time (1,066 women); includes 169 minority (81 Black or African American, non-Hispanic/Latino; 23 Asian, non-Hispanic/Latino; 36 Hispanic/Latino; 29 Two or more races, non-Hispanic/Latino), 10 international. Expenses: Contact institution. *Application deadline:* For fall admission, 1/17 for domestic students, 5/15 for international students; for spring admission, 10/15 for domestic students, 12/1 for international students. Applications are processed on a rolling basis. *Application fee:* $45. Electronic applications accepted. *Application Contact:* Coverley Beidleman, Assistant Director of Graduate Admissions, 410-704-5630, Fax: 410-704-3030, E-mail: cbeidleman@towson.edu. *Dean,* Dr. Laurie Mullen, 410-704-2570, Fax: 410-704-2733, E-mail: lmullen@towson.edu.

**College of Fine Arts and Communication** Students: 45 full-time (28 women), 127 part-time (103 women); includes 45 minority (19 Black or African American, non-Hispanic/Latino; 2 Asian, non-Hispanic/Latino; 14 Hispanic/Latino; 10 Two or more races, non-Hispanic/Latino), 5 international. Expenses: Contact institution. *Application deadline:* For fall admission, 1/17 for domestic students, 5/15 for international students; for spring admission, 10/15 for domestic students, 12/1 for international students. Applications are processed on a rolling basis. *Application fee:* $45. Electronic applications accepted. *Application Contact:* Coverley Beidleman, Assistant Director of Graduate Admissions, 410-704-5630, Fax: 410-704-3030, E-mail: cbeidleman@towson.edu. *Interim Dean,* Dr. Greg Faller, 410-704-3288, E-mail: gfaller@towson.edu.

**College of Health Professions** Students: 385 full-time (339 women), 102 part-time (88 women); includes 125 minority (70 Black or African American, non-Hispanic/Latino; 22 Asian, non-Hispanic/Latino; 17 Hispanic/Latino; 16 Two or more races, non-Hispanic/Latino), 6 international. Expenses: Contact institution. *Application deadline:* For fall admission, 1/17 for domestic students, 5/15 for international students; for spring admission, 10/15 for domestic students, 12/1 for international students. Applications are processed on a rolling basis. *Application fee:* $45. Electronic applications accepted. *Application Contact:* Coverley Beidleman, Assistant Director of Graduate Admissions, 410-704-5630, Fax: 410-704-3030, E-mail: cbeidleman@towson.edu. *Dean,* Dr. Lisa Plowfield, 410-704-2132, Fax: 410-704-3479, E-mail: lplowfield@towson.edu.

**College of Liberal Arts** Students: 189 full-time (154 women), 172 part-time (106 women); includes 94 minority (58 Black or African American, non-Hispanic/Latino; 11 Asian, non-Hispanic/Latino; 10 Hispanic/Latino; 15 Two or more races, non-Hispanic/Latino), 9 international. Expenses: Contact institution. *Application deadline:* For fall admission, 1/17 for domestic students, 5/15 for international students; for spring admission, 10/15 for domestic students, 12/1 for international students. Applications are processed on a rolling basis. *Application fee:* $45. Electronic applications accepted. *Application Contact:* Coverley Beidleman, Assistant Director of Graduate Admissions, 410-704-5630, Fax: 410-704-3030, E-mail: cbeidleman@towson.edu. *Dean,* Dr. Terry Cooney, 410-704-2128, E-mail: tcooney@towson.edu.

***Program in Leadership and Jewish Studies*** Students: 4 full-time (3 women), 12 part-time (5 women); includes 3 minority (2 Black or African American, non-Hispanic/Latino; 1 Hispanic/Latino). Expenses: Contact institution. *Application deadline:* For fall admission, 1/17 for domestic students, 5/15 for international students; for spring admission, 10/15 for domestic students, 12/1 for international students. Applications are processed on a rolling basis. *Application fee:* $45. Electronic applications accepted. *Application Contact:* Coverley Beidleman, Assistant Director of Graduate Admissions, 410-704-5630, Fax: 410-704-3030, E-mail: grads@towson.edu. *Program Director,* Prof. Jill Max, 410-704-7120, E-mail: jmax@towson.edu.

**Jess and Mildred Fisher College of Science and Mathematics** Students: 238 full-time (110 women), 354 part-time (152 women); includes 247 minority (131 Black or African American, non-Hispanic/Latino; 2 American Indian or Alaska Native, non-Hispanic/Latino; 64 Asian, non-Hispanic/Latino; 28 Hispanic/Latino; 22 Two or more races, non-Hispanic/Latino), 110 international. Expenses: Contact institution. *Application deadline:* For fall admission, 1/17 for domestic students, 5/15 for international students; for spring admission, 10/15 for domestic students, 12/1 for international students. Applications are processed on a rolling basis. *Application fee:* $45. Electronic applications accepted. *Application Contact:* Coverley Beidleman, Assistant Director of Graduate Admissions, 410-704-2113, Fax: 410-704-3030, E-mail: grads@towson.edu. *Dean,* Dr. David A. Vanko, 410-704-2121, Fax: 410-704-2604, E-mail: dvanko@towson.edu.

## TOYOTA TECHNOLOGICAL INSTITUTE AT CHICAGO, Chicago, IL 60637

**General Information** Proprietary, coed, graduate-only institution.

**GRADUATE UNITS**

**Program in Computer Science**

## TRENT UNIVERSITY, Peterborough, ON K9J 7B8, Canada

**General Information** Province-supported, coed, university. *Graduate housing:* Room and/or apartments available to single students; on-campus housing not available to married students. Housing application deadline: 7/10. *Research affiliation:* Watershed Science Centre (watershed studies), Ontario Power Generation, Inc. (acid rain deposition), Enbridge Consumers Gas (ozone depletion), Forensics Laboratory (DNA testing).

**GRADUATE UNITS**

**Graduate Studies** *Program availability:* Part-time.

***The Frost Centre for Canadian Studies and Indigenous Studies*** *Program availability:* Part-time.

## TREVECCA NAZARENE UNIVERSITY, Nashville, TN 37210-2877

**General Information** Independent-religious, coed, comprehensive institution. *Graduate housing:* On-campus housing not available.

**GRADUATE UNITS**

**Graduate Business Programs** *Program availability:* Evening/weekend, online learning. Electronic applications accepted.

**Graduate Counseling Program** *Program availability:* Part-time, evening/weekend. Electronic applications accepted.

**Graduate Education Program** *Program availability:* Part-time, evening/weekend, online learning. Electronic applications accepted.

**Graduate Instructional Design and Technology Program** *Program availability:* Online only. Electronic applications accepted.

**Graduate Leadership Programs** *Program availability:* Online learning. Electronic applications accepted.

**Graduate Physician Assistant Program**

**Graduate Religion Programs** *Program availability:* Part-time, online learning. Electronic applications accepted.

## TRIDENT UNIVERSITY INTERNATIONAL, Cypress, CA 90630

**General Information** Independent, coed, university.

**GRADUATE UNITS**

**College of Business Administration** *Program availability:* Part-time, evening/weekend, online learning. Electronic applications accepted.

**College of Education** *Program availability:* Part-time, evening/weekend, online learning. Electronic applications accepted.

**College of Health Sciences** *Program availability:* Part-time, evening/weekend, online learning. Electronic applications accepted.

**College of Information Systems** *Program availability:* Part-time, evening/weekend, online learning. Electronic applications accepted.

## TRINE UNIVERSITY, Angola, IN 46703-1764

**General Information** Independent, coed, comprehensive institution. *Graduate housing:* On-campus housing not available.

**GRADUATE UNITS**

**Lou Holtz Program in Leadership**

**Program in Business Administration**

**Program in Criminal Justice** *Program availability:* Part-time, evening/weekend, online only, 100% online, blended/hybrid learning. Electronic applications accepted.

**Program in Engineering Management**

**Program in Information Studies**

**Program in Physical Therapy**

**Program in Physician Assistant Studies**

## TRINITY BAPTIST COLLEGE, Jacksonville, FL 32221

**General Information** Independent-religious, coed, comprehensive institution. *Enrollment:* 12 part-time matriculated graduate/professional students (6 women). *Enrollment by degree level:* 12 master's. *Graduate faculty:* 6 full-time (1 woman), 5 part-time/adjunct (1 woman). *Tuition:* Part-time $320 per credit hour. *Required fees:* $65 per term. *Graduate housing:* On-campus housing not available. *Student services:* Writing training.

**Computer facilities:** 21 computers available on campus for general student use. A campuswide network can be accessed from student residence rooms. Online class registration is available.
Website: http://www.tbc.edu/

**General Application Contact:** Dr. Matthew Beemer, Senior Vice President, 904-596-2400, Fax: 904-596-2531, E-mail: mbeemer@tbc.edu.

**GRADUATE UNITS**

**Graduate Programs** *Program availability:* Online learning.

## TRINITY BIBLE COLLEGE AND GRADUATE SCHOOL, Ellendale, ND 58436

**General Information** Independent-religious, coed, comprehensive institution.

**GRADUATE UNITS**

**Graduate School**

## TRINITY CHRISTIAN COLLEGE, Palos Heights, IL 60463-0929

**General Information** Independent-religious, coed, comprehensive institution.

**GRADUATE UNITS**

**Program in Counseling Psychology** *Program availability:* Evening/weekend, online learning.

**Program in Special Education** *Program availability:* Evening/weekend. Electronic applications accepted.

## TRINITY COLLEGE, Toronto, ON M5S 1H8, Canada

**General Information** Independent-religious, coed, graduate-only institution. *Graduate housing:* Room and/or apartments available on a first-come, first-served basis to single students; on-campus housing not available to married students. Housing application deadline: 7/15.

**GRADUATE UNITS**

**Faculty of Divinity** *Program availability:* Part-time.

## TRINITY COLLEGE, Hartford, CT 06106-3100

**General Information** Independent, coed, comprehensive institution. *Graduate housing:* On-campus housing not available.

**GRADUATE UNITS**

**Graduate Programs** *Program availability:* Part-time, evening/weekend. Electronic applications accepted.

## TRINITY INTERNATIONAL UNIVERSITY, Deerfield, IL 60015-1284

**General Information** Independent-religious, coed, university. *Graduate housing:* Rooms and/or apartments available on a first-come, first-served basis to single and married students.

**GRADUATE UNITS**

**Trinity Evangelical Divinity School** *Program availability:* Part-time, online learning. Electronic applications accepted.

**Trinity Graduate School** *Program availability:* Part-time, evening/weekend, online learning. Electronic applications accepted.

**Trinity Law School** *Program availability:* Part-time, evening/weekend.

## TRINITY INTERNATIONAL UNIVERSITY FLORIDA, Davie, FL 33324

**General Information** Independent-religious, coed, graduate-only institution. *Enrollment by degree level:* 118 master's. *Graduate faculty:* 3 full-time (all women), 15 part-time/adjunct (all women). *Tuition:* Full-time $5040; part-time $720 per credit hour. *Required fees:* $900; $300 per semester. *Graduate housing:* On-campus housing not available. *Student services:* Campus employment opportunities, career counseling, services for students with disabilities.
Website: https://florida.tiu.edu/

**General Application Contact:** Deborah Wiles, Director of Academic Operations, 954-382-6416, Fax: 954-382-6420, E-mail: DWiles@tiu.edu.

**GRADUATE UNITS**

**Divinity School**

**Graduate School**

## TRINITY SCHOOL FOR MINISTRY, Ambridge, PA 15003-2397

**General Information** Independent-religious, coed, graduate-only institution. *Graduate housing:* On-campus housing not available.

**GRADUATE UNITS**

**Graduate Programs** *Program availability:* Part-time.

## TRINITY UNIVERSITY, San Antonio, TX 78212-7200

**General Information** Independent-religious, coed, comprehensive institution. *Enrollment:* 2,692 graduate, professional, and undergraduate students; 120 full-time matriculated graduate/professional students (78 women), 44 part-time matriculated graduate/professional students (27 women). *Enrollment by degree level:* 164 master's. *Graduate faculty:* 6 full-time (3 women), 22 part-time/adjunct (9 women). *Graduate housing:* On-campus housing not available. *Student services:* Campus employment opportunities, campus safety program, career counseling, exercise/wellness program, free psychological counseling, grant writing training, international student services, services for students with disabilities, teacher training, writing training. *Library facilities:* Elizabeth Huth Coates Library plus 1 other. *Collection:* Books: 688,626 (physical); Serial titles: 1,590 (physical), 120,000 (digital/electronic); Databases: 297. Weekly public service hours: 96; students can reserve study rooms.

**Computer facilities:** Computer purchase and lease plans are available. 500 computers available on campus for general student use. A campuswide network can be accessed. Online class registration is available.
Website: http://www.trinity.edu/

**GRADUATE UNITS**

**Department of Education** Students: 57 full-time (44 women), 4 part-time (2 women); includes 38 minority (6 Black or African American, non-Hispanic/Latino; 1 Asian, non-Hispanic/Latino; 26 Hispanic/Latino; 5 Two or more races, non-Hispanic/Latino), 2 international. Average age 36. *Faculty:* 1 (woman) full-time, 14 part-time/adjunct (6 women). Expenses: Contact institution. *Financial support:* Application deadline: 5/1; applicants required to submit FAFSA. In 2019, 42 master's awarded. *Program availability:* Part-time, evening/weekend. *Application Contact:* Office of Admissions, 210-999-7207, Fax: 210-999-8164, E-mail: admissions@trinity.edu. *Interim Chair,* Norvella Carter, 210-999-7506, Fax: 210-999-7592, E-mail: ncarter1@trinity.edu.

**Department of Health Care Administration** Students: 46 full-time (25 women), 39 part-time (25 women); includes 26 minority (5 Black or African American, non-Hispanic/Latino; 7 Asian, non-Hispanic/Latino; 11 Hispanic/Latino; 3 Two or more races, non-Hispanic/Latino). Average age 27. *Faculty:* 4 full-time (1 woman), 9 part-time/adjunct (3 women). Expenses: Contact institution. *Financial support:* Fellowships, institutionally sponsored loans, scholarships/grants, and unspecified assistantships available. Support available to part-time students. Financial award application deadline: 5/1; financial award applicants required to submit FAFSA. In 2019, 34 master's awarded. *Program availability:* Part-time, online learning. *Application deadline:* For fall admission, 6/1 for domestic students. Applications are processed on a rolling basis. *Application fee:* $50. Electronic applications accepted. *Application Contact:* Dr. Ed Schumacher, Professor/Chair, 210-999-8137, E-mail: hca@trinity.edu. *Professor/Chair,* Dr. Ed Schumacher, 210-999-8137, E-mail: hca@trinity.edu.

**School of Business** Students: 17 full-time (9 women); includes 4 minority (1 Asian, non-Hispanic/Latino; 2 Hispanic/Latino; 1 Two or more races, non-Hispanic/Latino), 1 international. Average age 23. Expenses: Contact institution. *Financial support:* Institutionally sponsored loans and scholarships/grants available. Financial award application deadline: 5/1; financial award applicants required to submit FAFSA. In 2019, 16 master's awarded. *Application deadline:* For fall admission, 2/1 for domestic and international students. Electronic applications accepted. *Application Contact:* Dr. Julie Persellin, Chair, Department of Accounting, 210-999-7230, E-mail: jpersell@trinity.edu. *Chair, Department of Accounting,* Dr. Julie Persellin, 210-999-7230, E-mail: jpersell@trinity.edu.

## TRINITY WASHINGTON UNIVERSITY, Washington, DC 20017-1094

**General Information** Independent-religious, women only, comprehensive institution. *Graduate housing:* Room and/or apartments available on a first-come, first-served basis to single students; on-campus housing not available to married students.

**GRADUATE UNITS**

**School of Business and Graduate Studies** *Program availability:* Part-time, evening/weekend.

**School of Education** *Program availability:* Part-time, evening/weekend.

**School of Nursing and Health Professions**

## TRINITY WESTERN UNIVERSITY, Langley, BC V2Y 1Y1, Canada

**General Information** Independent-religious, coed, comprehensive institution. *Enrollment:* 401 full-time matriculated graduate/professional students, 354 part-time matriculated graduate/professional students. *Enrollment by degree level:* 755 master's. *Graduate faculty:* 34 full-time (17 women), 57 part-time/adjunct (31 women). *Tuition:* Full-time $13,000 Canadian dollars; part-time $8700 Canadian dollars per semester hour. *Required fees:* $504 Canadian dollars; $336 Canadian dollars per semester hour. $168 Canadian dollars per semester. Tuition and fees vary according to course load, campus/location, program, reciprocity agreements and student level. *Graduate housing:* On-campus housing not available. *Student services:* Campus employment opportunities, campus safety program, career counseling, exercise/wellness program, free psychological counseling, international student services, low-cost health insurance, services for students with disabilities, teacher training, writing training.

**Computer facilities:** A campuswide network can be accessed from student residence rooms and from off campus.
Website: http://www.twu.ca/

**General Application Contact:** Tim Macfarlane, Senior Enrolment Advisor, 604-513-2121 Ext. 3046, E-mail: gradadmissions@twu.ca.

**GRADUATE UNITS**

**ACTS Seminaries** Students: 202 full-time (88 women), 184 part-time (79 women). Average age 35. *Faculty:* 13 full-time (0 women), 20 part-time/adjunct (3 women). Expenses: Contact institution. *Financial support:* Research assistantships, career-related internships or fieldwork, Federal Work-Study, institutionally sponsored loans, and scholarships/grants available. Financial award application deadline: 3/1; financial award applicants required to submit FAFSA. In 2019, 73 master's awarded. *Program availability:* Part-time. *Application deadline:* Applications are processed on a rolling basis. *Application fee:* $150 Canadian dollars for international students. Electronic applications accepted. *Application Contact:* Liisa Polkki, Director of Admissions, 604-513-2019, Fax: 604-513-2045, E-mail: acts@twu.ca. *ACTS Executive Director*, Ryan Klassen, E-mail: ryan.klassen@twu.ca.

**School of Graduate Studies** Students: 401 full-time, 354 part-time. Average age 28. 461 applicants, 68% accepted, 270 enrolled. *Faculty:* 34 full-time (17 women), 57 part-time/adjunct (31 women). Expenses: Contact institution. *Financial support:* Research assistantships, teaching assistantships, scholarships/grants, and unspecified assistantships available. Support available to part-time students. In 2019, 228 master's awarded. *Program availability:* Part-time, 100% online, blended/hybrid learning. *Application deadline:* Applications are processed on a rolling basis. *Application fee:* $150 Canadian dollars for international students. Electronic applications accepted. *Application Contact:* Phil Kay, Director of Graduate and International Admissions, 604-513-2121 Ext. 3444, E-mail: phil.kay@twu.ca.

***Master of Science in Nursing*** Average age 32. 43 applicants, 60% accepted, 12 enrolled. Expenses: Contact institution. *Financial support:* Research assistantships, teaching assistantships, scholarships/grants, and unspecified assistantships available. Support available to part-time students. *Program availability:* Part-time, 100% online, blended/hybrid learning. *Application deadline:* For spring admission, 10/1 for domestic and international students; for summer admission, 2/1 for domestic and international students. *Application fee:* $150 Canadian dollars for international students. Electronic applications accepted. *Application Contact:* Tim Macfarlane, Senior Enrolment Advisor, 604-513-2121 Ext. 3046, E-mail: tim.macfarlane@twu.ca. *Program Director*, Dr. Barb Astle, E-mail: barbara.astle@twu.ca.

## TRI-STATE BIBLE COLLEGE, South Point, OH 45680-8402

**General Information** Independent-religious, coed, comprehensive institution.

**GRADUATE UNITS**

**Graduate Program** Electronic applications accepted.

## TROY UNIVERSITY, Troy, AL 36082

**General Information** State-supported, coed, comprehensive institution. *Enrollment:* 16,436 graduate, professional, and undergraduate students; 1,080 full-time matriculated graduate/professional students (793 women), 2,332 part-time matriculated graduate/professional students (1,396 women). *Enrollment by degree level:* 3,238 master's, 107 doctoral, 67 other advanced degrees. *Graduate faculty:* 182 full-time (86 women), 76 part-time/adjunct (39 women). *International tuition:* $15,300 full-time. *Tuition, area resident:* Full-time $7650; part-time $2550 per semester hour. Tuition, state resident: full-time $7650; part-time $2550 per semester hour. Tuition, nonresident: full-time $15,300; part-time $5100 per semester hour. *Required fees:* $856; $352 per semester hour. $176 per semester. *Graduate housing:* Rooms and/or apartments available on a first-come, first-served basis to single and married students. Typical cost: $3300 per year ($6804 including board) for single students; $4140 per year ($7644 including board) for married students. Room and board charges vary according to housing facility selected. Housing application deadline: 3/1. *Student services:* Campus employment opportunities, campus safety program, career counseling, exercise/wellness program, free psychological counseling, international student services, low-cost health insurance, services for students with disabilities, teacher training, writing training. *Library facilities:* Lurleen B. Wallace Library (Troy Campus) plus 2 others. *Collection:* Books: 603,904 (physical), 277,690 (digital/electronic); Serial titles: 213 (physical), 134,396 (digital/electronic); Databases: 261. *Research affiliation:* Systemics Research Fund (protozoan symbionts), Birmingham Audubon Society (Alabama flora and fauna).

**Computer facilities:** 1,935 computers available on campus for general student use. A campuswide network can be accessed from student residence rooms and from off campus. Online class registration is available.
Website: http://www.troy.edu/

**General Application Contact:** Haley McKinnon, Director of Graduate Admissions, 334-670-3178, Fax: 334-670-3912, E-mail: hmckinnon@troy.edu.

**GRADUATE UNITS**

**Graduate School** Expenses: Contact institution. *Financial support:* Fellowships, research assistantships, teaching assistantships, career-related internships or fieldwork, Federal Work-Study, scholarships/grants, traineeships, tuition waivers, and unspecified assistantships available. Support available to part-time students. Financial award application deadline: 3/1; financial award applicants required to submit FAFSA. *Program availability:* Part-time, evening/weekend, 100% online, blended/hybrid learning. *Application deadline:* Applications are processed on a rolling basis. *Application fee:* $50. Electronic applications accepted. *Application Contact:* Jessica A. Kimbro, Assistant Director of Graduate Programs, 334-670-3189, Fax: 334-670-3912, E-mail: jacord@troy.edu. *Associate Provost/Dean*, Dr. Mary Anne C. Templeton, 334-670-3189, Fax: 334-670-3912, E-mail: mtempleton@troy.edu.

***College of Arts and Sciences*** Students: 166 full-time (88 women), 764 part-time (380 women); includes 346 minority (261 Black or African American, non-Hispanic/Latino; 4 American Indian or Alaska Native, non-Hispanic/Latino; 18 Asian, non-Hispanic/Latino; 45 Hispanic/Latino; 1 Native Hawaiian or other Pacific Islander, non-Hispanic/Latino; 17 Two or more races, non-Hispanic/Latino), 33 international. Average age 33. 627 applicants, 92% accepted, 329 enrolled. *Faculty:* 51 full-time (14 women), 24 part-time/adjunct (7 women). Expenses: Contact institution. *Financial support:* In 2019–20, 473 students received support. Fellowships, research assistantships, teaching assistantships, career-related internships or fieldwork, Federal Work-Study, scholarships/grants, traineeships, tuition waivers, and unspecified assistantships available. Support available to part-time students. Financial award application deadline: 3/1; financial award applicants required to submit FAFSA. In 2019, 238 master's awarded. *Program availability:* Part-time, evening/weekend, online learning. *Application deadline:* Applications are processed on a rolling basis. *Application fee:* $50. Electronic applications accepted. *Application Contact:* Haley McKinnon, Director of Graduate Admissions, 334-670-3178, Fax: 334-670-3733, E-mail: hmckinnon@troy.edu. *Dean*, Dr. Steven Taylor, 334-670-3399, Fax: 334-670-3673, E-mail: sltaylor@troy.edu.

***College of Business*** Students: 208 full-time (113 women), 694 part-time (350 women); includes 278 minority (236 Black or African American, non-Hispanic/Latino; 2 American Indian or Alaska Native, non-Hispanic/Latino; 5 Asian, non-Hispanic/Latino; 20 Hispanic/Latino; 2 Native Hawaiian or other Pacific Islander, non-Hispanic/Latino; 13 Two or more races, non-Hispanic/Latino), 31 international. Average age 34. 487 applicants, 91% accepted, 322 enrolled. *Faculty:* 44 full-time (14 women), 3 part-time/adjunct (0 women). Expenses: Contact institution. *Financial support:* In 2019–20, 437 students received support, including 5 research assistantships; fellowships, teaching assistantships, career-related internships or fieldwork, Federal Work-Study, scholarships/grants, traineeships, tuition waivers, and unspecified assistantships also available. Support available to part-time students. Financial award application deadline: 3/1; financial award applicants required to submit FAFSA. In 2019, 282 master's awarded. *Program availability:* Part-time, evening/weekend, 100% online, blended/hybrid learning. *Application deadline:* Applications are processed on a rolling basis. *Application fee:* $50. Electronic applications accepted. *Application Contact:* Haley McKinnon, Director of Graduate Admissions, 334-670-3178, Fax: 334-670-3733, E-mail: hmckinnon@troy.edu. *Dean*, Dr. Judson Edwards, 334-670-3989, Fax: 334-670-3708, E-mail: jcedwards@troy.edu.

***College of Communication and Fine Arts*** Students: 34 full-time (25 women), 80 part-time (57 women); includes 40 minority (35 Black or African American, non-Hispanic/Latino; 5 Hispanic/Latino). Average age 31. 69 applicants, 100% accepted, 53 enrolled. *Faculty:* 3 full-time (all women), 2 part-time/adjunct (0 women). Expenses: Contact institution. *Financial support:* In 2019–20, 36 students received support. Fellowships, research assistantships, teaching assistantships, career-related internships or fieldwork, Federal Work-Study, scholarships/grants, traineeships, tuition waivers, and unspecified assistantships available. Support available to part-time students. Financial award application deadline: 3/1; financial award applicants required to submit FAFSA. In 2019, 61 master's awarded. *Program availability:* Part-time, evening/weekend, online learning. *Application deadline:* For fall admission, 6/1 for international students; for spring admission, 10/15 for international students. Applications are processed on a rolling basis. *Application fee:* $50. Electronic applications accepted. *Application Contact:* Haley McKinnon, Director of Graduate Admissions, 334-670-3178, Fax: 334-670-3733, E-mail: hmckinnon@troy.edu. *Dean*, Dr. Larry Blocher, 334-670-3869, Fax: 334-670-3547, E-mail: lblocher@troy.edu.

***College of Education*** Students: 393 full-time (324 women), 521 part-time (416 women); includes 343 minority (285 Black or African American, non-Hispanic/Latino; 2 American Indian or Alaska Native, non-Hispanic/Latino; 8 Asian, non-Hispanic/Latino; 27 Hispanic/Latino; 21 Two or more races, non-Hispanic/Latino), 13 international. Average age 36. 386 applicants, 95% accepted, 230 enrolled. *Faculty:* 93 full-time (56 women), 40 part-time/adjunct (31 women). Expenses: Contact institution. *Financial support:* In 2019–20, 249 students received support. Fellowships, research assistantships, teaching assistantships, career-related internships or fieldwork, Federal Work-Study, scholarships/grants, traineeships, tuition waivers, and unspecified assistantships available. Support available to part-time students. Financial award application deadline: 3/1; financial award applicants required to submit FAFSA. In 2019, 313 master's, 23 other advanced degrees awarded. *Program availability:* Part-time, evening/weekend, online learning. *Application deadline:* For fall admission, 1/1 for domestic students, 6/1 for international students; for spring admission, 10/15 for international students. Applications are processed on a rolling basis. *Application fee:* $50. Electronic applications accepted. *Application Contact:* Haley McKinnon, Director of Graduate Admissions, 334-670-3178, Fax: 334-670-3733, E-mail: hmckinnon@troy.edu. *Dean*, Dr. Dionne Rosser-Mims, 334-670-3365, Fax: 334-670-3474, E-mail: drosser-mims@troy.edu.

***College of Health and Human Services*** Students: 279 full-time (243 women), 273 part-time (193 women); includes 189 minority (168 Black or African American, non-Hispanic/Latino; 1 American Indian or Alaska Native, non-Hispanic/Latino; 2 Asian, non-Hispanic/Latino; 13 Hispanic/Latino; 5 Two or more races, non-Hispanic/Latino), 10 international. Average age 33. 340 applicants, 91% accepted, 232 enrolled. *Faculty:* 36 full-time (24 women), 14 part-time/adjunct (9 women). Expenses: Contact institution. *Financial support:* In 2019–20, 116 students received support. Fellowships, research assistantships, teaching assistantships, career-related internships or fieldwork, Federal Work-Study, scholarships/grants, traineeships, tuition waivers, and unspecified assistantships available. Support available to part-time students. Financial award application deadline: 3/1; financial award applicants required to submit FAFSA. In 2019, 223 master's, 25 doctorates, 11 other advanced degrees awarded. *Program availability:* Part-time, evening/weekend, online learning. *Application deadline:* For fall admission, 5/1 for domestic students; for spring admission, 10/1 for domestic students; for summer admission, 3/1 for domestic students. Applications are processed on a rolling basis. *Application fee:* $50. Electronic applications accepted. *Application Contact:* Crystal Bishop, Director, Admissions & Records, 334-241-8631, E-mail: cdgodwin@troy.edu. *Dean*, Dr. Denise Green, 334-670-3712, Fax: 334-670-3743, E-mail: dmgreen@troy.edu.

## TRUETT MCCONNELL UNIVERSITY, Cleveland, GA 30528

**General Information** Independent-religious, coed, comprehensive institution. *Enrollment:* 3,055 graduate, professional, and undergraduate students; 38 full-time matriculated graduate/professional students (20 women), 32 part-time matriculated graduate/professional students (15 women). *Enrollment by degree level:* 70 master's. *Graduate faculty:* 17 full-time (7 women), 12 part-time/adjunct (2 women). *Tuition:* Full-time $6300; part-time $350 per credit hour. *Required fees:* $1010; $1010. Tuition and fees vary according to course load. *Graduate housing:* Rooms and/or apartments available on a first-come, first-served basis to single and married students. Typical cost: $5304 per year for single students; $5304 per year for married students. Room charges vary according to board plan and housing facility selected. Housing application deadline: 7/1. *Student services:* Campus employment opportunities, career counseling, exercise/wellness program, services for students with disabilities. *Library facilities:* Cofer Library.

**Computer facilities:** 40 computers available on campus for general student use. A campuswide network can be accessed. Online class registration is available.
Website: http://www.truett.edu/

**General Application Contact:** Timothy Agee, Graduate Admissions Coordinator, 706-865-2134 Ext. 4305, E-mail: tagee@truett.edu.

**GRADUATE UNITS**

**Balthasar Hubmaier School of Theology and Missions** Students: 8 full-time (2 women), 12 part-time (2 women); includes 1 minority (Hispanic/Latino), 2 international. Average age 36. 17 applicants, 29% accepted, 2 enrolled. Expenses: Contact institution. *Financial support:* Application deadline: 8/1; applicants required to submit FAFSA. In

2019, 4 master's awarded. *Program availability:* Part-time, 100% online. *Application deadline:* Applications are processed on a rolling basis. Electronic applications accepted. *Application Contact:* Timothy Agee, Graduate Admissions Coordinator, 706-865-2134 Ext. 4305, E-mail: tagee@truett.edu. *Dean*, Dr. Mael Disseau, 706-865-2134 Ext. 6606, E-mail: mdisseau@truett.edu.

**Hans Hut School of Business** Students: 13 full-time (5 women), 8 part-time (4 women); includes 3 minority (1 Asian, non-Hispanic/Latino; 2 Hispanic/Latino). Average age 34. 24 applicants, 67% accepted, 14 enrolled. Expenses: Contact institution. *Financial support:* Applicants required to submit FAFSA. In 2019, 5 master's awarded. *Program availability:* Part-time, online only, 100% online. *Application deadline:* For fall admission, 8/1 for domestic students; for spring admission, 12/1 for domestic students; for summer admission, 5/1 for domestic students. Applications are processed on a rolling basis. Electronic applications accepted. *Application Contact:* Timothy Agee, Graduate Admissions Coordinator, 706-865-2134 Ext. 4305, E-mail: tagee@truett.edu. *Dean*, Dr. Katherine Hyatt, 706-865-2134 Ext. 6504, E-mail: khyatt@truett.edu.

**The Leonhard Schiemer School of Psychology and Biblical Counseling** Students: 14 full-time (12 women), 9 part-time (6 women); includes 4 minority (1 Black or African American, non-Hispanic/Latino; 3 Hispanic/Latino). Average age 32. 17 applicants, 47% accepted, 6 enrolled. Expenses: Contact institution. *Financial support:* Applicants required to submit FAFSA. In 2019, 1 master's awarded. *Program availability:* Part-time. *Application deadline:* For fall admission, 8/1 for domestic students; for spring admission, 12/1 for domestic students; for summer admission, 5/1 for domestic students. Applications are processed on a rolling basis. Electronic applications accepted. *Application Contact:* Timothy Agee, Graduate Admissions Coordinator, 706-865-2134 Ext. 4305, E-mail: tagee@truett.edu. *Dean*, Dr. Holly Haynes, 706-865-2134 Ext. 6205, E-mail: hhaynes@truett.edu.

**The Peter and Gredel Walpot School of Education**

**Pilgram Marpeck School of Science, Technology, Engineering and Mathematics** Students: 3 full-time (1 woman); includes 1 minority (Hispanic/Latino). Average age 26. 2 applicants. Expenses: Contact institution. *Financial support:* Applicants required to submit FAFSA. *Program availability:* Part-time. *Application deadline:* For fall admission, 8/1 for domestic students; for spring admission, 12/1 for domestic students; for summer admission, 5/1 for domestic students. Applications are processed on a rolling basis. Electronic applications accepted. *Application Contact:* Timothy Agee, Graduate Admissions Coordinator, 706-865-2134 Ext. 4305, E-mail: tagee@truett.edu. *Dean*, Dr. Robert Bowen, 706-865-2134 Ext. 6400, E-mail: rbowen@truett.edu.

## TRUMAN STATE UNIVERSITY, Kirksville, MO 63501-4221

**General Information** State-supported, coed, comprehensive institution. CGS member. *Enrollment:* 5,231 graduate, professional, and undergraduate students; 199 full-time matriculated graduate/professional students (139 women), 37 part-time matriculated graduate/professional students (24 women). *Enrollment by degree level:* 226 master's, 10 other advanced degrees. *Graduate faculty:* 136 full-time (59 women). *International tuition:* $8018 full-time. Tuition, state resident: full-time $4630; part-time $385.50 per credit hour. Tuition, nonresident: full-time $8018; part-time $668 per credit hour. *Required fees:* $324. Full-time tuition and fees vary according to course level, course load, program and reciprocity agreements. *Graduate housing:* Rooms and/or apartments available on a first-come, first-served basis to single and married students. Typical cost: $7080 per year ($12,000 including board) for single students; $4473 per year for married students. Room and board charges vary according to housing facility selected. Housing application deadline: 5/1. *Student services:* Campus employment opportunities, campus safety program, career counseling, exercise/wellness program, free psychological counseling, grant writing training, international student services, multicultural affairs office, services for students with disabilities, teacher training, writing training. *Library facilities:* Pickler Memorial Library. *Collection:* Books: 491,954 (physical), 403,847 (digital/electronic); Serial titles: 300 (physical), 2,465 (digital/electronic); Databases: 107. Weekly public service hours: 105; students can reserve study rooms. *Research affiliation:* Gulf Coast Research Laboratory (marine science), Kirksville College of Osteopathic Medicine (biology).

**Computer facilities:** 1,056 computers available on campus for general student use. A campuswide network can be accessed. Online class registration is available.
Website: http://www.truman.edu/

**General Application Contact:** Bethany Gibson, Graduate Office and Academic Affairs Administrative Assistant, 660-785-4109, Fax: 660-785-7460, E-mail: gradinfo@truman.edu.

**GRADUATE UNITS**

**Office of Graduate Studies** Students: 198 full-time (138 women), 38 part-time (25 women); includes 17 minority (2 Black or African American, non-Hispanic/Latino; 12 Asian, non-Hispanic/Latino; 3 Hispanic/Latino). Average age 23. 113 applicants, 88% accepted, 77 enrolled. *Faculty:* 136 full-time (59 women). Expenses: Contact institution. *Financial support:* In 2019–20, 30 fellowships (averaging $500 per year), 19 research assistantships with full and partial tuition reimbursements (averaging $6,000 per year), 24 teaching assistantships with full and partial tuition reimbursements (averaging $8,000 per year) were awarded; career-related internships or fieldwork, Federal Work-Study, institutionally sponsored loans, scholarships/grants, and unspecified assistantships also available. Financial award application deadline: 5/1; financial award applicants required to submit FAFSA. In 2019, 169 master's awarded. *Application deadline:* For fall admission, 6/1 priority date for domestic and international students; for spring admission, 11/1 priority date for domestic and international students. Applications are processed on a rolling basis. *Application fee:* $40 ($0 for international students). Electronic applications accepted. *Application Contact:* Bethany Gibson, Graduate Office Administrative Assistant, 660-785-4109, Fax: 660-785-7460, E-mail: gradinfo@truman.edu. *Director of Graduate Studies*, Jeanne Harding, 660-785-4109, Fax: 660-785-7460, E-mail: jharding@truman.edu.

***School of Arts and Letters*** Electronic applications accepted.

***School of Business*** Electronic applications accepted.

***School of Health Sciences and Education*** Electronic applications accepted.

## TUFTS UNIVERSITY, Medford, MA 02155

**General Information** Independent, coed, university. CGS member. *Enrollment:* 11,878 graduate, professional, and undergraduate students; 5,161 full-time matriculated graduate/professional students (3,026 women), 659 part-time matriculated graduate/professional students (376 women). *Enrollment by degree level:* 2,473 master's, 3,036 doctoral, 311 other advanced degrees. *Graduate faculty:* 989 full-time (467 women), 557 part-time/adjunct (268 women). *Tuition:* Part-time $1799 per credit hour. Full-time tuition and fees vary according to degree level, program and student level. Part-time tuition and fees vary according to course load. *Graduate housing:* Room and/or apartments available on a first-come, first-served basis to single students; on-campus housing not available to married students. Housing application deadline: 4/15. *Student services:* Campus employment opportunities, campus safety program, career counseling, exercise/wellness program, international student services, services for students with disabilities, teacher training, writing training. *Library facilities:* Tisch Library plus 3 others. *Collection:* Books: 1.3 million (physical), 432,877 (digital/electronic); Serial titles: 1,012 (physical); Databases: 83,216. Weekly public service hours: 110; students can reserve study rooms. *Research affiliation:* Maine Medical Center (medicine), The Stockholm Environmental Institute (environmental science and policy), Caritas St. Elizabeth's Medical Center (medicine), Tufts Medical Center (medicine), Lahey Clinic Medical Center (medicine), Baystate Medical Center (medicine).

**Computer facilities:** Computer purchase and lease plans are available. 1,039 computers available on campus for general student use. A campuswide network can be accessed. Online class registration, Cloud storage for all students, staff, and faculty are available.
Website: http://www.tufts.edu/

**General Application Contact:** Information Contact, 617-628-5000.

**GRADUATE UNITS**

**Cummings School of Veterinary Medicine** Electronic applications accepted.

**The Fletcher School of Law and Diplomacy** *Program availability:* Online learning. Electronic applications accepted.

**The Gerald J. and Dorothy R. Friedman School of Nutrition Science and Policy** *Program availability:* Part-time. Electronic applications accepted.

**Graduate School of Arts and Sciences** *Program availability:* Part-time. Electronic applications accepted.

**Graduate School of Biomedical Sciences** Students: 208 full-time (125 women), 1 part-time; includes 50 minority (7 Black or African American, non-Hispanic/Latino; 23 Asian, non-Hispanic/Latino; 12 Hispanic/Latino; 8 Two or more races, non-Hispanic/Latino), 48 international. Average age 32. 788 applicants, 50 enrolled. *Faculty:* 197 full-time (72 women), 17 part-time/adjunct (4 women). Expenses: Contact institution. *Financial support:* In 2019–20, 170 research assistantships with full tuition reimbursements (averaging $35,000 per year) were awarded. Financial award application deadline: 12/1. In 2019, 24 master's, 34 doctorates awarded. *Application deadline:* For fall admission, 12/1 priority date for domestic and international students. *Application fee:* $90. Electronic applications accepted. *Application Contact:* Jeff Miller, Admissions Coordinator, 617-636-6767, Fax: 617-636-0375, E-mail: gsbs-admissions@tufts.edu. *Dean*, Dr. Dan Jay, 617-636-6767, Fax: 617-636-0375, E-mail: daniel.jay@tufts.edu.

**School of Dental Medicine**

**School of Engineering** *Program availability:* Part-time. Electronic applications accepted.

***The Gordon Institute*** *Program availability:* Part-time. Electronic applications accepted.

**School of Medicine**

**School of the Museum of Fine Arts at Tufts University** Students: 55 full-time. Average age 25. *Faculty:* 31 full-time (19 women), 23 part-time/adjunct (16 women). Expenses: Contact institution. *Financial support:* Fellowships, teaching assistantships, Federal Work-Study, and scholarships/grants available. Financial award application deadline: 1/15. In 2019, 44 master's, 15 other advanced degrees awarded. *Application deadline:* For fall admission, 1/15 priority date for domestic and international students. Applications are processed on a rolling basis. *Application fee:* $85. Electronic applications accepted. *Application Contact:* Office of Graduate Admissions, 617-627-3395, E-mail: gradadmissions@tufts.edu. *Associate Director of Graduate Programs*, Lisa Bynoe, 617-627-0031, E-mail: lisa.bynoe@tufts.edu.

## TULANE UNIVERSITY, New Orleans, LA 70118-5669

**General Information** Independent, coed, university. CGS member. *Enrollment:* 11,913 graduate, professional, and undergraduate students; 4,169 full-time matriculated graduate/professional students (2,315 women), 1,141 part-time matriculated graduate/professional students (684 women). *Enrollment by degree level:* 2,364 master's, 2,862 doctoral, 84 other advanced degrees. *Graduate faculty:* 74 full-time (39 women), 54 part-time/adjunct (36 women). *Tuition:* Full-time $57,004; part-time $3167 per credit hour. *Required fees:* $2086; $44.50 per credit hour. $80 per term. Tuition and fees vary according to course load, degree level and program. *Graduate housing:* Rooms and/or apartments available on a first-come, first-served basis to single and married students. Typical cost: $9660 per year for single students; $19,200 per year for married students. Room charges vary according to board plan, campus/location and housing facility selected. *Student services:* Campus employment opportunities, campus safety program, career counseling, child daycare facilities, exercise/wellness program, free psychological counseling, grant writing training, international student services, low-cost health insurance, multicultural affairs office, services for students with disabilities, teacher training, writing training. *Library facilities:* Howard Tilton Memorial Library plus 8 others. *Collection:* Books: 4.6 million (physical); Serial titles: 66,832 (physical). Study areas open 24 hours, 5–7 days a week; students can reserve study rooms. *Research affiliation:* New Orleans BioInnovation Center (NOBIC) (business consulting and start-up support, including educational events), Louisiana Cancer Research Consortium (treatment and prevention of cancer), Boehringer-Ingelheim (clinical research in coronary and pulmonary diseases, diabetes, and stroke), Blue Cross and Blue Shield of Louisiana (BCBSLA) (healthcare innovation including access, delivery, and outcomes), AbbVie (hepatitis and diabetes), Genentech (antiviral treatment and pulmonary disease).

**Computer facilities:** Computer purchase and lease plans are available. 556 computers available on campus for general student use. A campuswide network can be accessed. Online class registration is available.
Website: http://www.tulane.edu/

**General Application Contact:** Jennifer O'Brien-Brown, Program Manager, 504-247-1213, Fax: 504-865-6723, E-mail: ogps@tulane.edu.

**GRADUATE UNITS**

**A. B. Freeman School of Business** Students: 394 full-time (168 women), 379 part-time (162 women); includes 111 minority (41 Black or African American, non-Hispanic/Latino; 24 Asian, non-Hispanic/Latino; 38 Hispanic/Latino; 8 Two or more races, non-Hispanic/Latino), 427 international. Average age 28. 1,847 applicants, 72% accepted, 379 enrolled. *Faculty:* 49 full-time (15 women), 53 part-time/adjunct (7 women). Expenses: Contact institution. *Financial support:* In 2019–20, 233 students received support. Fellowships with tuition reimbursements available, research assistantships, teaching assistantships, career-related internships or fieldwork, Federal Work-Study, tuition waivers (full and partial), and unspecified assistantships available. Support available to part-time students. Financial award application deadline: 4/15; financial award applicants required to submit FAFSA. In 2019, 791 master's awarded. *Program availability:* Part-time, evening/weekend. *Application deadline:* For fall admission, 11/1 priority date for domestic students, 11/1 for international students; for winter admission,

1/6 for domestic and international students; for spring admission, 3/1 priority date for domestic students, 3/1 for international students; for summer admission, 5/5 for domestic students. Applications are processed on a rolling basis. *Application fee:* $125. Electronic applications accepted. *Application Contact:* Melissa Booth, Assistant Dean for Graduate Admissions, 800-223-5402, E-mail: freeman.admissions@tulane.edu. *Dean,* Ira Solomon, PhD, 504-865-5407, Fax: 504-865-5491, E-mail: businessdean@tulane.edu.

**School of Architecture** *Program availability:* Part-time.

**School of Liberal Arts** *Program availability:* Part-time. Electronic applications accepted.

***Roger Thayer Stone Center for Latin American Studies*** Electronic applications accepted.

**School of Medicine**

***Graduate Programs in Biomedical Sciences***

**School of Professional Advancement** *Program availability:* Part-time.

**School of Public Health and Tropical Medicine** *Program availability:* Part-time, evening/weekend, 100% online, synchronous sessions. Electronic applications accepted.

**School of Science and Engineering** *Program availability:* Part-time. Electronic applications accepted.

**School of Social Work** *Program availability:* Part-time. Electronic applications accepted.

## TUSCULUM UNIVERSITY, Greeneville, TN 37743-9997

**General Information** Independent-religious, coed, comprehensive institution. *Graduate housing:* On-campus housing not available.

**GRADUATE UNITS**

**Program in Business Administration** *Program availability:* Evening/weekend.

**Program in Curriculum and Instruction** *Program availability:* Evening/weekend.

**Program in Nursing** *Program availability:* Part-time.

**Program in Talent Development** *Program availability:* Online learning.

**Program in Teaching** *Program availability:* Evening/weekend.

## TUSKEGEE UNIVERSITY, Tuskegee, AL 36088

**General Information** Independent, coed, comprehensive institution. *Graduate housing:* Rooms and/or apartments available to single students and available on a first-come, first-served basis to married students. Housing application deadline: 5/1. *Research affiliation:* Boeing (engineering), Chevron (engineering), 3M Corporation (engineering), U.S. Department of Education (DOE) (agriculture), U.S. Department of Defense (agriculture).

**GRADUATE UNITS**

**Graduate Programs** *Program availability:* Part-time.

***Andrew F. Brimmer College of Business and Information Science***

***College of Agriculture, Environment and Nutrition Sciences***

***College of Arts and Sciences***

***College of Engineering***

***College of Veterinary Medicine, Nursing and Allied Health***

## TYNDALE UNIVERSITY COLLEGE & SEMINARY, Toronto, ON M2M 3S4, Canada

**General Information** Independent-religious, coed, comprehensive institution. *Graduate housing:* Room and/or apartments available on a first-come, first-served basis to single students; on-campus housing not available to married students.

**GRADUATE UNITS**

**Graduate Programs** *Program availability:* Part-time, online learning. Electronic applications accepted.

## UNIVERSITY OF ILLINOIS AT CHICAGO, Chicago, IL 60604-3968

**General Information** Independent, coed, graduate-only institution. *Enrollment by degree level:* 87 master's, 947 doctoral. *Graduate faculty:* 52 full-time (27 women), 139 part-time/adjunct (57 women). *International tuition:* $45,000 full-time. *Tuition, area resident:* Full-time $36,000; part-time $1200 per credit hour. Tuition, nonresident: full-time $45,000; part-time $1500 per credit hour. *Required fees:* $4654; $4282 $2141. Tuition and fees vary according to course load and program. *Graduate housing:* Rooms and/or apartments available on a first-come, first-served basis to single students and available to married students. *Student services:* Campus employment opportunities, campus safety program, career counseling, exercise/wellness program, free psychological counseling, international student services, low-cost health insurance, multicultural affairs office, services for students with disabilities, writing training. *Library facilities:* Louis L. Biro Law Library. *Collection:* Books: 46,081 (physical), 25,836 (digital/electronic); Serial titles: 1,187 (physical), 74,679 (digital/electronic); Databases: 71. Weekly public service hours: 96; students can reserve study rooms.

**Computer facilities:** 26 computers available on campus for general student use. A campuswide network can be accessed. Online class registration is available.
Website: http://www.jmls.edu/

**General Application Contact:** Chante Spann, Assistant Dean for Admissions, 800-537-4280, Fax: 312-427-5136, E-mail: admissions@jmls.edu.

## UNB FREDERICTON, Fredericton, NB E3B 5A3, Canada

**General Information** Province-supported, coed, university. *Enrollment:* 1,125 full-time matriculated graduate/professional students (494 women), 524 part-time matriculated graduate/professional students (352 women). *Enrollment by degree level:* 983 master's, 403 doctoral, 263 other advanced degrees. *Graduate faculty:* 428 full-time (151 women), 219 part-time/adjunct (45 women). *International tuition:* $12,435 Canadian dollars full-time. *Tuition, area resident:* Full-time $6975 Canadian dollars; part-time $3423 Canadian dollars per year. Tuition, province resident: full-time $6975 Canadian dollars; part-time $3423 Canadian dollars per year. Tuition, Canadian resident: full-time $6975 Canadian dollars; part-time $3423 Canadian dollars per year. *Required fees:* $92.25 Canadian dollars per term. Full-time tuition and fees vary according to degree level, campus/location, program, reciprocity agreements and student level. *Graduate housing:* Rooms and/or apartments available on a first-come, first-served basis to single and married students. Typical cost: $10,468 Canadian dollars per year ($0 Canadian dollars including board) for single students; $10,468 Canadian dollars per year ($0 Canadian dollars including board) for married students. Room and board charges vary according to board plan, campus/location and housing facility selected. Housing application deadline: 5/31. *Student services:* Campus employment opportunities, campus safety program, career counseling, child daycare facilities, exercise/wellness program, free psychological counseling, grant writing training, international student services, low-cost health insurance, multicultural affairs office, services for students with disabilities, teacher training, writing training. *Library facilities:* Harriet Irving Library plus 4 others. *Research affiliation:* Petroleum Research Atlantic Canada (petroleum), Atlantic Associate for Research in the Mathematical Sciences (mathematical sciences), Atlantic Hydrogen, Inc. (hydrogen), Pulp and Paper Research Institute of Canada (pulp and paper), National Research Council Institute for Information Technology (information technology), Huntsman Marine Science Centre (marine sciences).

**Computer facilities:** 935 computers available on campus for general student use. A campuswide network can be accessed from student residence rooms and from off campus. Online class registration is available.
Website: http://www.unb.ca/

**General Application Contact:** Dr. Drew Rendall, Dean of Graduate Studies, 506-458-7154, Fax: 506-453-4817, E-mail: drendall@unb.ca.

**GRADUATE UNITS**

**Faculty of Law (Fredericton)** Electronic applications accepted.

**School of Graduate Studies** Students: 864 full-time (358 women), 522 part-time (352 women), 553 international. *Faculty:* 428 full-time (151 women), 219 part-time/adjunct (45 women). Expenses: Contact institution. *Financial support:* Fellowships, research assistantships, teaching assistantships, scholarships/grants, tuition waivers, and unspecified assistantships available. Support available to part-time students. In 2019, 517 master's, 51 doctorates awarded. *Program availability:* Part-time, evening/weekend, blended/hybrid learning. *Application deadline:* 1/31 for domestic and international students. Applications are processed on a rolling basis. *Application fee:* $50 Canadian dollars. Electronic applications accepted. *Application Contact:* Jackie Seely, Program Assistant, 506-458-7390, Fax: 506-453-4817, E-mail: jseely@unb.ca. *Dean,* Dr. Drew Rendall, 506-458-7154, Fax: 506-453-4817, E-mail: drendall@unb.ca.

***Faculty of Arts - Saint John*** Students: 165 full-time (102 women), 34 part-time (14 women), 35 international. Average age 33. 198 applicants, 100% accepted, 198 enrolled. *Faculty:* 159 full-time (82 women), 1 (woman) part-time/adjunct. Expenses: Contact institution. *Financial support:* Fellowships, research assistantships, teaching assistantships, scholarships/grants, and unspecified assistantships available. Financial award application deadline: 1/31. In 2019, 32 master's, 3 doctorates awarded. *Program availability:* Part-time. *Application deadline:* For fall admission, 1/31 priority date for domestic students; for winter admission, 1/31 priority date for domestic students; for spring admission, 1/31 priority date for domestic students. Applications are processed on a rolling basis. *Application fee:* $50 Canadian dollars. Electronic applications accepted. *Application Contact:* Dr. John Kershaw, Acting Associate Dean of Graduate Studies, 506-447-3065, Fax: 506-453-4817, E-mail: kershaw@unb.ca. *Dean of Arts,* Dr. Joanne Wright, 506-458-7485, Fax: 506-453-5102, E-mail: jwright@unb.ca.

***Faculty of Business Administration*** Students: 73 full-time (27 women), 23 part-time (10 women), 40 international. Average age 32. *Faculty:* 32 full-time (11 women), 7 part-time/adjunct (3 women). Expenses: Contact institution. *Financial support:* Fellowships, research assistantships, and teaching assistantships available. Financial award application deadline: 1/15. In 2019, 31 master's awarded. *Program availability:* Part-time. *Application deadline:* For fall admission, 10/31 priority date for domestic and international students; for spring admission, 3/31 priority date for domestic and international students. *Application fee:* $50 Canadian dollars. Electronic applications accepted. *Application Contact:* Marilyn Davis, Acting Graduate Secretary, 506-453-4766, Fax: 506-453-3561, E-mail: mbacontact@unb.ca. *Director of Graduate Studies,* Dr. Donglei Du, 506-458-7353, Fax: 506-453-3561, E-mail: ddu@unb.ca.

***Faculty of Education*** Students: 52 full-time (40 women), 291 part-time (234 women), 10 international. Average age 39. *Faculty:* 29 full-time (19 women), 9 part-time/adjunct (6 women). Expenses: Contact institution. *Financial support:* Fellowships, research assistantships, teaching assistantships, and tuition waivers available. Financial award application deadline: 1/15. In 2019, 208 master's, 4 doctorates awarded. *Program availability:* Part-time, online learning. *Application deadline:* For fall admission, 8/31 priority date for domestic students, 1/31 priority date for international students; for winter admission, 1/31 priority date for domestic and international students; for spring admission, 1/31 for domestic students, 1/31 priority date for international students. *Application fee:* $50 Canadian dollars. Electronic applications accepted. *Application Contact:* Carol Ann Hatheway, Graduate Secretary, 506-451-6999, Fax: 506-453-3569, E-mail: hatheway@unb.ca. *Associate Dean,* Dr. David Wagner, 506-447-3294, Fax: 506-453-3569, E-mail: dwagner@unb.ca.

***Faculty of Engineering*** Students: 222 full-time (50 women), 36 part-time (6 women), 136 international. Average age 29. *Faculty:* 76 full-time (10 women). Expenses: Contact institution. *Financial support:* Fellowships, research assistantships, teaching assistantships, and career-related internships or fieldwork available. Financial award application deadline: 1/15. In 2019, 54 master's, 9 doctorates awarded. *Program availability:* Part-time. *Application deadline:* For fall admission, 3/1 priority date for domestic students. Applications are processed on a rolling basis. *Application fee:* $50 Canadian dollars. Electronic applications accepted. *Application Contact:* Dr. Chris Diduch, Dean, 506-453-4570, Fax: 506-453-5003, E-mail: diduch@unb.ca. *Dean,* Dr. Chris Diduch, 506-453-4570, Fax: 506-453-5003, E-mail: diduch@unb.ca.

***Faculty of Forestry and Environmental Management*** Students: 84 full-time (42 women), 16 part-time (5 women), 46 international. Average age 28. *Faculty:* 20 full-time (3 women), 6 part-time/adjunct (0 women). Expenses: Contact institution. *Financial support:* Fellowships, research assistantships, and teaching assistantships available. Financial award application deadline: 1/15. In 2019, 27 master's, 4 doctorates awarded. *Program availability:* Part-time. *Application deadline:* For fall admission, 3/1 for domestic students. Applications are processed on a rolling basis. *Application fee:* $50 Canadian dollars. Electronic applications accepted. *Application Contact:* Faith Sharpe, Graduate Secretary, 506-458-7520, Fax: 506-453-3538, E-mail: fsharpe@unb.ca. *Director of Graduate Studies,* Dr. Graham Forbes, 506-453-4929, Fax: 506-453-3538, E-mail: forbes@unb.ca.

***Faculty of Kinesiology*** Students: 35 full-time (17 women), 7 part-time (3 women), 3 international. Average age 30. *Faculty:* 20 full-time (8 women), 2 part-time/adjunct (0 women). Expenses: Contact institution. *Financial support:* Fellowships with tuition reimbursements, research assistantships, teaching assistantships, career-related internships or fieldwork, and scholarships/grants available. Financial award application deadline: 1/15. In 2019, 15 master's awarded. *Program availability:* Part-time. *Application deadline:* For winter admission, 1/31 for domestic students; for spring admission, 3/31 for domestic students. Applications are processed on a rolling basis. *Application fee:* $50 Canadian dollars. Electronic applications accepted. *Application Contact:* Leslie Harquail, Graduate Secretary, 506-453-4575, Fax: 506-453-3511, E-mail: harquail@unb.ca. *Dean,* Dr. Wayne Albert, 506-447-3101, Fax: 506-453-3511, E-mail: walbert@unb.ca.

***Faculty of Nursing*** Students: 14 full-time (13 women), 13 part-time (all women). Average age 36. *Faculty:* 41 full-time (37 women). Expenses: Contact institution. *Financial support:* Fellowships and research assistantships available. Financial award application deadline: 1/15. In 2019, 10 master's awarded. *Program availability:* Part-time, online learning. *Application deadline:* For winter admission, 1/2 priority date for domestic students. *Application fee:* $50 Canadian dollars. Electronic applications accepted. *Application Contact:* Tricia Canning, Graduate Secretary, 506-458 7650, Fax: 506-447-3057, E-mail: canningt@unb.ca. *Dean,* Lorna Butler, 506-458 7625, Fax: 506-447 3057, E-mail: Lorna.butler@unb.ca.

***Faculty of Science, Applied Science, and Engineering*** Students: 123 full-time (48 women), 23 part-time (13 women), 55 international. Average age 31. *Faculty:* 89 full-time (21 women), 1 part-time/adjunct (0 women). Expenses: Contact institution. *Financial support:* Fellowships, research assistantships, and teaching assistantships available. Financial award application deadline: 1/15. In 2019, 19 master's, 10 doctorates awarded. *Program availability:* Part-time. *Application deadline:* For fall admission, 3/1 priority date for domestic students. Applications are processed on a rolling basis. *Application fee:* $50 Canadian dollars. Electronic applications accepted. *Application Contact:* Heidi Stewart, Graduate Studies Coordinator, 506-458-7488, E-mail: scigrad@unb.ca. *Dean,* Dr. Gary Saunders, 506-453 4841, Fax: 506-453-3570, E-mail: gws@unb.ca.

## UNIFICATION THEOLOGICAL SEMINARY, Barrytown, NY 12507

**General Information** Independent-religious, coed, graduate-only institution. *Enrollment by degree level:* 84 master's, 24 doctoral. *Graduate faculty:* 4 full-time (1 woman), 9 part-time/adjunct (1 woman). *Tuition:* Full-time $9720; part-time $540 per credit. *Required fees:* $270; $15 per credit. $90 per semester. *Graduate housing:* On-campus housing not available. *Student services:* Campus employment opportunities, career counseling, free psychological counseling, international student services, writing training. *Library facilities:* Seminary Library. *Collection:* Books: 62,603 (physical), 65,806 (digital/electronic); Serial titles: 3 (physical), 6 (digital/electronic); Databases: 12. Weekly public service hours: 44.

**Computer facilities:** 5 computers available on campus for general student use. A campuswide network can be accessed. Online class registration is available. Website: http://www.uts.edu/

**General Application Contact:** Joy Theriot, Senior Admissions Counselor, 212-563-6647 Ext. 113, Fax: 212-563-6431, E-mail: j.theriot@uts.edu.

**GRADUATE UNITS**

**Graduate Programs** Students: 46 full-time (19 women), 62 part-time (24 women); includes 52 minority (27 Black or African American, non-Hispanic/Latino; 16 Asian, non-Hispanic/Latino; 4 Hispanic/Latino; 5 Two or more races, non-Hispanic/Latino), 34 international. Average age 44. *Faculty:* 4 full-time (1 woman), 9 part-time/adjunct (1 woman). Expenses: Contact institution. *Financial support:* In 2019–20, 108 students received support. Scholarships/grants available. Financial award application deadline: 6/15; financial award applicants required to submit FAFSA. In 2019, 3 master's, 7 doctorates awarded. *Program availability:* Part-time, evening/weekend, 100% online, blended/hybrid learning. *Application deadline:* For fall admission, 3/15 priority date for domestic and international students; for spring admission, 9/15 priority date for domestic and international students. Applications are processed on a rolling basis. *Application fee:* $30. Electronic applications accepted. *Application Contact:* Henry Christopher, Director of Admissions and Financial Aid, 212-563-6647 Ext. 105, Fax: 212-563-6431, E-mail: h.christopher@uts.edu. *Academic Dean,* Dr. Keisuke Noda, 212-563-6647 Ext. 101, Fax: 212-563-6431, E-mail: k.noda@uts.edu.

## UNIFORMED SERVICES UNIVERSITY OF THE HEALTH SCIENCES, Bethesda, MD 20814-4799

**General Information** Federally supported, coed, graduate-only institution. *Graduate housing:* On-campus housing not available. *Research affiliation:* National Library of Medicine, National Institutes of Health, Walter Reed Army Institute of Research, Armed Forces Institute of Pathology, U.S. Armed Forces Radiobiology Research Institute.

**GRADUATE UNITS**

**Daniel K. Inouye Graduate School of Nursing** Students: 170 full-time (98 women); includes 51 minority (21 Black or African American, non-Hispanic/Latino; 17 Asian, non-Hispanic/Latino; 11 Hispanic/Latino; 2 Native Hawaiian or other Pacific Islander, non-Hispanic/Latino). Average age 34. 88 applicants, 75% accepted, 66 enrolled. *Faculty:* 50 full-time (32 women), 1 part-time/adjunct (0 women). Expenses: Contact institution. *Financial support:* Robert Wood Johnson and Jonas scholars available. In 2019, 2 master's, 42 doctorates awarded. *Program availability:* Part-time. *Application deadline:* For winter admission, 2/15 for domestic students; for summer admission, 8/15 for domestic students. Electronic applications accepted. *Application Contact:* Maureen Jackson, Student Admissions Program Manager, 301-295-1055, E-mail: maureen.jackson.ctr@usuhs.edu. *Associate Dean for Academic Affairs,* Dr. Diane C. Seibert, 301-295-1080, Fax: 301-295-1707, E-mail: diane.seibert@usuhs.edu.

**F. Edward Hebert School of Medicine**

***Graduate Programs in the Biomedical Sciences and Public Health*** Electronic applications accepted.

**See Display below and Close-Up on page 633.**

## UNION COLLEGE, Barbourville, KY 40906-1499

**General Information** Independent-religious, coed, comprehensive institution. *Graduate housing:* Rooms and/or apartments available to single and married students.

**GRADUATE UNITS**

**Graduate Programs** *Program availability:* Part-time, evening/weekend.

## UNION COLLEGE, Lincoln, NE 68506-4300

**General Information** Independent-religious, coed, comprehensive institution. *Graduate housing:* Rooms and/or apartments available on a first-come, first-served basis to single and married students.

**GRADUATE UNITS**

**Physician Assistant Program** Electronic applications accepted.

## UNION INSTITUTE & UNIVERSITY, Cincinnati, OH 45206-1925

**General Information** Independent, coed, university.

**GRADUATE UNITS**

**Master of Arts Program** *Program availability:* Part-time, online only, 100% online. Electronic applications accepted.

**Master of Arts Program in Clinical Mental Health Counseling** *Program availability:* Part-time, online only, blended/hybrid learning. Electronic applications accepted.

**Master of Science Program in Healthcare Leadership**

**Master of Science Program in Organizational Leadership** *Program availability:* Part-time, online only, 100% online. Electronic applications accepted.

**PhD Program in Interdisciplinary Studies** *Program availability:* Part-time, online only, blended/hybrid learning. Electronic applications accepted.

## UNION PRESBYTERIAN SEMINARY, Richmond, VA 23227-4597

**General Information** Independent-religious, coed, graduate-only institution. *Graduate housing:* Rooms and/or apartments available on a first-come, first-served basis to single and married students. Housing application deadline: 6/30.

**GRADUATE UNITS**

**Graduate and Professional Programs** *Program availability:* Part-time, evening/weekend, online learning. Electronic applications accepted.

## UNION THEOLOGICAL SEMINARY IN THE CITY OF NEW YORK, New York, NY 10027-5710

**General Information** Independent-religious, coed, graduate-only institution. *Graduate housing:* Rooms and/or apartments available on a first-come, first-served basis to single and married students. Housing application deadline: 5/15.

**GRADUATE UNITS**

**Graduate and Professional Programs** *Program availability:* Part-time.

## UNION UNIVERSITY, Jackson, TN 38305-3697

**General Information** Independent-religious, coed, comprehensive institution. *Graduate housing:* Rooms and/or apartments available on a first-come, first-served basis to single and married students. Housing application deadline: 8/1.

**GRADUATE UNITS**

**College of Pharmacy** Electronic applications accepted.

**Institute for International and Intercultural Studies** *Program availability:* Part-time, evening/weekend. Electronic applications accepted.

**McAfee School of Business Administration** *Program availability:* Evening/weekend, online learning. Electronic applications accepted.

**School of Education** *Program availability:* Part-time, evening/weekend, online learning. Electronic applications accepted.

**School of Nursing** Electronic applications accepted.

**School of Social Work**

**School of Theology and Missions** *Program availability:* Part-time, evening/weekend, online learning. Electronic applications accepted.

## UNITED LUTHERAN SEMINARY, Gettysburg, PA 17325-1795

**General Information** Independent-religious, coed, graduate-only institution. *Enrollment by degree level:* 284 master's, 9 doctoral. *Graduate faculty:* 11 full-time (3 women), 9 part-time/adjunct (4 women). *Tuition:* Full-time $19,500; part-time $1950 per credit. Tuition and fees vary according to course load. *Graduate housing:* Rooms and/or apartments available on a first-come, first-served basis to single and married students. Typical cost: $4950 per year for single students; $12,000 per year for married students. Room charges vary according to housing facility selected. Housing application deadline: 4/1. *Student services:* Campus employment opportunities, exercise/wellness program, international student services, multicultural affairs office, services for students with disabilities, writing training. *Library facilities:* A.R. Wentz Library. *Collection:* Students can reserve study rooms.

**Computer facilities:** 10 computers available on campus for general student use. A campuswide network can be accessed from student residence rooms. Online class registration is available.
Website: http://www.unitedlutheranseminary.edu/

**General Application Contact:** Dr. Nancy E. Gable, Admissions Director, 717-338-3008 Ext. 3008, Fax: 334-3469, E-mail: ngable@uls.edu.

**GRADUATE UNITS**

**Graduate and Professional Programs** *Program availability:* Part-time, online learning. Electronic applications accepted.

## UNITED LUTHERAN SEMINARY, Philadelphia, PA 19119-1794

**General Information** Independent-religious, coed, graduate-only institution. *Graduate housing:* Rooms and/or apartments available on a first-come, first-served basis to single and married students. Housing application deadline: 5/15.

**GRADUATE UNITS**

**Graduate School** *Program availability:* Part-time, evening/weekend. Electronic applications accepted.

## UNITED STATES ARMY COMMAND AND GENERAL STAFF COLLEGE, Fort Leavenworth, KS 66027-2301

**General Information** Federally supported, coed, primarily men, graduate-only institution. *Graduate housing:* Rooms and/or apartments available to single and married students.

**GRADUATE UNITS**

**Graduate Program**

## UNITED STATES INTERNATIONAL UNIVERSITY–AFRICA, Nairobi 00800, Kenya

**General Information** Independent, coed, comprehensive institution. *Graduate housing:* Room and/or apartments available on a first-come, first-served basis to single students; on-campus housing not available to married students. Housing application deadline: 7/31.

**GRADUATE UNITS**

**School of Arts and Sciences** *Program availability:* Part-time, evening/weekend.

**School of Business Administration** *Program availability:* Part-time, evening/weekend.

## UNITED STATES MERCHANT MARINE ACADEMY, Kings Point, NY 11024-1699

**General Information** Federally supported, coed, comprehensive institution.

**GRADUATE UNITS**

**Graduate Program**

## UNITED STATES SPORTS ACADEMY, Daphne, AL 36526-7055

**General Information** Independent, coed, upper-level institution. *Graduate housing:* On-campus housing not available.

**GRADUATE UNITS**

**Graduate Programs** *Program availability:* Part-time, 100% online. Electronic applications accepted.

## UNITED STATES UNIVERSITY, San Diego, CA 92108

**General Information** Proprietary, coed, comprehensive institution.

**GRADUATE UNITS**

**Family Nurse Practitioner Program**

## UNITED TALMUDICAL SEMINARY, Brooklyn, NY 11211

**General Information** Independent-religious, men only, comprehensive institution.

**GRADUATE UNITS**

**Graduate Programs**

## UNITED THEOLOGICAL SEMINARY, Dayton, OH 45426

**General Information** Independent-religious, coed, graduate-only institution.

**GRADUATE UNITS**

**Graduate and Professional Programs** *Program availability:* Part-time, evening/weekend, online learning. Electronic applications accepted.

## UNITED THEOLOGICAL SEMINARY OF THE TWIN CITIES, New Brighton, MN 55112-2598

**General Information** Independent-religious, coed, graduate-only institution. *Graduate housing:* Rooms and/or apartments available on a first-come, first-served basis to single and married students.

**GRADUATE UNITS**

**Graduate Programs** *Program availability:* Part-time, evening/weekend.

## UNITY COLLEGE, Unity, ME 04988

**General Information** Independent, coed, comprehensive institution.

**GRADUATE UNITS**

**Program in Professional Science** *Program availability:* Online learning.

## UNIVERSIDAD ADVENTISTA DE LAS ANTILLAS, Mayagüez, PR 00681-0118

**General Information** Independent-religious, coed, comprehensive institution. *Graduate housing:* Rooms and/or apartments available on a first-come, first-served basis to single and married students.

**GRADUATE UNITS**

**EGECED Department** Electronic applications accepted.

## UNIVERSIDAD CENTRAL DEL CARIBE, Bayamón, PR 00960-6032

**General Information** Independent, coed, comprehensive institution. *Graduate housing:* On-campus housing not available.

**GRADUATE UNITS**

**Program in Substance Abuse Counseling**

**School of Medicine**

## UNIVERSIDAD DE LAS AMERICAS, A.C., 06700 Mexico City, Mexico

**General Information** Independent, coed, comprehensive institution.

**GRADUATE UNITS**

**Program in Business Administration**

**Program in Education**

**Program in International Organizations and Institutions**

**Program in Psychology**

## UNIVERSIDAD DE LAS AMÉRICAS PUEBLA, Puebla CP 72810, Mexico

**General Information** Independent, coed, university. CGS member. *Graduate housing:* On-campus housing not available. *Research affiliation:* Empacadora San Marcos S. A. de C. U. (food service), Volkswagen de Mexico S. A. de C. U. (mechanical engineering), Institute Mexicano del Tecnologa del agua (electronic engineering), Frugosa S. A. de C. U. (chemical engineering).

**GRADUATE UNITS**

**Division of Graduate Studies** *Program availability:* Part-time, evening/weekend.

***School of Business and Economics*** *Program availability:* Part-time, evening/weekend.

***School of Engineering*** *Program availability:* Part-time, evening/weekend.

***School of Humanities*** *Program availability:* Part-time, evening/weekend.

***School of Sciences*** *Program availability:* Part-time, evening/weekend.

***School of Social Sciences*** *Program availability:* Part-time, evening/weekend.

## UNIVERSIDAD DEL ESTE, Carolina, PR 00984

**General Information** Independent, coed, comprehensive institution.

**GRADUATE UNITS**

**Graduate School**

## UNIVERSIDAD DEL TURABO, Gurabo, PR 00778-3030

**General Information** Independent, coed, university. CGS member. *Graduate housing:* On-campus housing not available.

**GRADUATE UNITS**

**Graduate Programs** *Program availability:* Part-time, evening/weekend, 100% online, blended/hybrid learning. Electronic applications accepted.

***School of Business and Entrepreneurship*** *Program availability:* Part-time, evening/weekend. Electronic applications accepted.

***School of Engineering*** Electronic applications accepted.

***School of Health Sciences*** Electronic applications accepted.

***School of Social Sciences and Humanities*** Electronic applications accepted.

## UNIVERSIDAD DE MONTERREY, 66238 San Pedro Garza Garcia, NL, Mexico

**General Information** Independent-religious, coed, comprehensive institution.

**GRADUATE UNITS**

**Graduate Programs**

## UNIVERSIDAD METROPOLITANA, San Juan, PR 00928-1150

**General Information** Independent, coed, comprehensive institution. *Graduate housing:* On-campus housing not available. *Research affiliation:* University of Puerto Rico (physics, chemistry), University of Utah (computational chemistry), Howard University (computational chemistry), Berkeley National Laboratories (bioremediation), University Corporation for Atmospheric Research (computer science, atmospheric science), University of Colorado Boulder (computer science, biology).

**GRADUATE UNITS**

**School of Business Administration** *Program availability:* Part-time, evening/weekend. Electronic applications accepted.

**School of Education** *Program availability:* Part-time, evening/weekend. Electronic applications accepted.

**School of Environmental Affairs** *Program availability:* Part-time. Electronic applications accepted.

**School of Health Sciences**

**School of Social Sciences, Humanities and Communications**

## UNIVERSITÉ DE MONCTON, Moncton, NB E1A 3E9, Canada

**General Information** Province-supported, coed, comprehensive institution. *Graduate housing:* Rooms and/or apartments available on a first-come, first-served basis to single and married students.

**GRADUATE UNITS**

**Faculty of Administration** Students: 30 full-time (10 women), 24 international. Average age 26. 30 applicants, 100% accepted, 30 enrolled. *Faculty:* 27 full-time (11 women), 27 part-time/adjunct (8 women). Expenses: Contact institution. *Financial support:* In 2019–20, 7 fellowships (averaging $2,500 per year) were awarded; teaching assistantships and institutionally sponsored loans also available. Support available to part-time students. Financial award application deadline: 5/30. In 2019, 20 master's awarded. *Program availability:* Part-time, evening/weekend, 100% online. *Application deadline:* For fall admission, 6/1 for domestic students, 2/1 for international students; for winter admission, 11/15 for domestic students, 9/1 for international students; for spring admission, 3/31 for domestic students, 1/1 for international students; for summer admission, 3/31 for domestic students, 1/1 for international students. Applications are processed on a rolling basis. *Application fee:* $60. Electronic applications accepted. *Application Contact:* Natalie Allain, Admission Counselor, 506-858-4273, Fax: 506-858-4093, E-mail: natalie.allain@umoncton.ca. *Director*, Mohamed Zaher Bouaziz, 506-858-4110, Fax: 506-858-4093, E-mail: mohamed.zaher.bouaziz@umoncton.ca.

**Faculty of Arts and Social Sciences** *Program availability:* Part-time. Electronic applications accepted.

***School of Social Work***

**Faculty of Education** *Program availability:* Part-time.

***Graduate Studies in Education*** *Program availability:* Part-time.

**Faculty of Engineering**

**Faculty of Sciences** *Program availability:* Part-time. Electronic applications accepted.

**School of Food Science, Nutrition and Family Studies** *Program availability:* Part-time. Electronic applications accepted.

## UNIVERSITÉ DE MONTRÉAL, Montréal, QC H3C 3J7, Canada

**General Information** Province-supported, coed, university. *Graduate housing:* Room and/or apartments available on a first-come, first-served basis to single students; on-campus housing not available to married students. Housing application deadline: 2/1. *Research affiliation:* Centre Hospitalier Universitaire Mere-Enfant de l'Hopital Sainte-Justine, Centre de Recherche de L'Hopital Sacre-Coeur, Institut de Recherches Cliniques de Montreal, Institut de Cardiologie de Montreal, Institut Universitaire de geriatric de Montreal.

**GRADUATE UNITS**

**Department of Kinesiology** Electronic applications accepted.

**Faculty of Arts and Sciences** *Program availability:* Part-time. Electronic applications accepted.

***School of Criminology*** Electronic applications accepted.

***School of Industrial Relations*** *Program availability:* Part-time. Electronic applications accepted.

***School of Library and Information Sciences*** Electronic applications accepted.

***School of Psychoeducation*** *Program availability:* Part-time. Electronic applications accepted.

***School of Social Service*** *Program availability:* Part-time. Electronic applications accepted.

**Faculty of Dental Medicine** Electronic applications accepted.

**Faculty of Education** *Program availability:* Part-time, evening/weekend. Electronic applications accepted.

**Faculty of Environmental Design and Planning** Electronic applications accepted.

**Faculty of Law** *Program availability:* Part-time. Electronic applications accepted.

**Faculty of Medicine** Electronic applications accepted.

***Institute of Biomedical Engineering*** Electronic applications accepted.

***School of Speech Therapy and Audiology*** Electronic applications accepted.

**Faculty of Music** Electronic applications accepted.

**Faculty of Nursing** *Program availability:* Part-time. Electronic applications accepted.

**Faculty of Pharmacy** *Program availability:* Part-time. Electronic applications accepted.

**Faculty of Theology and Sciences of Religions** Electronic applications accepted.

**Faculty of Veterinary Medicine** Electronic applications accepted.

**School of Optometry** *Program availability:* Part-time. Electronic applications accepted.

## UNIVERSITÉ DE SAINT-BONIFACE, Saint-Boniface, MB R2H 0H7, Canada

**General Information** Independent-religious, coed, comprehensive institution.

**GRADUATE UNITS**

**Department of Education**

**Program in Canadian Studies**

## UNIVERSITÉ DE SHERBROOKE, Sherbrooke, QC J1K 2R1, Canada

**General Information** Independent, coed, university. *Graduate housing:* Room and/or apartments available to single students; on-campus housing not available to married students. Housing application deadline: 6/1. *Research affiliation:* Societe de Microelectronique Industrielle.

**GRADUATE UNITS**

**Faculty of Administration** *Program availability:* Part-time, evening/weekend.

**Faculty of Education** *Program availability:* Part-time, evening/weekend.

**Faculty of Engineering** *Program availability:* Part-time. Electronic applications accepted.

**Faculty of Law** *Program availability:* Part-time, evening/weekend. Electronic applications accepted.

**Faculty of Letters and Human Sciences** *Program availability:* Part-time.

***Institute of Management and Development of Cooperatives***

**Faculty of Medicine and Health Sciences** *Program availability:* Part-time. Electronic applications accepted.

***Graduate Programs in Medicine*** *Program availability:* Part-time. Electronic applications accepted.

**Faculty of Physical Education and Sports** *Program availability:* Part-time.

**Faculty of Sciences**

***Centre de Formation en Technologies de L'information*** Electronic applications accepted.

***Centre Universitaire de Formation en Environnement*** *Program availability:* Online learning. Electronic applications accepted.

**Faculty of Theology and Religious Studies** *Program availability:* Part-time, evening/weekend, online learning.

## UNIVERSITÉ DU QUÉBEC À CHICOUTIMI, Chicoutimi, QC G7H 2B1, Canada

**General Information** Province-supported, coed, university. CGS member. *Graduate housing:* Room and/or apartments available to single students; on-campus housing not available to married students.

**GRADUATE UNITS**

**Graduate Programs** *Program availability:* Part-time.

## UNIVERSITÉ DU QUÉBEC À MONTRÉAL, Montréal, QC H3C 3P8, Canada

**General Information** Province-supported, coed, university. CGS member. *Graduate housing:* Room and/or apartments available to single students; on-campus housing not available to married students. *Research affiliation:* Labopharm, Inc. (pharmacology), Hydro-Quebec (environmental sciences), Bell (computer sciences), Microcreatif (computer sciences), University Corporation for Atmospheric Research.

**GRADUATE UNITS**

**Graduate Programs** *Program availability:* Part-time.

## UNIVERSITÉ DU QUÉBEC À RIMOUSKI, Rimouski, QC G5L 3A1, Canada

**General Information** Province-supported, coed, comprehensive institution. CGS member. *Graduate housing:* Rooms and/or apartments available on a first-come, first-served basis to single and married students. *Research affiliation:* Institut des Sciences de la Mer de Rimouski (ISMER) (marine sciences), CRDT (territory development), Centre d'Etudes Nordiques (Nordicity), Quebec Ocean (oceans), Centre Recherche en Forestene (forestry).

**GRADUATE UNITS**

**Graduate Programs** *Program availability:* Part-time.

## UNIVERSITÉ DU QUÉBEC À TROIS-RIVIÈRES, Trois-Rivières, QC G9A 5H7, Canada

**General Information** Province-supported, coed, university. CGS member. *Graduate housing:* Room and/or apartments available to single students; on-campus housing not available to married students. Housing application deadline: 2/1.

**GRADUATE UNITS**

**Graduate Programs** *Program availability:* Part-time.

## UNIVERSITÉ DU QUÉBEC, ÉCOLE DE TECHNOLOGIE SUPÉRIEURE, Montréal, QC H3C 1K3, Canada

**General Information** Province-supported, coed, primarily men, comprehensive institution. CGS member. *Graduate housing:* Rooms and/or apartments available on a first-come, first-served basis to single and married students.

**GRADUATE UNITS**

**Graduate Programs** *Program availability:* Online learning.

## UNIVERSITÉ DU QUÉBEC, ÉCOLE NATIONALE D'ADMINISTRATION PUBLIQUE, Quebec, QC G1K 9E5, Canada

**General Information** Province-supported, coed, graduate-only institution. CGS member. *Graduate housing:* On-campus housing not available.

**GRADUATE UNITS**

**Graduate Programs in Public Administration** *Program availability:* Part-time.

## UNIVERSITÉ DU QUÉBEC EN ABITIBI-TÉMISCAMINGUE, Rouyn-Noranda, QC J9X 5E4, Canada

**General Information** Province-supported, coed, comprehensive institution. CGS member. *Graduate housing:* Room and/or apartments available on a first-come, first-served basis to single students; on-campus housing not available to married students. Housing application deadline: 3/1.

**GRADUATE UNITS**

**Graduate Programs** *Program availability:* Part-time.

## UNIVERSITÉ DU QUÉBEC EN OUTAOUAIS, Gatineau, QC J8X 3X7, Canada

**General Information** Province-supported, coed, university. CGS member. *Graduate housing:* Rooms and/or apartments available on a first-come, first-served basis to single and married students.

**GRADUATE UNITS**

**Graduate Programs** *Program availability:* Part-time, evening/weekend. Electronic applications accepted.

## UNIVERSITÉ DU QUÉBEC, INSTITUT NATIONAL DE LA RECHERCHE SCIENTIFIQUE, Québec, QC G1K 9A9, Canada

**General Information** Province-supported, coed, graduate-only institution. CGS member. *Enrollment by degree level:* 235 master's, 446 doctoral, 2 other advanced degrees. *Graduate faculty:* 150 full-time. *Graduate housing:* On-campus housing not available. *Student services:* Exercise/wellness program, free psychological counseling, international student services, low-cost health insurance, services for students with disabilities. *Library facilities:* Service de documentation et d'information specialisees (SDIS) plus 3 others. *Research affiliation:* Sigma Devtech Inc. (green technologies), MPB Technologies Inc. (communications, space, fusion technology, electromagnetics), Biosecur Lab. Inc. (creation and development of active antimicrobial ingredients).

**Computer facilities:** 500 computers available on campus for general student use. Online class registration is available.
Website: http://www.inrs.ca/

**General Application Contact:** Sean Otto, Registrar, 418-654-2518, Fax: 418-654-3858, E-mail: sean.otto@inrs.ca.

**GRADUATE UNITS**

**Graduate Programs** Students: 624 full-time (291 women), 59 part-time (24 women), 445 international. Average age 31. 139 applicants, 94% accepted, 107 enrolled. *Faculty:* 150 full-time. Expenses: Contact institution. *Financial support:* In 2019–20, fellowships (averaging $16,500 per year) were awarded; research assistantships and scholarships/grants also available. In 2019, 76 master's, 67 doctorates awarded. *Program availability:* Part-time. *Application deadline:* For fall admission, 3/30 for domestic and international students; for winter admission, 11/1 for domestic and international students; for spring admission, 3/1 for domestic and international students. *Application fee:* $45. Electronic applications accepted. *Application Contact:* Sean Otto, Registrar, 418-654-2518, Fax: 418-654-3858, E-mail: sean.otto@inrs.ca. *Acting Director of Research and Academic Affairs,* André St-Hilaire, 418-654-3113, E-mail: andre.st-hilaire@ete.inrs.ca.

***Armand-Frappier Santé Biotechnologie*** Students: 157 full-time (94 women), 9 part-time (4 women), 100 international. Average age 30. 23 applicants, 96% accepted, 21 enrolled. *Faculty:* 46 full-time. Expenses: Contact institution. *Financial support:* In 2019–20, fellowships (averaging $16,500 per year) were awarded; research assistantships also available. In 2019, 19 master's, 20 doctorates awarded. *Program availability:* Part-time. *Application deadline:* For fall admission, 3/30 for domestic and international students; for winter admission, 11/1 for domestic and international students; for spring admission, 3/1 for domestic and international students. *Application fee:* $45 Canadian dollars. Electronic applications accepted. *Application Contact:* Sean Otto, Registrar, 418-654-2518, Fax: 418-654-3858, E-mail: sean.otto@inrs.ca. *Director,* Claude Guertin, 450-687-5010, Fax: 450-686-5501, E-mail: claude.guertin@iaf.inrs.ca.

***Centre for Energie Materiaux Telecommunications*** Students: 208 full-time (61 women), 12 part-time (1 woman), 187 international. Average age 32. 36 applicants, 100% accepted, 29 enrolled. *Faculty:* 38 full-time. Expenses: Contact institution. *Financial support:* In 2019–20, fellowships (averaging $16,500 per year) were awarded; research assistantships and scholarships/grants also available. In 2019, 12 master's, 26 doctorates awarded. *Program availability:* Part-time. *Application deadline:* For fall admission, 3/30 for domestic and international students; for winter admission, 11/1 for domestic and international students; for spring admission, 3/1 for domestic and international students. *Application fee:* $45. Electronic applications accepted. *Application Contact:* Sean Otto, Registrar, 418-654-2518, Fax: 418-654-3858, E-mail: sean.otto@inrs.ca. *Director,* Ana Tavares, 514-228-6947, Fax: 450-929-8102, E-mail: ana.tavares@emt.inrs.ca.

***Centre for Urbanisation Culture Societe*** Students: 77 full-time (43 women), 24 part-time (11 women), 22 international. Average age 33. 27 applicants, 93% accepted, 20 enrolled. *Faculty:* 32 full-time. Expenses: Contact institution. *Financial support:* In 2019–20, fellowships (averaging $16,500 per year) were awarded; research assistantships also available. In 2019, 9 master's, 4 doctorates awarded. *Program availability:* Part-time. *Application deadline:* For fall admission, 3/30 for domestic and international students; for winter admission, 11/1 for domestic and international students; for spring admission, 3/1 for domestic and international students. *Application fee:* $45. Electronic applications accepted. *Application Contact:* Sean Otto, Registrar, 418-654-2518, Fax: 418-654-3858, E-mail: sean.otto@inrs.ca. *Director,* Helene Belleau, 514-499-4001, Fax: 514-499-4065, E-mail: helene.belleau@ucs.inrs.ca.

***Research Center–Water Earth Environment*** Students: 182 full-time (93 women), 14 part-time (8 women), 136 international. Average age 30. 53 applicants, 91% accepted, 37 enrolled. *Faculty:* 34 full-time. Expenses: Contact institution. *Financial support:* In 2019–20, fellowships (averaging $16,500 per year) were awarded; research assistantships also available. In 2019, 36 master's, 17 doctorates awarded. *Program availability:* Part-time. *Application deadline:* For fall admission, 3/30 for domestic and international students; for winter admission, 11/1 for domestic and international students; for spring admission, 3/1 for domestic and international students. *Application fee:* $45. Electronic applications accepted. *Application Contact:* Sean Otto, Registrar, 418-654-2518, Fax: 418-654-3858, E-mail: sean.otto@inrs.ca. *Acting Director,* André St-Hilaire, 418-654-3113, Fax: 418-654-2600, E-mail: andre.st-hilaire@ete.inrs.ca.

## UNIVERSITÉ SAINTE-ANNE, Church Point, NS B0W 1M0, Canada

**General Information** Province-supported, coed, comprehensive institution.

**GRADUATE UNITS**

**Program in Education** *Program availability:* Part-time.

## UNIVERSITY AT ALBANY, STATE UNIVERSITY OF NEW YORK, Albany, NY 12222-0001

**General Information** State-supported, coed, university. CGS member. *Enrollment:* 17,944 graduate, professional, and undergraduate students; 2,095 full-time matriculated graduate/professional students (1,263 women), 1,977 part-time matriculated graduate/professional students (1,280 women). *Enrollment by degree level:* 2,407 master's, 1,432 doctoral, 233 other advanced degrees. *Graduate faculty:* 625 full-time (248 women), 374 part-time/adjunct (175 women). *International tuition:* $23,530 full-time. *Tuition, area resident:* Full-time $11,530; part-time $480 per credit hour. Tuition, nonresident: full-time $23,530; part-time $980 per credit hour. *Required fees:* $2185; $96 per credit hour. Part-time tuition and fees vary according to course load and program. *Graduate housing:* On-campus housing not available. *Student services:* Campus employment opportunities, campus safety program, career counseling, child daycare facilities, exercise/wellness program, free psychological counseling, grant writing training, international student services, low-cost health insurance, multicultural affairs office, services for students with disabilities, teacher training, writing training. *Library facilities:* University Library plus 2 others. *Collection:* Books: 2.3 million (physical), 485,479 (digital/electronic); Serial titles: 128,734 (physical), 128,734 (digital/electronic); Databases: 391. Weekly public service hours: 113; students can reserve study rooms. *Research affiliation:* Naval Research Laboratories (organizational structures (public administration)), General Electric Corporate Research and Development Center (engineering), Whiteface Mountain Observatory (earth and atmospheric sciences), Woods Hole Oceanographic Institution (marine science and engineering), Wadsworth Laboratories, New York State Department of Health (biomedical sciences, epidemiology, environmental health).

**Computer facilities:** Computer purchase and lease plans are available. 500 computers available on campus for general student use. A campuswide network can be accessed. Online class registration is available.
Website: http://www.albany.edu/

**General Application Contact:** Michael DeRensis, Director, Graduate Admissions, 518-442-3980, Fax: 518-442-3922, E-mail: graduate@albany.edu.

**GRADUATE UNITS**

**College of Arts and Sciences** Students: 638 full-time (342 women), 564 part-time (302 women); includes 242 minority (53 Black or African American, non-Hispanic/Latino; 4 American Indian or Alaska Native, non-Hispanic/Latino; 58 Asian, non-Hispanic/Latino; 98 Hispanic/Latino; 1 Native Hawaiian or other Pacific Islander, non-Hispanic/Latino; 28 Two or more races, non-Hispanic/Latino), 335 international. 1,742 applicants, 42% accepted, 341 enrolled. *Faculty:* 338 full-time (123 women), 199 part-time/adjunct (102 women). Expenses: Contact institution. *Financial support:* Fellowships, research assistantships, teaching assistantships, career-related internships or fieldwork, Federal Work-Study, institutionally sponsored loans, traineeships, and unspecified assistantships available. Financial award applicants required to submit FAFSA. In 2019, 229 master's, 73 doctorates, 19 other advanced degrees awarded. *Program availability:* Part-time, evening/weekend, 100% online, blended/hybrid learning. *Application deadline:* For fall admission, 1/15 priority date for domestic students; for spring admission, 11/16 for domestic students. Applications are processed on a rolling basis. *Application fee:* $75. Electronic applications accepted. *Application Contact:* Michael DeRensis, Director, Graduate Admissions, 518-442-3980, Fax: 518-442-3922, E-mail: graduate@albany.edu. *Dean,* Jeanette Altarriba, 518-442-4654, Fax: 518-442-4651.

**College of Emergency Preparedness, Homeland Security and Cybersecurity** Students: 63 full-time (44 women), 127 part-time (93 women); includes 31 minority (9 Black or African American, non-Hispanic/Latino; 3 Asian, non-Hispanic/Latino; 18 Hispanic/Latino; 1 Two or more races, non-Hispanic/Latino), 22 international. Average age 27. 173 applicants, 77% accepted, 76 enrolled. *Faculty:* 25 full-time (9 women), 35 part-time/adjunct (11 women). Expenses: Contact institution. *Financial support:* Research assistantships, teaching assistantships, career-related internships or fieldwork, traineeships, and unspecified assistantships available. In 2019, 35 master's, 2 doctorates, 24 other advanced degrees awarded. *Program availability:* 100% online, blended/hybrid learning. *Application deadline:* For fall admission, 1/15 for domestic students; for spring admission, 11/15 for domestic students. *Application fee:* $75. Electronic applications accepted. *Application Contact:* Jennifer J Goodall, Vice Dean, 518-949-3283, E-mail: jgoodall@albany.edu. *Dean,* Dr. Robert Griffin, 518-442-5258, E-mail: rpgriffin@albany.edu.

**College of Engineering and Applied Sciences** Students: 188 full-time (48 women), 69 part-time (22 women); includes 15 minority (2 Black or African American, non-Hispanic/Latino; 11 Asian, non-Hispanic/Latino; 1 Hispanic/Latino; 1 Two or more races, non-Hispanic/Latino), 120 international. Average age 27. 381 applicants, 51% accepted, 59 enrolled. *Faculty:* 37 full-time (8 women), 7 part-time/adjunct (0 women). Expenses: Contact institution. *Financial support:* Fellowships, research assistantships, teaching assistantships, and Federal Work-Study available. Financial award application deadline: 4/1. In 2019, 147 master's, 3 doctorates awarded. *Program availability:* Part-time, blended/hybrid learning. *Application deadline:* For fall admission, 1/15 for domestic students; for spring admission, 11/15 for domestic students. *Application fee:* $75. Electronic applications accepted. *Application Contact:* Kim L. Boyer, Dean, 518-956-8240, Fax: 518-442-5367, E-mail: ceasinfo@albany.edu. *Dean,* Kim L. Boyer, 518-956-8240, Fax: 518-442-5367, E-mail: ceasinfo@albany.edu.

***College of Emergency Preparedness, Homeland Security and Cybersecurity*** Students: 63 full-time (44 women), 127 part-time (93 women); includes 41 minority (9 Black or African American, non-Hispanic/Latino; 13 Asian, non-Hispanic/Latino; 18 Hispanic/Latino; 1 Two or more races, non-Hispanic/Latino), 22 international. Average age 26. 173 applicants, 77% accepted, 76 enrolled. *Faculty:* 20 full-time (11 women), 40 part-time/adjunct (24 women). Expenses: Contact institution. *Financial support:* Research assistantships and teaching assistantships available. *Program availability:* Part-time, blended/hybrid learning. *Application Contact:* Robert Griffin, Dean, 518-442-5142, E-mail: rpgriffin@albany.edu. *Dean,* Robert Griffin, 518-442-5142, E-mail: rpgriffin@albany.edu.

**Nelson A. Rockefeller College of Public Affairs and Policy** Students: 149 full-time (85 women), 120 part-time (67 women); includes 52 minority (20 Black or African American, non-Hispanic/Latino; 8 Asian, non-Hispanic/Latino; 16 Hispanic/Latino; 8 Two or more races, non-Hispanic/Latino), 43 international. Average age 30. 310 applicants, 81% accepted, 110 enrolled. *Faculty:* 37 full-time (14 women), 22 part-time/adjunct (6 women). Expenses: Contact institution. *Financial support:* Fellowships, research assistantships, teaching assistantships, career-related internships or fieldwork, Federal Work-Study, and institutionally sponsored loans available. Financial award application deadline: 2/1. In 2019, 67 master's, 13 doctorates, 11 other advanced degrees awarded. *Program availability:* Part-time, 100% online, blended/hybrid learning. *Application deadline:* For fall admission, 1/15 priority date for domestic students, 5/1 for international students; for spring admission, 11/15 for domestic students. *Application fee:* $75. Electronic applications accepted. *Application Contact:* Karl R. Rethemeyer, Dean, 518-442-5283, E-mail: kretheme@albany.edu. *Dean,* Karl R. Rethemeyer, 518-442-5283, E-mail: kretheme@albany.edu.

**School of Business** Students: 265 full-time (92 women), 130 part-time (50 women); includes 121 minority (48 Black or African American, non-Hispanic/Latino; 2 American Indian or Alaska Native, non-Hispanic/Latino; 36 Asian, non-Hispanic/Latino; 29 Hispanic/Latino; 6 Two or more races, non-Hispanic/Latino), 33 international. 642 applicants, 74% accepted, 380 enrolled. *Faculty:* 55 full-time (21 women), 25 part-time/adjunct (2 women). Expenses: Contact institution. *Financial support:* Fellowships, research assistantships, career-related internships or fieldwork, and Federal Work-Study available. Financial award applicants required to submit FAFSA. In 2019, 241 master's awarded. *Program availability:* Part-time, evening/weekend, 100% online, blended/hybrid learning. *Application deadline:* For fall admission, 2/15 for domestic students, 5/1 for international students; for spring admission, 11/15 for domestic students. Applications are processed on a rolling basis. *Application fee:* $75. Electronic applications accepted. *Application Contact:* Michael DeRensis, Director, Graduate

Admissions, 518-442-3980, Fax: 518-442-3922, E-mail: graduate@albany.edu. *Dean*, Nilanjan Sen, 518-956-8370, E-mail: nsen@albany.edu.

**School of Criminal Justice** Students: 63 full-time (38 women), 18 part-time (15 women); includes 24 minority (11 Black or African American, non-Hispanic/Latino; 2 Asian, non-Hispanic/Latino; 10 Hispanic/Latino; 1 Two or more races, non-Hispanic/Latino), 13 international. Average age 27. 106 applicants, 61% accepted, 41 enrolled. *Faculty:* 16 full-time (5 women), 10 part-time/adjunct (4 women). Expenses: Contact institution. *Financial support:* Fellowships, research assistantships, teaching assistantships, career-related internships or fieldwork, Federal Work-Study, and institutionally sponsored loans available. Financial award application deadline: 4/1. In 2019, 39 master's, 4 doctorates awarded. *Program availability:* Part-time, blended/hybrid learning. *Application deadline:* For fall admission, 3/15 for domestic and international students; for spring admission, 11/15 for domestic students. *Application fee:* $75. Electronic applications accepted. *Application Contact:* Jane Champagne, Director, Graduate Admissions, 518-442-3980, Fax: 518-442-3922, E-mail: graduate@albany.edu. *Dean*, William Alex Pridemore, 518-442-5210, E-mail: pridemore@albany.edu.

**School of Education** Students: 375 full-time (287 women), 579 part-time (449 women); includes 173 minority (53 Black or African American, non-Hispanic/Latino; 29 Asian, non-Hispanic/Latino; 65 Hispanic/Latino; 1 Native Hawaiian or other Pacific Islander, non-Hispanic/Latino; 25 Two or more races, non-Hispanic/Latino), 74 international. Average age 30. 692 applicants, 64% accepted, 322 enrolled. *Faculty:* 53 full-time (28 women), 39 part-time/adjunct (24 women). Expenses: Contact institution. *Financial support:* Fellowships, career-related internships or fieldwork, and Federal Work-Study available. In 2019, 240 master's, 26 doctorates, 64 other advanced degrees awarded. *Program availability:* Part-time, evening/weekend, 100% online, blended/hybrid learning. *Application deadline:* For fall admission, 1/15 for domestic students; for spring admission, 11/15 for domestic students. *Application fee:* $75. Electronic applications accepted. *Application Contact:* Jason E Lane, Dean, 518-442-4988, E-mail: jlane@albany.edu. *Dean*, Jason E Lane, 518-442-4988, E-mail: jlane@albany.edu.

**School of Public Health** Students: 180 full-time (128 women), 288 part-time (211 women); includes 144 minority (51 Black or African American, non-Hispanic/Latino; 48 Asian, non-Hispanic/Latino; 27 Hispanic/Latino; 18 Two or more races, non-Hispanic/Latino), 57 international. 438 applicants, 71% accepted, 145 enrolled. *Faculty:* 47 full-time (27 women), 47 part-time/adjunct (21 women). Expenses: Contact institution. *Application deadline:* For fall admission, 1/15 for domestic students; for spring admission, 11/15 for domestic students. Applications are processed on a rolling basis. *Application fee:* $75. Electronic applications accepted. *Application Contact:* Michael DeRensis, Director, Graduate Admissions, 518-442-3980, Fax: 518-442-3922, E-mail: graduate@albany.edu. *Dean*, Dr. David Holtgrave, 518-485-5500, E-mail: dholtgrave@albany.edu.

**School of Social Welfare** Students: 254 full-time (219 women), 104 part-time (83 women); includes 110 minority (52 Black or African American, non-Hispanic/Latino; 13 Asian, non-Hispanic/Latino; 34 Hispanic/Latino; 11 Two or more races, non-Hispanic/Latino), 15 international. Average age 27. 348 applicants, 80% accepted, 170 enrolled. *Faculty:* 21 full-time (15 women), 21 part-time/adjunct (18 women). Expenses: Contact institution. *Financial support:* Fellowships, career-related internships or fieldwork, and Federal Work-Study available. Financial award application deadline: 2/15. In 2019, 154 master's, 5 doctorates awarded. *Program availability:* Part-time, evening/weekend, 100% online, blended/hybrid learning. *Application deadline:* For fall admission, 1/15 for domestic students; for spring admission, 11/15 for domestic students. *Application fee:* $75. Electronic applications accepted. *Application Contact:* Barbara Altrock, Assistant Director, Doctoral Program, E-mail: baltrock@albany.edu. *Dean*, Lynn Warner, 518-442-5324, E-mail: lwarner@albany.edu.

## UNIVERSITY AT BUFFALO, THE STATE UNIVERSITY OF NEW YORK, Buffalo, NY 14260

**General Information** State-supported, coed, university. CGS member. *Enrollment:* 31,923 graduate, professional, and undergraduate students; 6,187 full-time matriculated graduate/professional students (3,188 women), 3,590 part-time matriculated graduate/professional students (1,809 women). *Enrollment by degree level:* 4,764 master's, 4,739 doctoral, 274 other advanced degrees. *Graduate faculty:* 1,679 full-time (640 women), 168 part-time/adjunct (60 women). *International tuition:* $23,100 full-time. *Tuition, area resident:* Full-time $11,310; part-time $471 per credit hour. Tuition, state resident: full-time $11,310; part-time $471 per credit hour. Tuition, nonresident: full-time $23,100; part-time $963 per credit hour. *Required fees:* $2820. *Graduate housing:* Rooms and/or apartments available on a first-come, first-served basis to single and married students. Typical cost: $8521 per year ($14,631 including board) for single students. Housing application deadline: 5/1. *Student services:* Campus employment opportunities, campus safety program, career counseling, child daycare facilities, exercise/wellness program, free psychological counseling, international student services, low-cost health insurance, multicultural affairs office, services for students with disabilities, teacher training, writing training. *Library facilities:* Lockwood Memorial Library plus 11 others. *Collection:* Books: 3.4 million (physical), 826,650 (digital/electronic); Serial titles: 2,352 (physical), 175,278 (digital/electronic); Databases: 383. Weekly public service hours: 168; study areas open 24 hours, 5–7 days a week; students can reserve study rooms. *Research affiliation:* Hauptman-Woodward Medical Research Institute, Roswell Park Cancer Institute, Veterans Administration Medical Center, Calspan-University of Buffalo Research Center.

**Computer facilities:** 3,061 computers available on campus for general student use. A campuswide network can be accessed. Online class registration is available.
Website: http://www.buffalo.edu/

**General Application Contact:** Danielle D. Ianni, Director of Enrollment Operations, 716-645-3482, Fax: 716-645-6998, E-mail: ddianni@buffalo.edu.

**GRADUATE UNITS**

**Graduate School** *Program availability:* Part-time, evening/weekend, 100% online, blended/hybrid learning. Electronic applications accepted.

***College of Arts and Sciences*** *Program availability:* Part-time. Electronic applications accepted.

***Graduate Programs in Cancer Research and Biomedical Sciences at Roswell Park Cancer Institute*** Electronic applications accepted.

***Graduate School of Education*** Students: 557 full-time (401 women), 718 part-time (540 women); includes 219 minority (90 Black or African American, non-Hispanic/Latino; 4 American Indian or Alaska Native, non-Hispanic/Latino; 35 Asian, non-Hispanic/Latino; 61 Hispanic/Latino; 29 Two or more races, non-Hispanic/Latino), 79 international. Average age 33. 1,088 applicants, 64% accepted, 455 enrolled. *Faculty:* 71 full-time (46 women), 78 part-time/adjunct (52 women). Expenses: Contact institution. *Financial support:* In 2019–20, 85 students received support, including fellowships (averaging $10,970 per year), 40 research assistantships (averaging $18,240 per year); teaching assistantships, Federal Work-Study, institutionally sponsored loans, scholarships/grants, tuition waivers (full and partial), and unspecified assistantships also available. Support available to part-time students. Financial award applicants required to submit FAFSA. In 2019, 295 master's, 37 doctorates, 98 other advanced degrees awarded. *Program availability:* Part-time, 100% online, blended/hybrid learning. *Application deadline:* Applications are processed on a rolling basis. *Application fee:* $50. Electronic applications accepted. *Application Contact:* Ryan Taughrin, Director of Admissions, Office of Graduate Admissions, 716-645-2110, Fax: 716-645-7937, E-mail: gseinfo@buffalo.edu. *Dean*, Dr. Suzanne Rosenblith, 716-645-1354, Fax: 716-645-2479, E-mail: gseinfo@buffalo.edu.

***Jacobs School of Medicine and Biomedical Sciences*** Electronic applications accepted.

***School of Architecture and Planning*** Students: 210 full-time (95 women), 34 part-time (16 women); includes 57 minority (22 Black or African American, non-Hispanic/Latino; 13 Asian, non-Hispanic/Latino; 14 Hispanic/Latino; 8 Two or more races, non-Hispanic/Latino), 45 international. Average age 26. 316 applicants, 42% accepted, 97 enrolled. *Faculty:* 41 full-time (14 women), 22 part-time/adjunct (10 women). Expenses: Contact institution. *Financial support:* In 2019–20, 140 students received support, including 9 fellowships with full tuition reimbursements available (averaging $19,457 per year), 3 research assistantships with partial tuition reimbursements available (averaging $15,885 per year), 60 teaching assistantships with partial tuition reimbursements available (averaging $6,141 per year); career-related internships or fieldwork, Federal Work-Study, institutionally sponsored loans, scholarships/grants, health care benefits, tuition waivers (full and partial), and unspecified assistantships also available. Support available to part-time students. Financial award application deadline: 3/1; financial award applicants required to submit FAFSA. In 2019, 76 master's, 1 doctorate, 4 other advanced degrees awarded. *Program availability:* Part-time. *Application deadline:* For fall admission, 1/1 priority date for domestic and international students. Applications are processed on a rolling basis. *Application fee:* $75. Electronic applications accepted. *Application Contact:* Kevin P. Donovan, Director of Graduate Recruitment, 716-829-5224, Fax: 716-829-3256, E-mail: kpd2@buffalo.edu. *Dean*, Robert G. Shibley, 716-829-3981, Fax: 716-829-2297, E-mail: dean@ap.buffalo.edu.

***School of Dental Medicine*** Electronic applications accepted.

***School of Engineering and Applied Sciences*** *Program availability:* Part-time, evening/weekend, 100% online, blended/hybrid learning. Electronic applications accepted.

***School of Law*** Students: 439 full-time (233 women), 3 part-time (2 women); includes 92 minority (29 Black or African American, non-Hispanic/Latino; 2 American Indian or Alaska Native, non-Hispanic/Latino; 20 Asian, non-Hispanic/Latino; 28 Hispanic/Latino; 13 Two or more races, non-Hispanic/Latino), 22 international. Average age 27. 859 applicants, 47% accepted, 137 enrolled. *Faculty:* 53 full-time (27 women), 70 part-time/adjunct (28 women). Expenses: Contact institution. *Financial support:* In 2019–20, 396 students received support. Federal Work-Study, institutionally sponsored loans, scholarships/grants, tuition waivers (full and partial), and unspecified assistantships available. Financial award application deadline: 3/1; financial award applicants required to submit FAFSA. In 2019, 7 master's, 147 doctorates awarded. *Application deadline:* For fall admission, 3/1 priority date for domestic and international students. Applications are processed on a rolling basis. *Application fee:* $85. Electronic applications accepted. *Application Contact:* Lindsay Gladney, Vice Dean for Admissions, 716-645-2907, Fax: 716-645-6676, E-mail: law-admissions@buffalo.edu. *Dean*, Aviva Abramovsky, 716-645-2052, E-mail: aabramov@buffalo.edu.

***School of Management*** *Program availability:* Part-time, evening/weekend. Electronic applications accepted.

***School of Nursing*** *Program availability:* Part-time, 100% online. Electronic applications accepted.

***School of Pharmacy and Pharmaceutical Sciences*** Students: 580 full-time (333 women), 26 part-time (12 women); includes 217 minority (26 Black or African American, non-Hispanic/Latino; 186 Asian, non-Hispanic/Latino; 5 Hispanic/Latino), 82 international. Average age 24. 720 applicants, 24% accepted, 170 enrolled. *Faculty:* 44 full-time (13 women), 6 part-time/adjunct (4 women). Expenses: Contact institution. *Financial support:* In 2019–20, 267 students received support, including 35 research assistantships with full tuition reimbursements available (averaging $26,000 per year); scholarships/grants also available. Financial award application deadline: 3/1; financial award applicants required to submit FAFSA. In 2019, 10 master's, 144 doctorates awarded. *Application deadline:* For fall admission, 2/1 priority date for domestic and international students. Applications are processed on a rolling basis. *Application fee:* $50. Electronic applications accepted. *Application Contact:* Dr. Jennifer M. Rosenberg, Associate Dean, 716-645-2825 Ext. 1, Fax: 716-829-6568, E-mail: prepharm@buffalo.edu. *Dean*, Dr. James M. O'Donnell, 716-645-2823, Fax: 716-829-6568.

***School of Public Health and Health Professions*** *Program availability:* Part-time. Electronic applications accepted.

***School of Social Work*** *Program availability:* Part-time, blended/hybrid learning, Coursework Online & Field Education in Agency. Electronic applications accepted.

## UNIVERSITY OF ADVANCING TECHNOLOGY, Tempe, AZ 85283-1042

**General Information** Proprietary, coed, primarily men, comprehensive institution. *Graduate housing:* Room and/or apartments available on a first-come, first-served basis to single students; on-campus housing not available to married students.

**GRADUATE UNITS**

**Master of Science Program in Technology** Electronic applications accepted.

## THE UNIVERSITY OF AKRON, Akron, OH 44325

**General Information** State-supported, coed, university. CGS member. *Graduate housing:* Room and/or apartments available on a first-come, first-served basis to single students; on-campus housing not available to married students. Housing application deadline: 3/1.

**GRADUATE UNITS**

**Graduate School** *Program availability:* Part-time, evening/weekend. Electronic applications accepted.

***Buchtel College of Arts and Sciences*** *Program availability:* Part-time, evening/weekend. Electronic applications accepted.

***College of Business Administration*** *Program availability:* Part-time, evening/weekend. Electronic applications accepted.

***College of Education*** *Program availability:* Part-time. Electronic applications accepted.

***College of Engineering*** *Program availability:* Part-time, evening/weekend. Electronic applications accepted.

***College of Health Professions*** Electronic applications accepted.

***College of Polymer Science and Polymer Engineering*** *Program availability:* Part-time, evening/weekend. Electronic applications accepted.

**School of Law** *Program availability:* Part-time, evening/weekend. Electronic applications accepted.

## THE UNIVERSITY OF ALABAMA, Tuscaloosa, AL 35487

**General Information** State-supported, coed, university. CGS member. *Enrollment:* 38,100 graduate, professional, and undergraduate students; 3,294 full-time matriculated graduate/professional students (1,807 women), 1,783 part-time matriculated graduate/professional students (1,177 women). *Enrollment by degree level:* 3,015 master's, 2,011 doctoral, 51 other advanced degrees. *Graduate faculty:* 1,049 full-time (427 women), 95 part-time/adjunct (46 women). *Tuition, area resident:* Full-time $10,780; part-time $440 per credit hour. Tuition, nonresident: full-time $30,250; part-time $1550 per credit hour. *Graduate housing:* On-campus housing not available. *Student services:* Campus employment opportunities, campus safety program, career counseling, child daycare facilities, exercise/wellness program, free psychological counseling, grant writing training, international student services, low-cost health insurance, multicultural affairs office, services for students with disabilities, teacher training, writing training. *Library facilities:* Amelia Gayle Gorgas Library plus 8 others. *Collection:* Books: 3.3 million (physical), 1.8 million (digital/electronic); Serial titles: 137,451 (physical), 203,341 (digital/electronic); Databases: 580. Weekly public service hours: 141; study areas open 24 hours, 5–7 days a week; students can reserve study rooms. *Research affiliation:* Mercedes-Benz (automotive engineering), Alabama Power (utilities), TDK Corp. (materials science), Nucor Steel (materials science), Boeing (aerospace, manufacturing), Lockheed Martin Corporation (business analytics).

**Computer facilities:** 2,500 computers available on campus for general student use. A campuswide network can be accessed. Online class registration is available.
Website: http://www.ua.edu/

**General Application Contact:** Patrick D. Fuller, Senior Graduate Admissions Counselor, 205-348-5923, Fax: 205-348-0400, E-mail: patrick.d.fuller@ua.edu.

**GRADUATE UNITS**

**Graduate School** Students: 4 full-time (2 women), 6 part-time (3 women); includes 1 minority (Black or African American, non-Hispanic/Latino), 1 international. Average age 41. *Faculty:* 959 full-time (380 women), 19 part-time/adjunct (11 women). Expenses: Contact institution. *Financial support:* Fellowships with tuition reimbursements, research assistantships with tuition reimbursements, teaching assistantships with tuition reimbursements, career-related internships or fieldwork, Federal Work-Study, institutionally sponsored loans, scholarships/grants, traineeships, health care benefits, tuition waivers (full and partial), and unspecified assistantships available. Support available to part-time students. Financial award application deadline: 2/15; financial award applicants required to submit FAFSA. In 2019, 2 doctorates awarded. *Program availability:* Part-time, evening/weekend, online learning. *Application deadline:* For fall admission, 7/1 priority date for domestic students, 3/15 for international students; for spring admission, 11/1 priority date for domestic students, 7/1 for international students. Applications are processed on a rolling basis. *Application fee:* $50 ($60 for international students). Electronic applications accepted. *Application Contact:* Lesley Campbell, Director of Graduate Recruitment, 205-348-0051, Fax: 205-348-0400, E-mail: lesley.campbell@ua.edu. *Dean*, Dr. Susan Carvalho, 205-348-5921, Fax: 205-348-0400, E-mail: scarvalho@ua.edu.

***Capstone College of Nursing*** Students: 117 full-time (99 women), 190 part-time (164 women); includes 98 minority (69 Black or African American, non-Hispanic/Latino; 1 American Indian or Alaska Native, non-Hispanic/Latino; 10 Asian, non-Hispanic/Latino; 12 Hispanic/Latino; 6 Two or more races, non-Hispanic/Latino). Average age 40. 322 applicants, 42% accepted, 124 enrolled. *Faculty:* 32 full-time (30 women), 2 part-time/adjunct (1 woman). Expenses: Contact institution. *Financial support:* Scholarships/grants available. Financial award application deadline: 6/15; financial award applicants required to submit FAFSA. In 2019, 84 master's, 53 doctorates awarded. *Program availability:* Part-time, online learning. *Application deadline:* For fall admission, 3/1 priority date for domestic students. Applications are processed on a rolling basis. *Application fee:* $50 ($60 for international students). Electronic applications accepted. *Application Contact:* Vickie L. Samuel, Graduate Recruitment and Retention Liaison, 205-348-8163, Fax: 205-348-6674, E-mail: vsamuel@ua.edu. *Dean*, Dr. Suzanne Prevost, 205-348-1040, Fax: 205-348-5559, E-mail: sprevost@ua.edu.

***College of Arts and Sciences*** Students: 935 full-time (531 women), 82 part-time (43 women); includes 166 minority (71 Black or African American, non-Hispanic/Latino; 6 American Indian or Alaska Native, non-Hispanic/Latino; 17 Asian, non-Hispanic/Latino; 43 Hispanic/Latino; 29 Two or more races, non-Hispanic/Latino), 196 international. Average age 28. 1,387 applicants, 38% accepted, 273 enrolled. *Faculty:* 361 full-time (132 women), 3 part-time/adjunct (2 women). Expenses: Contact institution. *Financial support:* Career-related internships or fieldwork, Federal Work-Study, institutionally sponsored loans, scholarships/grants, and unspecified assistantships available. Support available to part-time students. Financial award applicants required to submit FAFSA. In 2019, 275 master's, 77 doctorates awarded. *Program availability:* Part-time, online learning. *Application fee:* $50 ($60 for international students). Electronic applications accepted. *Application Contact:* Patrick D. Fuller, Senior Graduate Admissions Counselor, 205-348-5923, Fax: 205-348-0400, E-mail: patrick.d.fuller@ua.edu. *Dean*, Dr. Joseph Messina, 205-348-5972, Fax: 205-348-0272, E-mail: jpmessina@ua.edu.

***College of Communication and Information Sciences*** Students: 201 full-time (141 women), 205 part-time (147 women); includes 74 minority (43 Black or African American, non-Hispanic/Latino; 1 American Indian or Alaska Native, non-Hispanic/Latino; 2 Asian, non-Hispanic/Latino; 18 Hispanic/Latino; 10 Two or more races, non-Hispanic/Latino), 29 international. Average age 32. 322 applicants, 77% accepted, 139 enrolled. *Faculty:* 88 full-time (36 women), 2 part-time/adjunct (1 woman). Expenses: Contact institution. *Financial support:* In 2019–20, 70 students received support. Fellowships with tuition reimbursements available, research assistantships with tuition reimbursements available, teaching assistantships with tuition reimbursements available, institutionally sponsored loans, health care benefits, and unspecified assistantships available. Financial award application deadline: 2/15. In 2019, 155 master's, 8 doctorates awarded. *Application deadline:* For fall admission, 2/15 priority date for domestic and international students; for winter admission, 11/1 priority date for international students; for spring admission, 11/1 priority date for domestic students. Applications are processed on a rolling basis. *Application fee:* $50 ($60 for international students). Electronic applications accepted. *Application Contact:* Allison Payne, Executive Assistant, 205-348-4786, E-mail: allison.s.payne@ua.edu. *Dean*, Dr. Mark Nelson, 205-348-4787, E-mail: mnelson@ua.edu.

***College of Education*** Students: 362 full-time (273 women), 483 part-time (346 women); includes 228 minority (162 Black or African American, non-Hispanic/Latino; 3 American Indian or Alaska Native, non-Hispanic/Latino; 10 Asian, non-Hispanic/Latino; 28 Hispanic/Latino; 2 Native Hawaiian or other Pacific Islander, non-Hispanic/Latino; 23 Two or more races, non-Hispanic/Latino), 50 international. Average age 36. 404 applicants, 71% accepted, 194 enrolled. *Faculty:* 115 full-time (62 women), 6 part-time/adjunct (2 women). Expenses: Contact institution. *Financial support:* In 2019–20, 119 students received support. Research assistantships with tuition reimbursements available, teaching assistantships with tuition reimbursements available, career-related internships or fieldwork, Federal Work-Study, institutionally sponsored loans, scholarships/grants, and unspecified assistantships available. Financial award applicants required to submit FAFSA. In 2019, 148 master's, 84 doctorates, 20 other advanced degrees awarded. *Program availability:* Part-time, online learning. *Application deadline:* For fall admission, 7/1 for domestic and international students; for spring admission, 11/15 for domestic students, 11/17 for international students. Applications are processed on a rolling basis. *Application fee:* $50 ($60 for international students). *Application Contact:* Dr. Kathy S. Wetzel, Assistant Dean for Student Services, 205-348-1154, Fax: 205-348-0080, E-mail: kwetzel@bamaed.ua.edu. *Dean*, Dr. Peter Hlebowitsh, 205-348-6052, E-mail: peter.hleb@ua.edu.

***College of Engineering*** Students: 254 full-time (46 women), 50 part-time (5 women); includes 21 minority (11 Black or African American, non-Hispanic/Latino; 3 Asian, non-Hispanic/Latino; 4 Hispanic/Latino; 3 Two or more races, non-Hispanic/Latino), 152 international. Average age 27. 327 applicants, 39% accepted, 65 enrolled. *Faculty:* 123 full-time (15 women). Expenses: Contact institution. *Financial support:* In 2019–20, 229 students received support, including fellowships with full tuition reimbursements available (averaging $16,022 per year), research assistantships with full tuition reimbursements available (averaging $16,022 per year), teaching assistantships with full tuition reimbursements available (averaging $16,022 per year); career-related internships or fieldwork, Federal Work-Study, and institutionally sponsored loans also available. Financial award application deadline: 2/15. In 2019, 57 master's, 36 doctorates awarded. *Program availability:* Part-time, online learning. *Application deadline:* For fall admission, 7/1 for domestic students, 4/15 for international students; for spring admission, 11/15 for domestic students, 9/1 for international students. Applications are processed on a rolling basis. *Application fee:* $50 ($60 for international students). Electronic applications accepted. *Application Contact:* Dr. Susan Carvalho, Dean, 205-348-8280, Fax: 205-348-0400, E-mail: secarvalho@ua.edu. *Dean*, Dr. Charles Karr, 205-348-6405, Fax: 205-348-8573.

***College of Human Environmental Sciences*** Students: 176 full-time (130 women), 413 part-time (309 women); includes 142 minority (78 Black or African American, non-Hispanic/Latino; 2 American Indian or Alaska Native, non-Hispanic/Latino; 13 Asian, non-Hispanic/Latino; 30 Hispanic/Latino; 1 Native Hawaiian or other Pacific Islander, non-Hispanic/Latino; 18 Two or more races, non-Hispanic/Latino), 11 international. Average age 32. 366 applicants, 74% accepted, 206 enrolled. *Faculty:* 64 full-time (45 women), 2 part-time/adjunct (both women). Expenses: Contact institution. *Financial support:* In 2019–20, 44 students received support. Fellowships with tuition reimbursements available, research assistantships with full tuition reimbursements available, teaching assistantships with full tuition reimbursements available, career-related internships or fieldwork, Federal Work-Study, institutionally sponsored loans, and scholarships/grants available. In 2019, 283 master's, 3 doctorates awarded. *Program availability:* Part-time, evening/weekend, online learning. *Application deadline:* For fall admission, 7/6 for domestic students. Applications are processed on a rolling basis. *Application fee:* $50 ($60 for international students). Electronic applications accepted. *Application Contact:* Patrick D. Fuller, Admissions Officer, 205-348-5923, Fax: 205-348-0400, E-mail: patrick.d.fuller@ua.edu. *Dean*, Dr. Stuart Usdan, 205-348-6250, Fax: 205-348-3789, E-mail: susdan@ches.ua.edu.

***Culverhouse College of Business*** Students: 472 full-time (196 women), 123 part-time (51 women); includes 86 minority (44 Black or African American, non-Hispanic/Latino; 4 American Indian or Alaska Native, non-Hispanic/Latino; 12 Asian, non-Hispanic/Latino; 14 Hispanic/Latino; 1 Native Hawaiian or other Pacific Islander, non-Hispanic/Latino; 11 Two or more races, non-Hispanic/Latino), 59 international. Average age 28. 956 applicants, 60% accepted, 242 enrolled. *Faculty:* 85 full-time (14 women). Expenses: Contact institution. *Financial support:* In 2019–20, 183 students received support. Fellowships with tuition reimbursements available, research assistantships with tuition reimbursements available, teaching assistantships with tuition reimbursements available, career-related internships or fieldwork, Federal Work-Study, institutionally sponsored loans, and scholarships/grants available. Support available to part-time students. Financial award application deadline: 2/5. In 2019, 432 master's, 13 doctorates awarded. *Program availability:* Part-time, evening/weekend, online learning. *Application deadline:* For fall admission, 4/15 priority date for domestic and international students. Applications are processed on a rolling basis. *Application fee:* $60 ($75 for international students). Electronic applications accepted. *Application Contact:* Jan Jones, Director, Specialized Master's Programs, 205-348-6517, E-mail: jjones@culverhouse.ua.edu. *Associate Dean*, Dr. Sharif Melouk, 205-348-3217, E-mail: smelouk@culverhouse.ua.edu.

***School of Social Work*** Students: 334 full-time (303 women), 75 part-time (60 women); includes 141 minority (116 Black or African American, non-Hispanic/Latino; 2 American Indian or Alaska Native, non-Hispanic/Latino; 3 Asian, non-Hispanic/Latino; 15 Hispanic/Latino; 5 Two or more races, non-Hispanic/Latino), 9 international. Average age 31. 388 applicants, 61% accepted, 170 enrolled. *Faculty:* 34 full-time (28 women), 4 part-time/adjunct (3 women). Expenses: Contact institution. *Financial support:* In 2019–20, 21 students received support. Research assistantships with full tuition reimbursements available, teaching assistantships with full tuition reimbursements available, career-related internships or fieldwork, scholarships/grants, traineeships, health care benefits, and unspecified assistantships available. Financial award application deadline: 2/1; financial award applicants required to submit FAFSA. In 2019, 247 master's, 3 doctorates awarded. *Program availability:* Part-time, blended/hybrid learning. *Application deadline:* For fall admission, 2/1 priority date for domestic and international students; for spring admission, 9/1 priority date for domestic and international students; for summer admission, 2/1 priority date for domestic and international students. *Application fee:* $50 ($60 for international students). Electronic applications accepted. *Application Contact:* Jennifer Thomas, Dean's Assistant, 205-348-3924, Fax: 205-348-9419, E-mail: jennifer.l.thomas@ua.edu. *Professor and Interim Dean*, Dr. Lesley Reid, 205-348-3924, Fax: 205-348-9419, E-mail: lwreid@ua.edu.

**The University of Alabama School of Law** Students: 390 full-time (187 women), 50 part-time (12 women); includes 80 minority (43 Black or African American, non-Hispanic/Latino; 3 American Indian or Alaska Native, non-Hispanic/Latino; 8 Asian, non-

Hispanic/Latino; 19 Hispanic/Latino; 1 Native Hawaiian or other Pacific Islander, non-Hispanic/Latino; 6 Two or more races, non-Hispanic/Latino), 11 international. Average age 27. 500 applicants, 98% accepted, 170 enrolled. *Faculty:* 5 full-time (0 women). Expenses: Contact institution. *Financial support:* Applicants required to submit FAFSA. In 2019, 46 master's, 135 doctorates awarded. *Application deadline:* Applications are processed on a rolling basis. *Application fee:* $40. Electronic applications accepted. *Application Contact:* Brandi Russell, Assistant Director for Admissions, 205-348-7945, E-mail: brussell@law.ua.edu. *Dean and Professor*, Mark E. Brandon, 205-348-5117, Fax: 205-348-3077, E-mail: mbrandon@law.ua.edu.

## THE UNIVERSITY OF ALABAMA AT BIRMINGHAM, Birmingham, AL 35294

**General Information** State-supported, coed, university. CGS member. *Enrollment:* 22,080 graduate, professional, and undergraduate students. *Enrollment by degree level:* 4,914 master's, 2,639 doctoral, 238 other advanced degrees. *Graduate housing:* On-campus housing not available. *Student services:* Campus employment opportunities, campus safety program, career counseling, exercise/wellness program, free psychological counseling, grant writing training, international student services, low-cost health insurance, multicultural affairs office, services for students with disabilities, teacher training, writing training. *Library facilities:* Lister Hill Library plus 2 others. *Collection:* Books: 1.5 million (physical), 510,501 (digital/electronic); Databases: 451. Students can reserve study rooms. *Research affiliation:* Southern Research Institute (cancer therapeutics, biodefense).

**Computer facilities:** A campuswide network can be accessed from student residence rooms and from off campus. Online class registration is available.
Website: http://www.uab.edu/

**General Application Contact:** Jesse Keppley, Director of Student and Academic Services, 205-996-5696, E-mail: jkeppley@uab.edu.

**GRADUATE UNITS**

**Collat School of Business** Students: 138 full-time (64 women), 566 part-time (257 women); includes 199 minority (134 Black or African American, non-Hispanic/Latino; 1 American Indian or Alaska Native, non-Hispanic/Latino; 34 Asian, non-Hispanic/Latino; 13 Hispanic/Latino; 17 Two or more races, non-Hispanic/Latino), 62 international. Average age 33. 309 applicants, 64% accepted, 142 enrolled. *Faculty:* 65 full-time (19 women), 3 part-time/adjunct (all women). Expenses: Contact institution. *Financial support:* In 2019–20, 2 research assistantships (averaging $5,000 per year), 4 teaching assistantships (averaging $5,000 per year) were awarded; career-related internships or fieldwork and unspecified assistantships also available. Financial award applicants required to submit FAFSA. In 2019, 232 master's awarded. *Program availability:* Part-time, evening/weekend, blended/hybrid learning. *Application deadline:* For fall admission, 8/1 for domestic and international students; for spring admission, 12/1 for domestic and international students; for summer admission, 5/1 for domestic and international students. Applications are processed on a rolling basis. *Application fee:* $60 ($75 for international students). Electronic applications accepted. *Application Contact:* Susan Noblitt Banks, Director of Graduate School Operations, 205-934-8227, Fax: 205-934-8413, E-mail: gradschool@uab.edu. *Dean*, Dr. Eric Jack, 205-934-8800, Fax: 205-934-8886, E-mail: ejack@uab.edu.

**College of Arts and Sciences** Students: 578 full-time (311 women), 216 part-time (129 women); includes 159 minority (98 Black or African American, non-Hispanic/Latino; 2 American Indian or Alaska Native, non-Hispanic/Latino; 19 Asian, non-Hispanic/Latino; 19 Hispanic/Latino; 21 Two or more races, non-Hispanic/Latino), 177 international. Average age 30. 985 applicants, 44% accepted, 206 enrolled. *Faculty:* 308 full-time (128 women), 6 part-time/adjunct (2 women). Expenses: Contact institution. *Financial support:* Fellowships, research assistantships, teaching assistantships, career-related internships or fieldwork, Federal Work-Study, and institutionally sponsored loans available. Support available to part-time students. In 2019, 185 master's, 44 doctorates awarded. *Program availability:* Part-time, evening/weekend, online learning. *Application deadline:* Applications are processed on a rolling basis. Electronic applications accepted. *Application Contact:* Susan Noblitt Banks, Director of Graduate School Operations, 205-934-8227, Fax: 205-934-8413, E-mail: gradschool@uab.edu. *Dean*, Dr. Robert E. Palazzo, 205-934-5643, E-mail: thecollege@uab.edu.

**Joint Health Sciences** Students: 338 full-time (212 women), 17 part-time (11 women); includes 106 minority (59 Black or African American, non-Hispanic/Latino; 1 American Indian or Alaska Native, non-Hispanic/Latino; 17 Asian, non-Hispanic/Latino; 15 Hispanic/Latino; 14 Two or more races, non-Hispanic/Latino), 64 international. Average age 27. 534 applicants, 17% accepted, 55 enrolled. *Faculty:* 250 full-time (93 women), 21 part-time/adjunct (3 women). Expenses: Contact institution. *Financial support:* Fellowships, research assistantships, and health care benefits available. Electronic applications accepted. *Application Contact:* Graduate School, 205-934-8227, E-mail: gradschool@uab.edu.

**School of Dentistry** Students: 235 full-time (101 women), 1 (woman) part-time; includes 44 minority (14 Black or African American, non-Hispanic/Latino; 2 American Indian or Alaska Native, non-Hispanic/Latino; 24 Asian, non-Hispanic/Latino; 3 Hispanic/Latino; 1 Two or more races, non-Hispanic/Latino), 2 international. Average age 25. *Faculty:* 56 full-time (23 women), 18 part-time/adjunct (7 women). Expenses: Contact institution. In 2019, 12 master's, 54 doctorates awarded. *Application deadline:* For fall admission, 11/15 priority date for domestic students. *Application fee:* $50. Electronic applications accepted. *Application Contact:* Dr. Steven J. Filler, Director of Dentistry Admissions, 205-934-3387, Fax: 205-934-0209. *Dean*, Dr. Michael S. Reddy, 205-934-4720, Fax: 205-934-9283.

**School of Education** Students: 213 full-time (178 women), 524 part-time (421 women); includes 241 minority (209 Black or African American, non-Hispanic/Latino; 1 American Indian or Alaska Native, non-Hispanic/Latino; 11 Asian, non-Hispanic/Latino; 8 Hispanic/Latino; 12 Two or more races, non-Hispanic/Latino), 17 international. Average age 34. 292 applicants, 65% accepted, 107 enrolled. *Faculty:* 54 full-time (38 women), 3 part-time/adjunct (2 women). Expenses: Contact institution. *Financial support:* Fellowships, career-related internships or fieldwork, and Federal Work-Study available. Support available to part-time students. In 2019, 243 master's, 21 doctorates, 69 other advanced degrees awarded. *Program availability:* Part-time, evening/weekend, online learning. *Application deadline:* Applications are processed on a rolling basis. *Application fee:* $45 ($60 for international students). Electronic applications accepted. *Application Contact:* Susan Noblitt Banks, Director of Graduate School Operations, 205-934-8227, Fax: 205-934-8413, E-mail: gradschool@uab.edu. *Dean*, Dr. Deborah L. Voltz, 205-934-5322.

**School of Engineering** Students: 176 full-time (45 women), 407 part-time (80 women); includes 129 minority (90 Black or African American, non-Hispanic/Latino; 1 American Indian or Alaska Native, non-Hispanic/Latino; 13 Asian, non-Hispanic/Latino; 16 Hispanic/Latino; 9 Two or more races, non-Hispanic/Latino), 151 international. Average age 34. 385 applicants, 58% accepted, 117 enrolled. *Faculty:* 41 full-time (6 women), 27 part-time/adjunct (5 women). Expenses: Contact institution. *Financial support:* In 2019–20, 126 students received support, including 40 fellowships with full tuition reimbursements available (averaging $27,017 per year), 57 research assistantships with full and partial tuition reimbursements available, 12 teaching assistantships; institutionally sponsored loans also available. Support available to part-time students. In 2019, 140 master's, 12 doctorates awarded. *Program availability:* Part-time, evening/weekend, 100% online, blended/hybrid learning. *Application deadline:* For fall admission, 8/1 for domestic and international students; for spring admission, 12/1 for domestic and international students; for summer admission, 5/1 for domestic and international students. Applications are processed on a rolling basis. *Application fee:* $50 ($60 for international students). Electronic applications accepted. *Application Contact:* Jesse Keppley, Director of Student and Academic Services, 205-996-5696, Fax: 205-934-8413, E-mail: gradschool@uab.edu. *Interim Dean*, Dr. Timothy M Wick, 205-975-5890, Fax: 205-934-8437, E-mail: tmwick@uab.edu.

**School of Health Professions** Students: 740 full-time (539 women), 182 part-time (123 women); includes 159 minority (87 Black or African American, non-Hispanic/Latino; 3 American Indian or Alaska Native, non-Hispanic/Latino; 36 Asian, non-Hispanic/Latino; 17 Hispanic/Latino; 1 Native Hawaiian or other Pacific Islander, non-Hispanic/Latino; 15 Two or more races, non-Hispanic/Latino), 28 international. Average age 30. 1,015 applicants, 56% accepted, 417 enrolled. *Faculty:* 113 full-time (65 women), 8 part-time/adjunct (2 women). Expenses: Contact institution. *Financial support:* Fellowships, research assistantships, teaching assistantships, career-related internships or fieldwork, Federal Work-Study, institutionally sponsored loans, scholarships/grants, traineeships, and unspecified assistantships available. Support available to part-time students. In 2019, 252 master's, 41 doctorates awarded. *Program availability:* Part-time, online learning. *Application fee:* $0 ($60 for international students). Electronic applications accepted. *Application Contact:* Susan Noblitt Banks, Director of Graduate School Operations, 205-934-8227, Fax: 205-934-8413, E-mail: gradschool@uab.edu. *Dean*, Dr. Harold P. Jones, 205-934-5149, Fax: 205-934-2412, E-mail: jonesh@uab.edu.

**School of Medicine** Students: 780 full-time (346 women); includes 177 minority (33 Black or African American, non-Hispanic/Latino; 6 American Indian or Alaska Native, non-Hispanic/Latino; 71 Asian, non-Hispanic/Latino; 3 Hispanic/Latino; 64 Two or more races, non-Hispanic/Latino). Average age 25. 3,768 applicants, 7% accepted, 186 enrolled. *Faculty:* 107 full-time (54 women), 47 part-time/adjunct (24 women). Expenses: Contact institution. *Financial support:* In 2019–20, 233 students received support. Career-related internships or fieldwork and scholarships/grants available. Financial award application deadline: 5/1; financial award applicants required to submit FAFSA. In 2019, 181 doctorates awarded. *Application deadline:* For fall admission, 11/1 for domestic students. *Application fee:* $80. Electronic applications accepted. *Application Contact:* Dr. Selwyn M. Vickers, Senior Vice President/Dean, School of Medicine, 205-934-1111, Fax: 205-934-0333. *Senior Vice President/Dean, School of Medicine*, Dr. Selwyn M. Vickers, 205-934-1111, Fax: 205-934-0333.

**School of Nursing** Students: 228 full-time (165 women), 1,393 part-time (1,234 women); includes 398 minority (267 Black or African American, non-Hispanic/Latino; 4 American Indian or Alaska Native, non-Hispanic/Latino; 52 Asian, non-Hispanic/Latino; 41 Hispanic/Latino; 34 Two or more races, non-Hispanic/Latino), 3 international. Average age 33. 1,027 applicants, 55% accepted, 421 enrolled. *Faculty:* 86 full-time (79 women), 42 part-time/adjunct (35 women). Expenses: Contact institution. *Financial support:* In 2019–20, 23 fellowships (averaging $34,685 per year), 12 research assistantships (averaging $9,042 per year), 2 teaching assistantships (averaging $22,000 per year) were awarded; scholarships/grants, traineeships, health care benefits, and unspecified assistantships also available. Support available to part-time students. In 2019, 557 master's, 19 doctorates awarded. *Program availability:* Part-time, online only, blended/hybrid learning. *Application deadline:* For fall admission, 2/24 for domestic students; for summer admission, 10/15 for domestic students. *Application fee:* $50. Electronic applications accepted. *Application Contact:* John Updegraff, Director of Student Affairs, 205-975-3370, Fax: 205-934-5490, E-mail: jupde22@uab.edu. *Dean*, Dr. Doreen C. Harper, 205-934-5360, Fax: 205-934-1894, E-mail: dcharper@uab.edu.

**School of Optometry** Students: 211 full-time (147 women), 10 part-time (8 women); includes 49 minority (10 Black or African American, non-Hispanic/Latino; 2 American Indian or Alaska Native, non-Hispanic/Latino; 31 Asian, non-Hispanic/Latino; 6 Hispanic/Latino), 11 international. Average age 29. 342 applicants, 35% accepted, 52 enrolled. *Faculty:* 205 full-time (141 women). Expenses: Contact institution. *Financial support:* In 2019–20, 44 students received support. Federal Work-Study, scholarships/grants, and out-of-state tuition offsets available. Financial award application deadline: 5/1; financial award applicants required to submit FAFSA. In 2019, 3 master's, 50 doctorates awarded. *Application deadline:* For fall admission, 4/1 for domestic students. Applications are processed on a rolling basis. Electronic applications accepted. *Application Contact:* Gerald Simon, Director, Optometry Student Affairs, 205-975-0739, Fax: 205-934-6458, E-mail: gsimonod@uab.edu. *Dean*, Dr. Kelly K. Nichols, 205-975-9935, Fax: 205-934-6758, E-mail: nicholsk@uab.edu.

**School of Public Health** Students: 277 full-time (194 women), 206 part-time (153 women); includes 140 minority (61 Black or African American, non-Hispanic/Latino; 6 American Indian or Alaska Native, non-Hispanic/Latino; 49 Asian, non-Hispanic/Latino; 9 Hispanic/Latino; 15 Two or more races, non-Hispanic/Latino), 85 international. Average age 31. 297 applicants, 61% accepted, 67 enrolled. *Faculty:* 67 full-time (38 women). Expenses: Contact institution. *Financial support:* Fellowships, research assistantships, teaching assistantships, career-related internships or fieldwork, traineeships, and unspecified assistantships available. Financial award application deadline: 3/1; financial award applicants required to submit FAFSA. In 2019, 133 master's, 19 doctorates awarded. *Program availability:* Part-time, 100% online, blended/hybrid learning. *Application deadline:* For fall admission, 4/1 priority date for domestic and international students; for spring admission, 11/1 for domestic students; for summer admission, 4/1 for domestic students. Applications are processed on a rolling basis. *Application fee:* $0 ($60 for international students). Electronic applications accepted. *Application Contact:* Hannah VanSlambrouck, Director of Enrollment Management, 205-975-8688, Fax: 205-975-5484, E-mail: soph@uab.edu. *Dean*, Dr. Paul Erwin, 205-934-4993, Fax: 205-975-5484, E-mail: perwin@uab.edu.

## THE UNIVERSITY OF ALABAMA IN HUNTSVILLE, Huntsville, AL 35899

**General Information** State-supported, coed, university. CGS member. *Graduate housing:* Rooms and/or apartments available on a first-come, first-served basis to single and married students. Housing application deadline: 6/1. *Research affiliation:* Oak Ridge, Lawrence Livermore and Savannah River National Labs - Y12National Security Complex (neutron science, energy technologies, high-performance computing, systems biology, materials science at the nanoscale, national security), National Oceanic and Atmospheric Administration (NOAA) (climate modeling, weather and air quality research, oceans, satellites), Hudson Alpha Institute for Biotechnology (medical research, biotechnology, genomic research, molecular biology), U.S. Department of

Defense/U.S. Army Aviation and Missile Command (missile research, development and engineering and manufacturing technology), NASA/Marshall Space Flight Center/Goddard Space Flight Center (space science, earth science, information technology, materials science, optical science), Cummings Research Park/Boeing/ADTRAN/SAIC/Teledyne Brown Engineering/Lockheed Martin/Dynetics, Inc. (computer science, aerospace engineering, information systems, space systems, defense systems, informatics).

**GRADUATE UNITS**

**School of Graduate Studies** *Program availability:* Part-time. Electronic applications accepted.

***College of Arts, Humanities, and Social Sciences*** *Program availability:* Part-time. Electronic applications accepted.

***College of Business Administration*** *Program availability:* Part-time. Electronic applications accepted.

***College of Education*** *Program availability:* Part-time. Electronic applications accepted.

***College of Engineering*** *Program availability:* Part-time. Electronic applications accepted.

***College of Nursing*** *Program availability:* Part-time. Electronic applications accepted.

***College of Science*** *Program availability:* Part-time. Electronic applications accepted.

## UNIVERSITY OF ALASKA ANCHORAGE, Anchorage, AK 99508

**General Information** State-supported, coed, comprehensive institution. *Graduate housing:* Rooms and/or apartments available on a first-come, first-served basis to single and married students. Housing application deadline: 7/1. *Research affiliation:* Conoco Phillips (energy), Habitat for Humanity (project management), BP Alaska (energy), Municipality of Anchorage (government), Providence Hospital (health care).

**GRADUATE UNITS**

**College of Arts and Sciences** *Program availability:* Part-time.

**College of Business and Public Policy** *Program availability:* Part-time, evening/weekend.

**College of Health** *Program availability:* Part-time, evening/weekend.

***School of Nursing*** *Program availability:* Part-time, evening/weekend.

***School of Social Work*** *Program availability:* Part-time, evening/weekend, online learning. Electronic applications accepted.

**School of Education** *Program availability:* Part-time.

## UNIVERSITY OF ALASKA FAIRBANKS, Fairbanks, AK 99775-7520

**General Information** State-supported, coed, university. *Graduate housing:* Rooms and/or apartments available on a first-come, first-served basis to single and married students. Housing application deadline: 7/31. *Research affiliation:* Hilcorp (Oil Production), Cold Climate Housing Research Center (Cold Regions Housing), Alaska Native Tribal Health Consortium (Alaska Native Health), Alyeska (Oil Transport), Southcentral Foundation (Health Research), Pollock Conservation Cooperative Research Center (Fisheries Research), Institute of Northern Forestry, Alaska Cooperative Fishery and Wildlife Research Unit.

**GRADUATE UNITS**

**College of Engineering and Mines** *Program availability:* Part-time. Electronic applications accepted.

**College of Fisheries and Ocean Sciences** *Program availability:* Part-time, Zoom. Electronic applications accepted.

**College of Liberal Arts** *Program availability:* Part-time, 100% online, blended/hybrid learning. Electronic applications accepted.

**College of Natural Science and Mathematics** *Program availability:* Part-time. Electronic applications accepted.

**College of Rural and Community Development** *Program availability:* Part-time, evening/weekend, 100% online, blended/hybrid learning. Electronic applications accepted.

**Graduate School for Interdisciplinary Studies** *Program availability:* Part-time. Electronic applications accepted.

**School of Education** *Program availability:* 100% online, blended/hybrid learning. Electronic applications accepted.

**School of Management** *Program availability:* Part-time, 100% online, blended/hybrid learning. Electronic applications accepted.

**School of Natural Resources and Extension** *Program availability:* Part-time. Electronic applications accepted.

## UNIVERSITY OF ALASKA SOUTHEAST, Juneau, AK 99801

**General Information** State-supported, coed, comprehensive institution. *Graduate housing:* Rooms and/or apartments available on a first-come, first-served basis to single and married students. Housing application deadline: 5/1. *Research affiliation:* National Park Service (environmental resources, cultural studies), North Pacific Research Board (marine biology, oceanography), U.S. Department of Education (DOE) (teaching, early childhood education), Natural Science Foundation (marine biology), U.S. Department of Agriculture (USDA) (forest service), Alaska Department of Education (teaching).

**GRADUATE UNITS**

**Graduate Programs** *Program availability:* Part-time, evening/weekend, online learning. Electronic applications accepted.

## UNIVERSITY OF ALBERTA, Edmonton, AB T6G 2E1, Canada

**General Information** Province-supported, coed, university. CGS member. *Graduate housing:* Rooms and/or apartments available on a first-come, first-served basis to single and married students.

**GRADUATE UNITS**

**Faculty of Extension**

**Faculty of Graduate Studies and Research** *Program availability:* Part-time, evening/weekend. Electronic applications accepted.

***Facultè Saint Jean*** *Program availability:* Part-time, evening/weekend, online learning.

***Faculty of Nursing*** *Program availability:* Part-time.

***Faculty of Rehabilitation Medicine*** Electronic applications accepted.

***School of Library and Information Studies*** Electronic applications accepted.

**Faculty of Kinesiology, Sport, and Recreation** *Program availability:* Part-time.

**Faculty of Law** *Program availability:* Part-time. Electronic applications accepted.

**Faculty of Medicine and Dentistry** Electronic applications accepted.

***Graduate Programs in Medicine*** *Program availability:* Part-time.

***School of Dentistry***

**Faculty of Pharmacy and Pharmaceutical Sciences** Electronic applications accepted.

**Neuroscience and Mental Health Institute** Electronic applications accepted.

**School of Public Health**

***Centre for Health Promotion Studies*** *Program availability:* Part-time, online learning.

## UNIVERSITY OF ANTELOPE VALLEY, Lancaster, CA 93534

**General Information** Proprietary, coed, comprehensive institution.

**GRADUATE UNITS**

**Program in Business Management**

**Program in Criminal Justice**

## THE UNIVERSITY OF ARIZONA, Tucson, AZ 85721

**General Information** State-supported, coed, university. CGS member. *Graduate housing:* Rooms and/or apartments available on a first-come, first-served basis to single students and available to married students. Housing application deadline: 5/1. *Research affiliation:* Smithsonian Astrophysical Observatory (astronomy), Research Corporation (astronomy), National Center for Atmospheric Research (atmospheric physics), Kitt Peak National Observatory (astronomy), Argonne National Laboratory (physics).

**GRADUATE UNITS**

**College of Agriculture and Life Sciences** *Program availability:* Part-time. Electronic applications accepted.

***School of Animal and Comparative Biomedical Sciences*** Electronic applications accepted.

***School of Family and Consumer Sciences*** *Program availability:* Part-time. Electronic applications accepted.

***School of Natural Resources and the Environment*** Electronic applications accepted.

***School of Plant Sciences*** *Program availability:* Part-time. Electronic applications accepted.

**College of Architecture, Planning, and Landscape Architecture** *Program availability:* Part-time. Electronic applications accepted.

***School of Architecture*** Electronic applications accepted.

**College of Education** *Program availability:* Part-time, online learning. Electronic applications accepted.

**College of Engineering** *Program availability:* Part-time, online learning. Electronic applications accepted.

**College of Fine Arts** *Program availability:* Part-time. Electronic applications accepted.

***School of Art*** *Program availability:* Part-time. Electronic applications accepted.

***School of Dance*** Electronic applications accepted.

***School of Music*** *Program availability:* Part-time. Electronic applications accepted.

***School of Theatre, Film and Television*** Electronic applications accepted.

**College of Humanities** *Program availability:* Part-time. Electronic applications accepted.

**College of Medicine** *Program availability:* Part-time.

**College of Nursing** *Program availability:* Part-time, online learning. Electronic applications accepted.

**College of Optical Sciences** *Program availability:* Part-time. Electronic applications accepted.

**College of Pharmacy**

**College of Science** *Program availability:* Part-time. Electronic applications accepted.

**College of Social and Behavioral Sciences** *Program availability:* Part-time, evening/weekend. Electronic applications accepted.

***Center for Latin American Studies*** *Program availability:* Part-time. Electronic applications accepted.

***School of Anthropology*** *Program availability:* Part-time. Electronic applications accepted.

***School of Geography and Development*** *Program availability:* Part-time. Electronic applications accepted.

***School of Information*** *Program availability:* Part-time. Electronic applications accepted.

***School of Journalism*** *Program availability:* Part-time. Electronic applications accepted.

***School of Middle Eastern and North African Studies*** *Program availability:* Part-time, evening/weekend. Electronic applications accepted.

**Eller College of Management** *Program availability:* Evening/weekend. Electronic applications accepted.

**Graduate Interdisciplinary Programs** *Program availability:* Part-time.

**James E. Rogers College of Law** Electronic applications accepted.

**Mel and Enid Zuckerman College of Public Health** Electronic applications accepted.

## UNIVERSITY OF ARKANSAS, Fayetteville, AR 72701

**General Information** State-supported, coed, university. CGS member. *Enrollment:* 27,559 graduate, professional, and undergraduate students; 1,287 full-time matriculated graduate/professional students (718 women), 2,883 part-time matriculated graduate/professional students (1,443 women). *Graduate housing:* Room and/or apartments available on a first-come, first-served basis to single students; on-campus housing not available to married students. Typical cost: $4871 per year. *Student services:* Campus employment opportunities, campus safety program, career counseling, exercise/wellness program, free psychological counseling, international student services, low-cost health insurance, multicultural affairs office, services for students with disabilities, teacher training, writing training. *Library facilities:* David W. Mullins Library plus 4 others. *Collection:* Books: 2 million (physical), 703,745 (digital/electronic); Serial titles: 60,187 (physical), 173,320 (digital/electronic); Databases: 331. Weekly public service hours: 109. *Research affiliation:* Southern Regional Education Board, Southeastern Universities Research Association, Southern Regional Education Board Uncommon Facilities Program, Oak Ridge Associated Universities, Science Coalition, National Minority Graduate Feeder Project.

**Computer facilities:** Computer purchase and lease plans are available. 675 computers available on campus for general student use. A campuswide network can be accessed. Online class registration is available.

Website: http://www.uark.edu/

**GRADUATE UNITS**

**Graduate School** Students: 1,891 full-time (993 women), 1,754 part-time (838 women); includes 599 minority (217 Black or African American, non-Hispanic/Latino; 35 American Indian or Alaska Native, non-Hispanic/Latino; 78 Asian, non-Hispanic/Latino; 192 Hispanic/Latino; 3 Native Hawaiian or other Pacific Islander, non-Hispanic/Latino; 74 Two or more races, non-Hispanic/Latino), 723 international. 4,357 applicants, 29% accepted. *Faculty:* 1,206 full-time (492 women), 237 part-time/adjunct (122 women).

Expenses: Contact institution. *Financial support:* In 2019–20, 761 research assistantships, 484 teaching assistantships with full tuition reimbursements were awarded; fellowships with tuition reimbursements, career-related internships or fieldwork, Federal Work-Study, institutionally sponsored loans, scholarships/grants, traineeships, and unspecified assistantships also available. Support available to part-time students. Financial award application deadline: 4/1; financial award applicants required to submit FAFSA. In 2019, 983 master's, 222 doctorates, 31 other advanced degrees awarded. *Program availability:* Part-time, online learning. *Application deadline:* For fall admission, 8/1 for domestic students, 4/1 for international students; for spring admission, 12/1 for domestic students, 10/1 for international students; for summer admission, 4/15 for domestic students, 3/1 for international students. Applications are processed on a rolling basis. *Application fee:* $60. Electronic applications accepted. *Application Contact:* Patty Gamboa, Director, Graduate and International Recruitment and Admissions, 479-575-6247, Fax: 479-575-5908, E-mail: pgamboa@uark.edu. *Dean*, Dr. Kim LaScola Needy, 479-575-4401, Fax: 479-575-5908, E-mail: gradinfo@uark.edu.

***College of Education and Health Professions*** Students: 399 full-time (289 women), 612 part-time (418 women); includes 210 minority (97 Black or African American, non-Hispanic/Latino; 16 American Indian or Alaska Native, non-Hispanic/Latino; 16 Asian, non-Hispanic/Latino; 60 Hispanic/Latino; 1 Native Hawaiian or other Pacific Islander, non-Hispanic/Latino; 20 Two or more races, non-Hispanic/Latino), 40 international. 380 applicants, 71% accepted. Expenses: Contact institution. *Financial support:* In 2019–20, 110 research assistantships, 15 teaching assistantships were awarded; fellowships with tuition reimbursements, career-related internships or fieldwork, and Federal Work-Study also available. Support available to part-time students. Financial award application deadline: 4/1; financial award applicants required to submit FAFSA. In 2019, 266 master's, 77 doctorates, 13 other advanced degrees awarded. *Application deadline:* For fall admission, 8/1 for domestic students, 4/1 for international students; for spring admission, 12/1 for domestic students, 10/1 for international students; for summer admission, 4/15 for domestic students, 3/1 for international students. Applications are processed on a rolling basis. *Application fee:* $60. Electronic applications accepted. *Application Contact:* Aaron Abbott, Asst. Director for Graduate Recruitment, 479-575-8757, E-mail: aabbotte@uark.edu. *Dean*, Dr. Brian Primack, E-mail: bprimack@uark.edu.

***College of Engineering*** Students: 390 full-time (121 women), 472 part-time (116 women); includes 137 minority (42 Black or African American, non-Hispanic/Latino; 8 American Indian or Alaska Native, non-Hispanic/Latino; 26 Asian, non-Hispanic/Latino; 43 Hispanic/Latino; 2 Native Hawaiian or other Pacific Islander, non-Hispanic/Latino; 16 Two or more races, non-Hispanic/Latino), 276 international. 401 applicants, 82% accepted. Expenses: Contact institution. *Financial support:* In 2019–20, 198 research assistantships, 21 teaching assistantships were awarded; fellowships with tuition reimbursements, career-related internships or fieldwork, and Federal Work-Study also available. Support available to part-time students. Financial award application deadline: 4/1; financial award applicants required to submit FAFSA. In 2019, 235 master's, 33 doctorates awarded. *Application deadline:* For fall admission, 8/1 for domestic students, 4/1 for international students; for spring admission, 12/1 for domestic students, 10/1 for international students; for summer admission, 4/15 for domestic students, 3/1 for international students. Applications are processed on a rolling basis. *Application fee:* $60. Electronic applications accepted. *Application Contact:* Dr. Norman Dennis, Senior Associate Dean and University Professor, 479-575-6011, E-mail: ndennis@uark.edu. *Dean*, Dr. John R. English, 479-575-7455, E-mail: jre@uark.edu.

***Dale Bumpers College of Agricultural, Food and Life Sciences*** Students: 170 full-time (96 women), 137 part-time (84 women); includes 33 minority (9 Black or African American, non-Hispanic/Latino; 2 American Indian or Alaska Native, non-Hispanic/Latino; 15 Hispanic/Latino; 7 Two or more races, non-Hispanic/Latino), 75 international. 126 applicants, 78% accepted. Expenses: Contact institution. *Financial support:* In 2019–20, 167 research assistantships, 7 teaching assistantships were awarded; fellowships with tuition reimbursements, career-related internships or fieldwork, Federal Work-Study, scholarships/grants, and unspecified assistantships also available. Support available to part-time students. Financial award application deadline: 4/1; financial award applicants required to submit FAFSA. In 2019, 93 master's, 26 doctorates awarded. *Application deadline:* For fall admission, 8/1 for domestic students, 4/1 for international students; for spring admission, 12/1 for domestic students, 10/1 for international students; for summer admission, 4/15 for domestic students, 3/1 for international students. Applications are processed on a rolling basis. *Application fee:* $60. Electronic applications accepted. *Application Contact:* Dausen Garet Duncan, Coordinator of Recruitment, 479-575-2253, E-mail: dgduncan@uark.edu. *Dean*, Dr. Deacue Fields, 479-575-2034, E-mail: dcfields@uark.edu.

***J. William Fulbright College of Arts and Sciences*** Students: 605 full-time (330 women), 218 part-time (99 women); includes 126 minority (38 Black or African American, non-Hispanic/Latino; 5 American Indian or Alaska Native, non-Hispanic/Latino; 17 Asian, non-Hispanic/Latino; 41 Hispanic/Latino; 25 Two or more races, non-Hispanic/Latino), 144 international. 719 applicants, 55% accepted. Expenses: Contact institution. *Financial support:* In 2019–20, 143 research assistantships, 373 teaching assistantships with full tuition reimbursements were awarded; fellowships, career-related internships or fieldwork, Federal Work-Study, institutionally sponsored loans, and traineeships also available. Support available to part-time students. Financial award application deadline: 4/1; financial award applicants required to submit FAFSA. In 2019, 213 master's, 42 doctorates awarded. *Application deadline:* For fall admission, 8/1 for domestic students, 4/1 for international students; for spring admission, 12/1 for domestic students, 10/1 for international students; for summer admission, 4/15 for domestic students, 3/1 for international students. Applications are processed on a rolling basis. *Application fee:* $60. Electronic applications accepted. *Application Contact:* Dr. Todd G. Shields, Dean, 479-575-4804, Fax: 479-575-2642, E-mail: tshield@uark.edu. *Dean*, Dr. Todd G. Shields, 479-575-4804, Fax: 479-575-2642, E-mail: tshield@uark.edu.

***Sam M. Walton College of Business Administration*** Students: 170 full-time (72 women), 187 part-time (54 women); includes 56 minority (15 Black or African American, non-Hispanic/Latino; 2 American Indian or Alaska Native, non-Hispanic/Latino; 14 Asian, non-Hispanic/Latino; 20 Hispanic/Latino; 5 Two or more races, non-Hispanic/Latino), 60 international. Expenses: Contact institution. *Financial support:* In 2019–20, 64 research assistantships, 17 teaching assistantships were awarded; fellowships, career-related internships or fieldwork, and Federal Work-Study also available. Support available to part-time students. Financial award application deadline: 4/1; financial award applicants required to submit FAFSA. In 2019, 161 master's, 15 doctorates awarded. *Application deadline:* For fall admission, 8/1 for domestic students, 4/1 for international students; for spring admission, 12/1 for domestic students, 10/1 for international students; for summer admission, 4/15 for domestic students, 3/1 for international students. *Application fee:* $60. Electronic applications accepted. *Application Contact:* Dr. Matt Waller, Dean, 479-575-5949, Fax: 479-575-4435, E-mail: mwaller@walton.uark.edu. *Dean*, Dr. Matt Waller, 479-575-5949, Fax: 479-575-4435, E-mail: mwaller@walton.uark.edu.

**School of Law** Students: 293 full-time (107 women), 17 part-time (7 women); includes 53 minority (13 Black or African American, non-Hispanic/Latino; 8 American Indian or Alaska Native, non-Hispanic/Latino; 4 Asian, non-Hispanic/Latino; 16 Hispanic/Latino; 12 Two or more races, non-Hispanic/Latino). Expenses: Contact institution. *Financial support:* In 2019–20, fellowships with full tuition reimbursements (averaging $6,000 per year), 8 research assistantships (averaging $2,500 per year) were awarded; teaching assistantships, career-related internships or fieldwork, Federal Work-Study, and scholarships/grants also available. Support available to part-time students. Financial award application deadline: 4/1; financial award applicants required to submit FAFSA. In 2019, 24 master's, 104 doctorates awarded. *Application deadline:* For fall admission, 8/1 for domestic students, 4/1 for international students; for spring admission, 12/1 for domestic students, 10/1 for international students; for summer admission, 4/15 for domestic students, 3/1 for international students. Applications are processed on a rolling basis. *Application fee:* $60. Electronic applications accepted. *Application Contact:* Margaret E. Sova McCabe, Dean, 479-575-3873, E-mail: terri@uark.edu. *Dean*, Margaret E. Sova McCabe, 479-575-3873, E-mail: terri@uark.edu.

## UNIVERSITY OF ARKANSAS AT LITTLE ROCK, Little Rock, AR 72204-1099

**General Information** State-supported, coed, university. CGS member. *Graduate housing:* Room and/or apartments available on a first-come, first-served basis to single students; on-campus housing not available to married students. Housing application deadline: 9/1.

**GRADUATE UNITS**

**Graduate School** *Program availability:* Part-time, evening/weekend, online learning. Electronic applications accepted.

***Clinton School of Public Service***

***College of Arts, Letters, and Sciences*** *Program availability:* Part-time, evening/weekend.

***College of Business*** *Program availability:* Part-time, evening/weekend.

***College of Education and Health Professions*** *Program availability:* Part-time, evening/weekend.

***College of Social Sciences and Communication*** *Program availability:* Part-time, evening/weekend.

***George W. Donaghey College of Engineering and Information Technology*** *Program availability:* Part-time, evening/weekend.

**William H. Bowen School of Law** *Program availability:* Part-time, evening/weekend. Electronic applications accepted.

## UNIVERSITY OF ARKANSAS AT MONTICELLO, Monticello, AR 71656

**General Information** State-supported, coed, comprehensive institution. *Graduate housing:* Rooms and/or apartments guaranteed to single students and available on a first-come, first-served basis to married students. Housing application deadline: 8/15.

**GRADUATE UNITS**

**School of Education** *Program availability:* Part-time, evening/weekend, online learning. Electronic applications accepted.

**School of Forest Resources** *Program availability:* Part-time. Electronic applications accepted.

## UNIVERSITY OF ARKANSAS AT PINE BLUFF, Pine Bluff, AR 71601-2799

**General Information** State-supported, coed, comprehensive institution. *Graduate housing:* Room and/or apartments available on a first-come, first-served basis to single students; on-campus housing not available to married students. Housing application deadline: 8/1.

**GRADUATE UNITS**

**Division of Graduate Studies and Continuing Education**

**School of Agriculture, Fisheries and Human Sciences**

**School of Education** *Program availability:* Part-time, evening/weekend.

## UNIVERSITY OF ARKANSAS FOR MEDICAL SCIENCES, Little Rock, AR 72205-7199

**General Information** State-supported, coed, university. *Graduate housing:* Rooms and/or apartments available on a first-come, first-served basis to single and married students. Housing application deadline: 7/15. *Research affiliation:* National Center for Toxicological Research, Veterans Administration Hospital, Oak Ridge Associated Universities, Arkansas Children's Hospital.

**GRADUATE UNITS**

**College of Health Professions** *Program availability:* Part-time, online learning. Electronic applications accepted.

**College of Medicine** Electronic applications accepted.

**College of Nursing** *Program availability:* Part-time.

**College of Pharmacy** Electronic applications accepted.

**Fay W. Boozman College of Public Health** *Program availability:* Part-time. Electronic applications accepted.

**Graduate School** *Program availability:* Part-time. Electronic applications accepted.

## UNIVERSITY OF ARKANSAS-FORT SMITH, Fort Smith, AR 72913-3649

**General Information** State and locally supported, coed, comprehensive institution.

**GRADUATE UNITS**

**Program in Healthcare Administration** *Program availability:* Online learning.

## UNIVERSITY OF BALTIMORE, Baltimore, MD 21201-5779

**General Information** State-supported, coed, comprehensive institution. *Graduate housing:* On-campus housing not available.

**GRADUATE UNITS**

**Graduate School** *Program availability:* Part-time, evening/weekend, online learning. Electronic applications accepted.

***College of Public Affairs***

***Merrick School of Business*** *Program availability:* Part-time, evening/weekend, online learning. Electronic applications accepted.

***Yale Gordon College of Arts and Sciences*** *Program availability:* Part-time, evening/weekend. Electronic applications accepted.

**Joint University of Baltimore/Towson University (UB/Towson) MBA Program** *Program availability:* Part-time, evening/weekend, online learning.

**School of Law** Students: 488 full-time (245 women), 180 part-time (106 women); includes 240 minority (103 Black or African American, non-Hispanic/Latino; 49 Asian, non-Hispanic/Latino; 56 Hispanic/Latino; 32 Two or more races, non-Hispanic/Latino), 6 international. Average age 29. 1,122 applicants, 55% accepted, 221 enrolled. *Faculty:* 60 full-time (31 women), 74 part-time/adjunct (27 women). Expenses: Contact institution. *Financial support:* In 2019–20, 347 students received support. Research assistantships, teaching assistantships, career-related internships or fieldwork, Federal Work-Study, and scholarships/grants available. Support available to part-time students. Financial award application deadline: 4/1; financial award applicants required to submit FAFSA. In 2019, 206 doctorates awarded. *Program availability:* Part-time, evening/weekend. *Application deadline:* For fall admission, 7/30 for domestic students, 4/1 priority date for international students. Applications are processed on a rolling basis. *Application fee:* $60. Electronic applications accepted. *Application Contact:* Jeffrey L. Zavrotny, Assistant Dean for Admissions, 410-837-5809, Fax: 410-837-4188, E-mail: jzavrotny@ubalt.edu. *Dean,* Ronald Weich, 410-837-4458.

## UNIVERSITY OF BRIDGEPORT, Bridgeport, CT 06604

**General Information** Independent, coed, comprehensive institution. CGS member. *Graduate housing:* Rooms and/or apartments guaranteed to single students and available on a first-come, first-served basis to married students. Housing application deadline: 8/15. *Research affiliation:* Connecticut Medicine Research Consortia, Marine Biology Station, Burndy Library.

**GRADUATE UNITS**

**Acupuncture Institute** *Program availability:* Part-time. Electronic applications accepted.

**College of Chiropractic** Electronic applications accepted.

**College of Naturopathic Medicine** Electronic applications accepted.

**College of Public and International Affairs** *Program availability:* Part-time, evening/weekend.

**Fones School of Dental Hygiene** *Program availability:* Part-time, evening/weekend, online learning.

**Nutrition Institute** *Program availability:* Part-time, evening/weekend, online learning. Electronic applications accepted.

**Physician Assistant Institute**

**School of Arts and Sciences** *Program availability:* Part-time, evening/weekend. Electronic applications accepted.

**School of Business** *Program availability:* Part-time, evening/weekend. Electronic applications accepted.

**School of Education** *Program availability:* Part-time, evening/weekend. Electronic applications accepted.

**School of Engineering** *Program availability:* Part-time, evening/weekend, online learning. Electronic applications accepted.

**Shintaro Akatsu School of Design** *Program availability:* Part-time, evening/weekend. Electronic applications accepted.

## THE UNIVERSITY OF BRITISH COLUMBIA, Vancouver, BC V6T 1Z1, Canada

**General Information** Province-supported, coed, university. CGS member. *Graduate housing:* Rooms and/or apartments available on a first-come, first-served basis to single and married students. Housing application deadline: 3/1. *Research affiliation:* British Columbia Research (chemical and biological science technology), Forintek Canada (forest technology), National Research Council of Canada Institute of Machinery Research (machinery research), Pulp and Paper Research Institute of Canada, Pacific Environment Institute, Pacific Biological Station (fisheries and oceanography).

**GRADUATE UNITS**

**Faculty of Applied Science** *Program availability:* Part-time. Electronic applications accepted.

***Clean Energy Research Center***

***School of Architecture and Landscape Architecture*** Electronic applications accepted.

***School of Biomedical Engineering***

***School of Community and Regional Planning*** Electronic applications accepted.

***School of Nursing*** *Program availability:* Part-time. Electronic applications accepted.

**Faculty of Arts** Electronic applications accepted.

***Center for Digital Media***

***Institute for Gender, Race, Sexuality, and Social Justice***

***School of Journalism*** Electronic applications accepted.

***School of Library, Archival and Information Studies*** *Program availability:* Part-time. Electronic applications accepted.

***School of Music*** *Program availability:* Part-time. Electronic applications accepted.

***School of Social Work*** Electronic applications accepted.

***Vancouver School of Economics*** Electronic applications accepted.

**Faculty of Dentistry** *Program availability:* Part-time. Electronic applications accepted.

**Faculty of Education** *Program availability:* Part-time, evening/weekend, online learning. Electronic applications accepted.

***School of Kinesiology*** *Program availability:* Part-time. Electronic applications accepted.

**Faculty of Forestry** Electronic applications accepted.

**Faculty of Land and Food Systems** *Program availability:* Part-time. Electronic applications accepted.

**Faculty of Medicine** *Program availability:* Part-time.

***School of Audiology and Speech Sciences*** Electronic applications accepted.

***School of Population and Public Health*** *Program availability:* Online learning. Electronic applications accepted.

***School of Rehabilitation Sciences*** Electronic applications accepted.

**Faculty of Pharmaceutical Sciences** Electronic applications accepted.

**Faculty of Science** *Program availability:* Part-time. Electronic applications accepted.

***Institute for Resources, Environment and Sustainability*** Electronic applications accepted.

**Institute of Asian Research** Electronic applications accepted.

**Peter A. Allard School of Law** *Program availability:* Part-time. Electronic applications accepted.

**Sauder School of Business** *Program availability:* Part-time, evening/weekend. Electronic applications accepted.

## UNIVERSITY OF CALGARY, Calgary, AB T2N 1N4, Canada

**General Information** Province-supported, coed, university. CGS member. *Graduate housing:* Rooms and/or apartments available on a first-come, first-served basis to single and married students. Housing application deadline: 3/31. *Research affiliation:* Alta Telecommunications Research Centre, Alberta Sulphur Research, Calgary Society for Students with Learning Difficulties, Canadian Institute of Resources Law, Canadian Music Centre, Canadian Energy Research Institute.

**GRADUATE UNITS**

**Cumming School of Medicine** *Program availability:* Part-time. Electronic applications accepted.

**Faculty of Graduate Studies** *Program availability:* Part-time, evening/weekend, blended/hybrid learning. Electronic applications accepted.

***Faculty of Arts*** *Program availability:* Part-time, evening/weekend. Electronic applications accepted.

***Faculty of Kinesiology*** Electronic applications accepted.

***Faculty of Law***

***Faculty of Nursing*** *Program availability:* Part-time. Electronic applications accepted.

***Faculty of Science*** *Program availability:* Part-time.

***Faculty of Social Work*** Electronic applications accepted.

***Haskayne School of Business*** *Program availability:* Part-time, evening/weekend.

***The School of Public Policy*** *Program availability:* Part-time.

***Schulich School of Engineering*** *Program availability:* Part-time, evening/weekend. Electronic applications accepted.

***Werklund School of Education*** *Program availability:* Part-time, evening/weekend, online learning. Electronic applications accepted.

**Faculty of Veterinary Medicine**

**School of Architecture, Planning and Landscaping**

***Program in Environmental Design***

## UNIVERSITY OF CALIFORNIA, BERKELEY, Berkeley, CA 94720

**General Information** State-supported, coed, university. CGS member. *Graduate housing:* Rooms and/or apartments available to single and married students.

**GRADUATE UNITS**

**Graduate Division** *Program availability:* Part-time, blended/hybrid learning.

***College of Chemistry*** Electronic applications accepted.

***College of Engineering*** *Program availability:* Part-time, 100% online, blended/hybrid learning. Electronic applications accepted.

***College of Environmental Design*** Electronic applications accepted.

***College of Letters and Science*** Electronic applications accepted.

***College of Natural Resources***

***Graduate School of Journalism*** Electronic applications accepted.

***Graduate School of Public Policy*** Electronic applications accepted.

***Haas School of Business*** *Program availability:* Part-time, evening/weekend.

***School of Education*** Electronic applications accepted.

***School of Information*** Electronic applications accepted.

***School of Public Health*** *Program availability:* Blended/hybrid learning. Electronic applications accepted.

***School of Social Welfare*** Electronic applications accepted.

**School of Law**

**School of Optometry** Electronic applications accepted.

**UC Berkeley Extension** *Program availability:* Part-time, evening/weekend, online learning.

## UNIVERSITY OF CALIFORNIA, DAVIS, Davis, CA 95616

**General Information** State-supported, coed, university. CGS member. *Graduate housing:* Rooms and/or apartments available to single and married students. Housing application deadline: 4/1.

**GRADUATE UNITS**

**College of Engineering** *Program availability:* Part-time. Electronic applications accepted.

**Graduate School of Management** Students: 237 full-time (127 women), 262 part-time (107 women); includes 169 minority (8 Black or African American, non-Hispanic/Latino; 1 American Indian or Alaska Native, non-Hispanic/Latino; 117 Asian, non-Hispanic/Latino; 41 Hispanic/Latino; 1 Native Hawaiian or other Pacific Islander, non-Hispanic/Latino; 1 Two or more races, non-Hispanic/Latino), 154 international. Average age 27. 1,722 applicants, 29% accepted, 278 enrolled. Expenses: Contact institution. *Financial support:* Fellowships with full and partial tuition reimbursements, research assistantships with partial tuition reimbursements, teaching assistantships with partial tuition reimbursements, institutionally sponsored loans, scholarships/grants, health care benefits, tuition waivers (partial), and unspecified assistantships available. Support available to part-time students. Financial award application deadline: 3/1; financial award applicants required to submit FAFSA. In 2019, 236 master's awarded. *Program availability:* Part-time, evening/weekend, 100% online. *Application deadline:* For fall admission, 9/15 priority date for domestic and international students. Applications are processed on a rolling basis. *Application fee:* $125. Electronic applications accepted. *Application Contact:* Anna Palmer, MBA Director of Recruitment and Admissions, 530-752-6421, E-mail: admissions@gsm.ucdavis.edu. *Dean and Professor,* H. Rao Unnava, 530-752-4600, E-mail: admissions@gsm.ucdavis.edu.

**Graduate Studies** Electronic applications accepted.

**School of Law** Electronic applications accepted.

**School of Medicine** Electronic applications accepted.

**School of Veterinary Medicine**

## UNIVERSITY OF CALIFORNIA, HASTINGS COLLEGE OF THE LAW, San Francisco, CA 94102-4978

**General Information** State-supported, coed, graduate-only institution. *Graduate housing:* Rooms and/or apartments available on a first-come, first-served basis to single and married students. Housing application deadline: 7/1.

**GRADUATE UNITS**

**Graduate Programs** *Program availability:* 100% online, blended/hybrid learning. Electronic applications accepted.

## UNIVERSITY OF CALIFORNIA, IRVINE, Irvine, CA 92697

**General Information** State-supported, coed, university. CGS member. *Enrollment:* 36,908 graduate, professional, and undergraduate students; 5,929 full-time matriculated graduate/professional students (2,820 women), 484 part-time matriculated graduate/professional students (262 women). *Graduate housing:* Rooms and/or apartments available on a first-come, first-served basis to single and married students. *Student services:* Campus employment opportunities, campus safety program, career counseling, child daycare facilities, exercise/wellness program, free psychological counseling, grant writing training, international student services, low-cost health insurance, multicultural affairs office, services for students with disabilities, teacher training, writing training. *Library facilities:* Langson Library plus 4 others. *Collection:* Books: 2 million (physical), 1.3 million (digital/electronic); Serial titles: 4,309 (physical), 177,370 (digital/electronic); Databases: 1,652. Study areas open 24 hours, 5–7 days a week; students can reserve study rooms.

**Computer facilities:** 1,500 computers available on campus for general student use. A campuswide network can be accessed. Online class registration is available.
Website: http://www.uci.edu/

**General Application Contact:** Erika Wichmann, Student Affairs Officer, Graduate Division, 949-824-4611, Fax: 949-824-9096, E-mail: ewichman@uci.edu.

**GRADUATE UNITS**

**Claire Trevor School of the Arts** Students: 143 full-time (66 women), 4 part-time (2 women); includes 57 minority (16 Black or African American, non-Hispanic/Latino; 14 Asian, non-Hispanic/Latino; 11 Hispanic/Latino; 16 Two or more races, non-Hispanic/Latino), 16 international. Average age 31. 431 applicants, 13% accepted, 47 enrolled. Expenses: Contact institution. *Financial support:* Fellowships, teaching assistantships, institutionally sponsored loans, traineeships, health care benefits, and unspecified assistantships available. Financial award application deadline: 3/1; financial award applicants required to submit FAFSA. In 2019, 52 master's, 6 doctorates awarded. *Application deadline:* For fall admission, 1/15 for domestic and international students. Applications are processed on a rolling basis. *Application fee:* $120 ($140 for international students). Electronic applications accepted. *Application Contact:* Prof. Vincent Olivieri, Associate Dean, 949-824-5684, Fax: 949-824-2450, E-mail: olivieri@uci.edu. *Dean*, Dr. Stephen Barker, 949-824-8792, Fax: 949-824-2450, E-mail: barker@uci.edu.

**Donald Bren School of Information and Computer Sciences** Students: 756 full-time (235 women), 22 part-time (9 women); includes 121 minority (11 Black or African American, non-Hispanic/Latino; 1 American Indian or Alaska Native, non-Hispanic/Latino; 91 Asian, non-Hispanic/Latino; 13 Hispanic/Latino; 5 Two or more races, non-Hispanic/Latino), 499 international. Average age 26. 5,562 applicants, 18% accepted, 331 enrolled. Expenses: Contact institution. *Financial support:* Fellowships, research assistantships with full tuition reimbursements, teaching assistantships, institutionally sponsored loans, traineeships, health care benefits, and unspecified assistantships available. Financial award applicants required to submit FAFSA. In 2019, 256 master's, 38 doctorates awarded. *Application deadline:* For fall admission, 12/15 for domestic and international students. *Application fee:* $120 ($140 for international students). Electronic applications accepted. *Application Contact:* Kristine Bolcer, Director of Student Affairs, 949-824-5156, Fax: 949-824-4163, E-mail: kbolcer@uci.edu. *Dean*, Marios C. Papaefthymiou, 949-824-7427, E-mail: marios@uci.edu.

**Institute of Transportation Studies** Students: 8 full-time (3 women), 1 part-time (0 women); includes 1 minority (Asian, non-Hispanic/Latino), 7 international. Average age 33. Expenses: Contact institution. *Financial support:* Fellowships, research assistantships with full tuition reimbursements, teaching assistantships, institutionally sponsored loans, traineeships, health care benefits, and unspecified assistantships available. Financial award application deadline: 3/1. In 2019, 2 master's, 1 doctorate awarded. *Application deadline:* For fall admission, 1/15 for domestic and international students. *Application fee:* $120 ($140 for international students). *Application Contact:* Amelia Regan, Director, Transportation Science Program, 949-824-2611, E-mail: aregan@uci.edu. *Director*, Stephen G. Ritchie, 949-824-4214, E-mail: sritchie@uci.edu.

**Interdisciplinary Studies**

**The Paul Merage School of Business** Students: 724 full-time (335 women), 282 part-time (127 women); includes 555 minority (41 Black or African American, non-Hispanic/Latino; 10 American Indian or Alaska Native, non-Hispanic/Latino; 420 Asian, non-Hispanic/Latino; 81 Hispanic/Latino; 3 Native Hawaiian or other Pacific Islander, non-Hispanic/Latino), 174 international. Average age 29. 4,297 applicants, 26% accepted, 557 enrolled. Expenses: Contact institution. *Financial support:* Career-related internships or fieldwork, Federal Work-Study, institutionally sponsored loans, scholarships/grants, traineeships, health care benefits, and unspecified assistantships available. Support available to part-time students. Financial award application deadline: 3/1; financial award applicants required to submit FAFSA. In 2019, 512 master's, 7 doctorates awarded. *Program availability:* Part-time, evening/weekend. *Application deadline:* For fall admission, 1/2 priority date for domestic and international students. Applications are processed on a rolling basis. *Application fee:* $120 ($140 for international students). Electronic applications accepted. *Application Contact:* Eric Spangenberg, Dean, 949-824-8470, E-mail: ers@uci.edu. *Dean*, Eric Spangenberg, 949-824-8470, E-mail: ers@uci.edu.

**Programs in Health Sciences**

**Samueli School of Engineering** Students: 877 full-time (283 women), 37 part-time (13 women); includes 178 minority (16 Black or African American, non-Hispanic/Latino; 119 Asian, non-Hispanic/Latino; 33 Hispanic/Latino; 1 Native Hawaiian or other Pacific Islander, non-Hispanic/Latino; 9 Two or more races, non-Hispanic/Latino), 526 international. Average age 26. 3,710 applicants, 33% accepted, 281 enrolled. Expenses: Contact institution. *Financial support:* Fellowships with tuition reimbursements, research assistantships with full tuition reimbursements, teaching assistantships with tuition reimbursements, institutionally sponsored loans, traineeships, health care benefits, and unspecified assistantships available. Financial award application deadline: 3/1; financial award applicants required to submit FAFSA. In 2019, 282 master's, 97 doctorates awarded. *Program availability:* Part-time. *Application deadline:* For fall admission, 1/15 priority date for domestic students, 1/15 for international students. Applications are processed on a rolling basis. *Application fee:* $120 ($140 for international students). Electronic applications accepted. *Application Contact:* Jean Bennett, Director of Graduate Student Affairs, 949-824-6475, Fax: 949-824-8200, E-mail: jean.bennett@uci.edu. *Dean*, Gregory N. Washington, 949-824-4333, Fax: 949-824-8200, E-mail: engineering@uci.edu.

**School of Biological Sciences** Students: 365 full-time (210 women), 2 part-time (1 woman); includes 141 minority (9 Black or African American, non-Hispanic/Latino; 1 American Indian or Alaska Native, non-Hispanic/Latino; 65 Asian, non-Hispanic/Latino; 63 Hispanic/Latino; 3 Two or more races, non-Hispanic/Latino), 72 international. Average age 27. 1,056 applicants, 26% accepted, 120 enrolled. Expenses: Contact institution. *Financial support:* Fellowships with full tuition reimbursements, research assistantships with full tuition reimbursements, teaching assistantships with full tuition reimbursements, career-related internships or fieldwork, institutionally sponsored loans, scholarships/grants, traineeships, health care benefits, and unspecified assistantships available. Financial award application deadline: 3/1; financial award applicants required to submit FAFSA. In 2019, 71 master's, 36 doctorates awarded. *Application deadline:* For fall admission, 12/15 for domestic and international students. Applications are processed on a rolling basis. *Application fee:* $120 ($140 for international students). Electronic applications accepted. *Application Contact:* Prof. R. Michael Mulligan, Associate Dean, 949-824-8433, Fax: 949-824-4709, E-mail: rmmullig@uci.edu. *Dean*, Prof. Frank Laferla, 949-824-5315, Fax: 949-824-3035, E-mail: laferla@uci.edu.

**School of Education** Students: 214 full-time (154 women), 1 part-time (0 women); includes 109 minority (3 Black or African American, non-Hispanic/Latino; 57 Asian, non-Hispanic/Latino; 46 Hispanic/Latino; 3 Two or more races, non-Hispanic/Latino), 29 international. Average age 27. 432 applicants, 48% accepted, 149 enrolled. Expenses: Contact institution. *Financial support:* Fellowships, research assistantships with full tuition reimbursements, institutionally sponsored loans, traineeships, health care benefits, and unspecified assistantships available. Financial award application deadline: 3/1; financial award applicants required to submit FAFSA. In 2019, 141 master's, 8 doctorates awarded. *Program availability:* Part-time, evening/weekend. *Application deadline:* For fall admission, 1/2 priority date for domestic students, 1/2 for international students. *Application fee:* $120 ($140 for international students). Electronic applications accepted. *Application Contact:* Denise Earley, Assistant Director of Student Affairs, 949-824-4022, E-mail: denise.earley@uci.edu. *Dean*, Richard Arum, 949-824-2534, E-mail: richard.arum@uci.edu.

**School of Humanities** Students: 285 full-time (149 women), 2 part-time (1 woman); includes 96 minority (14 Black or African American, non-Hispanic/Latino; 1 American Indian or Alaska Native, non-Hispanic/Latino; 27 Asian, non-Hispanic/Latino; 36 Hispanic/Latino; 18 Two or more races, non-Hispanic/Latino), 49 international. Average age 32. 931 applicants, 12% accepted, 64 enrolled. Expenses: Contact institution. *Financial support:* Fellowships with tuition reimbursements, research assistantships with full tuition reimbursements, teaching assistantships with tuition reimbursements, institutionally sponsored loans, traineeships, health care benefits, and unspecified assistantships available. Financial award application deadline: 3/1; financial award applicants required to submit FAFSA. In 2019, 57 master's, 44 doctorates awarded. *Application deadline:* For fall admission, 1/15 for domestic and international students. Applications are processed on a rolling basis. *Application fee:* $120 ($140 for international students). Electronic applications accepted. *Application Contact:* Amy Fujitani, Director of Graduate Student Affairs, 949-824-4303, Fax: 949-824-1360, E-mail: amy.fujitani@uci.edu. *Dean*, Georges Van Den Abbeele, 949-824-5133, E-mail: gvandena@uci.edu.

**School of Law** Electronic applications accepted.

**School of Medicine** Students: 545 full-time (290 women), 34 part-time (13 women); includes 98 minority (8 Black or African American, non-Hispanic/Latino; 1 American Indian or Alaska Native, non-Hispanic/Latino; 59 Asian, non-Hispanic/Latino; 29 Hispanic/Latino; 1 Two or more races, non-Hispanic/Latino), 17 international. Average age 29. 283 applicants, 14% accepted, 27 enrolled. Expenses: Contact institution. *Financial support:* Fellowships, research assistantships with full tuition reimbursements, teaching assistantships, career-related internships or fieldwork, institutionally sponsored loans, traineeships, health care benefits, and unspecified assistantships available. Financial award application deadline: 3/1; financial award applicants required to submit FAFSA. In 2019, 30 master's, 125 doctorates awarded. *Application deadline:* For fall admission, 1/15 for domestic and international students. *Application fee:* $120 ($140 for international students). Electronic applications accepted. *Application Contact:* Leora Fellus, Graduate Studies Director, 949-824-1028, E-mail: lfellus@uci.edu. *Dean*, Dr. Michael Stamos, 949-824-1046, E-mail: mstamos@uci.edu.

**School of Physical Sciences** Students: 554 full-time (219 women), 2 part-time (0 women); includes 154 minority (7 Black or African American, non-Hispanic/Latino; 1 American Indian or Alaska Native, non-Hispanic/Latino; 70 Asian, non-Hispanic/Latino; 50 Hispanic/Latino; 26 Two or more races, non-Hispanic/Latino), 112 international. Average age 27. 1,157 applicants, 33% accepted, 152 enrolled. Expenses: Contact institution. *Financial support:* Fellowships, research assistantships with full tuition reimbursements, teaching assistantships, career-related internships or fieldwork, institutionally sponsored loans, traineeships, health care benefits, and unspecified assistantships available. Financial award application deadline: 3/1; financial award applicants required to submit FAFSA. In 2019, 66 master's, 76 doctorates awarded. *Application deadline:* For fall admission, 1/15 priority date for domestic and international students. Applications are processed on a rolling basis. *Application fee:* $120 ($140 for international students). Electronic applications accepted. *Application Contact:* Prof. Isabella Velicogna, Associate Dean, 949-824-5419, E-mail: isabella@uci.edu. *Dean*, James Bullock, 949-824-6022, E-mail: bullock@uci.edu.

**School of Social Ecology** Students: 353 full-time (258 women), 75 part-time (65 women); includes 214 minority (33 Black or African American, non-Hispanic/Latino; 1 American Indian or Alaska Native, non-Hispanic/Latino; 48 Asian, non-Hispanic/Latino; 113 Hispanic/Latino; 1 Native Hawaiian or other Pacific Islander, non-Hispanic/Latino; 18 Two or more races, non-Hispanic/Latino), 53 international. Average age 29. 885 applicants, 43% accepted, 175 enrolled. Expenses: Contact institution. *Financial support:* Fellowships, research assistantships with full tuition reimbursements, teaching assistantships, institutionally sponsored loans, traineeships, health care benefits, and unspecified assistantships available. Financial award application deadline: 3/1; financial award applicants required to submit FAFSA. In 2019, 145 master's, 14 doctorates awarded. *Application deadline:* For fall admission, 1/15 priority date for domestic students, 1/15 for international students. Applications are processed on a rolling basis. *Application fee:* $120 ($140 for international students). Electronic applications accepted. *Application Contact:* Jennifer Craig, Director of Graduate Student Services, 949-824-5918, E-mail: craigj@uci.edu. *Dean*, Nancy Guerra, 949-824-5466, Fax: 949-824-1845, E-mail: nguerra1@uci.edu.

**School of Social Sciences** Students: 457 full-time (211 women), 8 part-time (1 woman); includes 147 minority (15 Black or African American, non-Hispanic/Latino; 2 American Indian or Alaska Native, non-Hispanic/Latino; 48 Asian, non-Hispanic/Latino; 61 Hispanic/Latino; 1 Native Hawaiian or other Pacific Islander, non-Hispanic/Latino; 20

Two or more races, non-Hispanic/Latino), 126 international. Average age 30. 789 applicants, 29% accepted, 112 enrolled. Expenses: Contact institution. *Financial support:* Fellowships, research assistantships with full tuition reimbursements, teaching assistantships, institutionally sponsored loans, traineeships, health care benefits, and unspecified assistantships available. Financial award application deadline: 3/1; financial award applicants required to submit FAFSA. In 2019, 65 master's, 53 doctorates awarded. *Application deadline:* For fall admission, 1/15 priority date for domestic students, 1/15 for international students. Applications are processed on a rolling basis. *Application fee:* $120 ($140 for international students). Electronic applications accepted. *Application Contact:* Michael McBride, Associate Dean for Research and Graduate Studies, 949-824-7417, Fax: 949-824-2182, E-mail: mcbride@uci.edu. *Dean,* William M. Maurer, 949-824-6802, Fax: 949-824-0646, E-mail: wmmaurer@uci.edu.

***Institute for Mathematical Behavioral Sciences*** Students: 9 full-time (4 women); includes 3 minority (1 Asian, non-Hispanic/Latino; 2 Two or more races, non-Hispanic/Latino), 2 international. Average age 38. 12 applicants, 17% accepted. Expenses: Contact institution. *Financial support:* Fellowships, research assistantships with full tuition reimbursements, teaching assistantships, institutionally sponsored loans, traineeships, health care benefits, and unspecified assistantships available. Financial award application deadline: 3/1; financial award applicants required to submit FAFSA. In 2019, 2 master's, 1 doctorate awarded. *Application deadline:* For fall admission, 1/15 priority date for domestic students, 1/15 for international students. Applications are processed on a rolling basis. *Application fee:* $120 ($140 for international students). Electronic applications accepted. *Application Contact:* Joanna Kerner, Administrative Manager, 949-824-8651, Fax: 949-824-3733, E-mail: kernerj@uci.edu. *Interim Director,* Jean-Paul Carvalho, 949-824-3417, Fax: 949-824-3733, E-mail: jpcarv@uci.edu.

## UNIVERSITY OF CALIFORNIA, LOS ANGELES, Los Angeles, CA 90095

**General Information** State-supported, coed, university. CGS member. *Graduate housing:* Rooms and/or apartments available on a first-come, first-served basis to single and married students.

**GRADUATE UNITS**

**David Geffen School of Medicine** Electronic applications accepted.

**Graduate Division** Electronic applications accepted.

***College of Letters and Science*** Electronic applications accepted.

***Fielding School of Public Health*** Electronic applications accepted.

***Graduate School of Education and Information Studies*** *Program availability:* Part-time, evening/weekend. Electronic applications accepted.

***Henry Samueli School of Engineering and Applied Science*** *Program availability:* Evening/weekend, blended/hybrid learning. Electronic applications accepted.

***Institute of the Environment and Sustainability***

***International Institute*** Electronic applications accepted.

***Luskin School of Public Affairs*** Electronic applications accepted.

***School of Nursing*** Electronic applications accepted.

***School of the Arts and Architecture*** Electronic applications accepted.

***School of Theater, Film and Television*** Electronic applications accepted.

***UCLA Anderson School of Management*** Students: 1,033 full-time (377 women), 1,162 part-time (391 women); includes 768 minority (47 Black or African American, non-Hispanic/Latino; 3 American Indian or Alaska Native, non-Hispanic/Latino; 533 Asian, non-Hispanic/Latino; 105 Hispanic/Latino; 2 Native Hawaiian or other Pacific Islander, non-Hispanic/Latino; 78 Two or more races, non-Hispanic/Latino), 575 international. Average age 31. 6,394 applicants, 29% accepted, 932 enrolled. *Faculty:* 81 full-time (21 women), 110 part-time/adjunct (21 women). Expenses: Contact institution. *Financial support:* Fellowships, research assistantships with partial tuition reimbursements, teaching assistantships with partial tuition reimbursements, career-related internships or fieldwork, institutionally sponsored loans, and scholarships/grants available. Support available to part-time students. In 2019, 991 master's, 9 doctorates awarded. *Program availability:* Part-time, evening/weekend. *Application deadline:* For fall admission, 10/2 for domestic and international students; for winter admission, 1/8 for domestic and international students; for spring admission, 4/16 for domestic and international students. Applications are processed on a rolling basis. *Application fee:* $200. Electronic applications accepted. *Application Contact:* Alex Lawrence, Assistant Dean and Director of MBA Admissions, 310-825-6944, Fax: 310-825-8582, E-mail: mba.admissions@anderson.ucla.edu. *Dean and John E. Anderson Chair in Management,* Dr. Antonio Bernardo, 310-825-7982, Fax: 310-206-2073, E-mail: a.bernardo@anderson.ucla.edu.

**School of Dentistry** Electronic applications accepted.

**School of Law** Average age 24. 6,175 applicants, 22% accepted, 307 enrolled. Expenses: Contact institution. *Financial support:* In 2019–20, 783 students received support. Career-related internships or fieldwork, scholarships/grants, health care benefits, tuition waivers (full and partial), and unspecified assistantships available. Financial award application deadline: 3/2. In 2019, 193 master's, 317 doctorates awarded. *Application deadline:* For fall admission, 2/1 for domestic students. Applications are processed on a rolling basis. *Application fee:* $75. Electronic applications accepted. *Application Contact:* Admissions Office, 310-825-2080, E-mail: admissions@law.ucla.edu. *Dean/Professor of Law,* Jennifer L. Mnookin, 310-825-8202.

## UNIVERSITY OF CALIFORNIA, MERCED, Merced, CA 95343

**General Information** State-supported, coed, university. CGS member. *Enrollment:* 8,847 graduate, professional, and undergraduate students; 693 full-time matriculated graduate/professional students (315 women), 3 part-time matriculated graduate/professional students (all women). *Enrollment by degree level:* 57 master's, 639 doctoral. *Graduate faculty:* 252 full-time (103 women), 2 part-time/adjunct (0 women). *International tuition:* $26,544 full-time. *Tuition, area resident:* Full-time $11,442; part-time $5721 per semester. Tuition, state resident: full-time $11,442; part-time $5721 per semester. Tuition, nonresident: full-time $26,544; part-time $13,272 per semester. *Required fees:* $564 per semester. *Graduate housing:* On-campus housing not available. *Student services:* Campus employment opportunities, campus safety program, career counseling, child daycare facilities, exercise/wellness program, free psychological counseling, grant writing training, international student services, low-cost health insurance, multicultural affairs office, services for students with disabilities, teacher training, writing training. *Library facilities:* Kolligian Library. *Collection:* Books: 145,798 (physical), 2 million (digital/electronic); Serial titles: 99,476 (physical). Weekly public service hours: 97; students can reserve study rooms. *Research affiliation:* NASA (nanotechnology and engineering), National Science Foundation (STEM), National Institutes of Health (health and behavioral sciences), DARPA (STEM), Department of Defense (physics and engineering), Keck (bioengineering and nanotechnology).

**Computer facilities:** A campuswide network can be accessed. Online class registration, student calendar, 10Gb online cloud storage, free office software are available.
Website: http://www.ucmerced.edu/

**General Application Contact:** Tsu Ya, Director of Admissions and Academic Services, 209-228-4521, Fax: 209-228-6906, E-mail: tya@ucmerced.edu.

**GRADUATE UNITS**

**Graduate Division** Students: 693 full-time (315 women), 3 part-time (all women); includes 220 minority (12 Black or African American, non-Hispanic/Latino; 63 Asian, non-Hispanic/Latino; 128 Hispanic/Latino; 1 Native Hawaiian or other Pacific Islander, non-Hispanic/Latino; 16 Two or more races, non-Hispanic/Latino), 269 international. Average age 29. 840 applicants, 45% accepted, 157 enrolled. *Faculty:* 252 full-time (103 women), 2 part-time/adjunct (0 women). Expenses: Contact institution. *Financial support:* In 2019–20, 621 students received support, including 22 fellowships with full tuition reimbursements available (averaging $22,005 per year), 137 research assistantships with full tuition reimbursements available (averaging $21,420 per year), 462 teaching assistantships with full tuition reimbursements available (averaging $21,911 per year); scholarships/grants, traineeships, and health care benefits also available. Financial award application deadline: 1/15. In 2019, 55 master's, 63 doctorates awarded. *Application deadline:* For fall admission, 1/15 for domestic and international students. *Application fee:* $105 ($125 for international students). Electronic applications accepted. *Application Contact:* Tsu Ya, Director of Admissions and Academic Services, 209-228-4521, Fax: 209-228-6906, E-mail: tya@ucmerced.edu. *Interim Vice Provost and Graduate Dean,* Dr. Christopher T. Kello, 209-228-2408, Fax: 209-228-6906, E-mail: ckello@ucmerced.edu.

***School of Engineering*** Students: 244 full-time (83 women), 1 (woman) part-time; includes 56 minority (2 Black or African American, non-Hispanic/Latino; 20 Asian, non-Hispanic/Latino; 30 Hispanic/Latino; 1 Native Hawaiian or other Pacific Islander, non-Hispanic/Latino; 3 Two or more races, non-Hispanic/Latino), 153 international. Average age 28. 330 applicants, 32% accepted, 67 enrolled. *Faculty:* 60 full-time (16 women). Expenses: Contact institution. *Financial support:* In 2019–20, 205 students received support, including 6 fellowships with full tuition reimbursements available (averaging $22,005 per year), 76 research assistantships with full tuition reimbursements available (averaging $21,420 per year), 123 teaching assistantships with full tuition reimbursements available (averaging $21,911 per year); scholarships/grants, traineeships, and health care benefits also available. In 2019, 30 master's, 17 doctorates awarded. *Application deadline:* For fall admission, 1/15 for domestic and international students. *Application fee:* $105 ($125 for international students). Electronic applications accepted. *Application Contact:* Tsu Ya, Director of Admissions and Academic Services, 209-228-4521, Fax: 209-228-6906, E-mail: tya@ucmerced.edu. *Dean,* Dr. Mark Matsumoto, 209-228-4047, Fax: 209-228-4047, E-mail: mmatsumoto@ucmerced.edu.

***School of Natural Sciences*** Students: 255 full-time (104 women), 1 (woman) part-time; includes 83 minority (5 Black or African American, non-Hispanic/Latino; 25 Asian, non-Hispanic/Latino; 44 Hispanic/Latino; 9 Two or more races, non-Hispanic/Latino), 77 international. Average age 28. 292 applicants, 43% accepted, 54 enrolled. *Faculty:* 79 full-time (32 women). Expenses: Contact institution. *Financial support:* In 2019–20, 233 students received support, including 9 fellowships with full tuition reimbursements available (averaging $22,005 per year), 56 research assistantships with full tuition reimbursements available (averaging $21,420 per year), 168 teaching assistantships with full tuition reimbursements available (averaging $21,911 per year); scholarships/grants, traineeships, and health care benefits also available. In 2019, 13 master's, 23 doctorates awarded. *Application deadline:* For fall admission, 1/15 for domestic and international students. *Application fee:* $105 ($125 for international students). Electronic applications accepted. *Application Contact:* Tsu Ya, Director of Graduate Admissions and Academic Services, 209-228-4521, Fax: 209-228-6906, E-mail: tya@ucmerced.edu. *Dean,* Dr. Elizabeth Dumont, 209-228-4487, Fax: 209-228-4060, E-mail: edumont@ucmerced.edu.

***School of Social Sciences, Humanities and Arts*** Students: 194 full-time (128 women), 1 (woman) part-time; includes 81 minority (5 Black or African American, non-Hispanic/Latino; 18 Asian, non-Hispanic/Latino; 54 Hispanic/Latino; 4 Two or more races, non-Hispanic/Latino), 39 international. Average age 31. 218 applicants, 48% accepted, 36 enrolled. *Faculty:* 113 full-time (57 women), 2 part-time/adjunct (0 women). Expenses: Contact institution. *Financial support:* In 2019–20, 183 students received support, including 7 fellowships with full tuition reimbursements available (averaging $22,005 per year), 5 research assistantships with full tuition reimbursements available (averaging $21,420 per year), 171 teaching assistantships with full tuition reimbursements available (averaging $21,911 per year); scholarships/grants, traineeships, and health care benefits also available. In 2019, 12 master's, 23 doctorates awarded. *Application deadline:* For fall admission, 1/15 for domestic and international students. *Application fee:* $105 ($125 for international students). Electronic applications accepted. *Application Contact:* Tsu Ya, Director of Admissions and Academic Services, 209-228-4521, Fax: 209-228-6906, E-mail: tya@ucmerced.edu. *Dean,* Dr. Jeffrey Gilger, 209-228-4343, E-mail: jgilger@ucmerced.edu.

## UNIVERSITY OF CALIFORNIA, RIVERSIDE, Riverside, CA 92521-0102

**General Information** State-supported, coed, university. CGS member. *Graduate housing:* Rooms and/or apartments available on a first-come, first-served basis to single and married students. Housing application deadline: 6/1. *Research affiliation:* Los Alamos National Laboratory (botany and plant sciences, chemistry, earth sciences, physics), Brookhaven National Laboratory (chemistry, physics), U.S. Salinity Laboratory (environmental sciences, biochemistry), J. Paul Getty Museum (art history), Lawrence Livermore National Laboratory (anthropology), Fermi National Accelerator Laboratory (physics).

**GRADUATE UNITS**

**Graduate Division** *Program availability:* Part-time, evening/weekend. Electronic applications accepted.

***The A. Gary Anderson Graduate School of Management*** *Program availability:* Part-time, evening/weekend. Electronic applications accepted.

***Graduate School of Education*** Electronic applications accepted.

***School of Public Policy***

**School of Medicine**

## UNIVERSITY OF CALIFORNIA, SAN DIEGO, La Jolla, CA 92093

**General Information** State-supported, coed, university. CGS member. *Enrollment:* 38,396 graduate, professional, and undergraduate students; 6,294 full-time matriculated graduate/professional students (2,469 women), 745 part-time matriculated graduate/professional students (303 women). *Enrollment by degree level:* 3,563 master's, 3,476 doctoral. *Graduate housing:* Rooms and/or apartments available on a first-come, first-served basis to single and married students. *Student services:* Campus employment opportunities, campus safety program, career counseling, child daycare facilities, exercise/wellness program, free psychological counseling, grant writing training, international student services, low-cost health insurance, multicultural affairs office, services for students with disabilities, teacher training, writing training. *Library facilities:* Geisel Library plus 1 other. *Collection:* Books: 3.5 million (physical), 958,000 (digital/electronic). Study areas open 24 hours, 5–7 days a week; students can reserve study rooms. *Research affiliation:* Sanford Burnham Institute, National Oceanic and Atmospheric Administration (NOAA) Fisheries, Veterans Administration Medical Center, Scripps Research Institute, La Jolla Institute for Allergy and Immunology, Salk Institute for Biological Studies.

**Computer facilities:** A campuswide network can be accessed. Online class registration is available.
Website: http://www.ucsd.edu/

**General Application Contact:** Graduate Admissions Office, 858-534-3554, E-mail: gradadmissions@ucsd.edu.

**GRADUATE UNITS**

**Graduate Division** Students: 6,294 full-time (2,469 women), 745 part-time (303 women). 25,027 applicants, 27% accepted, 2,514 enrolled. Expenses: Contact institution. *Financial support:* Fellowships with tuition reimbursements, research assistantships with tuition reimbursements, teaching assistantships with partial tuition reimbursements, career-related internships or fieldwork, institutionally sponsored loans, scholarships/grants, traineeships, health care benefits, and unspecified assistantships available. Support available to part-time students. Financial award applicants required to submit FAFSA. In 2019, 1,928 master's, 535 doctorates awarded. *Application fee:* $105 ($125 for international students). Electronic applications accepted. *Application Contact:* Graduate Admissions, 858-534-3554, E-mail: gradadmissions@ucsd.edu. *Dean*, Dr. James Antony, 858-534-6655, E-mail: graduatedean@ucsd.edu.

***Division of Biological Sciences*** Students: 411 full-time (239 women), 7 part-time (3 women); includes 184 minority (8 Black or African American, non-Hispanic/Latino; 2 American Indian or Alaska Native, non-Hispanic/Latino; 109 Asian, non-Hispanic/Latino; 18 Hispanic/Latino; 47 Two or more races, non-Hispanic/Latino), 117 international. 569 applicants, 37% accepted, 146 enrolled. Expenses: Contact institution. *Financial support:* Fellowships with full tuition reimbursements, research assistantships with full tuition reimbursements, teaching assistantships with full tuition reimbursements, scholarships/grants, traineeships, and unspecified assistantships available. Financial award applicants required to submit FAFSA. In 2019, 30 doctorates awarded. *Application deadline:* For fall admission, 12/3 for domestic students. *Application fee:* $105 ($125 for international students). Electronic applications accepted. *Application Contact:* Melody Bayzar, Program Coordinator, 858-534-0181, E-mail: biogradprog@ucsd.edu. *Chair*, Andrew Chisholm, 858-534-7783.

***Rady School of Management*** Students: 416 full-time (226 women), 187 part-time (98 women). 2,851 applicants, 30% accepted, 324 enrolled. *Faculty:* 28 full-time (5 women), 5 part-time/adjunct (1 woman). Expenses: Contact institution. *Financial support:* Fellowships, teaching assistantships, and scholarships/grants available. Financial award applicants required to submit FAFSA. In 2019, 311 master's awarded. *Program availability:* Part-time, evening/weekend. *Application deadline:* Applications are processed on a rolling basis. *Application fee:* $200. Electronic applications accepted. *Application Contact:* Matthew Alex, Director of Graduate Recruitment and Admissions, 858-534-2777, E-mail: radygradadmissions@ucsd.edu. *Dean*, Lisa Ordonez, 858-822-0830, E-mail: lordonez@ucsd.edu.

***School of Global Policy and Strategy*** *Program availability:* Part-time. Electronic applications accepted.

**School of Medicine** Students: 530. Expenses: Contact institution. *Application Contact:* 858-534-3880, E-mail: somadmissions@ucsd.edu. *Associate Dean for Admissions*, Dr. Carolyn J. Kelly, MD.

**Skaggs School of Pharmacy and Pharmaceutical Sciences** Students: 252. Expenses: Contact institution. *Application Contact:* Dr. James McKerrow, Dean, 858-822-7801. *Dean*, Dr. James McKerrow, 858-822-7801.

## UNIVERSITY OF CALIFORNIA, SAN FRANCISCO, San Francisco, CA 94143

**General Information** State-supported, coed, graduate-only institution. CGS member. *Graduate housing:* Rooms and/or apartments available to single and married students.

**GRADUATE UNITS**

**Graduate Division** *Program availability:* Part-time.

***School of Nursing***

**School of Dentistry**

**School of Medicine** Electronic applications accepted.

**School of Pharmacy** Electronic applications accepted.

## UNIVERSITY OF CALIFORNIA, SANTA BARBARA, Santa Barbara, CA 93106-2014

**General Information** State-supported, coed, university. CGS member. *Graduate housing:* Rooms and/or apartments guaranteed to single students and available on a first-come, first-served basis to married students. Housing application deadline: 6/1. *Research affiliation:* California NanoSystems Institute, The Institute for Social, Behavioral and Economic Research, National Center for Ecological Analysis and Synthesis, The Institute for Collaborative Biotechnologies, Institute for Polymers and Organic Solids, Mitsubishi Chemical Center for Advanced Materials.

**GRADUATE UNITS**

**Graduate Division** Electronic applications accepted.

***College of Engineering*** Electronic applications accepted.

***College of Letters and Sciences*** Electronic applications accepted.

***Donald Bren School of Environmental Science and Management*** Electronic applications accepted.

***Gevirtz Graduate School of Education*** Electronic applications accepted.

## UNIVERSITY OF CALIFORNIA, SANTA CRUZ, Santa Cruz, CA 95064

**General Information** State-supported, coed, university. CGS member. *Graduate housing:* Rooms and/or apartments available on a first-come, first-served basis to single and married students. Housing application deadline: 5/20. *Research affiliation:* Center for Biomimetic MicroElectronic Systems (science and engineering), Center for Information Technology Research in the Interest of Society (science and engineering), Institute for Regenerative Medicine (science and engineering), Center for Adaptive Optics (science and engineering), Center for Biomolecular Science and Engineering (science and engineering), Institute for Quantitative Biology (science and engineering).

**GRADUATE UNITS**

**Division of Graduate Studies** Electronic applications accepted.

***Division of Humanities*** Electronic applications accepted.

***Division of Physical and Biological Sciences*** Electronic applications accepted.

***Division of Social Sciences*** Electronic applications accepted.

***Division of the Arts*** Electronic applications accepted.

**Jack Baskin School of Engineering** Students: 626 full-time (201 women), 38 part-time (8 women); includes 122 minority (9 Black or African American, non-Hispanic/Latino; 4 American Indian or Alaska Native, non-Hispanic/Latino; 65 Asian, non-Hispanic/Latino; 34 Hispanic/Latino; 10 Native Hawaiian or other Pacific Islander, non-Hispanic/Latino), 366 international. 2,083 applicants, 32% accepted, 223 enrolled. *Faculty:* 107 full-time (22 women), 13 part-time/adjunct (1 woman). Expenses: Contact institution. *Financial support:* Fellowships, research assistantships, teaching assistantships, institutionally sponsored loans, scholarships/grants, traineeships, health care benefits, and tuition waivers (full and partial) available. Financial award applicants required to submit FAFSA. In 2019, 181 master's, 46 doctorates awarded. *Program availability:* Part-time. *Application fee:* $105 ($125 for international students). Electronic applications accepted. *Application Contact:* BSOE Graduate Student Affairs Office, 831-459-3531, E-mail: bsoe-ga@rt.ucsc.edu. *Dean*, Dr. Alexander Wolf, E-mail: alw@ucsc.edu.

## UNIVERSITY OF CENTRAL ARKANSAS, Conway, AR 72035-0001

**General Information** State-supported, coed, university. CGS member. *Graduate housing:* Rooms and/or apartments available on a first-come, first-served basis to single and married students. Housing application deadline: 7/1. *Research affiliation:* 3M Corporation, State Farm Foundation (insurance), Arkansas Game and Fish Commission, Acxiom (math, computers), Arkansas Educational Television Network.

**GRADUATE UNITS**

**Graduate School** *Program availability:* Part-time, evening/weekend, online learning.

***College of Business Administration*** *Program availability:* Part-time, evening/weekend.

***College of Education*** *Program availability:* Part-time, evening/weekend, online learning. Electronic applications accepted.

***College of Fine Arts and Communication*** *Program availability:* Part-time. Electronic applications accepted.

***College of Health and Behavioral Sciences*** *Program availability:* Part-time, evening/weekend, online learning. Electronic applications accepted.

***College of Liberal Arts*** *Program availability:* Part-time. Electronic applications accepted.

***College of Natural Sciences and Math*** *Program availability:* Part-time. Electronic applications accepted.

## UNIVERSITY OF CENTRAL FLORIDA, Orlando, FL 32816

**General Information** State-supported, coed, university. CGS member. *Enrollment:* 69,525 graduate, professional, and undergraduate students; 4,285 full-time matriculated graduate/professional students (2,334 women), 4,977 part-time matriculated graduate/professional students (3,164 women). *Graduate faculty:* 1,736 full-time (740 women), 662 part-time/adjunct (377 women). *Graduate housing:* Room and/or apartments available on a first-come, first-served basis to single students; on-campus housing not available to married students. Housing application deadline: 3/1. *Student services:* Campus employment opportunities, campus safety program, career counseling, child daycare facilities, exercise/wellness program, free psychological counseling, grant writing training, international student services, low-cost health insurance, multicultural affairs office, services for students with disabilities, teacher training, writing training. *Library facilities:* University Libraries plus 3 others. *Collection:* Books: 1.6 million (physical), 221,333 (digital/electronic); Serial titles: 646 (physical), 53,148 (digital/electronic); Databases: 508. Weekly public service hours: 105; students can reserve study rooms.

**Computer facilities:** Computer purchase and lease plans are available. 4,233 computers available on campus for general student use. A campuswide network can be accessed. Online class registration is available.
Website: http://www.ucf.edu/

**General Application Contact:** Associate Director, Graduate Admissions, 407-823-2766, Fax: 407-823-6442, E-mail: gradadmissions@ucf.edu.

**GRADUATE UNITS**

**College of Arts and Humanities** Students: 235 full-time (132 women), 194 part-time (112 women); includes 121 minority (24 Black or African American, non-Hispanic/Latino; 1 American Indian or Alaska Native, non-Hispanic/Latino; 7 Asian, non-Hispanic/Latino; 81 Hispanic/Latino; 8 Two or more races, non-Hispanic/Latino), 13 international. Average age 33. 333 applicants, 71% accepted, 151 enrolled. *Faculty:* 297 full-time (157 women), 89 part-time/adjunct (40 women). Expenses: Contact institution. *Financial support:* In 2019–20, 132 students received support, including 37 fellowships with partial tuition reimbursements available (averaging $7,584 per year), 26 research assistantships with partial tuition reimbursements available (averaging $4,051 per year), 100 teaching assistantships with partial tuition reimbursements available (averaging $5,273 per year); career-related internships or fieldwork, Federal Work-Study, institutionally sponsored loans, scholarships/grants, health care benefits, tuition waivers (partial), and unspecified assistantships also available. Financial award application deadline: 3/1; financial award applicants required to submit FAFSA. In 2019, 77 master's, 9 doctorates, 20 other advanced degrees awarded. *Program availability:* Part-time, evening/weekend. *Application fee:* $30. Electronic applications accepted. *Application Contact:* Associate Director, Graduate Admissions, 407-823-2766, Fax: 407-823-6442, E-mail: gradadmissions@ucf.edu. *Dean*, Jeffrey Moore, 407-823-2573, E-mail: jeffrey.moore@ucf.edu.

***School of Performing Arts*** Students: 65 full-time (32 women), 20 part-time (5 women); includes 22 minority (6 Black or African American, non-Hispanic/Latino; 1 Asian, non-Hispanic/Latino; 12 Hispanic/Latino; 3 Two or more races, non-Hispanic/Latino), 1 international. Average age 31. 76 applicants, 64% accepted, 37 enrolled. Expenses: Contact institution. *Financial support:* In 2019–20, 35 students received support, including 6 fellowships with partial tuition reimbursements available (averaging $8,333 per year), 8 research assistantships with partial tuition reimbursements available (averaging $2,808 per year), 30 teaching assistantships with partial tuition reimbursements available (averaging $4,695 per year); career-related internships or fieldwork, Federal Work-Study, institutionally sponsored loans, health care benefits, tuition waivers (partial), and unspecified assistantships also available. Financial award application deadline: 3/1; financial award applicants required to submit FAFSA. In 2019, 17 master's awarded. *Program availability:* Part-time. *Application deadline:* For fall admission, 7/15 for domestic students; for spring admission, 12/1 for domestic students. *Application fee:* $30. Electronic applications accepted. *Application Contact:* Associate Director, Graduate Admissions, 407-823-2766, Fax: 407-823-6442, E-mail: gradadmissions@ucf.edu. *Director*, Dr. Michael Wainstein, 407-823-2519, Fax: 407-823-3378, E-mail: michael.wainstein@ucf.edu.

***School of Visual Arts and Design*** Students: 41 full-time (17 women), 5 part-time (2 women); includes 23 minority (6 Black or African American, non-Hispanic/Latino; 1 Asian, non-Hispanic/Latino; 15 Hispanic/Latino; 1 Two or more races, non-Hispanic/Latino), 2 international. Average age 30. 41 applicants, 56% accepted, 18 enrolled. Expenses: Contact institution. *Financial support:* In 2019–20, 22 students received support, including 10 fellowships with partial tuition reimbursements available (averaging $7,400 per year), 15 teaching assistantships with partial tuition reimbursements available (averaging $5,226 per year); scholarships/grants, health care benefits, and unspecified assistantships also available. Financial award application deadline: 3/1; financial award applicants required to submit FAFSA. In 2019, 5 master's awarded. *Program availability:* Part-time. *Application deadline:* For fall admission, 7/1 for domestic students. *Application fee:* $30. Electronic applications accepted. *Application Contact:* Associate Director, Graduate Admissions, 407-823-2766, Fax: 407-823-6442, E-mail: gradadmissions@ucf.edu. *Director*, Dr. Rudy McDaniel, 407-823-3145, E-mail: rudy@ucf.edu.

**College of Business Administration** Students: 234 full-time (114 women), 681 part-time (342 women); includes 411 minority (99 Black or African American, non-Hispanic/Latino; 71 Asian, non-Hispanic/Latino; 218 Hispanic/Latino; 23 Two or more races, non-Hispanic/Latino), 44 international. Average age 30. 673 applicants, 59% accepted, 324 enrolled. *Faculty:* 134 full-time (35 women), 24 part-time/adjunct (7 women). Expenses: Contact institution. *Financial support:* In 2019–20, 85 students received support, including 8 fellowships with partial tuition reimbursements available (averaging $4,275 per year), 32 research assistantships with partial tuition reimbursements available (averaging $5,175 per year), 57 teaching assistantships with partial tuition reimbursements available (averaging $7,445 per year); career-related internships or fieldwork, Federal Work-Study, institutionally sponsored loans, health care benefits, and tuition waivers (partial) also available. Financial award application deadline: 3/1; financial award applicants required to submit FAFSA. In 2019, 396 master's, 4 doctorates, 5 other advanced degrees awarded. *Program availability:* Part-time, evening/weekend. *Application fee:* $30. Electronic applications accepted. *Application Contact:* Associate Director, Graduate Admissions, 407-823-2766, Fax: 407-823-6442, E-mail: gradadmissions@ucf.edu. *Dean*, Dr. Paul Jarley, 407-823-5133, E-mail: pjarley@bus.ucf.edu.

***Dr. P. Phillips School of Real Estate*** 9 applicants. Expenses: Contact institution. *Financial support:* Application deadline: 3/1; applicants required to submit FAFSA. In 2019, 10 master's awarded. *Program availability:* Part-time. *Application deadline:* For fall admission, 7/1 for domestic students. *Application fee:* $30. Electronic applications accepted. *Application Contact:* Associate Director, Graduate Admissions, 407-823-2766, Fax: 407-823-6442, E-mail: gradadmissions@ucf.edu. *Chair and Director*, Dr. Ajai Singh, 407-823-5756, Fax: 407-823-6676, E-mail: ajai.singh@ucf.edu.

***Kenneth G. Dixon School of Accounting*** Students: 67 full-time (34 women), 42 part-time (23 women); includes 42 minority (3 Black or African American, non-Hispanic/Latino; 19 Asian, non-Hispanic/Latino; 17 Hispanic/Latino; 3 Two or more races, non-Hispanic/Latino), 4 international. Average age 26. 75 applicants, 51% accepted, 31 enrolled. Expenses: Contact institution. *Financial support:* In 2019–20, 18 students received support, including 18 teaching assistantships with partial tuition reimbursements available (averaging $5,509 per year); career-related internships or fieldwork, Federal Work-Study, institutionally sponsored loans, health care benefits, tuition waivers (partial), and unspecified assistantships also available. Financial award application deadline: 3/1; financial award applicants required to submit FAFSA. In 2019, 77 master's awarded. *Program availability:* Part-time, evening/weekend. *Application deadline:* For fall admission, 7/15 for domestic students; for spring admission, 12/1 for domestic students; for summer admission, 4/15 for domestic students. *Application fee:* $30. Electronic applications accepted. *Application Contact:* Associate Director, Graduate Admissions, 407-823-2766, Fax: 407-823-6442, E-mail: gradadmissions@ucf.edu. *Director*, Dr. Gregory Trompeter, 407-823-2876, Fax: 407-823-3881, E-mail: trompete@ucf.edu.

**College of Community Innovation and Education** Students: 1,071 full-time (782 women), 2,026 part-time (1,540 women); includes 1,377 minority (537 Black or African American, non-Hispanic/Latino; 5 American Indian or Alaska Native, non-Hispanic/Latino; 124 Asian, non-Hispanic/Latino; 609 Hispanic/Latino; 3 Native Hawaiian or other Pacific Islander, non-Hispanic/Latino; 99 Two or more races, non-Hispanic/Latino), 66 international. Average age 33. 2,325 applicants, 72% accepted, 1,090 enrolled. *Faculty:* 229 full-time (135 women), 203 part-time/adjunct (137 women). Expenses: Contact institution. *Financial support:* In 2019–20, 197 students received support, including 56 fellowships with partial tuition reimbursements available (averaging $5,343 per year), 93 research assistantships with partial tuition reimbursements available (averaging $6,305 per year), 121 teaching assistantships with partial tuition reimbursements available (averaging $6,453 per year); career-related internships or fieldwork, Federal Work-Study, institutionally sponsored loans, health care benefits, tuition waivers (partial), and unspecified assistantships also available. Financial award application deadline: 3/1; financial award applicants required to submit FAFSA. In 2019, 744 master's, 59 doctorates, 233 other advanced degrees awarded. *Program availability:* Part-time, evening/weekend. *Application fee:* $30. Electronic applications accepted. *Application Contact:* Associate Director, Graduate Admissions, 407-823-2766, Fax: 407-823-6442, E-mail: gradadmissions@ucf.edu. *Dean*, Dr. Pamela S. Carroll, 407-823-1463, E-mail: pamela.carroll@ucf.edu.

***School of Public Administration*** Students: 149 full-time (95 women), 497 part-time (347 women); includes 277 minority (128 Black or African American, non-Hispanic/Latino; 1 American Indian or Alaska Native, non-Hispanic/Latino; 13 Asian, non-Hispanic/Latino; 118 Hispanic/Latino; 1 Native Hawaiian or other Pacific Islander, non-Hispanic/Latino; 16 Two or more races, non-Hispanic/Latino), 9 international. Average age 33. 430 applicants, 79% accepted, 226 enrolled. Expenses: Contact institution. *Financial support:* In 2019–20, 6 students received support, including 1 fellowship with partial tuition reimbursement available (averaging $5,000 per year), 4 research assistantships with partial tuition reimbursements available (averaging $6,049 per year), 1 teaching assistantship with partial tuition reimbursement available (averaging $5,478 per year); career-related internships or fieldwork, Federal Work-Study, institutionally sponsored loans, health care benefits, tuition waivers (partial), and unspecified assistantships also available. Financial award application deadline: 3/1; financial award applicants required to submit FAFSA. In 2019, 106 master's, 26 other advanced degrees awarded. *Program availability:* Part-time, evening/weekend. *Application deadline:* For fall admission, 6/15 for domestic students; for spring admission, 11/1 for domestic students. *Application fee:* $30. Electronic applications accepted. *Application Contact:* Associate Director, Graduate Admissions, 407-823-2766, Fax: 407-823-6442, E-mail: gradadmissions@ucf.edu. *Director*, Dr. Naim Kapucu, 407-823-6096, Fax: 407-823-5651, E-mail: kapucu@ucf.edu.

***School of Teacher Education*** Students: 184 full-time (139 women), 411 part-time (363 women); includes 225 minority (78 Black or African American, non-Hispanic/Latino; 1 American Indian or Alaska Native, non-Hispanic/Latino; 16 Asian, non-Hispanic/Latino; 112 Hispanic/Latino; 18 Two or more races, non-Hispanic/Latino), 28 international. Average age 35. 448 applicants, 69% accepted, 206 enrolled. Expenses: Contact institution. *Financial support:* In 2019–20, 84 students received support, including 31 fellowships with partial tuition reimbursements available (averaging $6,054 per year), 30 research assistantships with partial tuition reimbursements available (averaging $7,002 per year), 58 teaching assistantships with partial tuition reimbursements available (averaging $7,452 per year); career-related internships or fieldwork, Federal Work-Study, institutionally sponsored loans, health care benefits, tuition waivers (partial), and unspecified assistantships also available. Financial award application deadline: 3/1; financial award applicants required to submit FAFSA. In 2019, 138 master's, 113 other advanced degrees awarded. *Program availability:* Part-time, evening/weekend. *Application deadline:* For fall admission, 7/15 for domestic students; for spring admission, 12/15 for domestic students. *Application fee:* $30. Electronic applications accepted. *Application Contact:* Associate Director, Graduate Admissions, 407-823-2766, Fax: 407-823-6442, E-mail: gradadmissions@ucf.edu. *Director*, Dr. Michael Hynes, 407-823-1768, E-mail: michael.hynes@ucf.edu.

**College of Engineering and Computer Science** Students: 999 full-time (232 women), 770 part-time (193 women); includes 455 minority (82 Black or African American, non-Hispanic/Latino; 2 American Indian or Alaska Native, non-Hispanic/Latino; 106 Asian, non-Hispanic/Latino; 240 Hispanic/Latino; 25 Two or more races, non-Hispanic/Latino), 682 international. Average age 30. 1,826 applicants, 67% accepted, 555 enrolled. *Faculty:* 208 full-time (29 women), 50 part-time/adjunct (3 women). Expenses: Contact institution. *Financial support:* In 2019–20, 602 students received support, including 170 fellowships with partial tuition reimbursements available (averaging $11,677 per year), 436 research assistantships with partial tuition reimbursements available (averaging $8,253 per year), 176 teaching assistantships with partial tuition reimbursements available (averaging $8,249 per year); career-related internships or fieldwork, Federal Work-Study, tuition waivers (partial), and unspecified assistantships also available. Financial award application deadline: 3/1; financial award applicants required to submit FAFSA. In 2019, 390 master's, 108 doctorates, 28 other advanced degrees awarded. *Program availability:* Part-time, evening/weekend. *Application deadline:* For fall admission, 7/15 for domestic students; for spring admission, 12/1 for domestic students. *Application fee:* $30. Electronic applications accepted. *Application Contact:* Associate Director, Graduate Admissions, 407-823-2766, Fax: 407-823-6442, E-mail: gradadmissions@ucf.edu. *Dean*, Dr. Michael Georgiopoulos, 407-823-2156, E-mail: michaelg@ucf.edu.

**College of Graduate Studies** Students: 74 full-time (36 women), 78 part-time (41 women); includes 56 minority (16 Black or African American, non-Hispanic/Latino; 10 Asian, non-Hispanic/Latino; 24 Hispanic/Latino; 6 Two or more races, non-Hispanic/Latino), 10 international. Average age 31. 121 applicants, 70% accepted, 67 enrolled. *Faculty:* 5 full-time (2 women), 1 (woman) part-time/adjunct. Expenses: Contact institution. *Financial support:* In 2019–20, 15 students received support, including 5 fellowships with partial tuition reimbursements available (averaging $10,000 per year), 12 research assistantships with partial tuition reimbursements available (averaging $6,910 per year), 3 teaching assistantships with partial tuition reimbursements available (averaging $10,251 per year); health care benefits also available. Financial award application deadline: 3/1; financial award applicants required to submit FAFSA. In 2019, 22 master's, 11 other advanced degrees awarded. *Application deadline:* For fall admission, 7/15 for domestic students; for spring admission, 12/1 for domestic students. *Application fee:* $30. Electronic applications accepted. *Application Contact:* Associate Director, Graduate Admissions, 407-823-2766, Fax: 407-823-6442, E-mail: gradadmissions@ucf.edu. *Vice President for Research/Dean, College of Graduate Studies*, Dr. Elizabeth Klonoff, 407-823-6432, Fax: 407-823-6442, E-mail: elizabeth.klonoff@ucf.edu.

***Nanoscience Technology Center*** Students: 27 full-time (11 women), 6 part-time (0 women); includes 20 minority (5 Black or African American, non-Hispanic/Latino; 5 Asian, non-Hispanic/Latino; 8 Hispanic/Latino; 2 Two or more races, non-Hispanic/Latino), 2 international. Average age 26. 26 applicants, 85% accepted, 15 enrolled. Expenses: Contact institution. *Financial support:* In 2019–20, 3 students received support, including 3 research assistantships (averaging $4,542 per year). *Application Contact:* Associate Director, Graduate Admissions, 407-823-2766, Fax: 407-823-6442, E-mail: gradadmissions@ucf.edu. *Vice President for Research/Dean, College of Graduate Studies*, Dr. Elizabeth Klonoff, 407-823-6432, Fax: 407-823-6442, E-mail: elizabeth.klonoff@ucf.edu.

**College of Health Professions and Sciences** Students: 505 full-time (411 women), 384 part-time (335 women); includes 353 minority (103 Black or African American, non-Hispanic/Latino; 34 Asian, non-Hispanic/Latino; 191 Hispanic/Latino; 25 Two or more races, non-Hispanic/Latino), 5 international. Average age 29. 824 applicants, 48% accepted, 182 enrolled. *Faculty:* 106 full-time (69 women), 68 part-time/adjunct (51 women). Expenses: Contact institution. *Financial support:* In 2019–20, 34 students received support, including 22 fellowships with partial tuition reimbursements available (averaging $7,236 per year), 7 research assistantships with partial tuition reimbursements available (averaging $4,755 per year), 7 teaching assistantships with partial tuition reimbursements available (averaging $5,641 per year); career-related internships or fieldwork, Federal Work-Study, institutionally sponsored loans, traineeships, health care benefits, tuition waivers (partial), and unspecified assistantships also available. Financial award application deadline: 3/1; financial award applicants required to submit FAFSA. In 2019, 318 master's, 37 doctorates, 22 other advanced degrees awarded. *Program availability:* Part-time, evening/weekend. *Application fee:* $30. Electronic applications accepted. *Application Contact:* Associate Director, Graduate Admissions, 407-823-2766, Fax: 407-823-6442, E-mail: gradadmissions@ucf.edu. *Interim Dean*, Dr. Jose Fernandez, 407-823-0171, E-mail: jose.fernandez@ucf.edu.

***School of Communication Sciences and Disorders*** Students: 189 full-time (183 women), 6 part-time (5 women); includes 63 minority (10 Black or African American, non-Hispanic/Latino; 7 Asian, non-Hispanic/Latino; 43 Hispanic/Latino; 3 Two or more races, non-Hispanic/Latino), 2 international. Average age 25. 297 applicants, 46% accepted, 27 enrolled. Expenses: Contact institution. *Financial support:* In 2019–20, 14 students received support, including 3 fellowships with partial tuition reimbursements available (averaging $5,200 per year), 6 research assistantships with partial tuition reimbursements available (averaging $5,084 per year), 6 teaching assistantships with partial tuition reimbursements available (averaging $5,668 per year); career-related internships or fieldwork, Federal Work-Study, institutionally sponsored loans, and unspecified assistantships also available. Financial award application deadline: 3/1; financial award applicants required to submit FAFSA. In 2019, 87 master's awarded. *Program availability:* Part-time, evening/weekend. *Application deadline:* For fall admission, 2/1 for domestic students; for spring admission, 10/1 for domestic students. *Application fee:* $30. Electronic applications accepted. *Application Contact:* Associate Director, Graduate Admissions, 407-823-2766, Fax: 407-823-6442, E-mail: gradadmissions@ucf.edu. *Program Coordinator*, Dr. Linda Rosa-Lugo, 407-823-4798, E-mail: csdgraduate@ucf.edu.

***School of Kinesiology and Physical Therapy*** Students: 151 full-time (88 women), 26 part-time (13 women); includes 66 minority (7 Black or African American, non-Hispanic/Latino; 13 Asian, non-Hispanic/Latino; 37 Hispanic/Latino; 9 Two or more races, non-Hispanic/Latino), 3 international. Average age 25. 76 applicants, 72% accepted, 18 enrolled. Expenses: Contact institution. *Financial support:* In 2019–20, 8 students received support, including 7 fellowships (averaging $3,371 per year), 1 teaching assistantship (averaging $5,476 per year). *Application Contact:* Associate Director, Graduate Admissions, 407-823-2766, Fax: 407-823-6442, E-mail: gradadmissions@ucf.edu. *Interim Dean*, Dr. Jose Fernandez, 407-823-0171, E-mail: jose.fernandez@ucf.edu.

***School of Social Work*** Students: 165 full-time (140 women), 352 part-time (317 women); includes 224 minority (86 Black or African American, non-Hispanic/Latino; 14 Asian, non-Hispanic/Latino; 111 Hispanic/Latino; 13 Two or more races, non-Hispanic/Latino). Average age 31. 451 applicants, 46% accepted, 137 enrolled. Expenses: Contact institution. *Financial support:* In 2019–20, 12 students received support, including 12 fellowships (averaging $10,000 per year), 1 research assistantship (averaging $2,780 per year); career-related internships or fieldwork, institutionally sponsored loans, and unspecified assistantships also available. Financial award application deadline: 3/1; financial award applicants required to submit FAFSA. In 2019, 178 master's, 19 other advanced degrees awarded. *Program availability:* Part-time, evening/weekend. *Application deadline:* For fall admission, 4/1 for domestic students. *Application fee:* $30. Electronic applications accepted. *Application Contact:* Associate Director, Graduate Admissions, 407-823-2766, Fax: 407-823-6442, E-mail: gradadmissions@ucf.edu. *Director*, Dr. Bonnie Yegidis, 407-823-2114, E-mail: bonnie.yegidis@ucf.edu.

**College of Medicine** Students: 130 full-time (80 women), 14 part-time (9 women); includes 57 minority (14 Black or African American, non-Hispanic/Latino; 11 Asian, non-Hispanic/Latino; 30 Hispanic/Latino; 2 Two or more races, non-Hispanic/Latino), 32 international. Average age 26. 293 applicants, 35% accepted, 61 enrolled. *Faculty:* 143 full-time (66 women), 22 part-time/adjunct (10 women). Expenses: Contact institution. *Financial support:* In 2019–20, 85 students received support, including 13 fellowships (averaging $17,508 per year), 84 research assistantships (averaging $5,909 per year), 43 teaching assistantships (averaging $6,320 per year). In 2019, 42 master's, 5 doctorates awarded. *Application Contact:* Associate Director, Graduate Admissions, 407-823-2766, Fax: 407-823-6442, E-mail: gradadmissions@ucf.edu. *Vice President for Medical Affairs/Dean*, Dr. Deborah C. German, 407-266-1000, E-mail: deb@ucf.edu.

**College of Nursing** Students: 88 full-time (82 women), 382 part-time (336 women); includes 153 minority (56 Black or African American, non-Hispanic/Latino; 2 American Indian or Alaska Native, non-Hispanic/Latino; 27 Asian, non-Hispanic/Latino; 60 Hispanic/Latino; 8 Two or more races, non-Hispanic/Latino). Average age 38. 319 applicants, 61% accepted, 139 enrolled. *Faculty:* 60 full-time (50 women), 95 part-time/adjunct (85 women). Expenses: Contact institution. *Financial support:* In 2019–20, 30 students received support, including 25 fellowships with partial tuition reimbursements available (averaging $10,218 per year), 3 research assistantships with partial tuition reimbursements available (averaging $4,815 per year), 3 teaching assistantships (averaging $6,050 per year); career-related internships or fieldwork, Federal Work-Study, institutionally sponsored loans, traineeships, and unspecified assistantships also available. Financial award application deadline: 3/1; financial award applicants required to submit FAFSA. In 2019, 97 master's, 14 doctorates, 16 other advanced degrees awarded. *Program availability:* Part-time, evening/weekend. *Application deadline:* For fall admission, 3/15 for domestic students; for spring admission, 10/15 for domestic students. *Application fee:* $30. Electronic applications accepted. *Application Contact:* Associate Director, Graduate Admissions, 407-823-2766, Fax: 407-823-6442, E-mail: gradadmissions@ucf.edu. *Dean*, Dr. Mary Lou Sole, 407-823-5496, Fax: 407-823-5675, E-mail: mary.sole@ucf.edu.

**College of Optics and Photonics** Students: 116 full-time (30 women), 18 part-time (2 women); includes 9 minority (2 Asian, non-Hispanic/Latino; 7 Hispanic/Latino), 83 international. Average age 28. 137 applicants, 37% accepted, 24 enrolled. *Faculty:* 39 full-time, 7 part-time/adjunct (2 women). Expenses: Contact institution. *Financial support:* In 2019–20, 104 students received support, including 24 fellowships with partial tuition reimbursements available (averaging $20,192 per year), 84 research assistantships with partial tuition reimbursements available (averaging $11,089 per year), 8 teaching assistantships with partial tuition reimbursements available (averaging $8,700 per year); career-related internships or fieldwork, Federal Work-Study, institutionally sponsored loans, health care benefits, tuition waivers (partial), and unspecified assistantships also available. Financial award application deadline: 3/1; financial award applicants required to submit FAFSA. In 2019, 25 master's, 6 doctorates awarded. *Program availability:* Part-time, evening/weekend. *Application deadline:* For fall admission, 7/15 for domestic students; for spring admission, 12/1 for domestic students. *Application fee:* $30. Electronic applications accepted. *Application Contact:* Associate Director, Graduate Admissions, 407-823-2766, Fax: 407-823-6442, E-mail: gradadmissions@ucf.edu. *Dean and Director*, Dr. Bahaa E. Saleh, 407-823-6817, E-mail: besaleh@creol.ucf.edu.

**College of Sciences** Students: 624 full-time (311 women), 117 part-time (62 women); includes 183 minority (33 Black or African American, non-Hispanic/Latino; 1 American Indian or Alaska Native, non-Hispanic/Latino; 37 Asian, non-Hispanic/Latino; 93 Hispanic/Latino; 19 Two or more races, non-Hispanic/Latino), 163 international. Average age 29. 1,255 applicants, 33% accepted, 212 enrolled. *Faculty:* 324 full-time (116 women), 44 part-time/adjunct (10 women). Expenses: Contact institution. *Financial support:* In 2019–20, 505 students received support, including 104 fellowships with partial tuition reimbursements available (averaging $7,410 per year), 166 research assistantships with partial tuition reimbursements available (averaging $8,104 per year), 366 teaching assistantships with partial tuition reimbursements available (averaging $8,758 per year); health care benefits also available. Financial award application deadline: 3/1; financial award applicants required to submit FAFSA. In 2019, 146 master's, 56 doctorates, 26 other advanced degrees awarded. *Application fee:* $30. Electronic applications accepted. *Application Contact:* Associate Director, Graduate Admissions, 407-823-2766, Fax: 407-823-6442, E-mail: gradadmissions@ucf.edu. *Dean*, Dr. Michael Johnson, 407-823-1911, E-mail: michael.johnson@ucf.edu.

***School of Policy, Security, and International Affairs*** Students: 40 full-time (14 women), 18 part-time (6 women); includes 10 minority (1 Black or African American, non-Hispanic/Latino; 1 Asian, non-Hispanic/Latino; 8 Hispanic/Latino), 18 international. Average age 30. 40 applicants, 75% accepted, 15 enrolled. Expenses: Contact institution. *Financial support:* In 2019–20, 24 students received support, including 4 fellowships (averaging $2,150 per year), 3 research assistantships (averaging $7,047 per year), 22 teaching assistantships (averaging $7,602 per year). *Application Contact:* Associate Director, Graduate Admissions, 407-823-2766, Fax: 407-823-6442, E-mail: gradadmissions@ucf.edu. *Dean*, Dr. Michael Johnson, 407-823-1911, E-mail: michael.johnson@ucf.edu.

**Nicholson School of Communication and Media** Students: 122 full-time (68 women), 96 part-time (42 women); includes 90 minority (19 Black or African American, non-Hispanic/Latino; 16 Asian, non-Hispanic/Latino; 45 Hispanic/Latino; 10 Two or more races, non-Hispanic/Latino), 21 international. Average age 26. 278 applicants, 67% accepted, 117 enrolled. *Faculty:* 96 full-time (38 women), 22 part-time/adjunct (12 women). Expenses: Contact institution. *Financial support:* In 2019–20, 25 students received support, including 6 fellowships (averaging $7,200 per year), 5 research assistantships (averaging $3,818 per year), 24 teaching assistantships (averaging $5,776 per year). *Application Contact:* Associate Director, Graduate Admissions, 407-823-2766, Fax: 407-823-6442, E-mail: gradadmissions@ucf.edu.

**Rosen College of Hospitality Management** Students: 87 full-time (56 women), 217 part-time (150 women); includes 94 minority (27 Black or African American, non-Hispanic/Latino; 7 Asian, non-Hispanic/Latino; 48 Hispanic/Latino; 12 Two or more races, non-Hispanic/Latino), 36 international. Average age 30. 267 applicants, 69% accepted, 148 enrolled. *Faculty:* 69 full-time (27 women), 28 part-time/adjunct (13 women). Expenses: Contact institution. *Financial support:* In 2019–20, 28 students received support, including 17 fellowships with partial tuition reimbursements available (averaging $8,751 per year), 2 research assistantships with partial tuition reimbursements available (averaging $7,486 per year), 18 teaching assistantships with partial tuition reimbursements available (averaging $8,468 per year); health care benefits also available. Financial award application deadline: 3/1; financial award applicants required to submit FAFSA. In 2019, 89 master's, 2 doctorates, 49 other advanced degrees awarded. *Program availability:* Part-time. *Application deadline:* For fall admission, 7/15 for domestic students; for spring admission, 12/1 for domestic students. *Application fee:* $30. Electronic applications accepted. *Application Contact:* Associate Director, Graduate Admissions, 407-823-2766, Fax: 407-823-6442, E-mail: gradadmissions@ucf.edu. *Dean*, Dr. Abraham C. Pizam, 407-903-8010, E-mail: abraham.pizam@ucf.edu.

## UNIVERSITY OF CENTRAL MISSOURI, Warrensburg, MO 64093

**General Information** State-supported, coed, comprehensive institution. CGS member. *Enrollment:* 11,229 graduate, professional, and undergraduate students; 787 full-time matriculated graduate/professional students (448 women), 1,459 part-time matriculated graduate/professional students (997 women). *Enrollment by degree level:* 1,977 master's, 25 doctoral, 244 other advanced degrees. *Graduate faculty:* 236 full-time (113 women), 97 part-time/adjunct (61 women). *International tuition:* $15,048 full-time. *Tuition, area resident:* Full-time $7524; part-time $313.50 per credit hour. Tuition, state resident: full-time $7524; part-time $313.50 per credit hour. Tuition, nonresident: full-time $15,048; part-time $627 per credit hour. *Required fees:* $915; $30.50 per credit hour. *Graduate housing:* Rooms and/or apartments available on a first-come, first-served basis to single and married students. Typical cost: $5612 per year ($8962 including board) for single students. Room and board charges vary according to board plan, campus/location and housing facility selected. Housing application deadline: 5/1. *Student services:* Campus employment opportunities, campus safety program, career counseling, child daycare facilities, exercise/wellness program, free psychological counseling, grant writing training, international student services, low-cost health insurance, multicultural affairs office, services for students with disabilities, teacher training, writing training. *Library facilities:* James C. Kirkpatrick Library plus 1 other. *Collection:* Books: 499,982 (physical), 268,431 (digital/electronic); Serial titles: 1,579 (physical), 89,008 (digital/electronic); Databases: 97. Weekly public service hours: 96; students can reserve study rooms.

**Computer facilities:** 6,395 computers available on campus for general student use. A campuswide network can be accessed. Online class registration is available. Website: http://www.ucmo.edu/

**General Application Contact:** Shellie Hewitt, Director, Graduate Student Services, 660-543-4621, E-mail: giss@ucmo.edu.

### GRADUATE UNITS

**The Graduate School** Students: 787 full-time (448 women), 1,459 part-time (997 women); includes 213 minority (72 Black or African American, non-Hispanic/Latino; 5 American Indian or Alaska Native, non-Hispanic/Latino; 27 Asian, non-Hispanic/Latino; 59 Hispanic/Latino; 50 Two or more races, non-Hispanic/Latino), 574 international. Average age 30. 1,477 applicants, 68% accepted, 664 enrolled. *Faculty:* 236 full-time (113 women), 97 part-time/adjunct (61 women). Expenses: Contact institution. *Financial support:* In 2019–20, 89 students received support. Research assistantships, teaching assistantships, career-related internships or fieldwork, Federal Work-Study, scholarships/grants, unspecified assistantships, and administrative and laboratory assistantships available. Support available to part-time students. Financial award application deadline: 4/1; financial award applicants required to submit FAFSA. In 2019, 831 master's, 93 other advanced degrees awarded. *Program availability:* Part-time, 100% online, blended/hybrid learning. *Application deadline:* For fall admission, 6/1 priority date for domestic and international students; for spring admission, 10/15 priority date for domestic and international students; for summer admission, 4/1 priority date for domestic and international students. Applications are processed on a rolling basis. *Application fee:* $30 ($75 for international students). Electronic applications accepted. *Application Contact:* Shellie Hewitt, Director of Graduate and International Student Services, 660-543-4621, Fax: 660-543-4778, E-mail: hewitt@ucmo.edu. *Director of Graduate and International Student Services*, Shellie Hewitt, 660-543-4621, Fax: 660-543-4778, E-mail: hewitt@ucmo.edu.

## UNIVERSITY OF CENTRAL OKLAHOMA, Edmond, OK 73034-5209

**General Information** State-supported, coed, comprehensive institution. CGS member. *Graduate housing:* Rooms and/or apartments available on a first-come, first-served basis to single and married students. *Research affiliation:* National Science Foundation, U.S. Department of Education (DOE), U.S. Department of Veteran Affairs, Oklahoma Department of Human Services, Oklahoma Idea Network of Biomedical Research Excellence, Oklahoma Small Business Administration.

### GRADUATE UNITS

**The Jackson College of Graduate Studies** *Program availability:* Part-time, evening/weekend. Electronic applications accepted.

***College of Business*** *Program availability:* Part-time. Electronic applications accepted.

***College of Education and Professional Studies*** *Program availability:* Part-time. Electronic applications accepted.
***College of Fine Arts and Design*** *Program availability:* Part-time, evening/weekend. Electronic applications accepted.
***College of Liberal Arts*** *Program availability:* Part-time. Electronic applications accepted.
***College of Mathematics and Science*** *Program availability:* Part-time. Electronic applications accepted.
***Forensic Science Institute*** Electronic applications accepted.

## UNIVERSITY OF CHARLESTON, Charleston, WV 25304-1099

**General Information** Independent, coed, comprehensive institution. *Graduate housing:* Rooms and/or apartments available on a first-come, first-served basis to single and married students. *Research affiliation:* Walmart (pharmacy).

**GRADUATE UNITS**

**Doctor of Executive Leadership Program** Electronic applications accepted.
**Master of Business Administration Program** *Program availability:* Part-time, evening/weekend. Electronic applications accepted.
**Master of Forensic Accounting Program** *Program availability:* Part-time, blended/hybrid learning. Electronic applications accepted.
**Master of Science in Strategic Leadership Program** Electronic applications accepted.
**Physician Assistant Program** Electronic applications accepted.
**School of Pharmacy** Electronic applications accepted.

## UNIVERSITY OF CHICAGO, Chicago, IL 60637-1513

**General Information** Independent, coed, university. CGS member. *Graduate housing:* Rooms and/or apartments available on a first-come, first-served basis to single and married students. *Research affiliation:* National Opinion Research Center (social science), Argonne National Laboratory (energy, materials), Marine Biological Laboratory (molecular biology), Fermilab (high-energy physics).

**GRADUATE UNITS**

**Booth School of Business** *Program availability:* Part-time, evening/weekend. Electronic applications accepted.
**Divinity School** Electronic applications accepted.
**Division of the Biological Sciences** Electronic applications accepted.
**Division of the Humanities** Electronic applications accepted.
**Division of the Physical Sciences** Electronic applications accepted.
**Division of the Social Sciences** Electronic applications accepted.
***Center for Latin American Studies*** Electronic applications accepted.
***Center for Middle Eastern Studies*** Electronic applications accepted.
**Graham School of Continuing Liberal and Professional Studies** *Program availability:* Part-time, evening/weekend. Electronic applications accepted.
**Harris School of Public Policy** *Program availability:* Part-time, evening/weekend. Electronic applications accepted.
**Institute for Molecular Engineering** Electronic applications accepted.
**The Law School** Electronic applications accepted.
**Pritzker School of Medicine** Electronic applications accepted.
**School of Social Service Administration** *Program availability:* Part-time, evening/weekend. Electronic applications accepted.

## UNIVERSITY OF CINCINNATI, Cincinnati, OH 45221

**General Information** State-supported, coed, university. CGS member. *Graduate housing:* Rooms and/or apartments available on a first-come, first-served basis to single and married students. *Research affiliation:* Cincinnati Children's Hospital Medical Center, Cincinnati Department of Veterans Affairs Medical Center, Shriners Hospitals for Children-Cincinnati.

**GRADUATE UNITS**

**Carl H. Lindner College of Business** Students: 476 full-time (204 women), 680 part-time (287 women); includes 151 minority (55 Black or African American, non-Hispanic/Latino; 1 American Indian or Alaska Native, non-Hispanic/Latino; 52 Asian, non-Hispanic/Latino; 27 Hispanic/Latino; 3 Native Hawaiian or other Pacific Islander, non-Hispanic/Latino; 13 Two or more races, non-Hispanic/Latino), 395 international. Average age 30. 1,871 applicants, 49% accepted, 456 enrolled. *Faculty:* 117 full-time (37 women), 28 part-time/adjunct (4 women). Expenses: Contact institution. *Financial support:* In 2019–20, 395 students received support, including 25 research assistantships with full and partial tuition reimbursements available (averaging $23,250 per year); teaching assistantships, scholarships/grants, tuition waivers (full and partial), and unspecified assistantships also available. Financial award application deadline: 3/15; financial award applicants required to submit FAFSA. In 2019, 587 master's, 7 doctorates awarded. *Program availability:* Part-time, evening/weekend, 100% online, blended/hybrid learning. *Application deadline:* For fall admission, 6/30 priority date for domestic students, 3/15 for international students; for spring admission, 12/15 for domestic students, 9/15 for international students; for summer admission, 4/15 for domestic and international students. Applications are processed on a rolling basis. *Application fee:* $65 ($70 for international students). Electronic applications accepted. *Application Contact:* Dona Clary, Executive Director, Graduate Programs, 513-556-3546, Fax: 513-558-7006, E-mail: dona.clary@uc.edu. *Dean,* Dr. Marianne Lewis, 513-556-7001, Fax: 513-556-4891, E-mail: marianne.lewis@uc.edu.
**College of Law** Electronic applications accepted.
**Graduate School** *Program availability:* Part-time, evening/weekend, online learning. Electronic applications accepted.
***College-Conservatory of Music*** Electronic applications accepted.
***College of Allied Health Sciences*** *Program availability:* Part-time.
***College of Design, Architecture, Art, and Planning*** *Program availability:* Part-time. Electronic applications accepted.
***College of Education, Criminal Justice, and Human Services*** *Program availability:* Part-time, online learning. Electronic applications accepted.
***College of Engineering and Applied Science*** *Program availability:* Part-time, 100% online. Electronic applications accepted.
***College of Medicine*** Electronic applications accepted.
***College of Nursing*** Students: 429 full-time (355 women), 1,547 part-time (1,390 women); includes 453 minority (226 Black or African American, non-Hispanic/Latino; 5 American Indian or Alaska Native, non-Hispanic/Latino; 68 Asian, non-Hispanic/Latino; 103 Hispanic/Latino; 3 Native Hawaiian or other Pacific Islander, non-Hispanic/Latino; 48 Two or more races, non-Hispanic/Latino), 15 international. Average age 36. 779 applicants, 78% accepted, 464 enrolled. *Faculty:* 62 full-time (55 women), 125 part-time/adjunct (114 women). Expenses: Contact institution. *Financial support:* In 2019–20, 103 students received support, including 9 fellowships with full tuition reimbursements available (averaging $18,595 per year), 7 research assistantships with full tuition reimbursements available (averaging $12,991 per year), 8 teaching assistantships with full tuition reimbursements available (averaging $12,991 per year); institutionally sponsored loans, scholarships/grants, traineeships, health care benefits, tuition waivers (partial), and unspecified assistantships also available. Support available to part-time students. Financial award application deadline: 4/1; financial award applicants required to submit FAFSA. In 2019, 518 master's, 47 doctorates awarded. *Program availability:* Part-time, 100% online, blended/hybrid learning. *Application deadline:* For fall admission, 4/1 priority date for domestic and international students; for spring admission, 9/1 priority date for domestic and international students; for summer admission, 2/1 priority date for domestic and international students. Applications are processed on a rolling basis. *Application fee:* $135 ($140 for international students). Electronic applications accepted. *Application Contact:* Office of Student Affairs, 513-558-8400, E-mail: nursingbearcats@uc.edu. *Dean,* Dr. Greer Glazer, 513-558-5330, Fax: 513-558-9030, E-mail: greer.glazer@uc.edu.
***McMicken College of Arts and Sciences*** *Program availability:* Part-time, evening/weekend.
**James L. Winkle College of Pharmacy** *Program availability:* Part-time.
***Division of Pharmaceutical Sciences*** *Program availability:* Part-time, evening/weekend, 100% online, blended/hybrid learning. Electronic applications accepted.
***Division of Pharmacy Practice***

## UNIVERSITY OF COLORADO BOULDER, Boulder, CO 80309

**General Information** State-supported, coed, university. CGS member. *Graduate housing:* Rooms and/or apartments available to single and married students. *Research affiliation:* National Institute of Standards and Technology (NIST), National Oceanic and Atmospheric Administration (NOAA), U.S. West Advanced Technologies, NASA, National Center for Atmospheric Research.

**GRADUATE UNITS**

***College of Arts and Sciences*** Electronic applications accepted.
***College of Engineering and Applied Science*** Electronic applications accepted.
***College of Media, Communication and Information*** Electronic applications accepted.
***College of Music*** Electronic applications accepted.
***School of Education*** Electronic applications accepted.
**Leeds School of Business** Electronic applications accepted.
**School of Law** Electronic applications accepted.

## UNIVERSITY OF COLORADO COLORADO SPRINGS, Colorado Springs, CO 80918

**General Information** State-supported, coed, university. CGS member. *Enrollment:* 12,180 graduate, professional, and undergraduate students; 387 full-time matriculated graduate/professional students (260 women), 1,543 part-time matriculated graduate/professional students (916 women). *Enrollment by degree level:* 1,566 master's, 241 doctoral, 123 other advanced degrees. *Graduate faculty:* 347 full-time (172 women), 446 part-time/adjunct (256 women). Tuition, state resident: full-time $628; part-time $628 per credit hour. Tuition, nonresident: full-time $1250; part-time $1230 per credit hour. Tuition and fees vary according to course load and program. *Graduate housing:* Room and/or apartments available on a first-come, first-served basis to single students; on-campus housing not available to married students. Typical cost: $11,940 per year ($15,416 including board). Room and board charges vary according to board plan, campus/location and housing facility selected. Housing application deadline: 3/15. *Student services:* Campus employment opportunities, campus safety program, career counseling, child daycare facilities, exercise/wellness program, free psychological counseling, grant writing training, international student services, low-cost health insurance, multicultural affairs office, services for students with disabilities, teacher training, writing training. *Library facilities:* Kraemer Family Library. *Collection:* Books: 330,823 (physical), 279,953 (digital/electronic); Serial titles: 1,326 (physical), 129,566 (digital/electronic); Databases: 166. Weekly public service hours: 108; students can reserve study rooms. *Research affiliation:* Georgia Institute of Technology (education), University of North Texas Health Science Center (psychology), National Institute of Arthritis and Musculoskeletal and Skin Diseases (NIAMS) (mechanical and aerospace engineering), National Geographic Society (geography and environmental studies), i-CORE (physics), Structured Material Industries, NJ (electrical and computer engineering).

**Computer facilities:** A campuswide network can be accessed. Online class registration, student portal, learning management system are available.
Website: http://www.uccs.edu/

**General Application Contact:** Sarah Elsey, Program Manager, Graduate School, 719-255-3072, Fax: 719-255-3045, E-mail: gradinfo@uccs.edu.

**GRADUATE UNITS**

**College of Business** Students: 66 full-time (29 women), 295 part-time (150 women); includes 88 minority (11 Black or African American, non-Hispanic/Latino; 18 Asian, non-Hispanic/Latino; 42 Hispanic/Latino; 17 Two or more races, non-Hispanic/Latino), 9 international. Average age 34. 117 applicants, 72% accepted, 63 enrolled. *Faculty:* 40 full-time (12 women), 48 part-time/adjunct (21 women). Expenses: Contact institution. *Financial support:* In 2019–20, 36 students received support, including 2 teaching assistantships (averaging $8,000 per year); career-related internships or fieldwork, Federal Work-Study, scholarships/grants, and unspecified assistantships also available. Support available to part-time students. Financial award application deadline: 3/1; financial award applicants required to submit FAFSA. In 2019, 97 master's awarded. *Program availability:* Part-time, evening/weekend, 100% online, blended/hybrid learning. *Application deadline:* For fall admission, 6/1 priority date for domestic and international students; for spring admission, 11/1 priority date for domestic and international students; for summer admission, 4/1 priority date for domestic and international students. Applications are processed on a rolling basis. *Application fee:* $60 ($100 for international students). Electronic applications accepted. *Application Contact:* Janice Dowsett, Director of Graduate Programs, 719-255-3070, E-mail: cobgrad@uccs.edu. *Dean,* Dr. Karen Markel, 719-255-3113, Fax: 719-255-4667, E-mail: kmarkel@uccs.edu.
**College of Education** Students: 168 full-time (123 women), 290 part-time (212 women); includes 120 minority (16 Black or African American, non-Hispanic/Latino; 1 American Indian or Alaska Native, non-Hispanic/Latino; 8 Asian, non-Hispanic/Latino; 67 Hispanic/Latino; 28 Two or more races, non-Hispanic/Latino), 7 international. Average age 35. 119 applicants, 87% accepted, 93 enrolled. *Faculty:* 34 full-time (23 women), 77 part-time/adjunct (59 women). Expenses: Contact institution. *Financial support:* In

2019–20, 110 students received support, including 2 research assistantships (averaging $14,200 per year); career-related internships or fieldwork, Federal Work-Study, scholarships/grants, and unspecified assistantships also available. Support available to part-time students. Financial award application deadline: 3/1; financial award applicants required to submit FAFSA. In 2019, 195 master's, 10 doctorates awarded. *Program availability:* Part-time, evening/weekend, 100% online, blended/hybrid learning. *Application deadline:* For fall admission, 1/15 priority date for domestic and international students; for spring admission, 11/1 priority date for domestic and international students. Applications are processed on a rolling basis. *Application fee:* $60 ($100 for international students). Electronic applications accepted. *Application Contact:* The College of Education Student Resource Office, 719-255-4996, E-mail: education@uccs.edu. *Dean*, Dr. Valerie Martin Conley, 719-255-4133, E-mail: vmconley@uccs.edu.

**College of Engineering and Applied Science** Students: 23 full-time (4 women), 256 part-time (52 women); includes 55 minority (9 Black or African American, non-Hispanic/Latino; 18 Asian, non-Hispanic/Latino; 17 Hispanic/Latino; 11 Two or more races, non-Hispanic/Latino), 75 international. Average age 33. 169 applicants, 67% accepted, 64 enrolled. *Faculty:* 50 full-time (11 women), 34 part-time/adjunct (6 women). Expenses: Contact institution. *Financial support:* In 2019–20, 44 students received support, including 43 research assistantships (averaging $20,000 per year), 50 teaching assistantships (averaging $4,970 per year); career-related internships or fieldwork, Federal Work-Study, institutionally sponsored loans, scholarships/grants, traineeships, and unspecified assistantships also available. Support available to part-time students. Financial award application deadline: 3/1; financial award applicants required to submit FAFSA. In 2019, 61 master's, 13 doctorates awarded. *Program availability:* Part-time, evening/weekend. *Application deadline:* For fall admission, 6/1 for domestic students, 4/1 for international students; for spring admission, 11/1 for domestic students, 10/1 for international students. Applications are processed on a rolling basis. *Application fee:* $60 ($100 for international students). *Application Contact:* Ali Langfels, Office of Student Support, 719-255-3544, E-mail: alangfel@uccs.edu. *Dean*, Dr. Donald Rabern, 719-255-3543, E-mail: drabern@uccs.edu.

**College of Letters, Arts and Sciences** Students: 64 full-time (53 women), 206 part-time (109 women); includes 69 minority (6 Black or African American, non-Hispanic/Latino; 2 American Indian or Alaska Native, non-Hispanic/Latino; 4 Asian, non-Hispanic/Latino; 35 Hispanic/Latino; 22 Two or more races, non-Hispanic/Latino), 7 international. Average age 30. 489 applicants, 34% accepted, 88 enrolled. *Faculty:* 103 full-time (48 women), 51 part-time/adjunct (24 women). Expenses: Contact institution. *Financial support:* In 2019–20, 126 students received support, including 10 fellowships (averaging $2,500 per year), 5 research assistantships (averaging $5,275 per year), 58 teaching assistantships (averaging $3,255 per year); career-related internships or fieldwork, Federal Work-Study, scholarships/grants, and unspecified assistantships also available. Support available to part-time students. Financial award application deadline: 3/1; financial award applicants required to submit FAFSA. In 2019, 73 master's, 3 doctorates awarded. *Program availability:* Part-time, evening/weekend, 100% online, blended/hybrid learning. *Application deadline:* For fall admission, 12/1 for domestic and international students. Applications are processed on a rolling basis. *Application fee:* $60 ($100 for international students). Electronic applications accepted. *Application Contact:* Sarah Elsey, Graduate School Program Manager, 719-255-3072, E-mail: gradinfo@uccs.edu. *Dean of the Graduate School*, Dr. Kelli Klebe, 719-255-3779, Fax: 719-255-3045, E-mail: kklebe@uccs.edu.

**Helen and Arthur E. Johnson Beth-El College of Nursing and Health Sciences** Students: 20 full-time (18 women), 295 part-time (261 women); includes 74 minority (14 Black or African American, non-Hispanic/Latino; 2 American Indian or Alaska Native, non-Hispanic/Latino; 16 Asian, non-Hispanic/Latino; 26 Hispanic/Latino; 1 Native Hawaiian or other Pacific Islander, non-Hispanic/Latino; 15 Two or more races, non-Hispanic/Latino). Average age 36. 147 applicants, 44% accepted, 49 enrolled. *Faculty:* 62 full-time (47 women), 77 part-time/adjunct (68 women). Expenses: Contact institution. *Financial support:* In 2019–20, 14 students received support, including 1 research assistantship (averaging $20,800 per year), 9 teaching assistantships (averaging $3,000 per year); career-related internships or fieldwork, Federal Work-Study, and scholarships/grants also available. Support available to part-time students. Financial award application deadline: 3/1; financial award applicants required to submit FAFSA. In 2019, 63 master's, 4 doctorates awarded. *Program availability:* Part-time, 100% online. *Application deadline:* For fall admission, 3/15 priority date for domestic students, 3/15 for international students; for spring admission, 8/15 for domestic and international students. Applications are processed on a rolling basis. *Application fee:* $60 ($100 for international students). Electronic applications accepted. *Application Contact:* Diane Busch, Program Assistant II, 719-255-4424, Fax: 719-255-4416, E-mail: dbusch@uccs.edu. *Nursing Department Chair*, Dr. Deborah Pollard, 719-255-3577, Fax: 719-255-4416, E-mail: dpollard@uccs.edu.

**School of Public Affairs** Students: 28 full-time (18 women), 194 part-time (127 women); includes 87 minority (19 Black or African American, non-Hispanic/Latino; 4 American Indian or Alaska Native, non-Hispanic/Latino; 6 Asian, non-Hispanic/Latino; 48 Hispanic/Latino; 10 Two or more races, non-Hispanic/Latino), 4 international. Average age 34. 89 applicants, 83% accepted, 58 enrolled. *Faculty:* 22 full-time (12 women), 20 part-time/adjunct (10 women). Expenses: Contact institution. *Financial support:* In 2019–20, 35 students received support. Career-related internships or fieldwork, Federal Work-Study, scholarships/grants, and tuition waivers available. Support available to part-time students. Financial award application deadline: 3/1; financial award applicants required to submit FAFSA. In 2019, 38 master's awarded. *Program availability:* Part-time, evening/weekend, 100% online, blended/hybrid learning. *Application deadline:* Applications are processed on a rolling basis. *Application fee:* $60 ($100 for international students). Electronic applications accepted. *Application Contact:* Stephani Hosain, Graduate Student Services Specialist, 719-255-4993, E-mail: shosain@uccs.edu. *Dean*, Dr. George Reed, 719-255-4109, E-mail: george.reed@uccs.edu.

## UNIVERSITY OF COLORADO DENVER, Denver, CO 80217-3364

**General Information** State-supported, coed, university. CGS member. *Enrollment:* 25,645 graduate, professional, and undergraduate students; 6,577 full-time matriculated graduate/professional students (4,047 women), 1,676 part-time matriculated graduate/professional students (1,059 women). *Enrollment by degree level:* 5,014 master's, 3,146 doctoral, 93 other advanced degrees. *Graduate faculty:* 4,253 full-time (2,378 women), 1,006 part-time/adjunct (594 women). Tuition and fees vary according to course load, program and reciprocity agreements. *Graduate housing:* Room and/or apartments available on a first-come, first-served basis to single students; on-campus housing not available to married students. *Student services:* Campus employment opportunities, campus safety program, career counseling, child daycare facilities, exercise/wellness program, free psychological counseling, international student services, low-cost health insurance, multicultural affairs office, services for students with disabilities, teacher training, writing training. *Library facilities:* Auraria Library plus 1 other. *Collection:* Weekly public service hours: 85; students can reserve study rooms. *Research affiliation:* The Children's Hospital (pediatrics), National Jewish Health (pediatrics, immunology, respiratory disease), Denver Health (trauma, primary care, under-served populations).

**Computer facilities:** 750 computers available on campus for general student use. A campuswide network can be accessed from student residence rooms and from off campus. Online class registration is available.
Website: http://www.ucdenver.edu/

**General Application Contact:** Graduate School Admissions, 303-556-2704, E-mail: admissions@ucdenver.edu.

**GRADUATE UNITS**

**Business School** *Program availability:* Part-time, evening/weekend, 100% online, blended/hybrid learning. Electronic applications accepted.

**College of Architecture and Planning** *Program availability:* Part-time. Electronic applications accepted.

**College of Arts and Media** *Program availability:* Part-time, evening/weekend. Electronic applications accepted.

**College of Engineering, Design and Computing** *Program availability:* Part-time, evening/weekend. Electronic applications accepted.

**College of Liberal Arts and Sciences** *Program availability:* Part-time, evening/weekend. Electronic applications accepted.

**College of Nursing** *Program availability:* Part-time, evening/weekend, online learning. Electronic applications accepted.

**Colorado School of Public Health** *Program availability:* Part-time. Electronic applications accepted.

**School of Dental Medicine** Electronic applications accepted.

**School of Education and Human Development** *Program availability:* Part-time, evening/weekend, online learning. Electronic applications accepted.

**School of Medicine** Electronic applications accepted.

**School of Public Affairs** *Program availability:* Part-time, evening/weekend, online learning. Electronic applications accepted.

**Skaggs School of Pharmacy and Pharmaceutical Sciences** *Program availability:* Online learning. Electronic applications accepted.

## UNIVERSITY OF CONNECTICUT, Storrs, CT 06269

**General Information** State-supported, coed, university. CGS member. *Graduate housing:* Rooms and/or apartments available on a first-come, first-served basis to single and married students. Housing application deadline: 4/1. *Research affiliation:* U.S. Navy–Submarine Medical Research Laboratory, Haskins Laboratories.

**GRADUATE UNITS**

**Graduate School** *Program availability:* Part-time, evening/weekend, online learning. Electronic applications accepted.

***College of Agriculture, Health and Natural Resources*** Electronic applications accepted.

***College of Liberal Arts and Sciences*** Electronic applications accepted.

***eCampus*** *Program availability:* Online learning.

***Neag School of Education*** Electronic applications accepted.

***School of Business*** Electronic applications accepted.

***School of Engineering*** Electronic applications accepted.

***School of Fine Arts*** Electronic applications accepted.

***School of Nursing*** Electronic applications accepted.

***School of Pharmacy*** Electronic applications accepted.

***School of Social Work*** Electronic applications accepted.

**Institute of Materials Science**

**School of Law** *Program availability:* Part-time. Electronic applications accepted.

## UNIVERSITY OF CONNECTICUT HEALTH CENTER, Farmington, CT 06030

**General Information** State-supported, coed, graduate-only institution. *Graduate housing:* On-campus housing not available.

**GRADUATE UNITS**

**Graduate School** *Program availability:* Part-time, evening/weekend.

**School of Dental Medicine** Electronic applications accepted.

**School of Medicine** Electronic applications accepted.

## UNIVERSITY OF DALLAS, Irving, TX 75062-4736

**General Information** Independent-religious, coed, university. *Enrollment:* 2,481 graduate, professional, and undergraduate students; 252 full-time matriculated graduate/professional students (106 women), 754 part-time matriculated graduate/professional students (322 women). *Enrollment by degree level:* 883 master's, 104 doctoral, 7 other advanced degrees. *Tuition:* Part-time $1250 per credit hour. *Graduate housing:* On-campus housing not available. *Student services:* Campus employment opportunities, career counseling, exercise/wellness program, international student services, services for students with disabilities, teacher training, writing training. *Library facilities:* Cowan-Blakley Memorial Library. *Collection:* Books: 240,269 (physical), 248,867 (digital/electronic); Serial titles: 283 (physical), 189 (digital/electronic); Databases: 219. Weekly public service hours: 99; students can reserve study rooms.

**Computer facilities:** Computer purchase and lease plans are available. 125 computers available on campus for general student use. A campuswide network can be accessed. Online class registration is available.
Website: http://www.udallas.edu/

**General Application Contact:** Breonna Collins, Director, Graduate Admissions and College of Business Enrollment Management, 972-721-5304, E-mail: bcollins@udallas.edu.

**GRADUATE UNITS**

**Ann and Joe O. Neuhoff School of Ministry** Students: 3 full-time (1 woman), 66 part-time (33 women); includes 17 minority (2 Asian, non-Hispanic/Latino; 15 Hispanic/Latino). Average age 47. 24 applicants, 75% accepted, 13 enrolled. *Faculty:* 5 full-time (2 women), 2 part-time/adjunct (1 woman). Expenses: Contact institution. *Financial support:* In 2019–20, 12 students received support. Scholarships/grants and unspecified assistantships available. Financial award application deadline: 7/1; financial award applicants required to submit FAFSA. In 2019, 15 master's awarded. *Program availability:* Part-time. *Application deadline:* For fall admission, 8/1 priority date for domestic and international students; for spring admission, 1/1 priority date for domestic and international students; for summer admission, 5/1 priority date for domestic and international students. Applications are processed on a rolling basis. *Application fee:* $25. Electronic applications accepted. *Application Contact:* Dr. Jodi Hunt, Director of Graduate Programs, 972-721-5810, E-mail: jhunt@udallas.edu. *Dean,* Dr. Theodore J. Whapham, 972-721-4068, E-mail: twhapham@udallas.edu.

**Braniff Graduate School of Liberal Arts** Students: 129 full-time (52 women), 157 part-time (86 women); includes 50 minority (10 Black or African American, non-Hispanic/Latino; 4 Asian, non-Hispanic/Latino; 33 Hispanic/Latino; 3 Two or more races, non-Hispanic/Latino), 19 international. Average age 32. 154 applicants, 84% accepted, 71 enrolled. Expenses: Contact institution. *Financial support:* In 2019–20, 164 students received support. Research assistantships, teaching assistantships, scholarships/grants, tuition waivers (full and partial), and unspecified assistantships available. Financial award application deadline: 2/15; financial award applicants required to submit FAFSA. In 2019, 64 master's, 8 doctorates awarded. *Program availability:* Part-time, 100% online, blended/hybrid learning. *Application deadline:* For fall admission, 7/15 priority date for domestic and international students; for spring admission, 11/15 priority date for domestic and international students; for summer admission, 2/15 priority date for domestic and international students. Applications are processed on a rolling basis. *Application fee:* $50. Electronic applications accepted. *Application Contact:* Breonna Collins, Director, Graduate Admissions, 972-721-5304, E-mail: bcollins@udallas.edu. *Dean,* Dr. Joshua Parens, 972-721 5241, E-mail: jparens@udallas.edu.

**Satish and Yasmin Gupta College of Business** Students: 120 full-time (53 women), 531 part-time (203 women); includes 353 minority (173 Black or African American, non-Hispanic/Latino; 1 American Indian or Alaska Native, non-Hispanic/Latino; 78 Asian, non-Hispanic/Latino; 92 Hispanic/Latino; 2 Native Hawaiian or other Pacific Islander, non-Hispanic/Latino; 7 Two or more races, non-Hispanic/Latino), 96 international. Average age 33. 291 applicants, 96% accepted, 141 enrolled. Expenses: Contact institution. *Financial support:* Research assistantships, teaching assistantships, scholarships/grants, and unspecified assistantships available. Support available to part-time students. Financial award application deadline: 2/15; financial award applicants required to submit FAFSA. In 2019, 302 master's, 4 doctorates awarded. *Program availability:* Part-time, evening/weekend, 100% online, blended/hybrid learning. *Application deadline:* Applications are processed on a rolling basis. *Application fee:* $50. Electronic applications accepted. *Application Contact:* Breonna Collins, Director, Graduate Admissions, 972-7215304, E-mail: bcollins@udallas.edu. *Dean,* Brett J.L. Landry, 972-721-5356, E-mail: blandry@udallas.edu.

## UNIVERSITY OF DAYTON, Dayton, OH 45469

**General Information** Independent-religious, coed, university. CGS member. *Graduate housing:* Room and/or apartments available on a first-come, first-served basis to single students; on-campus housing not available to married students. *Research affiliation:* California Institute of Technology (materials development), Dayton Area Graduate Studies Institute (materials testing), Kern Family Foundation (curriculum development), Ohio Aerospace Institute (engine analysis), Riverside Research Institute (radar and materials research), Southwest Research Institute (engineering services).

**GRADUATE UNITS**

**College of Arts and Sciences** *Program availability:* Part-time, evening/weekend, online learning. Electronic applications accepted.

**Department of Biology** Electronic applications accepted.

**Department of Chemical Engineering** *Program availability:* Part-time, online learning. Electronic applications accepted.

**Department of Chemistry and Biochemistry** *Program availability:* Part-time. Electronic applications accepted.

**Department of Civil and Environmental Engineering and Engineering Mechanics** *Program availability:* Part-time, blended/hybrid learning. Electronic applications accepted.

**Department of Communication** *Program availability:* Part-time, 100% online. Electronic applications accepted.

**Department of Computer Science** *Program availability:* Part-time. Electronic applications accepted.

**Department of Counselor Education and Human Services** *Program availability:* Part-time. Electronic applications accepted.

**Department of Educational Administration** *Program availability:* Part-time, blended/hybrid learning. Electronic applications accepted.

**Department of Electrical and Computer Engineering** *Program availability:* Part-time, blended/hybrid learning. Electronic applications accepted.

**Department of Electro-Optics and Photonics** Electronic applications accepted.

**Department of Engineering Management, Systems and Technology** *Program availability:* Part-time, 100% online, blended/hybrid learning. Electronic applications accepted.

**Department of English** *Program availability:* Part-time. Electronic applications accepted.

**Department of Health and Sport Science** *Program availability:* Part-time, 100% online. Electronic applications accepted.

**Department of Mathematics** *Program availability:* Part-time. Electronic applications accepted.

**Department of Mechanical and Aerospace Engineering** *Program availability:* Part-time, 100% online, blended/hybrid learning. Electronic applications accepted.

**Department of Physical Therapy** Electronic applications accepted.

**Department of Physician Assistant Education** Electronic applications accepted.

**Department of Religious Studies** *Program availability:* Part-time. Electronic applications accepted.

**Department of Teacher Education** *Program availability:* Part-time, 100% online. Electronic applications accepted.

**Master of Public Administration Program** *Program availability:* Part-time, evening/weekend. Electronic applications accepted.

**PhD Program in Educational Leadership** *Program availability:* Part-time. Electronic applications accepted.

**Program in Clinical Psychology** Electronic applications accepted.

**Program in General Psychology** Electronic applications accepted.

**Program in Materials Engineering** *Program availability:* Part-time, evening/weekend, blended/hybrid learning. Electronic applications accepted.

**School of Business Administration** *Program availability:* Part-time, evening/weekend, blended/hybrid learning. Electronic applications accepted.

**School of Education**

**School of Law** *Program availability:* Part-time, 100% online.

## UNIVERSITY OF DELAWARE, Newark, DE 19716

**General Information** State-related, coed, university. CGS member. *Graduate housing:* Rooms and/or apartments available to single and married students. Housing application deadline: 3/15. *Research affiliation:* Hagley Museum, Winterthur Museum, Longwood Gardens, Bartol Research Foundation.

**GRADUATE UNITS**

**Alfred Lerner College of Business and Economics** *Program availability:* Part-time, evening/weekend. Electronic applications accepted.

**Center for Energy and Environmental Policy** Electronic applications accepted.

**College of Agriculture and Natural Resources** *Program availability:* Part-time. Electronic applications accepted.

**College of Arts and Sciences** *Program availability:* Part-time, evening/weekend. Electronic applications accepted.

***School of Public Policy and Administration*** *Program availability:* Part-time, evening/weekend. Electronic applications accepted.

**College of Earth, Ocean, and Environment** Electronic applications accepted.

***School of Marine Science and Policy***

**College of Education and Human Development** *Program availability:* Part-time, evening/weekend. Electronic applications accepted.

***School of Education*** *Program availability:* Part-time, evening/weekend. Electronic applications accepted.

**College of Engineering** *Program availability:* Part-time, evening/weekend, online learning. Electronic applications accepted.

**College of Health Sciences** *Program availability:* Part-time, evening/weekend, online learning. Electronic applications accepted.

## UNIVERSITY OF DENVER, Denver, CO 80208

**General Information** Independent, coed, university. CGS member. *Enrollment:* 12,931 graduate, professional, and undergraduate students; 3,149 full-time matriculated graduate/professional students (2,177 women), 3,866 part-time matriculated graduate/professional students (2,344 women). *Enrollment by degree level:* 5,031 master's, 1,583 doctoral, 401 other advanced degrees. *Graduate faculty:* 751 full-time (367 women), 693 part-time/adjunct (379 women). *Graduate housing:* Rooms and/or apartments available on a first-come, first-served basis to single and married students. Housing application deadline: 5/1. *Student services:* Campus employment opportunities, campus safety program, career counseling, exercise/wellness program, free psychological counseling, international student services, low-cost health insurance, multicultural affairs office, services for students with disabilities, teacher training, writing training. *Library facilities:* Anderson Academic Commons plus 1 other. *Collection:* Books: 1.7 million (physical), 2.3 million (digital/electronic); Serial titles: 594,063 (physical), 218,954 (digital/electronic); Databases: 1,306. Weekly public service hours: 145; study areas open 24 hours, 5–7 days a week; students can reserve study rooms. *Research affiliation:* National Center for Atmospheric Research (infrared measurements).

**Computer facilities:** Computer purchase and lease plans are available. 150 computers available on campus for general student use. A campuswide network can be accessed. Online (class) learning management system available.
Website: http://www.du.edu/

**General Application Contact:** Office of Graduate Studies, 303-871-2706, Fax: 303-871-4942, E-mail: gradinfo@du.edu.

**GRADUATE UNITS**

**Daniel Felix Ritchie School of Engineering and Computer Science** Students: 30 full-time (11 women), 249 part-time (63 women); includes 60 minority (8 Black or African American, non-Hispanic/Latino; 16 Asian, non-Hispanic/Latino; 26 Hispanic/Latino; 10 Two or more races, non-Hispanic/Latino), 78 international. Average age 29. 462 applicants, 71% accepted, 149 enrolled. *Faculty:* 42 full-time (7 women), 8 part-time/adjunct (3 women). Expenses: Contact institution. *Financial support:* In 2019–20, 139 students received support, including 20 research assistantships with tuition reimbursements available (averaging $14,559 per year), 33 teaching assistantships with tuition reimbursements available (averaging $15,152 per year); Federal Work-Study, institutionally sponsored loans, scholarships/grants, health care benefits, and unspecified assistantships also available. Financial award application deadline: 2/15; financial award applicants required to submit FAFSA. In 2019, 86 master's, 14 doctorates awarded. *Application deadline:* Applications are processed on a rolling basis. *Application fee:* $65. Electronic applications accepted. *Application Contact:* Information Contact, 303-871-3787, E-mail: ritchieschool@du.edu. *Dean,* JB Holston, 303-871-3787, E-mail: jb.holston@du.edu.

**Daniels College of Business** Students: 284 full-time (102 women), 455 part-time (197 women); includes 178 minority (32 Black or African American, non-Hispanic/Latino; 5 American Indian or Alaska Native, non-Hispanic/Latino; 33 Asian, non-Hispanic/Latino; 82 Hispanic/Latino; 1 Native Hawaiian or other Pacific Islander, non-Hispanic/Latino; 25 Two or more races, non-Hispanic/Latino), 55 international. Average age 33. 821 applicants, 66% accepted, 260 enrolled. *Faculty:* 104 full-time (39 women), 38 part-time/adjunct (10 women). Expenses: Contact institution. *Financial support:* In 2019–20, 288 students received support. Teaching assistantships, career-related internships or fieldwork, Federal Work-Study, institutionally sponsored loans, scholarships/grants, and unspecified assistantships available. Support available to part-time students. Financial award application deadline: 2/15; financial award applicants required to submit FAFSA. In 2019, 399 master's awarded. *Program availability:* Part-time, evening/weekend, online learning. *Application deadline:* For fall admission, 10/15 priority date for domestic and international students; for spring admission, 9/15 priority date for domestic and international students. Applications are processed on a rolling basis. *Application fee:* $100. Electronic applications accepted. *Application Contact:* Information Contact, 303-732-6186, E-mail: daniels@du.edu. *Dean,* Dr. Vivek Choudhury, 303-871-3411, E-mail: vivek.choudhury@du.edu.

***Franklin L. Burns School of Real Estate and Construction Management*** Students: 7 full-time (5 women), 40 part-time (11 women); includes 12 minority (3 Black or African American, non-Hispanic/Latino; 3 Asian, non-Hispanic/Latino; 4 Hispanic/Latino; 2 Two or more races, non-Hispanic/Latino). Average age 32. 46 applicants, 78% accepted, 24 enrolled. *Faculty:* 7 full-time (1 woman), 5 part-time/adjunct (1 woman). Expenses: Contact institution. *Financial support:* In 2019–20, 41 students received support. Teaching assistantships with tuition reimbursements available, Federal Work-Study, institutionally sponsored loans, scholarships/grants, and unspecified assistantships available. Support available to part-time students. Financial award application deadline: 2/15; financial award applicants required to submit FAFSA. In 2019, 54 master's awarded. *Program availability:* Part-time, evening/weekend. *Application deadline:* For fall admission, 10/15 priority date for domestic and international students; for spring admission, 9/15 priority date for domestic and international students. Applications are processed on a rolling basis. *Application fee:* $100. Electronic applications accepted. *Application Contact:* Ceci Smith, Assistant to the Director, 303-871-2145, E-mail: ceci.smith@du.edu. *Associate Professor and Director*, Dr. Barbara Jackson, 303-871-3470, E-mail: barbara.jackson@du.edu.

***Reiman School of Finance*** Students: 32 full-time (11 women), 18 part-time (8 women); includes 12 minority (1 Black or African American, non-Hispanic/Latino; 3 Asian, non-Hispanic/Latino; 4 Hispanic/Latino; 1 Native Hawaiian or other Pacific Islander, non-Hispanic/Latino; 3 Two or more races, non-Hispanic/Latino), 13 international. Average age 27. 86 applicants, 59% accepted, 20 enrolled. *Faculty:* 17 full-time (4 women). Expenses: Contact institution. *Financial support:* In 2019–20, 34 students received support. Teaching assistantships with tuition reimbursements available, career-related internships or fieldwork, Federal Work-Study, institutionally sponsored loans, scholarships/grants, tuition waivers, and unspecified assistantships available. Support available to part-time students. Financial award application deadline: 2/15; financial award applicants required to submit FAFSA. In 2019, 34 master's awarded. *Program availability:* Part-time, evening/weekend. *Application deadline:* For fall admission, 10/15 priority date for domestic and international students; for spring admission, 9/15 priority date for domestic and international students. Applications are processed on a rolling basis. *Application fee:* $100. Electronic applications accepted. *Application Contact:* Claudia Walinder, Office Manager, 303-871-3322, E-mail: claudia.walinder@du.edu. *Professor and Director*, Dr. Conrad Ciccotello, 303-871-2282, E-mail: conrad.ciccotello@du.edu.

***School of Accountancy*** Students: 30 full-time (15 women), 22 part-time (14 women); includes 14 minority (1 Black or African American, non-Hispanic/Latino; 2 Asian, non-Hispanic/Latino; 8 Hispanic/Latino; 3 Two or more races, non-Hispanic/Latino), 9 international. Average age 27. 71 applicants, 65% accepted, 19 enrolled. *Faculty:* 16 full-time (7 women), 5 part-time/adjunct (1 woman). Expenses: Contact institution. *Financial support:* In 2019–20, 39 students received support. Teaching assistantships with tuition reimbursements available, career-related internships or fieldwork, Federal Work-Study, institutionally sponsored loans, scholarships/grants, and unspecified assistantships available. Support available to part-time students. Financial award application deadline: 2/15; financial award applicants required to submit FAFSA. In 2019, 93 master's awarded. *Program availability:* Part-time, evening/weekend. *Application deadline:* For fall admission, 10/15 priority date for domestic and international students; for spring admission, 9/15 priority date for domestic and international students. Applications are processed on a rolling basis. *Application fee:* $100. Electronic applications accepted. *Application Contact:* Mary Haynes, Administrative Assistant, 303-871-2032, E-mail: Mary.Haynes@du.edu. *Professor and Gilbert Endowed Chair*, Dr. Sharon Lassar, 303-871-2032, E-mail: slassar@du.edu.

**Division of Arts, Humanities and Social Sciences** Students: 118 full-time (86 women), 182 part-time (109 women); includes 62 minority (7 Black or African American, non-Hispanic/Latino; 2 American Indian or Alaska Native, non-Hispanic/Latino; 10 Asian, non-Hispanic/Latino; 31 Hispanic/Latino; 1 Native Hawaiian or other Pacific Islander, non-Hispanic/Latino; 11 Two or more races, non-Hispanic/Latino), 29 international. Average age 28. 1,127 applicants, 32% accepted, 141 enrolled. *Faculty:* 240 full-time (131 women), 4 part-time/adjunct (2 women). Expenses: Contact institution. *Financial support:* In 2019–20, 259 students received support, including 14 research assistantships with tuition reimbursements available (averaging $14,314 per year), 128 teaching assistantships with tuition reimbursements available (averaging $9,310 per year); career-related internships or fieldwork, Federal Work-Study, institutionally sponsored loans, scholarships/grants, and unspecified assistantships also available. Support available to part-time students. Financial award application deadline: 2/15; financial award applicants required to submit FAFSA. In 2019, 95 master's, 21 doctorates, 7 other advanced degrees awarded. *Program availability:* Part-time. *Application deadline:* Applications are processed on a rolling basis. *Application fee:* $65. Electronic applications accepted. *Application Contact:* Information Contact, 303-871-4449, E-mail: cahss@du.edu. *Dean*, Dr. Danny McIntosh, 303-871-4449, E-mail: daniel.mcintosh@du.edu.

***Lamont School of Music*** Students: 25 full-time (12 women), 78 part-time (38 women); includes 20 minority (3 Black or African American, non-Hispanic/Latino; 1 American Indian or Alaska Native, non-Hispanic/Latino; 3 Asian, non-Hispanic/Latino; 9 Hispanic/Latino; 4 Two or more races, non-Hispanic/Latino), 16 international. Average age 28. 186 applicants, 83% accepted, 58 enrolled. *Faculty:* 30 full-time (10 women), 30 part-time/adjunct (14 women). Expenses: Contact institution. *Financial support:* In 2019–20, 80 students received support, including 39 teaching assistantships with tuition reimbursements available (averaging $6,709 per year); career-related internships or fieldwork, Federal Work-Study, institutionally sponsored loans, scholarships/grants, tuition waivers, and unspecified assistantships also available. Support available to part-time students. Financial award application deadline: 2/15; financial award applicants required to submit FAFSA. In 2019, 33 master's, 7 other advanced degrees awarded. *Program availability:* Part-time. *Application deadline:* For fall admission, 1/15 priority date for domestic and international students. Applications are processed on a rolling basis. *Application fee:* $65. Electronic applications accepted. *Application Contact:* Stephen Campbell, Director of Admission, 303-871-6973, E-mail: stephen.l.campbell@du.edu. *Professor and Director*, Dr. Keith Ward, 303-871-6986, E-mail: Keith.Ward@du.edu.

***School of Art and Art History*** Students: 11 full-time (all women), 10 part-time (7 women); includes 6 minority (1 Black or African American, non-Hispanic/Latino; 1 Asian, non-Hispanic/Latino; 4 Hispanic/Latino). Average age 27. 21 applicants, 86% accepted, 12 enrolled. *Faculty:* 16 full-time (11 women), 6 part-time/adjunct (5 women). Expenses: Contact institution. *Financial support:* In 2019–20, 20 students received support, including 8 teaching assistantships with tuition reimbursements available (averaging $8,177 per year); research assistantships with tuition reimbursements available, career-related internships or fieldwork, Federal Work-Study, institutionally sponsored loans, scholarships/grants, and unspecified assistantships also available. Support available to part-time students. Financial award application deadline: 2/15; financial award applicants required to submit FAFSA. In 2019, 13 master's awarded. *Program availability:* Part-time. *Application deadline:* For fall admission, 1/31 priority date for domestic and international students. Applications are processed on a rolling basis. *Application fee:* $65. Electronic applications accepted. *Application Contact:* Jason Kellermeyer, Coordinator of Academic Programs, 303-871-2846, E-mail: jason.kellermeyer@du.edu. *Associate Professor and Director*, Annabeth Headrick, 303-871-3574, E-mail: annabeth.headrick@du.edu.

**Division of Natural Sciences and Mathematics** Students: 28 full-time (15 women), 119 part-time (45 women); includes 23 minority (3 Black or African American, non-Hispanic/Latino; 1 Asian, non-Hispanic/Latino; 13 Hispanic/Latino; 6 Two or more races, non-Hispanic/Latino), 18 international. Average age 28. 293 applicants, 40% accepted, 54 enrolled. *Faculty:* 91 full-time (29 women), 14 part-time/adjunct (7 women). Expenses: Contact institution. *Financial support:* In 2019–20, 143 students received support, including 28 research assistantships with tuition reimbursements available (averaging $14,868 per year), 80 teaching assistantships with tuition reimbursements available (averaging $18,251 per year); career-related internships or fieldwork, institutionally sponsored loans, scholarships/grants, and unspecified assistantships also available. Support available to part-time students. Financial award application deadline: 2/15; financial award applicants required to submit FAFSA. In 2019, 52 master's, 19 doctorates awarded. *Program availability:* Part-time, evening/weekend. *Application deadline:* Applications are processed on a rolling basis. *Application fee:* $65. Electronic applications accepted. *Application Contact:* Kirsten Norwood, Executive Assistant to the Dean, 303-871-2693, E-mail: kirsten.norwood@du.edu. *Dean*, Dr. Andrei Kutateladze, 303-871-2995, E-mail: andrei.kutateladze@du.edu.

**DU/Iliff Joint PhD Program in the Study of Religion** Students: 19 full-time (7 women), 20 part-time (9 women); includes 5 minority (2 Black or African American, non-Hispanic/Latino; 1 Asian, non-Hispanic/Latino; 2 Hispanic/Latino), 4 international. Average age 38. 41 applicants, 46% accepted, 8 enrolled. *Faculty:* 7 part-time/adjunct (3 women). Expenses: Contact institution. *Financial support:* In 2019–20, 26 students received support, including 10 teaching assistantships (averaging $4,000 per year); scholarships/grants and unspecified assistantships also available. Financial award application deadline: 1/15. In 2019, 9 doctorates, 1 other advanced degree awarded. *Program availability:* Part-time. *Application deadline:* For fall admission, 1/15 priority date for domestic and international students. Applications are processed on a rolling basis. *Application fee:* $65. Electronic applications accepted. *Application Contact:* Information Contact, 303-765-3136, E-mail: jointphd@iliff.edu. *Manager, DU/Iliff Joint PhD Program*, Rhonda Eaker, 303- 765-3136, E-mail: Rhonda.Eaker@du.edu.

**Graduate School of Professional Psychology** Students: 243 full-time (192 women), 84 part-time (44 women); includes 95 minority (18 Black or African American, non-Hispanic/Latino; 1 American Indian or Alaska Native, non-Hispanic/Latino; 18 Asian, non-Hispanic/Latino; 46 Hispanic/Latino; 1 Native Hawaiian or other Pacific Islander, non-Hispanic/Latino; 11 Two or more races, non-Hispanic/Latino), 9 international. Average age 27. 953 applicants, 27% accepted, 137 enrolled. *Faculty:* 23 full-time (15 women), 16 part-time/adjunct (9 women). Expenses: Contact institution. *Financial support:* In 2019–20, 249 students received support, including 20 teaching assistantships with tuition reimbursements available (averaging $2,835 per year); career-related internships or fieldwork, Federal Work-Study, institutionally sponsored loans, scholarships/grants, unspecified assistantships, and clinical assistantships also available. Support available to part-time students. Financial award application deadline: 2/15; financial award applicants required to submit FAFSA. In 2019, 117 master's, 35 doctorates, 152 other advanced degrees awarded. *Application deadline:* For fall admission, 1/11 for domestic and international students. *Application fee:* $65. Electronic applications accepted. *Application Contact:* Julie Schellman, Director of Enrollment, 303-871-2908, E-mail: Julie.Schellman@du.edu. *Dean*, Dr. Shelly Smith-Acuna, 303-871-3880, Fax: 303-871-4220, E-mail: shelly.smith-acuna@du.edu.

**Graduate School of Social Work** Students: 887 full-time (806 women), 212 part-time (191 women); includes 343 minority (85 Black or African American, non-Hispanic/Latino; 13 American Indian or Alaska Native, non-Hispanic/Latino; 26 Asian, non-Hispanic/Latino; 174 Hispanic/Latino; 3 Native Hawaiian or other Pacific Islander, non-Hispanic/Latino; 42 Two or more races, non-Hispanic/Latino), 5 international. Average age 29. 1,439 applicants, 86% accepted, 494 enrolled. *Faculty:* 44 full-time (33 women), 80 part-time/adjunct (70 women). Expenses: Contact institution. *Financial support:* In 2019–20, 504 students received support. Research assistantships, teaching assistantships, scholarships/grants, and unspecified assistantships available. Support available to part-time students. Financial award application deadline: 2/15; financial award applicants required to submit FAFSA. In 2019, 294 master's, 5 doctorates, 75 other advanced degrees awarded. *Program availability:* Part-time, evening/weekend, online learning. *Application deadline:* For fall admission, 1/15 priority date for domestic and international students. Applications are processed on a rolling basis. *Application fee:* $65. Electronic applications accepted. *Application Contact:* Roberto Garcia, Executive Director, Enrollment, 303-871-2602, E-mail: gsswadmission@du.edu. *Morris Endowed Dean and Professor*, Dr. Amanda Moore McBride, 303-871-2203, E-mail: gssw.communications@du.edu.

**Josef Korbel School of International Studies** Students: 208 full-time (112 women), 24 part-time (13 women); includes 50 minority (11 Black or African American, non-Hispanic/Latino; 10 Asian, non-Hispanic/Latino; 15 Hispanic/Latino; 14 Two or more races, non-Hispanic/Latino), 20 international. Average age 27. 718 applicants, 70% accepted, 88 enrolled. *Faculty:* 41 full-time (15 women), 14 part-time/adjunct (2 women). Expenses: Contact institution. *Financial support:* In 2019–20, 161 students received support, including 4 teaching assistantships with tuition reimbursements available (averaging $16,875 per year); research assistantships with tuition reimbursements available, career-related internships or fieldwork, Federal Work-Study, institutionally sponsored loans, scholarships/grants, and unspecified assistantships also available. Support available to part-time students. Financial award application deadline: 2/15; financial award applicants required to submit FAFSA. In 2019, 134 master's, 2 doctorates, 26 other advanced degrees awarded. *Program availability:* Part-time. *Application deadline:* For fall admission, 1/23 priority date for domestic and international students; for winter admission, 11/1 for domestic and international students. Applications are processed on a rolling basis. *Application fee:* $65. Electronic applications accepted. *Application Contact:* Admissions Contact, 303-871-2324, E-mail: korbeladm@du.edu. *Dean*, Dr. Fritz Mayer, 303-871-6338, E-mail: frederick.mayer@du.edu.

***Institute for Public Policy Studies*** Students: 13 full-time (8 women), 1 (woman) part-time; includes 4 minority (2 Black or African American, non-Hispanic/Latino; 2 Hispanic/Latino), 2 international. Average age 27. 70 applicants, 70% accepted, 8 enrolled. *Faculty:* 2 full-time (0 women), 1 part-time/adjunct (0 women). Expenses: Contact institution. *Financial support:* In 2019–20, 11 students received support, including 1 teaching assistantship with tuition reimbursement available (averaging $7,500 per year); Federal Work-Study, scholarships/grants, and unspecified assistantships also available. Financial award application deadline: 2/15; financial award applicants required to submit FAFSA. In 2019, 10 master's awarded. *Application deadline:* For fall admission, 1/23 priority date for domestic and international students; for winter admission, 11/1 priority date for domestic and international students. Applications are processed on a rolling basis. *Application fee:* $65. Electronic applications accepted. *Application Contact:* Institute for Public Policy Studies, E-mail: ipps@du.edu. *Director*, Dr. Richard Caldwell, 303-871-2468, Fax: 303-871-3066, E-mail: richard.caldwell@du.edu.

**Morgridge College of Education** Students: 477 full-time (385 women), 492 part-time (378 women); includes 266 minority (59 Black or African American, non-Hispanic/Latino; 7 American Indian or Alaska Native, non-Hispanic/Latino; 36 Asian, non-Hispanic/Latino; 128 Hispanic/Latino; 2 Native Hawaiian or other Pacific Islander, non-Hispanic/Latino; 34 Two or more races, non-Hispanic/Latino), 58 international. Average age 31. 1,252 applicants, 68% accepted, 420 enrolled. *Faculty:* 54 full-time (38 women),

28 part-time/adjunct (16 women). Expenses: Contact institution. *Financial support:* In 2019–20, 698 students received support, including 19 research assistantships with tuition reimbursements available (averaging $11,372 per year), 3 teaching assistantships with tuition reimbursements available (averaging $4,333 per year); career-related internships or fieldwork, Federal Work-Study, institutionally sponsored loans, scholarships/grants, and unspecified assistantships also available. Support available to part-time students. Financial award application deadline: 2/15; financial award applicants required to submit FAFSA. In 2019, 222 master's, 46 doctorates, 129 other advanced degrees awarded. *Program availability:* Part-time, evening/weekend, online learning. *Application deadline:* Applications are processed on a rolling basis. *Application fee:* $65. Electronic applications accepted. *Application Contact:* Jodi Dye, Director of Admissions, 303-871-2510, E-mail: jodi.dye@du.edu. *Dean,* Dr. Karen Riley, 303-871-3665, E-mail: karen.riley@du.edu.

**Sturm College of Law** Students: 792 full-time (424 women), 136 part-time (85 women); includes 204 minority (29 Black or African American, non-Hispanic/Latino; 1 American Indian or Alaska Native, non-Hispanic/Latino; 33 Asian, non-Hispanic/Latino; 112 Hispanic/Latino; 29 Two or more races, non-Hispanic/Latino), 29 international. Average age 29. 2,489 applicants, 53% accepted, 326 enrolled. *Faculty:* 60 full-time (31 women), 29 part-time/adjunct (10 women). Expenses: Contact institution. *Financial support:* In 2019–20, 683 students received support, including 6 teaching assistantships with tuition reimbursements available (averaging $33,333 per year); career-related internships or fieldwork, Federal Work-Study, institutionally sponsored loans, scholarships/grants, unspecified assistantships, and tutorships also available. Support available to part-time students. Financial award application deadline: 2/15; financial award applicants required to submit FAFSA. In 2019, 66 master's, 238 doctorates, 68 Certificates awarded. *Program availability:* Part-time, evening/weekend. *Application deadline:* Applications are processed on a rolling basis. *Application fee:* $65. Electronic applications accepted. *Application Contact:* Yvonne Cherena-Pacheco, Associate Director of Admissions, 303-871-6151, E-mail: admissions@law.du.edu. *Dean,* Dr. Bruce Smith, 303-871-6103, E-mail: bsmith@law.du.edu.

**University College** Students: 59 full-time (33 women), 1,893 part-time (1,210 women); includes 545 minority (133 Black or African American, non-Hispanic/Latino; 16 American Indian or Alaska Native, non-Hispanic/Latino; 64 Asian, non-Hispanic/Latino; 252 Hispanic/Latino; 4 Native Hawaiian or other Pacific Islander, non-Hispanic/Latino; 76 Two or more races, non-Hispanic/Latino), 78 international. Average age 32. 1,290 applicants, 91% accepted, 752 enrolled. *Faculty:* 104 part-time/adjunct (52 women). Expenses: Contact institution. *Financial support:* In 2019–20, 56 students received support. Teaching assistantships available. Financial award applicants required to submit FAFSA. In 2019, 457 master's, 181 other advanced degrees awarded. *Program availability:* Part-time, evening/weekend, 100% online, blended/hybrid learning. *Application deadline:* For fall admission, 6/19 priority date for domestic students, 6/14 priority date for international students; for winter admission, 10/25 priority date for domestic students, 9/27 priority date for international students; for spring admission, 2/7 priority date for domestic students, 1/10 priority date for international students; for summer admission, 4/24 priority date for domestic students, 3/27 priority date for international students. Applications are processed on a rolling basis. *Application fee:* $75. Electronic applications accepted. *Application Contact:* Admission Team, 303-871-2291, E-mail: ucoladm@du.edu. *Dean,* Dr. Michael McGuire, 303-871-3518, E-mail: michael.mcguire@du.edu.

## UNIVERSITY OF DETROIT MERCY, Detroit, MI 48221

**General Information** Independent-religious, coed, university. *Graduate housing:* Room and/or apartments available on a first-come, first-served basis to single students; on-campus housing not available to married students.

**GRADUATE UNITS**

**College of Business Administration** *Program availability:* Part-time, evening/weekend, 100% online, blended/hybrid learning. Electronic applications accepted.

**College of Engineering and Science** *Program availability:* Part-time, evening/weekend. Electronic applications accepted.

**College of Health Professions**

**College of Liberal Arts and Education** *Program availability:* Part-time, evening/weekend.

**School of Architecture**

**School of Dentistry**

**School of Law** *Program availability:* Part-time.

## UNIVERSITY OF DUBUQUE, Dubuque, IA 52001-5099

**General Information** Independent-religious, coed, comprehensive institution. *Graduate housing:* Rooms and/or apartments available on a first-come, first-served basis to single students and available to married students.

**GRADUATE UNITS**

**Program in Business Administration** *Program availability:* Part-time, evening/weekend. Electronic applications accepted.

**Program in Communication** *Program availability:* Part-time, evening/weekend. Electronic applications accepted.

**University of Dubuque Theological Seminary** *Program availability:* Part-time, 100% online, blended/hybrid learning. Electronic applications accepted.

## UNIVERSITY OF EAST-WEST MEDICINE, Sunnyvale, CA 94085-3922

**General Information** Proprietary, coed, graduate-only institution. *Graduate housing:* On-campus housing not available.

**GRADUATE UNITS**

**Graduate Programs**

## UNIVERSITY OF EVANSVILLE, Evansville, IN 47722

**General Information** Independent-religious, coed, comprehensive institution. *Graduate housing:* Room and/or apartments available to single students; on-campus housing not available to married students. *Research affiliation:* The New American Colleges and Universities (higher education administration), Independent Colleges of Indiana (higher education administration), Council of Independent Colleges (higher education administration), Military Family Research Institute (higher education administration).

**GRADUATE UNITS**

**Center for Adult Education** *Program availability:* Part-time, evening/weekend.

**College of Education and Health Sciences**

***School of Health Sciences*** *Program availability:* Part-time, evening/weekend.

## UNIVERSITY OF FAIRFAX, Vienna, VA 22182

**General Information** Proprietary, coed, graduate-only institution.

**GRADUATE UNITS**

**Graduate Programs**

## THE UNIVERSITY OF FINDLAY, Findlay, OH 45840-3653

**General Information** Independent-religious, coed, comprehensive institution. *Enrollment:* 4,714 graduate, professional, and undergraduate students; 636 full-time matriculated graduate/professional students (419 women), 554 part-time matriculated graduate/professional students (318 women). *Graduate housing:* Room and/or apartments available on a first-come, first-served basis to single students; on-campus housing not available to married students. *Student services:* Campus employment opportunities, campus safety program, career counseling, exercise/wellness program, free psychological counseling, international student services, low-cost health insurance, multicultural affairs office, services for students with disabilities, writing training. *Library facilities:* Shafer Library plus 4 others. *Collection:* Books: 82,484 (physical), 428,266 (digital/electronic); Serial titles: 356 (physical), 96,301 (digital/electronic); Databases: 197. Weekly public service hours: 74. *Research affiliation:* The Ohio State University Research Foundation (biology), Rollin M. Gerstacker Foundation (environmental research), U.S. Department of Agriculture (USDA) (wildlife research), U.S. Department of Education (DOE) (technology innovation, bilingual teaching research), U.S. Department of Health and Human Services (terrorism preparedness).

**Computer facilities:** 151 computers available on campus for general student use. A campuswide network can be accessed. Online class registration is available.
Website: http://www.findlay.edu/

**General Application Contact:** Amber Feehan, Assistant Director of Graduate Admissions, 419-434-6933, Fax: 419-434-4898, E-mail: feehan@findlay.edu.

**GRADUATE UNITS**

**Office of Graduate Admissions** Students: 688 full-time (430 women), 553 part-time (308 women), 170 international. Average age 28. 865 applicants, 31% accepted, 235 enrolled. Expenses: Contact institution. *Financial support:* In 2019–20, 10 research assistantships with partial tuition reimbursements (averaging $7,200 per year), 35 teaching assistantships with partial tuition reimbursements (averaging $7,200 per year) were awarded; Federal Work-Study, institutionally sponsored loans, and unspecified assistantships also available. Financial award applicants required to submit FAFSA. In 2019, 363 master's, 141 doctorates awarded. *Program availability:* Part-time, evening/weekend, 100% online, blended/hybrid learning. *Application deadline:* Applications are processed on a rolling basis. Electronic applications accepted. *Application Contact:* Amber Feehan, Graduate Admissions Counselor, 419-434-6933, Fax: 419-434-4898, E-mail: feehan@findlay.edu. *Director of Admissions, Interim,* Dave M. Emsweller, 419-434-4578, E-mail: emsweller@findlay.edu.

## UNIVERSITY OF FLORIDA, Gainesville, FL 32611

**General Information** State-supported, coed, university. CGS member. *Graduate housing:* Rooms and/or apartments available on a first-come, first-served basis to single and married students. *Research affiliation:* Los Alamos National Laboratory (high magnetic field research), National Center for Automated Information Research (law and business data), Oracle Corporation (database management), IBM (information infrastructure), Association of Universities for Research in Astronomy (Gemini multinational telescope).

**GRADUATE UNITS**

**College of Dentistry**

**College of Medicine** Electronic applications accepted.

**College of Veterinary Medicine** *Program availability:* Part-time.

**Graduate School** *Program availability:* Part-time, evening/weekend, online learning. Electronic applications accepted.

***College of Agricultural and Life Sciences*** *Program availability:* Part-time. Electronic applications accepted.

***College of Design, Construction and Planning*** *Program availability:* Part-time, online learning. Electronic applications accepted.

***College of Education*** *Program availability:* Part-time, evening/weekend, online learning. Electronic applications accepted.

***College of Health and Human Performance*** *Program availability:* Part-time. Electronic applications accepted.

***College of Journalism and Communications*** *Program availability:* Part-time, online learning. Electronic applications accepted.

***College of Liberal Arts and Sciences*** *Program availability:* Part-time. Electronic applications accepted.

***College of Nursing*** *Program availability:* Part-time. Electronic applications accepted.

***College of Pharmacy*** *Program availability:* Part-time, evening/weekend, online learning. Electronic applications accepted.

***College of Public Health and Health Professions*** *Program availability:* Part-time. Electronic applications accepted.

***College of The Arts*** *Program availability:* Online learning. Electronic applications accepted.

***Herbert Wertheim College of Engineering*** *Program availability:* Part-time, online learning. Electronic applications accepted.

***School of Natural Resources and Environment*** Electronic applications accepted.

***Warrington College of Business Administration*** *Program availability:* Part-time, evening/weekend, online learning. Electronic applications accepted.

**Levin College of Law** Electronic applications accepted.

## UNIVERSITY OF FORT LAUDERDALE, Lauderhill, FL 33313

**General Information** Independent-religious, coed, comprehensive institution.

**GRADUATE UNITS**

**Graduate Program**

## UNIVERSITY OF GEORGIA, Athens, GA 30602

**General Information** State-supported, coed, university. CGS member. *Graduate housing:* Rooms and/or apartments available on a first-come, first-served basis to single and married students. *Research affiliation:* Skidaway Institute of Oceanography, Southeast Water Laboratory, Russell Research Laboratory, Organization for Tropical Studies.

**GRADUATE UNITS**

**Biomedical and Health Sciences Institute**

**College of Agricultural and Environmental Sciences** Electronic applications accepted.
***Institute of Plant Breeding, Genetics and Genomics***
**College of Education** Electronic applications accepted.
**College of Engineering**
**College of Environment and Design**
**College of Family and Consumer Sciences** Electronic applications accepted.
**College of Pharmacy** Electronic applications accepted.
**College of Public Health**
***Institute of Gerontology***
**College of Veterinary Medicine** Electronic applications accepted.
**Eugene P. Odum School of Ecology** Electronic applications accepted.
**Franklin College of Arts and Sciences** Electronic applications accepted.
***Artificial Intelligence Center*** Electronic applications accepted.
***Hugh Hodgson School of Music*** Electronic applications accepted.
***Institute for Women's Studies***
***Lamar Dodd School of Art*** Electronic applications accepted.
**Grady College of Journalism and Mass Communication** Electronic applications accepted.
**Institute of Bioinformatics**
**School of Law** Electronic applications accepted.
**School of Public and International Affairs** Electronic applications accepted.
**School of Social Work** *Program availability:* Part-time, evening/weekend. Electronic applications accepted.
**Terry College of Business** Electronic applications accepted.
***J.M. Tull School of Accounting*** Electronic applications accepted.
**Warnell School of Forestry and Natural Resources** Electronic applications accepted.

## UNIVERSITY OF GUAM, Mangilao, GU 96923

**General Information** Territory-supported, coed, comprehensive institution. *Graduate housing:* Room and/or apartments available on a first-come, first-served basis to single students; on-campus housing not available to married students. Housing application deadline: 5/1. *Research affiliation:* Bernice Pauahi Bishop Museum (science, cultural preservation), Pilar Project, Inc. (salvage of artifacts, archaeology), Cancer Research Center of Hawaii (cancer research).

**GRADUATE UNITS**

**Office of Graduate Studies** *Program availability:* Part-time.
***College of Liberal Arts and Social Sciences*** *Program availability:* Part-time.
***College of Natural and Applied Sciences***
***School of Business and Public Administration*** *Program availability:* Part-time.
***School of Education*** *Program availability:* Part-time.

## UNIVERSITY OF GUELPH, Guelph, ON N1G 2W1, Canada

**General Information** Province-supported, coed, university. *Graduate housing:* Rooms and/or apartments available to single and married students. Housing application deadline: 5/28.

**GRADUATE UNITS**

**Office of Graduate and Postdoctoral Studies** Students: 2,765 full-time (1,629 women), 204 part-time (129 women). *Faculty:* 736. Expenses: Contact institution. *Financial support:* Fellowships with full tuition reimbursements, research assistantships, teaching assistantships with full tuition reimbursements, career-related internships or fieldwork, Federal Work-Study, institutionally sponsored loans, scholarships/grants, tuition waivers (full), unspecified assistantships, and bursaries available. Support available to part-time students. *Program availability:* Part-time, evening/weekend, online learning. *Application deadline:* Applications are processed on a rolling basis. *Application fee:* $110. Electronic applications accepted. *Application Contact:* Nick Pankerichan, Manager, Graduate Admission and Marketing, 519-824-4120 Ext. 56198, Fax: 519-766-0143, E-mail: gradonln@uoguelph.ca. *Assistant VP - Graduate Studies*, Dr. B Bradshaw, 519-824-4120 Ext. 58460, E-mail: bbradsha@uoguelph.ca.
***Collaborative International Development Studies*** *Program availability:* Part-time.
***College of Arts*** *Program availability:* Part-time.
***College of Biological Science*** *Program availability:* Part-time. Electronic applications accepted.
***College of Management and Economics***
***College of Physical and Engineering Science*** *Program availability:* Part-time.
***College of Social and Applied Human Sciences*** *Program availability:* Part-time.
***Ontario Agricultural College*** *Program availability:* Part-time, online learning.
**Ontario Veterinary College**
***Graduate Programs in Veterinary Sciences***

## UNIVERSITY OF HARTFORD, West Hartford, CT 06117-1599

**General Information** Independent, coed, comprehensive institution. CGS member. *Enrollment:* 6,773 graduate, professional, and undergraduate students; 704 full-time matriculated graduate/professional students (441 women), 1,231 part-time matriculated graduate/professional students (732 women). *Enrollment by degree level:* 1,554 master's, 357 doctoral, 24 other advanced degrees. *Graduate faculty:* 149 full-time (76 women), 72 part-time/adjunct (42 women). *Tuition:* Full-time $23,700; part-time $645 per credit. *Required fees:* $510; $510 per unit. Tuition and fees vary according to course load, degree level and program. *Graduate housing:* On-campus housing not available. *Student services:* Campus employment opportunities, career counseling, free psychological counseling, international student services, low-cost health insurance, multicultural affairs office, services for students with disabilities. *Library facilities:* Mortensen Library plus 1 other. *Collection:* Books: 287,556 (physical), 4,624 (digital/electronic); Serial titles: 56,360 (digital/electronic); Databases: 213. Weekly public service hours: 104.

**Computer facilities:** 400 computers available on campus for general student use. A campuswide network can be accessed. Online class registration, student Web pages are available.
Website: http://www.hartford.edu/

**General Application Contact:** Erica Brilhart, Director of Graduate Admissions, 860-768-4371, Fax: 860-768-5160, E-mail: brilhart@mail.hartford.edu.

**GRADUATE UNITS**

**Barney School of Business** Students: 75 full-time (40 women), 665 part-time (340 women); includes 193 minority (62 Black or African American, non-Hispanic/Latino; 1 American Indian or Alaska Native, non-Hispanic/Latino; 64 Asian, non-Hispanic/Latino; 55 Hispanic/Latino; 11 Two or more races, non-Hispanic/Latino), 33 international. Average age 33. 212 applicants, 81% accepted, 134 enrolled. *Faculty:* 27 full-time (11 women), 10 part-time/adjunct (1 woman). Expenses: Contact institution. *Financial support:* In 2019–20, 40 research assistantships (averaging $3,600 per year) were awarded; fellowships, career-related internships or fieldwork, and scholarships/grants also available. Financial award application deadline: 5/1. In 2019, 196 master's awarded. *Program availability:* Part-time, evening/weekend. *Application deadline:* Applications are processed on a rolling basis. *Application fee:* $45. Electronic applications accepted. *Application Contact:* Erica Brilhart, Director of Graduate Admissions, 860-768-5102, E-mail: gradstudy@hartford.edu. *Interim Dean*, Stephen Mulready, 860-768-4243, Fax: 860-768-4198.

**College of Arts and Sciences** Students: 159 full-time (120 women), 217 part-time (160 women); includes 114 minority (38 Black or African American, non-Hispanic/Latino; 1 American Indian or Alaska Native, non-Hispanic/Latino; 19 Asian, non-Hispanic/Latino; 42 Hispanic/Latino; 14 Two or more races, non-Hispanic/Latino), 17 international. Average age 29. 325 applicants, 54% accepted, 98 enrolled. *Faculty:* 32 full-time (17 women), 19 part-time/adjunct (9 women). Expenses: Contact institution. *Financial support:* In 2019–20, 15 research assistantships (averaging $2,000 per year), 29 teaching assistantships (averaging $2,600 per year) were awarded; fellowships, career-related internships or fieldwork, Federal Work-Study, and tuition waivers (partial) also available. Support available to part-time students. Financial award application deadline: 6/1; financial award applicants required to submit FAFSA. In 2019, 86 master's, 38 doctorates awarded. *Program availability:* Part-time, evening/weekend. *Application deadline:* For fall admission, 7/1 priority date for domestic students; for spring admission, 12/1 for domestic students. Applications are processed on a rolling basis. *Application fee:* $45. Electronic applications accepted. *Application Contact:* Renee Murphy, Assistant Director of Graduate Admissions, 860-768-4371, Fax: 860-768-5160, E-mail: rmurphy@hartford.edu. *Dean*, Dr. Joseph C. Voelker, 860-768-4103, Fax: 860-768-5043, E-mail: voelker@hartford.edu.

**College of Education, Nursing, and Health Professions** Students: 230 full-time (160 women), 240 part-time (210 women); includes 104 minority (36 Black or African American, non-Hispanic/Latino; 1 American Indian or Alaska Native, non-Hispanic/Latino; 14 Asian, non-Hispanic/Latino; 44 Hispanic/Latino; 9 Two or more races, non-Hispanic/Latino), 20 international. Average age 33. 111 applicants, 91% accepted, 85 enrolled. *Faculty:* 30 full-time (20 women), 24 part-time/adjunct (18 women). Expenses: Contact institution. *Financial support:* In 2019–20, 4 research assistantships (averaging $4,500 per year) were awarded; teaching assistantships, institutionally sponsored loans, and unspecified assistantships also available. Financial award application deadline: 6/1; financial award applicants required to submit FAFSA. In 2019, 137 master's, 8 doctorates, 8 other advanced degrees awarded. *Program availability:* Part-time, evening/weekend. *Application deadline:* Applications are processed on a rolling basis. *Application fee:* $45. Electronic applications accepted. *Application Contact:* Susan Brown, Assistant Dean of Academic Services, 860-768-4692, Fax: 860-768-5043, E-mail: brown@hartford.edu. *Dean*, Dr. Dorothy A. Zeiser, 860-768-4649, Fax: 860-768-5043.

**College of Engineering, Technology and Architecture** Students: 44 full-time (15 women), 78 part-time (9 women); includes 29 minority (9 Black or African American, non-Hispanic/Latino; 1 American Indian or Alaska Native, non-Hispanic/Latino; 3 Asian, non-Hispanic/Latino; 15 Hispanic/Latino; 1 Two or more races, non-Hispanic/Latino), 24 international. Average age 29. 84 applicants, 65% accepted, 27 enrolled. *Faculty:* 13 full-time (0 women), 14 part-time/adjunct (2 women). Expenses: Contact institution. *Financial support:* In 2019–20, 24 fellowships (averaging $2,500 per year), 1 research assistantship (averaging $5,000 per year), 2 teaching assistantships (averaging $8,200 per year) were awarded; Federal Work-Study and unspecified assistantships also available. Support available to part-time students. Financial award application deadline: 6/1; financial award applicants required to submit FAFSA. In 2019, 50 master's awarded. *Program availability:* Part-time, evening/weekend. *Application deadline:* Applications are processed on a rolling basis. *Application fee:* $45. Electronic applications accepted. *Application Contact:* Laurie Granstrand, Manager of Student Services, 860-768-4858, E-mail: granstran@hartford.edu. *Dean*, Louis Manzione, 860-768-4112, Fax: 860-768-5073.

**Hartford Art School** Students: 41 full-time (21 women); includes 13 minority (2 Black or African American, non-Hispanic/Latino; 3 Asian, non-Hispanic/Latino; 6 Hispanic/Latino; 2 Two or more races, non-Hispanic/Latino), 1 international. Average age 37. 22 applicants, 18% accepted, 2 enrolled. *Faculty:* 3 full-time (1 woman), 2 part-time/adjunct (0 women). Expenses: Contact institution. *Financial support:* In 2019–20, 10 fellowships with partial tuition reimbursements (averaging $6,000 per year) were awarded; teaching assistantships and Federal Work-Study also available. Support available to part-time students. Financial award application deadline: 6/1; financial award applicants required to submit FAFSA. In 2019, 21 master's awarded. *Program availability:* Part-time. *Application deadline:* For fall admission, 3/1 priority date for domestic students. Applications are processed on a rolling basis. *Application fee:* $45. Electronic applications accepted. *Application Contact:* Ellen Carey, Director, 860-768-4616, Fax: 860-768-5160, E-mail: ecarey@mail.hartford.edu. *Dean*, Power Boothe, 860-768-4391.

**The Hartt School** Students: 155 full-time (85 women), 31 part-time (13 women); includes 22 minority (3 Black or African American, non-Hispanic/Latino; 7 Asian, non-Hispanic/Latino; 5 Hispanic/Latino; 7 Two or more races, non-Hispanic/Latino), 86 international. Average age 27. 186 applicants, 58% accepted, 49 enrolled. *Faculty:* 36 full-time (5 women), 31 part-time/adjunct (13 women). Expenses: Contact institution. *Financial support:* Fellowships, teaching assistantships, and Federal Work-Study available. Support available to part-time students. Financial award application deadline: 6/1; financial award applicants required to submit FAFSA. In 2019, 46 master's, 7 doctorates, 10 other advanced degrees awarded. *Program availability:* Part-time. *Application deadline:* For fall admission, 4/1 priority date for domestic students. Applications are processed on a rolling basis. *Application fee:* $45. Electronic applications accepted. *Application Contact:* Lynne Johnson, Director of Admissions, 860-768-4115, Fax: 860-768-4441, E-mail: johnson@hartford.edu. *Dean*, Dr. Malcolm Morrison, 860-768-4468, E-mail: morrison@mail.hartford.edu.

## UNIVERSITY OF HAWAII AT HILO, Hilo, HI 96720-4091

**General Information** State-supported, coed, comprehensive institution. *Graduate housing:* Rooms and/or apartments available on a first-come, first-served basis to single and married students.

**GRADUATE UNITS**

**Program in Clinical Psychopharmacology** Electronic applications accepted.
**Program in Counseling Psychology**
**Program in Education** *Program availability:* Part-time, evening/weekend. Electronic applications accepted.

**Program in Hawaiian and Indigenous Language and Culture Revitalization** Electronic applications accepted.

**Program in Hawaiian Language and Literature** Electronic applications accepted.

**Program in Indigenous Language and Culture Education** Electronic applications accepted.

**Program in Nursing Practice** Electronic applications accepted.

**Program in Pharmaceutical Sciences** Electronic applications accepted.

**Program in Pharmacy** Electronic applications accepted.

**Program in Teaching** Electronic applications accepted.

**Program in Tropical Conservation Biology and Environmental Science** Electronic applications accepted.

## UNIVERSITY OF HAWAII AT MANOA, Honolulu, HI 96822

**General Information** State-supported, coed, university. CGS member. *Graduate housing:* Rooms and/or apartments available to single and married students. Housing application deadline: 5/1. *Research affiliation:* Hawaiian Volcano Observatory (geology, geophysics), Honolulu Academy of Arts, East-West Center (communication, geography, economics), U.S. Geological Survey (USGS), Hawaii Agriculture Research Center, Bernice Pauahi Bishop Museum (anthropology, zoology).

**GRADUATE UNITS**

**John A. Burns School of Medicine** *Program availability:* Part-time.

***Graduate Programs in Biomedical Sciences*** *Program availability:* Part-time.

**Office of Graduate Education** *Program availability:* Part-time. Electronic applications accepted.

***College of Arts and Humanities*** *Program availability:* Part-time.

***College of Education*** *Program availability:* Part-time, evening/weekend.

***College of Engineering*** *Program availability:* Part-time.

***College of Languages, Linguistics and Literature*** *Program availability:* Part-time.

***College of Natural Sciences*** *Program availability:* Part-time.

***College of Social Sciences*** *Program availability:* Part-time, evening/weekend.

***College of Tropical Agriculture and Human Resources*** *Program availability:* Part-time.

***Hawai'inuiakea School of Hawaiian Knowledge*** *Program availability:* Part-time.

***School of Nursing and Dental Hygiene*** *Program availability:* Part-time, online learning.

***School of Ocean and Earth Science and Technology*** *Program availability:* Part-time.

***School of Pacific and Asian Studies*** *Program availability:* Part-time.

***School of Social Work*** *Program availability:* Part-time.

***School of Travel Industry Management*** *Program availability:* Part-time. Electronic applications accepted.

***Shidler College of Business*** *Program availability:* Part-time, evening/weekend.

**School of Architecture** *Program availability:* Part-time.

**William S. Richardson School of Law**

## UNIVERSITY OF HOLY CROSS, New Orleans, LA 70131-7399

**General Information** Independent-religious, coed, comprehensive institution. *Graduate housing:* On-campus housing not available.

**GRADUATE UNITS**

**Graduate Programs** *Program availability:* Part-time, evening/weekend, online learning.

## UNIVERSITY OF HOUSTON, Houston, TX 77204

**General Information** State-supported, coed, university. CGS member. *Graduate housing:* Rooms and/or apartments available on a first-come, first-served basis to single and married students. *Research affiliation:* Keck Consortium.

**GRADUATE UNITS**

**Bauer College of Business** *Program availability:* Part-time, evening/weekend. Electronic applications accepted.

**College of Education** Students: 381 full-time (303 women), 539 part-time (410 women); includes 541 minority (221 Black or African American, non-Hispanic/Latino; 5 American Indian or Alaska Native, non-Hispanic/Latino; 88 Asian, non-Hispanic/Latino; 203 Hispanic/Latino; 1 Native Hawaiian or other Pacific Islander, non-Hispanic/Latino; 23 Two or more races, non-Hispanic/Latino), 50 international. Average age 35. 511 applicants, 68% accepted, 255 enrolled. *Faculty:* 89 full-time (65 women), 7 part-time/adjunct (6 women). Expenses: Contact institution. *Financial support:* In 2019–20, 47 students received support, including 2 fellowships with full tuition reimbursements available (averaging $2,000 per year), 63 research assistantships with full tuition reimbursements available (averaging $11,567 per year), 60 teaching assistantships with full tuition reimbursements available (averaging $9,267 per year); career-related internships or fieldwork, Federal Work-Study, institutionally sponsored loans, scholarships/grants, traineeships, health care benefits, and unspecified assistantships also available. Support available to part-time students. Financial award application deadline: 2/1; financial award applicants required to submit FAFSA. In 2019, 223 master's, 37 doctorates awarded. *Program availability:* Part-time, evening/weekend, 100% online, blended/hybrid learning. *Application fee:* $80 ($75 for international students). Electronic applications accepted. *Application Contact:* Bridgette Jones, Director of Student Affairs, 713-743-2978, E-mail: bajones5@uh.edu. *Dean*, Dr. Robert H. McPherson, 713-743-5003, Fax: 713-743-9870, E-mail: bmcph@uh.edu.

**College of Liberal Arts and Social Sciences** *Program availability:* Part-time, online learning. Electronic applications accepted.

***Jack J. Valenti School of Communication*** *Program availability:* Part-time. Electronic applications accepted.

**College of Natural Sciences and Mathematics** *Program availability:* Part-time, online learning. Electronic applications accepted.

**College of Nursing** Students: 18 full-time (12 women), 33 part-time (32 women); includes 30 minority (13 Black or African American, non-Hispanic/Latino; 4 Asian, non-Hispanic/Latino; 12 Hispanic/Latino; 1 Native Hawaiian or other Pacific Islander, non-Hispanic/Latino). Average age 36. 38 applicants, 74% accepted, 20 enrolled. *Faculty:* 8 full-time (7 women). Expenses: Contact institution. *Financial support:* In 2019–20, 19 students received support. Federal Work-Study, scholarships/grants, and unspecified assistantships available. Support available to part-time students. Financial award application deadline: 7/1; financial award applicants required to submit FAFSA. In 2019, 12 master's awarded. *Application deadline:* For fall admission, 6/1 for domestic and international students; for spring admission, 11/1 for domestic and international students; for summer admission, 4/1 for domestic and international students. *Application fee:* $75. Electronic applications accepted. *Application Contact:* Tammy N. Whatley, Student Affairs Director, 832-842-8220, E-mail: tnwhatley@uh.edu. *Dean*, Dr. Kathryn Tart, 832-842-8200, E-mail: kmtart@uh.edu.

**College of Optometry** *Program availability:* Part-time. Electronic applications accepted.

**College of Pharmacy** *Program availability:* Part-time. Electronic applications accepted.

**College of Technology** *Program availability:* Part-time. Electronic applications accepted.

**Conrad N. Hilton College of Hotel and Restaurant Management** *Program availability:* Part-time. Electronic applications accepted.

**Cullen College of Engineering** *Program availability:* Part-time.

**Gerald D. Hines College of Architecture and Design** Students: 92 full-time (40 women), 6 part-time (2 women); includes 23 minority (1 Black or African American, non-Hispanic/Latino; 1 American Indian or Alaska Native, non-Hispanic/Latino; 9 Asian, non-Hispanic/Latino; 9 Hispanic/Latino; 3 Two or more races, non-Hispanic/Latino), 20 international. Average age 28. 192 applicants, 45% accepted, 47 enrolled. *Faculty:* 15 full-time (4 women), 13 part-time/adjunct (3 women). Expenses: Contact institution. *Financial support:* In 2019–20, 8 students received support, including 8 research assistantships with tuition reimbursements available (averaging $1,358 per year), 5 teaching assistantships (averaging $3,487 per year); career-related internships or fieldwork, institutionally sponsored loans, scholarships/grants, and unspecified assistantships also available. Financial award application deadline: 1/1; financial award applicants required to submit FAFSA. In 2019, 21 master's awarded. *Application deadline:* For fall admission, 2/1 priority date for domestic students, 2/1 for international students. Applications are processed on a rolling basis. *Application fee:* $50. Electronic applications accepted. *Application Contact:* Trang Phan, Assistant Dean, 713-743-2400, Fax: 713-743-2358, E-mail: tphan@uh.edu. *Dean*, Patricia Belton Oliver, 713-743-2400, Fax: 713-743-2358, E-mail: poliver@central.uh.edu.

**Graduate College of Social Work** *Program availability:* Part-time.

**Hobby School of Public Affairs** Students: 36 full-time (25 women), 6 part-time (2 women); includes 19 minority (5 Black or African American, non-Hispanic/Latino; 3 Asian, non-Hispanic/Latino; 11 Hispanic/Latino), 4 international. Average age 25. 43 applicants, 79% accepted, 23 enrolled. *Faculty:* 5 full-time (0 women), 4 part-time/adjunct (2 women). Expenses: Contact institution. *Financial support:* In 2019–20, 53 students received support. Fellowships, research assistantships, teaching assistantships, career-related internships or fieldwork, Federal Work-Study, institutionally sponsored loans, scholarships/grants, traineeships, and unspecified assistantships available. Support available to part-time students. Financial award application deadline: 6/15; financial award applicants required to submit FAFSA. In 2019, 14 master's awarded. *Program availability:* Part-time. *Application deadline:* For fall admission, 6/15 for domestic and international students; for spring admission, 12/1 for domestic and international students. Applications are processed on a rolling basis. *Application fee:* $75 ($125 for international students). Electronic applications accepted. *Application Contact:* Scott Mason, Program Manager 2, 713-743-5572, Fax: 713-743-3978, E-mail: smason@uh.edu. *Founding Dean*, Kirk Watson, Fax: 713-743-3978, E-mail: kpwatson@uh.edu.

**Kathrine G. McGovern College of the Arts**

***Moores School of Music*** *Program availability:* Part-time. Electronic applications accepted.

***School of Art*** Electronic applications accepted.

***School of Theatre and Dance*** *Program availability:* Part-time. Electronic applications accepted.

**University of Houston Law Center** Students: 626 full-time (323 women), 124 part-time (56 women); includes 297 minority (45 Black or African American, non-Hispanic/Latino; 2 American Indian or Alaska Native, non-Hispanic/Latino; 75 Asian, non-Hispanic/Latino; 154 Hispanic/Latino; 1 Native Hawaiian or other Pacific Islander, non-Hispanic/Latino; 20 Two or more races, non-Hispanic/Latino), 32 international. Average age 26. 2,628 applicants, 35% accepted, 209 enrolled. *Faculty:* 56 full-time (23 women), 166 part-time/adjunct (54 women). Expenses: Contact institution. *Financial support:* In 2019–20, 570 students received support, including 35 fellowships (averaging $3,215 per year); research assistantships, career-related internships or fieldwork, Federal Work-Study, scholarships/grants, and tuition waivers (full and partial) also available. Support available to part-time students. Financial award application deadline: 3/15; financial award applicants required to submit FAFSA. In 2019, 65 master's, 231 doctorates awarded. *Program availability:* Part-time, evening/weekend. *Application deadline:* For fall admission, 2/15 for domestic and international students. Applications are processed on a rolling basis. Electronic applications accepted. *Application Contact:* Pilar Mensah, Assistant Dean for Admissions, 713-743-2280, Fax: 713-743-2194, E-mail: lpmensah@central.uh.edu. *Dean and Professor of Law*, Leonard M. Baynes, 713-743-2100, Fax: 713-743-2122, E-mail: lbaynes@central.uh.edu.

## UNIVERSITY OF HOUSTON–CLEAR LAKE, Houston, TX 77058-1002

**General Information** State-supported, coed, comprehensive institution. CGS member. *Graduate housing:* Rooms and/or apartments available on a first-come, first-served basis to single students and available to married students. *Research affiliation:* NASA–Johnson Space Center (computer science, computer engineering), Baylor College of Medicine (life sciences), Schlumberger (ergonomic software).

**GRADUATE UNITS**

**School of Business** *Program availability:* Part-time, evening/weekend. Electronic applications accepted.

**School of Education** *Program availability:* Part-time, evening/weekend. Electronic applications accepted.

**School of Human Sciences and Humanities** *Program availability:* Part-time, evening/weekend.

**School of Science and Computer Engineering** *Program availability:* Part-time, evening/weekend.

## UNIVERSITY OF HOUSTON - DOWNTOWN, Houston, TX 77002

**General Information** State-supported, coed, comprehensive institution. *Enrollment:* 14,640 graduate, professional, and undergraduate students; 132 full-time matriculated graduate/professional students (76 women), 1,372 part-time matriculated graduate/professional students (802 women). *Enrollment by degree level:* 1,504 master's. *Graduate faculty:* 74 full-time (27 women), 22 part-time/adjunct (10 women). *International tuition:* $13,734 full-time. *Tuition, area resident:* Full-time $6948; part-time $386 per credit hour. Tuition, state resident: full-time $6948; part-time $386 per credit hour. Tuition, nonresident: full-time $13,644; part-time $758 per credit hour. *Required fees:* $1326; $1172. Tuition and fees vary according to program. *Graduate housing:* On-campus housing not available. *Student services:* Campus employment opportunities, campus safety program, career counseling, exercise/wellness program, free psychological counseling, international student services, low-cost health insurance, multicultural affairs office, services for students with disabilities, teacher training. *Library* *facilities:* W. I. Dykes Library. *Collection:* Study areas open 24 hours, 5–7 days a week; students can reserve study rooms.

**Computer facilities:** A campuswide network can be accessed from off campus. Online class registration is available.
Website: http://www.uhd.edu/

**General Application Contact:** Ceshia Love, Director of Admissions, 713-221-8093, Fax: 713-221-8658, E-mail: gradadmissions@uhd.edu.

**GRADUATE UNITS**

**College of Humanities and Social Sciences** Students: 36 full-time (29 women), 113 part-time (86 women); includes 99 minority (57 Black or African American, non-Hispanic/Latino; 1 American Indian or Alaska Native, non-Hispanic/Latino; 2 Asian, non-Hispanic/Latino; 32 Hispanic/Latino; 7 Two or more races, non-Hispanic/Latino), 2 international. Average age 38. 82 applicants, 83% accepted, 54 enrolled. *Faculty:* 16 full-time (3 women), 4 part-time/adjunct (2 women). Expenses: Contact institution. *Financial support:* Federal Work-Study and scholarships/grants available. Financial award application deadline: 4/1; financial award applicants required to submit FAFSA. In 2019, 39 master's awarded. *Program availability:* Part-time, evening/weekend, 100% online. *Application deadline:* For fall admission, 8/9 for domestic students; for spring admission, 12/2 for domestic students; for summer admission, 5/17 for domestic students. *Application fee:* $35 ($80 for international students). Electronic applications accepted. *Application Contact:* Ceshia Love, Director, Admissions, 713-221-8093, Fax: 713-223-7408, E-mail: gradadmissions@uhd.edu. *Dean,* Dr. DoVeanna Fulton, 713-221-8009, Fax: 713-223-7465, E-mail: fultond@uhd.edu.

**College of Public Service** Students: 33 full-time (22 women), 82 part-time (60 women); includes 78 minority (24 Black or African American, non-Hispanic/Latino; 2 Asian, non-Hispanic/Latino; 51 Hispanic/Latino; 1 Two or more races, non-Hispanic/Latino), 4 international. Average age 35. 46 applicants, 89% accepted, 36 enrolled. *Faculty:* 24 full-time (14 women), 2 part-time/adjunct (both women). Expenses: Contact institution. *Financial support:* Federal Work-Study and scholarships/grants available. Financial award application deadline: 4/1; financial award applicants required to submit FAFSA. In 2019, 39 master's awarded. *Program availability:* Part-time, evening/weekend, 100% online. *Application fee:* $35 ($80 for international students). Electronic applications accepted. *Application Contact:* Ceshia Love, Director of Admissions, 713-221-8093, Fax: 713-223-7408, E-mail: gradadmissions@uhd.edu. *Dean,* Dr. Jonathan Schwartz, 713-221-5720, Fax: 713-226-5274, E-mail: schwartzj@uhd.edu.

**College of Sciences and Technology** Students: 62 full-time (25 women), 95 part-time (41 women); includes 88 minority (23 Black or African American, non-Hispanic/Latino; 36 Asian, non-Hispanic/Latino; 27 Hispanic/Latino; 2 Two or more races, non-Hispanic/Latino), 28 international. Average age 33. 67 applicants, 88% accepted, 40 enrolled. *Faculty:* 14 full-time (7 women). Expenses: Contact institution. *Financial support:* Federal Work-Study and scholarships/grants available. Financial award application deadline: 4/1; financial award applicants required to submit FAFSA. In 2019, 51 master's awarded. *Program availability:* Part-time, evening/weekend. *Application deadline:* For fall admission, 8/9 for domestic students, 5/1 for international students; for spring admission, 12/2 for domestic students; for summer admission, 6/1 for domestic students, 4/1 for international students. *Application fee:* $35 ($80 for international students). Electronic applications accepted. *Application Contact:* Ceshia Love, Director of Admissions, 713-221-8093, Fax: 713-221-8658, E-mail: gradadmissions@uhd.edu. *Dean,* Dr. J. Akif Uzman, 713-221-8019, E-mail: st_dean@uhd.edu.

**Marilyn Davies College of Business** Students: 1 full-time (0 women), 1,082 part-time (615 women); includes 852 minority (412 Black or African American, non-Hispanic/Latino; 1 American Indian or Alaska Native, non-Hispanic/Latino; 105 Asian, non-Hispanic/Latino; 310 Hispanic/Latino; 4 Native Hawaiian or other Pacific Islander, non-Hispanic/Latino; 20 Two or more races, non-Hispanic/Latino), 37 international. Average age 34. 457 applicants, 89% accepted, 311 enrolled. *Faculty:* 20 full-time (3 women), 16 part-time/adjunct (6 women). Expenses: Contact institution. *Financial support:* Federal Work-Study and scholarships/grants available. Financial award application deadline: 4/1; financial award applicants required to submit FAFSA. In 2019, 427 master's awarded. *Program availability:* Part-time, evening/weekend, online only, 100% online. *Application deadline:* For fall admission, 7/15 for domestic students. *Application fee:* $35 ($80 for international students). Electronic applications accepted. *Application Contact:* Ceshia Love, Director of Admissions, 713-221-8093, Fax: 713-223-7408, E-mail: gradadmissions@uhd.edu. *Dean,* Dr. Charles E. Gengler, 713-221-8179, Fax: 713-221-8675, E-mail: genglerc@uhd.edu.

## UNIVERSITY OF HOUSTON–VICTORIA, Victoria, TX 77901-4450

**General Information** State-supported, coed, upper-level institution. *Graduate housing:* On-campus housing not available.

**GRADUATE UNITS**

**School of Arts and Sciences** *Program availability:* Part-time, evening/weekend, 100% online, blended/hybrid learning. Electronic applications accepted.

**School of Business Administration** *Program availability:* Part-time, evening/weekend, online learning. Electronic applications accepted.

**School of Education, Health Professions and Human Development** *Program availability:* Part-time, evening/weekend, online learning. Electronic applications accepted.

## UNIVERSITY OF IDAHO, Moscow, ID 83844-2282

**General Information** State-supported, coed, university. CGS member. *Enrollment:* 11,926 graduate, professional, and undergraduate students; 1,411 full-time matriculated graduate/professional students (620 women), 714 part-time matriculated graduate/professional students (312 women). *Enrollment by degree level:* 1,270 master's, 847 doctoral, 35 other advanced degrees. *Graduate faculty:* 444 full-time (148 women), 34 part-time/adjunct (14 women). Tuition, state resident: full-time $7753.80; part-time $502 per credit hour. Tuition, nonresident: full-time $26,990; part-time $1571 per credit hour. *Required fees:* $2122.20; $47 per credit hour. *Graduate housing:* Rooms and/or apartments available on a first-come, first-served basis to single and married students. *Student services:* Campus employment opportunities, campus safety program, career counseling, exercise/wellness program, free psychological counseling, grant writing training, international student services, low-cost health insurance, multicultural affairs office, services for students with disabilities, writing training. *Library facilities:* University of Idaho Library plus 1 other. *Collection:* Books: 1.5 million (physical), 1.3 million (digital/electronic); Serial titles: 109,553 (physical), 177,970 (digital/electronic). *Research affiliation:* Battelle Energy Alliance LLC (energy research), Columbia River Inter-Tribal Fish Commission (fish research), J. A. and Kathryn Albertson Foundation, Inc. (education), Howard Hughes Medical Institute (undergraduate research education), M. J. Murdock Charitable Trust (equipment support), Prograno (plant sciences).

**Computer facilities:** 510 computers available on campus for general student use. A campuswide network can be accessed. Online class registration is available.
Website: http://www.uidaho.edu/

**GRADUATE UNITS**

**College of Graduate Studies** Students: 1,090 full-time (472 women), 704 part-time (307 women); includes 213 minority (18 Black or African American, non-Hispanic/Latino; 29 American Indian or Alaska Native, non-Hispanic/Latino; 31 Asian, non-Hispanic/Latino; 103 Hispanic/Latino; 32 Two or more races, non-Hispanic/Latino), 308 international. Average age 32. 1,549 applicants, 58% accepted, 527 enrolled. *Faculty:* 415 full-time (133 women), 24 part-time/adjunct (10 women). Expenses: Contact institution. *Financial support:* Fellowships, research assistantships, teaching assistantships, career-related internships or fieldwork, Federal Work-Study, institutionally sponsored loans, scholarships/grants, and tuition waivers (full and partial) available. Support available to part-time students. Financial award applicants required to submit FAFSA. In 2019, 487 master's, 54 doctorates, 36 other advanced degrees awarded. *Program availability:* Online learning. *Application deadline:* For fall admission, 7/30 for domestic students, 5/15 for international students; for spring admission, 12/1 for domestic students, 10/15 for international students. Applications are processed on a rolling basis. *Application fee:* $60 ($70 for international students). Electronic applications accepted. *Application Contact:* Dr. Jerry McMurtry, Dean of the College of Graduate Studies, 208-885-2647, E-mail: cogs@uidaho.edu. *Dean of the College of Graduate Studies,* Dr. Jerry McMurtry, 208-885-2647, E-mail: cogs@uidaho.edu.

***College of Agricultural and Life Sciences*** Students: 121 full-time (69 women), 43 part-time (21 women). Average age 30. 145 applicants, 34% accepted, 31 enrolled. Expenses: Contact institution. *Financial support:* Research assistantships, teaching assistantships, career-related internships or fieldwork, and Federal Work-Study available. Support available to part-time students. Financial award application deadline: 12/1; financial award applicants required to submit FAFSA. In 2019, 40 master's, 9 doctorates awarded. *Application deadline:* For fall admission, 7/30 for domestic students; for spring admission, 12/1 for domestic students. Applications are processed on a rolling basis. *Application fee:* $60 ($70 for international students). Electronic applications accepted. *Application Contact:* Dr. Michael Parrella, Dean, 208-885-6681, E-mail: ag@uidaho.edu. *Dean,* Dr. Michael Parrella, 208-885-6681, E-mail: ag@uidaho.edu.

***College of Art and Architecture*** Students: 73 full-time, 10 part-time. Average age 28. 105 applicants, 76% accepted, 38 enrolled. Expenses: Contact institution. *Financial support:* Applicants required to submit FAFSA. In 2019, 32 master's awarded. *Application deadline:* For fall admission, 7/30 for domestic students; for spring admission, 12/1 for domestic students. Applications are processed on a rolling basis. *Application fee:* $60. Electronic applications accepted. *Application Contact:* Dr. Shauna Corry, Dean, 208-885-4409, E-mail: caa@uidaho.edu. *Dean,* Dr. Shauna Corry, 208-885-4409, E-mail: caa@uidaho.edu.

***College of Business and Economics*** Students: 50 full-time, 5 part-time. Average age 30. 40 applicants, 65% accepted, 19 enrolled. *Faculty:* 11. Expenses: Contact institution. *Financial support:* Research assistantships, teaching assistantships, Federal Work-Study, and scholarships/grants available. Support available to part-time students. Financial award applicants required to submit FAFSA. In 2019, 33 master's awarded. *Application deadline:* For fall admission, 7/30 for domestic students; for spring admission, 12/1 for domestic students. Applications are processed on a rolling basis. *Application fee:* $60. Electronic applications accepted. *Application Contact:* Dr. Marc Chopin, Dean, 208-885-6478, E-mail: cbe@uidaho.edu. *Dean,* Dr. Marc Chopin, 208-885-6478, E-mail: cbe@uidaho.edu.

***College of Education, Health and Human Sciences*** Students: 189 full-time (116 women), 215 part-time (143 women). Average age 35. 221 applicants, 86% accepted, 137 enrolled. *Faculty:* 57 full-time, 5 part-time/adjunct. Expenses: Contact institution. *Financial support:* Teaching assistantships and Federal Work-Study available. Support available to part-time students. Financial award applicants required to submit FAFSA. In 2019, 128 master's, 14 doctorates, 33 other advanced degrees awarded. *Application deadline:* For fall admission, 7/30 for domestic students; for spring admission, 12/1 for domestic students. Applications are processed on a rolling basis. *Application fee:* $60. Electronic applications accepted. *Application Contact:* Dr. Philip Scruggs, Interim Dean, 208-885-6772, E-mail: ehhs@uidaho.edu. *Interim Dean,* Dr. Philip Scruggs, 208-885-6772, E-mail: ehhs@uidaho.edu.

***College of Engineering*** Students: 230 full-time (35 women), 210 part-time (30 women). Average age 33. 397 applicants, 55% accepted, 93 enrolled. *Faculty:* 83. Expenses: Contact institution. *Financial support:* Fellowships, research assistantships, teaching assistantships, career-related internships or fieldwork, and Federal Work-Study available. Support available to part-time students. Financial award applicants required to submit FAFSA. In 2019, 81 master's, 11 doctorates awarded. *Application deadline:* For fall admission, 7/30 for domestic students; for spring admission, 12/1 for domestic students. Applications are processed on a rolling basis. *Application fee:* $60. Electronic applications accepted. *Application Contact:* Dr. Larry Stauffer, Dean, 208-885-6470, E-mail: deanengr@uidaho.edu. *Dean,* Dr. Larry Stauffer, 208-885-6470, E-mail: deanengr@uidaho.edu.

***College of Letters, Arts and Social Sciences*** Students: 153 full-time (69 women), 55 part-time (36 women). Average age 32. 237 applicants, 46% accepted, 74 enrolled. *Faculty:* 64. Expenses: Contact institution. *Financial support:* Fellowships, research assistantships, teaching assistantships, and Federal Work-Study available. Support available to part-time students. Financial award applicants required to submit FAFSA. In 2019, 72 master's, 1 doctorate awarded. *Application deadline:* For fall admission, 7/30 for domestic students; for spring admission, 12/1 for domestic students. Applications are processed on a rolling basis. *Application fee:* $60. Electronic applications accepted. *Application Contact:* Dr. Sean Quinlan, Dean, 208-885-6426, E-mail: class@uidaho.edu. *Dean,* Dr. Sean Quinlan, 208-885-6426, E-mail: class@uidaho.edu.

***College of Natural Resources*** Students: 147 full-time (83 women), 133 part-time (57 women). Average age 33. 184 applicants, 73% accepted, 96 enrolled. *Faculty:* 55 full-time, 6 part-time/adjunct. Expenses: Contact institution. *Financial support:* Fellowships, research assistantships, teaching assistantships, and Federal Work-Study available. Support available to part-time students. Financial award applicants required to submit FAFSA. In 2019, 79 master's, 6 doctorates awarded. *Program availability:* Online learning. *Application deadline:* For fall admission, 7/30 for domestic students; for spring admission, 12/1 for domestic students. Applications are processed on a rolling basis. *Application fee:* $60. Electronic applications accepted. *Application Contact:* Dr. Dennis Becker, Dean, 208-885-8981, Fax: 208-885-5534, E-mail: cnr@uidaho.edu. *Dean,* Dr. Dennis Becker, 208-885-8981, Fax: 208-885-5534, E-mail: cnr@uidaho.edu.

***College of Science*** Students: 132 full-time (48 women), 36 part-time (10 women). Average age 30. 220 applicants, 43% accepted, 39 enrolled. *Faculty:* 78. Expenses:

Contact institution. *Financial support:* Applicants required to submit FAFSA. In 2019, 21 master's, 13 doctorates awarded. *Application deadline:* Applications are processed on a rolling basis. *Application fee:* $60. Electronic applications accepted. *Application Contact:* Dr. Ginger Carney, Dean, 208-885-6195, E-mail: science@uidaho.edu. *Dean*, Dr. Ginger Carney, 208-885-6195, E-mail: science@uidaho.edu.

**College of Law** Students: 322 full-time (148 women), 10 part-time (5 women). Average age 29. *Faculty:* 30 full-time, 10 part-time/adjunct. Expenses: Contact institution. *Financial support:* Career-related internships or fieldwork, Federal Work-Study, and institutionally sponsored loans available. Financial award applicants required to submit FAFSA. *Application deadline:* For fall admission, 3/15 priority date for domestic students. Applications are processed on a rolling basis. Electronic applications accepted. *Application Contact:* Jerrold Long, Dean, 208-885-4977, E-mail: uilaw@uidaho.edu. *Dean*, Jerrold Long, 208-885-4977, E-mail: uilaw@uidaho.edu.

## UNIVERSITY OF ILLINOIS AT CHICAGO, Chicago, IL 60607-7128

**General Information** State-supported, coed, university. CGS member. *Graduate housing:* Room and/or apartments available on a first-come, first-served basis to single students; on-campus housing not available to married students. Housing application deadline: 3/1. *Research affiliation:* Chicago Manufacturing Technology Extension Center (manufacturing research and development, industrial research), Eastern Cooperative Oncology Group (clinical cancer research), Argonne National Laboratory (battery performance), National Surgical Adjuvant Breast and Bowel Project (prevention of breast cancer).

### GRADUATE UNITS

**College of Applied Health Sciences** *Program availability:* Part-time. Electronic applications accepted.

**College of Architecture, Design and the Arts** *Program availability:* Part-time, evening/weekend. Electronic applications accepted.

***School of Architecture*** Electronic applications accepted.

***School of Art and Art History*** *Program availability:* Part-time, evening/weekend. Electronic applications accepted.

***School of Design*** Electronic applications accepted.

**College of Dentistry** Electronic applications accepted.

**College of Education** *Program availability:* Part-time, evening/weekend. Electronic applications accepted.

**College of Engineering** *Program availability:* Part-time, evening/weekend. Electronic applications accepted.

**College of Liberal Arts and Sciences** *Program availability:* Part-time, evening/weekend. Electronic applications accepted.

***School of Literatures, Cultural Studies and Linguistics*** *Program availability:* Part-time. Electronic applications accepted.

**College of Medicine** *Program availability:* Part-time.

**College of Nursing** *Program availability:* Part-time. Electronic applications accepted.

**College of Pharmacy**

**College of Urban Planning and Public Affairs** *Program availability:* Part-time, evening/weekend. Electronic applications accepted.

**Jane Addams College of Social Work** *Program availability:* Part-time. Electronic applications accepted.

**Liautaud Graduate School of Business** *Program availability:* Part-time, evening/weekend. Electronic applications accepted.

**Program in Learning Sciences**

**Program in Neuroscience**

**School of Public Health** *Program availability:* Part-time. Electronic applications accepted.

***Division of Community Health Sciences*** *Program availability:* Part-time. Electronic applications accepted.

***Division of Environmental and Occupational Health Sciences*** *Program availability:* Part-time. Electronic applications accepted.

***Division of Health Policy and Administration*** *Program availability:* Part-time. Electronic applications accepted.

***Epidemiology and Biostatistics Division*** *Program availability:* Part-time. Electronic applications accepted.

***UIC John Marshall Law School*** Students: 775 full-time (452 women), 259 part-time (144 women); includes 334 minority (114 Black or African American, non-Hispanic/Latino; 2 American Indian or Alaska Native, non-Hispanic/Latino; 66 Asian, non-Hispanic/Latino; 123 Hispanic/Latino; 29 Two or more races, non-Hispanic/Latino), 8 international. 1,655 applicants, 70% accepted, 332 enrolled. *Faculty:* 52 full-time (27 women), 139 part-time/adjunct (57 women). Expenses: Contact institution. *Financial support:* In 2019–20, 614 students received support. Federal Work-Study, scholarships/grants, and tuition waivers (full and partial) available. Support available to part-time students. Financial award application deadline: 3/30; financial award applicants required to submit FAFSA. In 2019, 28 master's, 232 doctorates awarded. *Program availability:* Part-time, evening/weekend, 100% online, blended/hybrid learning. *Application deadline:* For fall admission, 4/1 priority date for domestic and international students; for spring admission, 11/15 priority date for domestic and international students. Applications are processed on a rolling basis. Electronic applications accepted. *Application Contact:* Chante Spann, Assistant Dean for Admissions, 800-537-4280, Fax: 312-427-5136, E-mail: admissions@jmls.edu. *Dean*, Darby Dickerson, 312-427-2737 Ext. 828, E-mail: ddickerson@jmls.edu.

## UNIVERSITY OF ILLINOIS AT SPRINGFIELD, Springfield, IL 62703-5407

**General Information** State-supported, coed, comprehensive institution. CGS member. *Enrollment:* 4,275 graduate, professional, and undergraduate students; 568 full-time matriculated graduate/professional students (274 women), 1,082 part-time matriculated graduate/professional students (527 women). *Enrollment by degree level:* 1,589 master's, 30 doctoral, 31 other advanced degrees. *Graduate faculty:* 158 full-time (68 women), 37 part-time/adjunct (22 women). *Tuition, area resident:* Full-time $7896; part-time $329 per credit hour. Tuition, nonresident: full-time $16,200; part-time $675 per credit hour. *Required fees:* $2735.60; $130.65 per credit hour. *Graduate housing:* Rooms and/or apartments available on a first-come, first-served basis to single and married students. Housing application deadline: 5/1. *Student services:* Campus employment opportunities, campus safety program, career counseling, child daycare facilities, exercise/wellness program, free psychological counseling, international student services, low-cost health insurance, multicultural affairs office, services for students with disabilities, teacher training, writing training. *Library facilities:* Norris L Brookens Library plus 1 other. *Collection:* Books: 342,013 (physical), 240,597 (digital/electronic); Serial titles: 8,456 (physical), 18,139 (digital/electronic); Databases: 179. Weekly public service hours: 90; students can reserve study rooms. *Research affiliation:* Council of Public Liberal Arts Colleges (COPLAC), Interuniversity Consortium for Political and Social Research, Council of Undergraduate Research, The Nature Conservancy, Illinois Flood Plan Restoration.

**Computer facilities:** 560 computers available on campus for general student use. A campuswide network can be accessed from student residence rooms and from off campus. Online class registration is available.
Website: http://www.uis.edu/

**General Application Contact:** Dr. Cecelia Cornell, Associate Vice Chancellor for Graduate Education, 888-977-4847, Fax: 217-206-7230, E-mail: ccorn1@uis.edu.

### GRADUATE UNITS

**Graduate Programs** Students: 503 full-time (273 women), 941 part-time (470 women); includes 334 minority (160 Black or African American, non-Hispanic/Latino; 87 Asian, non-Hispanic/Latino; 62 Hispanic/Latino; 25 Two or more races, non-Hispanic/Latino), 286 international. Average age 33. 1,701 applicants, 54% accepted, 325 enrolled. *Faculty:* 211 full-time (97 women), 36 part-time/adjunct (19 women). Expenses: Contact institution. *Financial support:* In 2019–20, 3 research assistantships with full tuition reimbursements (averaging $10,562 per year), 4 teaching assistantships with full tuition reimbursements (averaging $10,652 per year) were awarded; fellowships, career-related internships or fieldwork, Federal Work-Study, scholarships/grants, health care benefits, and unspecified assistantships also available. Support available to part-time students. Financial award application deadline: 11/15; financial award applicants required to submit FAFSA. In 2019, 588 master's, 29 other advanced degrees awarded. *Program availability:* Part-time, 100% online, blended/hybrid learning. *Application deadline:* Applications are processed on a rolling basis. *Application fee:* $60 ($75 for international students). Electronic applications accepted. *Application Contact:* Dr. Cecelia Cornell, Associate Vice Chancellor for Graduate Education, 217-206-7230, Fax: 217-206-7623, E-mail: ccorn1@uis.edu. *Associate Vice Chancellor for Graduate Education*, Dr. Cecelia Cornell, 217-206-7230, Fax: 217-206-7623, E-mail: ccorn1@uis.edu.

***College of Business and Management*** Students: 143 full-time (63 women), 154 part-time (60 women); includes 68 minority (23 Black or African American, non-Hispanic/Latino; 25 Asian, non-Hispanic/Latino; 14 Hispanic/Latino; 6 Two or more races, non-Hispanic/Latino), 89 international. Average age 31. 360 applicants, 48% accepted, 70 enrolled. *Faculty:* 30 full-time (9 women), 6 part-time/adjunct (2 women). Expenses: Contact institution. *Financial support:* In 2019–20, research assistantships with full tuition reimbursements (averaging $10,562 per year), teaching assistantships with full tuition reimbursements (averaging $10,652 per year) were awarded; fellowships, career-related internships or fieldwork, Federal Work-Study, scholarships/grants, health care benefits, and unspecified assistantships also available. Support available to part-time students. Financial award application deadline: 11/15; financial award applicants required to submit FAFSA. In 2019, 132 master's awarded. *Program availability:* Part-time, 100% online, blended/hybrid learning. *Application deadline:* Applications are processed on a rolling basis. *Application fee:* $60 ($75 for international students). Electronic applications accepted. *Application Contact:* Dr. Somnath Bhattacharya, Dean, 217-206-6533, Fax: 217-206-7541, E-mail: cbmdean@uis.edu. *Dean*, Dr. Somnath Bhattacharya, 217-206-6533, Fax: 217-206-7541, E-mail: cbmdean@uis.edu.

***College of Education and Human Services*** Students: 73 full-time (67 women), 158 part-time (126 women); includes 61 minority (45 Black or African American, non-Hispanic/Latino; 9 Hispanic/Latino; 7 Two or more races, non-Hispanic/Latino), 6 international. Average age 34. 145 applicants, 59% accepted, 42 enrolled. *Faculty:* 21 full-time (14 women), 13 part-time/adjunct (9 women). Expenses: Contact institution. *Financial support:* In 2019–20, research assistantships with full tuition reimbursements (averaging $10,562 per year), teaching assistantships with full tuition reimbursements (averaging $10,652 per year) were awarded; fellowships, career-related internships or fieldwork, Federal Work-Study, scholarships/grants, health care benefits, and unspecified assistantships also available. Support available to part-time students. Financial award application deadline: 11/15; financial award applicants required to submit FAFSA. In 2019, 88 master's, 6 other advanced degrees awarded. *Program availability:* Part-time, 100% online, blended/hybrid learning. *Application deadline:* Applications are processed on a rolling basis. *Application fee:* $60 ($75 for international students). Electronic applications accepted. *Application Contact:* Dr. James Ermatinger, Interim Dean, 217-206-6784, Fax: 217-206-6775, E-mail: jerma2@uis.edu. *Interim Dean*, Dr. James Ermatinger, 217-206-6784, Fax: 217-206-6775, E-mail: jerma2@uis.edu.

***College of Liberal Arts and Sciences*** Students: 156 full-time (69 women), 279 part-time (91 women); includes 93 minority (17 Black or African American, non-Hispanic/Latino; 53 Asian, non-Hispanic/Latino; 18 Hispanic/Latino; 5 Two or more races, non-Hispanic/Latino), 154 international. Average age 31. 737 applicants, 55% accepted, 121 enrolled. *Faculty:* 106 full-time (47 women), 2 part-time/adjunct (1 woman). Expenses: Contact institution. *Financial support:* In 2019–20, research assistantships with full tuition reimbursements (averaging $10,562 per year), teaching assistantships with full tuition reimbursements (averaging $10,652 per year) were awarded; fellowships, career-related internships or fieldwork, Federal Work-Study, scholarships/grants, health care benefits, and unspecified assistantships also available. Support available to part-time students. Financial award application deadline: 11/15; financial award applicants required to submit FAFSA. In 2019, 219 master's awarded. *Program availability:* Part-time, 100% online, blended/hybrid learning. *Application deadline:* Applications are processed on a rolling basis. *Application fee:* $60 ($75 for international students). Electronic applications accepted. *Application Contact:* Dr. Michael Lemke, Interim Dean, 217-206-6512, Fax: 217-206-6217, E-mail: mlemk1@uis.edu. *Interim Dean*, Dr. Michael Lemke, 217-206-6512, Fax: 217-206-6217, E-mail: mlemk1@uis.edu.

***College of Public Affairs and Administration*** Students: 131 full-time (74 women), 350 part-time (193 women); includes 112 minority (75 Black or African American, non-Hispanic/Latino; 9 Asian, non-Hispanic/Latino; 21 Hispanic/Latino; 7 Two or more races, non-Hispanic/Latino), 37 international. Average age 34. 459 applicants, 55% accepted, 92 enrolled. *Faculty:* 41 full-time (18 women), 9 part-time/adjunct (3 women). Expenses: Contact institution. *Financial support:* In 2019–20, research assistantships with full tuition reimbursements (averaging $10,562 per year), teaching assistantships with full tuition reimbursements (averaging $10,652 per year) were awarded; fellowships, career-related internships or fieldwork, Federal Work-Study, scholarships/grants, health care benefits, and unspecified assistantships also available. Support available to part-time students. Financial award application deadline: 11/15; financial award applicants required to submit FAFSA. In 2019, 149 master's, 23 other advanced degrees awarded. *Program availability:* Part-time, 100%

online, blended/hybrid learning. *Application deadline:* Applications are processed on a rolling basis. *Application fee:* $60 ($75 for international students). Electronic applications accepted. *Application Contact:* Dr. Robert Smith, Dean, 217-206-6523, Fax: 217-206-7807, E-mail: cpaa@uis.edu. *Dean*, Dr. Robert Smith, 217-206-6523, Fax: 217-206-7807, E-mail: cpaa@uis.edu.

## UNIVERSITY OF ILLINOIS AT URBANA-CHAMPAIGN, Champaign, IL 61820

**General Information** State-supported, coed, university. CGS member. *Graduate housing:* Rooms and/or apartments available to single and married students. *Research affiliation:* Midwest Universities Research Association, Sandia National Laboratories, National Center for Atmospheric Research.

**GRADUATE UNITS**

**College of Law**

**College of Veterinary Medicine**

**Graduate College**

***College of Agricultural, Consumer and Environmental Sciences***

***College of Applied Health Sciences***

***College of Education*** *Program availability:* Part-time, online learning.

***College of Engineering*** *Program availability:* Part-time, evening/weekend, online learning.

***College of Fine and Applied Arts***

***College of Liberal Arts and Sciences*** *Program availability:* Online learning.

***College of Media***

***Gies College of Business*** *Program availability:* Online learning.

***School of Information Sciences*** *Program availability:* Part-time, online learning.

***School of Labor and Employment Relations***

***School of Social Work***

**Illinois Informatics Institute**

## UNIVERSITY OF INDIANAPOLIS, Indianapolis, IN 46227-3697

**General Information** Independent-religious, coed, comprehensive institution. CGS member. *Graduate housing:* Rooms and/or apartments available on a first-come, first-served basis to single and married students.

**GRADUATE UNITS**

**Graduate Programs** *Program availability:* Part-time, evening/weekend, online learning.

***Center for Aging and Community*** *Program availability:* Part-time, evening/weekend, online learning.

***College of Applied Behavioral Sciences***

***College of Health Sciences***

***School of Business*** *Program availability:* Part-time, evening/weekend.

***School of Education*** *Program availability:* Part-time, evening/weekend.

***School of Nursing*** Electronic applications accepted.

***Shaheen College of Arts and Sciences*** *Program availability:* Part-time, evening/weekend.

## THE UNIVERSITY OF IOWA, Iowa City, IA 52242-1316

**General Information** State-supported, coed, university. CGS member. *Graduate housing:* Rooms and/or apartments available on a first-come, first-served basis to single and married students.

**GRADUATE UNITS**

**College of Dentistry**

**College of Law** Students: 447 full-time (201 women); includes 86 minority (17 Black or African American, non-Hispanic/Latino; 21 Asian, non-Hispanic/Latino; 34 Hispanic/Latino; 14 Two or more races, non-Hispanic/Latino), 24 international. Average age 24. 1,204 applicants, 59% accepted, 166 enrolled. *Faculty:* 43 full-time (19 women), 39 part-time/adjunct (13 women). Expenses: Contact institution. *Financial support:* In 2019–20, 327 students received support, including 327 fellowships with tuition reimbursements available (averaging $19,022 per year), 124 research assistantships with partial tuition reimbursements available (averaging $2,175 per year); career-related internships or fieldwork, scholarships/grants, and health care benefits also available. Financial award applicants required to submit FAFSA. In 2019, 9 master's, 141 doctorates awarded. *Application deadline:* For fall admission, 5/1 priority date for domestic and international students. Applications are processed on a rolling basis. *Application fee:* $40. Electronic applications accepted. *Application Contact:* Collins Byrd, Assistant Dean of Enrollment Management, 319-335-9095, Fax: 319-335-9646, E-mail: law-admissions@uiowa.edu. *Dean*, Kevin Washburn, 319-335-9034, Fax: 319-335-9019, E-mail: kevin-washburn@uiowa.edu.

**College of Pharmacy** Electronic applications accepted.

**Graduate College** *Program availability:* Part-time, evening/weekend, online learning. Electronic applications accepted.

***College of Education*** Electronic applications accepted.

***College of Engineering*** Electronic applications accepted.

***College of Liberal Arts and Sciences*** *Program availability:* Part-time, online learning. Electronic applications accepted.

***College of Nursing*** Electronic applications accepted.

***College of Public Health*** Electronic applications accepted.

***School of Library and Information Science*** Electronic applications accepted.

**Roy J. and Lucille A. Carver College of Medicine** *Program availability:* Part-time. Electronic applications accepted.

***Graduate Programs in Medicine*** *Program availability:* Part-time. Electronic applications accepted.

**Tippie College of Business** Electronic applications accepted.

## UNIVERSITY OF JAMESTOWN, Jamestown, ND 58405

**General Information** Independent-religious, coed, comprehensive institution.

**GRADUATE UNITS**

**Program in Education**

**Program in Physical Therapy**

## THE UNIVERSITY OF KANSAS, Lawrence, KS 66045

**General Information** State-supported, coed, university. CGS member. *Enrollment:* 27,552 graduate, professional, and undergraduate students; 3,111 full-time matriculated graduate/professional students (1,672 women), 1,691 part-time matriculated graduate/professional students (974 women). *Enrollment by degree level:* 3,113 master's, 4,281 doctoral, 200 other advanced degrees. *International tuition:* $23,950 full-time. Tuition, state resident: full-time $9989. Tuition, nonresident: full-time $23,950. *Required fees:* $984; $81.99 per credit hour. Tuition and fees vary according to course load, campus/location and program. *Graduate housing:* Room and/or apartments guaranteed to single students; on-campus housing not available to married students. Typical cost: $6084 per year ($10,350 including board). Room and board charges vary according to board plan and housing facility selected. Housing application deadline: 3/1. *Student services:* Campus employment opportunities, campus safety program, career counseling, child daycare facilities, exercise/wellness program, free psychological counseling, grant writing training, international student services, low-cost health insurance, multicultural affairs office, services for students with disabilities, teacher training, writing training. *Library facilities:* Watson Library plus 11 others. *Collection:* Books: 4.7 million (physical), 1 million (digital/electronic). Weekly public service hours: 168; study areas open 24 hours, 5–7 days a week; students can reserve study rooms.

**Computer facilities:** 1,500 computers available on campus for general student use. A campuswide network can be accessed. Online class registration, online payments are available.
Website: http://www.ku.edu/

**General Application Contact:** Graduate Studies, 785-864-8040, Fax: 785-864-7209, E-mail: graduate@ku.edu.

**GRADUATE UNITS**

**Graduate Studies** Students: 3,111 full-time (1,672 women), 1,691 part-time (974 women); includes 884 minority (233 Black or African American, non-Hispanic/Latino; 44 American Indian or Alaska Native, non-Hispanic/Latino; 154 Asian, non-Hispanic/Latino; 261 Hispanic/Latino; 4 Native Hawaiian or other Pacific Islander, non-Hispanic/Latino; 188 Two or more races, non-Hispanic/Latino), 891 international. Average age 31. 4,831 applicants, 56% accepted, 1,708 enrolled. Expenses: Contact institution. *Financial support:* Fellowships, research assistantships, teaching assistantships, career-related internships or fieldwork, Federal Work-Study, institutionally sponsored loans, scholarships/grants, traineeships, and unspecified assistantships available. Support available to part-time students. Financial award application deadline: 4/15; financial award applicants required to submit FAFSA. In 2019, 1,754 master's, 368 doctorates, 599 other advanced degrees awarded. *Program availability:* Part-time, evening/weekend, online learning. *Application fee:* $65 ($85 for international students). Electronic applications accepted. *Application Contact:* Abby Ehling, Assistant Director of Graduate Admissions, 785-864-3140, Fax: 785-864-7209, E-mail: graduate@ku.edu. *Dean of Graduate Studies*, Audrey Lamb, 785-864-8040, E-mail: lamb@ku.edu.

***College of Liberal Arts and Sciences*** Students: 1,462 full-time (796 women), 227 part-time (132 women); includes 277 minority (58 Black or African American, non-Hispanic/Latino; 24 American Indian or Alaska Native, non-Hispanic/Latino; 43 Asian, non-Hispanic/Latino; 91 Hispanic/Latino; 1 Native Hawaiian or other Pacific Islander, non-Hispanic/Latino; 60 Two or more races, non-Hispanic/Latino), 375 international. Average age 30. 2,107 applicants, 40% accepted, 431 enrolled. Expenses: Contact institution. *Financial support:* Fellowships, research assistantships with partial tuition reimbursements, teaching assistantships with tuition reimbursements, career-related internships or fieldwork, Federal Work-Study, institutionally sponsored loans, scholarships/grants, traineeships, and unspecified assistantships available. Support available to part-time students. Financial award applicants required to submit FAFSA. In 2019, 297 master's, 145 doctorates, 72 other advanced degrees awarded. *Program availability:* Part-time, evening/weekend, online learning. *Application fee:* $65 ($85 for international students). Electronic applications accepted. *Application Contact:* Kristine Latta, Director of the College Office of Graduate Affairs, 785-864-1784, E-mail: klatta@ku.edu. *Dean, College of Liberal Arts and Sciences*, Carl W. Lejuez, 785-864-3661, E-mail: clejuez@ku.edu.

***School of Architecture and Design*** Students: 97 full-time (48 women), 34 part-time (18 women); includes 21 minority (4 Black or African American, non-Hispanic/Latino; 6 Asian, non-Hispanic/Latino; 4 Hispanic/Latino; 7 Two or more races, non-Hispanic/Latino), 26 international. Average age 26. 101 applicants, 60% accepted, 33 enrolled. Expenses: Contact institution. *Financial support:* Fellowships, research assistantships, teaching assistantships, career-related internships or fieldwork, scholarships/grants, health care benefits, and unspecified assistantships available. Financial award application deadline: 1/15; financial award applicants required to submit FAFSA. In 2019, 70 master's, 2 doctorates, 8 other advanced degrees awarded. *Program availability:* Part-time. *Application deadline:* For fall admission, 1/15 priority date for domestic and international students; for summer admission, 1/15 priority date for domestic and international students. *Application fee:* $65 ($85 for international students). Electronic applications accepted. *Application Contact:* Joan Weaver, Graduate Admissions Contact, 785-864-3709, E-mail: jweaver@ku.edu. *Dean*, Frank Zilm, 816-561-7186, E-mail: frankzilm@ku.edu.

***School of Business*** Students: 276 full-time (121 women), 358 part-time (133 women); includes 140 minority (33 Black or African American, non-Hispanic/Latino; 6 American Indian or Alaska Native, non-Hispanic/Latino; 32 Asian, non-Hispanic/Latino; 33 Hispanic/Latino; 2 Native Hawaiian or other Pacific Islander, non-Hispanic/Latino; 34 Two or more races, non-Hispanic/Latino), 44 international. Average age 31. 435 applicants, 74% accepted, 277 enrolled. Expenses: Contact institution. *Financial support:* Fellowships, research assistantships, teaching assistantships, career-related internships or fieldwork, Federal Work-Study, and unspecified assistantships available. Financial award application deadline: 1/15; financial award applicants required to submit FAFSA. In 2019, 331 master's, 3 doctorates awarded. *Program availability:* Part-time, evening/weekend. *Application deadline:* For fall admission, 1/15 priority date for domestic and international students. *Application fee:* $65 ($85 for international students). Electronic applications accepted. *Application Contact:* Andrea Noltner, Graduate Admissions Contact, 785-864-7556, E-mail: anoltner@ku.edu. *Dean*, Dr. L. Paige Fields, 785-864-7546, E-mail: paige.fields@ku.edu.

***School of Education*** Students: 415 full-time (273 women), 689 part-time (491 women); includes 216 minority (83 Black or African American, non-Hispanic/Latino; 5 American Indian or Alaska Native, non-Hispanic/Latino; 23 Asian, non-Hispanic/Latino; 60 Hispanic/Latino; 1 Native Hawaiian or other Pacific Islander, non-Hispanic/Latino; 44 Two or more races, non-Hispanic/Latino), 110 international. Average age 33. 732 applicants, 69% accepted, 336 enrolled. Expenses: Contact institution. *Financial support:* Fellowships, research assistantships, teaching assistantships, career-related internships or fieldwork, scholarships/grants, and unspecified assistantships available. Financial award application deadline: 2/1. In 2019, 376 master's, 74 doctorates, 79 other advanced degrees awarded. *Program availability:* Part-time, online learning. *Application fee:* $65 ($85 for international students). Electronic applications accepted. *Application Contact:* Kim Huggett, Graduate Student Services Manager, 785-864-4510, E-mail: khuggett@ku.edu. *Dean*, Dr. Rick J. Ginsberg, 785-864-4297, E-mail: ginsberg@ku.edu.

***School of Engineering*** Students: 376 full-time (99 women), 211 part-time (69 women); includes 84 minority (16 Black or African American, non-Hispanic/Latino; 3 American Indian or Alaska Native, non-Hispanic/Latino; 25 Asian, non-Hispanic/Latino; 25 Hispanic/Latino; 15 Two or more races, non-Hispanic/Latino), 214 international. Average age 29. 525 applicants, 61% accepted, 143 enrolled. Expenses: Contact institution. *Financial support:* Fellowships, research assistantships, teaching assistantships, career-related internships or fieldwork, Federal Work-Study, scholarships/grants, and unspecified assistantships available. In 2019, 160 master's, 45 doctorates, 12 other advanced degrees awarded. *Program availability:* Part-time, evening/weekend, online learning. *Application fee:* $65 ($85 for international students). Electronic applications accepted. *Application Contact:* Amy Wierman, Assistant to the Dean, 785-864-2930, E-mail: awierman@ku.edu. *Dean*, Dr. Arvin Agah, 785-864-2930, E-mail: agah@ku.edu.

***School of Music*** Students: 148 full-time (74 women), 25 part-time (19 women); includes 12 minority (1 Black or African American, non-Hispanic/Latino; 5 Asian, non-Hispanic/Latino; 4 Hispanic/Latino; 2 Two or more races, non-Hispanic/Latino), 56 international. Average age 30. 265 applicants, 57% accepted, 72 enrolled. Expenses: Contact institution. *Financial support:* Fellowships, research assistantships, teaching assistantships, scholarships/grants, and unspecified assistantships available. In 2019, 48 master's, 33 doctorates awarded. *Application fee:* $65 ($85 for international students). Electronic applications accepted. *Application Contact:* Terri Morris, Graduate Services Coordinator, 785-864-3422, E-mail: tlmorris@ku.edu. *Dean*, Dr. Robert Walzel, 785-864-3421, E-mail: robert.walzel@ku.edu.

***School of Pharmacy*** Students: 75 full-time (37 women), 16 part-time (6 women); includes 12 minority (1 Black or African American, non-Hispanic/Latino; 5 Asian, non-Hispanic/Latino; 4 Hispanic/Latino; 2 Two or more races, non-Hispanic/Latino), 39 international. Average age 28. 149 applicants, 28% accepted, 23 enrolled. Expenses: Contact institution. *Financial support:* Fellowships, research assistantships, teaching assistantships, career-related internships or fieldwork, scholarships/grants, traineeships, and unspecified assistantships available. In 2019, 18 master's, 15 doctorates awarded. *Application fee:* $65 ($85 for international students). Electronic applications accepted. *Application Contact:* Patti Steffan, Graduate Admissions Contact, 785-864-3893, E-mail: psteffan@ku.edu. *Dean*, Kenneth L. Audus, 785-864-3591, E-mail: audus@ku.edu.

***School of Social Welfare*** Students: 279 full-time (229 women), 59 part-time (50 women); includes 87 minority (24 Black or African American, non-Hispanic/Latino; 3 American Indian or Alaska Native, non-Hispanic/Latino; 11 Asian, non-Hispanic/Latino; 31 Hispanic/Latino; 18 Two or more races, non-Hispanic/Latino), 4 international. Average age 30. 265 applicants, 94% accepted, 177 enrolled. Expenses: Contact institution. *Financial support:* Fellowships, research assistantships, teaching assistantships, Federal Work-Study, scholarships/grants, and tuition waivers (partial) available. Support available to part-time students. Financial award application deadline: 1/17; financial award applicants required to submit FAFSA. In 2019, 163 master's, 4 doctorates awarded. *Program availability:* Part-time, online learning. *Application deadline:* For fall admission, 1/15 for domestic and international students. *Application fee:* $65 ($85 for international students). Electronic applications accepted. *Application Contact:* Georgiana Spear, Graduate Admissions Contact, 785-864-0115, E-mail: gspear@ku.edu. *Dean*, Michelle Carney, 785-864-5975, E-mail: mmcarney@ku.edu.

***William Allen White School of Journalism and Mass Communications*** Students: 23 full-time (14 women), 80 part-time (59 women); includes 18 minority (5 Black or African American, non-Hispanic/Latino; 8 Hispanic/Latino; 5 Two or more races, non-Hispanic/Latino), 10 international. Average age 33. 58 applicants, 71% accepted, 32 enrolled. Expenses: Contact institution. *Financial support:* Fellowships, research assistantships, teaching assistantships, career-related internships or fieldwork, scholarships/grants, and unspecified assistantships available. Support available to part-time students. Financial award application deadline: 2/1; financial award applicants required to submit FAFSA. In 2019, 44 master's, 2 doctorates awarded. *Program availability:* Part-time. *Application deadline:* For fall admission, 1/1 priority date for domestic and international students; for spring admission, 8/1 for domestic and international students; for summer admission, 5/15 for domestic and international students. *Application fee:* $65 ($85 for international students). Electronic applications accepted. *Application Contact:* Jammie A. Johnson, Graduate Advisor/Administrative Assistant, 785-864-7649, E-mail: jamjohn@ku.edu. *Dean*, Ann Brill, 785-864-4755, E-mail: abrill@ku.edu.

**School of Law** Students: 313 full-time (165 women), 27 part-time (7 women); includes 58 minority (15 Black or African American, non-Hispanic/Latino; 5 American Indian or Alaska Native, non-Hispanic/Latino; 14 Asian, non-Hispanic/Latino; 22 Hispanic/Latino; 2 Two or more races, non-Hispanic/Latino), 15 international. Average age 25. 604 applicants, 56% accepted, 114 enrolled. *Faculty:* 29 full-time (16 women), 15 part-time/adjunct (6 women). Expenses: Contact institution. *Financial support:* In 2019–20, 5 fellowships (averaging $1,866 per year), 69 research assistantships (averaging $1,154 per year), 5 teaching assistantships (averaging $980 per year) were awarded; career-related internships or fieldwork, Federal Work-Study, institutionally sponsored loans, scholarships/grants, and unspecified assistantships also available. Financial award application deadline: 2/15; financial award applicants required to submit FAFSA. In 2019, 103 doctorates awarded. *Program availability:* Part-time. *Application deadline:* For fall admission, 4/1 priority date for domestic students, 4/1 for international students. Applications are processed on a rolling basis. *Application fee:* $55. Electronic applications accepted. *Application Contact:* Steven Freedman, Assistant Dean for Admissions, 866-220-3654, E-mail: admitlaw@ku.edu. *Dean*, Stephen W. Mazza, 785-864-4550, Fax: 785-864-5054.

**University of Kansas Medical Center** Students: 1,614 full-time (953 women), 491 part-time (381 women); includes 443 minority (48 Black or African American, non-Hispanic/Latino; 8 American Indian or Alaska Native, non-Hispanic/Latino; 162 Asian, non-Hispanic/Latino; 114 Hispanic/Latino; 2 Native Hawaiian or other Pacific Islander, non-Hispanic/Latino; 109 Two or more races, non-Hispanic/Latino), 93 international. Average age 28. *Faculty:* 1,477. Expenses: Contact institution. In 2019, 171 master's, 375 doctorates, 30 other advanced degrees awarded. *Application Contact:* Dr. Robert Simari, Executive Vice Chancellor, 913-588-1440, E-mail: rsimari@kumc.edu. *Executive Vice Chancellor*, Dr. Robert Simari, 913-588-1440, E-mail: rsimari@kumc.edu.

***School of Health Professions*** Students: 477 full-time (350 women), 65 part-time (60 women); includes 71 minority (9 Black or African American, non-Hispanic/Latino; 2 American Indian or Alaska Native, non-Hispanic/Latino; 17 Asian, non-Hispanic/Latino; 28 Hispanic/Latino; 1 Native Hawaiian or other Pacific Islander, non-Hispanic/Latino; 14 Two or more races, non-Hispanic/Latino), 17 international. Average age 27. *Faculty:* 118. Expenses: Contact institution. In 2019, 68 master's, 103 doctorates, 24 other advanced degrees awarded. *Application Contact:* Dr. Abiodun Akinwuntan, Dean, 913-588-5235, Fax: 913-588-5254, E-mail: aakinwuntan@kumc.edu. *Dean*, Dr. Abiodun Akinwuntan, 913-588-5235, Fax: 913-588-5254, E-mail: aakinwuntan@kumc.edu.

***School of Medicine*** Students: 1,080 full-time (550 women), 159 part-time (79 women); includes 307 minority (25 Black or African American, non-Hispanic/Latino; 4 American Indian or Alaska Native, non-Hispanic/Latino; 124 Asian, non-Hispanic/Latino; 77 Hispanic/Latino; 77 Two or more races, non-Hispanic/Latino), 74 international. Average age 27. *Faculty:* 1,294. Expenses: Contact institution. In 2019, 77 master's, 224 doctorates, 2 other advanced degrees awarded. *Application Contact:* Dr. Akinlolu Ojo, Executive Dean, E-mail: aojo@kumc.edu. *Executive Dean*, Dr. Akinlolu Ojo, E-mail: aojo@kumc.edu.

***School of Nursing*** Students: 57 full-time (53 women), 267 part-time (242 women); includes 65 minority (14 Black or African American, non-Hispanic/Latino; 2 American Indian or Alaska Native, non-Hispanic/Latino; 21 Asian, non-Hispanic/Latino; 9 Hispanic/Latino; 1 Native Hawaiian or other Pacific Islander, non-Hispanic/Latino; 18 Two or more races, non-Hispanic/Latino), 2 international. Average age 35. *Faculty:* 65. Expenses: Contact institution. *Financial support:* Research assistantships with tuition reimbursements, teaching assistantships with tuition reimbursements, scholarships/grants, and traineeships available. Financial award application deadline: 3/1; financial award applicants required to submit FAFSA. In 2019, 26 master's, 48 doctorates, 5 other advanced degrees awarded. *Program availability:* Part-time, 100% online, blended/hybrid learning. *Application deadline:* For fall admission, 4/1 for domestic and international students; for spring admission, 9/1 for domestic and international students. *Application fee:* $75. Electronic applications accepted. *Application Contact:* Dr. Pamela K. Barnes, Associate Dean, Student Affairs and Enrollment Management, 913-588-1619, Fax: 913-588-1615, E-mail: pbarnes2@kumc.edu. *Professor and Dean*, Dr. Sally Maliski, 913-588-1601, Fax: 913-588-1660, E-mail: smaliski@kumc.edu.

## UNIVERSITY OF KENTUCKY, Lexington, KY 40506-0032

**General Information** State-supported, coed, university. CGS member. *Graduate housing:* Rooms and/or apartments available to single and married students. *Research affiliation:* Continuous Electron Beam Accelerator Facility (high-energy physics), Battelle–Pacific Northwest National Laboratory (environmental sciences), Oak Ridge National Laboratory (nuclear physics), National Institute of Occupational Health and Safety (environmental health), National Drug Addiction Center (drug abuse and prevention).

**GRADUATE UNITS**

**College of Dentistry** Electronic applications accepted.

**College of Law** Electronic applications accepted.

**College of Medicine** Electronic applications accepted.

**Graduate School** *Program availability:* Part-time, evening/weekend. Electronic applications accepted.

***College of Agriculture, Food and Environment*** *Program availability:* Part-time. Electronic applications accepted.

***College of Arts and Sciences*** *Program availability:* Part-time. Electronic applications accepted.

***College of Communication and Information*** *Program availability:* Part-time. Electronic applications accepted.

***College of Design*** Electronic applications accepted.

***College of Education*** *Program availability:* Part-time, evening/weekend. Electronic applications accepted.

***College of Engineering*** *Program availability:* Part-time. Electronic applications accepted.

***College of Fine Arts*** *Program availability:* Part-time, evening/weekend. Electronic applications accepted.

***College of Health Sciences*** *Program availability:* Part-time. Electronic applications accepted.

***College of Nursing*** Electronic applications accepted.

***College of Public Health*** Electronic applications accepted.

***College of Social Work*** Electronic applications accepted.

***Gatton College of Business and Economics*** *Program availability:* Part-time, evening/weekend. Electronic applications accepted.

***Graduate School Programs from the College of Medicine*** Electronic applications accepted.

***Martin School of Public Policy and Administration*** *Program availability:* Part-time, evening/weekend, 100% online. Electronic applications accepted.

***Patterson School of Diplomacy and International Commerce*** Electronic applications accepted.

## UNIVERSITY OF KING'S COLLEGE, Halifax, NS B3H 2A1, Canada

**General Information** Province-supported, coed, comprehensive institution. *Graduate housing:* Room and/or apartments available on a first-come, first-served basis to single students; on-campus housing not available to married students. Housing application deadline: 4/1.

**GRADUATE UNITS**

**Graduate and Advanced Programs**

## UNIVERSITY OF LA VERNE, La Verne, CA 91750-4443

**General Information** Independent, coed, university. *Enrollment:* 4,484 graduate, professional, and undergraduate students; 1,614 full-time matriculated graduate/professional students (1,024 women), 1,441 part-time matriculated graduate/professional students (1,030 women). *Enrollment by degree level:* 2,516 master's, 266 doctoral, 273 other advanced degrees. *Graduate faculty:* 105 full-time (59 women), 164 part-time/adjunct (92 women). *Graduate housing:* Room and/or apartments available on a first-come, first-served basis to single students; on-campus housing not available to married students. *Student services:* Campus employment opportunities, campus safety program, career counseling, exercise/wellness program, free psychological counseling, international student services, low-cost health insurance, multicultural affairs office, services for students with disabilities, teacher training, writing training. *Library facilities:* Wilson Library. *Collection:* Students can reserve study rooms. *Research affiliation:* San Antonio Community Hospital, Riverside Community Hospital, Presbyterian Intercommunity Hospital, Huntington Memorial Hospital (health services management), Southern California Healthcare Systems, Methodist Hospital of Southern California.

**Computer facilities:** A campuswide network can be accessed. Online class registration, MyLaVerne (online) are available.
Website: http://www.laverne.edu/

**General Application Contact:** Graduate Admission Office, 909-448-4444, E-mail: gradadmission@laverne.edu.

**GRADUATE UNITS**

**College of Arts and Sciences** Students: 131 full-time (98 women), 29 part-time (23 women); includes 92 minority (7 Black or African American, non-Hispanic/Latino; 15 Asian, non-Hispanic/Latino; 61 Hispanic/Latino; 9 Two or more races, non-Hispanic/Latino), 2 international. Average age 28. *Faculty:* 14 full-time (9 women), 11 part-time/adjunct (4 women). Expenses: Contact institution. *Financial support:* Career-related internships or fieldwork, institutionally sponsored loans, scholarships/grants, and unspecified assistantships available. Financial award application deadline: 3/2; financial award applicants required to submit FAFSA. *Program availability:* Part-time. *Application deadline:* Applications are processed on a rolling basis. *Application Contact:* Graduate Admissions, 909-448-4444, E-mail: gradadmission@laverne.edu. *Interim Dean, College of Arts and Sciences*, Dr. Brian Clocksin, 909-448-4184, E-mail: bclocksin@laverne.edu.

**College of Business and Public Management** Students: 716 full-time (376 women), 516 part-time (314 women); includes 640 minority (93 Black or African American, non-Hispanic/Latino; 119 Asian, non-Hispanic/Latino; 387 Hispanic/Latino; 5 Native Hawaiian or other Pacific Islander, non-Hispanic/Latino; 36 Two or more races, non-Hispanic/Latino), 348 international. Average age 33. *Faculty:* 44 full-time (22 women), 52 part-time/adjunct (15 women). Expenses: Contact institution. *Financial support:* Career-related internships or fieldwork, institutionally sponsored loans, and scholarships/grants available. Financial award application deadline: 3/2; financial award applicants required to submit FAFSA. *Program availability:* Part-time, evening/weekend, online learning. *Application deadline:* Applications are processed on a rolling basis. Electronic applications accepted. *Application Contact:* Graduate Admissions, 909-448-4444, E-mail: gradadmission@laverne.edu. *Dean, College of Business and Public Management*, Dr. Abe Helou, 909-448-4455, E-mail: ihelou@laverne.edu.

**College of Law** *Program availability:* Part-time, evening/weekend. Electronic applications accepted.

**LaFetra College of Education** Students: 565 full-time (440 women), 825 part-time (647 women); includes 918 minority (75 Black or African American, non-Hispanic/Latino; 67 Asian, non-Hispanic/Latino; 733 Hispanic/Latino; 4 Native Hawaiian or other Pacific Islander, non-Hispanic/Latino; 39 Two or more races, non-Hispanic/Latino), 8 international. Average age 34. *Faculty:* 29 full-time (21 women), 77 part-time/adjunct (62 women). Expenses: Contact institution. *Financial support:* Federal Work-Study, institutionally sponsored loans, and scholarships/grants available. Financial award application deadline: 3/2; financial award applicants required to submit FAFSA. *Program availability:* Part-time, evening/weekend, 100% online, blended/hybrid learning. *Application deadline:* Applications are processed on a rolling basis. *Application Contact:* Graduate Admission, 909-448-4444, E-mail: gradadmission@laverne.edu. *Dean of LaFetra College of Education*, Dr. Kimberly White-Smith, 909-448-4583, E-mail: kwhite-smith@laverne.edu.

**Regional and Online Campuses** Students: 426 full-time (312 women), 654 part-time (460 women); includes 675 minority (71 Black or African American, non-Hispanic/Latino; 2 American Indian or Alaska Native, non-Hispanic/Latino; 66 Asian, non-Hispanic/Latino; 494 Hispanic/Latino; 6 Native Hawaiian or other Pacific Islander, non-Hispanic/Latino; 36 Two or more races, non-Hispanic/Latino), 1 international. Average age 36. *Faculty:* 18 full-time (11 women), 76 part-time/adjunct (42 women). Expenses: Contact institution. *Financial support:* Application deadline: 3/2; applicants required to submit FAFSA. *Program availability:* Part-time, evening/weekend. *Application deadline:* Applications are processed on a rolling basis. *Application Contact:* Graduate Admission Office, 909-448-4444, E-mail: gradadmission@laverne.edu. *Interim Dean*, Dr. Nelly Kazman, 909-448-4995, E-mail: nkazman@laverne.edu.

## UNIVERSITY OF LETHBRIDGE, Lethbridge, AB T1K 3M4, Canada

**General Information** Province-supported, coed, university. *Graduate housing:* Rooms and/or apartments available on a first-come, first-served basis to single and married students. Housing application deadline: 4/1. *Research affiliation:* Plains Midstream Canada ULC, Pacific Forestry Institution.

**GRADUATE UNITS**

**School of Graduate Studies** *Program availability:* Part-time, evening/weekend. Electronic applications accepted.

## UNIVERSITY OF LOUISIANA AT LAFAYETTE, Lafayette, LA 70504

**General Information** State-supported, coed, university. CGS member. *Enrollment:* 16,933 graduate, professional, and undergraduate students; 1,135 full-time matriculated graduate/professional students (605 women), 1,178 part-time matriculated graduate/professional students (675 women). *Enrollment by degree level:* 1,807 master's, 473 doctoral, 33 other advanced degrees. *Graduate faculty:* 319 full-time (115 women), 18 part-time/adjunct (11 women). *Tuition, area resident:* Full-time $5511; part-time $1630 per credit hour. Tuition, state resident: full-time $5511; part-time $1630 per credit hour. Tuition, nonresident: full-time $19,239; part-time $2409 per credit hour. *Required fees:* $46,637. *Graduate housing:* Rooms and/or apartments available on a first-come, first-served basis to single and married students. *Student services:* Campus employment opportunities, campus safety program, career counseling, child daycare facilities, free psychological counseling, international student services, low-cost health insurance, services for students with disabilities. *Library facilities:* Edith Garland Dupre Library. *Collection:* Books: 1.5 million (physical), 529,730 (digital/electronic); Serial titles: 26,860 (physical), 171,673 (digital/electronic); Databases: 232. Students can reserve study rooms. *Research affiliation:* National Wetlands Research Center (biology, wetlands restoration), Louisiana Universities Marine Consortium (marine biology), U.S. Fish and Wildlife Service (ecology), Army Corps of Engineers (wetlands), U.S. Geological Survey (USGS), U.S. Department of Agriculture (USDA).

**Computer facilities:** 413 computers available on campus for general student use. A campuswide network can be accessed. Online class registration is available.
Website: http://www.louisiana.edu/

**General Application Contact:** Dr. Mary Farmer-Kaiser, Dean, 337-482-6965, Fax: 337-482-1333, E-mail: kaiser@louisiana.edu.

**GRADUATE UNITS**

**BI Moody III College of Business Administration** *Program availability:* Part-time, evening/weekend.

**College of Education** *Program availability:* Part-time. Electronic applications accepted.

**College of Engineering** *Program availability:* Part-time, evening/weekend. Electronic applications accepted.

**College of Liberal Arts** *Program availability:* Part-time. Electronic applications accepted.

**College of Nursing and Allied Health Professions** Electronic applications accepted.

**College of Sciences** *Program availability:* Part-time. Electronic applications accepted.

***School of Geosciences*** *Program availability:* Part-time. Electronic applications accepted.

**College of the Arts** Electronic applications accepted.

***School of Architecture and Design*** Electronic applications accepted.

***School of Music*** Electronic applications accepted.

## UNIVERSITY OF LOUISIANA AT MONROE, Monroe, LA 71209-0001

**General Information** State-supported, coed, university. *Enrollment:* 8,489 graduate, professional, and undergraduate students; 1,000 full-time matriculated graduate/professional students (735 women), 610 part-time matriculated graduate/professional students (471 women). *Enrollment by degree level:* 1,017 master's, 545 doctoral, 48 other advanced degrees. *Graduate faculty:* 103 full-time (53 women), 30 part-time/adjunct (16 women). *Tuition, area resident:* Full-time $6489. Tuition, state resident: full-time $6489. Tuition, nonresident: full-time $18,989. *Required fees:* $2748. Tuition and fees vary according to course load and program. *Graduate housing:* Room and/or apartments available on a first-come, first-served basis to single students; on-campus housing not available to married students. Typical cost: $7855 (including board). Room and board charges vary according to board plan and housing facility selected. Housing application deadline: 5/1. *Student services:* Campus employment opportunities, career counseling, child daycare facilities, exercise/wellness program, free psychological counseling, international student services, services for students with disabilities, writing training. *Library facilities:* University Library. *Collection:* Books: 218,492 (physical), 293,246 (digital/electronic); Serial titles: 245 (physical), 198,009 (digital/electronic); Databases: 104. Students can reserve study rooms. *Research affiliation:* Juvenile Diabetes Research Foundation (pharmacology), Philip Morris, Inc. (medicinal chemistry), Harvard Hughes Medical Institute (biology), Xenoport, Inc. (pharmaceutics), U.S. Army Corps of Engineers (toxicology, environmental science), National Center for Toxicological Research (toxicology).

**Computer facilities:** Computer purchase and lease plans are available. A campuswide network can be accessed. Online class registration is available.
Website: http://www.ulm.edu/

**General Application Contact:** Juri Thompson, Coordinator of Graduate Admissions, 318-342-1084, Fax: 318-342-1042, E-mail: gradadmissions@ulm.edu.

**GRADUATE UNITS**

**Graduate School** Students: 1,000 full-time (735 women), 610 part-time (471 women); includes 484 minority (333 Black or African American, non-Hispanic/Latino; 11 American Indian or Alaska Native, non-Hispanic/Latino; 49 Asian, non-Hispanic/Latino; 42 Hispanic/Latino; 2 Native Hawaiian or other Pacific Islander, non-Hispanic/Latino; 47 Two or more races, non-Hispanic/Latino), 60 international. Average age 30. 1,034 applicants, 50% accepted, 343 enrolled. *Faculty:* 103 full-time (53 women), 30 part-time/adjunct (16 women). Expenses: Contact institution. *Financial support:* In 2019–20, 632 students received support. Research assistantships, teaching assistantships, career-related internships or fieldwork, Federal Work-Study, scholarships/grants, and unspecified assistantships available. Support available to part-time students. Financial award application deadline: 2/15; financial award applicants required to submit FAFSA. In 2019, 271 master's, 113 doctorates awarded. *Program availability:* Part-time, evening/weekend, 100% online, blended/hybrid learning. *Application deadline:* For fall admission, 8/1 for domestic students, 6/1 for international students; for spring admission, 1/1 for domestic students, 11/1 for international students; for summer admission, 6/1 for domestic students, 3/1 for international students. Applications are processed on a rolling basis. *Application fee:* $40. Electronic applications accepted. *Application Contact:* Juri Thompson, Coordinator of Graduate Admissions, 318-342-1084, Fax: 318-342-1042, E-mail: jthompson@ulm.edu. *Dean*, Dr. Sushma Krishnamurthy, 318-342-1036, Fax: 318-342-1042, E-mail: krishnamurthy@ulm.edu.

***College of Arts, Education, and Sciences*** Students: 184 full-time (141 women), 315 part-time (256 women); includes 150 minority (109 Black or African American, non-Hispanic/Latino; 2 American Indian or Alaska Native, non-Hispanic/Latino; 7 Asian, non-Hispanic/Latino; 15 Hispanic/Latino; 17 Two or more races, non-Hispanic/Latino), 7 international. Average age 35. 397 applicants, 56% accepted, 115 enrolled. *Faculty:* 26 full-time (11 women), 14 part-time/adjunct (8 women). Expenses: Contact institution. *Financial support:* In 2019–20, 178 students received support. Research assistantships with full tuition reimbursements available, teaching assistantships with full tuition reimbursements available, career-related internships or fieldwork, Federal Work-Study, scholarships/grants, and unspecified assistantships available. Support available to part-time students. Financial award application deadline: 2/15; financial award applicants required to submit FAFSA. In 2019, 77 master's, 7 doctorates awarded. *Program availability:* Part-time, evening/weekend, 100% online, blended/hybrid learning. *Application deadline:* For fall admission, 8/1 for domestic students, 6/1 for international students; for spring admission, 1/1 for domestic students, 11/1 for international students; for summer admission, 6/1 for domestic students, 3/1 for international students. Applications are processed on a rolling basis. *Application fee:* $40. Electronic applications accepted. *Application Contact:* Dr. Chris Michaelides, Associate Dean, 318-342-1243, Fax: 318-342-1755, E-mail: cmichaelides@ulm.edu. *Dean*, Dr. John Pratte, 318-342-1238, Fax: 318-342-1755, E-mail: pratte@ulm.edu.

***College of Business and Social Sciences*** Students: 152 full-time (113 women), 156 part-time (111 women); includes 141 minority (111 Black or African American, non-Hispanic/Latino; 3 American Indian or Alaska Native, non-Hispanic/Latino; 5 Asian, non-Hispanic/Latino; 10 Hispanic/Latino; 12 Two or more races, non-Hispanic/Latino), 19 international. Average age 29. 263 applicants, 60% accepted, 113 enrolled. *Faculty:* 24 full-time (8 women), 2 part-time/adjunct (0 women). Expenses: Contact institution. *Financial support:* In 2019–20, 133 students received support. Research assistantships with full tuition reimbursements available, teaching assistantships with full tuition reimbursements available, career-related internships or fieldwork, Federal Work-Study, scholarships/grants, and unspecified assistantships available. Financial award application deadline: 2/15; financial award applicants required to submit FAFSA. In 2019, 86 master's awarded. *Program availability:* Part-time, evening/weekend, 100% online, blended/hybrid learning. *Application deadline:* For fall admission, 8/1 for domestic students, 6/1 for international students; for spring admission, 1/1 for domestic students, 11/1 for international students; for summer admission, 6/1 for domestic students, 3/1 for international students. Applications are processed on a rolling basis. *Application fee:* $40. Electronic applications accepted. *Application Contact:* Dr. Ronald Berry, Dean, 318-342-1103, E-mail: rberry@ulm.edu. *Dean*, Dr. Ronald Berry, 318-342-1103, E-mail: rberry@ulm.edu.

***College of Health Sciences*** Students: 293 full-time (253 women), 138 part-time (104 women); includes 102 minority (71 Black or African American, non-Hispanic/Latino; 4 American Indian or Alaska Native, non-Hispanic/Latino; 5 Asian, non-Hispanic/Latino; 11 Hispanic/Latino; 2 Native Hawaiian or other Pacific Islander, non-Hispanic/Latino; 9 Two or more races, non-Hispanic/Latino), 5 international. Average age 31. 358

applicants, 37% accepted, 112 enrolled. *Faculty:* 34 full-time (24 women), 14 part-time/adjunct (8 women). Expenses: Contact institution. *Financial support:* In 2019–20, 191 students received support. Research assistantships with full tuition reimbursements available, teaching assistantships with full tuition reimbursements available, career-related internships or fieldwork, Federal Work-Study, scholarships/grants, and unspecified assistantships available. Financial award application deadline: 2/15; financial award applicants required to submit FAFSA. In 2019, 111 master's, 2 doctorates awarded. *Program availability:* Part-time, evening/weekend, online learning. *Application deadline:* For fall admission, 8/1 for domestic students, 6/1 for international students; for spring admission, 1/1 for domestic students, 11/1 for international students; for summer admission, 6/1 for domestic students, 3/1 for international students. Applications are processed on a rolling basis. *Application fee:* $40. Electronic applications accepted. *Application Contact:* Dr. Donald Simpson, Dean, 318-342-3312, E-mail: dsimpson@ulm.edu. *Dean*, Dr. Donald Simpson, 318-342-3312, E-mail: dsimpson@ulm.edu.

***College of Pharmacy*** Students: 371 full-time (228 women), 1 part-time (0 women); includes 91 minority (42 Black or African American, non-Hispanic/Latino; 2 American Indian or Alaska Native, non-Hispanic/Latino; 32 Asian, non-Hispanic/Latino; 6 Hispanic/Latino; 9 Two or more races, non-Hispanic/Latino), 29 international. Average age 24. 147 applicants, 66% accepted, 86 enrolled. *Faculty:* 19 full-time (10 women). Expenses: Contact institution. *Financial support:* In 2019–20, 130 students received support. Research assistantships with full tuition reimbursements available, career-related internships or fieldwork, Federal Work-Study, scholarships/grants, and unspecified assistantships available. Financial award application deadline: 2/15; financial award applicants required to submit FAFSA. In 2019, 104 doctorates awarded. *Application deadline:* For fall admission, 3/1 for domestic and international students; for spring admission, 9/1 for domestic and international students. Applications are processed on a rolling basis. Electronic applications accepted. *Application Contact:* Dr. Kevin Baer, Director of Graduate Studies and Research, 318-342-1698, E-mail: baer@ulm.edu. *Dean*, Dr. Glenn Anderson, 318-342-1600, E-mail: ganderson@ulm.edu.

## UNIVERSITY OF LOUISVILLE, Louisville, KY 40292-0001

**General Information** State-supported, coed, university. CGS member. *Enrollment:* 21,670 graduate, professional, and undergraduate students; 4,077 full-time matriculated graduate/professional students (2,169 women), 1,582 part-time matriculated graduate/professional students (798 women). *Enrollment by degree level:* 2,798 master's, 2,651 doctoral, 210 other advanced degrees. *Graduate faculty:* 1,728 full-time (726 women), 922 part-time/adjunct (527 women). *International tuition:* $27,114 full-time. *Tuition, area resident:* Full-time $13,000; part-time $723 per credit hour. Tuition, state resident: full-time $13,000; part-time $723 per credit hour. Tuition, nonresident: full-time $27,114; part-time $1507 per credit hour. *Required fees:* $196. Tuition and fees vary according to program and reciprocity agreements. *Graduate housing:* Rooms and/or apartments available on a first-come, first-served basis to single and married students. Typical cost: $3240 per year for single students; $3240 per year for married students. Room charges vary according to housing facility selected. *Student services:* Campus employment opportunities, campus safety program, career counseling, exercise/wellness program, free psychological counseling, grant writing training, international student services, low-cost health insurance, multicultural affairs office, services for students with disabilities, teacher training, writing training. *Library facilities:* William F. Ekstrom Library plus 6 others. *Collection:* Books: 1.6 million (physical), 215,864 (digital/electronic); Serial titles: 2,158 (physical), 90,689 (digital/electronic); Databases: 338. Weekly public service hours: 97; study areas open 24 hours, 5–7 days a week; students can reserve study rooms. *Research affiliation:* Ford Motor Company, General Electric Company (GE), Oak Ridge National Laboratory, Argonne National Laboratory.

**Computer facilities:** Computer purchase and lease plans are available. 400 computers available on campus for general student use. A campuswide network can be accessed. Online class registration is available.
Website: http://www.louisville.edu/

**General Application Contact:** Shabeer Hussain Amirali, Director of Graduate Admissions and Enrollment Management, 502-852-3108, E-mail: gradadm@louisville.edu.

**GRADUATE UNITS**

**Graduate School** Students: 4,077 full-time (2,169 women), 1,582 part-time (798 women); includes 1,318 minority (543 Black or African American, non-Hispanic/Latino; 9 American Indian or Alaska Native, non-Hispanic/Latino; 278 Asian, non-Hispanic/Latino; 262 Hispanic/Latino; 5 Native Hawaiian or other Pacific Islander, non-Hispanic/Latino; 221 Two or more races, non-Hispanic/Latino), 465 international. Average age 30. 7,326 applicants, 34% accepted, 1,671 enrolled. *Faculty:* 1,728 full-time (726 women), 922 part-time/adjunct (527 women). Expenses: Contact institution. In 2019, 1,443 master's, 549 doctorates, 119 other advanced degrees awarded. *Application fee:* $65. Electronic applications accepted. *Application Contact:* Dr. Barbara Clark, Acting Associate Dean, 502-852-6498, Fax: 502-852-3111, E-mail: gradadm@louisville.edu. *Acting Dean and Acting Vice Provost for Graduate Affairs*, Dr. Paul J. DeMarco, 502-852-0788, Fax: 502-852-2365, E-mail: paul.demarco@louisville.edu.

***College of Arts and Sciences*** Students: 506 full-time (254 women), 185 part-time (81 women); includes 137 minority (56 Black or African American, non-Hispanic/Latino; 15 Asian, non-Hispanic/Latino; 33 Hispanic/Latino; 33 Two or more races, non-Hispanic/Latino), 110 international. Average age 33. 578 applicants, 46% accepted, 183 enrolled. *Faculty:* 378 full-time (160 women), 263 part-time/adjunct (150 women). Expenses: Contact institution. *Financial support:* In 2019–20, 427 students received support, including 10 research assistantships with full tuition reimbursements available (averaging $18,000 per year), 243 teaching assistantships with full tuition reimbursements available (averaging $18,000 per year); health care benefits, tuition waivers (full), and unspecified assistantships also available. In 2019, 160 master's, 54 doctorates, 68 other advanced degrees awarded. *Program availability:* Part-time, 100% online, blended/hybrid learning. *Application deadline:* Applications are processed on a rolling basis. *Application fee:* $65. Electronic applications accepted. *Application Contact:* Dr. David Norvil Brown, Associate Dean for Graduate Education, 502-852-8966, Fax: 502-852-6888, E-mail: david.brown@louisville.edu. *Dean*, Dr. David Owen, 502-852-6490, Fax: 502-852-6888, E-mail: david.owen@louisville.edu.

***College of Business*** Students: 335 full-time (119 women), 60 part-time (29 women); includes 104 minority (49 Black or African American, non-Hispanic/Latino; 2 American Indian or Alaska Native, non-Hispanic/Latino; 24 Asian, non-Hispanic/Latino; 20 Hispanic/Latino; 9 Two or more races, non-Hispanic/Latino), 32 international. Average age 32. 455 applicants, 71% accepted, 263 enrolled. *Faculty:* 78 full-time (23 women), 50 part-time/adjunct (19 women). Expenses: Contact institution. *Financial support:* In 2019–20, 136 students received support. Career-related internships or fieldwork, scholarships/grants, and unspecified assistantships available. Financial award application deadline: 8/1; financial award applicants required to submit FAFSA. In 2019, 181 master's, 5 doctorates awarded. *Program availability:* Part-time, evening/weekend, 100% online, blended/hybrid learning. *Application deadline:* For fall admission, 6/1 priority date for domestic students, 5/1 priority date for international students; for spring admission, 4/1 priority date for domestic students. Applications are processed on a rolling basis. *Application fee:* $50. Electronic applications accepted. *Application Contact:* Richard Germain, Associate Dean, 502-852-4680, E-mail: richard.germain@louisville.edu. *Associate Dean*, Richard Germain, 502-852-4680, E-mail: richard.germain@louisville.edu.

***College of Education and Human Development*** Students: 425 full-time (245 women), 625 part-time (348 women); includes 300 minority (166 Black or African American, non-Hispanic/Latino; 2 American Indian or Alaska Native, non-Hispanic/Latino; 24 Asian, non-Hispanic/Latino; 64 Hispanic/Latino; 2 Native Hawaiian or other Pacific Islander, non-Hispanic/Latino; 42 Two or more races, non-Hispanic/Latino), 23 international. Average age 33. 470 applicants, 73% accepted, 244 enrolled. *Faculty:* 93 full-time (56 women), 171 part-time/adjunct (104 women). Expenses: Contact institution. *Financial support:* In 2019–20, 565 students received support, including 5 fellowships with full tuition reimbursements available (averaging $21,024 per year), 30 research assistantships with full tuition reimbursements available (averaging $21,024 per year), 14 teaching assistantships with full tuition reimbursements available (averaging $21,024 per year); scholarships/grants, traineeships, health care benefits, and unspecified assistantships also available. Financial award application deadline: 2/1; financial award applicants required to submit FAFSA. In 2019, 395 master's, 37 doctorates, 13 other advanced degrees awarded. *Program availability:* Part-time, evening/weekend, 100% online, blended/hybrid learning. *Application deadline:* For fall admission, 6/1 priority date for domestic students, 5/1 priority date for international students; for spring admission, 10/1 priority date for domestic students, 11/1 priority date for international students; for summer admission, 3/1 priority date for domestic students, 4/1 priority date for international students. Applications are processed on a rolling basis. *Application fee:* $65. Electronic applications accepted. *Application Contact:* Dr. Margaret Penetcost, Assistant Dean for Graduate Student Success, 502-852-2628, Fax: 502-852-1417, E-mail: gedadm@louisville.edu. *Interim Dean*, Dr. Amy A. Lingo, 502-852-3235, E-mail: cehdinfo@louisville.edu.

***Kent School of Social Work*** Students: 385 full-time (333 women), 96 part-time (73 women); includes 143 minority (75 Black or African American, non-Hispanic/Latino; 2 American Indian or Alaska Native, non-Hispanic/Latino; 8 Asian, non-Hispanic/Latino; 26 Hispanic/Latino; 2 Native Hawaiian or other Pacific Islander, non-Hispanic/Latino; 30 Two or more races, non-Hispanic/Latino), 7 international. Average age 32. 313 applicants, 77% accepted, 176 enrolled. *Faculty:* 33 full-time (22 women), 90 part-time/adjunct (73 women). Expenses: Contact institution. *Financial support:* In 2019–20, 53 students received support, including 1 fellowship with full tuition reimbursement available (averaging $20,000 per year), 7 research assistantships with full tuition reimbursements available (averaging $20,000 per year), 1 teaching assistantship with full tuition reimbursement available (averaging $20,000 per year); scholarships/grants, health care benefits, and unspecified assistantships also available. Financial award application deadline: 5/15; financial award applicants required to submit FAFSA. In 2019, 243 master's, 4 doctorates awarded. *Program availability:* Part-time, evening/weekend, 100% online, blended/hybrid learning. *Application deadline:* For fall admission, 5/30 for domestic and international students; for spring admission, 9/30 for domestic and international students; for summer admission, 2/28 for domestic and international students. Applications are processed on a rolling basis. *Application fee:* $65. Electronic applications accepted. *Application Contact:* Sarah Caragianis, Program Manager, MSSW Admissions, 502-852-0414, Fax: 502-852-0422, E-mail: sarah.caragianis@louisville.edu. *Dean*, Dr. David Jenkins, 502-852-3944, Fax: 502-852-0422, E-mail: d.jenkins@louisville.edu.

***School of Music*** Students: 56 full-time (19 women), 3 part-time (1 woman); includes 10 minority (2 Black or African American, non-Hispanic/Latino; 1 American Indian or Alaska Native, non-Hispanic/Latino; 4 Asian, non-Hispanic/Latino; 2 Hispanic/Latino; 1 Two or more races, non-Hispanic/Latino), 8 international. Average age 27. 75 applicants, 76% accepted, 31 enrolled. *Faculty:* 41 full-time (13 women), 33 part-time/adjunct (16 women). Expenses: Contact institution. *Financial support:* In 2019–20, 40 students received support, including 2 fellowships with full tuition reimbursements available (averaging $12,000 per year), 12 teaching assistantships with full tuition reimbursements available (averaging $12,000 per year); Federal Work-Study, scholarships/grants, health care benefits, tuition waivers (full), and unspecified assistantships also available. Financial award application deadline: 3/1. In 2019, 23 master's awarded. *Program availability:* Part-time. *Application fee:* $65. Electronic applications accepted. *Application Contact:* Laura Angermeier, Admissions Counselor/Senior Advising Counselor, 502-852-1623, Fax: 502-852-0520, E-mail: leange01@louisville.edu. *Dean, School of Music*, Dr. Teresa L. Reed, 502-852-6907, Fax: 502-852-0520, E-mail: teresa.reed@louisville.edu.

***School of Nursing*** Students: 164 full-time (140 women), 47 part-time (39 women); includes 45 minority (21 Black or African American, non-Hispanic/Latino; 5 Asian, non-Hispanic/Latino; 9 Hispanic/Latino; 10 Two or more races, non-Hispanic/Latino), 4 international. Average age 33. 84 applicants, 63% accepted, 48 enrolled. *Faculty:* 49 full-time (46 women), 91 part-time/adjunct (86 women). Expenses: Contact institution. *Financial support:* In 2019–20, 47 students received support, including 2 fellowships with full tuition reimbursements available (averaging $20,000 per year), 9 research assistantships with full tuition reimbursements available (averaging $20,000 per year), 3 teaching assistantships with full tuition reimbursements available (averaging $15,000 per year); scholarships/grants, health care benefits, unspecified assistantships, and Jonas Nurse Leader Fellowships also available. Financial award application deadline: 10/1; financial award applicants required to submit FAFSA. In 2019, 25 master's, 5 doctorates awarded. *Program availability:* Part-time, blended/hybrid learning. *Application deadline:* For fall admission, 1/15 priority date for domestic and international students; for summer admission, 10/15 priority date for domestic students. *Application fee:* $60. Electronic applications accepted. *Application Contact:* Trish Hart, MA, Assistant Dean for Student Affairs, 502-852-5825, Fax: 502-852-8783, E-mail: trish.hart@louisville.edu.

***School of Public Health and Information Sciences*** Students: 143 full-time (95 women), 111 part-time (65 women); includes 77 minority (37 Black or African American, non-Hispanic/Latino; 23 Asian, non-Hispanic/Latino; 7 Hispanic/Latino; 10 Two or more races, non-Hispanic/Latino), 48 international. Average age 33. 190 applicants, 66% accepted, 75 enrolled. *Faculty:* 40 full-time (17 women), 8 part-time/adjunct (3 women). Expenses: Contact institution. *Financial support:* In 2019–20, 128 students received support, including 6 fellowships with full tuition reimbursements available (averaging $20,000 per year), 43 research assistantships with full tuition reimbursements available (averaging $20,000 per year), 2 teaching assistantships with full tuition reimbursements available (averaging $20,000 per year); career-related internships or fieldwork, Federal Work-Study, scholarships/grants, health care benefits, and unspecified assistantships also available. Support available to part-time students. Financial award application deadline: 6/30; financial award applicants required to submit FAFSA. In 2019, 49 master's, 12 doctorates awarded. *Program availability:* Part-time, evening/weekend, 100% online. *Application deadline:* For fall admission, 7/1 for domestic students, 3/1 for international students; for spring admission, 11/1 for domestic students, 10/1 for international students. Applications are processed on a rolling basis. *Application fee:* $65. Electronic applications accepted. *Application Contact:* Vicki Lewis, Administrative Assistant, 502-852-1798, Fax: 502-852-3294, E-mail: vicki.lewis@louisville.edu. *Professor and Dean*, Dr. Craig Elliot Blakely, 502-852-3297, Fax: 502-852-3291, E-mail: craig.blakely@louisville.edu.

**J. B. Speed School of Engineering** Students: 313 full-time (70 women), 352 part-time (98 women); includes 117 minority (33 Black or African American, non-Hispanic/Latino; 1 American Indian or Alaska Native, non-Hispanic/Latino; 35 Asian, non-Hispanic/Latino; 23 Hispanic/Latino; 25 Two or more races, non-Hispanic/Latino), 173 international. Average age 29. 301 applicants, 53% accepted, 123 enrolled. *Faculty:* 110 full-time (19 women), 29 part-time/adjunct (6 women). Expenses: Contact institution. *Financial support:* In 2019–20, 251 students received support. Fellowships, research assistantships, teaching assistantships, scholarships/grants, health care benefits, and unspecified assistantships available. Financial award application deadline: 1/1. In 2019, 259 master's, 25 doctorates, 26 other advanced degrees awarded. *Program availability:* 100% online, blended/hybrid learning. *Application deadline:* For fall admission, 5/1 priority date for domestic and international students; for spring admission, 11/1 priority date for domestic and international students; for summer admission, 3/1 priority date for domestic and international students. Applications are processed on a rolling basis. *Application fee:* $65. Electronic applications accepted. *Application Contact:* Dr. Katherine Markuson, Director of Graduate Affairs, 502-852-6278, E-mail: katherine.markuson@louisville.edu. *Associate Dean for Research and Graduate Studies*, Dr. Kevin Walsh, 502-852-0826, E-mail: kevin.walsh@louisville.edu.

**Louis D. Brandeis School of Law** *Program availability:* Part-time. Electronic applications accepted.

**School of Dentistry** Students: 523 full-time (255 women), 3 part-time (1 woman); includes 144 minority (29 Black or African American, non-Hispanic/Latino; 61 Asian, non-Hispanic/Latino; 37 Hispanic/Latino; 17 Two or more races, non-Hispanic/Latino), 21 international. Average age 27. 196 applicants, 94% accepted, 143 enrolled. *Faculty:* 74 full-time (32 women), 67 part-time/adjunct (22 women). Expenses: Contact institution. *Financial support:* In 2019–20, 15 students received support, including 1 fellowship with full tuition reimbursement available (averaging $15,000 per year); scholarships/grants also available. Financial award application deadline: 3/15; financial award applicants required to submit FAFSA. In 2019, 24 master's, 115 doctorates awarded. *Application deadline:* For fall admission, 1/1 for domestic and international students. Applications are processed on a rolling basis. *Application fee:* $65. Electronic applications accepted. *Application Contact:* Jami Campbell, Assistant Director of Admissions, 502-852-5081, Fax: 502-852-1210, E-mail: dmdadms@louisville.edu. *Dean*, Dr. T. Gerry Bradley, 502-852-5295, E-mail: t0brad03@exchange.louisville.edu.

**School of Interdisciplinary and Graduate Studies** Students: 36 full-time (21 women), 14 part-time (5 women); includes 5 minority (1 Black or African American, non-Hispanic/Latino; 3 Hispanic/Latino; 1 Two or more races, non-Hispanic/Latino), 10 international. Average age 32. 27 applicants, 70% accepted, 14 enrolled. Expenses: Contact institution. *Financial support:* In 2019–20, 35 students received support, including 120 fellowships with full tuition reimbursements available (averaging $20,000 per year); scholarships/grants, health care benefits, unspecified assistantships, and Diversity scholarships also available. Financial award application deadline: 1/1; financial award applicants required to submit FAFSA. In 2019, 3 master's, 1 doctorate awarded. *Program availability:* Part-time. *Application deadline:* For fall admission, 7/1 priority date for domestic students, 5/1 priority date for international students; for winter admission, 7/1 priority date for domestic students, 5/1 for international students; for spring admission, 12/1 priority date for domestic students, 11/1 for international students; for summer admission, 4/1 priority date for domestic students, 4/1 for international students. Applications are processed on a rolling basis. *Application fee:* $65. Electronic applications accepted. *Application Contact:* Dr. Barbara Clark, Acting Associate Dean of the Graduate School, 502-852-6498, Fax: 502-852-3111, E-mail: gradadm@louisville.edu. *Acting Vice Provost for Graduate Affairs, Acting Dean of the Graduate School*, Dr. Paul J. DeMarco, 502-852-0788, Fax: 502-852-2365, E-mail: paul.demarco@louisville.edu.

**School of Medicine** Students: 893 full-time (457 women), 26 part-time (15 women); includes 200 minority (60 Black or African American, non-Hispanic/Latino; 1 American Indian or Alaska Native, non-Hispanic/Latino; 74 Asian, non-Hispanic/Latino; 28 Hispanic/Latino; 37 Two or more races, non-Hispanic/Latino), 30 international. Average age 27. 4,175 applicants, 10% accepted, 271 enrolled. *Faculty:* 760 full-time (298 women), 99 part-time/adjunct (43 women). Expenses: Contact institution. *Financial support:* In 2019–20, 191 students received support, including 25 research assistantships with full tuition reimbursements available (averaging $25,000 per year); fellowships, scholarships/grants, health care benefits, and unspecified assistantships also available. Financial award application deadline: 7/1; financial award applicants required to submit FAFSA. In 2019, 84 master's, 180 doctorates awarded. *Application deadline:* For fall admission, 10/15 priority date for domestic students. Applications are processed on a rolling basis. *Application fee:* $75. *Application Contact:* Dr. Stephen F. Wheeler, Associate Dean for Admissions, 502-852-5193, Fax: 502-852-0302, E-mail: sfwhee01@louisville.edu. *Dean, School of Medicine*, Dr. Toni M. Ganzel, 502-852-1499, Fax: 502-852-1484, E-mail: meddean@louisville.edu.

## UNIVERSITY OF LYNCHBURG, Lynchburg, VA 24501-3199

**General Information** Independent-religious, coed, comprehensive institution. *Graduate housing:* Room and/or apartments available on a first-come, first-served basis to single students; on-campus housing not available to married students.

**GRADUATE UNITS**

**Graduate Studies** *Program availability:* Part-time, evening/weekend. Electronic applications accepted.

## UNIVERSITY OF MAINE, Orono, ME 04469

**General Information** State-supported, coed, university. CGS member. *Enrollment:* 11,561 graduate, professional, and undergraduate students; 1,286 full-time matriculated graduate/professional students (755 women), 567 part-time matriculated graduate/professional students (398 women). *Enrollment by degree level:* 1,204 master's, 464 doctoral, 185 other advanced degrees. *International tuition:* $26,388 full-time. *Tuition, area resident:* Full-time $8100; part-time $450 per credit hour. Tuition, state resident: full-time $8100; part-time $450 per credit hour. Tuition, nonresident: full-time $26,388; part-time $1466 per credit hour. *Required fees:* $1257; $278 per semester. Tuition and fees vary according to course load. *Graduate housing:* Rooms and/or apartments available on a first-come, first-served basis to single and married students. Typical cost: $8320 per year ($9370 including board) for single students; $8320 per year for married students. Room and board charges vary according to board plan and housing facility selected. Housing application deadline: 8/1. *Library facilities:* Fogler Library. *Collection:* Books: 1.6 million (physical), 1.2 million (digital/electronic); Serial titles: 53,449 (physical), 143,082 (digital/electronic); Databases: 360. Weekly public service hours: 101; students can reserve study rooms. *Research affiliation:* Jackson Laboratory (medical genetics), Bigelow Laboratories for Ocean Sciences (marine science), Mount Desert Island Biological Laboratory (marine molecular biology), Sensor Research Development Corporation (electrical sensors), Maine Medical Center Research Institute (clinical medicine), Maine Institute for Human Genetics (medical genetics).

**Computer facilities:** Computer purchase and lease plans are available. 600 computers available on campus for general student use. A campuswide network can be accessed. Online class registration, online housing and financial aid information are available. Website: http://www.umaine.edu/

**General Application Contact:** Scott G. Delcourt, Assistant Vice President for Graduate Studies and Senior Associate Dean, 207-581-3291, Fax: 207-581-3232, E-mail: graduate@maine.edu.

**GRADUATE UNITS**

**Graduate School** Students: 1,286 full-time (755 women), 567 part-time (398 women); includes 141 minority (19 Black or African American, non-Hispanic/Latino; 26 American Indian or Alaska Native, non-Hispanic/Latino; 28 Asian, non-Hispanic/Latino; 44 Hispanic/Latino; 24 Two or more races, non-Hispanic/Latino), 222 international. Average age 33. 1,718 applicants, 65% accepted, 687 enrolled. *Faculty:* 652 full-time (227 women), 232 part-time/adjunct (100 women). Expenses: Contact institution. *Financial support:* In 2019–20, 831 students received support, including 14 fellowships with full tuition reimbursements available (averaging $22,400 per year), 378 research assistantships with full tuition reimbursements available (averaging $18,200 per year), 287 teaching assistantships with full tuition reimbursements available (averaging $16,000 per year); career-related internships or fieldwork, Federal Work-Study, institutionally sponsored loans, scholarships/grants, tuition waivers (full and partial), and unspecified assistantships also available. Support available to part-time students. Financial award application deadline: 3/1; financial award applicants required to submit FAFSA. In 2019, 351 master's, 69 doctorates, 62 other advanced degrees awarded. *Program availability:* Part-time, evening/weekend, 100% online, blended/hybrid learning. *Application deadline:* For fall admission, 1/15 priority date for domestic and international students; for spring admission, 11/15 priority date for domestic and international students. Applications are processed on a rolling basis. *Application fee:* $65. Electronic applications accepted. *Application Contact:* Scott G. Delcourt, Assistant Vice President for Graduate Studies/Senior Associate Dean, 207-581-3291, Fax: 207-581-3232, E-mail: graduate@maine.edu. *Assistant Vice President for Graduate Studies/Senior Associate Dean*, Scott G. Delcourt, 207-581-3291, Fax: 207-581-3232, E-mail: graduate@maine.edu.

***Climate Change Institute*** Students: 6 full-time (5 women); includes 2 minority (1 Hispanic/Latino; 1 Two or more races, non-Hispanic/Latino), 1 international. Average age 27. 14 applicants, 86% accepted, 4 enrolled. *Faculty:* 39 full-time (11 women). Expenses: Contact institution. *Financial support:* In 2019–20, 26 students received support, including 26 research assistantships with full tuition reimbursements available (averaging $15,200 per year); teaching assistantships with full tuition reimbursements available, institutionally sponsored loans, tuition waivers (full and partial), and unspecified assistantships also available. Financial award application deadline: 3/1; financial award applicants required to submit FAFSA. In 2019, 5 master's awarded. *Program availability:* Part-time. *Application deadline:* For fall admission, 11/1 priority date for domestic and international students; for spring admission, 2/1 priority date for domestic and international students. Applications are processed on a rolling basis. *Application fee:* $65. Electronic applications accepted. *Application Contact:* Dr. Karl Kreutz, Graduate Coordinator, 207-581-3011, E-mail: karl.kreutz@maine.edu. *Director*, Dr. Paul Mayewski, 207-581-3019, Fax: 207-581-1203, E-mail: paul.mayewski@maine.edu.

***College of Education and Human Development*** Students: 209 full-time (159 women), 366 part-time (288 women); includes 28 minority (5 Black or African American, non-Hispanic/Latino; 6 American Indian or Alaska Native, non-Hispanic/Latino; 7 Asian, non-Hispanic/Latino; 7 Hispanic/Latino; 3 Two or more races, non-Hispanic/Latino), 5 international. Average age 37. 340 applicants, 94% accepted, 236 enrolled. *Faculty:* 35 full-time (19 women), 47 part-time/adjunct (34 women). Expenses: Contact institution. *Financial support:* In 2019–20, 18 students received support, including 9 teaching assistantships with full tuition reimbursements available (averaging $15,200 per year); career-related internships or fieldwork, Federal Work-Study, institutionally sponsored loans, scholarships/grants, and unspecified assistantships also available. Support available to part-time students. Financial award application deadline: 3/1. In 2019, 86 master's, 5 doctorates, 38 other advanced degrees awarded. *Program availability:* Part-time, evening/weekend. *Application deadline:* For fall admission, 1/15 priority date for domestic students. Applications are processed on a rolling basis. *Application fee:* $65. Electronic applications accepted. *Application Contact:* Scott G. Delcourt, Senior Associate Dean of the Graduate School, 207-581-3291, Fax: 207-581-3232, E-mail: graduate@maine.edu. *Dean*, Dr. Mary Gresham, 207-581-2441, Fax: 207-581-2423.

***College of Engineering*** Students: 108 full-time (29 women), 30 part-time (5 women); includes 11 minority (2 Black or African American, non-Hispanic/Latino; 1 American Indian or Alaska Native, non-Hispanic/Latino; 3 Asian, non-Hispanic/Latino; 4 Hispanic/Latino; 1 Two or more races, non-Hispanic/Latino), 54 international. Average age 29. 116 applicants, 76% accepted, 41 enrolled. *Faculty:* 52 full-time (8 women), 5 part-time/adjunct (0 women). Expenses: Contact institution. *Financial support:* In 2019–20, 120 students received support, including 4 fellowships (averaging $22,650 per year), 48 research assistantships (averaging $20,700 per year), 22 teaching assistantships (averaging $16,300 per year); Federal Work-Study, institutionally sponsored loans, scholarships/grants, tuition waivers (full and partial), and unspecified assistantships also available. Financial award application deadline: 3/1. In 2019, 25 master's, 3 doctorates awarded. *Program availability:* Part-time. *Application deadline:* For fall admission, 2/1 priority date for domestic students. Applications are processed on a rolling basis. *Application fee:* $65. Electronic applications accepted. *Application Contact:* Scott G. Delcourt, Assistant Vice President for Graduate Studies and Senior Associate Dean, 207-581-3291, Fax: 207-581-3232, E-mail: graduate@maine.edu. *Dean*, Dr. Dana Humphrey, 207-581-2217, Fax: 207-581-2220, E-mail: dana.humphrey@umit.maine.edu.

**College of Liberal Arts and Sciences** Students: 269 full-time (129 women), 51 part-time (26 women); includes 40 minority (7 Black or African American, non-Hispanic/Latino; 5 American Indian or Alaska Native, non-Hispanic/Latino; 7 Asian, non-Hispanic/Latino; 13 Hispanic/Latino; 8 Two or more races, non-Hispanic/Latino), 60 international. Average age 31. 436 applicants, 54% accepted, 126 enrolled. *Faculty:* 147 full-time (46 women), 42 part-time/adjunct (14 women). Expenses: Contact institution. *Financial support:* In 2019–20, 250 students received support, including 13 fellowships (averaging $19,200 per year), 35 research assistantships (averaging $17,500 per year), 160 teaching assistantships (averaging $16,200 per year); career-related internships or fieldwork, Federal Work-Study, institutionally sponsored loans, scholarships/grants, and tuition waivers (full and partial) also available. Support available to part-time students. Financial award application deadline: 3/1. In 2019, 52 master's, 18 doctorates, 7 other advanced degrees awarded. *Program availability:* Part-time, evening/weekend. *Application deadline:* For fall admission, 2/1 priority date for domestic students. Applications are processed on a rolling basis. *Application fee:* $65. Electronic applications accepted. *Application Contact:* Scott G. Delcourt, Assistant Vice President for Graduate Studies and Senior Associate Dean, 207-581-3291, Fax: 207-581-3232, E-mail: graduate@maine.edu. *Dean*, Dr. Emily Haddad, 207-581-1954, Fax: 207-581-1947, E-mail: emily.haddad@maine.edu.

***College of Natural Sciences, Forestry, and Agriculture*** Students: 503 full-time (348 women), 58 part-time (42 women); includes 47 minority (4 Black or African American, non-Hispanic/Latino; 9 American Indian or Alaska Native, non-Hispanic/Latino; 9 Asian, non-Hispanic/Latino; 16 Hispanic/Latino; 9 Two or more races, non-Hispanic/Latino), 83 international. Average age 30. 567 applicants, 56% accepted, 178 enrolled. *Faculty:* 193 full-time (86 women), 122 part-time/adjunct (45 women). Expenses: Contact institution. *Financial support:* In 2019–20, 347 students received support, including 7 fellowships (averaging $23,900 per year), 190 research assistantships (averaging $19,700 per year), 93 teaching assistantships (averaging $16,000 per year); career-related internships or fieldwork, Federal Work-Study, institutionally sponsored loans, scholarships/grants, health care benefits, tuition waivers (full and partial), and unspecified assistantships also available. Support available to part-time students. Financial award application deadline: 3/1. In 2019, 145 master's, 30 doctorates, 6 other advanced degrees awarded. *Program availability:* Part-time, evening/weekend. *Application deadline:* For fall admission, 2/1 priority date for domestic students. Applications are processed on a rolling basis. *Application fee:* $65. Electronic applications accepted. *Application Contact:* Scott G. Delcourt, Assistant Vice President for Graduate Studies and Senior Associate Dean, 207-581-3291, Fax: 207-581-3232, E-mail: graduate@maine.edu. *Interim Dean*, Dr. Fred Servello, 207-581-3206, Fax: 207-581-3207.

***Graduate School of Biomedical Science and Engineering*** Students: 47 full-time (26 women), 1 part-time (0 women); includes 2 minority (1 Hispanic/Latino; 1 Two or more races, non-Hispanic/Latino), 9 international. Average age 30. 111 applicants, 17% accepted, 15 enrolled. *Faculty:* 182 full-time (60 women). Expenses: Contact institution. *Financial support:* In 2019–20, 47 students received support, including 1 fellowship with tuition reimbursement available (averaging $34,000 per year), 41 research assistantships with full tuition reimbursements available (averaging $20,000 per year), 5 teaching assistantships with full tuition reimbursements available (averaging $15,825 per year); career-related internships or fieldwork, scholarships/grants, and unspecified assistantships also available. Financial award application deadline: 3/1; financial award applicants required to submit FAFSA. In 2019, 7 doctorates awarded. *Application deadline:* For fall admission, 1/1 priority date for domestic and international students. Applications are processed on a rolling basis. *Application fee:* $65. Electronic applications accepted. *Application Contact:* Scott G Delcourt, Assistant Vice President for Graduate Studies and Senior Associate Dean, 207-581-3291, Fax: 207-581-3232, E-mail: graduate@maine.edu. *Assistant Vice President for Graduate Studies and Senior Associate Dean*, Scott G Delcourt, 207-581-3291, Fax: 207-581-3232, E-mail: graduate@maine.edu.

***The Maine Business School*** Students: 50 full-time (16 women), 53 part-time (20 women); includes 4 minority (2 American Indian or Alaska Native, non-Hispanic/Latino; 1 Hispanic/Latino; 1 Two or more races, non-Hispanic/Latino), 8 international. Average age 33. 94 applicants, 97% accepted, 60 enrolled. *Faculty:* 14 full-time (4 women), 6 part-time/adjunct (1 woman). Expenses: Contact institution. *Financial support:* In 2019–20, 30 students received support, including 4 teaching assistantships with full tuition reimbursements available (averaging $15,825 per year); career-related internships or fieldwork, Federal Work-Study, institutionally sponsored loans, scholarships/grants, tuition waivers (full and partial), and unspecified assistantships also available. Financial award application deadline: 3/1; financial award applicants required to submit FAFSA. In 2019, 25 master's, 4 other advanced degrees awarded. *Program availability:* Part-time, evening/weekend, online learning. *Application deadline:* For fall admission, 7/1 priority date for domestic and international students; for spring admission, 12/1 priority date for domestic and international students; for summer admission, 4/1 priority date for domestic and international students. Applications are processed on a rolling basis. *Application fee:* $65. Electronic applications accepted. *Application Contact:* Scott G. Delcourt, Assistant Vice President for Graduate Studies and Senior Associate Dean, 207-581-3291, Fax: 207-581-3232, E-mail: graduate@maine.edu. *Dean of Undergraduate School of Business*, Faye Gilbert, 207-581-1963, E-mail: faye.gilbert@maine.edu.

**University of Maine School of Law** Students: 262 full-time (134 women); includes 25 minority (3 Black or African American, non-Hispanic/Latino; 3 American Indian or Alaska Native, non-Hispanic/Latino; 8 Asian, non-Hispanic/Latino; 10 Hispanic/Latino; 1 Two or more races, non-Hispanic/Latino), 11 international. Average age 30. 582 applicants, 55% accepted, 96 enrolled. *Faculty:* 22 full-time (12 women), 42 part-time/adjunct (15 women). Expenses: Contact institution. *Financial support:* In 2019–20, 165 students received support, including 40 fellowships (averaging $4,000 per year), 5 research assistantships (averaging $1,000 per year), 6 teaching assistantships with partial tuition reimbursements available (averaging $2,500 per year); Federal Work-Study, scholarships/grants, and unspecified assistantships also available. Financial award application deadline: 6/30; financial award applicants required to submit FAFSA. In 2019, 76 doctorates awarded. *Program availability:* Part-time. *Application deadline:* For fall admission, 7/15 for domestic students, 6/1 for international students; for spring admission, 11/15 for international students. Applications are processed on a rolling basis. Electronic applications accepted. *Application Contact:* Caroline Wilshusen, Associate Dean of Admissions, 207-780-4341, Fax: 207-780-4239, E-mail: lawadmissions@maine.edu. *Dean*, Leigh Saufley, 207-780-4344, Fax: 207-780-4239, E-mail: lawdean@maine.edu.

## UNIVERSITY OF MAINE AT FARMINGTON, Farmington, ME 04938

**General Information** State-supported, coed, comprehensive institution. *Enrollment:* 1,930 graduate, professional, and undergraduate students; 106 part-time matriculated graduate/professional students (92 women). *Enrollment by degree level:* 106 master's. *Graduate faculty:* 9 full-time (7 women), 12 part-time/adjunct (11 women). *Student services:* Career counseling, exercise/wellness program, free psychological counseling, low-cost health insurance, services for students with disabilities. *Library facilities:* Mantor Library plus 1 other. *Collection:* Books: 53,312 (physical), 610,721 (digital/electronic); Serial titles: 145 (physical), 101,125 (digital/electronic); Databases: 200. Weekly public service hours: 88; students can reserve study rooms.

**Computer facilities:** Computer purchase and lease plans are available. 220 computers available on campus for general student use. A campuswide network can be accessed. Online class registration is available.
Website: http://www.umf.maine.edu/

**General Application Contact:** Dori Beane, Administrative Specialist, 207-778-7502, Fax: 207-778-8134, E-mail: gradstudies@maine.edu.

**GRADUATE UNITS**

**Graduate Programs in Education** Average age 36. *Faculty:* 9 full-time (7 women), 11 part-time/adjunct (10 women). Expenses: Contact institution. *Financial support:* Applicants required to submit FAFSA. In 2019, 26 master's awarded. *Program availability:* Part-time, evening/weekend, 100% online, blended/hybrid learning. *Application deadline:* For fall admission, 8/10 for domestic students; for spring admission, 1/5 for domestic students; for summer admission, 4/10 for domestic students. Applications are processed on a rolling basis. Electronic applications accepted. *Application Contact:* Kenneth Lewis, Director of Educational Outreach, 207-778-7502, Fax: 207-778-7066, E-mail: gradstudies@maine.edu. *Associate Dean for Graduate and Continuing Education*, Dr. Erin L Connor, 207-778 Ext. 7502, E-mail: erin.l.connor@maine.edu.

## UNIVERSITY OF MANAGEMENT AND TECHNOLOGY, Arlington, VA 22209-1609

**General Information** Proprietary, coed, comprehensive institution. *Enrollment:* 342 graduate, professional, and undergraduate students; 88 full-time matriculated graduate/professional students (30 women), 28 part-time matriculated graduate/professional students (9 women). *Graduate faculty:* 69 full-time (10 women). *Tuition:* Full-time $7020; part-time $390 per credit hour. *Required fees:* $90; $30 per semester. *Graduate housing:* On-campus housing not available. *Student services:* Career counseling, international student services. *Collection:* Books: 9,104 (physical), 569 (digital/electronic); Serial titles: 1,008 (physical), 25,739 (digital/electronic); Databases: 73.

**Computer facilities:** A campuswide network can be accessed. Online class registration is available.
Website: http://www.umtweb.edu/

**General Application Contact:** Kenny Hickey, Admissions, 703-516-0035, Fax: 703-516-0985, E-mail: admissions@umtweb.edu.

**GRADUATE UNITS**

**Program in Business Administration** *Program availability:* Part-time, 100% online. Electronic applications accepted.

**Program in Computer Science** *Program availability:* Part-time, evening/weekend, online learning. Electronic applications accepted.

**Program in Criminal Justice** *Program availability:* Part-time, evening/weekend, online learning.

**Program in Engineering Management**

**Program in Health Administration**

**Program in Homeland Security**

**Program in Information Technology**

**Program in Management** *Program availability:* Part-time, evening/weekend, online learning. Electronic applications accepted.

**Program in Public Administration**

## THE UNIVERSITY OF MANCHESTER, Manchester M13 9PL, United Kingdom

**General Information** Public, coed, comprehensive institution.

**GRADUATE UNITS**

**Manchester Institute of Education**

**School of Arts, Languages and Cultures**

**School of Biological Sciences**

**School of Chemical Engineering and Analytical Science**

**School of Chemistry**

**School of Computer Science**

**School of Dentistry**

**School of Earth and Environmental Sciences**

**School of Electrical and Electronic Engineering**

**School of Environment, Education and Development**

**School of Law**

**School of Materials**

**School of Mathematics**

**School of Mechanical, Aerospace and Civil Engineering**

**School of Medicine**

**School of Nursing, Midwifery and Social Work**

**School of Pharmacy and Pharmaceutical Sciences**

**School of Physics and Astronomy**

**School of Psychological Sciences**

**School of Social Sciences**

**The University of Manchester - Grad School Programmes** Students: 13,395. Expenses: Contact institution. *Financial support:* Scholarships/grants available. *Program availability:* Blended/hybrid learning. *Application deadline:* For summer admission, 6/30 for domestic and international students. Applications are processed on a rolling basis. *Application fee:* 50 British pounds. Electronic applications accepted. *Application Contact:* Daniel Annoot, International Officer, 44 161 306 1634, E-mail: international@manchester.ac.uk.

## UNIVERSITY OF MANITOBA, Winnipeg, MB R3T 2N2, Canada

**General Information** Province-supported, coed, university. CGS member. *Graduate housing:* Rooms and/or apartments available to single and married students. *Research affiliation:* Canada Department of Agriculture Research Station, Freshwater Institute, Atomic Energy of Canada, Manitoba Department of Mines, Resources, and Environmental Management, Northern Scientific Training Program (Northern studies), Taiga Biological Research Trust.

**GRADUATE UNITS**

**Dr. Gerald Niznick College of Dentistry**

**Faculty of Graduate Studies** *Program availability:* Part-time.
***Asper School of Business***
***Clayton H. Riddell Faculty of Environment, Earth, and Resources***
***College of Nursing***
***College of Pharmacy***
***College of Rehabilitation Sciences***
***College Universitaire de Saint Boniface***
***Desautels Faculty of Music***
***Faculty of Agricultural and Food Sciences***
***Faculty of Architecture***
***Faculty of Arts***
***Faculty of Education***
***Faculty of Engineering***
***Faculty of Kinesiology and Recreation Management***
***Faculty of Law*** Electronic applications accepted.
***Faculty of Science***
***Faculty of Social Work***
***Interdisciplinary Programs***
**Max Rady College of Medicine** *Program availability:* Part-time. Electronic applications accepted.
***Graduate Programs in Medicine*** *Program availability:* Part-time.

## UNIVERSITY OF MARY, Bismarck, ND 58504-9652

**General Information** Independent-religious, coed, comprehensive institution. *Graduate housing:* Room and/or apartments available on a first-come, first-served basis to single students; on-campus housing not available to married students. Housing application deadline: 7/15.

**GRADUATE UNITS**

**Gary Tharaldson School of Business** *Program availability:* Part-time, evening/weekend. Electronic applications accepted.

**Liffrig Family School of Education and Behavioral Sciences**

**School of Health Sciences** Electronic applications accepted.

***Division of Nursing*** *Program availability:* Part-time, evening/weekend, online learning. Electronic applications accepted.

## UNIVERSITY OF MARY HARDIN-BAYLOR, Belton, TX 76513

**General Information** Independent-religious, coed, comprehensive institution. *Enrollment:* 3,846 graduate, professional, and undergraduate students; 310 full-time matriculated graduate/professional students (190 women), 175 part-time matriculated graduate/professional students (118 women). *Enrollment by degree level:* 282 master's, 203 doctoral. *Graduate faculty:* 84 full-time (48 women), 28 part-time/adjunct (13 women). *Tuition:* Full-time $16,200; part-time $10,800 per credit hour. *Required fees:* $1350; $75 per credit hour. $50 per term. Tuition and fees vary according to course load and degree level. *Graduate housing:* On-campus housing not available. *Student services:* Campus employment opportunities, career counseling, exercise/wellness program, free psychological counseling, international student services, multicultural affairs office, services for students with disabilities, teacher training. *Library facilities:* Townsend Memorial Library. *Collection:* Books: 195,754 (physical), 29,300 (digital/electronic); Serial titles: 236 (physical), 399,560 (digital/electronic); Databases: 145. Weekly public service hours: 99; students can reserve study rooms.

**Computer facilities:** Computer purchase and lease plans are available. 275 computers available on campus for general student use. A campuswide network can be accessed. Online class registration is available.
Website: http://www.umhb.edu/

**General Application Contact:** Katherine Moore, Assistant Director, Graduate Admissions, 254-295-4924, E-mail: kmoore@umhb.edu.

**GRADUATE UNITS**

**Graduate Studies in Accounting** Students: 11 full-time (5 women), 5 part-time (3 women); includes 6 minority (1 Asian, non-Hispanic/Latino; 5 Hispanic/Latino). Average age 29. 10 applicants, 60% accepted, 3 enrolled. *Faculty:* 19 full-time (5 women), 3 part-time/adjunct (all women). Expenses: Contact institution. *Financial support:* In 2019–20, 16 students received support. Federal Work-Study, unspecified assistantships, and scholarships for some active duty military personnel available. Support available to part-time students. Financial award applicants required to submit FAFSA. *Program availability:* Evening/weekend. *Application deadline:* For fall admission, 6/1 for domestic students, 4/30 for international students; for spring admission, 11/1 for domestic students, 9/30 for international students. Applications are processed on a rolling basis. *Application fee:* $35 ($135 for international students). Electronic applications accepted. *Application Contact:* Mary Bosquez, Graduate Admissions Specialist, 254-295-4834, E-mail: mbosquez@umhb.edu. *Associate Dean, Graduate Programs in McLane College of Business*, Dr. Nancy Bonner, 254-295-4884, E-mail: nbonner@umhb.edu.

**Graduate Studies in Business Administration** Students: 13 full-time (3 women), 20 part-time (12 women); includes 11 minority (5 Black or African American, non-Hispanic/Latino; 1 Asian, non-Hispanic/Latino; 4 Hispanic/Latino; 1 Two or more races, non-Hispanic/Latino), 6 international. Average age 35. 44 applicants, 57% accepted, 10 enrolled. *Faculty:* 19 full-time (5 women), 3 part-time/adjunct (all women). Expenses: Contact institution. *Financial support:* In 2019–20, 23 students received support. Federal Work-Study, institutionally sponsored loans, unspecified assistantships, and scholarships for some active duty military personnel available. Support available to part-time students. Financial award applicants required to submit FAFSA. In 2019, 26 master's awarded. *Program availability:* Part-time, evening/weekend. *Application deadline:* For fall admission, 6/1 for domestic students, 4/30 priority date for international students; for spring admission, 11/1 for domestic students, 9/30 priority date for international students. Applications are processed on a rolling basis. *Application fee:* $35 ($135 for international students). Electronic applications accepted. *Application Contact:* Katherine Moore, Assistant Director, Graduate Admissions, 254-295-4924, E-mail: kmoore@umhb.edu. *Associate Dean, Graduate Programs in McLane College of Business*, Dr. Nancy Bonner, 254-295-4884, E-mail: nbonner@umhb.edu.

**Graduate Studies in Counseling** Students: 54 full-time (41 women), 23 part-time (19 women); includes 36 minority (13 Black or African American, non-Hispanic/Latino; 1 American Indian or Alaska Native, non-Hispanic/Latino; 1 Asian, non-Hispanic/Latino; 18 Hispanic/Latino; 3 Two or more races, non-Hispanic/Latino). Average age 31. 57 applicants, 75% accepted, 25 enrolled. *Faculty:* 6 full-time (3 women), 4 part-time/adjunct (2 women). Expenses: Contact institution. *Financial support:* In 2019–20, 58 students received support. Federal Work-Study, unspecified assistantships, and scholarships for some active duty military personnel available. Support available to part-time students. Financial award applicants required to submit FAFSA. In 2019, 32 master's awarded. *Program availability:* Part-time, evening/weekend. *Application deadline:* For fall admission, 6/1 for domestic students, 4/30 priority date for international students; for spring admission, 11/1 for domestic students, 9/30 priority date for international students. Applications are processed on a rolling basis. *Application fee:* $35 ($135 for international students). Electronic applications accepted. *Application Contact:* Katherine Moore, Assistant Director, Graduate Admissions, 254-295-4924, E-mail: kmoore@umhb.edu. *Interim Director, Graduate Counseling*, Dr. Ty Leonard, 254-295-5532, E-mail: hleonard@umhb.edu.

**Graduate Studies in Education** Students: 45 full-time (31 women), 81 part-time (59 women); includes 57 minority (38 Black or African American, non-Hispanic/Latino; 17 Hispanic/Latino; 2 Two or more races, non-Hispanic/Latino). Average age 41. 14 applicants, 86% accepted, 9 enrolled. *Faculty:* 13 full-time (7 women), 6 part-time/adjunct (0 women). Expenses: Contact institution. *Financial support:* In 2019–20, 126 students received support. Federal Work-Study and scholarships for some active duty military personnel available. Support available to part-time students. Financial award application deadline: 6/1; financial award applicants required to submit FAFSA. In 2019, 20 master's, 18 doctorates awarded. *Program availability:* Part-time, evening/weekend. *Application deadline:* For fall admission, 6/1 for domestic students, 4/30 priority date for international students; for spring admission, 11/1 for domestic students, 9/30 priority date for international students. Applications are processed on a rolling basis. *Application fee:* $35 ($135 for international students). Electronic applications accepted. *Application Contact:* Katherine Moore, Assistant Director, Graduate Admissions, 254-295-4924, E-mail: kmoore@umhb.edu. *Director, Graduate Programs in Education*, Dr. Todd Kunders, 254-295-4579, E-mail: tkunders@umhb.edu.

**Graduate Studies in Exercise Physiology** Students: 6 full-time (3 women), 26 part-time (11 women); includes 8 minority (2 Black or African American, non-Hispanic/Latino; 5 Hispanic/Latino; 1 Two or more races, non-Hispanic/Latino), 1 international. Average age 27. 21 applicants, 81% accepted, 10 enrolled. *Faculty:* 10 full-time (3 women). Expenses: Contact institution. *Financial support:* In 2019–20, 27 students received support. Federal Work-Study, unspecified assistantships, and scholarships for some active duty military personnel available. Support available to part-time students. Financial award application deadline: 6/1; financial award applicants required to submit FAFSA. In 2019, 21 master's awarded. *Program availability:* Part-time, 100% online. *Application deadline:* For fall admission, 6/1 for domestic students, 4/30 priority date for international students; for spring admission, 11/1 for domestic students, 9/30 priority date for international students. Applications are processed on a rolling basis. *Application fee:* $35 ($135 for international students). Electronic applications accepted. *Application Contact:* Katherine Moore, Assistant Director, Graduate Admissions, 254-295-4924, E-mail: kmoore@umhb.edu. *Director, MS Ed in Exercise Physiology Program*, Dr. Lem Taylor, 254-295-4895, E-mail: ltaylor@umhb.edu.

**Graduate Studies in Information Systems** Students: 46 full-time (17 women), 11 part-time (6 women); includes 3 minority (all Asian, non-Hispanic/Latino), 49 international. Average age 26. 245 applicants, 75% accepted, 14 enrolled. *Faculty:* 20 full-time (6 women), 2 part-time/adjunct (both women). Expenses: Contact institution. *Financial support:* In 2019–20, 46 students received support. Federal Work-Study, unspecified assistantships, and scholarships for some active duty military personnel available. Support available to part-time students. Financial award applicants required to submit FAFSA. In 2019, 30 master's awarded. *Program availability:* Part-time, evening/weekend. *Application deadline:* For fall admission, 6/1 for domestic students, 4/30 priority date for international students; for spring admission, 11/1 for domestic students, 9/30 priority date for international students. Applications are processed on a rolling basis. *Application fee:* $35 ($135 for international students). Electronic applications accepted. *Application Contact:* Katherine Moore, Assistant Director, Graduate Admissions, 254-295-4924, E-mail: kmoore@umhb.edu. *Professor, Graduate Program Director, Master of Science in Information Systems Program*, Dr. James King, 254-295-4404, E-mail: jking@umhb.edu.

**Graduate Studies in Nursing** Students: 22 full-time (20 women), 9 part-time (8 women); includes 15 minority (4 Black or African American, non-Hispanic/Latino; 3 Asian, non-Hispanic/Latino; 7 Hispanic/Latino; 1 Two or more races, non-Hispanic/Latino), 1 international. Average age 36. 26 applicants, 62% accepted, 15 enrolled. *Faculty:* 8 full-time (all women), 5 part-time/adjunct (3 women). Expenses: Contact institution. *Financial support:* In 2019–20, 24 students received support. Federal Work-Study, unspecified assistantships, and scholarships for some active duty military personnel available. Support available to part-time students. Financial award applicants required to submit FAFSA. In 2019, 17 master's, 2 other advanced degrees awarded. *Program availability:* Evening/weekend. *Application deadline:* For fall admission, 6/1 for domestic students, 4/30 priority date for international students; for spring admission, 11/1 for domestic students, 9/30 priority date for international students. Applications are processed on a rolling basis. *Application fee:* $35 ($135 for international students). Electronic applications accepted. *Application Contact:* Katherine Moore, Assistant Director, Graduate Admissions, 254-295-4924, E-mail: kmoore@umhb.edu. *Director, Master of Science in Nursing Program & Assistant Professor*, Dr. Elizabeth Jimenez, 254-295-4769, E-mail: ejimenez@umhb.edu.

**Graduate Studies in Physical Therapy** Students: 113 full-time (70 women); includes 28 minority (4 Black or African American, non-Hispanic/Latino; 7 Asian, non-Hispanic/Latino; 17 Hispanic/Latino). Average age 25. 337 applicants, 27% accepted, 40 enrolled. *Faculty:* 8 full-time (7 women), 10 part-time/adjunct (5 women). Expenses: Contact institution. *Financial support:* In 2019–20, 113 students received support. Federal Work-Study, unspecified assistantships, and scholarships for some active duty military personnel available. Financial award applicants required to submit FAFSA. In 2019, 34 doctorates awarded. *Application deadline:* For fall admission, 6/1 for domestic students, 4/30 priority date for international students; for spring admission, 11/1 for domestic students, 9/30 priority date for international students. Applications are processed on a rolling basis. *Application fee:* $35 ($135 for international students). Electronic applications accepted. *Application Contact:* Katherine Moore, Assistant Director, Graduate Admissions, 254-295-4924, E-mail: kmoore@umhb.edu. *Director, Doctor of Physical Therapy Program/Associate Professor*, Dr. Barbara Gresham, 254-295-4921, E-mail: bgresham@umhb.edu.

## UNIVERSITY OF MARYLAND, BALTIMORE, Baltimore, MD 21201

**General Information** State-supported, coed, graduate-only institution. CGS member. *Enrollment by degree level:* 2,171 master's, 3,531 doctoral, 177 other advanced degrees. *Graduate faculty:* 1,951 full-time (917 women), 933 part-time/adjunct (609 women). *Graduate housing:* Rooms and/or apartments available on a first-come, first-served basis to single and married students. *Student services:* Campus employment opportunities, campus safety program, career counseling, exercise/wellness program, free psychological counseling, grant writing training, international student services, low-cost health insurance, services for students with disabilities, writing training. *Library facilities:* Health Sciences and Human Services Library plus 1 other. *Collection:* Books:

292,010 (physical), 50,988 (digital/electronic); Serial titles: 306,853 (physical), 162,832 (digital/electronic); Databases: 206. Students can reserve study rooms. *Research affiliation:* University of Maryland Medical System (medical research), University of Maryland Biotechnology Institute (biology), University of Maryland BioPark (biology).

**Computer facilities:** Online class registration is available.
Website: http://www.umaryland.edu/

**General Application Contact:** Keith T. Brooks, Director, Graduate Enrollment Affairs, 410-706-7131, Fax: 410-706-3473, E-mail: kbrooks@umaryland.edu.

**GRADUATE UNITS**

**Francis King Carey School of Law** *Program availability:* Part-time, evening/weekend, 100% online. Electronic applications accepted.

**Graduate School** *Program availability:* Part-time, evening/weekend, online learning. Electronic applications accepted.

***School of Social Work*** Electronic applications accepted.

**Professional and Advanced Education Programs in Dentistry** Students: 582 full-time (301 women), 4 part-time (2 women); includes 282 minority (58 Black or African American, non-Hispanic/Latino; 140 Asian, non-Hispanic/Latino; 54 Hispanic/Latino; 30 Two or more races, non-Hispanic/Latino), 28 international. Average age 27. 1,322 applicants, 75% accepted, 159 enrolled. Expenses: Contact institution. *Financial support:* Career-related internships or fieldwork, Federal Work-Study, scholarships/grants, and traineeships available. Financial award application deadline: 3/1; financial award applicants required to submit FAFSA. In 2019, 132 doctorates, 23 Certificates awarded. *Application deadline:* Applications are processed on a rolling basis. *Application fee:* $85. Electronic applications accepted. *Application Contact:* Dr. Judith A. Porter, Assistant Dean for Admissions and Recruitment, 410-706-7472, Fax: 410-706-0945, E-mail: ddsadmissions@umaryland.edu. *Dean,* Dr. Mark A. Reynolds, 410-706-7461.

**Professional Program in Pharmacy** Electronic applications accepted.

**School of Medicine** Students: 1,119 full-time (701 women), 90 part-time (63 women); includes 446 minority (82 Black or African American, non-Hispanic/Latino; 254 Asian, non-Hispanic/Latino; 67 Hispanic/Latino; 43 Two or more races, non-Hispanic/Latino), 61 international. Average age 26. 6,152 applicants, 14% accepted, 345 enrolled. Expenses: Contact institution. *Financial support:* In 2019–20, research assistantships with partial tuition reimbursements (averaging $25,000 per year) were awarded; fellowships, Federal Work-Study, scholarships/grants, health care benefits, and unspecified assistantships also available. Financial award application deadline: 3/1; financial award applicants required to submit FAFSA. In 2019, 61 master's, 262 doctorates awarded. *Program availability:* Part-time. Electronic applications accepted. *Application Contact:* Dr. E. Albert Reece, Dean and Vice President for Medical Affairs, 410-706-7410, Fax: 410-706-0235, E-mail: deanmed@som.umaryland.edu. *Dean and Vice President for Medical Affairs,* Dr. E. Albert Reece, 410-706-7410, Fax: 410-706-0235, E-mail: deanmed@som.umaryland.edu.

**University of Maryland School of Nursing** Students: 539 full-time (463 women), 586 part-time (506 women); includes 485 minority (259 Black or African American, non-Hispanic/Latino; 3 American Indian or Alaska Native, non-Hispanic/Latino; 124 Asian, non-Hispanic/Latino; 66 Hispanic/Latino; 1 Native Hawaiian or other Pacific Islander, non-Hispanic/Latino; 32 Two or more races, non-Hispanic/Latino), 18 international. Average age 33. 964 applicants, 54% accepted, 347 enrolled. *Faculty:* 130 full-time (117 women), 125 part-time/adjunct (114 women). Expenses: Contact institution. *Financial support:* In 2019–20, 257 students received support, including 31 research assistantships with full and partial tuition reimbursements available (averaging $25,000 per year), 21 teaching assistantships with full and partial tuition reimbursements available (averaging $19,000 per year); scholarships/grants, traineeships, and unspecified assistantships also available. Support available to part-time students. Financial award application deadline: 3/1; financial award applicants required to submit FAFSA. In 2019, 197 master's, 114 doctorates, 12 other advanced degrees awarded. *Program availability:* Part-time. *Application deadline:* For fall admission, 11/1 priority date for domestic and international students; for spring admission, 12/15 for domestic and international students; for summer admission, 9/1 for domestic and international students. Applications are processed on a rolling basis. *Application fee:* $75. Electronic applications accepted. *Application Contact:* Larry Fillian, Associate Dean of Student and Academic Services, 410-706-6298, E-mail: lfillian@umaryland.edu. *Dean,* Dr. Jane Kirschling, 410-706-4359, E-mail: kirschling@umaryland.edu.

## UNIVERSITY OF MARYLAND, BALTIMORE COUNTY, Baltimore, MD 21250

**General Information** State-supported, coed, university. CGS member. *Enrollment:* 13,602 graduate, professional, and undergraduate students; 1,255 full-time matriculated graduate/professional students (578 women), 1,219 part-time matriculated graduate/professional students (623 women). *Enrollment by degree level:* 1,621 master's, 738 doctoral, 120 other advanced degrees. *Graduate faculty:* 454 full-time, 114 part-time/adjunct. *International tuition:* $1132 full-time. *Tuition, area resident:* Full-time $659. Tuition, state resident: full-time $659. Tuition, nonresident: full-time $1132. *Required fees:* $140; $140 per credit hour. *Graduate housing:* Room and/or apartments available on a first-come, first-served basis to single students; on-campus housing not available to married students. Typical cost: $6966 per year ($11,836 including board). Housing application deadline: 6/1. *Student services:* Campus employment opportunities, campus safety program, career counseling, child daycare facilities, exercise/wellness program, free psychological counseling, grant writing training, international student services, low-cost health insurance, multicultural affairs office, services for students with disabilities, teacher training, writing training. *Library facilities:* Albin O. Kuhn Library and Gallery. *Collection:* Books: 1.3 million (physical), 172,520 (digital/electronic); Serial titles: 27,505 (physical), 185,984 (digital/electronic); Databases: 388. Weekly public service hours: 94; study areas open 24 hours, 5–7 days a week; students can reserve study rooms. *Research affiliation:* Sciences Applications International Corporation (information systems and technology), Halliburton Energy Services, IBM (computers and information technology), BouMatic (dairy industry), Pfizer, Inc. (pharmaceuticals), Fujitsu Laboratories of America (information technology and communications).

**Computer facilities:** Computer purchase and lease plans are available. 1,065 computers available on campus for general student use. A campuswide network can be accessed. Online class registration, billing, housing, parking, degree audit and advising are available.
Website: http://www.umbc.edu/

**General Application Contact:** Kathryn Nee, Coordinator of Domestic Admissions, 410-455-2944, E-mail: nee@umbc.edu.

**GRADUATE UNITS**

**The Graduate School** Students: 1,255 full-time (578 women), 1,219 part-time (623 women); includes 729 minority (304 Black or African American, non-Hispanic/Latino; 5 American Indian or Alaska Native, non-Hispanic/Latino; 250 Asian, non-Hispanic/Latino; 113 Hispanic/Latino; 4 Native Hawaiian or other Pacific Islander, non-Hispanic/Latino; 53 Two or more races, non-Hispanic/Latino), 712 international. Average age 31. 2,925 applicants, 58% accepted, 814 enrolled. *Faculty:* 454 full-time, 114 part-time/adjunct. Expenses: Contact institution. *Financial support:* In 2019–20, 597 students received support, including 21 fellowships with tuition reimbursements available (averaging $18,909 per year), 341 research assistantships with tuition reimbursements available (averaging $18,909 per year), 302 teaching assistantships with tuition reimbursements available (averaging $18,909 per year); career-related internships or fieldwork, Federal Work-Study, scholarships/grants, traineeships, health care benefits, and unspecified assistantships also available. Financial award applicants required to submit FAFSA. In 2019, 624 master's, 81 doctorates, 128 other advanced degrees awarded. *Program availability:* 100% online. *Application deadline:* For fall admission, 1/1 for international students; for spring admission, 5/1 for international students. Applications are processed on a rolling basis. *Application fee:* $50. Electronic applications accepted. *Application Contact:* Kathryn Nee, Coordinator of Domestic Admissions, 410-455-2944, E-mail: nee@umbc.edu.

***College of Arts, Humanities and Social Sciences*** Students: 323 full-time (215 women), 523 part-time (366 women); includes 299 minority (136 Black or African American, non-Hispanic/Latino; 3 American Indian or Alaska Native, non-Hispanic/Latino; 71 Asian, non-Hispanic/Latino; 62 Hispanic/Latino; 3 Native Hawaiian or other Pacific Islander, non-Hispanic/Latino; 24 Two or more races, non-Hispanic/Latino), 42 international. Average age 34. 758 applicants, 54% accepted, 248 enrolled. *Faculty:* 254 full-time, 74 part-time/adjunct. Expenses: Contact institution. *Financial support:* In 2019–20, 182 students received support, including 6 fellowships (averaging $19,000 per year), 93 research assistantships (averaging $19,000 per year), 83 teaching assistantships (averaging $19,000 per year); career-related internships or fieldwork, scholarships/grants, health care benefits, and unspecified assistantships also available. Financial award applicants required to submit FAFSA. In 2019, 220 master's, 27 doctorates, 60 other advanced degrees awarded. *Program availability:* Part-time, evening/weekend, online learning. *Application deadline:* For fall admission, 1/1 for international students; for spring admission, 5/1 for international students. Applications are processed on a rolling basis. *Application fee:* $50. Electronic applications accepted. *Application Contact:* Kathryn Nee, Coordinator of Domestic Admissions, 410-455-2944, E-mail: nee@umbc.edu. *Dean,* Dr. Scot E. Casper, 410-455-2385, Fax: 410-455-1095, E-mail: casper@umbc.edu.

***College of Engineering and Information Technology*** Students: 712 full-time (265 women), 625 part-time (223 women); includes 367 minority (144 Black or African American, non-Hispanic/Latino; 2 American Indian or Alaska Native, non-Hispanic/Latino; 157 Asian, non-Hispanic/Latino; 44 Hispanic/Latino; 1 Native Hawaiian or other Pacific Islander, non-Hispanic/Latino; 19 Two or more races, non-Hispanic/Latino), 585 international. Average age 30. 1,739 applicants, 63% accepted, 438 enrolled. *Faculty:* 125 full-time (39 women), 110 part-time/adjunct (21 women). Expenses: Contact institution. *Financial support:* In 2019–20, 296 students received support, including 11 fellowships with full tuition reimbursements available (averaging $21,750 per year), 155 research assistantships with full tuition reimbursements available (averaging $19,250 per year), 130 teaching assistantships with full tuition reimbursements available (averaging $16,750 per year); career-related internships or fieldwork, Federal Work-Study, scholarships/grants, health care benefits, tuition waivers (partial), and unspecified assistantships also available. Support available to part-time students. Financial award application deadline: 6/30; financial award applicants required to submit FAFSA. In 2019, 347 master's, 36 doctorates, 66 other advanced degrees awarded. *Program availability:* Part-time. *Application deadline:* For fall admission, 6/1 for domestic students, 1/1 for international students; for spring admission, 11/1 for domestic students, 6/1 for international students. Applications are processed on a rolling basis. *Application fee:* $70. Electronic applications accepted. *Application Contact:* Kathryn Nee, Coordinator of Domestic Admissions, 410-455-2944, E-mail: nee@umbc.edu. *Dean and Professor,* Dr. Keith J. Bowman, 410-455-3270, Fax: 410-455-3559, E-mail: kjb@umbc.edu.

***College of Natural and Mathematical Sciences*** Students: 215 full-time (94 women), 64 part-time (27 women); includes 58 minority (20 Black or African American, non-Hispanic/Latino; 21 Asian, non-Hispanic/Latino; 7 Hispanic/Latino; 10 Two or more races, non-Hispanic/Latino), 85 international. Average age 29. 421 applicants, 45% accepted, 79 enrolled. *Faculty:* 100 full-time, 10 part-time/adjunct. Expenses: Contact institution. *Financial support:* In 2019–20, 185 students received support, including 4 fellowships (averaging $18,909 per year), 88 teaching assistantships with full tuition reimbursements available (averaging $18,909 per year). In 2019, 44 master's, 18 doctorates, 2 other advanced degrees awarded. *Program availability:* Part-time. *Application deadline:* Applications are processed on a rolling basis. *Application fee:* $50. Electronic applications accepted. *Application Contact:* Kathryn Nee, Coordinator of Domestic Admissions, 410-455-2944, E-mail: nee@umbc.edu. *Dean,* Dr. William R. LaCourse, 410-455-5827, Fax: 410-455-5831, E-mail: lacourse@umbc.edu.

***Erickson School of Aging Studies*** Students: 5 full-time (4 women), 7 part-time (all women); includes 5 minority (4 Black or African American, non-Hispanic/Latino; 1 Asian, non-Hispanic/Latino). Average age 32. 7 applicants, 57% accepted, 1 enrolled. *Faculty:* 4 full-time (1 woman), 7 part-time/adjunct (1 woman). Expenses: Contact institution. *Financial support:* In 2019–20, 1 student received support, including 1 teaching assistantship with full tuition reimbursement available (averaging $21,600 per year). Financial award applicants required to submit FAFSA. In 2019, 13 master's awarded. *Program availability:* Part-time. *Application deadline:* For fall admission, 6/1 for domestic students; for spring admission, 12/1 for domestic students. Applications are processed on a rolling basis. *Application fee:* $50. Electronic applications accepted. *Application Contact:* Michelle Howell, Administrative Assistant, 443-543-5607, E-mail: mhowell@umbc.edu. *Graduate Program Director,* Bill Holman, 443-543-5603, E-mail: holman1@umbc.edu.

## UNIVERSITY OF MARYLAND, COLLEGE PARK, College Park, MD 20742

**General Information** State-supported, coed, university. CGS member. *Graduate housing:* On-campus housing not available. *Research affiliation:* Battelle–Pacific Northwest National Laboratory, Canon U.S. Life Sciences, Inc. (technology development and analysis), Bill and Melinda Gates Foundation (international aid and outreach), Lockheed Martin Corporation (science and technology), BAE Systems (science and technology).

**GRADUATE UNITS**

**Academic Affairs** *Program availability:* Part-time, evening/weekend, online learning. Electronic applications accepted.

***A. James Clark School of Engineering*** *Program availability:* Part-time, evening/weekend, online learning.

***College of Agriculture and Natural Resources*** *Program availability:* Part-time, evening/weekend. Electronic applications accepted.

***College of Arts and Humanities*** *Program availability:* Part-time, evening/weekend. Electronic applications accepted.

***College of Behavioral and Social Sciences*** *Program availability:* Part-time, evening/weekend. Electronic applications accepted.

***College of Computer, Mathematical and Natural Sciences*** *Program availability:* Part-time, evening/weekend, online learning.

***College of Education*** *Program availability:* Part-time, evening/weekend, online learning. Electronic applications accepted.

***College of Information Studies*** *Program availability:* Part-time, evening/weekend. Electronic applications accepted.

***Philip Merrill College of Journalism*** *Program availability:* Part-time, evening/weekend. Electronic applications accepted.

***Robert H. Smith School of Business*** *Program availability:* Part-time, evening/weekend, online learning. Electronic applications accepted.

***School of Architecture, Planning and Preservation*** *Program availability:* Part-time, evening/weekend. Electronic applications accepted.

***School of Public Health*** *Program availability:* Part-time, evening/weekend. Electronic applications accepted.

***School of Public Policy*** *Program availability:* Part-time, evening/weekend, online learning. Electronic applications accepted.

## UNIVERSITY OF MARYLAND EASTERN SHORE, Princess Anne, MD 21853

**General Information** State-supported, coed, university. CGS member. *Graduate housing:* Room and/or apartments available to single students; on-campus housing not available to married students.

**GRADUATE UNITS**

**Graduate Programs** *Program availability:* Part-time, evening/weekend. Electronic applications accepted.

***School of Pharmacy***

## UNIVERSITY OF MARYLAND GLOBAL CAMPUS, Adelphi, MD 20783

**General Information** State-supported, coed, comprehensive institution. *Enrollment:* 58,281 graduate, professional, and undergraduate students; 90 full-time matriculated graduate/professional students (54 women), 12,029 part-time matriculated graduate/professional students (6,605 women). *Enrollment by degree level:* 11,331 master's, 185 doctoral, 603 other advanced degrees. *Graduate faculty:* 209 full-time (91 women), 3,530 part-time/adjunct (1,654 women). *Graduate housing:* On-campus housing not available. *Student services:* Career counseling, international student services, services for students with disabilities, writing training. *Library facilities:* Library plus 1 other. *Collection:* Books: 1,234 (physical), 94,961 (digital/electronic); Serial titles: 207,528 (digital/electronic); Databases: 127. Weekly public service hours: 77.

**Computer facilities:** Computer purchase and lease plans are available. 510 computers available on campus for general student use. A campuswide network can be accessed. Online class registration is available.
Website: http://www.umuc.edu/

**General Application Contact:** Admissions, 800-888-8682, E-mail: Studentsfirst@umgc.edu.

**GRADUATE UNITS**

**University of Maryland Global Campus** Students: 90 full-time (54 women), 12,029 part-time (6,605 women); includes 6,820 minority (4,687 Black or African American, non-Hispanic/Latino; 48 American Indian or Alaska Native, non-Hispanic/Latino; 768 Asian, non-Hispanic/Latino; 909 Hispanic/Latino; 44 Native Hawaiian or other Pacific Islander, non-Hispanic/Latino; 364 Two or more races, non-Hispanic/Latino), 308 international. Average age 36. 6,364 applicants, 100% accepted, 2,363 enrolled. *Faculty:* 209 full-time (91 women), 3,530 part-time/adjunct (1,654 women). Expenses: Contact institution. *Financial support:* Scholarships/grants available. Support available to part-time students. Financial award application deadline: 6/1; financial award applicants required to submit FAFSA. In 2019, 4,456 master's, 46 doctorates, 481 other advanced degrees awarded. *Program availability:* Part-time, evening/weekend, online learning. *Application deadline:* Applications are processed on a rolling basis. *Application fee:* $50. Electronic applications accepted. *Application Contact:* Admissions, 800-888-8682, E-mail: studentsfirst@umgc.edu. *Senior Vice President and Chief Academic Officer,* Blakely Pomietto, E-mail: cao-office@umgc.edu.

## UNIVERSITY OF MARY WASHINGTON, Fredericksburg, VA 22401-5358

**General Information** State-supported, coed, comprehensive institution. *Graduate housing:* Room and/or apartments available on a first-come, first-served basis to single students; on-campus housing not available to married students.

**GRADUATE UNITS**

**College of Business** *Program availability:* Part-time-only, evening/weekend. Electronic applications accepted.

**College of Education** *Program availability:* Part-time, evening/weekend. Electronic applications accepted.

## UNIVERSITY OF MASSACHUSETTS AMHERST, Amherst, MA 01003

**General Information** State-supported, coed, university. CGS member. *Graduate housing:* Rooms and/or apartments available on a first-come, first-served basis to single and married students. Housing application deadline: 6/15.

**GRADUATE UNITS**

**Graduate School** *Program availability:* Part-time, evening/weekend. Electronic applications accepted.

***College of Education*** *Program availability:* Part-time, online learning. Electronic applications accepted.

***College of Engineering*** *Program availability:* Part-time. Electronic applications accepted.

***College of Humanities and Fine Arts*** *Program availability:* Part-time. Electronic applications accepted.

***College of Natural Sciences*** *Program availability:* Part-time. Electronic applications accepted.

***College of Nursing*** *Program availability:* Part-time, online learning. Electronic applications accepted.

***College of Social and Behavioral Sciences*** *Program availability:* Part-time. Electronic applications accepted.

***Interdisciplinary Programs*** *Program availability:* Part-time. Electronic applications accepted.

***Isenberg School of Management*** *Program availability:* Part-time, evening/weekend, online learning. Electronic applications accepted.

***School of Public Health and Health Sciences*** *Program availability:* Part-time, evening/weekend, online learning. Electronic applications accepted.

## UNIVERSITY OF MASSACHUSETTS BOSTON, Boston, MA 02125-3393

**General Information** State-supported, coed, university. CGS member. *Enrollment:* 15,989 graduate, professional, and undergraduate students; 1,275 full-time matriculated graduate/professional students (836 women), 1,854 part-time matriculated graduate/professional students (1,268 women). *Enrollment by degree level:* 2,049 master's, 834 doctoral, 246 other advanced degrees. *Graduate faculty:* 689 full-time (343 women), 446 part-time/adjunct (280 women). *Graduate housing:* On-campus housing not available. *Student services:* Campus employment opportunities, campus safety program, career counseling, child daycare facilities, exercise/wellness program, free psychological counseling, international student services, low-cost health insurance, multicultural affairs office, services for students with disabilities, teacher training, writing training. *Library facilities:* Joseph P. Healey Library. *Collection:* Books: 384,946 (physical), 607,630 (digital/electronic); Serial titles: 8,312 (physical), 101,013 (digital/electronic); Databases: 180. *Research affiliation:* New England Aquarium (environmental sciences), Dana Farber/Harvard Cancer Center (biomedical sciences), John F. Kennedy Presidential Library (history).

**Computer facilities:** 350 computers available on campus for general student use. A campuswide network can be accessed. Online class registration is available.
Website: http://www.umb.edu/

**General Application Contact:** Graduate Admissions Coordinator, 617-287-6400, Fax: 617-287-6236, E-mail: graduate.admissions@umb.edu.

**GRADUATE UNITS**

**College of Advancing and Professional Studies** *Program availability:* Online learning. Electronic applications accepted.

**College of Education and Human Development** *Program availability:* Part-time, evening/weekend. Electronic applications accepted.

**College of Liberal Arts** *Program availability:* Part-time, evening/weekend. Electronic applications accepted.

**College of Management** *Program availability:* Part-time, evening/weekend. Electronic applications accepted.

**College of Nursing and Health Sciences** *Program availability:* Part-time, evening/weekend. Electronic applications accepted.

**College of Public and Community Service** *Program availability:* Part-time, evening/weekend.

**College of Science and Mathematics** *Program availability:* Part-time, evening/weekend. Electronic applications accepted.

**Graduate School of Global Inclusion and Social Development** Electronic applications accepted.

**McCormack Graduate School of Policy and Global Studies** *Program availability:* Part-time, evening/weekend. Electronic applications accepted.

**School for the Environment** Electronic applications accepted.

## UNIVERSITY OF MASSACHUSETTS DARTMOUTH, North Dartmouth, MA 02747-2300

**General Information** State-supported, coed, university. *Enrollment:* 8,154 graduate, professional, and undergraduate students; 646 full-time matriculated graduate/professional students (331 women), 1,026 part-time matriculated graduate/professional students (573 women). *Enrollment by degree level:* 1,025 master's, 544 doctoral, 103 other advanced degrees. *Graduate faculty:* 314 full-time (143 women), 140 part-time/adjunct (94 women). *Tuition, area resident:* Full-time $16,390; part-time $682.92 per credit. Tuition, state resident: full-time $16,390; part-time $682.92 per credit. Tuition, nonresident: full-time $29,578; part-time $1232.42 per credit. *Required fees:* $575. *Graduate housing:* Room and/or apartments available on a first-come, first-served basis to single students; on-campus housing not available to married students. Housing application deadline: 3/14. *Student services:* Campus employment opportunities, campus safety program, career counseling, exercise/wellness program, free psychological counseling, grant writing training, international student services, low-cost health insurance, multicultural affairs office, services for students with disabilities, teacher training, writing training. *Library facilities:* Claire T. Carney Library. *Collection:* Books: 179,835 (physical), 97,780 (digital/electronic); Serial titles: 1,336 (physical), 130,988 (digital/electronic); Databases: 140. Students can reserve study rooms. *Research affiliation:* National Oceanic and Atmospheric Administration (NOAA) (marine science and technology), National Science Foundation (biology), Health Resources Service Administration (nursing), Office of Naval Research (ONR) (engineering), Woods Hole Oceanographic Institution (marine science and technology), National Institute of Aerospace (engineering).

**Computer facilities:** Computer purchase and lease plans are available. 400 computers available on campus for general student use. A campuswide network can be accessed. Online class registration is available.
Website: http://www.umassd.edu/

**General Application Contact:** Scott Webster, Director of Graduate Studies and Admission, 508-999-8604, Fax: 508-999-8183, E-mail: graduate@umassd.edu.

**GRADUATE UNITS**

**Graduate School** Students: 646 full-time (331 women), 1,026 part-time (573 women); includes 319 minority (86 Black or African American, non-Hispanic/Latino; 4 American Indian or Alaska Native, non-Hispanic/Latino; 75 Asian, non-Hispanic/Latino; 110 Hispanic/Latino; 44 Two or more races, non-Hispanic/Latino), 248 international. Average age 32. 2,268 applicants, 69% accepted, 577 enrolled. *Faculty:* 314 full-time (143 women), 140 part-time/adjunct (94 women). Expenses: Contact institution. *Financial support:* In 2019–20, 39 fellowships (averaging $14,449 per year), 122 research assistantships (averaging $10,154 per year), 107 teaching assistantships (averaging $10,181 per year) were awarded; tuition waivers (full and partial), unspecified assistantships, and doctoral writing support, doctoral support also available. Financial award application deadline: 3/1; financial award applicants required to submit FAFSA. In 2019, 397 master's, 83 doctorates, 66 other advanced degrees awarded. *Program* *availability:* Part-time, 100% online, blended/hybrid learning. *Application deadline:* For fall admission, 8/15 for domestic students, 7/15 for international students; for spring admission, 11/1 for domestic students, 10/1 for international students. *Application fee:* $60. Electronic applications accepted. *Application Contact:* Scott Webster, Director of Graduate Studies and Admissions, 508-999-8604, Fax: 508-999-8183, E-mail: graduate@umassd.edu. *Director of Graduate Studies and Admissions*, Scott Webster, 508-999-8604, Fax: 508-999-8183, E-mail: graduate@umassd.edu.

***Charlton College of Business*** Students: 131 full-time (57 women), 332 part-time (173 women); includes 90 minority (25 Black or African American, non-Hispanic/Latino; 1 American Indian or Alaska Native, non-Hispanic/Latino; 30 Asian, non-Hispanic/Latino; 24 Hispanic/Latino; 10 Two or more races, non-Hispanic/Latino), 66 international. Average age 34. 307 applicants, 96% accepted, 173 enrolled. *Faculty:* 43 full-time (15 women), 21 part-time/adjunct (6 women). Expenses: Contact institution. *Financial support:* In 2019–20, 2 teaching assistantships (averaging $5,250 per year) were awarded; tuition waivers (partial) and unspecified assistantships also available. Financial award application deadline: 3/1; financial award applicants required to submit FAFSA. In 2019, 153 master's, 35 other advanced degrees awarded. *Program availability:* Part-time, 100% online, blended/hybrid learning. *Application deadline:* Applications are processed on a rolling basis. *Application fee:* $60. Electronic applications accepted. *Application Contact:* Scott Webster, Director of Graduate Studies and Admissions, 508-999-8604, Fax: 508-999-8183, E-mail: graduate@umassd.edu. *Assistant Dean of Graduate Programs*, Melissa Pacheco, 508-999-8543, Fax: 508-999-8646, E-mail: mpacheco@umassd.edu.

***College of Arts and Sciences*** Students: 126 full-time (93 women), 286 part-time (177 women); includes 81 minority (19 Black or African American, non-Hispanic/Latino; 1 American Indian or Alaska Native, non-Hispanic/Latino; 15 Asian, non-Hispanic/Latino; 33 Hispanic/Latino; 13 Two or more races, non-Hispanic/Latino), 28 international. Average age 33. 256 applicants, 79% accepted, 142 enrolled. *Faculty:* 190 full-time (95 women), 76 part-time/adjunct (49 women). Expenses: Contact institution. *Financial support:* In 2019–20, 24 fellowships (averaging $14,250 per year), 25 research assistantships (averaging $11,947 per year), 47 teaching assistantships (averaging $10,549 per year) were awarded; tuition waivers (full and partial), unspecified assistantships, and doctoral support, doctoral writing support also available. Financial award application deadline: 3/1; financial award applicants required to submit FAFSA. In 2019, 123 master's, 11 doctorates, 21 other advanced degrees awarded. *Program availability:* Part-time, 100% online, blended/hybrid learning. *Application deadline:* For fall admission, 8/15 for domestic students, 7/15 for international students; for spring admission, 11/1 for domestic students, 10/1 for international students. *Application fee:* $60. Electronic applications accepted. *Application Contact:* Scott Webster, Director of Graduate Studies and Admissions, 508-999-8604, Fax: 508-999-8183, E-mail: graduate@umassd.edu. *Dean, College of Arts and Sciences*, Pauline Entin, 508-999-8352, E-mail: pentin@umassd.edu.

***College of Engineering*** Students: 138 full-time (43 women), 155 part-time (40 women); includes 37 minority (7 Black or African American, non-Hispanic/Latino; 10 Asian, non-Hispanic/Latino; 15 Hispanic/Latino; 5 Two or more races, non-Hispanic/Latino), 134 international. Average age 28. 415 applicants, 81% accepted, 98 enrolled. *Faculty:* 59 full-time (17 women), 6 part-time/adjunct (1 woman). Expenses: Contact institution. *Financial support:* In 2019–20, 13 fellowships (averaging $14,860 per year), 68 research assistantships (averaging $5,905 per year), 49 teaching assistantships (averaging $10,378 per year) were awarded; tuition waivers (full and partial), unspecified assistantships, and doctoral support, doctoral writing support also available. Financial award application deadline: 3/1; financial award applicants required to submit FAFSA. In 2019, 97 master's, 11 doctorates, 10 other advanced degrees awarded. *Program availability:* Part-time, 100% online, blended/hybrid learning. *Application deadline:* For fall admission, 8/15 for domestic students, 7/15 for international students; for spring admission, 11/1 for domestic students, 10/1 for international students. *Application fee:* $60. Electronic applications accepted. *Application Contact:* Scott Webster, Director of Graduate Studies and Admissions, 508-999-8406, Fax: 508-999-8183, E-mail: graduate@umassd.edu. *Dean, College of Engineering*, Jean VanderGheynst, 508-999-8539, Fax: 508-999-9137, E-mail: jvandergheynst@umassd.edu.

***College of Visual and Performing Arts*** Students: 27 full-time (22 women), 22 part-time (15 women); includes 6 minority (1 Asian, non-Hispanic/Latino; 4 Hispanic/Latino; 1 Two or more races, non-Hispanic/Latino), 6 international. Average age 32. 85 applicants, 53% accepted, 13 enrolled. *Faculty:* 38 full-time (21 women), 15 part-time/adjunct (11 women). Expenses: Contact institution. *Financial support:* In 2019–20, 1 teaching assistantship (averaging $2,040 per year) was awarded; tuition waivers (partial) also available. Financial award application deadline: 3/1; financial award applicants required to submit FAFSA. In 2019, 16 master's awarded. *Program availability:* Part-time. *Application deadline:* For fall admission, 8/15 for domestic students, 7/15 for international students; for spring admission, 10/15 for domestic students, 9/15 for international students. *Application fee:* $60. Electronic applications accepted. *Application Contact:* Scott Webster, Director of Graduate Studies and Admissions, 508-999-8604, Fax: 508-999-8183, E-mail: graduate@umassd.edu. *Dean, College of Visual and Performing Arts*, Lawrence Jenkens, 508-999-9286, E-mail: lawrence.jenkens@umassd.edu.

***School for Marine Science and Technology*** Students: 16 full-time (12 women), 33 part-time (14 women); includes 2 minority (1 Hispanic/Latino; 1 Two or more races, non-Hispanic/Latino), 7 international. Average age 31. 23 applicants, 70% accepted, 6 enrolled. *Faculty:* 15 full-time (1 woman). Expenses: Contact institution. *Financial support:* In 2019–20, 2 fellowships (averaging $14,166 per year), 29 research assistantships (averaging $18,572 per year), 1 teaching assistantship (averaging $18,500 per year) were awarded; tuition waivers (full and partial) and doctoral support also available. Financial award application deadline: 3/1; financial award applicants required to submit FAFSA. In 2019, 7 master's, 2 doctorates awarded. *Program availability:* Part-time. *Application deadline:* For fall admission, 9/1 for domestic students, 10/1 for international students; for spring admission, 11/15 priority date for domestic students, 10/15 priority date for international students. *Application fee:* $60. Electronic applications accepted. *Application Contact:* Scott Webster, Director of Graduate Studies and Admissions, 508-999-8604, Fax: 508-999-8183, E-mail: graduate@umassd.edu. *Dean, School for Marine Science and Technology*, Steven Lohrenz, 508-910-6550, E-mail: slohrenz@umassd.edu.

***University of Massachusetts School of Law–Dartmouth*** Students: 206 full-time (102 women), 74 part-time (42 women); includes 77 minority (24 Black or African American, non-Hispanic/Latino; 2 American Indian or Alaska Native, non-Hispanic/Latino; 10 Asian, non-Hispanic/Latino; 29 Hispanic/Latino; 12 Two or more races, non-Hispanic/Latino), 6 international. Average age 29. 1,143 applicants, 55% accepted, 113 enrolled. *Faculty:* 19 full-time (10 women), 14 part-time/adjunct (5 women). Expenses: Contact institution. *Financial support:* Application deadline: 3/1; applicants required to submit FAFSA. In 2019, 47 doctorates awarded. *Program availability:* Part-time, evening/weekend. *Application deadline:* For fall admission, 6/30 priority date for domestic students, 5/30 priority date for international students. *Application fee:* $60. Electronic applications accepted. *Application Contact:* Nancy Hebert, Assistant Director of Law School Recruiting and Marketing, 508-985-1110, Fax: 508-985-1175, E-mail: lawadmissions@umassd.edu. *Assistant Dean*, Daniel Fitzpatrick, 508-985-1109, Fax: 508-985-1175, E-mail: lawadmissions@umassd.edu.

## UNIVERSITY OF MASSACHUSETTS LOWELL, Lowell, MA 01854

**General Information** State-supported, coed, university. CGS member. *Graduate housing:* Rooms and/or apartments available on a first-come, first-served basis to single students and available to married students. Housing application deadline: 4/1.

**GRADUATE UNITS**

**College of Fine Arts, Humanities and Social Sciences**

***School of Criminology and Justice Studies*** *Program availability:* Part-time, evening/weekend. Electronic applications accepted.

**College of Health Sciences** *Program availability:* Part-time.

***School of Nursing***

**College of Sciences** *Program availability:* Part-time, evening/weekend.

**Francis College of Engineering** *Program availability:* Part-time, evening/weekend.

**Graduate School of Education** *Program availability:* Part-time, evening/weekend, online learning. Electronic applications accepted.

**Manning School of Business** *Program availability:* Part-time, evening/weekend.

## UNIVERSITY OF MASSACHUSETTS MEDICAL SCHOOL, Worcester, MA 01655-0115

**General Information** State-supported, coed, graduate-only institution. CGS member. *Enrollment by degree level:* 21 master's, 1,166 doctoral, 10 other advanced degrees. *Graduate faculty:* 1,284 full-time (547 women), 423 part-time/adjunct (278 women). *Graduate housing:* On-campus housing not available. *Student services:* Campus employment opportunities, campus safety program, career counseling, child daycare facilities, exercise/wellness program, free psychological counseling, grant writing training, international student services, low-cost health insurance, multicultural affairs office, services for students with disabilities, teacher training, writing training. *Library facilities:* Lamar Soutter Library. *Collection:* Books: 25,389 (physical), 52,893 (digital/electronic); Serial titles: 9,225 (physical), 5,000 (digital/electronic); Databases: 304. Weekly public service hours: 82; study areas open 24 hours, 5–7 days a week. *Research affiliation:* Abbott Bioresearch Center (biomedical research and training), Charles River Laboratories (pre-clinical biomedical research).

**Computer facilities:** 107 computers available on campus for general student use. A campuswide network can be accessed. Online class registration is available.
Website: http://www.umassmed.edu/

**General Application Contact:** Karen Lawton, Director of Admissions, 508-856-2323, Fax: 508-856-3629, E-mail: admissions@umassmed.edu.

**GRADUATE UNITS**

**Graduate School of Biomedical Sciences** Students: 344 full-time (198 women), 1 (woman) part-time; includes 73 minority (12 Black or African American, non-Hispanic/Latino; 1 American Indian or Alaska Native, non-Hispanic/Latino; 45 Asian, non-Hispanic/Latino; 15 Hispanic/Latino), 120 international. Average age 29. 581 applicants, 23% accepted, 56 enrolled. *Faculty:* 1,258 full-time (525 women), 372 part-time/adjunct (238 women). Expenses: Contact institution. *Financial support:* In 2019–20, 22 fellowships with full tuition reimbursements (averaging $33,061 per year), 322 research assistantships with full tuition reimbursements (averaging $32,850 per year) were awarded; institutionally sponsored loans and scholarships/grants also available. Financial award application deadline: 5/15. In 2019, 6 master's, 49 doctorates awarded. *Application deadline:* For fall admission, 12/1 for domestic and international students. Applications are processed on a rolling basis. *Application fee:* $80. Electronic applications accepted. *Application Contact:* Dr. Kendall Knight, Assistant Vice Provost for Admissions, 508-856-5628, Fax: 508-856-3659, E-mail: kendall.knight@umassmed.edu. *Dean*, Dr. Mary Ellen Lane, 508-856-4018, E-mail: maryellen.lane@umassmed.edu.

**Graduate School of Nursing** Students: 176 full-time (152 women), 33 part-time (27 women); includes 61 minority (21 Black or African American, non-Hispanic/Latino; 1 American Indian or Alaska Native, non-Hispanic/Latino; 18 Asian, non-Hispanic/Latino; 20 Hispanic/Latino; 1 Native Hawaiian or other Pacific Islander, non-Hispanic/Latino). Average age 32. 131 applicants, 66% accepted, 58 enrolled. *Faculty:* 26 full-time (22 women), 51 part-time/adjunct (40 women). Expenses: Contact institution. *Financial support:* In 2019–20, 103 students received support. Scholarships/grants available. Support available to part-time students. Financial award application deadline: 5/15; financial award applicants required to submit FAFSA. In 2019, 28 master's, 34 doctorates, 1 other advanced degree awarded. *Program availability:* Blended/hybrid learning. *Application deadline:* For fall admission, 12/1 priority date for domestic students. Applications are processed on a rolling basis. *Application fee:* $100. Electronic applications accepted. *Application Contact:* Diane Brescia, Admissions Coordinator, 508-856-3488, Fax: 508-856-5851, E-mail: diane.brescia@umassmed.edu. *Dean*, Dr. Joan Vitello-Cicciu, 508-856-5081, Fax: 508-856-6552, E-mail: joan.vitello@umassmed.edu.

**School of Medicine** Students: 643 full-time (369 women); includes 204 minority (28 Black or African American, non-Hispanic/Latino; 2 American Indian or Alaska Native, non-Hispanic/Latino; 153 Asian, non-Hispanic/Latino; 20 Hispanic/Latino; 1 Native Hawaiian or other Pacific Islander, non-Hispanic/Latino), 2 international. Average age 26. 4,094 applicants, 9% accepted, 162 enrolled. *Faculty:* 1,258 full-time (525 women), 372 part-time/adjunct (238 women). Expenses: Contact institution. *Financial support:* In 2019–20, 197 students received support, including 14 fellowships with full tuition reimbursements available (averaging $33,061 per year), 57 research assistantships with full tuition reimbursements available (averaging $32,850 per year); institutionally sponsored loans, scholarships/grants, and tuition waivers (partial) also available. Financial award application deadline: 3/31; financial award applicants required to submit CSS PROFILE or FAFSA. In 2019, 125 doctorates awarded. *Application deadline:* For fall admission, 12/1 for domestic students. Applications are processed on a rolling basis. *Application fee:* $100. Electronic applications accepted. *Application Contact:* Jennifer Lee Shea, Admissions Coordinator, 508-856-2323, Fax: 508-856-3629, E-mail: admissions@umassmed.edu. *Dean/Provost/Executive Deputy Chancellor*, Dr. Terence R. Flotte, 508-856-8000, E-mail: terry.flotte@umassmed.edu.

## UNIVERSITY OF MEMPHIS, Memphis, TN 38152

**General Information** State-supported, coed, university. CGS member. *Enrollment:* 21,685 graduate, professional, and undergraduate students; 1,930 full-time matriculated graduate/professional students (1,145 women), 2,250 part-time matriculated graduate/professional students (1,449 women). *Enrollment by degree level:* 2,535 master's, 1,476 doctoral, 169 other advanced degrees. *Graduate faculty:* 526 full-time (221 women), 158 part-time/adjunct (71 women). *International tuition:* $16,128 full-time. *Tuition, area resident:* Full-time $9216; part-time $512 per credit hour. Tuition, state resident: full-time $9216; part-time $512 per credit hour. Tuition, nonresident: full-time $12,672; part-time $704 per credit hour. *Required fees:* $1530; $85 per credit hour. Tuition and fees vary according to program. *Graduate housing:* Rooms and/or apartments available on a first-come, first-served basis to single and married students. Typical cost: $9962 (including board) for single students; $9962 (including board) for married students. Room and board charges vary according to board plan and housing facility selected. *Student services:* Campus employment opportunities, campus safety program, career counseling, child daycare facilities, exercise/wellness program, free psychological counseling, grant writing training, international student services, multicultural affairs office, services for students with disabilities, teacher training, writing training. *Library facilities:* McWherter Library plus 4 others. *Collection:* Books: 900,408 (physical), 458,374 (digital/electronic); Serial titles: 17,630 (physical), 243,557 (digital/electronic); Databases: 398. Weekly public service hours: 91; students can reserve study rooms. *Research affiliation:* Memphis Bioworks Foundation, FedEx Corp, Oak Ridge National Laboratory, St. Jude Children's Research Hospital, Medtronic Inc., Urban Child Institute.

**Computer facilities:** 1,255 computers available on campus for general student use. A campuswide network can be accessed. Online class registration is available. Website: http://www.memphis.edu/

**General Application Contact:** Dr. Robin Poston, Dean of the Graduate School, 901-678-5739, Fax: 901-678-0378, E-mail: graduateschool@memphis.edu.

**GRADUATE UNITS**

**Cecil C. Humphreys School of Law** Students: 347 (177 women); includes 97 minority (69 Black or African American, non-Hispanic/Latino; 4 American Indian or Alaska Native, non-Hispanic/Latino; 11 Asian, non-Hispanic/Latino; 13 Hispanic/Latino). Average age 24. 647 applicants, 55% accepted, 132 enrolled. *Faculty:* 24 full-time (10 women). Expenses: Contact institution. *Financial support:* In 2019–20, 171 students received support. Fellowships, research assistantships, teaching assistantships, career-related internships or fieldwork, Federal Work-Study, scholarships/grants, and tuition waivers (partial) available. Support available to part-time students. Financial award application deadline: 5/1; financial award applicants required to submit FAFSA. In 2019, 1 doctorate awarded. *Program availability:* Part-time. *Application deadline:* For fall admission, 3/15 priority date for domestic and international students. Applications are processed on a rolling basis. *Application fee:* $0 ($40 for international students). Electronic applications accepted. *Application Contact:* Dr. Sue Ann McClellan, Assistant Dean for Law Admissions, Recruiting and Scholarships, 901-678-5403, Fax: 901-678-0741, E-mail: smcclell@memphis.edu. *Dean,* Katharine Traylor Schaffzin, 901-678-1623, Fax: 901-678-5210, E-mail: ktschffz@memphis.edu.

**Graduate School** Students: 1,930 full-time (1,145 women), 2,250 part-time (1,449 women); includes 1,460 minority (995 Black or African American, non-Hispanic/Latino; 6 American Indian or Alaska Native, non-Hispanic/Latino; 215 Asian, non-Hispanic/Latino; 161 Hispanic/Latino; 2 Native Hawaiian or other Pacific Islander, non-Hispanic/Latino; 81 Two or more races, non-Hispanic/Latino), 431 international. Average age 31. 2,624 applicants, 86% accepted, 1,191 enrolled. *Faculty:* 526 full-time (221 women), 158 part-time/adjunct (71 women). Expenses: Contact institution. *Financial support:* Fellowships with full tuition reimbursements, research assistantships with full tuition reimbursements, teaching assistantships with full tuition reimbursements, career-related internships or fieldwork, Federal Work-Study, institutionally sponsored loans, scholarships/grants, and unspecified assistantships available. Support available to part-time students. Financial award application deadline: 2/1; financial award applicants required to submit FAFSA. In 2019, 948 master's, 241 doctorates, 177 other advanced degrees awarded. *Program availability:* Part-time, evening/weekend, 100% online, blended/hybrid learning. *Application deadline:* For fall admission, 7/1 for domestic students, 5/1 for international students; for spring admission, 12/1 for domestic students, 9/15 for international students. Applications are processed on a rolling basis. *Application fee:* $35 ($60 for international students). Electronic applications accepted. *Application Contact:* Dr. Brian Meredith, Associate Dean of the Graduate School, 901-678-1404, Fax: 901-678-0378, E-mail: graduateadmissions@memphis.edu. *Dean of the Graduate School,* Dr. Robin Poston, 901-678-5739, Fax: 901-678-0378, E-mail: graduateschool@memphis.edu.

***College of Arts and Sciences*** Students: 622 full-time (368 women), 366 part-time (208 women); includes 297 minority (182 Black or African American, non-Hispanic/Latino; 45 Asian, non-Hispanic/Latino; 45 Hispanic/Latino; 25 Two or more races, non-Hispanic/Latino), 167 international. Average age 31. 492 applicants, 83% accepted, 211 enrolled. *Faculty:* 199 full-time (69 women), 35 part-time/adjunct (18 women). Expenses: Contact institution. *Financial support:* Fellowships with full tuition reimbursements, research assistantships with full tuition reimbursements, teaching assistantships with full tuition reimbursements, career-related internships or fieldwork, Federal Work-Study, institutionally sponsored loans, scholarships/grants, tuition waivers (full and partial), and unspecified assistantships available. Financial award application deadline: 2/1; financial award applicants required to submit FAFSA. In 2019, 225 master's, 58 doctorates, 36 other advanced degrees awarded. *Program availability:* Part-time, evening/weekend, 100% online, blended/hybrid learning. *Application deadline:* Applications are processed on a rolling basis. *Application fee:* $35 ($60 for international students). Electronic applications accepted. *Application Contact:* Dr. Abby Parrill-Baker, Dean, 901-678-2251, Fax: 901-678-4831, E-mail: aparrill@memphis.edu. *Dean,* Dr. Abby Parrill-Baker, 901-678-2251, Fax: 901-678-4831, E-mail: aparrill@memphis.edu.

***College of Communication and Fine Arts*** Students: 144 full-time (74 women), 113 part-time (65 women); includes 68 minority (36 Black or African American, non-Hispanic/Latino; 7 Asian, non-Hispanic/Latino; 18 Hispanic/Latino; 7 Two or more races, non-Hispanic/Latino), 20 international. Average age 32. 241 applicants, 73% accepted, 89 enrolled. *Faculty:* 87 full-time (35 women), 8 part-time/adjunct (3 women). Expenses: Contact institution. *Financial support:* Research assistantships with full tuition reimbursements, teaching assistantships with full tuition reimbursements, career-related internships or fieldwork, Federal Work-Study, institutionally sponsored loans, scholarships/grants, and unspecified assistantships available. Financial award application deadline: 2/1; financial award applicants required to submit FAFSA. In 2019, 59 master's, 10 doctorates, 5 other advanced degrees awarded. *Program availability:* Part-time, online learning. *Application deadline:* Applications are processed on a rolling basis. *Application fee:* $35 ($60 for international students). Electronic applications accepted. *Application Contact:* Dr. Anne Hogan, Dean, 901-678-2350, Fax: 901-678-5118, E-mail: anne.hogan@memphis.edu. *Dean,* Dr. Anne Hogan, 901-678-2350, Fax: 901-678-5118, E-mail: anne.hogan@memphis.edu.

***College of Education*** Students: 223 full-time (177 women), 730 part-time (553 women); includes 452 minority (372 Black or African American, non-Hispanic/Latino; 2 American Indian or Alaska Native, non-Hispanic/Latino; 23 Asian, non-Hispanic/Latino; 40 Hispanic/Latino; 15 Two or more races, non-Hispanic/Latino), 10 international. Average age 35. 520 applicants, 86% accepted, 295 enrolled. *Faculty:* 55 full-time (37 women), 38 part-time/adjunct (26 women). Expenses: Contact institution. *Financial support:* Research assistantships with full tuition reimbursements, teaching assistantships with full tuition reimbursements, career-related internships or fieldwork, Federal Work-Study, scholarships/grants, tuition waivers (partial), and unspecified assistantships available. Financial award application deadline: 2/1; financial award applicants required to submit FAFSA. In 2019, 162 master's, 49 doctorates, 63 other advanced degrees awarded. *Program availability:* Part-time, evening/weekend, 100% online, blended/hybrid learning. *Application deadline:* Applications are processed on a rolling basis. *Application fee:* $35 ($60 for international students). Electronic applications accepted. *Application Contact:* Stormey Warren, Graduate Programs, 901-678-2363, Fax: 901-678-4778, E-mail: shutsell@memphis.edu. *Dean,* Dr. Kandi Hill-Clarke, 901-678-5495, Fax: 901-678-4778, E-mail: k.hill-clarke@memphis.edu.

***College of Professional and Liberal Studies*** Students: 17 full-time (9 women), 123 part-time (86 women); includes 89 minority (80 Black or African American, non-Hispanic/Latino; 1 Asian, non-Hispanic/Latino; 5 Hispanic/Latino; 3 Two or more races, non-Hispanic/Latino), 1 international. Average age 41. 89 applicants, 80% accepted, 49 enrolled. *Faculty:* 1 full-time, 1 (woman) part-time/adjunct. Expenses: Contact institution. *Financial support:* Research assistantships with full tuition reimbursements, teaching assistantships with tuition reimbursements, Federal Work-Study, scholarships/grants, and unspecified assistantships available. Financial award application deadline: 2/3; financial award applicants required to submit FAFSA. In 2019, 25 master's, 5 other advanced degrees awarded. *Program availability:* Part-time, evening/weekend, online learning. *Application deadline:* For fall admission, 7/1 for domestic students, 5/1 for international students; for spring admission, 11/1 for domestic students, 9/15 for international students. Applications are processed on a rolling basis. *Application fee:* $35 ($60 for international students). Electronic applications accepted. *Application Contact:* Dr. Richard Irwin, Executive Dean, 901-678-2716, E-mail: rirwin@memphis.edu. *Executive Dean,* Dr. Richard Irwin, 901-678-2716, E-mail: rirwin@memphis.edu.

***Fogelman College of Business and Economics*** Students: 267 full-time (131 women), 505 part-time (222 women); includes 273 minority (135 Black or African American, non-Hispanic/Latino; 2 American Indian or Alaska Native, non-Hispanic/Latino; 102 Asian, non-Hispanic/Latino; 23 Hispanic/Latino; 1 Native Hawaiian or other Pacific Islander, non-Hispanic/Latino; 10 Two or more races, non-Hispanic/Latino), 162 international. Average age 31. 406 applicants, 85% accepted, 205 enrolled. *Faculty:* 38 full-time (7 women), 20 part-time/adjunct (0 women). Expenses: Contact institution. *Financial support:* Fellowships, research assistantships with full tuition reimbursements, teaching assistantships with full tuition reimbursements, career-related internships or fieldwork, Federal Work-Study, scholarships/grants, and unspecified assistantships available. Financial award application deadline: 2/1; financial award applicants required to submit FAFSA. In 2019, 243 master's, 3 doctorates, 50 other advanced degrees awarded. *Program availability:* Part-time, evening/weekend, online learning. *Application deadline:* For fall admission, 7/1 for domestic students, 5/1 for international students; for winter admission, 9/15 for international students; for spring admission, 12/1 for domestic students. *Application fee:* $35 ($60 for international students). Electronic applications accepted. *Application Contact:* Dr. Chuck Pierce, Associate Dean for Academic Programs and Research, 901-678-4620, Fax: 901-678-3759, E-mail: chuck.pierce@memphis.edu. *Dean,* Dr. Damon Fleming, 901-678-2457, Fax: 901-678-4705, E-mail: damon.fleming@memphis.edu.

***Herff College of Engineering*** Students: 99 full-time (26 women), 90 part-time (22 women); includes 31 minority (7 Black or African American, non-Hispanic/Latino; 1 American Indian or Alaska Native, non-Hispanic/Latino; 17 Asian, non-Hispanic/Latino; 5 Hispanic/Latino; 1 Two or more races, non-Hispanic/Latino), 98 international. Average age 30. 104 applicants, 75% accepted, 43 enrolled. *Faculty:* 39 full-time (6 women), 5 part-time/adjunct (1 woman). Expenses: Contact institution. *Financial support:* Fellowships with full tuition reimbursements, research assistantships with full tuition reimbursements, teaching assistantships with full tuition reimbursements, career-related internships or fieldwork, Federal Work-Study, scholarships/grants, tuition waivers (full and partial), and unspecified assistantships available. Financial award application deadline: 2/1; financial award applicants required to submit FAFSA. In 2019, 27 master's, 7 doctorates, 3 other advanced degrees awarded. *Program availability:* Part-time. *Application deadline:* For fall admission, 8/1 for domestic students, 5/1 for international students; for spring admission, 12/1 for domestic students, 9/15 for international students; for summer admission, 5/1 for domestic students. *Application fee:* $35 ($60 for international students). Electronic applications accepted. *Application Contact:* Dr. Russell Deaton, Associate Dean of Academic Affairs and Administration, 901-678-2175, Fax: 901-678-5030, E-mail: rjdeaton@memphis.edu. *Dean,* Dr. Richard Joseph Sweigard, 901-678-4306, Fax: 901-678-4180, E-mail: rjswgard@memphis.edu.

***Kemmons Wilson School of Hospitality and Resort Management*** Students: 27 full-time (12 women), 35 part-time (12 women); includes 24 minority (20 Black or African American, non-Hispanic/Latino; 2 Asian, non-Hispanic/Latino; 2 Two or more races, non-Hispanic/Latino), 2 international. Average age 27. 54 applicants, 81% accepted, 24 enrolled. *Faculty:* 6 full-time (2 women), 3 part-time/adjunct (1 woman). Expenses: Contact institution. *Financial support:* Research assistantships, teaching assistantships, career-related internships or fieldwork, Federal Work-Study, scholarships/grants, and unspecified assistantships available. Support available to part-time students. Financial award application deadline: 2/1; financial award applicants required to submit FAFSA. In 2019, 30 master's awarded. *Program availability:* Part-time, online learning. *Application deadline:* For fall admission, 7/1 for domestic students, 5/1 for international students; for spring admission, 12/1 for domestic students, 9/1 for international students; for summer admission, 5/1 for domestic students, 2/1 for international students. *Application fee:* $35 ($60 for international students). Electronic applications accepted. *Application Contact:* Dr. Radesh Palakurthi, Dean, 901-678-3430, E-mail: rplkrthi@memphis.edu. *Dean,* Dr. Radesh Palakurthi, 901-678-3430, E-mail: rplkrthi@memphis.edu.

***School of Communication Sciences and Disorders*** Students: 127 full-time (117 women), 20 part-time (17 women); includes 19 minority (10 Black or African American, non-Hispanic/Latino; 5 Asian, non-Hispanic/Latino; 3 Hispanic/Latino; 1 Two or more races, non-Hispanic/Latino), 4 international. Average age 25. 88 applicants, 95% accepted, 35 enrolled. *Faculty:* 17 full-time (15 women), 3 part-time/adjunct (2 women). Expenses: Contact institution. *Financial support:* Research assistantships with full tuition reimbursements, Federal Work-Study, scholarships/grants, and unspecified assistantships available. Financial award application deadline: 2/1; financial award applicants required to submit FAFSA. In 2019, 21 master's, 17 doctorates awarded. *Program availability:* Part-time. *Application deadline:* For fall admission, 2/1 priority date for domestic students. Applications are processed on a rolling basis. *Application fee:* $35 ($60 for international students). Electronic applications accepted. *Application Contact:* Dr. Lisa Mendel, Interim Associate Dean of Graduate Studies, 901-678-5800, E-mail: lmendel@memphis.edu. *Dean,* Dr. Linda Jarmulowicz, 901-678-5800, Fax: 901-525-1282, E-mail: ljrmlwcz@memphis.edu.

***School of Health Studies*** Students: 56 full-time (44 women), 42 part-time (33 women); includes 39 minority (24 Black or African American, non-Hispanic/Latino; 4 Asian, non-Hispanic/Latino; 4 Hispanic/Latino; 2 Native Hawaiian or other Pacific Islander, non-Hispanic/Latino; 5 Two or more races, non-Hispanic/Latino), 6 international. Average age 29. 63 applicants, 84% accepted, 37 enrolled. *Faculty:* 19 full-time (11 women), 2 part-time/adjunct (1 woman). Expenses: Contact institution. *Financial support:* Research assistantships, teaching assistantships, career-related internships or fieldwork, Federal Work-Study, scholarships/grants, and unspecified assistantships available. Financial award application deadline: 2/1; financial award applicants required to submit FAFSA. In 2019, 38 master's, 2 other advanced degrees awarded. *Program availability:* 100% online. *Application deadline:* For fall admission, 4/15 priority date for domestic students; for spring admission, 10/15 priority date for domestic students; for summer admission, 4/15 priority date for domestic students. *Application fee:* $35 ($60 for international students). *Application Contact:* Dr. Richard Bloomer, Dean, 901-678-4316, Fax: 901-678-3591, E-mail: rbloomer@memphis.edu. *Dean,* Dr. Richard Bloomer, 901-678-4316, Fax: 901-678-3591, E-mail: rbloomer@memphis.edu.

***School of Public Health*** Students: 126 full-time (80 women), 77 part-time (60 women); includes 70 minority (40 Black or African American, non-Hispanic/Latino; 17 Asian, non-Hispanic/Latino; 9 Hispanic/Latino; 4 Two or more races, non-Hispanic/Latino), 29 international. Average age 30. 105 applicants, 97% accepted, 67 enrolled. *Faculty:* 20 full-time (7 women), 10 part-time/adjunct (4 women). Expenses: Contact institution. *Financial support:* Research assistantships with full tuition reimbursements, Federal Work-Study, scholarships/grants, and unspecified assistantships available. Financial award application deadline: 2/1; financial award applicants required to submit FAFSA. In 2019, 47 master's, 9 doctorates awarded. *Program availability:* Part-time, evening/weekend, online learning. *Application deadline:* For fall admission, 4/1 for domestic students; for spring admission, 11/1 for domestic students. *Application fee:* $35 ($60 for international students). Electronic applications accepted. *Application Contact:* Dr. Marian Levy, Associate Dean, 901-678-4514, E-mail: mlevy@memphis.edu. *Dean,* Dr. James Gurney, 901-678-1673, E-mail: jggurney@memphis.edu.

**Loewenberg College of Nursing** Students: 19 full-time (17 women), 281 part-time (254 women); includes 104 minority (87 Black or African American, non-Hispanic/Latino; 5 Asian, non-Hispanic/Latino; 7 Hispanic/Latino; 5 Two or more races, non-Hispanic/Latino), 2 international. Average age 34. 117 applicants, 79% accepted, 48 enrolled. *Faculty:* 21 full-time (19 women), 11 part-time/adjunct (10 women). Expenses: Contact institution. *Financial support:* Federal Work-Study and scholarships/grants available. Financial award application deadline: 2/1; financial award applicants required to submit FAFSA. In 2019, 71 master's, 3 other advanced degrees awarded. *Program availability:* Part-time, evening/weekend, online learning. *Application deadline:* For fall admission, 2/15 for domestic and international students; for spring admission, 10/1 for domestic and international students. *Application fee:* $35 ($60 for international students). *Application Contact:* Dr. Lin Zhan, Dean, 901-678-2020, E-mail: lzhan@memphis.edu. *Dean,* Dr. Lin Zhan, 901-678-2020, E-mail: lzhan@memphis.edu.

## UNIVERSITY OF MIAMI, Coral Gables, FL 33124

**General Information** Independent, coed, university. CGS member. *Graduate housing:* On-campus housing not available. *Research affiliation:* Howard Hughes Medical Institute (biology), The Buoniconti Fund: Miami Project to Cure Paralysis (paralysis research), Organization for Tropical Studies, National Center for Atmospheric Research (atmospheric science).

**GRADUATE UNITS**

**Graduate School** *Program availability:* Part-time, evening/weekend, online learning. Electronic applications accepted.

***College of Arts and Sciences*** *Program availability:* Part-time, evening/weekend. Electronic applications accepted.

***College of Engineering*** *Program availability:* Part-time, evening/weekend. Electronic applications accepted.

***Frost School of Music*** Electronic applications accepted.

***Miller School of Medicine*** Students: 1,396 full-time (805 women), 61 part-time (48 women); includes 683 minority (86 Black or African American, non-Hispanic/Latino; 169 Asian, non-Hispanic/Latino; 295 Hispanic/Latino; 133 Two or more races, non-Hispanic/Latino), 105 international. Average age 26. 9,683 applicants, 6% accepted, 323 enrolled. *Faculty:* 1,470 full-time (560 women), 92 part-time/adjunct (58 women). Expenses: Contact institution. *Financial support:* Fellowships with partial tuition reimbursements, research assistantships with partial tuition reimbursements, teaching assistantships, career-related internships or fieldwork, Federal Work-Study, institutionally sponsored loans, scholarships/grants, and tuition waivers (full and partial) available. Support available to part-time students. Financial award applicants required to submit FAFSA. In 2019, 169 master's, 279 doctorates awarded. *Application deadline:* For fall admission, 12/1 priority date for domestic and international students. Applications are processed on a rolling basis. *Application fee:* $95. Electronic applications accepted. *Application Contact:* Dr. John L. Bixby, Vice Provost, 305-243-7587, Fax: 305-243-3593, E-mail: jbixby@med.miami.edu. *Executive Vice President and CEO of UHealth,* Dr. Henri Ford, 305-243-5677, Fax: 305-243-1698, E-mail: eabraham@miami.edu.

***Rosenstiel School of Marine and Atmospheric Science*** *Program availability:* Part-time. Electronic applications accepted.

***School of Architecture*** Electronic applications accepted.

***School of Communication*** *Program availability:* Part-time. Electronic applications accepted.

***School of Education and Human Development*** Students: 280 full-time (156 women), 208 part-time (154 women); includes 279 minority (94 Black or African American, non-Hispanic/Latino; 3 American Indian or Alaska Native, non-Hispanic/Latino; 10 Asian, non-Hispanic/Latino; 164 Hispanic/Latino; 8 Two or more races, non-Hispanic/Latino), 42 international. Average age 31. 598 applicants, 39% accepted, 139 enrolled. *Faculty:* 54 full-time (31 women). Expenses: Contact institution. *Financial support:* Fellowships, research assistantships, teaching assistantships, scholarships/grants, health care benefits, tuition waivers (full and partial), and unspecified assistantships available. Support available to part-time students. Financial award application deadline: 3/1; financial award applicants required to submit FAFSA. In 2019, 159 master's, 14 doctorates awarded. *Program availability:* 100% online. *Application deadline:* For fall admission, 10/1 for international students. *Application fee:* $85. Electronic applications accepted. *Application Contact:* Dr. Walter Secada, Vice Dean, 305-284-2102, Fax: 305-284-9395, E-mail: wsecada@miami.edu. *Vice Dean,* Dr. Walter Secada, 305-284-2102, Fax: 305-284-9395, E-mail: wsecada@miami.edu.

***School of Nursing and Health Studies*** *Program availability:* Part-time. Electronic applications accepted.

***University of Miami School of Law*** Students: 1,101 full-time (544 women), 89 part-time (43 women); includes 544 minority (68 Black or African American, non-Hispanic/Latino; 3 American Indian or Alaska Native, non-Hispanic/Latino; 27 Asian, non-Hispanic/Latino; 406 Hispanic/Latino; 40 Two or more races, non-Hispanic/Latino), 102 international. Average age 25. 2,576 applicants, 62% accepted, 360 enrolled. *Faculty:* 83 full-time (45 women), 93 part-time/adjunct (20 women). Expenses: Contact institution. *Financial support:* Fellowships, research assistantships, career-related internships or fieldwork, Federal Work-Study, institutionally sponsored loans, scholarships/grants, and unspecified assistantships available. Financial award application deadline: 3/1; financial award applicants required to submit FAFSA. *Application deadline:* For fall admission, 7/31 for domestic and international students. Applications are processed on a rolling basis. *Application fee:* $60. Electronic applications accepted. *Application Contact:* Joseph Matthews, Associate Director of Student Recruitment, 305-284-6746, Fax: 305-284-3084, E-mail: jmatthews@law.miami.edu. *Associate Dean of Admissions and Enrollment Management,* Katrin Hussmann Schroll, 305-284-2527, Fax: 305-284-3084, E-mail: kschroll@law.miami.edu.

***Miami Business School*** *Program availability:* Part-time, evening/weekend, 100% online, blended/hybrid learning. Electronic applications accepted.

## UNIVERSITY OF MICHIGAN, Ann Arbor, MI 48109

**General Information** State-supported, coed, university. CGS member. *Graduate housing:* Rooms and/or apartments available on a first-come, first-served basis to single and married students.

**GRADUATE UNITS**

**College of Engineering** *Program availability:* Part-time, 100% online, blended/hybrid learning. Electronic applications accepted.

**College of Pharmacy** Electronic applications accepted.

**Gerald R. Ford School of Public Policy** Students: 282 full-time (149 women); includes 91 minority (23 Black or African American, non-Hispanic/Latino; 1 American Indian or Alaska Native, non-Hispanic/Latino; 26 Asian, non-Hispanic/Latino; 30 Hispanic/Latino; 11 Two or more races, non-Hispanic/Latino), 38 international. Average age 27. 663 applicants, 65% accepted, 114 enrolled. *Faculty:* 43 full-time (17 women), 36 part-time/adjunct (14 women). Expenses: Contact institution. *Financial support:* In 2019–20, 203 students received support, including 169 fellowships with tuition reimbursements available, 33 teaching assistantships with tuition reimbursements available; research assistantships, career-related internships or fieldwork, traineeships, health care benefits, and unspecified assistantships also available. Financial award application deadline: 1/15; financial award applicants required to submit FAFSA. In 2019, 116 master's, 3 doctorates awarded. *Application deadline:* For fall admission, 1/15 priority date for domestic students, 1/15 for international students. *Application fee:* $75 ($90 for international students). Electronic applications accepted. *Application Contact:* Beth Soboleski, Director, Admissions and Recruiting, 734-764-0453, Fax: 734-647-7486, E-mail: fspp-admissions@umich.edu. *Dean of Public Policy,* Michael S. Barr, 734-764-2258, E-mail: ford.school.dean@umich.edu.

**Law School** Electronic applications accepted.

**Medical School** Electronic applications accepted.

**Rackham Graduate School** Students: 8,243 full-time (3,747 women), 714 part-time (310 women); includes 1,822 minority (345 Black or African American, non-Hispanic/Latino; 17 American Indian or Alaska Native, non-Hispanic/Latino; 667 Asian, non-Hispanic/Latino; 556 Hispanic/Latino; 1 Native Hawaiian or other Pacific Islander, non-Hispanic/Latino; 236 Two or more races, non-Hispanic/Latino), 3,610 international. Average age 27. 29,264 applicants, 27% accepted, 3,175 enrolled. Expenses: Contact institution. *Financial support:* Fellowships with full and partial tuition reimbursements, research assistantships with full and partial tuition reimbursements, teaching assistantships with full and partial tuition reimbursements, career-related internships or fieldwork, Federal Work-Study, scholarships/grants, traineeships, health care benefits, and unspecified assistantships available. Support available to part-time students. In 2019, 2,270 master's, 824 doctorates, 151 other advanced degrees awarded. *Program availability:* 100% online, blended/hybrid learning, Covid impacts - emergent formats. *Application deadline:* Applications are processed on a rolling basis. *Application fee:* $75 ($90 for international students). Electronic applications accepted. *Application Contact:* Admissions Office, 734-764-8129, E-mail: rackadmis@umich.edu. *Dean/Vice Provost for Academic Affairs, Graduate Studies,* Dr. Michael J. Solomon, 734-764-4400.

***College of Literature, Science, and the Arts*** Electronic applications accepted.

***Penny W. Stamps School of Art and Design*** Electronic applications accepted.

***Program in Biomedical Sciences (PIBS)*** Electronic applications accepted.

***School of Kinesiology*** Electronic applications accepted.

***School of Music, Theatre, and Dance*** Electronic applications accepted.

***School of Nursing*** *Program availability:* Part-time, online learning.

**Ross School of Business** *Program availability:* Part-time, evening/weekend. Electronic applications accepted.

**School for Environment and Sustainability** Electronic applications accepted.

**School of Dentistry** Electronic applications accepted.

**School of Education** Electronic applications accepted.

**School of Information** *Program availability:* Part-time. Electronic applications accepted.

**School of Public Health** *Program availability:* Evening/weekend. Electronic applications accepted.

**School of Social Work** Electronic applications accepted.

**Taubman College of Architecture and Urban Planning** Electronic applications accepted.

## UNIVERSITY OF MICHIGAN–DEARBORN, Dearborn, MI 48128

**General Information** State-supported, coed, comprehensive institution. *Enrollment:* 9,195 graduate, professional, and undergraduate students; 490 full-time matriculated graduate/professional students (190 women), 1,746 part-time matriculated graduate/professional students (629 women). *Enrollment by degree level:* 2,131 master's, 55 doctoral, 50 other advanced degrees. *Graduate faculty:* 323 full-time (132 women), 230 part-time/adjunct (99 women). *Student services:* Campus employment opportunities, campus safety program, career counseling, child daycare facilities, exercise/wellness program, free psychological counseling, grant writing training, international student services, low-cost health insurance, multicultural affairs office, services for students with disabilities, teacher training, writing training. *Library facilities:* Mardigian Library. *Collection:* Books: 189,535 (physical), 705,108 (digital/electronic); Serial titles: 310 (physical), 116,547 (digital/electronic); Databases: 847. Weekly public service hours: 95; students can reserve study rooms. *Research affiliation:* Henry W. Patton Center for Engineering Education and Practice, Center for Lightweighting Automotive Materials and Processing, Center for Electric Drive Transportation, DTE Power Electronics and Electric Drives Lab, Cybersecurity Center (CCERO).

**Computer facilities:** Computer purchase and lease plans are available. 750 computers available on campus for general student use. A campuswide network can be accessed. Online class registration, tuition and application payments accepted online are available. Website: http://www.umdearborn.edu/

**General Application Contact:** Office of Graduate Studies, 313-583-6321, E-mail: umd-graduatestudies@umich.edu.

**GRADUATE UNITS**

**College of Arts, Sciences, and Letters** Students: 41 full-time (30 women), 71 part-time (41 women); includes 37 minority (16 Black or African American, non-Hispanic/Latino; 12 Asian, non-Hispanic/Latino; 9 Hispanic/Latino), 3 international. Average age 31. 110 applicants, 58% accepted, 28 enrolled. *Faculty:* 55 full-time (28 women), 20 part-time/adjunct (10 women). Expenses: Contact institution. *Financial support:* Scholarships/grants and non-resident tuition scholarships available. Financial award application deadline: 3/1; financial award applicants required to submit FAFSA. In 2019, 38 master's awarded. *Program availability:* Part-time, evening/weekend. *Application deadline:* For fall admission, 8/1 priority date for domestic students, 5/1 priority date for international students; for winter admission, 12/1 priority date for domestic students, 9/1 priority date for international students; for spring admission, 4/1 priority date for domestic students, 1/1 priority date for international students. Applications are processed on a rolling basis. *Application fee:* $60. Electronic applications accepted. *Application Contact:* Office of Graduate Studies, 313-583-6321, E-mail: umd-graduatestudies@umich.edu. *Dean*, Dr. Martin Hershock, 313-593-5490, E-mail: mhershoc@umich.edu.

**College of Business** Students: 98 full-time (42 women), 471 part-time (202 women); includes 140 minority (31 Black or African American, non-Hispanic/Latino; 5 American Indian or Alaska Native, non-Hispanic/Latino; 53 Asian, non-Hispanic/Latino; 33 Hispanic/Latino; 18 Two or more races, non-Hispanic/Latino), 74 international. Average age 31. 472 applicants, 57% accepted, 135 enrolled. *Faculty:* 40 full-time (17 women), 9 part-time/adjunct (6 women). Expenses: Contact institution. *Financial support:* Scholarships/grants and non-resident tuition scholarships available. Financial award application deadline: 3/1; financial award applicants required to submit FAFSA. In 2019, 149 master's awarded. *Program availability:* Part-time, evening/weekend, 100% online. *Application deadline:* For fall admission, 8/1 priority date for domestic students, 5/1 priority date for international students; for winter admission, 12/1 priority date for domestic students, 9/1 priority date for international students; for spring admission, 4/1 priority date for domestic students, 1/1 priority date for international students. Applications are processed on a rolling basis. *Application fee:* $60. Electronic applications accepted. *Application Contact:* Joan Doherty, Academic Advisor/Counselor, 313-593-5460, E-mail: umd-gradbusiness@umich.edu. *Dean*, Dr. Raju Balakrishnan, 313-593-5460, E-mail: umd-cob-dean@umich.edu.

**College of Education, Health, and Human Services** Students: 18 full-time (14 women), 197 part-time (157 women); includes 49 minority (27 Black or African American, non-Hispanic/Latino; 9 Asian, non-Hispanic/Latino; 9 Hispanic/Latino; 1 Native Hawaiian or other Pacific Islander, non-Hispanic/Latino; 3 Two or more races, non-Hispanic/Latino), 7 international. Average age 33. 136 applicants, 70% accepted, 55 enrolled. *Faculty:* 16 full-time (11 women), 18 part-time/adjunct (12 women). Expenses: Contact institution. *Financial support:* Career-related internships or fieldwork and scholarships/grants available. Financial award application deadline: 3/1; financial award applicants required to submit FAFSA. In 2019, 71 master's, 1 doctorate awarded. *Program availability:* Part-time, evening/weekend, 100% online, blended/hybrid learning. *Application deadline:* For fall admission, 8/1 priority date for domestic students, 5/1 priority date for international students; for winter admission, 12/1 priority date for domestic students, 9/1 priority date for international students; for spring admission, 4/1 priority date for domestic students, 1/1 priority date for international students. Applications are processed on a rolling basis. *Application fee:* $60. Electronic applications accepted. *Application Contact:* Dr. Paul Fossum, Director, Master's Programs, 313-593-0982, E-mail: pfossum@umich.edu. *Dean*, Dr. Ann Lampkin-Williams, 313-593-5090, E-mail: lampkin@umich.edu.

**College of Engineering and Computer Science** Students: 333 full-time (104 women), 1,007 part-time (229 women); includes 192 minority (46 Black or African American, non-Hispanic/Latino; 2 American Indian or Alaska Native, non-Hispanic/Latino; 90 Asian, non-Hispanic/Latino; 41 Hispanic/Latino; 13 Two or more races, non-Hispanic/Latino), 511 international. Average age 28. 1,700 applicants, 48% accepted, 328 enrolled. *Faculty:* 80 full-time (11 women), 42 part-time/adjunct (4 women). Expenses: Contact institution. *Financial support:* In 2019–20, 327 students received support. Research assistantships with full tuition reimbursements available, teaching assistantships with full tuition reimbursements available, career-related internships or fieldwork, scholarships/grants, health care benefits, and non-residential student scholarships available. Support available to part-time students. Financial award application deadline: 3/1; financial award applicants required to submit FAFSA. In 2019, 455 master's, 4 doctorates awarded. *Program availability:* Part-time, evening/weekend, 100% online. *Application deadline:* For fall admission, 8/1 priority date for domestic students, 5/1 priority date for international students; for winter admission, 12/1 priority date for domestic students, 9/1 priority date for international students; for spring admission, 4/1 priority date for domestic students, 1/1 priority date for international students. Applications are processed on a rolling basis. *Application fee:* $60. Electronic applications accepted. *Application Contact:* Office of Graduate Studies Staff, 313-583-6321, E-mail: umd-graduatestudies@umich.edu. *Dean*, Dr. Anthony England, 313-593-5290, E-mail: cecsdeansoffice@umich.edu.

## UNIVERSITY OF MICHIGAN–FLINT, Flint, MI 48502-1950

**General Information** State-supported, coed, comprehensive institution. CGS member. *Enrollment:* 7,297 graduate, professional, and undergraduate students; 606 full-time matriculated graduate/professional students (430 women), 819 part-time matriculated graduate/professional students (549 women). *Enrollment by degree level:* 859 master's, 502 doctoral, 64 other advanced degrees. *Graduate faculty:* 302 full-time (161 women), 248 part-time/adjunct (154 women). *International tuition:* $15,776 full-time. *Tuition, area resident:* Full-time $10,544. Tuition, state resident: full-time $10,544. Tuition, nonresident: full-time $15,776. Tuition and fees vary according to degree level. *Graduate housing:* Room and/or apartments available on a first-come, first-served basis to single students; on-campus housing not available to married students. Typical cost: $7596 per year ($10,656 including board). Room and board charges vary according to board plan and housing facility selected. *Student services:* Campus employment opportunities, campus safety program, career counseling, child daycare facilities, exercise/wellness program, free psychological counseling, international student services, services for students with disabilities, teacher training, writing training. *Library facilities:* Frances Willson Thompson Library plus 1 other. *Collection:* Books: 228,601 (physical), 195,382 (digital/electronic); Serial titles: 1,862 (physical), 238,105 (digital/electronic); Databases: 1,849. Weekly public service hours: 96; students can reserve study rooms.

**Computer facilities:** Computer purchase and lease plans are available. 502 computers available on campus for general student use. A campuswide network can be accessed. Online class registration is available.
Website: http://www.umflint.edu/

**General Application Contact:** Matt Bohlen, Associate Director Graduate Programs, 810-762-3171, Fax: 810-766-6789, E-mail: bmaki@umflint.edu.

**GRADUATE UNITS**

**College of Arts and Sciences** Students: 54 full-time (21 women), 85 part-time (35 women); includes 24 minority (9 Black or African American, non-Hispanic/Latino; 1 American Indian or Alaska Native, non-Hispanic/Latino; 4 Asian, non-Hispanic/Latino; 8 Hispanic/Latino; 2 Two or more races, non-Hispanic/Latino), 37 international. Average age 32. 297 applicants, 57% accepted, 22 enrolled. *Faculty:* 96 full-time (48 women), 43 part-time/adjunct (22 women). Expenses: Contact institution. *Financial support:* Federal Work-Study, scholarships/grants, and unspecified assistantships available. Support available to part-time students. Financial award application deadline: 3/1; financial award applicants required to submit FAFSA. In 2019, 65 master's awarded. *Program availability:* Part-time. *Application deadline:* For fall admission, 8/1 for domestic students, 5/1 for international students; for winter admission, 11/15 for domestic students, 10/1 for international students; for spring admission, 3/15 for domestic students, 1/1 for international students; for summer admission, 5/15 for domestic students. Applications are processed on a rolling basis. *Application fee:* $55. Electronic applications accepted. *Application Contact:* Matt Bohlen, Associate Director of Graduate Programs, 810-762-3171, Fax: 810-766-6789, E-mail: bmaki@umich.edu. *Dean*, Dr. Susan Gano-Phillips, 810-762-3234, Fax: 810-762-3006, E-mail: sganop@umich.edu.

**College of Health Sciences** Students: 283 full-time (194 women), 80 part-time (56 women); includes 57 minority (15 Black or African American, non-Hispanic/Latino; 1 American Indian or Alaska Native, non-Hispanic/Latino; 15 Asian, non-Hispanic/Latino; 16 Hispanic/Latino; 10 Two or more races, non-Hispanic/Latino), 19 international. Average age 29. 486 applicants, 49% accepted, 133 enrolled. *Faculty:* 34 full-time (26 women), 45 part-time/adjunct (22 women). Expenses: Contact institution. *Financial support:* Federal Work-Study, scholarships/grants, and unspecified assistantships available. Support available to part-time students. Financial award application deadline: 3/1; financial award applicants required to submit FAFSA. In 2019, 43 master's, 77 doctorates awarded. *Program availability:* Part-time, 100% online. *Application deadline:* For fall admission, 8/1 for domestic students, 5/1 for international students; for winter admission, 11/15 for domestic students, 10/1 for international students; for spring admission, 3/15 for domestic students, 1/1 for international students. Applications are processed on a rolling basis. *Application fee:* $55. Electronic applications accepted. *Application Contact:* Matt Bohlen, Associate Director of Graduate Programs, 810-762-3171, Fax: 810-766-6789, E-mail: mbohlen@umflint.edu. *Dean*, Dr. Donna Fry, 810-237-6503, Fax: 810-237-6532, E-mail: donnafry@umflint.edu.

**Graduate Programs** Students: 10 full-time (6 women), 107 part-time (69 women); includes 42 minority (34 Black or African American, non-Hispanic/Latino; 3 American Indian or Alaska Native, non-Hispanic/Latino; 2 Asian, non-Hispanic/Latino; 2 Hispanic/Latino; 1 Two or more races, non-Hispanic/Latino), 2 international. Average age 40. 79 applicants, 75% accepted, 27 enrolled. *Faculty:* 8 full-time (3 women), 13 part-time/adjunct (8 women). Expenses: Contact institution. *Financial support:* Fellowships, Federal Work-Study, scholarships/grants, and unspecified assistantships available. Support available to part-time students. Financial award application deadline: 3/1; financial award applicants required to submit FAFSA. In 2019, 48 master's awarded. *Program availability:* Part-time, evening/weekend, online learning. *Application deadline:* For fall admission, 8/1 for domestic students, 5/1 for international students; for winter admission, 11/15 for domestic students, 10/1 for international students; for spring admission, 3/15 for domestic students, 1/1 for international students; for summer admission, 5/15 for domestic students. Applications are processed on a rolling basis. *Application fee:* $55. Electronic applications accepted. *Application Contact:* Matt Bohlen, Associate Director of Graduate Admissions, 810-762-3171, Fax: 810-766-6789, E-mail: mbohlen@umflint.edu. *Dean of Graduate Programs*, Stephen W Turner, 810-762-3171, Fax: 810-766-6789, E-mail: swturner@umflint.edu.

**School of Education and Human Services** Students: 31 full-time (20 women), 160 part-time (125 women); includes 47 minority (36 Black or African American, non-Hispanic/Latino; 2 Asian, non-Hispanic/Latino; 5 Hispanic/Latino; 4 Two or more races, non-Hispanic/Latino), 1 international. Average age 38. 103 applicants, 71% accepted, 48 enrolled. *Faculty:* 18 full-time (11 women), 20 part-time/adjunct (13 women). Expenses: Contact institution. *Financial support:* Federal Work-Study, scholarships/grants, and unspecified assistantships available. Support available to part-time students. Financial award application deadline: 3/1; financial award applicants required to submit FAFSA. In 2019, 60 master's awarded. *Program availability:* Part-time, mixed mode format. *Application deadline:* For fall admission, 7/1 for domestic students, 4/1 for international students; for winter admission, 11/15 for domestic students, 10/1 for international students; for spring admission, 3/15 for domestic students, 1/1 for international students. Applications are processed on a rolling basis. *Application fee:* $55. Electronic applications accepted. *Application Contact:* Matt Bohlen, Associate Director of Graduate Admissions, 810-762-3171, Fax: 810-766-6789, E-mail: mbohlen@umflint.edu. *Dean*, Dr. Bob Barnett, 810-766-6878, Fax: 810-766-6891, E-mail: rbarnett@umflint.edu.

**School of Management** Students: 29 full-time (14 women), 196 part-time (99 women); includes 59 minority (27 Black or African American, non-Hispanic/Latino; 3 American Indian or Alaska Native, non-Hispanic/Latino; 10 Asian, non-Hispanic/Latino; 11 Hispanic/Latino; 8 Two or more races, non-Hispanic/Latino), 19 international. Average age 36. 150 applicants, 75% accepted, 56 enrolled. *Faculty:* 25 full-time (4 women), 11 part-time/adjunct (3 women). Expenses: Contact institution. *Financial support:* Federal Work-Study, scholarships/grants, and unspecified assistantships available. Support available to part-time students. Financial award application deadline: 3/1; financial award applicants required to submit FAFSA. In 2019, 75 master's, 1 other advanced degree awarded. *Program availability:* Part-time, evening/weekend, mixed mode format. *Application deadline:* For fall admission, 8/1 for domestic students, 5/1 for international students; for winter admission, 11/15 for domestic students, 10/1 for international students; for spring admission, 3/15 for domestic students, 1/1 for international students;

for summer admission, 5/15 for domestic students. Applications are processed on a rolling basis. *Application fee:* $55. Electronic applications accepted. *Application Contact:* Matt Bohlen, Associate Director of Graduate Admissions, 810-762-3171, Fax: 810-766-6789, E-mail: mbohlen@umflint.edu. *Dean, School of Management*, Dr. Scott Johnson, 810-762-6579, Fax: 810-237-6685, E-mail: scotjohn@umflint.edu.

**School of Nursing** Students: 198 full-time (174 women), 188 part-time (162 women); includes 55 minority (6 Black or African American, non-Hispanic/Latino; 3 American Indian or Alaska Native, non-Hispanic/Latino; 21 Asian, non-Hispanic/Latino; 18 Hispanic/Latino; 1 Native Hawaiian or other Pacific Islander, non-Hispanic/Latino; 6 Two or more races, non-Hispanic/Latino), 1 international. Average age 37. 140 applicants, 84% accepted, 75 enrolled. *Faculty:* 32 full-time (31 women), 80 part-time/adjunct (71 women). Expenses: Contact institution. *Financial support:* Federal Work-Study, scholarships/grants, and unspecified assistantships available. Support available to part-time students. Financial award application deadline: 3/1; financial award applicants required to submit FAFSA. In 2019, 52 master's, 22 doctorates, 8 other advanced degrees awarded. *Program availability:* Part-time, evening/weekend, 100% online. *Application deadline:* For fall admission, 7/1 for domestic students, 5/1 for international students; for winter admission, 11/15 for domestic students, 10/1 for international students; for spring admission, 3/15 for domestic students, 1/1 for international students; for summer admission, 5/15 for domestic students. Applications are processed on a rolling basis. *Application fee:* $55. Electronic applications accepted. *Application Contact:* Matt Bohlen, Director of Graduate Admissions, 810-762-3171, Fax: 810-766-6789, E-mail: mbohlen@umflint.edu. *Director*, Dr. Constance J. Creech, 810-762-3420, Fax: 810-766-6851, E-mail: ccreech@umflint.edu.

## UNIVERSITY OF MINNESOTA, DULUTH, Duluth, MN 55812-2496

**General Information** State-supported, coed, comprehensive institution. *Graduate housing:* Room and/or apartments available to single students; on-campus housing not available to married students. Housing application deadline: 3/1. *Research affiliation:* Environmental Protection Agency Environmental Research Laboratory (aquatic biology), Minnesota Geological Survey, Northeastern Minnesota National Historical Center (local history), U.S. Forest Service, Northcentral Forest Experiment Station.

**GRADUATE UNITS**

**Graduate School** *Program availability:* Part-time, evening/weekend, online learning.

***College of Education and Human Service Professions*** *Program availability:* Part-time, evening/weekend, online learning.

***College of Liberal Arts*** *Program availability:* Part-time.

***Labovitz School of Business and Economics*** *Program availability:* Part-time, evening/weekend.

***School of Fine Arts*** *Program availability:* Part-time.

***Swenson College of Science and Engineering*** *Program availability:* Part-time, evening/weekend, online learning.

**Medical School** *Program availability:* Part-time.

## UNIVERSITY OF MINNESOTA ROCHESTER, Rochester, MN 55904

**General Information** State-supported, coed, comprehensive institution.

**GRADUATE UNITS**

**Graduate Programs**

## UNIVERSITY OF MINNESOTA, TWIN CITIES CAMPUS, Minneapolis, MN 55455-0213

**General Information** State-supported, coed, university. CGS member. *Graduate housing:* Rooms and/or apartments available on a first-come, first-served basis to single and married students. Housing application deadline: 5/1.

**GRADUATE UNITS**

**Carlson School of Management** *Program availability:* Part-time, evening/weekend, 100% online, blended/hybrid learning. Electronic applications accepted.

**College of Pharmacy** *Program availability:* Part-time.

**College of Science and Engineering** *Program availability:* Part-time, evening/weekend, 100% online, blended/hybrid learning. Electronic applications accepted.

***School of Mathematics*** *Program availability:* Part-time. Electronic applications accepted.

***School of Physics and Astronomy*** *Program availability:* Part-time.

***Technological Leadership Institute*** *Program availability:* Evening/weekend. Electronic applications accepted.

**College of Veterinary Medicine** *Program availability:* Part-time. Electronic applications accepted.

**Graduate School** *Program availability:* Part-time, evening/weekend, online learning. Electronic applications accepted.

***College of Biological Sciences*** *Program availability:* Part-time. Electronic applications accepted.

***College of Design*** Electronic applications accepted.

***College of Education and Human Development*** Students: 1,473 full-time (1,078 women), 544 part-time (378 women); includes 465 minority (128 Black or African American, non-Hispanic/Latino; 11 American Indian or Alaska Native, non-Hispanic/Latino; 129 Asian, non-Hispanic/Latino; 114 Hispanic/Latino; 1 Native Hawaiian or other Pacific Islander, non-Hispanic/Latino; 82 Two or more races, non-Hispanic/Latino), 222 international. Average age 32. 1,879 applicants, 60% accepted, 854 enrolled. *Faculty:* 166 full-time (92 women). Expenses: Contact institution. *Financial support:* In 2019–20, 86 fellowships, 255 research assistantships with full tuition reimbursements (averaging $12,177 per year), 212 teaching assistantships with full tuition reimbursements (averaging $13,056 per year) were awarded; scholarships/grants and tuition waivers (partial) also available. Financial award applicants required to submit FAFSA. In 2019, 612 master's, 105 doctorates, 81 other advanced degrees awarded. *Program availability:* Part-time. *Application fee:* $75 ($95 for international students). *Application Contact:* Schee Moua, Director of Graduate Education, 612-626-7356, E-mail: scmoua@umn.edu. *Dean*, Dr. Jean K. Quam, 612-626-9252, Fax: 612-626-7496, E-mail: jquam@umn.edu.

***College of Food, Agricultural and Natural Resource Sciences*** Students: 456 full-time, 152 part-time; includes 60 minority (12 Black or African American, non-Hispanic/Latino; 5 American Indian or Alaska Native, non-Hispanic/Latino; 18 Asian, non-Hispanic/Latino; 25 Hispanic/Latino), 173 international. *Faculty:* 741 full-time (180 women). Expenses: Contact institution. *Financial support:* Fellowships, research assistantships, teaching assistantships, career-related internships or fieldwork, institutionally sponsored loans, scholarships/grants, health care benefits, tuition waivers (full), and unspecified assistantships available. Support available to part-time students. Financial award application deadline: 12/15. *Program availability:* Part-time. *Application deadline:* For fall admission, 12/15 priority date for domestic and international students; for spring admission, 10/15 for domestic and international students. Applications are processed on a rolling basis. *Application fee:* $75 ($95 for international students). Electronic applications accepted. *Application Contact:* Marie Monter, Graduate Programs Specialist, 612-624-2748, E-mail: cfansgradcc@umn.edu. *Associate Dean for Research and Graduate Programs*, Dr. Gregory J. Cuomo, 612-625-1158, E-mail: cfansgradcc@umn.edu.

***College of Liberal Arts*** *Program availability:* Part-time, evening/weekend. Electronic applications accepted.

***Humphrey School of Public Affairs*** Students: 388 full-time (245 women), 92 part-time (57 women); includes 106 minority (41 Black or African American, non-Hispanic/Latino; 12 American Indian or Alaska Native, non-Hispanic/Latino; 24 Asian, non-Hispanic/Latino; 29 Hispanic/Latino), 55 international. Average age 30. 422 applicants, 88% accepted, 189 enrolled. *Faculty:* 33 full-time (17 women), 27 part-time/adjunct (12 women). Expenses: Contact institution. *Financial support:* In 2019–20, 247 students received support, including fellowships with tuition reimbursements available (averaging $12,000 per year), research assistantships with tuition reimbursements available (averaging $26,000 per year), teaching assistantships with tuition reimbursements available (averaging $18,000 per year); career-related internships or fieldwork, scholarships/grants, health care benefits, tuition waivers (full and partial), and unspecified assistantships also available. Financial award application deadline: 1/15; financial award applicants required to submit FAFSA. In 2019, 170 master's awarded. *Program availability:* Part-time. *Application deadline:* For fall admission, 4/1 for domestic and international students. *Application fee:* $75 ($95 for international students). Electronic applications accepted. *Application Contact:* Jacob Merrifield, Admissions Program Manager, 612-624-3800, Fax: 612-626-0002, E-mail: jmerrifi@umn.edu. *Associate Dean*, Laura Bloomberg, 612-625-0608, Fax: 612-626-0002, E-mail: bloom004@umn.edu.

***School of Nursing*** *Program availability:* Part-time, online learning.

**Law School** Students: 667 full-time (347 women); includes 106 minority (4 Black or African American, non-Hispanic/Latino; 1 American Indian or Alaska Native, non-Hispanic/Latino; 33 Asian, non-Hispanic/Latino; 45 Hispanic/Latino; 1 Native Hawaiian or other Pacific Islander, non-Hispanic/Latino; 22 Two or more races, non-Hispanic/Latino), 52 international. 2,129 applicants, 39% accepted, 236 enrolled. *Faculty:* 67 full-time (25 women), 147 part-time/adjunct (52 women). Expenses: Contact institution. *Financial support:* In 2019–20, 545 students received support. Fellowships, research assistantships, career-related internships or fieldwork, Federal Work-Study, institutionally sponsored loans, and scholarships/grants available. Financial award application deadline: 7/1; financial award applicants required to submit FAFSA. In 2019, 158 doctorates awarded. *Application deadline:* For fall admission, 7/15 for domestic students. Applications are processed on a rolling basis. *Application fee:* $60. Electronic applications accepted. *Application Contact:* Robin Ingli, Director of Admissions, 612-625-3487, Fax: 612-625-2011, E-mail: jdadmissions@umn.edu. *Dean*, Garry W. Jenkins, 612-625-4841.

**Medical School** *Program availability:* Part-time, evening/weekend.

**School of Dentistry**

**School of Public Health** *Program availability:* Part-time, online learning. Electronic applications accepted.

***Division of Environmental Health Sciences*** *Program availability:* Part-time. Electronic applications accepted.

## UNIVERSITY OF MISSISSIPPI, University, MS 38677

**General Information** State-supported, coed, university. CGS member. *Enrollment:* 21,617 graduate, professional, and undergraduate students; 1,945 full-time matriculated graduate/professional students (1,058 women), 832 part-time matriculated graduate/professional students (519 women). *Enrollment by degree level:* 1,183 master's, 1,526 doctoral, 68 other advanced degrees. *Graduate faculty:* 878 full-time (386 women), 217 part-time/adjunct (118 women). Tuition, state resident: full-time $8718; part-time $484.25 per credit hour. Tuition, nonresident: full-time $24,990; part-time $1388.25 per credit hour. *Required fees:* $100; $4.16 per credit hour. *Graduate housing:* Rooms and/or apartments available on a first-come, first-served basis to single and married students. Typical cost: $6264 per year ($10,734 including board) for single students. Room and board charges vary according to board plan and housing facility selected. *Student services:* Campus employment opportunities, campus safety program, career counseling, exercise/wellness program, free psychological counseling, international student services, multicultural affairs office, services for students with disabilities, teacher training, writing training. *Library facilities:* J. D. Williams Library plus 1 other. *Collection:* Books: 1.1 million (physical), 828,315 (digital/electronic); Serial titles: 41,289 (physical), 144,204 (digital/electronic); Databases: 380. Weekly public service hours: 109; students can reserve study rooms. *Research affiliation:* Mississippi Geographic Alliance, Mississippi Research Consortium, Mississippi-Alabama Sea Grant Consortium, Oak Ridge Associated Universities, Southeastern Universities Research Association, Mississippi Space Grant Consortium.

**Computer facilities:** 259 computers available on campus for general student use. A campuswide network can be accessed. Online class registration is available.
Website: http://www.olemiss.edu/

**General Application Contact:** Tameka Smith, Graduate Activities Specialist for Admissions, 662-915-7474, Fax: 662-915-7577, E-mail: gschool@olemiss.edu.

**GRADUATE UNITS**

**Graduate School** Students: 1,945 full-time (1,058 women), 832 part-time (519 women); includes 589 minority (360 Black or African American, non-Hispanic/Latino; 4 American Indian or Alaska Native, non-Hispanic/Latino; 69 Asian, non-Hispanic/Latino; 110 Hispanic/Latino; 3 Native Hawaiian or other Pacific Islander, non-Hispanic/Latino; 43 Two or more races, non-Hispanic/Latino), 377 international. Average age 28. *Faculty:* 866 full-time (379 women), 194 part-time/adjunct (87 women). Expenses: Contact institution. *Financial support:* Fellowships, research assistantships, teaching assistantships, career-related internships or fieldwork, Federal Work-Study, institutionally sponsored loans, scholarships/grants, traineeships, tuition waivers (full), and unspecified assistantships available. Financial award application deadline: 3/1; financial award applicants required to submit FAFSA. In 2019, 699 master's, 328 doctorates, 46 other advanced degrees awarded. *Program availability:* Part-time. *Application deadline:* For fall admission, 2/1 priority date for domestic students; for spring admission, 10/1 for domestic students. Applications are processed on a rolling basis. *Application fee:* $50. Electronic applications accepted. *Application Contact:* Tameka Smith, Graduate Activities Specialist for Admissions, 662-915-7474, Fax: 662-915-6557. *Dean*, Dr. Annette Kluck, 662-915-7474, Fax: 662-915-7577, E-mail: gschool@olemiss.edu.

***College of Liberal Arts*** Students: 509 full-time (258 women), 55 part-time (21 women); includes 89 minority (40 Black or African American, non-Hispanic/Latino; 13 Asian, non-Hispanic/Latino; 25 Hispanic/Latino; 11 Two or more races, non-Hispanic/Latino), 157 international. Average age 29. *Faculty:* 481 full-time (215 women), 71 part-time/adjunct (40 women). Expenses: Contact institution. *Financial support:* Fellowships, research assistantships, teaching assistantships, career-related internships or fieldwork, Federal Work-Study, institutionally sponsored loans, scholarships/grants, and unspecified assistantships available. Financial award application deadline: 3/1; financial award applicants required to submit FAFSA. In 2019, 119 master's, 51 doctorates awarded. *Program availability:* Part-time. *Application deadline:* Applications are processed on a rolling basis. *Application fee:* $50. Electronic applications accepted. *Application Contact:* Tameka Smith, Graduate Activities Specialist for Admissions, 662-915-7474, Fax: 662-915-7577, E-mail: gschool@olemiss.edu. *Dean*, Dr. Lee Michael Cohen, 662-915-7177, Fax: 662-915-5792, E-mail: libarts@olemiss.edu.

***School of Accountancy*** Students: 229 full-time (105 women), 12 part-time (4 women); includes 33 minority (9 Black or African American, non-Hispanic/Latino; 3 American Indian or Alaska Native, non-Hispanic/Latino; 1 Asian, non-Hispanic/Latino; 12 Hispanic/Latino; 8 Native Hawaiian or other Pacific Islander, non-Hispanic/Latino), 7 international. Average age 23. Expenses: Contact institution. *Application Contact:* Tameka Smith, Graduate Activities Specialist for Admissions, 662-915-7474, Fax: 662-915-7577, E-mail: gschool@olemiss.edu. *Dean, School of Accountancy*, Dr. W. Mark Wilder, 662-915-7468, Fax: 662-915-7483, E-mail: umaccy@olemiss.edu.

***School of Applied Sciences*** Students: 188 full-time (149 women), 37 part-time (18 women); includes 47 minority (35 Black or African American, non-Hispanic/Latino; 2 American Indian or Alaska Native, non-Hispanic/Latino; 1 Asian, non-Hispanic/Latino; 5 Hispanic/Latino; 1 Native Hawaiian or other Pacific Islander, non-Hispanic/Latino; 3 Two or more races, non-Hispanic/Latino), 23 international. Average age 26. Expenses: Contact institution. *Application Contact:* Temeka Smith, Graduate Activities Specialist for Admissions, 662-915-7474, Fax: 662-915-7577, E-mail: gschool@olemiss.edu. *Dean of Applied Sciences*, Dr. Peter Grandjean, 662-915-7900, Fax: 662-915-7901, E-mail: applsci@olemiss.edu.

***School of Business Administration*** Expenses: Contact institution. In 2019, 83 master's, 11 doctorates awarded. *Application Contact:* Temeka Smith, Graduate Activities Specialist for Admissions, 662-915-7474, Fax: 662-915-7577, E-mail: gschool@olemiss.edu. *Dean*, Dr. Ken Cyree, 662-915-5820, Fax: 662-915-5821, E-mail: info@bus.olemiss.edu.

***School of Education*** Expenses: Contact institution. *Financial support:* Scholarships/grants available. Financial award application deadline: 3/1; financial award applicants required to submit FAFSA. In 2019, 180 master's, 57 doctorates, 37 other advanced degrees awarded. *Application deadline:* Applications are processed on a rolling basis. *Application fee:* $50. Electronic applications accepted. *Application Contact:* Temeka Smith, Graduate Activities Specialist for Admissions, 662-915-7474, Fax: 662-915-7577, E-mail: gschool@olemiss.edu. *Dean*, Dr. David Rock, 662-915-7063, Fax: 662-915-7249, E-mail: soe@olemiss.edu.

***School of Engineering*** Students: 104 full-time (23 women), 19 part-time (5 women); includes 10 minority (3 Black or African American, non-Hispanic/Latino; 6 Asian, non-Hispanic/Latino; 1 Hispanic/Latino), 72 international. Average age 30. Expenses: Contact institution. In 2019, 36 master's, 17 doctorates awarded. *Application Contact:* Temeka Smith, Graduate Activities Specialist for Admissions, 662-915-7474, Fax: 662-915-7577, E-mail: gschool@olemiss.edu. *Dean*, Dr. David Puleo, 662-915-5780, Fax: 662-915-5387, E-mail: engineer@olemiss.edu.

***School of Journalism and New Media*** Students: 42 full-time (26 women), 23 part-time (19 women); includes 13 minority (6 Black or African American, non-Hispanic/Latino; 4 Hispanic/Latino; 3 Two or more races, non-Hispanic/Latino), 4 international. Average age 26. *Faculty:* 33 full-time (15 women), 19 part-time/adjunct (8 women). Expenses: Contact institution. In 2019, 18 master's awarded. *Application deadline:* Applications are processed on a rolling basis. *Application fee:* $50. Electronic applications accepted. *Application Contact:* Tameka Smith, Graduate Activities Specialist for Admission, 662-915-7474, Fax: 662-915-7577, E-mail: gschool@olemiss.edu. *Interim Dean*, Dr. Debora Wenger, 662-915-7146, Fax: 662-915-7765, E-mail: jour-imc@olemiss.edu.

***School of Pharmacy*** Students: 223 full-time (137 women), 215 part-time (137 women); includes 71 minority (29 Black or African American, non-Hispanic/Latino; 1 American Indian or Alaska Native, non-Hispanic/Latino; 31 Asian, non-Hispanic/Latino; 4 Hispanic/Latino; 6 Two or more races, non-Hispanic/Latino), 90 international. Average age 25. *Faculty:* 68 full-time (33 women), 13 part-time/adjunct (5 women). Expenses: Contact institution. *Financial support:* Fellowships, research assistantships, teaching assistantships, career-related internships or fieldwork, Federal Work-Study, institutionally sponsored loans, scholarships/grants, tuition waivers (full), and unspecified assistantships available. Financial award application deadline: 3/1; financial award applicants required to submit FAFSA. In 2019, 29 master's, 13 doctorates awarded. *Program availability:* Part-time. *Application deadline:* Applications are processed on a rolling basis. *Application fee:* $50. Electronic applications accepted. *Application Contact:* Temeka Smith, Graduate Activities Specialist for Admissions, 662-915-7474, Fax: 662-915-7577, E-mail: gschool@olemiss.edu. *Dean, School of Pharmacy*, Dr. David Allen, 662-915-7265, Fax: 662-9155704, E-mail: sopdean@olemiss.edu.

**School of Law** Students: 411 full-time (195 women), 7 part-time (3 women); includes 131 minority (67 Black or African American, non-Hispanic/Latino; 1 American Indian or Alaska Native, non-Hispanic/Latino; 6 Asian, non-Hispanic/Latino; 47 Hispanic/Latino; 10 Two or more races, non-Hispanic/Latino), 2 international. Average age 25. *Faculty:* 29 full-time (11 women), 14 part-time/adjunct (6 women). Expenses: Contact institution. *Financial support:* Fellowships, research assistantships, teaching assistantships, career-related internships or fieldwork, Federal Work-Study, institutionally sponsored loans, and scholarships/grants available. Support available to part-time students. Financial award application deadline: 3/1; financial award applicants required to submit FAFSA. In 2019, 1 master's, 108 doctorates awarded. *Application deadline:* Applications are processed on a rolling basis. *Application fee:* $50. Electronic applications accepted. *Application Contact:* Temeka Smith, Graduate Activities Specialist for Admissions, 662-915-7474, Fax: 662-915-7577, E-mail: gschool@olemiss.edu. *Dean, School of Law*, Dr. Susan Duncan, 662-915-7361, Fax: 662-915-6895, E-mail: lawadmin@olemiss.edu.

## UNIVERSITY OF MISSISSIPPI MEDICAL CENTER, Jackson, MS 39216-4505

**General Information** State-supported, coed, upper-level institution. *Graduate housing:* On-campus housing not available. *Research affiliation:* NASA-Stennis Space Center (imaging technology), Catfish Genetics Research Unit (immunology), Oak Ridge National Laboratory (physiology, biomedical engineering), Gulf Coast Research Laboratory (microbiology).

**GRADUATE UNITS**

**School of Dentistry**

**School of Graduate Studies in Health Sciences** Students: 191 full-time (103 women), 20 part-time (14 women); includes 84 minority (41 Black or African American, non-Hispanic/Latino; 25 Asian, non-Hispanic/Latino; 10 Hispanic/Latino; 8 Two or more races, non-Hispanic/Latino), 1 international. 346 applicants, 42% accepted, 125 enrolled. *Faculty:* 211 full-time (85 women). Expenses: Contact institution. *Financial support:* In 2019–20, 60 students received support, including research assistantships with full and partial tuition reimbursements available (averaging $28,000 per year), teaching assistantships (averaging $28,000 per year). Financial award application deadline: 4/15; financial award applicants required to submit FAFSA. In 2019, 80 master's, 20 doctorates awarded. *Program availability:* Part-time, online only, 100% online. *Application deadline:* For fall admission, 6/1 for domestic and international students; for spring admission, 10/1 for domestic and international students; for summer admission, 4/1 for domestic and international students. Applications are processed on a rolling basis. *Application fee:* $25. Electronic applications accepted. *Application Contact:* Michael Ryan, Associate Dean, 601-984-1842, Fax: 601-815-9440, E-mail: mjryan@umc.edu. *Associate Dean*, Sydney Murphy, PhD, 601-984-1206, Fax: 601-815-9440, E-mail: smurphy@umc.edu.

**School of Health Related Professions** *Program availability:* Part-time.

**School of Medicine** *Program availability:* Part-time. Electronic applications accepted.

**School of Nursing** *Program availability:* Part-time, evening/weekend, online learning. Electronic applications accepted.

## UNIVERSITY OF MISSOURI, Columbia, MO 65211

**General Information** State-supported, coed, university. CGS member. *Graduate housing:* Rooms and/or apartments available on a first-come, first-served basis to single and married students. Housing application deadline: 12/1.

**GRADUATE UNITS**

**College of Veterinary Medicine**

***Graduate Programs in Veterinary Medicine***

**Office of Research and Graduate Studies** *Program availability:* Part-time, evening/weekend.

***College of Agriculture, Food and Natural Resources*** *Program availability:* Part-time.

***College of Arts and Science*** *Program availability:* Part-time.

***College of Education*** *Program availability:* Part-time, evening/weekend.

***College of Engineering*** *Program availability:* Part-time.

***College of Human Environmental Sciences*** *Program availability:* Part-time.

***Harry S Truman School of Public Affairs*** Electronic applications accepted.

***Informatics Institute*** Electronic applications accepted.

***Robert J. Trulaske, Sr. College of Business*** *Program availability:* Part-time.

***School of Journalism*** *Program availability:* Part-time. Electronic applications accepted.

***School of Social Work*** *Program availability:* Part-time. Electronic applications accepted.

***Sinclair School of Nursing*** *Program availability:* Part-time. Electronic applications accepted.

**School of Health Professions**

**School of Law**

**School of Medicine** *Program availability:* Part-time.

***Graduate Programs in Medicine*** *Program availability:* Part-time.

## UNIVERSITY OF MISSOURI–KANSAS CITY, Kansas City, MO 64110-2499

**General Information** State-supported, coed, university. CGS member. *Graduate housing:* Room and/or apartments available on a first-come, first-served basis to single students; on-campus housing not available to married students. *Research affiliation:* Children's Mercy Hospital (health sciences), Truman Medical Center (health sciences), Veterans Administration Hospital (health sciences), Midwest Research Institute (health sciences), St. Luke's Hospital (health sciences).

**GRADUATE UNITS**

**College of Arts and Sciences** *Program availability:* Part-time, evening/weekend. Electronic applications accepted.

***School of Social Work*** *Program availability:* Part-time, evening/weekend.

**Conservatory of Music and Dance** *Program availability:* Part-time.

**Henry W. Bloch School of Management** *Program availability:* Part-time, evening/weekend. Electronic applications accepted.

**School of Biological Sciences** *Program availability:* Part-time, evening/weekend.

**School of Computing and Engineering** *Program availability:* Part-time.

**School of Dentistry**

**School of Education** *Program availability:* Part-time, evening/weekend.

**School of Graduate Studies** Electronic applications accepted.

**School of Law** *Program availability:* Part-time. Electronic applications accepted.

**School of Medicine**

**School of Nursing and Health Studies** *Program availability:* Part-time, online learning.

**School of Pharmacy** *Program availability:* Online learning. Electronic applications accepted.

## UNIVERSITY OF MISSOURI–ST. LOUIS, St. Louis, MO 63121

**General Information** State-supported, coed, university. CGS member. *Enrollment:* 16,007 graduate, professional, and undergraduate students; 816 full-time matriculated graduate/professional students (546 women), 1,838 part-time matriculated graduate/professional students (1,251 women). *Enrollment by degree level:* 1,729 master's, 704 doctoral, 221 other advanced degrees. *Graduate faculty:* 352 full-time (170 women), 270 part-time/adjunct (154 women). *International tuition:* $22,108 full-time. *Tuition, area resident:* Full-time $9005.40; part-time $6003.60 per credit hour. Tuition, state resident: full-time $9005.40; part-time $6003.60 per credit hour. Tuition, nonresident: full-time $22,108; part-time $14,738.40 per credit hour. Tuition and fees vary according to course load. *Graduate housing:* Rooms and/or apartments available on a first-come, first-served basis to single and married students. Typical cost: $5450 per year ($9550 including board) for single students; $5450 per year ($9550 including board) for married students. Housing application deadline: 7/1. *Student services:* Campus employment opportunities, campus safety program, career counseling, child daycare facilities, exercise/wellness program, free psychological counseling, grant writing training, international student services, low-cost health insurance, multicultural affairs office, services for students with disabilities, teacher training, writing training.

*Library facilities:* Thomas Jefferson Library plus 1 other. *Collection:* Books: 1.3 million (physical), 211,129 (digital/electronic); Serial titles: 20,879 (physical), 190,950 (digital/electronic); Databases: 276. Weekly public service hours: 82; students can reserve study rooms. *Research affiliation:* Express Scripts (business), St. Louis Zoo (biology), Missouri Botanical Garden (biology), Donald Danforth Plant Science Center (biology).

**Computer facilities:** Computer purchase and lease plans are available. 1,752 computers available on campus for general student use. A campuswide network can be accessed. Online class registration is available.
Website: http://www.umsl.edu/

**General Application Contact:** Graduate Admissions, 314-516-5458, Fax: 314-516-6996, E-mail: gradadm@umsl.edu.

**GRADUATE UNITS**

**College of Arts and Sciences** *Program availability:* Part-time, evening/weekend. Electronic applications accepted.

**College of Business Administration** *Program availability:* Part-time, evening/weekend. Electronic applications accepted.

**College of Education** *Program availability:* Part-time, evening/weekend. Electronic applications accepted.

**College of Nursing** *Program availability:* Part-time. Electronic applications accepted.

**College of Optometry** Electronic applications accepted.

**Department of Theatre and Dance**

**Graduate School** *Program availability:* Part-time, evening/weekend. Electronic applications accepted.

**School of Social Work** *Program availability:* Part-time. Electronic applications accepted.

## UNIVERSITY OF MOBILE, Mobile, AL 36613

**General Information** Independent-religious, coed, comprehensive institution. *Graduate housing:* Room and/or apartments available on a first-come, first-served basis to single students; on-campus housing not available to married students. Housing application deadline: 8/15.

**GRADUATE UNITS**

**Graduate Studies** *Program availability:* Part-time, evening/weekend, online learning. Electronic applications accepted.

## UNIVERSITY OF MONTANA, Missoula, MT 59812

**General Information** State-supported, coed, university. CGS member. *Graduate housing:* Rooms and/or apartments available on a first-come, first-served basis to single and married students. *Research affiliation:* Arthur Carhart National Wilderness Training Center (environmental research), Nature Center at Ft. Missoula Museum (environmental research), Rocky Mountain National Laboratories (medical research), Community Hospital Medical Center (medical research), Aldo Leopold Wilderness Institute (forestry).

**GRADUATE UNITS**

**Alexander Blewett III School of Law**

**Graduate School** *Program availability:* Part-time.

***College of Forestry and Conservation***

***College of Health Professions and Biomedical Sciences***

***College of Humanities and Sciences*** *Program availability:* Part-time.

***College of Visual and Performing Arts***

***Phyllis J. Washington College of Education and Human Sciences*** *Program availability:* Part-time.

***School of Business Administration*** *Program availability:* Part-time, evening/weekend, online learning.

***School of Journalism*** Electronic applications accepted.

## UNIVERSITY OF MONTEVALLO, Montevallo, AL 35115

**General Information** State-supported, coed, comprehensive institution. *Enrollment:* 2,559 graduate, professional, and undergraduate students; 123 full-time matriculated graduate/professional students (106 women), 179 part-time matriculated graduate/professional students (141 women). *Enrollment by degree level:* 159 master's. *International tuition:* $22,464 full-time. *Tuition, area resident:* Full-time $10,512; part-time $438 per contact hour. Tuition, state resident: full-time $10,512; part-time $438 per credit hour. Tuition, nonresident: full-time $22,464; part-time $936 per credit hour. *Graduate housing:* Rooms and/or apartments guaranteed to single students and available on a first-come, first-served basis to married students. Typical cost: $6596 per year ($9810 including board) for single students. *Student services:* Campus employment opportunities, campus safety program, career counseling, free psychological counseling, international student services, low-cost health insurance, services for students with disabilities, writing training. *Library facilities:* Carmichael Library. *Collection:* Students can reserve study rooms.

**Computer facilities:** 340 computers available on campus for general student use. A campuswide network can be accessed. Online class registration is available.
Website: http://www.montevallo.edu/

**GRADUATE UNITS**

**College of Arts and Sciences** Students: 56 full-time (54 women), 3 part-time (2 women); includes 5 minority (2 Black or African American, non-Hispanic/Latino; 1 American Indian or Alaska Native, non-Hispanic/Latino; 1 Native Hawaiian or other Pacific Islander, non-Hispanic/Latino; 1 Two or more races, non-Hispanic/Latino). Expenses: Contact institution. *Financial support:* Federal Work-Study, scholarships/grants, and unspecified assistantships available. In 2019, 26 master's awarded. *Program availability:* Part-time, evening/weekend. *Application deadline:* For fall admission, 7/15 for domestic students; for spring admission, 11/15 for domestic students. *Application fee:* $30. *Application Contact:* Tonja Battle, Administrative Assistant, 205-665-6508, E-mail: battletl@montevallo.edu. *Dean,* Dr. Mary Beth Armstrong, 205-665-6508.

**College of Education** Students: 59 full-time (46 women), 149 part-time (118 women); includes 52 minority (41 Black or African American, non-Hispanic/Latino; 1 Asian, non-Hispanic/Latino; 3 Hispanic/Latino; 7 Two or more races, non-Hispanic/Latino), 1 international. Expenses: Contact institution. *Financial support:* Federal Work-Study, scholarships/grants, and unspecified assistantships available. In 2019, 83 master's awarded. *Program availability:* Part-time, evening/weekend. *Application deadline:* For fall admission, 7/15 for domestic students; for spring admission, 11/15 for domestic students. *Application fee:* $30. *Application Contact:* Colleen Kennedy, Graduate Program Assistant, 205-665-6350, E-mail: ckennedy@montevallo.edu. *Interim Dean,* Dr. Charlotte Daughhetee, 205-665-6360, E-mail: daughc@montevallo.edu.

**Stephens College of Business** Students: 8 full-time (6 women), 27 part-time (21 women); includes 8 minority (6 Black or African American, non-Hispanic/Latino; 1 Asian, non-Hispanic/Latino; 1 Hispanic/Latino), 1 international. Expenses: Contact institution. In 2019, 23 master's awarded. *Program availability:* Part-time, evening/weekend. *Application deadline:* For fall admission, 7/15 for domestic students; for spring admission, 11/15 for domestic students. *Application fee:* $30. *Application Contact:* Dr. Stephen H. Craft, Dean, 205-665-6540, E-mail: scob@montevallo.edu. *Dean,* Dr. Stephen H. Craft, 205-665-6540, E-mail: scob@montevallo.edu.

## UNIVERSITY OF MOUNT OLIVE, Mount Olive, NC 28365

**General Information** Independent-religious, coed, comprehensive institution.

**GRADUATE UNITS**

**Graduate Programs** *Program availability:* Online learning.

## UNIVERSITY OF MOUNT UNION, Alliance, OH 44601-3993

**General Information** Independent-religious, coed, comprehensive institution. *Graduate housing:* Rooms and/or apartments available on a first-come, first-served basis to single and married students. Housing application deadline: 4/13.

**GRADUATE UNITS**

**Program in Educational Leadership** *Program availability:* Part-time, online only, 100% online. Electronic applications accepted.

**Program in Physical Therapy** Electronic applications accepted.

**Program in Physician Assistant Studies** Electronic applications accepted.

## UNIVERSITY OF NEBRASKA AT KEARNEY, Kearney, NE 68849-0001

**General Information** State-supported, coed, comprehensive institution. CGS member. *Enrollment:* 6,279 graduate, professional, and undergraduate students; 222 full-time matriculated graduate/professional students (170 women), 1,168 part-time matriculated graduate/professional students (801 women). *Enrollment by degree level:* 1,331 master's, 59 other advanced degrees. *Graduate faculty:* 221 full-time (95 women). *International tuition:* $10,242 full-time. *Tuition, area resident:* Full-time $4662; part-time $259 per credit hour. Tuition, nonresident: full-time $10,242; part-time $569 per credit hour. *Required fees:* $1222; $381.50 per term. Full-time tuition and fees vary according to course load, campus/location and program. *Graduate housing:* Rooms and/or apartments available on a first-come, first-served basis to single and married students. Typical cost: $6453 per year for single students; $6453 per year for married students. Room charges vary according to board plan, campus/location and housing facility selected. Housing application deadline: 6/15. *Student services:* Campus employment opportunities, campus safety program, career counseling, child daycare facilities, exercise/wellness program, free psychological counseling, grant writing training, international student services, low-cost health insurance, multicultural affairs office, services for students with disabilities, teacher training, writing training. *Library facilities:* Calvin T. Ryan Library.

**Computer facilities:** A campuswide network can be accessed. Online class registration, online degree audit, online personal information update, online bill viewing and payment, online financial aid awards and acceptance are available.
Website: http://www.unk.edu/

**General Application Contact:** Linda Johnson, Director, Graduate Admissions and Programs, 800-717-7881, Fax: 308-865-8837, E-mail: gradstudies@unk.edu.

**GRADUATE UNITS**

**College of Arts and Sciences** Students: 52 full-time (36 women), 512 part-time (341 women); includes 74 minority (9 Black or African American, non-Hispanic/Latino; 1 American Indian or Alaska Native, non-Hispanic/Latino; 10 Asian, non-Hispanic/Latino; 41 Hispanic/Latino; 13 Two or more races, non-Hispanic/Latino), 3 international. Average age 34. 163 applicants, 93% accepted, 111 enrolled. *Faculty:* 137 full-time (52 women). Expenses: Contact institution. *Financial support:* In 2019–20, 17 students received support, including 5 research assistantships with full tuition reimbursements available (averaging $10,500 per year), 12 teaching assistantships with full tuition reimbursements available (averaging $10,500 per year); career-related internships or fieldwork, scholarships/grants, health care benefits, and unspecified assistantships also available. Support available to part-time students. Financial award application deadline: 2/28; financial award applicants required to submit FAFSA. In 2019, 174 master's awarded. *Program availability:* Part-time, evening/weekend, 100% online, blended/hybrid learning. *Application deadline:* For fall admission, 7/10 for domestic students, 5/10 for international students; for spring admission, 11/10 for domestic students, 9/10 for international students; for summer admission, 4/10 for domestic students, 1/10 for international students. Applications are processed on a rolling basis. *Application fee:* $45. Electronic applications accepted. *Application Contact:* Linda Johnson, Director, Graduate Admissions and Programs, 800-717-7881, Fax: 308-865-8837, E-mail: gradstudies@unk.edu. *Dean,* Dr. Ryan Teten, 308-865-8881, E-mail: tetenrl@unk.edu.

**College of Business and Technology** Students: 14 full-time (8 women), 41 part-time (18 women); includes 6 minority (3 Black or African American, non-Hispanic/Latino; 2 Hispanic/Latino; 1 Native Hawaiian or other Pacific Islander, non-Hispanic/Latino), 3 international. Average age 31. 18 applicants, 100% accepted, 14 enrolled. *Faculty:* 42 full-time (19 women). Expenses: Contact institution. *Financial support:* In 2019–20, 2 research assistantships with full tuition reimbursements (averaging $10,980 per year), 1 teaching assistantship with full tuition reimbursement (averaging $10,980 per year) were awarded; career-related internships or fieldwork, scholarships/grants, health care benefits, and unspecified assistantships also available. Support available to part-time students. Financial award application deadline: 2/28; financial award applicants required to submit FAFSA. In 2019, 10 master's awarded. *Program availability:* Part-time, evening/weekend, 100% online, blended/hybrid learning. *Application deadline:* For fall admission, 7/10 for domestic students, 5/10 for international students; for spring admission, 11/10 for domestic students, 9/10 for international students; for summer admission, 4/10 for domestic students, 1/10 for international students. *Application fee:* $45. Electronic applications accepted. *Application Contact:* Linda Johnson, Director, Graduate Admissions and Programs, 800-717-7881, Fax: 308-865-8837, E-mail: gradstudies@unk.edu. *Dean, College of Business and Technology,* Dr. Timothy E. Jares, 308-865-8342, Fax: 308-865-8387, E-mail: jareste@unk.edu.

**College of Education** Students: 155 full-time (127 women), 616 part-time (438 women); includes 60 minority (5 Black or African American, non-Hispanic/Latino; 6 Asian, non-Hispanic/Latino; 36 Hispanic/Latino; 1 Native Hawaiian or other Pacific Islander, non-Hispanic/Latino; 12 Two or more races, non-Hispanic/Latino), 24 international. Average age 43. 269 applicants, 75% accepted, 148 enrolled. *Faculty:* 42 full-time (24 women). Expenses: Contact institution. *Financial support:* In 2019–20, 29 research assistantships with full tuition reimbursements (averaging $10,980 per year), 16 teaching assistantships with full tuition reimbursements (averaging $10,980 per year) were awarded; career-related internships or fieldwork, scholarships/grants, health care benefits, and unspecified assistantships also available. Support available to part-time students. Financial award application deadline: 2/28; financial award applicants required to submit FAFSA. In 2019, 268 master's, 22 Ed Ss awarded. *Program availability:* Part-time, evening/weekend, 100% online, blended/hybrid learning. *Application deadline:* For fall admission, 7/10 for domestic students, 5/10 for international students; for spring admission, 11/10 for domestic students, 9/10 for international students; for summer admission, 4/10 for domestic students, 1/10 for international students. Applications are processed on a rolling basis. *Application fee:* $45. Electronic applications accepted. *Application Contact:* Linda Johnson, Director, Graduate Admissions and Programs, 800-717-7881, Fax: 308-865-8837, E-mail: johnsonli@unk.edu. *Dean*, Dr. Mark J Reid, 308-865-8502, E-mail: reidm@unk.edu.

## UNIVERSITY OF NEBRASKA AT OMAHA, Omaha, NE 68182

**General Information** State-supported, coed, university. CGS member. *Graduate housing:* Room and/or apartments available on a first-come, first-served basis to single students; on-campus housing not available to married students.

**GRADUATE UNITS**

**Graduate Studies** *Program availability:* Part-time, evening/weekend, online learning. Electronic applications accepted.

***College of Arts and Sciences*** *Program availability:* Part-time, evening/weekend, online learning. Electronic applications accepted.

***College of Business Administration*** *Program availability:* Part-time, evening/weekend. Electronic applications accepted.

***College of Communication, Fine Arts and Media*** *Program availability:* Part-time, evening/weekend. Electronic applications accepted.

***College of Education*** *Program availability:* Part-time, evening/weekend. Electronic applications accepted.

***College of Information Science and Technology*** *Program availability:* Part-time, evening/weekend. Electronic applications accepted.

***College of Public Affairs and Community Service*** *Program availability:* Part-time, evening/weekend, online learning. Electronic applications accepted.

## UNIVERSITY OF NEBRASKA–LINCOLN, Lincoln, NE 68588

**General Information** State-supported, coed, university. CGS member. *Graduate housing:* Rooms and/or apartments available on a first-come, first-served basis to single and married students. Housing application deadline: 7/1. *Research affiliation:* U.S. Department of Agriculture (USDA), U.S. Department of Defense, NASA, National Science Foundation, National Institutes of Health, U.S. Meat Animal Research Center.

**GRADUATE UNITS**

**College of Law** Electronic applications accepted.

**Graduate College** *Program availability:* Part-time, evening/weekend, online learning. Electronic applications accepted.

***College of Agricultural Sciences and Natural Resources*** Electronic applications accepted.

***College of Architecture*** Electronic applications accepted.

***College of Arts and Sciences*** Electronic applications accepted.

***College of Business Administration*** *Program availability:* Part-time, evening/weekend. Electronic applications accepted.

***College of Education and Human Sciences*** Electronic applications accepted.

***College of Engineering*** Electronic applications accepted.

***College of Fine and Performing Arts*** Electronic applications accepted.

***College of Journalism and Mass Communications*** *Program availability:* Online learning. Electronic applications accepted.

## UNIVERSITY OF NEBRASKA MEDICAL CENTER, Omaha, NE 68198

**General Information** State-supported, coed, upper-level institution. CGS member. *Research affiliation:* UNeMed Corporation (biotechnology).

**GRADUATE UNITS**

**College of Allied Health Professions**

***Division of Physical Therapy Education***

***Division of Physician Assistant Education*** Electronic applications accepted.

**College of Dentistry** Electronic applications accepted.

**College of Medicine** Electronic applications accepted.

**College of Pharmacy** Electronic applications accepted.

**College of Public Health** *Program availability:* Part-time, online learning. Electronic applications accepted.

**Department of Biostatistics** *Program availability:* Part-time. Electronic applications accepted.

**Department of Epidemiology** *Program availability:* Part-time. Electronic applications accepted.

**Department of Health Promotion, Social and Behavioral Health** *Program availability:* Part-time. Electronic applications accepted.

**Department of Health Services Research and Administration** *Program availability:* Part-time, 100% online, blended/hybrid learning. Electronic applications accepted.

**Department of Pharmaceutical Sciences** Electronic applications accepted.

**Environmental Health, Occupational Health and Toxicology Graduate Program** Electronic applications accepted.

**Interdisciplinary Graduate Program in Biomedical Sciences** Electronic applications accepted.

**Medical Sciences Interdepartmental Area** *Program availability:* Part-time. Electronic applications accepted.

**PhD in Nursing Program** *Program availability:* Part-time, blended/hybrid learning. Electronic applications accepted.

**Program in Biomedical Informatics** *Program availability:* Part-time. Electronic applications accepted.

**Program in Emergency Preparedness** *Program availability:* Part-time, 100% online, blended/hybrid learning. Electronic applications accepted.

## UNIVERSITY OF NEVADA, LAS VEGAS, Las Vegas, NV 89154

**General Information** State-supported, coed, university. CGS member. *Enrollment:* 30,457 graduate, professional, and undergraduate students; 2,394 full-time matriculated graduate/professional students (1,426 women), 1,486 part-time matriculated graduate/professional students (941 women). *Enrollment by degree level:* 2,600 master's, 1,151 doctoral, 129 other advanced degrees. *Graduate faculty:* 528 full-time (193 women), 167 part-time/adjunct (92 women). *Required fees:* $153; $17 per credit. $351 per semester. Tuition and fees vary according to course load, program and reciprocity agreements. *Graduate housing:* Rooms and/or apartments available on a first-come, first-served basis to single and married students. Housing application deadline: 7/1. *Student services:* Campus employment opportunities, campus safety program, career counseling, child daycare facilities, exercise/wellness program, free psychological counseling, grant writing training, international student services, low-cost health insurance, multicultural affairs office, services for students with disabilities, teacher training, writing training. *Library facilities:* Lied Library plus 4 others. *Collection:* Weekly public service hours: 101; students can reserve study rooms. *Research affiliation:* Tesla (effluent remediation), Teledyne Brown Engineering (aerospace engineering), Eli Lilly and Company (clinical trials), Cryolife (clinical trials), Metawater (water treatment).

**Computer facilities:** 2,100 computers available on campus for general student use. A campuswide network can be accessed from student residence rooms and from off campus. Online class registration is available.
Website: http://www.unlv.edu/

**General Application Contact:** Garland David Beasley, Recruitment and Admissions Specialist, 702-895-4543, Fax: 702-895-4180, E-mail: gradrecruitment@unlv.edu.

**GRADUATE UNITS**

**Graduate College** Students: 2,394 full-time (1,426 women), 1,486 part-time (941 women); includes 1,619 minority (312 Black or African American, non-Hispanic/Latino; 16 American Indian or Alaska Native, non-Hispanic/Latino; 326 Asian, non-Hispanic/Latino; 695 Hispanic/Latino; 18 Native Hawaiian or other Pacific Islander, non-Hispanic/Latino; 252 Two or more races, non-Hispanic/Latino), 363 international. Average age 33. 2,735 applicants, 57% accepted, 1,111 enrolled. *Faculty:* 528 full-time (193 women), 167 part-time/adjunct (92 women). Expenses: Contact institution. *Financial support:* In 2019–20, 1,060 students received support, including 11 fellowships with full tuition reimbursements available (averaging $20,909 per year), 386 research assistantships with full tuition reimbursements available (averaging $15,331 per year), 703 teaching assistantships with full tuition reimbursements available (averaging $15,974 per year); institutionally sponsored loans, scholarships/grants, health care benefits, and unspecified assistantships also available. Financial award application deadline: 3/15; financial award applicants required to submit FAFSA. In 2019, 1,074 master's, 159 doctorates, 48 other advanced degrees awarded. *Program availability:* Part-time. *Application deadline:* For fall admission, 8/1 for domestic students, 5/1 for international students; for spring admission, 11/1 for domestic students, 10/1 for international students. *Application fee:* $60 ($95 for international students). Electronic applications accepted. *Application Contact:* Elizabeth Jost, Senior Admissions Analyst, 702-895-5412, E-mail: elizabeth.jost@unlv.edu. *Dean*, Dr. Kathryn Korgan, 702-895-0446, Fax: 702-895-4180, E-mail: kate.korgan@unlv.edu.

***College of Education*** Students: 582 full-time (422 women), 603 part-time (440 women); includes 549 minority (127 Black or African American, non-Hispanic/Latino; 4 American Indian or Alaska Native, non-Hispanic/Latino; 59 Asian, non-Hispanic/Latino; 267 Hispanic/Latino; 9 Native Hawaiian or other Pacific Islander, non-Hispanic/Latino; 83 Two or more races, non-Hispanic/Latino), 35 international. Average age 34. 533 applicants, 77% accepted, 325 enrolled. *Faculty:* 76 full-time (39 women), 43 part-time/adjunct (37 women). Expenses: Contact institution. *Financial support:* In 2019–20, 120 students received support, including 43 research assistantships with full tuition reimbursements available (averaging $15,567 per year), 79 teaching assistantships with full tuition reimbursements available (averaging $17,319 per year); institutionally sponsored loans, scholarships/grants, health care benefits, and unspecified assistantships also available. Financial award application deadline: 3/15; financial award applicants required to submit FAFSA. In 2019, 398 master's, 29 doctorates, 19 other advanced degrees awarded. *Program availability:* Part-time. *Application fee:* $60 ($95 for international students). Electronic applications accepted. *Application Contact:* Dr. Kim Metcalf, Dean, 702-895-3375, Fax: 702-895-4068, E-mail: education.dean@unlv.edu. *Dean*, Dr. Kim Metcalf, 702-895-3375, Fax: 702-895-4068, E-mail: education.dean@unlv.edu.

***College of Fine Arts*** Students: 138 full-time (66 women), 35 part-time (23 women); includes 55 minority (9 Black or African American, non-Hispanic/Latino; 2 American Indian or Alaska Native, non-Hispanic/Latino; 13 Asian, non-Hispanic/Latino; 23 Hispanic/Latino; 8 Two or more races, non-Hispanic/Latino), 24 international. Average age 32. 157 applicants, 64% accepted, 69 enrolled. *Faculty:* 52 full-time (15 women), 26 part-time/adjunct (12 women). Expenses: Contact institution. *Financial support:* In 2019–20, 98 students received support, including 35 research assistantships with full tuition reimbursements available (averaging $15,000 per year), 59 teaching assistantships with full tuition reimbursements available (averaging $14,313 per year); institutionally sponsored loans, scholarships/grants, health care benefits, and unspecified assistantships also available. Financial award application deadline: 3/15; financial award applicants required to submit FAFSA. In 2019, 58 master's, 6 doctorates awarded. *Program availability:* Part-time. *Application fee:* $60 ($95 for international students). Electronic applications accepted. *Application Contact:* Dr. Nancy Uscher, Dean/Professor, 702-895-4210, Fax: 702-895-4194, E-mail: fine.arts.dean@unlv.edu. *Dean/Professor*, Dr. Nancy Uscher, 702-895-4210, Fax: 702-895-4194, E-mail: fine.arts.dean@unlv.edu.

***College of Liberal Arts*** Students: 241 full-time (159 women), 85 part-time (40 women); includes 108 minority (13 Black or African American, non-Hispanic/Latino; 2 American Indian or Alaska Native, non-Hispanic/Latino; 13 Asian, non-Hispanic/Latino; 55 Hispanic/Latino; 1 Native Hawaiian or other Pacific Islander, non-Hispanic/Latino; 24 Two or more races, non-Hispanic/Latino), 14 international. Average age 32. 482 applicants, 26% accepted, 78 enrolled. *Faculty:* 98 full-time (40 women), 6 part-time/adjunct (4 women). Expenses: Contact institution. *Financial support:* In 2019–20, 237 students received support, including 6 fellowships with full tuition reimbursements available (averaging $20,833 per year), 73 research assistantships with full tuition reimbursements available (averaging $15,753 per year), 158 teaching assistantships with full tuition reimbursements available (averaging $15,206 per year); institutionally sponsored loans, scholarships/grants, health care benefits, and unspecified assistantships also available. Financial award application deadline: 3/15; financial award applicants required to submit FAFSA. In 2019, 50 master's, 25 doctorates awarded. *Program availability:* Part-time. *Application fee:* $60 ($95 for international students). Electronic applications accepted. *Application Contact:* Dr. Jennifer Keene, Dean, 702-895-3401, Fax: 702-895-4097, E-mail: liberalarts.dean@unlv.edu. *Dean*, Dr. Jennifer Keene, 702-895-3401, Fax: 702-895-4097, E-mail: liberalarts.dean@unlv.edu.

***College of Sciences*** Students: 179 full-time (81 women), 48 part-time (20 women); includes 55 minority (2 Black or African American, non-Hispanic/Latino; 22 Asian, non-Hispanic/Latino; 22 Hispanic/Latino; 9 Two or more races, non-Hispanic/Latino),

35 international. Average age 31. 186 applicants, 36% accepted, 47 enrolled. *Faculty:* 74 full-time (17 women), 6 part-time/adjunct (0 women). Expenses: Contact institution. *Financial support:* In 2019–20, 179 students received support, including 1 fellowship with full tuition reimbursement available (averaging $20,000 per year), 40 research assistantships with full tuition reimbursements available (averaging $19,409 per year), 138 teaching assistantships with full tuition reimbursements available (averaging $19,618 per year); institutionally sponsored loans, scholarships/grants, health care benefits, and unspecified assistantships also available. Financial award application deadline: 3/15; financial award applicants required to submit FAFSA. In 2019, 13 master's, 14 doctorates awarded. *Program availability:* Part-time. *Application fee:* $60 ($95 for international students). Electronic applications accepted. *Application Contact:* Dr. Eric Chronister, Dean, 702-895-3487, Fax: 702-895-4159, E-mail: sciences.dean@unlv.edu. *Dean*, Dr. Eric Chronister, 702-895-3487, Fax: 702-895-4159, E-mail: sciences.dean@unlv.edu.

***Greenspun College of Urban Affairs*** Students: 366 full-time (247 women), 183 part-time (139 women); includes 317 minority (89 Black or African American, non-Hispanic/Latino; 2 American Indian or Alaska Native, non-Hispanic/Latino; 34 Asian, non-Hispanic/Latino; 140 Hispanic/Latino; 4 Native Hawaiian or other Pacific Islander, non-Hispanic/Latino; 48 Two or more races, non-Hispanic/Latino), 11 international. Average age 33. 358 applicants, 81% accepted, 212 enrolled. *Faculty:* 39 full-time (20 women), 28 part-time/adjunct (11 women). Expenses: Contact institution. *Financial support:* In 2019–20, 101 students received support, including 38 research assistantships with full tuition reimbursements available (averaging $14,492 per year), 67 teaching assistantships with full tuition reimbursements available (averaging $13,240 per year); institutionally sponsored loans, scholarships/grants, health care benefits, and unspecified assistantships also available. Financial award application deadline: 3/15; financial award applicants required to submit FAFSA. In 2019, 170 master's, 13 doctorates, 16 other advanced degrees awarded. *Program availability:* Part-time. *Application fee:* $60 ($95 for international students). Electronic applications accepted. *Application Contact:* Dr. Robert Ulmer, Dean, 702-895-0628, Fax: 702-895-3291, E-mail: urbanaffairs.dean@unlv.edu. *Dean*, Dr. Robert Ulmer, 702-895-0628, Fax: 702-895-3291, E-mail: urbanaffairs.dean@unlv.edu.

***Howard R. Hughes College of Engineering*** Students: 166 full-time (48 women), 91 part-time (21 women); includes 72 minority (9 Black or African American, non-Hispanic/Latino; 1 American Indian or Alaska Native, non-Hispanic/Latino; 21 Asian, non-Hispanic/Latino; 30 Hispanic/Latino; 11 Two or more races, non-Hispanic/Latino), 111 international. Average age 30. 182 applicants, 75% accepted, 64 enrolled. *Faculty:* 66 full-time (10 women), 4 part-time/adjunct (1 woman). Expenses: Contact institution. *Financial support:* In 2019–20, 153 students received support, including 3 fellowships with full tuition reimbursements available (averaging $21,667 per year), 52 research assistantships with full tuition reimbursements available (averaging $16,202 per year), 98 teaching assistantships with full tuition reimbursements available (averaging $16,903 per year); institutionally sponsored loans, scholarships/grants, health care benefits, and unspecified assistantships also available. Financial award application deadline: 3/15; financial award applicants required to submit FAFSA. In 2019, 65 master's, 12 doctorates, 1 other advanced degree awarded. *Program availability:* Part-time. *Application fee:* $60 ($95 for international students). Electronic applications accepted. *Application Contact:* Dr. Rama Venkat, Dean, 702-895-3699, Fax: 702-895-4059, E-mail: engineering.dean@unlv.edu. *Dean*, Dr. Rama Venkat, 702-895-3699, Fax: 702-895-4059, E-mail: engineering.dean@unlv.edu.

***Lee Business School*** Students: 271 full-time (120 women), 166 part-time (68 women); includes 188 minority (15 Black or African American, non-Hispanic/Latino; 1 American Indian or Alaska Native, non-Hispanic/Latino; 77 Asian, non-Hispanic/Latino; 70 Hispanic/Latino; 25 Two or more races, non-Hispanic/Latino), 72 international. Average age 31. 246 applicants, 67% accepted, 108 enrolled. *Faculty:* 40 full-time (9 women), 13 part-time/adjunct (3 women). Expenses: Contact institution. *Financial support:* In 2019–20, 25 students received support, including 25 teaching assistantships with full tuition reimbursements available (averaging $11,200 per year); institutionally sponsored loans, scholarships/grants, health care benefits, and unspecified assistantships also available. Financial award application deadline: 3/15; financial award applicants required to submit FAFSA. In 2019, 191 master's, 8 other advanced degrees awarded. *Program availability:* Part-time. *Application fee:* $60 ($95 for international students). Electronic applications accepted. *Application Contact:* Dr. Paulette Tandy, Dean, 702-895-3362, Fax: 702-895-4090, E-mail: business.dean@unlv.edu. *Dean*, Dr. Paulette Tandy, 702-895-3362, Fax: 702-895-4090, E-mail: business.dean@unlv.edu.

***School of Integrated Health Sciences*** Students: 197 full-time (99 women), 22 part-time (8 women); includes 86 minority (6 Black or African American, non-Hispanic/Latino; 1 American Indian or Alaska Native, non-Hispanic/Latino; 34 Asian, non-Hispanic/Latino; 30 Hispanic/Latino; 1 Native Hawaiian or other Pacific Islander, non-Hispanic/Latino; 14 Two or more races, non-Hispanic/Latino), 11 international. Average age 28. 88 applicants, 43% accepted, 26 enrolled. *Faculty:* 22 full-time (10 women), 12 part-time/adjunct (7 women). Expenses: Contact institution. *Financial support:* In 2019–20, 56 students received support, including 24 research assistantships with full tuition reimbursements available (averaging $16,521 per year), 32 teaching assistantships with full tuition reimbursements available (averaging $15,257 per year); institutionally sponsored loans, scholarships/grants, health care benefits, and unspecified assistantships also available. Financial award application deadline: 3/15; financial award applicants required to submit FAFSA. In 2019, 20 master's, 39 doctorates awarded. *Program availability:* Part-time. *Application fee:* $60 ($95 for international students). Electronic applications accepted. *Application Contact:* Dr. Ronald T. Brown, Dean, 702-895-3693, Fax: 702-895-1356, E-mail: ihs.dean@unlv.edu. *Dean*, Dr. Ronald T. Brown, 702-895-3693, Fax: 702-895-1356, E-mail: ihs.dean@unlv.edu.

***School of Nursing*** Students: 44 full-time (41 women), 111 part-time (96 women); includes 48 minority (9 Black or African American, non-Hispanic/Latino; 16 Asian, non-Hispanic/Latino; 15 Hispanic/Latino; 1 Native Hawaiian or other Pacific Islander, non-Hispanic/Latino; 7 Two or more races, non-Hispanic/Latino), 1 international. Average age 38. 218 applicants, 33% accepted, 63 enrolled. *Faculty:* 15 full-time (13 women), 9 part-time/adjunct (8 women). Expenses: Contact institution. *Financial support:* In 2019–20, 2 students received support, including 1 research assistantship with full tuition reimbursement available (averaging $20,250 per year), 1 teaching assistantship with full tuition reimbursement available (averaging $20,250 per year); institutionally sponsored loans, scholarships/grants, health care benefits, and unspecified assistantships also available. Financial award application deadline: 3/15; financial award applicants required to submit FAFSA. In 2019, 19 master's, 14 doctorates, 2 other advanced degrees awarded. *Program availability:* Part-time, 100% online, blended/hybrid learning. *Application fee:* $60 ($95 for international students). Electronic applications accepted. *Application Contact:* Dr. Angela Amar, Dean/Professor, 702-895-3906, Fax: 702-895-4807, E-mail: nursing.dean@unlv.edu. *Dean/Professor*, Dr. Angela Amar, 702-895-3906, Fax: 702-895-4807, E-mail: nursing.dean@unlv.edu.

***School of Public Health*** Students: 100 full-time (66 women), 54 part-time (40 women); includes 77 minority (22 Black or African American, non-Hispanic/Latino; 1 American Indian or Alaska Native, non-Hispanic/Latino; 17 Asian, non-Hispanic/Latino; 21 Hispanic/Latino; 2 Native Hawaiian or other Pacific Islander, non-Hispanic/Latino; 14 Two or more races, non-Hispanic/Latino), 13 international. Average age 32. 74 applicants, 77% accepted, 39 enrolled. *Faculty:* 26 full-time (11 women), 10 part-time/adjunct (5 women). Expenses: Contact institution. *Financial support:* In 2019–20, 38 students received support, including 1 fellowship with full tuition reimbursement available (averaging $20,000 per year), 24 research assistantships with full tuition reimbursements available (averaging $14,146 per year), 10 teaching assistantships with full tuition reimbursements available (averaging $12,135 per year); institutionally sponsored loans, scholarships/grants, health care benefits, and unspecified assistantships also available. Financial award application deadline: 3/15; financial award applicants required to submit FAFSA. In 2019, 38 master's, 4 doctorates, 2 other advanced degrees awarded. *Program availability:* Part-time. *Application fee:* $60 ($95 for international students). Electronic applications accepted. *Application Contact:* Dr. Shawn Gerstenberger, Dean, 702-895-5090, Fax: 702-895-5184, E-mail: sph.dean@unlv.edu. *Dean*, Dr. Shawn Gerstenberger, 702-895-5090, Fax: 702-895-5184, E-mail: sph.dean@unlv.edu.

***William F. Harrah College of Hospitality*** Students: 38 full-time (25 women), 88 part-time (46 women); includes 33 minority (7 Black or African American, non-Hispanic/Latino; 2 American Indian or Alaska Native, non-Hispanic/Latino; 15 Asian, non-Hispanic/Latino; 7 Hispanic/Latino; 2 Two or more races, non-Hispanic/Latino), 33 international. Average age 35. 125 applicants, 54% accepted, 53 enrolled. *Faculty:* 17 full-time (7 women), 4 part-time/adjunct (2 women). Expenses: Contact institution. *Financial support:* In 2019–20, 34 students received support, including 4 research assistantships with full tuition reimbursements available (averaging $14,375 per year), 30 teaching assistantships with full tuition reimbursements available (averaging $13,500 per year); institutionally sponsored loans, scholarships/grants, health care benefits, and unspecified assistantships also available. Financial award application deadline: 3/15; financial award applicants required to submit FAFSA. In 2019, 29 master's, 3 doctorates awarded. *Program availability:* Part-time, evening/weekend, 100% online, blended/hybrid learning. *Application fee:* $60 ($95 for international students). Electronic applications accepted. *Application Contact:* Dr. Stowe Shoemaker, Dean, 702-895-3308, Fax: 702-895-4109, E-mail: hospitality.dean@unlv.edu. *Dean*, Dr. Stowe Shoemaker, 702-895-3308, Fax: 702-895-4109, E-mail: hospitality.dean@unlv.edu.

**School of Dental Medicine** Students: 369 full-time (154 women), 1 (woman) part-time; includes 154 minority (7 Black or African American, non-Hispanic/Latino; 1 American Indian or Alaska Native, non-Hispanic/Latino; 89 Asian, non-Hispanic/Latino; 36 Hispanic/Latino; 1 Native Hawaiian or other Pacific Islander, non-Hispanic/Latino; 20 Two or more races, non-Hispanic/Latino), 3 international. Average age 29. 1,543 applicants, 11% accepted, 80 enrolled. Expenses: Contact institution. *Financial support:* Federal Work-Study, institutionally sponsored loans, scholarships/grants, health care benefits, and unspecified assistantships available. Support available to part-time students. Financial award application deadline: 3/15; financial award applicants required to submit FAFSA. In 2019, 6 master's, 93 doctorates, 5 other advanced degrees awarded. *Program availability:* Part-time, evening/weekend, online learning. *Application deadline:* For fall admission, 1/1 for domestic and international students; for summer admission, 3/1 for domestic students. Applications are processed on a rolling basis. *Application fee:* $75. Electronic applications accepted. *Application Contact:* Dr. Christine C. Ancajas, Assistant Dean of Admissions and Student Affairs, 702-774-2522, Fax: 702-774-2521, E-mail: christine.ancajas@unlv.edu. *Assistant Dean of Admissions and Student Affairs*, Dr. Christine C. Ancajas, 702-774-2522, Fax: 702-774-2521, E-mail: christine.ancajas@unlv.edu.

**School of Medicine** Expenses: Contact institution. *Application Contact:* Marc Kahn, Dean of the UNLV School of Medicine, 1-7028951296, E-mail: deansoffice@medicine.unlv.edu. *Dean of the UNLV School of Medicine*, Marc Kahn, 1-7028951296, E-mail: deansoffice@medicine.unlv.edu.

**William S. Boyd School of Law** Students: 375 full-time (202 women), 69 part-time (33 women); includes 158 minority (33 Black or African American, non-Hispanic/Latino; 1 American Indian or Alaska Native, non-Hispanic/Latino; 22 Asian, non-Hispanic/Latino; 82 Hispanic/Latino; 20 Two or more races, non-Hispanic/Latino), 7 international. Average age 26. 947 applicants, 27% accepted, 130 enrolled. *Faculty:* 39 full-time (24 women), 53 part-time/adjunct (18 women). Expenses: Contact institution. *Financial support:* In 2019–20, 331 students received support, including 27 fellowships, 48 research assistantships (averaging $957 per year), 29 teaching assistantships (averaging $1,028 per year); scholarships/grants also available. Support available to part-time students. Financial award application deadline: 3/15. In 2019, 121 doctorates awarded. *Program availability:* Part-time, evening/weekend, blended/hybrid learning. *Application deadline:* For fall admission, 3/15 for domestic and international students. Applications are processed on a rolling basis. *Application fee:* $50. Electronic applications accepted. *Application Contact:* Dr. Brain Wall, Assistant Dean for Admissions and Financial Aid, 702-895-1350, Fax: 702-895-2414, E-mail: brian.wall@unlv.edu. *Dean*, Dr. Daniel W. Hamilton, 702-895-1876, Fax: 702-895-1095, E-mail: daniel.hamilton@unlv.edu.

## UNIVERSITY OF NEVADA, RENO, Reno, NV 89557

**General Information** State-supported, coed, university. CGS member. *Graduate housing:* Rooms and/or apartments available on a first-come, first-served basis to single and married students. Housing application deadline: 5/16. *Research affiliation:* National Institutes of Health (nursing), Desert Research Institute (natural resource sciences, environmental sciences).

**GRADUATE UNITS**

**Graduate School** *Program availability:* Part-time, evening/weekend, online learning. Electronic applications accepted.

***College of Agriculture, Biotechnology and Natural Resources*** Electronic applications accepted.

***College of Business*** *Program availability:* Part-time, online learning. Electronic applications accepted.

***College of Education*** Electronic applications accepted.

***College of Engineering*** Electronic applications accepted.

***College of Liberal Arts*** *Program availability:* Part-time, evening/weekend, online learning. Electronic applications accepted.

***College of Science*** Electronic applications accepted.

***Division of Health Sciences*** Electronic applications accepted.

***Donald W. Reynolds School of Journalism*** Electronic applications accepted.

School of Medicine

## UNIVERSITY OF NEW BRUNSWICK SAINT JOHN, Saint John, NB E2L 4L5, Canada

**General Information** Province-supported, coed, comprehensive institution. *Enrollment by degree level:* 153 master's, 19 doctoral. *Graduate faculty:* 133 full-time (60 women). *International tuition:* $12,435 Canadian dollars full-time. *Tuition, area resident:* Full-time $6975 Canadian dollars; part-time $3423 Canadian dollars per year. Tuition, province resident: full-time $6975 Canadian dollars; part-time $3423 Canadian dollars per year. Tuition, Canadian resident: full-time $6975 Canadian dollars; part-time $3423 Canadian dollars per year. *Required fees:* $132.75 Canadian dollars; $92.25 Canadian dollars per term. Tuition and fees vary according to campus/location, program and student level. *Graduate housing:* Rooms and/or apartments available on a first-come, first-served basis to single and married students. Typical cost: $4588 Canadian dollars per year ($5388 Canadian dollars including board) for single students; $14,400 Canadian dollars per year ($14,400 Canadian dollars including board) for married students. Room and board charges vary according to board plan and housing facility selected. Housing application deadline: 3/31. *Student services:* Campus employment opportunities, campus safety program, career counseling, child daycare facilities, exercise/wellness program, free psychological counseling, grant writing training, international student services, low-cost health insurance, multicultural affairs office, services for students with disabilities, teacher training, writing training. *Library facilities:* Hans W. Klohn Commons. *Collection:* Students can reserve study rooms. *Research affiliation:* Cook Aquaculture (aquaculture), Horizon Health (health research), Dalhousie Medicine New Brunswick (cancer and general health), Fisheries and Oceans Canada (biology/ecology), New Brunswick Community College (health research).

**Computer facilities:** 100 computers available on campus for general student use. A campuswide network can be accessed from student residence rooms and from off campus. Online class registration is available.
Website: http://www.unb.ca/

**General Application Contact:** Dr. Lilly Both, Acting Associate Dean of Graduate Studies, 506-648-5620, Fax: 506-648-5769, E-mail: lboth@unb.ca.

**GRADUATE UNITS**

**Department of Biology** Students: 30 full-time (18 women), 9 part-time (5 women), 8 international. *Faculty:* 20 full-time (7 women). Expenses: Contact institution. *Financial support:* Fellowships, research assistantships, teaching assistantships, scholarships/grants, and unspecified assistantships available. Financial award application deadline: 1/15. In 2019, 10 master's, 7 doctorates awarded. *Program availability:* Part-time. *Application deadline:* For fall admission, 2/15 for domestic and international students. Applications are processed on a rolling basis. *Application fee:* $50 Canadian dollars. Electronic applications accepted. *Application Contact:* Stacey Hines, Secretary, 506-648 5565, Fax: 506-648-5811, E-mail: shines@unb.ca. *Director of Graduate Studies*, Dr. Jeff Houlahan, 506-648 5967, Fax: 506-648-5811, E-mail: jeffhoul@unb.ca.

**Department of Psychology** Students: 12 full-time (8 women), 1 part-time (0 women), 1 international. *Faculty:* 10 full-time (6 women). Expenses: Contact institution. *Financial support:* Fellowships, research assistantships, teaching assistantships, and unspecified assistantships available. Support available to part-time students. Financial award application deadline: 2/1. In 2019, 4 master's awarded. *Program availability:* Part-time. *Application deadline:* For fall admission, 1/15 priority date for domestic students. *Application fee:* $50. Electronic applications accepted. *Application Contact:* Mary Miernicki, Administrative Assistant, 506-648-5640, Fax: 506-648-5780, E-mail: Mary.Miernicki@unb.ca. *Director of Graduate Studies*, Dr. Mary Ann Campbell, 506-648 5969, Fax: 506-648-5780, E-mail: mcampbel@unb.ca.

**Department of Social Science**

**Faculty of Business** Students: 97 full-time (47 women), 14 part-time (7 women), 89 international. *Faculty:* 25 full-time (4 women). Expenses: Contact institution. *Financial support:* In 2019–20, 4 students received support. Career-related internships or fieldwork and scholarships/grants available. Financial award application deadline: 1/15. In 2019, 76 master's awarded. *Program availability:* Part-time. *Application deadline:* For fall admission, 5/31 for domestic students, 7/15 for international students. *Application fee:* $100. Electronic applications accepted. *Application Contact:* Tammy Morin, Secretary, 506-648-5746, Fax: 506-648-5574, E-mail: tmorin@unbsj.ca. *Director of Graduate Studies*, Dr. Shelley Rinehart, 506-648-5902, Fax: 506-648-5574, E-mail: rinehart@unb.ca.

## UNIVERSITY OF NEW ENGLAND, Biddeford, ME 04005-9526

**General Information** Independent, coed, comprehensive institution. *Enrollment:* 7,483 graduate, professional, and undergraduate students; 2,689 full-time matriculated graduate/professional students (1,843 women), 487 part-time matriculated graduate/professional students (391 women). *Enrollment by degree level:* 1,402 master's, 1,590 doctoral, 184 other advanced degrees. *Graduate faculty:* 172 full-time (100 women), 143 part-time/adjunct (76 women). *Graduate housing:* On-campus housing not available. *Student services:* Campus employment opportunities, campus safety program, career counseling, exercise/wellness program, free psychological counseling, international student services, low-cost health insurance, multicultural affairs office, services for students with disabilities, teacher training, writing training. *Library facilities:* Jack S. Ketchum Library plus 1 other. *Collection:* Books: 135,000 (physical), 1.2 million (digital/electronic); Serial titles: 140,000 (digital/electronic); Databases: 200. Weekly public service hours: 146; study areas open 24 hours, 5–7 days a week; students can reserve study rooms.

**Computer facilities:** Computer purchase and lease plans are available. 91 computers available on campus for general student use. A campuswide network can be accessed. Online class registration is available.
Website: http://www.une.edu/

**General Application Contact:** Scott Steinberg, Vice President of University Admissions, 207-221-4225, Fax: 207-523-1925, E-mail: ssteinberg@une.edu.

**GRADUATE UNITS**

**College of Arts and Sciences** Students: 16 full-time (12 women), 9 part-time (6 women); includes 1 minority (Black or African American, non-Hispanic/Latino). Average age 28. *Faculty:* 31 full-time (18 women), 1 part-time/adjunct (0 women). Expenses: Contact institution. *Financial support:* Fellowships, research assistantships, teaching assistantships, career-related internships or fieldwork, scholarships/grants, traineeships, and unspecified assistantships available. Financial award application deadline: 5/1; financial award applicants required to submit FAFSA. In 2019, 12 master's awarded. *Program availability:* Part-time. *Application deadline:* Applications are processed on a rolling basis. Electronic applications accepted. *Application Contact:* Scott Steinberg, Vice President of University Admissions, 207-221-4225, Fax: 207-523-1925, E-mail: ssteinberg@une.edu. *Dean, College of Arts and Sciences*, Dr. Jonathan H. Millen, 207-602-2371, E-mail: jmillen@une.edu.

**College of Dental Medicine** Students: 250 full-time (137 women); includes 73 minority (12 Black or African American, non-Hispanic/Latino; 4 American Indian or Alaska Native, non-Hispanic/Latino; 38 Asian, non-Hispanic/Latino; 10 Hispanic/Latino; 2 Native Hawaiian or other Pacific Islander, non-Hispanic/Latino; 7 Two or more races, non-Hispanic/Latino), 4 international. Average age 27. *Faculty:* 28 full-time (14 women), 27 part-time/adjunct (4 women). Expenses: Contact institution. *Financial support:* Application deadline: 5/1; applicants required to submit FAFSA. In 2019, 63 doctorates awarded. *Application deadline:* For fall admission, 11/1 for domestic and international students. Electronic applications accepted. *Application Contact:* Scott Steinberg, Vice President of University Admissions, 207-221-4225, Fax: 207-523-1925, E-mail: ssteinberg@une.edu. *Dean, College of Dental Medicine*, Dr. Jon Ryder, 207-221-4702, Fax: 207-523-1915, E-mail: jryder2@une.edu.

**College of Graduate and Professional Studies** Students: 1,001 full-time (795 women), 470 part-time (378 women); includes 306 minority (211 Black or African American, non-Hispanic/Latino; 12 American Indian or Alaska Native, non-Hispanic/Latino; 61 Asian, non-Hispanic/Latino; 14 Hispanic/Latino; 4 Native Hawaiian or other Pacific Islander, non-Hispanic/Latino; 4 Two or more races, non-Hispanic/Latino). Average age 36. *Faculty:* 2 full-time (1 woman), 63 part-time/adjunct (44 women). Expenses: Contact institution. *Financial support:* Application deadline: 5/1; applicants required to submit FAFSA. In 2019, 614 master's, 85 doctorates, 79 other advanced degrees awarded. *Program availability:* Part-time, evening/weekend, online only, 100% online. *Application deadline:* Applications are processed on a rolling basis. Electronic applications accepted. *Application Contact:* Nicole Lindsay, Director of Online Admissions, 207-221-4966, E-mail: nlindsay1@une.edu. *Dean of the College of Graduate and Professional Studies*, Dr. Martha Wilson, 207-221-4985, E-mail: mwilson13@une.edu.

**College of Osteopathic Medicine** Students: 710 full-time (391 women); includes 135 minority (3 Black or African American, non-Hispanic/Latino; 1 American Indian or Alaska Native, non-Hispanic/Latino; 113 Asian, non-Hispanic/Latino; 5 Hispanic/Latino; 13 Two or more races, non-Hispanic/Latino), 20 international. Average age 27. *Faculty:* 46 full-time (22 women), 27 part-time/adjunct (11 women). Expenses: Contact institution. *Financial support:* Application deadline: 5/1; applicants required to submit FAFSA. In 2019, 180 doctorates awarded. *Application deadline:* For fall admission, 3/1 for domestic students. *Application Contact:* Scott Steinberg, Vice President of University Admissions, 207-221-4225, Fax: 207-523-1925, E-mail: ssteinberg@une.edu. *Dean, College of Osteopathic Medicine*, Dr. Jane Carreiro, 207-602-2460, E-mail: jcarreiro@une.edu.

**College of Pharmacy** Students: 219 full-time (147 women); includes 45 minority (21 Black or African American, non-Hispanic/Latino; 19 Asian, non-Hispanic/Latino; 4 Hispanic/Latino; 1 Two or more races, non-Hispanic/Latino), 1 international. Average age 25. *Faculty:* 22 full-time (13 women), 2 part-time/adjunct (1 woman). Expenses: Contact institution. *Financial support:* Application deadline: 5/1; applicants required to submit FAFSA. In 2019, 91 doctorates awarded. *Application deadline:* For fall admission, 3/1 for domestic students. Applications are processed on a rolling basis. Electronic applications accepted. *Application Contact:* Scott Steinberg, Vice President of University Admissions, 207-221-4225, Fax: 207-523-1925, E-mail: ssteinberg@une.edu. *Dean, College of Pharmacy*, Dr. Robert L. McCarthy, 207-221-4365, E-mail: rmccarthy2@une.edu.

**Westbrook College of Health Professions** Students: 493 full-time (361 women), 8 part-time (7 women); includes 59 minority (3 Black or African American, non-Hispanic/Latino; 2 American Indian or Alaska Native, non-Hispanic/Latino; 36 Asian, non-Hispanic/Latino; 10 Hispanic/Latino; 2 Native Hawaiian or other Pacific Islander, non-Hispanic/Latino; 6 Two or more races, non-Hispanic/Latino), 2 international. Average age 27. *Faculty:* 42 full-time (32 women), 23 part-time/adjunct (16 women). Expenses: Contact institution. *Financial support:* Application deadline: 5/1; applicants required to submit FAFSA. In 2019, 154 master's, 58 doctorates awarded. *Program availability:* Part-time. *Application deadline:* Applications are processed on a rolling basis. Electronic applications accepted. *Application Contact:* Scott Steinberg, Vice President of University Admissions, 207-221-4225, Fax: 207-523-1925, E-mail: ssteinberg@une.edu. *Dean, Westbrook College of Health Professions*, Dr. Karen T. Pardue, 207-221-4361, E-mail: kpardue@une.edu.

## UNIVERSITY OF NEW HAMPSHIRE, Durham, NH 03824

**General Information** State-supported, coed, university. CGS member. *Enrollment:* 14,784 graduate, professional, and undergraduate students. *Enrollment by degree level:* 1,591 master's, 586 doctoral, 42 other advanced degrees. *Graduate housing:* Rooms and/or apartments available on a first-come, first-served basis to single and married students. Housing application deadline: 7/15. *Student services:* Campus employment opportunities, campus safety program, career counseling, child daycare facilities, exercise/wellness program, free psychological counseling, grant writing training, international student services, low-cost health insurance, multicultural affairs office, services for students with disabilities, teacher training, writing training. *Library facilities:* Dimond Library plus 4 others. *Collection:* Books: 916,824 (physical), 1.2 million (digital/electronic); Serial titles: 31,506 (physical), 1.3 million (digital/electronic); Databases: 513. Weekly public service hours: 117; students can reserve study rooms.

**Computer facilities:** Computer purchase and lease plans are available. 320 computers available on campus for general student use. A campuswide network can be accessed from student residence rooms and from off campus. Online class registration is available.
Website: http://www.unh.edu/

**General Application Contact:** Dovev L. Levine, Assistant Dean, 603-862-3000, Fax: 603-862-0275, E-mail: grad.school@unh.edu.

**GRADUATE UNITS**

**Graduate School** Students: 1,450 full-time (863 women), 956 part-time (544 women); includes 181 minority (45 Black or African American, non-Hispanic/Latino; 1 American Indian or Alaska Native, non-Hispanic/Latino; 48 Asian, non-Hispanic/Latino; 57 Hispanic/Latino; 1 Native Hawaiian or other Pacific Islander, non-Hispanic/Latino; 29 Two or more races, non-Hispanic/Latino), 346 international. Average age 31. 2,199 applicants, 62% accepted, 689 enrolled. *Faculty:* 581. Expenses: Contact institution. *Financial support:* In 2019–20, 27 fellowships with full and partial tuition reimbursements, 166 research assistantships with full and partial tuition reimbursements, 454 teaching assistantships with full and partial tuition reimbursements were awarded; Federal Work-Study, scholarships/grants, traineeships, health care benefits, tuition waivers (full and partial), and unspecified assistantships also available. Support available to part-time students. Financial award application deadline: 3/1; financial award applicants required to submit FAFSA. In 2019, 754 master's, 95 doctorates, 65 other advanced degrees awarded. *Program availability:* Part-time, evening/weekend, 100% online, blended/hybrid learning. *Application deadline:* For fall admission, 7/1 priority date for domestic students, 4/1 priority date for international students; for spring admission, 2/1 priority date for domestic students, 11/1 priority date for international students; for summer admission, 4/1 priority date for domestic and international students. Applications are processed on a rolling basis. *Application fee:* $65. Electronic applications accepted. *Application Contact:* Dovev Levine, Assistant Dean, 603-862-2234, E-mail: dovev.levine@unh.edu. *Interim Dean*, Dr. Cari Moorhead, 603-862-3005, Fax: 603-862-0275, E-mail: cari.moorhead@unh.edu.

***Carsey School of Public Policy*** Students: 12 full-time (8 women), 50 part-time (27 women); includes 9 minority (4 Black or African American, non-Hispanic/Latino; 2 Hispanic/Latino; 3 Two or more races, non-Hispanic/Latino), 2 international. Average age 32. 48 applicants, 65% accepted, 10 enrolled. Expenses: Contact institution. *Financial support:* In 2019–20, 13 students received support. Fellowships, research assistantships, teaching assistantships, and scholarships/grants available. Financial award application deadline: 2/15. In 2019, 28 master's awarded. *Program availability:* Part-time. *Application deadline:* For fall admission, 8/15 for domestic students; for spring admission, 12/15 for domestic students; for summer admission, 4/15 for domestic students. *Application fee:* $65. Electronic applications accepted. *Application Contact:* Robin Husslage, Administrative Assistant, 603-862-2338, E-mail: robin.husslage@unh.edu. *Director*, Michael Swack, 603-862-2821, Fax: 603-862-0275, E-mail: michael.swack@unh.edu.

***College of Engineering and Physical Sciences*** Students: 356 full-time (113 women), 158 part-time (57 women); includes 31 minority (5 Black or African American, non-Hispanic/Latino; 1 American Indian or Alaska Native, non-Hispanic/Latino; 10 Asian, non-Hispanic/Latino; 9 Hispanic/Latino; 6 Two or more races, non-Hispanic/Latino), 214 international. Average age 28. 639 applicants, 56% accepted, 126 enrolled. Expenses: Contact institution. *Financial support:* In 2019–20, 372 students received support, including 14 fellowships, 121 research assistantships, 197 teaching assistantships; career-related internships or fieldwork, Federal Work-Study, scholarships/grants, and tuition waivers also available. Support available to part-time students. Financial award application deadline: 2/15; financial award applicants required to submit FAFSA. In 2019, 99 master's, 42 doctorates, 9 other advanced degrees awarded. *Program availability:* Part-time, evening/weekend. *Application deadline:* For fall admission, 4/1 for domestic students; for spring admission, 12/1 priority date for domestic students. *Application fee:* $65. Electronic applications accepted. *Application Contact:* Rebecca Kibler, 603-862-3778, E-mail: rebecca.kibler@unh.edu. *Chair*, Radim Bartos, 603-862-3792.

***College of Health and Human Services*** Students: 491 full-time (431 women), 192 part-time (153 women); includes 59 minority (23 Black or African American, non-Hispanic/Latino; 7 Asian, non-Hispanic/Latino; 19 Hispanic/Latino; 10 Two or more races, non-Hispanic/Latino), 6 international. Average age 30. 602 applicants, 61% accepted, 211 enrolled. Expenses: Contact institution. *Financial support:* In 2019–20, 61 students received support, including 2 research assistantships, 35 teaching assistantships; fellowships, career-related internships or fieldwork, Federal Work-Study, scholarships/grants, and tuition waivers (full and partial) also available. Support available to part-time students. Financial award application deadline: 2/15. In 2019, 427 master's, 23 doctorates, 51 other advanced degrees awarded. *Program availability:* Part-time, evening/weekend. *Application deadline:* For fall admission, 7/1 for domestic students, 4/1 for international students; for spring admission, 12/1 for domestic students; for summer admission, 6/1 for domestic students. *Application fee:* $65. Electronic applications accepted. *Application Contact:* Jane Dodge, 603-862-0965, E-mail: jane.dodge@unh.edu. *Chair*, Don Robin, 603-862-3836.

***College of Liberal Arts*** Students: 213 full-time (142 women), 230 part-time (169 women); includes 23 minority (6 Black or African American, non-Hispanic/Latino; 8 Asian, non-Hispanic/Latino; 6 Hispanic/Latino; 3 Two or more races, non-Hispanic/Latino), 18 international. Average age 33. 295 applicants, 64% accepted, 106 enrolled. Expenses: Contact institution. *Financial support:* In 2019–20, 177 students received support, including 5 fellowships, 2 research assistantships, 106 teaching assistantships; career-related internships or fieldwork, Federal Work-Study, scholarships/grants, and tuition waivers (full and partial) also available. Support available to part-time students. Financial award application deadline: 2/15; financial award applicants required to submit FAFSA. In 2019, 182 master's, 22 doctorates, 8 other advanced degrees awarded. *Program availability:* Part-time. *Application deadline:* For fall admission, 4/15 for domestic students; for spring admission, 12/1 for domestic students; for summer admission, 4/15 for domestic students. *Application fee:* $65. Electronic applications accepted. *Application Contact:* Brigitte Bailey, 603-862-3052, E-mail: brigitte.bailey@unh.edu. *Chair*, Brigitte Bailey, 603-862-3052.

***College of Life Sciences and Agriculture*** Students: 98 full-time (60 women), 71 part-time (40 women); includes 11 minority (1 Black or African American, non-Hispanic/Latino; 1 Asian, non-Hispanic/Latino; 6 Hispanic/Latino; 3 Two or more races, non-Hispanic/Latino), 23 international. Average age 27. 178 applicants, 34% accepted, 50 enrolled. Expenses: Contact institution. *Financial support:* In 2019–20, 117 students received support, including 3 fellowships, 23 research assistantships, 91 teaching assistantships; career-related internships or fieldwork, Federal Work-Study, scholarships/grants, and tuition waivers (full and partial) also available. Support available to part-time students. Financial award application deadline: 2/15; financial award applicants required to submit FAFSA. In 2019, 32 master's, 6 doctorates awarded. *Program availability:* Part-time. *Application deadline:* For fall admission, 1/1 priority date for domestic students, 4/1 for international students; for spring admission, 10/15 for domestic students. *Application fee:* $65. Electronic applications accepted. *Application Contact:* Madison Ferreri,, 603-862-1-4122, E-mail: grad.school@unh.edu. *Chair*, Alison Paglia, 603-862-1-4103.

***Interdisciplinary Programs*** Students: 94 full-time (50 women), 74 part-time (44 women); includes 19 minority (6 Black or African American, non-Hispanic/Latino; 2 Asian, non-Hispanic/Latino; 5 Hispanic/Latino; 1 Native Hawaiian or other Pacific Islander, non-Hispanic/Latino; 5 Two or more races, non-Hispanic/Latino), 16 international. Average age 33. 112 applicants, 73% accepted, 50 enrolled. Expenses: Contact institution. *Financial support:* In 2019–20, 62 students received support, including 4 fellowships, 15 research assistantships, 13 teaching assistantships. Financial award application deadline: 2/15. In 2019, 62 master's, 7 doctorates, 27 other advanced degrees awarded. *Program availability:* Part-time. *Application deadline:* For fall admission, 2/15 priority date for domestic students, 4/1 for international students; for winter admission, 12/1 priority date for domestic students. *Application fee:* $65. Electronic applications accepted. *Application Contact:* Dovev Levine, Assistant Dean, 603-862-3000, E-mail: grad.school@unh.edu. *Dean*, Dr. Cari Moorhead, 603-862-3000, E-mail: grad.school@unh.edu.

**Graduate School Manchester Campus** Students: 118 full-time (56 women), 110 part-time (47 women); includes 23 minority (4 Black or African American, non-Hispanic/Latino; 5 Asian, non-Hispanic/Latino; 13 Hispanic/Latino; 1 Two or more races, non-Hispanic/Latino), 39 international. Average age 32. 231 applicants, 78% accepted, 64 enrolled. Expenses: Contact institution. *Financial support:* In 2019–20, 11 students received support, including 1 teaching assistantship; fellowships, research assistantships, Federal Work-Study, scholarships/grants, health care benefits, and unspecified assistantships also available. Support available to part-time students. Financial award application deadline: 2/15; financial award applicants required to submit FAFSA. In 2019, 47 master's, 3 other advanced degrees awarded. *Program availability:* Part-time, evening/weekend. *Application deadline:* For fall admission, 6/1 for domestic students, 4/1 for international students; for spring admission, 12/1 for domestic students. *Application fee:* $65. Electronic applications accepted. *Application Contact:* Candice Morey, Educational Programs Coordinator, 603-641-4313, E-mail: unhm.gradcenter@unh.edu. *Educational Programs Coordinator*, Candice Morey, 603-641-4313, E-mail: unhm.gradcenter@unh.edu.

***Peter T. Paul College of Business and Economics*** Students: 155 full-time (54 women), 195 part-time (69 women); includes 31 minority (4 Black or African American, non-Hispanic/Latino; 16 Asian, non-Hispanic/Latino; 9 Hispanic/Latino; 2 Two or more races, non-Hispanic/Latino), 32 international. Average age 32. 220 applicants, 78% accepted, 120 enrolled. Expenses: Contact institution. *Financial support:* In 2019–20, 93 students received support, including 1 fellowship, 3 research assistantships, 12 teaching assistantships; career-related internships or fieldwork, Federal Work-Study, scholarships/grants, and tuition waivers (full and partial) also available. Support available to part-time students. Financial award application deadline: 2/15. In 2019, 134 master's awarded. *Program availability:* Part-time, evening/weekend. *Application deadline:* For fall admission, 6/15 for domestic students; for spring admission, 12/15 for domestic students. *Application fee:* $65. Electronic applications accepted. *Application Contact:* Tara Hunter, 603-862-3326, E-mail: tara.hunter@unh.edu. *Chair*, Stephen Ciccone, 603-862-3343.

***School of Marine Science and Ocean Engineering*** Students: 24 full-time (11 women), 5 part-time (1 woman); includes 1 minority (Hispanic/Latino), 10 international. Average age 29. 29 applicants, 62% accepted, 12 enrolled. Expenses: Contact institution. *Financial support:* In 2019–20, 25 students received support, including 2 fellowships, 18 research assistantships, 5 teaching assistantships; Federal Work-Study, scholarships/grants, and tuition waivers (full and partial) also available. Support available to part-time students. Financial award application deadline: 2/15. In 2019, 4 master's, 1 doctorate, 6 other advanced degrees awarded. *Application deadline:* For fall admission, 7/1 for domestic students, 4/1 for international students; for spring admission, 12/1 for domestic students. *Application fee:* $65. Electronic applications accepted. *Application Contact:* Laura Gustafson, Administrative Assistant, 603-862-0672, E-mail: laura.gustafson@unh.edu. *Chair*, Martin Wosnik, 603-862-1891.

**School of Law** *Program availability:* Part-time, 100% online, limited residential. Electronic applications accepted.

## UNIVERSITY OF NEW HAVEN, West Haven, CT 06516

**General Information** Independent, coed, comprehensive institution. CGS member. *Enrollment:* 6,793 graduate, professional, and undergraduate students; 1,285 full-time matriculated graduate/professional students (612 women), 591 part-time matriculated graduate/professional students (267 women). *Enrollment by degree level:* 1,826 master's, 30 doctoral, 20 other advanced degrees. *Graduate faculty:* 128 full-time (39 women), 98 part-time/adjunct (28 women). *Graduate housing:* Room and/or apartments available on a first-come, first-served basis to single students; on-campus housing not available to married students. *Student services:* Campus employment opportunities, campus safety program, career counseling, free psychological counseling, international student services, low-cost health insurance, multicultural affairs office, services for students with disabilities, writing training. *Library facilities:* Marvin K. Peterson Library.

**Computer facilities:** Computer purchase and lease plans are available. A campuswide network can be accessed. Online class registration, computer repair services are available.
Website: http://www.newhaven.edu/

**General Application Contact:** Selina O'Toole, Senior Associate Director of Graduate Admissions, 203-932-7337, E-mail: SOToole@newhaven.edu.

**GRADUATE UNITS**

**Graduate School** Students: 1,285 full-time (612 women), 591 part-time (267 women); includes 383 minority (177 Black or African American, non-Hispanic/Latino; 3 American Indian or Alaska Native, non-Hispanic/Latino; 79 Asian, non-Hispanic/Latino; 116 Hispanic/Latino; 3 Native Hawaiian or other Pacific Islander, non-Hispanic/Latino; 5 Two or more races, non-Hispanic/Latino), 682 international. Average age 28. 3,175 applicants, 77% accepted, 711 enrolled. Expenses: Contact institution. *Financial support:* Research assistantships with partial tuition reimbursements, teaching assistantships with partial tuition reimbursements, Federal Work-Study, scholarships/grants, and unspecified assistantships available. Financial award applicants required to submit FAFSA. In 2019, 731 master's, 3 doctorates, 19 other advanced degrees awarded. *Program availability:* Part-time, evening/weekend. *Application deadline:* Applications are processed on a rolling basis. *Application fee:* $50. Electronic applications accepted. *Application Contact:* Selina O'Toole, Senior Associate Director of Graduate Admissions, 203-932-7337, E-mail: SOToole@newhaven.edu.

***College of Arts and Sciences*** Students: 172 full-time (120 women), 35 part-time (23 women); includes 51 minority (25 Black or African American, non-Hispanic/Latino; 7 Asian, non-Hispanic/Latino; 18 Hispanic/Latino; 1 Native Hawaiian or other Pacific Islander, non-Hispanic/Latino), 41 international. Average age 27. 291 applicants, 77% accepted, 88 enrolled. Expenses: Contact institution. *Financial support:* Research assistantships with partial tuition reimbursements, teaching assistantships with partial tuition reimbursements, Federal Work-Study, scholarships/grants, and unspecified assistantships available. Support available to part-time students. Financial award application deadline: 5/1; financial award applicants required to submit FAFSA. In 2019, 85 master's, 2 other advanced degrees awarded. *Program availability:* Part-time, evening/weekend. *Application deadline:* Applications are processed on a rolling basis. *Application fee:* $50. Electronic applications accepted. *Application Contact:* Selina O'Toole, Senior Associate Director of Graduate Admissions, 203-932-7337, E-mail: SOToole@newhaven.edu. *Interim Dean*, Dr. Michael Rossi, 203-932-7125, E-mail: mrossi@newhaven.edu.

***Henry C. Lee College of Criminal Justice and Forensic Sciences*** Students: 294 full-time (172 women), 250 part-time (113 women); includes 134 minority (63 Black or African American, non-Hispanic/Latino; 1 American Indian or Alaska Native, non-Hispanic/Latino; 15 Asian, non-Hispanic/Latino; 51 Hispanic/Latino; 2 Native Hawaiian or other Pacific Islander, non-Hispanic/Latino; 2 Two or more races, non-Hispanic/Latino), 47 international. Average age 31. 471 applicants, 82% accepted, 206 enrolled. Expenses: Contact institution. *Financial support:* Research assistantships with partial tuition reimbursements, teaching assistantships with partial tuition reimbursements, Federal Work-Study, scholarships/grants, and unspecified assistantships available. Support available to part-time students. Financial award applicants required to submit FAFSA. In 2019, 233 master's, 3 doctorates, 11 other advanced degrees awarded. *Program availability:* Part-time, evening/weekend, 100% online, blended/hybrid learning. *Application deadline:* Applications are processed on a rolling basis. *Application fee:* $50. Electronic applications accepted. *Application Contact:* Selina O'Toole, Senior Associate Director of Graduate Admissions, 203-932-7337, E-mail: SOToole@newhaven.edu. *Acting Dean*, Dr. David Schroeder, 203-931-2959, E-mail: DSchroeder@newhaven.edu.

***Pompea College of Business*** Students: 261 full-time (117 women), 89 part-time (35 women); includes 89 minority (38 Black or African American, non-Hispanic/Latino; 1 American Indian or Alaska Native, non-Hispanic/Latino; 27 Asian, non-Hispanic/Latino; 22 Hispanic/Latino; 1 Two or more races, non-Hispanic/Latino), 110 international. Average age 28. 351 applicants, 93% accepted, 151 enrolled. Expenses: Contact institution. *Financial support:* Research assistantships with partial tuition reimbursements, teaching assistantships with partial tuition reimbursements, Federal Work-Study, scholarships/grants, and unspecified assistantships available. Support available to part-time students. Financial award application deadline: 5/1; financial award applicants required to submit FAFSA. In 2019, 126 master's, 4 other advanced degrees awarded. *Program availability:* Part-time, evening/weekend. *Application deadline:* Applications are processed on a rolling basis. *Application fee:* $50. Electronic applications accepted. *Application Contact:* Selina O'Toole, Senior Associate Director of Graduate Admissions, 203-932-7337, E-mail: SOToole@newhaven.edu. *Dean*, Dr. Brian Kench, 203-932-7115, E-mail: bkench@newhaven.edu.

***Tagliatela College of Engineering*** Students: 463 full-time (129 women), 143 part-time (41 women); includes 50 minority (16 Black or African American, non-Hispanic/Latino; 1 American Indian or Alaska Native, non-Hispanic/Latino; 22 Asian, non-Hispanic/Latino; 10 Hispanic/Latino; 1 Two or more races, non-Hispanic/Latino), 445 international. Average age 26. 1,825 applicants, 72% accepted, 188 enrolled. Expenses: Contact institution. *Financial support:* Research assistantships with partial tuition reimbursements, teaching assistantships with partial tuition reimbursements, Federal Work-Study, scholarships/grants, and unspecified assistantships available. Support available to part-time students. Financial award applicants required to submit FAFSA. In 2019, 213 master's, 1 other advanced degree awarded. *Program availability:* Part-time, evening/weekend. *Application deadline:* Applications are processed on a rolling basis. *Application fee:* $50. Electronic applications accepted. *Application Contact:* Selina O'Toole, Senior Associate Director of Graduate Admissions, 203-932-7337, E-mail: SOToole@newhaven.edu. *Dean and Vice Provost for Research*, Dr. Ronald Harichandran, 203-932-7167, E-mail: rharichandran@newhaven.edu.

**School of Health Sciences** Students: 95 full-time (74 women), 74 part-time (55 women); includes 59 minority (35 Black or African American, non-Hispanic/Latino; 8 Asian, non-Hispanic/Latino; 15 Hispanic/Latino; 1 Two or more races, non-Hispanic/Latino), 39 international. Average age 32. 237 applicants, 84% accepted, 78 enrolled. Expenses: Contact institution. *Application deadline:* Applications are processed on a rolling basis. *Application fee:* $50. Electronic applications accepted. *Application Contact:* Selina O'Toole, Senior Associate Director of Graduate Admissions, 203-932-7337, E-mail: SOToole@newhaven.edu. *Dean*, Dr. Summer McGee, 203-479-4104, E-mail: SMcGee@newhaven.edu.

## UNIVERSITY OF NEW MEXICO, Albuquerque, NM 87131-2039

**General Information** State-supported, coed, university. CGS member. *Enrollment:* 22,793 graduate, professional, and undergraduate students; 2,073 full-time matriculated graduate/professional students, 1,979 part-time matriculated graduate/professional students. *Enrollment by degree level:* 2,135 master's, 1,734 doctoral, 183 other advanced degrees. *Graduate faculty:* 758 full-time (346 women), 72 part-time/adjunct (37 women). *International tuition:* $23,292 full-time. Tuition, state resident: full-time $7633; part-time $972 per year. Tuition, nonresident: full-time $22,586; part-time $3840 per year. *Required fees:* $8608. Tuition and fees vary according to course level, course load, degree level, program and student level. *Graduate housing:* Rooms and/or apartments available on a first-come, first-served basis to single and married students. Typical cost: $4890 (including board) for single students. Housing application deadline: 7/16. *Student services:* Campus employment opportunities, campus safety program, career counseling, child daycare facilities, exercise/wellness program, free psychological counseling, grant writing training, international student services, low-cost health insurance, multicultural affairs office, services for students with disabilities, teacher training, writing training. *Library facilities:* College of University Libraries and Learning Sciences plus 7 others. *Collection:* Students can reserve study rooms. *Research affiliation:* Phillips Laboratory, Oak Ridge National Laboratory, Sandia National Laboratories, New Mexico Consortium, Los Alamos National Laboratory, Lovelace Respiratory Research Institute.

**Computer facilities:** Computer purchase and lease plans are available. 990 computers available on campus for general student use. A campuswide network can be accessed. Online class registration is available.
Website: http://www.unm.edu/

**General Application Contact:** Deborah Kieltyka, Associate Director, Admissions, 505-277-3140, Fax: 505-277-6686, E-mail: deborahk@unm.edu.

**GRADUATE UNITS**

**Anderson School of Management** Students: 523 part-time (266 women); includes 240 minority (8 Black or African American, non-Hispanic/Latino; 18 American Indian or Alaska Native, non-Hispanic/Latino; 19 Asian, non-Hispanic/Latino; 187 Hispanic/Latino; 8 Two or more races, non-Hispanic/Latino), 27 international. Average age 30. 398 applicants, 52% accepted, 185 enrolled. *Faculty:* 62 full-time (27 women), 41 part-time/adjunct (17 women). Expenses: Contact institution. *Financial support:* In 2019–20, 78 students received support, including 58 fellowships (averaging $15,746 per year), 16 research assistantships with partial tuition reimbursements available (averaging $15,400 per year); career-related internships or fieldwork, Federal Work-Study, scholarships/grants, and unspecified assistantships also available. Support available to part-time students. Financial award application deadline: 6/1; financial award applicants required to submit FAFSA. In 2019, 292 master's awarded. *Program availability:* Part-time, evening/weekend. *Application deadline:* For fall admission, 4/1 priority date for domestic students, 5/1 priority date for international students; for spring admission, 10/1 priority date for domestic and international students; for summer admission, 2/1 priority date for domestic and international students. Applications are processed on a rolling basis. *Application fee:* $100 ($70 for international students). Electronic applications accepted. *Application Contact:* Lisa Beauchene-Lawson, Supervisor, Graduate Admissions and Advisement, 505-277-3290, E-mail: andersongrad@unm.edu. *Dean*, Dr. Mitzi Montoya, 505-277-1792, E-mail: mitzimontoya@unm.edu.

**Graduate Studies** *Program availability:* Part-time, evening/weekend, online only, 100% online, blended/hybrid learning. Electronic applications accepted.

***College of Arts and Sciences*** *Program availability:* Part-time. Electronic applications accepted.

***College of Education and Human Sciences*** *Program availability:* Part-time, evening/weekend. Electronic applications accepted.

***College of Fine Arts*** *Program availability:* Part-time.

***College of Pharmacy*** *Program availability:* Part-time. Electronic applications accepted.

***College of University Libraries and Learning Sciences*** *Program availability:* Part-time, evening/weekend, online learning. Electronic applications accepted.

***Health Sciences Center***

***School of Architecture and Planning*** Electronic applications accepted.

***School of Engineering*** Students: 746 full-time (170 women); includes 211 minority (16 Black or African American, non-Hispanic/Latino; 8 American Indian or Alaska Native, non-Hispanic/Latino; 31 Asian, non-Hispanic/Latino; 142 Hispanic/Latino; 1 Native Hawaiian or other Pacific Islander, non-Hispanic/Latino; 13 Two or more races, non-Hispanic/Latino), 241 international. Average age 32. 559 applicants, 60% accepted, 178 enrolled. *Faculty:* 94 full-time (18 women), 42 part-time/adjunct (7 women). Expenses: Contact institution. *Financial support:* In 2019–20, 7 fellowships with full and partial tuition reimbursements (averaging $25,715 per year), 280 research assistantships with full and partial tuition reimbursements (averaging $27,408 per year), 62 teaching assistantships with full and partial tuition reimbursements (averaging $24,945 per year) were awarded; career-related internships or fieldwork, Federal Work-Study, scholarships/grants, health care benefits, tuition waivers (full and partial), and unspecified assistantships also available. Financial award application deadline: 3/1; financial award applicants required to submit FAFSA. In 2019, 211 master's, 56 doctorates awarded. *Program availability:* Part-time, 100% online, blended/hybrid learning. *Application deadline:* For fall admission, 1/15 priority date for domestic and international students; for spring admission, 7/14 priority date for domestic and international students. Applications are processed on a rolling basis. *Application fee:* $50 ($70 for international students). Electronic applications accepted. *Application Contact:* Prof. Charles Fleddermann, Associate Dean for Academic Affairs and Community Engagement, 505-277-5522, Fax: 505-277-1422, E-mail: cbf@unm.edu. *Dean*, Christos Christodoulou, 505-277-5522, Fax: 505-277-1422, E-mail: christos@unm.edu.

***School of Public Administration*** *Program availability:* Part-time, evening/weekend, online learning. Electronic applications accepted.

**School of Law** Electronic applications accepted.

**School of Medicine** Electronic applications accepted.

## UNIVERSITY OF NEW ORLEANS, New Orleans, LA 70148

**General Information** State-supported, coed, university. *Graduate housing:* Rooms and/or apartments available on a first-come, first-served basis to single and married students. *Research affiliation:* John C. Stennis Space Center (acoustics, computer science), Northrop Grumman Corporation (engineering), TJ Watson Research Center-IBM (chemistry), Paratek Microwave, Inc. (nanotechnology), Applied Research Lab-Penn State University (engineering), Lockheed Martin Corporation (materials).

**GRADUATE UNITS**

**Graduate School** *Program availability:* Part-time, evening/weekend. Electronic applications accepted.

***College of Business Administration*** *Program availability:* Part-time, evening/weekend. Electronic applications accepted.

***College of Engineering*** *Program availability:* Part-time. Electronic applications accepted.

***College of Liberal Arts, Education and Human Development*** *Program availability:* Part-time, evening/weekend. Electronic applications accepted.

***College of Sciences*** *Program availability:* Part-time, evening/weekend. Electronic applications accepted.

## UNIVERSITY OF NORTH ALABAMA, Florence, AL 35632-0001

**General Information** State-supported, coed, comprehensive institution. *Graduate housing:* Rooms and/or apartments available on a first-come, first-served basis to single and married students.

**GRADUATE UNITS**

**Anderson College of Nursing** *Program availability:* Part-time, online only, 100% online, blended/hybrid learning. Electronic applications accepted.

**College of Arts and Sciences** *Program availability:* Part-time, 100% online. Electronic applications accepted.

**College of Business** *Program availability:* Part-time, 100% online, blended/hybrid learning. Electronic applications accepted.

**College of Education** *Program availability:* Part-time, 100% online, blended/hybrid learning. Electronic applications accepted.

## UNIVERSITY OF NORTH CAROLINA ASHEVILLE, Asheville, NC 28804-3299

**General Information** State-supported, coed, comprehensive institution. *Enrollment:* 3,600 graduate, professional, and undergraduate students; 1 full-time matriculated graduate/professional student, 11 part-time matriculated graduate/professional students (7 women). *Enrollment by degree level:* 12 master's. *Graduate faculty:* 4 full-time (1 woman), 2 part-time/adjunct (0 women). *International tuition:* $21,236 full-time. *Tuition, area resident:* Full-time $4914. Tuition, state resident: full-time $4914. Tuition, nonresident: full-time $21,236. *Required fees:* $3108.50. *Graduate housing:* Room and/or apartments available on a first-come, first-served basis to single students; on-campus housing not available to married students. Typical cost: $7000 per year ($11,000 including board). Room and board charges vary according to housing facility selected. Housing application deadline: 5/1. *Student services:* Campus employment opportunities, campus safety program, career counseling, exercise/wellness program, free psychological counseling, international student services, low-cost health insurance, multicultural affairs office, services for students with disabilities, writing training. *Library facilities:* Ramsey Library. *Collection:* Books: 260,675 (physical), 863,561 (digital/electronic); Serial titles: 188 (physical), 71,396 (digital/electronic); Databases: 275. Weekly public service hours: 99; students can reserve study rooms.

**Computer facilities:** Computer purchase and lease plans are available. 802 computers available on campus for general student use. A campuswide network can be accessed. Online class registration is available.
Website: http://www.unca.edu/

**General Application Contact:** Lilly Augspurger, Administrative Assistant, 828-251-6099, E-mail: laugspur@unca.edu.

**GRADUATE UNITS**

**Master of Liberal Arts and Sciences Program** Students: 1 full-time (0 women), 11 part-time (7 women); includes 1 minority (Two or more races, non-Hispanic/Latino). Average age 42. *Faculty:* 4 full-time (1 woman), 2 part-time/adjunct (0 women). Expenses: Contact institution. *Financial support:* In 2019–20, 3 students received support. Scholarships/grants and tuition waivers for UNC faculty/staff available. Financial award applicants required to submit FAFSA. In 2019, 8 master's, 5 Graduate Certificates awarded. *Program availability:* Part-time. *Application fee:* $60. *Application Contact:* Lilly Augspurger, Administrative Assistant, 828-251-6099, E-mail: laugspur@unca.edu. *Graduate Council Chair*, Dr. Michael Neelon, 828-250-2359, E-mail: mneelon@unca.edu.

## THE UNIVERSITY OF NORTH CAROLINA AT CHAPEL HILL, Chapel Hill, NC 27599

**General Information** State-supported, coed, university. CGS member. *Enrollment:* 30,151 graduate, professional, and undergraduate students; 8,741 full-time matriculated graduate/professional students (5,083 women), 1,644 part-time matriculated graduate/professional students (795 women). *Enrollment by degree level:* 4,565 master's, 5,818 doctoral, 2 other advanced degrees. *Graduate faculty:* 3,753 full-time (1,844 women), 309 part-time/adjunct (167 women). *Graduate housing:* Rooms and/or apartments available on a first-come, first-served basis to single and married students. *Student services:* Campus employment opportunities, campus safety program, career counseling, child daycare facilities, exercise/wellness program, free psychological counseling, grant writing training, international student services, low-cost health insurance, multicultural affairs office, services for students with disabilities, teacher training, writing training. *Library facilities:* Davis Library plus 12 others. *Collection:* Books: 7.5 million (physical), 1.4 million (digital/electronic); Serial titles: 224,227 (digital/electronic); Databases: 1,285. Weekly public service hours: 140; study areas open 24 hours, 5–7 days a week; students can reserve study rooms. *Research affiliation:* Research Triangle Institute, Centers for Disease Control (CDC), Triangle Universities Nuclear Laboratory.

**Computer facilities:** Computer purchase and lease plans are available. 449 computers available on campus for general student use. A campuswide network can be accessed. Online class registration is available.
Website: http://www.unc.edu/

**GRADUATE UNITS**

**Eshelman School of Pharmacy** Electronic applications accepted.

**Graduate School** Students: 5,343 full-time (3,362 women), 696 part-time (465 women); includes 1,421 minority (412 Black or African American, non-Hispanic/Latino; 14 American Indian or Alaska Native, non-Hispanic/Latino; 350 Asian, non-Hispanic/Latino; 379 Hispanic/Latino; 3 Native Hawaiian or other Pacific Islander, non-Hispanic/Latino; 263 Two or more races, non-Hispanic/Latino), 886 international. Average age 29. 12,769 applicants, 31% accepted, 1,969 enrolled. *Faculty:* 1,896 full-time (872 women), 104 part-time/adjunct (41 women). Expenses: Contact institution. *Financial support:* Fellowships with full and partial tuition reimbursements, research assistantships with full and partial tuition reimbursements, teaching assistantships with full and partial tuition reimbursements, career-related internships or fieldwork, Federal Work-Study, institutionally sponsored loans, scholarships/grants, traineeships, health care benefits, and unspecified assistantships available. Support available to part-time students. Financial award applicants required to submit FAFSA. In 2019, 1,203 master's, 537 doctorates awarded. *Program availability:* Online learning. *Application deadline:* For fall admission, 12/12 priority date for domestic and international students. Applications are processed on a rolling basis. *Application fee:* $85. Electronic applications accepted. *Application Contact:* Director of Admissions and Enrolled Students. *Dean.*

***College of Arts and Sciences*** *Program availability:* Part-time. Electronic applications accepted.

***Gillings School of Global Public Health*** Students: 1,204 full-time (884 women), 212 part-time (148 women); includes 391 minority (113 Black or African American, non-Hispanic/Latino; 130 Asian, non-Hispanic/Latino; 86 Hispanic/Latino; 62 Two or more races, non-Hispanic/Latino), 190 international. Average age 29. 2,442 applicants, 47% accepted, 524 enrolled. *Faculty:* 234 full-time (140 women), 476 part-time/adjunct (274 women). Expenses: Contact institution. *Financial support:* Fellowships, research assistantships, teaching assistantships, career-related internships or fieldwork, Federal Work-Study, scholarships/grants, traineeships, health care benefits, and unspecified assistantships available. Financial award application deadline: 12/11; financial award applicants required to submit FAFSA. In 2019, 272 master's, 88 doctorates awarded. *Program availability:* Part-time, 100% online, blended/hybrid learning. *Application deadline:* For fall admission, 2/1 for domestic and international students. *Application fee:* $90. Electronic applications accepted. *Application Contact:* Johnston King, Enrollment Management Coordinator, 919-962-6314, Fax: 919-966-6352, E-mail: sph-osa@unc.edu. *Dean*, Dr. Barbara K. Rimer, 919-966-3215, Fax: 919-966-7678.

***Hussman School of Journalism and Media*** Students: 68 full-time (45 women), 82 part-time (58 women); includes 35 minority (13 Black or African American, non-Hispanic/Latino; 1 American Indian or Alaska Native, non-Hispanic/Latino; 4 Asian, non-Hispanic/Latino; 1 Hispanic/Latino; 16 Two or more races, non-Hispanic/Latino), 9 international. Average age 34. 205 applicants, 49% accepted, 73 enrolled. *Faculty:* 30 full-time (15 women), 5 part-time/adjunct (4 women). Expenses: Contact institution. *Financial support:* In 2019–20, 60 students received support, including 41 fellowships with full tuition reimbursements available (averaging $17,901 per year), 4 research assistantships with full tuition reimbursements available (averaging $17,465 per year); scholarships/grants and health care benefits also available. Financial award application deadline: 12/15; financial award applicants required to submit FAFSA. In 2019, 32 master's, 5 doctorates, 24 other advanced degrees awarded. *Program availability:* Part-time, all course instruction online, plus two on-campus experiences totaling seven days. *Application fee:* $95. Electronic applications accepted. *Application Contact:* Casey Hart, Assistant Director, Graduate Studies, 919-843-9471, Fax: 919-962-0620, E-mail: mjgrad@unc.edu. *Dean*, Susan King, 919-962-1204, Fax: 919-962-0620, E-mail: susanking@unc.edu.

***School of Education*** *Program availability:* Part-time. Electronic applications accepted.

***School of Government*** Electronic applications accepted.

***School of Information and Library Science*** Students: 227 full-time (163 women), 31 part-time (18 women); includes 42 minority (9 Black or African American, non-Hispanic/Latino; 1 American Indian or Alaska Native, non-Hispanic/Latino; 9 Asian, non-Hispanic/Latino; 11 Hispanic/Latino; 12 Two or more races, non-Hispanic/Latino), 56 international. Average age 28. 269 applicants, 73% accepted, 80 enrolled. *Faculty:* 30 full-time (12 women), 46 part-time/adjunct (23 women). Expenses: Contact institution. *Financial support:* In 2019–20, 59 fellowships with full tuition reimbursements (averaging $2,565 per year), 46 research assistantships with full tuition reimbursements (averaging $3,528 per year), 7 teaching assistantships with full tuition reimbursements (averaging $22,917 per year) were awarded; career-related internships or fieldwork, Federal Work-Study, scholarships/grants, health care benefits, and unspecified assistantships also available. Financial award application deadline: 12/10. In 2019, 125 master's, 17 doctorates, 2 other advanced degrees awarded. *Program availability:* Part-time, 100% online, blended/hybrid learning. *Application deadline:* For fall admission, 12/10 priority date for domestic and international students; for spring admission, 10/8 for domestic and international students; for summer admission, 3/10 for domestic and international students. Applications are processed on a rolling basis. *Application fee:* $90. Electronic applications accepted. *Application Contact:* Lara Bailey, Student Services Coordinator, 919-962-7601, Fax: 919-962-8071, E-mail: bailey@email.unc.edu. *Dean*, Dr. Gary Marchionini, 919-962-8363, Fax: 919-962-8071, E-mail: gary@ils.unc.edu.

***School of Social Work*** *Program availability:* Part-time. Electronic applications accepted.

**Kenan-Flagler Business School** *Program availability:* Evening/weekend, online learning. Electronic applications accepted.

**School of Dentistry** Electronic applications accepted.

**School of Law** Electronic applications accepted.

**School of Medicine** Electronic applications accepted.

**School of Nursing** *Program availability:* Part-time. Electronic applications accepted.

## THE UNIVERSITY OF NORTH CAROLINA AT CHARLOTTE, Charlotte, NC 28223-0001

**General Information** State-supported, coed, university. CGS member. *Enrollment:* 29,615 graduate, professional, and undergraduate students; 2,569 full-time matriculated graduate/professional students (1,329 women), 2,976 part-time matriculated graduate/professional students (1,866 women). *Enrollment by degree level:* 3,413 master's, 1,073 doctoral, 1,059 other advanced degrees. *Graduate faculty:* 921 full-time (413 women), 111 part-time/adjunct (67 women). Tuition, state resident: full-time $4337. Tuition, nonresident: full-time $17,771. *Required fees:* $3093. Tuition and fees vary according to course load, degree level and program. *Graduate housing:* Room and/or apartments available on a first-come, first-served basis to single students; on-campus housing not available to married students. Typical cost: $8850 per year ($12,650 including board). Room and board charges vary according to board plan and housing facility selected. Housing application deadline: 6/1. *Student services:* Campus employment opportunities, campus safety program, career counseling, exercise/wellness program, free psychological counseling, international student services, low-cost health insurance, multicultural affairs office, services for students with disabilities, teacher training, writing training. *Library facilities:* J. Murrey Atkins Library plus 1 other. *Collection:* Books: 745,390 (physical), 1.1 million (digital/electronic); Serial titles: 23,751 (physical), 132,424 (digital/electronic); Databases: 600. Study areas open 24 hours, 5–7 days a week; students can reserve study rooms. *Research affiliation:* McGraw Hill Education (special education and child development), SAS Institute (computer science), SURVICE Engineering Company (physics, optical sciences), Health Resources and Services Administration (public health sciences), National Science Foundation (bioinformatics, genomics), HDR Engineering, Inc. of the Carolinas (civil and environmental engineering).

**Computer facilities:** 1,600 computers available on campus for general student use. A campuswide network can be accessed. Online class registration is available.
Website: http://www.uncc.edu/

**General Application Contact:** Kathy B. Giddings, Director of Graduate Admissions, 704-687-5503, Fax: 704-687-1668, E-mail: gradadm@uncc.edu.

**GRADUATE UNITS**

**Belk College of Business** Students: 270 full-time (115 women), 377 part-time (116 women); includes 169 minority (71 Black or African American, non-Hispanic/Latino; 1 American Indian or Alaska Native, non-Hispanic/Latino; 44 Asian, non-Hispanic/Latino; 39 Hispanic/Latino; 1 Native Hawaiian or other Pacific Islander, non-Hispanic/Latino; 13 Two or more races, non-Hispanic/Latino), 162 international. Average age 31. 547 applicants, 73% accepted, 273 enrolled. *Faculty:* 86 full-time (27 women), 5 part-time/adjunct (2 women). Expenses: Contact institution. *Financial support:* In 2019–20, 67 students received support, including 62 research assistantships (averaging $9,611 per year), 5 teaching assistantships (averaging $15,500 per year); career-related internships or fieldwork, institutionally sponsored loans, scholarships/grants, and unspecified assistantships also available. Support available to part-time students. Financial award application deadline: 3/1; financial award applicants required to submit FAFSA. In 2019, 313 master's, 5 doctorates, 12 other advanced degrees awarded. *Program availability:* Part-time, evening/weekend. *Application deadline:* For fall admission, 3/1 priority date for domestic students; for spring admission, 10/1 priority date for domestic students. Applications are processed on a rolling basis. *Application fee:* $75. Electronic applications accepted. *Application Contact:* Kathy B. Giddings, Director of Graduate Admissions, 704-687-5503, Fax: 704-687-1668, E-mail: gradadm@uncc.edu. *Dean*, Dr. Steven Ott, 704-687-7577, Fax: 704-687-1393, E-mail: cob-dean@uncc.edu.

***Turner School of Accountancy*** Students: 58 full-time (23 women), 21 part-time (11 women); includes 20 minority (4 Black or African American, non-Hispanic/Latino; 6 Asian, non-Hispanic/Latino; 10 Hispanic/Latino), 6 international. Average age 27. 106 applicants, 63% accepted, 56 enrolled. *Faculty:* 12 full-time (3 women), 1 part-time/adjunct (0 women). Expenses: Contact institution. *Financial support:* Research assistantships, teaching assistantships, career-related internships or fieldwork, institutionally sponsored loans, scholarships/grants, and unspecified assistantships available. Support available to part-time students. Financial award application deadline: 3/1; financial award applicants required to submit FAFSA. In 2019, 71 master's awarded. *Program availability:* Part-time, evening/weekend. *Application deadline:* For fall admission, 3/1 priority date for domestic students; for spring admission, 10/1 priority date for domestic students; for summer admission, 5/1 for domestic students. Applications are processed on a rolling basis. *Application fee:* $75. Electronic applications accepted. *Application Contact:* Kathy B. Giddings, Director of Graduate Admissions, 704-687-5503, Fax: 704-687-1668, E-mail: gradadm@uncc.edu. *Director*, Dr. Hughlene Burton, 704-687-7696, E-mail: haburton@uncc.edu.

**Cato College of Education** Students: 239 full-time (194 women), 1,247 part-time (1,023 women); includes 511 minority (356 Black or African American, non-Hispanic/Latino; 2 American Indian or Alaska Native, non-Hispanic/Latino; 19 Asian, non-Hispanic/Latino; 93 Hispanic/Latino; 41 Two or more races, non-Hispanic/Latino), 19 international. Average age 34. 1,234 applicants, 77% accepted, 730 enrolled. *Faculty:* 122 full-time (77 women), 36 part-time/adjunct (28 women). Expenses: Contact institution. *Financial support:* In 2019–20, 49 students received support, including 32 research assistantships (averaging $11,562 per year), 12 teaching assistantships (averaging $6,842 per year); career-related internships or fieldwork, institutionally sponsored loans, scholarships/grants, unspecified assistantships, and administrative assistantships also available. Support available to part-time students. Financial award application deadline: 3/1; financial award applicants required to submit FAFSA. In 2019, 266 master's, 42 doctorates, 255 other advanced degrees awarded. *Program availability:* Part-time, evening/weekend, 100% online, blended/hybrid learning. *Application deadline:* Applications are processed on a rolling basis. *Application fee:* $75. Electronic applications accepted. *Application Contact:* Kathy B. Giddings, Director of Graduate Admissions, 704-687-5503, Fax: 704-687-1668, E-mail: gradadm@uncc.edu. *Interim Dean & Profession*, Dr. Teresa Petty, 704-687-0995, E-mail: tmpetty@uncc.edu.

**College of Arts and Architecture** Students: 79 full-time (35 women), 7 part-time (2 women); includes 25 minority (11 Black or African American, non-Hispanic/Latino; 3 Asian, non-Hispanic/Latino; 8 Hispanic/Latino; 3 Two or more races, non-Hispanic/Latino), 13 international. Average age 26. 119 applicants, 87% accepted, 36 enrolled. *Faculty:* 46 full-time (20 women), 4 part-time/adjunct (0 women). Expenses: Contact institution. *Financial support:* In 2019–20, 21 students received support, including 12 research assistantships (averaging $6,113 per year), 9 teaching assistantships (averaging $3,206 per year); career-related internships or fieldwork, institutionally sponsored loans, unspecified assistantships, and administrative assistantship also available. Support available to part-time students. Financial award application deadline: 3/1; financial award applicants required to submit FAFSA. In 2019, 62 master's awarded. *Program availability:* Part-time. *Application deadline:* Applications are processed on a rolling basis. *Application fee:* $75. Electronic applications accepted. *Application Contact:* Kathy B. Giddings, Director of Graduate Admissions, 704-687-5503, Fax: 704-687-1668, E-mail: gradadm@uncc.edu. *Dean of the College of Arts + Architecture*, Brook Muller, 704-687-0100, E-mail: bmuller7@uncc.edu.

***School of Architecture*** Students: 79 full-time (35 women), 7 part-time (2 women); includes 25 minority (11 Black or African American, non-Hispanic/Latino; 3 Asian, non-Hispanic/Latino; 8 Hispanic/Latino; 3 Two or more races, non-Hispanic/Latino), 13 international. Average age 26. 119 applicants, 87% accepted, 36 enrolled. *Faculty:* 25 full-time (11 women), 4 part-time/adjunct (0 women). Expenses: Contact institution. *Financial support:* In 2019–20, 20 students received support, including 12 research assistantships (averaging $6,113 per year), 8 teaching assistantships (averaging $3,170 per year); institutionally sponsored loans, scholarships/grants, unspecified assistantships, and administrative assistantship also available. Financial award application deadline: 3/1; financial award applicants required to submit FAFSA. In 2019, 62 master's awarded. *Application deadline:* For fall admission, 1/15 priority date for domestic students. Applications are processed on a rolling basis. *Application fee:* $75. Electronic applications accepted. *Application Contact:* Kathy B. Giddings, Director of Graduate Admissions, 704-687-5503, Fax: 704-687-1668, E-mail: gradadm@uncc.edu. *Director, Graduate School Programs*, Peter Wong, 704-687-0134, E-mail: plwong@uncc.edu.

**College of Computing and Informatics** Students: 659 full-time (234 women), 229 part-time (81 women); includes 100 minority (35 Black or African American, non-Hispanic/Latino; 1 American Indian or Alaska Native, non-Hispanic/Latino; 36 Asian, non-Hispanic/Latino; 19 Hispanic/Latino; 1 Native Hawaiian or other Pacific Islander, non-Hispanic/Latino; 8 Two or more races, non-Hispanic/Latino), 661 international. Average age 26. 1,585 applicants, 45% accepted, 258 enrolled. *Faculty:* 75 full-time (26 women), 16 part-time/adjunct (3 women). Expenses: Contact institution. *Financial support:* In 2019–20, 236 students received support, including 11 fellowships (averaging $42,149 per year), 74 research assistantships (averaging $9,801 per year), 148 teaching assistantships (averaging $5,507 per year); career-related internships or fieldwork, institutionally sponsored loans, scholarships/grants, and unspecified assistantships also available. Support available to part-time students. Financial award application deadline: 3/1; financial award applicants required to submit FAFSA. In 2019, 296 master's, 28 doctorates, 23 other advanced degrees awarded. *Program availability:* Part-time, evening/weekend. *Application deadline:* Applications are processed on a rolling basis. *Application fee:* $75. Electronic applications accepted. *Application Contact:* Kathy B. Giddings, Director of Graduate Admissions, 704-687-5503, Fax: 704-687-1668, E-mail: gradadm@uncc.edu. *Dean*, Dr. Fatma Mili, 704-687-8450, E-mail: fmili@uncc.edu.

**College of Health and Human Services** Students: 399 full-time (324 women), 255 part-time (205 women); includes 219 minority (141 Black or African American, non-Hispanic/Latino; 27 Asian, non-Hispanic/Latino; 34 Hispanic/Latino; 1 Native Hawaiian or other Pacific Islander, non-Hispanic/Latino; 16 Two or more races, non-Hispanic/Latino), 14 international. Average age 32. 827 applicants, 53% accepted, 275 enrolled. *Faculty:* 85 full-time (58 women), 24 part-time/adjunct (22 women). Expenses: Contact institution. *Financial support:* In 2019–20, 86 students received support, including 33 research assistantships (averaging $7,155 per year), 42 teaching assistantships (averaging $10,254 per year); fellowships, career-related internships or fieldwork, institutionally sponsored loans, scholarships/grants, traineeships, unspecified assistantships, and administrative assistantships also available. Support available to part-time students. Financial award application deadline: 3/1; financial award applicants required to submit FAFSA. In 2019, 258 master's, 17 doctorates, 16 other advanced degrees awarded. *Program availability:* Part-time, evening/weekend, 100% online, blended/hybrid learning. *Application deadline:* Applications are processed on a rolling basis. *Application fee:* $75. Electronic applications accepted. *Application Contact:* Kathy B. Giddings, Director of Graduate Admissions, 704-687-5503, Fax: 704-687-1668, E-mail: gradadm@uncc.edu. *Dean*, Dr. Catrine Tudor-Locke, 704-687-7917, E-mail: tudor-locke@uncc.edu.

***School of Nursing*** Students: 126 full-time (96 women), 142 part-time (127 women); includes 70 minority (48 Black or African American, non-Hispanic/Latino; 8 Asian, non-Hispanic/Latino; 9 Hispanic/Latino; 5 Two or more races, non-Hispanic/Latino), 1 international. Average age 35. 347 applicants, 37% accepted, 104 enrolled. Expenses: Contact institution. *Financial support:* In 2019–20, 6 students received support, including 4 research assistantships (averaging $4,856 per year), 2 teaching assistantships (averaging $3,615 per year); career-related internships or fieldwork, institutionally sponsored loans, scholarships/grants, traineeships, and unspecified assistantships also available. Support available to part-time students. Financial award application deadline: 3/1; financial award applicants required to submit FAFSA. In 2019, 102 master's, 10 doctorates, 10 other advanced degrees awarded. *Program availability:* Part-time, blended/hybrid learning. *Application deadline:* Applications are processed on a rolling basis. *Application fee:* $75. Electronic applications accepted. *Application Contact:* Kathy B. Giddings, Director of Graduate Admissions, 704-687-5503, Fax: 704-687-1668, E-mail: gradadm@uncc.edu. *Director*, Dr. Dena Evans, 704-687-7974, E-mail: devans37@uncc.edu.

***School of Social Work*** Students: 142 full-time (125 women), 42 part-time (36 women); includes 82 minority (50 Black or African American, non-Hispanic/Latino; 8 Asian, non-Hispanic/Latino; 18 Hispanic/Latino; 6 Two or more races, non-Hispanic/Latino). Average age 29. 269 applicants, 58% accepted, 93 enrolled. *Faculty:* 15 full-time (11 women), 12 part-time/adjunct (all women). Expenses: Contact institution. *Financial support:* In 2019–20, 14 students received support, including 12 research assistantships (averaging $2,503 per year); career-related internships or fieldwork, Federal Work-Study, institutionally sponsored loans, scholarships/grants, unspecified assistantships, and administrative assistantship also available. Support available to part-time students. Financial award application deadline: 2/1; financial award applicants required to submit FAFSA. In 2019, 89 master's awarded. *Program availability:* Part-time. *Application deadline:* Applications are processed on a rolling basis. *Application fee:* $75. Electronic applications accepted. *Application Contact:* Kathy B. Giddings, Director of Graduate Admissions, 704-687-5503, Fax: 704-687-1668, E-mail: gradadm@uncc.edu. *Director of the School of Social Work*, Dr. Schnavia Smith Hatcher, 704-687-7938, E-mail: schnavia.hatcher@uncc.edu.

**College of Liberal Arts and Sciences** Students: 464 full-time (282 women), 329 part-time (199 women); includes 187 minority (77 Black or African American, non-Hispanic/Latino; 1 American Indian or Alaska Native, non-Hispanic/Latino; 27 Asian, non-Hispanic/Latino; 54 Hispanic/Latino; 28 Two or more races, non-Hispanic/Latino), 118 international. Average age 29. 693 applicants, 57% accepted, 231 enrolled. *Faculty:* 379 full-time (177 women), 17 part-time/adjunct (9 women). Expenses: Contact institution. *Financial support:* In 2019–20, 306 students received support, including 16 fellowships (averaging $46,051 per year), 114 research assistantships (averaging $9,831 per year), 175 teaching assistantships (averaging $11,113 per year); career-related internships or fieldwork, institutionally sponsored loans, scholarships/grants, and administrative assistantships also available. Support available to part-time students. Financial award applicants required to submit FAFSA. In 2019, 214 master's, 46 doctorates, 35 other advanced degrees awarded. *Program availability:* Part-time, evening/weekend. *Application deadline:* Applications are processed on a rolling basis. *Application fee:* $75. Electronic applications accepted. *Application Contact:* Kathy B. Giddings, Director of Graduate Admissions, 704-687-5503, Fax: 704-687-1668, E-mail: gradadm@uncc.edu. *Dean*, Dr. Nancy A. Gutierrez, 704-687-0081, E-mail: ngutierr@uncc.edu.

**The Graduate School** Students: 97 full-time (49 women), 137 part-time (66 women); includes 71 minority (25 Black or African American, non-Hispanic/Latino; 33 Asian, non-Hispanic/Latino; 10 Hispanic/Latino; 3 Two or more races, non-Hispanic/Latino), 75 international. Average age 32. 472 applicants, 38% accepted, 85 enrolled. *Faculty:* 5 full-time (all women), 1 (woman) part-time/adjunct. Expenses: Contact institution. *Financial support:* In 2019–20, 206 students received support, including 115 research assistantships (averaging $10,135 per year), 85 teaching assistantships (averaging $9,864 per year); career-related internships or fieldwork, institutionally sponsored loans, scholarships/grants, traineeships, unspecified assistantships, and administrative assistantships also available. Support available to part-time students. Financial award application deadline: 3/1; financial award applicants required to submit FAFSA. In 2019, 74 master's, 35 other advanced degrees awarded. *Program availability:* Part-time, evening/weekend. *Application deadline:* For fall admission, 3/1 priority date for domestic students; for spring admission, 10/1 priority date for domestic students; for summer admission, 5/1 priority date for domestic students. Applications are processed on a rolling basis. *Application fee:* $75. Electronic applications accepted. *Application Contact:* Kathy B. Giddings, Director of Graduate Admissions, 704-687-5503, Fax: 704-687-1668, E-mail: gradadm@uncc.edu. *Dean and Associate Provost*, Dr. Thomas L. Reynolds, 704-687-7248, E-mail: gradadm@uncc.edu.

**William States Lee College of Engineering** Students: 335 full-time (83 women), 181 part-time (31 women); includes 56 minority (16 Black or African American, non-Hispanic/Latino; 3 American Indian or Alaska Native, non-Hispanic/Latino; 16 Asian, non-Hispanic/Latino; 16 Hispanic/Latino; 5 Two or more races, non-Hispanic/Latino), 308 international. Average age 28. 619 applicants, 69% accepted, 126 enrolled. *Faculty:* 122 full-time (22 women), 8 part-time/adjunct (2 women). Expenses: Contact institution. *Financial support:* In 2019–20, 251 students received support, including 7 fellowships (averaging $46,500 per year), 136 research assistantships (averaging $9,241 per year), 106 teaching assistantships (averaging $9,072 per year); career-related internships or fieldwork, institutionally sponsored loans, scholarships/grants, and unspecified assistantships also available. Support available to part-time students. Financial award application deadline: 3/1; financial award applicants required to submit FAFSA. In 2019, 209 master's, 39 doctorates, 5 other advanced degrees awarded. *Program availability:* Part-time, evening/weekend, blended/hybrid learning. *Application deadline:* Applications are processed on a rolling basis. *Application fee:* $75. Electronic applications accepted. *Application Contact:* Kathy B. Giddings, Director of Graduate Admissions, 704-687-5503, Fax: 704-687-1668, E-mail: gradadm@uncc.edu. *Interim Dean*, Dr. Ronald E. Smelser, 704-687-8244, E-mail: rsmelser@uncc.edu.

## THE UNIVERSITY OF NORTH CAROLINA AT GREENSBORO, Greensboro, NC 27412-5001

**General Information** State-supported, coed, university. CGS member. *Graduate housing:* Room and/or apartments available to single students; on-campus housing not available to married students. Housing application deadline: 5/15. *Research affiliation:* Moses Cone Memorial Hospital, North Carolina Zoological Park, North Carolina Baptist Hospital.

**GRADUATE UNITS**

**Graduate School** *Program availability:* Part-time, evening/weekend, online learning. Electronic applications accepted.

***Bryan School of Business and Economics*** *Program availability:* Part-time. Electronic applications accepted.

***College of Arts and Sciences*** *Program availability:* Part-time. Electronic applications accepted.

***School of Education*** *Program availability:* Part-time, evening/weekend. Electronic applications accepted.

***School of Health and Human Sciences*** Electronic applications accepted.

***School of Music, Theatre and Dance*** Electronic applications accepted.

***School of Nursing*** Electronic applications accepted.

## THE UNIVERSITY OF NORTH CAROLINA AT PEMBROKE, Pembroke, NC 28372-1510

**General Information** State-supported, coed, comprehensive institution. CGS member. *Graduate housing:* Room and/or apartments available to single students; on-campus housing not available to married students. Housing application deadline: 4/15.

**GRADUATE UNITS**

**The Graduate School** Students: 1,345; includes 247 minority (121 Black or African American, non-Hispanic/Latino; 107 American Indian or Alaska Native, non-Hispanic/Latino; 5 Asian, non-Hispanic/Latino; 14 Hispanic/Latino). Average age 28.

*Faculty:* 145 full-time, 52 part-time/adjunct. Expenses: Contact institution. *Financial support:* In 2019–20, 40 research assistantships with partial tuition reimbursements (averaging $9,000 per year) were awarded; career-related internships or fieldwork, scholarships/grants, and unspecified assistantships also available. Support available to part-time students. Financial award application deadline: 8/4; financial award applicants required to submit FAFSA. In 2019, 366 master's awarded. *Program availability:* Part-time, evening/weekend, 100% online, blended/hybrid learning. *Application deadline:* For fall admission, 3/15 priority date for domestic and international students; for spring admission, 10/15 priority date for domestic and international students. Applications are processed on a rolling basis. *Application fee:* $55 ($60 for international students). Electronic applications accepted. *Application Contact:* Gary Locklear, Executive Assistant, 910-521-6271, Fax: 910-521-6751, E-mail: grad@uncp.edu. *Dean,* Dr. Irene P. Aiken, 910-521-6271, Fax: 910-521-6751, E-mail: grad@uncp.edu.

***School of Business*** *Program availability:* Part-time, evening/weekend.

***School of Education*** *Program availability:* Part-time, evening/weekend.

## UNIVERSITY OF NORTH CAROLINA SCHOOL OF THE ARTS, Winston-Salem, NC 27127-2738

**General Information** State-supported, coed, comprehensive institution. *Graduate housing:* Room and/or apartments available on a first-come, first-served basis to single students. Housing application deadline: 5/1.

**GRADUATE UNITS**

**School of Design and Production** Electronic applications accepted.

**School of Filmmaking** Electronic applications accepted.

**School of Music** Electronic applications accepted.

## THE UNIVERSITY OF NORTH CAROLINA WILMINGTON, Wilmington, NC 28403-3297

**General Information** State-supported, coed, comprehensive institution. CGS member. *Enrollment:* 17,499 graduate, professional, and undergraduate students; 1,036 full-time matriculated graduate/professional students (734 women), 1,595 part-time matriculated graduate/professional students (1,119 women). *Enrollment by degree level:* 2,333 master's, 191 doctoral, 107 other advanced degrees. *Graduate faculty:* 500 full-time (239 women). *Tuition, area resident:* Full-time $4719; part-time $326 per credit hour. Tuition, state resident: full-time $4719; part-time $326 per credit hour. Tuition, nonresident: full-time $18,548; part-time $1099 per credit hour. *Required fees:* $2738. Tuition and fees vary according to program. *Graduate housing:* Room and/or apartments available on a first-come, first-served basis to single students; on-campus housing not available to married students. Typical cost: $6790 per year ($10,897 including board). Room and board charges vary according to board plan and housing facility selected. Housing application deadline: 4/30. *Student services:* Campus employment opportunities, campus safety program, career counseling, exercise/wellness program, free psychological counseling, international student services, low-cost health insurance, multicultural affairs office, services for students with disabilities. *Library facilities:* William Madison Randall Library. *Collection:* Books: 482,109 (physical), 418,670 (digital/electronic); Serial titles: 3,636 (physical), 100,047 (digital/electronic); Databases: 358. Weekly public service hours: 137; study areas open 24 hours, 5–7 days a week; students can reserve study rooms. *Research affiliation:* Seatox Research Inc. (biotechnology research and development), CMS Technology (seafood technology and safety), A-1 Biochem Labs (pharmaceuticals development), O.TM Biotech (environmental testing), OCIS Biotechnology (pharmaceuticals development).

**Computer facilities:** Computer purchase and lease plans are available. 1,141 computers available on campus for general student use. A campuswide network can be accessed. Online class registration is available.
Website: http://www.uncw.edu/

**General Application Contact:** Kimberly Harris, Administrative Specialist, Graduate School, 910-962-7449, Fax: 910-962-3787, E-mail: harrisk@uncw.edu.

**GRADUATE UNITS**

**Cameron School of Business** Students: 224 full-time (106 women), 387 part-time (188 women); includes 95 minority (33 Black or African American, non-Hispanic/Latino; 3 American Indian or Alaska Native, non-Hispanic/Latino; 15 Asian, non-Hispanic/Latino; 30 Hispanic/Latino; 14 Two or more races, non-Hispanic/Latino), 20 international. Average age 31. 443 applicants, 79% accepted, 326 enrolled. *Faculty:* 88 full-time (30 women). Expenses: Contact institution. *Financial support:* Scholarships/grants and unspecified assistantships available. Financial award application deadline: 1/1; financial award applicants required to submit FAFSA. In 2019, 124 master's awarded. *Program availability:* Part-time, 100% online, blended/hybrid learning. *Application deadline:* Applications are processed on a rolling basis. *Application fee:* $75. Electronic applications accepted. *Application Contact:* Candace Wilhelm, Graduate Programs Coordinator, 910-962-3903, Fax: 910-962-2184, E-mail: wilhelmc@uncw.edu. *Dean,* Dr. Robert Burrus, 910-962-3226, Fax: 910-962-3815, E-mail: burrusr@uncw.edu.

**Center for Marine Science** Students: 9 full-time (6 women), 10 part-time (6 women). Average age 24. 5 applicants, 100% accepted, 5 enrolled. *Faculty:* 8 full-time (2 women). Expenses: Contact institution. *Financial support:* Scholarships/grants available. Financial award application deadline: 1/1; financial award applicants required to submit FAFSA. In 2019, 5 master's awarded. *Program availability:* Part-time. *Application deadline:* For fall admission, 7/1 for domestic students; for spring admission, 10/31 for domestic students. Applications are processed on a rolling basis. *Application fee:* $75. Electronic applications accepted. *Application Contact:* Dr. Stephen Skrabal, Director, 910-962-7160, E-mail: skrabals@uncw.edu. *Director,* Dr. Stephen Skrabal, 910-962-7160, E-mail: skrabals@uncw.edu.

**College of Arts and Sciences** Students: 290 full-time (207 women), 351 part-time (223 women); includes 106 minority (30 Black or African American, non-Hispanic/Latino; 5 American Indian or Alaska Native, non-Hispanic/Latino; 4 Asian, non-Hispanic/Latino; 43 Hispanic/Latino; 24 Two or more races, non-Hispanic/Latino), 12 international. Average age 28. 574 applicants, 59% accepted, 255 enrolled. *Faculty:* 245 full-time (103 women). Expenses: Contact institution. *Financial support:* Research assistantships, teaching assistantships, Federal Work-Study, scholarships/grants, unspecified assistantships, and tuition remission available. Support available to part-time students. Financial award application deadline: 1/1; financial award applicants required to submit FAFSA. In 2019, 202 master's, 2 doctorates, 21 other advanced degrees awarded. *Program availability:* Part-time. *Application deadline:* Applications are processed on a rolling basis. *Application fee:* $75. Electronic applications accepted. *Application Contact:* Kimberly Harris, Administrative Specialist, Graduate School, 910-962-7449, Fax: 910-962-3787, E-mail: harrisk@uncw.edu. *Interim Dean,* Dr. Rich Ogle, 910-962-7232, Fax: 910-962-3114, E-mail: ogler@uncw.edu.

**Interdisciplinary Program in Computer Science and Information Systems** Students: 11 full-time (5 women), 13 part-time (2 women); includes 2 minority (1 Asian, non-Hispanic/Latino; 1 Two or more races, non-Hispanic/Latino), 10 international. Average age 30. 23 applicants, 52% accepted, 6 enrolled. *Faculty:* 10 full-time (2 women). Expenses: Contact institution. *Financial support:* Scholarships/grants and unspecified assistantships available. Financial award application deadline: 1/1; financial award applicants required to submit FAFSA. In 2019, 8 master's awarded. *Application deadline:* For fall admission, 6/1 for domestic students; for spring admission, 11/15 for domestic students. Applications are processed on a rolling basis. *Application fee:* $75. Electronic applications accepted. *Application Contact:* Candace Wilhelm, Graduate Coordinator, 910-962-3903, Fax: 910-962-7457, E-mail: wilhelmc@uncw.edu. *Program Coordinator,* Dr. Clayton Ferner, 910-962-7552, E-mail: cferner@uncw.edu.

**School of Health and Applied Human Sciences** Students: 18 full-time (12 women), 33 part-time (22 women); includes 11 minority (4 Black or African American, non-Hispanic/Latino; 5 Hispanic/Latino; 2 Two or more races, non-Hispanic/Latino). Average age 28. 17 applicants, 88% accepted, 13 enrolled. *Faculty:* 16 full-time (9 women). Expenses: Contact institution. *Financial support:* Scholarships/grants and unspecified assistantships available. Financial award application deadline: 1/1; financial award applicants required to submit FAFSA. In 2019, 15 master's awarded. *Program availability:* Part-time. *Application deadline:* For fall admission, 7/1 for domestic students; for spring admission, 11/15 for domestic students; for summer admission, 3/15 for domestic students. Applications are processed on a rolling basis. *Application fee:* $75. Electronic applications accepted. *Application Contact:* Dr. Anne Glass, Program Coordinator, 910-962-7509, E-mail: glassa@uncw.edu. *Director,* Dr. Steve Elliott, 910-962-2115, Fax: 910-962-7073, E-mail: elliotts@uncw.edu.

**School of Nursing** Students: 171 full-time (156 women), 423 part-time (387 women); includes 117 minority (73 Black or African American, non-Hispanic/Latino; 6 American Indian or Alaska Native, non-Hispanic/Latino; 12 Asian, non-Hispanic/Latino; 16 Hispanic/Latino; 1 Native Hawaiian or other Pacific Islander, non-Hispanic/Latino; 9 Two or more races, non-Hispanic/Latino). Average age 38. 527 applicants, 57% accepted, 199 enrolled. *Faculty:* 51 full-time (46 women). Expenses: Contact institution. *Financial support:* Scholarships/grants available. Financial award application deadline: 1/1; financial award applicants required to submit FAFSA. In 2019, 149 master's, 9 doctorates awarded. *Program availability:* Part-time, 100% online, blended/hybrid learning. *Application deadline:* For fall admission, 4/15 for domestic students. Applications are processed on a rolling basis. *Application fee:* $75. Electronic applications accepted. *Application Contact:* Dr. Sarah Hubbell, MSN Graduate Coordinator, 910-962-0561, E-mail: hubbells@uncw.edu. *Director,* Dr. Linda Haddad, 910-962-7410, Fax: 910-962-3723, E-mail: haddadl@uncw.edu.

**School of Social Work** Students: 110 full-time (98 women), 24 part-time (17 women); includes 31 minority (10 Black or African American, non-Hispanic/Latino; 2 Asian, non-Hispanic/Latino; 15 Hispanic/Latino; 1 Native Hawaiian or other Pacific Islander, non-Hispanic/Latino; 3 Two or more races, non-Hispanic/Latino). Average age 29. 113 applicants, 72% accepted, 47 enrolled. *Faculty:* 12 full-time (7 women). Expenses: Contact institution. *Financial support:* Teaching assistantships and scholarships/grants available. Financial award application deadline: 1/1; financial award applicants required to submit FAFSA. In 2019, 69 master's awarded. *Program availability:* Part-time. *Application deadline:* For fall admission, 4/15 for domestic students; for summer admission, 4/15 for domestic students. Applications are processed on a rolling basis. *Application fee:* $75. Electronic applications accepted. *Application Contact:* Dr. Kristin Bolton, MSW Coordinator, 910-962-2308, Fax: 910-962-7283, E-mail: boltonk@uncw.edu. *Director,* Dr. Stacey Kolomer, 910-962-2853, Fax: 910-962-7283, E-mail: kolomers@uncw.edu.

**Watson College of Education** Students: 157 full-time (126 women), 354 part-time (274 women); includes 143 minority (93 Black or African American, non-Hispanic/Latino; 12 American Indian or Alaska Native, non-Hispanic/Latino; 5 Asian, non-Hispanic/Latino; 16 Hispanic/Latino; 2 Native Hawaiian or other Pacific Islander, non-Hispanic/Latino; 15 Two or more races, non-Hispanic/Latino), 1 international. Average age 35. 263 applicants, 78% accepted, 160 enrolled. *Faculty:* 52 full-time (35 women). Expenses: Contact institution. *Financial support:* Scholarships/grants and unspecified assistantships available. Financial award application deadline: 1/1; financial award applicants required to submit FAFSA. In 2019, 155 master's, 17 doctorates awarded. *Program availability:* Part-time. *Application deadline:* Applications are processed on a rolling basis. *Application fee:* $75. Electronic applications accepted. *Application Contact:* Kimberly Harris, Administrative Specialist, Graduate School, 910-962-7449, Fax: 910-962-3787, E-mail: harrisk@uncw.edu. *Dean,* Dr. Van Dempsey, 910-962-3354, Fax: 910-962-4081, E-mail: dempseyv@uncw.edu.

## UNIVERSITY OF NORTH DAKOTA, Grand Forks, ND 58202

**General Information** State-supported, coed, university. CGS member. *Graduate housing:* Rooms and/or apartments guaranteed to single students and available on a first-come, first-served basis to married students. *Research affiliation:* U.S. Department of Agriculture (USDA), Human Nutrition Research Center, Neuropsychiatric Research Institute (neurosciences), Environmental Energy Research Center.

**GRADUATE UNITS**

**Graduate School** *Program availability:* Part-time, evening/weekend, online learning. Electronic applications accepted.

***College of Arts and Sciences*** *Program availability:* Part-time, online learning. Electronic applications accepted.

***College of Business and Public Administration*** *Program availability:* Part-time, evening/weekend, online learning. Electronic applications accepted.

***College of Education and Human Development*** *Program availability:* Part-time, evening/weekend, online learning. Electronic applications accepted.

***College of Nursing and Professional Disciplines*** *Program availability:* Part-time, evening/weekend, online learning. Electronic applications accepted.

***John D. Odegard School of Aerospace Sciences*** *Program availability:* Part-time, evening/weekend, online learning. Electronic applications accepted.

***School of Engineering and Mines*** *Program availability:* Part-time. Electronic applications accepted.

**School of Law**

**School of Medicine and Health Sciences** *Program availability:* Online learning.

## UNIVERSITY OF NORTHERN BRITISH COLUMBIA, Prince George, BC V2N 4Z9, Canada

**General Information** Province-supported, coed, university. *Graduate housing:* Room and/or apartments available on a first-come, first-served basis to single students; on-campus housing not available to married students. Housing application deadline: 2/15. *Research affiliation:* Houston Forest Products (forestry–wood debris management), TRC Cedar Ltd. (forestry–cyanolicen growth rate study), Remote Law Online Systems Corporation (computer science), Canadian Natural Oils Ltd. (chemistry–oil fractionation), Stella Jones, Inc. (forestry–Douglas fir cores), Insurance Corporation of British Columbia (moose involved in highway traffic accidents).

**GRADUATE UNITS**

**Office of Graduate Studies** *Program availability:* Part-time, evening/weekend, online learning.

## UNIVERSITY OF NORTHERN COLORADO, Greeley, CO 80639

**General Information** State-supported, coed, university. CGS member. *Graduate housing:* Rooms and/or apartments available on a first-come, first-served basis to single and married students. Housing application deadline: 5/30.

**GRADUATE UNITS**

**Graduate School** *Program availability:* Part-time, evening/weekend, online learning. Electronic applications accepted.

***College of Education and Behavioral Sciences*** *Program availability:* Part-time, online learning.

***College of Humanities and Social Sciences*** *Program availability:* Part-time. Electronic applications accepted.

***College of Natural and Health Sciences*** Electronic applications accepted.

***College of Performing and Visual Arts*** *Program availability:* Part-time. Electronic applications accepted.

***Monfort College of Business***

## UNIVERSITY OF NORTHERN IOWA, Cedar Falls, IA 50614

**General Information** State-supported, coed, comprehensive institution. CGS member. *Graduate housing:* Rooms and/or apartments available on a first-come, first-served basis to single and married students.

**GRADUATE UNITS**

**Graduate College** *Program availability:* Part-time, evening/weekend. Electronic applications accepted.

***College of Business Administration*** *Program availability:* Part-time, evening/weekend.

***College of Education*** *Program availability:* Part-time, evening/weekend. Electronic applications accepted.

***College of Humanities, Arts and Sciences*** *Program availability:* Part-time, evening/weekend. Electronic applications accepted.

***College of Social and Behavioral Sciences*** *Program availability:* Part-time, evening/weekend. Electronic applications accepted.

## UNIVERSITY OF NORTH FLORIDA, Jacksonville, FL 32224

**General Information** State-supported, coed, comprehensive institution. CGS member. *Graduate housing:* Room and/or apartments available on a first-come, first-served basis to single students; on-campus housing not available to married students. Housing application deadline: 6/1.

**GRADUATE UNITS**

**Brooks College of Health** *Program availability:* Part-time, evening/weekend. Electronic applications accepted.

***School of Nursing*** *Program availability:* Part-time. Electronic applications accepted.

**Coggin College of Business** *Program availability:* Part-time, evening/weekend. Electronic applications accepted.

**College of Arts and Sciences** *Program availability:* Part-time, evening/weekend. Electronic applications accepted.

**College of Computing, Engineering, and Construction** *Program availability:* Part-time. Electronic applications accepted.

***School of Computing*** *Program availability:* Part-time. Electronic applications accepted.

***School of Engineering*** *Program availability:* Part-time.

**College of Education and Human Services** *Program availability:* Part-time, evening/weekend. Electronic applications accepted.

## UNIVERSITY OF NORTH GEORGIA, Dahlonega, GA 30597

**General Information** State-supported, coed, comprehensive institution. *Enrollment:* 19,748 graduate, professional, and undergraduate students; 194 full-time matriculated graduate/professional students (151 women), 471 part-time matriculated graduate/professional students (314 women). *Enrollment by degree level:* 555 master's, 109 doctoral, 1 other advanced degree. *Graduate faculty:* 79 full-time (41 women), 7 part-time/adjunct (5 women). *Graduate housing:* Room and/or apartments available on a first-come, first-served basis to single students; on-campus housing not available to married students. Housing application deadline: 2/1. *Student services:* Campus employment opportunities, campus safety program, career counseling, exercise/wellness program, free psychological counseling, international student services, multicultural affairs office, services for students with disabilities, teacher training, writing training. *Library facilities:* Library Technology Center plus 4 others. *Collection:* Books: 195,525 (physical), 433,929 (digital/electronic); Serial titles: 168 (physical); Databases: 298. Weekly public service hours: 94; students can reserve study rooms. *Research affiliation:* Northeast Georgia Medical Center, Morehouse School of Medicine, St. Joseph's Hospital, Mettler Electronic Corporation.

**Computer facilities:** 3,500 computers available on campus for general student use. A campuswide network can be accessed. Online class registration is available.
Website: http://www.ung.edu/

**General Application Contact:** Cory Thornton, Director of Graduate Admissions, 706-867-2077, E-mail: cory.thornton@ung.edu.

**GRADUATE UNITS**

**Department of Counseling** Expenses: Contact institution.

**Department of Criminal Justice** Students: 2 full-time (1 woman), 24 part-time (18 women); includes 10 minority (2 Black or African American, non-Hispanic/Latino; 2 Asian, non-Hispanic/Latino; 3 Hispanic/Latino; 3 Two or more races, non-Hispanic/Latino). Average age 32. Expenses: Contact institution. *Application Contact:* Cory Thornton, Director of Graduate Admissions, 706-867-2077, E-mail: cory.thornton@ung.edu. *Department Head,* Dr. Douglas Orr, 706-867-3084, E-mail: douglas.orr@ung.edu.

**Department of History, Anthropology and Philosophy** Expenses: Contact institution. *Application Contact:* Cory Thornton, Director of Graduate Admissions, 706-867-2077, E-mail: cory.thornton@ung.edu. *Department Head,* Dr. Jeff Pardue, 678-717-3867.

**Department of Physical Therapy** Students: 95 full-time (72 women), 4 part-time (3 women); includes 9 minority (1 Asian, non-Hispanic/Latino; 6 Hispanic/Latino; 2 Two or more races, non-Hispanic/Latino), 6 international. Average age 26. *Faculty:* 8 full-time (4 women). Expenses: Contact institution. *Application deadline:* For summer admission, 10/1 for domestic students. Applications are processed on a rolling basis. *Application fee:* $50. Electronic applications accepted. *Application Contact:* Cory Thornton, Director of Graduate Admissions, 706-867-2077, E-mail: cory.thornton@ung.edu. *Department Head,* Dr. Susan Klappa, E-mail: susan.klappa@ung.edu.

**DNP Program**

**Doctor of Education Program in Higher Education Leadership and Practice** Expenses: Contact institution.

**Ed S in Educational Leadership Program** Students: 3 full-time (all women), 8 part-time (2 women); includes 6 minority (4 Black or African American, non-Hispanic/Latino; 1 Hispanic/Latino; 1 Two or more races, non-Hispanic/Latino). Average age 39. 30 applicants, 93% accepted, 18 enrolled. *Faculty:* 1 (woman) full-time, 38 part-time/adjunct (32 women). Expenses: Contact institution. *Financial support:* Application deadline: 3/17; applicants required to submit FAFSA. *Program availability:* Part-time, evening/weekend, blended/hybrid learning. *Application deadline:* For fall admission, 7/15 for domestic students. *Application fee:* $40. Electronic applications accepted. *Application Contact:* Cory Thornton, Director of Graduate Admissions, 706-867-2077, E-mail: cory.thornton@ung.edu. *Dean,* Dr. Sheri Hardee, 706-864-1998, E-mail: susan.ayres@ung.edu.

**Master of Arts in Teaching Program** Students: 20 part-time (15 women); includes 3 minority (2 Hispanic/Latino; 1 Two or more races, non-Hispanic/Latino). Average age 28. Expenses: Contact institution. *Application deadline:* For summer admission, 2/1 for domestic students. *Application fee:* $40. Electronic applications accepted.

**Program in Athletic Training** Students: 7 full-time (5 women), 1 part-time (0 women). Average age 24. *Faculty:* 15 full-time (6 women), 3 part-time/adjunct (all women). Expenses: Contact institution. *Application deadline:* For summer admission, 4/1 priority date for domestic students. *Application fee:* $40. Electronic applications accepted. *Application Contact:* Cory Thornton, Director of Graduate Admissions, 706-867-2077, E-mail: cory.thornton@ung.edu. *Dean,* Dr. Sheri Hardee, 706-864-1998, E-mail: sheri.hardee@ung.edu.

**Program in Curriculum and Instruction** Expenses: Contact institution.

**Program in Early Childhood Education** Expenses: Contact institution. *Application deadline:* For fall admission, 7/24 for domestic students; for spring admission, 12/12 for domestic students; for summer admission, 4/26 for domestic students. *Application fee:* $40. Electronic applications accepted.

**Program in Family Nurse Practitioner** Students: 70 part-time (61 women); includes 17 minority (3 Black or African American, non-Hispanic/Latino; 8 Asian, non-Hispanic/Latino; 4 Hispanic/Latino; 1 Native Hawaiian or other Pacific Islander, non-Hispanic/Latino; 1 Two or more races, non-Hispanic/Latino). Average age 34. 3 applicants, 33% accepted. Expenses: Contact institution. *Financial support:* Application deadline: 3/17; applicants required to submit FAFSA. *Application deadline:* For summer admission, 2/28 for domestic students. *Application fee:* $40. Electronic applications accepted.

**Program in Human Services and Delivery Administration** Expenses: Contact institution.

**Program in International Affairs** Expenses: Contact institution.

**Program in Kinesiology** Expenses: Contact institution.

**Program in Middle Grades Math and Science** Expenses: Contact institution.

**Program in Nursing Education** Students: 16 part-time (all women); includes 1 minority (Black or African American, non-Hispanic/Latino). Average age 40. Expenses: Contact institution. *Financial support:* Application deadline: 3/17; applicants required to submit FAFSA. In 2019, 2 master's awarded. *Program availability:* Part-time, evening/weekend, online only, Online program, with minimal campus visits required.

**Program in Public Administration** Expenses: Contact institution.

## UNIVERSITY OF NORTH TEXAS, Denton, TX 76203

**General Information** State-supported, coed, university. CGS member. *Graduate housing:* Rooms and/or apartments available on a first-come, first-served basis to single and married students. Housing application deadline: 9/1. *Research affiliation:* Delta and Pine Land Company (natural science), Semiconductor Research Corporation (materials science), Tech America (technology transfer), National Business Incubation Association (entrepreneurship), International Economic Development Council (economic growth).

**GRADUATE UNITS**

**Toulouse Graduate School** *Program availability:* Part-time, evening/weekend, online learning. Electronic applications accepted.

## UNIVERSITY OF NORTH TEXAS AT DALLAS, Dallas, TX 75241

**General Information** State-supported, coed, comprehensive institution.

**GRADUATE UNITS**

**College of Law**

**Graduate School**

## UNIVERSITY OF NORTH TEXAS HEALTH SCIENCE CENTER AT FORT WORTH, Fort Worth, TX 76107-2699

**General Information** State-supported, coed, graduate-only institution. CGS member. *Graduate housing:* On-campus housing not available. *Research affiliation:* Myogen, Inc. (cardiac research), My-tech, Inc. (cardiovascular research), Novopharm, Inc. (gene control), Ethnobotanical Product Investigation Consortium (natural plant products), Genelink (familial DNA depository), Botanical Research Institutions of Texas.

**GRADUATE UNITS**

**Graduate School of Biomedical Sciences**

**School of Health Professions**

**School of Public Health** *Program availability:* Part-time, evening/weekend, 100% online. Electronic applications accepted.

**Texas College of Osteopathic Medicine** Electronic applications accepted.

## UNIVERSITY OF NORTHWESTERN OHIO, Lima, OH 45805-1498

**General Information** Independent, coed, comprehensive institution.

**GRADUATE UNITS**

**Graduate College** *Program availability:* Evening/weekend, online learning.

## UNIVERSITY OF NORTHWESTERN–ST. PAUL, St. Paul, MN 55113-1598

**General Information** Independent-religious, coed, comprehensive institution. *Graduate housing:* On-campus housing not available. *Student services:* Campus safety program, career counseling, international student services, multicultural affairs office, services for students with disabilities, writing training. *Library facilities:* Berntsen Resource Center. *Collection:* Books: 86,024 (physical), 363,470 (digital/electronic); Serial titles: 627

(physical), 52,723 (digital/electronic); Databases: 106. Students can reserve study rooms.

**Computer facilities:** 200 computers available on campus for general student use. A campuswide network can be accessed. Online class registration, network file space, personal website, integrated student portal, b/w and color printing, virtual labs are available.
Website: http://www.unwsp.edu/

**General Application Contact:** Tami Treder, Graduate Admission Counselor, 651-628-3351, E-mail: tjtreder@unwsp.edu.

**GRADUATE UNITS**

**Master of Arts in Education Program** *Program availability:* Part-time, evening/weekend, online learning. Electronic applications accepted.

**Master of Arts in Human Services Program** *Program availability:* Part-time, evening/weekend, online learning. Electronic applications accepted.

**Master of Arts in Theological Studies Program** *Program availability:* Part-time, evening/weekend, online learning. Electronic applications accepted.

**Master of Business Administration Program** *Program availability:* Part-time, evening/weekend, online learning. Electronic applications accepted.

**Master of Divinity Program** *Program availability:* Part-time, evening/weekend, online learning. Electronic applications accepted.

**Master of Organizational Leadership Program** *Program availability:* Part-time, evening/weekend, online learning. Electronic applications accepted.

## UNIVERSITY OF NOTRE DAME, Notre Dame, IN 46556

**General Information** Independent-religious, coed, university. CGS member. *Graduate housing:* Rooms and/or apartments available on a first-come, first-served basis to single and married students. Housing application deadline: 5/1. *Research affiliation:* Space Telescope Science Institute, Brookhaven National Laboratory, Fermi National Accelerator Laboratory, Argonne National Laboratory.

**GRADUATE UNITS**

**The Graduate School** *Program availability:* Part-time. Electronic applications accepted.

***College of Arts and Letters*** *Program availability:* Part-time. Electronic applications accepted.

***College of Engineering*** Electronic applications accepted.

***College of Science*** Electronic applications accepted.

***Keough School of Global Affairs***

***Kroc Institute for International Peace Studies*** Electronic applications accepted.

***School of Architecture*** Electronic applications accepted.

**Institute for Educational Initiatives** Electronic applications accepted.

**The Law School** Electronic applications accepted.

**Mendoza College of Business** Students: 647 full-time (208 women), 47 part-time (29 women); includes 98 minority (20 Black or African American, non-Hispanic/Latino; 23 Asian, non-Hispanic/Latino; 36 Hispanic/Latino; 1 Native Hawaiian or other Pacific Islander, non-Hispanic/Latino; 18 Two or more races, non-Hispanic/Latino), 152 international. Average age 28. 1,495 applicants, 57% accepted, 534 enrolled. *Faculty:* 90 full-time (19 women), 47 part-time/adjunct (11 women). Expenses: Contact institution. *Financial support:* In 2019–20, 594 students received support. Fellowships available. Financial award application deadline: 2/28; financial award applicants required to submit FAFSA. In 2019, 501 master's awarded. *Application deadline:* Applications are processed on a rolling basis. Electronic applications accepted. *Application Contact:* Brian Connelly, Director of Marketing & Admissions, 574-631-1394, E-mail: bconnel2@nd.edu. *Martin J. Gillen Dean, and the Bernard J. Hank Professor of Finance,* Dr. Martijn Cremers, 574-631-1691, Fax: 574-631-4825, E-mail: mcremers@nd.edu.

## UNIVERSITY OF OKLAHOMA, Norman, OK 73019-0390

**General Information** State-supported, coed, university. CGS member. *Enrollment:* 31,207 graduate, professional, and undergraduate students; 2,851 full-time matriculated graduate/professional students (1,467 women), 3,345 part-time matriculated graduate/professional students (1,825 women). *Enrollment by degree level:* 4,238 master's, 1,929 doctoral, 29 other advanced degrees. *Graduate faculty:* 1,041 full-time (369 women), 53 part-time/adjunct (23 women). *International tuition:* $21,242.40 full-time. Tuition, state resident: full-time $6583.20; part-time $274.30 per credit hour. Tuition, nonresident: full-time $21,242; part-time $885.10 per credit hour. *Required fees:* $1994.20; $72.55 per credit hour. $126.50 per semester. Tuition and fees vary according to course load and degree level. *Graduate housing:* Rooms and/or apartments available on a first-come, first-served basis to single and married students. Typical cost: $5123 per year ($9739 including board) for single students; $8472 per year ($13,088 including board) for married students. Room and board charges vary according to board plan, campus/location and housing facility selected. Housing application deadline: 5/9. *Student services:* Campus employment opportunities, campus safety program, career counseling, child daycare facilities, exercise/wellness program, free psychological counseling, grant writing training, international student services, low-cost health insurance, multicultural affairs office, services for students with disabilities, teacher training, writing training. *Library facilities:* Bizzell Memorial Library plus 5 others. *Collection:* Books: 4.4 million (physical), 1.4 million (digital/electronic); Serial titles: 71,289 (physical), 128,934 (digital/electronic); Databases: 311. Weekly public service hours: 114; students can reserve study rooms. *Research affiliation:* National Oceanic and Atmospheric Administration (NOAA)/National Severe Storms Laboratory (weather), Nanowave Technologies, Inc. (radar), Department of the Interior South Central Region Climate Science Center (climate science), Weathernews Americas (weather), Sandia National Laboratories (national security), U.S. Department of Transportation Southern Plains Transportation Center (transportation infrastructure).

**Computer facilities:** Computer purchase and lease plans are available. 4,500 computers available on campus for general student use. A campuswide network can be accessed. Online class registration is available.
Website: http://www.ou.edu/

**General Application Contact:** Dr. Randall S. Hewes, Dean, Graduate College, 405-325-3811, Fax: 405-325-5346, E-mail: gradinfo@ou.edu.

**GRADUATE UNITS**

**Christopher C. Gibbs College of Architecture** *Program availability:* Part-time. Electronic applications accepted.

***Division of Architecture*** *Program availability:* Part-time. Electronic applications accepted.

***Division of Interior Design*** *Program availability:* Part-time. Electronic applications accepted.

***Division of Landscape Architecture*** Electronic applications accepted.

***Division of Regional and City Planning*** *Program availability:* Part-time. Electronic applications accepted.

***Haskell and Irene Lemon Division of Construction Science*** *Program availability:* Part-time. Electronic applications accepted.

**College of Arts and Sciences** *Program availability:* Part-time, evening/weekend, online learning. Electronic applications accepted.

***Anne and Henry Zarrow School of Social Work*** *Program availability:* Part-time, evening/weekend. Electronic applications accepted.

***School of Library and Information Studies*** *Program availability:* Part-time, evening/weekend, 100% online, blended/hybrid learning. Electronic applications accepted.

**College of Atmospheric and Geographic Sciences** *Program availability:* Part-time. Electronic applications accepted.

***School of Meteorology*** Electronic applications accepted.

**College of Law** *Program availability:* Part-time, 100% online. Electronic applications accepted.

**College of Professional and Continuing Studies** *Program availability:* Part-time, 100% online, blended/hybrid learning. Electronic applications accepted.

**David L. Boren College of International Studies** *Program availability:* Part-time, online courses with an 8-10 day study abroad. Electronic applications accepted.

**Gallogly College of Engineering** *Program availability:* Part-time. Electronic applications accepted.

***School of Aerospace and Mechanical Engineering*** *Program availability:* Part-time. Electronic applications accepted.

***School of Chemical, Biological and Materials Engineering*** *Program availability:* Part-time. Electronic applications accepted.

***School of Civil Engineering and Environmental Science*** *Program availability:* Part-time. Electronic applications accepted.

***School of Computer Science*** *Program availability:* Part-time. Electronic applications accepted.

***School of Electrical and Computer Engineering*** *Program availability:* Part-time. Electronic applications accepted.

***School of Industrial and Systems Engineering*** Electronic applications accepted.

***Stephenson School of Biomedical Engineering*** *Program availability:* Part-time. Electronic applications accepted.

**Gaylord College of Journalism and Mass Communication** *Program availability:* Part-time. Electronic applications accepted.

**Graduate College** *Program availability:* Part-time, evening/weekend, blended/hybrid learning. Electronic applications accepted.

**Jeannine Rainbolt College of Education** *Program availability:* Part-time, evening/weekend. Electronic applications accepted.

**Mewbourne College of Earth and Energy** *Program availability:* Part-time, evening/weekend. Electronic applications accepted.

***ConocoPhillips School of Geology and Geophysics*** *Program availability:* Part-time. Electronic applications accepted.

***Mewbourne School of Petroleum and Geological Engineering*** *Program availability:* Part-time, evening/weekend. Electronic applications accepted.

**Price College of Business** *Program availability:* Part-time, evening/weekend, 100% online. Electronic applications accepted.

***Division of Management Information Systems*** *Program availability:* Part-time, evening/weekend. Electronic applications accepted.

***John T. Steed School of Accounting*** *Program availability:* Part-time, 100% online. Electronic applications accepted.

**Weitzenhoffer Family College of Fine Arts** Electronic applications accepted.

***Helmerich School of Drama*** Electronic applications accepted.

***School of Dance*** Electronic applications accepted.

***School of Music*** Electronic applications accepted.

***School of Visual Arts*** Electronic applications accepted.

## UNIVERSITY OF OKLAHOMA HEALTH SCIENCES CENTER, Oklahoma City, OK 73190

**General Information** State-supported, coed, upper-level institution. CGS member. *Graduate housing:* Rooms and/or apartments available on a first-come, first-served basis to single and married students. *Research affiliation:* Veterans Administration Medical Center (clinical and applied medicine), University of Oklahoma Medical Center, Peggy and Charles Stephenson Oklahoma Cancer Center (cancer research), Oklahoma Medical Research Foundation, Dean A. McGee Eye Institute (ophthalmology), Oklahoma Children's Memorial Hospital (pediatrics).

**GRADUATE UNITS**

**College of Dentistry** Electronic applications accepted.

**College of Medicine** Electronic applications accepted.

**College of Pharmacy**

**Graduate College** *Program availability:* Part-time, evening/weekend.

***College of Allied Health*** *Program availability:* Part-time.

***College of Nursing*** *Program availability:* Part-time.

***Hudson College of Public Health*** *Program availability:* Part-time.

## UNIVERSITY OF OREGON, Eugene, OR 97403

**General Information** State-supported, coed, university. CGS member. *Graduate housing:* Rooms and/or apartments available to single and married students. *Research affiliation:* Oregon Research Institute, Battelle–Pacific Northwest National Laboratory, National Renewable Energy Laboratory (NREL), Stanford Linear Accelerator Center, Naval Research Laboratories.

**GRADUATE UNITS**

**Graduate School** *Program availability:* Part-time, evening/weekend.

***Charles H. Lundquist College of Business*** *Program availability:* Part-time, evening/weekend.

***College of Arts and Sciences*** *Program availability:* Part-time, evening/weekend.

***College of Design*** *Program availability:* Part-time, evening/weekend.

***College of Education*** *Program availability:* Part-time.

***School of Journalism and Communication*** *Program availability:* Part-time.

***School of Music*** *Program availability:* Part-time.

**School of Law**

## UNIVERSITY OF OTTAWA, Ottawa, ON K1N 6N5, Canada

**General Information** Province-supported, coed, university. *Graduate housing:* Rooms and/or apartments available on a first-come, first-served basis to single and married students. Housing application deadline: 3/15. *Research affiliation:* IBM (performance analytics software, supercomputing), General Electric Company (GE) (hardware, imaging, medical devices), Rio Tinto Alcan (aluminum and aluminum products), Pratt and Whitney Canada (turbine engines, advanced materials, aerospace), Wright Medical Technology Canada (orthopedic medical devices), Air Products and Chemicals Inc. (industrial gases (hydrogen), performance materials, equipment and technology).

**GRADUATE UNITS**

**Faculty of Graduate and Postdoctoral Studies** *Program availability:* Part-time, evening/weekend. Electronic applications accepted.

***Faculty of Arts*** *Program availability:* Part-time, evening/weekend. Electronic applications accepted.

***Faculty of Education*** *Program availability:* Online learning. Electronic applications accepted.

***Faculty of Engineering*** Electronic applications accepted.

***Faculty of Health Sciences*** *Program availability:* Part-time, evening/weekend. Electronic applications accepted.

***Faculty of Law*** *Program availability:* Part-time, evening/weekend. Electronic applications accepted.

***Faculty of Medicine*** Electronic applications accepted.

***Faculty of Science*** *Program availability:* Part-time, evening/weekend. Electronic applications accepted.

***Faculty of Social Sciences*** *Program availability:* Part-time, evening/weekend. Electronic applications accepted.

***Telfer School of Management*** *Program availability:* Part-time, evening/weekend. Electronic applications accepted.

## UNIVERSITY OF PENNSYLVANIA, Philadelphia, PA 19104

**General Information** Independent, coed, university. CGS member. *Enrollment:* 22,432 graduate, professional, and undergraduate students; 11,053 full-time matriculated graduate/professional students (5,787 women), 1,959 part-time matriculated graduate/professional students (1,269 women). *Enrollment by degree level:* 7,003 master's, 5,843 doctoral, 166 other advanced degrees. *Graduate housing:* Rooms and/or apartments available on a first-come, first-served basis to single and married students. *Student services:* Campus employment opportunities, campus safety program, career counseling, child daycare facilities, exercise/wellness program, free psychological counseling, international student services, low-cost health insurance, multicultural affairs office, services for students with disabilities, writing training. *Library facilities:* Van Pelt Library plus 13 others. *Collection:* Books: 6.7 million (physical), 2 million (digital/electronic); Serial titles: 282,857 (physical), 279,206 (digital/electronic). Study areas open 24 hours, 5–7 days a week; students can reserve study rooms. *Research affiliation:* Children's Hospital of Philadelphia, The Wistar Institute (anatomy and biology), BioAdvance, Regional Nanotechnology Center.

**Computer facilities:** Computer purchase and lease plans are available. A campuswide network can be accessed. Online class registration, billing information, financial aid application, status, academic records, student services are available.
Website: http://www.upenn.edu/

**GRADUATE UNITS**

**Annenberg School for Communication** Students: 68 full-time (43 women), 1 (woman) part-time; includes 17 minority (6 Black or African American, non-Hispanic/Latino; 4 Asian, non-Hispanic/Latino; 5 Hispanic/Latino; 2 Two or more races, non-Hispanic/Latino), 18 international. Average age 30. 247 applicants, 6% accepted, 11 enrolled. *Faculty:* 18 full-time (7 women), 7 part-time/adjunct (2 women). Expenses: Contact institution. *Financial support:* In 2019–20, 80 students received support. In 2019, 17 doctorates awarded. *Application fee:* $70. *Application Contact:* Joanne Murray, Assistant Dean for Graduate Studies, 215-573-6349, Fax: 215-898-2024, E-mail: joanne.murray@asc.upenn.edu. *Dean*, John L. Jackson, Jr..

**Graduate School of Education** Students: 1,126 full-time (798 women), 390 part-time (284 women); includes 487 minority (204 Black or African American, non-Hispanic/Latino; 109 Asian, non-Hispanic/Latino; 123 Hispanic/Latino; 51 Two or more races, non-Hispanic/Latino), 396 international. Average age 31. 3,105 applicants, 51% accepted, 888 enrolled. *Faculty:* 68 full-time (28 women), 47 part-time/adjunct (24 women). Expenses: Contact institution. In 2019, 559 master's, 77 doctorates awarded. *Program availability:* Part-time, evening/weekend, online learning. *Application fee:* $75. Electronic applications accepted. *Application Contact:* Dr. Pam Grossman, Dean, 215-898-7014, Fax: 215-746-6884. *Dean*, Dr. Pam Grossman, 215-898-7014, Fax: 215-746-6884.

***Division of Educational Linguistics*** Students: 159 full-time (134 women), 14 part-time (11 women); includes 19 minority (2 Black or African American, non-Hispanic/Latino; 12 Asian, non-Hispanic/Latino; 3 Hispanic/Latino; 2 Two or more races, non-Hispanic/Latino), 140 international. Average age 26. 488 applicants, 43% accepted, 106 enrolled. Expenses: Contact institution. *Financial support:* Fellowships, research assistantships, teaching assistantships, Federal Work-Study, scholarships/grants, health care benefits, and unspecified assistantships available. In 2019, 91 master's, 6 doctorates awarded. *Program availability:* Part-time. *Application deadline:* For fall admission, 12/8 priority date for domestic and international students. Applications are processed on a rolling basis. *Application fee:* $75. Electronic applications accepted. *Application Contact:* Kristina Lewis, Program Manager, 215-898-5212, E-mail: klewi@upenn.edu. *Program Manager*, Kristina Lewis, 215-898-5212, E-mail: klewi@upenn.edu.

***Division of Education Policy*** Students: 37 full-time (30 women), 6 part-time (4 women); includes 12 minority (9 Black or African American, non-Hispanic/Latino; 2 Asian, non-Hispanic/Latino; 1 Hispanic/Latino), 7 international. Average age 27. 224 applicants, 56% accepted, 36 enrolled. Expenses: Contact institution. *Financial support:* In 2019–20, 13 students received support. Fellowships, research assistantships, teaching assistantships, Federal Work-Study, scholarships/grants, and health care benefits available. In 2019, 24 master's, 3 doctorates awarded. *Program availability:* Part-time. *Application deadline:* For fall admission, 12/8 priority date for domestic and international students. Applications are processed on a rolling basis. *Application fee:* $75. Electronic applications accepted. *Application Contact:* Krista Featherstone, Program Manager, 215-573-8075, E-mail: kfeat@upenn.edu. *Program Manager*, Krista Featherstone, 215-573-8075, E-mail: kfeat@upenn.edu.

***Division of Higher Education*** Students: 105 full-time (50 women), 44 part-time (31 women); includes 59 minority (29 Black or African American, non-Hispanic/Latino; 11 Asian, non-Hispanic/Latino; 14 Hispanic/Latino; 5 Two or more races, non-Hispanic/Latino), 7 international. Average age 37. 308 applicants, 55% accepted, 65 enrolled. Expenses: Contact institution. *Financial support:* In 2019–20, 24 students received support. Fellowships, research assistantships, teaching assistantships, Federal Work-Study, scholarships/grants, health care benefits, and unspecified assistantships available. In 2019, 53 master's, 33 doctorates awarded. *Program availability:* Part-time. *Application deadline:* For fall admission, 12/8 priority date for domestic and international students. *Application fee:* $80. Electronic applications accepted. *Application Contact:* Dr. Ross Aikins, Program Manager, 215-898-8398, E-mail: raikins@upenn.edu. *Program Manager*, Dr. Ross Aikins, 215-898-8398, E-mail: raikins@upenn.edu.

***Division of Human Development and Quantitative Methods*** Students: 201 full-time (168 women), 12 part-time (11 women); includes 60 minority (25 Black or African American, non-Hispanic/Latino; 15 Asian, non-Hispanic/Latino; 15 Hispanic/Latino; 5 Two or more races, non-Hispanic/Latino), 90 international. Average age 28. 759 applicants, 47% accepted, 163 enrolled. Expenses: Contact institution. *Financial support:* In 2019–20, 95 students received support. Fellowships, research assistantships, teaching assistantships, career-related internships or fieldwork, Federal Work-Study, scholarships/grants, health care benefits, and unspecified assistantships available. In 2019, 152 master's, 6 doctorates awarded. *Program availability:* Part-time-only, evening/weekend. *Application deadline:* For fall admission, 12/8 priority date for domestic and international students. Applications are processed on a rolling basis. *Application fee:* $75. Electronic applications accepted. *Application Contact:* Dr. Elizabeth Mackenzie, Program Manager, 215-898-4176, E-mail: emackenz@upenn.edu. *Program Manager*, Dr. Elizabeth Mackenzie, 215-898-4176, E-mail: emackenz@upenn.edu.

***Division of Literacy, Culture, and International Education*** Students: 73 full-time (60 women), 30 part-time (25 women); includes 35 minority (5 Black or African American, non-Hispanic/Latino; 11 Asian, non-Hispanic/Latino; 13 Hispanic/Latino; 6 Two or more races, non-Hispanic/Latino), 32 international. Average age 32. 415 applicants, 48% accepted, 70 enrolled. Expenses: Contact institution. *Financial support:* In 2019–20, 44 students received support. Fellowships, research assistantships, teaching assistantships, Federal Work-Study, scholarships/grants, and health care benefits available. In 2019, 71 master's, 6 doctorates awarded. *Program availability:* Part-time. *Application deadline:* For fall admission, 12/8 priority date for domestic and international students. Applications are processed on a rolling basis. *Application fee:* $75. Electronic applications accepted. *Application Contact:* Dr. Alex Posecznick, Program Manager, 215-573-3947, E-mail: alpos@upenn.edu. *Program Manager*, Dr. Alex Posecznick, 215-573-3947, E-mail: alpos@upenn.edu.

***Division of Teaching, Learning, and Leadership*** Students: 234 full-time (158 women), 117 part-time (92 women); includes 113 minority (49 Black or African American, non-Hispanic/Latino; 18 Asian, non-Hispanic/Latino; 29 Hispanic/Latino; 17 Two or more races, non-Hispanic/Latino), 57 international. Average age 33. 800 applicants, 64% accepted, 290 enrolled. Expenses: Contact institution. *Financial support:* In 2019–20, 13 students received support. Fellowships, research assistantships, teaching assistantships, Federal Work-Study, scholarships/grants, health care benefits, and unspecified assistantships available. In 2019, 125 master's, 5 doctorates awarded. *Program availability:* Part-time. *Application deadline:* For fall admission, 12/8 priority date for domestic and international students. Applications are processed on a rolling basis. *Application fee:* $75. Electronic applications accepted. *Application Contact:* Administrative Coordinator, 215-898-4176. *Program Manager*, Dr. Veronica Aplenc, 215-898-2566, E-mail: vaplenc@upenn.edu.

**Perelman School of Medicine** Students: 1,791 full-time (986 women), 143 part-time (91 women); includes 826 minority (112 Black or African American, non-Hispanic/Latino; 3 American Indian or Alaska Native, non-Hispanic/Latino; 387 Asian, non-Hispanic/Latino; 245 Hispanic/Latino; 3 Native Hawaiian or other Pacific Islander, non-Hispanic/Latino; 76 Two or more races, non-Hispanic/Latino), 123 international. 9,423 applicants, 9% accepted, 430 enrolled. *Faculty:* 3,309 full-time (1,408 women), 624 part-time/adjunct (271 women). Expenses: Contact institution. In 2019, 89 master's, 94 doctorates awarded. *Application Contact:* Laura Harlan, Director, Admissions, 215-898-8000, E-mail: lharlan@pennmedicine.upenn.edu. *Senior Vice Dean for Education*, Dr. Suzanne Rose, 215-898-8034.

***Biomedical Graduate Studies*** Students: 922 full-time (539 women), 141 part-time (90 women); includes 389 minority (43 Black or African American, non-Hispanic/Latino; 3 American Indian or Alaska Native, non-Hispanic/Latino; 172 Asian, non-Hispanic/Latino; 137 Hispanic/Latino; 2 Native Hawaiian or other Pacific Islander, non-Hispanic/Latino; 32 Two or more races, non-Hispanic/Latino), 99 international. 2,423 applicants, 14% accepted, 183 enrolled. *Faculty:* 1,191 full-time (364 women). Expenses: Contact institution. In 2019, 62 master's, 94 doctorates awarded. *Application Contact:* Aislinn Wallace, Associate Director, 215-746-6349. *Director*, Dr. Kelly Jordan-Sciutto, 215-898-1585.

***Center for Clinical Epidemiology and Biostatistics*** Students: 92 full-time (59 women), 2 part-time (1 woman); includes 42 minority (15 Black or African American, non-Hispanic/Latino; 21 Asian, non-Hispanic/Latino; 5 Hispanic/Latino; 1 Two or more races, non-Hispanic/Latino). Average age 35. 40 applicants, 90% accepted, 31 enrolled. *Faculty:* 102 full-time (49 women), 39 part-time/adjunct (25 women). Expenses: Contact institution. *Financial support:* In 2019–20, 50 students received support, including 50 fellowships with tuition reimbursements available (averaging $57,000 per year); research assistantships, teaching assistantships, and tuition waivers also available. Financial award application deadline: 12/1. In 2019, 27 master's awarded. *Program availability:* Part-time. *Application deadline:* For fall admission, 12/1 priority date for domestic students, 12/1 for international students. Electronic applications accepted. *Application Contact:* Jennifer Kuklinski, Program Coordinator, 215-573-2382, E-mail: jkuklins@pennmedicine.upenn.edu. *Director*, Dr. Harold Feldman, 215-573-0901.

**School of Arts and Sciences** Students: 1,686 full-time (815 women), 361 part-time (220 women); includes 343 minority (91 Black or African American, non-Hispanic/Latino; 122 Asian, non-Hispanic/Latino; 80 Hispanic/Latino; 50 Two or more races, non-Hispanic/Latino), 760 international. Average age 30. 6,438 applicants, 17% accepted, 610 enrolled. *Faculty:* 501 full-time (178 women), 22 part-time/adjunct (10 women). Expenses: Contact institution. In 2019, 517 master's, 185 doctorates, 11 other advanced degrees awarded. *Program availability:* Part-time, evening/weekend. *Application fee:* $80. *Application Contact:* Patricia Rea, Associate Director for Admissions, E-mail: patrea@sas.upenn.edu. *Dean*, Steven J. Fluharty.

***College of Liberal and Professional Studies*** Students: 240 full-time (161 women), 290 part-time (180 women); includes 91 minority (31 Black or African American, non-Hispanic/Latino; 31 Asian, non-Hispanic/Latino; 14 Hispanic/Latino; 15 Two or more races, non-Hispanic/Latino), 136 international. Average age 33. 955 applicants, 44% accepted, 272 enrolled. Expenses: Contact institution. In 2019, 203 master's awarded. *Application Contact:* Nora Lewis, Vice Dean, Professional and Liberal Education, 215-898-7326, E-mail: nlewis@sas.upenn.edu. *Vice Dean, Professional and Liberal Education*, Nora Lewis, 215-898-7326, E-mail: nlewis@sas.upenn.edu.

***Fels Institute of Government*** Students: 15 full-time (9 women), 49 part-time (24 women); includes 19 minority (8 Black or African American, non-Hispanic/Latino; 6 Asian, non-Hispanic/Latino; 5 Hispanic/Latino), 3 international. Average age 33. 664 applicants, 44% accepted, 130 enrolled. Expenses: Contact institution. *Financial support:* Application deadline: 1/1. In 2019, 67 master's, 3 other advanced degrees awarded. *Program availability:* Part-time, evening/weekend.

***Joseph H. Lauder Institute of Management and International Studies*** Electronic applications accepted.

**School of Dental Medicine**

**School of Engineering and Applied Science** Students: 1,630 full-time (556 women), 593 part-time (229 women); includes 456 minority (40 Black or African American, non-Hispanic/Latino; 1 American Indian or Alaska Native, non-Hispanic/Latino; 298 Asian, non-Hispanic/Latino; 77 Hispanic/Latino; 40 Two or more races, non-Hispanic/Latino), 1,216 international. Average age 25. 10,541 applicants, 23% accepted, 1,062 enrolled. *Faculty:* 124 full-time (22 women), 27 part-time/adjunct (4 women). Expenses: Contact institution. In 2019, 661 master's, 65 doctorates awarded. *Program availability:* Part-time. *Application deadline:* For fall admission, 12/15 for domestic and international students. *Application fee:* $80. Electronic applications accepted. *Application Contact:* Associate director of Graduate Admissions, 215- 898-4542, Fax: 215- 573-5577, E-mail: admissions1@seas.upenn.edu. *Dean,* Vijay Kumar, E-mail: seasdean@seas.upenn.edu.

**School of Nursing** Students: 249 full-time (211 women), 471 part-time (418 women); includes 199 minority (57 Black or African American, non-Hispanic/Latino; 77 Asian, non-Hispanic/Latino; 45 Hispanic/Latino; 20 Two or more races, non-Hispanic/Latino), 14 international. Average age 32. 587 applicants, 60% accepted, 282 enrolled. *Faculty:* 60 full-time (52 women), 33 part-time/adjunct (29 women). Expenses: Contact institution. In 2019, 321 master's, 15 doctorates awarded. *Program availability:* Part-time, online learning. *Application Contact:* Sylvia English, Admissions Officer, Enrollment Management, 215-898-8439, Fax: 215-573-8439, E-mail: sylviaj@nursing.upenn.edu. *Dean,* Dr. Antonia M. Villarruel, 215-898-4271, Fax: 215-573-8439, E-mail: amvillar@nursing.upenn.edu.

**School of Social Policy and Practice** *Program availability:* Part-time, 100% online, blended/hybrid learning. Electronic applications accepted.

**School of Veterinary Medicine** Students: 476 full-time (400 women), 5 part-time (4 women); includes 79 minority (5 Black or African American, non-Hispanic/Latino; 28 Asian, non-Hispanic/Latino; 34 Hispanic/Latino; 12 Two or more races, non-Hispanic/Latino), 6 international. Average age 26. 1,238 applicants, 10% accepted, 121 enrolled. *Faculty:* 110 full-time (54 women), 58 part-time/adjunct (41 women). Expenses: Contact institution. In 2019, 121 doctorates awarded. *Application fee:* $75. *Application Contact:* Andrew M. Hoffman, Dean. *Dean,* Andrew M. Hoffman.

**Stuart Weitzman School of Design** Students: 777 full-time (470 women), 10 part-time (7 women); includes 113 minority (21 Black or African American, non-Hispanic/Latino; 40 Asian, non-Hispanic/Latino; 41 Hispanic/Latino; 11 Two or more races, non-Hispanic/Latino), 472 international. Average age 27. 1,797 applicants, 47% accepted, 352 enrolled. *Faculty:* 41 full-time (16 women), 17 part-time/adjunct (5 women). Expenses: Contact institution. *Financial support:* In 2019–20, 29 students received support. In 2019, 291 master's, 6 doctorates, 53 other advanced degrees awarded. *Program availability:* Part-time. *Application fee:* $80. *Application Contact:* Lauren Hoover, Admissions & Recruitment Coordinator, Graduate Admissions, E-mail: lhoover@design.upenn.edu. *Dean,* Frederick Steiner.

**University of Pennsylvania Carey Law School** Students: 772 full-time (387 women); includes 244 minority (52 Black or African American, non-Hispanic/Latino; 1 American Indian or Alaska Native, non-Hispanic/Latino; 85 Asian, non-Hispanic/Latino; 55 Hispanic/Latino; 51 Two or more races, non-Hispanic/Latino), 42 international. Average age 27. 6,483 applicants, 15% accepted, 235 enrolled. *Faculty:* 86 full-time (32 women), 160 part-time/adjunct (59 women). Expenses: Contact institution. *Financial support:* In 2019–20, 398 students received support. Fellowships, research assistantships, teaching assistantships, career-related internships or fieldwork, Federal Work-Study, institutionally sponsored loans, and scholarships/grants available. Financial award application deadline: 3/1; financial award applicants required to submit CSS PROFILE or FAFSA. In 2019, 24 master's, 250 doctorates awarded. *Application deadline:* For fall admission, 3/1 for domestic and international students. Applications are processed on a rolling basis. *Application fee:* $80. Electronic applications accepted. *Application Contact:* Renee Post, Associate Dean of Admissions and Financial Aid, 215-898-7400, Fax: 215-898-9606, E-mail: contactadmissions@law.upenn.edu. *Dean,* Theodore W. Ruger, 215-898-7463, Fax: 215-573-2025, E-mail: deanruger@law.upenn.edu.

**Wharton School** *Program availability:* Evening/weekend. Electronic applications accepted.

***The Wharton MBA Program for Executives*** *Program availability:* Evening/weekend.

## UNIVERSITY OF PHILOSOPHICAL RESEARCH, Los Angeles, CA 90027

**General Information** Proprietary, coed, graduate-only institution.

**GRADUATE UNITS**

**Master's in Consciousness Studies Program** Electronic applications accepted.

**Master's in Transformational Psychology Program** Electronic applications accepted.

## UNIVERSITY OF PHOENIX - BAY AREA CAMPUS, San Jose, CA 95134-1805

**General Information** Proprietary, coed, comprehensive institution. *Graduate housing:* On-campus housing not available.

**GRADUATE UNITS**

**College of Criminal Justice and Security**

**College of Education** *Program availability:* Evening/weekend, online learning. Electronic applications accepted.

**College of Information Systems and Technology** *Program availability:* Evening/weekend. Electronic applications accepted.

**College of Nursing** *Program availability:* Evening/weekend, online learning. Electronic applications accepted.

**College of Social Sciences** *Program availability:* Evening/weekend.

**School of Business** *Program availability:* Evening/weekend, online learning. Electronic applications accepted.

## UNIVERSITY OF PHOENIX - CENTRAL VALLEY CAMPUS, Fresno, CA 93720-1552

**General Information** Proprietary, coed, comprehensive institution.

**GRADUATE UNITS**

**College of Education**

**College of Human Services**

**College of Information Systems and Technology**

**College of Nursing**

**School of Business**

## UNIVERSITY OF PHOENIX - DALLAS CAMPUS, Dallas, TX 75251

**General Information** Proprietary, coed, comprehensive institution. *Graduate housing:* On-campus housing not available.

**GRADUATE UNITS**

**College of Criminal Justice and Security** *Program availability:* Online learning. Electronic applications accepted.

**College of Education**

**College of Information Systems and Technology** *Program availability:* Evening/weekend. Electronic applications accepted.

**School of Business** *Program availability:* Evening/weekend, online learning. Electronic applications accepted.

## UNIVERSITY OF PHOENIX - HAWAII CAMPUS, Honolulu, HI 96813-3800

**General Information** Proprietary, coed, comprehensive institution. *Graduate housing:* On-campus housing not available.

**GRADUATE UNITS**

**College of Education** *Program availability:* Evening/weekend. Electronic applications accepted.

**College of Information Systems and Technology** *Program availability:* Evening/weekend. Electronic applications accepted.

**College of Nursing** *Program availability:* Evening/weekend. Electronic applications accepted.

**School of Business** *Program availability:* Evening/weekend. Electronic applications accepted.

## UNIVERSITY OF PHOENIX - HOUSTON CAMPUS, Houston, TX 77079-2004

**General Information** Proprietary, coed, comprehensive institution. *Graduate housing:* On-campus housing not available.

**GRADUATE UNITS**

**College of Education**

**College of Information Systems and Technology** *Program availability:* Evening/weekend, online learning. Electronic applications accepted.

**College of Nursing** *Program availability:* Online learning. Electronic applications accepted.

**School of Business** *Program availability:* Evening/weekend, online learning. Electronic applications accepted.

## UNIVERSITY OF PHOENIX - LAS VEGAS CAMPUS, Las Vegas, NV 89135

**General Information** Proprietary, coed, comprehensive institution. *Graduate housing:* On-campus housing not available.

**GRADUATE UNITS**

**College of Education** *Program availability:* Evening/weekend. Electronic applications accepted.

**College of Human Services** *Program availability:* Online learning. Electronic applications accepted.

**College of Information Systems and Technology** *Program availability:* Evening/weekend. Electronic applications accepted.

**School of Business** *Program availability:* Evening/weekend, online learning. Electronic applications accepted.

## UNIVERSITY OF PHOENIX–ONLINE CAMPUS, Phoenix, AZ 85034-7209

**General Information** Proprietary, coed, comprehensive institution. *Graduate housing:* On-campus housing not available.

**GRADUATE UNITS**

**College of Education** *Program availability:* Evening/weekend, online learning. Electronic applications accepted.

**College of Health Sciences and Nursing** *Program availability:* Evening/weekend, online learning. Electronic applications accepted.

**College of Information Systems and Technology** *Program availability:* Evening/weekend, online learning. Electronic applications accepted.

**College of Justice and Security** *Program availability:* Evening/weekend, online learning. Electronic applications accepted.

**College of Social Science** *Program availability:* Evening/weekend, online learning. Electronic applications accepted.

**School of Advanced Studies** *Program availability:* Evening/weekend, online learning. Electronic applications accepted.

**School of Business** *Program availability:* Evening/weekend, online learning. Electronic applications accepted.

## UNIVERSITY OF PHOENIX - PHOENIX CAMPUS, Tempe, AZ 85282-2371

**General Information** Proprietary, coed, comprehensive institution. CGS member. *Graduate housing:* On-campus housing not available.

**GRADUATE UNITS**

**College of Criminal Justice and Security** *Program availability:* Evening/weekend, online learning. Electronic applications accepted.

**College of Education** *Program availability:* Evening/weekend, online learning. Electronic applications accepted.

**College of Health Sciences and Nursing** *Program availability:* Evening/weekend, online learning. Electronic applications accepted.

**College of Social Sciences** *Program availability:* Evening/weekend, online learning. Electronic applications accepted.

**School of Business** *Program availability:* Evening/weekend, online learning. Electronic applications accepted.

## UNIVERSITY OF PHOENIX - SACRAMENTO VALLEY CAMPUS, Sacramento, CA 95833-4334

**General Information** Proprietary, coed, comprehensive institution. *Graduate housing:* On-campus housing not available.

**GRADUATE UNITS**

**College of Education** *Program availability:* Evening/weekend. Electronic applications accepted.

**College of Information Systems and Technology** *Program availability:* Evening/weekend. Electronic applications accepted.

**College of Nursing** *Program availability:* Evening/weekend. Electronic applications accepted.

**School of Business** *Program availability:* Evening/weekend. Electronic applications accepted.

## UNIVERSITY OF PHOENIX - SAN ANTONIO CAMPUS, San Antonio, TX 78230

**General Information** Proprietary, coed, comprehensive institution.

**GRADUATE UNITS**

**College of Criminal Justice and Security**

**College of Education**

**College of Information Systems and Technology**

**College of Nursing**

**School of Business**

## UNIVERSITY OF PHOENIX - SAN DIEGO CAMPUS, San Diego, CA 92123

**General Information** Proprietary, coed, comprehensive institution. *Graduate housing:* On-campus housing not available.

**GRADUATE UNITS**

**College of Education** *Program availability:* Evening/weekend. Electronic applications accepted.

**College of Information Systems and Technology** *Program availability:* Evening/weekend. Electronic applications accepted.

**College of Nursing** *Program availability:* Evening/weekend. Electronic applications accepted.

**School of Business** *Program availability:* Evening/weekend. Electronic applications accepted.

## UNIVERSITY OF PIKEVILLE, Pikeville, KY 41501

**General Information** Independent-religious, coed, comprehensive institution. *Enrollment:* 2,262 graduate, professional, and undergraduate students; 851 full-time matriculated graduate/professional students (453 women), 7 part-time matriculated graduate/professional students (2 women). *Enrollment by degree level:* 70 master's, 785 doctoral, 2 other advanced degrees. *Graduate faculty:* 43 full-time (18 women), 15 part-time/adjunct (8 women). *Graduate housing:* Room and/or apartments available on a first-come, first-served basis to single students; on-campus housing not available to married students. Typical cost: $8050 (including board). Housing application deadline: 5/1. *Student services:* Campus employment opportunities, campus safety program, career counseling, exercise/wellness program, free psychological counseling, international student services, low-cost health insurance, services for students with disabilities. *Library facilities:* Allara Library plus 2 others. *Collection:* Books: 63,935 (physical), 294,261 (digital/electronic); Serial titles: 115 (physical), 86,810 (digital/electronic); Databases: 124. Weekly public service hours: 105; students can reserve study rooms.

**Computer facilities:** 308 computers available on campus for general student use. A campuswide network can be accessed.
Website: http://www.upike.edu/

**General Application Contact:** John Yancey, Director of Admissions, 606-218-5251, Fax: 606-218-5255, E-mail: johnyancey@upike.edu.

**GRADUATE UNITS**

**Coleman College of Business** Students: 51 full-time (23 women), 7 part-time (2 women); includes 12 minority (6 Black or African American, non-Hispanic/Latino; 6 Asian, non-Hispanic/Latino). Average age 31. *Faculty:* 5 part-time/adjunct (2 women). Expenses: Contact institution. *Financial support:* In 2019–20, 19 students received support, including 15 teaching assistantships with full tuition reimbursements available; university employee grants also available. Financial award application deadline: 2/15; financial award applicants required to submit FAFSA. In 2019, 27 master's awarded. *Program availability:* Part-time, evening/weekend, online only, 100% online. *Application deadline:* For fall admission, 8/15 for domestic students, 7/1 for international students. Applications are processed on a rolling basis. *Application fee:* $50. *Application Contact:* Cathy Maynard, Secretary, Business and Economics, 606-218-5020, Fax: 606-218-5031, E-mail: cathymaynard@upike.edu. *Dean,* Dr. Howard V. Roberts, 606-218-5019, Fax: 606-218-5031, E-mail: howardroberts@upike.edu.

**Kentucky College of Optometry** Students: 236 full-time (155 women); includes 43 minority (10 Black or African American, non-Hispanic/Latino; 2 American Indian or Alaska Native, non-Hispanic/Latino; 19 Asian, non-Hispanic/Latino; 12 Hispanic/Latino). Average age 25. 460 applicants, 38% accepted, 62 enrolled. *Faculty:* 15 full-time (5 women). Expenses: Contact institution. *Financial support:* Fellowships available. Financial award application deadline: 7/1; financial award applicants required to submit FAFSA. *Application deadline:* For fall admission, 3/31 for domestic students. *Application Contact:* Casey Price, Coordinator of Admissions, 606-218-5517, E-mail: caseyprice@upike.edu. *Dean,* Dr. Michael Bacigalupi, 606-218-5510, E-mail: mbacigalupi@upike.edu.

**Kentucky College of Osteopathic Medicine** Students: 551 full-time (267 women); includes 131 minority (5 Black or African American, non-Hispanic/Latino; 1 American Indian or Alaska Native, non-Hispanic/Latino; 105 Asian, non-Hispanic/Latino; 15 Hispanic/Latino; 5 Native Hawaiian or other Pacific Islander, non-Hispanic/Latino). Average age 25. 3,763 applicants, 6% accepted, 134 enrolled. *Faculty:* 24 full-time (9 women), 35 part-time/adjunct (13 women). Expenses: Contact institution. *Financial support:* In 2019–20, 11 students received support, including 11 fellowships with full and partial tuition reimbursements available (averaging $28,169 per year); scholarships/grants also available. Financial award application deadline: 8/1; financial award applicants required to submit FAFSA. In 2019, 119 doctorates awarded. *Application deadline:* For fall admission, 5/1 for domestic students. Applications are processed on a rolling basis. *Application fee:* $75. *Application Contact:* Michael Kennedy, Senior Recruiter, 606-218-5257, E-mail: michaelkennedy@upike.edu. *Dean,* Dr. Dana Shaffer, 606-218-5410, E-mail: danashaffer@upike.edu.

**Patton College of Education** Students: 12 full-time (7 women). Average age 33. *Faculty:* 10 part-time/adjunct (6 women). Expenses: Contact institution. *Financial support:* Application deadline: 2/1; applicants required to submit FAFSA. In 2019, 37 master's awarded. *Program availability:* Part-time, evening/weekend, online only, 100% online. *Application deadline:* For fall admission, 8/15 for domestic students. Applications are processed on a rolling basis. *Application fee:* $50. *Application Contact:* Fairy Coleman, Administrative Assistant, 606-218-5314, E-mail: fairycoleman@upike.edu. *Division Chair,* Dr. Coletta Parsley, 606-218-5318, E-mail: colettaparsley@upike.edu.

## UNIVERSITY OF PITTSBURGH, Pittsburgh, PA 15260

**General Information** State-related, coed, university. CGS member. *Enrollment:* 28,391 graduate, professional, and undergraduate students; 7,259 full-time matriculated graduate/professional students (4,063 women), 1,776 part-time matriculated graduate/professional students (1,099 women). *Enrollment by degree level:* 3,748 master's, 5,075 doctoral, 212 other advanced degrees. *Graduate faculty:* 4,492 full-time (1,977 women), 748 part-time/adjunct (354 women). *Student services:* Campus employment opportunities, campus safety program, career counseling, exercise/wellness program, free psychological counseling, international student services, low-cost health insurance, services for students with disabilities, writing training. *Library facilities:* Hillman Library plus 16 others. *Collection:* Books: 3.8 million (physical), 1.7 million (digital/electronic); Serial titles: 108,837 (physical), 268,771 (digital/electronic); Databases: 584. Weekly public service hours: 145; study areas open 24 hours, 5–7 days a week; students can reserve study rooms. *Research affiliation:* National Institutes of Health, National Science Foundation, General Electric Company (GE), Shire, Phillips.

**Computer facilities:** Computer purchase and lease plans are available. 1,128 computers available on campus for general student use. A campuswide network can be accessed. Online class registration, online class listings, online tuition payment are available.
Website: http://www.pitt.edu/

**General Application Contact:** Information Contact, 412-624-4141, E-mail: graduate@pitt.edu.

**GRADUATE UNITS**

**Graduate School of Public and International Affairs** Students: 260 full-time (156 women), 158 part-time (95 women); includes 49 minority (26 Black or African American, non-Hispanic/Latino; 7 Asian, non-Hispanic/Latino; 14 Hispanic/Latino; 2 Two or more races, non-Hispanic/Latino), 77 international. Average age 31. 544 applicants, 81% accepted, 163 enrolled. *Faculty:* 33 full-time (11 women), 10 part-time/adjunct (5 women). Expenses: Contact institution. *Financial support:* In 2019–20, 162 students received support, including 17 fellowships with full tuition reimbursements available (averaging $16,060 per year), 15 research assistantships with full tuition reimbursements available (averaging $16,060 per year); scholarships/grants also available. Financial award application deadline: 2/1. In 2019, 154 master's, 1 doctorate awarded. *Program availability:* Part-time, evening/weekend, 100% online. *Application deadline:* For fall admission, 2/1 priority date for domestic students, 1/15 priority date for international students; for spring admission, 11/1 priority date for domestic students, 8/1 priority date for international students; for summer admission, 3/1 priority date for domestic students, 1/15 priority date for international students. *Application fee:* $50. Electronic applications accepted. *Application Contact:* Dr. Michael Rizzi, Director of Student Services, 412-648-7643, Fax: 412-648-7641, E-mail: rizzim@pitt.edu. *Dean,* Dr. John Keeler, 412-648-7605, Fax: 412-648-7601, E-mail: gspia@pitt.edu.

**Graduate School of Public Health** Students: 428 full-time (308 women), 129 part-time (96 women); includes 131 minority (34 Black or African American, non-Hispanic/Latino; 44 Asian, non-Hispanic/Latino; 31 Hispanic/Latino; 1 Native Hawaiian or other Pacific Islander, non-Hispanic/Latino; 21 Two or more races, non-Hispanic/Latino), 110 international. Average age 28. 1,494 applicants, 52% accepted, 210 enrolled. *Faculty:* 154 full-time (81 women), 37 part-time/adjunct (23 women). Expenses: Contact institution. *Financial support:* In 2019–20, 200 students received support, including 118 research assistantships (averaging $20,500 per year), 5 teaching assistantships (averaging $18,500 per year); career-related internships or fieldwork, institutionally sponsored loans, scholarships/grants, traineeships, health care benefits, and unspecified assistantships also available. Support available to part-time students. Financial award applicants required to submit FAFSA. In 2019, 180 master's, 39 doctorates awarded. *Program availability:* Part-time, evening/weekend. *Application deadline:* For fall admission, 1/15 for domestic and international students. Applications are processed on a rolling basis. *Application fee:* $135. Electronic applications accepted. *Application Contact:* Karrie A. Lukin, Admissions Manager, 412-624-3003, Fax: 412-624-3755, E-mail: presutti@pitt.edu. *Interim Dean, Graduate School of Public Health,* A. Everette James, III, 412-624-3001, Fax: 412-624-3013.

**Katz Graduate School of Business** Students: 449 full-time (220 women), 306 part-time (116 women); includes 92 minority (23 Black or African American, non-Hispanic/Latino; 36 Asian, non-Hispanic/Latino; 23 Hispanic/Latino; 10 Two or more races, non-Hispanic/Latino), 278 international. Average age 30. 1,695 applicants, 48% accepted, 313 enrolled. *Faculty:* 95 full-time (30 women), 30 part-time/adjunct (10 women). Expenses: Contact institution. *Financial support:* Research assistantships, teaching assistantships, Federal Work-Study, scholarships/grants, health care benefits, and unspecified assistantships available. Financial award application deadline: 6/1; financial award applicants required to submit FAFSA. In 2019, 319 master's awarded. *Program availability:* Part-time, evening/weekend. *Application deadline:* For fall admission, 4/1 priority date for domestic students, 2/1 priority date for international students. *Application fee:* $50. *Application Contact:* Thomas Keller, Director of MBA Admissions, 412-648-1700, Fax: 412-648-1659, E-mail: mba@katz.pitt.edu. *Dean,* Dr. Arjang A. Assad, 412-648-1556, Fax: 412-648-1552, E-mail: aassad@katz.pitt.edu.

**Kenneth P. Dietrich School of Arts and Sciences** *Program availability:* Part-time. Electronic applications accepted.

***Center for Bioethics and Health Law*** Students: 5 full-time (all women), 5 part-time (4 women); includes 1 minority (Asian, non-Hispanic/Latino), 1 international. Average age 32. 6 applicants, 67% accepted, 4 enrolled. *Faculty:* 11 full-time (4 women), 4 part-time/adjunct (1 woman). Expenses: Contact institution. *Financial support:* Scholarships/grants available. Financial award application deadline: 3/1. In 2019, 7 master's awarded. *Program availability:* Part-time. *Application deadline:* For fall admission, 3/1 priority date for domestic and international students. Applications are processed on a rolling basis. *Application fee:* $50. Electronic applications accepted. *Application Contact:* Jody Stockdill, Administrative Assistant, 412-648-7007, Fax: 412-648-2649, E-mail: joc10@pitt.edu. *Director,* Dr. Lisa S. Parker, PhD, 412-648-7007, Fax: 412-648-2649, E-mail: lisap@pitt.edu.

***Center for Neuroscience*** Electronic applications accepted.

**School of Computing and Information** *Program availability:* Part-time, evening/weekend, 100% online. Electronic applications accepted.

**School of Dental Medicine** Electronic applications accepted.

**School of Education** Students: 391 full-time (293 women), 357 part-time (259 women); includes 137 minority (68 Black or African American, non-Hispanic/Latino; 19 Asian, non-Hispanic/Latino; 32 Hispanic/Latino; 1 Native Hawaiian or other Pacific Islander, non-Hispanic/Latino; 17 Two or more races, non-Hispanic/Latino), 80 international. Average age 32. 741 applicants, 76% accepted, 329 enrolled. *Faculty:* 80 full-time (55 women), 2 part-time/adjunct (1 woman). Expenses: Contact institution. *Financial support:* In 2019–20, fellowships with full and partial tuition reimbursements (averaging $20,250 per year), teaching assistantships with full and partial tuition reimbursements (averaging $19,480 per year) were awarded; research assistantships with full and partial tuition reimbursements, career-related internships or fieldwork, Federal Work-Study, institutionally sponsored loans, scholarships/grants, health care benefits, tuition waivers (full and partial), and unspecified assistantships also available. Support available to part-time students. Financial award applicants required to submit FAFSA. In 2019, 223 master's, 70 doctorates awarded. *Program availability:* Part-time, evening/weekend, 100% online, blended/hybrid learning. *Application deadline:* For fall admission, 1/15 priority date for domestic students, 1/14 for international students; for spring admission, 11/1 priority date for domestic students, 10/1 for international students; for summer admission, 1/15 for domestic and international students. Applications are processed on a rolling basis. *Application fee:* $50. Electronic applications accepted. *Application Contact:* Wesley Alan Vaina, Director of Admissions and Enrollment, 412-648-7362, Fax: 412-648-1899, E-mail: wvaina@pitt.edu. *Renée and Richard Goldman Dean*, Dr. Valerie Kinloch, 412-648-1780, Fax: 412-648-1899, E-mail: vkinloch@pitt.edu.

**School of Health and Rehabilitation Sciences** Students: 801 full-time (614 women), 52 part-time (41 women); includes 109 minority (18 Black or African American, non-Hispanic/Latino; 1 American Indian or Alaska Native, non-Hispanic/Latino; 40 Asian, non-Hispanic/Latino; 25 Hispanic/Latino; 25 Two or more races, non-Hispanic/Latino), 56 international. Average age 25. 2,043 applicants, 40% accepted, 372 enrolled. *Faculty:* 122 full-time (73 women), 22 part-time/adjunct (14 women). Expenses: Contact institution. *Financial support:* In 2019–20, 52 students received support, including 1 fellowship with full tuition reimbursement available (averaging $30,000 per year), 39 research assistantships with tuition reimbursements available (averaging $28,460 per year), 2 teaching assistantships with full tuition reimbursements available (averaging $18,000 per year); scholarships/grants and traineeships also available. Financial award applicants required to submit FAFSA. In 2019, 219 master's, 89 doctorates awarded. *Program availability:* Part-time, 100% online, blended/hybrid learning. Electronic applications accepted. *Application Contact:* Jessica Maguire, Director of Admissions, 412-383-6557, Fax: 412-383-6535, E-mail: maguire@pitt.edu. *Dean*, Dr. Anthony Delitto, 412-383-6560, Fax: 412-383-6535, E-mail: delitto@pitt.edu.

**School of Law** *Program availability:* Part-time, online learning. Electronic applications accepted.

**School of Medicine** *Program availability:* Part-time, blended/hybrid learning. Electronic applications accepted.

**School of Nursing** Students: 152 full-time (126 women), 188 part-time (143 women); includes 38 minority (13 Black or African American, non-Hispanic/Latino; 21 Asian, non-Hispanic/Latino; 4 Hispanic/Latino), 13 international. Average age 31. 250 applicants, 51% accepted, 102 enrolled. *Faculty:* 55 full-time (44 women), 5 part-time/adjunct (4 women). Expenses: Contact institution. *Financial support:* In 2019–20, 196 students received support, including 21 fellowships (averaging $12,195 per year), 12 research assistantships (averaging $15,010 per year), 48 teaching assistantships (averaging $11,302 per year); scholarships/grants, unspecified assistantships, and Matching Funds also available. Financial award application deadline: 6/1; financial award applicants required to submit FAFSA. In 2019, 55 master's, 30 doctorates awarded. *Program availability:* Part-time. *Application deadline:* For fall admission, 6/1 priority date for domestic students, 2/15 priority date for international students. *Application fee:* $50. Electronic applications accepted. *Application Contact:* Laurie Lapsley, Graduate Administrator, 412-624-9670, Fax: 412-624-2409, E-mail: lapsleyl@pitt.edu. *Dean/Professor*, Dr. Jacqueline Dunbar-Jacob, 412-624-7838, Fax: 412-624-2401, E-mail: dunbar@pitt.edu.

**School of Pharmacy** *Program availability:* Part-time. Electronic applications accepted.

**School of Social Work** *Program availability:* Part-time. Electronic applications accepted.

**Swanson School of Engineering** *Program availability:* Part-time. Electronic applications accepted.

**University Center for International Studies** *Program availability:* Part-time, evening/weekend, online learning.

## UNIVERSITY OF PORTLAND, Portland, OR 97203-5798

**General Information** Independent-religious, coed, comprehensive institution. *Graduate housing:* Room and/or apartments available on a first-come, first-served basis to single students; on-campus housing not available to married students. *Research affiliation:* Portland Area Nursing Consortium, Kaiser Center Health Resources.

**GRADUATE UNITS**

**Department of Communication Studies** *Program availability:* Part-time, evening/weekend. Electronic applications accepted.

**Dr. Robert B. Pamplin, Jr. School of Business** *Program availability:* Part-time, evening/weekend. Electronic applications accepted.

**School of Education** *Program availability:* Part-time, evening/weekend. Electronic applications accepted.

**School of Nursing** *Program availability:* Part-time, evening/weekend. Electronic applications accepted.

**Shiley School of Engineering** *Program availability:* Part-time, evening/weekend. Electronic applications accepted.

## UNIVERSITY OF PRINCE EDWARD ISLAND, Charlottetown, PE C1A 4P3, Canada

**General Information** Province-supported, coed, comprehensive institution. *Graduate housing:* Room and/or apartments available on a first-come, first-served basis to single students; on-campus housing not available to married students. *Research affiliation:* National Research Council of Canada Institute for Nutrisciences and Health, PEI Food Technology Centre, Agriculture Canada Research Station, Diagnostic Chemicals, Ltd., Canadian Food Inspection Agency, AquaHealth.

**GRADUATE UNITS**

**Atlantic Veterinary College** *Program availability:* Part-time.

**Faculty of Arts** *Program availability:* Part-time.

**Faculty of Education** *Program availability:* Part-time.

**Faculty of Science**

## UNIVERSITY OF PROVIDENCE, Great Falls, MT 59405

**General Information** Independent-religious, coed, comprehensive institution. *Graduate housing:* On-campus housing not available.

**GRADUATE UNITS**

**Graduate Studies** *Program availability:* Part-time, online learning. Electronic applications accepted.

## UNIVERSITY OF PUERTO RICO AT MAYAGÜEZ, Mayagüez, PR 00681-9000

**General Information** Commonwealth-supported, coed, university. *Graduate housing:* On-campus housing not available. *Research affiliation:* U.S. Department of Education (DOE) (STEM education), National Endowment for the Humanities, Tropical Agriculture Research Station (agriculture), Corporation for the Development and Administration of Marine Resources of Puerto Rico (marine science), National Science Foundation.

**GRADUATE UNITS**

**Graduate Studies** *Program availability:* Part-time, evening/weekend. Electronic applications accepted.

***College of Agricultural Sciences*** *Program availability:* Part-time.

***College of Arts and Sciences*** *Program availability:* Part-time.

***College of Business Administration*** *Program availability:* Part-time, evening/weekend. Electronic applications accepted.

***College of Engineering*** *Program availability:* Part-time. Electronic applications accepted.

## UNIVERSITY OF PUERTO RICO AT RIO PIEDRAS, San Juan, PR 00931-3300

**General Information** Commonwealth-supported, coed, university. *Graduate housing:* Room and/or apartments available to single students; on-campus housing not available to married students. Housing application deadline: 6/15. *Research affiliation:* U.S. Department of Education (DOE) (social sciences, general studies, physics, biology), U.S. Department of Health and Human Services (social sciences, biology), National Science Foundation (ecology, biology), Ocean Conservancy (ecology, biology), Ford International (ecology).

**GRADUATE UNITS**

**College of Business Administration** *Program availability:* Part-time.

**College of Education** *Program availability:* Part-time.

**College of Humanities** *Program availability:* Part-time.

**College of Natural Sciences** *Program availability:* Part-time.

**College of Social Sciences** *Program availability:* Part-time.

***Graduate School of Rehabilitation Counseling*** *Program availability:* Part-time.

***Graduate School of Social Work*** *Program availability:* Part-time.

***School of Public Administration*** *Program availability:* Part-time.

**Graduate School of Information Sciences and Technologies** *Program availability:* Part-time.

**Graduate School of Planning** *Program availability:* Part-time.

**School of Architecture** *Program availability:* Part-time.

**School of Communication** *Program availability:* Part-time.

**School of Law** *Program availability:* Part-time, evening/weekend.

## UNIVERSITY OF PUERTO RICO - MEDICAL SCIENCES CAMPUS, San Juan, PR 00936-5067

**General Information** Commonwealth-supported, coed, primarily women, university. *Graduate housing:* On-campus housing not available.

**GRADUATE UNITS**

**Graduate School of Public Health** *Program availability:* Part-time.

**School of Dental Medicine** Electronic applications accepted.

**School of Health Professions** Electronic applications accepted.

**School of Medicine** Electronic applications accepted.

***Biomedical Sciences Graduate Program*** Electronic applications accepted.

**School of Nursing** Electronic applications accepted.

**School of Pharmacy** *Program availability:* Part-time, evening/weekend. Electronic applications accepted.

## UNIVERSITY OF PUGET SOUND, Tacoma, WA 98416

**General Information** Independent, coed, comprehensive institution. *Graduate housing:* On-campus housing not available.

**GRADUATE UNITS**

**School of Education** *Program availability:* Part-time. Electronic applications accepted.

**School of Occupational Therapy** Electronic applications accepted.

**School of Physical Therapy** Electronic applications accepted.

## UNIVERSITY OF REDLANDS, Redlands, CA 92373-0999

**General Information** Independent, coed, comprehensive institution. *Graduate housing:* Rooms and/or apartments available on a first-come, first-served basis to single students and available to married students. Housing application deadline: 8/19. *Research affiliation:* Environmental Systems Research Institute (geographic information systems).

**GRADUATE UNITS**

**College of Arts and Sciences** Electronic applications accepted.

***School of Music*** *Program availability:* Part-time.

**School of Business** *Program availability:* Evening/weekend.

**School of Education** *Program availability:* Part-time, evening/weekend.

## UNIVERSITY OF REGINA, Regina, SK S4S 0A2, Canada

**General Information** Province-supported, coed, university. *Enrollment:* 1,067 full-time matriculated graduate/professional students (539 women), 710 part-time matriculated graduate/professional students (502 women). *Enrollment by degree level:* 1,411 master's, 299 doctoral, 40 other advanced degrees. *Graduate faculty:* 497 full-time (210 women), 220 part-time/adjunct (80 women). *Tuition:* Full-time $6684 Canadian dollars. *Required fees:* $100 Canadian dollars; $3351.45 Canadian dollars per trimester. $1117.15 Canadian dollars per semester. Tuition and fees vary according to course level, course load, degree level and program. *Graduate housing:* Rooms and/or apartments available on a first-come, first-served basis to single and married students.

Typical cost: $9828 Canadian dollars per year ($12,186 Canadian dollars including board) for single students; $11,652 Canadian dollars per year for married students. Room and board charges vary according to board plan, campus/location and housing facility selected. *Student services:* Campus employment opportunities, campus safety program, career counseling, child daycare facilities, exercise/wellness program, free psychological counseling, grant writing training, international student services, low-cost health insurance, multicultural affairs office, services for students with disabilities, teacher training, writing training. *Library facilities:* Dr. John Archer Library plus 5 others. *Collection:* Books: 805,505 (physical), 1.4 million (digital/electronic); Serial titles: 139,749 (physical), 155,436 (digital/electronic); Databases: 395. Weekly public service hours: 105; students can reserve study rooms. *Research affiliation:* TR Labs (telecommunications), Regional Centre of Expertise on Education for Sustainable Development in Saskatchewan (sustainable development), Petroleum Technology Research Center (green energy technologies), Saskatchewan Population Health and Evaluation Research Unit (health research), Canadian Plains Research Centre (CPRC) (climate change adaptation), Prairie Adaptation Research Collaborative (climate change and adaptation options).

**Computer facilities:** 412 computers available on campus for general student use. A campuswide network can be accessed. Online class registration is available. Website: http://www.uregina.ca/

**General Application Contact:** Mandy Kiel, Faculty Administrator, 306-585-5187, Fax: 306-337-2444, E-mail: grad.studies@uregina.ca.

**GRADUATE UNITS**

**Faculty of Graduate Studies and Research** Students: 1,067 full-time (539 women), 710 part-time (502 women). Average age 30. 4,549 applicants, 15% accepted, 451 enrolled. *Faculty:* 497 full-time (210 women), 220 part-time/adjunct (80 women). Expenses: Contact institution. *Financial support:* In 2019–20, 739 fellowships, 287 teaching assistantships were awarded; research assistantships, career-related internships or fieldwork, institutionally sponsored loans, scholarships/grants, traineeships, unspecified assistantships, and travel awards, Grauate scholarship base funds, SIES and donor funded schols also available. Financial award application deadline: 9/30. In 2019, 442 master's, 33 doctorates, 22 other advanced degrees awarded. *Program availability:* Part-time, evening/weekend. *Application deadline:* For fall admission, 2/15 for domestic and international students; for winter admission, 7/15 for domestic and international students; for spring admission, 10/15 for domestic and international students. Applications are processed on a rolling basis. *Application fee:* $100. Electronic applications accepted. *Application Contact:* Mandy Kiel, Faculty Administrator, 306-585-5187, Fax: 306-337-2444, E-mail: grad.admin@uregina.ca. *Dean*, Dr. Nick Jones, 306-585-5185, Fax: 306-337-2444, E-mail: grad.dean@uregina.ca.

***Faculty of Arts*** Students: 111 full-time (82 women), 20 part-time (14 women). Average age 30. 244 applicants, 20% accepted. *Faculty:* 117 full-time (47 women), 33 part-time/adjunct (16 women). Expenses: Contact institution. *Financial support:* In 2019–20, 147 students received support, including 66 fellowships, 43 teaching assistantships (averaging $2,552 per year); research assistantships, career-related internships or fieldwork, Federal Work-Study, scholarships/grants, unspecified assistantships, and travel award and Graduate Scholarship base funds also available. Support available to part-time students. Financial award application deadline: 9/30. In 2019, 37 master's, 1 doctorate awarded. *Program availability:* Part-time. *Application deadline:* Applications are processed on a rolling basis. *Application fee:* $100. Electronic applications accepted. *Application Contact:* Dr. Troni Grande, Acting Assoc Dean, Graduate Studies, 306-585-4570, E-mail: troni.grande@uregina.ca. *Dean*, Dr. Richard Kleer, 306-585-4895, Fax: 306-585-5368, E-mail: arts.dean@uregina.ca.

***Faculty of Education*** Students: 97 full-time (71 women), 221 part-time (170 women). Average age 30. 198 applicants, 37% accepted. *Faculty:* 50 full-time (35 women), 81 part-time/adjunct (55 women). Expenses: Contact institution. *Financial support:* In 2019–20, 215 students received support, including 134 fellowships with tuition reimbursements available, 27 teaching assistantships (averaging $2,552 per year); research assistantships, career-related internships or fieldwork, Federal Work-Study, scholarships/grants, unspecified assistantships, and travel award and Graduate Scholarship Base funds also available. Support available to part-time students. Financial award application deadline: 9/30. In 2019, 100 master's, 5 doctorates, 1 other advanced degree awarded. *Program availability:* Part-time. *Application deadline:* For fall admission, 2/15 for domestic and international students; for winter admission, 10/15 for domestic and international students; for spring admission, 2/15 for domestic and international students. Applications are processed on a rolling basis. *Application fee:* $100. Electronic applications accepted. *Application Contact:* Linda Jiang, Graduate Program Coordinator, 306-585-4506, Fax: 306-585-5387, E-mail: edgrad@uregina.ca. *Aoociate Dean, Graduate Programs*, Dr. Twyla Salm, 306-585-4604, Fax: 306-585-5387, E-mail: Twyla.Salm@uregina.ca.

***Faculty of Engineering and Applied Science*** Students: 262 full-time (70 women), 42 part-time (13 women). Average age 30. 689 applicants, 14% accepted. *Faculty:* 47 full-time (6 women), 21 part-time/adjunct (2 women). Expenses: Contact institution. *Financial support:* In 2019–20, 318 students received support, including 180 fellowships with tuition reimbursements available, 70 teaching assistantships (averaging $2,552 per year); research assistantships, career-related internships or fieldwork, Federal Work-Study, scholarships/grants, traineeships, unspecified assistantships, and Graduate scholarship base funds, SIES and other donor funded schols also available. Support available to part-time students. Financial award application deadline: 9/30. In 2019, 80 master's, 12 doctorates awarded. *Program availability:* Part-time. *Application deadline:* For fall admission, 1/31 for domestic and international students; for winter admission, 7/31 for domestic and international students. Applications are processed on a rolling basis. *Application fee:* $100. Electronic applications accepted. *Application Contact:* Colleen Walsh, Graduate and Co-operative Education Coordinator, 306-585-5416, Fax: 306-585-4556, E-mail: engg@uregina.ca. *Acting Dean*, Dr. Amr Henni, 306-585-4960, Fax: 306-585-4556, E-mail: Amr.Henni@uregina.ca.

***Faculty of Kinesiology and Health Studies*** Students: 28 full-time (14 women), 9 part-time (3 women). Average age 30. 31 applicants, 35% accepted. *Faculty:* 20 full-time (9 women), 24 part-time/adjunct (10 women). Expenses: Contact institution. *Financial support:* In 2019–20, 32 students received support, including 14 fellowships, 7 teaching assistantships (averaging $2,552 per year); research assistantships, career-related internships or fieldwork, Federal Work-Study, scholarships/grants, unspecified assistantships, and Travel Award and Graduate Scholarship Base funds also available. Support available to part-time students. Financial award application deadline: 9/30. In 2019, 8 master's, 1 doctorate awarded. *Program availability:* Part-time. *Application deadline:* Applications are processed on a rolling basis. *Application fee:* $100 Canadian dollars. Electronic applications accepted. *Application Contact:* Dr. Larena Hoeber, Associate Dean, Graduate Studies and Research, 306-585-4363, Fax: 306-585-4854, E-mail: khs.gsr-assocdean@uregina.ca. *Dean*, Dr. Harold Riemer, 306-585-4535, Fax: 306-585-4854, E-mail: khs.dean@uregina.ca.

***Faculty of Media, Art, and Performance*** Students: 32 full-time (22 women), 11 part-time (7 women). Average age 30. 62 applicants, 27% accepted. *Faculty:* 45 full-time (27 women), 10 part-time/adjunct (4 women). Expenses: Contact institution. *Financial support:* In 2019–20, 110 students received support, including 69 fellowships with tuition reimbursements available, 12 teaching assistantships (averaging $2,552 per year); research assistantships, career-related internships or fieldwork, scholarships/grants, and travel award and Graduate Scholarship Base funds also available. Support available to part-time students. Financial award application deadline: 9/30. In 2019, 11 master's awarded. *Program availability:* Part-time. *Application deadline:* For fall admission, 1/15 for domestic and international students. *Application fee:* $100. Electronic applications accepted. *Application Contact:* Dr. Kathleen Irwin, Associate Dean, Graduate and Research, 306-585-5519, Fax: 306-585-5544, E-mail: kathleen.irwin@uregina.ca. *Dean*, Dr. Rae Staseson, 306-585-5510, Fax: 306-585-5544, E-mail: Map.Dean@uregina.ca.

***Faculty of Nursing*** Students: 19 full-time (17 women), 36 part-time (29 women). Average age 30. 59 applicants, 54% accepted. *Faculty:* 18 full-time (15 women), 11 part-time/adjunct (10 women). Expenses: Contact institution. *Financial support:* In 2019–20, 40 students received support, including 36 fellowships, 2 teaching assistantships (averaging $2,552 per year); career-related internships or fieldwork, Federal Work-Study, scholarships/grants, unspecified assistantships, and travel Award and Graduate Scholarship Base Funds also available. Support available to part-time students. Financial award application deadline: 9/30. In 2019, 14 master's awarded. *Application deadline:* For fall admission, 3/15 for domestic and international students. *Application fee:* $100 Canadian dollars. Electronic applications accepted. *Application Contact:* Gillian Borys, Graduate Program Assistant, 306-337-3355, Fax: 306-337-8493, E-mail: gillian.borys@uregina.ca. *Associate Dean, Graduate Programs and Research*, Dr. Joan Wagner, 306-585-4070, Fax: 306-337-8493, E-mail: joan.wagner@uregina.ca.

***Faculty of Science*** Students: 266 full-time (113 women), 26 part-time (11 women). Average age 25. 534 applicants, 15% accepted. *Faculty:* 89 full-time (20 women), 50 part-time/adjunct (7 women). Expenses: Contact institution. *Financial support:* In 2019–20, 203 students received support, including 92 fellowships with tuition reimbursements available, 64 teaching assistantships (averaging $2,552 per year); research assistantships, career-related internships or fieldwork, Federal Work-Study, scholarships/grants, unspecified assistantships, and travel award and Graduate Scholarship Base funds also available. Support available to part-time students. Financial award application deadline: 9/30. In 2019, 57 master's, 13 doctorates awarded. *Program availability:* Part-time. *Application deadline:* Applications are processed on a rolling basis. *Application fee:* $100. Electronic applications accepted. *Application Contact:* Dr. Cory Butz, Associate Dean for Research, 306-585-4201, Fax: 306-585-4291, E-mail: cory.butz@uregina.ca. *Dean*, Dr. Douglas Farenick, 306-337-2110, Fax: 306-585-4291, E-mail: douglas.farenick@uregina.ca.

***Faculty of Social Work*** Students: 17 full-time (13 women), 58 part-time (50 women). Average age 30. 88 applicants, 28% accepted. *Faculty:* 26 full-time (19 women), 115 part-time/adjunct (84 women). Expenses: Contact institution. *Financial support:* In 2019–20, 61 students received support, including 51 fellowships, 6 teaching assistantships (averaging $2,552 per year); research assistantships, career-related internships or fieldwork, Federal Work-Study, scholarships/grants, unspecified assistantships, and travel award and Graduate Scholarship base funds also available. Support available to part-time students. Financial award application deadline: 9/30. In 2019, 32 master's awarded. *Program availability:* Part-time. *Application deadline:* For fall admission, 1/31 for domestic and international students. *Application fee:* $100. Electronic applications accepted. *Application Contact:* Dr. Nuelle Novik, Graduate Program Coordinator, 306-585-4573, Fax: 306-585-4872, E-mail: nuelle.novik@uregina.ca. *Dean*, Dr. Cathy Rocke, 306-585-4037, Fax: 306-585-5691, E-mail: sw.dean@uregina.ca.

***Johnson-Shoyama Graduate School of Public Policy*** Students: 116 full-time (71 women), 202 part-time (155 women). Average age 30. 328 applicants, 50% accepted. *Faculty:* 9 full-time (4 women), 19 part-time/adjunct (8 women). Expenses: Contact institution. *Financial support:* In 2019–20, 78 students received support, including 33 fellowships, 15 teaching assistantships (averaging $2,552 per year); research assistantships, career-related internships or fieldwork, Federal Work-Study, scholarships/grants, unspecified assistantships, and travel award and Graduate Scholarship Base funds also available. Support available to part-time students. Financial award application deadline: 9/30. In 2019, 67 master's, 12 other advanced degrees awarded. *Program availability:* Part-time. *Application deadline:* For fall admission, 5/1 for domestic and international students; for winter admission, 10/1 for domestic and international students. *Application fee:* $100. Electronic applications accepted. *Application Contact:* John Bird, Academic Advisor, 306-585-5469, Fax: 306-585-5461, E-mail: john.bird@uregina.ca. *Executive Director*, Dr. Doug Moen, 306-585-4921, Fax: 306-585-5461, E-mail: doeg.moen@uregina.ca.

***Kenneth Levene Graduate School of Business*** Students: 120 full-time (66 women), 45 part-time (27 women). Average age 30. 354 applicants, 45% accepted. *Faculty:* 41 full-time (15 women), 17 part-time/adjunct (7 women). Expenses: Contact institution. *Financial support:* In 2019–20, 138 students received support, including 58 fellowships, 8 teaching assistantships (averaging $2,552 per year); research assistantships, career-related internships or fieldwork, Federal Work-Study, scholarships/grants, unspecified assistantships, and travel award and Graduate Scholarship Base funds also available. Support available to part-time students. Financial award application deadline: 9/30. In 2019, 49 master's, 7 other advanced degrees awarded. *Program availability:* Part-time. *Application deadline:* For fall admission, 3/1 for domestic and international students; for winter admission, 7/1 for domestic and international students; for spring admission, 10/1 for domestic and international students; for summer admission, 10/1 for domestic and international students. Applications are processed on a rolling basis. *Application fee:* $100. Electronic applications accepted. *Application Contact:* Dr. Adrian Pitariu, Associate Dean, Research and Graduate Programs, 306-585-6294, Fax: 306-585-5361, E-mail: business.AD.levene@uregina.ca. *Dean*, Dr. Gina Grandy, 306-585-4435, Fax: 306-585-5361, E-mail: business.levene@uregina.ca.

## UNIVERSITY OF RHODE ISLAND, Kingston, RI 02881

**General Information** State-supported, coed, university. CGS member. *Enrollment:* 18,098 graduate, professional, and undergraduate students; 1,849 full-time matriculated graduate/professional students (1,171 women), 889 part-time matriculated graduate/professional students (520 women). *Enrollment by degree level:* 1,273 master's, 1,425 doctoral, 40 other advanced degrees. *Graduate faculty:* 675 full-time (335 women), 5 part-time/adjunct (2 women). *International tuition:* $26,512 full-time. *Tuition, area resident:* Full-time $13,734; part-time $763 per credit. Tuition, state resident: full-time $13,734; part-time $763 per credit. Tuition, nonresident: full-time $26,512; part-time $1473 per credit. *Required fees:* $1780; $52 per credit. $35 per term. One-time fee: $165. *Graduate housing:* Rooms and/or apartments available on a first-come, first-served basis to single and married students. Housing application deadline: 5/1. *Student services:* Campus employment opportunities, campus safety program, career counseling, free psychological counseling, international student services, low-cost health insurance, multicultural affairs office, teacher training. *Library facilities:* Robert L. Carothers Library and Learning Commons plus 3 others. *Collection:* Study areas open 24 hours, 5–7 days a week; students can reserve study rooms. *Research affiliation:* Sustainable Coastal Communities and Ecosystems (SUCCESS)-Leader with Associates, Rhode Island Network for Molecular Toxicology, Rhode Island Teacher Education Renewal (RITER), U.S. Department of Agriculture (USDA) (food stamp nutrition education).

**Computer facilities:** Computer purchase and lease plans are available. 2,500 computers available on campus for general student use. A campuswide network can be accessed from student residence rooms and from off campus. Online class registration is available.
Website: http://www.uri.edu/

**General Application Contact:** Graduate School Main Number, 401-874-2262, E-mail: urigrad@etal.uri.edu.

**GRADUATE UNITS**

**Graduate School** Students: 1,849 full-time (1,171 women), 889 part-time (520 women); includes 352 minority (76 Black or African American, non-Hispanic/Latino; 8 American Indian or Alaska Native, non-Hispanic/Latino; 132 Asian, non-Hispanic/Latino; 95 Hispanic/Latino; 5 Native Hawaiian or other Pacific Islander, non-Hispanic/Latino; 36 Two or more races, non-Hispanic/Latino), 265 international. 2,049 applicants, 46% accepted, 663 enrolled. *Faculty:* 675 full-time (340 women), 5 part-time/adjunct (3 women). Expenses: Contact institution. *Financial support:* In 2019–20, 184 research assistantships with full tuition reimbursements (averaging $9,152 per year), 338 teaching assistantships with full tuition reimbursements (averaging $14,078 per year) were awarded; unspecified assistantships also available. Financial award application deadline: 2/1; financial award applicants required to submit FAFSA. In 2019, 585 master's, 253 doctorates, 100 other advanced degrees awarded. *Program availability:* Part-time, evening/weekend, 100% online, blended/hybrid learning. *Application deadline:* For fall admission, 7/15 for domestic students, 2/1 for international students; for spring admission, 11/15 for domestic students, 7/15 for international students. *Application fee:* $65. Electronic applications accepted. *Application Contact:* Graduate Admissions, 401-874-2262, E-mail: urigrad@etal.uri.edu. *Dean of the Graduate School,* Dr. Brenton L DeBoef, 401-874-9480, Fax: 401-874-5072, E-mail: bdeboef@uri.edu.

***Alan Shawn Feinstein College of Education and Professional Studies*** Students: 43 full-time (28 women), 111 part-time (88 women); includes 17 minority (8 Black or African American, non-Hispanic/Latino; 2 American Indian or Alaska Native, non-Hispanic/Latino; 2 Asian, non-Hispanic/Latino; 4 Hispanic/Latino; 1 Two or more races, non-Hispanic/Latino), 6 international. 89 applicants, 58% accepted, 41 enrolled. *Faculty:* 23 full-time (15 women). Expenses: Contact institution. *Financial support:* In 2019–20, 3 research assistantships with tuition reimbursements (averaging $12,018 per year), 5 teaching assistantships with tuition reimbursements (averaging $17,520 per year) were awarded; unspecified assistantships also available. In 2019, 43 master's, 10 doctorates awarded. *Application Contact:* Dr. R. Anthony Rolle, Dean, 401-277-5489, E-mail: anthony_rolle@uri.edu. *Dean,* Dr. R. Anthony Rolle, 401-277-5489, E-mail: anthony_rolle@uri.edu.

***College of Arts and Sciences*** Students: 201 full-time (99 women), 256 part-time (139 women); includes 50 minority (13 Black or African American, non-Hispanic/Latino; 1 American Indian or Alaska Native, non-Hispanic/Latino; 14 Asian, non-Hispanic/Latino; 16 Hispanic/Latino; 1 Native Hawaiian or other Pacific Islander, non-Hispanic/Latino; 5 Two or more races, non-Hispanic/Latino), 42 international. 325 applicants, 67% accepted, 124 enrolled. *Faculty:* 226 full-time (105 women), 1 part-time/adjunct (0 women). Expenses: Contact institution. *Financial support:* In 2019–20, 14 research assistantships with tuition reimbursements (averaging $10,061 per year), 128 teaching assistantships with tuition reimbursements (averaging $16,874 per year) were awarded; unspecified assistantships also available. Financial award applicants required to submit FAFSA. In 2019, 130 master's, 25 doctorates, 36 other advanced degrees awarded. *Program availability:* Part-time, evening/weekend. *Application fee:* $65. Electronic applications accepted. *Application Contact:* Dr. Jeannette Riley, Dean, E-mail: jen_riley@uri.edu. *Dean,* Dr. Jeannette Riley, E-mail: jen_riley@uri.edu.

***College of Business*** Students: 84 full-time (40 women), 212 part-time (101 women); includes 42 minority (14 Black or African American, non-Hispanic/Latino; 1 American Indian or Alaska Native, non-Hispanic/Latino; 13 Asian, non-Hispanic/Latino; 10 Hispanic/Latino; 1 Native Hawaiian or other Pacific Islander, non-Hispanic/Latino; 3 Two or more races, non-Hispanic/Latino), 23 international. 218 applicants, 71% accepted, 93 enrolled. *Faculty:* 62 full-time (30 women), 1 (woman) part-time/adjunct. Expenses: Contact institution. *Financial support:* In 2019–20, 20 teaching assistantships with tuition reimbursements (averaging $13,599 per year) were awarded. Financial award applicants required to submit FAFSA. In 2019, 102 master's, 3 doctorates, 14 other advanced degrees awarded. *Program availability:* Part-time, evening/weekend. *Application fee:* $65. Electronic applications accepted. *Application Contact:* Lisa Lancellotta, Coordinator, MBA Programs, 401-874-4241, Fax: 401-874-4312, E-mail: mba@uri.edu. *Dean,* Dr. Maling Ebrahimpour, 401-874-4348, Fax: 401-874-4312, E-mail: mebrahimpour@uri.edu.

***College of Engineering*** Students: 127 full-time (32 women), 81 part-time (16 women); includes 21 minority (6 Black or African American, non-Hispanic/Latino; 1 American Indian or Alaska Native, non-Hispanic/Latino; 6 Asian, non-Hispanic/Latino; 5 Hispanic/Latino; 3 Two or more races, non-Hispanic/Latino), 76 international. 144 applicants, 71% accepted, 62 enrolled. *Faculty:* 67 full-time (14 women), 1 part-time/adjunct (0 women). Expenses: Contact institution. *Financial support:* In 2019–20, 50 research assistantships with full tuition reimbursements (averaging $9,726 per year), 31 teaching assistantships with full tuition reimbursements (averaging $10,292 per year) were awarded. Financial award applicants required to submit FAFSA. In 2019, 79 master's, 16 doctorates, 2 other advanced degrees awarded. *Program availability:* Part-time. *Application fee:* $65. Electronic applications accepted. *Application Contact:* Dr. Raymond Wright, Dean, 401-874-2186, Fax: 401-782-1066, E-mail: dean@egr.uri.edu. *Dean,* Dr. Raymond Wright, 401-874-2186, Fax: 401-782-1066, E-mail: dean@egr.uri.edu.

***College of Health Sciences*** Students: 286 full-time (227 women), 92 part-time (74 women); includes 38 minority (8 Black or African American, non-Hispanic/Latino; 14 Asian, non-Hispanic/Latino; 12 Hispanic/Latino; 4 Two or more races, non-Hispanic/Latino), 9 international. 850 applicants, 23% accepted, 79 enrolled. *Faculty:* 83 full-time (61 women), 2 part-time/adjunct (1 woman). Expenses: Contact institution. *Financial support:* In 2019–20, 11 research assistantships with tuition reimbursements (averaging $7,991 per year), 46 teaching assistantships with tuition reimbursements (averaging $12,939 per year) were awarded. Financial award applicants required to submit FAFSA. In 2019, 109 master's, 47 doctorates awarded. *Program availability:* Part-time, evening/weekend, 100% online, blended/hybrid learning. *Application fee:* $65. Electronic applications accepted. *Application Contact:* Dr. Gary Liguori, Dean, 401-874-9330, E-mail: gliguori@uri.edu. *Dean,* Dr. Gary Liguori, 401-874-9330, E-mail: gliguori@uri.edu.

***College of Nursing*** Students: 51 full-time (47 women), 72 part-time (65 women); includes 21 minority (9 Black or African American, non-Hispanic/Latino; 5 Asian, non-Hispanic/Latino; 4 Hispanic/Latino; 2 Native Hawaiian or other Pacific Islander, non-Hispanic/Latino; 1 Two or more races, non-Hispanic/Latino), 6 international. 32 applicants, 88% accepted, 21 enrolled. *Faculty:* 27 full-time (26 women). Expenses: Contact institution. *Financial support:* In 2019–20, 7 teaching assistantships with tuition reimbursements (averaging $13,376 per year) were awarded. Financial award application deadline: 2/1; financial award applicants required to submit FAFSA. In 2019, 34 master's, 9 doctorates, 1 other advanced degree awarded. *Program availability:* Part-time, evening/weekend, 100% online, blended/hybrid learning. *Application deadline:* For fall admission, 2/15 for domestic students, 2/1 for international students; for spring admission, 10/15 for domestic students, 7/15 for international students. *Application fee:* $65. Electronic applications accepted. *Application Contact:* Dr. Denise Coppa, Associate Professor/Interim Associate Dean for Graduate Programs, 401-874-5036, E-mail: dcoppa@uri.edu. *Dean,* Dr. Barbara Wolfe, 401-874-5324, E-mail: bwolfe@uri.edu.

***College of Pharmacy*** Students: 807 full-time (556 women), 13 part-time (7 women); includes 143 minority (14 Black or African American, non-Hispanic/Latino; 2 American Indian or Alaska Native, non-Hispanic/Latino; 70 Asian, non-Hispanic/Latino; 41 Hispanic/Latino; 16 Two or more races, non-Hispanic/Latino), 54 international. *Faculty:* 53 full-time (34 women). Expenses: Contact institution. *Financial support:* In 2019–20, 15 research assistantships with tuition reimbursements (averaging $8,916 per year), 17 teaching assistantships with tuition reimbursements (averaging $11,829 per year) were awarded. Financial award application deadline: 2/1; financial award applicants required to submit FAFSA. In 2019, 4 master's, 121 doctorates awarded. *Program availability:* Part-time. *Application fee:* $65. Electronic applications accepted. *Application Contact:* Dr. E. Paul Larrat, Dean/Professor, 401-874-5003, Fax: 401-874-2181, E-mail: larrat@uri.edu. *Dean/Professor,* Dr. E. Paul Larrat, 401-874-5003, Fax: 401-874-2181, E-mail: larrat@uri.edu.

***College of the Environment and Life Sciences*** Students: 188 full-time (108 women), 43 part-time (25 women); includes 22 minority (8 Black or African American, non-Hispanic/Latino; 1 American Indian or Alaska Native, non-Hispanic/Latino; 7 Asian, non-Hispanic/Latino; 2 Hispanic/Latino; 1 Native Hawaiian or other Pacific Islander, non-Hispanic/Latino; 3 Two or more races, non-Hispanic/Latino), 39 international. 222 applicants, 52% accepted, 75 enrolled. *Faculty:* 101 full-time (42 women). Expenses: Contact institution. *Financial support:* In 2019–20, 53 research assistantships with tuition reimbursements (averaging $8,336 per year), 70 teaching assistantships with tuition reimbursements (averaging $14,045 per year) were awarded. Financial award applicants required to submit FAFSA. In 2019, 74 master's, 17 doctorates, 19 other advanced degrees awarded. *Program availability:* Part-time. *Application fee:* $65. Electronic applications accepted. *Application Contact:* Dr. John Kirby, Dean, 401-874-2957, Fax: 401-874-4017, E-mail: jdkirby@uri.edu. *Dean,* Dr. John Kirby, 401-874-2957, Fax: 401-874-4017, E-mail: jdkirby@uri.edu.

***Graduate School of Oceanography*** Students: 59 full-time (34 women), 9 part-time (5 women); includes 2 minority (1 Asian, non-Hispanic/Latino; 1 Hispanic/Latino), 10 international. 87 applicants, 55% accepted, 18 enrolled. *Faculty:* 31 full-time (12 women). Expenses: Contact institution. *Financial support:* In 2019–20, 36 research assistantships with tuition reimbursements (averaging $9,988 per year), 13 teaching assistantships with tuition reimbursements (averaging $11,857 per year) were awarded. Financial award application deadline: 1/15; financial award applicants required to submit FAFSA. In 2019, 10 master's, 5 doctorates awarded. *Program availability:* Part-time. *Application deadline:* For fall admission, 1/15 for domestic and international students. *Application fee:* $65. Electronic applications accepted. *Application Contact:* Dr. David Smith, Professor of Oceanography/Associate Dean for Academic Affairs, 401-874-6172, E-mail: dcsmith@uri.edu. *Dean,* Dr. Bruce Corliss, 401-874-6222, Fax: 401-874-6931, E-mail: bruce.corliss@gso.uri.edu.

## UNIVERSITY OF RICHMOND, University of Richmond, VA 23173

**General Information** Independent, coed, comprehensive institution. *Graduate housing:* On-campus housing not available.

**GRADUATE UNITS**

**Robins School of Business** *Program availability:* Part-time, evening/weekend. Electronic applications accepted.

**School of Law** Electronic applications accepted.

## UNIVERSITY OF RIO GRANDE, Rio Grande, OH 45674

**General Information** Independent, coed, comprehensive institution. *Graduate housing:* Room and/or apartments available on a first-come, first-served basis to single students; on-campus housing not available to married students.

**GRADUATE UNITS**

**Graduate School** *Program availability:* Part-time.

## UNIVERSITY OF ROCHESTER, Rochester, NY 14627

**General Information** Independent, coed, university. CGS member. *Graduate housing:* Rooms and/or apartments available on a first-come, first-served basis to single and married students. *Research affiliation:* General Motors (chemical engineering, mechanical engineering, biomedical engineering), American Heart and Lung Associations (biochemistry/biophysics, cardiovascular research, environmental toxicology, oral biology, pulmonary medicine, pathology, pharmacology and physiology), Bausch & Lomb (optics, ophthalmology), Fermilab, Jet Propulsion Laboratory, and Lawrence Livermore National Laboratory (physics and astronomy, laser energetics), Johnson & Johnson (biology, neurosurgery, ophthalmology, psychiatry), IBM (computer science, electrical engineering, computer engineering).

**GRADUATE UNITS**

**Eastman School of Music** *Program availability:* Part-time.

**Hajim School of Engineering and Applied Sciences** Students: 624 full-time (158 women), 14 part-time (4 women); includes 66 minority (14 Black or African American, non-Hispanic/Latino; 1 American Indian or Alaska Native, non-Hispanic/Latino; 26 Asian, non-Hispanic/Latino; 16 Hispanic/Latino; 9 Two or more races, non-Hispanic/Latino), 396 international. Average age 26. 2,368 applicants, 37% accepted, 216 enrolled. *Faculty:* 98 full-time (16 women). Expenses: Contact institution. *Financial* *support:* Fellowships, research assistantships, teaching assistantships, career-related internships or fieldwork, scholarships/grants, traineeships, health care benefits, tuition waivers, and unspecified assistantships available. Support available to part-time students. In 2019, 202 master's, 36 doctorates awarded. *Application fee:* $60. Electronic applications accepted. *Application Contact:* Gretchen Briscoe, Assistant Dean of Graduate Education and Postdoctoral Affairs, AS&E, 585-275-2059, E-mail: gretchen.briscoe@rochester.edu. *Dean, Hajim School of Engineering and Applied Sciences/Professor of Electrical and Computer Engineering,* Dr. Wendi Heinzelman, 585-273-3958, E-mail: wendi.heinzelman@rochester.edu.

***Institute of Optics*** Students: 123 full-time (29 women), 6 part-time (2 women); includes 21 minority (3 Black or African American, non-Hispanic/Latino; 9 Asian, non-Hispanic/Latino; 5 Hispanic/Latino; 4 Two or more races, non-Hispanic/Latino), 68 international. Average age 26. 191 applicants, 51% accepted, 42 enrolled. *Faculty:* 18 full-time (1 woman). Expenses: Contact institution. *Financial support:* In 2019–20, 134 students received support, including 27 fellowships with full and partial tuition reimbursements available (averaging $31,796 per year), 84 research assistantships with full and partial tuition reimbursements available (averaging $29,282 per year), 23 teaching assistantships with full and partial tuition reimbursements available (averaging $1,813 per year); career-related internships or fieldwork, scholarships/grants, health care benefits, tuition waivers (full and partial), and unspecified assistantships also available. In 2019, 30 master's, 9 doctorates awarded. *Program availability:* Part-time. *Application fee:* $60. Electronic applications accepted. *Application Contact:* Kai Davies, Graduate Program Coordinator, 585-275-7629, E-mail: kai.davies@rochester.edu. *Director of the Institute of Optics; Professor,* Scott Carney, 585-274-0113, E-mail: scott.carney@rochester.edu.

**Margaret Warner Graduate School of Education and Human Development** *Program availability:* Part-time, evening/weekend.

**School of Arts and Sciences** Students: 730 full-time (304 women), 14 part-time (6 women); includes 93 minority (11 Black or African American, non-Hispanic/Latino; 1 American Indian or Alaska Native, non-Hispanic/Latino; 28 Asian, non-Hispanic/Latino; 36 Hispanic/Latino; 17 Two or more races, non-Hispanic/Latino), 308 international. Average age 28. 2,395 applicants, 25% accepted, 174 enrolled. *Faculty:* 284 full-time (88 women). Expenses: Contact institution. *Financial support:* Fellowships, research assistantships, teaching assistantships, career-related internships or fieldwork, Federal Work-Study, institutionally sponsored loans, scholarships/grants, traineeships, health care benefits, tuition waivers, and unspecified assistantships available. Support available to part-time students. In 2019, 158 master's, 77 doctorates awarded. Electronic applications accepted. *Application Contact:* Gretchen Briscoe, Assistant Dean of Graduate Enrollment and Postdoctoral Affairs, AS&E, 585-275-5029, E-mail: gretchen.briscoe@rochester.edu. *Dean of the School of Arts and Sciences and Professor of Biology,* Gloria Culver, 585-273-5000, E-mail: gloria.culver@rochester.edu.

***Goergen Institute for Data Science*** Students: 66 full-time (29 women), 6 part-time (2 women); includes 9 minority (1 Black or African American, non-Hispanic/Latino; 5 Asian, non-Hispanic/Latino; 2 Hispanic/Latino; 1 Two or more races, non-Hispanic/Latino), 52 international. Average age 26. 544 applicants, 33% accepted, 39 enrolled. Expenses: Contact institution. *Financial support:* In 2019–20, 4 students received support, including 4 teaching assistantships (averaging $1,500 per year); tuition waivers (partial) also available. In 2019, 22 master's awarded. *Application deadline:* For fall admission, 4/15 priority date for domestic and international students. *Application fee:* $60. Electronic applications accepted. *Application Contact:* Lisa Altman, Education Program Coordinator, 585-275-5288, E-mail: lisa.altman@rochester.edu. *Director,* Mujdat Cetin, 585-276-5061, E-mail: mujdat.cetin@rochester.edu.

**School of Medicine and Dentistry** *Program availability:* Part-time. Electronic applications accepted.

***Graduate Programs in Medicine and Dentistry*** *Program availability:* Part-time. Electronic applications accepted.

**School of Nursing** *Program availability:* Part-time, 100% online, blended/hybrid learning. Electronic applications accepted.

**Simon Business School** *Program availability:* Part-time, evening/weekend. Electronic applications accepted.

## UNIVERSITY OF ST. AUGUSTINE FOR HEALTH SCIENCES, San Marcos, CA 92069

**General Information** Proprietary, coed, graduate-only institution. *Graduate housing:* On-campus housing not available.

**GRADUATE UNITS**

**Graduate Programs** *Program availability:* Part-time, evening/weekend, online learning.

## UNIVERSITY OF ST. FRANCIS, Joliet, IL 60435-6169

**General Information** Independent-religious, coed, comprehensive institution. *Enrollment:* 3,079 graduate, professional, and undergraduate students; 257 full-time matriculated graduate/professional students (186 women), 870 part-time matriculated graduate/professional students (697 women). *Enrollment by degree level:* 892 master's, 140 doctoral, 95 other advanced degrees. *Graduate faculty:* 36 full-time (24 women), 91 part-time/adjunct (62 women). *Tuition:* Part-time $748 per credit hour. *Required fees:* $125 per semester. Part-time tuition and fees vary according to degree level and program. *Graduate housing:* Room and/or apartments available on a first-come, first-served basis to single students; on-campus housing not available to married students. *Student services:* Campus employment opportunities, campus safety program, career counseling, exercise/wellness program, free psychological counseling, international student services, multicultural affairs office, services for students with disabilities, teacher training. *Library facilities:* Brown Library. *Collection:* Books: 88,389 (physical), 16,299 (digital/electronic); Serial titles: 1,942 (physical), 109 (digital/electronic); Databases: 128. Weekly public service hours: 74; study areas open 24 hours, 5–7 days a week; students can reserve study rooms.

**Computer facilities:** 560 computers available on campus for general student use. A campuswide network can be accessed. Online class registration, billing and payment are available.
Website: http://www.stfrancis.edu/

**General Application Contact:** Sandee Sloka, Director Adult & Graduate Admissions, 800-735-7500, Fax: 815-740-3431, E-mail: ssloka@stfrancis.edu.

**GRADUATE UNITS**

**College of Arts and Sciences** *Program availability:* Part-time. Electronic applications accepted.

**College of Business and Health Administration** *Program availability:* Part-time, evening/weekend, 100% online, blended/hybrid learning. Electronic applications accepted.

**College of Education** *Program availability:* Part-time, evening/weekend, 100% online, blended/hybrid learning. Electronic applications accepted.

**Leach College of Nursing** *Program availability:* Part-time, evening/weekend, 100% online. Electronic applications accepted.

## UNIVERSITY OF SAINT FRANCIS, Fort Wayne, IN 46808-3994

**General Information** Independent-religious, coed, comprehensive institution. *Enrollment:* 2,249 graduate, professional, and undergraduate students; 235 full-time matriculated graduate/professional students (167 women), 230 part-time matriculated graduate/professional students (164 women). *Enrollment by degree level:* 423 master's, 37 doctoral, 5 other advanced degrees. *Graduate faculty:* 31 full-time (19 women), 30 part-time/adjunct (15 women). *Tuition:* Full-time $9450; part-time $525 per semester hour. *Required fees:* $330 per semester. Tuition and fees vary according to course load, degree level, campus/location and program. *Graduate housing:* Room and/or apartments available on a first-come, first-served basis to single students; on-campus housing not available to married students. Typical cost: $10,968 (including board). Housing application deadline: 7/1. *Student services:* Campus employment opportunities, campus safety program, career counseling, exercise/wellness program, free psychological counseling, multicultural affairs office, services for students with disabilities. *Library facilities:* Lee and Jim Vann Library. *Collection:* Books: 64,995 (physical), 239,068 (digital/electronic); Serial titles: 799 (physical), 36,336 (digital/electronic); Databases: 111. Weekly public service hours: 86; students can reserve study rooms.

**Computer facilities:** Computer purchase and lease plans are available. 105 computers available on campus for general student use. A campuswide network can be accessed. Online class registration is available.
Website: http://www.sf.edu/

**General Application Contact:** Kyle Richardson, Associate Director of Enrollment Management, 260-399-7700 Ext. 6310, E-mail: krichardson@sf.edu.

**GRADUATE UNITS**

**Graduate School** Students: 235 full-time (167 women), 230 part-time (164 women); includes 94 minority (47 Black or African American, non-Hispanic/Latino; 3 American Indian or Alaska Native, non-Hispanic/Latino; 11 Asian, non-Hispanic/Latino; 23 Hispanic/Latino; 10 Two or more races, non-Hispanic/Latino), 2 international. Average age 33. 197 applicants, 97% accepted, 128 enrolled. *Faculty:* 31 full-time (19 women), 30 part-time/adjunct (15 women). Expenses: Contact institution. *Financial support:* Applicants required to submit FAFSA. In 2019, 180 master's, 1 other advanced degree awarded. *Program availability:* Part-time, evening/weekend, 100% online, blended/hybrid learning. *Application deadline:* For fall admission, 7/1 for international students; for spring admission, 11/1 for international students; for summer admission, 3/1 for international students. Applications are processed on a rolling basis. Electronic applications accepted. *Application Contact:* Kyle Richardson, Associate Director of Enrollment Management, 260-399-7700 Ext. 6310, E-mail: krichardson@sf.edu. *Associate Vice President of Academic Affairs,* Tricia Bugajski, 260-399-7700 Ext. 6008, E-mail: tbugajski@sf.edu.

***Keith Busse School of Business and Entrepreneurial Leadership*** Students: 59 full-time (40 women), 105 part-time (63 women); includes 43 minority (24 Black or African American, non-Hispanic/Latino; 2 American Indian or Alaska Native, non-Hispanic/Latino; 4 Asian, non-Hispanic/Latino; 7 Hispanic/Latino; 6 Two or more races, non-Hispanic/Latino), 1 international. Average age 36. 90 applicants, 100% accepted, 56 enrolled. *Faculty:* 1 full-time (0 women), 19 part-time/adjunct (6 women). Expenses: Contact institution. *Financial support:* Applicants required to submit FAFSA. In 2019, 98 master's awarded. *Program availability:* Part-time, evening/weekend, online only, 100% online. *Application deadline:* Applications are processed on a rolling basis. Electronic applications accepted. *Application Contact:* Kyle Richardson, Associate Director of Enrollment Management, 260-399-7700 Ext. 6310, Fax: 260-399-8152, E-mail: krichardson@sf.edu. *KBSOBEL Division Director,* Eye-Lynn Clarke, 260-399-7700 Ext. 8315, E-mail: eclarke@sf.edu.

## UNIVERSITY OF SAINT JOSEPH, West Hartford, CT 06117-2700

**General Information** Independent-religious, coed, primarily women, comprehensive institution. *Graduate housing:* Room and/or apartments available on a first-come, first-served basis to single students; on-campus housing not available to married students. Housing application deadline: 6/1.

**GRADUATE UNITS**

**Department of Biology** *Program availability:* Part-time, online learning. Electronic applications accepted.

**Department of Business Administration** *Program availability:* Part-time, evening/weekend. Electronic applications accepted.

**Department of Chemistry** *Program availability:* Part-time, evening/weekend, online learning. Electronic applications accepted.

**Department of Counseling and Applied Behavioral Studies** *Program availability:* Part-time, evening/weekend. Electronic applications accepted.

**Department of Education** *Program availability:* Part-time, evening/weekend. Electronic applications accepted.

**Department of Nursing** *Program availability:* Part-time, evening/weekend. Electronic applications accepted.

**Department of Nutrition and Public Health** *Program availability:* Part-time, evening/weekend, online learning. Electronic applications accepted.

**Program in Marriage and Family Therapy** *Program availability:* Part-time, evening/weekend. Electronic applications accepted.

**Program in Social Work**

**Program in Special Education** *Program availability:* Part-time, evening/weekend. Electronic applications accepted.

**School of Pharmacy and Physician Assistant Studies** Electronic applications accepted.

## UNIVERSITY OF SAINT MARY, Leavenworth, KS 66048-5082

**General Information** Independent-religious, coed, comprehensive institution. *Enrollment:* 1,240 graduate, professional, and undergraduate students; 462 full-time matriculated graduate/professional students (284 women), 110 part-time matriculated graduate/professional students (81 women). *Enrollment by degree level:* 452 master's, 120 doctoral. *Graduate housing:* Room and/or apartments available on a first-come, first-served basis to single students; on-campus housing not available to married students. Typical cost: $7455 per year. *Student services:* Career counseling, free psychological counseling. *Library facilities:* Keleher Learning Commons. *Collection:* Books: 45,000 (physical), 10,500 (digital/electronic); Serial titles: 15 (physical), 38,459 (digital/electronic); Databases: 63. Weekly public service hours: 67; students can reserve study rooms.

**Computer facilities:** 30 computers available on campus for general student use. A campuswide network can be accessed. Online class registration is available. Website: http://www.stmary.edu/

**General Application Contact:** Dr. Ron Logan, Graduate Dean, 913-345-8288, Fax: 913-345-2802, E-mail: loganr@stmary.edu.

**GRADUATE UNITS**

**Graduate Programs** Students: 395 full-time (255 women), 61 part-time (40 women); includes 90 minority (25 Black or African American, non-Hispanic/Latino; 1 American Indian or Alaska Native, non-Hispanic/Latino; 13 Asian, non-Hispanic/Latino; 38 Hispanic/Latino; 4 Native Hawaiian or other Pacific Islander, non-Hispanic/Latino; 9 Two or more races, non-Hispanic/Latino), 10 international. Average age 32. Expenses: Contact institution. *Financial support:* Unspecified assistantships available. Financial award applicants required to submit FAFSA. In 2019, 167 master's, 41 doctorates awarded. *Program availability:* Part-time, evening/weekend, online learning. *Application deadline:* Applications are processed on a rolling basis. Electronic applications accepted. *Application Contact:* Dr. Michelle Metzinger, Provost and Vice President of Academics, E-mail: michelle.metzinger@stmary.edu. *Provost and Vice President of Academics*, Dr. Michelle Metzinger, E-mail: michelle.metzinger@stmary.edu.

## UNIVERSITY OF SAINT MARY OF THE LAKE–MUNDELEIN SEMINARY, Mundelein, IL 60060

**General Information** Independent-religious, men only, graduate-only institution. *Graduate housing:* Room and/or apartments guaranteed to single students; on-campus housing not available to married students. Housing application deadline: 8/1.

**GRADUATE UNITS**

**Graduate and Professional Programs** Electronic applications accepted.

## UNIVERSITY OF ST. MICHAEL'S COLLEGE, Toronto, ON M5S 1J4, Canada

**General Information** Independent-religious, coed, graduate-only institution. *Graduate housing:* Rooms and/or apartments available on a first-come, first-served basis to single and married students. Housing application deadline: 8/15.

**GRADUATE UNITS**

**Faculty of Theology** *Program availability:* Part-time. Electronic applications accepted.

## UNIVERSITY OF ST. THOMAS, St. Paul, MN 55105-1096

**General Information** Independent-religious, coed, university. *Graduate housing:* Room and/or apartments available on a first-come, first-served basis to single students; on-campus housing not available to married students. Housing application deadline: 5/1.

**GRADUATE UNITS**

**College of Arts and Sciences** *Program availability:* Part-time, evening/weekend.

**College of Education, Leadership and Counseling** *Program availability:* Part-time, evening/weekend, 100% online, blended/hybrid learning. Electronic applications accepted.

***Graduate School of Professional Psychology*** *Program availability:* Part-time, evening/weekend. Electronic applications accepted.

**Opus College of Business**

**The Saint Paul Seminary School of Divinity** *Program availability:* Part-time, evening/weekend. Electronic applications accepted.

**School of Engineering** *Program availability:* Part-time, evening/weekend. Electronic applications accepted.

**School of Law** *Program availability:* 100% online. Electronic applications accepted.

**School of Social Work** *Program availability:* Part-time, evening/weekend, 100% online, blended/hybrid learning. Electronic applications accepted.

## UNIVERSITY OF ST. THOMAS, Houston, TX 77006-4696

**General Information** Independent-religious, coed, comprehensive institution. *Enrollment:* 3,517 graduate, professional, and undergraduate students; 317 full-time matriculated graduate/professional students (153 women), 1,001 part-time matriculated graduate/professional students (714 women). *Enrollment by degree level:* 1,074 master's, 140 doctoral, 4 other advanced degrees. *Graduate faculty:* 151 full-time (68 women), 177 part-time/adjunct (100 women). *Tuition:* Full-time $30,800; part-time $1163 per credit hour. *Required fees:* $250; $210 per semester. One-time fee: $660. Tuition and fees vary according to degree level and program. *Graduate housing:* Room and/or apartments available on a first-come, first-served basis to single students; on-campus housing not available to married students. Typical cost: $1795 per year ($2940 including board). Room and board charges vary according to board plan and housing facility selected. *Student services:* Campus employment opportunities, campus safety program, career counseling, exercise/wellness program, international student services, services for students with disabilities. *Library facilities:* Doherty Library. *Collection:* Books: 262,245 (physical), 2,496 (digital/electronic); Serial titles: 74,347 (physical), 74,347 (digital/electronic); Databases: 274. Weekly public service hours: 100; students can reserve study rooms.

**Computer facilities:** Computer purchase and lease plans are available. 74 computers available on campus for general student use. A campuswide network can be accessed. Online class registration is available. Website: http://www.stthom.edu/

**General Application Contact:** Grad Programs, 713-942-5932, E-mail: gradprograms@stthom.edu.

**GRADUATE UNITS**

**Cameron School of Business** Students: 116 full-time (67 women), 131 part-time (73 women); includes 110 minority (18 Black or African American, non-Hispanic/Latino; 19 Asian, non-Hispanic/Latino; 68 Hispanic/Latino; 5 Two or more races, non-Hispanic/Latino), 72 international. Average age 31. 155 applicants, 82% accepted, 57 enrolled. *Faculty:* 17 full-time (7 women), 9 part-time/adjunct (4 women). Expenses: Contact institution. *Financial support:* Research assistantships, scholarships/grants, unspecified assistantships, and state work-study, institutional employment available. Support available to part-time students. Financial award application deadline: 8/1; financial award applicants required to submit FAFSA. In 2019, 48 master's awarded. *Program availability:* Part-time, evening/weekend, online learning. *Application deadline:* For fall admission, 8/1 for domestic students, 7/1 for international students; for spring admission, 12/1 for domestic students, 11/1 for international students; for summer admission, 5/1 for domestic students, 4/1 for international students. Applications are processed on a rolling basis. *Application fee:* $35. Electronic applications accepted. *Application Contact:* Dr. David Schein, 713-942-5936, Fax: 713-525-2110, E-mail: scheind@stthom.edu. *Dean, Cameron School of Business*, Dr. Mario Enzler, 713-525-2120, Fax: 713-525-2110, E-mail: enzlerm@stthom.edu.

**Center for Faith and Culture** Students: 9 part-time (5 women); includes 3 minority (1 Asian, non-Hispanic/Latino; 1 Hispanic/Latino; 1 Two or more races, non-Hispanic/Latino). Average age 49. *Faculty:* 2 full-time (0 women), 1 part-time/adjunct (0 women). Expenses: Contact institution. *Financial support:* Applicants required to submit FAFSA. In 2019, 1 master's awarded. *Application Contact:* Dr. Stuart Squires, Associate Director, E-mail: Squires@stthom.edu. *Director of the Center for Faith and Culture*, Fr. Binh Quach, E-mail: quach@stthom.edu.

**Center for Thomistic Studies** Students: 10 full-time (2 women), 29 part-time (4 women); includes 9 minority (2 Asian, non-Hispanic/Latino; 5 Hispanic/Latino; 2 Two or more races, non-Hispanic/Latino), 4 international. Average age 35. 23 applicants, 96% accepted, 6 enrolled. *Faculty:* 7 full-time (1 woman), 1 part-time/adjunct (0 women). Expenses: Contact institution. *Financial support:* In 2019–20, 6 students received support, including 2 fellowships with full and partial tuition reimbursements available (averaging $15,000 per year); research assistantships, teaching assistantships, scholarships/grants, tuition waivers, and unspecified assistantships also available. Financial award application deadline: 2/1; financial award applicants required to submit FAFSA. In 2019, 2 master's awarded. *Application deadline:* Applications are processed on a rolling basis. *Application fee:* $50. Electronic applications accepted. *Application Contact:* Valerie Hall, Administrative Assistant II, 713-525-3591, Fax: 713-942-3464, E-mail: hallvl@stthom.edu. *Assistant Professor*, Brian T Carl, Fax: 713-942-3464, E-mail: carlbt@stthom.edu.

**Program in Liberal Arts** Students: 12 full-time (6 women), 28 part-time (18 women); includes 19 minority (5 Black or African American, non-Hispanic/Latino; 2 Asian, non-Hispanic/Latino; 11 Hispanic/Latino; 1 Two or more races, non-Hispanic/Latino), 1 international. Average age 36. 14 applicants, 93% accepted, 11 enrolled. *Faculty:* 29 full-time (12 women), 23 part-time/adjunct (16 women). Expenses: Contact institution. *Financial support:* Applicants required to submit FAFSA. In 2019, 23 master's awarded. *Program availability:* Part-time, evening/weekend. *Application deadline:* Applications are processed on a rolling basis. *Application fee:* $35. Electronic applications accepted. *Application Contact:* Kate Henderson, Program Coordinator, 713-525-3556, Fax: 713-525-6924, E-mail: mla@stthom.edu. *Director*, Dr. Thomas Behr, 713-525-6951, E-mail: behrt@stthom.edu.

**Saint John Paul II Institute**

**School of Arts and Sciences** Students: 8 full-time (4 women), 94 part-time (67 women); includes 87 minority (1 Black or African American, non-Hispanic/Latino; 2 Asian, non-Hispanic/Latino; 84 Hispanic/Latino), 9 international. Average age 44. 164 applicants, 70% accepted, 58 enrolled. *Faculty:* 44 full-time (14 women), 49 part-time/adjunct (15 women). Expenses: Contact institution. *Financial support:* Fellowships, research assistantships, teaching assistantships, career-related internships or fieldwork, Federal Work-Study, institutionally sponsored loans, scholarships/grants, tuition waivers, and unspecified assistantships available. Support available to part-time students. Financial award application deadline: 7/15; financial award applicants required to submit FAFSA. In 2019, 35 master's awarded. *Program availability:* Part-time-only, evening/weekend. *Application deadline:* For fall admission, 7/15 priority date for domestic and international students; for spring admission, 12/15 priority date for domestic and international students; for summer admission, 4/15 priority date for domestic and international students. Applications are processed on a rolling basis. *Application fee:* $35. Electronic applications accepted. *Application Contact:* Christopher S Cheek, Graduate Admissions Manager, 713-525-3817, E-mail: cheekc@stthom.edu. *Executive Dean of the School of Arts and Sciences*, George A. Harne, PhD, 713-942-3419, E-mail: harneg@stthom.edu.

**School of Education and Human Services** Students: 89 full-time (66 women), 547 part-time (467 women); includes 448 minority (167 Black or African American, non-Hispanic/Latino; 1 American Indian or Alaska Native, non-Hispanic/Latino; 21 Asian, non-Hispanic/Latino; 248 Hispanic/Latino; 1 Native Hawaiian or other Pacific Islander, non-Hispanic/Latino; 10 Two or more races, non-Hispanic/Latino), 12 international. Average age 37. *Faculty:* 25 full-time (16 women), 41 part-time/adjunct (25 women). Expenses: Contact institution. *Financial support:* Application deadline: 4/15. In 2019, 328 master's awarded. *Program availability:* Part-time, evening/weekend, online learning. *Application deadline:* Applications are processed on a rolling basis. *Application fee:* $35. Electronic applications accepted. *Application Contact:* Alfredo G Gomez, 713-525-3540, E-mail: gomezag@stthom.edu. *Dean*, Dr. Paul C. Paese, 713-942-5999, Fax: 713-525-3871, E-mail: paesep@stthom.edu.

**School of Nursing** Students: 1 (woman) full-time, 14 part-time (11 women); includes 7 minority (5 Black or African American, non-Hispanic/Latino; 2 Asian, non-Hispanic/Latino). Average age 50. 30 applicants, 27% accepted, 7 enrolled. *Faculty:* 2 full-time (both women), 3 part-time/adjunct (all women). Expenses: Contact institution. *Financial support:* Scholarships/grants and $2000 scholarship awarded to DNP students entering in Fall 2019 available. *Program availability:* Part-time, online learning. *Application deadline:* For fall admission, 8/16 for domestic students. Applications are processed on a rolling basis. *Application fee:* $75. Electronic applications accepted. *Application Contact:* Sara N Johnson, Senior Nursing Admissions Counselor, 713-313-6067, Fax: 713-831-7802, E-mail: snjohnso@stthom.edu. *Dean and Professor*, Dr. Poldi Tschirch, 713-525-6991, Fax: 713-713-831-7802, E-mail: tschirp@stthom.edu.

**School of Theology** Students: 80 full-time (3 women), 78 part-time (29 women); includes 64 minority (5 Black or African American, non-Hispanic/Latino; 24 Asian, non-Hispanic/Latino; 34 Hispanic/Latino; 1 Two or more races, non-Hispanic/Latino), 25 international. Average age 38. 20 applicants, 100% accepted, 20 enrolled. *Faculty:* 7 full-time (2 women), 7 part-time/adjunct (1 woman). Expenses: Contact institution. *Financial support:* In 2019–20, 9 students received support. Applicants required to submit FAFSA. In 2019, 15 master's awarded. *Program availability:* Part-time-only, online learning. *Application deadline:* For fall admission, 7/30 for domestic students, 7/15 for international students; for spring admission, 12/15 for domestic students, 12/1 for international students; for summer admission, 5/1 for domestic students, 4/15 for international students. Applications are processed on a rolling basis. *Application fee:* $25. Electronic applications accepted. *Application Contact:* Beth Puayu, Assistant to the Dean, 713-654-5706, E-mail: puyaum@stthom.edu. *Division Dean*, Fr. Paul E. Lockey, 713-654-5760, E-mail: lockeyp@stthom.edu.

## UNIVERSITY OF SAN DIEGO, San Diego, CA 92110-2492

**General Information** Independent-religious, coed, university. *Enrollment:* 9,181 graduate, professional, and undergraduate students; 1,606 full-time matriculated graduate/professional students (1,041 women), 1,507 part-time matriculated graduate/professional students (851 women). *Enrollment by degree level:* 2,052 master's, 1,061 doctoral. *Graduate faculty:* 171 full-time (74 women), 232 part-time/adjunct (116 women). *Graduate housing:* Room and/or apartments available on a first-come, first-served basis to single students; on-campus housing not available to married students. Typical cost: $4970 per year ($6924 including board). Housing application deadline: 5/1. *Student services:* Campus employment opportunities, campus safety program, career counseling, child daycare facilities, exercise/wellness program, free psychological counseling, international student services, low-cost health insurance, multicultural affairs office, services for students with disabilities, teacher training. *Library facilities:* Helen K. and James S. Copley Library plus 1 other. *Collection:* Books: 453,355 (physical), 899,809 (digital/electronic); Serial titles: 10,956 (physical), 150,056 (digital/electronic); Databases: 402. Weekly public service hours: 116; students can reserve study rooms. *Research affiliation:* Leon R. Hubbard Hatchery (marine science), Tijuana River National Estuarine Research Reserve (marine science), Old Globe Theater (dramatic arts), Southwest Fisheries Science Center (marine science), Hubbs-SeaWorld Research Institute (marine science).

**Computer facilities:** Computer purchase and lease plans are available. 1,066 computers available on campus for general student use. A campuswide network can be accessed. Online class registration is available.
Website: http://www.sandiego.edu/

**General Application Contact:** Erika Garwood, Associate Director of Graduate Admissions, 619-260-4524, Fax: 619-260-4158, E-mail: grads@sandiego.edu.

**GRADUATE UNITS**

**College of Arts and Sciences** Students: 34 full-time (20 women), 29 part-time (14 women); includes 24 minority (3 Black or African American, non-Hispanic/Latino; 8 Asian, non-Hispanic/Latino; 9 Hispanic/Latino; 4 Two or more races, non-Hispanic/Latino), 2 international. Average age 29. *Faculty:* 15 full-time (5 women), 4 part-time/adjunct (2 women). Expenses: Contact institution. *Financial support:* In 2019–20, 55 students received support, including 14 fellowships with full tuition reimbursements available; career-related internships or fieldwork, Federal Work-Study, institutionally sponsored loans, scholarships/grants, and unspecified assistantships also available. Support available to part-time students. Financial award application deadline: 4/1; financial award applicants required to submit FAFSA. In 2019, 30 master's awarded. *Program availability:* Part-time, evening/weekend. *Application deadline:* Applications are processed on a rolling basis. *Application fee:* $45. Electronic applications accepted. *Application Contact:* Erika Garwood, Associate Director of Graduate Admissions, 619-260-4524, Fax: 619-260-4158, E-mail: grads@sandiego.edu. *Dean*, Dr. Noelle Norton, 619-260-4545.

**Division of Professional and Continuing Education** Students: 329 part-time (82 women); includes 141 minority (28 Black or African American, non-Hispanic/Latino; 2 American Indian or Alaska Native, non-Hispanic/Latino; 20 Asian, non-Hispanic/Latino; 83 Hispanic/Latino; 2 Native Hawaiian or other Pacific Islander, non-Hispanic/Latino; 6 Two or more races, non-Hispanic/Latino). Average age 39. 265 applicants, 86% accepted, 130 enrolled. *Faculty:* 2 full-time (1 woman), 17 part-time/adjunct (1 woman). Expenses: Contact institution. *Financial support:* Application deadline: 4/1; applicants required to submit FAFSA. In 2019, 168 master's awarded. *Program availability:* Part-time-only, evening/weekend, 100% online. *Application deadline:* For fall admission, 8/3 for domestic and international students; for spring admission, 12/2 for domestic and international students; for summer admission, 4/22 for domestic and international students. Applications are processed on a rolling basis. *Application fee:* $45. Electronic applications accepted. *Application Contact:* Erika Garwood, Associate Director of Graduate Admissions, 619-260-4524, Fax: 619-260-4158, E-mail: grads@sandiego.edu. *Assoc. Provost for Professional Education and Online Dev.*, Dr. Chell Roberts, 619-260-4585, Fax: 619-260-2961, E-mail: continuinged@sandiego.edu.

**Hahn School of Nursing and Health Science** Students: 252 full-time (202 women), 288 part-time (227 women); includes 261 minority (53 Black or African American, non-Hispanic/Latino; 2 American Indian or Alaska Native, non-Hispanic/Latino; 106 Asian, non-Hispanic/Latino; 76 Hispanic/Latino; 24 Two or more races, non-Hispanic/Latino), 24 international. Average age 34. *Faculty:* 28 full-time (23 women), 43 part-time/adjunct (32 women). Expenses: Contact institution. *Financial support:* In 2019–20, 284 students received support. Institutionally sponsored loans, scholarships/grants, and traineeships available. Support available to part-time students. Financial award application deadline: 4/1; financial award applicants required to submit FAFSA. In 2019, 174 master's, 47 doctorates awarded. *Program availability:* Part-time, evening/weekend. *Application deadline:* Applications are processed on a rolling basis. *Application fee:* $55. Electronic applications accepted. *Application Contact:* Erika Garwood, Associate Director of Graduate Admissions, 619-260-4524, Fax: 619-260-4158, E-mail: grads@sandiego.edu. *Dean, Hahn School of Nursing and Health Science*, Dr. Jane Georges, 619-260-4550, Fax: 619-260-6814, E-mail: nursing@sandiego.edu.

**Joan B. Kroc School of Peace Studies** Students: 73 full-time (58 women), 18 part-time (16 women); includes 49 minority (6 Black or African American, non-Hispanic/Latino; 6 Asian, non-Hispanic/Latino; 19 Hispanic/Latino; 18 Two or more races, non-Hispanic/Latino), 15 international. Average age 31. *Faculty:* 10 full-time (3 women), 2 part-time/adjunct (1 woman). Expenses: Contact institution. *Financial support:* In 2019–20, 79 students received support. Career-related internships or fieldwork, Federal Work-Study, institutionally sponsored loans, scholarships/grants, and unspecified assistantships available. Support available to part-time students. Financial award application deadline: 4/1; financial award applicants required to submit FAFSA. In 2019, 58 master's awarded. *Program availability:* Part-time, evening/weekend. Electronic applications accepted. *Application Contact:* Erika Garwood, Associate Director of Graduate Admissions, 619-260-4524, Fax: 619-260-4158, E-mail: grads@sandiego.edu. *Dean, Kroc School of Peace Studies*, Dr. Patricia Marquez, 619-260-7919, E-mail: krocschool@sandiego.edu.

**School of Business** Students: 194 full-time (71 women), 177 part-time (71 women); includes 116 minority (9 Black or African American, non-Hispanic/Latino; 26 Asian, non-Hispanic/Latino; 73 Hispanic/Latino; 8 Two or more races, non-Hispanic/Latino), 51 international. Average age 31. *Faculty:* 36 full-time (7 women), 20 part-time/adjunct (7 women). Expenses: Contact institution. *Financial support:* In 2019–20, 221 students received support. Career-related internships or fieldwork, Federal Work-Study, institutionally sponsored loans, and scholarships/grants available. Support available to part-time students. Financial award application deadline: 4/1; financial award applicants required to submit FAFSA. In 2019, 233 master's awarded. *Program availability:* Part-time, evening/weekend. *Application fee:* $125. Electronic applications accepted. *Application Contact:* Erika Garwood, Associate Director of Graduate Admissions, 619-260-4524, Fax: 619-260-4158, E-mail: grads@sandiego.edu. *Interim Dean*, Dr. Barbara Lougee, 619-260-4886, E-mail: sbadean@sandiego.edu.

**School of Law** Students: 711 full-time (410 women), 82 part-time (43 women); includes 254 minority (29 Black or African American, non-Hispanic/Latino; 7 American Indian or Alaska Native, non-Hispanic/Latino; 70 Asian, non-Hispanic/Latino; 122 Hispanic/Latino; 3 Native Hawaiian or other Pacific Islander, non-Hispanic/Latino; 23 Two or more races, non-Hispanic/Latino), 27 international. Average age 27. 2,971 applicants, 250 enrolled. *Faculty:* 43 full-time (16 women), 69 part-time/adjunct (21 women). Expenses: Contact institution. *Financial support:* In 2019–20, 624 students received support. Career-related internships or fieldwork, Federal Work-Study, institutionally sponsored loans, and scholarships/grants available. Support available to part-time students. Financial award application deadline: 3/1; financial award applicants required to submit FAFSA. In 2019, 52 master's, 181 doctorates awarded. *Program availability:* Part-time, evening/weekend. *Application deadline:* For fall admission, 7/31 for domestic students. Applications are processed on a rolling basis. Electronic applications accepted. *Application Contact:* Jorge Garcia, Assistant Dean, JD Admissions, 619-260-4528, Fax: 619-260-2218, E-mail: jdinfo@sandiego.edu. *Dean*, Dr. Stephen C. Ferruolo, 619-260-4527, E-mail: lawdean@sandiego.edu.

**School of Leadership and Education Sciences** Students: 364 full-time (293 women), 506 part-time (378 women); includes 389 minority (51 Black or African American, non-Hispanic/Latino; 1 American Indian or Alaska Native, non-Hispanic/Latino; 70 Asian, non-Hispanic/Latino; 221 Hispanic/Latino; 2 Native Hawaiian or other Pacific Islander, non-Hispanic/Latino; 44 Two or more races, non-Hispanic/Latino), 26 international. Average age 31. *Faculty:* 35 full-time (19 women), 74 part-time/adjunct (52 women). Expenses: Contact institution. *Financial support:* In 2019–20, 480 students received support. Career-related internships or fieldwork, Federal Work-Study, institutionally sponsored loans, scholarships/grants, unspecified assistantships, and stipends available. Support available to part-time students. Financial award application deadline: 4/1; financial award applicants required to submit FAFSA. In 2019, 370 master's, 13 doctorates awarded. *Program availability:* Part-time, evening/weekend. *Application fee:* $45. *Application Contact:* Erika Garwood, Associate Director of Graduate Admissions, 619-260-4524, Fax: 619-260-4158, E-mail: grads@sandiego.edu. *Dean*, Dr. Nicholas Ladany, 619-260-4540, Fax: 619-260-6835, E-mail: nladany@sandiego.edu.

**Shiley-Marcos School of Engineering** Students: 67 part-time (10 women); includes 34 minority (5 Black or African American, non-Hispanic/Latino; 11 Asian, non-Hispanic/Latino; 15 Hispanic/Latino; 3 Two or more races, non-Hispanic/Latino), 2 international. Average age 34. 65 applicants, 86% accepted, 37 enrolled. *Faculty:* 2 full-time (0 women), 3 part-time/adjunct (0 women). Expenses: Contact institution. *Financial support:* In 2019–20, 5 students received support. Institutionally sponsored loans and scholarships/grants available. Financial award application deadline: 4/1; financial award applicants required to submit FAFSA. In 2019, 30 master's awarded. *Program availability:* Part-time, evening/weekend. *Application deadline:* For fall admission, 8/3 for domestic students; for spring admission, 12/2 for domestic students; for summer admission, 4/13 for domestic students. Applications are processed on a rolling basis. *Application fee:* $45. Electronic applications accepted. *Application Contact:* Erika Garwood, Associate Director of Graduate Admissions, 619-260-4524, Fax: 619-260-4158, E-mail: grads@sandiego.edu. *Dean*, Dr. Chell Roberts, 619-260-4627, E-mail: croberts@sandiego.edu.

## UNIVERSITY OF SAN FRANCISCO, San Francisco, CA 94117

**General Information** Independent-religious, coed, university. *Enrollment:* 10,636 graduate, professional, and undergraduate students; 3,519 full-time matriculated graduate/professional students (2,310 women), 515 part-time matriculated graduate/professional students (339 women). *Enrollment by degree level:* 3,215 master's, 819 doctoral. *Graduate faculty:* 233 full-time (130 women), 239 part-time/adjunct (140 women). *Graduate housing:* Room and/or apartments available on a first-come, first-served basis to single students; on-campus housing not available to married students. Housing application deadline: 5/1. *Student services:* Campus employment opportunities, career counseling, exercise/wellness program, free psychological counseling, international student services, low-cost health insurance, multicultural affairs office, services for students with disabilities, teacher training, writing training. *Library facilities:* Gleeson Library|Geschke Center plus 1 other. *Collection:* Books: 532,484 (physical), 758,493 (digital/electronic); Serial titles: 7,804 (physical), 146,187 (digital/electronic); Databases: 344. Weekly public service hours: 136; study areas open 24 hours, 5–7 days a week; students can reserve study rooms. *Research affiliation:* NASA-Ames Research Center.

**Computer facilities:** Computer purchase and lease plans are available. 257 computers available on campus for general student use. A campuswide network can be accessed. Online class registration is available.
Website: http://www.usfca.edu/

**General Application Contact:** Office of Graduate Enrollment, 415-422-2090, E-mail: graduate@usfca.edu.

**GRADUATE UNITS**

**College of Arts and Sciences** Students: 980 full-time (510 women), 66 part-time (49 women); includes 390 minority (73 Black or African American, non-Hispanic/Latino; 4 American Indian or Alaska Native, non-Hispanic/Latino; 105 Asian, non-Hispanic/Latino; 151 Hispanic/Latino; 8 Native Hawaiian or other Pacific Islander, non-Hispanic/Latino; 49 Two or more races, non-Hispanic/Latino), 317 international. Average age 28. 2,752 applicants, 50% accepted, 521 enrolled. *Faculty:* 78 full-time (35 women), 52 part-time/adjunct (23 women). Expenses: Contact institution. *Financial support:* Fellowships, research assistantships, teaching assistantships, career-related internships or fieldwork, Federal Work-Study, institutionally sponsored loans, scholarships/grants, and tuition waivers (partial) available. Support available to part-time students. Financial award application deadline: 8/1; financial award applicants required to submit FAFSA. In 2019, 459 master's awarded. *Program availability:* Part-time, evening/weekend. *Application fee:* $55. Electronic applications accepted. *Application Contact:* Mark Landerghini, Information Contact, 415-422-5101, Fax: 415-422-5134, E-mail: asgraduate@usfca.edu. *Dean*, Dr. Marcelo Camperi, 415-422-6373.

**School of Education** Students: 925 full-time (702 women), 135 part-time (90 women); includes 592 minority (76 Black or African American, non-Hispanic/Latino; 2 American Indian or Alaska Native, non-Hispanic/Latino; 129 Asian, non-Hispanic/Latino; 311 Hispanic/Latino; 12 Native Hawaiian or other Pacific Islander, non-Hispanic/Latino; 62 Two or more races, non-Hispanic/Latino), 64 international. Average age 31. 1,031 applicants, 75% accepted, 418 enrolled. *Faculty:* 46 full-time (34 women), 72 part-time/adjunct (54 women). Expenses: Contact institution. *Financial support:* Fellowships, research assistantships, and teaching assistantships available. Financial award application deadline: 3/2; financial award applicants required to submit FAFSA. In 2019, 373 master's, 14 doctorates awarded. *Program availability:* Part-time, evening/weekend. *Application deadline:* For fall admission, 3/1 priority date for domestic and international students; for spring admission, 10/15 priority date for domestic and international students. Applications are processed on a rolling basis. *Application fee:* $55. Electronic applications accepted. *Application Contact:* Amy Fogliani, Director of Admission, 415-422-5467, E-mail: schoolofeducation@usfca.edu. *Dean*, Dr. Shabnam Koirala-Azad, 415-422-6525.

**School of Law** Students: 367 full-time (214 women), 141 part-time (64 women); includes 232 minority (27 Black or African American, non-Hispanic/Latino; 55 Asian, non-Hispanic/Latino; 113 Hispanic/Latino; 4 Native Hawaiian or other Pacific Islander, non-Hispanic/Latino; 33 Two or more races, non-Hispanic/Latino), 52 international. Average age 28. 1,598 applicants, 61% accepted, 213 enrolled. *Faculty:* 33 full-time (19 women), 25 part-time/adjunct (6 women). Expenses: Contact institution. *Financial* *support:* Career-related internships or fieldwork, Federal Work-Study, and institutionally sponsored loans available. Support available to part-time students. Financial award application deadline: 3/2; financial award applicants required to submit FAFSA. In 2019, 37 master's, 118 doctorates awarded. *Program availability:* Part-time, evening/weekend. *Application deadline:* For fall admission, 4/1 for domestic students. Applications are processed on a rolling basis. *Application fee:* $60. Electronic applications accepted. *Application Contact:* Alan P. Guerrero, Director of Admissions, 415-422-2975, E-mail: lawadmissions@usfca.edu. *Dean*, Susan Freiwald.

**School of Management** Students: 586 full-time (332 women), 30 part-time (15 women); includes 271 minority (30 Black or African American, non-Hispanic/Latino; 1 American Indian or Alaska Native, non-Hispanic/Latino; 108 Asian, non-Hispanic/Latino; 99 Hispanic/Latino; 4 Native Hawaiian or other Pacific Islander, non-Hispanic/Latino; 29 Two or more races, non-Hispanic/Latino), 156 international. Average age 31. 1,075 applicants, 68% accepted, 323 enrolled. *Faculty:* 33 full-time (9 women), 30 part-time/adjunct (7 women). Expenses: Contact institution. *Financial support:* Federal Work-Study and scholarships/grants available. Financial award application deadline: 3/2; financial award applicants required to submit FAFSA. In 2019, 364 master's awarded. *Program availability:* Part-time, evening/weekend, online learning. *Application fee:* $55. Electronic applications accepted. *Application Contact:* Terra Cole Brown, Assistant Director of Graduate Recruiting and Admissions, E-mail: tcolebrown@usfca.edu. *Interim Dean*, Dr. Charles T. Moses, E-mail: management@usfca.edu.

**School of Nursing and Health Professions** Students: 661 full-time (552 women), 143 part-time (121 women); includes 508 minority (71 Black or African American, non-Hispanic/Latino; 223 Asian, non-Hispanic/Latino; 163 Hispanic/Latino; 8 Native Hawaiian or other Pacific Islander, non-Hispanic/Latino; 43 Two or more races, non-Hispanic/Latino), 28 international. Average age 33. 1,404 applicants, 34% accepted, 248 enrolled. *Faculty:* 47 full-time (34 women), 61 part-time/adjunct (51 women). Expenses: Contact institution. *Financial support:* Institutionally sponsored loans available. Financial award application deadline: 3/2. In 2019, 359 master's, 33 doctorates awarded. *Program availability:* Part-time, 100% online, blended/hybrid learning. *Application deadline:* Applications are processed on a rolling basis. Electronic applications accepted. *Application Contact:* Dr. Margaret Baker, Dean, 415-422-6681, Fax: 415-422-6877, E-mail: nursing@usfca.edu. *Dean*, Dr. Margaret Baker, 415-422-6681, Fax: 415-422-6877, E-mail: nursing@usfca.edu.

## UNIVERSITY OF SASKATCHEWAN, Saskatoon, SK S7N 5A2, Canada

**General Information** Province-supported, coed, university. *Graduate housing:* Rooms and/or apartments available on a first-come, first-served basis to single and married students. *Research affiliation:* Canada Agriculture (agriculture research), Saskatchewan Research Council, University Hospital (cancer research), Innovation Place, Vaccine and Infectious Disease Organization/InterVac Laboratory (vaccinology and immunotherapeutics), Canadian Light Source.

**GRADUATE UNITS**

**College of Dentistry** Electronic applications accepted.

**College of Graduate and Postdoctoral Studies** *Program availability:* Part-time. Electronic applications accepted.

***College of Agriculture and Bioresources*** *Program availability:* Part-time.

***College of Arts and Science*** *Program availability:* Part-time. Electronic applications accepted.

***College of Education*** *Program availability:* Part-time. Electronic applications accepted.

***College of Engineering*** *Program availability:* Part-time. Electronic applications accepted.

***College of Kinesiology***

***College of Law*** *Program availability:* Part-time.

***College of Nursing*** *Program availability:* Part-time.

***College of Pharmacy and Nutrition***

***Edwards School of Business*** *Program availability:* Part-time.

***School of Environment and Sustainability***

***School of Public Policy***

***Toxicology Centre***

**College of Medicine**

**Western College of Veterinary Medicine**

## THE UNIVERSITY OF SCRANTON, Scranton, PA 18510

**General Information** Independent-religious, coed, comprehensive institution. CGS member. *Graduate housing:* Room and/or apartments available on a first-come, first-served basis to single students; on-campus housing not available to married students. *Research affiliation:* Allied Services (rehabilitation), Lackawanna River Corridor Association (environment), Universidad Iberoamericana (counseling and human services), Wyoming Valley Health Care System (nursing), Community Medical Center (health services), National Health Management Center (health care management).

**GRADUATE UNITS**

**College of Arts and Sciences** *Program availability:* Part-time, evening/weekend, 100% online. Electronic applications accepted.

**Kania School of Management**

**Panuska College of Professional Studies**

## UNIVERSITY OF SIOUX FALLS, Sioux Falls, SD 57105-1699

**General Information** Independent-religious, coed, comprehensive institution. *Graduate housing:* Rooms and/or apartments available on a first-come, first-served basis to single and married students.

**GRADUATE UNITS**

**Fredrikson School of Education** *Program availability:* Part-time, evening/weekend.

**Vucurevich School of Business** *Program availability:* Part-time, evening/weekend.

## UNIVERSITY OF SOUTH AFRICA, Pretoria 0003, South Africa

**General Information** Private, coed, university.

**GRADUATE UNITS**

**College of Agriculture and Environmental Sciences**

**College of Economic and Management Sciences**

**College of Human Sciences**

**College of Law**

**College of Science, Engineering and Technology**

**Graduate School of Business Leadership**

**Institute for Science and Technology Education**

## UNIVERSITY OF SOUTH ALABAMA, Mobile, AL 36688-0002

**General Information** State-supported, coed, university. CGS member. *Enrollment:* 14,397 graduate, professional, and undergraduate students; 3,847 full-time matriculated graduate/professional students (3,014 women), 949 part-time matriculated graduate/professional students (774 women). *Enrollment by degree level:* 3,446 master's, 1,173 doctoral, 177 other advanced degrees. *Graduate faculty:* 310 full-time (171 women), 143 part-time/adjunct (122 women). *Tuition, area resident:* Part-time $442 per credit hour. Tuition, state resident: full-time $10,608; part-time $442 per credit hour. Tuition, nonresident: full-time $21,216; part-time $884 per credit hour. *Graduate housing:* Room and/or apartments available on a first-come, first-served basis to single students; on-campus housing not available to married students. Typical cost: $4100 per year ($7800 including board). Room and board charges vary according to board plan and housing facility selected. Housing application deadline: 4/1. *Student services:* Campus employment opportunities, campus safety program, career counseling, exercise/wellness program, free psychological counseling, grant writing training, international student services, low-cost health insurance, multicultural affairs office, services for students with disabilities, teacher training, writing training. *Library facilities:* Marx Library plus 4 others. *Research affiliation:* Dauphin Island Marine Laboratory (marine sciences), Gynecologic Oncology Group (oncology), Eastern Cooperative Oncology Group (oncology), Radiation Therapy Oncology Group (oncology), National Institutes of Health (biomedical science), American College of Surgeons Oncology Group (oncology).

**Computer facilities:** Computer purchase and lease plans are available. A campuswide network can be accessed. Online class registration is available.
Website: http://www.southalabama.edu/

**General Application Contact:** Dr. Harold Pardue, Dean, Graduate School; Associate Vice President, Academic Affairs, 251-461-1600, Fax: 251-461-1513, E-mail: hpardue@southalabama.edu.

**GRADUATE UNITS**

**College of Arts and Sciences** Students: 177 full-time (114 women), 30 part-time (17 women); includes 53 minority (38 Black or African American, non-Hispanic/Latino; 1 American Indian or Alaska Native, non-Hispanic/Latino; 4 Asian, non-Hispanic/Latino; 3 Hispanic/Latino; 7 Two or more races, non-Hispanic/Latino), 6 international. Average age 28. 98 applicants, 97% accepted, 66 enrolled. *Faculty:* 76 full-time (31 women), 8 part-time/adjunct (5 women). Expenses: Contact institution. *Financial support:* Research assistantships, teaching assistantships, career-related internships or fieldwork, Federal Work-Study, institutionally sponsored loans, scholarships/grants, and unspecified assistantships available. Support available to part-time students. Financial award application deadline: 3/31; financial award applicants required to submit FAFSA. In 2019, 61 master's, 3 doctorates awarded. *Program availability:* Part-time, evening/weekend. *Application deadline:* Applications are processed on a rolling basis. *Application fee:* $60. Electronic applications accepted. *Application Contact:* Dr. Eric Loomis, Associate Dean; Graduate Director, College of Arts and Sciences, 251-460-7811, Fax: 251-461-1744, E-mail: ejloomis@southalabama.edu. *Dean, College of Arts and Sciences*, Dr. Andrzej Wierzbicki, 251-460-6280, Fax: 251-460-7928, E-mail: awierzbicki@southalabama.edu.

**College of Education and Professional Studies** Students: 338 full-time (249 women), 121 part-time (91 women); includes 141 minority (109 Black or African American, non-Hispanic/Latino; 3 American Indian or Alaska Native, non-Hispanic/Latino; 7 Asian, non-Hispanic/Latino; 10 Hispanic/Latino; 1 Native Hawaiian or other Pacific Islander, non-Hispanic/Latino; 11 Two or more races, non-Hispanic/Latino), 7 international. Average age 32. 163 applicants, 98% accepted, 128 enrolled. *Faculty:* 37 full-time (24 women), 10 part-time/adjunct (8 women). Expenses: Contact institution. *Financial support:* Fellowships, research assistantships, teaching assistantships, career-related internships or fieldwork, Federal Work-Study, institutionally sponsored loans, scholarships/grants, and unspecified assistantships available. Support available to part-time students. Financial award application deadline: 3/31; financial award applicants required to submit FAFSA. In 2019, 136 master's, 18 doctorates, 5 other advanced degrees awarded. *Program availability:* Part-time, evening/weekend. *Application deadline:* For fall admission, 8/18 for domestic students, 7/18 for international students; for spring admission, 1/10 for domestic students, 12/10 for international students; for summer admission, 5/31 for domestic students. Applications are processed on a rolling basis. *Application fee:* $35. Electronic applications accepted. *Application Contact:* Dr. John Kovaleski, Associate Dean, Director of Graduate Studies, College of Education and Professional Studies, 251-380-2738, Fax: 251-380-2758, E-mail: jkovales@southalabama.edu. *Dean, College of Education and Professional Studies*, Dr. Andrea Kent, 251-380-2738, Fax: 251-380-2748, E-mail: akent@southalabama.edu.

**College of Engineering** Students: 48 full-time (14 women), 29 part-time (6 women); includes 11 minority (4 Black or African American, non-Hispanic/Latino; 3 Asian, non-Hispanic/Latino; 3 Hispanic/Latino; 1 Two or more races, non-Hispanic/Latino), 18 international. Average age 30. 62 applicants, 79% accepted, 27 enrolled. *Faculty:* 20 full-time (2 women), 1 part-time/adjunct (0 women). Expenses: Contact institution. *Financial support:* Fellowships, research assistantships, teaching assistantships, career-related internships or fieldwork, Federal Work-Study, institutionally sponsored loans, scholarships/grants, and unspecified assistantships available. Support available to part-time students. Financial award application deadline: 3/31; financial award applicants required to submit FAFSA. In 2019, 24 master's, 4 doctorates awarded. *Program availability:* Part-time. *Application deadline:* For fall admission, 7/1 priority date for domestic students, 6/15 priority date for international students; for spring admission, 12/1 priority date for domestic students, 11/1 priority date for international students; for summer admission, 5/1 priority date for domestic students, 4/1 priority date for international students. Applications are processed on a rolling basis. *Application fee:* $35. Electronic applications accepted. *Application Contact:* Brenda Poole, Academic Records Specialist, 251-460-6140, Fax: 251-460-6343, E-mail: engineering@southalabama.edu. *Dean, College of Engineering*, Dr. John Usher, 251-460-6140, Fax: 251-460-6343, E-mail: engineering@southalabama.edu.

**College of Medicine** Students: 336 full-time (172 women); includes 93 minority (35 Black or African American, non-Hispanic/Latino; 7 American Indian or Alaska Native, non-Hispanic/Latino; 38 Asian, non-Hispanic/Latino; 9 Hispanic/Latino; 1 Native Hawaiian or other Pacific Islander, non-Hispanic/Latino; 3 Two or more races, non-Hispanic/Latino), 14 international. Average age 25. 15 applicants. *Faculty:* 227 full-time (68 women), 3 part-time/adjunct (2 women). Expenses: Contact institution. *Financial support:* Fellowships, research assistantships, teaching assistantships, career-related internships or fieldwork, institutionally sponsored loans, scholarships/grants, and unspecified assistantships available. Support available to part-time students. Financial award application deadline: 3/31; financial award applicants required to submit FAFSA. In 2019, 89 doctorates awarded. *Application fee:* $75. Electronic applications accepted. *Application Contact:* Mark Scott, Director of Admissions, College of Medicine, 251-460-7176, Fax: 251-460-6278, E-mail: mscott@southalabama.edu. *Vice President for*

*Medical Affairs/Dean of the College of Medicine*, Dr. John V. Marymont, 251-341-3030, Fax: 251-341-3994, E-mail: jmarymont@southalabama.edu.

**College of Nursing** Students: 2,311 full-time (2,024 women), 716 part-time (636 women); includes 955 minority (613 Black or African American, non-Hispanic/Latino; 28 American Indian or Alaska Native, non-Hispanic/Latino; 121 Asian, non-Hispanic/Latino; 123 Hispanic/Latino; 4 Native Hawaiian or other Pacific Islander, non-Hispanic/Latino; 66 Two or more races, non-Hispanic/Latino). Average age 35. 884 applicants, 93% accepted, 624 enrolled. *Faculty:* 72 full-time (66 women), 116 part-time/adjunct (103 women). Expenses: Contact institution. *Financial support:* Fellowships, research assistantships, teaching assistantships, career-related internships or fieldwork, Federal Work-Study, institutionally sponsored loans, scholarships/grants, and unspecified assistantships available. Support available to part-time students. Financial award application deadline: 3/31; financial award applicants required to submit FAFSA. In 2019, 744 master's, 157 doctorates, 94 other advanced degrees awarded. *Program availability:* Part-time, online learning. *Application deadline:* For fall admission, 2/15 priority date for domestic students, 1/15 priority date for international students; for spring admission, 7/15 priority date for domestic students, 6/15 priority date for international students; for summer admission, 11/15 priority date for domestic students, 10/15 priority date for international students. Applications are processed on a rolling basis. *Application fee:* $100. Electronic applications accepted. *Application Contact:* Jennifer Bouvier, Academic Advisor II, 251-445-9400, Fax: 251-445-9416, E-mail: jcamp@southalabama.edu. *Dean, College of Nursing*, Dr. Heather Hall, 251-445-9400, Fax: 251-445-9416, E-mail: heatherhall@southalabama.edu.

**Graduate School** Students: 29 full-time (21 women), 12 part-time (6 women); includes 7 minority (5 Black or African American, non-Hispanic/Latino; 1 Asian, non-Hispanic/Latino; 1 Two or more races, non-Hispanic/Latino), 2 international. Average age 28. 9 applicants, 89% accepted, 8 enrolled. *Faculty:* 11 full-time (2 women). Expenses: Contact institution. *Financial support:* Fellowships, research assistantships, teaching assistantships, career-related internships or fieldwork, Federal Work-Study, institutionally sponsored loans, scholarships/grants, and unspecified assistantships available. Support available to part-time students. Financial award application deadline: 3/31; financial award applicants required to submit FAFSA. In 2019, 3 master's, 7 doctorates awarded. *Program availability:* Part-time, evening/weekend. *Application fee:* $50. Electronic applications accepted. *Application Contact:* DeAnna Cobb, Assistant Director, Graduate School Services, 251-460-6310, E-mail: deannacobb@southalabama.edu. *Dean, Graduate School*, Dr. John Harold Pardue, 251-460-6310, E-mail: hpardue@southalabama.edu.

**Mitchell College of Business** Students: 107 full-time (58 women), 22 part-time (12 women); includes 26 minority (15 Black or African American, non-Hispanic/Latino; 1 American Indian or Alaska Native, non-Hispanic/Latino; 8 Asian, non-Hispanic/Latino; 2 Two or more races, non-Hispanic/Latino), 7 international. Average age 33. 54 applicants, 96% accepted, 49 enrolled. *Faculty:* 13 full-time (4 women). Expenses: Contact institution. *Financial support:* Fellowships, research assistantships, teaching assistantships, career-related internships or fieldwork, Federal Work-Study, institutionally sponsored loans, scholarships/grants, and unspecified assistantships available. Support available to part-time students. Financial award application deadline: 3/31; financial award applicants required to submit FAFSA. In 2019, 33 master's, 4 doctorates awarded. *Program availability:* Part-time, evening/weekend. *Application deadline:* For fall admission, 7/15 for domestic and international students; for spring admission, 12/1 for domestic and international students; for summer admission, 1/31 for domestic students, 10/15 for international students. *Application fee:* $35. Electronic applications accepted. *Application Contact:* Dr. Gwendolyn Pennywell, Assistant Dean of Graduate Studies, Mitchell College of Business, 251-460-6418, Fax: 251-460-6529, E-mail: mcobgraduate@southalabama.edu. *Dean, Mitchell College of Business*, Dr. Bob Wood, 251-460-6419, Fax: 251-460-6529, E-mail: bgwood@southalabama.edu.

**Pat Capps Covey College of Allied Health Professions** Students: 418 full-time (336 women), 1 (woman) part-time; includes 27 minority (5 Black or African American, non-Hispanic/Latino; 5 American Indian or Alaska Native, non-Hispanic/Latino; 7 Asian, non-Hispanic/Latino; 5 Hispanic/Latino; 1 Native Hawaiian or other Pacific Islander, non-Hispanic/Latino; 4 Two or more races, non-Hispanic/Latino), 26 international. Average age 24. 796 applicants, 44% accepted, 139 enrolled. *Faculty:* 36 full-time (30 women), 7 part-time/adjunct (6 women). Expenses: Contact institution. *Financial support:* Fellowships, research assistantships, teaching assistantships, career-related internships or fieldwork, Federal Work-Study, institutionally sponsored loans, scholarships/grants, and unspecified assistantships available. Support available to part-time students. Financial award application deadline: 3/31; financial award applicants required to submit FAFSA. In 2019, 92 master's, 54 doctorates awarded. *Application deadline:* Applications are processed on a rolling basis. *Application fee:* $75. Electronic applications accepted. *Application Contact:* Dr. Susan Gordon-Hickey, Interim Dean, College of Allied Health, 251-445-9250, Fax: 251-445-9259, E-mail: gordonhickey@southalabama.edu. *Interim Dean, College of Allied Health*, Dr. Susan Gordon-Hickey, 251-445-9250, Fax: 251-445-9259, E-mail: gordonhickey@southalabama.edu.

**School of Computing** Students: 83 full-time (26 women), 18 part-time (5 women); includes 22 minority (13 Black or African American, non-Hispanic/Latino; 1 American Indian or Alaska Native, non-Hispanic/Latino; 3 Asian, non-Hispanic/Latino; 1 Hispanic/Latino; 1 Native Hawaiian or other Pacific Islander, non-Hispanic/Latino; 3 Two or more races, non-Hispanic/Latino), 28 international. Average age 32. 61 applicants, 82% accepted, 25 enrolled. *Faculty:* 18 full-time (3 women). Expenses: Contact institution. *Financial support:* Fellowships, research assistantships, teaching assistantships, Federal Work-Study, institutionally sponsored loans, scholarships/grants, and unspecified assistantships available. Support available to part-time students. Financial award application deadline: 3/31; financial award applicants required to submit FAFSA. In 2019, 29 master's, 2 doctorates awarded. *Program availability:* Part-time, evening/weekend. *Application deadline:* For fall admission, 7/15 priority date for domestic students, 6/15 priority date for international students; for spring admission, 12/1 priority date for domestic students, 11/1 priority date for international students; for summer admission, 5/1 priority date for domestic students, 4/1 priority date for international students. Applications are processed on a rolling basis. *Application fee:* $45. Electronic applications accepted. *Application Contact:* Dr. Debra Chapman, Director of Graduate Studies, Assistant Professor, School of Computing, 251-460-1599, Fax: 251-460-7274, E-mail: dchapman@southalabama.edu. *Dean, Professor, School of Computing*, Dr. Alec Yasinsac, 251-460-6390, Fax: 251-460-7274, E-mail: yasinsac@southalabama.edu.

## UNIVERSITY OF SOUTH CAROLINA, Columbia, SC 29208

**General Information** State-supported, coed, university. CGS member. *Graduate housing:* Rooms and/or apartments available to single and married students. *Research affiliation:* E.I. du Pont de Nemours and Company (engineering, chemical engineering), Westinghouse/Savannah River Corporation (environmental restoration, hazardous waste remediation), Motorola Corporation–Energy Production Division (electrochemical engineering), Glaxo-Wellcome (pharmaceuticals), NCR Corporation (electrical and computer engineering).

**GRADUATE UNITS**

**The Graduate School** *Program availability:* Part-time, evening/weekend, online learning. Electronic applications accepted.

***Arnold School of Public Health*** *Program availability:* Part-time, online learning. Electronic applications accepted.

***College of Arts and Sciences*** *Program availability:* Part-time, evening/weekend. Electronic applications accepted.

***College of Education*** *Program availability:* Part-time, evening/weekend, online learning. Electronic applications accepted.

***College of Engineering and Computing*** *Program availability:* Part-time, evening/weekend, online learning. Electronic applications accepted.

***College of Hospitality, Retail, and Sport Management*** *Program availability:* Part-time, online learning. Electronic applications accepted.

***College of Information and Communications***

***College of Nursing*** *Program availability:* Part-time, online learning. Electronic applications accepted.

***College of Social Work*** *Program availability:* Part-time. Electronic applications accepted.

***Darla Moore School of Business*** *Program availability:* Part-time, evening/weekend, online learning. Electronic applications accepted.

***School of Music*** *Program availability:* Part-time. Electronic applications accepted.

***School of the Environment*** *Program availability:* Part-time, online learning. Electronic applications accepted.

**School of Law**

**School of Medicine** Electronic applications accepted.

**South Carolina College of Pharmacy** *Program availability:* Part-time. Electronic applications accepted.

## UNIVERSITY OF SOUTH CAROLINA AIKEN, Aiken, SC 29801

**General Information** State-supported, coed, comprehensive institution. *Enrollment:* 3,720 graduate, professional, and undergraduate students; 46 full-time matriculated graduate/professional students (26 women), 191 part-time matriculated graduate/professional students (95 women). *Enrollment by degree level:* 237 master's. *Graduate faculty:* 24 full-time (16 women), 6 part-time/adjunct (5 women). *International tuition:* $29,760 full-time. *Tuition, area resident:* Full-time $13,734; part-time $572.25 per credit hour. Tuition, state resident: full-time $13,734; part-time $572.25 per credit hour. Tuition, nonresident: full-time $29,760; part-time $1240 per credit hour. *Required fees:* $13 per credit hour. $25 per semester. Tuition and fees vary according to course load and program. *Graduate housing:* Room and/or apartments available on a first-come, first-served basis to single students; on-campus housing not available to married students. Typical cost: $5192 per year ($7946 including board). Room and board charges vary according to board plan. *Student services:* Campus employment opportunities, campus safety program, career counseling, child daycare facilities, exercise/wellness program, free psychological counseling, grant writing training, international student services, multicultural affairs office, services for students with disabilities, teacher training, writing training. *Library facilities:* Gregg-Graniteville Library. *Collection:* Books: 132,606 (physical), 345,793 (digital/electronic); Serial titles: 16,359 (physical), 128,203 (digital/electronic); Databases: 220. Weekly public service hours: 78; students can reserve study rooms. *Research affiliation:* VA Boston Healthcare System (Post Traumatic Stress Disorder (PTSD)), Dwight D. Eisenhower Army Medical Center (neuroscience), University of South Florida (psychology), Baruch College of the City University of New York (psychology), Illinois Institute of Technology (psychology), University of Rochester (psychology).

**Computer facilities:** 550 computers available on campus for general student use. A campuswide network can be accessed. Online class registration is available. Website: http://www.usca.edu/

**General Application Contact:** Dan Robb, Associate Vice Chancellor for Enrollment Management, 803-641-3487, Fax: 803-641-3727, E-mail: danr@usca.edu.

**GRADUATE UNITS**

**Master of Education in Educator Leadership**

**Program in Applied Clinical Psychology** Students: 17 full-time (16 women), 8 part-time (5 women); includes 3 minority (1 Black or African American, non-Hispanic/Latino; 1 Hispanic/Latino; 1 Two or more races, non-Hispanic/Latino), 1 international. Average age 26. 38 applicants, 29% accepted, 7 enrolled. *Faculty:* 8 full-time (6 women), 1 part-time/adjunct (0 women). Expenses: Contact institution. *Financial support:* In 2019–20, 20 students received support, including 18 research assistantships with partial tuition reimbursements available (averaging $3,788 per year), 5 teaching assistantships with partial tuition reimbursements available (averaging $2,857 per year); career-related internships or fieldwork, Federal Work-Study, scholarships/grants, tuition waivers (partial), and unspecified assistantships also available. Financial award application deadline: 3/1; financial award applicants required to submit FAFSA. In 2019, 16 master's awarded. *Program availability:* Part-time. *Application deadline:* For fall admission, 6/1 priority date for domestic and international students. Applications are processed on a rolling basis. *Application fee:* $45 ($100 for international students). Electronic applications accepted. *Application Contact:* Dan Robb, Associate Vice Chancellor for Enrollment Management, 803-641-3487, Fax: 803-641-3727, E-mail: danr@usca.edu. *Director*, Dr. Jane Stafford, 803-641-3358, Fax: 803-641-3720, E-mail: jstafford@usca.edu.

**Program in Business Administration** Students: 27 full-time (8 women), 167 part-time (79 women); includes 45 minority (25 Black or African American, non-Hispanic/Latino; 4 Asian, non-Hispanic/Latino; 11 Hispanic/Latino; 5 Two or more races, non-Hispanic/Latino), 3 international. Average age 36. 185 applicants, 70% accepted, 96 enrolled. *Faculty:* 10 full-time (5 women). Expenses: Contact institution. *Financial support:* In 2019–20, 6 students received support. Scholarships/grants and tuition waivers (partial) available. Support available to part-time students. Financial award application deadline: 3/1; financial award applicants required to submit FAFSA. In 2019, 16 master's awarded. *Program availability:* Part-time, online only, 100% online. *Application deadline:* For fall admission, 8/3 for domestic and international students; for spring admission, 12/16 for domestic and international students. Applications are processed on a rolling basis. *Application fee:* $45 ($100 for international students). Electronic applications accepted. *Application Contact:* Dan Robb, Associate Vice Chancellor for Enrollment Management, 803-641-3487, Fax: 803-641-3727, E-mail: danr@usca.edu. *Dean for School of Business Administration*, Dr. Michael J. Fekula, 803-641-3340, E-mail: mickf@usca.edu.

**Program in Educational Technology** Students: 1 (woman) full-time, 8 part-time (3 women). Average age 37. 3 applicants, 67% accepted, 2 enrolled. *Faculty:* 2 full-time (1 woman). Expenses: Contact institution. *Financial support:* In 2019–20, 5 students received support. Fellowships with partial tuition reimbursements available, career-related internships or fieldwork, Federal Work-Study, scholarships/grants, tuition waivers (partial), and unspecified assistantships available. Support available to part-time students. Financial award application deadline: 3/1; financial award applicants required to submit FAFSA. In 2019, 2 master's awarded. *Program availability:* Part-time, online only, 100% online. *Application deadline:* Applications are processed on a rolling basis. *Application fee:* $45 ($100 for international students). Electronic applications accepted. *Application Contact:* Dan Robb, Associate Vice Chancellor for Enrollment Management, 803-641-3487, Fax: 803-641-3727, E-mail: danr@usca.edu. *Educational Technology Program Coordinator,* Dr. Erin Besser, 803-641-3712, E-mail: erinbe@usca.edu.

## UNIVERSITY OF SOUTH CAROLINA UPSTATE, Spartanburg, SC 29303-4999

**General Information** State-supported, coed, comprehensive institution. *Enrollment:* 6,306 graduate, professional, and undergraduate students; 11 full-time matriculated graduate/professional students (7 women), 444 part-time matriculated graduate/professional students (382 women). *Enrollment by degree level:* 356 master's, 1 other advanced degree. *Graduate faculty:* 15 full-time (11 women), 6 part-time/adjunct (4 women). *Tuition, area resident:* Full-time $6867; part-time $572.25 per semester. Tuition, nonresident: full-time $14,880; part-time $1240 per semester hour. *Required fees:* $35; $35 per term. $25.50 per term. Tuition and fees vary according to course load and program. *Graduate housing:* On-campus housing not available. *Student services:* Campus employment opportunities, campus safety program, career counseling, exercise/wellness program, free psychological counseling, grant writing training, international student services, low-cost health insurance, multicultural affairs office, services for students with disabilities, teacher training, writing training. *Library facilities:* University of South Carolina Upstate Library.

**Computer facilities:** 450 computers available on campus for general student use. A campuswide network can be accessed. Online class registration is available. Website: http://www.uscupstate.edu/

**General Application Contact:** Dr. Tina Herzberg, Director of Graduate Education Programs, 864-503-5572, Fax: 864-503-5574, E-mail: therzberg@uscupstate.edu.

**GRADUATE UNITS**

**Graduate Programs** Students: 23 full-time (15 women), 432 part-time (375 women); includes 68 minority (42 Black or African American, non-Hispanic/Latino; 6 Asian, non-Hispanic/Latino; 12 Hispanic/Latino; 8 Two or more races, non-Hispanic/Latino), 3 international. Average age 24. *Faculty:* 15 full-time (11 women), 6 part-time/adjunct (4 women). Expenses: Contact institution. *Financial support:* Institutionally sponsored loans and institutional work-study available. Financial award application deadline: 7/15; financial award applicants required to submit FAFSA. In 2019, 11 master's awarded. *Program availability:* Part-time, evening/weekend. *Application deadline:* Applications are processed on a rolling basis. *Application fee:* $50. Electronic applications accepted. *Application Contact:* Donette Stewart, Associate Vice Chancellor for Enrollment Services, 864-503-5280, E-mail: dstewart@uscupstate.edu. *Director of Graduate Programs,* Dr. Tina Herzberg, 864-503-5572, Fax: 864-503-5573, E-mail: therzberg@uscupstate.edu.

## UNIVERSITY OF SOUTH DAKOTA, Vermillion, SD 57069

**General Information** State-supported, coed, university. CGS member. *Graduate housing:* Room and/or apartments available on a first-come, first-served basis to single students; on-campus housing not available to married students. Housing application deadline: 5/1.

**GRADUATE UNITS**

**Graduate School** *Program availability:* Part-time, evening/weekend, 100% online, blended/hybrid learning. Electronic applications accepted.

***Beacom School of Business*** *Program availability:* Part-time, evening/weekend, 100% online, blended/hybrid learning. Electronic applications accepted.

***College of Arts and Sciences*** *Program availability:* Part-time, online learning. Electronic applications accepted.

***College of Fine Arts*** Electronic applications accepted.

***Sanford School of Medicine*** *Program availability:* Part-time.

***School of Education*** *Program availability:* Part-time, evening/weekend, 100% online, blended/hybrid learning. Electronic applications accepted.

***School of Health Sciences*** *Program availability:* Part-time.

***School of Law*** *Program availability:* Part-time. Electronic applications accepted.

## UNIVERSITY OF SOUTHERN CALIFORNIA, Los Angeles, CA 90089

**General Information** Independent, coed, university. CGS member. *Graduate housing:* Rooms and/or apartments available on a first-come, first-served basis to single and married students. *Research affiliation:* SETI Institute (astronomy/astrobiology), Rancho Los Amigos Medical Center (medicine), Children's Hospital Los Angeles (medicine), Doheny Eye Institute (medicine), House Ear Institute (medicine), Jet Propulsion Laboratory (engineering and technology).

**GRADUATE UNITS**

**Graduate School** Electronic applications accepted.

***Annenberg School for Communication and Journalism*** Students: 702 full-time, 147 part-time; includes 261 minority (88 Black or African American, non-Hispanic/Latino; 1 American Indian or Alaska Native, non-Hispanic/Latino; 78 Asian, non-Hispanic/Latino; 58 Hispanic/Latino; 4 Native Hawaiian or other Pacific Islander, non-Hispanic/Latino; 32 Two or more races, non-Hispanic/Latino), 294 international. Average age 25. 1,852 applicants, 37% accepted, 389 enrolled. *Faculty:* 104 full-time, 122 part-time/adjunct. Expenses: Contact institution. *Financial support:* In 2019–20, 28 fellowships with full and partial tuition reimbursements (averaging $32,000 per year), 16 research assistantships with partial tuition reimbursements (averaging $15,000 per year), 6 teaching assistantships with full tuition reimbursements (averaging $22,287 per year) were awarded; career-related internships or fieldwork, Federal Work-Study, institutionally sponsored loans, scholarships/grants, health care benefits, tuition waivers (full and partial), and unspecified assistantships also available. Support available to part-time students. Financial award application deadline: 1/1; financial award applicants required to submit FAFSA. In 2019, 482 master's, 13 doctorates awarded. *Program availability:* Part-time, evening/weekend, online learning. *Application deadline:* For fall admission, 12/1 priority date for domestic and international students; for spring admission, 3/1 priority date for domestic students, 1/1 priority date for international students; for summer admission, 1/1 priority date for domestic and international students. Applications are processed on a rolling basis. *Application fee:* $90. Electronic applications accepted. *Application Contact:* Allyson Hill, Associate Dean for Admissions, 213-821-0770, Fax: 213-740-1933, E-mail: ascadm@usc.edu. *Dean,* Willow Bay, 213-740-6180, Fax: 213-740-3772, E-mail: ascdean@usc.edu.

***Dana and David Dornsife College of Letters, Arts and Sciences*** Electronic applications accepted.

***Gould School of Law***

***Herman Ostrow School of Dentistry*** Electronic applications accepted.

***Leonard Davis School of Gerontology*** *Program availability:* Part-time, online learning. Electronic applications accepted.

***Marshall School of Business*** Electronic applications accepted.

***Roski School of Art and Design*** Electronic applications accepted.

***Rossier School of Education*** Electronic applications accepted.

***School of Architecture*** Electronic applications accepted.

***School of Cinematic Arts*** Electronic applications accepted.

***School of Dramatic Arts*** Electronic applications accepted.

***School of Pharmacy***

***Sol Price School of Public Policy*** Electronic applications accepted.

***Suzanne Dworak-Peck School of Social Work*** Electronic applications accepted.

***Thornton School of Music*** *Program availability:* Part-time, evening/weekend. Electronic applications accepted.

***Viterbi School of Engineering*** *Program availability:* Part-time, online learning. Electronic applications accepted.

**Keck School of Medicine** Students: 1,816 full-time (1,115 women), 95 part-time (73 women); includes 1,094 minority (112 Black or African American, non-Hispanic/Latino; 10 American Indian or Alaska Native, non-Hispanic/Latino; 615 Asian, non-Hispanic/Latino; 249 Hispanic/Latino; 12 Native Hawaiian or other Pacific Islander, non-Hispanic/Latino; 96 Two or more races, non-Hispanic/Latino), 169 international. Average age 25. 10,438 applicants, 12% accepted, 599 enrolled. *Faculty:* 514 full-time (175 women), 59 part-time/adjunct (31 women). Expenses: Contact institution. *Financial support:* Fellowships, research assistantships, teaching assistantships, career-related internships or fieldwork, Federal Work-Study, institutionally sponsored loans, scholarships/grants, traineeships, and health care benefits available. Support available to part-time students. Financial award applicants required to submit FAFSA. In 2019, 421 master's, 34 doctorates, 196 other advanced degrees awarded. *Application deadline:* Applications are processed on a rolling basis. *Application fee:* $90. Electronic applications accepted. *Application Contact:* Marisela Zuniga, Department Business Administrator, 323-442-1607, Fax: 323-442-1199, E-mail: mzuniga@usc.edu. *Dean,* Dr. Laura Mosqueda, 323-442-1900.

***Graduate Programs in Medicine*** Students: 1,070 full-time (754 women), 95 part-time (73 women); includes 631 minority (67 Black or African American, non-Hispanic/Latino; 10 American Indian or Alaska Native, non-Hispanic/Latino; 322 Asian, non-Hispanic/Latino; 160 Hispanic/Latino; 11 Native Hawaiian or other Pacific Islander, non-Hispanic/Latino; 61 Two or more races, non-Hispanic/Latino), 168 international. Average age 26. 2,397 applicants, 38% accepted, 413 enrolled. *Faculty:* 514 full-time (175 women), 59 part-time/adjunct (31 women). Expenses: Contact institution. *Financial support:* Fellowships, research assistantships, teaching assistantships, career-related internships or fieldwork, Federal Work-Study, institutionally sponsored loans, scholarships/grants, traineeships, and health care benefits available. Support available to part-time students. Financial award applicants required to submit CSS PROFILE or FAFSA. In 2019, 421 master's, 34 doctorates awarded. *Application deadline:* Applications are processed on a rolling basis. *Application fee:* $90. Electronic applications accepted. *Application Contact:* Marisela Zuniga, Administrative Coordinator, 323-442-1607, Fax: 323-442-1199, E-mail: mzuniga@usc.edu. *Associate Dean for Graduate Affairs,* Dr. Ite Offringa, 323-442-1607, Fax: 323-442-1199, E-mail: ilaird@usc.edu.

**Program in Neuroscience** Electronic applications accepted.

## UNIVERSITY OF SOUTHERN INDIANA, Evansville, IN 47712-3590

**General Information** State-supported, coed, comprehensive institution. CGS member. *Graduate housing:* Room and/or apartments available on a first-come, first-served basis to single students; on-campus housing not available to married students. Housing application deadline: 3/1.

**GRADUATE UNITS**

**Graduate Studies** *Program availability:* Part-time, evening/weekend. Electronic applications accepted.

***College of Liberal Arts*** *Program availability:* Part-time, evening/weekend. Electronic applications accepted.

***College of Nursing and Health Professions*** *Program availability:* Part-time, blended/hybrid learning. Electronic applications accepted.

***Pott College of Science, Engineering, and Education*** *Program availability:* Part-time, evening/weekend. Electronic applications accepted.

***Romain College of Business*** *Program availability:* Part-time, evening/weekend. Electronic applications accepted.

## UNIVERSITY OF SOUTHERN MAINE, Portland, ME 04103

**General Information** State-supported, coed, comprehensive institution. CGS member. *Enrollment:* 8,429 graduate, professional, and undergraduate students; 707 full-time matriculated graduate/professional students (480 women), 710 part-time matriculated graduate/professional students (504 women). *Enrollment by degree level:* 1,058 master's, 267 doctoral, 91 other advanced degrees. *Graduate faculty:* 99 full-time (57 women), 56 part-time/adjunct (35 women). *Tuition, area resident:* Full-time $864; part-time $432 per credit hour. Tuition, state resident: full-time $864; part-time $432 per credit hour. Tuition, nonresident: full-time $2372; part-time $1186 per credit hour. *Required fees:* $141; $108 per credit hour. Tuition and fees vary according to course load. *Graduate housing:* Rooms and/or apartments available on a first-come, first-served basis to single and married students. Housing application deadline: 5/1. *Student services:* Campus employment opportunities, campus safety program, career counseling, exercise/wellness program, free psychological counseling, international student services, low-cost health insurance, multicultural affairs office, services for students with disabilities, teacher training, writing training. *Library facilities:* Glickman Library plus 3 others.

**Computer facilities:** Computer purchase and lease plans are available. 219 computers available on campus for general student use. A campuswide network can be accessed. Online class registration is available. Website: http://www.usm.maine.edu/

**General Application Contact:** Mary Sloan, Assistant Dean of Graduate Studies, 207-780-4812, Fax: 207-780-4969, E-mail: gradstudies@usm.maine.edu.

**GRADUATE UNITS**

**College of Arts, Humanities, and Social Sciences** *Program availability:* Part-time, evening/weekend, online learning. Electronic applications accepted.

***School of Music***

**College of Management and Human Service**

***Muskie School of Public Service*** *Program availability:* Part-time, evening/weekend, online learning. Electronic applications accepted.

***School of Business*** *Program availability:* Part-time, evening/weekend. Electronic applications accepted.

***School of Education and Human Development*** *Program availability:* Part-time, evening/weekend, online learning. Electronic applications accepted.

***School of Social Work*** *Program availability:* Part-time, evening/weekend. Electronic applications accepted.

**College of Science, Technology, and Health** *Program availability:* Part-time, evening/weekend. Electronic applications accepted.

***School of Nursing*** *Program availability:* Part-time. Electronic applications accepted.

**Lewiston-Auburn College**

## UNIVERSITY OF SOUTHERN MISSISSIPPI, Hattiesburg, MS 39406-0001

**General Information** State-supported, coed, university. CGS member. *Enrollment:* 14,133 graduate, professional, and undergraduate students; 1,373 full-time matriculated graduate/professional students (874 women), 1,105 part-time matriculated graduate/professional students (742 women). *Enrollment by degree level:* 1,412 master's, 981 doctoral, 85 other advanced degrees. *Tuition, area resident:* Full-time $4393; part-time $488 per credit hour. Tuition, nonresident: full-time $5393; part-time $600 per credit hour. *Required fees:* $6 per semester. *Graduate housing:* On-campus housing not available. *Student services:* Campus employment opportunities, campus safety program, career counseling, child daycare facilities, exercise/wellness program, free psychological counseling, grant writing training, international student services, low-cost health insurance, multicultural affairs office, services for students with disabilities, teacher training, writing training. *Library facilities:* Cook Memorial Library plus 4 others. *Collection:* Books: 1.4 million (physical), 331,932 (digital/electronic); Serial titles: 27,243 (physical), 118,798 (digital/electronic); Databases: 200. Weekly public service hours: 117; students can reserve study rooms. *Research affiliation:* Oak Ridge Associated Universities.

**Computer facilities:** Computer purchase and lease plans are available. 436 computers available on campus for general student use. A campuswide network can be accessed. Online class registration is available.
Website: http://www.usm.edu/

**General Application Contact:** Elisabeth McBride, Associate Director for Graduate Admissions, 601-266-5137, Fax: 601-266-5138, E-mail: graduateschool@usm.edu.

**GRADUATE UNITS**

**College of Arts and Sciences** Students: 579 full-time (291 women), 387 part-time (203 women); includes 202 minority (111 Black or African American, non-Hispanic/Latino; 6 American Indian or Alaska Native, non-Hispanic/Latino; 36 Asian, non-Hispanic/Latino; 39 Hispanic/Latino; 10 Two or more races, non-Hispanic/Latino), 117 international. 860 applicants, 39% accepted, 196 enrolled. Expenses: Contact institution. *Financial support:* Fellowships, research assistantships with full tuition reimbursements, teaching assistantships with full tuition reimbursements, Federal Work-Study, institutionally sponsored loans, scholarships/grants, health care benefits, and unspecified assistantships available. Financial award application deadline: 3/15; financial award applicants required to submit FAFSA. In 2019, 186 master's, 84 doctorates awarded. *Program availability:* Part-time, evening/weekend, online learning. *Application deadline:* For fall admission, 8/1 for domestic students, 6/1 for international students; for spring admission, 1/1 for domestic students, 11/1 for international students. Applications are processed on a rolling basis. *Application fee:* $60. Electronic applications accepted. *Application Contact:* Dr. Chris Winstead, Dean, 601-266-4315, E-mail: CAS.Dean@usm.edu. *Dean,* Dr. Chris Winstead, 601-266-4315, E-mail: CAS.Dean@usm.edu.

***School of Biological, Environmental and Earth Sciences*** Students: 77 full-time (41 women), 26 part-time (14 women); includes 11 minority (5 Black or African American, non-Hispanic/Latino; 1 Asian, non-Hispanic/Latino; 4 Hispanic/Latino; 1 Two or more races, non-Hispanic/Latino), 22 international. 105 applicants, 33% accepted, 25 enrolled. Expenses: Contact institution. *Financial support:* Research assistantships, teaching assistantships, Federal Work-Study, scholarships/grants, health care benefits, and unspecified assistantships available. Financial award applicants required to submit FAFSA. *Program availability:* 100% online, blended/hybrid learning. *Application deadline:* For fall admission, 8/15 for domestic students; for spring admission, 1/15 for domestic students; for summer admission, 5/15 for domestic students. *Application fee:* $60. Electronic applications accepted. *Application Contact:* Dr. Jake Schaefer, Director, 601-266-4748, Fax: 601-266-6541, E-mail: Jake.Schaefer@usm.edu. *Director,* Dr. Jake Schaefer, 601-266-4748, Fax: 601-266-6541, E-mail: Jake.Schaefer@usm.edu.

***School of Communication*** Students: 30 full-time (23 women), 35 part-time (23 women); includes 11 minority (8 Black or African American, non-Hispanic/Latino; 1 American Indian or Alaska Native, non-Hispanic/Latino; 1 Asian, non-Hispanic/Latino; 1 Hispanic/Latino), 15 international. 38 applicants, 45% accepted, 4 enrolled. Expenses: Contact institution. *Financial support:* Fellowships with full tuition reimbursements, research assistantships, teaching assistantships with full tuition reimbursements, Federal Work-Study, institutionally sponsored loans, scholarships/grants, health care benefits, and unspecified assistantships available. Financial award application deadline: 3/15; financial award applicants required to submit FAFSA. In 2019, 10 master's, 7 doctorates awarded. *Program availability:* Part-time. *Application deadline:* For fall admission, 3/1 priority date for domestic students, 3/1 for international students; for spring admission, 1/10 priority date for domestic and international students. Applications are processed on a rolling basis. *Application fee:* $60. Electronic applications accepted. *Application Contact:* Dr. John Meyer, Director, 601-266-4271, Fax: 601-266-4275, E-mail: John.Meyer@usm.edu. *Director,* Dr. John Meyer, 601-266-4271, Fax: 601-266-4275, E-mail: John.Meyer@usm.edu.

***School of Computing Sciences and Computer Engineering*** Students: 31 full-time (6 women), 8 part-time (2 women); includes 11 minority (1 Black or African American, non-Hispanic/Latino; 8 Asian, non-Hispanic/Latino; 1 Hispanic/Latino; 1 Two or more races, non-Hispanic/Latino), 22 international. 68 applicants, 37% accepted, 11 enrolled. Expenses: Contact institution. *Financial support:* Research assistantships with full tuition reimbursements, teaching assistantships with full tuition reimbursements, Federal Work-Study, institutionally sponsored loans, scholarships/grants, health care benefits, and unspecified assistantships available. Financial award application deadline: 3/15; financial award applicants required to submit FAFSA. In 2019, 19 master's awarded. *Application deadline:* Applications are processed on a rolling basis. *Application fee:* $60. Electronic applications accepted. *Application Contact:* Andrew H. Sung, Director, 601-266-4949, Fax: 601-266-5829. *Director,* Andrew H. Sung, 601-266-4949, Fax: 601-266-5829.

***School of Criminal Justice, Forensic Science, and Security*** Students: 2 full-time (both women), 3 part-time (1 woman); includes 1 minority (Black or African American, non-Hispanic/Latino). 18 applicants, 11% accepted. Expenses: Contact institution. *Financial support:* Research assistantships with full tuition reimbursements, teaching assistantships with full tuition reimbursements, career-related internships or fieldwork, Federal Work-Study, institutionally sponsored loans, scholarships/grants, health care benefits, and unspecified assistantships available. Financial award application deadline: 3/15; financial award applicants required to submit FAFSA. In 2019, 6 master's awarded. *Program availability:* Part-time. *Application deadline:* For fall admission, 3/15 priority date for domestic students, 3/15 for international students; for spring admission, 1/10 priority date for domestic and international students. Applications are processed on a rolling basis. *Application fee:* $60. Electronic applications accepted. *Application Contact:* Tera Wright, Manager of Graduate Admissions, 601-266-4509, Fax: 601-266-4391. *Director,* Dr. Lisa Nored, 601-266-4509, Fax: 601-266-4391.

***School of Humanities*** Students: 62 full-time (37 women), 38 part-time (15 women); includes 4 minority (1 Black or African American, non-Hispanic/Latino; 1 American Indian or Alaska Native, non-Hispanic/Latino; 1 Asian, non-Hispanic/Latino; 1 Two or more races, non-Hispanic/Latino), 2 international. 92 applicants, 53% accepted, 28 enrolled. Expenses: Contact institution. *Application fee:* $60. *Application Contact:* Dr. Matthew Casey, Director, 601-266-4333, E-mail: matthew.casey@usm.edu. *Director,* Dr. Matthew Casey, 601-266-4333, E-mail: matthew.casey@usm.edu.

***School of Mathematics and Natural Sciences*** Students: 46 full-time (16 women), 4 part-time (1 woman); includes 4 minority (2 Black or African American, non-Hispanic/Latino; 1 American Indian or Alaska Native, non-Hispanic/Latino; 1 Two or more races, non-Hispanic/Latino), 23 international. 73 applicants, 36% accepted, 11 enrolled. Expenses: Contact institution. *Application fee:* $60. Electronic applications accepted. *Application Contact:* Dr. Bernd Schroeder, Director, 601-4664394, E-mail: Bernd.Schroeder@usm.edu. *Director,* Dr. Bernd Schroeder, 601-4664394, E-mail: Bernd.Schroeder@usm.edu.

***School of Music*** Students: 83 full-time (43 women), 57 part-time (13 women); includes 20 minority (12 Black or African American, non-Hispanic/Latino; 1 American Indian or Alaska Native, non-Hispanic/Latino; 4 Hispanic/Latino; 3 Two or more races, non-Hispanic/Latino), 37 international. 103 applicants, 53% accepted, 24 enrolled. Expenses: Contact institution. *Financial support:* Fellowships with full tuition reimbursements, research assistantships, teaching assistantships with full tuition reimbursements, Federal Work-Study, institutionally sponsored loans, scholarships/grants, health care benefits, tuition waivers (partial), and unspecified assistantships available. Financial award application deadline: 2/1; financial award applicants required to submit FAFSA. In 2019, 20 master's, 9 doctorates awarded. *Program availability:* Blended/hybrid learning. *Application deadline:* For fall admission, 6/1 for domestic students; for spring admission, 11/1 for domestic students; for summer admission, 3/1 for domestic students. Applications are processed on a rolling basis. *Application fee:* $60. *Application Contact:* Dr. Jay Dean, Director, 601-266-4001, E-mail: Jay.Dean@usm.edu. *Director,* Dr. Jay Dean, 601-266-4001, E-mail: Jay.Dean@usm.edu.

***School of Ocean Science and Engineering*** Students: 75 full-time (37 women), 17 part-time (10 women); includes 10 minority (1 Black or African American, non-Hispanic/Latino; 1 American Indian or Alaska Native, non-Hispanic/Latino; 3 Asian, non-Hispanic/Latino; 3 Hispanic/Latino; 2 Two or more races, non-Hispanic/Latino), 13 international. 66 applicants, 29% accepted, 13 enrolled. Expenses: Contact institution. *Application fee:* $60. Electronic applications accepted. *Application Contact:* Dr. Robert Griffit, Director, 601-266-4294, E-mail: Joe.Griffitt@usm.edu. *Director,* Dr. Robert Griffit, 601-266-4294, E-mail: Joe.Griffitt@usm.edu.

***School of Performing and Visual Arts*** Students: 23 full-time (14 women); includes 2 minority (both Black or African American, non-Hispanic/Latino), 1 international. 42 applicants, 19% accepted, 8 enrolled. Expenses: Contact institution. *Application fee:* $60. Electronic applications accepted. *Application Contact:* Stacy Reischman Fletcher, Director, 601-266-4994, E-mail: Stacy.ReischmanFletcher@usm.edu. *Director,* Stacy Reischman Fletcher, 601-266-4994, E-mail: Stacy.ReischmanFletcher@usm.edu.

***School of Polymer Science and Engineering*** Students: 68 full-time (21 women), 5 part-time (2 women); includes 5 minority (2 Asian, non-Hispanic/Latino; 3 Hispanic/Latino), 15 international. 56 applicants, 52% accepted, 16 enrolled. Expenses: Contact institution. *Financial support:* Fellowships, research assistantships with full tuition reimbursements, teaching assistantships with full tuition reimbursements, Federal Work-Study, scholarships/grants, health care benefits, and unspecified assistantships available. Financial award application deadline: 3/15; financial award applicants required to submit FAFSA. In 2019, 6 master's, 13 doctorates awarded. *Application deadline:* For fall admission, 3/1 priority date for domestic students, 3/1 for international students. Applications are processed on a rolling basis. *Application fee:* $60. Electronic applications accepted. *Application Contact:* Dr. Derek Patton, Director, 601-266-4229. *Director,* Dr. Derek Patton, 601-266-4229.

***School of Social Sciences and Global Studies*** Students: 37 full-time (22 women), 99 part-time (61 women); includes 30 minority (18 Black or African American, non-Hispanic/Latino; 2 American Indian or Alaska Native, non-Hispanic/Latino; 1 Asian, non-Hispanic/Latino; 8 Hispanic/Latino; 1 Two or more races, non-Hispanic/Latino), 9 international. 96 applicants, 44% accepted, 27 enrolled. Expenses: Contact institution. *Program availability:* Part-time, evening/weekend, 100% online, blended/hybrid learning. *Application deadline:* Applications are processed on a rolling basis. *Application fee:* $60. Electronic applications accepted. *Application Contact:* Dr. Edward Sayre, Director, 601-266-4310, E-mail: edward.sayre@usm.edu. *Director,* Dr. Edward Sayre, 601-266-4310, E-mail: edward.sayre@usm.edu.

**College of Business and Economic Development** Students: 117 full-time (52 women), 101 part-time (44 women); includes 44 minority (29 Black or African American, non-Hispanic/Latino; 1 American Indian or Alaska Native, non-Hispanic/Latino; 2 Asian, non-Hispanic/Latino; 6 Hispanic/Latino; 6 Two or more races, non-Hispanic/Latino), 6 international. 244 applicants, 41% accepted, 96 enrolled. Expenses: Contact institution. *Financial support:* Research assistantships with full tuition reimbursements, teaching assistantships with full tuition reimbursements, Federal Work-Study, institutionally sponsored loans, scholarships/grants, and health care benefits available. Support available to part-time students. Financial award application deadline: 3/15; financial award applicants required to submit FAFSA. In 2019, 85 master's awarded. *Program availability:* Part-time. *Application deadline:* For fall admission, 8/1 priority date for domestic students, 6/1 for international students; for spring admission, 1/1 priority date for domestic students, 11/1 for international students. Applications are processed on a rolling basis. *Application fee:* $60. Electronic applications accepted. *Application Contact:* Dr. J. Bret Becton, Dean, 601-266-4659, Fax: 601-266-5814, E-mail: bret.becton@usm.edu. *Dean*, Dr. J. Bret Becton, 601-266-4659, Fax: 601-266-5814, E-mail: bret.becton@usm.edu.

***School of Accountancy*** Students: 16 full-time (11 women); includes 2 minority (1 Black or African American, non-Hispanic/Latino; 1 Two or more races, non-Hispanic/Latino). 27 applicants, 26% accepted, 7 enrolled. Expenses: Contact institution. *Financial support:* Research assistantships with full tuition reimbursements, Federal Work-Study, institutionally sponsored loans, scholarships/grants, health care benefits, and unspecified assistantships available. Support available to part-time students. Financial award application deadline: 3/15; financial award applicants required to submit FAFSA. In 2019, 20 master's awarded. *Program availability:* Part-time. *Application deadline:* For fall admission, 8/1 priority date for domestic students, 6/1 for international students; for spring admission, 1/1 priority date for domestic students, 11/1 for international students. Applications are processed on a rolling basis. *Application fee:* $60. Electronic applications accepted. *Application Contact:* Dr. Marv Bouillon, Director, 601-266-4641. *Director*, Dr. Marv Bouillon, 601-266-4641.

***School of Finance*** Students: 14 full-time (6 women), 1 (woman) part-time; includes 7 minority (6 Black or African American, non-Hispanic/Latino; 1 Hispanic/Latino). 18 applicants, 61% accepted, 10 enrolled. Expenses: Contact institution. *Financial support:* Application deadline: 3/15; applicants required to submit FAFSA. In 2019, 10 master's awarded. *Program availability:* Part-time. *Application deadline:* For fall admission, 8/1 for domestic students, 6/1 for international students; for spring admission, 1/1 for domestic students, 11/1 for international students. Applications are processed on a rolling basis. *Application fee:* $60. Electronic applications accepted. *Application Contact:* Dr. Kimberly Goodwin, Director, 601-266-4649. *Director*, Dr. Kimberly Goodwin, 601-266-4649.

***School of Management*** Students: 36 full-time (18 women), 84 part-time (39 women); includes 23 minority (14 Black or African American, non-Hispanic/Latino; 1 American Indian or Alaska Native, non-Hispanic/Latino; 1 Asian, non-Hispanic/Latino; 5 Hispanic/Latino; 2 Two or more races, non-Hispanic/Latino), 5 international. 133 applicants, 39% accepted, 44 enrolled. Expenses: Contact institution. *Financial support:* Applicants required to submit FAFSA. *Application deadline:* Applications are processed on a rolling basis. *Application fee:* $60. Electronic applications accepted. *Application Contact:* Dr. SherRhonda Gibbs, Director, E-mail: SherRhonda.Gibbs@usm.edu. *Director*, Dr. SherRhonda Gibbs, E-mail: SherRhonda.Gibbs@usm.edu.

***School of Marketing*** Students: 51 full-time (17 women), 16 part-time (5 women); includes 13 minority (8 Black or African American, non-Hispanic/Latino; 1 Asian, non-Hispanic/Latino; 1 Hispanic/Latino; 3 Two or more races, non-Hispanic/Latino), 1 international. 71 applicants, 48% accepted, 28 enrolled. Expenses: Contact institution. *Financial support:* Research assistantships with full tuition reimbursements, teaching assistantships with full tuition reimbursements, career-related internships or fieldwork, Federal Work-Study, scholarships/grants, health care benefits, and unspecified assistantships available. Financial award application deadline: 3/1; financial award applicants required to submit FAFSA. In 2019, 16 master's awarded. *Program availability:* Part-time, online learning. *Application deadline:* For fall admission, 8/1 for domestic students, 3/1 for international students; for spring admission, 1/3 for domestic and international students. Applications are processed on a rolling basis. *Application fee:* $60. Electronic applications accepted. *Application Contact:* Dr. Jamye Foster, Director, E-mail: Jamye.Foster@usm.edu. *Director*, Dr. Jamye Foster, E-mail: Jamye.Foster@usm.edu.

**College of Education and Human Sciences** Students: 334 full-time (266 women), 560 part-time (451 women); includes 257 minority (201 Black or African American, non-Hispanic/Latino; 4 American Indian or Alaska Native, non-Hispanic/Latino; 10 Asian, non-Hispanic/Latino; 23 Hispanic/Latino; 19 Two or more races, non-Hispanic/Latino), 5 international. 1,165 applicants, 29% accepted, 281 enrolled. Expenses: Contact institution. *Financial support:* Research assistantships with full tuition reimbursements, teaching assistantships with full tuition reimbursements, career-related internships or fieldwork, Federal Work-Study, institutionally sponsored loans, scholarships/grants, health care benefits, and unspecified assistantships available. Financial award application deadline: 3/15; financial award applicants required to submit FAFSA. In 2019, 238 master's, 30 doctorates, 24 other advanced degrees awarded. *Program availability:* Part-time. *Application deadline:* For fall admission, 3/1 priority date for domestic students, 3/1 for international students; for spring admission, 11/1 priority date for domestic students, 11/1 for international students. Applications are processed on a rolling basis. *Application fee:* $60. Electronic applications accepted. *Application Contact:* Dr. Trent Gould, Dean, 601-266-4224, Fax: 601-266-4175, E-mail: trent.gould@usm.edu. *Dean*, Dr. Trent Gould, 601-266-4224, Fax: 601-266-4175, E-mail: trent.gould@usm.edu.

***School of Child and Family Sciences*** Students: 35 full-time (27 women), 57 part-time (all women); includes 33 minority (22 Black or African American, non-Hispanic/Latino; 3 American Indian or Alaska Native, non-Hispanic/Latino; 7 Hispanic/Latino; 1 Two or more races, non-Hispanic/Latino), 1 international. 130 applicants, 21% accepted, 25 enrolled. Expenses: Contact institution. *Financial support:* Fellowships, research assistantships with full tuition reimbursements, career-related internships or fieldwork, Federal Work-Study, institutionally sponsored loans, scholarships/grants, health care benefits, and unspecified assistantships available. Financial award application deadline: 3/15; financial award applicants required to submit FAFSA. In 2019, 32 master's awarded. *Program availability:* Part-time, online learning. *Application deadline:* For fall admission, 3/1 priority date for domestic students, 3/1 for international students; for spring admission, 1/1 priority date for domestic and international students. Applications are processed on a rolling basis. *Application fee:* $60. Electronic applications accepted. *Application Contact:* Pat Sims, Director, 601-266-6990, Fax: 601-266-4680. *Director*, Pat Sims, 601-266-6990, Fax: 601-266-4680.

***School of Education*** Students: 57 full-time (45 women), 289 part-time (215 women); includes 104 minority (88 Black or African American, non-Hispanic/Latino; 1 Asian, non-Hispanic/Latino; 9 Hispanic/Latino; 6 Two or more races, non-Hispanic/Latino), 7 international. 385 applicants, 30% accepted, 96 enrolled. Expenses: Contact institution. *Program availability:* Part-time, evening/weekend, 100% online, blended/hybrid learning. *Application fee:* $60. *Application Contact:* Dr. Kyna Shelley, Director, 601-266-4578, E-mail: kyna.shelley@usm.edu. *Director*, Dr. Kyna Shelley, 601-266-4578, E-mail: kyna.shelley@usm.edu.

***School of Kinesiology and Nutrition*** Students: 32 full-time (20 women), 28 part-time (24 women); includes 13 minority (10 Black or African American, non-Hispanic/Latino; 3 Two or more races, non-Hispanic/Latino), 1 international. 88 applicants, 44% accepted, 24 enrolled. Expenses: Contact institution. *Program availability:* Part-time, evening/weekend, online learning. *Application fee:* $60. Electronic applications accepted. *Application Contact:* Dr. Melissa Thompson, Director, 601-266-6325, E-mail: M.Thompson@usm.edu. *Director*, Dr. Melissa Thompson, 601-266-6325, E-mail: M.Thompson@usm.edu.

***School of Library and Information Science*** Students: 56 full-time (48 women), 123 part-time (102 women); includes 39 minority (34 Black or African American, non-Hispanic/Latino; 4 Hispanic/Latino; 1 Two or more races, non-Hispanic/Latino), 3 international. 107 applicants, 51% accepted, 46 enrolled. Expenses: Contact institution. *Financial support:* Fellowships with tuition reimbursements, research assistantships with full tuition reimbursements, teaching assistantships with full tuition reimbursements, career-related internships or fieldwork, Federal Work-Study, institutionally sponsored loans, scholarships/grants, health care benefits, and unspecified assistantships available. Financial award application deadline: 3/15; financial award applicants required to submit FAFSA. In 2019, 53 master's awarded. *Program availability:* Part-time, evening/weekend, online learning. *Application deadline:* For fall admission, 3/15 priority date for domestic students, 3/15 for international students; for spring admission, 1/10 priority date for domestic and international students. Applications are processed on a rolling basis. *Application fee:* $60. Electronic applications accepted. *Application Contact:* Dr. Theresa Welsh, Director, 601-266-4236, Fax: 601-266-5774. *Director*, Dr. Theresa Welsh, 601-266-4236, Fax: 601-266-5774.

***School of Psychology*** Students: 103 full-time (75 women), 14 part-time (all women); includes 20 minority (8 Black or African American, non-Hispanic/Latino; 1 American Indian or Alaska Native, non-Hispanic/Latino; 2 Asian, non-Hispanic/Latino; 3 Hispanic/Latino; 6 Two or more races, non-Hispanic/Latino), 2 international. 282 applicants, 15% accepted, 37 enrolled. Expenses: Contact institution. *Financial support:* Research assistantships with full tuition reimbursements, teaching assistantships with full tuition reimbursements, career-related internships or fieldwork, Federal Work-Study, institutionally sponsored loans, scholarships/grants, health care benefits, and unspecified assistantships available. Financial award application deadline: 3/15; financial award applicants required to submit FAFSA. In 2019, 34 master's, 23 doctorates awarded. *Application deadline:* Applications are processed on a rolling basis. *Application fee:* $60. *Application Contact:* Dr. Sara Jordan, Director, 601-266-4177, E-mail: d.olmi@usm.edu. *Director*, Dr. Sara Jordan, 601-266-4177, E-mail: d.olmi@usm.edu.

***School of Social Work*** Students: 75 full-time (68 women), 27 part-time (25 women); includes 43 minority (37 Black or African American, non-Hispanic/Latino; 4 Hispanic/Latino; 2 Two or more races, non-Hispanic/Latino), 1 international. 179 applicants, 42% accepted, 58 enrolled. Expenses: Contact institution. *Financial support:* Research assistantships with tuition reimbursements, teaching assistantships with tuition reimbursements, career-related internships or fieldwork, Federal Work-Study, scholarships/grants, health care benefits, and unspecified assistantships available. Financial award application deadline: 3/15; financial award applicants required to submit FAFSA. In 2019, 53 master's awarded. *Program availability:* Part-time. *Application deadline:* For fall admission, 4/1 priority date for domestic and international students; for spring admission, 1/10 priority date for domestic and international students. Applications are processed on a rolling basis. *Application fee:* $60. Electronic applications accepted. *Application Contact:* Dr. Jerome Kolbo, Director, 601-266-5913, E-mail: jerome.kolbo@usm.edu. *Director*, Dr. Jerome Kolbo, 601-266-5913, E-mail: jerome.kolbo@usm.edu.

**College of Nursing and Health Professions** Students: 315 full-time (246 women), 30 part-time (20 women); includes 92 minority (71 Black or African American, non-Hispanic/Latino; 6 Asian, non-Hispanic/Latino; 5 Hispanic/Latino; 10 Two or more races, non-Hispanic/Latino), 28 international. 469 applicants, 34% accepted, 83 enrolled. Expenses: Contact institution. *Financial support:* Fellowships with full tuition reimbursements, research assistantships with full tuition reimbursements, teaching assistantships with full tuition reimbursements, career-related internships or fieldwork, Federal Work-Study, institutionally sponsored loans, scholarships/grants, health care benefits, and unspecified assistantships available. Financial award application deadline: 3/15; financial award applicants required to submit FAFSA. In 2019, 106 master's, 40 doctorates awarded. *Program availability:* Part-time, evening/weekend. *Application deadline:* For fall admission, 3/1 for domestic and international students; for spring admission, 1/10 priority date for domestic and international students. Applications are processed on a rolling basis. *Application fee:* $60. Electronic applications accepted. *Application Contact:* Dr. Lachel Story, Executive Associate Dean, 601-266-56485. *Executive Associate Dean*, Dr. Lachel Story, 601-266-56485.

***School of Health Professions*** Students: 58 full-time (41 women), 8 part-time (3 women); includes 25 minority (18 Black or African American, non-Hispanic/Latino; 2 Asian, non-Hispanic/Latino; 2 Hispanic/Latino; 3 Two or more races, non-Hispanic/Latino), 22 international. 125 applicants, 32% accepted, 23 enrolled. Expenses: Contact institution. *Financial support:* Research assistantships with full tuition reimbursements, teaching assistantships with full tuition reimbursements, career-related internships or fieldwork, Federal Work-Study, institutionally sponsored loans, scholarships/grants, health care benefits, and unspecified assistantships available. Financial award application deadline: 3/15; financial award applicants required to submit FAFSA. In 2019, 19 master's awarded. *Program availability:* Part-time, evening/weekend. *Application deadline:* For fall admission, 3/1 priority date for domestic and international students; for spring admission, 1/10 priority date for domestic and international students. Applications are processed on a rolling basis. *Application fee:* $60. Electronic applications accepted. *Application Contact:* Hwanseok Choi, Director, 601-266-5435, Fax: 601-266-5043, E-mail: hwanseok.choi@usm.edu. *Director*, Hwanseok Choi, 601-266-5435, Fax: 601-266-5043, E-mail: hwanseok.choi@usm.edu.

***School of Leadership and Advanced Practice Nursing*** Students: 175 full-time (126 women), 22 part-time (17 women); includes 54 minority (43 Black or African American, non-Hispanic/Latino; 3 Asian, non-Hispanic/Latino; 2 Hispanic/Latino; 6 Two or more races, non-Hispanic/Latino), 3 international. 161 applicants, 24% accepted, 27 enrolled. Expenses: Contact institution. *Financial support:* Research assistantships with full tuition reimbursements, teaching assistantships, Federal Work-Study, institutionally sponsored loans, scholarships/grants, traineeships, health care benefits, and unspecified assistantships available. Financial award application deadline: 3/15; financial award applicants required to submit FAFSA. In 2019, 60 master's, 33 doctorates, 2 other advanced degrees awarded. *Program availability:* Part-time, evening/weekend. *Application deadline:* For fall admission, 3/15 priority date for domestic students, 5/1 for international students; for spring admission, 1/10 priority date for domestic and international students. Applications are processed on a rolling basis. *Application fee:* $60. Electronic applications accepted. *Application Contact:* Dr. Lachel Story, Director, 601-266-6485, Fax: 601-266-5927, E-mail: lachel.story@usm.edu. *Director*, Dr. Lachel Story, 601-266-6485, Fax: 601-266-5927, E-mail: lachel.story@usm.edu.

***School of Speech and Hearing Sciences*** Students: 82 full-time (79 women); includes 13 minority (10 Black or African American, non-Hispanic/Latino; 1 Asian, non-Hispanic/Latino; 1 Hispanic/Latino; 1 Two or more races, non-Hispanic/Latino), 3 international. 183 applicants, 44% accepted, 35 enrolled. Expenses: Contact institution. *Financial support:* Research assistantships with full and partial tuition reimbursements, teaching assistantships with full and partial tuition reimbursements, career-related internships or fieldwork, Federal Work-Study, institutionally sponsored loans, scholarships/grants, health care benefits, and unspecified assistantships available. Financial award application deadline: 3/15; financial award applicants required to submit FAFSA. In 2019, 27 master's, 7 doctorates awarded. *Application deadline:* For fall admission, 3/1 for domestic and international students; for spring admission, 1/10 priority date for domestic and international students. *Application fee:* $60. Electronic applications accepted. *Application Contact:* Dr. Edward Goshorn, Chair, 601-266-5217, E-mail: Edward.Goshorn@usm.edu. *Chair*, Dr. Edward Goshorn, 601-266-5217, E-mail: Edward.Goshorn@usm.edu.

***Center for Science and Mathematics Education*** Students: 6 full-time (4 women), 14 part-time (11 women); includes 7 minority (4 Black or African American, non-Hispanic/Latino; 2 Asian, non-Hispanic/Latino; 1 Hispanic/Latino), 3 international. 7 applicants, 29% accepted, 2 enrolled. Expenses: Contact institution. *Financial support:* Fellowships with full tuition reimbursements, research assistantships with full tuition reimbursements, teaching assistantships with full tuition reimbursements, Federal Work-Study, scholarships/grants, health care benefits, and unspecified assistantships available. Financial award application deadline: 3/15; financial award applicants required to submit FAFSA. In 2019, 7 master's, 7 doctorates awarded. *Program availability:* Part-time, evening/weekend. *Application deadline:* For fall admission, 3/15 priority date for domestic students, 3/15 for international students; for spring admission, 1/10 priority date for domestic and international students. Applications are processed on a rolling basis. *Application fee:* $60. Electronic applications accepted. *Application Contact:* Dr. Julie Cwikla, Director, 601-266-4739, Fax: 601-266-4741, E-mail: Julie.Cwilka@usm.edu. *Director*, Dr. Julie Cwikla, 601-266-4739, Fax: 601-266-4741, E-mail: Julie.Cwilka@usm.edu.

**School of Interdisciplinary Studies and Professional Development** Students: 29 full-time (22 women), 98 part-time (56 women); includes 49 minority (44 Black or African American, non-Hispanic/Latino; 1 Asian, non-Hispanic/Latino; 4 Hispanic/Latino), 1 international. 61 applicants, 36% accepted, 18 enrolled. Expenses: Contact institution. *Financial support:* Research assistantships, teaching assistantships, Federal Work-Study, scholarships/grants, health care benefits, and unspecified assistantships available. Financial award applicants required to submit FAFSA. *Program availability:* Part-time, evening/weekend, 100% online, blended/hybrid learning. *Application deadline:* For fall admission, 8/15 for domestic students; for spring admission, 1/15 for domestic students; for summer admission, 5/15 for domestic students. Applications are processed on a rolling basis. *Application fee:* $60. Electronic applications accepted. *Application Contact:* Dr. Heather Annulis, Director, 228-214-3517, E-mail: Heather.Annulis@usm.edu. *Director*, Dr. Heather Annulis, 228-214-3517, E-mail: Heather.Annulis@usm.edu.

## UNIVERSITY OF SOUTH FLORIDA, Tampa, FL 33620-9951

**General Information** State-supported, coed, university. CGS member. *Enrollment:* 44,231 graduate, professional, and undergraduate students; 6,595 full-time matriculated graduate/professional students (3,655 women), 4,140 part-time matriculated graduate/professional students (2,745 women). *Enrollment by degree level:* 6,778 master's, 3,921 doctoral, 36 other advanced degrees. *Graduate faculty:* 1,185 full-time (493 women), 65 part-time/adjunct (27 women). *Graduate housing:* Room and/or apartments available on a first-come, first-served basis to single students; on-campus housing not available to married students. Housing application deadline: 8/22. *Student services:* Campus employment opportunities, campus safety program, career counseling, child daycare facilities, exercise/wellness program, free psychological counseling, grant writing training, international student services, low-cost health insurance, multicultural affairs office, services for students with disabilities, teacher training, writing training. *Library facilities:* Tampa Campus Library plus 5 others. *Collection:* Books: 1.8 million (physical), 652,513 (digital/electronic); Serial titles: 537 (physical), 58,975 (digital/electronic); Databases: 939. Weekly public service hours: 116; study areas open 24 hours, 5–7 days a week; students can reserve study rooms. *Research affiliation:* Moffitt Cancer Center (medicine (primarily oncology)), Jaeb Center for Health Research (medicine), Florida Orthopaedic Institute (medicine), James A. Haley & Bay Pines VA Hospitals (medicine), Florida Institute of Oceanography (marine science), National Science Foundation ICORPS (engineering, marine science, physics).

**Computer facilities:** 825 computers available on campus for general student use. A campuswide network can be accessed. Online class registration is available. Website: http://www.usf.edu/

**General Application Contact:** Dr. Dwayne Smith, Senior Vice Provost and Dean, Office of Graduate Studies, 813-974-2846, Fax: 813-974-5762, E-mail: gradliaison@grad.usf.edu.

**GRADUATE UNITS**

**College of Arts and Sciences** Students: 1,122 full-time (600 women), 591 part-time (379 women); includes 365 minority (85 Black or African American, non-Hispanic/Latino; 2 American Indian or Alaska Native, non-Hispanic/Latino; 49 Asian, non-Hispanic/Latino; 187 Hispanic/Latino; 1 Native Hawaiian or other Pacific Islander, non-Hispanic/Latino; 41 Two or more races, non-Hispanic/Latino), 361 international. Average age 31. 1,898 applicants, 39% accepted, 429 enrolled. *Faculty:* 363 full-time (139 women), 7 part-time/adjunct (3 women). Expenses: Contact institution. *Financial support:* In 2019–20, 318 students received support, including 2 research assistantships with tuition reimbursements available (averaging $13,650 per year); career-related internships or fieldwork, Federal Work-Study, institutionally sponsored loans, scholarships/grants, tuition waivers (full and partial), and unspecified assistantships also available. Support available to part-time students. Financial award applicants required to submit FAFSA. In 2019, 373 master's, 117 doctorates awarded. *Program availability:* Part-time, evening/weekend, online learning. *Application fee:* $30. Electronic applications accepted. *Application Contact:* Susan Hall, Executive Assistant to the Dean, 813-974-0853, Fax: 813-974-5911, E-mail: hall@usf.edu. *Dean*, Dr. Eric Eisenberg, 813-974-2804, Fax: 813-974-5911, E-mail: eisenberg@usf.edu.

***School of Geosciences*** Students: 93 full-time (43 women), 48 part-time (23 women); includes 24 minority (8 Black or African American, non-Hispanic/Latino; 6 Asian, non-Hispanic/Latino; 5 Hispanic/Latino; 5 Two or more races, non-Hispanic/Latino), 42 international. Average age 31. 107 applicants, 50% accepted, 23 enrolled. *Faculty:* 33 full-time (6 women). Expenses: Contact institution. *Financial support:* In 2019–20, 45 students received support, including 3 research assistantships (averaging $12,345 per year), 25 teaching assistantships with tuition reimbursements available (averaging $12,807 per year); unspecified assistantships also available. Financial award application deadline: 3/1. In 2019, 14 master's, 11 doctorates awarded. *Program availability:* Part-time, evening/weekend. *Application deadline:* For fall admission, 2/15 priority date for domestic students, 2/15 for international students; for spring admission, 10/15 priority date for domestic students, 9/15 for international students; for summer admission, 2/15 priority date for domestic students, 1/15 for international students. *Application fee:* $30. Electronic applications accepted. *Application Contact:* Dr. Ruiliang Pu, Associate Professor and Graduate Program Coordinator, 813-974-1508, Fax: 813-974-5911, E-mail: rpu@usf.edu. *Professor and Chair*, Dr. Mark Rains, 813-974-3310, Fax: 813-974-5911, E-mail: mrains@usf.edu.

***School of Information*** Students: 108 full-time (77 women), 182 part-time (137 women); includes 83 minority (23 Black or African American, non-Hispanic/Latino; 7 Asian, non-Hispanic/Latino; 49 Hispanic/Latino; 4 Two or more races, non-Hispanic/Latino). Average age 32. 141 applicants, 86% accepted, 71 enrolled. *Faculty:* 15 full-time (7 women). Expenses: Contact institution. *Financial support:* In 2019–20, 62 students received support. Unspecified assistantships available. Financial award application deadline: 6/30. In 2019, 128 master's awarded. *Program availability:* Part-time, evening/weekend, online learning. *Application deadline:* For fall admission, 6/1 priority date for domestic students, 5/1 for international students; for spring admission, 10/15 priority date for domestic students, 9/15 for international students. Applications are processed on a rolling basis. *Application fee:* $30. Electronic applications accepted. *Application Contact:* Dr. Randy Borum, Graduate Program Director, 813-974-3520, Fax: 813-974-6840, E-mail: wborum@usf.edu. *Director and Associate Professor*, Dr. Jim Andrews, 813-974-2108, Fax: 813-974-6840, E-mail: jimandrews@usf.edu.

***School of Interdisciplinary Global Studies*** Students: 37 full-time (10 women), 20 part-time (10 women); includes 12 minority (5 Black or African American, non-Hispanic/Latino; 2 Asian, non-Hispanic/Latino; 4 Hispanic/Latino; 1 Two or more races, non-Hispanic/Latino), 17 international. Average age 34. 48 applicants, 67% accepted, 20 enrolled. *Faculty:* 14 full-time (3 women). Expenses: Contact institution. *Financial support:* In 2019–20, 9 students received support, including 18 teaching assistantships with tuition reimbursements available (averaging $12,390 per year); unspecified assistantships also available. Financial award application deadline: 4/1. In 2019, 7 master's, 2 doctorates awarded. *Program availability:* Part-time, evening/weekend. *Application deadline:* For fall admission, 1/5 for domestic and international students; for spring admission, 10/15 for domestic students, 9/15 for international students. Applications are processed on a rolling basis. *Application fee:* $30. Electronic applications accepted. *Application Contact:* Dr. Steven Roach, Professor and Director of Graduate Studies, 813-974-9753, E-mail: sroach@usf.edu. *Associate Professor and SIGS Director*, Dr. Scott Solomon, 813-974-6394, E-mail: msolomon@usf.edu.

***School of Public Affairs*** Expenses: Contact institution. *Application Contact:* Susan Hall, Executive Assistant to the Dean, 813-974-0853, Fax: 813-974-5911, E-mail: hall@usf.edu. *Dean*, Dr. Eric Eisenberg, 813-974-2804, Fax: 813-974-5911, E-mail: eisenberg@usf.edu.

***Zimmerman School of Advertising and Mass Communications*** Students: 24 full-time (20 women), 20 part-time (17 women); includes 8 minority (4 Black or African American, non-Hispanic/Latino; 4 Hispanic/Latino), 20 international. Average age 26. 28 applicants, 79% accepted, 14 enrolled. *Faculty:* 11 full-time (6 women). Expenses: Contact institution. *Financial support:* In 2019–20, 6 students received support, including 9 teaching assistantships with tuition reimbursements available (averaging $10,513 per year); unspecified assistantships also available. Financial award application deadline: 2/28. In 2019, 12 master's awarded. *Program availability:* Part-time, evening/weekend. *Application deadline:* For fall admission, 2/15 priority date for domestic and international students. *Application fee:* $30. Electronic applications accepted. *Application Contact:* Dr. Art Ramirez, Jr., Associate Director, 813-974-2591, Fax: 813-974-2592, E-mail: aramirez2@usf.edu. *Director and Senior Instructor*, Dr. Wayne Garcia, 813-498-1925, Fax: 813-974-2592, E-mail: wgarcia@usf.edu.

**College of Behavioral and Community Sciences** Students: 598 full-time (522 women), 314 part-time (252 women); includes 287 minority (93 Black or African American, non-Hispanic/Latino; 2 American Indian or Alaska Native, non-Hispanic/Latino; 24 Asian, non-Hispanic/Latino; 149 Hispanic/Latino; 1 Native Hawaiian or other Pacific Islander, non-Hispanic/Latino; 18 Two or more races, non-Hispanic/Latino), 19 international. Average age 28. 1,155 applicants, 38% accepted, 321 enrolled. *Faculty:* 106 full-time (72 women), 4 part-time/adjunct (3 women). Expenses: Contact institution. *Financial support:* In 2019–20, 240 students received support. In 2019, 374 master's, 32 doctorates awarded. *Application Contact:* Francisco Vera, Assistant Director for Graduate Admissions, 813-974-2829, E-mail: fvera@usf.edu. *Dean*, Dr. Julianne Serovich, 813-974-1990, Fax: 813-974-2365, E-mail: jserovich@usf.edu.

***School of Aging Studies*** Students: 23 full-time (16 women), 4 part-time (all women); includes 4 minority (1 Black or African American, non-Hispanic/Latino; 1 Asian, non-Hispanic/Latino; 2 Two or more races, non-Hispanic/Latino). Average age 28. 25 applicants, 48% accepted, 6 enrolled. *Faculty:* 9 full-time (4 women). Expenses: Contact institution. *Financial support:* In 2019–20, 6 students received support, including 2 research assistantships with tuition reimbursements available (averaging $15,690 per year), 13 teaching assistantships with tuition reimbursements available (averaging $13,503 per year). Financial award application deadline: 2/3. In 2019, 6 master's, 3 doctorates awarded. *Program availability:* Part-time, evening/weekend. *Application deadline:* For fall admission, 12/11 priority date for domestic and international students; for spring admission, 10/15 for domestic students, 9/15 for international students; for summer admission, 2/15 for domestic students, 1/15 for international students. *Application fee:* $30. Electronic applications accepted. *Application Contact:* Brent Small, Professor, 813-974-9746, Fax: 813-974-9754, E-mail: bsmall@usf.edu. *Director and Professor*, Dr. Cathy L. McEvoy, 813-974-1940, Fax: 813-974-9754, E-mail: cmcevoy@usf.edu.

***School of Social Work*** Students: 143 full-time (132 women), 79 part-time (69 women); includes 86 minority (42 Black or African American, non-Hispanic/Latino; 1 American Indian or Alaska Native, non-Hispanic/Latino; 7 Asian, non-Hispanic/Latino; 34 Hispanic/Latino; 2 Two or more races, non-Hispanic/Latino), 3 international. Average age 30. 184 applicants, 42% accepted, 48 enrolled. *Faculty:* 14 full-time (13 women). Expenses: Contact institution. *Financial support:* In 2019–20, 53 students received support, including 1 research assistantship with tuition reimbursement available (averaging $9,001 per year); unspecified assistantships also available. Financial award application deadline: 3/15; financial award applicants required to submit FAFSA. In 2019, 138 master's awarded. *Program availability:* Part-time, evening/weekend. *Application deadline:* For fall admission, 2/15 priority date for domestic students, 2/15 for international students; for spring admission, 10/15 for domestic students, 9/15 for international students; for summer admission, 2/15 for domestic students, 1/15 for international students. Applications are processed on a rolling basis. *Application fee:* $30. Electronic applications accepted. *Application Contact:* Dr. Chris Simmons, MSW Chair and Instructor, 813-974-4306, E-mail:

csimmon4@usf.edu. *Professor and Director*, Dr. Riaan van Zyl, 813-974-4194, Fax: 813-974-4675, E-mail: nanpark@usf.edu.

**College of Education** Students: 438 full-time (331 women), 753 part-time (552 women); includes 330 minority (149 Black or African American, non-Hispanic/Latino; 3 American Indian or Alaska Native, non-Hispanic/Latino; 29 Asian, non-Hispanic/Latino; 123 Hispanic/Latino; 2 Native Hawaiian or other Pacific Islander, non-Hispanic/Latino; 24 Two or more races, non-Hispanic/Latino), 128 international. Average age 35. 795 applicants, 65% accepted, 355 enrolled. *Faculty:* 87 full-time (54 women). Expenses: Contact institution. *Financial support:* In 2019–20, 260 students received support, including 9 fellowships with full tuition reimbursements available (averaging $15,000 per year), 2 research assistantships with full tuition reimbursements available (averaging $15,000 per year); career-related internships or fieldwork, Federal Work-Study, institutionally sponsored loans, scholarships/grants, health care benefits, and unspecified assistantships also available. Support available to part-time students. Financial award applicants required to submit FAFSA. In 2019, 241 master's, 64 doctorates, 15 other advanced degrees awarded. *Program availability:* Part-time, evening/weekend, online learning. *Application deadline:* For fall admission, 2/15 for domestic students, 1/2 for international students; for spring admission, 10/15 for domestic students, 6/1 for international students. *Application fee:* $30. Electronic applications accepted. *Application Contact:* Dr. Diane Briscoe, Coordinator of Graduate Studies, 813-974-1804, Fax: 813-974-3391, E-mail: briscoe@usf.edu. *Dean*, Dr. Colleen S. Kennedy, 813-974-3400, Fax: 813-974-3826.

**College of Engineering** Students: 842 full-time (237 women), 256 part-time (55 women); includes 156 minority (37 Black or African American, non-Hispanic/Latino; 36 Asian, non-Hispanic/Latino; 72 Hispanic/Latino; 11 Two or more races, non-Hispanic/Latino), 759 international. Average age 27. 1,915 applicants, 44% accepted, 277 enrolled. *Faculty:* 136 full-time (22 women), 1 part-time/adjunct (0 women). Expenses: Contact institution. *Financial support:* In 2019–20, 169 students received support. Career-related internships or fieldwork, Federal Work-Study, scholarships/grants, health care benefits, and unspecified assistantships available. Financial award application deadline: 3/1. In 2019, 454 master's, 62 doctorates awarded. *Program availability:* Part-time, evening/weekend. *Application deadline:* For fall admission, 2/15 for domestic students, 1/2 priority date for international students; for spring admission, 10/15 for domestic students, 6/1 priority date for international students. Applications are processed on a rolling basis. *Application fee:* $30. Electronic applications accepted. *Application Contact:* Dr. Sanjukta Bhanja, Associate Dean for Academic Affairs, 813-974-4755, Fax: 813-974-5094, E-mail: bhanja@usf.edu. *Dean*, Dr. Robert Bishop, 813-974-3864, Fax: 813-974-5094, E-mail: robertbishop@usf.edu.

**College of Graduate Studies** Students: 70 full-time (15 women), 161 part-time (32 women); includes 112 minority (32 Black or African American, non-Hispanic/Latino; 1 American Indian or Alaska Native, non-Hispanic/Latino; 24 Asian, non-Hispanic/Latino; 51 Hispanic/Latino; 4 Two or more races, non-Hispanic/Latino), 4 international. Average age 34. 101 applicants, 76% accepted, 54 enrolled. *Faculty:* 1 (woman) full-time. Expenses: Contact institution. *Financial support:* In 2019–20, 20 students received support. Teaching assistantships available. Financial award application deadline: 2/1; financial award applicants required to submit FAFSA. In 2019, 133 master's awarded. *Program availability:* Part-time, evening/weekend, online learning. *Application deadline:* For fall admission, 2/15 for domestic and international students; for spring admission, 10/15 for domestic students, 9/15 for international students; for summer admission, 2/15 for domestic and international students. *Application fee:* $30. Electronic applications accepted. *Application Contact:* Paul Crawford, Associate Director for Graduate Admissions, 813-974-8800, E-mail: pjcrawford@usf.edu. *Senior Vice Provost and Dean of the Office of Graduate Studies*, Dr. Dwayne Smith, 813-974-7359, Fax: 813-974-5762, E-mail: mdsmith8@usf.edu.

**College of Marine Science** Students: 67 full-time (39 women), 21 part-time (12 women); includes 10 minority (1 Black or African American, non-Hispanic/Latino; 6 Hispanic/Latino; 3 Two or more races, non-Hispanic/Latino), 16 international. Average age 30. 79 applicants, 25% accepted, 17 enrolled. *Faculty:* 27 full-time (8 women). Expenses: Contact institution. *Financial support:* In 2019–20, 41 students received support, including 45 research assistantships with partial tuition reimbursements available (averaging $14,199 per year), 10 teaching assistantships with partial tuition reimbursements available (averaging $14,196 per year); health care benefits and unspecified assistantships also available. Financial award application deadline: 1/15. In 2019, 14 master's, 14 doctorates awarded. *Program availability:* Part-time. *Application deadline:* For fall admission, 1/10 for domestic and international students; for spring admission, 10/1 for domestic and international students. Applications are processed on a rolling basis. *Application fee:* $30. Electronic applications accepted. *Application Contact:* Dr. David F. Naar, Associate Professor and Director of Academic Affairs, 727-553-1637, Fax: 727-553-1189, E-mail: naar@usf.edu. *Dean*, Dr. Jacqueline E. Dixon, 727-553-3369, Fax: 727-553-1189, E-mail: jdixon@usf.edu.

**College of Nursing** Students: 265 full-time (207 women), 687 part-time (594 women); includes 343 minority (113 Black or African American, non-Hispanic/Latino; 1 American Indian or Alaska Native, non-Hispanic/Latino; 60 Asian, non-Hispanic/Latino; 141 Hispanic/Latino; 1 Native Hawaiian or other Pacific Islander, non-Hispanic/Latino; 27 Two or more races, non-Hispanic/Latino), 2 international. Average age 33. 955 applicants, 44% accepted, 343 enrolled. *Faculty:* 34 full-time (28 women), 2 part-time/adjunct (1 woman). Expenses: Contact institution. *Financial support:* In 2019–20, 181 students received support, including 7 research assistantships with tuition reimbursements available (averaging $18,935 per year), 29 teaching assistantships with tuition reimbursements available (averaging $30,814 per year); tuition waivers (partial) and unspecified assistantships also available. Financial award application deadline: 2/1; financial award applicants required to submit FAFSA. In 2019, 281 master's, 80 doctorates awarded. *Program availability:* Part-time. *Application deadline:* For fall admission, 12/15 for domestic and international students; for spring admission, 10/1 for domestic students, 9/15 for international students. *Application fee:* $30. Electronic applications accepted. *Application Contact:* Dr. Denise Maguire, Vice Dean, Graduate Programs, 813-396-9962, E-mail: dmaguire@health.usf.edu. *Dean, College of Nursing*, Dr. Victoria Rich, 813-974-8939, Fax: 813-974-5418, E-mail: victoriarich@health.usf.edu.

**College of Public Health** Expenses: Contact institution. *Application Contact:* Dr. Dwayne Smith, Senior Vice Provost and Dean, Office of Graduate Studies, 813-974-2846, Fax: 813-974-5762, E-mail: mdsmith3@usf.edu.

**College of Public Health** *Program availability:* Part-time, evening/weekend, 100% online, blended/hybrid learning. Electronic applications accepted.

**College of The Arts** Students: 177 full-time (92 women), 38 part-time (18 women); includes 55 minority (11 Black or African American, non-Hispanic/Latino; 9 Asian, non-Hispanic/Latino; 25 Hispanic/Latino; 10 Two or more races, non-Hispanic/Latino), 52 international. Average age 27. 204 applicants, 43% accepted, 65 enrolled. *Faculty:* 50 full-time (17 women), 3 part-time/adjunct (0 women). Expenses: Contact institution. *Financial support:* In 2019–20, 125 students received support. Unspecified assistantships available. In 2019, 89 master's, 2 doctorates awarded. *Program availability:* Part-time, evening/weekend. *Application deadline:* For fall admission, 1/15 for domestic and international students; for spring admission, 10/15 for domestic students, 9/15 for international students; for summer admission, 2/15 for domestic students, 1/15 for international students. *Application fee:* $30. Electronic applications accepted. *Application Contact:* Prof. Barton Lee, Senior Associate Dean, 813-974-2301, Fax: 813-974-2091, E-mail: blee@usf.edu. *Dean*, Dr. James S. Moy, 813-974-7380, Fax: 813-974-2091, E-mail: moy@usf.edu.

***School of Architecture and Community Design*** Students: 74 full-time (40 women), 19 part-time (8 women); includes 33 minority (7 Black or African American, non-Hispanic/Latino; 9 Asian, non-Hispanic/Latino; 14 Hispanic/Latino; 3 Two or more races, non-Hispanic/Latino), 19 international. Average age 26. 59 applicants, 39% accepted, 17 enrolled. *Faculty:* 8 full-time (0 women). Expenses: Contact institution. *Financial support:* In 2019–20, 43 students received support, including 3 teaching assistantships with tuition reimbursements available (averaging $9,360 per year); Federal Work-Study, scholarships/grants, and unspecified assistantships also available. In 2019, 42 master's awarded. *Application deadline:* For fall admission, 2/1 priority date for domestic students, 2/1 for international students. Applications are processed on a rolling basis. *Application fee:* $30. Electronic applications accepted. *Application Contact:* Mildred Abreu, Academic Advisor, 813-974-1216, Fax: 813-974-2557, E-mail: abreu@arch.usf.edu. *Director and Professor, School of Architecture and Community Design*, Dr. Robert MacLeod, 813-974-6015, Fax: 813-974-2557, E-mail: rmacleod@arch.usf.edu.

***School of Art and Art History*** Students: 45 full-time (25 women), 1 (woman) part-time; includes 11 minority (1 Black or African American, non-Hispanic/Latino; 8 Hispanic/Latino; 2 Two or more races, non-Hispanic/Latino), 4 international. Average age 30. 69 applicants, 32% accepted, 20 enrolled. *Faculty:* 17 full-time (8 women). Expenses: Contact institution. *Financial support:* In 2019–20, 42 students received support, including 37 teaching assistantships with partial tuition reimbursements available (averaging $9,440 per year); scholarships/grants, health care benefits, and unspecified assistantships also available. Support available to part-time students. Financial award application deadline: 2/15; financial award applicants required to submit FAFSA. In 2019, 13 master's awarded. *Program availability:* Part-time. *Application deadline:* For fall admission, 1/15 priority date for domestic students, 2/1 for international students. *Application fee:* $30. Electronic applications accepted. *Application Contact:* Prof. Neil Bender, Associate Professor and Graduate Program Director, 813-974-2360, Fax: 813-974-9226, E-mail: nb2@usf.edu. *Director*, Prof. Wallace Wilson, 813-974-2360, Fax: 813-974-9226, E-mail: wwilson2@usf.edu.

***School of Music*** Students: 58 full-time (27 women), 18 part-time (9 women); includes 11 minority (3 Black or African American, non-Hispanic/Latino; 3 Hispanic/Latino; 5 Two or more races, non-Hispanic/Latino), 29 international. Average age 28. 76 applicants, 55% accepted, 28 enrolled. *Faculty:* 23 full-time (7 women), 1 part-time/adjunct (0 women). Expenses: Contact institution. *Financial support:* In 2019–20, 40 students received support, including 1 research assistantship with tuition reimbursement available (averaging $15,724 per year), 46 teaching assistantships with tuition reimbursements available (averaging $10,099 per year); unspecified assistantships also available. Financial award application deadline: 2/15. In 2019, 34 master's, 2 doctorates awarded. *Program availability:* Part-time, evening/weekend. *Application deadline:* For fall admission, 2/15 priority date for domestic students, 2/1 for international students; for spring admission, 10/15 for domestic students, 9/15 for international students; for summer admission, 2/15 for domestic students, 1/15 for international students. *Application fee:* $30. Electronic applications accepted. *Application Contact:* Dr. David Williams, Associate Director/Associate Professor of Music Education, 813-974-9166, Fax: 813-974-8721, E-mail: davidw@usf.edu. *Director*, Dr. Karen Bryan, 813-974-2311, Fax: 813-974-8721, E-mail: kmbryan@usf.edu.

**Innovative Education** Expenses: Contact institution. *Application Contact:* Owen Hooper, Director, Summer and Alternative Calendar Programs, 813-974-6917, E-mail: hooper@usf.edu. *Associate Vice President and Assistant Vice Provost*, Dr. Cynthia DeLuca, 813-974-3077, Fax: 813-974-7061, E-mail: deluca@usf.edu.

**Morsani College of Medicine** Students: 1,314 full-time (694 women), 272 part-time (172 women); includes 634 minority (112 Black or African American, non-Hispanic/Latino; 7 American Indian or Alaska Native, non-Hispanic/Latino; 289 Asian, non-Hispanic/Latino; 194 Hispanic/Latino; 2 Native Hawaiian or other Pacific Islander, non-Hispanic/Latino; 30 Two or more races, non-Hispanic/Latino), 50 international. Average age 26. 8,974 applicants, 11% accepted, 567 enrolled. *Faculty:* 200 full-time (85 women), 39 part-time/adjunct (17 women). Expenses: Contact institution. *Financial support:* In 2019–20, 749 students received support. In 2019, 362 master's, 226 doctorates awarded. *Program availability:* Part-time. *Application deadline:* For fall admission, 2/1 priority date for domestic students, 2/1 for international students. *Application fee:* $30. Electronic applications accepted. *Application Contact:* Dr. Bob Deschenes, Vice Dean, Educational Affairs, 813-974-6393, E-mail: rdeschen@health.usf.edu. *Dean*, Dr. Charles J. Lockwood, 813-974-0533, Fax: 813-974-4990, E-mail: cjlockwood@health.usf.edu.

***School of Physical Therapy*** Students: 137 full-time (86 women); includes 29 minority (6 Black or African American, non-Hispanic/Latino; 9 Asian, non-Hispanic/Latino; 13 Hispanic/Latino; 1 Two or more races, non-Hispanic/Latino). Average age 24. 1,190 applicants, 4% accepted, 46 enrolled. *Faculty:* 12 full-time (7 women). Expenses: Contact institution. *Financial support:* In 2019–20, 64 students received support. Teaching assistantships available. In 2019, 44 doctorates awarded. *Application deadline:* For fall admission, 6/1 for domestic students, 1/1 for international students; for spring admission, 10/15 for domestic students, 9/15 for international students. *Application fee:* $30. Electronic applications accepted. *Application Contact:* Dr. Gina Maria Musolino, Associate Professor and Coordinator for Clinical Education, 813-974-2254, Fax: 813-974-8915, E-mail: gmusolin@health.usf.edu. *Director*, Dr. William S. Quillen, 813-974-9863, Fax: 813-974-8915, E-mail: wquillen@health.usf.edu.

**Muma College of Business** Students: 854 full-time (332 women), 485 part-time (191 women); includes 281 minority (78 Black or African American, non-Hispanic/Latino; 2 American Indian or Alaska Native, non-Hispanic/Latino; 65 Asian, non-Hispanic/Latino; 117 Hispanic/Latino; 1 Native Hawaiian or other Pacific Islander, non-Hispanic/Latino; 18 Two or more races, non-Hispanic/Latino), 517 international. Average age 30. 1,720 applicants, 57% accepted, 492 enrolled. *Faculty:* 76 full-time (21 women), 2 part-time/adjunct (0 women). Expenses: Contact institution. *Financial support:* In 2019–20, 300 students received support. Career-related internships or fieldwork, scholarships/grants, health care benefits, and unspecified assistantships available. Financial award applicants required to submit FAFSA. In 2019, 602 master's, 42 doctorates awarded. *Program availability:* Part-time, evening/weekend. *Application deadline:* For fall admission, 1/2 for domestic and international students; for spring admission, 10/1 for domestic students, 9/15 for international students. *Application fee:* $30. Electronic applications accepted. *Application Contact:* Dr. Jacqueline Reck,

Professor/Interim Associate Dean, 813-974-6721, Fax: 813-974-6528, E-mail: jreck@usf.edu. *Dean*, Dr. Moez Limayem, 813-974-4281, Fax: 813-974-3030, E-mail: mlimayem@usf.edu.

***Center for Entrepreneurship*** *Program availability:* Part-time, evening/weekend. Electronic applications accepted.

***Lynn Pippenger School of Accountancy*** Students: 69 full-time (31 women), 28 part-time (14 women); includes 34 minority (2 Black or African American, non-Hispanic/Latino; 1 American Indian or Alaska Native, non-Hispanic/Latino; 7 Asian, non-Hispanic/Latino; 18 Hispanic/Latino; 6 Two or more races, non-Hispanic/Latino), 8 international. Average age 24. 104 applicants, 59% accepted, 49 enrolled. *Faculty:* 11 full-time (5 women). Expenses: Contact institution. *Financial support:* In 2019–20, 55 students received support, including 18 teaching assistantships with tuition reimbursements available (averaging $12,273 per year); scholarships/grants, health care benefits, and unspecified assistantships also available. Financial award applicants required to submit FAFSA. In 2019, 50 master's awarded. *Program availability:* Part-time, evening/weekend. *Application deadline:* For fall admission, 3/1 priority date for domestic students, 3/1 for international students; for spring admission, 10/1 for domestic students, 9/15 for international students; for summer admission, 2/15 for domestic and international students. *Application fee:* $30. Electronic applications accepted. *Application Contact:* Stacee Bender, Academic Services Administrator, 813-974-4516, E-mail: staceebender@usf.edu. *Interim Director, School of Accountancy*, Dr. Uday Murthy, 813-974-6516, Fax: 813-974-6528, E-mail: umurthy@usf.edu.

**Patel College of Global Sustainability** Students: 82 full-time (56 women), 75 part-time (49 women); includes 34 minority (8 Black or African American, non-Hispanic/Latino; 4 Asian, non-Hispanic/Latino; 17 Hispanic/Latino; 5 Two or more races, non-Hispanic/Latino), 43 international. Average age 29. 121 applicants, 79% accepted, 65 enrolled. *Faculty:* 1 full-time (0 women). Expenses: Contact institution. *Financial support:* In 2019–20, 35 students received support. In 2019, 93 master's awarded. *Application deadline:* For fall admission, 6/1 for domestic students, 5/1 for international students; for spring admission, 10/15 for domestic students, 9/15 for international students. Electronic applications accepted. *Application Contact:* Dr. Govindan Parayil, Dean, 813-974-9694, E-mail: gparayil@usf.edu. *Dean*, Dr. Govindan Parayil, 813-974-9694, E-mail: gparayil@usf.edu.

**USF Health Taneja College of Pharmacy** Students: 398 full-time (234 women), 7 part-time (3 women); includes 180 minority (33 Black or African American, non-Hispanic/Latino; 72 Asian, non-Hispanic/Latino; 59 Hispanic/Latino; 2 Native Hawaiian or other Pacific Islander, non-Hispanic/Latino; 14 Two or more races, non-Hispanic/Latino), 13 international. Average age 25. 465 applicants, 44% accepted, 112 enrolled. *Faculty:* 32 full-time (18 women), 1 part-time/adjunct (0 women). Expenses: Contact institution. *Financial support:* In 2019–20, 159 students received support. Scholarships/grants available. In 2019, 11 master's, 91 doctorates awarded. *Program availability:* Part-time, 100% online, blended/hybrid learning. *Application deadline:* For fall admission, 6/1 for domestic and international students; for spring admission, 10/15 for domestic students, 9/15 for international students; for summer admission, 2/15 for domestic and international students. Applications are processed on a rolling basis. *Application fee:* $30. Electronic applications accepted. *Application Contact:* Dr. Amy Schwartz, Admissions Recruiter, 813-974-4652, E-mail: jlambert2@usf.edu.

## UNIVERSITY OF SOUTH FLORIDA, ST. PETERSBURG, St. Petersburg, FL 33701

**General Information** State-supported, coed, comprehensive institution. *Graduate housing:* Rooms and/or apartments available on a first-come, first-served basis to single and married students.

**GRADUATE UNITS**

**College of Arts and Sciences** *Program availability:* Part-time, online learning. Electronic applications accepted.

**College of Education** *Program availability:* Part-time. Electronic applications accepted.

**Kate Tiedemann College of Business** *Program availability:* Part-time. Electronic applications accepted.

## UNIVERSITY OF SOUTH FLORIDA SARASOTA-MANATEE, Sarasota, FL 34243

**General Information** State-supported, coed, comprehensive institution.

**GRADUATE UNITS**

**College of Business** *Program availability:* Part-time, evening/weekend. Electronic applications accepted.

**College of Hospitality and Technology Leadership** *Program availability:* Part-time. Electronic applications accepted.

**College of Liberal Arts and Social Sciences** *Program availability:* Part-time, 100% online, blended/hybrid learning. Electronic applications accepted.

## THE UNIVERSITY OF TAMPA, Tampa, FL 33606-1490

**General Information** Independent, coed, comprehensive institution. *Graduate housing:* Rooms and/or apartments available on a first-come, first-served basis to single and married students. Housing application deadline: 5/1. *Research affiliation:* Tampa General Hospital (nursing).

**GRADUATE UNITS**

**Program in Creative Writing** *Program availability:* Part-time. Electronic applications accepted.

**Program in Criminology and Criminal Justice** Electronic applications accepted.

**Program in Exercise and Nutrition Science** *Program availability:* Part-time, evening/weekend. Electronic applications accepted.

**Program in Nursing** *Program availability:* Part-time, evening/weekend. Electronic applications accepted.

**Programs in Education** *Program availability:* Part-time, evening/weekend. Electronic applications accepted.

**Sykes College of Business** *Program availability:* Part-time, evening/weekend. Electronic applications accepted.

## THE UNIVERSITY OF TENNESSEE, Knoxville, TN 37996

**General Information** State-supported, coed, university. CGS member. *Graduate housing:* Room and/or apartments available on a first-come, first-served basis to single students; on-campus housing not available to married students. Housing application deadline: 2/1. *Research affiliation:* Intel Corporation (computational science), Boeing (mechanical and aerospace engineering), Eastman Chemical (chemical engineering, chemistry), Mars, Inc. (materials science and engineering, polymer science, food science), DuPont (biofuels), Goodyear (chemical engineering; materials science and engineering; polymer science).

**GRADUATE UNITS**

**College of Law** Electronic applications accepted.

**Graduate School** *Program availability:* Part-time, evening/weekend, online learning. Electronic applications accepted.

***College of Agricultural Sciences and Natural Resources*** *Program availability:* Part-time, online learning. Electronic applications accepted.

***College of Architecture and Design*** Electronic applications accepted.

***College of Arts and Sciences*** *Program availability:* Part-time, evening/weekend. Electronic applications accepted.

***College of Business Administration*** *Program availability:* Part-time, online learning. Electronic applications accepted.

***College of Communication and Information*** *Program availability:* Part-time, evening/weekend, online learning. Electronic applications accepted.

***College of Education, Health and Human Sciences*** *Program availability:* Part-time, evening/weekend, online learning. Electronic applications accepted.

***College of Nursing*** *Program availability:* Part-time. Electronic applications accepted.

***College of Social Work*** *Program availability:* Part-time, online learning. Electronic applications accepted.

***College of Veterinary Medicine***

***Tickle College of Engineering*** Students: 893 full-time (197 women), 217 part-time (44 women); includes 128 minority (30 Black or African American, non-Hispanic/Latino; 2 American Indian or Alaska Native, non-Hispanic/Latino; 43 Asian, non-Hispanic/Latino; 33 Hispanic/Latino; 1 Native Hawaiian or other Pacific Islander, non-Hispanic/Latino; 19 Two or more races, non-Hispanic/Latino), 365 international. Average age 29. 990 applicants, 39% accepted, 226 enrolled. *Faculty:* 209 full-time (29 women), 13 part-time/adjunct (1 woman). Expenses: Contact institution. *Financial support:* In 2019–20, 949 students received support, including 176 fellowships with full tuition reimbursements available (averaging $18,134 per year), 561 research assistantships with full tuition reimbursements available (averaging $23,396 per year), 212 teaching assistantships with full tuition reimbursements available (averaging $19,998 per year); career-related internships or fieldwork, Federal Work-Study, institutionally sponsored loans, health care benefits, and unspecified assistantships also available. Financial award application deadline: 2/1; financial award applicants required to submit FAFSA. In 2019, 215 master's, 108 doctorates awarded. *Program availability:* Part-time, online learning. *Application deadline:* For fall admission, 2/1 priority date for domestic and international students; for spring admission, 6/15 for domestic and international students; for summer admission, 10/15 for domestic and international students. Applications are processed on a rolling basis. *Application fee:* $60. Electronic applications accepted. *Application Contact:* Dr. Ozlem Kilic, Associate Dean of Student Affairs, 865-974-2454, Fax: 865-974-9871, E-mail: okilic@utk.edu. *Dean*, Dr. Janis P. Terpenny, 865-974-5321, Fax: 865-974-8890, E-mail: terpenny@utk.edu.

## THE UNIVERSITY OF TENNESSEE AT CHATTANOOGA, Chattanooga, TN 37403-2598

**General Information** State-supported, coed, comprehensive institution. CGS member. *Graduate housing:* Room and/or apartments available on a first-come, first-served basis to single students; on-campus housing not available to married students. Housing application deadline: 6/1. *Research affiliation:* UT Law Enforcement Innovation Center (criminal justice), Highland Biological Field Station (biology and environmental science), Tennessee Valley Authority (engineering), Gulf Coast Research Laboratory (biology and environmental science), Tennessee Coalition against Domestic and Sexual Violence (criminal justice).

**GRADUATE UNITS**

**Department of Health and Human Performance** Students: 65 full-time (42 women), 1 (woman) part-time; includes 16 minority (10 Black or African American, non-Hispanic/Latino; 1 Asian, non-Hispanic/Latino; 4 Hispanic/Latino; 1 Two or more races, non-Hispanic/Latino), 1 international. Average age 25. 36 applicants, 100% accepted, 29 enrolled. *Faculty:* 21 full-time (13 women), 10 part-time/adjunct (7 women). Expenses: Contact institution. *Financial support:* Research assistantships with tuition reimbursements, teaching assistantships with tuition reimbursements, career-related internships or fieldwork, scholarships/grants, and unspecified assistantships available. Support available to part-time students. Financial award application deadline: 7/1; financial award applicants required to submit FAFSA. In 2019, 32 master's awarded. *Application deadline:* For fall admission, 6/15 priority date for domestic students, 7/1 for international students; for spring admission, 11/1 priority date for domestic students, 11/1 for international students. Applications are processed on a rolling basis. *Application fee:* $35 ($40 for international students). Electronic applications accepted. *Application Contact:* Dr. Joanne Romagni, Dean of the Graduate School, 423-425-4478, Fax: 423-425-5223, E-mail: joanne-romagni@utc.edu. *Department Head*, Dr. Marisa Colston, 423-425-4743, E-mail: marisa-colston@utc.edu.

**Department of Occupational Therapy** Students: 70 full-time (65 women), 1 (woman) part-time; includes 4 minority (2 Asian, non-Hispanic/Latino; 2 Two or more races, non-Hispanic/Latino). Average age 24. 29 applicants, 83% accepted, 24 enrolled. *Faculty:* 6 full-time (all women), 1 (woman) part-time/adjunct. Expenses: Contact institution. *Financial support:* Fellowships, research assistantships, career-related internships or fieldwork, scholarships/grants, and unspecified assistantships available. Support available to part-time students. Financial award application deadline: 7/1; financial award applicants required to submit FAFSA. In 2019, 24 doctorates awarded. *Application deadline:* For fall admission, 6/15 priority date for domestic students, 7/1 for international students; for spring admission, 11/1 priority date for domestic students, 11/1 for international students. Applications are processed on a rolling basis. *Application fee:* $35 ($40 for international students). Electronic applications accepted. *Application Contact:* Dr. Joanne Romagni, Dean of the Graduate School, 423-425-4478, Fax: 423-425-5223, E-mail: joanne-romagni@utc.edu. *Department Head*, Susan McDonald, 423-425-5759, E-mail: susan-mcdonald@utc.edu.

**Department of Political Science and Public Service** Students: 21 full-time (15 women), 12 part-time (7 women); includes 5 minority (4 Black or African American, non-Hispanic/Latino; 1 Asian, non-Hispanic/Latino). Average age 30. 17 applicants, 82% accepted, 13 enrolled. *Faculty:* 12 full-time (5 women), 4 part-time/adjunct (0 women). Expenses: Contact institution. *Financial support:* Research assistantships, career-related internships or fieldwork, scholarships/grants, and unspecified assistantships available. Support available to part-time students. Financial award application deadline: 7/1; financial award applicants required to submit FAFSA. In 2019, 12 master's, 1 other advanced degree awarded. *Program availability:* Part-time, evening/weekend. *Application deadline:* For fall admission, 6/15 priority date for domestic students, 7/1 for international students; for spring admission, 11/1 priority date for domestic students, 11/1 for international students. Applications are processed on a rolling basis. *Application fee:* $35 ($40 for international students). Electronic applications accepted. *Application Contact:* Dr. Joanne Romagni, Dean of the Graduate School, 423-425-4478, Fax: 423-425-5223, E-mail: joanne-romagni@utc.edu. *Department Head*, Dr. Michelle D. Deardorf, 423-425-4231, Fax: 423-425-2373, E-mail: michelle-deardorff@utc.edu.

**Engineering Management and Technology Program** Students: 10 full-time (4 women), 44 part-time (6 women); includes 9 minority (4 Black or African American, non-Hispanic/Latino; 1 Asian, non-Hispanic/Latino; 2 Hispanic/Latino; 2 Two or more races, non-Hispanic/Latino), 9 international. Average age 33. 24 applicants, 88% accepted, 8 enrolled. Expenses: Contact institution. *Financial support:* Research assistantships, teaching assistantships, career-related internships or fieldwork, scholarships/grants, and unspecified assistantships available. Support available to part-time students. Financial award application deadline: 7/1; financial award applicants required to submit FAFSA. In 2019, 21 master's, 1 other advanced degree awarded. *Program availability:* 100% online, blended/hybrid learning. *Application deadline:* For fall admission, 6/15 priority date for domestic students, 7/1 for international students; for spring admission, 11/1 priority date for domestic students, 11/1 for international students. Applications are processed on a rolling basis. *Application fee:* $35 ($40 for international students). Electronic applications accepted. *Application Contact:* Dr. Joanne Romagni, Dean of the Graduate School, 423-425-4478, Fax: 423-425-5223, E-mail: joanne-romagni@utc.edu. *Department Head*, Dr. Ahad Nasab, 423-425-4032, Fax: 423-425-5818, E-mail: Ahad-Nasab@utc.edu.

**Program in Accountancy** Students: 12 full-time (10 women), 9 part-time (7 women); includes 1 minority (Black or African American, non-Hispanic/Latino). Average age 27. 23 applicants, 70% accepted, 12 enrolled. *Faculty:* 11 full-time (5 women), 5 part-time/adjunct (2 women). Expenses: Contact institution. *Financial support:* Research assistantships, teaching assistantships, career-related internships or fieldwork, scholarships/grants, and unspecified assistantships available. Support available to part-time students. Financial award application deadline: 7/1; financial award applicants required to submit FAFSA. In 2019, 11 master's awarded. *Program availability:* Part-time, evening/weekend. *Application deadline:* For fall admission, 6/15 priority date for domestic students, 7/1 for international students; for spring admission, 11/1 priority date for domestic students, 11/1 for international students. Applications are processed on a rolling basis. *Application fee:* $35 ($40 for international students). Electronic applications accepted. *Application Contact:* Dr. Joanne Romagni, Dean of the Graduate School, 413-425-4478, Fax: 423-425-5223, E-mail: randy-walker@utc.edu. *Department Head*, Dr. Dan Hollingsworth, 423-425-4664, Fax: 423-425-5255, E-mail: dan-hollingsworth@utc.edu.

**Program in Business Administration** Students: 47 full-time (24 women), 202 part-time (95 women); includes 51 minority (14 Black or African American, non-Hispanic/Latino; 1 American Indian or Alaska Native, non-Hispanic/Latino; 14 Asian, non-Hispanic/Latino; 7 Hispanic/Latino; 15 Two or more races, non-Hispanic/Latino), 8 international. Average age 30. 109 applicants, 90% accepted, 63 enrolled. Expenses: Contact institution. *Financial support:* Research assistantships, teaching assistantships, career-related internships or fieldwork, scholarships/grants, health care benefits, tuition waivers (partial), and unspecified assistantships available. Support available to part-time students. Financial award application deadline: 7/1; financial award applicants required to submit FAFSA. In 2019, 120 master's awarded. *Program availability:* Part-time, evening/weekend, 100% online. *Application deadline:* For fall admission, 6/15 priority date for domestic students, 7/1 for international students; for spring admission, 11/1 priority date for domestic students, 11/1 for international students. Applications are processed on a rolling basis. *Application fee:* $35 ($40 for international students). Electronic applications accepted. *Application Contact:* Dr. Joanne Romagni, Dean of the Graduate School, 423-425-4478, Fax: 423-425-5223, E-mail: joanne-romagni@utc.edu. *Director of Graduate Programs*, Elizabeth Bell, 423-425-2326, Fax: 423-425-5255, E-mail: elizabeth-bell@utc.edu.

**Program in Computational Science** Students: 11 full-time (0 women), 14 part-time (2 women); includes 5 minority (2 Black or African American, non-Hispanic/Latino; 3 Asian, non-Hispanic/Latino), 13 international. Average age 35. 4 applicants, 100% accepted, 2 enrolled. Expenses: Contact institution. *Financial support:* Research assistantships, career-related internships or fieldwork, scholarships/grants, and unspecified assistantships available. Support available to part-time students. Financial award application deadline: 7/1; financial award applicants required to submit FAFSA. In 2019, 3 doctorates awarded. *Application deadline:* For fall admission, 6/15 priority date for domestic students, 7/1 for international students; for spring admission, 11/1 priority date for domestic students, 11/1 for international students. Applications are processed on a rolling basis. *Application fee:* $35 ($40 for international students). Electronic applications accepted. *Application Contact:* Dr. Joanne Romagni, Dean of the Graduate School, 423-425-4478, Fax: 423-425-5223, E-mail: joanne-romagni@utc.edu. *Department Head*, Dr. Luay Wahsheh, 423-425-4361, Fax: 423-425-5311, E-mail: luay-a-wahsheh@utc.edu.

**Program in Computer Science** Students: 27 full-time (7 women), 31 part-time (10 women); includes 16 minority (4 Black or African American, non-Hispanic/Latino; 2 Asian, non-Hispanic/Latino; 6 Hispanic/Latino; 4 Two or more races, non-Hispanic/Latino), 6 international. Average age 29. 35 applicants, 71% accepted, 16 enrolled. Expenses: Contact institution. *Financial support:* Research assistantships, teaching assistantships, career-related internships or fieldwork, scholarships/grants, health care benefits, and unspecified assistantships available. Support available to part-time students. Financial award application deadline: 7/1; financial award applicants required to submit FAFSA. In 2019, 18 master's awarded. *Program availability:* Part-time, 100% online. *Application deadline:* For fall admission, 6/15 priority date for domestic students, 7/1 for international students; for spring admission, 11/1 priority date for domestic students, 11/1 for international students. Applications are processed on a rolling basis. *Application fee:* $35 ($40 for international students). Electronic applications accepted. *Application Contact:* Dr. Joanne Romagni, Dean of the Graduate School, 423-425-4478, Fax: 423-425-5223, E-mail: joanne-romagni@utc.edu. *Department Head*, Dr. Luay Wahsheh, 423-425-4361, Fax: 423-425-5311, E-mail: luay-a-wahsheh@utc.edu.

**Program in Counseling** Students: 37 full-time (29 women), 16 part-time (12 women); includes 10 minority (4 Black or African American, non-Hispanic/Latino; 1 Asian, non-Hispanic/Latino; 3 Hispanic/Latino; 2 Two or more races, non-Hispanic/Latino). Average age 29. 41 applicants, 63% accepted, 12 enrolled. *Faculty:* 3 full-time (2 women), 2 part-time/adjunct (both women). Expenses: Contact institution. *Financial support:* Research assistantships, career-related internships or fieldwork, scholarships/grants, and unspecified assistantships available. Support available to part-time students. Financial award application deadline: 7/1; financial award applicants required to submit FAFSA. In 2019, 21 master's awarded. *Application deadline:* For fall admission, 6/15 priority date for domestic students, 7/1 for international students; for spring admission, 11/1 priority date for domestic students, 11/1 for international students. Applications are processed on a rolling basis. *Application fee:* $35 ($40 for international students). Electronic applications accepted. *Application Contact:* Dr. Joanne Romagni, Dean of the Graduate School, 423-425-4478, Fax: 423-425-4052, E-mail: joanne-romagni@utc.edu. *Director*, Dr. Elizabeth O'Brien, 423-425-4544, E-mail: elizabeth-o'brien@utc.edu.

**Program in Criminal Justice** Students: 18 full-time (11 women), 9 part-time (4 women); includes 6 minority (3 Black or African American, non-Hispanic/Latino; 1 Hispanic/Latino; 2 Two or more races, non-Hispanic/Latino). Average age 28. 16 applicants, 88% accepted, 13 enrolled. Expenses: Contact institution. *Financial support:* Research assistantships, teaching assistantships, career-related internships or fieldwork, scholarships/grants, and unspecified assistantships available. Support available to part-time students. Financial award application deadline: 7/1; financial award applicants required to submit FAFSA. In 2019, 9 master's awarded. *Program availability:* Part-time. *Application deadline:* For fall admission, 6/15 priority date for domestic students, 7/1 for international students; for spring admission, 11/1 priority date for domestic students, 11/1 for international students. Applications are processed on a rolling basis. *Application fee:* $35 ($40 for international students). Electronic applications accepted. *Application Contact:* Dr. Joanne Romagni, Dean of the Graduate School, 423-425-4478, Fax: 423-425-5223, E-mail: joanne-romagni@utc.edu. *Graduate Coordinator*, Dr. Christina Policastro, 423-425-5752, Fax: 423-425-2251, E-mail: Christina-Policastro@utc.edu.

**Program in Engineering** Students: 29 full-time (4 women), 27 part-time (3 women); includes 9 minority (4 Black or African American, non-Hispanic/Latino; 2 Asian, non-Hispanic/Latino; 1 Hispanic/Latino; 1 Native Hawaiian or other Pacific Islander, non-Hispanic/Latino; 1 Two or more races, non-Hispanic/Latino), 19 international. Average age 29. 39 applicants, 74% accepted, 16 enrolled. Expenses: Contact institution. *Financial support:* Research assistantships, teaching assistantships, career-related internships or fieldwork, scholarships/grants, health care benefits, and unspecified assistantships available. Support available to part-time students. Financial award application deadline: 7/1; financial award applicants required to submit FAFSA. In 2019, 22 master's awarded. *Program availability:* Part-time. *Application deadline:* For fall admission, 6/15 priority date for domestic students, 7/1 for international students; for spring admission, 11/1 priority date for domestic students, 11/1 for international students. Applications are processed on a rolling basis. *Application fee:* $35 ($40 for international students). Electronic applications accepted. *Application Contact:* Dr. Joanne Romagni, Dean of the Graduate School, 423-425-4478, Fax: 423-425-5223, E-mail: joanne-romagni@utc.edu. *Dean*, Dr. Daniel Pack, 423-425-2256, Fax: 423-425-5311, E-mail: daniel-pack@utc.edu.

**Program in English** Students: 15 full-time (9 women), 16 part-time (14 women); includes 4 minority (2 Black or African American, non-Hispanic/Latino; 1 Asian, non-Hispanic/Latino; 1 Native Hawaiian or other Pacific Islander, non-Hispanic/Latino). Average age 33. 15 applicants, 100% accepted, 10 enrolled. *Faculty:* 51 full-time (27 women), 22 part-time/adjunct (17 women). Expenses: Contact institution. *Financial support:* Research assistantships, teaching assistantships, career-related internships or fieldwork, scholarships/grants, health care benefits, and unspecified assistantships available. Support available to part-time students. Financial award application deadline: 7/1; financial award applicants required to submit FAFSA. In 2019, 8 master's awarded. *Program availability:* Part-time. *Application deadline:* For fall admission, 6/15 priority date for domestic students, 7/1 for international students; for spring admission, 11/1 priority date for domestic students, 11/1 for international students. Applications are processed on a rolling basis. *Application fee:* $35 ($40 for international students). Electronic applications accepted. *Application Contact:* Dr. Joanne Romagni, Dean of the Graduate School, 423-425-4478, Fax: 423-425-5223, E-mail: joanne-romagni@utc.edu. *Department Head*, Dr. Andrew McCarthy, 423-425-4615, Fax: 423-425-2282, E-mail: andrew-mccarthy@utc.edu.

**Program in Environmental Science** Students: 13 full-time (7 women), 14 part-time (9 women); includes 2 minority (1 Black or African American, non-Hispanic/Latino; 1 Hispanic/Latino). Average age 27. 10 applicants, 90% accepted, 6 enrolled. Expenses: Contact institution. *Financial support:* Research assistantships, teaching assistantships, career-related internships or fieldwork, scholarships/grants, and unspecified assistantships available. Support available to part-time students. Financial award application deadline: 7/1; financial award applicants required to submit FAFSA. In 2019, 17 master's awarded. *Program availability:* Part-time. *Application deadline:* For fall admission, 6/15 priority date for domestic students, 7/1 for international students; for spring admission, 11/1 priority date for domestic students, 11/1 for international students. Applications are processed on a rolling basis. *Application fee:* $35 ($40 for international students). Electronic applications accepted. *Application Contact:* Dr. Joanne Romagni, Dean of the Graduate School, 423-425-4478, Fax: 423-425-5223, E-mail: joanne-romagni@utc.edu. *Department Head*, Dr. John Tucker, 423-425-4341, Fax: 423-425-2285, E-mail: john-tucker@utc.edu.

**Program in Learning and Leadership** Students: 93 part-time (56 women); includes 22 minority (18 Black or African American, non-Hispanic/Latino; 1 American Indian or Alaska Native, non-Hispanic/Latino; 2 Hispanic/Latino; 1 Two or more races, non-Hispanic/Latino). Average age 44. 11 applicants, 100% accepted, 8 enrolled. *Faculty:* 5 full-time (1 woman), 1 part-time/adjunct (0 women). Expenses: Contact institution. *Financial support:* Research assistantships, career-related internships or fieldwork, scholarships/grants, and unspecified assistantships available. Support available to part-time students. Financial award application deadline: 7/1; financial award applicants required to submit FAFSA. In 2019, 10 doctorates awarded. *Application deadline:* For fall admission, 6/15 priority date for domestic students, 7/1 for international students; for spring admission, 11/1 priority date for domestic students, 11/1 for international students. Applications are processed on a rolling basis. *Application fee:* $35 ($40 for international students). Electronic applications accepted. *Application Contact:* Dr. Joanne Romagni, Dean of the Graduate School, 423-425-4478, Fax: 423-425-5223, E-mail: joanne-romagni@utc.edu. *Director*, Dr. David Rausch, 423-425-5270, E-mail: utclead@utc.edu.

**Program in Mathematics** Students: 4 full-time (all women), 6 part-time (1 woman); includes 3 minority (1 Asian, non-Hispanic/Latino; 1 Hispanic/Latino; 1 Two or more races, non-Hispanic/Latino), 1 international. Average age 35. 9 applicants, 78% accepted, 6 enrolled. *Faculty:* 27 full-time (10 women), 6 part-time/adjunct (2 women). Expenses: Contact institution. *Financial support:* Research assistantships and teaching assistantships available. Financial award application deadline: 7/1; financial award applicants required to submit FAFSA. In 2019, 3 master's awarded. *Program availability:* Part-time. *Application deadline:* For fall admission, 6/15 for domestic students, 7/1 for international students; for spring admission, 11/1 for domestic and international students. Applications are processed on a rolling basis. *Application fee:* $35 ($40 for international students). Electronic applications accepted. *Application Contact:* Dr. Joanne Romagni, Dean of the Graduate School, 423-425-4478, Fax: 423-425-5223, E-mail: joanne-romagni@utc.edu. *Department Head*, Dr. Christopher Cox, 423-425-5680, E-mail: Chris-Cox@utc.edu.

**Program in Physical Therapy** Students: 105 full-time (75 women); includes 7 minority (1 Black or African American, non-Hispanic/Latino; 2 Asian, non-Hispanic/Latino; 2 Hispanic/Latino; 2 Two or more races, non-Hispanic/Latino). Average age 24. 37 applicants, 97% accepted, 36 enrolled. *Faculty:* 12 full-time (6 women). Expenses: Contact institution. *Financial support:* Research assistantships, teaching assistantships, career-related internships or fieldwork, scholarships/grants, and unspecified assistantships available. Support available to part-time students. Financial award application deadline: 7/1; financial award applicants required to submit FAFSA. In 2019, 34 doctorates awarded. *Application deadline:* For fall admission, 6/15 priority date for domestic students, 7/1 for international students; for spring admission, 11/1 priority date for domestic students, 11/1 for international students. Applications are processed on a rolling basis. *Application fee:* $35 ($40 for international students). Electronic applications accepted. *Application Contact:* Dr. Joanne Romagni, Dean of the Graduate School, 423-425-4478, Fax: 423-425-5223, E-mail: joanne-romagni@utc.edu. *Department Head,* Dr. Nancy Fell, 423-425-2240, Fax: 423-425-2380, E-mail: Nancy-Fell@utc.edu.

**Program in Psychology** Students: 44 full-time (35 women), 4 part-time (3 women); includes 6 minority (1 Black or African American, non-Hispanic/Latino; 3 Hispanic/Latino; 2 Two or more races, non-Hispanic/Latino), 1 international. Average age 25. 98 applicants, 24% accepted, 20 enrolled. *Faculty:* 17 full-time (10 women), 4 part-time/adjunct (2 women). Expenses: Contact institution. *Financial support:* Research assistantships, teaching assistantships, career-related internships or fieldwork, scholarships/grants, and unspecified assistantships available. Support available to part-time students. Financial award application deadline: 7/1; financial award applicants required to submit FAFSA. In 2019, 26 master's awarded. *Program availability:* Part-time. *Application deadline:* For fall admission, 6/15 priority date for domestic students, 7/1 for international students; for spring admission, 11/1 priority date for domestic students, 11/1 for international students. Applications are processed on a rolling basis. *Application fee:* $35 ($40 for international students). Electronic applications accepted. *Application Contact:* Dr. Joanne Romagni, Dean of the Graduate School, 423-425-4478, Fax: 423-425-5223, E-mail: joanne-romagni@utc.edu. *Department Head,* Dr. Brian O'Leary, 423-425-4283, Fax: 423-425-4284, E-mail: Boleary@utc.edu.

**Program in Social Work** Students: 30 full-time (28 women), 3 part-time (all women); includes 8 minority (5 Black or African American, non-Hispanic/Latino; 1 Asian, non-Hispanic/Latino; 2 Hispanic/Latino). Average age 29. 38 applicants, 68% accepted, 19 enrolled. *Faculty:* 8 full-time (all women), 8 part-time/adjunct (7 women). Expenses: Contact institution. *Financial support:* Career-related internships or fieldwork, scholarships/grants, and unspecified assistantships available. Support available to part-time students. Financial award application deadline: 7/1; financial award applicants required to submit FAFSA. In 2019, 11 master's awarded. *Application deadline:* For fall admission, 6/15 priority date for domestic students, 7/1 for international students; for spring admission, 11/1 priority date for domestic students, 11/1 for international students. Applications are processed on a rolling basis. *Application fee:* $35 ($40 for international students). Electronic applications accepted. *Application Contact:* Dr. Joanne Romagni, Dean of the Graduate School, 423-425-4478, Fax: 423-425-5223, E-mail: joanne-romagni@utc.edu. *Coordinator,* Dr. Amy Doolittle, 423-425-5563, E-mail: amy-doolittle@utc.edu.

**School of Education** Students: 28 full-time (18 women), 63 part-time (44 women); includes 20 minority (10 Black or African American, non-Hispanic/Latino; 1 American Indian or Alaska Native, non-Hispanic/Latino; 1 Asian, non-Hispanic/Latino; 3 Hispanic/Latino; 5 Two or more races, non-Hispanic/Latino). Average age 32. 59 applicants, 78% accepted, 24 enrolled. *Faculty:* 21 full-time (14 women), 16 part-time/adjunct (15 women). Expenses: Contact institution. *Financial support:* Research assistantships, teaching assistantships, career-related internships or fieldwork, institutionally sponsored loans, scholarships/grants, and unspecified assistantships available. Support available to part-time students. Financial award application deadline: 7/1; financial award applicants required to submit FAFSA. In 2019, 42 master's, 7 other advanced degrees awarded. *Program availability:* Part-time. *Application deadline:* For fall admission, 6/15 for domestic students, 7/1 for international students; for spring admission, 11/1 for domestic and international students. Applications are processed on a rolling basis. *Application fee:* $35 ($40 for international students). Electronic applications accepted. *Application Contact:* Dr. Joanne Romagni, Dean of the Graduate School, 423-425-4478, Fax: 423-425-5223, E-mail: joanne-romagni@utc.edu. *Director,* Dr. Renee Murley, 423-425-4684, Fax: 423-425-5380, E-mail: renee-murley@utc.edu.

**School of Nursing** Students: 78 full-time (49 women), 51 part-time (43 women); includes 24 minority (11 Black or African American, non-Hispanic/Latino; 2 American Indian or Alaska Native, non-Hispanic/Latino; 4 Asian, non-Hispanic/Latino; 5 Hispanic/Latino; 2 Two or more races, non-Hispanic/Latino). Average age 34. 50 applicants, 100% accepted, 46 enrolled. *Faculty:* 32 full-time (29 women), 14 part-time/adjunct (10 women). Expenses: Contact institution. *Financial support:* Teaching assistantships, career-related internships or fieldwork, and scholarships/grants available. Support available to part-time students. Financial award application deadline: 7/1; financial award applicants required to submit FAFSA. In 2019, 38 master's, 16 doctorates, 2 other advanced degrees awarded. *Program availability:* 100% online. *Application deadline:* For fall admission, 6/15 priority date for domestic students, 7/1 for international students; for spring admission, 11/1 priority date for domestic students, 11/1 for international students. Applications are processed on a rolling basis. *Application fee:* $35 ($40 for international students). Electronic applications accepted. *Application Contact:* Dr. Joanne Romagni, Dean of the Graduate School, 423-425-4478, Fax: 423-425-5223, E-mail: joanne-romagni@utc.edu. *Director,* Dr. Chris Smith, 423-425-4665, Fax: 423-425-4668, E-mail: chris-smith@utc.edu.

## THE UNIVERSITY OF TENNESSEE AT MARTIN, Martin, TN 38238

**General Information** State-supported, coed, comprehensive institution. *Enrollment:* 7,296 graduate, professional, and undergraduate students; 146 full-time matriculated graduate/professional students (109 women), 312 part-time matriculated graduate/professional students (220 women). *Enrollment by degree level:* 458 master's. *Graduate faculty:* 113. *International tuition:* $23,040 full-time. *Tuition, area resident:* Full-time $9096; part-time $505 per credit hour. Tuition, state resident: full-time $9096; part-time $505 per credit hour. Tuition, nonresident: full-time $15,136; part-time $841 per credit hour. *Required fees:* $1520; $85 per credit hour. Part-time tuition and fees vary according to course load. *Graduate housing:* Rooms and/or apartments available on a first-come, first-served basis to single and married students. Typical cost: $2920 per year ($6396 including board) for single students; $4580 per year for married students. Housing application deadline: 3/1. *Student services:* Campus employment opportunities, campus safety program, career counseling, child daycare facilities, exercise/wellness program, free psychological counseling, international student services, low-cost health insurance, multicultural affairs office, services for students with disabilities, teacher training, writing training. *Library facilities:* Paul Meek Library. *Collection:* Books: 280,270 (physical), 114,346 (digital/electronic); Serial titles: 44,595 (physical), 220,785 (digital/electronic); Databases: 370. Weekly public service hours: 92; study areas open 24 hours, 5–7 days a week. *Research affiliation:* U.S. Department of Education (DOE) (academic extensions), National Writing Project (humanities), U.S. Department of Health and Human Services (infant health), U.S. Department of Justice (criminal justice), The University of Tennessee Research Foundation (science and technology), Oak Ridge National Laboratory (science, technology, engineering, and math (STEM)).

**Computer facilities:** 1,157 computers available on campus for general student use. A campuswide network can be accessed. Online class registration, online fee payments, degree progress, financial aid data, housing applications, transcripts are available. Website: http://www.utm.edu/

**General Application Contact:** Jolene L. Cunningham, Student Services Specialist, 731-881-7012, Fax: 731-881-7499, E-mail: jcunningham@utm.edu.

**GRADUATE UNITS**

**Graduate Programs** Students: 146 full-time (109 women), 312 part-time (220 women); includes 80 minority (61 Black or African American, non-Hispanic/Latino; 4 Asian, non-Hispanic/Latino; 5 Hispanic/Latino; 10 Two or more races, non-Hispanic/Latino). Average age 32. 549 applicants, 60% accepted, 236 enrolled. *Faculty:* 113. Expenses: Contact institution. *Financial support:* In 2019–20, 168 students received support, including 10 research assistantships with full tuition reimbursements available (averaging $7,666 per year), 16 teaching assistantships with full tuition reimbursements available (averaging $7,695 per year); scholarships/grants and tuition waivers (full and partial) also available. Financial award application deadline: 2/1; financial award applicants required to submit FAFSA. In 2019, 116 master's awarded. *Program availability:* Part-time, 100% online, blended/hybrid learning. *Application deadline:* For fall admission, 7/28 priority date for domestic and international students; for spring admission, 12/17 priority date for domestic and international students; for summer admission, 5/10 priority date for domestic and international students. Applications are processed on a rolling basis. *Application fee:* $30 ($130 for international students). Electronic applications accepted. *Application Contact:* Jolene L. Cunningham, Student Services Specialist, 731-881-7012, Fax: 731-881-7499, E-mail: jcunningham@utm.edu. *Interim Dean of Graduate Studies,* Dr. Joseph Mehlhorn, 731-881-7012, Fax: 731-881-7499, E-mail: graduatestudies@utm.edu.

***College of Agriculture and Applied Sciences*** Students: 9 full-time (5 women), 52 part-time (37 women); includes 4 minority (2 Black or African American, non-Hispanic/Latino; 1 Hispanic/Latino; 1 Two or more races, non-Hispanic/Latino). Average age 30. 72 applicants, 65% accepted, 23 enrolled. *Faculty:* 17. Expenses: Contact institution. *Financial support:* In 2019–20, 23 students received support, including 1 research assistantship with full tuition reimbursement available (averaging $9,802 per year), 2 teaching assistantships with full tuition reimbursements available (averaging $6,912 per year); scholarships/grants and tuition waivers (full and partial) also available. Financial award application deadline: 2/1; financial award applicants required to submit FAFSA. In 2019, 23 master's awarded. *Program availability:* Part-time, 100% online, blended/hybrid learning. *Application deadline:* For fall admission, 7/28 priority date for domestic and international students; for spring admission, 12/17 priority date for domestic and international students; for summer admission, 5/10 priority date for domestic and international students. Applications are processed on a rolling basis. *Application fee:* $30 ($130 for international students). Electronic applications accepted. *Application Contact:* Jolene L. Cunningham, Student Services Specialist, 731-881-7012, Fax: 731-881-7499, E-mail: jcunningham@utm.edu. *Dean,* Dr. Todd Winters, 731-881-7250, E-mail: winters@utm.edu.

***College of Business and Global Affairs*** Students: 12 full-time (10 women), 63 part-time (27 women); includes 15 minority (7 Black or African American, non-Hispanic/Latino; 3 Asian, non-Hispanic/Latino; 2 Hispanic/Latino; 3 Two or more races, non-Hispanic/Latino). Average age 34. 95 applicants, 40% accepted, 36 enrolled. *Faculty:* 28. Expenses: Contact institution. *Financial support:* In 2019–20, 39 students received support, including 5 research assistantships with full tuition reimbursements available (averaging $7,289 per year), 7 teaching assistantships with full tuition reimbursements available (averaging $7,831 per year); scholarships/grants and tuition waivers (full and partial) also available. Financial award application deadline: 2/1; financial award applicants required to submit FAFSA. In 2019, 31 master's awarded. *Program availability:* Part-time, 100% online, blended/hybrid learning. *Application deadline:* For fall admission, 7/28 priority date for domestic and international students; for spring admission, 12/17 priority date for domestic and international students; for summer admission, 5/10 priority date for domestic and international students. Applications are processed on a rolling basis. *Application fee:* $30 ($130 for international students). Electronic applications accepted. *Application Contact:* Jolene L. Cunningham, Student Services Specialist, 731-881-7012, Fax: 731-881-7499, E-mail: jcunningham@utm.edu. *Interim Dean,* Dr. Katie High, 731-881-7227, Fax: 731-881-7241, E-mail: khigh@utm.edu.

***College of Education, Health and Behavioral Sciences*** Students: 125 full-time (94 women), 175 part-time (140 women); includes 59 minority (50 Black or African American, non-Hispanic/Latino; 1 Asian, non-Hispanic/Latino; 2 Hispanic/Latino; 6 Two or more races, non-Hispanic/Latino). Average age 32. 370 applicants, 65% accepted, 169 enrolled. *Faculty:* 39. Expenses: Contact institution. *Financial support:* In 2019–20, 90 students received support, including 3 research assistantships with full tuition reimbursements available (averaging $7,121 per year), 7 teaching assistantships with full tuition reimbursements available (averaging $7,784 per year); scholarships/grants and tuition waivers (full and partial) also available. Financial award application deadline: 2/1; financial award applicants required to submit FAFSA. In 2019, 55 master's awarded. *Program availability:* Part-time, online only, 100% online. *Application deadline:* For fall admission, 7/28 priority date for domestic and international students; for spring admission, 12/17 priority date for domestic and international students; for summer admission, 5/10 priority date for domestic and international students. Applications are processed on a rolling basis. *Application fee:* $30 ($130 for international students). Electronic applications accepted. *Application Contact:* Jolene L. Cunningham, Student Services Specialist, 731-881-7012, Fax: 731-881-7499, E-mail: jcunningham@utm.edu. *Dean,* Cynthia West, 731-881-7127, Fax: 731-881-7975, E-mail: cwest@utm.edu.

***College of Humanities and Fine Arts*** Students: 22 part-time (16 women); includes 2 minority (both Black or African American, non-Hispanic/Latino). Average age 38. 12 applicants, 67% accepted, 8 enrolled. *Faculty:* 18 full-time (7 women). Expenses: Contact institution. *Financial support:* In 2019–20, 16 students received support, including 1 research assistantship with full tuition reimbursement available (averaging $9,048 per year); teaching assistantships with full tuition reimbursements available, scholarships/grants, and tuition waivers (full and partial) also available. Financial award application deadline: 2/1; financial award applicants required to submit FAFSA. In 2019, 7 master's awarded. *Program availability:* Part-time, blended/hybrid learning. *Application deadline:* For fall admission, 7/28 priority date for domestic and international students; for spring admission, 12/15 priority date for domestic and international students; for summer admission, 5/10 priority date for domestic and international students. Applications are processed on a rolling basis. *Application fee:* $30 ($130 for international students). Electronic applications accepted. *Application Contact:* Jolene L. Cunningham, Student Services Specialist, 731-881-7012, Fax: 731-881-7499, E-mail: jcunningham@utm.edu. *Dean,* Dr. Lynn Alexander, 731-881-7490, Fax: 731-881-7276, E-mail: lalexand@utm.edu.

## THE UNIVERSITY OF TENNESSEE HEALTH SCIENCE CENTER, Memphis, TN 38163-0002

**General Information** State-supported, coed, upper-level institution. CGS member. *Graduate housing:* On-campus housing not available. *Research affiliation:* Saint Jude's Children's Research Hospital, Veterans Administration Medical Center, University of Memphis, LeBonheur Children's Medical Center.

**GRADUATE UNITS**

**College of Dentistry** Electronic applications accepted.

**College of Graduate Health Sciences** Electronic applications accepted.

**College of Health Professions** *Program availability:* Part-time, evening/weekend, online learning. Electronic applications accepted.

**College of Medicine** Electronic applications accepted.

**College of Nursing** Students: 226 full-time (187 women), 28 part-time (26 women); includes 80 minority (63 Black or African American, non-Hispanic/Latino; 15 Asian, non-Hispanic/Latino; 2 Hispanic/Latino). Average age 33. 652 applicants, 20% accepted, 104 enrolled. *Faculty:* 62 full-time (55 women), 7 part-time/adjunct (2 women). Expenses: Contact institution. *Financial support:* In 2019–20, 112 students received support, including 16 research assistantships (averaging $229,578 per year); Federal Work-Study, institutionally sponsored loans, scholarships/grants, and tuition waivers (partial) also available. Financial award application deadline: 3/15; financial award applicants required to submit FAFSA. In 2019, 86 doctorates, 2 Certificates awarded. *Program availability:* Part-time, blended/hybrid learning. *Application deadline:* For fall admission, 1/15 for domestic students; for spring admission, 8/15 for domestic students. *Application fee:* $70. Electronic applications accepted. *Application Contact:* Glynis Blackard, Assistant Dean for Student Affairs, 901-448-6139, Fax: 901-448-4121, E-mail: gblackar@uthsc.edu. *Dean,* Dr. Wendy Likes, 901-448-6135, Fax: 901-448-4121, E-mail: wlikes@uthsc.edu.

**College of Pharmacy** Electronic applications accepted.

## THE UNIVERSITY OF TENNESSEE–OAK RIDGE NATIONAL LABORATORY, Oak Ridge, TN 37830-8026

**General Information** State-supported, coed, graduate-only institution. *Research affiliation:* Oak Ridge National Laboratory.

**GRADUATE UNITS**

**Graduate Program in Genome Science and Technology** Electronic applications accepted.

## THE UNIVERSITY OF TEXAS AT ARLINGTON, Arlington, TX 76019

**General Information** State-supported, coed, university. CGS member. *Graduate housing:* Rooms and/or apartments available on a first-come, first-served basis to single and married students. *Research affiliation:* Texas Health Resources (medical technologies), Center for Innovation (technology development and commercialization), Facebook (energy efficient electronic systems), U.S. Department of Energy (bioengineering), National Science Foundation (materials science and engineering), Texas Instruments (medical technologies).

**GRADUATE UNITS**

**Graduate School** *Program availability:* Part-time, evening/weekend, online learning.

***College of Architecture, Planning and Public Affairs*** *Program availability:* Part-time, evening/weekend, online learning. Electronic applications accepted.

***College of Business*** *Program availability:* Part-time, evening/weekend, online learning. Electronic applications accepted.

***College of Education***

***College of Engineering*** *Program availability:* Part-time, evening/weekend, online learning.

***College of Liberal Arts*** *Program availability:* Part-time, evening/weekend.

***College of Nursing and Health Innovation*** *Program availability:* Part-time, evening/weekend, online learning.

***College of Science*** *Program availability:* Part-time, evening/weekend.

***School of Social Work*** *Program availability:* Part-time, evening/weekend, online learning. Electronic applications accepted.

## THE UNIVERSITY OF TEXAS AT AUSTIN, Austin, TX 78712-1111

**General Information** State-supported, coed, university. CGS member. *Graduate housing:* Rooms and/or apartments available to single students and available on a first-come, first-served basis to married students.

**GRADUATE UNITS**

**Dell Medical School**

**Graduate School** *Program availability:* Part-time, evening/weekend. Electronic applications accepted.

***Cockrell School of Engineering*** *Program availability:* Part-time, evening/weekend. Electronic applications accepted.

***College of Communication*** *Program availability:* Part-time. Electronic applications accepted.

***College of Education*** *Program availability:* Part-time. Electronic applications accepted.

***College of Fine Arts*** *Program availability:* Part-time. Electronic applications accepted.

***College of Liberal Arts*** *Program availability:* Part-time. Electronic applications accepted.

***College of Natural Sciences*** *Program availability:* Part-time. Electronic applications accepted.

***College of Pharmacy*** Electronic applications accepted.

***Institute for Cellular and Molecular Biology***

***The Institute for Neuroscience*** Electronic applications accepted.

***Jackson School of Geosciences*** *Program availability:* Part-time. Electronic applications accepted.

***Lyndon B. Johnson School of Public Affairs*** *Program availability:* Part-time. Electronic applications accepted.

***McCombs School of Business*** Electronic applications accepted.

***Michener Center for Writers*** Electronic applications accepted.

***School of Architecture*** Electronic applications accepted.

***School of Information*** *Program availability:* Part-time. Electronic applications accepted.

***School of Nursing*** *Program availability:* Part-time. Electronic applications accepted.

***Steve Hicks School of Social Work*** *Program availability:* Part-time.

**School of Law** Students: 985 full-time (462 women); includes 301 minority (36 Black or African American, non-Hispanic/Latino; 4 American Indian or Alaska Native, non-Hispanic/Latino; 74 Asian, non-Hispanic/Latino; 149 Hispanic/Latino; 38 Two or more races, non-Hispanic/Latino), 27 international. Average age 24. 5,803 applicants, 18% accepted, 280 enrolled. *Faculty:* 94 full-time (36 women), 198 part-time/adjunct (55 women). Expenses: Contact institution. *Financial support:* In 2019–20, 870 students received support. Career-related internships or fieldwork, scholarships/grants, and tuition waivers (full) available. Financial award application deadline: 1/15; financial award applicants required to submit FAFSA. In 2019, 297 doctorates awarded. *Application deadline:* For spring admission, 3/1 for domestic students. Applications are processed on a rolling basis. *Application fee:* $70. Electronic applications accepted. *Application Contact:* Mathiew Le, Assistant Dean of Admissions & Financial Aid, 512-232-1200, E-mail: admissions@law.utexas.edu. *Dean,* Ward Farnsworth, 512-232-1120, E-mail: wfarnsworth@law.utexas.edu.

## THE UNIVERSITY OF TEXAS AT DALLAS, Richardson, TX 75080

**General Information** State-supported, coed, university. CGS member. *Enrollment:* 29,543 graduate, professional, and undergraduate students; 5,715 full-time matriculated graduate/professional students (2,488 women), 2,717 part-time matriculated graduate/professional students (1,177 women). *Enrollment by degree level:* 6,891 master's, 1,541 doctoral. *Graduate faculty:* 564 full-time (131 women), 238 part-time/adjunct (75 women). *Tuition, area resident:* Full-time $16,504. Tuition, state resident: full-time $16,504. Tuition, nonresident: full-time $34,266. Tuition and fees vary according to course load. *Graduate housing:* Rooms and/or apartments available on a first-come, first-served basis to single and married students. Typical cost: $7224 per year ($11,112 including board) for single students; $7224 per year ($11,112 including board) for married students. Housing application deadline: 5/31. *Student services:* Campus employment opportunities, campus safety program, career counseling, child daycare facilities, exercise/wellness program, free psychological counseling, grant writing training, international student services, low-cost health insurance, multicultural affairs office, services for students with disabilities, teacher training, writing training. *Library facilities:* Eugene McDermott Library plus 1 other. *Collection:* Books: 567,164 (physical), 1.5 million (digital/electronic); Serial titles: 77,304 (physical), 165,725 (digital/electronic); Databases: 596. Weekly public service hours: 152; study areas open 24 hours, 5–7 days a week; students can reserve study rooms.

**Computer facilities:** Computer purchase and lease plans are available. 170 computers available on campus for general student use. A campuswide network can be accessed. Online class registration is available.
Website: http://www.utdallas.edu/

**General Application Contact:** Dr. Juan E Gonzalez, Dean of Graduate Studies, 972-883-2234, Fax: 972-883-4308, E-mail: graduatestudies@utdallas.edu.

**GRADUATE UNITS**

**Erik Jonsson School of Engineering and Computer Science** Students: 1,711 full-time (492 women), 538 part-time (140 women); includes 249 minority (32 Black or African American, non-Hispanic/Latino; 139 Asian, non-Hispanic/Latino; 64 Hispanic/Latino; 14 Two or more races, non-Hispanic/Latino), 1,706 international. Average age 27. 6,263 applicants, 23% accepted, 635 enrolled. *Faculty:* 152 full-time (17 women), 41 part-time/adjunct (8 women). Expenses: Contact institution. *Financial support:* In 2019–20, 608 students received support, including 43 fellowships (averaging $4,082 per year), 373 research assistantships with partial tuition reimbursements available (averaging $24,016 per year), 217 teaching assistantships with partial tuition reimbursements available (averaging $17,130 per year); career-related internships or fieldwork, Federal Work-Study, institutionally sponsored loans, scholarships/grants, and unspecified assistantships also available. Support available to part-time students. Financial award application deadline: 4/30; financial award applicants required to submit FAFSA. In 2019, 774 master's, 89 doctorates awarded. *Program availability:* Part-time, evening/weekend. *Application deadline:* For fall admission, 7/15 for domestic students, 5/1 priority date for international students; for spring admission, 11/15 for domestic students, 9/1 priority date for international students. Applications are processed on a rolling basis. *Application fee:* $50 ($100 for international students). Electronic applications accepted. *Application Contact:* Dr. Stephanie G Adams, Dean, 972-883-2974, Fax: 972-883-2813, E-mail: sgadams@utdallas.edu. *Dean,* Dr. Stephanie G Adams, 972-883-2974, Fax: 972-883-2813, E-mail: sgadams@utdallas.edu.

**Naveen Jindal School of Management** Students: 2,572 full-time (1,116 women), 1,703 part-time (765 women); includes 901 minority (130 Black or African American, non-Hispanic/Latino; 7 American Indian or Alaska Native, non-Hispanic/Latino; 509 Asian, non-Hispanic/Latino; 180 Hispanic/Latino; 2 Native Hawaiian or other Pacific Islander, non-Hispanic/Latino; 73 Two or more races, non-Hispanic/Latino), 2,362 international. Average age 30. 5,311 applicants, 42% accepted, 1,329 enrolled. *Faculty:* 110 full-time (23 women), 128 part-time/adjunct (33 women). Expenses: Contact institution. *Financial support:* In 2019–20, 214 students received support, including 2 fellowships (averaging $1,000 per year), 30 research assistantships with partial tuition reimbursements available (averaging $35,627 per year), 166 teaching assistantships with partial tuition reimbursements available (averaging $17,420 per year); career-related internships or fieldwork, Federal Work-Study, institutionally sponsored loans, scholarships/grants, and unspecified assistantships also available. Support available to part-time students. Financial award application deadline: 4/30; financial award applicants required to submit FAFSA. In 2019, 2,189 master's, 19 doctorates awarded. *Program availability:* Part-time, evening/weekend, online learning. *Application deadline:* For fall admission, 7/15 for domestic students, 5/1 priority date for international students; for spring admission, 11/15 for domestic students, 9/1 priority date for international students. Applications are processed on a rolling basis. *Application fee:* $50 ($100 for international students). Electronic applications accepted. *Application Contact:* Dr. Monica Powell, Senior Associate Dean, Graduate Programs, 972-883-6595, Fax: 972-883-6425, E-mail: jindal@utdallas.edu. *Dean,* Dr. Hasan Pirkul, 972-883-2705, Fax: 972-883-2799, E-mail: hpirkul@utdallas.edu.

**School of Arts and Humanities** Students: 123 full-time (76 women), 116 part-time (71 women); includes 62 minority (14 Black or African American, non-Hispanic/Latino; 3 American Indian or Alaska Native, non-Hispanic/Latino; 9 Asian, non-Hispanic/Latino; 25 Hispanic/Latino; 11 Two or more races, non-Hispanic/Latino), 27 international. Average age 40. 130 applicants, 60% accepted, 59 enrolled. *Faculty:* 48 full-time (19 women), 11 part-time/adjunct (6 women). Expenses: Contact institution. *Financial support:* In 2019–20, 87 students received support, including 9 fellowships (averaging $5,074 per year), 14 research assistantships with partial tuition reimbursements available (averaging $26,575 per year), 69 teaching assistantships with partial tuition reimbursements available (averaging $14,961 per year); Federal Work-Study, institutionally sponsored loans, scholarships/grants, and unspecified assistantships also available. Support available to part-time students. Financial award application deadline: 4/30; financial award applicants required to submit FAFSA. In 2019, 30 master's, 16 doctorates awarded. *Program availability:* Part-time, evening/weekend. *Application deadline:* For fall admission, 7/15 for domestic students, 5/1 priority date for international students; for spring admission, 11/15 for domestic students, 9/1 priority date for international students. Applications are processed on a rolling basis. *Application fee:* $50 ($100 for international students). Electronic applications accepted. *Application Contact:* Dr. John Gooch, Associate Dean of Graduate Studies, 972-883-2756, Fax: 972-883-2989, E-mail: john.gooch@utdallas.edu. *Interim Dean*, Dr. Nils Roemer, 972-883-2984, Fax: 972-883-2989, E-mail: nroemer@utdallas.edu.

**School of Arts, Technology, and Emerging Communication** Students: 40 full-time (20 women), 14 part-time (5 women); includes 11 minority (4 Black or African American, non-Hispanic/Latino; 3 Asian, non-Hispanic/Latino; 3 Hispanic/Latino; 1 Two or more races, non-Hispanic/Latino), 16 international. Average age 34. 85 applicants, 20% accepted, 14 enrolled. *Faculty:* 22 full-time (10 women), 2 part-time/adjunct (0 women). Expenses: Contact institution. *Financial support:* In 2019–20, 36 students received support, including 10 research assistantships with partial tuition reimbursements available (averaging $26,280 per year), 26 teaching assistantships with partial tuition reimbursements available (averaging $15,886 per year); career-related internships or fieldwork, Federal Work-Study, institutionally sponsored loans, scholarships/grants, and unspecified assistantships also available. Support available to part-time students. Financial award application deadline: 4/30; financial award applicants required to submit FAFSA. In 2019, 8 master's awarded. *Application deadline:* For fall admission, 7/15 for domestic students, 5/1 priority date for international students; for spring admission, 11/15 for domestic students, 9/1 priority date for international students. Applications are processed on a rolling basis. *Application fee:* $50 ($100 for international students). Electronic applications accepted. *Application Contact:* Dr. Kim Knight, Associate Dean for Graduate Studies, 972-883-4346, E-mail: kak102020@utdallas.edu. *Dean*, Dr. Anne Balsamo, 972-883-4376, E-mail: atecdean@utdallas.edu.

**School of Behavioral and Brain Sciences** Students: 543 full-time (449 women), 73 part-time (52 women); includes 163 minority (21 Black or African American, non-Hispanic/Latino; 1 American Indian or Alaska Native, non-Hispanic/Latino; 62 Asian, non-Hispanic/Latino; 55 Hispanic/Latino; 24 Two or more races, non-Hispanic/Latino), 73 international. Average age 27. 853 applicants, 26% accepted, 176 enrolled. *Faculty:* 58 full-time (29 women), 25 part-time/adjunct (22 women). Expenses: Contact institution. *Financial support:* In 2019–20, 126 students received support, including 3 fellowships (averaging $2,250 per year), 46 research assistantships with partial tuition reimbursements available (averaging $28,327 per year), 79 teaching assistantships with partial tuition reimbursements available (averaging $19,242 per year); career-related internships or fieldwork, Federal Work-Study, institutionally sponsored loans, scholarships/grants, and unspecified assistantships also available. Support available to part-time students. Financial award application deadline: 4/30; financial award applicants required to submit FAFSA. In 2019, 206 master's, 29 doctorates awarded. *Program availability:* Part-time, evening/weekend. *Application deadline:* For fall admission, 7/15 for domestic students, 5/1 priority date for international students; for spring admission, 11/15 for domestic students, 9/1 priority date for international students. Applications are processed on a rolling basis. *Application fee:* $50 ($100 for international students). Electronic applications accepted. *Application Contact:* Dr. Robert D. Stillman, Associate Dean of Graduate Programs, 214-905-3106, Fax: 972-883-3491, E-mail: stillman@utdallas.edu. *Dean*, Dr. Steven L Small, 972-883-2355, Fax: 972-883-2491, E-mail: small@utdallas.edu.

**School of Economic, Political and Policy Sciences** Students: 208 full-time (108 women), 148 part-time (80 women); includes 117 minority (32 Black or African American, non-Hispanic/Latino; 1 American Indian or Alaska Native, non-Hispanic/Latino; 23 Asian, non-Hispanic/Latino; 50 Hispanic/Latino; 11 Two or more races, non-Hispanic/Latino), 91 international. Average age 34. 390 applicants, 47% accepted, 102 enrolled. *Faculty:* 62 full-time (14 women), 10 part-time/adjunct (0 women). Expenses: Contact institution. *Financial support:* In 2019–20, 97 students received support, including 3 fellowships (averaging $2,333 per year), 11 research assistantships with partial tuition reimbursements available (averaging $19,233 per year), 80 teaching assistantships with partial tuition reimbursements available (averaging $13,501 per year); career-related internships or fieldwork, Federal Work-Study, institutionally sponsored loans, scholarships/grants, and unspecified assistantships also available. Support available to part-time students. Financial award application deadline: 4/30; financial award applicants required to submit FAFSA. In 2019, 104 master's, 31 doctorates awarded. *Program availability:* Part-time, evening/weekend. *Application deadline:* For fall admission, 7/15 for domestic students, 5/1 priority date for international students; for spring admission, 11/15 for domestic students, 9/1 priority date for international students. Applications are processed on a rolling basis. *Application fee:* $50 ($100 for international students). Electronic applications accepted. *Application Contact:* Dr. Banks Miller, Associate Dean for Graduate Programs, 972-883-2930, Fax: 972-883-6297, E-mail: millerbp@utdallas.edu. *Dean*, Dr. Jennifer S Holmes, 972-883-6852, Fax: 972-883-6297, E-mail: jholmes@utdallas.edu.

**School of Interdisciplinary Studies** Students: 17 full-time (14 women), 16 part-time (10 women); includes 17 minority (5 Black or African American, non-Hispanic/Latino; 5 Asian, non-Hispanic/Latino; 4 Hispanic/Latino; 3 Two or more races, non-Hispanic/Latino), 1 international. Average age 35. 35 applicants, 54% accepted, 12 enrolled. *Faculty:* 3 full-time (2 women), 4 part-time/adjunct (2 women). Expenses: Contact institution. *Financial support:* Research assistantships with partial tuition reimbursements, teaching assistantships with partial tuition reimbursements, career-related internships or fieldwork, Federal Work-Study, institutionally sponsored loans, and scholarships/grants available. Support available to part-time students. Financial award application deadline: 4/30; financial award applicants required to submit FAFSA. In 2019, 6 master's awarded. *Program availability:* Part-time, evening/weekend. *Application deadline:* For fall admission, 7/15 for domestic students, 5/1 priority date for international students; for spring admission, 11/15 for domestic students, 9/1 priority date for international students. Applications are processed on a rolling basis. *Application fee:* $50 ($100 for international students). Electronic applications accepted. *Application Contact:* Jillian Duquaine-Watson, Program Head - Interdisciplinary Studies, 972-883-2350, Fax: 972-883-2440, E-mail: jmw087000@utdallas.edu. *Dean*, Dr. George Fair, 972-883-2350, Fax: 972-883-2440, E-mail: gwfair@utdallas.edu.

**School of Natural Sciences and Mathematics** Students: 501 full-time (213 women), 109 part-time (54 women); includes 119 minority (9 Black or African American, non-Hispanic/Latino; 66 Asian, non-Hispanic/Latino; 32 Hispanic/Latino; 12 Two or more races, non-Hispanic/Latino), 324 international. Average age 30. 945 applicants, 28% accepted, 156 enrolled. *Faculty:* 109 full-time (17 women), 17 part-time/adjunct (4 women). Expenses: Contact institution. *Financial support:* In 2019–20, 407 students received support, including 2 fellowships with partial tuition reimbursements available (averaging $750 per year), 110 research assistantships with partial tuition reimbursements available (averaging $25,264 per year), 287 teaching assistantships with partial tuition reimbursements available (averaging $18,094 per year); career-related internships or fieldwork, Federal Work-Study, institutionally sponsored loans, scholarships/grants, and unspecified assistantships also available. Support available to part-time students. Financial award application deadline: 4/30. In 2019, 140 master's, 44 doctorates awarded. *Program availability:* Part-time, evening/weekend. *Application deadline:* For fall admission, 7/15 for domestic students, 5/1 priority date for international students; for spring admission, 11/15 for domestic students, 9/1 priority date for international students. Applications are processed on a rolling basis. *Application fee:* $50 ($100 for international students). Electronic applications accepted. *Application Contact:* Dr. Mihaela Stefan, Associate Dean for Graduate Studies, 972-883-6581, Fax: 972-883-6371, E-mail: mihaela@utdallas.edu. *Interim Dean*, Dr. A. Dean Sherry, 972-883-2416, Fax: 972-883-6371, E-mail: sherry@utdallas.edu.

## THE UNIVERSITY OF TEXAS AT EL PASO, El Paso, TX 79968-0001

**General Information** State-supported, coed, university. CGS member. *Graduate housing:* Room and/or apartments available on a first-come, first-served basis to single students; on-campus housing not available to married students.

**GRADUATE UNITS**

**Graduate School** *Program availability:* Part-time, evening/weekend, online learning. Electronic applications accepted.

***College of Business Administration*** *Program availability:* Part-time, evening/weekend, online learning. Electronic applications accepted.

***College of Education*** *Program availability:* Part-time, evening/weekend, online learning. Electronic applications accepted.

***College of Engineering*** *Program availability:* Part-time, evening/weekend. Electronic applications accepted.

***College of Health Sciences*** *Program availability:* Part-time, evening/weekend, online learning. Electronic applications accepted.

***College of Liberal Arts*** *Program availability:* Part-time, evening/weekend, online learning. Electronic applications accepted.

***College of Science*** *Program availability:* Part-time, evening/weekend. Electronic applications accepted.

***School of Nursing*** *Program availability:* Online learning. Electronic applications accepted.

## THE UNIVERSITY OF TEXAS AT SAN ANTONIO, San Antonio, TX 78249-0617

**General Information** State-supported, coed, university. CGS member. *Graduate housing:* Room and/or apartments available on a first-come, first-served basis to single students; on-campus housing not available to married students. *Research affiliation:* Air Force Research Laboratory (information assurance and security), Carnegie Mellon University/National Security Agency (computer security), National Science Foundation (virtual reality, computer architecture, real-time systems), Cancer Prevention and Research Institute of Texas (chemistry), Army Research Laboratory (computer science, management science and statistics, electrical engineering), CPS Energy (engineering).

**GRADUATE UNITS**

**College of Architecture, Construction and Planning** *Program availability:* Part-time. Electronic applications accepted.

**College of Business** *Program availability:* Part-time, evening/weekend. Electronic applications accepted.

**College of Education and Human Development** *Program availability:* Part-time, evening/weekend, online learning. Electronic applications accepted.

**College of Engineering** *Program availability:* Part-time, evening/weekend. Electronic applications accepted.

**College of Liberal and Fine Arts** Electronic applications accepted.

**College of Public Policy** *Program availability:* Part-time, evening/weekend. Electronic applications accepted.

**College of Sciences** Electronic applications accepted.

**Joint PhD Program in Translational Science** *Program availability:* Part-time. Electronic applications accepted.

## THE UNIVERSITY OF TEXAS AT TYLER, Tyler, TX 75799-0001

**General Information** State-supported, coed, comprehensive institution. *Enrollment:* 1,081 full-time matriculated graduate/professional students (711 women), 1,559 part-time matriculated graduate/professional students (1,122 women). *Enrollment by degree level:* 2,095 master's, 466 doctoral, 79 other advanced degrees. *Graduate faculty:* 179 full-time (85 women), 33 part-time/adjunct (17 women). *Graduate housing:* Rooms and/or apartments available on a first-come, first-served basis to single and married students. Typical cost: $4745 per year for single students; $4745 per year for married students. *Student services:* Campus employment opportunities, campus safety program, career counseling, exercise/wellness program, free psychological counseling, grant writing training, services for students with disabilities, teacher training, writing training. *Library facilities:* Robert Muntz Library. *Research affiliation:* Embassy of Arab Republic of Egypt Cultural and Education Bureau (electrical engineering), TransAtlantic Lines, Inc. (civil engineering), American Society of Civil Engineers (civil engineering), McGraw-Hill Company (civil engineering), Renaissance Society of America (art history), American Lung Association of the Central States (biology).

**Computer facilities:** A campuswide network can be accessed from student residence rooms and from off campus. Online class registration is available.
Website: http://www.uttyler.edu/

**General Application Contact:** Office of Graduate Admissions, 903-566-7457, Fax: 903-566-7492, E-mail: ogs@uttyler.edu.

**GRADUATE UNITS**

**Ben and Maytee Fisch College of Pharmacy** Students: 313 full-time (191 women), 18 part-time (10 women); includes 214 minority (95 Black or African American, non-Hispanic/Latino; 64 Asian, non-Hispanic/Latino; 48 Hispanic/Latino; 7 Two or more races, non-Hispanic/Latino), 4 international. Average age 27. 133 applicants, 57% accepted, 75 enrolled. *Faculty:* 22 full-time (9 women), 3 part-time/adjunct (1 woman). Expenses: Contact institution. In 2019, 64 doctorates awarded. *Application Contact:* Jennifer Engel, Admissions Representative, 903-565-5777, E-mail: pharmacy@uttyler.edu. *Dean*, Dr. Lane J. Brunner, 903-566-6153, E-mail: lbrunner@uttyler.edu.

**College of Arts and Sciences** Students: 83 full-time (57 women), 102 part-time (69 women); includes 49 minority (15 Black or African American, non-Hispanic/Latino; 3

Asian, non-Hispanic/Latino; 22 Hispanic/Latino; 9 Two or more races, non-Hispanic/Latino), 4 international. Average age 33. 105 applicants, 88% accepted, 62 enrolled. *Faculty:* 46 full-time (20 women), 5 part-time/adjunct (1 woman). Expenses: Contact institution. *Financial support:* In 2019–20, 7 students received support. Fellowships, research assistantships, teaching assistantships, and Federal Work-Study available. Support available to part-time students. Financial award application deadline: 7/1; financial award applicants required to submit FAFSA. In 2019, 62 master's awarded. *Program availability:* Part-time, evening/weekend, online learning. *Application deadline:* Applications are processed on a rolling basis. Electronic applications accepted. *Application Contact:* Dr. Neil Gray, Dean, 903-566-7368. *Dean,* Dr. Neil Gray, 903-566-7368.

**College of Education and Psychology** Students: 250 full-time (191 women), 399 part-time (343 women); includes 185 minority (35 Black or African American, non-Hispanic/Latino; 2 American Indian or Alaska Native, non-Hispanic/Latino; 12 Asian, non-Hispanic/Latino; 115 Hispanic/Latino; 21 Two or more races, non-Hispanic/Latino), 10 international. Average age 35. 249 applicants, 55% accepted, 119 enrolled. *Faculty:* 23 full-time (12 women), 13 part-time/adjunct (7 women). Expenses: Contact institution. *Financial support:* Research assistantships, teaching assistantships, career-related internships or fieldwork, Federal Work-Study, institutionally sponsored loans, and scholarships/grants available. Support available to part-time students. Financial award application deadline: 4/1; financial award applicants required to submit FAFSA. In 2019, 308 master's awarded. *Program availability:* Part-time, evening/weekend. *Application fee:* $0 ($50 for international students). *Application Contact:* Dr. Wes Hickey, Dean, 903-565-5669, E-mail: whickey@uttyler.edu. *Dean,* Dr. Wes Hickey, 903-565-5669, E-mail: whickey@uttyler.edu.

***School of Education*** Students: 119 full-time (88 women), 316 part-time (276 women); includes 118 minority (25 Black or African American, non-Hispanic/Latino; 1 American Indian or Alaska Native, non-Hispanic/Latino; 5 Asian, non-Hispanic/Latino; 74 Hispanic/Latino; 13 Two or more races, non-Hispanic/Latino), 2 international. Average age 37. 119 applicants, 97% accepted, 89 enrolled. *Faculty:* 11 full-time (7 women), 7 part-time/adjunct (4 women). Expenses: Contact institution. *Financial support:* In 2019–20, 2 research assistantships (averaging $12,000 per year) were awarded; scholarships/grants also available. Financial award application deadline: 7/1. In 2019, 214 master's awarded. *Program availability:* Part-time, evening/weekend. *Application deadline:* For fall admission, 8/17 priority date for domestic students, 7/1 priority date for international students; for spring admission, 12/21 priority date for domestic students, 11/1 priority date for international students. Applications are processed on a rolling basis. *Application fee:* $25 ($50 for international students). Electronic applications accepted. *Application Contact:* Dr. Frank Dykes, Interim Director, 903-565-5772, E-mail: fdykes@uttyler.edu. *Interim Director,* Dr. Frank Dykes, 903-565-5772, E-mail: fdykes@uttyler.edu.

**College of Engineering** Students: 19 full-time (2 women), 15 part-time (6 women); includes 9 minority (1 Black or African American, non-Hispanic/Latino; 1 Asian, non-Hispanic/Latino; 7 Hispanic/Latino), 10 international. Average age 29. 44 applicants, 55% accepted, 9 enrolled. *Faculty:* 16 full-time (2 women). Expenses: Contact institution. *Financial support:* In 2019–20, 9 research assistantships with tuition reimbursements (averaging $2,333 per year), 11 teaching assistantships (averaging $2,333 per year) were awarded. Financial award application deadline: 7/1; financial award applicants required to submit FAFSA. In 2019, 25 master's awarded. *Program availability:* Part-time. *Application deadline:* Applications are processed on a rolling basis. *Application fee:* $25 ($50 for international students). Electronic applications accepted. *Application Contact:* Dr. Javier Kypuros, Dean, 903-566-6121, E-mail: jkypuros@uttyler.edu. *Dean,* Dr. Javier Kypuros, 903-566-6121, E-mail: jkypuros@uttyler.edu.

**College of Nursing and Health Sciences** Students: 171 full-time (139 women), 375 part-time (320 women); includes 188 minority (61 Black or African American, non-Hispanic/Latino; 1 American Indian or Alaska Native, non-Hispanic/Latino; 31 Asian, non-Hispanic/Latino; 75 Hispanic/Latino; 20 Two or more races, non-Hispanic/Latino), 11 international. Average age 36. 205 applicants, 72% accepted, 119 enrolled. *Faculty:* 39 full-time (32 women), 7 part-time/adjunct (6 women). Expenses: Contact institution. *Financial support:* Fellowships, research assistantships, and teaching assistantships available. In 2019, 106 master's, 21 doctorates awarded. *Program availability:* Part-time, evening/weekend, online learning. *Application deadline:* Applications are processed on a rolling basis. Electronic applications accepted. *Application Contact:* Dr. Yong Tai Wang, Dean, 903-566-7075, Fax: 903-566-7075, E-mail: ywang@uttyler.edu. *Dean,* Dr. Yong Tai Wang, 903-566-7075, Fax: 903-566-7075, E-mail: ywang@uttyler.edu.

**Soules College of Business** Students: 278 full-time (156 women), 705 part-time (420 women); includes 399 minority (136 Black or African American, non-Hispanic/Latino; 6 American Indian or Alaska Native, non-Hispanic/Latino; 63 Asian, non-Hispanic/Latino; 174 Hispanic/Latino; 20 Two or more races, non-Hispanic/Latino), 30 international. Average age 35. 455 applicants, 87% accepted, 215 enrolled. *Faculty:* 33 full-time (10 women), 5 part-time/adjunct (2 women). Expenses: Contact institution. *Financial support:* Research assistantships and career-related internships or fieldwork available. Financial award application deadline: 7/1. In 2019, 554 master's, 10 doctorates awarded. *Program availability:* Part-time, evening/weekend, online learning. *Application deadline:* Applications are processed on a rolling basis. *Application fee:* $0 ($50 for international students). Electronic applications accepted. *Application Contact:* Dr. Robert Beatty, Dean, 903-566-7360. *Dean,* Dr. Robert Beatty, 903-566-7360.

## THE UNIVERSITY OF TEXAS HEALTH SCIENCE CENTER AT HOUSTON, Houston, TX 77225-0036

**General Information** State-supported, coed, upper-level institution. *Graduate housing:* On-campus housing not available.

**GRADUATE UNITS**

**Cizik School of Nursing** *Program availability:* Part-time. Electronic applications accepted.

**McGovern Medical School** Electronic applications accepted.

**MD Anderson UTHealth Graduate School** Electronic applications accepted.

**School of Biomedical Informatics** Students: 53 full-time (32 women), 227 part-time (107 women); includes 135 minority (34 Black or African American, non-Hispanic/Latino; 1 American Indian or Alaska Native, non-Hispanic/Latino; 53 Asian, non-Hispanic/Latino; 41 Hispanic/Latino; 1 Native Hawaiian or other Pacific Islander, non-Hispanic/Latino; 5 Two or more races, non-Hispanic/Latino), 54 international. Average age 31. 163 applicants, 80% accepted, 86 enrolled. *Faculty:* 39 full-time (15 women), 4 part-time/adjunct (0 women). Expenses: Contact institution. *Financial support:* In 2019–20, 102 students received support, including 58 research assistantships (averaging $20,191 per year), 7 teaching assistantships (averaging $3,568 per year); career-related internships or fieldwork, institutionally sponsored loans, scholarships/grants, health care benefits, and unspecified assistantships also available. Support available to part-time students. Financial award application deadline: 5/1; financial award applicants required to submit FAFSA. In 2019, 44 master's, 2 doctorates awarded. *Program availability:* Part-time, 100% online, blended/hybrid learning. *Application deadline:* For fall admission, 7/1 for domestic and international students; for winter admission, 12/1 for domestic and international students; for spring admission, 11/1 for domestic and international students; for summer admission, 3/1 for domestic and international students. Applications are processed on a rolling basis. *Application fee:* $60. Electronic applications accepted. *Application Contact:* Jaime N Hargrave, Director, Student Affairs, 713-500-3920, Fax: 713-500-0360, E-mail: jaime.n.hargrave@uth.tmc.edu. *Dean/Chair in Informatics Excellence,* Dr. Jiajie Zhang, 713-500-3922, E-mail: jiajie.zhang@uth.tmc.edu.

**School of Dentistry** Electronic applications accepted.

**School of Public Health** *Program availability:* Part-time. Electronic applications accepted.

## THE UNIVERSITY OF TEXAS HEALTH SCIENCE CENTER AT SAN ANTONIO, San Antonio, TX 78229-3900

**General Information** State-supported, coed, upper-level institution. CGS member. *Research affiliation:* University Hospital, Southwest Research Institute, Southwest Foundation for Biomedical Research, Veterans Administration Hospital.

**GRADUATE UNITS**

**Graduate School of Biomedical Sciences**

**Joe R. and Teresa Lozano Long School of Medicine** Electronic applications accepted.

**School of Health Professions**

**School of Nursing** *Program availability:* Part-time.

**UT Health San Antonio School of Dentistry** Students: 509 full-time (272 women), 27 part-time (13 women); includes 268 minority (15 Black or African American, non-Hispanic/Latino; 108 Asian, non-Hispanic/Latino; 126 Hispanic/Latino; 7 Native Hawaiian or other Pacific Islander, non-Hispanic/Latino; 12 Two or more races, non-Hispanic/Latino), 27 international. Average age 27. 1,448 applicants, 15% accepted, 100 enrolled. *Faculty:* 100 full-time (41 women), 83 part-time/adjunct (20 women). Expenses: Contact institution. *Financial support:* In 2019–20, 90 students received support, including 1 fellowship (averaging $50,000 per year), 1 research assistantship (averaging $6,156 per year), 86 teaching assistantships (averaging $15,434 per year); Federal Work-Study also available. Financial award application deadline: 7/15; financial award applicants required to submit FAFSA. In 2019, 25 master's, 100 doctorates, 44 other advanced degrees awarded. *Application deadline:* For fall admission, 10/1 for domestic students. Applications are processed on a rolling basis. *Application fee:* $100. Electronic applications accepted. *Application Contact:* Dr. Kay Malone, Director of Admissions, 210-567-3180, Fax: 210-567-6721, E-mail: dsadmissions@uthscsa.edu. *Director of Admissions,* Dr. Kay Malone, 210-567-3180, Fax: 210-567-6721, E-mail: dsadmissions@uthscsa.edu.

## THE UNIVERSITY OF TEXAS HEALTH SCIENCE CENTER AT TYLER, Tyler, TX 75708

**General Information** State-supported, coed, graduate-only institution.

**GRADUATE UNITS**

**School of Community and Rural Health**

**School of Medical Biological Sciences**

## THE UNIVERSITY OF TEXAS MD ANDERSON CANCER CENTER, Houston, TX 77030

**General Information** State-supported, coed, upper-level institution. CGS member.

**GRADUATE UNITS**

**School of Health Professions**

## THE UNIVERSITY OF TEXAS MEDICAL BRANCH, Galveston, TX 77555

**General Information** State-supported, coed, comprehensive institution. CGS member. *Graduate housing:* Rooms and/or apartments available on a first-come, first-served basis to single and married students. *Research affiliation:* Shriners Hospitals (burns and wound healing).

**GRADUATE UNITS**

**Graduate School of Biomedical Sciences** Electronic applications accepted.

**School of Health Professions** Electronic applications accepted.

**School of Medicine**

**School of Nursing** *Program availability:* Part-time, online learning. Electronic applications accepted.

## THE UNIVERSITY OF TEXAS OF THE PERMIAN BASIN, Odessa, TX 79762-0001

**General Information** State-supported, coed, comprehensive institution. *Graduate housing:* Rooms and/or apartments available on a first-come, first-served basis to single and married students. Housing application deadline: 6/15.

**GRADUATE UNITS**

**Office of Graduate Studies** *Program availability:* Part-time, evening/weekend.

***College of Arts and Sciences*** *Program availability:* Part-time, evening/weekend.

***College of Business*** *Program availability:* Part-time, evening/weekend.

***School of Education***

## THE UNIVERSITY OF TEXAS RIO GRANDE VALLEY, Edinburg, TX 78539

**General Information** State-supported, coed, university. CGS member. *Enrollment:* 29,113 graduate, professional, and undergraduate students; 1,500 full-time matriculated graduate/professional students (882 women), 2,302 part-time matriculated graduate/professional students (1,528 women). *Enrollment by degree level:* 3,263 master's, 530 doctoral, 9 other advanced degrees. *Graduate faculty:* 438 full-time (168 women), 64 part-time/adjunct (40 women). *International tuition:* $13,321 full-time. *Tuition, area resident:* Full-time $5959; part-time $440 per credit hour. Tuition, state resident: full-time $5959. Tuition, nonresident: full-time $5959. *Required fees:* $1169; $185 per credit hour. *Graduate housing:* Rooms and/or apartments available on a first-come, first-served basis to single and married students. Typical cost: $8252 (including board) for single students. Housing application deadline: 7/1. *Student services:* Campus employment opportunities, campus safety program, career counseling, child daycare facilities, exercise/wellness program, free psychological counseling, international student services, services for students with disabilities, teacher training, writing training. *Library facilities:* University Library plus 4 others. *Collection:* Books: 546,403 (digital/electronic); Serial titles: 47,627 (digital/electronic); Databases: 230. Students can reserve study rooms. *Research affiliation:* Robert Wood Johnson (health science), Lockheed Martin Corporation (manufacturing engineering), Texas Instruments (curriculum and instruction), Pfizer, Inc. (health disparities), Howard Hughes Medical Institute (medical science), Boeing (engineering).

**Computer facilities:** Computer purchase and lease plans are available. A campuswide network can be accessed. Online class registration is available.
Website: http://www.utrgv.edu/

**General Application Contact:** Stephanie Ozuna, Assoc Dir Graduate Studies, 956-665-3558, E-mail: stephanie.ozuna@utrgv.edu.

**GRADUATE UNITS**

**College of Education and P-16 Integration** *Program availability:* Part-time, evening/weekend. Electronic applications accepted.

**College of Engineering and Computer Science** *Program availability:* Part-time, blended/hybrid learning. Electronic applications accepted.

**College of Fine Arts**

***School of Art*** Students: 5 full-time (4 women), 16 part-time (13 women); includes 19 minority (1 Asian, non-Hispanic/Latino; 18 Hispanic/Latino). Average age 33. 3 applicants, 67% accepted, 1 enrolled. *Faculty:* 4 full-time (0 women). Expenses: Contact institution. In 2019, 9 master's awarded.

***School of Music*** Students: 13 full-time (4 women), 4 part-time (1 woman); includes 11 minority (all Hispanic/Latino), 4 international. Average age 30. 11 applicants, 64% accepted, 5 enrolled. *Faculty:* 20 full-time (6 women), 2 part-time/adjunct (0 women). Expenses: Contact institution. In 2019, 5 master's awarded.

**College of Health Affairs** *Program availability:* Part-time, evening/weekend.

***School of Rehabilitation Services and Counseling*** Students: 99 full-time (80 women), 113 part-time (93 women); includes 192 minority (1 Black or African American, non-Hispanic/Latino; 2 Asian, non-Hispanic/Latino; 189 Hispanic/Latino), 3 international. Average age 31. 41 applicants, 93% accepted, 34 enrolled. *Faculty:* 16 full-time (10 women), 2 part-time/adjunct (both women). Expenses: Contact institution. *Financial support:* In 2019–20, 60 students received support, including 12 research assistantships (averaging $25,500 per year), 10 teaching assistantships (averaging $12,600 per year); career-related internships or fieldwork, Federal Work-Study, institutionally sponsored loans, scholarships/grants, traineeships, and unspecified assistantships also available. In 2019, 39 master's, 7 doctorates awarded. *Program availability:* Part-time, evening/weekend. *Application deadline:* For fall admission, 3/15 for domestic and international students; for spring admission, 10/15 for domestic and international students; for summer admission, 3/15 for domestic and international students. *Application fee:* $50. Electronic applications accepted. *Application Contact:* Dr. Elizabeth Chavez-Palacios, Clinical Assistant Professor/Graduate Coordinator, 956-665-3734, Fax: 956-665-5237, E-mail: elizabeth.palacios@utrgv.edu. *Director/Professor*, Dr. Bruce Reed, 956-665-7036, Fax: 956-665-5237, E-mail: bruce.reed@utrgv.edu.

***School of Social Work*** Students: 78 full-time (65 women), 105 part-time (93 women); includes 176 minority (4 Black or African American, non-Hispanic/Latino; 172 Hispanic/Latino), 1 international. Average age 30. 64 applicants, 89% accepted, 41 enrolled. *Faculty:* 11 full-time (6 women), 15 part-time/adjunct (10 women). Expenses: Contact institution. In 2019, 68 master's awarded.

**College of Health Professions**

**College of Liberal Arts** *Program availability:* Part-time, evening/weekend.

**College of Sciences** *Program availability:* Part-time, evening/weekend. Electronic applications accepted.

***School of Earth, Environmental, and Marine Sciences*** Students: 48 full-time (25 women), 20 part-time (10 women); includes 33 minority (1 Asian, non-Hispanic/Latino; 32 Hispanic/Latino), 15 international. Average age 27. 22 applicants, 82% accepted, 14 enrolled. *Faculty:* 7 full-time (2 women). Expenses: Contact institution. In 2019, 14 master's awarded.

***School of Mathematical and Statistical Sciences*** Students: 26 full-time (10 women), 31 part-time (18 women); includes 42 minority (1 American Indian or Alaska Native, non-Hispanic/Latino; 41 Hispanic/Latino), 3 international. Average age 30. 31 applicants, 97% accepted, 15 enrolled. *Faculty:* 20 full-time (1 woman). Expenses: Contact institution. In 2019, 19 master's awarded.

**Robert C. Vackar College of Business and Entrepreneurship** *Program availability:* Part-time, evening/weekend.

**School of Medicine** Students: 204 full-time (103 women); includes 135 minority (22 Black or African American, non-Hispanic/Latino; 25 Asian, non-Hispanic/Latino; 76 Hispanic/Latino; 12 Native Hawaiian or other Pacific Islander, non-Hispanic/Latino). Average age 26. Expenses: Contact institution.

**School of Nursing** Students: 20 full-time (15 women), 124 part-time (100 women); includes 117 minority (37 Black or African American, non-Hispanic/Latino; 9 Asian, non-Hispanic/Latino; 71 Hispanic/Latino). Average age 38. 47 applicants, 96% accepted, 31 enrolled. *Faculty:* 15 full-time (12 women), 4 part-time/adjunct (all women). Expenses: Contact institution.

## THE UNIVERSITY OF TEXAS SOUTHWESTERN MEDICAL CENTER, Dallas, TX 75390

**General Information** State-supported, coed, graduate-only institution. CGS member. *Graduate housing:* Rooms and/or apartments available on a first-come, first-served basis to single and married students.

**GRADUATE UNITS**

**Southwestern Graduate School of Biomedical Sciences** Electronic applications accepted.

***Division of Basic Science*** Electronic applications accepted.

**Southwestern Medical School** Electronic applications accepted.

**Southwestern School of Health Professions**

## THE UNIVERSITY OF THE ARTS, Philadelphia, PA 19102-4944

**General Information** Independent, coed, comprehensive institution. *Graduate housing:* Room and/or apartments available to single students; on-campus housing not available to married students. Housing application deadline: 6/1. *Research affiliation:* The Franklin Institute (general science education), Philadelphia Museum of Art (arts and culture), School District of Philadelphia (education), Ben Franklin Technology Partners (high tech department and creative/cultural production in Philadelphia).

**GRADUATE UNITS**

**College of Art, Media and Design** *Program availability:* Part-time. Electronic applications accepted.

**College of Performing Arts** *Program availability:* Part-time.

***School of Dance***

***School of Music*** *Program availability:* Part-time. Electronic applications accepted.

## UNIVERSITY OF THE CUMBERLANDS, Williamsburg, KY 40769-1372

**General Information** Independent-religious, coed, university. *Graduate housing:* Room and/or apartments available on a first-come, first-served basis to single students; on-campus housing not available to married students.

**GRADUATE UNITS**

**Graduate Programs in Education** *Program availability:* Part-time, evening/weekend, online learning. Electronic applications accepted.

**Hutton School of Business** *Program availability:* Part-time, online learning. Electronic applications accepted.

**Program in Christian Studies** *Program availability:* Part-time, evening/weekend, online learning. Electronic applications accepted.

**Program in Clinical Psychology** *Program availability:* Part-time, evening/weekend, online learning.

**Program in Physician Assistant Studies** Electronic applications accepted.

**Program in Professional Counseling** *Program availability:* Part-time, evening/weekend, online learning. Electronic applications accepted.

## UNIVERSITY OF THE DISTRICT OF COLUMBIA, Washington, DC 20008-1175

**General Information** District-supported, coed, comprehensive institution. CGS member.

**GRADUATE UNITS**

**College of Agriculture, Urban Sustainability and Environmental Sciences**

**College of Arts and Sciences** *Program availability:* Part-time, evening/weekend.

**David A. Clarke School of Law** Students: 120 full-time (85 women), 133 part-time (85 women); includes 177 minority (118 Black or African American, non-Hispanic/Latino; 26 Asian, non-Hispanic/Latino; 25 Hispanic/Latino; 8 Two or more races, non-Hispanic/Latino), 3 international. Average age 32. 531 applicants, 36% accepted, 79 enrolled. *Faculty:* 21 full-time (15 women), 26 part-time/adjunct (14 women). Expenses: Contact institution. *Financial support:* In 2019–20, 155 students received support, including 48 fellowships (averaging $4,250 per year), 4 research assistantships (averaging $3,000 per year), 46 teaching assistantships (averaging $3,000 per year); Federal Work-Study and scholarships/grants also available. Financial award application deadline: 3/15; financial award applicants required to submit FAFSA. In 2019, 65 doctorates awarded. *Program availability:* Part-time, evening/weekend. *Application deadline:* For fall admission, 3/15 priority date for domestic and international students. Applications are processed on a rolling basis. *Application fee:* $35. Electronic applications accepted. *Application Contact:* Jino Ray, Associate Dean of Admission, 202-274-7336, Fax: 202-274-5583, E-mail: jino.ray@udc.edu. *Dean*, Renee M. Hutchins, 202-274-7346, Fax: 202-274-5583, E-mail: renee.hutchins@udc.edu.

**School of Business and Public Administration** *Program availability:* Part-time, evening/weekend.

**School of Engineering and Applied Sciences**

## UNIVERSITY OF THE FRASER VALLEY, Abbotsford, BC V2S 7M8, Canada

**General Information** Province-supported, coed, comprehensive institution. *Enrollment:* 9,839 graduate, professional, and undergraduate students; 46 full-time matriculated graduate/professional students (32 women), 38 part-time matriculated graduate/professional students (27 women). *Enrollment by degree level:* 75 master's, 9 other advanced degrees. *Graduate faculty:* 23 full-time (13 women). *International tuition:* $25,000 Canadian dollars full-time. *Tuition, area resident:* Part-time $570.74 Canadian dollars per credit. Tuition, province resident: part-time $570.74 Canadian dollars per credit. Tuition, Canadian resident: part-time $570.74 Canadian dollars per credit. *Required fees:* $18.11 Canadian dollars per credit. One-time fee: $195.59 Canadian dollars full-time. *Graduate housing:* Room and/or apartments available on a first-come, first-served basis to single students; on-campus housing not available to married students. Typical cost: $6040 Canadian dollars (including board). Housing application deadline: 5/15. *Student services:* Campus employment opportunities, campus safety program, career counseling, exercise/wellness program, free psychological counseling, grant writing training, international student services, low-cost health insurance, services for students with disabilities, writing training. *Library facilities:* Peter Jones Library plus 3 others. *Collection:* Books: 159,000 (physical), 311,000 (digital/electronic). Students can reserve study rooms.

**Computer facilities:** Online class registration is available.
Website: http://www.ufv.ca/

**General Application Contact:** Educational Advisors, 604-854-4528, Fax: 604-855-7614, E-mail: advising@ufv.ca.

**GRADUATE UNITS**

**Graduate Studies** Students: 46 full-time (32 women), 38 part-time (27 women); includes 26 minority (all American Indian or Alaska Native, non-Hispanic/Latino). Average age 40. 65 applicants, 89% accepted, 58 enrolled. *Faculty:* 23 full-time (13 women). Expenses: Contact institution. *Financial support:* Research assistantships, scholarships/grants, health care benefits, and bursaries available. Financial award application deadline: 5/10. In 2019, 27 master's awarded. *Program availability:* Evening/weekend. *Application deadline:* For fall admission, 1/31 priority date for domestic students, 4/1 priority date for international students; for winter admission, 8/31 priority date for domestic students; for spring admission, 12/31 priority date for domestic students. *Application fee:* $75 Canadian dollars ($250 Canadian dollars for international students). Electronic applications accepted. *Application Contact:* Educational Advisors, 604-854-4528, Fax: 604-855-7614, E-mail: advising@ufv.ca. *Associate Vice President for Research, Engagement and Graduate Studies*, Dr. Garry Fehr, 604-504-4074, E-mail: Garry.Fehr@ufv.ca.

## UNIVERSITY OF THE INCARNATE WORD, San Antonio, TX 78209-6397

**General Information** Independent-religious, coed, comprehensive institution. *Enrollment:* 8,175 graduate, professional, and undergraduate students; 2,185 full-time matriculated graduate/professional students (1,305 women), 622 part-time matriculated graduate/professional students (325 women). *Enrollment by degree level:* 1,266 master's, 1,541 doctoral. *Graduate faculty:* 133 full-time (74 women), 84 part-time/adjunct (38 women). *Tuition:* Full-time $11,520; part-time $960 per credit hour. *Required fees:* $1128; $94 per credit hour. Tuition and fees vary according to degree level, campus/location, program and student level. *Graduate housing:* Room and/or apartments available on a first-come, first-served basis to single students; on-campus housing not available to married students. Typical cost: $7520 per year ($12,824 including board). Room and board charges vary according to board plan and housing facility selected. Housing application deadline: 5/1. *Student services:* Campus employment opportunities, campus safety program, career counseling, exercise/wellness program, free psychological counseling, grant writing training, international student services, low-cost health insurance, multicultural affairs office, services for students with disabilities, teacher training, writing training. *Library facilities:* J. E. and M. E. Mabee Library plus 1 other. *Collection:* Books: 159,953 (physical), 60,292 (digital/electronic); Serial titles: 1,063 (physical), 86,652 (digital/electronic); Databases: 206. Weekly public service hours: 105.

**Computer facilities:** Computer purchase and lease plans are available. 406 computers available on campus for general student use. A campuswide network can be accessed. Online class registration is available.
Website: http://www.uiw.edu/

**General Application Contact:** Jessica Delarosa, Director of Admissions, 210-805-2543, Fax: 210-829-3921, E-mail: jsdelaro@uiwtx.edu.

**GRADUATE UNITS**

**College of Humanities, Arts, and Social Sciences** Students: 10 full-time (7 women), 7 part-time (5 women); includes 13 minority (all Hispanic/Latino), 1 international. 9 applicants, 100% accepted, 8 enrolled. *Faculty:* 1 full-time (0 women), 6 part-time/adjunct (1 woman). Expenses: Contact institution. *Financial support:* Research assistantships, scholarships/grants, tuition waivers (full and partial), and unspecified assistantships available. Financial award applicants required to submit FAFSA. *Program availability:* Part-time, evening/weekend. *Application deadline:* Applications are processed on a rolling basis. *Application fee:* $20. Electronic applications accepted. *Application Contact:* Jessica Delarosa, Director of Admissions, 210-829-6005, Fax: 210-829-3921, E-mail: admis@uiwtx.edu. *Dean,* Dr. Kevin Vichcales, 210-829-2759, Fax: 210-829-3830, E-mail: vichcale@uiwtx.edu.

**Dreeben School of Education** Students: 86 full-time (56 women), 107 part-time (66 women); includes 114 minority (15 Black or African American, non-Hispanic/Latino; 3 Asian, non-Hispanic/Latino; 92 Hispanic/Latino; 4 Two or more races, non-Hispanic/Latino), 34 international. 49 applicants, 92% accepted, 22 enrolled. *Faculty:* 9 full-time (5 women), 6 part-time/adjunct (3 women). Expenses: Contact institution. *Financial support:* In 2019–20, 4 research assistantships were awarded; Federal Work-Study, scholarships/grants, tuition waivers (partial), and unspecified assistantships also available. Financial award applicants required to submit FAFSA. In 2019, 19 master's, 18 doctorates awarded. *Program availability:* Part-time, evening/weekend. *Application deadline:* Applications are processed on a rolling basis. *Application fee:* $20. Electronic applications accepted. *Application Contact:* Jessica Delarosa, Director of Admissions, 210-829-6005, Fax: 210-829-3921, E-mail: admis@uiwtx.edu. *Dean,* Dr. Denise Staudt, 210-829-2761, Fax: 210-829-2765, E-mail: staudt@uiwtx.edu.

**Feik School of Pharmacy** Students: 365 full-time (254 women), 8 part-time (7 women); includes 273 minority (26 Black or African American, non-Hispanic/Latino; 79 Asian, non-Hispanic/Latino; 160 Hispanic/Latino; 1 Native Hawaiian or other Pacific Islander, non-Hispanic/Latino; 7 Two or more races, non-Hispanic/Latino), 17 international. 108 applicants, 97% accepted, 92 enrolled. *Faculty:* 21 full-time (15 women), 1 (woman) part-time/adjunct. Expenses: Contact institution. *Financial support:* Research assistantships, Federal Work-Study, scholarships/grants, and unspecified assistantships available. Financial award applicants required to submit FAFSA. In 2019, 91 doctorates awarded. *Application deadline:* For fall admission, 12/1 for domestic and international students. *Application fee:* $50. Electronic applications accepted. *Application Contact:* Dr. Amy Diepenbrock, Assistant Dean, Student Affairs, 210-883-1060, Fax: 210-822-1521, E-mail: diepenbr@uiwtx.edu. *Dean,* Dr. David Maize, 210-883-1000, Fax: 210-822-1516, E-mail: maize@uiwtx.edu.

**H-E-B School of Business and Administration** Students: 203 full-time (105 women), 27 part-time (11 women); includes 148 minority (22 Black or African American, non-Hispanic/Latino; 2 American Indian or Alaska Native, non-Hispanic/Latino; 6 Asian, non-Hispanic/Latino; 113 Hispanic/Latino; 1 Native Hawaiian or other Pacific Islander, non-Hispanic/Latino; 4 Two or more races, non-Hispanic/Latino), 27 international. 137 applicants, 95% accepted, 83 enrolled. *Faculty:* 20 full-time (10 women), 9 part-time/adjunct (3 women). Expenses: Contact institution. *Financial support:* Research assistantships, Federal Work-Study, scholarships/grants, tuition waivers (partial), and unspecified assistantships available. Financial award applicants required to submit FAFSA. In 2019, 136 master's awarded. *Program availability:* Part-time, evening/weekend. *Application deadline:* Applications are processed on a rolling basis. *Application fee:* $20. Electronic applications accepted. *Application Contact:* Jessica Delarosa, Director of Admissions, 210-8296005, Fax: 210-829-3921, E-mail: admis@uiwtx.edu. *Dean,* Dr. Forrest Aven, 210-805-5884, Fax: 210-805-3564, E-mail: aven@uiwtx.edu.

**Ila Faye Miller School of Nursing and Health Professions** Students: 104 full-time (71 women), 6 part-time (5 women); includes 68 minority (24 Black or African American, non-Hispanic/Latino; 1 American Indian or Alaska Native, non-Hispanic/Latino; 2 Asian, non-Hispanic/Latino; 40 Hispanic/Latino; 1 Two or more races, non-Hispanic/Latino), 2 international. 30 applicants, 100% accepted, 20 enrolled. *Faculty:* 13 full-time (9 women), 1 (woman) part-time/adjunct. Expenses: Contact institution. *Financial support:* Research assistantships, Federal Work-Study, scholarships/grants, tuition waivers (partial), and unspecified assistantships available. Financial award applicants required to submit FAFSA. In 2019, 19 master's, 20 doctorates awarded. *Program availability:* Part-time, evening/weekend. *Application deadline:* Applications are processed on a rolling basis. *Application fee:* $20. Electronic applications accepted. *Application Contact:* Jessica Delarosa, Director of Admissions, 210-8296005, Fax: 210-829-3921, E-mail: admis@uiwtx.edu. *Dean,* Dr. Holly Cassells, 210-829-3982, Fax: 210-829-3174, E-mail: cassells@uiwtx.edu.

**Rosenberg School of Optometry** Students: 258 full-time (187 women); includes 158 minority (8 Black or African American, non-Hispanic/Latino; 2 American Indian or Alaska Native, non-Hispanic/Latino; 89 Asian, non-Hispanic/Latino; 58 Hispanic/Latino; 1 Two or more races, non-Hispanic/Latino), 4 international. 91 applicants, 99% accepted, 69 enrolled. *Faculty:* 17 full-time (5 women). Expenses: Contact institution. *Financial support:* Fellowships, Federal Work-Study, and scholarships/grants available. Financial award applicants required to submit FAFSA. In 2019, 65 doctorates awarded. *Application deadline:* For fall admission, 5/1 for domestic students. *Application fee:* $50. Electronic applications accepted. *Application Contact:* Jill Mohr, Director of Admissions and Student Services, 210-883-1190, Fax: 210-883-1191, E-mail: mohr@uiwtx.edu. *Dean,* Dr. Timothy Wingert, 210-883-1195, Fax: 210-283-6890, E-mail: twingert@uiwtx.edu.

**School of Mathematics, Science, and Engineering** Students: 19 full-time (17 women), 5 part-time (3 women); includes 14 minority (1 Black or African American, non-Hispanic/Latino; 13 Hispanic/Latino), 3 international. 15 applicants, 87% accepted, 5 enrolled. *Faculty:* 2 full-time (1 woman), 1 part-time/adjunct (0 women). Expenses: Contact institution. *Financial support:* Research assistantships, Federal Work-Study, scholarships/grants, tuition waivers (partial), and unspecified assistantships available. Financial award applicants required to submit FAFSA. In 2019, 18 master's awarded. *Program availability:* Part-time, evening/weekend. *Application deadline:* Applications are processed on a rolling basis. *Application fee:* $20. Electronic applications accepted. *Application Contact:* Jessica Delarosa, Director of Admissions, 210-8296005, Fax: 210-829-3921, E-mail: admis@uiwtx.edu. *Dean,* Dr. Carlos A. Garcia, 210-829-2717, Fax: 210-829-3153, E-mail: cagarci9@uiwtx.edu.

**School of Media and Design** Students: 21 full-time (11 women), 5 part-time (4 women); includes 16 minority (2 Black or African American, non-Hispanic/Latino; 14 Hispanic/Latino), 3 international. 7 applicants, 100% accepted, 6 enrolled. *Faculty:* 6 full-time (3 women), 2 part-time/adjunct (0 women). Expenses: Contact institution. *Financial support:* Federal Work-Study, scholarships/grants, tuition waivers (partial), and unspecified assistantships available. Financial award applicants required to submit FAFSA. In 2019, 9 master's awarded. *Program availability:* Part-time, evening/weekend. *Application deadline:* Applications are processed on a rolling basis. *Application fee:* $20. Electronic applications accepted. *Application Contact:* Jessica Delarosa, Director of Admissions, 210-8296005, Fax: 210-829-3921, E-mail: admis@uiwtx.edu. *Dean,* Dr. Sharon Welkey, 210-829-6091, Fax: 210-829-3196, E-mail: welkey@uiwtx.edu.

**School of Osteopathic Medicine** Students: 513 full-time (304 women), 2 part-time (both women); includes 323 minority (33 Black or African American, non-Hispanic/Latino; 1 American Indian or Alaska Native, non-Hispanic/Latino; 122 Asian, non-Hispanic/Latino; 145 Hispanic/Latino; 22 Two or more races, non-Hispanic/Latino). 574 applicants, 75% accepted, 207 enrolled. *Faculty:* 9 full-time (5 women), 1 part-time/adjunct (0 women). Expenses: Contact institution. *Financial support:* Research assistantships, career-related internships or fieldwork, scholarships/grants, and unspecified assistantships available. Financial award applicants required to submit FAFSA. In 2019, 31 master's awarded. *Application deadline:* For fall admission, 9/1 for domestic students; for spring admission, 3/15 for domestic students. Applications are processed on a rolling basis. *Application fee:* $50. Electronic applications accepted. *Application Contact:* Sonia Winney, Admissions Coordinator, 210-283-6998, E-mail: winney@uiwtx.edu. *Dean,* Dr. Robyn Phillips-Madson, E-mail: rmadson@uiwtx.edu.

**School of Physical Therapy** Students: 103 full-time (57 women), 57 part-time (38 women); includes 91 minority (12 Black or African American, non-Hispanic/Latino; 17 Asian, non-Hispanic/Latino; 62 Hispanic/Latino). 68 applicants, 100% accepted, 55 enrolled. *Faculty:* 16 full-time (9 women), 10 part-time/adjunct (8 women). Expenses: Contact institution. *Financial support:* Scholarships/grants and unspecified assistantships available. Financial award applicants required to submit FAFSA. In 2019, 75 doctorates awarded. *Application deadline:* For fall admission, 10/1 priority date for domestic students. *Application fee:* $50. *Application Contact:* Christina Immel, Director of Enrollment, 210-283-6918, E-mail: cimmel@uiwtx.edu. *Dean,* Dr. Caroline Goulet, 210-283-6924, E-mail: goulet@uiwtx.edu.

**School of Professional Studies** Students: 503 full-time (236 women), 385 part-time (175 women); includes 571 minority (124 Black or African American, non-Hispanic/Latino; 5 American Indian or Alaska Native, non-Hispanic/Latino; 35 Asian, non-Hispanic/Latino; 382 Hispanic/Latino; 3 Native Hawaiian or other Pacific Islander, non-Hispanic/Latino; 22 Two or more races, non-Hispanic/Latino), 1 international. 670 applicants, 99% accepted, 296 enrolled. *Faculty:* 16 full-time (12 women), 41 part-time/adjunct (18 women). Expenses: Contact institution. *Financial support:* Scholarships/grants and unspecified assistantships available. Financial award applicants required to submit FAFSA. In 2019, 429 master's, 5 doctorates awarded. *Program availability:* Part-time, evening/weekend, 100% online, blended/hybrid learning. *Application deadline:* Applications are processed on a rolling basis. Electronic applications accepted. *Application Contact:* Julie Weber, Director of Marketing and Recruitment, 210-318-1876, Fax: 210-829-2756, E-mail: eapadmission@uiwtx.edu. *Dean,* Vincent Porter, 210-8292770, E-mail: porterv@uiwtx.edu.

## UNIVERSITY OF THE PACIFIC, Stockton, CA 95211-0197

**General Information** Independent, coed, university. CGS member. *Graduate housing:* Rooms and/or apartments available on a first-come, first-served basis to single and married students. Housing application deadline: 7/1. *Research affiliation:* Lawrence Hall of Science.

**GRADUATE UNITS**

**Arthur A. Dugoni School of Dentistry** Electronic applications accepted.

**College of the Pacific**

**Conservatory of Music**

**Eberhardt School of Business** *Program availability:* Part-time.

**Gladys L. Benerd School of Education**

**McGeorge School of Law** *Program availability:* Part-time, evening/weekend. Electronic applications accepted.

**School of Engineering and Computer Science** Electronic applications accepted.

**Thomas J. Long School of Pharmacy and Health Sciences**

## UNIVERSITY OF THE PEOPLE, Pasadena, CA 91101

**General Information** Private, coed, comprehensive institution.

**GRADUATE UNITS**

**Master of Business Administration Program** *Program availability:* Online learning.

## UNIVERSITY OF THE POTOMAC, Washington, DC 20005

**General Information** Proprietary, coed, comprehensive institution.

**GRADUATE UNITS**

**Program in Business Administration** *Program availability:* Online learning.

## UNIVERSITY OF THE SACRED HEART, San Juan, PR 00914-0383

**General Information** Independent-religious, coed, comprehensive institution. *Graduate housing:* Room and/or apartments available on a first-come, first-served basis to single students; on-campus housing not available to married students. Housing application deadline: 5/31.

**GRADUATE UNITS**

**Graduate Programs** *Program availability:* Part-time, evening/weekend.

## UNIVERSITY OF THE SCIENCES, Philadelphia, PA 19104-4495

**General Information** Independent, coed, university. CGS member. *Graduate housing:* On-campus housing not available. *Research affiliation:* Progenra (molecular biology), Encapsulation Systems (analytical chemistry), Johnson & Johnson (cell biology), Ortho-McNeil Pharmaceuticals, Inc. (pharmacy), Polymedix (computational chemistry).

**GRADUATE UNITS**

**Doctor of Physical Therapy Program** *Program availability:* Part-time, evening/weekend, online learning.

**Philadelphia College of Pharmacy**

**Program in Bioinformatics** *Program availability:* Part-time, evening/weekend.

**Program in Biomedical Writing** *Program availability:* Part-time, evening/weekend, online learning.

**Program in Cell Biology and Biotechnology** *Program availability:* Part-time, evening/weekend.

**Program in Chemistry, Biochemistry and Pharmacognosy** *Program availability:* Part-time.

**Program in Health Policy** *Program availability:* Part-time, evening/weekend, online learning.

**Program in Health Psychology**

**Program in Occupational Therapy** *Program availability:* Online learning. Electronic applications accepted.

**Program in Pharmaceutical and Healthcare Business** *Program availability:* Part-time, evening/weekend, online learning.

**Program in Pharmaceutics** *Program availability:* Part-time.

**Program in Pharmacology and Toxicology**

**Program in Pharmacy Administration** *Program availability:* Part-time.

**Program in Public Health** *Program availability:* Part-time, evening/weekend, online learning.

## THE UNIVERSITY OF THE SOUTH, Sewanee, TN 37383-1000

**General Information** Independent-religious, coed, comprehensive institution. *Enrollment:* 1,768 graduate, professional, and undergraduate students; 59 full-time matriculated graduate/professional students (21 women), 12 part-time matriculated graduate/professional students (8 women). *Enrollment by degree level:* 70 master's, 1 other advanced degree. *Graduate faculty:* 11 full-time (4 women), 8 part-time/adjunct (3 women). *Graduate housing:* Rooms and/or apartments available on a first-come, first-served basis to single and married students. *Student services:* Campus employment opportunities, campus safety program, career counseling, child daycare facilities, free psychological counseling, international student services, multicultural affairs office, writing training. *Library facilities:* Jessie Ball duPont Library. *Collection:* Books: 522,116 (physical), 574,014 (digital/electronic); Serial titles: 4,136 (physical), 23,827 (digital/electronic); Databases: 351. Study areas open 24 hours, 5–7 days a week; students can reserve study rooms.

**Computer facilities:** 150 computers available on campus for general student use. A campuswide network can be accessed from student residence rooms and from off campus. Online class registration is available.
Website: http://www.sewanee.edu/

**GRADUATE UNITS**

**School of Theology** Students: 59 full-time (21 women), 6 part-time (3 women); includes 3 minority (1 Black or African American, non-Hispanic/Latino; 2 Hispanic/Latino), 6 international. Average age 40. *Faculty:* 11 full-time (4 women), 8 part-time/adjunct (3 women). Expenses: Contact institution. *Financial support:* Institutionally sponsored loans and scholarships/grants available. Support available to part-time students. Financial award application deadline: 4/30. In 2019, 24 master's, 5 doctorates awarded. *Program availability:* Part-time. *Application deadline:* For fall admission, 7/1 for domestic students, 2/1 for international students. Applications are processed on a rolling basis. Electronic applications accepted. *Application Contact:* Walker Adams, Director of Recruitment and Admission, 931-598-1283, E-mail: theologyadmissions@sewanee.edu. *Dean,* James F. Turrell, 931-598-1288, Fax: 931-598-1412, E-mail: deansot@sewanee.edu.

**Sewanee School of Letters** Students: 40 part-time (24 women); includes 5 minority (1 Black or African American, non-Hispanic/Latino; 1 Asian, non-Hispanic/Latino; 1 Hispanic/Latino; 2 Two or more races, non-Hispanic/Latino). Average age 42. *Faculty:* 3 full-time (1 woman), 7 part-time/adjunct (4 women). Expenses: Contact institution. *Financial support:* Institutionally sponsored loans and scholarships/grants available. In 2019, 16 master's awarded. *Program availability:* Part-time. *Application deadline:* For summer admission, 4/15 for domestic students. Applications are processed on a rolling basis. Electronic applications accepted. *Application Contact:* April R. Alvarez, Associate Director of the School of Letters, 931-598-1636, E-mail: sletters@sewanee.edu. *Director of the School of Letters,* Justin Taylor, 931-598-1636, E-mail: sletters@sewanee.edu.

## UNIVERSITY OF THE SOUTHWEST, Hobbs, NM 88240-9129

**General Information** Independent-religious, coed, comprehensive institution. *Graduate housing:* On-campus housing not available.

**GRADUATE UNITS**

**Graduate Programs** *Program availability:* Part-time, evening/weekend, online learning. Electronic applications accepted.

## UNIVERSITY OF THE VIRGIN ISLANDS, St. Thomas, VI 00802

**General Information** Territory-supported, coed, comprehensive institution. *Enrollment:* 2,088 graduate, professional, and undergraduate students; 55 full-time matriculated graduate/professional students (45 women), 183 part-time matriculated graduate/professional students (143 women). *Enrollment by degree level:* 159 master's, 79 doctoral. *Graduate faculty:* 18 full-time (10 women), 16 part-time/adjunct (9 women). *Tuition, area resident:* Full-time $6948; part-time $386 per credit hour. Tuition, territory resident: part-time $386 per credit hour. Tuition, nonresident: full-time $13,230; part-time $735 per credit hour. *Required fees:* $508; $254 per semester. *Graduate housing:* On-campus housing not available. *Student services:* Campus employment opportunities, career counseling, child daycare facilities, exercise/wellness program, services for students with disabilities. *Library facilities:* Ralph M. Paiewonsky Library. *Collection:* Study areas open 24 hours, 5–7 days a week; students can reserve study rooms.

**Computer facilities:** 500 computers available on campus for general student use. A campuswide network can be accessed. Online class registration is available.
Website: http://www.uvi.edu/

**General Application Contact:** Charmaine L. Smith, Director of Admissions, 340-692-4070, E-mail: hsmithc@uvi.edu.

**GRADUATE UNITS**

**College of Liberal Arts and Social Sciences** *Program availability:* Part-time, evening/weekend. Electronic applications accepted.

**College of Science and Mathematics** Electronic applications accepted.

**School of Business** *Program availability:* Part-time, evening/weekend. Electronic applications accepted.

**School of Business, Social Sciences, Marine and Environmental Sciences** Students: 40 full-time (33 women), 60 part-time (47 women); includes 61 minority (52 Black or African American, non-Hispanic/Latino; 1 American Indian or Alaska Native, non-Hispanic/Latino; 5 Hispanic/Latino; 3 Two or more races, non-Hispanic/Latino), 8 international. Average age 32. 57 applicants, 95% accepted, 38 enrolled. *Faculty:* 14 full-time (9 women), 7 part-time/adjunct (3 women). Expenses: Contact institution. *Financial support:* In 2019–20, 14 students received support, including 3 fellowships, 7 research assistantships, 4 teaching assistantships; scholarships/grants also available. Financial award application deadline: 4/15; financial award applicants required to submit FAFSA. *Program availability:* Part-time, evening/weekend. *Application deadline:* For fall admission, 4/30 for domestic and international students; for spring admission, 10/30 for domestic and international students. *Application fee:* $25. Electronic applications accepted. *Application Contact:* Charmaine L. Smith, Director of Admissions, 340-692-4070, E-mail: hsmithc@uvi.edu.

**School of Education** Students: 13 full-time (10 women), 110 part-time (84 women); includes 79 minority (75 Black or African American, non-Hispanic/Latino; 3 Hispanic/Latino; 1 Native Hawaiian or other Pacific Islander, non-Hispanic/Latino), 19 international. Average age 46. 42 applicants, 98% accepted, 24 enrolled. *Faculty:* 2 full-time, 10 part-time/adjunct (6 women). Expenses: Contact institution. *Financial support:* In 2019–20, 1 student received support. Fellowships, research assistantships, teaching assistantships, and scholarships/grants available. Financial award application deadline: 4/15; financial award applicants required to submit FAFSA. In 2019, 6 master's, 6 doctorates awarded. *Program availability:* Part-time, evening/weekend. *Application deadline:* For fall admission, 4/30 for domestic and international students; for spring admission, 10/30 for domestic and international students. *Application fee:* $25. Electronic applications accepted. *Application Contact:* Charmaine M. Smith, Director of Admissions, 340-692-4070, E-mail: csmith@uvi.edu. *Dean,* Dr. Karen Brown, 340-693-1321, Fax: 340-693-1335, E-mail: karen.brown@uvi.edu.

## UNIVERSITY OF THE WEST, Rosemead, CA 91770

**General Information** Independent, coed, comprehensive institution. *Graduate housing:* Rooms and/or apartments guaranteed to single students and available on a first-come, first-served basis to married students. Housing application deadline: 9/22.

**GRADUATE UNITS**

**Department of Business Administration** *Program availability:* Part-time, evening/weekend.

**Department of Psychology** *Program availability:* Part-time, evening/weekend.

**Department of Religious Studies** *Program availability:* Part-time, evening/weekend.

**Program in Buddhist Chaplaincy**

## THE UNIVERSITY OF TOLEDO, Toledo, OH 43606-3390

**General Information** State-supported, coed, university. CGS member. *Graduate housing:* Room and/or apartments available to single students; on-campus housing not available to married students. *Research affiliation:* Merck & Company, Inc. (pharmaceutical research), Midwest Astronomical Data Reduction and Analysis Facility (astronomy), Edison Industrial Systems Center (systems integration, quality control, mathematical modeling), Ohio Aerospace Institute (aerospace research), National Renewable Energy Laboratory (NREL) (thin films, photovoltaics), NASA–Glen Research Center at Lewis Field (aerospace engineering).

**GRADUATE UNITS**

**College of Graduate Studies** *Program availability:* Part-time, evening/weekend, online learning. Electronic applications accepted.

***College of Business and Innovation*** *Program availability:* Part-time, evening/weekend. Electronic applications accepted.

***College of Communication and the Arts*** Electronic applications accepted.

***College of Engineering*** *Program availability:* Part-time, evening/weekend, online learning. Electronic applications accepted.

***College of Health and Human Services*** Electronic applications accepted.

***College of Languages, Literature and Social Sciences*** *Program availability:* Part-time. Electronic applications accepted.

***College of Medicine and Life Sciences*** *Program availability:* Part-time, evening/weekend. Electronic applications accepted.

***College of Natural Sciences and Mathematics*** *Program availability:* Part-time. Electronic applications accepted.

***College of Nursing*** *Program availability:* Part-time, online learning. Electronic applications accepted.

***College of Pharmacy and Pharmaceutical Sciences*** Electronic applications accepted.

***College of Social Justice and Human Service***

***Judith Herb College of Education*** *Program availability:* Part-time, evening/weekend. Electronic applications accepted.

**College of Law** Students: 233 full-time (127 women), 62 part-time (36 women); includes 53 minority (16 Black or African American, non-Hispanic/Latino; 10 Asian, non-Hispanic/Latino; 16 Hispanic/Latino; 1 Native Hawaiian or other Pacific Islander, non-Hispanic/Latino; 10 Two or more races, non-Hispanic/Latino), 1 international. Average age 28. 443 applicants, 66% accepted, 104 enrolled. *Faculty:* 22 full-time (7 women), 12 part-time/adjunct (9 women). Expenses: Contact institution. *Financial support:* In 2019–20, 243 students received support. Research assistantships, career-related internships or fieldwork, Federal Work-Study, and scholarships/grants available. Support available to part-time students. Financial award application deadline: 8/1; financial award applicants required to submit FAFSA. In 2019, 3 master's, 80 doctorates, 9 Certificates awarded. *Program availability:* Part-time, evening/weekend. *Application deadline:* For fall admission, 8/1 priority date for domestic students, 7/31 for international students; for winter admission, 11/15 for domestic students. Applications are processed on a rolling basis. Electronic applications accepted. *Application Contact:* Jessica Mehl, Assistant Dean of Law Admissions, 419-530-4131, Fax: 419-530-4345, E-mail: law.admissions@utoledo.edu. *Dean,* D. Benjamin Barros, 419-530-2379, Fax: 419-530-4526, E-mail: ben.barros@utoledo.edu.

## UNIVERSITY OF TORONTO, Toronto, ON M5S 1A1, Canada

**General Information** Province-supported, coed, university. CGS member. *Graduate housing:* Rooms and/or apartments available on a first-come, first-served basis to single students and available to married students. *Research affiliation:* Fields Institute for Research in Mathematical Sciences, Canadian Institute for Theoretical Astrophysics, Royal Ontario Museum, Pontifical Institute of Medieval Studies, Hospital for Sick Children, Center for Addiction and Mental Health.

**GRADUATE UNITS**

**Faculty of Medicine** Electronic applications accepted.

***Institute of Health Policy, Management and Evaluation*** Electronic applications accepted.

***Institute of Medical Science*** Electronic applications accepted.

**School of Graduate Studies** *Program availability:* Part-time, evening/weekend. Electronic applications accepted.

***Advanced Design and Manufacturing Institute*** *Program availability:* Part-time. Electronic applications accepted.

***Department of Nursing Science*** *Program availability:* Part-time. Electronic applications accepted.

***Department of Public Health Sciences*** *Program availability:* Part-time. Electronic applications accepted.

***Faculty of Applied Science and Engineering*** *Program availability:* Part-time.

***Faculty of Arts and Science*** *Program availability:* Part-time. Electronic applications accepted.

***Faculty of Dentistry*** Electronic applications accepted.

***Faculty of Forestry*** Electronic applications accepted.

***Faculty of Information*** *Program availability:* Part-time. Electronic applications accepted.

***Faculty of Kinesiology and Physical Education*** Electronic applications accepted.

***Faculty of Law*** *Program availability:* Part-time. Electronic applications accepted.

***Faculty of Music*** *Program availability:* Part-time. Electronic applications accepted.

***Faculty of Social Work*** *Program availability:* Part-time. Electronic applications accepted.

***John H. Daniels Faculty of Architecture, Landscape, and Design*** Electronic applications accepted.

***Leslie Dan Faculty of Pharmacy*** *Program availability:* Part-time. Electronic applications accepted.

***Munk School of Global Affairs*** Electronic applications accepted.

***Ontario Institute for Studies in Education*** *Program availability:* Part-time, evening/weekend.

***Rotman School of Management*** *Program availability:* Part-time, evening/weekend.

## THE UNIVERSITY OF TULSA, Tulsa, OK 74104-3189

**General Information** Independent, coed, university. CGS member. *Enrollment:* 4,387 graduate, professional, and undergraduate students; 593 full-time matriculated graduate/professional students (273 women), 141 part-time matriculated graduate/professional students (44 women). *Enrollment by degree level:* 447 master's, 293 doctoral. *Graduate faculty:* 162 part-time/adjunct. *Tuition:* Full-time $22,896; part-time $1272 per credit hour. *Required fees:* $6 per credit hour. Tuition and fees vary according to course load and program. *Graduate housing:* Rooms and/or apartments available on a first-come, first-served basis to single and married students. Housing application deadline: 7/1. *Student services:* Campus employment opportunities, campus safety program, career counseling, exercise/wellness program, free psychological counseling, grant writing training, international student services, low-cost health insurance, multicultural affairs office, services for students with disabilities, teacher training, writing training. *Library facilities:* McFarlin Library plus 1 other. *Collection:* Books: 761,545 (physical), 538,954 (digital/electronic); Serial titles: 5,249 (physical), 71,240 (digital/electronic); Databases: 226. Weekly public service hours: 89; study areas open 24 hours, 5–7 days a week; students can reserve study rooms. *Research affiliation:* Network of Excellence in Training (NEXT) (petrophysics), Chevron Texaco (petroleum engineering).

**Computer facilities:** Computer purchase and lease plans are available. 710 computers available on campus for general student use. A campuswide network can be accessed. Online class registration is available.
Website: http://www.utulsa.edu/

**General Application Contact:** Dr. Brenton McLaury, Vice Provost for Research/Dean of the Graduate School, 918-631-2336, Fax: 918-631-2156, E-mail: grad@utulsa.edu.

**GRADUATE UNITS**

**College of Law** Students: 283 full-time (142 women), 24 part-time (11 women); includes 88 minority (13 Black or African American, non-Hispanic/Latino; 15 American Indian or Alaska Native, non-Hispanic/Latino; 4 Asian, non-Hispanic/Latino; 13 Hispanic/Latino; 1 Native Hawaiian or other Pacific Islander, non-Hispanic/Latino; 42 Two or more races, non-Hispanic/Latino), 2 international. Average age 28. 621 applicants, 57% accepted, 118 enrolled. *Faculty:* 25 full-time (14 women), 11 part-time/adjunct (3 women). Expenses: Contact institution. *Financial support:* In 2019–20, 251 students received support. Federal Work-Study and scholarships/grants available. Support available to part-time students. Financial award application deadline: 8/1; financial award applicants required to submit FAFSA. In 2019, 5 master's, 88 doctorates, 27 Certificates awarded. *Program availability:* Part-time. *Application deadline:* For fall admission, 7/31 priority date for domestic and international students; for spring admission, 12/1 priority date for domestic students, 12/1 for international students; for summer admission, 4/22 for domestic and international students. Applications are processed on a rolling basis. *Application fee:* $30. Electronic applications accepted. *Application Contact:* April M. Fox, Associate Dean of Admissions and Financial Aid, 918-631-2406, Fax: 918-631-3126, E-mail: april-fox@utulsa.edu. *Dean,* Prof. Lyn Suzanne Entzeroth, 918-631-2400, Fax: 918-631-3126, E-mail: lyn-entzeroth@utulsa.edu.

**Graduate School** *Program availability:* Part-time, evening/weekend. Electronic applications accepted.

***College of Engineering and Natural Sciences*** *Program availability:* Part-time. Electronic applications accepted.

***Collins College of Business*** *Program availability:* Part-time, evening/weekend, 100% online. Electronic applications accepted.

***Kendall College of Arts and Sciences*** *Program availability:* Part-time, evening/weekend. Electronic applications accepted.

***Oxley College of Health Sciences*** Electronic applications accepted.

## UNIVERSITY OF UTAH, Salt Lake City, UT 84112-1107

**General Information** State-supported, coed, university. CGS member. *Enrollment:* 32,818 graduate, professional, and undergraduate students; 6,514 full-time matriculated graduate/professional students (3,099 women), 1,819 part-time matriculated graduate/professional students (838 women). *Enrollment by degree level:* 4,218 master's, 4,115 doctoral. *Graduate faculty:* 1,225 full-time (452 women), 169 part-time/adjunct (56 women). Tuition, state resident: full-time $7085; part-time $272.51 per credit hour. Tuition, nonresident: full-time $24,937; part-time $959.12 per credit hour. *Required fees:* $880.52; $880.52 per semester. Tuition and fees vary according to degree level, program and student level. *Graduate housing:* Rooms and/or apartments available on a first-come, first-served basis to single and married students. Typical cost: $7725 per year ($11,844 including board) for single students; $1182 per year for married students. Room and board charges vary according to board plan and housing facility selected. Housing application deadline: 4/26. *Student services:* Campus employment opportunities, campus safety program, career counseling, child daycare facilities, exercise/wellness program, free psychological counseling, grant writing training, international student services, low-cost health insurance, multicultural affairs office, services for students with disabilities, teacher training, writing training. *Library facilities:* J. Willard Marriott Library plus 3 others. *Collection:* Books: 2.5 million (physical), 1.5 million (digital/electronic); Serial titles: 480 (physical), 10,075 (digital/electronic); Databases: 321. Students can reserve study rooms. *Research affiliation:* Watson Laboratory (pharmaceutical research), Myriad Genetics (pharmaceutical research/manufacturing), Neuropsychiatric Institute (brain research, mental health and substance abuse treatment), ARUP Laboratories (medical research), John A. Moran Eye Center (vision treatment and research).

**Computer facilities:** Computer purchase and lease plans are available. 1,099 computers available on campus for general student use. A campuswide network can be accessed. Online class registration, online classes are available.
Website: http://www.utah.edu/

**General Application Contact:** Graduate Admissions, 801-581-8761, Fax: 801-585-7864, E-mail: graduate@sa.utah.edu.

**GRADUATE UNITS**

**Graduate School** *Program availability:* Part-time, evening/weekend, 100% online, blended/hybrid learning. Electronic applications accepted.

***College of Architecture and Planning*** Students: 110 full-time (51 women), 11 part-time (5 women); includes 31 minority (5 Asian, non-Hispanic/Latino; 20 Hispanic/Latino; 6 Two or more races, non-Hispanic/Latino), 19 international. Average age 29. *Faculty:* 17 full-time (9 women), 9 part-time/adjunct (1 woman). Expenses: Contact institution. *Financial support:* In 2019–20, 28 fellowships (averaging $11,286 per year), 6 research assistantships (averaging $19,333 per year), 50 teaching assistantships (averaging $9,220 per year) were awarded. Financial award application deadline: 2/1; financial award applicants required to submit FAFSA. In 2019, 45 master's awarded. *Application fee:* $55 ($65 for international students). Electronic applications accepted. *Application Contact:* Lorilie Spegar, Academic Advisor, Recruitment and Admissions, 801-585-2361, Fax: 801-581-8217, E-mail: recruitment@arch.utah.edu. *Dean,* Dr. Keith Diaz Moore, 801-585-1766, Fax: 801-581-8217, E-mail: diazmoore@utah.edu.

***College of Education*** Students: 304 full-time (235 women), 295 part-time (204 women); includes 155 minority (13 Black or African American, non-Hispanic/Latino; 1 American Indian or Alaska Native, non-Hispanic/Latino; 21 Asian, non-Hispanic/Latino; 88 Hispanic/Latino; 5 Native Hawaiian or other Pacific Islander, non-Hispanic/Latino; 27 Two or more races, non-Hispanic/Latino), 13 international. Average age 34. *Faculty:* 72 full-time (51 women), 19 part-time/adjunct (11 women). Expenses: Contact institution. *Financial support:* In 2019–20, 53 fellowships (averaging $6,189 per year), 21 research assistantships (averaging $10,143 per year), 35 teaching assistantships (averaging $12,514 per year) were awarded. Financial award applicants required to submit FAFSA. In 2019, 174 master's, 30 doctorates awarded. *Application Contact:* Elaine Clark, Dean, 801-581-8221, E-mail: el.clark@utah.edu. *Dean,* Elaine Clark, 801-581-8221, E-mail: el.clark@utah.edu.

***College of Engineering*** Students: 960 full-time (212 women), 330 part-time (49 women); includes 134 minority (6 Black or African American, non-Hispanic/Latino; 1 American Indian or Alaska Native, non-Hispanic/Latino; 60 Asian, non-Hispanic/Latino; 41 Hispanic/Latino; 2 Native Hawaiian or other Pacific Islander, non-Hispanic/Latino; 24 Two or more races, non-Hispanic/Latino), 541 international. Average age 28. 1,779 applicants, 37% accepted, 360 enrolled. *Faculty:* 202 full-time (29 women), 15 part-time/adjunct (1 woman). Expenses: Contact institution. *Financial support:* In 2019–20, 228 students received support, including 49 fellowships (averaging $11,184 per year), 547 research assistantships (averaging $13,718 per year), 195 teaching assistantships (averaging $11,949 per year); tuition waivers and unspecified assistantships also available. Financial award application deadline: 12/15. In 2019, 370 master's, 111 doctorates awarded. *Program availability:* Part-time. *Application deadline:* For fall admission, 12/15 priority date for domestic and international students. Applications are processed on a rolling basis. *Application fee:* $30 ($45 for international students). Electronic applications accepted. *Application Contact:* Amy Arkwright, Academic Program Coordinator, 801-585-0370, Fax: 801-581-8692, E-mail: amy.arkwright@utah.edu. *Dean,* Dr. Richard B. Brown, 801-581-6912, Fax: 801-581-6912, E-mail: brown@utah.edu.

***College of Fine Arts*** Students: 111 full-time (62 women), 61 part-time (48 women); includes 21 minority (1 Black or African American, non-Hispanic/Latino; 1 American Indian or Alaska Native, non-Hispanic/Latino; 8 Asian, non-Hispanic/Latino; 7 Hispanic/Latino; 4 Two or more races, non-Hispanic/Latino), 22 international. Average age 32. *Faculty:* 77 full-time (37 women), 18 part-time/adjunct (5 women). Expenses: Contact institution. *Financial support:* In 2019–20, 1 fellowship (averaging $5,000 per year), 91 teaching assistantships (averaging $17,648 per year) were awarded. Financial award application deadline: 2/1; financial award applicants required to submit FAFSA. In 2019, 36 master's, 12 doctorates awarded. *Application Contact:* Sarah Reichel, Academic Coordinator, Graduate Studies, 801-585-6972, E-mail: sarah.reichel@utah.edu. *Dean,* John W. Scheib, 801-581-3887, Fax: 801-581-3066.

***College of Health*** Students: 541 full-time (395 women), 59 part-time (42 women); includes 89 minority (5 Black or African American, non-Hispanic/Latino; 23 Asian, non-Hispanic/Latino; 46 Hispanic/Latino; 2 Native Hawaiian or other Pacific Islander, non-Hispanic/Latino; 13 Two or more races, non-Hispanic/Latino), 21 international. Average age 29. *Faculty:* 71 full-time (37 women), 7 part-time/adjunct (4 women). Expenses: Contact institution. *Financial support:* In 2019–20, 11 fellowships (averaging $13,181 per year), 57 research assistantships (averaging $14,684 per year), 72 teaching assistantships (averaging $16,306 per year) were awarded. In 2019, 149 master's, 85 doctorates awarded. *Application Contact:* Dr. Shari Lindsey, Assistant Dean of Students, 801-581-5580, Fax: 801-581-5580, E-mail: shari.lindsey@health.utah.edu. *Dean,* Dr. David H. Perrin, 801-581-8537, Fax: 801-581-5580, E-mail: david.perrin@health.utah.edu.

***College of Humanities*** Students: 175 full-time (105 women), 55 part-time (23 women); includes 40 minority (2 Black or African American, non-Hispanic/Latino; 2 American Indian or Alaska Native, non-Hispanic/Latino; 10 Asian, non-Hispanic/Latino; 20

Hispanic/Latino; 6 Two or more races, non-Hispanic/Latino), 32 international. Average age 32. *Faculty:* 87 full-time (45 women), 5 part-time/adjunct (1 woman). Expenses: Contact institution. *Financial support:* In 2019–20, 22 fellowships (averaging $15,818 per year), 6 research assistantships (averaging $22,333 per year), 141 teaching assistantships (averaging $18,177 per year) were awarded. In 2019, 35 master's, 23 doctorates awarded. *Application Contact:* Dr. Stuart Culver, Dean, 801-581-6214. *Dean,* Dr. Stuart Culver, 801-581-6214.

***College of Mines and Earth Sciences*** Students: 78 full-time (25 women), 42 part-time (27 women); includes 11 minority (1 Black or African American, non-Hispanic/Latino; 1 Asian, non-Hispanic/Latino; 6 Hispanic/Latino; 3 Two or more races, non-Hispanic/Latino), 26 international. Average age 30. *Faculty:* 39 full-time (9 women), 1 part-time/adjunct (0 women). Expenses: Contact institution. In 2019, 17 master's, 18 doctorates awarded. *Application Contact:* Anita Austin Tromp, Executive Assistant, 801-585-9344, E-mail: anita.austin@utah.edu. *Dean,* Dr. Darryl P. Butt, 801-581-8767, E-mail: darryl.butt@utah.edu.

***College of Nursing*** Students: 330 full-time (264 women), 61 part-time (51 women); includes 63 minority (5 Black or African American, non-Hispanic/Latino; 15 Asian, non-Hispanic/Latino; 26 Hispanic/Latino; 3 Native Hawaiian or other Pacific Islander, non-Hispanic/Latino; 14 Two or more races, non-Hispanic/Latino), 7 international. Average age 35. *Faculty:* 49 full-time (47 women), 9 part-time/adjunct (7 women). Expenses: Contact institution. *Financial support:* In 2019–20, 57 fellowships (averaging $7,667 per year), 12 research assistantships (averaging $6,750 per year), 20 teaching assistantships (averaging $5,300 per year) were awarded. In 2019, 18 master's, 100 doctorates awarded. *Program availability:* Part-time, online learning. *Application fee:* $55 ($65 for international students). *Application Contact:* Carrie Radmall, Associate Director of Student Services, 801-581-3414, E-mail: carrie.radmall@nurs.utah.edu. *Dean,* Barbara Wilson, PhD, 801-581-8262, E-mail: barbara.wilson@nurs.utah.edu.

***College of Pharmacy*** Students: 243 full-time (144 women), 20 part-time (9 women); includes 82 minority (6 Black or African American, non-Hispanic/Latino; 48 Asian, non-Hispanic/Latino; 15 Hispanic/Latino; 13 Two or more races, non-Hispanic/Latino), 21 international. Average age 27. *Faculty:* 35 full-time (16 women). Expenses: Contact institution. *Financial support:* In 2019–20, 15 research assistantships (averaging $15,600 per year), 2 teaching assistantships (averaging $7,000 per year) were awarded. In 2019, 1 master's, 69 doctorates awarded. Electronic applications accepted. *Application Contact:* Dallas Nelson, Senior Academic Advisor, 801-581-5384, E-mail: dallas.nelson@pharm.utah.edu. *Dean,* Dr. Randall T. Peterson, 801-587-3064, E-mail: randall.peterson@pharm.utah.edu.

***College of Science*** Students: 359 full-time (145 women), 86 part-time (35 women); includes 54 minority (1 Black or African American, non-Hispanic/Latino; 22 Asian, non-Hispanic/Latino; 21 Hispanic/Latino; 10 Two or more races, non-Hispanic/Latino), 125 international. Average age 27. *Faculty:* 123 full-time (22 women), 2 part-time/adjunct (1 woman). Expenses: Contact institution. *Financial support:* In 2019–20, 20 fellowships (averaging $12,700 per year), 162 research assistantships (averaging $10,961 per year), 183 teaching assistantships (averaging $17,186 per year) were awarded. In 2019, 70 master's, 64 doctorates awarded. *Application Contact:* Lisa Batchelder, Student Services and Administration Manager, 801-581-3374, E-mail: office@science.utah.edu. *Dean,* Dr. Peter Trapa, 801-581-6958, E-mail: ptrapa@math.utah.edu.

***College of Social and Behavioral Science*** Students: 304 full-time (176 women), 166 part-time (82 women); includes 76 minority (5 Black or African American, non-Hispanic/Latino; 9 Asian, non-Hispanic/Latino; 44 Hispanic/Latino; 2 Native Hawaiian or other Pacific Islander, non-Hispanic/Latino; 16 Two or more races, non-Hispanic/Latino), 60 international. Average age 31. *Faculty:* 113 full-time (43 women), 11 part-time/adjunct (1 woman). Expenses: Contact institution. *Financial support:* In 2019–20, 15 fellowships (averaging $15,667 per year), 46 research assistantships (averaging $14,587 per year), 130 teaching assistantships (averaging $13,908 per year) were awarded. In 2019, 152 master's, 37 doctorates awarded. *Application Contact:* Bobbi Davis, Student Services Director, 801-581-7579, E-mail: bobbi.davis@utah.edu. *Dean,* Cynthia Berg, 801-581-8620, E-mail: cynthia.berg@csbs.utah.edu.

***College of Social Work*** Students: 301 full-time (233 women), 21 part-time (17 women); includes 69 minority (6 Black or African American, non-Hispanic/Latino; 5 American Indian or Alaska Native, non-Hispanic/Latino; 9 Asian, non-Hispanic/Latino; 37 Hispanic/Latino; 3 Native Hawaiian or other Pacific Islander, non-Hispanic/Latino; 9 Two or more races, non-Hispanic/Latino), 2 international. Average age 32. 262 applicants, 79% accepted, 155 enrolled. *Faculty:* 24 full-time (13 women), 13 part-time/adjunct (11 women). Expenses: Contact institution. *Financial support:* In 2019–20, 150 students received support, including 48 fellowships (averaging $4,083 per year), 17 research assistantships (averaging $7,412 per year), 3 teaching assistantships (averaging $8,667 per year); career-related internships or fieldwork, scholarships/grants, traineeships, and unspecified assistantships also available. Financial award application deadline: 3/30; financial award applicants required to submit FAFSA. In 2019, 155 master's, 7 doctorates awarded. *Program availability:* Part-time, evening/weekend, online learning. *Application deadline:* For fall admission, 4/1 priority date for domestic students. *Application fee:* $55. Electronic applications accepted. *Application Contact:* Elizabeth Perez, Director of Academic Advising, 801-585-1596, E-mail: elizabeth.perez@utah.edu. *Dean,* Dr. Martell L. Teasley, 801-581-6194, E-mail: martell.teasley@utah.edu.

***David Eccles School of Business*** Average age 25. Expenses: Contact institution. *Financial support:* Fellowships with partial tuition reimbursements, research assistantships with partial tuition reimbursements, teaching assistantships with tuition reimbursements, scholarships/grants, tuition waivers (full and partial), and unspecified assistantships available. Financial award applicants required to submit FAFSA. In 2019, 797 master's, 11 doctorates awarded. *Program availability:* Part-time, evening/weekend. *Application fee:* $55 ($65 for international students). Electronic applications accepted. *Application Contact:* Director of Graduate Admissions, 801-585-7366. *Dean,* Dr. Taylor Randall, 801-587-3869, E-mail: dean@eccles.utah.edu.

**School of Dentistry** Students: 194 full-time (54 women); includes 42 minority (2 Black or African American, non-Hispanic/Latino; 16 Asian, non-Hispanic/Latino; 17 Hispanic/Latino; 7 Two or more races, non-Hispanic/Latino). Average age 27. 503 applicants, 10% accepted, 51 enrolled. *Faculty:* 12 full-time (2 women), 1 part-time/adjunct (0 women). Expenses: Contact institution. *Financial support:* In 2019–20, 13 students received support. Scholarships/grants available. Financial award application deadline: 5/15; financial award applicants required to submit FAFSA. In 2019, 27 doctorates awarded. *Application deadline:* For fall admission, 10/1 for domestic students. *Application fee:* $90. *Application Contact:* Julie Oyler, Office of Admissions, 801-585-0718, Fax: 801-585-6485, E-mail: julie.oyler@hsc.utah.edu. *Dean,* Dr. Wyatt R. Hume, DDS, 801-587-1208, E-mail: wyatt.hume@hsc.utah.edu.

**School of Medicine**

**S.J. Quinney College of Law** Students: 306 full-time (140 women), 2 part-time (1 woman); includes 61 minority (13 Black or African American, non-Hispanic/Latino; 3 American Indian or Alaska Native, non-Hispanic/Latino; 11 Asian, non-Hispanic/Latino; 26 Hispanic/Latino; 1 Native Hawaiian or other Pacific Islander, non-Hispanic/Latino; 7 Two or more races, non-Hispanic/Latino), 3 international. Average age 28. 761 applicants, 41% accepted, 102 enrolled. *Faculty:* 44 full-time (18 women), 53 part-time/adjunct (22 women). Expenses: Contact institution. *Financial support:* In 2019–20, 155 students received support, including 129 fellowships with partial tuition reimbursements available (averaging $8,000 per year), 60 research assistantships with partial tuition reimbursements available (averaging $8,000 per year); scholarships/grants and unspecified assistantships also available. Financial award application deadline: 3/10; financial award applicants required to submit FAFSA. In 2019, 4 master's, 85 doctorates awarded. *Program availability:* Evening/weekend. *Application deadline:* For fall admission, 3/10 for domestic and international students. Applications are processed on a rolling basis. *Application fee:* $60. Electronic applications accepted. *Application Contact:* Reyes Aquilar, Associate Director for Admission and Financial Aid, 801-581-6563, E-mail: reyes.aguilar@law.utah.edu. *Dean and Professor of Law,* Elizabeth Ann Kronk Warner, 801-581-6571, E-mail: elizabeth.warner@law.utah.edu.

## UNIVERSITY OF VALLEY FORGE, Phoenixville, PA 19460

**General Information** Independent-religious, coed, comprehensive institution.

**GRADUATE UNITS**

**Program in Christian Leadership**

**Program in Music Technology** *Program availability:* Online learning.

**Program in Theology**

**Program in Worship Studies**

## UNIVERSITY OF VERMONT, Burlington, VT 05405

**General Information** State-supported, coed, university. CGS member. *Graduate housing:* On-campus housing not available. *Research affiliation:* Miner Institute (animal sciences).

**GRADUATE UNITS**

**Graduate College** *Program availability:* Part-time, 100% online, blended/hybrid learning. Electronic applications accepted.

***College of Agriculture and Life Sciences*** *Program availability:* Part-time. Electronic applications accepted.

***College of Arts and Sciences*** *Program availability:* Part-time. Electronic applications accepted.

***College of Education and Social Services*** *Program availability:* Part-time, evening/weekend. Electronic applications accepted.

***College of Engineering and Mathematical Sciences*** *Program availability:* Part-time. Electronic applications accepted.

***College of Nursing and Health Sciences*** Electronic applications accepted.

***Grossman School of Business*** *Program availability:* Part-time. Electronic applications accepted.

***The Rubenstein School of Environment and Natural Resources*** *Program availability:* Part-time. Electronic applications accepted.

**The Robert Larner, MD College of Medicine** Electronic applications accepted.

***Graduate Programs in Medicine*** *Program availability:* 100% online. Electronic applications accepted.

## UNIVERSITY OF VICTORIA, Victoria, BC V8W 2Y2, Canada

**General Information** Province-supported, coed, university. *Graduate housing:* Rooms and/or apartments available on a first-come, first-served basis to single and married students. Housing application deadline: 2/1. *Research affiliation:* Dominion Astrophysical Observatory, Bamfield Marine Research Station (marine biology), Tri-University Meson Facility, Canada/France/Hawaii Telescope Observatory, Institute of Ocean Sciences (geography, oceanography).

**GRADUATE UNITS**

**Faculty of Graduate Studies** *Program availability:* Part-time, online learning. Electronic applications accepted.

***Faculty of Education***

***Faculty of Engineering***

***Faculty of Fine Arts***

***Faculty of Human and Social Development***

***Faculty of Humanities***

***Faculty of Science*** Electronic applications accepted.

***Faculty of Social Sciences***

***Peter B. Gustavson School of Business*** *Program availability:* Part-time. Electronic applications accepted.

**Faculty of Law** *Program availability:* Part-time. Electronic applications accepted.

## UNIVERSITY OF VIRGINIA, Charlottesville, VA 22903

**General Information** State-supported, coed, university. CGS member. *Graduate housing:* Rooms and/or apartments available on a first-come, first-served basis to single and married students. Housing application deadline: 6/1. *Research affiliation:* Oak Ridge National Laboratory (energy), National Institute of Aerospace, Jefferson National Accelerator Facility (nuclear physics), Federal Executive Institute (leadership development), National Radio Astronomy Observatory, The Judge Advocate General's School, U.S. Army (law).

**GRADUATE UNITS**

**College and Graduate School of Arts and Sciences** *Program availability:* Part-time. Electronic applications accepted.

**Curry School of Education** Electronic applications accepted.

**Darden School of Business** Electronic applications accepted.

**Data Science Institute**

**Frank Batten Sr. School of Leadership and Public Policy** Electronic applications accepted.

**McIntire School of Commerce** Electronic applications accepted.

**School of Architecture** Electronic applications accepted.

**School of Engineering and Applied Science** *Program availability:* Part-time, online learning. Electronic applications accepted.

**School of Law** Electronic applications accepted.

**School of Medicine** Electronic applications accepted.

**School of Nursing** *Program availability:* Part-time. Electronic applications accepted.

## UNIVERSITY OF WASHINGTON, Seattle, WA 98195

**General Information** State-supported, coed, university. CGS member. *Graduate housing:* Rooms and/or apartments available on a first-come, first-served basis to single and married students. Housing application deadline: 5/1. *Research affiliation:* Fred Hutchinson Cancer Research Center, Children's Hospital and Regional Medical Center (pediatric research).

**GRADUATE UNITS**

**Graduate School** *Program availability:* Part-time, evening/weekend, online learning. Electronic applications accepted.

***College of Arts and Sciences*** *Program availability:* Part-time, evening/weekend. Electronic applications accepted.

***College of Built Environments*** *Program availability:* Part-time, evening/weekend. Electronic applications accepted.

***College of Education*** *Program availability:* Part-time, evening/weekend. Electronic applications accepted.

***College of Engineering*** Students: 1,787 full-time (591 women), 1,026 part-time (326 women); includes 610 minority (44 Black or African American, non-Hispanic/Latino; 3 American Indian or Alaska Native, non-Hispanic/Latino; 343 Asian, non-Hispanic/Latino; 119 Hispanic/Latino; 3 Native Hawaiian or other Pacific Islander, non-Hispanic/Latino; 98 Two or more races, non-Hispanic/Latino), 1,091 international. Average age 27. 8,636 applicants, 30% accepted, 968 enrolled. Expenses: Contact institution. *Financial support:* In 2019–20, 115 fellowships with full tuition reimbursements (averaging $33,540 per year), 761 research assistantships with full tuition reimbursements (averaging $34,990 per year), 297 teaching assistantships with full tuition reimbursements (averaging $33,460 per year) were awarded; Federal Work-Study, institutionally sponsored loans, scholarships/grants, health care benefits, tuition waivers (full), unspecified assistantships, and stipend supplements also available. Support available to part-time students. In 2019, 724 master's, 184 doctorates awarded. *Program availability:* Part-time, online learning. *Application fee:* $85. Electronic applications accepted. *Application Contact:* Mike Engh, Assistant Director, Academic Affairs, 206-685-3714, Fax: 206-685-0666, E-mail: enghmw@uw.edu. *Frank & Julie Jungers Dean of Engineering*, Dr. Nancy Allbritton, 206-543-1829, Fax: 206-685-0666, E-mail: nlallbr@uw.edu.

***College of the Environment*** Electronic applications accepted.

***Evans School of Public Policy and Governance*** *Program availability:* Part-time, evening/weekend. Electronic applications accepted.

***Information School*** Students: 394 full-time (249 women), 283 part-time (198 women); includes 154 minority (33 Black or African American, non-Hispanic/Latino; 8 American Indian or Alaska Native, non-Hispanic/Latino; 71 Asian, non-Hispanic/Latino; 38 Hispanic/Latino; 4 Native Hawaiian or other Pacific Islander, non-Hispanic/Latino), 184 international. Average age 30. 1,205 applicants, 47% accepted, 307 enrolled. *Faculty:* 49 full-time (30 women), 33 part-time/adjunct (19 women). Expenses: Contact institution. *Financial support:* In 2019–20, 73 students received support, including 14 fellowships with full tuition reimbursements available (averaging $46,977 per year), 90 research assistantships with full tuition reimbursements available (averaging $22,137 per year), 70 teaching assistantships with full tuition reimbursements available (averaging $22,849 per year); Federal Work-Study, institutionally sponsored loans, scholarships/grants, health care benefits, tuition waivers (full and partial), and unspecified assistantships also available. Support available to part-time students. Financial award application deadline: 10/1; financial award applicants required to submit FAFSA. In 2019, 234 master's, 5 doctorates awarded. *Program availability:* Part-time, evening/weekend, 100% online coursework with required attendance at on-campus orientation at start of program. *Application deadline:* For fall admission, 12/1 priority date for domestic and international students. *Application fee:* $85. Electronic applications accepted. *Application Contact:* Kari Brothers, Admissions Counselor, 206-616-5541, Fax: 206-616-3152, E-mail: kari683@uw.edu. *Dean*, Dr. Anind Dey, E-mail: anind@uw.edu.

***Michael G. Foster School of Business*** *Program availability:* Part-time, evening/weekend, blended/hybrid learning. Electronic applications accepted.

***School of Dentistry***

***School of Law***

***School of Medicine*** *Program availability:* Part-time. Electronic applications accepted.

***School of Nursing*** *Program availability:* Part-time.

***School of Public Health*** Students: 818 full-time (588 women), 190 part-time (144 women); includes 344 minority (63 Black or African American, non-Hispanic/Latino; 16 American Indian or Alaska Native, non-Hispanic/Latino; 195 Asian, non-Hispanic/Latino; 64 Hispanic/Latino; 6 Native Hawaiian or other Pacific Islander, non-Hispanic/Latino), 161 international. Average age 31. 1,850 applicants, 45% accepted, 394 enrolled. *Faculty:* 243 full-time (130 women), 211 part-time/adjunct (99 women). Expenses: Contact institution. *Financial support:* Fellowships with full and partial tuition reimbursements, research assistantships with full and partial tuition reimbursements, teaching assistantships with full and partial tuition reimbursements, career-related internships or fieldwork, Federal Work-Study, institutionally sponsored loans, scholarships/grants, traineeships, health care benefits, tuition waivers (full and partial), and unspecified assistantships available. Support available to part-time students. In 2019, 300 master's, 60 doctorates awarded. *Program availability:* Part-time, evening/weekend, blended/hybrid learning. *Application fee:* $85. Electronic applications accepted. *Application Contact:* Student and Academic Services, 206-685-3057, E-mail: sphsas@uw.edu. *Dean*, Hilary Godwin.

***School of Social Work*** *Program availability:* Evening/weekend, online learning.

**School of Pharmacy**

## UNIVERSITY OF WASHINGTON, BOTHELL, Bothell, WA 98011

**General Information** State-supported, coed, comprehensive institution. *Graduate housing:* Room and/or apartments available on a first-come, first-served basis to single students; on-campus housing not available to married students. Housing application deadline: 5/1. *Research affiliation:* Bill and Melinda Gates Foundation (improving health and reducing poverty in developing countries, providing opportunities to succeed in school and life in the U.S.), Carnegie Corporation of New York (doing real and permanent good in this world by creating ladders on which the aspiring can rise), American Institutes for Research (labor market success), Michael and Susan Dell Foundation (portfolio network scale-up project), William and Flora Hewlett Foundation (planning for the state education agency of the future), Walton Family Foundation (student-based allocation systems).

**GRADUATE UNITS**

**Master of Arts in Cultural Studies Program** *Program availability:* Evening/weekend. Electronic applications accepted.

**Master of Arts in Policy Studies Program** *Program availability:* Evening/weekend. Electronic applications accepted.

**Program in Computing and Software Systems** *Program availability:* Part-time, evening/weekend. Electronic applications accepted.

**Program in Creative Writing and Poetics**

**Program in Education** *Program availability:* Part-time, evening/weekend. Electronic applications accepted.

**Program in Nursing** *Program availability:* Part-time. Electronic applications accepted.

**School of Business** *Program availability:* Part-time, evening/weekend. Electronic applications accepted.

## UNIVERSITY OF WASHINGTON, TACOMA, Tacoma, WA 98402-3100

**General Information** State-supported, coed, comprehensive institution. *Graduate housing:* Room and/or apartments available on a first-come, first-served basis to single students; on-campus housing not available to married students. Housing application deadline: 5/14. *Research affiliation:* City of Tacoma/Port of Tacoma (water quality and sustainability studies), South Sound Public and Private Schools (internships and educational research).

**GRADUATE UNITS**

**Graduate Programs** *Program availability:* Part-time, evening/weekend. Electronic applications accepted.

## UNIVERSITY OF WATERLOO, Waterloo, ON N2L 3G1, Canada

**General Information** Province-supported, coed, university. *Graduate housing:* Rooms and/or apartments available on a first-come, first-served basis to single and married students. *Research affiliation:* Waterloo Maple, Inc. (symbolic computation research), Bell Canada, GM Canada, IBM, COM DEV International (telecommunications), Nortel (telecommunications).

**GRADUATE UNITS**

**Graduate Studies and Postdoctoral Affairs** *Program availability:* Part-time, evening/weekend, online learning. Electronic applications accepted.

***Faculty of Applied Health Sciences*** *Program availability:* Part-time. Electronic applications accepted.

***Faculty of Arts*** *Program availability:* Part-time, evening/weekend. Electronic applications accepted.

***Faculty of Engineering*** *Program availability:* Part-time, evening/weekend, online learning. Electronic applications accepted.

***Faculty of Environment*** *Program availability:* Part-time. Electronic applications accepted.

***Faculty of Mathematics*** Electronic applications accepted.

***Faculty of Science*** *Program availability:* Part-time. Electronic applications accepted.

## THE UNIVERSITY OF WEST ALABAMA, Livingston, AL 35470

**General Information** State-supported, coed, comprehensive institution. *Enrollment:* 5,653 graduate, professional, and undergraduate students; 3,282 full-time matriculated graduate/professional students (2,667 women), 132 part-time matriculated graduate/professional students (83 women). *Enrollment by degree level:* 2,929 master's, 76 doctoral, 409 other advanced degrees. *Graduate faculty:* 50 full-time (28 women), 110 part-time/adjunct (62 women). *Required fees:* $380; $130. *Graduate housing:* Room and/or apartments available on a first-come, first-served basis to single students; on-campus housing not available to married students. Housing application deadline: 5/1. *Student services:* Campus employment opportunities, campus safety program, career counseling, exercise/wellness program, free psychological counseling, international student services, services for students with disabilities. *Library facilities:* Julia Tutwiler Library plus 1 other. *Collection:* Books: 209,776 (physical), 2,121 (digital/electronic); Serial titles: 41,804 (physical), 108,967 (digital/electronic); Databases: 174. Weekly public service hours: 96; students can reserve study rooms.

**Computer facilities:** 400 computers available on campus for general student use. A campuswide network can be accessed. Online class registration is available.
Website: http://www.uwa.edu/

**General Application Contact:** Dr. B. J. Kimbrough, Dean of Graduate Studies, 205-652-3647, Fax: 205-652-3670, E-mail: bkimbrough@uwa.edu.

**GRADUATE UNITS**

**School of Graduate Studies** Students: 3,282 full-time (2,667 women), 132 part-time (83 women); includes 1,270 minority (1,139 Black or African American, non-Hispanic/Latino; 30 American Indian or Alaska Native, non-Hispanic/Latino; 7 Asian, non-Hispanic/Latino; 40 Hispanic/Latino; 5 Native Hawaiian or other Pacific Islander, non-Hispanic/Latino; 49 Two or more races, non-Hispanic/Latino), 29 international. Average age 34. 1,002 applicants, 92% accepted, 737 enrolled. *Faculty:* 50 full-time (28 women), 110 part-time/adjunct (62 women). Expenses: Contact institution. *Financial support:* In 2019–20, 22 teaching assistantships (averaging $7,344 per year) were awarded; Federal Work-Study, scholarships/grants, and unspecified assistantships also available. Support available to part-time students. Financial award application deadline: 3/1; financial award applicants required to submit FAFSA. In 2019, 848 master's, 140 other advanced degrees awarded. *Program availability:* Part-time, evening/weekend, 100% online. *Application deadline:* Applications are processed on a rolling basis. *Application fee:* $40. Electronic applications accepted. *Application Contact:* Dr. B. J. Kimbrough, Dean of Graduate Studies, 205-652-3647, Fax: 205-652-3670, E-mail: bkimbrough@uwa.edu. *Dean of Graduate Studies*, Dr. B. J. Kimbrough, 205-652-3647, Fax: 205-652-3670, E-mail: bkimbrough@uwa.edu.

***College of Business and Technology*** Students: 179 full-time (115 women), 6 part-time (2 women); includes 112 minority (105 Black or African American, non-Hispanic/Latino; 1 American Indian or Alaska Native, non-Hispanic/Latino; 1 Hispanic/Latino; 1 Native Hawaiian or other Pacific Islander, non-Hispanic/Latino; 4 Two or more races, non-Hispanic/Latino), 9 international. Average age 31. 96 applicants, 97% accepted, 59 enrolled. *Faculty:* 1 full-time (0 women), 16 part-time/adjunct (10 women). Expenses: Contact institution. *Financial support:* Federal Work-Study and scholarships/grants available. Support available to part-time students. Financial award application deadline: 3/1; financial award applicants required to submit FAFSA. In 2019, 24 master's awarded. *Program availability:* Part-time, evening/weekend, 100% online. *Application deadline:* Applications are processed on a rolling basis. *Application fee:* $40. Electronic applications accepted. *Application Contact:* Dr. Aliquippa Allen, Dean of College of Business and

Technology, 205-652-3564, Fax: 205-652-3776, E-mail: aallen@uwa.edu. *Dean of College of Business and Technology*, Dr. Aliquippa Allen, 205-652-3564, Fax: 205-652-3776, E-mail: aallen@uwa.edu.

***College of Education*** Students: 2,881 full-time (2,435 women), 102 part-time (71 women); includes 1,086 minority (978 Black or African American, non-Hispanic/Latino; 27 American Indian or Alaska Native, non-Hispanic/Latino; 5 Asian, non-Hispanic/Latino; 34 Hispanic/Latino; 4 Native Hawaiian or other Pacific Islander, non-Hispanic/Latino; 38 Two or more races, non-Hispanic/Latino), 16 international. Average age 35. 785 applicants, 93% accepted, 592 enrolled. *Faculty:* 35 full-time (25 women), 88 part-time/adjunct (51 women). Expenses: Contact institution. *Financial support:* In 2019–20, 2 teaching assistantships (averaging $7,344 per year) were awarded; Federal Work-Study, scholarships/grants, and unspecified assistantships also available. Support available to part-time students. Financial award application deadline: 3/1; financial award applicants required to submit FAFSA. In 2019, 757 master's, 140 other advanced degrees awarded. *Program availability:* Part-time, evening/weekend, 100% online. *Application deadline:* Applications are processed on a rolling basis. *Application fee:* $40. Electronic applications accepted. *Application Contact:* Dr. B. J. Kimbrough, Dean of Graduate Studies, 205-652-3647, Fax: 205-652-3670, E-mail: bkimbrough@uwa.edu. *Dean of Graduate Studies*, Dr. B. J. Kimbrough, 205-652-3647, Fax: 205-652-3670, E-mail: bkimbrough@uwa.edu.

***College of Liberal Arts*** Students: 39 full-time (36 women), 6 part-time (5 women); includes 21 minority (18 Black or African American, non-Hispanic/Latino; 1 Hispanic/Latino; 2 Two or more races, non-Hispanic/Latino), 1 international. Average age 26. 24 applicants, 92% accepted, 20 enrolled. *Faculty:* 7 full-time (2 women), 7 part-time/adjunct (5 women). Expenses: Contact institution. *Financial support:* In 2019–20, 3 teaching assistantships (averaging $7,344 per year) were awarded; Federal Work-Study, scholarships/grants, and unspecified assistantships also available. Support available to part-time students. Financial award application deadline: 3/1; financial award applicants required to submit FAFSA. In 2019, 2 master's awarded. *Program availability:* Part-time, evening/weekend, 100% online. *Application deadline:* Applications are processed on a rolling basis. *Application fee:* $40. Electronic applications accepted. *Application Contact:* Dr. Mark Davis, Dean of College of Liberal Arts, 205-652-3570, Fax: 205-652-3717, E-mail: mdavis@uwa.edu. *Dean of College of Liberal Arts*, Dr. Mark Davis, 205-652-3570, Fax: 205-652-3717, E-mail: mdavis@uwa.edu.

***College of Natural Sciences and Mathematics*** Students: 153 full-time (63 women), 18 part-time (5 women); includes 39 minority (30 Black or African American, non-Hispanic/Latino; 1 American Indian or Alaska Native, non-Hispanic/Latino; 4 Hispanic/Latino; 4 Two or more races, non-Hispanic/Latino), 3 international. Average age 29. 62 applicants, 97% accepted, 53 enrolled. *Faculty:* 10 full-time (2 women), 5 part-time/adjunct (0 women). Expenses: Contact institution. *Financial support:* In 2019–20, 8 teaching assistantships (averaging $7,344 per year) were awarded; Federal Work-Study, scholarships/grants, and unspecified assistantships also available. Support available to part-time students. Financial award application deadline: 3/1; financial award applicants required to submit FAFSA. In 2019, 65 master's awarded. *Program availability:* Part-time, evening/weekend, 100% online. *Application deadline:* Applications are processed on a rolling basis. *Application fee:* $40. Electronic applications accepted. *Application Contact:* Dr. John McCall, Dean of College of Natural Sciences and Mathematics, 205-652-3412, Fax: 205-652-3831, E-mail: jmccall@uwa.edu. *Dean of College of Natural Sciences and Mathematics*, Dr. John McCall, 205-652-3412, Fax: 205-652-3831, E-mail: jmccall@uwa.edu.

## THE UNIVERSITY OF WESTERN ONTARIO, London, ON N6A 3K7, Canada

**General Information** Province-supported, coed, university. CGS member. *Graduate housing:* Rooms and/or apartments available on a first-come, first-served basis to single and married students.

**GRADUATE UNITS**

**Faculty of Law**

**Ivey Business School** Electronic applications accepted.

**School of Graduate and Postdoctoral Studies** *Program availability:* Part-time, evening/weekend, online learning. Electronic applications accepted.

***Center for the Study of Theory and Criticism***

***Don Wright Faculty of Music*** *Program availability:* Part-time.

***Faculty of Arts and Humanities*** *Program availability:* Part-time.

***Faculty of Health Sciences***

***Faculty of Information and Media Studies***

***Faculty of Science*** *Program availability:* Part-time, online learning.

***Faculty of Social Science*** *Program availability:* Part-time, evening/weekend.

**Schulich School of Medicine and Dentistry**

## UNIVERSITY OF WESTERN STATES, Portland, OR 97230-3099

**General Information** Independent, coed, graduate-only institution. *Graduate housing:* On-campus housing not available. *Research affiliation:* Oregon Center for Complimentary and Alternative Medicine in Craniofacial Disorders (complimentary and alternative medicine), Consortial Center for Chiropractic Research (Palmer College of Chiropractic) (chiropractic).

**GRADUATE UNITS**

**Professional Program**

## UNIVERSITY OF WEST FLORIDA, Pensacola, FL 32514-5750

**General Information** State-supported, coed, comprehensive institution. CGS member. *Graduate housing:* Room and/or apartments available on a first-come, first-served basis to single students; on-campus housing not available to married students. *Research affiliation:* Pensacola Bay Area Convention and Visitors Bureau (Pensacola tourism study), Software Engineering Research Consortium (Motorola, Northrup Grumman through Ball State University) (software engineering), University of Southern Mississippi Consortium on Coastal Estuarine Research (microbial biofilms and coastal estuarine research).

**GRADUATE UNITS**

**College of Arts, Social Sciences, and Humanities** *Program availability:* Part-time, evening/weekend.

***Division of Anthropology and Archaeology***

**College of Business** *Program availability:* Part-time, evening/weekend.

**College of Education and Professional Studies** *Program availability:* Part-time, evening/weekend.

***Ed D Programs*** *Program availability:* Part-time, evening/weekend.

**Hal Marcus College of Science and Engineering** *Program availability:* Part-time, evening/weekend.

**Usha Kundu, MD College of Health** *Program availability:* Part-time.

***School of Nursing*** *Program availability:* Part-time, evening/weekend.

## UNIVERSITY OF WEST GEORGIA, Carrollton, GA 30118

**General Information** State-supported, coed, comprehensive institution. CGS member. *Enrollment:* 13,238 graduate, professional, and undergraduate students; 538 full-time matriculated graduate/professional students (404 women), 1,811 part-time matriculated graduate/professional students (1,447 women). *Enrollment by degree level:* 1,599 master's, 174 doctoral, 576 other advanced degrees. *Graduate faculty:* 266 full-time (134 women). Tuition and fees vary according to course load, degree level, program and reciprocity agreements. *Graduate housing:* Rooms and/or apartments available on a first-come, first-served basis to single and married students. Typical cost: $4900 per year ($9668 including board) for single students; $4900 per year ($9668 including board) for married students. Room and board charges vary according to board plan and housing facility selected. Housing application deadline: 6/1. *Student services:* Campus employment opportunities, campus safety program, career counseling, exercise/wellness program, free psychological counseling, international student services, multicultural affairs office, services for students with disabilities, teacher training, writing training. *Library facilities:* Irvine Sullivan Ingram Library plus 1 other. *Collection:* Weekly public service hours: 110; students can reserve study rooms.

**Computer facilities:** 1,200 computers available on campus for general student use. A campuswide network can be accessed. Online class registration is available.
Website: http://www.westga.edu/

**General Application Contact:** Dr. Toby Ziglar, Assistant Dean of the Graduate School, 678-839-1394, Fax: 678-839-1395, E-mail: graduate@westga.edu.

**GRADUATE UNITS**

**College of Arts and Humanities** Students: 26 full-time (14 women), 64 part-time (40 women); includes 14 minority (9 Black or African American, non-Hispanic/Latino; 1 American Indian or Alaska Native, non-Hispanic/Latino; 2 Hispanic/Latino; 2 Two or more races, non-Hispanic/Latino). Average age 32. 24 applicants, 100% accepted, 21 enrolled. *Faculty:* 67 full-time (36 women). Expenses: Contact institution. *Financial support:* Fellowships, research assistantships, teaching assistantships, career-related internships or fieldwork, Federal Work-Study, institutionally sponsored loans, scholarships/grants, and unspecified assistantships available. Support available to part-time students. Financial award application deadline: 4/1; financial award applicants required to submit FAFSA. *Program availability:* Part-time, evening/weekend, 100% online, blended/hybrid learning. *Application deadline:* For fall admission, 8/1 for domestic students, 6/1 for international students; for spring admission, 11/15 for domestic students, 10/15 for international students; for summer admission, 5/15 for domestic students, 3/30 for international students. Applications are processed on a rolling basis. *Application fee:* $40. Electronic applications accepted. *Application Contact:* Dr. Toby Ziglar, Assistant Dean of the Graduate School, 678-839-1394, Fax: 678-839-1395, E-mail: graduate@westga.edu. *Dean and Professor of Theatre*, Dr. Pauline Gagnon, 678-839-5450, E-mail: pgagnon@westga.edu.

**College of Education** Students: 281 full-time (205 women), 1,441 part-time (1,161 women); includes 505 minority (413 Black or African American, non-Hispanic/Latino; 1 American Indian or Alaska Native, non-Hispanic/Latino; 14 Asian, non-Hispanic/Latino; 46 Hispanic/Latino; 31 Two or more races, non-Hispanic/Latino), 3 international. Average age 35. 610 applicants, 85% accepted, 327 enrolled. *Faculty:* 39 full-time (23 women). Expenses: Contact institution. *Financial support:* Fellowships, research assistantships, teaching assistantships, career-related internships or fieldwork, Federal Work-Study, institutionally sponsored loans, scholarships/grants, and unspecified assistantships available. Support available to part-time students. Financial award application deadline: 4/1; financial award applicants required to submit FAFSA. *Program availability:* Part-time, evening/weekend, 100% online, blended/hybrid learning. *Application deadline:* For fall admission, 7/21 for domestic students, 6/1 for international students; for spring admission, 11/30 for domestic students, 10/15 for international students; for summer admission, 4/15 for domestic students, 3/30 for international students. Applications are processed on a rolling basis. *Application fee:* $40. Electronic applications accepted. *Application Contact:* Dr. Toby Ziglar, Assistant Dean of the Graduate School, 678-839-1394, Fax: 678-839-1395, E-mail: graduate@westga.edu. *College of Education Dean*, Dr. Dianne Hoff, 678-839-5430, E-mail: dhoff@westga.edu.

**College of Science and Mathematics** Students: 14 full-time (9 women), 71 part-time (20 women); includes 25 minority (12 Black or African American, non-Hispanic/Latino; 9 Asian, non-Hispanic/Latino; 2 Hispanic/Latino; 2 Two or more races, non-Hispanic/Latino), 13 international. Average age 29. 75 applicants, 73% accepted, 40 enrolled. *Faculty:* 47 full-time (16 women). Expenses: Contact institution. *Financial support:* Fellowships, research assistantships, teaching assistantships, career-related internships or fieldwork, Federal Work-Study, institutionally sponsored loans, scholarships/grants, and unspecified assistantships available. Support available to part-time students. Financial award application deadline: 4/1; financial award applicants required to submit FAFSA. *Program availability:* Part-time, evening/weekend, 100% online, blended/hybrid learning. *Application deadline:* For fall admission, 6/1 for domestic and international students; for spring admission, 11/15 for domestic students, 10/15 for international students; for summer admission, 4/1 for domestic students, 3/30 for international students. Applications are processed on a rolling basis. *Application fee:* $40. Electronic applications accepted. *Application Contact:* Dr. Toby Ziglar, Assistant Dean of the Graduate School, 678-839-1394, Fax: 678-839-1395, E-mail: graduate@westga.edu. *Interim Dean and Professor of Theatre*, Dr. Pauline Gagnon, 678-839-5450, E-mail: pgagnon@westga.edu.

**College of Social Sciences** Students: 88 full-time (60 women), 94 part-time (62 women); includes 72 minority (66 Black or African American, non-Hispanic/Latino; 4 Hispanic/Latino; 2 Two or more races, non-Hispanic/Latino), 4 international. Average age 34. 56 applicants, 79% accepted, 26 enrolled. *Faculty:* 48 full-time (22 women). Expenses: Contact institution. *Financial support:* Fellowships, research assistantships, teaching assistantships, career-related internships or fieldwork, Federal Work-Study, institutionally sponsored loans, scholarships/grants, and unspecified assistantships available. Support available to part-time students. Financial award application deadline: 4/1; financial award applicants required to submit FAFSA. *Program availability:* Part-time, evening/weekend, 100% online, blended/hybrid learning. *Application deadline:* For fall admission, 7/15 for domestic students, 6/1 for international students; for spring admission, 11/30 for domestic students, 10/15 for international students; for summer admission, 5/15 for domestic students, 3/30 for international students. Applications are processed on a rolling basis. *Application fee:* $40. Electronic applications accepted. *Application Contact:* Dr. Toby Ziglar, Assistant Dean of the Graduate School, 678-839-1394, Fax: 678-839-1395, E-mail: graduate@westga.edu. *Professor of Mass Comm and Interim Dean*, Dr. Amber Smallwood, 678-839-5170, E-mail: amksmall@westga.edu.

**Richards College of Business** Students: 49 full-time (36 women), 103 part-time (58 women); includes 55 minority (47 Black or African American, non-Hispanic/Latino; 2 Asian, non-Hispanic/Latino; 6 Hispanic/Latino), 8 international. Average age 29. 106 applicants, 92% accepted, 67 enrolled. *Faculty:* 38 full-time (15 women). Expenses: Contact institution. *Financial support:* Fellowships, research assistantships, teaching assistantships, career-related internships or fieldwork, Federal Work-Study, institutionally sponsored loans, scholarships/grants, and unspecified assistantships available. Support available to part-time students. Financial award application deadline: 4/1; financial award applicants required to submit FAFSA. *Program availability:* Part-time, evening/weekend, 100% online, blended/hybrid learning. *Application deadline:* For fall admission, 7/15 for domestic students, 6/1 for international students; for spring admission, 11/15 for domestic students, 10/15 for international students; for summer admission, 5/15 for domestic students, 3/30 for international students. Applications are processed on a rolling basis. *Application fee:* $40. Electronic applications accepted. *Application Contact:* Dr. Toby Ziglar, Assistant Dean of the Graduate School, 678-839-1394, Fax: 678-839-1395, E-mail: graduate@westga.edu. *Dean & Sewell Chair of Private Enterprise*, Dr. Faye McIntyre, 678-839-6467, E-mail: busn@westga.edu.

**Tanner Health System School of Nursing** Students: 5 full-time (all women), 113 part-time (106 women); includes 21 minority (18 Black or African American, non-Hispanic/Latino; 1 Hispanic/Latino; 2 Two or more races, non-Hispanic/Latino). Average age 39. 183 applicants, 55% accepted, 74 enrolled. *Faculty:* 12 full-time (all women). Expenses: Contact institution. *Financial support:* Fellowships, research assistantships, teaching assistantships, career-related internships or fieldwork, Federal Work-Study, institutionally sponsored loans, scholarships/grants, and unspecified assistantships available. Support available to part-time students. Financial award application deadline: 4/1; financial award applicants required to submit FAFSA. *Program availability:* Evening/weekend, 100% online, blended/hybrid learning. *Application deadline:* For fall admission, 2/1 for domestic and international students. Applications are processed on a rolling basis. *Application fee:* $40. Electronic applications accepted. *Application Contact:* Dr. Toby Ziglar, Assistant Dean of the Graduate School, 678-839-1394, Fax: 678-839-1395, E-mail: graduate@westga.edu. *Dean and Professor*, Jenny Schuessler, 678-839-6552, E-mail: nurs@westga.edu.

## UNIVERSITY OF WEST LOS ANGELES, Inglewood, CA 90301

**General Information** Proprietary, coed, upper-level institution. *Graduate housing:* On-campus housing not available.

**GRADUATE UNITS**

**School of Business**

**School of Law** *Program availability:* Part-time, evening/weekend. Electronic applications accepted.

## UNIVERSITY OF WINDSOR, Windsor, ON N9B 3P4, Canada

**General Information** Province-supported, coed, university. *Graduate housing:* Rooms and/or apartments available on a first-come, first-served basis to single and married students. Housing application deadline: 6/7. *Research affiliation:* Daimler/Chrysler Automotive Research and Development Centre.

**GRADUATE UNITS**

**Faculty of Graduate Studies** *Program availability:* Part-time, evening/weekend. Electronic applications accepted.

***Faculty of Arts and Social Sciences*** *Program availability:* Part-time. Electronic applications accepted.

***Faculty of Education*** *Program availability:* Part-time, evening/weekend. Electronic applications accepted.

***Faculty of Engineering*** *Program availability:* Part-time. Electronic applications accepted.

***Faculty of Human Kinetics*** *Program availability:* Part-time. Electronic applications accepted.

***Faculty of Nursing*** Electronic applications accepted.

***Faculty of Science*** *Program availability:* Part-time. Electronic applications accepted.

***GLIER-Great Lakes Institute for Environmental Research*** Electronic applications accepted.

***Odette School of Business*** *Program availability:* Evening/weekend. Electronic applications accepted.

## THE UNIVERSITY OF WINNIPEG, Winnipeg, MB R3B 2E9, Canada

**General Information** Province-supported, coed, comprehensive institution. *Graduate housing:* On-campus housing not available.

**GRADUATE UNITS**

**Faculty of Graduate Studies** Students: 240 full-time (138 women), 160 part-time (137 women). 667 applicants, 23% accepted, 70 enrolled. Expenses: Contact institution. *Financial support:* In 2019–20, 126 fellowships (averaging $7,760 per year), 11 research assistantships (averaging $7,250 per year) were awarded; teaching assistantships, career-related internships or fieldwork, scholarships/grants, and traineeships also available. Support available to part-time students. In 2019, 13 master's awarded. *Program availability:* Part-time. *Application deadline:* For fall admission, 2/1 for domestic and international students; for winter admission, 7/1 for domestic and international students; for spring admission, 12/1 for domestic and international students. *Application fee:* $100 Canadian dollars ($120 Canadian dollars for international students). Electronic applications accepted. *Application Contact:* Dagmawit Habtemariam, Graduate Studies Recruitment, Enrolment and Student Tracking Officer, 204-786-9309, Fax: 204-774-4134, E-mail: d.habtemariam@uwinnipeg.ca. *Dean of Arts and Sciences*, Dr. Mavis Reimer, 204-988-7625, E-mail: m.reimer@uwinnipeg.ca.

**Faculty of Theology** *Program availability:* Part-time.

## UNIVERSITY OF WISCONSIN–EAU CLAIRE, Eau Claire, WI 54702-4004

**General Information** State-supported, coed, comprehensive institution. CGS member. *Graduate housing:* Room and/or apartments available on a first-come, first-served basis to single students; on-campus housing not available to married students. Housing application deadline: 5/1. *Research affiliation:* Geological Survey of Canada (geology), Chevron Phillips Chemical Company (chemistry), Excel Energy (geography), American Chemical Society Petroleum Research Fund (chemistry, geology), ASIANetwork (anthropology, biology, geography), Research Corporation (chemistry).

**GRADUATE UNITS**

**College of Arts and Sciences** Electronic applications accepted.

**College of Business** Electronic applications accepted.

**College of Education and Human Sciences** Electronic applications accepted.

**College of Nursing and Health Sciences** Electronic applications accepted.

## UNIVERSITY OF WISCONSIN–GREEN BAY, Green Bay, WI 54311-7001

**General Information** State-supported, coed, comprehensive institution. *Graduate housing:* Room and/or apartments available on a first-come, first-served basis to single students; on-campus housing not available to married students. Housing application deadline: 5/1. *Research affiliation:* Wisconsin Space Grant Consortium (space and aerospace science), UW Sea Grant Institute (Great Lakes and ocean sustainability and stewardship), UW System Applied Research Program (biogas generation), UW Extension Solid and Hazardous Waste Education Center (sustainable use of natural resources), Abbott Laboratories (anaerobic digestion systems).

**GRADUATE UNITS**

**Graduate Studies** *Program availability:* Part-time, evening/weekend, 100% online. Electronic applications accepted.

## UNIVERSITY OF WISCONSIN–LA CROSSE, La Crosse, WI 54601-3742

**General Information** State-supported, coed, comprehensive institution. CGS member. *Enrollment:* 10,558 graduate, professional, and undergraduate students; 409 full-time matriculated graduate/professional students (257 women), 526 part-time matriculated graduate/professional students (310 women). *Enrollment by degree level:* 729 master's, 168 doctoral, 38 other advanced degrees. *Graduate faculty:* 94 full-time (37 women), 44 part-time/adjunct (37 women). *Graduate housing:* Room and/or apartments available on a first-come, first-served basis to single students; on-campus housing not available to married students. Housing application deadline: 5/1. *Student services:* Campus employment opportunities, campus safety program, career counseling, child daycare facilities, exercise/wellness program, free psychological counseling, grant writing training, international student services, low-cost health insurance, multicultural affairs office, services for students with disabilities, teacher training, writing training. *Library facilities:* Murphy Library plus 1 other. *Collection:* Books: 482,242 (physical), 906,635 (digital/electronic); Serial titles: 8,751 (physical), 133,564 (digital/electronic); Databases: 251. Weekly public service hours: 107; students can reserve study rooms.

**Computer facilities:** A campuswide network can be accessed. Online class registration is available.
Website: http://www.uwlax.edu/

**General Application Contact:** Jennifer Weber, Senior Student Services Coordinator Graduate Admissions, 608-785-8939, E-mail: admissions@uwlax.edu.

**GRADUATE UNITS**

**College of Arts, Social Sciences, and Humanities** Students: 53 full-time (40 women), 101 part-time (74 women); includes 39 minority (10 Black or African American, non-Hispanic/Latino; 1 American Indian or Alaska Native, non-Hispanic/Latino; 10 Asian, non-Hispanic/Latino; 10 Hispanic/Latino; 8 Two or more races, non-Hispanic/Latino), 2 international. Average age 28. 137 applicants, 64% accepted, 69 enrolled. *Faculty:* 9 full-time (6 women), 10 part-time/adjunct (all women). Expenses: Contact institution. *Financial support:* Research assistantships with partial tuition reimbursements, Federal Work-Study, scholarships/grants, health care benefits, and tuition waivers (partial) available. Support available to part-time students. Financial award applicants required to submit FAFSA. In 2019, 66 master's awarded. *Application fee:* $56. Electronic applications accepted. *Application Contact:* Jennifer Weber, Senior Student Services Coordinator Graduate Admissions, 608-785-8939, E-mail: admissions@uwlax.edu. *Dean*, Dr. Karl Kunkel, 608-785-8113, Fax: 608-785-8119, E-mail: kkunkel@uwlax.edu.

**College of Science and Health** Students: 356 full-time (217 women), 279 part-time (112 women); includes 60 minority (7 Black or African American, non-Hispanic/Latino; 1 American Indian or Alaska Native, non-Hispanic/Latino; 27 Asian, non-Hispanic/Latino; 13 Hispanic/Latino; 12 Two or more races, non-Hispanic/Latino), 39 international. Average age 28. 1,271 applicants, 28% accepted, 264 enrolled. *Faculty:* 82 full-time (30 women), 18 part-time/adjunct (15 women). Expenses: Contact institution. *Financial support:* Research assistantships with tuition reimbursements, Federal Work-Study, scholarships/grants, health care benefits, and tuition waivers (partial) available. Support available to part-time students. Financial award applicants required to submit CSS PROFILE or FAFSA. In 2019, 179 master's, 41 doctorates awarded. *Application fee:* $56. Electronic applications accepted. *Application Contact:* Jennifer Weber, Senior Student Services Coordinator Graduate Admissions, 608-785-8939, E-mail: admissions@uwlax.edu. *Interim Dean*, Dr. Mark Sandheinrich, 608-785-8261, Fax: 608-785-8221, E-mail: msandheinrich@uwlax.edu.

**School of Education** Students: 146 part-time (124 women); includes 11 minority (1 Black or African American, non-Hispanic/Latino; 1 American Indian or Alaska Native, non-Hispanic/Latino; 6 Hispanic/Latino; 3 Two or more races, non-Hispanic/Latino). Average age 35. 92 applicants, 99% accepted, 87 enrolled. *Faculty:* 3 full-time (1 woman), 16 part-time/adjunct (12 women). Expenses: Contact institution. *Financial support:* Research assistantships, Federal Work-Study, scholarships/grants, health care benefits, and tuition waivers (partial) available. Support available to part-time students. Financial award application deadline: 3/15; financial award applicants required to submit FAFSA. In 2019, 85 master's, 4 other advanced degrees awarded. *Program availability:* Part-time, evening/weekend. *Application deadline:* Applications are processed on a rolling basis. Electronic applications accepted. *Application Contact:* Jennifer Weber, Senior Student Services Coordinator Graduate Admissions, 608-785-8939, E-mail: admissions@uwlax.edu. *Dean, School of Education*, Marcie Wycoff-Horn, 608-785-6786, E-mail: mwycoff-horn@uwlax.edu.

## UNIVERSITY OF WISCONSIN–MADISON, Madison, WI 53706-1380

**General Information** State-supported, coed, university. CGS member. *Graduate housing:* Rooms and/or apartments available on a first-come, first-served basis to single and married students. *Research affiliation:* Morgridge Institute for Research (life sciences: biological sciences), WiCell Research Institute (life sciences: biological sciences), University of Wisconsin Hospitals and Clinics (life sciences: health and medical sciences), William S. Middleton Memorial Veterans Hospital (life sciences: health and medical sciences), Universities Research Association, Inc. (physical and earth sciences: physics and astronomy), U.S. Department of Agriculture (USDA), Dairy Forage Center (life sciences: agriculture).

**GRADUATE UNITS**

**Graduate School** *Program availability:* Part-time, evening/weekend, 100% online, blended/hybrid learning. Electronic applications accepted.

***College of Agricultural and Life Sciences*** *Program availability:* Part-time. Electronic applications accepted.

***College of Engineering*** Students: 1,373 full-time (349 women), 485 part-time (101 women); includes 226 minority (30 Black or African American, non-Hispanic/Latino; 1 American Indian or Alaska Native, non-Hispanic/Latino; 87 Asian, non-

Hispanic/Latino; 79 Hispanic/Latino; 1 Native Hawaiian or other Pacific Islander, non-Hispanic/Latino; 28 Two or more races, non-Hispanic/Latino), 897 international. Average age 27. 5,754 applicants, 30% accepted, 510 enrolled. *Faculty:* 204 full-time (40 women). Expenses: Contact institution. *Financial support:* In 2019–20, 1,197 students received support, including 75 fellowships with full tuition reimbursements available, 725 research assistantships with full tuition reimbursements available, 351 teaching assistantships with full tuition reimbursements available; career-related internships or fieldwork, Federal Work-Study, institutionally sponsored loans, scholarships/grants, health care benefits, and unspecified assistantships also available. Support available to part-time students. Financial award application deadline: 12/1; financial award applicants required to submit FAFSA. In 2019, 497 master's, 166 doctorates awarded. *Program availability:* Part-time, 100% online, blended/hybrid learning. *Application deadline:* Applications are processed on a rolling basis. *Application fee:* $75 ($81 for international students). Electronic applications accepted. *Application Contact:* Information Contact, 608-262-2433, Fax: 608-265-9505, E-mail: admissions@grad.wisc.edu. *Dean,* Dr. Ian M. Robertson, 608-262-3482, Fax: 608-262-6400, E-mail: engr-dean_engr@wisc.edu.

***College of Letters and Science*** *Program availability:* Part-time, evening/weekend, online learning. Electronic applications accepted.

***Gaylord Nelson Institute for Environmental Studies*** *Program availability:* Part-time. Electronic applications accepted.

***School of Education***

***School of Human Ecology*** Electronic applications accepted.

***Wisconsin School of Business*** Students: 462 full-time (174 women), 125 part-time (37 women); includes 71 minority (8 Black or African American, non-Hispanic/Latino; 2 American Indian or Alaska Native, non-Hispanic/Latino; 31 Asian, non-Hispanic/Latino; 17 Hispanic/Latino; 13 Two or more races, non-Hispanic/Latino), 131 international. Average age 29. 859 applicants, 48% accepted, 303 enrolled. *Faculty:* 291 full-time (76 women), 45 part-time/adjunct (16 women). Expenses: Contact institution. *Financial support:* In 2019–20, 222 students received support, including 8 fellowships with full tuition reimbursements available (averaging $22,140 per year), 19 research assistantships with full tuition reimbursements available (averaging $20,304 per year), 96 teaching assistantships with full tuition reimbursements available (averaging $14,375 per year); career-related internships or fieldwork, scholarships/grants, health care benefits, and unspecified assistantships also available. Support available to part-time students. In 2019, 284 master's, 9 doctorates awarded. *Program availability:* Part-time, evening/weekend. *Application deadline:* For fall admission, 7/15 for domestic and international students; for winter admission, 1/10 for domestic and international students; for spring admission, 3/1 for domestic and international students; for summer admission, 4/27 for domestic and international students. Applications are processed on a rolling basis. *Application fee:* $75 ($81 for international students). Electronic applications accepted. *Application Contact:* Betsy Kacizak, Director of Admissions and Recruiting, Full-time MBA Program, 608-262-4000, E-mail: betsy.kacizak@wisc.edu. *Associate Dean of the MBA and Masters Programs,* Dr. Enno Siemsen, 608-890-3130, E-mail: esiemsen@wisc.edu.

**Law School** *Program availability:* Part-time, evening/weekend. Electronic applications accepted.

**School of Medicine and Public Health** Electronic applications accepted.

**School of Nursing** *Program availability:* Part-time. Electronic applications accepted.

**School of Pharmacy** Electronic applications accepted.

**School of Veterinary Medicine**

## UNIVERSITY OF WISCONSIN–MILWAUKEE, Milwaukee, WI 53201-0413

**General Information** State-supported, coed, university. CGS member. *Graduate housing:* Rooms and/or apartments available on a first-come, first-served basis to single and married students. Housing application deadline: 5/1. *Research affiliation:* GE Healthcare (informatics, biomedical imaging), Veolia Water S. A. (water research), We Energies (environment, wind turbine technology), Rockwell Automation (informatics, sensors and devices, materials), Johnson Controls (environment, advanced automation).

**GRADUATE UNITS**

**Graduate School** *Program availability:* Part-time, evening/weekend. Electronic applications accepted.

***College of Engineering and Applied Science*** *Program availability:* Part-time. Electronic applications accepted.

***College of Health Sciences*** *Program availability:* Part-time.

***College of Letters and Science*** *Program availability:* Part-time. Electronic applications accepted.

***College of Nursing*** *Program availability:* Part-time. Electronic applications accepted.

***Helen Bader School of Social Welfare*** *Program availability:* Part-time. Electronic applications accepted.

***Joseph J. Zilber School of Public Health*** *Program availability:* Part-time. Electronic applications accepted.

***Lubar School of Business*** *Program availability:* Part-time, evening/weekend. Electronic applications accepted.

***Peck School of the Arts*** *Program availability:* Part-time. Electronic applications accepted.

***School of Architecture and Urban Planning*** *Program availability:* Part-time. Electronic applications accepted.

***School of Education*** *Program availability:* Part-time. Electronic applications accepted.

***School of Freshwater Sciences*** Electronic applications accepted.

***School of Information Studies*** *Program availability:* Part-time. Electronic applications accepted.

## UNIVERSITY OF WISCONSIN–OSHKOSH, Oshkosh, WI 54901

**General Information** State-supported, coed, comprehensive institution. *Graduate housing:* Room and/or apartments available on a first-come, first-served basis to single students; on-campus housing not available to married students.

**GRADUATE UNITS**

**Graduate Studies** *Program availability:* Part-time, evening/weekend. Electronic applications accepted.

***College of Business*** *Program availability:* Part-time. Electronic applications accepted.

***College of Education and Human Services*** *Program availability:* Part-time, evening/weekend. Electronic applications accepted.

***College of Letters and Science*** *Program availability:* Part-time, evening/weekend. Electronic applications accepted.

***College of Nursing*** *Program availability:* Part-time. Electronic applications accepted.

## UNIVERSITY OF WISCONSIN–PARKSIDE, Kenosha, WI 53141-2000

**General Information** State-supported, coed, comprehensive institution. *Enrollment:* 4,420 graduate, professional, and undergraduate students; 151 full-time matriculated graduate/professional students (73 women), 331 part-time matriculated graduate/professional students (158 women). *Enrollment by degree level:* 481 master's, 1 other advanced degree. *Graduate faculty:* 46 full-time (21 women), 2 part-time/adjunct (0 women). *International tuition:* $18,767 full-time. *Tuition, area resident:* Full-time $9173; part-time $509.64 per credit. Tuition, state resident: full-time $9173; part-time $509.64 per credit. Tuition, nonresident: full-time $18,767; part-time $1042.64 per credit. *Required fees:* $1123.20; $63.64 per credit. Tuition and fees vary according to campus/location, program and reciprocity agreements. *Graduate housing:* Room and/or apartments available on a first-come, first-served basis to single students; on-campus housing not available to married students. Typical cost: $4562 per year ($8200 including board). Room and board charges vary according to board plan and housing facility selected. Housing application deadline: 6/1. *Student services:* Campus employment opportunities, campus safety program, career counseling, child daycare facilities, exercise/wellness program, free psychological counseling, international student services, low-cost health insurance, multicultural affairs office, services for students with disabilities. *Library facilities:* UWP Library. *Collection:* Books: 406,756 (physical); Serial titles: 1,277 (physical). Weekly public service hours: 75; students can reserve study rooms.

**Computer facilities:** 376 computers available on campus for general student use. A campuswide network can be accessed. Online class registration, online tutoring; online advising are available.
Website: http://www.uwp.edu/

**General Application Contact:** Richard Barth, Interim AVC of Enrollment Services and Director of Admissions, 262-595-2355, Fax: 262-595-2630, E-mail: admissions@uwp.edu.

**GRADUATE UNITS**

**College of Business, Economics, and Computing** *Program availability:* Part-time, evening/weekend. Electronic applications accepted.

**College of Natural and Health Sciences** *Program availability:* Part-time. Electronic applications accepted.

## UNIVERSITY OF WISCONSIN–PLATTEVILLE, Platteville, WI 53818-3099

**General Information** State-supported, coed, comprehensive institution. *Enrollment:* 8,240 graduate, professional, and undergraduate students; 63 full-time matriculated graduate/professional students (40 women), 674 part-time matriculated graduate/professional students (282 women). *Enrollment by degree level:* 737 master's. *Graduate housing:* On-campus housing not available. *Student services:* Campus employment opportunities, campus safety program, career counseling, child daycare facilities, exercise/wellness program, free psychological counseling, grant writing training, international student services, multicultural affairs office, services for students with disabilities, teacher training, writing training. *Library facilities:* Karrmann Library plus 1 other. *Collection:* Books: 167,304 (physical), 59,292 (digital/electronic); Serial titles: 1,151 (physical), 44,687 (digital/electronic); Databases: 123. Weekly public service hours: 87.

**Computer facilities:** 200 computers available on campus for general student use. A campuswide network can be accessed from student residence rooms and from off campus. Online class registration is available.
Website: http://www.uwplatt.edu/

**General Application Contact:** Dee Dunbar, School of Graduate Studies, 608-342-1322, E-mail: gradstudies@uwplatt.edu.

**GRADUATE UNITS**

**School of Graduate Studies** *Program availability:* Part-time, evening/weekend, online learning. Electronic applications accepted.

***College of Engineering, Mathematics and Science*** *Program availability:* Part-time.

***College of Liberal Arts and Education*** *Program availability:* Part-time, evening/weekend. Electronic applications accepted.

***Distance Learning Center*** *Program availability:* Part-time, evening/weekend. Electronic applications accepted.

## UNIVERSITY OF WISCONSIN–RIVER FALLS, River Falls, WI 54022

**General Information** State-supported, coed, comprehensive institution. *Graduate housing:* Room and/or apartments available on a first-come, first-served basis to single students; on-campus housing not available to married students.

**GRADUATE UNITS**

**Outreach and Graduate Studies** *Program availability:* Part-time. Electronic applications accepted.

***College of Agriculture, Food, and Environmental Sciences*** *Program availability:* Part-time. Electronic applications accepted.

***College of Arts and Science*** *Program availability:* Part-time. Electronic applications accepted.

***College of Business and Economics*** Electronic applications accepted.

***College of Education and Professional Studies*** *Program availability:* Part-time.

## UNIVERSITY OF WISCONSIN–STEVENS POINT, Stevens Point, WI 54481-3897

**General Information** State-supported, coed, comprehensive institution. *Graduate housing:* Room and/or apartments available on a first-come, first-served basis to single students; on-campus housing not available to married students.

**GRADUATE UNITS**

**College of Fine Arts and Communication** *Program availability:* Part-time.

***Division of Communication*** *Program availability:* Part-time.

**College of Letters and Science**

**College of Natural Resources** *Program availability:* Part-time.

**College of Professional Studies** *Program availability:* Part-time.

***School of Communication Sciences and Disorders***

***School of Education*** *Program availability:* Part-time.

***School of Health Care Professions***

***School of Health Promotion and Human Development*** *Program availability:* Part-time.

## UNIVERSITY OF WISCONSIN–STOUT, Menomonie, WI 54751

**General Information** State-supported, coed, comprehensive institution. *Graduate housing:* Room and/or apartments available on a first-come, first-served basis to single students; on-campus housing not available to married students.

**GRADUATE UNITS**

**Graduate School** *Program availability:* Part-time, online learning. Electronic applications accepted.

***College of Arts, Humanities and Social Sciences***

***College of Education, Health and Human Sciences*** *Program availability:* Part-time, online learning. Electronic applications accepted.

***College of Management***

***College of Science, Technology, Engineering and Mathematics*** *Program availability:* Part-time, online learning. Electronic applications accepted.

## UNIVERSITY OF WISCONSIN–SUPERIOR, Superior, WI 54880-4500

**General Information** State-supported, coed, comprehensive institution. *Graduate housing:* Rooms and/or apartments available on a first-come, first-served basis to single students and available to married students. Housing application deadline: 7/1. *Research affiliation:* Great Lakes Indian Fish and Wildlife Commission, Wisconsin Department of Natural Resources (biology), Environmental Protection Agency (biology), The Mexican National Institute for Ecology (biology), The Mexican Marine National Park Service (biology), Coastal Zone Management Institute and Authority of Belize (biology), Fisheries Department, Government of Belize (biology).

**GRADUATE UNITS**

**Graduate Division** *Program availability:* Part-time, evening/weekend, online learning. Electronic applications accepted.

## UNIVERSITY OF WISCONSIN–WHITEWATER, Whitewater, WI 53190-1790

**General Information** State-supported, coed, comprehensive institution. CGS member. *Graduate housing:* Rooms and/or apartments available on a first-come, first-served basis to single students and available to married students. Housing application deadline: 9/1. *Research affiliation:* Generac Power Systems (manufacturing), American Ag-Tec International (international marketing), American Family Insurance (insurance), R.A. Smith and Associates (civil engineering), Sho-Deen (property management and development), Webco Industries, Inc. (lightning radioactive transfer).

**GRADUATE UNITS**

**School of Graduate Studies** *Program availability:* Part-time, evening/weekend, online learning. Electronic applications accepted.

***College of Arts and Communications*** *Program availability:* Part-time, evening/weekend, online learning. Electronic applications accepted.

***College of Business and Economics*** *Program availability:* Part-time, evening/weekend, online learning. Electronic applications accepted.

***College of Education and Professional Studies*** *Program availability:* Part-time, evening/weekend, online learning. Electronic applications accepted.

***College of Letters and Sciences*** *Program availability:* Part-time, evening/weekend. Electronic applications accepted.

## UNIVERSITY OF WYOMING, Laramie, WY 82071

**General Information** State-supported, coed, university. CGS member. *Graduate housing:* Rooms and/or apartments available on a first-come, first-served basis to single and married students.

**GRADUATE UNITS**

**College of Agriculture and Natural Resources** *Program availability:* Part-time. Electronic applications accepted.

**College of Arts and Sciences** *Program availability:* Part-time. Electronic applications accepted.

***School of Politics, Public Affairs and International Studies*** *Program availability:* Part-time. Electronic applications accepted.

**College of Business** *Program availability:* Part-time, evening/weekend, online learning.

**College of Education** *Program availability:* Online learning. Electronic applications accepted.

***Science and Mathematics Teaching Center*** Electronic applications accepted.

**College of Engineering and Applied Science** *Program availability:* Part-time. Electronic applications accepted.

**College of Health Sciences** *Program availability:* Part-time, online learning. Electronic applications accepted.

***Division of Communication Disorders*** *Program availability:* Part-time, online learning. Electronic applications accepted.

***Division of Kinesiology and Health*** *Program availability:* Part-time, online learning. Electronic applications accepted.

***Division of Social Work***

***Fay W. Whitney School of Nursing*** *Program availability:* Part-time, online learning.

***School of Pharmacy*** *Program availability:* Online learning.

**College of Law** Electronic applications accepted.

**Graduate Program in Molecular and Cellular Life Sciences**

**Program in Ecology**

## UNIVERSITÉ LAVAL, Québec, QC G1K 7P4, Canada

**General Information** Independent, coed, university. *Graduate housing:* Room and/or apartments available on a first-come, first-served basis to single students; on-campus housing not available to married students. *Research affiliation:* Centre Hospitalier Universitaire de Quebec (biomedical research), Institut National d'optique (optics and photonics), Centre de Developpement de la Geomatique (applied geomatics), Institut Maurice-Lamontagne (oceanography), Forintek Canada (forestry and wood processing), Societe des pades de Sciences Naturelles du Quebec (biology).

**GRADUATE UNITS**

**Faculty of Administrative Sciences** *Program availability:* Part-time, online learning. Electronic applications accepted.

**Faculty of Agricultural and Food Sciences** *Program availability:* Part-time. Electronic applications accepted.

**Faculty of Architecture, Planning and Visual Arts** Electronic applications accepted.

***School of Architecture*** *Program availability:* Part-time. Electronic applications accepted.

***School of Visual Arts*** Electronic applications accepted.

**Faculty of Dentistry** Electronic applications accepted.

**Faculty of Education** *Program availability:* Part-time. Electronic applications accepted.

**Faculty of Forestry, Geography and Geomatics** Electronic applications accepted.

**Faculty of Law** *Program availability:* Part-time. Electronic applications accepted.

**Faculty of Letters** *Program availability:* Part-time. Electronic applications accepted.

**Faculty of Medicine** *Program availability:* Part-time. Electronic applications accepted.

**Faculty of Music** Electronic applications accepted.

**Faculty of Nursing** Electronic applications accepted.

**Faculty of Pharmacy** *Program availability:* Part-time. Electronic applications accepted.

**Faculty of Philosophy** Electronic applications accepted.

**Faculty of Sciences and Engineering** *Program availability:* Part-time. Electronic applications accepted.

**Faculty of Social Sciences** *Program availability:* Part-time. Electronic applications accepted.

***School of Psychology*** Electronic applications accepted.

***School of Social Work*** Electronic applications accepted.

**Faculty of Theology and Religious Sciences** Electronic applications accepted.

**Québec Institute for Advanced International Studies** Electronic applications accepted.

## UNIVERSITÉ TÉLUQ, Québec, QC G1K 9H5, Canada

**General Information** Province-supported, coed, comprehensive institution. *Graduate housing:* On-campus housing not available.

**GRADUATE UNITS**

**Graduate Programs** *Program availability:* Part-time.

## UPPER IOWA UNIVERSITY, Fayette, IA 52142-1857

**General Information** Independent, coed, comprehensive institution. *Graduate housing:* Room and/or apartments available to single students.

**GRADUATE UNITS**

**Master of Education Program**

**Online Master's Programs** *Program availability:* Part-time, online learning. Electronic applications accepted.

## URBANA UNIVERSITY–A BRANCH CAMPUS OF FRANKLIN UNIVERSITY, Urbana, OH 43078-2091

**General Information** Independent, coed, comprehensive institution. *Graduate housing:* Room and/or apartments available on a first-come, first-served basis to single students; on-campus housing not available to married students.

**GRADUATE UNITS**

**College of Education and Sports Studies** *Program availability:* Part-time, evening/weekend.

**College of Nursing and Allied Health**

**College of Social and Behavioral Sciences**

**Division of Business Administration** *Program availability:* Part-time, evening/weekend.

## URSHAN GRADUATE SCHOOL OF THEOLOGY, Florissant, MO 63031

**General Information** Independent-religious, coed, graduate-only institution.

**GRADUATE UNITS**

**Graduate Programs** *Program availability:* Online learning.

## URSULINE COLLEGE, Pepper Pike, OH 44124-4398

**General Information** Independent-religious, coed, primarily women, comprehensive institution. *Enrollment:* 1,116 graduate, professional, and undergraduate students; 210 full-time matriculated graduate/professional students (188 women), 185 part-time matriculated graduate/professional students (148 women). *Enrollment by degree level:* 324 master's, 14 doctoral, 55 other advanced degrees. *Graduate faculty:* 19 full-time (15 women), 45 part-time/adjunct (29 women). *Tuition:* Full-time $18,784; part-time $1174 per credit hour. *Required fees:* $320; $240 per unit. One-time fee: $100. Tuition and fees vary according to course level and program. *Graduate housing:* Room and/or apartments available on a first-come, first-served basis to single students; on-campus housing not available to married students. Typical cost: $13,870 (including board). Housing application deadline: 8/20. *Student services:* Campus employment opportunities, career counseling, exercise/wellness program, free psychological counseling, multicultural affairs office, services for students with disabilities, teacher training, writing training. *Library facilities:* Ralph M. Besse Library. *Collection:* Books: 92,462 (physical), 351,238 (digital/electronic); Serial titles: 284 (physical), 59,448 (digital/electronic); Databases: 162. Weekly public service hours: 94; students can reserve study rooms.

**Computer facilities:** 120 computers available on campus for general student use. A campuswide network can be accessed. Online class registration is available.
Website: http://www.ursuline.edu/

**General Application Contact:** Melanie Steele, Director, Graduate Admission, 440-646-8119, Fax: 440-684-6138, E-mail: graduateadmissions@ursuline.edu.

**GRADUATE UNITS**

**School of Graduate and Professional Studies** Students: 210 full-time (188 women), 189 part-time (152 women); includes 113 minority (78 Black or African American, non-Hispanic/Latino; 2 American Indian or Alaska Native, non-Hispanic/Latino; 16 Asian, non-Hispanic/Latino; 8 Hispanic/Latino; 9 Two or more races, non-Hispanic/Latino). Average age 37. 275 applicants, 98% accepted, 127 enrolled. *Faculty:* 19 full-time (15 women), 45 part-time/adjunct (29 women). Expenses: Contact institution. *Financial support:* In 2019–20, 49 students received support. Federal Work-Study, scholarships/grants, and tuition waivers (partial) available. Financial award application deadline: 3/1; financial award applicants required to submit FAFSA. In 2019, 150 master's, 2 doctorates awarded. *Program availability:* Part-time, 100% online. *Application deadline:* For fall admission, 8/1 priority date for domestic students. Applications are processed on a rolling basis. *Application fee:* $25. Electronic applications accepted. *Application Contact:* Melanie Steele, Director, Graduate Admission, 440-646-8146, Fax: 440-684-6138, E-mail: graduateadmissions@ursuline.edu. *Dean*, Dr. Elizabeth Kavran, 440-449-2015, E-mail: ekavran@ursuline.edu.

## UTAH STATE UNIVERSITY, Logan, UT 84322

**General Information** State-supported, coed, university. CGS member. *Graduate housing:* Rooms and/or apartments available on a first-come, first-served basis to single and married students. *Research affiliation:* Boeing Aerospace and Engineering (science and engineering), Duke Energy Corporation (engineering), Kennecott Copper Corporation (natural resources), Kraft Foods, Inc. (agriculture), National Endowment for Financial Education (education).

**GRADUATE UNITS**

**School of Graduate Studies** *Program availability:* Part-time, evening/weekend, online learning.

***Caine College of the Arts***

***College of Agriculture and Applied Sciences*** *Program availability:* Part-time, online learning.

***College of Engineering*** *Program availability:* Part-time, evening/weekend. Electronic applications accepted.

***College of Humanities and Social Sciences*** *Program availability:* Part-time, evening/weekend, online learning.

***College of Science*** *Program availability:* Part-time, evening/weekend.

***Emma Eccles Jones College of Education and Human Services*** *Program availability:* Part-time, evening/weekend, online learning.

***Jon M. Huntsman School of Business*** *Program availability:* Part-time, evening/weekend, online learning.

***S.J. and Jessie E. Quinney College of Natural Resources*** *Program availability:* Part-time.

## UTAH VALLEY UNIVERSITY, Orem, UT 84058-5999

**General Information** State-supported, coed, comprehensive institution. *Enrollment:* 41,728 graduate, professional, and undergraduate students; 194 full-time matriculated graduate/professional students (117 women), 340 part-time matriculated graduate/professional students (135 women). *Enrollment by degree level:* 517 master's, 17 other advanced degrees. Tuition and fees vary according to program. *Graduate housing:* On-campus housing not available. *Student services:* Campus employment opportunities, campus safety program, career counseling, child daycare facilities, exercise/wellness program, free psychological counseling, grant writing training, international student services, low-cost health insurance, multicultural affairs office, services for students with disabilities, teacher training. *Library facilities:* Utah Valley University Library plus 1 other. *Collection:* Books: 194,315 (physical), 341,537 (digital/electronic); Serial titles: 16,301 (physical), 602,769 (digital/electronic); Databases: 220. Students can reserve study rooms.

**Computer facilities:** A campuswide network can be accessed. Online class registration is available.
Website: http://www.uvu.edu/

**General Application Contact:** Shauna Reher, Administrative Assistant, 801-863-7348, E-mail: graduate_studies@uvu.edu.

**GRADUATE UNITS**

**MBA Program** Students: 32 full-time (9 women), 121 part-time (25 women); includes 19 minority (1 Black or African American, non-Hispanic/Latino; 2 Asian, non-Hispanic/Latino; 14 Hispanic/Latino; 2 Two or more races, non-Hispanic/Latino), 3 international. Average age 30. 190 applicants, 38% accepted, 73 enrolled. Expenses: Contact institution. *Financial support:* Applicants required to submit FAFSA. In 2019, 100 master's awarded. *Program availability:* Part-time, evening/weekend. *Application deadline:* For fall admission, 2/1 priority date for domestic and international students. Applications are processed on a rolling basis. *Application fee:* $45. Electronic applications accepted. *Application Contact:* Matthew Moon, Admissions and Marketing Coordinator, E-mail: mmoon@uvu.edu. *Director*, Bill Neal, 801-863-6148, E-mail: william.neal@uvu.edu.

**Program in Cybersecurity** Students: 4 full-time (1 woman), 25 part-time (3 women); includes 6 minority (2 Black or African American, non-Hispanic/Latino; 1 Asian, non-Hispanic/Latino; 2 Hispanic/Latino; 1 Two or more races, non-Hispanic/Latino). Average age 35. 27 applicants, 41% accepted, 11 enrolled. *Faculty:* 2 full-time. Expenses: Contact institution. *Financial support:* Applicants required to submit FAFSA. *Program availability:* Part-time. *Application Contact:* Shauna Reher, Administrative Assistant, 801-863-7348, E-mail: graduate_studies@uvu.edu. *Director*, Robert Jorgensen, 801-863-5282, E-mail: robert.jorgensen@uvu.edu.

**Program in Education** Students: 14 full-time (12 women), 81 part-time (53 women); includes 17 minority (1 Black or African American, non-Hispanic/Latino; 2 American Indian or Alaska Native, non-Hispanic/Latino; 10 Hispanic/Latino; 1 Native Hawaiian or other Pacific Islander, non-Hispanic/Latino; 3 Two or more races, non-Hispanic/Latino). Average age 35. 5 applicants, 40% accepted, 2 enrolled. Expenses: Contact institution. *Financial support:* Scholarships/grants available. Financial award application deadline: 5/1; financial award applicants required to submit FAFSA. In 2019, 22 master's awarded. *Program availability:* Part-time. *Application deadline:* For fall admission, 1/10 for domestic and international students. Applications are processed on a rolling basis. *Application fee:* $45. Electronic applications accepted. *Application Contact:* LynnEl Springer, Admin Support III, 801-863-8228. *Director of Graduate Studies*, Deborah Escalante, 801-863-8228.

**Program in Nursing** *Program availability:* Part-time, online learning. Electronic applications accepted.

**Program in Social Work**

## UTICA COLLEGE, Utica, NY 13502-4892

**General Information** Independent, coed, comprehensive institution. *Enrollment:* 4,947 graduate, professional, and undergraduate students; 990 full-time matriculated graduate/professional students (538 women), 484 part-time matriculated graduate/professional students (265 women). *Enrollment by degree level:* 1,086 master's, 339 doctoral, 36 other advanced degrees. *Graduate faculty:* 65 full-time (28 women). *Graduate housing:* Room and/or apartments available on a first-come, first-served basis to single students; on-campus housing not available to married students. Housing application deadline: 3/1. *Student services:* Campus employment opportunities, campus safety program, career counseling, international student services, low-cost health insurance, services for students with disabilities. *Library facilities:* Frank E. Gannett Memorial Library. *Collection:* Books: 307,523 (physical); Serial titles: 267,023 (physical). Students can reserve study rooms.

**Computer facilities:** 430 computers available on campus for general student use. A campuswide network can be accessed. Online class registration is available.
Website: http://www.utica.edu/

**General Application Contact:** John D. Rowe, Director of Graduate Admissions, 315-792-3824, Fax: 315-792-3003, E-mail: jrowe@utica.edu.

**GRADUATE UNITS**

**Department of Physical Therapy** Students: 86 full-time (46 women), 386 part-time (253 women); includes 246 minority (17 Black or African American, non-Hispanic/Latino; 220 Asian, non-Hispanic/Latino; 8 Hispanic/Latino; 1 Native Hawaiian or other Pacific Islander, non-Hispanic/Latino), 4 international. Average age 34. 240 applicants, 98% accepted, 232 enrolled. *Faculty:* 10 full-time (4 women). Expenses: Contact institution. *Financial support:* Career-related internships or fieldwork, scholarships/grants, tuition waivers (partial), and unspecified assistantships available. Support available to part-time students. Financial award application deadline: 3/15; financial award applicants required to submit FAFSA. In 2019, 299 doctorates awarded. *Program availability:* Part-time, evening/weekend, online learning. *Application deadline:* Applications are processed on a rolling basis. *Application fee:* $50. Electronic applications accepted. *Application Contact:* John D. Rowe, Director of Graduate Admissions, 315-792-3824, Fax: 315-792-3003, E-mail: jrowe@utica.edu. *Director*, Dr. Ashraf Elazzazi, 315-792-3313, E-mail: aelazza@utica.edu.

**Graduate Certificate Programs**

**MBA in Economic Crime and Fraud Management** Students: 50 full-time (35 women), 14 part-time (6 women); includes 17 minority (6 Black or African American, non-Hispanic/Latino; 1 American Indian or Alaska Native, non-Hispanic/Latino; 5 Asian, non-Hispanic/Latino; 4 Hispanic/Latino; 1 Two or more races, non-Hispanic/Latino). Average age 33. 31 applicants, 61% accepted, 17 enrolled. *Faculty:* 4 full-time (0 women). Expenses: Contact institution. *Financial support:* Career-related internships or fieldwork, scholarships/grants, tuition waivers (partial), and unspecified assistantships available. Support available to part-time students. Financial award application deadline: 3/15; financial award applicants required to submit FAFSA. In 2019, 49 master's awarded. *Program availability:* Part-time, evening/weekend, online learning. *Application deadline:* Applications are processed on a rolling basis. *Application fee:* $50. Electronic applications accepted. *Application Contact:* John D. Rowe, Director of Graduate Admissions, 315-792-3824, Fax: 315-792-3003, E-mail: jrowe@utica.edu. *Director of Economic Crime Graduate Programs*, Dr. R. Bruce McBride, 315-792-3808, E-mail: rmcbride@utica.edu.

**MBA Program in Management**

**MPS Program in Cyber Policy and Risk Analysis**

**Program in Accountancy** Students: 9 full-time (6 women), 3 part-time (2 women); includes 5 minority (1 Black or African American, non-Hispanic/Latino; 1 Asian, non-Hispanic/Latino; 3 Hispanic/Latino). Average age 25. 11 applicants, 64% accepted, 6 enrolled. *Faculty:* 3 full-time (1 woman). Expenses: Contact institution. *Financial support:* Career-related internships or fieldwork, scholarships/grants, tuition waivers (partial), and unspecified assistantships available. Support available to part-time students. Financial award application deadline: 3/15; financial award applicants required to submit FAFSA. In 2019, 13 master's awarded. *Program availability:* Part-time, evening/weekend. *Application deadline:* Applications are processed on a rolling basis. *Application fee:* $50. Electronic applications accepted. *Application Contact:* John D. Rowe, Director of Graduate Admissions, 315-792-3824, Fax: 315-792-3003, E-mail: jrowe@utica.edu. *MBA Director*, Dr. Zhaodan Huang, 315-792-3247, E-mail: zhuang@utica.edu.

**Program in Cybersecurity** Students: 280 full-time (75 women), 88 part-time (32 women); includes 97 minority (52 Black or African American, non-Hispanic/Latino; 1 American Indian or Alaska Native, non-Hispanic/Latino; 15 Asian, non-Hispanic/Latino; 23 Hispanic/Latino; 6 Two or more races, non-Hispanic/Latino). Average age 34. 232 applicants, 78% accepted, 148 enrolled. *Faculty:* 5 full-time (0 women), 8 part-time/adjunct (0 women). Expenses: Contact institution. *Financial support:* Application deadline: 3/15; applicants required to submit FAFSA. In 2019, 155 master's awarded. *Program availability:* Part-time, evening/weekend, 100% online. *Application deadline:* Applications are processed on a rolling basis. Electronic applications accepted. *Application Contact:* John D. Rowe, Director of Graduate Admissions, 315-792-3824, Fax: 315-792-3003, E-mail: jrowe@utica.edu. *Chair*, Joseph Giordano, 315-792-2521.

**Program in Data Science**

**Program in Economic Crime and Fraud Management** *Program availability:* Part-time, evening/weekend, 100% online. Electronic applications accepted.

**Program in Health Care Administration** *Program availability:* Part-time, evening/weekend, online learning. Electronic applications accepted.

**Program in Nursing**

**Program in Occupational Therapy** Students: 88 full-time (80 women), 1 part-time (0 women); includes 10 minority (2 Black or African American, non-Hispanic/Latino; 2 Asian, non-Hispanic/Latino; 5 Hispanic/Latino; 1 Two or more races, non-Hispanic/Latino), 1 international. Average age 25. 65 applicants, 98% accepted, 57 enrolled. *Faculty:* 7 full-time (all women). Expenses: Contact institution. *Financial support:* Career-related internships or fieldwork, scholarships/grants, tuition waivers (partial), and unspecified assistantships available. Support available to part-time students. Financial award application deadline: 3/15; financial award applicants required to submit FAFSA. In 2019, 59 master's awarded. *Program availability:* Part-time, evening/weekend. *Application deadline:* Applications are processed on a rolling basis. *Application fee:* $50. Electronic applications accepted. *Application Contact:* John D. Rowe, Director of Graduate Admissions, 315-792-3824, Fax: 315-792-3003, E-mail: jrowe@utica.edu. *Director*, Cora Bruns, 315-792-3125, E-mail: cbruns@utica.edu.

**Teacher Education Programs** Students: 58 full-time (36 women), 20 part-time (13 women); includes 10 minority (3 Black or African American, non-Hispanic/Latino; 1 Asian, non-Hispanic/Latino; 4 Hispanic/Latino; 2 Two or more races, non-Hispanic/Latino). Average age 28. 85 applicants, 65% accepted, 46 enrolled. *Faculty:* 10 full-time (7 women). Expenses: Contact institution. *Financial support:* Career-related internships or fieldwork, scholarships/grants, tuition waivers (partial), and unspecified assistantships available. Support available to part-time students. Financial award application deadline: 3/15; financial award applicants required to submit FAFSA. In 2019, 17 master's awarded. *Application deadline:* Applications are processed on a rolling basis. *Application fee:* $50. Electronic applications accepted. *Application Contact:* John D. Rowe, Director of Graduate Admissions, 315-792-3824, Fax: 315-792-3003, E-mail: jrowe@utica.edu. *Dean of Health Professions and Education*, Dr. Patrice Hallock, 315-792-3162, E-mail: phallock@utica.edu.

## VALDOSTA STATE UNIVERSITY, Valdosta, GA 31698

**General Information** State-supported, coed, university. CGS member. *Graduate housing:* Rooms and/or apartments available on a first-come, first-served basis to single and married students. Housing application deadline: 7/1.

**GRADUATE UNITS**

**College of Nursing and Health Sciences** *Program availability:* Part-time, online learning. Electronic applications accepted.

**Department of Communication Sciences and Disorders** Electronic applications accepted.

**Department of Curriculum, Leadership, and Technology** *Program availability:* 100% online, blended/hybrid learning. Electronic applications accepted.

**Department of Elementary Education** *Program availability:* Part-time, evening/weekend, blended/hybrid learning. Electronic applications accepted.

**Department of English** *Program availability:* Part-time, 100% online, blended/hybrid learning. Electronic applications accepted.

**Department of Political Science** *Program availability:* Part-time, evening/weekend, online learning. Electronic applications accepted.

**Department of Psychology, Counseling, and Family Therapy** *Program availability:* Part-time, evening/weekend, 100% online, blended/hybrid learning. Electronic applications accepted.

**Department of Social Work** *Program availability:* Part-time, evening/weekend, online learning.

**Langdale College of Business** *Program availability:* Part-time, evening/weekend, 100% online, blended/hybrid learning. Electronic applications accepted.

**Program in Library and Information Science** *Program availability:* 100% online.

## VALLEY CITY STATE UNIVERSITY, Valley City, ND 58072

**General Information** State-supported, coed, comprehensive institution. *Enrollment:* 1,665 graduate, professional, and undergraduate students; 5 full-time matriculated graduate/professional students (3 women), 125 part-time matriculated graduate/professional students (97 women). *Enrollment by degree level:* 130 master's. *Graduate faculty:* 23 full-time (13 women), 11 part-time/adjunct (5 women). *International tuition:* $402 full-time. *Tuition, area resident:* Full-time $402; part-time $402 per credit. Tuition, state resident: full-time $402; part-time $402 per credit. Tuition, nonresident: full-time $402; part-time $402 per credit. *Required fees:* $75.96; $75.96 per credit. *Graduate housing:* On-campus housing not available. *Student services:* Campus safety program, career counseling, free psychological counseling, services for students with disabilities, teacher training, writing training. *Library facilities:* Allen Memorial Library. *Collection:* Books: 77,906 (physical), 140,050 (digital/electronic); Serial titles: 1,301 (physical), 29,378 (digital/electronic); Databases: 86. Weekly public service hours: 61; students can reserve study rooms.

**Computer facilities:** Computer purchase and lease plans are available. 1,200 computers available on campus for general student use. A campuswide network can be accessed. Online class registration is available.
Website: http://www.vcsu.edu/

**General Application Contact:** Misty Lindgren, Coordinator of Extended Learning, 701-845-7303, Fax: 701-845-7190, E-mail: misty.lindgren@vcsu.edu.

**GRADUATE UNITS**

**Online Graduate Programs** Students: 5 full-time (3 women), 125 part-time (97 women); includes 6 minority (1 Black or African American, non-Hispanic/Latino; 2 American Indian or Alaska Native, non-Hispanic/Latino; 2 Asian, non-Hispanic/Latino; 1 Two or more races, non-Hispanic/Latino). Average age 35. 26 applicants, 85% accepted, 21 enrolled. *Faculty:* 23 full-time (13 women), 11 part-time/adjunct (5 women). Expenses: Contact institution. *Financial support:* In 2019–20, 51 students received support. Scholarships/grants, tuition waivers (full and partial), and unspecified assistantships available. Financial award application deadline: 3/15; financial award applicants required to submit FAFSA. In 2019, 45 master's awarded. *Program availability:* Part-time, evening/weekend, online only, 100% online. *Application deadline:* For fall admission, 7/24 for domestic and international students; for spring admission, 12/11 for domestic and international students; for summer admission, 5/2 for domestic and international students. Applications are processed on a rolling basis. *Application fee:* $35. Electronic applications accepted. *Application Contact:* Misty Lindgren, Coordinator of Extended Learning, 701-845-7303, Fax: 701-845-7190, E-mail: misty.lindgren@vcsu.edu. *Dean of Graduate Studies & Extended Learning,* Dr. James Boe, 701-845-7304, E-mail: jim.boe@vcsu.edu.

## VALPARAISO UNIVERSITY, Valparaiso, IN 46383

**General Information** Independent-religious, coed, comprehensive institution. CGS member. *Graduate housing:* Rooms and/or apartments available on a first-come, first-served basis to single and married students. Housing application deadline: 8/1.

**GRADUATE UNITS**

***College of Business*** *Program availability:* Part-time, evening/weekend, online learning. Electronic applications accepted.

***College of Nursing and Health Professions*** *Program availability:* Part-time, evening/weekend, online learning. Electronic applications accepted.

## VAN ANDEL INSTITUTE GRADUATE SCHOOL, Grand Rapids, MI 49503

**General Information** Private, coed, graduate-only institution. *Enrollment by degree level:* 27 doctoral. *Graduate faculty:* 37 full-time (10 women). *Tuition:* Full-time $25,000. *Graduate housing:* On-campus housing not available. *Student services:* Career counseling, exercise/wellness program, grant writing training, international student services, low-cost health insurance, services for students with disabilities, teacher training, writing training. *Library facilities:* Van Andel Institute Library. *Collection:* Study areas open 24 hours, 5–7 days a week.

**Computer facilities:** 4 computers available on campus for general student use. A campuswide network can be accessed from student residence rooms and from off campus. Online class registration is available.
Website: https://vaigs.vai.org/

**General Application Contact:** Christy Mayo, Director of Enrollment and Records, 616-234-5722, Fax: 616-234-5709, E-mail: christy.mayo@vai.org.

**GRADUATE UNITS**

**PhD Program** Electronic applications accepted.

## VANCOUVER ISLAND UNIVERSITY, Nanaimo, BC V9R 5S5, Canada

**General Information** Province-supported, coed, comprehensive institution. *Graduate housing:* Room and/or apartments available on a first-come, first-served basis to single students; on-campus housing not available to married students. Housing application deadline: 3/5.

**GRADUATE UNITS**

**Master of Business Administration Program** *Program availability:* Part-time. Electronic applications accepted.

## VANCOUVER SCHOOL OF THEOLOGY, Vancouver, BC V6T 1L4, Canada

**General Information** Independent-religious, coed, graduate-only institution. *Enrollment by degree level:* 117 master's, 1 doctoral, 16 other advanced degrees. *Graduate faculty:* 11 full-time (3 women), 12 part-time/adjunct (6 women). *Graduate housing:* Rooms and/or apartments available on a first-come, first-served basis to single and married students. Housing application deadline: 3/15. *Student services:* Campus employment opportunities, campus safety program, career counseling, free psychological counseling, international student services, low-cost health insurance, services for students with disabilities, writing training. *Library facilities:* H.R. MacMillan Library.
Website: http://www.vst.edu/

**General Application Contact:** Julie Lees, Recruitment, 604-822-6502, E-mail: jlees@vst.edu.

**GRADUATE UNITS**

**Graduate and Professional Programs** *Program availability:* Part-time, online learning. Electronic applications accepted.

## VANDERBILT UNIVERSITY, Nashville, TN 37240-1001

**General Information** Independent, coed, university. CGS member. *Enrollment:* 13,131 graduate, professional, and undergraduate students; 5,281 full-time matriculated graduate/professional students (3,050 women), 1,026 part-time matriculated graduate/professional students (730 women). *Enrollment by degree level:* 2,746 master's, 3,527 doctoral, 34 other advanced degrees. *Graduate faculty:* 1,081 full-time (362 women), 18 part-time/adjunct (7 women). *Tuition:* Full-time $51,018; part-time $2087 per hour. *Required fees:* $542. Tuition and fees vary according to program. *Graduate housing:* On-campus housing not available. *Student services:* Campus employment opportunities, campus safety program, career counseling, child daycare facilities, exercise/wellness program, free psychological counseling, grant writing training, international student services, low-cost health insurance, multicultural affairs office, services for students with disabilities, teacher training, writing training. *Library facilities:* Jean and Alexander Heard Library plus 7 others. *Collection:* Books: 3.1 million (physical), 1.7 million (digital/electronic); Databases: 3,700. *Research affiliation:* Medtronic, Incorporated (medical research), Celgene Corporation (biopharmaceuticals), Sandhill Scientific, Inc. (medical research), Westat, Inc. (research and evaluation), Amgen (medicine), Boston Scientific Corporation (health science and technology).

**Computer facilities:** A campuswide network can be accessed. Online class registration, productivity and educational software are available.
Website: http://www.vanderbilt.edu/

**General Application Contact:** Walter B. Bieschke, Program Coordinator for Graduate Admissions, 615-322-0236, Fax: 615-343-9936, E-mail: vandygrad@vanderbilt.edu.

**GRADUATE UNITS**

**Center for Medicine, Health, and Society** Students: 9 full-time (7 women), 3 part-time (2 women); includes 5 minority (3 Black or African American, non-Hispanic/Latino; 2 Two or more races, non-Hispanic/Latino). Average age 23. 21 applicants, 86% accepted, 9 enrolled. *Faculty:* 8 full-time (5 women). Expenses: Contact institution. *Financial support:* Federal Work-Study, scholarships/grants, and health care benefits available. Financial award application deadline: 1/15; financial award applicants required to submit CSS PROFILE or FAFSA. In 2019, 15 master's awarded. *Application deadline:* For fall admission, 1/15 for domestic and international students. Electronic applications accepted. *Application Contact:* JuLeigh Petty, Acting Director/Director of Graduate Studies, 615-322-6725, Fax: 615-322-2731, E-mail: juleigh.petty@vanderbilt.edu. *Director,* Dr. Jonathan Metzl, 615-343-2504, Fax: 615-343-8889, E-mail: jonathan.metzl@vanderbilt.edu.

**Department of Anthropology** Students: 25 full-time (16 women); includes 4 minority (1 Black or African American, non-Hispanic/Latino; 3 Hispanic/Latino), 9 international. Average age 32. 48 applicants, 8% accepted, 3 enrolled. *Faculty:* 13 full-time (4 women). Expenses: Contact institution. *Financial support:* Fellowships with tuition reimbursements, research assistantships with full tuition reimbursements, teaching assistantships with full tuition reimbursements, career-related internships or fieldwork, Federal Work-Study, institutionally sponsored loans, scholarships/grants, and health care benefits available. Financial award application deadline: 1/15; financial award applicants required to submit CSS PROFILE or FAFSA. In 2019, 5 master's, 2 doctorates awarded. *Application deadline:* For fall admission, 1/15 for domestic and international students. Electronic applications accepted. *Application Contact:* John Janusek, Director of Graduate Studies, 615-343-6120, E-mail: john.w.janusek@vanderbilt.edu. *Chair,* Dr. Beth Conklin, 615-343-6120, Fax: 615-343-0230, E-mail: beth.a.conklin@vanderbilt.edu.

**Department of Biological Sciences** Students: 56 full-time (28 women); includes 12 minority (3 Black or African American, non-Hispanic/Latino; 2 Asian, non-Hispanic/Latino; 4 Hispanic/Latino; 3 Two or more races, non-Hispanic/Latino), 13 international. Average age 27. 63 applicants, 27% accepted, 6 enrolled. *Faculty:* 21 full-time (5 women). Expenses: Contact institution. *Financial support:* Fellowships with tuition reimbursements, research assistantships with full tuition reimbursements, teaching assistantships with full tuition reimbursements, Federal Work-Study, institutionally sponsored loans, scholarships/grants, traineeships, and health care benefits available. Financial award application deadline: 1/15; financial award applicants required to submit CSS PROFILE or FAFSA. In 2019, 1 master's, 8 doctorates awarded. *Application deadline:* For fall admission, 1/15 for domestic and international students. Electronic applications accepted. *Application Contact:* Julian Hillyer, Director of Graduate Studies, 615-343-2065, E-mail: julian.hillyer@vanderbilt.edu. *Chair,* Dr. Douglas McMahon, 615-322-2008, Fax: 615-343-6707, E-mail: douglas.g.mcmahon@vanderbilt.edu.

**Department of Biomedical Informatics** Students: 22 full-time (9 women), 1 (woman) part-time; includes 8 minority (1 Black or African American, non-Hispanic/Latino; 5 Asian, non-Hispanic/Latino; 1 Hispanic/Latino; 1 Two or more races, non-Hispanic/Latino). Average age 31. 57 applicants, 25% accepted, 7 enrolled. *Faculty:* 28 full-time (6 women). Expenses: Contact institution. *Financial support:* Fellowships with tuition reimbursements, research assistantships with tuition reimbursements, teaching assistantships with tuition reimbursements, Federal Work-Study, institutionally sponsored loans, scholarships/grants, traineeships, and health care benefits available. Financial award application deadline: 1/15; financial award applicants required to submit CSS PROFILE or FAFSA. In 2019, 6 master's, 2 doctorates awarded. *Program availability:* Part-time. *Application deadline:* For fall admission, 1/15 for domestic and international students. Electronic applications accepted. *Application Contact:* Cynthia Gadd, Director of Graduate Studies, 615-936-1050, Fax: 615-936-1427, E-mail: cindy.gadd@vanderbilt.edu. *Chair,* Dr. Kevin Johnson, 615-936-1423, Fax: 615-936-1427, E-mail: kevin.johnson@vanderbilt.edu.

**Department of Chemistry** Students: 109 full-time (56 women); includes 28 minority (8 Black or African American, non-Hispanic/Latino; 4 Asian, non-Hispanic/Latino; 11 Hispanic/Latino; 5 Two or more races, non-Hispanic/Latino), 8 international. Average age 26. 238 applicants, 26% accepted, 18 enrolled. *Faculty:* 22 full-time (4 women). Expenses: Contact institution. *Financial support:* Fellowships with tuition reimbursements, research assistantships with full tuition reimbursements, teaching assistantships with full tuition reimbursements, Federal Work-Study, institutionally sponsored loans, scholarships/grants, traineeships, and health care benefits available. Financial award application deadline: 1/15; financial award applicants required to submit CSS PROFILE or FAFSA. In 2019, 4 master's, 11 doctorates awarded. *Application deadline:* For fall admission, 1/15 for domestic and international students. Electronic applications accepted. *Application Contact:* Carmello Rizzo, Director of Graduate Studies, 615-322-2861, Fax: 615-322-4936, E-mail: c.rizzo@vanderbilt.edu. *Chair,* Dr. David Cliffel, 615-343-3937, Fax: 615-322-4936, E-mail: d.cliffel@vanderbilt.edu.

**Department of Earth and Environmental Sciences** Students: 16 full-time (10 women); includes 2 minority (both Hispanic/Latino). Average age 26. 20 applicants, 20% accepted, 1 enrolled. *Faculty:* 8 full-time (1 woman). Expenses: Contact institution. *Financial support:* Fellowships with tuition reimbursements, research assistantships with tuition reimbursements, teaching assistantships with full tuition reimbursements, career-related internships or fieldwork, Federal Work-Study, institutionally sponsored loans, and health care benefits available. Financial award application deadline: 1/15; financial award applicants required to submit CSS PROFILE or FAFSA. In 2019, 3 master's awarded. *Application deadline:* For fall admission, 1/15 for domestic and international students. Electronic applications accepted. *Application Contact:* David Furbish, Director of Graduate Studies, 615-322-2137, E-mail: david.j.furbish@vanderbilt.edu. *Chair,* Dr. Steven Goodbred, 615-322-2976, E-mail: g.gualda@vanderbilt.edu.

**Department of Economics** Students: 113 full-time (55 women), 5 part-time (1 woman); includes 9 minority (2 Asian, non-Hispanic/Latino; 4 Hispanic/Latino; 3 Two or more races, non-Hispanic/Latino), 83 international. Average age 26. 532 applicants, 39% accepted, 48 enrolled. *Faculty:* 28 full-time (3 women). Expenses: Contact institution. *Financial support:* Fellowships, teaching assistantships, career-related internships or fieldwork, Federal Work-Study, institutionally sponsored loans, scholarships/grants, and health care benefits available. Financial award application deadline: 1/15; financial award applicants required to submit CSS PROFILE or FAFSA. In 2019, 18 master's, 6 doctorates awarded. *Application deadline:* For fall admission, 1/15 for domestic and international students; for spring admission, 11/1 for domestic students. Applications are processed on a rolling basis. Electronic applications accepted. *Application Contact:* Mattias Polborn, Director of Graduate Studies, 615-322-8113, Fax: 615-343-8495, E-mail: mattias.polborn@vanderbilt.edu. *Chair,* Dr. Peter Rousseau, 615-343-2466, Fax: 615-343-8495, E-mail: peter.l.rousseau@vanderbilt.edu.

**Department of English** Students: 41 full-time (26 women); includes 15 minority (11 Black or African American, non-Hispanic/Latino; 1 Asian, non-Hispanic/Latino; 1 Hispanic/Latino; 2 Two or more races, non-Hispanic/Latino), 4 international. Average age 28. 168 applicants, 11% accepted, 12 enrolled. *Faculty:* 30 full-time (21 women). Expenses: Contact institution. *Financial support:* Fellowships, research assistantships, teaching assistantships with full tuition reimbursements, Federal Work-Study, institutionally sponsored loans, scholarships/grants, and health care benefits available. Financial award application deadline: 1/15; financial award applicants required to submit CSS PROFILE or FAFSA. In 2019, 7 master's, 4 doctorates awarded. *Application deadline:* For fall admission, 1/15 for domestic and international students. Electronic applications accepted. *Application Contact:* Vera Kutzinski, Director of Graduate Studies, 615-322-2541, Fax: 615-343-8028, E-mail: vera.kutzinski@vanderbilt.edu. *Chair,* Dr. Dana Nelson, 615-322-2541, Fax: 615-343-8028, E-mail: dana.d.nelson@vanderbilt.edu.

**Department of Frech** Students: 12 full-time (7 women); includes 2 minority (1 Hispanic/Latino; 1 Two or more races, non-Hispanic/Latino), 1 international. Average age 29. 15 applicants, 13% accepted, 1 enrolled. *Faculty:* 14 full-time (9 women). Expenses: Contact institution. *Financial support:* Fellowships, teaching assistantships, career-related internships or fieldwork, Federal Work-Study, institutionally sponsored loans, scholarships/grants, and health care benefits available. Financial award application deadline: 1/15; financial award applicants required to submit CSS PROFILE or FAFSA. In 2019, 2 master's, 1 doctorate awarded. *Application deadline:* For fall admission, 1/15 for domestic and international students. Electronic applications accepted. *Application Contact:* Nathalie Debrauwere-Miller, Director of Graduate Studies, 615-322-6900, Fax: 615-343-6909, E-mail: n.debrau@vanderbilt.edu. *Chair,* Dr. Lynn Ramey, 615-322-6900, Fax: 615-343-6909, E-mail: lynn.ramey@vanderbilt.edu.

**Department of Germanic and Slavic Languages** Students: 22 full-time (15 women); includes 2 minority (1 Black or African American, non-Hispanic/Latino; 1 Hispanic/Latino), 3 international. Average age 30. 6 applicants, 83% accepted, 3 enrolled. *Faculty:* 7 full-time (4 women). Expenses: Contact institution. *Financial support:* Fellowships, teaching assistantships, career-related internships or fieldwork, Federal Work-Study, institutionally sponsored loans, scholarships/grants, and health care benefits available. Financial award application deadline: 1/15; financial award applicants required to submit CSS PROFILE or FAFSA. In 2019, 3 doctorates awarded. *Application deadline:* For fall admission, 1/15 for domestic and international students. Electronic applications accepted. *Application Contact:* Meike Werner, Director of Graduate Studies, 615-875-9065, Fax: 615-343-7258, E-mail: meike.werner@Vanderbilt.Edu. *Chair,* Dr. Lutz Koepnick, 615-322-2611, Fax: 615-343-7258, E-mail: lutz.koepnick@vanderbilt.edu.

**Department of History** Students: 48 full-time (23 women), 1 part-time (0 women); includes 8 minority (1 Black or African American, non-Hispanic/Latino; 1 American Indian or Alaska Native, non-Hispanic/Latino; 4 Hispanic/Latino; 2 Two or more races, non-Hispanic/Latino), 12 international. Average age 29. 124 applicants, 17% accepted, 8 enrolled. *Faculty:* 36 full-time (12 women). Expenses: Contact institution. *Financial support:* Fellowships with full tuition reimbursements, teaching assistantships with full tuition reimbursements, Federal Work-Study, institutionally sponsored loans, scholarships/grants, and health care benefits available. Financial award application deadline: 1/15; financial award applicants required to submit CSS PROFILE or FAFSA. In 2019, 2 master's, 11 doctorates awarded. *Application deadline:* For fall admission, 1/15 for domestic and international students. Electronic applications accepted. *Application Contact:* Samira Sheikh, Director of Graduate Studies, 615-322-4740, Fax: 615-343-6002, E-mail: samira.sheikh@vanderbilt.edu. *Chair,* Dr. Joel Harrington, 615-322-2575, Fax: 615-343-6002, E-mail: joel.harrington@vanderbilt.edu.

**Department of Mathematics** Students: 38 full-time (3 women); includes 1 minority (Two or more races, non-Hispanic/Latino), 21 international. Average age 26. 127 applicants, 13% accepted, 7 enrolled. *Faculty:* 30 full-time (2 women). Expenses: Contact institution. *Financial support:* Fellowships, research assistantships with full tuition reimbursements, teaching assistantships with full tuition reimbursements, Federal Work-Study, institutionally sponsored loans, scholarships/grants, and health care benefits available. Financial award application deadline: 1/15; financial award applicants required to submit CSS PROFILE or FAFSA. In 2019, 1 master's, 7 doctorates awarded. *Application deadline:* For fall admission, 1/1 for domestic and international students. Electronic applications accepted. *Application Contact:* Alexander Powell, Director of Graduate Studies, 615-322-6650, Fax: 315-343-0215, E-mail: alexander.m.powell@vanderbilt.edu. *Chair,* Dr. Mike Neamtu, 615-322-6672, Fax: 615-343-0215, E-mail: mike.neamtu@vanderbilt.edu.

**Department of Philosophy** Students: 22 full-time (12 women), 1 (woman) part-time; includes 9 minority (1 Black or African American, non-Hispanic/Latino; 2 Asian, non-Hispanic/Latino; 2 Hispanic/Latino; 4 Two or more races, non-Hispanic/Latino), 3 international. Average age 27. 107 applicants, 10% accepted, 7 enrolled. *Faculty:* 14 full-time (4 women). Expenses: Contact institution. *Financial support:* Fellowships with full tuition reimbursements, teaching assistantships with full tuition reimbursements, Federal Work-Study, institutionally sponsored loans, scholarships/grants, and health care benefits available. Financial award application deadline: 1/15; financial award applicants required to submit CSS PROFILE or FAFSA. In 2019, 3 master's, 2 doctorates awarded. *Application deadline:* For fall admission, 1/15 for domestic and international students. Electronic applications accepted. *Application Contact:* Kelly Oliver, Director of Graduate Studies, 615-343-0334, Fax: 615-343-7259, E-mail: kelly.oliver@vanderbilt.edu. *Chair,* Dr. Robert Talisse, 615-343-5349, Fax: 615-343-7259, E-mail: robert.talisse@vanderbilt.edu.

**Department of Physics and Astronomy** Students: 41 full-time (9 women); includes 10 minority (4 Black or African American, non-Hispanic/Latino; 6 Hispanic/Latino), 7 international. Average age 27. 58 applicants, 28% accepted, 8 enrolled. *Faculty:* 24 full-time (4 women). Expenses: Contact institution. *Financial support:* Fellowships, research assistantships with full tuition reimbursements, teaching assistantships with full tuition reimbursements, career-related internships or fieldwork, Federal Work-Study, and institutionally sponsored loans available. Financial award application deadline: 1/15; financial award applicants required to submit CSS PROFILE or FAFSA. In 2019, 8 doctorates awarded. *Application deadline:* For fall admission, 1/1 for domestic and international students. Electronic applications accepted. *Application Contact:* Julia Velkovska, Director of Graduate Studies, 615-322-2828, E-mail: julia.velkovska@vanderbilt.edu. *Chair,* Dr. Shane Hutson, 615-343-9980, E-mail: shane.hutson@Vanderbilt.Edu.

**Department of Political Science** Students: 44 full-time (24 women); includes 3 minority (1 Black or African American, non-Hispanic/Latino; 1 Asian, non-Hispanic/Latino; 1 Two or more races, non-Hispanic/Latino), 14 international. Average age 29. 178 applicants, 11% accepted, 8 enrolled. *Faculty:* 20 full-time (7 women). Expenses: Contact institution. *Financial support:* Fellowships with full tuition reimbursements, research assistantships with full tuition reimbursements, teaching assistantships with full tuition reimbursements, Federal Work-Study, institutionally sponsored loans, scholarships/grants, and health care benefits available. Financial award application deadline: 1/15; financial award applicants required to submit CSS PROFILE or FAFSA. In 2019, 5 master's, 2 doctorates awarded. *Application deadline:* For fall admission, 1/15 for domestic and international students. Electronic applications accepted. *Application Contact:* Emily Ritter, Director of Graduate Studies, 615-936-9795, Fax: 615-343-6003, E-mail: emily.h.ritter@vanderbilt.edu. *Chair,* Dr. Alan Wiseman, 615-322-6222, Fax: 615-343-6003, E-mail: alan.wiseman@vanderbilt.edu.

**Department of Religion** Students: 54 full-time (37 women); includes 18 minority (11 Black or African American, non-Hispanic/Latino; 2 Asian, non-Hispanic/Latino; 4 Hispanic/Latino; 1 Two or more races, non-Hispanic/Latino), 8 international. Average age 34. 113 applicants, 13% accepted, 6 enrolled. *Faculty:* 26 full-time (10 women). Expenses: Contact institution. *Financial support:* Fellowships, teaching assistantships, Federal Work-Study, institutionally sponsored loans, health care benefits, and tuition waivers (full and partial) available. Support available to part-time students. Financial award application deadline: 1/15; financial award applicants required to submit CSS PROFILE or FAFSA. In 2019, 7 master's, 6 doctorates awarded. *Application deadline:* For fall admission, 12/15 for domestic and international students. Electronic applications accepted. *Application Contact:* Karen Eardley, Administrative Assistant, 615-343-3977, Fax: 615-343-9957, E-mail: karen.eardley@vanderbilt.edu. *Chair and Director of Graduate Studies,* Dr. James Byrd, Jr., 615-343-9977, Fax: 615-343-9957, E-mail: james.p.byrd@vanderbilt.edu.

**Department of Sociology** Students: 32 full-time (27 women); includes 11 minority (6 Black or African American, non-Hispanic/Latino; 4 Asian, non-Hispanic/Latino; 1 Hispanic/Latino), 2 international. Average age 28. 95 applicants, 11% accepted, 4 enrolled. *Faculty:* 16 full-time (6 women). Expenses: Contact institution. *Financial support:* Fellowships with full tuition reimbursements, research assistantships, teaching assistantships with full tuition reimbursements, Federal Work-Study, institutionally sponsored loans, scholarships/grants, and health care benefits available. Financial award application deadline: 1/15; financial award applicants required to submit CSS PROFILE or FAFSA. In 2019, 6 master's, 2 doctorates awarded. *Application deadline:* For fall admission, 1/15 for domestic and international students. Electronic applications accepted. *Application Contact:* Lijun Song, Director of Graduate Studies, 615-322-1731, Fax: 615-322-7505, E-mail: lijun.song@vanderbilt.edu. *Chair,* Dr. Larry Isaac, 615-322-7626, Fax: 615-322-7505, E-mail: larry.isaac@vanderbilt.edu.

**Department of Spanish and Portuguese** Students: 24 full-time (12 women); includes 6 minority (1 Black or African American, non-Hispanic/Latino; 5 Hispanic/Latino), 12 international. Average age 31. 33 applicants, 15% accepted, 4 enrolled. *Faculty:* 11 full-time (4 women). Expenses: Contact institution. *Financial support:* Fellowships, teaching assistantships with full tuition reimbursements, Federal Work-Study, institutionally sponsored loans, and health care benefits available. Financial award application deadline: 1/15; financial award applicants required to submit CSS PROFILE or FAFSA. In 2019, 3 master's, 1 doctorate awarded. *Application deadline:* For fall admission, 1/15 for domestic and international students. Electronic applications accepted. *Application Contact:* Jose Cardenas Bunsen, Director of Graduate Studies, 615-322-6930, Fax: 615-343-7260, E-mail: jose.cardenas-bunsen@Vanderbilt.Edu. *Chair,* Andres Zamora, 615-322-6930, Fax: 615-343-7260, E-mail: andres.zamora@vanderbilt.edu.

**Divinity School** *Program availability:* Part-time. Electronic applications accepted.

**Peabody College** *Program availability:* Part-time, evening/weekend, online courses with semester immersions on campus. Electronic applications accepted.

**PhD Program in Special Education** Students: 127 full-time (119 women), 3 part-time (all women); includes 23 minority (1 Black or African American, non-Hispanic/Latino; 7 Asian, non-Hispanic/Latino; 9 Hispanic/Latino; 6 Two or more races, non-Hispanic/Latino), 13 international. Average age 27. 40 applicants, 23% accepted, 6 enrolled. *Faculty:* 16 full-time (11 women). Expenses: Contact institution. *Financial support:* Fellowships with full tuition reimbursements, research assistantships with full tuition reimbursements, teaching assistantships with full tuition reimbursements, Federal Work-Study, institutionally sponsored loans, traineeships, and health care benefits available. Financial award application deadline: 1/15; financial award applicants required to submit CSS PROFILE or FAFSA. In 2019, 13 doctorates awarded. *Application deadline:* For fall admission, 12/1 for domestic and international students. Electronic applications accepted. *Application Contact:* Dr. Robert Hodapp, Director of Graduate Studies, 615-322-8150, Fax: 615-343-1570, E-mail: robert.hodapp@vanderbilt.edu. *Chair,* Dr. Joseph Wehby, 615-322-8150, Fax: 615-343-1570, E-mail: joseph.wehby@vanderbilt.edu.

**Program in Community Research and Action** Students: 31 full-time (24 women); includes 14 minority (7 Black or African American, non-Hispanic/Latino; 2 Asian, non-Hispanic/Latino; 2 Hispanic/Latino; 3 Two or more races, non-Hispanic/Latino), 4 international. Average age 30. 84 applicants, 11% accepted, 5 enrolled. Expenses: Contact institution. *Financial support:* In 2019–20, 16 students received support. Fellowships, research assistantships with full tuition reimbursements available, teaching assistantships with full tuition reimbursements available, Federal Work-Study, scholarships/grants, health care benefits, tuition waivers, and unspecified assistantships available. Financial award application deadline: 1/15; financial award applicants required to submit FAFSA. In 2019, 2 doctorates awarded. *Application deadline:* For fall admission, 12/1 for domestic and international students. Electronic applications accepted. *Application Contact:* Brian Christens, Director of Graduate Studies, 615-322-6881, Fax: 615-322-1141, E-mail: b.christens@vanderbilt.edu. *Chair,* Paul Speer, 615-322-3117, Fax: 615-322-1769, E-mail: paul.w.speer@vanderbilt.edu.

**Program in Creative Writing** Students: 16 full-time (11 women); includes 8 minority (1 Black or African American, non-Hispanic/Latino; 3 Asian, non-Hispanic/Latino; 3 Hispanic/Latino; 1 Two or more races, non-Hispanic/Latino), 1 international. Average age 27. 331 applicants, 3% accepted, 6 enrolled. *Faculty:* 29 full-time (20 women). Expenses: Contact institution. *Financial support:* Fellowships, teaching assistantships, Federal Work-Study, institutionally sponsored loans, and health care benefits available. Financial award application deadline: 1/15; financial award applicants required to submit CSS PROFILE or FAFSA. In 2019, 2 master's awarded. *Application deadline:* For fall admission, 1/15 for domestic and international students. Electronic applications accepted. *Application Contact:* Katherine Daniels, Director of Graduate Studies, 615-322-2541, E-mail: kate.daniels@vanderbilt.edu. *Chair,* Dr. Dana Nelson, 615-322-2541, E-mail: dana.d.nelson@vanderbilt.edu.

**Program in Human Genetics** Students: 19 full-time (14 women); includes 3 minority (2 Asian, non-Hispanic/Latino; 1 Two or more races, non-Hispanic/Latino), 5 international. Average age 26. *Faculty:* 32 full-time (10 women). Expenses: Contact institution. *Financial support:* Fellowships, research assistantships, Federal Work-Study, institutionally sponsored loans, traineeships, and health care benefits available. Financial award application deadline: 1/15; financial award applicants required to submit CSS PROFILE or FAFSA. In 2019, 3 doctorates awarded. *Application deadline:* For fall admission, 1/15 for domestic and international students. Electronic applications accepted. *Application Contact:* Todd Edwards, Director of Graduate Studies, 615-322-3652, E-mail: todd.l.edwards@vanderbilt.edu. *Director,* Dr. David Samuels, 615-343-7870, Fax: 615-322-1453, E-mail: david.c.samuels@vanderbilt.edu.

**Program in Latin American Studies** Students: 4 full-time (2 women); includes 1 minority (Hispanic/Latino). Average age 26. 19 applicants, 26% accepted, 3 enrolled. *Faculty:* 53 full-time (20 women). Expenses: Contact institution. *Financial support:* Teaching assistantships with full tuition reimbursements, Federal Work-Study, institutionally sponsored loans, and health care benefits available. Financial award application deadline: 1/15; financial award applicants required to submit CSS PROFILE or FAFSA. In 2019, 2 master's awarded. *Application deadline:* For fall admission, 1/15 for domestic and international students. Electronic applications accepted. *Application Contact:* Nicolette M. Kostiw, Assistant Director/Director of Graduate Studies, 615-322-2527, Fax: 615-343-6002, E-mail: nicolette.m.wilhide@vanderbilt.edu. *Director,* Dr. Edward Fischer, 615-322-2527, Fax: 615-343-6002, E-mail: edward.f.fischer@vanderbilt.edu.

**Program in Leadership and Policy Studies** Students: 30 full-time (20 women), 1 (woman) part-time; includes 13 minority (5 Black or African American, non-Hispanic/Latino; 4 Asian, non-Hispanic/Latino; 2 Hispanic/Latino; 2 Two or more races, non-Hispanic/Latino). Average age 31. 90 applicants, 16% accepted, 6 enrolled. *Faculty:* 15 full-time (7 women). Expenses: Contact institution. *Financial support:* Fellowships with full tuition reimbursements, research assistantships with full tuition reimbursements, teaching assistantships with full tuition reimbursements, Federal Work-Study, institutionally sponsored loans, scholarships/grants, traineeships, and health care benefits available. Financial award application deadline: 1/15; financial award applicants required to submit CSS PROFILE or FAFSA. In 2019, 3 doctorates awarded. *Application deadline:* For fall admission, 12/1 for domestic and international students. Electronic applications accepted. *Application Contact:* Sean Corcoran, Director of Graduate Studies, 615-322-8021, Fax: 615-343-7094, E-mail: sean.corcoran@vanderbilt.edu. *Chair,* Carolyn Heinrich, 615-322-1169, Fax: 615-343-7094, E-mail: carolyn.j.heinrich@vanderbilt.edu.

**Program in Learning, Teaching and Diversity** Students: 42 full-time (36 women), 1 part-time (0 women); includes 15 minority (4 Black or African American, non-Hispanic/Latino; 5 Asian, non-Hispanic/Latino; 2 Hispanic/Latino; 4 Two or more races, non-Hispanic/Latino), 4 international. Average age 32. 90 applicants, 16% accepted, 6 enrolled. *Faculty:* 19 full-time (10 women), 2 part-time/adjunct (both women). Expenses: Contact institution. *Financial support:* Fellowships with partial tuition reimbursements, research assistantships with full tuition reimbursements, teaching assistantships with full tuition reimbursements, Federal Work-Study, institutionally sponsored loans, scholarships/grants, traineeships, and health care benefits available. Financial award application deadline: 1/15; financial award applicants required to submit CSS PROFILE or FAFSA. In 2019, 4 doctorates awarded. *Application deadline:* For fall admission, 12/1 for domestic and international students. Electronic applications accepted. *Application Contact:* Llana Horn, Director of Graduate Studies, 615-322-5884, Fax: 615-322-8014, E-mail: llana.horn@vanderbilt.edu. *Chair,* Dr. Deborah Rowe, 615-322-8044, Fax: 615-322-8014, E-mail: deborah.w.rowe@vanderbilt.edu.

**Program in Liberal Arts and Science** Students: 1 full-time (0 women), 27 part-time (19 women); includes 5 minority (3 Black or African American, non-Hispanic/Latino; 2 Two or more races, non-Hispanic/Latino). Average age 41. 8 applicants, 88% accepted, 4 enrolled. Expenses: Contact institution. *Financial support:* Institutionally sponsored loans and tuition waivers (partial) available. In 2019, 9 master's awarded. *Program availability:* Part-time. *Application deadline:* For fall admission, 1/15 priority date for domestic students, 1/15 for international students; for spring admission, 11/15 for domestic and international students. Applications are processed on a rolling basis. *Application Contact:* Andrea Hearn, Director, 615-875-5831, Fax: 615-343-8702, E-mail: andrea.l.hearn@vanderbilt.edu. *Director,* Andrea Hearn, 615-875-5831, Fax: 615-343-8702, E-mail: andrea.l.hearn@vanderbilt.edu.

**Program in Nursing Science** Students: 28 full-time (26 women), 2 part-time (both women); includes 7 minority (1 Asian, non-Hispanic/Latino; 3 Hispanic/Latino; 3 Two or more races, non-Hispanic/Latino). Average age 37. 20 applicants, 40% accepted, 6 enrolled. *Faculty:* 22 full-time (20 women), 3 part-time/adjunct (all women). Expenses: Contact institution. *Financial support:* Fellowships with full tuition reimbursements, research assistantships with full tuition reimbursements, teaching assistantships with full tuition reimbursements, career-related internships or fieldwork, Federal Work-Study, institutionally sponsored loans, scholarships/grants, health care benefits, and tuition waivers (full and partial) available. Financial award application deadline: 1/15; financial award applicants required to submit CSS PROFILE or FAFSA. In 2019, 5 doctorates awarded. *Application deadline:* For fall admission, 1/15 for domestic and international students. Electronic applications accepted. *Application Contact:* Judy Vesterfelt, Program Manager, 615-322-7410, E-mail: judy.vesterfelt@vanderbilt.edu. *Director of Graduate Studies,* Sheila Ridner, 615-322-3800, Fax: 615-343-5898, E-mail: sheila.ridner@vanderbilt.edu.

**Program in Psychological Sciences** Students: 82 full-time (48 women); includes 9 minority (1 Black or African American, non-Hispanic/Latino; 2 Asian, non-Hispanic/Latino; 3 Hispanic/Latino; 3 Two or more races, non-Hispanic/Latino), 29 international. Average age 26. 520 applicants, 3% accepted, 10 enrolled. *Faculty:* 51 full-time (22 women). Expenses: Contact institution. *Financial support:* Fellowships with full tuition reimbursements, research assistantships with full tuition reimbursements, teaching assistantships with full tuition reimbursements, career-related internships or fieldwork, Federal Work-Study, institutionally sponsored loans, scholarships/grants, traineeships, and health care benefits available. Financial award application deadline: 1/15; financial award applicants required to submit CSS PROFILE or FAFSA. In 2019, 6 doctorates awarded. *Application deadline:* For fall admission, 12/1 for domestic and international students. Electronic applications accepted. *Application Contact:* Dr. Rene Marois, Chair, 615-322-2874, Fax: 615-343-5027, E-mail: r.marois@vanderbilt.edu. *Chair,* Bethany Rittle-Johnson, 615-322-8301, Fax: 615-343-9494, E-mail: Bethany.rittle-johnson@vanderbilt.edu.

**School of Engineering** *Program availability:* Part-time. Electronic applications accepted.

**School of Medicine** *Faculty:* 115 full-time (44 women), 2 part-time/adjunct (0 women). Expenses: Contact institution. *Financial support:* Institutionally sponsored loans and scholarships/grants available. Financial award application deadline: 3/1; financial award applicants required to submit FAFSA. *Application deadline:* For fall admission, 11/15 for domestic and international students. *Application fee:* $50. *Application Contact:* Dr. Jeffrey R. Balser, Dean, School of Medicine, 615-936-3030, E-mail: jeffrey.balser@vanderbilt.edu. *Dean, School of Medicine,* Dr. Jeffrey R. Balser, 615-936-3030, E-mail: jeffrey.balser@vanderbilt.edu.

**Vanderbilt Law School** Electronic applications accepted.

**Vanderbilt University Owen Graduate School of Management** *Program availability:* Evening/weekend.

**Vanderbilt University School of Nursing** Students: 600 full-time (527 women), 295 part-time (267 women); includes 203 minority (64 Black or African American, non-Hispanic/Latino; 5 American Indian or Alaska Native, non-Hispanic/Latino; 38 Asian, non-Hispanic/Latino; 59 Hispanic/Latino; 2 Native Hawaiian or other Pacific Islander, non-Hispanic/Latino; 35 Two or more races, non-Hispanic/Latino), 1 international. Average age 30. 1,548 applicants, 48% accepted, 521 enrolled. *Faculty:* 134 full-time (120 women), 30 part-time/adjunct (26 women). Expenses: Contact institution. *Financial support:* In 2019–20, 645 students received support. Scholarships/grants available. Financial award application deadline: 3/15; financial award applicants required to submit FAFSA. In 2019, 354 master's, 63 doctorates, 3 other advanced degrees awarded. *Program availability:* Part-time, blended/hybrid learning. *Application deadline:* For fall admission, 11/1 priority date for domestic and international students. Applications are processed on a rolling basis. *Application fee:* $50. Electronic applications accepted. *Application Contact:* Patricia Peerman, Assistant Dean for Enrollment Management, 615-322-3800, Fax: 615-343-0333, E-mail: vusn-admissions@vanderbilt.edu. *Dean,* Dr. Linda Norman, 615-343-8876, Fax: 615-343-7711, E-mail: linda.norman@vanderbilt.edu.

## VANDERCOOK COLLEGE OF MUSIC, Chicago, IL 60616-3731

**General Information** Independent, coed, comprehensive institution. *Graduate housing:* Rooms and/or apartments available on a first-come, first-served basis to single and married students. Housing application deadline: 6/1.

**GRADUATE UNITS**

**Master of Music Education Program** *Program availability:* Part-time.

## VANGUARD UNIVERSITY OF SOUTHERN CALIFORNIA, Costa Mesa, CA 92626

**General Information** Independent-religious, coed, comprehensive institution. *Graduate housing:* On-campus housing not available.

**GRADUATE UNITS**

**Graduate Program in Clinical Psychology** *Program availability:* Part-time, evening/weekend. Electronic applications accepted.

**Graduate Program in Nursing** *Program availability:* Part-time, evening/weekend, blended/hybrid learning.

**Graduate Program in Organizational Psychology**

**Graduate Programs in Education** *Program availability:* Evening/weekend. Electronic applications accepted.

**Graduate Programs in Religion** *Program availability:* Part-time, evening/weekend, 100% online, blended/hybrid learning. Electronic applications accepted.

## VAUGHN COLLEGE OF AERONAUTICS AND TECHNOLOGY, Flushing, NY 11369

**General Information** Independent, coed, primarily men, comprehensive institution.

**GRADUATE UNITS**

**Graduate Programs**

## VERMONT COLLEGE OF FINE ARTS, Montpelier, VT 05602

**General Information** Independent, coed, graduate-only institution. *Enrollment by degree level:* 348 master's. *Graduate faculty:* 125 part-time/adjunct (67 women). *Tuition:* Full-time $25,864; part-time $880 per credit. *Required fees:* $1322; $661 per term. Tuition and fees vary according to program. *Graduate housing:* Room and/or apartments available on a first-come, first-served basis to single students; on-campus housing not available to married students. Typical cost: $2142 (including board). Room and board charges vary according to board plan. *Student services:* Campus safety program, international student services, services for students with disabilities. *Library facilities:* The Gary Library. *Collection:* Books: 60,000 (physical), 110,000 (digital/electronic); Serial titles: 250 (physical), 250 (digital/electronic); Databases: 10. Weekly public service hours: 40; students can reserve study rooms.

**Computer facilities:** 26 computers available on campus for general student use. A campuswide network can be accessed from student residence rooms and from off campus.
Website: http://www.vcfa.edu/

**General Application Contact:** Ann Cardinal, Director of Student Recruitment, 802-828-8589, E-mail: admissions@vcfa.edu.

**GRADUATE UNITS**

**Graduate Studies in Art and Design Education** Electronic applications accepted.

**International MFA in Creative Writing and Literary Translation Program**

**MFA in Film Program** Electronic applications accepted.

**MFA in Graphic Design Program** Electronic applications accepted.

**MFA in Music Composition Program**

**MFA in Visual Art Program** Electronic applications accepted.

**MFA in Writing and Publishing Program**

**MFA in Writing for Children and Young Adults Program** Electronic applications accepted.

**MFA in Writing Program**

## VERMONT LAW SCHOOL, South Royalton, VT 05068-0096

**General Information** Independent, coed, graduate-only institution. *Graduate housing:* On-campus housing not available.

**GRADUATE UNITS**

**Graduate and Professional Programs** *Program availability:* Part-time. Electronic applications accepted.

***Master's Programs*** *Program availability:* Part-time, 100% online, blended/hybrid learning.

## VERMONT TECHNICAL COLLEGE, Randolph Center, VT 05061-0500

**General Information** State-supported, coed, comprehensive institution.

**GRADUATE UNITS**

**Program in Computer Software Engineering**

## VICTORIA UNIVERSITY, Toronto, ON M5S 1K7, Canada

**General Information** Independent-religious, coed, graduate-only institution. *Graduate housing:* Rooms and/or apartments available on a first-come, first-served basis to single and married students. Housing application deadline: 6/30.

**GRADUATE UNITS**

**Emmanuel College** Electronic applications accepted.

## VILLANOVA UNIVERSITY, Villanova, PA 19085-1699

**General Information** Independent-religious, coed, university. CGS member. *Graduate housing:* On-campus housing not available.

**GRADUATE UNITS**

**Charles Widger School of Law** *Program availability:* Part-time, evening/weekend. Electronic applications accepted.

**College of Engineering** *Program availability:* Part-time, evening/weekend, online learning. Electronic applications accepted.

**Graduate School of Liberal Arts and Sciences** *Program availability:* Part-time, evening/weekend, 100% online. Electronic applications accepted.

**M. Louise Fitzpatrick College of Nursing** *Program availability:* Part-time, online learning. Electronic applications accepted.

**Villanova School of Business** Students: 73 full-time (33 women), 1,011 part-time (385 women); includes 205 minority (44 Black or African American, non-Hispanic/Latino; 1 American Indian or Alaska Native, non-Hispanic/Latino; 72 Asian, non-Hispanic/Latino; 59 Hispanic/Latino; 29 Two or more races, non-Hispanic/Latino), 25 international. Average age 33. 503 applicants, 81% accepted, 297 enrolled. *Faculty:* 100 full-time (37 women), 34 part-time/adjunct (5 women). Expenses: Contact institution. *Financial support:* Research assistantships and scholarships/grants available. Financial award application deadline: 6/30; financial award applicants required to submit FAFSA. In 2019, 462 master's awarded. *Program availability:* 100% online, blended/hybrid learning, residency orientation programs and international study. *Application deadline:* For fall admission, 7/31 for domestic and international students; for spring admission, 11/30 for domestic and international students; for summer admission, 4/30 for domestic and international students. Applications are processed on a rolling basis. *Application fee:* $65. Electronic applications accepted. *Application Contact:* Claire Bruno, Assistant Dean, Graduate Admissions, 610-519-6745, E-mail: claire.bruno@villanova.edu. *Dean,* Dr. Joyce E. A. Russell, 610-519-6082, E-mail: joyce.russell@villanova.edu.

## VIRGINIA BAPTIST COLLEGE, Fredericksburg, VA 22407

**General Information** Independent, coed, comprehensive institution.

**GRADUATE UNITS**

**Graduate Programs**

## VIRGINIA BEACH THEOLOGICAL SEMINARY, Virginia Beach, VA 23464

**General Information** Independent-religious, coed, graduate-only institution. *Graduate housing:* On-campus housing not available.

**GRADUATE UNITS**

**Graduate Programs** *Program availability:* Online learning. Electronic applications accepted.

## VIRGINIA COMMONWEALTH UNIVERSITY, Richmond, VA 23284-9005

**General Information** State-supported, coed, university. CGS member. *Graduate housing:* Room and/or apartments available on a first-come, first-served basis to single students; on-campus housing not available to married students. *Research affiliation:* Virginia Biotechnology Research Park.

**GRADUATE UNITS**

**Graduate School** *Program availability:* Part-time, evening/weekend. Electronic applications accepted.

***College of Humanities and Sciences*** *Program availability:* Part-time, evening/weekend. Electronic applications accepted.

***L. Douglas Wilder School of Government and Public Affairs***

***School of Allied Health Professions*** *Program availability:* Part-time. Electronic applications accepted.

***School of Business*** *Program availability:* Part-time, evening/weekend. Electronic applications accepted.

***School of Education*** *Program availability:* Part-time. Electronic applications accepted.

***School of Engineering*** Electronic applications accepted.

***School of Life Sciences*** Electronic applications accepted.

***School of Nursing*** *Program availability:* Part-time, evening/weekend, online learning. Electronic applications accepted.

***School of Social Work*** Electronic applications accepted.

***School of the Arts*** *Program availability:* Part-time. Electronic applications accepted.

**Medical College of Virginia-Professional Programs** *Program availability:* Part-time. Electronic applications accepted.

***School of Dentistry*** Electronic applications accepted.

***School of Medicine*** Electronic applications accepted.

***School of Pharmacy*** *Program availability:* Part-time. Electronic applications accepted.

**Program in Pre-Medical Basic Health Sciences** Electronic applications accepted.

## VIRGINIA INTERNATIONAL UNIVERSITY, Fairfax, VA 22030

**General Information** Proprietary, coed, comprehensive institution. *Research affiliation:* Apple Federal Credit Union (financial management).

**GRADUATE UNITS**

**School of Business** *Program availability:* Part-time, online learning. Electronic applications accepted.

**School of Computer Information Systems** *Program availability:* Part-time, online learning. Electronic applications accepted.

**School of Education** *Program availability:* Part-time, online learning. Electronic applications accepted.

**School of Public and International Affairs**

## VIRGINIA POLYTECHNIC INSTITUTE AND STATE UNIVERSITY, Blacksburg, VA 24061

**General Information** State-supported, coed, university. CGS member. *Enrollment:* 36,383 graduate, professional, and undergraduate students; 5,033 full-time matriculated graduate/professional students (2,251 women), 2,050 part-time matriculated graduate/professional students (807 women). *Enrollment by degree level:* 3,373 master's, 3,710 doctoral. *Graduate faculty:* 2,036 full-time (734 women), 20 part-time/adjunct (11 women). Tuition, state resident: full-time $13,700; part-time $761.25 per credit hour. Tuition, nonresident: full-time $27,614; part-time $1534 per credit hour. *Required fees:* $886.50 per term. Tuition and fees vary according to campus/location and program. *Graduate housing:* Room and/or apartments available on a first-come, first-served basis to single students; on-campus housing not available to married students. Typical cost: $5044 per year. *Student services:* Campus employment opportunities, campus safety program, career counseling, exercise/wellness program, free psychological counseling, grant writing training, international student services, low-cost health insurance, multicultural affairs office, services for students with disabilities, teacher training, writing training. *Library facilities:* Newman Library plus 2 others. *Collection:* Study areas open 24 hours, 5–7 days a week. *Research affiliation:* Virginia Tech Carilion School of Medicine and Research Institute, Commonwealth Center for Advanced Manufacturing (CCAM), Wellcome Trust Centre for Neuroimaging (health research), Virginia Biosciences Health Research Corporation (health research), Transport Canada (transportation), Elanco Animal Health (agriculture).

**Computer facilities:** A campuswide network can be accessed. Online class registration is available.
Website: http://www.vt.edu/

**General Application Contact:** Graduate Admissions and Academic Progress, 540-231-8636, E-mail: grads@vt.edu.

**GRADUATE UNITS**

**Graduate School** Students: 5,033 full-time (2,251 women), 2,050 part-time (807 women); includes 1,302 minority (368 Black or African American, non-Hispanic/Latino; 10 American Indian or Alaska Native, non-Hispanic/Latino; 389 Asian, non-Hispanic/Latino; 320 Hispanic/Latino; 2 Native Hawaiian or other Pacific Islander, non-Hispanic/Latino; 213 Two or more races, non-Hispanic/Latino), 2,024 international. Average age 30. 7,862 applicants, 50% accepted, 2,007 enrolled. *Faculty:* 2,036 full-time (734 women), 20 part-time/adjunct (11 women). Expenses: Contact institution. In 2019, 1,501 master's, 629 doctorates awarded. *Program availability:* Part-time, evening/weekend, 100% online, blended/hybrid learning. *Application deadline:* For fall admission, 8/1 for domestic students, 4/1 for international students; for spring admission, 1/1 for domestic students, 9/1 for international students. Applications are processed on a rolling basis. *Application fee:* $75. Electronic applications accepted. *Application Contact:* Dr. Janice Austin, Assistant Dean and Director, Admissions & Academic Progress, 540-231-8636, E-mail: grads@vt.edu. *Vice President and Dean for Graduate Education,* Dr. Karen P. DePauw, 540-231-6691, E-mail: grads@vt.edu.

***College of Agriculture and Life Sciences*** Students: 364 full-time (213 women), 106 part-time (68 women); includes 79 minority (29 Black or African American, non-Hispanic/Latino; 1 American Indian or Alaska Native, non-Hispanic/Latino; 13 Asian, non-Hispanic/Latino; 16 Hispanic/Latino; 20 Two or more races, non-Hispanic/Latino), 106 international. Average age 28. 314 applicants, 57% accepted, 130 enrolled. *Faculty:* 246 full-time (83 women). Expenses: Contact institution. *Financial support:* In 2019–20, 248 research assistantships with full tuition reimbursements (averaging $20,360 per year), 127 teaching assistantships with full tuition reimbursements (averaging $18,183 per year) were awarded; fellowships, scholarships/grants, and unspecified assistantships also available. Financial award application deadline: 3/1; financial award applicants required to submit FAFSA. In 2019, 92 master's, 59 doctorates awarded. *Application deadline:* For fall admission, 8/1 for domestic students, 4/1 for international students; for spring admission, 1/1 for domestic students, 9/1 for international students. Applications are processed on a rolling basis. *Application fee:* $75. Electronic applications accepted. *Application Contact:* Crystal Tawney, Administrative Assistant, 540-231-4152, Fax: 540-231-4163, E-mail: cdtawney@vt.edu. *Dean,* Dr. Alan L. Grant, 540-231-4152, Fax: 540-231-4163, E-mail: algrant@vt.edu.

***College of Architecture and Urban Studies*** Students: 304 full-time (156 women), 180 part-time (77 women); includes 90 minority (40 Black or African American, non-Hispanic/Latino; 19 Asian, non-Hispanic/Latino; 24 Hispanic/Latino; 7 Two or more races, non-Hispanic/Latino), 130 international. Average age 33. 475 applicants, 72% accepted, 126 enrolled. *Faculty:* 145 full-time (58 women), 2 part-time/adjunct (1 woman). Expenses: Contact institution. *Financial support:* In 2019–20, 2 fellowships with full tuition reimbursements (averaging $24,875 per year), 35 research assistantships with full tuition reimbursements (averaging $16,344 per year), 126 teaching assistantships with full tuition reimbursements (averaging $11,525 per year) were awarded; scholarships/grants and unspecified assistantships also available. Financial award application deadline: 3/1; financial award applicants required to submit FAFSA. In 2019, 130 master's, 23 doctorates awarded. *Application deadline:* For fall admission, 8/1 for domestic students, 4/1 for international students; for spring admission, 1/1 for domestic students, 9/1 for international students. Applications are processed on a rolling basis. *Application fee:* $75. Electronic applications accepted. *Application Contact:* Christine Mattsson-Coon, Executive Assistant, 540-231-6416, Fax: 540-231-6332, E-mail: cmattsso@vt.edu. *Dean*, Dr. Richard Blythe, 540-231-6416, Fax: 540-231-6332, E-mail: richbl1@vt.edu.

***College of Engineering*** Students: 1,881 full-time (495 women), 326 part-time (70 women); includes 264 minority (51 Black or African American, non-Hispanic/Latino; 2 American Indian or Alaska Native, non-Hispanic/Latino; 96 Asian, non-Hispanic/Latino; 69 Hispanic/Latino; 46 Two or more races, non-Hispanic/Latino), 1,247 international. Average age 27. 4,014 applicants, 44% accepted, 658 enrolled. *Faculty:* 447 full-time (90 women), 6 part-time/adjunct (2 women). Expenses: Contact institution. *Financial support:* In 2019–20, 47 fellowships with full tuition reimbursements (averaging $19,703 per year), 1,163 research assistantships with full tuition reimbursements (averaging $20,602 per year), 554 teaching assistantships with full tuition reimbursements (averaging $16,333 per year) were awarded; scholarships/grants and unspecified assistantships also available. Financial award application deadline: 3/1; financial award applicants required to submit FAFSA. In 2019, 489 master's, 200 doctorates awarded. *Application deadline:* For fall admission, 8/1 for domestic students, 4/1 for international students; for spring admission, 1/1 for domestic students, 9/1 for international students. Applications are processed on a rolling basis. *Application fee:* $75. Electronic applications accepted. *Application Contact:* Linda Perkins, Executive Assistant, 540-231-9752, Fax: 540-231-3031, E-mail: lperkins@vt.edu. *Dean*, Dr. Julia Ross, 540-231-9752, Fax: 540-231-3031, E-mail: rjulie@vt.edu.

***College of Liberal Arts and Human Sciences*** Students: 571 full-time (405 women), 351 part-time (223 women); includes 176 minority (103 Black or African American, non-Hispanic/Latino; 3 American Indian or Alaska Native, non-Hispanic/Latino; 18 Asian, non-Hispanic/Latino; 31 Hispanic/Latino; 1 Native Hawaiian or other Pacific Islander, non-Hispanic/Latino; 20 Two or more races, non-Hispanic/Latino), 93 international. Average age 34. 865 applicants, 55% accepted, 336 enrolled. *Faculty:* 452 full-time (241 women), 1 (woman) part-time/adjunct. Expenses: Contact institution. *Financial support:* In 2019–20, 3 fellowships with full tuition reimbursements (averaging $7,621 per year), 34 research assistantships with full tuition reimbursements (averaging $15,645 per year), 370 teaching assistantships with full tuition reimbursements (averaging $18,225 per year) were awarded; scholarships/grants and unspecified assistantships also available. Financial award application deadline: 3/1; financial award applicants required to submit FAFSA. In 2019, 270 master's, 63 doctorates awarded. *Application deadline:* For fall admission, 8/1 for domestic students, 4/1 for international students; for spring admission, 1/1 for domestic students, 9/1 for international students. Applications are processed on a rolling basis. *Application fee:* $75. Electronic applications accepted. *Application Contact:* Chelsea Blanchet, Executive Assistant, 540-231-6779, Fax: 540-231-7157, E-mail: bchels1@vt.edu. *Dean*, Dr. Laura Belmonte, 540-231-6779, Fax: 540-231-7157, E-mail: belmonte@vt.edu.

***College of Natural Resources and Environment*** Students: 178 full-time (83 women), 69 part-time (43 women); includes 41 minority (6 Black or African American, non-Hispanic/Latino; 9 Asian, non-Hispanic/Latino; 22 Hispanic/Latino; 4 Two or more races, non-Hispanic/Latino), 29 international. Average age 31. 134 applicants, 63% accepted, 65 enrolled. *Faculty:* 84 full-time (20 women). Expenses: Contact institution. *Financial support:* In 2019–20, 3 fellowships with full tuition reimbursements (averaging $33,250 per year), 90 research assistantships with full tuition reimbursements (averaging $20,262 per year), 45 teaching assistantships with full tuition reimbursements (averaging $17,795 per year) were awarded; scholarships/grants also available. Financial award application deadline: 3/1; financial award applicants required to submit FAFSA. In 2019, 93 master's, 13 doctorates awarded. *Application deadline:* For fall admission, 8/1 for domestic students, 4/1 for international students; for spring admission, 1/1 for domestic students, 9/1 for international students. Applications are processed on a rolling basis. *Application fee:* $75. Electronic applications accepted. *Application Contact:* Arlice Banks, Executive Assistant, 540-231-7051, Fax: 540-231-7664, E-mail: arbanks@vt.edu. *Dean*, Dr. Paul M. Winistorfer, 540-231-5481, Fax: 540-231-7664, E-mail: pstorfer@vt.edu.

***College of Science*** Students: 544 full-time (221 women), 37 part-time (15 women); includes 75 minority (14 Black or African American, non-Hispanic/Latino; 1 American Indian or Alaska Native, non-Hispanic/Latino; 20 Asian, non-Hispanic/Latino; 31 Hispanic/Latino; 9 Two or more races, non-Hispanic/Latino), 216 international. Average age 27. 962 applicants, 33% accepted, 138 enrolled. *Faculty:* 375 full-time (118 women), 2 part-time/adjunct (1 woman). Expenses: Contact institution. *Financial support:* In 2019–20, 5 fellowships with full tuition reimbursements (averaging $25,988 per year), 281 research assistantships with full tuition reimbursements (averaging $15,597 per year), 370 teaching assistantships with full tuition reimbursements (averaging $18,225 per year) were awarded; unspecified assistantships also available. Financial award application deadline: 3/1; financial award applicants required to submit FAFSA. In 2019, 75 master's, 69 doctorates awarded. *Application deadline:* For fall admission, 8/1 for domestic students, 4/1 for international students; for spring admission, 1/1 for domestic students, 9/1 for international students. Applications are processed on a rolling basis. *Application fee:* $75. Electronic applications accepted. *Application Contact:* Allison Craft, Executive Assistant, 540-231-6394, Fax: 540-231-3380, E-mail: crafta@vt.edu. *Dean*, Dr. Sally C. Morton, 540-231-5422, Fax: 540-231-3380, E-mail: scmorton@vt.edu.

***Intercollege*** Students: 203 full-time (86 women), 745 part-time (218 women); includes 278 minority (64 Black or African American, non-Hispanic/Latino; 119 Asian, non-Hispanic/Latino; 59 Hispanic/Latino; 1 Native Hawaiian or other Pacific Islander, non-Hispanic/Latino; 35 Two or more races, non-Hispanic/Latino), 93 international. Average age 33. 603 applicants, 78% accepted, 327 enrolled. Expenses: Contact institution. *Financial support:* In 2019–20, 4 fellowships with full and partial tuition reimbursements (averaging $17,088 per year), 153 research assistantships with full tuition reimbursements (averaging $23,076 per year), 27 teaching assistantships with full tuition reimbursements (averaging $19,900 per year) were awarded; scholarships/grants also available. Financial award application deadline: 3/1; financial award applicants required to submit FAFSA. In 2019, 138 master's, 20 doctorates awarded. *Application deadline:* For fall admission, 8/1 for domestic students, 4/1 for international students; for spring admission, 1/1 for domestic students, 9/1 for international students. Applications are processed on a rolling basis. *Application fee:* $75. Electronic applications accepted. *Application Contact:* Dr. Janice Austin, 540-231-6691, E-mail: grads@vt.edu. *Vice President and Dean for Graduate Education*, Dr. Karen P. DePauw, 540-231-7581, Fax: 540-231-1670, E-mail: kpdepauw@vt.edu.

***Pamplin College of Business*** Students: 236 full-time (101 women), 201 part-time (67 women); includes 137 minority (29 Black or African American, non-Hispanic/Latino; 57 Asian, non-Hispanic/Latino; 32 Hispanic/Latino; 19 Two or more races, non-Hispanic/Latino), 82 international. Average age 32. 410 applicants, 59% accepted, 173 enrolled. *Faculty:* 145 full-time (39 women), 2 part-time/adjunct (0 women). Expenses: Contact institution. *Financial support:* In 2019–20, 1 fellowship with full tuition reimbursement (averaging $17,499 per year), 7 research assistantships with full tuition reimbursements (averaging $18,246 per year), 60 teaching assistantships with full tuition reimbursements (averaging $19,940 per year) were awarded; scholarships/grants and unspecified assistantships also available. Financial award application deadline: 3/1; financial award applicants required to submit FAFSA. In 2019, 181 master's, 8 doctorates awarded. *Program availability:* Part-time, evening/weekend, 100% online, blended/hybrid learning. *Application deadline:* For fall admission, 8/1 for domestic students, 4/1 for international students; for spring admission, 1/1 for domestic students, 9/1 for international students. Applications are processed on a rolling basis. *Application fee:* $75. Electronic applications accepted. *Application Contact:* Kimberly Ridpath, Executive Assistant, 540-231-9647, Fax: 540-231-4487, E-mail: ridpathk@vt.edu. *Dean*, Dr. Robert T. Sumichrast, 540-231-6601, Fax: 540-231-4487, E-mail: busdean@vt.edu.

**Virginia-Maryland College of Veterinary Medicine** Students: 583 full-time (422 women), 34 part-time (26 women); includes 142 minority (28 Black or African American, non-Hispanic/Latino; 3 American Indian or Alaska Native, non-Hispanic/Latino; 23 Asian, non-Hispanic/Latino; 35 Hispanic/Latino; 53 Two or more races, non-Hispanic/Latino), 28 international. Average age 26. 85 applicants, 87% accepted, 54 enrolled. *Faculty:* 132 full-time (79 women), 6 part-time/adjunct (5 women). Expenses: Contact institution. *Financial support:* In 2019–20, 3 fellowships with full and partial tuition reimbursements (averaging $2,668 per year), 33 research assistantships with full tuition reimbursements (averaging $19,301 per year), 30 teaching assistantships with full tuition reimbursements (averaging $21,932 per year) were awarded; scholarships/grants also available. Financial award application deadline: 3/1; financial award applicants required to submit FAFSA. In 2019, 33 master's, 137 doctorates awarded. *Application deadline:* For fall admission, 8/1 for domestic students, 4/1 for international students; for spring admission, 1/1 for domestic students, 9/1 for international students. Applications are processed on a rolling basis. *Application fee:* $75. Electronic applications accepted. *Application Contact:* Sheila Steele, Executive Assistant, 540-231-7910, Fax: 540-231-3505, E-mail: ssteele@vt.edu. *Dean*, Dr. Daniel Givens, 540-231-7910, Fax: 540-231-3505, E-mail: gdaniel@vt.edu.

**Virginia Tech Carilion School of Medicine and Research Institute** Students: 169 full-time (69 women), 1 part-time (0 women); includes 20 minority (4 Black or African American, non-Hispanic/Latino; 15 Asian, non-Hispanic/Latino; 1 Hispanic/Latino). Average age 26. *Faculty:* 10 full-time (6 women), 1 (woman) part-time/adjunct. Expenses: Contact institution. *Financial support:* Scholarships/grants available. In 2019, 37 doctorates awarded. *Application deadline:* For fall admission, 12/1 for domestic students. Electronic applications accepted. *Application Contact:* Lee Learman, MD, Dean, 540-526-2559. *Dean*, Lee Learman, MD, 540-526-2559.

**VT Online**

## VIRGINIA STATE UNIVERSITY, Petersburg, VA 23806-0001

**General Information** State-supported, coed, comprehensive institution. *Graduate housing:* Room and/or apartments available on a first-come, first-served basis to single students; on-campus housing not available to married students. Housing application deadline: 5/1. *Research affiliation:* Medical College of Virginia/Virginia Commonwealth University (biology), The College of William and Mary (biology), University of Massachusetts (biology), Rolls Royce USA (engineering), C-CAM Technologies (engineering).

**GRADUATE UNITS**

**College of Graduate Studies** *Program availability:* Part-time, evening/weekend.

***College of Education***

***College of Engineering and Technology***

***College of Humanities and Social Sciences*** *Program availability:* Part-time, evening/weekend.

***College of Natural and Health Sciences***

## VIRGINIA THEOLOGICAL SEMINARY, Alexandria, VA 22304

**General Information** Independent-religious, coed, graduate-only institution. *Graduate housing:* Rooms and/or apartments available on a first-come, first-served basis to single and married students. Housing application deadline: 5/1.

**GRADUATE UNITS**

**Graduate and Professional Programs** *Program availability:* Part-time.

## VIRGINIA UNION UNIVERSITY, Richmond, VA 23220-1170

**General Information** Independent-religious, coed, comprehensive institution. *Enrollment:* 304 full-time matriculated graduate/professional students (108 women), 29 part-time matriculated graduate/professional students (12 women). *Enrollment by degree level:* 286 master's, 47 doctoral. *Graduate faculty:* 9 full-time (2 women), 11 part-time/adjunct (2 women). *Graduate housing:* Room and/or apartments available on a first-come, first-served basis to single students; on-campus housing not available to married students. *Student services:* Career counseling, low-cost health insurance. *Library facilities:* L. Douglas Wilder Learning Resource Center and Library plus 1 other. *Collection:* Books: 123,475 (physical), 66,271 (digital/electronic); Databases: 100. Weekly public service hours: 41; students can reserve study rooms.

**Computer facilities:** 237 computers available on campus for general student use. A campuswide network can be accessed from student residence rooms. Online class registration is available.
Website: http://www.vuu.edu/

**General Application Contact:** Kimberly Clark, Registrar, 804-257-5715, E-mail: kaclark@vuu.edu.

**GRADUATE UNITS**

**Evelyn R. Syphax School of Education, Psychology and Interdisciplinary Studies**

**Samuel DeWitt Proctor School of Theology** *Program availability:* Part-time, evening/weekend.

## VIRGINIA UNIVERSITY OF INTEGRATIVE MEDICINE, Fairfax, VA 22031

**General Information** Private, coed, graduate-only institution. *Enrollment by degree level:* 304 master's, 32 doctoral. *Graduate faculty:* 11 full-time (4 women), 19 part-time/adjunct (7 women). *Tuition:* Part-time $300 per credit. *Graduate housing:* On-campus housing not available. *Student services:* Campus employment opportunities, campus safety program, career counseling, international student services, services for students with disabilities. *Library facilities:* Main library plus 1 other.

**Computer facilities:** 6 computers available on campus for general student use. A campuswide network can be accessed.
Website: http://www.vuim.edu/

**General Application Contact:** CHAD EGRESI, 703-323-5690 Ext. 102, E-mail: cegresi@vuim.edu.

**GRADUATE UNITS**
**Graduate Programs**

## VIRGINIA UNIVERSITY OF LYNCHBURG, Lynchburg, VA 24501-6417

**General Information** Independent-religious, coed, comprehensive institution. *Graduate housing:* Room and/or apartments available on a first-come, first-served basis to single students; on-campus housing not available to married students. Housing application deadline: 9/5.

**GRADUATE UNITS**
**Graduate Programs** *Program availability:* Online learning.

## VIRGINIA WESLEYAN UNIVERSITY, Virginia Beach, VA 23455

**General Information** Independent-religious, coed, comprehensive institution.

**GRADUATE UNITS**
**Graduate Studies** *Program availability:* Online learning.

## VITERBO UNIVERSITY, La Crosse, WI 54601-4797

**General Information** Independent-religious, coed, comprehensive institution. *Graduate housing:* Room and/or apartments available on a first-come, first-served basis to single students; on-campus housing not available to married students. Housing application deadline: 4/2.

**GRADUATE UNITS**
**Graduate Program in Nursing** *Program availability:* Part-time. Electronic applications accepted.
**Graduate Programs in Education** *Program availability:* Part-time, evening/weekend. Electronic applications accepted.
**Master of Arts in Servant Leadership Program** *Program availability:* Part-time, evening/weekend. Electronic applications accepted.
**Master of Business Administration Program** *Program availability:* Part-time, evening/weekend. Electronic applications accepted.
**Master of Science in Mental Health Counseling Program** *Program availability:* Part-time, evening/weekend. Electronic applications accepted.

## WAGNER COLLEGE, Staten Island, NY 10301-4495

**General Information** Independent, coed, comprehensive institution. *Graduate housing:* Room and/or apartments available on a first-come, first-served basis to single students; on-campus housing not available to married students. Housing application deadline: 4/1. *Research affiliation:* Staten Island University Hospital.

**GRADUATE UNITS**
**Division of Graduate Studies** *Program availability:* Part-time, evening/weekend. Electronic applications accepted.
***Evelyn L. Spiro School of Nursing*** *Program availability:* Part-time, evening/weekend. Electronic applications accepted.
***Nicolais School of Business*** *Program availability:* Part-time, evening/weekend.

## WAKE FOREST UNIVERSITY, Winston-Salem, NC 27109

**General Information** Independent, coed, university. CGS member. *Graduate housing:* On-campus housing not available.

**GRADUATE UNITS**
**Graduate School of Arts and Sciences** *Program availability:* Part-time. Electronic applications accepted.
**School of Business** *Program availability:* Evening/weekend. Electronic applications accepted.
**School of Law** Electronic applications accepted.
**School of Medicine** Electronic applications accepted.
***Graduate Programs in Medicine*** Electronic applications accepted.
**Virginia Tech-Wake Forest University School of Biomedical Engineering and Sciences** Electronic applications accepted.

## WALDEN UNIVERSITY, Minneapolis, MN 55401

**General Information** Proprietary, coed, university. CGS member.

**GRADUATE UNITS**
**Graduate Programs** *Program availability:* Part-time, evening/weekend, online only, 100% online. Electronic applications accepted.
***Richard W. Riley College of Education and Leadership*** *Program availability:* Part-time, evening/weekend, online only, 100% online. Electronic applications accepted.
***School of Counseling*** *Program availability:* Part-time, evening/weekend, online only, 100% online. Electronic applications accepted.
***School of Health Sciences*** *Program availability:* Part-time, evening/weekend, online only, 100% online. Electronic applications accepted.
***School of Information Systems and Technology*** *Program availability:* Part-time, evening/weekend, online only, 100% online. Electronic applications accepted.
***School of Management*** *Program availability:* Part-time, evening/weekend, online only, 100% online. Electronic applications accepted.
***School of Nursing*** *Program availability:* Part-time, evening/weekend, online only, 100% online. Electronic applications accepted.
***School of Psychology*** *Program availability:* Part-time, evening/weekend, online only, 100% online. Electronic applications accepted.
***School of Public Policy and Administration*** *Program availability:* Part-time, evening/weekend, online only, 100% online. Electronic applications accepted.
***School of Social Work and Human Services*** *Program availability:* Part-time, evening/weekend, online only, 100% online. Electronic applications accepted.

## WALDORF UNIVERSITY, Forest City, IA 50436

**General Information** Independent-religious, coed, comprehensive institution.

**GRADUATE UNITS**
**Program in Organizational Leadership**

## WALLA WALLA UNIVERSITY, College Place, WA 99324

**General Information** Independent-religious, coed, comprehensive institution. *Graduate housing:* Rooms and/or apartments available on a first-come, first-served basis to single and married students.

**GRADUATE UNITS**
**Graduate Studies** *Program availability:* Part-time, evening/weekend. Electronic applications accepted.
***Center for Cinema, Religion, and Worldview***
***School of Education and Psychology*** *Program availability:* Part-time. Electronic applications accepted.
***Wilma Hepker School of Social Work and Sociology*** *Program availability:* Part-time. Electronic applications accepted.

## WALSH COLLEGE OF ACCOUNTANCY AND BUSINESS ADMINISTRATION, Troy, MI 48083

**General Information** Independent, coed, upper-level institution. *Enrollment:* 1,811 graduate, professional, and undergraduate students; 33 full-time matriculated graduate/professional students (14 women), 1,025 part-time matriculated graduate/professional students (520 women). *Enrollment by degree level:* 1,058 master's. *Graduate faculty:* 22 full-time (8 women), 36 part-time/adjunct (14 women). *Tuition:* Full-time $22,059; part-time $7353 per credit hour. *Required fees:* $175 per semester. *Graduate housing:* On-campus housing not available. *Student services:* Career counseling, international student services, services for students with disabilities, writing training. *Library facilities:* Vollbrecht Library. *Collection:* Books: 25,320 (physical), 350,000 (digital/electronic); Serial titles: 125 (physical), 103,500 (digital/electronic); Databases: 132. Weekly public service hours: 40.

**Computer facilities:** 200 computers available on campus for general student use. A campuswide network can be accessed. Online class registration, Campus Wifi are available.
Website: http://www.walshcollege.edu/

**General Application Contact:** Karen Mahaffy, Executive Director, Admissions and Enrollment Services, 248-823-1216, Fax: 248-823-1611, E-mail: kmahaffy@walshcollege.edu.

**GRADUATE UNITS**
**Graduate Programs** *Program availability:* Part-time, evening/weekend, 100% online, blended/hybrid learning, on-ground. Electronic applications accepted.

## WALSH UNIVERSITY, North Canton, OH 44720-3396

**General Information** Independent-religious, coed, comprehensive institution. CGS member. *Enrollment:* 2,694 graduate, professional, and undergraduate students. *Enrollment by degree level:* 490 master's, 69 doctoral, 2 other advanced degrees. *Graduate housing:* Room and/or apartments available on a first-come, first-served basis to single students; on-campus housing not available to married students. Housing application deadline: 7/15. *Student services:* Campus employment opportunities, campus safety program, career counseling, exercise/wellness program, free psychological counseling, international student services, low-cost health insurance, multicultural affairs office, services for students with disabilities, teacher training, writing training. *Library facilities:* Brother Edmond Drouin Library. *Collection:* Books: 97,575 (physical), 254,114 (digital/electronic); Serial titles: 995 (physical), 82,413 (digital/electronic); Databases: 167. Weekly public service hours: 79. *Research affiliation:* North Canton Public Schools (straight A grants (student development)), Research Foundation of the Carolinas (surgery), Akron General Health System (patient satisfaction), Mercy Medical Center (orthopedics, nursing, physical therapy), Akron Children's Hospital (orthopedics).

**Computer facilities:** 336 computers available on campus for general student use. A campuswide network can be accessed. Online class registration is available.
Website: http://www.walsh.edu/

**General Application Contact:** Audra Dice, Director of Graduate Admissions, 330-490-7181, Fax: 330-490-7165, E-mail: adice@walsh.edu.

**GRADUATE UNITS**
**Doctor of Nursing Practice**
**Doctor of Physical Therapy** Students: 95 full-time (66 women); includes 3 minority (1 Black or African American, non-Hispanic/Latino; 2 Two or more races, non-Hispanic/Latino). Average age 25. 201 applicants, 25% accepted, 30 enrolled. *Faculty:* 7 full-time (5 women), 1 (woman) part-time/adjunct. Expenses: Contact institution. *Financial support:* In 2019–20, 3 students received support. Unspecified assistantships available. Financial award application deadline: 12/31; financial award applicants required to submit FAFSA. In 2019, 31 doctorates awarded. *Application deadline:* For fall admission, 10/1 priority date for domestic students. Electronic applications accepted. *Application Contact:* Mona McAuliffe, Associate Director of Graduate Admissions, 330-490-7406, Fax: 330-490-7406, E-mail: mmcauliffe@walsh.edu. *Program Director*, Dr. Leigh Murray, 330-490-7259, E-mail: lmurray@walsh.edu.
**Master of Arts in Counseling and Human Development (CHD)** Students: 38 full-time (30 women), 36 part-time (28 women); includes 7 minority (5 Black or African American, non-Hispanic/Latino; 1 Asian, non-Hispanic/Latino; 1 Two or more races, non-Hispanic/Latino), 3 international. Average age 28. 43 applicants, 84% accepted, 19 enrolled. *Faculty:* 6 full-time (5 women), 8 part-time/adjunct (7 women). Expenses: Contact institution. *Financial support:* In 2019–20, 5 students received support. Research assistantships and unspecified assistantships available. Financial award application deadline: 12/31. In 2019, 27 master's awarded. *Program availability:* Part-time, evening/weekend, blended/hybrid learning. *Application deadline:* For fall admission, 7/15 priority date for domestic students. Applications are processed on a rolling basis. Electronic applications accepted. *Application Contact:* Dr. Lisa Zimmerman, Program Director, 330-490-7266, E-mail: lzimmerman@walsh.edu. *Program Director*, Dr. Lisa Zimmerman, 330-490-7266, E-mail: lzimmerman@walsh.edu.
**Master of Arts in Education** Students: 15 full-time (7 women), 53 part-time (41 women); includes 1 minority (Black or African American, non-Hispanic/Latino). Average age 32. 28 applicants, 71% accepted, 18 enrolled. *Faculty:* 4 full-time (2 women). Expenses: Contact institution. *Financial support:* In 2019–20, 1 student received support. Unspecified assistantships available. Financial award application deadline: 12/31; financial award applicants required to submit FAFSA. In 2019, 36 master's awarded. *Program availability:* Part-time, online only, 100% online. *Application deadline:* For fall admission, 7/15 priority date for domestic students. Applications are processed on a rolling basis. Electronic applications accepted. *Application Contact:* Dr. David

Brobeck, Graduate Education Program Director, 330-490-7385, Fax: 330-490-7385, E-mail: dbrobeck@walsh.edu. *Graduate Education Program Director*, Dr. David Brobeck, 330-490-7385, Fax: 330-490-7385, E-mail: dbrobeck@walsh.edu.

**Master of Arts in Theology Program** Students: 2 full-time (1 woman), 11 part-time (5 women); includes 1 minority (Black or African American, non-Hispanic/Latino). Average age 45. *Faculty:* 2 full-time (0 women), 1 part-time/adjunct (0 women). Expenses: Contact institution. *Financial support:* Unspecified assistantships available. Financial award application deadline: 12/31; financial award applicants required to submit FAFSA. In 2019, 4 master's awarded. *Program availability:* Part-time, evening/weekend, 100% online. *Application deadline:* For fall admission, 7/15 for domestic students. Applications are processed on a rolling basis. Electronic applications accepted. *Application Contact:* Dr. Chris Seeman, Graduate Program Director, 330-244-4665, E-mail: cseeman@walsh.edu. *Graduate Program Director*, Dr. Chris Seeman, 330-244-4665, E-mail: cseeman@walsh.edu.

**Master of Business Administration** Students: 60 full-time (32 women), 128 part-time (67 women); includes 23 minority (12 Black or African American, non-Hispanic/Latino; 1 American Indian or Alaska Native, non-Hispanic/Latino; 1 Asian, non-Hispanic/Latino; 9 Two or more races, non-Hispanic/Latino), 4 international. Average age 39. 158 applicants, 50% accepted, 51 enrolled. *Faculty:* 11 full-time (6 women), 9 part-time/adjunct (4 women). Expenses: Contact institution. *Financial support:* In 2019–20, 4 students received support. Unspecified assistantships available. Financial award application deadline: 12/31; financial award applicants required to submit FAFSA. In 2019, 52 master's awarded. *Program availability:* Part-time, evening/weekend, online only, 100% online. *Application deadline:* For fall admission, 7/15 priority date for domestic students. Applications are processed on a rolling basis. Electronic applications accepted. *Application Contact:* Dr. Rajshekhar Javalgi, Dean, DeVille School of Business, 330-4907048, E-mail: rjavalgi@walsh.edu. *Dean, DeVille School of Business*, Dr. Rajshekhar Javalgi, 330-4907048, E-mail: rjavalgi@walsh.edu.

**Master of Occupational Therapy** Students: 61 full-time (54 women); includes 3 minority (2 Black or African American, non-Hispanic/Latino; 1 Asian, non-Hispanic/Latino), 1 international. Average age 25. 90 applicants, 67% accepted, 33 enrolled. *Faculty:* 5 full-time (all women). Expenses: Contact institution. *Financial support:* Unspecified assistantships available. Financial award application deadline: 8/28; financial award applicants required to submit FAFSA. *Application deadline:* For fall admission, 10/15 for domestic and international students. *Application Contact:* Marcie Erickson, Graduate Admissions Counselor, 330-490-7418, E-mail: merickson@walsh.edu. *Program Director*, Dr. Stephanie Bachman, 330-490-7522, E-mail: sbachman@walsh.edu.

**Master of Science in Nursing** Students: 80 full-time (68 women), 83 part-time (73 women); includes 12 minority (5 Black or African American, non-Hispanic/Latino; 1 Asian, non-Hispanic/Latino; 6 Two or more races, non-Hispanic/Latino). Average age 35. 76 applicants, 93% accepted, 55 enrolled. *Faculty:* 5 full-time (4 women), 11 part-time/adjunct (10 women). Expenses: Contact institution. *Financial support:* In 2019–20, 1 student received support. Research assistantships available. Financial award application deadline: 12/31; financial award applicants required to submit FAFSA. In 2019, 38 master's, 2 doctorates awarded. *Program availability:* Part-time, 100% online, blended/hybrid learning. *Application deadline:* Applications are processed on a rolling basis. Electronic applications accepted. *Application Contact:* Dr. Janet Finneran, Director of Graduate Nursing Programs, 330-2444759, Fax: 330-4907206, E-mail: jfinneran@walsh.edu. *Dean, Byers School of Nursing*, Dr. Judy Kreye, 330-2444757, Fax: 330-4907206, E-mail: jkreye@walsh.edu.

## WARNER PACIFIC UNIVERSITY, Portland, OR 97215-4099

**General Information** Independent-religious, coed, comprehensive institution. *Graduate housing:* On-campus housing not available.

**GRADUATE UNITS**

**Graduate Programs** *Program availability:* Part-time, evening/weekend.

## WARNER UNIVERSITY, Lake Wales, FL 33859

**General Information** Independent-religious, coed, comprehensive institution. *Graduate housing:* Room and/or apartments available on a first-come, first-served basis to single students; on-campus housing not available to married students.

**GRADUATE UNITS**

**School of Business** *Program availability:* Part-time, evening/weekend, online learning. Electronic applications accepted.

**School of Education** *Program availability:* Part-time, evening/weekend, online learning. Electronic applications accepted.

## WARREN WILSON COLLEGE, Asheville, NC 28815-9000

**General Information** Independent-religious, coed, comprehensive institution. *Enrollment:* 791 graduate, professional, and undergraduate students; 87 full-time matriculated graduate/professional students (60 women). *Enrollment by degree level:* 76 master's. *Graduate faculty:* 25 full-time (13 women). *Tuition:* Full-time $18,800. *Graduate housing:* Room and/or apartments guaranteed to single students; on-campus housing not available to married students. Typical cost: $1200 (including board). Housing application deadline: 3/10. *Library facilities:* Pew Learning Center and Ellison Library.

**Computer facilities:** A campuswide network can be accessed. Online class registration, home directory and public html for each user, word processing, GIS, Statistical Analysis are available.
Website: http://www.warren-wilson.edu/

**General Application Contact:** Trish Marshall, MFA Program Manager, 828-771-3717, Fax: 828-771-3717.

**GRADUATE UNITS**

**Master of Arts Program in Critical and Historical Craft Studies** Electronic applications accepted.

**MFA Program for Writers** Electronic applications accepted.

## WARTBURG THEOLOGICAL SEMINARY, Dubuque, IA 52004-5004

**General Information** Independent-religious, coed, graduate-only institution. *Graduate housing:* Rooms and/or apartments available on a first-come, first-served basis to single and married students. Housing application deadline: 4/30. *Research affiliation:* Menighetsfakultet, Augustana Theologische Hochschule.

**GRADUATE UNITS**

**Graduate and Professional Programs** *Program availability:* Online learning. Electronic applications accepted.

## WASHBURN UNIVERSITY, Topeka, KS 66621

**General Information** City-supported, coed, comprehensive institution. *Graduate housing:* Room and/or apartments available on a first-come, first-served basis to single students; on-campus housing not available to married students.

**GRADUATE UNITS**

**College of Arts and Sciences** *Program availability:* Part-time, evening/weekend. Electronic applications accepted.

**School of Applied Studies** *Program availability:* Part-time, evening/weekend, online learning.

**School of Business** *Program availability:* Part-time, evening/weekend. Electronic applications accepted.

**School of Law** Electronic applications accepted.

**School of Nursing** *Program availability:* Part-time.

## WASHINGTON ADVENTIST UNIVERSITY, Takoma Park, MD 20912

**General Information** Independent-religious, coed, comprehensive institution. *Graduate housing:* Rooms and/or apartments available on a first-come, first-served basis to single and married students. Housing application deadline: 8/1.

**GRADUATE UNITS**

**MBA Program** *Program availability:* Part-time, evening/weekend, online learning.

**Program in Counseling Psychology** *Program availability:* Part-time.

**Program in Health Care Administration** *Program availability:* Part-time. Electronic applications accepted.

**Program in Nursing - Business Leadership** *Program availability:* Part-time.

**Program in Nursing - Education** *Program availability:* Part-time.

**Program in Professional Counseling Psychology** *Program availability:* Part-time.

**Program in Public Administration** *Program availability:* Part-time.

**Program in Religion** *Program availability:* Part-time.

## WASHINGTON & JEFFERSON COLLEGE, Washington, PA 15301

**General Information** Independent, coed, comprehensive institution.

**GRADUATE UNITS**

**Graduate and Continuing Studies**

## WASHINGTON AND LEE UNIVERSITY, Lexington, VA 24450

**General Information** Independent, coed, comprehensive institution. *Research affiliation:* Future of Privacy Forum (data privacy, data security, and related fields).

**GRADUATE UNITS**

**School of Law** Electronic applications accepted.

## WASHINGTON STATE UNIVERSITY, Pullman, WA 99164

**General Information** State-supported, coed, university. CGS member. *Graduate housing:* Rooms and/or apartments available on a first-come, first-served basis to single and married students. Housing application deadline: 3/1. *Research affiliation:* Battelle–Pacific Northwest National Laboratory (biochemistry, engineering).

**GRADUATE UNITS**

**Carson College of Business** *Program availability:* Online learning.

**College of Agricultural, Human, and Natural Resource Sciences** *Program availability:* Part-time, online learning. Electronic applications accepted.

***School of Economic Sciences*** Electronic applications accepted.

***School of Food Science*** *Program availability:* Part-time. Electronic applications accepted.

***School of the Environment***

**College of Arts and Sciences** Electronic applications accepted.

***School of Biological Sciences***

***School of Music*** *Program availability:* Part-time. Electronic applications accepted.

***School of Politics, Philosophy and Public Affairs*** *Program availability:* Online learning. Electronic applications accepted.

***School of the Environment***

**College of Education** Electronic applications accepted.

**College of Nursing**

**College of Pharmacy and Pharmaceutical Sciences**

**College of Veterinary Medicine** Students: 530 full-time (405 women); includes 80 minority (1 American Indian or Alaska Native, non-Hispanic/Latino; 16 Asian, non-Hispanic/Latino; 4 Hispanic/Latino; 1 Native Hawaiian or other Pacific Islander, non-Hispanic/Latino; 58 Two or more races, non-Hispanic/Latino), 3 international. Average age 24. 1,499 applicants, 14% accepted, 135 enrolled. *Faculty:* 24 full-time (5 women), 50 part-time/adjunct (12 women). Expenses: Contact institution. *Financial support:* In 2019–20, 446 students received support, including 28 fellowships with full tuition reimbursements available, 87 research assistantships with full tuition reimbursements available (averaging $27,018 per year), 34 teaching assistantships with full tuition reimbursements available (averaging $27,018 per year); career-related internships or fieldwork, Federal Work-Study, institutionally sponsored loans, scholarships/grants, traineeships, health care benefits, and unspecified assistantships also available. Support available to part-time students. Financial award application deadline: 1/31; financial award applicants required to submit FAFSA. In 2019, 18 master's, 126 doctorates awarded. *Application deadline:* For fall admission, 9/15 for domestic and international students; for spring admission, 8/1 for international students. *Application fee:* $65. Electronic applications accepted. *Application Contact:* Stacey Poler, Recruitment Officer, 509-335-6133, E-mail: s.poler@wsu.edu. *Dean*, Dr. Dori Borjesson, 509-3359515, E-mail: dori.borjesson@wsu.edu.

**The Edward R. Murrow College of Communication** Electronic applications accepted.

**Elson S. Floyd College of Medicine**

**Voiland College of Engineering and Architecture**

***The Gene and Linda Voiland School of Chemical Engineering and Bioengineering***

***School of Electrical Engineering and Computer Science*** *Program availability:* Part-time.

***School of Mechanical and Materials Engineering*** *Program availability:* Part-time. Electronic applications accepted.

## WASHINGTON UNIVERSITY IN ST. LOUIS, St. Louis, MO 63130-4899

**General Information** Independent, coed, university. CGS member. *Graduate housing:* Rooms and/or apartments available on a first-come, first-served basis to single and married students.

**GRADUATE UNITS**

**Brown School** Students: 282 full-time (226 women); includes 90 minority (40 Black or African American, non-Hispanic/Latino; 10 American Indian or Alaska Native, non-Hispanic/Latino; 26 Asian, non-Hispanic/Latino; 13 Hispanic/Latino; 1 Native Hawaiian or other Pacific Islander, non-Hispanic/Latino). Average age 24. *Faculty:* 54 full-time (31 women), 87 part-time/adjunct (61 women). Expenses: Contact institution. *Financial support:* In 2019–20, 90 research assistantships were awarded; fellowships, teaching assistantships, career-related internships or fieldwork, Federal Work-Study, scholarships/grants, and unspecified assistantships also available. Support available to part-time students. Financial award applicants required to submit FAFSA. *Application deadline:* For fall admission, 12/15 priority date for domestic and international students; for winter admission, 3/1 priority date for domestic and international students. Applications are processed on a rolling basis. Electronic applications accepted. *Application Contact:* Office of Admissions and Recruitment, 314-935-6676, Fax: 314-935-4859, E-mail: brownadmissions@wustl.edu. *Director of Admissions and Recruitment*, Jamie L. Adkisson-Hennessey, 314-935-3524, Fax: 314-935-4859, E-mail: jadkisson@wustl.edu.

**The Graduate School** Electronic applications accepted.

***Division of Biology and Biomedical Sciences*** Electronic applications accepted.

**Olin Business School** Electronic applications accepted.

**Sam Fox School of Design and Visual Arts**

***Graduate School of Art*** Electronic applications accepted.

**School of Engineering and Applied Science** *Program availability:* Part-time, evening/weekend. Electronic applications accepted.

**School of Law** Students: 978 full-time (483 women), 17 part-time (8 women). Average age 26. 4,129 applicants, 25% accepted, 229 enrolled. *Faculty:* 82 full-time (41 women), 87 part-time/adjunct (28 women). Expenses: Contact institution. *Financial support:* Career-related internships or fieldwork, Federal Work-Study, institutionally sponsored loans, scholarships/grants, and health care benefits available. Support available to part-time students. Financial award applicants required to submit FAFSA. In 2019, 235 doctorates awarded. *Application deadline:* Applications are processed on a rolling basis. Electronic applications accepted. *Application Contact:* Mary Ann Clifford, Assistant Dean for Admissions, 314-935-4525, E-mail: applylaw@wustl.edu. *Dean of the Law School, Howard and Caroline Cayne Distinguished Professor of Law*, Nancy Staudt, 314-935-6420.

**School of Medicine** Electronic applications accepted.

***Division of Biostatistics*** *Program availability:* Part-time. Electronic applications accepted.

## WATKINS COLLEGE OF ART, DESIGN, & FILM, Nashville, TN 37228

**General Information** Independent, coed, comprehensive institution.

**GRADUATE UNITS**

**Program in Film** *Program availability:* Evening/weekend.

## WAYLAND BAPTIST UNIVERSITY, Plainview, TX 79072-6998

**General Information** Independent-religious, coed, comprehensive institution. *Enrollment:* 4,827 graduate, professional, and undergraduate students; 71 full-time matriculated graduate/professional students (41 women), 985 part-time matriculated graduate/professional students (519 women). *Enrollment by degree level:* 1,027 master's, 29 doctoral. *Graduate faculty:* 142 full-time (52 women), 375 part-time/adjunct (155 women). *Tuition:* Full-time $728; part-time $728 per semester. *Required fees:* $1218. Tuition and fees vary according to degree level, campus/location and program. *Graduate housing:* Rooms and/or apartments available on a first-come, first-served basis to single and married students. Typical cost: $3354 per year ($8342 including board) for single students. *Student services:* Campus employment opportunities, campus safety program, career counseling, free psychological counseling, international student services, services for students with disabilities, teacher training, writing training. *Library facilities:* J.E. and L.E. Mabee Learning Resource Center. *Collection:* Books: 130,903 (physical), 49,479 (digital/electronic); Serial titles: 555,663 (digital/electronic); Databases: 104.

**Computer facilities:** Computer purchase and lease plans are available. 840 computers available on campus for general student use. A campuswide network can be accessed from student residence rooms and from off campus. Online class registration is available.
Website: http://www.wbu.edu/

**General Application Contact:** Amanda Stanton, Coordinator of Graduate Studies, 806-291-3423, Fax: 806-291-1953, E-mail: stanton@wbu.edu.

**GRADUATE UNITS**

**Graduate Programs** Students: 71 full-time (41 women), 985 part-time (519 women); includes 635 minority (236 Black or African American, non-Hispanic/Latino; 4 American Indian or Alaska Native, non-Hispanic/Latino; 35 Asian, non-Hispanic/Latino; 291 Hispanic/Latino; 18 Native Hawaiian or other Pacific Islander, non-Hispanic/Latino; 51 Two or more races, non-Hispanic/Latino), 6 international. Average age 40. 230 applicants, 94% accepted, 155 enrolled. *Faculty:* 142 full-time (52 women), 375 part-time/adjunct (155 women). Expenses: Contact institution. *Financial support:* Federal Work-Study, institutionally sponsored loans, and scholarships/grants available. Support available to part-time students. Financial award application deadline: 5/1; financial award applicants required to submit FAFSA. In 2019, 391 master's awarded. *Program availability:* Part-time, evening/weekend, 100% online, blended/hybrid learning. *Application deadline:* Applications are processed on a rolling basis. *Application fee:* $50. Electronic applications accepted. *Application Contact:* Amanda Stanton, Coordinator of Graduate Studies, 806-291-3423, Fax: 806-291-1950, E-mail: stanton@wbu.edu. *Vice President of Academics*, Dr. Cindy McClenegan, 806-291-3410, Fax: 806-291-1953, E-mail: hallb@wbu.edu.

## WAYNESBURG UNIVERSITY, Waynesburg, PA 15370-1222

**General Information** Independent-religious, coed, comprehensive institution. *Graduate housing:* Room and/or apartments available on a first-come, first-served basis to single students; on-campus housing not available to married students. Housing application deadline: 8/1.

**GRADUATE UNITS**

**Graduate and Professional Studies** *Program availability:* Part-time, evening/weekend. Electronic applications accepted.

## WAYNE STATE COLLEGE, Wayne, NE 68787

**General Information** State-supported, coed, comprehensive institution. CGS member. *Graduate housing:* Room and/or apartments available on a first-come, first-served basis to single students; on-campus housing not available to married students. *Research affiliation:* Nebraska Business Development Center, Social Sciences Research Center.

**GRADUATE UNITS**

**Department of Health, Human Performance and Sport** *Program availability:* Part-time, evening/weekend. Electronic applications accepted.

**School of Business and Technology** *Program availability:* Part-time, evening/weekend, online learning.

**School of Education and Counseling** *Program availability:* Part-time, evening/weekend.

## WAYNE STATE UNIVERSITY, Detroit, MI 48202

**General Information** State-supported, coed, university. CGS member. *Enrollment:* 26,844 graduate, professional, and undergraduate students. *Enrollment by degree level:* 5,062 master's, 3,748 doctoral, 280 other advanced degrees. *Tuition:* Full-time $34,567. *Graduate housing:* Rooms and/or apartments available on a first-come, first-served basis to single and married students. *Student services:* Campus employment opportunities, campus safety program, career counseling, child daycare facilities, exercise/wellness program, free psychological counseling, grant writing training, international student services, multicultural affairs office, services for students with disabilities, teacher training, writing training. *Library facilities:* David Adamany Undergraduate Library plus 5 others. *Collection:* Books: 1.7 million (physical), 1.1 million (digital/electronic); Serial titles: 60,832 (physical), 112,521 (digital/electronic); Databases: 700. Weekly public service hours: 138; study areas open 24 hours, 5–7 days a week. *Research affiliation:* Detroit Medical Center, Henry Ford Health System, John A. Dingell VA Medical Center, Karmanos Cancer Institute.

**Computer facilities:** A campuswide network can be accessed. Online class registration is available.
Website: http://www.wayne.edu/

**General Application Contact:** Sherry Quinn, Office of Graduate Admissions, 313-577-8141, Fax: 313-625-6053, E-mail: gradadmissions@wayne.edu.

**GRADUATE UNITS**

**College of Education** Students: 450 full-time (344 women), 683 part-time (497 women); includes 454 minority (326 Black or African American, non-Hispanic/Latino; 7 American Indian or Alaska Native, non-Hispanic/Latino; 18 Asian, non-Hispanic/Latino; 49 Hispanic/Latino; 54 Two or more races, non-Hispanic/Latino), 34 international. Average age 35. 944 applicants, 30% accepted, 198 enrolled. *Faculty:* 47. Expenses: Contact institution. *Financial support:* In 2019–20, 301 students received support, including 3 fellowships with tuition reimbursements available (averaging $22,500 per year), 6 research assistantships with tuition reimbursements available (averaging $20,633 per year); teaching assistantships with tuition reimbursements available, Federal Work-Study, scholarships/grants, traineeships, health care benefits, and unspecified assistantships also available. Support available to part-time students. Financial award applicants required to submit FAFSA. In 2019, 323 master's, 33 doctorates, 71 other advanced degrees awarded. *Program availability:* Part-time, evening/weekend, 100% online, blended/hybrid learning. *Application deadline:* For fall admission, 6/1 priority date for domestic students, 5/1 for international students; for winter admission, 10/1 priority date for domestic students, 9/1 priority date for international students; for spring admission, 2/1 priority date for domestic students, 1/1 priority date for international students. *Application fee:* $50. Electronic applications accepted. *Application Contact:* Paul W. Johnson, Assistant Dean of Academic Services, 313-577-1606, E-mail: askcoe@wayne.edu. *Dean*, Dr. R. Douglas Whitman, 313-577-1620, E-mail: dwhitman@wayne.edu.

***Division of Administrative and Organizational Studies*** Students: 80 full-time (57 women), 243 part-time (182 women); includes 172 minority (143 Black or African American, non-Hispanic/Latino; 6 Asian, non-Hispanic/Latino; 12 Hispanic/Latino; 11 Two or more races, non-Hispanic/Latino), 10 international. Average age 40. 206 applicants, 28% accepted, 40 enrolled. *Faculty:* 8. Expenses: Contact institution. *Financial support:* In 2019–20, 98 students received support, including 4 research assistantships with tuition reimbursements available (averaging $19,967 per year); fellowships with tuition reimbursements available, scholarships/grants, and unspecified assistantships also available. Support available to part-time students. Financial award applicants required to submit FAFSA. In 2019, 48 master's, 9 doctorates, 42 other advanced degrees awarded. *Program availability:* Part-time, evening/weekend. *Application deadline:* Applications are processed on a rolling basis. *Application fee:* $50. Electronic applications accepted. *Application Contact:* Dr. Mary L. Waker, Graduate Admissions Officer, 313-577-1601, Fax: 313-577-7904, E-mail: m.waker@wayne.edu. *Assistant Dean*, Dr. William Hill, 313-577-9316, E-mail: ad2107@wayne.edu.

***Division of Teacher Education*** Students: 97 full-time (70 women), 208 part-time (166 women); includes 86 minority (48 Black or African American, non-Hispanic/Latino; 5 American Indian or Alaska Native, non-Hispanic/Latino; 4 Asian, non-Hispanic/Latino; 14 Hispanic/Latino; 15 Two or more races, non-Hispanic/Latino), 7 international. Average age 36. 213 applicants, 28% accepted, 41 enrolled. *Faculty:* 18. Expenses: Contact institution. *Financial support:* In 2019–20, 62 students received support, including 2 fellowships (averaging $23,750 per year), 1 research assistantship with tuition reimbursement available (averaging $23,960 per year); Federal Work-Study, scholarships/grants, and unspecified assistantships also available. Support available to part-time students. Financial award applicants required to submit FAFSA. In 2019, 107 master's, 9 doctorates, 10 other advanced degrees awarded. *Program availability:* Part-time, evening/weekend. *Application deadline:* Applications are processed on a rolling basis. *Application fee:* $50. Electronic applications accepted. *Application Contact:* Dr. Mary L. Waker, Graduate Admissions Officer, 313-577-1601, Fax: 313-577-7904, E-mail: m.waker@wayne.edu. *Assistant Dean for Teacher Education*, Dr. Roland Coloma, 313-577-0902, E-mail: rscoloma@wayne.edu.

***Division of Theoretical and Behavioral Foundations*** Students: 199 full-time (171 women), 142 part-time (107 women); includes 135 minority (90 Black or African American, non-Hispanic/Latino; 2 American Indian or Alaska Native, non-Hispanic/Latino; 6 Asian, non-Hispanic/Latino; 16 Hispanic/Latino; 21 Two or more races, non-Hispanic/Latino), 10 international. Average age 32. 364 applicants, 25% accepted, 72 enrolled. *Faculty:* 10. Expenses: Contact institution. *Financial support:* In 2019–20, 92 students received support, including 1 fellowship (averaging $20,000 per year), 1 research assistantship with tuition reimbursement available (averaging $19,967 per year); teaching assistantships, Federal Work-Study, scholarships/grants, health care benefits, and unspecified assistantships also available. Support available to part-time students. Financial award applicants required to submit FAFSA. In 2019, 101 master's, 11 doctorates, 19 other advanced degrees awarded. *Program availability:* Part-time, evening/weekend. *Application deadline:* Applications are processed on a rolling basis. *Application fee:* $50. Electronic applications accepted. *Application Contact:* Dr. Mary L Waker, Graduate Admissions Officer, 313-577-1601,

Fax: 313-577-7904, E-mail: m.waker@wayne.edu. *Assistant Dean,* Dr. William Hill, 313-577-9316, E-mail: ad2107@wayne.edu.

**College of Engineering** Students: 601 full-time (178 women), 388 part-time (107 women); includes 137 minority (50 Black or African American, non-Hispanic/Latino; 57 Asian, non-Hispanic/Latino; 19 Hispanic/Latino; 11 Two or more races, non-Hispanic/Latino), 536 international. Average age 29. 1,774 applicants, 34% accepted, 203 enrolled. *Faculty:* 118. Expenses: Contact institution. *Financial support:* In 2019–20, 484 students received support, including 22 fellowships with tuition reimbursements available (averaging $20,144 per year), 72 research assistantships with tuition reimbursements available (averaging $21,706 per year), 86 teaching assistantships with tuition reimbursements available (averaging $20,780 per year); Federal Work-Study, scholarships/grants, health care benefits, tuition waivers (full and partial), and unspecified assistantships also available. Support available to part-time students. Financial award applicants required to submit FAFSA. In 2019, 423 master's, 43 doctorates, 5 other advanced degrees awarded. *Program availability:* Part-time, evening/weekend. *Application deadline:* For fall admission, 7/15 priority date for domestic students, 5/15 priority date for international students; for winter admission, 11/1 priority date for domestic students, 10/1 priority date for international students; for spring admission, 2/1 priority date for domestic students, 1/1 priority date for international students. Applications are processed on a rolling basis. *Application fee:* $50. Electronic applications accepted. *Application Contact:* Graduate Program Coordinator, E-mail: engineeringgradadmissions@eng.wayne.edu. *Dean,* Dr. Farshad Fotouhi, 313-577-3776, E-mail: fotouhi@wayne.edu.

***Division of Engineering Technology*** Students: 8 full-time (0 women), 5 part-time (0 women); includes 4 minority (3 Black or African American, non-Hispanic/Latino; 1 Asian, non-Hispanic/Latino), 5 international. Average age 31. 13 applicants, 69% accepted, 2 enrolled. *Faculty:* 5. Expenses: Contact institution. *Financial support:* In 2019–20, 3 students received support. Career-related internships or fieldwork and scholarships/grants available. Financial award applicants required to submit FAFSA. In 2019, 11 master's awarded. *Application deadline:* For fall admission, 6/1 priority date for domestic students, 5/1 priority date for international students; for winter admission, 10/1 priority date for domestic students, 9/1 priority date for international students; for spring admission, 2/1 priority date for domestic students, 1/1 priority date for international students. Applications are processed on a rolling basis. *Application fee:* $50. Electronic applications accepted. *Application Contact:* Rob Carlson, Graduate Program Coordinator, 313-577-9615, E-mail: rcarlson@wayne.edu. *Division Chair,* Dr. Ece Yaprak, 313-577-0875, E-mail: yaprak@eng.wayne.edu.

**College of Fine, Performing and Communication Arts** *Program availability:* Online learning. Electronic applications accepted.

**College of Liberal Arts and Sciences** *Program availability:* Part-time, evening/weekend, online learning. Electronic applications accepted.

**College of Nursing** Students: 134 full-time (118 women), 216 part-time (187 women); includes 98 minority (51 Black or African American, non-Hispanic/Latino; 24 Asian, non-Hispanic/Latino; 6 Hispanic/Latino; 17 Two or more races, non-Hispanic/Latino), 18 international. Average age 33. 425 applicants, 37% accepted, 95 enrolled. *Faculty:* 27. Expenses: Contact institution. *Financial support:* In 2019–20, 104 students received support, including 39 fellowships with tuition reimbursements available (averaging $6,456 per year), 1 research assistantship (averaging $24,950 per year), 5 teaching assistantships with tuition reimbursements available (averaging $25,000 per year); scholarships/grants, health care benefits, and unspecified assistantships also available. Support available to part-time students. Financial award application deadline: 3/1; financial award applicants required to submit FAFSA. In 2019, 58 master's, 31 doctorates awarded. *Program availability:* Part-time. *Application deadline:* For fall admission, 1/31 for domestic students; for winter admission, 11/1 for domestic students. Applications are processed on a rolling basis. *Application fee:* $50. Electronic applications accepted. *Application Contact:* Dr. Laurie M Lauzon Clabo, Dean, College of Nursing, 313-577-4082, E-mail: laurie.lauzon.clabo@wayne.edu. *Dean, College of Nursing,* Dr. Laurie M Lauzon Clabo, 313-577-4082, E-mail: laurie.lauzon.clabo@wayne.edu.

**Eugene Applebaum College of Pharmacy and Health Sciences** *Program availability:* Part-time, evening/weekend. Electronic applications accepted.

**Law School** Students: 393 full-time (197 women), 41 part-time (20 women); includes 63 minority (38 Black or African American, non-Hispanic/Latino; 6 American Indian or Alaska Native, non-Hispanic/Latino; 9 Asian, non-Hispanic/Latino; 5 Hispanic/Latino; 5 Two or more races, non-Hispanic/Latino), 8 international. Average age 26. 741 applicants, 44% accepted, 119 enrolled. *Faculty:* 40 full-time (17 women), 52 part-time/adjunct (23 women). Expenses: Contact institution. *Financial support:* In 2019–20, 326 students received support. Federal Work-Study and scholarships/grants available. Support available to part-time students. Financial award application deadline: 6/30; financial award applicants required to submit FAFSA. In 2019, 4 master's awarded. *Program availability:* Part-time, evening/weekend. *Application deadline:* For fall admission, 7/1 for domestic students. Applications are processed on a rolling basis. Electronic applications accepted. *Application Contact:* Kathy Fox, Assistant Dean of Admissions, 313-577-3937, Fax: 313-993-8129, E-mail: lawinquire@wayne.edu. *Dean and Professor of Law,* Richard A. Bierschbach, 313-577-3933, E-mail: rbierschbach@wayne.edu.

**Mike Ilitch School of Business** Students: 259 full-time (146 women), 1,156 part-time (521 women); includes 413 minority (233 Black or African American, non-Hispanic/Latino; 1 American Indian or Alaska Native, non-Hispanic/Latino; 79 Asian, non-Hispanic/Latino; 58 Hispanic/Latino; 42 Two or more races, non-Hispanic/Latino), 74 international. Average age 30. 1,106 applicants, 40% accepted, 272 enrolled. *Faculty:* 29. Expenses: Contact institution. *Financial support:* In 2019–20, 199 students received support, including 1 fellowship with tuition reimbursement available (averaging $20,000 per year), 7 research assistantships with tuition reimbursements available (averaging $22,129 per year), 2 teaching assistantships with tuition reimbursements available (averaging $19,967 per year); scholarships/grants, health care benefits, and unspecified assistantships also available. Support available to part-time students. Financial award applicants required to submit FAFSA. In 2019, 386 master's, 3 doctorates, 50 other advanced degrees awarded. *Program availability:* Part-time, evening/weekend. *Application deadline:* For fall admission, 7/1 for domestic students, 5/1 priority date for international students; for winter admission, 11/1 for domestic students, 9/1 priority date for international students; for spring admission, 3/1 for domestic students, 1/1 priority date for international students. Applications are processed on a rolling basis. *Application fee:* $50. Electronic applications accepted. *Application Contact:* Kiantee N. Rupert-Jones, Assistant Dean, 313-577-4511, E-mail: ag2233@wayne.edu. *Dean, School of Business Administration,* Dr. Robert Forsythe, 313-577-4501, E-mail: robert.forsythe@wayne.edu.

**School of Information Sciences** *Program availability:* Part-time, evening/weekend, 100% online, blended/hybrid learning. Electronic applications accepted.

**School of Medicine** Students: 1,425 full-time (687 women), 139 part-time (80 women); includes 545 minority (116 Black or African American, non-Hispanic/Latino; 14 American Indian or Alaska Native, non-Hispanic/Latino; 290 Asian, non-Hispanic/Latino; 89 Hispanic/Latino; 36 Two or more races, non-Hispanic/Latino), 100 international. Average age 26. 11,061 applicants, 4% accepted, 418 enrolled. *Faculty:* 214. Expenses: Contact institution. *Financial support:* In 2019–20, 1,150 students received support, including 54 fellowships with tuition reimbursements available (averaging $24,438 per year), 102 research assistantships with tuition reimbursements available (averaging $26,944 per year), 1 teaching assistantship (averaging $19,267 per year); Federal Work-Study, scholarships/grants, health care benefits, and unspecified assistantships also available. Support available to part-time students. Financial award applicants required to submit FAFSA. In 2019, 96 master's, 29 doctorates, 307 other advanced degrees awarded. Electronic applications accepted. *Application Contact:* Dr. Kevin Sprague, Associate Dean of Admissions, 313-577-1466, Fax: 313-577-9420, E-mail: kevin.sprague@med.wayne.edu. *Dean,* Dr. Mark E. Schweitzer, 313-577-1335, Fax: 313-577-8777, E-mail: mark.schweitzer@med.wayne.edu.

**School of Social Work** Students: 474 full-time (410 women), 156 part-time (134 women); includes 259 minority (187 Black or African American, non-Hispanic/Latino; 1 American Indian or Alaska Native, non-Hispanic/Latino; 18 Asian, non-Hispanic/Latino; 26 Hispanic/Latino; 27 Two or more races, non-Hispanic/Latino), 16 international. Average age 30. 729 applicants, 20% accepted. *Faculty:* 27. Expenses: Contact institution. *Financial support:* In 2019–20, 139 students received support, including 4 fellowships with tuition reimbursements available (averaging $21,875 per year), 7 research assistantships with tuition reimbursements available (averaging $22,429 per year), 1 teaching assistantship with tuition reimbursement available (averaging $19,967 per year); scholarships/grants and unspecified assistantships also available. Financial award applicants required to submit FAFSA. In 2019, 315 master's, 2 doctorates, 20 other advanced degrees awarded. *Program availability:* Part-time, evening/weekend, 100% online, blended/hybrid learning. *Application deadline:* For fall admission, 12/18 for domestic students; for spring admission, 4/1 for domestic students. Applications are processed on a rolling basis. *Application fee:* $50. Electronic applications accepted. *Application Contact:* Anwar Najor-Durack, Assistant Dean for Student Affairs, 313-577-4409, E-mail: ac1724@wayne.edu. *Dean and Professor,* Sheryl Kubiak, 313-577-4409, E-mail: spk@wayne.edu.

## WEBBER INTERNATIONAL UNIVERSITY, Babson Park, FL 33827-0096

**General Information** Independent, coed, comprehensive institution. *Enrollment:* 735 graduate, professional, and undergraduate students; 65 full-time matriculated graduate/professional students (33 women), 5 part-time matriculated graduate/professional students (2 women). *Enrollment by degree level:* 70 master's. *Graduate faculty:* 10 full-time (5 women), 2 part-time/adjunct (0 women). *Tuition:* Full-time $17,496; part-time $8746 per year. *Graduate housing:* Room and/or apartments available on a first-come, first-served basis to single students; on-campus housing not available to married students. Typical cost: $10,143 per year. Room charges vary according to board plan and housing facility selected. Housing application deadline: 8/1. *Student services:* Campus employment opportunities, campus safety program, career counseling, exercise/wellness program, international student services, services for students with disabilities. *Library facilities:* Grace and Roger Babson Library. *Collection:* Books: 1,041 (physical); Databases: 127. Weekly public service hours: 70; students can reserve study rooms.

**Computer facilities:** 92 computers available on campus for general student use. A campuswide network can be accessed. Online class registration is available.
Website: http://www.webber.edu/

**General Application Contact:** Amanda Amico, Admissions Counselor, 863-638-2910, Fax: 863-638-1591, E-mail: AmicoAC@webber.edu.

**GRADUATE UNITS**

**Graduate School of Business** Students: 65 full-time (33 women), 5 part-time (2 women); includes 19 minority (13 Black or African American, non-Hispanic/Latino; 1 Asian, non-Hispanic/Latino; 5 Hispanic/Latino), 7 international. Average age 28. 86 applicants, 47% accepted, 31 enrolled. *Faculty:* 10 full-time (5 women), 2 part-time/adjunct (0 women). Expenses: Contact institution. *Financial support:* Scholarships/grants and unspecified assistantships available. Financial award application deadline: 8/1; financial award applicants required to submit FAFSA. In 2019, 41 master's awarded. *Program availability:* Part-time, evening/weekend, 100% online, blended/hybrid learning. *Application deadline:* For fall admission, 8/1 for domestic students, 6/1 for international students; for spring admission, 1/1 for domestic students. Applications are processed on a rolling basis. Electronic applications accepted. *Application Contact:* Amanda Amico, Admissions Counselor, 863-638-2910, Fax: 863-638-1591, E-mail: admissions@webber.edu. *Dean,* Dr. Charles Shieh, 863-638-2971, E-mail: ShiehCS@webber.edu.

## WEBER STATE UNIVERSITY, Ogden, UT 84408-1001

**General Information** State-supported, coed, comprehensive institution. *Enrollment:* 29,843 graduate, professional, and undergraduate students; 339 full-time matriculated graduate/professional students (203 women), 460 part-time matriculated graduate/professional students (252 women). *Enrollment by degree level:* 700 master's, 33 doctoral, 66 other advanced degrees. *Graduate faculty:* 100 full-time (45 women), 18 part-time/adjunct (9 women). *Tuition, area resident:* Full-time $7197; part-time $4981 per credit. Tuition, state resident: full-time $7197; part-time $4981 per credit. Tuition, nonresident: full-time $16,560; part-time $11,589 per credit. *Required fees:* $643 per semester. One-time fee: $60. Tuition and fees vary according to course load and program. *Graduate housing:* Room and/or apartments available on a first-come, first-served basis to single students; on-campus housing not available to married students. Typical cost: $8400 (including board). Room and board charges vary according to board plan and housing facility selected. *Student services:* Campus employment opportunities, campus safety program, career counseling, child daycare facilities, exercise/wellness program, free psychological counseling, grant writing training, international student services, low-cost health insurance, multicultural affairs office, services for students with disabilities, teacher training, writing training. *Library facilities:* Stewart Library. *Collection:* Books: 498,531 (physical); Serial titles: 425 (physical); Databases: 223,410. *Research affiliation:* Raytheon Training Corporation (education).

**Computer facilities:** Computer purchase and lease plans are available. 650 computers available on campus for general student use. A campuswide network can be accessed from student residence rooms and from off campus. Online class registration is available.
Website: http://www.weber.edu/

**General Application Contact:** Scott Teichert, Director of Admissions, 801-626-7670, Fax: 801-626-6045, E-mail: scottteichert@weber.edu.

**GRADUATE UNITS**

**College of Social and Behavioral Sciences** Students: 9 full-time (7 women), 24 part-time (11 women); includes 5 minority (1 American Indian or Alaska Native, non-Hispanic/Latino; 3 Hispanic/Latino; 1 Two or more races, non-Hispanic/Latino). Average age 34. *Faculty:* 4 full-time (1 woman). Expenses: Contact institution. *Financial support:* In 2019–20, 4 students received support. Scholarships/grants available. Financial award application deadline: 4/1; financial award applicants required to submit FAFSA. In 2019, 9 master's awarded. *Program availability:* Part-time, evening/weekend, online only, 100% online. *Application deadline:* For fall admission, 7/29 for domestic students; for spring admission, 12/11 for domestic students; for summer admission, 4/1 for domestic students. Applications are processed on a rolling basis. *Application fee:* $60 ($90 for international students). *Application Contact:* Faye Medd, Enrollment Director, 801-626-6146, Fax: 801-626-6145, E-mail: fmedd@weber.edu. *Interim Dean*, Dr. Julie Rich, 801-626-6282, E-mail: jrich@weber.edu.

**Dumke College of Health Professions** Students: 214 full-time (146 women), 43 part-time (28 women); includes 18 minority (3 Black or African American, non-Hispanic/Latino; 1 American Indian or Alaska Native, non-Hispanic/Latino; 1 Asian, non-Hispanic/Latino; 9 Hispanic/Latino; 4 Two or more races, non-Hispanic/Latino), 4 international. Average age 35. *Faculty:* 22 full-time (12 women), 3 part-time/adjunct (2 women). Expenses: Contact institution. *Financial support:* In 2019–20, 74 students received support. Scholarships/grants available. Financial award application deadline: 4/1; financial award applicants required to submit FAFSA. In 2019, 104 master's awarded. *Program availability:* Part-time, evening/weekend, 100% online. *Application deadline:* For fall admission, 3/15 for domestic students, 2/20 for international students. *Application fee:* $60 ($90 for international students). Electronic applications accepted. *Application Contact:* Ann Gessel, Office Manager, 801-626-7127, Fax: 801-626-7683, E-mail: anngessel@weber.edu. *Dean*, Dr. Yasmin Simonian, 801-626-7117, Fax: 801-626-7683, E-mail: ysimonian@weber.edu.

***School of Nursing*** Students: 85 full-time (73 women), 18 part-time (16 women); includes 6 minority (1 Asian, non-Hispanic/Latino; 4 Hispanic/Latino; 1 Two or more races, non-Hispanic/Latino). Average age 38. *Faculty:* 14 full-time (13 women), 2 part-time/adjunct (both women). Expenses: Contact institution. *Financial support:* In 2019–20, 16 students received support. Scholarships/grants available. Financial award application deadline: 4/1; financial award applicants required to submit FAFSA. In 2019, 52 master's awarded. *Program availability:* Part-time, evening/weekend, online only, 100% online. *Application deadline:* For fall admission, 4/1 priority date for domestic students. *Application fee:* $60 ($90 for international students). Electronic applications accepted. *Application Contact:* Robert Holt, Director of Enrollment, 801-626-7774, Fax: 801-626-6397, E-mail: rholt@weber.edu. *MSN & DNP Program Director*, Dr. Deborah Juff, 801-626-7833, Fax: 801-626-6397, E-mail: djudd@weber.edu.

**Goddard School of Business and Economics** Students: 76 full-time (31 women), 169 part-time (59 women); includes 19 minority (4 Asian, non-Hispanic/Latino; 13 Hispanic/Latino; 2 Two or more races, non-Hispanic/Latino), 4 international. Average age 35. *Faculty:* 17 full-time (4 women), 4 part-time/adjunct (0 women). Expenses: Contact institution. *Financial support:* In 2019–20, 45 students received support. Scholarships/grants available. Financial award application deadline: 4/1; financial award applicants required to submit FAFSA. In 2019, 123 master's, 20 other advanced degrees awarded. *Program availability:* Part-time, evening/weekend. *Application deadline:* For fall admission, 5/1 for domestic students; for spring admission, 9/1 for domestic students. *Application fee:* $60 ($90 for international students). Electronic applications accepted. *Application Contact:* Mara Sikkink, Coordinator of Academic Advisement, 801-626-6534, Fax: 801-626-6747, E-mail: marasikkink@weber.edu. *Dean*, Dr. Mathew Mouritsen, 801-626-7307, Fax: 801-626-6687, E-mail: gsbe@weber.edu.

***School of Accounting and Taxation*** Students: 32 full-time (11 women), 16 part-time (8 women); includes 6 minority (3 Asian, non-Hispanic/Latino; 3 Hispanic/Latino), 1 international. Average age 29. *Faculty:* 6 full-time (1 woman). Expenses: Contact institution. *Financial support:* In 2019–20, 27 students received support. Scholarships/grants available. Financial award application deadline: 4/1; financial award applicants required to submit FAFSA. In 2019, 39 master's awarded. *Program availability:* Part-time, evening/weekend. *Application deadline:* For fall admission, 8/1 for domestic students; for spring admission, 12/1 for domestic students; for summer admission, 4/1 for domestic students. *Application fee:* $60 ($90 for international students). Electronic applications accepted. *Application Contact:* Dr. Larry A. Deppe, Graduate Coordinator, 801-626-7838, Fax: 801-626-7423, E-mail: ldeppe1@weber.edu. *Program Director*, Dr. Ryan Pace, 801-626-7562, Fax: 801-626-7423, E-mail: rpace@weber.edu.

**Jerry and Vickie Moyes College of Education** Students: 30 full-time (23 women), 86 part-time (65 women); includes 10 minority (2 Black or African American, non-Hispanic/Latino; 1 American Indian or Alaska Native, non-Hispanic/Latino; 6 Hispanic/Latino; 1 Two or more races, non-Hispanic/Latino), 6 international. Average age 35. *Faculty:* 22 full-time (12 women), 3 part-time/adjunct (2 women). Expenses: Contact institution. *Financial support:* In 2019–20, 27 students received support. Institutionally sponsored loans, scholarships/grants, tuition waivers (full and partial), and unspecified assistantships available. Support available to part-time students. Financial award application deadline: 4/1; financial award applicants required to submit FAFSA. In 2019, 51 master's awarded. *Program availability:* Part-time, evening/weekend. *Application deadline:* For fall admission, 5/15 for domestic students; for spring admission, 9/15 for domestic students; for summer admission, 1/15 for domestic students. *Application fee:* $60 ($90 for international students). *Application Contact:* Nathan Alexander, College of Education Recruiter, 801-626-8124, Fax: 801-626-7427, E-mail: nathanalexander@weber.edu. *Dean*, Dr. Kristi Hadley, 801-626-6272, Fax: 801-626-7427, E-mail: kristihadley@weber.edu.

**Masters of Electrical Engineering** Students: 4 full-time (0 women), 3 part-time (0 women), 1 international. Average age 27. *Faculty:* 4 full-time (0 women). Expenses: Contact institution. *Financial support:* In 2019–20, 2 students received support. *Program availability:* Part-time. *Application deadline:* For fall admission, 5/7 for domestic and international students; for spring admission, 11/7 for domestic and international students. *Application fee:* $60 ($65 for international students). Electronic applications accepted. *Application Contact:* Scott Teichert, Director of Admissions, 801-626-7670, Fax: 801-626-6045, E-mail: scottteichert@weber.edu. *Department Chair*, Dr. Justin B. Jackson, 801-626-6078, E-mail: justinjackson@weber.edu.

**Telitha E. Lindquist College of Arts and Humanities** Students: 16 full-time (12 women), 69 part-time (48 women); includes 11 minority (2 Asian, non-Hispanic/Latino; 4 Hispanic/Latino; 5 Two or more races, non-Hispanic/Latino), 3 international. Average age 34. *Faculty:* 21 full-time (10 women), 3 part-time/adjunct (2 women). Expenses: Contact institution. *Financial support:* In 2019–20, 13 students received support. Scholarships/grants and tuition waivers (full and partial) available. Financial award application deadline: 4/1; financial award applicants required to submit FAFSA. In 2019, 37 master's awarded. *Program availability:* Part-time, evening/weekend. *Application deadline:* For fall admission, 4/1 for domestic students. *Application fee:* $60 ($90 for international students). Electronic applications accepted. *Application Contact:* Scott Teichert, Director of Admissions, 801-626-7670, Fax: 801-626-6045, E-mail: scottteichert@weber.edu. *Assoc. Dean, College of Arts and Humanities*, Dr. Amanda Sowerby, 801-626-6424, Fax: 801-626-7422, E-mail: arts_humanities@weber.edu.

## WEBSTER UNIVERSITY, St. Louis, MO 63119-3194

**General Information** Independent, coed, comprehensive institution. *Graduate housing:* Room and/or apartments available on a first-come, first-served basis to single students; on-campus housing not available to married students. Housing application deadline: 4/1. *Research affiliation:* Literacy Investment for Tomorrow.

**GRADUATE UNITS**

**College of Arts and Sciences** *Program availability:* Part-time, evening/weekend, online learning.

***Institute for Human Rights and Humanitarian Studies***

**George Herbert Walker School of Business and Technology** *Program availability:* Part-time, evening/weekend, online learning.

**Leigh Gerdine College of Fine Arts** *Program availability:* Part-time, evening/weekend.

**School of Communications** *Program availability:* Part-time, evening/weekend, online learning.

**School of Education** *Program availability:* Part-time, online learning.

## WEILL CORNELL MEDICINE, New York, NY 10065

**General Information** Independent, coed, graduate-only institution. *Graduate housing:* Rooms and/or apartments guaranteed to single students and available on a first-come, first-served basis to married students. Housing application deadline: 4/30. *Research affiliation:* Memorial Sloan-Kettering Cancer Center (cancer), Houston Methodist Hospital (general medicine and surgery), The Rockefeller University (biomedical research), New York Methodist (general medicine and surgery), Hospital for Special Surgery (orthopedics), Burke Medical Research Institute (neurology).

**GRADUATE UNITS**

**Weill Cornell Graduate School of Medical Sciences** Electronic applications accepted.

**Weill Cornell/Rockefeller/Sloan-Kettering Tri-Institutional MD-PhD Program** Electronic applications accepted.

## WELCH COLLEGE, Gallatin, TN 37066

**General Information** Independent-religious, coed, comprehensive institution.

**GRADUATE UNITS**

**Program in Theology and Ministry** *Program availability:* Online learning.

## WENTWORTH INSTITUTE OF TECHNOLOGY, Boston, MA 02115-5998

**General Information** Independent, coed, comprehensive institution. *Graduate housing:* Room and/or apartments available on a first-come, first-served basis to single students; on-campus housing not available to married students. Housing application deadline: 5/1.

**GRADUATE UNITS**

**Department of Architecture** Electronic applications accepted.

**Master of Engineering in Civil Engineering Program** *Program availability:* Part-time-only, evening/weekend. Electronic applications accepted.

**Master of Science in Applied Computer Science Program** *Program availability:* Part-time, online only, 100% online. Electronic applications accepted.

**Master of Science in Construction Management Program** *Program availability:* Part-time-only, evening/weekend, 100% online, blended/hybrid learning. Electronic applications accepted.

**Master of Science in Facility Management Program** *Program availability:* Part-time, evening/weekend, online only, 100% online, blended/hybrid learning. Electronic applications accepted.

**Online Master of Science in Technology Management Program** *Program availability:* Part-time-only, evening/weekend, online only, 100% online. Electronic applications accepted.

## WESLEYAN COLLEGE, Macon, GA 31210-4462

**General Information** Independent-religious, Undergraduate: women only; graduate: coed, comprehensive institution. *Graduate housing:* On-campus housing not available.

**GRADUATE UNITS**

**Department of Business and Economics**

**Department of Education** *Program availability:* Part-time. Electronic applications accepted.

## WESLEYAN UNIVERSITY, Middletown, CT 06459

**General Information** Independent, coed, university. CGS member. *Graduate housing:* Rooms and/or apartments available on a first-come, first-served basis to single and married students. Housing application deadline: 7/1. *Research affiliation:* Woods Hole Oceanographic Institution, Cold Spring Harbor Laboratory.

**GRADUATE UNITS**

**Graduate Liberal Studies Program** *Program availability:* Part-time, evening/weekend. Electronic applications accepted.

**Graduate Studies** Electronic applications accepted.

## WESLEY BIBLICAL SEMINARY, Jackson, MS 39206

**General Information** Independent-religious, coed, graduate-only institution.

**GRADUATE UNITS**

**Graduate Programs** *Program availability:* Part-time. Electronic applications accepted.

## WESLEY COLLEGE, Dover, DE 19901-3875

**General Information** Independent-religious, coed, comprehensive institution. *Graduate housing:* On-campus housing not available.

**GRADUATE UNITS**

**Business Program** *Program availability:* Part-time, evening/weekend.

**Education Program** *Program availability:* Part-time, evening/weekend.

**Environmental Studies Program** *Program availability:* Part-time, evening/weekend.

**Nursing Program** *Program availability:* Part-time, evening/weekend. Electronic applications accepted.

**Occupational Therapy Program**

## WESLEY THEOLOGICAL SEMINARY, Washington, DC 20016-5690

**General Information** Independent-religious, coed, graduate-only institution. *Graduate faculty:* 23 full-time (5 women), 8 part-time/adjunct (4 women). *Graduate housing:* Rooms and/or apartments available to single and married students. Housing application deadline: 7/1. *Student services:* Career counseling, free psychological counseling, low-cost health insurance. *Library facilities:* Library at Wesley Theological Seminary.
Website: http://www.wesleyseminary.edu/

**General Application Contact:** Rev. Michael W. Armstrong, Director of Admissions, 202-885-8653, Fax: 202-885-8605, E-mail: admis@wesley.action.org.

**GRADUATE UNITS**

**Graduate and Professional Programs** *Program availability:* Part-time.

## WEST CHESTER UNIVERSITY OF PENNSYLVANIA, West Chester, PA 19383

**General Information** State-supported, coed, comprehensive institution. CGS member. *Enrollment:* 17,669 graduate, professional, and undergraduate students; 1,018 full-time matriculated graduate/professional students (739 women), 1,845 part-time matriculated graduate/professional students (1,245 women). *Enrollment by degree level:* 2,552 master's, 202 doctoral, 109 other advanced degrees. *Graduate housing:* Room and/or apartments available on a first-come, first-served basis to single students; on-campus housing not available to married students. Housing application deadline: 5/1. *Student services:* Campus employment opportunities, campus safety program, career counseling, exercise/wellness program, free psychological counseling, international student services, multicultural affairs office, services for students with disabilities, teacher training. *Library facilities:* Francis Harvey Green Library plus 1 other. *Collection:* Books: 715,684 (physical), 1.2 million (digital/electronic); Serial titles: 1,528 (physical), 135,694 (digital/electronic); Databases: 271. Weekly public service hours: 134; study areas open 24 hours, 5–7 days a week. *Research affiliation:* Pennsylvania Equine Toxicology and Research Laboratory (chemistry), Temple University Collaborative on Community Inclusion of Individuals with Psychiatric Disabilities (social work), University of Pennsylvania (social work), University of Connecticut Human Rights Institute Research Program on Economic and Social Rights (social work), The Soldier's Project (social work), Independent Blue Cross (IBC) (nursing).

**Computer facilities:** Computer purchase and lease plans are available. 2,547 computers available on campus for general student use. A campuswide network can be accessed. Online class registration, virtual software are available.
Website: http://www.wcupa.edu/

**General Application Contact:** Alana Luttermoser, Executive Director of Graduate Admissions (Interim), 610-436-2943, Fax: 610-436-2763, E-mail: GradSchool@wcupa.edu.

**GRADUATE UNITS**

**College of Arts and Humanities** Students: 47 full-time (26 women), 113 part-time (75 women); includes 23 minority (8 Black or African American, non-Hispanic/Latino; 1 Asian, non-Hispanic/Latino; 10 Hispanic/Latino; 4 Two or more races, non-Hispanic/Latino), 4 international. 109 applicants, 85% accepted, 47 enrolled. Expenses: Contact institution. *Financial support:* Federal Work-Study, scholarships/grants, and unspecified assistantships available. Financial award application deadline: 2/15; financial award applicants required to submit FAFSA. *Application deadline:* For fall admission, 7/1 for international students; for spring admission, 10/15 for international students; for summer admission, 3/15 for international students. Applications are processed on a rolling basis. *Application fee:* $50. Electronic applications accepted. *Application Contact:* Office of Graduate Studies, 610-436-2943, Fax: 610-436-2763, E-mail: gradstudy@wcupa.edu. *Dean,* Jen Bacon, PhD, 610-436-3326, E-mail: JBacon@wcupa.edu.

**College of Business and Public Management** Students: 184 full-time (97 women), 727 part-time (383 women); includes 238 minority (145 Black or African American, non-Hispanic/Latino; 2 American Indian or Alaska Native, non-Hispanic/Latino; 22 Asian, non-Hispanic/Latino; 49 Hispanic/Latino; 20 Two or more races, non-Hispanic/Latino), 4 international. 494 applicants, 87% accepted, 309 enrolled. Expenses: Contact institution. *Financial support:* Federal Work-Study, scholarships/grants, and unspecified assistantships available. Financial award application deadline: 2/15; financial award applicants required to submit FAFSA. *Application deadline:* For fall admission, 7/1 for international students; for spring admission, 10/15 for international students; for summer admission, 3/15 for international students. Applications are processed on a rolling basis. *Application fee:* $50. Electronic applications accepted. *Application Contact:* Office of Graduate Studies, 610-436-2943, Fax: 610-436-2763, E-mail: gradstudy@wcupa.edu. *Dean,* Dr. Evan Leach, 610-436-2930, E-mail: eleach@wcupa.edu.

***The School of Business at West Chester University*** Students: 64 full-time (23 women), 431 part-time (185 women); includes 99 minority (44 Black or African American, non-Hispanic/Latino; 1 American Indian or Alaska Native, non-Hispanic/Latino; 16 Asian, non-Hispanic/Latino; 30 Hispanic/Latino; 8 Two or more races, non-Hispanic/Latino). 228 applicants, 91% accepted, 161 enrolled. Expenses: Contact institution. *Financial support:* Federal Work-Study, scholarships/grants, and unspecified assistantships available. Financial award application deadline: 2/15. *Program availability:* Part-time, evening/weekend, online only, 100% online. *Application deadline:* For fall admission, 7/1 for international students; for spring admission, 10/15 for international students; for summer admission, 3/15 for international students. Applications are processed on a rolling basis. *Application fee:* $50. Electronic applications accepted. *Application Contact:* Office of Graduate Studies, 610-436-2943, Fax: 610-436-2763, E-mail: gradstudy@wcupa.edu.

**College of Education and Social Work** Students: 401 full-time (331 women), 579 part-time (499 women); includes 247 minority (166 Black or African American, non-Hispanic/Latino; 1 American Indian or Alaska Native, non-Hispanic/Latino; 14 Asian, non-Hispanic/Latino; 39 Hispanic/Latino; 27 Two or more races, non-Hispanic/Latino), 6 international. 652 applicants, 75% accepted, 294 enrolled. Expenses: Contact institution. *Financial support:* Federal Work-Study, scholarships/grants, and unspecified assistantships available. Financial award application deadline: 2/15; financial award applicants required to submit FAFSA. *Program availability:* Part-time, evening/weekend, 100% online, blended/hybrid learning. *Application deadline:* For fall admission, 7/1 for international students; for spring admission, 10/15 for international students; for summer admission, 3/15 for international students. Applications are processed on a rolling basis. *Application fee:* $50. Electronic applications accepted. *Application Contact:* Office of Graduate Studies, 610-436-2943, Fax: 610-436-2763, E-mail: gradstudy@wcupa.edu. *Interim Dean,* Dr. Cheryl Neale-McFall, Ph.D., LPC, NCC, 610-436-2321, E-mail: CNEALE-MCFALL@WCUPA.EDU.

**College of Health Sciences** Students: 247 full-time (195 women), 209 part-time (178 women); includes 120 minority (81 Black or African American, non-Hispanic/Latino; 16 Asian, non-Hispanic/Latino; 16 Hispanic/Latino; 7 Two or more races, non-Hispanic/Latino), 13 international. 632 applicants, 58% accepted, 166 enrolled. Expenses: Contact institution. *Financial support:* Federal Work-Study, scholarships/grants, and unspecified assistantships available. Financial award application deadline: 2/15; financial award applicants required to submit FAFSA. *Application deadline:* For fall admission, 7/1 for international students; for spring admission, 10/15 for international students; for summer admission, 3/15 for international students. Applications are processed on a rolling basis. *Application fee:* $50. Electronic applications accepted. *Application Contact:* Office of Graduate Studies, 610-436-2943, Fax: 610-436-2763, E-mail: gradstudy@wcupa.edu. *Interim Dean,* Dr. Scott Heinerichs, 610-436-2825, E-mail: shenerichs@wcupa.edu.

**College of the Sciences and Mathematics**

**School of Music**

## WESTCLIFF UNIVERSITY, Irvine, CA 92606

**General Information** Proprietary, coed, comprehensive institution.

**GRADUATE UNITS**

**College of Business**

**College of Education**

## WEST COAST UNIVERSITY, North Hollywood, CA 91606

**General Information** Proprietary, coed, comprehensive institution.

**GRADUATE UNITS**

**Graduate Programs**

## WESTERN CAROLINA UNIVERSITY, Cullowhee, NC 28723

**General Information** State-supported, coed, university. CGS member. *Enrollment:* 12,167 graduate, professional, and undergraduate students; 808 full-time matriculated graduate/professional students (550 women), 836 part-time matriculated graduate/professional students (549 women). *Enrollment by degree level:* 1,385 master's, 209 doctoral, 50 other advanced degrees. *Graduate faculty:* 233 full-time (110 women), 36 part-time/adjunct (17 women). *International tuition:* $7421 full-time. *Tuition, area resident:* Full-time $2217.50; part-time $1664 per semester. Tuition, state resident: full-time $2217.50; part-time $1664 per semester. Tuition, nonresident: full-time $7421; part-time $5566 per semester. *Required fees:* $5598; $1954 per semester. Tuition and fees vary according to course load, campus/location and program. *Graduate housing:* Room and/or apartments available on a first-come, first-served basis to single students; on-campus housing not available to married students. Housing application deadline: 5/1. *Student services:* Campus employment opportunities, campus safety program, career counseling, child daycare facilities, exercise/wellness program, free psychological counseling, international student services, low-cost health insurance, multicultural affairs office, services for students with disabilities, teacher training, writing training. *Library facilities:* Hunter Library. *Collection:* Weekly public service hours: 96; study areas open 24 hours, 5–7 days a week; students can reserve study rooms. *Research affiliation:* North Carolina Center for the Advancement of Teaching.

**Computer facilities:** Computer purchase and lease plans are available. A campuswide network can be accessed. Online class registration is available.
Website: http://www.wcu.edu/

**General Application Contact:** Admissions Specialist, 828-227-7398, Fax: 828-227-7480, E-mail: grad@email.wcu.edu.

**GRADUATE UNITS**

**Graduate School** *Program availability:* Part-time, evening/weekend, 100% online, blended/hybrid learning.

***College of Arts and Sciences*** *Program availability:* Part-time, evening/weekend. Electronic applications accepted.

***College of Business*** *Program availability:* Part-time, evening/weekend, online learning.

***College of Education and Allied Professions*** *Program availability:* Part-time, evening/weekend, online learning.

***College of Engineering and Technology*** *Program availability:* Part-time, evening/weekend, online learning.

***College of Fine and Performing Arts*** *Program availability:* Part-time.

***College of Health and Human Sciences*** *Program availability:* Part-time, evening/weekend.

## WESTERN COLORADO UNIVERSITY, Gunnison, CO 81231

**General Information** State-supported, coed, comprehensive institution.

**GRADUATE UNITS**

**Graduate Programs in Education** *Program availability:* Online learning.

**Program in Creative Writing** *Program availability:* Online learning.

**Program in Environmental Management** *Program availability:* Online learning.

## WESTERN CONNECTICUT STATE UNIVERSITY, Danbury, CT 06810-6885

**General Information** State-supported, coed, comprehensive institution. *Enrollment:* 5,631 graduate, professional, and undergraduate students; 67 full-time matriculated graduate/professional students (42 women), 582 part-time matriculated graduate/professional students (447 women). *Enrollment by degree level:* 569 master's, 64 doctoral, 16 other advanced degrees. *Graduate housing:* Rooms and/or apartments available on a first-come, first-served basis to single and married students. Housing application deadline: 4/1. *Student services:* Campus employment opportunities, career counseling, child daycare facilities, exercise/wellness program, free psychological counseling, international student services, low-cost health insurance, multicultural affairs office, services for students with disabilities, teacher training, writing training. *Library facilities:* Ruth Haas Library plus 1 other. *Collection:* Books: 204,701 (physical), 240,140 (digital/electronic); Serial titles: 302 (physical), 67,162 (digital/electronic); Databases: 188. Weekly public service hours: 144; students can reserve study rooms. *Research affiliation:* Smithsonian Institution Affiliations Program, The Jane Goodall Institute, Center for Financial Forensics and Information Security, New England Educational Assessment Network, American Society for Microbiology.

**Computer facilities:** 1,042 computers available on campus for general student use. A campuswide network can be accessed. Online class registration, online payment are available.
Website: http://www.wcsu.edu/

**General Application Contact:** Dr. Chris Shankle, Associate Director of Graduate Studies, 203-837-9005, Fax: 203-837-8326, E-mail: shanklec@wcsu.edu.

**GRADUATE UNITS**

**Division of Graduate Studies** *Program availability:* Part-time.

***Ancell School of Business*** *Program availability:* Part-time.

***Maricostas School of Arts and Sciences*** *Program availability:* Part-time.
***School of Professional Studies*** *Program availability:* Part-time.
***School of Visual and Performing Arts*** *Program availability:* Part-time.

## WESTERN GOVERNORS UNIVERSITY, Salt Lake City, UT 84107

**General Information** Independent, coed, comprehensive institution. *Graduate housing:* On-campus housing not available.

**GRADUATE UNITS**

**College of Business** *Program availability:* Evening/weekend, online learning. Electronic applications accepted.
**College of Health Professions** *Program availability:* Evening/weekend, online learning. Electronic applications accepted.
**College of Information Technology** *Program availability:* Online learning.
**Teachers College** *Program availability:* Evening/weekend, online learning. Electronic applications accepted.

## WESTERN ILLINOIS UNIVERSITY, Macomb, IL 61455-1390

**General Information** State-supported, coed, comprehensive institution. CGS member. *Graduate housing:* Rooms and/or apartments available on a first-come, first-served basis to single and married students. *Research affiliation:* National Council of Teachers of English (English and journalism), Petroleum Research Fund (chemistry), Bayer Crop Services (agriculture), McDonald's Corporation (education), The Ceres Trust (agriculture), Quad Cities Manufacturing Lab (engineering).

**GRADUATE UNITS**

**School of Graduate Studies** *Program availability:* Part-time, online learning. Electronic applications accepted.
***College of Arts and Sciences*** *Program availability:* Part-time. Electronic applications accepted.
***College of Business and Technology*** *Program availability:* Part-time. Electronic applications accepted.
***College of Education and Human Services*** *Program availability:* Part-time, evening/weekend, online learning. Electronic applications accepted.
***College of Fine Arts and Communication*** *Program availability:* Part-time. Electronic applications accepted.
***Illinois Institute for Rural Affairs*** Electronic applications accepted.

## WESTERN KENTUCKY UNIVERSITY, Bowling Green, KY 42101

**General Information** State-supported, coed, comprehensive institution. CGS member. *Graduate housing:* Room and/or apartments guaranteed to single students; on-campus housing not available to married students. Housing application deadline: 4/1. *Research affiliation:* Bowling Green Field Station for Animal Studies (U.S. Fish and Wildlife Service), Roybal Center (gerontology).

**GRADUATE UNITS**

**Graduate School** *Program availability:* Part-time, evening/weekend, online learning.
***College of Education and Behavioral Sciences*** *Program availability:* Part-time, evening/weekend, online learning.
***College of Health and Human Services*** *Program availability:* Part-time, evening/weekend.
***Gordon Ford College of Business*** *Program availability:* Part-time, evening/weekend.
***Ogden College of Science and Engineering*** *Program availability:* Part-time, evening/weekend.
***Potter College of Arts and Letters*** *Program availability:* Part-time, evening/weekend, online learning.

## WESTERN MICHIGAN UNIVERSITY, Kalamazoo, MI 49008

**General Information** State-supported, coed, university. CGS member. *Graduate housing:* Rooms and/or apartments available on a first-come, first-served basis to single and married students. Housing application deadline: 7/1. *Research affiliation:* Argonne National Laboratory (particle physics), Central States Universities, Inc., Ames Research Center (manufacturing education), Copper Development Association, Inc. (plastics extrusion), Pharmacia and Upjohn Company (electron microscopy), Flowserve Corporation (mechanical pumps and seals).

**GRADUATE UNITS**

**Graduate College** *Program availability:* Part-time, evening/weekend.
***College of Arts and Sciences*** *Program availability:* Part-time.
***College of Education and Human Development*** *Program availability:* Part-time.
***College of Engineering and Applied Sciences*** *Program availability:* Part-time.
***College of Fine Arts*** *Program availability:* Part-time.
***College of Health and Human Services*** *Program availability:* Part-time.
***Haworth College of Business*** *Program availability:* Part-time.

## WESTERN MICHIGAN UNIVERSITY COOLEY LAW SCHOOL, Lansing, MI 48901-3038

**General Information** Independent, coed, graduate-only institution. *Graduate housing:* On-campus housing not available.

**GRADUATE UNITS**

**Graduate Programs** *Program availability:* Part-time, evening/weekend, 100% online, blended/hybrid learning. Electronic applications accepted.

## WESTERN MICHIGAN UNIVERSITY HOMER STRYKER MD SCHOOL OF MEDICINE, Kalamazoo, MI 49007

**General Information** Graduate-only institution.

**GRADUATE UNITS**

**MD Program**

## WESTERN NEW ENGLAND UNIVERSITY, Springfield, MA 01119

**General Information** Independent, coed, university. *Graduate housing:* Rooms and/or apartments available to single and married students. Housing application deadline: 3/9. *Research affiliation:* New England Center for Children (applied behavior analysis).

**GRADUATE UNITS**

**College of Arts and Sciences** *Program availability:* Part-time-only, evening/weekend, online learning. Electronic applications accepted.
**College of Business** *Program availability:* Part-time, evening/weekend, online learning. Electronic applications accepted.
**College of Engineering** *Program availability:* Part-time, evening/weekend, online learning. Electronic applications accepted.
**College of Pharmacy and Health Sciences** Electronic applications accepted.
**School of Law** *Program availability:* Part-time, evening/weekend. Electronic applications accepted.

**See Display on page 618 and Close-Up on page 635.**

## WESTERN NEW MEXICO UNIVERSITY, Silver City, NM 88062-0680

**General Information** State-supported, coed, comprehensive institution. *Graduate housing:* Rooms and/or apartments available on a first-come, first-served basis to single and married students. Housing application deadline: 6/30.

**GRADUATE UNITS**

**Graduate Division** *Program availability:* Part-time, evening/weekend, online learning. Electronic applications accepted.
***School of Business*** *Program availability:* Part-time, online learning. Electronic applications accepted.
***School of Education*** *Program availability:* Part-time, online learning. Electronic applications accepted.

## WESTERN OREGON UNIVERSITY, Monmouth, OR 97361

**General Information** State-supported, coed, comprehensive institution. *Graduate housing:* Room and/or apartments available on a first-come, first-served basis to single students; on-campus housing not available to married students. *Research affiliation:* Teaching Research Institute (education).

**GRADUATE UNITS**

**Graduate Programs** *Program availability:* Part-time, evening/weekend, online learning.
***College of Education*** *Program availability:* Part-time, evening/weekend, online learning.
***College of Liberal Arts and Sciences*** *Program availability:* Part-time, evening/weekend.

## WESTERN SEMINARY - PORTLAND, Portland, OR 97215-3367

**General Information** Independent-religious, coed, graduate-only institution. *Graduate housing:* On-campus housing not available.

**GRADUATE UNITS**

**Graduate Programs** *Program availability:* Part-time, evening/weekend, online learning.

## WESTERN SEMINARY–SACRAMENTO CAMPUS, Rocklin, CA 95765

**General Information** Independent-religious, coed, graduate-only institution.

**GRADUATE UNITS**

**Graduate Certificate Programs** *Program availability:* Online learning.
**Graduate Diploma Programs**
**Master of Divinity Program**
**Program in Biblical and Theological Studies**
**Program in Marital and Family Therapy**
**Program in Ministry and Leadership**

## WESTERN SEMINARY - SAN JOSE CAMPUS, Milpitas, CA 95035

**General Information** Independent-religious, coed, graduate-only institution. *Graduate housing:* On-campus housing not available.

**GRADUATE UNITS**

**Graduate Programs** *Program availability:* Part-time, evening/weekend, online learning. Electronic applications accepted.

## WESTERN STATE COLLEGE OF LAW AT WESTCLIFF UNIVERSITY, Irvine, CA 92618-3601

**General Information** Proprietary, coed, graduate-only institution. *Enrollment by degree level:* 350 doctoral. *Graduate faculty:* 21 full-time (13 women), 36 part-time/adjunct (14 women). *Tuition:* Full-time $42,860; part-time $28,660 per year. *Graduate housing:* On-campus housing not available. *Student services:* Campus employment opportunities, career counseling, free psychological counseling, international student services, services for students with disabilities. *Library facilities:* Western State College of Law Library. *Collection:* Books: 51,828 (physical); Serial titles: 1,011 (physical); Databases: 12. Weekly public service hours: 133; students can reserve study rooms.

**Computer facilities:** 12 computers available on campus for general student use. Online class registration is available.
Website: http://www.wsulaw.edu/

**General Application Contact:** Rhonda Cohen, Director of Admissions, 714-459-1108, Fax: 714-441-1748, E-mail: adm@wsulaw.edu.

**GRADUATE UNITS**

**Professional Program** *Program availability:* Part-time, evening/weekend. Electronic applications accepted.

## WESTERN THEOLOGICAL SEMINARY, Holland, MI 49423-3622

**General Information** Independent-religious, coed, graduate-only institution. *Enrollment by degree level:* 289 master's, 46 doctoral. *Graduate faculty:* 19 full-time (5 women), 13 part-time/adjunct (5 women). *Tuition:* Full-time $1580; part-time $8910 per credit hour. *Required fees:* $100; $100 per semester. *Graduate housing:* Rooms and/or apartments available on a first-come, first-served basis to single and married students. Housing application deadline: 7/1. *Student services:* Campus employment opportunities, services for students with disabilities, writing training. *Library facilities:* Cook Library plus 1 other. *Collection:* Books: 86,079 (physical); Serial titles: 185 (physical). Students can reserve study rooms.

**Computer facilities:** 16 computers available on campus for general student use. A campuswide network can be accessed from student residence rooms. Online class registration is available.
Website: http://www.westernsem.edu/

**General Application Contact:** Jill English, Director of Admissions, 616-392-8555, Fax: 616-392-7717, E-mail: jill.english@westernsem.edu.

**GRADUATE UNITS**

**Graduate and Professional Programs** *Program availability:* Part-time, 100% online, blended/hybrid learning. Electronic applications accepted.

### WESTERN UNIVERSITY OF HEALTH SCIENCES, Pomona, CA 91766-1854

**General Information** Independent, coed, graduate-only institution. *Enrollment by degree level:* 585 master's, 3,207 doctoral. *Graduate faculty:* 309 full-time (154 women), 127 part-time/adjunct (69 women). Tuition and fees vary according to course level, course load, degree level, program and student level. *Graduate housing:* Rooms and/or apartments available on a first-come, first-served basis to single and married students. *Student services:* Campus employment opportunities, campus safety program, career counseling, exercise/wellness program, free psychological counseling, grant writing training, international student services, low-cost health insurance, services for students with disabilities. *Library facilities:* Harriet K & Philip Pumerantz Library plus 1 other. *Collection:* Books: 20,863 (physical), 2,351 (digital/electronic); Serial titles: 734 (physical), 45,612 (digital/electronic); Databases: 78. Weekly public service hours: 91; students can reserve study rooms. *Research affiliation:* Fulgent (biomedical research), Neuralstem (biomedical research), Kaiser Permanente (biomedical research), Novo Nordisk (biomedical research), Zeavision LLC (biomedical research), Aspire Biomet, Inc (cancer research).

**Computer facilities:** 56 computers available on campus for general student use. A campuswide network can be accessed. Online class registration is available.
Website: http://www.westernu.edu/

**General Application Contact:** Admissions Office, 909-469-5335, Fax: 909-469-5570, E-mail: admissions@westernu.edu.

**GRADUATE UNITS**

**College of Dental Medicine** Students: 283 full-time (147 women); includes 185 minority (7 Black or African American, non-Hispanic/Latino; 2 American Indian or Alaska Native, non-Hispanic/Latino; 105 Asian, non-Hispanic/Latino; 43 Hispanic/Latino; 28 Two or more races, non-Hispanic/Latino), 7 international. Average age 28. 2,548 applicants, 8% accepted, 74 enrolled. *Faculty:* 45 full-time (21 women), 21 part-time/adjunct (7 women). Expenses: Contact institution. *Financial support:* In 2019–20, 8 students received support. Scholarships/grants available. Financial award application deadline: 3/2; financial award applicants required to submit FAFSA. In 2019, 68 doctorates awarded. *Application deadline:* For fall admission, 12/1 for domestic and international students. Applications are processed on a rolling basis. *Application fee:* $60. Electronic applications accepted. *Application Contact:* Marie Anderson, Admissions Counselor, 909-469-5290, Fax: 909-469-5570, E-mail: mesparza@westernu.edu. *Dean,* Dr. Steven Friedrichsen, 909-706-3911, E-mail: sfriedrichsen@westernu.edu.

**College of Graduate Nursing** Students: 287 full-time (231 women), 23 part-time (18 women); includes 220 minority (13 Black or African American, non-Hispanic/Latino; 4 American Indian or Alaska Native, non-Hispanic/Latino; 101 Asian, non-Hispanic/Latino; 77 Hispanic/Latino; 1 Native Hawaiian or other Pacific Islander, non-Hispanic/Latino; 24 Two or more races, non-Hispanic/Latino), 6 international. Average age 32. 696 applicants, 28% accepted, 121 enrolled. *Faculty:* 21 full-time (17 women), 44 part-time/adjunct (34 women). Expenses: Contact institution. *Financial support:* In 2019–20, 23 students received support. Career-related internships or fieldwork and scholarships/grants available. Support available to part-time students. Financial award application deadline: 3/2; financial award applicants required to submit FAFSA. In 2019, 77 master's, 12 doctorates awarded. *Program availability:* Part-time, evening/weekend, blended/hybrid learning. *Application deadline:* Applications are processed on a rolling basis. *Application fee:* $60. Electronic applications accepted. *Application Contact:* Office of Admissions, 909-469-5335, E-mail: admissions@westernu.edu. *Dean,* Dr. Mary Lopez, 909-706-3860, Fax: 909-469-5521, E-mail: mlopez@westernu.edu.

**College of Health Sciences** Students: 354 full-time (243 women), 23 part-time (18 women); includes 230 minority (14 Black or African American, non-Hispanic/Latino; 3 American Indian or Alaska Native, non-Hispanic/Latino; 82 Asian, non-Hispanic/Latino; 91 Hispanic/Latino; 2 Native Hawaiian or other Pacific Islander, non-Hispanic/Latino; 38 Two or more races, non-Hispanic/Latino). Average age 28. 2,873 applicants, 10% accepted, 158 enrolled. *Faculty:* 25 full-time (17 women), 17 part-time/adjunct (10 women). Expenses: Contact institution. *Financial support:* In 2019–20, 76 students received support. Career-related internships or fieldwork, scholarships/grants, and traineeships available. Financial award application deadline: 3/2; financial award applicants required to submit FAFSA. In 2019, 102 master's, 56 doctorates awarded. *Program availability:* Blended/hybrid learning. *Application deadline:* Applications are processed on a rolling basis. Electronic applications accepted. *Application Contact:* Office of Admissions, 909-469-5650, Fax: 909-469-5570, E-mail: admissions@westernu.edu. *Interim Dean,* Dr. Dee Schilling, 909-469-5300, Fax: 909-469-5438, E-mail: dschilling@westernu.edu.

**College of Optometry** Students: 315 full-time (231 women); includes 216 minority (7 Black or African American, non-Hispanic/Latino; 1 American Indian or Alaska Native, non-Hispanic/Latino; 124 Asian, non-Hispanic/Latino; 46 Hispanic/Latino; 2 Native Hawaiian or other Pacific Islander, non-Hispanic/Latino; 36 Two or more races, non-Hispanic/Latino), 14 international. Average age 27. 416 applicants, 38% accepted, 69 enrolled. *Faculty:* 30 full-time (15 women), 4 part-time/adjunct (2 women). Expenses: Contact institution. *Financial support:* In 2019–20, 31 students received support. Career-related internships or fieldwork, scholarships/grants, and traineeships available. Financial award application deadline: 3/2; financial award applicants required to submit FAFSA. In 2019, 86 doctorates awarded. *Application deadline:* For fall admission, 5/1 for domestic and international students. Applications are processed on a rolling basis. *Application fee:* $65. Electronic applications accepted. *Application Contact:* Marie Anderson, Director of Admissions, 909-469-5485, Fax: 909-469-5570, E-mail: admissions@westernu.edu. *Dean,* Dr. Elizabeth Hoppe, 909-706-3497, E-mail: ehoppe@westernu.edu.

**College of Osteopathic Medicine of the Pacific** Students: 1,321 full-time (632 women); includes 678 minority (21 Black or African American, non-Hispanic/Latino; 2 American Indian or Alaska Native, non-Hispanic/Latino; 466 Asian, non-Hispanic/Latino; 90 Hispanic/Latino; 2 Native Hawaiian or other Pacific Islander, non-Hispanic/Latino; 97 Two or more races, non-Hispanic/Latino), 24 international. Average age 27. 5,235 applicants, 14% accepted, 318 enrolled. *Faculty:* 71 full-time (32 women), 18 part-time/adjunct (5 women). Expenses: Contact institution. *Financial support:* In 2019–20, 139 students received support. Career-related internships or fieldwork and scholarships/grants available. Financial award application deadline: 3/2; financial award applicants required to submit FAFSA. In 2019, 328 doctorates awarded. *Application deadline:* For fall admission, 2/1 for domestic and international students. Applications are processed on a rolling basis. *Application fee:* $65. Electronic applications accepted. *Application Contact:* Martha Alfaro, Assistant Director of Admissions, 909-469-5332, Fax: 909-469-5570, E-mail: mhuizar@westernu.edu. *Dean,* Dr. Paula Crone, 541-259-0206, Fax: 541-259-0201, E-mail: pcrone@westernu.edu.

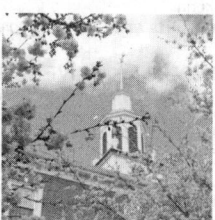

**College of Pharmacy** Students: 526 full-time (359 women), 7 part-time (5 women); includes 385 minority (18 Black or African American, non-Hispanic/Latino; 280 Asian, non-Hispanic/Latino; 40 Hispanic/Latino; 47 Two or more races, non-Hispanic/Latino), 30 international. Average age 28. 523 applicants, 61% accepted, 134 enrolled. *Faculty:* 38 full-time (16 women), 7 part-time/adjunct (3 women). Expenses: Contact institution. *Financial support:* In 2019–20, 53 students received support, including 15 teaching assistantships with full tuition reimbursements available (averaging $21,000 per year); research assistantships and scholarships/grants also available. Financial award application deadline: 3/2; financial award applicants required to submit FAFSA. In 2019, 9 master's, 137 doctorates awarded. Electronic applications accepted. *Application Contact:* Office of Admission, 909-469-5335, E-mail: admissions@westernu.edu. *Dean,* Dr. Daniel Robinson, 909-469-5533, Fax: 909-469-5539, E-mail: drobinson@westernu.edu.

**College of Podiatric Medicine** Students: 153 full-time (53 women); includes 96 minority (7 Black or African American, non-Hispanic/Latino; 60 Asian, non-Hispanic/Latino; 15 Hispanic/Latino; 1 Native Hawaiian or other Pacific Islander, non-Hispanic/Latino; 13 Two or more races, non-Hispanic/Latino), 1 international. Average age 27. 454 applicants, 27% accepted, 49 enrolled. *Faculty:* 11 full-time (7 women), 5 part-time/adjunct (1 woman). Expenses: Contact institution. *Financial support:* In 2019–20, 28 students received support. Career-related internships or fieldwork, scholarships/grants, and traineeships available. Financial award application deadline: 3/2; financial award applicants required to submit FAFSA. In 2019, 27 doctorates awarded. *Application deadline:* For fall admission, 6/30 for domestic and international students. Applications are processed on a rolling basis. Electronic applications accepted. *Application Contact:* Marie Anderson, Director of Admissions, 909-469-5485, Fax: 909-469-5570, E-mail: admissions@westernu.edu. *Dean,* Dr. Kathleen Satterfield, 909-706-3933, E-mail: vsatterfield@westernu.edu.

**College of Veterinary Medicine** Students: 414 full-time (323 women); includes 200 minority (11 Black or African American, non-Hispanic/Latino; 1 American Indian or Alaska Native, non-Hispanic/Latino; 56 Asian, non-Hispanic/Latino; 92 Hispanic/Latino; 1 Native Hawaiian or other Pacific Islander, non-Hispanic/Latino; 39 Two or more races, non-Hispanic/Latino), 3 international. Average age 27. 817 applicants, 33% accepted, 108 enrolled. *Faculty:* 55 full-time (26 women), 10 part-time/adjunct (5 women). Expenses: Contact institution. *Financial support:* In 2019–20, 20 students received support. Career-related internships or fieldwork, institutionally sponsored loans, scholarships/grants, and veterans' educational benefits available. Financial award application deadline: 3/2; financial award applicants required to submit FAFSA. In 2019, 103 doctorates awarded. *Application deadline:* For fall admission, 9/15 for domestic and international students. Electronic applications accepted. *Application Contact:* Karen Hutton-Lopez, Director of Admissions, 909-469-5650, Fax: 909-469-5570, E-mail: admissions@westernu.edu. *Dean,* Dr. Phil Nelson, 909-469-5661, Fax: 909-469-5635, E-mail: pnelson@westernu.edu.

**Graduate College of Biomedical Sciences** Students: 74 full-time (45 women), 12 part-time (6 women); includes 69 minority (6 Black or African American, non-Hispanic/Latino; 32 Asian, non-Hispanic/Latino; 21 Hispanic/Latino; 1 Native Hawaiian or other Pacific Islander, non-Hispanic/Latino; 9 Two or more races, non-Hispanic/Latino), 1 international. Average age 26. 346 applicants, 23% accepted, 66 enrolled. *Faculty:* 8 full-time (1 woman), 7 part-time/adjunct (2 women). Expenses: Contact institution. *Financial support:* In 2019–20, 31 students received support. Scholarships/grants available. Financial award application deadline: 3/2; financial award applicants required to submit FAFSA. In 2019, 38 master's awarded. *Application deadline:* Applications are processed on a rolling basis. *Application fee:* $50. Electronic applications accepted. *Application Contact:* Daniell Mendoza, Office of Admissions, 909-469-5541, Fax: 909-469-5335, E-mail: admissions@westernu.edu. *Acting Dean of Graduate College of Biomedical Sciences,* Dr. Guru Betageri, 909-469-5682, E-mail: gbetageri@westernu.edu.

## WESTERN WASHINGTON UNIVERSITY, Bellingham, WA 98225-5996

**General Information** State-supported, coed, comprehensive institution. CGS member. *Graduate housing:* Rooms and/or apartments available on a first-come, first-served basis to single and married students. Housing application deadline: 5/1. *Research affiliation:* Teck Cominco Ltd., Research Corporation, Dreyfus Foundation, Golden Associates, American Metals Technology, NARSAD (mental health).

**GRADUATE UNITS**

**Graduate School** *Program availability:* Part-time. Electronic applications accepted.

***College of Business and Economics*** *Program availability:* Part-time, evening/weekend. Electronic applications accepted.

***College of Fine and Performing Arts*** *Program availability:* Part-time. Electronic applications accepted.

***College of Humanities and Social Sciences*** *Program availability:* Part-time. Electronic applications accepted.

***College of Sciences and Technology*** Electronic applications accepted.

***Huxley College of the Environment*** *Program availability:* Part-time. Electronic applications accepted.

***Woodring College of Education*** *Program availability:* Part-time, online learning. Electronic applications accepted.

## WESTFIELD STATE UNIVERSITY, Westfield, MA 01086

**General Information** State-supported, coed, comprehensive institution. *Graduate housing:* On-campus housing not available.

**GRADUATE UNITS**

**College of Graduate and Continuing Education** *Program availability:* Part-time, evening/weekend.

## WEST LIBERTY UNIVERSITY, West Liberty, WV 26074

**General Information** State-supported, coed, comprehensive institution. *Enrollment:* 2,496 graduate, professional, and undergraduate students; 123 full-time matriculated graduate/professional students (74 women), 187 part-time matriculated graduate/professional students (120 women). *Enrollment by degree level:* 310 master's. *Graduate faculty:* 27 full-time (13 women), 18 part-time/adjunct (9 women). *Graduate housing:* Room and/or apartments available on a first-come, first-served basis to single students; on-campus housing not available to married students. *Student services:* Campus employment opportunities, campus safety program, career counseling, exercise/wellness program, free psychological counseling, grant writing training, international student services, services for students with disabilities, writing training. *Library facilities:* Paul N. Elbin Library.

**Computer facilities:** Computer purchase and lease plans are available. A campuswide network can be accessed. Online class registration is available.
Website: http://www.westliberty.edu/

**General Application Contact:** Sara Sweeney, Director of Graduate Studies, 304-336-8015, E-mail: sara.sweeney@westliberty.edu.

**GRADUATE UNITS**

**College of Education and Human Performance** *Program availability:* Part-time, evening/weekend. Electronic applications accepted.

**College of Sciences**

**Gary E. West College of Business**

**School of Professional Studies**

## WESTMINSTER COLLEGE, New Wilmington, PA 16172-0001

**General Information** Independent-religious, coed, comprehensive institution. *Graduate housing:* On-campus housing not available.

**GRADUATE UNITS**

**The Bill and Vieve Gore School of Business**

**School of Education**

**School of Nursing and Health Sciences**

**Schools of Arts and Sciences**

## WESTMINSTER COLLEGE, Salt Lake City, UT 84105-3697

**General Information** Independent, coed, comprehensive institution. *Graduate housing:* Room and/or apartments available on a first-come, first-served basis to single students; on-campus housing not available to married students. *Research affiliation:* International Psychotherapy Institute (clinical training), Zions Bank (entrepreneurship).

**GRADUATE UNITS**

**The Bill and Vieve Gore School of Business** *Program availability:* Part-time, evening/weekend, blended/hybrid learning. Electronic applications accepted.

**School of Arts and Sciences** *Program availability:* Part-time, evening/weekend. Electronic applications accepted.

**School of Education** *Program availability:* Part-time, evening/weekend. Electronic applications accepted.

**School of Nursing and Health Sciences** Electronic applications accepted.

## WESTMINSTER SEMINARY CALIFORNIA, Escondido, CA 92027-4128

**General Information** Independent-religious, coed, primarily men, graduate-only institution. *Graduate housing:* On-campus housing not available.

**GRADUATE UNITS**

**Programs in Theology** *Program availability:* Part-time, evening/weekend.

## WESTMINSTER THEOLOGICAL SEMINARY, Philadelphia, PA 19118

**General Information** Independent-religious, coed, primarily men, graduate-only institution. *Graduate housing:* Room and/or apartments available on a first-come, first-served basis to single students; on-campus housing not available to married students.

**GRADUATE UNITS**

**Graduate and Professional Programs** *Program availability:* Part-time.

## WEST TEXAS A&M UNIVERSITY, Canyon, TX 79015

**General Information** State-supported, coed, comprehensive institution. CGS member. *Graduate housing:* Room and/or apartments available on a first-come, first-served basis to single students; on-campus housing not available to married students. *Research affiliation:* Owens Corning (sports exercise), Pantex (chemistry), Agriculture Experiment Station (agriculture), Engineering Experiment Station (math, science).

**GRADUATE UNITS**

**College of Agriculture and Natural Sciences** *Program availability:* Part-time. Electronic applications accepted.

**College of Business** *Program availability:* Part-time, evening/weekend, 100% online, blended/hybrid learning. Electronic applications accepted.

**College of Education and Social Sciences** *Program availability:* Part-time, evening/weekend, online learning. Electronic applications accepted.

**College of Fine Arts and Humanities** *Program availability:* Part-time, evening/weekend. Electronic applications accepted.

***School of Music*** *Program availability:* Part-time. Electronic applications accepted.

**College of Nursing and Health Sciences** *Program availability:* Part-time, evening/weekend. Electronic applications accepted.

**Program in Interdisciplinary Studies** *Program availability:* Part-time, evening/weekend. Electronic applications accepted.

**School of Engineering, Computer Science and Mathematics** *Program availability:* Part-time. Electronic applications accepted.

## WEST VIRGINIA SCHOOL OF OSTEOPATHIC MEDICINE, Lewisburg, WV 24901-1196

**General Information** State-supported, coed, graduate-only institution. *Enrollment by degree level:* 809 doctoral. *Graduate faculty:* 55 full-time (31 women), 1 part-time/adjunct (0 women). *Tuition, area resident:* Full-time $22,472. Tuition, nonresident: full-time $53,710. *Required fees:* $1200. *Graduate housing:* On-campus housing not available. *Student services:* Campus employment opportunities, campus safety program, career counseling, exercise/wellness program, multicultural affairs office, services for students with disabilities. *Library facilities:* James R. Stookey Library. *Collection:* Books: 4,786 (physical), 1,449 (digital/electronic); Serial titles: 9 (physical), 6,023 (digital/electronic); Databases: 21. Weekly public service hours: 93; study areas open 24 hours, 5–7 days a week; students can reserve study rooms.

**Computer facilities:** 19 computers available on campus for general student use. A campuswide network can be accessed from off campus.
Website: http://www.wvsom.edu/

**General Application Contact:** Ronnie Collins, Director of Admissions, 304-647-6336, Fax: 304-647-6384, E-mail: rcollins@osteo.wvsom.edu.

**GRADUATE UNITS**

**Professional Program** Electronic applications accepted.

## WEST VIRGINIA STATE UNIVERSITY, Institute, WV 25112-1000

**General Information** State-supported, coed, comprehensive institution. *Graduate housing:* Rooms and/or apartments available on a first-come, first-served basis to single and married students. Housing application deadline: 9/1.

**GRADUATE UNITS**

**Biotechnology Graduate Program** Electronic applications accepted.

**Master of Science Program in Law Enforcement and Administration** Electronic applications accepted.

**Media Studies Graduate Program** Electronic applications accepted.

## WEST VIRGINIA UNIVERSITY, Morgantown, WV 26506

**General Information** State-supported, coed, university. CGS member. *Graduate housing:* Rooms and/or apartments available on a first-come, first-served basis to single and married students. Housing application deadline: 1/22. *Research affiliation:* NASA IV and V Center (software verification/validation), Research Partnership for an Energy Secure America (energy research), Florida Agricultural and Mechanical University (plasma physics), University of Pittsburgh/Carnegie Mellon University (energy research), National Energy Technology Laboratory (fossil energy and environmental research), Federal Bureau of Investigation (FBI) (biometrics research).

**GRADUATE UNITS**

**College of Business and Economics** *Program availability:* Part-time, online learning. Electronic applications accepted.

**College of Creative Arts** *Program availability:* Part-time. Electronic applications accepted.

**College of Education and Human Services** *Program availability:* Part-time, evening/weekend, online learning. Electronic applications accepted.

**College of Law** *Program availability:* Part-time. Electronic applications accepted.

**College of Physical Activity and Sport Sciences** Electronic applications accepted.

**Davis College of Agriculture, Forestry and Consumer Sciences** *Program availability:* Part-time. Electronic applications accepted.

**Eberly College of Arts and Sciences** *Program availability:* Part-time, evening/weekend, online learning. Electronic applications accepted.

***School of Social Work*** *Program availability:* Part-time.

**Reed College of Media** *Program availability:* Part-time, online learning. Electronic applications accepted.

**School of Dentistry** Electronic applications accepted.

**School of Medicine** *Program availability:* Part-time, evening/weekend. Electronic applications accepted.

**School of Nursing** *Program availability:* Part-time, online learning. Electronic applications accepted.

**School of Pharmacy** Electronic applications accepted.

**School of Public Health** *Program availability:* Part-time, online learning.

**Statler College of Engineering and Mineral Resources** *Program availability:* Part-time. Electronic applications accepted.

## WEST VIRGINIA WESLEYAN COLLEGE, Buckhannon, WV 26201

**General Information** Independent-religious, coed, comprehensive institution. *Graduate housing:* Room and/or apartments available to single students; on-campus housing not available to married students.

**GRADUATE UNITS**

**MBA Program** *Program availability:* Part-time, evening/weekend.

**Program in Creative Writing**

**School of Exercise Science and Athletic Training**

**School of Nursing**

## WHEATON COLLEGE, Wheaton, IL 60187-5593

**General Information** Independent-religious, coed, comprehensive institution. CGS member. *Enrollment:* 3,004 graduate, professional, and undergraduate students; 256 full-time matriculated graduate/professional students (153 women), 289 part-time matriculated graduate/professional students (146 women). *Enrollment by degree level:* 422 master's, 123 doctoral. *Graduate faculty:* 35 full-time (11 women), 23 part-time/adjunct (15 women). *Tuition:* Full-time $16,800; part-time $700 per credit hour. Tuition and fees vary according to degree level and program. *Graduate housing:* Rooms and/or apartments available on a first-come, first-served basis to single and married students. Typical cost: $6660 per year for single students; $11,810 per year for married students. Room charges vary according to board plan and housing facility selected. *Student services:* Campus employment opportunities, campus safety program, career counseling, exercise/wellness program, free psychological counseling, grant writing training, international student services, multicultural affairs office, services for students with disabilities, writing training. *Library facilities:* Buswell Memorial Library. *Collection:* Books: 359,725 (physical), 167,199 (digital/electronic); Serial titles: 352 (physical), 6,146 (digital/electronic); Databases: 170. Weekly public service hours: 94; students can reserve study rooms.

**Computer facilities:** 325 computers available on campus for general student use. A campuswide network can be accessed. Online class registration, financial information, degree requirements evaluation are available.
Website: http://www.wheaton.edu/

**General Application Contact:** Terrance Campbell, Director of Graduate Admissions, 630-752-5195, E-mail: graduate.admissions@wheaton.edu.

**GRADUATE UNITS**

**Graduate School** *Program availability:* Part-time. Electronic applications accepted.

***Humanitarian and Disaster Leadership Program*** *Program availability:* Part-time. Electronic applications accepted.

## WHEELING JESUIT UNIVERSITY, Wheeling, WV 26003-6295

**General Information** Independent-religious, coed, comprehensive institution. *Graduate housing:* Rooms and/or apartments available on a first-come, first-served basis to single and married students.

**GRADUATE UNITS**

**Department of Business** *Program availability:* Part-time, evening/weekend. Electronic applications accepted.

**Department of Education** *Program availability:* Part-time, evening/weekend, online learning. Electronic applications accepted.

**Department of Nursing** *Program availability:* Part-time, evening/weekend, online learning. Electronic applications accepted.

**Department of Physical Therapy** Electronic applications accepted.

**Department of Social Sciences** *Program availability:* Part-time, evening/weekend. Electronic applications accepted.

## WHITTIER COLLEGE, Whittier, CA 90608-0634

**General Information** Independent, coed, comprehensive institution. *Graduate housing:* On-campus housing not available.

**GRADUATE UNITS**

**Graduate Programs** *Program availability:* Part-time, evening/weekend.

## WHITWORTH UNIVERSITY, Spokane, WA 99251-0001

**General Information** Independent-religious, coed, comprehensive institution. *Enrollment:* 2,776 graduate, professional, and undergraduate students; 152 full-time matriculated graduate/professional students (98 women), 262 part-time matriculated graduate/professional students (193 women). *Enrollment by degree level:* 386 master's, 28 other advanced degrees. *Graduate faculty:* 37 full-time (18 women), 16 part-time/adjunct (3 women). *Tuition:* Full-time $11,970; part-time $3990 per credit. Tuition and fees vary according to course load and program. *Graduate housing:* Room and/or apartments available on a first-come, first-served basis to single students; on-campus housing not available to married students. Typical cost: $7450 per year ($12,800 including board). Room and board charges vary according to board plan and housing facility selected. Housing application deadline: 5/1. *Student services:* Campus employment opportunities, career counseling, exercise/wellness program, grant writing training, international student services, multicultural affairs office, services for students with disabilities, teacher training, writing training. *Library facilities:* Harriet Cheney Cowles Library. *Collection:* Weekly public service hours: 97; students can reserve study rooms.

**Computer facilities:** 280 computers available on campus for general student use. A campuswide network can be accessed from student residence rooms and from off campus. Online class registration, learning management system are available.
Website: http://www.whitworth.edu/

**General Application Contact:** Susan L Cook, Continuing Studies & Graduate Admissions, 509-777-3222, E-mail: graduateandcsadmissions@whitworth.edu.

**GRADUATE UNITS**

**Graduate Studies in Theology** *Program availability:* Part-time, evening/weekend. Electronic applications accepted.

**School of Business** *Program availability:* Part-time, evening/weekend. Electronic applications accepted.

**School of Education** *Program availability:* Part-time, evening/weekend, online learning.

## WICHITA STATE UNIVERSITY, Wichita, KS 67260

**General Information** State-supported, coed, university. CGS member. *Enrollment:* 16,052 graduate, professional, and undergraduate students; 1,200 full-time matriculated graduate/professional students (693 women), 1,572 part-time matriculated graduate/professional students (821 women). *Enrollment by degree level:* 1,816 master's, 488 doctoral, 468 other advanced degrees. *Graduate faculty:* 399 full-time (159 women), 20 part-time/adjunct (12 women). *Graduate housing:* Rooms and/or apartments available on a first-come, first-served basis to single and married students. *Student services:* Campus employment opportunities, campus safety program, career counseling, child daycare facilities, exercise/wellness program, free psychological counseling, grant writing training, international student services, low-cost health insurance, multicultural affairs office, services for students with disabilities, teacher training, writing training. *Library facilities:* Ablah Library plus 2 others. *Collection:* Books: 188,268 (physical), 763,530 (digital/electronic); Serial titles: 31,502 (physical), 270,605 (digital/electronic); Databases: 366. Study areas open 24 hours, 5–7 days a week; students can reserve study rooms. *Research affiliation:* Spirit Aerosystems (aerospace engineering), General Atomics (aerospace engineering), Wesley Medical Center (industrial and manufacturing engineering), NASA (aerospace engineering), Airbus (aerospace engineering), NetApp (computer engineering).

**Computer facilities:** 1,500 computers available on campus for general student use. A campuswide network can be accessed. Online class registration, learning management system are available.
Website: http://www.wichita.edu/

**General Application Contact:** Jordan Oleson, Assistant Director of Graduate Admissions, 316-978-3095, Fax: 316-978-3253, E-mail: jordan.oleson@wichita.edu.

**GRADUATE UNITS**

**Graduate School** *Program availability:* Part-time, evening/weekend, 100% online, blended/hybrid learning. Electronic applications accepted.

***College of Applied Studies*** *Program availability:* Part-time, evening/weekend, 100% online, blended/hybrid learning.

***College of Engineering*** *Program availability:* Part-time, evening/weekend.

***College of Fine Arts*** *Program availability:* Part-time.

***College of Health Professions*** *Program availability:* Part-time.

***Fairmount College of Liberal Arts and Sciences*** *Program availability:* Part-time, evening/weekend, 100% online, blended/hybrid learning.

***Institute for Interdisciplinary Creativity***

***W. Frank Barton School of Business*** *Program availability:* Part-time, evening/weekend.

## WIDENER UNIVERSITY, Chester, PA 19013-5792

**General Information** Independent, coed, comprehensive institution. CGS member. *Enrollment:* 6,601 graduate, professional, and undergraduate students; 1,666 full-time matriculated graduate/professional students (1,040 women), 1,615 part-time matriculated graduate/professional students (1,357 women). *Enrollment by degree level:* 1,567 master's, 1,594 doctoral, 120 other advanced degrees. *Graduate faculty:* 160 full-time (99 women), 202 part-time/adjunct (129 women). *Tuition:* Full-time $48,750; part-time $917 per credit hour. Tuition and fees vary according to class time, degree level, campus/location and program. *Graduate housing:* Rooms and/or apartments available on a first-come, first-served basis to single and married students. Housing application deadline: 5/30. *Student services:* Campus employment opportunities, career counseling, child daycare facilities, exercise/wellness program, free psychological counseling, international student services, multicultural affairs office, services for students with disabilities, teacher training, writing training. *Library facilities:* Wolfgram Memorial Library. *Research affiliation:* Small Business Administration, Riverfront Development Corporation (engineering, management), Advanced Technology Center (engineering).

**Computer facilities:** A campuswide network can be accessed from student residence rooms and from off campus. Online class registration is available.
Website: http://www.widener.edu/

**General Application Contact:** Amanda Scarpa, Director of Graduate Admissions & Enrollment, 610-499-4282, Fax: 610-499-4676, E-mail: gel@widener.edu.

**GRADUATE UNITS**

**College of Arts and Sciences** *Program availability:* Part-time, evening/weekend.

**Commonwealth Law School** *Program availability:* Part-time. Electronic applications accepted.

**Delaware Law School** *Program availability:* Part-time, 100% online.

**Graduate Programs in Engineering** *Program availability:* Part-time, evening/weekend. Electronic applications accepted.

**School of Business Administration** *Program availability:* Part-time, evening/weekend, 100% online, blended/hybrid learning. Electronic applications accepted.

**School of Human Service Professions** *Program availability:* Part-time, evening/weekend, 100% online, blended/hybrid learning.

***Center for Education*** *Program availability:* Part-time, evening/weekend. Electronic applications accepted.

***Center for Social Work Education***

***Institute for Graduate Clinical Psychology*** Electronic applications accepted.

***Institute for Physical Therapy Education***

**School of Nursing** *Program availability:* Part-time, evening/weekend. Electronic applications accepted.

## WILBERFORCE UNIVERSITY, Wilberforce, OH 45384

**General Information** Independent-religious, coed, comprehensive institution.

**GRADUATE UNITS**

**Program in Rehabilitation Counseling**

## WILFRID LAURIER UNIVERSITY, Waterloo, ON N2L 3C5, Canada

**General Information** Province-supported, coed, comprehensive institution.

**GRADUATE UNITS**

**Faculty of Graduate and Postdoctoral Studies** *Program availability:* Part-time, evening/weekend. Electronic applications accepted.

***Faculty of Arts*** *Program availability:* Part-time. Electronic applications accepted.

***Faculty of Music*** Electronic applications accepted.

***Faculty of Science*** Electronic applications accepted.

***Lazaridis School of Business and Economics*** *Program availability:* Part-time, evening/weekend. Electronic applications accepted.

***Lyle S. Hallman Faculty of Social Work*** *Program availability:* Part-time. Electronic applications accepted.

***School of International Policy and Governance***

**Laurier Brantford** Electronic applications accepted.

**Waterloo Lutheran Seminary** *Program availability:* Part-time. Electronic applications accepted.

## WILKES UNIVERSITY, Wilkes-Barre, PA 18766-0002

**General Information** Independent, coed, comprehensive institution. *Enrollment:* 4,680 graduate, professional, and undergraduate students; 481 full-time matriculated graduate/professional students (334 women), 2,196 part-time matriculated graduate/professional students (1,719 women). *Enrollment by degree level:* 2,104 master's, 573 doctoral. *Graduate housing:* On-campus housing not available. *Student services:* Campus employment opportunities, career counseling, free psychological counseling, international student services, low-cost health insurance, multicultural affairs office, services for students with disabilities. *Library facilities:* Eugene S. Farley Library. *Collection:* Books: 173,872 (physical), 338,879 (digital/electronic); Serial titles: 71,253 (digital/electronic); Databases: 131. Students can reserve study rooms.

**Computer facilities:** Computer purchase and lease plans are available. 1,015 computers available on campus for general student use. A campuswide network can be accessed. Online class registration is available.
Website: http://www.wilkes.edu/

**GRADUATE UNITS**

**College of Graduate and Professional Studies** Students: 450 full-time (300 women), 1,879 part-time (1,424 women); includes 365 minority (155 Black or African American, non-Hispanic/Latino; 3 American Indian or Alaska Native, non-Hispanic/Latino; 64 Asian, non-Hispanic/Latino; 90 Hispanic/Latino; 53 Two or more races, non-Hispanic/Latino), 5 international. Average age 35. Expenses: Contact institution. *Program availability:* Part-time, 100% online, blended/hybrid learning.

***College of Science and Engineering*** Students: 10 full-time (2 women), 9 part-time (1 woman); includes 3 minority (all Hispanic/Latino), 2 international. Average age 31. Expenses: Contact institution. *Financial support:* Unspecified assistantships available. *Program availability:* Part-time. *Application Contact:* Dr. Prahlad Murthy, Interim Dean, 570-408-4617, E-mail: prahlad.murthy@wilkes.edu. *Interim Dean,* Dr. Prahlad Murthy, 570-408-4617, E-mail: prahlad.murthy@wilkes.edu.

***Jay S. Sidhu School of Business and Leadership*** Students: 14 full-time (4 women), 68 part-time (33 women); includes 16 minority (5 Black or African American, non-Hispanic/Latino; 2 Asian, non-Hispanic/Latino; 6 Hispanic/Latino; 3 Two or more races, non-Hispanic/Latino), 2 international. Average age 30. Expenses: Contact institution. *Financial support:* Unspecified assistantships available. *Program availability:* Part-time, evening/weekend, 100% online, blended/hybrid learning. *Application Contact:* Dr. Abel Adekola, 570-408-4701, E-mail: abel.adekola@wilkes.edu.

***Nesbitt School of Pharmacy*** Students: 275 full-time (179 women); includes 48 minority (1 Black or African American, non-Hispanic/Latino; 1 American Indian or Alaska Native, non-Hispanic/Latino; 24 Asian, non-Hispanic/Latino; 4 Hispanic/Latino; 18 Two or more races, non-Hispanic/Latino), 1 international. Average age 22. Expenses: Contact institution. *Application Contact:* Dr. Scott Stolte, 570-408-4911, E-mail: scott.stolte@wilkes.edu.

***Passan School of Nursing*** Students: 39 full-time (35 women), 535 part-time (453 women); includes 198 minority (130 Black or African American, non-Hispanic/Latino; 1 American Indian or Alaska Native, non-Hispanic/Latino; 26 Asian, non-Hispanic/Latino; 27 Hispanic/Latino; 14 Two or more races, non-Hispanic/Latino). Average age 40. Expenses: Contact institution. *Program availability:* Part-time, 100% online. *Application Contact:* Dr. Deborah Zbegner, 570-408-4086, E-mail: deborah.zbegner@wilkes.edu.

***School of Education*** Students: 65 full-time (47 women), 1,190 part-time (877 women); includes 80 minority (11 Black or African American, non-Hispanic/Latino; 1 American Indian or Alaska Native, non-Hispanic/Latino; 9 Asian, non-Hispanic/Latino; 44 Hispanic/Latino; 15 Two or more races, non-Hispanic/Latino). Average age 35. Expenses: Contact institution. *Financial support:* Unspecified assistantships available. *Program availability:* Part-time, evening/weekend, 100% online, blended/hybrid learning. *Application Contact:* Dr. Rhonda Rabbitt, 570-408-3408, E-mail: rhonda.rabbitt@wilkes.edu.

## WILLAMETTE UNIVERSITY, Salem, OR 97301-3931

**General Information** Independent-religious, coed, comprehensive institution. *Graduate housing:* Room and/or apartments available on a first-come, first-served basis to single students; on-campus housing not available to married students. Housing application deadline: 6/1.

**GRADUATE UNITS**

**Atkinson Graduate School of Management** Students: 100 full-time (32 women), 118 part-time (62 women); includes 63 minority (13 Black or African American, non-Hispanic/Latino; 1 American Indian or Alaska Native, non-Hispanic/Latino; 18 Asian, non-Hispanic/Latino; 21 Hispanic/Latino; 1 Native Hawaiian or other Pacific Islander, non-Hispanic/Latino; 9 Two or more races, non-Hispanic/Latino), 10 international. Average age 30. 165 applicants, 81% accepted, 77 enrolled. *Faculty:* 19 full-time (6 women), 23 part-time/adjunct (8 women). Expenses: Contact institution. *Financial support:* In 2019–20, 200 students received support. Federal Work-Study, scholarships/grants, and unspecified assistantships available. Financial award application deadline: 5/1; financial award applicants required to submit FAFSA. In 2019, 110 master's awarded. *Program availability:* Part-time, evening/weekend. *Application deadline:* 5/1 priority date for domestic and international students. Applications are processed on a rolling basis. Electronic applications accepted. *Application Contact:* David Cortez, Assistant Director of Recruitment, 503-370-6792, Fax: 503-370-3011, E-mail: dcortez@willamette.edu. *Dean, Professor of Applied Statistics and Information Systems,* Dr. Michael L. Hand, 503-370-6790, Fax: 503-370-3011, E-mail: mhand@willamette.edu.

**College of Law** *Program availability:* Part-time. Electronic applications accepted.

## WILLIAM & MARY, Williamsburg, VA 23187-8795

**General Information** State-supported, coed, university. CGS member. *Enrollment:* 8,773 graduate, professional, and undergraduate students; 1,636 full-time matriculated graduate/professional students (841 women), 766 part-time matriculated graduate/professional students (410 women). *Enrollment by degree level:* 1,368 master's, 1,001 doctoral, 33 other advanced degrees. *Graduate faculty:* 727 full-time (304 women), 180 part-time/adjunct (77 women). *Graduate housing:* Room and/or apartments available on a first-come, first-served basis to single students; on-campus housing not available to married students. *Student services:* Campus employment opportunities, campus safety program, career counseling, child daycare facilities, exercise/wellness program, free psychological counseling, grant writing training, international student services, low-cost health insurance, multicultural affairs office, services for students with disabilities, teacher training, writing training. *Library facilities:* Earl Gregg Swem Library plus 5 others. *Collection:* Books: 1.4 million (physical), 2.6 million (digital/electronic); Serial titles: 40,730 (physical), 201,557 (digital/electronic); Databases: 645. Weekly public service hours: 110; study areas open 24 hours, 5–7 days a week; students can reserve study rooms. *Research affiliation:* Colonial Williamsburg (archaeology, history), Thomas Jefferson National Accelerator Facility (nuclear physics), Court Records Solutions (law and technology), AidData (global aid flows and development finance), James City County Business and Technology Incubator (economic development), Center for Excellence in Aging and Geriatric Health (public policy, kinesiology).

**Computer facilities:** Computer purchase and lease plans are available. 400 computers available on campus for general student use. A campuswide network can be accessed. Online class registration is available.
Website: http://www.wm.edu/

**GRADUATE UNITS**

**Raymond A. Mason School of Business** Students: 425 full-time (138 women), 437 part-time (170 women); includes 212 minority (79 Black or African American, non-Hispanic/Latino; 4 American Indian or Alaska Native, non-Hispanic/Latino; 56 Asian, non-Hispanic/Latino; 38 Hispanic/Latino; 1 Native Hawaiian or other Pacific Islander, non-Hispanic/Latino; 34 Two or more races, non-Hispanic/Latino), 118 international. Average age 32. 1,109 applicants, 69% accepted, 348 enrolled. *Faculty:* 39 full-time (11 women), 12 part-time/adjunct (2 women). Expenses: Contact institution. *Financial support:* In 2019–20, 215 students received support. Fellowships and scholarships/grants available. Financial award application deadline: 3/15; financial award applicants required to submit FAFSA. In 2019, 467 master's awarded. *Program availability:* Part-time, evening/weekend, 100% online. *Application deadline:* For fall admission, 11/16 for domestic and international students; for winter admission, 1/18 for domestic and international students; for spring admission, 5/16 for domestic and international students; for summer admission, 7/15 for domestic students. *Application fee:* $100. Electronic applications accepted. *Application Contact:* Amanda K. Barth, Director, Full-time MBA Admissions, 757-221-2944, Fax: 757-221-2958, E-mail: amanda.barth@mason.wm.edu. *Dean,* Dr. Lawrence Pulley, 757-221-2891, Fax: 757-221-2937, E-mail: larry.pulley@mason.wm.edu.

**School of Education** Students: 189 full-time (143 women), 326 part-time (243 women); includes 121 minority (47 Black or African American, non-Hispanic/Latino; 15 Asian, non-Hispanic/Latino; 41 Hispanic/Latino; 18 Two or more races, non-Hispanic/Latino), 16 international. Average age 35. 568 applicants, 62% accepted, 250 enrolled. *Faculty:* 50 full-time (31 women), 37 part-time/adjunct (20 women). Expenses: Contact institution. *Financial support:* In 2019–20, 128 students received support, including 1 fellowship with full tuition reimbursement available (averaging $20,000 per year), 88 research assistantships with full tuition reimbursements available (averaging $19,888 per year); teaching assistantships, scholarships/grants, and unspecified assistantships also available. Financial award application deadline: 1/15; financial award applicants required to submit FAFSA. In 2019, 126 master's, 33 doctorates, 7 other advanced degrees awarded. *Program availability:* Part-time, evening/weekend, Coursework is online with required residencies. *Application deadline:* For fall admission, 1/15 for domestic and international students; for spring admission, 10/1 for domestic and international students. *Application fee:* $50. Electronic applications accepted. *Application Contact:* Dorothy Smith Osborne, Senior Assistant Dean for Academic Programs and Student Services, 757-221-2317, E-mail: dsosbo@wm.edu. *Dean,* Dr. Robert C. Knoeppel, 757-221-2317, E-mail: rknoeppel@wm.edu.

**Virginia Institute of Marine Science** Students: 80 full-time (60 women), 5 part-time (2 women); includes 10 minority (1 Black or African American, non-Hispanic/Latino; 1 Asian, non-Hispanic/Latino; 3 Hispanic/Latino; 5 Two or more races, non-

Hispanic/Latino), 12 international. Average age 28. 80 applicants, 28% accepted, 20 enrolled. *Faculty:* 51 full-time (14 women), 1 part-time/adjunct (0 women). Expenses: Contact institution. *Financial support:* In 2019–20, 74 students received support, including research assistantships with full tuition reimbursements available (averaging $22,500 per year), teaching assistantships with full tuition reimbursements available (averaging $22,500 per year). Financial award application deadline: 1/5; financial award applicants required to submit FAFSA. In 2019, 9 master's, 11 doctorates awarded. *Application deadline:* For fall admission, 1/5 for domestic students, 1/6 for international students. *Application fee:* $50. Electronic applications accepted. *Application Contact:* John M. Griffin, Asst. Director for Admissions & Student Affairs, 804-684-7105, Fax: 804-684-7881, E-mail: admissions@vims.edu. *Dean/Director,* Dr. John T. Wells, 804-684-7103, Fax: 804-684-7009, E-mail: wells@vims.edu.

**William & Mary Law School** Students: 632 full-time (350 women), 8 part-time (4 women); includes 82 minority (28 Black or African American, non-Hispanic/Latino; 24 Asian, non-Hispanic/Latino; 10 Hispanic/Latino; 20 Two or more races, non-Hispanic/Latino), 58 international. Average age 25. 3,464 applicants, 33% accepted, 280 enrolled. *Faculty:* 49 full-time (24 women), 109 part-time/adjunct (30 women). Expenses: Contact institution. *Financial support:* In 2019–20, 597 students received support, including 15 fellowships with partial tuition reimbursements available (averaging $4,000 per year), 185 research assistantships (averaging $1,854 per year), 41 teaching assistantships (averaging $4,012 per year); career-related internships or fieldwork, scholarships/grants, and tuition waivers also available. Financial award application deadline: 2/15; financial award applicants required to submit FAFSA. In 2019, 36 master's, 230 doctorates awarded. *Application deadline:* For fall admission, 3/1 priority date for domestic and international students. Applications are processed on a rolling basis. Electronic applications accepted. *Application Contact:* Dexter A. Smith, Associate Dean for Admissions, 757-221-3785, Fax: 757-221-3261, E-mail: dsmith05@wm.edu. *Dean/Professor,* A Benjamin Spencer, 757-221-3790, Fax: 757-221-3261, E-mail: spencer@wm.edu.

## WILLIAM CAREY UNIVERSITY, Hattiesburg, MS 39401

**General Information** Independent-religious, coed, comprehensive institution. *Graduate housing:* Room and/or apartments available on a first-come, first-served basis to single students; on-campus housing not available to married students. Housing application deadline: 8/15.

**GRADUATE UNITS**

**College of Osteopathic Medicine**
**Department of Psychology and Graduate Counseling** *Program availability:* Part-time.
**School of Business** *Program availability:* Part-time.
**School of Education** *Program availability:* Part-time.
**School of Nursing** *Program availability:* Part-time.
**School of Pharmacy**

## WILLIAM JAMES COLLEGE, Newton, MA 02459

**General Information** Independent, coed, primarily women, upper-level institution. *Graduate housing:* On-campus housing not available.

**GRADUATE UNITS**

**Graduate Programs** Electronic applications accepted.

## WILLIAM JESSUP UNIVERSITY, Rocklin, CA 95765

**General Information** Independent-religious, coed, comprehensive institution.

**GRADUATE UNITS**

**Program in Teaching** *Program availability:* Evening/weekend.

## WILLIAM JEWELL COLLEGE, Liberty, MO 64068-1843

**General Information** Independent, coed, comprehensive institution.

**GRADUATE UNITS**

**Department of Education**

## WILLIAM PATERSON UNIVERSITY OF NEW JERSEY, Wayne, NJ 07470-8420

**General Information** State-supported, coed, comprehensive institution. CGS member. *Graduate housing:* Room and/or apartments available on a first-come, first-served basis to single students; on-campus housing not available to married students. Housing application deadline: 5/1. *Research affiliation:* Sun Chemical (chemistry), Arysta Life Sciences (biology).

**GRADUATE UNITS**

**College of Education**
**College of Humanities and Social Sciences**
**College of Science and Health**
**College of the Arts and Communication**
**Cotsakos College of Business**

## WILLIAM PENN UNIVERSITY, Oskaloosa, IA 52577-1799

**General Information** Independent-religious, coed, comprehensive institution.

**GRADUATE UNITS**

**College for Working Adults** *Program availability:* Online learning.

## WILLIAMS BAPTIST UNIVERSITY, Walnut Ridge, AR 72476

**General Information** Independent-religious, coed, comprehensive institution.

**GRADUATE UNITS**

**Graduate Programs**

## WILLIAMS COLLEGE, Williamstown, MA 01267

**General Information** Independent, coed, comprehensive institution. *Enrollment:* 2,134 graduate, professional, and undergraduate students; 29 full-time matriculated graduate/professional students (19 women). *Enrollment by degree level:* 29 master's. *Graduate faculty:* 24. *Tuition:* Full-time $55,140. *Graduate housing:* Room and/or apartments available on a first-come, first-served basis to single students; on-campus housing not available to married students. Typical cost: $7350 per year. Room charges vary according to board plan. Housing application deadline: 4/15. *Student services:* Campus employment opportunities, campus safety program, career counseling, exercise/wellness program, free psychological counseling, international student services, low-cost health insurance, multicultural affairs office, services for students with disabilities, writing training. *Library facilities:* Sawyer Library plus 2 others. *Collection:* Books: 1 million (physical); Serial titles: 272 (physical), 126,699 (digital/electronic). Weekly public service hours: 118; study areas open 24 hours, 5–7 days a week; students can reserve study rooms. *Research affiliation:* Clark Art Institute.

**Computer facilities:** 1,000 computers available on campus for general student use. A campuswide network can be accessed. Online class registration is available.
Website: http://www.williams.edu/

**General Application Contact:** Karen E. Kowitz, Program Administrator, 413-458-0596, E-mail: kekowitz@williams.edu.

**GRADUATE UNITS**

**Graduate Program in the History of Art** Electronic applications accepted.

## WILLIAMSON COLLEGE, Franklin, TN 37067

**General Information** Independent-religious, coed, comprehensive institution.

**GRADUATE UNITS**

**Program in Organizational Leadership** *Program availability:* Evening/weekend.

## WILLIAM WOODS UNIVERSITY, Fulton, MO 65251-1098

**General Information** Independent-religious, coed, comprehensive institution. *Graduate housing:* On-campus housing not available.

**GRADUATE UNITS**

**Graduate and Adult Studies** *Program availability:* Part-time, evening/weekend. Electronic applications accepted.

## WILMINGTON COLLEGE, Wilmington, OH 45177

**General Information** Independent-religious, coed, comprehensive institution. *Graduate housing:* On-campus housing not available.

**GRADUATE UNITS**

**Department of Education** *Program availability:* Part-time.

## WILMINGTON UNIVERSITY, New Castle, DE 19720-6491

**General Information** Independent, coed, university. *Graduate housing:* On-campus housing not available.

**GRADUATE UNITS**

**College of Business** *Program availability:* Part-time, evening/weekend. Electronic applications accepted.
**College of Education** *Program availability:* Part-time, evening/weekend. Electronic applications accepted.
**College of Health Professions** *Program availability:* Part-time. Electronic applications accepted.
**College of Social and Behavioral Sciences** *Program availability:* Part-time, evening/weekend. Electronic applications accepted.
**College of Technology** *Program availability:* Part-time, evening/weekend. Electronic applications accepted.

## WILSON COLLEGE, Chambersburg, PA 17201-1285

**General Information** Independent-religious, coed, primarily women, comprehensive institution.

**GRADUATE UNITS**

**Graduate Programs** *Program availability:* Evening/weekend. Electronic applications accepted.

## WINEBRENNER THEOLOGICAL SEMINARY, Findlay, OH 45840

**General Information** Independent-religious, coed, graduate-only institution. *Enrollment by degree level:* 49 master's, 4 doctoral. *Graduate faculty:* 6 full-time (3 women), 4 part-time/adjunct (0 women). *Tuition:* Full-time $9450; part-time $525 per credit. Tuition and fees vary according to course load, degree level and program. *Graduate housing:* On-campus housing not available. *Student services:* Campus safety program, career counseling, free psychological counseling, international student services, multicultural affairs office, services for students with disabilities, writing training. *Library facilities:* Shafer Library plus 1 other. *Collection:* Books: 42,350 (physical), 43 (digital/electronic); Serial titles: 2 (physical), 4 (digital/electronic). Weekly public service hours: 95; study areas open 24 hours, 5–7 days a week; students can reserve study rooms.

**Computer facilities:** 224 computers available on campus for general student use. A campuswide network can be accessed from student residence rooms and from off campus. Online class registration is available.
Website: http://www.winebrenner.edu/

**General Application Contact:** Amy Kinney, Director of Enrollment Management, 419-434-4241, E-mail: admissions@winebrenner.edu.

**GRADUATE UNITS**

**Graduate Programs** *Program availability:* Part-time, 100% online, blended/hybrid learning. Electronic applications accepted.

## WINGATE UNIVERSITY, Wingate, NC 28174

**General Information** Independent-religious, coed, comprehensive institution. *Graduate housing:* Rooms and/or apartments available on a first-come, first-served basis to single and married students. Housing application deadline: 8/15.

**GRADUATE UNITS**

**Department of Physical Therapy**
**Harris Department of Physician Assistant Studies**
**Porter B. Byrum School of Business** *Program availability:* Part-time, evening/weekend. Electronic applications accepted.
**School of Pharmacy** Electronic applications accepted.
**School of Sport Sciences** Electronic applications accepted.
**Thayer School of Education** *Program availability:* Part-time, evening/weekend.

## WINONA STATE UNIVERSITY, Winona, MN 55987

**General Information** State-supported, coed, comprehensive institution. *Graduate housing:* Room and/or apartments available to single students; on-campus housing not available to married students. Housing application deadline: 3/2.

**GRADUATE UNITS**

**College of Education** *Program availability:* Part-time, evening/weekend.
**College of Liberal Arts** *Program availability:* Part-time.
**College of Nursing and Health Sciences** *Program availability:* Part-time, online learning.

## WINSTON-SALEM STATE UNIVERSITY, Winston-Salem, NC 27110-0003

**General Information** State-supported, coed, comprehensive institution. *Graduate housing:* On-campus housing not available.

**GRADUATE UNITS**

**Department of Occupational Therapy** Electronic applications accepted.

**Department of Physical Therapy** Electronic applications accepted.

**MAT Program** *Program availability:* Part-time, evening/weekend, online learning. Electronic applications accepted.

**Program in Business Administration** *Program availability:* Part-time, evening/weekend, online learning. Electronic applications accepted.

**Program in Computer Science and Information Technology** *Program availability:* Part-time. Electronic applications accepted.

**Program in Health Administration**

**Program in Nursing** *Program availability:* Part-time, evening/weekend, online learning. Electronic applications accepted.

**Program in Rehabilitation Counseling** *Program availability:* Part-time, online learning. Electronic applications accepted.

## WINTHROP UNIVERSITY, Rock Hill, SC 29733

**General Information** State-supported, coed, comprehensive institution. CGS member. *Enrollment:* 5,813 graduate, professional, and undergraduate students; 338 full-time matriculated graduate/professional students (273 women), 763 part-time matriculated graduate/professional students (635 women). *Enrollment by degree level:* 787 master's, 46 other advanced degrees. *Graduate faculty:* 126 full-time (67 women), 13 part-time/adjunct (8 women). *Tuition, area resident:* Full-time $7659; part-time $641 per credit hour. Tuition, state resident: full-time $7659; part-time $641 per credit hour. Tuition, nonresident: full-time $14,753; part-time $1234 per credit hour. *Graduate housing:* Rooms and/or apartments available on a first-come, first-served basis to single and married students. Housing application deadline: 3/1. *Student services:* Campus employment opportunities, campus safety program, career counseling, exercise/wellness program, free psychological counseling, international student services, low-cost health insurance, multicultural affairs office, services for students with disabilities. *Library facilities:* Dacus Library plus 1 other. *Collection:* Books: 295,558 (physical), 187,817 (digital/electronic); Serial titles: 3,474 (physical), 53,319 (digital/electronic); Databases: 87. Weekly public service hours: 144; study areas open 24 hours, 5–7 days a week; students can reserve study rooms.

**Computer facilities:** Computer purchase and lease plans are available. 620 computers available on campus for general student use. A campuswide network can be accessed. Online class registration, university services are available.
Website: http://www.winthrop.edu/

**General Application Contact:** The Graduate School, 800-411-7041, Fax: 803-323-2204, E-mail: gradschool@winthrop.edu.

**GRADUATE UNITS**

**College of Arts and Sciences** *Program availability:* Part-time. Electronic applications accepted.

**College of Business Administration** *Program availability:* Part-time, evening/weekend, online learning. Electronic applications accepted.

**College of Education** *Program availability:* Part-time. Electronic applications accepted.

**College of Visual and Performing Arts** *Program availability:* Part-time. Electronic applications accepted.

## WISCONSIN LUTHERAN COLLEGE, Milwaukee, WI 53226-9942

**General Information** Independent-religious, coed, comprehensive institution.

**GRADUATE UNITS**

**College of Adult and Graduate Studies**

## WISCONSIN SCHOOL OF PROFESSIONAL PSYCHOLOGY, Milwaukee, WI 53225-4960

**General Information** Independent, coed, graduate-only institution. *Graduate housing:* On-campus housing not available.

**GRADUATE UNITS**

**Program in Clinical Psychology** *Program availability:* Part-time, evening/weekend.

## WITTENBERG UNIVERSITY, Springfield, OH 45501-0720

**General Information** Independent-religious, coed, comprehensive institution.

**GRADUATE UNITS**

**Graduate Program**

## WONGU UNIVERSITY OF ORIENTAL MEDICINE, Las Vegas, NV 89123

**General Information** Private, coed, graduate-only institution. *Enrollment by degree level:* 46 master's. *Graduate faculty:* 18 part-time/adjunct (11 women). *Tuition:* Full-time $11,320; part-time $2830 per quarter. *Required fees:* $520; $520 per quarter. $130 per quarter. One-time fee: $150. Tuition and fees vary according to course load, program and student level. *Graduate housing:* On-campus housing not available. *Student services:* Campus employment opportunities, career counseling, international student services. *Library facilities:* Wongu University Library plus 1 other. *Collection:* Books: 2,221 (physical). Weekly public service hours: 40.

**Computer facilities:** 2 computers available on campus for general student use. A campuswide network can be accessed. Online class registration is available.
Website: http://www.wongu.org/

**General Application Contact:** Admission Coordinator, 702-463-2122, E-mail: start@wongu.edu.

**GRADUATE UNITS**

**Graduate Program** *Program availability:* Part-time. Electronic applications accepted.

## WON INSTITUTE OF GRADUATE STUDIES, Glenside, PA 19038

**General Information** Proprietary, coed, graduate-only institution. *Enrollment by degree level:* 52 master's, 19 other advanced degrees. *Graduate faculty:* 10 full-time (8 women), 43 part-time/adjunct (29 women). *Tuition:* Full-time $15,000; part-time $7500 per credit. *Required fees:* $750; $600 per credit. Tuition and fees vary according to degree level and program. *Student services:* Career counseling, writing training. *Library facilities:* Won Institute of Graduate Studies Library plus 1 other. *Collection:* Books: 4,987 (physical), 5 (digital/electronic); Databases: 3. Students can reserve study rooms.

**Computer facilities:** 4 computers available on campus for general student use. A campuswide network can be accessed. Online class registration is available.
Website: http://www.woninstitute.edu/

**General Application Contact:** Jennifer Cake, Enrollment Management Counselor, 215-884-8942 Ext. 219, Fax: 215-884-9002, E-mail: jennifer.cake@woninstitute.edu.

**GRADUATE UNITS**

**Acupuncture Studies Program** Electronic applications accepted.

**Program in Chinese Herbal Medicine** Electronic applications accepted.

**Won Buddhist Studies Program** *Program availability:* Part-time.

## WOODBURY UNIVERSITY, Burbank, CA 91504-1052

**General Information** Independent, coed, comprehensive institution. *Graduate housing:* Room and/or apartments available on a first-come, first-served basis to single students; on-campus housing not available to married students.

**GRADUATE UNITS**

**School of Architecture**

**School of Business** *Program availability:* Part-time, evening/weekend.

## WOODS HOLE OCEANOGRAPHIC INSTITUTION, Woods Hole, MA 02543-1541

**General Information** Independent, coed, graduate-only institution. CGS member. *Graduate housing:* Rooms and/or apartments guaranteed to single students and available on a first-come, first-served basis to married students.

**GRADUATE UNITS**

**MIT/WHOI Joint Program in Oceanography/Applied Ocean Science and Engineering** Electronic applications accepted.

## WORCESTER POLYTECHNIC INSTITUTE, Worcester, MA 01609-2280

**General Information** Independent, coed, university. CGS member. *Graduate housing:* Rooms and/or apartments available on a first-come, first-served basis to single and married students. *Research affiliation:* American Institutes for Research (educational software), United States Advanced Battery Consortium LLC (advanced battery recycling), SRI International (educational software), Toyota Motor Company (automotive safety technology), MathWorks Inc. (Internet of Things (IoT)), University of Massachusetts Medical School at Worcester (basic transitional and clinical medical research).

**GRADUATE UNITS**

**Graduate Admissions** *Program availability:* Part-time, evening/weekend, 100% online, blended/hybrid learning. Electronic applications accepted.

***Foisie Business School*** *Program availability:* Part-time, evening/weekend, 100% online, blended/hybrid learning. Electronic applications accepted.

## WORCESTER STATE UNIVERSITY, Worcester, MA 01602-2597

**General Information** State-supported, coed, comprehensive institution. *Enrollment:* 6,204 graduate, professional, and undergraduate students; 173 full-time matriculated graduate/professional students (149 women), 699 part-time matriculated graduate/professional students (536 women). *Enrollment by degree level:* 579 master's, 293 other advanced degrees. *Graduate faculty:* 42 full-time (30 women), 38 part-time/adjunct (20 women). *International tuition:* $3042 full-time. *Tuition, area resident:* Full-time $3042; part-time $169 per credit hour. Tuition, state resident: full-time $3042; part-time $169 per credit hour. Tuition, nonresident: full-time $3042; part-time $169 per credit hour. *Required fees:* $2754; $153 per credit hour. *Graduate housing:* On-campus housing not available. *Student services:* Campus employment opportunities, campus safety program, career counseling, exercise/wellness program, free psychological counseling, international student services, low-cost health insurance, multicultural affairs office, services for students with disabilities, teacher training, writing training. *Library facilities:* Learning Resource Center. *Collection:* Books: 129,248 (physical), 173,109 (digital/electronic); Serial titles: 202 (physical), 151,915 (digital/electronic); Databases: 287. Weekly public service hours: 100.

**Computer facilities:** Computer purchase and lease plans are available. A campuswide network can be accessed. Online class registration is available.
Website: http://www.worcester.edu/

**General Application Contact:** Sara Grady, Associate Dean, Graduate and Continuing Education, 508-929-8130, Fax: 508-929-8100, E-mail: sara.grady@worcester.edu.

**GRADUATE UNITS**

**Graduate School** Students: 140 full-time (120 women), 142 part-time (96 women); includes 39 minority (14 Black or African American, non-Hispanic/Latino; 11 Asian, non-Hispanic/Latino; 11 Hispanic/Latino; 3 Two or more races, non-Hispanic/Latino), 10 international. Average age 29. 104 applicants, 100% accepted, 91 enrolled. *Faculty:* 34 full-time (21 women), 14 part-time/adjunct (8 women). Expenses: Contact institution. *Financial support:* Career-related internships or fieldwork, scholarships/grants, and unspecified assistantships available. Support available to part-time students. Financial award application deadline: 3/1; financial award applicants required to submit FAFSA. In 2019, 84 master's awarded. *Application deadline:* For fall admission, 3/1 for domestic and international students; for spring admission, 11/1 for domestic and international students; for summer admission, 3/1 for domestic and international students. Applications are processed on a rolling basis. *Application fee:* $50. Electronic applications accepted. *Application Contact:* Sara Grady, Associate Dean, Graduate Studies and Professional Development, 508-929-8130, Fax: 508-929-8100, E-mail: sara.grady@worcester.edu. *Associate Vice President for Continuing Education/Dean of the Graduate Studies,* Dr. Roberta Kyle, 508-929-8811, Fax: 508-929-8100, E-mail: rkyle@worcester.edu.

## WORLD MISSION UNIVERSITY, Los Angeles, CA 90020

**General Information** Independent-religious, coed, comprehensive institution.

**GRADUATE UNITS**

**Graduate Programs** *Program availability:* Online learning.

## WRIGHT GRADUATE UNIVERSITY FOR THE REALIZATION OF HUMAN POTENTIAL, Elkhorn, WI 53121

**General Information** Independent, coed, graduate-only institution.

**GRADUATE UNITS**

**Graduate Programs**

## THE WRIGHT INSTITUTE, Berkeley, CA 94704-1796

**General Information** Independent, coed, graduate-only institution. *Graduate housing:* On-campus housing not available.

**GRADUATE UNITS**

**Doctoral Program in Clinical Psychology** Electronic applications accepted.

**Master of Arts in Counseling Psychology Program** *Program availability:* Part-time, evening/weekend. Electronic applications accepted.

## WRIGHT STATE UNIVERSITY, Dayton, OH 45435

**General Information** State-supported, coed, university. CGS member. *Graduate housing:* Rooms and/or apartments available on a first-come, first-served basis to single and married students. *Research affiliation:* Wright-Patterson Air Force Base (research and development, systems and logistics), Veterans Administration Medical Center, Scott-Kettering Magnetic Resonance Research Laboratory (medical science), Edison Biotechnology Center, Edison Materials Technology Center (processing).

**GRADUATE UNITS**

**Boonshoft School of Medicine**

**Graduate School** *Program availability:* Part-time, evening/weekend, 100% online, blended/hybrid learning. Electronic applications accepted.

***College of Education and Human Services*** *Program availability:* Part-time, evening/weekend.

***College of Engineering and Computer Science*** *Program availability:* Part-time, evening/weekend.

***College of Liberal Arts*** *Program availability:* Part-time.

***College of Nursing and Health*** *Program availability:* Part-time, evening/weekend.

***College of Science and Mathematics*** *Program availability:* Part-time, evening/weekend.

***Raj Soin College of Business*** *Program availability:* Part-time, evening/weekend.

**School of Professional Psychology**

## WYCLIFFE COLLEGE, Toronto, ON M5S 1H7, Canada

**General Information** Independent-religious, coed, graduate-only institution. *Graduate housing:* Rooms and/or apartments guaranteed to single students and available on a first-come, first-served basis to married students. Housing application deadline: 5/1.

**GRADUATE UNITS**

**Division of Advanced Degree Studies** *Program availability:* Part-time.

**Division of Basic Degree Studies** *Program availability:* Part-time.

## XAVIER UNIVERSITY, Cincinnati, OH 45207

**General Information** Independent-religious, coed, university. *Graduate housing:* On-campus housing not available.

**GRADUATE UNITS**

**College of Arts and Sciences** *Program availability:* Part-time. Electronic applications accepted.

**College of Professional Sciences**

***School of Education*** Electronic applications accepted.

***School of Nursing*** *Program availability:* Part-time, evening/weekend. Electronic applications accepted.

**Williams College of Business** *Program availability:* Part-time, evening/weekend. Electronic applications accepted.

## XAVIER UNIVERSITY OF LOUISIANA, New Orleans, LA 70125

**General Information** Independent-religious, coed, comprehensive institution. *Graduate housing:* Room and/or apartments available on a first-come, first-served basis to single students; on-campus housing not available to married students. Housing application deadline: 5/1.

**GRADUATE UNITS**

**College of Pharmacy** Electronic applications accepted.

**Graduate School** *Program availability:* Part-time, evening/weekend. Electronic applications accepted.

***Institute for Black Catholic Studies*** *Program availability:* Part-time. Electronic applications accepted.

## YALE UNIVERSITY, New Haven, CT 06520

**General Information** Independent, coed, university. CGS member. *Graduate housing:* Rooms and/or apartments available on a first-come, first-served basis to single and married students. Housing application deadline: 6/1. *Research affiliation:* Howard Hughes Medical Institute, J.B. Pierce Foundation (environmental physiology), Haskins Laboratories (speech, hearing, reading).

**GRADUATE UNITS**

**Graduate School of Arts and Sciences** *Program availability:* Part-time.

***School of Engineering and Applied Science*** *Program availability:* Part-time.

**School of Architecture** Electronic applications accepted.

**School of Art** Electronic applications accepted.

**School of Drama** Electronic applications accepted.

**School of Music** Students: 232 full-time (105 women); includes 47 minority (3 Black or African American, non-Hispanic/Latino; 22 Asian, non-Hispanic/Latino; 15 Hispanic/Latino; 7 Two or more races, non-Hispanic/Latino). Average age 25. 1,481 applicants, 12% accepted, 116 enrolled. *Faculty:* 29 full-time (9 women), 31 part-time/adjunct (7 women). Expenses: Contact institution. *Financial support:* In 2019–20, 211 students received support, including 211 fellowships (averaging $38,000 per year); Federal Work-Study, scholarships/grants, and unspecified assistantships also available. Financial award application deadline: 5/30; financial award applicants required to submit FAFSA. In 2019, 73 master's, 6 doctorates, 30 ADs awarded. *Application deadline:* For fall admission, 12/1 for domestic and international students. *Application fee:* $150. Electronic applications accepted. *Application Contact:* Suzanne M. Stringer, Director of Student Services, 203-432-1962, Fax: 203-432-7448, E-mail: suzanne.stringer@yale.edu. *Dean,* Robert Blocker, 203-432-4160, Fax: 203-432-7542.

**School of Nursing** *Program availability:* Part-time, online learning. Electronic applications accepted.

**School of the Environment** Students: 310 full-time. Average age 26. 600 applicants, 150 enrolled. *Faculty:* 32 full-time, 50 part-time/adjunct. Expenses: Contact institution. *Financial support:* In 2019–20, 230 students received support. Fellowships, research assistantships, teaching assistantships, career-related internships or fieldwork, Federal Work-Study, institutionally sponsored loans, scholarships/grants, and health care benefits available. Support available to part-time students. Financial award application deadline: 2/15; financial award applicants required to submit FAFSA. In 2019, 152 master's, 15 doctorates awarded. *Program availability:* Part-time. *Application deadline:* For fall admission, 12/15 priority date for domestic and international students. *Application fee:* $80. Electronic applications accepted. *Application Contact:* Wendi Hicks, Director of Enrollment Management, 800-825-0330, Fax: 203-432-5528, E-mail: fesinfo@yale.edu. *Carl W. Knobloch, Jr. Dean at the Yale School of the Environment,* Dr. Ingrid C. Burke, 203-432-5109, Fax: 203-432-3051.

**Yale Divinity School** *Program availability:* Part-time. Electronic applications accepted.

**Yale Law School** Students: 628 full-time (322 women). Average age 25. 3,284 applicants, 7% accepted, 212 enrolled. *Faculty:* 93 full-time, 164 part-time/adjunct. Expenses: Contact institution. *Financial support:* Application deadline: 3/15; applicants required to submit FAFSA. *Application deadline:* For fall admission, 2/28 for domestic students. Applications are processed on a rolling basis. *Application fee:* $85. Electronic applications accepted. *Application Contact:* Craig Janecek, Assistant Dean of Admissions, 203-432-4995, E-mail: admissions.law@yale.edu. *Dean,* Heather Gerken, 203-432-1660.

**Yale School of Management**

**Yale School of Medicine** *Program availability:* Part-time. Electronic applications accepted.

***Yale School of Public Health*** Students: 534 full-time (386 women); includes 156 minority (24 Black or African American, non-Hispanic/Latino; 83 Asian, non-Hispanic/Latino; 30 Hispanic/Latino; 19 Two or more races, non-Hispanic/Latino), 220 international. Average age 25. 1,300 applicants, 220 enrolled. *Faculty:* 161 full-time (71 women), 121 part-time/adjunct (57 women). Expenses: Contact institution. *Financial support:* Fellowships with full tuition reimbursements, research assistantships with full tuition reimbursements, teaching assistantships with full tuition reimbursements, career-related internships or fieldwork, institutionally sponsored loans, scholarships/grants, and tuition waivers available. Support available to part-time students. Financial award application deadline: 3/1; financial award applicants required to submit FAFSA. In 2019, 250 master's, 12 doctorates awarded. *Application deadline:* For fall admission, 12/15 for domestic and international students; for summer admission, 12/15 for domestic and international students. Applications are processed on a rolling basis. *Application fee:* $135. Electronic applications accepted. *Application Contact:* Mary Keefe, Director of Admissions, 203-785-2844, E-mail: ysph.admissions@yale.edu. *Dean and Anna M.R. Lauder Professor of Public Health,* Dr. Sten Vermund, E-mail: sten.vermund@yale.edu.

## YESHIVA BETH MOSHE, Scranton, PA 18505-2124

**General Information** Independent-religious, men only, comprehensive institution.

**GRADUATE UNITS**

**Graduate Programs**

## YESHIVA DERECH CHAIM, Brooklyn, NY 11218

**General Information** Independent-religious, men only, comprehensive institution.

**GRADUATE UNITS**

**Graduate Program**

## YESHIVA KARLIN STOLIN, Brooklyn, NY 11204

**General Information** Independent-religious, men only, comprehensive institution. *Graduate housing:* On-campus housing not available.

**GRADUATE UNITS**

**Graduate Programs**

## YESHIVA OF NITRA RABBINICAL COLLEGE, Mount Kisco, NY 10549

**General Information** Independent-religious, men only, comprehensive institution.

**GRADUATE UNITS**

**Graduate Programs**

## YESHIVA SHAAR HATORAH TALMUDIC RESEARCH INSTITUTE, Kew Gardens, NY 11418-1469

**General Information** Independent-religious, men only, comprehensive institution.

**GRADUATE UNITS**

**Graduate Programs**

## YESHIVATH VIZNITZ, Monsey, NY 10952

**General Information** Independent-religious, men only, comprehensive institution.

**GRADUATE UNITS**

**Graduate Programs**

## YESHIVATH ZICHRON MOSHE, South Fallsburg, NY 12779

**General Information** Independent-religious, men only, comprehensive institution.

**GRADUATE UNITS**

**Graduate Programs** *Program availability:* Part-time.

## YESHIVA UNIVERSITY, New York, NY 10033-3201

**General Information** Independent, coed, university. *Graduate housing:* On-campus housing not available.

**GRADUATE UNITS**

**Azrieli Graduate School of Jewish Education and Administration** *Program availability:* Part-time, evening/weekend.

**Benjamin N. Cardozo School of Law** *Program availability:* 100% online. Electronic applications accepted.

**Bernard Revel Graduate School of Jewish Studies** *Program availability:* Part-time.

**Ferkauf Graduate School of Psychology** *Program availability:* Part-time.

**The Katz School** *Program availability:* Part-time, online learning.

**Sy Syms School of Business** *Program availability:* Part-time.

**Wurzweiler School of Social Work** *Program availability:* Part-time, evening/weekend.

## YORK COLLEGE OF PENNSYLVANIA, York, PA 17403-3651

**General Information** Independent, coed, comprehensive institution. *Enrollment:* 4,305 graduate, professional, and undergraduate students; 43 full-time matriculated graduate/professional students (21 women), 226 part-time matriculated graduate/professional students (143 women). *Enrollment by degree level:* 225 master's, 38 doctoral, 6 other advanced degrees. *Graduate faculty:* 25 full-time (15 women), 19 part-time/adjunct (12 women). *Graduate housing:* On-campus housing not available. *Student services:* Campus employment opportunities, campus safety program, career counseling, exercise/wellness program, free psychological counseling, international student services, services for students with disabilities, writing training. *Library facilities:* Schmidt Library.

**Computer facilities:** A campuswide network can be accessed from student residence rooms and from off campus. Online class registration is available.
Website: http://www.ycp.edu/

**General Application Contact:** Sueann Robbins, Director of Graduate and Transfer Admission, 717-815-2257, Fax: 717-849-1607, E-mail: admissions@ycp.edu.

**GRADUATE UNITS**

**Graduate Programs in Behavioral Sciences and Education** Students: 111 part-time (85 women); includes 3 minority (1 Asian, non-Hispanic/Latino; 1 Hispanic/Latino; 1 Two or more races, non-Hispanic/Latino), 1 international. Average age 32. 41 applicants, 95% accepted, 32 enrolled. *Faculty:* 3 full-time (2 women), 8 part-time/adjunct (6 women). Expenses: Contact institution. *Financial support:* Scholarships/grants available. Financial award applicants required to submit FAFSA. In 2019, 20 master's awarded. *Program availability:* Part-time, evening/weekend, online learning. *Application deadline:* For fall admission, 7/15 priority date for domestic students; for spring admission, 11/15 priority date for domestic students; for summer admission, 4/15 priority date for domestic students. Applications are processed on a rolling basis. Electronic applications accepted. *Application Contact:* Sueann Robbins, Director, Graduate Admission, 717-815-2257, E-mail: srobbins@ycp.edu. *Director, Graduate Programs in Behavioral Science and Education,* Dr. Joshua D. DeSantis, 717-815-1936, E-mail: jdesant1@ycp.edu.

**Graham School of Business** Students: 10 full-time (3 women), 73 part-time (27 women); includes 11 minority (6 Black or African American, non-Hispanic/Latino; 1 Asian, non-Hispanic/Latino; 3 Hispanic/Latino; 1 Two or more races, non-Hispanic/Latino), 2 international. Average age 32. *Faculty:* 15 full-time (7 women), 4 part-time/adjunct (3 women). Expenses: Contact institution. *Financial support:* In 2019–20, 3 students received support. Scholarships/grants available. Financial award applicants required to submit FAFSA. In 2019, 25 master's awarded. *Program availability:* Part-time, evening/weekend. *Application deadline:* For fall admission, 7/15 priority date for domestic students, 5/1 for international students; for spring admission, 11/15 priority date for domestic students, 9/1 for international students; for summer admission, 4/15 priority date for domestic students. Applications are processed on a rolling basis. Electronic applications accepted. *Application Contact:* MBA Office, 717-815-1491, Fax: 717-600-3999, E-mail: mba@ycp.edu. *MBA Director,* Nicole Cornell Sadowski, 717-815-1491, Fax: 717-600-3999, E-mail: ncornell@ycp.edu.

**The Stabler Department of Nursing** Students: 30 full-time (15 women), 36 part-time (30 women); includes 9 minority (1 Black or African American, non-Hispanic/Latino; 6 Asian, non-Hispanic/Latino; 1 Hispanic/Latino; 1 Two or more races, non-Hispanic/Latino), 1 international. Average age 34. 61 applicants, 46% accepted, 23 enrolled. *Faculty:* 6 full-time (all women), 5 part-time/adjunct (4 women). Expenses: Contact institution. *Financial support:* In 2019–20, 1 student received support. Scholarships/grants available. Financial award applicants required to submit FAFSA. In 2019, 24 master's awarded. *Program availability:* Part-time. Electronic applications accepted. *Application Contact:* Allison Malachosky, Administrative Assistant, 717-815-2290, Fax: 717-849-1651, E-mail: amalacho@ycp.edu. *Director, Graduate Programs in Nursing,* Colleen Marshall-Fantaski, 717-815-1791, Fax: 717-849-1651, E-mail: cfantaski@ycp.edu.

## YORK COLLEGE OF THE CITY UNIVERSITY OF NEW YORK, Jamaica, NY 11451

**General Information** State and locally supported, coed, comprehensive institution.

**GRADUATE UNITS**

**School of Arts and Sciences**

**School of Health Sciences and Professional Programs**

## YORK UNIVERSITY, Toronto, ON M3J 1P3, Canada

**General Information** Province-supported, coed, university. CGS member. *Graduate housing:* Rooms and/or apartments available on a first-come, first-served basis to single and married students. *Research affiliation:* Imperial Oil Limited, National Palace Museum, Unicorn Children's Foundation (developmental and learning disorders), Smithsonian Institution (astronomy, physics, space), Beijing Municipality (management training), German Academic Exchange (German studies).

**GRADUATE UNITS**

***Faculty of Graduate Studies*** *Program availability:* Part-time, evening/weekend. Electronic applications accepted.

***Faculty of Education*** *Program availability:* Part-time. Electronic applications accepted.

***Faculty of Fine Arts*** *Program availability:* Part-time. Electronic applications accepted.

***Faculty of Health***

***Faculty of Liberal Arts and Professional Studies***

***Faculty of Science*** *Program availability:* Part-time, evening/weekend.

***Glendon Campus***

***Lassonde School of Engineering***

***Osgoode Hall Law School*** *Program availability:* Part-time, evening/weekend. Electronic applications accepted.

***Schulich School of Business*** *Program availability:* Part-time, evening/weekend. Electronic applications accepted.

## YO SAN UNIVERSITY OF TRADITIONAL CHINESE MEDICINE, Los Angeles, CA 90066

**General Information** Private, coed, graduate-only institution. *Graduate housing:* On-campus housing not available.

**GRADUATE UNITS**

**Program in Acupuncture and Traditional Chinese Medicine** *Program availability:* Part-time, online learning.

## YOUNGSTOWN STATE UNIVERSITY, Youngstown, OH 44555-0001

**General Information** State-supported, coed, comprehensive institution. CGS member. *Graduate housing:* Room and/or apartments available on a first-come, first-served basis to single students; on-campus housing not available to married students. *Research affiliation:* Ohio Supercomputer Center (computational chemistry and physics), Northeast Ohio Medical University (medicine), Parker-Hannifin Corporation (engineering technology), Ohio Mass Spectrometry Consortium (chemistry and biology), BioRemedial Technologies Inc. (environmental bioremediation).

**GRADUATE UNITS**

**College of Graduate Studies** *Program availability:* Part-time, evening/weekend.

***Beeghly College of Education*** *Program availability:* Part-time, evening/weekend.

***Bitonte College of Health and Human Services*** *Program availability:* Part-time, evening/weekend.

***Cliffe College of Creative Arts and Communication*** *Program availability:* Part-time, evening/weekend.

***College of Liberal Arts and Social Sciences*** *Program availability:* Part-time.

***College of Science, Technology, Engineering and Mathematics*** *Program availability:* Part-time, evening/weekend.

***Williamson College of Business Administration*** *Program availability:* Part-time, evening/weekend.

# CLOSE-UPS OF INSTITUTIONS OFFERING GRADUATE AND PROFESSIONAL WORK

# CHAPMAN UNIVERSITY

## *Graduate Studies*

CHAPMAN UNIVERSITY

### Programs of Study

Chapman University offers the Juris Doctor (law); the Ph.D. in education; the Ph.D. in computational and data sciences; the Doctor of Physical Therapy (D.P.T.); the Doctor of Pharmacy (Pharm.D.); Master of Medical Sciences (MMS) PA; the Master of Arts (M.A.) in English, film studies, international studies, war and society, leadership development, marriage and family therapy, counseling, school psychology, special education, teaching (elementary), teaching (secondary), and teaching music education; the Master of Fine Arts (M.F.A.) in creative writing, documentary filmmaking, film production, film and television producing, production design, and screenwriting; the Master of Music (M.M.) in keyboard collaborative arts; and the Master of Science (M.S.) in accounting, communication sciences and disorders, computational and data sciences, economic systems design, food science, health and strategic communication, and pharmaceutical sciences. Also offered are the Master of Business Administration and the Executive M.B.A. With its emphasis on collaboration, Chapman University offers the following dual-degree and joint programs: the English M.A./ Creative Writing M.F.A., the J.D./M.B.A., the M.B.A./M.F.A. in film and television producing, the J.D./M.F.A. in film and television producing, and the M.B.A./M.S. in food science. Many of the degree programs offer specializations.

Public school credential programs include multiple subject, multiple subject with bilingual emphasis, single subject, special education credentials mild/moderate and moderate/severe preliminary, special education credentials mild/moderate and moderate/severe Level II. Credential programs can be combined with one of the degree programs in education. The counseling and school psychology programs are offered with or without the LPCC.

Required units vary with each degree; however, each program comprises courses that best prepare students to advance their career or enter a new profession. Program requirements include advancement to degree candidacy after the completion of 12 units. Many programs require a comprehensive examination, taken at the end of or during the final semester of course work, yet some programs offer a thesis project option in place of the comprehensive examination. One or two internship courses that provide practical experience in the student's field are required for some programs. Course work from other accredited institutions may be transferred; a maximum of 6 credits may be applied to a program. At least 24 credits must be taken in residence.

Research projects are essential to many degree programs and are undertaken in research courses or through cooperative education. Because class sizes are kept small, students can readily communicate with faculty members about research projects and general academic work.

### Research Facilities

Academic and research centers and institutes include the nationally recognized A. Gary Anderson Center for Economic Research; the Economic Science Institute; Albert Schweitzer Institute; Ludie and David C. Henley Social Sciences Research Laboratory; Walter Schmid Center for International Business; Center for Global Law and Development; Ralph W. Leatherby Center for Entrepreneurship Business Ethics; C. Larry Hoag Center for Real Estate and Finance; John Fowles Center for Creative Writing; Barry and Phyllis Rodgers Center for Holocaust Education; the Francis Smith Center for Individual and Family Therapy for psychological counseling and research; a state-of-the-art human performance laboratory and research vivarium; and food science and nutrition food-tasting and research laboratories. The entire campus is a WiFi hotspot, and there are Dell PC and Macintosh computer laboratories. The Chapman University Leatherby Libraries contain more than 291,000 volumes, more than 59,000 full-text electronic journals, more than 15,000 electronic books, and 800 print journals, and 21,000 audio/visual items (DVDs, videos, CDs, and other media). Chapman has the largest collection of Albert Schweitzer memorabilia in the western United States.

### Financial Aid

Many financial aid opportunities are available for qualified students, including Chapman University Fellowships and loans, which are based on need and academic achievement; graduate assistantships; residence life positions; employment; California State Graduate Fellowships; Federal Direct Student Loans; Benefits for Veterans and Dependents; and an employer-paid tuition plan. More than 93 percent of Chapman graduate students benefit from some form of financial aid and 34 percent receive department fellowship assistance. Students interested in any of these opportunities should contact the Graduate Financial Aid Office at 714-628-2730.

### Cost of Study

Tuition varies by program. Part-time and full-time students, as well as California and non-California residents, are charged the same tuition rate. Tuition for a full-time student (9 credits per semester) is approximately $14,000 to $50,000 per academic year, depending on the student's program. Books and personal expenses add to annual costs.

### Living and Housing Costs

Chapman offers limited housing for graduate students. Off-campus housing is available.

### Student Group

Graduate study programs enroll close to 1,900 students each year. Courses are scheduled so that both full- and part-time students can attend. Many students have been working in their field and bring practical experience to the classroom; they come from many states and countries, and about 50 percent are women. Students who choose to enroll at Chapman want a small-campus atmosphere, personalized attention, superior faculty, and the education that will enable them to succeed in a highly competitive professional world. Opportunities for graduates are plentiful due to the concentration of business and industry in Orange County and throughout Southern California. Potential employers of future Chapman graduates sit on many institutional advisory boards.

### Location

Located in Orange County, California, the University is just minutes from major recreation and entertainment venues, including Disneyland, Angel Stadium, Honda Center, and some of the most beautiful beaches in the world. The campus is nestled on the edge of a historic residential neighborhood—coffee shops, brew pubs, boutiques, and restaurants are all within walking distance of campus.

### The University

Chapman is an independent, private institution and has provided liberal arts and professional education of distinction since its founding in 1861. It has continued to meet the needs of its students with fine academic programs and individualized attention. Undergraduate and graduate degree programs are offered. The graduate curricula are designed to offer advanced study in specific disciplines to broaden and deepen a student's knowledge. Faculty members include distinguished academicians and noted professional practitioners.

Chapman is accredited by and is a member of the Western Association of Schools and Colleges. It is also a member of the Independent Colleges of Southern California, the College Entrance Examination Board, the Western College Association, the Association of Independent California Colleges and Universities, the American Council on Education, the American Association of Colleges for Teacher Education, the Division of Higher Education of the Christian Church (Disciples of Christ), and the American Assembly of Collegiate Schools of Business. The College of Educational Studies is accredited by the Teacher Education Accreditation Council. Its teacher training and credential programs are accredited by the California Commission on Teacher Credentialing. The school psychology program is approved by the National Association of School Psychologists. The physical therapy program is accredited by the Commission on Accreditation in the Physical Therapy Education of the American Physical Therapy Association and by the Physical Therapy Examining Committee of the Board of Medical Quality Assurance of the State of California. The M.B.A. programs are fully accredited by AACSB International—The Association to Advance Collegiate Schools of Business. The School of Law is fully approved by the American Bar Association. The marriage and family therapy program is accredited by COAMFTE, the Commission on Accreditation for Marriage and Family Therapy Education of AAMFT, the American Association for Marriage and Family Therapy. The communication sciences and disorders program is accredited by the Council of Academic Accreditation of ASHA, the American Speech-Language-Hearing Association. The Doctor of Pharmacy and M.M. in keyboard collaborative arts are under consideration by and pending approval from their respective accrediting bodies.

**Applying**

Students are admitted in the fall, spring, and summer for most programs. Applicants should submit applicable fees and a completed Application for Graduate Studies (students must apply online through the Apply Yourself application); official transcripts of all postsecondary work, showing the completion of a bachelor's degree or master's degree (if a master's degree is required by the program of interest); scores on the GMAT, GRE, MCAT, PCAT, MAT, or CSET; TOEFL, PTE, or IELTS scores, for international students; two letters of recommendation; a resume; and a statement of intent. Departments, however, should be consulted for specific program requirements.

To apply to the following programs, the Centralized Application System is required: Doctor of Physical Therapy (PTCAS), Doctor of Pharmacy (PHARMCAS), M.S. in communication sciences and disorders (CSDCAS), and M.S. in athletic training (ATCAS).

**Correspondence and Information**

Office of Graduate Admission
Argyros Forum, Room 213
Chapman University
Orange, California 92866
United States
Phone: 714-997-6711
888-CU-APPLY (toll-free)
Fax: 714-997-6713
E-mail: gradadmit@chapman.edu
Website: http://www.chapman.edu

## PROGRAM DIRECTORS

**Accounting: Jim Dusserre, EMBA '11, Assistant Director, Graduate Business Programs Darryl Stevens, Assistant ,Dean of M.B.A. Programs, Argyros School of Business and Economics; Ph.D., USC. he left.**

**Athletic Training: Jason Bennett, Director of Athletic Training Program, College of Educational Studies; D.A., Middle Tennessee.**

**Business Administration: Darryl Stevens, Assistant Dean of M.B.A. Programs, Argyros School of Business and Economics; Ph.D., USC.**

**Communication Sciences and Disorders: Judy K. Montgomery retired, Professor of Education; Ph.D., Claremont.**

**Computational and Data Sciences: Hesham El-Askary, Associate Professor and Director, Computation and Data Sciences Graduate Programs; Ph.D., George Mason.**

**Creative Writing: Anna Leahy, Ph.D, Professor of English; Ph.D., Ohio University.**

**Economic Systems Design: Stephen Rassenti, Professor of Economics and Mathematics and Director, Economic Science Institute; Ph.D., Arizona.**

**Education (Ph.D.): Dawn Hunter, Professor of Education; Ph.D., Maryland, College Park.**

**Educational Psychology: Kelly Kennedy, Associate Professor; Ph.D., California, Santa Barbara.**

**English: Anna Leahy, Ph.D, Professor of English; Ph.D., Ohio University.**

**Film Production, Film and Television Producing, Screenwriting, Production Design, Documentary Filmmaking, M.B.A./M.F.A. Film and Television Producing, Film Studies, and J.D./M.F.A. Film and Television Producing: Barbara Doyle, Professor of Film and Television and Chair, Graduate Conservatory; Ed.M., Harvard.**

**Food Science: Anuradha Prakash, Associate Professor of Food Science and Program Director, Department of Physical Sciences; Ph.D., Ohio State.**

**Health and Strategic Communication: Jennifer Bevan, Associate Professor of Communication Studies and Director, Health and Strategic Communication Program; Ph.D., Georgia.**

**International Studies: Lynn Horton, Associate Professor and Program Director of International Studies Program; Ph.D., Texas at Austin.**

**Keyboard Collaborative Arts: Louise Thomas, Associate Dean and Program Director; D.M., USC.**

**Law: Tom Campbell, Professor, School of Law; Ph.D., Chicago, J.D., Harvard.**

**Leadership Development: Whitney McIntyre Miller, Professor and Program Director; Ph.D., University of San Diego.**

**Pharmaceutical Sciences: Keyvakous Parang, Associate Dean of Research, Graduate Studies, and Global Affairs; Ph.D., Alberta.**

**Pharmacy: Ronald Jordan, Dean, School of Pharmacy; B.S., Rhode Island.**

**Physical Therapy: Jaclyn Brechter, Chair, Department of Physical Therapy; Ph.D., USC.**

**Physician Assistant: Jennifer Grumet, Assistant Professor, PA Studies; M.D., USC**

**Psychology: Brennan Peterson, Associate Professor of Psychology and Program Director of Marriage and Family Therapy; Ph.D., Virginia Tech.**

**School Counseling: John Brady, Associate Professor and Coordinator of Counselor Education Programs; Ph.D., US International.**

**Special Education: Jody Brown; M.S., Redlands.**

**Teaching and Multiple Subject Credential: Keith Howard, Assistant Professor and Director, Graduate Degree and Credential Programs in Teaching; Ph.D., USC.**

**Teaching and Single Subject Credential: Keith Howard, Assistant Professor and Director, Graduate Degree and Credential Programs in Teaching; Ph.D., USC.**

**Teaching Music Education: Keith Howard, Assistant Professor and Director, Graduate Degree and Credential Programs in Teaching; Ph.D., USC.**

**War and Society: Kyle Longley, Professor of History, Department of History; Ph.D., University of Kentucky.**

A bustling Attallah Piazza is the centerpiece of Chapman University's picturesque Southern California campus.

# ROBERT MORRIS UNIVERSITY
## *Graduate Programs*

### Programs of Study

Robert Morris University (RMU) offers more than thirty graduate degree programs, including two Doctor of Philosophy (Ph.D.) programs — information systems and communications, and instructional management and leadership — and the Doctor of Nursing Practice (D.N.P.) offered as an adult nurse practitioner, family nurse practitioner, or psychiatric and mental health nurse practitioner. Master's programs available include the Master of Business Administration (M.B.A.) as well as Master of Science (M.S.) degrees in business education, counseling psychology, cyber investigations and intelligence, cybersecurity and information assurance, data analytics, engineering management, instructional management and leadership, Internet information systems, health services administration, healthcare analytics, healthcare systems administration, human resource management, nonprofit leadership, nursing education, nursing leadership, organizational leadership, taxation, web and mobile information systems. Master of Education (M.Ed.) degrees are available in literacy and special education, and Master of Science in Nursing (M.S.N.) degrees area available in nursing education, nursing leadership, and as a dual degree with the M.B.A. The university also offers a variety of online graduate certificates.

### Research Facilities

Facilities supporting the graduate programs at Robert Morris University include nine open-access computer laboratories, two physical libraries, and an electronic library offering an array of research databases. Classrooms have been equipped with advanced computer and presentation technology equipment to facilitate teaching and learning.

To support a large number of holdings, the library has a state-of-the-art searchable catalog system. The RMU Electronic Library offers continual off-campus access to more than 100 major research databases. The library is a member of numerous resource-sharing consortia that greatly extend the amount of materials available to support graduate education.

### Financial Aid

Graduate loans are available for those who qualify. Students are encouraged to file the Free Application for Federal Student Aid (FAFSA). Robert Morris University participates in the Federal Family Education Loan (FFEL) Program and also offers various interest-free payment plans, as well as third-party billing and corporate reimbursement programs.

### Cost of Study

Tuition varies by program. Visit http://sfs.rmu.edu/tuition-fee-schedules/2020-2021-tuition-fees for current tuition rates and fees.

### Student Group

RMU enrolls approximately 1,000 students in its graduate degree programs, with an equal number of men and women. Students come from diverse professional and academic backgrounds.

### Location

Robert Morris University is located on a 230-acre campus in suburban Moon Township, 17 miles west of downtown Pittsburgh and 15 minutes from Pittsburgh International Airport. Many graduate programs and classes are also offered online or at the RMU downtown campus at the Heinz 57 Center.

### The University

Robert Morris University is located on a 230-acre campus in suburban Moon Township, 17 miles west of downtown Pittsburgh and 15 minutes from Pittsburgh International Airport. The city is an important corporate hub for financial and banking industries, health care, and industrial and high-tech engineering and manufacturing, providing a wide selection of employment opportunities as well as the cultural and commercial opportunities of a major city. Many graduate programs and classes are also offered online to help drive positive change locally, nationally, and globally.

### Applying

The graduate programs admit students on a rolling admission basis. However, students are encouraged to submit all required materials at least two months prior to the start of their desired term of entry. Applications can be filed for free through the University's website.

### Correspondence and Information

Office of Graduate Admissions
Robert Morris University
6001 University Boulevard
Moon Township, Pennsylvania 15108-1189
United States
Phone: 800-762-0097 (toll-free)
graduateadmissions@rmu.edu
Website: http://www.rmu.edu/graduate

### FULL-TIME FACULTY (2019)

**Mary Ann Rafoth, Ph.D., Provost and Sr. V.P., Academic Affairs**

#### SCHOOL OF BUSINESS

Michelle Patrick, Ph.D., Dean
Ira Abdullah, Ph.D.
Anna Abdulmanova, Ph.D.
Artemisia Apostolopoulou, Ph.D.
Robert Beaves, Ph.D.
Scott Branvold, M.A., Ed.D.
Lois Bryan, D.Sc., C.P.A.
Hasan Celik, M.A.
Yun Chu, Ph.D.
John Clark, Ph.D.
Steven Clinton, Ph.D.
Michele Cole, J.D., Ph.D.
Daria Crawley, Ph.D.
Zane Dennick-Ream, M.B.A.
Riza Emekter, Ph.D.
Frank Flanegin, Ph.D.
Eliada Griffin El, Ph.D.
Jeffery Guiler, Ph.D.
David Hess, M.B.A., C.P.A.
Steven Hodaszy, J.D.
Albena Ivanova, Ph.D.
Derya Jacobs, Ph.D.
Cathleen Jones, D.Sc.
Ersem Karadag, Ph.D.
Gregory Krivacek, Ph.D., C.P.A.
Jill Kurp, Ph.D.
Denise Letterman, M.B.A.
Chia-Jung Lin, Ph.D.
Patrick Litzinger, Ph.D.
Jianyu Ma, Ph.D.
Carol MacPhail, M.S.
Dean Manna, Ph.D.
Richard Mills, Ph.D.
Marcel Minutolo, Ph.D.
Kihyun Park, Ph.D.
Jacob Peng, Ph.D.
Jodi Potter, Ph.D.
Yasmin Purohit, Ph.D.
Stanko Racic, Ph.D.
Ronald Rubenfield, M.B.A.
Denis Rudd, Ed.D., FMP
Tapan Seth, Ph.D.
Zhaoyun Shangguan, Ph.D.
James Shock, D.B.A.
Alan Smith, Ph.D., C.P.G.S.
Louis Swartz, J.D.
David Synowka, Ph.D.
Yanbin Tu, Ph.D.
Prasad Reddy Vemala Venkata Siva, Ph.D.
Qin Yang, Ph.D.
Qiongyao Zhang, Ph.D.

#### SCHOOL OF ENGINEERING, MATHEMATICS AND SCIENCE

Maria Kalevitch, Ph.D., Dean
Jameela Al-Jaroodi, Ph.D.
Sushil Acharya, Dr.Eng.
Paul Badger, Ph.D.
Gavin Buxton, Ph.D.
Benjamin Campbell, Ph.D.
Rika Carlsen, Ph.D.
Adam Combs, Ph.D.
Kathleen Donoghue, M.S.Ed.
William Dress, Ph.D.
Heather Elfen, Ph.D.
Ergin Erdem, Ph.D., CMfgE
Christophe Groendyke, Ph.D.
Catherine Hanna, Ph.D.
Sarajane Hill, M.S.
Melissa Hillwig, Ph.D.
E. Gregory Holdan, Ph.D.
David Hudak, Ph.D.
Won Joo, Ph.D.
Nader Kesserwan, M.Sc.
Kenneth LaSota, Ph.D.
Allen Lias, Ph.D.
Priyadarshan Manohar, Ph.D.

Matthew Maurer, Ph.D.
Jeffrey Mitchell, Ph.D.
Luis Monterrubio Salazar, Ph.D., CMfgE
Allen Renfro, Ph.D.
Anthony Robins, Ph.D.
Sang Ho Shim, Ph.D.
Daniel Short, Ph.D.
Arif Sirinterlikci, Ph.D., CMfgE
Sue Spade, M.S.
Lewis Stein, D.P.M.
Monica VanDieren, Ph.D.
Qian Zhao, Ph.D..

**SCHOOL OF INFORMATICS, HUMANITIES AND SOCIAL SCIENCES**

Amjad Ali, Ph.D., Dean
Stuart Allen, Ph.D.
Andrew Ames, M.F.A.
Daniel Barr, Ph.D.
Jeanne Baugh, Ed.D.
Natalya Bromall, Ph.D.
Barbara Burgess-Lefebvre, M.F.A.
Donna Cellante, Ed.D.
Gary Davis, D.Sc.
M. Kathryn Dennick-Brecht, Ed.D.
Justin DePlato, Ph.D.
Peter Draus, Ed.D.
Michele Edwards, Ph.D.
Soren Fanning, Ph.D.
Arthur Grant, Ph.D.
Timothy Hadfield, M.F.A.
Philip Harold, Ph.D.
Francis Hartle, D.Sc.
Christine Holtz, M.F.A.
Diane Igoche, Ph.D.
Ann Jabro, Ph.D.
Timothy Jones, Ph.D.
Edward Karshner, Ph.D.
Mary Catherine Kiliany, M.S.
Frederick Kohun, Ph.D.
Leslie Koren, M.F.A.
Paul Kovacs, Ph.D.
Joseph Laverty, Ph.D.
John Lawson, Ph.D.
Carolina Loyola-Garcia, M.F.A.
Min Lu, Ph.D.
Petros Malakyan, Ph.D.
John McCarthy, Ph.D.
Julianne Michalenko, M.S.
Sushma Mishra, Ph.D.
Anthony Moretti, Ph.D.
James O'Roark, Ph.D.
Sylvia Pamboukian, Ph.D.
Sun-A Park, Ph.D.
Karen Paullet, D.Sc.
Jamie Pinchot, D.Sc.
Koren Pinson, Ph.D.
Michael Quigley, Ph.D.
Jon Radermacher, M.F.A.
Constance Ruzich, Ph.D.
Donald Seaton, J.D.
Robert Skovira, Ph.D.
John Stewart, Ph.D.
Elizabeth Stork, Ph.D.
Diane Todd, Ph.D.
Lazarina Topuzova, Ph.D.
A. Helena Vanhala, Ph.D.
Wenli Wang, Ph.D.
Ping Wang, Ph.D.
Chad Wertley, Ph.D.
Hyla Willis, M.F.A.
David Wood, Ph.D.
Peter Wu, Ph.D.
Chen Yang, Ph.D.
Zhou Yang, Ph.D.

**SCHOOL OF NURSING, EDUCATION AND HUMAN STUDIES**

D. Mark Meyers, Ph.D., Dean
Carianne Bernadowski, Ph.D.
James Bernauer, Ed.D.
Angela Bires, Ed.D.
Lynda Davidson, Ph.D.
Terri Devereaux, Ph.D.
Vicki Donne, D.Ed.
Nadine Englert, Ph.D.
Stephen Foreman, Ph.D.
Diane Frndak, Ph.D.
Richard Fuller, D.Ed.
Mary E Guimond, Ph.D.
Holly Hampe, D.Sc.
Mary Hansen, Ph.D.
Jillian Harrington, Ed.D.
Carla Haser, Ph.D.
Susan Hellier, Ph.D.
Kirstyn Kameg, D.N.P.
Jessica Kamerer, Ed.D.
Judith Kaufmann, Dr.PH
Beatrice Kunka, Ed.D.
Lisa Locasto, D.N.P., R.N.
Donna Mason, M.S.
Samantha Monda, Ph.D.
Joyce Ott, D.N.P.
Neha Pandit, Ph.D.
Susan Parker, Ph.D.
Stephen Paul, Ph.D.
Katrina Pyo, Ph.D.
Denise Ramponi, D.N.P.
Margaret Rateau, Ph.D.
Luann Richardson, Ph.D.
Carl Ross, Ph.D.
Janice Sarasnick, Ph.D.
Ashlee Shields, Ph.D.
Janene Szpak, D.N.P., R.N.
Nathan Taylor, Ph.D.
Lawrence Tomei, Ed.D.
William Wentling, D.Sc.
David Wheeler, Ph.D.
John Zeanchock, Ed.D.
Ying Zhang, Ph.D.
Shamika Zyhier, Ph.D.

**UNIVERSITY LIBRARY**

Timothy Schlak, Ph.D., Dean
David Bennett, M.L.S.
Christopher Devine, M.A., M.L.S.
Abiodun Ibraheem, M.L.I.S.
Jacqueline Klentzin, Ph.D.
Donald Luisi, M.L.S.
Chloe Mills, M.A., M.L.I.S.
Emily Paladino, M.L.I.S.

RMU's suburban Pittsburgh campus spreads across 230 scenic acres that were once the grounds of a country estate.

# *UNIFORMED SERVICES UNIVERSITY OF THE HEALTH SCIENCES*

## *F. Edward Hébert School of Medicine*
## *Graduate Program in Emerging Infectious Diseases*

**Program of Study**

The Uniformed Services University of the Health Sciences (USUHS) offers several Graduate Programs in Biomedical Sciences.

**Emerging Infectious Diseases Program:** This Program has two academic tracks within the field of emerging infectious diseases: microbiology and immunology, or preventive medicine/parasitology, with primary interest in the pathogenesis, host response, pathology and epidemiology of infectious diseases. **Molecular and Cell Biology Program:** This Interdisciplinary Ph.D. Program offers training to address many of the fundamental questions of modern biology ranging from protein- nucleic acid interactions to cytokines, growth factors, and developmental biology. **Neuroscience Program:** This Interdisciplinary Ph.D. Program is for students with a strong background in the biological, behavioral, and/or physical sciences to understand and explore CNS processes, with focuses in traumatic brain injury, developmental disorders, epilepsy, and addiction. The Center for Health Professions Education (CHPE) is an interdisciplinary program that offers three certificates and two degrees and targets practicing health professionals in our system. **Foundations in Health Professions Education (FHPE):** The FHPE is a certificate program designed to be a stepping stone toward the MHPE or PhD in HPE.

**Master of Health Professions Education (MHPE):** The MHPE program provides broad scholarly experience in the theory and practice of HPE by providing learners with the opportunity to participate in a series of formal courses, conduct original research, and obtain practical experiences to further enhance their leadership and educator skills. **Doctor of Philosophy in Health Professions Education (PhD in HPE)** is meant to serve those select students who desire to be at the forefront of the scholarship, leadership, and teaching of health professions students and residents. Although a master's degree (e.g., MHPE, MPH, MEd, or MS degree) is not a prerequisite for the PhD in HPE, it is highly desirable.**Department of Medical and Clinical Psychology:** Doctoral Programs and research in medical psychology and clinical psychology emphasize the application of psychology to behavioral medicine and to clinical psychology.

**Department of Medical History:** A Master of Military Medical History (MMH) Program is offered to U.S. Army officers. The program is designed to meet the needs of the Army officers in the Medical Services Corps MOS 70H, to prepare the officer to be an instructor in professional military medical educational programs, and for utilization as a field historian for specific military medical issues. **Department of Preventive Medicine and Biometric:** Graduate Programs in public health are offered at the master's and doctoral levels. The Master of Public Health (MPH), Master of Tropical Medicine and Hygiene (MTM&H), Master of Science in Public Health (MSPH), Master of Science in Vector Biology, and the Master of Healthcare Administration and Policy (MHAP) programs are designed for students with at least 3 years of experience in a health-related field. The department also offers Doctoral degrees in Public Health, Vector Biology/Parasitology and Environmental/Occupational Health.

**The Physician Scientist (M.D./Ph.D.) Program:** This program is designed to prepare physician scientists who will lead the military biomedical research community and make valuable contributions to the advancement of their respective fields through research, patient care, and teaching. In our Program, graduate studies normally will be completed before medical studies. At the end of his/her 3rd year in the Program, the students are commissioned in one of the Uniformed Services which marks the beginning of the student's military service.

Each program permits considerable flexibility in the choice of courses and research areas; training programs are tailored to meet the individual requirements of each student. Students in the programs conduct their research under the direction of faculty members in laboratories that are located in the medical school. During the first year of study, students begin formal course work. Each student is required to take laboratory training rotations in the research laboratories of program faculty members. By the end of the first year, students select a research area and a faculty thesis adviser. During the second year, students complete requirements for advancement to candidacy, including required course work and passage of the qualifying examination. After advancement to candidacy, each student develops an original research project and prepares and defends a written dissertation under the guidance of his or her faculty adviser and advisory committee.

**Research Facilities**

USUHS has several academic and research centers to provide laboratories support for a variety of research projects.

The Human Performance Laboratory (HPL) is a research laboratory located within the Department of Military and Emergency Medicine. It is an interdisciplinary laboratory where research scientists trained in exercise physiology, nutritional biochemistry, sports psychology, immunology, endocrinology, and psychology work with physicians, medical students, graduate students, and others to investigate various aspects of human performance and stress physiology.

The Center for the Study of Traumatic Stress (CSTS) is a new public-private partnership working to increase knowledge of the consequences of trauma and disaster and to apply this knowledge to helping people cope with traumatic events. The Center provides education, consultation and training to our nation and its communities on the effects of trauma and disaster and individual and organizational recovery following these events while maintaining a wide-ranging, vigorous research program to extend our knowledge of the consequences of event-related stress.

The Center for Prostate Disease Research (CSDR) is the only free-standing prostate cancer research center in the U.S. This 20,000 square foot state-of-the-art basic science laboratory facility is attracting the best and brightest to study the disease. Using blood and tissues collected from volunteering military beneficiaries, the CPDR laboratory has amassed a large bank of prostate cancer specimens that are serving to unravel the genetics of the disease.

The Center for Neuroscience and Regenerative Medicine (CNRM) is a federal medical research program that has transformed collaborative interactions between the U.S. Department of Defense and the National Institutes of Health, Walter Reed Army Medical Center, and the National Naval Medical Center. Congress established CNRM to bring together the expertise of physicians and scientists at these collaborating institutions in the National Capital area to develop innovative approaches to brain injury diagnosis and recovery.

Armed Forces Radiobiology Research Institute (AFRRI), a tri-service laboratory chartered in 1961, conducts research in the field of radiobiology and related matters essential to the operational and medical support of the U.S. Department of Defense and the military services. The institute collaborates with other governmental facilities, academic institutions, and civilian laboratories in the United States and other countries. Its findings have broad military and civilian applications.

The Walter Reed Army Institute of Research (WRAIR), which is the largest, most diverse, and oldest laboratory in the US Army Medical Research and Materiel Command, conducts research on a range of militarily relevant issues, including naturally occurring infectious diseases, combat casualty care, operational health hazards, and medical defense against biological and chemical weapons. WRAIR is the Department of Defense's lead agency for infectious disease research and a crucial source of research support for medical product development. Despite WRAIR's focus on the military, its research has been used to solve nonmilitary medical problems around the world.

The National Institutes of Health (NIH) is the steward of medical and behavioral research for the Nation. Its mission is science in pursuit of fundamental knowledge about the nature and behavior of living systems and the application of that knowledge to extend healthy life and reduce the burdens of illness and disability. The goals of the agency are as follows: 1) foster fundamental creative discoveries, innovative research strategies, and their applications as a basis to advance significantly the Nation's capacity to protect and impdrove health; 2) develop, maintain, and renew scientific human and physical resources that will assure the Nation's capability to prevent disease; 3) expand the knowledge base in medical and associated sciences in order to enhance the Nation's economic well-being and ensure a continued high return on the public investment in research; and 4) exemplify and promote the highest level of scientific integrity, public accountability, and social responsibility in the conduct of science.

**Financial Aid and Cost of Study**

USUHS provides an attractive package of financial support that is administered as a federal salary. This support is available on a competitive basis to all civilian graduate students. Awards are made on an annual basis and are renewable for up to three years. In addition to this base support, health insurance and transit benefits are provided if needed. Students are not required to pay any tuition or fees. Civilian students incur no obligation to the United States government for service after completion of their graduate training programs. Students are required to maintain health insurance.

**Student Group**

USUHS has an active and growing graduate program; approximately 300 students are enrolled, from diverse backgrounds, who come from many states, and about 50 percent of them are women. In addition to the graduate and medical programs in the medical school, the nursing school has graduate programs for nurse practitioners and nurse anesthetists.

**Student Outcomes**

Graduates hold faculty, research associate, postdoctoral, science policy, and other positions in universities, medical schools, government, and industrial research institutions. The vast majority of USU Ph.D. graduates take positions with federal research labs in the National Capital Region and other parts of the country. They serve within the Military Health System, the Pentagon, around the world in various positions and in the Public Health Service. USU graduates are currently employed at the National Institutes of Health, Indian Health Service, Food and Drug Administration, Centers for Disease Control and Prevention, and the U.S. Department of Agriculture.

**Location**

The region is a center of education and research and is home to five major universities, four medical schools, the National Library of Medicine and the National Institutes of Health (next to the USUHS campus), Walter Reed National Military Medical Center, the Armed Forces Institute of Pathology, the Library of Congress, the Smithsonian Institution, the National Bureau of Standards, and many other private and government research centers. The Metro subway system has a station near campus and provides a convenient connection from the University to museums and cultural attractions of downtown Washington. The University is within an easy distance of three major airports, Baltimore Washington International, Reagan International, and Dulles International. Both Reagan and Dulles International airports are accessible from the campus via Metro subway.

**The University**

The University was established by Congress in 1972 to provide a comprehensive education in medicine to those who demonstrate potential for careers as Medical Corps officers in the uniformed services. Graduate programs in the basic medical sciences are offered to both civilian and military students and are an essential part of the academic environment at the University. Uniformed Services University subscribes fully to the policy of equal educational opportunity and accepts students on a competitive basis without regard to race, color, sex, age, or creed.

**Applying**

Civilian applicants are accepted as full-time students only. Each applicant must have a bachelor's degree from an accredited academic institution. A strong background in science with courses in several of the following disciplines—biochemistry, biology, chemistry, mathematics, physics, physiology, and psychology—is desirable. Applicants must arrange for official transcripts of all prior college-level courses taken to be sent to the Office of Graduate Education. **The GRE is optional for Fall 2021 Admission. Not submitting the GRE will not be counted against an applicant. Applicants submitting GREs will not be given preference over those without GREs. Please disregard any information that states the GRE is required for graduate admission.** Applicants must also arrange for letters of recommendation from 3 people who are familiar with their academic work to be emailed to the University. For full consideration and evaluation for support, completed applications should be received by **December 1** for matriculation in late August. Late applications are evaluated on a space-available basis. There is no application fee. Students may complete an application at https://registrar.usuhs.edu.

**For information about the USUHS Graduate Programs:**
Uniformed Services University
Graduate Education Office
4301 Jones Bridge Road, A1045
Bethesda, Maryland 20814-4799
graduateprogram@usuhs.edu

Tina Finley
Program Specialist
4301 Jones Bridge Road
Bethesda, Maryland 20814-4799
Phone: 301-295-3642
netina.finley@usuhs.edu

## PROGRAM DIRECTORS

Neuroscience – Kimberly Byrnes, PhD - Microglial and macrophage-based chronic inflammation after traumatic brain and spinal cord injury; noninvasive imaging of post-injury metabolic and inflammatory events. (https://www.usuhs.edu/nes)

Emerging Infectious Diseases - D. Scott Merrell, Ph.D. - Basic Biology of Bacterial, Viral, or Parasite Diseases; Microbiome, Bacterial stress response and adaptation, Polymicrobial interactions. (https://www.usuhs.edu/eid)

Molecular & Cell Biology – Tharun Sundaresan, PhD - Mechanism of mRNA decay; Molecular basis of cancer. (https://www.usuhs.edu/mcb)

Medical & Clinical Psychology - Tracy Sbrocco, Ph.D. - health disparities; obesity, anxiety disorders. (CPS https://www.usuhs.edu/mps/clinical-psychology) MPS (https://www.usuhs.edu/mps/medical-psychology)

Preventive Medicine & Biostatistics - Cara H. Olsen, MS, DrPH (Director) – Biostatistics, Public health (https://www.usuhs.edu/pmb)

Medicine/Health Professions Education - Steven J. Durning, MD, PhD - General internal medicine. (https://www.usuhs.edu/hpe)

## Programs of Study

A better job, financial security, and personal satisfaction are just some of the end goals for students seeking to earn an advanced degree through graduate study at Western New England University. From business to communication, creative writing to behavior analysis, and programs for teachers and engineers, students gain essential skills and expertise for success in their careers.

Programs in Communication, Accounting, and Curriculum and Instruction are offered entirely online and were developed specifically for that delivery model. Most of the Business and Engineering master's programs follow a blended model, allowing students to study completely online or attend select live sessions on campus. This flexibility enables working professionals to learn at their own pace. Education programs are offered in late afternoon and early evening to accommodate the schedules of working teachers. The low-residency M.F.A. in Creative Writing program includes four short-term residencies with author mentors, and the M.S. in Sport Leadership and Coaching includes two short-term residencies.

The University is regionally accredited by the New England Commission of Higher Education.

The **College of Arts and Sciences** offers the following graduate programs:

- Master of Arts in Communication with a public relations concentration
- Master of Arts in English for Teachers
- Master of Arts in Mathematics for Teachers
- Master of Education in Curriculum and Instruction
- Master of Fine Arts in Creative Writing
- Master of Science in Applied Behavior Analysis
- Ph.D. in Behavior Analysis

The **College of Business** offers the following graduate programs:

- Master of Business Administration (M.B.A.)
- Master of Science in Accounting (M.S.A.)
- M.S.A. with Forensic Accounting and Fraud Investigation concentration
- Master of Science in Organizational Leadership (M.S.O.L.)
- Master of Science in Sport Leadership and Coaching (M.S.L.C)
- J.D./M.B.A. dual degree program
- J.D./M.S.A. dual degree program
- J.D./M.S.O.L. dual degree program
- J.D./M.S.L.C. dual degree program
- Pharm.D./M.B.A. dual degree program
- Pharm.D./M.S.O.L. dual degree program

The **College of Engineering** offers these graduate programs:

- Master of Science in Civil Engineering (M.S.C.E.)
- Master of Science in Construction Management (M.S.C.M.)
- Master of Science in Electrical Engineering (M.S.E.E.)
- M.S.E.E. with Mechatronics concentration
- Master of Science in Engineering Management (M.S.E.M.)
- Master of Science in Industrial Engineering (M.S.I.E.)
- Master of Science in Mechanical Engineering (M.S.M.E.)
- M.S.M.E. with Mechatronics concentration
- M.S.E.M./M.B.A. combined degree program
- Ph.D. in Engineering Management
- J.D./M.S.E.M. dual degree program

The University also offers programs though the College of Pharmacy and Health Sciences and the Law School. These include the Juris Doctor, the Doctor of Pharmacy, and the Doctor of Occupational Therapy.

## Financial Aid

To be considered for financial aid, a student must have final approval into a degree program and be enrolled in a minimum of 3 credits per term. Financial need-based resources, including grants and low-interest federal loans, may be available for eligible students.

## Cost of Study

Western New England University is committed to keeping a high-quality private education affordable for its students. Western New England's graduate tuition rates are some of the most affordable in the region. Tuition for graduate programs is as follows:

**College of Arts and Sciences:**

- Online M.Ed.: $724 per credit
- M.A.E.T., and M.A.M.T.: $401 per credit
- M.A. in Communication: $840 per credit
- M.F.A. in Creative Writing: $673 per credit
- M.S. in Applied Behavior Analysis: $1,203 per credit
- Ph.D. in Behavior Analysis: $1,434 per credit

**College of Business:**

- M.B.A., M.S.A., M.S.O.L., and M.S.L.C.: $919 per credit

**College of Engineering:**

- M.S.C.E., M.S.C.M., M.S.E.E., M.S.E.M., M.S.I.E., and M.S.M.E.: $1,203 per credit
- Ph.D. in Engineering Management: $1,434 per credit

## Living and Housing Costs

Graduate students have the option of living on campus. Housing costs range between $9,000 and $11,015, depending upon the apartment type and duration (10 to 12 months).

## Career Development

The Career Development Center assists students and alumni with career planning, occupational exploration, and job search strategies. The center's staff members implement the University's strong commitment to the development of a student's career decision-making by providing individual career advising and assistance in identifying career options.

The Career Development Center staff brings students in contact with employers through dynamic on-campus recruiting, employer information sessions, and career fairs. In addition, students are assisted with resources for part-time and summer employment. A weekly newsletter is published online at www.wne.edu/careercenter and serves as one tool for alerting students to employment opportunities, internships, recruiting schedules, and career-related workshops and activities.

## Location

Western New England University's beautiful 215-acre suburban campus is located in Springfield, Massachusetts, the cultural urban center of the western part of the state. Perhaps best known as the birthplace of basketball and home of the Naismith Memorial Basketball Hall of Fame, Springfield is midway between New York and Boston and on the road between New York and Canada. Springfield is ideally located for travel in all directions, and there is convenient access from the University to both the Mass Pike and Interstate 91.

## Faculty

With an average class size of 20, students work closely with the University's full-time faculty members who bring outstanding professional and academic credentials to the classroom. On average, 85 percent of graduate courses are taught by full-time faculty members. Ninety percent of the faculty hold terminal degrees in their field.

Additional details about the faculty for specific departments/programs can be found at wne.edu.

## The University

Originally established in 1919 to serve working adults, Western New England University is renowned for its innovative programs, culture of collaboration, and faculty members who are focused on student success. Today that commitment continues through the University's graduate programs on campus and online.

Accredited by AACSB International, the College of Business is widely respected throughout the region for the caliber of its flagship M.B.A. program, sought-after M.S.A. degree, and dynamic new offering in organizational leadership. The College of Arts and Sciences offers high-quality master's programs for teachers at an affordable tuition rate and an immersive M.F.A. in Creative Writing program. The College's master's and doctoral programs in Behavior Analysis have positioned the University as a global leader in research and education in that discipline. The thriving College of Engineering is recognized as an educational leader by major corporations in the northeast who seek out graduates of the University's master's and combined engineering/business and law degree programs.

## Applying

Western New England University has a rolling admissions policy for most programs, not a set admission deadline. Admission decisions are typically released within one to two weeks of an application being complete. The University urges prospective students to apply as early as possible in relation to the anticipated start date. Most of the graduate programs offer multiple entry points annually. Graduate students can apply online at www.wne.edu/gradapp.

## Correspondence and Information

Office of Graduate Admissions
Western New England University
1215 Wilbraham Road
Springfield, Massachusetts 01119
United States
Phone: 413-782-1517
800-325-1122, Ext. 1517 (toll-free)
E-mail: study@wne.edu
Website: wne.edu/grad

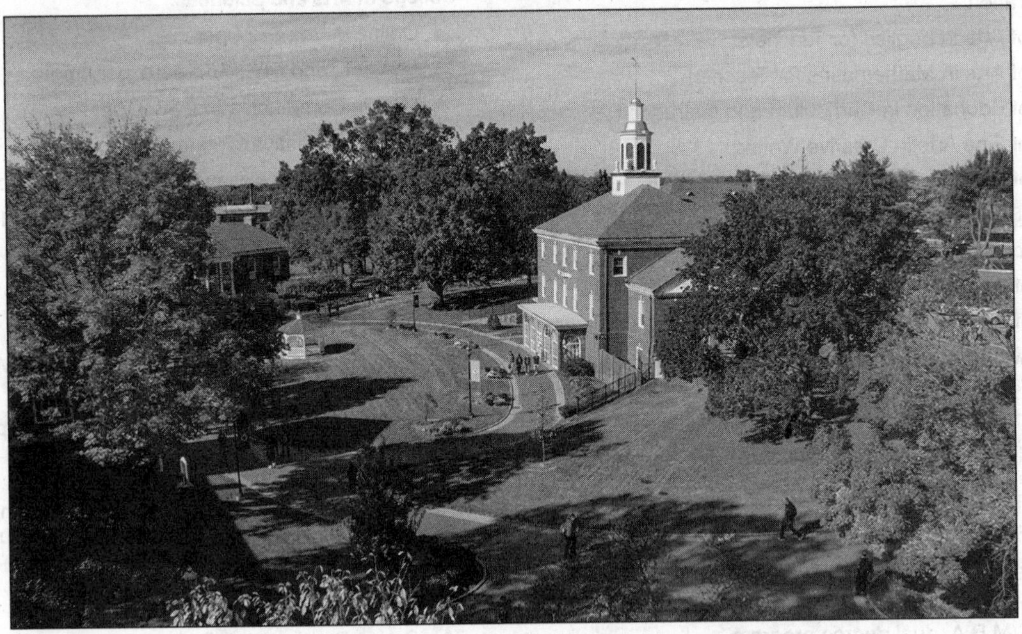

# APPENDIXES

# Institutional Changes Since the 2020 Edition (Graduate)

Following is an alphabetical listing of institutions that have recently closed, merged with other institutions, or changed their names or status. In the case of a name change, the former name appears first, followed by the new name.

Antioch University (Midwest Yellow Springs, OH): *closed.*

Argosy University, Atlanta (Atlanta, GA): *closed.*

Argosy University, Chicago (Chicago, IL): *closed.*

Argosy University, Hawaii (Honolulu, HI): *closed.*

Argosy University, Los Angeles (Los Angeles, CA): *closed.*

Argosy University, Northern Virginia (Arlington, VA): *closed.*

Argosy University, Orange County (Orange, CA): *closed.*

Argosy University, Phoenix (Phoenix, AZ): *closed.*

Argosy University, Seattle (Seattle, WA): *closed.*

Argosy University, Tampa (Tampa, FL): *closed.*

Argosy University, Twin Cities (Eagan, MN): *closed.*

College of Saint Elizabeth (Morristown, NJ): *name changed to Saint Elizabeth University.*

College of St. Joseph (Rutland, VT): *closed.*

Concordia University (Portland, OR): *closed.*

Elmhurst College (Elmhurst, IL): *name changed to Elmhurst University.*

The John Marshall Law School (Chicago, IL): *closed; acquired by University of Illinois at Chicago; name changed to UIC John Marshall Law School.*

Marygrove College (Detroit, MI): *closed.*

Nebraska Christian College of Hope International University (Papillion, NE): *closed.*

Northwest Christian University (Eugene, OR): *name changed to Bushnell University.*

Notre Dame de Namur University (Belmont, CA): *closed.*

Silver Lake College of the Holy Family (Manitowoc, WI): *closed.*

University of South Florida Sarasota-Manatee (Sarasota, FL): *to merge with University of South Florida Main Campus.*

University of South Florida, St. Petersburg (St. Petersburg, FL): *to merge with University of South Florida Main Campus.*

Watkins College of Art, Design, and Film (Nashville, TN): *to merge with Belmont University.*

# Abbreviations Used in the Guides

The following list includes abbreviations of degree names used in the profiles in the 2020 edition of the guides. Because some degrees (e.g., Doctor of Education) can be abbreviated in more than one way (e.g., D.Ed. or Ed.D.), and because the abbreviations used in the guides reflect the preferences of the individual colleges and universities, the list may include two or more abbreviations for a single degree.

## DEGREES

A Mus D — Doctor of Musical Arts
AC — Advanced Certificate
AD — Artist's Diploma
Doctor of Arts
ADP — Artist's Diploma
Adv C — Advanced Certificate
AGC — Advanced Graduate Certificate
AGSC — Advanced Graduate Specialist Certificate
ALM — Master of Liberal Arts
AM — Master of Arts
AMBA — Accelerated Master of Business Administration
APC — Advanced Professional Certificate
APMPH — Advanced Professional Master of Public Health
App Sc — Applied Scientist
App Sc D — Doctor of Applied Science
AstE — Astronautical Engineer
ATC — Advanced Training Certificate
Au D — Doctor of Audiology
B Th — Bachelor of Theology
CAES — Certificate of Advanced Educational Specialization
CAGS — Certificate of Advanced Graduate Studies
CAL — Certificate in Applied Linguistics
CAPS — Certificate of Advanced Professional Studies
CAS — Certificate of Advanced Studies
CATS — Certificate of Achievement in Theological Studies
CE — Civil Engineer
CEM — Certificate of Environmental Management
CET — Certificate in Educational Technologies
CGS — Certificate of Graduate Studies
Ch E — Chemical Engineer
Clin Sc D — Doctor of Clinical Science
CM — Certificate in Management
CMH — Certificate in Medical Humanities
CMM — Master of Church Ministries
CMS — Certificate in Ministerial Studies
CNM — Certificate in Nonprofit Management
CPC — Certificate in Publication and Communication
CPH — Certificate in Public Health
CPS — Certificate of Professional Studies
CScD — Doctor of Clinical Science
CSD — Certificate in Spiritual Direction
CSS — Certificate of Special Studies
CTS — Certificate of Theological Studies
D Ac — Doctor of Acupuncture
D Admin — Doctor of Administration
D Arch — Doctor of Architecture
D Be — Doctor in Bioethics
D Com — Doctor of Commerce
D Couns — Doctor of Counseling
D Des — Doctorate of Design
D Div — Doctor of Divinity
D Ed — Doctor of Education
D Ed Min — Doctor of Educational Ministry
D Eng — Doctor of Engineering
D Engr — Doctor of Engineering
D Ent — Doctor of Enterprise
D Env — Doctor of Environment
D Law — Doctor of Law
D Litt — Doctor of Letters
D Med Sc — Doctor of Medical Science
D Mgt — Doctor of Management
D Min — Doctor of Ministry
D Miss — Doctor of Missiology
D Mus — Doctor of Music
D Mus A — Doctor of Musical Arts
D Phil — Doctor of Philosophy
D Prof — Doctor of Professional Studies
D Ps — Doctor of Psychology
D Sc — Doctor of Science
D Sc D — Doctor of Science in Dentistry
D Sc IS — Doctor of Science in Information Systems
D Sc PA — Doctor of Science in Physician Assistant Studies
D Th — Doctor of Theology
D Th P — Doctor of Practical Theology
DA — Doctor of Accounting
Doctor of Arts
DACM — Doctor of Acupuncture and Chinese Medicine
DAIS — Doctor of Applied Intercultural Studies
DAOM — Doctorate in Acupuncture and Oriental Medicine
DAT — Doctorate of Athletic Training
Professional Doctor of Art Therapy
DBA — Doctor of Business Administration
DBH — Doctor of Behavioral Health
DBL — Doctor of Business Leadership
DC — Doctor of Chiropractic
DCC — Doctor of Computer Science
DCD — Doctor of Communications Design
DCE — Doctor of Computer Engineering
DCJ — Doctor of Criminal Justice
DCL — Doctor of Civil Law
Doctor of Comparative Law
DCM — Doctor of Church Music
DCN — Doctor of Clinical Nutrition
DCS — Doctor of Computer Science
DDN — Diplôme du Droit Notarial
DDS — Doctor of Dental Surgery
DE — Doctor of Education
Doctor of Engineering
DED — Doctor of Economic Development
DEIT — Doctor of Educational Innovation and Technology
DEL — Doctor of Executive Leadership
DEM — Doctor of Educational Ministry
DEPD — Diplôme Études Spécialisées
DES — Doctor of Engineering Science
DESS — Diplôme Études Supérieures Spécialisées
DET — Doctor of Educational Technology
DFA — Doctor of Fine Arts
DGP — Diploma in Graduate and Professional Studies
DGS — Doctor of Global Security
DH Sc — Doctor of Health Sciences
DHA — Doctor of Health Administration
DHCE — Doctor of Health Care Ethics
DHL — Doctor of Hebrew Letters
DHPE — Doctorate of Health Professionals Education
DHS — Doctor of Health Science
DHSc — Doctor of Health Science
DIT — Doctor of Industrial Technology
Doctor of Information Technology
DJS — Doctor of Jewish Studies
DLS — Doctor of Liberal Studies
DM — Doctor of Management
Doctor of Music
DMA — Doctor of Musical Arts
DMD — Doctor of Dental Medicine
DME — Doctor of Manufacturing Management
Doctor of Music Education
DMFT — Doctor of Marital and Family Therapy
DMH — Doctor of Medical Humanities
DML — Doctor of Modern Languages
DMP — Doctorate in Medical Physics
DMPNA — Doctor of Management Practice in Nurse Anesthesia
DN Sc — Doctor of Nursing Science

| | |
|---|---|
| DNAP | Doctor of Nurse Anesthesia Practice |
| DNP | Doctor of Nursing Practice |
| DNP-A | Doctor of Nursing Practice - Anesthesia |
| DNS | Doctor of Nursing Science |
| DO | Doctor of Osteopathy |
| DOL | Doctorate of Organizational Leadership |
| DOM | Doctor of Oriental Medicine |
| DOT | Doctor of Occupational Therapy |
| DPA | Diploma in Public Administration |
| | Doctor of Public Administration |
| DPDS | Doctor of Planning and Development Studies |
| DPH | Doctor of Public Health |
| DPM | Doctor of Plant Medicine |
| | Doctor of Podiatric Medicine |
| DPPD | Doctor of Policy, Planning, and Development |
| DPS | Doctor of Professional Studies |
| DPT | Doctor of Physical Therapy |
| DPTSc | Doctor of Physical Therapy Science |
| Dr DES | Doctor of Design |
| Dr NP | Doctor of Nursing Practice |
| Dr OT | Doctor of Occupational Therapy |
| Dr PH | Doctor of Public Health |
| Dr Sc PT | Doctor of Science in Physical Therapy |
| DRSc | Doctor of Regulatory Science |
| DS | Doctor of Science |
| DS Sc | Doctor of Social Science |
| DScPT | Doctor of Science in Physical Therapy |
| DSI | Doctor of Strategic Intelligence |
| DSJS | Doctor of Science in Jewish Studies |
| DSL | Doctor of Strategic Leadership |
| DSNS | Doctorate of Statecraft and National Security |
| DSS | Doctor of Strategic Security |
| DSW | Doctor of Social Work |
| DTL | Doctor of Talmudic Law |
| | Doctor of Transformational Leadership |
| DV Sc | Doctor of Veterinary Science |
| DVM | Doctor of Veterinary Medicine |
| DWS | Doctor of Worship Studies |
| EAA | Engineer in Aeronautics and Astronautics |
| EASPh D | Engineering and Applied Science Doctor of Philosophy |
| ECS | Engineer in Computer Science |
| Ed D | Doctor of Education |
| Ed DCT | Doctor of Education in College Teaching |
| Ed L D | Doctor of Education Leadership |
| Ed M | Master of Education |
| Ed S | Specialist in Education |
| Ed Sp | Specialist in Education |
| EDB | Executive Doctorate in Business |
| EDM | Executive Doctorate in Management |
| EE | Electrical Engineer |
| EJD | Executive Juris Doctor |
| EMBA | Executive Master of Business Administration |
| EMFA | Executive Master of Forensic Accounting |
| EMHA | Executive Master of Health Administration |
| EMHCL | Executive Master in Healthcare Leadership |
| EMIB | Executive Master of International Business |
| EMIR | Executive Master in International Relations |
| EML | Executive Master of Leadership |
| EMPA | Executive Master of Public Administration |
| EMPL | Executive Master in Policy Leadership |
| | Executive Master in Public Leadership |
| EMS | Executive Master of Science |
| EMTM | Executive Master of Technology Management |
| Eng | Engineer |
| Eng Sc D | Doctor of Engineering Science |
| Engr | Engineer |
| Exec MHA | Executive Master of Health Administration |
| Exec Ed D | Executive Doctor of Education |
| Exec MBA | Executive Master of Business Administration |
| Exec MPA | Executive Master of Public Administration |
| Exec MPH | Executive Master of Public Health |
| Exec MS | Executive Master of Science |
| Executive MA | Executive Master of Arts |
| G Dip | Graduate Diploma |
| GBC | Graduate Business Certificate |
| GDM | Graduate Diploma in Management |
| GDPA | Graduate Diploma in Public Administration |
| GEMBA | Global Executive Master of Business Administration |
| GM Acc | Graduate Master of Accountancy |
| GMBA | Global Master of Business Administration |
| GP LL M | Global Professional Master of Laws |
| GPD | Graduate Performance Diploma |
| GSS | Graduate Special Certificate for Students in Special Situations |
| IEMBA | International Executive Master of Business Administration |
| IMA | Interdisciplinary Master of Arts |
| IMBA | International Master of Business Administration |
| IMES | International Master's in Environmental Studies |
| Ingeniero | Engineer |
| JCD | Doctor of Canon Law |
| JCL | Licentiate in Canon Law |
| JD | Juris Doctor |
| JM | Juris Master |
| JSD | Doctor of Juridical Science |
| | Doctor of Jurisprudence |
| | Doctor of the Science of Law |
| JSM | Master of the Science of Law |
| L Th | Licentiate in Theology |
| LL B | Bachelor of Laws |
| LL CM | Master of Comparative Law |
| LL D | Doctor of Laws |
| LL M | Master of Laws |
| LL M in Tax | Master of Laws in Taxation |
| LL M CL | Master of Laws in Common Law |
| M Ac | Master of Accountancy |
| | Master of Accounting |
| | Master of Acupuncture |
| M Ac OM | Master of Acupuncture and Oriental Medicine |
| M Acc | Master of Accountancy |
| | Master of Accounting |
| M Acct | Master of Accountancy |
| | Master of Accounting |
| M Accy | Master of Accountancy |
| M Actg | Master of Accounting |
| M Acy | Master of Accountancy |
| M Ad | Master of Administration |
| M Ad Ed | Master of Adult Education |
| M Adm | Master of Administration |
| M Adm Mgt | Master of Administrative Management |
| M Admin | Master of Administration |
| M ADU | Master of Architectural Design and Urbanism |
| M Adv | Master of Advertising |
| M Ag | Master of Agriculture |
| M Ag Ed | Master of Agricultural Education |
| M Agr | Master of Agriculture |
| M App Comp Sc | Master of Applied Computer Science |
| M App St | Master of Applied Statistics |
| M Appl Stat | Master of Applied Statistics |
| M Aq | Master of Aquaculture |
| M Ar | Master of Architecture |
| M Arch | Master of Architecture |
| M Arch I | Master of Architecture I |
| M Arch II | Master of Architecture II |
| M Arch E | Master of Architectural Engineering |
| M Arch H | Master of Architectural History |
| M Bioethics | Master in Bioethics |
| M Cat | Master of Catechesis |
| M Ch E | Master of Chemical Engineering |
| M Cl D | Master of Clinical Dentistry |
| M Cl Sc | Master of Clinical Science |
| M Comm | Master of Communication |
| M Comp | Master of Computing |
| M Comp Sc | Master of Computer Science |
| M Coun | Master of Counseling |
| M Dent | Master of Dentistry |
| M Dent Sc | Master of Dental Sciences |
| M Des | Master of Design |
| M Des S | Master of Design Studies |
| M Div | Master of Divinity |
| M E Sci | Master of Earth Science |
| M Ec | Master of Economics |

| | |
|---|---|
| M Econ | Master of Economics |
| M Ed | Master of Education |
| M Ed T | Master of Education in Teaching |
| M En | Master of Engineering |
| M En S | Master of Environmental Sciences |
| M Eng | Master of Engineering |
| M Eng Mgt | Master of Engineering Management |
| M Engr | Master of Engineering |
| M Ent | Master of Enterprise |
| M Env | Master of Environment |
| M Env Des | Master of Environmental Design |
| M Env E | Master of Environmental Engineering |
| M Env Sc | Master of Environmental Science |
| M Ext Ed | Master of Extension Education |
| M Fin | Master of Finance |
| M Geo E | Master of Geological Engineering |
| M Geoenv E | Master of Geoenvironmental Engineering |
| M Geog | Master of Geography |
| M Hum | Master of Humanities |
| M IDST | Master's in Interdisciplinary Studies |
| M Jur | Master of Jurisprudence |
| M Kin | Master of Kinesiology |
| M Land Arch | Master of Landscape Architecture |
| M Litt | Master of Letters |
| M Mark | Master of Marketing |
| M Mat SE | Master of Material Science and Engineering |
| M Math | Master of Mathematics |
| M Mech E | Master of Mechanical Engineering |
| M Med Sc | Master of Medical Science |
| M Mgmt | Master of Management |
| M Mgt | Master of Management |
| M Min | Master of Ministries |
| M Mtl E | Master of Materials Engineering |
| M Mu | Master of Music |
| M Mus | Master of Music |
| M Mus Ed | Master of Music Education |
| M Music | Master of Music |
| M Pet E | Master of Petroleum Engineering |
| M Pharm | Master of Pharmacy |
| M Phil | Master of Philosophy |
| M Phil F | Master of Philosophical Foundations |
| M Pl | Master of Planning |
| M Plan | Master of Planning |
| M Pol | Master of Political Science |
| M Pr Met | Master of Professional Meteorology |
| M Prob S | Master of Probability and Statistics |
| M Psych | Master of Psychology |
| M Pub | Master of Publishing |
| M Rel | Master of Religion |
| M Sc | Master of Science |
| M Sc A | Master of Science (Applied) |
| M Sc AC | Master of Science in Applied Computing |
| M Sc AHN | Master of Science in Applied Human Nutrition |
| M Sc BMC | Master of Science in Biomedical Communications |
| M Sc CS | Master of Science in Computer Science |
| M Sc E | Master of Science in Engineering |
| M Sc Eng | Master of Science in Engineering |
| M Sc Engr | Master of Science in Engineering |
| M Sc F | Master of Science in Forestry |
| M Sc FE | Master of Science in Forest Engineering |
| M Sc Geogr | Master of Science in Geography |
| M Sc N | Master of Science in Nursing |
| M Sc OT | Master of Science in Occupational Therapy |
| M Sc P | Master of Science in Planning |
| M Sc Pl | Master of Science in Planning |
| M Sc PT | Master of Science in Physical Therapy |
| M Sc T | Master of Science in Teaching |
| M SEM | Master of Sustainable Environmental Management |
| M Serv Soc | Master of Social Service |
| M Soc | Master of Sociology |
| M Sp Ed | Master of Special Education |
| M Stat | Master of Statistics |
| M Sys E | Master of Systems Engineering |
| M Sys Sc | Master of Systems Science |
| M Tax | Master of Taxation |
| M Tech | Master of Technology |
| M Th | Master of Theology |
| M Trans E | Master of Transportation Engineering |
| M U Ed | Master of Urban Education |
| M Urb | Master of Urban Planning |
| M Vet Sc | Master of Veterinary Science |
| MA | Master of Accounting |
| | Master of Administration |
| | Master of Arts |
| MA Comm | Master of Arts in Communication |
| MA Ed | Master of Arts in Education |
| MA Ed/HD | Master of Arts in Education and Human Development |
| MA Islamic | Master of Arts in Islamic Studies |
| MA Min | Master of Arts in Ministry |
| MA Miss | Master of Arts in Missiology |
| MA Past St | Master of Arts in Pastoral Studies |
| MA Ph | Master of Arts in Philosophy |
| MA Psych | Master of Arts in Psychology |
| MA Sc | Master of Applied Science |
| MA Sp | Master of Arts (Spirituality) |
| MA Th | Master of Arts in Theology |
| MA-R | Master of Arts (Research) |
| MAA | Master of Applied Anthropology |
| | Master of Applied Arts |
| | Master of Arts in Administration |
| MAAA | Master of Arts in Arts Administration |
| MAAD | Master of Advanced Architectural Design |
| MAAE | Master of Arts in Art Education |
| MAAPPS | Master of Arts in Asia Pacific Policy Studies |
| MAAS | Master of Arts in Aging and Spirituality |
| MAASJ | Master of Arts in Applied Social Justice |
| MAAT | Master of Arts in Applied Theology |
| MAB | Master of Agribusiness |
| | Master of Applied Bioengineering |
| | Master of Arts in Business |
| MABA | Master's in Applied Behavior Analysis |
| MABC | Master of Arts in Biblical Counseling |
| MABE | Master of Arts in Bible Exposition |
| MABL | Master of Arts in Biblical Languages |
| MABM | Master of Agribusiness Management |
| MABS | Master of Arts in Biblical Studies |
| MABT | Master of Arts in Bible Teaching |
| MAC | Master of Accountancy |
| | Master of Accounting |
| | Master of Arts in Communication |
| | Master of Arts in Counseling |
| MACC | Master of Arts in Christian Counseling |
| MACCT | Master of Accounting |
| MACD | Master of Arts in Christian Doctrine |
| MACE | Master of Arts in Christian Education |
| MACH | Master of Arts in Church History |
| MACI | Master of Arts in Curriculum and Instruction |
| MACIS | Master of Accounting and Information Systems |
| MACJ | Master of Arts in Criminal Justice |
| MACL | Master of Arts in Christian Leadership |
| | Master of Arts in Community Leadership |
| MACM | Master of Arts in Christian Ministries |
| | Master of Arts in Christian Ministry |
| | Master of Arts in Church Music |
| | Master of Arts in Counseling Ministries |
| MACML | Master of Arts in Christian Ministry and Leadership |
| MACN | Master of Arts in Counseling |
| MACO | Master of Arts in Counseling |
| MAcOM | Master of Acupuncture and Oriental Medicine |
| MACP | Master of Arts in Christian Practice |
| | Master of Arts in Church Planting |
| | Master of Arts in Counseling Psychology |
| MACS | Master of Applied Computer Science |
| | Master of Arts in Catholic Studies |
| | Master of Arts in Christian Studies |
| MACSE | Master of Arts in Christian School Education |
| MACT | Master of Arts in Communications and Technology |
| MAD | Master in Educational Institution Administration |
| | Master of Art and Design |
| MADR | Master of Arts in Dispute Resolution |

| | |
|---|---|
| MADS | Master of Applied Disability Studies |
| MAE | Master of Aerospace Engineering |
| | Master of Agricultural Economics |
| | Master of Agricultural Education |
| | Master of Applied Economics |
| | Master of Architectural Engineering |
| | Master of Art Education |
| | Master of Arts in Education |
| | Master of Arts in English |
| MAEd | Master of Arts Education |
| MAEE | Master of Agricultural and Extension Education |
| MAEL | Master of Arts in Educational Leadership |
| MAEM | Master of Arts in Educational Ministries |
| MAEP | Master of Arts in Economic Policy |
| | Master of Arts in Educational Psychology |
| MAES | Master of Arts in Environmental Sciences |
| MAET | Master of Arts in English Teaching |
| MAF | Master of Arts in Finance |
| MAFE | Master of Arts in Financial Economics |
| MAFM | Master of Accounting and Financial Management |
| MAFS | Master of Arts in Family Studies |
| MAG | Master of Applied Geography |
| MAGU | Master of Urban Analysis and Management |
| MAH | Master of Arts in Humanities |
| MAHA | Master of Arts in Humanitarian Assistance |
| MAHCM | Master of Arts in Health Care Mission |
| MAHG | Master of American History and Government |
| MAHL | Master of Arts in Hebrew Letters |
| MAHN | Master of Applied Human Nutrition |
| MAHR | Master of Applied Historical Research |
| MAHS | Master of Arts in Human Services |
| MAHSR | Master in Applied Health Services Research |
| MAIA | Master of Arts in International Administration |
| | Master of Arts in International Affairs |
| MAICS | Master of Arts in Intercultural Studies |
| MAIDM | Master of Arts in Interior Design and Merchandising |
| MAIH | Master of Arts in Interdisciplinary Humanities |
| MAIOP | Master of Applied Industrial/Organizational Psychology |
| MAIS | Master of Arts in Intercultural Studies |
| | Master of Arts in Interdisciplinary Studies |
| | Master of Arts in International Studies |
| MAIT | Master of Administration in Information Technology |
| MAJ | Master of Arts in Journalism |
| MAJCS | Master of Arts in Jewish Communal Service |
| MAJPS | Master of Arts in Jewish Professional Studies |
| MAJS | Master of Arts in Jewish Studies |
| MAL | Master of Athletic Leadership |
| MALA | Master of Arts in Liberal Arts |
| MALCM | Master in Arts Leadership and Cultural Management |
| MALD | Master of Arts in Law and Diplomacy |
| MALER | Master of Arts in Labor and Employment Relations |
| MALL | Master of Arts in Language Learning |
| MALLT | Master of Arts in Language, Literature, and Translation |
| MALP | Master of Arts in Language Pedagogy |
| MALS | Master of Arts in Liberal Studies |
| MAM | Master of Acquisition Management |
| | Master of Agriculture and Management |
| | Master of Applied Mathematics |
| | Master of Arts in Management |
| | Master of Arts in Ministry |
| | Master of Arts Management |
| | Master of Aviation Management |
| MAMC | Master of Arts in Mass Communication |
| | Master of Arts in Ministry and Culture |
| | Master of Arts in Ministry for a Multicultural Church |
| MAME | Master of Arts in Missions/Evangelism |
| MAMFC | Master of Arts in Marriage and Family Counseling |
| MAMFT | Master of Arts in Marriage and Family Therapy |
| MAMHC | Master of Arts in Mental Health Counseling |
| MAMS | Master of Applied Mathematical Sciences |
| | Master of Arts in Ministerial Studies |
| | Master of Arts in Ministry and Spirituality |
| MAMT | Master of Arts in Mathematics Teaching |
| MAN | Master of Applied Nutrition |
| MANT | Master of Arts in New Testament |
| MAOL | Master of Arts in Organizational Leadership |
| MAOM | Master of Acupuncture and Oriental Medicine |
| | Master of Arts in Organizational Management |
| MAOT | Master of Arts in Old Testament |
| MAP | Master of Applied Politics |
| | Master of Applied Psychology |
| | Master of Arts in Planning |
| | Master of Psychology |
| | Master of Public Administration |
| MAP Min | Master of Arts in Pastoral Ministry |
| MAPA | Master of Arts in Public Administration |
| MAPC | Master of Arts in Pastoral Counseling |
| MAPE | Master of Arts in Physics Education |
| MAPM | Master of Arts in Pastoral Ministry |
| | Master of Arts in Pastoral Music |
| | Master of Arts in Practical Ministry |
| MAPP | Master of Arts in Public Policy |
| MAPS | Master of Applied Psychological Sciences |
| | Master of Arts in Pastoral Studies |
| | Master of Arts in Public Service |
| MAPW | Master of Arts in Professional Writing |
| MAQRM | Master's of Actuarial and Quantitative Risk Management |
| MAR | Master of Arts in Reading |
| | Master of Arts in Religion |
| Mar Eng | Marine Engineer |
| MARC | Master of Arts in Rehabilitation Counseling |
| MARE | Master of Arts in Religious Education |
| MARL | Master of Arts in Religious Leadership |
| MARS | Master of Arts in Religious Studies |
| MAS | Master of Accounting Science |
| | Master of Actuarial Science |
| | Master of Administrative Science |
| | Master of Advanced Study |
| | Master of American Studies |
| | Master of Animal Science |
| | Master of Applied Science |
| | Master of Applied Statistics |
| | Master of Archival Studies |
| MASA | Master of Advanced Studies in Architecture |
| MASC | Master of Arts in School Counseling |
| MASD | Master of Arts in Spiritual Direction |
| MASE | Master of Arts in Special Education |
| MASF | Master of Arts in Spiritual Formation |
| MASJ | Master of Arts in Systems of Justice |
| MASLA | Master of Advanced Studies in Landscape Architecture |
| MASM | Master of Aging Services Management |
| | Master of Arts in Specialized Ministries |
| MASS | Master of Applied Social Science |
| MASW | Master of Aboriginal Social Work |
| MAT | Master of Arts in Teaching |
| | Master of Arts in Theology |
| | Master of Athletic Training |
| | Master's in Administration of Telecommunications |
| Mat E | Materials Engineer |
| MATCM | Master of Acupuncture and Traditional Chinese Medicine |
| MATDE | Master of Arts in Theology, Development, and Evangelism |
| MATDR | Master of Territorial Management and Regional Development |
| MATE | Master of Arts for the Teaching of English |
| MATESL | Master of Arts in Teaching English as a Second Language |
| MATESOL | Master of Arts in Teaching English to Speakers of Other Languages |
| MATF | Master of Arts in Teaching English as a Foreign Language/Intercultural Studies |
| MATFL | Master of Arts in Teaching Foreign Language |
| MATH | Master of Arts in Therapy |

| | |
|---|---|
| MATI | Master of Administration of Information Technology |
| MATL | Master of Arts in Teaching of Languages |
| | Master of Arts in Transformational Leadership |
| MATM | Master of Arts in Teaching of Mathematics |
| MATRN | Master of Athletic Training |
| MATS | Master of Arts in Theological Studies |
| | Master of Arts in Transforming Spirituality |
| MAUA | Master of Arts in Urban Affairs |
| MAUD | Master of Arts in Urban Design |
| MAURP | Master of Arts in Urban and Regional Planning |
| MAW | Master of Arts in Worship |
| MAWSHP | Master of Arts in Worship |
| MAYM | Master of Arts in Youth Ministry |
| MB | Master of Bioinformatics |
| MBA | Master of Business Administration |
| MBA-AM | Master of Business Administration in Aviation Management |
| MBA-EP | Master of Business Administration–Experienced Professionals |
| MBAA | Master of Business Administration in Aviation |
| MBAE | Master of Biological and Agricultural Engineering |
| | Master of Biosystems and Agricultural Engineering |
| MBAH | Master of Business Administration in Health |
| MBAi | Master of Business Administration–International |
| MBAICT | Master of Business Administration in Information and Communication Technology |
| MBC | Master of Building Construction |
| MBE | Master of Bilingual Education |
| | Master of Bioengineering |
| | Master of Bioethics |
| | Master of Biomedical Engineering |
| | Master of Business Economics |
| | Master of Business Education |
| MBEE | Master in Biotechnology Enterprise and Entrepreneurship |
| MBET | Master of Business, Entrepreneurship and Technology |
| MBI | Master in Business Informatics |
| MBIOT | Master of Biotechnology |
| MBiotech | Master of Biotechnology |
| MBL | Master of Business Leadership |
| MBLE | Master in Business Logistics Engineering |
| MBME | Master's in Biomedical Engineering |
| MBMSE | Master of Business Management and Software Engineering |
| MBOE | Master of Business Operational Excellence |
| MBS | Master of Biblical Studies |
| | Master of Biological Science |
| | Master of Biomedical Sciences |
| | Master of Bioscience |
| | Master of Building Science |
| | Master of Business and Science |
| | Master of Business Statistics |
| MBST | Master of Biostatistics |
| MBT | Master of Biomedical Technology |
| | Master of Biotechnology |
| | Master of Business Taxation |
| MBV | Master of Business for Veterans |
| MC | Master of Classics |
| | Master of Communication |
| | Master of Counseling |
| MC Ed | Master of Continuing Education |
| MC Sc | Master of Computer Science |
| MCA | Master of Commercial Aviation |
| | Master of Communication Arts |
| | Master of Criminology (Applied) |
| MCAM | Master of Computational and Applied Mathematics |
| MCC | Master of Computer Science |
| MCD | Master of Communications Disorders |
| | Master of Community Development |
| MCE | Master in Electronic Commerce |
| | Master of Chemistry Education |
| | Master of Christian Education |
| | Master of Civil Engineering |
| | Master of Control Engineering |
| MCEM | Master of Construction Engineering Management |
| MCEPA | Master of Chinese Economic and Political Affairs |
| MCHE | Master of Chemical Engineering |
| MCIS | Master of Communication and Information Studies |
| | Master of Computer and Information Science |
| | Master of Computer Information Systems |
| MCIT | Master of Computer and Information Technology |
| MCJ | Master of Criminal Justice |
| MCL | Master in Communication Leadership |
| | Master of Canon Law |
| | Master of Christian Leadership |
| | Master of Comparative Law |
| MCM | Master of Christian Ministry |
| | Master of Church Music |
| | Master of Communication Management |
| | Master of Community Medicine |
| | Master of Construction Management |
| | Master of Contract Management |
| MCMin | Master of Christian Ministry |
| MCMM | Master in Communications and Media Management |
| MCMP | Master of City and Metropolitan Planning |
| MCMS | Master of Clinical Medical Science |
| MCN | Master of Clinical Nutrition |
| MCOL | Master of Arts in Community and Organizational Leadership |
| MCP | Master of City Planning |
| | Master of Community Planning |
| | Master of Counseling Psychology |
| | Master of Cytopathology Practice |
| | Master of Science in Quality Systems and Productivity |
| MCPD | Master of Community Planning and Development |
| MCR | Master in Clinical Research |
| MCRP | Master of City and Regional Planning |
| | Master of Community and Regional Planning |
| MCRS | Master of City and Regional Studies |
| MCS | Master of Chemical Sciences |
| | Master of Christian Studies |
| | Master of Clinical Science |
| | Master of Combined Sciences |
| | Master of Communication Studies |
| | Master of Computer Science |
| | Master of Consumer Science |
| MCSE | Master of Computer Science and Engineering |
| MCSL | Master of Catholic School Leadership |
| MCSM | Master of Construction Science and Management |
| MCT | Master of Commerce and Technology |
| MCTM | Master of Clinical Translation Management |
| MCTP | Master of Communication Technology and Policy |
| MCTS | Master of Clinical and Translational Science |
| MCVS | Master of Cardiovascular Science |
| MD | Doctor of Medicine |
| MDA | Master of Dietetic Administration |
| MDB | Master of Design-Build |
| MDE | Master in Design Engineering |
| | Master of Developmental Economics |
| | Master of Distance Education |
| | Master of the Education of the Deaf |
| MDH | Master of Dental Hygiene |
| MDI | Master of Disruptive Innovation |
| MDM | Master of Design Methods |
| | Master of Digital Media |
| MDP | Master in Sustainable Development Practice |
| | Master of Development Practice |
| MDR | Master of Dispute Resolution |
| MDS | Master in Data Science |
| | Master of Dental Surgery |
| | Master of Design Studies |
| | Master of Digital Sciences |
| MDSPP | Master in Data Science for Public Policy |

| | |
|---|---|
| ME | Master of Education |
| | Master of Engineering |
| | Master of Entrepreneurship |
| ME Sc | Master of Engineering Science |
| ME-PD | Master of Education–Professional Development |
| MEA | Master of Educational Administration |
| | Master of Engineering Administration |
| MEAE | Master of Entertainment Arts and Engineering |
| MEAP | Master of Environmental Administration and Planning |
| MEB | Master of Energy Business |
| MEBD | Master in Environmental Building Design |
| MEBT | Master in Electronic Business Technologies |
| MEC | Master of Electronic Commerce |
| Mech E | Mechanical Engineer |
| MEDS | Master of Environmental Design Studies |
| MEE | Master in Education |
| | Master of Electrical Engineering |
| | Master of Energy Engineering |
| | Master of Environmental Engineering |
| MEECON | Master of Energy Economics |
| MEEM | Master of Environmental Engineering and Management |
| MEENE | Master of Engineering in Environmental Engineering |
| MEEP | Master of Environmental and Energy Policy |
| MEERM | Master of Earth and Environmental Resource Management |
| MEH | Master in Humanistic Studies |
| | Master of Environmental Health |
| | Master of Environmental Horticulture |
| MEHS | Master of Environmental Health and Safety |
| MEIM | Master of Entertainment Industry Management |
| | Master of Equine Industry Management |
| MEL | Master of Educational Leadership |
| | Master of Engineering Leadership |
| | Master of English Literature |
| MELP | Master of Environmental Law and Policy |
| MEM | Master of Engineering Management |
| | Master of Environmental Management |
| | Master of Marketing |
| MEME | Master of Engineering in Manufacturing Engineering |
| | Master of Engineering in Mechanical Engineering |
| MENR | Master of Environment and Natural Resources |
| MENVEGR | Master of Environmental Engineering |
| MEP | Master of Engineering Physics |
| MEPC | Master of Environmental Pollution Control |
| MEPD | Master of Environmental Planning and Design |
| MER | Master of Employment Relations |
| MERE | Master of Entrepreneurial Real Estate |
| MERL | Master of Energy Regulation and Law |
| MES | Master of Education and Science |
| | Master of Engineering Science |
| | Master of Environment and Sustainability |
| | Master of Environmental Science |
| | Master of Environmental Studies |
| | Master of Environmental Systems |
| MESM | Master of Environmental Science and Management |
| MET | Master of Educational Technology |
| | Master of Engineering Technology |
| | Master of Entertainment Technology |
| | Master of Environmental Toxicology |
| METM | Master of Engineering and Technology Management |
| MEVE | Master of Environmental Engineering |
| MF | Master of Finance |
| | Master of Forestry |
| MFA | Master of Financial Administration |
| | Master of Fine Arts |
| MFALP | Master of Food and Agriculture Law and Policy |
| MFAS | Master of Fisheries and Aquatic Science |
| MFC | Master of Forest Conservation |
| MFCS | Master of Family and Consumer Sciences |
| MFE | Master of Financial Economics |
| | Master of Financial Engineering |
| | Master of Forest Engineering |
| MFES | Master of Fire and Emergency Services |
| MFG | Master of Functional Genomics |
| MFHD | Master of Family and Human Development |
| MFM | Master of Financial Management |
| | Master of Financial Mathematics |
| MFPE | Master of Food Process Engineering |
| MFR | Master of Forest Resources |
| MFRC | Master of Forest Resources and Conservation |
| MFRE | Master of Food and Resource Economics |
| MFS | Master of Food Science |
| | Master of Forensic Sciences |
| | Master of Forest Science |
| | Master of Forest Studies |
| | Master of French Studies |
| MFST | Master of Food Safety and Technology |
| MFT | Master of Family Therapy |
| MFWCB | Master of Fish, Wildlife and Conservation Biology |
| MFYCS | Master of Family, Youth and Community Sciences |
| MGA | Master of Global Affairs |
| | Master of Government Administration |
| | Master of Governmental Administration |
| MGBA | Master of Global Business Administration |
| MGC | Master of Genetic Counseling |
| MGCS | Master of Genetic Counselor Studies |
| MGD | Master of Graphic Design |
| MGE | Master of Geotechnical Engineering |
| MGEM | Master of Geomatics for Environmental Management |
| | Master of Global Entrepreneurship and Management |
| MGIS | Master of Geographic Information Science |
| | Master of Geographic Information Systems |
| MGM | Master of Global Management |
| MGMA | Master of Greenhouse Gas Management and Accounting |
| MGP | Master of Gestion de Projet |
| MGPS | Master of Global Policy Studies |
| MGREM | Master of Global Real Estate Management |
| MGS | Master of Gender Studies |
| | Master of Gerontological Studies |
| | Master of Global Studies |
| MH | Master of Humanities |
| MH Sc | Master of Health Sciences |
| MHA | Master of Health Administration |
| | Master of Healthcare Administration |
| | Master of Hospital Administration |
| | Master of Hospitality Administration |
| MHB | Master of Human Behavior |
| MHC | Master of Mental Health Counseling |
| MHCA | Master of Health Care Administration |
| MHCD | Master of Health Care Design |
| MHCI | Master of Human-Computer Interaction |
| MHCL | Master of Health Care Leadership |
| MHCM | Master of Health Care Management |
| MHE | Master of Health Education |
| | Master of Higher Education |
| | Master of Human Ecology |
| MHE Ed | Master of Home Economics Education |
| MHEA | Master of Higher Education Administration |
| MHHS | Master of Health and Human Services |
| MHI | Master of Health Informatics |
| | Master of Healthcare Innovation |
| MHID | Master of Healthcare Interior Design |
| MHIHIM | Master of Health Informatics and Health Information Management |
| MHIIM | Master of Health Informatics and Information Management |
| MHK | Master of Human Kinetics |
| MHM | Master of Healthcare Management |
| MHMS | Master of Health Management Systems |
| MHP | Master of Health Physics |
| | Master of Heritage Preservation |
| | Master of Historic Preservation |
| MHPA | Master of Heath Policy and Administration |

| | |
|---|---|
| MHPCTL | Master of High Performance Coaching and Technical Leadership |
| MHPE | Master of Health Professions Education |
| MHR | Master of Human Resources |
| MHRD | Master in Human Resource Development |
| MHRIR | Master of Human Resources and Industrial Relations |
| MHRLR | Master of Human Resources and Labor Relations |
| MHRM | Master of Human Resources Management |
| MHS | Master of Health Science |
| | Master of Health Sciences |
| | Master of Health Studies |
| | Master of Hispanic Studies |
| | Master of Human Services |
| | Master of Humanistic Studies |
| MHSA | Master of Health Services Administration |
| MHSM | Master of Health Systems Management |
| MI | Master of Information |
| | Master of Instruction |
| MI Arch | Master of Interior Architecture |
| MIA | Master of Interior Architecture |
| | Master of International Affairs |
| MIAA | Master of International Affairs and Administration |
| MIAM | Master of International Agribusiness Management |
| MIAPD | Master of Interior Architecture and Product Design |
| MIB | Master of International Business |
| MIBS | Master of International Business Studies |
| MICLJ | Master of International Criminal Law and Justice |
| MICM | Master of International Construction Management |
| MID | Master of Industrial Design |
| | Master of Industrial Distribution |
| | Master of Innovation Design |
| | Master of Interior Design |
| | Master of International Development |
| MIDA | Master of International Development Administration |
| MIDP | Master of International Development Policy |
| MIDS | Master of Information and Data Science |
| MIE | Master of Industrial Engineering |
| MIF | Master of International Forestry |
| MIHTM | Master of International Hospitality and Tourism Management |
| MIJ | Master of International Journalism |
| MILR | Master of Industrial and Labor Relations |
| MIM | Master in Ministry |
| | Master of Information Management |
| | Master of International Management |
| | Master of International Marketing |
| MIMFA | Master of Investment Management and Financial Analysis |
| MIMLAE | Master of International Management for Latin American Executives |
| MIMS | Master of Information Management and Systems |
| | Master of Integrated Manufacturing Systems |
| MIP | Master of Infrastructure Planning |
| | Master of Intellectual Property |
| | Master of International Policy |
| MIPA | Master of International Public Affairs |
| MIPD | Master of Integrated Product Design |
| MIPER | Master of International Political Economy of Resources |
| MIPM | Master of International Policy Management |
| MIPP | Master of International Policy and Practice |
| | Master of International Public Policy |
| MIPS | Master of International Planning Studies |
| MIR | Master of Industrial Relations |
| | Master of International Relations |
| MIRD | Master of International Relations and Diplomacy |
| MIRHR | Master of Industrial Relations and Human Resources |
| MIS | Master of Imaging Science |
| | Master of Industrial Statistics |
| | Master of Information Science |
| | Master of Information Systems |
| | Master of Integrated Science |
| | Master of Interdisciplinary Studies |
| | Master of International Service |
| | Master of International Studies |
| MISE | Master of Industrial and Systems Engineering |
| MISKM | Master of Information Sciences and Knowledge Management |
| MISM | Master of Information Systems Management |
| MISW | Master of Indigenous Social Work |
| MIT | Master in Teaching |
| | Master of Industrial Technology |
| | Master of Information Technology |
| | Master of Initial Teaching |
| | Master of International Trade |
| MITA | Master of Information Technology Administration |
| MITM | Master of Information Technology and Management |
| MJ | Master of Journalism |
| | Master of Jurisprudence |
| MJ Ed | Master of Jewish Education |
| MJA | Master of Justice Administration |
| MJM | Master of Justice Management |
| MJS | Master of Judaic Studies |
| | Master of Judicial Studies |
| | Master of Juridical Studies |
| MK | Master of Kinesiology |
| MKM | Master of Knowledge Management |
| ML | Master of Latin |
| | Master of Law |
| ML Arch | Master of Landscape Architecture |
| MLA | Master of Landscape Architecture |
| | Master of Liberal Arts |
| MLAS | Master of Laboratory Animal Science |
| | Master of Liberal Arts and Sciences |
| MLAUD | Master of Landscape Architecture in Urban Development |
| MLD | Master of Leadership Development |
| | Master of Leadership Studies |
| MLE | Master of Applied Linguistics and Exegesis |
| MLER | Master of Labor and Employment Relations |
| MLI Sc | Master of Library and Information Science |
| MLIS | Master of Library and Information Science |
| | Master of Library and Information Studies |
| MLM | Master of Leadership in Ministry |
| MLPD | Master of Land and Property Development |
| MLRHR | Master of Labor Relations and Human Resources |
| MLS | Master of Leadership Studies |
| | Master of Legal Studies |
| | Master of Liberal Studies |
| | Master of Library Science |
| | Master of Life Sciences |
| | Master of Medical Laboratory Sciences |
| MLSCM | Master of Logistics and Supply Chain Management |
| MLT | Master of Language Technologies |
| MLTCA | Master of Long Term Care Administration |
| MLW | Master of Studies in Law |
| MLWS | Master of Land and Water Systems |
| MM | Master of Management |
| | Master of Mediation |
| | Master of Ministry |
| | Master of Music |
| MM Ed | Master of Music Education |
| MM Sc | Master of Medical Science |
| MM St | Master of Museum Studies |
| MMA | Master of Marine Affairs |
| | Master of Media Arts |
| | Master of Musical Arts |
| MMAL | Master of Maritime Administration and Logistics |
| MMAS | Master of Military Art and Science |
| MMB | Master of Microbial Biotechnology |
| MMC | Master of Manufacturing Competitiveness |

| | |
|---|---|
| | Master of Mass Communications |
| MMCM | Master of Music in Church Music |
| MMCSS | Master of Mathematical Computational and Statistical Sciences |
| MME | Master of Management in Energy |
| | Master of Manufacturing Engineering |
| | Master of Mathematics Education |
| | Master of Mathematics for Educators |
| | Master of Mechanical Engineering |
| | Master of Mining Engineering |
| | Master of Music Education |
| MMEL | Master's in Medical Education Leadership |
| MMF | Master of Mathematical Finance |
| MMFC/T | Master of Marriage and Family Counseling/Therapy |
| MMFT | Master of Marriage and Family Therapy |
| MMG | Master of Management |
| MMH | Master of Management in Hospitality |
| | Master of Medical Humanities |
| MMI | Master of Management of Innovation |
| MMIS | Master of Management Information Systems |
| MML | Master of Managerial Logistics |
| MMM | Master of Manufacturing Management |
| | Master of Marine Management |
| | Master of Medical Management |
| MMP | Master of Marine Policy |
| | Master of Medical Physics |
| | Master of Music Performance |
| MMPA | Master of Management and Professional Accounting |
| MMQM | Master of Manufacturing Quality Management |
| MMR | Master of Marketing Research |
| MMRM | Master of Marine Resources Management |
| MMS | Master in Migration Studies |
| | Master of Management Science |
| | Master of Management Studies |
| | Master of Manufacturing Systems |
| | Master of Marine Studies |
| | Master of Materials Science |
| | Master of Mathematical Sciences |
| | Master of Medical Science |
| | Master of Medieval Studies |
| MMSE | Master of Manufacturing Systems Engineering |
| MMSM | Master of Music in Sacred Music |
| MMT | Master in Marketing |
| | Master of Math for Teaching |
| | Master of Music Therapy |
| | Master's in Marketing Technology |
| MMus | Master of Music |
| MN | Master of Nursing |
| | Master of Nutrition |
| MN NP | Master of Nursing in Nurse Practitioner |
| MNA | Master of Nonprofit Administration |
| | Master of Nurse Anesthesia |
| MNAE | Master of Nanoengineering |
| MNAL | Master of Nonprofit Administration and Leadership |
| MNAS | Master of Natural and Applied Science |
| MNCL | Master of Nonprofit and Civic Leadership |
| MNCM | Master of Network and Communications Management |
| MNE | Master of Nuclear Engineering |
| MNL | Master in International Business for Latin America |
| MNM | Master of Nonprofit Management |
| MNO | Master of Nonprofit Organization |
| MNPL | Master of Not-for-Profit Leadership |
| MNpS | Master of Nonprofit Studies |
| MNR | Master of Natural Resources |
| MNRD | Master of Natural Resources Development |
| MNRES | Master of Natural Resources and Environmental Studies |
| MNRM | Master of Natural Resource Management |
| MNRMG | Master of Natural Resource Management and Geography |
| MNRS | Master of Natural Resource Stewardship |
| MNS | Master of Natural Science |
| MNSE | Master of Natural Sciences Education |
| MO | Master of Oceanography |
| MOD | Master of Organizational Development |
| MOGS | Master of Oil and Gas Studies |
| MOL | Master of Organizational Leadership |
| MOM | Master of Organizational Management |
| | Master of Oriental Medicine |
| MOR | Master of Operations Research |
| MOT | Master of Occupational Therapy |
| MP | Master of Physiology |
| | Master of Planning |
| MP Ac | Master of Professional Accountancy |
| MP Acc | Master of Professional Accountancy |
| | Master of Professional Accounting |
| | Master of Public Accounting |
| MP Aff | Master of Public Affairs |
| MP Th | Master of Pastoral Theology |
| MPA | Master of Performing Arts |
| | Master of Physician Assistant |
| | Master of Professional Accountancy |
| | Master of Professional Accounting |
| | Master of Public Administration |
| | Master of Public Affairs |
| MPAC | Master of Professional Accounting |
| MPAID | Master of Public Administration and International Development |
| MPAP | Master of Physician Assistant Practice |
| | Master of Public Administration and Policy |
| | Master of Public Affairs and Politics |
| MPAS | Master of Physician Assistant Science |
| | Master of Physician Assistant Studies |
| MPC | Master of Professional Communication |
| MPD | Master of Product Development |
| | Master of Public Diplomacy |
| MPDS | Master of Planning and Development Studies |
| MPE | Master of Physical Education |
| MPEM | Master of Project Engineering and Management |
| MPFM | Master of Public Financial Management |
| MPH | Master of Public Health |
| MPHE | Master of Public Health Education |
| MPHM | Master in Plant Health Management |
| MPHS | Master of Population Health Sciences |
| MPHTM | Master of Public Health and Tropical Medicine |
| MPI | Master of Public Informatics |
| MPIA | Master of Public and International Affairs |
| MPL | Master of Pastoral Leadership |
| MPM | Master of Pastoral Ministry |
| | Master of Pest Management |
| | Master of Policy Management |
| | Master of Practical Ministries |
| | Master of Professional Management |
| | Master of Project Management |
| | Master of Public Management |
| MPNA | Master of Public and Nonprofit Administration |
| MPNL | Master of Philanthropy and Nonprofit Leadership |
| MPO | Master of Prosthetics and Orthotics |
| MPOD | Master of Positive Organizational Development |
| MPP | Master of Public Policy |
| MPPA | Master of Public Policy Administration |
| | Master of Public Policy and Administration |
| MPPAL | Master of Public Policy, Administration and Law |
| MPPGA | Master of Public Policy and Global Affairs |
| MPPM | Master of Public Policy and Management |
| MPR | Master of Public Relations |
| MPRTM | Master of Parks, Recreation, and Tourism Management |
| MPS | Master of Pastoral Studies |
| | Master of Perfusion Science |
| | Master of Planning Studies |
| | Master of Political Science |
| | Master of Preservation Studies |
| | Master of Prevention Science |
| | Master of Professional Studies |
| | Master of Public Service |
| MPSA | Master of Public Service Administration |
| MPSG | Master of Population and Social Gerontology |

| | |
|---|---|
| MPSIA | Master of Political Science and International Affairs |
| MPSL | Master of Public Safety Leadership |
| MPT | Master of Pastoral Theology |
| | Master of Physical Therapy |
| | Master of Practical Theology |
| MPVM | Master of Preventive Veterinary Medicine |
| MPW | Master of Professional Writing |
| | Master of Public Works |
| MQF | Master of Quantitative Finance |
| MQM | Master of Quality Management |
| | Master of Quantitative Management |
| MQS | Master of Quality Systems |
| MR | Master of Recreation |
| | Master of Retailing |
| MRA | Master in Research Administration |
| | Master of Regulatory Affairs |
| MRC | Master of Rehabilitation Counseling |
| MRCP | Master of Regional and City Planning |
| | Master of Regional and Community Planning |
| MRD | Master of Rural Development |
| MRE | Master of Real Estate |
| | Master of Religious Education |
| MRED | Master of Real Estate Development |
| MREM | Master of Resource and Environmental Management |
| MRLS | Master of Resources Law Studies |
| MRM | Master of Resources Management |
| MRP | Master of Regional Planning |
| MRRD | Master in Recreation Resource Development |
| MRS | Master of Religious Studies |
| MRSc | Master of Rehabilitation Science |
| MRUD | Master of Resilient Design |
| MS | Master of Science |
| MS Cmp E | Master of Science in Computer Engineering |
| MS Kin | Master of Science in Kinesiology |
| MS Acct | Master of Science in Accounting |
| MS Accy | Master of Science in Accountancy |
| MS Aero E | Master of Science in Aerospace Engineering |
| MS Ag | Master of Science in Agriculture |
| MS Arch | Master of Science in Architecture |
| MS Arch St | Master of Science in Architectural Studies |
| MS Bio E | Master of Science in Bioengineering |
| MS Bm E | Master of Science in Biomedical Engineering |
| MS Ch E | Master of Science in Chemical Engineering |
| MS Cp E | Master of Science in Computer Engineering |
| MS Eco | Master of Science in Economics |
| MS Econ | Master of Science in Economics |
| MS Ed | Master of Science in Education |
| MS Ed Admin | Master of Science in Educational Administration |
| MS El | Master of Science in Educational Leadership and Administration |
| MS En E | Master of Science in Environmental Engineering |
| MS Eng | Master of Science in Engineering |
| MS Engr | Master of Science in Engineering |
| MS Env E | Master of Science in Environmental Engineering |
| MS Exp Surg | Master of Science in Experimental Surgery |
| MS Mat SE | Master of Science in Material Science and Engineering |
| MS Met E | Master of Science in Metallurgical Engineering |
| MS Mgt | Master of Science in Management |
| MS Min | Master of Science in Mining |
| MS Min E | Master of Science in Mining Engineering |
| MS Mt E | Master of Science in Materials Engineering |
| MS Otol | Master of Science in Otolaryngology |
| MS Pet E | Master of Science in Petroleum Engineering |
| MS Sc | Master of Social Science |
| MS Sp Ed | Master of Science in Special Education |
| MS Stat | Master of Science in Statistics |
| MS Surg | Master of Science in Surgery |
| MS Tax | Master of Science in Taxation |
| MS Tc E | Master of Science in Telecommunications Engineering |
| MS-R | Master of Science (Research) |
| MSA | Master of School Administration |
| | Master of Science in Accountancy |
| | Master of Science in Accounting |
| | Master of Science in Administration |
| | Master of Science in Aeronautics |
| | Master of Science in Agriculture |
| | Master of Science in Analytics |
| | Master of Science in Anesthesia |
| | Master of Science in Architecture |
| | Master of Science in Aviation |
| | Master of Sports Administration |
| | Master of Surgical Assisting |
| MSAA | Master of Science in Astronautics and Aeronautics |
| MSABE | Master of Science in Agricultural and Biological Engineering |
| MSAC | Master of Science in Acupuncture |
| MSACC | Master of Science in Accounting |
| MSACS | Master of Science in Applied Computer Science |
| MSAE | Master of Science in Aeronautical Engineering |
| | Master of Science in Aerospace Engineering |
| | Master of Science in Applied Economics |
| | Master of Science in Applied Engineering |
| | Master of Science in Architectural Engineering |
| MSAEM | Master of Science in Aerospace Engineering and Mechanics |
| MSAF | Master of Science in Aviation Finance |
| MSAG | Master of Science in Applied Geosciences |
| MSAH | Master of Science in Allied Health |
| MSAL | Master of Sport Administration and Leadership |
| MSAM | Master of Science in Applied Mathematics |
| MSANR | Master of Science in Agriculture and Natural Resources |
| MSAS | Master of Science in Administrative Studies |
| | Master of Science in Applied Statistics |
| | Master of Science in Architectural Studies |
| MSAT | Master of Science in Accounting and Taxation |
| | Master of Science in Advanced Technology |
| | Master of Science in Athletic Training |
| MSB | Master of Science in Biotechnology |
| MSBA | Master of Science in Business Administration |
| | Master of Science in Business Analysis |
| MSBAE | Master of Science in Biological and Agricultural Engineering |
| | Master of Science in Biosystems and Agricultural Engineering |
| MSBCB | Master's in Bioinformatics and Computational Biology |
| MSBE | Master of Science in Biological Engineering |
| | Master of Science in Biomedical Engineering |
| MSBENG | Master of Science in Bioengineering |
| MSBH | Master of Science in Behavioral Health |
| MSBM | Master of Sport Business Management |
| MSBME | Master of Science in Biomedical Engineering |
| MSBMS | Master of Science in Basic Medical Science |
| MSBS | Master of Science in Biomedical Sciences |
| MSBTM | Master of Science in Biotechnology and Management |
| MSC | Master of Science in Commerce |
| | Master of Science in Communication |
| | Master of Science in Counseling |
| | Master of Science in Criminology |
| | Master of Strategic Communication |
| MSCC | Master of Science in Community Counseling |
| MSCD | Master of Science in Communication Disorders |
| | Master of Science in Community Development |
| MSCE | Master of Science in Chemistry Education |
| | Master of Science in Civil Engineering |
| | Master of Science in Clinical Epidemiology |
| | Master of Science in Computer Engineering |
| | Master of Science in Continuing Education |
| MSCEE | Master of Science in Civil and Environmental Engineering |
| MSCF | Master of Science in Computational Finance |
| MSCH | Master of Science in Chemical Engineering |
| MSChE | Master of Science in Chemical Engineering |
| MSCI | Master of Science in Clinical Investigation |
| MSCID | Master of Science in Community and International Development |

| | |
|---|---|
| MSCIS | Master of Science in Computer and Information Science |
| | Master of Science in Computer and Information Systems |
| | Master of Science in Computer Information Science |
| | Master of Science in Computer Information Systems |
| MSCIT | Master of Science in Computer Information Technology |
| MSCJ | Master of Science in Criminal Justice |
| MSCJA | Master of Science in Criminal Justice Administration |
| MSCJS | Master of Science in Crime and Justice Studies |
| MSCLS | Master of Science in Clinical Laboratory Studies |
| MSCM | Master of Science in Church Management |
| | Master of Science in Conflict Management |
| | Master of Science in Construction Management |
| | Master of Supply Chain Management |
| MSCMP | Master of Science in Cybersecurity Management and Policy |
| MSCNU | Master of Science in Clinical Nutrition |
| MSCP | Master of Science in Clinical Psychology |
| | Master of Science in Community Psychology |
| | Master of Science in Computer Engineering |
| | Master of Science in Counseling Psychology |
| MSCPE | Master of Science in Computer Engineering |
| MSCPharm | Master of Science in Pharmacy |
| MSCR | Master of Science in Clinical Research |
| MSCRP | Master of Science in City and Regional Planning |
| | Master of Science in Community and Regional Planning |
| MSCS | Master of Science in Clinical Science |
| | Master of Science in Computer Science |
| | Master of Science in Cyber Security |
| MSCSD | Master of Science in Communication Sciences and Disorders |
| MSCSE | Master of Science in Computer Science and Engineering |
| MSCTE | Master of Science in Career and Technical Education |
| MSD | Master of Science in Dentistry |
| | Master of Science in Design |
| | Master of Science in Dietetics |
| MSDM | Master of Security and Disaster Management |
| MSE | Master of Science Education |
| | Master of Science in Economics |
| | Master of Science in Education |
| | Master of Science in Engineering |
| | Master of Science in Engineering Management |
| | Master of Software Engineering |
| | Master of Special Education |
| | Master of Structural Engineering |
| MSECE | Master of Science in Electrical and Computer Engineering |
| MSED | Master of Sustainable Economic Development |
| MSEE | Master of Science in Electrical Engineering |
| | Master of Science in Environmental Engineering |
| MSEH | Master of Science in Environmental Health |
| MSEL | Master of Science in Educational Leadership |
| MSEM | Master of Science in Engineering and Management |
| | Master of Science in Engineering Management |
| | Master of Science in Engineering Mechanics |
| | Master of Science in Environmental Management |
| MSENE | Master of Science in Environmental Engineering |
| MSEO | Master of Science in Electro-Optics |
| MSES | Master of Science in Embedded Software Engineering |
| | Master of Science in Engineering Science |
| | Master of Science in Environmental Science |
| | Master of Science in Environmental Studies |
| | Master of Science in Exercise Science |
| MSESE | Master of Science in Energy Systems Engineering |
| MSET | Master of Science in Educational Technology |
| | Master of Science in Engineering Technology |
| MSEV | Master of Science in Environmental Engineering |
| MSF | Master of Science in Finance |
| | Master of Science in Forestry |
| MSFA | Master of Science in Financial Analysis |
| MSFCS | Master of Science in Family and Consumer Science |
| MSFE | Master of Science in Financial Engineering |
| MSFM | Master of Sustainable Forest Management |
| MSFOR | Master of Science in Forestry |
| MSFP | Master of Science in Financial Planning |
| MSFS | Master of Science in Financial Sciences |
| | Master of Science in Forensic Science |
| MSFSB | Master of Science in Financial Services and Banking |
| MSFT | Master of Science in Family Therapy |
| MSGC | Master of Science in Genetic Counseling |
| MSH | Master of Science in Health |
| | Master of Science in Hospice |
| MSHA | Master of Science in Health Administration |
| MSHCA | Master of Science in Health Care Administration |
| MSHCPM | Master of Science in Health Care Policy and Management |
| MSHE | Master of Science in Health Education |
| MSHES | Master of Science in Human Environmental Sciences |
| MSHFID | Master of Science in Human Factors in Information Design |
| MSHFS | Master of Science in Human Factors and Systems |
| MSHI | Master of Science in Health Informatics |
| MSHP | Master of Science in Health Professions |
| MSHR | Master of Science in Human Resources |
| MSHRL | Master of Science in Human Resource Leadership |
| MSHRM | Master of Science in Human Resource Management |
| MSHROD | Master of Science in Human Resources and Organizational Development |
| MSHS | Master of Science in Health Science |
| | Master of Science in Health Services |
| | Master of Science in Homeland Security |
| MSHSR | Master of Science in Human Security and Resilience |
| MSI | Master of Science in Information |
| | Master of Science in Instruction |
| | Master of System Integration |
| MSIA | Master of Science in Industrial Administration |
| | Master of Science in Information Assurance |
| MSIDM | Master of Science in Interior Design and Merchandising |
| MSIE | Master of Science in Industrial Engineering |
| MSIEM | Master of Science in Information Engineering and Management |
| MSIM | Master of Science in Industrial Management |
| | Master of Science in Information Management |
| | Master of Science in International Management |
| MSIMC | Master of Science in Integrated Marketing Communications |
| MSIMS | Master of Science in Identity Management and Security |
| MSIS | Master of Science in Information Science |
| | Master of Science in Information Studies |
| | Master of Science in Information Systems |
| | Master of Science in Interdisciplinary Studies |
| MSISE | Master of Science in Infrastructure Systems Engineering |
| MSISM | Master of Science in Information Systems Management |
| MSISPM | Master of Science in Information Security Policy and Management |
| MSIST | Master of Science in Information Systems Technology |
| MSIT | Master of Science in Industrial Technology |
| | Master of Science in Information Technology |
| | Master of Science in Instructional Technology |
| MSITM | Master of Science in Information Technology Management |

| | |
|---|---|
| MSJ | Master of Science in Journalism |
| | Master of Science in Jurisprudence |
| MSJC | Master of Social Justice and Criminology |
| MSJFP | Master of Science in Juvenile Forensic Psychology |
| MSJJ | Master of Science in Juvenile Justice |
| MSJPS | Master of Science in Justice and Public Safety |
| MSK | Master of Science in Kinesiology |
| MSL | Master in the Study of Law |
| | Master of School Leadership |
| | Master of Science in Leadership |
| | Master of Science in Limnology |
| | Master of Sports Leadership |
| | Master of Strategic Leadership |
| | Master of Studies in Law |
| MSLA | Master of Science in Legal Administration |
| MSLB | Master of Sports Law and Business |
| MSLFS | Master of Science in Life Sciences |
| MSLP | Master of Speech-Language Pathology |
| MSLS | Master of Science in Library Science |
| MSLSCM | Master of Science in Logistics and Supply Chain Management |
| MSLT | Master of Second Language Teaching |
| MSM | Master of Sacred Ministry |
| | Master of Sacred Music |
| | Master of School Mathematics |
| | Master of Science in Management |
| | Master of Science in Medicine |
| | Master of Science in Organization Management |
| | Master of Security Management |
| | Master of Strategic Ministry |
| | Master of Supply Management |
| MSMA | Master of Science in Marketing Analysis |
| MSMAE | Master of Science in Materials Engineering |
| MSMC | Master of Science in Management and Communications |
| | Master of Science in Mass Communications |
| MSME | Master of Science in Mathematics Education |
| | Master of Science in Mechanical Engineering |
| | Master of Science in Medical Ethics |
| MSMHC | Master of Science in Mental Health Counseling |
| MSMIT | Master of Science in Management and Information Technology |
| MSMLS | Master of Science in Medical Laboratory Science |
| MSMOT | Master of Science in Management of Technology |
| MSMP | Master of Science in Medical Physics |
| | Master of Science in Molecular Pathology |
| MSMS | Master of Science in Management Science |
| | Master of Science in Marine Science |
| | Master of Science in Medical Sciences |
| MSMSE | Master of Science in Manufacturing Systems Engineering |
| | Master of Science in Material Science and Engineering |
| | Master of Science in Material Science Engineering |
| | Master of Science in Mathematics and Science Education |
| MSMus | Master of Sacred Music |
| MSN | Master of Science in Nursing |
| MSNA | Master of Science in Nurse Anesthesia |
| MSNE | Master of Science in Nuclear Engineering |
| MSNS | Master of Science in Natural Science |
| | Master of Science in Nutritional Science |
| MSOD | Master of Science in Organization Development |
| | Master of Science in Organizational Development |
| MSOEE | Master of Science in Outdoor and Environmental Education |
| MSOES | Master of Science in Occupational Ergonomics and Safety |
| MSOH | Master of Science in Occupational Health |
| MSOL | Master of Science in Organizational Leadership |
| MSOM | Master of Science in Oriental Medicine |
| MSOR | Master of Science in Operations Research |
| MSOT | Master of Science in Occupational Technology |
| | Master of Science in Occupational Therapy |
| MSP | Master of Science in Pharmacy |
| | Master of Science in Planning |
| | Master of Speech Pathology |
| | Master of Sustainable Peacebuilding |
| MSPA | Master of Science in Physician Assistant |
| MSPAS | Master of Science in Physician Assistant Studies |
| MSPC | Master of Science in Professional Communications |
| MSPE | Master of Science in Petroleum Engineering |
| MSPH | Master of Science in Public Health |
| MSPHR | Master of Science in Pharmacy |
| MSPM | Master of Science in Professional Management |
| | Master of Science in Project Management |
| MSPNGE | Master of Science in Petroleum and Natural Gas Engineering |
| MSPPM | Master of Science in Public Policy and Management |
| MSPS | Master of Science in Pharmaceutical Science |
| | Master of Science in Political Science |
| | Master of Science in Psychological Services |
| MSPT | Master of Science in Physical Therapy |
| MSRA | Master of Science in Recreation Administration |
| MSRE | Master of Science in Real Estate |
| | Master of Science in Religious Education |
| MSRED | Master of Science in Real Estate Development |
| | Master of Sustainable Real Estate Development |
| MSRLS | Master of Science in Recreation and Leisure Studies |
| MSRM | Master of Science in Risk Management |
| MSRMP | Master of Science in Radiological Medical Physics |
| MSRS | Master of Science in Radiological Sciences |
| | Master of Science in Rehabilitation Science |
| MSS | Master of Security Studies |
| | Master of Social Science |
| | Master of Social Services |
| | Master of Sports Science |
| | Master of Strategic Studies |
| | Master's in Statistical Science |
| MSSA | Master of Science in Social Administration |
| MSSCM | Master of Science in Supply Chain Management |
| MSSD | Master of Arts in Software Driven Systems Design |
| | Master of Science in Sustainable Design |
| MSSE | Master of Science in Software Engineering |
| | Master of Science in Special Education |
| MSSEM | Master of Science in Systems and Engineering Management |
| MSSI | Master of Science in Security Informatics |
| | Master of Science in Strategic Intelligence |
| MSSIS | Master of Science in Security and Intelligence Studies |
| MSSL | Master of Science in School Leadership |
| MSSLP | Master of Science in Speech-Language Pathology |
| MSSM | Master of Science in Sports Medicine |
| | Master of Science in Systems Management |
| MSSP | Master of Science in Social Policy |
| MSSS | Master of Science in Safety Science |
| | Master of Science in Systems Science |
| MSST | Master of Science in Security Technologies |
| MSSW | Master of Science in Social Work |
| MSSWE | Master of Science in Software Engineering |
| MST | Master of Science and Technology |
| | Master of Science in Taxation |
| | Master of Science in Teaching |
| | Master of Science in Technology |
| | Master of Science in Telecommunications |
| | Master of Science Teaching |
| MSTC | Master of Science in Technical Communication |
| | Master of Science in Telecommunications |
| MSTCM | Master of Science in Traditional Chinese Medicine |
| MSTE | Master of Science in Telecommunications Engineering |
| | Master of Science in Transportation Engineering |
| MSTL | Master of Science in Teacher Leadership |

| | |
|---|---|
| MSTM | Master of Science in Technology Management |
| | Master of Science in Transfusion Medicine |
| MSTOM | Master of Science in Traditional Oriental Medicine |
| MSUASE | Master of Science in Unmanned and Autonomous Systems Engineering |
| MSUD | Master of Science in Urban Design |
| MSUS | Master of Science in Urban Studies |
| MSW | Master of Social Work |
| MSWE | Master of Software Engineering |
| MSWREE | Master of Science in Water Resources and Environmental Engineering |
| MT | Master of Taxation |
| | Master of Teaching |
| | Master of Technology |
| | Master of Textiles |
| MTA | Master of Tax Accounting |
| | Master of Teaching Arts |
| | Master of Tourism Administration |
| MTC | Master of Technical Communications |
| MTCM | Master of Traditional Chinese Medicine |
| MTD | Master of Training and Development |
| MTE | Master in Educational Technology |
| | Master of Technological Entrepreneurship |
| MTESOL | Master in Teaching English to Speakers of Other Languages |
| MTHM | Master of Tourism and Hospitality Management |
| MTI | Master of Information Technology |
| MTID | Master of Tangible Interaction Design |
| MTL | Master of Talmudic Law |
| MTM | Master of Technology Management |
| | Master of Telecommunications Management |
| | Master of the Teaching of Mathematics |
| | Master of Transformative Ministry |
| | Master of Translational Medicine |
| MTMH | Master of Tropical Medicine and Hygiene |
| MTMS | Master in Teaching Mathematics and Science |
| MTOM | Master of Traditional Oriental Medicine |
| MTPC | Master of Technical and Professional Communication |
| MTR | Master of Translational Research |
| MTS | Master of Theatre Studies |
| | Master of Theological Studies |
| MTW | Master of Teaching Writing |
| MTWM | Master of Trust and Wealth Management |
| MUA | Master of Urban Affairs |
| MUAP | Master's of Urban Affairs and Policy |
| MUCD | Master of Urban and Community Design |
| MUD | Master of Urban Design |
| MUDS | Master of Urban Design Studies |
| MUEP | Master of Urban and Environmental Planning |
| MUP | Master of Urban Planning |
| MUPD | Master of Urban Planning and Development |
| MUPP | Master of Urban Planning and Policy |
| MUPRED | Master of Urban Planning and Real Estate Development |
| MURP | Master of Urban and Regional Planning |
| | Master of Urban and Rural Planning |
| MURPL | Master of Urban and Regional Planning |
| MUS | Master of Urban Studies |
| Mus M | Master of Music |
| MUSA | Master of Urban Spatial Analytics |
| MVP | Master of Voice Pedagogy |
| MVS | Master of Visual Studies |
| MWBS | Master of Won Buddhist Studies |
| MWC | Master of Wildlife Conservation |
| MWR | Master of Water Resources |
| MWS | Master of Women's Studies |
| | Master of Worship Studies |
| MWSc | Master of Wildlife Science |
| Nav Arch | Naval Architecture |
| Naval E | Naval Engineer |
| ND | Doctor of Naturopathic Medicine |
| | Doctor of Nursing |
| NE | Nuclear Engineer |
| Nuc E | Nuclear Engineer |
| OD | Doctor of Optometry |
| OTD | Doctor of Occupational Therapy |
| PBME | Professional Master of Biomedical Engineering |
| PC | Performer's Certificate |
| PD | Professional Diploma |
| PGC | Post-Graduate Certificate |
| PGD | Postgraduate Diploma |
| Ph L | Licentiate of Philosophy |
| Pharm D | Doctor of Pharmacy |
| PhD | Doctor of Philosophy |
| PhD Otol | Doctor of Philosophy in Otolaryngology |
| PhD Surg | Doctor of Philosophy in Surgery |
| PhDEE | Doctor of Philosophy in Electrical Engineering |
| PMBA | Professional Master of Business Administration |
| PMC | Post Master Certificate |
| PMD | Post-Master's Diploma |
| PMS | Professional Master of Science |
| | Professional Master's |
| Post-Doctoral MS | Post-Doctoral Master of Science |
| Post-MSN Certificate | Post-Master of Science in Nursing Certificate |
| PPDPT | Postprofessional Doctor of Physical Therapy |
| Pro-MS | Professional Science Master's |
| Professional MA | Professional Master of Arts |
| Professional MBA | Professional Master of Business Administration |
| Professional MS | Professional Master of Science |
| PSM | Professional Master of Science |
| | Professional Science Master's |
| Psy D | Doctor of Psychology |
| Psy M | Master of Psychology |
| Psy S | Specialist in Psychology |
| Psya D | Doctor of Psychoanalysis |
| S Psy S | Specialist in Psychological Services |
| Sc D | Doctor of Science |
| Sc M | Master of Science |
| SCCT | Specialist in Community College Teaching |
| ScDPT | Doctor of Physical Therapy Science |
| SD | Specialist Degree |
| SJD | Doctor of Juridical Sciences |
| SLPD | Doctor of Speech-Language Pathology |
| SM | Master of Science |
| SM Arch S | Master of Science in Architectural Studies |
| SMACT | Master of Science in Art, Culture and Technology |
| SMBT | Master of Science in Building Technology |
| SP | Specialist Degree |
| Sp Ed | Specialist in Education |
| Sp LIS | Specialist in Library and Information Science |
| SPA | Specialist in Arts |
| Spec | Specialist's Certificate |
| Spec M | Specialist in Music |
| Spt | Specialist Degree |
| SSP | Specialist in School Psychology |
| STB | Bachelor of Sacred Theology |
| STD | Doctor of Sacred Theology |
| STL | Licentiate of Sacred Theology |
| STM | Master of Sacred Theology |
| tDACM | Transitional Doctor of Acupuncture and Chinese Medicine |
| TDPT | Transitional Doctor of Physical Therapy |
| Th D | Doctor of Theology |
| Th M | Master of Theology |
| TOTD | Transitional Doctor of Occupational Therapy |
| VMD | Doctor of Veterinary Medicine |
| WEMBA | Weekend Executive Master of Business Administration |
| XMA | Executive Master of Arts |